dir./ect etc.
dissim./ilated etc.
dist. distinct;
    distinguished
distrib./utive etc.
Du./tch

E English
Eccl./esiastical etc.
Ecol./ogy etc.
Econ./omics etc.
EFris. East Frisian
Egypt./ian
E. Ind. East Indian, of
    the East Indies
Electr./icity etc.
elem./entary etc.
ellipt./ical(ly)
emphat./ic(ally)
Engin./eering etc.
Engl. England; English
Entom./ology etc.
equiv./alent
erron./eous(ly)
esp./ecial(ly)
Eth./ics etc.
etym./ology etc.
euphem./ism etc.
Eur./ope(an)
ex./ample
exagg./eration etc.
exc./ept
excl. exclamation etc.;
    exclusive etc.
expr./essing etc.

F French
f. from
fam./iliar etc.
fem./inine
Fenc./ing
fig./urative(ly)
Finn./ish
Flem./ish
foll./owing entry
Footb./all
form./ation
Fortif./ication
Fr./ench
Frank./ish
freq./uent(ly)
frequent./ative(ly)
fut./ure (tense)

G German
Gael. GAELIC 1

Gallo-Rom./an
gen. general etc.;
    genitive
Geog./raphy etc.
Geol./ogy etc.
Geom./etry etc.
Ger./man
Gk Greek (classical if
    not otherwise
    described)
Gmc Germanic
Goth./ic
Gram./mar etc.

Hawk./ing
Heb./rew
Her./aldry etc.
Hind./ustani
Hist. historical; history
Horol./ogy etc.
Hort./iculture etc.
Hung./arian
Hunt./ing

i. intransitive
Icel./andic
IE Indo-European
illit./erate etc.
imit./ative etc.
immed./iate(ly)
imper./ative
impers./onal
improp./er(ly)
incept./ive
incl including;
    inclusive
Ind. of the subcontinent
    comprising India,
    Pakistan, and
    Bangladesh
ind. indicative; indirect
indecl./inable
indef./inite
inf./initive
infl./uence etc.
instr./umental (case)
int./erjection
interrog./ative(ly)
intr./ansitive
ints. interjections
Ir./ish (language or
    usage)
iron./ical(ly)
irreg./ular(ly)
It./alian

(other wise described)
lang./uage
LDu. Low Dutch
LG Low German
LHeb. Late Hebrew
Ling./uistics etc.
lit./eral(ly)
LL Late Latin

M Middle (with
    languages)
Magn./etism etc.
masc./uline
Math./ematics etc.
MDa. Middle Danish
MDu. Middle Dutch
ME Middle English
Mech./anics etc.
Med./icine etc.
med./ieval
metaph./or etc.
Metaphys./ics etc.
metath./esis etc.
Meteorol./ogy etc.
Mex./ican
MFlem. Middle
    Flemish
MHG Middle High
    German
Mil./itary etc.
Min./eralogy etc.
mistransl./ation
MLG Middle Low
    German
mod./ern
Mount./aineering
MSw. Middle Swedish
Mus./ic etc.
Myth./ology etc.

n. noun
N. Amer. North
    America(n)
Nat. National
Naut./ical etc.
neg./ative(ly)
N. Engl. north of
    England
neut./er
nom./inative

(continued on back endpaper)

THE
CONCISE OXFORD
DICTIONARY

THE
CONCISE OXFORD
DICTIONARY

OF
CURRENT ENGLISH

BASED ON

The Oxford English Dictionary

AND ITS SUPPLEMENTS

FIRST EDITED BY

H. W. Fowler and F. G. Fowler

SEVENTH EDITION

Edited by J. B. Sykes

OXFORD

AT THE CLARENDON PRESS

Oxford University Press, Walton Street, Oxford OX2 6DP

Oxford New York Toronto
Delhi Bombay Calcutta Madras Karachi
Petaling Jaya Singapore Hong Kong Tokyo
Nairobi Dar es Salaam Cape Town
Melbourne Auckland

and associated companies in
Beirut Berlin Ibadan Nicosia

Oxford is a trademark of Oxford University Press

© Oxford University Press, 1964, 1976, 1982

Published in the United States by
Oxford University Press, New York

First edition 1911
New edition (revised) 1929
Third edition (with Addenda) 1934
Fourth edition 1951
Fifth edition 1964
Sixth edition 1976
Seventh edition 1982
Reprinted 1982, 1983 (twice), 1984 (twice)
1985, 1986, 1987

British Library Cataloguing in Publication Data
The Concise Oxford dictionary.—7th ed.
1. English language—Dictionaries
I. Sykes, J. B.
423 PE1625
ISBN 0-19-861131-5
ISBN 0-19-861132-3 Thumb Index

Printed in Great Britain
at the University Printing House, Oxford
by David Stanford
Printer to the University

CONTENTS

PREFACE TO THE SEVENTH EDITION

THE preparation of the seventh edition of the *Concise Oxford Dictionary* has not involved such extensive changes as did that of the sixth, but consideration has nevertheless been given to several thousand points that have come to my attention since 1976, and many of these have led to further improvements and additions. I am again indebted for a wealth of suggestions to colleagues, friends, and many correspondents; among the latter, special mention should be made of the regular contributions from Mr A. R. Babcock of Summit, New Jersey; Mr J. W. Gardner of Bath; Dr I. Grafe of London; Mr V. Petti of Stockholm; and Mr N. Yamagishi of Hirakata City, Japan.

The information provided by the dictionary has been augmented in this edition by the markings **D** and **R**, whose meaning is explained on page viii.

J.B.S.

April, 1981

From the
PREFACE TO THE SIXTH EDITION

IN this sixth edition of the *Concise Oxford Dictionary* the changes made include revisions and additions resulting from a detailed scrutiny of the whole work, as well as modifications of typography and format to allow greater ease of use. Such a thorough recension has been possible because I have had access to the reference library and the very large collection of examples built up for the *Supplement to the Oxford English Dictionary* now in course of publication, and to the advice of members of the OED department and other officers of the Oxford University Press.

The opportunity has been taken to eliminate some matter that can no longer be regarded as pertaining to current English, to add many new words, phrases, and meanings that have entered the language in recent years (including technical expressions found in general literature), to increase the contribution from the English-speaking world outside the British Isles, to incorporate the appendix of abbreviations into the main list, to systematize the definitions of interrelated terms, to eliminate some duplication of definitions, to expand some unduly concise wordings, and to add an enlarged Introduction (which the reader is strongly recommended to study) explaining the use of the dictionary.

J.B.S.

July, 1975

From the
PREFACE TO THE FIRST EDITION

THE book is designed as a dictionary, and not as an encyclopaedia; that is, the uses of words and phrases as such are its subject-matter, and it is concerned with giving information about the things for which those words and phrases stand only so far as correct use of the words depends upon knowledge of the things. The degree of this dependence varies greatly with the kind of word treated, the difference between cyclopaedic and dictionary treatment varies with it, and the line of distinction is accordingly a fluctuating and dubious one. It is to the endeavour to discern and keep to this line that we attribute whatever peculiarities we are conscious of in this dictionary as compared with others of the same size. One of these peculiarities is the large amount of space given to the common words that no one goes through the day without using scores or hundreds of times, often disposed of in a line or two on the ground that they are plain and simple and that every one knows all about them by the light of nature, but in fact entangled with other words in so many alliances and antipathies during their perpetual knocking about the world that the idiomatic use of them is far from easy; chief among such words are the prepositions, the conjunctions, the pronouns, and such 'simple' nouns and verbs as *hand* and *way*, *go* and *put*. Another peculiarity is the use, copious for so small a dictionary, of illustrative sentences as a necessary supplement to definition when a word has different senses between which the distinction is fine, or when a definition is obscure and unconvincing until exemplified; these sentences often are, but still more often are not, quotations from standard authors; they are meant to establish the sense of the definition by appeal not to external authority, but to the reader's own consciousness, and therefore their source, even when authoritative, is not named. A third and a fourth peculiarity are the direct results of the preceding ones; if common words are to be treated at length, and their uses to be copiously illustrated, space must be saved both by the curtest possible treatment of all that are either uncommon or fitter for the encyclopaedia than the dictionary, and by the severest economy of expression—amounting to the adoption of telegraphese—that readers can be expected to put up with.

H.W.F.
F.G.F.

June, 1911

INTRODUCTION

THIS introduction is designed to help the reader understand the way in which information is presented in the *Concise Oxford Dictionary*, where, as the name suggests, compactness has been a primary aim. Although many changes have been made in the sixth and seventh editions, users acquainted with previous editions will not find much that is unfamiliar as regards the style.

I. *Vocabulary*

The general aims of the dictionary have remained as they were specified by the original editors. The words, phrases, and meanings given are those current in the English of the present day—either in living use, or familiar through their occurrence in frequently quoted literature of the past. The attitude taken, however, is now essentially descriptive rather than prescriptive: that is, the dictionary seeks to record what is found to exist in the educated use of modern English. Restricted usage is regularly shown by usage labels such as (literary) and (colloq.) or subject labels such as (Law) and (Cricket); see paragraph IV. Admission has also been granted to many vulgar or slang expressions that are often met in print, or heard, at the present time. Two categories of deprecated usage have been identified by special markings in the seventh edition: **D** (= disputed) indicates a use that, although widely found, is still the subject of much adverse comment by a significant number of educated writers; **R** (= racially offensive) indicates a use that is regarded as offensive by members of a particular ethnic or religious group. Limitations of space make it impossible to include every possible and legitimate derivative (e.g. compounds of obvious meaning such as *boiler-room*, the obvious literal senses where the figurative meaning is more important, the less common adverbs in -*ly*, or phrase-based compounds such as *arm-twisting* from *twist a person's arm*). Likewise, standard grammatical procedures such as the attributive use of nouns, or the intransitive use of transitive verbs as notional passives (*the car handles well*) are not often mentioned. The reader in search of a broader canvas of English words and their history is recommended to consult the twelve-volume *Oxford English Dictionary* and its Supplements on which this work is based, the intermediate abridgement in the *Shorter Oxford English Dictionary*, the encyclopaedic matter in the *Oxford Illustrated Dictionary*, and such specialized works as the Oxford Companions to art, English literature, music, and the theatre.

II. *Arrangement of dictionary entries*

For conciseness, derivatives and compounds are often put in the entry headed by their first element, even if this brings them out of their alphabetical position. It is therefore advisable to seek any word in its alphabetical place and then (if necessary) in the entry for its first part, for example *ant-eater* under *ant, playboy* under *play*². Cross-references are provided where the placing of a word may not be obvious; here, as in all other cross-references, the word to which reference is necessary is printed in SMALL CAPITALS. Raised figures (as in PLAY²) are used to distinguish two or more entry words having the same spelling; plain figures (as in FLOW 3) refer to bold-type arabic sense-numbers (see paragraph III). There are separate entries for the principal prefixes and suffixes, and cross-reference to these is often made for the explanation of derivative forms; for instance, most adverbs in *-ly* are entered with -LY², and similarly for nouns in -NESS, and verbs in -IZE (1) etc. (where the figure indicates the specific meaning among those listed in the entry for -IZE). Cross-references are also used to clarify the sense of an ambiguous word in a definition (as PIKE³, the fish, at *jack*¹ 6), to indicate an entry where further relevant information may be found (as LIBEL at *slander*), and to lead to definitions of phrases such as *let* SLEEP²*ing dogs lie*, which are usually defined under only one of their constituent words; such a phrase or compound is not itself a sense of the entry word unless preceded by an equals sign (for example *paper*¹ . . . = NEWS*paper* implies that 'paper' can mean 'newspaper'; *hare* . . . BELGIAN *hare*; = ELECTRIC *hare* implies that 'hare' alone can mean 'electric hare' but not 'Belgian hare').

III. *Structure of entries*
The entry word (headword) is printed in **bold** type, or in ***bold italic*** if it is not yet naturalized in English and is usually found in italics in printed matter. Alternative forms are shown either by the use of parentheses as at **rac(c)oon** (where the position of the entry implies that the spelling *racoon* is given preference over *raccoon*) or by placing them, either in full or abbreviated, after a comma (**carcass, carcase**; **pygmy, pigmy**; **organize, -ise**). These are followed by any necessary indication of the · pronunciation where it cannot be shown in the headword itself (see 'Pronunciation' below), by the italic abbreviation for the part or parts of speech (*n.* for noun, etc.), and by an indication of any irregular inflexions (see 'Inflexion' below). The order of senses is normally based on frequency and convenience rather than historical evolution. The definitions of the senses of a word are separated by commas if very close in meaning, by semicolons if somewhat more distinct, and by bold-type arabic numbers (**1.**) if quite distinct. When an entry deals with more than one part of speech, the relevant part-of-speech abbreviation follows **1.**, and any subsequent number where it changes. Derivatives are in **bold** type (often partly replaced by the swung dash—see paragraph v—and by small capitals—see paragraph II); defined compounds and phrases in **semi-bold** (or in ***bold italic*** where not yet naturalized); examples and expressions defined by cross-reference, in *italic*. Definitions may include words in *italic* that are normally used with the headword in the

sense concerned: '**contingent** . . . incidental *to*' implies that the idiomatic construction for this sense is *contingent to*; '**soak** . . . place or leave or lie in or *in* liquid' implies that either *soak* or *soak in water* etc. can be used for this sense; '**gather** . . . infer, deduce, (*that*)' implies that the word *gather* may, but need not, be used with a clause beginning with the conjunction *that*. Italicized examples may include words in ordinary (roman) type that are replaceable by others: *pull* one's *weight* covers *pull my weight, pull his weight*, and so on; *pull* person's *leg* is used similarly, where the person is not the subject of the verb. The etymology is at the end of the entry, in square brackets [ ] (see 'Etymology' below). Round brackets ( ) may be used anywhere in the entry to enclose letters or words that are optional or explanatory, for example definitions that are explanatory rather than formal; '(of . . .)' often precedes the definition of a verb or adjective to indicate the type of noun to which it can be applied, and a definition of a transitive verb may be followed by words in round brackets indicating the type of noun that occurs as its object. The expression 'in vbl senses' denotes 'in senses that may be deduced from the meanings of the corresponding verb'; 'abs.' refers to the use of a transitive verb without object, an adjective without noun, etc. (see ABSOLUTELY). Systematic names of animals and plants are given where they are appropriate as a guide to further information in specialized books on mammals, ferns, etc. (Here, as in definitions, 'etc.' is used to denote other items of the same general kind.)

IV. *Usage and subject labels*
Words (usually abbreviated) in round brackets ( ) preceding a definition are used to show that all or some of the senses are restricted to a particular type of discourse or subject field in current English. The principal usage labels are (colloq.): colloquial, not used in formal discourse, but widely used and entirely acceptable in informal circumstances; (sl.): slang, used only in certain circumstances (see SLANG); (joc.): jocular, used only in humorous or playful style; (derog.): derogatory, used only contemptuously; (vulg.): vulgar, used only by those who have no wish to be thought either polite or educated; (arch.): archaic, used only in old-fashioned (or religious or legal) speech or writing; (literary): in sense 2 as given at LITERARY. See back endpaper for the geographical restrictions denoted by the symbols * and ||. The many subject labels, such as (Law), (Math.), (Naut.) (see the list of 'Abbreviations and Symbols used in the Dictionary' on endpapers), show that a word or sense is current only in a particular field of activity. When preceding all numbered senses, labels apply to the whole entry; when coming at the start of a numbered sense, or of an entry without numbers, they apply as far as the next label, if any; otherwise, as far as the next label or the next semicolon or full stop. Proprietary terms are treated as described in the note on p. xx.

V. *The swung dash*
A considerable amount of space is saved by the swung dash ∼, which stands for the headword of the entry (or any of the alternative spellings of

the headword) or for that part of it which precedes the vertical rule: for example, in the entry at **hair**, ~ stands for *hair*, ~*'brush* for *hair'brush*, (-)~*ed* for *haired* or *-haired*; at **hungr|y**, ~*y* stands for *hungry*, ~*ily* for *hungrily*. Where the headword begins or ends with a hyphen, the swung dash does not include that hyphen (at **inter-**, ~*stellar* = *interstellar*, but ~*-city* = *inter-city*); a capital or small letter preceding the swung dash replaces an initial small or capital letter in the headword (at **genesis**, *G*~ = *Genesis*; at **Renaissance**, *r*~ = *renaissance*). Any indication of pronunciation or stress corresponding to the relevant part of the headword is transmitted by the swung dash unless cancelled by a respelling in round brackets or by a new stress (thus ~A'TION cancels the main stress on the first syllable of **co'git|ate**, **to'ler|ate**, etc.); otherwise, the normal pronunciation rules are implied (at **impact**, ~**ion** is pronounced *-shon*; the second *c* in *caecitis* is pronounced s as usual before *i*, although in **caec|um** it is pronounced k; the plural ~*e* (= *nebulae*) at **nebula** is pronounced ně'būlē (see 'Pronunciation')).

VI. *Hyphenation*
There is great variety in the use of the hyphen in English, especially between British and American styles, and there are few clearly defined rules on the subject. To clarify the intention in this dictionary (which conforms essentially to the British style), a hyphen that falls at the end of a line is repeated at the start of the next line to make clear that it is not simply the result of the printing convention whereby any word so divided is hyphenated.

VII. *Entries for abbreviations in general use*
These are to be found in their alphabetical places among ordinary words, the ampersand (&) being treated as if written 'and'. There are frequent variations in the presence or absence of capitals and full stops in abbreviations, and no attempt is made to show all possible forms. Abbreviations not in general use but employed in this dictionary are listed on the endpapers.

PRONUNCIATION

The pronunciation given in this dictionary is the standard one 'without any accent', associated especially with Southern England (sometimes called 'Received Pronunciation'). No attempt is made here to show the many variations heard in educated speech in Northern England, the rest of the British Isles, the United States, and the rest of the English-speaking world. Further information may be sought in dictionaries concerned primarily with pronunciation.

Where possible, the pronunciation is shown in the bold type of the headword that begins each entry, or of a derivative within an entry. If not, part or all of the word is respelt in round brackets ( ) immediately following it. Occasionally a group of forms is followed by a comma and then by a respelling that relates to the whole group. The pronunciation of a derivative formed by a suffix printed in small capitals is often to be found by means of the marking or respelling at the suffix entry. No attempt is made to show syllables or to indicate suitable points of division of words at the end of printed lines.

I. *With respelling*

Respelling in round brackets is according to the following scheme, which also shows corresponding symbols in the International Phonetic Alphabet. See section IV below for the use of the stress-mark ´.

Consonants

		IPA				IPA
b	as in (băt)	b	ng	as in (sĭng)		ŋ
ch	as in (chĭn)	tʃ	ngg	as in (fĭ′ngger) =		
d	as in (dŏg)	d		finger		ŋg
dh	as in (dhĕn) = then	ð	p	as in (pĕt)		p
f	as in (făt)	f	r	as in (răt)		r
g	(except after n) as in		s	as in (sĭp)		s
	(gō)	g	sh	as in (shĭp)		ʃ
h	(except after c, d, s, t,		t	as in (tĭp)		t
	z) as in (hăt)	h	th	as in (thĭn)		θ
j	as in (jăm)	dʒ	v	as in (văn)		v
k	as in (kĭt)	k	w	as in (wĭn)		w
l	as in (lŏt)	l	y	as in (yĕt)		j
m	as in (măt)	m	z	as in (zĭp)		z
n	as in (nĕt)	n	zh	as in (vĭ′zhon)		
ṅ	(French nasalization)			= vision		ʒ
	as in (gär′sawṅ) =		χ	(Scots etc.) as in (lŏχ)		
	garçon etc.	(æ̃, õ, etc.)		= loch		x

Vowels

		IPA				IPA
ā	as in (fāt) = fate	eɪ	ō	as in (gōt) = goat		əʊ
ă	as in (făt)	æ	ŏ	as in (gŏt)		ɒ
a	as in (agō′)	ə	o	as in (flă′gon)		ə
ah	as in (bah)	ɑ	oi	as in (boil)		ɔɪ
ār	as in (fār) = fare	eə(r)	oo	as in (boot)		u
âr	as in (fâr)	ɑ(r)	oŏ	as in (boŏk)		ʊ
aw	as in (paw)	ɔ	oor	as in (poor)		ʊə(r)
ē	as in (mēt) = meet	i	ôr	as in (pôrt)		ɔ(r)
ĕ	as in (mĕt)	e	ow	as in (brow)		aʊ
e	as in (tō′ken)	ə	owr	as in (sowr) = sour		aʊə(r)
ēr	as in (fēr) = fear	ɪə(r)	ū	as in (dū) = due		ju
êr	as in (fêr) = fur	ɜ(r)	ŭ	as in (dŭg)		ʌ
er	as in (tā′ker)	ə(r)	u	as in (bō′nus)		ə
ī	as in (bīt) = bite	aɪ	ūr	as in (pūr) = pure		jʊə(r)
ĭ	as in (bĭt)	ɪ		See ṅ (under 'Consonants'		
i	as in (bā′sin)	ə		above) for French nasalized		
īr	as in (fīr) = fire	aɪə(r)		vowels.		

Vowels such as ă may be pronounced in two ways, e.g. either as ā or as ă (pă′trĭot); similarly (zĕ′brȧ). Vowel combinations in -r include the consonantal value of r when followed by another vowel in the next syllable or word (*fearing*, *fear it*). Apart from this, the vowels *a, e, i, o, u,* and *er* are usually indistinguishable except in very precise speech.

II. *Without respelling*

Words or parts of words that are not respelt are pronounced in accordance with the foregoing scheme—for example: **bă′nĭsh, stū′dĭō, rĭ′nger,** but **fĭ′nger** (-ngg-), **dă′nger** (-nj-)—together with the symbols and values stated in the following seven rules.

1. ė = ĭ (**nā′kėd**)
    îr = ẽr (**bîrth**)
    ûr = ẽr (**bûrn**)
    ȳ = ī (**rėlȳ′**)
    y̆ = ĭ (**dū′ty̆**)
    ȳr = īr (**tȳre**)
    ŷr = ẽr (**myŷr′tle**)

2. e final is silent (**ă′ctĭve, āpe, galôr′e;** cf. **rĕ′cĭpė**); **-le** final after a consonant = -*el* (**cā′ble, stā′ple, mă′ntle**).

3. Unmarked vowels (other than final **e**), if not respelt and not part of a compound vowel (**ah** etc.), correspond to *a* etc. above (**agō′, tō′ken, bā′sin, flă′gon, bō′nus**); **y** (except in **yr**) – y (consonant); **ar** etc. = *er* (**partĭ′cŭlar, mā′ker, tā′pir, sai′lor, lĕ′mur, zĕ′phyr**).

4. A doubled consonant is pronounced as single (**sĭ′lly̆, hă′ppen, bŭ′tter, bŭtt**). This applies also to the combinations **ck** (= k), **cq, dg(e, i, y), dj, sc(e, i, y), tch, xc(e, i, y), xs, ârr, arr,** etc.

5. The following letters and combinations have the values shown:

    ae = ē (**ae′gĭs**)
    ai = ā (**pain**)
    air = âr (**fair**)
    au = aw (**maul**)
    aur = ôr (**dī′nosaur**)
    ay = ā (**say**)
    c before **e, i, y̆, ȳ** is 'soft' and = s (**īce, cĭ′ty̆, ī′cy̆, cȳ′der**), elsewhere is 'hard' and = k (**cŏb, crȳ, ârc**)
    ea = ē (**mean**)
    ear = ēr (**fear**)
    ee = ē (**meet**)
    eer = ēr (**beer**)
    eu = ū (**feud**)
    ew = ū (**few**)

g before **e, i, y̌, ȳ** is 'soft' and = j (**āge, gǐn, ôr′gy̌, gȳbe**), elsewhere is 'hard' and = g (**gāme, bǎg, ôr′gan**)
ie = ē (**thief**)
ier = ēr (**pier**)
n before 'hard' **c, k, q, x** = ng (**zǐnc, ǔ′ncle, tǎnk, bǎ′nquėt, mǐnx**)
oa = ō (**boat**)
oar = ôr (**boar**)
ou = ow (**bound**)
our = owr (**sour**)
oy = oi (**boy**)
ph ≠ f (**phō′tō**)
qu = kw (**quǐt**)
tion = shon (**nā′tion, nǎ′tional**)
wh = w (**whǐch**) or (by some speakers) hw (not shown in respelling)
x = ks (**fǒx**)

6. The following combinations, beginning a word, have the values shown:
kn- = n (**knǒt**)
rh- = r (**rhȳme**)
wr- = r (**wrǐst**)

7. The following, ending a word, have the values shown:
-age = ǐj (**vǐ′llage**)
-ate = at (**dě′lǐcate**) or (by some speakers) ǐt
-e (see 2 above)
-ey = ǐ (**dǒ′nkey**)
-le (see 2 above)
-nch = nch or nsh (**trěnch**)
-ous = us (**fūr′ǐous**), and similarly for **-ously̌, -ousnėss**
-sm = zem (**spǎ′sm**)
-ture = cher or (sometimes, esp. in less common words) tūr

Note that all the above rules may be overridden by respelling, for example **dǔ′lly̌** (-l-lǐ), **break** (-āk), **gět** (g-), **quay** (kē), **fā′vour** (-ver), **grā′teful** (-tf-), **ahea′d** (a-hě′d), **lōō′phōle** (-p-h-), the hyphen being used to make it clear that letters are to be taken separately and not as parts of combined symbols.

Where a word has no marking at all, its pronunciation will be found within the entry (**housewife**), or (in the case of a cross-reference) at the principal word. Acronyms are usually pronounced either as words (if thus shown by respelling) or as sequences of letters; other abbreviations are usually pronounced as their full forms. See 'Inflexion' below for a description of the pronunciations of inflected forms of words.

The occasional accents on letters as in **attaché**, **fête**, should not be confused with pronunciation markings.

III. *Alternative pronunciations*

Semicolons in the respelling separate different parts of the word, as in **brea'thalȳser** (brĕ'-; -zer). Alternative accepted pronunciations are always respelt and are separated by commas. Where the second alternative covers a shorter part of the word than the first, the remainder is understood to be common to both, e.g. **a'lways** (aw'lwāz, -ĭz) is pronounced aw'lwāz or aw'lwĭz.

Unstressed vowels often have a reduced value, for example (ū) becoming (yo͞o) in **cîr'cūlar**. The combinations of (ĭ) with preceding c, s, t; d, g, j; z, when followed by a vowel, are often palatalized into (sh, j, zh) respectively (as is normal in *acacia, Alsatian*, etc.); similarly, (ĭ) followed by a vowel tends to become consonantal (y), and (tū), (dū) tend to become (cho͞o) or (cho͝o), (jo͞o) or (jo͝o), when not beginning a word or stressed syllable.

In speech at normal speed the indeterminate vowel in words ending in **-ble**, **-den**, **-gon**, **-sm**, **-thm**, **-tory**, and the like, is often barely discernible.

IV. *Stress*

The usual main stress is shown by a stress-mark ' after the stressed vowel. No attempt is made to show secondary stress, and even the main stress may change when the word is used in different positions, e.g. *Chi'nese, i'deal* attributively, *Chine'se, ide'al* predicatively, or when a compound is used in different positions.

Unless otherwise shown, the stress falls on the first part of a hyphenated compound; it is usually on the second part of a compound written as two words. Where the swung dash ∼ (see Introduction, paragraph v) is used, it may be followed immediately by a stress-mark to indicate a stress on the syllable it represents, or a suffix may have the stress-mark; otherwise, the stress is the same as in the word or part-word represented by the swung dash.

INFLEXION

The following are the rules for the formation of normal inflected forms of nouns, adjectives, adverbs, and verbs, and are applicable except where a different form is shown in round brackets ( ) in the dictionary entry immediately after the part-of-speech abbreviation *n., a., v., v.t.*, etc. The absence of any such different form is to be taken (for example at **virus** *n.*, **jacket** *v.t.*, and **parallel²** *v.t.*) as implying that the inflected forms are in accordance with the rules given below; the word *or* indicates the existence of more than one accepted form, not necessarily arranged in order of decreasing frequency of occurrence.

In these rules, 'sibilant wds' denotes all words ending in the sound of s (or x), z, sh (or ch), or zh (or j); '-o wds' denotes all words ending in the letter *o* except those in *-oo*; '-e wds' denotes all words ending in a silent *e*;

and '-*y* wds' denotes all words ending in the letter *y* preceded by a consonant, together with those in -*quy*.

I. *Plural of nouns*

Sibilant wds add -*es*, pronounced (ĭz), -*e* wds dropping the *e*: *boxes, cases, mazes, porches*; -*y* wds change -*y* into -*ies*, pronounced (ĭz): *puppies*, or (īz): *skies*; -*o* wds add -*s* or -*es*, pronounced (-z), as shown in round brackets in the dictionary for all such words except those where no plural is in use (e.g. *blanco, quattrocento*); other nouns add -*s*, pronounced (s) after voiceless consonants (*books, cats, cliffs, faiths, hopes*) and (z) after voiced consonants and vowel sounds (*bags, hoods, knaves, scythes, tubs, views, ways*). A compound consisting of a noun followed by a word other than a noun usually adds the plural ending to the noun (*courts martial, passers-by*). Abbreviations etc. add -*s* (*MPs, 1960s*) or sometimes '*s*; a few use a doubled letter (*pp.* = *pages*); some abbreviations of units remain unchanged (*m.* = *mile* or *miles*).

II. *Possessive of nouns*

Singular nouns add '*s*, pronounced (-ĭz) for sibilant wds (*fox's, goose's, witch's*), (s) after other voiceless consonants (*book's, cat's*), and (z) after other voiced consonants and vowel sounds (*boy's, dog's, man's*). Plural nouns not ending in the sound of s or z are treated like singular nouns (*men's, women's, sheep's*). Plural nouns ending in the sound of s or z add an apostrophe without change of pronunciation (*books', cats', boys', beaux'*); the same is sometimes done with singular nouns of this type (*for goodness' sake*). Abbreviations etc. add '*s* (*MP's*, in plural *MPs'*; *1960's*).

III. *Comparative and superlative of adjectives and adverbs*

The syllables -ER³ and -EST¹ are added to adjectives and adverbs of one syllable (*bolder, boldest; faster, fastest*), -*e* wds dropping the *e* (*braver, bravest; later, latest*), and a final single consonant (except *h, w*, or *x*) being doubled, without change of pronunciation, if preceded by a single-letter vowel (*grimmer, fattest; bigger* pr. bĭ'ger). The same applies to adjectives of two syllables that are -*y* wds, the *y* becoming *i* (*happier, luckiest*; similarly for some -*ey* wds such as *gooey: gooier*), to some adverbs of this type, especially *early*; to adjectives of two syllables ending in -*er*, -*le* after a consonant, or -*ow* (*cleverer, tenderest, nobler, simplest, narrower, mellowest*); and to negative forms of adjectives of all the types mentioned so far (*unfairest, ignobler, unluckiest*). The comparative and superlative of all other adjectives and adverbs must (except where otherwise shown), and those of any adjective or adverb may, be formed by prefixing *more* and *most* (*more beautiful, most splendid, most unfair, more brave, most nobly*). Similar rules apply to the formation of derived adjectives in -ISH¹ (*fattish, biggish, yellowish*; but *prettyish*).

IV. *Third person singular present indicative of verbs*
Sibilant wds (-*e* wds dropping the *e*) and -*o* wds add -*es*, pronounced (ĭz)
and (z) respectively: *pushes, places, goes;* -*y* wds change -*y* into -*ies*,
pronounced (ĭz): *carries,* or (īz): *cries;* other verbs add -*s*, pronounced (s)
after voiceless consonants (*bakes, cuts, peeps*) and (z) after voiced
consonants and vowel sounds (*begs, boos, fades, rubs, stays, ties, wallows*).

V. *Past tense and past participle of verbs*
-*e* wds add -*d* (*moved, tied, glued*); -*y* wds change -*y* into -*ied*, pronounced
(ĭd): *carried,* or (īd): *cried;* other verbs add -*ed;* the final -*ed* is pronounced
(ĭd) after the sound of t or d (*trusted, hated, ended, faded*), (t) after other
voiceless consonants (*baked, peeped, pushed*), and (d) after other voiced consonants and vowel sounds (*absorbed, booed, seemed, stayed, vetoed, wallowed*).
A final single consonant is often doubled (cf. paragraph III above), but
this is always indicated in the dictionary by (**-bb-**) etc. (*rubbed, tinned,
mimicked, preferred; sagged, tugged,* pr. -gd). There are many irregular forms;
if the past tense and past participle are different, they are separated by a
semicolon (**ran; run**); a single form stands for both (**brought, cut,
found**). In archaic and poetical use, -*ed* after a voiceless consonant may
be written -*t*, the consonant never being doubled (*blest, kist, wrapt*). Some
past participles when used as adjectives have different forms (*drunken*) or
pronunciations in (-ĭd) (*blessed, learned*); this pronunciation also occurs in
archaic and poetical use (*the hornèd Moon*) and for some derived adverbs in
-*edly* (*advisedly*). Similar rules apply to the formation of derived nouns in
-*ER*[1] (*carrier, winner*) and adjectives in -*ABLE* (*carriable, winnable*).

VI. *Present participle and gerund of verbs*
All verbs add -*ing* (*fishing, playing, studying*), -*e* wds (except those in -*ee*, -*ie*,
-*oe*) dropping the *e* (*dancing, moving, gluing; seeing*). A final single consonant
is often doubled (cf. paragraph III above), but this is always indicated in
the dictionary by (**-bb-**) etc. (*rubbing, tinning, mimicking, sitting, preferring;
sagging, tugging,* pr. -gĭng).

VII. *Archaic second and third person singular of verbs*
These are formed in -(*e*)*st* for the second person singular present and past
(*playest, canst, hearest, hear'st; madest, knewest, haddest, hadst, wouldst*), and
-(*e*)*th* for the third person singular present indicative (*goeth, saith*). They
are retained in some religious, legal, poetical, and dialectal usage.

ETYMOLOGY

The word-derivations given in this dictionary are based almost entirely
on those by Dr G. W. S. Friedrichsen in the previous edition of the *Concise
Oxford Dictionary* and in the 1973 printing of the *Shorter Oxford English
Dictionary*, but he does not bear any responsibility for the exact formula-
tions used here. More detailed information may be sought in the latter of

those works and in the *Oxford Dictionary of English Etymology* by Onions, Friedrichsen, and Burchfield (1966).

The etymology is given in square brackets [ ] at the end of nearly every entry. It begins with 'f.' (= from) or 'f. as' (= formed from the same source as) except where the word is traced back to Middle English or Old English, or where in the immediate source (foreign) language it has exactly the same form as in English (in which case that form is not repeated in the etymology: at **formula**, [L . . .] means [from Latin *formula* . . .]; at **basis**, [L f. Gk . . .] means [from Latin *basis* from Greek *basis* . . .]). Thereafter, the word may be traced back to earlier forms in other languages (preceded by 'f.') or in the same language (usually placed in round brackets). Where no form is given after the name of a language (other than immediate sources as above, as far as the first comma), it is understood to be the same as in the next language mentioned: at **high**, 'OS, OHG *hōh*' implies that the Old Saxon form is also *hōh*. Where no meaning is given for a form, it is understood to be the same as for the last one previously given in the etymology: at **knave**, 'OE *cnafa* boy, servant, = OHG *knabo*' implies that the Old High German form also had those meanings. Where no meaning is given for the first form in an etymology, it is understood to be the same as the first listed meaning of the English word.

There are frequent cross-references to other entries which represent component parts of a word, or which share some aspect of the derivation; these are printed in SMALL CAPITALS. An asterisk (*) precedes any form that is not recorded in known documents, but merely inferred to have existed.

Where the exact path of derivation is uncertain, the word 'or' is used: for instance, many English words have corresponding forms in both French and Latin and present a special problem in that we cannot be certain whether the word was adopted from one or the other, or from both at different times or by different persons. At **inclement**, 'f. F *inclément* or f. L *inclemens*', and at **hostility**, 'f. F *hostilité* or f. LL *hostilitas*', indicate situations of this kind.

Where the origin of a word cannot be reliably established at all, it is described as 'uncertain' or 'unknown', even if there are frequently-repeated speculative derivations (as with *pommy*). In such cases the century in which the word was first used in English is stated.

'After' introduces a word or form or language that has served as a basis for analogical formation.

The source of derivatives within an entry is usually indicated by printing in small capitals the suffixes such as -NESS, -LY¹, -LY², -ATION, -IZE (3), which are explained in their alphabetical places; the raised figures refer to different entries for suffixes spelt alike, and the figures in round brackets to particular senses of the suffix concerned. 'Hence' is used to introduce a derivative of the entry word itself (*brewer* from *brew*¹) or of one or all of its numbered senses (*briefly* from *brief*³ 1; *bringer* from *bring*

1–3); 'whence' introduces a derivative of one particular sense, separated only by semicolons, of that word (*careenage* from the first sense of *careen*); 'so' introduces a derivative formed from a predecessor given in the etymology of the entry word (*Carnivora* from Latin *carnivorus*, like *carnivorous*); 'hence or cogn.' introduces two or more derivatives describable partly by 'hence' and partly by 'so' (*censorial* from Latin, *censorship* from English *censor*).

An equals sign (=) precedes forms in other languages that are cognates rather than sources. The description of a form as F (French), G (German), and so on, does not necessarily imply that it is still current, or so spelt, in that language, nor does OF (Old French) or the like imply that it is now obsolete.

Words are usually given their customary dictionary forms for each language, e.g. verbs in the infinitive (French, German, Latin, etc.), first person singular present indicative (Greek), third person singular perfect (Semitic languages), but the English translation is not made to correspond grammatically to each of these.

'ME' (Middle English) refers to the period 1150–1500, no distinction being made between early and late ME; 'OE' (Old English) to the period before 1150. Words of Gmc (Germanic) or WG (West Germanic) origin that have come down from OE or ME are illustrated, so far as possible, by some or all of the forms known or inferred for the older stages of the cognate dialects, usually in the order OS (Old Saxon), OHG (Old High German), ON (Old Norse), and Goth. (Gothic), followed by reconstructed Germanic and IE (Indo-European) forms where appropriate: **hard** . . . [OE *h(e)ard*, = OS *hard*, OHG *hart*, ON *harthr*, Goth. *hardus* f. Gmc **hardhuz* f. IE **kratus*]. In OE, OS, ON, and Goth., the letters thorn and edh (or letters corresponding to them) are both represented by *th*; in OS the plain *b* and *d* are used irrespective of their phonetic value in that dialect; but in Gmc forms, *bh*, *dh*, and *th* are written where appropriate Long vowels are denoted in ON (as also in Icelandic, Irish, and Magyar) by an acute accent (*á*), but in other languages by a macron (*ā*). LDu. (Low Dutch) stands for Low German and Dutch regarded as a linguistic unit.

Words of Romance origin are referred to their immediate source, usually F (French) or OF (Old French before 1400), and thence briefly to earlier sources where known; Rom. (Romanic) denotes the vernacular descendants of Latin that gave rise to French, Spanish, Italian, etc. L (Latin) without prefix denotes classical Latin before about AD 200; OL (Old Latin) Latin before about 75 BC; LL (Late Latin) about AD 200–600; med. L (medieval Latin) about 600–1500; mod. L (modern Latin) since about 1500.† French nouns of Latin origin normally represent the Latin accusative case, but in this dictionary the Latin nominative is cited, followed by the genitive where necessary to show the relevant stem. Here, as elsewhere, a sequence of two forms in one language without

† Gk (Greek) is similarly classified.

punctuation indicates one word in different cases, tenses, or the like. For example, **hearse** . . . [ME, f. OF *herse* harrow f. med. L *erpica* f. Rom. *herpica f. L (*h*)*irpex -picis* large rake f. Samnite (*h*)*irpus* wolf . . .] traces the chain of derivation through Middle English to the Old French *herse* 'harrow', the medieval Latin *erpica* and the inferred Romanic form *herpica* 'harrow', the Latin *hirpex* or *irpex*, genitive *hirpicis* or *irpicis*, 'large rake', and the Samnite word *hirpus* or *irpus* 'wolf'. Latin vowels are left unmarked as to quantity, except for the -*ēre* of the second conjugation, and -*ĕre* of third-conjugation verbs otherwise identical with these.

Greek and Russian words are transliterated in accordance with Appendix II. The Latin form of a word derived through Latin from Greek is usually omitted, being either identical with the transliterated Greek or obtainable from it according to the following scheme:

Greek	Latin	Greek	Latin
-a (m. & f. acc. sing.)	-em	ō	o
ai	ae	-oi (nom. pl.)	-i
ē	e	oi (elsewhere)	oe
-ē, -ēs (1st decl. nom.)	-a	-on	-um
ei	i *or* e	-ōn (nom.)	-o
gg	ng	-os (masc. nom.)	-us
gk	nc	-os (gen.)	-is
gx	nx	ou	u
k	c	u (exc. in diphthong)	y

The first element of a compound word is often referred to a prefix entry, and the remainder treated separately within round brackets; meanings given within the bracket belong to the simple word, those of the compound being added if necessary outside it. Thus at **convene** '[. . . f. L con(*venire vent-* come) assemble, agree, fit]' indicates that *convene* is derived from the Latin *convenire* to assemble, which is from the Latin prefix *con-* (explained in a separate entry) and *venire* to come; the supine stem *vent-* and the senses 'agree, fit' are added for the elucidation of **convention** and **convenience**, which are referred to CONVENE.

The first element of a Greek compound thus treated is sometimes written in the Latin transliteration to assist reference to the prefix entry; for example, at **synagogue**, *sunagō* appears as 'syn(*agō* bring)' in order to refer to the prefix entry SYN-.

NOTE ON PROPRIETARY TERMS

THIS dictionary includes some words which are or are asserted to be proprietary names or trade marks. Their inclusion does not imply that they have acquired for legal purposes a non-proprietary or general significance, nor is any other judgement implied concerning their legal status. In cases where the editor has some evidence that a word is used as a proprietary name or trade mark this is indicated by the letter **P**, but no judgement concerning the legal status of such words is made or implied thereby.

A

A, a¹, (ā) *n.* (*pl.* **As** *or* **A's**). first letter of alphabet; (Mus.) sixth note in diatonic scale of C major; first hypothetical person or example; highest class (of road, academic marks, population as regards affluence, etc.); **from A to Z**, over the entire range, completely; **from A to B**, from any place to some other place (*use* one's *car simply as a means of getting from A to B*); (Alg., usu. *a*) first known quantity; **A1** (ā wŭ′n), (Naut.) first-class (vessel in Lloyd's Register of Shipping), (colloq.) excellent, first-rate; **A1, A2**, etc., standard paper-sizes each half the previous one, e.g. A4 = 297 × 210 mm., A5 = 210 × 148 mm.

a², **an¹**, (*a, an; or, when stressed,* ā, ăn) *a.* (Called the *indefinite article*; unemphatic substitute for) one, some, any; one like (*a Daniel*); one single (*could not see a thing, reduce unemployment at a stroke*), (after all of, etc.) the same (*all of a size*); (distrib.) in, to, or for, each (£*40 a year, twice a day, seven a side,* where *a* is orig. = foll.). For usage see AN¹. [weakening of OE *ān* one]

a³ *prep.* (usu. as *pref.*) on (*afire, afoot*); to (*ashore*); towards (*aback, aside, a-starboard*); in (*nowadays*); in the process of (w. vbl ns. passively (*a-building*) or actively esp. w. go, set (*he went a-begging, they set the bells a--ringing*) and w. vbs. in same sense (*abuzz, aflutter*)). [weakening of OE prep. *an, on* (see ON¹)]

a- *pref.* **1.** f. OE *a-*, orig. *ar-*, away, on, up, out, (*arise*). **2.** f. ME *a-* f. OE *an, on,* prep. (see prec.). **3.** f. ME *a-* f. OE *of* prep. (*akin*). **4.** f. ME *a-* (= OF pref. *a-*), either directly f. L *ad* to, at (*ascend*) or thr. F. *a-* (*agree*); many wds derived in the latter way have been later assim. to L spelling, as *address, aggrieve*. **5.** f. ME *a-*, = OF *a-,* f. L *ab* from, away, (*abridge*). **6.** f. ME, AF *a-* = OF *e-, es-* f. L *ex* out, utterly, (*affray*). **7.** f. Gk *a-,* not, without—derived directly (*agnostic, amoral*), thr. L (*apetalous*), or thr. L and F (*adamant, amethyst*); usu. AN- bef. vowel or *h*.

-a *suf.* forming: **1.** ns. f. Gk, L, and Rom. fem. sing., as *idea* (Gk), *arena* (L), *piazza* (It.), *duenna* (Sp.), esp. names of animals and plants, ancient or Latinized mod. (*hyena, dahlia*), oxides (*alumina*), geog. names (*Africa*), and feminine names, ancient or Latinized mod. (*Lydia, Hilda*). **2.** *pl.* ns. [f. Gk and L neut. pl.] (*phenomena, genera*), esp. names, often f. mod. L, of Zool. groups (*Carnivora*). **3.** colloq. or sl. for *of* (*coupla, kinda, pinta*) or *have* (*mighta*) or *to* (*oughta*).

A. *abbr.* ‖(Of films) certified as suitable for adult audiences but possibly not for children; ampere(s); ångström(s); answer; Associate of; atomic (energy etc.).

a *abbr.* atto-.

AA *abbr.* *Alcoholics Anonymous; anti-aircraft; ‖Automobile Association; ‖(of films) to be seen only by persons over 14.

AAA *abbr.* ‖Amateur Athletic Association; *American Automobile Association.

A. & M. *abbr.* (Hymns) Ancient and Modern.

A. & R. *abbr.* artists and recording (*or* repertoire).

aar′dvark (ār′d-) *n.* termite-eating nocturnal African mammal. [Afrik. (*aarde* earth, *vark* pig)]

aar′dwol\|f (ār′dwŏŏlf) *n.* (*pl.* ~ves). insectivorous African mammal of hyena family. [Afrik. (*aarde* earth, *wolf* wolf)]

Aaron's beard (ārŏnz-) *n.* popular name for several plants, esp. a St. John's wort (*Hypericum calycinum*). [ref. to Ps. 133: 2]

Aaron's röd (ārŏnz-) *n.* popular name for several tall plants, esp. a mullein (*Verbascum thapsus*). [ref. to Num. 17: 8]

A'asia *abbr.* Australasia.

aa′svogel (ah′sfōgel) *n.* S. Afr. vulture. [Afrik. (*aas* carrion, *vogel* bird)]

*AAU *abbr.* Amateur Athletic Union.

ab- *pref.* off, away, from (*abduct, abnormal, abuse*). [F or f. L]

AB *abbr.* able rating or seaman [f. *able-bodied*]; *Bachelor of Arts [f. L *Artium Baccalaureus*].

ă′ba, abaya (abā′ya), **ă′bba**, *n.* sleeveless outer garment as worn by Arabs. [f. Arab. '*abā*′]

‖**ä′băc** *n.* nomogram. [f. F *abaque* f. L ABACUS]

ă′baca *n.* (plant yielding) Manila hemp. [f. Sp. *abacá*]

abă′ck *adv.* backwards, behind; (Naut., of square sails) pressed against mast by head wind; **taken** ~, (of ship) with sails in that state; **take** ~, (fig.) surprise, disconcert. [OE *on bæc* (as A³, BACK¹)]

ă′bac\|us *n.* (*pl.* ~uses, *or* ~i *pr.* -sī). **1.** calculating frame with balls sliding on wires or in grooves, used before adoption of the nine figures and zero, and still in elementary teaching. **2.** (Archit.) upper member of capital, supporting architrave. [L, f. Gk *abax abakos* slab, drawing-board, f. Heb. '*ābāk* dust]

Abă′ddon (a-) *n.* hell; the Devil (Rev. 9:11). [Heb., = destruction]

aba′ft (-ah′-) *adv. & prep.* (Naut.) **1.** *adv.* in stern half of ship. **2.** *prep.* nearer stern than, aft of. [f. A³ + *baft* f. OE *bæftan* (*be* BY¹, *æftan* behind)]

*ăbalō′nĕ *n.* edible mollusc of genus *Haliotis*, with ear-shaped shell lined with mother-of-pearl; ormer, sea-ear. [f. Amer. Sp. *abulón*]

abă′ndon¹ *v.t.* give up to another's control or mercy; yield one*self* completely to a passion or impulse; give up (possession, habit, game); forsake (person, post, ship). [ME, f. OF *abandoner* (*à bandon* under control f. Rom. *bando-onis f. med. L *bandum,* var. of LL *bannus, bannus*')]

abă′ndon² (abā′ndon, ăbah′ndawn) *n.* careless freedom of manner, letting oneself go. [F; see prec.]

abă′ndoned (-ond) *a.* forsaken; profligate. [p.p. of ABANDON¹]

abă′ndonee′ *n.* (Law). one to whom anything is relinquished, esp. underwriter entitled to salvage a wreck. [f. ABANDON¹ + -EE]

abă′ndonment *n.* giving up or forsaking; being forsaken; self-surrender; careless freedom of manner, impulsiveness. [f. F *abandonnement* (as ABANDON¹; see -MENT)]

aba′se *v.t.* lower, humiliate, debase; hence ~MENT (-sm-) *n.* [ME, f. OF *abaisser* (*a* = A- 4, *baissier* to lower f. Rom. *bassiare f. LL *bassus* short of stature); infl. by BASE³]

aba′sh *v.t.* (usu. in *pass.*) embarrass, disconcert; hence ~MENT *n.* [ME, f. OF *esbair* (*es-* = A- 6, *baïr* astound or *baer* yawn)]

aba′sk (-ah′-) *adv.* basking. [f. A³ + BASK]

abā′te *v.* **1.** *v.t. & i.* diminish; make or grow less. **2.** *v.t.* do away with (nuisance); lower (price); deduct (specified or unspecified part of price); mitigate (violence, pain); weaken (energy). **3.** (Law). quash (writ or action). **4.** So ~MENT (-tm-) *n.* [ME, f. OF *abatre, batre*. Rom. **abbatt(u)ere* (A- 4, L *batt(u)ere* beat)]

ă′batis, abă′ttis, *n.* (*pl.* same *or* ~es). defence made of felled trees with boughs pointing outwards; hence ~ED² (-st) *a.* [F (*abatre* fell; see prec.)]

ă′battoir (-twăr) *n.* slaughterhouse. [F (as prec.; see -ORY)]

abaya, abba. See ABA.

ă′bbacy̆ *n.* office, jurisdiction, or tenure, of an abbot or abbess. [ME, f. eccl. L *abbacia* (*abbat*- ABBOT; see -ACY)]

Abbā′sid (*a*-) *a.* & *n.* (member) of dynasty of caliphs ruling in Baghdad 750–1258. [f. *Abbas*, Muhammad's uncle d. 652 + -ID³]

abbā′tial (-shăl) *a.* of an abbey, abbot, or abbess. [F, or f. med. L *abbatialis* (as ABBOT; see -IAL)]

abbé (ă′bā) *n.* Frenchman (orig. abbot) entitled to wear ecclesiastical dress, with or without official duties. [F, f. eccl. L *abbas abbatis* ABBOT]

ă′bbĕss *n.* head of abbey of nuns. [ME, f. OF *abbesse* f. eccl. L *abbatissa* (as ABBOT; see -ESS¹)]

Abbevi′llian (ăbv-) *a.* & *n.* (culture) of earliest palaeolithic period in Europe. [F (-*ien*), f. *Abbeville* in N. France; see -IAN]

ă′bbey *n.* building(s) occupied by monks or nuns under an abbot or abbess; the monks or nuns as a body; church or house that was once an abbey or part of it; **the A∿**, ||(esp.) Westminster Abbey. [ME, f. OF *abbeie* etc. f. med. L *abbatia* ABBACY]

ă′bbot *n.* head of abbey of monks. [OE *abbod* etc., f. eccl. L *abbas -atis* f. Gk *abbas* father f. Aram. *'abbā*]

abbrē′viate¹ *a.* relatively short. [ME, f. LL *abbreviatus* (as foll.; see -ATE²)]

abbrē′vi|āte² *v.t.* make short (usu. of writing part of word for whole; occas. of story etc.); so ∿A′TION *n.* [ME, f. LL *abbreviare* shorten (*ab* or *ad*, *brevis* short) + -ATE³; cf. ABRIDGE]

ABC (ābēsē′) *n.* the alphabet (*as easy as ABC*); rudiments of any subject; alphabetical guide. [f. A + B + C]

ABC *abbr.* Australian Broadcasting Commission; *American Broadcasting Company.

ă′bdic|āte *v.t.* renounce formally or by default (a power, office, duty, right, or abs., esp. of the crown); so ∿A′TION *n.* [f. L AB(*dicare* declare) + -ATE³]

ăbdomĕn (ă′bdo-, ăbdō′-) *n.* **1.** (Anat.) belly, part of body containing stomach, bowels, and other digestive organs. **2.** (Zool.) hinder part of insect, crustacean, spider, etc. [L]

ăbdŏ′minal *a.* of the abdomen (in either sense). [f. mod. L *abdominalis* f. L. *abdomin*- stem of prec. + -AL]

ăbdŏ′minous *a.* corpulent. [f. L *abdomin*- stem of ABDOMEN + -OUS]

abdŭ′ct *v.t.* kidnap (child); take away (esp. woman) by illegal force or fraud; (of muscle etc.) draw (limb etc.) away from middle line of body etc.; so ∿ION, ∿OR, *ns.* [f. L AB(*ducere duct*- draw)]

abea′m *adv.* on a line at right angles to ship's or aircraft's length; opposite middle *of* (ship etc.). [A³ + BEAM¹]

ābēcēdār′ian *a.* & *n.* **1.** *a.* arranged alphabetically. **2.** *n.* person learning the alphabet or rudiments of a subject. [f. LL *abecedarius* (*a, b, c, d*; see -ARY¹) + -AN]

abē′d *adv.* (arch.) in bed. [OE (as A³, BED¹)]

abele (abē′l, ā′bel) *n.* the white poplar, *Populus alba*. [f. Du. *abeel* f. OF *abel*, earlier *aubel* f. med. L *albellus* dim. of *albus* white]

A′berdeen (ă′-) *n.* ∿ (**Angus**), (animal of) Scottish breed of polled black beef cattle; ∿ (**terrier**), Scotch terrier. [∿ in Scotland]

Aberdō′nian (ă-) *a.* & *n.* (native or inhabitant) of Aberdeen. [f. med. L *Aberdonia* + -IAN]

Abernĕ′thy̆ (ă-) *n.* hard biscuit flavoured with caraway seeds. [prob. f. John ∿, Engl. surgeon d. 1831]

abĕ′rr|ant *a.* straying from moral standard; (esp. Biol.) diverging from normal type; so ∿ANCE, ∿ANCY, *ns.* [f. L AB(*errare* stray); see -ANT]

ăberrā′tion *n.* **1.** a straying from the path (lit. or fig.); breaking of rules; moral slip; temporary lapse of memory; deviation from type. **2.** (Opt.) non--convergence of rays from a point to one focus. **3.** (Astron.) apparent displacement of celestial body from its true position, caused by observer's motion. [f. L *aberratio* (as prec.; see -ATION)]

abě′t *v.t.* (-tt-). encourage or assist (offence or offender; esp. *aid and abet*); so ∿MENT, ∿tER¹, (esp. Law) ∿tOR, *ns.* [ME, f. OF *abeter* (*à* to, *beter* BAIT¹)]

ab extra (ăb ĕ′kstra) *adv.* from outside. [LL]

abey′|ance (-bā′-) *n.* state of suspension or temporary disuse; (of rights etc.) dormant condition liable to revival (usu. *be in* or *fall into abeyance*); hence ∿ANT *a.* [f. AF *abeiance* f. OF *abeer* (*à* to, *beer* f. med. L *batare* gape)]

abhŏ′r *v.t.* (-rr-). regard with disgust and hatred. [ME, f. F *abhorrer* or f. L AB(*horrēre* shudder)]

abhŏ′rrence *n.* detestation; detested thing. [f. foll. + -ENCE]

abhŏ′rrent *a.* (Of conduct etc.) inspiring disgust, hateful, *to* (person etc.); not according *to* (abhorrent *to the spirit of the law*); (arch.) feeling disgust; ∿ **from**, inconsistent with. [f. as ABHOR; see -ENT]

abī′dance *n.* continuance, dwelling (*in*); abiding (*by* rules etc.). [f. foll. + -ANCE]

abī′de *v.* (abo′de *pr.* -ō′d, *or* ∿d). **1.** *v.i.* remain, continue; (arch.) dwell; ∿ **by** (*past* and *p.p.* usu. ∿d), remain faithful to, act upon (terms, promise). **2.** *v.t.* encounter, sustain; submit to, suffer; (*neg.* or *interrog.*, with *n.* or *inf.*) put up with, tolerate; (arch.) wait for. [OE *ābīdan* (A- 1, *bīdan* BIDE)]

abī′ding *a.* enduring, permanent; hence ∿LY² *adv.* [f. prec. + -ING²]

a′bigail *n.* lady's-maid. [character in Beaumont & Fletcher's *Scornful Lady*; cf. 1 Sam. 25]

abī′lity̆ *n.* sufficient power, capacity (*to do* something); legal competency (to act); cleverness, talent, mental power, (*his undoubted ability; his manifold abilities*). [ME f. OF *ablete* f. L *habilitas -tatis* (*habilis* deft; see -TY¹)]

-abī′lity̆ *suf.* forming *ns.* f. *adjs.* in -ABLE (*communicability*). [f. F -*abilité* or f. L -*abilitas*; see -ITY]

ab initio (ăb ĭnĭ′shĭō) *adv.* from the beginning. [L]

ābīo|gĕ′nĕsis *n.* spontaneous generation; supposed origin of life by formation of organic from inorganic substances; hence ∿GE′NIC *a.* [f. A- 7 + Gk *bios* life + GENESIS]

ābiŏ′tic *a.* devoid of life. [f. A- 7 + BIOTIC]

ă′bjĕct *a.* brought low, miserable; craven, degraded, despicable, self-abasing; hence ∿LY² *adv.*, ∿NESS *n.* [ME, f. L *abjectus* p.p. of AB(*icĕre* = *jacĕre* throw)]

abjĕ′ction *n.* state of misery or degradation. [ME f. OF, or f. L *abjectio* (as prec.; see -ION)]

abjur′e (-joor′) *v.t.* Renounce on oath (an opinion, heresy, cause, claim, claimant); swear perpetual absence from (one's country etc.); so **ăbjur**A′TION *n.* [f. L AB(*jurare* swear)]

ăblā′te *v.t.* remove by ablation. [back-form. f. foll.]

ăblā′tion *n.* (Surg.) removal of any part of body; (Geol.) wasting or erosion of a glacier, iceberg, or rock by melting or water action; (Astronaut.) evaporation or melting of part of outer surface of spacecraft through heating by friction with atmosphere. [F, or f. LL *ablatio* f. L AB(*lat*- p.p. st. of *ferre* carry)]

a′blative *a.* & *n.* (Gram.) ∿ (**case**), case of (esp. Latin) nouns etc., expressing source, agent, cause, or instrument, of action, = *from* or *by* w. the noun etc.; **ablative** ABSOLUTE. [ME, f. OF *ablatif -ive* or f. L *ablativus* (as prec.; see -IVE)]

a′blaut (-owt) *n.* vowel change in related words in (esp. the parent Indo-European language, arising out of differences of accent and stress, and surviving e.g. in *sing, sang, sung*. [G]

ăblā′ze *adv.* & *pred. a.* on fire; glittering; excited. [f. A³ + BLAZE¹]

a′ble *a.* **1.** talented, clever; competent, having the means or power (*to*) (esp. used w. parts of *be* to supply the deficiencies of *can*, e.g. *shall be able to* as that of *can*); legally qualified. **2.** ∿-**bodied**, fit, skilled; ∿(-**bodied**) **rating, seaman**, one able to perform all duties. **3.** Hence **ā′ blY²** *adv.*, capably, cleverly. [ME, f. OF *hable*, *able* f. L *habilis* handy (*habēre* to hold)]

-able *suf.* forming *adjs.*, in wds formed at early date freq. w. act. sense (*comfortable, suitable*), now always w. pass. sense: 'that can, may, must, be —d' (*eatable, execrable, forgivable, payable*), 'that can be made the subject of' (*dutiable, objectionable*), 'that is relevant to or in accordance with' (*fashionable, seasonable, serviceable*). [F, or f. L -*a*- of first conjug. +-*bilis* (see -BLE), in F extended to vbs. of all conjugs.; in E now appended even to native vbs. as *bearable*, nouns as *clubbable*, and phrasal vbs. as *get-at-able*, prob. f. confusion w. prec.]

abloo'm *adv. & pred. a.* in or into bloom. [f. A³ +BLOOM¹]

ablu'sh *adv. & pred. a.* blushing. [f. A³+BLUSH¹]

ablu'tion (-lōō'-) *n.* (usu. in *pl.*) ceremonial washing of person, hands, or sacred vessels; water that has been used for this; (joc.) ordinary personal washing; ||building containing washing-places etc. in camp, ship, etc.; hence ∿ARY¹ *a.* [ME f. OF, or f. LL AB(*lutio* f. *luere lut-* wash; see -ION)]

a'bly *adv.* See ABLE.

-ably *suf.* forming advs. corresp. to adjs. in -*able*. [f. -ABLE+-LY²]

ABM *abbr.* anti-ballistic-missile missile.

a'bnegate *v.t.* deny oneself (something); renounce (a right or belief). [f. L AB(*negare* deny) +-ATE³]

abnega'tion *n.* denial; renunciation (of doctrine); (self-)∿, self-sacrifice. [f. OF, or f. LL *abnegatio* (as prec.; see -ATION)]

abno'rmal *a.* exceptional, irregular; deviating from type; relating to what is abnormal (*abnormal psychology*); hence **abnorma'lity** *n.*, the quality or an instance of it, ∿ITY² *adv* [earlier and F *anormal*, *anomal* f. Gk *anōmalos* ANOMALOUS, assoc. w. L *abnormis*; see foll.]

abnor'mity *n.* irregularity; a monstrosity. [f. L AB(*normis* f. *norma* rule) +-ITY]

A'bo (ă'-), **ă'bō**, *n.* (*pl.* ∿s) & *a.* (Austral. sl., often derog.) Aboriginal. [abbr.]

aboar'd *adv. & prep.* on or into ship, aircraft, train, *bus, etc. (*ship* etc. either expressed or implied); alongside, near; all ∿! (call that warns of imminent departure; |ME, f. A³+BOARD¹ & F *à bord*|

abo'de¹ *n.* dwelling-place, house; stay, habit of dwelling (*make one's abode*). [vbl n. of ABIDE; cf. *ride, rode, road*]

abo'de². See ABIDE.

abo'lish *v.t.* end existence of (custom, institution); hence ∿ABLE *a.*, ∿ER¹, ∿MENT, *ns.* [ME, f. F *abolir* (-ISH³) f. L *abolēre* destroy]

aboli'tion *n.* abolishing, being abolished (esp. w. ref. to capital punishment, or (Hist.) Negro slavery, and the movement against it, whence ∿ISM(3), ∿IST(2), *ns.*). [F, or f. L *abolitio* (as prec.; see -ION)]

aboma'sum *n.* (*pl.* ∿a). fourth STOMACH of ruminant. [mod. L, f. AB- +OMASUM]

A-bomb (ā'bŏm) *n.* atomic bomb. [f. A (for ATOMIC) +BOMB]

abo'minab|le *a.* detestable, odious; morally or physically loathsome; (by exagg.) unpleasant (*abominable weather*); A∿le Snowman, yeti, unidentified anthropoid or ursine animal alleged to exist in Himalayas; hence ∿LY² *adv.* [ME f. OF, f. L *abominabilis* f. AB(*ominari* f. OMEN) deprecate; see -ABLE]

abo'minate *v.t.* loathe; (by exagg.) dislike. [f. L *abominari* (as prec.) +-ATE³]

abomina'tion *n.* loathing; odious or degrading habit or act; an object of disgust (*to*). [ME f. OF (as ABOMINATE; see -ATION)]

abori'ginal *a. & n.* **1.** *a.* (Of races and natural objects) indigenous, existing in a land at the dawn of history, or before arrival of colonists; of the Australian Aboriginals; hence ∿ITY (-ă'l-) *n.*, ∿LY² *adv.* **2.** *n.* aboriginal inhabitant, esp. (usu. A∿) of Australia. [f. as foll. +-AL]

abori'gine *n.* (usu. in *pl.*, *pr.* -ēz or -ĭz). aboriginal inhabitant. (usu. A∿) of Australia; aboriginal plant or animal. [L *aborigines* pl., prob. f. phr. *ab origine* from the beginning]

*****abor'ning** *adv. & pred. a.* (while) being born or produced. [f. A³ +BORN+-ING²]

abor't *v. & n.* **1.** *v.i.* undergo abortion; (Biol.) remain undeveloped, shrink away. **2.** *v.t.* cause abortion of; (fig.) cause to end fruitlessly; stop (growth, disease) in early stages. **3.** *v.t. & i.* (Aeron. & Astronaut.) terminate (flight), stop, abandon, or destroy (rocket etc.), fail to complete flight. **4.** Hence ∿ÏFA'CIENT *a. & n.*, (drug or other agent) causing abortion. **5.** *n.* (Aeron. & Astronaut.) unsuccessful (flight by) rocket etc.; termination of such flight. [f. L AB(*oriri ort-* be born) miscarry]

abor'ted *a.* untimely born; undeveloped; (Biol.) rudimentary (*thorns are aborted branches*). [f. prec. +-ED¹ (2)]

abor'tion *n.* miscarriage of birth, esp. if deliberately induced; causing of this, illegally, whence ∿IST (1) *n.*; (Med.) delivery of (prob. non-viable) foetus in first 28 weeks of pregnancy; arrested development of any organ; dwarfed or misshapen creature; failure of a project or action. [f. L *abortio* (as ABORT; see -ION)]

abor'tive *a.* resulting in abortion; (Biol., of organ etc.) rudimentary, arrested in development; fruitless, unsuccessful; hence ∿LY² (-vlĭ) *adv.*, ∿NESS (-vn-) *n.* [ME, f. OF *abortif -ive* f. L *abortivus* (as ABORT, -IVE)]

abou'l|ia, abū'l|ia, *n.* loss of will-power (as mental disorder); hence ∿IC *a.* [f. Gk *a-* not+*boule* will]

abou'nd *v.i.* be plentiful; be rich in; teem or be infested (*with*). [ME, f. OF *abunder* etc. f. L AB(*undare* f. *unda* wave) overflow]

abou't *adv. & prep.* **1.** all round from outside (*compass it about; go a long way about; He is about my path;* BEAT¹ *about the bush*); all round from a centre (*look,* LAY⁰, *about you*). **2.** somewhere near (HANG¹ *about; people or objects about us; have or keep one's* WIT²*s about one*); carried with (*have no money about me*); here and there (*in* a place, or abs.) (*measles is about; move,* ORDER², *about*); PUT¹ *about; dotted about the fields; man about* TOWN); **out and ∿**, (of person, esp. after illness) engaging in normal outdoor activity; **up and ∿**, arisen after sleep or illness. **3.** near in number, scale, degree, etc., (*about half, fifty, right, midnight, my size, the best*); (colloq., in iron. understatement or comparison; *I'm about tired of this; about as exciting as cold semolina*). **4.** facing in opposite direction (RIGHT¹ *about turn* or *face; the wrong way about*); **∿ turn** or ***face** (as Mil. command). **5.** in rotation (*take turns about; on duty* (*week* and) *week about*). **6.** occupied in action (*send him about his* BUSINESS; *what are you about?*); **am ∿ to do**, am on the point of doing (so all vbs. forming fut. participles). **7.** in connection with, on the subject of, (*quarrels, a book, about money; something wrong about it; have read, do not know, about it;* SET¹, SEE¹, GO¹, *about*); in relation to (*symmetry about a line or plane*); **how about,** = WHAT *about;* **what** thing **is** (all) ∿, (colloq.) its essential nature or purpose. **8.** in the course of events (*I brought it about; it came about*). **9.** (Naut.) on or to the opposite tack (*go about; put about*). [OE *onbūtan* (*on būtan, būtan* BUT¹)]

about-fa'ce *n., & v.i.* (make) reversal of direction, opinion, policy, or behaviour. [f. Mil. commands (ABOUT & ∿)]

abo've (-ŭ'v) *adv., prep., a., & n.* **1.** *adv.* at or to a higher point; overhead; on high; upstream; upstairs; in heaven. **2.** on the upper side; in preceding part of book or article (*as was remarked above; the above--mentioned facts*); in addition (*over and above*). **3.** *prep.* over, on the top of, higher than (*above average,* PAR¹; *heard above the din; head above water*); ∿ **ground**, (fig.) alive; *above one's* HEAD¹; ∿ **oneself**, carried away by high spirits, conceit, etc.; ∿-**boar'd** *adv. & pred. a.*, undisguised(ly), fair(ly), open(ly) [metaph. f. card-playing]. **4.** more than (*above a hundred*); upstream from; further north than; (arch.) to an earlier time than (*not traced above the third century*); out of reach of (*above criticism, suspicion, my understanding*); too great or good for (*above meanness, ideas above one's station*); more important than (*above all (else)*); of higher rank than. **5.**

a. preceding, previous (*the above statements*). **6.** *n.* that which is above. [f. A³ + OE *bufan* (*be* BY¹, *ufan* above)]

ab ovo (ăb ō′vō) *adv.* (relating tediously) from the very beginning. [L, = from the egg]

Abp. *abbr.* Archbishop.

ăbracadă′bra *n.* spell, magic formula; gibberish. [cabbalistic word supposed when written triangularly, and worn, to cure fevers etc.; L f. Gk]

abrā′de *v.t.* scrape off, wear away, injure, (skin, rock, fabric, etc.) by rubbing. [f. L AB(*radere ras-* scrape)]

A′brahăm-măn (ā′bra-h-) *n.* (*pl.* **-men**). (Hist.) wandering beggar of 16th c., usu. feigning insanity; **sham Abraham,** feign illness or insanity. [perh. after Luke 16]

abrā′sion (-zhon) *n.* scraping off, wearing away, (of skin, rock, etc.); damaged area resulting from this. [f. L *abrasio* (as ABRADE; see -ION)]

abrā′sive *a.* & *n.* **1.** (substance) capable of rubbing or grinding down. **2.** *a.* tending to graze the skin; (fig.) tending to hurt person's feelings. [f. as prec. + -IVE]

ăbreă′ct|ion *n.* (Psych.) free expression and release of a previously repressed emotion; hence ~IVE *a.*, **ăbreă′ct** *v.t.* release by abreaction. [f. AB-+REAC-TION, after G *abreagierung*]

abrea′st (-ĕ′st) *adv.* side by side and facing the same way; keeping up, not behind, (*of* or *with* progress, thought, etc.). [ME, f. A³ + BREAST¹]

abrī′dge *v.t.* condense (book, film, etc.); curtail (liberty); (arch.) deprive (person *of*). [ME, f. OF *abreg(i)er* f. LL *abbreviare* ABBREVIATE²]

abri′dgement, -dgm-, (-jm-) *n.* shortening (of book etc.); curtailment (of rights); epitome, abstract. [f. F *abrégement* (as prec.; see -MENT)]

abroa′ch *adv.* & *pred. a.* (Of cask) pierced, so as to let the liquor run. [ME, f. AF *abroche* f. OF *abrochier* (as A-4, BROACH¹)]

abroa′d (-aw′d) *adv.* **1.** in or to foreign lands; **from ~,** from another country. **2.** broadly, in different directions (*scattered abroad*); in motion, current, (*there is a rumour abroad*). **3.** (arch.) out of doors; in error. [ME, f. A³ + BROAD]

a′brogāte *v.t.* repeal, cancel, (law, custom); so **ăbrogA′TION** *n.* [f. L AB(*rogare* propose law) + -ATE³]

abrŭ′pt *a.* sudden, hasty; disconnected, not smooth (*abrupt manner of speaking*); steep, precipitous; (Bot.) truncated; (Geol., of strata) suddenly cropping out; hence ~LY² *adv.*, ~NESS *n.* [f. L *abruptus* p.p. of AB(*rumpere* break)]

abrŭ′ption *n.* breaking away of part from a mass. [f. L *abruptio* (as prec.; see -ION)]

abs- *pref.* = AB-. [var. of L *ab-* used before *c, q, t*]

ă′bscèss *n.* localized collection of pus formed in the body by disintegration of tissue. [f. L *abscessus* a going away f. ABS(*cedere cess-* go)]

abscī′ssa *n.* (*pl.* ~s or ~e). (Math.) part of line between fixed point on it and ordinate drawn to it from any other point; coordinate measured parallel to *x*-axis. [mod. L *abscissa* (*linea*) fem. p.p. of AB(*scindere sciss-* cut)]

absci′ssion (-shon) *n.* cutting off; (Bot.) natural separation. [f. L *abscissio* (as prec.; see -ION)]

abscō′nd *v.i.* depart secretly; flee from the law; hence ~ER¹ *n.* [f. L ABS(*condere* stow)]

ă′bseil (-sāl, -zīl) *n.*, & *v.i.* (make) descent of steep rock-face by using doubled rope fixed at higher point. [f. G *abseilen* (*ab* down, *seil* rope)]

ă′bsence *n.* being away from a place or person; time of being away; non-existence or lack *of*; inattention due to thought of other things (*esp. absence of mind*). [ME f. OF, f. L *absentia* (absent- ABSENT¹)]

ă′bsent¹ *a.* **1.** not present (~ **from,** at another place than; ~ **voter,** one who votes by post because absent from usual voting-place); not existing. **2.** inattentive, abstracted in mind; hence ~LY² *adv.*, ~-mĭ′ndED² *a.*, ~-mĭ′ndĕdLY² *adv.*, ~-mĭ′ndĕdNESS, ~NESS, *ns.* [ME f. OF, f. L *absens absentis* part. of AB(*esse* be)]

absĕ′nt² *v.refl.* keep one*self* away; withdraw one*self*. [ME, f. OF *absenter* or f. LL *absentare* (absent- ABSENT¹)]

ăbsentee′ *n.* person not present; ABSENT¹ voter; person, esp. landlord, habitually living elsewhere; hence ~ISM(2) *n.*, practice of being an absentee, practice of workers, pupils, etc., of absenting themselves from work, esp. frequently or without good reason. [f. ABSENT² + -EE]

ă′bsinth *n.* wormwood, the plant or its essence; ~(e), a green liqueur made (at least orig.) from wine and wormwood. [f. F *absinthe* f. L f. Gk *apsinthion*]

absit omen (ăbsĭt ō′mĕn) *int.* may suggested foreboding not become fact. [L, = may this (evil) omen be absent]

ă′bsolute (-ōōt, -ūt) *a.* **1.** complete, perfect. **2.** pure; ~ **alcohol** (free from water). **3.** unrestricted, independent (~ **majority,** more than half, majority over all rivals combined); ruling arbitrarily, despotic. **4.** not in usu. grammatical relation; **ablative** ~ in L, **accusative** ~ in G, **genitive** ~ in Gk, **nominative** ~ **or** ~ **construction** in E, noun and participle (or E infinitive) used as adverbial clause (*dinner being over, we left the table; let us toss for it, loser to pay*). **5.** not relative or comparative; unqualified, unconditional; (Philos.) self-existent and conceivable without relation to other things (**the** ~, that which is absolute); absolute MAGNITUDE, ~ **music,** self-dependent instrumental music devoid of literary etc. suggestions; ~ **pitch,** (Mus.) (1) ability to recognize or reproduce the pitch of a note, (2) fixed standard of pitch defined by rate of vibration; ~ **temperature** (measured from absolute ZERO). **6.** Hence ~NESS (-tn-) *n.* [ME, f. L *absolutus* p.p. (see ABSOLVE); infl. by OF *absolut*]

ă′bsolutelў (-ōōtlĭ,-ūtlĭ) *adv.* **1.** independently, in and by itself; arbitrarily, without external control. **2.** without qualification; (esp. Gram.) without the usual accompaniments (*transitive verb used* ~, without its object). **3.** unconditionally; positively, actually, (*it absolutely exploded*); conclusively; completely, quite; (w. neg.) at all; (colloq., *pr.* -ōō′-) quite so, yes. [f. prec. + -LY²]

ăbsolu′tion (-lōō′-, -lū′-) *n.* formal setting-free from guilt, sentence, or obligation; ecclesiastical declaration of forgiveness of sins; remission of penance; forgiveness. [ME f. OF, f. L *absolutio -onis* (as ABSOLVE; see -ION)]

ă′bsolut|ism (-lōō-, -lū-) *n.* (Theol.) doctrine that God acts absolutely in the matter of salvation; (Polit.) principle of absolute government; philosophy of the absolute; hence ~IST(2) *n.* [f. ABSOLUTE + -ISM]

absō′lve (-z-) *v.t.* set or pronounce free (*from* blame, *of* sin, *from* obligation, or abs.); acquit, pronounce not guilty. [f. L AB(*solvere solut-* loosen)]

absōr′b (-s-, -z-) *v.t.* swallow up, incorporate (**be** ~**ed by,** lose one's identity in); engross the attention of; take in (fluid, food, knowledge); reduce intensity of (heat, light, sound, particles, impact, etc.) by physical or chemical action; consume (income, labour, strength, etc.); hence ~ABLE *a.*, ~ABI′LITY, ~ER¹(2), *ns.* [ME, f. F *absorber* or f. L AB(*sorbēre sorpt-* suck in)]

absōr′bed (-sōr′bd, -z-) *a.* intensely engaged or interested; hence ~LY² (-bĭdlĭ) *adv.* [p.p. of prec.]

absōr′b|ent (-s-, -z-) *a.* & *n.* **1.** *a.* having tendency to absorb; ***ent cotton,** cotton wool; hence ~ENCY *n.* **2.** *n.* substance of this kind; one of the vessels in plants and animals (e.g. root tips) that absorb nutriment. [f. L (as ABSORB); see -ENT]

absōr′bing (-s-, -z-) *a.* engrossing, intensely interesting; hence ~LY² *adv.* [f. ABSORB + -ING³]

absōr′pt|ion (-s-, -z-) *n.* disappearance through incorporation in something else; mental engrossment; process of absorbing fluid, light, etc.; hence ~IVE *a.*, ~IVENESS (-vn-) *n.* [L *absorptio* (as ABSORB; see -ION)]

ăbsqua′tūlāte (-ō′-) *v.i.* (joc.) depart; decamp. [joc. after *abscond, squattle* decamp, *perambulate*]

abstai′n (-s-) *v.i.* **1.** restrain oneself (*from*); (esp.) refrain from alcohol. **2.** decline to use one's vote. **3.** Hence ∼ER¹ *n.*, ∼ING² *a.* [ME, f. AF *astener* f. OF *astenir* f. L ABS(*tinēre tent-* = *tenēre* hold)]

ăbstē'mious *a.* (Of persons, habits, etc.) sparing, moderate, not self-indulgent, esp. in food and drink; hence ∼LY² *adv.*, ∼NESS *n.* [f. L *abstemius* (ABS-, *temetum* strong drink) + -OUS]

ăbstē'ntion *n.* abstaining (*from*, or abs.), (esp.) not using one's vote. [F, or f. LL *abstentio -onis* (as ABSTAIN; see -ION)]

ăbstēr'|gent *a.* & *n.* cleansing (substance); so ∼SION (-shon) *n.*, ∼SIVE *a.* [f. L ABS(*tergēre ters-* wipe); see -ENT]

ă'bstinence *n.* abstaining (*from* any pleasure etc.); continence; partial fasting; (**total**) ∼, going without alcohol; = foll. [ME f. OF, f. L *abstinentia* (as ABSTINENT; see -ENCE)]

ă'bstinency *n.* habit of abstaining from pleasure, food, etc. [f. as prec.; see -ENCY]

ă'bstinent *a.* practising abstinence; hence ∼LY² *adv.* [ME f. OF, f. L (as ABSTAIN; see -ENT)]

ă'bstrăct¹ *a.* **1.** separated from matter, practice, or particular examples; not concrete; ∼ **noun** (denoting quality or state); **the** ∼, ideal or theoretical way of regarding things. **2.** idealistic, not practical; abstruse; (Art etc.) free from representational qualities (∼ **expressionism**, ACTION painting). **3.** Hence ∼LY² *adv.*, ∼NESS *n.* [ME f. OF, or f. L *abstractus* p.p. of ABS(*trahere* draw)]

ă'bstrăct² *n.* brief statement of content of book etc., summary; abstraction or abstract term; abstract painting etc. [as prec.]

ăbstră'ct³ *v.t.* deduct, remove; (euphem.) steal; disengage (attention etc.) *from*; consider abstractly; summarize; hence ∼OR *n.* [f. ABSTRACT¹]

ăbstră'ctĕd *a.* withdrawn in thought; not attending; hence ∼LY² *adv.*, ∼NESS *n.* [p.p. of prec.]

ăbstră'ction *n.* taking away, withdrawal; (euphem.) stealing; process of stripping an idea of its concrete accompaniments; an idea so stripped, something visionary; piece of abstract art, whence ∼ISM (3), ∼IST (2), *ns.*; absence of mind. [F, or f. L *abstractio* (as ABSTRACT¹; see -ION)]

ăbstru'se (-ōō's) *a.* hard to understand, profound; hence ∼LY² (-slī) *adv.*, ∼NESS (-sn-) *n.* [F, or f. L ABS(*trusus* p.p. of *trudere* push)]

ăbsŭr'd *a.* incongruous, inappropriate; unreasonable; ridiculous, silly; hence ∼LY² *adv.* [f. F *absurde* or f. L *absurdus* (AB-, *surdus* deaf, dull)]

ăbsŭr'dĭtÿ *n.* Folly, unreasonableness; absurd statement or act. [f. F *absurdité* or f. LL *absurditas* (as ABSURD; see -ITY)]

abu'lia, abu'lic. See ABOULIA.

abŭ'ndance *n.* quantity more than enough, plenty; overflowing emotion (*abundance of the heart*); relative quantity or number (of plants, substances, etc.) present; affluence, wealth; call undertaking to make nine tricks in solo whist. [ME, f. OF (*h*)*abundançe* f. L *abundantia* (as foll.; see -ANCE)]

abŭ'ndant *a.* more than enough, plentiful; rich (*in*); hence ∼LY² *adv.* [ME, f. L (as ABOUND; see -ANT)]

ab urbe condĭta (ăb ĕrbĭ kŏ'ndĭta) *adv.* (Of date) reckoning from the foundation of Rome in 753 BC. [L, = from the founding of the city]

abŭ'se¹ (-z) *v.t.* misuse, make bad use of; maltreat; speak insultingly or unkindly to or of. [ME, f. OF *abuser* f. Rom. *abusare f. L AB(*uti us-* USE²)]

abŭ's|e² *n.* **1.** misuse, perversion, (*of*); unjust or corrupt practice. **2.** reviling; insulting or unkind speech. **3.** Hence ∼IVE *a.* [ME, f. OF *abus* or f. L *abusus* (as prec.)]

abŭ't *v.* (-tt-). **1.** *v.i.* (Of estates or countries) have common boundary, border on; (of part of building) end *on* or *against*, lean *on*. **2.** *v.t.* abut on. [sense 'border upon' f. OF *abouter* (BUTT⁴); sense 'end on' f. AL *abuttare* (OF *but* end)]

abŭ'tment *n.* lateral support (esp. of arch or bridge);

point of junction between such support and thing supported. [f. prec. + -MENT]

abŭ'tter *n.* (Law). owner of adjoining property. [f. ABUT + -ER¹]

abÿ(e)' *v.t.* (abou'ght *pr.* -aw't). (arch.) redeem, pay the penalty of, (offence). [OE *ābycgan* redeem (as A- 1, BUY)]

abÿ'sm *n.* (arch. or poet.) = ABYSS. [ME, f. OF *abi(s)me* f. med. L *abysmus* assim. (to -ISM) of *abyssus* ABYSS]

abÿ'smal (-z-) *a.* bottomless (esp. fig.; *abysmal ignorance*); (colloq.) extremely bad (*his taste is abysmal*); hence ∼LY² *adv.* [f. prec. + -AL]

abÿ'ss *n.* bottomless chasm, deep gorge; immeasurable depth, esp. fig. (*abyss of despair*); primal chaos. [ME, f. LL f. Gk *abussos* bottomless (a- not, *bussos* depth)]

abÿ'ssal *a.* at or of ocean depths or floor; (Geol.) plutonic. [f. prec. + -AL]

ac- *pref.* **1.** Assim. form of AD- before *c, k, q.* **2.** Erron. for a- [of various orig.; see A-], as in *acknowledge.* **3.** See AD- 2.

-ăc *suf.* forming *adjs.* (*cardiac, iliac, maniac*), which are often also (or only) used as *ns.* (cf. -ACAL). [f. F *-aque* or L *-acus* or Gk *-akos* adj. suf.]

AC *abbr.* ‖Aircraftman; (*or* **a.c.**) alternating current; before Christ [f. L *ante Christum*]; Companion of the Order of Australia.

a/c *abbr.* account. [f. *account current* (ACCOUNT² 3)]

Ac *symb.* actinium.

acā'cia (-sha) *n.* tree or shrub of genus *Acacia*, some members of which yield gum ARABIC; (**false**) ∼, the locust-tree (*Robinia pseudoacacia*), grown for ornament. [L, f. Gk *akakia*]

a'cadēme *n.* (literary). college, university; **grove(s) of A**∼, (fig.) university environment. [f. Gk *Akadēmos* (see ACADEMY); improp. transf., perh. from Milton's 'grove of Academe', *Paradise Regained* iv. 244]

ăcadĕ'm|ic *a.* & *n.* **1.** *a.* scholarly; of a university etc. (*academic dress; academic* YEAR). **2.** abstract, unpractical, theoretical, cold, merely logical, (Art) conventional, over-formal, whence ∼ICISM (3); ∼ICALLY *adv.* **3.** of the philosophy of Plato; sceptical. **4.** Hence ∼ICALLY *adv.* **5.** *n.* member of a university; scholarly person. [f. F *académique* or f. L *academicus* (as ACADEMY; see -IC)]

ăcadĕ'mical *a.* & *n.* **1.** *a.* belonging to a college or university. **2.** *n.* (in *pl.*) university costume. [f. prec. + -AL]

ăcadēmī'cian (-shan) *n.* member of an Academy, esp. of the Royal Academy of Arts or the Académie française or the USSR Academy of Sciences. [f. F *académicien* (as ACADEMIC; see -ICIAN)]

Acā'demy (*a-*) *n.* **1.** garden near Athens where Plato taught; Plato's followers or philosophical system (cf. GARDEN, LYCEUM, PORCH). **2.** (*a*∼). place of study; secondary school, esp. in Sc. school-names. **3.** place for special training (*Royal Military Academy*). **4.** society for cultivating literature, art, music, science, etc., of which membership is an honour, esp. the Royal Academy (of Arts). [f. F *académie* or f. L f. Gk *akadēmeia* (*Akadēmos* the man or demigod f. whom Plato's garden was named)]

Acā'dian (*a-*) *a.* & *n.* (native or inhabitant) of Nova Scotia; descendant of Nova Scotian immigrants in Louisiana. [f. F *Acadie* Nova Scotia + -AN]

-acal *suf.* forming *adjs.* (*heliacal*); often used to distinguish them from *ns.* in -AC (*maniac, maniacal*). [f. -AC + -AL]

acă'nthus *n.* herbaceous plant of genus *Acanthus*, with prickly leaves; (Gk Archit.) conventional representation of its leaf. [L, f. Gk *akanthos* (*akantha* thorn perh. f. *akē* sharp point)]

a cappĕ'lla (ă-, ah-) *a.* & *adv.* (Of choral music) unaccompanied. [It., = in church style]

a'carid *n.* & *a.* (mite or tick) of order Acarida, esp. of family Acaridae. [f. mod. L *acarida* (*acarus* f. Gk *akari* mite; see -ID³)]

acár'pous *a.* (Bot.) not producing fruit. [f. A- 7 + Gk *karpos* fruit + -OUS]

∥ACAS (ā'kăs) *abbr.* Advisory, Conciliation, and Arbitration Service.

acătalě'ctic *a.* & *n.* (Pros.) (line) that is complete, not catalectic. [f. LL *acatalecticus* f. Gk *akatalēktos* (as A- 7, CATALECTIC)]

Accadian. See AKKADIAN.

ăccě'de (ăks-) *v.i.* (abs. or w. *to*). **1.** enter upon an office; become monarch. **2.** join a party; become part of a country; assent to an opinion or policy; formally accept a treaty etc. [ME, f. L AC(*cedere cess-* go)]

accělerǎ'nd|ō (aks-, ăch-) *adv., a.,* & *n.* (*pl.* ∼os *or* ∼i). (Mus.) (passage performed) with gradual increase of speed. [It.]

accě'lerāte (aks-) *v.* **1.** *v.t.* make quicker (*accelerated motion*); cause to move faster or happen earlier. **2.** *v.i.* (Of motion or process) become swifter; begin to move more quickly. [f. L AC(*celerare* f. *celer* swift) + -ATE[3]]

accělerā'tion (aks-) *n.* **1.** making quicker; being made quicker; (of vehicle) ability to gain speed. **2.** (Phys.) rate of change of velocity per unit time. [f. F *accélération* or f. L *acceleratio* (as ACCELERATE; see -ION)]

accě'leratīve (aks-) *a.* tending to increase speed, quickening. [f. ACCELERATE + -IVE]

accě'lerātor (aks-) *n.* thing that increases anything's speed, esp. pedal in motor vehicle for this purpose; substance that speeds up a chemical reaction; (Phys.) apparatus for imparting high speeds to charged particles. [f. ACCELERATE + -OR]

accělerǒ'měter (aks-) *n.* instrument for measuring acceleration or vibrations. [f. ACCELERATE + -O- + -METER]

ǎ'ccent[1] (ǎ'ks-) *n.* **1.** prominence given to syllable by stress or (in some languages) by pitch; mark used with letter to show quality of vowel, metrical stress, speech stress, distinction of homonyms, etc. **2.** individual, local or national mode of pronunciation; modulation to express feeling; (in *pl.*) person's (mode of) speech. **3.** rhythmical stress in verse or prose, whence **accě'ntuAL** (aks-) *a.* **4.** recurrent or other stress in music. **5.** intensity, sharp emphasis (*on*); distinctive character; a contrasting detail. [F, or f. L *accentus* (AC-, *cantus* song) repr. Gk *prosōidia* (PROSODY)]

ăccě'nt[2] (ăks-) *v.t.* pronounce with accent, emphasize (word or syllable); put written accents on; (fig.) accentuate. [f. F *accenter* (as prec.)]

accě'ntor (aks-) *n.* bird of genus *Prunella*, e.g. HEDGE[1]--sparrow. [cf. med. L *accentor*, f. L *ad* to + *cantor* singer]

ăccě'ntū|āte (ăks-) *v.t.* emphasize, heighten; make conspicuous; hence ∼A'TION *n.* [f. med. L *accentuare* (as ACCENT[1]) + -ATE[3]]

accě'pt (aks-) *v.t.* & (arch., w. *of*) *v.i.* **1.** consent to receive (person, something offered, or abs.); answer affirmatively (invitation, suitor). **2.** regard with favour. **3.** tolerate; submit to (*accept the umpire's decision*); receive as adequate or valid (*will accept your explanation; slot machine accepts only pennies; accept service of writ*); allow the truth of, believe; ∼ed **opinion** (generally held to be correct). **4.** undertake (office); take responsibility for, agree to meet, (draft or bill of exchange). **5.** Hence ∼ER[1] *n.* [ME, f. OF *accepter* or f. L *acceptare* f. AC(*cipere cept-* = *capere* take)]

accě'pt|able (aks-) *a.* worth accepting; pleasing, welcome; tolerable (*acceptable risk*); hence or cogn. ∼ABLY *adv.,* ∼ABI'LITY, ∼ableNESS (-beln-), *ns.* [ME f. OF, f. LL *acceptabilis* (as ACCEPT; see -ABLE)]

accě'ptance (aks-) *n.* **1.** consent to receive (gift, thing delivered, payment, pleasure, duty); favourable reception (*of* person or thing, *by* or *with* person); affirmative answer to invitation. **2.** approval, belief; toleration. **3.** engagement to meet a bill; a bill so accepted. [F (*accepter* f. as ACCEPT; see -ANCE)]

accě'ptant (aks-) *a.* ∼ **of,** willingly accepting [F (as prec.; see -ANT)]

ăccěptā'tion (ăks-) *n.* a particular sense, or the generally recognized meaning, of a word or phrase.

[ME f. OF, f. med. L *acceptatio* (as ACCEPT; see -ATION)]

accě'ptor (aks-) *n.* one who accepts a bill; (Phys.) atom or molecule able to receive an extra electron, esp. impurity in a semiconductor; (Chem.) substance able to combine with another; (Electr.) circuit able to accept a given frequency. [f. ACCEPT + -OR]

ǎ'ccěss (ǎ'ks-) *n.* **1.** approach; ∼ **(to),** right or means of approaching or reaching. **2.** being approached (*easy of access*); ∼ **time,** (Computers) time needed to retrieve stored information. **3.** passage, channel, doorway. **4.** attack or outburst (*of* illness, anger, emotion). [ME, f. OF *acces* or f. L *accessus* f. AC(*cedere cess-* go)]

accě'ssary̆ (aks-) *n.* & *a.* = ACCESSORY 2. [f. med. L. *accessarius* (as ACCEDE; see -ARY[1])]

accě'ss|ible (aks-) *a.* able to be reached, entered, influenced, or understood; ∼**ible to,** able to be reached etc. by; hence ∼IBI'LITY *n.,* ∼IBLY *adv.* [F, or f. LL *accessibilis* (as ACCEDE; see -IBLE)]

accě'ssion (aksě'shon) *n.,* & *v.t.* **1.** *n.* entering upon an office (esp. the throne) or condition (as manhood). **2.** being added; thing added (e.g. book *to* library), increase, addition; (Law) improvement or natural growth of property. **3.** assent; formal acceptance of treaty etc. **4.** *v.t.* record addition of (book etc.) to library. [F, or f. L *accessio -onis* (as ACCEDE; see -ION)]

accě'ssor|y̆ (aks-) *a.* & *n.* **1.** *a.* additional; (of thing) subordinately contributing, dispensable; adventitious. **2.** *a.* & *n.* (one) that helps in or is privy *to* any act, esp. a crime; ∼y̆ **before, after, the fact,** helping to plan, conceal, it. **3.** *n.* (esp. in *pl.*) accessory thing, accompaniment; minor fitting or attachment; small article of (esp. woman's) dress, whence ∼IZE (5) *v.t.* [f. med. L *accessorius* (as ACCEDE; see -ORY)]

acciaccatu'ra (achahkatōō'ra) *n.* (Mus.) grace-note performed quickly before an essential note of a melody. [It.]

ǎ'ccidence (ǎ'ks-) *n.* part of grammar dealing with the variable forms of words. [f. med. L sense of L *accidentia* (tr. Gk *parepomena*) neut. pl. of *accidens* (as foll.); see -ENCE]

ǎ'ccident (ǎks-) *n.* **1.** event that is without apparent cause or unexpected; **chapter of** ∼**s,** *the* unforeseen course of events, *a* sequence of misfortunes. **2.** unintentional act, chance, misfortune, (*by accident*); unlucky event, esp. one causing injury or damage, (*accident-PRONE*). **3.** irregularity in structure; property or quality not essential to our conception of a substance (so of material qualities of bread and wine after transubstantiation); mere accessory. [ME f. OF, f. LL *accidens* f. L AC(*cidere* = *cadere* fall); see -ENT]

ǎccidě'ntal (ǎks-) *a.* & *n.* **1.** *a.* happening by chance, undesignedly, or unexpectedly, whence ∼LY[2] *adv.;* occasional. **2.** *a.* & *n.* (thing) not essential to a conception; subsidiary; (Mus.) ∼ **(sharp, flat, natural),** sign attached to single note, not in key signature. [ME, f. LL *accidentalis* (as prec.; see -AL)]

ǎ'ccidie (ǎ'ks-), **acě'dia,** *ns.* laziness, torpor; apathy. [ME f. AF *accidie* f. OF *accide* f. med. L *acidia* alt. f. LL *acedia* f. Gk *akēdia* listlessness]

acclai'm *v.t.,* & *n.* **1.** *v.t.* welcome or applaud enthusiastically; (w. obj. & compl.) hail as (king, winner, saviour; *acclaimed him king*). **2.** *n.* (shout of) applause or welcome. [ME, f. L AC(*clamare* shout), sp. assim. to *claim*]

ǎcclamā'tion *n.* loud and eager assent to a proposal (*voted, carried, by acclamation*); (usu. in *pl.*) shouting in a person's honour. [f. L *acclamatio* (as prec.; see -ATION)]

acclimāte (ǎ'klī-, aklī'-) *v.t.* acclimatize; hence ∼**acclimatA'TION** *n.* [f. F *acclimater* (à to, *climat* CLIMATE)]

ǎccli̅mā'tion *n.* acclimatization. [irreg. f. prec.]

acclī'matīz|e, -īs|e (-īz), *v.t.* & *i.* habituate (animals, plants, one*self*), become habituated, to new climate or surroundings; hence ∼A'TION *n.* [f. F *acclimater* (see ACCLIMATE) + -IZE]

accli'vit|ў *n.* upward slope; hence ∿ous *a.* [f. L *acclivitas* f. AC(*clivis* f. *clivus* slope); see -ITY]

ccolāde (ă'-, -ā'd) *n.* **1.** sign at bestowal of knight-hood, now usu. stroke on shoulder with flat of sword; (fig.) bestowal of praise, acknowledgement of merit. **2.** (Mus.) vertical line or brace coupling staves. [F, f. Prov. *acolada* f. Rom. **accollare* embrace (as AC-, L *collum* neck); see -ADE]

acco'mmodāte *v.t.* **1.** adapt (thing or person *to* another); harmonize; reconcile, settle differences between. **2.** equip, supply, (person *with*); oblige, confer favour on; provide lodging or room for. [f. L AC(*commodare* f. *commodus* fitting) + -ATE³]

accŏ'mmodāting *a.* obliging, easy to deal with; compliant; hence ∿LY² *adv.* [f. prec. + -ING²]

accŏmmodā'tion *n.* **1.** adjustment (e.g. of lens of eye to focus for various distances); adaptation of any-thing or oneself to a purpose or meaning different from the original. **2.** settlement, compromise. **3.** serviceable thing, convenience; loan of money; (in *sing.* or **pl.*) lodgings, living premises; (in *pl.*) **seat in vehicle etc. **4.** ∿ **address** (used on letters to person unable or unwilling to give permanent address); *accommodation* BILL⁴; ∿ **ladder** (up side of ship from small boat); ∿ **road** (for access to place not on public road). [F, or f. L *accommodatio -onis* (as ACCOMMODATE; see -ATION)]

acco'mpaniment (-ŭ'm-) *n.* **1.** appendage, accom-panying thing. **2.** (Mus.) subsidiary part, usu. instru-mental, supporting solo instrument or voice, choir, etc. [f. F *accompagnement* (as ACCOMPANY; see -MENT)]

acco'mpan|ў (-ŭ'm-) *v.t.* **1.** supplement (a thing *with*, as word with blow); go or be put or be found with; escort, attend; (of thing) coexist with, characterize. **2.** (Mus.) support (singer, player, chorus) by perform-ing subsidiary part, whence ∿(ў)ist (1) *n.* [ME, f. F *accompagner* (à to, OF *compaing* COMPANION¹), assim. to COMPANY]

acco'mplice (-ŭ'-, -ŏ'-) *n.* partner in crime. [f. ME and F *complice* (prob. by assoc. w. prec.), f. LL *complex complicis* confederate (cf. COMPLICATE)]

acco'mplish (-ŭ'-, -ŏ'-) *v.t.* perform, complete; succeed in doing; hence ∿ED¹ (-sht) *a.*, clever, skilled, well trained or educated. [ME, f. OF *acomplir* f. Rom. **ACcomplēre* f. I. *complēre* COMPLETE²; see -ISH²]

acco'mplishment (-ŭ'-, -ŏ'-) *n.* fulfilment, com-pletion; thing done or attained, achievement; acquired skill, esp. social. [ME, f. prec. + -MENT]

acco'mpt. Var. (arch.) of ACCOUNT¹,²

accŏr'd¹ *v.* **1.** *v.i.* (Esp. of thing) be in harmony or consistent (*with*, or abs.). **2.** *v.t.* grant (permission, request, etc.); give (welcome etc.). [ME, f. OF *acorder* f. Rom. **AC(cordare* f. L *cor cordis* heart)]

accŏr'd² *n.* **1.** consent, mutual agreement; **with one** ∿, all agreeing. **2.** treaty of peace; harmonious correspondence in colour, pitch, tone, etc. **3.** volition (*of one's own accord*). [ME, f. OF *acord* (*acorder*; see prec.)]

accŏr'dance *n.* conformity, agreement, (*in accordance with*). [ME, f. OF *acordance* (as ACCORD¹; see -ANCE)]

accŏr'dant *a.* in tune, agreeing, (*with*, or abs.); hence ∿LY² *adv.* [ME, f. OF *acordant* (as ACCORD¹; see -ANT)]

accŏr'ding *adv.* **1.** ∿ **as**, in proportion as (of a process varying with another), in a manner depending on which of certain alternatives is true. **2.** ∿ **to**, in a manner consistent with or degree proportioned to (*value them according to their merits*), as stated by. [f. ACCORD¹ + -ING²]

accŏr'dingly *adv.* as the (stated) circumstances suggest; therefore; ∿ **as**, according as. [f. prec. + -LY²]

accŏr'dion *n.* portable musical instrument having bellows, metal reeds, and keyboard and/or key-buttons; ∿ **pleat**, ∿ **wall**, (folding like bellows of accordion); hence ∿IST (3) *n.* [f. G *akkordion* f. It. *accordare* to tune]

acco'st *v.t.* approach and address, esp. boldly; open

conversation with; (of prostitute) solicit. [f. F *accoster* f. It. *accostare* f. Rom. **AC(costare* f. L *costa* rib; see COAST¹)]

accouchement (ăkōō'shmahn) *n.* childbirth; lying in. [F. (*accoucher* act as midwife; see -MENT)]

accouch|eur (ăkōōsher') *n.* (*fem.* ∿**euse** *pr.* -er'z). man who acts as midwife. [F (as prec.)]

accou'nt¹ *v.* **1.** *v.t.* consider, regard as, (w. obj. & compl. or inf.; *account him a hero, wise, to be guilty*). **2.** *v.i.* ∿ **for**, give reckoning of (money held in trust), answer for (conduct, performance of duty), explain the cause of, serve as explanation of (*that accounts for it*), (Sport) be responsible for the death, defeat, dismissal, etc., of. [ME, f. OF *aconter* (a- AC-, *conter* COUNT²)]

accou'nt² *n.* **1.** reckoning of debit and credit, in money or service (**money of** ∿, name of sum of money not repr. by actual coin etc.); statement of moneys or goods or services received and expended, with balance (*render* or *send in, pay* or *settle, an account*); *account* RENDERed; **keep** ∿**s**, enter all expenditure for comparison with income; **settle** or **square** ∿**s with,** receive or pay the balance due from or to, (fig.) have revenge on; **on** ∿, as interim payment; on one's **own** ∿, for and at one's own purposes and risk; **on** ∿ **of,** because of; **on no** ∿, under no circumstances, certainly not. **2.** favourable result of the reckoning, profit; **turn to** (**good**) ∿, make useful. **3.** business relationship involving reckoning of debit and credit, esp. with bank or with firm granting credit; **current** ∿ (formerly ∿ **current**) (at bank in order to withdraw money on demand); DEPOSIT¹ *account*; **joint** ∿ (held by two or more persons in conjunction); **on** ∿, debited by firm instead of being paid for im-mediately. **4.** periodic settlement of accounts on Stock Exchange; ∿ **day** (when this takes place). **5.** statement of administration as required by creditor, or of discharge of any responsibility; answering for conduct (*demand, render, an account; call to account*); **gone to his** ∿, dead; **give a good** ∿ **of** oneself, be successful, make favourable impression. **6.** considera-tion (*take into account* or *take account of*; *leave out of account* or *take no account of*); importance (*of some* or *no account*). **7.** narration, report, description, (*of* event, person, etc.); performance (*of* piece of music etc.); **by all** ∿**s,** in everyone's opinion. [ME, f. OF *acont* (*aconter*; see prec.)]

accou'nt|able *a.* bound to give account, responsible, (*for* things, *to* persons, *or* abs.); explicable; hence ∿ABI'LITY, ∿**able**NESS (-beln-), *ns.*, ∿ABLY *adv.* [f. ACCOUNT² + -ABLE]

accou'nt|ant *n.* professional keeper and inspector of accounts; |CHARTERED *accountant*; TURF *accountant*; hence ∿ANCY *n.*, profession or duties of an account-ant. [law F, f. pres. part. of OF *aconter* ACCOUNT¹; see -ANT]

accou'nting *n.* in vbl senses; process or art of keeping and verifying accounts. [f. ACCOUNT¹ + -ING¹]

||**accou'tre, *accou'ter,** (-ōō'ter) *v.t.* (usu. in *p.p.*) attire, equip, esp. with special costume. [F f. *accoutrer* f. OF *acoustrer* (A- 4, *cousture* sewing; cf. CON-, SUTURE)]

||**accou'trement, *accou'terment,** (-ōō't-) *n.* (usu. in *pl.*) equipment, trappings; (Mil.) soldier's outfit other than weapons and garments. [F (as prec.; see -MENT)]

accrĕ'dit *v.t.* gain belief or influence for (adviser, statement, etc.); send out (ambassador etc.) with credentials to person, *to* or *at* a court or government; attribute (thing *to* person), credit (person *with* thing); hence ∿A'TION *n.* [f. F AC(*créditer* f. *crédit* CREDIT¹)]

accrĕ'dited *a.* (Of person or organization) officially recognized; (of belief) generally accepted, orthodox; (of cattle, milk, etc.) having guaranteed quality. [p.p. of prec.]

accrē'te *v.* **1.** *v.i.* grow together or into one; form round or on *to*, as round a nucleus. **2.** *v.t.* attract (such additions). [f. L AC(*crescere cret-* grow)]

accrē'tion *n.* growth by organic enlargement; growing of separate things into one; product of such growing; (adhesion of) extraneous matter added to anything; (Law) (1) = ACCESSION, (2) increase of legacy etc. by share of failing co-legatee. [f. L *accretio* (as prec.; see -ION)]

accru|e' (-ōō') *v.i.* come (*to* person, *from* a thing) as natural increase, advantage, result (esp. of interest on invested money); hence ～AL 2 *n.*, ～ED[1] (2) (-ōō'd) *a.* [ME, f. AF *acru*, p.p. of *acreistre* increase f. L *accrescere* ACCRETE]

accū'ltur|āte (-cher-) *v.t. & i.* adapt to, adopt, a different culture; hence ～A'TION *n.*, ～ATIVE *a.* [f. AC- +CULTURE+-ATE[3]]

accū'mūlāte *v.* **1.** *v.t.* heap up, gradually get increasing number or quantity of (lit., or fig. of a fortune, ill will, etc.); produce or acquire thus. **2.** *v.i.* grow numerous, form an increasing mass or quantity (lit. or fig.; *dirt, disasters, had accumulated*). [f. L *AC(cumulare* f. *cumulus* heap)+-ATE[3]]

accūmūlā'tion *n.* accumulating or being accumulated; growth of capital by continued interest; taking of higher and lower university degrees simultaneously; accumulated mass (*of* snow, papers, property, etc.). [f. L *accumulatio* (as prec.; see -ION)]

accū'mūlative *a.* arising from accumulation (*accumulative proof, evidence*); arranged so as to accumulate; acquisitive, given to hoarding; hence ～LY[2] (-vlǐ) *adv.* [f. ACCUMULATE+-IVE]

accū'mūlātor *n.* one who accumulates things; ‖rechargeable electric cell; bet placed on a sequence of events, winnings and stake from each being staked on next; storage register in computer. [f. ACCUMULATE +-OR]

a'ccūr|āte *a.* careful, precise; in exact conformity with a standard or with truth; hence ～ACY *n.*, ～ateLY[2] (-tlǐ) *adv.* [f. L *accuratus* done carefully, p.p. of AC(*curare* f. *cura* care); see -ATE[2]]

accūr'sed, (arch.) **accūr'st,** *a.* lying under a curse, ill-fated; involving misery; (colloq.) execrable, detestable. [p.p. of *accurse*, f. A-1+CURSE[2]; cf. AD-2]

accū'sal (-z-) *n.* accusation. [f. ACCUSE+-AL 2]

ăccūsā'tion (-z-) *n.* accusing; being accused; a charge of offence or crime; indictment. [ME f. OF, f. L *accusatio -onis* (as ACCUSE; see -ATION)]

accū'sative (-z-) *a. & n.* (Gram.) ～(*case*), case of nouns etc., expressing goal of motion or obj. of action (in uninflected languages, applied to the wd that stands as obj., though with no mark of case); *accusative* ABSOLUTE; hence **accūsatī'v**AL (-z-) *a.*, ～LY[2] (-vlǐ) *adv.* [ME, f. OF *accusatif -ive* or f. L (*casus*) *accusativus*, transl. Gk (*ptōsis*) *aitiatikē*]

accūsatōr'ial (-z-) *a.* ～ procedure etc. (in which prosecutor and judge are not the same, opp. *inquisitorial*). [f. as foll. +-AL]

accū'satory (-z-) *a.* (Of language, manner, etc.) conveying or implying accusation. [f. L *accusatorius* (as foll.; see -ORY)]

accū's|e (-z) *v.t.* **1.** charge with a fault, indict, (person *as* offender or *of* offence); **the** ～ed (person, esp. on criminal charge). **2.** lay the blame on. **3.** (arch.) betray, disclose. **4.** Hence ～ER[1] *n.*, ～INGLY *adv.* [ME *acuse* f. OF *ac(c)user* f. L AC(*cusare* f. *causa* CAUSE[1])]

accū'stom *v.t.* make (one*self*, or person or thing) used *to*; hence ～ED[2] (-md) *a.*, (esp.) customary, usual. [ME, f. OF *acostumer* (A-4, *costume* CUSTOM); *accustomed* also f. obs. sense 'make usual']

āce *n.* **1.** the 'one' on cards, dice, or dominoes; card etc. so marked (‖～ **up one's sleeve, *～ in the hole,** something effective kept in reserve); **play** one's ～, use one's best resource. **2.** (Lawn Tennis etc.) stroke (esp. service) that opponent cannot return; point thus scored. **3.** smallest possible amount, hair's breadth, (*within an ace of collapse*). **4.** pilot who has brought down many enemy aircraft; one who excels at something, champion. [ME, f. OF f. L *as* unity, AS[2]]

-ā'cea (-sha) *suf.* forming pl. names of orders and classes of animals (*Crustacea*); cf. -ACEAN. [neut. pl. of L adj. suf. *-aceus* of the nature of]

-ā'ceae (-sǐē) *suf.* forming pl. names of families of plants (*Rosaceae*). [fem. pl. of L adj. suf. *-aceus* (see prec.)]

-ā'cean (-shan) *suf.* forming *adjs.*, = -ACEOUS, and *ns.* as sing. of names in -ACEA (*crustacean*). [f. L *-aceus* (see -ACEA)+-AN]

acē'dia. See ACCIDIE.

Acě'ldama (ak-, as-) *n.* field of bloodshed; scene of slaughter. [Acts 1: 19; ME, f. Gk *Akeldama* f. Aram. *ḥ⁴ḳēl d⁴mā* field of blood]

-ā'ceous (-shus) *suf.* forming *adjs.* (*carbonaceous, herbaceous*), esp. from *ns.* in -ACEA, -ACEAE (*crustaceous, rosaceous*). [f. L *-aceus* (see -ACEA)+-OUS]

acē'phalous *a.* headless; having no chief; (Zool.) having no part of body specially organized as head; (Bot.) with head aborted or cut off; (Pros.) lacking syllable(s) in first foot. [f. med. L f. Gk *akephalos* headless (*a-* not, *kephalē* head)+-OUS]

acēr'b|(ic) *a.* astringently sour, harsh-tasting; bitter or sharp in speech, manner, or temper; so ～ITY *n.* [f. L *acerbus* sour-tasting, -IC]

acě'sc|ent *a.* turning sour; somewhat sour (lit. or fig.); so ～ENCE *n.* [F, or f. L *acescere* become sour; see -ENT]

ăcětā'būl|um *n.* (*pl.* ～a). **1.** (Rom. Ant.) cup to hold vinegar. **2.** (Zool.) cup-shaped sucker of cuttlefish etc.; socket for head of thigh-bone, or of leg in insects. [ME f. L (*acetum* vinegar, *-abulum* dim. of *-abrum* holder)]

ăcětā'lděhyde *n.* = ALDEHYDE 1. [f. ACETIC + ALDEHYDE]

a'cětāte *n.* salt or ester of acetic acid, esp. its cellulose ester used to make textiles, gramophone records, etc.; ～ **fibre,** ～ **silk,** (made artificially from cellulose acetate). [f. foll. +-ATE[1] (3)]

acē'tic *a.* pertaining to vinegar; ～ **acid,** the acid (CH₃COOH) that gives vinegar its characteristic taste. [f. F *acétique* f. L *acetum* vinegar; see -IC]

a'cěto- *comb. form.* (Chem.) acetic, acetyl, (*acetonitrile*). [f. as prec. +-o-]

a'cětōne *n.* colourless volatile liquid ketone valuable as solvent of organic compounds. [f. prec. +-ONE]

a'cětous *a.* having the qualities of vinegar; producing vinegar; sour. [f. LL *acetosus* sour (as ACETIC; see -OUS)]

a'cětyl *n.* (Chem.) the radical of acetic acid; ～**cho'line,** compound serving to transmit impulses from nerve fibres; ～ **silk,** = ACETATE *silk.* [f. ACETIC + -YL]

acě'tylēne *n.* colourless hydrocarbon gas, C₂H₂, burning with bright flame, used esp. in lighting and welding. [f. ACETIC+-YL+-ENE]

Achae'an (akē'-) *a. & n.* (inhabitant) of Achaea in ancient Greece; (in Homer) Greek. [f. L f. Gk *Akhaios*+-AN]

Achae'menid (akē'-) *a. & n.* (member) of ruling dynasty in Persia 553–330 BC. [f. Gk *Akhaimenidēs* (*Akhaimenēs*, Pers. king; see -ID[3])]

acharnement (ashār'nmahn) *n.* ferocity; gusto. [F]

āche[1] (āk) *v.i.* suffer or be source of continuous or prolonged dull pain or mental distress. [ME, f. OE *acan*; pr. after foll.]

āche[2] (āk) *n.* continuous or prolonged dull pain; hence **ā'chy**[2] (ā'kǐ) *a.* [ME, f. OE *æce*; pr. after prec.]

achē'ne (akē'n) *n.* (Bot.) small dry one-seeded fruit that does not open, e.g. strawberry pip. [f. mod. L *achaenium* (A-7, Gk *khainō* gape)]

Acheu'lian, -lèan, (ashōō'-) *a. & n.* (culture) of the palaeolithic period in Europe etc. following the Abbevillian and preceding the Mousterian. [F (*-éen*), f. St-*Acheul* in N. France, where remains of it were found]

à cheval (ah shevah'l) *adv.* with one foot on each side; (of gambling stake) risked equally on two chances. [F, on horseback]

achie've|e *v.* **1.** *v.t.* accomplish, carry out; acquire; reach (success, glory, one's objective); hence ～ABLE *a.* **2.** *v.i.* attain desired level of performance. **3.** Hence ~ER[1] *n.* [ME, f. OF *achever* f. phr. *a chief* to a head; see A- 4, CHIEF[1]]

achie'vement (-vm-) *n.* completion, accomplishment; thing accomplished; (Psych.) performance in test; (Her.) escutcheon with adjuncts, or bearing, esp. in memory of a distinguished feat, or = HATCHMENT. [f. prec. + -MENT, or f. F *achèvement*]

Achi'llês (aki'lēz) *n. Achilles'* HEEL[1]; *Achilles* TENDON. [L, name of Gk hero in Homer's *Iliad*, invulnerable except in heel]

achromǎ't|ic (ǎk-) *a.* (Opt.) free from colour; transmitting light without decomposing it into constituent colours; hence ~ICALLY *adv.*; ~ī'CITY, ~ISM (2) (akrō'ma-), *ns.* [f. F *achromatique* f. Gk *akhrōmatos* (as A- 7, CHROMATIC); see -IC]

achy. See ACHE[2].

a'cid[1] *a.* sharp-tasting, sour (||~ **drop,** kind of sweetmeat with acid taste); (fig.) biting, severe, unpleasant, whence ~LY[2] *adv.*; (Chem.) having the essential properties of an ACID[2]; (Geol.) containing much silica; so **aci'd**ITY *n.*, (esp.) excessively acid condition of stomach. [f. F *acide* or f. L *acidus* (*acēre* be sour)]

a'cid[2] *n.* **1.** sour substance; (Chem.) one of a class of substances that neutralize are and neutralized by alkalis, and contain hydrogen that can be replaced by metals, and of which the principal types are sour and able to corrode or dissolve metals; ~ **radical** (formed by removal of hydrogen or hydroxyl groups from acid); ~ **test** (in which acid is applied to test for gold etc., often fig. of severe or conclusive test); **put the** ~ **on,** (Austral. sl.) seek to extract loan, favour, etc., from. **2.** (sl.) the drug LSD; ~**-head,** user of this. **3.** Hence **aci'd**IC *a.* (Chem. & Geol.), **aci'd**IFY *v.t.*, **ǎcidi'**METER, **ǎcidi'**METRY, *ns.* [f. prec.]

ǎcidō's|is *n.* (*pl.* ~es *pr.* -ēz) (Path.) over-acid condition of blood or body tissues. [f. prec. + -OSIS]

aci'dūlāte *v.t.* make somewhat acid. [f. L *acidulus* (dim. of *acidus* sour) + -ATE[3]]

aci'dūlous *a.* somewhat acid. [f. as prec. + -OUS]

a'cin|us *n.* (*pl.* ~i *pr.* -ī). (one of the small berries that make up) compound fruit such as blackberry; seed of grape or berry; (Anat.) racemose gland, or terminus of duct in it. [L, = berry, kernel]

-a'cious (-shus) *suf.* forming *adjs.* w. sense 'inclined to' (*pugnacious*), 'abounding in' (*capacious*). [f. L *-ax -acis*, added chiefly to vbl stems to form *adjs.*, + -OUS]

-a'city *suf.* forming *ns.* of quality corresponding to *adjs.* in -ACIOUS. [f. F *-acité* or f. L *-acitas -tatis*]

ǎck-ǎ'ck *a.* & *n.* (colloq.) anti-aircraft (gun etc.). [formerly signallers' name for letters *AA*]

a'ckee, ǎ'kee, *n.* tropical tree (*Blighia sapida*); its fruit, edible when cooked. [f. Kru *ákee*]

||ǎck ě'mma *adv.* & *n.* (colloq.) = A.M. [formerly signallers' name for letters *AM*]

acknow'lĕdge (aknŏ'lĭj) *v.t.* agree to the truth of; own (person etc. *to be* something); own to knowing, take notice of; recognize the authority or claims of; express appreciation of, reward (a service); announce receipt of; recognize in legal form. [f. obs. KNOWLEDGE *v.* after obs. *acknow* (A- 2, KNOW[1]), or from obs. *n. acknowledge*]

acknow'lĕdgement, -dgm-, (aknŏ'lĭjm-) *n.* act of acknowledging; thing given or done in return for a service, message, etc.; (esp., in *pl.*) author's statement of indebtedness to others. [f. prec. + -MENT]

acli'nic *a.* ~ **line,** magnetic equator, on which magnetic needle has no dip. [f. Gk *aklinēs* (a- not, *klinō* bend) + -IC]

a'cmē *n.* highest point; point or period of perfection. [Gk, = highest point]

a'cnē *n.* skin eruption characterized by red pimples. [mod. L, f. erron. Gk *aknas* for *akmas* acc. pl. of *akmē* facial eruption; cf. prec.]

a'colyte *n.* church officer attending priest; attendant, assistant; beginner. [ME, f. OF *acolyt* or f. eccl. L *acolytus* f. Gk *akolouthos* follower]

a'conite *n.* poisonous plant of genus *Aconitum*, esp.

monkshood or wolfsbane; drug obtained from this; **winter** ~, yellow-flowered winter plant of genus *Eranthis*; hence **ǎconi'tic** *a.* (Chem.), **aco'nit**INE[5] *n.*, a poisonous alkaloid got from aconite. [f. F *aconit* or f. L *aconitum* f. Gk *akoniton*]

a'corn *n.* fruit of the oak; ~ **barnacle,** ~ **shell,** multi-valve cirriped living on rocks; ~ **worm,** a primitive marine worm. [OE *æcern*, cogn. w. *æcer* ACRE, later assoc. w. OAK and CORN[1]]

acǒtȳlē'don *n.* plant with no distinct seed-leaves; hence ~OUS *a.* [f. mod. L *acotyledones* pl.; see A- 7, COTYLEDON]

acou'st|ic (-ōō'-) *a.* relating to sound or sense of hearing; (of building materials) used for soundproofing; (of a mine) that can be exploded by sound waves transmitted under water; (Mus. etc., of instrument or recording) not electric; hence ~ICAL *a.*, ~ICALLY *adv.*, ~ī'CIAN *n.*, ~ICS *n. pl.*, acoustical properties (of room etc.), (usu. treated as *sing.*) science of sound. [f. Gk *akoustikos* (*akouō* hear; see -IC)]

acquai'nt *v.t.* make (person, one*self*) familiar (*with* circumstances, *that*); ~ **with,** make (person) aware of (facts etc.); **be** ~ **ed with,** have personal knowledge of (person or thing). [ME, f. OF *acointier* f. LL *accognitare* (AC-, *cognoscere cognit-* come to know)]

acquai'ntance *n.* **1.** knowledge more than mere recognition and usu. less than intimacy (*with* person or thing); **make the** ~ **of,** come to know). **2.** person with whom one is acquainted. **3.** Hence ~SHIP (-s-sh-) *n.*, = sense 1. [ME, f. OF *acontance* (as prec.; see -ANCE)]

acquě'st *n.* (Law) property gained otherwise than by inheritance. [obs. F, f. Rom. *acquaesitum* neut. p.p. (as n.) of **acquaerere* ACQUIRE]

acquie'sc|e *v.i.* agree, esp. tacitly; raise no objection; ~**e in,** accept (arrangements, conclusions); hence ~ENCE *n.*, ~ENT *a.* [f. L AC(*quiescere* rest)]

acquir'e *v.t.* gain by and for oneself; come into possession (lit. or fig.) of; ~**d characteristic,** (Biol.) one caused by environment, not inherited; ~**d taste,** (object of) liking gained by experience; hence ~MENT (ir'm) *n.*, (esp.) mental attainment. [ME, f. OF *aquerre* f. Rom. **acquaerere* f. L AC(*quirere quisit-* = *quaerere* seek)]

acquisi'tion (-z-) *n.* act of acquiring; thing acquired, useful or welcome addition; so **acqui'sit**IVE (-z-) *a.*, keen to acquire things, **acqui'sitive**NESS (-zĭtĭvn-) *n.* [f. L *acquisitio* (as prec.; see -ION)]

acqui't *v.t.* (-tt-). declare (person) not guilty (*of* offence), (arch.) pay (a debt), ~ one*self of,* discharge (duty, responsibility); ~ one*self,* perform one's part *well, ill,* etc. [ME, f. OF *aquiter* f. med. L *acquitare* pay debt (as AC-, QUIT[11])]

acqui'ttal *n.* deliverance from a charge by verdict etc.; performance (of duty). [f. prec. + -AL]

acqui'ttance *n.* payment of debt; release from debt; receipt in full. [ME, f. OF *aquitance* (as ACQUIT; see -ANCE)]

a'ore (kor) *n.* measure of land, 4,840 sq. yds. or about 4,050 sq. metres; piece of tilled or enclosed land, field, (**land of broad** ~**s,** Yorkshire; GOD'S Acre); (in *pl.*, fig.) large area; hence (~)ā'cred (-erd) *a.*, ~AGE (1) *n.* [OE *æcer*, = OHG *ackar*, ON *akr*, Goth. *akrs*, f. Gmc **akraz* f. IE **agros*]

a'crid *a.* (~**er,** ~**est**). bitterly pungent, irritating, corrosive; bitter in temper or manner; hence **acri'd**ITY *n.* [irreg. f. L *acer acris* keen + -ID[1], prob. after *acid*]

a'cridine (-ēn) *n.* colourless crystalline compound got from coal tar, source of dyes and drugs. [f. prec. + -INE]

ǎcrīflā'vine (-īn, -ēn) *n.* reddish powder used as antiseptic. [irreg. f. prec. + FLAVINE]

a'crimony *n.* bitterness of temper or manner; hence **ǎcrimō'ni**OUS *a.*, **ǎcrimō'nious**LY[2] (-ĭuslĭ) *adv.* [f. F *acrimonie* or f. L *acrimonia* pungency (as ACRID; see -MONY)]

a'crobǎt *n.* performer of spectacular gymnastic feats,

e.g. rope-walking; (fig.) one who changes position nimbly in argument; hence **ăcrobă′tıc** *a.*, **ăcrobă′t-ıcally** *adv.*, **ăcrobă′tıcs** *n.*, (doing of) acrobatic feats (also = AEROBATICS). [f. F *acrobate* f. Gk *akrobatēs* (*akron* summit, *bainō* walk)]

ă′crogen *n.* (Bot.) cryptogamous plant having perennial stem with growing point at extremity, e.g. fern or moss; hence **acrŏ′gĕnous** *a.* [f. Gk *akron* tip + -GEN]

ăcromĕ′galў *n.* (Med.) excessive growth of hands, feet, and face, caused by excessive activity of pituitary gland. [f. F *acromégalie* f. Gk *akron* extremity + *megas megal-* great; see -Y[1]]

acrŏ′nўc(h)al (-ĭk-) *a.* happening at nightfall (esp. of rising or setting of stars); hence ∼LY[2] *adv.* [f. Gk *akronukhos* (*akron* peak, *nux nuktos* night) + -AL]

ă′cronўm *n.* word formed from initial letters of other words (*Ernie, laser, Nato, radar, Unesco*). [f. Gk *akron* end + -*onum-* = *onoma* name]

acrŏ′pĕtal *a.* (Bot.) developing from below upwards; hence ∼LY[2] *adv.* [f. Gk *akron* tip + L *petere* seek + -AL]

ăcrophŏ′bia *n.* (Psych.) morbid dread of heights. [f. Gk *akron* peak + -PHOBIA]

acrŏ′polis *n.* citadel or upper fortified part of Greek city, esp. of Athens. [f. Gk *akropolis* (*akron* summit, *polis* city)]

acro′ss (-ŏ′s, -aw′s) *adv.* & *prep.* **1.** forming a cross with, making angles with, (obj. expressed or understood: *a line drawn across* or *across the road*); GET[1] *across.* **2.** into contact with; COME, RUN[1], *across.* **3.** from side to side (of) (*run across, across the road; stretched across, across the road; half a mile across*); COME *across with;* ∼ **the board** *a.* & *adv.*, general(ly), all-embracing(ly). **4.** on the other side (of) (*by this time he is across* (*the Channel*)); PUT[1] (*it*) *across.* [ME f. OF *a croix, en croix*, later regarded as f. A[3] + CROSS[1]]

acrŏ′stic *n.* poem or other composition in which the initial (**single** ∼), the initial and final (**double** ∼), or the initial, middle, and final (**triple** ∼) letters of the lines make words; word-puzzle so made. [f. F *acrostiche* or f. Gk *akrostikhis* (*akron* end, *stikhos* row, line of verse), assim. to -IC]

acrў′lic *a.* & *n.* ∼ **acid**, unsaturated organic acid from which synthetic substances are derived by polymerization; ∼ (**fibre, plastic, resin**), synthetic substance of this kind. [f. *acrolein* (f. L *acer acris* pungent + *olēre* to smell + -IN) + -YL + -IC]

ăct[1] *n.* **1.** thing done, deed (*act of* GOD; *act of* GRACE); this as outward sign of a condition etc. (*act of faith*); ∼ (short prayer) **of contrition; Acts** (**of the Apostles**), NT book following Gospels. **2.** process of doing, operation (*in the very act of; caught in the act*). **3.** decree passed by a legislative body etc., statute; verificatory legal document (esp. *act and deed*). **4.** main division of a play; one of a series of short performances in circus or variety programme; performer(s) of this; **get into the** ∼, (sl.) become participant (esp. for profit); **put on an** ∼, (colloq.) show off, talk for display, pretend. **5.** (Hist.) thesis publicly defended by candidate for university degree. [ME, f. OF *acte* and L *actus, -um* (see foll.)]

ăct[2] *v.* **1.** *v.t.* portray (incident or story) by actions; ∼ **out**, translate (ideas etc.) into action. **2.** perform the part of (character in a play or in life) (*act Othello; act the* FOOL[1]). **3.** *v.i.* perform actions, behave (*generously*, etc.); ∼ (serve) **as** *interpreter;* ∼ **for** *me* (be my representative) *in the matter;* ∼ (**up**)**on** (execute) *a suggestion;* ∼ **up**, (colloq.) misbehave, give trouble; ∼ **up to** (put into practice) *a principle.* **4.** perform special functions (*the policeman declined to act; the brake refused to act*); perform a play or part, be actor or actress; exert energy or influence (*on; alcohol acts on the brain; acid acts on metal*). [partly f. L *agere act-* do; partly f. prec.]

ACT *abbr.* Australian Capital Territory.

ACTH *abbr.* adrenocorticotrophic hormone.

ă′cting *a.* & *n.* **1.** In vbl senses. **2.** *a.* (Before title etc.) doing duty temporarily (*Acting Captain*); doing alone duties nominally shared with others (*Acting Manager*).

3. *n.* art or occupation of performing parts in plays, films, etc.; ∼ **copy** (for actors' use, with stage-directions and cuts). [f. ACT[2] + -ING[2,1]]

ăctı′nia *n.* (*pl.* ∼**e**). sea ANEMONE, esp. of genus *Actinia.* [mod. L, f. Gk *aktis -inos* ray; see -IA[2]]

ă′ctinide *n.* (Chem.) any element in the series of fifteen starting with actinium. [f. ACTINIUM + -IDE as in *lanthanide*]

ă′ctinism *n.* property of short-wavelength radiant energy by which chemical changes are produced as in photography; hence **ăctı′nıc** *a.* [f. Gk *aktis -inos* ray + -ISM]

ăctı′nium *n.* (Chem.) radioactive metallic element found in pitchblende. [f. as prec. + -IUM]

ăctinŏ′mĕter *n.* instrument for measuring intensity of radiation. [f. Gk *aktis -inos* ray + -O- + -METER]

ăctinomŏr′phic *a.* (Biol.) radially symmetrical. [f. as prec. + Gk *morphē* form + -IC]

ăctinomўcē′tēs (-ēz) *n.* group of minute organisms of order Actinomycetales, thought to be filamentous bacteria. [f. as prec. + *mycetes* (Gk *mukēs -ētos* mushroom)]

ă′ction *n.*, & *v.t.* **1.** *n.* process of acting, exertion of energy or influence, (*men of action; put into action; action of an acid on metal*); **take** ∼, begin to act; **out of** ∼, not working. **2.** thing done, act. **3.** (Theatr.) series of events represented; (sl.) principal activity or operations. **4.** mode or style of movement (*action of a player, of a horse*); mechanism of piano or other instrument. **5.** legal process; engagement between opposing forces (*killed in action*); **go into** ∼, (fig.) start work. **6.** ∼ **committee, group** (formed to take active steps, esp. in politics); ∼ **painting** (with paint applied by artist's random or spontaneous actions); ∼ **stations**, positions taken up by troops, sailors, etc., before going into action. **7.** *v.t.* bring a legal action against. [ME f. OF, f. L *actio -onis* (as ACT[2]; see -ION)]

ă′ctionab|le *a.* affording ground for an action at law; hence ∼LY[2] *adv.* [f. prec. + -ABLE]

ă′ctiv|āte *v.t.* make active; (Phys.) make radioactive; ∼**ated carbon**, carbon, esp. charcoal, treated to increase its adsorptive power; ∼**ated sludge**, aerated sewage containing aerobic bacteria; hence ∼A′TION, ∼ātor, *ns.* [f. foll. + -ATE[3]]

ă′ctive *a.* & *n.* **1.** *a.* given to action; working, effective; practical, diligent; radioactive; able to rotate plane of vibration of polarized light; ∼ **carbon** = ACTIVATED *carbon; active* LIST[1]; ∼ **service**, full-time service in armed forces; ∼ **volcano** (likely to erupt, not extinct). **2.** (Gram.) ∼ **voice**, that comprising all forms of intransitive verbs, and those forms of transitive verbs that attribute the action of the verb to the person or thing whence it proceeds (the logical subject), as *We saw him;* (of verb etc.) in active voice; cf. MIDDLE[1], PASSIVE. **3.** Hence ∼LY[2] (-vlĭ) *adv.*, ∼NESS (-vn-) *n.* **4.** *n.* (Gram.) active voice or form of verb. [ME, f. OF *actif -ive* or f. L *activus* (as ACT[2]; see -IVE)]

ă′ctiv|ism *n.* policy of vigorous action in politics etc.; hence ∼IST (2) *n.* [f. ACTIVE + -ISM]

ăctı′vitў *n.* exertion of energy; state or quality of being active; diligence, nimbleness; = RADIOACTIVITY; (esp. in *pl.*) actions, occupations. [f. F *activité* or f. LL *activitas* (as ACTIVE; see -ITY)]

ă′cton *n.* (Hist.) jacket of quilted cotton worn under mail; mail-plated jacket of leather etc. [ME, f. OF *auqueton* padding, padded jacket, prob. f. Prov. *alcoton* cotton f. Arab. *alḳuṭun* (the cotton)]

ă′ct|or *n.* performer of part in play, film, etc.; hence ∼RESS[1] *n.*, ∼rěssȳ[2] *a.*, affectedly theatrical. [L, = doer, actor (as ACT[2]; see -OR[2])]

ACTU *abbr.* Australian Council of Trade Unions.

ă′ctual (-kchŏŏal) *a.* existing in fact, real; present, current. [ME f. OF *actuel* f. LL *actualis* (*actus* vbl n. f. *agere* ACT[2]; see -AL)]

ăctuă′litў (-kchŏŏă′-) *n.* reality; realism; (in *pl.*) existing conditions. [ME, f. OF *actualité* entity or f. med. L *actualitas* (as prec.; see -ITY)]

a'ctuallỹ (-kchŏŏa-) *adv.* as a fact, really; at present, for the time being; as a matter of fact, even (strange as it may seem). [f. ACTUAL + -LY²]

a'ctuarỹ *n.* expert in statistics, esp. one who calculates insurance risks and premiums; hence **actūar'iAL** *a.* [f. L *actuarius* bookkeeper (*actus*; see ACTUAL, -ARY¹)]

a'ctūlāte *v.t.* communicate motion to (machine etc.); cause operation of (electrical device etc.); be motive for action of (person); hence ∼A'TION, ∼ātOR, *ns.* [f. med. L *actuare* (*actus*; see ACTUAL, -ATE³)]

acū'itỹ *n.* sharpness, acuteness (lit. or fig., of needle, senses, understanding). [f. F *acuité* or f. med. L *acuitas* (*acuere* sharpen; see ACUTE, -ITY)]

acū'leate *a.* pointed, incisive; (Zool.) having a sting; (Bot.) prickly. [f. L *aculeatus* sting, dim. of *acus* needle; see -ATE²)]

acūmen (akū'-, ā'kū-) *n.* keen insight or discernment, penetration. [L *acumen -minis* anything sharp (*acuere* sharpen; see ACUTE)]

acū'minate *a.* (Biol.) tapering to a point. [f. L *acuminatus* pointed (as prec.; see -ATE²)]

a'cūpŭncture *n.* (Med.) (orig. Chinese) method of pricking skin or tissues with needles as treatment for various conditions. [f. L *acu* with a needle + PUNCTURE]

acu'shla (-ŏŏ'-) *n.* (Ir.) darling. [f. Ir. *a cuisle* O pulse (of my heart)!]

acū'te *a.* (∼r, ∼st). **1.** sharp, pointed; penetrating (*an acute critic*); (of angle) less than a right angle. **2.** (Of disease) coming sharply to a crisis, opp. CHRONIC; (of controversy, difficulty, shortage) critical, serious; (of sensation, senses) keen; (of sound) high, shrill. **3.** ∼ accent, mark (') placed over letters in some languages to show quality, vowel length, pronunciation (e.g. *maté*), etc. **4.** Hence ∼LY² (-tlī) *adv.*, ∼NESS (-tn-) *n.* [f. L *acutus* p.p. of *acuere* sharpen (*acus* needle)]

ACW *abbr.* Aircraftwoman.

-acỹ *suf.*, branch of suf. -CY forming *ns.* of state or quality (*accuracy, advocacy, conspiracy, diplomacy, episcopacy, fallacy, lunacy, obstinacy, piracy, primacy, supremacy*); see also -CRACY. [f. or after F *-acie* or L *-acia* or *-atia* or Gk *-ateia*]

a'cỹl *n.* (Chem.) acid RADICAL. [G (as ACID², -YL)]

ad *n.* (colloq.) advertisement; advertising. [abbr.]

ad- *pref.* **1.** [(thr. OF *a-* or) f. L *ad* to] w. sense of motion or direction to, reduction or change into, addition, adherence, increase, or intensification; usu. assim. to *ac-* bef. *c, k, q,* and similarly to *af-* etc. bef. *f, g, l, n, p, r, s, t;* reduced to *a-* bef. *sc, sp, st.* **2.** [f. *a-* repr. *prefs.* other than *ad-*] (*accurse, admiral, advance, affray*).

ad *suf.* **1.** forming *ns.* (*a*) [f. Gk *-as -ada*]: in collective numerals (*myriad, triad*); in fem. patronymics (*Dryad, Naiad*); in names of poems (*Iliad,* and by anal. *Dunciad;* so *jeremiad*). (*b*) [f. F *-ade*] (*ballad, salad*); see the more usual -ADE 1. **2.** (Biol.) invented to form *adjs.* and *advs.* w. sense 'towards' (part indicated by main element of wd): *caudad* towards the tail [L *cauda* tail].

AD *abbr.* of the Christian era. [f. ANNO DOMINI]

a'dage *n.* traditional maxim, proverb of common experience. [F, f. L *adagium* (*ad* to, root of *aio* say)]

da'gio (adah'jyŏ) *adv., a.,* & *n.* (*pl.* ∼s). (Mus.) (movement) in slow time; ∼ **dancing,** kind involving feats of balance etc. [It.]

A'dam¹ (ă'-) *n.* first man, in Hebrew tradition; **not know** person **from** ∼, have no knowledge of his appearance; **old** ∼, sinful nature innate in a person; ∼'s **ale** or **wine,** water; ∼'s **apple,** projection of thyroid cartilage of larynx, esp. as prominent in men. [f. Heb. 'ādām man]

A'dam² (ă'-) *a.* of the decorative style of architecture and furniture created by the Scottish brothers Robert and James *Adam* (18th c.).

a'damant *n.* & *a.* **1.** *n.* (arch.) diamond or other hard substance; hence **adamă'ntINE²** *a.* **2.** *a.* unyielding to requests. [f. OF *adamaunt* f. L f. Gk *adamas -mant-* untameable (*a-* not, *damaō* to tame)]

A'damīte (ă'd-) *n.* human being as descendant of Adam; member of sect living naked like Adam. [f. ADAM¹ + -ITE¹]

adă'pt *v.* **1.** *v.t.* fit, adjust, (a thing *to* another); make suitable (*to* or *for* a purpose); modify, alter, (*adapted from the Bible story*); hence or cogn. ∼ABI'LITY *n.*, ∼ABLE *a.*, (esp.) able to adapt oneself to new surroundings, ∼ABLY *adv.*, **ădaptA'TION** *n.*, (esp., Biol.) process by which organism or species becomes adjusted to its environment, ∼ER¹, ∼OR, *ns.*, (esp.) device allowing connection of pieces of equipment not orig. designed to be connected, ∼IVE *a.* **2.** *v.i.* adapt oneself (*to* conditions). [f. F *adapter* f. L AD(*aptare* f. *aptus* fit)]

ADC *abbr.* aide-de-camp.

ad captandum (vulgus) (ăd kăptă'ndum vŭlgus) *adv.* & *a.* (designed) to appeal to the emotions (of the rabble). [L, = for alluring (the crowd)]

ădd *v.t.* & *i.* **1.** join (one thing *to* another) as increase or supplement (*add your efforts to mine; add insult to injury;* ∼ **in,** include; *this* ∼s **to** (increases) *our difficulties;* say further (*he added a remark*). **2.** unite two or more numbers to get number equal to their total amount; ∼ **up,** find the sum of, amount *to,* (colloq.) make sense. **3.** Hence ∼'ED¹ *a.* (∼ed **value tax** = VALUE added *tax*). [ME, f. L AD(*dere dit-* = *dare* put)]

a'ddăx *n.* large antelope of N. Africa, with twisted horns. [L, f. African wd]

addě'nd|um *n.* (*pl.* ∼a). thing (esp. omitted thing) to be added; appendix, addition; (esp., in *pl.*) additional matter at end of book. [L, gerundive of *addere* ADD]

a'dder *n.* small venomous snake, esp. common viper; DEATH *adder,* **horned** ∼, PUFF¹-*adder,* species of Viperidae; **deaf as an** ∼, completely deaf; ∼'s **tongue,** kind of fern (*Ophioglossum*). [OE *nædre,* = OS *nādra,* OHG *nātara,* ON *nathra,* Goth. *nadrs; n-* lost in ME by wrong division of *a naddre,* cf. APRON, AUGER, UMPIRE]

addi'ct¹ *v.t.* (esp. in *pass.*) devote, apply habitually or compulsively, (*to* a practice); hence ∼ION *n.*, (esp.) condition of taking drug excessively and being unable to cease doing so without adverse effects, ∼IVE *a.*, causing addiction and dependence. [f. L AD(*dicere dict-* say) assign]

a'ddict² *n.* person addicted to a habit, esp. one dependent on a (specified) drug (*drug addict, heroin addict*); (colloq.) enthusiastic devotee of sport or pastime (*film addict*). [f. prec.]

A'ddison (ă'd-) *n.* ∼'s **disease** (characterized by progressive anaemia and debility and brown discoloration of the skin). [first recognized by T. *Addison,* Engl. physician d. 1860]

addi'tion *n.* **1.** process of adding; **in** ∼, as an added thing etc. (*to*). **2.** Thing added (*a useful addition*). [ME f. OF, or f. L *additio* (as ADD; see -ITION)]

addi'tional *a.* added, supplementary; hence ∼LY² *adv.* [f. prec. + -AL]

a'dditive *a.* & *n.* **1.** *a.* to be added; characterized by addition (*additive process*). **2.** *n.* thing to be added, esp. substance added to another so as to give it specific qualities. [f. LL *additivus* (as ADD; see -IVE)]

a'ddle *a.* & *v.* **1.** *a.* empty, vain; muddled, unsound, (*addle-brained, addle-head*); (of egg) addled. **2.** *v.t.* muddle, confuse. **3.** *v.i.* (Of egg) become addled. [OE *adela* filth (MLG *adele*) used as *a.,* then as v.]

a'ddled (ă'dĕld) *a.* made addle; (of egg) rotten, producing no chick. [f. ADDLE *a.,* assim. to p.p. form, app. bef. *addle* v. existed]

addrĕ'ss¹ *v.t.* **1.** direct in speech or writing (*address remarks, a protest, petition,* etc. *to* person; ∼ one**self to,** speak or write to. **2.** write directions for delivery (esp. name and place of residence etc. of intended recipient) on (envelope etc.). **3.** speak or write to, esp. deliver a speech to, (person, audience); direct one's attention to. **4.** apply (one*self* to a task); (Golf) take aim at, prepare to hit, (ball). [ME, f. OF *adresser* f. Rom. *AD(drictiare* f. *drictus* = L *directus* DIRECT²)]

addrĕ'ss² *n.* **1.** superscription of letter; name of place to which letters etc. for a person or firm are directed; number etc. giving position of information in computer; place of residence. **2.** discourse delivered to audience. **3.** readiness, skill, dexterity. **4.** (arch.) manner in conversation. **5.** (in *pl.*) courteous approach, courtship (*pay* one's *addresses to*). [f. prec. & F *adresse*]

ăddrĕssee' *n.* person to whom something (esp. a letter) is addressed. [f. ADDRESS¹ + -EE]

Addrĕ'ssograph, a-, (-ahf) *n.* (**P**) machine for printing addresses on envelopes. [f. ADDRESS² + -O- + -GRAPH]

addŭ'c|e *v.t.* cite as proof or instance; hence ∼IBLE *a.* [f. L AD(*ducere* duct- lead)]

addŭ'ct *v.t.* draw (limb etc.) towards middle line of body etc.; so ∼ION *n.* [f. as prec.]

-āde *suf.* forming *ns.* **1.** [f. or after F *-ade* f. Prov., Sp., or Port. *-ada* or It. *-ata* f. L *-ata* fem. sing. p.p. of vbs in *-are*] w. senses (1) action done (*blockade, tirade*); (2) body concerned in action or process (*cavalcade*); (3) product of material or action (*arcade, lemonade, masquerade*). **2.** [f. F *-ade* f. Gk *-as -ada*] (*decade*); cf. -AD 1. **3.** [f. Sp. or Port. *-ado*, masc. form of 1 above] w. senses (1)–(3) (*brocade*) or 'person concerned' (*renegade*).

ă'denine (-ēn) *n.* crystalline base found in some glands and as constituent of DNA. [f. G *adenin* f. as foll.; see -INE⁵]

ă'dĕnoids (-z) *n. pl.* (Path.) mass of enlarged lymphatic tissue between back of nose and throat, often hindering speaking and breathing; hence **ădĕnoi'd**AL *a.* [f. Gk *adēn -enos* gland + -OID]

ădĕnō'ma *n.* (*pl.* ∼s *or* ∼ta). glandlike benign tumour. [mod. L, f. Gk *adēn* gland + -OMA]

adĕ'nosine *n.* nucleoside found in muscle, from which compounds providing muscular energy are derived. [f. ADENINE + RIBOSE]

adĕpt¹ (ă'd-, adĕ'-) *a.* thoroughly proficient (*at or in*). [f. L *adeptus* p.p. of AD(*ipisci* attain)]

ă'dĕpt² *n.* skilled performer, expert. [f. prec.]

ă'dĕqua|te *a.* proportionate (*to* the requirements); sufficient, satisfactory; barely sufficient; hence ∼ACY *n.,* ∼ateLY² (-tlĭ) *adv.* [f. L *adaequatus* p.p. of ADAequare make equal (*aequus*); see -ATE²]

ad eundem (ăd ĕū'ndĕm) *adv.* (admitted) to the same degree or rank at another university or institution. [L, = to the same]

à deux (ah dĕr') *adv.* & *a.* for two; between two. [F]

ad fin. *abbr.* at or near the end. [f. L *ad finem*]

adhēr'e (ad-h-) *v.i.* stick fast *to* (substance); give support *to* (agreement, opinion, party); behave according *to* (rule, plan, promise). [f. F *adhérer* or f. L AD(*haerēre* haes- stick)]

adhēr'|ent (ad-h-) *a.* & *n.* **1.** *a.* sticking (*to* substance); adhering *to* (rule etc.); so ∼ENCE *n.* **2.** *n.* supporter (*of* party etc.). [f. F *adhérent* (as prec.; see -ENT)]

adhē'sion (ad-hē'zhon) *n.* adhering (lit. or fig.; give one's ∼ **to,** declare acceptance of); maintenance of contact between wheels and road or rail; (Path.) unnatural union of surfaces due to inflammation. [f. F *adhésion* or f. L *adhaesio* (as ADHERE; see -ION)]

adhē'sive (ad-h-) *a.* & *n.* having the property of adhering, sticky, (substance); *adhesive* TAPE; hence ∼LY² (-vlĭ) *adv.,* ∼NESS (-vn-) *n.* [f. F *adhésif -ive* (as ADHERE; see -IVE)]

adhi'bit (ad-h-) *v.t.* affix; apply, administer, (remedy); hence **ădhĭbi'**TION (ăd-h-) *n.* [f. L AD(*hibēre* hibit- = *habēre* have)]

ad hoc (ăd hŏ'k) *adv.* & *a.* for this particular purpose; special(ly). [L]

ad hominem (ăd hŏ'mĭnĕm) *adv.* & *a.* personal; (of argument) appealing to feelings not reason. [L, = to the person]

ādiăbă't|ic *a.* & *n.* (Phys.) **1.** *a.* impassable to heat; occurring without heat entering or leaving system; hence ∼ICALLY *adv.* **2.** *n.* curve or formula for adiabatic phenomena. [f. Gk *adiabatos* impassable (*a-* not, *diabainō* pass)]

ādiǎ'ntum *n.* fern of genus *Adiantum*, e.g. true maiden hair; (pop.) black maidenhair, a spleenwort. [L, f Gk *adianton* maidenhair (*a-* not, *diantos* wettable)]

adieu' (adū') *int.* & *n.* (*pl.* ∼s, ∼x, *pr.* adū'z) goodbye. [ME f. OF (*à* to, *Dieu* God)]

ad infinitum (ăd ĭnfinī'tum) *adv.* without limit, fo ever. [L]

ad interim (ăd ĭ'ntĕrĭm) *adv.* & *a.* for the meantime [L]

ă'dipocēre *n.* greyish fatty or soapy substance gener ated in dead bodies subjected to moisture. [f. I *adipocire* f. L *adeps adipis* fat + -o- + F *cire* wax f. L *cera*

ă'dipōse *a.* pertaining to fat, fatty; ∼ **tissue,** fat -containing connective tissue in animals; hence **ădipō'sITY** *n.* [f. mod. L *adiposus* (*adeps -ipis* fat; se∈ -OSE¹)]

ă'dĭt *n.* (In mines) horizontal entrance or passage means of approach. [f. L AD(*itus* f. *ire it-* go)]

Adj. *abbr.* Adjutant.

adjā'c|ent *a.* lying near, contiguous (*to*); so ∼ENCY *n* adjā'cence lie); see -ENT]

ă'djĕctive *a.* & *n.* **1.** *a.* additional, not standing by itself, dependent; ∼ **dye** (which needs mordant to fix it); ∼ **law,** subsidiary part of law, enforcemen procedure. **2.** *n.* word or phrase naming an attribute added to a noun to describe the thing etc. more fully hence **ădjĕctī'**VAL *a.* (also euphem. for expletive adj.). [ME, f. OF *adjectif -ive* f. LL *adjectivus* f. L AD(*jicere* ject- = *jacēre* throw); see -IVE]

adjoi'n *v.t.* be contiguous with; (arch.) = ADD l. [ME f. OF *ajoindre, ajoign-* f. L AD(*jungere* junct- join)]

adjour'n (ajĕr'n) *v.* **1.** *v.t.* put off, postpone; break off for later resumption. **2.** *v.i.* (Of persons met together) suspend joint proceedings and separate; transfer meeting *to* another place. **3.** Hence ∼MENT *n.* [ME, f OF *ajorner* (a- AD-, *jorn* day f. LL *diurnum* day f. L *diurnus* DIURNAL); cf. JOURNAL, JOURNEY]

adjŭ'dg|e *v.t.* adjudicate (a matter); pronounce judicially (*that* a thing is; a thing *to be*); award judicially (thing *to* person); (arch.) condemn (person *to* penalty or to do); hence ∼(**e**)MENT (-jm-) *n.* [ME, f OF *ajuger* f. L *adjudicare* (see foll.)]

adju'dic|āte (ajōō'-) *v.* **1.** *v.t.* decide judicially regard ing (claim etc.); pronounce (person *to be* bankrupt etc.). **2.** *v.i.* act as judge in court, tribunal, competi tion, etc. **3.** Hence ∼A'TION, ∼ātOR, *ns.,* ∼ātIVE *a.* [f. L AD(*judicare* f. *judex -icis* judge) + -ATE³]

ă'djŭnct *n.* thing subordinate or incidental (*to* or *of*); assistant, subordinate person, esp. with temporary appointment only; (Gram.) amplification of the predicate, subject, etc.; (Logic) non-essential attri bute; hence **adjŭ'nct**IVE *a.* [f. L *adjunctus*; see ADJOIN]

adjur'e (ajoor') *v.t.* charge (person) under oath (*to* do); request earnestly; hence **ădjur**A'TION (ăjoor-) *n.* [ME, f. L AD(*jurare* swear) in LL sense 'put person to an oath']

adjŭ'st *v.* **1.** *v.t.* arrange, put in order; regulate, esp. by small amount; assess (loss or damages); harmonize (discrepancies); adapt (*to* standard or purpose). **2.** *v.i.* adapt oneself (*to* one's environment etc.). **3.** Hence ∼ABLE *a.,* ∼ER¹, ∼MENT, *ns.* [f. F *adjuster* refash. (after *juste* JUST¹) of OF *ajoster* f. Rom. **adjuxtare* f. L *juxta* near]

ă'djutage, ă'j-, (ă'jōō-) *n.* mouthpiece of artificial fountain. [F *aj*(*o*)*utage* (*ajouter* add, join, f. OF *ajoster*; see prec., -AGE)]

ă'djut|ant (ă'jōō-) *n.* **1.** assistant; (Mil.) officer who assists superior officers by communicating orders, conducting correspondence, etc., whence ∼ANCY *n.;* A∼ant-**General,** high-ranking Army administra tive officer. **2.** ∼ant (**bird**), giant Indian stork. [f. L *adjutare* frequent. of *adjuvare* (see foll.) + -ANT]

ă'djuvant (ă'jōō-) *a.* & *n.* helpful, auxiliary, (person or thing). [F, or f. L AD(*juvare* jut- help); see -ANT]

Adlēr'ian (ăd-) *a.* (n.) (disciple) of Adler or his system of psychology. [f. A. *Adler,* Austrian psychologist d. 1937 + -IAN]

ăd lĭ'b *adv.*, *a.*, & *v.i.* (**-bb-**). **1.** *adv.* to any desired extent. **2.** (*ad-lib*). *a.*, & *v.i.* (colloq.) (speak) without preparation; improvise(d). [abbr. of foll.]

ad libitum (ăd lĭ'bĭtum) *adv.* = prec. [L, = according to pleasure]

ad litem (ăd lī'tĕm) *a.* (Of guardian etc.) appointed for a lawsuit. [L]

Adm. *abbr.* Admiral.

ă'd|măn *n.* (*pl.* ∼**men**). one who produces advertisements commercially. [f. AD + MAN[1]]

||**ă'dmăss** *n.* section of the community that is readily influenced by advertising etc. [f. AD + MASS[2]]

admea'sure (-mĕ'zher) *v.t.* apportion, assign in due shares; so ∼MENT *n.* [ME, f. OF *amesurer* f. med. L AD(*mensurare* MEASURE[1])]

ă'dmin *n.* (colloq.) administration. [abbr.]

admi'nicle *n.* thing that helps; (Law) corroboratory evidence; hence **ădminĭ'cūlAR**[1] *a.* [f. L *adminiculum* prop]

admi'nister *v.* **1.** *v.t.* manage (affairs); formally give out (sacrament, justice) or present (oath) *to*; furnish, give, (thing *to*); apply (remedies *to*); hence **admi'nistRABLE** *a.* **2.** *v.i.* act as administrator; (arch.) contribute *to* (one's comfort etc.). [ME, f. OF *aministrer* f. L AD(*ministrare* MINISTER[2])]

admi'nistrāte *v.t.* & *i.* administer. [f. L *administrare* (see prec) + -ATE[3]]

admĭnistrā'tion *n.* management (*of* business); management of public affairs, government; the ministry, the Government; *President's period of office; (Law) management of deceased person's estate (**letters of** ∼, authority to administer estate of an intestate; cf. *probate*); administering (*of* justice, oath, etc.); application (*of* remedies). [ME f. OF, or f. L *administratio* (as prec.; see -ATION)]

admĭ'nistrative *a.* pertaining to management of affairs; hence ∼LY[2] (-vlĭ) *adv.* [f. F *administratif -ive* or f. L *administrativus* (as prec.; see -IVE)]

admĭ'nistrā|tor *n.* manager (of business or public affairs); one capable of organizing; one who performs official duties (of religion, justice, etc.); applier or giver (*of*); (Law) one authorized to manage estate for legal owner during minority, absence, etc., or estate of one who dies without appointing competent executors; hence ∼torSHIP, ∼TRIX, *ns.* [L (as ADMINISTER; see -OR)]

ă'dmirab|le *a* worthy of admiration; excellent; A∼le Crichton (krī'ton), one who excels in many things [f. J. Crichton, Scottish scholar, poet, athlete d. 1585]; hence ∼LY[2] *adv.* [F, f. L *admirabilis* (as ADMIRE; see -ABLE)]

ă'dmiral *n.* **1.** commander-in-chief of a country's navy (||**Lord High A**∼, title of sovereign); naval officer of high rank, commander of fleet or squadron; **A**∼ **of the Fleet** (***Fleet A**∼), ∼, **vice-**∼, **rear-** -∼, the four grades of such officers. **2. red** ∼, **white** ∼, species of butterfly. **3.** Hence ∼SHIP *n.* [ME, f. OF *a*(*d*)*mira*(*i*)*l* etc. f. med. L *a*(*d*)*miralis* etc., f. Arab. '*amīr* commander (cf. AMIR), assoc. w. prec.]

ă'dmiraltý *n.* **1.** ||(*A*∼; Hist. exc. in titles). department administering the Navy. **2.** (Law). trial and decision of maritime questions and offences. [ME, f. OF *admiral*(*i*)*té* as prec.; see -TY[1])]

ădmirā'tion *n.* pleased contemplation; (arch.) wonder; respect, warm approval; object of this (*was the admiration of the whole town*); **to** ∼, marvellously. [F, or f. L *admiratio* (as foll.; see -ATION)]

admir'|e *v.t.* regard with pleased surprise, respect, or approval; (arch.) wonder at; (colloq.) express admiration of (*forgot to admire her cat*); hence ∼ER[1] *n.*, (esp., woman's) suitor, ∼ING[2] *a.*, showing or feeling admiration. [f. F *admirer* or f. L AD(*mirari* wonder at)]

admĭ'ss|ible *a.* (Of idea or plan) worthy of being accepted or considered; (Law) allowable as judicial evidence; capable of being admitted (*to* office or position); hence ∼IBI'LITY *n.* [F, or f. med. L *admissibilis* (as ADMIT; see -IBLE)]

admĭ'ss|ion (-shon) *n.* admitting, being admitted, (*to*); charge for this; acknowledgement (*of* error etc.); so ∼IVE *a.* [ME, f. L *admissio* (as foll.; see -ION)]

admĭ't *v.* (**-tt-**). **1.** *v.t.* let in, permit (person etc.) entrance or access (*to* place, class, privilege, etc.), whence ∼tABLE *a.*; accept as valid or true, whence ∼tĕdLY[2] *adv.*; acknowledge, confess, (thing *to be, that* it is, *to* being, or abs.); (of enclosed space) have room for. **2.** *v.i.* ∼ **of,** leave room for, be open to, (doubt, improvement). [ME, f. L AD(*mittere* miss- send)]

admĭ'ttance *n.* admitting, being admitted (usu. to a place; *no admittance except on business*); (Electr.) reciprocal of IMPEDANCE. [f. ADMIT + -ANCE]

admĭ'x *v.* **1.** *v.t.* add as an ingredient. **2.** *v.t.* & *i.* mingle (*with* something). **3.** So ∼tURE *n.*, admixing, thing added (esp. minor ingredient). [f. AD- + MIX]

admŏ'nish *v.t.* urge (person *to do, that* he should do); give advice to; reprove; warn (*of* a thing); so ∼MENT *n.* [ME, f. OF *amonester* f. Rom. *admonestare unexpl. alt. of L AD(*monēre* monit- warn); assim. to L wd and -ISH[2]]

ădmoni'tion *n.* admonishing; warning; reproof; so **admŏ'nitORY** *a.* [ME, f. OF *amonition* f. L *admonitio -onis* (as prec.; see -ITION)]

ad nauseam (ăd naw'sĭăm, -z-) *adv.* to a disgusting extent. [L, = to sickness]

ădnŏ'minal *a.* (Gram.) attached to a noun. [f. L *adnomen -minis* (= AGNOMEN) + -AL]

ado' (*u*dōō') *n.* (*pl.* ∼**s**). action, business, fuss, (**without more** ∼, forthwith); difficulty. [orig. in *much ado* = much to do, f. north. ME *at do* (= *to do*) f. ON *at* AT as sign of inf. + DO[1]]

-ado *suf.* forming *ns.* (*desperado*); cf. -ADE 3. [f. Sp. or Port. *-ado* f. L *-atus* p.p. of vbs. in *are*]

adō'be (-ō'bĭ, -ō'b) *n.* unburnt sun-dried brick; clay from which such bricks can be made. [Sp. f. Arab.]

ădolě'sc|ent *n.* & *a.* (person) growing up, between childhood and manhood or womanhood; so ∼ENCE *n.* [ME f. OF, f. L *adolescere* grow up + -ENT]

Adō'nis (ad-) *n.* handsome young man; ∼ **blue,** species of butterfly (*Lysandra bellargus*). [name of youth loved by Venus; L f. Gk, f. Phoen. *adōn* lord]

adō'pt *v t* (**person**) into a relationship he did not previously occupy, esp. *as* one's child; take (idea etc.) from someone else; choose, take up; ||(of local authority) accept responsibility for maintenance of (road etc.); approve, accept, (report etc.); hence ∼ABLE *a.*, ∼ION *n.* [f. F *adopter* or f. L AD(*optare* choose)]

adō'ptive *a.* due to adoption (*adoptive son, father*); hence ∼LY[2] (-vlĭ) *adv.* [ME, f. OF *adoptif -ive* f. L *adoptivus* (as prec.; see -IVE)]

adōr'|e *v.t.* regard with deep respect and affection; worship as divine; (RC Ch.) offer reverence to (Host etc.); (colloq.) like greatly; so ∼ABLE *a.*, ∼ABLY *adv.*, **ădorA'TION** *n.* [ME, f. OF *aourer* f. L AD(*orare* pray) worship]

adōr'er *n.* worshipper; ardent admirer. [f. prec. + -ER[1]]

adōr'n *v.t.* add beauty or lustre to; furnish with ornament(s); so ∼MENT *n.* [ME, f. OF *ao*(*u*)*rner* f. L AD(*ornare* furnish, deck)]

adow'n *adv.* & *prep.* (arch. or poet.) = DOWN[3,4]. [OE *adūn*(*e*), earlier *ofdūne* (as OF, cf. A- 3; *dūne* dat. of *dūn* hill, DOWN[1])]

ADP *abbr.* adenosine diphosphate; automatic data processing.

ad personam (ăd persō'năm) *adv.* to the person; personal. [L]

ad rem (ăd rě'm) *adv.* & *a.* to the point; to the purpose. [L, = to the matter]

adrē'nal *a.* *n.* **1.** *a.* at or near the kidneys; ∼ **glands,** ductless glands on or above kidneys, secreting ADRENALIN. **2.** *n.* adrenal gland. [f. AD- + RENAL]

adrē'nalin(*P), **-ine,** *n.* hormone secreted by adrenal glands, affecting circulation and muscular action, and causing excitement and stimulation; same substance got from animals or by synthesis, used as stimulant. [f. prec. + -IN, -INE[5]]

adrēnocŏrticotrŏ′p(h)|ic *a.* ∿ic **hormone**, ∿IN, hormone secreted by pituitary gland and stimulating adrenal cortex. [f. ADRENAL + CORTEX + -TROPHIC, -TROPIC]

adri′ft *adv.* & *pred. a.* drifting; exposed to the elements or (fig.) the circumstances; (colloq.) unfastened, out of touch, out of order, ill-informed. [f. A³ + DRIFT¹]

adroi′t *a.* dextrous; skilful; hence ∿LY² *adv.*, ∿NESS *n.* [F (*à droit* according to right)]

ădscītī′tious (-ĭ′shŭs) *a.* adopted from without; supplemental. [f. L AD(*sciscere scit-* incept. of *scire* know) + -ITIOUS²]

ădsōr′b *v.t.* (Usu. of solid) hold (molecules of a gas or liquid or solute) to its surface; so ∿ATE¹ (5) *n.*, ∿ENT *a.* & *n.*, **ădsōr′ptION** *n.* [f. AD-, after *absorb*]

ă′dsŭm *int.* (As answer in roll-call etc.) I am present. [L]

ă′dūl|āte *v.t.* flatter obsequiously; so ∿A′TION, ∿ātoR, *ns.*, ∿ātorY *a.* [f. L *adulari* fawn on + -ATE³]

Adŭ′llamīte (ad-) *n.* member of a dissident political group. [orig. of Liberal rebels 1866; f. cave of *Adullam* (1 Sam. 22: 1, 2) + -ITE¹]

adŭlt (ă′d-, adŭ′lt) *a.* & *n.* **1.** (one who is) grown up; ∿ **education** (for those over usual school age). **2.** *a.* mature, fully developed. **3.** Hence ∿HOOD (-t-h-) *n.*, ∿LY² *adv.* [f. L *adultus* p.p. of *adolescere* grow up; cf. ADOLESCENT]

adŭ′lterant *a.* & *n.* (substance) used in adulterating. [f. as foll. + -ANT]

adŭ′lterate¹ *a.* tainted by adultery; spurious, base. [f. L *adulteratus* p.p. of *adulterare*; see foll., -ATE²]

adŭ′lter|āte² *v.t.* debase (esp. foods) by admixture of other substances; so ∿A′TION, ∿ātoR, *ns.* [f. L *adulterare* corrupt (*adulter* adulterer) + -ATE³]

adŭ′lter|er *n.* one guilty of adultery; so ∿ESS¹ *n.* [f. obs. v. *adulter* f. OF *avoutrer* f. L *adulterare* (see prec.), + -ER¹]

adŭ′lterīne *a.* (born) of adultery; spurious; illegal. [f. L *adulterinus* (*adulter*; see foll., -INE¹)]

adŭ′lter|ў *n.* voluntary sexual intercourse of married person other than with spouse; so ∿ous *a.*, ∿ousLY² *adv.* [ME, f. OF *avoutrie* etc. (*avoutre* adulterer f. L *adulter*); assim. to L *adulterium*]

ă′dumbrāte *v.t.* represent in outline; faintly indicate; typify, foreshadow; overshadow; hence or cogn. **ădumbrA′TION** *n.*, **adŭ′mbratIVE** *a.* [f. L AD(*umbrare* f. *umbra* shade) + -ATE³]

adŭ′st *a.* (arch.) scorched, parched; sunburnt; gloomy, melancholy. [ME, f. F *aduste* or f. L *adustus* p.p. of AD(*urere* burn)]

ad valorem (ăd valōr′ĕm) *adv.* & *a.* (Of taxes) in proportion to estimated value of goods. [L, = according to the value]

adva′nce¹ (-vah′-) *v.* **1.** *v.t.* move or put forward; promote, help on, (plan, person); bring forward (claim, suggestion); bring (event) to earlier date; pay (money) before it is due; lend (money); raise (price); so ∿MENT (-sm-) *n.* (esp. of promotion of plan or person). **2.** *v.i.* move forward; make progress; rise (in price); (in *p.p.*) far on in progress (*the work is well advanced*), ahead of the times (*advanced ideas*); ||∿d **level**, GCE examination for university entrance qualification; ∿d **studies** (in higher branches of a subject). [ME, f. OF *avancer* f. Rom. *abantiare* f. LL *abante* in front f. L *ab* away + *ante* before]

adva′nce² (-vah′-) *n.* going forward; progress; (esp. in *pl.*) friendly or amorous approach; rise in price; payment beforehand; loan; in ∿, ahead in place or time; ∿ **booking** (made before day of journey, performance, etc.); ∿ **copy** (of book etc., supplied before date of publication); ∿ **guard** (preceding main body of army). [f. prec. & F *avance* n. (as prec.)]

adva′ntage¹ (-vah′-) *n.* **1.** better position, precedence, superiority (*gain an advantage over*); **have the** ∿ of, have better position than; **you have the** ∿ **of me**, (esp.) you know me but I do not know you; **take** ∿ **of**, avail oneself of (circumstance), outwit (person)

esp. unfairly, (euphem.) seduce; **take at** ∿, (arch.) take (person) by surprise; **to** ∿, in a way to exhibit the merits (*was seen, heard, to advantage*). **2.** benefit, profit, (*it could be shortened with advantage*; **turn to** ∿ benefit from); beneficial feature. **3.** (Tennis). next point won after deuce; ∿ **in, out**, (to server, receiver of service). **4.** Hence **ădvantā′geous** (-jus) *a.*, **ădvantā′geous**LY² (-jus-) *adv.* [ME, f. OF *avantage* (*avant* in front f. LL *abante*; see ADVANCE¹)]

adva′ntage² (-vah′-) *v.t.* be beneficial or favourable to; further, promote. [ME, f. prec. or F *avantager*]

advě′ct|ion *n.* (Meteorol.) heat transfer by horizontal flow of air; hence ∿IVE *a.* [f. L *advectio* f. AD(*vehere vect-* carry); see -ION]

ă′dvent *n.* arrival of important person or thing; (A∿) season before Christmas; (A∿) coming or second coming of Christ, whence A∿ISM (3), A∿IST (2), *ns.*, (tenets of) member of a sect believing in the imminent millennium of Christ. [OE, f. OF *advent, auvent* f. L *adventus* arrival f. AD(*venire vent-* come)]

ădventī′tious (-shŭs) *a.* coming from outside; accidental, casual; ||(Law, of property) coming from a stranger or by collateral, not direct, succession; (Biol.) occurring in an unusual place; hence ∿LY² *adv.* [f. L *adventicius* (as prec.; see -ITIOUS¹)]

advě′nture¹ *n.* daring enterprise; unexpected or exciting incident; commercial speculation; hazardous activity; ∿ **playground** (where children are provided with waste materials etc. as basis for play); hence ∿SOME¹ (-chers-) *a.* [ME, f. OF *aventure* f. Rom. *adventura* (*res* thing) about to happen (as ADVENT]

advě′nture² *v.* **1.** *v.i.* incur risk; dare to go or come (*into, upon,* a place); dare to enter (*up*)on (undertaking). **2.** *v.t.* (arch.) hazard, imperil, (one*self,* thing). [ME, f. OF *aventurer* (as prec.)]

advě′ntur|er (-cher-) *n.* one who seeks adventures; mercenary soldier; speculator; one who lives by his wits; hence ∿ESS¹ *n.* [f. F *aventurier* (as ADVENTURE²; see -ER¹)]

advě′ntur|ism (-cher-) *n.* tendency to take risks in foreign policy etc.; hence ∿IST (2) *n.* [f. ADVENTURE + -ISM]

advě′nturous (-cher-) *a.* rash, venturesome; filled with adventures; enterprising; hence ∿LY² *adv.* [ME, f. OF *aventuros* (as ADVENTURE¹; see -OUS)]

ă′dvěrb *n.* word or phrase that modifies or qualifies another word (esp. adjective, verb, or other adverb) or a word-group, expressing a relation of place, time, circumstance, manner, cause, degree, etc. (*gently, so, now, accordingly, here, why*); hence **advě′rb**IAL *a.* [f. F *adverbe* or f. L *adverbium* (ad to, *verbum* word, VERB) transl. of Gk *epirrhēma*]

ad verbum (ăd věr′bum) *adv.* & *a.* verbatim. [L, = to the word]

ă′dversарў *n.* opponent, antagonist; enemy; **the A**∿, the Devil. [ME, f. OF *adversarie* f. L *adversarius* (*adversus*; see ADVERSE, -ARY¹)]

advě′sative *a.* (Of words etc.) expressing opposition or antithesis; hence ∿LY² (-vlĭ) *adv.* [f. F *adversatif -ive* or f. LL *adversativus* (*adversari* oppose f. *adversus*; see foll., -IVE)]

ă′dvěrse *a.* contrary, hostile, (*to*); hurtful, injurious, (*to*); (arch.) placed opposite; hence ∿LY² (-slĭ) *adv.* [ME, f. OF *advers* f. L *adversus* p.p. of AD(*vertere versturn*)]

advě′sitў *n.* condition of adverse fortune; misfortune. [ME, f. OF *adversité* f. L *adversitas -tatis* (as prec.; see -ITY)]

||**ă′dvěrt¹** *n.* (colloq.) advertisement. [abbr.]

advě′rt² *v.i.* refer *to* (in speaking or writing). [ME, f. OF *avertir* f. Rom. *advertire* (as ADVERSE)]

ă′dvertīs|e (-z) *v.* **1.** *v.t.* make (thing, one*self,* or abs.) generally or publicly known; (esp.) describe (goods) publicly with view to increasing sales; notify (person *of* thing, *that*). **2.** *v.i.* ∿**e for**, ask for by public notice. **3.** Hence ∿ER¹ *n.* [ME, f. OF *avertir* (st. -iss-); see ADVERT², -ISH²]

advĕr'tisement (-sm-) *n.* public announcement (esp. in newspapers, on posters, by television, etc.); advertising; (arch.) notice to readers in book etc. [earlier *avert-* f. F *avertissement* (as prec.; see -MENT)]

advī'ce *n.* opinion given or offered as to future action (take ∼, seek it esp. from legal etc. expert, or act according to it when given); information given, news; formal notice of transaction; (in *pl.*) communications from a distance. [ME f. OF *avis* f. Rom. **advisum* f. L *ad* to + *visum* p.p. of *vidēre* see]

advī's|able (-z-) *a.* to be recommended; expedient; hence ∼ABI'LITY, ∼**able**NESS (-beln-), *ns.*, ∼ABLY *adv.* [f. foll. + -ABLE]

advī's|e (-z) *v.t.* & *i.* offer advice (to); recommend (*they advise caution; advised me to rest*); inform, notify, (*of thing, that*); *consult *with*; hence ∼ER[1], ∼OR, *ns.*, (esp.) person habitually consulted, *person advising students. [ME, f. OF *aviser* f. Rom. **advisare* f. L *ad* to, *visare* frequent. of *vidēre* see]

advī'sed (-zd) *a.* deliberate, considered, whence ∼LY[2] (-ĭ'zĭdlĭ) *adv.*; judicious (ILL-*advised*). [p.p. of prec.]

advī'sory (-z-) *a.* giving advice; consisting in giving advice. [f. ADVISE + -ORY]

ădvocaa't (-ah't) *n.* liqueur of eggs, sugar, and brandy. [Du., = ADVOCATE('s drink)]

ă'dvocacy *n.* function of an advocate; pleading in support of [ME, f. OF *a*(*d*)*vocacie* f. med. L *advocatia* (as foll.; see -ACY)]

ă'dvocate[1] *n.* one who pleads for another; one who speaks in favour *of* (proposal etc.) (DEVIL'*s advocate*); professional pleader in courts of justice, (Sc.) barrister (**Faculty of A∼s**, Scottish bar; **Lord A∼**, principal law-officer of Crown in Scotland); hence ∼SHIP (-tsh-) *n.*, **ă'dvocā**TORY *a.* [ME f. OF *avocat* f. L *advocatus* p.p. (as n.) of AD(*vocare* call)]

ă'dvocate[2] *v.t.* plead for, defend; recommend, support (policy etc.). [f. prec.]

‖advow'son (-z-) *n.* right of presentation to a benefice. [ME, f. AF *a*(*d*)*voweson* f. OF *avoeson* f. L *advocatio -onis* (as ADVOCATE[1]; see -ION)]

advt. *abbr.* advertisement.

ă'dȳt|um *n.* (*pl.* ∼a). innermost part of a temple; private chamber, sanctum. [L, f. Gk *aduton* neut. (as n.) of *adutos* impenetrable (*a-* not, *duō* enter)]

ădze, *ădz, *n.,* & *v.t.* (dress or cut with) tool for cutting away surface of wood, like axe with arched blade at right angles to handle. [OE *adesa*, of unkn. orig.]

-ae *pl. suf.* used in names of animal and plant families (*Folidae, Rosaceae*) and (esp ‖) instead of -*as* in pl. of many non-naturalized or unfamiliar ns. in -*a* derived f. L or Gk (*larvae*, mathematical *formulae, actiniae*). [f. pl. -*ae* of L ns. in -*a* or pl. -*ai* of some Gk ns.]

ae'dīle *n.* Roman magistrate who superintended public buildings and other matters; hence ∼SHIP (-lsh-) *n.* [f. L *aedilis* (*aedes* building; see -IL)]

ae'gis *n.* protection, impregnable defence; **under the** ∼ (auspices) **of.** [L, f. Gk *aigis* mythical shield of Zeus or Athene]

‖ae'grŏtăt *n.* certificate that university student is too ill to attend examination etc.; examination pass awarded for this reason. [L, = he is sick (*aeger*)]

-ae'mia, *-ē'mia, *suf.* forming *ns.* denoting that a substance is (excessively) present in the blood (*bacteriaemia, pyaemia*). [mod. L, f. Gk -*aimia* (*haima* blood; see -IA[1])]

aeō'lian, *ēō'lian, *a.* **1.** wind-borne; ∼ **harp**, stringed instrument producing musical sounds on exposure to wind. **2.** **Aeolian mode**, (Mus.) (1) ancient Greek MODE, (2) ninth of church modes (with A as final and E as dominant). [f. L *Aeolius*: sense 1 f. *Aeolus* god of winds f. Gk *Aiolos*; sense 2 f. *Aeolis* Gk colony district in Asia Minor f. Gk *Aiolis*; see -AN]

Aeō'lic *a.* & *n.* (dialect) of Aeolia. [f. as prec. 2 + -IC]

aeolō'tropy *n.* change of physical properties consequent on change of orientation; anisotropy. [f. Gk *aiolos* changeful + -*tropia* turning; see -Y[1]]

ae'on, ē'on, *n.* an age of the universe, immeasurable

period; eternity; (Platonic & Gnostic Philos.) a power existing from eternity, emanation or phase of the supreme deity. [f. eccl. L f. Gk *aiōn* age]

aepȳŏr'nis *n.* extinct giant flightless bird of genus *Aepyornis*, like moa. [mod. L, f. Gk *aipus* high + *ornis* bird]

aer'|āte (āī'-) *v.t.* expose to mechanical or chemical action of air; charge with carbon dioxide (‖*aerated water*); hence ∼A'TION, ∼ātOR, *ns.* [f. L *aer* AIR[1] + -ATE[3], after F *aérer*]

aer'ial (āī'-) *a.* & *n.* **1.** *a.* (or āēr'ial). of air, gaseous; thin as air, ethereal; immaterial, imaginary; hence ∼ITY (-ă'l-) *n.* **2.** of or in the atmosphere, atmospheric; existing, moving, happening, in the air; ∼ **cableway, railway, ropeway,** system of overhead cables from which cars or containers are suspended, usu. driven electrically; hence ∼IST *n.*, high-wire or trapeze artist. **3.** by or from aircraft (*aerial bombardment, photography, TORPEDO*). **4.** Hence ∼LY[2] *adv.* **5.** *n.* wire or rod used to transmit or receive radio waves. [f. L f. Gk *aerios* (*aēr* air) + -AL]

aerie. See EYRIE.

aer'ifŏrm (āī'-) *a.* of the form of air, gaseous; unsubstantial, unreal. [f. L *aer* AIR[1] + -I- + -FORM]

aero- (āī'ō) *comb. form.* **1.** air, as: ∼**bio'logy,** study of airborne micro-organisms, pollen, spores, etc., esp. as agents of infection; ∼**dyna'mics,** study of interaction between air and solid bodies moving through it (so ∼**dyna'mic** *a.,* ∼**dyna'micist** *n.*); **aero'logy** (-ŏ'l-), study of atmosphere away from ground (hence ∼**lo'gical** *a.*); ∼**nau'tics,** science, art, or practice of aerial navigation (hence ∼**nau'tic**(**al**) *adjs.*); **aero'nomy** (-ŏ'n-), science of upper atmosphere. **2.** aircraft, as: ∼**-engine** (for propelling aircraft); ‖**aer'ofoil** [FOIL[1]], aircraft wing, fin, or tailplane. [f. Gk *aero-* (*aēr* air)]

aerobā'tics (āī'-) *n. pl.* (usu. treated as *sing.*) feats of expert and usu. spectacular flying of aircraft. [f. prec. + ACROBATICS]

aer'|ōbe (āī'-) *n.* micro-organism living only in presence of free oxygen from the air; hence ∼ō'BIC *a.* [f. F *aérobie* f. as AERO- + Gk *bios* life]

‖aer'odrōme (āī'-) *n.* (arch.) = AIR[1]*field.* [f. AERO- + -DROME]

aer'olite (āī'-) *n.* stony meteorite. [f. AERO- + -LITE]

‖aer'oplāne (āī'-) *n.* mechanically driven winged heavier-than-air flying machine. [f. F *aéroplane* (as AERO-, PLANE[3])]

aer'osol (āī'-) *n.* system of colloidal particles dispersed in gas (e.g. fog or smoke); (container of) substance packed under pressure with device for releasing it as fine spray. [f. AERO- + SOL[3]]

aer'ospace (āī'-) *n.* Earth's atmosphere and outer space; technology of aviation in this region. [f. AERO- + SPACE[1]]

aeru'ginous (ērōō'-) *a.* of the nature or colour of verdigris. [f. L *aeruginosus* (*aerugo -inis* verdigris f. *aes aeris* bronze; see -OUS)]

Aescūlā'pian *a.* of medicine or physicians. [f. L *Aesculapius* f. Gk *Asklēpios* god of medicine + -IAN]

aesthēte *n.* professed admirer of the beautiful; ‖(at university) studious person (opp. HEARTY). [f. Gk *aisthētēs* one who perceives (as foll.), or f. foll. after *athlete* f. *athletic*]

aesthĕ't|ic *a.* & *n.* **1.** *a.* belonging to the appreciation of the beautiful; having such appreciation; in accordance with principles of good taste; hence ∼ICALLY *adv.*, ∼ICISM (3) *n.*, ∼ICS *n.*, philosophy of the beautiful or of art. **2.** *n.* set of principles of good taste and appreciation of beauty. [f. Gk *aisthētikos* (*aisthanomai* perceive; see -ETIC)]

aestival, *estival, (ě'stĭval, ěstī'val) *a.* belonging to or appearing in summer. [ME f. OF *estival,* f. L *aestivalis* f. *aestivus* (*aestus* heat); see -IVE, -AL]

ae'stiv|āte (ē'-) *v.i.* spend the summer, esp. (Zool.) in state of torpor; hence ∼A'TION *n.,* (esp., Bot.) arrangement of petals in flower-bud before expansion (cf. VERNATION). [f. L *aestivare* + -ATE[3]]

aetatis (ētā′tĭs, ītah′tĭs) a. (abbr. **aet., aetat.**) of or at the age of (aet. 17). [L]

ae′ther. Var. of ETHER 1, 2.

aetiŏ′logȳ, *ētiŏ′logȳ, n. assignment of a cause; philosophy of causation; (Med.) science of the causes of disease; hence **aetiŏ′gIC**(AL) adjs., **aetiŏ′gICALLY** adv. [f. LL f. Gk aitiologia (aitia cause; see -LOGY)]

af- pref., assim. form of AD- before f.

AF abbr. audio frequency.

afar′ adv. at, to, a distance (esp. afar off); **from ∼,** from a distance. [ME, f. A- 2, 3 + FAR[1]]

||AFC abbr. Air Force Cross; Association Football Club.

ă′ffable a. (Of person) easy to approach and converse with; courteous, esp. to inferiors; hence or cogn. **ăffABI′LITY** n., **ă′ffabLY[2]** adv. [F, f. L affabilis f. AF(fari speak); see -ABLE]

affair′ n. **1.** thing to be done; concern, business, matter, (that is my affair; the Dreyfus affair); love affair; (colloq.) thing, happening; **∼ of honour,** duel to settle question of honour. **2.** (in pl.) ordinary pursuits of life; business dealings; public matters (current affairs, world affairs). [ME, f. AF afere f. OF afaire (à faire to do); cf. ADO]

affaire (de cœur) (ăfār′ dĕ kēr′) n. love affair. [F]

affairé (ăfār′ā) a. busy; involved. [F]

affĕ′ct[1] v.t. assume (character) (affect the free thinker); use by preference; pretend to have or feel (indifference etc.); pretend (to do). [f. F affecter or f. L affectare aim at, frequent. of AF(ficere fect- = facere do) influence]

affĕ′ct[2] v.t. **1.** move, touch, (in mind); hence **∼ING[2]** a., **∼INGLY** adv. **2.** produce (material) effect on; (of disease etc.) attack; (in pass., arch.) be assigned to. [f. F affecter or f. L affect- (see prec.)]

ă′ffect[3] n. (Psych.) feeling, emotion, desire, esp. as leading to action. [f. G affekt f. L affectus disposition (aficere; see AFFECT[1])]

ăffĕcta′tion n. studied display of; artificiality of manner; pretence. [F, or f. L affectatio (as AFFECT[1]; see -ATION)]

affĕ′ctĕd a. In vbl senses; artificially assumed or displayed, pretended; (of person) full of affectation, artificial, whence **∼LY[2]** adv., **∼NESS** n.; (w. adv.) disposed, inclined, (towards, or abs.). [p.p. of AFFECT[1,2]]

affĕ′ction n. affecting; being affected; mental state, emotion, whence **∼AL** a.; mental disposition; goodwill, kindly feeling, love, (for, towards); bodily state due to any influence; (esp.) malady, disease. [ME f. OF, f. L affectio -onis (as AFFECT[2]; see -ION)]

affĕ′ctionate a. loving, fond; (of thing) showing love or tenderness; hence **∼LY[2]** (-tlĭ) adv., **∼NESS** (-tn-) n. [f. F affectionné or f. med. L affectionatus (as AFFECTION; see -ATE[2])]

affĕ′ctive a. pertaining to the affections, emotional; (Psych.) pertaining to affects; hence **ăffĕcti′VITY** n. [f. F affectif -ive f. LL affectivus (as AFFECT[2]; see -IVE)]

ă′ffenpinscher (-nsher) n. (animal of) small breed of dog like griffon. [G (affe monkey, pinscher terrier)]

ă′fferent a. (Physiol.) conducting inwards or upwards (afferent nerves, vessels) (opp. efferent). [f. L AF(ferre bring); see -ENT]

affi′ance[1] n. (arch.) faith, trust, (in); (arch.) pledging of faith, esp. in marriage. [ME, f. OF afiance (see foll.)]

affi′ance[2] v.t. (usu. in pass.) promise to give (person) solemnly in marriage. [f. OF afiancer (afiance f. afier f. med. L AF(fidare f. fidus trusty); see -ANCE]

***affi′ant** n. maker of affidavit. [F, pres. part. of afier (see prec.)]

affiche (ăfē′sh) n. notice affixed to wall etc. [F (afficher post up)]

ăffidā′vĭt n. written statement, confirmed by oath, to be used as judicial evidence (deponent made or swore or took an affidavit). [med. L, = has stated on oath, f. affidare (see AFFIANCE[2])]

affi′liāte v.t., & n. **1.** v.t. (Of institution) adopt (persons as members, societies as branches); attach

(persons, societies) to, connect (them) with, (a society); so **affiliā′TION** n. (||**affiliation order,** legal order that putative father of illegitimate child must help to support it). **2.** n. affiliated person or organization. [f. med. L AFfiliare adopt (filius son) + -ATE[3]]

affi′ned (-nd) a. related, connected. [f. affine a. f. I affinis related (see foll.) + -ED[1]]

affi′nĭtȳ n. relationship, relations, esp. by marriage structural resemblance (between animals, plants, languages); (fig.) similarity of character suggesting relationship, family likeness; liking, attraction person having attraction for another; (Chem.) tendency of certain substances to combine with others. [ME, f. OF afinité f. L affinitas -tatis (AFfinis related, lit. bordering on, f. finis border; see -ITY)]

affir′m v. **1.** v.t. assert strongly, state as a fact; (Law) confirm, ratify, (judgement). **2.** v.i. make formal declaration; esp. (Law) make affirmation. **3.** Hence **∼ABLE, ∼atORY,** adjs. [ME, f. OF afermer f. L AFfirmare (firmus strong)]

affirmā′tion n. affirming; (Law) solemn declaration by person who conscientiously declines taking an oath. [F, or f. L affirmatio (as prec.; see -ATION)]

affir′mative a. & n. **1.** a. affirming, answering that a thing is so; (of vote) expressing approval; (Logic) asserting that a proposition is valid; hence **∼LY[2]** (-vlĭ) adv. **2.** n. that which affirms; **answer in the ∼,** say that thing is so. [ME f. OF affirmatif -ive f. LL affirmativus (as prec.; see -IVE)]

affi′x[1] v.t. fix, fasten, (thing to, on; lit. or fig.); impress (seal, stamp); add in writing (signature, postscript). [f. F affixer or f. med. L affixare frequent. of L AF(figere fix- fix)]

ă′ffix[2] n. appendage, addition; (Gram.) addition placed at the beginning (prefix) or end (suffix) of root, stem, or word, or in body of word (infix), to modify its meaning. [f. F affixe f. L affigere (as prec.)]

affi′xture n. affixing. [f. AFFIX[1], after fixture]

afflā′tus n. divine impulse (esp. poetic); inspiration. [L, f. AF(flare flat- blow)]

affli′ct v.t. distress with bodily or mental suffering; **∼ed with,** suffering from. [ME, f. L afflictare, or afflict- p.p. st. of AF(fligere flict- dash)]

affli′ct|ion n. misery, distress; (cause of) pain or calamity; so **∼IVE** a. [ME f. OF, f. L afflictio -onis (as prec.; see -ION)]

ă′fflu|ent (-lŏō-) a. & n. **1.** a. flowing freely, copious; abounding (esp. in riches); wealthy; **∼ent society,** one in which material wealth is widely distributed; hence or cogn. **∼ENCE** n., **∼entLY[2]** adv. **2.** n. tributary stream. **3.** So **ă′fflŭx** n., flow towards a point, influx. [ME f. OF, f. L AF(fluere flux- flow); see -ENT]

affor′ce v.t. reinforce (group of persons, e.g. jury) by adding experts. [ME, f. OF aforcier (a to, FORCE[1])]

affor′d v.t. provide; (of thing) yield supply of; **can ∼,** have means for or be rich enough to do, be in a position to do (can't afford to let him think so), be able to spare. [ME, f. OE geforthian promote (as Y-, FORTH), assim. to wds in AF-]

affŏ′rest v.t. convert into forest; plant with trees; so **∼A′TION** n. [f. med. L AFforestare (foresta FOREST)]

affrā′nchise (-z) v.t. release from servitude or obligation. [f. OF afranchir (as ENFRANCHISE, w. pref. A- 4)]

affray′ n. breach of the peace by fighting or rioting in public. [ME, f. AF afrayer v. f. OF esfreer, f. Rom. *EX[1]fridare (Gmc *frithuz peace)]

affrei′ghtment (-rā′t-) n. hiring of ship to carry cargo. [f. affreight v. hire ship to carry cargo f. F AF(fréter f. fret FREIGHT); see -MENT]

ă′ffricate n. (Phonet.) combination of plosive with immediately following fricative or spirant, e.g. ch. [f. L AF(fricare rub); see -ATE[2]]

affri′ght (-ī′t) v.t., & n. (arch.) fright(en). [f. A- 1 + FRIGHT 2]

affro′nt (-ŭ′nt) v.t., & n. **1.** v.t. insult openly; offend modesty or self-respect of; face, confront. **2.** n. open insult (feel it an affront; offer an affront to). [ME, f. OF

afronter slap in the face, insult, f. Rom. ***AF**frontare f. L frons frontis face]

affu′sion (-zhon) n. pouring on (esp. of water on body in baptism). [F, or f. LL affusio f. L AF(fundere fuspour); see -ION]

A′fghăn (ă′fgăn) n. native, inhabitant, or language (Pashto), of Afghanistan; (a∿) knitted and sewn woollen blanket or shawl; ∿ **hound,** hunting dog with long silky hair. [f. Pashto afghānī]

aficionado (afĭsyonah′dō) n. (pl. ∿s). devotee of bullfighting; devotee of any sport or pastime. [Sp.]

afie′ld adv. in the field; away from home, to or at a distance. [OE (as A³, FIELD)]

afir′e adv. & pred. a. on fire (lit. or fig.). [ME, f. A³ + FIRE¹]

află′me adv. & pred. a. in flames (lit. or fig.). [f. A⁰ + FLAME¹]

ä′flatŏxin n. carcinogen produced by the mould Aspergillus flavus. [f. Aspergillus + flavus + TOXIN]

***AFL-CIO** abbr. American Federation of Labor and Congress of Industrial Organizations.

afloa′t adv. & pred. a. floating in water or air; at sea, on board ship; full of or covered with water; out of debt; in full swing; in general circulation, current. [OE (as A⁰, FLOAT¹)]

||**AFM** abbr. Air Force Medal.

a fond (ah faw′n) adv. thoroughly, fully. [F, = to bottom]

afoo′t adv. & pred. a. astir, on the move; in operation or employment; (arch.) on one's own feet. [ME, f. A³ + FOOT¹]

afor′e adv. & prep. (Naut.) in front (of) (afore the mast); (arch.) previously. [OE onforan (as A³, FORE²)]

afor′e- comb. form. before, previously, (aforementioned, aforesaid); ∿**thought,** premeditated (malice aforethought). [f. prec.]

a fortiori (ā fŏrtiŏr′ī) adv. & a. with yet stronger reason; more conclusively. [L]

***afou′l** adv. foul (fall, run, afoul of). [f. A³ + FOUL]

afrai′d pred. a. alarmed, frightened, (of, lest, that, or abs.); ∿ (of the consequences, and therefore unwilling) **to** do a thing; **I'm** ∿, (colloq.) I admit with (real or politely simulated) regret (I'm afraid I'm late; I'm afraid there's none left). [ME, p.p. of obs. affray v. f. AF]

afrayer f. OF esfreer (see AFFRAY)

ä′freet, ä′frit, (-rēt) n. evil demon in Muslim mythology. [f. Arab. 'ifrīt]

afre′sh adv. anew, with fresh beginning. [f. A- 3 + FRESH]

A′fric (ă′f-) a. & n. (arch. or poet.) (Of) Africa. [f. L Africus African]

A′frican (ă′f-) a. & n. (native, esp. dark-skinned, or inhabitant) of Africa; (S. Afr.) Bantu; *Black; ∿ **violet,** saintpaulia; hence ∿ISM (3, 4), ∿IST (2, 3), ns., ∿IZE (3) v.t., make African, place under control of African Blacks. [f. L Africanus (Africa; see -AN)]

Afrikaa′ns (ăfrĭkah′ns) n. language derived from Dutch, used in S. Africa. [Du., = African]

ăfrīkä′nder n. S. Afr. breed of cattle or sheep; (S. Afr.) kind of gladiolus. [f. Afrik. Afrikaander alt. of Du. Afrikaner after Hollander etc.]

Afrika′ner (ăfrĭkah′ner) n. Afrikaans-speaking white person in S. Africa, esp. of Dutch descent; afrikander. [Afrik., f. as prec.]

A′frō (ă′f-) a. (Of hair style) long and bushy, as naturally grown by some Blacks. [f. foll., or abbr. of AFRICAN; see -O]

A′fr(ō)- (ă′f-) comb. form. African, as: Aframerican, Afro--American, (esp. of Amer. Blacks); Afro-Asian, Afro--Asiatic. [f. L Afr Afr- African]

ăfrōrmō′sia (-z-) n. (Afr. tree of genus Afrormosia yielding) wood like teak in appearance, used for furniture. [mod. L, f. AFRO- + Ormosia genus of trees]

aft (ahft) adv. (Naut. & Aeron.) in or near or to or towards stern or tail. [prob. alt. f. ME baft (see ABAFT) on anal. of AFTER]

a′fter¹ (ahf′-) adv., prep., & conj. **1.** adv. behind in place

(Jill came tumbling after, look before and after); later in time (soon after; a week after). **2.** prep. in pursuit or quest of (run, inquire, after him; hanker after; he is after a job); behind (shut the door after you); about, concerning (ask after her, her health etc.; LOOK after). **3.** following in time, later than, (*a quarter after ten o'clock); ∿ **you** (formula in yielding precedence); ∿ **you with,** (colloq.) may I have next turn at; ∿ **six months,** when six months have or had elapsed; **time** ∿ **time** (& sim. phrs.), many places (etc.) in succession. **4.** in view of (after such behaviour); notwithstanding (after all my efforts); next in importance to; according to (after a FASHION; after one's own HEART); in imitation of (person, word, etc.) (a picture after Rubens; 'aesthete' is formed after 'athlete'); in allusion to (named after). **5.** ∿ **all,** in spite of all that has happened or has been said etc. (after all, what does it matter?) or of one's exertions, expectations, etc., (he tried for an hour and failed after all; so you have come after all!). **6.** conj. in or at the time subsequent to that when (after he went, goes, has gone, had gone). [OE æfter, = OS, OHG aftar, ON aptr, Goth. aftra, Gmc f. *af- (cogn. w. Gk apo or opisō) + compar. suf. *-ter]

a′fter² (ah′-) a. **1.** later, following, (in after years); (Naut.) nearer stern (after cabins, mast; after-PEAK¹), whence ∿MOST a. **2.** ∿**birth,** placenta and foetal membrane discharged after birth; ∿**care,** attention given after a stay in hospital, prison, etc.; ∿**effect,** effect that follows after an interval or after the primary action of something; ∿**glow,** radiance (lit. or fig.) remaining after removal of source; ∿**grass,** = AFTERMATH (lit.); ∿**image** (retained by sense--organ, esp. eye, and producing sensation after cessation of stimulus); ∿**life,** life at a later time or after death; ∿**light,** hindsight; ∿**pains** (caused by contraction of womb after childbirth); ∿**shave** a. & n., (lotion) for use after shaving; ∿**taste** (remaining or recurring after eating or drinking); ∿**thought,** something that is thought of or added later; ∿**word,** concluding remarks in book, esp. by person other than its author. [f. prec.]

a′ftermath (ah′-; -äth, -ahth) n. grass growing after mowing or harvest; (fig.) consequences (the aftermath of war). [f. prec. + math mowing f. OE mæth f. Gmc *mē- MOW²]

afternoo′n (ah-) n. time from noon or lunch-time to evening (lit. or fig.; in or during the afternoon; on Wednesday afternoon; the afternoon of life); this time spent in a particular way; afternoon TEA. [f. AFTER¹ 3 + NOON]

a′fters (ah′-; -z) n. pl. (colloq.) course following main course at meal. [f. AFTER¹ or AFTER²]

a′fterwards (-z), ***a′fterward,** (ah′-) adv. later, subsequently. [OE æflunwearde a. (æftan AFT, -WARD) + -s³]

ag- pref., assim. form of AD- before g.

Ag symb. silver. [f. L argentum]

a′ga (ah′ga) n. (In Muslim countries, esp. under Ottoman Empire) commander, chief; **Aga Khan,** spiritual leader of Ismaili Muslims. [f. Turk. aǧa master]

agai′n (-ĕ′n, -ā′n) adv. **1.** another time, once more; ∿ **and** ∿, **time and** (time) ∿, repeatedly; **back** ∿, **home** ∿, **quite well** ∿, to or in original position or condition; **come** ∿, (esp.) make second effort, (as imper., colloq.) what did you say?; NOW and again; **as much** ∿, twice as much; **half as much** or **many** ∿, one-and-a-half times as much or many. **2.** further, besides (again, what about the children?); on the other hand (I might, and again I might not); in accordance or response (glasses rang again; the loaded table groaned again). [orig. north. form of ME ayen etc., f. OE ongēan, ongægn, etc., OS angegin, OHG ingagan, f. Gmc (as ON¹, *gagan-, *gagin- straight)]

agai′nst (-ĕ′n-, -ā′n-) prep. **1.** in opposition to (fight against; I am against him; hanging; arson is against the law; against the CLOCK¹, the GRAIN 5; OVER against); to the disadvantage of (his age is against him); in contrast to (against a dark background; 99 as against 102 yesterday). **2.** in anticipation of or preparation for (against his coming; against a rainy day; protected against the cold; warned against pickpockets); in return for (issued against payment of the fee); into collision or in contact with (ran against a rock; lean, stand, against the wall; UP against). [f. ME ayenes etc. (ayen AGAIN; see -s³), +-t as in amidst, amongst, betwixt, whilst]

a'gama n. Old World lizard like iguana. [Carib]

aga'mic a. (Zool.) characterized by absence of sexual action. [f. as AGAMOUS + -IC]

agamo|ge'nesis n. (Biol.) asexual reproduction; so ~**gene'tic** a. [f. as foll. + Gk genesis birth]

a'gamous a. (Biol.) without (distinguishable) sexual organs. [f. LL f. Gk agamos (a- not, gamos marriage) + -ous]

agapa'nthus n. S. Afr. ornamental lily of genus Agapanthus, with blue or white flowers. [mod. L, f. Gk agapē love + anthos flower]

aga'pe¹ adv. & pred. a. gaping; open-mouthed with wonder or expectation. [f. A³ + GAPE]

a'gapē² n. love-feast held by early Christians in connection with Lord's Supper; (Theol.) Christian love, charity. [Gk, = brotherly love]

agape'mone n. abode of free love. [f. A~, name of a community founded in Somerset c. 1850, believed to practise free love; irreg. f. Gk agapē love + monē abode]

a'gar-(-a'gar) n. seaweed of various kinds, esp. Ceylon moss; gelatinous substance made from this and used in food, bacterial cultures, etc. [Malay]

a'garic n. fungus of family Agaricaceae, with cap and stalk, incl. common mushroom; FLY¹ agaric. [f. L f. Gk agarikon]

a'gate n. one of several varieties of hard usu. banded chalcedony; coloured toy marble resembling this. [f. F agate, -the, f. L f. Gk akhatēs]

aga'vē n. (Bot.) plant of genus Agave, with spiny leaves, flowering only once, e.g. American aloe. [L, f. Gk Agauē, proper name in myth (agauos illustrious)]

aga'ze adv. gazing. [ME, f. A³ + GAZE]

a'gba n. kind of W. Afr. timber. [Yoruba]

age¹ n. **1.** length of past life or of existence; **be your** ~, (colloq.) act sensibly; **look** one's ~, look as old as one really is; MENTAL¹, READING, age; **moon's** ~, time elapsed since new moon; **of an** ~ **with**, of same age as. **2.** duration or period of life required for a purpose; **come of** ~, reach adult status (esp. in Law at 18, formerly 21); age of CONSENT², of DISCRETION; **over** ~, (1) old enough, (2) too old; **under** ~, not old enough, esp. not yet of adult status. **3.** latter part of life (peevishness of age); ~ **before beauty,** children must give precedence to their elders. **4.** a generation; (Hist.) great period (Age of REASON¹; brazen, BRONZE, GOLDEN, IRON¹, SILVER¹, STONE, age; MIDDLE¹ Ages); (colloq., esp. in pl.) long time (waiting for ages); ~**-long,** ~**-old,** having existed for a very long time. **5.** (Geol.) period of time, esp. one shorter than an EPOCH, corresp. to STAGE¹ in rocks; ICE¹-age. [ME f. OF, f. Rom. *aetaticum f. L aetas -atis age; see -AGE]

age² v.t. & i. (part. ~**ing** or aging, pr. ā'jǐng). (cause or allow to) grow old or mature or show effects of passage of time; begin to appear older (he's aged a lot recently); hence **a'g(e)**ING¹ (ā'jǐng) n., change of properties occurring in some metals after heat treatment or cold working. [f. prec.]

-age (-ĭj) suf. forming ns. w. sense: (1) aggregate or number of (coverage, the peerage, acreage); (2) function or condition (bondage, a peerage); (3) action (breakage, spillage); (4) fees payable for, cost of using, (porterage, postage); (5) place, abode, (anchorage, orphanage, parsonage); (6) product of action (dosage, wreckage). [OF, f. Rom. *-aticum (*aetaticum AGE, *coraticum COURAGE), f. L -aticum neut. of adj. suf. -aticus -ATIC]

aged a. **1.** (ā'jĭd). having lived long, old; hence **a'ged**NESS n. **2.** (ājd). of the age of (aged ten); that has been subjected to ageing; (of horse) over six years old. [p.p. of AGE²]

a'geless (-jl-) a. never growing or appearing old or outmoded. [f. AGE¹ + -LESS]

a'gency n. **1.** active operation, action (moral, free, agency); intervening action (fertilized by the agency of insects); action personified (an invisible agency). **2.** function of an agent or representative; business establishment of an agent (employment, news, agency); specialized department of United Nations. [f. med. L. agentia f. L agere do; see -ENCY]

age'nda n. things to be done; (list of) items of business to be considered at a meeting. [L, neut. pl. of gerundive of agere do; now usu. treated as sing.]

a'gent n. **1.** one who or that which exerts power or produces an effect (**free** ~, one whose actions are not subject to another's control); (cause of) natural force or effect on matter (oxidizing agent). **2.** one who acts for another in business, politics, etc., (estate, insurance, secret, agent); spy; **law** ~, (Sc.) solicitor; ~**-general,** London representative of Australian state or Canadian province. **3.** So **age'nt**IAL (-shal) a. [f. L agere do; see -ENT]

agent provocateur (ahzhahn prŏvŏkatēr') n. (pl. -ts -rs pr. same). person employed to detect suspected offenders by tempting them to overt action. [F, = provocative agent]

aggiornament|o (ajōrnamĕ'ntō) n. (pl. ~**i** pr. -ē). bringing up to date, esp. of RC Church policy. [It.]

agglo'mer|ate¹ v.t. & i. collect into a mass; accumulate in a disorderly way; hence ~**A'TION** n., ~**ATIVE** a. [f. L AGglomerare (glomus -meris ball) + -ATE³]

agglo'merate² a. & n. (collected into) a mass; (Geol.) mass of volcanic fragments united under heat (cf. CONGLOMERATE). [f. as prec.; see -ATE¹,²]

agglu'tin|ate (-lōō'-) v.t. & i. unite as with glue; (of language) combine simple words without change of form to express compound ideas; (Biol.) cause or undergo coalescence (of bacteria, erythrocytes, etc.); hence ~**A'TION** n., ~**ATIVE** a., ~**IN** n., (Biol.) substance causing agglutination. [f. L AGglutinare (gluten -tinis glue) + -ATE³]

aggra'ndize, -ise (-ĭz), v.t. increase power, rank, wealth, of (person, State); make appear greater than the reality; hence ~**MENT** (-zm-) n. [f. F agrandir (st. -iss-), prob. f. It. AG (grandire f. L grandis large); assim. to vbs in -IZE]

a'ggrav|ate v.t. increase gravity of (illness, offence, etc.); (colloq.) exasperate (person); so ~**A'TION** n. [(prob. f. F aggraver) f. L AGgravare make heavy (gravis) + -ATE³]

a'ggregate¹ a. & n. **1.** a. collected into one body; collective, total, (CORPORATION aggregate); (Bot., of fruit) formed from carpels of one flower (e.g. raspberry). **2.** n. sum total; assemblage (**in the** ~, as a whole); broken stone etc. used in making concrete; mass of particles in soil etc.; (Geol.) mass of minerals formed into one rock. [f. L AGgregare herd together (grex gregis flock); see -ATE¹,²]

a'ggreg|ate² v.t. & i. collect together; unite (individual to company); (colloq.) amount to (specified total); hence ~**A'TION** n., ~**ATIVE** a. [f. as prec. + -ATE³]

aggre'ss|ion (-shon) n. act of beginning quarrel or war; unprovoked attack; (Psych.) hostile or destructive tendency or behaviour; so ~**OR** n. [f. F agression or f. L aggressio attack f. AG (gredi = gradi walk); see -ION]

aggre'ssive a. **1.** of aggression; offensive. **2.** disposed to attack; forceful, self-assertive. **3.** Hence ~**LY²** (-vlĭ) adv., ~**NESS** (-vn-) n. [f. as prec.; see -IVE]

aggrie've v.t. (usu. in pass.) grieve, distress; oppress, treat unfairly. [ME, f. OF agrever make heavier f. Rom. *AG (grevare) GRIEVE¹]

a'ggro n. (sl.) deliberate trouble-making. [abbr. of AGGRAVATION or AGGRESSION; see -O]

agha'st (agah'st) a. (usu. pred.) terrified; struck with amazement. [ME, p.p. of obs. v. agast, gast frighten; see GHASTLY]

a'gile a. quick-moving, nimble, active; hence or cogn. **agi'l**ITY n., ~**LY²** (-l-lĭ) adv. [F, f. L agilis (agere do; see -IL)]

agi'n (ag-) prep. (joc. or dial.) against; ~ **the**

government, uncooperative. [corrupt. of (AGAIN obs. prep. =) AGAINST]

a'gio n. (pl. ∽s). percentage charged on exchange of paper money into cash, or of one currency into another more valuable; excess value of one currency over another; money-exchange business. [f. It. *aggio*]

a'giotage n. money-exchange business; speculation in stocks; stock-jobbing. [F (*agioter* f. as prec. + connecting -*t*-; see -AGE)]

agi'st v.t. take in livestock to feed; charge (land or its owner) with a public burden; so ∽MENT n. [f. OF *agister* (à to, *gister* lodge f. Rom. *jacitare* frequent. of L *jacēre* lie)]

a'gitāte v. **1.** v.t. shake, move; disturb, excite, (feelings, person); revolve mentally, discuss, debate, (plan etc.). **2.** v.i. keep up an agitation (*for* or *against*). [f. L *agitare* frequent. of *agere* drive + -ATE³]

agitā'tion n. shaking, moving; (mental or physical) commotion, disturbance; debate, discussion; keeping of a matter constantly before the public. [F, or f. L *agitatio* as prec.; see -ATION)]

ăgita'tō (-ah'-) adv. (Mus.) in an agitated manner. [It.]

a'gitātor n. one who agitates, esp. politically; apparatus for shaking or mixing liquid etc. [L (as AGITATE; see -OR)]

a'gitpröp (ă'j-, ă'g-) n. (system of) Russian Communist propaganda. [Russ. (as AGITATION, PROPAGANDA)]

a'glĕt n. **1.** metal tag of a lace; metallic ornament of dress. **2.** = AIGUILLETTE. [ME, f. F *aiguillette* dim. of *aiguille* needle f. LL *acucula* dim. of *acus* needle]

agley' (-ā', -ē') adv. (Sc.) askew, awry; GANG² *agley*. [f. A³ + Sc. *gley* squint]

aglow' (-ō') adv. & pred. a. glowing(ly). [f. A³ + GLOW]

AGM abbr. annual general meeting.

a'gnail n. torn skin at root of finger-nail; soreness resulting from this. [OE *angnægl* f. GMC (*ang*- tight, painful, *nægl* NAIL¹ 3, hard excrescence fixed in the flesh); mod. sense, and form *hangnail*, result from pop. etym., *nail* being taken as NAIL¹ 1]

a'gnāte n. & a. (one who is) descended esp. by male line from same male ancestor (cf. COGNATE); descended from same forefather, of same clan or nation; (fig.) akin, of same nature; hence **ăgnā'tic** a., **ăgnā'tion** n. [f. L *agnatus* (*ad* to, *gnatus* born p.p. of (*g*)*nasci* f. stem *gen*- beget)]

ăgnō'mĕn n. (Rom. Ant.) fourth name occas. given as honour (see COGNOMEN); nickname. [L (as AG-, (*g*)*nomen* name)]

ăgnō'stic n. & a. (adherent) of the view that nothing is known, or likely to be known, of the existence of God or of anything beyond material phenomena; hence ∽ISM (3) n. [f. A- 7 + GNOSTIC]

Agnus Dei (ăgnŭs dē'ī, -ōōs dā'ē) n. part of RC Mass beginning *Agnus Dei*; figure of lamb bearing cross or flag, as emblem of Christ; cake of wax stamped with such figure and blessed by Pope. [L, = lamb of God]

ago' adv. past, gone by, (ten years *ago*); **long ∽**, long since. [ME (*ago*, *agone*), p.p. of obs. v. *ago* (A- 1, GO¹)]

ago'g adv. & pred. a. eager, expectant. [f. F en gogues (en in, pl. of *gogue* fun; orig. unkn.)]

ago'nic a. ∽ **line**, line of zero magnetic declination. [f. Gk *agōnios* without angle (*a*- not, *gōnia* angle) + -IC]

ăgoni'st|ic a. polemical, combative; hence ∽ICALLY adv. [f. LL f. Gk *agōnistikos* (*agōnistēs* contestant f. *agōn* contest); see -IST, -IC]

a'goniz|e, -īs|e (-īz) v. **1.** v.i. suffer agony, writhe in anguish; contend, wrestle (lit. or fig.). **2.** v.t. cause agony to; (in *p.p.*) expressing agony (*agonized look*); hence ∽INGLY adv. [f. F *agoniser* or f. LL *agonizare* f. Gk *agōnizomai* contend (*agōn* contest)]

a'gony n. extreme mental or physical suffering (||∽ **column**, (colloq.) = PERSONAL *column*; **death ∽**, **last ∽**, pangs of death); severe struggle. [ME, f. OF *agonie* or f. LL f. Gk *agōnia* (*agōn* contest; see -Y¹)]

ăgoraphō'b|ia n. (Psych.) morbid dread of public places or open spaces (opp. *claustrophobia*); hence ∽IC

a. & n. [mod. L, f. Gk *agora* place of assembly, market-place + -PHOBIA]

agou'ti, -ty̆, agu'ti, (-gōō'-) n. rodent of genus *Dasyprocta* or *Myoprocta* of Central and S. America, related to guinea-pig. [f. F *agouti* or Sp. *aguti* f. Tupi *aguti*]

AGR abbr. advanced gas-cooled (nuclear) reactor.

ā'grapha n. pl. sayings of Christ not recorded in canonical Gospels. [Gk, = unwritten things]

agrā'rian a. & n. **1.** a. relating to landed property; relating to cultivated land. **2.** n. advocate of redistribution of landed property. [f. L *agrarius* (*ager agri* land; see -ARY¹) + -AN]

agree' v. **1.** v.i. consent (*to* proposal, statement, *to* do); **∽ to differ** or **disagree**, no longer try to convince each other. **2.** hold similar opinion (*with* person *that* or *about*); **be ∽d**, have reached similar opinion. **3.** become or be in harmony (*with* person); **∽ on**, decide by mutual consent. **4.** **∽ with**, suit constitution of (*this work, lobster, the climate, does not agree with him*). **5.** (Gram.) have same number, gender, case, or person. **6.** v.t. bring into harmony; ||reach agreement concerning (*agree a price*); consent to or approve of (proposal, terms, etc.). [ME, f. OF *agreer* f. Rom. *AGgratare* make agreeable (*gratus*)]

agree'ab|le (-rǐ'ǎbel) a. pleasing (*to*, or abs.); (colloq., of person) willing to agree (*to* a thing, *to* doing, or abs.); conformable *to*; hence ∽leNESS (-beln-) n., ∽LY² adv. (∽ly **surprised**, surprised and pleased). [ME, f. OF *agreable* (*agreer* AGREE; see -ABLE)]

agree'ment n. mutual understanding; covenant, treaty; (Law) arrangement undertaken by and legally binding on parties; holding of similar opinion; state of being harmonious; (Gram.) having the same number, gender, case, or person. [ME, f. OF (as AGREE; see -MENT)]

agre'stic a. rural, rustic; uncouth. [f. L *agrestis* (*ager* field) + -IC]

a'gribusinèss (-bĭzn-) n. group of industries dealing with farming produce and services. [f. AGRICULTURE + BUSINESS]

a'gricülture n. science or practice of cultivating the soil and rearing animals; hence **ăgricŭ'ltur**AL a., **ăgricŭ'ltur(al)**IST (3) ns., (-cher-). [F, or f. L *agricultura* (*ager agri* field, *cultura* CULTURE)]

a'grimony n. perennial plant of genus *Agrimonia*, esp. *A. eupatoria* with small yellow flowers; HEMP *agrimony*. [ME, f. OF *aigremoine* f. L *agrimonia* alt. of *argemonia* f. Gk *argemōnē* poppy]

agro'nom| y̆ n. science of soil management and crop production; so **ăgrono'mic**(AL) *adjs.*, **agrono'mi**cs, ∽IST (3), ns. F *agronomie* (*agronome* agriculturist f. Gk *agros* land + -*nomos* f. *nemō* arrange); see -Y¹]

agrou'nd adv. & pred. a. (Of ship) on the bottom of shallow water (*be, run, aground*). [ME, f. A³ + GROUND¹]

ā'gü|e n. malarial fever, with cold, hot, and sweating stages; shivering fit (lit. or fig.); hence **ā'güED²** (-ūd), ∽ISH¹, *adjs.* [ME f. OF, f. med. L *acuta* (*febris* fever) ACUTE]

aguti. See AGOUTI.

ah int. expr. sorrow or regret (*ah me!*), surprise, pleasure, admiration, entreaty, remonstrance, dislike, boredom, contempt, mockery; *ah* WELL⁴. [ME f. OF *a*]

AH abbr. in the year of the Hegira; of the Muslim era. [f. L *anno Hegirae*]

aha' (ahhah', a-hah') int. expr. surprise, triumph, mockery, irony. [ME, f. AH + HA¹]

ahea'd (a-hĕ'd) adv. **1.** farther forward in space or time; **∽ of**, farther advanced than (lit. or fig.). **2.** in the line of one's forward motion (*breakers ahead*); straight forwards; GO¹ *ahead*. [orig. Naut., f. A³ + HEAD¹]

ahĕ'm (a-h-) int. (used to attract attention, express disapproval, or gain time). [lengthened form of HEM³]

ahi'msa (a-hǐ'msah) n. (Hindu, Buddhist, & Jainist Philos.) doctrine of non-violence or non-killing. [Skr. (*a* without, *himsa* injury)]

ăhistŏ'ric(al) *adjs.* not historic(al); unrelated to history. [f. A- 7 + HISTORIC(AL)]

ahoy' (*a*-h-) *int.* (Naut.) used in hailing. [f. AH + HOY²]

à huis clos (ah wē klō') *adv.* in private. [F, = with closed doors]

ahŭ'll (*a*-h-) *adv.* (Naut.) with sails taken in and helm lashed on lee side. [f. A³ + HULL²]

a'ï (ah'ï) *n.* three-toed sloth of S. America, of genus *Bradypus.* [f. Tupi *ai*, repr. its cry]

AI *abbr.* artificial insemination.

aid¹ *v.t.* help (person *to* do, or abs.); promote (recovery etc.). [ME, f. OF *aïdier* f. L *adjutare* frequent. of AD(*juvare jut*- help)]

aid² *n.* help; helper; material source of help (*teaching aid*; FOREIGN aid; *aids and appliances*); (Hist.) grant of subsidy or tax to king; **in ~ of**, in support of; **what's (all) this in ~ of?**, (colloq.) what is the purpose of this?; PRAY *in aid.* [ME, f. OF *aïde* f. Rom. **adjuta* fem. p.p. (as *n.*) of *adjuvare* AID¹]

AID *abbr.* *Agency for International Development; artificial insemination by donor.

aide *n.* = foll.; *assistant. [abbr.]

aide-de-camp (ād-dɛkah'n) *n.* (*pl.* **aides-de-camp** *pr.* same). officer acting as confidential assistant to senior officer. [F]

aide-mémoire (ā'dmĕmwâr) *n.* (book or document serving as) an aid to the memory; (Diplom.) memorandum. [F (*aider* to help, *mémoire* memory)]

aigrĕtte (ā'-, -ĕ't) *n.* egret; its white plume; tuft of feathers or hair; spray of gems etc. [F]

ai'guille (-gwēl) *n.* sharp peak of rock, esp. in Alps. [F (see AGLET)]

aiguillĕ'tte (āgwilĕ't) *n.* tagged point hanging from shoulder upon breast of some uniforms. [F (see AGLET)]

AIH *abbr.* artificial insemination by husband.

ai'kidō (ī'-) *n.* Japanese form of self-defence using attacker's energy against him without injuring him. [Jap. (*ai* mutual, *ki* mind, *dō* way)]

ail *v.* **1.** *v.t.* (arch., in 3rd person *act.* w. pron. subj.) trouble, afflict, (*what ails him?*). **2.** *v.i.* be ill; hence ~'MENT *n.*, (esp. slight) illness. [OE *egl*(*i*)*an* (*egle* troublesome, Goth. *agls* disgraceful)]

ai'lerŏn *n.* hinged flap on rear edge of aeroplane wing, used to control sideways balance. [F, dim. of *aile* wing f. L *ala*]

ai'ling *a.* ill, esp. often ill; (fig.) in poor condition. [f. AIL + -ING²]

ailuro- (ilūr'o) *comb. form.* cat, as ~PHIL(E), ~PHOBE, *ns.* & *adjs.*, ~PHO'BIA *n.* [f. Gk *ailouros* cat + -o-]

aim¹ *v.* **1.** *v.t.* direct (blow, missile, act, remark, *at*); ~ **at**, point (gun etc.) towards. **2.** *v.i.* take aim (~ **high**, show ambition); intend or try (*to* do, *at* doing); ~ **at**, (fig.) seek to attain (*aim at a bishopric*). [ME, partly f. OF *amer* f. L *aestimare* reckon, partly f. OF *ae*(*s*)*mer* f. Rom. *ADaestimare]

aim² *n.* directing of weapon, missile, etc. at object (**take ~**, direct weapon etc. thus); design, purpose, object aimed at; hence ~'LESS *a.*, ~'lĕssLY² *adv.*, ~'lĕssNESS *n.* [ME, f. prec.]

ain't. See BE, HAVE¹.

air¹ *n.* **1.** invisible gaseous substance enveloping earth, mixture mainly of oxygen and nitrogen, breathed by all land animals and plants; the earth's atmosphere; free or unconfined space in atmosphere (*birds of the air*; *in the open air*); CLEAR² *the air*; *give person *the* ~, (sl.) dismiss him; **in the ~**, (of opinions, feelings) spreading about, (of projects etc.) uncertain; **on the ~**, broadcast(ing) by radio or television; **take the ~**, go out of doors; THIN¹ *air.* **2.** the atmosphere as place of (esp. warlike) operations with aeroplanes etc.; **by ~**, in or by aircraft. **3.** breeze, light wind. **4.** appearance (*an air of absurdity*); bearing, gesture, (*with a triumphant air*); confident bearing (*does things with an air*); (esp. in *pl.*) affected manner, pretentiousness, (*gave himself airs*; *airs and* GRACEs). **5.** (Mus.) melody, tune, esp., in harmonized composition, predominant (usu. soprano) part. **6.** ~ **bag**, safety device filling with air to protect occupants of motor car in collision; ~**-bed,**

inflated mattress; ~**-bladder,** one filled with air ir animals or plants; ~'**borne,** transported by air, (o aircraft) in the air after taking off (*the squadron was soor airborne*); ~ **brake,** (1) brake worked by air pressure (2) movable flap to retard aircraft; ~**-brick** (perforated for ventilation); ~'**brush,** device fo spraying paint by means of compressed air; ~'**bus,** aircraft providing passenger service like bus; **Air Chief Marshal** (see *Air Marshal*); ||*air* COMMODORE ~**-conditioned,** (of room, building, etc.) having the air in it cleaned and brought to required humidity (and temperature); ~**-conditioner,** ~**-conditioning,** (apparatus for) this process; ~**-cooled** (by a current of cool air); *air* CORRIDOR; ~'**craft,** aeroplane(s), helicopter(s), (occas. also) airship(s) and balloon(s); ~'**craft-carrier,** ship that carries and serves as a base for aeroplanes; ~'**craftman,** ~'**craftwoman,** lowest rank in (W)RAF; ~'**crew,** crew manning an aircraft; ~**-cushion,** (1) cushion inflated with air, (2) layer of air supporting vehicle of hovercraft type; ~ **ferry,** transport of cars etc. over water by aircraft; ~'**field,** area of land where aircraft are kept and may take off and land; *~'**foil,** = AERO*foil*; ~ **force** (||ROYAL *Air Force*), branch of armed forces for attack and defence in the air; ~'**frame,** body of aircraft as dist. from engine(s); ~'**glow,** radiation from upper atmosphere, detectable at night; ~'**gun** (using compressed air to propel missile); ~ **hostess,** stewardess in passenger aircraft; ~**-jacket** (inflated, to support wearer in water); ||~ **letter,** sheet of light paper that may be sent cheaply by airmail; ~'**lift,** (*n.*) transport of troops, supplies, etc. by air, esp. in emergency, (*v.t.*) transport thus; ~ **line,** pipe supplying air to diver etc.; ~'**line,** line of aircraft for public service; ~ **liner,** large passenger aircraft; ~'**lock,** (1) stoppage of flow in pump or pipe caused by air, (2) compartment with double doors for entering or leaving vessel under pressure; ~'**mail,** (*n.*) mail carried by air, (*v.t.*) send thus; ~'**man,** man who flies in an aircraft, esp. as pilot or member of crew, member of RAF below commissioned rank; **Air Marshal,** RAF officer of high rank, below Air Chief Marshal and above Air Vice-Marshal; ~'**minded,** interested in aviation; ~'**miss,** narrow escape from collision between aircraft; **Air Officer,** RAF officer above rank of Group Captain; *~'**plane,** aeroplane; ~ **pocket,** apparent vacuum in air causing aircraft to drop some distance; ~'**port,** airfield, esp. one fully equipped, usu. with customs-house, at which passengers by air embark or disembark; ~'**post,** = *airmail*; ~ **power,** ability to defend and attack by means of aircraft, missiles, etc.; ~ **pump** (for pumping air into or out of a vessel); ~ **raid,** attack by aircraft; ~ **rifle** (as *airgun*); ||~'**screw,** propeller of aircraft; ~**-sea rescue** (from the sea by aircraft); ~'**ship,** flying machine lighter than air; ~'**sick,** affected with nausea due to motion of aircraft; ~'**space,** air above country etc., esp. considered as subject to its jurisdiction; ~ **speed,** speed of aircraft etc. relative to the air through which it is moving; ~'**strip,** strip of ground used or usable for landing and take-off of aircraft; ~ **terminal,** place in a town where transport is provided to and from airport; ~'**tight,** impermeable to air; ~**-to-~,** from one aircraft to another in flight; ~ **traffic controller,** person at airport who gives radio instructions to pilots wishing to take off or land; **Air Vice-Marshal** (see *Air Marshal*); ~'**way,** (1) ventilating passage in mine, (2) route regularly followed by aircraft; ~'**woman,** woman who flies in an aircraft, esp. as pilot or member of crew, member of WRAF below commissioned rank; ~'**worthy,** (of aircraft) fit to fly. [senses 1-3 ME f. OF, f. L f. Gk *aēr*; sense 4 F, prob. f. OF *aire* place, disposition f. L *area*; sense 5 f. It. *aria*]

air² *v.t.* **1.** expose to open air, ventilate; finish drying at fire or in heated ~'**ing cupboard,** whence ~'**ER**² *n.*, frame for drying clothes etc. **2.** parade (qualities, fine clothes); make public (grievances, theories). **3.** ~ one**self**, go out in fresh air. [f. prec.]

Air'edāle (ār'd-) *n.* large rough-coated terrier. [~ in W. Yorkshire]

air'lèss *a.* stuffy; breezeless, still. [f. AIR¹ + -LESS]

air'ȳ *a.* **1.** aerial, lofty; breezy. **2.** superficial, flippant; immaterial, unsubstantial; of thin texture. **3.** light in movement; sprightly; graceful, delicate. **4.** Hence **air'ĭLY²** *adv.*, **air'ĭNESS** *n.* **5.** ~**-fairy**, (colloq.) delicate or light as a fairy, nonchalant, (derog.) fanciful or unsubstantial. [f. AIR¹ + -Y²]

aisle (īl) *n.* part of church, esp. one parallel to and divided by pillars from the main nave, choir, or transept; passage between rows of pews or seats; hence **aisl**ED² (īld), ~LESS (ī'l-l-), *adjs.* [ME f. OF *ele*, f. L *ala* wing; confus. w. *island* and F *aile* wing]

||**aĭt,** ||**eyot,** (āt) *n.* small isle, esp. in a river. [f. OE *iggath* etc. f. īeg ISLAND + dim. suf.]

aitch *n.* name of letter H; **drop** one's ~**es**, fail to pronounce initial *h* in words. [ME f. OF *ache* f. L **ahha*]

||**ai'tchbône** *n.* (cut of beef lying over) buttock or rump bone. [ME *nage-*, *nache-bone* buttock f. OF *nage*, *nache* f. LL (pl.) *naticas* f. L *natis*, *-es* buttock(s); for loss of *n-* cf. ADDER, APRON]

ajar'¹ *adv.* & *pred. a.* (Of door) slightly open. [f. A³ + obs. *char* f. OE *cerr* a turn]

ajar'² *adv.* out of harmony. [f. A³ + JAR¹]

AJC *abbr.* Australian Jockey Club.

ajutage. See ADJUTAGE.

AK *abbr.* Alaska; Knight of the Order of Australia.

*a.k.a. *abbr.* also known as.

AKC *abbr.* Associate of King's College, London.

ā'kee. See ACKEE.

aki'mbō *adv.* (Of the arms) with hands on hips and elbows turned outwards. [ME *in kenebowe*, prob. f. ON **i keng boginn* bent in a curve; assim. to A³]

aki'n *pred. a.* related by blood; (fig.) of similar or kindred character. [f. A- 3 + KIN]

Akkā'diăn, Accā'diăn, (ak-) *n.* & *a.* (Semitic language) of Akkad in ancient Babylonia. [f. *Akkad* + -IAN]

akvavit. See AQUAVIT.

al- *pref.*, assim. form of AD- before *l*.

-al *suf.* **1.** forming adjs. f. (or f. *ns.* f.) L (*central, general, postal, regimental, sensational*) or L (*colossal, rhomboidal, tropical*; cf. also -IAL, -ICAL) or f. F. *ns.* (*tidal*) [f. F *-el* or f. L *-alis* adj. suf. cogn. w. *aris* (AR¹)]. **2.** forming *ns* [f. F *-aille* or f. (or after) L *-alis* etc. used as *n.*] (*animal, cardinal, rival*), esp. of vbl action (*arrival, proposal, recital, trial, withdrawal*).

AL *abbr.* Alabama.

Al *symb.* aluminium.

à la (ah lah) *prep.* after the manner of; ~ *russe*, in the Russian manner. [F, f. À LA MODE]

Ala. *abbr.* Alabama.

ā'labast|er (-bah-) *n.* & *a.* **1.** *n.* translucent usu. white form of gypsum, often carved into ornaments; hence ~rINE¹ (-ah's-) *a.* **2.** *a.* of alabaster; like alabaster in whiteness or smoothness. [ME, f. OF *alabastre* f. L *alabaster, -trum*, f. Gk *alabast(r)os*]

à la carte (ah lah kār't) *adv.* & *a.* by the bill of fare; ordered as separately priced item(s) from menu, not as part of table d'hôte meal. [F]

ală'ck *int.* (arch.) expr. regret or surprise, esp. in phr. ~**-a-day.** [prob. f. AH + LACK]

ală'crĭtÿ *n.* briskness, cheerful readiness. [f. L *alacritas* (*alacer* brisk; see -ITY)]

Ală'ddĭn (a-) *n.* ~**'s cave,** place of great riches; ~**'s lamp,** talisman enabling holder to gratify any wish. [character in *Arabian Nights*]

à la mode (ah lah mō'd) *adv.* & *a.* in the fashion, fashionable; (of beef) braised in wine; *(of food) served with ice cream. [F, = in the fashion]

ală'nna(h) *int.* (Ir.) of address or endearment. [f. Ir. *a leanbh* my child!]

à la page (ah lah pah'zh) *adv.* up to date; in the latest fashion. [F]

ā'lar *a.* pertaining to wings; winglike, wing-shaped; axillary. [f. L *alaris* (*ala* wing; see -AR¹)]

alār'm¹ *n.* **1.** warning sound giving notice of danger; warning (*give, raise, the alarm*). **2.** frightened anticipation of danger; uneasiness. **3.** mechanism that sounds the alarm (*burglar alarm*); apparatus that rings at set time; ~ (**clock**), clock with this; cf. ALARUM. [ME, f. OF *alarme* f. It. *allarme* (*all' arme!* to arms)]

alār'm² *v.t.* arouse to sense of danger; disturb; agitate with fear (*alarmed at, that, to find* etc.); hence ~ING² *a.*, ~INGLY *adv.* [f. prec.]

alār'm|ist *n.* one who raises alarms on slight grounds; panic-monger; so ~ISM (1) *n.* [f. ALARM¹ + -IST]

alār'um *n.* Var. of ALARM¹; ~**s and excursions**, (joc., f. old stage-direction) confused noise and bustle.

ala's (-ă's, -ah's) *int.* expr. grief, pity, concern. [ME, f. OF *a las(se)* (*a* ah, *las(se)* f. L *lassus* weary)]

Alas. *abbr.* Alaska.

Alā'ska (a-) *n.* **baked** ~, sponge-cake and ice cream in meringue covering. [name of northernmost state of US]

Ala'stor (alah's-) *n.* avenging deity, nemesis. [f. Gk *alastōr* (*a-* not, *last-* f. *lath-* forget)]

ā'lāte *a.* having wings or winglike appendages. [f. L *alatus* (*ala* wing; see -ATE²)]

ălb *n.* white vestment reaching to feet, worn by Christian priests etc. [OE *albe* f. eccl. L *alba* fem. (as n.) of L *albus* white]

ā'lbacŏre *n.* **1.** large W. Ind. species of tunny. **2.** one of various other related fish. [f. Port. *albacor, -cora*, f. Arab. *al* the + *bakr* young camel or *bakūr* premature, precocious]

Albā'nian (ăl-) *a.* & *n.* (native, inhabitant, or language) of Albania. [f. *Albania* in SE Europe + -AN]

albā'ta *n.* white metal, German silver. [f. L *albata* whitened (*albus* white)]

ā'lbatrŏss *n.* one of a family of long-winged birds allied to petrels, inhabiting Pacific and Southern Oceans; ||(Golf) hole played in three strokes under par or bogey. [alt. (after L *albus* white) of 17th-c. *alcatras*, applied to various sea-birds, f. Sp. and Port. *alcatraz*, var. of Port. *alcatruz* f. Arab. *alḳādūs* the pitcher (*al* the, *ḳādūs* f. Gk *kados* jar)]

ălbē'dō *n.* (*pl.* ~s). fraction of incident radiation reflected by a surface. [eccl. L, = whiteness, f. L *albus* white]

albē'it (awl-) *conj.* (literary). though (*he tried, albeit without success*). [f. ALL + BE + IT¹, = let it be completely true that]

ā'lbert *n.* watch-chain with crossbar. [f. Prince *Albert*, consort of Queen Victoria, d. 1861]

ălbē'scent *a.* growing white; shading into white. [f. L *albescere* (*albus* white); see -ESCENT]

Albĭgĕ'ns|ēs (ăl-; -z) *n. pl.* members of Manichaean sect in S. France in 11th–13th c.; hence ~IAN *a.* [L, f. *Albi* in S. France]

ălbī'nō (-bē'-) *n.* (*pl.* ~s). person or animal having congenital absence of colouring pigment in skin and hair, which are white, and eyes, which are usu. pink and unduly sensitive to light; plant lacking normal colouring; hence **ă'lbĭn**ISM (5) *n.*, **ălbĭnŏ'tɪc** *a.* [Sp. & Port., orig. of white Negroes, f. *albo* (L *albus*) white + *-ino* (-INE¹)]

A'lbĭon (ă'l-) *n.* (poet. or rhet.) (Orig. Greek and Roman name for) Britain; **perfidious** ~, England (f. F *la perfide Albion* w. ref. to her alleged treachery to other nations). [OE f. L, f. Celt. **Albio*]

ā'lbīte *n.* white or soda felspar. [f. L *albus* white + -ITE¹]

ā'lbum *n.* **1.** blank book for insertion of autographs, stamps, photographs, etc. **2.** holder for set of gramophone records; set of records; one record comprising several pieces of music etc. [L, = blank tablet, neut. of *albus* white]

ā'lbūmèn *n.* white of egg; (Bot.) endosperm, substance found between skin and germ of many seeds, usu. the eatable part. [L *albumen -minis* white of egg (*albus* white)]

ä´lbūmĭn *n.* any of a class of water-soluble proteins found in egg-white, milk, blood, etc.; hence **ȧlbū´mĭn**ous *a.* [f. F *albumine* f. L *albumin-* (see prec.)]

ȧlbū´mĭnoid *n.* complex protein forming framework of organs and tissues of animals and plants. [f. L (as prec.) +-OID]

ȧlbūmĭnū´r´ia *n.* presence of proteins in the urine, usu. as symptom of kidney disease. [f. L (as ALBUMIN) +-URIA]

ȧlbū´r´num *n.* = SAP¹*wood*. [L (*albus* white)]

alcahest. Var. of ALKAHEST.

ȧlcā´ic *a.* & *n.* **1.** *a.* of verse metre in four-line stanza invented by Alcaeus. **2.** *n.* (in *pl.*) alcaic verses. [f. LL f. Gk *alkaikos* (*Alkaios* Alcaeus, lyric poet of Mitylene *c.* 600 BC; see -IC)]

alca´lde (ahlkah´ldä) *n.* magistrate or mayor in Spanish, Portuguese, or Latin-Amer. town. [Sp., f. Arab. *al-ḳāḍī* the judge (see CADI)]

ä´lchem|y̆ (-k-) *n.* medieval forerunner of chemistry, esp. pursuit of transmutation of baser metals into gold or silver; (fig.) transformation like those sought in alchemy; hence or cogn. **älchĕ´m**IC(AL) (-k-) *adjs.*, ∼IST (3) *n.*, ∼IZE (1) *v.t.* [ME, f. OF *alkemie, alkamie* f. med. L *alchimia, -emia,* f. Arab. *alkīmīā* (*al* the, *kīmīā* f. Gk *khēmia, -meia* art of transmuting metals)]

älcheri´nga (-ngga) *n.* 'golden age' in mythology of some Australian Aboriginals. [Aboriginal, = dream-time]

ä´lcohŏl *n.* **1.** (**ethyl**) ∼, colourless volatile inflammable liquid, intoxicant present in wine, beer, whisky, etc., also used as solvent, fuel, etc. **2.** any liquor containing this. **3.** (Chem.) one of large class of compounds of same type as ethyl alcohol. [F or med. L, f. Arab. *al-kuḥl* (*al* the, *kuḥl* KOHL)]

ȧlcohŏ´lic *a.* & *n.* **1.** *a.* of, relating to, containing, caused by, alcohol. **2.** *n.* person addicted to excessive consumption of alcohol. [f. prec. +-IC]

ä´lcohŏlism *n.* continual heavy drinking of alcoholic liquor; diseased condition resulting from this. [f. mod. L *alcoholismus* (as ALCOHOL; see -ISM)]

ȧlcohŏlŏ´|mĕter *n.* instrument for measuring alcoholic strength of spirits; hence ∼METRY *n.* [f. ALCOHOL +-O-+-METER]

Alcoran, Alkoran, (ȧlkorah´n, ȧ´l-) *n.* (arch.) Koran. [ME f. OF, f. Arab. *al-ḳur´ān* the reading, the recitation (see KORAN)]

ä´lcōve *n.* (vaulted) recess in room-wall, subsidiary room thus formed; recess in garden wall or hedge; (arch.) summer-house. [F, f. Sp. *alcoba* f. Arab. *al-ḳubba* (*al* the, *ḳubba* vault)]

ä´ldĕhy̆de *n.* **1.** colourless volatile fluid with suffocating smell, obtained by oxidation of alcohol, acetaldehyde. **2.** one of a class of compounds of this type. **3.** Hence **äldĕhy̆´d**IC *a.* [abbr. of mod. L *alcohol dehydrogenatum* alcohol deprived of hydrogen]

al dente (ȧl dĕ´ntĭ) *a.* (Of pasta etc.) cooked so as to be still firm when bitten. [It., lit. 'to the tooth']

a´lder (aw´l-) *n.* tree of genus *Alnus*, related to birch; one of various other similar trees not related; ∼ **buckthorn,** shrub of buckthorn genus. [OE *alor, aler,* = MLG *aller,* OHG *elira, erila,* ON *ölr,* cogn. w. L *alnus,* w. euphonic *d*]

a´lder|man (aw´l-) *n.* (*pl.* ∼**men**). (chiefly Hist.) co-opted member of English county or borough council, next in dignity to Mayor; (US & Austral.) elected governor of city; hence ∼**mä´n**IC *a.,* ∼**man**SHIP *n.* [f. OE *aldor* patriarch (*ald* old, *-or,* n. suf.) +MAN¹]

a´ldermanry̆ (aw´l-) *n.* (Hist.) district having its own alderman; rank of alderman. [ME, f. prec. +-RY]

A´lderney (aw´l-) *a.* & *n.* (animal) of breed of dairy cattle from *Alderney* or elsewhere in the Channel Islands.

A´ldīne (aw´l-) *a.* of or by Aldus Manutius, Venetian printer of 16th c., who introduced italic type. [f. mod. L *Aldinus* (*Aldus;* see -INE¹)]

A´ldĭs (aw´l-) *n.* ∼ **lamp,** hand lamp for signalling in Morse code. [f. A.C.W. ∼, inventor]

ä´ldrĭn *n.* white crystalline chlorinated hydrocarbon used as insecticide. [f. K. *Alder,* Ger. chemist d. 1958 +-IN]

āle *n.* (arch. exc. as trade wd). beer (REAL² *ale*); ∼**´cost,** costmary; ∼**´house,** (Hist.) house at which ale was retailed; ***∼**´wife,** one of several species of fish allied to herring. [OE *alu,* = ON *öl*]

ālēatŏr´ĭc, ā´lēatory̆, *adjs.* depending on the throw of a die or on chance; (Mus. & Art) involving random choice by performer. [f. L *aleatorius* (*aleator* dice-player f. *alea* die); see -IC, -Y²]

alee´ *adv.* & *pred. a.* on the lee or sheltered side of ship; to leeward. [ME, f. A³+LEE]

ā´lēgar *n.* sour ale; malt vinegar. [f. ALE, after VINEGAR]

alĕ´mbĭc *n.* apparatus formerly used in distilling; (fig.) means of transmutation. [ME f. OF, f. med. L *alembicus* f. Arab. *al-´inbīḳ* (*al* the, *´inbīḳ* still f. Gk *ambix -ikos* cup, cap of a still)]

alĕ´mbĭc|ātĕd *a.* (Of literary style) over-refined, as if by distillation; so ∼A´TION *n.* [f. prec. +-ATE³+-ED¹]

a´lĕph (ah´-) *n.* first letter of Hebrew alphabet. [f. Heb. *´ālĕp,* prob. f. ALPHA]

alĕr´t *a., n.,* & *v.t.* **1.** *a.* watchful, vigilant; lively, nimble; hence ∼LY² *adv.,* ∼NESS *n.* **2.** *n.* warning call, alarm; (period of) warning of air raid etc.; **on the** ∼, on the look-out against danger or attack. **3.** *v.t.* make alert, warn. [f. F *alerte* f. It. *all´ erta* (*alla* to the, *erta* watch-tower)]

-ā´lēs (-z) *suf.* forming pl. names of orders of plants (*Rosales*). [pl. of L adj. suf. *-alis* (see -AL)]

aleur´on, aleur´ōne, (-lūr´-) *n.* protein found as granules in seeds of plants etc. [f. Gk *aleuron* flour]

||A lĕvel (ā´-) *n.* = ADVANCE*d level* (in GCE). [abbr.]

älĕxa´nders (-ĭgzah´nderz) *n.* umbelliferous plant (*Smyrnium olusatrum*), formerly used in salads. [OE, f. med. L *alexandrum*]

Alĕxa´ndrian (älĭgzah´-) *a.* of Alexandria, esp. as chief centre of Hellenistic literature in 3rd and 2nd c. BC; (of writer) imitative, or fond of recondite learning. [f. *Alexandria* in Egypt, founded by *Alexander* the Great]

älĕxa´ndrīne (-ĭgz-) *a.* & *n.* ∼ (**verse**), iambic line of six feet or twelve syllables. [f. F *alexandrin* f. *Alexandre* Alexander (the Great), subj. of an OF poem in this metre]

alĕxä´ndrīte (-ĭgz-) *n.* green variety of chrysoberyl. [f. Tsar *Alexander* I of Russia + -ITE¹ (2)]

alĕ´xĭn, -ine, *n.* one of a class of proteins found in blood serum and capable of destroying bacteria etc. [G, f. Gk *alexō* ward off; see -IN, -INE⁵]

alĕ´xĭphär´mic *a.* & *n.* (having the quality of) an antidote. [earlier *-ac* f. F *alexipharmaque* f. Gk *alexiphar-makon* remedy for poison (*alexō* ward off, *pharmakon* poison)]

ä´lfa *n.* N. Afr. esparto grass. [f. Arab. *ḥalfā´*]

älfa´lfa *n.* lucerne. [Sp., f. Arab. *al-faṣfaṣa,* a green fodder]

älfrĕ´scō *adv.* & *a.* in the open air (*lunched alfresco; an alfresco lunch*). [f. It. *al fresco* in the fresh (air)]

ä´lg|a *n.* (usu. in *pl.* ∼**ae** *pr.* -jē, -gē). (Bot.) primitive cryptogam, e.g. seaweeds, some plankton, water bloom; hence ∼AL, ∼OID, ∼olŏ´gicAL, *adjs.,* ∼ĭCIDE (1), ∼ŏ´LOGIST, ∼´LOGY, *ns.* [L]

ä´lgĕbr|a *n.* branch of mathematics dealing with properties of numbers and quantities by means of letters and other general symbols; system of this based on given axioms; hence ∼ä´ic(AL) *adjs.,* ∼ä´icALLY *adv.,* ∼(ā)IST (3) *ns.* [It., Sp., med. L, f. Arab. *al-jabr* (*al* the, *jabr* reunion of broken parts f. *jabara* reunite)]

-ä´lgia (-ja) *suf.* (Med.) denoting pain in a specified part (*neuralgia*); hence **-ä´lg**IC *n.* [Gk *algos* pain; see -IA¹)]

ä´lgĭcīde. See ALGA.

ä´lgĭd *a.* (esp. Med.) cold, chilly; hence **älgĭ´d**ITY *n.* [f. L *algidus* (*algēre* be cold; see -ID¹)]

älgĭ´nic *a.* ∼ **acid,** insoluble colloidal acid found in salts in some algae; hence **ä´lgĭn**ATE¹ (3) *n.* [f. ALGA+-IN+-IC]

A'gŏl (ă'-) *n.* algebraic computer language. [f. ALGORITHMIC + L(ANGUAGE)]

ălgolă'gn|ia *n.* sexual perversion in which pleasure is got from inflicting pain on oneself or others; hence ~IC *a.* & *n.* [mod. L, f. G *algolagnie* f. Gk *algos* pain + *lagneia* lust]

ălgŏ'logy̆ etc. See ALGA.

Algŏ'nquian (-kwĭ-, -kĭ-), **-nkĭan**, (ăl-) *a.* & *n.* (member or language) of a large group of N. Amer. Indian tribes. [f. *Algonquin* people + -IAN]

ă'lgorĭsm, ă'lgorĭthm (-dhĕm), *ns.* **1.** Arabic (decimal) notation of numbers. **2.** process or rules for (esp. machine) calculation etc.; hence **ălgorĭ'thmIC** (-dh-) *a.* [ME, f. OF *augori(s)me* f. med. L *algorismus* f. Arabicized Pers. *al-Ķuwārizmī* man of Ķuwārizm, surname of a 9th-c. mathematician; assim. to -ISM and F *algorithme*, Gk *arithmos* number]

ălguazi'l (-gw-) *n.* Spanish warrant-officer or sergeant. [Sp., f. Arab. *al-wazīr* (*al-* the; see VIZIER)]

Alhă'mbr|a (ăl-) *n.* palace of Moorish kings at Granada; hence ~E'SQUE *a.* [Sp., f. Arab. *al-ḥamrā'* the red (f. name of founder, 1273)]

ā'lias *adv.* & *n.* (name by which one is or has been) called at other times. [L, = at another time, otherwise]

ă'libī *n.* & *v.* **1.** *n.* plea that when an alleged act took place one was elsewhere; (colloq.) excuse of any kind. **2.** *v.i.* & *t.* (colloq.) offer excuse (for) [L, = elsewhere]

A'lice (ă'-) *n.* ~-in-Wo'nderland, (attrib.) fantastic, absurd. [heroine of two books by L. Carroll]

ălicy̆'clic *a.* (Chem.) combining the structural properties of aliphatic and cyclic compounds. [f. G *alicyclisch* (as ALIPHATIC, CYCLIC)]

ă'lidāde *n.* (Surv. & Astron.) instrument for determining directions. [F, & ME f. med. L, f. Arab. *al-'iḍāda* the revolving radius ('*aḍud* upper arm)]

ā'lien *a.* & *n.* **1.** *a.* not one's own; foreign, under foreign allegiance (*alien* PRIORY); differing in nature (*from*, *to*); out of harmony; repugnant (*to*). **2.** *n.* non-naturalized foreigner; a being from another world; (arch.) person excluded (*from*); hence ~AGE (2) *n.* [ME f. OF, f. L *alienus* belonging to another (*alius*)]

ā'lien|āte *v.t.* estrange; transfer ownership of; turn away, divert, (*from*); hence or cogn. ~ABLE *a.*, ~A'TION *n.*, (esp., Theatr.) objectivity of spectator's reaction, sought by some dramatists, ~ātor *n.* [ME, f. L *alienare* (as prec.) + -ATE³]

ā'lien|ism *n.* (arch.) study and treatment of mental diseases, psychiatry; hence ~IST (3) *n.* (esp. *legal adviser on psychiatric problems). [f. ALIEN + -ISM]

ā'lifŏrm *a.* wing-shaped. [f. mod. L *aliformis* f. L *ala* wing (see FORM)]

ali'ght¹ (-ī't) *v.i.* dismount (*from* horse); descend (*from* vehicle); settle, come to earth, from the air. [OE *ālīhtan* (A- 1, *līhtan* LIGHT⁵)]

ali'ght² (-ī't) *pred. a.* on fire; lighted up. [ME, prob. f. phr. *on a light* (= lighted) *fire*]

ali'gn (-ī'n), **ali'ne**, *v.t.* place or lay in a line; bring into line, (esp.) bring three or more points into a straight line; (Polit. etc.) place in relation of agreement or alliance with others; hence ~MENT (-ī'nm-) *n.* [f. F *aligner* f. phr. *à ligne* into LINE²]

ali'ke *adv.* & *pred. a.* **1.** *adv.* in like manner. **2.** *a.* similar, like; indistinguishable. [ME, f. OE *gelīc* and ON *glíkr* (LIKE¹)]

ă'liment *n.* food; (fig.) support, mental sustenance; hence **ălimĕ'ntAL** *a.* [ME f. F, or f. L *alimentum* (*alere* nourish; see -MENT)]

ălimĕ'ntary̆ *a.* nourishing; performing functions of nutrition; providing maintenance; ~ canal (transmitting food through medium from mouth to anus). [f. L *alimentarius* (as prec.; see -ARY¹)]

ălimentā'tion *n.* nourishment; maintenance. [F, or f. med. L *alimentatio* (*alimentare*, as ALIMENT; see -ATION)]

ă'limony̆ *n.* **1.** (arch.) maintenance. **2.** allowance due to woman from (ex-)husband after divorce or legal separation, or during proceedings for these. [f. L *alimonia* nutriment (*alere* nourish)]

alī'ne etc. See ALIGN.

A'-line (ā'-) *a.* (Of garment) having narrow waist or shoulders and somewhat flared skirt. [f. A + LINE² 14]

ălipha'tic *a.* (Chem.) related to fats; of organic compounds in which carbon atoms form open chains, not rings. [f. Gk *aleiphar -atos* fat + IC]

ă'liquŏt *a.* & *n.* ~ (**part**), part contained by the whole an integral number of times, integral factor; (loosely) any known fraction of a whole. [f. F *aliquote* f. L *aliquot* some, so many]

-ă'lity̆ *suf.* forming *ns.*, w. senses as -ITY (*banality*, *generality*). [f. -AL + -ITY]

alī've *a.* (usu. *pred.*) **1.** living; **any man** ~ (whatever); **man** ~! (colloq. expletive); **keep the matter** ~ (still under discussion); **microphone is** ~ (switched on and working); **wire is** ~ (electrically charged). **2.** fully responsive *to* (an idea etc.). **3.** ~ (**and kicking**), (colloq.) active, brisk; **look** ~, (colloq.) be brisk. **4.** swarming *with* (*river alive with boats*). **5.** Hence ~NESS (-vn-) *n.* [OE *on līfe* (as A³, LIFE)]

alī'zarin *n.* red colouring matter of madder; (*attrib.*, of a dye) derived from or similar in action to this pigment. [f. F *alizarine* (*alizari* madder f. Arab. *al-'iṣara* pressed juice f. '*aṣara* to press fruit); see -IN]

-'lkahĕst (-a-h-) *n.* universal solvent sought by alchemists (lit. or fig.) [sham Arab., prob. invented by Paracelsus]

ă'lkal|ī *n.* (*pl.* ~is *or* ~ies). one of a class of substances that neutralize and are neutralized by acids, and form caustic or corrosive solutions in water, including caustic soda, caustic potash, and ammonia; other substance with similar but weaker properties, e.g. sodium carbonate; ~i metals, those whose hydroxides are alkalis, members of the sodium group; hence ~IFY *v.t.*, **ălkali'METER**, **ălkali'METRY**, ~I'NITY *n*. [ME f. med. L, f. Arab. *al-ḳalī* calcined ashes (*ḳala* fry)]

ă'lkaloid *n.* one of a large group of nitrogenous bases of vegetable origin, many used as drugs, e.g. morphine, quinine, strychnine. [f. G (as prec.; see -OID)]

ălkalō's|is *n.* (*pl.* ~es *pr.* -ēz). (Path.) over-alkaline condition of blood or body tissues. [f. ALKALI + -OSIS]

ă'lkāne *n.* (Chem.) = PARAFFIN 2. [f. ALKYL + -ANE 2]

ă'lkanet *n.* (plant, *Alkanna tinctoria*, whose root yields) a red dye. [ME, f. Sp. *alcaneta* dim. of *alcana* f. Arab. *al-ḥinnā'* the henna shrub]

ă'lkēne *n.* (Chem.) = OLEFIN. [f. ALKYL + -ENE 1]

Alkoran. See ALCORAN.

ă'lkyd *n.* any of a group of synthetic resins derived from various alcohols and acids. [f. ALKYL + ACID²]

ă'lkȳl *a.* derived from or related to a paraffin hydrocarbon, esp. by replacement or removal of hydrogen atom. [f. G *alkohol* ALCOHOL + -YL]

all (awl) *a.*, *n.*, & *adv.* **1.** *a.* whole amount, quantity, or extent of (*all day; all England; all his life; and all* THAT¹; *take it all*); ~ **hail**, *int.* of greeting (*to*) [*hail* = health]; **get away from it** ~ (from everyday tasks and worries); *stop* ~ **this** (this excessive) *grumbling*; *all the* TIME¹ 9; *all the* WAY 3. **2.** greatest possible (*ran with all speed*). **3.** (w. *pl.*) entire number of (*all men; all ten men; his children are all boys; admirals all; all the others*); **All Fools' Day** 1 Apr.; *all* FOURS; *All* HALLOW'S; *all* HAND¹S; ~ **kind(s) of,** ~ **manner of,** many different kinds of; **All Saints' Day,** 1 Nov.; **All Souls' Day,** 2 Nov. **4.** any whatever (*beyond all doubt; disclaim all knowledge of; gave up all idea of winning*). **5.** *n.* all persons concerned (*all were agreed*); *all* SUCH 11; **one and** ~, ~ **and sundry,** all individually and collectively. **6.** (In games) for each side (*score was two goals all*); LOVE¹ all. **7.** ~ **of,** the whole of (*take all of it*), every one of (*all of us*), (colloq.) as much as (*all of seven feet tall; walked all of two miles*), (colloq.) affected by (*was all of a dither*). **8.** everything (*that is all; all is lost*); one's whole property (*he lost his all*); ~ **but** *adv.*, everything short of (*all but impossible; he was all but drowned*); ~ **in** ~, (1) taken as a whole, (2) of supreme importance; ∼ **one**, a matter of indifference (*it is all one to me*); all UP; ∼ **very fine** or **very well**, (colloq. phr. expr. dissatisfaction, or rejection of consolation etc.); **and** ∼ (the rest); **at** ∼, (usu. w. neg. or interrog.) in any way or to any extent (*not at all*; *did you see him at all?*; *occurs very rarely if at all*); **in** ∼, in total number. **9.** *adv.* entirely, quite, (*dressed all in white*; *all covered with mud*; *all round the room*; *all the better*; *was all smiles*; *all at once*; *all too soon*; *an all-powerful dictator*; *the all-important thing*); (colloq.) very (*went all high-falutin*); ∼ **for**, (colloq.) strongly in favour of (*am all for fair play*); *what* thing *is all* ABOUT; *all* ALONG; **All Blacks**, (colloq.) New Zealand international Rugby Union football team; ∼ **in**, exhausted; ∼ **out**, involving all one's strength or resources; *going* ∼ **out** (at full speed); *all* OVER 8, 10, 13; ∼ **right**, (*adv.*) as desired, satisfactorily, certainly (*that's the man all right*), (*int.*) I assent to your order or proposal, (*pred. a.*) safe and sound, in good condition, satisfactory, acceptable (*a* BIT[2] *of all right*); ∼ **round**, (1) in all respects, (2) for each person present etc.; *all* SET[3]; *all* SQUARE[2]; (*not*) *all* THAT[1] 3; ∼ **there**, (colloq.) not deficient in intellect etc.; ∼ **the same**, (*adv.*) in spite of this, notwithstanding (*he was punished all the same*, in spite of extenuating circumstances etc.), (*pred. a.*) just the same, making no difference (*if it's all the same to you*, if you don't mind). **10.** ∼-**American**, representing whole of, or only, America or US; *∼-**around**, = *all-round*; ∼-**clear′**, signal that danger or difficulty is over; ∼-**ele′ctric**, using only electricity for heating and lighting; *∼-**fired**, (sl.) extreme(ly), excessive(ly); ∼-**in**, inclusive of all; ∼-**in wrestling** (with few or no restrictions); ∼-**o′verish**, (colloq.) indisposed all over the body; ∼-**purpose**, suitable for several uses; ∼-**red**, (Hist.) entirely on British territory (usu. coloured red in maps); ∼-**round**, having ability in many departments; ∼-**rou′nder**, one able to perform several tasks (esp. ‖in sports); ∼-**sorts**, miscellany, esp. of liquorice sweets; ∼-**time**, (of record) hitherto unsurpassed; ∼-**up**, total (weight of aircraft) incl. crew, passengers, cargo, etc., when in air. [OE *all*, *eall*, = OS, OHG *al*, ON *allr*, Goth. *alls*, prob. f. Gmc *alnaz]

alla bre′ve (brā′vā). See BREVE.

ălla cappĕ′lla. Var. of A CAPPELLA.

A′llah (ă′la) *n.* Muslim name of God. [f. Arab. ′*allāh* contr. of *al-′ilāh* (*al* the, *ilāh* god)]

ăllā′nto‖is *n.* (*pl.* ∼**ides** *pr.* -ĭdēz). (Zool.) foetal membrane in mammal, bird, or reptile. [mod. L, f. Gk *allantoeidēs* sausage-shaped]

allay′ *v.t.* alleviate (pain, hunger, etc.); diminish (fears, pleasure, etc.). [OE *ālecgan* (as A- 1, LAY[3])]

ăllēgā′tion *n.* alleging; (esp. unproved) assertion. [ME f. F, or f. L *allegatio* (*allegare* allege; see -ATION)]

allē′g‖e *v.t.* affirm, esp. without proof, (thing, *that*); advance as argument or excuse; hence ∼ED[1] (-ĕ′jd) *a.*, ∼**ĕd**LY[2] *adv.*, (used in statements for which author disclaims responsibility). [ME, f. AF *alegier*, OF *esligier* f. Rom. *EX[1]*litigare* clear at law; confused in sense w. L *allegare* (see prec.)]

allē′giance (-jəns) *n.* duty of subject to sovereign or government; loyalty (lit. or fig.). [ME, f. AF *alligeance f. OF *ligeance* (as LIEGE; see -ANCE); perh. assoc. w. ALLIANCE]

ă′llĕgor‖y̆ *n.* narrative description of a subject under guise of another having similarities to it, e.g. Bunyan's *Pilgrim's Progress* describing life as journey; picture in which meaning is symbolically represented; emblem; hence or cogn. **ăllĕgō′r**IC(AL) *adjs.*, ∼IST (1) *n.*, ∼IZE (1) *v.t.* [ME f. OF *allegorie* f. L f. Gk *allēgoria* (*allos* other, *-agoria* speaking)]

ăllĕgrĕ′tto *adv.*, *a.*, & *n.* (*pl.* ∼**s**). (Mus.) (movement) in fairly brisk time. [It., dim. of ALLEGRO]

ălle′grō (-lā′-, -lĕ′-) *adv.*, *a.*, & *n.* (*pl.* ∼**s**). (Mus.) (movement) in brisk time. [It., = lively, gay]

ă′llēle, **ă′llĕl**, **allē′lomŏrph**, *ns.* (gene determining) one of two alternative Mendelian characters. [(*allele*

f. G *allel* abbr. of) *allelomorph* f. Gk *allēl*- one another + -o- + *morphē* form]

ăllĕlu′ia, **-u′ya**, **hăllĕlu′jah**, (-lŏ̄ō′ya) *n.* (song of) praise to God; (RC Ch.) part of mass including this. [ME f. eccl. L f. (Septuagint) Gk *allēlouia* f. Heb. *hallĕlūyāh* praise ye the Lord]

ă′llemande (ă′lmahnd) *n.* name of several German dances; music for one of these, esp. as suite movement; country-dance figure. [F, = German (dance)]

ă′llergen *n.* substance that causes allergic reaction; hence **ăllergĕ′n**IC *a.* [f. ALLERGY + -GEN (1)]

ă′llergy̆ *n.* (Med.) unusual sensitiveness to the action of particular foods, pollens, insect-bites, etc.; (colloq.) antipathy; hence **allĕr′g**IC *a.*, relating to or characterized by allergy, (colloq.) sensitive (esp. antipathetic) *to*. [f. G *allergie*, after *energie* ENERGY, f. Gk *allos* other]

allē′viāte *v.t.* lessen; make less burdensome or severe; hence ∼A′TION, ∼**ā**tOR, *ns.*, ∼**ā**tIVE, ∼**ā**tORY *adjs.* [f. LL *alleviare* lighten f. L AL(*levare* raise) + -ATE[3]]

ă′lley[1] *n.* walk or passage, esp. in park or garden; (∼(-way), narrow street or passage (up one's ∼, = *up* one's STREET); enclosure for skittles, bowling, etc.; side strip added to tennis singles court when doubles are played. [ME, f. OF *alee* walking, passage (*aler* go f. L *ambulare* walk)]

ă′lley[2]. See ALLY[3].

‖**Alley′nian** (ală′n-) *a.* & *n.* (past or present member) of Dulwich College. [f. E. *Alleyn*, founder of the college d. 1626 + -IAN]

ălliā′ceous (-shŭs) *a.* of the genus ALLIUM; smelling or tasting of garlic etc. [f. mod. L *alliaceus* f. L *allium* garlic; see -ACEOUS]

alli′ance *n.* union by marriage; kinship; (esp. of countries) joining in pursuit of common interests; league, association; community in nature or qualities; (Biol.) group of allied families. [ME, f. OF *aliance* (as ALLY[1]; see -ANCE)]

a′llied (-īd) *a.* See ALLY[1].

ă′lligātor *n.* Amer. loricate reptile of genus *Alligator*; other large American or Chinese loricate; skin of such an animal; ∼ **clip** (with teeth for gripping); ∼ **pear**, avocado; ∼ **tortoise**, snapping turtle. [f. Sp. *el lagarto* the lizard f. L *lacerta*]

alli′terāte *v.i.* (use words that) begin with same letter or sound; hence ∼IVE *a.* [back-form. f. foll.; see -ATE[3]]

ăllitĕrā′tion *n.* commencement of adjacent or closely connected words with same letter or sound (*cool*, *calm*, *and collected*; *sing a song of sixpence*). [f. mod. L AL(*literatio* f. *littera* letter; see -ATION)]

ă′llium *n.* plant of genus *Allium*, incl. garlic, onions, leeks, and various garden flowers. [L, = garlic]

ăllo- *comb. form.* other (*allogamy*, *allopathy*). [f. Gk *allos* other]

ă′lloc‖āte *v.t.* assign, devote, (*to* person or purpose); assign to a place; hence or cogn. ∼ABLE *a.*, ∼A′TION *n.* [f. med. L *allocare* (*locus* place) + -ATE[3]]

ăllocū′tion *n.* formal or hortatory address. [f. L *allocutio* f. AL(*loqui locut*- speak; see -ION)]

al(l)ō′di‖um *n.* (Hist.) estate held in absolute ownership, without acknowledgement to a superior; so ∼AL *a.* [f. med. L f. Frank. *allōd- entire property (as ALL, *ōd* estate)]

ăllō′gamy̆ *n.* (Bot.) cross-fertilization. [f. ALLO- + Gk -*gamia* f. *gamos* marriage]

ă′llomŏrph *n.* one of two or more alternative forms of a morpheme; hence **ăllomŏ̄r′ph**IC *a.* [f. ALLO- + MORPHEME]

ă′llopath *n.* one who practises allopathy. [f. F *allopathe* back-form. f. *allopathie* = foll.]

ăllŏ′path‖y̆ *n.* treatment of disease by usual means, i.e. by inducing an opposite condition (opp. *homoeopathy*); hence **ăllopă′th**IC *a.*, ∼IST (3) *n.* [G *allopathie* (as ALLO-, -PATHY)]

ă′llophōne *n.* one of the variant sounds forming a phoneme; hence **ăllophō′n**IC *a.* [f. ALLO- + PHONEME]

allŏ′t *v.t.* (-tt-). distribute or deal by lot or with authority; apportion (*to*). [f. OF *aloter* (*a* to, LOT)]

allŏt'ment *n.* apportioning; share allotted to one; one's lot in life; ||small portion of usu. public land let out for cultivation. [f. prec. + -MENT]

ä'llotrōpe *n.* one form of a substance which exhibits allotropy. [back-form. f. foll.]

ällŏ'tropȳ *n.* existence of several forms of a chemical element in same state (gas, liquid, solid) but with different physical or chemical properties; hence **ällotrŏ'pic**(AL) *adjs.* [f. Gk *allotropos* of another form (*allos* different, *tropos* manner f. *trepō* to turn)]

ällŏttee' *n.* one to whom allotment is made. [f. ALLOT + -EE]

allow' *v.* 1. *v.t.* admit (thing *to be*, *that*); permit (practice, person *to* do); indulge one*self* in (conduct); *consider, assert, (that)*; give (limited quantity or sum; *allow him £200 a year*); add or deduct in consideration of something; hence ∼ABLE *a.* 2. *v.i.* admit *of*; ∼ **for**, take into consideration, make addition or deduction corresponding to. [ME, orig. = 'praise', f. OF *alouer* f. L AL*laudare* praise & med. L AL*locare* place]

allow'ance[1] *n.* tolerance (*of*); limited quantity or sum esp. of money or food; money paid to cover special expenses (*entertainment, family, allowance*); deduction, discount; **make** ∼(**s**) **for**, allow for (esp. mitigating circumstances). [ME, f. OF *alouance* (as prec.; see -ANCE)]

allow'ance[2] *v.t.* make allowance to (person); supply in limited quantities. [f. prec.]

alloy'[1] (ă'loi, aloi') *n.* mixture composed wholly or mainly of metals; inferior metal mixed esp. with gold or silver (lit. or fig.). [f. F *aloi* f. OF *aloier, aleier* combine f. L AL*ligare* bind]

alloy'[2] (ă'loi, aloi') *v.t.* mix (metals); debase by admixture; moderate. [f. F *aloyer* (*aloi*; see prec.)]

a'llseed (aw'l-) *n.* any of various plants producing much seed. [f. ALL + SEED]

a'llspīce (aw'l-) *n.* pimento, dried ground berry of *Pimenta officinalis*, supposed to combine flavour of cinnamon, nutmeg, and cloves; plant yielding this; one of various other aromatic shrubs. [f. ALL + SPICE]

allu'de (-ū'd, -ōō'd) *v.i.* refer covertly, transiently, or indirectly, *to* (something assumed known); refer in any manner *to*. [f. L AL(*ludere lus-* play)]

allūr'e *v.t.*, & *n.* 1. *v.t.* tempt, entice, win over, (*to, from*, person, place, conduct); fascinate, charm; hence ∼MENT (-ūr'm-) *n.* 2. *n.* personal charm, attractiveness. [ME, f. OF *alure* attract (a AD-, *luere* LURE[1])]

allu'sion (-lū'zhon, -lōō'zhon) *n.* covert, passing, or indirect reference (*to*), any reference *to*. [F, or f. LL *allusio* (as ALLUDE; see -ION)]

allu'sive (-ū'-, -ōō'-) *a.* containing an allusion (*to*); containing many allusions; hence ∼LY[2] (-vlĭ) *adv.*, ∼NESS (-vn-) *n.* [as prec.; see -IVE]

allu'vial (-ū'-, -ōō'-) *a.* & *n.* 1. *a.* pertaining to alluvium. 2. *n.* alluvial (esp. gold-bearing) deposit. [f. ALLUVIUM + -AL]

allu'vion (-ū'-, -ōō'-) *n.* wash of sea or river against shore or banks; flood; matter deposited by flood, esp. alluvium; (Law) formation of new land by water's action. [F, f. L AL*luvio-onis* (*luere* wash)]

allu'vi|um (-ū'-, -ōō'-) *n.* (*pl.* ∼a or ∼ums). deposit of earth, sand, etc., left by flood, esp. in river valley or delta. [L, neut. of AL*luvius* a. (*luere* wash)]

ally[1] (ăli', ă'lī) *v.t.* (*attrib. p.p. usu. pr.* ă'līd). combine or unite for special purpose *to* or *with* (esp. of marriage and alliance with foreign States); (in *p.p.*) pertaining to allied forces or States, esp. (*A-*) to Britain and her allies in wars of 1914–18 and 1939–45; **allied to**, (of thing) related to, connected with. [ME, f. OF *al(e)ier* f. L AL*ligare* bind; cf. ALLOY[1]]

ă'lly[2] *n.* person, State, etc., allied with another. [f. prec.]

ă'lly[3], **ă'lley**[2], *n.* choice playing-marble of marble, alabaster, or glass. [perh. dim. of ALABASTER]

-ally *suf.* forming *advs.* f. *adjs.* in -AL; cf. -LY[2].

ă'llȳl *n.* (Chem.) unsaturated univalent radical, C₃H₅. [f. L *allium* garlic + -YL]

älmacă'ntar. See ALMUCANTAR.

Alma Ma'ter (ă-; mā'-, mah'-) *n.* Title used of universities and schools by their past and present pupils. [L, = bounteous mother]

a'lmanăc, (rare) **-ăck,** (aw'l-, ŏ'l-) *n.* annual calendar of months and days, usu. with astronomical data and other information. [ME, f. med. L *almanac*(*h*) f. LGk *almenikhiaka*]

ă'lmandīne *n.* violet-tinted garnet. [F, alt. of obs. *alabandine* f. med. L *alabandina* (*Alabanda*, ancient city in Asia Minor)]

almī'ghtȳ (awlmī'tĭ) *a.* & *adv.* 1. *a.* having all possible power (esp. *Almighty God*; **the A**∼, God); (sl.) very great. 2. *adv.* (sl.) exceedingly. [OE *ælmihtig* (as ALL 9, MIGHTY)]

almīr'ah (-*a*) *n.* (Ind.) wardrobe, movable cupboard. [f. Urdu *almari* f. Port. *almario* f. L *armarium* closet, chest (*arma* utensils)]

a'lmond (ah'm-) *n.* kernel of stone-fruit borne by two trees (**sweet, bitter,** ∼), varieties of *Amygdalus communis*, allied to plum and peach; either tree; ∼ **eyes** (apparently almond-shaped). [ME, f. OF *alemande* etc. f. med. L *amandula* f. L *amygdala* f. Gk *amugdalē*; assoc. w. *wds* in AL-]

almon|er (ah'm-, ă'lm-) *n.* official distributor of alms, whence ∼RY (3) *n.*; ||social worker attached to hospital, seeing to after-care of patients [ME, f. AF *aumoner*, OF *aumonier* f. Rom. *almosinarius* f. med. L *eleēmosynarius* (as ALMS; see -ARY[1])]

a'lmost (aw'l-) *adv.* all but; as the nearest thing to. [OE *ælmǣst* for the most part (as ALL, MOST)]

alms (ahmz) *n.* (usu. as *sing.*) charitable relief of the poor; charitable donation; ∼**folk**, ∼**man**, person(s) supported by alms; ∼**house**, one founded by charity for reception of poor. [OE *ælmysse, -messe,* f. Gmc *almōsan*(*i*)*na* f. Rom. *almosina*, alt. after *alimonia* (see ALIMONY) f. LL f. Gk *eleēmosunē* compassionateness (*eleēmōn* a. f. *eleos* compassion)]

älmucă'ntar,-mac-, *n.* line of constant altitude above the horizon. [ME, f. med. L *almucantarath* or F *almucantara* etc., f. Arab. *almuḳanṭarāt* sundial (*ḳanṭara* arch)]

alŏ'dium. See ALLODIUM.

ă'lōe *n.* plant of genus *Aloe*, with erect spikes of flowers, and leaves yielding bitter juice; (in *pl.*) purgative drug procured from juice of aloes; one of various other plants, e.g. agave. [OE *al*(*e*)*we* f. L f. Gk *aloē*]

älŏě'tic *a.* & *n.* (medicine) containing aloes [f. Gk *aloē* on false anal. of diuretic etc.]

alo'ft (ŏ-, aw') *adv.* & *pred. a.* high up (lit., esp. Naut., or fig.); upward. [ME, f. ON *á lopt*(*i*) (*á* in, on, to, *lopt* air); cf. LIFT, LOFT]

alŏ'gical *a.* non-logical; opposed to logic. [A- 7 + LOGICAL]

alo'ha *int.* (used in Hawaii at greeting or parting); *A∼ State,* Hawaii. [Hawaiian, = love]

alo'ne *pred. a.,* & *adv.* 1. *a.* not with others (*this fact alone would discredit him*); **go it** ∼, act by oneself without assistance; **LEAVE**[2] *alone*; **LET**[2] *alone*. 2. standing by oneself (*in opinion* etc.). 3. *adv.* only, exclusively, (*you alone can help me*). [ME, f. ALL + ONE]

alŏ'ng *adv.* & *prep.* 1. from end to end (of); through any part of the length (of). 2. *adv.* onward (GET[1], MOVE[2], RUN[1], *along*); in(to) more advanced state (*coming along nicely*); in company or conjunction (*with*) (GO[1] *along with*); with a person (*take a torch along; I'll be along in ten minutes*); **all** ∼, all the time; ∼**shore,** by the shore, along and on the shore; ∼**side,** close to side of ship, pier, etc.; ∼**si'de of,** side by side with (lit. or fig.). [OE *andlang* f. WG *and-* opposite + *lang-* extended, LONG[1]]

aloo'f *adv.* & *n.* 1. *adv.* away, apart, (lit. or fig.; *stand, keep, hold, aloof*). 2. *a.* distant, unsympathetic; hence ∼LY[2] *adv.*, ∼NESS *n.* [orig. Naut., f. A[3] + LUFF]

älopē'cia *n.* (Med.) baldness, complete or partial. [L, f. Gk *alōpekia* fox-mange (*alōpēx* fox; see -IA[1])]

alou'd *adv.* audibly, not silently or in a whisper (THINK *aloud*); (arch.) loudly. [f. A[3] + LOUD]

alow' (-ō') *adv.* (Naut.) in or into lower part of vessel. [f. A³+LOW¹ 2]

ălp *n.* mountain-peak, esp. (in *pl., Alps*) those in Switzerland and adjacent countries; (in Switzerland) green pasture-land on mountainside. [orig. pl., f. F f. L *Alpes* f. Gk *Alpeis*]

ălpă′ca *n.* kind of llama with long woolly hair; its wool; fabric made from the wool, with or without other fibres. [Sp., f. Quechua *alpako* (*pako* reddish--brown)]

ălpărga′ta (-gah′-) *n.* light canvas shoe with plaited fibre sole, espadrille. [Sp.]

ă′lpenhŏrn *n.* long wooden horn used by Alpine herdsmen. [G, = Alp-horn]

ă′lpenstŏck *n.* long iron-tipped staff used in mountain-climbing. [G, = Alp-stick]

ă′lpha *n.* first Greek letter (A, α) = a (**A∼ and Omega,** beginning and end); first-class mark in examination (∼ **plus,** superlatively good); (Astron.) chief star in a constellation; ∼ **particles,** ∼ **rays,** helium nuclei emitted by radioactive substances (orig. regarded as rays). [ME f. L f. Gk]

ă′lphabĕt *n.* set of letters used in a language (*Russian alphabet*) or symbols or signs for them (*Morse,* deaf--and-dumb, *alphabet*); **phonetic** ∼ (used to represent sounds of speech); hence ∼IC(AL) *adjs.,* ∼ICALLY *adv.,* (-ĕ′-) (esp. of order of letters or words), ∼IZE (3) *v.t.* [f. LL *alphabetum* f. Gk *alpha, bēta,* first two letters of alphabet]

ălphabĕ′ric, ălphanūmĕ′ric(al), *adjs.* containing both alphabetic and numerical symbols. [f. ALPHA-BETIC+NUMERICAL]

A′lpīne (ă′-) *a.* & *n.* **1.** *a.* of the Alps or any lofty mountains. **2.** *n.* plant native or suited to mountain districts. [f. L *Alpinus* (*Alpes*; see ALP, -INE¹)]

A′lpin|ist (ă′-) *n.* Alpine climber; so ∼ISM (2) *n.* [f. F *alpiniste* (as prec.; see -IST)]

alrea′dў (awlrĕ′dĭ) *adv.* before this or that time; as early as this. [f. ALL 9+READY]

alright (erron.) = *all right* (ALL 9).

ALS *abbr.* autograph letter signed.

Alsă′ce (ă-) *n.* dry white wine. [∼ in E. France]

Alsā′tia (ălsā′sha) *n.* (Hist.) precinct of White Friars in London as sanctuary for debtors and criminals. [med., L, = prec., as being a much disputed territory]

||Alsā′tian (ălsā′shan) *n.* (animal of) a breed of wolfhound. [f. *Alsatia* (= ALSACE)+-AN]

ă′lsīke *n.* species of clover (*Trifolium hybridum*). [f. A∼ in Sweden]

a′lsō (aw′l-) *adv.* in addition, besides; ∼**-ran** *n.,* horse or dog not placed in first three in race, (fig.) person(s) who failed to win distinction. [OE *alswā* (as ALL 9, SO¹)]

ălt *n.* (Mus.) high note; **in** ∼, in octave beginning with G above treble staff, (fig., arch.) in exalted mood. [f. It. *alto* ALTO f. L *altus* high]

Alta. *abbr.* Alberta.

a′ltar (aw′l-, ŏ′l-) *n.* flat-topped block for offerings to deity; Communion table; **lead to the** ∼, marry (woman); ∼**-piece,** reredos, esp. a painting. [OE *altar, -er,* Gmc f. LL *altar*(*e*), *-ium* f. L *altus* high]

ăltă′zĭmuth *n.* instrument for determining altitude and azimuth of heavenly bodies. [f. ALTITUDE+AZIMUTH]

a′lter (aw′l-, ŏ′l-) *v.t.* & *i.* change in characteristics, position, etc.; *castrate or spay; so ∼ABLE *a.,* ∼A′TION *n.* [ME, f. OF *alterer* f. LL *alterare* f. L *alter* other]

a′lterative (aw′l-, ŏ′l-) *a.* & *n.* **1.** *a.* tending to alter. **2.** *a.* & *n.* (medicine, treatment) that alters bodily processes. [ME, f. med. L *alterativus* (as prec.; see -ATIVE)]

a′lterc|āte (aw′l-, ŏ′l-) *v.i.* dispute hotly, wrangle, (*with*); so ∼A′TION *n.* [f. L *altercari*+-ATE³]

alter ego (ălter ĕ′gō) *n.* (*pl.* ∼*s*). intimate friend. [L, = other self]

altêr′n|ant (awl-, ŏl-) *a.* alternating; hence ∼ANCE *n.* [f. L *alternare;* see foll., -ANT]

altêr′nate¹ (awl-, ŏl-) *a.* & *n.* **1.** *a.* (Of things of two kinds) coming each after one of the other kind (∼ **leaves, angles,** those placed alternately on the two sides of stem, line); (of sequence etc.) consisting of alternate things; (w. *pl.,* of one class of things) every second one (*comes on alternate days*); alternative; hence ∼LY² (-tlĭ) *adv.* **2.** *n.* deputy; substitute. [f. L *alternatus* p.p. of *alternare* do things by turns (*alternus* every other f. *alter* other); see -ATE²]

a′ltern|āte² (aw′l-, ŏ′l-) *v.* **1.** *v.t.* arrange, perform, (two sets of things) alternately; interchange (one thing) alternately *with* or by another. **2.** *v.i.* (Of two things) succeed each other by turns; (of a whole) consist of alternate things (∼**ating current,** electric current reversing its direction at regular intervals); (of one class of things) appear alternately *with* another. **3.** So ∼A′TION *n.* (∼**ation of generations,** reproduction by alternate processes, e.g. sexual and asexual), ∼**ātor** *n.,* dynamo giving alternating current. [f. as prec.+-ATE³]

altêr′native (awl-, ŏl-) *a.* & *n.* **1.** *a.* (Of two things) mutually exclusive; (of one or more things) available in place of another (**the** ∼ **society,** group of persons dissociating themselves from conventional social practices); hence ∼LY² (-vlĭ) *adv.* **2.** *n.* liberty to choose between two or more things; one of two or more possibilities. [f. F *alternatif -ive* or f. med. L *alternativus* (as prec.; see -ATIVE)]

ă′lthŏrn (-t-h-) *n.* (Usu. high-pitched) wind instrument of saxhorn family. [G (as ALT, HORN¹)]

althou′gh (awldhō′) *conj.* = THOUGH 1, 3. [ME, f. ALL 9+THOUGH]

ă′ltimĕter *n.* instrument for showing height above sea level, esp. aneroid barometer in aircraft. [f. L *altus* high+-I-+-METER]

ă′ltĭtūde *n.* height (of object, esp. above sea level or horizon); depth; (Geom.) length of perpendicular from vertex to base; (fig.) eminence. [ME, f. L *altitudo* (*altus* high; see -TUDE)]

ă′ltō *n.* (*pl.* ∼*s*). (Mus.) highest adult male voice, above tenor; female voice of similar range, contralto; singer with alto voice; part written for alto voice; second-highest-pitched member of a group of similar instruments; ∼ **clef** (placing middle C on middle line of staff). [It. *alto* (*canto*) high (singing)]

ăltōcŭ′mŭl|us (*pl.* ∼**i** *pr.* -ī). (Meteorol.) clouds like cumulus but at higher level. [mod. L, f. L *altus* high+-O-+CUMULUS]

altogĕ′ther (awltogĕ′dh-, ŏl-) *adv.* & *n.* **1.** *adv.* totally; on the whole. **2.** *n.* (colloq.) **in the** ∼, nude. [ME, f. ALL+TOGETHER]

ăltō-rèlie′vō *n.* (*pl.* ∼*s*). (sculpture in) high RELIEF². [It.]

ăltōstra′t|us (-ā′-, -ah′-) *n.* (*pl.* ∼**i** *pr.* -ī). (Meteorol.) clouds forming continuous layer at medium altitude. [mod. L, f. L *altus* high+-O-+STRATUS]

ăltri′cial (-shal) *a.* (Of bird) whose young have to be fed by parents after hatching. [f. L *altrix altricis* fem. nourisher (*altor* f. *alere altus* nourish; see -TRIX)+-IAL]

ă′ltru|ism (-rŏō-) *n.* regard for others as a principle of action; unselfishness; hence ∼IST (2) *n.,* ∼**i′st**IC *a.,* ∼**i′st**ICALLY *adv.* [f. F *altruisme* f. It. *altrui* somebody else f. Rom. *alteri huic* to this other; see -ISM]

ă′lum *n.* double sulphate of aluminium and potassium; one of a series of similar compounds. [ME f. OF, f. L *alumen aluminis*]

alū′mina *n.* aluminium oxide. [f. L *alumen* alum, after *soda* etc.]

||ălūmī′nium, *alū′mĭnum, *n.* silvery light ductile and malleable metallic element, not tarnished by air; ∼ **bronze,** alloy of this with copper. [*aluminium* alt. (after *sodium* etc.) f. *aluminum,* earlier *alumium* f. ALUM+-IUM]

alū′mĭniz|e, -īs|e (-īz) *v.t.* coat with aluminium; hence ∼A′TION *n.* [f. prec.+-IZE]

***alŭ′mn|us** *n.* (*pl.* ∼**i** *pr.* -ī; *fem.* ∼**a,** *pl.* ∼**ae**). former pupil or student (lit. or fig.). [L, = nursling, pupil (*alere* nourish)]

älvē'olar *a.* of tooth-socket; (Phonet., of consonant) pronounced with tongue-tip at or near ridge of teeth, e.g. *n, s, t.* [f. foll. + -AR[1]]

älvē'ol|us *n.* (*pl.* ∼i *pr.* -ī). small cavity; socket of tooth; cell of honeycomb; terminal air-sac of lung; so ∼ATE[2] *a.* [L, dim. of *alveus* cavity]

a'lways (aw'lwāz, -ĭz), (arch.) **a'lway** (aw'-), *adv.* at all times; on all occasions; whatever the circumstances (*I can always sleep on the floor*); repeatedly (*they are always complaining*). [ME, prob. distrib. gen. f. ALL + WAY + 's 1)]

ä'lÿssum *n.* one of various cruciferous plants of genus *Alyssum* etc. with usu. yellow or white flowers. [f. L f. Gk *alusson*]

am. See BE.

AM *abbr.* amplitude modulation; *Master of Arts [f. L *Artium Magister*]; Member of the Order of Australia; in the year of the world [f. L *anno mundi*].

a.m. *abbr.* before noon. [f. L *ante meridiem*]

Am *symb.* americium.

AMA *abbr.* American Medical Association; Australian Medical Association.

ämadavā't, ävadavā't, *n.* small Indian songbird (*Estrilda amandava*). [f. *Ahmadabad* in India]

ä'madou (-ōō) *n.* tinder from fungi. [F f. mod. Prov., lit. = lover (because quickly afire) f. L (as AMATEUR)]

a'mah (ah'ma) *n.* (China etc.) nursemaid. [f. Port. *ama* nurse]

amai'n *adv.* (arch. or poet.) vehemently; in all haste. [f. A[3] + MAIN[2]]

amä'lgam *n.* mixture of a metal with mercury (*gold amalgam*); plastic mixture of any substances (lit. or fig.). [ME, f. F *amalgame* or f. med. L *amalgama*, prob. f. Gk *malagma* an emollient]

amä'lgam|āte *v.t.* & *i.* mix; unite (classes, societies, companies, ideas, etc.); (of metals) alloy with mercury; hence ∼A'TION *n.*, amalgamating or being amalgamated, merging of two or more business concerns into one. [f. med. L *amalgamare* (as prec.) + -ATE[3]]

amänuē'ns|is *n.* (*pl.* ∼es *pr.* -sēz). one who writes from dictation or copies manuscript; literary assistant. [L, a. (as n.) f. (*servus*) *a manu* secretary + -*ensis* belonging to]

ä'maränth *n.* imaginary unfading flower, whence **amara'nth|INE[1]** *a.*; flower of genus *Amaranthus*, e.g. prince's feather and love-lies-bleeding; purple colour. [f. F *amarante* or mod. L *amaranthus* f. L f. Gk *amarantos* everlasting (*a*- not, *marainō* wither), alt. after *polyanthus* etc.]

ämarÿ'llis *n.* bulbous S. Afr. plant of genus *Amaryllis*; one of various related plants. [L f. Gk *Amaryllis*, name of a country girl]

amä'ss *v.t.* heap together; accumulate (esp. riches). [f. F *amasser* or f. med. L *amassare* f. Rom. *AD(massare* f. L *massa* MASS[2])]

ä'mateur (-tūr, -tēr) *n.* one who is fond *of* (thing); one who practises a thing (esp. an art or game) only as a pastime, esp. unpaid player etc. (opp. *professional*); hence ∼ISH[1] *a.*, having the faults of amateurs' work, unskilful in execution, ∼ISM (2) *n.* [F, f. It. *amatore* f. L *amator* -*oris* lover (*amare* love)]

Ama'ti (ahmah'tē) *n.* violin or cello made by *Amati* family in Cremona *c.* 1550–1700.

ä'mative *a.* disposed to loving. [f. med. L *amativus* f. L *amare* love; see -ATIVE]

ä'matorÿ *a.* pertaining to a lover or to sexual love. [f. L *amatorius* (*amare* love; see -ORY)]

ämaur|ō'sis *n.* (*pl.* ∼oses *pr.* -ēz). partial or total loss of sight from disease of optic nerve; hence ∼o'TIC *a.* [mod. L, f. Gk (*amauroō* darken f. *amauros* dim; see -OSIS)]

amā'ze *v.t.*, & *n.* **1.** *v.t.* overwhelm with wonder (*amazed at, that, to find* etc.); hence ∼MENT (-zm-) *n.* **2.** *n.* (arch. or poet.) amazement. [ME, f. OE *āmasod* p.p. of *āmasian*, of uncert. orig.]

A'maz|on (ä'-) *n.* one of a fabulous race of female warriors in Scythia and elsewhere; female warrior (lit. or fig.); (*a*∼) tall, strong, or athletic woman; hence ∼ō'nIAN *a.* [ME f. L f. Gk (prob. foreign word, but explained by Greeks as *a*- not + *mazos* breast, from removal of right breast to facilitate use of bow)]

ämbā'gēs (-z) *n. pl.* indirect or roundabout paths (lit. or fig.). [ME f. OF f. L (*amb*- both ways, *agere* drive)]

ämbä'ssador *n.* diplomat sent by one sovereign or State on mission to another; diplomat of highest rank permanently representing sovereign or State at foreign court or government (*ambassador-at-LARGE*); official messenger; hence **ämbassadō'r'IAL** *a.* [ME, f. F *ambassadeur* f. It. *ambasciator* f. Rom. *ambactiator* (*ambactiare* f. med. L *ambactia* charge, office, f. Gmc *ambahtaz* f. L *ambactus* servant, of Gaulish orig.)]

ämbä'ssadress *n.* female ambassador; ambassador's wife. [f. prec. + -ESS[1]]

ä'mbätch *n.* tropical Afr. tree with very light spongy wood. [Ethiopic]

ä'mber *n.* & *a.* **1.** *n.* yellow translucent fossil resin; yellow traffic light shown as caution between red (= *stop*) and green (= *go*). **2.** *a.* made of or coloured like amber; *∼-jack, large game-fish of W. Atlantic. [ME, f. OF *ambre* f. Arab. '*anbar* ambergris, amber]

ä'mbergris (-īs, -ēs) *n.* waxlike odoriferous substance found floating in tropical seas, and in intestines of sperm whale. [ME, f. OF *ambre gris* grey AMBER]

ambiance (ahñbïah'ńs) *n.* surroundings, milieu. [F (as AMBIENT; see -ANCE)]

ämbidě'xtrous, -terous, *a.* able to use left and right hands equally well; (fig.) working in either of two media (e.g. verse and prose); deceitful; hence **ämbi-dě'xtě'RITY** *n.*, ∼LY[2] *adv.*, ∼NESS *n.* [f. LL *ambidexter* (*ambi*- on both sides, *dexter* right-handed) + -OUS]

ä'mbi|ent *a.* surrounding; hence ∼ENCE *n.*, (esp.) surroundings. [f. F *ambiant* or f. L *ambiens* -*entis* pres. part. of *ambire* go round (*ambi*- on both sides, *ire* go)]

ämbigū'ïtÿ *n.* double meaning; instance of this; expression capable of more than one meaning. [ME, f. OF *ambiguité* or f. L *ambiguitas* (as foll.; see -ITY)]

ämbi'guous *a.* obscure; having double meaning; of doubtful classification; of uncertain issue; hence ∼LY[2] *adv.*, ∼NESS *n.* [f. L *ambiguus* doubtful f. *ambigere* (*ambi*- both ways, *agere* drive) + -OUS]

ä'mbit *n.* precincts; bounds; scope, extent. [ME, f. L *ambitus* circuit (*ambire*; see AMBIENT)]

ämbi'tion *n.* ardent desire for distinction; aspiration (*to be, to do*); object of such desire. [ME f. OF, f. L *ambitio* -*onis* (*ambire ambut*- canvass for votes; see AMBIENT, -ION)]

ämbi'tious (-shŭs) *a.* full of ambition; strongly desirous (*of* a thing, *to* do); showing ambition (*an ambitious attempt*); hence ∼LY[2] *adv.*, ∼NESS *n.* [ME, f. OF *ambitieus* f. L *ambitiosus* (as prec.; see -ITIOUS[2])]

ämbi'val|ence, ∼|**encÿ,** *ns.* (Psych.) coexistence in one person of the emotional attitudes of love and hate, or other opposite feelings, towards the same object or situation; so ∼ENT *a.* [f. G *ambivalenz* f. L *ambo* both, after EQUIVALENCE, -CY]

ämbivě'rsion (-shon) *n.* (Psych.) balance between introversion and extroversion; hence **ä'mbivêrt** *n.*, person having such balance. [f. L *ambi*- on both sides + -*version* after EXTROVERSION, INTROVERSION]

ä'mble (-z), & *n.* **1.** *v.i.* (Of horse etc.) move by lifting two feet on one side together; ride an ambling horse; ride at an easy pace; move in a way suggesting an ambling horse. **2.** *pl.* gait of ambling horse; easy pace. [ME, f. OF *ambler* f. L *ambulare* walk]

ämblÿ'ō'pïa *n.* impaired vision without apparent change in eye; hence ∼ō'pIC *a.* [Gk (*ambluōpos n.*, *amblus* dull + *ōps ōpos* eye; see -IA[1])]

ä'mbō *n.* (*pl.* ∼s, or ∼nes *pr.* -ō'nēz). pulpit in early Christian church etc. [med. L, f. Gk *ambōn* rim (in med. Gk = pulpit)]

ämboy'na *n.* ornamental wood of an Asian tree. [*A*∼ Island in Indonesia]

ämbrō'si|a (-zïa, -zhya) *n.* **1.** (Gk & Rom. Myth.)

ambry · 28 · Amish

food of the gods; anything delightful to taste or smell;
so ∿AL a. 2. food of certain bees and beetles. [L, f.
Gk, = elixir of life (ambrotos immortal)]
ǎ′mbrỹ. See AUMBRY.
ǎmbs-ā′ce (-mz-) n. (arch.) lowest throw at dice, pair
of aces; bad luck; worthlessness. [ME, f. OF ambes as f.
L ambo both + as ACE]
ǎ′mbŭlance n. conveyance for sick or injured persons
(*∿-chaser, (sl.) one who seeks profit through
lawsuits for others' personal injuries); mobile hospital
following army. [F (as foll.; see -ANCE)]
ǎ′mbŭlant a. (Med.) (Of treatment) not confining
patient to bed; (of patient) able to walk about, not
confined to bed. [f. L ambulare walk; see -ANT]
ǎ′mbŭlatorỹ a. & n. 1. a. pertaining to walking;
adapted for walking; movable; not permanent;
= prec. 2. n. place for walking; arcade, esp. in apse;
cloister. [f. L ambulatorius (ambulare walk; see -ORY)]
ǎmbuscā′de n., & v.t. & i. (lie or conceal in, attack
from) ambush. [f. F embuscade f. It. imboscata or Sp.
emboscada (imboscare; see AMBUSH², -ADE)]
ǎ′mbush¹ (-ŏŏsh) n. concealment of troops, troops
concealed, in a wood etc. (lie in ambush); attack from
such position; (gen.) lying in wait. [ME, f. OF
embusche (embuschier; see foll.)]
ǎ′mbush² (-ŏŏsh) v.t. & i. lie in wait (for); attack from
ambush. [ME, f. OF embuschier f. Rom. *IM¹(boscare f.
*boscus BUSH¹)]
AMDG abbr. to the greater glory of God. [f. L ad
majorem Dei gloriam]
*amē′ba. See AMOEBA.
âme damnée (ahm dah′nā) n. (pl. -es -es pr. same).
devoted adherent. [F, = damned soul]
ameer′. See AMIR.
amē′lior āte v.t. & i. (cause to) become better; hence
∿A′TION, ∿ātOR, ns., ∿atIVE a. [f. MELIORATE after F
améliorer alt. f. OF ameillorer (meilleur f. L melior -oris
better)]
amē′n (ah-, ā-) int. & n. (saying of) 'so be it' esp. at
end of prayer etc.; say ∿ (assent) to. [ME f. eccl. L
f. Gk f. Heb. 'āmēn certainly]
amē′n|able a. (Of person) responsible (to law etc., or
abs.); (of thing) subject or liable to; responsive,
tractable; hence ∿ABI′LITY, ∿ableNESS (-beln-), ns.,
∿ABLY adv. [AF (Law), f. F amener bring to (a- AD-,
mener bring f. L L minare drive animals f. L minari
threaten); see -ABLE]
amē′nd v.t. correct error in (document); make
proposed minor improvements in (motion etc. under
discussion); make better; so ∿MENT n., minor improvement in document, e.g. added article in US
Constitution. [ME, f. OF amender f. Rom. *admendare
f. L emendare EMEND]
amende honorable (amahnd ŏnŏrah′bl) n. (pl. -es
-es pr. same). public or open apology and reparation.
[F, = honourable reparation]
amē′nds (-z) n. reparation, restitution, compensation,
(make amends). [ME, f. OF amendes penalties, fine, pl.
of amende reparation (amender AMEND)]
amē′nitỹ n. pleasantness (of place, person, etc.; ||∿
bed, bed available in hospital to give more privacy
for small payment); (usu. in pl.) pleasant feature.
[ME, f. OF amenité or f. L amoenitas (amoenus pleasant;
see -ITY)]
||āmĕnorrhoe′a, *-rrhe′a, (-rē′a) n. (Path.) ab-
normal absence of menstruation. [f. A- 7 + MENO-
+ Gk -rrhoia (rheō flow)]
amĕnt¹ (ā′mĕ-, amĕ′-) n. person with congenital
mental deficiency; so āmē′ntIA¹ (-sha) n. [f. L amens
-ent- mad (a away from, mens mentis mind)]
amē′nt², amē′nt|um (pl. ∿a), ns. catkin. [L,
= thong]
amĕr′ce v.t. fine; punish in any way; hence or cogn.
amĕr′cIABLE a., ∿MENT (-sm-) n. [ME amercy, f. AF
amercier (a et, merci MERCY)]
Amĕ′rican (a-) a. & n. 1. a. belonging to continent of
America (usu. in comb., as Latin-American); belonging

to the United States; ||∿ cloth, cotton cloth
enamelled or waterproofed with shiny surface; American INDIAN; ∿ organ, harmonium with suction-
-operated instead of blown reeds; *∿ plan (charging
for hotel-room with inclusion of meals); ∿ tiger,
jaguar. 2. n. native of America of Old-World descent;
citizen of United States; English language as spoken
in United States. 3. Hence Amĕ′rica′NA (a-) n. pl. [f.
mod. L Americanus (America f. Latinized name of
Amerigo Vespucci, It. navigator d. 1512; see -AN)]
Amĕ′ricanism (a-) n. word or sense or phrase
peculiar to or originating from United States; attachment to or sympathy with the United States. [f.
prec. + -ISM]
Amĕ′ricanize (a-), -ise (-īz), v.t. & i. naturalize as an
American; make or become American in character.
[f. as prec. + -IZE]
amerĭ′cium (-ĭ′sĭ-, -ĭ′shĭ-) n. (Chem.) artificially
made transuranic radioactive metallic element. [f.
America (where first made) + -IUM]
A′merind, Ameri′ndian, (ă-) adjs. & ns. American
Indian or Eskimo; so Ameri′ndIC (ă-) a. [port-
manteau wds]
à merveille (ah mārvā′y) adv. admirably, wonderfully. [F, lit. 'to a marvel']
ǎ′mĕthÿst n. precious stone, purple or violet quartz;
hence ∿INE¹ (-ĭ′s-) a. [ME, f. OF ametiste f. L f. Gk
amethustos not drunken, the stone being supposed to
prevent intoxication]
Amhǎ′ric (ă-) n. & a. (of the) official and trade
language of Ethiopia. [f. Amhara, Ethiopian province
+ -IC]
ǎ′miable a. feeling and inspiring friendliness; lovable;
hence āmiABI′LITY, ∿NESS (-beln-), ns., ǎ′miabLY²
adv. [ME f. OF, f. LL amicabilis amicable; confused
w. F aimable lovable]
āmiǎ′nt(h)us n. mineral variety of asbestos, splitting
into flexible fibres. [L, f. Gk amiantos undefiled (a- not,
miainō defile) i.e. purified by fire, being incombustible;
for -h- cf. AMARANTH]
ǎ′mic|able a. not hostile; done in a friendly spirit;
hence ∿ABI′LITY, ∿ableNESS (-beln-), ns., ∿ABLY
adv. [f. LL amicabilis (amicus friend; see -ABLE)]
ǎ′mice¹ n. square of white linen worn by celebrant
priests, formerly on head, now on neck and shoulders.
[ME, f. med. L amicia, -sia; earlier amit f. OF, f. L
amictus garment]
ǎ′mice² n. cap, hood, or cape, of religious orders.
[ME, f. OF aumusse f. med. L almucia etc., of unkn.
orig.]
amicus curiae (amīkus kūr′iē) n. (pl. -ci pr. -sī).
friend of the (law)court, disinterested adviser. [mod.
L]
ami′d(st) prep. in the middle of (lit. or fig.); in the
course of. [ME amidde(s) f. OE on ON¹ + oblique case of
MID¹; -st w. adv. gen. -s + -t as in AGAINST]
ǎ′mide n. (Chem.) compound formed from ammonia
by replacing one (or occas. more than one) hydrogen
atom by metal or acid radical. [f. AMMONIA + -IDE]
ǎ′midone n. synthetic analgesic drug, methadone. [f.
AMINE + d(iphenyl) + -ONE]
ami′dships, *-ĭp, adv. in or into middle of ship (lit. or
fig.). [f. MIDSHIP(S) after AMID]
ami′dst. See AMID.
ǎ′mine (-ēn) n. (Chem.) compound formed from
ammonia by replacing one or more hydrogen atoms
by alkyl or other non-acidic radical. [f. AMMONIA +
-INE⁵]
aminō-ā′cĭd (-ēn-) n. (Chem.) organic acid containing the group NH₂ derived from ammonia, esp. as
constituent of proteins. [f. AMINE + ACID²]
amir′ (-ēr′), ameer′ n. Title of various Muslim
rulers; hence ∿ATE¹ (1) n. [f. Arab. 'amīr commander
(amara command); cf. EMIR]
A′mish (ah′-, ā′-) a. belonging to a strict US
Mennonite sect. [prob. f. G amisch f. J. Amen 17th c.
Swiss preacher; see -ISH¹]

amī′ss adv. & pred. a. out of order; wrong(ly); inappropriate(ly) (come, go, amiss); take ~, take offence at (thing). [ME, prob. f. ON á mis so as to miss (á on, mis cogn. w. MIS-¹, MISS²)]

ǎ′mĭtў n. friendship, friendly relationship. [ME, f. OF amitié f. Rom. *amicitas -tatis f. L amicus friend; see -ITY]

ǎ′mmèter n. instrument for measuring electric current, esp. in amperes. [f. AMPERE + -METER]

ǎ′mmō n. (colloq.) ammunition. [abbr.]

ǎmmō′nia n. colourless gas with pungent smell and strong alkaline reaction, nitrogen trihydride, NH₃; (liquid) ~, ~ water, solution of ammonia in water. [mod. L, f. SAL AMMONIAC]

ǎmmoni′acal a. pertaining to ammonia or sal ammoniac. [f. ME ammoniac, f. OF (arm-, amm-) f. L f. Gk ammōniakos of Ammon (cf. SAL AMMONIAC), + -AL]

ǎmmō′niāted a. combined or treated with ammonia.

ǎ′mmonīte n. fossil cephalopod of order Ammonoidea, with flat spiral shell. [f. mod. L ammonites, after med. L cornu Ammonis, = L Ammonis cornu (Pliny), horn of (Jupiter) Ammon; see -ITE¹ (2)]

ǎmmō′nium n. univalent radical of ammonia salts. [mod. L (as AMMONIA; scc -IUM)]

ǎmmūni′tion n. military projectiles (bullets, shells, grenades, etc.) and propellants; (fig.) facts, arguments, etc., used in attack or defence. [f. obs. F amunition, corrupt. of (la) munition (the) MUNITION]

ǎmnē′s|ĭa (-z-) n. loss of memory; hence ~ĭAC n., ~ĭC a. & n. [mod. L, f. Gk, = forgetfulness]

ǎ′mnĕstў n., & v.t. 1. n. general pardon, esp. for political offence. 2. v.t. give amnesty to. [f. F amnestie or f. L f. Gk amnēstia oblivion]

ǎmniocĕntē′s|ĭs n. (pl. ~es pr. -ēz). (Med.) sampling of amniotic fluid by insertion of hollow needle. [f. foll. + -o- + Gk kentēsis pricking (kentō to prick)]

ǎ′mni|ŏn n. (pl. ~a). (Zool. & Physiol.) innermost membrane enclosing foetus before birth; hence ~o′TIC a. [Gk, = caul (dim. of amnos lamb)]

amoe′b|a (-mē′-), *amē′b|a, n. (pl. ~as or ~ae). single-celled aquatic protozoan, perpetually changing shape; hence ~IC, ~OID, adjs. [mod. L, f. Gk amoibē change]

ǎmoebē′an (-mēb-) a. (Esp. of verse dialogue) alternately answering. [f. L f. Gk amoibaios interchanging (as prec.) + -AN]

amŏ′k, amŭ′ck, adv. run ~, run about in frenzied thirst for blood (lit. or fig.). [f. Malay amok rushing in frenzy]

amo′ng(st) (-mŭ′-) prep. in the assemblage of, surrounded by; in the general practice or views of (there is honour among thieves); in the number of (reckoned among his best works); within the limits of (collectively or distributively: fine pounds among us; divided among us); in comparison with (one among many); by joint action of (kill him among you); by reciprocal action of; quarrelled ~ themselves, with one another. [OE ongemang (on ON, gemang assemblage, cf. MINGLE); -st w. adv. gen. -s + -t as in AGAINST]

Amŏntilla′dō (a-; -lah′-) n. (pl. ~s). medium dry sherry of a matured type. [Sp. (Montilla in Spain, -ado = -ATE²)]

ǎmō′ral a. unconcerned with, or outside, morals; non-moral. [f. A- 7 + MORAL]

amorett|o (ǎmŏrĕ′tō) n. (pl. ~i pr. -ē). a Cupid. [It., dim. of amore love f. L (as AMOUR)]

ǎ′morist n. one who professes (esp. sexual) love; one who writes of love. [L amor or F amour love + -IST]

amorō′sō n. (pl. ~s). full rich type of sherry. [Sp., = amorous]

ǎ′morous a. inclined to (esp. sexual) love; in love of or pertaining to love; hence ~LY² adv., ~NESS n. [ME f. OF, f. med. L amorosus f. L amor love; see -OUS]

amŏr′ph|ous a. shapeless; (Min. & Chem.) uncrystallized; unorganized; hence ~ousLY² adv., ~ousNESS n. [f. mod. L amorphus f. Gk amorphos shapeless (a- not, morphē form) + -OUS]

amŏr′tiz|e, -īs|e (-īz), v.t. transfer (land) to corporation in mortmain; extinguish (debt, usu. by means of sinking-fund); gradually write off initial cost of (assets); hence ~A′TION n. [ME, f. OF amortir (st. -iss-) f. Rom. *admortire (ad to, mort- death)]

amou′nt¹ v.i. be equivalent (in total value, quantity, significance, etc.) to. [ME, f. OF amunter (amont upward, lit. uphill, f. L ad montem)]

amou′nt² n. total to which a thing amounts; full value, significance, etc.; quantity; any ~, a great deal (of); no ~ of, not even the greatest possible amount of. [f. prec.]

amour′ (-oor′) n. love affair, esp. secret one. [F, = love, f. L amor amoris]

amourĕ′tte (-oor-) n. petty love affair. [F, dim. of amour; see prec.]

amour propre (ǎmoor prŏ′pr) n. self-esteem; vanity. [F]

ǎmp n. (colloq.) ampere; amplifier. [abbr.]

AMP abbr. adenosine monophosphate.

ǎmpĕlŏ′psĭs n. climbing plant allied to vine, esp. Virginia creeper. [mod. L, f. Gk ampelos vine + opsis appearance]

ǎ′mperage (-ār-) n. (Electr.) strength of current in amperes. [f. AMPERE + -AGE]

ǎ′mpere (-ār) n. (Electr.) fundamental unit of current. [f. A. M. Ampère, Fr. physicist d. 1836]

ǎ′mpersǎnd n. the sign & (= and, L et). [corrupt. of '& per se (i.e. by itself) and', the old way of naming and explaining the character &]

ǎmphě′tamine (-ĭn, -ēn) n. synthetic stimulant and decongestant drug. [f. alpha-methyl-phenethylamine]

ǎmphi- comb. form. both; of both kinds; on both sides; around. [Gk]

Amphi′bia (ǎ-) n. pl. class of Vertebrata, intermediate between reptiles and fishes, incl. frogs, newts, etc., able to live on land or in water. [mod. L f. Gk, neut. pl. of amphibios (AMPHI-, bios life)]

ǎmphi′bian a. & n. (animal) living both on land and in water; (Zool.) (member) of the Amphibia; (tank, aircraft, etc.) adapted to operate on both land and water. [f. as prec. + -AN]

ǎmphi′bŏlogy n. branch of zoology treating of Amphibia. [f. as prec. + -o- + -LOGY]

ǎmphi′bious a. living both on land and in water; connected with or operating on both land and water; (Mil.) involving co-operation of sea and land (and occas. air) forces organized for invasion, (of forces) trained for such action; having a twofold life, connected with two classes, etc.; hence ~LY² adv. [f. AMPHIBIA + -OUS]

ǎmphibŏ′logy n. quibble; ambiguous wording. [ME, f. OF amphibologie f. LL amphibologia for L f. Gk amphibolia ambiguity]

ǎ′mphĭbrǎch (-k) n. (Pros.) foot consisting of one long syllable between two short; hence **ǎmphĭbrǎ′chic** (-k-) a. [f. L amphibrachys, -us f. Gk amphibrakhus short at both ends (as AMPHI-, brakhus short)]

ǎmphi′ctўon n. delegate to amphictyonic council; the A~s, the Greek amphictyonic council. [f. Gk AMPHIKtuones pl. dwellers around]

ǎmphi′ctў|onў n. association of tribes etc. for common welfare esp. in ancient Greece; so ~ŏ′NIC a. [f. Gk amphiktuonia (as AMPHI-; see -Y¹)]

ǎmphi′gamous a. (Bot.) without distinct sexual organs. [f. F amphigame (as AMPHI-, Gk gamos marriage) + -OUS]

ǎmphigour′i, ǎmphi′gorў, n. nonsensical verse etc. composition. [F amphigouri, of uncert. orig.]

ǎmphimi′x|ĭs n. (pl. ~es pr. -ēz). (Biol.) fusion of gametes from two individuals in sexual reproduction; so **ǎmphimi′ctIC** a. [mod. L, f. as AMPHI- + Gk mixis mingling]

ǎmphiŏ′xus n. lancelet of genus Branchiostoma. [mod. f. as AMPHI- + Gk oxus sharp]

ǎ′mphipod n. small usu. marine crustacean of order Amphipoda, with feet of two kinds, e.g. sandhopper. [f. AMPHI- + Gk pous podos foot]

ămphĭ'prostÿle *a.* & *n.* (building) with portico at each end. [f. L f. Gk AMPHI(*prostulos* PROSTYLE)]

ămphĭsbae'na *n.* fabulous serpent with head at each end; (Zool.) wormlike lizard of genus *Amphisbaena*. [ME f. L, f. Gk *amphisbaina* (*amphis* both ways, *bainō* go)]

||**ă'mphĭtheatre, *-ter,** (-ĭater) *n.* oval or circular building, with seats rising in tiers round central open space; large circular hollow; semicircular gallery in a theatre; (fig.) scene of a contest. [f. L f. Gk *amphitheatron* (as AMPHI-, THEATRE)]

ă'mphora *n.* (*pl.* ～e *or* ～s). Greek or Roman two-handled vessel. [L, f. Gk *amphoreus*]

ămphotĕ'rĭc *a.* (Chem.) capable of reacting as acid and base. [f. Gk *amphoteros* compar. of *amphō* both +-IC]

ă'mple *a.* (～r, ～st). spacious; extensive; abundant, copious; (euphem.) stout; quite enough; hence ～NESS (-peln-) *n.*, **ă'mpLY²** *adv.* [ME f. F, f. L *amplus*]

ă'mplĭ|fÿ *v.* **1.** *v.t.* enhance; increase loudness of (sounds), strength of (electrical signals), etc., whence ～fīER¹ *n.*; enlarge (story, statement). **2.** *v.i.* expatiate. **3.** Hence ～FICA'TION *n.* [ME, f. OF *amplifier* f. L *amplificare* (as AMPLE; see -FY)]

ă'mplĭtūde *n.* **1.** breadth; abundance; wide range. **2.** (Phys.) maximum extent of vibration or oscillation from position of equilibrium; (Electr.) maximum departure from average of alternating current or wave; ～ **modulation** (in which amplitude of carrier wave is varied). [F, or f. L *amplitudo* (as AMPLE; see -TUDE)]

ă'mpoule (-ōōl) *n.* (Med.) small sealed glass vessel to contain materials before injection [F, f. as foll.]

ămpŭ'lla *n.* (*pl.* ～e). Roman two-handled globular flask; vessel for sacred uses; (Zool. & Physiol.) dilated end of vessel, canal, or duct. [L]

ă'mpūt|āte *v.t.* cut off (part of animal body etc., esp. limb because of injury or disease); hence ～A'TION, ～ātOR, *ns.*, ～EE¹ *n.*, one who has lost limb etc. by amputation. [f. L *amputare* (*amb-* about, *putare* prune) +-ATE³]

amŭ'ck. See AMOK.

ă'mŭlĕt *n.* thing worn as charm against evil (lit. or fig.). [f. L *amuletum*; orig. unkn.]

amŭ's|e (-z) *v.t.* **1.** interest *with* pleasant trifling matters; ～e one**self,** pass time in small diversions. **2.** make (person) laugh or smile (*be amused with, by, at, that, to find* etc.). **3.** Hence ～IVE *a.* [ME, f. OF *amuser* cause to MUSE² (causal *a* to, *muser* stare)]

amŭ'sement (-zm-) *n.* pleasant diversion; causing of laughter or smiles; pastime; ||～ **arcade,** place for recreation with automatic game-machines etc. [F (*amuser*; see prec., -MENT)]

ă'mÿl *n.* (Chem.) radical, C_5H_{11}, derived from pentane. [f. L *amylum* starch, from which oil containing it was distilled]

ămÿlāse (-s, -z) *n.* diastase. [f. prec. +-ASE]

ămÿlŏ'psĭn *n.* pancreatic enzyme that converts starch into sugar. [f. AMYL after *pepsin*]

A'mÿtāl (ă'-) *n.* (P) white crystalline powder used as sedative and hypnotic, esp. as sodium salt. [f. Chem. name *isoamylethyl barbituric acid*]

an¹ (*an or, when stressed,* ăn) *a.* See ʌ²; *an* is the form generally used before words beginning with vowel sounds (*an egg, an hour, an MP*), and sometimes used before words beginning with *h* in unstressed syllable (*an historical novel, an hypothesis*).

ăn² *conj.* (arch. or dial.) if. [ME weakening of AND]

an- *pref.* **1.** f. OE, ME *an* = on (*anon, anent*). **2.** assim. form of AD- before *n.* **3.** f. Gk ANA- (*anode*). **4.** f. Gk *an-* = *a-* not (A- 7) (*anarchy*).

-an *suf.* forming *adjs.* (often used as *ns.*) esp. f. names of places, systems, Zool. classes or orders, and founders (*Australasian, Chilean, Anglican, crustacean, crocodilian, Lutheran*); cf. also -ANE, -EAN, -IAN, -ICIAN. [f. or after F -*ain*, -(*i*)*en* or f. L -*anus*]

a'na (ah'-) *n.* **1.** (as *pl.*) anecdotes, literary gossip, about a person. **2.** (as *sing.*) collection of person's memorable sayings. [= -ANA]

äna- *pref.* (usu. **an-** bef. vowel) w. sense 'up' (*androm ous*), 'back' (*anamnesis*), 'again' (*anabaptism*). [f. Gk an up]

-a'na (ah'-) *suf.* forming *pl. ns.*, w. sense 'anecdotes o publications or other items concerning persons places, or topics' (*Shakespeareana, Victoriana, Americana cricketana*). [neut. pl. of L -*anus*; cf. -AN]

ănabă'pt|ĭsm *n.* (Hist.) doctrine that persons bap tized as infants should be rebaptized as adults; se ～IST (2) *n.* [f. eccl. L f. Gk ANA(*baptismos* BAPTISM)]

ă'nabăs *n.* perchlike freshwater fish of genus *Anabas* able to leave water and ascend trees. [mod. L, f. Gk pres. part. of *anabainō* walk up]

ană'bas|ĭs *n.* (*pl.* ～es *pr.* -ēz). up-country march, esp that of Cyrus the younger into Asia, narrated b Xenophon. [Gk, = ascent, f. ANA(*bainō* go)]

ănabă'tĭc *a.* (Meteorol.) (Of wind) caused by ai flowing upwards; cf. KATABATIC. [f. Gk *anabatiko* ascending (as prec.; see -IC)]

ănabĭ|ō'sĭs *n.* (*pl.* -oses *pr.* -ō'sēz). (Biol.) ability t regain life after apparent death by drying etc.; state o reduced animation; so ～o'tic *a.* [mod. L, f. G *anabiōsis* (ANA*bioō* return to life; see -OSIS)]

ană'bolism *n.* (Biol.) constructive metabolism synthesis of complex substances for body tissues etc (opp. CATABOLISM); so **ănabō'lĬc** *a.* [f. Gk ANA(*bolē* *ballō* throw) ascent +-ISM]

ă'nabranch (-ahn-) *n.* (esp. Austral.) stream tha leaves river and re-enters it lower down. [f. ANASTO MOSE + BRANCH¹]

ănachrŏ'nĭc (-k-) *a.* involving anachronism; out o date. [f. foll. after *synchronic* etc.]

ană'chron|ĭsm (-k-) *n.* error in computing of time person or thing out of harmony with the time; relatin of an event, custom, or circumstance to a wrong period of time; hence ～ĭ'stĬc *a.* [f. F *anachronisme* or f Gk ANA(*khronismos* f. *khronos* time; see -ISM]

ănacolū'th|on *n.* (*pl.* ～a). sentence or construction lacking grammatical sequence; hence ～ĬC *a.* [LL, f Gk *anakolouthon* (as AN- 4, *akolouthos* following)]

ănacŏ'nda *n.* large tropical S. Amer. aquatic anc arboreal boa. [alt. of *anacondaia* f. Sinh. *henakandaye* whip-snake (*hena* lightning, *kanda* stem); orig. of snake in Sri Lanka (Ceylon)]

anăcrĕŏ'ntĭc *a.* & *n.* **1.** (poem) after the manner of Anacreon. **2.** *a.* convivial and amatory in tone. [f. L *anacreonticus* f. Gk *Anakreōn -ont-* Anacreon, Gk lyric poet à. 478 BC]

ănacru's|ĭs (-ōō'-) *n.* (*pl.* ～es *pr.* -ēz). (Pros.' unstressed syllable at beginning of verse; (Mus.' unstressed note(s) before first bar-line. [f. Gk ANA (*krousis* f. *krouō* strike)]

ană'dromous *a.* (Of fish) ascending rivers from sea to spawn. [f. Gk ANA(*dromos* -running) +-OUS]

anae'm|ia, *anē'm|ia, *n.* (Med.) deficiency of red blood-corpuscles or their haemoglobin, often causing pallor; PERNICIOUS *anaemia*; hence ～ĬC *a.* (lit., or fig. lacking vigour etc.). [mod. L, f. Gk *anaimia* (as AN- 4 -AEMIA)]

anaerōbe (anăr'-, ă'-) *n.* micro-organism that can on must live without free oxygen from the air; hence **ănaerō'bĬc** (-āī'-) *a.* [f. F *anaérobie* f. as AN- 4+ AEROBE]

ănaesthē'si|a (ănĭs-), ***ănĕs-,** (-zīa) *n.* absence o sensation, esp. artificially induced insensitivity to pain; hence ～ĭ'oLGY *n.* [mod. L, f. Gk *anaisthēsia* (as AN- 4, *aisthēsis* sensation; see -IA¹)]

ănaesthĕ'tĭc (ănĭs-), ***ănĕs-,** *a.* & *n.* (agent) that produces partial or complete insensitivity to pain etc.; **general** ～ (affecting whole body, usu. with loss of consciousness); **local** ～ (affecting limited part of body). [f. Gk *anaisthētos* insensible (as prec.) +-IC]

anae'sthet|ĭze, -īse (-ĭz), ***anē's-,** *v.t.* deprive of sensation (lit. or fig.); administer anaesthetic to; hence ～IST (1), ～IZA'TION, *ns.* [f. as prec. +-IZE]

ă'naglÿph *n.* embossed ornament in low relief; (Photog.) composite stereoscopic picture printed in

superimposed complementary colours; hence **ănagly'ph**ıc a. [f. Gk ANA(gluphē f. gluphō carve)]
nagnō'ris|is n. (pl. ~es pr. -ēz). recognition, dénouement in drama. [Gk anagnōrisis]
nagō'gē n. spiritual, allegorical, or mystical interpretation; hence **ănagō'g**ıc(AL) adjs. [eccl. L f. Gk, f. inagō lead up (AN- 3)]
'nagrăm n. transposition of letters of word or phrase, to form new word or phrase; hence or cogn. **ănagrammă'tı**c(AL) adjs., **ănagrä'mmat**ıze (1) v.t. [f. F anagramme or mod L anagramma, f. Gk ANA-+gramma -atos letter; cf. -GRAM]
'nal a. pertaining to or situated near the anus. [f. mod. L analis (as ANUS; see -AL)]
'nalĕcts, ănalĕ'cta, n. pl. literary gleanings. [L f. Gk analekta things gathered (ANAlegō pick up)]
nalĕ'ptic a. & n. restorative (medicine). [f. Gk analēptikos (ANAlambanō take back; see -ıc)]
nălgē'sıa (-z-, -s-) n. absence or relief of pain; so **ănălgē's**ıc a. & n., (drug) producing analgesia. [mod. L, f. Gk, = painlessness]
ä'nalōg. See ANALOGUE.
nalō'gıc a. of analogy. [f. F analogique or f. L f. Gk analogikos (as ANALOGUE; see -ıc)]
nalō'gıcal a. according to analogy; expressing an analogy; hence ~LY² adv. [f. as prec.; see -ıCAL]
nă'logıst n. one who argues from or seeks analogies. [f. foll. +-ıST]
nă'logıze, -ıse (-īz), v. 1. v.t. represent by analogy; show to be analogous. 2. v.i. Use analogy; be in harmony (with). [f. ANALOGY +-ıZE]
nă'logous a. similar, parallel, (to); showing analogy; hence ~LY² adv., ~NESS n. [f. L f. Gk analogos proportionate +-ous]
'nalŏgue (-g), *ă'nalŏg, n.** analogous or parallel word or thing (e.g. narrative); ~ **computer,** one using physical quantities (voltage, weight, length, etc.) to represent numbers. [F, f. Gk analogon neut. adj. (see prec.)]
nă'logÿ n. agreement, similarity, (to, with, between); analogue; (Logic) process of reasoning from parallel cases; (Philol.) imitation of existing words in forming inflexions or constructions of others, without the existence of corresponding intermediate stages; (Biol.) resemblance of function between organs essentially different. [f. F analogie or f. L f. Gk analogia proportion (as ANALOGOUS; see -Y¹)]
'nalȳs|e (-z), *ă'nalȳz|e, v.t.** examine minutely the constitution of; = PSYCHOANALYSE; (Chem.) ascertain constituents of (sample of mixture or compound); find or show the essence or structure of (book, music, etc.); (Gram.) resolve (sentence) into its grammatical elements; hence ~ABLE a., ~AND¹ n., person undergoing psychoanalysis, ~ER¹ n. [f. obs. analyse n. or f. F analyser (analyse n. f. med. L ANALYSIS)]
nă'lÿsis n. (pl. ana'lyses pr. -sēz). 1. resolution into simpler elements by analysing (opp. synthesis); statement of result of this; **in the final, last, ultimate,** ~, after all due consideration, in the end; **bowling** ~, (Cricket) statement usu. of overs and maiden overs bowled, runs conceded, and wickets taken, by bowler. 2. (Math.) use of algebra and calculus in problem-solving. 3. = PSYCHOANALYSIS. [med. L, f. Gk ANA(lusis f. luō set free)]
'nalÿst n. one skilled in (esp. chemical) analysis; = PSYCHOANALYST. [f. F analyste (analyser ANALYSE), after ns. in -iste -ıST f. vbs in -iser -ıZE)]
nalÿ'tıc a. pertaining to analysis; (Philol.) analytical. [f. LL f. Gk analutikos (as ANALYSIS; see -ıc)]
nalÿ'tical a. employing analytic methods; (Philol.) using separate words instead of inflexions; ~ **geometry** (using coordinates); hence ~LY² adv. [f. as prec.; see -ıCAL]
ä'nalÿze. See ANALYSE.
namnē's|is n. (pl. ~es pr. -ēz). recollection (esp. of a previous existence); patient's account of his medical history. [Gk, = remembrance]

ănamŏr'phos|is n. (pl. ~es pr. -ēz). distorted drawing or picture appearing regular from one point; so **ănamŏr'ph**ıc a. [Gk (ANAmorphoō transform f. morphē form; see -OSIS)]
ana'nas (-ah'n-) n. pineapple; pinguin. [F or Sp., f. Guarani anănă]
ană'ndrous a. (Bot.) having no stamens. [f. Gk anandros without males (an- not, anēr andros male) +-ous]
ä'napaest, *-pēst, n. (Pros.) foot consisting of two short syllables followed by one long; so **ănapae'st**ıc a. [f. L f. Gk ANA(paistos f. paiō strike) reversed (because reverse of dactyl)]
ănă'phora n. 1. (Rhet.) repetition of word or phrase at beginning of successive clauses; use of word referring to or replacing earlier word(s) (e.g. DO¹ 9), whence **ănaphŏ'r**ıc a. 3. (Eccl.) part of Eucharistic service where oblation is made. [L f. Gk, = repetition (as ANA-, pherō carry)]
ănăphrodi'sıăc (-z-) a. & n. (drug) reducing sexual desire. [f. AN- 4 + as APHRODISIAC]
ănaphȳlă'|xis n. (pl. ~xes pr. -ksēz). (Med.) hypersensitivity of tissues to second dose of antigen; hence ~ctıc a. [mod. L, f. F anaphylaxie f. as ANA-+Gk phulaxis guarding]
ănaptÿ'|xis n. (pl. ~xes pr. -ksēz). (Phonet.) development of vowel between two consonants (she went thataway); hence ~ctıc a. [mod. L, Gk ANA(ptuxis f. ptussō fold)]
ä'nărch (-k) n. 1. anarchist. 2. (poet.) leader of revolt. [f. Gk anarchos leaderless (as AN- 4, -arkhos ruling f. arkhō to rule)]
ä'narch|ÿ (-kī) n. absence of government in a society; political or social disorder; hence **anăr'ch**ıc(AL) (-k-) adjs., ~ISM (3), ~IST (2), ns., (adherent of) doctrine that all government should be abolished, ~ı'st**ıc a. [f. med. L f. Gk anarkhia (anarkhos; see prec.)]
ănastıgmă'tıc a. free from astigmatism; so [by backform. thr. G] **ănă'stıgmăt** n., lens, or lens-system made anastigmatic by correction. [f. AN- 4 +ASTIGMATIC]
ănastomō's|is n. (pl. ~es pr. -ēz). cross-connection of arteries, branches, rivers, etc.; so **ană'stomose** (-z) v.i., communicate by anastomosis. [mod. L f. Gk, f. ANAstomoō furnish with mouth (stoma); see -OSIS]
ană'strophe n. (Rhet.) inversion of usual order of words or clauses. [Gk ANA(strophē f. strephō to turn) turning back]
ană'thema n. accursed thing; curse of God; curse of Church, excommunicating a person or denouncing a doctrine; imprecation; detested thing or person (he, it, is anathema to me); so ~tıze v.t. & i., curse. [eccl. L f. excommunicated person, excommunication, L f. Gk = excommunicated thing devoted, (later) accursed thing (ANAtithēmi set up)]
ănatŏ'mical a. belonging to anatomy; structural; hence ~LY² adv. [f. F anatomique or f. LL anatomicus (as ANATOMY, -ıC); see -ıCAL]
ană'tomist n. dissecter of dead bodies; person skilled in anatomy; (fig.) analyser. [f. F anatomiste or med. L *anatomista as foll.; see -ıST]
ană'tomīze, -ıse (-īz), v.t. dissect; (fig.) analyse. [f. F anatomiser or med. L anatomizare f. anatomia (see foll., -ıZE)]
ană'tom|ÿ n. dissection of human body, animals, or plants; (science of) bodily structure of human beings, animals, or plants; (joc.) human body; (fig.) analysis. [f. F anatomie f. L f. LL f. Gk anatomia (as ANA-, -TOMY)]
ä'nburÿ n. soft tumour of horse or ox; disease of root-plants. [perh. f. ang- (cf. AGNAIL) +BERRY¹]
-ance suf. forming ns. of quality (or instance of it) (arrogance, protuberance, relevance, resemblance) or action (assistance, furtherance, penance). [f. or after F -ance f. L -antia, -entia; see -ANT, -ENT]
ä'ncĕst|or n. any person from whom one's father or mother is descended, forefather; hence ~RESS¹ n.

[ME, f. OF *ancestre* f. L *antecessor -oris* f. ANTE(*cedere cess-* go); see -OR]

ancĕ′stral *a.* belonging to or inherited from ancestors. [f. F *ancestral*; see prec., -AL]

ă′ncĕstrý *n.* (lineage of) ancestors, esp. noble or aristocratic; ancient descent. [ME, alt. f. OF *ancesserie* (as ANCESTOR; see -Y[1])]

ă′nchor[1] (-k-) *n.* **1.** heavy metal structure used to moor ship to sea-bottom etc. or balloon etc. to ground (at ∼, thus moored; **cast, come to,** (let down), **weigh** (take up), ∼; SHEET[3]-*anchor*); (fig.) source of confidence. **2.** ∼**man,** one playing vital part (at back of tug-of-war team, as last runner in relay race, as compère in broadcast programme, etc.); ∼**-plate,** heavy piece of timber or metal, e.g. as support for suspension-bridge cables; ∼**-ring,** TORUS (sense 4) of circular cross-section. [f. OE *ancor* etc. & OF *ancre* f. L *ancora* f. Gk *agkura*]

ă′nchor[2] (-k-) *v.* **1.** *v.t.* secure (ship) by means of anchor; fix firmly (lit. or fig.). **2.** *v.i.* cast anchor; be moored by means of anchor. [ME, f. OF *ancrer* f. med. L *anc(h)orare*]

ă′nchorage (-k-) *n.* (place for) anchoring; lying at anchor; (fig.) thing to depend upon. [f. ANCHOR[1] + -AGE]

ă′nchor|īte, ă′nchor|ĕt, (-k-) *n.* hermit, recluse; person of secluded habits; hence or cogn. ∼ESS[1] *n.,* ∼ĕ′tIC, ∼ĭ′tIC, *adjs.* [ME, f. med. L *anc(h)orita,* eccl. L *anchoreta* f. eccl. Gk *anakhōrētēs* (ANAkhōreō retire); see -ET[2]]

ănchově′ta *n.* small Pacific anchovy caught for use as bait or to make fish-meal. [Sp., dim. of *anchova* (cf. foll.)]

anchový (ă′ncho-, ănchō′-) *n.* small fish of herring family with rich flavour; ∼ **pear,** W. Ind. fruit like mango; ∼ **toast** (spread with paste made from anchovies). [f. Sp. & Port. *ancho(v)a,* of uncert. orig.]

ănchu′sa (-kū′-, -chōō′-) *n.* plant of genus *Anchusa,* akin to borage; related plant, e.g. bugloss. [L, f. Gk *agkhousa*]

anchylose etc. Var. of ANKYLOSE etc.

ancien régime (ahṅsyăṅ rāzhē′m) *n.* (*pl.* **-ns -es** *pr.* same). system of government in France before the Revolution; (transf.) a superseded regime. [F, = old rule]

ă′ncient[1] (-shĕnt) *a. & n.* **1.** *a.* belonging to times long past; ∼ **history** (esp. before fall of Western Roman Empire in 476, (fig.) something already long familiar); hence ∼LY[2] *adv.,* long ago. **2.** having existed, or lived, long; ∼ **lights,** window that neighbour may not deprive of light by building; ||∼ **monument,** old building etc. preserved usu. under Government control. **3.** *n.* (arch.) old man. **4. the A**∼ **of Days,** God; **the** ∼**s,** civilized nations of antiquity, esp. Greeks and Romans. **5.** Hence ∼NESS *n.* [ME f. AF *auncien,* f. OF *ancien,* f. Rom. **anti-, anteanus* (*ante* before; see -AN)]

ă′ncient[2] (-shĕnt) *n.* (arch.) = ENSIGN. [corrupt. of form *ensyne* etc. by assoc. w. *ancien* = prec.]

ănci′llarý *a.* subservient, subordinate, (*to*). [f. L *ancillaris* (*ancilla* maidservant; see -ARY[2])]

ă′ncon *n.* (Archit.) console, usu. of two volutes, (apparently) supporting cornice. [L, f. Gk *agkōn* elbow]

-ancÿ *suf.* forming *ns.* denoting quality (*constancy, relevancy*) or state (*expectancy, infancy*), but not action (cf. -ANCE). [f. or after L *-antia* (cf. -ENCY)]

and (and, an, or, when stressed, ănd) *conj.* (connecting words, clauses, or sentences, that are to be taken jointly; *cakes and buns; white and brown bread; buy and sell; two hundred and forty*); *better* ∼ (steadily) *better; she cried* ∼ *cried* (cried for a long time); *and* ALL; GOOD *and; miles* ∼ (very many) *miles;* NICE *and;* TRY *and; there are books* ∼ (different kinds of, good and bad) *books; two* ∼ *two,* (1) two added to two, (2) by twos; *move* ∼ (= if you move) *I shout; Britain and* (= in relation to) *the Common Market; A* **and/or** *B,* A or B or both. [OE *and,* = OS *anda, endi,* OHG *anti, enti,* f. IE *nṭha]

-ănd *suf.* See -ND[1].

ăndă′ntĕ *adv., a., & n.* (Mus.) (movement) moderately slow time. [It., part. of *andare* go]

ăndanti′nō (-tē′-) *adv., a., & n.* (*pl.* ∼**s**). (Mus. (movement) rather quicker (orig. slower) tha andante. [It., dim. of prec.]

ă′ndiron (-īern) *n.* metal stand for supporting burnin wood on hearth etc., FIRE[1]dog. [ME, f. OF *andier,* unkn. orig.; assim. to IRON[1]]

ăndroe′ci|um (-rē′-) *n.* (*pl.* ∼**a**). (Bot.) stamens take collectively. [mod. L, f. Gk *andro-* male + *oikion* house

ă′ndrogen *n.* male sex hormone or other substanc capable of developing and maintaining certain ma sexual characteristics; hence **ăndrogĕ′n**IC *a.* [f. G *andro-* male + -GEN]

ă′ndrogȳne *a. & n.* hermaphrodite (person). [OF, c f. L f. Gk *androgunos* (*anēr andros* male, *gunē* woman)

ăndrŏ′gȳn|ous *a.* hermaphrodite, whence ∼y[1] *n* (Bot.) with stamens and pistils in same flower c inflorescence. [f. prec. + -OUS]

ă′ndroid *n.* robot with apparently human form. [f Gk *andro-* male, man + -OID]

-ă′ndrous *suf.* (Bot.) forming *adjs.* w. sense 'havin specified male organs or stamens' (*monandrous*). [f mod. L f. Gk *-andros* (*anēr andros* male) + -OUS]

-āne *suf.* **1.** Var. of -AN, usu, w. differentiation (*germane humane, urbane*) but occas. alone (*mundane*). **2.** (Chem forming names of paraffins and other saturate hydrocarbons (*methane, propane*) [after -ene, -ine, etc.]

anear′ *adv. & prep.* (arch.) = NEAR[1]. [f. A-+NEAR[1]

ă′nĕcdōtage *n.* anecdotes; (joc., after *dotage*) garrul ous old age. [f. foll. + -AGE]

ă′nĕcdōt|e *n.* narrative (or painting etc.) of amusin or interesting incident; hence ∼(**al**)IST (3) *n.,* ∼AI ∼IC (-dŏ-), *adjs.* [F, or f. mod. L f. Gk *anekdota* thing unpublished (as AN- 4, *ekdotos* f. *ekdidōmi* publish)]

ănĕchō′ĭc (-kō′-) *a.* free from echo. [f. AN- 4 + ECHO[1] + -IC]

anē′le *v.t.* (arch.) anoint; give extreme unction tc [ME, f. AN- 1 + *elien* f. OE *ele* f. L *oleum* oil]

*anē′mia. See ANAEMIA.

anē′mo|graph (-ahf) *n.* instrument for recording o paper the direction and force of wind; henc ∼**grä′ph**IC *a.* [f. Gk *anemos* wind + -GRAPH]

ănĕmŏ′mĕter *n.* instrument for measuring force o wind; hence **ănĕmomĕ′tr**IC *a.,* **ănĕmŏ′metry** *n.* [f as prec. + -METER]

anĕ′monĕ *n.* plant of genus *Anemone,* akin to butter cup; **sea** ∼, large polyp with petal-like tentacle round mouth; **wood** ∼, wild kind of anemone, wind -flower. [f. L f. Gk *anemōnē* wind-flower (*anemos* wind)

ănĕmŏ′philous *a.* wind-pollinated. [f. Gk *anemo* wind + -PHILOUS]

anĕ′nt *prep.* (arch., joc., or Sc.) concerning. [OE ∼ *efen* on a level with]

-ā′nĕous *suf.* forming *adjs.* (*cutaneous, miscellaneous*). [f L *-aneus* + -OUS]

ă′neroid *a. & n.* (barometer) that measures air -pressure by its action on elastic lid of evacuated box not by height of fluid column. [f. F *anéroïde* f. Gk *a* not + *nēros* wet; see -OID]

*anesthesia, etc. See ANAESTHESIA, etc.

aneur′in (-nūr′-) *n.* vitamin B[1]. [f. anti- + polyneuriti + vitamin]

ă′neurȳsm, -ism, (-nūr′-) *n.* morbid dilatation of ar artery; hence **ăneurȳ′sm**AL, **-ĭ′sm**AL, (-nūrī′z-) *a* [f. Gk *aneurusma* (*aneurunō* widen out f. *eurus* wide)]

anew′ *adv.* again; in a different way. [ME, f. A- (3) + NEW[1]]

ănfrăctŭŏ′sitý *n.* circuitousness, intricacy, (lit. or fig.). [f. F *anfractuosité* f. LL *anfractuosus* f. L *anfractus* a bending; see -OSITY]

ă′ngarý (ă′ngg-) *n.* (Law). belligerent's right (subjec to compensation of loss) of seizing or destroying neutral property under military necessity. [f. F *angarie* f. L or LL *angaria* forced service f. Gk *aggareia* (*aggaros* courier f. Pers. *angaros*)]

angel (-nj-) *n.* **1.** divine attendant or messenger (good, evil, ~, attendant spirits; GUARDIAN *angel*); one of the lowest ORDER[1] of ninefold celestial hierarchy; **on the side of the ~s,** favouring the pleasanter or more spiritual view of a question, believing that good will prevail. **2.** lovely or innocent being; obliging or loving person; (sl.) financial backer of (esp. theatrical) enterprise; unexplained radar echo; ~(-**noble**), old English gold coin bearing figure of archangel Michael piercing dragon. **3.** ~ **cake,** ~ **food,** very light sponge cake; ~**fish,** one of various fish with winglike fins; ~**s, devils, -on-horseback,** savoury of oysters wrapped in slices of bacon. [ME, f. OF *angele* f. eccl. L *angelus* f. Gk *aggelos* messenger]

ange'lic (-nj-) *a.* pertaining to angels; like an angel in beauty or sublimity or power; **A~ Doctor,** St. Thomas Aquinas; hence ~AL *a.,* ~ALLY *adv.* [ME, f. F *angélique* or f. LL f. Gk *aggelikos* (as prec.; see -IC)]

ange'lica (-nj-) *n.* aromatic umbelliferous plant, used in cooking and medicine; its candied stalks. [f. med. L (*herba*) *angelica* angelic herb]

a'ngelus (-nj-) *n.* devotional exercise commemorating Incarnation, said by Roman Catholics at morning, noon, and sunset, at sound of ~ **bell.** [f. opening words *Angelus domini* (L, = the angel of the Lord)]

a'nger[1] (ă'ngg-) *n.* extreme displeasure. [ME, f. ON *angr* grief (**ang* narrow)]

a'nger[2] (ă'ngg-) *v.t.* make angry, enrage. [ME, f. ON *angra* vex (as prec.)]

A'ngevin (ă'nj-) *a. & n.* (native or inhabitant) of Anjou; (one) of the Plantagenets, including English kings from Henry II to Richard II. [F]

angi'na (pě'ctoris) (-nj-) *n.* pain in chest resulting from over-exertion when heart is diseased. [L, = spasm of the chest (*angina* quinsy f. Gk *agkhonē* strangling)]

a'ngiosperm (-nj-) *n.* flowering plant, with enclosed seeds, opp. *gymnosperm*; hence ~OUS (-ĕr'-) *a.* [f. Gk *aggeion* vessel + *sperma* seed]

a'ngle[1] (ă'nggel) *n.* space between two meeting lines or planes; inclination of two lines to each other (ACUTE, OBTUSE, RIGHT[1], *angle*); corner; sharp projection; direction from which photograph etc. is taken; (fig.) aspect from which a matter is considered; ~ **brackets,** brackets ⟨ ⟩ (see BRACKET[1] 2); ~**dozer,** bulldozer with blade set obliquely; ~**-iron,** piece of iron with L-shaped cross-section to strengthen framework; ~**-parking** (of cars obliquely to roadside). [ME f. OF, or f. L *angulus* dim. of **angus*]

a'ngle[2] (ă'nggel) *v.t. & i.* move or place obliquely; (colloq.) present (news etc.) from particular viewpoint; hence **a'ngl**ED[2] (ă'nggeld) *a.,* placed obliquely, having an angle (also in *comb.*). [f. prec.]

a'ngle[3] (ă'nggel) *n., & v.i.* **1.** *n.* (arch.) fish-hook; **brother of the ~,** angler. **2.** *v.i.* fish with hook and bait (*for,* or abs.; lit., or fig.: *angle for compliments, votes,* etc.). [OE *angul,* = OS, OHG *angul,* ON *öngull*]

A'ngle[4] (ă'nggel) *n.* member of tribe from Schleswig that settled in Eastern Britain in 5th c.; hence ~IAN *a.* [f. L *Anglus* f. Gmc **angli-* (OE *Engle;* cf. ENGLISH[1]). *Angul* a district of Schleswig (now in N. Germany) (as prec.)]

a'ngler (ă'ngg-) *n.* one who fishes with hook and line; ~(-**fish**), one of various fishes that prey upon small fish, attracting them by filaments attached to head and mouth. [f. ANGLE[3] + -ER[1]]

A'nglican (ă'ngg-) *a. & n.* (adherent) of the reformed Church of England or of any church in communion with it; hence ~ISM (3) *n.* [f. med. L *Anglicanus* (Magna Carta) f. *Anglicus* (Bede). Angl. ANGLE[4]]

a'nglice (ă'ngg-) *adv.* in English. [med. L]

A'nglicism (ă'ngg-) *n.* English idiom; Englishness; preference for what is English. [f. L *Anglicus* (see ANGLICAN) + -ISM]

A'nglicize, -ise, (ă'ngglĭsīz) *v.t.* make English in form or character. [f. as prec. + -IZE]

A'nglist (ă'ngg-) *n.* student of or scholar in English language or literature; hence **Angli'stics** (ăngg-) *n.* [G, f. L *Anglus* English; see -IST]

Anglo- (ăngg-) *comb. form.* English (*Anglo-Catholic*); of English origin (*an Anglo-American*); English or British and (*an Anglo-American agreement*). [mod. L, f. L *Anglus* English; see -O-]

Anglo-Ca'tholic (ăngg-) *a. & n.* (member) of party holding that the Church of England is a branch of the Catholic Church and rejecting its Protestant element. [f. prec. + CATHOLIC]

Angloce'ntric (ăngg-) *a.* centred on England. [f. ANGLO- + -CENTRIC]

Anglo-Fre'nch (ăngg-) *a. & n.* **1.** (of) French language as retained and separately developed in England after Norman Conquest. **2.** *a.* English (or British) and French. [f. ANGLO- + FRENCH]

Anglo-I'ndian (ăngglōi'-) *a. & n.* (person) of British birth but living or having lived long in India; (person) of mixed British and Indian parentage; (of word) adopted into English from an Indian language. [f. ANGLO- + INDIAN]

Anglo-La'tin (ăngg-) *a. & n.* (of) Latin as used in medieval England. [f. ANGLO- + LATIN]

Angloma'nia (ăngg-) *n.* excessive admiration of English customs; so **AngloMA'NIAC, A'ngloPHIL**(E), **A'nglo**PHOBE *n. & adjs.,* **AngloPHO'BIA** *n.,* (ăngg-). [f. ANGLO- + -MANIA]

Anglo-No'rman (ăngg-) *a. & n.* (of the) dialect of Normans as used in England after Norman Conquest. [f. ANGLO- + NORMAN]

a'nglophone (ăngg-) *a. & n.* English-speaking (person). [f. ANGLO-, after FRANCOPHONE]

Anglo-Sa'xon (ăngg-) *n. & a.* English Saxon (as distinct from Old Saxons of the continent); Old English (person, language) before Norman Conquest; **modern English, (colloq.) plain English; (person) of English descent (wherever found); hence ~ISM (2, 3, 4) *n.* [f. mod. L *Anglo-Saxones,* med. L *Angli Saxones* after OE *Angulseaxe, -an*]

ango'ra, (arch.) **ăngō'la,** (ăngg-) *n.* fabric made from hair of angora goat; ~ **cat, goat, rabbit,** (long--haired varieties); ~ (**wool**), mixture of sheep's wool and angora rabbit hair. [f. *Angora* (Ankara) in Turkey; *angola* is a corruption]

ăngostu'ra (ăngg-) *n.* ~ **bark,** aromatic bark formerly used as febrifuge and tonic; **A~ Bitters,** (P) kind of tonic first made in Angostura. [f. *Angostura,* town in Venezuela on the Orinoco, now Ciudad Bolívar]

a'ngrly̌ (ă'ngg-) *a.* showing anger, extremely displeased, resentful, (*at, about,* thing; *at, with,* person; *that, to find* etc.); (fig.) seeming to show anger (*an angry sky*); irritable; (of wound, sore, etc.) inflamed, painful; hence ~ILY[2] *adv.* [ME, f. ANGER[1] + -Y[1]]

angst (ă-) *n.* anxiety; feeling of guilt or remorse. [G]

a'ngström (ă'ngstrĕrm, ŏ'ng-) *n.* unit of wavelength measurement, 10^{-10} metre. [f. A. J. *Ångström,* Swedish physicist d. 1874]

a'nguine (ă'ngg-) *a.* snakelike. [f. L *anguinus* (*anguis* snake); see -INE[1]]

a'nguish (ă'nggw-) *n.* severe bodily or mental pain. [ME, f. OF *anguisse* choking f. L *angustia* tightness (*angustus* narrow); cf. -ISH[2]]

a'nguished (ă'nggwĭsht) *a.* suffering or expressing anguish. [p.p. of *anguish* v. f. OF *anguissier* f. eccl. L *angustiare* to distress f. as prec.]

a'ngular (ă'ngg-) *a.* **1.** having angles; sharp-cornered; lacking plumpness, smoothness, or suavity. **2.** placed in or at an angle; measured by angle (*angular distance;* ~ **momentum,** quantity of rotation of a body, product of its moment of inertia and angular velocity; ~ **velocity,** rate of change of angular position of rotating body). **3.** Hence ~ITY (-ă'r-) *n.,* ~LY[2] *adv.* [f. L *angularis* (*angulus* ANGLE[1]; see -AR[1])]

ănhe'dral *a. & n.* **1.** (Aeron.) (having) negative dihedral angle. **2.** *a.* (Of crystal etc.) not having normal external form. [f. AN- 4 + -HEDRAL]

änhȳ′dride n. (Chem.) substance obtained by removing the elements of water from a compound, esp. from an acid. [f. as foll. + -IDE]

änhȳ′dr|ous a. (Chem.) without water, esp. water of crystallization; so ∼ITE[1] (2) n., anhydrous calcium sulphate. [f. Gk *anudros* (as AN- 4, *hudōr* water) + -OUS]

änĭcŏ′nĭc a. (Of idol, symbol, etc.) not shaped in human or animal form. [f. AN- 4 + ICONIC]

ä′nĭcŭt, ä′nn-, n. river-dam in S. India built for irrigation purposes. [f. Tamil *aṇai-kaṭṭu* dam-building]

anī′gh (-ī′) adv. & prep. (arch.) = NEAR[1]. [f. NIGH after *anear*]

ä′nīle a. old-womanish; imbecile; so **anī′l**ITY n. [f. L *anilis* (*anus* old woman; see -IL)]

ä′nīline (-ēn, -īn) n. oily liquid got from coal tar, an organic base; ∼ **dye,** (1) one of numerous dyes made from aniline, (2) any synthetic dye. [f. G *anilin* f. *anil* indigo (whence orig. obtained) f. F or Port. f. Arab. *an-nīl* (*al* the, *nīl* f. Skr. *nīlī* indigo f. *nīla* dark blue); see -INE[5]]

ä′nĭma n. (Psych.) inner personality (opp. *persona*); feminine part of a man's personality. [L, = mind, soul]

änĭmadvē̄r′|t v.i. pass criticism or censure *on* (conduct, fault, etc.); so ∼SION (-shon) n. [f. L *animadvertere* f. *animus* mind + AD(*vertere vers-* turn)]

ä′nĭmal n. & a. **1.** n. organized being endowed (more or less perceptibly) with life, sensation, and voluntary motion; (esp.) such being other than man; (colloq.) **there is no such** ∼ (person or thing). **2.** quadruped; a brutish man. **3.** a. characteristic of animals; ∼ **magnetism,** (Hist.) mesmerism; ∼ **spirits,** natural exuberance. **4.** of animals as opp. to vegetables (*animal charcoal*); carnal, sensual. [L, f. *animale* neut. of *animalis* having breath (*anima* breath; see -AL)]

änĭma′lcŭle n. microscopic animal. [f. mod. L *animalculum* (*animal*; see prec., -CULE)]

ä′nĭmalism n. animal activity; sensuality; doctrine that humans are mere animals. [f. ANIMAL + -ISM]

änĭma′lĭtȳ n. animal nature or system; merely animal nature; the animal world. [f. F *animalité* f. L *animalita* a.; see -ITY)]

ä′nĭmalĭz|e, -īs|e (-īz), v.t. convert to animal substance; sensualize; hence ∼A′TION n. [f. ANIMAL + -IZE]

anima mundi (änĭma mŭ′ndī) n. power supposed to organize and regulate the material universe. [med. L, = soul of the world]

ä′nĭmate[1] a. living; lively. [f. L *animatus* p.p. of *animare* give life to (*anima* life, soul); see -ATE[2]]

ä′nĭmāt|e[2] v.t. breathe life into; enliven, make lively (*an animated discussion*); give (film etc.) appearance of movement by using quick succession of gradually varying drawings; encourage; inspire, actuate; hence ∼ēdLY[2] adv., **änĭma′TION** n., (esp.) state of being alive, ardour, vivacity, ∼OR n., (Cinemat.) artist who prepares animated cartoons. [f. as prec. + -ATE[3]]

ä′nĭmé (-mā) n. one of various resins, esp. W. Ind. resin used in making varnish. [F, of uncert. orig.]

ä′nĭm|ism n. doctrine of *anima mundi*; attribution of living soul to plants, inanimate objects, and natural phenomena; hence ∼IST (2) n., ∼ĭ′stIC a. [f. L *anima* life, soul + -ISM]

änĭmŏ′sĭtȳ n. spirit of enmity (*against, between, towards*). [ME, f. OF *animosité* or f. LL *animositas* (*animosus* spirited f. as foll.; see -OSITY)]

ä′nĭmus n. animating spirit; animosity shown in speech or action; (Psych.) masculine part of a woman's personality. [L, = spirit, mind]

ä′nĭon n. ion with negative charge that moves towards anode in presence of electric field (opp. CATION). [f. ANA- + ION]

änĭŏ′nĭc a. of anion(s); having an active anion. [f. prec. + -IC]

ä′nĭse n. umbelliferous plant (*Pimpinella anisum*) with aromatic seeds (see foll.). [ME, f. OF *anis* f. L f. Gk *anison* anise, dill]

ä′nĭseed n. seed of anise, used to flavour liqueurs and sweets. [ME, f. prec. + SEED]

änĭsĕ′tte (-z-) n. liqueur flavoured with aniseed. [I dim. of *anis* ANISE; see -ETTE]

änĭsotrŏ′p|ĭc a. having physical properties (e.g elasticity) that depend on direction; hence ∼ICALL adv., **änĭsŏ′trop**Y[1] n. [f. AN- 4 + ISOTROPIC]

ä′nker n. (Hist.) (cask containing) quantity of about gal. of wine. [LG & Du., f. med. L *anc(h)eria*]

änkh (ängk) n. keylike cross used in ancient Egypt a symbol of life. [Egypt., = life, soul]

ä′nkle n., & v.i. **1.** n. joint connecting foot with leg slender part between this and calf; ∼ **sock,** short soc just covering ankle. **2.** v.i. (sl.) walk. [ME, f. ON *ankul-* f. Gmc *ank-* f. IE *ang-* (as in ANGLE[1])]

ä′nklĕt n. ornament or fetter for ankle; *ankle sock. [prec. + -LET, after *bracelet*]

ä′nkўlōse (-ōz) v.t. & i. stiffen or unite by ankylosis [back-form. f. foll. after *anastomose* etc.]

änkўl|ō′sĭs n. (pl. ∼**oses** pr. -ō′sēz). formation of sti joint by consolidation of articulating surfaces; grow ing together of separate bones; hence ∼o′TIC a. [mod L, f. Gk *agkulōsis* (*agkuloō* crook; see -OSIS)]

ä′nlăce n. (arch.) short tapering two-edged dagger [ME, of unkn. orig.]

ä′nna n. former coin of India and Pakistan, one -sixteenth of rupee. [f. Hind. *ānā*]

ä′nnal n. annals of one year; record of one item i chronicle. [back-form. f. ANNALS]

ä′nnal|ist n. writer of annals; hence ∼ĭ′stIC a. [foll. + -IST]

ä′nnals (-z) n. pl. narrative of events year by year historical records. [f. F *annales* or f. L *annales* (*libri* yearly (books) (*annus* year; see -AL)]

ä′nnātes (-ts) n. pl. (RC Ch.) first year's revenue of se or benefice, paid to Pope. [f. F *annate* f. med. L *annate* year's proceeds (*annus* year; see -ADE)]

an(n)ä′ttō, anä′tta, n. orange-red dye from pulp o Central Amer. fruit, used for colouring cheese etc. [Carib name of the fruit-tree]

annea′l v.t., & n. **1.** v.t. toughen (glass or metals) b heating and usu. slow cooling; (fig.) toughen. **2.** n treatment by annealing. [OE *onǣlan* (on AN- 1, *ǣlar* burn, bake f. *āl* fire]

annĕ′ctent a. (Biol.) connecting (*annectent link*). [f. L *annectere* (see ANNEX[1], -ENT)]

ä′nnelid n. segmented worm of phylum Annelida, e.g earthworm; hence **annĕ′lid**AN a. & n. [f. F *annélide* o mod. L *annelida* pl. f. F *annelés* ringed animals (OF *ane* ring f. L *anellus* dim. of *anulus* ring)]

annĕ′x[1] v.t. add as subordinate part; append (*to book* etc.); take possession of (territory etc.), esp. (colloq.) take without right; attach as an attribute, addition, or consequence; so **ännĕx**A′TION n. [ME, f. OF *annexer* f. L AN(*nectere nex-* bind)]

ä′nnĕx[2], **-ĕxe,** n. addition to a document; (||usu. *-exe*) supplementary building, esp. for extra accommoda tion. [f. F *annexe* f. L *annexum* p.p. (as n.) of *annectere* bind; cf. prec.]

ä′nnĭcŭt. See ANICUT.

annī′hĭlāt|e (-nī′-) v.t. destroy largely or completely; (fig.) make insignificant; hence ∼OR n. [f. LL AN*nihilare* (*nihil* nothing) + -ATE[3]]

annĭhĭlā′tion (-nī′-) n. destruction etc. [f. prec.]; (Phys.) conversion of particle and antiparticle into radiation; (Theol.) destruction of soul as well as body, whence ∼ISM (2), ∼IST (2), ns. [F, or f. LL *annihilatio* (see prec., -ATION)]

annĭvē̄r′sarȳ n. yearly return of a date; celebration of this. [ME, f. L *anniversarius* (*annus* year, *versus* turned; see -ARY[1])]

Annō Dŏ′mĭnī (ă-) adv. & n. **1.** adv. in the year of our Lord, of the Christian era. **2.** n. (colloq.) advancing age (*suffering from Anno Domini*). [L, = in the year of the Lord]

ä′nnot|āte v.t. furnish (book etc.) with notes; hence or cogn. ∼ātABLE a., ∼A′TION n., ∼ātOR n. [f. L AN*notare* (*nota* mark) + -ATE[3]]

annou′nce v.t. make publicly known (*that*); make

known the approach of; make known (without words) to senses or mind, be sign of; hence ∼MENT (-sm-), **annou′ncer**[1] (esp. in broadcasting), *ns.* [ME, . OF *annoncer* f. L ANnuntiare (*nuntius* messenger)]

annoy′[1] *n.* (arch. or poet.) annoyance. [ME, f. OF anui, anoi f. Rom. **inodio* (see foll.)]

annoy′[2] *v.t.* **1.** cause slight anger or mental distress to; ɔe ∼ed (somewhat angry) *with* person, *about* or *at* hing, *that, to find* etc. **2.** molest, harass. **3.** So ∼ANCE *n.* ME, f. OF *anuier* etc., LL *inodiare*, f. Rom. **inodio* f. L *n odio* hateful]

annūal *a.* & *n.* **1.** & *n.* **1.** *a.* reckoned by the year; recurring yearly (∼ **ring**, ring in cross-section of tree, fish, etc., rom one year's growth); lasting for one year; hence ∼LY[2] *adv.* **2.** *n.* plant that lives only for a year; book etc. published in yearly numbers. [ME f. OF *annuel* f. LL *annualis* f. I. *annalis* (*annus* year; see -AL)]

annū′itant *n.* one who holds or receives an annuity. [f. oll. +-ANT, by assim. to *accountant* etc.]

annū′ity *n.* sum payable in respect of a particular year; yearly grant; investment of money entitling nvestor to series of equal annual sums. [ME, f. F annuité f. med. L *annuitas -tatis* f. L *annuus* yearly (as ANNUAL; see -ITY)]

annū′l *v.t.* (-ll-). abolish, cancel; declare invalid; hence ∼MENT *n.* [ME, f. OF *anuller* f. LL AN(*nullare* f. *nullus* none)]

′nnūlar *a.* ringlike; ∼ **eclipse** of sun (when moon, ɔrojected on sun's disc, leaves ring of light visible); hence ∼LY[2] *adv.* [f. F *annulaire* or f. L *annularis* *an*(*n*)*ulus* ring; see -AR[1])]

′nnūlate *a.* having, or marked with, or formed of, ings. [f. L *annulatus* (as ANNULUS; see -ATE[2])]

′nnūlet *n.* small ring; (Archit.) small fillet or band encircling column. [f. L (as foll.) +-ET[1]]

′nnūl|us *n.* (*pl.* ∼i *pr.* -ī). (esp. Math. & Biol.) ring. L *an*(*n*)*ulus*]

annū′nciāte (-shī-) *v.t.* proclaim; indicate as coming ɔr ready. [f. LL *annunciare* f. L *annuntiare* announce + ·ATE[3]]

annūnciā′tion *n.* announcement; (*A*∼) that of the Incarnation, made by Gabriel to Mary; (*A*∼) festival commemorating this, Lady Day, 25 March. [ME, f. ɔF *annonciation* f. LL *annuntiatio -onis* (as prec.; see ·ATION)]

annū′nciātor (-shī-) *n.* announcer; audible or visible ndicator of place where bell has been rung, position ɔf train, etc. [f. LL *annuntiator* (as prec.; see -OR)]

annus mirabilis (ănŭs mīrah′bĭlĭs) *n.* remarkable or auspicious year. [mod. L, = wonderful year]

nō′a *n.* small wild ox of Celebes. [name in Celebes]

′nōde *n.* (Electr.) positive electrode or terminal (opp. CATHODE); ∼ **ray**, beam of particles from anode of nigh-vacuum tube; hence **ā′nod**AL, **anō′d**IC, *adjs.* [f. Gk *anodos* way up (*ana* up, *hodos* way)]

′nodize, -ise (-īz), *v.t.* coat (metal) with protective ayer (e.g. of alumina) by making it anode in electrolysis. [f. ANODE +-IZE]

′nodȳne *a.* & *n.* (medicine etc.) able to assuage pain; anything) mentally soothing and harmless. [f. L f. Gk *anōdunos* painless (as AN- 4, *odunē* pain)]

nōē′s|is *n.* (*pl.* ∼es *pr.* -ēz). (Psych.) consciousness with sensation but without thought; so **ănōē′tic** *a.* [f. A- 7 + Gk *noēsis* understanding]

noi′nt *v.t.* apply ointment or oil to (esp. as religious ceremony at baptism or on consecration as priest or King); smear, rub; **the Lord's Anointed,** (1) Christ, (2) king by divine right. [ME, f. AF *anoint* a. f. OF *enoint* p.p. of *enoindre* f. L IN[1](*ungere* unct-)]

nōmali′stic *a.* (Astron.) of anomaly; ∼ **month** (between successive perigees of moon); ∼ **year** (between successive perihelia of earth). [f. Gk *anōmalos* (see foll.) +-IST +-IC]

nō′malous *a.* irregular; abnormal; hence ∼LY[2] *adv.*, ∼NESS *n.* [f. LL f. Gk *anōmalos* (as AN- 4, *homalos* even) +-OUS]

nō′malūre *n.* African rodent of genus *Anomalurus*,

with projecting scales on tail. [f. mod. L *anomalurus* f. Gk *anōmalos* ANOMALOUS + *oura* tail]

anō′malȳ *n.* irregularity of motion, behaviour, etc.; (Astron.) angular distance of planet or satellite from its last perihelion or perigee. [f. L f. Gk *anōmalia* (*anōmalos* ANOMALOUS; see -Y[1])]

ă′nomȳ, ă′nomie, *n.* lack of the usual social standards in group or person; hence **ano′m**IC *a.* [f. Gk *anomia* (*anomos* lawless); *-ie* f. F]

anō′n *adv.* (arch. or literary). soon, presently, (*will say more of this anon*); EVER *and anon.* [OE *on ān* into one, *on āne* in one]

anō′n. *abbr.* anonymous (author).

ănonā′ceous (-ā′shŭs) *a.* of the custard-apple family Annonaceae. [f. mod. L *An*(*n*)*ona* genus of edible fruits typical of family +-ACEOUS]

ă′nonȳm *n.* person who remains nameless; anonymous publication; pseudonym. [f. F *anonyme* f. Gk *anōnumos* (see foll.)]

anō′nȳmous *a.* of unknown name; of unknown or undeclared source or authorship; impersonal; hence ∼LY[2] *adv.*, **ănonȳ′m**ITY, ∼NESS, *ns.* [f. L f. Gk *anōnumos* nameless (as AN- 4, *onoma* name); see -OUS]

anō′phelēs (-z) *n.* mosquito of genus *Anopheles*, esp. one carrying malaria. [mod. L, f. Gk *anōphelēs* unprofitable]

ă′norăk *n.* skin or cloth hooded jacket for wear in polar regions; similar weatherproof garment for ordinary wear. [f. Greenland Eskimo *anoraq*]

ănorĕ′|xia *n.* (Path.) absence of appetite or desire; ∼xia **nervo′sa** (-ō-), condition of which chronic anorexia induced by emotional disturbance is a symptom; so ∼**ct**IC *a.* & *n.* [LL f. Gk (an- not, *orexis* appetite; see -IA[1])]

ănō′sm|ia (-z-) *n.* loss of sense of smell; hence ∼IC *a.* [mod. L f. as AN- 4 + Gk *osmē* smell + -IA[1]]

ano′ther (-ŭ′dh-) *pron.* (*pl.* **others**) & *a.* (*pl.* **other**). an additional (one) (*have another pear; have another;* YOU'*re another; after another month; after another six months*); a different (one) (*take this towel away and bring me another; another person than yourself; one man's* MEAT *is another man's poison;* ONE *another;* ||∼ **place,** the other House of Parliament (used in Commons to refer to Lords, and vice versa); some or any other (one) (*will not do another man's work*); ||unnamed additional party to legal action (*X versus Y and another*); ||(also **A. N. Other**) player unnamed or not yet selected; someone else (*another Solomon*); **such** ∼, another of the same sort. [ME, f. AN[1] + OTHER]

anō′vŭlant *a.* & *n.* (drug) preventing ovulation. [f. AN- 4 | OVULATION |-ANT]

ănŏxae′mia *n.* (Med.) defective oxygenation of the blood. [mod. L, f. as AN- 4 +OXYGEN +-AEMIA]

anō′x|ia *n.* (Med.) deficiency of oxygen in tissues; hence ∼IC *a.* [mod. L, f. as AN- 4 +OXYGEN +-IA[1]]

anschluss (ă′nshlōŏs) *n.* union, esp. annexation of Austria by Germany in 1938. [G (*anschliessen* join)]

ă′nserine *a.* of or like a goose; silly. [f. L *anserinus* (*anser* goose; see -INE[1])]

a′nswer[1] (ah′nser) *n.* something said or done to deal with a question, accusation, problem, etc.; **know all the** ∼**s,** (colloq.) be very experienced. [OE *andswaru* f. Gmc **andswarō* (**and-* against, **swar-*; cf. OE *swerian* swear)]

a′nswer[2] (ah′nser) *v.* **1.** *v.t.* make answer to (*answer me, my question*); ∼ (summons to) **the door, the telephone,** etc.; be satisfactory for (purpose etc.). **2.** *v.i.* make answer (*to*); be responsible (*for* person or thing); correspond (*to* description etc.); be satisfactory or successful; ∼ **to the name of,** be called; ∼ **back,** (colloq.) make impudent answer to rebuke etc. [OE *andswarian* (as prec.)]

a′nswerable (ah′nser-) *a.* responsible (*to* person, *for* person or thing); that can be answered. [f. prec. +-ABLE]

ănt *n.* small social hymenopterous insect proverbial for industry; **white** ∼, termite; ∼-**bear,** (1) tamanoir,

(2) aardvark; ~-eater, name of various mammals that live on ants, e.g. aardvark, echidna, pangolin; ~(s')-eggs, pupae or larvae of ants, used as animal food; ~'heap, ~'hill, (-t-h-) mound over ants' nest, conical nest of termites, (fig.) crowded dwelling; ~-lion, (larva of) nocturnal neuropterous insect that traps ants. [OE ǣmet(t)e, ēmete (see EMMET) f. WG *āmaitja (ā off, mait- cut)]

an't (ahnt) v.i. (arch.) = are not; (arch. colloq.) = am not; (arch. vulg.) = is not, has not, have not. [contr.]

ant-. See ANTI-.

-ant suf. forming adjs. denoting existence of action (pendant, repentant) or state (arrogant, expectant), and ns. denoting agent (assistant, celebrant, deodorant), usu. f. vbs. [f. or after F -ant or f. L -ant-, -ent-, pres. part. st. of vbs (cf. -ENT)]

äntä'cid a. & n. preventive or corrective of acidity (esp. in stomach). [f. ANT-+ACID²]

äntä'gonism n. active opposition (to, against, person or thing; between two). [f. F antagonisme (as foll.; see -ISM)]

äntä'gon|ist n. opponent; (Biol.) substance or organ that interferes with the action of another; hence ~i'stic a. [f. F antagoniste or f. LL antagonista f. Gk antagōnistēs (as foll.; see -IST)]

äntä'gonīze, -īse (-īz) v.t. (Of force etc.) counteract, tend to neutralize, (another); evoke hostility or opposition or enmity in. [f. Gk ANT(agōnizomai f. agōn contest; see -IZE)]

Antär'ctic (ă-) a. & n. (of) the south polar regions; ~ Circle, parallel of latitude 66° 33' S.; ~a n., continent mainly within Antarctic Circle. [ME, f. OF antartique or f. L f. Gk ANT(arktikos ARCTIC)]

ä'ntè n., & v.t. 1. n. (In poker etc.) stake put up by player before drawing cards; (transf.) advance payment. 2. v.t. put up as ante; *(transf.) bet, stake, pay up. [L, = before]

äntè- pref. forming ns. (ante-room), and adjs. with (antenatal) or without (ante-post) adj. ending, w. sense 'before, preceding'. [L ante prep. & adv., = before]

äntè-bĕ'llum a. occurring or existing before a (specified) war, esp. *the Civil War. [L (ante before, bellum war)]

äntècè'd|ent a. & n. 1. a. previous (to); presumptive, a priori; hence or cogn. ~ENCE n., ~entLY² adv. 2. n. preceding thing or circumstance; (Logic) the part of a conditional proposition on which the other part depends; (Gram.) noun, clause, sentence, to which a (usu. following and esp. relative) pronoun or adverb refers; (in pl.) past history (esp. of person). [ME f. F, or f. L ANTE(cedere go); see -ENT]

ä'ntèchāmber n. room leading to a more important one. [earlier anti-, f. F antichambre, f. It. anticamera (as ANTE-, CHAMBER)]

ä'ntèchâpel n. outer part at west end of college chapel. [f. ANTE-+CHAPEL]

ä'ntèdāte¹ n. date before the true time (esp. of writing). [f. ANTE-+DATE²]

äntèdā'te² v.t. affix, assign, an earlier (esp. than the true) date to (document, event); precede in time. [f. prec.]

äntèdilu'vian (-ū'-, -ōo'-) a. & n. 1. a. belonging, referring, appropriate, to the time before the Flood; (colloq.) utterly out of date. 2. n. old-fashioned or aged person. [f. ANTE-+L diluvium DELUGE+-AN]

ä'ntèlōpe n. (pl. same or ~s). deerlike ruminant animal, e.g. chamois, gazelle, gnu; leather made from its skin. [ME, f. OF antelop or f. med. L ant(h)alopus f. late Gk antholops, of unkn. orig.]

äntè-mōr'tem a. made before death. [L, = before death]

äntèmŭ'ndāne a. existing or occurring before creation of world. [f. ANTE-+L mundus world+-ANE]

äntènā'tal a. existing or occurring previous to birth; pertaining to the period of pregnancy. [f. ANTE-+NATAL]

äntè'nn|a n. 1. (pl. ~ae). sensory organ found in pairs on heads of insects, crustaceans, etc., feeler; (Bot.)

irritable process in male flower of some orchids; hence ~AL, ~ARY¹, adjs. 2. (pl. ~as). * = AERIAL 5. [L, = sail-yard]

äntènŭ'ptial (-shal) a. born, occurring, etc., before marriage. [f. LL ANTE(nuptialis NUPTIAL)]

äntèpè'ndi|um n. (pl. ~a). veil or hanging for front of altar. [med. L (ANTE-, pendēre hang)]

äntèpènŭ'lt a. & n. = foll. [abbr. of LL ANTE(paenult mus PENULT)]

äntèpènŭ'ltimate a. & n. last but two (esp. syllable [f. ANTE-+PENULTIMATE]

||äntè-pō'st a. (Of racing bets) made before th runners' numbers are made known. [f. ANTI +POST¹]

äntèprä'ndial a. before-dinner. [f. ANTE-+L prandium dinner+-AL]

äntēr'ior a. more to the front; prior (to); henc äntēriō'rITY n., ~LY² adv. [f. F antérieur or f. anterior, compar. f. ante before]

ä'ntè-room (-ōōm, -ŏōm) n. room leading to a mor important one; ||(Mil.) sitting-room in officers' mes [f. ANTE-+ROOM, after earlier ANTECHAMBER]

änthē'li|on (-h-) n. (pl. ~a). luminous halo projected o cloud or fog-bank opposite to sun. [Gk, neut. o anthēlios opposite to sun (as ANTI-, hēlios sun)]

änthĕlmi'ntic, -nthic, a. & n. (medicine) actin against parasitic (esp. intestinal) worms. [f. ANT +Gk helmins helminthos worm+-IC]

ä'nthem n. non-metrical musical setting of sacre words; composition for church use sung antiphonall song of praise or gladness; NATIONAL anthem. [O antefn, antifne f. LL antiphona ANTIPHON]

änthē'mi|on (-h-) n. (pl. ~a). flower-like ornament used i art. [Gk, = flower]

ä'nther n. (Bot.) part of stamen containing poller hence ~AL a. [f. F anthère or mod. L anthera, in 'medicine extracted from flowers' f. Gk anthēra flowery fem. a. f. anthos flower]

änther'idi|um n. (pl. ~a). (Bot.) male sex organ i cryptogams. [mod. L, f. anthera (as prec.)+Gk -idio dim. suf.]

änthŏ'log|ў n. choice collection of passages fror literature (esp. poems), songs, paintings, etc.; henc ~IST (1) n., ~IZE v.t. & i., compile anthology (of). [F anthologie or med. L f. Gk anthologia (anthos flowe -logia collection f. legō gather)]

änthozō'an a. & n. (marine animal) of the cla Anthozoa, including corals, sea anemones, etc. [mod. L Anthozoa. Gk anthos flower+zōia animals; se -AN]

ä'nthracēne n. aromatic hydrocarbon obtained in th distillation of coal tar. [f. Gk anthrax -akos coal+-ENE

ä'nthrac|īte n. non-bituminous hard variety of coa hence ~ī'tic a. [f. Gk anthrakitis a kind of coal (a prec.; see -ITE¹)]

ä'nthräx n. disease of sheep and cattle, transmissibl to man by infection from animals so affected. [LL Gk, = carbuncle]

änthropo-comb.form. human, mankind, as; ~ce'ntric a., ~ce'ntrism n., regarding man as central fact o universe; ~ge'nic, (1) of anthropogeny, (2) origi nated by man; ~geny, (-ŏ'j-), study of origin of man ~graphy (-ŏ'g-), science of geographical distributio of man. [f. Gk anthrōpos human being]

ä'nthropoid a. & n. 1. a. manlike in form; (colloq., o person) apelike. 2. n. being that is human in form only, esp. anthropoid ape. [f. Gk anthrōpoeidēs (as ANTHROPO-; see -OID)]

änthropŏ'log|ў n. study of mankind, esp. of it societies and customs; study of structure and evolu tion of man as an animal; hence änthropolŏ'gICA a., ~IST (3) n. [f. ANTHROPO-+-LOGY]

änthropŏ'mĕtrŷ n. measurement of the human body hence änthropomĕ'trIC a. [f. ANTHROPO-+-METRY

änthropomŏr'phic a. of the nature of anthropo morphism. [f. as foll. +-IC]

änthropomŏr'ph|ism n. attribution of human form

or personality to (god, animal, etc.); hence ∼IZE (4) *v.t.* [f. as foll. + -ISM]

anthropomor′phous *a.* of human form. [f. Gk ANTHROPOmorphos (*morphē* form) + -OUS]

anthropo′phag|ȳ *n.* cannibalism; hence ∼OUS *a.* [f. Gk ANTHROPOphagia (*phagō* eat)]

a′nti *n.* & *prep.* (person) opposed to (a certain policy etc.). [f. foll.]

anti- *pref.* (sometimes **ant-** before vowel or *h*) freely used to form *ns.* from *ns.* (*antibody, anticlimax, antipope*) and *adjs.* from *ns.* (*anti-aircraft, antitrust*) or from *adjs.* (*Antarctic, anticlerical, anticoagulant, anti-Semitic*), w. senses: 'opposite, against, preventing'; (Phys.) anti-particle of specified particle (*antineutrino, antiproton*); unlike the conventional form (*anti-hero, anti-novel*); (w. suf. *-ism, -ist*) (doctrine of) person opposed to (*antivivisectionism, -ist*). [f. or after Gk *anti-* against]

anti-air′craft (-ahft) *a.* [JACOBIN¹] for defence against hostile aircraft. [f. prec. + AIR¹*craft*]

a′ntiar *n.* upas tree of Java; poison obtained from it. [f. Jav. *antjar*]

antibiō′s|is *n.* (*pl.* ∼es *pr.* -ēz). condition of antagonism between (esp. micro-)organisms. [mod. L, f. F *antibiose* (as ANTI-, SYMBIOSIS)]

antibiō′tic *a.* & *n.* (substance) capable of destroying or injuring living organisms, esp. bacteria. [f. F *antibiotique* f. as ANTI- + Gk *biōtikos* fit for life (*bios* life; see -OTIC)]

a′ntibŏdy *n.* any of various proteins in the human or animal body, produced by and counteracting antigens. [transl. of G *antikörper* (as ANTI-, *körper* body)]

a′ntic *n.* & *a.* **1.** *n.* (usu. in *pl.*) grotesque or absurd posture or action. **2.** *a.* (arch.) grotesque, bizarre. [f. It. *antico* ANTIQUE, used as = grotesque]

antica′thōde *n.* target in X-ray tube on which electrons from cathode impinge. [f. ANTI- + CATHODE]

A′ntichrīst (ă′ntĭk-) *n.* enemy of Christ; great personal opponent of Christ expected by early Church to appear before end of world. [ME, f. OF *antecrist* f. eccl. L f. Gk ANTIkhristos (*Khristos* CHRIST)]

antichri′stian (-krĭ′styan) *a.* pertaining to Antichrist; opposed to Christianity. [f. prec., w. extended meaning]

antï′cipāt|e *v.t.* discuss, consider, use, spend, etc., before the due or natural time; forestall (person or thing); look forward to; (D) expect; hence ∼IVE, ∼ORY, *adjs.*, ∼OR *n.* [f. L *anticipare* (*anti-* for ANTE-, *-cipare* f. *capere* take) + -ATE³]

anticipā′tion *n.* **1.** action of anticipating; **thanking you in** ∼ (closing formula in letter of inquiry or request). **2.** (Mus.) introduction beforehand of part of chord about to follow. [F, or f. L *anticipatio* (as prec.; see -ATION)]

anticle′rical *a.* & *n.* (person) opposed to strong influence of clergy, esp. in politics; hence ∼ISM (3) *n.* [f. ANTI- + CLERICAL]

anticlī′max *n.* opposite of climax; ineffective end to anything which has suggested a climax; descent contrasting with previous rise; hence **anticlimă′ctic** *a.* [f. ANTI- + CLIMAX]

a′nticlīn|e *n.* (Geol.) ridge or fold from which strata slope down in opposite directions; so ∼AL (-ī′n-) *a.* [f. ANTI- + Gk *klinō* lean, after INCLINE²]

anticlō′ckwīse (-z) *adv.* & *a.* See CLOCK¹ 3.

anticoā′gŭlant *a.* & *n.* (drug) retarding or preventing clotting of blood. [f. ANTI- + COAGULANT]

anticonvŭ′lsant *a.* & *n.* (drug) retarding or preventing convulsions. [f. ANTI- + CONVULSANT]

anticy′cl|ōne *n.* system of winds rotating outwards from area of high barometric pressure; so ∼ŏ′nic *a.* [f. ANTI- + CYCLONE]

a′ntidŏt|e *n.* medicine etc. taken or given to counteract poison; (fig.) thing that counteracts an evil; hence ∼AL *a.* [F, or f. L *antidotum* neut. of ANTIdotos given against]

a′ntifreeze *n.* substance (usu. ethylene glycol) added

to water to lower its freezing-point, esp. for use in radiator of engine. [f. ANTI- + FREEZE]

ănti-g (-jē′) *a.* (Of clothing for astronaut etc.) designed to counteract effects of high acceleration. [f. ANTI- + *g* symb. for acceleration due to gravity]

a′ntigen *n.* substance (e.g. toxin) that stimulates production of antibodies when introduced into the body; hence **ăntigĕ′nic** *a.* [G (as ANTIBODY, -GEN)]

ănti-gră′vitȳ *n.* hypothetical force opposing gravity. [f. ANTI- + GRAVITY]

a′nti-hērō *n.* (*pl.* ∼es). (In novel etc.) hero of unconventional or non-traditional type. [f. ANTI- + HERO]

ăntihī′stamine (-ĭn, -ēn) *n.* & *a.* (substance) that counteracts effects of histamine, used esp. in cases of allergy. [f. ANTI- + HISTAMINE]

ănti-Jă′cobin *a.* & *n.* (person) opposed to Jacobins (1789) or to the French Revolution. [f. ANTI- + JACOBIN¹]

a′ntiknŏck (-ĭn-) *n.* substance added to motor fuel to prevent detonation. [f. ANTI- + KNOCK²]

ăntilŏ′garithm (-dhem), (colloq.) **ă′ntilŏg,** *ns.* number to which a logarithm belongs (*100 is the common antilogarithm of 2*). [f. ANTI- + LOGARITHM]

ănti′logȳ *n.* contradiction in terms. [f. F *antilogie* f. Gk *antilogia* (as ANTI-, -LOGY)]

ăntimaca′ssar *n.* (esp. Hist.) covering put over backs (and arms) of chairs etc., as protection from grease or as ornament. [f. ANTI- + MACASSAR (*oil*)]

a′ntimasque (-mahsk) *n.* grotesque interlude between acts of masque. [f. ANTI- + MASQUE]

a′ntimătter *n.* (hypothetical) matter composed solely of antiparticles. [f. ANTI- + MATTER¹]

ăntimonǎr′chical (-k-) *a.* opposed to monarchy. [f. ANTI- + MONARCHICAL]

a′ntimonȳ *n.* brittle silvery-white metallic element, used esp. in alloys; hence **ăntimō′nIAL, ăntimō′nIC, ăntimō′nIOUS,** *adjs.* [ME, f. med. L *antimonium* (11th c.), of unkn. orig.]

a′nting *n.* rubbing or placing of ants etc. in plumage by birds, perh. to kill parasites. [f. ANT + -ING¹]

a′ntinōde *n.* (Phys.) point or line of maximum amplitude in vibrating body. [f. ANTI- + NODE]

ăntinō′mian *a.* & *n.* **1.** *a.* opposed to the obligatoriness of moral law. **2.** *n.* one who maintains that moral law is not binding on Christians; hence ∼ISM (2) *n.* [f. med. L *Antinomi,* name of sect in Germany (1535) alleged to hold this opinion (as ANTI-, Gk *nomos* law) + -AN]

ănti′nomȳ *n.* contradiction in a law, or between two laws; conflict of authority; paradox. [f. L f. Gk ANTI(*nomia* f. *nomos* law)]

a′nti-nŏvel *n.* novel of unconventional or non-traditional type. [f. ANTI- + NOVEL¹]

a′ntiparticle *n.* (Phys.) elementary particle having same mass as given particle but opposite electric charge or magnetic moment. [f. ANTI- + PARTICLE]

ăntipa′st|ō (-pah′-) *n.* (*pl.* ∼i or ∼os). hors d'œuvre. [It.]

ăntipathĕ′tic *a.* opposed in nature or disposition (*to*); hence ∼AL, ∼ALLY *adv.* [f. as ANTIPATHY after *pathetic*]

ăntipa′thic *a.* of contrary character (*to*); (Med.) having or producing contrary symptoms. [f. foll. + -IC]

ănti′pathȳ *n.* constitutional or settled aversion (*to*; *for*; *between* persons etc.). [f. F *antipathie* or L *antipathia* f. Gk *antipatheia* f. ANTIpathēs opposed in feeling (*pathos -eos*)]

ănti-pĕrsonne′l *a.* (Of bomb etc.) designed to kill or injure human beings. [f. ANTI- + PERSONNEL]

ăntipĕr′spirant *a.* & *n.* (substance) tending to inhibit perspiration. [f. ANTI- + PERSPIRE + -ANT]

ăntiphlogī′stic *a.* & *n.* (medicine etc.) reducing inflammation. [f. ANTI- + PHLOGISTIC]

a′ntiphon *n.* verse of psalm etc. sung or recited usu. responsively by choir; (fig.) response. [f. eccl. L *antiphona,* fem. sing., f. Gk ANTIphōna (neut. pl. of *antiphōnos* responsive) f. *phōnē* sound]

For other words in *anti-* see ANTI-.

ănti'phonal *a.* & *n.* **1.** *a.* sung alternately; responsive; hence ~LY² *adv.* **2.** *n.* collection of antiphons. [f. prec. +-AL]

ănti'phonarў *n.* book of antiphons. [f. eccl. L *antiphonarium* (as ANTIPHON; see -ARY¹)]

ănti'phonў *n.* antiphonal singing; response, echo. [f. ANTIPHON +-Y¹]

ănti'pod|ēs (-z) *n. pl.* place(s) diametrically opposite (to each other), esp. Australasia as region on opposite side of earth to Europe; (w. back-form. *sing.* **ă'ntipōde**) exact opposite (*of, to*); hence ~AL, ~E'AN, *adjs.* [F, or LL f. Gk *antipodes* having the feet opposite, pl. of ANTI*pous* a. (*pous podos* foot)]

ă'ntipōle *n.* opposite pole; direct opposite. [f. ANTI- +POLE²]

ă'ntipōpe *n.* person set up as Pope in opposition to one (held by others to be) canonically chosen. [f. F *antipape* f. med. L *antipapa*, assim. to *pope*]

ăntiprō'tŏn *n.* (Phys.) antiparticle of proton. [f. ANTI- +PROTON]

ăntipўrĕ'tic *a.* & *n.* (drug) allaying or preventing fever. [f. ANTI- +PYRETIC]

ăntiquār'ian *a.* & *n.* **1.** *a.* connected with study of antiques or antiquities. **2.** *n.* antiquary. **3.** Hence ~ISM (2) *n.* [f. as foll. +-AN]

ă'ntiquarў *n.* student or collector of antiques or antiquities. [f. L *antiquarius* (*antiquus* ancient; see -ARY¹)]

ă'ntiquātĕd *a.* old-fashioned; out of date. [p.p. of *antiquate* v. f. *antiquate* a., f. eccl. L *antiquare* make old; see -ATE².³]

ănti'que (-ē'k) *a., n.,* & *v.t.* **1.** *a.* of old times; existing since old times; old-fashioned; archaic. **2.** *n.* relic of old times, esp. furniture etc. sought by collectors. **3.** *v.t.* make (furniture etc.) appear antique by artificial means. [F, or f. L *antiquus, anticus,* former, ancient (*ante* before)]

ănti'quitў *n.* ancientness (*a city of great antiquity*); old times, esp. time before Middle Ages; the ancients; (in *pl.*) customs, events, etc., of ancient times; (usu. in *pl.*) ancient relics. [ME, f. OF *antiquité* f. L *antiquitas -tatis* (*antiquus*; see prec., -ITY)]

ăntirrhi'num (-rī'-) *n.* = SNAPdragon (1). [L, f. Gk *antirrhinon* (*anti* counterfeiting, *rhis rhinos* nose, from resemblance of flower to animal's mouth)]

ăntisăbbatār'ian *a.* & *n.* (person) opposed to observance of the Sabbath. [f. ANTI- +SABBATARIAN]

ăntiscŏrbū'tic *a.* & *n.* (medicine) preventing or curing scurvy. [f. ANTI- +SCORBUTIC]

ăntiscri'ptural (-cher-, -choor-) *a.* opposed to Scripture. [f. ANTI- +SCRIPTURAL]

ănti-Sē'm|īte *a.* & *n.* (person) hostile to Jews; so **ănti-Sèmi'tic** *a.,* ~itism (3) *n.* [f. ANTI- +SEMITE]

ăntisē'psis *n.* process or principles of using antiseptics. [mod. L (as ANTI-, SEPSIS)]

ăntisē'ptic *a.* & *n.* **1.** *a.* counteracting sepsis, esp. by preventing growth of bacteria; scrupulously clean; sterile (lit. or fig.). **2.** *n.* antiseptic agent. [f. ANTI- +SEPTIC]

ă'ntisēr|um *n.* (*pl.* ~a). serum with high antibody content. [f. ANTI- +SERUM]

ăntisō'cial (-shal) *a.* opposed to principles or instincts on which society is based, or to normal social practices; not sociable. [f. ANTI- +SOCIAL]

ăntistă'tic *a.* counteracting the effects of static electricity. [f. ANTI- +STATIC]

ănti'strophē *n.* See STROPHE. [LL, f. Gk *antistrophē* (ANTI*strephō* turn against)]

ăntithē'|ism *n.* opposition to belief in existence of a God; hence ~IST (2) *n.* [f. ANTI- +THEISM]

ănti'thes|is *n.* (*pl.* ~es *pr.* -ēz). contrast of ideas expressed by parallelism of strongly contrasted words; opposition, contrast, (*of, between,* two things); direct opposite (*of, to*). [LL f. Gk (ANTITI*thēmi* set against)]

ăntithē'tic *a.* of the nature of antithesis; contrasted; consisting of two opposites; so ~AL *a.,* ~ALLY *adv.* [f. Gk *antithetikos* (as prec.; see -IC)]

ăntitŏ'x|in *n.* substance that neutralizes a toxin; so ~IC *a.* [f. ANTI- +TOXIN]

ă'ntitrāde *a.* & *n.* (wind) that blows in opposite direction to trade wind, at different altitude or place. [f. ANTI- +TRADE]

ăntitrinitār'ian *a.* & *n.* (person) opposed to doctrine of the Trinity. [f. ANTI- +TRINITARIAN]

*ăntitrŭ'st *a.* (Of law etc.) opposed to trusts or other monopolies. [f. ANTI- +TRUST 8]

ă'ntitype *n.* that which a type or symbol represents; one of the opposite type; hence **ăntitў'pICAL** *a.* [f. Gk ANTI*tupos* corresponding as an impression to the die (*tupos* stamp)]

ăntivēnē'ne, ăntivē'nin, *ns.* antitoxin, esp. against snake poison. [f. ANTI- +L *venenum* poison +-IN]

ăntivivisē'ction|ism *n.* opposition to vivisection or to experiments with animals; so ~IST (2) *n.* [f. ANTI- +VIVISECTION]

ă'ntler *n.* (branch of) horn of stag or other (usu. male) deer; hence (-)~ED² (-*lerd*) *a.* [ME f. AF, var. of OF *antoillier,* of unkn. orig.]

ăntonomā'sia (-z-) *n.* substitution of epithet etc. for proper name (e.g. *the Iron Duke* for 'the Duke of Wellington'); use of a proper name to express a general idea (e.g. *a Solomon* for 'a wise man'). [L f. Gk (*antonomazō* name instead f. as ANTI- +*onoma* name)]

ă'ntonўm *n.* word of contrary meaning to another, as *bad* to *good* (opp. *synonym*); hence **ăntŏ'nўm**OUS *a.* [f. F *antonyme* (as ANTI-, SYNONYM)]

- **ă'ntr|um** *n.* (*pl.* ~a). cavity in the body (esp. one in the upper jaw-bone); hence ~AL *a.* [L, f. Gk *antron* cave]

ā'nus *n.* excretory opening at end of alimentary canal. [L]

ă'nvil *n.* block (usu. iron) on which smith works metal; (Anat.) a bone of the ear, the incus. [OE *anfilte* etc., = OHG *anafalz,* f. Gmc **ana*on +vbl stem w. sense 'beat']

ănxi'etў (ăngz-) *n.* state of being anxious; concern about the future; earnest desire (*for* a thing, *to* do); (Psych.) morbid state of excessive uneasiness. [f. F *anxieté* or f. L *anxietas -tatis* (as foll.; see -TY¹)]

ă'nxious (ă'ngkshŭs) *a.* troubled, uneasy in mind, (*about*); earnestly desirous (*for* a thing, *to* do); causing anxiety; hence ~LY² *adv.* [f. L *anxius* (*angere* choke) + -OUS]

a'nў (ĕ'-) *a., pron.,* & *adv.* **1.** *a.* & *pron.* (With interrog. or neg. expressed or implied) one or some but no matter which (*have you any wool?; have you any of them?; cannot find any of them; hardly any difference; to avoid any delay;* **not having** ~, (colloq.) unwilling to participate); whichever (of all) is chosen (*any fool knows that; in any* CASE¹ **1**; *any* MORE; *at any* RATE¹; ~ **time,** (colloq.) at any time; *has* ~ **amount** (a great deal) *of money*); an appreciable or significant (*did not stay for any length of time*). **2.** *adv.* (Usu. w. compar. in neg. or interrog. context) at all, in some degree (*is that any better?; without being any the wiser*). [OE *ænig,* = OHG *einag,* f. Gmc **ain-* one + *-*ig* -Y²]

a'nўbŏdў (ĕ'-) *n.* & *pron.* whatever person; a person, no matter who, (~'s *game* etc., evenly balanced contest; ~'s **guess,** an unpredictable matter); a person of any kind; a person of importance. [f. ANY +BODY¹ (= person)]

a'nўhow (ĕ'-) *adv.* anyway; haphazardly (*does his work anyhow; things are all anyhow*). [f. ANY +HOW]

a'nўone (ĕ'nĭwŭn, -wun) *n.* & *pron.* anybody. [f. ANY +ONE]

*a'nўplāce (ĕ'-) *adv.* anywhere. [f. ANY +PLACE¹]

a'nўthing (ĕ'-) *n.* & *pron.* whatever thing; a thing, no matter which (~ **but,** far from; **like** ~, with great intensity etc.); a thing of any kind. [f. ANY +THING]

a'nўway (ĕ'-) *adv.* in any way; in any case; in any rate; (resuming after digression: *anyway, as I was saying*). [f. ANY +WAY]

a'nўwhere (ĕ'nĭwār) *adv.* & *pron.* (in or to) any place. [f. ANY +WHERE]

a'nўwise (ĕ'-; -z) *adv.* in any manner. [OE *on ænige wīsan* in any wise]

For other words in *anti-* see ANTI-.

Ắ'nzắc *n. & a.* **1.** (member) of the Australian and New Zealand Army Corps (1914–18); ∼ **Day,** 25 Apr. **2.** Australian or New Zealand (person, esp. serviceman). [f. initials]

ĂO *abbr.* Officer of the Order of Australia.

'AOK (āōkā') *a.* (colloq.) in perfect order. [f. *all systems OK*]

ĭ'orĭst *a. & n.* (Gram.) indefinite, not implying limitation; ∼ **(tense),** past tense merely denoting occurrence without limitation as to duration etc.; so **āorĭ'stĬC** *a.* [f. Gk *aoristos* indefinite (*a*- not, *horizō* define)]

āŏr'tǀa *n.* great artery or trunk of the arterial system, issuing from heart; hence ∼ĬC *a.* [f. Gk *aortē* (*a*(*e*)*irō* raise)]

ĭ'oudăd (ah'ōō-) *n.* N. Afr. wild or domesticated sheep (*Ammotragus tragelaphus*). [F, f. native name]

ă outrance (ah ōō'trahṅs) *adv.* to the death; to the bitter end. [F, = to the utmost]

ăp- *pref.* **1.** assim. form of AD- before *p.* **2.** See APO-.

'ap. *abbr.* apothecaries'.

ăpā'ce *adv.* (literary). swiftly, quickly. [f. OF *à pas* at (a considerable) PACE¹]

ăpā'che *n.* (*A*∼) (apă'chĭ). member of N. Amer. Indian tribe. **2.** (apă'sh). violent street ruffian, orig. in Paris; ∼ **dance,** a vigorous dance for two. [Mex. Sp.]

ĭ'panage, ă'pp-, *n.* provision for maintenance of younger children of kings etc.; perquisite, subsidiary title; natural accompaniment or attribute. [F, f. OF *apaner* dower f. med. L AP*panare* (*panis* bread) endow with means of subsistence; see -AGE]

ăpăr't *adv.* **1.** aside, separately, independently; ∼ **from,** not considering; **joking** ∼, seriously; SET¹ *apart*; **tell** ∼, distinguish between. **2.** to or at a distance. **3.** into pieces (*come apart*); **take** ∼, (fig.) analyse, deal with severely or thoroughly. [ME f. OF (*à* to, *part* side)]

ăpăr'theid (-t-hāt) *n.* (S. Afr.) (policy of) racial segregation; (fig.) similar segregation elsewhere. [Afrik. (as prec. -HOOD)]

ăpăr'tment *n.* single room in a house; **flat* (∼ **house,** block of flats); (in *pl.*) set of (usu. rented furnished) rooms. [f. F *appartement* f. It. *appartamento* (*appartare* separate f. *a parte* apart; see -MENT)]

ăpăthĕ'tǀic *a.* not feeling emotion; uninterested; hence ∼ICALLY *adv.* [f. foll., after *pathetic*]

ĭ'pathў *n.* insensibility to suffering; passionless existence; lack of interest or desire (*towards*). [f. F *apathie* f. L f. Gk *apatheia* (*apathēs* without feeling f. *a*- not + *pathos* suffering)]

ă'patĭte *n.* crystalline mineral of calcium phosphate and fluoride. [f. G *apatit* f. Gk *apatē* deceit (from its deceptive forms); see -ITE¹]

ăpe¹ *n.* **1.** tailless monkey, esp. anthropoid; any monkey; ∼**-man,** extinct primate intermediate between ape and man. **2.** imitator, mimic; apelike person; **go** ∼, (sl.) become crazy. [OE *apa*, = OHG *affo*, ON *api* f. Gmc **apan-*]

ăpe² *v.t.* imitate, mimic. [f. prec.]

ăpea'k *adv. & pred. a.* (Naut.) vertical(ly) (*oars apeak*). [f. F *à pic* (*à* at, *pic* PEAK¹)]

ăperçu (ăpĕrsū') *n.* summary, conspectus; an insight. [F, p.p. of *apercevoir* perceive]

ăpĕr'ient *a. & n.* laxative (medicine). [f. L *aperire* to open; see -ENT]

ăpĕriŏ'dĭc *a.* (Phys.) without a natural period. [f. A- 7 + PERIODIC¹]

ăpĕ'ritĭf (-ēf) *n.* alcoholic drink as appetizer. [f. F *apéritif* f. med. L *aperitivus* var. of LL *apertivus* f. L *aperire* to open; see -IVE]

ĭ'perture *n.* opening, gap; space through which light passes in optical or photographic instrument. [f. L *apertura* (as prec.; see -URE)]

ĭ'perў *n.* mimicry; ape-house. [f. APE¹ + -ERY]

ăpĕ'talous *a.* without petals. [f. mod. L f. Gk *apetalos* leafless (*a*- not, *petalon* leaf) + -OUS]

ā'pĕx *n.* (*pl.* ∼**es,** or **apices** *pr.* ā'pĭsēz). tip; top, climax; vertex (of triangle, cone); pointed end (of heart, lung, etc.). [L, = peak, tip]

‖APEX (ā'pĕks) *abbr.* Association of Professional, Executive, Clerical, and Computer Staff.

ă'pfelstrudel (-rōō-) *n.* baked spiced apples in flaky pastry. [G (*apfel* apple, STRUDEL)]

ăphaer'ĕsǀis (afēr'-) *n.* (*pl.* ∼**es** *pr.* -ēz). removal of letter or syllable at beginning of word (e.g. in derivation of ADDER). [LL, f. Gk *aphairesis* (as APO-, *haireō* take)]

ăphā'sǀia (-zĭa) *n.* loss of speech, or of understanding of language, owing to brain damage; hence ∼IC *a. & n.* [mod. L f. Gk, f. *aphatos* speechless (*a*- not, *pha*-speak; see -IA¹)]

ăphē'lǀion (-lyon, -lĭon) *n.* (*pl.* ∼**a**). point (of planet's or comet's orbit) farthest from sun. [Graecized f. mod. L *aphelium* f. Gk *aph' hēliou* from the sun]

ă'phĕsǀis *n.* (*pl.* ∼**es** *pr.* -ēz). gradual loss of unaccented vowel at beginning of word (e.g. of *e* from *esquire* to short *squire*); hence **aphĕ'tǀic** *a.* [Gk, = letting go (as APO-, *hiēmi* send)]

ă'phĭd *n.* plant-louse, small insect infesting and damaging plants, e.g. greenfly. [back-form. f. *aphides* (see foll.)]

ă'phĭs *n.* (*pl.* **aphides** *pr.* ā'fĭdēz). aphid, esp. of genus *Aphis* [mod. L (Linnaeus) f. Gk (1523), perh. misreading of *koris* bug]

ăphō'nǀia, ă'phonў, *n.* loss or absence of voice. [mod. L *aphonia* f. Gk (*aphōnos* voiceless f. *a*- not + *phōnē* voice; see -IA¹, -Y¹)]

ă'phorǀism *n.* short pithy statement or maxim; hence ∼IST (1) *n.,* **ăphori'stǀic** *a.,* ∼IZE (2) *v.i.* [f. F *aphorisme* or f. LL f. Gk *aphorismos* definition (AP*horizō* f. *horos* boundary; see -ISM)]

ăphrŏdi'sǀiăc (-z-) *a. & n.* (drug etc.) arousing sexual desire. [f. Gk *aphrodisiakos* (*aphrodisios* f. *Aphroditē* Gk goddess of love; see -AC)]

ăphў'llous *a.* (Bot.) naturally without leaves. [f. mod. L f. Gk *aphullos* (*a*- not, *phullon* leaf) + -OUS]

ā'piǀan *a.* pertaining to bees. [f. L *apianus* (*apis* bee; see -AN)]

āpiār'ian *a.* pertaining to bee-keeping. [f. as foll. + -AN]

ā'piarǀy *n.* place where bees are kept; hence ∼IST (1) *n.* [f. L *apiarium* (*apis* bee; see -ARY¹)]

ă'pical *a.* belonging to or at an apex; situated at the tip; hence ∼LY² *adv.* [f. L APEX -*icis* + -AL]

apices. See APEX.

ā'picǔlture *n.* bee-keeping; hence **āpicǔ'lturǀAL** *a.,* **āpicǔ'lturǀIST** (3) *n.,* (-cher-). [f. L *apis* bee, after *agriculture*]

apie'ce *adv.* severally, each (*had five pounds apiece*). [f. A² + PIECE¹]

ā'pish *a.* of the nature or appearance of an ape; apelike in manner, silly; hence ∼LY² *adv.,* ∼NESS *n.* [f. APE¹ + -ISH¹]

ăplanā'tǀic *a.* free from spherical aberration; so [by back-form. thr. G] **ā'planǀat** *n.,* lens, or lens-system, made aplanatic by correction. [f. Gk *aplanētos* free from error (*a*- not, *planaō* wander) + -IC]

aplā'sǀia (-z-) *n.* (Med.) congenital irregularity or absence of organ or structure; hence **aplā'stǀic** *a.* [mod. L, f. Gk (*a*- not, *plasis* formation); see -IA¹]

aplĕ'ntў *adv.* in plenty. [f. A³ + PLENTY]

aplŏ'mb (-m) *n.* self-possession. [F, = perpendicularity, f. *à plomb* according to plummet]

ăpnoe'a (-nē'a), *****ăpnē'a,** *n.* (Med.) cessation of breathing. [mod. L f. Gk *apnoia* (*apnous* breathless)]

ăpo- *pref.* (usu. **ap-** bef. vowel or *h*) w. sense 'away from' (*apogee*), 'separate' (*apocarpous*). [f. Gk *apo* from, away, un-, quite]

apŏ'calypse *n.* revelation, esp. that made to St. John in island of Patmos; book recording this; grand or violent event resembling those described in St. John's book; so **apŏcalў'ptǀic**(AL) *adjs.* [ME f. OF, f. eccl. L f. Gk *apokalupsis* (APO*kaluptō* uncover)]

ăpocăr'pous *a.* (Bot.) having carpels distinct. [f. APO-
+ Gk *karpos* fruit + -OUS]

ăpochromă'tic (-k-) *a.* free from spherical and
chromatic aberrations; so [by back-form. thr. G]
ă'pochromăt (-k-) *n.*, lens, or lens-system, made
apochromatic by correction. [f. APO- + CHROMATIC]

apŏ'copĕ *n.* removal of letter(s) or syllable(s) at end of
word (e.g. in derivation of CURIO). [LL, f. Gk
APO(*kopē* f. *koptō* cut)]

Apocr. *abbr.* Apocrypha.

ă'pocrine *a.* (Of gland) losing parts of cells when
secreting. [f. APO- + Gk *krinō* separate]

Apŏ'crȳpha (*a*-) *n.* books of Old Testament included
in Septuagint and Vulgate, but not in Hebrew Bible
and not in all modern Bibles. [ME, f. eccl. L *apocrypha*
(*scripta*) pl., hidden writings f. Gk *apokruphos*
(APO*kruptō* hide away)]

apŏ'crȳphal *a.* of the Apocrypha; of doubtful authenticity (esp. of some early Christian texts resembling
those of NT); invented (*apocryphal story*). [f. prec. +
-AL]

ă'podal *a.* without (or with undeveloped) feet or
ventral fins. [f. *apod* apodal creature f. Gk *apous*
footless (*a*- not, *pous podos* foot) + -AL]

ăpodi'ctic, -dei'ctic (-dī'-), *a.* of clear demonstration; clearly established. [f. L f. Gk *apodeiktikos* (APO-,
deiknumi show; see -IC)]

apŏ'dos|is *n.* (*pl.* ~es *pr.* -ēz). consequent clause of
conditional sentence. [LL, f. Gk (APO*didōmi* give
back)]

ă'pogee *n.* point (in orbit of moon, planet, or artificial
satellite) farthest from earth; (fig.) most distant or
highest point; hence **ăpogē'AN** *a.* [f. F *apogée* or f.
mod. L f. Gk APO*geion* away from earth (*gē* earth)]

ăpolau'stic *a.* seeking enjoyment. [f. Gk *apolaustikos*
(APO*lauō* enjoy; see -IC)]

ăpoli'tical *a.* unconcerned with or detached from
politics. [f. A- 7 + POLITICAL]

Apŏllinăr'is (*a*-) *n.* effervescent mineral water from
*Apollinaris*burg in the Rhineland.

Apŏ'llō (*a*-) *n.* (*pl.* ~s). young man of great beauty.
[L, f. Gk *Apollōn* name of sun-god]

Apŏllō'nian (ă-) *a.* of Apollo, Gk & Rom. sun-god,
patron of music and poetry; serene, thoughtful, self-
-disciplined. [f. L f. Gk *Apollōnios* (as prec.) + -AN]

Apŏ'llyon (*a*-) *n.* the Devil (Rev. 9:11). [L (Vulgate),
f. Gk *apolluōn* pres. part. of *apollumi* (APO-, *ollumi*
destroy)]

apŏlogĕ't|ic *a.* & *n.* **1.** *a.* regretfully acknowledging or
excusing fault or failure; diffident; vindicatory; hence
~ICALLY *adv.* **2.** *n.* (usu. in *pl.*) reasoned defence, esp.
of Christianity. [f. F *apologétique* f. LL f. Gk *apologētikos*
(APO*logeomai* speak in defence; see -IC)]

apŏ'logist *n.* one who defends (e.g. Christianity) by
argument. [f. F *apologiste* f. Gk *apologizomai* render
account (*apologos* account); see -IST]

apŏ'logīze, -īse (-īz), *v.i.* make an apology (*to* person,
for person or thing). [f. Gk (see prec.)]

ă'pologue (-g) *n.* moral fable. [F, or f. L f. Gk
APO(*logos* discourse) story]

apŏ'logy *n.* regretful acknowledgement of fault or
failure; assurance that no offence was intended;
explanation, vindication; poor or scanty
specimen of (*this apology for a letter*). [f. F *apologie* or f.
LL f. Gk *apologia* (as APOLOGETIC)]

ă'polune (-ōōn, -ūn) *n.* point in body's orbit about
moon where it is farthest from moon's centre. [f. APO-
+ L *luna* moon, after *apogee*]

ăpomi'x|is *n.* (*pl.* ~es *pr.* -ēz). (Biol.) reproduction
without fertilization; so **ăpomi'ctic** *a.* [mod. L, f. as
APO- + Gk *mixis* mingling]

ăpophă'tic *a.* (Theol.) (Of knowledge of God)
obtained by negation. [f. Gk APO*phatikos* negative]

ă'pophthĕgm (-ofthĕm, -othĕm), ***a'pothĕgm**
(-ĕm), *n.* terse saying; pithy maxim; hence ~ă'TIC

(-ofthĕg-, -othĕg-) *a.* [f. F *apophthegme* or mod. L f. Gk
apophthegma -*matos* (APO*phtheggomai* speak out)]

ăpŏplĕ'ct|ic *a.* pertaining to, causing, suffering from,
tending to, apoplexy; hence ~ICALLY *adv.* [f. F
apoplectique or f. LL f. Gk *apoplēktikos* (APO*plēssō* strik
completely; see -IC)]

ă'poplĕxȳ *n.* inability to feel and move, caused by
blockage or rupture of brain artery. [ME, f. OF
apoplexie f. LL f. Gk *apoplēxia* (as prec.)]

ăposēmă'tic *a.* (Zool.) (Of coloration, markings
etc.) serving to warn or repel. [f. APO- + Gk *sēmo*
sēmatos sign + -IC]

ăposiōpē's|is *n.* (*pl.* ~es *pr.* -ēz). (Rhet.) sudden
breaking-off in speech. [L f. Gk, f. APO(*siōpaō* keep
silent)]

apŏ'stasȳ *n.* abandonment of religious faith, vows
principles, or party. [ME, f. eccl. L f. NT Gk *apostasi*
(APO*stasis* defection f. *stat*- stand)]

apŏ'state *n.* & *a.* (one) guilty of apostasy; so **ăpostă't**
ICAL *a.* [ME f. OF, or f. eccl. L *apostata* f. Gk *apostatē*
deserter (as prec.)]

apŏ'statīze, -īse (-īz), *v.i.* become an apostate. [f
apostatazire (*apostata*; see prec.)]

ā pŏsteriŏr'ī (-ĕr-, -ēr-) *adv.* & *a.* (reasoning) from
effects to causes; inductive(ly). [L, = from wha
comes after]

apŏ'stil *n.* (arch.) marginal note. [f. F *apostill*
(*apostiller* v. f. *postille* POSTIL)]

apŏ'stle (-sel) *n.* **1.** messenger, esp. (A~) any of the
twelve whom Christ sent forth to preach Gospel; ~
-bird, one of various Austral. birds forming flocks o
about a dozen; A~s' Creed, simplest and prob
earliest form of Christian creed, anciently ascribed t
the Apostles; ~ **spoon** (with figure of Apostle on
handle). **2.** first successful Christian missionary in a
country (*St. Boniface, the Apostle of Germany*); leader o
reform (*apostle of temperance*). **3.** Hence ~SHIP *n.* [OF
apostle f. eccl. L f. Gk *apostolos* (APO*stellō* send forth)]

apŏ'stolate *n.* apostleship; leadership in reform. [f
eccl. *apostolatus* (as prec.; see -ATE[1])]

ăposto'lic *a.* pertaining to the Apostles (A~
Fathers, Christian leaders immediately after the
Apostles; *apostolic* SUCCESSION); of the character of ar
apostle (VICAR *apostolic*); of the Pope as successor of
St. Peter; hence ~AL *a.*, ~ALLY *adv.* [f. F *apostoliqu*
or eccl. L f. Gk *apostolikos* (as APOSTLE; see -IC)]

apŏ'stroph|e[1] *n.* exclamatory passage by orator or
poet, addressed to particular person (often dead or
absent) or thing; hence ~IZE (1, 2) *v.t.* & *i.* [L f. Gk
lit. 'turning away' (as foll.)]

apŏ'strophe[2] *n.* sign of omission of letters (*can't*) or
numbers (*the spirit of '76*, i.e. 1776), or of possessive
case (*a man's coat*) (plus *'s*). [F, or LL f. Gk
apostrophos adj. as n., accent of elision (APO*strephō* turn
away)]

apŏstrŏ'phic *a.* In senses of the above *ns.* [f. APO
STROPHE[1,2] + -IC]

apŏ'thecar|ȳ *n.* **1.** (arch.) druggist, pharmaceutica
chemist. **2.** ~ies' measure, weight, (||Hist.) sets of
units used in pharmacy for liquid volume (with fluic
OUNCE[1] of 8 drachms = 480 minims) and for weigh
(with OUNCE[1] of 8 drachms = 24 scruples = 480
grains) respectively. [ME, f. OF *apotecaire* f. LL
apothecarius f. L *apotheca* f. Gk *apothēkē* storehouse; see
-ARY[1]]

***apothegm.** See APOPHTHEGM.

ă'pothĕm *n.* (Geom.) line from centre of regula
polygon perpendicular to a side. [f. Gk APO(*tithēmi* se
place); cf. THEME]

apŏthĕō's|is *n.* (*pl.* ~es *pr.* -ēz). deification (lit. or
fig.); canonization; deified ideal or highest develop
ment; hence **apŏ'theos|IZE** (1) *v.t.* eccl. L, f. Gk
APO(*theoō* make a god of, f. *theos* god; see -OSIS)]

apotropă'ic *a.* having power to avert evil influence or
bad luck. [f. Gk (*tropaios* f. *trepō* turn) averting
evil + -IC]

appa'l (-aw'l) *v.t.* (-ll-). dismay, terrify; hence ~ING

a., (esp., colloq.) shocking, unpleasant. [ME, f. OF *apalir* grow pale; cf. PALE²]

'appa'll (-aw'l). Var. of prec.

Appaloo'sa (ă-) *n.* horse of N. Amer. breed with dark spots on light background. [f. *Opelousa* in Louisiana, or *Palouse*, river in Idaho]

'ppanage. See APANAGE.

apparat (ăperah't) *n.* Communist party machine in USSR and other countries. [Russ. f. G, = apparatus]

apparatchik (ăperah'chĭk) *n.* (*pl.* ∼ *sor* ∼ *i*). member of *apparat*; Communist agent. [Russ.]

apparā'tus *n.* equipment for doing something, e.g. gymnastics or scientific experiments; organs effecting a natural process; *apparat* or other political organization; ∼ (**criticus**), list of variant readings, materials for textual study of document. [L (AP*parare* make ready for; see -ATE¹)]

appä'rel¹ *v.t.* (‖-ll-). (arch.) attire, dress. [ME, f. OF *apareiller* f. Rom. *ADpariculare* make fit (*pariculum* dim. of *par* equal)]

appä'rel² *n.* **1.** (literary). clothing, dress. **2.** ornamental embroidery on some ecclesiastical vestments. [ME, f. OF *apareil* (*apareiller*; see prec.)]

ppä'rent *a.* manifest, palpable, (**heir** ∼, one whose right of inheritance cannot be superseded by birth of another heir; cf. PRESUMPTIVE); seeming; *apparent* MAGNITUDE; ∼ **time**, solar time; hence ∼LY² *adv.* [ME, f. OF *aparant* f. L (as APPEAR; see -ENT)]

ppari'tion *n.* appearance, esp. (as) of a supernatural being; ghost. [ME f. F, or f. L *apparitio* attendance (as APPEAR; see -ION)]

ppä'ritor *n.* officer of ecclesiastical synod or court. [L, = public servant (as APPEAR; see -OR)]

ppea'l¹ *v.* **1.** *v.i.* make request (*to* higher tribunal, or abs.) for alteration of decision of lower one (‖*appeal to the* COUNTRY); call attention *to* (evidence); make earnest request (*to* person, *for* thing or *to* do); address oneself *to* (person, etc.) for help or corroboration or decision; (Cricket) ask umpire whether batsman is out; (seek to) be attractive (*she does not appeal to me; films that appeal to depraved tastes*); hence ∼ING² *a.* **2.** *v.t.* remove (case) to higher court; hence ∼ABLE *a.* [ME, f. OF *apeler* f. L AP(*pellare* f. *pellere* drive) address]

ppea'l² *n.* act of appealing; request for public donations to support a cause; feature or quality that appeals (*has sex, snob, appeal*); right of appealing; **Court of A**∼(**s**) (hearing cases previously tried in inferior courts); LORD (*Justice*) *of Appeal*. [ME, f. OF *apel* (as prec.)]

ppear' *v.i.* become or be visible; present oneself formally or publicly; (Law) act as counsel; be published (*it appeared in the papers; new edition will appear*); be manifest; have the appearance of being, seem, (*you appear to forget; strange as it may appear; it appears that*). [ME, f. *aper-* stressed st. of *apareir* f. L AP*parēre* -*rit-* come in sight)]

ppear'ance *n.* **1.** act of appearing; **put in an** ∼, be present, esp. briefly. **2.** form as perceived (*has a prosperous appearance*); **to all** ∼(**s**), so far as can be seen; **keep up** or **save** ∼**s** (outward show of prosperity etc.). **3.** semblance. [ME, f. OF *aparance, ence*, f. LL *apparentia* (as prec.; see -ENCE)]

ppea'se (-z) *v.t.* make calm or quiet (strife, anger, person); (Polit.) try to conciliate or bribe (potential aggressor) by making concessions, freq. with implication of sacrifice of principles; soothe; satisfy (appetite, prejudice); hence ∼MENT (-zm-) *n.* [ME, f. AF *apeser*, OF *apaisier* (à *to, pais* PEACE)]

ppe'llant *n.* & *a.* (one) who appeals to higher court; = foll. [ME, f. F (as APPEAL¹; see -ANT)]

ppe'llate *a.* (Law). taking cognizance of appeals. [f. L *appellatus* (as APPEAL¹; see -ATE²)]

ppellā'tion *n.* name, title; nomenclature. [ME f. OF, f. L *appellatio -onis* (as APPEAL¹; see -ATION)]

ppe'llative *a.* (Of noun) designating a class, common (as opp. to *proper*). [f. LL *appellativus* (as APPEAL¹; see -ATIVE)]

appe'nd *v.t.* hang on, annex; add, esp. in writing. [f. L AP(*pendere* hang)]

appe'ndage *n.* thing attached, esp. (Zool.) leg etc. of arthropod; addition; accompaniment. [f. prec. + -AGE]

appe'ndant *a.* & *n.* (person or thing) attached in subordinate capacity (*to* another). [f. OF *apendant* (*apendre* f. as APPEND; see -ANT)]

appe'nd|ix *n.* (*pl.* ∼*ices pr.* -sēz, or ∼*ixes*). subsidiary addition (*to* book or document); (Anat.) small process developed from surface of any organ, esp. the vermiform process of the caecum; hence ∼(**ĭc**)E'CTOMY, ∼**ĭci'tis**, *ns.* [L *appendix -icis* (AP*pendere* APPEND)]

apperceiʹve (-sĕ'v) *v.t.* be conscious of perceiving; (Psych.) unite and assimilate (a perception) to ideas already possessed, and so comprehend and interpret. [ME (in obs. sense 'observe'), f. OF *aperceveir* f. Rom. *AP(percipere* f. L *percipere* PERCEIVE)]

äpperce'pt|ion *n.* mind's perception of itself; (Psych.) perception with recognition or identification by association with previous ideas; hence ∼IVE *a.* [f. F *aperception* f. mod. L *apperceptio -onis* (as prec.; see -ION)]

äppertaiʹn *v.i.* belong as possession or right *to*; be appropriate *to*; relate *to*. [ME, f. OF *apertenir* f. LL AP(*pertinēre* PERTAIN)]

ä'ppetence, -cy̆, *ns.* longing or desire *for*. [f. F *appétence* or f. L *appetentia* (AP*petere* seek after; see -ENCE, -ENCY)]

ä'ppetent *a.* eagerly desirous. [ME, f. L *appetere* (see prec., -ENT)]

ä'ppetīte *n.* desire, inclination, (*for*); desire to satisfy natural needs, esp. for food or sexual pleasure; so **appe'titive** *a.* [ME, f. OF *apetit* f. L *appetitus* (AP*petere* seek after; see -ITE²)]

ä'ppetizer, -iser (-z-), *n.* thing eaten or drunk to stimulate appetite. [f. *appetize* (back-form. f. foll.) + -ER¹ (2)]

ä'ppetizing, -isĭng (-z-), *a.* giving appetite. [f. F *appétissant* irreg. f. *appétit* f. as APPETITE]

applau'd *v.* **1.** *v.i.* express approval loudly, as by clapping hands. **2.** *v.t.* express approval of, praise. [f. L AP*plaudere -plaus-* clap hands]

applau'se (-z) *n.* approbation loudly expressed; marked approval. [f. med. L *applausus* (as prec.)]

ä'pple *n.* **1.** rounded firm edible juicy fruit of a tree of the genus *Malus*; any of various similar fleshy many-celled fruits; ∼ **of** the eye or one's eye, (orig.) pupil or eyeball, any cherished object. **2.** ∼ **brandy**, spoil his plans; ∼-**green**, yellowish green; ∼-**head**, rounded head of toy dog; *∼-**jack**, apple brandy; ∼-**pie bed** (with sheets so folded that one's legs cannot be stretched out); ∼-**pie order**, perfect order; *∼--**polisher**, (sl.) toady; ∼-**s** (**and pears**), ‖(rhyming sl.) stairs; ∼ **sauce**, apples stewed to a pulp, *(sl.)* insincere flattery, nonsense. [OE *æppel*, = OHG *apful*, ON *epli* f. Gmc *∼aplu-*]

appli'ance *n.* thing applied as means to an end; utensil, device, equipment; fire-engine. [f. APPLY + -ANCE]

ä'pplic|able *a.* capable of being applied; having reference, appropriate, (*to*); hence ∼ABI'LITY *n.*, ∼ABLY *adv.* [OF, or f. med. L *applicabilis* (as APPLY; see -ABLE)]

ä'pplicant *n.* one who applies (*for*). [f. foll. + -ANT]

äpplicā'tion *n.* **1.** putting of one thing to another; thing (e.g. medicament) so put. **2.** employment of means; bringing (*of* general rule etc.) to bear upon particular case. **3.** relevance, applicability; diligence; (making of) a request. [ME f. F, f. L *applicatio -onis* (as APPLY; see -ATION)]

ä'pplicātor *n.* device for applying something, esp. to the body. [f. prec. + -OR]

äppli'qué (-lě'kā) *n.* & *a.*, & *v.t.* (∼**d** *pr.* -ād). **1.** *n.* & *a.* (ornamental work) cut out from one material and affixed to surface of another (esp. in needlework). **2.** *v.t.* ornament thus. [F, p.p. of *appliquer* apply f. L *applicare*; see foll.]

applȳ' *v.* **1.** *v.t.* put close (*to*) or in contact; administer (remedy etc. *to*; lit. or fig.); devote (*to*); make use of (**applied**, put to practical use, opp. *theoretical* or *pure*; *applied* MATHEMATICS); use as relevant or suitable (*to*). **2.** *v.i.* have relevance (*to*); make formal request (*for* help etc. *to*); make request (*for* employment etc.). [ME, f. OF *aplier* f. L AP*plicare* fold, fasten to]

appŏggiatu'ra (-ōjatōō'ra) *n.* (Mus.) grace-note just above or below primary note, performed before it and delaying it. [It.]

appoi'nt *v.t.* fix (time, place, *for* purpose); prescribe, ordain; (Law) declare destination of (property, or abs.); assign to office (*appoint him governor, to govern, to be governor, appoint him*); WELL-, *badly*, ∿ed, furnished or equipped; hence ∿EE' *n.*, *∿IVE *a.* [ME, f. OF *apointer* (*à point* to a point)]

appoi'ntment *n.* appointing, esp. of time and place for meeting; office assigned; (usu. in *pl.*) equipment, furnishing, fittings. [ME, f. OF *apointement* (as prec.; see -MENT)]

appŏr't *n.* production of material objects by supposedly occult means at spiritualist seance; object thus produced. [ME (in obs. senses), f. OF *aport* (*aporter* f. *à* to, *porter* bring)]

appŏr'tion *v.t.* give as due share (*to*); portion out; hence ∿MENT *n.* [f. F *apportionner* or f. med. L *apportionare* (as AP-, PORTION)]

ă'pposite (-z-) *a.* well expressed; appropriate (*to*); hence ∿LY² (-tlī) *adv.*, ∿NESS (-tn-) *n.* [f. L *appositus* p.p. of AP (*ponere* put); see -ITE²]

apposi'tion (-z-) *n.* placing side by side; (Gram.) placing of word syntactically parallel with another, esp. addition of one noun to another (*William the Conqueror*); hence ∿AL *a.* [ME f. F, or f. LL *appositio* (as prec.; see -ITION)]

apprai's|e (-z) *v.t.* (Esp. of official valuer) value or fix price for; estimate; hence ∿AL, ∿eMENT (-zm-), ∿ER¹, *ns.*, ∿ABLE, ∿IVE, *adjs.* [f. APPRIZE by assim. to PRAISE]

apprē'ciab|le (-sha-) *a.* capable of being estimated; perceptible; considerable; hence ∿LY² *adv.* [F (*apprécier*; see foll., -ABLE)]

apprē'ci|āte (-shī-, -sī-) *v.* **1.** *v.t.* estimate worth, quality, amount, of; estimate rightly; understand, recognize, *that*; be sensitive to; esteem highly, be grateful for; raise in value; hence ∿ATIVE, ∿atORY, *adjs.* **2.** *v.i.* rise in value. [f. LL AP*pretiare* appraise (*pretium* price) +-ATE³]

apprēciā'tion (-shī-, -sī-) *n.* estimation, judgement; adequate recognition; rise in value; (usu. favourable) review of book etc. [F, f. LL *appretiatio -onis* (as prec.; see -ATION)]

ăpprĕhĕ'nd *v.t.* seize, arrest; perceive (by senses or intellect); understand; anticipate with fear. [f. F *appréhender* or L AP (*prehendere -hens-* lay hold of)]

ăpprĕhĕ'ns|ible *a.* capable of being grasped (by senses or intellect); hence ∿IBI'LITY *n.* [f. LL *apprehensibilis* (as prec.; see -IBLE)]

ăpprĕhĕ'nsion (-shən) *n.* seizure, arrest; grasping (of ideas), conception; understanding; uneasiness. [F, or f. LL *apprehensio* (as prec.; see -ION)]

ăpprĕhĕ'nsive *a.* pertaining to perception by senses or intellect; uneasy in mind, fearful, (*of* thing, *that* it may happen, *for* person, *for* his safety); (arch.) perceptive, intelligent; hence ∿LY² (-vlī) *adv.*, ∿NESS (-vn-) *n.* [f. F *appréhensif* or med. L *apprehensivus* (as prec.; see -IVE)]

apprĕ'ntice *n.*, & *v.t.* **1.** *n.* learner of a craft, bound to serve, and entitled to instruction from, his employer for specified term; (esp. of jockey) beginner, novice; hence ∿SHIP (-s-sh-) *n.* **2.** *v.t.* bind as apprentice. [ME, f. OF *aprentis* (*apprendre* learn, as APPREHEND), after wds in -*tis*, -*tif*, f. L -*tivus* (see -IVE)]

appri'se (-z) *v.t.* inform; **be** ∿**d** (aware) **of.** [f. F *appris* -*ise* p.p. of *apprendre* learn, teach, (as APPREHEND)]

appri'ze *v.t.* (arch.) appraise; esteem highly. [ME, f. OF *aprisier* (*à* to, *pris* PRICE)]

‖**ă'pprŏ** (-, colloq.) **on** ∿, on APPROVAL. [abbr. of *approval* or *approbation*]

approa'ch¹ *v.* **1.** *v.i.* come near(er) in space or time (Golf) play approach shot; (Aeron.) make approach **2.** *v.t.* be similar in character etc. to; come near to set about (task); approximate to; make tentative proposal to; attempt to influence or bribe; (arch. bring near; hence ∿ABI'LITY *n.*, ∿ABLE *a.*, (esp. friendly. [ME, f. OF *aproch(i)er* f. eccl. L AP*propiar* draw near (*propius* compar. of *prope* near)]

approa'ch² *n.* act or means of approaching; approximation; (Bridge) bidding method with gradual advance to final contract; (Golf) stroke, not from tee played to reach the green; (Aeron.) final part of flight before landing. [f. prec.]

*∗**ă'pprobāte** *v.t.* approve formally, sanction. [ME, f L AP*probare* test f. *probus* good) +-ATE³]

ăpprobā'tion *n.* sanction; approval; so **ă'pprobātIVE**, **ă'pprobātORY**, *adjs.* [ME f. OF, f. L *approbatio -onis* (as prec.; see -ATION)]

apprō'priate *a.* belonging or peculiar (*to*); suitable or proper (*to, for*); hence ∿LY² (-tlī) *adv.*, ∿NESS (-tn-) *n.* [f. LL *appropriatus* p.p. of AP*propriare* (*proprius* own) see -ATE²]

apprō'pri|āte *v.t.* take possession of; take to oneself esp. without authority; devote (money etc.) to special purposes; hence or cogn. ∿A'TION, ∿ătOR, *ns.* ∿ATIVE *a.* [f. prec.; see -ATE³]

appro'val *n.* act of approving; sanction; **on** ∿ (of goods supplied) to be returned if not satisfactory [f. foll. +-AL 2]

approv've *v.t.* & *i.* **1.** *v.t.* confirm, sanction; commend (arch.) show one*self* to be. **2.** *v.t.* & *i.* ∿ (**of**), pronounce or consider good or satisfactory, agree to; ∿**d school** (Hist.) community home for training of young offenders. [ME, f. OF *aprover*, f. L (as APPROBATE)]

approx. *abbr.* approximate(ly).

apprō'ximate¹ *a.* fairly correct, near to the actual hence ∿LY² (-tlī) *adv.* (**very** ∿**ly**, as only a rough approximation). [f. LL *approximatus* p.p. of AP*proxi mare* (*proximus* very near); see -ATE²]

apprō'xim|āte² *v.t.* & *i.* bring or come near but not exactly (*to* thing, esp. in quality, number, etc.); hence ∿A'TION *n.*, ∿ATIVE *a.* [f. prec.; see -ATE³]

appŭr'tĕnance *n.* (usu. in *pl.*) belonging; appendage accessory. [ME, f. AF *apurtenaunce*, OF *apertenance*, Rom. *∗appertinentia* (as APPERTAIN; see -ANCE)]

appŭr'tĕnant *a.* belonging, appertaining, pertinent (*to*). [ME, f. OF *apartenant* part. (as APPERTAIN)]

Apr. *abbr.* April.

après-ski (ăprăskē') *attrib. a.* & *n.* (worn or done at time after day's skiing at resort. [F]

ā'prĭcŏt *n.* (tree bearing) juicy stone-fruit allied to plum and peach; its colour when ripe, orange-pink [f. Port. *albricoque* or Sp. *albaricoque* f. Arab. *a* the+*barḳuḳ* f. Gk *praikokion* f. L *praecoquum* var. of *praecox* early-ripe; *apri-* after L *apricus* ripe, -*cot* by assim. to F *abricot*]

A'pril (ā'pril, -il) *n.* fourth month of year; ∿ **fool** person jokingly fooled on 1 Apr. (∿ *Fool's Day*); ∿ **weather**, alternating sunshine and showers. [ME f. L *Aprilis*]

ā priōr'ī *adv.* & *a.* (reasoning) from causes to effects deductive(ly); presumptive(ly); without investigation, as far as one knows; (of knowledge) obtained by deduction without sensory experience; hence ∿A'TION *n.*, ∿ATIVE *a.* [f. prec.; see -ATE³]

āpriōr'ISM *n.*, doctrine of a priori ideas. [L, = from what is before]

ā'pron n. **1.** garment worn in front of body to protect clothes; **tied to** ∿**-strings of** (*wife, mother,* etc.) unduly controlled by. **2.** official dress of this kind (*bishop's, freemason's, apron*); leather covering for legs in open carriage; endless conveyor-belt; hard -surfaced area on airfield, used for manœuvring and (un)loading aircraft; (Theatr.) advanced strip of stage for playing scenes in front of curtain. **3.** Hence ∿eD² (-nd) *a.*, ∿FUL 2 *n.* [ME *naperon* etc., f. OF of *nape* table-cloth f. L *mappa*; for loss of *n-* cf. ADDER

ăpropŏs (-pŏ', ă'propŏ) *adv.* & *a.* to the purpose

appropriate(ly); (abs.) incidentally, by the way; in respect of; (colloq.) concerning. [f. F à propos (à to, propos PURPOSE[1])]

pse n. large semicircular or polygonal recess, arched or dome-roofed, esp. at end of church; apsis. [f. L APSIS]

'psidal a. of the form of an apse; of apsides. [f. foll. + -AL]

'psi|s n. (pl. ~des pr. -dēz). point on orbit of planet, satellite, etc. nearest to or farthest from body round which it moves. [L, f. Gk (h)apsis -idos arch, vault]

pt a. suitable, appropriate; having a tendency (to do etc.); quick-witted (at); hence ~'LY[2] adv., ~'NESS n. [ME, f. L aptus fitted p.p. of apere fasten]

'pterous a. (Zool.) wingless; (Bot.) having no winglike expansions. [f. Gk apteros (a- not, pteron wing) + -OUS]

'pteryx n. flightless New Zealand bird of genus Apteryx, with rudimentary wings and no tail, kiwi. [mod. L, f. Gk a- not + pterux wing]

'ptitūde n. fitness; natural propensity or talent (for); ability, esp. (Psych.) to acquire a particular skill. [F, f. LL aptitudo -inis (as APT; see -TUDE)]

'qua n. the colour aquamarine. [abbr.]

qua- pref. denoting water, esp. w. ref. to aquatic entertainments or sports. [f. L aqua water]

'quacúlture n. cultivation of plants or breeding of animals in water. [f. AQUA-, after agriculture]

qua fór'tis n. (Chem.) nitric acid. [L, = strong water]

'qualŭng n., & v.i. 1. n. diver's portable breathing-apparatus with cylinders of compressed air strapped on back, feeding air automatically through mask or mouthpiece. 2. v.i. use this. [f. L aqua water + LUNG]

quamari'ne (-ē'n) n. bluish-green beryl; its colour. [f. L aqua marina sea water]

quanaut n. underwater explorer or swimmer. [f. AQUA- + Gk nautēs sailor]

'quaplāne n., & v.i. 1. n. board on which person rides, towed behind speedboat. 2. v.i. ride standing on aquaplane; (of vehicle) glide uncontrollably on water covering road surface. [f. L aqua water + PLANE[3]]

qua rē'gia n. (Chem.) mixture of nitric and hydrochloric acids, able to dissolve gold and platinum. [L, = royal water]

quarě'lle n. painting in thin usu. transparent water-colours. [F, f. It. acquarella water-colour dim. of acqua f. L aqua water]

quār'i|um n. (pl. ~ums or ~a). artificial pond or tank usu. with transparent sides, for keeping live aquatic plants and animals; place containing such tanks; hence **ä'quarIST** n., keeper of an aquarium. [f. neut. of L aquarius of water (aqua), after vivarium]

quar'i|us (a-) n. (person born under) sign of the ZODIAC, the Water-carrier; hence ~AN a. & n., (person) born under Aquarius. [L (as prec.; see -ARY[1])]

quá'tic a. & n. 1. a. growing or living in or near water; (of sports) conducted in or on water. 2. n. aquatic plant or animal; (in pl.) aquatic sports. [ME, f. F aquatique or f. L aquaticus (aqua water; see -ATIC)]

'quatint n. method of etching on copper with nitric acid; engraving so made. [f. F aquatinte f. It. acqua tinta coloured water]

quavi't, ăkvavi't, (-ē't) n. alcoholic spirit from potatoes etc. [Scand.]

qua vi'tae n. alcoholic spirits, esp. of the first distillation. [L, = water of life, orig. alchemists' term]

'quedŭct n. artificial channel, esp. elevated structure of masonry, for conveyance of water; (Physiol.) small canal, esp. in head of mammals. [f. L aquae ductus conduit (aqua water, ducere duct- lead)]

'quèous a. of water; containing water; (Geol.) produced by water (aqueous rocks); ~ **humour**, (Anat.) transparent fluid between lens of eye and cornea. [f. med. L aqueus f. L aqua water, + -OUS]

'quifer n. (Geol.) layer of rock or soil able to hold or

transmit much water. [f. L aqui- (aqua water) + -fer bearing (ferre bear)]

äquilē'gia n. (usu. blue-flowered) plant of genus Aquilegia, columbine. [mod. use of med. L wd, of unkn. orig.]

ä'quilīne a. of or like an eagle; (of nose) curved like eagle's beak. [f. L aquilinus (aquila eagle; see -INE[1])]

ar- pref., assim. form of AD- before r.

-ar[1] suf. forming (1) adjs. (angular, annular, linear, molecular, nuclear, titular) and ns. (scholar) [f. or after OF -aire or -ier or f. L -aris], (2) ns. (pillar) [f. F -er or f. L -ar, -are, neut. of -aris].

-ar[2] suf. forming ns. (bursar, exemplar, mortar, vicar). [f. OF -aire or -ier or f. L -arius, -arium]

-ar[3] suf. var. of -ER[1], -OR, (liar, pedlar).

AR abbr. Arkansas.

Ar symb. argon.

ARA abbr. Associate of the Royal Academy.

A'rab (ă'-) n. & a. 1. (one) of the Semitic people originally inhabiting Saudi Arabia and neighbouring countries, now the Middle East generally. 2. n. Arabian horse; **street arab**, (R) homeless child. [f. F Arabe f. L Arabs Arabis f. Gk Araps -abos f. Arab. 'arab]

ärabě'sque (-k) n. decoration with fanciful intertwining of leaves, scrollwork, etc.; (Mus.) passage or composition suggesting this decoration; (Ballet) posture in which body is bent forwards and supported on one leg with the other leg extended horizontally backwards, and arms are extended one forwards and one backwards. [F, f. It. arabesco (arabo Arab; see -ESQUE)]

Arā'bian (a-) a. & n. (native or inhabitant) of Arabia. [ME, f. OF arabi prob. f. Arab. 'arabī, or f. L Arab(i)us f. Gk Arabios, + -AN]

A'rabic (ă'-) a. & n. 1. a. of Arabia; **gum a~** (exuded by some kinds of acacia); **a~ numerals**, 1, 2, 3, etc. (opp. Roman numerals). 2. of the Arabs' language or literature. 3. n. language orig. of the Arabs, now spoken in much of N. Africa and Middle East. [ME, f. OF arabic f. L f. Gk Arabikos]

ä'rabis n. cruciferous plant of genus Arabis, with white or purple flowers. [med. L f. Gk, = Arabian]

A'rabīsm (ă'-) n. Arabic usage; Arab nationalism etc. [f. ARAB + -ISM]

A'rabist (ă'-) n. student of Arabic language or Arab civilization. [f. ARAB + -IST]

ä'rable a. & n. (land) ploughed or fit for ploughing; ||(of crops) that can be grown on arable. [F, or f. L arabilis (arare plough; see -ABLE)]

A'raby (ā'-) n. (poet.) Arabia. [f. OF Arabie f. L f. Gk Arabia]

ara'chnid (-k-) n. (Zool.) member of the class Arachnida, comprising spiders, scorpions, ticks, and mites. [f. F arachnide or mod. L arachnida f. Gk arakhnē spider; see -ID[3]]

arā'chnoid (-k-) a. & n. 1. a. (Bot.) covered with long cobweb-like hairs. 2. n. (Anat.) middle MENINX, between dura mater and pia mater. [f. mod. L arachnoides f. Gk arakhnoeidēs (arakhnē cobweb; see -OID)]

arā'k. See ARRACK.

A'raldīte (ă'-) n. (P) name of various epoxy resins used as strong cements, insulators, etc. [20th c.; orig. uncert.]

Aramā'ic (ă-) a. & n. (of) language of Syria, widely used as lingua franca by Jews and others in time of Christ; (of) northern branch of Semitic family of languages, including Syriac and Mandaean. [f. L f. Gk Aramaios of Aram (bibl. name of Syria); see -IC]

ärapai'ma (-pī'-) n. large S. Amer. food-fish of genus Arapaima, pirarucú. [Tupi]

ärapő'nga, -pŭ'nga, (-ngga) n. S. Amer. bell-bird. [f. Port.]

äraucār'ia n. evergreen tree of genus Araucaria, e.g. monkey-puzzle. [mod. L, f. Arauco, former province in Chile; see -ARY[1]]

âr'balest n. (Hist.) crossbow with special mechanism for drawing. [OE arblast f. OF arbaleste f. LL arcubalista (arcus bow, BALLISTA)]

ar̃′bit|er *n.* judge; arbitrator; one who has entire control (*of*); ∼**er elegantiar′um** (*or* **elega′ntiae**) (-shĭ-), judge of taste and etiquette (lit. of elegance); so ∼**ress**[1] *n.* [L]

ar̃′bitrag|e (-ahzh) *n.* traffic in bills of exchange or stocks to take advantage of different prices in other markets; so ∼**eur′** (-ahzhēr′) *n.*, one who engages in arbitrage. [F, f. *arbitrer* (as ARBITRATE); see -AGE]

ar̃′bitral *a.* pertaining to arbitration. [F, or f. LL *arbitralis* (ARBITER); see -AL]

ar̃bi′trament *n.* deciding of dispute by arbiter; authoritative decision. [ME, f. OF *arbitrement* f. med. L *arbitramentum* (as ARBITRATE; see -MENT)]

ar̃′bitrar|y̆ *a.* derived from mere opinion or random choice; capricious; unrestrained; despotic; hence ∼**ily**[2] *adv.*, ∼**iness** *n.* [f. L *arbitrarius* or F *arbitraire*; see ARBITER, -ARY[1]]

ar̃′bitrate *v.t & i.* decide by arbitration. [f. L *arbitrari* judge (ARBITER) + -ATE[3]]

ar̃bitra′tion *n.* settlement of a dispute by an arbitrator. [ME f. OF, f. L *arbitratio -onis* (as prec.; see -ATION)]

ar̃′bitrator *n.* one appointed by two parties to settle dispute; arbiter; hence ∼**ship** *n.* [ME f. LL, f. as prec. + -OR]

ar̃′bitress. See ARBITER.

ar̃′blast (-ahst). Var. of ARBALEST.

ar̃′bor[1] *n.* axle or spindle on which something revolves; *tool-holder in lathe etc. [f. F *arbre* tree, axis, f. L *arbor*; refash. on L]

*ar̃′bor[2]. See ARBOUR.

ar̃bora′ceous (-shŭs) *a.* treelike; wooded. [f. L *arbor* tree + -ACEOUS]

Ar̃′bor Day (ar̃′-) *n.* day set apart annually in US, Australia, and elsewhere for public tree-planting. [f. L *arbor* tree + DAY]

ar̃bor′eal *a.* of, living in, connected with, trees. [f. L *arboreus* (*arbor* tree) + -AL]

ar̃bor′eous *a.* wooded; arboreal. [f. as prec. + -OUS]

ar̃bore′sc|ent *a.* treelike in growth or general appearance; hence ∼**ENCE** *n.* [f. L *arborescere* grow into a tree (*arbor*); see -ESCENT]

ar̃bore′t|um *n.* (*pl.* ∼**a** *or* *∼**ums**). botanical tree-garden. [L (*arbor* tree)]

ar̃′bori|culture *n.* cultivation of trees and shrubs; hence ∼**cu̇′ltur**AL *a.*, ∼**cu̇′ltur**IST (3) *n.*, (-cher-). [f. L *arbor -oris* tree, after *agriculture*]

ar̃boriza′tion, -**īsa′tion** (-z-), *n.* treelike appearance of crystal etc. [f. as prec. + -IZE + -ATION]

ar̃bor vī′tae *n.* evergreen conifer of genus *Thuja*. [L, = tree of life]

||**ar̃′bour**, *ar̃′bor[2]**, (-er) *n.* bower, shady retreat with sides and roof formed mainly by trees or climbing plants; hence ∼**ED**[2] (-erd) *a.* [ME f. AF *erber*, f. OF *erbier* (*erbe* herb f. L *herba*; see -ARIUM]; phonetic change to *ar*- assisted by assoc. with L *arbor* tree]

ar̃bū′tus *n.* evergreen of genus *Arbutus*, e.g. strawberry-tree; *trailing ∼, mayflower. [L]

ar̃c *n.*, & *v.i.* (∼**ing** *pr.* ar̃′k-, ∼**ed** *pr.* ar̃kt). **1.** *n.* part of circumference of circle or other curve; (Electr.) luminous bridge formed by discharge between electrodes in gas; ∼ **lamp**, ∼ **light**, light sources using electric arc; ∼ **welding** (using electric arc to melt metals to be welded). **2.** *v.i.* form arc. [ME f. OF, f. L *arcus* arc, curve]

||**ARC** *abbr.* Agricultural Research Council.

ar̃ca′de *n.* passage arched over; any covered walk, esp. with shops etc. along one or both sides; ||AMUSEMENT *arcade* (Archit.) series of arches supporting or along wall; hence **ar̃ca′d**ED[2] *a.* [F, f. Prov. *arcada* or It. *arcata* f. Rom. *arca* ARCH[1]; see -ADE]

Arca′dian (ar̃-) *a.* & *n.* ideal(ly) rustic; hence ∼**ISM** *n.*, pastoral simplicity. [f. L *Arcadius* f. Gk *Arkadia* mountain district in Peloponnese, taken as ideal rustic paradise, + -AN]

Ar̃′cady̆ (ar̃′-) *n.* (poet.) ideal rustic paradise. [f. Gk *Arkadia* (see prec.)]

arcā′ne *a.* mysterious, secret; hence ∼**LY**[2] (-nlĭ) *adv*, ∼**NESS** (-n-n-) *n.* [F, or f. L *arcanus* (*arcēre* shut up f. ar̃ chest; see -ANE)]

arcā′n|um *n.* (usu. in *pl.* ∼**a**). mystery, secret. [neut. of *arcanus* (see prec.)]

ar̃ch[1] *n.* curved structure as support for bridge, roo floor, etc., or as ornament; curvature in shape of arch e.g. on inner side of foot; vault; **Court of Arche** (Eccl.) court of appeal for the province of Canterbury orig. held in the church of St. Mary-le-Bow (or 'of th Arches'); ∼′**way**, vaulted passage, arched entrance [ME, f. OF *arche* f. Rom. *arca, n. pl. by-form of *arcus* arc]

ar̃ch[2] *v.* **1.** *v.t.* furnish with or form into arch; span lik arch; *arched* SQUALL. **2.** *v.i.* form arch. [ME, f. prec.]

ar̃ch[3] *a.* consciously or affectedly playful or teasing hence ∼**LY**[2] *adv.*, ∼**NESS** *n.* [f. foll. (2), orig. in rogue etc.]

arch- *pref.* w. sense (1) chief, superior, (*archbisho* *archdiocese, archduke*), (2) pre-eminent, esp. extreme bad, (*arch-fiend*). [f. OE *arce-* or OF *arche-*, f. L f. G *arkhi-* etc. (*arkhos* chief)]

Archae′an, *Arche′an**, (ar̃k-) *a.* & *n.* (of) the earlie geological period. [f. Gk *arkhaios* ancient (*arkh* beginning) + -AN]

ar̃chae|ŏ′logy̆, *ar̃chĕ|ŏ′logy̆**, (-kĭ-) *n.* study o human antiquities, esp. of the prehistoric perio and usu. by excavation; **industrial** ∼**ology,** stud of machines etc. formerly used in industry; henc or cogn. ∼**olŏ′g**IC(AL) *adj*s., ∼**o′log**IST (3) *n* ∼**o′log**IZE (2) *v.i.* [f. mod. L f. Gk *arkhaiologia* ancien history (as prec.; see -LOGY)]

ar̃chaeŏ′pteryx (-kĭŏ′-) *n.* oldest known fossil bir with tail like reptile's. [f. Gk *arkhaios* ancient + *pter* wing]

ar̃chā′|ic (-k-) *a.* primitive; of early period in cultu or art (e.g. 7th–6th c. BC in Greece); antiquated; (word etc.) no longer in ordinary use, though retaine for special purposes; hence ∼**ICALLY** *adv.* [f. *archaïque* f. Gk *arkhaïkos* (as prec.; see -IC)]

ar̃chā′|ism (-k-) *n.* retention or imitation of the old o obsolete (esp. in language and art); archaic word o expression; hence ∼**IST** (1) *n.*, ∼**I′ST**IC *a.* [f. mod. L Gk *arkhaïsmos* (*arkhaïzō*; see foll., -ISM)]

ar̃chā′ize (-k-), -**īse** (-īz), *v.* **1.** *v.i.* imitate the archai **2.** *v.t.* render archaistic. [f. Gk *arkhaïzō* be old -fashioned (*arkhaios* ancient; see -IZE)]

ar̃′changel (-kānj-) *n.* angel of highest rank; one of th eighth ORDER[1] of ninefold celestial hierarchy; henc **archangĕ′l**IC (-kănj-) *a.* [OE, f. AF *archangele* f. ecc L f. eccl. Gk *arkhaggelos* (as ARCH-, ANGEL)]

ar̃chbi′shop *n.* chief bishop of province; hence **ar̃ch** BI′SHOPRIC *n.* [OE (as ARCH-, BISHOP)]

ar̃chdea′con *n.* Anglican clergyman next belo bishop; dignitary of similar rank in other Churche hence ∼**RY** (2, 3), ∼**SHIP**, *n*s. [OE *arce-, ercediacon* eccl. L f. eccl. Gk *arkhidiakonos* (as ARCH-, DEACON[2]

ar̃chdī′ocese *n.* see of an archbishop; so **ar̃ch** **diŏ′cès**AN *a.* [f. ARCH- + DIOCESE]

ar̃′ch|duke *n.* (*fem.* ∼**duchess**). (Hist.) chief duk (esp. as title of son of Emperor of Austria); hence o cogn. ∼**DU′CAL** *a.*, ∼**DUCHY** *n.* [f. OF *archeduc* f. med. *archidux -ducis* (as ARCH-, DUKE)]

*Archean. See ARCHAEAN.

ar̃chegŏ′ni|um (-kĭ-) *n.* (*pl.* ∼**a**). (Bot.) female se organ in mosses, ferns, etc. [mod. L, abbr. of G *archegonium* (*arkhe-* chief, *gonos* race)]

ar̃ch-ĕ′nemy̆ *n.* chief enemy; the Devil. [f. ARCH- (2 + ENEMY]

*archeology. See ARCHAEOLOGY.

ar̃′cher *n.* one who shoots with bow and arrows; (*A∼* the zodiacal sign Sagittarius; ∼**-fish**, E. Ind. fis shooting water from mouth to dislodge and catc insects; so **ar̃′ch**ERY (2) *n.* [AF, f. OF *archier* f. Rom *arcarius* f. L *arcus* bow; see -ARY[1]]

ar̃′chĕtyp|e (-k-) *n.* original model, prototype; typica specimen; (Psych.) primordial mental imag inherited by all; recurrent symbol or motif; so ∿AL, **ărchĕtў'pICAL** (-k-), *adjs.* [f. L f. Gk *arkhetupon* (*arkhe-* ARCH-, *tupos* stamp)]

ărch-fie'nd *n.* the Devil. [f. ARCH- (2) + FIEND]

ărchĭdĭă'con|al (-kĭ-) *a.* pertaining to an archdeacon; so ∿ATE¹ (1) *n.* [f. med. L *archidiaconalis* (as ARCH-, DIACONAL)]

ărchĭĕpĭ'scop|al (-kĭĭ-) *a.* pertaining to an archbishop; so ∿ATE¹ (1) *n.* [f. eccl. L f. Gk *arkhiepiskopos* archbishop + -AL]

ăr'chĭl (-ch-, -k-) *n.* (violet dye from) one of various kinds of lichen. [var. of ORCHIL]

ărchĭmă'ndrīte (-k-) *n.* superior of large monastery in Orthodox Church (often as honorary title of monastic priest). [F, or f. eccl. L *archimandrita* f. eccl. Gk *arkhimandritēs* (*arkhi-* ARCH-, *mandra* monastery)]

Archĭmē'dĕan (ārk-) *a.* of Archimedes (Greek mathematician d. 212 BC); ∿ **screw,** instrument raising water by turning of inclined screw. [f. LL *Archimedeus* + -AN]

Archĭmē'dēs (ārk-; -z) *n.* ∿' **principle** (that a body immersed in a fluid is subject to an upward force equal in magnitude to the weight of fluid it displaces). [see prec.]

ărchĭpĕ'lagō (-k-) *n.* (*pl.* ∿s *or* ∿es). sea with many islands; group of islands. [f. It. *arcipelago* f. Gk *arkhi-* chief + *pelagos* sea (orig. = the Aegean Sea)]

ăr'chĭtĕct (-kĭ-) *n.* designer of buildings, who prepares plans and superintends construction; designer of complex structure; the Creator; designer of ships etc.; (fig.) achiever (*architect of his own fortunes*). [f. F *architecte* f. It. *architetto*, or f. L *architectus* f. Gk *arkhitektōn* (*arkhi-* ARCH-, *tektōn* builder)]

ărchĭtĕctŏ'n|ĭc (-kĭ-) *a.* of architecture or architects; constructive; pertaining to systematization of knowledge; hence ∿ICS *n.* [f. L f. Gk *arkhitektonikos* (as prec.; see -IC)]

ăr'chĭtĕcture (-kĭ-) *n.* art or science of building; thing built; structure; style of building; construction; hence **ărchĭtĕ'ctural** (-kĭtĕ kchei-) *a.* [F, or f. L *architectura* (*architectus* ARCHITECT; see -URE)]

ăr'chĭtrāve (-k-) *n.* main beam resting immediately on abacus of column; the various parts surrounding doorway or window; moulding round exterior of arch. [F f. It. (*archi-* ARCH-, *trave* f. L *trabs trabis* beam)]

ăr'chĭve (-k-) *n.* (in *sing.* or usu. in *pl.*) place in which collected public or corporate records are stored; records so kept. [f. F *archives* pl. f. L *archi(v)a* f. Gk *arkheia* public records (*arkhē* government)]

ăr'chĭvist (-k-) *n.* keeper of archives. [f. prec. + -IST]

ăr'chĭvŏlt (-k-) *n.* lower curve of arch from impost to impost; band of mouldings on this. [f. F *archivolte* or It. *archivolto* (as ARC, VAULT¹)]

ăr'chlute (-ōōt, -ūt) *n.* theorbo. [f. F *archiluth* (as ARCH-, LUTE¹)]

ăr'chon (-k-) *n.* one of nine chief magistrates in ancient Athens; hence ∿SHIP *n.* [f. Gk *arkhōn* ruler (pres. part., as n., of *arkhō* rule)]

Ar'ctic (ār'-) *a.* & *n.* **1.** *a.* of the north polar regions (∿ **Circle,** parallel of latitude 66° 33′ N.); (*a*∿; colloq., of weather) very cold. **2.** *n.* Arctic regions; (*a*∿) *thick waterproof overshoe. [ME, f. OF *artique* f. L *ar(c)ticus* f. Gk *arktikos* (*arktos* bear, Ursa Major; see -IC)]

ăr'cŭate *a.* bent like a bow; arched. [f. L *arcuatus* p.p. of *arcuare* curve (*arcus* bow, curve); see -ATE²]

arcus senilis (ārkus sĕnī'lis) *n.* narrow opaque band often encircling cornea in old age. [L, lit. 'senile bow']

-ard, -art, *suf.* forming *ns.* (*placard, pollard, Spaniard, standard, wizard*), usu. depreciatory (*braggart, drunkard, dullard, sluggard*). [ME & OF, f. G -*hard, -hart* hardy (in proper names)]

ăr'dent *a.* **1.** burning; ∿ (alcoholic) **spirits. 2.** eager, zealous; (of person or feelings) fervent. **3.** Hence **ăr'dENCY** *n.*, ∿LY² *adv.* [ME, f. OF *ardant* f. L *ardens -entis* (*ardēre* burn); see -ANT]

||**ăr'dour,** *ăr'dor,** (-*er*) *n.* fierce heat; warm emotion; fervour, zeal, (*for*). [ME f. OF, f. L *ardor -oris* (*ardēre* burn; see -OR)]

ăr'dŭous *a.* hard to achieve or overcome; laborious; strenuous, energetic; (arch.) steep; hence ∿LY² *adv.*, ∿NESS *n.* [f. L *arduus* steep, difficult + -OUS]

āre¹ *n.* metric unit of square measure, 100 square metres. [F, f. L AREA]

are². See BE.

ār'ĕa *n.* **1.** superficial extent; region, tract; hence **ār'ĕAL** *a.* **2.** defined space for particular use (*parking area, picnic area*); subject field (*areas of discussion*); branch of study; scope, range; (*or* *∿way*) sunk court in front of house basement; *∿ code,** dialling code for another part of the country. [L, = vacant piece of level ground]

areca (ă'rĭka, arē'ka) *n.* tropical Asiatic palm-tree of genus *Areca*; ∿ **nut,** astringent seed of a species of areca. [Port., f. Malayalam *áḍekka*]

ăr'ĕg. See ERG².

arē'na *n.* central part of amphitheatre etc., in which contests take place; (fig.) scene of conflict, sphere of action; ∿ **stage** (Theatr., placed amid audience); ∿ **theatre,** theatre-in-the-round. [L (*h*)*arena* sand, sand-strewn place of combat]

ărĕnă'ceous (-shus) *a.* sandlike; sandy; growing in sand. [f. L *arenaceus* (as prec.; see -ACEOUS)]

aren't. See BE.

arē'ol|a *n.* (*pl.* ∿ae). interstice; (Anat.) circular pigmented area, e.g. that surrounding nipple or pupil; hence ∿AR¹ *a.* [L, dim. of AREA]

arê'te (-ā't) *n.* sharp ridge of mountain, esp. in Switzerland. [F, f. L *arista* ear of corn, fishbone, spine]

ăr'gala *n.* adjutant bird. [f. Hindi *hargīlā*]

ăr'gali *n.* large Asiatic wild sheep; bighorn. [Mongol]

ăr'gent *n.* & *a.* (esp. Her.) silver (colour). [F, f. L *argentum*]

argĕnti'ferous *a.* yielding silver. [f. L *argentum* + -I- + -FEROUS]

ăr'gĕntĭne *a.* of silver; silvery; the A∿, Argentina; whence **Argenti'nIAN** (ār-) *a.* & *n.* [f. F *argentin* (*argent* silver; see -INE¹); cf. the A∿ f. Sp.]

ăr'gil *n.* clay (esp. potter's); so ∿1A'ceous *a.*, or of like clay. [f. F *argile* f. L *argilla* f. Gk *argillos* (*argos* white)]

Ar'gĭve (ār'g-) *a.* & *n.* (inhabitant) of Argos in ancient Greece; Greek. [L *Argivus* f. Gk *Argeios*]

ăr'gle-bărgle *v.i.,* & *n.* = ARGY-BARGY. [corrupt. and redupl. of *argue*, as in *huggle*]

ăr'gol *n.* crude TARTAR¹ 1. [ME f. AF *argoile* of unkn. orig.]

ăr'gŏn *n.* (Chem.) gaseous element, an almost inert constituent of the atmosphere. [Gk, neut. of *argos* idle (*a-* not, *ergon* work)]

ăr'gosy *n.* (Hist. or poet.) large merchant-vessel, esp. of Ragusa or Venice; (poet.) ship, venture. [prob. f. It. *Ragusea* (*nave*) Ragusan (vessel)]

ăr'gŏt (-gō) *n.* jargon or slang of a class or group, formerly esp. of thieves. [F, of unkn. orig.]

ăr'gūe *v.* **1.** *v.t.* maintain by reasoning (*that*); (arch.) prove. **2.** *v.t.* treat (matter) by reasoning; persuade (*person into, out of*); ∿ **away,** get rid of by argument; argue the TOSS 8. **3.** prove; indicate. **4.** *v.i.* reason, reason contentiously, (*with, against*; *person*; *for, against, about, that*); hence ∿**ABLE** *a.* make clear, prove, accuse]

ăr'gūfy *v.i.* (colloq.) dispute excessively. [illit. ARGUE; cf. *speechify*]

ăr'gūment *n.* **1.** reason advanced (*for, against*; proposition *or* course of action); reasoning process; ∿ **from silence** (based on opponent's silence or on absence of evidence). **2.** debate, esp. heated one. **3.** summary of subject-matter of book etc. **4.** (Math.) independent variable determining value of function. [ME f. OF, f. L *argumentum* (*arguere*; see ARGUE, -MENT)]

ar̄gūměntā'tion *n.* methodical reasoning; debate. [F, f. L *argumentatio* (*argumentari* as prec.; see -ATION)]

ar̄gūmě'ntative *a.* using methodical reasoning; fond of arguing; hence ~LY² (-vlĭ) *adv.*, ~NESS (-vn-) *n.* [f. F *argumentatif* -*ive* or f. LL *argumentativus* (as prec.; see -ATIVE)]

argumentum e silentio (ār̄gūměntum ē sǐlě'nshǐŏ) *n.* = ARGUMENT *from silence.* [L]

Ar'gus (ār'-) *n.* watchful guardian; Asiatic pheasant; butterfly with ocellated wings; ~-eyed, vigilant. [ME f. L, f. Gk *Argos* mythical person with a hundred eyes]

ar̄gū'te *a.* (literary). sharp, shrewd; (of sounds) shrill; hence ~LY² (-tlĭ) *adv.*, ~NESS (-tn-) *n.* [ME, f. L *argutus* p.p. of *arguere* (see ARGUE)]

ar̄'gy-bar̄gy *n.* (joc.) dispute, wrangle. [orig. Sc.; cf. ARGLE-BARGLE, -Y³]

ar̄'ia *n.* (Mus.) long accompanied song for one voice in opera, oratorio, etc. [It.]

Ar'ian¹ (ār'-) *a.* & *n.* (holder) of the doctrine of Arius of Alexandria (4th c.), who denied full divinity of Christ; hence ~ISM (3) *n.* [f. eccl. L *Arianus* (*Arius* f. Gk *Arios, Areios*; see -AN)]

Ar'ian² (ār'-) *a.* & *n.* (person) born under Aries. [f. ARIES + -AN]

-ar'ian *suf.* forming *adjs.* and *ns.* (*agrarian, antiquarian, disciplinarian*), esp. w. sense '(member) of a sect etc.', believer in' (*humanitarian, Unitarian, vegetarian*). [f. L -*arius* (see -ARY¹) + -AN]

ä'rid *a.* dry, parched; (fig.) uninteresting; (Geog.) too dry to support vegetation; (of ground) barren, bare; hence **ari'dITY**, ~NESS, *ns.*, ~LY² *adv.* [f. F *aride* or f. L *aridus* (*arēre* be dry; see -ID¹)]

ar̄'iel *n.* species of gazelle in W. Asia and Africa. [f. Arab. '*aryal* stag]

Ar'ies (ār'ēz) *n.* (*pl.* same). (person born under) sign of the ZODIAC, the Ram; **first point of** ~, vernal EQUINOCTIAL point. [ME f. L, = ram]

ari'ght (-ī't) *adv.* rightly. [OE (as A³, RIGHT³)]

ä'ril *n.* (Bot.) extra seed-covering in certain plants, e.g. yew. [f. mod. L *arillus*; cf. med. L *arilli* dried grape-stones]

-ar'ious *suf.* forming *adjs.* (*gregarious, vicarious*). [f. L -*arius* (see -ARY¹) + -OUS]

ari'se (-z) *v.i.* (aro'se *pr.* -ō'z; ari'sen *pr.* -ĭ'zen). originate; be born; come into notice; result (*from, out of*); present itself; rise, esp. from the dead. [OE *ārīsan* (as A- 1, RISE¹)]

ari'sings (-zĭngz) *n. pl.* materials forming secondary or waste products of operations. [f. prec. + -ING¹ (2)]

ǎristŏ'cracy̆ *n.* government by the best or most outstanding citizens; State so governed; ruling body of nobles; class of nobles; the best representatives *of* (intellect etc.). [f. F *aristocratie* f. Gk *aristokratia* (*aristos* of nobles; class of nobles; see -CRACY)]

ǎ'ristŏcrăt *n.* one of the class of nobles. [f. F *aristocrate* (as foll.)]

ǎristŏcrǎ't|ic *a.* pertaining to or attached to aristocracy; grand; stylish; with distinguished bearing and manners; hence ~ICALLY *adv.* [f. F *aristocratique* f. Gk *aristokratikos* (as ARISTOCRACY; see -IC)]

Aristotē'lian (ă-) *a.* & *n.* (disciple or student) of the Greek philosopher Aristotle (d. 322 BC); logical, deductive. [f. L *Aristotelius, -eus,* f. Gk *Aristoteleios* (*Aristotelēs* Aristotle) + -AN]

ari'thmetic¹ *n.* science of numbers; knowledge of this; computation, use of numbers; hence **arithmeti'cIAN** *n.* [ME, f. OF *arismetique* f. Rom. *arismetica f. L *arithmetica* f. Gk *arithmētikē* (*tekhnē*) (art) of counting (*arithmeō* count f. *arithmos* number; see -IC)]

ǎrithmě'tic², -ic|al, *adjs.* of arithmetic; *arithmetic* MEAN¹; ~al progression, (series of numbers showing) increase or decrease by a constant quantity (e.g. 1, 2, 3, 4, etc., 9, 7, 5, 3, etc.). [f. L f. Gk *arithmētikos* (see prec.) + -AL]

-ar̄'ium *suf.* forming *ns.* usu. denoting place (*aquarium, planetarium*). [L, neut. of *adjs.* in -*arius* (see -ARY¹)]

Ariz. *abbr.* Arizona.

ar̄k *n.* chest, box; **Ark** (**of the Covenant** or **of Testimony**), chest or cupboard containing scrolls or tables of Jewish Law; NOAH'S ark (**have come out of the Ark**, (colloq.) be very antiquated). [OE *ærc*, = OHG *archa*, ON *örk*, Goth. *arka*, f. L *arca* chest]

Ark. *abbr.* Arkansas.

ar̄m¹ *n.* **1.** upper limb of human body from shoulder to hand; ~ **in** ~, (of two or more persons) with arms interlinked; **as long as my** or **your** ~, (colloq.) very long; **at** ~'**s length**, as far as arm can reach, far enough to avoid undue familiarity, (of dealings) with neither party controlled by the other; **on** one's ~, supported by it; **under** one's ~, between it and body; **in** ~s, (of child) too young to walk; **in** person's ~s, embraced by him; **with open** ~s, cordially; **within** ~'**s reach**, reachable by extending arm without moving from chair etc. **2.** forelimb of animal; flexible limb of invertebrate; sleeve of garment; side part of chair to support sitter's arm; large branch of tree; thing resembling arm (*arm of the sea*). **3.** ~**chair'** (with side supports); ~**'chair** *a.*, (fig.) theorizing, not practical or participating (*armchair critic, traveller*); ~'**hole** (through which arm is put into garment sleeve or out of sleeveless garment); ~'**pit**, hollow under arm at shoulder. **4.** Hence (-)ar̄mED² (-md) *a.*, ~'**ful** 2. *n.*, quantity that can be held by one or both arms, ~'LESS *a.* [OE, = OHG *arm*, ON *armr*, Goth. *arms* f. Gmc *armaz]

ar̄m² *n.* **1.** (usu. in *pl.*) weapon; = *firearm* (see FIRE¹ 8); **small** ~s, portable firearms, esp. rifles, pistols, light machine-guns, sub-machine-guns, etc.; ~s **race**, contest between nations in accumulating weapons; **bear** ~s, be armed, serve as soldier, have coat of arms; **in** ~s, armed; **lay down** one's, **take up,** ~s, cease, begin, fighting; **up in** ~s, actively rebelling (*against*, lit. or fig.; *about*, fig.). **2.** (in *pl.*) military profession. **3.** each kind of troops or branch of military services, infantry, cavalry, artillery, etc. **4.** (in *pl.*) heraldic devices; COAT *of arms*; [KING¹ *of Arms.* [ME, f. OF *armes* pl. f. L *arma* arms, fittings]

ar̄m³ *v.t.* **1.** furnish (person, one*self,* or abs.) with weapons; ~ed **neutrality** (of nations prepared for war); *armed* SERVICE¹'s. **2.** furnish with tools or other requisites or (fig.) advantages. **3.** render (bomb etc.) able to explode. [ME, f. OF *armer* f. L *armare* arm(s)]

ar̄ma'da (-ah'-) *n.* fleet of warships, esp. that sent by Spain against England in 1588. [Sp., f. Rom. *armata* army; see -ADE]

ar̄madi'llō *n.* (*pl.* ~s). burrowing mammal of S. America, with body encased in bony plates, and often with habit of rolling itself into ball when captured. [Sp., dim. of *armado* armed man f. L *armatus* p.p. of *armare* ARM³]

Armage'ddon (ar̄mag-) *n.* (scene of) ultimate or large-scale conflict. [Rev. 16: 16 (AV)]

ar̄'mament *n.* force equipped for war; (in *sing.* or *pl.*) military weapons and equipment, esp. guns on warship; process of equipping for war. [f. L *armamentum* (as ARM³; see -MENT)]

ar̄maměntar̄'i|um *n.* (*pl.* ~a). set of equipment available to physician etc. (also fig.). [L, = arsenal]

ar̄'mature *n.* defensive covering of animals or plants; internal framework to support sculpture etc. during construction; piece of soft iron placed in contact with poles of magnet, to preserve its power or transmit force to something; wire-wound core of dynamo or electric motor; moving part of electric bell etc.; (arch.) arms, armour. [F, f. L *armatura* armour (as ARM²; see -URE)]

arme blanche (ar̄m blah'nsh) *n.* (*pl.* **-es -es** *pr.* same). cavalry sword or lance; cavalry. [F, = white ARM²]

Arme'nian (ar̄-) *a.* & *n.* (native, inhabitant, or

language) of Armenia; (member) of reputedly Monophysite church established in Armenia *c.* 300. [f.
Armenia in USSR +-AN]

ar'miger *n.* person entitled to heraldic arms; hence ∼ous (-ĭ'j-) *a.* [L, = bearing arms (*arma* ARM²s, *gerere* bear)]

armi'llary *a.* pertaining to bracelets; ∼ **sphere**, (Hist.) skeleton celestial globe of metal rings representing equator, tropics, etc. [f. mod. L *armillaris* f. L *armilla* bracelet; see -ARY²]

Armi'nian (ār-) *a.* & *n.* (holder) of the doctrine of Arminius, Dutch Protestant theologian d. 1609, who opposed the views of Calvin, esp. on predestination; hence ∼ISM (3) *n.* [f. *Arminius*, Latinized f. *Harmensen*, +-AN]

ar'mistice *n.* cessation from hostilities (lit. or fig.); short truce; A∼ **Day**, 11 Nov., anniversary of the armistice of 1918 (now replaced by ‖Remembrance Sunday and *Veterans' Day). [F, or f. mod. L *armistitium* (*arma* arms, -*stitium* stoppage; cf. SOLSTICE)]

ar'mlet *n.* band worn round arm; small inlet of sea or branch of river. [f. ARM¹+-LET]

*‖ar'mor etc, See ARMOUR¹,² etc.

armŏr'ial *a.* pertaining to heraldic arms. [f. foll.+ -AL]

ar'mory̆¹ *n.* heraldry; hence ∼IST (3) *n.* [f. OF *armoierie*; see ARMOURY]

*ar'mory̆². See ARMOURY.

‖**ar'mour¹**, *ar'mor¹**, (-mer) *n.* **1.** (Hist.) defensive covering for the body worn in fighting. **2.** ∼(-plate), metal sheathing of warship, composed of plates (∼-clad, furnished with this); steel plates etc. protecting cars, tanks, etc., from projectiles; armoured vehicles collectively, e.g. tanks, armoured cars. **3.** diver's suit. **4.** defensive covering of animals or plants. **5.** heraldic devices. [ME, f. OF *armure* f. L *armatura* (see ARMATURE)]

‖**ar'mour²**, *ar'mor²**, (-mer) *v.t.* furnish with protective covering; toughen (glass); ∼ed **car, train,** etc., one with protective plates of steel etc., and (usu.) guns; ∼ed **division** etc., one equipped with armoured cars, tanks, etc. [f. prec.]

‖**ar'mourer**, *ar'morer**, (-mer-) *n.* maker or repairer of arms or armour; official in charge of ship's or regiment's arms. [f. AF *armurer*, OF -*urier*, (as ARMOUR¹; see -ER²)]

‖**ar'moury̆**, *ar'mory̆²**, (-erĭ) *n.* place where arms are kept, arsenal; array of weapons, resources, etc.; *drill hall; *armourer's workshop. [ME, f. OF *armoi(e)rie* (*armoier* to blazon f. *arme* ARM²); assim. to ARMOUR¹]

ar'my̆ *n.* organized force armed for fighting on land; *the military profession*; large number (*an army of locusts, of helpers*); organized body for a cause (*Salvation Army; Church Army*); ∼ **corps,** main subdivision of army in the field; ‖**A∼ List,** official list of commissioned officers; ∼-**worm**, larva of various moths and flies, gathering in large numbers. [ME, f. OF *armee* f. Rom. *armata* fem. p.p. of *armare* arm; see -Y⁴]

ar'nica *n.* composite plant of genus Arnica, e.g. mountain tobacco; medicine prepared from this, used for bruises etc. [mod. L, of unkn. orig.]

aroi'nt *v.* or *int.* (arch.) ∼ **thee**, begone. [17th c.; orig. unkn.]

arō'ma *n.* fragrance, sweet smell; subtle pervasive quality. [f. L f. Gk *arōma -atos* spice]

āroma't|ic *a.* & *n.* **1.** *a.* fragrant, spicy; (of smell) pleasantly pungent; (Chem.) of organic compounds containing rings of (usu. six) carbon atoms; *aromatic* VINEGAR; hence ∼ICALLY *adv.* **2.** *n.* aromatic substance. [ME, f. OF *aromatique* f. LL f. Gk *arōmatikos* (as AROMA; see -IC)]

arose. See ARISE.

arou'nd *adv.* & *prep.* **1.** *adv.* on every side, in every direction; round, round about; (colloq.) near at hand,

in existence; in various places, here and there, at random, (*fool around; shop around*); **have been** ∼, (colloq.) have gained worldly experience. **2.** *prep.* on or along the circuit of; on every side of, enveloping; here and there in or near; *round (the church around the corner*); *approximately at, approximately equal to. [f. A- 2+ROUND²]

arou's|e (-z) *v.t.* awake from sleep; stir into activity; call into existence (*his behaviour aroused suspicion*); so ∼AL *n.* [f. A- 1+ROUSE², after *arise*]

arow' (-ō') *adv.* in a row or line. [ME, f. A³+ROW¹]

ARP *abbr.* air-raid precautions.

arpě'ggio (-ĕ'jiō, -ĕ'jō) *n.* (*pl.* ∼s). (Mus.) sounding of notes of chord in (usu. rapid upward) succession, not simultaneously; chord so sounded. [It. (*arpeggiare* play harp, f. *arpa* harp)]

ar'quebus. See HARQUEBUS.

arr. *abbr.* arranged by; arrives.

ä'rrack, arä'k, *n.* alcoholic spirit, esp. distilled from coco sap or rice. [f. Arab. '*arak* sweat, alcoholic spirit from grapes or dates]

arrai'gn (-ā'n) *v.t.* indict before tribunal; accuse; find fault with, call in question, (action, statement); so ∼MENT *n.* [ME, f. AF *arainer* f. OF *araisnier* f. Rom. *Arationare* reason, talk reasonably f. L *ratio* -onis reason, discourse]

arrā'nge (-nj) *v.* **1.** *v.t.* put into order, adjust; (Mus.) adapt (composition) for different medium, instrumental or vocal; adapt (play etc.) for broadcasting; settle (dispute etc.); settle beforehand the order or manner of; plan, cause to occur. **2.** *v.i.* take steps, form plans, give instructions, (*arrange to be there, for the car to be there; arrange about it*); come to agreement (*with person, about thing*). [ME, f. OF *arangier* (*à* to, *rangier* RANGE¹)]

arra'ngement (-njm-) *n.* arranging or being arranged; condition or manner of being arranged; thing arranged; settlement of dispute etc.; (in *pl.*) plans, measures, (*make your own arrangements*). [F (as prec.; see -MENT)]

ä'rrant *a.* downright, complete, (*arrant liar, nonsense*); hence ∼LY² *adv.* [ME, var. of ERRANT, orig. in phrs. like *arrant* (=outlawed roving) *thief*]

ä'rras *n.* rich tapestry, (Hist.) hanging screen of this on wall(s) of room. [f. A∼, town in NE France famous for the fabric]

array'¹ *v.t.* marshal, dispose, (forces); (Law) empanel (jury); dress, esp. with display; adorn. [ME, f. AF *araier* f. *areer*, f. Rom. *Arredare* f. Gmc *rædh*-prepare]

array'² *n.* imposing or well-ordered series of persons or things; (Law) order of empanelling jury; (Math.) matrix; (Hist.) arming of militia; (poet.) outfit, dress. [ME, f. AF *arai* f. OF *arei* (*areer*; see prec.)]

arrear'|s *n. pl.* outstanding debts; what remains not done (*arrears of work*); **in** ∼(s), behindhand, esp. in payment; so ∼AGE (1, 2) *n.* [ME, orig. adv. f. OF *arere* f. med. L *adretro* (AD-, *retro* backwards); first used in phr. *in arrear*]

arrě'st¹ *v.t.* **1.** stop (growth, motion, moving person or thing, progress of disease, decay); ∼ **judgement**, (Law) stay proceedings after verdict, on ground of error. **2.** seize (person or ship), esp. by legal authority; catch (attention); catch attention of. **3.** Hence ∼ABLE *a.*, (esp.) of offence) such that offender may be arrested without warrant; so ∼A'TION *n.*; ∼ER¹; ∼OR, *ns.*, (esp.) device for retarding aircraft by hook and cable on landing; ∼MENT *n.*, (esp., Sc.) attachment of earnings. [ME, f. OF *arester* f. Rom. *Arrestare* remain, stop (REST³)]

arrě'st² *n.* **1.** stoppage, check; **cardiac** ∼, heart failure; ∼ **of judgement** (Law) (see prec.). **2.** seizure; legal apprehension; **under** ∼ (legal restraint). [ME, f. OF *arest(e)* (*arester*; see prec.)]

arrière-ban (ä'rierbăn) *n.* (Hist.) (calling together of) vassals summoned for military service. [F, f. Frank. *hariban (hari* army, *ban* proclamation)]

arrière-pensée (ărǐārpah'ṅsā) *n.* ulterior motive; mental reservation. [F]

a'rris *n.* (Archit.) sharp edge formed by angular contact of two plane or curved surfaces. [corrupt. f. F *areste*, mod. ARÊTE]

arri'val *n.* act of arriving; appearance upon scene; person or thing that has arrived; (**new**) ∼, (colloq.) new-born child. [ME, f. AF *arrivaille* (*arriver* as foll.; see -AL 2)]

arri've *v.i.* ∼ (**at, in,** etc.), come to destination (lit., or fig.: *arrive at conclusions*) or end of journey or specified point on journey; establish one's reputation or position; (colloq., of child) be born; (of thing) be brought; (of time) come. [ME, f. OF *ariver* f. Rom. *AR*ri*pare* come to shore (L *ripa*)]

arrí'viste (ărēvē'st) *n.* ambitious or self-seeking person, so **arrívisme** (ărēvē'zem) *n.*, behaviour of an *arriviste*. [F (*arriver* f. OF as prec.; see -IST)]

a'rrog|ant *a.* overbearing; presumptuous; aggressively haughty; hence or cogn. ∼ANCE, ∼ANCY, *ns.*, ∼antLY[2] *adv.* [ME f. OF (as foll.; see -ANT)]

a'rrog|āte *v.t.* claim unduly (thing *to* one*self*); attribute unjustly (*to* person); so ∼A'TION *n.* [f. L AR(*rogare* ask) + -ATE[3]]

arrondissement (ărŏndē'smahṅ) *n.* administrative subdivision of French department. [F]

a'rrow (-ō) *n.* pointed straight slender missile shot from bow; pointer etc. of similar shape; ∥**broad** ∼, mark distinguishing British Government stores, e.g. (formerly) prison clothing; ∼**-grass,** marsh plant of genus *Triglochin* with 3-barbed burst capsules; ∼**head,** pointed end of arrow, water-plant with sagittate leaves; ∼**root,** plant from which a nutritious starch is prepared; hence ∼Y[2] *a.* [OE *ar*(*e*)*we* f. ON *ör*, st. *arw-, f. Gmc *arhw- f. IE *arkw-]

*arroy'ō *n.* (*pl.* ∼s). brook, stream; gully. [Sp.]

∥**ārse**[1]**, *ăss**[2], *n.* (vulg.) buttocks, rump; ∼**-hole,** anus; ∼**-licking** *n.* & *a.*, toadying. [OE *ærs*, = OHG, ON *ars*, Gmc *arsaz, IE *órsos]

∥**ārse**[2]. Var. of ASS[3].

ār'senal *n.* government establishment for storage or manufacture of weapons and ammunition; store of weapons (lit. or fig.). [F, or f. It. *arzanale* f. Arab. *dār*-ṣinā'*a* (*dār* house, *sinā*'*a* art, industry f. *ṣana*'a fabricate)]

ār'senic *n.* (Chem.) brittle steel-grey semi-metallic element; (pop.) arsenic trioxide, white mineral substance, a violent poison; **red** ∼, realgar; hence **ārsē'ni**ous *a.* [ME f. OF, f. L f. Gk *arsenikon* yellow orpiment (identified with *arsenikos* male, but in fact) f. Arab. *al-zarnīḵ* (*al* the, *zarnīḵ* orpiment f. Pers. f. *zar* gold)]

ārsě'nic[2] *a.* pertaining to arsenic; (Chem.) containing arsenic with valence five. [f. prec. + -IC]

ārsě'nical *a.* & *n.* (drug) containing arsenic. [f. ARSENIC[1] + -AL]

ār'sine (-ēn) *n.* (Chem.) compound AsH₃, like phosphine but with arsenic in place of phosphorus. [f. ARSENIC[1] after *amine*]

ār's|is *n.* (*pl.* ∼es *pr.* -ēz). stressed syllable or part of metrical foot (opp. THESIS). [ME f. LL f. Gk, = lifting (*airō* raise)]

ār'son *n.* malicious setting on fire of house etc.; hence ∼IST *n.*, person guilty of arson. [legal AF, OF, f. med. L *arsio* -*onis* f. L *ardēre ars*- burn]

ārsphe'namine (-ēn, -ēn) *n.* drug formerly used in treating yaws and syphilis. [f. ARSENIC + PHENYL + AMINE]

ārsў-vēr'sў *adv.* (vulg.) back to front; upside down. [f. ARSE[1] + L *versus* p.p. of *vertere* turn, after *hurly-burly* etc.]

art[1]. See BE.

ārt[2] *n.* **1.** skill, esp. human skill as opposed to nature; (ability in) skilful execution as an object in itself; cunning; imitative or imaginative skill applied to design, as in paintings, architecture, etc. (WORK[1]s *of art*); (*attrib.*) pertaining to use of such skill (*art music; art needlework*); (in *pl.*) = FINE[2] *arts.* **2.** thing in which

---

skill may be exercised; (in *pl.*) certain branches of university or school study serving as preparation for later life or for more advanced studies, esp. languages, literature, philosophy, history, etc., as dist. from sciences; **Bachelor, Master, of Arts,** one who has attained a certain standard of proficiency in these at university. **3.** practical application of any science; industrial pursuit, craft. **4.** knack; stratagem. **5.** ∼s **and crafts,** decorative design and handicraft; ∼ **and part,** accessory, participant; ∼ **deco** (dě'kō), decorative art style of 1920s and 1930s; ∼**-form,** established form of composition (e.g. novel, sonata, sonnet), medium of artistic expression; ∼ **nouveau** (ār nōōvō') [F, = new art], art style of late 19th c. with ornamented and flowing designs; ∼ **paper** (coated with smooth-surfaced clay etc.); ∼ **union,** (Austral. & NZ) lottery (orig. with work of art as prize); ∼'**work,** illustrative matter in printed text. [ME f. OF, f. L *ars artis*]

-art. See -ARD.

art. *abbr.* article.

ār'těfăct, ār'ti-, *n.* product of human art and workmanship; (Archaeol.) product of prehistoric or aboriginal art as dist. from similar object naturally produced; (Biol. etc.) thing not naturally present, introduced during preparation or investigation. [f. L *arte* (abl. of *ars* art) + *factum* (neut. p.p. of *facere* make)]

ārtě'l *n.* collective enterprise of craftsmen etc. in Russia. [Russ.]

ārtēr'ial *a.* belonging to an artery; of the nature of or resembling an artery (esp. of important main roads etc.). [F (*artère* artery; see -AL)]

ārtēr'ializ|e, -īs|e (-īz), *v.t.* convert venous into arterial (blood) by exposure to oxygen in lungs; furnish with arterial sytem; hence ∼A'TION *n.* [f. prec. + -IZE]

ārtēr'iōle *n.* small artery adjoining capillaries. [F, dim. of *artère* ARTERY]

ārtēriōsclěr'ō'sis *n.* (*pl.* ∼o'ses *pr.* -ēz). hardening and thickening of walls of arteries, esp. in old age; hence ∼o'TIC *a.* [f. ARTERY + -O- + SCLEROSIS]

ār'ter|ў *n.* **1.** muscular-walled tube forming part of system by which blood is conveyed from heart (cf. VEIN) to all parts of body; hence ∼I'TIS *n.* **2.** (fig.) important channel of transport. [ME, f. L f. Gk *artēria* prob. f. *airō* raise]

ārtē'sian (-zhan) *a.* ∼ **well,** perpendicular boring into oblique strata, producing constant supply of water at surface with little or no pumping. [f. F *artésien* (*Artois*, old French province)]

ār'tful *a.* (Of person or action) crafty, deceitful; hence ∼LY[2] *adv.*, ∼NESS *n.* [f. ART[2] + -FUL]

ārthr|i'tis *n.* inflammation of joint(s); so ∼i'TIC *a.* & *n.* [L f. Gk (*arthron* joint; see -ITIS)]

ār'thropŏd *n.* (Zool.) animal of phylum Arthropoda, with segmented body and jointed limbs, e.g. insect, spider, crustacean. [f. Gk *arthron* joint + *pous podos* foot]

Arthūr'ian (ār-) *a.* relating to King Arthur or his knights. [f. *Arthur*, legendary British king + -IAN]

ār'tic *n.* (colloq.) articulated lorry. [abbr.]

ār'tichōke *n.* plant allied to thistle; (**globe**) ∼, its partly edible flower-head; **Jerusalem** ∼ [corrupt. of It. *girasole* sunflower] ∼, species of sunflower with edible tuberous roots. [f. It. *articiocco* alt. of *alcarcioffo f. Arab. *al-ḵarṣūfa*]

ār'ticle[1] *n.* **1.** separate portion of anything written; separate clause (of agreement etc.; *the* THIRTY-*nine Articles; articles of apprenticeship*); literary composition (other than fiction) forming part of magazine etc. but independent of others. **2.** particular part of speech; **∼ of faith,** basic point of belief. **3.** (Gram.) **definite** ∼, 'the'; **indefinite** ∼, 'a, an'; corresponding adj. in other languages. **4.** (arch.) **in the** ∼ (moment) of death. [ME f. OF, f. L *articulus* dim. of *artus* joint]

ār'ticle[2] *v.t.* bind by articles of apprenticeship. [f. prec.]

artic'ular *a.* pertaining to the joints. [ME, f. L *articularis* (as ARTICLE¹; see -AR¹)]

artic'ul|ate¹ *a.* jointed; distinctly jointed; with clearly distinguishable parts (*articulate speech*); able to express oneself fluently and coherently; hence ∿ACY, ∿ateNESS (-tn-), *ns.*, ∿ateLY² (-tlī) *adv.* [f. L *articulatus* (as prec.; see -ATE²)]

artic'ulat|e² *v.* **1.** *v.t.* (usu. in *pass.*) connect by joints; ∿ed **lorry** etc. (with flexibly connected sections). **2.** (usu. in *pass.*) mark with apparent joints. **3.** divide into words, pronounce, distinctly; utter. **4.** Hence ∿ORY *a.* (esp. of speech). **5.** *v.i.* speak distinctly; speak. **6.** form joint *with*. [f. as prec.; see -ATE³]

articula'tion *n.* act or mode of jointing; joint; act of speaking; articulate utterance, speech. [F, or f. L *articulatio* (articulare joint, as ARTICLE¹; see -ATION)]

ar'tifact. See ARTEFACT.

ar'tifice *n.* device, contrivance; (piece of) cunning; address, skill. [F, f. L *artificium* (ars artis art, -ficium making f. facere make)]

artif'icer *n.* craftsman; (Mil., Navy) skilled mechanic; inventor (*of*). [ME, f. AF, prob. alt. of OF *artificien*, f. as prec.]

artifi'cial (-shal) *a.* **1.** made by art; not natural (*artificial light, satellite*); ∿ **insemination,** injection of semen into womb by artificial means; ∿ **language** made from words etc. in several languages, esp. one meant for international use); ∿ **respiration,** restoration or initiation of breathing by manual or mechanical means. **2.** not real (*artificial flowers, limb*); ∿ **horizon,** dish of mercury etc. for use with sextant on land, gyroscopic device showing position of aircraft rel. to horizon plane; *artificial* KIDNEY, MOTHER¹; ∿ **silk,** (arch.) rayon. **3.** affected, insincere; factitious, not arising naturally. **4.** Hence **artificia'lity** (-shi-), ∿NESS, *ns.*, ∿IZE (3) *v.t.*, ∿LY² *adv.* [ME, f. OF *artificiel* or f. L *artificialis* (as ARTIFICE; see -AL)]

arti'llery *n.* large guns used in fighting on land; branch or arm of the service that uses these; hence **arti'llerist** (3), ∿**man,** *ns.* [ME, f. OF *artillerie* (artiller alt. of atiller, atirier equip, arm, f. à to, tire order; see -ERY)]

artisa'n (-z-) *n.* mechanic, skilled (esp. manual) worker; hence ∿ ATE¹ (4) *n.* [F, f. It. *artigiano* f. Rom. *artitianus* f. L *artitus* p.p. of artire instruct in arts; see -AN]

ar'tist *n.* one who practises one of the fine arts, esp. painting; one who makes his craft a fine art (*artist in words* etc.); artiste; (Austral. & NZ) devotee (usu. w. defining wd; *booze artist*); ∿**'s proof,** copy of engraving taken for the artist and valued as fresher than ordinary copies; hence ∿RY (5) *n.* [f. F *artiste* f. It. *artista* (arte ART²; see -IST)]

arti'ste (-tē'-) *n.* professional singer, dancer, etc. [F; see prec.]

artis'tic *a.* of art or artists; made or done with art; appreciative of art; having natural skill in art; hence ∿ICALLY *adv.* [f. prec. + -IC]

ar'tless *a.* not resulting from or displaying art; clumsy; guileless, ingenuous; hence ∿LY² *adv.*, ∿NESS *n.* [f. ART² + -LESS]

ar'ty *a.* (colloq.) (Of person, furniture, etc.) pretentiously or quaintly artistic; ∿-(and-)**crafty,** (joc.) (of furniture) remarkable rather than for specially artistic style than for usefulness or comfort [after the *Arts and Crafts* Exhibition Society founded 1888], (of person) arty. [f. ART² + -Y²]

Ar'yan (āi'-) *a.* & *n.* **1.** (arch.) Indo-European; Indo-Iranian. **2.** (of) the parent language of the Indo-European (esp. Indo-Iranian) family; (member) of the peoples speaking any of these languages; (improp., esp. in Nazi Germany) non-Jewish German. [f. Skr. *āryas* noble, earlier used as a national name]

a'ryl *a.* derived from or related to an aromatic hydrocarbon. [f. G *arryl* (as AROMATIC, -YL)]

as¹ (az or, when stressed, ăz) *adv., conj.,* & *rel. pron.* **1.** *adv.* (in main sentence, foll. by *as* in expressed or understood subord. clause). in the same degree (*I came as quickly as I could; is twice as big; I know that as well as you; we* MAY¹ *as well go*). **2.** *rel. adv.* or *conj.* (in subord. clause, with or without antecedent *as, so,* expressing degree; manner, etc., of the principal sentence): (degree) *you are as good as he* (see also GOOD 12); *it is not so* (or *as*) *easy as you think*; *as* (remarkably) *many or few as six*; *as recently as* (no longer ago than) *last week*; *quick as a flash he jumped out*; *fair as* (= though) *she is*; *try as he might, however hard he tried*; (*as*) *sure as fate* (and in many other proverbial expressions); (manner) *do as you like*; *as you well know*; *according as we decide*; *Olivier as Hamlet*; *did this as* (in the function of) *their legal representative; treat him as a stranger; you are, **as it were*** (= to a certain extent, or as if it were actually so), *compromised; friends as distinct from mere acquaintances; they rose as one man; late as usual; he smiled, as who should say* (arch., = as a man would smile who said); **as you were!** (order, esp. Mil., to return to previous position); (time) *it struck me as I was speaking; I knew him as a boy*; (reason) *as you are ready, we can go at once*; (result) *he so arranged matters as to suit everyone; be so good as to come*; (purpose) *turned aside so as to avoid meeting her*; (illustration) *cathedral cities, as Norwich.* **3.** *rel. pron.* that, who, which, (*I had the same trouble as you; such countries as Spain*; (vulg.) *it was him as did it*); (with antecedent inferred from main sentence) *he was a foreigner, as* (which fact) *they perceived from his accent; he was a playwright, as was his wife.* **4. as and when,** to the extent and at the time that, (colloq.) = IF *and when; as* FAR¹ *as*; **as for,** with regard to (*as for you, I despise you*); **as from,** (in formal dating; *prices will be raised as from 31 March*); *as* IF; **as (it) is,** in the existing state; *as* LONG² *as; as* MUCH; **as of,** *as from, as* at (date); *as* PER; *as* REGARD¹*s; as* SOON *as; as* SUCH 11; **as though,** = *as* IF; **as to,** with respect to (*said nothing as to hours, as to when he would come; as to you, I despise you*); **as was,** in the previously existing state; *as* WELL³ (*as*); **as yet,** up to this or that time (though not at some later time) (*has worked well as yet*). [reduced form of OE *alswā* ALSO]

ăs² *n.* (*pl.* **a'sses**). Roman copper coin. [L]

as- *pref.,* assim. form of AD- before s.

AS *abbr.* Anglo-Saxon.

As *symb.* arsenic.

ASA *abbr.* ||Amateur Swimming Association; *American Standards Association.

ăsafoe'tida (-fē't-), *-fē't-, n.* resinous plant gum with strong smell, formerly used in medicine. [ME f. med. L (*asa* f. Pers. *azā* mastic; *fetida* as FETID)]

a.s.a.p. *abbr.* as soon as possible.

ăsbe'stos (ăz-, ăs-) *n.* fibrous silicate mineral that can be woven into an incombustible fabric; this fabric; hence ∿INE² *a.* ∿o'sis *n.,* lung disease from inhaling asbestos particles. [ME, f. OF *a(l)beston* f. L f. Gk *asbeston* (acc.) unquenchable (*a-* not, *sbestos* f. *sbennumi* quench)]

a'scarid *n.* intestinal roundworm of family Ascaridae. [f. mod. L f. Gk *askaris*]

ascē'nd *v.* **1.** *v.i.* go or come up; (of thing) rise, be raised; (Print., of letter) have part projecting upwards, whence ∿ER¹ *n.,* such letter or part; slope upwards, lie along ascending slope; rise in thought, rank, or degree of quality; (of sound) rise in pitch; go back in point of time. **2.** *v.t.* go up, climb, (hill, stairs); go along (river) towards its source; mount upon (∿ **the throne,** become king or queen). [ME, f. L *ascendere*, AD (*scendere scens-* = *scandere* climb)]

ascē'ndancy, -ency, *ns.* dominant control (*over*). [f. foll. + -ANCY, -ENCY]

ascě'ndant *a. & n.* **1.** *a.* rising; (Astron.) rising towards zenith; (Astrol.) just above eastern horizon; predominant. **2.** *n.* (Astrol.) point of ecliptic that is ascendant at a given time; **in the ~**, supreme, dominating, (pop.) rising. **3.** ancestor. [ME f. OF, f. L (as ASCEND; see -ANT)]

ascě'nsion (-shŏn) *n.* act of ascending; (*A~*) ascent of Christ into Heaven on fortieth day after Resurrection (**A~ Day**, Thursday on which this is commemorated; **A~tide**, period of ten days from Ascension Day to Whitsun Eve); **right ~**, (Astron.) longitude measured along celestial equator; hence ~AL *a.* [ME f. OF, f. L *ascensio -onis* (as ASCEND; see -ION)]

ascě'nt *n.* act of ascending; upward movement, rise, (lit. or fig.); way by which one may ascend; upward slope; SONG *of Ascents*. [f. ASCEND, after *descent*]

ăscertai'n *v.t.* find out (for certain), get to know; hence ~ABLE *a.*, ~MENT *n.* [ME, f. OF *acertener*, st. *acertain-* (à to, CERTAIN)]

ascě's|is *n.* (*pl.* ~es *pr.* -ēz). practice of self-discipline. [f. Gk *askēsis* training (*askeō* exercise)]

ascě't|ic *a. & n.* **1.** *a.* severely abstinent, austere, esp. for spiritual benefit; having the appearance of an ascetic; hence ~ICALLY *adv.*, ~ICISM (2) *n.* **2.** *n.* one who practises severe self-discipline; (Eccl. Hist.) one who retired into solitude for this purpose. [f. med. L or f. Gk *askētikos* (*askētēs* monk f. *askeō* exercise; see -ET², -IC)]

ascī'dian *n.* (Zool.) tunicate of order Ascidiacea, esp. sea-squirt. [f. mod. L *Ascidia* f. Gk *askidion* dim. of *askos* wineskin + -AN]

ascī'tēs (-z) *n.* (*pl.* same). abdominal dropsy. [ME f. LL f. Gk (*askos* wineskin)]

Asclě'piad (a-) *n.* (Gk & L Pros.) verse of spondee, two (or three) choriambi, and iambus. [f. LL f. Gk *asklēpiadeios* (*Asklēpiadēs* Gk poet of 3rd c. BC, its inventor)]

ascŏr'bic *a.* ~ **acid**, vitamin C. [f. A- 7 + SCORBUTIC]

*ă'scŏt *n.* man's broad tie; broad scarf looped under chin. [*A~* in Berkshire, England, where race-meetings are held]

ascri'b|e *v.t.* regard as belonging (*to* person or cause); attribute, impute, (*to*); so ~ABLE *a.*, **ascri'ption** *n.*, (esp.) preacher's words ascribing praise to God at end of sermon. [ME, f. L *ascribere*, AD (*scribere* script- write)]

ă'sdic (-z-) *n.* earlier form of sonar. [f. initials of Anti-Submarine Detection Investigation Committee]

-āse *suf.* (Chem.) forming names of enzymes (*amylase*). [f. DIASTASE]

ASEAN (ă'sĭăn) *abbr.* Association of South East Asian Nations.

āsě'ĭtÿ *n.* (Metaphys.) independent or underived existence. [f. med. L *aseitas* f. L *a* from + *se* oneself; see -ITY]

āsě'psĭs *n.* absence of sepsis or of harmful bacteria; aseptic method in surgery. [f. A- 7 + SEPSIS]

āsě'ptic *a.* free from sepsis, esp. that caused by micro-organisms; (of wound, instrument, dressing) surgically sterile, sterilized; (of method etc.) aiming at the absence (rather than counteraction, cf. ANTISEPTIC) of septic matter. [f. A- 7 + SEPTIC]

āsě'xual *a.* **1.** (Biol.) without sex; (of reproduction) not involving fusion of gametes. **2.** without sexuality. **3.** Hence ~ITY (-ă'l-) *n.* [f. A- 7 + SEXUAL]

ăsh¹ *n.* **1.** forest-tree of genus *Fraxinus*, with silver-grey bark, pinnate foliage, and hard, tough, pale wood; its wood; MOUNTAIN *ash*. **2.** ~**key**, winged seed of the ash; ~**plant**, sapling of ash, used as stick etc. [OE *æsc* = OHG *ask*, ON *askr*, f. Gmc **askiz*]

ăsh² *n.* (freq. in *pl.*) powdery residue left after combustion of any substance (**lay in ~es**, burn to the ground; SACK¹*cloth and ashes*); (in *pl.*) remains of human body after cremation or disintegration, ||(*the A~es*, Cricket) trophy for winner of series of test matches between England and Australia; ashlike material ejected by volcano; ~**bin**, ***~'can**, dustbin; ~ **blonde**, (woman with) very fair (hair); ~'**pan**, tray under grate; ~'**tray**, receptacle for tobacco ash etc.; **Ash Wednesday**, first day of

Lent (from former custom of sprinkling ashes on penitents' heads). [OE *æsce*, = OHG *asca*, ON *aska*, Goth. *azgo*]

ashā'med (-md) *a.* (usu. *pred.*) embarrassed, disconcerted, by shame (*ashamed of having lied, that one lied*); ~ **for** *you* (on account of); ~ **to** *say* (reluctant, but not necessarily refusing). [OE *āscamod* p.p. of *āscamian* feel shame (as A- 1, SHAME²)]

ă'shen¹ *a.* pertaining to an ash-tree; (arch.) made of ash wood. [f. ASH¹ + -EN⁵]

ă'shen² *a.* of ashes; ash-coloured, grey, pale. [f. ASH² + -EN⁵]

ă'shět *n.* (Sc. & NZ). large plate or dish. [f. F *assiette*]

Ashkèna'z|ĭ (ă-; -ah'-) *n.* (*pl.* ~im). E. European Jew (cf. SEPHARDI); hence ~IC *a.* [mod. Heb., f. *Ashkenaz* (Gen. 10: 3)]

ă'shlar *n.* square-hewn stone(s); masonry constructed of this; similar masonry as facing to rubble or brick wall. [ME, f. OF *aisselier* f. L *axilla* dim. of *axis* board; see -AR²]

ă'sharing *n.* short upright boarding in garret, cutting off acute angle of roof with floor. [f. prec. + -ING¹]

ashŏr'e *adv.* to or on shore or land. [f. A³ + SHORE¹]

ă'shram *n.* (Ind.) place of religious retreat, hermitage. [f. Skr. *asrama* hermitage]

ă'shÿ *a.* = ASHEN²; covered with ashes. [f. ASH² + -Y²]

A'sian (ā'shan) *a. & n.* (native or inhabitant) of Asia, (person) descended from natives of Asia. [f. L f. Gk *Asianos* (*Asia*; see -AN)]

Asiă'tic (āshĭ-) *a. & n.* (R *of persons*) Asian. [f. L f. Gk *Asiatikos*; see -IC]

asī'de *adv. & n.* **1.** *adv.* to or on one side, away; ***~** (apart) **from**; SET¹ *aside*; **take ~** (esp. for private conversation). **2.** *n.* words spoken aside, esp. spoken by actor and heard by audience but supposed not to be heard by other actors; incidental remark of author etc. [orig. *on side*; see A³]

ă'sĭnĭne *a.* pertaining to asses; stupid; hence **ăsĭnī'n-ITY** *n.* [f. L *asininus* (*asinus* ass; see -INE¹)]

-asis *suf.* forming names of diseases (*psoriasis, satyriasis*). [L, f. Gk *-asis* in ns. of state f. vbs in *-aō*]

ask (ah-) *v.* **1.** *v.t.* call for an answer to or about (*ask (him) a question; ask (him) this, (him) who it is; ask him the time; ask (him) his name; ask a question of a person; ask him about it*); **I ~ you** (excl. of disgust etc.); **if you ~ me**, (colloq.) in my opinion; ~ **me another**, (colloq.) I do not know. **2.** seek to obtain from another person (*ask a favour of him; ask (him) a favour; asked £5 for the book; ask him for £5, to do it; ask that it may be done; ask to be allowed out; you have only to ask*); ~'**ing price** (set by seller); **for the** (mere) ~**ing. 3.** invite (person *to* dinner etc., or out or OVER); (arch., of thing) require. **4.** *v.i.* ~ **for**, seek to obtain or meet or be directed to (*ask (him) for it, seek is asking for you, for the coat office*); ~ **for it**, (sl.) = *ask for* TROUBLE etc., = OHG *eiscōn*, f. WG **aiskōjan*]

aska'nce, **aska'nt**, (-ă'n-, -ah'n-) *adv.* sideways, squinting (**look ~ at**, view suspiciously); with oblique meaning. [16th c., of unkn. orig.]

ăskā'rĭ *n.* E. African native soldier or policeman. [Arab. *'askarī* soldier]

askě'sĭs. Var. of ASCESIS.

askew' *adv. & pred. a.* oblique(ly); awry. [f. A³ + SKEW]

asla'nt (-ah'nt) *adv. & prep.* obliquely (across). [f. A³ + SLANT]

asleě'p *adv. & pred. a.* in or into a state of sleep (lit. or fig.); (euphem.) dead; (of limb) benumbed; (of top) spinning without apparent motion [f. A³ + SLEEP¹]

||A'slěf (ă'z-) *abbr.* Associated Society of Locomotive Engineers and Firemen.

aslŏ'pe *adv. & pred. a.* sloping, crosswise. [ME, of uncert. orig.]

ASM *abbr.* air-to-surface missile.

asō'cial (-shal) *a.* not social; antisocial; (colloq.) inconsiderate of or hostile to others. [f. A- 7 + SOCIAL]

ăsp *n.* small viper of S. Europe; viper of N. Africa and Arabia. [ME, f. OF *aspe* or f. L f. Gk *aspis*]

aspá'ragus *n.* plant of genus *Asparagus*; one species of this (*A. officinalis*) whose young shoots are eaten; this food; ∼ **fern,** decorative plant of genus *Asparagus*. [L, f. Gk *asparagos*]

ä'spĕct *n.* way of looking; looking or fronting in a given direction; side so fronting; phase; particular component of complicated matter; look, expression; appearance (esp. to the mind); (Gram.) verbal category or form expressing inception, duration, or completion, whence **äspĕ'ctūal** *a.*; (Astrol.) relative position of planets etc.; ∼ **ratio** (Aeron., of aerofoil span to mean chord; Telev., of picture width to height). [ME, f. L *aspectus* (ADspicere -spect- look at)]

ä'spen *n.* kind of poplar with especially tremulous leaves. [f. earlier name *asp* f. OE *æspe*, = OHG *aspa*, Gmc *aspōn, + -EN[5] forming adj. taken as n.]

äspergi'll|um *n.* (*pl.* ∼**ums** *or* ∼**a**). brush etc. for sprinkling holy water. [mod. L, f. L *aspergere* (*ad* to, *spargere* sprinkle) + -*illum* dim. suf.]

äspĕ'rity *n.* roughness; rough excrescence; harshness, sharpness, (of temper or tone). [ME, f. OF *asperité* or f. L *asperitas* (*asper* rough; see -ITY)]

aspĕr'se *v.t.* attack reputation of (person with allegations etc.); calumniate; so **aspĕr'sion** (-shon) *n.* (*cast aspersions on*). [ME, = besprinkle, f. L *aspergere -ers-*; see ASPERGILLUM]

äspersŏr'l|um *n.* (*pl.* ∼**a**). vessel for holy water. [med. L (as prec.; see -ORY)]

ä'sphält *n.,* & *v.t.* **1.** *n.* dark bituminous pitch from petroleum; mixture of this with sand etc. for surfacing roads etc.; hence **äsphä'ltic** *a.* **2.** *v.t.* surface (road etc.) with asphalt. [ME; ult. f. LL *asphalton, -um*, f. Gk *asphalton,* of foreign orig.]

ä'sphodĕl *n.* plant of genus *Asphodeline* or *Asphodelus*, of lily family; (poet.) immortal flower in Elysium. [f. L f. Gk *asphodelos*; cf. DAFFODIL]

äsphy̆'xi|a *n.* defective aeration of blood through impaired respiration; suffocation; hence ∼**ant** *a.* & *n.*, ∼**ate**[3] *v.t.* & *i.*, ∼**a'tion** *n.* [mod. L f. Gk *asphuxia* (*a-* not, *sphuxis* pulse); see -IA[1]]

ä'spic[1] *n.* (poet.) asp. [F, f. OF *aspide* f. L (as ASP); prob. infl. by F *piquer* to sting]

ä'spic[2] *n.* savoury meat jelly used as garnish or to contain game, eggs, etc. [F, = ASP, f. the colours of the jelly (compared to those of the asp)]

äspĭdi'stra *n.* foliage plant of genus *Aspidistra*, with broad tapering leaves, freq. grown as house plant. [mod. L f. Gk *aspis aspidos* shield]

aspirant (aspīr'-, ä'sper-) *a.* & *n.* (one) who aspires (*to, after, for*). [F, or f. L, as ASPIRE; see -ANT]

ä'spirate[1] *a.* & *n.* (consonant) pronounced with a breathing, blended with sound of *h*; sound of *h*. [f. L *aspiratus* p.p. of *aspirare*; see ASPIRE, -ATE[2]]

ä'spirăte[2] *v.t.* pronounce with a breathing; draw (fluid) by suction from vessel or cavity. [f. as prec. + -ATE[3]]

äspirā'tion *n.* drawing of breath; earnest desire (*for, to, after*); action of aspirating. [ME f. OF, or f. L *aspiratio* (as prec.; see -ATION)]

ä'spirātor *n.* apparatus for aspirating fluid. [f. L *aspirare*; see foll., -OR]

aspīr'e *v.i.* desire earnestly (*to, after*); rise high (usu. fig.). [ME, f. F *aspirer* or f. L *aspirare*, AD(*spirare* breathe)]

ä'spirin *n.* acetylsalicylic acid, an analgesic and febrifuge; tablet of this. [G, f. ACETYL + *spiraeic* (= salicylic) *acid* + -IN]

asqui'nt *adv.* & *pred. a.* (*look* etc.) on one side or from corner of eye or with squint. [ME, perh. f. A- + LDu. *schuinte* slant; cf. Du. *schuinte* slant]

ass[1] (äs, ahs) *n.* quadruped of horse genus with long ears, donkey, (esp. fig., as type of ignorance, stupidity, etc.); stupid person (**make an** ∼ **of,** make (person) look absurd or foolish); **asses' bridge,** PONS *asinorum*. [OE *assa*, f. OCelt. **as(s)in* f. L *asinus*]

*ass[2] (äs, ahs) *n.* (vulg.) = ARSE[1].

ass[3] (äs, ahs) *v.i.* (sl.) fool *about, around*. [f. ASS[1]]

assagai. See ASSEGAI.

assai (asah'ē) *adv.* (Mus.) very (*adagio assai*). [It.]

assai'l *v.t.* make hostile attack upon (lit. or fig.); make resolute start on (task); overwhelm (*with* questions etc.); hence ∼**ABLE** *a.*, ∼**ANT** *n.* [ME, f. OF *asaill-* stressed st. of *asalir* f. med. L *assalire* f. L Assilire (*salire salt-* leap)]

assä'ssin *n.* one who undertakes to kill treacherously; (Hist.) Muslim fanatic in time of Crusades, sent on murder errands by the Old Man of the Mountains or later leaders. [F, or f. med. L *assassinus* f. Arab. *ḥaššāšīn* f. *ḥaššāš* hashish-eater]

assä'ssin|āte *v.t.* kill (esp. political or religious leader) by treacherous violence; hence ∼**a'tion** *n.* (CHARACTER *assassination*), ∼**ātor** *n.* [f. med. L *assassinare* (*assassinus*; see prec.) + -ATE[3]]

assau'lt (-aw'lt, -ŏ'lt) *n.* hostile attack (lit. or fig.); rush against walls of fortress etc. (*carry by assault*); (Law) unlawful personal attack (even if only with menacing words), cf. BATTERY; (euphem.) rape (of woman); ∼ **craft,** portable boat for attack by water; hence ∼**ive** *a.* [ME, f. OF *asaut* f. Rom. *assaltus f. med. L (as ASSAIL)]

assau'lt[2] (-aw'lt, -ŏ'lt) *v.t.* make violent or hostile attack upon (lit. or fig.); attack (fortress) by sudden rush; (euphem.) rape (woman). [ME, f. OF *assauter* f. Rom. *assaltare spring at for I. AS(*sultare* frequent. of *salire* salt- leap)]

assay'[1] *n.* **1.** trial of metals or ore for quality; **A**∼ **Office** (awarding hallmarks). **2.** (Chem. etc.) determination of content of a substance. [ME, f. OF *assai*, var. of *essai* (see ESSAY[1])]

assay'[2] *v.t.* & *i.* test quality of (metals, ore); (Chem.) perform assay; show (content) on assay; (arch.) attempt (task, *to* do); hence ∼**ABLE** *a.* [ME, f. OF *assaier, essayer* (see ESSAY[2])]

ä'ssĕgai, ä'ssagai, (-gī) *n.* slender iron-tipped spear of hard wood, esp. missile of S. Afr. tribes. [f. obs. F *azagaie* or Port. *azagaia* f. Arab. *az-zaġāyah* (*al* the, *zaġāyah* spear)]

assĕ'mblage *n.* bringing or coming together; concourse of persons; collection of things; fitting together; object made of pieces fitted together; (Art) object made of unrelated things joined together. [f. foll. + -AGE]

assĕ'mbl|e *v.t.* & *i.* gather together, collect, arrange in order; (Mech.) fit together the parts of (machine, structure); hence ∼**ER**[1] *n.*, (esp.) routine for putting computer program together. [ME, f. OF *asembler* f. Rom. *assimulare bring together (L *ad* to, *simul* together)]

assĕ'mbly̆ *n.* gathering together; concourse; meeting for discussion, recreation, etc.; deliberative body, legislative council; military call to assemble, given by drum or bugle; assembling of a machine or structure or its parts; ∼ **line,** group of machines and workers progressively assembling some product; ∼**man,** member of legislative assembly; ∼ **room, shop,** place where a machine or its parts are assembled; ∼ **rooms** (in which dances etc. are held). [ME, f. OF *asemblee* fem. p.p. of *asembler* (see prec.)]

assĕ'nt[1] *v.i.* consent (*to* proposal, request); express agreement (*to* statement or opinion, or abs.); hence ∼**OR** *n.* (‖esp. election-candidate's supporter other than proposer and seconder). [ME, f. OF *asenter* f. Rom. *assentare f. L *assentari (ad* to, *sentire* think)]

assĕ'nt[2] *n.* (official) consent or sanction (**royal** ∼ of sovereign to bill passed by Parliament); (mental) acceptance. [ME, f. OF *as(s)ente* (as prec.)]

assĕ'ntient (-shĕnt, -shĕnt) *a.* & *n.* (person) that assents. [L *assentire* (as ASSENT[1]; see -ENT)]

assĕr't *v.t.* vindicate claim to (rights); give effect to (∼ oneself), insist on one's rights or opinions); declare; so ∼**IVE** *a.*, tending to assert (oneself), dogmatic, ∼**OR** *n.* [f. L AS(*serere sert-* join)]

assĕr'tion *n.* insistence on a right or opinion; (self-)∼, insistence on recognition of one's claims; declaration, positive statement. [ME f. F, or f. L *assertio* (as prec.; see -ION)]

asses. *pl.* of AS² or ASS¹,².

asse′ss *v.t.* fix amount of (taxes, fine); fix amount of and impose (*on* person or community); fine or tax (person, community, property, *in, at*, so much); estimate value of (esp. property for taxation); estimate magnitude or quality of; hence ∼ABLE *a.*, ∼MENT *n.* [ME, f. F *assesser* f. L AS(*sidēre* sess- = *sedēre* sit)]

asse′ssor *n.* one who sits as adviser to judge etc.; one who assesses taxes or estimates value of property for taxation or insurance purposes; hence ∼IAL (ăsĕsōr′-) *a.* [ME, f. OF *assessour* f. L *assessor* -*oris* assistant-judge (as prec.; see -OR); 2nd sense f. med. L]

a′ssĕt *n.* property available to meet debts; any possession; (person or thing having) any useful quality. [f. *assets* (taken as pl.), f. AF *asetz* f. OF *asez* enough f. Rom. *assatis* f. L *ad* to + *satis* enough]

∥ASSET *abbr.* Association of Supervisory Staffs, Executives, and Technicians.

asse′ver|āte *v.t.* solemnly declare; so ∼A′TION *n.* [f. L AS*severare* (*severus* serious) + -ATE³]

assi′bil|āte *v.t.* (Phonet. & Philol.) pronounce as or change to sibilant or fricative; hence ∼A′TION *n.* [f. L AS(*sibilare* hiss) + -ATE³]

assi′dūous *a.* persevering, diligent; attending closely; hence or cogn. **ăssĭdū′ITY**, ∼NESS, *ns.*, ∼LY² *adv.* [f. L *assiduus* (as ASSESS) + -OUS]

assi′gn¹ (-ī′n) *v.t.* **1.** allot as share (*to*); transfer formally (esp. personal property, *to*); hence ∼OR (asī′ner, asīnōr′) *n.* **2.** appoint (place etc. *to*); fix, specify; ascribe, refer, (event *to* date); ascribe (reason *to, for*, thing). **3.** Hence ∼ABLE *a.* [ME, f. OF *asi*(*g*)*ner* f. L AS*signare* mark out to (*signum* sign)]

assi′gn² (-ī′n) *n.* one to whom property or right is legally transferred. [ME, f. F *assigné* (see ASSIGNEE)]

ăssigna′tion *n.* apportionment; attribution *to*; formal transference; appointment (of time and place); illicit lovers' meeting; *∗∼ house*, brothel. [ME f. OF, f. L *assignatio -onis* (as ASSIGN¹; see -ATION)]

assignee′ (-īn-) *n.* one appointed to act for another; assign. [ME, f. OF *assigné*, p.p. of *assigner* ASSIGN¹]

assi′gnment (-ī′n-) *n.* allocation; legal transference, document effecting this; attribution; statement (of reasons); task allotted to person (∗esp. to student). [ME, f. OF *assignement* f. med. L *assignamentum* (as ASSIGN¹; see -MENT)]

assi′mil|āte *v.* **1.** *v.t.* make like (*to, with*); (Philol.) make (sound) more like another in same or contiguous word; absorb into the system (lit. or fig.). **2.** *v.i.* be so absorbed. **3.** Hence or cogn. ∼A′TION *n.*, *ns.*, ∼ABLE, ∼ATIVE, ∼atory, *adjs.* [ME, f. L AS*similare* (*similis* like) + -ATE³]

assi′st *v.* & *n.* **1.** *v.t.* help (person, process, person *in* doing); hence ∼ANCE *n.* (∥NATIONAL *Assistance*). **2.** *v.i.* take part (*in*); be present (*at*). **3.** *n.* ∗help; ∗act of helping; ∗(Baseball etc.) player's action in helping to put out opponent, score goal, etc. [ME, f. F *assister* f. L AS*sistere* take one's stand by]

assi′stant & *n.* **1.** *a.* helping; subordinate. **2.** *n.* helper; subordinate worker, esp. in shop to serve customers. [ME *assistent*, f. med. L *assistens -ent-* present (as assist); see -ANT, -ENT)]

assi′ze *n.* (Hist.) **1.** (usu. in *pl.*) periodical session in each county of England and Wales for administration of civil and criminal justice. **2.** statutory price of bread and ale. [ME, f. OF *as*(*s*)*ise*, fem. p.p. (as n.) of *aseeir* sit at, f. L *assidēre*; cf. ASSESS]

Assoc. *abbr.* Association.

asso′ciable (-sha-) *a.* that can be connected in thought (*with*); hence ∼ABI′LITY *n.* [F, f. *associer* (as foll.; see -ABLE)]

asso′ciate¹ (-shī-, -sī-) *a.* & *n.* **1.** *a.* joined in companionship, function, or dignity; allied **2.** *n.* partner;

companion; colleague; subordinate member of a body, institute, etc.; thing connected with another; hence ∼SHIP (-tsh-) *n.* [ME, f. L *associatus* p.p. of AS*sociare* (*socius* sharing, allied); see -ATE²]

asso′ci|āte² (-shī-, -sī-) *v.* **1.** *v.t.* join (persons, things, or one *with* another); connect as an idea; make one*self* a partner *in* (a matter); declare one*self* in agreement *with*. **2.** *v.i.* combine for common purpose; have frequent dealings (*with*). **3.** Hence ∼ATIVE, ∼atORY, *adjs.*, ∼ātOR *n.* [f. L *associare* (as prec.) + -ATE³]

assōcia′tion *n.* act of associating; organized body of persons for a joint purpose (**articles** or **deed of** ∼, document giving particulars of limited liability company); fellowship, companionship; mental connection between related ideas; (Chem.) loose aggregation of molecules; (Ecol.) group of associated plants; ∥A∼ **football**, kind played with round ball which may not be handled during play exc. by goalkeeper (cf. RUGBY); hence ∼AL *a.*, ∼ISM *n.*, theory accounting for mental phenomena by association of ideas. [F, or f. med. L *associatio* (as prec.; see -ATION)]

assoi′l *v.t.* (arch.) absolve from sin; acquit; release; atone for. [ME, f. AF *as*(*s*)*oili*(*e*)*r*, OF *assoil-* stressed stem of *asoldre* f. L (as ABSOLVE)]

ä′sson|ance *n.* resemblance of sound between two syllables; rhyming of one word with another in accented vowel and those that follow, but not in consonants (*sonnet, porridge*), or in consonants but not in vowels (*killed, cold*); so ∼ANT *a.*, ∼ATE³ *v.i.* [F, f. L AS*sonare* respond to (*sonus* sound); see -ANCE]

assor′t *v.* **1.** *v.t.* classify, arrange in sorts; group *with* others. **2.** *v.i.* suit *well* or *ill with*. [f. OF *assorter* (à to, *sorte* SORT¹)]

assor′tative *a.* assorting (esp. ∼ **mating**, not random but based on similarity of partners' characteristics etc.). [f. prec. + -ATIVE]

assor′tĕd *a.* of various sorts put together; **ill-**∼, not well matched. [p.p. of ASSORT]

assor′tment *n.* set of various sorts put together. [f. ASSORT + -MENT]

ASSR *abbr.* Autonomous Soviet Socialist Republic.

Asst. *abbr.* Assistant.

assuā′ge (asw-) *v.t.* calm, soothe, (person, feelings, pain); appease (appetite, desire); hence ∼MENT (-jm-) *n.* [ME, f. OF *as*(*s*)*ouagier* f. Rom. ∗AS*suaviare* f. L *suavis* sweet]

assū′m|e *v.t.* **1.** take or put on oneself (aspect, garment); ∼**ing,** taking much upon oneself, arrogant. **2.** undertake (office, duty). **3.** simulate (ignorance etc.); arrogate (credit etc.) *to* one*self*. **4.** take as being true, for purpose of argument or action. [ME, f. L AS(*sumere sumpt-* take)]

assū′mption *n.* **1.** act of assuming; thing assumed, arrogance. **2.** (A∼). reception of Virgin Mary bodily into Heaven; feast in honour of this (15 Aug.). [ME, f. OF *asompsion* or f. L *assumptio* (as ASSUME; see -ION)]

assū′mptive *a.* taken for granted; arrogant. [f. L *assumptivus* (as ASSUME; see -IVE)]

assur′ance (ashoor′-) *n.* formal guarantee; positive declaration that thing is true; ∥insurance, esp. of life; certainty; self-confidence; impudence. [ME, f. OF *aseürance* (*aseürer* as foll.; -ANCE)]

assur′e (ashoor′) *v.t.* make safe; ∥insure (esp. life); make certain, ensure the happening etc. of; make (person) sure (*of* fact; REST³ *assured*); tell (person) confidently (*of* a thing, *of* its being so, *that* it is so); hence **assur′ĕdLY²** (ashoor′-) *adv.*, certainly. [ME, f. OF *aseürer* f. Rom. ∗AS*securare* f. L *securus* safe, SECURE]

Assy′rian (a-) *a.* & *n.* (inhabitant or language) of Assyria. [f. L f. Gk *Assurios* of Assyria, ancient empire in Mesopotamia, + -IAN]

Assyriŏ′logy (a-) *n.* study of language, history, antiquities, of Assyria; hence ∼LOGIST *n.* [f. L f. Gk *Assuria* + -o- + -LOGY]

AST abbr. Atlantic Standard Time.

ästä′ble a. not stable; (Electr.) not having a stable state. [f. A- 7 + STABLE¹]

ästä′tic a. (Electr.) not tending to keep one position; ∿ **galvanometer**, one in which the effect of the earth's magnetic field on the needle is greatly reduced. [f. Gk *astatos* unstable (*a*- not, *sta*- stand) + -IC]

ä′statine (-ēn) n. (Chem.) artificial radioactive element, heaviest of halogen group. [f. as prec. + -INE⁵]

ä′ster n. composite plant of genus *Aster*, with showy radiated flowers, e.g. Michaelmas daisy; **China** ∿, flower of allied species, *Callistephus chinensis*. [L, f. Gk *astēr* star]

-ä′ster suf. forming ns. denoting poor quality (*criticaster*, *poetaster*) or (Bot.) incomplete resemblance (*oleaster*, *pinaster*). [L]

ä′sterisk n., & v.t. **1.** n. star-shaped symbol (*) used to mark words etc. for reference or distinction, or to replace omitted matter. **2.** v.t. mark with asterisk. [ME, f. LL f. Gk *asteriskos* dim., as ASTER]

ä′sterism n. cluster of stars; group of three asterisks (*∗*), calling attention. [f. Gk *asterismos* (as ASTER; see IEM)]

astĕr′n adv. (Naut. & Aeron.) aft; away to the rear (*of*); backwards. [f. A³ + STERN²]

ä′steroid n. one of the small planets revolving round sun mainly between orbits of Mars and Jupiter; (Zool.) starfish; hence ∿AL (-oi′d-) a. [f. Gk *asteroeidēs* (as ASTER; see -OID)]

ästhē′nia n. (Med.) loss of strength, debility. [mod. L, f. Gk *astheneia* (*asthenēs* weak; see -IA¹)]

ästhē′nic a. & n. **1.** (person) of lean and long-limbed build. **2.** a. of or characterized by asthenia. [f. prec. + -IC]

ä′sthma (-sm-) n. disease (esp. allergic) of respiration, esp. with paroxysms of difficult breathing. [ME f. med. L *asma*, f. Gk *asthma* -*matos* (*azō* breathe hard)]

ästhmä′t|ic (-sm-) a. & n. pertaining to or effective against asthma; (person) suffering from asthma; hence ∿ICALLY adv. [f. L f. Gk *asthmatikos* (as prec.; see -IC)]

A′sti (ä′-) n. still or (∿ **spümä′ntè**) sparkling Italian white wine. [∿ in Piedmont]

asti′gmatism n. structural defect in eye or lens, preventing rays of light from being brought to common focus; so **ästigma′tic** a. [f. A- 7 + Gk *stigma* -*matos* point + -IC]

asti′lbe n. white- or red-flowered perennial plant of genus *Astilbe*. [mod. L, f. Gk *a*- not + *stilbē* fem. of *stilbos* glittering; f. the inconspicuous (individual) flowers]

astir′ adv. & pred. a. in motion; out of bed; excited(ly). [f. A³ + STIR¹ 5]

ASTMS abbr. Association of Scientific, Technical, and Managerial Staffs.

astŏ′nish v.t. amaze; surprise greatly; hence ∿MENT n. [f. obs. *astone* f. OF *estoner* f. Gallo-Rom. *EX(tonare* thunder); see -ISH²]

astou′nd v.t. shock with alarm or surprise; amaze. [f. obs. *astound* a. = *astoned* p.p. of obs. *astone*; see prec.]

asträ′ddle adv. & pred. a. in a straddling position. [f. A³ + STRADDLE]

ä′stragal n. (Archit.) small moulding round top or bottom of column. [f. foll.]

asträ′galus n. (Anat. & Zool.) ankle-bone supporting tibia, talus; (Bot.) leguminous plant of genus *Astragalus*. [L, f. Gk *astragalos* ankle-bone, moulding, a plant]

ästrakhä′n (-an) n. dark curly fleece of young lambs from *Astrakhan* in Russia; cloth imitating this.

ä′stral a. connected with or consisting of stars; ∿ **body**, (Theosophy) ethereal counterpart of body, thought to survive death; ∿ **spirits** (formerly thought to inhabit heavenly bodies). [f. LL *astralis* (*astrum* star; see -AL)]

astray′ adv. & pred. a. out of the right way; (esp., fig.) in or into error or sin; **go** ∿, (fig.) be lost or

mislaid. [ME, f. OF *estraié* p.p. of *estraier* f. Rom. *extravagare* f. L *extra* out of bounds + *vagari* wander]

astrī′de adv. & prep. **1.** adv. with legs apart; with legs on either side (*of*) **2.** prep. astride of; extending across. [f. A³ + STRIDE 3]

astrī′ng|ent (-nj-) a. & n. **1.** a. causing contraction of body tissues, styptic; severe; austere; hence ∿ENCY n., ∿entLY² adv. **2.** n. astringent substance. [F, f. L *astringere* (ad to, *stringere* bind); see -ENT]

ä′strŏ- comb. form. star, heavenly body, as: ∿bo′tany, study of plants on celestial bodies; ∿dome, ∿hatch, domed window in aircraft for astronomical observations. [Gk (*astron* star)]

ä′strolābe n. instrument for measuring altitudes of stars etc. [ME, f. OF *astrelabe* f. med. L *astrolabium* f. Gk *astrolabon*, neut. (as n.) of ASTROlabos star-taking]

astrŏ′logy n. art of judging reputed occult influence of stars, planets, etc. on human affairs; so **astrŏ′-** **LOGER** n., **ästrolŏ′gic**(AL) adjs. [ME, f. OF *astrologie* f. L f. Gk ASTRO(*logia* -LOGY)]

ä′stronaut n. space traveller; hence or cogn. ∿ICAL a., ∿ICS n., science of space travel, (-aw′-). [f. ASTRO-, after *aeronaut*]

astrŏ′nomy n. science of the heavenly bodies; hence or cogn. ∿ER¹ (3) n., person who studies or practises astronomy, **ästronŏ′mic**(AL) adjs. (∿ical figures, **distances**, as enormous as those familiar to astronomers; ∿ical unit, earth's mean distance from sun, about 150 million kilometres; *astronomical* YEAR); **ästronŏ′mically** adv. [ME, f. OF *astronomie* f. L f. Gk *astronomia* f. ASTROnomos a. star-arranging (*nemō* arrange)]

ästrophy′sic|s (-ï′z-) n. branch of astronomy concerned with physics and chemistry of the heavenly bodies; hence ∿AL a., ∿IST (3) n. [f. ASTRO- + PHYSICS]

astū′te a. shrewd, sagacious; crafty; hence ∿LY² (-tlī) adv., ∿NESS (-tn-) n. [f. obs. F *astut* or L *astutus* (*astus* craft)]

asŭ′nder adv. (rhet.) apart. [OE *on sundran* into pieces; cf. SUNDER]

asÿ′lum n. sanctuary, place of refuge and safety, esp. for criminals, (**political** ∿, protection from arrest by another country; (Hist.) institution for shelter and support of afflicted (e.g. blind, deaf, and esp. insane) or destitute persons. [ME f. L f. Gk *asulon* refuge (*a*- not, *sulon* right of seizure)]

äsÿ′mmetry n. lack of symmetry; hence **äsÿm-** **me′tric**(AL) adjs. [f. Gk *asummetria* (*a*- not; see SYMMETRY)]

ä′sympt|ōte (-mpt-, -mt-) n. line that continually approaches given curve but does not meet it at a finite distance; hence ∿o′TIC a., ∿ŏ′TICALLY adv. [mod. L *asymptota* (*linea* line) f. Gk *asumptōtos* not falling together (*a*- not, *sun*- together, *ptōtos* falling f. *piptō* fall)]

äsÿ′nchronous (-ngk-) a. not synchronous; hence ∿LY² adv. [f. A- not + SYNCHRONOUS]

asÿ′ndet|on n. (*pl.* ∿a). (Rhet.) omission of conjunction; hence ∿IC (äsündě′t-) a. [mod. L, f. Gk *asundeton* neut. a. (*a*- not, *sundetos* bound together)]

at (or, when stressed, ăt) prep. **1.** Expr. exact, approximate, or vague position, lit. or fig. of condition, occasion, price, time, etc., (*meet at a point*; *wait at the corner*; *at the top*; *at Bath* (or any town etc. except those of public or private importance; cf. IN¹); *at school*; *at* HOME¹ *7*; *at SEA*; *at a distance*; *at* ARM¹*s length*; *sick at heart*; *at* HAND¹; *out at elbows*; *at work*; *at* ONE 3; *at* EASE¹; *at dinner*; *at* WAR¹; *at a standstill*; *play at fighting*; *good at repartee*; *at daggers drawn*; *at a disadvantage*; *at his* MERCY; *came at a run*; *sold at £1 each*; *at a low price*; *at* ONCE 4; *at short notice*; *at a* TOUCH²; *at midday*; *at Easter*; *at* (*the age of*) *70*; *at all events*; *at* ALL *8*; *at* BEST¹; *at* FIRST *6*; *at* LAST³ *8*; *at* LEAST *2*; *at* MOST *6*; *at* WORST *2*; *annoyed at finding*; *impatient at delay*); **at it**, at work or other activity; **where it's at**, (sl.) the (true) scene of action; **at that**, at that point, estimate, etc., (*leave it at that*, not do more), moreover (*lost in twenty moves, and to an amateur at*

at- *that*), nevertheless (*delayed ten minutes, but caught the train at that*). **2.** Expr. motion towards, lit. or fig., (*arrive at a place*; *get, rush, shoot, laugh, look, grumble, guess, hint, snatch, aim, at*). [OE *æt*, = OHG *az*, OS, ON, Goth. *at*, Gmc cogn. w. L *ad* to]

at- *pref.*, assim. form of AD- before *t*.

At *symb.* astatine.

ä'tabrine. See ATEBRIN.

ä'tarăxў, -ă'xia, *n.* stoical indifference; imperturbability; so **ătără'c**tIC, **ătără'x**IC, *adjs.* & *ns.*, tranquillizing (drug). [f. F *ataraxie* f. Gk *ataraxia* impassiveness]

ä'tavĭsm *n.* resemblance to remote ancestors rather than parents; reversion to earlier type; hence **ătavĭ'st**IC *a.* [f. F *atavisme* f. L *atavus* great-grandfather's grandfather; see -ISM]

ătă'xў, -xia, *n.* imperfect control of voluntary bodily functions; **locomotor** ∼, disease affecting co-ordination of movements; hence **ătă'x**IC *a.* [f. mod. L f. Gk *ataxia* (*a-* not, *taxis* order)]

||**ATC** *abbr.* air traffic control; Air Training Corps.

ate. See EAT.

-ate[1] (*at*, āt) *suf.* forming *ns.*, denoting (1) status or office (*doctorate, episcopate, marquisate*), (2) state or function (*curate, legate, magistrate, mandate*), (3) (Chem.) salt of acid w. corresp. name in *-ic* (*chlorate, nitrate*), (4) group (*electorate*), (5) product (*condensate, filtrate*). [f. or after OF *-at* or *-é*(*e*) or f. L *-atus* n. or p.p. (cf. foll.)]

-ate[2] (*at*, āt) *suf.* forming *adjs.* & *ns.* (*associate*[1], *delegate, desolate, duplicate*[1], *separate*[1]) or *adjs.* f. L or E *n.* or *adj.* (*cordate, insensate, Italianate*). [f. or after (F *-é* f.) L *-atus*_ p.p. of vbs. in *-are*]

-āte[3] *suf.* forming *vbs.* (*associate*[2], *camphorate, duplicate*[2], *fascinate, felicitate, hyphenate, separate*[2]). [f. or after (F *-er* f.) L *-are* (p.p. *-atus*); cf. prec.]

ä'tĕbrĭn (||P̄), **ä'tabrĭne** (*P). *n.* = QUINACRINE. [f. -ATE[1] (3) + BRINE]

atě'lier (-lyā) *n.* workshop, studio, esp. of artist or couturier. [F]

a tempo (ah tĕ'mpō) *adv.* (Mus.) in the previous tempo. [It., lit. 'in time']

Athanā'sian (ă-; -shạn) *a.* of Athanasius, bishop of Alexandria d. 373; ∼ **Creed**, that beginning *Quicunque vult*, = *Whosoever will*, formerly ascribed to Athanasius. [f. LL *Athanasius* + -AN]

ā'thĕ|**ism** *n.* disbelief in the existence of God or gods; godlessness; so ∼IST (2) *n.*, ∼ĭ'stIC *a.* [f. F *athéisme* f. Gk *atheos* without God (*a-* not, *theos* god); see -ISM]

ä'thelĭng *n.* (Hist.) prince or lord. [OE *ætheling*, = OHG *ediling* f. WG **athelinga* (**athal* family; see -ING[3])]

ăthĕmä'tĭc *a.* **1.** (Mus.) not based on the use of themes. **2.** (Gram., of form of verb) having suffix attached to stem without thematic vowel. [f. A- 7 + THEMATIC]

Athē'nian (*a-*) *a.* & *n.* (native or inhabitant) of Athens. [f. L *Atheniensis* (*Athenae* f. Gk *Athēnai* Athens, principal city of Greece) + -IAN]

ătherŏsclĕr|**ŏ'sis** *n.* (*pl.* ∼o'ses *pr.* -ēz). form of arteriosclerosis with fatty degeneration; hence ∼o'tIC *a.* [f. G (*-sklerose*) f. Gk *athērē* groats + -O- + SCLEROSIS]

athĭr'st *pred. a.* (literary). thirsty; eager (*for*). [OE *ofthyrst* for *ofthyrsted* p.p. of *ofthyrstan* be thirsty]

ä'thlĕte *n.* competitor or skilled performer in physical exercises; robust or vigorous person; ∼**'s foot**, contagious ringworm of the feet. [f. L *athleta* f. Gk *athlētēs* f. *athlein* contend for prize (*athlon*); see -ET[2]]

ăthlĕ't|**ĭc** *a.* & *n.* **1.** *a.* pertaining to athletes (*athletic* SPORTS) ; physically powerful; large and muscular in build; hence ∼ICALLY *adv.*, ∼**ĭc**ISM (2) *n.* **2.** *n.* (in *pl.*, occas. treated as *sing.*). practice of or competition in physical exercises (running, jumping, throwing, etc.); *physical sports and games of any kind. [f. F *athlétique* or f. L f. Gk *athlētikos* (as prec.; see -IC)]

athwar't (-ôr't) *adv.* & *prep.* across from side to side

(usu. obliquely); crosswise, perversely; in opposition (to); ∼**-hawse**, (Naut.) lying transversely in front o' anchored ship. [f. A[3] + THWART]

-atic (ătĭk, ä'tĭk) *suf.* forming *adjs.* & *ns.* (1) [f. F *-atiqu*ₑ or f. L *-aticus* f. p.p. st. *-at-* of vbs in *-are* + *-icus* (see -IC cf. -AGE)] (*aquatic, erratic, fanatic, lunatic*), (2) [f. F *-atique* or f. LL f. Gk *-atikos*] (*aromatic, idiomatic problematic*).

ati'lt *adv.* tilted and nearly falling; **run** or **ride** ∼ (arch., on horseback with thrust of lance; usu. fig.). [f A- + TILT[1]]

-a'tion *suf.* forming *ns.* denoting (1) vbl action, (2), instance of this, (3) resulting state, (4) resulting thing. (*alteration, civilization, constellation, creation, filtration flirtation, hesitation, plantation, preservation, starvation vexation, visitation*); cf. also -FICATION. [f. or after F, or f L *-atio -ationis* f. vbs in *-are* (see -ION)]

-ative (*a-*, ā-) *suf.* forming *adjs.* (*authoritative, imitative pejorative, qualitative, talkative*). [f. or after F *-atif -ativ*ₑ or f. L *-ativus* f. p.p. st. *-at-* of vbs in *-are* + *-ivus* (see -IVE; cf. -ATIC)]

Atlä'ntèan (*a-*) *a.* of or like Atlas, esp. w. ref. to strength. [f. L *Atlanteus* (as ATLAS) + -AN]

atlä'ntēs (-z) *n. pl.* (Archit.) male figures used a: pillars to support entablature. [Gk, pl. of ATLAS]

Atlä'ntĭc (*a-*) *a.* & *n.* (of or adjoining) the ocean between Europe and Africa to the east and America to the west; ∼ **Time**, standard time used in eastern Canada. [ME, f. L f. Gk *Atlantikos* (as ATLAS; see -IC), orig. of Atlas mountains, then of sea near W. Afr. coast]

atlăntosaur'us *n.* extinct gigantic reptile of genus *Atlantosaurus*. [mod. L, f. Gk (as foll., *sauros* lizard)]

ä'tlas *n.* book of maps or charts, orig. with figure of Atlas at front; (Anat.) uppermost cervical vertebra supporting skull. [L, f. Gk *Atlas -antos* Titan who held up pillars of universe, hence the mountains in N Africa, regarded as supporting the heavens]

atm. *abbr.* (Phys.) atmosphere(s).

ä'tmosphēre *n.* gaseous envelope surrounding heavenly body; that surrounding the earth; one surrounding any substance; mental or moral environment esp. artistic or emotional; pervading tone or mood, esp. attractive one; air (in any place), esp. w ref. to effects on those present; (Phys.) pressure exerted by atmosphere on earth's surface, taken a: unit of pressure, about 1 kg weight per sq. cm; hence **ătmosphĕ'r**IC(AL) *adjs.*, **ătmosphĕ'r**ICS *n. pl.* (interference with telecommunications, due to electric disturbances in atmosphere. [f. mod. L *atmosphaera* f. Gk *atmos* vapour; see SPHERE]

atoll (ä'tŏl, atŏ'l) *n.* ring-shaped coral reef enclosing lagoon. [f. Maldive *atolu*]

ä'tom *n.* smallest particle of a chemical element; thi: as source of atomic energy; very small portion or thing or quantity; (*attrib.*) = foll. (*atom bomb*); ∼**-smasher**, (colloq.) particle-ACCELERATOR. [ME, f OF *atome*, f. L f. Gk *atomos* indivisible]

atŏ'mĭc *a.* of or relating to atom(s); concerned with or using atomic energy or atomic bombs; ∼ **bomb** (deriving its destructiveness from atomic energy); ∼ **clock** (using atomic vibrations as standard of time); ∼ **energy**, nuclear energy; ∼ **mass**, = *atomic weight*; ∼ **number**, (of a chemical element) number of unit positive charges carried by the nucleus of its atom; ∼ **philosophy**, atomism; ∼ **pile**, nuclear REACTOR; ∼ **power**, nuclear power; ∼ **theory**, (1) (Philos.) = foll., (2) theory that chemical elements consist of atoms of definite relative weight uniting with those of other elements in fixed proportions; ∼ **warfare** (in which atomic bombs are used); ∼ **weight**, ratio between the mass of one atom of an element or isotope and one-twelfth of the weight of an atom of the isotope carbon 12; hence **atŏ'm**ICALLY *adv.* [f. mod. L *atomicus* (as prec.; see IC)]

ä'tom|**ism** *n.* (Philos.) theory that all matter consist: of minute individual particles; (Psych.) theory that mental states are made up of elementary units; hence ~IST (2) *n*., ~i'stic *a*. [f. ATOM + -ISM]

ă'tomīz|e, -īs|e (-īz), *v.t.* reduce to atoms or fine particles; hence ~A'TION *n*., ~ER¹ *n*., instrument for reducing liquids to fine spray. [f. ATOM + -IZE]

ă'tomy¹ *n*. (arch.) skeleton; emaciated body. [f. ANATOMY, taken as *an atomy*]

ă'tomy² *n*. (arch.) atom; tiny being. [prob. f. *atomi* pl. of L *atomus* ATOM, assoc. w. prec.]

atō'nal (ā-, a-) *a*. (Mus.) not written in any particular key or mode; hence **ătonă'lity** *n*. [f. A- 7 + TONAL]

atō'ne *v.i.* make amends; ~ **for**, expiate. [back-form. f. foll.]

atō'nement (-nm-) *n*. atoning; expiation, reparation for wrong or injury; reconciliation of God and man; **the A~**, expiation of mankind's sin by Christ; **Day of A~**, most solemn religious fast of Jewish year, eight days after Jewish New Year. [f. *at* ONE 3 + -MENT, after med. L *adunamentum* and earlier *onement* f. obs. v. *one* unite]

atō'nic *a*. without accent or stress; (Path.) lacking tone; so **ă'tony¹** *n*. [f. A- 7 + TONIC]

atō'p *adv.* & *prep.* on the top (*of* or of). [f. A³ + TOP¹]

-ator *suf.* See -OR.

-atory *suf.* See -ORY.

ATP *abbr.* adenosine triphosphate.

ătrabi'lious (-lyus) *a*. melancholy; ill-tempered; hence ~NESS *n*. [f. L *atra bilis* (black bile, transl. Gk *melagkholia* MELANCHOLY) + -OUS; cf. TEMPERAMENT]

ā'tri|um *n*. (*pl.* ~**a** or ~**ums**). central court of Roman house; cavity in body, esp. (Anat.) one of two upper cavities of heart that receive blood from veins; hence ~AL *a*. [L]

atrō'cious (-shus) *a*. extremely wicked; very bad (*atrocious weather*); hence ~LY² *adv.*, ~NESS *n*. [f. L *atrox -ocis* cruel + -OUS]

atrō'city *n*. extreme wickedness; atrocious deed; (colloq.) repellent act or thing. [f. F *atrocité* or f. L *atrocitas* (as prec.; see -ITY)]

ă'trophy *n*. & *v*. **1.** *n*. wasting away through under-nourishment or lack of use; emaciation (lit. or fig.). **2.** *v.t.* & *i*. (cause to) undergo atrophy. [f. F *atrophie* or f. LL f. Gk *atrophia* (a- not, *trophē* food); see -Y¹]

ā'tropine (-īn, -ēn) *n*. poisonous alkaloid found in deadly nightshade, used in medicine. [f. mod. L *Atropa belladonna* deadly nightshade f. Gk *Atropos* inflexible, name of one of the Fates; see -INE⁵]

*ă'ttaboy *int.* (sl.) expr. encouragement or admiration. [prob. corrupt. of *that's the boy!*]

attă'ch *v*. **1.** *v.t.* fasten (thing *to* another); join one*self* (*to* person, company, expedition); (usu. in *pass.*) bind in friendship, make devoted (*is deeply attached to her*); appoint for special or temporary duties; affix (im-material things, name, liability, etc., *to*); attribute (importance, meaning, etc. *to*); (Law) seize (person, property) by legal authority; hence ~ABLE *a*. **2.** *v.i.* be attributable (*no blame attaches to the bystanders*). [ME, f. OF *estachier* fasten f. Gmc **stakōn* f. **stak-* STAKE; in Law sense thr. OF *atachier*]

attă'ché (-shä) *n*. one attached to ambassador's staff (*military, press, attaché*); ~ **case**, small rectangular case for carrying documents etc. [F, p.p. of *attacher* (as prec.)]

attă'chment *n*. act of attaching; thing (to be) attached; means of attaching; affection, devotion; legal seizure. [ME, f. F *attachement* (*attacher* attach; see -MENT)]

attă'ck¹ *v*. **1.** *v.t.* act against with (esp. armed) force; seek to hurt or defeat; criticize adversely; act harmfully on; begin vigorous work on; hence ~ABLE *a*. **2.** *v.i.* make attack. **3.** Hence ~ER¹ *n*. [f. F *attaquer* f. It. *attaccare* ATTACH, join (battle)]

attă'ck² *n*. act of attacking; offensive operation or behaviour; (Mus.) action or manner of beginning piece, passage, etc.; sudden start of illness etc. (*bilious, heart, attack*; *an attack of the blues*); player(s) seeking to score goals etc. [f. prec., or f. F *attaque* f. It. *attacco*]

attai'n *v*. **1.** *v.t.* arrive at, reach; gain, accomplish; hence ~ABI'LITY *n*., ~ABLE *a*., ~ableNESS (-bԑln-) *n*. **2.** *v.i.* ~ **to**, arrive at by development or effort. [ME, f. AF *atain-, atein-*, OF *ataign-* st. of *ataindre* f. L AT*tingere* (*tangere* touch)]

attai'nder *n*. (Hist.) consequences of sentence of death or outlawry (forfeiture of estate, loss of civil rights); **bill of ~**, legislation inflicting attainder without trial. [ME f. AF, = OF *ateindre* ATTAIN used as n. (see -ER⁴)]

attai'nment *n*. act of attaining; thing attained, esp. (in *pl.*) personal achievements. [f. ATTAIN + -MENT]

attai'nt *v.t.* **1.** (Hist.) subject to attainder. **2.** (of disease etc.) strike, affect; taint. [ME, f. obs. *attaint a*. f. OF *ataint, ateint* p.p. f. as ATTAIN; confused in meaning with TAINT]

ă'ttar, ō'ttō¹, *n*. fragrant essential oil, esp. from rose--petals. [f. Pers. *'ular* f. Arab. ('*itr* perfume)]

atte'mper *v.t.* (arch.) modify by admixture; soothe, mollify; accommodate or attune *to*; hence ~MENT *n*. [ME, f. OF *atemprer* f. L AT(*temperare* TEMPER¹)]

atte'mpt¹ *v.t.* try (thing, action, *to* do); try to conquer (mountain, fortress) or accomplish; ~ **the life of**, (arch.) try to kill; hence ~ABLE *a*. [f. OF *attempter*, f. L AT(*temptare* TEMPT)]

atte'mpt² *n*. act of attempting (*to* do, at thing or doing, *on the life of, on the record*); endeavour; result of attempting, esp. unsuccessfully. [f. prec.]

atte'nd *v*. **1.** *v.i.* turn the mind *to*; apply oneself (*to*, or abs.). **2.** be present (*at*); wait *on*. **3.** *v.t.* wait on; escort, accompany; follow as result from (*attended with serious consequences*); be present at (lecture etc.); go regularly to (school, church, etc.). **4.** Hence ~ER¹ *n*. [ME, f. OF *atendre* f. L AT*tendere* -tent- stretch]

atte'ndance *n*. act of ATTENDING (senses 2 and 3; ||~ **centre**, place where young delinquents must attend regularly instead of being sent to prison; DANCE¹ *attendance*); number of persons present. [ME f. OF *atendance* (as prec.; see -ANCE)]

atte'ndant *a*. & *n*. **1.** *a*. waiting (*on*); accompanying (*attendant circumstances*). **2.** *n*. one who attends; person providing service (*cloakroom attendant*; **medical ~**, one's physician; **museum** etc. ~, custodian or guide). [ME f. OF (as ATTEND; see -ANT)]

atte'ntion *n*. & *int*. **1.** *n*. act of ATTENDING (sense 1; *give, pay, attention*); faculty of attending (sense 1; *attract attention*; *call, draw, attention to*); consideration, care; (in *pl.*) ceremonious politeness (**pay** one's ~**s** to, woo); (Mil.) erect attitude of readiness (*come to, stand at, attention*). **2.** *int*. A~!, order to take notice or to assume attitude of attention. [ME, f. L *attentio* (as ATTEND; see -ION)]

atte'ntive *a*. heedful; ATTENDING (sense 1) *to*; polite, assiduous; hence ~LY² (-vlī) *adv.*, ~NESS (-vn-) *n*. [ME, f. F *attentif -ive* f. *attente*, OF *atente*, fem. p.p. (as ATTEND; see -IVE]

atte'nū|āte¹ *v.t.* make thin; reduce in force, value, or virulence; reduce amplitude of (signal or current); so ~A'TION, ~ātor, *ns*. [f. L AT*tenuare* (*tenuis* thin) + -ATE³]

atte'nuate² *a*. slender; rarefied; tapering gradually. [f. L *attenuatus* p.p. of *attenuare* (see prec., -ATE²)]

atte'st *v*. **1.** *v.t.* certify validity of; enrol (recruit) for military service; ||~**ed cattle, milk,** (certified free from disease). **2.** *v.i.* bear witness *to*; (of recruit) enrol for military service. **3.** Hence ~OR *n*. [f. F *attester* f. L AT*testari* (*testis* witness)]

attestā'tion *n*. act of attesting; testimony. [F, or f. LL *attestatio* (as prec.; see -ATION)]

A'ttic¹ (ă'-) *a*. & *n*. of Athens or Attica; ~ (**dialect**), Greek as used by the ancient Athenians; ~ **salt, wit**, refined wit. [f. L f. Gk *Attikos*]

a'ttic² *n*. highest storey of house, usu. immediately under roof; room in this. [f. F *attique*, as prec.; orig. (Archit.) small order above a taller one]

A'tticism *n*. extreme elegance of speech. [f. Gk *Attikismos* (as ATTIC¹; see -ISM)]

attir'e v.t., & n. dress (esp. w. ref. to fine or formal or special clothing). [ME, f. OF atir(i)er equip f. à tire in order, of unkn. orig.]

a'ttitūde n. disposition of figure (in painting etc.); posture of body (**strike an** ∼, assume it theatrically); position of aircraft etc. relative to specified directions; settled behaviour, as indicating opinion; ∼ (**of mind**), settled mode of thinking; hence **ăttitū'din**AL a. [F, f. It. attitudine fitness, posture, f. LL aptitudo -dinis (aptus fit; see -TUDE)]

ăttitū'dinīze, -īse (-īz), v.i. practise or adopt attitudes; speak, write, behave, affectedly. [f. It. attitudine f. LL (as prec.) + -IZE]

attn. abbr. (for the) attention (of).

ă'ttō- pref. denoting factor of 10⁻¹⁸ (attometre). [f. Da. or Norw. atten eighteen + -o-]

attor'ney (-têr'-) n. **1.** one appointed to act for another in business or legal matters (**power of** ∼, authority to act thus); *qualified lawyer, esp. representing client in proceedings; *DISTRICT attorney; hence ∼SHIP (-nĭsh-) n. **2.** A∼-Ge'neral, chief legal officer of some countries and states. [ME, f. OF atorné p.p. (as n.) of atorner assign (à to, torner turn; see -Y⁴]

attră'ct v.t. draw or bring to oneself or itself (he attracted a crowd with his tricks; magnet attracts iron; publicity attracts new members); give or promise pleasure to (person); draw forth and fix on oneself (attention etc.); hence ∼ABLE a. [f. L AT(trahere tract- draw)]

attră'ctant a. & n. (substance) which attracts (esp. insects). [f. prec. + -ANT]

attră'ction n. act or faculty of drawing to oneself or itself (lit. or fig.); (Phys.) tendency of bodies to attract or approach each other (opp. repulsion); thing that attracts (fig.); (Gram.) influence of word in context to cause incorrect form of adjacent word. [F, or f. L attractio (as ATTRACT; see -ION)]

attră'ctive a. attracting or capable of attracting (esp. fig., interesting, pleasing); hence ∼LY² (-vlĭ) adv., ∼NESS (-vn-) n. [f. F attractif -ive f. LL attractivus (as ATTRACT; see -IVE)]

ă'ttribūte¹ n. quality ascribed to person or thing; material object recognized as appropriate to person or office; characteristic quality; (Gram.) attributive word. [ME, f. OF attribut or f. L attributum (ATtribuere -ut- assign)]

attri'būt|e² v.t. regard as belonging or appropriate to (author etc.); refer (effect to its cause); assign (to time or place); hence ∼ABLE a. [f. L as prec.]

ăttribū'tion n. act of attributing. [ME, f. OF, f. L attributio -onis (as ATTRIBUTE¹; see -ION)]

attri'būtive a. (Gram., of a. or n., opp. predicative) expressing an attribute (e.g. old in the old dog but not in the dog is old); hence ∼LY² (-vlĭ) adv. [f. F attributif -ive (as ATTRIBUTE¹; see -IVE)]

attri'tion n. friction; gradual wearing out (esp. Mil.; **war of** ∼, one whose outcome depends on which side can last longer); abrasion; (Theol.) sorrow for sin (short of contrition); hence ∼AL a. [ME, f. LL attritio (ATterere -trit- rub; see -ION)]

attū'ne v.t. bring into musical accord (to, lit. or fig.); tune (instrument). [f. AT- + TUNE 4]

Atty. abbr. Attorney.

ATV abbr. ||Associated Television.

ătÿ'pical a. not conforming to type; hence ∼LY² adv. [f. A- 2 + TYPICAL]

AU abbr. ångström unit; astronomical unit.

Au symb. gold. [f. L aurum]

aubade (ōbah'd) n. poem or piece of music appropriate to dawn. [F, f. Sp. albada (alba dawn)]

auberge (ōbār'zh) n. inn. [F]

au'bergine (ō'berzhēn) n. fruit of egg-plant, used as vegetable. [F, f. Cat. alberginia f. Arab. al-bādinjān f. Pers. bādinjān f. Skr. vātiṃgaṇa]

aubrie'tia, (erron.) **-rē'tia**, (-sha) n. spring-flowering dwarf perennial rock-plant of genus Aubrieta. [mod. L, f. Claude Aubriet, Fr. botanist d. 1743; see -IA¹]

au'burn a. reddish brown (usu. of person's hair).

[ME, orig. yellowish white, f. OF auborne, alborne, f. L alburnus whitish (albus white)]

AUC abbr. ab urbe condita.

au courant (ō kōō'rahn) pred. a. acquainted with or of what is going on; well-informed. [F, = in the (regular) course]

au'ction n., & v.t. **1.** n. public sale in which articles are sold to maker of highest bid; **all over the** ∼, (Austral. sl.) everywhere; **Dutch** ∼, sale in which price is reduced by auctioneer till a buyer is found. **2.** ∼ (**bridge**), form of bridge in which players bid for right to name trumps; sequence of bids made at bridge. **3.** v.t. sell by auction. [f. L auctio increase, auction (augēre auct- increase; see -ION)]

auctioneer' n. one whose business is to conduct auctions; hence ∼ING¹ (1) n. [f. prec. + -EER]

auda'cious (-shŭs) a. daring, bold; impudent; hence or cogn. ∼LY² adv., ∼NESS, **audA'CITY**, ns. [f. L audax -acis bold (audēre dare; see -ACIOUS)]

au'dible a. that can be heard; hence **aud**IBI'LITY, ∼NESS (-beln-), ns., **au'dib**LY² adv. [f. LL audibilis (audire hear; see -IBLE)]

au'dience n. hearing (**give** ∼, listen); formal interview (had audience of; had an audience with); persons within hearing; whole group of listeners or spectators; readers (of book, writer, etc.). [ME f. OF, f. L audientia (audire hear; see -ENCE)]

au'dile a. pertaining to sense of hearing. [f. L audire hear, after tactile]

au'diō n. (reproduction of) sound; ∼ **frequency** (comparable to that of normally audible sound); ∼ **typist** (who types direct from tape or other recording). [f. foll.]

au'diō- comb. form. hearing, as: ∼LOGY (-ŏ'l-) n., science of hearing, whence ∼LOGIST (-ŏ'l-) n.; ∼METER (-ŏ'm-) n., instrument for testing hearing; ∼PHILE n., devotee of high-fidelity sound reproduction; ∼vi'sual, using both sight and sound. [f. L audire hear + -o-]

au'dit n., & v.t. **1.** n. official examination of accounts; ∼ **ale** (of special quality, formerly brewed in English colleges, orig. for use on day of audit). **2.** v.t. conduct audit of; *attend (class) without intending to obtain credits. [ME, f. L auditus hearing (audire -it- hear)]

audi'tion n. **1.** n. power of hearing; listening; trial hearing or seeing of applicant for employment as singer, dancer, etc. **2.** v.t. & i. hear etc., be heard etc., as applicant. [F, or f. L auditio (audire -it- hear; see -ION)]

au'ditive a. concerned with hearing. [f. F auditif -ive (as prec.; see -IVE)]

audi'tor n. listener; one who audits accounts; hence ∼IAL a., one who audits accounts; hence ∼IAL a. [ME, f. AF auditour f. L auditor -oris (as prec.; see -OR)]

auditor'i|um n. (pl. ∼ums or ∼a), building or part of building occupied by audience. [L, neut. (as n.) of auditorius a. (see foll., -ORIUM)]

au'ditorў a. & n. **1.** a. concerned with hearing; received by the ear. **2.** n. (arch.) assembly of hearers, audience; auditorium. [f. L auditorius (as AUDITOR; see -ORY)]

au fait (ō fā') pred. a. conversant, instructed; **put** or **make** ∼ **with**, instruct in. [F]

au fond (ō faw'n) adv. at bottom, basically. [F]

Aug. abbr. August.

Augē'an a. filthy, like the stables of Augeas, which Hercules cleansed by diverting river Alpheus to flow through them. [f. L Augeas f. Gk Augeias + -AN]

au'ger (-g-) n. tool for boring holes in wood, having long shank with helical groove, cutting edge, and transverse handle; similar instrument for boring in soil. [OE nafogār (nafu NAVE¹, gār piercer); cf. OS, OHG nabugēr, ON nafarr; for loss of n- cf. ADDER]

aught¹ (awt) n. (arch. or poet.) anything. [OE āwiht etc.; = OS ēowiht, f. WG (as AYE², WIGHT)]

aught². See OUGHT¹.

au'gīte *n*. dark variety of pyroxene containing alumina. [f. L f. Gk *augītēs* (*augē* lustre; see -ITE¹)]

au'gment¹ *n*. (Gram.) vowel prefixed to past tenses in the older IE languages. [ME f. OF, or f. LL *augmentum* (as foll.)]

augmě'nt² *v.t.* & *i*. make or become greater; increase; ∼ed **interval** (Mus., greater by a semitone than corresp. major or perfect interval). [ME, f. F *augmenter* or f. LL *augmentare* increase f. L *augmentum* (*augēre* increase)]

augmentā'tion *n*. enlargement; growth; increase; (Mus.) repetition of passage in notes longer than those previously used. [ME f. F, f. LL *augmentatio -onis* (*augmentare*; see prec., -ATION)]

augmě'ntative *a*. having the property of increasing; (Gram., of affix or derived word) increasing in force the idea of the original word. [f. F *augmentatif -ive* or f. med. L *augmentativus* (as AUGMENT²; see -ATIVE)]

au grand sérieux (ō grahṅ sěrēěr') *adv*. quite seriously (*take it, him*, etc., *au grand sérieux*). [F]

au gratin. See GRATIN.

au'gur¹ *n*. Roman religious official who foretold future events by observing behaviour of birds etc.; soothsayer; hence ∼SHIP *n*. [L]

au'gur² *v*. **1.** *v.t.* foresee, predict; portend. **2.** *v.i.* ∼ well, ill, have good, bad, implications *for*. [f. prec.]

au'gural *a*. of augurs; significant as regards the future. [f. L *auguralis* (AUGUR¹; see -AL)]

au'gurŷ *n*. divination by omens; omen. [ME, f. OF *augurie* or f. L *augurium* (AUGUR¹)]

augŭ'st¹ *a*. majestic; venerable; noble; impressive; hence ∼LY² *adv*., ∼NESS *n*. [f. F *auguste* or L *augustus* consecrated, venerable]

Au'gust² *n*. eighth month of year. [OE, f. L *augustus* (see prec.), name of Augustus Caesar, first Roman emperor]

Augŭ'stan *a*. & *n*. **1.** *a*. connected with reign of Augustus Caesar, outstanding period of Latin literature; (of any national literature) classical (in Engl. literature 17th–18th c.). **2.** *n*. writer of the Augustan age of any literature. [f. L *Augustanus* (*Augustus*; see -AN)]

Augŭ'stine *n*. Augustinian friar. [ME, f. OF *augustin* f. L *Augustinus* (see foll.)]

Augŭstī'nian *a*. & *n*. **1.** *a*. of or relating to St. Augustine, a Doctor of the Church (d. 430), or his doctrines; belonging to a religious order observing rule derived from St. Augustine's writings. **2.** *n*. adherent of the doctrines of St. Augustine; one of the order of Augustinian friars. [f. L *Augustinus* Augustine +-IAN]

auk *n*. sea-bird of family Alcidae, e.g. great auk (flightless and extinct), little auk, guillemot, puffin, razorbill. [f. ON *álka*]

auld *a*. (Sc.) old; ∼ **lang syne** (-sīn), 'old long since', the days of long ago (esp. as title and refrain of song sung at parting etc.). [OE *ald*, Anglian form of OLD]

au'lic *a*. pertaining to a court. [f. F *aulique* or f. L f. Gk *aulikos* (*aulē* court; see -IC)]

au'mbrŷ, ă'mbrŷ, *n*. closed recess in wall of church; (Hist.) small cupboard. [ME, f. OF *almarie, armarie*, f. L *armarium* closet, chest (*arma* utensils)]

au naturel (ō nătŭrě'l) *adv*. & *pred. a*. uncooked; (cooked) in the most natural or simplest way. [F, = in the natural state]

aunt (ahnt) *n*. father's or mother's sister; uncle's wife; (colloq.) unrelated woman friend of children; **A**∼ **Sally,** game in which players throw sticks or balls at wooden dummy, (fig.) object of unreasonable attack; **my** (**sainted** etc.). ∼ (sl. excl. of surprise etc.); hence (colloq.) ∼'IE, ∼'Y³, *ns*. [ME, f. AF *aunte*, OF *ante* f. L *amita*]

au pair (ō p-) *a*. & *n*. (Of arrangements between two parties) paid for by mutual services (no money passing); ||∼ (**girl**), young (usu. foreign) woman helping with housework etc. in return for room and board. [F]

aur'a *n*. (*pl*. ∼e or ∼s). subtle emanation (from flowers etc.); atmosphere diffused by or attending person, place, etc. (esp. in mystical or spiritualistic use); (Path.) premonitory symptom in epilepsy etc.; hence **aur'al¹** [-AL] *a*. [ME f. L f. Gk, = breeze, breath]

aur'al² *a*. pertaining to or received by the ear; hence ∼LY² *adv*. [f. L *auris* ear +-AL]

aur'éate *a*. golden, gold-coloured; resplendent; (of language) highly ornamented. [ME, f. LL *aureatus* f. L *aureus* golden (*aurum* gold); see -ATE²]

aurě'ola, aur'éole, *n*. celestial crown of martyr etc.; glory round head or body of pictured divine figure; halo or ring round sun or moon. [ME; *aureola* (*corona*) L, = golden (crown), fem. of *aureolus* f. *aureus* (*aurum* gold); *aureole* f. OF f. L *aureola*]

auréomy'cin *n*. antibiotic used esp. in lung diseases. [f. L *aureus* golden + Gk *mukēs* fungus +-IN]

au revoir (ō revwār') *int*. & *n*. (goodbye) till we meet again. [F]

aur'ic *a*. pertaining to gold. [f. L *aurum* gold + -IC]

aur'icle *n*. external ear of animals; process shaped like lower lobe of ear; (Anat.) (small appendage to) atrium of heart. [f. foll.]

aurī'cūla *n*. species of primula, with ear-shaped leaves; mollusc of genus *Auricula*. [L, dim. of *auris* ear]

aurī'cūlar *a*. **1.** pertaining to the ear; ∼ **confession** (made privately in priest's ear). **2.** pertaining to auricle of heart; shaped like an auricle. **3.** Hence ∼LY² *adv*. [f. LL *auricularis* (AURICULA; see -AR¹)]

aurī'cūlate *a*. having ear-shaped appendages. [f. L AURICULA +-ATE²]

aurī'ferous *a*. yielding gold. [f. L *aurifer* (*aurum* gold); see -FEROUS]

Aurīgnā'cian (-shan) *a*. & *n*. (culture) of the palaeolithic period in Europe following the Mousterian and preceding the Solutrean. [F (-*ien*), f. *Aurignac* in SW France, where remains of it were found]

aur'īst *n*. ear specialist. [f. L *auris* ear +-IST]

aur'ŏchs (owr'ŏks, ōr'-) *n*. **1.** extinct European wild ox, urus. **2.** European bison, wisent. [G, f. OHG *ūrohso* (*ūr* urus, *ohso* ox)]

auror'a *n*. (*pl*. ∼s or ∼e). luminous atmospheric (prob. electrical) phenomenon, usu. of streamers radiating from above northern (∼ **bŏrēā'lis**) or southern (∼ **austrā'lis**) magnetic pole; dawn; (A∼) Roman goddess of dawn; hence **auror'AL** *a*. [L, = dawn, goddess of dawn]

auscultā'tion *n*. act of listening, esp. (Med.) to sounds of heart, lungs, etc.; so **auscŭ'ltatory** *a*. [f. L *auscultatio* (*auscultare* listen to; see -ATION)]

au sérieux (ō sěrēěr') *adv*. seriously (*take it, him*, etc., *au sérieux*). [F]

au'spicāte *v.t.* (arch.) inaugurate, initiate. [f. L *auspicari* prognosticate (*auspex*; see foll.) + -ATE³]

au'spice *n*. forecast; (in *pl*.) patronage (*under the auspices of*). [orig. 'observation of bird-flight in divination'; F, or f. L *auspicium* (*auspex* observer of birds f. *avis* bird)]

auspī'cious (-shus) *a*. of good omen, favourable; prosperous; hence ∼LY² *adv*., ∼NESS *n*. [f. prec. + -OUS]

Au'ssie (ŏ'zĭ, ŏ'sĭ) *n*. & *a*. (colloq.) Australia(n). [abbr.; see -IE]

austēr'e (ŏ-, aw-) *a*. (∼**r**, ∼**st**). harsh, stern; morally strict; severely simple; hence or cogn. ∼LY² (-ēr'lĭ) *adv*., ∼NESS (-ēr'n-) *n*., **austě'rITY** (ŏ-, aw-) *n*. (esp. of nation-wide economies). [ME f. OF, f. L f. Gk *austēros* severe]

Au'stin (ŏ'-, aw'-) *a*. & *n*. = AUGUSTINIAN. [contr. of AUGUSTINE]

au'stral (aw'-, ŏ'-) *a*. southern; (A∼) of Austral(as)ia (*Austral English*). [ME, f. L *australis* (*Auster* south wind; see -AL)]

Australā'sian (ŏ-, aw-; -shan) *a*. & *n*. (native or inhabitant) of Australasia. [f. *Australasia* Australia and islands of SW Pacific (f. F *Australasie* f. as *Australia + Asia*) + -AN]

Austrā'lian (ŏ-, aw-) *n.* & *a.* (native or inhabitant) of Australia; ~ **bear**, koala; ~ (**National**) **Rules**, form of football played with Rugby ball by teams of 18; ~ **terrier** (wire-haired Australian breed); hence ~ISM (2, 4) *n.* [f. F *australien* f. L (as AUSTRAL)]

Austrālopi'thec|us (ŏ-, aw-) *n.* small-brained fossil hominid of genus *Australopithecus*; hence ~INE[1] *n.* & *a.* [mod. L, f. L *australis* southern+-o-+Gk *pithēkos* ape]

au'tarchy̆ (-kǐ) *n.* absolute sovereignty, despotism; hence **autār'chIC**(AL) (-k-) *adjs.* [f. mod. L *autarchia* (as AUTO-, Gk *-arkhia* f. *arkhō* rule)]

au'tarky̆ *n.* self-sufficiency, esp. economic; hence **autār'kIC**(AL) *adjs.*, **au'tarkIST** (2) *n.* [f. Gk *autarkeia* (as AUTO-, *arkeō* suffice)]

authĕ'nt|ic *a.* reliable, trustworthy; of undisputed origin, genuine; (of church mode) having sounds comprised between final and its octave (cf. PLAGAL); hence ~ICALLY *adv.*, ~ï'cITY *n.* [ME, f. OF *autentique* f. LL f. Gk *authentikos* principal, genuine; see -IC]

authĕ'ntic|āte *v.t.* establish truth or authorship or validity or genuineness of; hence ~A'TION, ~ātOR, *ns.* [f. med. L *authenticare* (LL *authenticus*; see prec.)+-ATE[3]]

au'thor *n.*, & *v.t.* **1.** *n.* originator (*of* a condition of things, event, etc.); writer of book(s), essay(s), etc.; author's writings; hence ~ESS[1] *n.*, **authŏ'rIAL** *a.* **2.** *v.t.* be author of. [ME f. AF *autour*, OF *autor* f. L *auctor* (*augēre auct-* increase, originate, promote; see -OR)]

authŏritā'rian *a.* & *n.* (esp. Polit.) (person) favouring obedience to authority as opp. to individual liberty; tyrannical (person); (of State etc.) that is a dictatorship; hence ~ISM (3) *n.* [f. AUTHORITY+-ARIAN]

authŏ'ritative *a.* possessing or claiming authority; proceeding from competent authority; commanding, imperative; hence ~LY[2] (-vlǐ) *adv.*, ~NESS (-vn-) *n.* [f. foll.+-ATIVE]

authŏ'rity̆ *n.* power or right to enforce obedience; delegated power (*to* do, *for* an act, or abs.); person or (esp. in *pl.*) body having authority; personal influence, esp. over opinion; weight of testimony; book, quotation, considered as settling a question; evidence or declaration that may be cited in support of a statement (*on the authority of Plato*); person whose opinion is accepted, esp. expert in a subject (*an authority on bees*). [ME, f. OF *autorité* f. L *auctoritas* (*auctor*; see AUTHOR, -ITY)]

au'thoriz|e, **-is|e** (-ĭz), *v.t.* **1.** sanction; A~ed **Version**, English transl. of Bible (1611). **2.** give authority to, commission, (person *to* do). **3.** Hence ~A'TION *n.* [ME, f. OF *autoriser* f. med. L *auctorizare* (*auctor*; see AUTHOR, -IZE)]

au'thorship *n.* occupation or career as a writer; origin (*of* book). [f. AUTHOR+-SHIP]

au'tism *n.* morbid absorption in fantasy; mental condition esp. in children, preventing proper response to environment; hence **auti'stIC** *a.* [f. mod. L *autismus* (as AUTO-, -ISM)]

***au'tō** *n.* (*pl.* ~s). (colloq.) motor car. [abbr. of AUTOMOBILE]

au'to- *comb. form* (usu. aut- bef. vowel). self (*autism*); one's own (*autobiography*); by oneself, spontaneous, (*auto-suggestion*); by itself, automatic, (*automobile*). [f. or after Gk *auto-* f. *autos* self]

autobahn (aw'tobahn) *n.* (*pl.* ~s *or* ~en). German or Swiss motorway. [G (*auto* motor car, *bahn* path, road)]

autobiō'graph|y̆ *n.* writing the story of one's own life; story so written; hence ~ER[1] *n.*, **autobiŏgrā'phIC**(AL) *adjs.* [f. AUTO-+BIOGRAPHY]

***au'tocāde** *n.* motorcade. [f. AUTOMOBILE+CAVALCADE]

au'tocār *n.* (arch.) motor vehicle. [f. AUTO-+CAR]

autocĕ'phalous *a.* having its own head; (of bishop, church, etc.) independent. [f. Gk *autokephalos* (as AUTO-, *kephalē* head)+-OUS]

autŏ'chthon (-k-) *n.* (in *pl.* ~s, *or* ~es *pr.* -ēz) original or earliest known inhabitants; aborigines; hence ~AL, **autochthŏ'nIC**, ~OUS, (-k-) *adjs.* [Gk, = sprung from that land itself (as AUTO-, *khthōn -onos* land)]

au'toclāve *n.* strong vessel used for chemical reactions at high pressures and temperatures; sterilizer using high-pressure steam. [f. AUTO-+L *clavus* nail or *clavis* key]

au'tocōde *n.* machine code which computer itself can interpret. [f. AUTO-+CODE]

autŏ'cracy̆ *n.* absolute government by one person; controlling influence. [f. Gk *autokrateia* (as foll.)]

au'tocrăt *n.* absolute ruler; dictatorial person; so **autocră'tIC** *a.* [f. F *autocrate* f. Gk *autokratēs* (as AUTO-, *kratos* power)]

au'tocrŏss *n.* motor-racing across country or on unmade roads. [f. AUTOMOBILE+CROSS- (4)]

Au'tocūe *n.* (P) device showing television speaker the script as aid to memory. [f. AUTO-+CUE[1]]

au'tocy̆cle *n.* (arch.) bicycle with auxiliary engine. [f. AUTO-+CYCLE]

auto-da-fé (awtodahfā') *n.* (*pl.* **autos-da-fé**). sentence of the Inquisition; execution of this, esp. burning of heretic. [Port., = act of the faith]

au'todidăct *n.* self-taught person; so **autodidă'ctIC** *a.* [f. AUTO-+as DIDACTIC]

autŏ-ĕ'rotism *n.* sexual excitement generated without another person's stimulus; so **autō-ĕrŏ'tIC** *a.*, **autō--ĕrŏ'tICISM** *n.* [f. AUTO-+EROTISM]

autŏ'gamy̆ *n.* (Bot.) self-fertilization. [f. AUTO-+Gk *-gamia* f. *gamos* marriage]

autŏ'gĕnous *a.* self-produced; ~ **welding** (by melting edges together without adding different material). [f. AUTO-+-GENOUS]

autogīr'ō *n.* (*pl.* ~s). early form of helicopter with propeller and freely rotating horizontal vanes. [Sp. (as AUTO-, *giro* gyration)]

au'tograft (-ahft) *n.* (Surg.) graft from another part of same individual. [f. AUTO-+GRAFT[1]]

au'tograph (-ahf) *n.*, & *v.t.* **1.** *n.* manuscript in author's own handwriting; person's own hand-writing, esp. signature; document signed by its author. **2.** *v.t.* write with one's own hand; sign. [F, or f. LL f. Gk *autographon* neut. (as n.) of *autographos* (as AUTO-, *-graphos* written); cf. -GRAPH]

autŏ'graphy̆ *n.* writing with one's own hand; reproduction of writing or drawing by direct facsimile; so **autogră'phIC** *a.* [f. prec.+-Y[1]]

autogy̆r'ō *n.* Var. of AUTOGIRO.

au'tohárp *n.* kind of zither with mechanical device to allow playing of chords. [f. AUTO-+HARP[1]]

autŏ-immū'n|e *a.* (Med.) caused by the production of antibodies to substances naturally present; so ~ITY *n.* [f. AUTO-+IMMUNE]

autŏ-intŏxicā'tion *n.* (Med.) poisoning by toxin produced within the body. [f. AUTO-+INTOXICATION]

autŏ'ly̆sis *n.* destruction of body cells by their own enzymes; hence **autoly̆'tIC** *a.* [f. AUTO-+-LYSIS]

***au'tomăt** *n.* cafeteria in which meals etc. are provided from slot-machines; slot-machine. [G, f. F *automate*, as AUTOMATON]

au'tomāte *v.t.* subject to or operate by automation. [back-form. f. AUTOMATION]

automă'tic *a.* & *n.* **1.** *a.* working of itself, without direct human actuation; (of firearm) having mechanism for loading, firing, and ejecting until ammunition is exhausted or pressure on trigger ceases; is released; (of telephone system) operated by automatic switches; (of gear system in motor vehicle) operated automatically according to speed and acceleration; ~ **pilot**, device for keeping aircraft or ship on set course. **2.** done without thought, unconscious; unintelligent, merely mechanical, (*an automatic consequence*; *incurs automatic disqualification*). **3.** (Psych.) performed unconsciously or subconsciously; ~ **writing** (with planchette etc.). **4.** Hence **automă'tICALLY** *adv.*,

For other words in auto- see AUTO-.

automati'city *n.* **5.** *n.* automatic firearm, tool, etc.; (colloq.) vehicle with automatic gear system. [f. as AUTOMATON + -IC]

automā'tion *n.* automatic control of manufacture of product through successive stages; use of automatic equipment to save mental and manual labour. [irreg. f. prec. + -ATION]

autŏ'matism *n.* involuntary action; unthinking routine; (Psych.) action performed unconsciously or subconsciously, mental state accompanying such actions. [f. F *automatisme* (*automate* AUTOMATON; see -ISM)]

autŏ'matīze, -ise (-īz), *v.t.* make automatic; subject to automation. [f. AUTOMATIC + -IZE]

autŏ'mat|on *n.* (*pl.* ∿a *or* ∿ons). piece of mechanism with concealed motive power; organism, esp. person, whose actions are involuntary or without active intelligence. [L f. Gk, neut. (as n.) of AUTOmatos acting of itself]

*au'tomobile (-ēl) *n.* motor car. [F (as AUTO-, MOBILE)]

automō'tive *a.* concerned with motor vehicles. [f. AUTO- + MOTIVE¹]

autŏ'nom|y *n.* right of self-government; personal freedom; freedom of the will; hence *or* cogn. **autono'mic** *a.*, (esp. Physiol., functioning involuntarily), ∿IST (3) *n.*, ∿OUS *a.* [f. Gk *autonomia* f. AUTO(*nomos* law); see -Y¹]

au'topilot *n.* automatic pilot. [abbr.]

autopista (aw'topīsta) *n.* Spanish motorway. [Sp. (as AUTOMOBILE, *pista* track)]

autŏpsy̌ (aw'-, -ŏ'-) *n.* personal inspection; post-mortem examination; (fig.) critical dissection. [f. F *autopsie* or f. mod. L f. Gk *autopsia* (*autoptēs* eye-witness)]

autorā'diograph (-ahf) *n.* photograph of object, produced by radiation from radioactive material in the object; so **autorādiográ'phic** *a.*, **autorādiō'-GRAPHY** *n.* [f. AUTO- + RADIOGRAPH]

autoroute (aw'tŏrōōt) *n.* French motorway. [F (as AUTOMOBILE, ROUTE)]

autostrad|a (owtostrah'da) *n.* (*pl.* ∿e *pr.* -dä). Italian motorway. [It. (as AUTOMOBILE, *strada* road)]

auto-sugge'stion (-sŭjě'schon) *n.* hypnotic or subconscious suggestion from subject himself. [f. AUTO- + SUGGESTION]

autotě'lic *a.* having or being a purpose in itself. [f. AUTO- | Gk *telos* end + -IC]

autŏ'tomy̌ *n.* (Zool.) casting off of part(s) of body. [f. AUTO- + -TOMY]

autotŏ'x|in *n.* poisonous substance produced by changes within the organism; so ∿IC *a.* [f. AUTO- + TOXIN]

autotrŏ'phic *a.* self-nourishing; able to feed on simple substances. [f. AUTO- + Gk *trophos* feeder + -IC]

au'totype *n.* facsimile; photographic printing process for monochrome reproduction; print so made. [f. AUTO- + TYPE¹]

au'tumn (-m) *n.* third season of the year, in N. hemisphere September–November (Astron., from autumnal equinox to winter solstice); (fig.) season of maturity or incipient decay; ∿ **crocus**, plant of genus *Colchicum*, esp. meadow saffron; ∿ **tints**, brown and gold colours of dying leaves. [ME f. OF *automne* f. L *autumnus*]

autŭ'mnal *a.* of or like, appearing or occurring or done in, appropriate to, autumn (*autumnal tints* cf. prec.); autumnal EQUINOX); maturing or blooming in autumn; past prime of life. [f. L *autumnalis* (as prec.; see -AL)]

auxano'mēter *n.* instrument for measuring growth of plants. [f. Gk *auxanō* increase + -o- + -METER]

auxi'liar|y̌ (-gzĭ'lyerĭ) *a.* & *n.* (person or thing) that gives help (*to*; ∿y **troops**, ∿**ies**, (Mil.) foreign or allied troops in a belligerent nation's service); (of services or equipment) subsidiary; ∿y (**verb**), (Gram.) one used in forming tenses, moods, voices, of other verbs. [f. L *auxiliarius* (*auxilium* help; see -ARY²)]

au'xin *n.* substance which stimulates growth of plants, growth hormone. [G, f. Gk *auxō* increase + -IN]

AV *abbr.* audio-visual; Authorized Version.

ăvadavă't. See AMADAVAT.

avai'l¹ *v.* **1.** *v.i.* provide help; be of value or profit. **2.** *v.t.* help, benefit; ∿ **oneself of,** profit by, take advantage of. [ME, f. obs. *vail* v. f. stressed st. of OF *valoir* be worth f. L *valēre*]

avai'l² *n.* use, profit (usu. in neg. or interrog. phrs.: *of no avail, without avail, of what avail?*). [f. prec.]

avai'l|able *a.* capable of being used; at one's disposal; within one's reach; hence ∿ABI'LITY, ∿ableNESS (-beln-), *ns.*, ∿ABLY *adv.* [ME, f. AVAIL¹ + -ABLE]

ă'valanche (-ahnsh) *n.* & *v.* **1.** *n.* mass of snow, rock, and ice, descending mountain rapidly; (fig.) sudden onrush of anything. **2.** *v.t.* & *i.* carry or descend like avalanche. [F, alt. of dial. *lavanche* after *avaler* descend]

ăvant-gar'd|e (ăvahn-) *n.* & *a.* (of) pioneers or innovators in any art in a particular period; hence ∿ISM (3), ∿IST (2), *ns.* [F, = vanguard]

ă'varice *n.* greed for gain, cupidity; (fig.) eager desire to get or keep; hence **ăvari'cious** (-shus) *a.* [ME f. OF, f. L *avaritia* (*avarus* greedy; see -ICE)]

ava'st (-ah'st) *int.* (Naut.) stop, cease. [f. Du. *houd vast* hold fast]

ă'vatār *n.* **1.** (Hindu Myth.) descent of deity to earth in incarnate form. **2.** incarnation; manifestation; phase. [f. Skr. *avatāra* descent (*áva* down, *tar-* pass over)]

avau'nt *int.* (arch.) begone. [ME f. AF, f. OF *avant* f. Rom. *abante before f. L *ab* from | *ante* before]

a've (ah'vĭ, -vā) *int.* & *n.* **1.** *int.* welcome; farewell; **Ave** (**Maria**) (Hail, Mary), devotional recitation (cf. Luke 1:28 & 42) and prayer to the Virgin Mary. **2.** *n.* shout of welcome or farewell. [ME f. L, 2nd sing. imper. of *avēre* fare well]

Ave. *abbr.* Avenue.

avě'nge (-nj) *v.t.* inflict retribution, exact satisfaction, on behalf of (person, violated right, etc.); (in *pass.*) avenge oneself; take vengeance for (injury). [ME, f OF *avengier* (*à* to, *vengier* f. L *vindicare* vindicate)]

ă'vens (-z) *n.* one of various plants of genus *Geum*; **mountain** ∿, a related plant (*Dryas octopetala*). [ME f. OF *avence* (med. L *avencia*), of unkn. orig.]

avě'nturine *n.* brownish glass with copper crystals; variety of spangled quartz resembling this. [F, f. It. *avventurino* (*avventura* chance, from its accidental discovery)]

ă'venue *n.* way of approach (usu. fig.; *explore every avenue*); ||tree-lined approach to country house; road-way with trees or other objects at regular intervals; broad street. [F, fem. p.p. (as n.) of *avenir* f. L *advenire* come to]

avě'r *v.t.* (-rr-). assert, affirm. [ME, f. OF *averer* (a-AD-, L *verus* true)]

ă'verage¹ *n.* **1.** generally prevailing rate, degree, or amount; ordinary standard; middle estimate (*on the average*; ordinary *standard*; middle estimate (*on the* or *an*, *on*, *average*); **law of** ∿**s**, proposition that occurrence of one extreme will be matched by that of the other extreme so as to maintain the normal average. **2.** (esp. arithmetic) MEAN¹ 2; **batting** ∿, (Baseball) batter's safe hits per time at bat, (Cricket) bowling ∿, (Cricket) bowler's conceded runs per wicket taken. **3.** damage to or loss of insured ship or cargo; **general** ∿, deliberate partial sacrifice of insured ship or cargo to avoid total loss; **particular** ∿, partial damage to or loss of insured ship or cargo; ∿ **adjustment,** apportionment of liability resulting from average. [f. F *avarie* damage to ship or cargo, f. It. *avaria*. Arab. *'awārīya* damaged goods ('*awār* damage at sea, loss); *-age* after *damage*]

ă'verage² *a.* estimated by average; of the ordinary standard or kind; hence ∿LY² (-jlĭ) *adv.* [f. prec.]

ă'verage³ *v.t.* & *i.* estimate average of, esp. as arithmetic mean; estimate general standard of;

~ (**out at**), amount on an average to; do etc. on an average (*average six hours' work a day*). [f. as prec.]
avēr'ment *n.* positive statement, affirmation, esp. (Law) with offer of proof. [ME, f. AF, OF *aver(r)ement* (as AVER; see -MENT)]
avēr'se *pred. a.* opposed, disinclined, (*to, from*); hence ~NESS (-sn-) *n.* [f. L *aversus* (as AVERT)]
avēr'sion (-shon) *n.* **1.** dislike, unwillingness, (*to, from, for*); ~ **therapy** (designed to make patient averse to an existing habit). **2.** object of dislike (*my pet aversion*). [F, or f. L *aversio* (as AVERT; see -ION)]
avēr't *v.t.* turn away (eyes, thoughts, *from*); prevent, ward off, hence ~ABLE, ~IBLE, *adjs.* [ME, f. L *avertere* (a AB- away, *vertere vers-* turn); partly f. OF *avertir* f. Rom. **avertire*]
Avě'st|a (*a*-) *n.* See ZEND; hence ~AN, ~IC, *adjs.* & *ns.*, (ancient Iranian language) of the Avesta. [Pers.]
ā'vian *a.* pertaining to birds. [f. L *avis* bird + -AN]
ā'viarȳ *n.* large cage or building for keeping birds. [f. L *aviarium* (as prec.; see -ARY¹)]
ā'viāte *v.i.* & *t.* fly in aeroplane; pilot (aeroplane). [back-form. f. foll.]
āviā'tion *n.* art or practice of operating aeroplanes, helicopters, etc.; aircraft manufacture. [F, irreg. f. L *avis* bird; see -ATION]
ā'viā|tor *n.* airman or airwoman; so ~TRIX *n.* [f. F *aviateur* f. L *avis* bird; see -OR]
ā'vid *a.* eager, greedy (*of, for*); hence or cogn. **avī'dITY** *n.*, ~LY² *adv.* [f. F *avide* or f. L *avidus* (*avēre* crave; see -ID¹)]
ā'vifauna *n.* birds (of district, country) collectively. [f. L *avis* bird + FAUNA]
āviŏ'nics *n.* application of electronics in aviation. [f. AVIATION + ELECTRONICS]
āvitaminō's|is *n.* (*pl.* ~es *pr.* -ēz). (Path.) condition resulting from deficiency of one or more vitamins. [mod. L, f. as A- 7 + VITAMIN + -OSIS]
āvizā'ndum *n.* (Sc. Law). private consideration by judge etc. [med. L, gerund of *avizare* consider (as ADVISE)]
ăvoca'dō (-ah'-) *n.* (*pl.* ~s). ~ (**pear**), succulent rough-skinned pear-shaped tropical Amer. and W. Ind. fruit, alligator pear. [Sp., = advocate (pop. rendering of Aztec *ahuacatl*)]
ăvoca'tion *n.* minor occupation; (colloq.) vocation, calling. [f. L *avocatio* (*avocare* call away; see -ATION)]
ā'vocĕt *n.* wading bird with upturned bill. [f. F *avocette* f. It. *avosetta*]
Avoga'drō (ăvogah'-) *n.* ~**'s constant** or **number**, number of atoms in one gram-atom; ~**'s law** (that gases at same temperature and pressure have same number of molecules per unit volume). [f. A. ~, It. physicist d. 1856]
avoi'd *v.t.* keep away or refrain from (thing, do*ing*); escape, evade; (Law) defeat (pleading), quash (sentence); hence ~ABLE *a.*, ~ANCE *n.* [f. AF *avoider*, OF *evuider* clear out, get quit of (*es* out, *vuidier* f. *vuide* empty, VOID)]
ăvoirdŭpoi's (ăver-; -z) *a.* & *n.* ~ (**weight**), system of weights based on ~ **pound** of 16 ounces or 7,000 grains; bodily weight, heaviness. [ME, f. OF *aveir de peis* goods of weight (*aveir* f. L *habēre* have, *peis* see POISE)]
avou'ch *v.t.* & *i.* (arch. or rhet.) guarantee; affirm; confess; hence ~MENT *n.* [ME, f. OF *avochier* f. L AD(*vocare* call)]
avow' *v.t.* admit, confess; (in *refl.* and *pass.*) admit oneself to be (*avowed himself the author; the avowed author*); hence ~ABLE *a.*, ~AL *n.*, ~ĕDLY² *adv.* [ME, f. OF *avouer* acknowledge f. L AD(*vocare* call)]
avŭ'lsion (-shon) *n.* tearing away; (Law) sudden removal of land by flood etc. to another person's estate. [F, or f. L *avulsio* (*avellere avuls-* pluck away; see -ION)]
avŭ'ncŭlar *a.* of or resembling an uncle. [f. L *avunculus* maternal uncle (dim. of *avus* grandfather) + -AR¹]
aw *int.* *(Sc. & US).* expr. mild remonstrance, commiseration, disgust, etc. [imit.]

awai't (*a*-w-) *v.t.* wait for; (of thing) be in store for (*a surprise awaits you*). [ME, f. AF *awaitier*, OF *aguaitier* (a AD-, *waitier* WAIT¹)]
awā'ke¹ (*a*-w-) *v.* (*past* awo'ke *pr.* -ō'k; *p.p.* awo'ken *or* ~d). **1.** *v.i.* cease to sleep; (fig.) become active; ~ **to**, become conscious of. **2.** *v.t.* cause to cease sleeping (lit. or fig.). [OE *āwæcnan* and *āwacian* (as A- 2, WAKE¹)]
awā'ke² (*a*-w-) *pred. a.* no longer or not yet asleep; vigilant; WIDE *awake*; ~ **to**, aware of. [short for *awaken*, orig. p.p. of prec.]
awā'ken (*a*-w-) *v.t.* intr. & i. = AWAKE¹ (lit. or fig.), esp. (fig.) arouse (*to* a sense of), make aware. [OE *onwæcnan, āwæcnan, āwæcnian* (as A- 2, WAKE¹, WAKEN)]
awar'd¹ (*a*wōr'd) *v.t.* order to be given as payment, penalty, or prize; grant; assign. [ME, f. AF *awarder* f. ONF *eswarder* = OF *esguarder* consider, ordain, f. Rom. **eswardare* f. WG **ward-*; see WARD¹]
awar'd² (*a*wōr'd) *n.* judicial decision; payment, penalty, or prize awarded. [ME f. AF (*awarder*; see prec.)]
awār'e (*a*-w-) *pred. a.* conscious, not ignorant, having knowledge, (*of, that*); well-informed; hence ~NESS (-ār'n-) *n.* [OE *gewær*, = OS *giwar*, OHG *giwar, gawar*, WG f. as Y-, WARE²]
awa'sh (awŏ'-) *pred. a.* level with surface of water; carried or washed by the waves; flooded. [f. A³ + WASH¹]
away (*a*-w-) *adv., a., & n.* **1.** *adv.* to or at a distance (lit. or fig.) from the place, person, thing, in question (*go away; throw it away; give it away; he is away, five miles away*); FAR¹ *and away*; OUT *and away*; PUT¹, TURN¹, *away*. **2.** towards or into non-existence (*sound dies away; explain it away; idle one's time away*). **3.** constantly, persistently, continuously, (*laughing away; peg away; working away*). **4.** without delay; FIRE² *away*; RIGHT⁴ *away*; STRAIGHT *away*. **5.** ~ **with**, (*imper.*) go away with, take away; DO¹ *away with*; GET¹ *away with it*; MAKE¹ *away with*. **6.** *a.* played on opponents' ground etc. (*away match, win*). **7.** *n.* away match or win. [OE *onweg, aweg* on (the, his, one's) way; f. A³ + WAY]
awe *n., & v.t.* **1.** *n.* reverential fear or wonder (*stand in awe of; hold in awe*); ~**'stricken**, ~**'struck**, struck with awe; hence ~SOME¹ (aw's-) *a.* **2.** *v.t.* inspire with awe. [ME *age* f. ON *agi* f. Gme **ag-*]
awear'ȳ (*a*-w-) *pred. a.* (poet.) tired, weary, (*of*). [f. A- + WEARY]
awei'gh (awā') *pred. a.* (Of anchor) just lifted from ground in weighing. [f. A³ + WEIGH]
aw'ful *a.* inspiring awe; solemnly impressive; (colloq.) notable (esp. for badness) in its kind (*awful writing; has an awful lot of money*); hence ~NESS *n.* [f. AWE + -FUL]
aw'fullȳ *adv.* **1.** In adj. senses. **2.** (colloq., *pr.* aw'flĭ). extremely (*an awfully nice fellow; thanks awfully*). [f. prec. + -LY²]
awhee'l (awē'l) *adv. & pred. a.* on wheels, esp. cycling. [f. A³ + WHEEL¹]
awhī'le (awī'l) *adv.* for a short time. [OE *āne hwīle* a while]
aw'kward *a.* ill-adapted for use; clumsy (person, thing); bungling (~ **age**, callow adolescence; *awkward about it*); embarrassing; embarrassed (*felt awkward about it*); difficult or dangerous to deal with (*awkward customer, situation*); hence ~LY² *adv.*, ~NESS *n.* [f. obs. *awk* backhanded, untoward (ME, f. ON *afugr* turned the wrong way) + -WARD]
awl *n.* small pointed tool for pricking, esp. that used by shoemakers. [OE *æl*, = OHG *ala*, ON *alr*]
awn *n.* stiff bristle at top of grain-sheath of barley, oats, grasses, etc. [ME, f. ON *ögn* pl. *agnar*, = OHG *agana*, Goth. *ahana* chaff]
aw'ning *n.* sheet of canvas etc. as shelter against sun or rain, esp. on ship's deck. [17th c. (Naut.), of uncert. orig.]
awoke, -en. See AWAKE¹.
AWOL (ā'wŏl) *abbr.* absent without leave.
awrȳ' (arī') *adv. & a.* **1.** *adv.* crookedly, askew; amiss,

improperly; **go** ∿, go or do wrong. **2.** *a.* (usu. *pred.*) crooked (lit. or fig.). [ME, f. A³+WRY]

axe, *ax, *n.,* & *v.t.* **1.** *n.* chopping-tool, usu. of iron with steel edge and wooden handle (∿ **to grind,** private ends to serve); drastic reduction or elimination of expenditure, staff, etc.; ∿**-breaker,** hard--wooded Austral. tree. **2.** *v.t.* cut down drastically (costs, services); remove, eliminate, dismiss. [OE *æx,* = OS *akus,* OHG *ackus,* ON *öx,* Goth. *aqizi* f. Gmc **akuwizjō,* *akuzjō]

ä'xel *n.* jumping movement in skating. [f. *Axel* R. Paulsen, Norw. skater d. 1938]

axes. *pl.* of AXE or AXIS¹.

ä'xial *a.* forming or belonging to an axis; round an axis (*axial rotation, symmetry*); hence ∿ITY (-ă'l-) *n.,* ∿LY² *adv.* [f. AXIS¹+-AL]

ä'xil *n.* upper angle between leaf and stem it springs from, or between branch and trunk. [f. L AXILLA]

äxï'lla *n.* (*pl.* ∿e). armpit; axil. [L, = armpit, dim. of *ala,* **acsla,* wing]

ä'xillary *a.* pertaining to the armpit; (Bot.) in or growing from the axil. [f. AXILLA+-ARY¹]

axiö'log|y *n.* (Philos.) theory of value; hence **äxioLO'GICAL** *a.,* ∿IST (3) *n.* [f. F *axiologie* f. Gk *axia* value, see -LOGY]

ä'xiom *n.* established principle; (esp. Geom.) self--evident truth. [f. F *axiome* or f. L f. Gk *axiōma* (*axios* worthy)]

äxiöma't|ic *a.* self-evident; characterized by axioms; hence ∿ICALLY *adv.* [f. Gk *axiomatikos* (*axiōma* -*matos;* see prec., -IC)]

ä'xis¹ *n.* (*pl.* **a'xes** *pr.* -ēz). **1.** imaginary line about which a body rotates; imaginary line by revolution about which a plane figure is conceived as generating a solid; line dividing regular figure symmetrically. **2.** fixed reference line for measurement of coordinates etc. **3.** (Bot.) central column of inflorescence or other growth. **4.** (Anat.) second cervical vertebra. **5.** central part of organ or organism. **6.** (Polit. etc.) agreement or alliance between two or more countries intended to form a centre round which like-minded nations may rally; **the A∿,** (Hist.) (alliance of 1939 between) Germany and Italy, later extended to include Japan and other countries. [L, = axle, pivot]

ä'xis² *n.* white-spotted deer (*Axis axis*) of S. Asia. [L]

ä'xle *n.* spindle upon or with which wheel revolves; rod connecting pair of wheels of vehicle (orig. ∿--tree). [earliest in ME *axol tre* f. ON *öxull-tré*]

A'xminster (ă'-) *n.* ∿ carpet, machine-woven tufted kind with cut pile. [∿ in Devon]

ä'xolotl *n.* newtlike amphibian found in Mexican lakes. [Nahuatl (*atl* water, *xolotl* servant)]

ä'xon *n.* (Anat. & Zool.) long appendage of nerve cell, usu. carrying signals from it. [mod. L, f. Gk *axōn* axis]

ay¹, aye¹, (ī) *adv.* & *n.* (*pl.* ayes *pr.* īz). **1.** *adv.* (esp. arch., dial., Naut., or in formal voting). yes; ∿, ∿, **sir!,** (Naut.) I understand and will carry out your orders. **2.** *n.* affirmative answer or vote; **the ayes have it,** affirmative voters are in majority. [16th c.; prob. f. pron. *I* expr. assent]

ay² *int.* ∿ **me!** (expr. regret, sorrow, or pity). [ME; *ay me!* prob. after OF *aimi* etc.]

ay'ah (ī'*a*) *n.* native nurse or maidservant esp. of Europeans in India etc. [Anglo-Ind., f. Port. *aia* nurse, fem. of *aio* tutor]

ayatö'llah (īatö'la) *n.* Shiite religious leader in Iran. [Pers., f. Arab. = token of God]

aye¹ (ī). See AY¹.

aye² (ā) *adv.* (arch.) ever, always; at all times; **for** ∿, for ever. [ME, f. ON *ei, ey,* cogn. w. Goth. *aiws* age, eternity. f. Gmc *aiwaz]

ay'e-aye (ī'ī) *n.* squirrel-like cat-sized nocturnal tree--climbing lemur of Madagascar. [F, f. Malagasy *aiay*]

Ay'lesbury (ā'lzb-) *n.* (*pl.* ∿s). (bird of) breed of white domestic ducks. [∿ in Buckinghamshire]

Ayr'shire (ār'-) *n.* (animal of) breed of mainly white dairy cattle. [former Scottish county]

AZ *abbr.* Arizona.

azä'lea *n.* flowering shrubby plant of genus or subgenus *Azalea.* [mod. L f. Gk, fem. of *azaleos* dry (from the dry soil in which Linnaeus believed that it flourished)]

azē'otrope *n.* (Chem.) mixture of liquids with boiling--point remaining constant during distillation; hence **azēotrö'pic** *a.* [f. A- 7+Gk *zeö* boil+*tropos* turning]

Azi'lian (a-) *a.* & *n.* (of) the transitional period between the palaeolithic and neolithic ages in Europe. [f. Mas d'*Azil* in French Pyrenees, where remains of it were found]

a'zimuth *n.* arc of celestial great circle from zenith to horizon; arc of horizon between north or south point and point where the great circle passing through a heavenly body and at the zenith cuts the horizon; = BEARING 6; hence **äzimü'thAL** *a.* [ME, f. OF *azimut* f. Arab. *as-sumūt* (*al* the, *sumūt* pl. of *samt* way, direction)]

ä'zö- *pref.* (Chem.) containing two adjacent nitrogen atoms between carbon atoms. [f. F *azote* nitrogen f. Gk A- not+*zōē* live]

azö'ic *a.* having no trace of life; (Geol.) containing no organic remains. [irreg. f. Gk *azōos* (a- not, *zōē* life)+-IC]

A'ztec (ă'-) *a.* & *n.* (one) of the native people dominant in Mexico till the conquest by Cortes (1519); (of) their language. [f. F *Aztéque* or Sp. *Azteca* f. Nahuatl *aztecatl* men of the north]

ä'zure (-zher, -zhyer, -zūr) *n.* & *a.* **1.** *n.* sky blue; (Her.) blue; unclouded vault of heaven. **2.** *a.* sky-blue; (Her.) usu. after *n.*) blue; (fig.) cloudless, serene. [ME, f. OF *asur, azur* f. med. L *azzurum, azolum* f. Arab. *al*+*lāzaward* f. Pers. *lāžward* lapis lazuli]

ä'zygous *a.* & *n.* (Anat.) (organic part) not existing in pairs. [f. Gk *azugos* unyoked (a- not, *zugon* yoke)+-ous]

B

B, b, (bē) *n.* (*pl.* **Bs** *or* **B's**). second letter of alphabet; (Mus.) seventh note in diatonic scale of C major; second hypothetical person or example; second highest class (of road, academic marks, population as regards affluence, etc.); (Alg., usu. *b*) second known quantity; **B film** (made for use as supporting feature in cinema programme).

B. *abbr.* Bachelor; bel(s); bishop; black (pencil-lead); Blessed.

b. *abbr.* bay horse; billion; born; bowled by; bye.

B *symb.* boron.

BA *abbr.* Bachelor of Arts; British Academy; British Association.

Ba *symb.* barium.

baa (bah) *n.*, & *v.i.* (~ed *or* ~'d, *pr.* bahd). (esp. of sheep) bleat; ~-**lamb,** childish name for lamb. [imit.]

BAA *abbr.* British Airports Authority.

Bā'al *n.* (*pl.* ~**im**). Phoenician and Canaanite god; false god; hence ~ISM (3) *n.* [ME, f. Heb. *ba'al* lord]

baas (bahs) *n.* (S. Afr.) master (freq. as *voc.*). [Du.; cf. BOSS²]

baa'sskap (bah'skahp) *n.* (S. Afr.) domination, esp. of non-whites by whites. [Afrik.]

ba'ba (bah'bah) *n.* (**rum**) ~, rich sponge-cake soaked in rum syrup. [F]

ba'bacōōte (bah'-) *n.* woolly lemur of Madagascar, indri. [f. Malagasy *babakoto*]

bā'bbitt¹ *n.* soft alloy of tin, antimony, copper, and usu. lead; bearing-lining made of this. [f. I. *Babbitt,* Amer. inventor d. 1862]

Bā'bbitt² *n.* materialistic complacent business man; hence ~RY (4) *n.* [character in & title of novel (1922) by S. Lewis]

bā'bble¹ *v.* **1.** *v.i.* talk half-articulately, foolishly, incoherently, or excessively; (of stream etc.) murmur. **2.** *v.t.* divulge or repeat foolishly; reveal (secret). **3.** Hence ~MENT (-bĕlm-) *n.* [ME, f. MLG *babbelen,* or imit.]

bā'bble² *n.* imperfect, foolish, or childish speech; idle talk; murmur of water etc.; (Teleph.) unwanted interference from several other conversations. [f. prec.]

bā'bbler *n.* chatterer; teller of secrets; one of a large group of passerine birds with loud chattering voices. [f. BABBLE¹ + -ER¹]

bābe *n.* **1.** (poet.) young child, baby. **2.** inexperienced or guileless person (in *pl.* often *babes and sucklings, babes in the wood*); MILK¹ *for babes.* **3.** *(sl.)* young woman. [ME, imit. of child's *ba, ba*]

bā'bel *n.* scene of confusion; confusion of tongues; noisy assembly; meaningless noise; **tower of B**~, visionary plan. [ME, f. Heb. *bābel* Babylon f. Akkad. *bāb ili* gate of god; ref. to Gen. 11]

Ba'b|i (bah'-) *n.* (member of) Persian eclectic sect founded in 1844; = BAHA'I; hence ~ISM (3), ~IST (2), *ns.* [f. Pers. *Bab-*ed-Din, gate (= intermediary) of the Faith, whence the founder's usual title of (the) *Bab*]

bābirou'ssa, -ru'sa, -ru'ssa, (-rōō'-) *n.* E. Ind. wild hog with upturned hornlike tusks. [f. Malay *bābi* hog + *rūsa* deer]

baboo. See BABU.

babōō'n *n.* large African and Arabian monkey with doglike snout; ugly or uncouth person. [ME, f. OF *babuin* or med. L *babewynus,* of unkn. orig.]

babou'che (-ōō'sh) *n.* oriental heelless slipper. [F, f. Arab. *bābūj* f. Pers. *pāpūš* (*pā* foot, *pūš* covering)]

ba'bu, ba'boo, (bah'bōō) *n.* (Ind.) title of respect, esp. to Hindus; (Hist., derog.) English-writing Indian clerk; ~ **English** (ornate and somewhat unidiomatic). [f. Hindi *bābū*]

babu'l (-ōō'l) *n.* thorny mimosa of India. [Hind. & Pers.]

babu'shka (-ōō'-) *n.* head-scarf tied under chin. [Russ., = grandmother]

bā'bȳ *n.*, & *v.t.* **1.** *n.* very young child, esp. one not yet able to walk; **carry** or **hold the** ~, bear unwelcome responsibility; **it's your** ~, you must deal with it; **throw away the** ~ **with the bathwater,** reject essential with inessential; hence ~HOOD *n.* **2.** youngest member (*of* family, team, etc.); unduly childish person, whence ~ISH¹ *a.*; animal or thing small of its kind; (sl.) young woman, sweetheart; (sl.) person or thing. **3.** ~-**bouncer,** = *baby-jumper*; ~ **buggy,** **pram,* ||(*B- B-*; P) kind of push-chair; ~ **car,** motor car of small size and power; ~ **carriage,** pram; ~-**face,** (person having) smooth rounded face like baby's; ~-**farmer,** (usu. derog.) person who looks after babies for payment; ~ **grand,** small grand piano; ||~-**jumper,** hanging frame on springs, in which child is fastened to exercise limbs; ~-**sit** *v.i.,* act as ~-**sitter,** person looking after child while its parents are out; (sl.) young woman, sweetheart; (sl.) ~-**talk,** imperfect speech as used by or to young children; ~-**walker,** device for helping baby learning to walk. **4.** *v.t.* treat like baby. [ME, f. as BABE, -Y³]

Bā'bȳlon *n.* (rhet.) great and luxurious city; so **Bābȳlō'nian** *a.* [L, f. Gk *Babulōn* capital of Chaldea, f. Heb. *bābel*]

băccalaur'eate *n.* university degree of bachelor. [f. F. *baccalauréat* or f. med. L *baccalaureatus* (*baccalaureus* bachelor; see -ATE¹)]

bă'ccarat (-rah) *n.* gambling card-game, played by punters in turn against banker. [F]

bă'ccāte *a.* (Bot.) bearing berries; berry-shaped. [f. L *baccatus* berried (*bacca* berry; see -ATE²)]

Bă'cchanal (-ka-) *a.* & *n.* **1.** *a.* of or like Bacchus (Greek and Roman god of wine) or his rites; riotous, roistering. **2.** *n.* priest, priestess, votary, of Bacchus; noisy or drunken reveller or revelry. [f. L *bacchanalis* (*Bacchus* f. Gk *Bakkhos* god of wine; see -AL)]

Băcchanā'li|a (-ka-) *n. pl.* festival of Bacchus; drunken revelry; so ~AN *a.* & *n.,* riotous or drunken (person). [L, neut. pl. of *bacchanalis* (see prec.)]

Bă'cchant (-ka-) *n.* (*pl.* ~s, *or* ~es *pr.* bakă'ntēz) & *a.,* **Bacchante** (bă'kant, bakā'nt, bakă'ntī) *n. fem.* Bacchanal; hence **Bacchă'ntic** (-kă'-) *a.* [f. F *bacchante* f. L *bacchari* celebrate Bacchanal rites]

Bă'cchic (-kĭk) *a.* Bacchanal. [f. L f. Gk *bakkhikos* of Bacchus; see -IC]

||bă'ccy (-kĭ) *n.* (colloq.) tobacco. [abbr.]

băch *n.,* & *v.i.* (colloq.) **1.** *n.* (NZ) small hut or seaside house. **2.** *v.i.* live as bachelor. [abbr.]

bă'chelor *n.* unmarried man; (Hist.) young knight serving under another's banner (**knight** ~, knight not belonging to a special order); man or woman who has taken university etc. degree below that of Master (usu. the first degree in a faculty); ~'s **button**(s), one of various button-like flowers, esp. double buttercup; ~ **flat** (suitable for unmarried person); ~ **girl** (unmarried and living independently); ~ (**seal**), young male fur-seal with no mate; hence ~HOOD, ~SHIP, *ns.* [ME & OF *bacheler* aspirant to knighthood, f. Rom. **baccalaris,* in med. L altered to *baccalaureus,* w. pun on *bacca lauri* laurel berry]

baci'llary *a.* relating to or caused by bacilli. [f. BACILLUS + -ARY¹]

baci'llifŏrm *a.* rod-shaped. [f. as foll. + -I- + -FORM]

baci'll|us *n.* (*pl.* ~i *pr.* -ī). rod-shaped bacterium, esp.

one that causes disease by entering and multiplying in animal and other tissues; (loosely, usu. in *pl.*) any pathogenic bacterium. [LL, dim. of L *baculus* stick]

băck[1] *n.* & *a.* **1.** *n.* hinder surface of human body from shoulders to hips; **at the ~ of,** behind in support, pursuit, or concealment; **~ to ~,** with backs adjoining and opposite each other (e.g. of houses), (fig.) in succession; BEHIND person's *back*; **get** or **put** person's **~ up,** make him angry or stubborn; **give** or **make a ~,** bend down for leapfrog or wall-climbing; **on one's ~,** ill in bed; **on** person's **~,** (colloq.) harassing or annoying him; SEE[1] *the back of*; **turn** one's **~ on,** run away from, abandon, ignore; **with** one's **~ to the wall,** at bay, hard pressed. **2.** body as needing clothes or as weight-carrier; BREAK[1] one's *back*; **have on** one's **~,** be burdened with; **put** one's **~ into,** use all one's efforts on. **3.** surface of things corresponding to human back; **~** (outer surface) **of hand** (*know like the ~ of* one's *hand,* be entirely familiar with); **~** (rear surface) **of head, leg;** less active or important part; **~ of book,** spine or final page; **~ of knife,** non-cutting edge. **4.** upper surface of animal's body; similar ridge-shaped surface (*back of hill*); **~ of ship,** keel (*broke her back*). **5.** side or part normally more remote or away from spectator or direction of motion (*back of car, chair, door, house, mouth*); **at the ~ of** one's **mind,** in memory but not consciously thought of; *talk through the back of* one's NECK[1]; *back of* BEYOND; ***in ~** (of), behind. **6.** part of dress covering back esp. from shoulders to waist; hence **~'LESS** *a.*, (of dress) low-cut at back. **7. the B~s,** grounds on the Cam at back of some Cambridge colleges. **8.** (position of) defensive player in football etc. **9. ~'ache,** pain in one's back; **~'board** (esp. worn to support or straighten the back); **~'bone,** spine (*of* book), (fig.) main support, firmness of character; *to the ~*bone, thoroughly; **~-breaking,** extremely laborious; **~'rest,** support for the back; **~'scratcher,** implement for scratching one's own back, (fig.) one who performs mutual services for gain; **~'slapping,** (fig.) vigorously hearty; **~'stroke** (made by swimmer lying on back). **10.** *a.* (no compar.; superl. **~'most**). situated behind (*back street, teeth*); (Cricket) of playing BACK[3]; of the past; remote; inferior; overdue (*back pay*); reversed (*back flow*); (Phonet.) formed at back of mouth **11.** ‖**~-be'nch(er),** (occupant of) seat in House of Commons etc. used by member not entitled to sit on front bench; **~'blocks,** (Austral., NZ, etc.) land in remote and sparsely-inhabited interior; ‖**~-boiler** (behind domestic fire or cooking range); **~'chat,** (colloq.) impudent repartee; ‖**~'cloth,** (Theatr.) painted cloth at back of stage as main part of scenery; **~ country,** (Austral., NZ, etc.) area away from settled districts; **~ door,** (fig.) secret means of approach; **~-door** *a.*, (fig.) clandestine, underhand; **~'drop,** backcloth; **~'ground,** part of scene, picture, or description, that serves as setting to chief figures or objects and foreground, (fig.) obscurity or retirement, (fig.) person's cultural knowledge, education, experience, etc., information needed to understand problem etc., (Phys.) radiation from natural sources, (Radio) adventitiously received signals; **~** *ground heating* (for general warmth); **~** *ground music* (used as accompaniment in film etc.); **~'hand,** (Tennis etc.) (stroke) played with back of hand turned towards opponent; **~ha'nded,** delivered with back of hand or in opposite of usual direction, indirect, ambiguous (*backhanded compliment*); **~'hander,** backhand stroke, backhanded blow, indirect attack, (sl.) bribe; **~'list,** publisher's list of books still in print; **~'log,** reserves, arrears of unfulfilled orders, uncompleted work, etc.; **~'marker,** scratch man in race etc.; **~ number,** old issue of magazine etc., (sl.) out-of-date method or person; ***~'pack** *n.*, & *v.i.*, (travel with) rucksack etc.; *back* PASSAGE[1]; **~ room,** (fig.) place where (secret) research is done; **~ seat,** (fig., colloq.)

inferior or unimportant position; **~-seat driver,** one who rides in back seat of motor car and gives unwanted advice to its driver, (fig.) one who attempts to control without responsibility; **~'side,** buttocks; **~'sight,** that nearer stock of rifle etc., (Surv.) sight taken backwards; **~ slang,** form of slang in which words are spelt and pronounced backwards (cf. SLOP[3], YOB); **~'stage** *a.* & *adv.*, (Theatr.) behind the curtain, esp. in wings or dressing-rooms, (fig.) behind the scenes; **~ stairs,** **~-stair(s)** *a.*, (fig.) = *back-door*; **~'stay,** rope etc. downwards and aft from top of mast; ***~ talk,** backchat; **~'veld,** (S. Afr.) back country; **~'water,** still water beside stream and fed by its back flow, (fig.) (condition or place of) intellectual stagnation; **~'woods,** wholly or partly uncleared forest, remote or sparsely inhabited region; **~'woodsman,** inhabitant of backwoods, uncouth person, ‖(fig.) peer who rarely or never attends the House of Lords; **~'yard,** yard at back of house, (fig.) somewhere easily accessible (esp. one's *own backyard*). [OE *bæc,* = OS, ON *bak,* f. Gmc ***bakam*]

băck[2] *v.* **1.** *v.t.* act as or put a back, lining, support, or background, to; assist with money or argument, bet on success of, whence **~'ER**[1] *n.*; lie at back of; countersign, endorse. **2.** cause (horse, boat, car, etc.) to move backwards; **~ water,** reverse boat's forward motion with oars. **3.** *v.i.* go backwards; ***~ and fill,** move to and fro, vacillate. **4.** (Of wind) change direction counter-clockwise (cf. VEER[2]). **5. ~ down,** abandon claim; so **~-down** n.; **~ out,** (fig.) withdraw; **~ up,** help by subordinate action, (of running water) accumulate behind obstruction, ***form queue of vehicles etc. ***reverse (vehicle); **~-up** n., support, spare or reserve, ***queue of vehicles etc. (***~-up light,** reversing light). [f. prec.]

băck[3] *adv.* **1.** to the rear; away from what is considered the front; **~ and forth,** to and fro; ***~ of,** behind; **play ~,** (Cricket) step back to play defensive stroke. **2.** away from a promise (*go back on one's word*); in or into the past or an earlier or normal position or condition; home (*will be back at six*). **3.** in return (*pay back*); ANSWER[2] *back*; GET[1] *back*. **4.** at a distance (*back from the road*); in check (*keep back from*). **5. ~'bite** *v.t.,* slander, speak ill of; hence **~'biter; ~'comb** *v.t.,* comb (under-hair) back towards scalp; **~-cross** (of hybrid and one parent); **~'date** *v.t.,* put earlier date to, make retrospectively valid; **~'fill,** replace excavated earth etc. round foundations etc. placed in hole made; **~'fire** *v.i.,* premature explosion in cylinder or explosion in exhaust-pipe of vehicle engine; **~fir'e** *v.i.,* undergo backfire, (of plan etc.) recoil on originator, have opposite effect to what was intended; **~-formation,** (word got by) making from an existing supposed derivative (as *automation, lazy, pedlar*) a previously non-existent word (*automate, laze, peddle*) from which it might have come; **~'lash,** irregular recoil in machinery, excessive play between parts of machine, (fig.) excessive or violent reaction; **~-pe'dal** *v.i.,* work pedal backwards, (fig.) reverse one's previous action; **~-projection** (of picture from behind transparent screen for viewing or filming); **~-scattering** (of radiation in reverse direction); **~'slide** *v.i.,* relapse into sin or error; **~'space** *v.i.,* cause typewriter carriage (or 'golf ball') to move backwards one space; **~'stitch** *n.,* & *v.t.* & *i.,* sew(ing) with overlapping stitches; **~'track** *v.i.,* (fig.) = *back-pedal*; **~'wash,** motion of receding wave, repercussions. [f. ABACK]

băckgămmon (-gǎ'-, bǎ'-) *n.* game for two, played on special double board with dice and pieces like draughtsmen; most complete form of win in this. [f. BACK[3] (because pieces go back or re-enter) + GAMMON[2]]

bǎ'cking *n.* In vbl senses; body of supporters; material used to form thing's back or support; accompaniment to a singer. [f. BACK[2] + -ING[1]]

bǎ'cksheesh. Var. of BAKSHEESH.

bä´ckward(s) (-dz) *adv.*, **bä´ckward** *a.* **1.** *adv.* away from one's front (*look, lean*, etc.). *backwards*; **bend, fall, lean, over** ∿, go to opposite extreme, do one's utmost (*to agree* etc.)); back foremost (*walk* etc. *backwards*); (of thing's motion) back to starting-point (*flow, roll*, etc. *backward*); ∿ **and forwards**, in both directions alternately, to and fro. **2.** into a worse state (*go* etc. *backward*); into the past (*reckon* etc. *backwards*); reverse way (*spell* etc. *backwards*); **know** ∿, be entirely familiar with; **ring the bells** ∿ (from bass upwards). **3.** *a.* directed to rear or starting-point; reversed; reluctant, shy; behindhand, dull; hence **bä´ckward**NESS *n.* [f. *abackward*, later assoc. w. BACK¹; see ∿BACK(S)]

||**bäckwardä´tion** *n.* percentage paid by seller of stock for right of delaying delivery (cf. CONTANGO). [f. prec. used as v. + -ATION]

bä´con *n.* (piece of) cured back or side of pig; **bring home the** ∿, (colloq.) succeed in one's undertaking; **save** one's ∿, escape death or injury. [ME f. OF, f. Frank. *bako* = OHG *bahho* ham, flitch, f. Gmc **bakkon-*]

Bäco´nian *a.* & *n.* **1.** *a.* of Bacon or his philosophy; experimental, inductive. **2.** *n.* follower of Bacon; believer that Bacon was author of Shakespeare's plays. [f. Francis *Bacon*, Engl. philosopher d. 1626 + -IAN]

bäctēriŏ´log|ў *n.* science of bacteria; hence **bäctērio**LO´GICAL *a.* (∿ical **warfare,** deliberate use of bacteria to spread disease among enemy), ∿IST (3) *n.* [f. BACTERIUM + -O- + -LOGY]

bäctēri|ŏ´lўsis *n.* (*pl.* ∿o´lyses *pr.* -ēz). destruction of bacteria by antibodies; so ∿olў´TIC *a.*, capable of destroying bacteria. [f. BACTERIUM + -O- + -LYSIS]

bäctēr´iophage (-fāj, -fahzh) *n.* virus which destroys bacteria. [F, f. as foll. + -Gk *phagein* eat]

bäctēr´io|stä´sis *n.* (*pl.* ∿sta´ses *pr.* -ēz). inhibition of growth of bacteria without destroying them; hence ∿STA´TIC *a.* [f. foll. + -O- + -STASIS]

bäctēr´|ium *n.* (*pl.* ∿ia). microscopic unicellular plant of widely distributed class, esp. of kind which causes disease; hence ∿IAL *a.*, ∿ĬCIDE (1) *n.* [mod. L, f. Gk *baktērion* dim. of *baktron* stick]

Bä´ctrĭan *a.* of Bactria in central Asia; ∿ **camel** (with two humps). [f. L f. Gk *Baktrianos*; see -AN]

bäd *a.* & *adv.* (WORSE, WORST) & *n.* **1.** *a.* worthless (*bad cheque*); inferior; deficient (*bad light*); of poor quality (*bad driver, English, liar*); incorrect, not valid; counterfeit or debased (*bad* PENNY); unpleasant (*bad breath, weather*). **2.** bad BOOK¹*s,* BREAK²; ∿ **debt** (not recoverable); *bad* EGG¹, FAITH, FORM¹; *with a bad* GRACE; ||*bad* HAT; *bad* JOB¹; ***∿ lands,** extensive uncultivable eroded tracts; ∿ **law** (not sustainable); *bad* LOT, NEWS; **in a** ∿ **sense** (unfavourable); *bad* TEMPER²; **go** ∿, decay; **not** ∿, **not half** ∿, **not so** ∿, (colloq.) fairly or very good; **too** ∿, (colloq.) regrettable. **3.** noxious (*sweets are bad for your teeth*); wicked (***∿ man,** desperado; ***∿ mouth,** malicious gossip or criticism; ***∿-mouth** v.t., subject to this); offensive (*bad* LANGUAGE); painful (∿ **blood,** ill feeling; **a** ∿ **business,** an unfortunate matter); in ill health, injured, in pain, (*she is bad, worse, today; a bad leg*); **in a** ∿ **way,** ill or in trouble. **4.** (colloq., of things in no case good). notable, decided, pronounced, (*bad accident, blunder, headache*). **5.** (colloq.) regretful (*feel bad about it*). **6.** Hence ∿´DISH¹ *a.*, ∿´dў³ * adv.*, (colloq.) criminal, villain, ∿´LУ² *adv.* (WORSE, WORST), (esp.) by much (*badly beaten*), very much (*want a thing badly; hair badly needs cutting*), (colloq.) regretfully (*feel badly about it*), ∿´NESS *n.* **7.** *adv.* *(colloq.) badly. **8.** *n.* ill fortune (*take the bad with the good*); debit side of account (*£500 to the bad*); ruin (*go to the bad*); **in** ∿, (colloq.) in disfavour *with; from bad* to WORSE. [ME, perh. f. OE *bæddel* hermaphrodite, womanish man; for loss of *l* cf. MUCH, WENCH]

bä´de. See BID¹.

bädge *n.* distinctive mark worn as sign of office or

achievement or licensed employment or membership of a society; symbol; thing that reveals a quality or condition. [ME, of unkn. orig.]

bä´dger *n.*, & *v.t.* **1.** *n.* grey-coated strong-jawed fiercely defensive nocturnal burrowing hibernating plantigrade mammal of weasel family; fishing-fly, or painting or other brush, made of its hair; ∿**-baiting,** setting dogs to draw badger from its burrow or from a cask; ***B∿ State,** Wisconsin. **2.** *v.t.* pester as dogs worry a badger; torment, tease. [16th c., perh. f. BADGE + -ARD, w. ref. to its white forehead mark]

badinage (bä´dĭnahzh) *n.* humorous ridicule. [F (*badiner* to joke)]

ba´dmash (bŭ´dmahsh) *n.* (Ind.) rascal, hooligan. [Pers. & Urdu]

bä´dmĭnton *n.* **1.** summer drink of claret, soda, and sugar. **2.** game with net, rackets, and shuttlecock. [*B∿* in Avon]

Bae´dĕker (bā´d-) *n.* guidebook published by firm founded by Karl *Baedeker* (d. 1859); ∿ **raids,** German reprisal air raids in 1942 on places in England of cultural and historical importance.

bä´el *n.* thorny Indian tree with aromatic orange-like fruit. [f. Hindi *bel*, Marathi *bail*]

bä´ffle *v.t.*, & *n.* **1.** *v.t.* frustrate, reduce to perplexity, (person, curiosity, faculties); stop progress of (efforts, ship); hence ∿MENT (-fĕlm-) *n.* **2.** *n.* state of being baffled; ∿(-**plate**), **bä´ffle**R¹, plate hindering or regulating passage of fluid or gas or radiation through outlet or inlet (e.g. a damper); ∿**-board,** device to prevent spread of sound, esp. round loudspeaker cone to improve tone. [perh. conn. w. F *bafouer* ridicule, OF *beffer* mock]

bäg¹ *n.* **1.** receptacle of flexible material with closable opening at top (esp. w. prefixed word showing contents or purpose; DIPLOMATIC *bag,* GAME¹*bag,* HAND¹*bag,* KIT¹*bag, mailbag, travelling-bag,* VANITY *bag*); (w. such prefix understood) particular kind of this; hence ∿´FUL 2 *n.* **2.** contents of bag; MIXED *bag;* amount of game a sportsman has shot or caught (also fig.). **3.** ∿ **and baggage,** with all belongings; ∿ **of bones,** lean creature; (**whole**) ∿ **of tricks,** every device, everything, the whole lot; ***hold the** ∿, = *hold the* BABY; **in the** ∿, (colloq.) in one's possession or power, (as good as) secured; *let the* CAT¹ *out of the bag.* **4.** (in *pl.*) wealth, large amount, plenty; ||trousers. **5.** sac in animal body containing honey, poison, etc.; baggy place under eye etc.; (sl., derog.) woman (*old bag*); (sl.) distinctive mode of behaviour, esp. in playing jazz; (sl.) one's current interest. **6.** ∿´man, commercial traveller, (Austral.) tramp, *(sl.) agent who collects or distributes money for illicit purposes; ∿´**pipe(s),** reed-pipe wind instrument with bag as receptacle for air, melody pipe (chanter), and fixed-note pipes (drones), used in Scotland and elsewhere; ||∿´**wash,** (laundry that undertakes) rough unfinished washing of clothes; ∿**-wig,** 18th-c. wig with back hair enclosed in bag. [ME, perh. f. ON *baggi,* of unkn. orig.]

bäg² *v.* (-gg-). **1.** *v.t.* & *i.* (cause to) swell, bulge, or hang loosely. **2.** *v.t.* put in a bag, secure (game, whether lit. bagged or not), take possession of (*bag the best chair*), (euphem.) steal; ||(school sl.) claim on the ground of being first to do so (usu. *bags I, bags first innings!,* etc.). [f. prec.]

bäg³ *v.t.* (-gg-). cut thinned ears of corn etc. with reaping-hook. [17th c., also *badge;* orig. unkn.]

bagarre (bahgär´) *n.* scuffle, brawl. [F]

bagá´sse *n.* residue after extraction of juice from sugar-cane or sugar-beet. [F, f. Sp. *bagazo*]

bägatĕ´lle *n.* trifle, negligible amount; game in which small balls are struck into numbered holes on board with semicircular end; (Mus.) short unpretentious piece. [F, f. It. *bagatella* dim., perh. f. *baga* BAGGAGE]

*bä´gel (-g-) *n.* hard ring-shaped bread roll. [f. Yiddish *beygel*]

bä´ggage *n.* **1.** belongings with which one travels by sea or air (*or land); BAG¹ and baggage; *∿ car, luggage van; *∿ check, luggage-ticket; *∿ room, cloakroom; *∿ tag, luggage-label. 2. portable equipment of army; (fig.) mental equipment etc. 3. (joc.) good-for-nothing woman, saucy girl. [ME, f. OF bagage (baguer tie up or bagues bundles, perh. rel. to BAG¹; see -AGE)]

ba'gg|ȳ (-gĭ) a. puffed out, hanging in loose folds; hence ∿iNESS n. [f. BAG¹+-Y²]

ba'gnio (bah'nyō) n. (pl. ∿s). Oriental prison; brothel. [f. It. bagno f. L balneum bath]

băguĕ'tte (-gě't) n. (Archit.) small moulding of semicircular section, like astragal; gem cut in long rectangular shape; long narrow French loaf. [F, f. It. bacchetta dim. of bacchio f. L baculum staff]

bah int. expr. contempt. [prob. f. F]

Baha'dur (bahah'-) n. Title of respect appended in India to a person's name (and to other titles). [Hindi, = hero, f. Pers. (as foll.)]

Baha'|ī (bah-hah'ī) n. religious faith developed from Babı by Bahá'u'lláh (d. 1892), emphasizing unity of mankind and its religions, and seeking world peace; hence ∿ISM (3), ∿IST (2), ∿ITE¹ (1), ns. [f. Pers. bahā splendour]

Bahā'mian (ba-h-) a. & n. (native or inhabitant) of Bahamas. [f. Bahamas+-IAN]

baignoire (bā'nwār) n. box at theatre on level of stalls. [F, = bath-tub]

bail¹ n. 1. security given for released prisoner's appearance for trial; **forfeit** one's, (colloq.) **jump,** ∿, fail to appear for trial after being bailed; **give leg** ∿, (joc.) run away; ∿'sman (-z-), one who gives bail for another. 2. person(s) acting as surety for prisoner's appearance for trial; **go** ∿ **for,** (fig.) guarantee truth of. [ME f. OF bail custody (bailler take charge of f. L bajulare bear a burden f. bajulus carrier)]

bail² v.t. 1. deliver (goods) in trust for a purpose; hence ∿EE¹, ∿'OR, ns. 2. (Of magistrate etc.) release on security given for appearance; secure liberation of, by becoming bail or security for; ∿ **out,** thus liberate prisoner, (fig.) release from difficulty. 3. So ∿'ABLE a., ∿'MENT n. [f. OF bailler; see prec.]

bail³ n. 1. (Hist.) outer line of fortification; wall of castle or court within it. 2. bar separating horses in open stable; (Cricket) one of two cross-pieces over stumps; bar on typewriter holding paper against platen. [ME, f. OF bail(e), perh. f. bailler enclose, of unkn. orig.]

bail⁴ n. hoop-handle of kettle, pail, etc.; (esp. Austral.) frame holding cow's head at milking. [ME, prob. f. ON beygla (beygja to bend, bow)]

bail⁵ v. (Austral.) 1. v.t. ∿ **up,** secure (cow; see prec.); (of bushranger) make (person) hold up the arms to be robbed; buttonhole (person). 2. v.i. (Of victim) throw up the arms. [perh. f. OF bailler enclose; cf. BAIL³]

bail⁶, bāle³, v. 1. v.t. scoop water out or out of (boat etc.); hence **bai'lER¹** n., utensil for doing this. 2. v.i. **bale out, bail out,** (of airman) make emergency parachute descent from aircraft, (of surfer) leave surfboard. [f. obs. n. bail bucket f. F baille f. Rom. *bajula fem. of L bajulus carrier]

bai'ley¹ n. outer wall of castle; any of its inner defensive circuits; any of the courts enclosed between these; **Old B∿,** London Central Criminal Court, formerly standing in ancient bailey of city wall. [ME, var. of BAIL³]

Bai'ley² n. ∿ **bridge,** prefabricated kind made of lattice steel and designed for rapid construction. [f. Sir D. ∿, Engl. engineer b. 1901, its designer]

bai'lie n. Scottish municipal councillor serving as magistrate. [ME, f. OF bailli(s) BAILIFF]

bai'liff n. officer under sheriff executing writs and processes, and performing distraints and arrests; agent or steward of landlord; *official in court of law; (Hist. exc. in formal titles) sovereign's representative in a district, esp. chief officer of a hundred; first civil officer in Channel Islands. [ME, f. OF baillif obl. case

of baillis f. med. L bajulivus f. L bajulus carrier, manager]

bai'liwick n. district or jurisdiction of bailie or bailiff; (joc.) person's sphere of operations. [f. BAILIE+ WICK²]

bain-marie' (băn-) n. (pl. -ns- pr. same). vessel of hot water in which cooking-pans are slowly heated; DOUBLE¹ boiler. [F, transl. med. L balneum Mariae transl. Gk kaminos Marias furnace of Mary (supposed Jewish alchemist)]

Baira'm (bīrah'm) n. one of two annual Muslim festivals (**Lesser** and **Greater** ∿). [Turk. & Pers.]

bairn n. (Sc., N. Engl., or literary). child. [OE bearn, = OS, OHG, ON barn, f. Gmc *barnam, conn. w. *beran BEAR³]

bait¹ v. 1. v.t. torment (chained animal) by setting dogs at it; torment (helpless person) with jeers etc. 2. (arch.) give food to (horses on journey). 3. put (real or sham) food on or in (hook, trap, fishing-place). 4. v.i. (arch.) stop on journey to take food or rest. [ME, f. ON beita causal of bíta BITE¹; sense 3 prob. f. foll.]

bait² n. food to entice prey (**live** ∿, small fish so used); (fig.) an allurement, temptation; (arch.) halt in journey for refreshment or rest. [partly f. ON beita food, partly f. prec.]

∥**bait⁰.** See BATE³.

balze n. coarse usu. green woollen stuff with long nap used for coverings and linings. [f. F baies pl. fem. of bai chestnut-coloured, BAY⁶, treated as sing.; cf. BODICE]

ba'jra (bah'-) n. (Ind.) pearl millet or similar grain. [Hindi]

bāke v. & n. 1. v.t. cook by dry heat in closed place or on hot surface (not by direct exposure to fire); harden by heat; (of sun) ripen (fruit), tan (skin). 2. v.i. undergo the process of being baked; be cooked, hardened, tanned, etc. by heat. 3. ∿'**apple,** (Can.) (dried) cloudberry; ∿'**house,** house or room for baking bread; ∿**d beans,** haricot beans baked and usu. tinned with tomato sauce; ∿**d potato** (usu. cooked in its skin); **baking-powder,** mixture of sodium bicarbonate, cream of tartar, etc., used instead of yeast to make cakes etc. rise; **baking-soda,** sodium bicarbonate. 4. n. *party, esp. for eating baked food. [OE bacan, = OHG bachan, ON baka, f. Gmc *bak-, IE *bhog-]

bā'kelīte n. plastic made from formaldehyde and phenol etc. [f. G Bakelit f. name of L. H. Baekeland, Belgian-Amer. inventor d. 1944; see -ITE¹ (?)]

bā'ker n. one who bakes and sells bread; ∿'s **dozen,** thirteen [13th loaf being retailer's profit]; hence **bā'kery** (3) n. [OE bæcere (as BAKE, -ER¹)]

Ba'kewell (-kw-) n. ∿ **tart,** baked sweet of pastry with jam layer and almond paste. [∿ in Derbyshire]

ba'klava (bah'-) n. dessert of flaky pastry, honey, and nuts. [Turk.]

bă'ksheesh n. gratuity, tip, (give baksheesh to); alms. [ult. f. Pers. bakšīš (bakšīdan give)]

Balacla'va (-ah'-) n. ∿ (**helmet**), woollen covering for head and neck, worn orig. by soldiers on active service. [∿ in the Crimea, site of battle (1854)]

bălalai'ka (-lī'-) n. triangular-bodied guitar-like musical instrument with 2-4 strings, popular in Slav countries. [Russ.]

bă'lance¹ n. 1. weighing-apparatus with central pivot, beam, and two scales (TIP² the balance); spring or lever substitute for this; ∿(-**wheel**), speed-regulating gear of clock or watch; (B∿) the zodiacal sign Libra. 2. weighing of actions or opinions; wavering of fortune or chance; **in the** ∿, remaining uncertain. 3. power to decide (hold the balance); counterpoise, set-off; even distribution of weight or amount; ∿ **of mind,** sanity; ∿ **of nature,** constancy of conditions resulting from interaction of living things; ∿ **of power** (with no nation greatly disturbing another). 4. (Art etc.) harmony of design and proportion. 5. steady position; **keep** one's ∿, not fall;

lose one's ∼, fall physically or be upset mentally; **off** one's ∼, in danger of falling. **6.** preponderating weight or amount (*the balance of advantage lies with him*). **7.** (Accountancy). difference between credits and debits; statement of this (STRIKE *a balance*); ∼ **sheet**, written statement of it with details, esp. for public company; ∼ **of payments**, difference of value between payments into and out of a country, including INVISIBLE items; ∼ **of trade**, difference between exports and imports; **on** ∼, taking everything into consideration. **8.** difference between amount due and greater amount offered (*you may keep the balance*); (colloq.) rest, remainder. [ME f. OF, f. Rom. *bilancia* f. LL (*libra*) *bilanx bilancis* two-scaled (balance) (as BI-, *lanx* scale)]

ba'lance² *v.* **1.** *v.t.* weigh (a question, two arguments etc. against each other); match (thing) *with, by, against*, another; bring (thing, one*self*, or abs.) into, or keep in, equilibrium; equal or neutralize weight of; make up for; exclude undue preponderance of any constituent in (*balanced diet*). **2.** (Accountancy). compare debits and credits of (account); make entry necessary to equalize them in (account); settle (account) by paying deficit. **3.** *v.i.* oscillate, waver; (of account) have two sides equal. [f. F *balancer* (*balance*; see prec.)]

ba'las *n.* rose-coloured spinel ruby. [ME, f. OF *balais* f. med. L *balascus* f. Arab. *balakš* f. Pers. *Badakšān*, district of origin]

balata (bă'lǎ-, balah'-) *n.* Central Amer. tree of family Sapotaceae; its dried juice, used as substitute for gutta-percha. [S. Amer. Sp.]

Bálbri'ggan *n.* knitted cotton fabric used for underwear etc. [∼ in Ireland, where orig. made]

bǎ'lconӯ *n.* external balustraded platform with access from upper-floor window; (in theatre) tier of seats above dress-circle, usu. = gallery; *dress-circle; (in cinema etc.) upstairs seats. [f. It. *balcone* prob. f. Gmc *balkon* (as BALK¹, -OON)]

bald (bawld) *a.* with scalp wholly or partly hairless (*bald as a* COOT); **go** ∼**-headed,** (sl.) proceed (*at, for, into*) regardless of consequences); (of animal etc.) hairless, featherless, treeless, leafless, napless; (of horse etc.) marked with white, esp. on face (∼**-faced**); (of tyre, colloq.) having lost its tread by wear; (of style etc.) meagre, dull, (of bad qualities) undisguised, whence ∼'LY² *adv.*; ∼ **eagle** (white--crowned Amer. kind, used as emblem of US); ∼**'head,** ∼**'pate,** (person) with bald head, white--crowned Amer. widgeon; ∼'ING² *a.*, becoming bald; hence ∼'NESS *n.* [ME, perh. f. *ball-* white patch + -ED²]

ba'ldachin, -quin, (bǎ'ldǎkin, baw-) *n.* canopy projecting, suspended, or carried, over altar, throne, priest, etc. [orig. 'rich brocade', f. It. *baldacchino* (*Baldacco* Baghdad, its place of origin; see -INE¹)]

ba'lderdash (bawl'l-) *n.* jumble of words; nonsense. [earlier sense (16th c.) 'frothy liquid'; orig. unkn.]

ba'ldmoney (baw'ldmŭnĭ) *n.* aromatic white--flowered umbelliferous mountain plant (*Meum athamanticum*). [ME in sense 'gentian'; orig. unkn.]

ba'ldric (baw'l-) *n.* (Hist.) belt for sword, bugle, etc., hung from shoulder across body to opposite hip. [ME *baudry* f. OF *baudrei*; cf. MHG *balderich*]

bāle¹ *n.* (arch. & poet.) evil; destruction; woe, pain, misery. [OE *b(e)alu*, = OS *balu*, OHG *balo*, ON *böl* f. Gmc *balw-*]

bāl|e² *n.*, & *v.t.* (make up into) package of merchandise usu. wrapped in canvas etc. and corded or hooped; quantity in bale as measure (e.g. *500 lb. of cotton); hence ∼'ER¹ (2) *n.* [ME, prob. f. MDu. *bale*, ult. identical w. BALL¹]

bāle³. See BAIL⁶.

balee'n *n.* & *a.* whalebone; ∼ **whale**, kind that yields baleen. [OF *baleine* f. L *balaena* whale]

bā'lefīre (-lf-) *n.* (literary). funeral pyre; beacon-fire; bonfire. [f. OE *bǣl* & ON *bál* great fire + FIRE¹]

bā'leful (-lf-) *a.* pernicious, destructive; malignant; hence ∼LY² *adv.* [f. BALE¹ + -FUL]

bǎlibū'ntal *n.* (hat of) fine close-woven straw. [f. *Baliuag buntal* (*Baliuag* in Philippines + BUNTAL)]

Balǐnē'se (bah-; -z) *a.* & *n.* (*pl.* same). (native or language) of Bali. [f. *Bali* island in Indonesia + -ESE]

balk¹, baulk¹, (bawk, bawlk) *n.* ridge left unploughed between furrows; stumbling-block, hindrance; (usu. *baulk*) area marked on billiard table where ball may be exempt from direct stroke; roughly squared timber beam; tie-beam of house; (Baseball) illegal action of pitcher. [OE *balc* f. ON *bálkr* f. Gmc *balkuz*]

balk², baulk², (bawk, bawlk) *v.* **1.** *v.t.* shirk, ignore, miss, (topic, turn, duty, chance); hinder, thwart, disappoint, (balked their plans; *baulked of his prey*). **2.** *v.i.* jib, shy; hence ∼'Y² *a.*, reluctant, perverse. [f. prec.]

Ba'lkan (baw'l-) *a.* & *n.* **1.** *a.* of the peninsula in Europe bounded by the Adriatic, Aegean, and Black Seas; of its peoples and countries; hence ∼IZE (3) *v.t.*, divide (an area) into small antagonistic States. **2.** *n.* (in *pl.*) The Balkan countries.

ball¹ (bawl) *n.* **1.** solid or hollow sphere (**terrestrial** ∼, the earth; **three** ∼**s,** pawnbroker's sign). **2.** hard or soft, inflated or solid, large or small, sphere used in games (*ball is in your* COURT¹; **have the** ∼ **at** one's **feet,** have one's opportunity; **keep** one's **eye on the** ∼, remain alert; **keep the** ∼ **rolling,** do one's part in talk etc.; **start the** ∼ **rolling,** make a beginning; **on the** ∼, (colloq.) alert; **play** ∼, (colloq.) co-operate (*with*)); (Cricket) single delivery of it by bowler (NO¹--*ball*); (Baseball) single delivery of it by pitcher, esp. if outside specified limits and not struck at by batter, four such deliveries entitling batter to go to first base (*base on balls*). **3.** solid non-explosive missile (not always spherical) for cannon, rifle, pistol, etc.; hence ∼-PROOF² *a.* **4.** (in *pl.*, vulg.) testicles, (fig.) nonsense, muddle (*make a balls of*), unsuccessful attempt; ∼**s-up,** confusion, muddle; ∼**s up** *v.t.*, = BALL³ *up*. **5.** material gathered or wound in round mass, e.g. of snow, soil, wool, string, minced meat, animal medicine, (∼ **of fire,** very energetic etc. person; EYE¹*ball*; rounded part of hand or foot at base of thumb or big toe. **6.** ∼ (**and socket**) **joint,** form of joint with rounded end in concave cup or socket, having great freedom of movement; ∼**-bear'ing,** (Mech.) bearing avoiding friction by use of small balls, ball for this purpose; ∼**'boy** (retrieving balls in lawn tennis etc.; *∼ **clay,** pipeclay; ∼**'cock,** automatic device to control water level in cistern, with floating ball; ∼**-flower,** (Archit.) ornament resembling ball within hollow flower; *∼ **game,** baseball game; ∼ **lightning** (rare globular form); *∼**'park,** baseball ground (**not in the right** ∼*park,* nowhere near one's objective); ∼**-pen,** ∼**-point,** (pen) having tiny ball as its writing point. [ME, f. ON *böllr* f. Gmc *balluz*]

ball² (bawl) *n.* social assembly for dancing (so ∼**'room,** ∼*room dancing,* social dancing as recreation); **give a** ∼, be host at ball; **have** (oneself) **a** ∼, (sl.) enjoy oneself; **open the** ∼, (fig.) commence operations. [f. F *bal* (obs. *baler, baller,* f. LL *ballare* to dance f. Gk *ballō*)]

ball³ (bawl) *v.* **1.** *v.t.* squeeze or wind into a ball; ∼ **up,** (sl.) muddle, entangle. **2.** *v.i.* grow into a lump or lumps. [f. BALL¹]

bǎ'llad *n.* simple song, esp. sentimental or romantic or narrative composition of several verses, each sung to same melody, with accompaniment merely subordinate (∼ **metre,** COMMON¹ *metre*); poem in short stanzas narrating popular story; hence ∼EER', ∼-MONGER (usu. derog.), ∼RY (5), *ns.* [ME f. OF *balade* f. Prov. *balada* dancing-song (*balar* dance; see BALL², -ADE 1)]

balla'de (-ah'd) *n.* poem of one or more triplets of stanzas with 7, 8, or 10 lines, each ending with same refrain line, and envoy; (Mus.) lyrical instrumental piece. [earlier spelling and pronunc. of prec.]

bä'llast n., & v.t. **1.** n. heavy material placed in ship or balloon-car to secure stability; **in** ∼, (of ship) laden with ballast only or unladen. **2.** experience, principles, etc., that give stability to character. **3.** coarse stone etc. used to form bed of railway or substratum of road. **4.** (Electr.) device to stabilize current in circuit. **5.** v.t. furnish with ballast; make steady, or fill, with ballast. [16th c., f. LG or Scand.]

bälleri'na (-ē'na) n. female ballet-dancer, esp. (**prima** ∼) dancer taking one of the leading classical female roles in ballet. [It., fem. of ballerino dancing--master (ballare dance f. LL; see BALL²)]

bä'llet (-lā) n. theatrical performance of dancing and mime to music; company performing this; hence **bällé'tic** a., **bä'llétomāne** n., enthusiast of ballet, **bällétoMA'NIA** n. [F, f. It. balletto dim. of ballo BALL²]

balli'sta n. (pl. ∼e). ancient military engine for hurling great stones etc. [L, f. Gk ballō throw]

balli'st|ic a. of projectiles; moving under force of gravity only (∼ic missile, one which moves under gravity after initial powered and guided stage); hence ∼ICS n., science of projectiles or of firearms. [f. prec. + -IC]

bä'llocks n. pl. (vulg.) = BALL¹ 4. [OE bealluc dim. f. Gmc *ball- BALL¹]

ballon d'essai (bălawn dĕsā') n. (pl. -ns pr. same). experiment to see how new policy etc. will be received. [F, = trial balloon]

bä'llonėt n. air-compartment in balloon etc. to maintain pressure as buoyant gas is released. [f. F ballonnet, dim. of ballon (see foll., -ET¹)]

ballōō'n n. **1.** round or pear-shaped airtight envelope inflated with hot air or other gas lighter than ordinary air and so able to rise skywards, esp. one with car attached for passengers; BARRAGE balloon; **when the** ∼ **goes up,** when action or trouble begins. **2.** small rubber bag (to be) inflated with air as child's toy etc. **3.** anything hollow and inflated; (colloq.) balloon-shaped line enclosing words or thoughts of characters in strip cartoons etc.; large globular drinking-glass. **4.** ∼ **tyre,** low-pressure pneumatic tyre with large cross-section; ∼ **vine,** tropical Amer. vine with balloon-like pods. [f. F ballon or It. ballone large ball (balla ball; see -OON)]

balloo'n v. **1.** v.i. travel by balloon; (of gown, sail, etc.) swell out like balloon. **2.** v.t. hit or kick (ball etc.) high in the air. [f. prec.]

bä'llot n. (usu. secret) voting; small ball, ticket, or paper (∼-paper) used in voting; votes so recorded; lot-drawing; ∼-box (used in voting esp. to contain ballot-papers marked by voters and to preserve secrecy). [f. It. ballotta dim. of balla BALL¹]

bä'llot v. **1.** v.i. give (usu. secret) vote (∼ for, select (officials etc.) by ballot); draw lots (for precedence etc.). **2.** v.t. take ballot of. [f. It. ballottare (ballotta; see prec.)]

||**bä'lly** a. & adv. (sl.) euphem. form of BLOODY¹ as vague intensive (took the whole bally lot). [pronunc. of bl—y = bloody]

bä'llyhoō' n., & v.t. **1.** n. factitious vulgar or misleading or noisy publicity; showman's touting speech; bombastic nonsense. **2.** v.t. advertise, cajole, by ballyhoo. [20th c., orig. US; etym. unkn.]

bä'llyrăg v. (-gg-). (sl.) **1.** v.t. maltreat by jeering at or playing practical jokes on. **2.** v.i. indulge in horseplay. [18th c.; orig. unkn.]

balm (bahm) n. **1.** fragrant and medicinal exudation from certain trees; aromatic ointment for anointing, soothing pain, or healing; perfume, fragrance; healing or soothing influence, consolation. **2.** Asian and N. Afr. tree yielding balm; aromatic herb of genus Melissa; ∼ of Gilead [cf. Jer. 8:22], (1) (plant of genus Commiphora yielding) fragrant resin formerly much used as unguent, (2) balsam fir or poplar. [ME, f. OF ba(s)me f. L balsamum BALSAM]

ba'lm-crickėt (bah'm-) n. cicada. [earlier baum-, partial transl. of G baumgrille tree-cricket]

bälmö'ral n. round flat cap worn by some Scottish regiments. [f. B∼ Castle, royal residence in Grampian, Scotland]

ba'lm|ỹ (bah'mi) a. yielding balm; fragrant; soft, mild; soothing, healing; (sl.) crazy; hence ∼iLY² adv., ∼iNESS n. [f. BALM + -Y²]

bä'lnėarỹ a. pertaining to baths or bathing. [f. L balneum bath + -ARY¹]

bälneö'logỹ n. scientific study of bathing and medicinal springs. [f. as prec. + -O- + -LOGY]

balo'ney. See BOLONEY.

BALPA abbr. British Air Line Pilots' Association.

ba'lsa (baw'l-, bŏ'l-) n. Amer. tropical tree (Ochroma lagopus); ∼(-wood), its light strong wood, used for lifebelts etc.; raft or float. [Sp., = raft]

ba'lsam (baw'l-, bŏ'l-) n. **1.** resinous product = BALM (exudation or ointment); any of various other medicinal oleo-resins; Canada ∼ (from balsam fir, used in mounting for microscope). **2.** artificial ointment, esp. one of various substances dissolved in oil or turpentine. **3.** (fig.) healing or soothing agency. **4.** tree yielding balsam; flowering plant of genus Impatiens; ∼ apple, gourdlike plant with highly coloured fruit; ∼ fir, ∼ poplar, Amer. trees (Abies balsamea, Populus balsamifera) yielding balsam. **5.** Hence **balsă'mic, balsami'ferous**, (băl-, bawl-, bŏl-), adjs. [OE, f. L balsamum]

Ba'ltic (baw'l-, bŏ'l-) a. & n. **1.** ∼ (**Sea**), almost land--locked sea of NE Europe. **2.** a. of the branch of Indo--European languages that includes Lithuanian and Lettish. [f. med. L Balticus f. LL Balthae dwellers near the Baltic Sea; see -IC]

ba'ltimore (baw'l-, bŏ'l-) n. N. Amer. orange and black starling (Icterus galbula). [f. its colours' being those of coat of arms of Lord B∼, governor of Maryland d. 1632]

bä'luster n. short pillar with curving outline, esp. in balustrade; post helping to support rail; (in pl., arch.) banisters. [f. F balustre f. It. balaustro f. L f. Gk balaustion wild-pomegranate flower (from resemblance of shape)]

bälusträ'de n. row of balusters with rail or coping as ornamental parapet to terrace, balcony, etc. [F (as prec.; see -ADE)]

bambin|o (hămbē'nō) n. (pl. ∼i pr. -ē). image of infant Jesus in swaddling-clothes; (colloq.) young child in Italy. [It., dim. of bambo silly]

bämbōō' n. mainly tropical giant grass of genus Bambusa; its hollow jointed stem, used as stick or material or food; ∼ curtain, (Polit.) 'IRON¹ curtain' in respect of Communist China. [f. earlier bambous etc. taken as pl., f. Du bamboes, unexpl. alt. of Port. mambu f. Malay]

bämbōō'zle v.t. (sl.) hoax, mystify; cheat into doing something or out of property etc.; hence ∼MENT (-zelm-) n. [c. 1700, prob. of cant orig.]

băn¹ v.t. (-nn-). formally prohibit, interdict. [OE bannan summon, = OHG bannan, ON banna f. Gmc *bannan proclaim to be under penalty]

băn² n. formal or authoritative prohibition (on); tacit prohibition by public opinion; ecclesiastical anathema, interdict; curse supposed to have supernatural power; sentence of outlawry; (arch.) angry execration. [f. prec.]

banal (banah'l, -ă'l, bā'nal) a. commonplace, trite; hence or orig. **bană'lity** n., ∼LY² adv. [orig. in sense 'compulsory', hence 'common to all'; f. Gmc as BAN¹, -AL]

bana'na (-ah') n. tropical and subtropical fruit-tree (Musa sapientum); its pulpy fruit, finger-shaped with yellow skin when ripe, growing in clusters; ||**go** ∼**s**, (sl.) become crazy or angry; **hand of** ∼**s** (bunch, esp. 10–20, like fingers of hand); ∼**lander**, (Austral.) Queenslander; ∼ **republic**, (usu. derog.) small tropical country economically dependent on its fruit export; banana SPLIT². [Port. or Sp., f. name in Guinea]

banau'sic *a.* (derog.) suitable (only) for artisans; un-cultivated; materialistic. [f. Gk *banausikos* for artisans]

Bä'nburÿ *n.* ∼ **cake,** pastry filled with currant mixture. [∼ in Oxfordshire, where orig. made]

bănc *n.* in ∼, (Law) sitting as full court. [AF, = bench, f. med. L (as BANK³)]

bănd¹ *n.* **1.** flat strip of thin material; hoop or loop (of iron, RUBBER², etc.) put round a thing to keep it together; metal etc. ring round bird's leg to identify it; strip forming part of garment (shirt, hat, skirt, etc.); (in *pl.*) development of neckband or collar into two pendent strips in clerical, legal, or academic dress; (Mech.) belt connecting wheels or pulleys; stripe of colour or distinguishable material on object; range of values within a series; range of frequency or wave-length in spectrum; ∼'**box,** box of paper-covered cardboard or thin wood for millinery, orig. for neckbands, (*look as if* one *came out of a* ∼*box,* look extremely neat); ∼'**saw,** endless saw running over wheels; ∼'**width,** range of frequencies used in tele-communications. **2.** organized company of persons with common object, esp. robbers etc. (**B**∼ **of Hope,** total-abstinence association); *herd or flock. **3.** body of musicians, esp. wind-instrument performers (*brass band; dance band*); **the** ∼ **begins to play,** (fig.) matters become serious or exciting; BEAT¹ *the band;* ∼'**master,** conductor of band; ∼'**sman** (-z-), member of band; ∼'**stand,** covered outdoor plat-form for band etc.; ∼'**wagon,** wagon for band of musicians esp. in circus parade, (fig.) imaginary vehicle regarded as carrying a band of political leaders likely to be successful (*climb* or *jump on the* ∼*wagon,* seek to join the party etc. that seems likely to win). **4.** (arch.) thing that restrains, binds together, connects, or unites; BOND¹. [senses 1 & 4 ult. f. Gmc *bindan BIND¹. (4) (tie), ME f. ON, f. Gmc *bandam; (1) (strip), ME f. OF bande, bende, med. L benda f. Gmc *bendōn; (2, 3) (company), ME f. OF bande, med. L banda, prob. of Gmc orig.]

bănd² *v.t.* put a band on; mark with stripes, (in *p.p.,* Bot. & Zool.) marked with coloured bands or bars; form into a league (usu. refl., or abs. w. *together*). [f. F bander (*bande;* see prec.)]

bä'ndage *n.,* & *v.t.* **1.** *n.* strip of material for binding up wound etc., or for blindfolding. **2.** *v.t.* tie up with bandage. [F (*bande;* see BAND¹, -AGE)]

bändä'nna *n.* coloured handkerchief or neckerchief with yellow or white spots. [prob. Port., f. Hindi]

b. & b. *abbr.* bed and breakfast.

băndeau (bä'ndō, -ō') *n.* (*pl.* ∼**x** *pr.* -z). strip of material for binding woman's hair. [F]

banderilla (bănderi'lya) *n.* decorated dart thrust into bull's neck or shoulders during bullfight; so **ban-derillero** (bănderïlyär'ō) *n.* (*pl.* ∼**s**), bullfighter using banderillas. [Sp.]

bănderō'l(e) *n.* long narrow flag with cleft end, flown at mast-head; ornamental streamer on knight's lance; ribbon-like scroll or stone band with inscription. [f. F banderole f. It. banderuola dim. of bandiera BANNER]

bä'ndicōot *n.* ∼ (**rat**), (Ind.) large destructive rat (*Bandicota indica*), (Austral.) insectivorous and herbi-vorous marsupial of genus *Perameles.* [f. Telugu pandikokku pig-rat]

bä'ndit *n.* (*pl.* ∼**s** or bandi'tti). outlaw; lawless robber or murderer; gangster; hence ∼RY (4) *n.* [f. It. bandito (pl. -iti), p.p. (as n.) of bandire ban, = med. L bannire proclaim; see BANISH]

bä'ndŏg *n.* (Hist.) dog kept on chain. [ME, f. BAND¹+DOG¹]

băndoleer', -ier', *n.* shoulder-belt with loops or pockets for cartridges. [f. Du. bandelier or f. F bandoulière, prob. f. as BANDEROLE]

bä'ndÿ¹ *v.t.* ∼ (**about**), throw, strike, pass, to and fro (ball, or fig. stories, insults, etc.); discuss (names etc.), esp. disparagingly; give and take (blows etc.), ex-change (compliments etc.) *with* person. [perh. f. F bander take sides (*bande BAND¹* 2)]

bä'ndÿ² *a.* (Of legs) curved so as to be wide apart a' the knees; ∼**-legged,** having bandy legs. [perh. f obs. *bandy* curved stick]

bāne *n.* cause of ruin or trouble (*he is the bane of my life*) (poet.) ruin, woe; (arch., fig., or in comb., e.g *henbane,* RAT¹*sbane*) poison; ∼'**berry,** (bitter poison-ous berry of) plant of genus *Actaea;* hence ∼'FUL (-nf-*) *a.* [OE *bana,* = OHG *bano,* ON *bani* f. Gmc *banon]

băng¹ *v.t. & i.* strike or shut noisily; (cause to) make sound of blow or explosion; (sl.) copulate (with) hence ∼'ER¹ *n.,* (esp., sl.) sausage, noisy firework, noisy old car. [16th c., perh. f. Scand.]

băng² *n.* sharp blow; sound of a blow; report of gun; sound of explosion (BIG *bang;* **with a** ∼, successfully or impressively); (sl.) drug injection [cf. BHANG]; (sl.) copulation. [f. prec.]

băng³ *adv.* with sudden impact; abruptly; (colloq.) completely, exactly (*bang in the middle*); explosively (as conventional imitation of shot or explosion, lit. or fig., *bang went my hopes of success*); **go** ∼, shut etc. noisily, explode; ∼ **off,** (sl.) immediately; ∼ **on,** (sl.) exactly right; *∼**-up,** (sl.) first-class. [f. BANG¹]

băng⁴ *v.t.,* & *n.* **1.** *v.t.* cut (front hair) straight across forehead. **2.** *n.* fringe thus formed; ∼'**tail,** horse esp with tail cut straight across; ∼'*tail muster,* (Austral.) counting of cattle by cutting across tufts at tail-ends. [f. prec.]

bä'ngle (-nggel) *n.* rigid ring as bracelet or anklet. [f. Hindi *bangri* glass bracelet]

bä'nian, bä'nyan, *n.* Hindu trader; loose flannel jacket etc.; ∼ (**-tree**), Indian fig, branches of which root themselves over wide area. [Port. *banian* f. Gujarati *vāṇijo* man of trading caste, f. Skr.; applied orig. to one such tree under which banians had buil* pagoda]

bä'nish *v.t.* condemn (person) to removal (*from* place, esp. a country); dismiss from one's presence or mind; hence ∼MENT *n.* [ME, f. OF *banir* (-ISH²) f. Rom. *bannire* f. Gmc *bannjan (*bann- BAN¹)]

bä'nister, bä'nnister, *n.* (usu. in *pl.*) upright(s) supporting stair handrail; (in *pl.*) these uprights and rail together. [f. earlier *barrister,* corrupt. of BALUSTER]

bä'njō *n.* (*pl.* ∼**s** or ∼**es**). stringed musical instrument with neck and head like guitar and body made like tambourine, played with fingers or plectrum; hence ∼IST (3) *n.* [Negro corrupt. of earlier *bandore* ult. f. Gk *pandoura* three-stringed lute]

bănk¹ *n.* **1.** raised shelf of ground, slope; elevation in sea or river bed; artificial slope of road etc. enabling car etc. to maintain speed round a curve; (flat--topped) mass of cloud, fog, snow, etc. **2.** sloping margin of river, ground near river (**right, left,** ∼, to one looking down stream); edge of hollow place (e.g. top of mine-shaft). [ME, f. ON *banki f. Gmc *bankon; cf. BANK⁵, BENCH]

bănk² *v.t. & i.* contain or confine with bank(s); (of car or aeroplane or its occupant) travel with one side higher in rounding a curve; cause (car etc.) to do this; build (road etc.) higher at outer edge of bend to help fast cornering; ∼ (**up**), heap or rise into banks, pack tightly (fire, for slow burning). [f. prec.]

bănk³ *n.* **1.** establishment for custody of money, which it pays out on customer's order; **central** ∼, national (not commercial) bank; ||**the B**∼, Bank of England, issuing legal-tender notes, and having the Govern-ment as chief customer. **2.** small domestic receptacle for money; (Gaming) amount of money held by keeper of table; place for storing anything for future use (*blood bank; data bank*). **3.** ∼**-bill,** ||bill drawn by one bank on another, *banknote; ∼ **card,** = CHEQUE card; ∼ **holiday,** day on which banks are legally closed, ||usu. kept as general holiday also; ∼ **manager,** person in charge of local branch of bank; ∼'**note,** banker's promissory note (esp. from central bank) payable to bearer on demand and serving as money; ||**B**∼ **Rate,**

inimum lending rate; **~'roll*, (*n.*) roll of bank-
otes, funds, (*v.t.*, colloq.) support financially. [f. F
anque or f. It. *banca* f. med. L *banca, bancus*, f. Gmc
bank- bench; cf. BANK¹, ⁵]
ank⁴ *v.* **1.** *v.i.* keep BANK³, trade in money; keep
money *at* (or *with*) bank; (Gaming) be keeper of the
ank; ~ **on**, base one's hopes on, count upon, reckon
eliable. **2.** *v.t.* deposit (money etc.) in bank. [f. prec.]
ank⁵ *n.* row of keys, lights, switches, etc.; group of
imilar objects connected in line; tier *of* oars. [ME, f.
)F *banc* f. Gmc **bank-*; cf. BANK¹, BENCH]
'nkable *a.* that will be accepted at a BANK³; (fig.)
eliable. [f. BANK⁴ + -ABLE]
'nker¹ *n.* **1.** one who manages a BANK³; **let me be
our** ~ (lend the money you need); ~**'s card**, =
HEQUE *card*; *banker's* ORDER¹. **2.** (Gaming) keeper of
he bank; dealer in some games of chance; a gambling
ame of cards. **3.** result forecast identically (while
ther forecasts differ) in several football-pool entries
n one coupon. [f. F *banquier* (*banque* BANK³; see -ER²)]
'nker² *n.* fishing boat or fisherman off Newfound-
and; (Austral.) river flooded to top of banks. [f.
ANK¹ + -ER¹]
inke't *n.* auriferous conglomerate like pudding-
stone, found in S. Africa. [Du., = kind of hardbake
BANQUET¹)]
'uking *n.* In vbl senses of BANK², ⁴; fishing on a sea
ank (esp. off Newfoundland). [f. BANK¹, ², ⁴ + -ING¹]
'nkrŭpt *n.*, *a.*, & *v.t.* **1.** *n.* (Law) insolvent person
vhose estate is administered and distributed for
enefit of all his creditors; insolvent debtor. **2.** *a.*
nsolvent; undergoing legal process because of in-
olvency; (fig.) bereft *of* (some quality etc.); hence
~CY *n.* **3.** *v.t.* reduce to bankruptcy. [16th c., f. It.
anca rotta (BANK³, L *rumpere rupt-* break) broken
ench, assim. to L]
i'nksia *n.* flowering shrub of genus *Banksia*, orig.
Australian; ~ **rose**, small-flowered Chinese climbing
ose. [f. Sir J. *Banks*, Engl. naturalist d. 1820 + -IA¹]
'nner *n.* & *a.* **1.** *n.* cloth flag on pole used as standard
f king, knight, etc.; **join, follow, the** ~ **of**, (fig.)
dhere to the cause of. **2.** ensign (esp. on two poles or
rossbar) borne in religious or political demonstra-
ions; anything used as symbol of principles. **3.** *a.*
onspicuous (*banner headline* in newspaper); ***pre-
minent**. [ME, f. AF *banere*, OF *baniere*, f. Rom.
bundaria f. med. L *bandum* standard (BAND¹ 4), f.
Gmc]
i'nneret *n.* (Hist.) knight having vassals in the field
under his own banner; knighthood conferred on the
ield for valour. [ME & OF *baneret* (*baniere* BANNER; -*et*
as -ATE¹)]
'nnister. See BANISTER.
i'nnock *n.* (Sc. & N. Engl.) round flat loaf, usu.
unleavened. [OE *bannuc*, perh. f. Celt.]
inns (-z) *n. pl.* notice in church etc. of intended
marriage, read on three Sundays to give opportunity
f objection; **forbid the** ~, raise such objection. [pl.
f BAN²]
i'nquĕt¹ *n.* elaborate feast; dinner with speeches in
elebration of something or to further a cause. [F,
lim. of *banc* bench, BANK³]
i'nquĕt² *n.* **1.** *v.t.* regale (person). **2.** *v.i.* feast;
arouse; hence ~ER¹ *n.* [f. F *banqueter* (*banquet*; see
rec.)]
anquĕ'tte (-ngk-) *n.* raised step behind rampart etc.;
upholstered seat along wall. [F, f. It. *banchetta* dim. of
anca bench, BANK³]
i'nshee *n.* (Ir. & Sc.) female spirit whose wail
portends death in a house. [f. Ir. *bean sídhe* f. OIr. *ben
síde* woman of the fairies]
ănt *v.i.* (arch.) undergo banting treatment. [back-
form. f. BANTING; cf. -ING¹]
ă'ntam *n.* small kind of domestic fowl, of which the
cock is very pugnacious; small but spirited person;
~**weight** (Boxing; see BOX⁵*ing-weights*). [app. f.
Bāntān in Java (not their orig. home)]

bä'nter *n.* & *v.* **1.** *n.* humorous ridicule; good-
-humoured personal remarks. **2.** *v.t.* make fun of,
rally. **3.** *v.i.* talk jestingly. [17th c., of unkn. orig.]
bä'nting *n.* (arch.) treatment of obesity by abstinence
from sugar, starch, and fat. [f. W. *Banting*, Engl.
undertaker and dietitian d. 1878]
bä'ntling *n.* young child, brat. [16th c., perh. f. G
bänkling (*bank* bench; cf. BASTARD)]
Băntu' (-ōō′) *n.* (*pl.* ~ *or* ~**s**) & *a.* (member) of a group
of Negroid peoples in equatorial and southern Africa;
(group) of languages spoken by them. [Bantu, =
people]
Băntusta'n (-ōōstah′n) *n.* (S. Afr.) area reserved for
Bantu members of population. [f. BANTU + -*stan* as in
Hindustan]
bä'nxring *n.* Javanese squirrel-like insectivorous
animal, tree-shrew. [f. Jav. *bangsring*]
bä'nyan *n.* See BANIAN.
bänzai' (-zī′) *int.* form of greeting by Japanese to their
Emperor, cheer used in battle, etc. [Jap., = ten
thousand years (of life to you)]
bä'obäb *n.* orig. African tree (*Adansonia digitata*) with
enormously thick trunk and large fruit with edible
pulp. [L (1592), prob. f. an Afr. lang.]
BAOR *abbr.* British Army of the Rhine.
băp *n.* (esp. Sc.) large soft bread roll. [16th c.; orig.
unkn.]
bä'ptĭsm *n.* **1.** religious rite of immersing person in, or
sprinkling with, water in sign of purification and
(with Christians) of admission to the Church, generally accompanied by name-giving. **2.** (fig.) ~ **of
blood**, martyrdom of the unbaptized; ~ **of fire**,
soldier's first battle. **3.** naming of church bells and of
ships. So **băptĭ'smAL** (-z-) *a.* [ME, f. OF
ba(p)te(s)me f. eccl. L f. Gk *baptismos* (*baptizō* BAPTIZE;
see -ISM)]
bä'ptĭst *n.* one who baptizes, esp. John the Baptist;
(*B*~) one of a Christian religious body objecting to
infant baptism, and practising immersion. [ME, f.
OF *baptiste*. f. eccl. L f. Gk *baptistēs* (*baptizō*; see
BAPTIZE)]
bä'ptĭstery *n.* part of church (or, formerly, separate
building) used for baptism; (in Baptist chapel)
immersion receptacle for baptism. [ME, f. OF *bap-
tisterie* f. eccl. L f. Gk *baptistērion* bathing-place
(*baptizō*; see BAPTIZE)]
băptī'ze, -ī'se (-ī'z), *v.t.* administer baptism to
(person, or abs.); christen; name or nickname. [ME,
f. OF *baptisor* f. eccl. L *baptizare* f. Gk *baptizō* immerse,
baptize]
bär¹ *n.* **1.** long piece of rigid material (metal, wood,
etc.); oblong piece (of chocolate, soap, etc.); CROSS*bar*;
heating element of electric fire; ~**bell**, iron bar with
heavy ball at each end used in exercising; *bar*
TRACERY. **2.** strip of silver below clasp of medal as
additional distinction; band of colour etc. on surface
(~ *chart* etc., using bars to represent quantities);
(Her.) narrow horizontal stripe across field (~
sinister, erron. for BEND¹ or BATON *sinister*, supposed
sign of bastardy). **3.** rod or pole used to fasten or
confine or obstruct (window, door, grate, etc.;
behind ~**s**, in prison); barrier of any shape; sandbank or shoal at mouth of harbour or estuary. **4.**
immaterial barrier or obstacle; restriction; (Mus.)
vertical line (also ~**-line**) across staff dividing composition into sections of equal time-value, such
section; (Law) plea arresting action or claim. **5.** (In
lawcourt) place at which prisoner stands, (fig.) *bar of
conscience, opinion*, etc.; a particular court; **be called to
the** ~ (i.e. that at Inns of Court separating benchers
from others), be admitted a barrister; **be called
within the** ~ (i.e. that in courts within which QCs
plead), be appointed Queen's Counsel; **the** ~QCs,
barristers, profession or barrister; **the outer** ~, those
not QCs. **6.** rail dividing off space (e.g. in Parliament)
to which non-members may be admitted on business.
7. (In inn etc.) counter across which alcoholic

refreshments are served, space behind or room or premises containing it; ∼'**fly,** /person frequenting such places; *∼'**keep,** ||∼'**maid,** ∼'**man,** ∼'**tender,** attendant at such counter. **8.** place where anything is served across counter etc., esp. refreshments (COFFEE bar; SNACK-*bar*); specialized department in large shop (*heel bar; slipper bar*). [ME, f. OF *barre,* f. Rom. *barra of unkn. orig.]

bar² *v.t.* (-**rr**-). fasten (door etc.) with bar(s); keep (person) *in* or *out*; obstruct (path etc.); (Law) stay (process or party) by objection; exclude from consideration (cf. BAR⁵, BARRING); prohibit; ||(sl.) object to, dislike, (person, habit, etc.); mark with stripe(s). [ME, f. OF *barrer* (*barre*; see prec.)]

bar³ *n.* large Mediterranean food-fish (*Sciaena aquila*). [F]

bar⁴ *n.* (esp. Meteorol.) unit of pressure, 10⁵ newton per square metre, approx. one atmosphere. [f. Gk *baros* weight]

bar⁵ *prep.* except (*all over bar the shouting*); ∼ **three** etc., (in stating odds in Racing) except the three etc. horses already named (also ellipt. w. omission of *three* etc.). [imper. of BAR², prob. by anal. w. *except* etc.]

bǎrathē'a *n.* fine cloth made from wool (with or without silk or cotton). [19th c.; orig. unkn.]

barb¹ *n.,* & *v.t.* **1.** *n.* secondary backward-projecting point of arrow, fish-hook, etc.; (fig.) wounding quality or remark; beardlike filament at mouth of barbel or other fish; lateral filament branching from shaft of feather. **2.** *v.t.* furnish (arrow etc.) with barb; ∼ed **wire,** *∼'**wire,** (for fences and esp. as obstruction in war, with short pointed pieces of wire inserted at intervals). [ME, f. OF *barbe* f. L *barba* beard]

barb² *n.* breed of horse or pigeon imported from Barbary; (Austral.) black kelpie. [f. F *barbe* f. It. *barbero* of BARBARY]

Barbā'dian *a.* & *n.* (native or inhabitant) of Barbados. [f. *Barbados* in W. Indies + -IAN]

barbā'rian *n.* & *a.* rough, wild, or uncultured (person). [orig. of any foreigner w. different language or customs; f. F *barbarien* f. *barbare* (as BARBAROUS; see -IAN)]

barbā'r|ic *a.* rough, uncultured; like or of barbarians and their art or taste, unrestrained; hence ∼ICALLY *adv.* [ME, f. OF *barbarique* or f. L f. Gk *barbarikos* (*barbaros* foreign; see -IC)]

bar'barism *n.* (use of) word or action not in accordance with normal standards; absence of culture; ignorance and rudeness; instance of this. [f. F *barbarisme* f. L f. Gk *barbarismos* (*barbarizō* speak like a foreigner f. *barbaros* foreign; see -ISM)]

barbā'rity *n.* savage cruelty; instance of it. [f. as BARBAROUS + -ITY]

bar'bariz|e, -īs|e (-īz), *v.t.* & *i.* make or become barbarous; hence ∼A'TION *n.* [f. as foll. + -IZE]

bar'barous *a.* uncivilized; cruel; coarse; hence ∼LY² *adv.,* ∼NESS *n.* [orig. of any foreign language or people; f. L f. Gk *barbaros* foreign + -OUS]

Bar'bary *n.* (Old name of) western part of N. Africa; ∼ **ape,** macaque of N. Africa and Gibraltar. [ult. f. Arab. *barbar* BERBER]

bar'bēcūe *n.,* & *v.t.* **1.** *n.* metal frame for cooking meat above open fire; fireplace containing this; meat etc. thus cooked; open-air party at which such food is served. **2.** *v.t.* cook on barbecue. [f. Sp. *barbacoa* f. Haitian *barbacôa* wooden frame on posts]

bar'bel *n.* large European freshwater fish of genus *Barbus* with fleshy filaments hanging from mouth; such filament in any fish. [ME f. OF, f. LL *barbellus* dim. of *barbus* barbel (*barba* beard)]

bar'ber *n.,* & *v.t.* **1.** *n.* one who cuts men's hair and shaves or trims beards, men's hairdresser; ∼-**shop** *a.,* *(fig., colloq.) of close-harmony male quartet singing; ∼'**s itch, rash,** ringworm of face communicated by (unsterilized) shaving apparatus; ∼'**s pole** (spirally painted red and white and used as barber's sign). **2.** *v.t.* cut hair of; (fig.) cut (grass etc.) short.

[ME & AF, f. OF *barbeor* f. med. L *barbator* -*oris* (*barb* beard); see -OR, -ER²]

bar'berry *n.* shrub of genus *Berberis,* with spin shoots, yellow flowers, and oblong red berries; i berry. [ME, f. OF *berberis,* of unkn. orig.; assim. BERRY¹]

bar'bet *n.* tropical bird with bristle-tufts at base of bi [F (*barbe* beard; see -ET¹)]

barbe'tte *n.* platform in fort or ship from which gui fire over parapet etc. without embrasure. [F, dim. *barbe* beard; see -ETTE]

bar'bican *n.* outer defence of city or castle, esp. doub tower over gate or bridge. [ME, f. OF *barbacane,* ‹ unkn. orig.]

***bar'bital,** ||**bar'bitōne,** *ns.* soporific drug, verona [f. BARBITURIC + -*al* as in *veronal,* -ONE]

barbitū'ric *a.* (Chem.) ∼ **acid,** an acid, malon urea, from which various soporific and sedative dru are derived; hence **barbi'tūr**ATE¹ (3) *n.* [f. F *ba biturique* f. G *barbitur*(*säure* acid) f. woman's Christia name *Barbara*]

Bar'bizon *n.* ∼ **school,** coterie of mid-19th-c. Frenc naturalistic painters. [∼ near Paris]

barbō'la *n.* ∼ (**work**), embellishment of small articl by attachment of coloured models of flowers, frui etc. made from a plastic paste. [arbitr. from *barboti* clay slip for ornamenting pottery]

bar'būle *n.* filament branching from barb (of feathe as barb from shaft. [f. L *barbula* dim. of *barba* bear see -ULE]

bar'carōle, -ōlle, *n.* song of gondolier; music i imitation of it. [f. F *barcarolle* f. Venetian It. *barcaro* boatman's song (*barca* boat)]

Barcēlōna *n.* ∼ (**nut**), hazel-nut imported fro Spain etc. [∼ in Spain]

bard¹ *n.* **1.** Celtic minstrel; poet honoured at Eisted fod; hence ∼'IC *a.* **2.** (literary). poet; **the B**∼ (o Avon), Shakespeare; ∼ŏ'LATRY *n.,* excessiv admiration of Shakespeare. [f. Gael. & Ir. *bárd,* bardd, f. OCelt. *bardos]

bard² *n.,* & *v.t.* **1.** *n.* slice of bacon placed on meat game before roasting. **2.** *v.t.* cover with bards. [f. *barde,* orig. = horse's breastplate, ult. f. Arab.]

bar'dy *n.* (Austral.) edible wood-boring grub or i larva. [Aboriginal]

bāre¹ *a.* **1.** unclothed, uncovered; (of head) hatless; (c tree) leafless; unfurnished, unprotected, (of floo without carpet; undisguised (*lay bare the truth*); ur adorned (*bare facts, walls*); empty (*cupboard was bare* scanty (*a bare majority*); mere (*bare necessities of life*). ∼ **of,** unprovided with; **with** one's ∼ **hands,** n using tool or weapon. **3.** ∼'**back** *a.* & *adv.,* (esp.) o unsaddled horse; *∼'**faced,** (fig.) undisguised, ir pudent; ∼'**foot** *a.* & *adv.,* ∼'**footed** *a.,* without shoe or stockings; ∼**hea'ded,** without hat or cap. 4 Hence ∼'NESS (bār'n-) *n.* [OE *bær,* = OS, OHG ba ON *berr,* f. Gmc *bazaz f. IE *bhosós]

bāre² *v.t.* uncover, unsheathe; reveal (*bared its teeth in* snarl). [OE *barian* (*bær;* see prec.)]

bāre³. See BEAR³.

barège (barā'zh) *n.* & *a.* (of) silky gauze made fro wool etc. [F, f. *Barèges* in SW France, where orig made]

bar'ely (bār'li) *adv.* merely; only just; scarcely (*bare* escaped disaster); scantily (*barely furnished rooms*); (arch openly, explicitly. [f. BARE¹ + -LY²]

bar'gain (-gĭn) *n.* **1.** agreement on terms of a transac tion; **into** or ***in the** ∼, beyond the strict terms moreover; **make** or **strike a** ∼, come to terms; best bargain. **2.** thing acquired by such agreement; **good bad,** ∼, thing or result cheaply or dearly bough *make the* BEST¹ *of a bad bargain.* **3.** thing acquired o offered cheap, esp. in special shop-sale; ∼ **basemen** (in shop, where bargains are offered). [ME, f. O *bargaine* (*bargainier;* see foll.)]

bar'gain (-gĭn) *v.* **1.** *v.i.* discuss terms of a transactio (*with* person *for* thing, or abs.); ∼ **for** or (colloq.) on be prepared for, expect, (usu. w. neg. or *more than*: *did not bargain for* or *on her coming too*; *had more guests than I bargained for*); ∼ **on**, rely on. **2.** *v.t.* ∼ **away**, part with for a consideration. **3.** Hence ∼ER¹ *n*. [ME, f. OF *bargaignier*, prob. f. Gmc *borganjan (*borgan look after)]

arge *n*., & *v.i.* **1.** *n*. flat-bottomed freight-boat for canals, rivers, and harbours, with or without sails; large ornamental oared vessel for state occasions; ornamental house-boat (e.g. *College barge*); second boat of man-of-war; *∼'**man**, bargee; ∼-**pole** (for fending; *would not touch with a* ∼-*pole*, refuse to associate or be concerned with). **2.** *v.i.* lurch or rush heavily *into*, *against*, *about*; ∼ **in**, intrude. [ME f. OF, perh. f. med. L *barica* f. Gk *baris* Egyptian boat]

arge-board *n*. (Archit.) board or ornamental screen along edge of gable. [cf. med. L *bargus* gallows; BOARD¹]

bargee *n*. person in charge of or working on barge. [f. BARGE + -EE]

arilla *n*. plant of genus *Salsola* in Spain, Sicily, etc.; impure alkali made by burning either this or kelp. [Sp.]

a'ritone *n*. (Mus.) male voice between tenor and bass; singer with this voice; part written for baritone voice; member of a group of similar instruments, between tenor and bass; type of bass viol. [f. It. *baritono* f. Gk *barutonos* (*barus* heavy, *tonos* TONE¹)]

ar'ium *n*. (Chem.) white metallic element, of which baryta is the oxide; ∼ **meal**, mixture containing barium sulphate, used in radiography of alimentary canal. [f. BARYTA + -IUM]

ark¹ *n*. outer sheath of tree trunks and branches; this material used as TAN¹; ∼'**cloth** (made from inner bark of paper mulberry etc.). [ME, f. OIcel. *börkr bark-*, perh. rel. to BIRCH]

ark² *v.t.* strip bark from (tree); abrade (knuckles etc.). [f. prec.]

ark³ *n*. (poet.) ship, boat. [= BARQUE]

ark⁴ *n*. sharp explosive cry of dogs, foxes, squirrels; *his* ∼ *is worse than his bite*, he is irritable but harmless; hence ∼'LESS *a*. [f. foll.]

ark⁵ *v.i.* (Of dog etc.) utter bark; speak petulantly or imperiously; *act as tout; ∼ **at**, abuse; ∼ **up the wrong tree**, (fig.) be on wrong track, make effort in wrong direction; ∼'**ing** deer, muntjak; *barking* SQUIRREL. [OE *beorcan*, repr. earlier *berkan, perh. var. of BREAK¹]

arkentine. See BARQUENTINE.

ar'ker *n*. tout at auction, side-show, etc. [f. BARK⁵ + -ER¹]

ar'ley *n*. hardy awned cereal of genus *Hordeum* used as food and in making malt liquors and spirits; ∼-(**corn**), its grain (**John B**∼**corn**, malt liquor personified), (Hist.) length of its grain as measure (⅓ inch); PEARL¹ barley; ∼-**mow**, stack of barley; ∼ **sugar**, usu. twisted sweetmeat of boiled sugar; ∼-**water**, decoction of pearl barley for invalids etc. [OE *bærlic a*. f. *bære*, *bere* barley + -*lic* -LY¹]

arm *n*. froth on fermenting malt liquor; yeast, leaven. [f. OE *beorma* f. OLG *bermon]

ar'mecide *n*. & *a*. (giver of benefits that are) illusory, imaginary, disappointing. [name of Arabian-Nights prince whose feast to beggar was rich dish-covers with nothing below]

ar mi'tzvah (-tsva) *n*. (religious initiation ceremony for) Jewish boy aged 13. [Heb., = 'son of commandment']

ar'my *a*. full of barm; (sl.) crazy. [f. BARM + -Y²]

arn¹ *n*. roofed building for storing grain, hay, *livestock, *vehicles, etc., (derog.) large unadorned building; ∼ **dance**, kind of schottische; ∼-**door**, lit., or fig. target too large to be missed; ∼-**owl**, kind of owl frequenting barns; ∼'**storm**, act as ∼'**stormer**, itinerant actor (esp. given to ranting), *politician, or *aviator; ∼'**yard**, farmyard. [OE *bern*, *beren* (*bere* barley, *ern*, *ærn* house)]

barn² *n*. (Phys.) unit of nuclear cross-section, 10^{-28} square metre. [perh. f. phr. 'as big as a barn']

bar'nacle *n*. **1.** ∼ (**goose**), Arctic goose (*Anas leucopsis*) visiting Britain in winter. **2.** cirriped clinging to rock or by fleshy foot-stalk to ship's bottom; follower who cannot be shaken off. [ME, earlier *bernak*, med. L *bernaca*, of unkn. orig.]

bar'ney *n*. (colloq.) noisy quarrel. [perh. f. dial.]

ba'rograph (-ahf) *n*. self-recording barometer. [f. Gk *baros* weight + -O- + -GRAPH]

baro'meter *n*. instrument measuring atmospheric pressure used for forecasting weather and ascertaining height above sea-level; (fig.) *barometer of opinion* etc.; hence **bărome'tric**(AL) *adjs*., **barŏ'metry** *n*. [f. as prec. + -METER]

ba'ron *n*. member of the lowest order of British nobility; holder of similar foreign title; great merchant in a specified commodity (*beer baron*); powerful or influential person; (Hist.) one who held lands etc. from king, judge in Court of Exchequer; ∼ **of beef**, double sirloin undivided. [ME, f. AF *barun*, OF *baron* f. med. L *baro -onis* man, of unkn. orig.]

ba'ronage *n*. barons or nobles collectively; annotated list of barons or peers. [ME f. OF *barnage* (as prec.; see -AGE)]

ba'roness *n*. baron's wife or widow; woman holding rank of baron in her own right. [ME, f. OF *baronesse*; see BARON, -ESS¹]

ba'ronet *n*. member of lowest hereditary titled British order; hence ∼CY *n*. [ME, f. AL *baronettus* (as BARON; see -ET¹)]

ba'ronetage *n*. baronets collectively; annotated list of baronets. [f. prec. + -AGE; cf. BARONAGE]

baro'nial *a*. of, belonging to, befitting, baron(s); (Archit.) in turreted style used by Sc. land-owners. [f. foll. + -AL]

ba'rony *n*. domain, rank, tenure, of baron; (Ir.) division of county; (Sc.) large manor. [ME, f. OF *baronie* (as BARON; see -Y¹)]

barŏ'que (-k) *a*. & *n*. **1.** (of) certain stylistic tendencies in 17th–18th c. arts, characterized by exuberance and extravagance; (of mus. instrument) designed as in 17th–18th c. **2.** *a*. grotesque, whimsical. [F, orig. 'misshapen pearl']

barou'che (-ōō'sh) *n*. (Hist.) four-wheeled horse-drawn carriage with collapsible half-hood. [f. G (dial.) *barutsche* f. It. *baroccio* f. *biroccio f. LL *birotium* f. L *birotus* (BI- 1(a), *rota* wheel)]

barque (-k) *n*. vessel with aftermost mast fore-and-aft rigged and remaining (usu. two) masts square-rigged. [ME f. F, prob. f. Prov. f. L *barca* ship's boat]

bar'quentine, bar'k-, (bär'kenten) *n*. three-masted vessel with foremast square-rigged, and mizen fore-and-aft rigged. [f. prec., after *brigantine*]

bă'rrack¹ *n*. & *v.t.* **1.** (usu. in *pl*., often treated as *sing*.) building(s) in which soldiers are lodged (∼-**room lawyer**, pompously argumentative person; ∼-**square**, drill-ground near barracks); building in which many persons are similarly herded together; large building of severely dull or plain appearance. **2.** *v.t.* place in barracks. [f. F *baraque* f. It. *baracca* or Sp. *barraca* soldier's tent, of unkn. orig.]

bă'rrack² *v.i.* & *t.* (Of spectators at games etc.) shout or jeer (at). [app. f. BORAK]

bărracoo'n *n*. (Hist.) enclosure for slaves, convicts, etc. [f. Sp. *barracón* (as BARRACK¹; see -OON)]

bărracu'da (-ōō'da), **-cou'ta** (-ōō'ta), *n*. **1.** (usu. -*uda*) large voracious W. Ind. sea-fish of family Sphyraenidae. **2.** (usu. -*outa*) long slender food-fish of Pacific etc. (*Thyrsites atun*). [Amer. Sp. *barracuda*]

ba'rrage (-rahzh) *n*. **1.** artificial barrier in river etc. (esp. in Nile). **2.** (Mil.) barrier to enemy's offensive or defensive action, usu. made of artillery fire as intensively bombarded; (fig.) rapid succession (*of* questions etc.); ∼ **balloon**, large captive balloon supporting steel cable as part of barrier against aircraft. **3.** heat or deciding event in fencing, show-jumping, etc. [F (*barrer*; see BAR², -AGE)]

bărramŭ'ndi n. one of various Austral. freshwater food-fishes. [Aboriginal]

bă'rrator n. malicious raiser of discord; (Hist.) vexatious litigant. [ME, f. AF *baratour*, OF *barateor* trickster (*barater* f. Rom. *prattare exchange, cheat f. Gk *prattō* manage)]

bă'rratr|ў n. (Marine Law) fraud or gross and criminal negligence of master or crew to prejudice of ship's owners or users; (Hist.) vexatious litigation or incitement to it; trade in Church or State appointments; hence ∿ous a. [ME, f. OF *bar*(*a*)*terie* (*barat* deceit f. as BARRATOR)]

bă'rre n. waist-level horizontal bar to help dancers keep their balance when exercising. [F, = BAR¹]

bă'rrel¹ n. **1.** wooden vessel of hooped staves with flat ends and usu. outward-bulging sides, cask, (**over a ∿,** helpless; **scrape the ∿,** use one's last resources); contents of this; measure of capacity (variable, *c.* 30–40 gallons); revolving cylinder in capstan, watch, and other machines; cylindrical body or trunk of an object (e.g. fountain-pen); belly and loins of horse, etc.; metal tube of gun. **2. ∿-chested,** having a large rounded chest; ***∿house,** low-class saloon, unrestrained forceful jazz-playing; **∿-organ,** musical instrument with pin-studded cylinder turned by handle and mechanism opening pipes or striking metal tongues; **∿ vault** (with uniform concave roof). [ME, f. OF *baril,* perh. f. Rom. *barra (BAR¹)]

bă'rrel² v. (||-ll-). **1.** v.t. put in barrel(s). **2.** v.i. *(sl.) drive fast. [f. prec.]

bă'rren a. (∿er, ∿est) & n. **1.** a. not bearing, or incapable of bearing, children, young, fruit, vegetation, or produce, (∿wort, herb of genus *Epimedium,* thought to cause sterility); meagre, unprofitable, dull; hence ∿LY² adv., ∿NESS (-n-n-) n. **2.** n. barren tract of land, esp. (in *pl.*) in N. Amer. [ME, f. AF *barai*(g)*ne,* OF *barhaine* etc., of unkn. orig.]

bă'rrēt n. small flat cap, esp. biretta. [f. F *barrette* f. It. *baretta* (as BIRETTA)]

***barrĕ'tte** n. woman's bar-shaped clip or ornament for hair. [F, dim. of *barre* BAR¹]

bărrică'de¹ n. hastily erected rampart across street etc. of barrels, carts, stones, furniture, etc. during revolution; barrier (lit. or fig.). [F (*barrique* f. Sp. *barrica* cask f. as *barril* BARREL¹; see -ADE)]

bărrică'de² v.t. block (street etc.) with barricade; defend (place or person) with barricade. [f. prec.]

bă'rrier n. fence barring advance or preventing access; gate at railway station where tickets must be shown; obstacle, boundary, or agency that prevents communication, success, etc.; ∿ **cream** (to protect skin against damage, infection, etc.); ∿ **reef,** coral reef separated from adjacent land by broad deep channel; SOUND³ barrier. [ME f. AF *barrere,* OF *barriere* f. Rom. *barraria (*barra BAR¹)]

bă'r'ring prep. except, not including. [f. BAR² +-ING²]

bă'r'riō n. (*pl.* ∿s). Spanish-speaking quarter of US town or city. [Sp., = district of town]

bă'rrister n. ||(∿(-at-law), person called to bar and having right of practising as advocate in the higher courts; *lawyer. [16th c., f. BAR¹, perh. after *minister*]

bă'rrow¹ (-ō) n. (Archaeol.) grave-mound, tumulus. [OE *beorg,* = OS, OHG *berg,* f. Gmc *bergaz]

bă'rrow² (-ō) n. = HAND¹-barrow, WHEEL¹barrow; ||two-wheeled handcart (∿ **boy,** coster); metal frame with two wheels for transporting luggage etc.; quantity carried in barrow. [OE *bearwe* f. Gmc **barwōn,* conn. w. BEAR³]

Băr'săc n. somewhat sweet white Bordeaux wine. [∿ in SW France]

Bart. *abbr.* Baronet.

băr'ter¹ v. **1.** v.t. exchange (goods or intangible things) *for* other goods or *away,* ∿ **away,** part with for a (usu. unworthy) consideration. **2.** v.i. trade by exchange. [prob. f. OF *barater;* see BARRATOR]

băr'ter² n. traffic by exchange of goods (also fig., e.g. of talk). [f. prec.]

bărtīză'n n. battlemented parapet, or overhangin battlemented corner turret, at top of church tower c castle. [spurious form (Scott) f. *bertisene* illit. spellin of *bratticing;* see BRATTICE]

băr'ton n. (arch.) farmyard. [OE *bere-tūn* (*bere* barley *tūn* enclosure; see TOWN)]

||**Băr't's** n. (colloq.) St. Bartholomew's Hospital i London. [abbr.]

bă'rўŏn n. (Phys.) heavy elementary particle (nucleo or hyperon); hence **bărўŏ'n**IC a. [f. Gk *barus* heav + -ON]

bă'rўsphēre n. dense core of the earth, within th lithosphere. [f. Gk *barus* heavy + *sphaira* sphere]

barў'ta n. barium oxide or hydroxide; hence **barў't** a. [f. foll., after *soda* etc.]

barў'tēs (-z) n. native barium sulphate, heavy spa used in some white paints. [f. Gk *barus* heavy, part assim. to mineral names in *-ites*]

bă'rўtōne a. & n. (Gk Gram.) (word) with no or grav accent on last syllable. [f. Gk *barutonos* (see BAR TONE)]

bă'sal a. of, at, or forming, the base; fundamenta *basal* METABOLISM. [f. BASE¹ + -AL]

basalt (bă'sawlt, basaw'lt) n. **1.** dark igneous roc often in columnar strata; hence **basa'lt**IC (-saw'l-) *c* **2.** black porcelain invented by Wedgwood. [f. I *basaltes* var. of *basanites* f. Gk (*basanos* touchstone)]

bas bleu (bah blër') n. bluestocking. [F]

bă'scŭle n. lever apparatus used in ∿-**bridge,** kind drawbridge raised and lowered with counterpoise [F, earlier *bacule* see-saw (*battre* bump, *cul* buttocks)]

băse¹ n. **1.** that on which anything stands or depends support, foundation, (lit. or fig.); principle, starting -point; main or important ingredient of mixture material supporting film etc.; root or stem as origin c word or derivative; middle part of transistor. 2 (Archit.) part of column between shaft and pedest or pavement; (Her.) lowest part of shield. **3.** (Bot. & Zool.) end at which an organ is attached to trunk. **4.** (Geom.) line or surface on which plane or solid figur is regarded as standing. **5.** (Chem.) substanc capable of combining with an acid to form a sal (including, but wider than, ALKALI). **6.** (Mil.) tow or other area in rear of an army where drafts, stores hospitals, etc., are concentrated; operational head quarters. **7.** (Surv.) known line used as geometrica base for trigonometry. **8.** (Math.) starting-numbe for system of numeration or logarithms (as 10 i decimal counting). **9.** (Baseball). one of the fou stations that must be reached in turn when scoring run; **get to first ∿,** (fig.) achieve first step toward objective; **off ∿,** (fig.) mistaken. **10.** *∿'board skirting-board; ∿ **hit** (enabling batter to reach firs base safely); ∿'line, starting-point, (Tennis) line a each end of court, (Print.) = *the* LINE² 13; ∿'load permanent load on power supplies etc.; ∿'man fielder near a base in baseball. [F, or f. L f. Gk *bas* stepping]

băse² v.t. found (something *on*; establish (*firmly* etc.) ∿ oneself **on,** rely upon (in argument etc.); ∿**d on** -∿**d,** using as fundamental station or means (*sub marine based on* Malta; *land-based forces; computer-base accountancy*). [f. prec.]

băse³ a. **1.** morally low; cowardly, selfish, mean, o despicable; menial; hence ∿LY² (-slī) adv., ∿NES (-sn-) n. **2.** ∿'**born,** of low birth, illegitimate; ∿ coi (spurious, alloyed); ∿ **metals** (opposed to noble o precious). [ME in sense 'of small height', f. F *bas* i med. L *bassus* short (in L as cognomen)]

bă'seball (-sbawl) n. (ball used in) US national gam with teams of nine who in turn seek to strike bal thrown by opponent and traverse circuit of fou points called bases. [f. BASE¹ + BALL¹]

bă'seless (-sl-) a. groundless, unfounded; hence ∿LY adv., ∿NESS n. [f. BASE¹ + -LESS]

bă'sement (-sm-) n. lowest or fundamental part o structure; inhabited storey below ground level

prob. Du., perh. f. It. *basamento* base of column
basare BASE²)]
se'nji *n.* smallish rarely-barking African hunting-
dog. [Bantu]
ses. *pl.* of BASE¹ or BASIS.
sh *v.t.*, & *n.* **1.** *v.t.* strike heavily so as to smash in or
; make violent or persistent attack on. **2.** *n.* heavy
 low; (sl.) attempt (*have a bash*); (sl.) party, entertain-
nent. [ult. imit., perh. f. *bang, smash, dash,* etc.]
shaw'. Var. (arch.) of PASHA.
'shful *a.* shy, diffident; shamefaced, sheepish; hence
∽LY² *adv.*, ∽NESS *n.* [f. obs. *bash* v. (ABASH) + -FUL]
shi-bazou'k (-ōō'k) *n.* (Hist.) mercenary of Turk-
h irregulars, notorious for pillage and brutality. [f.
urk. *başıbozuk* irregular soldier]
'sic *a.* of, at, or forming, base; fundamental;
Chem.) having the properties of or containing a
ase; (Geol.) with low silica content; standard mini-
ıum (allowance, pay, etc.); (B∽) an easily learned
omputer language [*Beginners' All-Purpose
Symbolic Instruction Code*]; ∽ **weave** (consisting of
ults of organic bases); **B∽ English** (simplified form
ith select vocabulary of 850 words for international
se); ∽ **industry,** one of great economic importance;
⸱ **slag,** fertilizer containing phosphates formed as
y-product in steel manufacture; hence **bā'sICALLY**
dv. [f. DASE¹ + IC]
si'cit̄y *n.* (Chem.) number of equivalents of base
acting with one molecule of a particular acid. [f.
rec. + -ITY]
si'di|um *n.* (*pl.* ∽a). spore-bearing structure in
ome fungi. [mod. L, Gk *basidion* dim. of BASIS]
'sil (-z-) *n.* aromatic herb of genus *Ocimum,* esp.
weet ∽ and **bush** ∽, both culinary. [ME, f. OF
asile f. med. L f. Gk *basilikos* royal]
'silar *a.* of or at the base (esp. of skull). [f. mod. L
asilaris (BASIS; see -AR¹)]
si'lic|a *n.* oblong hall with double colonnade and
ose used for lawcourts and assemblies; such building
sed as Christian church; church with special
rivileges from Pope; hence ∽AN *a.* [L, f. Gk *basilikē
ikia, stoa*) royal (house, portico) f. *basileus* king; see
c]
'silisk (bā'z-) *n.* **1.** fabulous reptile hatched by
erpent from cock's egg, with lethal breath and look;
∽-glance etc., (fig.) evil eye, person or thing that
lasts (reputation etc.). **2.** (Her.) cockatrice; (Zool.)
mall American lizard of genus *Basiliscus,* with hollow
est inflated at will. [ME, f. L f. Gk *basiliskos* (dim. of
asileus* king) kinglet, serpent, golden-crested wren]
'sin *n.* hollow round metal or pottery vessel, less
eep than wide, and narrowing downwards, for
olding water etc., bowl, hollow depression; dock
ith floodgates; land-locked harbour; area drained
y river and tributaries; circular or oval valley;
Geol.) formation with strata dipping towards centre,
eposit (e.g. of coal) contained in this; hence ∽FUL 2
(lit., or sl. fig., = BELLYFUL). [ME, f. OF *bacin* f.
ied. L *ba(s)cinus,* perh. f. Gaulish]
'sinet *n.* (Hist.) light steel helmet. [ME, f. OF
acinet dim. (as prec.; see -ET¹)]
si'petal *a.* developing from above downwards;
ence ∽LY² *adv.* [f. BASIS + L *petere* seek + -AL]
'sis *n.* (*pl.* **ba'ses** *pr.* -sēz). main ingredient;
oundation; beginning; determining principle (*on a
urely friendly basis*); common ground for negotiation
tc. [L f. Gk, = BASE¹]
sk (bah-) *v.i.* revel in warmth and light (usu. *in the
un,* firelight, etc., fig. in popularity etc.); ∽'ing
hark, very large species of shark (*Cetorhinus maximus*),
ccustomed to lie near water surface. [ME, app. f.
ON *bathask* refl. of *batha* BATHE¹]
'skerville *n.* style of type (as used in this dictionary).
orig. designed by J. ∽, Engl. printer d. 1775]
'sket (bah'-) *n.* container made of plaited or
iterwoven osiers, cane, rushes, wire, etc.; ∽(ful),
uantity contained in it; (fig.) group or range of

similar things; structure resembling basket; (**type**)
∽, keybars of typewriter; net used, goal scored, in
basketball; (euphem., colloq.) bastard; ∽**ball,** (large
inflated ball used in) game played by teams of five or
six in which goal is scored when ball is thrown into net
fixed on ring 10 ft. above ground; ∽ **chair** (made of
wickerwork); ∽ (comprehensive) **clause;** ∽ **weave**
(resembling basket material in design); ∽**work,**
∽RY (5), (art of making) structure of interlaced
osiers etc. [AF & OF, AL *baskettum,* of unkn. orig.]
bā'snèt. Var. of BASINET.
bā'son. Var. (arch.) of BASIN.
Basque (băsk, bah-) *n.* & *a.* **1.** (native or language) of
Western Pyrenees. **2.** *n.* (*b*∽). short continuation of
bodice below waist; bodice having this. [F, f. L *Vasco
-onis*]
bă's-relief *n.* (sculpture in) low RELIEF². [earlier *basse
relieve,* f. It. *basso rilievo* low relief; later alt. to F form]
băss¹ *n.* (*pl.* ∽ *or* ∽'es). common perch; one of many
similar sea or freshwater fish with spiny fins. [earlier
barse f. OE *bærs,* f. MHG *bars*]
băss² *n.* inner bark of lime or palm tree used as fibre;
∽'wood, Amer. lime tree or its wood. [alt. f. BAST]
băss³ *a.* & *n.* **1.** *a.* deep-sounding; of or suited to bass
part; ∽ **clef** (placing F below middle C on second
highest line of staff); ∽ **viol,** viola da gamba,
double-bass. **2.** *n.* lowest part in harmonized music;
male voice of lowest range; singer with this voice; part
written for bass voice; low-pitched member of a
group of similar instruments; (colloq.) double-bass,
whence ∽'IST (3) *n.*; **figured** *or* **thorough** ∽, (1)
bass part with numerals etc. below to indicate the
proper harmony, (2) theory of harmony; GROUND¹
bass. [= BASE³, alt. after It. *basso*]
bă'ssèt *n.* ∽(-hound), short-legged hound for hunting
various small game. [F, dim. of *bas basse* low; see
BASE³]
bă'ssèt-hörn *n.* tenor clarinet with extended compass.
[G, transl. of F *cor de bassette* f. It. *corno di bassetto (corno
horn, di of, bassetto* dim. of *basso* BASE³)]
băssinė't *n.* hooded wicker cradle or pram. [F, dim. of
bassin BASIN]
bă'ss|ō *n.* (*pl.* ∽os *or* ∽i). man with bass voice; ∽o
ostina'to (-ah'-), = GROUND¹ *bass;* ∽o **profu'ndo,**
man with unusually deep bass voice. [It., = BASS³;
ostinato persistent, *profondo* deep]
bassoo'n *n.* bass instrument of oboe family, whence
∽IST (3) *n.*; its player; organ and harmonium stop of
similar quality. [f. F *basson* f. It. *bassone* (*basso* BASE³;
see -OON)]
basso-relievo (băsōrĕlyä'vō) *n.* (*pl.* ∽s). = BAS-
-RELIEF. [It.]
băst *n.* inner bark of lime (see BASS²); other flexible
fibrous bark. [OE *bæst* f. Gmc **bastaz*]
ba'stard (bah'-, bă'-) *a.* & *n.* **1.** *a.* born out of wedlock,
illegitimate; (of things) unauthorized, hybrid,
counterfeit; (Bot. & Zool.) closely resembling another
species; ∽ **title,** half-title; ∽ **wing,** (Zool.) rudimentary extra digit with quill-feathers. **2.** *n.* bastard
person; (S. Afr., also **bastaard**) person of mixed
race, Griqua; (colloq.) disliked or unfortunate person
or thing. [ME f. OF, f. med. L *bastardus,* perh. f. *bastum
pack-saddle; see -ARD]
bă'stardiz|e, -is|e (-īz), *v.t.* declare illegitimate;
hence ∽A'TION *n.* [f. prec. + -IZE]
ba'stardy (bah'-, bă'-) *n.* state of being bastard,
illegitimacy. [f. AF & OF *bastardie* (as BASTARD; see
-Y¹)]
băste¹ *v.t.* stitch loosely together, tack, (as preparation
for regular sewing). [ME, f. OF *bastir* sew lightly f.
Frank. **bastjan* f. Gmc **bastaz* (BAST)]
băste² *v.t.* moisten (roasting meat) with gravy or
melted fat to prevent drying. [16th c., of unkn. orig.]
băste³ *v.t.* thrash, cudgel. [perh. fig. use of prec.]
băsti'lle (-ē'l) *n.* (Hist.) fortress; prison. [ME f. OF
bastille, bastide f. Prov. *bastida* (*bastir* build); applied to
a 14th-c. prison-fortress in Paris, destroyed 1789]

băstīnā'dō n. (pl. ∽s or ∽es), & v.t. (punish or torture by) caning on soles of feet. [f. Sp. *bastonada* (*baston* BATON); see -ADO]

bă'stion n. projecting part of fortification, irregular pentagon with its base in the line (or at an angle) of the main works; similar natural rock formation; (fig.) institution serving as defence. [F, f. It. *bastione* (*bastire* build)]

băt¹ n. furry mammal of order Chiroptera flying esp. at nightfall, with forelimbs modified to carry membranous wings; **blind as a** ∽, completely blind; **have** ∽s **in the belfry**, (colloq.) be crazy or eccentric, whence BATS a.; **like a** ∽ **out of hell**, (sl.) very quickly; ∽'**wing sleeve** (with deep armhole and tight cuff). [16th c., alt. of ME *bakke* f. Scand.]

băt² n. & v. (-tt-). **1.** n. implement with handle, for striking ball in cricket, baseball, table tennis, etc.; **carry** one's ∽, (Cricket) be not out at end of side's completed innings; ‖**off** one's **own** ∽, (fig.) unaided; **right off the* ∽, immediately. **2.** act of using this; (usu. in pl.) object like table-tennis bat used to guide aircraft when taxiing; batsman (*a good* etc. *bat*). **3.** ∽'**sman**, user of cricket etc. bat, signaller using bats to guide aircraft; ∽*sman's wicket*, cricket pitch favouring batsmen; hence ∽'*smans*HIP n. **4.** v.i. use bat, have innings; (sl.) move (*along, around*, etc.). **5.** v.t. strike (as) with bat; ∽ **in**, (Baseball) effect scoring of (run) by batting. [ME, f. OE *batt* club, perh. partly f. OF *batte* club (*battre* strike)]

‖**băt**³ n. (sl.) pace of stroke or step (*went off at a rare bat*). [19th c., perh. f. BAT¹]

băt⁴ n. (sl.) spree, binge. [orig. uncert.; cf. BATTER⁴]

băt⁵ v.t. (-tt-). wink; **never** ∽**ted an eyelid**, (1) did not sleep a wink, (2) betrayed no emotion. [var. of obs. *bate* flutter]

bata'ta (-ah'ta) n. sweet POTATO. [Sp., f. Taino]

Batā'vian a. & n. (inhabitant) of ancient Batavia (between Rhine and Waal) or of modern Holland, Dutch(man). [f. L *Batavia* (*Batavi* the Batavians) + -AN]

bătch n., & v.t. **1.** n. loaves produced at one baking; quantity or number of things or persons coming at once and treated as a set; ∽ **production**, treating materials in batches, not continuously. **2.** v.t. arrange in batches. [ME, f. OE *bæcce* (*bacan* BAKE)]

bāte¹ v.t. restrain; **with** ∽**d breath**, anxiously. [f. ABATE]

‖**bāte**², ‖**bait**³, n. (sl.) rage (*was in an awful bate*). [f. BAIT¹ = state of baited person]

bă'teau (-tō) n. (pl. ∽x pr. -ōz). light river-boat, esp. flat-bottomed kind used in Canada. [F, = boat]

bă'teleur (-lêr) n. short-tailed Afr. and Arabian eagle (*Terathopius ecaudatus*). [F, = juggler]

Bā'tesian (-ts-) a. ∽ **mimicry** (in which edible species is protected by resemblance to harmful one). [f. H. W. *Bates*, Engl. naturalist d. 1892 + -IAN]

bath¹ (bahth; pl. pr. -dhz) n. **1.** immersion in liquid etc. for cleansing or therapy (*have, take, a bath*); BLOOD¹*-bath*; MUD-*bath*; SHOWER-*bath*; SUN-*bath*; TURKISH *bath*. **2.** water etc. for bathing in; surrounding medium for developing films, controlling temperature, etc. **3.** ∽(-**tub**), vessel for bathing in; BIRD-*bath*; EYE¹-*bath*. **4.** (usu. in pl.) building for bathing or swimming in. **5.** ∽ **cube**, **salts**, etc., (for softening or scenting bath-water); ***∽'**robe**, dressing-gown; ∽'**room**, room containing bath, (euphem.) lavatory. **6.** ‖**Order of the B**∽, order of knighthood, named from bath preceding knight's installation. **7.** (*B*∽). town in Avon named from hot springs; B∽ **brick**, preparation for cleaning metal; B∽ **bun**, round spiced kind with currants and icing; B∽ **chair** (wheeled, for invalid); *Bath* CHAP²; B∽ **Oliver**, unsweetened biscuit invented by Dr W. Oliver of Bath, d. 1764; B∽ **stone**, oolite building-stone. [OE *bæth*, = OHG *bad*, OS, ON *bath* f. Gmc *batham]

‖**bath**² (bahth) v. **1.** v.t. wash (child, invalid, animal,

etc.) in bath. **2.** v.i. take a bath, bath oneself. [prec.]

băth‖**e**¹ (-dh) v. **1.** v.t. immerse in liquid etc.; moist all over (*bathe* one's *eyes*); (of sunlight etc.) envelop. v.i. immerse oneself in water etc., ‖usu. as recreatic ∽'**ing beauty, belle**, attractive woman in bathin -suit; ∽'**ing-machine**, (Hist.) wheeled dressing-b drawn into sea for bathing from; ∽'**ing-su** -**costume**, garment worn when bathing. [C *bathian*, = OHG *badon*, ON *batha* f. Gmc **bath (*batham* BATH¹)]

‖**băthe**² (-dh) n. immersion in liquid, esp. in sea, riv or swimming-bath. [f. prec. 2]

bā'ther (-dh-) n. one who bathes; (in pl., Austra bathing-suit. [f. BATHE¹ + -ER¹]

bathĕ'tic a. marked by bathos. [irreg. f. Gk BATH after *pathos, pathetic*]

bă'tholith n. dome of intrusive igneous rock exten ing to unknown depth. [G, f. as foll. + -LITH]

bathŏ'mēter n. instrument used to ascertain depth water. [f. Gk *bathos* depth + -O- + -METER]

Bathō'nian a. & n. **1.** (native or inhabitant) of BAT **7. 2.** (Geol.) (of) subdivision of Jurassic typified * formations at Bath. [f. mod. L *Bathonia* Bath + -AN

bā'thŏs n. fall from sublime to commonplace; an climax; performance absurdly unequal to occasio [Gk, = depth]

bathŏ'tic a. marked by bathos. [irreg. f. prec. aft *chaos, chaotic*]

bă'thȳscăphe n. manned vessel for deep-sea divin with special buoyancy gear. [F, f. Gk *bathus* deep *skaphos* ship]

bă'thȳsphēre n. large strong submersible sphere f deep-sea observation. [f. Gk *bathus* deep + SPHERE]

batik (bă'tĭk, bătē'k) n. method (orig. in Java) printing coloured design on textiles by waxi parts not to be dyed; material so treated. [Jav., l 'painted']

bati'ste (-ē'st) n. & a. (of) fine light cotton or lin fabric like cambric. [F, f. *Baptiste* of Cambrai, fi maker]

bă't‖man n. (pl. ∽**men**; fem. ∽**woman** ∽**women**). (Mil.) officer's servant. [f. *bat* (OF *ba*(; f. Prov., f. med. L *bastum* pack-saddle) + MAN¹]

bă'ton n. staff of office, esp. field marshal's; constable (Her.) narrow truncated bend (∽ **sinister**, sign bastardy); (Mus.) conductor's wand for beati time, drum major's stick; (Horol.) short bar replaci some figures on dials. [f. F *bâton, baston* f. Ro **baston-* (**bastare* drive with stick f. LL *bastum* stick

batrā'chian (-k-) a. & n. **1.** a. of frogs and toads. **2.** & n. (one) of the Batrachia or Salientia, animals th cast off gills and tail. [f. Gk *batrakheios* (*batrakh* frog) + -AN]

băts a. (usu. pred.) (sl.) crazy. [f. BAT¹s *in the belfry*]

bă'tsman. See BAT².

battă'lion (-yon) n. large body of men in battle arr: (**God is for the big** ∽**s**, force prevails); unit infantry composed of several companies and formi part of brigade; large group of persons with simil tasks etc. [f. F *battaillon* f. It. *battaglione* (*battagl* BATTLE¹; cf. -OON)]

‖**bă'ttels** (-z) n. pl. college account at Oxford f board and provisions supplied, or for all colle expenses. [perh. f. obs. v. *battle* fatten f. obs. a. *bat* nutritious; cf. BATTEN³]

bă'tten¹ n. long narrow piece of squared timber; bar wood used for clamping boards of door etc.; strip wood carrying electric lamps; (Naut.) strip of woo or metal covering hatchway tarpaulin; hence ∽IN (6) n. [f. OF *batant* part. of *batre* beat (see BATTERY)

bă'tten² v.t. strengthen with battens; ∽ **dow** (Naut.) close (*the hatches*; see prec.). [f. prec.]

bă'tten³ v.i. feed gluttonously (*on*; grow fat; thrive, esp at expense of another. [f. ON *batna* get better (*ba* advantage)]

a'tter[1] *v.* **1.** *v.t.* & *i.* strike repeatedly so as to bruise or break (person, thing, or abs.; *against, at,* door etc.; *bout, down, in*); ~**ed baby** (with signs of repeated violence by adults); ~**ed wife** (subjected to repeated violence by her husband). **2.** *v.t.* operate against walls etc.) with artillery; (fig.) handle severely theory, person); beat out of shape, indent; ~**ing-ram,** swinging beam anciently used for breaching walls, sometimes with ram's-head end. [ME, f. AF *aterer* f. OF *batre* beat (see BATTERY)]

a'tter[2] *n.* runny mixture of flour and egg beaten up with milk or water for cooking; (Print.) area of damaged type. [ME, f. AF *batour* f. OF *bateüre (batre; ee* prec.)]

a'tter[3] *n.* (Baseball) player using bat. [f. BAT[2] + -ER[1]]

a'tter[4] *n.* (sl.) spree, binge. [19th c., orig. unkn.]

a'tter[5] *v.i.* & *n.* (have) receding slope from ground upwards. [ME, of unkn. orig.]

a'ttery *n.* **1.** (Law). infliction of blows, or of any menacing touch to clothes or person (esp. in phr. *issault and battery).* **2.** (Mil.) emplacement for one or more guns on land or ship; artillery unit of guns and men and vehicles. **3.** set of connected similar units of quipment; portable cell(s) supplying electricity; Psych.) series of tests, series of cages, etc., in which hens are confined for intensive laying, or poultry or cattle reared and fattened; (Baseball) pitcher and catcher. f. F *batterie (bat(t)re* strike f. L *battuere;* see -ERY)]

a'tting *n.* In vbl senses; cotton fibre prepared in heets for quilts etc. [f. BAT[2] + -ING[1]]

a'ttle[1] *n.* **1.** fight, esp. between large organized forces **do** ~**, join** ~**,** enter into combat; PITCH[2]*ed battle;* ~**royal,** battle in which several combatants or all available forces engage, free fight, (fig.) heated argument); victory in fighting (*the battle is to the strong; outh is half the* ~**,** a great help); (fig.) contest (*battle f wits).* **2.** ~**axe,** medieval or prehistoric weapon, colloq.) domineering or formidable (usu. middle-aged) woman; ~**cruiser,** heavy-gunned ship of higher speed and lighter armour than battleship; ~**cry,** war-cry, slogan; ~**dress,** soldier's etc. everyday uniform of blouse and trousers; ~ **fatigue,** = COMBAT *fatigue;* ~**field,** ~**ground,** scene of battle; ~**ship,** most heavily armed and armoured warship, designed to meet the most powerful ships in battle. ME, f. OF *bataille* f. Rom. **battalia* f. LL *battualia* pl. gladiatorial exercises f. L *battuere* beat; see -LE 2]

a'ttle[2] *n.* **1.** *v.i.* struggle (*with* or *against* difficulties, waves, opponent, etc., *for* one's rights etc.). **2.** *v.t.* ight (one's way etc.); **battle with.* [f. F *batailler bataille;* see prec.)]

a'ttledore (-teld-) *n.* **1.** (Hist.) wooden instrument ike canoe paddle used in washing, baking, etc. **2.** small racket used with shuttlecock in the game of ~ **and shuttlecock.** [15th c., perh. f. Prov. *batedor* beater (*batre* beat)]

a'ttlement (-tlm-) *n.* (usu. in *pl.*) alternately high and low parapet at top of wall, for defence of puilding; roof enclosed by this (*walking on the battle-ments*); hence ~ED[2] *a.* [f. OF *bataillier* furnish with amparts + -MENT]

a'ttue (bătū', -oo') *n.* driving of game by beaters cowards sportsmen; shooting-party on this plan; wholesale slaughter. [F, fem. p.p. (as *n.*) of *battre* beat . L *battuere*]

a'tty *a.* (sl.) crazy. [f. BAT[1] + -Y[2]]

atwoman. See BATMAN.

au'ble *n.* showy trinket; (Hist.) jester's emblem; trifle, toy; thing of no worth. [ME f. OF *ba(u)bel* child's toy, of unkn. orig.]

aud (bôd) *n.* unit of telegraphic signalling speed, corresp. to one dot etc. per second. [f. J. M. E. *Baudot,* Fr. engineer d. 1903]

au'haus (bow'hows) *n.* (principles of) a German school of architectural design (1919–33). [G (*bau* building, *haus* house)]

baulk[1,2]. See BALK[1,2].

bau'xite *n.* earthy mineral containing varying proportions of alumina, the chief commercial source of aluminium; hence **bauxi'tic** *a.* [F, f. *Les Baux* near Arles in S. France + -ITE[1] (2)]

bawbee (-ē', baw'-) *n.* (Sc.) halfpenny. [f. name of the laird of *Sillebawby,* 16th-c. Scots mint-master]

bawd *n.* procuress. [f. ME *bawdstrot* f. OF *baude(s)-tro(y)t* procuress]

baw'd|y *a.* & *n.* humorously indecent (talk); ~**y-house,** brothel; hence ~**iLY**[2] *adv.,* ~**iNESS** *n.* [f. prec. + -Y[2]]

bawl *v.t.* & *i.* speak or weep at top of voice; ~ **out,** (colloq.) reprimand severely. [imit.; cf. med. L *baulare* bark, Icel. *baula* (Sw. *böla*) to low]

bay[1] *n.* **1.** kind of laurel, esp. *Laurus nobilis;* (in *pl.*) wreath of its leaves won by conquerors or poets; fame as hero or poet. **2.** ~**berry,** fragrant W. Indian tree (*Pimenta acris*); ~**leaf,** (usu. dried) leaf of *L. nobilis* used as flavouring; ~ **rum,** perfume (esp. for the hair) distilled from rum and bayberry leaves. [f. OF *baie* f. L *baca* berry]

bay[2] *n.* part of sea filling wide-mouthed opening of land; recess in mountain range; ~ **salt,** salt crystals from evaporation of sea-water; **Bay State,* Massachusetts. [ME, f. OF *baie* f. OSp. *bahia*]

bay[3] *n.* division of wall between columns or buttresses; recess or compartment (**sick-**~**,** part of ship's deck used as hospital, any quarters for sick persons); partitioned or marked space forming a unit (*unloading bay*); space added to room by advancing window from wall line (~ **window,** window filling such space, (sl.) protuberant abdomen); ||railway line at station, ending in cul-de-sac and acting as starting--point or terminus for side-line, platform adjoining this. [ME, f. OF *baie* (*ba(y)er* gape f. med. L *batare*)]

bay[4] *n.* deep bark of large dog or of hounds in pursuit, esp. chorus raised as they draw close to quarry; **at** ~**,** in desperate situation; **bring to** ~**,** come close to (quarry); **hold, keep,** at ~**,** keep at a distance; **stand at** ~**,** turn against pursuers. [ME f. OF (*a*)*bai* f. *bayer; bayer* bark f. It. (*ab*)*baiare,* of imit. orig.]

bay[5] *v.i.* & *t.* (Of large dog) bark or howl (at). [ME f. OF (*a*)*baiier* bark f. It. (*ab*)*baiare,* of imit. orig.]

bay[6] *a.* & *n.* reddish-brown (horse) with black mane and tail. [f. OF *bai* f. L *badius*]

bayadère (-dār') *n.* Hindu dancing-girl (esp. at S.--Indian temple); striped textile fabric. [F, f. Port. *bailadeira* dancer)]

Bay'ard *n.* chivalrous person. [f. Seigneur de ~, Fr. soldier d. 1524]

bay'onet *n.* & *v.t.* **1.** *n.* stabbing blade attachable to rifle-muzzle; ~ **plug** etc., electric etc. plug with push-and-twist engagement of parts to prevent detachment by simple pull. **2.** *v.t.* stab with bayonet. [f. F *baïonnette,* perh. f. *Bayonne* in SW France, where first made; cf. -ET[1]]

bay'ou (bī'oo) *n.* marshy offshoot of river etc. in southern US. [Amer. F; cf. Choctaw *bayuk*]

bazaar' (-zār') *n.* oriental market; large shop selling fancy goods; sale of goods for charity. [f. Pers. *bāzār,* prob. through Turk. and It.]

*bazoo' *n.* (sl.) mouth. [19th c.; orig. unkn.]

bazoo'ka *n.* crude trombone-like musical instrument; anti-tank rocket-gun of similar form. [arbitr. name; cf. prec.]

BB *abbr.* double-black (pencil-lead).

*BBB *abbr.* Better Business Bureau.

BBC *abbr.* British Broadcasting Corporation; ~ **English** (standard upheld by BBC announcers).

bbl. *abbr.* barrels (esp. of oil).

BC *abbr.* BEFORE Christ; British Columbia; British Council.

BCE *abbr.* before the COMMON[1] Era.

BD *abbr.* Bachelor of Divinity.

Bde. *abbr.* (esp. Mil.) Brigade.

bde'llium (d-) *n.* (tree esp. of genus *Commiphora*

yielding) resin used as perfume etc. [L, f. Gk *bdellion* rendering Heb. *bᵉdhōlah*]

Bdr. *abbr.* Bombardier.

BDS *abbr.* Bachelor of Dental Surgery.

be(bē, bĭ) *v.* (*pres. ind.*: 1 **am** *pr.* ăm *or* am; 2 **art** (arch.) *pr.* ārt *or* ert; 3 **is** *pr.* iz; *pl.* & 2 *sing.* **are** *pr.* ār *or er*, *or* **be** (arch.; *powers that be*); *past ind.*: 1 and 3 **was** *pr.* wŏz *or* woz; 2 **wast** (arch.) *pr.* wŏst *or* wost, *or* **wert** (arch.) *pr.* wĕrt *or* wert; *pl.* & 2 *sing.* **were** *pr.* wĕr *or* wār *or* wer; *pres. subj.* **be**; *past. subj.* **were**, exc. 2 *sing.* **wert** (arch.); *imper.* **be**; *pres. part.* **being** *pr.* bē'ing; *p.p.* **been** *pr.* bēn *or* bĭn; colloq. abbr. forms: **'m** = *am*, **'s** = *is*, **'re** = *are*; **aren't** (ārnt) = *am not* (interrog.), *are not*; **isn't** (ĭ'zent) = *is not*; **wasn't** (wŏ'zent) = *was not*; **weren't** (wĕrnt *or* wārnt) = *were not*; **ain't** (colloq.) = *am not*, (vulg. or joc.) = *is not, are not.* **1.** (As full verb) exist, occur, live, (often with *there*; *God is, there is a God*; *there is a green hill far away*; *I think, therefore I am*; *can such things be?*; **to be or not to be,** should existence be terminated? (f. Shak. *Hamlet* III. i. 56); **Miss X that was,** her maiden name being X; **for the time being,** = *for the* PRESENT²; **be that as it may,** no matter what is the fact concerning that); remain, continue, (LET³ *it be*); (w. *adv.* or *adv. phr.*) occupy position in space or time (*is in the garden*; *her birthday is on Tuesday*), take or direct oneself (*be off!*; *are you for London?*; *is from Canada*), experience condition (*he is better today*), occupy oneself (*what are you about?*; *mice have been at the food*), hold view (*I am for, against, capital punishment*), (in perf. tenses) go (to place etc.) (*has been to Rome, in the matter*); (w. ind. obj.) befall (*woe is me*); (in *p.p.*, colloq.) called, visited, (*has anyone been?*); **been (and gone) and,** (colloq. phr. expr. protest or surprise; *you have been and moved my papers!*). **2.** (As cop. v., with *n.*, *a.*, or *adj. phr.*) have state or quality (*I am a man*; *he is ill*; *be of good courage*; *be quick about it*); coincide in identity with (*you are the man I want*; *today is Thursday*; *it is I*, colloq. *it is me*); (emphat.) form main constituent of (*Kingsley Martin was the 'New Statesman'*); amount to (*twice two is four*); cost (*how much are these pears?*); signify (*it is nothing to me*); act the part of (*Miss X is Desdemona*). **3.** (As aux. v.) (with *p.p.* of *v.t.* forming passives) (*this was done*); (arch., with *p.p.* of *v.i.* such as *fall, come, flee, grow,* forming perf. tenses) (*the sun is set*; *Babylon is fallen*); (with *pres. part. act.* forming progressive tenses act. and pass.) (*he is building a house*; *am leaving tomorrow*; *the house was building*); (with *pres. part. pass.* forming progressive tenses pass.) (*the house was being built*); (w. inf. expr. duty (*I am to inform you*), intention (*he is to be there*), possibility (*the house is to let*; *it was not to be found*), destiny (*they were never to meet again*)); *were* (w. inf. in hypothesis) (*if I were,* or *were I, to tell you*). **4. be-all (and end-all)** *n.*, whole being or essence (*of*); **be-in** *n.*, (sl.) usu. spontaneous meeting of hippies etc. in public place; **-to-be** *a.*, future (*his bride-to-be*). [*am, is,* f. Gmc **es-*; past forms f. Gmc **wes-*; *be, been, being* f. OE *bēon* f. IE **beu-*; *are, art* f. Gmc **ar-*]

be- *pref.* forming *vbs.* **1.** (to *v.t.*) all over, all round, (*beset, bemoan*). **2.** (to *v.t.*) thoroughly, excessively, (*begrudge, belabour*). **3.** (to *v.i.*, expr. transitive action) (*bemoan, bestride*). **4.** (to *a.* or *n.,* expr. transitive action) (*befool, befoul*). **5.** (to *n.*) = to call (so and so). **6.** (to *n.*) = to surround with, to affect with, to treat in the manner of, (*becloud, befriend*). **7.** (to *n.*, w. suf. *-ED²*) = having (*bejewelled, beribboned, bespectacled, bewigged*). [OE *be-,* weak form of *bī* BY¹ prep. & adv., as used in *bygone, by-law, byword,* etc.]

BE *abbr.* Bachelor of Education; Bachelor of Engineering; bill of exchange.

Be *symb.* beryllium.

BEA *abbr.* British Epilepsy Association; (formerly) British European Airways.

beach *n.*, & *v.t.* **1.** *n.* sea-shore or lake-shore covered with pebbles or sand; part of shore between high- and low-water marks. **2.** (arch.) water-worn pebbles or sand. **3.** **~-ball,** large inflated ball for games on beach;

∼**'comber,** (1) white man in Pacific Islands etc. wh lives by collecting jetsam, longshore vagrant, (2) lor wave rolling in from sea; ∼**-head,** fortified positic established on beach by landing forces [after *bridg head*]; ∼ **plum,** (edible fruit of) maritime N. Ame shrub (*Prunus maritima*). **4.** *v.t.* run or haul up (shi whale, etc.) on shore. [16th c., of unkn. orig.]

||**beach-la-mar'** *n.* commercial jargon English used W. Pacific. [corrupt. f. Port. *bicho do mar* BÊCHE-D -MER]

bea'con *n.* **1.** signal or signal-fire on pole or hi ||conspicuous hill suitable for this. **2.** signal statio radio station whose signal helps to fix position of sh or aircraft or spacecraft. **3.** signal light; guide warning; ||amber globe on pole marking some pede trian crossings. [OE *bēacn,* = OS *bōkan,* OHG *bouhhe* f. WG **baukna*]

bead¹ *n.* small rounded usu. perforated object f threading with others on string or wire, sewing o fabric, etc. (**tell** one's ∼**s,** use beads of rosary etc. i counting prayers); drop of liquid, bubble; small kno in foresight of gun (**draw a ∼ on,** take aim at); inn edge of pneumatic tyre gripping rim of whee (Archit.) moulding like a series of beads, or narro moulding of semicircular section; ∼**-roll,** list names, long series, (orig. of persons to be prayed for ∼**'sman** (-z-), (Hist.) pensioner bound to pray fo benefactor, almsman. [orig. 'prayer' (for which ori used), OE *gebed,* = OS *beda,* OHG *beta,* Goth. *bida,* Gmc **bedh-*; see BID¹]

bead² *v.* **1.** *v.t.* furnish with beads; string together. *v.i.* form or grow into beads. [f. prec.]

bea'ding *n.* in vbl senses; bead of tyre; (Archit.) BEAD¹. [f. BEAD¹,²+-ING¹]

||**bea'dle** *n.* ceremonial officer of church, college, ci company, etc.; (Hist.) parish officer appointed b vestry to keep order in church, etc.; (Sc.) church of cer attending on the minister; hence ∼-DOM (-deld *n.,* stupid officiousness, ∼-SHIP (-delsh-) *n.* [ME f. C bedel f. Rom. **bidellus,* of Gmc orig.; see -LE 1]

bea'dy *a.* (Of eyes) small and bright; covered wit beads or drops. [f. BEAD¹+-Y²]

bea'gle *n.* small hound, used for hare-hunting who field follows on foot; spy, informer, constabl **bea'gling,** hunting with beagles. [ME, f. C *beegueule* noisy person, prob. f. *beer* open wide+*gueu* throat]

beak¹ *n.* bird's horny projecting jaws (esp. in bird o prey, and when strong and hooked); similar mandible -end of other animals, e.g. turtle; hooked nose; pro jection at prow of ancient warship; spout; henc (-)∼ED² (-kt) *a.* [ME f. OF *bec* f. L *beccus,* of Cel origin]

||**beak²** *n.* (sl.) magistrate; schoolmaster. [19th c prob. f. thieves' cant]

bea'ker *n.* lipped cylindrical glass vessel for scientifi experiments; tumbler-shaped plastic vessel for drink ing from; tall wide-mouthed pottery drinking-vesse found in graves of European Bronze Age **B∼ Folk** (arch. or literary) large drinking-cup. [ME, f. O *bikarr* = OS *bikeri,* OHG *behhari* f. pop. L **bicariu* perh. f. Gk *bikos* drinking-bowl]

beam¹ *n.* **1.** long piece of squared timber or of meta supported at both ends, used in houses, ships, etc., (i **in** one's **eye,** fault great compared to another's; se Matt. 7:3); cylinder in loom on which warp or cloth i wound; chief timber of plough; bar of balance; shan of anchor; lever in engine connecting piston-rod an crank; main stem of stag's antlers; (in *pl.*) horizonta cross-timbers of ship supporting deck and joinin sides (**on her ∼-ends,** on her side, almost capsizing **on** one's **∼-ends,** (fig.) near end of resources); side o ship (*land on the port beam*); ship's breadth (**broad i the ∼,** (colloq.) having wide hips); *beam*-COMPASS* (es). **2.** ray or pencil of radiation; this as guide t aircraft or missile; course so indicated (**off a ∼,** (colloq.) mistaken; **on the ∼,** (colloq.) on the righ

For other words in be- *see* BE-.

track); directional flow of particles; radiance; bright look, smile. [OE *bēam* tree, = OS *bām*, OHG *boum* f. WG **bauma*; cf. ON *bathmr*, Goth. *bagms*]

beam² *v.* **1.** *v.t.* emit (light, affection, etc.); direct (radio signals etc., and fig.) *at*; hence ~ER¹ *n.*, (Cricket) ball bowled at batsman's head. **2.** *v.i.* shine; smile radiantly; hence ~ING² *a.* [f. prec.]

bea'my̆ *a.* (Of ship) broad-beamed. [f. BEAM¹ + -Y²]

bean *n.*, & *v.t.* **1.** *n.* (seed, used as food, of) leguminous plant bearing smooth usu. kidney-shaped seeds in long pods; **full of** ~s, (colloq.) in high spirits; **give** person ~s, (sl.) punish or scold him; **not a** ~, (sl.) no money; ||OLD *bean*; SPILL¹ *the beans*. **2.** similar seed of other plants (e.g. cocoa, coffee); *(sl.)* head. **3.** ~'pole, (fig.) tall thin person; ~'stalk, stem of bean plant. **4.** Hence *~'ERY *n.*, cheap restaurant. **5.** *v.t.* *(sl.) hit on head. [OE *bēan*, = OHG *bōna*, ON *baun* f. **baunō*]

||bea'nfeast *n.* employer's annual dinner given to employees; (colloq.) festival, celebration, merry time. [f. prec. + FEAST, beans and bacon being regarded as indispensable dish]

bea'nie *n.* small close-fitting hat worn on back of head. [perh. f. BEAN 'head' + -IE]

||bea'nō *n.* (*pl.* ~s). (sl.) beanfeast. [abbr. + -o]

bear¹ (bār) *n.* **1.** thick-furred plantigrade mammal of family Ursidae (**Great B**~, **Little B**~, constellations near north pole; **the B**~, Russia; **like a** ~ **with a sore head,** (colloq.) ill-tempered; **loaded for** ~, *(colloq.) fully prepared); child's toy like this animal (cf. TEDDY 2); rough, unmannerly, or uncouth person; (St. Exch.) one who sells for future delivery hoping to buy cheaper meanwhile (cf. BULL¹) [perh. w. ref. to selling bear's skin before killing bear]. **2.** ~-baiting, (Hist.) setting dogs to attack captive bear; ~'garden, (fig.) scene of tumult; ~-hug, powerful embrace; ~'leader, (fig.) rich young man's travelling tutor; ~ market (with falling prices); ~'s-breech, (Bot.) kind of acanthus; ~'s-ear, auricula; ~'s-foot, a hellebore (*Helleborus fetidus*); ~'s-grease, (arch.) pomade; ~'skin, (wrap etc.) of bear's skin, Guards' tall furry cap; *B~ State, Arkansas; hence ~'ish¹ *a.* [OE *bera*, = OHG *bero*, f. WG **bero*]

bear² (bār) *v.* (St. Exch.) **1.** *v.i.* speculate for a fall. **2.** *v.t.* produce fall in price of (stocks etc.). [f. prec.]

bear³ (bār) *v.* (bore, arch. bare; borne or born; in pass. born is used w. ref. to birth, but borne by w. name of mother). **1.** *v.t.* (poet. or formal). carry. **2.** carry visibly, show, be known by, (banner, device, arms, the marks *of*, name, relation or ratio *to*); ~ (away or off), win (prize etc.); ~ oneself (behave) well etc. **3.** bring something needed (*bear witness*; *bear person company*); ~ a hand, help. **4.** exercise (office, rule); carry in the mind (*bear a grudge*); ~ in mind, not forget. **5.** wear; ~ arms (as soldier, or of heraldic arms). **6.** (in *p.p.*). (in *comb.*) carried or transported by (AIR¹*borne*); be borne away (by external force or influence; or internal impulse); is borne in upon one, becomes one's conviction (*that*). **7.** ~ out, confirm (story etc.), confirm account etc. given by (person). **8.** sustain (weight, responsibility, cost); ~ a part in, share. **9.** stand (test etc.), endure (GRIN *and bear it*); (usu. w. neg. or interrog.) tolerate, put up with, (*cannot bear him*), admit of; hence ~'ABLE *a.* **10.** be fit for (*his language won't bear repeating*). **11.** ~ up, uphold, (abs.) not despair, (Naut.) sail to leeward; ~ with, treat forbearingly, tolerate patiently. **12.** give birth to; produce, yield (*land bears crops*, and abs.); ~ fruit, (fig.) have results. **13.** *v.i.* thrust, strive, apply weight, tend; diverge (*right, to the left*, etc.); ~ down, exert downward pressure; ~ down on, move rapidly or purposely towards; ~ hard on, oppress; ~ (up)on, be relevant to; bring to ~, apply, aim (gun etc.). [OE *beran*, = OS, OHG *beran*, ON *bera*, Goth. *bairan* f. Gmc **ber-* f. IE **bher-*]

beard¹ *n.* **1.** hair of man's lower face (excluding WHISKERS and MOUSTACHE); OLD *man's beard*. **2.** chin tuft of animal; gills of oyster; byssus of mollusc; beak--bristles of birds (*bearded* TIT¹); awn of grass. **3.** Hence ~ED², ~LESS, *adjs.* [OE, = OHG *bart* f. WG **bardha*]

beard² *v.t.* oppose openly, defy; ~ the lion in his den, (fig.) openly attack person on his own subject etc. [f. prec.]

bear'die *n.* (colloq.) bearded man. [f. BEARD¹ + -IE]

bear'er (bār'-) *n.* person or thing that carries or helps to carry; Indian palanquin-carrier (Hist.) or personal servant; carrier of equipment on safari etc.; bringer of letters or message; presenter of cheque; possessor of shares; (good etc.) ~, plant etc. that produces (well etc.). [f. BEAR³ + -ER¹]

bear'ing (bār'-) *n.* **1.** In vbl senses. **2.** outward behaviour; bodily attitude; endurability (*past bearing*). **3.** heraldic charge or device. **4.** relation, reference, aspect, (*consider it in all its bearings*; *what is the bearing of this on the argument?*). **5.** (usu. in *pl.*) part of machine that bears the friction, esp. between rotating shaft and its housing; BALL¹-*bearings*. **6.** direction in which a place etc. lies; (in *pl.*) relative position; have lost my ~s, do not know where I am. **7.** ~-rein, fixed rein from bit to saddle forcing horse to arch its neck. [f. BEAR³ + -ING¹]

Béarnai'se (bā-; -z) *a.* ~ sauce, rich usu. tarragon-flavoured white sauce. [F, fem. of *béarnais* of *Béarn* in SW France]

beast *n.* (esp. wild) animal (*beast of* BURDEN¹, *of* PREY¹); quadruped (*man and beast*); domesticated bovine animal; brutal man; disliked person or thing; the B~, Antichrist (mark of the B~, sign of heresy or evil nature); the ~, animal nature in man; hence ~IE *n.*, (Sc. or joc.) small animal. [ME, f. OF *beste* f. Rom. *besta* f. L *bestia*]

*beastings. See BEESTINGS.

bea'stl|y̆ *a.* **1.** like a beast or its ways; foul; sensual. **2.** unfit for human use, dirty; (colloq.) unpleasant, undesirable. **3.** Hence ~iNESS *n.* [f. BEAST + -LY¹]

bea'stly⁰ *adv.* (sl.) very (esp. of bad things), regrettably, (*beastly drunk, wet; raining beastly hard*). [f. BEAST + -LY²]

beat¹ *v.* (beat; BEATEN, or beat esp. in senses 3 and 4). **1.** *v.t.* & *i.* strike repeatedly (~ the air, strive in vain; ~ one's breast, in mourning or woe); remove dust from (carpet) by beating; knock loudly at door etc.); make (path) by trampling. **2.** inflict blows on; (of sun, rain, etc.) strike persistently (*on*, or abs.). **3.** *v.t.* overcome, surpass; ~ the band, (sl.) surpass everything; beat the CLOCK¹; ~ person to it, to the punch, etc., get there first (lit. or fig.); can you beat it? (sl., expr. surprise or amazement). **4.** exhaust (DEAD *beat*); be too hard for, perplex. **5.** *v.t.* & *i.* (of wings) move up and down; move rhythmically (*heart etc. beats or is beating*); ~ time, mark or follow time of music with baton, foot, etc. **6.** *v.i.* (Phys.) create BEAT² 4; (Naut.) sail to windward. **7.** *v.t.* shift, drive, alter, shape, deform, by blows; strike (bushes, water) to rouse game; ~ (up), make (eggs etc.) into frothy smooth mixture by vigorous stirring etc.; ||~ the bounds, mark parish boundaries by striking certain points with rods; ~ one's brains, search for ideas. **8.** *v.i.* & *t.* play on drum; *beat to* QUARTER¹s; *beat a* RETREAT; ~ it, (sl.) go away. **9.** ~ about, search (*for* excuse etc.); ~ about the bush, approach subject indirectly; ~ down, bargain with (seller), cause seller to lower (price); ~ in, crush; ~ off, drive back (attack etc.); ~ out, forge (metal), *defeat (one's competitors); ~ up, thrash (person) severely, collect (recruits etc.). [OE *bēatan* = OHG *bōzan*, ON *bauta* f. Gmc **bautan*]

beat² *n.* **1.** stroke on drum, signal so given. **2.** (Mus.) movement of conductor's baton; principal recurring accent; interval between two such accents. **3.** measured sequence of strokes or sounds; throbbing; strongly marked rhythm of popular music. **4.** (Phys.) pulsation due to combination of two sounds or electric currents of (slightly) different frequencies.

5. sentinel's or policeman's appointed course; area covered by this; one's habitual round. **6.** sportsman's area traversed in search of game. **7.** *(sl.) **the ~ of,** something surpassing (*did you ever see the beat of that?*). **8.** *(Journ.) scoop. [f. prec.]

beat³ *n.* & *a.* (one) of the ~ **generation** (young people with unconventional dress and behaviour as expression of social philosophy). [prob. f. p.p. of BEAT¹]

bea'ten *a.* In vbl senses; worn; (~ **track,** well-trodden way, lit. or fig.); shaped by the hammer; exhausted, dejected. [p.p. of BEAT¹]

bea'ter *n.* In vbl senses; person employed to rouse game; implement for beating carpets, eggs, etc. [f. BEAT¹ + -ER¹]

bēati'f¦ic *a.* making blessed; (colloq.) blissful (*beatific smile*); hence ~ICALLY *adv.* [f. F *béatifique* or f. L *beatificus* (*beatus* blessed; see -FIC)]

bèatifica'tion *n.* making or being blessed; (RC Ch.) first step to canonization, announcement that dead person is in bliss. [F, or f. eccl. L *beatificatio* (as foll.; see -ATION)]

bèa'tify *v.t.* make happy; (RC Ch.) announce beatification of. [f. F *béatifier* or f. eccl. L *beatificare* f. L *beatus* blessed; see -FY]

bea'ting *n.* In vbl senses; chastisement (*take a beating*); defeat (**take some, a lot of,** ~, be difficult to surpass). [f. BEAT¹ + -ING¹]

bèa'titūde *n.* blessedness; (in *pl.*) the declarations of blessedness in Matt. 5: 3–11; patriarchal title in Orthodox Church. [F, or f. L *beatitudo* (*beatus* blessed; see -TUDE)]

bea'tnik *n.* member of the BEAT³ generation. [f. BEAT³ + -*nik* after *sputnik*, perh. infl. by US use of Yiddish -*nik* agent-suf.]

beau (bō) *n.* (*pl.* ~x or ~s, *pr.* bōz). fop, dandy; ladies' man, admirer; *boy-friend, lover. [F, = handsome, f. L *bellus*]

Beau'fort (bō'f-) *n.* ~ **scale,** scale of wind speed ranging from 0 (calm) to 12 (hurricane over 73 m.p.h.). [f. Sir F. ~, Engl. admiral d. 1857]

beau geste (bō zhě'st) *n.* display of magnanimity. [F, = splendid gesture]

beau idé'al (bō-) *n.* one's highest or ideal type of excellence or beauty. [F *beau idéal* = ideal beauty, often misunderstood in E as = beautiful ideal; see BEAU, IDEAL]

Beau'jolais (bō'zholā) *n.* red or white burgundy wine from *Beaujolais* district of France.

beau mo'nde (bō maw'nd) *n.* fashionable society. [F]

Beaune (bōn) *n.* red burgundy wine from *Beaune* district of France.

beaut (būt) *n.* & *a.* (Austral., NZ, & US; sl.) beautiful (person or thing). [abbr. of BEAUTY]

beau'teous (bū'-) *a.* (rhet.) beautiful. [ME, f. BEAUTY + -OUS, after *bounteous, plenteous*]

beauti'cian (būti'shan) *n.* one who runs a beauty parlour; specialist in beauty treatment. [f. BEAUTY + -ICIAN]

beau'tiful (bū'-) *a.* delighting the eye or ear (*beautiful face, voice*); gratifying any taste (*beautiful poem, picture, roast beef, batting, batsman*); morally or intellectually impressive, charming, or satisfactory, (*beautiful patience, organization, specimen*; *~ **letters,** *belles-lettres*); hence ~LY² *adv.*, (esp., colloq.) excellently (*beautifully warm*; *that will do beautifully*). [f. BEAUTY + -FUL]

beau'ti¦fy (bū'-) *v.t.* make beautiful; adorn; hence ~FICA'TION, ~fIER¹ (1, 2), *ns.* [f. foll. + -FY]

beau'ty (bū'-) *n.* **1.** combination of qualities, as shape, proportion, colour, in human face or form, or in other objects, that delights the sight (~ **is only skin deep,** one cannot judge by appearances); combined qualities delighting the other senses, the moral sense, or the intellect. **2.** beautiful person or thing; exceptionally good specimen (*here is a beauty*); beautiful woman; beautiful feature, ornament, (**the ~ of it,** the particular point that gives satisfaction). **3.** ~ **parlour,**

establishment in which the art or trade of face massage, hairdressing, manicuring, applying cos metics, etc. is carried on; ~ **queen,** woman judgec most beautiful in a competition; ~ **sleep** (before midnight); ~ **spot,** (1) small patch placed or woman's face as foil to complexion, (2) beautifu locality; ~ **treatment,** use of cosmetics etc. tc enhance person's beauty. [ME, f. AF *beuté*, OF *bealté beauté*, f. Rom. *bellitas f. L (as BEAU); see -TY¹]

beaux. See BEAU.

beaux arts (bōz ār') *n.* & *a.* **1.** *n. pl.* fine arts. **2.** *a.* o classical decorative style maintained esp. in 19th c. by **École des Beaux-Arts** in Paris. [F *beaux-arts*]

beaux yeux (bōz yěr') *n.* person's favour; **for the ~ of,** just to gratify (-person). [F, = fine eyes]

bea'ver¹ *n.* (*pl.* same or ~s). amphibious broad-tailec soft-furred rodent of genus *Castor*, able to cut dowr trees and build dams, (**eager ~,** (colloq.) (over-) zealous person); its light-brown fur; hat of this; ~ (**cloth**), heavy woollen cloth like beaver fur B~**board,** (*P) kind of fibreboard; ~ **lamb,** lamb' wool made to look like beaver fur. [OE *be(o)for*, = OHG *bibar,* ON *bjórr* f. Gmc *bebruz f. IE **bhebhrú (*bhru* brown)]

bea'ver² *n.* (Hist.) lower face-guard of helmet. [f. OI *baviere* bib (*baver* slaver f. *beve* saliva f. Rom. *baba)]

bea'ver³ *n.* (sl.) bearded man. [20th c.; orig. uncert.]

bea'ver⁴ *v.i.* ~ **away,** work hard at. [f. BEAVER¹]

bē'bŏp *n.* kind of jazz music, with complex harmony and highly syncopated rhythm; hence ~pER¹ (3) *n* [imit. of typical phr.]

bèca'lm (-ah'm) *v.t.* (usu. in *pass.*) deprive (ship) o wind. [f. BE- 6 + CALM¹]

bèca'me. See BECOME.

bècau'se (-ŏ'z) *adv.* & *conj.* **1.** *adv.* by reason, or account, (*of*). **2.** *conj.* for the reason that, inasmucl as, since. [ME, f. BY¹ prep. + CAUSE¹, after OF *pai cause de* by reason of]

bèccafi'cò (-fē'-) *n.* (*pl.* ~s). small migrant bird eater in Italy. [It. *beccafico* peck, *fico* fig)]

béchamel (bě'sh-) *n.* kind of fine white sauce. [in vented by Marquis de B~, Fr. courtier d. 1703]

bêche-de-mer (bāshdemār') *n.* (*pl.* same or *bêches-pr.* same). **1.** holothurian animal eaten as a delicacy ir China. **2.** beach-la-mar. [F, alt. of *biche de mer* f. Port *bicho do mar* sea-worm]

běck¹ *n.* (N. Engl.) brook, mountain stream. [ME, f. ON *bekkr* f. Gmc *bakkiz]

běck² *n.* (literary) significant gesture, nod, etc.; the order implied by such gesture; **at** person's ~ **anc call,** having to obey his orders instantly. [f. *beck* v. f. BECKON]

bě'cket *n.* (Naut.) contrivance for rope-loop, hook, bracket, etc., for securing loose ropes, tackle, or spars [18th c.; orig. unkn.]

bě'ckon v. **1.** *v.t.* summon, call attention of, by gesture. **2.** *v.i.* make mute signal (*to* person). [OE *bīecnan bēcnan,* = OS *bōknian,* OHG *bouhnen* f. WG *baukniar (*baukna* BEACON)]

bèclou'd *v.t.* cover with clouds; obscure. [f. BE-6 + CLOUD 1]

bèco'm¦e (-ŭ'm) v. (**beca'me; beco'me**). **1.** *v.i.* come into being; **what has ~e of** (happened to) **him? 2.** (As cop. v., with *n., a.,* or *adj. phr.*) begin to be (*became known; became Prime Minister*). **3.** *v.t.* suit, befit (*it ill becomes you to complain*); adorn, look well on; hence ~ING² *a.* [OE *becuman* = OHG *biqueman,* Goth. *biquiman* f. Gmc **bi-* BE- + *kweman COME]

bě'cquerël (-ker-) *n.* (Phys.) unit of radioactivity, corresp. to one disintegration per second. [f. A. H. *Becquerel,* Fr. physicist d. 1908]

bĕd¹ *n.* **1.** thing to sleep or rest on; mattress (*feather bed* etc.); framework with mattress and coverings; animal's resting place, litter; use of bed; being in bed. **2.** ~ **and board,** (1) lodging and food, (2) connubia relations; ~ **and breakfast,** sleeping accommoda tion and food next morning, as offered to hotels etc.;

~ **of roses,** easy position; ~ **of sickness,** invalid state; **brought to** ~ (in childbirth, *of* child, or abs.); DIE² *in* one's *bed*; **go to** ~, retire for the night, (fig.) have sexual intercourse **with,** (of newspaper) go to press; **has got out of** ~ **on the wrong side,** is bad-tempered for the day; KEEP¹ one's *bed*; **lie in the** ~ one **has made,** accept consequences of one's acts; **make the** ~, arrange its coverings for further use; NARROW *bed*; **put to** ~, cause (child, newspaper, etc.) to go to bed; **take to** one's ~, become ill and have to remain in bed. **3.** *bed*BUG; ~'**chamber,** (arch. exc. in titles of sovereign's attendants) bedroom; ~'**clothes,** sheets, pillows, blankets, etc.; ~'**fast,** bedridden; ~'**fellow,** sharer of bed, (fig.) associate; ~'**jacket** (worn when sitting up in bed); ~**-linen,** sheets and pillowcases; ||~'**maker,** person tending rooms in college, hotel, etc.; ~'**pan,** invalid's utensil for urination or defecation when in bed; ~'**post,** upright support of bed (*between you and me and the* ~*post,* in strict confidence); ~**-rest,** confinement of patient to bed; ~**-ridden,** confined to bed by infirmity, (fig.) decrepit, [OE *bedreda* (*ridan* ride)]; ~'**roll,** (US & NZ) bedding rolled into a bundle; ~'**room,** room for sleeping in (sometimes w. ref. to sexual intimacy: ~*room comedy* etc.); ~'**side,** side of esp. invalid's bed; ~*side book* (for reading in bed); *good* ~*side manner* (of tactful doctor); ||~**-si'tting-room,** (colloq.) ~**-si'tter,** (sl.) ~**-si't,** combined bedroom and sitting-room; ~'**sock,** warm sock worn in bed; ~'**sore** (developed in invalid by lying in bed), ~'**spread,** cloth or sheet put over bed during day etc. when not in use; ~'**stead,** framework of bed; ~'**straw,** herbaceous plant of genus *Galium* once used as straw for beds, esp. (*Our*) *Lady's* ~*straw* (yellow-flowered species); ~'**table** (for use by person sitting up in bed); ~'**time,** hour for going to bed; ~**-wetting,** nocturnal enuresis. **4.** flat base on which anything rests; ~'**plate,** metal plate forming base of machine. **5.** garden bed (to be) filled with plants; place where osiers etc. are grown. **6.** bottom of sea, river, etc.; ~'**rock,** solid rock underlying alluvial deposits etc., (fig.) ultimate facts or principles of a theory, character, etc. **7.** foundation of road or railway; slates etc. of billiard-table. **8.** stratum; layer of oysters etc. [OE *hed*(*d*), = OS *hed, heddi,* OHG *betti,* Goth. *badi* f. Gmc **badhjam*]

bed² *v.t.* & *i.* (**-dd-**). **1.** ~ (**down**), put or go to bed; (fig.) have sexual intercourse in bed. **2.** *v.t.* ~ (**out**), plant in a garden bed. **3.** *v.t.* cover up or fix firmly in something. **4.** *v.t.* & *i.* arrange as, be or form, a layer. [OE *beddian* (*bedd*; see prec.)]

B.Ed. *abbr.* Bachelor of Education.

bedă'bble *v.t.* stain or splash with dirty liquid, blood, etc. [f. BE- 1 + DABBLE]

bedad' *int.* (Ir.) by God! [corrupt.; cf. GAD¹]

bedau'b *v.t.* smear with paint etc.; bedizen. [f. BE-1 + DAUB 1]

bedaz'zle *v.t.* completely dazzle; confuse (person); hence ~MENT (-zelm-) *n.* [f. BE- 2 + DAZZLE 1]

be'ddable *a.* sexually attractive. [f. BED² + -ABLE]

be'dder *n.* in vbl senses; plant suited for garden bed; ||(colloq.) college bedmaker. [f. BED² + -ER¹]

be'dding *n.* In vbl senses; mattress, bedclothes, etc.; litter for cattle, horses, etc.; bottom layer; (Geol.) (esp. visible) stratification; ~ **plant** (suitable for garden bed). [f. BED² + -ING¹]

bede'ck *v.t.* adorn. [f. BE- 1 + DECK²]

bede'guar (-gär) *n.* mosslike excrescence on rose-bush produced by insect's puncture. [f. F *bédegar* f. Pers. *bād-āwar* wind-brought]

||**bedel(l)** (bē'del, bedē'l) *n.* university official with chiefly processional duties. [= BEADLE]

bede'vil *v.t.* (||-ll-). treat with diabolical violence or abuse; possess, bewitch, spoil, confound; plague, afflict; hence ~MENT *n.* [f. BE- 6 + DEVIL¹]

bedew' *v.t.* cover or sprinkle with dew or dewlike water. [f. BE- 6 + DEW¹]

Be'dford *n.* ~ **cord,** woven fabric with prominent ridges in direction of warp. [~ in England]

bedi'ght (-ī't) *a.* (arch.) arrayed, adorned. [ME, p.p. of *bedight* v. (BE- 1; see DIGHT)]

bedi'm *v.t.* (**-mm-**). make (eyes, mind) dim. [f. BE- 4 + DIM 1]

bedi'zen *v.t.* deck out gaudily. [f. BE- 2 + obs. *dizen* deck out]

be'dlam *n.* madhouse; scene of uproar; hence ~ITE¹ (1) *n.*, (arch.) insane person. [f. hospital of St. Mary of *Bethlehem* in London]

Be'dlington *n.* ~ (**terrier**), narrow-headed sporting terrier with fairly long curly grey hair. [~ in Northumberland]

be'd(o)uin (-ōō-) *n.* (*pl.* same) & *a.* (Arab) of the desert; wandering (person). [ME, f. OF *beduin* ult. f. Arab. *badwiyyīn* (obl. case) dwellers in the desert (*badw* desert)]

bedra'ggle *v.t.* wet (dress etc.) by trailing it, or so that it trails or hangs limp; (esp. in *p.p.*) make (person) untidy or dishevelled. [f. BE- 2 + DRAGGLE]

Beds. *abbr.* Bedfordshire.

bee *n.* **1.** four-winged stinging social insect collecting nectar and pollen and producing wax and honey; insect of similar type; busy worker; **meeting for combined work or amusement; SPELLING-bee*; **have a** ~ **in** one's **bonnet,** be obsessed on some point. **2.** ~**-bread,** (honey and) pollen used as food by bees; ~**-eater,** bright-plumaged bird of family Meropidae; ~'**hive,** artificial habitation for bees, (fig.) domed structure resembling this, busy place; ~**-line,** straight line between two places, esp. if quickly traversed; ~**-master,** keeper of bees; ~ **orchis** (with bee-shaped flowers); ~'**s knees,** (sl.) something outstandingly good; **bee'swax** (-z-), WAX¹ secreted by bees as comb material, and used to polish wood; **bee'swing** (-z-), filmy second crust on old port wine. [OE *bēo,* = OHG *bīa,* ON *bý* f. Gmc **bīon*]

||**Beeb** *n.* (colloq.) the BBC. [abbr.]

beech *n.* smooth-barked glossy-leaved mast bearing forest tree of genus *Fagus*; ~('**wood**), its wood; (Austral.) one of various similar trees; ~**-fern,** kind of polypody; ~**-marten,** white-breasted marten found in S. Europe and Asia; ~'**mast,** fruit of beech; hence ~EN⁵, ~'Y², *adjs.* [OE *bēce* f. Gmc **bōkjōn*]

beef *n.* & *v.* **1.** *n.* (*pl.* ~s). flesh of ox, bull, or cow; (in person) size, muscle. **2.** (usu. in *pl.* **beeves** *pr.* -vz, or **~s*). ox(en), esp. fattened, or their carcasses. **3.** (sl., *pl.* ~s). complaint, protest. **4.** ~'**burger,** hamburger; **~'cake,* (sl.) display of sturdy masculine physique; ||~'**eater,** (colloq.) warder in Tower of London, or Yeoman of the Guard, [f. obs. sense 'well-fed menial']; ~'**steak,** thick slice of beef from hindquarters for grilling etc. (~*steak fungus,* red edible fungus resembling beef); ~ **tea,** stewed beef juice for invalids; ~**-wood,** red timber of various Austral. and W. Ind. trees. **5.** *v.i.* (sl.) complain. **6.** *v.t.* ~ **up,** (sl.) reinforce, strengthen. [ME, f. AF, OF *boef* f. L *bos bovis* ox]

bee'fy *a.* like beef; solid, muscular; hence ~iNESS *n.* [f. prec. + -Y²]

Bee'lzebub *n.* the Devil. [OE f. L, f. Gk *beelzeboub* & Heb. *ba'al z⁵būb* lord of flies, name of Philistine god]

been. See BE.

beep *n.,* & *v.i.* **1.** *n.* sound of motor-car horn; short high-pitched sound of various devices. **2.** *v.i.* emit beep; hence ~ER¹ *n.,* device emitting beep. [imit.]

beer *n.* alcoholic liquor (esp. of lighter kinds) from fermented malt etc. flavoured with hops etc.; glass of this (*two beers, please*); other fermented drink (GINGER *beer,* ROOT¹ *beer*); *beer and* SKITTLES; **small** ~, (lit.) weak beer, (fig.) trifling matters; **think** no **small** ~ **of,** have high opinion of; ~**-engine** (for drawing beer up from barrel or cellar); ~ **garden,** ~ **hall,** etc., (where beer is served); ||~'**house** (licensed for beer, not spirits); ~**-mat,** small table-mat for beer-glass; hence ~'Y² *a.,* (esp.) betraying influence of beer. [OE *bēor*, = MDu. *bēr*, OHG *bior*, WG, f. LL *biber* drink f. L *bibere*]

bee′stings, *bea′-, (-z) *n. pl.* first milk (esp. of cow after calving). [OE **bēsting* (*bēost*, OHG *biost*, of unkn. orig.)]

beeswax, beeswing. See BEE.

beet *n.* plant of genus *Beta* with succulent root (SUGAR--*beet*); (or ||~′root), root of beet, esp. crimson root of garden beet as vegetable. [OE *bēte*, = LG *beete*, OHG *bieza*, WG, f. L *beta*, perh. of Celt. orig.]

bee′tle[1] *n.* tool with heavy head and handle for ramming, crushing, driving wedges, etc.; machine for finishing cloth e.g. by beating; ~-**brain** etc., blockhead. [OE *bētel* f. Gmc **bautilaz* (**bautan* BEAT[1]; see -LE 1)]

bee′tle[2] *n.*, & *v.i.* **1.** *n.* insect of order Coleoptera, having front wings converted to hard wing-cases closing over back wings; (pop.) large black insect of this kind; (pop.) similar insect; **black-~**, common cockroach. **2.** short-sighted person; dice game in which beetle-figure is drawn or assembled; ~-**crusher**, large boot or foot. **3.** *v.i.* ~ **off**, (sl.) depart. [OE *bitula* biter (*bītan* BITE[1])]

bee′tle[3] *a.* projecting, shaggy, scowling, (*beetle brows*, *beetle-browed*). [ME, of unkn. orig.]

bee′tle[4] *v.i.* (Of brows or cliffs) overhang. [f. prec.]

bee′troot. See BEET.

beeves. See BEEF.

bee′zer *n.* (sl.) nose; person. [20th c.; orig. uncert.]

||BEF *abbr.* (Hist.) British Expeditionary Force.

befa′ll (-aw′l) *v.* (befe′ll; ~en). **1.** *v.i.* happen. **2.** *v.t.* happen to (person etc.). [OE *befeallan* (as BE- 2, *feallan* FALL[1])]

befi′t *v.t.* (-tt-). suit, be fitted or appropriate for; be incumbent on; hence ~tING[2] *a.* [f. BE- 2 + FIT[4]]

befo′g *v.t.* (-gg-). envelop in fog; confuse; obscure. [f. BE- 6 + FOG[2] 1]

befoo′l *v.t.* delude, make fool of. [f. BE- 4 + FOOL[1] 1]

befo′re *adv.*, *prep.*, & *conj.* **1.** *adv.* ahead (*go before*); in the front (*before and behind*); earlier than the time in question, already (*have heard this before*); in the past (*long before*). **2.** *prep.* in front of; ahead of; under the impulse of (*before the wind*; *recoil before the attack*; *carry all before you*); in presence of (*appear before judge*; *bow before authority*; ~ **God**, as God sees me, used as solemn asseveration); awaiting (*the future before them*); earlier than (~ **Christ**, (of date) reckoned backwards from birth of Jesus Christ); earlier than the coming of (future event); farther on than; rather than (*would starve before stealing*). **3.** *conj.* earlier than the time when; rather than that (*would starve before he stole*). [OE *beforan*, = OS *biforan*, OHG *bifora* f. Gmc *bi-*BY[1] + **forana* from the front (**fora* FOR)]

befo′rehand (-ôr′h-) *adv.* in anticipation; in advance; in readiness; **be** ~ **with**, anticipate, forestall. [ME, f. prec. + HAND[1]; cf. AF *avant main*]

befou′l *v.t.* make foul (lit. or fig.). [f. BE- 4 + FOUL[1]]

befrie′nd (-rĕ′nd) *v.t.* act as friend to; help, favour. [f. BE- 6 + FRIEND]

befu′ddle *v.t.* make drunk; confuse. [f. BE- 3 + FUDDLE 1]

beg *v.* (-gg-). **1.** *v.t.* ask for (food, money, etc., or abs.) as gift; ~ one's **bread**, live by begging. **2.** *v.i.* ask (*for* alms etc.); live by alms; (of dog) sit up with forepaws raised expectantly. **3.** *v.t.* & *i.* ask earnestly or humbly (thing, *for* thing, *of* person, person *to* do, *of* person to do, *that* something may be done; *begged to be allowed out*); ask formally (*beg leave*; *beg* PARDON[1]); take leave to do (*I beg to differ, enclose, announce,* etc.). **4.** ~ **off**, get (person) excused penalty etc., decline to take part etc.; ~ **the question**, assume truth of thing to be proved or thing equivalent to it, (pop.) evade difficulty; **go (a-)~ging**, (fig., of opportunity etc.) find no accepter, be unwanted. [ME, prob. f. OE *bedecian* f. Gmc **bedh-* base of BID[1]]

begă′d *int.* (colloq.) by God! [corrupt.] cf. GAD[1]]

begă′n. See BEGIN.

begă′t. See foll.

begĕ′t (-g-) *v.t.* (-tt-; bego′t, (arch.) bega′t; bego′tten). procreate (usu. of father, sometimes of father and mother); give rise to, occasion, (*beget doubt, strife*); hence ~tER[1] *n.* [OE *begietan*, = OS *bigetan* seize, OHG *bigezzan* receive; f. as BE- 1 + GET[1] procreate]

bĕ′ggar[1] *n.* one who begs; one who lives by begging; poor person (~**s must not** or **cannot be choosers** must take what is offered); (colloq.) person, fellow (*insolent beggar*; *poor little beggar!*). [ME, f. BEG + -AR[3]]

bĕ′ggar[2] *v.t.* reduce to poverty; outshine; exhaust resources of (*beggar description*); ~-**my-neighbour** card-game in which player seeks to capture opponent's cards (also fig. of national policy etc.). [f. prec.]

bĕ′ggarl|y̆ *a.* needy, poverty-stricken; intellectually poor; mean, sordid; ungenerous; hence ~iNESS *n.* [f. BEGGAR[1] + -LY[1]]

bĕ′ggary̆ *n.* extreme poverty. [f. BEGGAR[1] + -Y[1]]

bĕ′ghard (-gerd) *n.* (Hist.) male counterpart of BÉGUINE[1]. [f. med. L *beghardus* f. OF *bégard* (as BÉGUINE[1]; see -ARD)]

begi′n (-g-) *v.* (-nn-; bega′n; begu′n). **1.** *v.t.* perform first part of (*begin work*; *begin crying*; *begin to cry*; *it has begun to be done*, *it has been begun*); ~ **school**, attend it for first time. **2.** come to do at a certain time (*begin to feel ill*; *food was beginning to decay*; *this is beginning to get wearisome*). **3.** (colloq.) show any attempt or likelihood to (*can't*, *does not*, *begin to compete with him*). **4.** *v.i.* be the first to do something; take the first step (**beginning student*); start speaking; be begun (*meeting will begin at 7*); come into being, arise; have its commencement, nearest boundary, etc., (at some point in space or time); ~ **at**, start from; ~ (**up)on**, set to work at; ~ **with**, take first or as starting-point; **to** ~ **with**, as the first thing, in the first place. [OE *beginnan*, = OS, OHG *biginnan*, WG f. *bi-* BE- + Gmc **-ginnan*, of unkn. orig.]

begi′nner (-g-) *n.* in vbl senses; one just beginning to learn a skill etc.; ~'s **luck**, good luck supposed to attend beginner at games etc. [f. prec. + -ER[1]]

begi′nning (-g-) *n.* In vbl senses; time at which anything begins; source, origin; first part; **the** ~ **of the end**, first clear sign of final result. [f. BEGIN + -ING[1]]

begi′rd (-g-) *v.t.* (begir′t). (literary; esp. in *p.p.*) gird round, encircle. [OE *begyrdan* (as BE- 1, GIRD[1])]

bego′ne (-ŏ′n, -aw′n) *v.* (in *imper.* & *inf.* only). go away immediately. [f. BE + GONE]

bego′nia *n.* plant of genus *Begonia*, with coloured perianth but no petals, and often with brilliant foliage also. [f. M. *Bégon*, Fr. patron of science d. 1710 + -IA[1]]

begŏ′rra *int.* (Ir.) by God! [corrupt.]

begŏ′t(ten). See BEGET.

begri′me *v.t.* make grimy. [f. BE- 1 + GRIME 2]

begru′dge *v.t.* feel or show dissatisfaction at (thing); envy (person) the possession of. [f. BE- 2 + GRUDGE 1]

begui′le (-gī′l) *v.t.* delude; cheat (person *of*, *out of*, *or into* doing); charm, amuse; divert attention from (toil, passage of time); hence ~MENT (-gī′lm-) *n.* [f. BE- 2 + obs. *guile* to deceive]

béguine (bāgē′n) *n.* member of Netherlands religious lay sisterhood not bound by vows. [ME f. OF, f. L (le) *Bègue* 12th-c. priest who founded the order; cf. -INE[3]]

bĕgui′ne[2] (-gē′n) *n.* dance of W. Ind. orig.; its rhythm. [Amer. F, f. F *béguin* infatuation]

bĕ′gum (bā′-) *n.* Indian Muslim lady of high rank. [Urdu *begam* f. E. Turk. *bīgam* princess fem. of *big* prince; cf. BEY]

beha′lf (-ah′f) *n.* **on** or ***in** ~ **of,** in the interest of (person, principle, etc.), as representative of. [mixture of earlier phrs. *on his halve* and *bihalve him*, both = on his side; see BY[1], HALF]

behā′ve *v.i.* & *refl.* **1.** *v.i.* act or react (in specified way);

~ **towards**, treat (*well* etc.); ill-~d, well-~d, having bad, good, manners or conduct. **2.** (Of machine etc.) work (*well* etc.); (esp. to or of child) conduct oneself with propriety. **3.** *v. refl.* (esp. of or to child) show good manners. [f. BE- 2 + HAVE¹]

bĕhā'viour, *-ior, (-vyer) *n.* deportment, manners; way of conducting oneself (**be on** one's **good** or **best** ~, take care to behave well when being observed or tested); moral conduct, treatment shown to or towards others; way in which ship, machine, substance, etc., acts or works; (Psych.) response to stimulus (~ **therapy**, treatment of neurotic condition by gradual training to react normally); hence ~AL *a.* (~**al science**, study of human behaviour). [f. prec. after *demeanour* and obs. *haviour* f. *have*]

bĕhā'viour|ism, *-ior|-, (-vyer-) *n.* (Psych.) study of human actions by analysis into stimulus and response; doctrine that such study is the only valid method in psychology; hence ~IST (2) *n.,* ~i'stic *a.* [f. prec. + -ISM]

bĕhea'd (-hĕ'd) *v.t.* cut off the head of; kill thus. [OE *behēafdian* (be- (from) about, *hēafod* HEAD¹)]

bĕhĕ'ld. See BEHOLD.

bĕhĕ'moth *n.* enormous creature. [ME, f. Heb. *bᵉhēmōt* intensive pl. of *bᵉhēmāh* beast, perh. f. Egyptian *p-ehe-mau* water ox]

bĕhĕ'st *n.* (literary) command [OE *behǣs* f. Gmc *bihaissi- (*bi- BE-, *haitan bid, call)]

bĕhī'nd *adv., prep.,* & *n.* **1.** *adv.* & *prep.* in or to the rear (of); ~ person's **back**, without its knowledge, **put** ~ **one**, refuse to consider. **2.** on farther side (of); hidden (by) (*what is behind that remark?*); behind the SCENES. **3.** towards one's rear (*glance behind before moving off*); farther back in space or time (than; ~ **the times**, antiquated; **come from** ~, win after lagging; **fall** or **lag** ~, not keep up); past in relation to (*all that trouble is behind me*). **4.** in support of (*the man behind the project*); in an inferior position (to); remaining after departure of oneself (*leave behind*) or of others (*remain or stay behind*), later than; (~ **schedule** or **time**, unpunctual; in the tracks of; in arrear (*with payments* etc.). **5.** *n.* buttocks (Austral. Nat. Football) kick etc. scoring one point. [OE *behindan, bihindan* (*bi* BY¹, *hindan* from behind, *hinder* below = OHG *hintana* behind, Goth. *hintana* beyond)]

bĕhī'ndhănd (-d-h-) *adv.* & *pred. a.* in arrear (*with or in payments* etc.); out of date, behind time. [f. prec. + HAND¹; cf. BEFOREHAND]

behŏ'ld *v.t.* (*behĕld*) (arch. or literary), see, become aware of by sight; (in *imper.*, calling attention) behold, *a pale horse*; hence ~ER¹ *n.* [OE *bihaldan* (as BE- 2, *haldan* hold)]

bĕhŏ'lden *pred. a.* under obligation (*to*). [p.p (obs exc. in this use) of prec., − bound]

bĕhŏŏ'f *n.* (arch.) benefit, advantage (*to, for, on, (the) behoof of*). [OE *behōf*, = MDu. *behoef*, MHG *behuof*, WG (*bi- BE-, *hōf- cogn. w. HEAVE¹)]

bĕhŏŏ've, *bĕhŏŏ've, *v.t. impers.* be incumbent on (person) *to* (do something); (w. neg. etc.) befit (*it ill behoves me to complain*). [OE *behōfian* (*behōf*; see prec.)]

beige (bāzh) *n.* & *a.* (of) yellowish-grey colour of undyed and unbleached wool. [F, of unkn. orig.]

beigel. Var. of BAGEL.

bĕ'ing *n.* In vbl senses; existence (in ~, existing); constitution, nature, essence; anything (esp. person) that exists (**the Supreme B~**, God). [f. BE +-ING¹]

bĕjā'bers, bĕjā'bbers, (-z) *int.* (Ir.) by Jesus! [corrupt.]

bĕjew'elled, *-eled, (-ōōeld) *a.* adorned with jewels. [f. BE- 7 +JEWEL +-ED²]

bĕl *n.* unit used in comparison of power levels in electrical communication or intensities of sound, corresponding to an intensity ratio of 10 to 1; cf. DECIBEL. [f. A. G. *Bell*, Amer. inventor of telephone d. 1922]

|bĕlā'bour (-ber). ***bĕlā'bor,** *v.t.* thrash (lit. or fig.); labour (a subject). [f. BE- 2 +LABOUR² (exert one's strength)]

bĕlā'tĕd *a.* coming (too) late; overtaken by darkness. [p.p. of obs. *belate* delay (BE- 4, LATE¹)]

bĕlay' *v.t.,* & *n.* **1.** *v.t.* fix (running rope) round cleat, pin, rock, etc., to secure it; ~ (**there**)!, (Naut. sl.) stop!, enough!; ~**ing-pin**, fixed wooden or iron pin for belaying on. **2.** *n.* (spike of rock used for) act of belaying. [f. Du. *beleggen*]

bĕl ca'ntō (-ă'-, -ah'-) *n.* singing with full rich broad tone and accomplished vocal technique. [It., = fine song]

bĕlch *v.* & *n.* **1.** *v.i.* emit wind noisily from stomach through mouth. **2.** *v.t.* (Of gun, chimney, volcano, etc.) send out or up; utter forcibly. **3.** *n.* act of belching. [OE *belcettan* or *belcan*]

bĕ'lcher *n.* (arch.) neckerchief with white spots on blue ground. [f. J. *Belcher*, Engl. pugilist d. 1811]

bĕ'ldam(e) *n.* (arch.) old woman, hag; virago. [f. ME & OF *bel* beautiful + DAM², DAME]

bĕlea'guer (-ger) *v.t.* besiege (lit. or fig.). [f. Du. *belegeren* camp round (as BE- 6, *leger* a camp)]

bĕ'lemnīte *n.* tapering sharp-pointed fossil bone of extinct cuttlefish. [f. mod. L *belemnites* f. Gk *belemnon* dart +-ITE¹ (2)]

bel esprit (bĕl ĕsprē') *n.* (*pl.* **beaux esprits** *pr.* bōz ĕsprē'). witty person. [F, lit. fine mind]

bĕ'lfry *n.* bell tower, attached to church etc. or separate; bell space in church tower; BAT¹s *in the belfry.* [ME, f. OF *berfrei* f. Frank. *bergfridh-, prob. f. *hergan protect + *frithuz peace; alt. by assoc. w. *bell*]

Bĕ'lgian (-jən) *a.* & *n.* (native or inhabitant) of Belgium; ~ **hare**, dark-red long-eared breed of domestic rabbit. [f. *Belgium* + -AN]

Bĕ'lgic *a.* of the ancient Belgae of N. Gaul; of the Low Countries. [f. L *Belgicus* (*Belgae*; see -IC)]

Bĕlgrā'vi|a *n.* fashionable residential part of London S. of Knightsbridge; hence ~AN *a.* & *n.* [f. *Belgrave* Square in this district (*Belgrave* in Leicestershire) + -IA¹]

Bĕ'lial *n.* the Devil. [f. Heb. *bᵉliyya'al* worthless]

bĕli'e *v.t.* (**bely'ing**). give false notion of; fail to fulfil (promise etc.); fail to justify (hope etc.); fail to corroborate. [OE *belēogan* (as BE- 3, *lēogan* LIE²)]

bĕlie'f *n.* trust or confidence (*in*); acceptance of any received theology; acceptance of (thing, fact, statement, etc.) as true or existing (*belief in his honesty, that he is honest*; **beyond** ~, incredible; **to the best of my** ~, in my genuine opinion; thing believed; religion; firm opinion (*it is my belief that he did it*). [ME, f. OE *gelēafa* (as foll.)]

bĕlie'v|e *v.* **1.** *v.i.* have faith in (arch. *on*). **2.** put trust in truth of (statement), efficacy of (principle or system), advisability of (practice), existence of (thing). **3.** suppose, think, (*Mr Smith, I believe?*). **4.** Hence ~ER¹ *n.,* (esp.) adherent of a specified religion (OLD *Believer*); so ~ING² *a.* **5.** *v.t.* accept truth of (statement etc.); ~**e it or not, would you** ~**e it?**, (colloq.) it is surprising though true. **6.** accept veracity of (person); ~**e one's ears, eyes**, etc., accept that what one apparently hears, sees, etc., is true. **7.** be of opinion that; suppose, think, (*is believed to be in Rome*); **make** ~**e**, pretend (*to do or that*). **8.** Hence ~ABLE *a.* [OE *belȳfan, belēfan*, w. change of pref. f. *gelēfan*, = OS *gilōbian*, OHG *gilouben*, Goth. *galaubjan* f. Gmc *glaubjan hold dear, f. same root as LIEF]

bĕli'ke *adv.* (arch.) probably; perhaps. [f. BY¹ + LIKE¹ as n. = likelihood]

|Beli'sha (-ē'sha) *n.* ~ **beacon**, as BEACON 3 (marking pedestrian crossing). [f. L. Hore-*Belisha* d. 1957, Minister of Transport 1934]

bĕli'ttle *v.t.* make small, dwarf; depreciate; hence ~MENT (-tlm-) *n.* [f. BE- 4 + LITTLE]

bĕll¹ *n.* **1.** hollow object of cast metal in deep cup shape widening at lip made to emit clear musical sound when struck. **2.** stroke of bell, (Naut.) **one to eight** ~**s**, half-hours of watch; (Boxing etc.) signal for start or end of round. **3.** bell-shaped object or part; flower corolla (BLUE¹*bell*; CANTERBURY *bell*); any object designed to emit bell-like sound for calling attention etc.; (in *pl.*, Mus.) instrument like glockenspiel. **4. bear away the** ∼, be first, win; ∼, **book, and candle** (in allusion to eccl. cursing formula); **sound or clear as a** ∼, quite sound or clear (in other senses besides the acoustic). **5.** ∼**-bird,** one of various S. Amer. and Austral. birds with bell-like note; ∼**-bottomed,** (of trousers) bell-shaped below knee; *∼'boy,** page in hotel or club; ∼**-buoy** (with warning bell rung by waves' motion); *bell*-COT[1]; ∼**-flower,** herbaceous plant of genus *Campanula*; ∼**-founder, -founding, -foundry,** caster, casting, and manufactory, of large bells; ∼**-glass** (bell--shaped as cover for plants); ∼**-heather,** plant *Erica cinerea* or *E. tetralix*; *∼'hop,** (sl.) bellboy; ∼**s of Ireland,** plant (*Molluccella laevis*) with green bell--shaped calyx; ∼**-jar,** bell-shaped glass to cover instruments or contain gas in laboratory; ∼'**man,** (Hist.) town crier; ∼**-metal,** alloy of copper and tin (with more tin than in bronze) for bells; ∼**-pull,** cord or handle attached to bell-wire; ∼**-punch** (for punching ticket and making ringing sound at same time); ∼**-push,** button to operate electric bell; ∼**-ringer, -ringing,** (of church bells or handbells with changes etc.); ∼**-tent,** conical tent with central pole; ∼**-wether,** leading sheep of flock with bell on neck, ringleader; ∼**-wire,** wire pulled at door etc. to sound a bell. [OE *belle*, = MDu., MLG *belle*; a LG wd perh. related to BELL[3]]

bell[2] *v.* **1.** *v.t.* furnish with bell(s); ∼ **the cat,** take the danger of a common enterprise on oneself [f. fable of cat and mice]. **2.** *v.i.* widen *out* like bell lip. [f. prec.]

bell[3] *n.*, & *v.i.* (make the) cry of stag or buck at rutting--time. [OE *bellan* bark, bellow, = OHG *bellan*; cf. ON *belja* and BELLOW]

belladō'nna *n.* **1.** (Bot.) deadly nightshade, a poisonous plant (*Atropa belladonna*) with purple flowers and purple-black berries. **2.** (Med.) drug prepared from this. **3.** ∼ **lily,** S. Afr. amaryllis with white or pink flowers. [mod. L f. It., = fair lady, perh. because a cosmetic is made from it]

belle *n.* handsome woman; reigning beauty (*the belle of the ball, of New York*). [F, f. L *bella* fem. of *bellus* pretty]

belle époque (bĕl ĕpŏ'k) *n.* period of settled and comfortable life preceding war of 1914–18. [F, = fine period]

belle laide (bĕl lā'd) *n.* (*pl.* **belles laides** *pr.* same). woman who is ugly but fascinatingly so. [F (*belle* beautiful, *laide* ugly, fem. adjs.)]

belles-lettres (bĕl-lĕ'tr) *n. pl.* (occas. treated as *sing.*) studies or writings of the purely literary kind, (esp.) essays, criticisms, etc.; hence **bĕllĕ'trĭsM** (2), **bĕllĕ'trĭsT** (3), (-l-l-) *ns.*, **bĕllĕtrĭ'stĭc** (-l-l-) *a.* [F, = fine letters]

bĕllic|ōse *a.* inclined to fighting; hence ∼o'sĭTY *n.* [ME, f. L *bellicosus* (*bellum* war; see -IC, -OSE[1])]

bĕlli'gerence, -ency, *ns.* pugnacious behaviour; status of a belligerent. [f. foll.; see -ENCE, -ENCY]

bĕlli'gerent *a.* & *n.* (nation, party, or person) waging regular war as recognized by the law of nations; of such nation etc.; any opponent engaged in conflict; pugnacious. [f. L *belligerare* wage war (*bellum* war, *gerere* wage); see -ENT]

bĕ'llow (-ō) *v.* & *n.* **1.** *v.i.* roar like a bull; shout or roar with pain. **2.** *v.t.* utter loudly and usu. angrily. **3.** *n.* bellowing sound. [ME, of uncert. orig.; perh. related to BELL[3]]

bĕ'llows (-ōz) *n. pl.* (occas. treated as *sing*). **1.** portable or fixed contrivance for driving blast of air into a fire or through pipes of organ, reeds of harmonium, etc.; **pair of** ∼ (two-handled form for fire). **2.** expansible part of camera etc. [ME, prob. f. OE *belga* pl. of *bel[i]g*, *bæl(i)g* BELLY[1], abbr. of *blæstbel(i)g* blowing-bag]

bĕ'lly[1] *n.* **1.** cavity of human body below diaphragm with stomach and bowels and other contents, abdomen; front surface of body from waist to groin; womb; corresponding parts of animals. **2.** stomach; body as

needing food; appetite, gluttony. **3.** cavity of any thing, bulging part (concave or convex); front, inner or lower surface; surface of violin etc. across whic strings pass. **4.** ∼**ache,** (*n.*) colic, (*v.i.*, sl.) complai whiningly; ∼**-band** (below horse's belly, holdin shafts etc. in place); ∼**-button,** (colloq.) nave ∼**-dance,** oriental solo dance by woman, with muc abdominal movement; ∼**-flop,** (*n.*, & *v.i.*, colloq. dive landing flat on belly; ∼**-landing,** crash-landin of aircraft on belly without use of undercarriage ∼**-laugh,** deep unrestrained laugh. [OE *belig, bæl(i)g bag* (**balg-*, **belg-* swell)]

bĕ'lly[2] *v.t.* & *i.* ∼ (**out**), (usu. of sails) swell out. [prec.]

bĕ'llyful (-ŏŏl) *n.* as much as or more than one want of anything. [f. BELLY[1] + -FUL 2]

bĕlŏ'ng *v.i.* **1.** be rightly assigned *to* (as duty, righ possession, natural or usual accompaniment, exampl in classification, characteristic, part, member, in habitant, appendage); ∼ **to,** be member of (club household, grade of society, etc.). **2.** *be resident in o connected *with*. **3.** be rightly placed or classified (*in under,* etc.); fit a specified environment etc. [ME, app an intensive, f. BE- 2, of ME *longen* belong f. OE *langian* (*gelang* at hand)]

bĕlŏ'ngĭngs (-z) *n. pl.* person's movable property o luggage; (colloq.) person's relatives etc. [f. prec. + -ING[1]]

Bĕlŏrū'ssian, Byĕlŏ-, (-shan) *a.* & *n.* (native or lan guage) of Belorussia in western USSR. [f. *Belorussi* f. Russ. *Belorussiya* (*belyi* white, *Russiya* Russia) + -AN

belŏ'ved (as *a.* or *n.* usu. -ŭ'vĭd, as *p.p.* -ŭ'vd) *p.p., a., & n.* **1.** *p.p.*, & *a.* dearly loved (*of* or *by,* or abs.). **2.** *n.* beloved person. [f. obs. vb *belove* f. BE- 2 + LOVE[2]]

below (-ō') *adv.* & *prep.* **1.** *adv.* at or to a lower point downstream; downstairs (esp. Naut., **go** ∼, fron deck); (rhet.) on earth, in hell. **2.** *adv.* in lower rank (*th judge in the court below*); at foot of page, or in later par of book or article. **3.** *prep.* lower than; *below* PAR[1] STAIRS; *temperature is 20 below* (*freezing-point*). **4.** down stream from; further south than; at or to greate depth than; covered by, lower in amount, degree etc., than (*below* one's BREATH); of lower rank than unworthy of. [f. *be* BY[1] + LOW[1] *a.*]

bĕl pae'se (-ahā'zā) *n.* rich white mild creamy chees orig. from Italy. [It., = fair country]

bĕlt[1] *n.* **1.** encircling strip of cloth, leather, etc., wor round waist or baldric-wise to confine or suppor clothes or weapons etc.; ∼ **and braces** (w. ref. t policy of twofold security); **hit below the** ∼, figh unfairly; TIGHTEN one's *belt*; **under** one's ∼, eaten, o otherwise secured; SEAT-*belt*. **2.** belt worn as mark o rank by earl or knight, or by champion at boxing expert in judo, etc. **3.** strip of colour, special surface trees, etc., round or on anything; region (*cotton, wheat fever, commuter, belt*; GREEN[1] *belt*); flexible strip carryin machine-gun cartridges; endless strap connectin pulleys, whence ∼'ING[1] (3) *n.*; (sl.) heavy blow; *∼ line, *∼'way,* etc., railway or road around city [OE, = OHG *balz,* ON *belti* f. Gmc **baltjaz, *baltjōn f. L *balteus*]

bĕlt[2] *v.* **1.** *v.t.* put belt round; fasten on with belt; marl with belt of colour etc.; thrash with belt; hit hard; ∼ **out,** (sl.) utter forcibly. **2.** *v.i.* (sl.) rush; ∼ **up** (colloq.) wear seat-belt, (sl.) be quiet. [f. prec.]

Bĕ'ltāne *n.* (ancient Celtic festival on) May Day. [Gael. *bealltainn*]

bĕlu'ga (-lŏŏ'-) *n.* large kind of sturgeon; caviare from it; white whale. [f. Russ. *beluga, belukha* (*belyi* white)]

bĕ'lvēdēre *n.* raised turret or summer-house to view scenery from. [It. (*bel* beautiful, *vedere* see)]

bĕly'ing. See BELIE.

BEM *abbr.* British Empire Medal; bug-eyed monster.

bĕ'ma *n.* platform in ancient Athenian public assembly; reading platform in synagogue; sanctuary in Orthodox Church. [Gk]

For other words in *be-* **see** BE-.

emīr'e v.t. cover or stain with mud; (in pass.) be stuck in mud. [f. BE- 6 + MIRE¹]

emoa'n v.t. weep or express sorrow for or over. [f. BE- 3 + MOAN²]

emū'se (-z) v.t. stupefy; make (person) confused. [f. BE- 2 + MUSE²]

en¹ n. (Sc.) inner room (usu. of two-roomed cottage); **but and ~**, outer and inner rooms, cottage having only these. [ellipt. use of ben adv., within (OE binnan), BUT¹ outside]

en² n. (Sc.) mountain peak; high mountain. [f. Gael. beann]

ench n., & v.t. **1.** n. long seat of wood or stone; seat across boat. **2.** judge's seat; office of judge; lawcourt (||Queen's, King's, B~, division of High Court); (collect.) judges, magistrates; **on the ~**, serving as judge or magistrate. **3.** ||(Parl.) seat appropriated to certain group etc. (FRONT, BACK¹-, CROSS-, bench). **4.** *seat used by players not participating in a game for the time being. **5.** working-table in carpenter's shop, laboratory, etc. **6.** level ledge in masonry or earthwork, on hill-slope, etc. **7.** ~-mark, mark cut in rock etc. by surveyors to mark point in line of levels, (fig.) criterion or point of reference; ~ **seat** (across whole width of car); ~-warrant, one issued by a judge. **8.** v.t. exhibit (dog) at show; *retire (player) to bench. [OE benc, - OS banc, OHG hank, ON *benkr f. Gmc *bankiz; cf. BANK¹]

be'ncher n. senior member, sharing management, of Inns of Court; (Parl.) occupant of (specified) bench (BACK¹-, CROSS-, FRONT-, bencher). [f. prec. + -ER¹]

end¹ n. **1.** (Naut.) knot of various kinds (fisherman's, weaver's, etc., bend). **2.** (Her.) stripe from dexter chief to sinister base; ~ **sinister** (from sinister chief to dexter base, sign of bastardy). [OE bend band, bond, = Goth. bandi f. Gmc *bandjō (*band-, *bend-BIND¹); cf. BAND¹, BOND¹]

end² n. bending; curve in road, racecourse, etc., (**round the ~**, (colloq.) crazy); bent part of a thing; (in pl., colloq.) caisson disease, its painful symptoms; (sl.) spree. [f. foll.]

end³ v. (past bent; p.p. bent exc. in bended KNEE¹s). **1.** v.t. & i. force out of straightness; modify (rules etc.) to suit oneself; impart to (rigid object) or receive a curved or angular shape; **be'ntwood** (artificially curved for chairs etc.). **2.** v.t. bring to bear (energies, ears, eyes, oneself, etc. on, to); (in pass.) be determined (on thing or doing; on pleasure bent). **3.** (sl., esp. in p.p.) make illicit or dishonest, pervert. **4.** attach (cable, sail) with knot. **5.** v.t. & i. turn (steps, eyes) in new direction; incline from the perpendicular. **6.** v.i. bow, stoop, submit, (to or before); **catch** person ~'ing, (colloq.) take him at disadvantage. **7.** v.t. force to submit. **8.** Hence ~'ER¹ n. (esp., sl.) drinking-spree, ~'Y² a. (colloq.) flexible. [OE bendan = ON benda, f. Gmc *bandjan (*band-; cf. BEND¹)]

enea'th adv. & prep. **1.** (arch. & literary). below, under, underneath. **2.** prep. in manner unworthy of (person, one's status, etc.); ~ **contempt** etc., not worth despising etc. [OE binithan, bineothan (bi by¹, nithan, neothan below f. Gmc *nith-; cf. NETHER)]

enedi'cite n. **1.** blessing invoked; grace at table. **2.** (B~). canticle beginning Benedicite, omnia opera, from Song of 3 Children in Apocrypha. [ME f. L, = bless ye (benedicere; see BENEDICTION); omnia opera = all the works of the Lord)]

be'nedick n. newly married man, esp. confirmed bachelor who marries. [f. Benedick, character in Shak. Much Ado]

Benedi'ctine a. & n. (monk or nun) following rule established 529 by St. Benedict; (b~; pr. -ēn), liqueur of brandy flavoured with herbs, made orig. by Benedictine monks. [f. F bénédictine or mod. L benedictinus (Benedictus Benedict; see -INE¹)]

benedi'ction n. utterance of a blessing, generally at table, at end of church service, or as special RC service; a blessing, blessedness. [ME f. OF, f. L benedictio -onis (benedicere -dict- bless; see -ION)]

benedi'ctory a. of or expressing benediction. [f. L benedictus (see prec.) + -ORY after valedictory]

Benedi'ctus n. **1.** part of RC Mass beginning Benedictus qui venit (Blessed is he who cometh). **2.** canticle beginning Benedictus Dominus Deus (Blessed be the Lord God) from Luke 1: 68–79. [L, = blessed, p.p. of benedicere (see BENEDICTION)]

benefa'ction n. doing good; gift for charitable purpose. [f. LL benefactio (as BENEFIT¹; see -ION)]

be'nefact|or n. person who has given friendly aid; patron of or donor to a cause or charitable institution; hence ~RESS¹ n. [ME f. LL (as BENEFIT¹; see -OR)]

bene'fic a. having a favourable influence. [f. L beneficus (as BENEFIT¹; see -FIC)]

be'nefice n. church living; property held by an ecclesiastical officer, esp. by rector or vicar; hence ~ED² (-st) a. [ME f. OF, f. L beneficium favour (bene well + -fic- f. facere do)]

bene'ficent a. doing good; (showing) active kindness; hence or cogn. ~ENCE n., ~entLY² adv. [f. L beneficent- (beneficus BENEFIC; see -ENT)]

benefi'cial (-shal) a. advantageous; (Law) of, or having, the use or benefit of property etc.; hence ~LY² adv. [ME, f. F bénéficial or f. LL beneficialis (as BENEFICE; see -AL)]

benefi'ciary (-sheri) n. holder of church living; receiver of benefits, esp. under person's will. [f. L beneficiarius (as BENEFICE; see -ARY¹)]

beneficiā'tion n. treatment of raw materials, ores, etc., to improve their properties. [f. Sp beneficiar to benefit (beneficio f. L beneficium; so BENEFICE, -ATION)]

be'nefit¹ n. **1.** advantage; **for the ~ of**, on behalf of, (iron.) for the instruction or disadvantage of; **the ~ of the doubt**, assumption of innocence rather than guilt where neither is proved. **2.** allowance etc. to which person is entitled under insurance or social security (sickness, unemployment, supplementary, benefit); or as member of benefit-club or society; (Hist.) exemption from ordinary courts by the privilege of one's order (benefit of clergy); **without ~ of clergy**, (joc.) without formal marriage etc. **3.** performance at theatre, game, etc., of which proceeds go to particular player etc. **4.** ~-club, ~ society, (for mutual insurance against illness or effects of old age). [ME f. AF benfet, OF bienfet, f. L benefactum neut. p.p. of bene facere do well]

be'nefit² v. (*or -tt-). **1.** v.t. do good to. **2.** v.i. receive benefit (by, from). [f. prec.]

Be'nelux n. Belgium, the Netherlands, and Luxemburg in association as a regional economic group. [f. Belgium + Netherlands + Luxemburg]

bene'volent a. desirous of doing well; charitable (benevolent fund, society); kind and helpful; hence or cogn. ~ENCE n., ~entLY² adv. [ME, f. OF benivolent f. L bene volens -entis well wishing (velle wish)]

B. Eng. abbr. Bachelor of Engineering.

Benga'l (-nggaw'l) a. ~ **light**, kind of firework used for signals; ~ **quince**, bael; ~ **tiger**, the true tiger; so ~I a. & n., (native or language) of Bengal. [former Indian province, now consisting of Bangladesh and Indian state of W. Bengal]

benī'ghted (-nī't-) a. overtaken by night; in intellectual or moral darkness; ignorant; (fig.) of obs. benight v. f. BE- 6 + NIGHT]

benī'gn (-ī'n) a. gracious, gentle; (of climate etc.) mild; fortunate, salutary; (Med.) mild, not malignant; hence **benī'gn**ITY n., ~LY² adv. [ME, f. OF benigne fem., f. L benignus prob. f. *benigenus (bene well, -genus born); cf. MALIGN]

benī'gn|ant a. kind or gracious to inferiors; salutary; (Med.) = prec.; hence ~ANCY n., ~antLY² adv. [18th c., f. prec. or L benignus, after malignant]

be'nison (-z-) n. (arch.) a blessing. [ME, f. OF beneiçun etc. f. L benedictio -onis BENEDICTION]

Be'njamin¹ n. youngest (and favourite) son. [name of youngest son of Jacob (Gen. 43 etc.)]

be'njamin² n. = BENZOIN; ~ **tree**, (1) tree yielding benzoin, (2) spicebush. [corrupt. of BENZOIN]

bĕ'nnĕt *n.* **1.** See HERB *bennet.* **2.** = BENT[1] 2.
bĕ'nni *n.* sesame plant; ∼**seed,** sesame seed. [f.
Mende *bene*]
bĕ'nnÿ[1] *n.* (sl.) overcoat. [abbr. of *benjamin,* perh. f. a
tailor's name]
bĕ'nnÿ[2] *n.* (sl.) Benzedrine. [abbr.]
bĕnt[1] *n.* **1.** stiff-stemmed reedy or rushlike grass. **2.** stiff
flower-stalk or old stalk of grasses. **3.** grass of genus
Agrostis. **4.** heath, unenclosed pasture. [ME, repr. OE
beonet- (in place-names), OS *binet,* OHG *binuz* f. WG
*binut-]
bĕnt[2] *n.* inclination, bias, tendency; **to the top of**
one's ∼, to heart's content. [prob. f. BEND[3] after
descend, descent, etc.]
bĕnt[3]. See BEND[3].
Bĕ'ntham|ism (-*ta*-, -*tha*-) *n.* utilitarian philosophy
based on measurability of pleasure and aim of
greatest happiness of the greatest number; so ∼ITE[1]
(1) *n.* [f. J. *Bentham,* Engl. philosopher d. 1832 + -ISM]
bĕ'nth|ŏs *n.* flora and fauna found at bottom of ocean
or lake; hence ∼IC *a.* [Gk, = depth of the sea]
bĕ'ntonīte *n.* kind of clay used as absorbent, filler, etc.
[f. Fort *Benton* in Montana + -ITE[1] (2)]
ben trovato (bĕn trovah'tō) *a.* well invented,
characteristic if not true. [It., = well found]
bĕ'ntwŏŏd. See BEND[3].
bĕnŭ'mb (-m) *v.t.* (Usu. of cold) make torpid,
insensible, powerless; paralyse (mind, action).
[earlier p.p. of ME *benimen* deprive f. OE *beniman* (*bi*-
BE-, *niman* take)]
Bĕ'nzĕdrine (-ēn, -īn) *n.* (P) amphetamine. [f.
BENZOIC + EPHEDRINE]
bĕ'nzĕn|e *n.* aromatic liquid got from
coal and petroleum, used as solvent, fuel, and in
manufacture of plastics etc.; ∼**e ring,** arrangement
of 6 carbon atoms in benzene molecule; hence ∼OID
a. [f. BENZOIC + -ENE]
bĕ'nzine (-ēn) *n.* mixture of liquid hydrocarbons got
from petroleum and used as solvent, esp. in dry-
-cleaning. [f. foll. + -INE[5]]
bĕ'nzŏin (gum) ∼, fragrant aromatic resin of E.
Asian tree of genus *Styrax*; (Chem.) white crystalline
constituent of this; hence **bĕnzŏ'IC** *a.* [earlier *benjoin*
thr. F etc. f. Rom. *lobenjoi* f. Arab. *lubān jāwī* incense of
Java (*lo-* being dropped in Rom. as if the def. article)]
bĕ'nzŏl, -ōle, *n.* benzene, esp. unrefined. [f. BENZOIC
+ -OL]
bĕquea'th (-dh) *v.t.* leave (personal estate *to* person;
cf. DEVISE) by will; transmit (example etc.) to posterity. [OE *becwethan* (as BE- 3, *cwethan* say; cf.
QUOTH)]
bĕquĕ'st *n.* bequeathing; thing bequeathed. [ME, f.
BE- + obs. *quiste* f. OE -*cwiss, cwide* saying]
bĕrā'te *v.t.* scold. [f. BE- 1 + RATE[3]]
Bĕr'ber *n.* & *a.* (member) of the N. Afr. stock
including the aboriginal races, speaking allied
languages; language of Berber people. [f. Arab.
barbar]
bĕr'beris *n.* plant of genus *Berberis,* barberry. [med. L
& OF, of unkn. orig.]
berceuse (bārsĕr'z) *n.* cradle-song; (Mus.) piece in
this style. [F]
bĕrea've *v.t.* **1.** (bere'ft). rob, dispossess, *of* (usu.
immaterial things, e.g. life, hope). **2.** (∼d). leave
desolate (esp. in *p.p.*); (of death etc.) deprive *of* a
relation, wife, etc.; hence ∼MENT (-vm-) *n.* [OE
berēafian (as BE- 2, REAVE)]
bĕrĕ'ft. See prec.
bĕ'ret (bĕ'rā, -rĭ) *n.* round flat felt or cloth cap. [F, f.
dial. & Prov. *berret*; cf. BIRETTA]
bĕrg[1] *n.* = ICEBERG. [abbr.]
bĕrg[2] *n.* (S. Afr.) mountain or hill (esp. in comb.); ∼
wind, hot dry northerly wind blowing in coastal
regions. [Afrik. f. Du.]
bĕr'gamăsque (-sk) *n.* dance like tarantella. [f.
Bergamo in Italy]
bĕr'gamŏt[1] *n.* citrus tree (*Citrus bergamia*); perfume

extracted from rind of its fruit; aromatic herb, esp
Mentha citrata. [as prec.]
bĕr'gamŏt[2] *n.* kind of fine pear. [f. F *bergamotte* f. It
bergamotta f. Turk. *begarmud* prince's pear]
ber'gschrund (bār'kshrŏŏnt) *n.* (Mount.) crevasse o▪
gap at junction of steep upper slope with glacier o▪
névé. [G]
bĕr'gÿlt (-g-) *n.* red sea-fish, the Norway haddock
[perh. f. ON *berg* rock]
bĕrhÿ'me (-rī'm) *v.t.* (arch.) write verses about
lampoon. [f. BE- 3 + RHYME[2]]
bĕrĭbĕ'ri *n.* mainly tropical polyneuritic diseas▪
caused by deficiency of vitamin B_1, esp. in rice-base▪
diet. [Sinh., f. *beri* weakness]
bĕrk, bĭrk, bŭrk(e), *n.* (sl.) fool. [abbr. of *Berkeley* o▪
Berkshire Hunt, rhyming sl. for *cunt*]
Berkelei'an (bārklē'an) *n.* & *a.* (follower) of Berkeley
or his philosophy, which denied the objective existence of the material world. [f. G. *Berkeley,* Ir
philosopher d. 1753; see -IAN]
bĕr'kelium (bĕrkē'lium, bĕr'kl-) *n.* (Chem.) artificially
made transuranic radioactive metallic element
[mod. L, f. *Berkeley* in California (where first made)
+ -IUM]
Berks. *abbr.* Berkshire.
bĕrli'n, bĕrli'ne (-ē'n), *n.* four-wheeled covered carriage with hooded seat behind; so **Bĕrli'nER**[1] (4) *n.* [f.
Berlin in Germany (-*ine* thr. F)]
bĕrm *n.* narrow ledge, esp. in fortification betwee▪
ditch and base of parapet; narrow path or grass stri▪
beside road. [f. F *berme* f. Du. *berm,* prob. cogn. w. ON
barmr brim]
Bermū'd|a *n.* ∼**a rig,** (Naut., with high tapering sai▪
called ∼**ian mainsail**); ∼**as,** ∼**a shorts,** knee-
-length shorts; hence ∼IAN *a.* & *n.* [∼ (Islands) in W
Atlantic]
Bĕr'nardine *a.* & *n.* = CISTERCIAN. [f. St. *Bernard* o▪
Clairvaux, Fr. churchman d. 1153, who founded a
branch of the order, + -INE[1]]
bĕ'rry[1] *n.* small roundish juicy fruit without stone
(Bot.) fruit with seeds enclosed in pulp (e.g. gooseberry, tomato, banana); egg in fish or lobster roe; (sl.)
||pound, *dollar; hence (-)**bĕ'rrīED**[2] (-ĭd) *a.* [OE
beri(g)*e,* = OS, OHG *beri,* ON *ber,* Goth. *basi* f. Gm▪
*basj-, *bazj-]
bĕ'rry[2] *v.i.* form berry; go gathering berries. [f. prec.]
bersaglieri (bārsahlyā'ē) *n. pl.* highly traine▪
Italian infantry, orig. riflemen. [It.]
bĕr'sĕrk *n.* & *a.* **1.** *n.* ∼(**er**), wild Norse warrio▪
fighting with mad frenzy. **2.** *a.* (*or* bersĕr'k, -z-). wild,
frenzied, (esp. *go berserk*). [f. Icel. *berserkr* prob. f. *bern-*
BEAR[1] + *serkr* coat]
bĕrth[1] *n.* adequate sea-room (*give* WIDE *berth to*); room
for ship to swing at anchor; ship's place at wharf;
proper place for anything; sleeping-place in ship,
train, etc.; situation, appointment. [prob. f. naut. use
of BEAR[3] + -TH[1]]
bĕrth[2] *v.* **1.** *v.t.* moor (ship) in suitable place; provide
sleeping-place for. **2.** *v.i.* (Of ship) come to mooring.
[f. prec.]
bĕr'tha *n.* deep falling collar or small cape on dress.
[F *berthe* (*Berthe* Bertha, woman's Christian name)]
bĕr'ÿl *n.* transparent precious stone, pale-green, light
blue, yellow, or white; mineral species including this,
emerald, and aquamarine. [ME f. OF, f. L f. Gk
bērullos]
bĕrÿ'llium *n.* very light hard white metallic element.
[f. prec. + -IUM]
bĕsee'ch *v.t.* (besought *pr.* -saw't, or ∼ed). ask
earnestly for; entreat (person, person *that* or *to* do or
for thing); hence ∼ING[2] *a.,* suppliant. [ME, f. *bi-* BE-
2 + seek etc. SEEK]
bĕsee'm *v.t.* (arch.; impers.) suit; be fitting or creditable to. [f. BE- 2 + SEEM]
bĕsĕ't *v.t.* (-**tt**-; beset), hem in; occupy and make
impassable (road beset); (of difficulties, doubts, temp-
tations, etc). assail, encompass; ∼**ting sin** (that

especially or most frequently tempts one); hence ∼MENT n. [OE besettan, = OS bisettian, OHG bisezzan, Goth. bisatjan f. Gmc *bi- BE- 1 + *satjan SET¹]

beshrew' (-rōō') v.t. (arch., as mock-heroic imprecation). the Devil etc. take (me, person, or thing). [f. BE- 2 + obs. shrew to curse f. SHREW]

besi'de prep. close to, by, near; on a level with; compared with; wide of (beside the mark, point, question, etc.); ∼ oneself, distraught. [OE be sīdan (as BY¹, SIDE¹)]

besi'des (-dz) adv. & prep. in addition (to); moreover; otherwise, else, (than). [f. prec. + -s³]

besie'ge v.t. invest, lay siege to; crowd round; assail with requests; hence ∼ER¹ n. [ME, f. assiege (by substitution of pref. BE-), f. OF asegier f. Rom. *AS(sedicare f. *sedicum siege)]

beslá'ver, beslŏ'bber, vbs. t. slaver on or over; flatter fulsomely. [f. BE- 1 + SLAVER², SLOBBER]

besmear' v.t. smear with greasy or sticky stuff; (fig.) sully (reputation etc.). [f. OE bismierwan (bi- BE- 1, smierwan SMEAR v.)]

besmĭr'ch v.t. soil, discolour; dim brightness of; (fig.) sully (reputation etc.). [f. BE- 1 + SMIRCH]

be'som (bē'z-, bī'-) n. broom made of twigs tied round stick; (prov., derog.) woman. [OE besema, = OS besmo, OHG besamo , f. WG *hesmo]

besŏ't v t (-tt-). (usu. in p.p.) stupefy mentally or morally; infatuate. [f. BE- 4 + SOT]

besought. See BESEECH.

bespá'ngle (-ă'nggel) v.t. cover with spangles. [f. BE- 6 + SPANGLE]

bespá'tter v.t. spatter (object) all over; spatter (liquid etc.) about; cover with abuse or flattery. [f. BE- 1 + SPATTER]

bespea'k v.t. (past bespo'ke pr. -ō'k, p.p. bespo'ke as adj., otherwise bespo'ken). engage beforehand; order (goods); suggest; be evidence of; (literary) speak to; bespoke tailor, overcoat, etc., (seller of) clothes made to order, opp. ready-made clothes etc. [OE bisprecan, = OS besprekan, OHG bisprohhan; see DE 3, SPEAK]

bespe'ctacled (-keld) a. wearing spectacles. [f. BE- 7 + SPECTACLE + -ED²]

bespo'ke(n). See BESPEAK.

bespre'nt a. (arch.) sprinkled (with). [ME, p.p. of obs. besprenge f. OE besprengan (as BE- 1, sprengan sprinkle; see SPRENT)]

bespri'nkle v.t. sprinkle or strew over (with; lit. or fig.); sprinkle (liquid etc.) over. [ME, f. BE- 3 + sprenkel freq. of sprengen besprinkle (as prec.)]

Be'ssemer a. ∼ process (formerly much used for removing carbon, silicon, etc., from molten pig-iron by passage of air, thus converting it to a material suitable for steel-making). [f. Sir H. ∼, Engl. engineer d. 1898]

best¹ a., adv., & n. 1. a. (superl. of GOOD). of the most excellent or outstanding or desirable kind (the best friend I have; the best thrashing he ever had; the best bedroom; the best thing to do would be to leave); best BUY; ∼ end, rib end of neck of lamb etc. for cooking; put one's ∼ foot forward, go at full pace, exert all one's efforts; ∼ girl, (colloq.) sweetheart; ∼ man, bridegroom's chief attendant at wedding; ∼ part, most of; ∼ seller, (author of) book with large sale; ∼ way (shortest, surest, easiest, etc.). 2. adv. (superl. of WELL³). in the best manner; to the greatest degree; most usefully (is best ignored); as ∼ one can or may, as well as one is able to do under the circumstances; had ∼, would find it wisest to. 3. n. that which is best; victory; ∼ of three games, winning 2; get or have the ∼ of it, win fight or argument; give person ∼, admit his superiority. 4. chief advantage or merit (that is the best of knowing French; bring out the best in person). 5. the best persons or things. 6. all the ∼ (expr. good will); at ∼, on the most hopeful view; at its, one's, ∼, in the best state; at the ∼ of times, even in the most favourable circumstances; do one's ∼ (to win etc.),

do all one can; did it (all) for the ∼, with good intentions; it was (all) for the ∼, desirable in the end; look one's ∼ (most attractive); make the ∼ of it, things, a bad bargain, etc., be as contented as possible; make the ∼ of one's opportunities, way, oneself, etc., do as well as possible, progress as fast as possible, etc.; one's (Sunday) ∼, best clothes; six of the ∼, vigorous caning; to the ∼ of one's ability, belief, power, etc., so far as one can do, judge, etc.; with the ∼ (of them), as well as anyone. [OE betest a., bet(o)st adv., = OS best, OHG bezzisto, ON beztr, Goth. batists f. Gmc *batistaz superl. of *bat-; cf. BETTER¹]

best² (colloq.) defeat, outwit. [f. prec.]

bestea'd (-ě'd) v.t. & i. (arch.) avail, help. [f. BE- 2 + stead v. f. STEAD]

beste'ad a. (arch.) (ill, hard, sore, etc.) situated, circumstanced. [ME, f. BE- 2 + stad f. ON staddr p.p. of stethja place]

be'stial a. of or like a beast or beasts; brutish; barbarous; savage; depraved, lustful; hence or cogn. ∼ITY (-ă'l-) n., (esp.) unnatural form of copulation between person and animal, ∼IZE (3) v.t., ∼LY² adv. [ME f. OF, f. LL bestialis (bestia beast; see -AL)]

be'stiary n. medieval moralizing treatise on beasts. [f. med. L bestiarium f. L bestia beast; see -ARY¹]

bestir' v. refl. (-rr-). exert, rouse, (oneself). [f. BE- 2 + STIR¹ v.]

bestow' (-ō') v.t. deposit; lodge; confer (thing) (up)on (person) as gift; hence ∼AL, ∼MENT, ns. [ME, f. BE- 2 + OE stow a place]

bestrew' (-rōō') v.t. (p.p. ∼ed or ∼n). strew (surface) with; scatter (things) about; lie scattered over. [OE bestrēowian (as BE- 1, STREW)]

bestri'dden. See foll.

bestri'de v.t. (bestro'de; bestri'dden). get or sit on (horse, chair, etc.) with legs astride; stand astride over. [OE bestrīdan (as BE- 3, STRIDE v.)]

bestro'de. See foll.

bět v. (-tt-; ∼ or ∼'ted) & n. 1. v.i. & t. risk one's money etc., risk (an amount etc.) against another's, risk money etc. thus against (person), by agreeing to forfeit it if doubtful event does not result in specified way (on or against result or competitor, that a thing will happen; you ∼, (colloq.) you may take it as certain); (colloq.) feel sure (I bet he's forgotten it). 2. n. act of betting; sum of money bet; (colloq.) course of action (your best bet is to call tomorrow); (colloq.) opinion (my bet is that he won't come). [16th c., of uncert. orig.; perh. v. f. n., f. abet n., in sense 'instigation, support of a cause']

be'ta n. second Greek letter (B, β) = b; (Astron.) second brightest star in a constellation; second-class mark in examination (∼ plus, ∼ minus, rather better, worse, than average second-class); ∼ particles, ∼ rays, fast-moving electrons emitted by radioactive substances (orig. regarded as rays). [ME f. L f. Gk]

betä'ke v. refl. (betoo'k; ∼n). ∼ oneself to, go to (place or person). [ME, f. BE- 2 + TAKE¹]

be'tatron n. (Phys.) apparatus for accelerating electrons in circular path. [f. BETA + -TRON]

be'tel n. leaf of evergreen plant Piper betle, chewed in the East with areca-nut parings; ∼-nut, the areca nut. [Port., f. Malayalam veṭṭila]

bête noire (bāt nwär) n. (pl. bêtes noires pr. same). particularly disliked person or thing. [F, = black beast]

be'thel n. Nonconformist chapel; seamen's church. [f. Heb. bēt-'ēl house of God (Gen. 28: 17–19)]

bethe'sda (-z-) n. Nonconformist chapel. [John 5: 2]

bethi'nk v. refl. (bethou'ght pr. -thaw't). ∼ oneself or (arch.) one, reflect, stop to think, remind oneself of, how, or that. [OE bithencan = OS bithenkian, OHG bidenken, Goth. bithagkjan, Gmc (*bi- BE-, *thankjan THINK)]

beti'de v.i. & t. (only in inf. & 3 sing. pres. subj.) happen (whate'er may betide); happen to (woe betide him who etc., orig. a curse, now usu. as warning). [ME, f. BE-2 + obs. *tide* befall f. OE *tīdan*]

betī′mes (-mz) *adv.* early in day, year, life, etc.; in good time. [ME, f. obs. *betime* (BY¹, TIME¹) + -s³]

bêtise (bātē′z) *n.* foolish or ill-timed remark or action; piece of folly. [F]

betō′ken *v.t.* augur, indicate; suggest, be token of. [OE. *bitācnian* (as BE- 2, *tācnian* signify f. as TOKEN)]

bĕ′tonў *n.* purple-flowered plant (*Stachys officinalis*); one of various similar plants (**water** ∼; **wood** ∼). [ME, f. OF *betoine* f. pop. L *betonia* for L *betonica* f. *vettonica* perh. f. name of Iberian tribe]

betōō′k. See BETAKE.

betray′ *v.t.* give up treacherously (person or thing *to* enemy); be disloyal to; lead astray; reveal treacherously or involuntarily; be evidence or symptom of; hence ∼AL *n.* [ME f. BE- 2 + obs. *tray* f. OF *trair* f. Rom. **tradire* f. L *tradere* hand over]

betrō′th (-ō′dh) *v.t.* (usu. in *p.p.*). bind with promise to marry; hence ∼AL *n.*, ∼ED¹ (-dhd) *a.* & *n.* [ME, f. BE- 6 + *trouthe*, *treuthe* TRUTH, later assim. to TROTH]

bĕ′tter¹ *a.*, *adv.*, & *n.* **1.** *a.* (*compar.* of GOOD). of a more excellent or outstanding or desirable kind; partly or fully recovered from illness; ∼ **feelings**, conscience; ∼ **half**, (joc.) wife; ∼ **part**, most *of*; **for** ∼ (**or**) **for worse**, on terms of accepting all results, whatever the (unpredictable) outcome; **no** ∼ **than**, practically, merely (*no* ∼ *than she should be*, of doubtful virtue). **2.** *adv.* (*compar.* of WELL³). in a better manner; to a greater degree; more usefully (*is better ignored*); ∼ **than** (number etc.), above; **go one** ∼, outbid etc. by one, (fig.) outdo person, **outdo (person); **had** ∼, (colloq.) ∼, would find it wiser to; *better* OFF; KNOW¹ *better than*; THINK *better of*. **3.** *n.* that which is better (*change for the better*); **get the** ∼ **of**, defeat, outwit; **think** (all) **the** ∼ **of**, have higher opinion of; person who is more skilful etc. than oneself; (in *pl.*) persons of higher rank than oneself. [f. OE *betera*, OS *betiro*, OHG *bezziro*, ON *betri*, Goth. *batiza* f. Gmc **batizon* (**bat-* cogn. w. BOOT²; see -ER³)]

bĕ′tter² *v.t.* amend, improve; surpass (a feat etc.); ∼ oneself, get better situation, wages, etc., hence ∼MENT *n.*, improvement, enhanced value (of real property) arising from local improvements. [ME f. prec.]

bĕ′tter³, **bĕ′ttor**, *n.* one who bets. [f. BET + -ER¹, -OR]

bĕ′tting *n.* In vbl senses; odds offered (lit. or fig.); ∼-**shop**, bookmaker's shop or office. [f. BET + -ING¹]

bĕtwee′n *prep.* & *adv.* in, into, along, or across, a space, line, interval, or route, bounded by (any number of, esp. two, points, lines, dates, etc.; *between* TIME¹*s*, WHILE¹*s*); separating (*difference between right and wrong*; **stand** ∼, act as mediator or protector); connecting; (**in**) ∼, intermediately in place, time, amount, or order (to); owing partly to, partaking of the nature of, shared by, (each); to and from (*runs between London and Brighton*); reciprocally on the part of (*agreement between us*); confined to (*choose between*); separated (**far** ∼, at wide intervals); ||∼-**maid**, servant assisting two others, e.g. cook and housemaid. [OE *betwēonum* f. Gmc **bi* BY¹ + **twēon* (**twihnai*, ult. rel. to TWO)]

bĕtwi′xt *prep.* & *adv.* (poet., arch., or dial.) between; ∼ **and between**, (colloq.) intermediate(ly). [ME, f. OE *betwēohs*, *betwēox*, etc. f. Gmc **bi* BY¹ + **twisk*-twofold (**twa* TWO, **-isk* -ISH¹); cf. AGAINST]

BeV *abbr.* billion (= 10⁹) electron-volts.

bĕ′vel¹ *n.* joiner's and mason's tool for adjusting angles; slope from horizontal or vertical; sloping surface; ∼ **gear** (working one shaft from another at angle to it by ∼ **wheels**, toothed wheels with working face oblique to axis). [f. OF **bevel* (*baïf* open--mouthed f. *baer* gape; cf. BAY³)]

bĕ′vel² *v.t.* & *i.* (||-ll-). impart bevel to, slant. [f. prec.]

bĕ′verage *n.* (formal or joc.) liquid for drinking. [ME, f. OF *be*(*u*)*vrage* f. Rom. **biberaticum* f. L *bibere* drink; see -AGE]

bĕ′vў *n.* company (orig. of ladies, roes, quails, larks). [15th c.; orig. unkn.]

bewai′l *v.t.* wail over; mourn for. [f. BE- 3 + WAIL v.]

bewā′r′**e** *v.i.* & *t.* (only in *imper.* and *inf.*) be cautious, take heed, (of); take heed *of*, *lest*, *how*, *that* . . . *not*. [f. BE + WARE²]

bewi′lder *v.t.* lead astray; perplex, confuse; hence ∼MENT *n.* [f. BE- 2 + obs. *wilder* lose one's way]

bewi′tch *v.t.* affect by magic, put a spell on; delight exceedingly. [ME, f. BE- 2 + OE *wiccian* enchant (*wicca* WITCH)]

bewray′ (bīrā′) *v.t.* (arch.) reveal, esp. involuntarily. [ME, f. BE- 2 + obs. *wray* accuse f. OE *wrēgan*, = OS *wrōgian*, OHG *ruogen*, ON *rœgja* f. Gmc **wrōgjan*]

bey (bā) *n.* (Hist.) Turkish governor; **Bey of Tunis**, ruler of Tunisia; ∼′**lic** *n.*, bey's province or jurisdiction. [Turk.]

bèyŏ′nd *adv.*, *prep.*, & *n.* **1.** *adv.* & *prep.* at or to the farther side (of); past, outside; later than; out of reach, comprehension, or range, of (*it is beyond me*; living beyond one's means; *beyond repair*; *beyond* MEASURE¹); surpassing; not subject to (*beyond argument*; *beyond question*); more (than) (*this is beyond a joke*). **2.** *n.* the ∼, the future life, the unknown; **the back of** ∼, very remote or out-of--the-way place. [OE *beg*(*e*)*ondan* (be BY¹, *g*(*e*)*ondan* f. Gmc **jandana* f. **jand-*, see YON, YONDER)]

bezant (bĕ′za-, bizā′-) *n.* **1.** (Hist.) gold or silver coin, orig. minted at Byzantium. **2.** (Her.) gold roundel. [ME, f. OF *besanz* *-ant* f. L *Byzantius* adj. of *Byzantium*]

bĕ′zel *n.* sloped edge of chisel etc.; oblique faces of cut gem; groove holding watch-glass or gem; rim holding glass etc. cover. [f. OF **besel*, of unkn. orig.]

bĕzi′que (-ē′k) *n.* card-game for two, with double pack of 64 cards (ace to seven only); combination of queen of spades and jack of diamonds in this game. [f. F *bésigue*, perh. f. Pers. *bāzīgar* juggler]

bĕ′zoar *n.* concretion with hard nucleus found in stomach or intestines of certain animals (chiefly ruminants), formerly believed antidotal. [ult. f. Pers. *pādzahr* antidote, Arab. *bāzahr*]

bĕzō′nian *n.* (arch.) rascal, beggarly fellow. [f. It. *bisogno* & Sp. *bisoño* need + -IAN]

||**b.f.** (bēē′f) *n.* (euphem.) bloody fool. [abbr.]

b.f. *abbr.* **bold face; brought forward.

||**B′ham** *abbr.* Birmingham.

bhăng (bă-) *n.* Indian hemp; its leaves etc. used as narcotic and intoxicant. [f. Port. *bangue*, Pers. *bang*, & Urdu etc. *bhāng* f. Skr. *bhaṅgā*]

bha′ral (bŭ′-) *n.* Himalayan wild sheep. [Hindi]

b.h.p. *abbr.* brake horsepower.

bī- *pref.* (often **bin-** before vowel) to *adjs.* & *ns.*, forming other *adjs.* & *ns.* **1.** *adjs.*, w. sense (a) having two (bilateral, bilingual, binaural), (b) doubly, in two ways, (biconcave) etc., (c) (Bot. & Zool.) twice over, i.e. divided into similarly divided parts, (bipinnate), (d) lasting for two, appearing etc. every two, (biennial), (e) appearing etc. twice in, (biannual, bimonthly), (f) joining two (bi-parietal). **2.** *ns.*, w. sense (a) thing having two (biplane), (b) (Chem.) salt having twice the proportion of acid to base molecules indicated by the simple word (bicarbonate, bisulphate). [L]

Bi *symb.* bismuth.

bīă′nnūal *a.* appearing etc. twice a year. [f. BI- 1(e) + ANNUAL] Hence ∼LY *adv.*

bī′as¹ *n.* **1.** (Bowls). lopsided form of a bowl, its oblique course. **2.** inclination, predisposition (towards); prejudice; influence. **3.** (Statistics) distortion of result by neglected factor. **4.** (Dressmaking etc.) **cut on the** ∼, cut obliquely across the warp; ∼ **binding**, strip so cut, used to finish edges etc. [f. F *biais* f. LL *bifax* looking two ways f. as BI- + L *facies* face]

bī′as² *v.t.* (-s- or -ss-). give a bias to; influence (usu. unfairly); inspire with prejudice. [f. prec.]

bīă′thlon *n.* athletic contest in which competitors engage in skiing and shooting. [f. BI- 1(a), after PENTATHLON]

For other words in *be-* **see** BE-.

biā'xial *a.* having two (optic) axes. [f. BI- 1(a) + AXIAL]

bib¹ *n.* edible sea-fish (*Trisopterus luscus*) akin to cod, with inflatable head-membrane. [f. foll.]

bib² *n.* piece of cloth etc. put under child's chin to keep dress-front clean; top front part of apron or overall (**best** ∼ **and tucker**, best clothes). [perh. f. foll.]

bib³ *v.i.* (-bb-). (arch.) drink much or often; hence ∼'bᴇʀ¹ *n.* [ME, perh. f. L *bibere* drink]

bi'b-côck *n.* tap with bent nozzle fixed at end of pipe. [perh. f. BIB² + COCK¹]

bi'belot (bĕ'blō) *n.* small curio or artistic trinket. [F]

Bī'ble *n.* **1.** Christian scriptures of the Old and New Testament; copy of them; particular edition of them (BISHOPS', BREECHES, PRINTERS', VINEGAR, WICKED, *Bible*). **2.** scriptures of other religion; authoritative book. **3.** *∼ belt, reputedly puritanical area of S. and central US; ∼ oath (taken on the Bible); ∼-pounding, -punching, -thumping, etc., (sl.) aggressively expounding or following the Bible. [ME f. OF, f. eccl. L f. Gk *biblia* books pl. of *biblion*, orig. dim. of *biblos, bublos* papyrus]

bi'blical *a.* of, concerning, contained in, the Bible; resembling the language of the Bible; hence ∼ʟʏ² *adv.* [f. prec. + -ICAL]

bibliŏ'graph|ў *n.* history or description of books, their authorship, editions, etc.; book containing such details; list of books etc. of any author, printer, country, subject; hence or cogn. ∼ᴇʀ¹ *n.*, **bibliogrā'ph**ɪᴄ(ᴀʟ) *adjs.*, ∼ɪᴢᴇ (1) *v.t.* [f. F (*-phie*) or f. mod. L f. Gk *bibliographia* (*biblion* book; see BIBLE, -GRAPHY)]

bi'bliománcў *n.* divination by books, esp. by the Bible. [f. Gk *biblion* book (see BIBLE) + -O- + -MANCY]

bibliomā'ni|a *n.* craze for collecting books; hence ∼ᴀᴄ *n.* [f. as prec. + -MANIA]

bi'bliophil, -phīle, *n.* lover of books; collector of books; hence **bibliophi'lɪᴄ** *a.*, **bibliŏ'phɪlʏ¹** *n.* [f. F *bibliophile* (as prec.; see -PHIL, -PHILE)]

bi'bliopole *n.* seller of (esp. rare) books; so **bibliŏ'polʏ¹** *n.* [f. L f. Gk *bibliopōlēs* (*biblion* book, *pōlēs* seller)]

bi'bŭlous *a.* addicted to drinking alcoholic liquor; hence ∼ʟʏ² *adv.* [f. L *bibulus* freely drinking (*bibere* drink) + -OUS]

bică'meral *a.* having two (legislative) chambers. [f. BI- 1(a) + L *camera* chamber + -AL]

bicăr'b *n.* (colloq.) = foll. 2. [abbr.]

bicār'bonăte *n.* **1.** (Chem.) salt containing double proportion of carbon dioxide. **2.** (pop.) sodium bicarbonate, used as antacid, in baking-powder, etc. [f. BI- 2(b) + CARBONATE¹]

bice *n.* ∼ or blue ∼, green ∼, pigments made from blue, green, basic copper carbonate; similar pigment made from smalt etc.; dull shade of blue or green given by these. [orig. = brownish grey, f. OF *bis* dark grey, of unkn. orig.]

bicéntenarў (-sĕntĕ'-, -sĕ'ntĭ-) *a. & n.* (festival) of the two-hundredth anniversary. [f. BI- 1(d) + CENTENARY]

bicénte'nnial *a. & n.* **1.** *a.* lasting, occurring every, two hundred years. **2.** *n.* = prec. [f. BI- 1(d) + CENTENNIAL]

bice'phalous *a.* two-headed. [f. BI- 1(a) + -CEPHALOUS]

bi'cĕps *n.* muscle with double head or attachment, esp. that which bends elbow; muscularity. [L, = two-headed, f. as BI- 1(a) + -*ceps* (*caput* head)]

bi'cker *v.i.* quarrel, wrangle; (of stream, rain, etc.) brawl, patter; (of flame, light, etc.) flash, flicker. [ME *biker, beker*, of unkn. orig.]

bicŏ'ncāve (-n-k-) *a.* (Of lens etc.) concave, convex, on both sides. [f. BI- 1(b) + CONCAVE, CONVEX]

bicŭ'ltural (-cher-) *a.* having or combining two cultures. [f. BI- 1(a) + CULTURAL]

bicŭ'spid *a. & n.* (tooth) with two cusps, human premolar. [f. BI- 1(a) + L *cuspis* -*idis* sharp point]

bi'cӯcle *n., & v.i.* (ride on) two-wheeled pedal-driven road vehicle; ∼-**chain**, chain transmitting power from bicycle pedals to wheel; ∼-**clip** (used to confine cyclist's trouser-leg at ankle); ∼-**pump**, portable pump for inflating tyres of bicycle; hence **bi'cÿclɪsᴛ** (1) *n.* [F, f. BI- 2(a) + Gk *kuklos* wheel]

bid¹ *v.* (-**dd-**). **1.** *v.t.* (arch. or poet.; *past* **bade** *pr.* băd, *or* ∼; *p.p.* ∼ *or* ∼'**den**). command to, tell to, (*bid the soldiers shoot; do as you are bid*); proclaim (defiance etc.); invite (*bidden guest*; ∼'**ding-prayer**, one inviting congregation to join in, now usu. a group of intercessory prayers); salute (person) with *welcome, farewell,* etc. **2.** *v.i. & t.* (*past & p.p.* ∼). (esp. at auction) offer price, offer (a certain price) *for*; offer to do work etc. for stated price; (Cards) make a BID² of or in, make a bid on the basis of (one's hand), make a bid; ∼ **fair to** do, show promise of doing; hence ∼'**d**ᴇʀ¹ *n.* [OE *biddan* ask, = OS *biddian*, OHG *bitten*, ON *hithja*, Goth. *bidjan* f. Gmc *bidhjan* pray, & OE *bēodan* offer, command, OS *biodan*, OHG *biotan*, ON *bjótha*, Goth. *biudan*, IE *bh(e)udh-*]

bid² *n.* offer of price, esp. at auction; offer made for stated price, TENDER² 3, (**make a** ∼ **for**, (fig.) make an attempt to secure); (Cards) statement of number of tricks player proposes to win in specified suit or no-trumps; attempt, effort. [f. prec.]

bi'dd|able *a.* obedient; (of hand or suit at cards) suitable for being bid; hence ∼ᴀʙɪ'ʟɪᴛʏ *n.* [f. BID¹ + -ABLE]

bi'dden. See BID¹.

bi'ddɪng *n.* In vbl senses, the offers at auction; (Cards) the bids made; a command. [f. BID¹ + -ING¹]

bi'ddỳ *n.* (sl., derog.) woman. [pet-form of woman's Christian name *Bridget*]

bi'ddỳ-biddỳ *n.* (NZ) (bur of) the piripiri. [corrupt. of Maori PIRIPIRI]

bide *v.i. & v.t.* ∼ one's **time,** await best opportunity. *v.i.* (arch. or dial.) remain. [OE *bīdan*, = OS *bīdan*, OHG *bītan*, ON *bítha*, Goth. *beidan* f. Gmc *bīdhan*]

bi'det (bē'dā) *n.* low bath for washing, esp. of the genital region. [F, = pony]

bi'donville *n.* shanty-town built of oil drums etc. [F (*bidon* oil drum, petrol tin, *ville* town)]

Bie'dermeier (-mī-) *a.* (derog.) conventional; bourgeois. [f. *Biedermaier* fictitious Ger. poet (1854), applied to a style of furniture etc. in Germany 1815–1848]

biĕ'nnial *a. & n.* **1.** *a.* lasting, recurring every, two years; hence ∼ʟʏ² *adv.* **2.** *n.* (Bot.) plant that springs one year, and flowers, fructifies, and perishes, the next. [f. L *biennis* (as BI- 1(d), *annus* year) + -AL]

biĕ'nni|um *n.* (*pl.* ∼**ums** *or* ∼**a**). period of two years. [L (as prec.)]

bier *n.* movable frame on which coffin or corpse is placed, or taken to grave. [OE *bēr*, = OS, OHG *bāra* f. WG **bērō* f. Gmc **beran* BEAR³]

biff *n., & v.t.* (sl.) **1.** *n.* smart blow. **2.** *v.t.* strike (person). [imit.]

‖bi'ffin *n.* deep-red cooking-apple. [= *beefing* f. BEEF + -ING¹ (3), w. ref. to the colour]

bi'fīd *a.* divided by deep cleft into two halves. [f. L BI(*fidus* f. st. of *findere* cleave)]

bifō'cal *a. & n.* **1.** *a.* having two foci (esp. of combined distant and near vision spectacles). **2.** *n.* (in *pl.*) bifocal spectacles. [f. BI- 1(b) + FOCAL]

bi'furcāte *v.t. & i.* divide into two branches, fork. [f. med. L *bifurcare* f. L *bifurcus* two-forked (as BI-, *furca* fork), + -ATE³]

bifurcā'tion *n.* division into two branches; point of such division; such branches or one of them. [f. prec. + -ATION]

big *a. & adv.* **1.** *a.* of considerable size, amount, intensity, etc. (usu. without emotional implications of *great; elected by a big majority;* **in a** ∼ **way,** on a large scale, (colloq.) with great enthusiasm, display, etc.); of largest, larger than usual, size (*big drum,* GAME¹ 8, *toe*); (more) grown up (*you're a big boy now*); elder (*big brother, sister*); **too** ∼ **for** one's **boots** or **breeches,**

(sl.) conceited. **2.** advanced in pregnancy (esp. of animals or fig., *big with consequences*); important (*the big fight, league, race*); **a ~ man** (in eminence or range of operation); **~ money,** large amounts, high profit or pay; **the Big Three, Four,** etc., the predominant few. **3.** boastful (*big words*); (colloq.) generous; (colloq.) ambitious (*have big ideas; the big* IDEA); (colloq.) outstanding (*his big opportunity, my big moment*). **4. ~ band,** large group playing jazz etc.; **~ bang,** assumed violent event creating the universe; ||**Big Ben,** great bell, clock, and tower, of Houses of Parliament; ***Big Board,** (colloq.) New York Stock Exchange; **Big Brother,** all-powerful dictator simulating benevolence [Orwell's *1984*]; **~ bud,** plant disease caused by gall-mite; **~ bug,** (sl.) bigwig; **~ business,** (persons concerned in) commerce on the grand scale (freq. with sinister implications); **~ Chief, ~ Daddy,** (sl.) bigwig; ***~ deal!,** (sl., iron.) I am not impressed; **~ dipper,** ||fairground switch-back, ***Great BEAR**[1]; **~ end,** end of connecting-rod that encircles crankpin; **~ gun,** (sl.) bigwig; **~'-head,** (colloq.) conceit(ed person); **~-hearted,** generous; **~'horn,** Rocky Mountains sheep; **~ house,** principal house in a village etc., (sl.) prison; **~-mouthed,** boastful; **~ name,** famous person; **~ noise, ~ pot, ~ shot,** (sl.) bigwig; **the ~ smoke,** ||(sl.) London, (orig. Austral. Aboriginal) a large town; **~ stick,** display of force; *big* STIFF; **~ time,** (sl.) highest rank among entertainers etc.; **~ top,** main tent at circus; **~ tree,** giant sequoia; **~ wheel,** Ferris wheel, *****(sl.) bigwig; **~'wig,** (colloq.) important person. **5.** Hence **~'**NESS *n.* **6.** *adv.* in a big manner; **come, go, over ~** (with great effect); **look, talk, ~** (boastfully); **think ~** (ambitiously). [ME, of unkn. orig.]

bi'gamist *n.* person guilty of bigamy. [f. foll. + -IST]

bi'gam|ў *n.* crime of going through form of marriage while previous marriage is still in existence; hence **~**OUS *a.* [ME, f. OF *bigamie* (-Y[1]) (*bigame* bigamous f. LL *bigamus* f. as BI- + Gk *gamos* marriage)]

bight (bīt) *n.* loop of rope; curve or recess of coast, river, etc. [OE *byht,* MLG *bucht* f. Gmc ******b*(*e*)*ug-*; see BOW[3]]

bi'got *n.* obstinate and intolerant adherent of a creed or view; hence **~**ED[2] *a.,* **~**RY (4, 5) *n.* [16th c. f. F; orig. unkn.]

Bihár'ĭ *a.* & *n.* (native or language) of Bihar. [Hindi, f. *Bihar* in India + -I]

bijou (bē'zhōō) *n.* (*pl.* **~x** *pr.* same) & *a.* **1.** *n.* jewel, trinket. **2.** *a.* small and elegant. [F]

bijouterie (bēzhōō'terē) *n.* jewellery, trinkets, etc. [F; see prec. and -ERY]

bik|e *n.,* & *v.i.* (colloq.) (use) bicycle or motor cycle; hence ***~**ER[1] (1) *n.* [abbr.]

biki'ni (-ē'-) *n.* scanty two-piece beach garment worn by women; **~ briefs** etc., women's briefs of similar design. [f. *B~,* atoll in Marshall Islands in Pacific where atomic bomb was exploded 1946]

bilā'teral *a.* **1.** of, on, with, two sides; **~ symmetry** (about a plane). **2.** affecting or between two parties, countries, etc. **3.** Hence **~**LY[2] *adv.* [f. BI- 1(a) + L *latus lateris* side + -AL]

bi'lberry *n.* (small blue fruit of) dwarf hardy N. European shrub (*Vaccinium myrtillus*) growing on heaths and stony moors and in mountain woods. [cf. Da. *böllebær*]

bi'lbō *n.* (*pl.* **~s** or **~es**). (Hist.) sword of notable temper. [f. *Bilboa* = Bilbao in Spain]

bi'lbōes (-ōz) *n. pl.* (Hist.) iron bar with sliding shackles for prisoner's ankles. [16th c.; orig. unkn.]

Bildungsroman (bĭ'ldōongzrŏmahn) *n.* novel dealing with one person's early life and development. [G]

bīle *n.* brownish-yellow bitter fluid secreted by liver to aid digestion; derangement of the bile; (fig.) peevishness; **~-duct** (conveying bile to duodenum). [F, f. L *bilis*]

bilge[1] *n.* nearly horizontal part of ship's bottom, inside

or out; filth that collects inside the bilge; (sl.) nonsense, rot; **~-keel,** timber or plate fastened under bilge to prevent rolling; **~-water,** stinking water collected in bilge. [prob. var. of BULGE[1]]

bilge[2] *v.* **1.** *v.t.* stave in the bilge of. **2.** *v.i.* spring a leak in the bilge; bulge, swell out. [f. prec.]

bilhár'zia *n.* tropical flatworm of genus *Bilharzic* parasitic in human pelvic region; bilharziasis; hence **bilhárzī'**ASIS *n.,* chronic disease produced by its presence, schistosomiasis. [mod. L, f. T. *Bilharz,* Ger physician d. 1862 + -IA[2]]

bi'liary (-lyerĭ) *a.* of the bile. [f. F *biliaire*; see BILE -ARY[2]]

bīli'ngual (-ĭ'nggwal) *a.* & *n.* **1.** *a.* having, speaking (fluently), spoken or written in, two languages; hence **~**ISM (1) *n.* **2.** *n.* person able to speak two languages esp. fluently. [f. L *bilinguis* (as BI- 1(a), *lingua* tongue, -AL)]

bi'lious (-lyus) *a.* liable to, affected by, causing, or arising from, derangement of the bile; (fig.) peevish having bilious TEMPERAMENT; hence **~**LY[2] *adv.,* **~**NESS *n.* [f. L *biliosus* (*bilis* bile; see -OUS)]

-bi'litў. See -ABILITY, -IBILITY, -UBILITY. [f. as -BLE -ITY]

bilk *v.t.* evade payment of (creditor, bill); cheat; give the slip to. [orig. uncert., perh. = BALK[2]; earliest use (17th c.) in cribbage; = spoil opponent's score]

bill[1] *n.* **1.** (Hist.) weapon like halberd with hool instead of blade. **2. ~**('hook), concave-edged lopping implement for pruning etc. [OE *bil,* = OS *bil* OHG *bill* f. WG ******bilja*]

bill[2] *n.* bird's beak (esp. when slender, flattened, or weak, and in pigeons and web-footed birds); muzzle of platypus; narrow promontory; point of anchor -fluke; hence (-)**~**ED[2] (-ld) *a.* [OE *bile,* of unkn. orig.]

bill[3] *v.i.* (Of doves) stroke bill with bill; exchange caresses (esp. *bill and coo*). [f. prec.]

bill[4] *n.* **1.** draft of proposed law; (Law) written statement of (esp. plaintiff's) case; TRUE bill. **2.** note o charges for goods supplied or services rendered amount thus owed; *****banknote; poster, placard (programme of) entertainment. **3. ~** (**of exchange**) written order to pay sum on given date to drawer or to named payee; **accommodation ~** (to raise money on credit). **4. ~ of fare,** menu, (fig.) programme; **~ of health,** certificate regarding infectious disease on ship or in port at time of sailing (*clean ~ of health,* certificate that there is no disease also fig. of person or thing examined and found in good condition); *bill of* INDICTMENT; **~ of lading,** shipmaster's detailed receipt to consignor, *****waybill **~ of mortality,** (Hist.) weekly statement of deaths in and near London; ||**~ of quantities,** detailed statement of work, prices, dimensions, etc., for the erection of a building; *Bill of* RIGHT*s*[3]; **~ of sale,** certificate of transfer of personal property, esp borrower's certificate that chattel is pledged as security. **5. ~'board,** large outdoor board for advertisements; ***~'fold,** wallet for banknotes; **~'head,** printed account form; **~'poster, ~'sticker,** person who pastes up placards. [ME f AF *bille,* AL *billa,* prob. alt. of med. L *bulla* seal, document, BULL[3]]

bill[5] *v.t.* announce, put in the programme (**~ed to appear** etc., announced as going to); advertise *as* send note of charges to. [f. prec.]

bi'llabŏng *n.* (Austral.) river branch that forms backwater or stagnant pool. [f. Aboriginal *Billibang* Bell River (*billa* water)]

bi'llêt[1] *n.* order requiring person to board and lodge the soldier etc. bearing it; place where troops etc. are lodged; destination (**every bullet has its ~,** hits only by providential order); appointment, situation [ME f. AF *billette,* AL *billetta,* dim. of *billa* BILL[4]; see -ET[1]]

bi'llêt[2] *v.t.* quarter (soldiers etc.) *on* (town, house-holder, etc.), *in, at*; (of householder) provide (soldier

etc.) with board and lodging; hence ∼EE′, ∼ER¹, *ns.*
[f. prec.]

bi′llet³ *n.* thick piece of firewood; small bar of metal;
(Archit.) short roll inserted at intervals in hollow
moulding. [ME, f. F *billette* and *billot* dims. of *bille*
tree-trunk f. med. L *billa*, *billus*, prob. of Celt. orig.]

billet-doux (bilidōō′) *n.* (*pl.* billets- *pr.* -ōō′z). (joc.)
love-letter. [F]

bi′lliard|s (-lyerdz) *n.* game played with cues and
three balls on oblong smooth cloth-covered table;
||**bar** ∼s, variant in which balls are to be struck into
holes on table; ∼-**ball**, ∼-**cue**, ∼-**room**, ∼-**table**,
kinds used for billiards; ∼-**marker**, attendant, or
apparatus for, keeping the score. [orig. pl., f. F *billard*
billiards, cue, dim. of *bille*; see BILLET³]

bi′llingsgāte (-z-) *n.* abuse, violent invective. [17th
c., from the scolding of fish-sellers in *B*∼ market,
London]

bi′llion (-yon) *a.* & *n.* (for *pl.* usage see HUNDRED). ||a
million million; a thousand million; *∼air′e*, person
possessing a thousand million dollars [after MILLION-
AIRE]; hence ∼TH² *a.* & *n.* [F (as BI-, MILLION)]

bi′llon *n.* alloy of gold or silver with predominating
amount of base metal. [F (*bille* BILLET³)]

bi′llow (-ō) *n.*, & *v.i.* **1.** *n.* great wave; (poet., in *sing.* or
pl.) the sea; (fig.) anything that sweeps along as if in
waves; hence ∼Y² *a.* **2.** *v.i.* rise or move or swell in
billows. [f. ON *bylgja* f. Gmc *bulg*-, *belg*- swell]

billy¹ *n.* (orig. Austral. & NZ) cylindrical tin etc. or
enamelled container used as kettle, cooking-pot,
food-carrier, etc. [perh. f. Aboriginal *billa* water]

bi′llỹ² *n.* **1.** = BILLY-GOAT. **2.** *∼* (**club**), policeman's
truncheon. [f. *B*∼, pet-form of man's Christian name
William]

bi′llỹcăn *n.* = BILLY¹. [f. BILLY¹ + CAN¹]

||**bi′llỹcŏck** *n.* (arch.) bowler hat. [said to have been
orig. designed for *William Coke* 1850]

bi′llỹ-goat *n.* male goat. [f. as BILLY² + GOAT]

bi′llỹ-ō(h) (-ō) *n.* (colloq.) **like** ∼ (intensive phr.):-
ruining like ∼ (very hard), *fighting like* ∼ (fiercely).
[19th c.; orig. unkn.]

bilō′bate, bi′lōbed (-ōbd) *adjs.* having two lobes. [f.
BI- 1(a) + LOBE + -ATE², -ED²]

bi′ltŏng *n.* (S. Afr.) strips of sun-dried lean meat.
[Afrik. (*bil* buttock, whence it is cut, *tong* tongue,
which it looks like)]

Bim *n.* (colloq.) inhabitant of Barbados. [19th c.; orig.
unkn.]

BIM *abbr.* British Institute of Management.

bi′manal, bi′manous, *adjs.* having two hands. [f. BI-
1(a) + L *manus* hand + -AL, -OUS]

bimba′shi (-ah′-) *n.* Turkish major or naval commander. [Turk., = head of a thousand (*bin* thousand,
baş head)]

bi′mbō *n.* (*pl.* ∼s or ∼es). (sl., usu. derog.) person;
woman. [It., = little child]

bimĕta′llic *a.* **1.** of two metals; ∼ **strip** (in thermostat etc., made of two bands of metals with different
thermal expansion, thus bending when heated, in a
way that can be used to control temperature). **2.**
using gold and silver as legal tender to any amount at
fixed ratio to each other; hence **bimĕ′tall**ISM (3),
bimĕ′tallIST (2), *ns.* [f. F *bimétallique* (as BI- 1(a),
METALLIC)]

bimĭllenarỹ (-mǐlě′-, -mǐ′lǐ-) *a.* & *n.* (festival) of the
two-thousandth anniversary. [f. BI- 1(d) + MIL-
LENARY]

bimo′nthlỹ (-mŭ′-) *a.* & *n.* (periodical) produced or
occurring every two months or twice a month. [f. BI-
1(d, e) + MONTHLY]

bin *n.* receptacle for corn, coal, bottled wine, etc.;
receptacle for household rubbish, litter, etc.; ||canvas
receptacle used in hop-picking. [OE *bin(n)*, *binne* f.
OBrit. **benna*, or f. med. L *benna* f. Gaulish]

bin-. See BI-.

bi′narỹ *a.* & *n.* dual, of or involving pairs; ∼ **fission**,
(Biol.) division of cell or organism into two parts;

(Mus.) ∼ **form** (of movement in two sections), ∼
measure (of two beats to bar); ∼ (**star**), system of
two stars revolving round each other; ∼ **compound**
(Chem., of two elements or radicals); ∼ **digit**, one of
two (usu. 0 and 1) used in *binary* SCALE³. [f. LL *binarius*
(*bini* two together; see -ARY¹)]

bi′nate *a.* (Bot.) composed of two equal parts; growing in pairs. [f. mod. L *binatus* f. L *bini* (as prec.; see
-ATE²)]

bīnaur′al *a.* of, used with, both ears (*binaural stethoscope*); (of sound) recorded by two microphones and
usu. transmitted separately to the two ears. [f. BI- +
AURAL²]

bind¹ *v.* (**bound;** see also BOUNDEN). **1.** *v.t.* tie; fasten,
attach, *to* or *on* or *together*. **2.** put in bonds, restrain;
obstruct (*fog*-, *snow-bound*); fasten or hold together;
constipate; (esp. Cookery) cause to cohere; **bound
up**, closely associated *with*. **3.** be obligatory, exercise
authority, impose constraint or duty, *on*; indenture as
apprentice; ratify (bargain etc.); (in *pass.*) be required
by duty, be certain, *to* (do something); ∼ (**over**),
subject to legal obligation, promise, etc.; **I'll be
bound**, (fig.) I guarantee truth of (statement), I feel
certain. **4.** (sl.) bore, weary. **5.** ∼ (**up**), bandage;
encircle (head etc.) *with*, wreathe (material) *round*, *on*;
edge with braid, iron, etc.; fasten sheets of (book),
fasten (sheets of book), into (usu. stiff) cover. **6.** *v.i.*
(Of snow etc.) cohere, stick; be prevented from
moving freely; (sl.) complain. [OE *bindan*, = OS
bindan, OHG *bintan*, ON *binda*, Goth *bindan* f. IE
*bhendh-]

bind² *n.* = BINE; (Mus.) = TIE² 5; (sl.) nuisance, bore;
**position that prevents free action; **in a* ∼, (sl.) in
difficulty. [f. prec.]

bi′nder *n.* In vbl senses; bookbinder; cementing
substance; tie-beam; bondstone in wall; machine for
reaping and binding grain into sheaves; loose cover
for unbound newspapers etc. [f. BIND¹ + -ER¹]

bi′ndery *n.* bookbinder's workshop. [f. prec. + -ERY
(3)]

bi′ndi-eye (-ī) *n.* (Austral.) small herb with burlike
fruit. [20th c.; orig. unkn.]

bi′nding¹ *a.* obligatory (*on*). [f. BIND¹ + -ING³]

bi′nding² *n.* In vbl senses; book-cover; tape, braid,
etc., for protecting raw edges. [f. BIND¹ + -ING¹]

*bi′ndle *n.* (colloq.) tramp's bundle or bedding etc.
[prob. corrupt. of BUNDLE¹]

bi′ndweed *n.* convolvulus; other climbing plant, e.g.
honeysuckle. [f. BIND¹ + WEED]

bīne *n.* flexible shoot; stem of climbing plant, esp. the
hop. [orig. dial. form of BIND²]

Bi′net(-Simo′n) (bě′nā sēmaw′n) *a.* = scale, test,
(for measuring intelligence). [f. A. *Binet* d. 1911 and
T. *Simon* d. 1961, Fr. psychologists]

binge (-nj) *n.* (sl.) drinking-bout, spree. [prob. orig.
dial., = soak]

bi′ngō¹ (-nggō) *n.* (*pl.* ∼s). popular gambling game
like lotto, played esp. in public halls, with cards
divided into numbered squares, in which player first
covering all or specified set of numbers on card wins
prize. [perh. f. winner's excl.; cf. dial. *bing*, imit.]

bi′ngō² (-nggō) *int.* expr. sudden action or event, esp.
winning of game of bingo (see prec.). [imit. of sudden
sound]

bi′nnacle *n.* receptacle for ship's compass. [earlier
bittacle, ME, f. Sp. *bitácula* or Port. *bitacola* f. L
habitaculum habitation (*habitare* inhabit)]

bīnŏ′cular *a.* & *n.* **1.** *a.* adapted for or using two eyes.
2. *n.* (usu. in *pl.*) field- or opera-glasses for use with
both eyes. [f. L *bini* two together + *oculus* eye + -AR¹]

bīnō′mial *a.* & *n.* (algebraic sum or difference)
consisting of two terms (∼ **theorem**, formula for
finding any power of a binomial without multiplying
at length); = BINOMINAL (name). [f. F *binôme* or mod.
L *binomium* (as BI-, Gk *nomos* part, portion) + -AL]

bīnō′minal *a.* composed of or using two names; ∼
system (of scientific nomenclature by genus and

species). [f. L *binominis* (BI- 1(a), *nomen -inis* name) + -AL]

bint *n.* (colloq., usu. derog.) girl; woman. [Arab., = daughter, girl]

bǐ'ntūrǒng *n.* S. Asian prehensile-tailed civet (*Arctictis binturong*). [Malay]

bio- *comb. form.* (1) life (*biography*); (2) biological (*biomathematics*); (3) of living beings (*bioscience*). [f. Gk *bios* (course of) human life]

biochě'm|ĭstrў (-kě'-) *n.* study of chemical or physico-chemical processes and products involved in life phenomena of plants and animals; hence ∼ICAL *a.*, ∼IST (3) *n.* [f. prec. + CHEMISTRY]

biocoen|ō'sĭs (-sēn-), *-cēn|-, *n.* (*pl.* ∼oses *pr.* -ō'sēz). association of organisms forming a community; relationship existing between such organisms; hence ∼ŏ'LOGY *n.*, ∼O'TIC *a.* [mod. L, f. BIO- + Gk *koinōsis* sharing (*koinos* common)]

biŏdègrā'dable *a.* capable of being decomposed by living matter, esp. by bacteria; so **biŏdègrād**ABI'LITY, **biŏdègrad**A'TION, *ns.* [f. BIO- + DEGRADE + -ABLE]

biŏfee'dbăck *n.* technique of using feedback of a normally automatic bodily response to a stimulus, in order to acquire voluntary control of the response. [f. BIO- + FEEDBACK]

biŏgě'nēsĭs *n.* hypothesis that living matter arises only from living matter; synthesis of chemical substances by living matter; hypothetical development of living matter from complex inanimate substances; hence **biŏgěně'tɪc** *a.* [f. BIO- + Gk *genesis* birth]

biŏgě'nic *a.* produced by living matter. [f. BIO- + -GENIC]

biŏ'graphў *n.* written life of a person; branch of literature dealing with persons' lives; life-course of a living (usu. human) being; so **biŏ'GRAPHER** *n.*, **biō**GRA'PHIC(AL) *adjs.* [f. F *biographie* or mod. L f. med. Gk *biographia* (as BIO-, -GRAPHY)]

biŏlŏ'gĭcal *a.* of or relating to biology or life phenomena; ∼ **clock**, innate mechanism controlling rhythmic activities of an organism; ∼ **control** (of pest by introducing a natural enemy of it); ∼ **warfare**, use of organisms against an enemy, esp. of bacteria to spread disease; hence ∼LY² *adv.* [f. BIOLOGY + -ICAL]

biŏ'log|ў *n.* science of life, dealing with morphology, physiology, anatomy, behaviour, origin, and distribution, of animals and plants; hence ∼IST (3) *n.* [f. F f. G *biologie* (as BIO-, -LOGY)]

biŏlumině'sc|ence (-lōo-, -lū-) *n.* emission of light by living organisms; hence ∼ENT *a.* [f. BIO- + LUMINESCENCE]

bĭ'ōmăss *n.* total quantity or weight of organisms in a given area. [f. BIO- + MASS²]

biŏmăthĕmă'tĭcs *n.* science of the application of mathematics to biology. [f. BIO- + MATHEMATICS]

biŏ'mĕtrў *n.*, **biomě'trics** *n. pl.* (usu. treated as *sing.*) science of the application of statistical methods to biological facts; so **biomě'trɪc**(AL) *adjs.*, **biomĕtrɪ'cɪan** *n.* [f. BIO- + -METRY]

bǐ'omŏrph *n.* decorative form representing living object; hence ∼IC (-ŏr'-) *a.* [f. BIO- + Gk *morphē* form]

biŏ'nic *a.* relating to bionics; having mechanical body-parts, or superhuman powers resulting from these. [f. foll.; see -IC]

biŏ'nics *n. pl.* (usu. treated as *sing.*) study of mechanical systems that function like (parts of) living beings. [f. BIO- after *electronics*]

biŏnŏ'mics *n. pl.* (usu. treated as *sing.*) branch of biology dealing with organisms' habits and modes of life in their natural environment. [f. BIO-, after ECONOMICS]

biophў'sĭc|s (-z-) *n. pl.* (usu. treated as *sing.*) science of the application of the laws of physics to biological phenomena; hence ∼AL *a.*, ∼IST (3) *n.* [f. BIO- + PHYSICS]

bǐ'ōpsў *n.* examination of tissue cut from the living body; removal of such tissue. [f. F *biopsie* f. Gk *bios* life + *opsis* sight, after *necropsy*]

bǐ'orhỹthm *n.* any of the recurring cycles of physical, emotional, and intellectual activity said to occur in people's lives. [f. BIO- + RHYTHM]

bǐ'oscōpe *n.* (S. Afr.) cinema. [f. BIO- + -SCOPE]

bǐ'ōsphēre *n.* regions of earth's crust and atmosphere in which living matter is found. [f. G *biosphäre* (as BIO-, SPHERE)]

biosў'nthěs|ĭs *n.* (*pl.* ∼es *pr.* -ēz). production of chemical substance by living organism. [f. BIO- + SYNTHESIS]

biō'ta *n.* animal and plant life of a region. [mod. L; cf. Gk *biotē* life]

biō'tic *n.* relating to life or to living things. [f. F *biotique* or f. LL f. Gk *biōtikos* (*bios* life; see -IC)]

biŏtin *n.* crystalline vitamin in yeast etc., controlling growth. [G, f. Gk *bios* life + -IN]

bipártĭsăn (-zǎ'n, -pä'r't-) *a.* of or involving two (political) parties. [f. BI- 1(a) + PARTISAN¹]

bipär'tĭte *a.* having two parts; (of treaty, contract, etc.) drawn up in two corresponding parts; shared by or involving two parties. [f. L *bipartitus* f. BI(*partire* PART²)]

bǐ'pěd *a.* & *n.* two-footed (animal); so **bǐ'pědAL** *a.* [f. L *bipes -edis* (as BI- 1(a), *pes pedis* foot)]

bǐpi'nnate *a.* having lobes that themselves have lobes. [f. BI- 1(c) + PINNATE]

bǐ'plāne *n.* aeroplane having two sets of wings, one above the other. [f. BI- 1(a) + PLANE³]

bǐpō'lar *a.* having two poles or extremities. [f. BI- 1(a) + POLAR]

bîrch *n.*, & *v.t.* **1.** *n.* smooth-barked slender-branched northern forest tree of genus *Betula*; ∼('wood), its wood; (NZ) one of various similar trees; ∼bark, bark of *B. papyrifera* for canoes etc., *such canoe; ∼(-rod), bundle of birch twigs used to flog delinquents; hence ∼EN⁵ *a.* **2.** *v.t.* flog with birch. [OE *bi(e)rce*, = OHG *birka* f. Gmc *berkjōn*]

bîrd *n.*, & *v.i.* **1.** *n.* feathered vertebrate with two wings and two feet; game-bird; (sl.) young woman; (colloq.) person; (sl.) prison (sentence) [f. rhyming sl. *birdlime* = time]. **2.** (fig.) **a** ∼ **in the hand**, something certain; ∼ **is** or **has flown**, prisoner etc. has escaped; ∼s **of a feather**, people of like character; (strictly) **for the** ∼s, (sl.) trivial, uninteresting; **get the** ∼, (sl.) be dismissed, be hissed and booed; **kill two** ∼s **with one stone**, achieve two aims at once; **like a** ∼, without difficulty or hesitation; **little** ∼, unnamed informant (*told me* etc.); OLD *bird*. **3.** ∼ **of paradise**, New Guinea bird with beautiful brilliantly coloured plumage; ∼ **of passage**, migrant, (fig.) transient visitor; *bird of* PREY¹. **4.** ∼-**bath**, basin in garden etc. with water for birds to bathe in; ∼'**brain(ed)**, stupid or flighty (person); ∼'**cage**, wire cage for bird(s), object of similar design; ∼-**call**, bird's natural call, instrument imitating it; ∼ **cherry**, wild cherry (*Prunus padus*); *∼ **dog**, retriever (lit., or fig. of person); ∼-**fancier**, one who knows about, collects, breeds, or deals in, birds; *bird*LIME¹; ∼ **sanctuary**, area where birds are protected and helped to breed; ∼'**seed**, special seeds given to caged birds; ∼'s-**eye**, plant (esp. ||germander speedwell) with small bright round flowers, pattern with many small spots; ∼'s-**eye view**, view from overhead *of* town etc. or (fig.) *of* subject; ∼'s-**foot**, plant like foot of bird, esp. of genus *Lotus* with claw-shaped pods; ∼'s **nest**, nest of bird (∼'s *nest soup*, made from edible kind of S. Asian swift's nest); ∼'s-**nesting** (-zn-), hunting for birds' nests, usu. to get eggs; ∼-**song**, musical cry of bird(s); ∼-**strike**, collision between bird and aircraft; ∼-**table**, raised platform on which food for birds is placed; ∼-**watcher**, one who observes birds in their natural surroundings; ∼-**watching**, this occupation; hence ∼(-**watch**) *v.i.* [OE *brid*, of unkn. orig.]

bîr'die *n.* little bird; (Golf) hole played in one stroke under par or bogey. [f. prec. + -IE]

For other words in bi- see BI-.

bĭrefrĭ'ng|ent (-nj-) *a.* (Phys.) having double RE-FRACTION; so ∼ENCE *n.* [f. BI- 1 (b) + REFRINGENT]

bĭr'ēme *n.* ancient galley with two banks of oars. [f. L *biremis* (as BI- 1 (a), *remus* oar)]

bĭrĕ'tta *n.* square cap of various colours (cf. ZUC-CHETTO) worn by RC and other clergymen. [f. It. *berretta* or Sp. *birreta* fem. dims. corresp. to Prov. BERET f. LL *birrus* cape]

bĭrk. See BERK.

Bĭr'ó *n.* (*pl.* ∼s). (P) (make of) ball-point pen. [f. L. *Biró*, Hung. inventor]

bĭrth *n.* **1.** emergence of young from body of mother; **give ∼ to,** produce (young) thus, also fig.; **new ∼,** (Theol.) spiritual regeneration. **2.** coming into existence; origin, beginning; parentage, descent, inherited position; noble lineage. **3.** ∼ **certificate,** official document giving date and place of person's birth; ∼ **control,** (practice of) methods of preventing undesired pregnancy; ∼**'day,** (anniversary of) day of one's birth; ∼*day card, party, present,* (given on this); ||∼*day honours,* titles etc. given on sovereign's (official) birthday; ∼*day suit,* (joc.) state of nakedness; ∼**'mark,** unusual mark on one's body at or from birth, usu. an irregularly-shaped blotch of brown or dark red skin; ∼ **pill,** contraceptive pill; ∼**'place** (at which one was born); ∼ **rate,** number of births per thousand of population per year etc ; ∼**'right,** rights or possessions belonging to one as eldest son, as born in a certain status or country, or as a human being. [ME, f. ON *byrth*, Goth. *gabaurths* f. Gmc **gaburthiz* f. stem **ber-* BEAR[3] + -TH[1]]

BIS *abbr.* Bank for International Settlements.

bĭ'scuit (-kǐt) *n.* & *a.* **1.** *n.* ||piece of usu. unleavened cake or bread of various materials, usu. crisp, dry, hard, and in small flat thin shape; TAKE[1] *the biscuit.* **2.** *soft round cake like scone. **3.** porcelain etc. after firing but before glazing and painting. **4.** one of three square sections of soldier's mattress. **5.** *n.* & *a.* (of) light-brown colour. [ME, f. OF *bescoit* etc. f. med. L **bscoctus* twice baked f. L *bis* + *coctus* p.p. of *coquere* cook]

bise (bēz) *n.* keen dry N. wind in Switzerland, S. France, etc. [ME f. OF]

bĭsĕ'ct *v.t.* cut or divide into two (prop. equal) parts; hence **bĭsĕ'ction** *n.* [f. BI- + L *secare* sect- cut]

bĭsĕ'ctor *n.* bisecting line. [f. as prec. + -OR]

bĭsĕ'xūal *a.* of two sexes; having both sexes in one individual; (of person) sexually attracted by members of both sexes; hence ∼ITY (ŭ'-) *n.* [f. BI- 1 (a) + SEXUAL]

bish *n.* (sl.) mistake. [20th c.; orig. unkn.]

bĭ'shop *n.* clergyman consecrated as governor of diocese and possessing powers of confirming, instituting, and ordaining (*bishop* SUFFRAGAN); chess piece with mitre-shaped top; mulled and spiced wine; **Bishops' Bible** (version of 1568); ∼ **sleeve,** full sleeve gathered at wrist. [OE *bisc(e)op*, = OS *biskop*, OHG *biscof*, ON *biskup* f. pop. L **biscopus* f. eccl. L f. Gk *episkopos* overseer (as EPI-, -*skopos* -looking)]

bĭ'shopric *n.* office or diocese of bishop. [OE *bisceoprīce* (as prec., *rīce* realm)]

bĭsk. See BISQUE[3].

Bĭ'smárck (-z-) *n.* ∼ **herring** (marinaded fillet served cold). [f. Prince O. von ∼, Ger. statesman d. 1898]

bismi'llah (-a-) *int.* (used by Muslims before action). [Arab., = in the name of Allah]

bĭ'smuth (-z-) *n.* reddish-white easily fusible metallic element; compound of it used medicinally. [f. mod. L *bisemutum,* latinization of G *wismut,* of unkn. orig.]

bĭ'son *n.* (*pl.* same). wild ox of two species of genus *Bison,* European (also called *wisent*) and American (also called *buffalo*). [ME f. L, f. Gmc **wisand-*]

bisque[1] (-k) *n.* (Tennis) right of scoring one point without winning it, at any time in the set; (Croquet) right of playing extra turn; (Golf) handicap stroke to be taken when desired. [F; etym. unkn.]

bisque[2] (-k) *n.* unglazed white porcelain used in statuettes. [f. BISCUIT]

bisque[3] (-k), **bisk,** *n.* rich soup made from shellfish etc. [F; etym. unkn.]

bissĕ'xtīle *a.* & *n.* leap(-year). [f. LL *bi(s)sextilis* (*annus*), (year) containing the *bis sextus dies* or doubled 24 Feb. (sixth day before calends of March)]

bĭstā'ble *a.* having two stable states. [f. BI- 1 (a) + STABLE[1]]

bĭ'stŏrt *n.* herb with twisted root and cylindrical spike of flesh-coloured flowers. [f. F *bistorte* or f. med. L *bistorta* (*bis* twice + *torta* fem. p.p. of *torquēre* twist)]

bĭ'stourў (-terĭ) *n.* surgeon's scalpel. [f. F *bistouri, bistorie,* orig. = dagger; orig. unkn.]

||**bĭ'stre** (-ter), ***bĭ'ster,** *n.* & *a.* brown pigment prepared from soot; (of) its colour. [F; orig. unkn.]

bĭ'strō (bē'-) *n.* (*pl.* ∼s). small bar or restaurant. [F]

bĭsŭ'lphāte, *-**f-,** *n.* (Chem.) salt containing double proportion of sulphate radical. [f. BI- 2 (b) + SULPHATE]

bit[1] *n.* boring-piece of drill, cutting-iron of plane, nipping-part of pincers etc.; part of key that engages with lock-lever; copper head of soldering-iron; mouthpiece of bridle; **take the ∼ between** one's **teeth,** (fig.) escape from control. [OE *bite,* = OS *biti,* OHG *biz,* ON *bit* f. Gmc **bitiz* (**bītan* BITE[1])]

bit[2] *n.* **1.** morsel of food; (small) piece or quantity or portion of anything; **∼ by ∼,** gradually. 2. (colloq.) **a ∼,** somewhat (*feeling a bit tired*); **a ∼ of,** rather (*a bit of a coward*), a small or unimportant (*only a bit of a book*), a small quantity of (*here's a bit of advice*), a fair quantity of (*takes a bit of remembering*); **a ∼ of all right,** very pleasing person or thing; ∼**s and pieces,** ∼**s and bobs,** odds and ends; ∼**s of,** poor little (*children, furniture*); **do** one's ∼, contribute service or money to a cause; **every ∼ as,** quite as; **not a ∼** (of it), not at all; to ∼**s,** into small fragments. **3.** (colloq.) *a short time* (*wait a bit*) or distance (*move up a bit*); small coin; *amount of 12½ cents (*two, four, six, bits*). **4.** (colloq.) ∼ (**part,** small part in a play or film. **5.** (sl.) ∼ (of stuff), young woman. [OE *bita,* = OHG *bizzo,* ON *biti* f. Gmc **biton* (**bītan* BITE[1])]

bit[3] *v.t.* (-tt-). put bit into mouth of (horse); restrain. [f. BIT[1]]

bit[4] *n.* (Computers etc.) unit of information expressed as choice between two possibilities. [f. BINARY + DIGIT]

bit[5]. See BITE[1].

bitch *n.* & *v.* **1.** *n.* female dog; ∼ (**fox, otter, wolf**), female fox etc.; (derog.) woman, esp. lewd or malicious or treacherous one (SON *of a bitch*); (colloq.) unpleasant or difficult thing; hence ∼'*y*[2] *a.,* immoral, spiteful, ill-tempered. **2.** *v.i.* be spiteful or unfair; (colloq.) grumble. **3.** *v.t.* be spiteful or unfair to; ∼ (**up**), (colloq.) muddle. [OE *bicce,* rel. to ON *bikkja*]

bite[1] *v.* (**bit**; **bi'tten,** occas. **bit**). **1.** *v.t.* cut into or nip with the teeth; ∼ **off** etc., detach with the teeth. **2.** (Of snake, mosquito, flea, etc.) wound with sting or maxilla; **bitten with,** infected by (enthusiasm etc.); **what's biting you?,** (colloq.) what is worrying you? **3.** cause gnawing, smarting, etc., pain to (*frost-bitten*). **4.** (Of wheel, screw, anchor, etc.) grip; (of sword) penetrate. **5.** (usu. in *pass.*) take in, swindle; **once bitten twice shy,** being cheated or deluded promotes later caution. **6.** *v.i.* snap *at*; accept bait (lit. or fig.); have (desired) adverse effect. **7.** ∼ **back,** restrain (speech etc.) by biting the lips; ∼ **on the bullet,** be stoical; ∼ **the dust,** (rhet.) fall and die; ∼ **the hand that feeds** one, injure a benefactor; ∼ person's **head off,** respond curtly or angrily; *bite* one's LIP[1]; ∼ **off more than one can chew,** attempt too ambitious a task; **something to ∼ on,** (esp. fig.) enough to get a grip or understanding. [OE *bītan,* = OS *bītan,* OHG *bīzan,* ON *bīta,* Goth. *beitan* f. Gmc **bītan*]

bīte[2] *n.* **1.** act of, wound made by, piece detached by, biting; ***put the ∼ on,** (sl.) borrow or extort money from. **2.** food to eat; small meal. **3.** taking of bait by fish; grip, hold, (lit. or fig.); bringing together of teeth in occlusion; (fig.) incisiveness, pungency. [f. prec.]

bi′ter *n.* In vbl senses; **the** ~ **bit**, swindler himself duped. [f. BITE¹ + -ER¹]

bi′ting *a.* In vbl senses; pungent, stinging (*biting wind*); sarcastic; hence ~LY² *adv.* [f. BITE¹ + -ING²]

bi′tten. See BITE¹.

bi′tter *a.* & *n.* 1. *a.* tasting like wormwood or quinine, opp. *sweet,* (~-**apple,** colocynth; ~ **orange,** SEVILLE orange); (of beer) much flavoured with hops, opp. *mild*; unwelcome to the mind (*know from bitter experience*; **the** ~ **end,** last extremity; *bitter* PILL¹). **2.** caused by or showing mental pain (*a bitter rejoinder*); full of affliction or resentment; virulent, relentless; biting, harsh; piercingly cold. **3.** Hence ~LY² *adv.,* ~NESS *n.* **4.** *n.* bitterness; (in *pl.*) liquors impregnated with wormwood etc. used to promote appetite or digestion or as flavourings; ||bitter beer; ~-**sweet,** sweet(ness) with bitter after-taste or element (lit. or fig.), woody NIGHTSHADE. [OE *biter,* = OS, OHG *bittar,* ON *bitr,* Goth. *baitrs,* prob. f. Gmc *bītan* BITE¹; *the bitter end* may be f. Naut., where the wds mean the last part of a cable left round the bitts when the rest is overboard]

bi′tterling *n.* small carplike freshwater fish from Central Europe. [G (*bitter* BITTER, -*ling* -LING¹)]

bi′ttern *n.* marsh bird of genus *Botaurus* allied to herons, esp. one known for male's booming note in breeding-season. [ME, f. OF *butor* f. Rom. **butaurus* f. L *butio* bittern + *taurus* bull; -*n* perh. f. assoc. w. HERN]

bitts *n. pl.* (Naut.) pair of posts on deck for fastening cables etc. [ME, prob. f. LG; cf. LG, Du. *beting*]

bi′tty *a.* made up of unrelated bits, scrappy. [f. BIT² + -Y²]

bi′tūmen *n.* **1.** any of various brown or black mixtures of tarlike hydrocarbons derived from petroleum naturally or by distillation; (Austral. colloq.) tarred road. **2.** So **bitū′minous** *a.*; **bituminous coal,** kind burning with smoky flame. [L *bitumen -minis*]

bitū′miniz|e, -īs|e (-īz), *v.t.* convert into, impregnate or cover with, bitumen; hence ~A′TION *n.* [f. prec. + -IZE (3, 5)]

bivā′lent *a.* (Chem.) having a valence of two. [f. BI-1(a) + *valent-* pres. part. st. f. as VALENCE²]

bi′valve *a.* & *n.* **1.** *a.* (Biol.) having two valves. **2.** *a.* & *n.* (mollusc) with hinged double shell, e.g. oyster. [f. BI-1(a) + VALVE]

bi′vouac (-ŏŏ-) *v.i.* (-ck-), & *n.* (remain, esp. for the night, in) temporary encampment without tents. [F, prob. f. Swiss G *beiwacht* additional guard at night (formed by citizens' patrol in Aargau and Zurich)]

bi′vvy *n.* (sl.) shelter; small tent. [abbr. of prec.]

bi-wee′kly *a.* & *n.* (periodical) produced or occurring every two weeks or twice a week. [f. BI-1(d, e) + WEEKLY]

bi-year′ly *a.* & *adv.* (produced or occurring) every two years or twice a year. [f. BI-1(d, e) + YEARLY]

biz *n.* (colloq.) business. [abbr.]

bizar′re (-zär′) *a.* eccentric, fantastic, grotesque; so ~**rie** (-rerē) *n.,* bizarre quality [-ERY]. [F, = handsome, brave, f. Sp & Port. *bizarro,* f. Basque *bizarra* beard]

bk. *abbr.* book.

Bk *symb.* berkelium.

BL *abbr.* Bachelor of Law; bill of lading; British Leyland; British Library.

bl. *abbr.* barrel; black.

blăb *v.* (-bb-) & *n.* **1.** *v.t.* & *i.* talk or tell foolishly or indiscreetly, reveal, let out, (secrets etc., or abs.); hence ~′bER¹ *n.* **2.** *n.* person who blabs. [v. f. n., ME; cf. OHG *blabbizōn,* prob. f. Gmc **blab-* imit.]

blăck¹ *a.* **1.** opposite to white, colourless from the absence or complete absorption of all light (like coal or soot); so near this as to have no distinguishable colour; very dark-coloured (~ **in the face,** purple with strangulation, exertion, or passion). **2.** dark-skinned (usu. *B*~) pertaining to Negroes;

dark-clothed; (of sky, cloud, deep water, etc.) dusky, gloomy; (of hands, clothes) dirty; (as distinguishing epithet) *black bear, pine, snake, vulture, black- -backed gull,* etc. **3.** deadly, sinister, wicked, hateful, (*black-hearted*; *black ingratitude*; **not so** ~ **as** one **is painted,** better than one's reputation); dismal (*black despair*); angry, sulky, threatening, (*black looks*); implying disgrace or condemnation; presenting tragedy or bitter reality in comic terms (*black comedy, humour, joke*; performed by blackleg labour; (of goods etc.) not to be handled by workers on strike; contravening economic regulations (*black market*). **4.** B~ **Africa** (south of Sahara, where Blacks predominate); ~ **and blue,** discoloured by bruises; B~ **and Tans,** armed force recruited to fight Sinn Fein 1921, wearing mixture of military and constabulary uniforms; ~ **and white,** written etc. in black ink on white paper, (of film etc.) not in colour, (fig.) comprising only opposite extremes; (*down*) *in* ~ *and white,* recorded in writing or print; ~ **art,** magic [partly f. *black* in sense 'wicked', partly by assoc. w. med. L *nigromantia* corrupt. of *necromantia* NECROMANCY]; ~ **ball** (placed in ballot-box etc. to reject candidate); whence ~′**ball** *v.t.,* reject by this or other means of voting; ~-**beetle,** common cockroach; ~ **belt,** region in US where Blacks predominate, (holder of) mark of proficiency in judo; ~′**berry,** dark-fruited bramble or its fruit (*plentiful as* ~*berries,* as plentiful as can be; ~′*berrying,* gathering them); ~′**bird,** European songbird of thrush family, **grackle or similar bird, (Hist.) kidnapped Negro or Polynesian on slave-ship (~′*birding,* trade in these); ~′**board** (with black or dark surface, used in schools etc. for writing or drawing on in chalk); ~ **body,** (Phys.) hypothetical perfect absorber and radiator; **in** person's ~ **books,** out of favour with him; ~ **box,** (1) flight-recorder in aircraft, (2) apparatus of unknown internal design; ~′**boy,** Austral. tree with thick dark trunk and head of spearlike leaves; ~ **bread,** coarse rye bread; *black* BRYONY; ~′**buck,** Ind. or S. Afr. antelope; ||~ **cap,** (Hist.) cap worn by judge when sentencing to death; ~′**cap,** bird with black-topped head, esp. a warbler (*Sylvia atricapilla*); *black* CATTLE; ||~-**coat worker,** clerk etc. (opp. industrial employee); ~′**cock,** male of black grouse (cf. GREY-*hen*); ~ **coffee** (without milk or cream); ||B~′ **Country,** smoky grimy district in Staffs. and W. Midlands; *black* CURRANT; ~ **damp,** = CHOKE¹-*damp; Black* DEATH; *black* DIAMOND; ~ **dog,** sulks, melancholy mood; ~′**earth,** chernozem; ~ **eye** (with surrounding skin discoloured by bruise, or with dark iris), whence ~-*eyed*; ~-**eyed Susan,** flower with light petals and dark centre, esp. of genus *Rudbeckia*; ~-**face,** (1) dark-faced sheep, (2) make- -up for Negro role; ~′**fellow,** (Hist.) Australian Aboriginal; ~′**fish,** (1) one of several dark-coloured species of fish (e.g. tautog), (2) salmon just after spawning; *black* FLAG⁴; ~′**fly,** thrips or aphid infesting plants; B~ **Friar,** Dominican [f. their black cloaks]; *black* FROST; ~ **game,** ~ **grouse,** a European GROUSE¹ (*Lyrurus tetrix*); ~′**head,** (1) bird with black head, esp. scaup, (2) black-topped pimple in hair follicle on face etc.; ~ **hole,** (Astron.) region from which no matter or radiation can escape, (esp. Mil.) place of confinement for punishment; ~ **ice,** thin hard transparent ice; *black* IVORY; ~′**jack,** (1) tarred- -leather vessel for alcoholic liquor, (2) pirates' black flag, (3) *flexible loaded bludgeon, (4) *vingt-et-un;* ~′**lead** *v.t.,* & *n.,* (polish with) graphite [named from its making marks like lead]; ~′**leg,** (1) swindler esp. on turf, (2) || = SCAB 3, (*v.i.* & *t.*) act as blackleg, betray or injure thus [origin of senses unknown]; *black* LEOPARD; ~ **letter,** old heavy style of type; ~ **light,** invisible ultraviolet or infra-red radiation; ~′**list** (of persons under suspicion, liable to punishment or unfavourable treatment, etc.); ~′**list** *v.t.,* enter name of (person) on black list; *black* MAGIC; ~′**mail** *v.t.,* & *n.,* compel, compulsion, to make payment or action in return for concealment of discreditable secrets etc., (fig.) use (of) threats or moral pressure [f. obs. *mail* rent, OE *māl* f. ON *mál* agreement, perh. = OHG *mahal* assembly]; **B~ Maria,** vehicle for taking prisoners from and to gaol; ~ **mark** (of discredit against one's name); ~ **market,** (place of) illegitimate traffic in officially controlled goods or currencies or in commodities in short supply (~ *marketeer,* one who engages in this); ~ **Mass,** (1) travesty of the mass said to be used in the cult of Satanism, (2) Requiem Mass; **B~ Monk,** Benedictine; **B~ **Muslim,** member of Negro sect proposing separation of Blacks and Whites; *black* MUSTARD, NIGHTSHADE; **B~ **Panther,** one of a group of extremist fighters for Blacks' rights; *black* PEPPER[1]; **B~ Pope,** head of Jesuits; **B~ Power,** movement in secret support of civil rights etc. of Blacks; ~ **pudding** (sausage-shaped, of blood, suet, etc.); ||**B~ Rod,** gentleman usher of Lord Chamberlain's department, House of Lords, etc.; **B~ Sash,** (S. Afr.) women's anti-apartheid organization; ~ **sheep,** scoundrel, unsatisfactory member (*of* family etc.); ~'**shirt,** Fascist [f. It. Fascist uniform]; ~'**smith,** smith working in iron; ~'**spot,** place of danger or difficulty, esp. area with high accident rate etc.; *black* SQUALL, SWAN; ~ **tea** (fully fermented before drying); ~'**thorn,** (1) thorny shrub bearing white flowers before leaves and small plums or sloes (~*thorn winter,* time of its flowering, cold with NE winds), (2) cudgel or walking-stick of its wood; ~ **tie,** man's black bow-tie worn with dinner-jacket; **~'**top,** type of road surfacing; ~ **tracker,** (Austral.) Aboriginal employed to help find persons lost or hiding in the bush; ~ **velvet,** mixture of stout and champagne, (Austral. & NZ sl.) dark-skinned woman; *black* VOMIT; ||**B~ Watch,** Royal Highland Regiment [f. their dark-coloured tartan]; ~**-water fever,** tropical disease caused by malarial infection, with dark urine; ~ **widow,** common Amer. spider, the female of which devours its mate. **5.** Hence ~'ISH[1] *a.,* ~'LY[2] *adv.,* ~'NESS *n.* [OE *blæc,* = OHG *blah-,* of unkn. orig.]

blăck[2] *n.* black colour; black pigment; black clothes or material (*dressed in black*); fungus or smut in wheat etc.; the black colour in roulette and rouge-et-noir; black ball in snooker etc.; (player of) black men in chess etc.; credit side of account (**in the ~,** solvent); (usu. *B~*) Negro or (Austral.) Aboriginal, whence ~'Y[3] *n.* (sl.). [f. prec.]

blăck[3] *v.t.* **1.** make black, polish with blacking; declare (goods etc.) 'black'. **2.** ~ **out,** (*v.t.*) obliterate or obscure, extinguish all lights in, obscure (windows etc.) to prevent any light being seen from outside, esp. from the air, (*v.i.*) undergo black-out. **3.** ~-**out** *n.,* blacking out or being blacked out, period when obscuring of lights is compulsory, sudden darkening of theatre stage, loss of radio reception through fading or jamming, prevention of release of information, temporary complete loss of consciousness or failure of memory, aviator's temporary blindness etc. esp. resulting from centrifugal force when a sudden turn is made. [f. BLACK[1]]

blă'ckamoor (-oor, -ōr) *n.* Negro; dark-skinned person. [f. BLACK[1] + MOOR[2]]

blă'ckavīsed (-zd) *a.* (arch.) dark-complexioned. [f. BLACK[1] + F *vis* face]

blă'cken *v.t.* & *i.* make or become black(er) or dark(er); speak evil of, defame, (person's character). [ME, f. BLACK[1] + -EN[6]]

blă'ckguard (blă'gård) *n., a.,* & *v.t.* **1.** *n.* & *a.* scoundrel(ly); foul-mouthed (person); hence ~LY[1] *a.* **2.** *v.t.* call blackguard; abuse scurrilously. [f. BLACK[1] + GUARD[1]; orig. collect. *n.* and applied to menials of royal household, camp-followers, bodyguard, criminals, vagrants]

blă'cking *n.* in vbl senses; paste or liquid for blacking or polishing boots etc. [f. BLACK[1] + -ING[1]]

Blă'ckwŏŏd *n.* (Bridge). convention of bidding four

and five no-trumps to find number of aces and kings held by partner. [f. E.F. ~, 20th-c. Amer. bridge-player]

blă'dder *n.* **1.** membranous bag in human and other animal bodies, containing urine, bile (*gall-bladder*), air, etc., (esp. the urinary bladder); this or part of it or similar object prepared for various uses, inflated, etc. **2.** (fig.) anything inflated and hollow; wordy person, windbag; inflated pericarp or vesicle in plants and seaweeds (~**-wrack,** common seaweed with these in its fronds). [OE *blǣdre,* = OS *blādara,* OHG *blātara,* ON *blắthra* f. Gmc **blǣdrōn* (**blǣ-* BLOW[1])]

blāde *n.* **1.** flat spear-shaped leaf esp. of grass and cereals; whole of such plants before ear comes (*in the blade*); (Bot.) broad thin part of leaf apart from petiole. **2.** flattened part of oar, bat, spade, paddle-wheel, turbine, propeller, etc.; cutting-piece of sword, chisel, knife, etc.; sword; (**razor-**~, flat piece of metal with usu. two sharp edges, used in safety razor; ~(-**bone),** flat bone, esp. shoulder-blade as joint of meat or otherwise; (Archaeol.) long narrow FLAKE[2]. **3.** jovial, dashing, etc., fellow. **4.** Hence (-)**blā'dED**[2] *a.* [OE *blæd,* = OHG *blat,* ON *blath* f. Gmc **bladham* perh. f. **blō-* BLOW[3]]

||**blae'berry** (blā'-) *n.* = BILBERRY. [ME, f. *blae* (Sc. and N. Engl. dial. f. ME *blo* f. ON *blár* f. Gmc; see BLUE[1]) + BERRY[1]]

blăg *n.,* & *v.t.* (-**gg**-). rob(bery), esp. with violence. [19th c.; orig. unkn.]

blague (blahg) *n.* humbug, claptrap; hence **blagueur** (blahgēr') *n.,* pretentious talker. [F]

blah(-blah) *n.* (colloq.) pretentious nonsense. [imit.]

blain *n.* inflamed swelling or sore on skin. [OE *blegen,* = LG *bleien* f. WG **blegen*]

blāme[1] *v.t.* find fault with (*for* offence etc.) (**be to ~,** deserve censure; **I don't ~ you,** (colloq.) I think your action was justifiable); fix the responsibility on; (colloq.) ~ **thing on** person, hold him responsible for it; hence ~'ABLE (-ma-) *a.* [ME, f. OF *bla(s)mer* f. pop. L *blastemare* f. eccl. L *blasphemare* reproach f. Gk *blasphēmeō* blaspheme]

blāme[2] *n.* censure; responsibility for bad result (*lay the blame on; bear the blame*). [ME, f. OF *blame* (*blamer,* see prec.)]

blā'meful (-mf-) *a.* deserving blame. [ME, f. BLAME[2] + -FUL]

blā'meless (-ml-) *a.* innocent; hence ~LY[2] *adv.,* ~NESS *n.* [ME, f. BLAME[2] + -LESS]

blā'meworth|y (-mwērdhĭ) *a.* deserving blame; hence ~iNESS *n.* [f. BLAME[2] + -WORTHY]

blanch (-ah-) *v.* **1.** *v.t.* make white by withdrawing colour, peeling (almonds esp. by scalding), or depriving (plants) of light, immerse (food) in boiling water. **2.** *v.t.* & *i.* make or grow pale with fear, cold, etc. **3.** *v.t.* ~ **over,** palliate by misrepresentation. [ME, f. OF *blanchir* (*blanc* BLANK[1])]

blancma'nge (blamŏ'nzh) *n.* opaque jelly of (usu. flavoured and sweetened) cornflour and milk [ME, f. OF *blancmanger* (*blanc* white, BLANK[1], *manger* eat f. L *manducare* MANDUCATE)]

blā'ncō *n.,* & *v.t.* (Mil.) (treat with) white substance for whitening belts etc., or similar coloured substance. [f. F *blanc* white, BLANK[1]]

blănd *a.* gentle or suave in manner; mild; not irritating or stimulating; hence ~'LY[2] *adv.,* ~'NESS *n.* [f. L *blandus* soft, smooth]

blā'ndish *v.t.* flatter, coax; hence ~MENT *n.* (usu. in *pl.*), flattery, cajolery. [ME, f. OF *blandir* (-ISH[2]) f. L *blandiri* (*blandus* soft, smooth)]

blănk[1] *a.* **1.** (Of paper) not written or printed on; (of document) with spaces left for signature or details (~ **cheque,** with amount left for payee to fill in, hence = CARTE BLANCHE). **2.** empty, not filled, (*blank space*); ~ **cartridge** (without bullet, to make sound only); ~ **test** (done without specimen, to verify absence of effects of reagents etc.); *blank* WINDOW. **3.** having no interest, incident, result, or expression

(look ~, appear puzzled); unrelieved, sheer, (blank WALL); unrhymed (~ verse, esp. iambic pentameters). **4.** Hence ~LY² adv., ~NESS n. [ME, f. OF blanc white f. Rom. *blancus f. Gmc *blankaz]
blänk² n. lottery ticket that gains no prize (draw (a) ~, elicit no response, fail); space left to be filled up in document; empty surface or interval (one's mind, memory, etc., **is a** ~, has no impressions etc.); document having blank space(s) to be filled up; domino with one or both halves blank; coin-disc before stamping, metal or wooden block before final shaping; = BLANK¹ cartridge; dash written instead of word or letter, whence ~, ~ed (-kt), ~'ety, ||~'y, as euphem. substitutes for profane or abusive ns. and adjs. [f. prec.]
blänk³ v.t. screen off or out; cut out (metal blank); *defeat without allowing to score. [f. prec.]
blä'nkėt¹ n. & a. **1.** n. large piece of woollen etc. material used for warmth, esp. as bed-covering, horse-cloth, etc.; ~ **bath,** washing of patient in bed; ~ **stitch** (for finishing edges of blankets etc.); **electric** ~ (that can be connected to mains and heated by internal wiring); **wet** ~, gloomy person preventing others' enjoyment etc.; **born on the wrong side of the** ~, illegitimate; hence ~ING¹ (3) n. **2.** thick mass or layer (of fog, snow, etc.) that covers something; rubber sheet transferring impression from plate to paper etc. in offset printing. **3.** a. general rather than individual, covering all cases or classes, inclusive, (blanket term, agreement). [ME, f. OF blancquet, blanchet (blanc white, BLANK¹; see -ET¹)]
blä'nkėt² v.t. cover with blanket (lit. or fig.); stifle, keep quiet, (scandal, question, etc.); take wind from sails of (another craft) by passing to windward. [f. prec.]
blanquette (blahṅkě't) n. (Cookery). dish of white meat, e.g. veal, in white sauce. [F (as BLANKET¹)]
blä're v.i. & t., & n. (make) sound of trumpet; utter loudly. [ME, f. MDu. blaren, bleren, imit.]
blä'rney n., & v.t. & i. (use, subject to) cajoling talk; nonsense. [f. B~, Irish castle near Cork with stone said to confer cajoling tongue on whoever kisses it]
blasé (-ah'zā) a. cloyed with or tired of pleasure; unimpressed because of over-familiarity. [F]
blä̈sphē'me v. **1.** v.i. talk impiously. **2.** v.t. utter profanity about, revile. [ME, f. OF blasfemer f. eccl. L blasphemare f. Gk blasphēmeō; cf. BLAME¹]
blä'sphem|ў n. impious or profane talk; hence ~ous a. [ME, f OF blasfemie f. eccl. L f. Gk blasphēmia slander, blasphemy]
blast¹ (-ah-) n. **1.** strong gust of wind; sound of wind-instrument, car horn, whistle, etc.; current of air in smelting etc.; **at full** ~, (colloq.) working at maximum speed etc. **2.** destructive wave of highly compressed air spreading outwards from an explosion; (colloq.) severe reprimand. **3.** ~**furnace,** smelting furnace into which compressed hot air is driven; ~**hole** (containing explosive charge for blasting). [OE blǣst, = OHG blāst, ON blástr f. Gmc *blǣstaz (*blǣs-blow)]
blast² (-ah-) v. **1.** v.t. blow up (rocks etc.) with explosives; hence ~ER¹ n., (esp., fig.) heavy lofted golf-club for playing from bunker. **2.** v.i. ~ **off,** (of rocket etc.) take off from launching site; ~**-off** n., (initial thrust for) launching of rocket etc. **3.** v.t. wither, shrivel, blight, (plant, animal, limb, prosperity, character; esp., w. subj. God expr. or understood in curses, also abs. as int.; hence ~'ED¹ a. & adv. damnable, -bly). [f. prec.]
-bläst suf. (Biol.) embryonic cell (erythroblast; cf. -CYTE); germ layer of embryo (epiblast). [f. Gk blastos sprout]
blä'stūla n. (pl. ~e or *~s). (Biol.) hollow ball of cells formed by cleavage of ovum. [mod. L, f. Gk blastos sprout+dim. suf.; cf. -ULE]
blä't|ant a. noisy, vulgarly clamorous; flagrant, palpable; obtrusive, conspicuous; unashamed; hence

~ANCY n., ~antLY² adv. [wd used by Spenser (1596), perh. after Sc. blatand = bleating]
blather(skite). See BLETHER.
blāze¹ n. **1.** bright flame or fire; state of being on fire; (in pl., sl.) hell (go to blazes; what the blazes!; like ~s, with great energy). **2.** violent outburst (of passion etc.); glow of colour, bright display; (fig.) full light (blaze of publicity). [OE blǣse torch, f. Gmc *blasōn; ult. cogn. w. BLAZE³]
blāze² v.i. **1.** burn with flame (~ up, burst into blaze); be brilliantly lighted; burn with anger, excitement, etc., (~ up, burst out in anger). **2.** show bright colours; emit light; ~ away, fire continuously with rifles etc., work enthusiastically at anything; *blazing star, plant with brilliant star-shaped flowers esp. of genus Aletris. [f. prec.]
blāze³ n. white mark on animal's face; mark made on tree by chipping bark to mark route. [17th c.; = ON blesi, OHG blassa in same sense]
blāze⁴ v.t. mark (tree, path) by chipping bark; esp. blaze a trail (lit., show the way for others to follow, or fig.). [f. prec.]
blāze⁵ v.t. proclaim as with trumpet; ~ **abroad,** spread (news) about. [ME, f. MLG, MDu. blāzen blow; = ON blása, OHG blāsan, Goth. -blesan f. Gmc blǣsan (cf. BLAST¹) f. *blǣ- (BLOW¹)]
blā'zer n. coloured light unlined jacket worn by schoolchildren, sportsmen, etc.; man's plain jacket not matching trousers. [f. BLAZE²+-ER¹]
blā'zon¹ n. heraldic shield, coat of arms, bearings, or banner; correct description of these; record, description, esp. of virtues etc. [ME, f. OF blason shield, of unkn. orig.]
blā'zon² v.t. describe or paint (arms) heraldically; inscribe (object) with arms, names, etc., in colours or ornamentally; proclaim; hence ~MENT n. [ME, f. prec. and BLAZE⁵]
blā'zonrў n. (art of describing or painting) heraldic devices or armorial bearings; brightly coloured display. [f. prec.+-RY]
-ble suf. See -ABLE, -IBLE, -UBLE. [OF, f. L -bilis forming vbl adjs. act. or pass. f. vbs. or p.p. stems]
bleach v. & n. **1.** v.t. & i. whiten by exposure to sunlight or by chemical process; ~**'ing-powder,** chloride of lime, used esp. to remove colour from materials; hence ~ER¹ n., one who bleaches (esp. textiles), vessel or chemical used in bleaching, (usu. in pl.) outdoor uncovered plank-seat for spectators at sports ground. **2.** n. bleaching substance or process. [OE blǣcan, = ON bleikja f. Gmc *blaikjan (*blaik-white)]
bleak¹ n. small river-fish of various species, esp. Alburnus lucidus. [ME, prob. f. ON bleikja, OHG bleicha f. Gmc *blaikjōn (*blaik- white)]
bleak² a. bare, exposed, wind-swept; chilly; dreary, unpromising (bleak prospects). [16th c.; rel. to obs. adjs. bleach, blake (f. ON bleikr) pale; ult. f. Gmc *blaikaz; cf. BLEACH]
blear a., & v.t. (make) (eyes or mind) dim-sighted, dull, filmy; (make) indistinct in outline; hence ~'y² a.; ~(y)-eyed, having blear eyes or wits. [ME, cogn. w. MHG blerre blurred vision, LG blarr-, blerr-oged blear-eyed]
bleat v.i. & t., & n. (make) sheep's, goat's, or calf's, tremulous cry; speak (out) feebly or foolishly or plaintively. [OE blǣtan = OHG blāzen, Du. blaten; imit.]
blěb n. small blister or bubble on skin or in water or glass. [var. of BLOB]
blěd. See blEED.
bleed v. (bled) & n. **1.** v.i. emit blood (one's **heart** ~s, one is very sorrowful); suffer wounds or violent death (for cause etc.). **2.** (Of plant) emit sap; (of dye) come out in water or (Print.) be cut into when pages are trimmed. **3.** part with money, pay lavishly, suffer extortion. **4.** v.t. draw blood surgically from; (fig.) extort money from; (Print.) extend (illustration) to

cut edge of page, cut into printed area of when trimming; allow (fluid) to escape from closed system through valve etc., treat (system) thus. **5.** *n.* act of bleeding. [OE *blēdan,* = ON *blœtha* f. Gmc **blōdhjan* (**blōdham* BLOOD[1])]

blee′der *n.* In vbl senses; person inclined to bleed excessively from slight wound, haemophiliac; (vulg.) person (esp. unpleasant). [f. prec. + -ER[1]]

blee′ding *a.* & *adv.* In vbl senses; ‖(vulg. euphem.) = BLOODY 2, 4; ~ **heart,** pop. name of various plants, esp. of genus *Dicentra,* (colloq.) too soft-hearted person. [f. BLEED + -ING[2]]

bleep *n.,* & *v.i.* (emit) intermittent high-pitched sound, esp. as signal; hence ~ ER[1] (2) *n.* [imit.]

blě′mish[1] *v.t.* spoil the beauty or brightness (lit. or fig.) or perfection of. [ME, f. OF *ble*(*s*)*mir* (-ISH[2]) make pale, prob. of Gmc orig.]

blě′mish[2] *n.* physical or moral defect; stain, flaw. [f. prec.]

blench *v.i.* flinch, quail. [ME, f. OE *blencan,* ON *blekkja* deceive f. Gmc **blankjan;* for later senses cf. BLINK[1]]

blěnd[1] *v.t.* & *i.* (~′ed, poet. or rhet. **blent**). **1.** *v.t.* mix (things) together (esp. sorts of tea, spirit, tobacco, to get certain quality); mingle intimately *with;* mix (components) so as to be inseparable and indistinguishable. **2.** *v.i.* be blended *with;* become one, form harmonious compound; (esp. of colours) pass imperceptibly into each other. **3.** Hence ~ ER[1] (1, 2) *n.* [ME, prob. f. ON *blanda* mix]

blěnd[2] *n.* mixture made of various sorts of tea, spirits, wool, tobacco, etc.; portmanteau word. [f. prec.]

blěnde *n.* native zinc sulphide. [G (*blenden* deceive, ‘because while often resembling galena it yielded no lead’)]

Blě′nheim (-nĭm) *n.* kind of small red and white spaniel; ~ **Orange,** golden-coloured late-ripening apple. [f. Duke of Marlborough’s seat at Woodstock, Oxfordshire, named after his victory at ~ in Bavaria (1704)]

blě′nný *n.* spiny-finned sea-fish esp. of genus *Blennius.* [f. L *blennius* f. Gk *blennos* mucus, from mucous coating of its scales]

blěnt. See BLEND[1].

blěpharī′tis *n.* inflammation of eyelids. [f. Gk *blepharon* eyelid + -ITIS]

blě′sbŏk, -bŭck, *n.* large S. Afr. antelope (*Damaliscus albifrons*). [Afrik. (*bles* BLAZE[3], from white mark on forehead, *bok* goat)]

blěss *v.t.* (BLESSED *or* blest). consecrate (esp. food); sanctify by sign of cross (**not have a penny** to ~ oneself with, be impoverished, w. ref. to cross on silver penny); call holy, adore, (God); attribute one’s good fortune to (esp. one’s stars); (of father, priest, etc.) pronounce words held to bring divine or supernatural favour upon; invoke God’s favour on; make happy or successful (abs. or *with* something); (God) ~ **mē,** ~ **you,** ~ **my soul, I’m blest,** (excl. of surprise or pleasure or indignation, (God) ~ **you** also as well-wishing or to one who sneezes); *bless my* etc. HEART; (euphem.) = damn, curse, etc. [OE *blædsian, blēdsian, blētsian,* (*blōd* blood; hence mark with blood, consecrate); meaning infl. by wd’s being used at the conversion of the English to translate L *benedicere* praise]

blě′ssèd (usu. *pr.* blěst as *pred. a.*), **blěst** (usu. poet.), *a.* consecrated (*Blessed* SACRAMENT, VIRGIN); revered; fortunate (~ **with,** (esp. iron.) fortunate in the possession of); in paradise; (RC Ch.) beatified; blissful, bringing happiness (*blessed ignorance* etc.); (euphem.) cursed. [p.p. of prec.]

blě′ssèdnèss *n.* happiness; enjoyment of divine favour; **single** ~, (joc.) state of being unmarried (perversion of Shak. *Midsummer Night’s Dream* 1. i. 78). [f. prec. + -NESS]

blě′ssing *n.* declaration, invocation, or bestowal, of (esp. divine) favour; grace before or after food (*ask a*

blessing); gift of God, nature, etc., thing one is glad of; ~ **in disguise,** unwelcome but salutary experience, apparent misfortune that eventually does good. [f. BLESS + -ING[1]]

blě′ther, blă′ther, (-dh-) *v.i.,* & *n.* (talk) loquacious nonsense; hence **blă′therskīte, blě′therskăte,** (-dh-) *ns.,* blether(ing person). [ME *blather,* Sc. *blether,* f. ON *blathra* talk nonsense (*blathr* nonsense); derog. use of SKATE[1]]

blew. See BLOW[1,3].

blew′its (-ōō′-) *n.* late edible mushroom with lilac stem. [prob. f. BLUE[1]]

blight[1] (-īt) *n.* plant disease caused by fungoid parasite, mildew, rust, smut; ‖species of aphid; any obscure malignant influence; unsightly urban area. [17th c., of unkn. orig.]

blight[2] (-īt) *v.t.* affect with blight; exert baleful influence on, frustrate, wither, mar; hence ~ ER[1] *n.,* (esp., sl.) (usu. contemptible or annoying) person or thing. [f. prec.]

‖**Blī′ghty** (-ī′tĭ) *n.* (Army sl.) England, home, after foreign service (**a** ~ **one** etc., wound ensuring return to England). [Anglo-Ind. corrupt. of Hind. *bilāyatī, wilāyatī* foreign, European.]

‖**bli′mey** *int.* (**cor**) ~, (vulg.) expr. surprise, contempt, etc. [corrupt. of (*God*) *blind me!*]

blimp *n.* **1.** small non-rigid airship; barrage balloon; soundproof cover for cine-camera. **2.** ‖(**Colonel**) **Blimp,** character invented by the cartoonist David Low (d. 1963), representing a pompous, obese, elderly figure, pop. interpreted as type of dichard or reactionary; hence ~ **ERY** (4) *n.,* ~ **ISH**[1] *a.* [20th c., of uncert. orig.]

blind[1] *a.* & *adv.* **1.** *a.* without sight (~ **corner,** one round which motorist etc. cannot see; **turn a** or one’s ~ **eye to,** pretend not to notice); (Aeron.) without direct observation, using instruments only. **2.** without foresight, discernment, intellectual perception, or adequate information, (~ **to,** incapable of appreciating; one’s ~ **side,** direction in which one cannot see approach of danger etc.); reckless; not ruled by purpose (*blind forces*). **3.** concealed (*blind ditch;* ~-**stitch,** ‖ sewing visible on one side only, (*v.t.* & *i.*) sew thus); (of door, window, etc.) walled up; closed at one end (~ *alley,* cul-de-sac, unprofitable course of action; ~-*alley job* etc., one with no prospect of advancement); (Cookery) baked without filling; (sl.) drunk(en); **not a** ~ (**bit of**), (sl.) not the slightest. **4.** ~ **coal** (burning without flame); ~ **date,** social engagement between two persons of opposite sex who have not met before; ~ **god,** Eros or Cupid; ~ **gut,** caecum; *blind* HOOKEY; ~-**man’s buff,** game in which blindfold player tries to catch others, who push him about [f. obs. *buff* = buffet]; ~ **man’s holiday,** time just before lamps are lit; ~ **spot,** (Anat.) point of entry of optic nerve on retina, insensitive to light, (Radio) point of unusually weak reception, (fig.) area where vision or understanding is lacking; ~ **stamping, tooling,** (in bookbinding without use of colour or gold-leaf); ~′**worm,** slow-worm [f. small size of eyes]. **5.** Hence ~ LY[2] *adv.,* ~′NESS *n.* **6.** *adv.* blindly (*flying blind*); *bake it blind*); ~ **drunk,** insensible through drink; **go it** ~, act recklessly or without proper consideration. [OE, = OS *blind,* OHG *blint,* ON *blindr,* Goth. *blinds* f. Gmc **blindaz*]

blind[2] *v.* **1.** *v.t.* make unable to see, permanently or temporarily; rob of judgement, deceive, (~ **with science,** overawe by display of knowledge). **2.** *v.i.* ‖(sl.) go blindly or heedlessly (esp. in motor vehicle). **3.** Hence ~′ING[1] *n.,* (esp.) (process of covering newly made road with fine material to fill interstices. [ME, f. prec.]

blind[3] *n.* obstruction to sight or light; screen for window, esp. on rollers, (VENETIAN *blind*); ‖awning of shop-window; *screen for hunters; screen to keep cold air from radiator of vehicle; pretext; legitimate business concealing illegitimate one; ||(sl.) heavy drinking-bout; (Poker) stake put up before seeing one's cards. [f. prec.]

bli′nder *n.* In vbl senses; (colloq.) excellent performance in game; *(in *pl.*) blinkers. [f. BLIND² + -ER¹]

bli′ndfōld¹ *v.t.* deprive (eyes, person) of sight with bandage (lit. or fig.). [replacing (by assoc. w. FOLD²) ME *blindfellen* (FELL⁴) strike blind]

bli′ndfōld² *a.* & *adv.* with eyes bandaged; (Chess) without sight of board and men; without circumspection. [earlier p.p. *blindfelled*; see prec.]

bli′ndfōld³ *n.* bandage to prevent person from seeing; (fig.) obstruction to perception. [f. prec.]

blink¹ *v.* **1.** *v.i.* move the eyelids; look with eyes opening and shutting; shut the eyes for a moment, esp. involuntarily; shine with unsteady or intermittent light, cast momentary gleam; hence ∼ING² *a.* & *adv.*, ||(vulg. euphem.) = BLOODY¹ 2, 4. **2.** *v.t.* prevent (tears) by blinking; blink with (eyes); (fig.) ignore, shirk consideration of, (esp. *the fact*). [partly var. of *blenk* = BLENCH, partly f. MDu. *blinken* shine]

blink² *n.* blinking; momentary gleam or glimpse; = ICE¹*blink*; **on the** ∼, (sl.) out of order. [f. prec.]

bli′nker *n.*, & *v.t.* **1.** *n.* In vbl senses; (usu. in *pl.*) leather screen(s) on bridle preventing horse from seeing sideways. **2.** *v.t.* (esp. fig.) obscure with blinkers. [f. BLINK¹ + -ER¹]

blip *v.* (-pp-), & *n.* **1.** *v.t.* strike briskly. **2.** *n.* act or sound of blipping; small image of object on radar screen. **3.** *v.i.* make blip. [imit.]

bliss *n.* gladness, enjoyment; perfect joy or happiness; blessedness; being in heaven; hence ∼FUL *a.*, (esp.) happily oblivious (*blissful ignorance*). [OE *blīths*, *bliss*, = OS *blīdsea* f. Gmc *blīthsjō* (*blīthiz* BLITHE); sense infl. by BLESS]

bli′ster *n.* & *v.* **1.** *n.* thin vesicle on skin filled with serum, caused by friction, burning, etc.; similar swelling on surface of plant, metal, painted wood, (∼ **pack**, bubble pack); (Med.) anything applied to raise a blister; (sl.) annoying person; ∼ **copper** (almost pure); ∼ **gas**, poison gas causing blisters on skin. **2.** *v.t.* raise blister on; (fig.) attack sharply (*blistering criticism*). **3.**v.i. become covered with blisters. [ME, perh. f. OF *blestre*, *blo(u)stre* swelling, pimple]

blīthe (-dh) *a.* **1.** (chiefly poet.) gay, joyous; hence ∼'SOME¹ (-dhs-) *a.* **2.** careless, casual. **3.** Hence ∼'LY² (-dhlī) *adv.*, ∼'NESS (-dhn-) *n.* [OE *blīthe*, = OS *blīthi*, OHG *blīdi*, ON *blīthr*, Goth. *bleiths* f. Gmc **blīthiz*]

bli′thering (-dh-) *a.* (colloq.) senselessly talkative; utter, hopeless, (*blithering idiot*); contemptible. [f. *blither*, var. of BLETHER + -ING²]

B. Litt. *abbr.* Bachelor of Letters. [f. L *Baccalaureus Litterarum*]

blitz (-ts) *n.*, & *v.t.* (colloq.) **1.** *n.* intensive or sudden (esp. aerial) attack (lit. or fig.); *the* air raids on London in 1940. **2.** *v.t.* attack or damage or destroy by blitz. [abbr. of foll.]

bli′tzkrieg (-tsk-) *n.* violent campaign intended to bring about speedy victory. [G, = lightning war]

bli′zzard *n.* severe snowstorm. [US 'violent blow' (1829), 'snowstorm' (1859), perh. imit.]

bloat¹ *v.t.* cure (herring) by salting and smoking slightly. [f. obs. *bloat* soft and wet, perh. f. ON *blautr* soaked]

bloat² *v.t.* & *i.* inflate, swell; hence ∼'ED¹ *a.*, puffed up, esp. with gluttony, pride, excessive wealth, etc. [f. obs. *bloat* swollen, perh. f. ON *blautr* soft, flabby; cf. prec.]

bloa′ter *n.* herring cured by prec. [f. BLOAT¹ + -ER¹]

blōb *n.* drop of liquid; small roundish mass; spot of colour; (Cricket sl.) score of 0. [imit.; cf. BLEB]

blōc *n.* combination of parties, governments, groups, etc., to foster a particular interest; ∼ **vote** = BLOCK¹ *vote*. [F, = BLOCK¹]

blŏck¹ *n.* **1.** log of wood, tree-stump, (**chip off the old** ∼, child like his father esp. in character); large piece

of wood for chopping, beheading, or hammering on, or mounting horse from (***on the** ∼, being auctioned); mould for shaping hats on. **2.** pulley or system of pulleys mounted in case; *block and* TACKLE. **3.** piece of wood or metal engraved for printing on paper or fabric; (in *pl.*) set of wooden cubes etc. as child's toy. **4.** bulky or massive piece of anything; unhewn lump of rock; prepared piece of building-stone; (sl.) head (*knock* person's *block off*). **5.** compact mass of buildings bounded by (usu. four) streets (∼**-buster**, (sl.) huge bomb capable of destroying this, (fig.) thing of great power); ***area** between streets in town or suburb; ***length** of such area (*lives three blocks away*); large building (*block of flats*). **6.** stolid or hard-hearted person. **7.** obstruction; (Amer. Footb. etc.) blocking action; group of jammed vehicles unable to proceed; ∼ **system**, (Railways) system by which no train may enter a section that is not clear; **mental** or **psychological** ∼, particular mental inability due to subconscious emotional factors. **8.** (Cricket) spot on which batsman blocks ball, and rests bat before playing; (Athletics) = STARTING-*block*. **9.** (Austral. etc.) tract of land offered to individual settler by government; large area of land. **10.** large quantity of shares, seats, etc., esp. if treated as unit; set of sheets of paper for writing or drawing on, fastened together at edge; (*attrib.*) made or treated as a large unit (*block booking*, *grant*). **11.** ∼'**board**, plywood board with core of thin wooden strips; ∼ **capitals** (cf. *block letters*); ∼ **diagram** (showing general arrangement of parts of apparatus); ∼'**head**, stupid person; ∼ **heater**, storage heater; ∼'**house**, (1) one-storeyed timber building with loopholes used as fort, (2) house of squared logs, (3) reinforced concrete shelter; ∼ **letters** (without serifs, or with each letter separate as in print and usu. in capitals); ∼ **mountain** (formed by faults); ∼**-ship** (used to block a channel etc.); ∼ **tin**, refined tin cast in ingots; ∼ **vote** (in which voter has influence according to number of persons he represents). [ME, f. OF *bloc* f. MDu. *blok*, of unkn. orig.]

blŏck² *v.t.* **1.** obstruct (passage etc.); put obstacles in way of (progress etc.; ∼ **up**, **in**, confine); (Amer. Footb. etc.) intercept (opponent) with one's body; (esp. in *p.p.*) restrict use or conversion of (currency or other asset); (Cricket) stop (ball) with bat. **2.** emboss or impress design on (book cover); ∼ **out**, **in**, sketch roughly, plan. **3.** Hence ∼'AGE (3) *n.*, blocked(-up) state. [f. prec. or f. F *bloquer* (*bloc*; see prec.)]

blŏckā′de¹ *n.* surrounding of place, blocking of harbour etc., by hostile forces to prevent goods etc. from reaching or leaving it (**run** ∼, evade blocking force); ***obstruction** by snow etc. [f. prec. + -ADE, prob. after *ambuscade*]

blŏckā′de² *v.t.* subject to blockade (obstruct (passage, view, etc.). [f. prec.]

||**blŏnd** (sl.) man, fellow, chap. [Shelta]

blŏnd *a.* & *n.* **1.** *a.* (Of hair) light-coloured, flaxen; (of complexion) light-coloured. **2.** *n.* person having such hair and skin. [ME f. F, f. med. L *blondus*, *blundus* yellow, perh. of Gmc orig.]

blŏnde *a.* & *n.* (Of woman or woman's hair) blond. [F, fem. of *blond* (see prec.)]

blood¹ (-ŭd) *n.* **1.** liquid (usu. red) circulating in arteries and veins of higher animals; corresponding liquid in lower animals; one's blood BOIL²·5; one's ∼ **runs cold**, one is horrified; **first** ∼, first shedding of blood (in Boxing, or fig.); **out for** person's ∼, determined to defeat him; **taste** ∼, (fig.) be stimulated by early success. **2.** taking of life; guilt of bloodshed. **3.** passion, temperament, mettle, (**bad** ∼, ill feeling; ∼ **out of** (or **from**) **a stone**, pity from the pitiless or money from the avaricious; **in cold** ∼, without passion, deliberately; **his** ∼ **is up**, he is in a fighting mood). **4.** race, descent, parentage; BLUE¹ *blood*; **fresh** or **new** ∼, new members admitted to family, society, etc.; **young** ∼, younger member(s) of party etc.; **in** one's ~, fundamental in one's character (*the sea is in his blood*); *prince* etc. **of the** ~, royal. **5.** relationship, relations, (*own flesh and blood*; ~ **is thicker than water,** the tie of kinship is strong). **6.** dandy, man of fashion, (*young blood*). **7.** ||(esp. in *pl.*) blood-and-thunder story. **8.** ~ **and iron,** relentless use of military force (esp. as motto of Bismarckian policy); ~**-and-thunder,** sensational, melodramatic; ~ **bank,** place where supply of blood for transfusion is stored; ~**-bath,** massacre; ~**-brother** (by birth or ceremonial mingling of blood); ~ **count,** (counting of) number of corpuscles in a definite volume of blood; ~**-curdling,** so horrific as to seem to curdle the blood; *blood-*DONOR; ~ **feud** (between families of which one has killed or injured member(s) of the other); ~ **group,** any one of the (usu. four) types into which human blood may be divided according to its compatibility in transfusion; ~**-guilt,** responsibility for murder or death; ~**-heat,** ordinary temperature of human blood in health, about 98°F or 37°C; ~ **horse,** thoroughbred; ~'**hound,** large keen-scented dog formerly used to track cattle, criminals, etc., (fig.) detective; ~**-letting,** surgical removal of some of patient's blood, (joc.) bloodshed; ~**-lust** (for shedding of blood); ~**-money,** (1) reward to witness for securing capital sentence, (2) fine paid to next of kin for slaughter of relative; ~ **orange** (with red-streaked pulp); ~**-poisoning,** state resulting from presence of pathogenic bacteria in blood; *blood* PRESSURE; ~ **pudding,** black pudding; ~**-red,** red as blood; ~**-relation,** one related by blood, not by marriage; ~ **royal,** *the* royal family; ~'**shed,** spilling of blood, slaughter [f. phr. *to shed blood*]; ~'**shot,** (of eyeball) tinged with blood; *blood* SPAVIN; ~ **sports,** those involving bloodshed or killing of animals, esp. hunting; ~**-stained,** (1) stained with blood, (2) disgraced by bloodshed; ~'**stock,** thoroughbred horses; ~'**stone,** green chalcedony spotted or streaked with red; ~'**stream,** circulating blood; ~'**sucker,** leech, extortioner; ~ **test,** examination of blood for diagnosis etc.; ~'**thirsty,** eager for bloodshed; *blood* TRANSFUSION; ~**-vessel,** vein, artery, or capillary, conveying blood; ~'**worm,** bright-red midge-larva used as fishing bait; ~**-wort,** plant with red roots or leaves, esp. red-veined dock. **9.** Hence ~'ED² *a.* [OE *blōd,* = OS *blod,* OHG *bluot,* ON, Goth. *blōth* f. Gmc **blōdham*]

blood² (-ŭd) *v.t.* allow first taste of blood to (hound, or fig. of initiating persons). [f. prec.]

bloo′dless (-ŭ′-) *a.* without blood; unemotional; pale; without bloodshed; hence ~LY² *adv.* [f. BLOOD¹ + -LESS]

bloo′dy¹ (-ŭ′-) *a.* & *adv.* **1.** of, like, running or smeared with, blood (*bloody* FLUX; *bloody* SWEAT); red (~ **hand,** armorial device of baronet; B~ **Mary,** mixed drink of vodka and tomato juice); involving, loving, resulting from, bloodshed (~**-minded,** (colloq.) deliberately uncooperative; sanguinary, cruel. **2.** ||(In strong language) = DAMNED 2 etc. (*a bloody shame*), or as mere intensive (*not a bloody one*); unpleasant. **3.** Hence **bloo′diLY²** *adv.,* **bloo′diNESS** *n.* (-ŭ′-). **4.** *adv.* ||(As in 2) = DAMNED 3, confoundedly, very, or as intensive. [OE *blōdig* (as BLOOD¹, -Y²)]

bloo′dy² (-ŭ′-) *v.t.* make bloody; stain with blood. [f. prec.]

bloom¹ *n.* **1.** flower, esp. of plant grown or admired chiefly for the flower, florescence (*in bloom*); prime, perfection. **2.** flush, glow; delicate powdery deposit on grapes, plums, etc., freshness, (**take the** ~ **off,** make stale); cloudiness on shiny surface; (**water-**)~, scum formed by algae on water surface. [ME, f. ON *blóm, blómi,* OHG *bluomo,* OHG *bluomo, -ma,* Goth. *blōma* f. Gmc **blōmon, -ōn* (**blō-* BLOW³; cf. BLOSSOM¹)]

bloom² *v.* **1.** *v.i.* bear flowers, be in flower; come into, be in, full beauty; culminate, flourish. **2.** *v.t.* ||(Photog.) coat (lens) so as to reduce reflection from surface. [ME, f. prec.]

bloom³ *n.,* & *v.t.* **1.** *n.* mass of puddled iron hammered or squeezed into thick bar. **2.** *v.t.* make into bloom. **3.** Hence ~'ERY (3) *n.* [OE *blōma*]

||**bloo′mer¹** *n.* (sl.) blunder. [= BLOOMING *error*; see -ER¹]

||**bloo′mer²** *n.* large loaf with rounded diagonally slashed top. [20th c.; orig. uncert.]

bloo′mers (-z) *n. pl.* **1.** (Hist.) woman's costume with loose knee-length trousers. **2.** woman's undergarment of this shape; (colloq.) knickers. [f. Mrs A. *Bloomer,* Amer. social reformer d. 1894, who advocated similar costume]

bloo′ming *a.* & *adv.* In vbl senses; ||(sl. euphem.) = BLOODY¹ 2, 4. [f. BLOOM² + -ING²]

Bloo′msbury (-z-) *n.* & *a.* (associated with or similar to) early 20th-c. school (~ **group**) of writers and aesthetes living in Bloomsbury; intellectual, highbrow. [f. ~ in west-central London]

*bloo′per *n.* (colloq.) embarrassing error. [f. imit. *bloop* + -ER¹]

blo′ssom¹ *n.* flower, esp. as promising fruit; mass of flowers on fruit-tree etc. (*in blossom*); early stage of growth, promise; hence ~Y² *a.* [OE *blōstm(a),* cogn. w. MDu. *bloesem,* MLG *blōs(s)em* (cf. also ON *blómstr*), prob. f. as BLOOM¹]

blo′ssom² *v.i.* open into flower (lit., or fig.; *blossom out into a statesman*). [OE *blōstmian* (as prec.)]

blot¹ *n.* spot or stain of ink etc., dark patch; disfigurement, blemish; defect; disgraceful act or quality in good character. [ME, prob. f. Scand., cf. Icel. *blettr* spot, stain]

blot² *v.t.* & *i.* (-tt-). spot or stain with ink (~ one's *copy-book,* (colloq.) spoil one's character or record, commit an indiscretion); smudge; (of pen, ink) make blots; disgrace; ~ **out,** obliterate (writing), obscure (view), exterminate, destroy; dry with ~'ting-**paper,** absorbent paper for drying wet ink, whence ~'tER¹ (2) *n.,* (esp. pad of this, *temporary recording--book, e.g. police charge-sheet). [f. prec.]

blotch *n.* discoloured or inflamed patch on skin; irregular patch of ink or colour; hence ~'Y² *a.* [17th c., f. obs. *plotch* and BLOT¹]

blŏ′ttŏ *a.* ||(sl.) very drunk. [20th c.; perh. f. BLOT¹]

blouse (-z) *n.,* & *v.t.* **1.** *n.* (esp. French) workman's or peasant's loose linen or cotton garment, usu. belted at waist. **2.** woman's loose upper garment, usu. tucked into skirt or trousers at waist; upper part of soldier's or airman's battledress. **3.** *v.t.* make (bodice etc.) loose like blouse. [19th c., F, of unkn. orig.]

blou′son (blōō′zawn) *n.* short blouse-shaped jacket. [F]

blow¹ (-ō) *v.* (**blew** *pr.* blōō; ~**n** exc. in sense 'cursed') **1.** *v.i.* (Of wind, air, or imper.s.) move along, act as air-current, (*blow great* GUNs); send directed air--current from mouth (~ **hot and cold,** vacillate); puff, pant; (US & Austral. colloq.) boast; be driven or sounded by blowing; (sl.) depart suddenly; (of whale) eject air and water; (of electric filament or fuse) melt when overloaded; (of food-tin etc.) swell from internal gas pressure. **2.** *v.t.* work bellows of (organ; esp. in *pass.*); exhaust of breath; send out by breathing (*blow air into;* ~ **a kiss,** kiss one's hand and wave it to distant person); drive by blowing; make or shape (bubble, glass) by blowing air in; sound (wind instrument, note or signal *on* or *with* it; ~ one's **own trumpet,** praise oneself); direct air-current at (*blow fingers, fire*); clear (nose, egg) by air-current. **3.** send flying (*off* etc.) by explosion; cause (electric fuse etc.) to melt under overload; break into (safe etc.) with explosives; (sl.) depart suddenly from; (sl.) reveal (*blow the* GAFF²); ~ person's **mind,** (sl.) cause him to have drug-induced hallucinations or similar experience; ~ one's **top** or ***stack,** (colloq.) show great anger. **4.** (Of flies) deposit eggs in; (sl.) curse, confound, (*I'll be blowed if* etc.; esp. in *imper.* ~ **you, Jack,** I don't care about you) and abs. (*oh blow!*); (sl.) squander, spend (money) recklessly (cf. BLUE⁴).

5. ~**-ball,** globular seed-head of dandelion etc.; ~**-dry,** arrange (hair) while drying it with hand--held blower; ~**-fish,** kind able to inflate its body when frightened etc.; ~**'fly,** meat-fly, bluebottle; ~**-hard,** boastful (person); ~**-hole,** hole for blowing or breathing through, nostril of whale etc., vent for air, smoke, etc., in tunnel etc.; ~**'lamp** (for directing very hot flame on a selected spot); ~**'pipe,** tube for heating flame by blowing air or other gas into it, tube used in glass-blowing, tube for propelling arrows or darts by blowing; ~**'torch,** = *blowlamp*. **6.** ~ **in,** break inwards by explosion, (colloq.) come in unexpectedly; ~ **on, upon,** make stale, discredit; ~ **out,** (*v.t.*) extinguish by blowing, send outwards by explosion (~ *out* one's *brains*, shoot oneself in the head), (*v.i.*) (of tyre) burst, (of fuse etc.) melt; so ~--*out* n., (also, colloq.) large meal; ~ **over,** pass off without serious consequences; ~ **up,** (*v.t.*) send upwards or shatter by explosion, (colloq.) reprove, inflate, (colloq.) enlarge (photograph etc.), exaggerate, (*v.i.*) arise, come to notice, be shattered by explosion, lose one's temper; ~**-up** n., explosion, (colloq.) enlargement (of photograph etc.). [OE *blāwan,* = OHG *blā(h)an* f. IE **bhlā-*]

blow² (-ō) *n.* blowing; inhaling of fresh air; blowing of flute, one's nose, etc.; = FLY¹*-blow;* **boast(er).* [f. prec.]

blow³ (-ō) *v.i.* (**blew** *pr.* blōō; ~**n**). (arch.) burst into or be in flower. [OE *blōwan,* = OS *blōjan,* OHG *bluojan* f. Gmc **blō-;* cf. *blade,* BLOOM¹]

blow⁴ (-ō) *n.* (arch.) blossoming (*in full blow* etc.). [f. prec.]

blow⁵ (-ō) *n.* **1.** hard stroke with fist, instrument, etc.; **at one** ~, by a single stroke, in one operation; ~**-by-**~, (of description etc.) giving all details in sequence; **come to** ~**s,** begin fighting; **strike a** ~ **for, against,** help, oppose. **2.** disaster, shock, (*to* person). [15th c., of unkn. orig.]

blow'er (-ō'er) *n.* in vbl senses; apparatus for increasing a fire's draught, e.g. sheet of iron across fireplace; (colloq.) telephone. [f. BLOW¹ + -ER¹]

blown. See BLOW¹·³.

blow'y̆ (-ō'ĭ) *a.* windy, wind-swept. [f. BLOW¹ + -Y²]

blow'zy̆ *a.* red-faced, coarse-looking; slatternly. [f. obs. *blowze* beggar's wench; orig. unkn.]

blŭb *v.i.* (**-bb-**). (sl.) shed tears. [abbr. of BLUBBER³]

blŭ'bber¹ *n.* **1.** whale fat; SEA *blubber.* **2.** weeping. [ME, perh. imit. (obs. meanings 'foaming, bubble')]

blŭ'bber² *a.* (Of lips) swollen, protruding. [earlier *blabber, blobber,* imit.]

blŭ'bber³ *v.t.* & *i.* utter with sobs; weep noisily; wet, disfigure, swell, (face) with weeping. [f. BLUBBER¹]

blu'chers (-ōō'kerz) *n. pl.* (Hist.) strong leather half--boots or high shoes. [f. G. L. von *Blücher,* Prussian general d. 1819]

blŭ'dgeon (-ŭ'jon) *n.,* & *v.t.* **1.** *n.* heavy-headed stick. **2.** *v.t.* strike repeatedly with bludgeon; coerce. [18th c., of unkn. orig.]

blŭ'dger *n.* (Austral. & NZ sl.) hanger-on; loafer; hence [as back-form.] **blŭdge** *v.i.,* avoid work, impose *on.* [orig. Engl. sl., = pimp, f. obs. *bludgeoner* f. prec.; see -ER¹]

blue¹ (blōō) *a.* **1.** of the colour between green and violet in the spectrum, coloured like the clear sky or deep sea (also of things much paler, darker, etc., e.g. smoke, distant hills, bruises); with blue-coloured skin through cold, fear, anger, etc.; wearing blue clothes; (as distinguishing epithet) *blue fox, vitriol,* etc. **2.** sad, depressed; (of state of affairs etc.) dismal; (of music) characteristic of the blues; belonging to a particular political party, in UK usu. Conservative; (of woman, arch.) that is a bluestocking; (of talk, film, etc.) indecent or profane. **3.** ~ **baby** (with congenital cyanosis from heart defect); ~ **bag** (for lawyer's brief); ~**'bell,** any of several plants with blue bell--shaped flowers, esp. (Sc.) light-blue-flowered *Campanula,* harebell, (Engl.) wild hyacinth; ~**'berry,**

(blue fruit of) one of several plants of genus *Vaccinium;* ~**-bird,** N. Amer. song-bird of genus *Sialis,* with blue back; ~ **blood,** noble birth; B~ **Book,** Parliamentary or Privy-Council report, ***book giving personal details of US government officials; ~**'bottle,** dark blue cornflower, large buzzing fly with blue body, (Austral.) Portuguese man-of-war; ~ **cheese** (with veins of blue mould); ~**-chip,** [f. high-valued blue chips in Poker] of highest quality, (St. Exch., of shares) constituting a fairly reliable investment, though less secure than gilt-edged; ||~**-coat** boy, girl, school, (pupil in) charity school, esp. Christ's Hospital; ~**-collar** worker, manual or industrial (opp. office) worker; *blue* DAHLIA; ~ **devils,** mood of depression; *blue* ENSIGN; ~ **eye** (with blue iris); ~**-eyed** boy, (colloq.) pet, favourite; ~**'fish,** a voracious game--fish (*Pomatomus saltatrix*); *blue* FUNK¹; ***~**'gill,** a freshwater sunfish; ***~ **grass,** a bluish-coloured grass, esp. of Kentucky; ~ **ground,** dark usu. blue soil in which diamonds are found in S. Africa etc.; ~ **gum,** kind of eucalyptus tree, esp. *Eucalyptus globulus;* ~**'jacket,** seaman in Navy; ***~ **laws,** severe puritanical laws of kind alleged to have been in force among early colonists of New England; ||B~**'mantle,** one of four pursuivants of English College of Arms; ~ **metal,** broken blue stone for road-making; **once in a** ~ **moon,** very rarely; ~ **mould,** a fungus in food, esp. in certain cheeses when mature; *blue* MURDER¹; ***B~**-nose,** (colloq.) Nova-Scotian, puritanical person; ~ **pencil** (used in making corrections, obliterations, etc.); ~**-pencil** *v.t.* (||*-ll-*), mark etc. with blue pencil, make cuts in, censor; B~ **Peter,** blue flag with white square, hoisted by ship before sailing; ~ **pill,** mercurial aperient; ~**'print,** (*n.*) blue photographic print representing final stage of engineering or other plans, (fig.) detailed plan of work to be done, ***(*v.t.*) work out (programme etc.); ~ **ribbon,** ribbon of the Garter, greatest honour in any sphere, sign of teetotalism; *blue* ROAN¹, ROCK¹; ||~ **rod,** official of order of St. Michael & St. George; ***~**-sky laws** (preventing sales to gullible investors); ~**'stocking,** woman having or affecting literary tastes and learning [Blue Stocking Society, met about 1750 to talk on literature etc., some of the men wearing ordinary blue (not dress) stockings]; ~**'streak,** (colloq.) fast-moving thing or person; ~**'stone,** copper sulphate; ~**'throat,** thrush of genus *Erithacus; blue* TIT¹, VITRIOL; ~ **water,** open sea; ~ **whale,** a rorqual, largest known living animal. **4.** Hence **blu'ish** 2 (blōō'-) *a.,* ~**'ness** (-ōō'n-) *n.* [ME, f. OF *bleu* f. Rom. **blavus* f. OE **blæwaz*]

blue² (blōō) *n.* blue colour; blue pigment; blue powder used to whiten laundry; blue clothes or material (*dressed in blue*); blue butterfly; blue ball in snooker etc.; **the** ~, the clear sky (BOLT¹ *from the blue; out of the* ~, unexpectedly); the sea; ||**the** B~**s,** the Royal Horse Guards; colour or member of a political party, in UK usu. Conservative; (colloq.) one who has represented his university colours, esp. Oxford (**dark** ~) or Cambridge (**light** ~), in a sport (**get one's** ~, be chosen as representative); (Austral. sl.) argument, row; (in *pl.*) melancholy; (in *pl.,* sometimes treated as *sing.*) (type of) melancholy song of Amer. Negro origin. [f. prec.]

blu|e³ (blōō) *v.t.* (*part.* ~**eing** *or* ~**ing,** *pr.* -ōō'ĭ-). make blue; treat with laundering blue. [f. BLUE¹]

blu|e⁴ (blōō) *v.t.* (*part.* ~**eing** *or* ~**ing,** *pr.* -ōō'ĭ-). (sl.) squander (money). [perh. var. of BLOW¹]

Blue'beard (blōō'-) *n.* person who murders several wives in succession, or has mysterious or horrible things to conceal. [f. character in fairy-tale told in F (*Barbe-bleue*) by Perrault]

*****blu'et** (blōō'-) *n.* blue-flowered plant of genus *Houstonia.* [f. BLUE¹ + -ET¹]

blu'ey (blōō-) *n.* (Austral.) bushman's bundle (HUMP *bluey*); (colloq.) blue summons-paper or cattle-dog. [f. BLUE¹ + -Y²]

bluff¹ *a.* (Of ship's bows, cliffs) having perpendicular broad front; (of person or his manner) abrupt, blunt, frank, hearty; hence ~'LY² *adv.*, ~'NESS *n.* [17th c. Naut. wd, of unkn. orig.]

bluff² *n.* headland or cliff with perpendicular broad face. [f. prec.]

bluff³ *v.* **1.** *v.i.* make pretence of strength to gain advantage etc. **2.** *v.t.* deceive (opponent, rival) thus. [19th c., orig. in Poker; earlier sense 'blindfold', f. Du. *bluffen* brag]

bluff⁴ *n.* act of bluffing (**call** person's ~, challenge his attempt to deceive by bluffing); threats designed to operate without action. [19th c., orig. in Poker; earlier sense 'horse's blinker', prob. f. prec.]

bluish. See BLUE¹ 4.

blu'nder¹ *v.* **1.** *v.i.* move blindly, stumble, (*along*; ~ **upon**, find by chance); make gross mistake. **2.** *v.t.* mismanage; ~ **away**, waste or lose by mismanagement. [ME, prob. f. Scand.; cf. MSw. *blundra* shut the eyes]

blu'nder² *n.* stupid or careless mistake. [prob. f. prec., but found earlier]

blu'nderbuss *n.* (Hist.) short gun with large bore firing many balls or slugs. [alt. of Du. *donderbus* thunder gun, assoc. w. BLUNDER¹]

blung|e (-nj) *v.t.* (Pottery). mix (clay, bone, flint--powder, etc.) with water by revolving machinery; hence ~'ER¹ (2) *n.* [after *plunge*, *blend*]

blunt *a.*, *n.*, & *v.t.* **1.** *a.* dull, not sensitive; without sharp edge or point; outspoken; uncompromising (*a blunt refusal to go*); hence ~'LY² *adv.*, ~'NESS *n.* **2.** *n.* (arch. sl.) ready money. **3.** *v.t.* make blunt(er). [ME, perh. f. Scand. (ON *blunda* shut the eyes; cf. BLUNDER¹)]

blur¹ *n.* smear of ink etc.; dimness, confused effect. [16th c.; perh. rel. to BLEAR]

blur² *v.t.* & *i.* (**-rr-**). smear (clear writing etc.) with ink etc.; sully, disfigure; make or become indistinct, efface; dim (perception etc.). [as prec.]

blurb *n.* publisher's (usu. eulogistic) brief description of book printed on its jacket or in advertisements elsewhere; descriptive or commendatory matter. [coined by G. Burgess, Amer. humorist d. 1951]

blurt *v.t.* burst *out* with, utter abruptly. [prob. imit.]

blush *v.i.* become red in the face with shame or other emotion (*at* sight or word, *with* or *for* joy or usu. shame); be ashamed (*blush to own* etc.); be red or pink. [ME, f. OE *blyscan*]

blush² *n.* **1.** glance, glimpse; **at** (**the**) **first** ~, on first glimpse or impression. **2.** reddening of face in shame etc. (*put to the blush*); **spare** person's ~es, not embarrass him by praise. **3.** rosy glow, flush of light. [f. prec.]

blu'sher *n.* cosmetic used to give colour to the face. [f. BLUSH¹ +-ER¹]

blu'ster *v.i.* (Of wind, waves, person) storm boisterously. [16th c.; ult. imit.]

blu'ster² *n.* boisterous blowing; noisy self-asserting talk, threats; hence ~-Y² *a.* [f. prec.]

BM *abbr.* Bachelor of Medicine; British Museum.

BMA *abbr.* British Medical Association.

B. Mus. *abbr.* Bachelor of Music.

Bn. *abbr.* (esp. Mil.) Battalion.

bn. *abbr.* billion.

BNC *abbr.* Brasenose College, Oxford.

bo¹ *int.* = BOO. [imit.]

*bo² *n.* (Form of address, =) mate, old chap. [19th c., perh. f. BOY]

BO *abbr.* (colloq.) body odour.

bo'a *n.* **1.** large S. Amer. non-poisonous snake of genus *Boa* etc. killing by compression; Old-World python; woman's long fur or feather throat-wrap. **2.** ~ **constrictor,** Brazilian species of boa; python. [L]

BOAC *abbr.* (formerly) British Overseas Airways Corporation.

boar *n.* uncastrated male pig; its flesh; WILD *boar*; male guinea-pig etc. [OE *bār*, = OS *bērswīn*, OHG *bēr* f. WG **baira*]

board¹ *n.* **1.** long thin usu. fairly narrow piece of sawn timber; slab made of one or more such pieces of wood etc., bare or covered with cloth, leather, etc., used for various purposes, as in games, for posting notices, etc., (BLACK¹*board*, *chessboard*, *notice-board*, SPRING²-*board*; ACROSS *the board*); (in *pl.*) theatre stage, actor's profession; material compressed from wood fibres etc. into stiff sheets; = STRAW¹-*board*; *~ **foot**, 144 cu. in. (of timber); *~'**walk**, footway (orig.) made of boards. **2.** table (ABOVE-*board*; SWEEP¹ *the board*); table spread for meals; food served, daily meals provided at contract price or in return for services (esp. *board and lodging*); council-table, councillors, committee (‖**B**~ **of Customs and Excise,** ‖**B**~ **of Inland Revenue,** government departments; *~ **of trade,** chamber of commerce); body of examiners or interviewers; directors of company (~'**room,** their meeting-place). **3.** ship's side: **go by the** ~, (of mast etc.) fall overboard, (fig.) be entirely neglected; **on** ~ = ABOARD, esp. on or into ship, aircraft, train, bus, etc. **4.** (Naut.) distance covered in one tack. [OE *bord*, f. two distinct Gmc wds meaning (1) board (2) border, respectively f. Gmc *bordham and *bordhaz; reinforced in ME by F *bord*, ON *borth*]

board² *v.* **1.** *v.t.* cover or close (*up*) with boards. **2.** *v.t.* & *i.* provide (lodger or daily guest) with, (of lodger etc.) receive, stated meals at fixed rate (~ **out,** eat away from home, place (destitute etc. child) in family; ~ **with,** be lodger boarding in house of); bring (candidate etc.) before board of interviewers. **3.** *v.t.* come alongside (ship, usu. to attack); force one's way on board (ship, or abs.); go on board (ship, aircraft, train, bus, etc.). **4.** (Of ship) tack. [f. prec.]

boar'der *n.* one who boards (sense 2) with someone, esp. pupil at boarding-school; one who boards an enemy ship. [f. prec. +-ER¹]

boar'ding *n.* In vbl senses; ~-**house,** ~-**school,** in which persons, schoolchildren, board (sense 2)). [f. BOARD² +-ING¹]

boart. See BORT.

boast¹ *n.* excessively proud statement; cause of pride; hence ~'FUL *a.*, ~'FULLY *adv.*, ~'FULNESS *n.* [ME f. AF *bost*; orig. unkn.]

boast² *v.* **1.** *v.i.* praise oneself; make boasts *of* or *about*. **2.** *v.t.* possess as thing to be proud of. **3.** Hence ~'ER¹ *n.* [ME f. AF *boster (as prec.)]

boat¹ *n.* **1.** small open oared or engined or sailing vessel, fishing-vessel, mail packet, or small steamer, (BURN² one's *boats*; MISS² *the boat*; **push the** ~ **out,** (colloq.) celebrate; ROCK³ *the boat*; **in the same** ~, in same predicament, with like risks etc.; **ship's** ~ (carried on board ship); **take to the** ~s, use ship's boats to escape from sinking ship etc., (fig.) precipitously abandon one's undertaking); **large sea--going vessel; boat-shaped utensil for sauce etc. **2.** ~-**bill,** S. Amer. heron with bill like overturned boat; ~-**deck** (from which ship's boats are launched); ~ **drill,** exercise of launching ship's boats; ~-**hook,** long pole with hook and spike; ~-**house,** shed at water's edge for housing boat(s); ~'**load,** as many or as much as a boat can hold; ~'**man,** one who hires out his boat(s), one who provides transport by boat; ~ **people,** refugees leaving a country by sea; ~ **race** (between rowing crews, esp. between Oxford and Cambridge Universities); ~'**swain,** bo's'n, bo'sun; **bosun** (bō'sun), ship's officer in charge of sails, rigging, etc., and summoning men to duty (~*swain's chair,* wooden seat suspended from ropes for work on side of ship or building); ~-**train** (timed to catch or meet boat); ~-**yard** (where boats are built and stored). **3.** Hence ~'FUL 2 *n.* [OE *bāt*, = ON *beit* f. Gmc **bait-*]

boat² *v.i.* go in boat; amuse oneself thus (*boating man*); hence ~'ER¹ *n.*, hard flat straw hat (as formerly worn for boating). [f. prec.]

boate'l. See BOTEL.

bob¹ *n.* & *v.* (**-bb-**). **1.** *n.* weight on pendulum, plumb-line, or kite-tail; knot of hair, tassel-shaped curl (∿-**wig**, wig with short curls, opp. to *full--bottomed wig*); CHERRY-*bob*; = BOB-SLEIGH; short line at end of stanza; horse's docked tail; bobbed hair; *∿*cat, Amer. short-tailed lynx; ∿'tail, (horse or dog with) docked tail; RAG¹*tag and bobtail.* **2.** *v.t.* cut (woman's or child's hair) to hang short of shoulders. **3.** *v.i.* ride on bob-sleigh. [ME; orig. unkn.]

‖bŏb² *n.* (*pl.* same). (sl.) shilling; five decimal pence, 5p. [19th c.; orig. unkn.]

bŏb³ *v.i.* (-bb-). **1.** move up and down, dance, rebound; curtsy; ∿ **up** (**like a cork**), (fig.) emerge suddenly, become active or conspicuous again after defeat. **2.** ∿ **for,** try to catch with the mouth (fruit floating or hanging). [14th c.; app. imit.]

bŏb⁴ *n.* jerk, bouncing movement; curtsy; (Bell-ringing) one of several kinds of change in long peals. [f. prec.]

‖bŏb⁵ *n.* dry, wet, ∿, cricketing, boating, Etonian; ∿'s **your uncle,** (sl.) all is well. [prob. f. pet-form of man's Christian name *Robert*]

bŏ'bbin *n.* cylinder from which thread, yarn, wire, etc., is unwound as wanted; reel, spool; small bar and string for raising door-latch; ∿-**lace** (made by hand with thread wound on bobbins). [f. F *bobine*]

bŏ'bbinĕt *n.* machine-made cotton net (imitating lace made with bobbins on pillow). [f. prec. + NET¹]

‖bŏ'bbish *a.* (sl.) brisk, well. [f. BOB³ + -ISH¹]

bŏ'bble *n.* small woolly ball as ornament or trimming. [dim. of BOB¹]

‖bŏ'bby¹ *n.* **1.** (colloq.) policeman [f. Sir *Robert* Peel, Engl. statesman d. 1850]. **2.** ∿ (**calf**), unweaned calf slaughtered soon after birth. [f. as BOB⁵ + -Y³]

bŏ'bby² *n.* *∿ pin, flat hairpin; ∿ socks, short socks covering ankle; ∿-soxer, (usu. derog.) adolescent girl wearing bobby socks. [f. BOB¹ + -Y³]

bŏ'bbў-dä'zzler *n.* remarkable or excellent thing or person. [dial., rel. to DAZZLE]

bŏ'blĕt *n.* bob-sleigh for two persons. [f. BOB¹ + -LET]

bŏ'bolink *n.* N. Amer. song-bird (*Dolichonyx oryzivorus*). [orig. *Bob* (*o'*) *Lincoln*; imit. of its call]

bŏ'b-sleigh (-lā) *n.* (one of) two short sledges coupled, used in tobogganing and for drawing logs; mechanically steered and braked sledge. [f. BOB(¹?) + SLEIGH, SLED]

bŏ'bstay *n.* rope holding bowsprit down. [f. BOB(³?) + STAY²]

bŏ'b-white *n.* N. Amer. quail of genus *Colinis.* [imit. of its call]

boca'ge (-ah'zh) *n.* representation of silvan scenery in ceramics. [F, f. OF *boscage* (see BOSCAGE)]

Bŏche (-sh) *n.* & *a.* (sl., derog.) German [F sl., orig. = rascal; applied to Germans in 1914–18 war]

bŏck *n.* strong dark-coloured German beer; glass of (any) beer. [F f. G abbr. of *Eimbockbier* (*Einbeck* in Hanover, *bier* BEER)]

‖bŏd *n.* (sl.) person. [f. BODY¹]

BOD *abbr.* biochemical oxygen demand.

bŏde *v.* **1.** *v.t.* foresee, foretell, (evil); portend, foreshow. **2.** *v.i.* promise *well* or *ill.* **3.** Hence bŏ'dING¹, ∿'MENT (-dm-), *ns.* [OE *bodian* (*boda* messenger, = OS *bodo*, OHG *boto*, ON *bothi* f. Gmc *budhon*)]

bŏ'deful (-df-) *a.* ominous, presageful. [19th c., f. *bode* omen + -FUL]

bodĕ'ga *n.* cellar or shop selling wine. [Sp., f. L f. Gk *apothēkē* storehouse]

bŏdge. Var. of BOTCH.

Bŏdhisa'ttva (-disah'-) *n.* (Buddhism). one who is able to reach nirvana but delays doing so through compassion for human suffering. [Skr., = one whose essence is perfect knowledge]

bŏ'dice *n.* upper part of woman's dress, down to waist; woman's undergarment for same part of body. [orig. *pair of bodies* = whalebone corset]

bŏ'dilĕss *a.* incorporeal; separated from the body. [f. BODY¹ + -LESS]

bŏ'dily¹ *a.* of or affecting the human body or physical nature [f. BODY¹ + -LY¹]

bŏ'dilў² *adv.* with the whole bulk, as a whole; in the body, in person. [f. BODY¹ + -LY²]

bŏ'dkin *n.* blunt thick needle with large eye for drawing tape etc. through hem; long pin for fastening hair; small pointed instrument for piercing cloth, removing piece of type for correction, etc.; ‖(arch.) person squeezed between two others (*ride bodkin*). [ME, perh. f. Celt.]

Bŏ'dleian¹ (-lĭan) *n.*, Bŏdlei'an² (-lē'an) *n.*, (colloq.) Bŏ'dley *n.* (of) the Library of Oxford University. [f. Sir T. *Bodley*, Engl. diplomat d. 1613, who re-founded it 1603, + -AN]

Bodŏ'ni *n.* style of type for printing and typewriting. [f. G. ∿, It. printer d. 1813]

bŏ'dў¹ *n.* **1.** man or animal as material organism (**keep** ∿ **and soul together,** manage to remain alive; (**dead**) ∿, corpse; **over my dead** ∿, (colloq.) entirely without my assent. **2.** trunk apart from head and limbs; main portion (stem, hull, nave, etc.; *of* motor car, document, etc.); majority. **3.** human being, person, (HEIR *of the* or one's *body; good sort of body, anybody,* etc.). **4.** aggregate of persons (*governing body*), things, or substance (*body of ore, of water*; **in a** ∿, all together; *body* CORPORATE, POLITIC); society, league, military force; collection *of* facts etc. **5.** piece of matter (**heavenly** ∿, sun, star, etc.); bulk, quantity; comparative solidity or substantial character or flavour (*wine of good body*); thing perceptible to senses. **6.** ∿-**blow,** (fig.) severe set-back; ∿-**building,** strengthening the body esp. by exercise; ∿-**colour,** opaque pigment; ∿-**guard,** escort or personal guard of dignitary etc.; ∿**line bowling,** (Cricket) persistent fast bowling on leg side threatening batsman's body; ∿ **odour,** (esp. unpleasant) smell of the body; ∿--**servant,** valet; ∿-**snatcher,** (Hist.) illicit exhumer of corpses for dissection; ∿ **stocking,** woman's under-garment covering trunk and legs; ∿'**work,** structure of vehicle body. **7.** Hence (-)bŏ'diED² (-ĭd) *a.* [OE *bodig,* corresp. to OHG *botah*; orig. unkn.]

bŏ'dў² *v.t.* ∿ **forth,** give mental shape to, exhibit in outward shape, typify. [f. prec.]

Boeŏ'tian (beō'shan) *a.* & *n.* crass or dull (person). [f. *Boeotia* in ancient Greece, proverbial for stupidity of inhabitants, + -AN]

Boer (bō'er, boor) *n.* & *a.* (of) Dutch or Dutch--descended S. African(s). [Du.; see BOOR]

bŏ'ffin *n.* (sl.) person engaged in (esp. technical) research. [20th c.; orig. unkn.]

Bŏ'fors (-z) *n.* ∿ (**gun**), type of light anti-aircraft gun [∿ in Sweden]

bŏg¹ *n.* **1.** (piece of) wet spongy ground (∿ **violet** etc. plant growing in bogs; ‖(sl.) lavatory. **2.** ∿-**bean** = BUCK¹*bean;* ∿ **myrtle,** shrub with fragrant leaves found in bogs; ∿ **oak,** ancient oak preserved in black state in peat; *bog* SPAVIN; ∿-**trotter,** (derog.) Irishman. **3.** Hence ∿'gy² (-gĭ) *a.* [f. Ir. or Gael. *bogach* (*bog* soft)]

bŏg² *v.t.* (-gg-). (usu. in *pass.*) submerge in bog (lit., or fig.: *bogged down in* or *by difficulties*). [f. prec.]

bŏ'gey¹ (-gĭ) *n.* score that good golf-player should do hole or course in. [perh. f. BOGY as imaginary person]

bŏgey². See BOGY.

bŏ'gle *v.i.* hesitate, demur, *at* or *about*; equivocate; be startled or baffled. [prob. f. dial. *boggle* BOGY]

‖bŏ'gie (-gĭ) *n.* undercarriage with two or more wheel-pairs, pivoted below end of rail vehicle. [19th c.; north. dial. wd, of unkn. orig.]

bŏ'gle *n.* bugbear; scarecrow; phantom; goblin. [orig. Sc. 16th c.), prob. rel. to BOGY]

bŏ'gus *a.* sham, fictitious, spurious. [19th c. US wd orig. unkn.]

bŏ'gў, bŏ'gey², (-gĭ) *n.* the Devil; ∿ (**man**), evil spirit goblin; bugbear. [19th c., orig. as proper name; cf BOGLE]

BOGLE

bŏhea' *n.* black tea of lowest quality (last crop of season). [f. *Bu-i* (Wuyi) Hills in China]

Bŏhē'mĭan *a.* & *n.* **1.** (native or inhabitant) of Bohemia; Czech. **2.** socially unconventional (person); person, esp. artist or writer, of free-and-easy habits, manners, and sometimes morals; hence **bŏhē'mĭan-ism** (2) *n.* [f. *Bohemia* + -AN; sense 2 f. F *bohémien* gypsy]

⁕bŏ'hŭnk *n.* (sl.) immigrant from central or SE Europe; rough fellow. [app. f. prec. + HUNGARIAN]

ɔoil¹ *n.* inflamed suppurating swelling caused by infection of hair follicle etc. [OE *bȳl(e)*, = OS *būla*, OHG *būlla* bladder f. WG *⁕būlja*]

ɔoil² *v.* **1.** *v.i.* bubble up, undulate, (of liquid at the temperature at which it changes into vapour, or of containing vessel: *kettle is boiling*); (of sea etc., feelings, person) seethe, be agitated, like boiling water or its vessel; be cooked by boiling; **blood ∼s** (with indignation; *it makes my blood boil*); **∼ down to**, amount to, signify basically; **∼ over**, overflow by boiling; **∼'ing** (hot), (colloq.) very hot; **keep the pot ∼ing**, get a living. **2.** *v.t.* bring (liquid, vessel) to temperature at which it boils; manufacture (soap etc.) thus; subject to heat of boiling water, cook thus; **∼ down**, reduce by boiling (lit. or fig.); **∼ed shirt**, dress shirt with starched front; ‖**∼ed sweet**, sweetmeat made of boiled sugar. [ME, f. AF *boiller*, OF *boillir*, f. L *bullire* to bubble (*bulla* bubble)]

ɔoil² *n.* boiling, boiling-point, (*on, at, to, the boil*). [f. prec.]

ɔoi'ler *n.* In vbl senses (*soap-boiler*); vessel for boiling, esp. for making steam under pressure; water-tank attached to fire etc. in house; metal tub for boiling laundry; vegetable, fowl, etc., suited to boiling; **∼-plate**, rolled steel for making boilers, ⁕(fig.) stereotyped writings esp. as syndicated for newspapers; **∼ suit**, one-piece garment combining overalls and shirt. [f. BOIL² + -ER¹]

ɔoi'ling *n.* In vbl senses; **the whole ∼**, (sl.) the whole lot; **∼-point**, temperature at which liquid (esp. water) boils, (fig.) high excitement. [f. BOIL² + -ING¹]

ɔoi'sterous *a.* violent, rough, (wind, sea, behaviour, speech, persons); noisily cheerful; hence **∼LY²** *adv.*, **∼NESS** *n.* [var. of ME. *boistous*, of unkn. orig.]

ŏō'las *n.* (as *sing.* or *pl.*) S. Amer. etc. missile consisting of balls connected by a strong cord (when thrown bringing down quarry by entangling limbs). [Sp. & Port., pl. of *bola* ball]

ɔold *a.* **1.** courageous, enterprising, confident; forward, immodest; **make** (**so**) **∼** (**as**), presume, venture, (*to do*). **2.** vigorous, free, well-marked, clear, (*bold imagination, drawing, description, features, headland*, etc.). **3.** **∼**(-face, -faced), (of type) having a heavy or conspicuous face, as **bŏld** in this entry. **4.** Hence **∼LY²** *adv.*, **∼NESS** *n.* [OE *bald*, – OS, OHG *bald*, ON *ballr* dangerous f. Gmc *⁕balthaz*]

ŏōle¹ *n.* stem or trunk of tree. [ME, f. ON *bolr*, perh. rel. to BALK¹]

ŏōle² *n.* fine compact earthy clay. [f. LL BOLUS]

ɔolĕ'ction *a.* & *n.* (moulding) placed above or round panel etc. [18th c.; orig. unkn.]

ɔoler'ŏ (-ār'ō) *n.* (*pl.* **∼s**). Spanish dance; music for it; (*or* bŏ'lerō) woman's short open jacket with or without sleeves. [Sp.]

ŏō'lĭde *n.* large meteor, fire-ball. [F, f. L f. Gk *bolis -idos* missile]

ɔoll *n.* rounded seed-vessel, as in flax or cotton; **∼-weevil**, small destructive insect infesting cotton-plant. [ME, f. MDu. *bolle*; see BOWL¹]

ŏō'llard *n.* post on ship or quay for securing ropes to; short post on traffic island. [ME, perh. f. ON *bolr* BOLE¹ + -ARD]

ŏō'llix *v.t.* (vulg.) bungle, confuse. [f. foll.]

ŏō'llix², **bŏ'llocks.** Vars. of BALLOCKS.

ɔolo'gna (-nya) *n.* = *Bologna* SAUSAGE. [f. *B*∼ in Italy]

ɔolŏ'mĕter *n.* electrical instrument for measuring heat radiation; hence **bolŏ'METRY** *n.*, **bŏlomĕ'trıc** *a.*

ɔolŏ'ney, balŏ'ney, *n.* **1.** (sl.) humbug, nonsense. **2.** ⁕Bologna SAUSAGE. [20th c.; orig. uncert.]

Bŏ'lshĕv‖ĭk *n.* (Hist.) advocate of proletarian dictatorship in Russia by soviets, Russian communist; (pop.) socialist revolutionary; hence **∼ISM** (3) *n.*, **∼IST** (2) *n.*, **∼IZE** (3) *v.t.* [Russ., = member of majority, one who (in 1903) favoured extreme measures, f. *bol' she* greater]

Bŏ'lshie, -shȳ, *n.* & *a.* (sl.) **1.** *n.* Bolshevik. **2.** *a.* of Bolsheviks; left-wing; uncooperative. [abbr.]

bŏ'lster¹ *n.* long (esp. under-)pillow across bed or couch; pad or support in machine or instrument. [OE, = OHG *bolstar*, ON *bolstr* f. Gmc *⁕bolstraz* (*⁕bolg-* swell)]

bŏ'lster² *v.t.* **∼** (**up**), support with bolster, (fig.) prop, aid. [f. prec.]

bŏ'lster³ *n.* chisel for cutting bricks. [20th c.; orig. uncert.]

bŏlt¹ *n.* short heavy arrow of crossbow (**have shot my ∼**, have done all I can); discharge of lightning (**∼ from the blue**, complete surprise); door-fastening of sliding bar and socket on jamb, lintel, or threshold; sliding piece of lock or rifle-breech; metal pin with head for holding things together, usu. riveted or with nut; (as measure) roll of fabric, bundle of osiers; **∼-rope** (round sail-edge to prevent tearing). [OE, = MLG *bolte*, OHG *bolz*; ult. orig. unkn.]

bŏlt² *v.* **1.** *v.i.* & *t.* dart off or away, (of horse) escape from control; run to seed; (cause fox, rabbit, etc. to) escape from hole or burrow; gulp down hastily without chewing; ⁕(Polit.) break away, refuse to support party or policy; **∼-hole**, (fig.) means of escape. **2.** *v.t.* fasten (door etc.) with bolt, keep *in* or *out* by bolting door; fasten together with bolts; **∼-on** *a.*, (of car parts etc.) able to be fixed thus. [f. prec.]

bŏlt³ *n.* act of bolting (see prec.); sudden start; running away. [f. prec.]

bŏlt⁴ *adv.* **∼ upright**, rigidly erect (like a bolt). [f. BOLT¹]

bŏlt⁵, boult, (bōlt) *v.t.* sift; investigate. [ME f. OF *bul(e)ter*, prob. f. ⁕*bureter* = It. *burattare*, of unkn. orig.]

bŏ'lter *n.* In vbl senses; horse apt to bolt; (or **bou'lter** *pr.* same) sieve, sifting machine. [f. BOLT²,⁵ + -ER¹]

bŏ'lus *n.* large pill; quantity of food at moment of swallowing. [LL, f. Gk *bōlos* clod]

bŏ'ma *n.* (E. Afr.) defensible enclosure; police or military post; magistrate's office. [Swahili]

bŏmb (-m) *n.* & *v.* **1.** *n.* high-explosive or incendiary material or smoke or gas etc. in container fired from gun, or thrown or deposited by hand, or dropped from aircraft, and exploded by impact or by time mechanism; *atomic bomb, hydrogen bomb, the* ∼; atomic or hydrogen bomb as supreme weapon; **like a ∼**, (colloq.) very successfully. **2.** mass of lava discharged from volcano; (sl.) large sum of money; (sl.) drugged cigarette; ⁕(colloq.) a failure. **3.** **∼-bay**, compartment in aircraft to hold bombs; **∼-disposal**, removal and detonation of unexploded and delayed-action bombs; **∼-happy**, (colloq.) suffering from shell-shock; *bomb*-PROOF²; **∼'shell**, artillery bomb (esp. fig., cause of great surprise; *news came as a bomb-shell* etc.); **∼-sight**, device in aircraft for aiming bombs; **∼-site**, area where buildings have been destroyed by bombs. **4.** *v.t.* attack with bombs; **∼ out**, (esp. in *p.p.*) drive by bombs out of a building etc. *N.v.i.* throw or drop bombs; (sl.) fail; hence **∼'ER¹** (-mer) *n.*, (sl.) aircraft used for bombing; **∼ jacket** (tightly gathered at waist and cuffs). [f. F *bombe* f. It. *bomba* f. L Gk *bombos* hum]

bŏmbär'd *v.t.* attack with heavy guns; (Phys.) subject (substance) to stream of high-speed particles; (fig.) assail persistently *with* abuse, argument, etc.; hence **∼MENT** *n.* [f. F *bombarder* (*bombarde* f. med. L *bombarda* stone-throwing engine prob. f. L *bombus*; see prec.]

bŏ'mbard² *v.t.* bass shawm. [ME, f. OF *bombarde*]

bŏmbardier' *n.* **1.** ‖artillery non-commissioned officer. **2.** ⁕aimer and releaser of bombs from aircraft. **3.** **∼ beetle** (audibly releasing unpleasant vapour when alarmed). [F, f. as BOMBARD¹; see -IER]

bŏ'mbardon *n.* (Mus.) low-pitched brass wind instrument; organ stop imitating this. [f. It. *bombardone* (*bombardo* bassoon, -*one*; see -OON)]

bombasine. See BOMBAZINE.

bŏ'mbast *n.* pompous or extravagant language; hence **bŏmbă'stic** *a.*, **bŏmbă'stically** *adv.* [f. earlier *bombace* cotton wool f. F f. med. L *bombax -acis* alt. f. *bombyx*; see BOMBAZINE]

Bŏmbay dŭ'ck *n.* bummalo, esp. as relish. [corrupt. of *bombil*; see BUMMALO]

bŏ'mbazine, -sine, (-zēn) *n.* twilled dress-material of worsted with or without silk or cotton, esp. black kind formerly much used for mourning. [f. F. *bombasin* f. med. L *bombacinum* f. LL *bombycinus* silken (*bombyx -ycis* silk or silkworm f. Gk *bombux*)]

bombe (bawnb) *n.* (Cookery). cone-shaped or cup-shaped dish or confection, freq. frozen. [F, = BOMB]

bomber. See BOMB 5.

bŏ'mbilāte, bŏ'mbināte, *vbs. i.* (literary). hum, buzz. [f. med. L *bombilare, bombinare* buzz f. L *bombus* (see BOMB) + -ATE[3]]

bŏmbŏr'a *n.* (Austral.) dangerous sea area with waves breaking over submerged reef. [Aboriginal]

bōna fī'dé *a.* & *adv.* genuine(ly), sincere(ly). [L, abl. sing. of foll.]

bōna fī'dēs (-z) *n.* honest intention, sincerity. [L, = good faith]

bonă'nza *n.* & *a.* **1.** *n.* prosperity, good luck; large output (esp. of mines); unexpected success (orig. in mining), run of luck. **2.** *a.* greatly prospering or productive. [orig. US f. Sp., = fair weather f. L *bonus* good]

bona vacantia (bōna vakă'ntĭa) *n.* (Law). goods without apparent owner. [L, = ownerless goods]

bŏ'n-bŏn *n.* piece of confectionery, sweet. [F (*bon* good f. L *bonus*)]

||**bŏnce** *n.* large playing-marble; (sl.) head. [19th c.; orig. unkn.]

bŏnd[1] *n.* **1.** thing that ties another down or together; (in *pl.*) thing restraining bodily freedom, imprisonment, (*burst* one's *bonds*). **2.** restraining or uniting force; adhesion; (Chem.) linkage between atoms in a molecule. **3.** binding engagement, agreement, (*his word is as good as his bond*); deed by which person binds himself to pay another; government's or public company's documentary promise to repay borrowed money, usu. with interest, debenture; insurance policy; ∼ (**paper**), high-quality writing-paper suitable for bonds; ∼-**washing**, dividend-stripping. **4.** **in** ∼, (of goods) stored under charge of Customs in 'bonded warehouse' till importer pays duty. **5.** (Bricklaying). one of various methods (*English bond, Flemish bond*, etc.) of holding wall together by making bricks overlap; ∼'**stone**, stone or brick running through wall. [ME var. of BAND[1]]

bŏnd[2] *v.t.* bind together (bricks etc., see prec.; resin etc. with fibres); connect with bond; place goods in bond. [f. prec.]

bŏnd[3] *a.* (arch.) in serfdom or slavery; hence ∼'**maid**, ∼'**man**, ∼'**servant**, ∼'**service**, ∼'**slave**, ∼'-**woman**. [adj. use of ME *bonde* f. OE *bonda* husbandman f. ON *bóndi* = *bóandi*, part. of *búa, bóa* dwell]

bŏ'ndage *n.* serfdom, slavery; subjection to constraint, influence, obligation, etc. [ME, f. AL *bondagium*; see prec. and -AGE; infl. by BOND[1]]

bŏ'ndéd *a.* (Of goods) placed in bond; (of warehouse) for such goods; (of debt) secured by bonds; (of material) reinforced by or cemented to another. [f. BOND[1] + -ED[2]]

bŏ'nds|man (-z-) *n.* (*pl.* ∼**men**) slave (lit. or fig.). [var. of *bondman* (BOND[3]) as though f. *bond's* gen. of BOND[1]]

bŏne[1] *n.* **1.** one of the pieces of hard tissue making up vertebrate animal's skeleton; (in *pl.*) the body (**feel in** one's ∼**s**, feel sure; **make old** ∼**s**, live to old age), its remains (*his bones were laid*); body's hard, solid, or essential part (*flesh and bone*; **bare** ∼**s**, mere essentials;

close to or **near the** ∼, (1) destitute, (2) indecent; **to the** ∼, penetratingly, to the bare minimum; **work** one's **fingers to the** ∼, work very hard); (Austral.) bone used by Aboriginals in spells to cause sickness or death (*point the bone*). **2.** material of which bones consist; similar substance, e.g. ivory, dentine, whalebone; thing made of bone, e.g. domino; (in *pl.*) dice, castanets; strip of stiff substance in corset etc. **3.** subject of dispute (*bone of contention*; *bone to pick with someone*); **make no** ∼**s**, not hesitate or scruple. **4.** ∼ **china**, (made of clay mixed with ash from bones); ∼-**dry**, quite dry; *∼'**fish**, large game-fish with many small bones; ∼'**head**(ed), (sl.) stupid (person); ∼ **idle, lazy**, utterly idle or lazy; ∼-**meal**, crushed or ground bones used esp. as fertilizer; ∼-**oil**, dark oil got by carbonizing bones; ∼-**seeking**, (Med.) tending to be deposited in the bones; ∼-**setter**, one who sets broken or dislocated bones, esp. without being qualified surgeon; ∼-**shaker**, jolting vehicle, (Hist.) bicycle without rubber tyres; ∼-**spavin** ∼ **weary**, utterly weary; ∼-**yard**, (sl.) cemetery. [OE *bān*, = OS *bēn*, OHG, ON *bein* f. Gmc *bainam*]

bŏne[2] *v.* 1. *v.t.* take out the bones from (meat, fish). **2.** stiffen with bone. **3.** (sl.) steal. **4.** *v.i.* *∼ up on*, study intensively. [f. prec.; sense 3 perh. diff. wd]

bŏ'ner *n.* (sl.) stupid mistake. [f. BONE[1] + -ER[1]]

bŏ'nfire *n.* large open-air fire to celebrate event (|||B∼ **Night,** 5 Nov.; cf. GUY[2]) or as signal; fire for consuming rubbish (**make a** ∼ **of**, destroy by burning). [earlier *bonefire* f. BONE[1] (bones being the chief material formerly used) + FIRE[1]]

bŏ'ngō[1] (-nggō) *n.* (*pl.* same or ∼**s**). large striped African antelope. [cf. Bangi *mbangani*, Lingala *mongu*]

bŏ'ngō[2] (-nggō) *n.* (*pl.* ∼**s** or ∼**es**). one of pair of small drums usu. held between knees and played with fingers. [Amer. Sp. *bongó*]

bonhomie (bŏ'nomē) *n.* geniality; good-natured friendliness. [F (*bonhomme* good fellow, -*ie* = -Y[1])]

bŏ'nhomous (-nom-) *a.* showing bonhomie. [f. prec. + -OUS]

Bŏ'niface *n.* keeper of inn etc. [character in Farquhar's *Beaux' Stratagem* (1707)]

bŏ'n|ism *n.* doctrine that the world is good, but not the best possible; so ∼IST (2) *n.* [f. L *bonus* good + -ISM]

bŏni'tō (-ē'-) *n.* (*pl.* ∼**s**). large mackerel-like fish. [Sp.]

bŏ'nkers (-z) *a.* (sl.) crazy. [20th c.; orig. unkn.]

bon mot (bawn mō', bŏn-) *n.* (*pl.* **bons mots** *pr.* same or -mō'z). witty saying. [F]

bonne bouche (bŏn bōō'sh) *n.* (*pl.* ∼**s** or **bonnes bouches,** *pr.* same). titbit, esp. to end up with. [F (*bonne* fem. good, *bouche* mouth)]

bŏ'nnét *n.* **1.** woman's or child's outdoor head-dress with strings; (man's or boy's) round brimless Scotch cap (BEE in one's *bonnet*); Amer. Indian's ceremonial head-dress; ∼ **rouge** (F, *pr.* bŏnă rōō'zh), red cap as revolutionary symbol. **2.** cowl of chimney etc.; protective cap in various machines, |||hinged cover over engine of motor vehicle; (Naut.) additional canvas laced to sail-foot; ∼-**head**, = SHOVEL-head (1); ∼-**monkey**, Ind. macaque wit' bonnet-like tuft of hair; hence ∼ED[2] *a.* [ME, f. OF *bonet* short for *chapel de bonet* cap of some kind of material (med. L *bonetus*)]

bŏ'nn|ỹ *a.* **1.** (chiefly Sc. & N. Engl.) comely. **2.** healthy-looking; pleasing. **3.** Hence ∼ILY[2] *adv.* [16th c.; perh. f. F *bon* good]

bŏ'nsai (-sī) *n.* (method of cultivating) artificially dwarfed potted plant or small tree. [Jap.]

bŏ'nspiel *n.* (esp. Sc.) curling-match (usu. between two clubs). [16th c., perh. f. LG]

bŏ'nt(e)bŏk *n.* (S. Afr.) reddish white-faced antelope. [Afrik. (*bont* spotted, *bok* BUCK[1])]

bon ton (bawn taw'n) *n.* good breeding; the fashionable world. [F, lit. good tone]

bŏ'nus *n.* something to the good, into the bargain;

extra dividend or issue to shareholders of company, distribution of profits to insurance-policy-holders, gratuity to employees beyond their normal pay. [joc. or ignorant use of L *bonus, bonum* good (thing)] **bon vivant** (bawn vēvah'n) *n.* gourmand. [F, lit. good liver (*vivre* to live)] **bon viveur** (bawn vēvēr') *n.* one who lives luxuriously. [pseudo-F] **bon voyage** (bawn vwahyah'z) *int.* of farewell to departing traveller. [F] **bō'nÿ** *a.* of or like bone(s); big-boned with little flesh; (of fish) having bones rather than cartilage. [f. BONE¹ + -Y²] **bönze** *n.* Japanese or Chinese Buddhist priest. [F, or f. Port. *bonzo* perh. f. Jap. *bonzō* f. Chin. *fanseng* religious person, or f. Jap. *bō-zi* f. Chin. *fasi* teacher of the law] **bō'nzer** *a.* (Austral. sl.) excellent, first-rate. [perh. f. BONANZA] **boo** *int., n.,* & *v.t.* & *i.* expr., (make) sound of, disapproval or contempt (**can't say ~ to a goose,** is very shy or timid); jeer at (speaker, performer, announcement, etc.). [imit.] **boob** *n.,* & *v.i.* (sl.) **1.** simpleton; (make) mistake. **2.** *n.* (in *pl.*; prob. f. BUB¹). woman's breasts. [abbr. of BOOBY] **boo'boo** *n.* (sl.) mistake. [f. prec.] **boo'book** *n.* (Austral.) medium-sized brown spotted owl. [imit.] **boo'bÿ** *n.* **1.** silly or stupid or childish person; small gannet. **2.** **~hatch,* (sl.) mental hospital; *~ prize,* awarded to least competitor or lowest scorer in contest of any kind; *~ trap,* thing placed on top of door ajar to fall on first opener, (Mil.) apparently harmless device concealing explosive charge designed to go off when tampered with; *~-trap v.t.,* place booby trap(s) in or on. [prob. f. Sp. *bobo* (in both senses 1) f. L *balbus* stammering] **boo'dle** *n.* (sl.) money, esp. for political bribery. [f. Du. *boedel* possessions] **boogie-woo'gie** (-gǐ-; -gǐ) *n.* style of playing blues on piano, marked by persistent bass rhythm. [20th c.; orig. unkn.] **book¹** *n.* **1.** portable written or printed work filling a number of sheets fastened together, usu. with sheets sewn or pasted hingewise and enclosed in cover (**closed ~,** thing of which one has no understanding); literary composition that would fill such a set of sheets (or several) if printed; telephone directory; (colloq.) magazine. **2.** anything from which one may learn (**throw the ~ at,** make all possible charges against); imaginary record, list, etc., (**~ of fate,** future as being predetermined; **~ of life,** list of those who shall be saved); **the** (**good**) **~,** the Bible (*swear on the book; people of the B~,* Jews); main division of literary work or of Bible; **~** (**of words**) = LIBRETTO; script of play. **3.** back-hinged set of blank sheets for writing accounts, notes, exercises, etc., in; (in *pl.*) society's records, trader's accounts; bets on a horse-race etc. or at a race-meeting (*make a book;* **in my ~,** as I see the matter; **suits my ~,** is convenient to me); set of tickets, stamps, matches, cheques, pieces of cloth, six tricks at cards, etc., bound up or collected. **4. bring to ~,** call to account; **go by the ~,** (according to rules); **in** person's **bad** or **black, good, ~s,** in disfavour, favour, with him; **not in the ~,** disallowed; **on the ~s,** in list of members etc.; **read** person **like a ~,** understand his motives etc. fully; **speak by the ~** (with correct information); **speak** or **talk like a ~** (in formal phrases); **speak without ~,** give facts from memory; **take a leaf out of** person's **~,** imitate him. **5. ~'binder, -ding,** binder, binding, of books; **~'case** (-k-k-), case containing shelves for books; **~ club,** society whose members can buy selected books on special terms; **~-ends,** pair of usu. ornamental pieces to keep row of books upright; **~'keeper, -ping,** (-k-k-) one who keeps, (art or business of) keeping, accounts of trader, public

office, etc.; **~'land,** (Hist.) area of common land granted by charter to private owner; **~-learned,** knowing books (but lacking practical experience); **~-learning** or **-lore,** mere theory; **~'maker,** **~'making,** (1) compiler, compiling, of books (esp. for mercenary motives), (2) professional betting (person); **~'man,** literary man; **~'mark(er),** strip of leather, paper, etc., to mark place in book; **~'mobile* (-ēl), mobile library; **~ page,** (1) page of book, (2) page of newspaper etc. on which reviews of books appear; **~-plate,** ex-libris; ||**~-post,** transmission of books by post at especially low rates; **~-rest,** adjustable support for open book on table; **~'seller,** dealer in books; **~'shop** (where books are sold); ||**~'stall** (for sale of books out of doors or in station etc.); **~'store,* bookshop; ||**~ token,** voucher for sum of money to buy book(s); **~-trough,** V-shaped rack for display of books on table etc., to show titles; **~ value,** value of a commodity as entered in firm's books (opp. *market value*); **~'work,** study of books (opp. *practical work*); **~'worm,** larva of moth or beetle eating its way through books, (fig.) person devoted to reading. **6.** Hence **~'IE** *n.,* (colloq.) bookmaker (2); **~'ISH** *a.,* addicted to reading books, studious, getting knowledge from books only, literary rather than colloquial; **~'LET** *n.,* small book (usu. paper-covered). [OE *bōc,* = OHG *buoh,* ON *bók* f. Gmc **bōks,* usu. taken to be cogn. w. BEECH] **book²** *v.* **1.** *v.t.* enter in book or list; engage (seat etc.) in advance, (guest, supporter, etc.) for some occasion; enter name of (person engaging seat, offender, suspect, etc.); issue railway etc. ticket to (person) (whence **~'ing-clerk,** ||**-hall,** ||**-office**); (in *p.p.,* sl.) caught, unable to escape. **2.** *v.i.* obtain ticket for journey etc.; **~ in,** register at hotel etc. [OE *bōcian* (as prec.)] **boo'ksÿ** *a.* (colloq.) having literary or bookish pretensions. [f. pl. of BOOK¹ + -Y²] **Boo'lean** *a.* **~ algebra** etc., abstract system of postulates and symbols applicable to logical problems. [f. G. *Boole,* Engl. mathematician d. 1864 + -AN] **boom¹** *n.* long pole with one end fixed, to support sail-foot, camera, microphone, etc.; floating barrier of timber across river or harbour mouth. [Du., = BEAM¹] **boom²** *v.i.,* & *n.* (make, speak etc. with) deep resonant sound; hum, buzz; SONIC *boom.* [imit.] **boom³** *v.i.,* & *n.* (Esp. of commercial venture), prosper, etc.; (show) sudden activity or development; **~ town,** town undergoing sudden growth due to boom, hence **~'LET** *n.* [19th c.; US wd, perh. f. prec. (cf. *make things hum*)] **boo'mer** *n.* large male kangaroo; N. Amer. mountain beaver; large wave. [f. BOOM² + -ER¹] **boo'meräng** *n.,* & *v.i.* **1.** *n.* Australian thin curved hardwood missile, usu. of kind that can be thrown so as to return to its thrower; (fig.) scheme etc. that recoils on its author. **2.** *v.i.* act as a boomerang; (fig.) recoil on originator. [Aboriginal name, perh. modified] **boo'msläng** *n.* (S. Afr.) large tree-snake. [Afrik. (*boom* tree, *slang* snake)] **boon¹** *n.* request, thing asked for; favour, gift; blessing, advantage. [ME, orig. = prayer f. ON *bón* f. Gmc **bōniz,* f. unkn. orig.] **boon²** *a.* congenial, jolly, (*boon companion*). [ME, f. OF *bon* f. L *bonus* good] **boo'ndock* *n.* (sl., usu. in *pl.*) rough or isolated country. [f. Tagalog *bundok* mountain] **boo'ndoggle* *n.,* & *v.i.* (engage in) trivial or unnecessary work. [20th c.; orig. unkn.] **boor** *n.* clumsy or ill-bred person; hence **~'ISH¹** *a.* [f. LG *būr* or Du. *boer* farmer; cf. BOWER³] **boost** *v.t.,* & *n.* **1.** *v.t.* (colloq.) push from below; assist. **2.** increase reputation, value, etc., of (person, scheme, commodity, etc.) by praise, advertising, etc. **3.** raise

voltage in electric circuit etc.); amplify (radio signal). **4.** *n.* act or process of boosting; scheme of advertisement; resulting advance in value etc. [19th c. US wd; orig. unkn.]
boo'ster *n.* device for boosting voltage or signal strength; auxiliary engine or rocket to give initial acceleration; (Med.) dose increasing or renewing effect of earlier one. [f. prec. + -ER¹]
boot¹ *n.*, & *v.t.* **1.** *n.* outer foot-covering, esp. of leather, coming (*well) above ankle; covering to protect lower part of horse's leg; ~ and saddle [corrupt. of F *boute-selle* place saddle], cavalry signal to mount; DIE² *in* one's *boots*; **get, give, the ~,** (sl.) be dismissed, dismiss, from employment; HEART *in* one's *boots*; **like old ~s,** (sl.) tremendously; **put the ~ in,** kick brutally, take decisive action; *too* BIG *for* one's *boots*; **the ~ is on the other leg** or **foot,** truth or responsibility is just the other way round; **you bet your ~s,** (sl.) it is quite certain; hence ~'ED² *a.* **2.** (Hist.) instrument of torture encasing the foot. **3.** (Hist.) luggage-receptacle in coach under guard's and coachman's seats; ||luggage-receptacle at back (or occas. front) of motor car. **4.** *~'black,* shoeblack; *~ camp* (sl., for basic training of naval recruits); ~-faced, grim or expressionless; ~'jack, contrivance for pulling boots off; ~'lace, cord or leather strip for lacing boots; ~'leg, smuggle(d) (esp. of liquor), illicitly sold; ~'licker, toady; ~'straps, (fig.) unaided effort (*raise oneself by one's own bootstraps*); ~-tree, mould for keeping boot in shape. **5.** *v.t.* kick; (sl.) kick or drive (person) *out* (*of* house, employment, etc.). [ME, f. ON *bóti* or f. OF *bote*, of unkn. orig.]
boot² *n.* **to ~,** as well, to the good, additionally. [OE *bōt*, = OS *bōta*, OHG *buoza*, ON *bót*, Goth. *bōta* f. Gmc *bōtō* remedy (*bōt-, *bāt-; cf. BETTER¹, BEST)]
boot³ *v.t.* (arch.; usu. *impers.* and abs.). do good, avail (*what boots it to repeat how time is slipping underneath our feet?*). [ME, f. prec.]
bootee' *n.* woman's short lined boot; infant's woollen etc. boot. [f. BOOT¹ + -EE; cf. *coatee*]
booth (-dh) *n.* temporary shelter of canvas etc.; covered stall in market, tent at fair, etc.; (partly) enclosed area for telephoning, voting, sitting in restaurant, etc. [ME, f. Old East Norse *bóth* (*bóa* dwell; cf. BOND³, BOWER¹)]
boo'tless *a.* unavailing. [OE *bótléas*; see BOOT², -LESS]
||**boots** *n.* hotel servant who cleans boots and shoes, carries luggage, etc. [pl. of BOOT¹]
boo'ty *n.* plunder or profit acquired in common and to be divided; gain, prize. [ME, f. MLG *būte, buite* exchange, of uncert. orig.]
booz|e *v.i.,* & *n.* **1.** *v.i.* drink (alcoholic liquor) habitually or excessively. **2.** *n.* (esp. alcoholic) drink; drinking-bout. **3.** Hence ~'ER¹ *n.,* one who boozes, ||(sl.) public house; ~'Y² *a.,* addicted to drink, intoxicated. [earlier *bouse, bowse,* f. MDu. *būsen* drink to excess]
bop *n.* = BEBOP; hence ~'PER¹ (3), ~'STER, *ns.* [abbr.]
bo-pee'p *n.* game of hiding and suddenly reappearing, played with young child. [f. BO¹ + PEEP²]
bŏr'a¹ *n.* cold dry NE wind blowing in the upper Adriatic. [It. dial., f. L *boreas* north wind; see BOREAL]
bŏr'a² *n.* (Austral.) rite of admission to manhood among Aborigines. [Aboriginal]
bora'cic *a.* of borax (~ *acid,* boric acid). [f. med. L BORAX *boracis* + -IC]
bo'rage (bŏ'-, bŭ'-) *n.* blue-flowered hairy-leaved plant used in salads etc. [f. OF *bourrache* f. med. L *borrago* f. Arab. '*abu 'āraķ* father of sweat (from its use as a diaphoretic)]
bŏr'ăk *n.* (Austral. & NZ sl.) nonsense; banter. [Aboriginal Austral.]
bŏr'āte *n.* salt of boric acid. [f. BORIC + -ATE¹]
bŏr'ăx *n.* sodium borate as native deposit or purified white powder or crystals. [ME f. OF *boras* f. med. L *borax* f. Arab. *būraķ* f. Pers. *būrah*]

bŏr'azŏn *n.* hard oxidation-resistant form of boron nitride. [f. BORON + AZO- nitrogen + -*on*]
bŏrbory'gm|us *n.* (*pl.* ~**i** *pr.* -ī). rumbling of gas in intestines; hence ~IC *a.* [mod. L f. Gk]
Bŏrdeau'x (-dō') *n.* (*pl.* same *pr.* -ōz). red (claret) or white wine esp. from district of Bordeaux; ~ **mixture,** fungicide for fruit-trees etc. [~ in SW France]
***bŏrdĕ'l,** *bŏrdĕ'llō* (*pl.* -**os**), *ns.* brothel. [ME, (f. It. *bordello*) f. OF *bordel* small farm, dim. of *borde* f. Gallo-Rom. *borda* f. Frank. *bord* BOARD¹]
bŏr'der¹ *n.* **1.** side, edge, boundary or part near it; frontier of country; **the B~,** boundary and adjoining districts between England and Scotland, N. Ireland and Irish Republic, US and Mexico, etc.; **B~ terrier,** small rough-haired kind. **2.** continuous bed round garden or part of it; distinct edging for strength or ornament or definition round anything; ~ **print** (with design running parallel to edge of fabric). **3.** ~**land,** district on either side of border, (fig.) intermediate condition (e.g. between sleeping and waking), debatable ground; ~**line,** (*n.*) line of demarcation, (*a.*) on the borderline (~*line case,* e.g. one verging on obscenity or insanity). [ME f. OF *bordure,* f. Rom. **bordare* (**bordus* f. Gmc **bordhaz*; cf. BOARD¹, -URE)]
bŏr'der² *v.t.* & *i.* put or be a border to; ~ (**on**), adjoin, resemble, come close to being. [ME, f. prec.]
bŏrdereau' (-dō') *n.* (*pl.* ~**x** *pr.* -z). memorandum of contents, docket. [F]
bŏr'derer *n.* dweller on or near frontier, esp. that between England and Scotland. [f. BORDER¹ + -ER¹ (4)]
bŏr'dūre *n.* (Her.) border round edge of shield. [ME form of BORDER¹]
bore¹ *v.t.* **1.** *v.t.* make hole in, usu. with revolving tool; hollow out (tube etc.) evenly; make (hole, one's way), by boring, persistent pushing, or excavation. **2.** *v.i.* (Of racehorse) push another horse out of the way; drill a well (for oil etc.). [OE *borian,* = OHG *borōn* ON *bora* f. Gmc **borōn*]
bore² *n.* hollow of firearm barrel or of cylinder in internal combustion engine; diameter of this, calibre. ~('hole), deep narrow hole made in earth to find water etc. [partly f. prec., partly f. ON *bora* borehole f. Gmc **borōn*]
bore³ *n.* nuisance (usu. as *pred.*); tiresome or dull person. [18th c.; orig. unkn.; early contexts suggest F deriv.]
bore⁴ *v.t.* weary by tedious talk or dullness. [app. f. contemporary BORE³]
bore⁵ *n.* tide-wave with steep front moving up some estuaries and bays; eagre. [ME, perh. f. ON *bára* wave]
bore⁶. See BEAR³.
bŏr'eal *a.* of the North or the Arctic or the north wind. [ME, f. F *boréal* or f. LL *borealis* f. L f. Gk *Boreas* god of north wind; see -AL]
bŏr'ecōle (bŏr'k-) *n.* = KALE. [f. Du. *boerenkool* peasant's cabbage]
bŏr'edom (bŏr'd-) *n.* being bored, ennui. [f. BORE³ + -DOM]
bŏr'er *n.* in vbl senses; boring worm, mollusc, or insect. [f. BORE¹ + -ER¹]
bŏr'ic *a.* of boron; ~ **acid** (derived from borax and used as mild antiseptic). [f. BORON + -IC]
bŏrn *a.* having come into existence by birth; destined to be (*born rich, tired, to be hanged, a poet; a ~ orator, an orator ~,* by natural ability); utter, hopeless, (*born fool idiot*); (in comb.) as (*English-born, first-born*) ~ **again,** regenerate; *born and bred* (see BREED¹); ~ **of,** owing origin to; **not ~ yesterday,** (fig.) far from foolish; **in all my ~ days,** (colloq.) in my life hitherto. [p.p. of BEAR³]
bŏrne. See BEAR³.
borné (bŏr'nā) *a.* having limitations, of limited ideas, narrow-minded. [F]

Bor'nhŏlm (-ōm) *n.* ～ **disease**, epidemic virus disease with intercostal pain. [～ in Denmark]

ŏro- *comb. form.* boron, as: **boroflu'oride, boro-si'licate**, etc., salts containing boron. [f. foll.]

ŏr'ŏn *n.* non-metallic solid element (brown amorphous powder or black crystals). [f. BORAX w. ending of *carbon*, which it resembles in some respects]

ŏrō'nia *n.* (Austral.) sweet-scented shrub of genus *Boronia.* [f. F. *Borone*, It. botanist d. 1794 + -IA¹]

o'rough (bŭ'rō) *n.* **1.** (Hist.) ‖town with corporation and privileges conferred by royal charter; town sending member(s) to parliament. **2.** administrative area in Greater London. **3.** ‖pocket ～, (Hist.) borough where election was controlled by private person or family; ‖rotten ～, (Hist.) borough no longer having real constituency. **4.** *town or village; *one of five parts of New York City; *(in Alaska) county. [OE *burg, burh*, = OS *burg*, OHG *burug*, ON *borg*, Goth. *baurgs* f. Gmc *burgs cogn. w. *bergan shelter; cf. BURGH]

orough-E'nglish (bŭrŏǐ'nggl-) *n.* (Hist.) tenure in some parts of England whereby youngest son inherited all lands and tenements. [ME, f. AF (*tenure en*) *Burgh Engloys* English borough (tenure); so called as not existing in France]

o'rrow (ō) *v.t. & i.* get temporary use of (money or property to be returned; *from* or *of* person); adopt, use without being the true or original owner or inventor, derive from another, import from an alien source; (Golf) (1) play ball uphill to roll back, (2) allow for wind or slope; ～ed **light**, (1) reflected light, (2) internal window; *borrowed* PLUME¹s or *plumage*; ～ed **time**, unexpected extension esp. of life; hence ～ER¹, ～ING¹ (2), *ns.* [OE *borgian* give a pledge (= OHG *borgēn* take heed) f. *borg* (= OS *borg*) pledge, f. root of Gmc *bergan protect (cf. prec.)]

orsch (-sh), **bŏrtsch** (-ch), *n.* highly seasoned Russian or Polish soup of various ingredients including beetroot and cabbage. [f. Russ. *borshch*]

Bŏr'stal *n.* institution to which young offenders may be sent for reformative training. [～ in Kent]

ŏrt, boart, *n.* diamond fragments made in cutting; diamond malformed in the making. [f. Du. *boort*]

ŏr'zoi *n.* large Russian wolfhound with usu. white silky coat. [Russ. (*borzyi* swift)]

o'scage, -kage, *n.* masses of trees or shrubs; wooded scenery. [ME, f. OF *boscage* f. Gallo-Rom. *boscaticus (*bŏsŏos; cf. BUSH¹, AUK)]

ŏsh¹ *n. & int.* (sl.) nonsense, foolish talk. [f. Turk. *boş* empty]

ŏsh² *n.* lower sloping part of blast-furnace shaft, from belly to hearth. [17th c.; orig. unkn.]

ŏ'sie (-zi) *n.* (Austral.) ～. [f. B. J. T. Bosanquet, Engl. cricketer d. 1936 + -IE]

ŏ'skage. See BOSCAGE.

ŏ'sky *a.* wooded, bushy. [f. ME *bosk* thicket + -Y²]

ŏ's'n. See BOAT¹*swain*

bo'som (bŏŏ'z-) *n.* **1.** person's breast; *(in *pl.*) woman's breasts; enclosure formed by breast and arms. **2.** breast of dress, space between dress and breast; *shirt-front; surface of lake, sea, ground, etc.; `enfolding relationship (*bosom of one's family, of the church*); the heart, thoughts, desires, etc. (～ **friend**, intimate); hence ～Y² *a.*, (of woman) having prominent bosom. [OE *bōsm*, = OS *bōsom*, OHG *buosam* f. WG *bōsm-, perh. f. *bōhsm- f. *bōg- (cf. BOUGH)]

bŏ'sŏn (-z-) *n.* (Phys.) particle obeying relations stated by Bose and Einstein, with integral spin. [f. S. N. Bose, Ind. physicist d. 1974 + -ON]

bŏss¹ *n.* protuberance; round metal knob or stud on centre of shield or ornamental work; (Archit.) carved or sculptured projection at intersecting-point of ribs; (Geol.) large mass of igneous rock; (Mech.) enlarged part of shaft. [ME, f. OF *boce* f. Rom. *bokja, *botja, of unkn. orig.]

bŏss² *n.* (colloq.) ～(-**man**), master, person in authority, overseer; *manager of political organization, whence ～'ISM (3) *n.*; hence ～'Y² *a.*, domineering. [19th c.; US wd f. Du. *baas* master]

bŏss³ *v.t.* (sl.) be master or manager of; give orders to (～ person **about**, continually give peremptory orders to him). [f. prec.]

‖**bŏss⁴** *n.*, & *v.t.* **1.** *n.* (sl.) ～(-**shot**), bad shot or guess, miss; bungle, mess; ～-**eyed**, (sl.) blind in one eye, cross-eyed, crooked, one-sided. **2.** *v.t.* (sl.) miss, bungle. [19th c.; orig. unkn.]

bŏssa nŏ'va *n.* Brazilian dance like samba; music for it. [f. Port. *bossa* tendency + *nova* fem. of *novo* new]

Bŏ'ston *n.* ～ **terrier**, small smooth-haired terrier. [～ in Massachusetts]

bō'sun, bo'sun. See BOAT¹*swain.*

Bŏ'swĕll (-z-) *n.* biographer like James ～ d. 1795, writer of Samuel Johnson's life; hence **Bŏswĕ'll**IAN (-z-) *a.*, ～ISM (3) *n.*, ～IZE (4) *v.i.*

bŏt(t) *n.* parasitic worm infesting horses etc., larva of ～-**fly**. [prob. of LG orig.]

bot. *abbr.* bottle; bought.

bŏ'tan|**ў¹** *n.* science of structure, physiology, classification, and distribution of plants; so **botā'n**ICAL, (arch.) **botā'n**IC, *adjs.*, ～IST (3) *n.*, ～IZE (2) *v.i.*, (esp.) study plants where they grow. [f. *botanic* f. F *botanique* or LL f. Gk *botanikos* (*botanē* plant); see -IC, -Y¹]

Bŏ'tanў² *a. & n.* ～ (**wool**), merino wool, esp. from Australia. [f. ～ *Bay*, New S. Wales, named from the variety of its flora]

botā'rgo *n.* (*pl.* ～**es** or ～**s**) relish of mullet or tunny roe. [f. It. *bottarga* f. Egypt. Arab. *baṭārikh* fish-roe, of Coptic orig.]

bŏtch *n.*, & *v.t. & i.* (make a) clumsy patch; spoil(t) or bungle(d) work; repair badly. [ME, of unkn. orig.]

botě'l, boatě'l, *n.* hotel for boat-owners; ship serving as hotel. [f. BOAT¹ + HOTEL]

bŏth *a., pron., & adv.* **1.** *a. & pron.* the two (and not only one) (both (the) brothers are dead; both (of the brothers) are dead; the brothers are both dead); ‖(～ **ways**, (Racing) = EACH *way*; have it ～ **ways**, choose now one now the other of alternatives or contradictories to suit one's argument etc. **2.** *adv.* with equal truth in two (or arch. more) cases (*both brother and sister are dead; she is both shrewd and buried; both God and man and beast*). [ME, f. ON *báthir* etc. (= OS *bethia*, OHG *bēde*), extended form of base root; by OE *bēgen* both]

hŏ'ther¹ (dh-) *v, & int.* **1.** *v.t.* give trouble to; worry; ～ **oneself**, one's **head**, be anxious (*about*); **can't be** ～**ed**, will not make the effort needed. **2.** *v.i.* worry or trouble oneself (*to do, about*); be concerned *with*. **3.** *v.t.* (subj.) & *int.* (colloq., expr. impatience). confound, damn. [18th c., Anglo-Ir., perh. f. POTHER]

bŏ'ther² (-dh-) *n.* (cause of) worry, fuss, minor trouble; worried state. [f. prec.]

bŏthera'tion (-dh-) *n.* & *int.* **1.** *n.* prec. **2.** *int.* = BOTHER¹. [f. BOTHER¹ + -ATION]

bŏ'thersome (-dh-) *a.* annoying, troublesome. [f. BOTHER¹ + -SOME¹]

bŏ'thў, -ie, (Sc.) hut, cottage; one-roomed building in which labourers are lodged. [18th c.; orig. unkn.; perh. rel. to BOOTH]

bō'-tree *n.* sacred pipal tree of India. [repr. Sinh. *bogaha* f. *bo* = Pali and Skr. *bodhi* perfect knowledge + *gaha* tree (Buddha's enlightenment having occurred beneath such a tree)]

bŏtt. See BOT.

bŏ'ttle¹ *n.* **1.** narrow-necked vessel, usu. of glass or plastic for storing liquid; amount of liquid in it; act or habit of drinking alcoholic liquor (**on the** ～, addicted to drink; **over a** ～, while drinking; = FEED¹*ing*-*bottle*; = HOT¹-*water bottle*; metal cylinder for liquefied gas. **2.** ～-**brush**, cylindrical brush for cleaning bottles, plant with flower of this shape; ～-**fed**, fed with milk from feeding-bottle, with mother's milk; ～-**glass**, coarse dark-green glass; ～-**green**,

dark green; ∿-**neck**, (fig.) narrow stretch or restricted outlet of road, anything obstructing an even flow of production etc.; ∿-**nose**, swollen nose; ∿-**nosed**, (of dolphin, whale) with bottle-shaped snout; ∿-**opener**, device for opening bottles of beer etc.; ∿-**party** (to which each guest brings bottle of wine etc.), drinking-party; ∿-**tree**, Austral. tree with swollen bottle-shaped trunk; ∿-**washer**, (colloq.) factotum, underling. [ME, f. OF *botele*, *botaille* f. med. L *butticula* dim. of LL *buttis* BUTT[1]]

bŏ'ttle² *v.t.* store in bottle(s); preserve (fruit etc.) in jars; (in *p.p.*, sl.) drunk; ∿ **up**, conceal, restrain for a time, (resentment etc.), entrap or keep entrapped (enemy forces etc.). [f. prec.]

bŏ'ttom¹ *n.* & *a.* **1.** *n.* lowest point or part, part on which thing rests (∿ **up**, upside-down; ∿**s up!**, call to drain one's glass); buttocks; seat (of chair); ∿ **falls out**, collapse occurs; **knock the** ∿ **out of**, prove (thing) worthless. **2.** ground under water of sea, lake, etc., (**go, send, to the** ∿, sink; **touch** ∿, reach bottom of water with feet, (fig.) be at the lowest or worst point or on firm facts), whence ∿LESS *a.*, without bottom, baseless, inexhaustible, (*the* ∿*less pit*, hell); low-lying land. **3.** (person occupying) less honourable end of table, class, etc.; farthest or inmost point (*bottom of garden*, HEART, *bay*). **4.** keel, horizontal part near keel, hull, ship esp. as cargo-carrier (*in British bottoms*). **5.** basis, origin, (**be at the** ∿ **of**, cause); essential character, reality, (**at** ∿, basically, essentially; **get to the** ∿ **of**, fully investigate and explain). **6.** *a.* lowest, last (**bet one's** ∿ **dollar**, (sl.) stake all); ∿ **dog**, = UNDERDOG; ∿ **drawer**, ||(fig.) woman's store of clothes etc. in preparation for marriage; ||*bottom* GEAR; hence ∿MOST (-m-m-) *a.* [OE *botm*, = OS *bodom* f. Gmc **buthm-*, **buthn-*]

bŏ'ttom² *v.* **1.** *v.t.* put bottom to (saucepan, chair); touch bottom of, find the extent or real nature of; base (argument etc.) *on*. **2.** *v.i.* reach or touch bottom; ∿ (**out**), reach lowest level. [f. prec.]

bŏ'ttomrӯ *n.*, & *v.t.* **1.** *n.* system of lending money to shipowner for purposes of voyage on security of ship, lender losing the money if ship is lost. **2.** *v.t.* pledge (ship) thus. [f. BOTTOM¹ = ship+-RY, after Du. *bodemerij*]

bŏ'tūlism *n.* (Med.) poisoning by a bacillus found esp. in infected sausages or tinned food etc. [f. G *botulismus* f. L *botulus* sausage; see -ISM (5)]

bou'clé (bōō'klā) *n.* yarn of looped or curled ply; fabric of this. [F, = buckled, curled]

bou'doir (bōō'dwār) *n.* (woman's) small private room. [F, lit. sulking-place (*bouder* sulk)]

bou'ffant (bōō'fahn) *a.* (Of dress, hair, etc.) puffed out. [F]

bougainvi'llaea (bōōgan-) *n.* tropical plant of genus *Bougainvillaea*, with large bright-coloured bracts almost concealing flowers. [f. L. A. de *Bougainville*, Fr. navigator d. 1811+-A 1]

bough (bow) *n.* tree-branch (esp. one of the chief branches). [OE *bōg*, *bōh*, = OHG *buog*, ON *bógr* shoulder of an animal f. Gmc **bōguz*]

bought. See BUY.

bou'ghten (baw'ten) *a.* (dial. & US) purchased at shop, opp. home-made. [var. p.p. of BUY]

bougie (bōō'zhē) *n.* wax candle; thin flexible surgical instrument for exploring, dilating, etc., the passages of the body. [F, f. Arab. *Bujiya* Algerian town with wax trade]

bouillabai'sse (bōōyabā's) *n.* rich fish-stew, orig. from Provence. [F]

bouilli (bōōyē') *n.* stewed or boiled meat. [F, = boiled]

bou'illon (bōō'yawn) *n.* broth, thin soup. [F (*bouillir* to boil)]

bou'lder (bō'l-) *n.* large water-worn or weather-worn stone; ∿ **clay**, (Geol.) mixture of boulders etc. in clay as glacial formation. [short for *boulderstone*, ME f. Scand.]

bou'lè¹ *n.* legislative body of ancient or modern Greece. [Gk *boulē* senate]

boule² (bōōl) *n.* French form of bowls, played on rough ground with usu. metal balls. [F, = BOWL²]

boule³. See BUHL.

bou'levārd (bōō'-) *n.* broad street with rows of trees along it; **broad main road. [F, f. G *bollwerk* BULWARK, orig. of promenade on demolished fortification]

boulle. See BUHL.

boult. See BOLT⁵.

boulter. See BOLTER.

bounç|e¹ *v.i.* & *t.* **1.** (cause to) rebound; (sl., of cheque) be returned by bank when there are no funds to meet it; **(sl.) dismiss. **2.** throw oneself *about* or *up*; rush (noisily, angrily, etc.) *into* or *out of* (room), in or out; talk big; hustle (person) by bluff or assumptions *into* doing or *out of* (something). **3.** Hence ∿'ING² *a.*, big and healthy, boisterous, ∿'ᵧ² *a.* [ME *bunsen* beat, thump, perh. imit., or f. LG *bunsen*, Du. *bons* thump]

bounce² *n.* rebound(ing power); ejection; boast, exaggeration, swagger. [f. prec.]

bou'ncer *n.* In vbl senses; (Cricket) bumper; (sl. person employed to expel troublesome persons from public house etc. [f. BOUNCE¹+-ER¹]

bound¹ *n.* limit of territory (BEAT¹ *the bounds*); (usu. in *pl.*) limitation, restriction, (||out of ∿s, beyond limits set by rules of school etc.); hence ∿'LESS *a.* [ME, f. AF *bounde*, OF *bonde* etc., f. med. L *bodina* earlier *butina*, of unkn. orig.]

bound² *v.t.* set bounds to, limit, (esp. in *pass.* w. *by*); be the boundary of. [f. prec.]

bound³ *v.i.* (Of ball etc.) recoil from wall or ground; bounce; (of living thing, wave, etc.) spring, leap; advance lightly. [f. F *bondir* (orig. of sound) f. Rom. **bombitire* var. of LL *bombitare* f. L *bombus* hum]

bound⁴ *n.* springy movement upward or forward (*b* LEAP²s *and bounds*); (of ball etc.) recoil, bounce. [f. *bond* (bound; see prec.)]

bound⁵ *a.* ready to start or having started (*for*) moving in specified direction (*northbound*). [ME f. ON *búinn* p.p. of *búa* get ready; *-d* euphonic, or partly after foll.]

bound⁶. See BIND¹.

bou'ndary *n.* limit-line; (Cricket) hit to limit of field scoring 4 or 6 runs; ∿ **layer** (of fluid adjacent to body moving through it); ∿ **rider**, (Austral. & NZ) rider round sheep or cattle station mending fences etc. [f. dial. *bounder* f. BOUND²+-ER¹, perh. after *limitary*]

bou'nden *a.* (Of duty etc.) obligatory. [arch. p.p. of BIND¹]

bou'nder *n.* In vbl senses; (sl.) (ill-bred) person, cad. [f. BOUND²,³+-ER¹]

bou'ntĕous *a.* (rhet.) beneficent, liberal; freely bestowed; hence ∿LY² *adv.*, ∿NESS *n.* [ME, f. OF *bontif* (*bonté* BOUNTY)+-OUS, after *plenteous*]

bou'ntiful *a.* = prec. (**Lady B**∿, beneficent lady of neighbourhood [character in Farquhar's *Beaux Stratagem* (1707)]); ample; hence ∿LY² *adv.* [f. foll.+-FUL]

bou'ntӯ *n.* munificence, liberality in giving; gift (**king's, queen's,** ∿, (Hist.) former sum made to mother of triplets; **Queen Anne's** ∿, (Hist.) fund for augmenting poor benefices; sum paid to encourage trade enterprise, or for killing dangerous animals etc. gratuity to recruits on enlistment. [ME, f. OF *bonté* f. L *bonitas* -*tatis* (*bonus* good; see -TY¹)]

bouquet (bōōkā', bō-, bōō'kā) *n.* bunch of flowers esp. for carrying at ceremony; (fig.) piece of praise; perfume of wine; ∿ **garni**, bunch of herbs for flavouring. [F, f. dial. var. of OF *bos*, *bois* wood; see -ET¹]

bou'quetin (bōō'k-) *n.* Alpine ibex. [F, f. OF *bo estaign* f. MHG *steinbock* (as STONE, BUCK¹)]

****bour'bon¹** (ber'-, boor'-) *n.* whisky distilled from maize and rye. [f. B∿ County, Kentucky, where first made]

Bour'bon² (boor'-) n. *reactionary; ~ **biscuit** (chocolate-flavoured with chocolate-cream filling). [f. the ~ family, whose descendants founded dynasties in France and Spain]

Bour'don (boor'-) n. low-pitched stop in organ or harmonium; lowest bell in peal of bells; drone pipe of bagpipe. [F, = bagpipe-drone, f. Rom. *burdo -onis*, imit.]

bour'geois (boor'zhwah) n. & a. (member) of middle class; (person) of humdrum or conventional middle--class ideas; selfish(ly) materialist; capitalist(ic). [F; see BURGESS]

bourgeoisie' (boorzhwahzē') n. the middle or bourgeois class. [F]

bourn¹ (boorn, bōrn) n. small stream. [ME, S. Engl. var. of BURN¹]

bourn², bourne, (boorn, bōrn) n. (arch.) limit; goal. [f. F *borne* f. OF *bodne* BOUND¹]

bourrée' (boor'ā) n. (music for) old lively dance like gavotte. [F]

bourse (boors) n. money-market, esp. (B~) Paris equivalent of Stock Exchange. [F, = purse, f. med. L *bursa*; cf. PURSE¹]

boustrophē'don (bow-, boo-) a. & adv. (written) from right to left and from left to right in alternate lines. [Gk, adv. = as ox turns in ploughing (*bous* ox, -*strophos*, STROPHE turning, -*don* adv. suf.)]

bout n. spell of turn at work or exercise; spell of drinking or illness; trial of strength, wrestling- or box- ing-match. [16th c., app. same as obs. *bought* bending]

bouti'que (boote'k) n. small shop or department selling (esp. fashionable) clothes or accessories. [F, = small shop, f. L (as BODEGA)]

boutonnière (bootŏnyār') n. spray of flowers worn in buttonhole. [F]

bouzou'ki (boozoo'-) n. Greek form of mandoline. [f. mod. Gk *mpouzouki* pr. b-]

bō'vine a. of or like an ox, esp. in stupidity or slowness; of the genus *Bos* of ruminants. [f. LL *bovinus* f. L *bos bovis* ox; see -INE¹]

bō'vver n. (sl.) deliberate trouble-making; ~ **boy,** violent hooligan. [cockney pr. of BOTHER²]

bow¹ (bō) n. **1.** curve; rainbow. **2.** weapon for shooting arrows with string joining ends of curved piece of wood etc. (**two strings to** one's ~, a twofold resource; *draw the* LONG¹*bow*; = SADDLE-*bow*; rod with stretched horsehair for playing violin etc., single passage of this across strings; = BAIL⁴; metal ring forming handle of scissors, key, etc.; *side-piece of spectacle-frame*. **3.** KEY¹-*knot* (1) with single or double loop; ribbon etc. so tied. **4.** ~-**compass(es),** compasses with jointed legs; ~'**fin,** voracious Amer. freshwater fish; ~ **head,** Greenland whale; ~**-legged,** ~**-legs,** (having) bandy legs; ~'**man,** archer; ~**-saw,** narrow saw stretched like bowstring on light frame; ~'**shot,** distance to which bow can send arrow; ~'**string** n., & v.t., (strangle with) string of bow (former Turkish method of execution); ~**-tie,** necktie (to be) tied in shape of bow (sense 3); ~**-wi'ndow,** curved bay window. [OE *boga*, = OS, mod. G *bogen*, ON *bogi* f. Gmc *bugon* (*bug*- BOW³)]

bow² (bō) v.t. use the bow on (violin etc., or abs.). [f. prec.]

bow³ v. **1.** v.i. submit (*to the inevitable* etc.); ~ (**down**), bend or kneel in sign of submission or reverence *to* or *before*; incline head or body in salutation, assent, etc., (~**ing acquaintance,** slight degree of acquaintance that stops at this); ~ **out,** make one's exit (esp. formally); *bow and* SCRAPE. **2.** v.t. express (thanks etc.), usher *in* or *out*, by bowing; cause to bend (lit. or fig., *knee, head, back* etc. for burden, *will*); ~ **down,** crush, make stoop, (esp. *bowed down by* or *with* care etc.). [OE *būgan*, f. OHG *biogan*, ON *bjúga*, Goth. *biugan* f. Gmc *beugan*, cf. BOW¹]

bow⁴ n. bending of head or body in salutation, assent, etc.; **make** one's ~, make formal entrance or exit; **take a** ~, acknowledge applause. [f. prec.]

bow⁵ n. (often in *pl.*) fore-end of boat or ship from

where it begins to curve inwards (**on the** ~, within 45° of the point right ahead; **shot across the** ~**s,** (fig.) warning); rower nearest the bow; ~'**man** (stationed in bow); ~ **wave** (set up at bows of moving ship or in front of body moving in air). [f. LG *boog*, Du. *boeg*, ship's bow, orig. shoulder; see BOUGH]

bow'dler|īze, -īse (-īz), v.t. expurgate (book etc.); hence ~**ISM** (3), ~**īZA'TION,** ns. [f. T. *Bowdler* (d. 1825), expurgator of Shakespeare, + -IZE (4)]

bow'el n. division of alimentary canal below stomach, intestine, gut, (*bowel* MOTION¹); (in *pl.*, arch.) pity, tender feelings, (*bowels of mercy* etc.); (in *pl.*) inner- most parts (*bowels of the earth*). [ME, f. OF *buel* etc. f. L *botellus* dim. of *botulus* sausage]

bow'er¹ n., & v.t. **1.** n. place closed in with foliage, arbour, summer-house, whence ~Y²a.; (poet.) inner room; ~**-bird,** Austral. bird of the bird-of-paradise family constructing elaborate runs adorned with feathers, shells, etc. during courtship. **2.** v.t. embower. [OE *būr*, = OS, OHG, ON *būr* f. Gmc *būraz* (*bū- dwell)]

bow'er² n. ~(-**anchor**), either of two anchors (**best** ~ and **small** ~) carried at ship's bow; ~(-**cable**), cable of bower-anchor. [f. BOW⁵ + -ER¹]

bow'er³ n. one of two cards (**right** ~, jack of trumps, **left** ~, jack of same colour) at euchre and similar games. [f. G *bauer* peasant, jack at cards, cogn. w. Du. *boer*; see BOOR]

*****bow'erÿ** n. district (orig. **the B**~, street in New York City) known as resort of drunks and down-and-outs. [f. Du. *bouwerij* farm]

bow'ie (bō'ī) n. ~ (**knife**), long knife with blade double-edged at point used as weapon by Amer. pioneers. [f. J. *Bowie*, Amer. soldier d. 1836]

bowl¹ (bōl) n. basin, esp. deep-shaped or for liquid; (arch.) drinking-vessel; contents of a bowl; *bowl-shaped region; bowl-shaped part of tobacco- -pipe, spoon, balance,* etc.; amphitheatre; hence ~'**FUL** 2 n. [OE *bolle, bolla*, = OS *bollo*, OHG *bolla* f. Gmc *bul-* swell]

bowl² (bōl) n. **1.** wooden or hard rubber ball made slightly out of spherical shape to make it run on curved course. **2.** flattened or spherical wooden ball at skittles. **3.** (in *pl.*, usu. treated as *sing.*) game played with bowls (sense 1) on grass, or with round balls in room. [ME & F *boule* f. L *bulla* bubble]

bowl³ (bōl) v.t. & i. **1.** play bowls or skittles; roll (ball, hoop, etc.) along ground; go along by revolving or by means of wheels; go *along, go fast and smoothly;* ~ **over,** knock down, (fig.) disconcert, render help- less, impress greatly. **2.** (Cricket). deliver (*ball, over,* or abs.); knock *down* (wicket); ~ (**out**), dismiss (bats- man) by knocking down wicket with delivered ball; ~ **out,** dismiss (side). [f. prec.]

bow'ler¹ (bō-) n. player at bowls; (Cricket) fieldsman who bowls. [f. prec. + -ER¹]

‖**bow'ler²** (bō'-) n. ~ (**hat**), hard felt hat with rounded crown; ~**-hat** v.t. (-*tt*-), (sl.) retire from the army etc. [f. B~, hatter, who designed it 1850]

bow'line (bō'-) n. rope from weather side of square sail to bow; ~ (**knot**), simple knot for forming non--slipping loop at end of rope. [ME, f. MLG *bōline* = MDu. *boechlijne* (as BOW⁵, LINE²)]

bow'ling (bō'-) n. In vbl senses; ~**-alley,** long enclosure for playing skittles, building containing such; ~**-crease,** (Cricket) line from behind which bowler delivers ball; ~**-green,** lawn for playing bowls. [f. BOWL³ + -ING²]

bowman. See BOW¹,⁵.

bow'ser (-z-) n. tanker for fuelling aircraft etc. (Austral. & NZ) petrol pump. [P]

bowsprit (bō'-) n. spar running out from ship's stem to which forestays are fastened. [ME, f. MLG *bōgsprēt* = MDu. *boechspriet* (as BOW⁵, SPRIT)]

Bow Street (bō'-) n. (Hist.) London street containing chief metropolitan police-court; ~ **officer, runner,** London policeman.

bow'-wow *int.* & *n.* dog's bark or imitation of it; (childish colloq.) dog. [imit.]

bow'yăng (bō'-) *n.* (Austral. & NZ) band or strap round trouser-leg below knee. [f. dial. *bowy-yangs* etc.]

bow'yer (bō'-) *n.* maker or seller of archers' bows. [f. BOW¹ + -YER]

böx¹ *n.* evergreen shrub or small tree of genus *Buxus*, esp. one of a species with small dark leathery leaves, much used in garden borders; ∼('wood), its wood, used by turners and engravers; (Austral.) tree with similar wood; ∼ **elder,** Amer. maple (*Acer negundo*). [OE, f. L *buxus*, Gk *puxos*]

böx² *n.* **1.** container (usu. with lid, rectangular or cylindrical, for solids) of wood, metal, cardboard, etc.; boxful, quantity contained in box; coachman's seat; = LETTER-*box*, *MAIL³*box*, MONEY-*box*, POST²- -*office box*, etc.; receptacle at newspaper office for replies to advertisement; the ∼, (colloq.) television (set); *in the* WRONG *box*. **2.** separate compartment in theatre, restaurant, etc.; compartment for horse in stable or vehicle (HORSE¹-*box*; **loo'se** ∼, one in which it can move about); = CALL²-*box*, JURY-*box*, SENTRY- -*box*, SIGNAL²-*box*, ||TELEPHONE-*box*, WITNESS-*box*, etc.; small country house for use when fishing, shooting, etc.; protective case for piece of mechanism; cricketer's light shield to protect genitals. **3.** confined area; space enclosed by printed lines; (Football, colloq.) penalty area; (Baseball) area occupied by batter or pitcher. **4.** ∼ **barrage** (on all sides of an area, to prevent escape from it); ∼ **camera,** simple box-shaped hand camera; *∼'**car,** closed railway goods wagon; ∼ **coat,** heavy overcoat (for coachman etc.); ∼ **girder** (made of plates fastened in box shape); ||∼ **junction,** yellow-striped road area which vehicle must not enter if it cannot leave immediately; ∼-**kite,** tailless kite with light rectangular frame at each end; ∼ **number** (to identify box in newspaper office or post office); ∼-**office** (for booking seats in theatre etc., (fig.) entertainment etc. likely to attract audiences); ∼ **pew** (enclosed like box); ∼-**pleat** (of two parallel contrary pleats forming raised band); ||∼-**room** (in which boxes, trunks, etc. are stored); ∼ **score,** tabulated results of baseball etc. game; ∼-**spanner** (with head fitting over nut etc.); ∼-**spring,** one of set of vertical springs in mattress; ∼ **tortoise** (that can enclose itself entirely within shell); ∼-**wallah,** (India) dealer or pedlar. **5.** Hence ∼'FUL 2 *n.*, ∼'Y² *a.* [OE, prob. f. *bux f. LL *buxis* -*id*- var. of L PYXIS box of boxwood]

böx³ *v.t.* provide with or put into a box; ∼ **the compass,** (Naut.) recite the points in correct order, (fig.) make complete revolution and end where one began (in politics, argument, etc.); ∼-**haul,** veer ship round on keel for lack of room; ∼ **in,** confine and restrict movement of; ∼ **up,** confine uncomfortably, muddle. [f. prec.]

böx⁴ *n.* slap with hand on ear(s). [ME, of unkn. orig.]

böx⁵ *v.t.* & *i.* slap (person's ears); fight (person, or abs.) with fists (usu. in padded gloves, as sport); ∼ **clever,** (sl.) behave cleverly; ∼'**ing-glove,** padded glove worn in boxing; ∼'**ing-weight,** weight at which boxers are matched (British amateur scale, somewhat modified for professionals, wrestlers, weight-lifters, and in other countries: *heavyweight* no limit, *light heavyweight* or *cruiserweight* 81 kg, *middleweight* 75 kg, *light middleweight* 71 kg, *welterweight* 67 kg, *light welterweight* 63¾ kg, *lightweight* 60 kg, *featherweight* 57 kg, *bantamweight* 54 kg, *flyweight* 51 kg, *light flyweight* 48 kg). [f. prec.]

Böx and Cöx *n.* two persons who are never together, never at home at the same time; two persons who take turns in a part, position, etc. (also as *a.*, *adv.*, & *v.i.*). [name of play (1847) by J. M. Morton, in which two persons unknowingly become tenants of same room]

bö'xcalf (-kahf) *n.* chrome-tanned calfskin with hatched grain. [after Joseph *Box*, London bootmaker *c.* 1890]

bö'xer *n.* one who boxes (BOX⁵); (*B*∼, Hist.) member o Chinese anti-foreign secret society; medium-size smooth-haired kind of dog derived from German bull dog; ∼ **shorts,** men's loose underpants. [f. BOX⁵ + -ER¹]

||**Bö'xing Day** *n.* first weekday after Christmas. [o which Christmas-boxes were traditionally given, obs. sense of BOX³ f. (money-)BOX²]

boy *n.* & *int.* **1.** *n.* male child; young man; (as familia *voc.*, **my** ∼; also to dog); **old** ∼ (see OLD 7); mal native servant, labourer. **2.** ∼-**and-girl,** juvenil (romance etc.); ∼-**friend,** girl's or woman's usual o preferred male companion; ∼-**meets-girl,** conven tional (romance etc.); ∼ **scout,** = SCOUT¹ 2; ||∼'s -**love,** southernwood; **the** ∼, (arch. sl.) champagn the ∼**s,** group of men esp. with similar interests grown-up sons of family; ∼**s will be** ∼**s,** juvenil behaviour must be tolerated; **jobs for the** ∼**s,** assurance of gain for one's friends. **3.** Hence ∼'HOO *n.*, ∼'ISH¹ *a.*, (esp.) high-spirited. **4.** *int.* (**oh**) ∼ (expr surprise, excitement, etc.). [ME, = servant, perh. AF **abuié,* *embuié fettered f. LL IM¹*boiare* (L *boi* fetter; see BUOY¹)]

böyär' *n.* (Hist.) member of aristocratic order i Russia. [f. Russ. *boyarin* grandee]

boy'cott *v.t.,* & *n.* **1.** *v.t.* combine to punish or coerc (person, class, nation) by systematic refusal of socia or commercial relations; refuse to handle (goods etc. with this aim. **2.** *n.* such treatment. [f. Capt. C. C *Boycott,* Irish land-agent d. 1897, so treated f. 1880]

Boyle *n.* ∼'**s law** (that gas pressure and volume ar inversely proportional at constant temperature). [Robert ∼, Brit. scientist d. 1691]

boy'ō *n.* (*pl.* ∼**s**). (colloq., Welsh & Ir.) boy (esp. *voc.*). [f. BOY]

boy'senbĕrry (-z-, -s-) *n.* (fruit of) a hybrid of severa species of bramble. [f. R. *Boysen,* 20th-c. Amer horticulturist + BERRY¹]

***bö'zō** *n.* (*pl.* ∼**s**). (sl.) person, fellow. [20th c.; orig unkn.]

BP *abbr.* boiling-point; British Petroleum; Britisl Pharmacopoeia.

Bp. *abbr.* Bishop.

BPC *abbr.* British Pharmaceutical Codex.

B.Phil. *abbr.* Bachelor of Philosophy.

Bq *abbr.* becquerel.

BR *abbr.* British Rail.

Br. *abbr.* British; Brother.

br. *abbr.* brown.

Br *symb.* bromine.

bra (-ah) *n.* brassière. [abbr.]

brāce¹ *n.* **1.** thing that clasps, tightens, supports unites, or secures; ||(in *pl.*) straps to support trouser from shoulders; wire device for straightening teeth. **2** connecting mark in printing ({ or }); (Mus.) simila mark connecting staves to be performed at same time (*pl.* same) pair, couple, (of dogs, game, pistols, etc. of persons). **3.** strengthening-piece of iron or timbe in building; (Naut.) rope attached to yard fo trimming sail (*splice the* MAIN³ *brace*); ∼ **and bit** revolving tool for boring. [ME, f. OF *brace* two arm f. L *bracchia* (pl.) arms, some senses f. foll.]

brāce² *v.t.* fasten tightly, stretch, string up, giv firmness to, invigorate, (∼ one**self**, ∼ **up,** prepar for effort); support; (Naut.) move (sail) by braces [ME, partly f. OF *bracier* embrace, partly f. prec.]

brā'celĕt (-sl-) *n.* ornamental band, chain, etc., fo wrist or arm; (sl.) handcuff. [ME f. OF, dim. of *brace* f. L *bracchiale* (*bracchium* arm)]

brā'cer¹ *n.* in vbl senses; (colloq.) pick-me-up. [BRACE² + -ER¹]

brā'cer² *n.* wrist-guard of archer, fencer, etc. [ME, OF *brasseüre* (*bras* arm, -*eüre* -URE)]

brā'chial (-kĭ-) *a.* of the arm (*brachial artery*); like a arm. [f. L *brachialis* (*bracchium* arm; see -AL]

brā'chiāte (-kĭ-) *v.i.* (Of ape) move by using the arm to swing from branch to branch; hence ∼A'TION ∼ātor, *ns.* [f. L *brachium* arm + -ATE³]

brachio|saur'us (-kĭ-) *n.* huge dinosaur of genus *Brachiosaurus*, with forelegs longer than hind legs; so **∼pŏd** (-ă'kĭ-) *n.*, invertebrate of phylum Brachiopoda like bivalve mollusc (esp. as fossil). [mod. L., f. Gk *brakhiōn* arm + *sauros* lizard, *pous podos* foot]

brachi'stochrōne (-kĭ'stokr-) *n.* curve between two points along which body moves in shorter time than for any other curve. [f. Gk *brakhistos* shortest + *khronos* time]

brăchў- (-k-) *comb. form.* short, as: **∼cepha'lic, ∼ce'phalous,** having a short or broad head; **∼logy** (braki'lojĭ), (over-)conciseness of expression. [f. Gk *brakhus* short]

orä'cken *n.* kind of large fern abundant on heaths, hillsides, etc.; mass of such ferns. [north. ME, f. ON *brakni*]

orä'ckĕt¹ *n.* **1.** flat-topped projection from wall serving as support to statue, arch, etc.; shelf with slanting under-prop for hanging against wall; wooden or metal angular support; support of lamp, projecting from wall. **2.** mark used in pairs ( ), [ ], { } (cf. BRACE¹), ⟨ ⟩, for enclosing words, figures, etc.; skating-figure resembling {. (Mil. etc.) distance between two shots either side of target in range-finding; group bracketed together as similar (*social bracket*) or falling between certain limits (*income bracket*). [f. F *braguette* or Sp. *bragueta* codpiece dim. of F *brague* f. Prov. *braga* f. L *braca*, pl. *bracae* breeches]

brä'ckĕt² *v.t.* enclose in brackets as parenthetic, spurious, or (Math.) having spec. relations to what precedes or follows, etc.; couple (names etc.) with brace, imply connection or equality between; (Mil. etc.) place two shots one short of and one beyond (target) in range-finding. [f. prec.]

orä'ckĭsh *a.* (Of water) slightly salt. [f. obs. *brack* a. f. MLG, MDu. *brac* + -ISH¹]

brăct *n.* (usu. small) leaf or scale below calyx. [f. L *bractea* thin plate, gold-leaf]

orăd *n.* thin flat small-headed nail. [var. of ME *brod* goad, pointed instrument, f. ON *broddr* spike]

brä'dawl *n.* small non-spiral boring-tool. [f. prec. + AWL]

|Brä'dshaw *n.* (Hist.) timetable of (esp. British) passenger trains. [f. G. ∼, Brit. printer d. 1853, first publisher of *Bradshaw's Railway Guide*]

brä'dў- *comb. form.* slow, as: **∼car'dia,** abnormally slow heart-action; **∼seism** (-sīzem), slow rise and fall of earth's crust. [f. Gk *bradus* slow]

brae (-ā) *n.* (Sc.) steep bank, hillside. [ME, f. ON *brá* eyelash, = OS, OHG *brāwa* eyebrow; for sense cf. BROW]

brăg *n.,* & *v.i,* & *t.* (**-gg-**). boast, boasting; card-game like poker. [ME, orig. a = spirited, boastful, of unkn. orig.]

brăggadō'cĭō (-shĭō) *n.* (*pl.* **∼s**). empty boasting. [formed by Spenser 1590 as name (meaning boaster) on prec. or foll. and It. augment. suf. *-occio*]

brä'ggart *n.* & *a.* (person) given to bragging. [f. F *bragard* (*braguer* BRAG; see -ARD)]

Brah'ma¹ *n.* supreme Hindu deity; divine reality of which world is manifestation. [Skr., = creator]

brahmapu'tra (-ōō't-), **brah'ma²,** *n.* (bird of) large Asian breed of domestic fowl. [f. river *Brahmaputra* in India, whence brought]

brah'min, -man, *n.* member of Hindu priestly caste; ***B∼,** (colloq.) highly cultured or intellectual aloof person; hence **brahmi'nic**(AL), **-mä'nic**(AL), *adjs.,* **∼ism** (3) *n.* (f. Skr. *brāhmaṇas* (*brahmaṇ* priest))

braid¹ *n.* entwined hair, plait; band etc. entwined with the hair; silk, thread, etc., woven into a band; hence ∼'ING¹ (3, 6) *n.* [f. foll.]

braid² *v.t.* plait, interweave, (hair, flowers, thread); arrange (hair) in braids; confine (hair etc.) with ribbon etc.; trim, edge, with braid. [OE *bregdan,* = OS *bregdan,* OHG *brettan,* ON *bregtha* f. Gmc *bregdhan*]

brail *n.,* & *v.t.* (haul up with) small rope(s) on sail-edges for trussing sails before furling. [ME, f. OF *brai(e)l* f. med. L *bracale* girdle (*bracae* breeches; see -AL 2)]

Braille *n.,* & *v.t.* **1.** *n.* system of writing and printing for the blind, in which the characters are represented by raised dots. **2.** *v.t.* print or transcribe in Braille characters. [f. L. ∼, Fr. teacher d. 1852, its inventor]

brain *n.,* & *v.t.* **1.** *n.* convoluted nervous tissue in skull of vertebrates (in *sing.* of the whole as an organ, in *pl.* of the substance esp. as food; BLOW¹ *out* one's *brains*); centre of sensation, thought, etc., (BEAT¹, CUDGEL, RACK³, one's *brains; get* or **have on the** ∼, be constantly thinking of (person or thing); TURN¹ person's *brain*); (source of) intellectual power, whence ∼'LESS *a.* (PICK² person's *brains*); (colloq.) clever person, (in *pl.*) the cleverest person in a group; electronic device comparable to brain. **2.** **∼-child,** (colloq.) product of thought; ∼ **drain,** (colloq.) loss of intellectual or highly trained workers by emigration; **∼-fag,** mental exhaustion; ∼ **fever,** inflammation of the brain; **∼-fever bird,** Ind. cuckoo with maddeningly persistent cry; **∼-pan,** (colloq.) skull; ∼'**power,** mental ability or intelligence; **∼-stem,** medulla oblongata; ∼'**storm,** violent symptoms of mental disturbance, *(colloq.) brainwave; ***∼'storming,** spontaneous discussion in search for new ideas; **∼s trust,** group of experts giving impromptu answers to questions; *∼ **trust,** group of experts guiding or advising the government; **∼-teaser, ∼-twister,** difficult puzzle esp. for amusement; ∼'**washing,** systematic replacement of established ideas in person's mind by new ones (so ∼'**wash** *v.t.*); ∼'**wave,** electrical impulse in brain, (colloq.) sudden bright idea; ∼'**work,** mental activity. **3.** *v.t.* dash out brains of. [OE *brægen,* = MLG *bregen,* f. WG **bragna*]

brai'nў *a.* intellectually clever or active. [f. prec. + -Y²]

braise (-z) *v.t.* cook (meat etc.) slowly over liquid in closed container. [f. F *braiser* (*braise* live coals)]

brake¹ *n.* bracken [ME, perh. shortened f. BRACKEN, *-en* being taken to be the pl. ending]

brake² *n.* thicket, brushwood. [ME, f. OE *bracu,* MLG *brake* branch, stump]

brake³ *n.* toothed instrument for braking flax and hemp; ∼ **(-harrow),** heavy harrow; instrument for peeling off willow-bark, baker's kneading-machine. [ME, MLG, MDu., = flax-brake, cogn. w. BREAK¹]

brake⁴ *v.t.* crush (flax, hemp) by beating. [f. prec.]

brake⁵ *n.* apparatus for checking (usu. rotary) motion (**apply** or **put on the ∼,** lit., or fig. moderate one's enthusiasm); ∼**-block,** block holding brake-shoe; ∼**-drum,** cylinder attached to wheel receiving pressure of brake-shoe; ∼ **fluid,** liquid used in hydraulic brake; ∼ **horsepower,** engine horsepower measured in terms of force needed to brake it; ∼ **lining,** piece of fabric to increase friction of brake-shoe; ∼'**man,** man in charge of brake(s); ∼**-shoe,** part of brake coming in contact with wheel etc.; ||∼'**sman,** = brakeman; ∼**-van,** railway carriage from which train's brakes can be controlled; hence ∼'LESS (-kl-) *a.* [prob. f. obs. *brake* in sense machine-handle or similar]

brake⁶ *v.t.* retard (wheel, car, train etc.) with brake; apply brake. [f. prec.]

brake⁷ *n.* large wagonette; estate car. [var. of BREAK³]

brake⁸. see BREAK¹.

brä'mble *n.* rough prickly shrub of genus *Rubus* with long trailing shoots, esp. blackberry-bush; blackberry; hence **brä'mblў²** *a.* [OE *bræmbel* (earlier *bræmel*); see BROOM]

brä'mbling *n.* brightly coloured finch (*Fringilla montifringilla*). [f. G *brämling* prob. f. WG **brām-* (cf. prec.)]

Brä'mley *n.* ∼(**'s seedling,** large green variety of cooking apple. [f. M. ∼, Engl. butcher in whose garden it may have first grown *c.* 1850]

brän *n.* husks of grain separated from flour after grinding; ||~**-tub** (filled with bran into which children dip for toys etc.). [ME f. OF, of unkn. orig.]

branch¹ (-ah-) *n.* limb springing from tree or bough; lateral extension or subdivision of mountain-range, river, road, railway, family, genus, subject of knowledge, or argument; local establishment of library, bank or other business, etc.; nozzle of fireman's hose; hence (-)~ED² (-cht) *a.*, ~´LET *n.*, ~´Y² *a.* [ME, f. OF *branche*, f. LL *branca* paw]

branch² (-ah-) *v.i.* put branches *out*, *forth*; spread or spring *out*, tend *away* or *off*, diverge *into*. [f. prec.]

brä´nchi|ae, brä´nchi|a, (-ngk-) *n. pl.* gills; hence ~AL, ~ATE², *adjs.* [L *branchia*, pl. *-ae*, f. Gk *bragkhia* pl.]

bränd¹ *n.* burning or charred log or stick, (poet.) torch, (~ **from the burning**, rescued person, convert); permanent mark deliberately made by hot iron; stigma (~ **of Cain**, blood-guilt); trade mark, goods of particular make or trade mark (lit. or fig.); iron stamp for burning-in a mark; (poet.) sword; kind of blight in which leaves look burnt; ~**-new´**, conspicuously or completely new. [OE, = OHG *brant*, ON *brandr* f. Gmc **brandaz* (**bran-* BURN²)]

bränd² *v.t.* burn with hot iron (penally, or to show ownership or quality); apply (mark) thus; label with trade mark; impress on memory; stigmatize. [f. prec.]

brä´ndish *v.t.* wave about, flourish, (weapon, etc.) in display or threat. [f. OF *brandir* (-ISH²) f. Rom. **brandire* f. Gmc **brand-* sword-blade]

brä´ndling *n.* red earthworm with rings of brighter colour, used as bait. [f. BRAND¹ + -LING¹ 1]

brä´ndy *n.* strong spirit distilled from wine, or from fermented fruit-juice (*apple* etc. *brandy*); ||~**-ball**, kind of brandy-flavoured sweet; ~**-snap**, rolled gingerbread wafer. [earlier *brand(e)wine* f. Du. *brandewijn* burnt (distilled) wine]

bränk-ûr´sine *n.* bear's-breech, kind of acanthus. [f. F *branche* ursine, med. L *branca ursina* bear's claw; see BRANCH¹, URSINE]

brän-new´. Var. of BRAND¹-*new*.

*bränt. See BRENT.

bräsh¹ *n.* loose broken rock or ice; hedge refuse, clippings, etc. [18th c., of unkn. orig.]

bräsh² *a.* (colloq.) rash; cheeky, saucy; vulgarly self-assertive; hence ~´LY² *adv.*, ~´NESS *n.* [orig. dial., perh. f. RASH²]

bräsh³ *n.* eruption of fluid from stomach. [16th c., perh. imit.]

brass (-ahs) *n.*, *a.*, & *v.* **1.** *n.* yellow alloy of copper and zinc (**as bold as** ~, excessively bold or self-assured); inscribed monumental or sepulchral tablet of brass (~**-rubbing,** cf. RUB¹ 3); (horse-)~, brass ornament worn by draught-horse; brass block used for design etc. on book-cover; (Mus.) brass wind-instruments; brassware; ||(sl.) money; (sl.) prostitute; effrontery; (**top**) ~, (colloq.) = (highest-ranking) officers or *brass hats* (also of leaders in industry, politics, etc.). **2.** *a.* made of brass; ~ **band**, set of musicians with brass (and percussion) instruments; ~ **farthing**, least possible amount; ||~ **hat**, (sl.) officer of high rank with gold braid on cap; ~ **plate** (on door, gate, or window-ledge, with name, trade, etc.); ~ **rags**, sailors' cleaning cloths (*part* ~ *rags*, (sl.) cease friendship *with*); ~ **tacks**, (sl.) actual details, real business, (*get down to brass tacks*); ~´**ware**, utensils etc. made of brass. **3.** *v.i.* (sl.) pay *up.* **4.** *v.t.* ~ **off**, (in *p.p.*, sl.) fed up. [OE *bræs*, = MLG *bras* of unkn. orig.]

brä´ssage *n.* mint-charge for coining money. [F, f. *brasser* stir melted metals together, brew, f. pop. L **braciare* f. L *brace* kind of grain]

brä´ssärd *n.* badge worn on arm; band worn on sleeve, esp. with uniform. [F (*bras* arm; see -ARD)]

brä´sserie *n.* beer saloon; restaurant serving beer with food. [F, = brewery (*brasser* brew)]

brä´ssica *n.* plant of genus *Brassica* (cabbage, turnip, etc.). [L, = cabbage]

brä´ssie, -ў², *n.* wooden-headed golf-club with brass sole. [f. BRASS + -IE]

brä´ssière (-syār, -zyer) *n.* woman's undergarment worn to support breasts. [F]

bra´ss|ў¹ (-ah-) *a.* like brass in colour, sound, or taste; impudent; pretentious; hence ~ĬLY² *adv.*, ~ĬNESS *n.* [f. BRASS + -Y²]

brä´ssў². See BRASSIE.

brät *n.* (usu. derog.) child. [perh. abbr. f. Sc. *bratchart* hound, or f. *brat* rough garment]

brä´ttice *n.* wooden partition or shaft-lining in coal -mine. [ME, = temporary breastwork on parapet f. AF *breteske*, OF *bretesche* f. med. L *brittisca* f. OE *brittisc* BRITISH]

brava´dō (-vah´-) *n.* (occas. *pl.* ~**es** *or* ~**s**). show o boldness. [f. Sp. *bravata* (*bravo*; cf. foll., -ADO)]

brä´ve¹ *a.* & *n.* **1.** *a.* able to face and endure danger o pain; (literary) splendid, spectacular, admirable (*make a brave show*); hence ~´LY² (-vlĭ) *adv.* **2.** *n.* Amer Indian warrior. [ME f. F, f. It. or Sp. *bravo*, f. Rom **brabus* (**brabarus* f. L *barbarus* BARBAROUS)]

brä´ve² *v.t.* defy, encounter with bravery; ~ **it out** behave defiantly under suspicion or blame. [f. F *braver* (as prec.)]

brä´verў *n.* brave conduct or nature; (literary) splendour. [f. F *braverie* or It. *braveria* (as prec.; se -ERY)]

bra´vō¹ (-ah´-) *n.* (*pl.* ~**es** *or* ~**s**). hired ruffian desperado. [It.; see BRAVE¹]

bra´vō² (-ah´-) *n.* (*pl.* ~**s**) & *int.* cry of approval, esp to actor etc. [F f. It.]

bravur´a (-oor´a, -ūr´a) *n.* brilliant or ambitious performance; passage or style of (esp. vocal) music requiring exceptional powers. [It.]

braw *a.* (Sc.) fine, good. [var. of *brawf* BRAVE¹]

brawl¹ *n.*, & *v.* (engage in) noisy quarrel; (of stream run noisily; hence ~´ER¹ *n.* [ME, f. OProv. *braular* rel. to BRAY¹]

brawn *n.* muscle, lean flesh; muscularity; pig's head etc. boiled, chopped, and moulded. [ME, f. AF *braun* OF *braon* Gmc **brādon* roast flesh]

braw´n|ў *a.* strong, muscular; hence ~ĬNESS *n.* [f. prec. + -Y²]

bray¹ *n.* & *v.* **1.** *n.*, & *v.i.* (make) the cry, or a sound like the cry, of an ass; (make) sound of harshly played trumpet. **2.** *v.t.* utter harshly. [ME, f. OF *braire* f. Rom. **bragere*, perh. f. Celt.]

bray² *v.t.* pound, beat small, esp. with pestle and mortar. [ME, f. AF *braier*, OF *breier* f. Gmc **brekan* BREAK¹]

brâze¹ *v.t.*, & *n.* **1.** *v.t.* solder with alloy of brass and zinc. **2.** *n.* brazed joint. [f. F *braser* solder (*braise* live coals)]

brä´zen¹ *a.* made of brass; strong, yellow, or harsh-sounding, as brass; ~(**-faced**), shameless; hence ~´LY² *adv.*, ~´NESS (-n-n-) *n.* [OE *bræsen* (*bræs* brass; se EN⁵)]

brä´zen² *v.t.* ~ **out**, face or undergo impudently (esp. ~ **it out**, be unashamed of one's misbehaviour) [f. prec.]

brä´zi|er¹ (-zĭer, -zher) *n.* worker in brass; hence ~ERY (1) *n.* [ME, prob. f. BRASS + -IER, after *glass*, *glazier*]

brä´zier² (-zĭer, -zher) *n.* pan or stand for holding lighted coals as portable heater. [f. F *brasier* (*braise* hot coals)]

Brazi´l *n.* ~(**-nut**), large three-sided nut from S. Amer. tree; ~(**-wood**), hard red wood from tropical tree of genus *Caesalpinia*, yielding dyes; hence ~IAN *a.* & *n.* [~ in S. America, named from ~-*wood* f. ME *brasile* f. med. L *brasilium*]

BRCS *abbr.* British Red Cross Society.

breach¹ *n.* **1.** breaking or neglect (*of* rule, duty, contract, someone's privileged rights); ~ **of the peace**, riot or affray; ~ **of promise**, (esp.) breaking of promise to marry); breaking of relations, separation, estrangement, quarrel. **2.** broken state; gap, esp. in fortifications made by artillery; **stand in the** ~, bear brunt of attack, lit. or fig.; **step into the** ~, give help in crisis. [ME f. OF *breche* f. Gallo-Rom. *brecca f. Frank. *breka, Gmc *brekan BREAK¹]

breach² *v.t.* break through, make gap in. [f. prec.]

bread (-ĕd) *n.*, & *v.t.* **1.** *n.* flour moistened, kneaded, and baked, usu. with leaven (BLACK¹, BROWN¹, WHITE¹, *bread*); ~ **and butter,** bread slices spread with butter, necessary food, a livelihood, routine work to ensure an income; ~-**and-butter letter** (of thanks for hospitality, sent by departed guest); ~ **and circuses,** public provision of food and entertainment; ~ **and milk,** broken bread in hot boiled milk; ~ **and scrape,** stingily buttered bread; ~ **and water,** plainest possible diet; *cast bread upon* WATER¹s; ~ **and wine,** Eucharist; ~ **buttered on both sides,** easy prosperity; **know which side** one's ~ **is buttered** (where one's advantage lies). **2.** necessary food (**break** ~, (arch.) take food; **break-ing of** ~, Eucharist; (**daily**) ~, livelihood; **eat the** ~ **of,** be subjected to (*affliction* etc.); **take the** ~ **out of** person's **mouth,** take away his living by competition etc.); (sl.) money. **3.** ~-**basket,** (sl.) stomach; ~-**bin,** container for loaves; ~'**board** (for cutting bread on or (sl.) making flat model of electric circuit etc.); ~'**crumb,** crumb of loaf, (esp. in *pl.*) bread crumbled for use in cooking; ~ **fruit** (of tropical tree *Artocarpus incisa,* with white pulp like new bread); *~'**line,** queue of poor people waiting to receive food, (fig.) subsistence level; *bread* ROLL¹; ~ **sauce,** milk sauce thickened with breadcrumbs; ~-**stick,** long thin roll of crisp bread; ~'**stuffs,** (1) grain flour, (2) articles of bread; ~-**winner,** person whose work supports a family. **4.** *v.t.* coat with breadcrumbs for cooking. [OE *brēad,* = OS *brōd,* OHG *brōt,* ON *brauth* f. Gmc **braudham,* of unkn. orig.]

breadth (-ĕd-) *n.* broadness, measurement from side to side; piece (of cloth etc.) of full breadth; extent, distance, room; (fig.) largeness, freedom from limitations (*of* mind, view, etc.); liberality, catholicity, toleration; (Art) unity of whole, achieved by disregard of unnecessary detail; hence ~'WAYS, ~'WISE, *advs.* [f. obs. *brede,* OE *brǣdu,* OHG *breitī,* ON *breidd,* Goth. *braidei* f. Gmc *braidjōn abstr. n. f. *braidh-BROAD, + -TH¹ after *length* etc.]

break¹ (-āk) *v.t.* & *i.* (**broke** *pr.* -ōk, (arch.) **brakei** BROKEN, see also BROKE). **1.** (Of a whole) make or become discontinuous otherwise than by cutting or tearing, divide or disperse into two or more parts, (*break* BULK¹, *the* INN¹; ~ *a set,* sell its parts separately); (of waves) curl over and disintegrate in foam; (of prices) fall suddenly; (of weather) change suddenly esp. after settled period; (of troops) disperse in confusion; (of clouds) show gap; disconnect (electric circuit); subject (vowel) to fracture. **2.** crack, graze, (*broken heads*); shatter (*break a window*); break bone in (arm, back, leg, etc.), fracture or dislocate (neck; ~ **the back of,** do hardest or greatest part of, overburden (person); *break on the* WHEEL¹); make by separating obstacles (*a trail, a way,* etc.); penetrate by breaking (*break open;* ~**ing and entering,** house-breaking); surpass (record); cause to cease or be discontinuous (*break gloom, spell, journey, silence,* STEP², one's *fast*); (of voice) change tone with emotion or at manhood; change (banknote etc.) for coins; unfurl (flag etc.); defeat object of (strike); solve (cipher etc.); disprove (alibi); (Tennis) win a game against (opponent's service); (Boxing, usu. as command from referee) come out of clinch; have interval between spells of work (*we broke for coffee*). **3.** (Of a part) disconnect or become separate from something otherwise than by cutting (~ **with,** quarrel or cease relations with); dismiss (officer); (of bowled ball in Cricket) deviate from original direction on pitching. **4.** make a way, come, produce, with effort, suddenness, violence, etc., (*break into* house, *out of* prison, *through* obstacles); (of day) dawn; (of storm) begin violently; reveal, (of news) be revealed; escape, emerge

from, (prison, bounds, cover(t); *break free* or *loose*); fail to rejoin (ship) after absence on leave; ~ **into,** suddenly begin to utter, perform, etc., (*laughter, a run, tears*), establish oneself in (profession); *break* WIND¹ 6. **5.** make or become weak, disable, discourage, destroy, cease, exhaust, (~ **bank,** exhaust its resources or its limit of payment; ~ **blow, fall,** weaken its effect); make or become bankrupt; tame, subdue, (*break* one's or person's HEART, *will, spirit; break resistance, a rebellion;* ~ **a habit,** be no longer subject to it; ~ person etc. **of a habit,** make him no longer subject to it; ~ **horse** (**to the rein**), make him accustomed to it); make of no effect, act contrary to (*law, contract,* one's *promise,* one's WORD¹). **6.** ~ **away,** make or become free or separate; ~'**away,** (*n.*) breaking away, secession, false start in race, (Rugby Footb.) outside second-row forward, (Austral.) stampede, (*a.*) that breaks away or has broken away; ~ **down,** collapse, fail, cease to function, demolish, decompose, suppress (resistance), analyse (total) into components, lose self-control; ~'**down** *n.,* collapse, failure of mechanical action or health or (esp. mental) power, analysis, disintegration; ~ **even,** emerge from transaction etc. with neither gain nor loss; ~ **in,** intrude forcibly esp. as thief (whence ~-*in n.*), interrupt, accustom to habit, tame, discipline, wear etc. until comfortable; ~ **in on,** disturb, interrupt; ~ **off,** detach by breaking, bring to an end, cease; ~ **out,** open up and remove contents (esp. of cargo), begin suddenly or violently, burst from restraint or concealment (whence ~-*out n.*), release (run-up flag), become covered *in* (*a rash* etc.), exclaim; ~'**through** *n.,* act of breaking through obstacle etc., major advance in knowledge etc.; ~ **up,** disband, depart, disconcert, break into small pieces, become feeble, be convulsed (*with laughter* etc.), (conversation etc.), (of weather) = sense 1; ~'**up** *n.,* disintegration, decay, collapse, dispersal. **7.** ~ **crop** (grown to avoid continual growing of cereals); ~-**front** *a.,* (of furniture) with front not in a continuous line; ~-**line,** (Print.) last line of paragraph (usu. not of full length); ~'**neck** *a.,* dangerous (pace); ~'**water,** object (esp. groyne or pier) resisting force of waves; ~'**wind,** (Austral.) wind-break. **8.** Hence ~'ADLE *a.,* & *n.* in *pl.,* (things) easily broken, ~'AGE (3) *n.* [OE *brecan,* = OS *brekan,* OHG *brehhan,* Goth. *brikan* f. Gmc *brekan]

break² (-āk) *n.* breaking (~ **of day,** dawn); escape from prison; sudden dash, (Cricket) deviation of ball on pitching; (Bill. etc.) points scored continuously; gap, broken place, interruption of continuity; (Electr.) breaking of circuit; (Jazz) short unaccompanied passage; short spell of recreation or refreshment between periods of work etc. (esp. *coffee-break, tea-break*); (colloq.) a fair chance, piece of good luck; (**bad**) ~, (colloq.) unfortunate remark or ill-judged action, piece of ill luck; EVEN² *break.* [f. prec.]

break³ (-āk) *n.* carriage-frame without body, for breaking-in young horses; = BRAKE⁷. [perh. = *brake* framework, 17th c., of unkn. orig.]

brea'ker¹ (-ā'k-) *n.* In vbl senses (esp. in comb., as *horse-breaker*); heavy ocean-wave breaking on coast or over reefs. [f. BREAK¹ + -ER²]

brea'ker² (-ā'k-) *n.* (Naut.) small keg. [f. Sp. *bareca, barrica* cask, cogn. w. BARREL¹]

brea'kfast (brĕ'k-) *n.,* & *v.i.* (take) first meal of day; WEDDING *breakfast.* [f. BREAK¹ interrupt + FAST²]

brea'king (-ā'k-) *n.* In vbl senses; (of vowel) = FRACTURE 2; ~**point,** (at which thing or person gives way under stress); ~**strength,** maximum stress that a body can withstand without breaking. [f. BREAK¹ + -ING¹]

bream¹ *n.* (*pl.* same). yellowish arch-backed freshwater fish of genus *Abramis;* (**sea-**) ~, similarly shaped sea-fish of family Sparidae, esp. porgy or POMFRET 2; *sunfish of genus *Lepomis* etc. [ME, f. OF *bre(s)me* f. Frank. **brachsima,* OS *bressemo,* OHG *brahsema*]

bream² v.t. (Hist.) clean (ship's bottom) by burning and scraping. [prob. f. LG, cogn. w. BROOM]

breast¹ (-ĕst) n. **1.** either of the two milk-secreting organs on upper front of woman's body; corresponding usu. rudimentary part of man's body; (fig.) source of nourishment. **2.** upper front of human body or of coat, dress, etc.; corresponding part of animals; CHIMNEY-*breast*; heart, emotions, thoughts, (**make a clean ~ of**, confess fully); BEAT¹ one's *breast*. **3.** ~'**bone**, thin flat vertical bone or cartilage in chest connecting ribs; ~-**drill** (pushed with breast to press against workpiece); ~-**fed, -feeding**, (at mother's breast, opp. from bottle); ~-**high**, high as the breast, (submerged) to the breast, (of scent) so strong that hounds race with heads up; ~-**pin** (jewelled etc., worn in tie); ~'**plate**, vestment or piece of armour covering breast, lower shell of turtle, tortoise, etc., inscription-plate on coffin; ~-**stroke**, stroke made while swimming on the breast by extending the arms in front and sweeping them back; ~-**wall** (confining a bank of earth); ~-**wheel**, water-wheel with water admitted near axle; ~'**work**, temporary breast-high defence or parapet. **4.** Hence (-)~'ED² a. [OE *brēost*, = OS *briost*, ON *brjóst* f. Gmc **breustam*]

breast² (-ĕst) v.t. oppose the breast to; face, contend with, (waves, hill); climb (hill); *breast the* TAPE. [f. prec.]

brea'stsümmer (-ĕ'st-) n. beam across broad opening, sustaining superstructure. [f. BREAST¹ + SUMMER²]

breath (-ĕth) n. exhalation as perceptible to sight or smell or hearing (**below** or **under** one's ~, in a whisper); slight movement of air; whiff of perfume etc.; air taken into and expelled from lungs (**draw ~**, breathe, live; **a ~ of** (brief time in or small amount of) **fresh air; waste ~**, talk in vain; **keep** or **save** one's **~ to cool** one's **porridge, save** one's ~, abstain from useless talk; **~ of life**, a necessity); process of respiration (**catch, hold,** one's ~, in fear or absorbing emotion); one respiration (*say* inconsistent things *in the same breath*); power of breathing (**out of ~**, not able to breathe quick enough after exertion; **take ~**, pause to rest; **take** person's **~ away**, make him breathless with delight, surprise, etc.; so ~-**taking** a.); whisper, murmur, (*not a breath of suspicion*); **~ test** (given with breathalyser). [OE *brǣth* f. Gmc **brāthaz* f. IE **bhrēlos* (**bhrē-* burn)]

brea'thalŷser, *-ŷzer, (brĕ'-; -zer) n. instrument measuring amount of alcohol in breath; so **brea'thalŷse** (brĕ'-; -z) v.t., carry out such measurement on. [f. BREATH + ANALYSE + -ER¹]

breathe (-ēdh) v. **1.** v.i. take air into and expel it from the lungs (**~ down** person's **neck**, be close behind him esp. in pursuit or from mistrust); be or seem alive; take breath, pause, (**~ again, freely,** recover from fear etc., be at ease); (of wine, fabric) be exposed to fresh air; sound, speak, (of wind) blow, softly (**~ upon**, tarnish, taint). **2.** v.t. send out or take in (as if) with breathed air (**~** one's **last**, die); utter (**not ~ a word of,** keep quite secret); exhibit (*breathe defiance, simplicity*); allow (horse etc.) to breathe, give rest after exertion. [ME, f. BREATH]

brea'ther (-ĕ'dh-) n. In vbl senses; short spell of exercise; brief pause for rest; safety-vent in crankcase etc. [f. prec. + -ER¹]

brea'thing (-ĕ'dh-) n. In vbl senses; (Gk Gram.) **rough, smooth, ~**, signs (cf. Appendix II) indicating that initial vowel or rho is or is not aspirated; ~-**space**, time to breathe, pause. [f. BREATHE + -ING¹]

brea'thlèss (-ĕ'th-) a. panting; holding the breath through excitement etc.; unstirred by wind; hence ~LY² adv., ~NESS n. [f. BREATH + -LESS]

brea'th|ŷ (-ĕ'thǐ) a. (Of singing-voice) with sound of emission of breath; hence ~iNESS n. [f. BREATH + -Y²]

brĕ'ccia (-cha) n. rock of angular stones etc. cemented by lime etc.; hence **brĕ'cciATE³** (-chǐ-) v.t., form into breccia. [It., = gravel, f. Gmc **brekan* BREAK¹]

brĕd. See BREED¹.

brĕde. Var. (arch.) of BRAID¹.

breech n., & v.t. **1.** n. (**pair of**) ~es (brǐ'chǐz), short trousers esp. fastened below knee, now used esp. for riding or in court costume etc. (**B~es Bible,** Geneva Bible of 1560 with *breeches* for *aprons* in Gen. 3: 7; ~'**es-buoy,** lifebuoy on rope with canvas breeches for user's legs); trousers or knickerbockers; *too* BIG *for* one's *breeches;* WEAR¹ *the breeches.* **2.** buttocks (arch. exc. w. ref. to baby's position at or before birth); **birth** (with buttocks foremost). **3.** part of cannon behind bore, back part of rifle or gun barrel; ~-**block** (closing breech aperture in gun); ~-**loader, -loading,** (gun) loaded at breech, not through muzzle. **4.** v.t. (arch.) put (boy) into breeches instead of petticoats. [OE *brōc,* pl. *brēc* (treated as sing. in MĔ), = OS *brōk,* OHG *bruoh,* ON *brók* f. Gmc **brōks*]

breed¹ v.t. & i. (**bred**). **1.** bear, generate, (offspring); propagate (**~ in,** always mate with or marry near relations); yield, produce, result in; cause to propagate, raise, (cattle, domestic animals); **bred in the bone,** hereditary. **2.** train up (*bred to the law*); bring up; arise, spread; **bred and born** or **born and bred,** by birth and upbringing. **3.** (Phys.) create (fissile material) by nuclear reaction. **4.** Hence ~ER¹ n.; **~er reactor,** nuclear reactor that can create more fissile material than it consumes in the chain reaction. [OE *brēdan,* = OHG *bruotan* f. WG **brōdjan* (**brōd-* BROOD¹)]

breed² n. **1.** stock of animals etc. within a species, having similar appearance and usu. developed by deliberate selection. **2.** race, lineage. **3.** sort, kind. [f. prec.]

bree'ding n. In vbl senses; result of training, behaviour; good manners. [f. BREED¹ + -ING¹]

breeks n. pl. (Sc.) Var. of *breeches* (BREECH 1).

breeze¹ n. gadfly. [OE *briosa,* of unkn. orig.]

breeze² n., & v.i. **1.** n. gentle wind; (on Beaufort scale) wind of 4-31 m.p.h.; wind blowing from land at night or sea during day; (sl.) easy task; (sl.) quarrel, display of temper; **get, have, put, the ~** (= WIND¹ 6) **up;** ~'**way,** roofed outdoor passage; hence ~'LESS (-zl-) a. **2.** v.i. (colloq.) go like a breeze, move *along* or *come in* in lively or offhand manner. [prob. f. OSp. & Port. *briza* NE wind]

breeze³ n. small cinders etc. used with sand and cement in making ~-**blocks** (lightweight building blocks). [?f. F *braise* live coals]

bree'z|ŷ a. wind-swept; pleasantly windy; fresh, lively, jovial; careless; hence ~ILY² adv., ~iNESS n. [f. BREEZE² + -Y²]

brĕ'msstrahlung (-mzshtrahlŏŏng) n. (Phys.) radiation due to retardation of charged particle by electric field, esp. of nucleus. [G, = braking radiation]

Brĕn n. ~ (**gun**), light-weight quick-firing machine-gun. [f. *Brno* in Czechoslovakia (where orig. made) + *Enfield* in England (where later made)]

brĕnt, *brănt, ~(-**goose**), smallest species of wild goose (*Bernicla brenta*), visiting Britain in winter. [16th c., of unkn. orig.]

brethren. See BROTHER.

Brĕ'ton a. & n. (native, or Celtic language) of Brittany. [OF, = BRITON]

brĕ'tzel. Var. of PRETZEL.

brĕve n. **1.** (Hist.) authoritative letter from sovereign or pope. **2.** (Mus.) note = two semibreves, now rarely used (**alla ~** pr. ălăbrā'vă, time signature indicating 2 or 4 minim beats in bar). **3.** written or printed mark (˘) of short or unstressed vowel. [ME, var. of BRIEF¹]

brĕ'vèt n., & v.t. **1.** n. document conferring a privilege from sovereign or government, esp. rank without corresponding pay in army (*brevet rank, major*). **2.** v.t. confer brevet rank on. [ME f. OF, dim. of *bref* BRIEF¹]

brĕ'viarŷ n. (RC Ch.) book containing the service for

each day, to be recited by those in orders. [f. L *breviarium* summary (*breviare* abridge); see ABBREVIATE², -ARY¹]

brĕ'vĭtў *n.* compact written or spoken expression, conciseness; short span (*of* life etc.). [f. AF *breveté*, OF *brieveté* (*bref* BRIEF¹; see -ITY)]

brew¹ (-ōō) *v.t. & i.* make (beer etc.) by infusion, boiling, and fermentation; make (tea etc.) by infusion or mixture (∼ **up,** make tea); undergo these processes; concoct, bring about, set in train; grow to ripeness, fester, gather force, (usu. of evil results; *mischief is brewing*); hence ∼'ER¹, ∼'ERY (3), *ns.* (esp. w. ref. to beer etc.). [OE *brēowan*, = OS *breuwan*, OHG *briuwan*, ON *brugga* f. Gmc **breu(w)an*]

brew² (-ōō) *n.* process of brewing; amount brewed at once; (quality of) what is brewed (*a good strong brew*). [f. prec.]

‖**brew'ster** (-ōō'-) *n.* **B∼ Sessions,** magistrates' sessions for issue of licences to permit trade in alcoholic liquors. [f. obs. *brewster* (orig. female) brewer; see -STER]

bri'ar¹,². See BRIER¹,².

Brĭar'd *n.* sheep-dog of a French breed. [F adj. (BRIE)]

bribe¹ *n.* money etc. offered to procure (often illegal or dishonest) action or decision in favour of giver. [f. foll.]

brĭb|e² *v.t.* persuade by bribe (*to* do); (abs.) practise bribery; hence ∼'ABLE *a.*, ∼'ERY (4) *n.* [ME f. OF *hriber, brimber* beg, of unkn. orig.]

bri'c-à-bràc *n.* miscellaneous old ornaments, furniture, trinkets, etc. [F, f. obs. *à bric et à brac* at random]

brick¹ *n. & a.* **1.** *n.* clay kneaded, moulded, and baked or sun-dried; small usu. rectangular block of this (**drop a ∼,** (sl.) say indiscreet thing; *bricks without* STRAW¹; **like a load** or **ton of ∼s,** (colloq.) with crushing weight or force); similar block of concrete etc.; brick-shaped loaf, block of tea, ice cream, etc.; child's toy building-block; (sl.) generous or loyal person. **2.** ∼'**bat,** piece of brick, esp. as missile [BAT²], (fig.) uncomplimentary remark; ∼'**field** (in which bricks are made); ∼'**fielder,** (Austral.) hot dry N. wind; ∼'**layer,** workman building with bricks; *brick*- -NOG¹; ∼'**red** (of) the red colour of bricks; *brick* WALL; ∼'**work,** building in brick; ∼'**yard,** place where bricks are made. **3.** Hence ∼'IE *n.*, (sl.) bricklayer. **4.** *a.* built of brick (*brick* WALL), of the red colour of bricks. [ME, f. MLG, MDu. *bri(c)ke,* of unkn. orig.]

brick² *v.t.* block *up* (window etc.), close *in,* with brickwork. [f. prec.]

brī'dal *a.* of bride or wedding; hence ∼LY² *adv.* [orig. n., = wedding-feast, f. OE *brýd-ealu* (*brýd* BRIDE, *ealu* ALE-drinking)]

bride *n.* woman on her wedding-day and for some time before and after it; ∼**-cake,** wedding-cake; ∼**-price,** money etc. paid to bride's family esp. in primitive societies. [OE *brýd,* = OS *brūd,* OHG *brūt,* ON *bruthr,* Goth. *brūths* f. Gmc **brūdhiz*]

bri'degroom (-dg-) *n.* man on his wedding-day and for some time before and after it. [OE *brýdguma* (as BRIDE, *guma* man, assim. to GROOM)]

bri'desmaid (-dz-) *n.* unmarried woman or girl (usu. one of several) attending bride at wedding. [earlier *bridemaid,* f. BRIDE + MAID]

bri'dewell (-dw-) *n.* (arch.) prison, reformatory. [f. St. *Bride's Well* in London, near which such a building stood]

bridge¹ *n.* **1.** structure carrying road, path, railway, etc., across stream, ravine, road, railway, etc.; ∼ **of asses,** = PONS *asinorum;* ∼ **of boats** (over boats moored abreast); BURN² one's *bridges;* **cross a ∼ when** one **comes to it,** deal with a problem when and if it arises. **2.** raised platform from which ship is directed; upper bony part of nose; upright piece over which strings of violin etc. are stretched; (Bill.) long stick with device at end to support cue, support for cue

formed with hand; bridgework; LAND¹*-bridge.* **3.** ∼'**head,** post held on far side of river or other obstacle, facing enemy's position; ∼ **passage,** (Mus. etc.) transition between main subjects; ∼'**work,** partial denture supported by teeth on each side. [OE *brycg,* = OS *bruggia,* OHG *brucca,* ON *brygg ja* f. Gmc **brug jō*]

bridg|e² *v.t.* be or make bridge over; span as if with bridge; ∼**ing loan** (made to cover short interval between buying a house etc. and selling another). [OE *brycgian* (as prec.)]

bridge³ *n.* card-game derived from whist, in which one player's cards are exposed and are played by his partner; (esp.) AUCTION *bridge* or CONTRACT¹ *bridge;* ∼ **roll,** small soft bread roll. [19th c.; orig. unkn.]

bri'dle¹ *n.* headgear to control horse, including headstall, bit, and rein; (Naut.) mooring-cable; (Physiol.) ligament checking motion of a part; ∼**-path, -road, -way,** (fit for riders but not for vehicles). [OE *brīdel,* = OHG *brittil,* WG f. as BRAID², + -LE 1]

bri'dle² *v.* **1.** *v.t.* put bridle on (horse etc.); curb, hold in, bring under control. **2.** *v.i.* ∼ (**up**), express offence, resentment, etc., (as if) by throwing up head and drawing in chin. [OE *brīdlian* (as prec.)]

bridōō'n *n.* snaffle and rein of military bridle. [f. F *bridon* (*bride* bridle; see -OON)]

Brie *n.* kind of soft cheese. [∼ in N. France]

brief¹ *n.* Pope's letter on matter of discipline to person or community (less formal than bull); (Law) summary of facts and law-points of a case drawn up for counsel (**hold a ∼ for,** be retained as counsel for, be obliged to argue in favour of); ‖piece of employment for barrister (DOCK⁵ *brief,* WATCH²*ing brief*), whence ∼'LESS *a.;* *(Law) statement of arguments to support case; instructions given to aircraft crews etc.; ‖∼**-bag** (in which barrister carries briefs); ∼**-case,** flat rectangular case for documents etc. [ME f. AF *bref,* OF *brief,* f. LL *breve* dispatch, note, neut. of L *brevis* short]

brief² *v.t.* ‖instruct (barrister) by brief; instruct (aircraft crews etc.) with regard to raid etc.; instruct or inform thoroughly in advance. [f. prec.]

brief³ *a. & n.* **1.** *a.* of short duration; concise in expression (be ∼, speak in few words; **in ∼,** in short); hence ∼'LY² *adv ;* ∼'NESS *n.* **2.** *n.* (in *pl.*) men's short underpants, women's short knickers. [ME f. AF *bref,* OF *brief,* f. L *brevis* short]

bri'er¹, bri'ar¹, *n.* prickly bush, esp. of wild rose; ∼**-rose,** dog-rose; **sweet-∼,** wild rose with small fragrant leaves and flowers; hence ∼Y² *a.* [OE *brēr, brēr,* of unkn. orig.]

bri'er², bri'ar², *n.* white heath (*Erica arborea*) of S. Europe; tobacco pipe made from its root. [19th c. *bruyer* f. F *bruyère* heath f. Gallo-Rom. **brucaria* (**brūcus* f. Gaulish **brūko*); assim. to prec.]

brig¹ *n.* two-masted square-rigged vessel, with additional lower fore-and-aft sail on gaff and boom to mainmast; *prison, esp. in warship [abbr. of BRIGANTINE]

brig² Sc. & N. Engl. var. of BRIDGE¹.

Brig. *abbr.* Brigadier.

brigā'de *n., & v.t.* **1.** *n.* subdivision of army; ‖infantry unit consisting usu. of 3 battalions and forming part of a division; corresponding armoured unit. **2.** organized or uniformed band of workers (*fire brigade*). **3.** *v.t.* form into brigade. [F, f. It. *brigata* company (*brigare* be busy with, f. *briga* strife); see -ADE]

brigadier' *n.* (formerly also ∼**-general**) officer commanding a brigade, (titular rank granted to) staff officer of similar standing, above colonel and below major-general. [F; see prec., -IER]

bri'galow (-ō) *n.* (Austral.) one of various acacia trees. [Aboriginal]

bri'gand *n.* member of robber band living by pillage and ransom; hence or cogn. ∼AGE (3), ∼ISM (2), ∼RY (5), *ns.,* ∼ISH¹ *a.* [ME f. OF, f. It. *brigante* (*brigare;* see BRIGADE)]

bri'gandine *n.* coat of mail, esp. made of iron rings or plates within canvas etc. [ME f. OF, or f. It. *brigantina* (as prec.; see -INE⁴)]

bri'gantine (-ēn) *n.* two-masted vessel with square--rigged foremast and fore-and-aft-rigged mainmast. [f. OF *brigandine* or f. It. *brigantino* (*brigante*; see BRIGAND)]

bright¹ (-īt) *a.* & *adv.* **1.** *a.* emitting or reflecting much light, shining, (∼ **lights,** urban places of entertainment; ∼'**work,** polished metal on ships etc.); lit up with joy, hope, etc.; (of colour) intense, shining; illustrious; vivacious; quick-witted; clever, talented, (*bright boy, idea*); hence ∼'EN⁶ (*up*) *v.t.* & *i.*, ∼'ISH¹ 2 *a.*, ∼'LY² *adv.*, ∼'NESS *n.* **2.** *adv.* brightly (*moon shines bright*); ∼ **and early,** very early in the morning. [OE *beorht,* adv. *beorhte,* = OS, OHG *beraht,* ON *bjartr,* Goth. *berhts.* Gmc **berhtaz*]

Bright² (-īt) *n.* ∼'**s disease,** one of various forms of degeneration of the kidneys. [f. R. ∼, Engl. physician d. 1858]

brill *n.* European flat-fish (*Scophthalmus rhombus*) resembling turbot. [15th c.; orig. unkn.]

bri'lli|ant¹ (-lya-) *a.* bright, sparkling; illustrious, striking; highly talented; showy; hence ∼ANCE, ∼ANCY, *ns.*, ∼**ant**LY² *adv.* [f. F *brillant* part. of *briller* shine, f. It. *brillare,* of unkn. orig.]

bri'lliant² (-lya-) *n.* diamond of finest cut and brilliance; ∼ **shape** (with two horizontal surfaces joined by facets). [f. F as prec. used as n.]

bri'lliantine (-lyantēn) *n.* cosmetic for making hair smooth and glossy; *shiny dress fabric. [f. F *brillantine* (as BRILLIANT¹; see -INE⁴)]

brim¹ *n.* edge or lip of cup, bowl, or hollow; projecting edge of hat; ∼-**full,** full to the brim; hence ∼'LESS, ∼**med²** (-md), *adjs.* [ME *brimme,* of unkn. orig.; cf. ON *barmr* brim, MHG *brem* border]

brim² *v.t.* & *i.* (**-mm-**). fill or be full to the brim (lit. or fig.); ∼ **over,** overflow (lit. or fig.). [f. prec.]

brim³ *n.* (US & Austral.) Var. of BREAM¹.

bri'mstone *n.* **1.** (arch.) sulphur. **2.** fuel of hell-fire; ∼ (**butterfly, moth**), kind that is yellow like sulphur; hence **bri'mston**Y² *a.* [ME, prob. f. OE *bryne* burning+STONE]

bri'ndled (-děld), **bri'ndle,** *a.* brownish or tawny with streaks of other colour. [*brindled* (whence back--form. *brindle*) alt. of *brinded* f. earlier *brended* f. *brend,* perh. of Scand. orig.]

brine *n.,* & *v.t.* **1.** *n.* water saturated or nearly so with salt; the sea; ∼-**pan,** salt-pan; hence **bri'ny²** *a.* (the **briny,** ||(sl.) the sea). **2.** *v.t.* steep in or saturate with brine. [OE *brīne,* = MDu. *brīne,* of unkn. orig.]

bring *v.t.* (**brought** *pr.* -awt). **1.** cause to come, come with or convey by carrying, leading, impelling, or attracting, (∼-**and-buy** *sale* etc., at which customers bring things for sale and buy what is brought by others); be sold for (price); cause, result in; prefer (charge), initiate (legal action), adduce (argument); cause to become (*bring low*); cause despite reluctance (*cannot bring myself to believe, to do it*), **2.** ∼ **home to** person, convict or convince him of; ∼ **into being,** cause to exist; ∼ **into play,** cause to operate; ∼ **into the world,** give birth to; *bring to* BEAR², *to* BOOK¹; ∼ **to mind,** (cause oneself to) remember; ∼ **to pass,** cause to happen. **3.** ∼ **about,** cause to happen, reverse (ship); ∼ **back,** call to mind; ∼ **down,** kill or wound, cause (penalty) to fall *on,* abase, make (flying bird, aircraft, etc.) fall, lower (price etc.), continue (record) *to* a point; ∼ **the house down,** ∼ **down the house,** (Theatr.) get loud applause; ∼ **forth,** give birth to, produce, cause; ∼ **forward,** draw attention to, move to earlier date or time, transfer from previous page or account; ∼ **in,** introduce (custom, fashion, topic, legislation), produce as profit or increase, adduce, pronounce (verdict; person *guilty, not guilty*); ∼ **off,** rescue from wreck etc., conduct (attempt) successfully; ∼ **on,** cause, cause discussion of, advance progress of; ∼ **out,** express, exhibit

clearly, introduce (girl) to society, publish, make known; ∼ **over,** convert to one's own side; ∼ **round,** restore to consciousness, bring incidentally or informally, win over (*to* other person's opinion); ∼ **through,** save (sick person); ∼ **to,** check motion of, (abs.) come to a stop, restore to consciousness; ∼ **under,** subdue; ∼ **up,** supervise training of (child) in habits, manners, etc., cause to appear in court, anchor (ship), (abs.) come to a stop, call attention to, vomit; ∼ **up to date,** provide with what is needed to deal with latest developments; *bring up the* REAR¹. **4.** Hence ∼'ER¹ *n.* [OE *bringan,* = OS, OHG *bringan,* Goth. *briggan* f. Gmc **brengan*]

bri'njal (-awl) *n.* (Ind. & Afr.) aubergine [ult. f. Port. *berinjela* f. as AUBERGINE]

brink *n.* edge of steep place; border of water, esp. when steep (**shiver on the** ∼, hesitate to plunge, usu. fig.); verge (*of* discovery, ruin, eternity, etc.); *the* verge of war; ∼'**manship,** art of advancing to the very brink of war etc. but not engaging in it. [ME, f. ON **brenkōn* (OIcel. *brekka* slope), of unkn. orig.]

bri'ny. See BRINE.

brio (brē'ō) *n.* vivacity. [It.]

bri'oche (brē'ōsh) *n.* small round sweet cake made with light yeast dough. [F]

briquë'tte, briquë't, (-kě't) *n.* block of compressed coal-dust. [F *briquette,* dim. of *brique* brick]

brisk *a.* & *v.* **1.** *a.* (Esp. of movement) active, lively, (*brisk pace, trade, wind* etc.); enlivening, keen, (*air* etc.); hence ∼'EN⁶ *v.t.* & *i.*, ∼'LY² *adv.*, ∼'NESS *n.* **2.** *v.t.* & *i.* ∼ (**up**), make or become brisk. [prob. f. F BRUSQUE]

bri'skét *n.* breast of animals (esp. as joint of meat). [f. AF **brusket, brisket,* OF *bruschet* etc., perh. f. ON *brjósk;* see -ET¹]

bri'sling (-s-, -z-) *n.* small herring or sprat. [Norw. & Da., = sprat]

bri'stle¹ (-ĭ'sel) *n.* one of stiff hairs on pig's back and sides; short stiff hair of other animals, man's short--cropped beard, or plants; short stiff piece of wire etc.; ∼**tail,** wingless insect of order Thysanura; ∼**worm,** polychaete; hence **bri'stly²** (-ĭ'slĭ) *a.* [ME, prob. f. OE **brystel,* *byrstel f. *byrst* (= OHG, ON *burst*) +-LE 1]

bri'stle² (-ĭ'sel) *v.i.* & *t.* (cause to) stand upright (hair etc.); ∼ (**up**), raise or rise like bristles or into roughness; show temper, prepare for fight; be thickly set *with* hair, difficulties, etc. [f. prec.]

bri'stling (-sl-). Var. of BRISLING.

Bri'stol *n.* **1.** ∼ **board,** kind of fine pasteboard for drawing on; (**shipshape and**) ∼ **fashion,** (Naut. or transf.) with all in good order. **2.** (*b*∼; in *pl.*, sl.) woman's breasts. [∼ in England; sense 2 rhyming sl. f. *Bristol cities* = *titties*]

Brit *n.* (colloq.) British person. [abbr.]

Brit. *abbr.* Britain; British.

Britā'nnia (-nya) *n.* personification of Britain, usu. as woman with shield, helmet, and trident; ∼ **metal,** alloy of tin, antimony, and copper, resembling silver; ∼ **silver** (about 96%, pure). [L, also *Brittan(n)ia* = Gk *Brettania* (*Brettanoi* Britons; see BRITISH)]

Britā'nnic *a.* of Britain (chiefly in phr. *Her* or *His Britannic Majesty*). [f. L *Britannicus* (as prec.; see -IC)]

Bri'ticism, Bri'tishism, *n.* idiom used in Gt. Britain and not in US etc. [f. foll. +-ISM (4); -*icism* after *gallicism*]

Bri'tish *a.* of (Great) Britain or its inhabitants or language; *English; **the** ∼, (*pl.*) British people; ∼ **English** (esp. as contrasted with language of US etc.); *British* LEGION, THERMAL *unit*; ∼ **warm,** kind of short military overcoat. [OE *Brettisc* etc. f. *Bret* (L *Britto* or OCelt. **Britto(s)*); see -ISH¹]

Bri'tisher *n.* (US etc. term for) British subject esp. of British descent. [f. prec. +-ER¹; cf. *foreigner*]

Bri'tishism. See BRITICISM.

Bri'ton *n.* one of the people living in S. Britain before the Roman conquest; native or inhabitant of Great Britain, or (Hist.) the British Empire. [ME & OF *Breton* f. L *Britto -onis* f. OCelt. **Britto(s)*]

brĭt'tle a. & n. **1.** a. apt to break, fragile; insecure; hard-natured; ~**-star**, kind of starfish; hence ~LY² (-tel-lĭ), **brĭt'tLY²**, advs., ~NESS (-teln-) n. **2.** n. brittle sweet made from nuts and melted sugar. [ME, f. brytf. Gmc *brut- break up]

brĭ'tzka, -tzska, (-ĭ'tska) n. open carriage with calash top and space for reclining. [f. Pol. bryczka dim. of bryka goods wagon]

brize (-ēz). Var. of BREEZE¹.

bro. abbr. brother.

broach¹ n. roasting-spit; octagonal church-spire rising from tower without parapet; boring-bit. [ME f. OF broche f. Rom. *brocca spike f. L brocc(h)us in brocci dentes projecting teeth; cf. BROOCH]

broach² v.t. pierce (cask) to draw liquor, begin drawing (liquor); open and start using contents of (bale, box, cargo, etc.); begin discussion of (subject). [ME, f. OF brocher f. Rom. deriv. of prec.]

broach³ v.t. & i. ~ (to), veer or cause (ship) to veer and present side to wind and waves. [18th c.; orig. unkn.]

broad (-awd) a., n., & adv. **1.** a. large across, wide, not narrow; (appended to measurement) = in breadth (6 ft. broad); extensive (broad ACRES); as ~ as it is long, without preference for either aspect. **2.** full, clear, main, explicit, (broad daylight, facts, distinction, hint); somewhat coarse (broad story), strongly dialectal etc. (broad Yorkshire, Scots), whence ~'NESS n., generalized (broad rule; in the broadest sense of the word); tolerant (B~ Church, Anglican churchmen favouring comprehensiveness and not pressing doctrines); bold in effect or style. **3.** broad ARROW; ~ bean, (large flat seed of) an edible bean; ~**-brow,** (colloq.) person with broad interests; ~**'cloth,** fine twilled woollen or worsted cloth, plain-woven cotton etc. cloth, [phr. in Act of Parl. 1482 kept as name for quality rather than width]; *~ jump, long jump; ~**-leaved,** (of tree) deciduous but hard-timbered; ~**'loom,** (carpet) woven in broad width; ~**mi'nded(ness),** (condition of) being tolerant or liberal in thought or opinion; broad PENNANT; ~**'sheet,** large sheet of paper printed on one side only; ~**'side,** (1) = broadside above, (2) ship's side above water between bow and quarter (~side on, to, with this presented, transversely), (3) (discharge of) all guns on one side of ship, (fig.) powerful verbal attack; ~**'sword,** broad-bladed cutting-sword; ~**'tail,** caracul sheep, its lamb's fur; ~**'way,** a broad road; *B~'way, New York theatre life. **4.** n. the broad part (broad of the back), ||(in E. Anglia) large piece of fresh water formed by widening of river; *(sl.) woman, prostitute. **5.** adv. broadly, fully (broad awake). **6.** Hence ~'EN⁶ v.t. & i., ~'LY², ~'WAY3, ~'WISE, advs. [OE brād, − OS brēd, OHG breit, ON breithr, Goth. braiths f. Gmc *braidhaz]

broa'dcast (-aw'dkah-) a., adv., v. (-cast or -casted; -cast), & n. **1.** a. (Of seed) scattered freely, not in drills or rows, (fig.) widely disseminated. **2.** adv. in broadcast manner. **3.** v.t. sow or disseminate thus; dio seminate (news, music, etc.) by radio or television. **4.** v.i. speak, sing, play, etc., for radio or television transmission. **5.** Hence ~ER¹ n. **6.** n. transmission by radio or television. [f. prec. + CAST¹ p.p.]

||Broa'dmoor (-aw'-; -oor, -ōr) n. institution at Broadmoor for treatment of mental patients under special conditions (formerly housing insane criminals). [~ in Berkshire]

Brŏ'bdĭngnăg n. land of giants; hence ~IAN (-ă'g-) a. [place in Swift's Gulliver's Travels]

brocā'de n., & v.t. **1.** n. fabric woven with raised patterns, orig. of added metal threads. **2.** v.t. work with raised pattern. [f. Sp. & Port. brocado f. It. broccato & F brocart (It. brocco twisted thread; see -ADE)]

brŏ'ccoli n. hardy variety of cauliflower; (sprouting) ~, form of this which produces many small heads. [It., pl. of broccolo cabbage-top dim. of brocco; see BROACH¹]

brŏch (-ŏk, -ŏχ) n. prehistoric circular stone tower in N. Scotland and adjacent islands. [f. ON borg castle]

brochě'tte (-shě't) n. skewer on which chunks of meat are cooked. [F, dim. of broche BROACH¹]

brō'chure (-sher, -shūr) n. booklet, pamphlet, esp. giving information about place etc. [F, lit. 'stitching' (brocher stitch; see -URE)]

brŏck n. badger. [OE broc(c) f. OBrit. brokkos]

brŏ'ckĕt n. second-year male red deer with straight horns. [ME, f. AF *broquet dim. of broque (= broche BROACH¹); see -ET¹]

brō'derer n. (arch.) embroiderer (now only as guild-name). [f. obs. brouder etc. f. OF (see EMBROIDER) + -ER¹]

broderie anglaise (brōdrĭ ahnglā'z) n. open embroidery on linen, cambric, etc.; fabric so embroidered. [F, = English embroidery]

brōgue¹ (-ōg) n. rough shoe of untanned leather; strong outdoor shoe with ornamental perforated bands. [f. Gael. & Ir. brōg f. ON brók]

brōgue² (-ōg) n. dialectal, esp. Irish, accent. [18th c., orig. unkn.; perh. allusively f. prec.]

broi'der(ў). Var. (arch.) of EMBROIDER(Y).

broil¹ v.t. & i. cook (meat) or be cooked on fire of gridiron; make or be very hot (of person in sun etc.); hence ~'ER¹ n., young chicken reared for broiling, apparatus or compartment for broiling, very hot day; ~**'er house,** building for rearing broiler chickens in close confinement. [ME, f. OF bruler burn f. Rom. *brustulare]

broil² n. (arch.) quarrel; tumult. [f. obs. broil to muddle; cf. EMBROIL]

brōke past & p.p. of BREAK¹; as p.p. arch. exc. (colloq.) ruined, without money; *go for ~, (sl.) exert strenuous efforts.

brō'ken a. In vbl senses; ~ chord, (Mus.) chord in which notes are performed successively not simultaneously; ~ cloud (covering large part of sky); ~ colour (mixed or juxtaposed closely with another); ~**-down,** used or worn and hence broken or about to break; ~ English etc. (imperfect); ~ ground (uneven); ~**-hearted,** crushed by grief; ~ home (of family lacking one parent esp. through divorce or separation); ~ line (made up of dashes); ~ man (reduced to despair); broken REED¹; ~ sleep (disturbed and intermittent); ~ tea, tea-siftings; ~ time, (esp. working) time reduced by interruptions; ~ water (choppy); ~**-winded,** (of horse) disabled by ruptured air-cells in lungs; hence ~LY² adv., ~NESS (-n-n-) n. [p.p. of BREAK¹]

brō'ker n. middleman in business; agent, commissioner; pawnbroker; stockbroker; ||person licensed to sell or appraise distrained goods; hence ~AGE n., (esp.) broker's fee or commission. [ME f. AF brocour = Prov. abrocador, of unkn. orig.]

brō'king n. broker's trade, acting as broker. [f. obs. broke v. (cf. prec.) + -ING¹]

brō'lga n. (Austral.) species of crane (Grus rubicunda) often seen in pairs. [Aboriginal]

||brō'llў n. **1.** (colloq.) umbrella. **2.** (sl.) parachute. [abbr.]

brŏm-. See BROMO-.

brōme n. oatlike grass of genus Bromus. [f. mod. L Bromus f. Gk brōmos]

bromē'lia, -iad, ns. Amer. plant of family Bromeliaceae (e.g. of genus Bromelia) usu. with spiny leaves, e.g. pineapple. [f. O. Bromel, Sw. botanist d. 1705 + -IA¹]

brō'mic a. containing bromine in chem. combination, esp. ~ acid (HBrO₃); hence **brō'mATE¹** (3) n. [f. BROMINE + -IC]

brō'mide n. binary compound of bromine, used in various preparations as sedative; commonplace bore, trite remark; ~ paper, photographic printing paper coated with silver bromide emulsion. [f. foll. + -IDE]

brō'mine (-ēn) n. non-metallic element, a poisonous dark liquid with rank smell; hence **brō'mISM** (5) n. [f. F brome. Gk brōmos stink + -INE⁵]

brōmo-, (esp. bef. vowel) **brōm-,** *comb. form.* (Chem.) bromine. [f. prec. + -o-]

*brŏnc *n.* (colloq.) = BRONCO. [abbr.]

brŏ'nchia (-k-) *n. pl.* ramifications of bronchi in lungs. [LL f. Gk (*brogkhos* windpipe)]

brŏ'nchial (-k-) *a.* of bronchi or bronchia. [f. prec. + -AL]

brŏ'nchiŏle (-k-) *n.* minute branch of bronchus. [f. mod. L *bronchiola dim. of BRONCHIA]

brŏnch|ī'tĭs (-k-) *n.* inflammation of bronchial mucous membrane; hence ∿ī'tĭc *a.* & *n.* [mod. L, f. BRONCHUS + -ITIS]

brŏ'ncho- (-k-) *comb. form.* bronchi, bronchia, throat, as: ∿cele (-sēl), goitre; ∿scope, instrument for inspecting interior of bronchi. [f. foll.]

brŏ'nch|us (-k-) *n.* (*pl.* ∿i *pr.* -kī). either of two main divisions of windpipe. [LL, as BRONCHIA]

brŏ'ncō *n.* (*pl.* ∿s). wild or half-tamed horse of California etc.; *∿-buster, (sl.) breaker-in of broncos. [Sp., = rough]

brŏntosaur'us *n.* herbivorous large dinosaur of genus *Brontosaurus* of the Jurassic and Cretaceous periods. [f. Gk *brontē* thunder + -o- + *sauros* lizard]

*Brŏnx *n.* cocktail of gin, vermouth, and orange-juice; ∿ cheer, (sl.) sound of contempt or derision made with tongue between lips. [∿ in New York]

brŏnze *n.,* *a.,* & *v.* **1.** *n.* brown alloy chiefly of copper and tin (B∿ Age, time when weapons and tools were usu. made of bronze); work of art made of bronze; bronze medal; colour of bronze; hence **brŏ'nzy²** *a.* **2.** *a.* made of or coloured like bronze; ∿ medal, medal of bronze usu. awarded as third prize. **3.** *v.t.* & *i.* give bronzelike surface to; make or become brown, tan. [F, f. It. *bronzo,* prob. f. Pers. *birinj* copper]

brooch (-ō-) *n.* ornament with hinged pin and catch, usu. worn fastened to woman's dress etc. or as badge etc. [ME *broche* = BROACH¹]

brŏŏd¹ *n.* young birds etc. from one hatching; (usu. derog. or joc.) human family, children; bee or wasp larvae; group of related things; ∿-mare etc. (kept for breeding). [OE *brōd,* cogn. w. MDu. *broet,* OHG *bruot* f. Gmc **brōd-* (**brō-* warm, heat)]

brŏŏd² *v.i.* sit as hen on eggs; (of night etc.) hang close over or (up)on; meditate (esp. resentfully) (*on* or *over,* or abs.). [f. prec.]

brŏŏ'der *n.* heated house for chicks, piglets, etc. [f. prec. + -ER¹]

brŏŏ'd|ў *a.* (Of hen) wishing to incubate eggs; (fig.) feeling depressed; hence ∿ĭNESS *n.* [f. BROOD¹ + -Y²]

brŏŏk¹ *n.* small stream; ∿'lime, kind of speedwell common in ditches; ∿'weed, small herb of genus *Samolus* found in wet places; hence ∿'LET *n.* [OE *brōc,* = MLG *brōk,* OHG *bruoh* marsh, WG, of unkn. orig.; ∿*lime* f. OE *hleomoce* name of the plant]

brŏŏk² *v.t.* (literary; usu. w. neg.) tolerate (insult etc.); admit of (delay etc.). [OE *brūcan,* = OS *brūkan,* OHG *brūhhan,* Goth. *brūkjan* f. Gmc **brūk-* use f. IE **bhrug-*]

brŏŏm *n.* yellow-flowered shrub of genus *Cytisus* or *Genista;* sweeping-implement usu. on long handle (**new** ∿, newly appointed person eager to sweep away abuses); ∿'rape, brown leafless parasitic plant growing on roots of broom etc. [L *rapum* tuber]; ∿'stick, handle of broom (allegedly ridden on through the air by witches, and jumped over by parties to sham marriage). [OE *brōm,* = MLG *brām;* cf. BRAMBLE]

Bros. *abbr.* Brothers (esp. in title of firm)

||**brŏse** (-z) *n.* dish of oatmeal with boiling water or milk poured on it; **Athole** ∿, mixture of whisky, oatmeal, and honey. [Sc. form of *brewis* broth. ME f. OF *bro(u)ez* (*breu* f.). Rom. *brodo f. Gmc *brotham BROTH)]

broth (-ŏ-, -aw-) *n.* unclarified meat or fish stock; thin soup made from it; meat stock as nutrient medium for bacteria; ∿ of a boy, (Ir.) good fellow. [OE, = ON *broth,* OHG *brod* f. Gmc *brotham (**bru-* BREW; see -TH¹)]

brŏ'thel *n.* house etc. where prostitutes may be visited. [orig. ∿-*house* f. ME *brothel* worthless man, prostitute, f. OE *brēothan* go to ruin]

bro'ther (-ŭ'dh-) *n.* **1.** son of same parents or (also half-∿) same parent as another person. **2.** man who is a close friend, fellow citizen, countryman, associate, or equal. **3.** (*pl.* **brethren** *pr.* brĕ'dhrĭn). man who is a fellow member of religious society (LAY² *brother*), trade union, regiment, guild, order, profession, etc.; official of certain companies etc.; ELDER¹ *brother.* **4.** (*pl.* also **brethren**). (As title) member of religious order. **5.** ∿ **german** (having same parents); ∿ **uterine** (having same mother only); ∿**-in-law,** brother of one's husband or wife, husband of one's sister(-in-law); ||*Brother* JONATHAN. **6.** *Brother²* *a.* & *adv.* [OE *brōthor,* = OS *brōthar,* OHG *bruodar,* ON *brōthir,* Goth. *brōthar* f. Gmc *brōthar f. IE *bhrātēr]

bro'therhŏŏd (-ŭ'dh-) *n.* relationship (as) between brothers; companionship; (members of) association for mutual help etc.; community of feeling; *trade union esp. of railwaymen; *(members of) a profession. [ME, alt. f. *brotherrede* f. OE *brōthor-ræden,* cf. (KIND)RED) after wds in -HOOD, -HEAD]

brougham (-ōŏm, -ōō'am) *n.* (Hist.) one-horse (or electric) closed carriage; motor car with driver's seat open. [f. Lord *B*∿ d. 1868]

brought. See BRING.

brouhaha (brōō'hah-hah) *n.* commotion, sensation; hubbub, uproar. [F]

brow *n.* **1.** eyebrow (KNIT one's *brows*); forehead; (colloq.) level of intellect [after *highbrow* etc.]; hence (-)∿ED² (-owd) *a.* edge, projection, of cliff etc., top of hill in road. [OE *brū* f. Gmc *brūs f. IE *bhrūs]

brow'beat *v.t.* (-beat; -beaten). bully or intimidate with looks and words. [f. BROW + BEAT¹]

brown¹ *a.* **1.** of the colour given by mixing red, yellow, and black, or by toasting bread; (as distinguishing epithet) *brown bear, willow;* dark-skinned, sun-tanned. **2.** ∿ **bread** (of unbolted flour); ∿ **coal,** lignite; ∿ **eye** (with brown iris); ∿ **goods,** household furniture such as television sets, kettles, opp. *white goods; brown* HOLLAND; ∿ **paper,** unbleached kind used for packing etc.; *brown* STUDY¹ 4; ∿ **sugar** (partly refined); **do** ∿, (sl.) cheat. **3.** Hence ∿'ISH¹ *a.;* ∿'NESS (-n-n-) *n.* [OE *brūn,* = OS, OHG *brūn,* ON *brúnn* f. Gmc *brūnaz]

brown² *n.* brown colour; brown pigment; brown clothes or material (*dressed in brown*); brown butterfly; brown ball in snooker etc.; ||**the** ∿, brown mass of flying game-birds; *fire into the* ∿, let fly into a covey without singling out a bird, (transf.) shoot at random into a mass. [f. prec.]

brown³ *v.t.* & *i.* make or become brown by roasting, sunburn, etc.; ||∿ed off, (sl.) bored, fed up; ∿-out *n.,* partial black-out or power cut. [f. BROWN¹]

Brow'nian *a.* ∿ **movement** *n.,* irregular oscillation of microscopic particles suspended in a fluid. [f. R. *Brown,* Sc. botanist d. 1858, + -IAN]

brow'nie *n.* benevolent shaggy goblin said to haunt house and do household work secretly; (*B*∿) member of junior branch of Guides; (Austral. & NZ) sweet currant-bread; *square of rich cake with nuts. [f. BROWN¹ + -IE]

brow'ning *n.* browned sugar or flour used to colour gravy etc. [f. BROWN³ + -ING¹]

*brow'nstōne *n.* kind of reddish-brown sandstone used for building (in front elevation); house faced with brown. [f. BROWN¹ + STONE]

browse¹ (-z) *n.* twigs, young shoots, etc., as fodder for cattle; act of browsing. [earlier *brouse* f. OF *brost* young shoot f. Gmc]

browse² (-z) *v.t.* & *i.* **1.** feed on; crop, (leaves, twigs, scanty vegetation). **2.** *v.i.* feed thus; (fig.) read desultorily. [f. F *broster* (*brost;* see prec.)]

brr (br-r) *int.* expr. shivering. [imit.]

BRS *abbr.* British Road Services.

brucĕllō'sĭs (brōō-) *n.* disease caused by bacteria of

genus *Brucella* (undulant fever in man, contagious abortion in cattle etc.). [f. *Brucella* (f. Sir D. *Bruce*, Sc. physician d. 1931) +-OSIS]

Bru'in (-ōō'-) *n.* (Personal name for) bear. [ME f. Du., = BROWN¹, name in *Reynard the Fox*]

bruise¹ (-ōōz) *n.* injury by blow to body (also to fruit etc.) discolouring skin. [f. foll.]

bruise² (-ōōz) *v.t.* injure by blow that discolours skin without breaking it or a bone (of human or animal body, also fruit, plant, etc.); crush, grind small; (fig.) hurt mentally; *bruised* REED¹. [ME, f. OE *brȳsan* crush, reinforced by AF *bruser*, OF *bruisier* break]

brui'ser (-ōō'z-) *n.* In vbl senses; prize-fighter. [f. prec. +-ER¹]

bruit¹ (-ōōt) *n.* (arch.) report, rumour. [F, = noise (*bruire* roar)]

bruit² (-ōōt) *v.t.* (arch. or US) spread (report) *abroad* or *about*. [f. prec.]

||**Brŭm** *n.* (colloq.) Birmingham (England); hence ∼'mie *n.*, person from Birmingham. [abbr. of BRUMMAGEM]

brŭ'mby *n.* (Austral.) wild or unbroken horse. [19th c.; orig. unkn.]

brume (-ōōm) *n.* (literary). mist, fog. [F, f. L *bruma* winter]

Brŭ'mmagem *a.* counterfeit; cheap and showy. [dial. form of *Birmingham*, England, w. ref. to counterfeit coins and plated goods once made there]

bru'mous (-ōō'-) *a.* wintry; foggy. [f. F *brumeux* f. LL *brumosus* rainy (as BRUME; see -OUS)]

brŭnch *n.* (colloq.) single meal instead of breakfast and lunch. [portmanteau wd]

brunĕt (-ōō-) *n.* & *a.* dark-skinned (white person). [F, dim. of *brun* BROWN¹; see -ET¹]

brunĕtte (-ōō-) *n.* & *a.* dark-skinned and/or brown-haired (white woman). [F, fem. of prec.; see -ETTE]

brŭnt *n.* chief stress *of* shock, attack, etc. (usu. in phr. *bear the brunt of*). [ME; orig. unkn.]

brŭsh¹ *n.* **1.** (arch. exc. US, Austral., etc.) undergrowth, thicket, small trees and shrubs growing *or* (in US) cut in faggots; land covered with such growth; (Austral.) dense forest. **2.** implement of bristles, hair, wire, etc., set in wood etc. for scrubbing or sweeping; bunch of hairs etc. in straight handle, quill, etc., for painting, drawing, writing, etc.; one of pair of thin sticks with long wire bristles for striking drum, cymbal, etc. **3.** bushy tail, esp. of fox; brushlike tuft. **4.** (Electr.) brushlike discharge of sparks; piece of carbon or metal ending in wire or strips securing good metallic connection; movable strip of conducting material for making and breaking connection. **5.** (Austral. & NZ sl.) girl, young woman. **6.** application of brush, brushing; short sharp encounter (*with*), skirmish, graze. **7.** ∼'fire (small-scale) *war*; ∼ turkey, (Austral.) large mound-building bird; ∼'wood, undergrowth, thicket, cut or broken twigs etc.; ∼'work, painter's (style of) manipulation of brush. **8.** Hence ∼LESS *a.*, not requiring use of brush; ∼'Y² *a.* [sense 1 ME, f. AF *brousse*, OF *brosse*, *broce*, sense 6 f. foll., other senses ME f. OF *brosse*, *broisse*, perh. both f. Rom. **bruscia*]

brŭsh² *v.t.* & *i.* **1.** move briskly (esp. *by, through, against*); sweep or scrub clean, put in order, with brush; graze or touch in passing; remove (dust etc.) with brush; treat (surface) with brush to change its nature or appearance; ∼ed aluminium (lustreless); ∼ed fabric (with nap raised). **2.** ∼ aside, dismiss or dispose of curtly or lightly; ∼ off, dismiss, rebuff; ∼-off *n.*, dismissal; ∼ over, paint lightly; ∼ up, furbish, renew one's acquaintance with (subject); so ∼-up *n.* [f. prec.]

brusque (-ōōsk, -ŭ-) *a.* blunt, offhand, abrupt, (of or in manner, speech); hence ∼'LY² *adv.*, ∼'NESS, ∼'rie (-skerē) [-ERY], *ns.* [F, f. It. *brusco* sour, as n. butcher's broom f. Rom. **bruscum*]

Brŭ'ssels (-z) *n.* ∼ carpet (with wool pile and stout linen back); ∼ lace, rich pillow-lace or needle-point;

∼ sprouts, edible buds of the cabbage *Brassica oleracea gemmifera*. [∼ in Belgium]

brut (brōōt) *a.* (Of wine) unsweetened. [F]

bru'tal (-ōō'-) *a.* coarse; savagely cruel; merciless (*brutal frankness*); hence ∼ISM (2), **brutä'lity** (-ōō-), *ns.*, ∼IZE (1, 3) *v.t.* & *i.*, ∼LY² *adv.* [F, or f. med. L *brutalis* (*brutus* BRUTE; see -AL)]

brute (-ōōt) *a.* & *n.* **1.** *a.* not possessing capacity to reason; stupid, sensual, beastlike, cruel, or passionate (person, act, motive, etc.); unconscious, merely material, (*brute force, matter*). **2.** brute person or beast; (colloq.) disliked person. **3.** Hence ∼'HOOD (-t-h-) *n.*, **bru'tish** 1 (-ōō'-) *a.* [f. F *brut(e)* f. L *brutus* stupid]

brȳo'log|ȳ *n.* study of mosses; hence ∼IST (3) *n.* [f. Gk *bruon* moss+-O-+-LOGY]

brȳ'onȳ *n.* climbing plant of genus *Bryonia*; **black** ∼, similar plant (*Tamus communis*). [f. L f. Gk *bruōnia*]

brȳ'ophyte *n.* moss or liverwort. [f. mod. L *Bryophyta* f. Gk *bruon* moss+*phuton* plant]

brȳozō'|an *a.* & *n.* (member) of phylum Bryozoa of aquatic animals forming colonies; hence ∼ō'LOGY *n.* [f. Gk *bruon* moss+*zōia* animals+-AN]

Brȳthŏ'nic *a.* & *n.* (language) of the Celts of S. Britain. [f. W *Brython* Britons f. OCelt. **Brittones*, +-IC]

BS *abbr.* **Bachelor of Science; Bachelor of Surgery; British Standard.

||**BSA** *abbr.* Birmingham Small Arms (Company).

B.Sc. *abbr.* Bachelor of Science.

BSI *abbr.* British Standards Institution.

BST *abbr.* British Summer Time (1968–71); British Summer Time.

Bt. *abbr.* Baronet.

B.th.u., B.t.u., *abbr.* British thermal unit(s).

bu. *abbr.* bushel(s).

bŭb¹ *n.* (usu. in *pl.*) woman's breast. [f. earlier *bubby*; cf. dial. G *bübbi* teat]

*bŭb² *n.* (colloq.) (word of address to) boy, man. [f. earlier *bubby*, perh. childish form of BROTHER or f. G *bube* boy]

bū'bal *n.* N. Afr. and Arabian antelope (*Alcelaphus buselaphus*). [f. L f. Gk *boubalos* oxlike antelope]

bū'bble¹ *n.* **1.** spherical or hemispherical envelope of liquid enclosing air etc.; air-filled cavity in liquid, or in solidified liquid, as glass or amber; transparent domed canopy, unsubstantial or visionary project, enterprise, etc. (SOUTH *Sea Bubble*). **2.** sound or appearance of boiling. **3.** ∼ and **squeak**, cold meat or potatoes fried with chopped vegetables; ∼ **bath** (in which water is made to foam by perfumed toilet preparation); ∼ car, small motor car with transparent dome; *bubble* CHAMBER; ∼ **gum**, chewing-gum that can be blown into large bubbles; ∼ **pack**, small package enclosing goods in transparent material on backing. **4.** Hence **bŭ'bbly²** *a.*, & *n.* ||(sl.) champagne. [ME, prob. imit.]

bū'bble² *v.i.* send up, rise in, make the sound of, bubbles (lit. or fig.; ∼ **(over)**, be exuberant *with* laughter, anger, etc.; (colloq.) splutter. [ME, prob. imit.]

bŭ'bblȳ-jŏck *n.* (Sc.) turkey-cock. [f. *bubbly* (imit., BUBBLE¹) +*Jock* = *Jack* = *Jack*]

bū'b|ō *n.* (*pl.* ∼**oes**). inflamed swelling in glandular part, esp. groin or armpit; hence ∼ō'NIC *a.* (esp. ∼onic plague, contagious bacterial disease characterized by presence of buboes), ∼ō'NOCELE *n.*, hernia of groin. [L, f. Gk *boubōn* groin]

bŭ'ccal *a.* of the cheek; of or in the mouth. [f. L *bucca* cheek +-AL]

bŭccanee'r *n.*, & *v.i.* (be) pirate, orig. of the Spanish-American coasts; (be) unscrupulous adventurer; hence ∼ISH¹ *a.* [f. F *boucanier* f. *boucaner* cure meat on a *boucan* (i.e. barbecue), f. Tupi *mukem*]

bŭ'ccinātor (-ksī-) *n.* flat thin cheek-muscle. [L, f. *buccinare* blow trumpet (*buccina*); see -OR]

Bu'chman|ism (bōō'k- or bŭ'k-) *n.* (usu. derog.) theories or practice of the Oxford Group Movement; so ∼ITE¹ *a.* [f. F. *Buchman*, Amer. evangelist d. 1961 +-ISM]

bŭck¹ *n.* **1.** male of fallow-deer, roe-deer, reindeer, chamois, antelope, hare, rabbit, ferret, or rat; (arch.) dandy; (*attrib.*, *sl.*) male (*buck nigger*, derog.), *(Mil.) of lowest rank (*buck private* etc.). **2.** ~'**bean**, bog--plant with white or pinkish flowers; ~'**eye**, (*n.*) shrub or tree of genus *Aesculus*, its nut or fruit, (*a.*) *showy but not impressive; *B~**eye State**, Ohio; *~ **fever**, nervousness when called on to act; ~--**horn**, horn of buck as material for knife-handles etc.; ~**-hound**, small variety of staghound; ~ **rarebit**, Welsh rarebit with poached egg; ~'**shot**, coarse shot; ~'**skin**, (leather made of) buck's or similar skin, thick smooth cotton or woollen cloth; ~'**thorn**, thorny shrub with cathartic berries, esp. of genus *Rhamnus*; ~**-tooth**, tooth that projects. [OE *buc* male deer, = OHG *boc*, ON *bukkr* f. Gmc *bukkaz*, and OE *bucca* male goat, f. ON *bukkon*]

bŭck² *v.* **1.** *v.i.* (Of horse) jump vertically with back arched and feet drawn together. **2.** *v.t.* ~ (**off**), throw (rider or burden) thus; *oppose, resist. [f. prec.]

bŭck³ *v.i.* & *t.* (sl.) ~ (**up**), make haste, become or make vigorous or cheerful (esp. in *imper.*); (in *p.p.*) encouraged, elated. [f. BUCK¹ in sense *dandy*]

bŭck⁴ *n.* basket for trapping eels. [19th c.; orig. unkn.]

bŭck⁵ *n.* body of cart; *~'**board**, (vehicle with) body formed by plank on wheels. [perh. f. obs. *bouk* belly, f. OE *būc* f. Gmc *būkaz*]

bŭck⁶ *n.* conversation; boastful talk. [f. Hindi *buk buk*]

bŭck⁷ *n.* (sl.) article placed as reminder before player whose turn it is to deal at poker; **pass the ~**, (colloq.) shift responsibility (*to* another). [19th c.; orig. unkn.]

bŭck⁸ *n.* (US & Austral. sl.) dollar; **a fast ~**, easy money. [19th c.; orig. unkn.]

bŭck⁹ *n.* *saw-horse; vaulting-horse. [f. Du. (*zaag*)*boc*]

bŭ'ckĕt¹ *n.* **1.** round open vessel with handle, for drawing, holding, or carrying water etc.; ~(**ful**), amount contained in this; (in *pl.*) large quantities (of rain, tears, etc.). **2.** compartment of water-wheel; scoop of dredger or grain-elevator. **3. kick the ~**, (sl.) die [perh. f. obs. *bucket* beam, yoke]; ~ **seat** (with rounded back to fit one person); ~**-shop**, office for gambling in stocks, speculating on markets, etc. [ME & AF *buket*, *buquet*, perh. f. OE *būc* pitcher; see -ET¹]

bŭ'ckĕt² *v.i.* & *t.* move or drive jerkily or bumpily; (of rain etc.) pour down heavily. [f. prec.]

bŭ'ckle¹ *n.* flat frame with hinged pin, for securing a strap, belt, etc.; similarly shaped ornament on shoe etc. [ME, f. OF *boucle* f. L *buccula* cheek-strap of helmet (*bucca* cheek; see -ULE)]

bŭ'ckle² *v.t.* & *i.* **1.** fasten (*up*, *on*, etc.) with buckle; ~ (**down**) **to**, prepare for, set about, (work etc.); ~ **to**, get to work, make vigorous start. **2.** ~ (**up**), (cause to) give way, crumple up, under longitudinal pressure. [f. prec.; in sense 2 f. F *boucler* bulge]

bŭ'ckler *n.* (Hist.) small round shield usu. held by a handle; (Bot.) shield-fern. [ME, f. OF *bocler* lit. 'having a boss' (*boucle* BOSS¹; see -ER²)]

Bŭ'ckley's (-lĭz) *n.* & *a.* (Austral. & NZ colloq.) ~ (**chance**), little or no chance. [19th c.; orig. uncert.]

bŭ'ckling *n.* smoked herring. [f. G *bückling* bloater]

bŭ'ckŏ *n.* (*pl.* ~es) & *a.* (Naut. sl.) swaggering or domineering (fellow). [BUCK¹+-o]

bŭ'ckram *n.* & *a.* coarse linen or cloth stiffened with gum or paste; stiff(ness) in manner; **men in ~**, figment (Shak. *1 Henry IV* II. iv. 210–50). [ME, AF *bukeram*, OF *boquerant*, perh. f. *Bokhara* in central Asia]

Bŭcks. *abbr.* Buckinghamshire.

||**bŭ'ckshee** *n.*, *a.*, & *adv.* (sl.) **1.** *n.* something in addition to the usual allowance; something extra or free. **2.** *a.* & *adv.* gratuitous(ly), free of charge. [corrupt. of BAKSHEESH]

bŭ'ckwheat *n.* cereal plant of genus *Fagopyrum*, whose seed is used esp. for horse and poultry food, and in US for breakfast pancakes. [f. MDu. *boecweite* beech wheat, its grains being shaped like beechmast]

būcŏ'l|ic *a.* & *n.* **1.** *a.* of shepherds, pastoral, rustic; hence ~ICALLY *adv.* **2.** *n.* (usu. in *pl.*) pastoral poem, e.g. Virgil's eclogues. [f. L f. Gk *boukolikos* (*boukolos* herdsman f. *bous* ox)]

bŭd¹ *n.* rudiment of shoot, foliage, or flower; leaf or flower not fully open; (Zool.) asexual growth later separating to form new animal; anything still undeveloped; **in ~**, putting forth buds; **nip in the ~**, (fig.) destroy at early stage of development. [ME, of unkn. orig.]

bŭd² *v.i.* & *t.* (-dd-). put forth buds; begin to grow or develop (*budding lawyer*, *cricketer*); (Zool.) form (as) bud; (Hort.) graft bud of (plant) on to another plant. [f. prec.]

*bŭd³ *n.* (colloq.) = BUDDY (esp. as *voc.*). [abbr.]

Bu'ddh|a (bōō'da) *n.* title of successive teachers past and future of the Asian religion ~ISM (3) *n.*, esp. of its founder, the Ind. philosopher Gautama (5th c. BC); hence ~IST (2) *n.* & *a.*, ~**i'st**IC(AL) *adjs.* [Skr., = enlightened, p.p. of *budh* know]

bŭ'ddleia (-lĭa) *n.* shrub or tree of genus *Buddleia*, with fragrant lilac or yellow flowers. [f. A. *Buddle*, Engl. botanist d. 1715 + -IA¹]

bŭ'ddy *n.*, & *v.i.* (colloq.) **1.** *n.* (often as *voc.*) brother, companion, friend. **2.** *v.i.* ~ (**up**), become friendly. [perh. corrupt. of *brother*, or var. of BUTTY¹]

bŭdge *v.* (In neg. sentences). **1.** *v.i.* make slightest movement; change opinion. **2.** *v.t.* compel to budge. [f. F *bouger* stir f. Rom. *bullicare* frequent. of L *bullire* boil]

bŭ'dgerigâr *n.* Austral. grass parakeet, often kept as cage-bird. [Aboriginal, = good cockatoo]

bŭ'dgĕt *n.* & *v.* **1.** *n.* annual estimate of revenue and expenditure of a country or organization; private person's or family's similar estimate; amount of money needed or available; (*attrib.*) inexpensive; **on a ~**, avoiding undue expense; ~ **account, plan**, (with revolving credit and regular payments); hence ~ARY¹ *a.* **2.** (arch.) quantity of material etc., esp. written or printed matter. **3.** *v.i.* & *t.* ~ (**for**), allow or arrange for in budget. [ME = pouch, f. OF *bougette* dim. of *bouge* leather bag f. L *bulga* (f. Gaulish) knapsack; cf. BULGE¹]

bŭ'dgie *n.* (colloq.) = BUDGERIGAR. (abbr.; see -IE)

bŭff¹ *n.* & *a.* (of) velvety dull-yellow ox-leather; human skin (**in the ~**, naked); (of) dull-yellow colour (**the B~s**, former East Kent Regiment, from colour of facings); (colloq.) enthusiast [orig. for watching fires, f. buff uniforms formerly worn by New York volunteer firemen]; ~**-stick**, stick covered with buff for polishing. [orig. sense 'buffalo', prob. f. F *buffle*]

bŭff² *v.t.* polish (metal, finger-nails, etc.); make (leather) velvety like buff. [f. prec.]

bŭ'ffalō *n.* (*pl.* ~es, or same), & *v.t.* **1.** *n.* ox esp. of one of three species: *Bubalus bubalis* of Asia, *Syncerus caffer* of S. Africa, and *Bison bison* of N. America; ||member of a sociable and benevolent organization (*Royal Antediluvian Order of Buffaloes*); amphibious tank. **2.** ~ **chips**, dried dung of buffalo etc. as fuel; *~ **grass**, prairie grass formerly common on buffalo pastures; *~ **robe**, lined trimmed hide of buffalo as rug etc. **3.** *v.t.* *(sl.) overawe, outwit. [prob. f. Port. *bufalo* f. LL *bufalus* f. L f. Gk *boubalos* antelope, wild ox]

bŭ'ffer¹ *n.* & *v.t.* **1.** *n.* apparatus for deadening impact, esp. ||of railway vehicles; (Chem.) substance tending to maintain constant acidity of solution; intermediate store in computer; ~ **solution** (Chem., containing buffer); ~ **state**, small State between two possible belligerents, diminishing chance of hostilities; ~ **stock**, reserve of commodity to offset price fluctuations. **2.** *v.t.* act as buffer to; (Chem.) treat with buffer. [perh. f. obs. *buff* v., imit. of sound of soft body struck, + -ER¹]

bŭ'ffer² *n.* (sl.) (**old**) ~, (old-fashioned or incompetent) fellow. [18th c., prob. f. as prec. or w. sense 'stutterer']

bŭ′ffĕt[1] n., & v.t. (strike with) blow of or as of hand; (of fate etc.) knock, hurt, plague; contend with (waves etc.); hence ~ING[1] (1, 2) n., beating, repeated blows, (Aeron.) irregular oscillation, caused by air eddies, of any part of an aircraft. [ME f. OF, dim. of bufe blow]

bu′ffĕt[2] (bŏŏ′fā) n. **1.** (or bŭ′fĭt). sideboard or recessed cupboard for china, plate, etc. **2.** (place offering) service of food from sideboard or counter where guests or customers serve themselves; ~ **car**, railway coach serving light meals; ~ **meal** (served from sideboard etc.). [F, f. OF bufet stool, of unkn. orig.]

bŭ′fflehead (-fĕlhĕd) n. N. Amer. duck with seemingly over-large head. [f. obs. buffle BUFFALO + HEAD[1]]

buffo (bŏŏ′fō) n. (pl. ~s) & a. burlesque, comic, (actor). [It.]

buffoo′n n., & v.i. (play the) wag, jester, or mocker; hence ~ERY (4) n., ~ISH[1] a. [f. F bouffon f. It. buffone f. med. L buffo clown f. Rom. *buffare puff; see -OON]

bŭg n., & v.t. (-gg-). **1.** n. hemipterous insect, esp. (be′d)~, flat evil-smelling blood-sucking one (Cimex lectularius) infesting beds; *any small insect. **2.** (sl.) micro-organism, esp. virus, or disease caused by it; (person having) obsession; enthusiast; concealed microphone; defect in machine or plan. **3.** BIG bug; ~-eyed, with bulging eyes; ~'house, (sl.) (n.) mental hospital, (a.) *crazy; ~-hunter, (colloq.) entomologist. **4.** v.t. (sl.) install concealed microphone in, listen to by this means; *annoy, bother. **5.** v.i. (sl.) *~ out, leave quickly. [17th c.; orig. unkn.]

bŭ′gaboo, bŭ′gbear (-bār), ns. object of baseless fear; false belief used to intimidate or dissuade; bête noire, cause of annoyance. [bugbear f. obs. bug + BEAR[1]; bugaboo prob. dial.]

bŭ′gger (-g-) n. & v. **1.** n. person who commits buggery. **2.** (vulg.) (esp. unpleasant) person or thing; = DAMN 3; ~-all, nothing. **3.** v.t. commit buggery with. **4.** v.t. & i. (vulg.) = DAMN 2; ~ about, around, persecute, mess about (with); ~ off, go away; ~ (up), ruin, spoil. [ME f. MDu., f. OF bougre, orig. 'heretic' f. med. L Bulgarus Bulgarian (member of Greek Church)]

bŭ′ggerу (-g-) n. sodomy; (Law) bestiality; to ~, (vulg.) = to the DEVIL[1] 8. [ME, f. MDu. buggerie f. OF bougere (as prec.; see -Y[1])]

Bŭ′ggins (-gĭnz) n. ~'s turn, appointment by rotation rather than by merit. ['typical' name used generically]

bŭ′ggy[1] (-gĭ) a. infested with bugs. [f. BUG + -Y[2]]

bŭ′ggy[2] (-gĭ) n. light horse-drawn vehicle for one or two persons; small sturdy motor vehicle (beach, dune, etc. buggy); *pram. [18th c.; orig. unkn.]

bŭ′gle[1] n. & v. **1.** n. ~-horn), brass instrument like small trumpet used by huntsmen and for military signals. **2.** v.i. sound bugle. **3.** v.t. sound (call) on bugle. **4.** Hence **bŭ′glER**[1], **bŭ′glET**[1], ns. [ME, orig. = 'buffalo', f. OF f. L buculus dim. of bos ox]

bŭ′gle[2] n. creeping plant of genus Ajuga with usu. blue flowers. [ME, f. LL bugula]

bŭ′gle[3] n. tube-shaped glass bead sewn on dress etc. for ornament. [16th c.; orig. unkn.]

bŭ′gloss n. plant allied to borage, of various genera, VIPER's bugloss. [f. F buglosse or L f. Gk bouglōssos ox-tongued]

buhl, boule[3]**, boulle,** (bŏŏl) n. & a. (inlaid with) brass, tortoise-shell, etc., cut in ornamental patterns for inlaying. [buhl Germanized) f. A. C. Boule, Fr. wood-carver d. 1732]

build[1] (bĭ-) v. (built pr. bĭ-, arch. ~'ed). **1.** v.t. construct by putting parts or material together (house, ship, nest, vehicle, fire, road, or other structure large or intricate relative to the user); (in p.p.) having specified build (sturdily built, clinker-built, etc.); ~ in, round, up, surround with houses etc., block up; lay (material) in(to wall etc.) as part of structure; built-in, forming integral part of structure, (fig.) personality, etc.; built-up, (1) increased in height etc. by addition of parts, (2) composed of separately

prepared parts, (3, of locality) fully occupied by houses etc. **2.** establish, make (up) or accumulate gradually; base (hopes etc.); ~ up, increase in size or strength, praise, boost; ~'up n., favourable description in advance, gradual approach to a climax or maximum. **3.** v.i. ~ on, rely on; ~ up, gradually establish itself. [OE byldan (bold dwelling f. Gmc *budwell; cf. BOWER[1], BOOTH)]

build[2] (bĭ-) n. style of construction, make; proportions of human body (sturdy build etc.). [f. prec.]

bui′lder (bĭ′-) n. In vbl senses; master builder, contractor for building houses. [f. BUILD[1] + -ER[1]]

bui′lding (bĭ′-) n. In vbl senses; permanent fixed thing built for occupation (house, school, factory, stable, etc.); ~ line, limit relative to frontage beyond which owner may not build; ||~ society (accepting investments at interest, and lending to persons buying houses etc.). [f. BUILD[1] + -ING[1]]

built. See BUILD[1].

bŭlb n. globular base of stem of lily, onion, etc., sending roots downwards and leaves etc. upwards; compressible globular rubber attachment for pneumatic operation of syringe etc.; (Anat.) roundish swelling of any cylindrical organ, as of hair-root or spinal cord; dilated part of glass tube, e.g. reservoir of thermometer; (glass container of) electric lamp; so ~'ous a., of, having, like, bulb(s), (esp. of plant) growing from a bulb. [f. L bulbus f. Gk bolbos onion]

bu′lbul (bŏŏ′lbŏŏl) n. Asian song-thrush; singer, poet. [Pers. f. Arab., of imit. orig.]

Bu′lgar n. native or inhabitant of Bulgaria; so **Bŭlgā′r**IAN a. & n., (native, inhabitant, or language) of Bulgaria. [f. med. L Bulgarus f. OBulg. Blŭgarinŭ]

bŭlge[1] n. convex part, irregular swelling, tendency to swell out, on flat or flatter surface or line; bilge of ship; (colloq.) temporary increase in volume or numbers; (Mil.) salient; (sl.) advantage (esp. in phr. have, or get, the ~ on, have, get, the advantage over); hence **bŭ′lgу**[2] a. [ME, f. OF boulge, bouge f. L bulga; see BUDGET]

bŭlge[2] v.i. & t. swell outwards; be replete; extend (bag etc.) by stuffing it. [f. prec.]

buli′mia n. (Med.) morbid hunger. [mod. L f. Gk boulimia (bous ox, limos hunger)]

bŭlk[1] n. cargo (break ~, begin unloading; in ~, loose, not in package); large quantity (save money by posting in bulk); large shape, person, or body; size, magnitude; great size, mass, large mass; roughage; the greater part or number of; ~ buying, buying in large amounts, purchase by one buyer of all or most of a producer's output. [sense 'cargo' f. OIcel. búlki; sense 'mass' etc. perh. alt. f. obs. bouk (cf. BUCK[5])]

bŭlk[2] **1.** v.i. seem in respect of size or importance (bulk large, larger). **2.** v.t. combine (consignments etc.); make (book, textile yarn, etc.) seem thicker by suitable treatment. [f. prec.]

bŭ′lkhead (-hĕd) n. upright partition separating compartments in ship, aircraft, vehicle, etc. [f. bulk stall f. ON bálkr + HEAD[1]]

bŭ′lk|ў a. of great or too great size; unwieldy; hence ~ILY adv., ~iNESS n. [f. BULK[1] + -Y[2]]

bull[1] n. & a. **1.** n. uncastrated male of ox 2, or any bovine animal (~ in a china shop, reckless or clumsy destroyer; take the ~ by the horns, meet difficulty boldly); male of whale, elephant, and other large animals; (B~) the zodiacal sign Taurus; *(sl.) policeman. **2.** (St. Exch.). one who buys, hoping to sell at higher price later (cf. BEAR[2]); hence ~ISH[1] a., (also, fig.) optimistic. **3.** = bull's-eye (of target). **4.** a. like that of a bull (bull head, neck). **5.** ~ ant, (Austral.) = bulldog ant; ~-at-a-gate, directly attacking; ~'dog (of powerful and courageous large-headed smooth-haired breed, tenacious and courageous (person), (colloq.) (Oxf. & Camb.) University proctor's attendant; ~dog ant, (Austral.) large ant with vicious sting; ~dog clip, fastener with strong closure; ~'**doze** v.t., (colloq.) clear with bulldozer, make one's *way* forcibly, intimidate, coerce; ~'**dozer,** powerful tractor with broad vertical blade in front, used for clearing ground etc.; *~-**fiddle,** (colloq.) double-bass; ~'**fight(ing),** Spanish etc. sport of baiting and usu. killing bull with horsemen etc.; ~'**finch,** (1) strong-beaked handsome-plumaged songbird, (2) quickset hedge with ditch [perh. f. 'bull fence']; ~'**frog,** large Amer. frog with bellowing cry; ~'**head,** small big-headed fish, esp. MILLER's thumb; ~-**headed,** obstinate, impetuous, blundering; ~-**horn,** megaphone; ~ **market** (with rising prices); ~-**nose(d),** with rounded end; ~-**of-the-bog,** bittern; *~'**pen,** exercise area for baseball pitchers; *~-**pine,** ponderosa; ~ **point,** (colloq.) point of superiority; ~-**puncher,** (Austral.) bullock-driver; ~'**ring,** arena for bullfight; ~'**roarer,** flat strip of wood tied to a string, making a roaring sound when whirled round, used esp. in religious rites of Australian Aboriginals; *~ **session,** informal group discussion; ~'**s-eye,** boss of glass formed at centre of blown glass sheet, hemispherical piece or thick disc of glass as light in ship's deck or side, hemispherical lens, (lantern) with such lens, small circular window, centre of target, large round peppermint sweetmeat; ~'**shit,** (vulg.) nonsense, BULL[6]; ~-**terrier,** dog of short-haired breed that is cross between bulldog and terrier; ||~'**trout,** salmon trout. [ME, f. ON *boli* = MLG, MDu. *bulle*]

bull² (bŏŏl) v.i. & t. act or treat violently etc.; (St. Exch.) speculate for a rise; raise price of (stocks etc.). [f. prec.]

bull³ (bŏŏl) n. papal edict. [ME, f. OF *bulle* f. L *bulla* rounded object, in med. L 'seal']

bull⁴ (bŏŏl) n. (Irish) ~, expression containing contradiction in terms or implying ludicrous inconsistency. [17th c.; orig. unkn.]

bull⁵ (bŏŏl) n. drink made of water flavoured by being put in empty spirit cask. [19th c.; orig. unkn.]

bull⁶ (bŏŏl) n. (sl.) unnecessary routine tasks or discipline; nonsense; trivial or insincere talk or writing; *bad blunder. [f. BULL⁴]

bull⁷ (bŏŏl) n. deck-game in which small flat sandbags are thrown on an inclined board marked with numbered squares. [19th c.; orig. unkn.]

bu'llace (bŏŏ'lĭs) n. species of wild (or semi-cultivated) plum-tree (*Prunus insititia*) or its fruit. [ME, f. OF *buloce, beloce* f. Rom. *bulluca* sloe]

bu'llāte (bŏŏ'-) a. (Bot. etc.) having blisters. [f. med. L *bullatus* f. L *bulla* bubble; see -ATE²]

bu'ller (bŏŏ'-) n. (sl.) = BULL¹*dog* (proctor's attendant). [f. *bulldog* + -ER¹ (5)]

bu'llet (bŏŏ'-) n. missile of lead etc. (usu. round, or cylindrical and pointed) used in rifles, revolvers, etc.; ~-**head(ed),** (with) round head; *bullet-PROOF²*. [f. F *boulet, boulette* dim. of *boule* ball f. L *bulla* bubble; cf. -ET¹]

bu'llĕtĭn (bŏŏ'-) n. short official statement or broadcast report of public event or news or of invalid's condition; *board, notice-board. [F, f. It. *bullettino* dim. of *bulletta* passport dim. of *bulla* seal, BULL³]

Bu'llĭ (bŏŏ'-) n. (Austral.) type of soil used for cricket pitches etc. [~ in New South Wales]

bu'llion (bŏŏl'yon) n. metal, esp. gold or silver, before (or as valued apart from) coining or manufacture. [AF, = mint, var. of OF *bouillon* f. Rom. *bullio -onis* (*bullire* BOIL²; see -ION)]

bu'llock¹ (bŏŏ'-) n. bull after castration; ~-**cart,** cart drawn by bullock(s). [OE *bulluc,* dim. of BULL¹; see -OCK]

bu'llock² (bŏŏ'-) v.t. make one's *way* with heavy violence. [f. prec.]

bu'llocky (bŏŏ'-) n. (Austral. & NZ colloq.) bullock-driver. [f. BULLOCK¹ + -Y³]

bu'lly (bŏŏ'-) n. person who uses strength or power to

coerce others by fear; (arch.) pimp; ~(-**boy),** hired ruffian. [orig. as term of endearment, prob. f. MDu. *boele* lover]

bu'lly² (bŏŏ'-) v.t. persecute, oppress, physically or morally, by (threat of) superior force; frighten *into* or *out of.* [f. prec.]

bu'lly³ (bŏŏ'-) a. & int. (sl.) very good, first-rate; ~ **for you, him,** etc., bravo. [perh. f. BULLY¹]

bu'lly⁴ (bŏŏ'-) n., & v.i. (Hockey). **1.** n. procedure for putting ball in play, beginning with threefold striking of two opposing players' sticks. **2.** v.i. ~ **off,** start play in this way. [19th c., perh. f. *bully* scrum in Eton football; orig. unkn.]

bu'lly⁵ (bŏŏ'-) n. ~ (**beef),** corned beef. [f. F *bouilli* boiled beef (*bouillir* BOIL²)]

bu'llyrag (bŏŏ'-) Var. of BALLYRAG.

bu'lly tree (bŏŏ'-) n. = BALATA. [corrupt.]

bu'ln-buln (bŏŏ'-; -bŏŏ-) n. (Austral.) lyre-bird. [Aboriginal, imit.]

bu'lrŭsh (bŏŏl'-) n. kind of tall rush (*Scirpus lacustris*); cat's tail of genus *Typha*; (OT) papyrus plant. [perh. f. BULL¹ = large, coarse, as in *bullfrog, bulltrout,* etc.]

bu'lwark (bŏŏl'-) n. rampart, earthwork, etc.; mole, breakwater; person, principle, etc., that acts as a defence; ship's side above deck. [ME, f. MLG, MDu. *bolwerk;* see BOLE¹, WORK¹]

bŭm¹ n. **1.** (sl.) buttocks. **2.** ||~(-**bailiff**), (Hist.) bailiff employed for arrests [from touching debtor on the back]; ~-**boat** (plying with fresh provisions etc. for ships); ~-**sucker, -sucking,** ||(sl.) toady(ing). [ME *bom,* of unkn. orig.]

*bŭm² n., a., & v. (-mm-). (sl.) **1.** n. habitual loafer or tramp; lazy dissolute person; **on the ~,** vagrant, begging; ~ **rap,** imprisonment on false charge; ~'s **rush,** forcible ejection. **2.** a. of poor quality; ~ **steer,** false information. **3.** v.i. loaf, wander *around,* be a bum. **4.** v.t. get by begging, cadge. [prob. abbr. or back-form. f. BUMMER]

||**bŭ'mble¹** n. self-important official; hence ~DOM (-bëld-). [f. *Bumble,* name of beadle in Dickens's *Oliver Twist;* earlier = jumble, blunderer]

bŭ'mble² v.i. make buzz or hum; ramble *on* in speaking; move or act ineptly or flounderingly. [f. BOOM² + -LE, and partly f. prec. in earlier sense 'blunderer']

bŭ'mble-bee n. large loud-humming bee of genus *Bombus.* [f. prec. + BEE]

bŭ'mble-pŭppy n. unskilful bridge, whist, etc.; game with tennis-ball attached by string to pole. [19th c.; orig. unkn., but cf. BUMBLE²]

||**bŭmf** n. (sl.) toilet-paper; (usu. derog.) papers, documents. [abbr. of *bum-fodder* (BUM¹, FODDER)]

bŭ'mmalō n. (pl. same). small fish (*Harpodon nehereus*) of S. Asian coasts. [perh. f. Marathi *bombíl(a)*]

bŭmmaree' n. (Hist.) middleman at Billingsgate fish-market, London; self-employed licensed porter at Smithfield meat-market, London. [18th c.; orig. unkn.]

*bŭ'mmer n. idler, loafer; unpleasant occurrence. [19th c.; perh. f. G *bummler*]

bŭmp¹ v. & adv. **1.** v.t. push, throw down, (box etc.) *against* or *on* (wall, person, floor, etc.); hurt (one's head etc.) by striking it (*against,* on, or abs.); overtake in boat-race (~'**ing-race;** see foll.); *displace; ~ (**off),** (sl.) murder; ~ **up,** (colloq.) increase (prices etc.). **2.** v.i. come with a bump *against;* go *along* with repeated bumps; (of liquid) boil explosively; ~ **into,** (colloq.) meet by chance. **3.** adv. with a bump, suddenly, violently, (*come, go,* etc., *bump;* cf. BANG³). [16th c., imit., perh. f. Scand.]

bŭmp² n. **1.** dull-sounding blow, knock, collision; (on races where boats start at fixed intervals) overtaking (and touching) of boat by next in line, giving victory to latter (~-**supper,** celebration of success in bumping-races); ~-**ball,** (Cricket) ball hit hard on ground close to bat and coming to fieldsman like possible catch. **2.** swelling caused by bump; uneven patch on road, cricket-pitch, etc.; (Phren.) prominence on skull, faculty supposedly indicated by it, esp. ∼ **of locality**, supposed faculty of recognizing places and finding one's way; (rising air current causing) irregularity in aircraft's motion; (sl.) dancer's forward thrust of abdomen; hence -'Y² *a.* [f. prec.]

bump² *n.*, & *v.i.* (make) bittern's cry. [imit.]

bu'mper *n.* In vbl senses; brim-full glass of wine; anything unusually large or abundant or excellent (usu. attrib.: *bumper harvest, audience*); bar attached to (usu. front or back of) motor vehicle to reduce damage in collisions (∼-to-∼, travelling very close together); *railway buffer; (Cricket) ball that rises high after pitching. [f. BUMP¹ + -ER¹]

∥**bumph.** Var. of BUMF.

bu'mpkin *n.* rustic or awkward fellow. [perh. f. Du. *boomken* little tree or MDu. *bommekijn* little barrel]

bu'mptious (-pshus) *a.* self-assertive, offensively conceited; hence ∼LY² *adv.*, ∼NESS *n.* [joc., f. BUMP¹ after *fractious*]

bun *n.* **1.** small soft round sweet bread or cake with currants etc.; ∥∼-**fight**, (sl.) tea-party; ∼ **in the oven** (sl.), child conceived; **hot cross** ∼ (marked with cross and eaten, usu. hot, on Good Friday); TAKE¹ *the bun.* **2.** (Sc.) rich fruit cake or currant bread. **3.** hair dressed in bun shape. [ME, of unkn. orig.]

bu'na (bū'-, boo'-) *n.* synthetic rubber made by polymerization of butadiene. [G (as BUTADIENE, *natrium* sodium)]

Bu'nbury *n.* fictitious excuse for making visit or avoiding obligation. [f. use in Wilde's *Importance of Being Earnest*]

bunch¹ *n.* cluster of things growing or fastened together (*bunch of flowers, grapes, keys*); lot, collection, (*best of the bunch*); (sl.) gang, group; ∼ **grass**, N. Amer. grass growing in clumps; hence ∼'Y² *a.* [ME; orig. unkn.]

bunch² *v.* **1.** *v.t.* make into bunch(es); gather (material) into close folds. **2.** *v.i.* form group or crowd. [f. prec.]

***bu'nco** *n.* (*pl.* ∼s), & *v.t.* (sl.) swindle (esp. by card-sharping or confidence trick); ∼-**steerer**, swindler. [perh. f. Sp. *banca* a card-game]

buncombe. Var. of BUNKUM.

bund *n.* (In Far East) embankment, causeway, quay. [f. Hind. *band*, f. Pers.]

bu'nder *n.* (Ind.) landing-place, quay, harbour; ∼-**boat** (used for coastal and harbour work). [f. Hind. *bandar*, f. Pers.]

Bundestag (bōō'ndeztahg) *n.* Lower House of Parliament in Federal Republic of Germany. [G (*bund* federation, *tagen* confer)]

bu'ndle¹ *n.* **1.** collection of things loosely fastened together (esp. clothes, papers, or odds and ends in handkerchief or paper); set of sticks, rods, etc., bound up; set of parallel fibres, NERVES, etc. **2.** (sl.) large amount of money; **do** or **go a** ∼ **on**, be very fond of (thing). [ME, perh. f. OE *byndelle* a binding, but also f. LG & Du. *bundel*]

bu'ndle² *v.* **1.** *v.t.* tie in or make *up* into a bundle; throw confusedly *into* any receptacle; put or send (esp. person) in a hurry or unceremoniously *out, off, away*, etc. **2.** *v.t.* & *i.* ∼ **up**, dress warmly or cumbersomely. **3.** *v.i.* sleep clothed *with* another person (esp. as local custom during courtship). [f. prec.]

bu'ndobust *n.* (Ind.) arrangements, organization. [f. Hind. *band-o-bast* tying and binding]

bung¹ *n.* stopper, esp. large cork stopping hole in cask; brewer or publican; ∼-**ho'** (excl. at parting or as toast); ∼-**hole** (for filling or emptying cask). [f. MDu. *bonghe*]

bung² *v.t.* stop (cask) with bung (∼ed **up**, closed, blocked); (sl.) throw, toss. [f. prec.]

bung³ *a.* (Austral. & NZ sl.) dead; ruined, useless. [Aboriginal]

bu'ngalow (-nggalō) *n.* one-storeyed house; hence

∼OID *a.*, (usu. derog.) resembling a bungalow, consisting of bungalows. [orig. in India, f. Gujarati *bangalo* f. Hind. *banglā* belonging to Bengal]

bu'ngle (-nggel) *v.i.* & *t.*, & *n.* (make) clumsy work, confusion; blunder over, fail to accomplish, (task); hence ∼ER¹ *n.* [imit.; cf. BUMBLE²]

bu'nion (-yon) *n.* swelling on foot, esp. at first joint of big toe. [f. OF *buignon* (*buigne* bump on head)]

bunk¹ *n.* sleeping-berth, esp. one of two or more arranged one above another; ∼-**bed**, piece of furniture comprising two bunks. [19th c.; orig. unkn.]

bunk² *v.i.*, & *n.* (sl.) (**do a**) ∼, make off, vanish. [19th c.; orig. unkn.]

bunk³ *n.* (sl.) nonsense, humbug. [abbr. of BUNKUM]

bu'nker *n.*, & *v.t.* **1.** *n.* container for fuel; (Golf) pit containing sand etc. and constituting a hazard; (Mil.) reinforced underground shelter. **2.** *v.t.* fill bunkers of (ship etc.); (usu. in *p.p.*) trap in bunker, (fig.) bring into difficulties. [19th c.; orig. unkn.]

bu'nkum *n.* nonsense; ostentatious talking. [orig. *buncombe*, f. *Buncombe* County in N. Carolina, whose member spoke needlessly in Congress *c.* 1820 to impress his constituents]

bu'nny *n.* (Child's name for) rabbit; ∼ (**girl**), club hostess wearing costume suggestive of rabbit. [f. *bun* rabbit + -Y³]

Bu'nsen *n.* ∼ **burner** (burning air with gas for heating substances in chemical laboratories etc.). [f. R. W. ∼, Ger. chemist d. 1899]

bunt¹ *n.* cavity or baggy part of fishing-net, sail, etc.; ∼'**line** (confining bunt when furling sail). [16th c.; orig. unkn.]

bunt² *n.* disease of wheat caused by smut-ball fungus of genus *Tilletia*. [18th c.; orig. unkn.]

bunt³ *v.* & *n.* **1.** *v.t.* & *i.* push with head or horns, butt. **2.** *v.t.* *(Baseball)* stop (ball) with bat without swinging. **3.** *n.* act of bunting. [19th c.; cf. BUTT⁴]

bu'ntal *n.* straw from talipot palm. [Tagalog]

bu'nting¹ *n.* bird of sub-family Emberizinae, allied to finches. [ME; orig. unkn.]

bu'nting² *n.* (loosely-woven fabric used for) flags and festive decorations. [18th c.; orig. unkn.]

bu'nya *n.* (Austral.) tall tree (*Araucaria bidwillii*) bearing large nutritious cones. [Aboriginal]

bu'nyip *n.* (Austral.) fabulous monster of swamps and lagoons. [Aboriginal]

buoy¹ (boi) *n.* anchored float showing navigable course or reefs etc.; (**li'fe**)∼, device (usu. ring) to keep person afloat; hence ∼'AGE (1, 3, 4) *n.* [ME, prob. f. MDu. *bo(e)ye*, perh. f. OF *boie* chain f. L *boia*, pl. *boiae* f. Gk *boeiai* (*dorai*) ox-hides, ox-leather straps]

buoy² (boi) *v.t.* **1.** ∼ (**up**), keep afloat; sustain (person, courage, etc.), uplift, encourage. **2.** mark (*out*) with buoy(s). [sense 1 f. Sp. *boyar* (see BUOYANT); sense 2 f. prec.]

buo'yancy (boi'-) *n.* floating power on liquid or in air; resilience, recuperative power, (of spirits, also of stock-market prices, etc.); cheerfulness. [f. foll.; see -ANCY]

buo'yant (boi'-) *a.* apt to float, rise, keep up, or recover; able to keep things up; light-hearted; hence ∼LY² *adv.* [f. F *buoyant* or Sp. *boyante* part. of *boyar* float (*boya* BUOY¹), f. base + -ANT)]

bur, burr³, *n.* (any plant with) clinging seed-vessel or flower; person hard to shake off; = BURR¹ 1; ∼ **oak**, N. Amer. oak with large fringed acorn-cups. [ME; cf. Da. *burre* bur, burdock, Sw. *kard-borre* burdock]

bu'rble *v.i.* speak ramblingly; make murmuring noise; (Aeron.) of air-flow; break up into turbulence. [19th c., imit.]

bu'rbot *n.* eel-like flat-headed bearded freshwater fish (*Lota lota*). [ME; cf. OF *barbote*]

bur'den¹ *n.* load (lit., or of labour, duty, sorrow, etc.); ∼ **of proof**, obligation to prove one's assertion); obligatory expense; (also arch. **bur'then** *pr.* -dh-) ship's carrying-capacity, tonnage; bearing of loads (*ship*, *beast*, *of burden*); refrain, chorus, of song [partly f. BOURDON]; chief theme or gist of poem, book, speech, etc.; hence ∿SOME¹ *a*. [OE *byrthen*, = OS *burthinnia* f. WG **burthinnja* (**burthi*- BIRTH, **-innja* -EN³); for -*d*- cf. *murder*]

bur'den², (arch.) **bur'then** (-dh-), *v.t.* load (lit. or fig.), encumber; oppress. [f. prec.]

bur'dock *n.* coarse weed of genus *Arctium*, with prickly flower-heads and docklike leaves. [f. BUR + DOCK¹]

bureau (būr'ō, -ō') *n.* (*pl.* ∿x *or* ∿s, *pr.* -ōz). **1.** ‖writing-desk with drawers; *chest of drawers. **2.** office or department for transacting specific business; government department. [F, = desk, orig. its baize covering, f. OF *burel* (*bure*, *buire* dark brown f. Rom. *burius dark red f. L *burrus* bright red f. Gk *purros* red)]

bureau'|cracy (būrŏ'-) *n.* government by central administration; officialism or officials of such government; so ∿CRAT (būr'o-) *n.*, (esp. unimaginative) official in bureaucracy, ∿crā'tic (būr'o-) *a.*, ∿cratIZE (3) *v.t.* [f. F *bureaucratie* (as prec.; see -CRACY)]

bur̆ĕ'tte, ***būr̆ĕ't**, *n.* graduated glass tube with end-tap for measuring small quantities of liquid in chemical analysis. [F]

*bur̄g *n.* (colloq.) town or city. [see BOROUGH]

bur'gage *n.* (Hist.) tenure of land in town on yearly rent. [ME, f. med. L *burgagium* (*burgus* BOROUGH; see -AGE)]

burgee' *n.* triangular or swallow-tailed flag bearing colours or emblem of yacht club or sailing club. [19th c.; perh. for *∿'*s flag*, with ∿ = 'owner' f. F *bourgeois* f. OF *burgeis* (see BURGESS)]

bur'geon (-jŏn) *n.*, & *v.i.* (literary). (put forth, spring forth as) young shoot(s); bud; (fig.) begin to grow rapidly. [ME, f. OF *bor-*, *burjon* f. Rom. *burrio -onis f. LL *burra* wool]

*bur'ger (-g-) *n.* (colloq.) hamburger; (in comb.) food resembling hamburger (*beefburger*, *nutburger*). [abbr.]

bur'gess *n.* ‖inhabitant of borough with full municipal rights, citizen; ‖(Hist.) member of parliament for borough, corporate town, or university; *borough magistrate or governor. [ME f. OF *burgeis* f. Rom. *burgensis f. LL *burgus* BOROUGH]

burgh (bŭ'rŏ) *n.* (Sc.) borough, chartered town; hence ∿AL (bĕr'gal) *a.* [Sc. form of BOROUGH]

bur'gher (-ger) *n.* freeman or citizen of a foreign town; (S. Afr., Hist.) citizen of a Boer republic; descendant of Dutch or Portuguese colonist in Sri Lanka. [f. G or Du. *burger* (*burg* BOROUGH; see -ER¹)]

bur'glar *n.* one who enters building illegally (in Engl. law formerly by night only) with intent to commit felony; hence ∿Y¹ *n.*, **bur̄glār'ious** *a.*, *∿IZE (1) *v.t.* [f. legal AF *burgler* = AL *burg(u)lator*, f. *burg-pillage]

bur'gle *v.* **1.** *v.i.* commit burglary. **2.** *v.t.* rob by burglary. [19th c.; back-form. f. prec.]

bur'gomaster (-ah-) *n.* mayor of Dutch or Flemish town. [f. Du. *burgemeester* (*burg* BOROUGH), assim. to MASTER¹]

bur̆ĕ'gonĕt *n.* (Hist.) visored helmet. [f. F *bourguignotte* perh. fem. of *bourguignot* Burgundian (*Bourgogne* Burgundy); assim. to -ET¹]

burgoo' *n.* (Naut. sl.) porridge; *soup or stew for outdoor meal. [f. Arab. *burģul* f. Turk. *bulgur* bruised grain]

bur'grāve *n.* (Hist.) ruler of town or castle. [f. G *burggraf* (*burg* BOROUGH, *graf* COUNT³ f. OLG *grēve*)]

bur'gundy *n.* (usu. red) wine of Burgundy in E. France; similar wine from other countries; red colour of such wine.

bu'rhel (-rĕl). Var. of BHARAL.

bu'rial (bĕ'-) *n.* burying, esp. of dead body; funeral; (Archaeol.) instance of burial; ∿-ground, cemetery; ∿-service, religious ceremony at funeral. [ME, erron. formed as sing. of OE *byrgels* f. Gmc *burgisli (**burg-* BURY, **-isli*; cf. RIDDLE¹)]

bur̄'in *n.* tool for engraving on copper or wood; (Archaeol.) chisel-pointed flint tool. [F]

bur̆k. See BERK.

bur̄'ka *n.* Muslim woman's long enveloping garment worn in public. [Hind., f. Arab. *burḳa'*]

burke¹ *v.t.* avoid, smother, (publicity, inquiry); hush up, suppress, (rumour). [f. W. *Burke*, executed in 1829 for smothering people to sell bodies for dissection]

‖**Burke²** *n.* (colloq.) (Used for) '∿'s Peerage etc.' [f. John ∿, compiler d. 1848]

burl *n.* knot in wool or cloth or *wood. [ME, f. OF *bourle* tuft of wool, dim. of *bourre* coarse wool f. LL *burra* wool]

bur'lăp *n.* coarse canvas esp. of jute for sacking etc.; similar material for dress or furnishing. [17th c.; orig. unkn.]

burlě'sque (-k) *a.* & *n.*, & *v.t.* **1.** imitative, imitation, imitate, for purpose of deriding or amusing; bombast(ic), mock-serious(ness); caricature, parody, esp. (of) literary or dramatic work. **2.** *n.* *variety show freq. featuring strip-tease. [F, f. It. *burlesco* (*burla* mockery; see -ESQUE)]

bur'ly *a.* sturdy; big and strong; hence ∿ıNESS *n.* [ME *borli*(*ch*) prob. f. OE *bŭrlic fit for the BOWER¹; see -LY¹]

Bur'man *a.* & *n.* = foll. [f. *Burma* + -AN]

Bur̆me'se (-z) *a.* & *n.* (*pl.* same). (native or language) of Burma. [f. *Burma* + -ESE]

burn¹ *n.* (Sc.) small stream. [OE *burna* etc., = MDu. *borne*, & Gmc *brunnon, -*az*; cf. BOURN¹]

burn² *v.t.* & *i.* (∿t *or* ∿ed). **1.** consume, be consumed, waste, by fire, (of heat, person heating, or heated thing; ∿ one's **boats** or **bridges**, commit oneself irrevocably to a course); blaze or glow with fire; use energy of (propellant, nuclear fuel); **money to** ∿ (in great abundance). **2.** give or cause to give light (of lamp, candles, gas, oil, electricity, etc.); burn CANDLE *at both ends*, DAYLIGHT, *the midnight* OIL¹. **3.** put or be put to death by fire. **4.** subject (clay, chalk, etc.) to heat for a purpose; harden (bricks), make (lime, charcoal) by heat; ∿ *sacrifice*, make (hole etc.) by heat (**money ∿s hole in pocket**, one is eager to spend it). **6.** injure or damage, be injured or damaged, by fire, sun's rays, or great heat (∿ one's **fingers**, suffer for meddling or rashness); char or scorch in cooking, (cause to) adhere to pan etc. and char; cauterize, brand; eat, make acid etc. eat, its way (*into* material). **7.** parch, colour, with heat or sunlight (*brown*, *dry*, etc., or abs.). **8.** give or feel sensation or pain (as) of heat; ears ∿ (esp., allegedly, when one is talked of). **9.** make or be hot or passionate; glow, rage, yearn; (sl.) drive fast. **10.** ∿ **away**, diminish to nothing by burning; ∿ **down**, burn less vigorously as fuel fails, destroy (building) by burning; ∿ **in**, imprint by burning (lit. or fig.); ∿ **low** (nearly out); ∿ **out**, burn away, (make) fail by burning, consume contents of by burning (also fig.), make homeless by burning of house; ∿ **up**, get rid of by fire, flash into blaze, *(sl.) be or make furious. **11.** ∿'**ing-glass**, lens to concentrate sun's rays on object and burn it; ∿t **almond** (enclosed in burnt sugar); ∿t **cork** (used to blacken face etc.); ∿t **ochre**, SIENNA, UMBER, (calcined to deeper colour); ∿t **offering**, sacrifice offered by burning. [OE *birnan* v.i., *bærnan* v.t., f. Gmc **bren-* etc.]

burn³ *n.* sore or mark made by burning; provision of thrust by engine of spacecraft; (US etc.) forest area cleared by burning; (sl.) cigarette; (sl.) car race. [f. prec.]

bur'ner *n.* In vbl senses: part of lamp, gas cooker, etc., that shapes the flame; **on the front, back,** ∿, (sl.) receiving much, little, attention. [f. BURN² + -ER¹]

bur'net *n.* brown-flowered plant of genus *Sanguisorba* or *Poterium*; diurnal moth, greenish-black with crimson spots on wings. [f. obs. *burnet* a. dark brown f. OF *burnete*; see BRUNET]

||**Bur'nham** (-nam) *n.* ~ **scale**, national salary scale (since 1924) for teachers in maintained schools. [f. Lord ~, chairman of committee which recommended this scale]

bur'ning *a.* In vbl senses; ardent (*burning desire*); flagrant (*burning shame*); hotly discussed, exciting, (*burning question*); ~ **bush**, (1) one of various shrubs with red fruits or red autumn leaves (w. ref. to Exod. 3:2), (2) fraxinella. [f. BURN² + -ING²]

bur'nish *v.t.* polish by rubbing. [ME, f. OF *burnir* = *brunir* (*brun* BROWN¹); see -ISH²]

bur'nou's (-ōō's) *n.* Arab or Moorish hooded cloak. [F, f. Arab. *burnus* f. Gk *birros* cloak]

burnt. See BURN².

burp *n.*, & *v.i.* & *t.* (sl.) (cause to) belch; *~ **gun**, automatic pistol. [imit.]

burr¹ *n.* **1.** rough edge left on cut or punched metal or paper; surgeon's or dentist's small drill. **2.** siliceous rock used for millstones; whetstone; kind of limestone. **3.** rough sounding of letter *r*; whirring sound. **4.** coronet of deer's antler. [var. of BUR]

burr² *v.t.* & *i.* pronounce with burr; speak indistinctly; make whirring sound. [f. prec.]

burr³. See BUR.

bu'rrawäng (-a-w-) *n.* (Austral.) (nut of) a palmlike tree of genus *Macrozamia*. [f. Mount *Budawang* in New South Wales]

*bu'rro *n.* (*pl.* ~s). (colloq.) small donkey used as pack-animal. [Sp.]

bu'rrow (-ō) *n.*, & *v.i.* & *t.* (make or live in) hole excavated in earth, as of foxes, rabbits, etc.; make by excavating (hole, one's way); hide oneself; ~ **into**, (fig.) investigate mysteries etc. of; hence ~ER¹ *n.* [ME, app. var. of BOROUGH]

bur's|a *n.* (*pl.* ~ae *or* ~as). (Anat. & Zool.) sac or saclike cavity to lessen friction; hence ~AL *a.*, ~I' TIS *n.* [med. L, = bag; cf. PURSE¹]

bur'sar *n.* treasurer; person in charge of funds and other property of college etc.; holder of bursary; hence ~SHIP *n.*, (csp.) endowment given to student. [f. F *boursier* or (in first sense) med. L *bursarius* (BURSA; see -AR²)]

bursar'ial *a.* of bursar(y). [f. prec. + -AL]

bur'sary *n.* bursarship; bursar's room in college etc. [f. med. L *bursaria* (as BURSAR; see -ARY¹)]

bursi'tis. See BURSA.

burst¹ *v.t.* & *i.* (burst). **1.** fly by expansion of contents or internal pressure, or break (containing case), violently asunder; split; be rent about to burst because of excitement etc. **2.** get away from or through, make way *out* or *in*, or express one's feelings, by force or suddenly (*river bursts banks*). **3.** open, come open, or be opened, forcibly (*abscess, bud, cloud, bursts; burst door, door bursts, open*). **4.** fill or be full to overflowing. **5.** appear or come suddenly (*burst into flame, upon the view; sun burst out*). **6.** suffer bursting of (some part; *burst a blood-vessel*, (fig.) one's sides *with laughing*). **7.** ~ **in**, come in abruptly, break in by violence; ~ **into**, suddenly begin to utter etc. (song, laughter, tears); ~ **out**, go out abruptly, exclaim, suddenly begin (laughing etc.). [OE *berstan*, = OS, OHG *brestan*, ON *bresta* f. Gmc *brestan*]

burst² *n.* bursting, split; sudden issuing forth (*burst of flame*), explosion, outbreak, (lit. or fig., *burst of applause, firing*); = SPURT¹; ~'**proof**, (of door lock) able to withstand violent impact. [f. prec.]

burthen. See BURDEN¹,².

bur'ton¹ *n.* light handy two-block tackle. [f. ME BRETON tackles]

||**bur'ton²** *n.* (sl.) **go for a** ~, be lost, destroyed, or killed. [20th c.; perh. f. *Burton* ale f. B~-*on-Trent* in Staffordshire]

bu'ry (bě'rĭ) *v.t.* **1.** deposit (corpse etc.) in earth, tomb, or sea; lose by death (*has buried three husbands*); put under ground (*bury alive*; ~ **the hatchet** or *tomahawk*, cease to quarrel); hide (treasure etc.) in earth; cover up, submerge; ~ing-**beetle**, sexton

beetle; ~**ing-ground**, ~**ing-place**, cemetery. **2.** put away, forget; consign to obscurity; put out of sight (face *in* hands, hands *in* pockets); involve deeply (*bury* oneself *in* one's *work*). [OE *byrgan* f. WG *burgjan* (*burg-* st. of Gmc *bergan* shelter, protect; cf. BURIAL)]

bus *n.* (*pl.* ~'ses) & *v.* (*-ss-*). **1.** large passenger vehicle running on fixed route; (colloq.) aeroplane, motor car, etc.; MISS² *the bus*; ~'**bar**, (Electr.) system of conductors carrying all power to or from a station; *~'**boy**, waiter's assistant; ~-**conductor**, (1) conductor of bus, (2) busbar; ||~ **lane**, strip of road for use mainly by buses; ~'**man**, driver of a bus (~*man's holiday*, leisure time spent in same kind of occupation as one's regular work); ~-**shelter**, roadside structure for protection against rain etc. for persons waiting for bus; *bus* STATION; ~-**stop**, regular stopping-place of bus. **2.** *v.i.* go by bus. **3.** *v.t.* *transport by bus (esp. schoolchildren to counteract racial segregation). [abbr. of OMNIBUS]

||**bu'sby** (-z-) *n.* tall fur cap of hussars and guardsmen. [18th c.; orig. unkn.]

bush¹ (bŏŏ-) *n.* **1.** shrub or clump of shrubs with stems of moderate length (BEAT¹ *about the bush*); bunch of ivy as ancient vintner's sign (*good wine needs no* ~, only the inferior needs advertisement); luxuriant growth of hair etc. **2.** woodland, forest, untilled district, (esp. in Australia, NZ, Afr.); **go** ~, (Austral.) leave one's usual surroundings, run wild. **3.** ~-**baby**, galago; *bush* BASIL; ~'**buck**, small S. Afr. antelope; ~'**craft**, skill in living in the bush; ~-**fighting**, fighting in the bush, guerrilla warfare; ~ **jacket**, belted cotton jacket; ~ **lawyer**, (NZ) a bramble, (Austral. & NZ) layman pretending to legal knowledge; *~ **league**, minor baseball league; B~'**man**, aboriginal or language of a S. Afr. people [after Du. *boschjesman* (*bosch* bush)]; ~'**man**, dweller, farmer, or traveller in the Australian bush; ~'**manship**, bushcraft; ~'**master**, venomous S. Amer. snake; ~-**ranger**, (Hist.) Australian brigand living in the bush; ~ **shirt**, = *bush jacket*; ~ **sickness**, disease of animals due to lack of cobalt in soil; ~ **telegraph**, rapid spreading of information, rumour, etc.; ~'**veld** (-fĕlt), veld composed largely of bush, wooded region in Transvaal; ~-**whacker**, one who clears land of bush, backwoodsman, *(Hist.) deserter or guerrilla. [ME, partly f. OE *bysc*, partly f. ON *buski*, partly (cf. BOSKY) f. OF *bos(c)*, all ult. f. Gmc *busk-*]

bush² (bŏŏ-) *n.*, & *v.t.* **1.** *n.* metal lining of axle-hole or other circular orifice; perforated plug; box or bearing in which shaft revolves; (Electr.) insulating sleeve. **2.** *v.t.* furnish with bush. [f. MDu. *busse* BOX²]

bushed (bŏŏsht) *a.* (Austral. & NZ colloq.) lost in the bush, bewildered; *(colloq.) tired out. [f. BUSH¹ + -ED²]

bu'shel¹ (bŏŏ'-) *n.* measure of capacity (||8 gallons, *32 quarts) for corn, fruit, ||liquids, etc., (hide one's **light under a** ~, conceal one's merits); hence ~FUL 2 *n.* [ME, f. OF *buissiel* etc., perh. of Gaulish orig.]

*bu'shel² (bŏŏ'-) *v.t.* & *i.* mend or alter (clothes). [perh. f. G *bosseln* do odd jobs]

bu'shido (bŏŏ'shē-) *n.* code of honour and morals evolved by the samurai. [Jap., = military knight's way]

bu'shing (bŏŏ'-) *n.* = BUSH². [f. BUSH² + -ING¹ (3)]

bu'shy¹ (bŏŏ'-) *n.* (Austral. & NZ) dweller in the bush. [f. BUSH¹ + -Y³]

bu'shy² (bŏŏ'-) *a.* having many bushes; growing thickly; covered with bush; hence ~INESS *n.* [f. BUSH¹ + -Y²]

busily. See BUSY¹.

bu'siness (bĭ'zn-) *n.* **1.** task, duty, province, (**make it one's** ~, undertake *to*); cause of coming (*what is your business?*). **2.** habitual occupation, profession, trade; **~ as usual**, things will proceed normally despite disturbances; *business* CARD²; *~ **cycle**, trade cycle; ~ **hours** (of regular work, of shop or office opening);

∼ **studies,** training in economics, management, etc.; *∼ **suit,** lounge suit; BIG *business;* **in** ∼, trading or dealing, (fig.) able to begin operations. **3.** serious work; ∼ **end,** (colloq.) working end of tool etc.; **get down to** ∼, begin in earnest; **mean** ∼, be in earnest; **on** ∼, with definite purpose, esp. one relating to business (sense 2). **4.** thing needing attention, agenda, (*the business of the day, meeting,* etc.); dealings with men and matters. **5.** difficult matter (*what a business it is!*; *make a great business of it*). **6.** thing that concerns one, that one may meddle with; **mind your own, go about your, send about his,** ∼ (expr. reproof of meddlesomeness, or dismissal); **has no** ∼ to (no right); **like nobody's** ∼, (colloq.) extraordinarily. **7.** (derog.) concern, affair, structure, (*sick of the whole business*; *a lath-and-plaster business*); (sl.) all that is available (cf. WORK¹ 9). **8.** (Theatr.) action on stage. **9.** buying and selling, trade, (*doing a great business*; *good stroke of business*); ∼ **man, woman,** (engaged in trade or commerce); ∼ **is** ∼, commercial considerations have priority; **do** person's ∼, (sl.) ruin or kill him. **10.** commercial house, firm. **11.** Hence ∼-LIKE *a.*, practical, systematic. [OE *bisignis* (as BUSY¹, -NESS)]

bü′sker *n.* itinerant musician or actor, esp. performing in street; so **bü′sk**ING¹,² *a.* & *n.* [f. *busk* peddle etc. (perh. f. obs. F *busquer* seek)]

bü′skin *n.* thick-soled boot lending height to ancient Athenian tragic actor; (fig.) tragic drama; (Hist.) half-boot; hence ∼ED² (-nd) *a.* [prob. f. OF *bouzequin*, var. of *bro(u)sequin*, of unkn. orig.]

büss *n.*, & *v.t.* (arch. or *colloq.) kiss. [earlier *bass* n. & v.; cf. F *baiser*, f. L *basiare*]

büst¹ *n.* **1.** sculpture of person's head, shoulders, and chest. **2.** upper front of body, bosom, esp. of woman; circumference of this; hence ∼′Y² *a.*, (of woman) having prominent bust. [f. F *buste* f. It. *busto*, of unkn. orig.]

büst² *n.* & *v.* (∼′ed *or* ∼). (colloq.) **1.** *n.* sudden failure; worthless thing; bad hand at cards; drinking-bout. **2.** *v.t.* & *i.* burst, break; dismiss, reduce to lower rank; arrest; ∼ **up,** explode, bring or come to collapse; ∼-**up** *n.*, explosion, quarrel, collapse; hence ∼′ER *n.*, (esp.) violent gale, (sl., as form of usu. disrespectful address) mate, fellow. [f. BURST¹,²]

büst³, bü′stĕd, *adjs.* (colloq.) broken, burst, collapsed; bankrupt. [f. prec.]

bü′stard *n.* large swift-running bird of genus *Otis.* [ME, perh. f. AF *bustarde,* mixture of OF *bistarde, oustarde,* both f. L *avis tarda* slow bird (the inappropriate adj. unexplained)]

bü′stee *n.* (Ind.) shanty town, slum. [f. Hind. *bastī* dwelling]

bü′stle¹ (-sel) *v.* **1.** *v.i.* bestir oneself; make show of activity, hurry *about*; hence **bü′stl**ING² (-sl-) *a.*, full of activity. **2.** *v.t.* make (person) hurry or work hard. [perh. var. of obs. *buskle* frequent. of obs. *busk* prepare (ON *búask* refl. of *búa* prepare; cf. BOUND⁵); see -LE 3]

bü′stle² (-sel) *n.* excited activity, fuss. [f. prec.]

bü′stle³ (-sel) *n.* (Hist.) pad or frame puffing out top of woman's skirt at back. [18th c.; orig. unkn.]

bu′sÿ¹ (bĭ′zĭ) *a.* & *n.* **1.** *a.* occupied, working, engaged, with attention concentrated, (*in, with, at*; also, prep. being dropped, with vbl n. now looking like part.: *he was busy packing*); full of activity or detail; (of telephone line) engaged; unresting, ever employed, (*busy as a bee*); fussy, meddlesome, prying; ∼**body,** meddlesome person, mischief-maker; ∼ **Lizzie,** house-plant of genus *Impatiens*; hence **bu′s**ĬLY² (bĭ′z-) *adv.*, ∼NESS *n.* **2.** *n.* (sl.) detective. [OE *bisig*, = MLG, MDu. *besich,* of unkn. orig.]

bu′sÿ² (bĭ′zĭ) *v.t.* occupy (esp. one*self*, one's *hands,* etc.), keep busy, (*with, in, at, about, doing,* or abs.). [OE *bisgian* (as prec.)]

but¹ (*or, when stressed,* bŭt) (orig. *adv.* & *prep.* = outside, without; developed into *conj.*, under which most mod. uses belong; is now *adv., prep.*, negative *rel. pron.*,

& *conj.*; clear distinction of these is not possible here). **1.** only, no more than, (*she is but a child*; *it was used but once*; *I can but do it*). **2.** except, if not, short of, except that, if it were not that, short of the condition that, (*they are all wrong but he* or *him*; *no one but me* or *I*; *but for you, but that you came, I should have drowned*; *never saw her but once*; *he all but did it*; *what can he do but die?*; *nothing would content him but I must come*); last, next, etc. ∼ **one, two,** etc., if one, two, etc., were excluded from the count. **3.** other(wise) than (*cannot choose but, cannot but, do it*); ANYTHING *but.* **4.** who or that not (*no one but knows that*). **5.** without the result etc. that (*never rains but it pours*; *justice was never done but someone complained*). **6.** rather than so-and-so shall prove untrue (*it shall go HARD but I will get there*); that not (*not such a fool but knows that*). **5.** without the result etc. that (*never rains but it pours*; *justice was never done but someone complained*). **6.** rather than so-and-so shall prove untrue (*it shall go HARD but I will get there*); that not (*not such a fool but knows that*). **5.** without the result etc. that (*never rains but it pours*; *justice was never done but someone complained*). **6.** rather than so-and-so shall prove untrue (*it shall go HARD but I will get there*); that not (*not such a fool but knows that*) —also *but that, but what*—*he can see the reason*). **7.** to say (that) not (*who knows but that*—also (colloq.) *but what*—*it is true*?; NOT *but that* or *what*). **8.** ∼ **that,** (after neg.) that (*I don't deny, doubt, but that*). **9.** ∼ (**then, yet**), on the contrary, nevertheless, however, on the other hand, moreover, yet. **10.** (Introducing emphasized word) *it must be used always, but always.* [OE *be-ūtan, būtan, būta* outside, without, = OS *biūtan,* OHG *biūzan* f. WG **be, *bi* BY¹ + **ūtana* from outside]

bŭt² *n.* & *v.t.* (-tt-). **1.** *n.* an objection (*ifs and buts*). **2.** *v.t.* utter or use ('but'); ∼ **me no** ∼**s,** do not raise objections. [f. prec.]

bŭt³. See BEN¹.

būtadī′ēne *n.* (Chem.) gas used in making synthetic rubber. [f. BUTANE + DI-² + -ENE; cf. BUNA]

bū′tāne *n.* (Chem.) hydrocarbon of the paraffin series, C_4H_{10}, used in liquefied form as fuel. [f. BUTYL + -ANE]

butch (bŏŏ-) *n.* (often *attrib.*) (sl.) tough youth or man; mannish woman; *∼ **haircut,** crew cut. [perh. abbr. of foll.]

bu′tcher (bŏŏ′-) *n.* **1.** one who slaughters animals for food; dealer in meat (**the** ∼, **the baker, the candlestick-maker,** people of all trades); *(colloq.) seller of sweets etc. on train; judge, general, etc., who has men killed needlessly or brutally. **2.** ∼-**bird,** shrike esp. of genus *Lanius*; ∼-**boots,** high boots without tops; ∼'**s-broom,** low spiny-leaved evergreen shrub; ∼'**s** (**hook**), (rhyming sl.) a look; ∼'**s meat** (excluding poultry, game, and bacon etc.). **3.** Hence ∼LY¹ *a.* [ME, f. OF *bo(u)chier* (*boc* BUCK¹)]

bu′tcher² (bŏŏ′-) *v.t.* slaughter or cut up (animal); kill (people) wantonly or cruelly; ruin by bad performance etc. [f. prec.]

bu′tcherÿ (bŏŏ′-) *n.* slaughterhouse; butcher's trade; needless or cruel slaughter of people. [ME, f. OF *boucherie* (as BUTCHER¹; see -Y¹)]

bu′tler *n.* servant in charge of wine-cellar and plate etc.; principal manservant. [ME, f. AF *buteler,* OF *bouteillier*; see BOTTLE¹, -ER² (2)]

bŭtt¹ *n.* cask, esp. as measure of wine or ale. [f. AL *butta, bota,* AF *but,* f. OF *bo(u)t* f. LL *buttis*]

bŭtt² *n.* ∼(-end), thicker end, esp. of tool or weapon; trunk of tree, esp. part just above ground; ∼(-end), remnant; stub of cigar or cigarette; flat-fish (sole, plaice, turbot); ∼(-end), square end of plank meeting a similar one; *(sl.) buttocks; ∼ **weld** (in which pieces are joined end to end). [ME, (a) f. MLG, MDu. *but* flat-fish (see HALIBUT, TURBOT), (b) = Du. *bot* stumpy]

bŭtt³ *n.* **1.** mound behind target; grouse-shooter's stand screened by low turf or stone wall; (in *pl.*) shooting-range; target. **2.** aim, object; object of (ridicule etc.), object of teasing and ridicule (*make a butt of* person). [ME, f. OF *but* goal, of unkn. orig.]

bŭtt⁴ *v.i.* & *t.*, & *n.* **1.** push with head; ∼ **in,** (fig.) intervene, meddle; *∼**i′nsky,** (sl.) meddler. **2.** *v.i.* & *t.* meet end to end (*butt against, upon*); come, place (timber etc.), end to end (*butt against* wall etc.). [ME, f. AF *buter,* OF *boter* f. Gmc **buttan* sprout; infl. by prec. and ABUT]

*bŭtte *n.* conspicuous isolated hill, esp. one with steep or clifflike sides. [F, = mound]

bŭ'tter[1] *n.* **1.** edible fatty substance made from cream by churning, used on bread and in cookery, (**look as if ~ would not melt in** one's **mouth**, seem demure; **melted ~**, (also) sauce of butter, flour, etc.); substance of similar consistency or look (COCOA[2] *butter*; PEA*nut butter*; **vegetable ~**, such substance got from plant); fulsome flattery. **2. ~-and-eggs,** plant with two yellows in flower, e.g. toadflax; **~-ball,** (1) piece of butter moulded into a ball, (2) *bufflehead [because very fat in autumn]; **~-bean,** (1) yellow--podded bean, (2) dried white Lima bean; **~bur,** plant of genus *Petasites* with large soft leaves; **~-cream,** mixture of butter, sugar, etc., as filling or topping for cake; **~cup,** yellow-flowered plant of genus *Ranunculus*; **~fingers,** person likely to drop things or unable to catch ball etc.; **~-fish,** slippery kind, of various species; **~-knife,** blunt knife for cutting butter at table; **~milk,** somewhat acid liquid fat left after churning butter; **~ muslin,** thin loosely woven cloth with fine mesh, used orig. for wrapping butter; **~-nut,** N. Amer. (oily nut of) tree *Juglans cinerea*; **~scotch,** kind of toffee made chiefly with butter and sugar; **~wort,** fleshy-leaved violet--flowered bog-plant, *Pinguicula vulgaris.* [OE *butere*, = OHG *butera*, WG f. L *butyrum* f. Gk *bouturon*]

bŭ'tter[2] *v.t.* spread, cook, serve, with butter (**fine words ~ no parsnips,** mere protestations do not alter facts; see BREAD 1); **~ up,** flatter. [f. prec.]

bŭ'tterfly *n.* diurnal insect of order Lepidoptera with large often showy wings erect when at rest and knobbed antennae (**break a ~ on the wheel,** use needless destructive force); (in *pl.,* colloq.) nervous tremors (esp. *in stomach* etc.); showy or frivolous person; **~-fish,** fish (esp. a blenny) with variegated colours or broad fins; **~-nut** (Mech., with wings to be turned by thumb and finger); **~ stroke** (Swimming, in which both arms are lifted at same time); **~ valve** (with hinged semicircular plates). [OE *buttor-flēoge* (as BUTTER[1], FLY[1])]

bŭ'ttery[1] *n.* place in college etc. where provisions are kept and supplied. [ME, f. AF **buterie, boterie* butt--store (as BUTT[1]; see -ERY)]

bŭ'ttery[2] *a.* like or containing butter; hence **~INESS** *n.* [f. BUTTER[1] + -Y[2]]

bŭ'ttock *n.* either of two fleshy protuberances on lower rear part of human body; corresponding part of animal, ||manœuvre in wrestling using buttock or hip. [f. butt ridge + -OCK]

bŭ'tton[1] *n.* **1.** knob or disc sewn to garment to fasten it by passing through buttonhole, or for ornament, or attached as badge, (**a ~ short,** (colloq.) mentally deficient; ***on the ~,** precisely); thing of little value. **2.** bud; mushroom not yet open. **3.** knob etc. pressed to operate electric bell etc.; small rounded object; terminal knob (on fencing foil, making it harmless; also as ornament). **4. ~ chrysanthemum** (with many small round flower-heads); **~ day,** (Austral.) FLAG[4]-*day* (but with buttons not flags); **~hole,** (*n.*) slit made to receive fastening button, ||flower(s) worn in coat-lapel buttonhole, (*v.t.*) make buttonholes in, hold by coat or waistcoat button, detain (reluctant listener); **~hole stitch,** looped stitch for edging button-holes; **~hook** (for pulling button into place); **~stick,** appliance to protect cloth in button--polishing; **~-through,** (of dress) fastening by buttons over its whole length; ***~-tree,** ***~-wood,** plane-tree. **5.** Hence (-) **~ED**[2] (-nd), **~LESS,** **~Y**[2], *adjs.* [ME, f. OF *bouton* f. Rom. *bottone (*bottare f. Gmc *button sprout)]

bŭ'tton[2] *v.* **1.** *v.t.* furnish with button(s). **2.** *v.t. & i.* **~ (up),** fasten with buttons, (fig.) complete satisfactorily, (in *p.p.,* of person) taciturn; ***~** one's **lip,** (sl.) remain silent. [f. prec.]

bŭ'ttons (-z) *n.* liveried page-boy. [f. BUTTON[1] (from rows of buttons on his jacket)]

bŭ'ttress *n.,* & *v.t.* **1.** *n.* support built against wall etc. (FLYING[2] *buttress*); prop (lit. or fig.); buttress-like projection of hill. **2.** *v.t.* **~ (up),** support (lit. or fig.) with buttress, by argument, etc. [ME, f. OF (*ars*) *bouterez* thrusting (arch) f. *bouteret* f. *bouter* BUTT[4]]

bŭ'tty[1] *n.* **1.** (colloq.) mate, chum, companion. **2.** middleman between mine-proprietor and miners; **~-gang** (of men undertaking part of large job, sharing profits equally). **3.** barge etc. towed by another. [19th c., perh. f. BOOTY in phr. *play booty* join in sharing plunder]

||**bŭ'tty**[2] *n.* (dial.) slice of bread and butter; sandwich. [f. BUTTER[1] + -Y[3]]

bŭ'tyl *n.* (Chem.) radical, C_4H_9, derived from butane; **~ rubber,** kind of synthetic rubber. [f. foll. + -YL]

bŭty'ric *a.* (Chem.) **~ acid,** colourless syrupy liquid acid (C_3H_7COOH) found in rancid butter; hence **bŭ'tyrATE** (3) *n.* [f. L *butyrum* BUTTER[1] + -IC]

bŭ'xom *a.* plump and comely; hence **~NESS** *n.* [earlier sense *pliant,* ME f. st. of OE *būgan* BOW[3] + -SOME[1]]

buy (bī) *v.t.* (**bought** *pr.* bawt), & *n.* **1.** *v.t.* obtain in exchange for money etc.; serve to procure (*money cannot buy happiness*); get by some sacrifice (*dearly bought*); win over (person) by bribery etc.; (sl.) accept, believe, be deceived by, suffer, receive as punishment etc. (**~ it,** be killed). **2. ~ in,** buy a stock of, withdraw at auction by naming higher price than highest offered; **~ into,** obtain share in by payment; **~ off,** pay to get rid of (claim, claimant, blackmailer); **~ out,** pay (person) to give up post, property, etc.; **~** oneself **out,** obtain release by payment; **~ over,** bribe; **~ up,** buy as much as possible of, absorb (other firm etc.) by purchase. **3.** Hence **~'ER**[1] *n.,* (esp.) agent who selects and purchases stock for a large shop etc.; **~er's** or **~ers' market,** one in which goods are plentiful and cheap. **4.** *n.* purchase (**best ~,** that giving best results in proportion to price; **good ~,** a favourable bargain, thing cheaply bought). [OE *bycgan,* = OS *buggian,* ON *hyggja,* Goth. *bugjan* f. Gmc *bugjan]

buzz[1] *n.* hum of bee etc.; sound of buzzer; sound of people talking, stir, general movement; rumour; confused low sound; (sl.) telephone call; **~-bomb,** (colloq.) flying bomb; ***~-saw,** circular saw; **~-word,** catchword, slogan. [f. foll.]

buzz[2] *v.i. & t.* make humming sound; signal with buzzer; move or hover *about* busily; (sl.) go *off* quickly; (of place) sound confusedly; (colloq.) throw hard; fly fast and very close to (another aircraft). [imit.]

bu'zzard *n.* raptorial bird of genus *Buteo*; *turkey buzzard; (ME, f. OF *busard, buson* f. L *buteo -onis* falcon; see -ARD]

bu'zzer *n.* in vbl senses; whistle or hooter; electric buzzing-machine for sending signals. [f. BUZZ[2] + -ER[1]]

BVM *abbr.* Blessed Virgin Mary.

bwa'na (-ah'-) *n.* (Afr.) master, sir. [Swahili]

BWI *abbr.* (Hist.) British West Indies.

by[1] *prep. & adv.* **1.** *prep.* (bī or, when unstressed, bǐ). near, at or to side of, about person or in possession of, in company of, in region of, slightly inclining to, (*come here by me*; STAND[1] *by*; ABIDE *by*; *have not got it by me*; COME *by*); **by** oneself, alone (& see 4); **north by east,** between N. and NNE; **north-east by east,** between NE and ENE; **by the head, stern,** (of ship) deeper in water there. **2.** along, in passing along, through, via, avoiding, passing, outstripping, (*by nearest road*; *by the* WAY; *by the* BYE[1]; *travel by Paris, by sea*; *pass him by, go by him*). **3.** during, in the circumstances of, (*by day, night, daylight*). **4.** through the agency, means, instrumentality, or causation of, owing to, in such a manner, with, (*know, say, by* HEART; *multiply, divide, 12 by 2 to get 24, 6; 3 ft. by 2 ft.* (lengths in two directions); *lead by the hand*; *set by the ears* (EAR[1] 1); *go, be known, by the name of*; *what do you mean by that?*; *by all, no,* MEAN[3]*s*; *live by bread*; *do it by one's deputy*; *have children by* (man as father, woman as mother);

colt by (sire); *approved, written, made, by; novel by Scott, play by Shaw; no light to read by; case goes by default; begin, end, by doing; by* WAY *of; cautious by nature;* **by cheque** etc., in credit entries; *by chance; by dint of; by reason of; by* VIRTUE *of*); **by oneself,** without help or prompting (& see 1). **5.** as soon as, not later than, *(by now, next week, tomorrow, the time (that) he gets here*); according to, after, from, *(by* ROTE; *by* RIGHT[3]; *by* RIGHT[3]*s; take warning, example, by; by your* LEAVE[1]; *judge by appearances; ten minutes by the clock; sell, buy, by retail, the yard, the packet; paid by the hour;* **by the dozen** etc., in at least that quantity). **6.** with succession of, succeeding, *(by* DEGREES, *by hundreds,* **getting worse by the minute, day by day, year by year, man by man,* LITTLE *by little,* ONE *by one,* TWO *by two*); **by and by,** (*adv.*) before long, (*n.*) the future. **7.** to the extent of *(missed by a foot; too clever by* HALF 2; *better by far*). **8.** concerning, in respect of, *(do one's duty by; do as you would be done by; French by blood, Jones by name; pull up by the roots;* (colloq.) *all right by me*). **9.** as surely as one believes in *(by God;* SWEAR *by*). **10.** *adv.* (bī). near (STAND[1] *by; lives close by*). **11.** aside, in reserve, (PUT[1] *by,* LAY[3] *by*). **12.** past *(they marched by; all that is gone by*). **13.** ~ **and large,** on the whole, everything considered, (orig. Naut., to the wind and off it); **by'gone,** (*a.*) past, antiquated, (*n.,* in *pl.*) past offences *(let bygones be bygones,* forgive and forget), domestic objects of the past; **by'line,** line in newspaper etc. naming writer of article, (Assoc. Footb.) goal-line; **by'stander,** spectator. [OE *bī, bi, be,* = OS, OHG *bī, bi,* Goth. *bi* f. Gmc *bi]

bȳ[2], bȳe[2], *a.* subordinate, incidental, secondary; side, out-of-the-way; **by-blow,** (1) side-blow not at main opponent, (2) bastard child; **by-effect,** side-effect; *by-*ELECTION; **by-form,** collateral form of word etc.; **by-lane,** side lane; **by'name,** sobriquet, nickname; **by'pass,** (*n.*) secondary channel for gas etc. to allow flow when main channel is blocked; road passing round town or to centre to provide alternative route for through traffic, (*v.t.*) provide with bypass, avoid; **by'path,** secluded path, minor branch of subject; **by--play,** subsidiary action in play (lit. or fig.); **by--product,** incidental or secondary product of manufacture etc.; **by-road,** minor road; **by-street,** side-street; **byway,** by-road or bypath; **by'word,**

proverb, person etc. taken as typical of a (usu. bad) quality *(a byword for laziness* etc.). [f. prec.]

bȳ[3] *n.* Var. of foll.

bȳe[1] *n.* something subordinate **(by the by** or **bye,** incidentally, parenthetically); (Cricket) run scored from ball that passes batsman without being hit, **leg-~,** from one that touches batsman; (Golf) hole(s) remaining after decision of match; (being) unpaired competitor in game etc. [f. BY[1], as *n.*]

bȳe[2]. See BY[2].

bȳe[3] *int.* (colloq.) = GOODBYE. [abbr.]

bȳe'-bȳe[1], bȳe'-bȳes (bī'bīz), *n.* (Child's wd for) sleep, bed. [ME, f. sound used in lullabies]

bȳe-bȳe'[2] *int.* (colloq.) = GOODBYE. [childish corrupt.]

Byelorussian. See BELORUSSIAN.

bȳ'-law, bȳe'-law, *n.* ‖regulation made by local authority or corporation; regulation of company etc. [ME, prob. f. obs. *byrlaw* local custom (ON *býjar* gen. sing. of *býr* town, but assoc. w. BY[2]; *lagu LAW)]

bȳre *n.* cow-shed. [OE *bȳre,* perh. cogn. w. BOWER[1]]

Bȳrŏ'nĭc *a.* characteristic of Byron or his romantic poetry. [f. Lord *Byron,* Engl. poet d. 1824 + -IC]

bўssĭnŏ's‖ĭs *n.* (*pl.* **-es** *pr.* -ēz). (Path.) lung disease due to prolonged inhalation of textile fibre dust. [mod. L, f. Gk *bussinos* made of byssus + -OSIS]

bў'ssus *n.* (Hist.) fine textile fibre and fabric of flax; tuft of silky filaments by which some molluscs adhere to rock. [ME f. L, f. Gk *bussos*]

bȳte *n.* group of binary digits in computer. [20th c., perh. based on BIT[4] and BITE[2]]

by'wŏner (bī'wō-, bā'vō-) *n.* (S. Afr.) holder of land under *métayage* system. [Afrik. (*by* with, *woon* live; see -ER[1])]

Bȳză'ntīne *a.* & *n.* **1.** (inhabitant) of Byzantium or the E. Roman Empire; (Archit. etc.) of style developed in the Eastern Empire. **2.** *a.* like Byzantine politics; complicated; inflexible; underhand. [f. F *byzantin* or f. L *Byzantinus* (*Byzantium,* later Constantinople and now Istanbul; see -INE[1])]

Bȳză'ntĭn‖ism *n.* style and methods of architecture etc. developed in Byzantine Empire; so ~IST (3) *n.* [f. prec. + -ISM]

C

, c, (sē) *n.* (*pl.* **Cs** *or* **C's**). third letter of alphabet; (Mus.) first note of natural major scale; third hypothetical person or example; third highest class (of academic marks, population as regards affluence, etc.); (Alg., usu. *c*) third known quantity; (as Roman numeral) 100 (**cc** 200, **cd** 400, **cm** 900); ||**C3** (sē thrē´), lowest medical grade in war of 1914–18, (colloq.) unfit, worthless.

, *abbr.* Cape; Celsius, Centigrade; ||COMMAND² Paper (second series, 1870–99); Conservative; coulomb(s).

, *abbr.* about [L *circa*]; caught by; cent(s); centi-; century; chapter; cold; colt; cubic.

, *symb.* carbon; copyright (also ©).

, *abbr.* (Austral. & NZ) care of.

A *abbr.* California; (Sc. & Can.) chartered accountant.

a. *abbr. circa.*

a *symb.* calcium.

aaba. Var. of KAABA.

ab *n.* taxi or (Hist.) hackney carriage; shelter or compartment for driver of train, lorry, or cranc; ∨'man, driver of cab; ||∿-rank, place where cabs are authorized to wait. [abbr. of CABRIOLET]

AB *abbr.* Citizens' Advice Bureau; *Civil Aeronautics Board.

aba'l *n.* secret intrigue; political clique, faction; (Hist.) committee of five ministers under Charles II, whose surnames happened to begin with C, A, B, A, and L. [f. F *cabale* f. med. L *cabala*, CABBALA]

abala. See CABBALA.

aballer'o (-lyär'ö) *n.* (*pl.* ∿s). Spanish gentleman. [Sp.; see CAVALIER]

caba'na (-ah'-) *n.* shelter at beach or swimming-pool. [f. Sp. *cabaña* f. LL (as CABIN)]

a'baret (rā) *n.* entertainment provided in restaurant etc. while customers are at table. [F, = wooden structure, tavern]

a'bbage *n.* green culinary vegetable, variety of *Brassica oleracea*, with leaves forming a round heart or head; (colloq.) person without ambition or interests; ∿-palm, tree with edible cabbage like terminal bud, ∿-rose, double rose with large round compact flower; ∿-tree, = cabbage-palm; ∿ white, butterfly of genus *Pieris* feeding on cabbage leaves; hence **ca'bbagy²** (-iji) *a.* [earlier *cabache, -oche* f. OF (Picard) *caboche* head, OF *cabocc*, of unkn. orig.]

ab(b)al|a (kabah'la) *n.* Jewish oral tradition; mystic interpretation, esoteric doctrine, occult lore; hence ∿ISM (3), ∿IST (2), *ns.*, ∿ĭ'STIC *a.* [med. L, f. Rabbinical Heb. *ḳabbālā* tradition]

a'bby *n.* (colloq.) cab-driver. [t. CAB + -Y³]

a'ber *n.* roughly trimmed tree-trunk used in Sc. Highland sport of tossing the ∿. [f. Gael. *cabar* pole]

a'bin *n.,* & *v.t.* **1.** *n.* small poor dwelling or shelter; room or compartment in ship or aircraft or spacecraft for passengers or crew, or in aircraft for cargo; driver's cab; ∿-boy (waiting on officers or passengers); ∿ class, intermediate class of accommodation in ship; ∿ cruiser, power-driven vessel with cabin and living accommodation. **2.** *v.t.* (esp. in *b.p.*) confine in small space, cramp. [ME f. OF *cabane* f. Prov. *cabana* f. LL *capanna, cavanna*]

a'binet *n.* **1.** case or cupboard with drawers, shelves, etc., for storing or displaying articles; piece of furniture containing radio or television set etc. **2.** (Polit.; **C**∿). inner circle of ministers controlling Government policy; || **C**∿ **Minister,** one of them; |SHADOW¹ Cabinet. **3.** (arch.) small private room. **4.** ∿-maker, skilled joiner; ||∿ photograph (about 6 by 4 inches); ∿ pudding, steamed

pudding with dried fruit. [f. prec. + -ET¹, infl. by F *cabinet*]

ca'ble¹ *n.* **1.** strong thick rope of hemp or wire; (Naut.) chain of anchor, (as measure) 200 yards; (esp. submarine or underground telegraph) line containing insulated wires; cablegram; (Archit.) rope-shaped ornament. **2.** ∿-car (moved by endless cable); ∿-laid, (of rope) having three triple strands; ∿ railway (along which cars or carriages are drawn by endless cable moved by fixed engine); ∿ (stitch), knitted pattern looking like twisted rope; ∿way, transporting-system with usu. elevated cable. [ME f. AF, ONF *cable* f. OF *chable*, or f. Prov. *cable*, f. LL *cap(u)lum* halter f. Arab. *ḥabl*]

ca'ble² *v.t.* & *i.* furnish or fasten with cable; (Archit.) fill with cables; transmit (message), communicate, inform (person), by submarine cable. [f. prec.]

ca'blegram (-belg-) *n.* message by submarine cable. [f. CABLE¹ + -GRAM]

ca'bochon (-sh-) *n.* gem polished but not faceted; **en** ∿, (of gem) so treated. [F, dim. of *caboche*; see CABBAGE]

caboo'dle *n.* (sl.) **the whole** ∿, the lot, the whole number or quantity, (of persons or things). [19th c. US, perh. f. phr. *kit and boodle*]

caboo'se *n.* cooking-room on ship's deck; *guard's van, car on goods train for workmen etc. [f. Du. *cabūse*, of unkn. orig.]

ca'botage (-ahzh, -īj) *n.* coastal trade; reservation to a country of (esp. air) traffic operation within its territory. [F (*caboter* to coast, perh. f. Sp. *cabo* CAPE²; see -AGE)]

cabotin (kahbotă'n) *n.* (*fem.* ∿ *e* pr.-ē'n). second-rate actor [F, = strolling player, perh. f. as prec., from blance to vessels travelling from port to port]

ca'briole *n.* kind of curved leg characteristic of Queen Anne and Chippendale furniture. [F, f. *cabrioler, caprioler* f. It. *capriolare* to leap in the air; from resemblance to leaping animal's foreleg (see CAPRIOLE)]

cabriole't (-lā) *n.* (Hist.) light two-wheeled hooded one-horse chaise; motor car with folding top. [F, f. *cabriole* goat's leap (cf. CAPRIOLE), applied to its motion; cf. -ET¹]

ca'ca'nny (kah-) *n.* go-slow, trade-union policy of limiting output. [Sc., = proceed warily; see CALL¹ 5, CANNY]

caca'o (-ah'ö, -ā'ö) *n.* (*pl.* ∿s). seed of orig. tropical Amer. tree, from which cocoa and chocolate are made; ∿(-tree), this tree (*Theobroma cacao*). [Sp., f. Nahuatl *oaca(uult* tree)]

ca'chalot (-sh-, -lŏt, -lō) *n.* sperm whale. [F, f. Sp. & Port. *cachalote*; orig. unkn.]

cache (kăsh) *n.,* & *v.t.* **1.** *n.* hiding-place for treasure, provisions, ammunition, etc.; what is hidden in a cache. **2.** *v.t.* place in cache. [F (*cacher* to hide)]

cachectic. See CACHEXIA.

ca'chet (-shā) *n.* distinguishing mark; internal evidence of authenticity; prestige; (Med.) small case of gelatine etc. enclosing dose of medicine, capsule. [F (*cacher* press f. Rom. *coacticare* f. L *coactare* constrain)]

cache'xia, -xy, (-kě'-) *n.* chronic debility of body or mind; so **cache'ctic** (-kě'-) *a.* [f. F *cachexie* or f. LL f. Gk *kakhexia* (*kakos* bad, *hexis* habit; see -IA¹, -Y¹)]

ca'chinnate (-kă-) *v.i.* (literary). laugh loudly; so ∿A'TION (3), ∿atory *a.* [f. L *cachinnare* f. -ATE³]

ca'cholong (-sh-) *n.* kind of opal. [F, f. Mongolian *kashchilon* beautiful stone]

ca'chou (-shoo) *n.* catechu; lozenge to sweeten breath. [F, f. Port. *cachu* f. Malay *kāchu*; cf. CATECHU]

cachu'cha (-ōō'-) n. Spanish solo dance. [Sp.]
caci'que (-sē'k) n. W. Ind. or Amer. Ind. native chief;
political boss in Spain or Latin America; hence
caci'quism (-sē'k-) n., government by caciques. [Sp.,
f. Carib.]
căck-hă'ndĕd a. (colloq.) left-handed; clumsy. [f.
dial. cack excrement + HAND¹ + -ED²]
că'ckle v. & n. 1. v.i., & n. (make) clucking of hen after
laying; (indulge in) noisy inconsequential talk; (give)
loud silly laugh; cut the ∼, (colloq.) come to the
point. 2. v.t. say cacklingly. [ME, prob. f. MLG,
MDu. kākelen, imit.]
căcodē'mon, -ae'mon, n. evil spirit; malignant person. [f. Gk kakodaimōn (kakos bad, daimōn spirit)]
că'codȳl n. (Chem.) radical formed from arsenic
and methyl, occurring in malodorous compounds;
hence căcodȳ'lic a. [f. Gk kakōdēs stinking (kakos
bad) + -YL]
cacoēpȳ (kakō'-, kă'-) n. bad pronunciation (opp.
orthoepy). [f. Gk kak(o)epeia (kakos bad, epos word); see
-Y¹]
cacoethes (kăkōē'thēz) n. itch for doing something
inadvisable; ∼ scribe'ndi, irresistible desire to
write. [L, f. Gk kakoēthes neut. a. (kakos bad, ēthos
disposition)]
caco'graphȳ n. bad handwriting or spelling; hence
caco'GRAPHER n., căcoGRA'PHIC(AL) adjs. [f. Gk
kakos bad, after orthography]
caco'logȳ n. bad choice of words or pronunciation.
[f. LL f. Gk kakologia vituperation (kakos bad; see
-LOGY)]
că'comistle (-sel) n. racoon-like animal of southern
N. America. [f. Amer. Sp. cacomixtle f. Nahuatl
tlacomiztli]
caco'phon|y n. discordant sound; so ∼ous a.[f. F
cacophonie f. Gk kakophōnia f. kakophōnos (kakos bad,
phōnē sound); see -Y¹]
că'ct|us n. (pl. ∼i pr. -ī, or ∼uses). succulent plant of
family Cactaceae, with thick fleshy stem, usu. spines
but no leaves, and brilliantly coloured flowers; ∼us
dahlia, kind of dahlia with rolled-back flower-rays
resembling cactus flower; hence ∼A'CEOUS, ∼AL,
∼OID, adjs. [L, f. Gk kaktos cardoon]
căcū'minal a. (Phonet.) pronounced with tongue-
-tip curled up towards hard palate. [f. L cacuminare
make pointed (cacumen -minis tree-top) + -AL]
căd n. vulgar ill-bred person; person guilty or capable
of ungentlemanly conduct, blackguard, whence
∼'DISH¹ a. [abbr. of CADDIE in sense 'odd-job man']
cadă'stral a. of or showing extent, value, and ownership, of land for taxation. [F, f. cadastre register of
property f. Prov. cadastro f. It. catast(r)o, earlier
catastico f. late Gk katastikhon list, register (kata
stikhon line by line)]
cadă'ver n. (esp. Med.) corpse; so cadă'verIC a. [ME
f. L (cadere fall)]
cadă'verous a. corpselike; deathly pale. [f. L cadaver-
osus as prec.; see -OUS)]
că'ddie, că'ddy², n., & v.i. 1. n. golfer's attendant
for carrying clubs etc.; ∼ car or cart, light two-
-wheeled trolley for transporting golf clubs during
game. 2. container for small objects ready for use.
3. v.i. act as caddie. [orig. Sc., f. F CADET]
că'ddis n. ∼-fly, feebly flying freq. nocturnal insect
of order Trichoptera, living near water; ∼-worm,
larva of caddis-fly etc., living in water and making
cylindrical case of sticks etc., used as fishing-bait.
[17th c., of unkn. orig.]
că'ddish. See CAD.
că'ddȳ¹ n. small box for holding tea. [earlier catty
weight of 1⅓ lb., f. Malay kātī]
că'ddȳ². See CADDIE.
că'denc|e n. rhythm; measured movement, esp. of
sound; fall of voice, esp. at end of sentence etc.;
intonation; close of musical phrase; hence ∼ED²
(-st) a. [ME f. OF *cadence f. It. cadenza f. pop. L
*cadentia f. L cadere fall; see -ENCE]

că'dencȳ n. status of younger branch of family. [f. a
prec.; see -ENCY]
cadĕ'ntial (-shal) a. of cadence or cadenza. [f. a
CADENCE + -IAL]
cadĕ'nza n. (Mus.) passage for solo instrument or
voice, usu. near close of movement, sometimes improvised. [It.; see CADENCE]
cadĕ't n. younger son; student in naval or military or
air force college; member of corps receiving elementary military or police training; (NZ) young man
learning sheep-farming; hence ∼SHIP n. [F, f
Gascon dial. capdet f. Rom. *capitellus dim. of L
caput head]
cădg|e v. 1. v.i. go about begging. 2. v.t. get by begging
or sponging. 3. Hence ∼'ER¹ n. [19th c., earlier =
?bind, carry; orig. unkn.]
ca'dĭ (kah'-, kā'-) n. judge in Muslim country. [f
Arab. ḳāḍī (ḳaḍā to judge)]
Cădmē'an a. ∼ victory, = PYRRHIC² victory. [f. L f
Gk Kadmeios (Kadmos Cadmus; see foll.)]
că'dmium n. bluish-white metallic element, physi
cally resembling tin; ∼ cell, voltaic cell used a
standard of e.m.f.; ∼ yellow, intense yellow pig
ment containing cadmium sulphide. [f. obs
cadmia calamine f. L f. Gk kadm(e)ia (gē) Cadmear
(earth), f. Cadmus legendary founder of Thebes; see
-IUM]
cadre (kah'der, kahdr, kă'drĭ) n. (Mil. etc.) per
manent establishment of unit forming nucleus fo
expansion at need; (member of) group of worker
promoting interests of Communist Party. [F, f. It
quadro f. L quadrus square]
cadū'c|eus n. (pl. ∼ei pr. -iī). Ancient Greek o
Roman herald's wand, esp. as carried by messenger
-god Hermes or Mercury. [L, f. Doric Gk karuk(e)ion
(kērux herald)]
cadū'c|ous a. (Zool. & Bot.), of organs and parts
falling off early; so ∼ITY n. [f. L caducus falling
(cadere fall) + -OUS]
caecī'lian (sĭs-) a. & n. (Zool.) (member) of orde
Apoda of amphibians, mainly tropical and wormlike
lacking limbs or scales and lizard + AN]
cae'c|um (sē'-), *cē'c|um, n. (pl. ∼a). blind end o
first part of large intestine; hence ∼AL a., ∼I'TI
(sĭ-) n. [L, for intestinum caecum f. caecus blind, transl
of Gk tuphlon enteron]
Caenozoic. See CAINOZOIC.
Caerns. abbr. Caernarvonshire (former county in
Wales).
Caerphi'llȳ (kār-, kâr-, ker-) n. kind of mild white
cheese. [∼ in Wales]
Cae'sar (sē'z-) n. any of the Roman emperors, esp
from Augustus to Hadrian; autocrat; (Med. sl.
(case of) Caesarean section; ∼'s wife, person
required to be above suspicion. [L, family name o
Gaius Julius ∼, Roman statesman d. 44 BC]
Caesăr'ean, -ian, (sĭz-) a. & n. 1. a. of Caesar or the
Caesars, imperial; ∼ birth, operation, section
delivery of child by cutting walls of abdomen [from
story that Julius Caesar was so delivered]. 2. n
adherent of Caesar or of an autocratic system; se
Cae'sarism (3), Cae'sarist (2), (sē'z-) ns. 3
Caesarean operation. [f. L Caesarianus; see -EAN, -IAN
cae'sious (sē'z-) a. (Bot.) bluish or greyish green
[f. L caesius + -OUS]
cae'sium, *cē'sium, (sē'z-) n. soft silver-white ele
ment of alkali-metal group. [as prec. f. its spectrum
lines; see -IUM]
caesūr'|a (sĭz-) n. (Gk & L Pros.) break betwee
words within a metrical foot; (mod. Pros.) pause nea
middle of line; hence ∼AL a. [L (caedere caes- cut
see -URE)]
*CAF abbr. cost and freight.
cafăr'd (kahfăr') n. melancholia. [F, = cockroach
hypocrite]
café¹, cafe, (kă'fā, kă'fĭ, joc. or vulg. kăf) n. coffee
-house, tea-shop, restaurant, *bar; ∼ society

regular patrons of fashionable restaurants and night-clubs. [F, = coffee(-house)]
café² (kă'fā) n. ~ **au lait** (ō lā), coffee with milk, colour of this; ~ **noir** (nwâr), coffee without milk. [F, as prec.; *noir* = black]
căfĕtēr'ia n. restaurant in which customers fetch food and drink from the counter. [f. Amer. Sp. *cafetería* coffee-shop]
||**căff** n. (sl.) café. [abbr.]
că'ffeine (-fēn, -fīĭn) n. vegetable alkaloid stimulant found in coffee and tea plants. [f. F *caféine* (*café* coffee; see -INE⁵)]
Caffre. See KAFFIR.
căftăn, k-, (kă'ftăn, kăftah'n) n. Eastern man's long tunic with waist girdle; woman's long loose dress; loose shirt. [f. Turk. *ḳaftān*, partly thr. F *cafetan*]
cāge n., & v.t. **1.** n. fixed or portable prison, of wire or barred, esp. for birds or animals or prisoners of war; prison (lit. or fig.); (Mining) frame for hoisting and lowering men, wagons, etc.; compartment for passengers etc. in lift; open framework of various kinds; ~-**bird,** bird (of kind customarily) kept in cage. **2.** v.t. place or keep in cage. [ME f. OF, f. L *cavea*]
cā'gey, cā'gy, a. (**ca'gier, ca'giest**). (colloq.) shrewd; wary; secretive; uncommunicative; hence **cā'gILY** adv., **cā'geyNESS** (-jĭn-), **cā'gINESS,** ns. [20th c. US; orig. unkn.]
cagou'le (-ōō'l) n. hooded thin windproof garment worn in mountaineering etc. [F]
*****cahoo't** (ka-h-) n. (sl., usu. in *pl.*) company, partnership; collusion; **in** ~s, in league *with*. [19th c.; orig. uncert.]
cai'man. See CAYMAN.
Cain n. **raise** ~, (colloq.) make a disturbance, create trouble. [f. ~, eldest son of Adam (Gen. 4)]
Cainozō'ic (kīn-), **Caen-** (sēn-), *****Cēn-,** a. & n. (Geol.) (of) the third geological era; Tertiary or Quaternary. [f. Gk *kainos* new + *zōion* animal + -IC]
cai'que (kaē'k, kiē'k) n. light rowing-boat on Bosporus; Levantine sailing-ship. [F, f. It. *caicco* f. Turk. *ḳayiḳ*]
cairn n. pyramid of rough stones as memorial, to mark path, etc.; ~ (**terrier**), small short-legged longish-bodied shaggy-coated terrier (perh. f. its being used to hunt among cairns). [f. Gael. *carn*]
cair'ngŏrm (-n-g-) n. yellow or wine-coloured semi-precious stone. [found on C~, mountain in Scotland (Gael. *carn gorm* blue cairn)]
caisson (kā'son, kasōō'n) n. **1.** ammunition chest or wagon. **2.** large watertight chamber open at bottom, from which water is kept out by air pressure, used in laying foundations under water; floating vessel used as dock gate; ~ **disease,** sickness caused by too rapid decompression of workers in compressed air (as in caissons etc.). [F (f. It. *cassone*), assim. to *caisse* CASE²; see -OON]
cai'tiff n. & a. (poet. or arch.) base or despicable (person); coward(ly). [ME, f. OF *caitif, chaitif,* f. Rom. *captivus* f. L *captivus* CAPTIVE]
cajō'l|e v.t. persuade by flattery, deceit, etc., (*into* doing, *out of* something); coax something *out of* person; hence ~e**MENT** (-lm-), ~e**RY** (4), ns. [f. F *cajoler*]
cāke n. & v. **1.** n. sweet usu. unleavened bread with other ingredients besides flour, e.g. currants, spice, butter, eggs, sugar; quantity of this baked in thick disc or ornamental shape (**slice of the** ~, (fig.) participation in benefits); (Sc. & N. Engl.) thin oaten bread (**land of** ~s, Scotland); flattish compact mass of other food (*fish cake*, PANCAKE) or of any compressed substance (||CATTLE-*cake*; *cake of soap, wax, tobacco*). **2.** ~s **and ale,** merry-making; ~'**walk,** (1) dance developed from Negro contest in graceful walking with cake for prize, (2) easy task; **go** or **sell like hot** ~s (very readily); piece of ~, (colloq.) something easy or pleasant; TAKE¹ *the cake*; **cannot have** one's ~ **and eat it,** cannot eat one's

~ **and have it,** cannot enjoy both alternatives. **3.** v.t. & i. form into compact mass; cover *with* hardened mass (*caked with dirt*). [ME, f. ON *kaka*]
Cal. abbr. California.
cal. abbr. calorie(s).
Că'labâr n. ~ **bean,** poisonous seed of tropical Afr. climbing plant yielding medicinal extract. [~ in Nigeria]
că'labăsh n. gourd whose shell serves for holding liquid etc.; (fruit of) tropical Amer. tree of genus *Crescentia,* whose fruit is so used; pipe etc. made from these or of like shape. [f. F *calebasse* f. Sp. *calabaza,* perh. f. Pers. *karbuz* melon]
*****călaboo'se** n. prison, lock-up. [f. Negro F *calabouse* f. Sp. *calabozo* dungeon]
călabre'se (-ā'sā) n. variety of sprouting broccoli. [It., = Calabrian]
călamă'ncō n. (*pl.* ~es). (Hist.) glossy woollen material chequered on one side. [16th c., of unkn. orig.]
călamă'nder n. hard wood of E. Ind. tree of genus *Diospyros,* used in furniture. [19th c.; orig unkn., perh. conn. w. Sinh. *kalu-madīriya*]
că'lamarỹ n. cuttlefish with long tapering internal shell, esp. squid of genus *Loligo*. [f. med. L *calamarium* pen case f. L *calamarius* (*calamus* pen; see -ARY¹)]
că'lamine n. native zinc carbonate; pink powder of zinc carbonate or oxide etc. used in lotion or ointment. [ME f. F, f. med. L *calamina* alt. f. L *cadmia*; see CADMIUM]
că'lamint n. mintlike herb or shrub of genus *Calamintha*. [ME, f. OF *calament* f. med. L *calamentum* f. LL f. Gk *kalaminthē*]
cală'mit|ỹ n. adversity; deep distress; grievous disaster; *****~y-howler,** C~y **Jane,** prophet of disaster; so ~ous a. [ME, f. F *calamité* f. L *calamitas -tatis*; see -ITY]
calando (kală'ndō) adv. (Mus.) gradually decreasing in speed and volume. [It., = slackening]
cală'ndria n. closed vessel carrying tubes and serving as heat-exchanger etc. [Sp., = lark]
cală'sh n. (Hist.) light low-wheeled carriage with removable folding hood; carriage hood; (Can.) two-wheeled horse-drawn vehicle; (Hist.) woman's hooped silk hood. [f. F *calèche* f. G *kalesche* f. Pol. *kolaska* or Czech *kolesa*]
călc- comb. form. lime, as. ~-**sinter,** crystalline deposit from calcareous springs, travertine; ~-**spar,** calcite; ~-**tuff,** porous calcareous deposit. [f. G *kalk* f. L CALX]
călcă'ne|um n. (*pl.* ~a). heel-bone. [L]
călcā'r'eous, -ious, a. of or containing calcium carbonate. [f. L *calcarius* (CALX; see -ARY¹) + OUS]
călceolā'ria n. S. Amer. plant of genus *Calceolaria,* with slipper-shaped flower. [mod. L, f. L *calceolus* dim. of *calceus* shoe + -aria fem. (-ARY¹)]
că'lceolāte a. (Bot.) slipper-shaped. [f. as prec. + -ATE²]
calces. See CALX.
călcĭ'ferous a. yielding calcium carbonate. [f. L CALX lime + -I- + -FEROUS]
că'lc|ify v.t. & i. convert to or be converted into calcium carbonate; harden by deposit of calcium salts; petrify; hence ~i'FIC a., ~iFICA'TION n. [f. as prec. + -FY]
că'lcin|e v. **1.** v.t. reduce to quicklime or friable substance by roasting or burning; desiccate; refine by consuming baser part; burn to ashes. **2.** v.i. undergo any of these processes. **3.** Hence **calcinA'TION** n. [ME, f. OF *calciner* or f. med. L *calcinare* f. LL *calcina* lime f. L CALX]
că'lcite n. crystalline calcium carbonate. [f. G *calcit* f. L CALX lime; see -ITE¹]
că'lcium n. greyish-white metallic element whose oxide is quicklime and whose oxides occur widely as calcium carbonate. [f. L CALX lime + -IUM]
că'lcŭl|āte v. **1.** v.t. ascertain by mathematics;

ascertain esp. beforehand (nature of event, date, etc.) by exact reckoning. **2.** *v.t.* & *i.* plan deliberately; rely (*up*)*on*; (in *pres. part.* and *p.p.*) shrewd, cold--blooded, selfish; (in *p.p.*) apt, fit, suitable, *to* do. **3.** *v.t.* *(colloq.) suppose, believe. **4.** Hence ∼ABLE, ∼ATIVE, *adjs.* [f. LL *calculare* (as CALCULUS)+-ATE³]
căl·cūlā'tion *n.* (result got by) calculating; forecast. [ME f. OF, f. LL *calculatio -onis* (as prec.; see -ATION)]
că'lcūlātor *n.* In vbl senses; set of tables for use in calculation; calculating-machine. [ME f. L (as CALCULATE; see -OR)]
că'lcūlous *a.* (Med.) of or suffering from calculus. [f. L *calculosus* (as foll.; see -OUS)]
că'lcūl|us *n.* (*pl.* ∼i *pr.* -ī, *or* ∼uses). **1.** (Med.) stone, concretion in some part of body (*renal* etc. *calculus*). **2.** (Math. etc.) particular method of calculation or reasoning (*calculus of probabilities, variations*); (esp.) = INFINITESIMAL *calculus*; DIFFERENTIAL, INTEGRAL, *calculus*. [L, = small stone (-ULE) used in reckoning on abacus]
calder'a (kahldār'a) *n.* deep cauldron-like cavity on summit of volcano. [Sp., f. LL *caldaria* boiling--pot]
caldron. See CAULDRON.
Cālĕdŏ'nian *a.* & *n.* (native) of ancient Scotland; (usu. joc. or Hist. exc. in titles of institutions) Scots(man); (Geol.) (of) episode of mountain--formation in Europe in the Palaeozoic era. [f. L *Caledonia* northern Britain+-AN]
călĕfă'cient (-shent) *a.* & *n.* (Med.) (substance) producing warmth. [f. L *calefacere* (*calēre* be warm, *facere* make)+-ENT]
călĕfă'ctorў *a.* & *n.* **1.** *a.* producing warmth. **2.** *n.* warm room in monastery. [f. LL *calefactorius* f. as prec.; see -ORY]
că'lĕndar *n.*, & *v.t.* **1.** *n.* system by which beginning, length, and subdivision of year are fixed (*calendar* MONTH, YEAR); table(s) with months, weeks, and festivals etc., of a given year, or with dates important for certain classes (*gardener's calendar*); adjustable device showing the day's date etc.; register or list, esp. of canonized saints, cases for trial, *matters for debate, or documents chronologically arranged with summaries; hence **calĕ'ndr**IC(AL) *adjs.* **2.** *v.t.* register or enter in calendar; arrange, analyse, and index (documents). [ME, f. AF *calender*, OF *calendier*, f. L *calendarium* account-book (as CALENDS; see -AR²)]
că'lĕnder¹ *n.*, & *v.t.* **1.** *n.* machine in which cloth, paper, etc., is pressed by rollers to glaze or smooth it. **2.** *v.t.* press in calender. [f. F *calandre*(*r*), of unkn. orig.]
că'lĕnder² *n.* mendicant dervish. [f. Pers. *ḳalandar*]
că'lĕnds (-z) *n. pl.* first of month in ancient-Roman calendar; **on, till, the Greek C**∼, never, for ever. [ME, f. OF *calendes* f. L *kalendae* (*kal- proclaim); from proclaiming of order of days]
calĕ'ndūla *n.* marigold or other plant of genus *Calendula*, with large yellow or orange flowers. [mod. L, dim. of *calendae* (as prec.), perh. = little clock]
că'lĕnture *n.* tropical delirium of sailors, who think the sea as green fields. [F, f. Sp. *calentura* fever (*calentar* be hot f. Rom. *calentare f. L *calēre* be warm)]
calf¹ (kahf) *n.* (*pl.* calves *pr.* kahvz). **1.** young bovine animal, esp. domestic cow, for first year (*cow* in or *with* ∼, pregnant; FATted *calf*; **golden** ∼, wealth as object of worship (Exod. 32)); ∼('skin), calf--leather, esp. in bookbinding and shoemaking. **2.** young elephant, whale, etc. (Naut.) floating piece of ice detached from iceberg etc. **3.** ∼-**love**, immature romantic affection; hence ∼'HOOD *n.*, ∼'ISH¹ 1 *a.* [OE *cælf*, = OS *calf*, OHG *kalb* f. WG *kalbha]
calf² (kahf) *n.* (*pl.* calves *pr.* kahvz). fleshy hinder part of leg below knee; hence -**calv**ED² (kahvd) *a.* [ME, f. ON *kálfi*, of unkn. orig.]
Că'liban *n.* man of degraded bestial nature. [character in Shak. *The Tempest*]
că'libr|āte *v.t.* find calibre of; calculate irregularities of (tube, gauge) before graduating; graduate

(gauge) with allowance for irregularities; correlate readings of (instrument etc.) with a standard; hence ∼A'TION, ∼ātOR, *ns.* [f. foll.+-ATE³]
||**calibre** (kă'lĭber, kalē'ber), *că'liber, *n.* **1.** internal diameter of gun or any tube; diameter of bullet or shell. **2.** weight of character, standing, importance; ability (*we need a man of your calibre*). [f. F *calibre* f. Sp. or f. It. *calibro*, f. Arab. *ḳālib* mould]
calices. See CALIX.
cali'chĕ (-ē'-) *n.* mineral deposit in dry areas of N. & S. America, esp. Chile saltpetre. [Amer. Sp.]
că'licle *n.* (Biol.) small cuplike body; so **cali'cūl**AR¹ *a.* [f. L *caliculus* dim. of *calix* cup]
că'licō *n.* (*pl.* ∼es *or* *∼s) & *a.* **1.** *n.* cotton cloth, esp. plain white unprinted, bleached or unbleached (∼--**printer**, -**printing**, producer, production, of coloured patterns on calico); *printed cotton fabric. **2.** *a.* of calico; *multicoloured, piebald. [earlier *calicut*, f. name of town in India]
Calif. *abbr.* California.
călifŏ'rnium *n.* (Chem.) artificially made transuranic radioactive metallic element. [f. *California* (where first made)+-IUM]
că'lipăsh, că'lipee, *ns.* gelatinous substances in turtle regarded as delicacies (-*ash*, dull green next to upper shell; -*ee*, light yellow next to lower shell). [17th c., perh. W. Ind. or alt. f. Sp. *carapacho* CARAPACE]
că'liper. See CALLIPER.
că'liph *n.* (esp. Hist.) Muslim chief civil and religious ruler; hence ∼ATE¹ *n.* [ME, f. OF *caliphe* f. Arab. *ḳalīfa* successor (i.e. of Muhammad)]
călisthĕ'nic. Var. of CALLISTHENIC.
că'li|x *n.* (*pl.* ∼ces *pr.* -sēz) cuplike cavity or organ. [L, = cup; cf. CALYX]
***calk.** See CAULK.
call¹ (kawl) *v.t.* & *i.* **1.** cry, shout, speak loudly, (lit. or fig.); (of bird etc.) utter characteristic note; cry *out*; cry *to* (person); (of cricket umpire) disallow ball from (bowler); (Cards) name (suit, contract) in bidding; attempt to predict result of tossing coin etc.; pay brief visit (*at* house, port, station, etc., (*up*)*on* person; *in*); read *over* (names to ascertain owners' presence); *call the* ROLL¹, TUNE; ∼ **for,** open, demand, require, need, go to a place to get; ∼ **off,** cancel (engagement etc.), order (pursuer, attacker) to desist; ∼ (**up**)**on,** invoke, appeal to, request or require (*to* act, speak, etc.). **2.** summon (*for* help); demand presence of (taxi, witness, actor after curtain); invite to pastorate; communicate (with) by radio or telephone; *call to* ACCOUNT; ∼ **into being,** create; *call* person's BLUFF⁴; ∼ **to mind** etc., recollect; ∼ **to order,** request to be orderly, declare (meeting) open; ∼ **into play,** give scope for; ∼ **in question,** dispute; ∼ **away,** divert, distract; ∼ **down,** invoke, reprimand; ∼ **forth,** elicit; ∼ **in,** withdraw from circulation, seek advice from; ∼ **out,** elicit, challenge to duel, order (workers) to strike, summon to action (esp. troops to aid the civil authorities); *call over the* COALS; ∼ **up,** imagine, recollect, summon (esp. to talk by telephone, to serve in army etc., whence ∼--**up** *n.*). **3.** rouse from sleep; fix time for (*call a meeting*); announce as ensuing (*call a halt,* lit. or fig.); urge, invite, nominate, (*duty, pleasure, calls*; ||*call to the* BAR¹); *call attention to; call to witness*). **4.** name, describe as, (*call a* SPADE *a spade*; *call him John*; ∼ person **names,** abuse him in speech); consider, regard or estimate as, (*I call that mean*); *call it a* DAY, QUITS; ∼ (thing) one's **own,** possess. **5.** (Sc.) drive (animal, vehicle, etc.). **6.** Hence ∼'ABLE *a.* [OE *ceallian* f. ON *kalla*, = MLG, MDu. *kallen*, OHG *kallōn* talk (*kallōjan f. Gmc *kal)]
call² (kawl) *n.* **1.** shout, cry; special cry of bird etc., imitation of this, instrument imitating it; signal on bugle etc., signalling-whistle; short resp. formal visit; **pay a** ∼, make this (*pay a call on him; pay him a call*), (colloq.) go to lavatory. **2.** invitation, summons, (to

actor etc. to appear for rehearsal, performance, or applause; ||to the BAR¹; from God, conscience, or congregation, to be pastor); duty, need, occasion, (*no call to blush*); demand *for* (money, esp. lent or unpaid capital; wares) or *on* (one's *purse*, *time*, etc.); (St. Exch.) option of buying stock at fixed price at given date; (Cards) player's right or turn to make a bid, bid etc. thus made; act of telephoning, conversation over telephone. **3. at** ∿, **on** ∿, ready or available when wanted, (of money lent) repayable on demand; **within** ∿, near enough to be summoned by calling. **4. ||∿-box**, structure containing public telephone; ∿**-boy**, prompter's attendant summoning actors; ∿**-day**, **-night**, (on which students are called to the bar); ∿**-girl**, prostitute accepting appointments by telephone; ∿ **of nature**, need to urinate or defecate; ∿**-over**, (1) = ROLL¹-*call*, (2) reading aloud of a list of betting prices (in sporting club etc.); ∿**-sign(al)** (indicating identity of radio transmitter); [ME, f. prec.]

că'lla *n.* aquatic plant of genus *Calla*; ∿ (**lily**), (pop.) arum lily. [mod. L]

ca'ller¹ (kaw'-) *n.* In vbl senses; person who pays call or visit, makes telephone call, announces numbers in bingo etc., or gives directions in square dance. [f. CALL¹ + -ER¹]

ca'ller² *a.* (Sc.) (Of fish) fresh, not decaying; (of air) cool. [var. of ME *calver*, perh. f. OE *calwer* curds]

calli'graph|y *n.* beautiful handwriting; handwriting; so **calli'GRAPHER**, ∿IST (1), *ns.*, **calliGRA'PHIC** *a.* [f. Gk *kalligraphia* (*kallos* beauty; see -GRAPHY)]

ca'lling (kaw'-) *n.* In vbl senses; divine summons to salvation or self-devotion; occupation, profession, trade; *∿-**card**, = *visiting*-CARD². [f. CALL¹ + -ING¹]

***calli'ope** *n.* set of steam whistles producing musical notes, played by keyboard like that of organ. [f. name of Muse of epic poetry, Gk *Kalliopē*, lit. beautiful--voiced]

că'l(l)iper *n.*, & *v.t.* **1. a.** ∿ **compasses** or ∿**s**, compasses with bowed legs for measuring diameter of convex bodies, or with out-turned points for measuring cavities; ∿ (**splint**), metal support for leg. **2.** *v.t.* measure with callipers. [app. var. of CALIBRE]

cállipy'gian, **cállipy'gous**, *adjs.* having well--shaped buttocks. [f. Gk *kallipugos* (*kallos* beauty, *pugē* buttocks) + -IAN, -OUS]

állisthě'n|ic *a.* suitable for producing strength and grace; hence ∿ICS *n. pl.*, gymnastic exercises to achieve bodily health and grace of movement [f. Gk *kallos* beauty + *sthenos* strength + -IC]

ca'llop *n.* (Austral.) golden perch. [Aboriginal]

cállő'sity *n.* abnormal hardness and thickness of skin; hardened insensitive part, lump. [f. F *callosité* or f. L *callositas* (as foll.; see -ITY)]

ca'llous *a.* & *n.* **1. a.** (Physiol. & Zool., of skin) hardened, hard; (of person, heart, etc.) unfeeling, insensitive, whence ∿LY² *adv.*, ∿NESS *n.* **2. n.** callus. [ME, f. L *callosus* (as CALLUS; see -OUS) or F *calleux*]

ca'llow (-ō) *a.* unfledged; raw, inexperienced; hence ∿LY² *adv.*, ∿NESS *n.* [OE *calu* f. WG **kalwaz*, prob. f. L *calvus* bald]

állu'na (-ōō'-) *n.* common heather, of genus *Calluna*. [mod. L, f. Gk *kallunō* beautify (*kallos* beauty)]

ca'llus *n.* (Physiol.) thickened part of skin or soft tissue; (Path.) bony material formed when bone--fracture heals; (Bot.) new tissue over wound. [L]

calm¹ (kahm) *n.* stillness, serenity, (of weather, air, sea, the mind, social or political conditions); windless period. [ME, perh. f. pop. L **calma* f. LL f. Gk *kauma* heat]

calm² (kahm) *a.* & *v.* **1. a.** tranquil, quiet, windless, (lit. or fig.); (colloq.) self-confident, impudent, (*pretty calm of him*); hence ∿'LY² *adv.*, ∿'NESS *n.* **2.** *v.t.* make calm, quiet, pacify. **3.** *v.i.* ∿ (**down**), become calm. [ME, f. med. L *calmus* f. as prec.]

almative (kă'lm-, kah'm-) *a.* & *n.* (Med.) calming (agent), sedative. [f. prec. + -ATIVE]

că'lomĕl *n.* mercurous chloride, esp. when used as purgative. [mod. L, perh. f. Gk *kalos* beautiful + *melas* black]

Că'lor *n.* (P) ∿ **gas**, liquefied butane etc. under pressure in containers for domestic use. [L *calor* heat]

că'loric *n.* & *a.* **1.** *n.* heat, esp. (Hist.) when regarded as a fluid. **2.** *a.* pertaining to heat or calories. [f. F *calorique* (L *calor* heat; see -IC)]

că'lorie *n.* (Phys.) unit of quantity of heat, the amount needed to raise temperature of one gram (**small** ∿) or one kilogram (**large** or **great** ∿) of water one degree C; large calorie as unit of energy value of foods. [F, arbitr. f. L *calor* heat + -*ie* (-Y¹)]

că'lori'fic *a.* producing heat; ∿ **value**, amount of heat given by specified quantity of fuel. [f. L *calorificus* (*calor* heat; see -I-, -FIC)]

că'lori'mĕter *n.* apparatus for measuring heat; hence **călorimĕ'tric** *a.*, **călori'METRY** *n.* [f. L *calor* heat + -I- + -METER]

că'lorỹ Var. of CALORIE.

calő'tte *n.* skull-cap of RC priests etc. [F, dim. of *cale* caul]

cálque (-k) *n.* (Philol.) loan-translation (*of* or *on*). [F, = copy, tracing (*calquer* trace f. It. f. L *calcare* tread)]

***Căltĕ'ch** (-k) *n.* California Institute of Technology. [abbr.]

că'ltrop, **-ap**, *n.* (Hist.) four-spiked iron ball thrown on ground to impede cavalry horses; (Her.) representation of this; (Bot.) plant with spined caltrop--like flower-heads, which catch or entangle feet. [ME, f. OF *kauketrape*, *chauchetrape* (*chauchier* tread, *trappe* trap); (Bot.) f. OE *calcatrippe* f. med. L *calcatrippa*]

că'lūmĕt *n.* Amer. Ind. clay-bowled reed-stemmed tobacco-pipe; symbol of peace. [F, dial. var. of *chalumeau* f. LL *calamellus* dim. of *calamus* reed]

calŭ'mni|āte *v.t.* slander; hence or cogn. ∿A'TION, ∿ATOR, *ns.*, ∿ATORY *a.* [f. L *calumniari* + -ATE³]

că'lumny *n.*, & *v.t.* **1. n.** malicious misrepresentation; false charge; slanderous report; so **calŭ'mnious** *a.* **2.** *v.t.* slander. [f. L *calumnia*]

că'lvadōs *n.* apple brandy. [f. C∿, department of Normandy, France]

Că'lvarỹ *n.* place or (RC Ch.) representation of Crucifixion. [ME, f. LL *calvaria* skull (*calvus* bald), transl. of Gk *golgotha*, Aram. *gulgúltá* (Matt. 27; 33)]

calve (kahv) *v.i.* & *t.* give birth to calf; (esp. in *pass.*) give birth to (calf); (of iceberg etc.) break off mass of ice. [OE *c(e)alfian* (*cælf* CALF¹)]

-calved See CALF².

calves. See CALF¹,².

Că'lvin|ism *n.* theology of Calvin or his followers; adherence to this; hence ∿IST (2) *n.*, ∿I'stic(AL) *adjs.*, ∿IZE (4) *v.i.* & *t.* [f. F *calvinisme* or mod. L -*ismus* f. J. *Calvin*, Fr. theologian d. 1564]

călx *n.* (pl. **ca'lces** *pr.* -sēz). powder or friable substance left when a metal or mineral has been burnt. [L *calx calcis* lime, prob. f. Gk *khalix*, pebble, limestone]

calỹ'psō *n.* (pl. ∿s). (usu. spontaneous topical) W. Ind. song in Afr. rhythm. [20th c.; orig. unkn.]

că'l|yx *n.* (pl. ∿yces *pr.* -īsēz, or ∿yxes). (Bot.) whorl of leaves forming outer case of bud or envelope of flower; (Biol.) = CALIX. [L, f. Gk *kalux* case of bud, husk (cf. *kaluptō* hide)]

căm *n.* projecting part of wheel etc. in machinery, shaped to convert circular into reciprocal or variable motion; ∿'**shaft** carrying cam(s). [f. Du. *kam* comb; cf. Du. *kamrad* cog-wheel]

cămara'derie (-ah'd-) *n.* mutual trust and sociability of comrades. [F]

cămarĭ'lla *n.* cabal, clique. [Sp., dim. of *camara* chamber]

cămaron (kămarō'n, kă'marən) *n.* freshwater shrimp or prawn like crayfish. [Sp., = shrimp]

Camb. *abbr.* Cambridge.

că'mber *n.* & *v.* **1.** *n.* slight convexity above, arched form, (of beam, deck, road from side to side, aircraft wing, etc.); sideways inclination of motor vehicle's wheel. **2.** *v.i.* & *t.* have, or impart to (beam etc.), such convexity. [f. F *cambre, chambre* arched, *cambrer* to arch, f. L *camurus* curved inwards]

Că'mberwĕll *n.* ~ **Beauty,** brown butterfly with yellow-bordered wings. [~ in London]

că'mbist *n.* expert in, manual of, financial exchange; dealer in bills of exchange. [f. F *cambiste* f. It. *cambista* (*cambio* CHANGE[1])]

că'mbium *n.* (Bot.) cellular tissue from which growth of xylem and phloem occurs. [med. L, = (ex)CHANGE[1]]

Cămbō'dian *a.* & *n.* (native or language) of Cambodia (Kampuchea). [f. *Cambodia* in SE Asia + -AN]

Că'mbrian *a.* & *n.* Welsh(man); (Geol.) (of) earliest Palaeozoic period or system. [f. L *Cambria* var. of *Cumbria* f. W *Cymry* Welshmen or *Cymru* Wales (OCelt. *Kombroges* compatriots)]

că'mbric *n.* fine white linen; similar cotton fabric. [f. *Kamerijk,* Flem. form of *Cambrai* in N. France, where orig. made]

Că'mbridge *n.* ~ **blue,** light blue. [~, university town in England]

Cambs. *abbr.* Cambridgeshire.

căme[1] *n.* grooved slip of lead as used in lattice windows. [app. = Sc. *calm* casting-mould]

căme[2]. See COME.

că'mel *n.* large hornless ruminant long-necked cushion-footed quadruped with (Arabian) one hump or (Bactrian) two humps (SWALLOW[1] *a camel*); shade of fawn colour; machine for floating a ship; ~**-back,** inferior rubber for tyres; ~('s)**-hair,** made of camel's hair or (paint-brushes) of squirrel's tail hairs. [OE, f. L f. Gk *kamēlos,* f. Semitic]

cămeleer' *n.* camel-driver. [f. prec. + -EER]

camĕ'llia *n.* shrub of genus *Camellia,* esp. flowering evergreen from China and Japan. [f. J. *Camellus* or *Kamel,* 17th-c. Jesuit and botanist + -IA[1]]

camelopârd (kă'me-, kamĕ'-) *n.* giraffe. [f. L *camelopardus* f. Gk *camēlopardalis* (as CAMEL, PARD[1])]

că'melrў *n.* troops mounted on camels. [f. CAMEL + -RY]

Că'membert (-mahnbār) *n.* kind of small soft rich cheese. [~ in Normandy, France, where orig. made]

că'mĕō *n.* (*pl.* ~s). small piece of relief-carving in stone (onyx, agate, etc.) usu. with colour-layers utilized to give background; relief design of similar form; short literary sketch or acted scene. [ME, f. OF *camahieu* etc. & med. L *cammaeus*]

că'mera *n.* **1.** apparatus for taking photographs or television pictures; **on** ~, in act of being filmed; ~**man,** one who operates a camera professionally, esp. in cinema or television; ~ **obscur'a,** darkened box with aperture for projecting image of distant object on screen within; ~**-shy,** not liking to be photographed. **2.** *in* ~, (1, Law) in judge's private room, (2) privately, not in public. [L, = vault, f. Gk *kamara* thing with arched cover]

cămerli'ngō, -lĕ'n-, (-nggō) *n.* (*pl.* ~s). Pope's chamberlain and financial secretary; treasurer of the Sacred College. [It. *camerlingo* f. Frank., see CHAMBERLAIN]

‖**că'miknickers** (-ĭnĭkerz) *n. pl.* woman's one-piece close-fitting undergarment. [f. CAMISOLE + KNICKERS]

că'mion *n.* dray; lorry; bus. [F]

că'misōle *n.* (arch.) under-bodice, usu. embroidered. [F, f. It. *camiciola* or Sp. *camisola* (*camicia, camisa* shirt; see CHEMISE)]

că'mlĕt *n.* (arch.) light cloth of various materials for cloaks etc. [orig. a costly Eastern material, ME, f. OF *cham-, camelot* perh. ult. f. Arab. *ḳamla(t)* nap; assoc. w. CAMEL]

că'momīle, ch- (k-), *n.* aromatic composite plant of genus *Anthemis* or *Matricaria* with flowers used as

tonic; ~ **tea,** infusion of the flowers. [ME, f. OF *camomille* f. LL *c(h)amomilla* f. Gk *khamaimēlon* earth-apple (f. apple-smell of flowers)]

că'mouflage (-ŏōflahzh, -ŏf-) *n.,* & *v.t.* **1.** *n.* disguise of guns, ships, etc., effected by obscuring with splashes of various colours, smoke-screens, foliage, etc.; means of disguise or evasion. **2.** *v.t.* hide by camouflage. [F (*camoufler* (sl.) disguise f. It. *camuffare* disguise, deceive; see -AGE)]

cămp[1] *n.* **1.** place where troops are lodged or trained; military life (*court and camp*); (arch.) army on campaign; (remains of) ancient fortified site; temporary quarters of nomads, gypsies, detainees, holiday-makers, Scouts, Guides, or travellers; (persons) camping out; (S. Afr.) portion of veld fenced off for pasture on farms; (Austral. & NZ) assembly place of sheep or cattle; adherents of a doctrine or party. **2.** ~**-bed, -chair,** etc., (folding and portable); ~'**craft,** skill in living in camp; ~**-fever,** typhus; ~**-fire,** open-air fire in camp etc.; *~ **fire girl,** member of a recreational and training organization; ~**-follower,** non-military worker or hanger-on in camp, disciple of group or theory; *~**-meeting,** religious open-air or tent meeting often lasting several days; ~'**site,** place for camping; ~**-stool,** light stool with folding legs. [F, f. It. *campo* f. L *campus* level ground]

cămp[2] *v.i.* encamp, lodge in camp; ~ (**out**), lodge in temporary quarters or in the open; (Austral. & NZ, of sheep or cattle) flock together esp. for rest. [f. F *campes* (as prec.)]

cămp[3] *a., n.,* & *v.* **1.** *a.* affected, effeminate; homosexual; exaggerated, bizarre. **2.** *n.* camp behaviour; hence ~'Y[2] *a.* **3.** *v.i.* & *t.* behave or do in a camp way, ~ **it up,** overact. [20th c.; orig. uncert.]

cămpai'gn (-ā'n) *n.,* & *v.i.* **1.** *n.* series of military operations in a definite area or with one objective or forming the whole or a distinct part of a war; military service in the field (*on campaign*); organized course of action, esp. (Polit. etc.) attempt to arouse public interest, esp. before an election. **2.** *v.i.* serve on or conduct campaign; hence ~ER[1] *n.* (**old** ~er, veteran, person skilled in adapting himself to circumstances). [f. F *campagne* open country, f. It. *campagna* f. LL *campania;* cf. CHAMPAIGN]

cămpani'le (-nē'-) *n.* bell-tower, usu. detached, esp. in Italy. [It. (*campana* bell)]

cămpanŏ'|logўn *n.* subject of bells (founding, ringing etc.); hence ~LOGER, ~LOGIST, *ns.,* ~LO'GICAL *a.* [f. mod. L *campanologia* f. LL *campana* bell + -LOGY]

cămpă'nūla *n.* plant of genus *Campanula,* with bell-shaped flowers, usu. blue, pink, or white. [mod. L, dim. of *campana* bell; see -ULE]

cămpă'nūlate *a.* (Bot. & Zool.) bell-shaped. [f. as prec. + -ATE[2]]

Cămpea'chў *n.* ~ **wood,** LOG[1]wood. [f. *Campeche* in Mexico, whence first exported]

că'mper *n.* In vbl senses; motor vehicle used as living-accommodation when camping. [f. CAMP[2] + -ER[1]]

că'mphor *n.* whitish translucent crystalline volatile substance with aromatic smell and bitter taste, used in pharmacy and as insect-repellent; hence **cămphŏ'ric** *a.* [ME, f. OF *camphore* or med. L *camphora,* f. Arab. *kāfūr* f. Skr. *karpūram*]

că'mphorāte *v.t.* impregnate or treat with camphor. [f. prec. + -ATE[3]]

că'mpion *n.* plant of genus *Silene, Melandrium,* or *Lychnis,* with notched flowers. [transl. of Gk *lukhnis stephanōmatikē* a plant used for garlands, perh. f. obs. *campion* CHAMPION]

că'mpus *n.* grounds of university or college; university as teaching etc. institution. [L, = field]

că'mwŏŏd *n.* hard red W. Afr. wood yielding dye. [perh. f. Temne]

căn[1] *n.,* & *v.t.* (**-nn-**). **1.** *n.* metal vessel for liquids, usu. with handle; **carry** or **take the** ~ (**back**), (sl.) bear the responsibility or blame. **2.** jacket for nuclear fuel rod; *metal container (~ **of worms,** complex and largely uninvestigated topic); *(sl.) lavatory; (sl.) prison. **3.** tin-plate container for hermetic sealing (to preserve meat, fish, fruit, drink, etc.); ∿**-opener**, tool for opening cans. **4.** *v.t.* put into a can; preserve thus; (sl.) desist from. **5.** Hence (-)∿'**nER**[1] *n.*, ∿'**nERY** (3) *n.*, canning-factory. [OE *canne*, = OHG *channa*, ON *kanna*, Gmc or f. LL *canna*]

can² (*or, when stressed*, kăn) *v. aux.* (*pres.* **can** exc. 2 *sing.* (arch.) **canst**, *neg.* **ca'nnot**, (colloq.) **can't** *pr.* kahnt; *past* **could** *pr.* kud *or* kŏŏd exc. 2 *sing.* (arch.) **couldst** *pr.* kŏŏdst *or* **couldest** *pr.* kŏŏ'dĭst, *neg.* **could not**, (colloq.) **couldn't** *pr.* kŏŏ'dĕnt; no other parts used). be able to; have right to; (colloq.) be permitted to (*all right, you can go*); know how to (*can you play bridge, speak French?*); could, feel inclined to (*could laugh for joy*; *could you please ring?; really couldn't think of it*); (ellipt.) *will do what I can, how could you?*, (I) ∿ **do** (it), (that) **could be** (so). [OE *cunnan*, = OS *cunnan*, OHG *kunnan*, ON *kunna*, Goth. *kunnan* (preterite-present vbs.) know f. IE]

Can. *abbr.* Canada; Canadian.

Ca'naan (-nan) *n.* land of promise; heaven. [ancient name of W. Palestine; eccl. L f. eccl. Gk *Khanaan* f. Heb. *kᵉna'an*]

Ca'nada *n.* Canada BALSAM; ∿ **goose**, N. Amer. wild goose (*Branta canadensis*); hence **Canā'dIAN** *a.* & *n.* [∿ in N. America]

anaille (kanah'ē) *n.* the rabble, the populace. [F, f. It. *canaglia* pack of dogs (*cane* dog)]

a'nakin. Var. of CANNIKIN.

anā'l *n.* duct in plant or animal body for food, liquid, air, etc.; artificial watercourse for inland navigation or irrigation; (on planet Mars) seasonal marking, like a narrow line when observed from the Earth; (Zool.) groove in shell for protrusion of mollusc's breathing-tube; ∿ **boat**, long narrow boat for use on canals; ∿ **ray**, beam of particles moving to cathode of high-vacuum tube. [ME f. OF, earlier *chanel* f. L *canalis* or It. *canale*]

a'naliz|e, -ĭs|e (-īz), *v.t.* make canal through; convert (river) into canal; provide with canals; (fig.) give desired direction etc. to; hence ∿A'TION *n.* [f. F. *canaliser* (CANAL; see -IZE)]

a'napé (-pǐ) *n.* **1.** piece of bread, toast, etc., with small savoury on top. **2.** sofa. [F]

anārd (kanär'd, kă'närd) *n.* false report, hoax; extra surface attached to aircraft for stability or control. [F, = duck]

anarese. Var. of KANARESE.

anār'ȳ *n.* yellow-feathered song-bird, the finch *Serinus canarius;* (Hist.) sweet wine from Canary Islands; ∿(-**coloured**), ∿-**yellow**, bright yellow; ∿ **creeper**, yellow-flowered climbing plant, *Tropaeolum peregrinum;* ∿-**seed** (used as food for canaries and other cage-birds). [f. *Canary* Islands f. F *Canarie* f. Sp. & L *Canaria* (*canis* dog), one of the islands being noted in Roman times for large dogs]

anā'sta *n.* card-game of Uruguayan origin, resembling rummy; meld of seven cards in it. [Sp., = basket]

anā'ster *n.* tobacco prepared by coarsely breaking the dried leaves. [orig. the rush basket container; f. Sp. *canastro*, f. med. L **canastrum*, f. Gk *kanastron*; see CANISTER]

'ncăn (-n-k-) *n.* high-kicking dance by woman with display of legs and petticoats. [F]

'ncel *v.* (||-ll-). **1.** *v.t.* obliterate, cross out; annul, make void, abolish; countermand, revoke order or arrangements for, neutralize; balance, make up for; efface (postage stamp) to prevent further use; (Math.) strike out (same factor) from numerator and denominator, from two sides of equation, etc.; (Mus.) return to natural pitch after (sharp or flat). **2.** *v.i.* ∿ (**out**), neutralize each other. **3.** Hence ∿LA'TION *n.* [ME, f. F *canceller* f. L *cancellare* (*cancelli* cross-bars, lattice)]

'ncel² *n.* countermand; postal cancellation;

(Print.) suppression and reprinting of leaf or leaves set up, the suppressed or the substituted leaf or leaves; *(Mus.) natural-sign. [f. prec.]

că'ncellate, că'ncellāted, *adjs.* (Biol.) marked with crossing lines; (of bone) porous. [f. as foll. + -ATE² (+ -ED¹)]

că'ncellous *a.* (Of bone) porous. [f. L *cancelli* lattice + -OUS]

că'ncer *n.* **1.** (C∿). sign of the ZODIAC, the Crab; TROPIC *of Cancer*. **2.** (Path.) (condition in which there is) malignant tumour from uncontrolled growth of tissue, tending to spread and to recur when removed; (fig.) evil (corruption etc.) acting similarly; ∿ **stick**, (sl.) cigarette; hence ∿OUS *a.* [ME f. L, = crab, cancer, after Gk *karkinos;* cf. CARCINOMA]

că'ncroid *a.* & *n.* **1.** *a.* crablike; like cancer. **2.** *n.* crustacean of crab family; mild form of cancer. [f. as prec. + -OID]

c & b *abbr.* caught and bowled by.

candela (kă'ndĭla, -ē'la) *n.* unit of luminous intensity in the international system. [L, = CANDLE]

cǎndēla'br|um (-ă'-, -ah'-) *n.* (*pl.* ∿**a** *or* ***∿**ums**; also *sing.* ∿**a**, *pl.* ∿**as**). large, usu. branched, candlestick or lamp-holder; ∿**um tree**, tropical Afr. tree with foliage shaped like candelabrum. [L (*candela* CANDLE)]

cǎnde'sc|ent *a.* glowing (as) with white heat; hence ∿ENCE *n.* [f. L *candere* be white; see -ESCENT]

că'ndĭd *a.* frank, not hiding one's thoughts; (arch.) unbiased; ∿ **camera**, small camera for taking informal pictures of persons freq. without their knowledge (so ∿ **photograph** etc.); hence ∿LY² *adv.*, ∿NESS *n.* [f. F *candide* or L *candidus* white (*candēre;* see prec.)]

că'ndĭdacȳ *n.* candidature. [f. foll. + -ACY]

că'ndĭdate (-*at*, -āt) *n.* one who seeks or is nominated for, appointment to an office or honour or membership; person or thing thought likely to gain any position; examinee. [f. F *candidat* or f. L *candidatus* white-robed (Roman candidates wearing white, f. *candidus* (*candēre* be white); see -ATE²]

||**că'ndĭdature** *n.* standing for election, being candidate. [F (as prec.; see -URE)]

că'ndle *n.*, & *v.t.* **1.** *n.* cylinder of wax, tallow, etc., enclosing wick, for giving light by burning; ∿(**power**), unit of luminous intensity; **Roman** ∿, firework in form of tube discharging coloured balls. **2.** BELL¹, *book, and candle;* **burn the** ∿ **at both ends**, exhaust one's strength or resources through under-taking too much; **can't, is not to, hold a** ∿ **to**, is not to be compared with, is much inferior to; **game not worth the** ∿, result not justifying the cost or trouble. **3.** ∿**berry-myrtle**, ∿**berry-tree**, trees yielding wax and oil used for candles; ∿-**light**, (1) light of candles, (2) dusk; ∿**stick**, support for (usu. single) candle; ∿-**tree** (with long candle-like fruit); ∿**wick**, (material with raised usu. tufted pattern in) thick soft cotton yarn. **4.** *v.t.* test (egg) for freshness etc. by holding between eye and light. [OE *candel* f. L *candela* (*candēre* shine)]

Că'ndlemas (delm-) *n.* feast of Purification of Virgin Mary and presentation of Christ in Temple, when candles are blessed (2 Feb.). [OE *Candelmæsse* (as CANDLE, MASS¹)]

||**că'ndour** (-der), *****că'ndor**, prec. candid behaviour or action; frankness. [f. F *candeur* or f. L *candor* whiteness (*candēre;* see -OR)]

C. & W. *abbr.* country-and-western.

că'ndȳ *n.*, & *v.t.* **1.** *n.* (**sugar-**/∿), crystallized sugar made by repeated boiling and slow evaporation; ***sweetmeat (COUGH² *candy*); ∿-**floss**, mass of fluffy spun sugar; ***∿-**store**, sweet-shop; ∿-**stripe**(d), pattern(ed) in alternate stripes of white and colour. **2.** *v.t.* preserve by coating and impregnating with sugar (*candied* PEEL³). [earlier *sugar candy* f. F *sucre candi* f. Arab. *sükkar ḳandī* (*ḳand* sugar f. Pers. *kand* f. Skr. *khaṇḍa* sugar in pieces)]

că'ndȳtŭft *n.* plant of genus *Iberis* with white, pink, or purple flowers in flat tufts. [f. obs. *Candy* (*Candia* Crete) +TUFT]

cāne¹ *n*. **1.** hollow jointed stem of giant reeds and grasses (*bamboo cane*) or solid stem of slender palms (*rattan, Malacca*, etc.); SUGAR-*cane*; material of such stems for wickerwork etc.; this stem or a length of it used as walking-stick or instrument of punishment or to support plant; any slender walking-stick. **2.** *~-**brake**, tract of land overgrown with canes; ~ **chair** (with seat of woven cane strips); ~-**sugar** (obtained from the sugar-cane); *cane*-TRASH. [ME f. OF, f. L f. Gk *kanna* reed f. Semitic]

cāne² *v.t.* beat with cane, whence **cā′nɪnɢ¹** (1) *n*.; weave cane into (chair etc.). [f. prec.]

căngue (kăng), **căng,** *n*. (Hist.) heavy wooden board worn round neck as punishment in China. [F. *cangue* f. Port. *canga* yoke, f. Vietnamese]

că′nīne *a*. & *n*. of or as of a dog or dogs; dog; ~ (**tooth**), one of the four strong pointed teeth between incisors and molars. [ME, f. *canin -ine* or f. L *caninus* (*canis* dog; see -INE¹)]

că′nister *n*. small container usu. of metal for tea, shot, etc. [f. L *canistrum* f. Gk *kanastron* wicker basket (*kanna* CANE¹)]

că′nker *n*., & *v.t.* **1.** *n*. ulcerous disease of animals; necrotic disease of plants; (fig.) corrupting influence; ~(-**worm**), caterpillar destroying buds and leaves; hence ~OUS *a*. **2.** *v.t.* consume with canker; infect, corrupt; (in *p.p.*) soured, malignant, crabbed. [OE *cancer* & ONF *cancre*, OF *chancre* f. L *cancer*; see CANCER, CHANCRE]

că′nna *n*. plant of genus *Canna*, with bright yellow, red, or orange flowers and ornamental leaves. [L; see CANE¹]

că′nnabis *n*. hemp plant of genus *Cannabis*; preparation of parts of it used as intoxicant or hallucinogen; ~ **resin,** sticky product esp. from flowering tops of female cannabis plant. [L f. Gk]

că′nned (-nd) *a*. In vbl senses; (sl.) drunk, (of music) recorded for reproduction. [p.p. of CAN¹]

că′nnel *n*. ~ (**coal**), bituminous coal burning with bright flame. [16th c.; orig. N. Engl.]

cănnellō′nī *n. pl.* rolls of pasta containing meat and seasoning. [It., augment. pl. of *cannello* stalk; see -OON]

că′nnelūre *n*. groove round bullet etc. [F (*canneler* f. *canne* reed, CANE¹; see -URE)]

că′nner(ȳ). See CAN¹.

că′nnibal *n*. & *a*. **1.** *n*. person who eats human flesh; animal that eats its own species; hence ~ISM (2) *n*., ~**ī′stɪc** *a*. **2.** *a*. of or having these habits. [orig. pl. *Canibales* f. Sp., var. of *Caribes* name of a W. Ind. nation]

că′nnibalīze, -īse (-īz), *v.t.* use (machine etc.) as source of spare parts for others. [f. prec. +-IZE (4)]

că′nnikin *n*. small can. [f. Du. *kanneken* (as CAN¹, -KIN)]

că′nnon¹ *n*. **1.** aircraft's automatic shell-firing gun; (Hist.; *pl.* usu. same) piece of ordnance, gun of kind that needs a mounting; ~-**ball**, (Hist.) projectile fired by cannon; ~-**bone**, tube-shaped bone between horse's hock and fetlock; ~-**fodder,** men regarded merely as material to be consumed in war. **2.** (Mech.) hollow cylinder moving independently on shaft. **3.** ~(-**bit**), smooth round bit for horse. **4.** ||(Bill.) hitting of two balls successively by player's ball. [f. F *canon* f. It. *cannone* great tube (*canna* CANE¹; see -OON); in sense 4 f. older CAROM]

||**că′nnon²** *v.i.* come into collision, strike obliquely, *against, into*; make cannon at billiards. [f. prec.]

cănnonā′de *n*., & *v.t.* **1.** *n*. continuous gunfire. **2.** *v.t.* bombard with cannon. [f. F *cannonade*, f. It. *cannonata* (as prec.; see -ADE)]

că′nnot. See CAN².

că′nnŭl|a *n*. (*pl.* ~**ae** or ~**as**). (Surg.) small tube for inserting into a cavity or tumour to allow fluid to enter or escape; hence ~ATE³ *v.t.*, introduce cannula into. [L, dim. of *canna* CANE¹]

că′nn|ȳ *a*. shrewd, worldly-wise, (esp. of Scots) thrifty;

circumspect (CA′CANNY); sly, pawky; hence ~ɪLY² *adv.*, ~ɪNESS *n*. [f. CAN² know + -Y²]

canoe′ (-ōō′) *n*., & *v.i.* (~**ing**). (go in, paddle) keelless boat propelled by paddle(s) (PADDLE² one's *own canoe*); hence ~ɪST (3) *n*. [f. Sp. and Haitian *canoa*]

că′non *n*. **1.** church decree; ~ **law,** eccl. law esp. from papal and council pronouncements. **2.** general law, rule, or principle; criterion; collection or list of sacred books etc. accepted as genuine; (list of) recognized genuine works of a particular author (*the Shakespeare canon*). **3.** part of Mass containing words of consecration; (Mus.) (style of) piece with different parts taking up same subject successively in strict imitation. **4.** member of cathedral chapter; MINOR *canon; canon* REGULAR; hence ~ESS¹, ~RY (2), *ns*. [OE f. L f. Gk *kanōn*, in ME also f. AF & OF *canun, -on*; in sense 4 ME, f. OF *canonie* f. eccl. L *canonicus*; cf. CANONICAL]

cañon. See CANYON.

canŏ′nĭc *a*. = foll.; so ~ATE¹ *n*., canonry. [OE, f. OF *canonique* or f. L f. Gk *kanonikos* (as CANON; see -IC)]

canŏ′nical *a*. & *n*. **1.** *a*. appointed by canon law (~ **hours,** times for prayer, or for celebration of marriage); included in canon of Scripture; authoritative, standard, accepted; (Mus.) in canon form; of a cathedral chapter or a member of it; hence ~LY² *adv*. **2.** *n*. (in *pl*.) canonical dress of clergy. [f. med. L *canonicalis*; see prec., -AL]

cănonĭ′cĭtȳ *n*. status of canonical book. [f. L *canonicus* canonical +-ITY]

că′nonist *n*. expert in canon law. [ME, f. F *canoniste* or f. med. L *canonista* (as CANON; see -IST)]

că′nonīz|e, -īs|e (-īz), *v.t.* admit formally to list of saints; regard as a saint; sanction by church authority; so ~A′TION *n*. [ME, f. med. L *canonizare* (as CANON; see -IZE)]

că′nonrȳ. See CANON 4.

canŏŏ′dle *v.i.* & *t.* (sl.) cuddle amorously, fondle [19th c.; US, of unkn. orig.]

Canŏ′pĭc *a*. ~ **jar, vase,** urn used for holding the entrails of an embalmed body in ancient Egyptian burial. [f. L *Canopicus*, f. *Canopus* in ancient Egypt; see -IC]

că′nopȳ *n*., & *v.t.* **1.** *n*. covering suspended or held over throne, bed, person, etc. (also fig. of any overhanging shelter, the sky, etc.); (Archit.) rooflike projection over niche etc.; expanding part of parachute; cover of cockpit in aircraft. **2.** *v.t.* supply or be canopy to [ME, f. med. L *canopeum* f. L f. Gk *kōnōpeion* mosquito-net *kōnōps* gnat)]

canŏ′rous *a*. melodious, resonant. [f. L *canoru. (canere* sing) + -OUS]

cănst. See CAN².

cănt¹ *n*. bevel, oblique face, of crystal, bank, etc.; push toss, movement, that partly or quite upsets; tilted or sloping position; ||~**rail,** timber etc. supporting railway-carriage roof. [ME, f. MLG *kant, kante* MDu. *cant,* point, side, edge, f. Rom. *canto f. L *cant(h)us* iron tire]

cănt² *v.* **1.** *v.t.* bevel off; tilt; turn over or upside down push or pitch sideways. **2.** *v.i.* take inclined position lie aslant; (Naut.) swing round. **3.** ~-**dog,** ~-**hook** iron hook at end of long handle, used for rolling logs [f. prec.]

cănt³ *n*., & *v.i.* **1.** *n*. (usu. derog.) language of clas: profession, sect, etc., jargon. **2.** ephemeral catch words; words used for fashion without being meant insincere use of words implying piety; hypocrisy. **3** *v.i.* use cant; ~**'ing arms,** (Her.) arms containin; allusion to name of bearer. [earlier of musical sound of intonation, and of beggars' whining, perh. f singing of religious mendicants; prob. f. L *cantar* frequent. of *canere* sing]

Cant. *abbr.* Canticles (OT)

Că′ntăb. *abbr.* of Cambridge University. [f. L *Canta brigiensis*]

cănta′bile (-ah′-) *adv.* & *n*. (Mus.) (piece) in smootł flowing style. [It., = singable]

Cantabri′gian n. & a. (member) of Cambridge (or *Harvard) University; (native or inhabitant) of Cambridge in England or *in Massachusetts. [f. L *Cantabrigia* Cambridge + -AN]

ca′ntal n. hard strong type of French cheese. [f. C~, department of Auvergne, France]

ca′ntaloup, -oupe, (-ōōp) n. small round ribbed melon with orange flesh. [F *cantaloup*, f. *Cantaluppi* near Rome, where first grown in Europe]

canta′nkerous a. bad-tempered, quarrelsome; hence ~LY² adv., ~NESS n. [perh. f. Ir. *cant* outbidding + *rancorous*]

canta′ta (-tah′-) n. (Mus.) choral work, kind of short oratorio, or lyric drama set to music but not intended for acting. [It. *cantata* (*aria*) sung (air) f. *cantare* sing]

Canta′te (-ah′-) n. canticle consisting of Ps. 98. [L, = sing ye, its first word]

cantatrice (kä′ntatrēs, -ē′chä) n. professional woman singer. [It. & F]

cantee′n n. provision and liquor shop in camp or barracks (**dry, wet,** ~, without, chiefly for, liquor); ‖bar, lunch-counter, etc. at outdoor entertainment or in large public or private institution; soldier's or camper's water-flask or set of eating and drinking utensils; case or chest of plate or cutlery for domestic use. [f. F *cantine* f. It. *cantina* cellar]

cante hondo (kahntĭ hŏ′ndō) n. type of usu. mournful Spanish song. [Sp., = deep song]

ca′nter n. & v. **1.** n. easy gallop; *win in a* ~, easily. **2.** v.i. (Of horse or rider) go at this pace. **3.** v.t. make (horse) go thus. [short for *Canterbury pace, gallop, trot,* etc., f. supposed easy pace of medieval pilgrims to Canterbury in Kent]

Ca′nterbury n. **1.** ~ **bell,** kind of campanula [f. bells of Canterbury pilgrims' horses]. **2.** (c~). stand with partitions for music etc. [~ in Kent]

antha′rides (-z) n. pl. (Med.) dried SPANISH fly. [pl. of L f. Gk *kantharis* Spanish fly]

a′nth‖us n. (pl. ~**i** pr. -ī). outer or inner corner of eye, where lids meet. [L, f. Gk *kanthos*]

a′nticle n. hymn; one of the Anglican Prayer-Book hymns; (C~ of) C~s, SONG of Solomon. [ME f. OF, or f. L *canticulum* dim. of *canticum* (*cantus* song f. *canere* sing)]

antile′na n. (Mus.) simple or sustained melody. [It.]

a′ntilever n. long bracket projecting from wall to support balcony etc.; beam or girder fixed at only one end; ~ **bridge** (with piers each of which has two cantilevers, and long girders connecting cantilevers of adjacent piers). [17th c.; orig. unkn.]

a′ntill′ate v.t. & i. chant, recite with musical tones; hence ~A′TION n. [f. L *cantillare* sing low (as CHANT) + -ATE⁰]

anti′na n. bar-room or wine-shop. [Sp. & It.]

a′ntle n. (arch.) piece or slice cut off; hind bow of saddle. [ME, f. AF *cantel*, OF *chantel* f. med. L *cantellus* dim. of L *cantus* CANT¹]

a′ntō n. (pl. ~s). division of long poem. [It., = song, f. L *cantus*]

anton¹ (kä′ntŏn, -ŏ′n) n. subdivision of country; State of Swiss confederation; (Her.) square division, less than a QUARTER¹, in upper (usu. dexter) corner of shield; hence ~AL a. [OF, = corner (as CANT¹; see -OON)]

anto′n² v.t. **1.** (käntŏ′n). divide into cantons. **2.** (kantōō′n). quarter (soldiers). [partly f. F *cantonner*, partly f. prec.]

antone′se (-z) a. & n. (pl. same). (native or inhabitant or Chinese dialect) of Canton. [f. *Canton* in China + -ESE]

anto′nment (-ōō′n-) n. lodging assigned to troops; (Ind.) permanent military station. [f. F *cantonnement* (as CANTON²; see -MENT)]

a′ntor n. leader of singing in church, precentor; precentor in synagogue. [L, = singer (*canere* cant-sing; see -OR)]

antōr′ial a. of the precentor; of N. side of choir (cf. DECANAL). [f. prec. + -IAL]

cantŏr′is a. (Mus.) to be sung by cantorial side in antiphonal singing (cf. DECANI). [L, gen. of CANTOR precentor]

ca′ntrip n. (Sc.) witch's trick; piece of mischief, playful act. [18th c.; orig. unkn.]

***Canu′ck** n. & a. (derog.) (French) Canadian (person or horse or pony). [app. f. *Canada*]

ca′nvas n., & v.t. (-s- or -ss-). **1.** n. (piece of) strong unbleached cloth of hemp, flax, or other coarse yarn, for sails, tents, painting on; a painting, esp. in oils; open kind of canvas used as basis for tapestry and embroidery; racing-boat's covered end (*win* **by a** ~, by narrow margin in racing); **under** ~, (1) in tent(s), (2) with sails spread; ~**-back,** N. Amer. wild duck *Aythya valisineria* (f. colour of back feathers). **2.** v.t. cover with canvas. [ME & ONF *canevas*, OF *chanevaz* f. Rom. **cannapaceum* f. **cannapum* f. L CANNABIS]

ca′nvass v. & n. **1.** v.t. & i. discuss thoroughly; solicit votes, solicit votes from (electors in constituency), ascertain sentiments of, ask custom of; ‖propose (plan etc.); *check validity of votes; hence ~ER¹ n. **2.** n. canvassing for or of votes. [f. prec., orig. = toss in a sheet, shake up, agitate, etc.]

ca′nyon, cañon, (kä′nyon) n. deep gorge, freq. with stream. [f. Sp. *cañón* tube (*caña* f. L *canna* CANE¹)]

cänzone′tta, cänzone′t, n. short light song; kind of madrigal. [It., dim. of *canzone* song f. L *cantio -onis* (*canere* sing)]

caou′tchouc (kow′chōōk) n. & a. (of) unvulcanized rubber. [F, f. Carib *cahuchu*]

cap¹ n. **1.** nurse's or woman servant's indoor head-dress; brimless soft esp. outdoor head-dress, usu. with peak; **the** ~ **fits,** (fig.) general remark is true of person in question; ~ **in hand,** (fig.) humbly; **set** one's ~ **at,** try to attract as suitor. **2.** special head-dress (college mortar-board, as part of Highland costume, or ‖awarded as sign of membership of sports team; ~ **and bells** (worn by professional jester); ~ **of liberty** (conical, given to Roman slave on emancipation, now (esp. French) Republican symbol); *cap of MAINTENANCE*); money collected in cap at fox-hunt etc. from those who are not subscribing members. **3.** covering like cap in shape, position, etc., natural (mushroom top, kneecap, etc.), or designed for various purposes (windmill top, toe-cap; device to seal bottle, protect nib of fountain pen or lens of camera, etc.; — DUTCH¹ *cap; — PERCUSSION cap*); ~ **sleeve** (extending only short distance from shoulder); ~**′stone,** top stone, coping. **4.** (mining) ~**′FUL 2** n., (esp.) passing gust of wind. [f. OE *cæppe* f. LL *cappa*, perh. f. L *caput* head]

cap² v.t. (-pp-). **1.** put cap on; (Sc. & NZ) confer university degree on; award cap to (player); protect (end of beam etc.) with metal etc., whence ~′PING¹ (3) n. **2.** lie on top of, form cap of; follow with another (~ **anecdote, quotation,** etc., produce another esp. better or apposite one; ~ **verses,** reply with verse beginning with the previous one's last letter. [f. prec.]

CAP abbr. Common Agricultural Policy.

cap. abbr. capital (letter); chapter [f. L *capitulum* or *caput*]

capabi′lity n. power *of* (action etc., acting etc.), *for* (being treated in some way), *to* (do something); undeveloped or unused faculty. [f. foll. + -ITY]

ca′pable a. susceptible, admitting, (*of*); ~ **of,** having the ability or fitness for; wicked enough for; gifted, able, competent; hence **ca′pabLY²** adv. [F, f. LL *capabilis* f. L *capere* hold; see -ABLE]

capa′cious (-shus) a. able to hold much; hence ~LY² adv., ~NESS n. [f. L *capax -acis* (*capere* hold) + -IOUS]

capa′citance n. (Electr.) **1.** ratio of the change in the electric charge of a body to the corresponding change in its potential. **2.** ability to store a charge of electricity, capacity. [f. CAPACITY + -ANCE]

capa′citāte *v.t.* render capable (*for, to* do); make legally competent. [f. CAPACITY + -ATE³]

capa′citor *n.* (Electr.) device having capacitance usu. consisting of conductors separated by insulator. [f. foll. + -OR]

capa′cǐtỹ *n.* **1.** power of containing, receiving, experiencing, or producing, (*capacity for heat, moisture,* etc.); maximum amount that can be contained, produced, etc.; **to** ∼, fully (*working to capacity*); (*attrib.*) fully occupying (*capacity audience* etc.). **2.** cubic content, e.g. of cylinders in engine, (**measure of** ∼, measure used for vessels and liquids, grain, etc.); mental power, faculty, talent; position, relative character, (*in a civil capacity; in my capacity as critic*); legal competency; (Electr.) capacitance, whence **capa′cǐt**(AT)IVE *a.* [ME, f. F *capacité* f. L *capacitas -tatis* (as CAPACIOUS; see -ITY)]

cǎp-à-pie′ (-apē′) *adv.* (arch.) from head to foot, (armed, ready, etc.). [f. OF *cap a pie*]

capa′rison *n.*, & *v.t.* **1.** *n.* (usu. in *pl.*) horse's trappings; equipment, outfit. **2.** *v.t.* put caparisons on. [f. obs. F *caparasson* f. Sp. *caparazón* saddle-cloth (*capa* CAPE¹)]

cāpe¹ *n.* short sleeveless cloak, either as separate garment or as fixed or detachable part of longer cloak or coat. [F, f. Prov. *capa* f. LL *cappa* CAP¹]

cāpe² *n.* headland, promontory. [ME, f. OF f. Prov. *cap* f. Rom. **capo* f. L *caput* head]

Cāpe³ *n.* the CAPE² of Good Hope; *the* province containing it; ∼ **cart,** (S. Afr.) two-wheeled horse--drawn cart; ∼ **Coloured,** (member) of COLOURED population of Cape Province; ∼ **doctor,** (S. Afr.) strong SE wind; ∼ **Dutch,** (arch.) Afrikaans; ∼ **gooseberry,** kind of ground-cherry, c∼′**skin,** soft leather from S. Afr. sheepskin; ∼ **smoke,** (Hist.) S. Afr. brandy. [f. prec.]

cǎp(e)lin *n.* small smeltlike fish used as cod-bait. [f. F f. Prov. *capelan; see* CHAPLAIN]

cā′per¹ *n.* bramble-like S. Eur. shrub (*Capparis spinosa*); (in *pl.*) its flower-buds pickled (esp. for *caper sauce*). [ME, & f. F *câpres,* f. L f. Gk *kapparis*; treated as pl., cf. CHERRY, PEA]

cā′per² *n.*, & *v.i.* **1.** *n.* frisky movement, leap; fantastic proceeding; (sl.) any activity or occupation; **cut a** ∼ or ∼**s,** = sense 2. **2.** *v.i.* move friskily, leap; hence ∼ER¹ *n.* [abbr. of CAPRIOLE]

cǎpercai′llie, -lzie (-lyǐ, -lzǐ), *n.* large kind of grouse (*Tetrao urogallus*), largest European gallinaceous bird. [f. Gael. *capull coille* horse of the wood]

cǎ′piäs *n.* (Law). writ commanding arrest of person named. [L, = you are to seize, 2 sing. pres. subj. of *capere* take]

cǎpillā′ritỹ *n.* (power of exerting) capillary attraction or repulsion. [f. F *capillarité*; see foll., -TY¹]

capi′llarỹ *a.* & *n.* of hair; hairlike, thin as hair; (tube) of minute or hairlike diameter (e.g. one of ramified blood-vessels intervening between arteries and veins); ∼ **attraction, repulsion,** (by which liquid is drawn up, down, in capillary tubes). [f. L *capillaris* (*capillus* hair; see -ARY²)]

cǎ′pital¹ *n.* head or cornice of pillar or column. [ME, f. OF *capitel* f. LL *capitellum* dim. of *caput* head]

cǎ′pital² *a.* & *n.* **1.** *a.* involving loss of life (*capital punishment*); punishable by death (*capital offence*); vitally injurious, fatal, (*capital error*). **2.** standing at the head; chief (∼ **city** or **town,** head town of country, county, etc.); important, leading, first-class; (colloq.) excellent, first-rate, (also as *int.* of approval); original, principal. **3.** Hence ∼LY² *adv.* **4.** (Of letter) having form and size used to begin sentence, name, etc. (*capital A* etc.); **with a** ∼ **A** etc., emphatically such (*life with a capital L*). **5.** *n.* capital letter; capital city or town. **6.** stock with which company or person enters into business; accumulated wealth esp. as used in further production; holders of this as a class; **make** ∼ **out of,** (fig.) turn to account. **7.** ∼ **gain,** profit from sale of investments or property; ∼ **goods,** goods (to be) used in producing commodities, opp. *consumer*

goods; *capital* LEVY; ∼ **ship,** battleship, or warship of similar class; ∼ **sum,** lump sum of money, esp payable to insured person; ∼ **territory** (containing capital city of a country); ∼ **transfer tax** (levied on transfer of capital by gift, bequest, etc.). [ME f. OF f. L *capitalis* (*caput -itis* head; see -AL)]

cǎ′pital|ism *n.* possession of capital or wealth; system in which private capital or wealth is used in production and distribution of goods; (Polit.) dominance of private owners of capital and production for profit hence or cogn. ∼IST (2) *n.* (freq. derog.), **cǎpi-talī′stic** *a.* [f. prec. + -ISM]

cǎ′pitalīz|e, - īs|e (-īz), *v.* **1.** *v.t.* convert into or provide with capital; compute or realize present value o (income); reckon (value of asset) by setting future benefits against cost of maintenance; write (letter) as capital, begin (word) with capital letter. **2.** *v.t.* & *i* ∼**e (on),** (fig.) turn to account, make use of to one's advantage. **3.** Hence ∼A′TION *n.* [f. F *capitaliser* (a CAPITAL²; see -IZE)]

cǎpitā′tion *n.* (levying of) tax or fee of so much a head; ∼ **grant** (of so much for every person fulfilling conditions). [F, or f. LL *capitatio* poll-tax (*caput -iti* head; see -ATION)]

Cǎ′pitol *n.* temple of Jupiter in ancient Rome *Congress or State legislature building. [ME f. OI *capitolie,* f. L *capitolium* (*caput* head)]

capi′tular *a.* of a cathedral chapter; (Anat.) of a terminal protuberance of bone. [f. LL *capitularis* f. Il *capitulum* CHAPTER; see -AR¹]

capi′tularỹ *n.* collection of ordinances, esp. of Frankish kings. [f. LL *capitularius* f. L (as prec.) see -ARY¹]

capi′tulāte *v.i.* surrender esp. on stated conditions. [f med. L *capitulare* draw up under headings (CAPIT ULUM) + -ATE³]

capitulā′tion *n.* capitulating; statement of mair divisions of subject; agreement, conditions. [f. LI *capitulatio* (as prec.; see -ATION)]

capi′tul|um *n.* (*pl.* ∼**a**). (Bot.) rounded or flattene flower-head of composite plant etc. [L, dim. of *capu* head]

cǎ′plin. See CAPELIN.

cǎ′pō (tǎ′stō) *n.* (*pl.* ∼**s**). device on stringed instru ment to adjust pitch of all strings simultaneously. [I It. *capo tasto* head stop]

cā′pon *n.* domestic cock castrated and fattened fo eating; hence ∼IZE (3) *v.t.* [OE f. AF *capun,* O *capon,* f. Rom. *cappone f. L *capo -onis*]

cǎponier′ *n.* covered passage across ditch of fort. [Sp. *caponera,* lin. pen for CAPONS]

capō′t *n.*, & *v.t.* (-tt-). **1.** *n.* (In piquet) winning of a tricks by one player. **2.** *v.t.* Score capot agains (opponent). [F]

capō′te *n.* soldier's, traveller's, etc., long cloak wit hood. [F, dim. of *cape* CAPE¹]

cappuccino (kahpŏochē′nō) *n.* (*pl.* ∼**s**). coffee wit milk, esp. made with espresso coffee. [It., = CAPU CHIN]

Capri′ (-ē′) *n.* ∼ **pants,** ∼**s,** women's close-fittin tapered trousers. [∼, island in Bay of Naples]

cǎ′pric *a.* (Chem.) ∼ **acid,** acid obtained from butter, coconut oil, etc. [f. L *caper -pri* goat + -IC (from its goatlike smell)]

capri′cciō (-ǐ′chiō) *n.* (*pl.* ∼**s**). (Mus.) lively (usu short) musical composition. [It.; see CAPRICE]

capriccioso (kaprǐchiō′sō) *adv.* (Mus.) in free an impulsive style. [It. (prec.; see -OUS)]

capri′ce (-ē′s) *n.* unaccountable change of mind o conduct; inclination to this; work of lively fancy in ai etc., esp. capriccio. [F, f. It. CAPRICCIO sudden star orig. 'horror']

capri′cious (-shus) *a.* guided by caprice, inconstan irregular, unpredictable; hence ∼LY² *adv.,* ∼NESS *n* [f. F *capricieux* f. It. CAPRICCIOSO]

Cǎ′pricōrn(us) *n.* sign of the ZODIAC, the Goa TROPIC *of Capricorn.* [(ME, f. OF *capricorne*.) f *capricornus* (*caper -pri* goat, *cornu* horn)]

că'prine a. of or like a goat. [ME, f. L caprinus (caper -pri goat; see -INE¹)]

:ă'priŏle n., & v.i. (give a) leap, caper; trained horse's high leap and kick without advancing. [F, f. It. capriola, capriolare leap (capriolo roebuck f. L capreolus dim. of caper goat)]

:aprŏ'ic a. (Chem.) ~ acid, acid found with capric and butyric acids in butter etc. [f. as CAPRIC, w. -oic for differentiation]

ăps. abbr. capital letters.

Că'psian a. & n. (of) a palaeolithic culture of N. Africa and S. Europe. [f. L Capsa = Gafsa in Tunisia + -IAN]

ă'psicum n. tropical plant of genus Capsicum, with pungent capsules and seeds; its fruit. [mod. L, perh. f. L capsa CASE²]

ă'psĭd¹ n. bug of family Capsidae, esp. one carrying plant disease. [f. mod. L Capsus a genus of them + -ID³]

ă'psĭd² n. shell or coat of some viruses. [f. F capside f. L capsa box; see -ID²]

ăpsi'z|e v. 1. v.t. upset, overturn, (boat). 2. v.i. be capsized. 3. Hence ~AL 2 n. [perh. ult. f. Sp. capuzar sink by the head (cabo head and chapuzar dive)]

ă'pstan n. revolving barrel with vertical axis, worked by men walking round and pushing horizontal bars, or by steam etc., for winding cable, halyard, etc.; revolving spindle on tape recorder etc.; ~ lathe (with revolving tool-holder). [f. Prov. cabestan, earlier cabestran (cabestre halter f. L capistrum f. capere seize)]

ă'psŭl|e n. & a. 1. n. (Physiol.) membranous envelope; (Bot.) dry seed-case opening when ripe by parting of valves; (Med.) small case of gelatine enclosing dose; metal bottle-top; detachable nose--cone of rocket etc. or cabin of spacecraft containing instruments or crew; hence ~AR¹ a. 2. a. highly condensed (description etc.). [F, f. L capsula (capsa CASE²; see -ULE)]

ă'psŭlize, -īse (-īz), v.t. put (information etc.) in compact form. [f. prec. + -IZE]

ăapt. abbr. Captain.

ă'ptain¹ (-tĭn) n. 1. chief, leader (~ of industry, industrial magnate); great soldier, strategist, experienced commander (||~-general, honorary officer esp. of artillery); (Army, *Air Force) officer of rank below major and above lieutenant; (Navy) officer commanding warship, officer of rank below commodore or rear admiral and above commander (||C~ of the Fleet, staff officer in charge of maintenance); *policeman ranking below chief officer; person in command of merchant or passenger ship; pilot of civil aircraft; ~'s biscuit, hard fancy biscuit. 2. foreman; ||head boy or girl at school, leader of side in games; *supervisor of waiters or bellboys. 3. Hence ~CY, ~SHIP, ns. [ME and OF capitain f. LL capitaneus chief (L caput capitis head)]

ă'ptain² (-tĭn) v.t. be captain of, lead. [f. prec.]

ă'ption n., & v.t. 1. n. heading of chapter, article, etc.; wording on cinema or television screen, appended to illustration or cartoon, etc.; (Law) certificate attached to or written on document. 2. v.t. provide with caption. [ME, f. L captio (capere capt- take; see -ION)]

ă'ptious (-shŭs) a. fond of taking exception or raising objections; hence ~LY² adv., ~NESS n. [ME, f. OF captieux or f. L captiosus (as prec.; see -IOUS)]

ă'ptiv|āte v.t. fascinate, charm; so ~A'TION n. [f. LL captivare take captive (as foll.) + -ATE³]

ă'ptive a. & n. (person or animal) taken prisoner, kept in confinement, under restraint, unable to escape; of or like prisoner (captive state); ~ audience unable to avoid being addressed etc.); ~ balloon held by rope from ground); so căpti'vity n. (the ~, of Jews in Babylon, 6th c. BC). [ME, f. L captivus capere capt- take; see -IVE)]

ă'ptor n. one who takes a captive or prize. [L (as prec.; see -OR)]

ă'pture n., & v.t. 1. n. seizing, taking possession of, capturing; thing or person captured. 2. v.t. take prisoner, seize as prize; put in permanently accessible form (could not capture the likeness); (Chess etc.) remove (man) from board; (Phys.) absorb (atomic particle); (of stream) divert upper course of (another) by encroaching on basin. [F, f. L captura (as prec.; see -URE)]

Că'pŭchĭn n. & a. Franciscan (friar) of new rule of 1528; (Hist.) woman's cloak and hood; c~ monkey, pigeon, (with head hair, head and neck feathers, like cowl). [F, f. It. cappuccino (cappuccio cowl f. cappa CAPE¹)]

caput mortuum (kăput mōr'tŭum) n. worthless residue. [L, = dead head; alch. term for residuum after distillation or sublimation]

căpўbăr'a n. large S. Amer. rodent (Hydrochoerus capybara) allied to guinea-pig. [Tupi]

căr n. 1. wheeled vehicle (of specified type; DINING-car, JAUNTing-car, ||TRAM¹car); = MOTOR car; *railway carriage or van; *lift-cage; passenger compartment of airship or balloon or cableway; (poet.) wheeled vehicle, chariot. 2. ~ coat, short coat designed esp. for car-drivers; *~'fare, passenger's fare to travel by bus etc.; *~'hop, (colloq.) waiter at drive-in restaurant etc.; ~'load, quantity that can be carried in a car, *minimum quantity of goods for which lower rate is charged for transport; ~'man, driver of van, carrier; ||~-park, space for parking cars; ~'port, roofed open-sided shelter for car; ~'sick, affected with nausea caused by motion of car. [ME f. AF & ONF carre, f. Rom. *carra, L carrum, carrus, f. OCelt. *karrom, *karros]

cărabineer', -ier', n. (Hist.) soldier with carbine; ||The C~s, Royal Scots Dragoon Guards. [f. F carabinier (carabine CARBINE; see -EER, -IER)]

carabini|ere (kărabĭnyăr'ĭ) n. (pl. ~eri pr. -ăr'ē). Italian soldier in corps serving as policemen. [It.]

că'racăl n. lynx of N. Africa and SW Asia (Felis caracal). [F or Sp., f. Turk. karakulak (kara black, kulak ear)]

că'racŏle n., & v.i. (Of horse or rider) (execute) half-turn(s) to right or left. [f. F caracole(r)]

că'racul, kă'rakul, (-ool) n. Asian sheep whose lambs have dark curled fleece; fur made from or resembling this. [Russ.]

cara'fe (-ä'f, -ah'f) n. glass bottle for water or wine at table, in bedroom, etc. [F, f. It. caraffa prob. f. Sp. garrafa f. Arab. ġarrāfa drinking vessel]

că'ramel n. burnt sugar or syrup used for colouring spirits etc.; toffee made with sugar melted and further heated; light-brown colour of caramel; hence -IZE (3) v.t. & i. [F, f. Sp. caramelo]

că'rapăce n. upper shell of tortoise or crustacean. [F, f. Sp. carapacho]

că'rat n. 1. measure of weight for precious stones, 200 milligrams. 2. measure of purity of gold, pure gold being 24 carats. [F, f. It. carato f. Arab. ķīrāt weight of four grains, f. Gk keration fruit of carob (dim. of keras horn)]

căravăn (kă'-, -vă'n) n., & v.i. (||-nn-). 1. n. company of merchants, pilgrims, etc., travelling together, esp. across desert in Asia or N. Africa; covered cart or carriage; ||dwelling-place on wheels, able to be towed by horse or car; ||~ park or site, place where caravans are parked as dwellings. 2. v.i. travel or live in caravan. [f. F caravane f. Pers. kārwān]

căravă'nserai (-rī) n. Eastern inn with inner court where caravans rest. [f. Pers. kārwānsarāy (as prec., SERAI)]

că'ravel, căr'vel, n. (Hist.) small light fast ship, chiefly Spanish and Portuguese of 15th-17th c. [f. F car(a)velle f. Port. caravela, f. Gk karabos horned beetle, crayfish, light ship]

că'raway (-a-wā) n. umbelliferous plant, Carum carvi, ~ seed, its fruit, used in cakes and as source of oil. [prob. f. OSp. alcarahueya f. Arab. alkarāwiyā, perh. f. Gk karon, kareon cumin]

carb *n.* (colloq.) carburettor. [abbr.]

car'bamāte *n.* salt or ester of an amide, $CONH_2OH$, of carbonic acid. [f. CARBONIC + AMIDE + -ATE¹ (3)]

car'bide *n.* binary compound of carbon; esp. (**calcium**) ~ (used in making acetylene gas). [f. CARBON + -IDE]

car'bine *n.* short firearm orig. for cavalry use. [earlier & F *carabine*, weapon of the *carabin* mounted musketeer]

car'bo- *comb. form.* carbon, as: CARBOHYDRATE, CARBOLIC, CARBOXYL. [f. CARBON + -O-]

car'bohy'drāte *n.* (Chem.) energy-producing organic compound of carbon with oxygen and hydrogen (e.g. starch, sugar, glucose). [f. CARBO- + HYDRATE¹]

car'bŏ'lic *a.* ~ **acid**, phenol; ~ **soap** (containing this). [f. CARBO- + -OL + -IC]

car'bon *n.* **1.** non-metallic chemical element occurring as diamond, graphite, and charcoal, in carbon dioxide and carbonates, and in all organic compounds; RADIO-*carbon*. **2.** carbon copy; carbon paper; (Electr.) rod of carbon in arc lamp. **3.** ~ **copy,** copy made with carbon paper, (fig.) exact copy; ~ **dating,** determination of age from decay of radio-carbon of ancient organic materials; ~ **dioxide,** gas formed by combustion of carbon and by breathing; ~ **disulphide,** colourless liquid used as solvent; ~ **14,** radioisotope used in carbon dating, with mass 14; ~ **monoxide,** very poisonous, colourless, almost odourless gas formed by incomplete combustion of carbon, occurring e.g. in exhaust of motor engines; ~ **paper,** thin paper thinly coated with carbon etc. for making copy of words written or typed; ~ **steel** (with properties depending mainly on amount of carbon present); ~ **tetrachloride,** colourless liquid used as solvent in dry cleaning etc. [f. F *carbone* f. L *carbo -onis* charcoal]

car'bonā'ceous (-sh*us*) *a.* of or like coal or charcoal; consisting of or containing carbon. [f. prec. + -ACEOUS]

car'bonā'de *n.* rich beef stew made with onions and beer. [F]

car'bonā'dō *n. (pl.* ~s). dark opaque kind of diamond used as abrasive etc. [Port.]

car'bonāte¹ *n.* salt of carbonic acid. [f. F *carbonat* f. mod. L *carbonatum* (as CARBON, -ATE¹ (3))]

car'bonāte² *v.t.* impregnate with carbon dioxide, aerate; convert into carbonate. [f. prec.]

car'bŏ'nic *a.* (Chem.) of carbon; ~ **acid,** weak acid formed from carbon dioxide and water; ~ **acid gas,** (arch.) carbon dioxide. [f. CARBON + -IC]

car'boni'ferous *a.* & *n.* producing coal; (*C*~, Geol.) (of the) Palaeozoic period or system, above Devonian and below Permian, often containing coal. [f. CARBON + -I- + -FEROUS]

car'boniz|e, -īs|e (-īz), *v.t.* convert into carbon; reduce to charcoal or coke; coat (paper) with carbon; hence ~A'TION *n.* [f. CARBON + -IZE]

Car'borŭ'ndum, c~, *n.* (*P) silicon carbide used as abrasive or refractory. [f. CARBON + CORUNDUM]

car'bŏ'xyl *n.* (Chem.) univalent group (—COOH) present in many organic acids; hence **carboxy'lic** *a.* [f. CARBO- + OXYGEN + -YL]

car'boy *n.* large globular glass bottle to contain liquids safely, usu. protected by frame. [f. Pers. *ḳarāba* large glass flagon]

car'bŭncle *n.* **1.** red precious stone, esp. garnet cut in boss shape. **2.** severe abscess, esp. on neck; face pimple; hence **carbŭ'ncŭlar**¹ *a.* [ME f. OF *charbucle* etc., f. L *carbunculus* small coal (*carbo* coal; see -UNCLE)]

car'būrā'tion *n.* process of charging air with spray of liquid hydrocarbon fuel. [f. foll. + -ATION]

car'būrē't *v.t.* (‖-tt-). combine (any element) chemically with carbon. [f. CARBON + -URET]

car'būrē'ttor, -tter, *esp. US* -tor, *n.* apparatus for carburation of air in petrol engines. [f. prec. + -OR, -ER¹]

car'cajou (-jōō, -zhōō) *n.* (Zool.) American glutton, wolverine. [F, app. of Amer. Ind. orig.]

car'canĕt *n.* (arch.) jewelled necklace or collar. [f. obs. & F *carcan,* f. Gmc *querkbann* chin-strap + -ET¹]

car'cass, ‖car'case, *n.* dead body of animal or bird; human body, (joc. or derog.) alive or (derog.) dead; animal's trunk without head or offal (~ **meat,** raw meat as dist. from corned or tinned meat); bones of cooked bird; worthless remains (*of*); skeleton, framework, (of building, ship, etc.); foundation of motor-vehicle tyre; (Hist.) spherical projectile filled with combustible material to ignite buildings etc. [ME f. AF *carcois* (OF *charcois*), & f. F *carcasse*; ult orig. unkn.]

carci'no|gen *n.* (Path.) cancer-producing substance so ~GE'NIC (1) *a.* [f. foll. + -GEN]

carcinō'ma *n. (pl.* ~**ta** *or* ~s). (Path.) cancer, esp malignant epithelial tumour. [L, f. Gk *karkinōme (karkinos* crab; see -OMA)]

card¹ *n.,* & *v.t.* (cleanse, comb, or scratch, with toothed instrument or wire-brush etc. for raising nap on cloth or for disentangling fibres of wool, hemp etc., before spinning; ~**'ing-wool** (short-stapled). [ME, f. OF *carde* f. Prov. *carda* (*cardar* tease, comb f pop. L *caritare* f. L *carere* card)]

card² *n.* **1.** = PLAYING-*card* (COURT¹-*card*; HOUSE¹ of *cards*; **on** or *****in** the **~**s, likely, possible; **play** one's **~**s **well,** act cleverly; **lay** or **put** (**all**) one's **~**s on **the table,** disclose all one's resources, plans, etc. SHOW¹ one's *cards*; ~ **up** one's **sleeve,** plan ir reserve); **~**s, card-game, card-playing; (*sure, safe doubtful,* etc.) **plan,** expedient; (colloq.) (*knowing, oda* etc.) **person;** (colloq.) eccentric person. **2.** flat piece of thick paper or thin pasteboard for various purposes POST²*card*; ticket of admission or membership; invitation; (**business**) ~ (with name and information about one's firm); (**visiting-**)~ (with name etc., sent or left in lieu of formal visit); BIRTH*day,* WEDDING-CHRISTMAS, etc., ~ (sent as notification or greeting to friends); programme of events at race-meeting etc., ~ for entering cricket scores; list of holes on golf course for entering player's scores; printed or written notice of rules, etc., for display; (in *pl.,* colloq.) employee' documents held by employer (**ask for, get,** one' **~**s, ask, be told, to leave one's employment). **3** **~'board,** pasteboard for cutting cards from or making boxes etc., (*attrib.,* fig.) insubstantial; **~ -carrying,** having valid membership (esp. of politica party); **~-game,** game using playing-cards; **~ index** (in which each item is entered on separate card); **~-i'ndex** *v.t.,* make card index of; **~ -playing,** use of playing-cards in game; **~-room** (in which games are played with cards); **~-sharp,** **~ -sharper,** swindler at card-games; **~-table,** (esp folding) table for card-playing; **~ vote,** = BLOCK vote, esp. in trade-union meetings. [ME, f. OE *carte* f L *charta* f. Gk *khartēs* papyrus-leaf]

Card. *abbr.* Cardinal.

car'damom, -mum, *n.* spice from the seed-capsule of E. Ind. plants, esp. *Elettaria cardamomum.* [f. *cardamomum* or F *cardamome*; Gk *kardamōmon (kardamo* cress, *amōmon* a spice plant)]

car'dan *a.* (Engin.) ~ **joint,** universal joint; ~ **shaf** (with universal joint at one or both ends). [f. G *Cardano,* It. mathematician d. 1576]

car'diăc *a.* & *n.* **1.** *a.* of the heart (*cardiac* ARREST²); *n.* upper orifice of stomach. **2.** *n.* person with heart disease. [f. F *cardiaque* f. L *cardiacus* f. Gk *kardiako (kardia* heart; see -AC)]

car'digan *n.* knitted woollen etc. jacket with or without sleeves. [named after 7th Earl of C~ d. 1868]

car'dinal *a.* & *n.* **1.** *a.* on which something hinges fundamental, important, (*cardinal* HUMOUR¹. ~ **numbers,** one, two, three, etc., as opp. to ordina numbers; ~ **points** (of compass), N., S., E., W *cardinal* VIRTUES¹, of deep scarlet (like cardinal cassock); (Zool.) of hinge of bivalve; **~-flowe** scarlet lobelia; hence **~LY²** *adv.* **2.** *n.* one of leadin dignitaries of RC Church, electing Pope; *cardinal* VICAR; hence ∿ATE[1], ∿SHIP, *ns*. **3.** small scarlet Amer. song-bird of genus *Richmondena*. **4.** (Hist.) woman's cloak, orig. of scarlet cloth with hood. [a. ME f. OF, f. L *cardinalis* (*cardo -inis* hinge; see -AL); n. OE f. OF, f. med. L *cardinalis*]

ăr'dio- *comb. form.* heart, as: ∿GRAM, record of heart movements, made by ∿GRAPH; so ∿GRAPHER, ∿GRAPHY, (-ŏ'g-); ∿LOGY (-ŏ'l-), study of the heart; ∿va'scular, involving heart and blood-vessels. [f. Gk *kardia* heart + -o-]

ărdōō'n *n*. thistle-like vegetable allied to globe artichoke. [f. F *cardon* (*carde* edible part of artichoke f. Prov. *cardo* f. Rom. **carda* f. L *cardu(u)s* thistle); see -OON]

:ards. *abbr.* Cardiganshire (former county in Wales).

ăre[1] *n*. **1.** trouble, anxiety (*care killed the* CAT[1]); occasion for these; serious attention, heed, caution, pains, (**take, have a, ∿,** be cautious, not neglect or fail); charge, protection, (*A* ∿ **of B,** at B's address); **take ∿ of,** ensure safety of, deal with, dispose of; thing to be done or seen to; = CHILD *care*. **2.** ∿**'free,** free from anxiety or responsibility; ∿-**laden,** ∿**'worn,** (with anxieties); ∿**'taker,** person hired to take charge, esp. of house in owner's absence, ||person looking after public building, (*attrib.*) exercising temporary control (*caretaker government*). [OE *caru*, = OS *kara*, OHG *chara*, ON *kor*, Goth. *kara* f. Gmc **karō*]

ăre[2] *v.i.* feel concern or interest (*for, about*); (usu. w. neg. expressed or implied) feel regard, deference, affection, liking, (*for, about*), be concerned *whether* etc., (often with expletive *a damn, a tinker's cuss,* etc.; **for all I ∿, I couldn't ∿ less, who ∿s?,** (colloq.) I am utterly uninterested or indifferent); be willing or wishful *to* (*should not care to be seen with him; would you care to try them?*); ∿ **for,** provide for, look after. [OE :arian, = OS *karon,* OHG *charōn,* Goth. *karōn* f. Gmc **karōjan,* or f. prec.]

aree'n *v.t.* & *i.* turn (ship) on side for cleaning, :aulking, etc., whence ∿AGE (4, 5) *n*.; (cause to) heel over; *(of vehicle etc.) career. [f. *careen* n. = careened position of ship f. F *carène* f. It. *carena* f. L *carina* keel]

areer' *n*., & *v.i.* **1.** *n*. swift course, impetus, (*in full, mid,* etc., *career*); course or progress through life or history; way of making a livelihood and advancing oneself (∿ **diplomat,** professional diplomat; ∿ **girl, woman,** woman who works permanently in a profession; ∿**s master, mistress,** teacher advising pupils on choice of career); hence ∿IST (3) *n.*, one ntent mainly on personal advancement and success n life. **2.** *v.i.* go swiftly or wildly. [f. F *carrière* f. It. *carriera* f. Prov. *-eira* f. Rom. **carraria* (*via*) carriage- -road) f. L *carrus* CAR]

ăr'eful (kār'f-) *a*. concerned *for*, taking care *of*; painstaking, watchful, cautious, (*to do, that,* etc.); done with or showing care; hence ∿LY[2] *adv.*, ∿NESS *n*. OE *carful* (as CARE[1], -FUL)]

ăr'eless (kār'l-) *a*. unconcerned, taking no heed *of*, ight-hearted; inattentive, negligent (*of*), thoughtless; ∥ffortless; inaccurate; hence ∿LY[2] *adv.*, ∿NESS *n*. [OE *carlēas* (as CARE[1], -LESS)]

arĕ'ss *n*., & *v.t.* **1.** *n*. fondling touch, kiss. **2.** *v.t.* bestow caress on; treat fondly or kindly. [f. F *caresse(r)* . It. *carezza* f. Rom. **caritia* f. L *carus* dear]

ăr'ĕt *n*. mark (⅄) placed below line or in margin to how place of omission. [L, = is lacking]

ăr'făx *n*. place where (usu. four) roads meet. [ME f. AF *carfuks*, OF *carrefurcs* f. pop. L **QUADRI(furcus* f. *urca* fork)]

ăr'gō *n*. (*pl.* ∿es *or* **∿s*). goods carried by ship, aircraft, or *motor vehicle; ∿ **boat** (carrying only or hiefly cargo); ∿ **cult,** (orig. in Pacific Islands) belief n forthcoming arrival of supernatural benefactors. Sp., f. as CHARGE[1]]

ăria'ma (-ah'-) *n*. Var. of SERIEMA.

Că'rĭb *n*. & *a*. (one) of aboriginal inhabitants of southern W. Ind. islands and adjacent coasts; their language. [f. Sp. *Caribe* f. Haitian]

Cărĭbbē'an *n*. & *a*. of the region occupied by the Caribs; of W. Indies; ∿ (**sea**), the part of the Atlantic between the southern W. Ind. islands and Central America. [f. prec. + -EAN]

că'ribou (-bōō) *n*. (*pl.* same). N. Amer. reindeer. [Can. F, prob. f. Amer. Ind.]

că'ricatŭr|e *n*., & *v.t.* **1.** *n*. grotesque representation of person or thing by exaggeration of characteristic traits, in picture, writing, or mime; ridiculously poor imitation or version; hence ∿AL *a.*, ∿IST (1) *n.* **2.** *v.t.* make or give a caricature of. [F, f. It. *caricatura* (*caricare* load, exaggerate; see CHARGE[1])]

car'ies (kār'ĭēz, kār'ēz) *n*. (*pl.* same). decay (of bones or teeth); hence **cārĭ̄ōGE'NIC** (1) *a*. [L]

carĭllon (karĭ'lyon, kă'rĭl(y)on) *n*. set of bells sounded either from keyboard or mechanically; tune played on bells; instrument (or part of organ) imitating peal of bells. [F, f. Rom. **quatrinio* peal of four bells]

carī'n|a *n*. (Biol.) ridge-shaped structure, esp. keel of bird's breastbone; hence ∿AL *a*. [L, = keel]

că'rĭnate *a*. (Of bird) having keeled breastbone (opp. *ratite*). [f. L *carinatus* keeled (*carina* keel; see -ATE[2])]

cărĭō'ca *n*. native of Rio de Janeiro; (music for) Brazilian dance like samba. [Port.]

cărĭōgĕ'nic. See CARIES.

căr'ĭous *a*. decayed (esp. of bones or teeth). [f. L *cariosus* (CARIES; see -OUS)]

căr'king *a*. (arch.) burdensome (*care* etc.). [part. of obs. *cark* v. f. ONF *carkier* f. Rom. **carcare* (**carricare* CHARGE[2])]

cărl *n*. (Sc.) man, fellow. [OE, f. ON *karl,* cogn. w. CHURL]

Căr'ley *n*. ∿ (**float**), large emergency raft on ship. [f. H. S. ∿, Amer. inventor (1903)]

căr'line *n*. plant of genus *Carlina*, allied to thistle. [F, f. med. L *carlina* perh. for *cardina* (L *cardo* thistle), assoc. w. *Carolus Magnus* Charlemagne]

Carlovingian. See CAROLINGIAN.

Căr'mĕlite *n*. & *a*. (member) of mendicant order of friars or of a similar order of nuns. [F, or f. med. L *carmelita* (Mt. *Carmel* in Palestine, place of foundation in 12th c.; see -ITE[1] (1))]

căr'minative *a*. & *n*. (drug) curing flatulence. [f. F *carminatif -ive* or med. L *carminare* heal (by incantation); see CHARM[1], -ATIVE]

căr'mine *n*. & *a*. (coloured like, colour of) crimson pigment made from cochineal. [f. F *carmin* or f. med. L *carminium* perh. f. *carmesinum* CRIMSON + *minium* cinnabar]

Carms. *abbr.* Carmarthenshire (former county in Wales).

Căr'naby Street *n*. (usu. *attrib.*) fashionable clothing for young people. [name of street in central London]

căr'nage *n*. great slaughter, esp. of human beings. [F, f. It. *carnaggio* f. med. L *carnaticum* f. L *caro carnis* flesh; see -AGE]

căr'nal *a*. sensual, fleshly, (**have ∿ knowledge of,** (Law) have sexual intercourse with); unsanctified, worldly; hence **cărna'lITY** *n.*, ∿IZE (3) *v.t.*, ∿LY[2] *adv.* [ME, f. LL *carnalis* (*caro*; see prec., -AL)]

cărnă'ssial *a*. & *n*. = SECTORIAL, 2, 3. [f. F *carnassier* carnivorous + -AL]

cărnā'tion[1] *n*. & *a*. (of) rosy pink colour. [F. f. It. *carnagione* f. LL *carnatio -onis* (as CARNAL; see -ATION) fleshiness]

cărnā'tion[2] *n*. cultivated clove pink. [in 16th c. also *coronation,* perh. the orig. form, later assim. to prec.]

cărnau'ba (-naw'-, -naōō'-, -now'-) *n*. Brazilian palm (*Copernicia cerifera*); its yellowish leaf-wax, used as polish etc. [Port.]

cărnē'lian. See CORNELIAN[1].

căr'net (-nā) *n*. permit to drive across frontier or use camping-site. [F, = notebook]

||**căr'ney.** See CARNY.

căr'nival n. festivities usual during period before Lent in RC countries; riotous revelry; *travelling circus or fair; festivities esp. occurring at regular date. [f. It. carne-, carnovale f. med. L carnelevarium etc. Shrove-tide, f. L caro carnis flesh + levare put away]

căr'nivorous a. feeding on flesh or other animal matter; (esp.) belonging to the Carnivora, (of plant) digesting animal substance; so **Cărni'vora** n. pl., large order of mainly carnivorous mammals (cats, dogs, foxes, bears, seals, etc.); **căr'ni**VORE n., carnivorous animal or plant. [f. L carnivorus (caro carnis flesh; see -vorous)]

∥căr'nÿ, căr'ney, v.t., & a. (colloq.) **1.** v.t. coax, wheedle. **2.** a. artful, sly. [19th c.; orig. unkn.]

că'rob n. horn-shaped edible pod of Mediterranean evergreen tree (∿-tree), Ceratonia siliqua. [f. obs. F car(r)obe f. med. L carrubia, -um f. Arab. ḳarrūba]

că'rol n. & v. (∥-ll-). **1.** n. joyous song, esp. Christmas hymn. **2.** v.t. & i. sing (as) carol; sing joyfully. [ME, f. OF carole(r), of unkn. orig.]

Cărolē'an, Că'rolīne, adjs. of the time of Charles I or II of England; **Caroline script** (Carolingian). [f. L Carolus Charles + -EAN, -INE[1]]

Căroli'ngian, Cārlovi'ngian, (-nj-) a. & n. (member) of second Frankish dynasty, founded by Charlemagne (d. 814); (style) of script developed in France at time of Charlemagne. [(Caro- after L Carolus Charles) f. F carlovingien f. Karl Charles after mérovingien MEROVINGIAN]

***că'rom** n., & v.i. **1.** n. cannon at billiards. **2.** v.i. make carom; strike and rebound off. [abbr. of carambole f. Sp. carambola]

că'rotēne n. orange or red substance formed in carrots etc. and acting as source of vitamin A; hence **carō'tēn**OID n., pigment of class including carotene. [f. G carotin f. L carota CARROT; see -ENE]

carō'tid a. & n. (of or near) one of the two great arteries carrying blood to head. [f. F carotide or mod. L carotides f. Gk. karōtides pl. (karoō stupefy, compression of these arteries being thought to cause stupor)]

carou's|e (-z) v.i., & n. (have or engage in) drinking-bout; drink heavily; hence ∿AL 2 n. [orig. as adv. = right out, in phr. drink carouse f. G gar aus trinken]

cărousē'l, *cărr-, (-ōōs-, -z-) n. (Hist.) kind of tournament; rotating delivery or conveyor system; *roundabout, merry-go-round. [f. F carrousel f. It. carosello]

cărp[1] n. (pl. same). freshwater fish of genus Cyprinus, esp. a species usu. bred in ponds. [ME, f. OF carpe f. Prov. or f. LL carpa]

cărp[2] v.i. talk querulously, find fault, (usu. at); (in pres. part., of tongue, criticism) captious. [obs. ME senses 'talk, say, sing', f. ON karpa to brag; mod. sense (16th c.) f. or infl. by L carpere pluck at, slander]

căr'pal. See CARPUS.

căr'pel n. (Bot.) one of the constituent units of a compound ovary; hence ∿LARY[1]. [f. F carpelle or mod. L carpellum f. Gk karpos fruit; see -LE 2]

căr'pènter n. & v. **1.** n. craftsman in woodwork (esp. of rough solid kinds as in ship or house building; cf. JOINER, CABINET-maker); ∿ **ant, bee,** kinds boring into trees; so **căr'pèntry** (2, 5) n. **2.** v.i. & t. do, or make by, carpenter's work, (fig.) construct, fit (things) together. [ME & AF; OF carpentier, f. LL carpentarius (carpentum wagon f. Gaulish; see -ER[2])]

căr'pèt n., & v.t. **1.** n. thick fabric for covering floor and stairs (**figure in the ∿**, pattern not immediately perceptible; **on the ∿**, (1, colloq.) being reprimanded, (2) under discussion [f. earlier use as table-cover]; RED carpet; **sweep under the ∿**, conceal (thing) in the hope that others will overlook or forget it); area of intensive bombing etc.; smooth, soft, or bright expanse of grass, flowers, etc. **2.** ∿**-bag,** travelling-bag, orig. made of carpet; ∿**-bagger,** political candidate etc. without local connections

(orig. northerner in southern US after 1865); ∿**-bed** garden bed with dwarf plants arranged in pattern; ∿**-knight,** (arch.) idler, ladies' man: ∿**-shark** (with carpet-like pattern on back); ∿ **slipper** (of kind with upper made orig. of carpet-like material); ∿**-snake,** large variegated Australian python; ∿**-sweeper,** household implement with revolving brush(es) for sweeping carpets. **3.** v.t. cover (as) with a carpet; whence ∿ING[1] (3) n.; (colloq.) reprimand, reprove. [ME, f. OF carpite or med. L carpita, f. obs. It. carpita woollen counterpane f. Rom. *carpire f. L carper pluck, pull to pieces]

cărphŏ'logy n. delirious fumbling with bedclothes etc. [f. Gk karphologia (karphos straw etc., legō pick; see -y[1])]

cărpo-[1] comb. form. carpus. [f. CARPUS + -O-]

cărpo-[2] comb. form. fruit, as **cărpŏ'**LOGY n. [f. Gk karpos fruit + -O-]

căr'p|us n. (pl. ∿**i** pr. -ī). part of skeleton between forearm or foreleg and metacarpus, eight small bones in higher vertebrates (in man, wrist; in horse, knee); hence ∿AL a. [mod. L, f. Gk karpos wrist]

că'rrack n. (Hist.) large merchant-ship equipped for warfare. [ME, f. F caraque f. Sp. carraca f. Arab. ḳarāḳir]

că'rrageen, -gheen, (-gēn) n. edible purple seaweed (Chondrus crispus) found in N. hemisphere. [f. Carra gheen in Ireland]

că'rrel n. **1.** (Hist.) small enclosure or study in cloister. **2.** small cubicle for reader in (stack-room of) library. [var. of CAROL in obs. sense]

că'rriage (-rĭj) n. **1.** conveying; transport; cost of conveying (∿ **forward,** carriage to be paid by receiver; ∿ **paid,** by sender); manner of carrying (head, body, etc.), bearing, deportment. **2.** wheeled vehicle for persons (HACKNEY, INVALID[1], ∥railway carriage); four-wheeled private vehicle drawn by two (∿ **and pair**) or more horses (**drive ∿ and six** etc., **through,** cf. COACH 4); ∥railway passenger vehicle (**gun-**)∿, wheeled support of gun; (Mech.) sliding etc. part of machinery to carry and move other parts, e.g. in typewriter. **3.** ∿ **clock** (portable in rectangular case with handle); ∿**-dog,** dalmatian; ∿ **trade** (trade with) those rich enough to own a private carriage; ∿**way,** part of road intended for vehicular traffic. **4.** Hence ∿ABLE (-ĭja-) a., (of road) available to carriages. [ME, f. ONF cariage (carier CARRY[1]; see -AGE)]

că'rrick bĕnd n. (Naut.) kind of knot to join ropes. [BEND[1]; carrick perh. f. CARRACK]

că'rrier n. **1.** In vbl. senses; person or company undertaking for hire the conveyance of goods or passengers (COMMON[1] carrier); substance used to support or convey pigment, catalyst, radioactive material, etc.; part of bicycle etc. for carrying luggage or a passenger; person or animal that without suffering from a disease or showing a hereditary characteristic transmits it to others; (Phys.) mobile electron or hole in a semiconductor; = aircraft-carrier. **2.** ∿(-**bag**), paper or plastic bag for shopping etc.; carrier PIGEON[1]; ∿ **wave,** continuous electromagnetic wave on which signal is superposed by modulation of amplitude or frequency. [f. CARRY[1] + -ER[1]]

că'rriole n. small open carriage for one; covered light cart; Canadian sledge. [F, f. It. carriuola, dim. of carr (CAR)]

că'rrion n. & a. **1.** n. dead putrefying flesh; anything vile, garbage, filth; ∿ **crow,** black crow (Corvus corone), feeding on carrion, small animals, etc. **2.** a. rotten, loathsome. [ME, f. AF & ONF caroine, -oign, OF charoigne, f. Rom. *caronia f. L caro flesh]

cărronă'de n. (Hist.) ship's short large-calibred gun. [f. Carron in Scotland, orig. place of making, + -ADE]

că'rrot n. umbelliferous plant (Daucus carota) with tapering orange-coloured edible root; the root, used as vegetable; the vegetable used as incentive to donkey, (fig.) means of persuasion; (in pl., sl.) redhair, red-haired person, whence ∼ʏ² *a*. [f. F *carotte* f. L *carota* f. Gk *karōton*]

că′rrȳ¹ *v*. **1.** *v.t.* transport in vehicle, ship, aircraft, hand, or mind, or on person, or (of wind etc.) by its own motion; ∼ **all before** one, succeed, overcome all opposition; *carry* COALs *to Newcastle*; *carrying--TRADE*; FETCH¹ *and carry*; *carry* WEIGHT¹. **2.** conduct (*pipes carry water*; *wires carry electric current*; *carry into effect*); ∼ person **back** (in thought to past time). **3.** transfer (figures to column of higher value); ∼ **forward,** transfer to new page or account. **4.** (Of gun etc.) propel to specified distance. **5.** be pregnant with (*she was carrying twins*). **6.** (Of motive, money, etc.) cause or enable to go *to*; (of day's journey etc.) bring *to*. **7.** prolong, continue, (*carry tower to 500 ft.*, *modesty to excess*, *joke too far*). **8.** win (prize; ∼ **the day,** succeed; ∼ **fortress** etc., capture it; ∼ **hearers with** one, persuade them); win victory or acceptance for (*carry* one's *point, a motion, bill*); (Golf) cause ball to pass beyond (bunker etc.). **9.** have with one, possess, (*arms, a watch,* etc.; *carry* one's BAT², CONVICTION; ∼ **with** one, remember); involve, imply, (*loans carry interest*; *principles carry consequences*); stock (goods for sale); (of newspaper) publish, esp. regularly; (of radio station etc.) broadcast, esp. regularly. **10.** hold in a certain way (*carry* one's *head* or *body*, oneself, *erect* etc.). **11.** endure weight of, support, (*ships carry sail*; *columns carry dome*); be major cause of effectiveness of (*he carries that department*). **12.** ∼**-all,** carriole, *car with sideways seats; ∼**-cot,** portable cot for baby. **13.** ∼ **away,** inspire, transport, deprive of self-control, (Naut.) lose (mast etc.) by breakage, break off or away; ∼ **off,** remove from life, remove by force, win, render acceptable or passable; ∼ **it off** (**well**), do well under difficulties; ∼ **on,** advance (process) by a stage, continue, conduct (conversation, business); ∼ **out,** put (principles, instructions, etc.) into practice; ∼ **over,** = *carry forward* (see sense 3), postpone (work etc.) to later time, (St. Exch.) keep over to next settling-day, whence ∼*-over* n.; ∼ **through,** bring safely out of difficulties, complete. **14.** *v.i.* (Of missile, sound, etc.) travel, penetrate; ∼ **on,** go on with what one is doing; (colloq.) behave strangely or violently, flirt (*with*); ∼**-on** *n.*, ∼**ing**(**s**)**-on,** (*sl.*) excitement, questionable behaviour, flirtation. [ME, f. AF & ONF *carier* (as CAR)]

că′rrȳ² *n*. act of carrying; (Golf) ball's flight before pitching; portage between rivers etc.; range of gun etc. [f. prec.]

cârse *n*. (Sc.) lowland beside river. [ME, perh. f. *carrs* swamps]

cart *n.*, & *v.t.* **1.** *n.* strong two-wheeled or four-wheeled usu. horse-drawn vehicle used in farming and for heavy goods; light two-wheeled one-horse vehicle for driving in; ‖**in the** ∼, (*sl.*) in an awkward or losing position; **put the** ∼ **before the horse,** reverse proper order, take effect for cause. **2.** ∼**-horse** (thickset and fit for heavy work), ∼**-load,** cartful, large quantity of anything; ∼**-road** or **-track** (too rough for carriages); ∼**-wheel,** wheel of cart, large coin or hat etc., lateral handspring with arms and legs extended; ∼**-wright,** maker of carts. **3.** Hence ∼′AGE (4), ∼′ER¹, ∼′FUL 2, *n*s. **4.** *v.t.* carry (as) in a cart; (*sl.*) carry (esp. cumbersome thing) over unduly long distance; (Cricket) hit hard; ∼ **off,** remove esp. by force. [ME, f. ON *kartr* cart & OE *cræt*, prob. infl. by AF & ONF *carete* dim. of *carre* CAR]

cârte *n.* Var. of QUART².

carte blanche (kârt blah′nsh) *n.* full discretionary power given to person; hand of cards without court--card. [F, = blank paper (as CARD², BLANK¹)]

cârte-de-visi′te (-zē′t) *n.* (arch.) small photograph for use as visiting-card. [F, = visiting-card]

cârtě′l *n.* manufacturers' union to control production, marketing arrangements, prices, etc.; political combination between parties; hence ∼IZE (3) *v.t.* & *i.*, combine to form a (business) cartel. [f. G *kartell* f. F *cartel* f. It. *cartello* dim. of *carta* CARD²]

Cârtē′sian (-zyan) *a*. & *n*. (follower) of Descartes or his philosophy or mathematical methods; ∼ **co-ordinates** (measured from intersecting straight axes); ∼ **diver** etc., toy that rises and falls in liquid when cover of vessel is subjected to varying pressure; hence ∼ISM (3) *n.* [f. mod. L *Cartesianus* (*Cartesius* name of René *Descartes*, Fr. philosopher d. 1650; see -IAN)]

Cârthagi′nian *a*. & *n*. (native or inhabitant) of Carthage; ∼ **peace,** treaty of peace that is very severe to the defeated contestant. [f. L *Carthago -ginis* Carthage, ancient city near Tunis + -IAN]

Cârthū′sian (-zyan) *a*. & *n*. (member) of order of monks founded by St. Bruno 1086; ‖(past or present member) of Charterhouse School (founded on site of Carthusian monastery). [f. med. L *Carthusianus* f. L *Cart*(*h*)*usia* (CHARTREUSE, near Grenoble); see -IAN]

car′tilage *n.* (structure in vertebrates made of) firm elastic tissue, gristle; **temporary** ∼ (in the young, changing later to bone); hence **cârtilă′gin**OID, **cârtilă′gin**OUS, *adjs*. [F, f. L *cartilago -ginis*]

cår′togram *n.* map with diagrammatic statistical information. [f. F *cartogramme* (*carte* map, CARD²; see -GRAM)]

cârtŏ′graphȳ *n.* map-drawing; hence **cârtŏ′-**GRAPHER *n.*, **cârto**GRA′PHIC(AL) *adjs*. [f. F *cartographie* (as prec.; see -GRAPHY)]

cår′tomăncȳ *n.* fortune-telling by playing-cards. [f. F *cartomancie* (*carte* CARD²; see -MANCY)]

cår′ton *n.* light cardboard etc. container for goods. [F, f. as foll.]

cârtoo′n *n.* & *v*. **1.** *n.* full-size drawing on stout paper as design for painting, tapestry, mosaic, etc.; full--page (or large) illustration, esp. satirical one on politics in newspaper or magazine; amusing drawing with or without caption; sequence of these in STRIP²; film made from a succession of drawings that simulate a cinema film; hence ∼IST (3) *n.* **2.** *v.i.* draw cartoon(s). **3.** *v.t.* represent (person etc.) in cartoon [f. It. *cartone* (*carta* CARD²; see -OON)]

cârtou′che (-ōō′sh) *n.* in architecture, scroll ornament e.g. volute of Ionic capital; tablet imitating, or drawing of, scroll with rolled-up ends, used ornamentally or bearing inscription; ornate frame; (Archaeol.) oval ring containing hieroglyphic names and titles of Egyptian kings etc. [F, = cartridge, f. It. *cartoccio* f. *carta* (CARD²)]

cår′tridge *n.* **1.** case containing charge of propellant explosive for firearms or blasting, with bullet or shot if for small arms (BLANK¹ *cartridge*); spool of film, magnetic tape, etc., in container; removable pick-up head of record-player; ink-container for insertion in pen. **2.** ∼**-belt** (with sockets for cartridges); ∼ **paper** (thick and rough, used for cartridges, for drawing, and for strong envelopes). [f. prec.]

c(**h**)**âr′tularȳ** (k-) *n.* collection of charters or records; place where these are kept. [f. med. L *c*(*h*)*artularium* (*c*(*h*)*artula* dim. of L *c*(*h*)*arta* CARD²; see -ARY¹)]

caruncle (kă′ru-, karŭ′-) *n.* fleshy excrescence, e.g. turkeycock's wattles. [obs. F, f. L *caruncula* (*caro carnis* flesh; see -UNCLE)]

cârve *v.* (*p.p.* ∼**d** or arch. **car′ven**). **1.** *v.t.* produce by cutting (statue, portrait, representation in relief or intaglio, inscription, design, or abs., *out of, in,* or *on*, material; *carve* one's *way*, lit. or fig.); change (material *into* something) by cutting; cover or adorn (material) *with* figures cut in it, cut designs etc., whence **cår′v**ING¹ (2) *n.* **2.** *v.i.* & *t.* cut up meat, cut up (meat etc.), at or for table (**carving knife,** long knife for this purpose); ∼ **out,** take from larger whole, make (career, name, etc.) *for* oneself by much effort; ∼ **up,** divide into several pieces, whence ∼**-up** *n.*, (*sl.*) sharing-out, esp. of booty. [OE *ceorfan* cut f. WG **kerfan*]

cår′vel *n.* See CARAVEL; ∼**-built,** with planks flush (cf. CLINKER³-*built*). [f. as CARAVEL]

cår′ver¹ *n.* In vbl senses; carving knife, (in *pl.*)

carving knife and fork; ||armchair in set of dining-
-room chairs. [f. CARVE + -ER¹]
***Cär′ver²** *n.* ~ **chair** (with arms, rush seat, and back
having horizontal and vertical spindles). [f. J. ~, first
governor of Plymouth Colony, d. 1621]
cärÿä′tid *n.* (*pl.* ~es *pr.* -ēz, *or* ~s). (Archit.) female
figure used as pillar to support entablature. [f. F
caryatide f. It. *cariatide* or f. L f. Gk *karuatis -idos* priestess
at Caryae (*Karuai*) in Laconia]
cärÿö′ps|ïs *n.* (*pl.* ~es *pr.* -ēz). (Bot.) one-seeded
indehiscent fruit with pericarp fused to seed-coat, as
in wheat and maize. [mod. L, f. Gk *karuon* nut + *opsis*
appearance]
Cäsanö′va (-z-, -s-) *n.* man engaging in promiscuous
love affairs. [f. G. J. ~ de Seingalt, It. adventurer d.
1798]
cä′sbah, kä′sbah, (-z-) *n.* (Arab quarter near) citadel
of N. Afr. city. [F *casbah* f. Arab. *ḳaṣ(a)ba* citadel]
cäscä′de *n.,* & *v.i.* **1.** *n.* (small) waterfall; section of
large broken waterfall; succession of electrical devices
or stages in a process; quantity of material etc. falling;
wavy arrangement of hanging lace etc. **2.** *v.i.* fall in or
like cascade. [F, f. It. *cascata* f. *cascare* to fall f. Rom.
cäscä′ra *n.* ~ (**sagrada** *pr.* -ah′da), bark of N.
Amer. buckthorn, used as purgative. [Sp., = sacred
bark]
cäse¹ *n.* **1.** instance of thing's occurring; actual state of
affairs (**is, is not, the** ~, is true, false; **as the** ~ **may
be,** according to the situation); position, circumstances, in which one is (**in good, evil,** ~, (arch.)
well, badly, off); matter being investigated by police,
social worker, etc.; (Med.) diseased condition of a
person, instance of any disease; *(colloq.) comical
person. **2.** (Law) cause or suit for trial; statement of
facts in cause *sub judice,* drawn up for higher court's
consideration (*judge states a case*); cause that has been
decided and may be cited (LEADING² *case*); sum of
arguments on one side (*that is our case;* **make out a** ~,
prove it); valid set of arguments (*have no case; there is a
case for doing nothing at present*). **3.** (Gram.) form of
noun, adjective, or pronoun, in inflected languages
expressing relation to some other word in sentence
(in uninflected languages, this relation itself apart
from form). **4. in** ~, if, in the event that, lest; (**just)
in** ~, against some possible occurrence; **in** ~ **of,** in
the event of; **in the** ~ **of,** as regards; **in any** ~,
whatever the fact is, whatever may happen; **in no** ~,
under no circumstances; **in that** ~, if that is true,
should that happen. **5.** ~-**book** (with record of legal
or medical cases; also fig.); ~ **history,** record of
person's ancestry, personal history, information
about patient, etc., for use in determining necessary
treatment etc.; ~-**law,** law as settled by decided
cases; ~-**load,** cases with which doctor etc. is concerned at one time; ~-**study,** (record of) attempt to
understand person etc. from collected information
about his development; ~′**work(er),** social work(er)
concerned with individuals or groups. [ME f. OF *cas*
f. L *casus* fall (*cadere cas-* to fall)]
cäse² *n.,* & *v.t.* **1.** *n.* what encloses or contains
something, box, bag, sheath, etc., (*bookcase, brief-case,
spectacle-case, suitcase*); glass box for showing specimens, curiosities, etc.; outer protective covering
part (of watch, sausage, seed-vessel, book, etc.); box
with appropriate contents (*dressing-case*); (Print.)
receptacle with compartments for type (**upper** ~,
capitals; **lower** ~, small letters). **2.** ~-**bound,** (of
book) in hard cover; ~-**harden** *v.t.,* harden surface
of, esp. give steel surface to (iron) by carbonizing,
(fig.) render callous; ~-**knife** (carried in sheath); ~-
-**shot,** (1) bullets in iron case fired from cannon, (2)
shrapnel. **3.** *v.t.* enclose in case; surround *with;* (sl.)
examine (house etc., esp. in preparation for robbery);
hence **cä′sing¹** (3) *n.* [ME, f. OF *casse, chasse,* f. L *capsa*
(*capere* hold)]
cä′sein (-sïïn, -sēn) *n.* protein of milk, the basis of
cheese. [f. L *caseus* cheese + -IN]

cä′semäte (-sm-) *n.* chamber in thickness of wall of
fortress, with embrasures; armoured enclosure for
guns in warship. [F, & f. It. *casamatta* or Sp. -*mata,* f.
camata, perh. f. Gk *khasma -atos* gap]
cä′sement (-sm-) *n.* metal or wooden vertically
hinged frame with glass forming (part of) window;
(poet. etc.) window: ~ **cloth,** plain fabric used for
curtains etc. [ME, f. AL *cassimentum* (*cassa* CASE²; see
-MENT)]
cä′séous *a.* of or like cheese. [f. L *caseus* cheese + -OUS]
cäsh¹ *n.,* & *v.t.* **1.** *n.* ready money, actual coins, notes,
etc., (opp. *credit,* ~ **on delivery,** forwarding of goods
against cash to be paid to postman or carrier; *cash*
DOWN³; HARD *cash*); (Banking etc.) coins, or coins and
banknotes, opp. cheques and orders; (colloq.)
wealth. **2.** ~-**account** (to which only cash is carried,
and from which all payments are made); ~-**book**
(for record of cash received and paid); ~ **and carry,**
(of goods) paid for in cash and removed by buyer, not
delivered, (of trader) dealing thus; ~ **crop** (to be sold,
not used as food etc.); ~ **desk** (where cash is taken in
shop etc.); ~ **flow,** movement of money as affecting
liquidity, or as measure of profitability; *cash* NEXUS; ~
payment (in ready money); ~ **price** (lowest, for
ready money); ~ **register,** mechanical till visibly
recording amount of each purchase, totalling receipts, etc. **3.** *v.t.* give or obtain cash for (note, cheque
etc.); (Bridge) lead (winning card); ~ **in,** pay into
bank etc.; ~ **in** (one's **checks,** (colloq.) die. **4.** *v.i.* ~
in on, realize profit on, (fig.) get advantage from. [f.
obs. F *casse* box or f. It. *cassa* f. L *capsa* CASE²]
cäsh² *n.* (*pl.* same). (Hist.) E. Ind. or Chinese small
coin. [ult. f. Port. *ca(i)xa* f. Tamil *kāsu* f. Skr. *karsha*]
cä′shew (-ōō) *n.* large tropical tree (*Anacardium
occidentale*); ~(-**nut**), its edible kidney-shaped nut. [f.
Port. f. Tupi (*a)caju*]
cäshier′¹ *n.* person in charge of bank's or business's
cash; person receiving payments in shop etc. [f. Du
cassier or f. F *caissier* (as CASH¹; see -IER)]
cäshier′² *v.t.* dismiss from service, esp. with disgrace
depose; (arch.) get rid of. [f. Flem. *kasseren* disband,
revoke, f. F *casser* f. L *quassare* QUASH]
cä′shmēre *n.* fine soft wool of Kashmir goat; imitation of it. [f. *Kashmir* in Asia]
cä′sïng. See CASE².
casi′nö (-sē′-) *n.* (*pl.* ~s). public room or building for
amusements, esp. gambling. [It., dim. of *casa* house f.
L *casa* cottage]
cask (kah-) *n.* barrel, esp. for alcoholic drinks; its
contents or capacity. [f. F *casque* or Sp. *casco* helmet]
ca′skèt (kah′-) *n.* small box or chest, often ornamental, for jewels, letters, cremated ashes, etc.
***rectangular coffin. [perh. f. AF form of OF *cassette* f
It. *cassetta* dim. of *cassa* f. L *capsa* CASE²; see -ET¹]
Cä′slon (-z-) *n.* style of type cut by the Caslons of
imitated from theirs. [f. W. ~, Engl. typographer d
1766 and his son d. 1778]
casque (käsk) *n.* (Hist. or poet.) helmet. [F, f
Sp. *casco*]
Cassä′ndra *n.* (esp. disregarded) prophet of disaster
[L f. Gk *Kas(s)andra,* daughter of Priam king of Troy
she was commended by Apollo to prophesy correctly
but not be believed]
cässa′ta (-ah′-) *n.* Neapolitan ice-cream with frui
and nuts. [It.]
cassä′tion *n.* annulment; **Court of C~,** court o
appeal in France etc. [ME f. F (*casser;* see QUASH
-ATION)]
cassa′va (-ah′-) *n.* tropical plant of genus *Manihot
with tuberous roots; its starch or flour; bread made
from these. [earlier *cas(s)avi* etc., f. Taino *casavi,* infl
by F *cassave*]
cä′sserōle *n.,* & *v.t.* **1.** *n.* covered heat-proof vessel in
which food is cooked and served; food thus prepared
2. *v.t.* cook in casserole. [F, f. *cassole* dim. of *casse* f
Prov. *cassa* f. LL *cattia,* pan f. Gk *kuathion* dim. o
kuathos cup]
cassė′tte *n.* container of film, magnetic tape

etc., for insertion into equipment. [F, dim. of *casse* CASE²]

că'ssia (-sĭa, -sha) *n.* inferior kind of cinnamon; plant of genus *Cassia*, yielding senna-leaves. [f. L f. Gk *kasia* f. Heb. *ḳᵉṣî̄ 'āh* bark like cinnamon]

că'ssis *n.* syrupy black-currant flavouring for drinks etc. [F, = black currant]

cassī'terīte *n.* native tin dioxide. [f. Gk *kassiteros* tin + -ITE¹ (2)]

că'ssock *n.* long close garment worn esp. by clergy and choristers; hence ∼ED² (-kt) *a.* [f. F *casaque* long coat f. It. *casacca* horseman's coat, prob. f. Turkic; cf. COSSACK]

cassoulet (kă'sŏōlā) *n.* ragout of meat and beans. [F, dim. of dial. *cassolo* stew-pan]

că'ssowarȳ (-o-) *n.* large flightless bird of genus *Casuarius*, related to emu. [f. Malay *kasuārī, kasavārī*]

cast¹ (kah-) *v.* (**cast**). **1.** *v.t.* move by throwing; ∼ **adrift**, leave to drift; *cast* ANCHOR¹; ∼ **ashore** (of waves etc.); ∼ **aspersions on**, utter them regarding (person etc.); ∼ **an eye**, glance; *cast the* LEAD¹, LOTS; ∼ **line, net**, throw it out into water etc. in fishing; ∼ **a shadow**, make it fall (*on*); ∼ **a spell on**, bewitch; ∼ **a vote**, give or deposit it; DIE¹ *is cast*. **2.** *v.i.* ∼ing **vote** (that decides between two equal parties) [f. obs. sense 'turn the scale']. **3.** *v.t.* throw off, get rid of, shed esp. in process of growth; (of horse) lose (shoe); ∼ **aside**, give up using, abandon. **4.** *v.t.* & *i.* reckon, calculate; calculate and record details of (horoscope). **5.** *v.t.* arrange; assign (actors) as characters; allocate roles in (play, film, etc., or abs.). **6.** shape, found, (plastic or liquid substance, esp. molten metal, by hardening in mould), form (figure, type, etc.) of metal; ∼ **iron**, hard alloy of iron, carbon, and silicon cast in mould; ∼-**iron** *a.*, made of this, (fig.) hard, unchangeable, impregnable; hence ∼ING¹ (2) *n.* **7.** ∼ **about** or (**a**)**round**, go this way and that in search, devise means, (*for, to do, how*); ∼ **away**, reject, (in *pass.*, of ship) be wrecked, see CASTAWAY; ∼ **down**, depress (cf. DOWNCAST²); ∼ **loose**, detach (oneself); *cast* in one's LOT *with*; ∼ **off**, abandon (so ∼-*off a.* & *n.*), (Knitting) take stitches off needle and loop each over next to finish edge, (Naut.) loosen and throw off (rope etc., or abs.), (Print.) estimate space taken in print by MS copy; ∼ **on**, (Knitting) make first row of loops on needle; ∼ **out**, expel; ∼ **up**, add (column of figures etc.), (of sea) deposit on shore. [ME, f. ON *kasta*]

cast² (kah-) *n.* **1.** throwing of missile etc.; distance so attained; throw or number thrown at dice; throw of net, sounding-lead, or fishing-line (also, in fishing, the gut with hook and fly, and *good, bad*, etc., place for casting); ∼-**net** (thrown out and immediately drawn in, not set). **2.** undigested food thrown up by hawk, owl, etc.; earth excreted by worm. **3.** set of actors taking parts in play, film, etc. **4.** form into which any work is thrown; model made by casting in mould; moulded mass of solidified material (*leg in a plaster cast*). **5.** twist, inclination; ∼ (**in the eye**), slight squint. **6.** tinge or shade of colour. **7.** type, quality, (esp. *cast of features, cast of mind*). [ME, f. prec.]

Căstā'lian *a.* of Castalia on Mt. Parnassus, fountain of the Muses; of the Muses. [f. L *Castalius* (*Castalia* f. & L *casualis* (*casus* CASE¹; see -AL)]

căstanĕ't *n.* (usu. in *pl.*) small concave piece of hardwood or ivory clicked or rattled in pairs as rhythmic accompaniment to dance etc. [f. Sp. *castañeta* dim. of *castaña* f. L *castanea* chestnut]

ca'staway (kah'sta-) *n.* & *a.* shipwrecked (person); (arch.) reprobate. [f. p.p. of CAST¹ + AWAY]

caste (kah-) *n.* Hindu hereditary class, with members socially equal, united in religion, and usu. following same trades, having no social intercourse with persons of other castes (∼ **mark**, symbol on forehead denoting this); more or less exclusive social class; this system; the position it confers (**lose** ∼, descend in social scale); (Zool.) form of a social insect having a

particular function. [f. Sp. and Port. *casta* lineage, race, breed, fem. of *casto* pure, CHASTE]

că'stellan *n.* (Hist.) governor of castle. [ME f. ONF *castelain* f. med. L *castellanus* (as CASTLE¹; see -AN)]

că'stell|ātĕd *a.* castle-like; battlemented; so ∼A'TION *n.* [f. med. L *castellatus* (as CASTLE¹; see -ATE², -ED¹)]

ca'ster (kah'-) *n.* In vbl senses; machine for casting type; see also CASTOR². [ME, f. CAST¹ + -ER¹]

că'stig|āte *v.t.* chastise, punish with blows or words; hence ∼A'TION, ∼ātor, *ns.*, ∼ātory *a.* [f. L *castigare* reprove (*castus* pure) + -ATE³]

Căsti'le (-ē'l) *n.* ∼ **soap**, fine hard white or mottled soap made with olive oil and soda. [f. as foll.]

Casti'lian *a.* & *n.* (native or inhabitant) of Castile; language of Castile, standard literary Spanish. [f. *Castile* in Spain + -IAN]

ca'stle¹ (kah'sel) *n.* large fortified building or set of buildings, stronghold, (**Englishman's house is his** ∼, none may force entrance); mansion that was once such; (Chess) = ROOK²; **the C**∼, (Ir. Hist.) viceroy's government and administration (with seat at Dublin Castle); ∼ **in the air**, ∼ **in Spain**, visionary project, day-dream; ∼-**nut**, (Mech.) one with notched extension for locking-pin; ∼ **pudding** (steamed or baked in small mould); hence **ca'stl**ED² (kah'seld) *a.* [f. AF & ONF *castel, chastel* f. L *castellum* dim. of *castrum* fort; see -LE 2]

ca'stle² (kah'sel) *v.i.* & *i.* (Chess). move rook to square next to king and king to other side of rook (∼ **the king**, or usu. abs.). [f. prec.]

ca'stor¹ (kah'-) *n.* substance obtained from beaver and used in medicine and perfumery; (arch. sl.) hat. [F or L, f. Gk *kastōr* beaver]

ca'stor², ca'ster, (kah'-) *n.* **1.** small bottle etc. with holes in top for sprinkling contents; ∼ **sugar**, white finely granulated kind. **2.** small swivelled wheel on leg of chair, table, etc.; ∼ **action**, swivelling of vehicle wheels to ensure stability. [f. CAST¹ + -OR, -ER¹]

ca'stor³ (kah'-) *n.* ∼ **oil**, oil from seeds (∼ **beans**) of the plant *Ricinus communis*, used as purgative and lubricant. [18th c., orig. uncert.: perh. so called as having succeeded CASTOR¹ in medical use]

căstr|ā'te *v.t.* remove testicles of; geld; deprive of vigour; expurgate (book); hence ∼A'TION *n.* (∼ation **complex**, (Psych.) child's anxiety over imagined loss of genitals), ∼ātIVE *a.* [f. L *castrare*) + -ATE³]

căstra'tǐ|ō (-rah'-) *n.* (*pl.* ∼*i pr.* -ē). (Hist.) adult male singer castrated in boyhood so as to retain soprano or alto voice. [It., p.p. of *castrare* f. as prec.]

Că'strō|ism *n.* political principles or actions of Fidel Castro or his followers; so ∼IST (2) *n.* [f. Fidel *Castro* Ruz, Cuban statesman b. 1927 + -ISM]

că'sual (-zhyŏŏ-, -zyŏŏ-) *a.* & *n.* accidental; irregular; undesigned; unmethodical; careless; (colloq.) unconcerned, uninterested, unceremonious; ∼ **clothes**, ∼**s**, informal clothes; ∼ (**labourer**), one without permanent employment, working when the chance comes, ∼ (**shoe**), low-heeled slip-on shoe; ||∼ **ward**, place for temporary accommodation of vagrants; ∼ **water**, (Golf) temporary accumulation of water (i.e. not one of the recognized hazards of the course); hence ∼LY² *adv.*, ∼NESS *n.* [ME, f. OF *casuel* & L *casualis* (*casus* CASE¹; see -AL)]

că'sualtȳ (-zhyŏŏ-, -zyŏŏ-) *n.* accident, mishap, disaster; person killed or injured in war or accident; thing lost or destroyed; (colloq.) = ∼ **department** or **ward**, part of hospital where casualties are attended to. [ME, f. med. L *casualitas* (as prec.; see -ITY), after *royalty* etc.]

căsuāri'na (-ē'na) *n.* (orig. Austral. and E. Ind.) tree of genus *Casuarina*, with jointed branches resembling gigantic horse-tails. [f. mod. L *casuarius* cassowary (from resemblance between branches and feathers)]

că'su|ist (-zhŏŏ-, -zū-) *n.* person, esp. theologian, who resolves cases of conscience, duty, etc.; sophist, quibbler; hence ∼i'stIC(AL) *adjs.*, ∼istRY (4) *n.* [f. F *casuiste* f. Sp. *casuista* f. L *casus* CASE¹; see -IST (3)]

casus belli (kāsus bĕ'lī, kahzus bĕ'lĭ) *n.* act or situation justifying or precipitating war. [L]

căt[1] *n.* **1.** small furry domesticated carnivorous quadruped, *Felis catus*; WILD *cat*; (colloq., derog.) spiteful or malicious woman; (sl.) person, esp. jazz enthusiast; any member of genus *Felis*, e.g. lion, tiger, leopard (esp. *the Cats, the great Cats*); catlike animal of other species (*civet cat, polecat*). **2.** ~('head), horizontal beam from each side of ship's bow for raising and carrying anchor. **3.** ~(-o'-nine-tails), (Hist.) rope whip with nine knotted lashes for flogging sailors, soldiers, or criminals. **4.** tapered short stick in game of tipcat. **5.** let the ~ out of the bag, reveal secret, esp. involuntarily; BELL[2] *the cat*; like a ~ on hot bricks, uneas(il)y; like something the ~ brought in, bedraggled; care killed the ~, (for all its nine lives; therefore,) be cheerful! (sim. *curiosity killed the cat*, do not be inquisitive); ~-and-dog *life* etc., full of quarrels; not a ~ in hell's chance, no chance whatever; see which way the ~ jumps, wait for opinion or result to declare itself; a ~ may look at a king, even inferiors must be allowed some privileges; enough to make a ~ laugh, extremely amusing; turn ~ in pan, change sides, be turncoat; ~ among the pigeons, violent intruder; rain ~s and dogs, very hard; not room to swing a ~, very confined space; has the ~ got your tongue?, (colloq.) why are you silent? **6.** ~'bird, bird with mewing cry (N. Amer. mocking-bird, Austral. bower-bird, etc.); CATBOAT; ||~ burglar (who enters by climbing wall to upper storey); ~'call, (n.) shrill whistle of disapproval at meetings etc., (v.i. & t.) make, reprove with, this; ~'door, small door that cat can itself open; ~'fish, (esp. freshwater) fish of sub-order Siluroides; CATGUT; ~'head (see sense 2); ~-ice, thin ice unsupported by water; ~-lap, (sl.) slops, tea, etc.; ~'lick, (colloq.) perfunctory wash; ~'mint, blue-flowered aromatic plant (*Nepeta cataria*); ~'nap *n.*, & *v.i.* (-*pp*-), (have) brief sleep in chair etc.; ~'nip, catmint; ~'s-cradle, child's game with string forming patterns between fingers; ~'s-eye, precious stone of Sri Lanka and Malabar, ||(C-; P) one of line of reflector studs on road; ||~'s-foot, ground ivy; ||~'s--meat, horse's or other flesh prepared and sold as food for cats; ~'s-paw, person used as tool by another, slight breeze rippling water in places; ~'s pyjamas, (sl.) = *cat's whiskers*; ~'s-tail, tall plant with long flat leaves; ~'suit, single garment from neck to feet, with trouser legs; ~'s whiskers, (sl.) something very fine; ~'walk, narrow footway along a bridge, among large engines, etc. **7.** Hence ~'HOOD (-t-h-) *n.*, ~ LIKE *a.* [OE *catt(e)*, = OHG *kazza*, ON *köttr*, f. LL *cattus, catta*; ME *catt(e)* reinforced by AF & ONF *cat* f. same source]

căt[2] *v.t.* (-*tt*-). (Naut.) raise (anchor, or abs.) from surface of water to cathead. [f. prec.]

cat-. See CATA-.

||**CAT** *abbr.* College of Advanced Technology.

căta-*pref.* (usu. **cat-** before vowel or *h*) meaning 'down' (*catadromous*), 'wrongly' (*catachresis*). [f. Gk *kata* down]

cată'bolism *n.* (Biol.) destructive metabolism, breakdown of complex substances in the body, (opp. ANABOLISM); so **cătăbŏ'lIC** *a.* [f. Gk *cată*(*bolē* a throwing) +-ISM]

cătachr|ē'sis (-k-) *n.* (*pl.* ~**eses** *pr.* -ē'sēz) incorrect use of words; hence ~**ĕ'stIC**(AL) *adjs.* [L f. Gk CATA(*khrēsis* f. *khraomai* use)]

cătaclă's|is *n.* (*pl.* ~**es** *pr.* -ēz). (Geol.) crushing of rocks; so **cătaclă'stIC** *a.* [mod. L, f. Gk CATA(*klasis* breaking)]

că'taclăsm *n.* violent break, disruption. [f. Gk CATA-(*klasma* f. *klaō* to break)]

că'taclўsm *n.* violent event; political or social upheaval; hence ~AL, ~IC, (-ĭ'zm-) *adjs.* [f. F *cataclysme* f. L f. Gk CATA(*klusmos* flood f. *kluzō* wash)]

cătacomb (-kōŏm, -kōm) *n.* subterranean

cemetery; (in *pl.*) the many Roman subterranean galleries with recesses excavated in sides for tombs; (in *pl.*) similar works elsewhere; cellar. [f. F *catacombes* f. LL *catacumbas* (name given in 5th c. to cemetery of St. Sebastian near Rome), of unkn. orig.]

cată'dromous *a.* (Of fish) descending to lower river or sea to spawn. [f. Gk CATA(*dromos* -running) + -OUS]

că'tafălque (-k) *n.* decorated structure to carry coffin or effigy of distinguished person during funeral service, or for a lying in state; structure on which coffin is drawn in procession. [F, f. It. *catafalco*, of unkn. orig.; cf. SCAFFOLD]

Că'talan *a.* & *n.* (native or language) of Catalonia in Spain. [F f. Sp.]

că'talāse (-s, -z) *n.* (Chem.) enzyme that catalyses reduction of hydrogen peroxide. [f. CATALYSIS + -ASE]

cătalĕ'ctic *a.* & *n.* (Pros.) (line) lacking one syllable in last foot. [f. LL f. Gk CATA(*lēktikos* ceasing f. *lēgō* cease; see -IC)]

că'talĕpsў *n.* trance or seizure with loss of sensation and consciousness accompanied by rigidity of the body; so **cătalĕ'ptIC** *a.* & *n.* [f. F *catalepsie* or f. LL *catalepsia* f. Gk CATA(*lēpsis* seizure); see -Y[1]]

*că't(t)alō *n.* (*pl.* ~**es** *or* ~**s**). cross between male buffalo and domestic cow. [f. CATTLE + BUFFALO]

că'talŏgue (-g), ***-lŏg**, *n.*, & *v.t.* (enumerate or enter in a) complete list, usu. alphabetical or under headings, and often with particulars added to items; ***university course-list** etc.; ~ **raisonné** (rāzonā'), descriptive catalogue with explanations or comments; hence **că'talŏg(u)ER**[1] (-ger) *n.* [F, f. LL f. Gk *katalogos* f. CATA(*legō* choose) enrol]

cată'lpa *n.* tree of genus *Catalpa*, with heart-shaped leaves, trumpet-shaped flowers, and long pods. [Amer. Ind. (Creek)]

că'talȳse, *că'talȳze, *v.t.* (Chem.) accelerate (process) or produce by catalysis. [f. foll. after *analyse*]

cată'lȳs|is *n.* (*pl.* ~**es** *pr.* -ēz). (Chem.) effect produced by a substance that, without itself undergoing change, aids a chemical change in other substances; hence **cătalȳ'tIC** *a.* [f. Gk CATA(*lusis* f. *luō* set free) dissolution]

că'talȳst *n.* substance causing catalysis; (fig.) thing or person that facilitates a change. [f. prec. after *analyst*]

cătamară'n *n.* raft or float of logs tied side by side, longest in middle; raft of two boats fastened side by side; sailing boat with two hulls side by side; (colloq.) quarrelsome woman. [f. Tamil *kaṭṭumaram* tied wood]

că'tamīte *n.* boy kept for homosexual practices; passive partner in sodomy. [f. L *catamitus* thr. Etruscan f. Gk *Ganumēdēs* Ganymede, cupbearer of Zeus]

cătamou'ntain (-tĭn) *n.* leopard, puma, or other tiger-cat; wild quarrelsome person. [ME, f. *cat of the mountain*]

cătană'nchè (-ngkĭ) *n.* plant of genus *Catananche*, with blue or yellow flowers. [mod. L, f. L *catanancē* plant used in love-potions f. Gk *katanagkē* (*kata* down, *anagkē* compulsion)]

că'taplĕxў *n.* sudden temporary paralysis due to fright etc.; hence **cătaplĕ'ctIC** *a.* [f. Gk CATA*plēxis* stupefaction]

că'tapŭlt *n.* & *v.* **1.** *n.* (Hist.) military machine for throwing heavy lever and ropes for discharging stones etc. **2.** ||boy's contrivance of forked stick and elastic for shooting small stones etc.; mechanical contrivance for launching glider, aircraft from deck of ship, etc. **3.** *v.t.* launch with catapult; fling forcibly (lit. or fig.). **4.** *v.i.* move (as if) from catapult. [f. F *catapulte* f. L *catapulta* f. Gk *katapeltēs* (*kata* CATA-, **pel-* cf. *pallō* hurl)]

cată'ract *n.* waterfall (prop. large and sheer; cf. CASCADE); downpour, rush of water; (Path.) progressive opacity of eye-lens. [f. L *cataracta* f. Gk *katarrhaktēs* down-rushing; in Path. sense prob. f. obs. sense *portcullis*]

cată'rrh (-är') *n.* inflammation of mucous membrane;

watery discharge in nose or throat due to this; hence **catăr'rh**AL (-ral) *a*. [f. F *catarrhe* f. LL *catarrhus* f. Gk *katarrhous* f. *katarrheō* (CATA-, *rheō* flow)]

că'tarrhĭne (-rĭn) *a*. & *n*. (Zool.) (monkey) having nostrils close together, and directed downwards. [f. Gk CATA- + *rhis rhinos* nose]

:ată'strophĕ *n*. sudden or widespread or noteworthy disaster; event subverting system of things; disastrous end, ruin; dénouement of drama; hence **catas-trŏ'ph**IC *a*., **catastrŏ'ph**ICALLY *adv*. [f. L *catastropha* f. Gk CATA(*strophē* turning f. *strephō* turn)]

:ată'stroph|ism *n*. (Geol.) theory that crustal changes have occurred in sudden violent and unusual events; so ∼IST (2) *n*. [f. prec. + -ISM]

:ătatŏ'nĭa *n*. schizophrenia with intervals of catalepsy and occas. violence; catalepsy; hence **catatŏ'n**IC *a*. & *n*. [f. G *katatonie* (as CATA-, TONE[1], -IA[1])]

:ataw'ba *n*. US variety of grape; white wine made from it. [f. River C∼ in Carolinas]

că'tboat *n*. sailing-boat with single mast placed well forward and carrying only one sail. [perh. f. *cat* former type of coaler in NE England, + BOAT[1]]

:ătch[1] *v*. (caught *pr*. kawt). **1.** *v.t.* capture, ensnare, make unable to escape; ∼ (**up**), overtake (∼ **up**, (abs.) make up arrears); lay hold of or hold *of* (*catch a* TARTAR[2]); be in time for (train etc., person about to depart); see (film), hear (broadcast), etc. **2.** surprise, detect, (*at* or *in*, or do*ing*; ∼ **me!**, **him!**, (iron.) you may be sure I etc. shall not); (in *pass.*, colloq.) become pregnant. **3.** hit (usu. *on* part specified; *caught him on the nose*; *caught him a blow* or *one*). **4.** *v.i.* (Of fire or combustible) begin to burn. **5.** become fixed or entangled, take hold, ∼ **at**, (seek to) grasp (*catch at a* STRAW[1]); ∼ **on**, (colloq.) (1) become popular, (2) understand what is meant. **6.** *v.t.* snatch (esp. ∼ **up**, **away**). **7.** intercept motion of and hold (*nail catches dress*; *put something to catch the drips*); (Cricket etc.) prevent (ball) from touching ground after striking the bat, ∼ (**out**), dismiss (batsman) by doing this; ∼ **out**, (fig.) detect in a mistake etc., take unawares. **8.** check suddenly (*catch* one's BREATH). **9.** receive, incur, be infected with, (*cold* or a COLD[2], *a fever*; a scolding, thrashing, or 'it'; a habit; *catch* one's DEATH, FIRE[1], *the* SUN). **10.** grasp with senses or mind (meaning, sound, tune, ∼ **a likeness**, see and reproduce it; ∼ **a glimpse of**, see for a moment; *catch* SIGHT[1] *of*). **11.** arrest, captivate, (attention, eye, fancy; ∼ **Speaker's eye**, succeed in being called on to speak in House of Commons). **12.** ∼**-all**, (thing) designed to catch or include various items; ∼**-as**-∼**-can**, wrestling style in which all holds are permissible; ∼ **crop**, crop grown between two staple crops (in position or time); ∼**'fly**, plant (esp. of genus *Silene*) with sticky stem; ∼**'penny** *a*., intended merely to sell readily, superficially attractive; ∼**-phrase**, one in frequent current use; ∥∼**-points** (to derail train etc., e.g. when running away down slope); ∼**'weight** *a*. & *n*., (Sports) unrestricted (as regards) weight; ∼**'word**, word so placed as to draw attention, first and last headwords repeated at top of dictionary etc. page, rhyming word in verse, last word (cue) of actor's speech, first word of page given at foot of previous one, word or phrase caught up and repeated esp. in connexion with party politics, slogan. **13.** Hence ∼'ABLE *a*. [ME, f. AF & ONF *cachier*, OF *chacier*, f. Rom. **captiare* for L *captare* try to catch; cf. CHASE[2]]

:ătch[2] *n*. **1.** act of catching; amount of fish etc. caught. **2.** (Cricket etc.) chance of or success in catching ball (**a good** or **safe** ∼, person skilful at catching). **3.** cunning question, deception, surprise; unexpected difficulty; ∼**-22**, (sl.) dilemma where victim cannot win [f. novel by J. Heller 1961]. **4.** contrivance for checking motion of door etc. **5.** thing or person caught or worth catching, esp. in matrimony by virtue of wealth etc., (**no** ∼, bad bargain, unwelcome acquisition). **6.** (Mus.) round for three or more equal

voices, occas. so devised as to produce punning or other humorous verbal combinations. [f. prec.]

că'tcher *n*. In vbl senses; (Baseball) fielder who stands behind batter. [f. CATCH[1] + -ER[1]]

că'tching *a*. In vbl senses; infectious; attractive, captivating. [f. CATCH[1] + -ING[2]]

că'tchment *n*. ∼ **area** (from which rainfall flows into river, reservoir, etc., (fig.) from which a hospital's patients, a school's pupils, etc. are drawn). [f. CATCH[1] + -MENT]

că'tchpōle, -pŏll, *n*. (Hist.) sheriff's officer. [OE *kæcepol* f. AF & ONF **cachepol*, OF *chacepol*, or f. AL *cacepollus* chase-fowl (as CATCH[1], L *pullus* fowl)]

că'tchup. Var. of KETCHUP.

că'tchў *a*. attractive; (of tune etc.) easily remembered. [f. CATCH[1] + -Y[2]]

cāte *n*. (arch.; usu. in *pl.*) choice food. [f. obs. *acate* purchase f. AF *acat*, OF *achat* f. *acater*, *achater* buy; see CATER[2]]

catèchě't|ĭc(al) (-kĕ'-) *adjs*. of or by oral teaching; according to a, or the Church, catechism; consisting of or proceeding by question and answer; hence ∼ICALLY *adv*., ∼ICS *n*. [f. eccl. Gk *katēkhētikos* (*katēkhētēs* oral teacher; see CATECHIZE, -IC, -AL)]

că'tĕchism (-k-) *n*. instruction by question and answer; published example of this, esp. on religious doctrine (**Church C∼**, Anglican; **Longer** and **Shorter C∼**, of Presbyterians); series of questions put to anyone; hence **catèchi'sm**AL (ki'z) *a*. [f. eccl. L *catechismus* (as foll.; scc -ISM)]

că'tèch|ize (-k-), **-ise** (-īz) *v.t.* instruct by question and answer, or by use of Church Catechism; put questions to, examine; so ∼IST (1), ∼**īz**ER[1], *ns*. [f. LL *catechizare* f. eccl. Gk *katēkhizō* (*katēkheō* make four f. as CATA-, *ēkheō* sound; see -IZE)]

că'tèchu (-ōō) *n*. gambier or similar vegetable extract, containing much tannin. [mod. L, f. Malay *kachu*]

cătèchū'mĕn (-kū'-) *n*. Christian convert under instruction before baptism. [ME, f. OF *catechumene* or eccl. L *catechumenus* f. pass. part. of Gk *katēkheō* (see CATECHIZE)]

cătègŏ'rĭcal *a*. unconditional, absolute; explicit, direct, plain-speaking; ∼ **imperative**, (Ethics) unconditional moral obligation derived from pure reason, bidding of conscience as ultimate moral law; hence ∼LY[2] *adv*. [f. F *catégorique* or f. LL f. Gk *katēgorikos*; see foll., -IC, -AL]

că'tègŏr|ў *n*. class, division; (Philos.) one of a possibly exhaustive set of classes among which all things might be distributed; one of the a priori conceptions applied by the mind to sense-impressions; any relatively fundamental philosophical concept; hence **catè-gŏr'ī**AL *a*., ∼IZE *v.t.*, place in category. [f. F *catégorie* or f. LL f. Gk *katēgoria* statement (*katēgoros* accuser)]

catē'n|a *n*. (*pl.* ∼**ae** or ∼**as**). connected series of patristic comments on Scripture, or of other things. [L, = chain; orig. *catena patrum* chain of the Fathers (of the Church)]

catē'nary *a*. & *n*. (like) curve formed by uniform chain hanging freely from two points not in same vertical line; ∼ **bridge**, suspension bridge hung from such chains. [f. L *catenarius* (*catena* chain; see -ARY[1])]

că'tèn|āte *v.t.* connect like links of chain; hence ∼A'TION *n*. [f. L *catenare* (as prec.) + -ATE[3]]

cā'ter[1] *n*. the four on dice. [f. F *quatre* f. L *quattuor* four]

cā'ter[2] *v.i.* purvey food; provide meals *for*; provide amusement, requisites, etc., *for*; pander *to* (evil inclinations); hence ∼ER[1] *n*., (esp.) one whose trade is to supply food for social events, ∼ING[1] *n*., such trade. [f. obs. *n. cater* (now *caterer*), f. *acater* f. AF *acatour* buyer f. *acater* buy f. Rom. **AC(captare* catch)]

cā'teran *n*. (Sc.) Highland irregular fighting-man, raider. [ME, f. med. L *cateranus* & f. Gael. *ceathairne* peasantry]

*cā'tercŏrner, -cŏrnered (-erd) *adv*. & *a*. (placed or situated) diagonally. [f. dial. adv. *cater* diagonally (cf. CATER[1]) + CORNER + -ED[2]]

că′ter-cousin (-kŭz-) *n.* (arch.) intimate friend. [perh. f. as CATER², w. ref. to boarding together]

că′terpillar *n.* larva of butterfly or moth; similar larva of various insects; (*C∼*; **P**) vehicle (also **C∼ tractor**) with endless articulated steel band (**C∼ track, tread**) passing round and worked by two wheels, to travel on rough ground. [perh. f. AF var. of OF *chatepelose* lit. hairy cat, infl. by obs. *piller* ravager]

că′terwaul *v.i.*, & *n.* (make) cat's screaming. [ME, f. CAT¹ + *-waul* etc. imit.]

că′tgŭt *n.* material used for strings of musical instruments and surgical sutures, made of twisted intestines of sheep, horse, or ass (not cat). [f. CAT¹ (reason unkn.) + GUT]

Cath. *abbr.* Cathedral; Catholic.

Că′thar *n.* (*pl.* ∼s, *or* ∼i *pr.* -ī). member of medieval sect seeking to achieve great purity; hence ∼ISM (3), ∼IST (2), *ns.* [f. med. L *Cathari* pl. f. Gk *katharoi* the pure]

cathăr′s|is *n.* (*pl.* ∼es *pr.* -ēz). **1.** (Med.) purgation. **2.** outlet to emotion afforded by drama etc. or (Psych.) by abreaction. [mod. L, f. Gk *katharsis* (*kathairō* cleanse); sense 2 f. Aristotle's *Poetics*]

cathăr′tic *a.* & *n.* **1.** (Med.) purgative (medicine). **2.** *a.* effecting catharsis. [f. LL f. Gk *kathartikos* (as prec.; see -IC)]

Cathay′ *n.* (arch. or poet.) the country China. [f. med. L *Cat(h)aya*]

cathe′ctic. See CATHEXIS.

cathe′dral *a.* & *n.* ∼ (**church**), principal church of diocese, with bishop's throne; ∼ **city**, one in which there is a cathedral. [ME a. f. OF, or f. LL *cathedralis* f. L f. Gk *kathedra* chair (as CATA-, *hed*- sit); see -AL]

Că′therine *n.* ∼ **wheel**, circular window with radial divisions, rotating firework, lateral handspring with arms and legs extended. [f. mod. L *Catharina* f. Gk *Aikaterina*, name of saint martyred on spiked wheel]

că′theter *n.* (Med.) tubular instrument for passing into body cavity to allow movement of fluid; hence ∼IZE (1) *v.t.*, introduce catheter into. [LL, f. Gk *kathetēr* (*kathiēmi* send down)]

cathĕto′meter *n.* instrument for measuring small vertical distances. [f. *cathetus* perpendicular line (L f. Gk as prec.) + -o- + -METER]

cathĕ′x|is *n.* (*pl.* ∼es *pr.* -ēz). (Psych.) concentration of mental energy in one channel; so **cathĕ′ctIC** *a.* [f. Gk *kathexis* retention]

că′thŏde *n.* (Electr.) negative electrode or terminal (opp. ANODE); ∼ **ray**, beam of electrons from cathode of high-vacuum tube caused by electric field, heat, radiation, etc.; ∼**-ray tube**, sealed evacuated vessel in which cathode rays produce luminous image on fluorescent screen; hence **că′thodAL, cathŏ′dIC**, *adjs.* [f. Gk *kathodos* descent (*kata* down, *hodos* way)]

că′tholic *a.* & *n.* **1.** *a.* universal; of interest or use to all men; all-embracing, of wide sympathies, broad-minded, tolerant; **C∼ Epistles** (of James etc., as not addressed to one person or church). **2. C∼ Church,** (orig.) whole body of Christians; ∼, belonging to or in accord with (a) this, (b) the church before separation into Greek or Eastern and Latin or Western, (c) the Latin Church after that separation (cf. ORTHODOX), (d) (often **Roman C∼**) the part of the Latin Church that remained under the Roman obedience after the Reformation, (e) any church (as the Anglican) claiming continuity with (b). **3. C∼ Apostolic Church,** IRVINGITES; **C∼ King, his C∼ Majesty,** (Hist.) King of Spain. **4.** Hence **cathŏ′lICALLY** *adv.*, (Eccl.) **cathŏ′lIcISM** (2, 3) *n.*, **cathŏli′cITY** *n.*, (Eccl.) **cathŏ′licIZE** (3) *v.t.*, ∼LY² *adv.* **5.** *n.* member of catholic church, esp. (C∼) Roman Catholic Church accepting jurisdiction of Pope as supreme head of that Church. [ME, f. OF *catholique* or f. LL f. Gk *katholikos* universal f. *kath′ holou* in general (*kata* in respect of, *holos* whole)]

cathŏ′licon *n.* universal remedy, panacea. [ME

f. F, f. mod. L *catholicum*, neut. (as n.) of LL *catholicus* (see prec.)]

Cătilīnā′r′ian *a.* & *n.* (one who engages in) conspiracy, esp. against government. [f. *Catiline*, Rom. conspirator d. 63 BC + -ARIAN]

că′tion *n.* ion with positive charge that moves towards cathode in presence of electric field (opp. ANION). [f. CATA- + ION]

cătiŏ′nic *a.* of cation(s); having an active cation. [f. prec. + -IC]

că′tkin *n.* cylindrical male or female inflorescence of willow, hazel, etc., usu. hanging and usu. downy or silky. [f. obs. Du. *katteken* kitten (as CAT¹, -KIN)]

cato′ptr|ic *a.* of mirror, reflector, or reflection; hence ∼ICS *n.* [f. Gk *katoptrikos* (*katoptron* mirror; see -IC)]

că′tsup. Var. of KETCHUP.

***că′ttalō.** See CATALO.

că′tterỹ *n.* place where cats are bred or looked after. [f. CAT¹ + -ERY]

că′ttish, că′ttỹ, *adjs.* catlike; (esp., fig.) sly and spiteful; hence **că′ttishLY², că′ttiLY²,** *advs.*, **că′ttishNESS, că′ttiNESS,** *ns.* [f. CAT¹ + -ISH¹, -Y²]

că′ttle *n. pl.* **1.** oxen (*cattle and sheep*; **black** ∼, oxen of Scottish and Welsh highland breeds, orig. black); (arch.) livestock. **2.** ∥∼**-cake,** concentrated food for cattle, in cake form; ∥∼**-grid,** *∼**-guard,** ditch covered by spaced bars to allow passage of vehicles and pedestrians but not cattle etc.; ∼**-lifter,** cattle-thief; *∼**-man,** one who tends or rears cattle; ∼-plague, rinderpest; *∼**-rustler,** cattle-thief ∼**-stop,** (NZ) = *cattle-grid*; *∼**-truck,** truck for transport of cattle, (fig.) crowded uncomfortable vehicle. [ME & AF, ONF *catel*, OF *chatel* (cf CHATTEL) f. as CAPITAL²; see -LE 2]

că′ttleya (-lĭa) *n.* Amer. epiphytic orchid of genus *Cattleya*, with handsome violet, pink, or yellow flowers. [mod. L, f. W. *Cattley*, Engl. patron of botany d. 1832; see -A 1]

că′ttỹ. See CATTISH.

că′ttỹcŏrner, -ered (-erd) Var. of CATER CORNER(ED).

Caucā′sian (-zĭan, -zhan) *a.* & *n.* (member) of the 'white' or light-skinned race of mankind; (native or inhabitant) of the Caucasus. [f. *Caucasus*, supposed place of origin + -IAN]

cau′cus *n.* (∥usu. derog.) local political usu. elective party committee for fighting elections, defining policy etc.; this system as a political power; (party meeting) [18th c. US, perh. f. Algonquin *cau′-cau-as′u* adviser]

cau′dal *a.* of, at, like, tail; of posterior part of body hence or cogn. ∼LY² *adv.*, **cau′dATE²** *a.* [f. mod. L *caudalis* f. L *cauda* tail; see -AL]

caudi′llō (kowdē′lyō) *n.* (*pl.* ∼s). (In Spanish-speaking countries) military or political leader. [Sp. f. LL *capitellum* dim. of *caput* head]

cau′dle *n.* (arch.) warm gruel with spice, sugar, and wine, for invalids. [ME, f. ONF *caudel*, OF *chaudel* med. L *caldellum* dim. of L *caldum* hot drink (*calidus* warm)]

caught. See CATCH¹.

caul *n.* **1.** (Hist.) woman's close-fitting indoor head-dress; plain back part of woman's indoor head-dress **2.** inner membrane enclosing foetus; portion of this occas. found on child's head at birth, thought to be of good omen; omentum [ME, perh. f. OF *cale* small cap]

∥**cau′ldron** (kaw′-, kŏ′-), **ca′l-** (kaw′-), *n.* large boiling-vessel (usu. of deep basin shape with hoop handle and removable lid). [ME, f. AF & ONF *caudron*, augment. (see -OON) f. Rom. *caldario,* f. *caldarium* hot bath (*calidus* hot)]

cau′liflower (kŏ′l-) *n.* variety of cabbage with large white flower-head; ∼ **cheese,** savoury dish containing mainly cauliflower and cheese; ∼ **ear,** ea (usu. boxer's) thickened by repeated blows. [earlie *cole-florie* etc., f. obs. F *chou fleuri* flowered cabbage assim. to COLE and FLOWER]

caulk, *calk, (kawk) *v.t.* stop up seams of (ship), stop up (seams), with oakum etc. and waterproofing material or by driving plate-junctions together; hence ∼ER¹ *n.* [f. OF dial. *cauquer* tread, press with force, f. L *calcare* tread (*calx* heel)]

cau'sal (-z-) *a.* of, acting as, expressing, due to, a cause or causes; of the nature of cause and effect; so **causä'l**ITY (-z-) *n.*, ∼LY² *adv.* [f. LL *causalis* (as CAUSE¹; see -AL)]

causä'tion (-z-) *n.* causing or producing an effect; relation of cause and effect; doctrine that all things have causes. [F, or f. L *causatio* pretext etc., in med. L action of causing, f. *causare* (CAUSE²); see -ATION]

cau'sative (-z-) *a.* acting as cause, productive *of*; (Gram.) expressing cause; hence ∼LY² (-vlĭ) *adv.* [ME, f. OF *causatif* or f. LL *causativus* (as prec.; see -ATIVE)]

cause¹ (-z) *n.* **1.** what produces an effect; antecedent(s) invariably and unconditionally followed by a certain phenomenon; person who, agent that, occasions something; ground, reason, motive, for action etc. (*no cause for complaint*); adequate motive or justification (esp. *show cause*); First C∼, the Creator of the universe; SECOND *cause*; hence ∼'LESS (-zl-) *a.* **2.** (Law). matter about which person goes to law; his case (*plead a cause*); lawsuit; ∼ **list** (of cases awaiting trial). **3.** side of any dispute espoused by person or party (lost ∼, hopeless undertaking; **make common ∼ with,** join side of); subject of interest (**good ∼,** movement deserving support); **in the ∼ of,** to defend or support. [ME f. OF, f. L *causa*]

caus|e² (-z) *v.t.* be the cause of, produce; induce, make, (person or thing *to do, to be* done); hence ∼ER¹ *n.* [ME, f. OF *causer* or med. L *causare, causari* f. L *causa* CAUSE¹]

cause (kŏz, koz) *adv.* & *conj.* (colloq.) = BECAUSE. [abbr.]

cause célèbre (kōz sălĕ'br) *n.* (*pl. causes célèbres pr.* same). lawsuit that attracts much attention. [F].

causerie (kō'zerī) *n.* (*pl. pr.* same). informal article or talk, esp. on literary subject. [F (*causer* talk)]

cau'seway (-zwā), (arch. or dial.) **cau'sey** (-zĭ), *n.* raised road across low or wet place or piece of water; raised footway by road. [earlier *cauce*(*way*) f. AF *cauce(*e*), ONF *caucié*(*e*) f. Rom. *culciata (*via*) f. L CALX lime(stone)]

cau'st|ic *a.* & *n.* (substance) that burns or corrodes organic tissue (∼ic **potash,** potassium hydroxide; ∼ic **soda,** sodium hydroxide), sarcastic, biting; (Phys.) (surface or curve) formed by intersection of rays reflected or refracted from curved surface; hence ∼ICALLY *adv.*, ∼ï'CITY *n.*, ∼ICIZE (3) *v.t.* [f. L f. Gk *kaustikos* (*kaustos* burnt f. *kaiō* burn; see -IC)]

cau'teriz|e, -ïs|e (-ĭz), *v.t.* sear with hot iron or caustic, in treatment of wound; (fig.) make callous; hence ∼A'TION *n.* [f. F *cautériser* f. LL *cauterizare* f. Gk *kautēriazō* (*kautērion* branding-iron f. *kaiō* burn; see -IZE)]

cau'tery *n.* metal instrument or caustic for searing tissue; cauterizing. [f. L f. Gk *kautērion*; see prec.]

cau'tion *n.*, & *v.t.* **1.** *n.* prudence, taking care, avoidance of rashness, attention to safety; (Sc. Law & US) BAIL¹, guarantee or guarantor; ∥∼ **money,** sum deposited as security for good conduct; hence **cau'tious** *a.*, **cau'tious**LY² *adv.*, (-shus-). **2.** warning; fact that acts as warning; warning and reprimand (*dismissed with a caution*); hence ∼ARY¹ *a.* **3.** (colloq.) surprising or amusing person or thing. **4.** *v.t.* warn (person; *against, to* or *not to* do); warn and reprove. [ME f. OF, f. L *cautio -onis* (*cavēre caut-* take heed; see -ION)]

ăvalcä'de *n.* company or procession of riders, motor cars, etc.; any procession. [F, f. It. *cavalcata* (*cavalcare* f. Rom. *caballicare f. L *caballus* pack-horse); ride f. Rom. *caballicare f. L *caballus* pack-horse; ride f. Rom. *caballicare; see -ADE)]

ăvalier' *n.* & *a.* **1.** *n.* courtly gentleman, gallant, esp. as escorting a lady; (Hist.; *C*∼) supporter of Charles I in Civil War; (arch.) horseman. **2.** *a.* offhand,

curt, supercilious; hence ∼LY² *adv.* [F, f. It. *cavaliere,* f. as CHEVALIER]

cavă'lly *n.* (arch.) large sea-fish of genus *Caranx* etc. [f. Sp. *caballo* horse, *caballa* mare f. L (as foll.)]

că'valry *n.* (usu. treated as *pl.*) soldiers on horseback or in motor vehicles; ∼**man,** soldier of cavalry regiment; ∼ **sword,** sabre; ∼ **twill,** strong fabric in double twill. [f. F *cavallerie* f. It. *cavalleria* (*cavallo* f. L *caballus* horse; see -ERY)]

căvati'na (-tē'-) *n.* short simple song; similar piece of instrumental music, usu. slow and emotional. [It.]

cäve¹ *n.* large natural underground hollow usu. with horizontal opening; ∥(Polit.) dissident group (cf. ADULLAMITE); (*attrib.*) living in caves; ∼**bear,** extinct species whose remains are found in caves; ∼**-dweller,** ∼**man,** (esp.) prehistoric man living in caves, (fig.) man of primitive or violent passions, instincts, and behaviour; ∼**-painting,** picture(s) of animals etc. on interior of cave esp. by prehistoric peoples. [ME f. OF, f. L *cava* (*cavus* hollow)]

căve² *v.t.* & *i.* **1.** hollow out, make into a cave; explore caves, whence **că'ver¹, că'ving¹** (1), *ns.* **2.** ∼ **in,** (cause to) subside or recede (of earth etc. over hollow, of wall yielding inwards); yield to pressure, submit, withdraw opposition; so ∼**-in** *n.* [sense 1 f. prec.; sense 2 prob. f. E. Anglian dial. *calve in*; cf. Flem. *inkalven,* Du. *afkalven,* in sim. sense]

∥**că've³** *int.* (school sl.) look out! (as warning cry); **keep** ∼, act as look-out. [1.,, = beware]

că'vĕat *n.* warning, proviso; (Law) process in court to suspend proceedings; ∼ *e'mptor,* let the buyer beware (he alone is responsible if he is disappointed). [L, = let him beware]

că'vendish *n.* tobacco softened, sweetened, and pressed into cakes. [prob. f. surname *C*∼]

că'vern *n.* underground hollow, (esp. vast) cave; dark hollow part; hence ∼ED² (-nd), ∼OUS, *adjs.* [ME, f. OF *caverne* or f. L *caverna* (*cavus* hollow)]

că'vĕsson *n.* strong nose-band used in taming troublesome horses. [f. F *caveçon* f. It. *cavezzone* augment. of *cavezza* halter f. Rom. *capitia f. med. L *capitium* head-covering f. L *caput capitis* head]

cavĕ'tt|ō *n.* (*pl.* ∼**i** *pr.* -ē). (Archit.) hollowed moulding with quadrantal cross-section. [It., dim. of *cavo* hollow f. L *cavus*]

căviäre, -är, (kă'-, -är') *n.* pickled roe of sturgeon etc., eaten as delicacy; ∼ **to the general,** [Shak. *Hamlet* II. ii. 457] good thing unappreciated by the ignorant. [early forms repr. It. *caviale* f. Turk. *ḥāvyār*]

că'vil *v.i.* (∥-ll-), *n.* (raise) captious or frivolous objection (*at, about*); hence ∼LER¹ *n.* [f. F *caviller* f. L *cavillari* (*cavilla* mockery)]

că'vit|y *n.* hollow place, hollow, empty space in a solid body; ∼ **wall,** double wall with internal cavity; hence **căvita'tion** *n.*, formation of cavity in a structure, or of bubbles in a liquid, or of a vacuum in a liquid. [f. F *cavité* or f. LL *cavitas* f. L *cavus* hollow; see -ITY]

cavor't *v.i.* (sl.) prance. [US wd, perh. f. CURVET]

că'vy *n.* S. Amer. rodent of family Caviidae, esp. guinea-pig. [f. mod. L *cavia* f. Galibi *cabiai*]

caw *n.*, & *v.i.* (make) cry of rook, crow, or raven. [imit.]

cay *n.* insular bank or reef of coral, sand, etc.; cf. KEY³. [f. Sp. *cayo* shoal, reef f. F *quai*; see QUAY]

cayĕ'nne ∼ (**pepper**), pungent red powder from capsicum plants, used for seasoning. [f. Tupi *kyynha,* assim. to *Cayenne* capital of French Guiana]

cay'man, cai'man, *n.* S. Amer. alligator, esp. of genus *Caiman.* [f. Sp. & Port. *caiman* f. Carib *acayuman*]

***cay'üse** (kī'-) *n.* Amer. Ind. pony. [Chinook]

ca'za (kah-) *n.* Turkish district under judge. [f. Turk. *kaza,* rel. to CADI]

CB *abbr.* citizens' band; ∥Companion (of the Order of) the Bath; confinement etc. to barracks.

*Cb *symb.* columbium.

CBC *abbr.* Canadian Broadcasting Corporation.

***CBD** *abbr.* cash before delivery.

‖**CBE** *abbr.* Commander (of the Order) of the British Empire.

‖**CBI** *abbr.* Confederation of British Industry.

***CBS** *abbr.* Columbia Broadcasting System.

‖**CC** *abbr.* Companion of the Order of Canada; ‖County Council(lor); Cricket Club.

c.c. *abbr.* carbon copy; cubic centimetre(s).

CCC *abbr.* Corpus Christi College.

‖**CCF** *abbr.* Combined Cadet Force.

‖**C.Chem.** *abbr.* chartered chemist.

CD *abbr.* civil defence; *Corps Diplomatique.*

‖**Cd.** *abbr.* COMMAND² Paper (third series, 1900–18).

cd *abbr.* candela.

Cd *symb.* cadmium.

Cdr. *abbr.* Commander.

Cdre. *abbr.* Commodore.

***CDT** *abbr.* Central Daylight Time.

CE *abbr.* Church of England; civil engineer; Common Era.

Ce *symb.* cerium.

cēanō'thus *n.* shrub of genus *Ceanothus,* with usu. blue flowers. [mod. L, f. Gk *keanōthos* kind of thistle]

cease¹ *v.* **1.** *v.i.* (literary). desist *from;* (of feelings, actions) come to an end. **2.** *v.t.* (literary), stop doing, being, etc. (or *to* do, be, etc.); bring to an end (strife, endeavours, etc.). **3.** (Mil.) ∼ **fire**, discontinue firing; ∼**fire** *n.,* signal to do this, time or period when hostilities are discontinued. [ME, f. OF *cesser* f. L *cessare* frequent. of *cedere cess-* yield]

cease² *n.* (literary). **without** ∼, ∼'LESS (-sl-) *a.,* not ceasing; hence ∼'lèssLY² (-sl-) *adv.* [f. OF *ces* (*cesser;* see prec.)]

cē'cĭty *n.* (poet., usu. fig.) blindness. [f. L *caecitas* (*caecus* blind; see -ITY)]

***cē'cum.** See CAECUM.

cē'dar *n.* evergreen coniferous tree of genus *Cedrus,* with fragrant durable wood; one of various similar trees; ∼(**wood**), wood of cedar, esp. of *Juniperus virginiana;* hence ∼**n** [-EN⁵] *a.* (poet.). [ME f. OF *cedre,* f. L f. Gk *kedros*]

cēde *v.t.* give up, grant, admit, surrender (territory). [f. F *céder* or f. L *cedere* yield]

cèdi'lla *n.* mark written under *c* (ç) to show that it is sibilant; similar mark under *s* in Turkish, etc. [f. Sp. *cedilla,* dim. of *zeda* f. Gk *zēta* letter Z]

‖**CEGB** *abbr.* Central Electricity Generating Board.

ceilidh (kā'lǐ) *n.* (esp. Sc. & Ir.) informal gathering for music, dancing, song, and story. [Gael.]

cei'ling (sē'-) *n.* lining of roof of room; top of room or other compartment; (Aeron.) maximum altitude a given aircraft can attain under specified conditions; altitude of base of cloud layer; upper limit of prices, wages, performance, etc.; (Naut.) inside planking of ship's bottom and sides. [f. *ceil* form ceiling for (perh. f. L *celare* hide) + -ING¹ (2)]

cē'ladon *n.* & *a.* willow green; grey-green glaze used on some pottery; Chinese pottery thus glazed. [F, f. name of character in D'Urfé's *L'Astrée*]

cē'landine *n.* one of two yellow-flowered plants, **greater** ∼ (*Chelidonium majus*) and **lesser** ∼ (*Ranunculus ficaria*). [ME and OF *celidoine* f. med. L *celidonia,* for L *chelidonia* (*herba* plant) f. Gk *khelidonion* (*khelidōn* the swallow); for *-n-* cf. *passenger*]

-cēle *comb. form.* (Path.) tumour (of specified part), as *gastrocele.* [f. Gk *kēlē* tumour]

cē'lēbrant *n.* officiating priest, esp. at Eucharist. [F, or f. L *celebrare* (see foll., -ANT)]

cē'lēbr|āte *v.* **1.** *v.t.* perform publicly and duly (religious ceremony etc.); officiate at (Eucharist); observe (festival), honour, with rites, festivities, etc.; praise widely, extol; (in *p.p.*) widely known. **2.** *v.i.* officiate at Eucharist; engage in festivities after success etc. **3.** So ∼A'TION, ∼ātor, *ns.,* ∼ātory *a.* [f. L *celebrare* (*celeber -bris* frequented, renowned) + -ATE³]

cē'lēbrity *n.* being famous; well-known person. [f. *célébrité* or f. L *celebritas* (*celeber;* see prec., -ITY)]

cělě'riăc *n.* variety of celery with root like turnip. [f. CELERY; *-ac* unexplained]

cělě'rĭtӯ *n.* (arch. or literary). swiftness (of living movement or agency). [ME, f. F *célérité* f. L *celeritas -tatis* (*celer* swift; see -ITY)]

cě'lerӯ *n.* plant (*Apium graveolens*) whose blanched stem is used as salad and vegetable; ∼ **pine**, Australasian tree with branchlets like celery leaves. [f. F *céleri* f. It. dial. *selleri* f. L f. Gk *selinon* parsley]

cělě'sta *n.* (Mus.) small keyboard instrument with hammers striking metal bars, giving notes like those of glockenspiel. [pseudo-L, f. F *céleste* (see foll.)]

cělě'ste *n.* organ and harmonium stop with soft tremulous tone; = prec. [f. F *céleste* heavenly f. L *caelestis* (*caelum* heaven)]

cělě'stial *a.* of the sky (*celestial equator, globe, map,* SPHERE); heavenly, divine, divinely good, beautiful, etc., whence ∼lӯ² *adv.;* **C**∼ **Empire**, (Hist.) China [transl. of native title]; ∼ **navigation** (using observed positions of heavenly bodies). [ME f. OF, f. med. L *caelestialis* f. L *caelestis* (see prec., -IAL)]

***cě'liăc.** See COELIAC.

cě'libate *a.* & *n.* (of) unmarried person, esp. one bound or resolved not to marry; so **cě'libACY** *n.* [f. F *célibat* or f. L *caelibatus* unmarried state (*caelebs -ibis* unmarried; see -ATE¹)]

cěll *n.* **1.** small room for one person in monastery; similar room for prisoner (**condemned** ∼ for person condemned to death); compartment in bees' comb; (Electr.) vessel containing electrodes for current-generation or electrolysis; hermit's one-roomed dwelling; (Hist.) dependent monastery or nunnery. **2.** enclosed cavity in organism or mineral; one of imaginary compartments of brain, assigned to various faculties; (Biol.) portion of protoplasm usu enclosed in membrane, ultimate element of organic structures; (fig., of group of persons) centre or nucleus of political (esp. revolutionary or subversive) activities. **3.** Hence (-)∼ED² (-ld) *a.* [ME f. OF *celle* or f. L *cella* storeroom etc.]

cě'llar *n.,* & *v.t.* (put or store in an) underground room; (**wine**-)∼, place in which wine is kept person's stock of wine (*keeps a good cellar*); hence ∼AGE¹) *n.,* ∼ER¹ *n.,* monastic officer in charge of wine etc [ME f. AF *celer,* OF *celier* f. LL *cellarium* storehouse (see prec., -AR², -ARY¹)]

cě'llarě't *n.* case or sideboard for holding winebottles in dining-room. [f. prec. + -ET¹]

cě'll|ō (-tsh-) *n.* (*pl.* ∼os). bass instrument like very large violin, 4-stringed, and held upright on floor by seated player; hence ∼IST (3) *n.* [abbr. of VIOLONCELLO]

Cě'llophāne, c-, *n.* (P) transparent wrapping materia made from viscose. [f. CELLULOSE + -O- + -*phane* (cf DIAPHANOUS)]

cě'llūlar *a.* of or having small compartments o cavities; porous; (Physiol.) of or consisting of cells; ∼ **blanket, shirt,** etc., (of open texture); ∼ **plan** (without distinct stem, leaves, etc.); hence **cěllū-lă'rITY** *n.* [f. F *cellulaire* f. L mod. L *cellularis;* see -AR¹]

cě'llūl|e *n.* (Anat.) small cell or cavity; hence o cogn. as derivs of CELL 2) ∼ATE², ∼OUS, *adjs.* ∼A'TION *n.* [F, or f. L *cellula* (*cella* cell; see -ULE)]

cěllūli'tis *n.* inflammation of cellular tissue. [f. a prec. + -ITIS]

cě'llŭloid *n.* plastic made from camphor and cellulos nitrate; piece of this; (fig.) cinema films. [irreg. f foll. + -OID]

cě'llŭlōse (-s, -z) *n.,* & *v.t.* **1.** *n.* (Chem.) carbohydrat forming main constituent of plant-cell walls anc textile fibres; (pop.) paint or lacquer consisting of esp cellulose acetate or nitrate in solution; hence **cěllū-lō'sIC** (-z-) *a.* **2.** *v.t.* treat with cellulose. [F (a CELLULE; see -OSE²)]

***cě'lom.** See COELOM.

Cě'lsius *a.* pertaining to the ∼ **scale** of tem perature, on which water freezes at 0° and boils a

100° under standard conditions. [f. A. ~, Sw. astronomer d. 1744]

Celt[1] (k-, s-) *n.* member of one of a group of W. Eur. peoples (incl. ancient Gauls and Britons; modern Bretons, Cornish, Gaels, Irish, Manx, Welsh). [f. L *Celtae* pl. f. Gk *Keltoi*]

celt[2] *n.* (Archaeol.) stone or metal chisel-edged prehistoric implement. [f. (?) L *celtes*]

Ce′ltic (k-, s-) *a.* & *n.* (language) of the Celts and kindred peoples; ~ **cross**, Latin cross with circle round centre; ~ **fringe**, the Highland Scots, Irish, Welsh, and Cornish, in relation to the rest of Britain; ~ **Sea**, sea area S. of Ireland & W. of Cornwall; ~ **twilight**, romantic fairy-tale atmosphere of Ir. folklore [f. title of Yeats's anthology]; hence ~ISM (2, 4) *n.*, ~IZE (2, 3) *v.i.* & *t.* [f. L *celticus* (as CELT[1]; see -IC) or F *celtique*]

ce′mbalō (ch-) *n.* (*pl.* ~s). harpsichord. [abbr. of CLAVICEMBALO]

cemē′nt *n.*, & *v.t.* **1.** *n.* substance applied as paste and hardening into stony consistency for binding together stones or bricks and for forming floors, walls, etc.; strong mortar of calcined lime and clay (**hydraulic** ~, kind hardening under water); any substance applied soft for sticking things together; substance for filling teeth; bony substance surrounding root of tooth; (fig.) principle that unites; ~**-mixer**, machine (usu. with revolving drum) for mixing cement with water. **2.** *v.t.* unite (as) with cement (lit. or fig.); apply cement to, line or cover with cement; hence **cemēnt**A′TION *n.*, (esp.) heating of iron with charcoal powder to form steel. [ME, f. OF *ciment* f. L *caementum* quarry stone (*caedere* hew; see -MENT)]

ce′metery (-trǐ) *n.* place for burials, other than a churchyard. [f. LL f. Gk *koimētērion* dormitory (*koimaō* put to sleep)]

∥C.Eng. *abbr.* chartered engineer.

*****ce′nobīte.** See COENOBITE.

ce′notaph (-ahf, -ǎf) *n.* sepulchral monument to person whose body is elsewhere; ∥**the** C~, (esp.) that in London commemorating the dead of the 1914–18 and 1939–45 wars; empty tomb. [f. F *cénotaphe* f. LL *cenotaphium* f. Gk *kenos* empty + *taphos* tomb]

cenō′te *n.* natural underground reservoir used as sacrificial well by Mayas. [Mex. Sp., f. Maya *conot*]

*****Cēnozō′ic.** See CAINOZOIC.

cense *v.t.* perfume or worship with burning incense. [ME, f. OF *encenser* INCENSE[2]]

ce′nser *n.* vessel in which incense is burnt, esp. one that is swung during religious ceremony. [ME f. AF, OF *censier* f. *encensier* (*encens* INCENSE[1]; see -ER[2] (2))]

ce′nsor *n.*, & *v.t.* **1.** *n.* person expressing opinions on other's morals and conduct. **2.** official with power to suppress whole or parts of books, plays, films, letters, news, etc. on grounds of obscenity, seditiousness, etc. **3.** (Rom. Hist.) magistrate who compiled censuses and supervised conduct. **4.** (Psych.) power by which certain unconscious ideas and memories are prevented from emerging into the consciousness. **5.** Hence or cogn. **cēnsōr′IAL** *a.*, ~SHIP *n.* **6.** *v.t.* act as censor (sense 2) of; make deletions or changes in. [L, f. *censēre* assess (see -OR); in sense 4 mistransl. of G *zensur* censorship]

cēnsōr′ious *a.* fault-finding, severely critical; hence ~LY[2] *adv.*, ~NESS *n.* [f. L *censorius* (CENSOR; see -ORY)+-OUS]

ce′nsure (-sher) *n.*, & *v.t.* **1.** *n.* adverse judgement, expression of disapproval, reprimand. **2.** *v.t.* criticize harshly and unfavourably; reprove; hence ~ABLE *a.* [ME f. OF, f. L *censura* (*censēre* assess; see -URE); v. f. F *censurer*]

ce′nsus *n.* official numbering of population or of a class of things, with various statistics. [L (*censēre* assess)]

cent *n.* **1.** See PER CENT. **2.** hundredth of US etc. dollar or other coin; coin of this value; typical small coin (*don't care a cent*). [F, or f. It. *cento* or L *centum* hundred]

cent. *abbr.* century.

∥ce′ntal *n.* weight of 100 lb., esp. of corn. [f. L *centum* hundred + -AL]

ce′ntaur *n.* (Gk Myth.) horse with human body, arms, and head, in place of its neck and head. [ME, f. L f. Gk *kentauros*, of unkn. orig.]

ce′ntaury *n.* plant of genus *Centaurium*, esp. *C. umbellatum*, formerly used in medicine. [f. LL *centauria*, *-ea*, f. L f. Gk *kentaur(e)ion* (*kentauros*, see prec.); said to have been discovered by the centaur Chiron]

centénā̄′ian *a.* & *n.* (person) a hundred or more years old. [f. as foll. + -AN]

ce′ntenarý (sĕntē′-, sĕ′ntǐ-) *a.* & *n.* (festival) of the hundredth anniversary. [f. L *centenarius* (*centeni* a hundred each f. *centum* hundred; see -ARY[1])]

centē′nnial *a.* & *n.* **1.** *a.* lasting, occurring every, hundred years; = prec.; *****C~ State,** Colorado (founded 1876). **2.** *n.* = prec. [f. L *centum* hundred, after *biennial*]

*****ce′nter**[1],[2]. See CENTRE[1],[2].

ce′ntering. See CENTRING.

centē′simal *a.* reckoning or reckoned by hundredths; hence ~LY[2] *adv.* [f. L *centesimus* hundredth (*centum* hundred) + -AL]

ce′nti- *comb. form.* hundred, hundredth, esp. of a unit in the metric system, as: *centi*GRAM[2], *centi*LITRE, CENTIMETRE. [f. L *centum* hundred + -I-]

ce′ntigrāde *a.* having a hundred degrees; esp. = CELSIUS. [F, f. L *centum* hundred + *gradus* step]

ce′ntime (sah′ntēm) *n.* one-hundredth of a franc. [F, f. L (as CENTESIMAL)]

∥ce′ntimētre (-ter), *****-mēter,** *n.* one-hundredth of a metre about 0.4 inch; (as unit of rainfall or pressure, cf. INCH[1]); ~**gram-second system** (using these as basic units of length, mass, and time). [f. CENTI-+METRE[2]]

ce′ntipede *n.* myriapod of class Chilopoda. [f. F *centipède* or f. L *centipeda* (*centum* hundred, *pes pedis* foot)]

ce′ntō[1] *n.* (*pl.* ~s). composition made up of quotations from other authors. [L, = patchwork garment]

Ce′ntō[2] *n.* Central Treaty Organization. [abbr.]

ce′ntral *a.* & **1.** *a.* of, in, at, from, containing, the centre; leading, principal, dominant, essential; **C~ America,** isthmus joining N. and S. America; *central* BANK[3]; ~ **heating,** method of warming a building by hot water or hot air or steam conveyed by pipes from *central source*, or by general system of radiators etc.; ~ **nervous system,** brain and spinal cord; **C~ Powers,** Germany and Austria-Hungary before 1914; **C~ Time,** standard time used in central Canada and US; hence **cēntrā′lITY,** ~NESS, *ns.*, ~LY[2] *adv.* **2.** *n.* *****telephone exchange. [F, or f. L *centralis* (*centrum* CENTRE[1]; see -AL)]

Cēntrā′lia *n.* remote central regions of Australia. [f. prec. + *Australia*]

ce′ntral|ism *n.* centralizing system; so ~IST (2) *n.* [f. CENTRAL+-ISM]

ce′ntralīz|e, -īs|e (-īz), *v.i.* & *t.* come or bring to a centre; concentrate (administration) at single centre; subject (State etc.) to this system; hence ~A′TION *n.* [f. CENTRAL+-IZE, or f. F *centraliser*]

∥ce′ntre[1] (-ter), *****ce′nter**[1], *n.* & *a.* **1.** *n.* middle point (equidistant from ends of line or from extremities of regular surface or body, or from all points on circumference of arc or circle or sphere); DEAD *centre*. **2.** point, pivot, axis, of revolution; (in lathe etc.) conical adjustable support for workpiece. **3.** point of concentration or dispersion, nucleus, source. **4.** place or group of buildings forming central point in district etc. or main area for an activity (*city*, DETENTION, HEALTH, *shopping*, *centre*). **5.** filling within chocolates etc. **6.** = CENTRING. **7.** (Mil.) main body of troops between wings. **8.** (Polit.) party or group holding moderate opinions. **9.** (Footb. & Hockey). middle player in line; kick or hit from wing to centre of pitch. **10.** ~ **of attraction,** (Phys.) point to which bodies tend by gravity, (fig.) person or thing drawing general attention; **~-bit**, boring tool with centre point and side cutters; **~board** (for lowering through boat's keel to prevent leeway); **~-fold**, centre spread that folds out; **~-forward**, **~-half**, middle player or position in forward, half-back, line; *centre of* GRAVITY, *of* MASS²; **~-piece**, ornament for middle of table, principal item; **~ of pressure**, point at which single force can be applied to balance pressure over whole surface; **~-second**, (clock or watch with) seconds hand mounted on centre arbor; **~ spread**, two facing middle pages of newspaper etc.; **~ three-quarter**, (Rugby Footb.) one of two middle players in line of three-quarters. **11.** Hence **cĕ'ntrı**c(AL) *adjs.*, **cĕntrı̆'**cıty *n.* **12.** *a.* at or of the centre; hence **~most** (-*erm*-) *a.* [ME, f. OF *centre* or f. L *centrum* f. Gk *kentron* sharp point]

||**cĕ'ntre²** (-*ter*), ***cĕ'nter²**, *v.* **1.** *v.i.* be concentrated *in*, (*up*)*on*, *at*, (D) (*a*)*round*. **2.** *v.t.* place in centre; mark with a centre; concentrate *in* etc.; (Footb. & Hockey) kick or hit (ball) from wing to centre of pitch. [f. prec.]

centreing. See CENTRING.

-cĕ'ntric *suf.* forming *adjs.* w. sense 'having a (specified) centre', as: ANTHROPOcentric, CONCENTRIC, ECCENTRIC, HELIOcentric. [after *concentric* etc. f. Gk *kentrikos* (as CENTRE¹; see -IC)]

cĕntrı̆'fŭgal (-rı̆'-; D sĕ'-) *a.* moving or tending to move from centre; **~ force** (with which body revolving round centre seems to tend to fly off); **~ machine** etc. (in which rotation causes centrifugal motion); hence **~ly²** *adv.* [f. mod. L *centrifugus* (*centrum* CENTRE¹, *-fugus* -fleeing f. *fugere* flee) +-AL]

cĕ'ntrı̆fŭge *n.*, & *v.t.* **1.** *n.* centrifugal machine rotating at very high speed, designed to separate solids from liquids, or liquids from other liquids (e.g. cream from milk). **2.** *v.t.* subject to centrifugal motion; separate by centrifuge; hence **cĕntrı̆fŭga'tıon** *n.* [F, f. as prec.]

cĕ'ntrı̆ng, cĕ'ntreı̆ng, cĕ'ntring, (-*ter*-) *n.* temporary framing used to support arch, dome, etc., while under construction. [f. CENTRE²+-ING¹]

cĕntri'pĕtal *a.* moving or tending to move towards centre (opp. CENTRIFUGAL); hence **~ly²** *adv.* [f. mod. L *centripetus* (*centrum* CENTRE¹, *-petus* -seeking f. *petere* seek) +-AL]

cĕ'ntrı̆st *n.* (Polit. etc.) holder of moderate views; so **~ism** (3) *n.* [f. CENTRE¹ +-IST]

cĕ'ntŭple *a.*, *n.*, & *v.* **1.** *a.* & *n.* hundredfold (amount). **2.** *v.t.* & *i.* multiply by a hundred. [F, or f. eccl. L *centuplus*, *centuplex* f. L *centum* hundred]

cĕntŭ'rion *n.* commander of century in ancient Roman army. [ME, f. L *centurio -onis* (as foll.)]

cĕ'ntŭrı̆ (-chĕrı̆) *n.* **1.** company in ancient Roman army, orig. of 100 men; political division for voting in ancient Rome. **2.** a hundred of something; hundred runs in one batsman's innings at cricket; hundred--year period reckoned successively from an accepted epoch, esp. from birth of Christ (**first ~**, 1–100, **twentieth ~**, 1901–2000, **second century** B.C., 200–101 BC, etc.); any hundred successive years; **~ plant**, agave, flowering only once in many years. [L *centuria* (*centum* hundred; see -Y¹)]

cĕp *n.* edible mushroom of genus *Boletus*. [f. F *cèpe* f. Gascon *cep*, f. L *cippus* stake]

cĕpha'lic *a.* of or in the head; **~ index**, quantity expr. ratio of head's greatest breadth and length. [f. F *céphalique* L f. Gk *kephalikos* (*kephalē* head; see -IC)]

-cĕpha'lic. See -CEPHALOUS.

cĕ'phalopŏd *n.* mollusc of class Cephalopoda, with distinct tentacled head, e.g. cuttlefish and octopus. [f. Gk *kephalē* head +-o +Gk *pous podos* foot]

cĕphalothŏ'răx *n.* fused head and thorax of spider, crab, etc. [f. as prec.+THORAX]

-cĕ'phalous, -cĕpha'lic, *comb. form.* (esp. Anthropol.) = -headed, as: BRACHY~, DOLICHO~. [f. Gk *kephalē* head +-OUS, -IC]

cĕ'phĕïd *n.* (Astron.) variable star with typical curve of brightness change, used to measure distances. [f. δ *Cephei* orig. example (*Cepheus* constellation f. name of mythical king) +-ID³]

cĕrǎ'm|ic *a.* & *n.* **1.** *a.* of (the art of) pottery; of (substances produced by) process of strong heating of clay etc. minerals. **2.** *n.* article made of pottery; substance made by firing clay etc. minerals at high temperatures. **3.** Hence **~ics**, **cĕ'ramist** (3), *ns.* [f. Gk *keramikos* (*keramos* pottery; see -IC)]

cĕrǎ'stēs (-z) *n.* horned viper of N. Africa etc. [L f. Gk *kerastēs* (*keras* horn)]

cĕrǎ'stium *n.* plant of genus *Cerastium*, with white flowers and often horn-shaped capsules. [mod. L, f. Gk *kerastēs* horned (*keras* horn)]

cĕrato-, kĕrato-, *comb. form.* horn; cornea. [f. Gk *keras -atos* horn]

Cĕr'berus *n.* sop to **~**, something to propitiate an official, guard, etc. [L, f. Gk *Kerberos* three-headed dog guarding entrance to Hades]

cĕre *n.* waxlike membrane at base of some birds' beaks. [f. L *cera* wax]

cĕr'ĕal *a.* & *n.* **1.** *a.* of corn or edible grain. **2.** *n.* (usu. in *pl.*) kind(s) of grain used for human food; food made from wheat, maize, or other cereal (usu. as breakfast dish). [f. L *cerealis* (*Ceres* goddess of agriculture; see -AL)]

cĕrĕbĕ'll|um *n.* smaller (posterior) part of brain; hence **~ar** *a.* [L, dim. of CEREBRUM]

cĕ'rĕbral *a.* of the brain; (of literature, music, etc.) appealing to the intellect rather than to the emotions; clever; intellectual; (Phonet.) cacuminal; **~ palsy**, spastic paralysis from brain damage before or at birth, with jerky or uncontrolled movements. [f. L *cerebrum* brain +-AL]

cĕrĕbrǎ'tion *n.* working of the brain, esp. **unconscious ~** (of results reached without conscious thought); hence **cĕ'rĕbrate³** *v.i.* [f. as prec.+ -ATION]

cĕrĕbro- *comb. form.* brain, as: **~-spi'nal**, of brain and spine; **~to'nic**, like ectomorph in temperament, with predominantly intellectual interests; **~-vas'-cular**, of the brain and its blood-vessels. [f. as foll.+-o-]

cĕ'rĕbrum *n.* principal (anterior) part of brain. [L]

cēr'cloth (sēr'klŏth, -awth) *n.* waxed cloth used as waterproof covering or (esp.) as winding-sheet. [earlier *cered cloth* f. *cere* to wax f. L *cerare* (*cera* wax)]

cĕr'ement (sēr'm-) *n.* (usu. in *pl.*; arch.) grave--clothes. [first used by Shak. in *Hamlet* (1602); app. f. prec.+-MENT]

cĕrĕmō'nial *a.* & *n.* **1.** *a.* with or of ritual or ceremony, formal; hence **~ism** (3), **~ist** (2), *ns.*, **~ly²** *adv.* **2.** *n.* system of rites; formalities proper to any occasion; observance of conventions; (RC Ch.) book containing order of ritual. [f. LL *caerimonialis* (as CEREMONY; see -AL)]

cĕrĕmō'nious *a.* addicted or showing addiction to ceremony, punctilious; hence **~ly²** *adv.*, **~ness** *n.* [f. F *cérémonieux* or f. LL *caerimoniosus* (as foll.; see -OUS)]

cĕ'rĕmon|y̆ *n.* outward rite or observance; empty form; formalities; punctilious behaviour; **Master of C~ies**, person in charge of ceremonies that are observed on state or public occasions, person introducing speakers at banquet or entertainers in variety show; **stand on ~y**, insist on observance of formalities; **without ~y**, informally, casually. [ME, f. OF *ceremonie* or f. L *caerimonia* religious worship]

Cerenkov. See CHERENKOV.·

cĕ'resin *n.* hard whitish wax used with or instead of beeswax. [f. mod. L *ceres* f. L *cera* wax, +-IN]

ceri'se (-ē'z, -ē's) *a.* & *n.* (of) a light clear red. [F, = CHERRY]

cēr'ium *n.* (Chem.) metallic element of lanthanide series. [f. *Ceres*, an asteroid discovered (1801) just previously, +-IUM]

cēr'mĕt *n.* heat-resistant alloy of ceramic with metal. [f. CERAMIC+METAL]

CERN (sĕrn) *abbr.* European Organization for Nuclear Research. [f. F *Conseil Européen pour la Recherche Nucléaire*, former title]

cēro- *comb. form.* wax, as: ∼**graphy** (-ŏ′g-), writing or designing on or with wax; ∼**pla′stic,** modelled in wax, of wax-modelling. [f. L *cera* or Gk *kēros* wax]

‖**cĕrt** *n.* (sl.) event or result certain to happen; horse certain to win race. [abbr. of CERTAIN(TY)]

cert. *abbr.* certificate: certified.

cĕr′tain (-tan, -tĭn) *a.* **1.** settled, unfailing; unerring, reliable; that may be reckoned on (**for** ∼, as a certainty; **make** ∼, = *make* SURE); indisputable, confident, convinced, (*of, that*); destined, undoubtedly going, *to do.* **2.** that might but need not or should not be specified (*a certain person; lady of a certain age*); some though not much (*felt a certain reluctance*); existing but probably unknown to reader or hearer (*a certain John Smith*); (as *pl. pron.*) some but not all. [ME f. OF, f. Rom. **certanus* f. L *certus* settled]

cĕr′tainly (-tan-, -tĭn-) *adv.* indubitably; infallibly; confidently; admittedly; (in answers) I admit it, no doubt, yes. [f. prec. + -LY[2]]

cĕr′tainty (-tan-, -tĭn-) *n.* undoubted fact (**bet on a** ∼, usu. dishonestly with secret knowledge of result; MORAL *certainty*), indubitable prospect; thing or person that may be relied on (*to do*); absolute conviction (*of, that*); **for a** ∼, beyond possibility of doubt. [ME f. AF *certainté*, OF *-eté* (as CERTAIN, TY[1])]

Cert. Ed. *abbr.* Certificate in Education.

cĕr′tes (-z) *adv.* (arch.) assuredly; I assure you. [ME f. OF, prob. f. Rom. **ad certas* for a certainty f. L (as CERTAIN)]

cĕr′tifiable *a.* able to be certified, (esp.) insane. [f. CERTIFY + -ABLE]

certi′ficate *n.,* & *v.t.* **1.** *n.* document formally attesting a fact, esp. birth, marriage, death, medical condition, abilities, fulfilment of requirements, ownership of shares, etc.; **C**∼ **of Secondary Education,** examination set for secondary-school pupils in England and Wales, certificate gained by passing it. **2.** *v.t.* (-āt) (esp. in *p.p.*) provide with or license or attest by certificate; hence **certifica′tion** *n.* [f. F *certificat* or f. med. L *certificatum* neut. p.p. (as n.) of *certificare* (see foll.)]

cĕr′tifȳ *v.t.* make formal statement of, declare by certificate; officially declare (person) insane; (arch.) inform with certainty; ∼**ied cheque** (value of which is guaranteed by bank); ***∼**ied mail** (whose delivery is recorded); ∼**ied milk** (guaranteed free from tuberculosis bacillus); ***∼**ied public accountant,** accountant holding certificate of professional competence. [ME, f. OF *certifier* f. med. L *certificare* f. L *certus* certain; see -FY]

certiorari (sĕrtiĕrār′ī, sĕrshiĕrār′ē) *n.* writ from higher court for records of case tried in lower. [LL, pass. of *certiorare* inform (*certior* compar. of *certus* certain)]

cĕr′titude *n.* feeling certain or convinced. [ME, f. LL *certitudo* (*certus* certain; see -TUDE)]

ceru′lēan (-ōō′-) *a.* deep-blue like clear sky. [f. L *caeruleus* sky-blue (*caelum* sky; see -EAN)]

ceru′m|ĕn (-ōō′-) *n.* yellow waxy substance in outer ear; hence ∼**inous** *a.* [mod. L, f. L *cera* wax]

ceruse (sēr′ōōs, sirōō′s) *n.* white LEAD[1]. [ME f. OF, f. L *cerussa,* perh. f. Gk *kēros* wax)]

cĕr′velat (-ah) *n.* kind of smoked pork sausage. [obs. F, f. It. *cervellata*]

cĕr′vical (-vī′-, sĕr′vĭ-) *a.* (Anat.) of neck; of cervix. [F, or f. mod. L *cervicalis,* f. L *cervix -icis* neck; see -AL]

cĕr′vine *a.* of or like deer. [f. L *cervinus* (*cervus* deer; see -INE[1])]

cĕr′vi|x *n.* (*pl.* ∼**ces** *pr.* -sēz) (Anat.) neck; necklike structure, esp. that of womb. [L]

*****Cesarean, -ian.** Vars. of CAESAREAN (in Med. sense).

Cĕsă′rĕvĭtch, -wĭtch, (-z-) *n.* (Hist.) eldest son of emperor of Russia; ‖(-w-) horse-race run annually at Newmarket. [f. Russ. *tsesarevich*]

*****cesium.** See CAESIUM.

cĕss[1] *n.* (Sc., Ir., India, etc.) tax, rate. [prop. *sess* for obs. *assess* n.; see ASSESS]

cĕss[2] *n.* (Ir.) **bad** ∼ **to,** may evil befall. [perh. f. prec.]

cĕssā′tion *n.* ceasing; pause. [ME, f. L *cessatio* (*cessare* CEASE[1]; see -ATION)]

cĕ′sser *n.* (Law). coming to an end, cessation, (*of* term, liability, etc.). [AF & OF, = CEASE[1]; see -ER[4]]

cĕ′ssion (-shon) *n.* ceding, giving up, (*of* rights, property, or esp. *of* territory by State). [ME f. OF, or f. L *cessio* (*cedere cess-* go away; see -ION)]

cĕ′ssionary (-shon-) *n.* = ASSIGN[2]. [f. LL *cessionarius* f. as prec.; see -ARY[1]]

cĕ′sspĭt *n.* pit for disposal of refuse; = foll. [f. foll. + PIT[1]]

cĕ′sspool *n.* underground chamber for temporary storage of liquid waste or sewage; (fig.) ∼ (= SINK[2]) **of iniquity** etc. [perh. alt., after POOL[1], f. earlier *cesperalle,* f. *suspiral* vent, water-pipe, f. OF *souspirail* air-hole f. as SUSPIRE; SEE -AL 2]

cĕ′stŏde, cĕ′stoid, *n.* (Zool.) ribbon-like intestinal worm, esp. tapeworm. [f. L f. Gk *kestos* girdle + -ODE, -OID]

CET *abbr.* Central European Time.

cētā′cean (-shan) *a.* & *n.* (member) of the mammalian order Cetacea, containing whales, dolphins, and porpoises; so **cetā′ceous** *a.* [f. mod. L *Cetacea* f. L *cetus* f. Gk *kētos* whale; see -ACEAN]

cē′tāne *n.* (Chem.) hydrocarbon ($C_{16}H_{34}$) of paraffin series, found in petroleum; ∼ **number,** quantity measuring ignition properties of diesel oil. [f. SPERMA-CETI, after *methane* etc.]

cĕ′terach (-k) *n.* fern of genus *Ceterach,* having backs of fronds covered with scales. [med. L, f. Pers. *šaytarak* f. Arab. *šaytaraj*]

ceteris paribus (kātĕrēs pār′ĭbus, sĕt-) *adv.* other things being equal or unchanged. [L]

Ceylo′n (sĭ-) *n.* ∼ **moss,** E. Ind. red seaweed (*Gracilaria lichenoides*); hence ∼E′SE (sĭlonē′z) *a.* & *n.* [island S. of India, now Sri Lanka]

‖**CF** *abbr.* Chaplain to the Forces.

c.f. *abbr.* carried forward.

cf. *abbr.* compare. [f. L *confer* imper.]

Cf *symb.* californium.

CFA *abbr.* African Financial Community. [f. F *Communauté financière d'Afrique*]

‖**CGM** *abbr.* Conspicuous Gallantry Medal.

CGS *abbr.* centimetre-gram-second; Chief of General Staff.

‖**CH** *abbr.* Companion of Honour.

ch. *abbr.* chapter; chestnut; church.

‖**cha** (-ah) *n.* (sl.) tea. [f. as CHAR[4]]

Chă′blis (shă′blē) *n.* a white burgundy wine. [∼ in E. France]

chāce. Var. (arch.) of CHASE[1,2].

cha-cha (chah′chah), **cha-cha-cha′** (chahchah-chah′), *n.,* & *v.i.* (perform) a ballroom dance with Latin-Amer. rhythm. [Amer. Sp.]

chaco′nne (sh-) *n.* (Mus.) (dance to) music on ground bass; composition in this style. [F, f. Sp. *chacona*]

‖**Chăd** *n.* (**Mr**) ∼, figure of a head above a wall, with caption protesting against shortages etc. [20th c.; orig. uncert.]

chae′tognăth (k-) *n.* small planktonic worm of phylum Chaetognatha, with spined head. [f. mod. L *Chaetognatha* f. Gk *khaitē* long hair + *gnathos* jaw; see -A]

chae′topŏd (k-) *n.* annelid of class Chaetopoda, with bristled feet. [f. as prec. + Gk *pous podos* foot]

chāfe *v.* & *n.* **1.** *v.t.* & *i.* rub (skin, to restore warmth or sensation); make or become sore or damaged by rubbing; irritate; become annoyed, fret. **2.** *n.* (sore made by) chafing; state of annoyance. [ME f. OF *chaufer* f. Rom. **calefare* f. L *calefacere* (*calēre* be hot, *facere* make)]

chā′fer *n.* large slow-moving beetle, esp. cockchafer. [OE *ceafor* & *cefer,* = OS *kever,* OHG *chevar,* f. Gmc **kabraz, *kebraz*]

chaff (-ahf) *n.* & *v.* **1.** *n.* husks of corn etc. separated by threshing or winnowing (**separate wheat from** ∼, (fig.) distinguish good from bad); chopped hay and straw as cattle-food; spurious substitute (**caught with** ∼, easily deceived or trapped); worthless stuff; strips of metal foil in air to obstruct radar detection; ∼-**cutter**, machine for chopping fodder; hence ∼′Y² *a.* **2.** *v.t.* chop (straw etc.). **3.** *v.t.* & *i.*, & *n.* banter. [OE *ceaf, cæf,* = OHG *keva* husk, prob. f. Gmc **kaf-*, **kef-* gnaw; sense 3 perh. f. CHAFE]

cha′ffer *v.* & *n.* **1.** *v.i.* & *t.* haggle, bargain; hence ∼ER¹ *n.* **2.** *n.* chaffering. [ME, f. OE *ceapfaru* (*ceap* bargain, *faru* journey)]

∥**cha′ffinch** *n.* common European finch (*Fringilla coelebs*). [f. OE *ceaffinc* (as CHAFF, FINCH)]

cha′fing-dish *n.* vessel with outer pan of hot water for keeping warm anything placed on it; dish with spirit-lamp etc. for cooking at table. [f. obs. sense of CHAFE = warm + -ING¹ + DISH¹]

Cha′gas (-ah′-) *n.* ∼′(s) **disease**, form of sleeping sickness transmitted by blood-sucking bugs. [f. C. ∼, Braz. physician d. 1934]

chagrin (shă′grĭn, shagrē′n) *n.*, & *v.t.* (affect with) acute vexation or mortification. [f. F *chagrin*(er), of uncert. orig.]

chain *n.*, & *v.t.* **1.** *n.* connected flexible series of metal or other links; (in *pl.*) fetters, confinement, restraining force; ornament or badge of office in form of chain worn round neck etc.; = BICYCLE-*chain,* TYRE-*chain,* WATCH¹-*chain.* **2.** sequence, series, set, (*of* proof, events, posts, mountains); group of associated shops, hotels, newspapers, etc.; figure in quadrille etc.; (Chem.) group of (esp. carbon) atoms joined in sequence in molecule. **3.** jointed metal-rod measuring-line; its length (66 ft.). **4.** ∼(-**shot**), (Hist.) two cannon-balls or half balls joined by chain for cutting masts etc. **5.** (Naut.) device for widening basis of shrouds beyond ship's sides. **6.** ∼-**armour** (made of interlaced rings); ∼ **bridge,** suspension bridge on chains; ∼ **drive** (Mech., with transmission by endless chains); ∼-**gang** (of convicts, chained together, or forced to work in chains); ∼-**gear** (transmitting motion by endless chain); ∼-**letter,** letter of which recipient is asked to make copies to be sent to a (named) number of others (these being asked to do the like); ∼-**link** *a.*, made of wire in diamond-shaped mesh; ∼-**mail,** chain-armour; ∼ **reaction,** (Chem.) reaction forming intermediate products which react with the original substance and are repeatedly renewed, (Phys.) series of fission reactions each initiated by neutrons from previous one, (fig.) series of events each due to previous one; ∼-**saw** (with teeth on endless chain); ∼-**shot** (see sense 4); ∼-**smoker,** one who smokes continually, esp. one who lights another cigarette or cigar from the end of the one last smoked; ∼-**stitch,** ornamental crochet or embroidery stitch like chain; ∼ **store,** one of a series of shops owned by one firm and selling the same class of goods; ∼-**wale,** = CHANNEL²; ∼-**wheel** (transmitting power by chain fitted to its edges). **7.** Hence ∼′LESS *a.*, ∼ (**up**), secure or confine with chain (lit. or fig.). [ME, f. OF *cha*(*e*)*ine* f. L *catena*]

chair *n.*, & *v.t.* **1.** *n.* separate seat for one, of various forms (ARM¹-, BATH¹-, DECK¹-, EASY, *chair;* **take a** ∼, sit down). **2.** seat of authority; professorship; ∥mayoralty (*alderman* etc. **past** or **above the** ∼, **below the** ∼, who has, has not, been mayor). **3.** seat or office of person presiding at meeting, public dinner, etc., (**be in the, take the** ∼, be chairman); chairman (*address, appeal to, the chair*). **4.** iron or steel socket holding railway rail in place. **5.** (Hist.) = SEDAN 1. **6.** * = ELECTRIC chair. **7.** ∼-**bed,** chair that unfolds into a bed; ∼-**borne,** (colloq.) administrative not active; ∼-**car,** railway carriage with chairs instead of long seats, parlour car; ∼-**lift,** series of chairs on endless cable for carrying passengers up mountain etc.; ∼′**man** etc. (see foll.); ∼′**person,**

chairman or chairwoman. **8.** *v.t.* install in chair, esp. of authority; ∥place (as if) in chair and carry aloft (winner of contest, election, etc.); act as chairman of, preside over, (meeting). [ME, f. AF *chaere,* OF *chaiere* f. L f. Gk *kathedra* (see CATHEDRAL)]

chair′man *n.* (*pl.* **chair′men;** *fem.* **chair′lady, chair′woman**). person chosen to preside over meeting; permanent president of committee, board of directors, firm, country, etc.; master of ceremonies at entertainment; (Hist.) one of two sedan-bearers; hence ∼SHIP *n.* [f. prec. + MAN¹]

chaise (shāz) *n.* **1.** (esp. Hist.) pleasure or travelling carriage, esp. light open carriage for one or two persons; POST²-*chaise.* **2.** ∼ **longue** (-lŏ′ngg) [F, = long chair], kind of low chair with seat long enough to support user's legs; ∼ **percée** (-pār′sā) [F, = pierced chair], chair incorporating chamber-pot. [F, var. of *chaire* f. as CHAIR]

chalā′za (k-) *n.* (*pl.* ∼**e**). one of two twisted membranous strips joining yolk to ends of egg. [mod. L f. Gk, = hailstone]

chālce′dony (k-) *n.* precious or semi-precious stone, a type of quartz, having many varieties such as agate, onyx, cornelian, chrysoprase. [ME, f. L *c*(*h*)*alcedonius* f. Gk *khalkēdōn*]

chālce′nter∣ic (k-) *a.* with bowels of bronze, tough; so ∼OUS *a.* [f. Gk *khalkenteros* (as foll., ENTERO-) + -IC]

chālcoli′thic (k-) *a.* (Archaeol.) of a period in which both stone and bronze implements are used. [f. Gk *khalkos* copper + *lithos* stone + -IC]

chālcopȳ′rite (k-) *n.* copper-iron sulphide ore. [f. Gk *khalkos* copper + PYRITE]

Chālde′an (k-) *a.* & *n.* **1.** (native or language) of ancient Chaldea or Babylonia. **2.** (exponent) of astrology. **3.** (member) of Uniat (formerly Nestorian) sect in Iran etc. [f. L f. Gk *Khaldaios* f. Assyr. *kaldu,* + -AN]

Chāldee′ (k-) *n.* = prec. 1; Aramaic as used in OT books. [ME, repr. L *Chaldaei* pl. (as prec.)]

cha′ldron (-awˈl-) *n.* measure for coals, approx. 36 bushels. [f. OF *chauderon* augment. (see -OON) of *chaud*(*i*)*ere* pot f. LL *caldaria* f. L *cal*(*i*)*dus* hot]

chā′let (shă′lā) *n.* Swiss mountain cowherd's hut; Swiss peasant's wooden cottage; house with widely overhanging roof; small villa; small house in holiday camp etc. [Swiss F]

chā′lice *n.* goblet; Eucharistic wine-cup; (poet.) flower-cup. [ME f. OF, f. L *calix -icis* cup]

chalk¹ (-awk) *n.* white soft earthy limestone used for burning into lime and for writing and drawing; coloured preparation of like texture used in crayons for drawing; (Geol.) strata consisting mainly of chalk; **as different as** ∼ **and** or **from cheese,** unlike in essentials; ∥**by a long** ∼, ∥**by long** ∼**s,** by far [f. use of chalk to mark score in games]. **2.** *∼**board,** blackboard; ∼-**pit,** quarry in which chalk is dug; ∼-**stone,** concretion of urates like chalk in tissues and joints esp. of hands and feet; ∼-**stripe**(**d**), (having) pattern of thin white stripes on dark background. [OE *cealc,* **cælc,* = OS *calc,* OHG *kalk,* WG f. L CALX]

chalk² (-awk) *v.t.* rub, mark, draw, write, write *up,* with chalk; ∼ **it up,** charge it (*to* my account etc.); ∼ **out,** sketch, plan as thing to be accomplished; ∼ **up,** register (success etc.). [f. prec.]

cha′lk∣ȳ (-awˈkĭ) *a.* abounding in or white as chalk; like or containing chalk-stones; hence ∼INESS *n.* [f. CHALK¹ + -Y²]

chā′llenge¹ (-nj) *n.* calling to respond, esp. sentry's call for password etc.; exception taken (e.g. to juryman); summons to take part in trial or contest, esp. to duel; demanding or difficult task; (Sport) invitation to contest, esp. issued to reigning champion; (Med.) test of immunity after immunization treatment. [ME & OF *c*(*h*)*alenge,* f. L *calumnia* calumny]

chā′llenge² (-nj) *v.t.* (Of sentry etc.) call to respond (lit. or fig.); take exception to (evidence, juryman), dispute, deny; claim (attention, admiration, etc.); invite to take part in contest, game, discussion, or duel; (Med.) test by challenge; (abs., usu. in *pres. part.*) offer interesting difficulties (*a challenging problem*); hence ~eABLE (-nja-) *a.*, ~ER[1] *n.* [ME, f. OF *c(h)alenger* f. L *calumniari* (*calumnia* calumny)]

chǎ'llis *n.* lightweight soft clothing fabric. [perh. f. surname]

chaly'bĕate (ka-) *a.* (Of mineral water or spring) impregnated with iron salts. [f. mod. L *chalybeatus* f. L *chalybs* f. Gk *khalups -ubos* steel; see -ATE[2]]

chǎm (k-) *n.* great ~, autocrat, dominant critic etc. (esp. Samuel Johnson). [F, f. Turki (as KHAN[1])]

chǎ'maephȳte (k-) *n.* (Bot.) plant whose buds are on or near the ground. [f. Gk *khamai* on the ground + -PHYTE]

chǎ'mber *n.* **1.** (poet. or arch., exc. in *comb.*) room, esp. bedroom. **2.** (in *pl.*) set of rooms in larger building, esp. in Inns of Court, let separately; judge's room for hearing cases not needing to be taken in court. **3.** (hall used by) deliberative or judicial body, one of the houses of a parliament (esp. SECOND *chamber, Chamber of Deputies*). **4.** = *chamber-pot.* **5.** cavity in body of animal or plant; enclosed space in machinery etc. (esp. part of gun-bore that contains charge); compartment in structure; (Phys.) apparatus designed to reveal tracks of ionizing particles by a visible effect (*bubble, cloud, spark, chamber*). **6.** C~ of Commerce, association to promote local commercial interests; ~ concert (of chamber music); *Chamber of* HORRORS; ~maid, housemaid at hotel etc., *housemaid; ~ music (for small group of instruments; ~-pot, receptacle for urine etc., used in bedroom. **7.** Hence (-)~ED[2] (-erd) *a.* (of tomb, containing a burial chamber). [ME f. OF *chambre* f. L CAMERA]

chǎ'mberlain (-lĭn) *n.* officer managing household of sovereign or great noble; treasurer of corporation etc.; ||**Lord Great C~** (**of England**), hereditary holder of a ceremonial office; ||**Lord C~** (**of the Household**), head of management of Royal Household, formerly licenser of plays; hence ~SHIP *n.* [ME, f. OF *chamberlain* etc., f. Frank. *kamerling f. OS *kamara* f. L (see prec., -LING[1])]

Cha'mbertin (shah'nbertǎn) *n.* a dry red burgundy wine. [~ in E. France]

chǎ'mbray (sh-) *n.* linen-finished gingham with white weft and coloured warp. [irreg. f. *Cambrai* (see CAMBRIC)]

chambré (shah'nbrā) *a.* (Of red wine) brought to room temperature. [F, p.p. of *chambrer* (*chambre* room; see CHAMBER)]

chamē'lĕ|on (k-) *n.* small prehensile-tailed long-tongued lizard with power of changing colour according to its surroundings and of living long without food; variable or inconstant person; hence ~ŏ'nIC *a.* [ME, f. L f. Gk *khamaileōn* (*khamai* on the ground, *leōn* lion)]

chǎ'mfer *v.t.*, & *n.* **1.** *v.t.* bevel symmetrically (right-angled edge or corner). **2.** *n.* surface so made. [back-form. f. *chamfering* f. F *chamfrain* f. *chant* edge (CANT[1]) + *fraint* broken (OF *fraindre* break f. L *frangere*)]

chǎ'mois (shǎ'mwah) *n.* (*pl.* same *pr.* -z). **1.** wild antelope of goat size, found in mountains of Europe and Asia. **2.** (or shǎ'mĭ) ~(-leather), soft pliable leather from sheep, goats, deer, etc., piece of this for polishing etc. [F; cf. Gallo-L *camox*]

chamomile. See CAMOMILE.

chǎmp[1] *v.t.* & *i.*, & *n.* munch (fodder) noisily; work (bit) noisily in teeth (~ing, ~ing at the bit, (fig.) restlessly impatient); (make) chewing action or noise. [prob. imit.]

chǎmp[2] *n.* (sl.) champion. [abbr.]

chǎmpā'gne (shǎmpā'n) *n.* white (esp. sparkling) wine from Champagne or elsewhere; pale straw colour. [f. C~, former province in E. France]

chǎ'mpaign (-ān) *n.* (literary). (expanse of) open country. [ME, f. OF *champagne* f. LL *campania*; cf. CAMPAIGN]

||**chǎ'mpers** (sh-; -z) *n.* (sl.) champagne. [f. CHAMPAGNE + -ER[1] (5) + -s[1]]

chǎ'mpert|y *n.* (Law) action of assisting a party in a suit in which one is not naturally interested, with view to receiving share of disputed property; hence ~ous *a.* [ME f. AF *champartie*, f. OF *champart* feudal lord's share of produce, f. L *campus* field + *pars* part]

chǎ'mpion *n.*, *a.*, *adv.*, & *v.t.* **1.** *n.* person who fights, argues, etc., for another or for a cause (||**King's, Queen's, C~,** or **C~ of England,** hereditary official at coronations). **2.** athlete, boxer, etc., animal, plant, etc., that has defeated all competitors (often attrib.: *champion boxer, turnip*); hence ~SHIP *n.* **3.** *a.* & *adv.* (colloq. or dial.) first-class, splendid(ly). **4.** *v.t.* support the cause of, argue in favour of, defend. [ME f. OF, f. med. L *campio -onis* fighter f. L *campus* field]

champlevé (shah'nlevā) *a.* & *n.* (enamel-work) in which hollows made in surface are filled with enamel colours. [F, = raised field]

chance[1] (-ah-) *n.* & *a.* **1.** *n.* way things happen of themselves, fortune; undesigned occurrence; opportunity, *esp. of escape etc.;* (Cricket) opportunity of dismissing a batsman; possibility; probability (esp. in *pl.; the chances are against it, are even*). **2.** absence of design or discoverable cause; course of events regarded as a power, fate, **game of** ~ (decided by luck not skill). **3. by** ~, as it happens or happened, without design; *the* MAIN[3] *chance*; OFF *chance*; **on the** ~, in view of the possibility (*of, that*); **stand a** ~, have a prospect of success etc.; **take a** or one's ~ (**on, with**), let things go as they may, consent to take what comes (as regards); **take a** ~, **take** ~**s,** behave riskily. **4.** *a.* fortuitous (*a chance companion, meeting*). [ME, f. AF *ch(e)aunce*, OF *chēance* (*chēoir* fall f. Rom. *cadēre f. L *cadere*; see -ANCE)]

chance[2] (ah) *v.* **1.** *v.i.* happen without intention (*that, to do*); ~ (**up**)**on,** happen to find, meet, etc. **2.** *v.t.* (colloq.) risk (esp. *chance it*); ~ one's **arm,** take one's (possibly slight) chance of doing something successfully. [ME, f. prec.]

cha'ncel (-ah'-) *n.* part of church near altar, reserved for clergy, choir, etc., and usu. enclosed. [ME f. OF, f. L *cancelli* lattice]

cha'ncellery (-ah'-) *n.* position, staff, department, official residence, of a chancellor; office attached to embassy or consulate. [ME, f. OF *chancellerie* (*chancelier*; see foll., -ERY)]

cha'ncellor (-ah'-) *n.* **1.** state or law official of various kinds; ||C~ (*of the* EXCHEQUER); ||C~ of Duchy of Lancaster, member of government (legally representative of Queen as Duke of Lancaster), often Cabinet Minister employed on non-departmental work; ||**Lord** (**High**) **C~** (presiding in House of Lords, Chancery Division, and Court of Appeal). **2.** bishop's law officer; C~ of Garter or other order (who seals commissions etc.); non-resident head of university; *president of chancery court; (Germany, Austria) chief minister of the State. **3.** Hence ~SHIP *n.* [OE f. AF *c(h)anceler*, OF *-ier* f. LL *cancellarius* porter, secretary (*cancelli* lattice)]

chance-mĕ'dley (-ah-) *n.* (Law) action, esp. homicide, mainly but not entirely unintentional; inadvertency. [f. AF *chance medlee*; see MEDDLE) mixed chance]

cha'ncery (-ah'-) *n.* ||(C~) Lord Chancellor's court, division of High Court of Justice (WARD[1] *in Chancery*); records office of order of knighthood; court of bishop's chancellor; *court of equity; chancellery of embassy; office for public records; **in** ~, (of boxer or wrestler) with head held under opponent's arm being pummelled. [ME, contracted f. CHANCELLERY]

chǎ'ncre (shǎ'ngker) *n.* ulcer in venereal disease etc. [F, f. L CANCER]

chǎ'ncroid (shǎ'ngk-) *n.* localized form of chancre. [f. prec. + -OID]

cha'ncǀy̆ (-ah'-) *a.* uncertain, risky; hence ∼ĭLY² *adv.*, ∼ĭNESS *n.* [f. CHANCE¹ + -Y²]
chǎndelier' (sh-) *n.* branched hanging support for several lights. [F *chandelle* f. as CANDLE)]
cha'ndler (-ah'-) *n.* dealer in candles, oil, soap, paint, and groceries (ǁcorn-∼, in corn; ship('s)-∼, in cordage, canvas, etc.); hence **cha'ndl**ERY (1) (-ah'-) *n.* [ME, f. AF *chaundeler*, OF *chandelier* (*chandelle*, as CANDLE; see -ER²)]
chǎnge¹ (-nj) *n.* **1.** making or becoming different; substitution of one for another, variety (*for a change*); hence ∼'FUL 1 (-jf-), ∼'LESS (-jl-), *adjs.* **2.** ǁC∼, 'C∼ [as if f. EXCHANGE¹], place where merchants meet (**on** C∼, engaged there). **3.** (Of moon) arrival at fresh phase, esp. at new moon; ∼ **of air,** different climate; ∼ (**of clothes**), second outfit in reserve; *change of* HEART; ∼ (**of life**), menopause; SEA *change.* **4.** money given for money in larger units or different currency; money returned as balance of that tendered in payment; **get no** ∼ **out of,** (sl.) fail to get the better of (in business, argument, etc.) or information from; **give** ∼, *****make** ∼, select money from till etc. and give it to buyer as change; = SMALL *change.* **5.** (Bell-ringing; usu. in *pl.*) different orders in which peal of bells can be rung; **ring the** ∼**s** (**on,** or abs.), (fig.) vary ways of expressing or doing thing. [ME, f. AF *chaunge*, OF *change* (*changer*; see foll.)]
chǎnge² (-nj) *v.* **1.** *v.t.* take or use another instead of (*change* one's *coat*); give up, get rid of, *for*; make different (often *to, into, from*); give or get money change for; put fresh clothes, coverings, etc., change from (*child, bed,* etc.); go from one to another of (*change houses, sides, trains*); give and receive, exchange, (*change places with; we changed places*). **2.** *v.i.* become different (often *to, into, from*) (of moon) arrive at fresh phase, esp. become new; change trains etc.; put on different (esp. evening) clothes. **3.** *change* COLOUR¹; ∼ **down,** engage lower gear in vehicle; ∼ one's **feet,** (colloq.) put on other shoes etc.; *change* FRONT; ∼ **gear,** engage different gear in vehicle; *change* HAND¹s, one's MIND²; ∼ **over** *v.t.* & *i.*, ∼**-over** *n.*, change from one system or situation to another; *change* STEP², *the* SUBJECT², one's TUNE; ∼ **up,** engage higher gear in vehicle. [ME, f. OF *changer* f. LL *cambiare*, L *cambire* barter, prob. of Celt. orig.]
cha'ngeǀable (-nja-) *a.* that can change or be changed; irregular, inconstant; hence ∼ABI'LITY (-ja-), ∼**able**NESS (-jabeln-), *ns.* [ME f. OF, f. as prec.; see -ABLE]
cha'ngeling (-njl-) *n.* thing or child believed to be substituted for another by stealth, esp. elf-child thus left by fairies. [f. CHANGE² + -LING¹]
chǎ'nnel¹ *n.,* & *v.t.* (ǁ-ll-). **1.** *n.* natural or artificial hollow bed of water; navigable part of waterway; piece of water, wider than strait, joining two larger pieces, usu. seas (ǁ**the** C∼, English Channel); tubular passage for liquid. **2.** course in which anything moves, direction, line; medium of communication, agency, (*through the usual channels*); circuit for telegraphic communication; (Broadcasting) band of frequencies sufficiently wide for transmission of signal, esp. as used for a particular programme; service using this; path for information; lengthwise strip on recording tape etc.; groove, flute. **3.** *v.t.* form channels in, groove; (fig.) guide, direct. [ME f. OF *chanel* f. L *canalis* CANAL]
chǎ'nnel² *n.* broad thick plank projecting horizontally from ship's side abreast of mast to widen basis for shrouds. [for CHAIN-*wale* (WALE); cf. *gunnel* for *gunwale*]
chǎ'nneǀlize, -īse (-īz), *v.t.* convey (as if) in a channel, guide. [f. CHANNEL¹ + -IZE]
chanson de geste (shahǹsawǹ de zhě'st) *n.* (*pl.* **-ns** *pr.* -ǹz). one of a group of medieval French epic poems. [F, = song of heroic deeds]
chant (-ah-) *n.* & *v.* **1.** *n.* song; (Mus.) short musical passage in two or more phrases each connected with

reciting note, for singing unmetrical words (psalms, canticles); measured monotonous song, musical recitation of words; sing-song intonation in talk. **2.** *v.i.* & *t.* sing; utter musically or rhythmically; intone, sing to a chant. [n. f. v., ME f. OF *chanter* sing, f. L *cantare* frequent. of *canere cant-* sing]
cha'nter (-ah'-) *n.* In vbl senses; melody-pipe, with finger-holes, of bagpipe. [f. prec. + -ER¹]
chanterě'lle (shah-) *n.* **1.** yellow funnel-shaped edible fungus, *Cantharellus cibarius.* **2.** (Mus.) highest-pitched string of banjo etc. [F, in sense 1 f. mod. L *cantharellus* dim. of *cantharus* f. Gk *kantharos* drinking-vessel, in sense 2 f. as CHANT]
chanteuse (shahǹtër'z) *n.* female singer of popular songs. [F]
cha'nticleer (-ah'-) *n.* (Personal name for) domestic cock. [ME, f. OF *chantecler* (as CHANT, CLEAR¹), name in *Reynard the Fox*]
Chanti'lly (shahǹtē'yĭ) *n.* delicate kind of bobbin-lace; sweetened whipped cream. [∼ near Paris]
cha'ntry (-ah'-) *n.* endowment for priest(s) to celebrate masses for founder's soul; priests, chapel, altar, so endowed. [ME, f. AF *chaunterie*, OF *chanterie* (*chanter* CHANT: see -ERY)]
chanty. Var. of SHANTY².
Chanukkah. Var. of HANUKKAH.
chǎ'ös (k-) *n.* formless primordial matter; utter confusion; hence **chǎö'tǀIC** (k-) *a.*, **chǎö'tǀ**ICALLY (k-) *adv.* [F or L, f. Gk *khaos; -otic* after *erotic* etc.]
chǎp¹ *v.* (-pp-) & *n.* **1.** *v.t.* & *i.* crack in fissures (usu. of skin or dry ground). **2.** *n.* (usu. in *pl.*) crack, open seam, esp. in skin, whence ∼'PY² *a.*; *****∼'stick,** part of cosmetic substance to prevent chaps. [ME, perh. rel. to MLG, MDu. *kappen* chop off]
chǎp² *n.* lower jaw or half of cheek, esp. of pig as food (*Bath chap*; ∼**-fallen,** with jaw hanging down, dispirited, dejected); see also CHOP³. [16th c., var. of CHOP³; orig. unkn.]
chǎp³ *n.* (colloq.) man, boy, fellow. [short for CHAP-MAN]
chap. *abbr.* chapter.
*****chǎpare'jŏs** (chǎ'parä'hŏs, sh-) *n. pl.* cowboy's leather overalls for legs. [Mex. Sp.]
*****chǎparrā'l** (ch-, sh-) *n.* dense tangled brushwood; ∼ **cock,** = ROAD¹*runner.* [Sp. (*chaparra* evergreen oak)]
chapā't(t)ĭ. See CHUPATTY.
chǎ'p-bŏŏk *n.* (Hist.) small pamphlet of tales, ballads, tracts, etc., hawked by chapmen. [19th c.; see CHAPMAN]
chāpe *n.* metal cap of scabbard-point; back-piece of buckle attaching to strap etc.; sliding loop on belt or strap. [ME f. OF, = cope, hood, f. as CAP¹]
chapeau-bras (shapŏbrah') *n.* (*pl.* **chapeaux--bras** *pr.* same). three-cornered flat silk hat carried under arm. [f. F *chapeau* hat + *bras* arm]
chǎ'pel *n.* place of Christian worship other than parish church or cathedral, esp. one attached to private house or institution (∼ **royal,** of royal palace); place for private worship in larger building, with altar, esp. part of cathedral etc. separately dedicated (LADY *chapel*); Anglican church subordinate to parish church, esp. ∼ **of ease** (for convenience of remote parishioners); ǁplace of worship of Nonconformist bodies; chapel service, attendance at chapel; (Print.) journeyman printers' association or meeting (**father of the** ∼, its president); ǁ∼ **of rest,** undertaker's mortuary; so ∼RY *n.,* district served by chapel. [ME f. OF *chapele* f. med. L *capella* dim. of *cappa* cloak (CAP¹); first chapel was sanctuary in which St. Martin's sacred cloak was kept by *cappellani* (see CHAPLAIN)]
chapelle ardente (shapěl ãrdah'ǹt) *n.* chamber prepared for lying-in-state of distinguished person and lit up with candles, torches, etc. [F, lit. 'burning chapel']
chǎ'perŏn (sh-) *n.,* & *v.t.* **1.** *n.* person who ensures propriety, esp. married or older woman accompanying

young unmarried woman on social occasions; hence ∿AGE *n.* **2.** *v.t.* act as chaperon to. [F, = hood, chaperon, dim. of *chape* cope f. as CAP¹]

chă'plain (-lĭn) *n.* clergyman officiating in private chapel of great person or institution, on board ship, or for regiment etc.; hence ∿CY *n.* [ME, f. AF & OF *c(h)apelain* f. med. L *cappellanus* (see CHAPEL)]

chă'plĕt *n.* wreath of flowers, leaves, gold, gems, etc., for head; string of beads for counting prayers (55, one-third of rosary number), or as necklace; bead--moulding. [ME f. OF *chapelet* dim. of *chapel* f. Rom. **cappellus* dim. of LL *cappa* CAP¹]

∥chă'p|man *n.* (*pl.* ∿men). (Hist.) pedlar. [OE *cēapman* (*cēap* barter; see CHEAP, MAN¹)]

chă'ppal *n.* Indian usu. leather sandal. [Hindi]

chă'ppie *n.* (colloq.) = CHAP³. [f. CHAP³ + -IE]

chă'ppy See CHAP¹.

*chăps (ch-, sh-) *n.* = CHAPAREJOS. [abbr.]

chă'pter *n.* **1.** main division of a book (∿ **and verse**, exact reference or authority); (fig.) limited subject, piece of narrative, etc. (*chapter of* ACCIDENTS); ∥Act of Parliament numbered as part of session's proceedings (Eliz. 2 1972 c. 60 = Gas Act, 1972). **2.** general meeting, or whole number, of certain appointed clergymen (canons) of collegiate or cathedral church or members of monastic or knightly order (∿ **house**, building used for such meetings or *for meetings etc. of students); division of printers' guild; *local branch of a society. [ME f. OF *chapitre* f. L *capitulum* dim. of *caput -itis* head]

chăr¹, chărr, *n.* (*pl.* same). small trout of genus *Salvelinus*. [17th c.; orig. unkn.]

chăr² *n.,* & *v.i.* (**-rr-**). **1.** *n.* ∥∿, ∥∿'lady, ∿'woman, woman hired by the hour or day or week to clean rooms in offices or ∥houses. **2.** *v.i.* work as charwoman. [earlier *chare* f. OE *cerr* a turn, *cierran* to turn]

chăr³ *v.t.* & *i.* (**-rr-**). burn to charcoal; scorch, blacken with fire. [app. back-form. f. CHARCOAL]

∥chăr⁴ *n.* (sl.) tea. [f. Chin. *cha*]

chă'rabănc (sha-, -ăng) *n.* (arch.) motor coach. [f. F *char à bancs* seated carriage]

chă'racter (kă'rĭk-) *n.,* & *v.t.* **1.** *n.* distinctive mark; (in *pl.*) inscribed letters or figures; graphic symbol, esp. denoting sound or idea; (arch.) style of such symbols used in a language; (Computers) group of symbols representing letter etc. **2.** characteristic (esp. Biol., of species etc.); collective peculiarities, sort, style; person's or race's idiosyncrasy, mental or moral qualities; distinction, individuality. **3.** moral strength, esp. if highly developed or evident; reputation, good reputation (∿ **reference, witness,** (attesting to this); ∿ **assassination,** malicious destruction of person's reputation); ∿ (**sketch,** brief) written description of person's qualities; testimonial. **4.** personage, personality; person portrayed in novel, drama, etc.; part played by actor or (arch.) hypocrite; **in, out of,** ∿, appropriate to these or not, (of action etc.) in accord or not with person's character. **5.** eccentric or noticeable person (*quite a character*); ∿ **actor** who impersonates eccentric or unusual persons. **6.** Hence ∿LESS *a.* **7.** *v.t.* (arch.) inscribe; describe. [ME, f. OF *caractere* f. L f. Gk *kharaktēr* stamp, impress]

chăracterī'st|ic (kărĭk-) *a.* & *n.* typical, distinctive, (trait, mark, quality); indicative of character; (Math.) integral part of logarithm; ∿ic **curve** (showing relation between interdependent quantities); ∿ic **radiation** (of wavelength peculiar to one substance); hence ∿ICALLY *adv.* [f. F *caractéristique* or f. med. L f. Gk *kharaktēristikos* (see prec., -IST, -IC)]

chă'racteriz|e (kă'rĭk-), -**īs|e** (-īz), *v.t.* describe character of; describe as; be characteristic of, impart character to; hence ∿A'TION *n.* [f. F *caractériser* or med. L *characterizare* f. Gk *kharaktērizō* (as CHARACTER; see -IZE)]

chăracterŏ'logy (kărĭk-) *n.* (Psych.) science of the development and variation of character. [f. G *charac-terologie* (as CHARACTER, -O-, -LOGY)]

chara'de (sharah'd) *n.* **1.** (in *pl.*, usu. treated as *sing.*) game of guessing word from written or acted clue given for each syllable and for the whole. **2.** such clue; (fig.) absurd pretence. [F, f. mod. Prov. *charrado* conversation (*charra* chatter)]

chăr'as *n.* narcotic resin from flower-heads of hemp, cannabis resin. [Hindi]

chăr'coal *n.* black porous residue of partly burnt wood, bones, etc., a form of carbon; ∿ **biscuit** (containing wood-charcoal to aid digestion); ∿**-burner,** maker of charcoal; ∿ (**grey**), dark grey. [ME, conn. w. COAL in sense 'charcoal']

chărd *n.* kind of beet with edible leaves and stalks. [f. F *carde,* and *chardon* thistle; cf. CARDOON]

chărge¹ *n.* **1.** appropriate quantity of material to put into receptacle, mechanism, etc., at one time, esp. of explosive for gun; (fig.) load; (colloq.) dose of drugs; (Her.) device, bearing. **2.** quantity of electricity carried by a body; energy stored chemically for conversion into electricity; process of charging battery. **3.** expense (*at his own charge*); price demanded for service or goods (*are his charges reasonable?*); obligation to pay. **4.** task, duty, commission; care, custody, (*of; nurse in charge of child, child in the charge of nurse;* CURATE-*in-charge;* ∥**give** person **in** ∿, hand him over to police; **take** ∿, assume control or direction *of,* (colloq., of things) get out of control, esp. with disastrous results); thing or person entrusted; minister's flock. **5.** exhortation, directions, orders; formal instruction by bishop to clergy, judge to jury, etc. **6.** accusation, esp. against prisoner brought for trial; **lay to** person's ∿, accuse him of; **put** person **on a** ∿, decide that he will be accused. **7.** rushing attack by soldiers, animal, etc. (**return to the** ∿, begin again, esp. in argument); (Mil.) signal sounded for such attack; attack made by throwing oneself against opponent in football etc. **8.** *∿ **account,** credit account at shop etc.; ∥∿**-hand,** workman in charge of others; ∥∿**-nurse,** nurse in charge of ward etc.; ∿**-sheet,** record of cases and charges made at police station. [ME f. OF, f. Rom. **carrica* f. LL *car(ri)care;* see foll.]

chărge² *v.* **1.** *v.t.* load or fill to the full or proper extent (vessel, gun with explosive); saturate (air with vapour or fig. *with* emotion, water with chemicals); give electric charge to (body); store energy in (battery etc.). **2.** entrust *with* (∿ **oneself with,** undertake). **3.** command *to do, exhort* **4.** accuse, impute, (person *with* action); make accusation *that*; debit (*charge it* (*up*) *to my account*), debit to one's account (*I'd like to charge this dress*). **5.** demand (price) *for*, demand (price) from (person). **6.** *v.t.* & *i.* make rushing attack (on); throw oneself (against). **7.** Hence ∿ABLE (-ăr'ja-) *a.* [ME f. OF *charger* f. LL *car(ri)care* load f. L *carrus* CAR]

chărgé (d'affaires) (shăr'zhă dăfār') *n.* (*pl.* **-gés** pr. same). ambassador's deputy; representative at minor court or government. [F, = in charge (of affairs)]

chăr'ger¹ *n.* (arch.) large flat dish. [ME f. AF *chargeour;* see CHARGE², -OR]

chăr'ger² *n.* In vbl senses; (Mil.) cavalry horse; (poet.) any horse. [f. CHARGE² + -ER¹]

chă'riot *n.,* & *v.t.* **1.** *n.* (poet.) stately or triumphal vehicle. **2.** (Hist.) four-wheeled carriage with back seats only; two-wheeled usu. horse-drawn vehicle used in ancient fighting and racing, whence ∿EER' *n.* **3.** *v.t.* (literary). convey as or in chariot. [ME f. OF, augment. of *char* CAR]

chari'sma (karī'z-) *n.* (*pl.* **-ta**). divinely conferred power or talent; capacity to inspire followers with devotion and enthusiasm; hence **chărismă'tic** (kărĭz-) *a.* [eccl. L, f. Gk *kharisma* (*kharis* favour, grace)]

chă'ritable *a.* generous in giving to the poor; connected with such giving; of or for charity; apt to judge favourably of persons, acts, and motives; hence ∿NESS

(-bɛln-) *n.*, **chă′ritabLY²** *adv.* [ME f. OF (*charité* = foll.; see -ABLE)]

chă′rity *n.* **1.** love of fellow men; kindness, affection; leniency in judging others. **2.** beneficence, liberality to those in need or distress, alms-giving (in *pl.*, acts of this), alms; trust for advancement of education etc.; institution for helping those in need, help so given; ~ **begins at home** (is due first to one's own family and friends); **cold as** ~ (in allusion to unsympathetic administration); ||**C~ Commission(er**s), board established to control charitable trusts; ~ **school** (supported by charitable contributions). [OE, f. OF *charité* f. L *caritas -tatis* (*carus* dear; see -ITY)]

charivar′i (sh-) *n.* medley of sounds, hubbub. [F, = serenade with pans, trays, etc., to unpopular person]

||**char′lădy**. See CHAR².

char′latan (sh-) *n.* false pretender to knowledge or skill, esp. in medicine; hence ~ISM (2), ~RY (5), *ns*. [F, f. It. *ciarlatano* (*ciarlare* babble)]

Charles's Wai′n (-lzĭz-) *n.* constellation Ursa Major or its seven bright stars. [OE *Carles wægn* the wain of Carl (Charles the Great, Charlemagne), perh. by assoc. of star Arcturus with legends of King Arthur and Charlemagne]

Char′leston (-ls-, -lz-) *n.*, & *v.i.* **1.** *n.* American dance with side-kicks from knee. **2.** *v.i.* dance this, kick thus. [~ in S. Carolina, US]

*****char′ley hŏrse** *n.* (sl.) stiffness or cramp in arm or leg. [19th c.; orig. uncert.]

char′lie *n.* (sl.) fool; person; ||(in *pl.*) woman's breasts; *inhabitant (esp. soldier) of (North) Vietnam. [dim. of name *Charles*; see -IE]

char′lock *n.* wild mustard, a yellow-flowered weed. [OE *cerlic*, of unkn. orig.]

char′lotte (sh-) *n.* pudding made of stewed fruit with casing or layers or covering of bread, biscuits, sponge--cake, or breadcrumbs, (*apple charlotte*); ~ **russe** (-rōō′s), custard etc. enclosed in sponge-cake or sponge biscuits. [F]

charm¹ *n.* **1.** word(s), act, or object supposedly having occult power (*against*), spell, (*work like a* ~, perfectly); thing worn to avert evil etc., amulet; trinket on bracelet etc. **2.** quality or feature that excites love or admiration; attractiveness, indefinable power of delighting; (in *pl.*, esp.) woman's sexual attractiveness; ~ **school**, place where women are taught graceful behaviour; hence ~′LESS *a.* [ME f. OF *charme*, f. L *carmen* song]

charm² *v.t.* bewitch, influence (as) by magic; bring (as) by magic (*charm secret, consent*, etc., *out of*); endow with seemingly magic power (*bear a charmed life*); captivate, delight, (*charmed with*); give pleasure to; hence ~′ING² *a.*, delightful. [ME, f. OF *charmer* (*charme*; see prec.)]

char′mer *n.* in vbl senses; pleasant or attractive person; SNAKE-*charmer*. [f. prec. + -ER¹]

charmeu′se (sharmē′z) *n.* soft smooth silky dress--fabric. [F, fem. of *charmeur* (as CHARM², -ER¹)]

char′nel-house *n.* house or vault in which dead bodies or bones are piled. [ME & OF *charnel* burying--place, f. med. L *carnale* f. LL *carnalis* CARNAL]

Cha′rollais, -olais, (shă′rolă) *n.* (animal of) breed of large white beef-cattle. [f. Monts du ~ in E. France]

Char′on (k-) *n.* (Gk Myth.) ferryman conveying souls across Styx to Hades. [L, f. Gk *Kharōn*]

char′poy *n.* (Ind.) light bedstead. [f. Hind. *chārpāi*]

charr. See CHAR¹.

chart *n.*, & *v.t.* **1.** *n.* navigator's sea map, showing coast outlines, rocks, shoals, etc.; air navigator's map; outline map showing special features; set of curves on graph etc. showing fluctuations in temperature, prices, etc.; sheet of tabulated or diagrammatic information, esp. (usu. in *pl.*) listing the currently most popular gramophone records. **2.** *v.t.* make chart of, map. [f. F *charte* f. L *charta* (CARD²)]

char′ter¹ *n.* written grant of rights by sovereign or legislature, esp. creation of borough, company, university, etc. (**Great C~**, Magna Charta); written constitution (of United Nations); deed conveying land; = CHARTER-PARTY; privilege, admitted right(s), (fig.) licence to misbehave; ~ **flight** (by chartered aircraft); ~-**member**, original member of society, corporation, etc. [ME f. OF *chartre*, f. L *chartula* dim. of *charta* (CARD²)]

char′ter² *v.t.* grant charter, give privilege, to (||~ed accountant, engineer, librarian, surveyor, etc., member of professional body that has royal charter; ~ed **libertine**, person allowed to do as he pleases); hire (ship, aircraft, vehicle, etc.); hence ~ER¹ *n.* [ME, f. prec.]

char′ter-părty *n.* deed between ship-owner and merchant for hire of ship and delivery of cargo. [f. F *charte partie* f. med. L *charta partita* divided charter, indenture]

Char′t|ism *n.* (Hist.) principles of UK reform movement of 1837–48; hence ~IST (2) *n.* [f. L *charta* charter + -ISM; name taken from the manifesto 'People's Charter']

chartreu′se (shărtrēr′z) *n.* green or yellow liqueur of brandy and aromatic herbs etc.; dish of fruit enclosed in jelly etc.; apple-green colour. [f. La Grande *Chartreuse* (Carthusian monastery near Grenoble)]

chartulary. See CARTULARY.

charwoman. See CHAR².

char′|ỹ *a.* cautious, wary *of*; shy *of* or sparing *in* doing; ungenerous (*chary of praise*); hence ~iLY² *adv.*, ~iNESS *n.* [OE *cearig*, = OS *carag*, OHG *karag* f. WG **karag*-(**karō* CARE¹; see -Y²)]

Chary′bdis (k-) *n.* See SCYLLA.

Chas. *abbr.* Charles.

chase¹ *n.* pursuit (**give** ~, go in pursuit); hunting, esp. as sport (*the chase*; WILD-*goose chase*); steeplechase; unenclosed hunting-land; animal, ship, etc., pursued; (Hist.) ~, ~-**gun**, ~-**port**, gun, port, in bow or stern for use while chasing or being chased. [ME f. OF *chace* f. Rom. **captia* (**captiare*; see foll.]

chase² *v.* **1.** *v.t.* pursue; drive *from, out of, to*, etc.; (colloq.) try to attain; (**go and**) ~ **oneself**, (colloq., usu. in *imper.*) depart; ~ **up**, (colloq.) pursue with specific purpose. **2.** *v.i.* hurry (*after*, etc.). [ME, f. OF *chacier* f. Rom. **captiare* for L *captare* frequent. of *capere* take; cf. CATCH¹]

chase³ *v.t.* emboss, engrave, (metal). [app. f. earlier *enchase* f. F *enchâsser* (as EN-¹, CASE²)]

chase⁴ *n.* part of gun enclosing bore; trench or groove cut to receive pipe etc. [f. F *chas* enclosed space f. Prov. *ca(u)s* f. med. L *capsum* thorax]

chase⁵ *n.* metal frame holding composed type for page or sheet. [f. F *châsse* f. L *capsa* (CASE²)]

cha′ser *n.* In vbl senses; horse for steeplechasing, chase-gun; *amorous pursuer of women; (colloq.) drink following drink of another kind, e.g. spirits after coffee, water or beer after spirits. [f. CHASE² + -ER¹]

Chasid. Var. of HASID.

cha′sm (kă′zem) *n.* deep fissure; wide difference of feeling, interests, etc., gulf; (arch.) hiatus. [f. L f Gk *khasma* gaping hollow]

chasse (shahs) *n.* liqueur taken after coffee etc. [F (*chasser* CHASE²)]

chassé (shă′să) *n.*, & *v.i.* (make) gliding step in dancing; ~ **croisé** (-krwah′zā), double *chassé*, (fig.) to-and-fro movement with change of position. [F, = chasing]

Chassid. Var. of HASID.

cha′ssis (shă′sĭ, -sē) *n.* (*pl.* same *pr.* -z). base-frame of gun-carriage, motor vehicle, etc.; metal frame to carry radio etc. equipment. [f. F *châssis* f. Rom. **capsicium* f. L *capsa* CASE²]

chaste *a.* abstaining from unlawful or immoral or from all sexual intercourse, pure, virgin; decent (of speech); restrained, severe, pure in taste or style, unadorned, simple; ~-**tree**, ornamental shrub

(*Vitex agnus-castus*), with blue or white flowers; hence ∼LY² (-tlǐ) *adv.* [ME f. OF, f. L *castus*]

châs′ten (-sen) *v.t.* discipline, punish by inflicting suffering; moderate; restrain, subdue. [f. obs. *chaste* v. (f. OF *chastier* f. L *castigare* CASTIGATE) + -EN⁶]

chăstī′se (-z) *v.t.* punish; thrash; hence ∼MENT (chăstī′zm-, chǎ′stīzm-) *n.* [ME, app. irreg. f. obs. vbs. *chaste, chasty* (see prec.) + -ISE³]

chǎ′stǐtў *n.* being chaste; virginity, celibacy; simplicity of style or taste; ∼ **belt,** garment designed to prevent woman from having sexual intercourse. [ME, f. OF *chasteté* f. L *castitas -tatis* (*castus* chaste; see -ITY)]

chǎ′sŭble (-z-) *n.* sleeveless vestment of celebrant at Mass or Eucharist. [ME f. OF *chesible*, later -*uble* f. F *chasuble* f. LL *casubla* irreg. f. L *casula* hooded cloak, little cottage, dim. of *casa* cottage]

chăt¹ *v.i.* & *t.* (-tt-), & *n.* (indulge in) easy familiar talk; ∼ (**up**), (sl.) chat to, esp. flirtatiously or with ulterior motive; ∼ **show,** = TALK *show.* [ME, f. CHATTER]

chăt² *n.* songbird of genus *Saxicola, Epthianura*, or *Icteria*, esp. STONE*chat*, WHIN¹*chat.* [prob. imit.]

château (shă′tō) *n.* (*pl.* -**x** *pr.* -z). large country house in France, esp. giving name to wine made near it. [F, f. OF *chastel* (CASTLE¹)]

chǎ′telaine (sh-) *n.* **1.** (Hist.) set of short chains attached to woman's belt for carrying keys, watch, pencil, etc. **2.** mistress of large house. [f. F *châtelaine*, fem. of -*ain* lord of a castle, f. med. L *castellanus* CASTELLAN]

chǎ′ttel *n.* movable possession (usu. in *pl.*, esp. *goods and chattels*); *∼ **mortgage,** conveyance of chattels by mortgage as security for debt. [ME f. OF *chatel*; see CATTLE]

chǎ′tter *v.i.*, & *n.* **1.** *v.i.* (Of bird) utter quick series of short notes; (of person) talk quickly, incessantly, foolishly, or inopportunely; (of teeth etc.) rattle together. **2.** *n.* any of these sounds; vibration of tool; ∼**box,** talkative person, esp. child. [ME, imit.; see -ER⁶]

chǎ′tt|ў¹ *a.* fond of chatting; resembling chat (*chatty letter*); hence ∼ĬLY² *adv.*, ∼ĬNESS *n.* [f. CHAT¹ + -Y²]

chǎ′ttў² *n.* (Ind.) earthenware water-pot. [f. Hindi *chātī*]

Chaucēr′ian *a.* & *n.* **1.** *a.* (in the style) of Chaucer. **2.** *n.* student of Chaucer's works. [f. G. *Chaucer*, Eng. poet d. 1400 + -IAN]

chaud-froid (shō′frwah′) *n.* dish of cold cooked meat or fish in jelly or sauce. [F (*chaud* hot, *froid* cold)]

chauffeur (shō′fer, shōfēr′) *n.* (*fem.* **chauffeuse** *pr.* -ērz), & *v.t.* **1.** *n.* person employed to drive a private or hired motor car. **2.** *v.t.* drive (car) as chauffeur; convey (person) by car. [F, = stoker]

chaulmoo′gra *n.* E. Ind. tree of various species of family Flacourtiaceae, whose seeds yield an oil formerly used in treatment of leprosy. [Bengali]

*chautau′qua (ch-, sh-) *n.* summer school or similar educational course. [f. C∼ in New York State]

chau′vin|ist (shō′v-) *n.* bellicose patriot; fervent supporter of a cause; **male** ∼**ist,** man showing excessive loyalty to other men and prejudice against women; so ∼ISM (3) *n.*, ∼ĭ′stIC *a.* [f. *Chauvin*, Napoleonic veteran, in the Cogniards' *Cocarde Tricolore* (1831), + -IST]

chaw *v.t.*, & *n.* (arch., dial., or vulg.) chew; ∼**-bacon,** (derog.) bumpkin. [var. of CHEW]

Ch.B. *abbr.* Bachelor of Surgery. [f. L *Chirurgiae Baccalaureus*]

Ch.Ch. *abbr.* Christ Church.

cheap *a.* & *adv.* **1.** *a.* low in price, value, or charge made (∼ **and nasty,** of low cost and bad quality; ∼′**jack,** (n.) hawker at fair etc., (a.) inferior, shoddy; *cheap* SKATE³; **dirt** ∼, very cheap(ly); **on the** ∼, cheaply); worth more than its cost; easily got or made (*cheap gibes*); (of money) available at low interest; worthless, of little account (**feel** ∼, (sl.) feel

ashamed or ill; **hold** ∼, despise). **2.** *adv.* cheaply (*got it cheap; going cheap*). **3.** Hence ∼′ISH (2) *a.*, ∼′LY² *adv.*, ∼′NESS *n.* [f. obs. phr. *good cheap* (*cheap* a bargain f. OE *cēap* barter, = OS *kōp*, OHG *kouf*, ON *kaup* f. Gmc *kaupaz* f. L *caupo* innkeeper)]

chea′pen *v.t.* & *i.* make or become cheap, depreciate, degrade. [f. prec. + -EN⁶]

cheat *n.* & *v.* **1.** *n.* trick, fraud, deception; swindler, deceiver; impostor; unfair player. **2.** *v.t.* deceive, trick (person *into* or *out of* thing); (arch.) beguile (time etc.). **3.** *v.i.* act fraudulently. [n. f. v., ME *chete* f. *achete*, var. of ESCHEAT²]

chea′ter *n.* In vbl senses; *(in *pl.*, sl.) spectacles. [f. prec. + -ER¹]

chĕck¹ *n.* **1.** (also as *int.*) (Announcement to opponent of) exposure of chess king to attack. **2.** sudden stopping or slowing of motion; rebuff, repulse; crack or flaw in timber. **3.** (Hunt.) loss of the scent. **4.** stoppage, pause; restraint on action (*keep in* ∼, under control); person or thing that restrains. **5.** control to secure accuracy; means or act of testing quality; token of identification for left luggage, seat-holder, etc.; mark of verification; *bill in restaurant. **6.** *counter at cards; **hand** or **pass in** one's ∼s, (colloq.) die. **7.** ∼**-action** (restraining piano hammer from striking string twice); ∼**-list,** (esp. complete) list for reference and verification; ∼**-nut,** LOCK²-nut; ∼**-point** (where documents, vehicles, etc., are checked or inspected); ∼**-rein** (attaching one horse's rein to another's bit, or preventing horse from lowering head); *∼**-room,** cloakroom in hotel or theatre, office for left luggage etc.; ∼**-valve** (allowing flow in one direction only); ∼′**weighman** (who checks weight of mined coal on behalf of miners). [ME, f. OF *eschec* f. med. L *scaccus* f. Arab. f. Pers. *šāh* king]

chĕck² *v.* & *int.* **1.** *v.t.* threaten (opponent's king) at chess. **2.** suddenly stop or slow the motion of. **3.** *v.i.* (Of hounds) stop on losing scent, or to make sure of it. **4.** *v.t.* restrain, curb; (colloq., of superior) find fault with, rebuke. **5.** *v.t.* & *i.* ∼ (**on, up, up on, ***out), test (statement, account, figures, employees, or abs.) by comparison etc., examine accuracy or condition of; *∼ (**out**), agree when compared; *∼ (**off**), mark with tick etc.; *deposit (luggage etc.) for storage or dispatch; ∼ **in,** register (prior to leaving by air) at airport; ∼ **in, out,** arrive at, depart from, hotel or factory, record such arrival or departure of (person); ∼**-in,** act of checking in; ∼**-out,** act of checking out, final check, pay-desk in supermarket etc.; ∼ **over, through,** (*adv.* or *prep.*), verify successive items of; ∼**-up,** careful (esp. medical) examination; hence **che′cker** *n.* [-ER¹]. **6.** *int.* *expr.* assent or agreement. [ME, f. OF *eschequier* play chess, give check to (*eschec*; see prec.)]

chĕck³ *n.* cross-lined pattern of small squares; fabric woven or printed with this; hence ∼ED² (-kt) *a.* [ME, prob. f. CHEQUER¹]

***chĕck⁴.** See CHEQUE.

chĕ′cker¹,²,³. See CHEQUER¹,², CHECK² 5.

chĕ′ckerbĕrrў *n.* (fruit of) the wintergreen *Gaultheria procumbens.* [f. *checkers* berries of service-tree + BERRY¹]

***chĕ′cker|s** (-z) *n. pl.* (usu. treated as *sing.*) the game of draughts; hence ∼(**man**) draughtsman. [f. pl. of CHEQUER¹]

chĕ′ckmāte *n.*, & *v.t.* **1.** *n.* (also as *int.*) (announcement to opponent of) inextricable check of king at chess; final defeat or deadlock. **2.** *v.t.* give checkmate to; defeat, frustrate. [ME, f. OF *eschec mat* (cf. CHECK¹) f. Pers. *šāh māt* king is dead]

Chĕ′ddar *n.* cheese made by piling curds and forming smooth mass. [∼ in Somerset, where first made]

cheek *n.*, & *v.t.* **1.** *n.* side-wall of mouth, side of face below eye; ∼**-bone,** that below eye; ∼ **by jowl,** close together, intimate; **to** one's **own** ∼, not shared with others; TONGUE¹ *in cheek*; **turn the other** ∼, accept attack etc. meekly, refuse to retaliate. **2.** impertinent

speech; cool confidence, effrontery, (*have the cheek to*).
3. side post of door etc.; (in *pl.*) jaws of vice, side-
-pieces of various parts of machines arranged in lateral pairs, (sl.) buttocks. **4.** *v.t.* address saucily. [OE
cē(a)ce f. WG **kækōn*, and OE *cēoce* f. WG **keuka*]
chee'k|ў *a.* insolent, impudent; hence ∼ily² *adv.*,
∼iness *n.* [f. prec. + -y²]
cheep *v.i.*, & *n.* (utter) shrill feeble note (as) of young
bird; **not a** ∼, (colloq.) not the slightest sound etc.
[imit.; cf. PEEP¹]
cheer¹ *n.* **1.** frame of mind (**what** ∼?, how do you
feel?; **be of good** ∼, be stout-hearted or hopeful);
food, fare, (**make good** ∼, feast). **2.** shout of
encouragement or applause (**three** ∼s, successive
united hurrahs, often *for* person or thing honoured;
two ∼s, (iron.) mild enthusiasm); ‖(in *pl.*,
colloq.) = CHEERIO; ∼-**leader,** one who leads cheers
of applause etc. [ME f. AF *chere* face etc., OF *chiere* f.
LL *cara* face f. Gk *kara* head]
cheer² *v.t.* & *i.* comfort, gladden; incite, urge *on*, esp.
by shouts; applaud; shout for joy; ∼ **up,** make or
become happier. [ME, f. prec.]
cheer'ful *a.* contented, in good spirits, hopeful;
bright, pleasant; willing, not reluctant; hence ∼ly²
adv., ∼ness *n.* [f. CHEER¹ + -FUL]
‖**cheeriŏ'** *int.* (colloq.) expr. good wishes on parting
or before drinking; goodbye. [f. CHEER²,
CHEERY + O²]
cheer'less *a.* dull, gloomy, dreary, miserable; hence
∼ly² *adv.*, ∼ness *n.* [f. CHEER¹ + -LESS]
cheer'lў *a.* & *adv.* **1.** *a.* (arch.) cheerful. **2.** *adv.* (esp.
Naut.) heartily, with a will. [f. CHEER¹ + -LY¹,²]
cheer'|ў *a.* lively, in good spirits; genial, cheering;
hence ∼ily² *adv.*, ∼iness *n.* [f. CHEER¹ + -Y²]
cheese¹ (-z) *n.* **1.** food made of pressed curds;
complete cake etc. of this within rind; *bread and cheese*;
CHALK¹ *and cheese*; GREEN¹ *cheese*; **hard** ∼, (sl.) bad
luck. **2.** fruit of mallow; round flat object, e.g. heavy
flat wooden disc used in skittles; (**big**) ∼, (sl.)
important person [perh. f. Hind. *chīz* thing]; DAMSON,
lemon, etc. ∼, conserve of the fruit with shape or
usu. consistency of (cream) cheese. **3.** ∼'**board** (from
which cheese is served); ∼'**burger,** hamburger with
cheese in or on it; ∼'**cake,** tart(let) of pastry filled
with sweetened curds, (colloq.) display of shapely
female body in advertisement etc.; ∼'**cloth,** BUTTER¹
muslin; ∼-**cutter,** knife with broad curved blade,
device for cutting cheese by pulling a wire through it;
∼-**fly** (breeding in cheese); ∼-**head,** squat cylindrical head of screw etc.; *cheese-MITE*; ∼'**monger,**
dealer in cheese, butter, etc.; ∼-**paring,** stingy,
stinginess; ∼ **straw,** thin cheese-flavoured strip of
pastry; ∼'**wood,** (hard yellowish wood of) Austral.
tree of genus *Pittosporum*. [OE *cēse* etc., = OS *kāsi*,
k(i)ēsi, OHG *chāsi*, WG **kāsi* f. L *caseus*]
cheese² (-z) *v.t.* (sl.) (Esp. in *imper.*) stop *it*, leave off;
‖∼**d** (**off**), bored, exasperated. [19th c.; orig. unkn.]
chee's|ў (-zī) *a.* like or tasting of cheese; (sl.) inferior,
cheap and nasty; hence ∼iness *n.* [f. CHEESE¹ + -Y²]
chee'tah (-*a*) *n.* swift-running spotted feline that can
be trained to hunt deer etc. [f. Hindi *cītā*, perh. f. Skr.
citraka speckled]
chēf (sh-) *n.* man who is (usu. chief) cook in hotel etc.
[F, = head]
chef-d'œuvre (shādĕr'vr) *n.* (*pl.* *chefs-* *pr.* same).
masterpiece. [F]
cheiro-. Var. of CHIRO-.
che'la¹ (chā'-) *n.* novice in course of qualifying for
initiation in esoteric Buddhism; disciple, pupil.
[Hindi, = servant]
chē'l|a² (k-) *n.* (*pl.* ∼**ae**). prehensile claw of crabs,
lobsters, scorpions, etc.; hence ∼ATE² *a.*, (esp., Chem.)
forming or having a group that loops round a central
ion, whence ∼ATE³ *v.t.*, ∼A'TION *n.* [mod. L, f. L *chele*
or f. Gk *khēlē* claw]
Chĕ'llèan (sh-) *a.* (Archaeol.) = ABBEVILLIAN. [f. F
chelléen (*Chelles* near Paris; see -AN)]

Chĕ'lsea (-sǐ) *n.* ∼ **bun,** kind of rolled currant-bun; ∼
pensioner, inmate of the Chelsea Royal Hospital for
old or disabled soldiers; ∼ **ware,** kind of porcelain
made at Chelsea in 18th c. [∼ in London]
Chĕltŏ'nian *a.* & *n.* (past or present member) of
Cheltenham College. [f. mod. L *Cheltonia* Cheltenham + -IAN]
chĕ'mical (k-) *a.* & *n.* **1.** *a.* of, made by, relating to
chemistry; (of lavatory) effecting decomposition of
waste by chemical process; *chemical* ENGINEER¹;
engineering, industrial application of chemistry; ∼
warfare (using poison gas and other chemicals)
hence ∼ly² *adv.* **2.** *n.* substance obtained by or used in
chemical process; **fine** ∼s, those used in small
amounts and fairly pure; **heavy** ∼s, bulk chemicals
used in industry and agriculture. [f. *chemic* alchemic f
F *chimique* or mod. L *chimicus, chymicus,* f. med. L
alchymicus (as ALCHEMY; see -IC) + -AL]
chĕ'micō- (k-) *comb. form.* chemical (and), as: ∼
-physical, pertaining to chemistry and physics. [f
chemic = prec. + -O-]
chĕmǐlūminĕ'sc|ence (k-; -lōō-, -lū-) *n.* emission of
light accompanying chemical reaction; hence ∼ent
a. [f. G (-*eszenz*) (as prec., LUMINESCENCE)]
chemin de fer (shĕmăn de fâr') *n.* form of baccarat
[F, = railway, lit. road of iron]
chemi'se (shĕmē'z) *n.* woman's loose-fitting under
garment or dress hanging straight from shoulders
[ME f. OF, f. LL *camisia* shirt]
chĕmǐsŏr'ption (k-) *n.* adsorption by chemical
action. [f. CHEMICAL + ADSORPTION]
chĕ'mist (k-) *n.* person skilled in chemistry; ‖dealer in
medicinal drugs, usu. also selling other medical goods
and toiletries. [earlier *chymist* f. F *chimiste* f. mod. L
chimista (*alchimista* ALCHEMIST)]
chĕ'mistrў (k-) *n.* science of the elements and
compounds and their laws of combination and
change resulting from interactions between substances in contact; (fig.) mysterious change or pro
cess. [f. prec. + -RY]
chĕmo- (k-) *comb. form.* chemical, as: ∼**sy'nthesis**
formation of carbohydrates from inorganic com
pounds without sunlight; ∼**the'rapy,** treatment of
disease by chemical means. [f. CHEMICAL + -O-]
*chĕ'murgў (k-) *n.* chemical and industrial use of
organic raw materials. [f. prec., after *metallurgy*]
cheni'lle (shĕnē'l) *n.* yarn with pile all round, used in
trimming furniture; fabric made with it. [F, = hairy
caterpillar f. L *canicula* dim. of *canis* dog]
chĕòngsă'm *n.* Chinese woman's garment with high
neck and slit skirt. [Chin.]
‖**chĕque** (-k), ***chĕck⁴,** *n.* written order to bank(er) to
pay named sum from drawer's account to bearer or
(order of) named person; form on which such order is
to be written; BLANK¹ *cheque*; ∼-**book,** book of form
for writing cheques, issued to bank's customer; ∼
card (issued by bank to guarantee honouring of any
cheque up to stated value); ***checking account**
current account at bank. [f. CHECK³ 5]
chĕ'quer¹ (-ker), **chĕ'cker¹,** *n.* (often in *pl.*) pattern
made of squares or with alternating colours; ∼
-board, (pattern resembling) chess-board. [ME, f.
EXCHEQUER]
chĕ'quer² (-ker), **chĕ'cker²,** *v.t.* mark with squares
esp. of alternate colours; variegate, break uniformity
of, (lit. or fig.; esp. in *p.p.*) undergoing varied
fortunes). [ME, f. prec.]
C(h)ĕrĕ'nkŏv (ch-; -f) *n.* ∼ **radiation** (emitted by
particles moving in a medium at speeds faster than
that of light in same medium). [f. P. A. ∼, Russ
physicist b. 1904]
chĕ'rish *v.t.* protect or tend (child, plant, etc.
lovingly; value, hold dear, cling to, (esp. hopes
feelings, etc.). [ME, f. OF *cherir* (*cher* f. L *carus* dear
see -ISH²)]
cher'nozĕm (-ăr'-) *n.* fertile humus-rich black soil of
S. Russia etc. [Russ. (*chernyĭ* black, *zemlya* earth)]

Cherokee (-ĕ'-, -ē') n. (member of) Amer. Ind. tribe formerly inhabiting much of southern US; ~ **rose,** fragrant white wild rose of southern US. [f. Cherokee *Tsárăgĭ*]

cheroot (sh-) n. cigar with both ends open. [f. F *cheroute* f. Tamil *shuruṭṭu* roll]

he'rry n. & a. **1.** n. small stone-fruit; tree of genus *Prunus* bearing this or grown for its ornamental flowers; ~(-**wood**), its wood; **two bites at a** ~, unenterprising or hesitant action; ~-**bob,** two cherries with joined stems (BOB[1]); ~ **brandy,** dark-red liqueur of brandy in which cherries have been steeped; ~-**laurel,** ‖common laurel (*Prunus lauro-cerasus*), *evergreen shrub (*P. caroliniana*); ~-**picker,** crane for raising and lowering persons; ~-**pie,** (1) pie made with cherries, (2) garden heliotrope. **2.** a. red, esp. of the colour of ripe cherries, (*cherry lips, ribbon*). [ME, f. ONF *cherise* (treated as pl.; cf. PEASE) f. med. L *ceresia* perh. f. L f. Gk *kerasos*]

he'r'sonēse (k-) n. (usu. poet. or rhet.) peninsula, esp. of Thrace west of Hellespont. [f. L f. Gk *khersonēsos* (*khersos* dry, *nēsos* island)]

hert n. flintlike form of quartz. [17th c.; orig. unkn.]

he'rub n. (*pl.* ~s *or* -**im**). angelic being; one of the second ORDER[1] of ninefold celestial hierarchy, gifted with knowledge; (Art) winged (head of) child; beautiful or innocent child; hence **cheru'b**IC (-ōō'-) a. [ME, f. OE *cherubin* and f. Heb. *k*[e]*rūb,* pl. *k*[e]*rūbîm*]

her'vil n. garden herb used to flavour soup, salad, etc. [OE *cerfille,* = OHG *kervela* f. L f. Gk *khairephullon*]

hes. *abbr.* Cheshire.

he'shire (*-er,* -ēr) n. grin like a ~ **cat** (broadly and fixedly); ~ **cheese,** kind like Cheddar, orig. made in Cheshire. [county in England]

hess n. game for two players with thirty-two ~-**men,** on ~-**board** chequered with sixty-four squares. [ME, f. OF *esches* pl. of *eschec* (CHECK[1])]

he'ssel n. cheese-making mould. [app. f. CHEESE[1] +WELL[1]]

hest n. **1.** large strong box; box for sailor's belongings; box for tools, medicines, etc.; treasury or coffer of institution, (fig.) the money in it; case of some commodity, esp. tea; ~ **of drawers,** piece of furniture with set of drawers in frame; ~ **of viols** (complete set, orig. kept in a chest). **2.** part of human or animal body enclosed in ribs; front surface of body from neck to waist; **get thing off** one's ~, (colloq.) relieve one's anxiety by disclosing something; **play close to** one's ~, (colloq.) be cautious or secretive about; ~-**protector,** flannel etc. worn on chest as protection against cold; ~-**voice** (of lowest speaking or singing register); hence ~'ED[2] a., ~'Y[2] a., (colloq.) inclined to, marked by, symptomatic of, chest disease, (colloq.) having a large chest or prominent breasts, *(sl.) arrogant. [OE *cest,* *cyst,* = OHG, ON *kista* f. Gmc *kistō(n) f. L f. Gk *kistē*]

he'sterfield n. sofa with padded seat, back, and ends; plain overcoat usu. with velvet collar. [f. 19th-c. Earl of C~]

he'stnut (-sn-) n. & a. **1.** n. tree, *Castanea sativa,* (also ~-**tree, Spanish** ~, or **sweet** ~); its glossy hard brown edible fruit; ~(-**wood**), its heavy wood; other tree of genus *Castanea;* = HORSE[1]-*chestnut;* small hard patch on horse's leg; stale joke or anecdote. **2.** n. & a. (of) chestnut colour, deep reddish-brown; (horse) of reddish-brown or yellowish-brown colour (**liver** ~, dark kind). [f. obs. *chesten* (f. OF *chastaine* f. L f. Gk *kastanea*) +NUT]

he'tnik n. guerrilla fighter in Balkans. [f. Serbian *četnik* (*četa* band, troop)]

heva'l-glass (sh-; -ahs) n. tall mirror swung on upright frame. [f. F *cheval* horse, frame]

hevalier' (sh-) n. member of certain orders of knighthood, or of French Legion of Honour etc.; (Hist.) title of Old and Young PRETENDERS; ~ *d'in-dustrie* (-dă'ndōōstrē), adventurer, swindler. [ME f. AF *chevaler,* OF *chevalier* f. med. L *caballarius* f. L *caballus* horse; see -IER, -EER]

chevaux de frise (shevō de frē'z) n. pl. (occas. treated as *sing.*) iron spikes set in timber etc. to repel cavalry etc. in war, or to guard fence or wall in peace. [F, lit. horses of Friesland; invented by 17th-c. Frisians who had no cavalry]

chevet (sheva') n. apsidal end of church, with attached group of apses. [F, = pillow, f. L *capitium* (*caput* head)]

Che'viot n. (animal of) breed of sheep from *Cheviot* Hills on border of England and Scotland; (c~) wool or cloth from it.

che'vron (sh-) n. **1.** (Her. & Archit.) bent bar of inverted V shape. **2.** badge in V shape (inverted or not) on sleeve of uniform indicating rank or length of service; V-shaped stripe. [ME f. OF, f. Rom. *caprione f. L *caper* goat; cf. L *capreoli* pair of rafters]

che'vrotain, -tin, (sh-) n. small deerlike animal of genus *Tragulus.* [F, dim. of OF *chevrot* dim. of *chèvre* goat]

che'vy. Var. of CHIVVY.

chew (-ōō) v. & n. **1.** *v.t.* & *i.* work (food etc., or abs.) between the teeth, grind to pulp or indent by repeated biting; turn *over* in mind, meditate *on* or *over;* discuss, talk *over; chew the* CUD; *~ **out,** (colloq.) reprimand; ~ **the rag** or **the fat,** (sl.) discuss a matter, ‖esp. reiterate an old grievance, grumble; **like a piece of** ~ed **string,** (colloq.) weary and weak; ~'**ing-gum,** preparation of sweetened and flavoured gums (*esp.* chicle), used for prolonged chewing, hence (-)~'ER[1] n. **2.** n. act of chewing; quid of tobacco; chewy sweetmeat. [OE *cēowan,* = OHG *kiuwan* f. WG *kewwan]

chew'y (-ōō'ĭ) a. suitable for chewing; needing to be chewed. [f. prec. +-Y[2]]

Cheyne–Stō'kes (-ānstō'ks) a. (Path.) ~ **breathing** etc. (with gradual decrease of movement to complete stop, followed by gradual increase). [f. J. *Cheyne,* Sc. physician d. 1836, and W. *Stokes,* Ir. physician d. 1878]

chez (shā) *prep.* at the house or home of. [F, f. OF *chiese* f. L *casa* cottage]

chi (kī) n. twenty-second Greek letter, (X ,χ) = kh, ch; ~-**rho',** monogram of chi and rho as first two letters of Gk *Khristos* Christ; ~-**squar'e,** method of comparing observed and theoretical values in Statistics. [ME, f. Gk *khī*]

Chiă'nti (k-) n. dry usu. red Italian wine. [~ in Tuscany, Italy]

chiăroscur'o (kyăroskoor'ō) n. (*pl.* ~s) treatment of light and shade in painting; light and shade effects in nature; use of contrast in literature etc.; (*attrib.*) half-revealed. [It (*chiaro* CLEAR[1]; *oscuro* dark, OBSCURE)]

chiă'smus (kĭă'z-) n. inversion in second phrase of order followed in first (*to stop too fearful and too faint to go*); hence **chiă'st**IC (kī-) a. [mod. L f. Gk *khiasmos* crosswise arrangement (*khiazō* mark with letter CHI)]

chibou'k, -que, (-ōō'k) n. long Turkish tobacco-pipe. [f. Turk. *çubuk* tube]

chic (shēk) n., & a. (**chic-er, chic-est**). **1.** n. stylishness, elegance in dress; skill, effectiveness. **2.** a. stylish, elegant. [F]

chica'ne (sh-) v. & n. **1.** *v.i.* use chicanery. **2.** *v.t.* cheat (person) *into, out of,* etc. **3.** n. chicanery; (Bridge) hand without trumps, or without cards of one suit; artificial barrier or obstacle on motor racecourse. [f. F *chicane*(r) quibble]

chica'nery n. trickery in legal matters; deception, quibbling. [f. F *chicanerie* (as prec.; see -ERY)]

***chica'nō** (ch-, sh-; -ā'-, -ah'-) n. (*pl.* ~s). American person of Mexican origin. [f. Sp. *mejicano* Mexican]

chi'chi (shē'shē) a. & n. frilly or showy (thing); fussy or affected (person, behaviour). [F]

chick[1] n. young bird before or after hatching; (sl.) young woman; ~**abi'ddy,** term of endearment used of or to child; ~'**weed,** small weed of genus *Stellaria* etc. [ME, f. CHICKEN]

chick[2] n. (Ind.) screen for doorway etc., made from split bamboo and twine. [f. Hindi *chik*]

*chi'ckadee *n.* Amer. titmouse of genus *Penthestes* or *Parus*, with dark-crowned head (lit., or fig. as term of endearment to woman). [imit.]

chi'ckèn *n.* (*pl.* ~s *or* ~), *a.*, & *v.i.* **1.** *n.* young bird, esp. of domestic fowl; (flesh of) domestic fowl as food; youthful person (esp. *is no chicken*); (sl.) game testing courage in face of danger; **count** one's ~s (**before they are hatched**), be over-optimistic or precipitate; MOTHER *Carey's chicken*; ~-**and-egg problem** (which first produced the other); ~-**breast**(ed), (having) malformed projection of breastbone; *chicken* CHOLERA; ~-**feed**, food for poultry, (colloq.) unimportant amount of money etc.; ~-**heart**(ed), ~-**liver**(ed), (with) no courage, such person; ~-**pox**, mild eruptive disease esp. of children; ~-**wire**, light wire netting with hexagonal mesh. **2.** *a.* (sl.) cowardly. **3.** *v.i.* ~ **out,** (sl.) withdraw through cowardice. [OE *cīcen, cÿcen,* f. Gmc *kiukīnam* cogn. w. COCK[1]; cf. -EN[1]]

chi'ckling *n.* common cultivated vetchling (*Lathyrus sativus*). [earlier *chicheling* dim. of ME & F *chiche* f. L *cicer* chick-pea]

chi'ck-pea *n.* dwarf pea (*Cicer arietinum*). [orig. *ciche pease,* f. as prec. + PEASE]

chi'cle (chi'-, che'-; -kel, -klē) *n.* milky juice of the balata, sapodilla, or similar tree, the basis of chewing-gum. [Amer. Sp., f. Nahuatl *tzictli*]

chi'corÿ *n.* blue-flowered plant (*Cichorium intybus*) cultivated for its salad leaves and its root; its root ground for use with or instead of coffee; *endive. [ME, f. obs. F *cicorée* endive f. med. L *cic(h)orea* f. L f. Gk *kikhorion* SUCCORY]

chid('den). See foll.

chide *v.t.* & *i.* (**chi'ded** *or* chid; **chi'ded** *or* **chi'dden** *or* chid. (arch. or literary). scold, rebuke. [OE *cīdan,* of unkn. orig.]

chief[1] *n.* **1.** leader, ruler; head of tribe, clan, etc.; head of a department, highest official; **C~ of Staff,** senior staff officer of a service or commander; hence ~'DOM, ~'SHIP, *ns.,* ~'LESS, ~'LY[1], *adjs.* **2. in** ~, (arch.) most of all, especially, (*for many reasons, and this one in chief*); -**in-**~, supreme (*Colonel, Commandant, Commander, Commodore, -in-Chief*), (Hist.) holding directly from the king (*tenant-in-chief*); EXAMINATION-*in-chief*. **3.** (Her.) upper third of shield. [ME f. OF *ch(i)ef* f. Rom. *capum f. L *caput* head]

chief[2] *a.* (usu. *attrib.*) formally leading or most important (*Chief Justice* etc.); first in importance, influence, etc.; prominent, leading; hence ~'LY[2] *adv.,* above all, mainly but not exclusively. [ME, f. prec.]

chie'ftain (-tan, -tĭn) *n.* captain of robbers; chief of tribe or clan; hence ~CY, ~ESS[1], ~SHIP, *ns.* [ME f. OF *chevetaine* f. LL *capitaneus* CAPTAIN[1]; assim. to CHIEF[1]]

chi'ff-chàff *n.* small European bird (*Phylloscopus collybita*) of warbler family. [imit.]

chi'ffŏn (sh-) *n.* & *a.* **1.** *n.* light diaphanous plain-woven fabric of silk, nylon, etc. **2.** *a.* (Of fabric) lightweight; (of pie etc.) light-textured. [F (*chiffe* rag)]

chiffonier' (sh-) *n.* movable low cupboard with sideboard top. [f. F *chiffonnier, -ière* rag-picker, chest of drawers for odds and ends]

chi'gger (-g-) *n.* **1.** = CHIGOE. **2.** harvest-bug. [var. of CHIGOE]

chi'gnon (shē'nyawn) *n.* coil or mass of hair at back of woman's head. [F, orig. = nape of neck]

chi'göe *n.* tropical flea, burrowing into skin. [Carib.]

chihua'hua (chĭwah'wa) *n.* (animal of) very small smooth-haired breed of dog, originating in Mexico. [C~ state and city in Mexico]

chi'lblain *n.* itching swelling on hand, foot, etc., from exposure to cold and poor blood-circulation; hence ~ED[2] (-nd) *a.* [f. CHILL[1] + BLAIN]

child *n.* (*pl.* **chi'ldren** *pr.* chĭ'-) **1.** young human being, boy or girl; unborn or newborn human being (**with** ~, pregnant); person who has not reached age of discretion; childish person; **this** ~, (sl.) I, me.

2. son or daughter (at any age) *of* (or w. *my* etc.) offspring; descendant (lit. or fig.), follower, or adherent *of* (*Children of* ISRAEL; *child of nature, of* WRATH *of God, of the Devil*); product *of.* **3.** ‖~ **benefit,** State benefit replacing family allowance; ~'**birth,** (arch. ~'**bed,** parturition; ~ **care,** (esp. local authority's care of children temporarily deprived of norma home life; ~ **guidance,** supervision of children' (esp. psychological) welfare; ~-**minder,** one who takes care of child esp. in absence of mother; ~ -**proof,** not able to be operated or damaged by child ~'s **play,** easy task. **4.** Hence ~'LESS, ~'LY[1] (poet.) *adjs.* [OE *cild* f. *kiltham]

Childe *n.* (arch.) youth of noble birth (*Childe Harold Roland*). [var. of prec.]

Chi'ldermas *n.* (arch.) festival of Holy Innocents 28 Dec. [OE *cilderamæsse* (*cildra* gen. pl. of *cild* CHILD *mæsse* MASS[1])]

chi'ldhŏŏd (-d-h-) *n.* state of being a child; time from birth to puberty; **second** ~, dotage. [OE *cildhād* (a CHILD, -HOOD)]

chi'ldish *a.* of or proper to a child; puerile, unsuitable for a grown person; hence ~LY[2] *adv.,* ~NESS *n.* [OF *cildisc* (as CHILD, -ISH[1])]

chi'ldlike *a.* having good qualities of child, as inno cence, frankness, etc. [f. CHILD + -LIKE]

chi'ldren. See CHILD.

Chi'lĕ *n.* ~ **pine,** monkey-puzzle; ~ **nitre** *or* **salt petre,** natural sodium nitrate; hence ~AN *a.* & *n* [~ in S. America]

chi'li. See CHILLI.

chi'liad (k-) *n.* a thousand; a thousand years. [f. LL Gk *khilias -ados;* see -AD 1]

chi'liãsm, chi'liäst, (k-) *ns.* doctrine of or belief in believer in, the millennium; hence **chiliä'stic** (k-) *a* [f. Gk *khiliasmos* & LL *chiliastes,* f. as prec.]

chill[1] *n.* cold sensation, lowered temperature of body feverish shivering, feverish cold (*catch a chill*); un pleasant coldness of air, water, etc., (**take the** ~ **off** warm slightly); depressing influence (*cast a chill over*) coldness of manner; hence ~'SOME[1] *a.* (literary). [O *c(i)ele* f. *kaliz (*kalan be cold); revived as f. CHILL[3]]

chill[2] *a.* (literary). unpleasantly cold to feel; feelin cold; unfeeling, unemotional, austere; hence ~'NES *n.* [app. f. p.p. of foll., after *cool, cold*]

chill[3] *v.t.* & *i.* make or become cold; deaden or destro with cold; depress, dispirit; harden (molten metal) b contact with cold material; preserve (meat etc.) a low temperature without freezing. [ME, of uncer orig., though prob. rel. to CHILL[1]]

chi'l(l)ï *n.* (*pl.* ~es). dried pod of capsicum (as relish or made into cayenne); ~ **con carne,** Mexican stew of chilli-flavoured minced beef. [f. Sp. *chile, chili* Aztec *chilli*]

chi'll|ÿ *a.* somewhat cold to feel; feeling somewha cold; sensitive to cold; not genial, cold-mannered hence ~'NESS *n.* [f. CHILL[1] + -Y[2]]

‖Chiltern Hŭ'ndreds (-z) *n. pl.* crown manor administration of which is nominal office unde Crown and so requires MP to vacate seat; **apply fo the** ~, resign from House of Commons. [f. *Chilter* Hills in S. England + HUNDRED 2 + s[1]]

chimaera. See CHIMERA.

chimb. See CHIME[3].

chime[1] *n.* set of attuned bells; series of sounds given b this; agreement, correspondence. [ME, prob. f. *chym(b)e bell,* perh. f. *chimbel f. OE *cimbal* f. L f. G *kumbalon* CYMBAL]

chime[2] *v.* **1.** *v.t.* make (bell) sound; ring chimes o (bells); show (hour) by chiming. **2.** *v.i.* (Of bells) rin chimes; be in agreement (*together, with,* or abs.); ~ **i** (1) join harmoniously (*with*), (2) interject remark [ME, rel. to prec.]

chime[3], **chimb** (-m), *n.* projecting rim at end of cask [ME; cf. MDu., MLG *kimme*]

chimĕr'a, -aer'a, (kĭmēr'a) *n.* **1.** (Gk Myth.) monste with lion's head, goat's body, and serpent's tai

2. bogy; thing of hybrid character; wild or fanciful conception; hence **chime̅'**rɪcᴀʟ (k-) *a*. **3.** (Biol.) organism formed by grafting etc. from tissues of different genetic origin. **4.** (Zool.) fish of family Chimaeridae. [f. L f. Gk *khimaira* she-goat, chimera]

chime̅r'e *n*. bishop's outer robe. [ME, perh. rel. to Sp. *zamarra* sheepskin cloak, It. *cimarra* long robe]

chi'mney *n*. **1.** channel carrying off smoke or steam of fire, furnace, engine, etc.; part of this above roof; glass tube providing draught for lamp-flame; natural vent, e.g. of volcano; (Mount.) narrow cleft by which cliff may be climbed. **2.** ∼-**breast,** projecting wall between chimney and room; ∼-**corner,** ∼-**nook,** warm seat within old-fashioned fireplace; ∼-**piece,** mantel-piece; ∼-**pot,** earthenware or metal pipe added to chimney-top (∼-*pot hat*, (arch.) tall silk hat); *chimney*-**stack**; ∼-**swallow,** ∼-**swift,** the swift *Chaetura pelagica*; ∼-**sweep,** person whose business is to remove soot from chimneys. [ME, f. OF *cheminée* f. LL *caminata* (? *camera*) (room) with a fireplace f. L f. Gk *kaminos* oven; see -ʏ⁴]

chimp *n*. (colloq.) = foll. [abbr.]

himpanzee' *n*. African ape of genus *Anthropopithecus*, animal most closely resembling man. [f. F *chimpanzé* f. Kongo]

chin *n*. **1.** front of lower jaw; **keep** one's ∼ **up,** remain cheerful; sᴛɪᴄᴋ¹ one's ∼ *out*; **take on the** ∼, (1) suffer severe blow from, (2) endure courageously; *∼ music, talk, chatter*; ∼-**strap** (for fastening hat etc. under chin); ∼-**wag** *n*., & *v.i*. (-gg-), (sl.) talk; hence ∼'ʟᴇss *a*., (fig.) lacking firmness of character, ∼ɴᴇᴅ² *a*. **2.** *(sl.) talk; insolence. [OE *cin(n)* = OS, OHG *kinni*, ON *kinn* chin, lower jaw, Goth. *kinnus* cheek f. Gmc **kinn-*]

chi'na¹ *a*. from China (*China* cʀᴇᴘᴇ, ᴀsᴛᴇʀ, etc.; ∼ **orange,** common orange, orig. from China; ∼ **silk,** light plain-woven silk fabric; ∼ **tea,** smoke-cured kind from small-leaved tea plant grown in China); ∼**town,** section of a town (esp. a seaport) in which the Chinese live as a colony. [∼, country in Asia]

chi'na² *n*. fine semi-transparent or white earthenware, porcelain; ∼(**ware**), things made of this; ∼-**closet** (for keeping or displaying one's china); ∼ **clay,** kaolin; ∼ (**plate**), (rhyming sl.) mate. [f. Pers. *chīnī* (as prec.)]

chi'nagraph (-ahf) *n*. kind of pencil that can write on china, glass, etc. [f. prec.+-ɢʀᴀᴘʜ]

Chi'naman *n*. (*pl*. -**men**). **1.** (arch. or derog.) a Chinese. **2.** (Cricket). off-break or googly by left-handed bowler. **3.** *(colloq.) ∼'s **chance,** very slight chance. [f. Cʜɪɴᴀ¹+ᴍᴀɴ¹]

*****chinch** *n*. ∼(-**bug**), bedbug; small insect (*Blissus leucopterus*) destroying grain. [f. Sp. *chinche* f. L *cimex* -*icis*]

hincherinchee' *n*. S. Afr. perennial white-flowered bulbous plant (*Ornithogalum thyrsoides*). [imit., f. the squeaky rubbing of its stalks]

Chinchi'lla *n*. small S. Amer. rodent of genus *Chinchilla*; its soft grey fur; breed of domestic cat or rabbit. [Sp., dim. of *chinche* bug, cʜɪɴᴄʜ (from supposed smell)]

chin-chi'n *int*. (colloq.) of greeting and farewell, and as toast. [f. Chin. *qingqing* (pr. ch-)]

Chi'ndit *n*. Allied fighter behind Japanese lines in Burma (1943-5). [f. Burm. *chinthé*, a mythical creature]

chine¹ *n*. deep narrow ravine in Isle of Wight and Dorset. [OE *cinu* chink etc., f. Gmc **ki-* burst open]

hine² *n*., & *v.t*. **1.** *n*. backbone; joint of meat containing animal's backbone or part of it; ridge, arête. **2.** *v.t*. cut through backbone of (carcass). [ME, f. OF *eschine* f. Rom. **skīna* f. Gmc **skin-* sʜɪɴ and L *spina* sᴘɪɴᴇ]

hine³ *n*. join of side and bottom of ship etc. [= cʜɪᴍᴇ³]

hiné (shēnā') *a*. (Of fabric) given mottled pattern of (supposedly) Chinese style by colouring warp before weaving. [F, p.p. of *chiner* (*Chine* China)]

Chinee' *n*. (sl.) Chinese person. [f. foll. taken as pl.]

Chine̅'se (-z) *a*. & *n*. (*pl*. same). (native or language) of China; person of Chinese descent; ∼ **boxes** (nested together); ∼ **cabbage** (lettuce-like species); ∼ **copy,** slavish imitation; ∼ **goose,** small brown or white domesticated goose; ∼ **gooseberry,** (NZ) (vine with) brown hairy fruit; ∼ **lantern,** (1) collapsible lantern of paper, (2) plant with inflated orange calyx; ∼ **puzzle,** intricate puzzle or problem; ∼ **wall,** (fig.) insurmountable barrier; ∼ **white,** white zinc oxide as pigment. [f. Cʜɪɴᴀ¹+-ᴇsᴇ]

chink¹ *n*. long narrow opening, slit, peep-hole; place not fully closed and admitting light etc. [16th c., rel. to cʜɪɴᴇ¹]

chink² *n*. & *v*. **1.** *n*. sound as of glasses or coins striking together. **2.** *v.i*. make this sound. **3.** *v.t*. cause (coin etc.) to make this sound. [imit.]

Chink³ *n*. (sl., derog.) a Chinese. [abbr.]

chinkerinchee'. Var. of cʜɪɴᴄʜᴇʀɪɴᴄʜᴇᴇ.

*****chi'nō** (-ē'-) *n*. (*pl*. ∼s). cotton twill cloth, usu. khaki-coloured; (in *pl*.) garment made of it. [Amer. Sp., = toasted]

Chino- *comb. form*. China, = Sɪɴᴏ-. [f. Cʜɪɴᴀ¹+-ᴏ-]

chinoi'serie (shīnwah'z-) *n*. imitation of Chinese motifs in furniture etc. [F]

chinoo̅'k *n*. warm dry wind which blows east of the Rocky Mountains; warm wet southerly wind west of them; ∼ **salmon,** large salmon of N. Pacific. [Amer. Ind. name of a tribe]

chintz (-ts) *n*. & *a*. (of) cotton cloth usu. fast-printed with particoloured pattern and usu. glazed; hence ∼'ʏ² *a*., (fig.) cheap, mean. [earlier *chints* pl. f. Hindi *chīnt* f. Skr. *citra* variegated]

chionodo̅'xa (k-) *n*. blue-flowered early-blooming plant of genus *Chionodoxa*, glory-of-the-snow. [mod. L, f. Gk *khiōn* snow+*doxa* glory]

chip¹ *n*. **1.** thin piece cut from wood or broken from stone etc. (*chip off the old* ʙʟᴏᴄᴋ¹; **have a** ∼ **on** one's **shoulder,** be touchy or embittered); thin slice of fruit, etc.; long slender piece of potato; small square of semiconductor used to make integrated circuit; ||(in *pl*.) potato chips fried (ꜰɪsʜ¹ *and chips*); *(in pl*.) potato cʀɪsᴘs. **2.** wood split into strips for making baskets, hats, etc.; ∼ (**basket**), basket made of these joined or woven. **3.** place on china etc. from which chip has been knocked off. **4.** counter, piece of money; **have had** one's ∼s, (sl.) be beaten etc.; **when the** ∼s **are down,** (colloq.) when it comes to the point. **5.** ∼'**board,** thin material made of compressed wood chips and resin; ∼ (**shot**), (Footb.) short upward kick, (Golf) short lofted approach-shot on to putting-green. [ME, f. OE *cipp, cyp* beam]

chip² *v*. (-pp-). **1.** *v.t*. cut (wood), break (stone, crockery), at surface or edge, whence ∼'ᴘɪɴɢ¹ (2) *n*.; shape thus; cut (potato) into chips; cut or break (piece etc.) *off*, *from*; carve (inscription); (colloq.) tease (a person); kick or hit with chip shot. **2.** *v.i*. be apt to break at edge; play chip shot. **3.** *v.i*. & *t*. ∼ **in,** (colloq.) interrupt speaker, contribute (money etc.). [prob. repr. OE **cippian*; cf. MLG, MDu., *kippen* hatch out]

chi'pmunk *n*. N. Amer. ground-squirrel. [Algonquian]

chipola'ta (-lah'-) *n*. small spicy sausage. [F, f. It. *cipollata* dish of onions (*cipolla* onion)]

Chi'ppendale *n*. elegant style of ornamented furniture. [f. T. ∼, Engl. cabinet-maker d. 1779]

*****chi'pper** *a*. cheerful. [perh. f. N. Engl. dial. *kipper* lively]

chi'ppie *n*. Var. of foll. 2.

chi'pply *a*. & *n*. **1.** *a*. (sl.) unwell; irritable; hence ∼ɪɴᴇss *n*. **2.** *n*. (colloq.) fish-and-chips shop; (sl.) promiscuous or delinquent young woman; (sl.) carpenter. [f. cʜɪᴘ¹·², +-ʏ²·³]

Chips *n*. (Naut. sl.) ship's carpenter. [pl. of cʜɪᴘ¹]

chir'al (k-) *a*. (Of crystal etc.) not superposable on its mirror image; hence ∼ɪᴛʏ (-ă'l-) *n*. [f. Gk *kheir* hand+-ᴀʟ]

chīr′o- (k-) *comb. form.* hand, as: ~**graphy** (-ŏ′g-), handwriting; ~**mancy**, palmistry. [f. Gk *kheir* hand+-o-]

chirŏ′pod|y̆ (kĭ-, shĭ-) *n.* treatment given to feet, esp. for corns, bunions, etc.; hence ~**IST** (3) *n.* [f. prec.+Gk *pous podos* foot+-Y¹]

chīroprä′ct|ic (k-) *n.* & *a.* (of) manipulation esp. of spinal column as method of curing some diseases; hence ~**OR** *n.*, one who practises chiropractic. [f. CHIRO-+Gk *praktikos* (cf. PRACTICAL)]

chīrŏ′pter|an (k-) *n.* member of mammal order Chiroptera, with membraned hands serving as wings, the bats; so ~**OUS** *a.* [f. CHIRO-+Gk *pteron* wing+-AN]

chîrp *v.i.* & *t.*, & *n.* (make) short sharp note (as) of small bird or of grasshopper etc.; utter (song), express (joy etc.), thus; talk merrily. [ME, earlier *chirk, chirt*; imit.]

chîr′p|y̆ *a.* (colloq.) lively, cheerful; hence ~**ĬLY²** *adv.*, ~**ĬNESS** *n.* [f. prec.+-Y²]

chîrr *v.i.*, & *n.* (make) prolonged trilling sound (as) of grasshopper. [imit.; cf. CHURR]

chi′rrup *v.i.*, & *n.* (make) series of chirps, twittering. [trilled form of CHIRP]

chi′sel (-z-) *n.*, & *v.t.* (||-ll-). **1.** *n.* tool having square bevelled end for shaping wood, stone, or metal; **cold** ~ (suitable for cutting cold metal). **2.** *v.t.* cut or shape with chisel (~**led** *features* etc., clear-cut); (sl.) defraud, treat unfairly; hence ~**ĬER¹** *n.* [ME f. ONF, f. Rom. **cisellum* f. LL *cisorium* f. L *caedere caes-*cut]

chit¹ *n.* young child; young, small, or slender woman (usu. derog.; *chit of a girl*). [ME, whelp, cub, kitten, perh. = dial. *chit* sprout]

chit² *n.* note or written paper; note of order, sum owed, etc. [earlier *chitty*, Anglo-Ind. f. Hindi *ciṭṭhī* pass f. Skr. *citra* mark]

chi′tal (-ē′t-) *n.* axis deer. [f. Hindi *cītal*]

chi′t-chăt *n.*, & *v.i.* (-tt-). (hold) light conversation; gossip. [redupl. of CHAT¹]

chi′tin (k-) *n.* substance forming horny constituent in exoskeleton of arthropods; hence ~**OUS** *a.* [f. F *chitine* irreg. f. Gk *khitōn*; see foll., -IN]

chi′ton (k-) *n.* **1.** mollusc of genus *Chiton*, with shell or overlapping plates. **2.** long woollen garment worn by ancient Greeks. [f. Gk *khitōn*]

chi′tterling *n.* (usu. in *pl.*) smaller intestines of pigs etc., esp. as cooked for food. [ME; orig. uncert.]

chiv *n.*, & *v.t.* (-vv-). (sl.) knife. [17th c.; orig. unkn.]

chi′valrous (sh-) *a.* of or as of the Age of Chivalry; of or as of the ideal knight, gallant, honourable, courteous, disinterested; quixotic; hence ~**LY²** *adv.* [ME, f. OF *chevalerous* (as CHEVALIER; see -OUS)]

chi′valr|y̆ (sh-) *n.* medieval knightly system with its religious, moral, and social code (*Age of Chivalry*); ideal knight's characteristics, courage and courtesy; inclination to defend or help weaker party; (arch.) body of horsemen, knights, or gallant gentlemen; (arch.) knightly skill; hence ~**ĬC** *a.* [ME f. OF *chevalerie* etc. f. med. L *caballerius* for LL *caballarius* horseman (as CAVALIER; see -RY)]

chīve *n.* small culinary herb (*Allium schoenoprasus*) allied to onion and leek. [ME f. OF *cive*, dial. **chive*, f. L *cepa* onion]

chi′vvy̆, chî′vy̆, *v.t.* pursue, harass. [f. *chevy* n. & v., prob. f. ballad of *Chevy Chase*, place on Scottish Border]

||chiz(z) *n.*, & *v.t.* (-zz-). (sl.) cheat, swindle. [f. CHISEL]

chlămy̆domō′nas (kl-) *n.* unicellular green freshwater alga of genus *Chlamydomonas*. [mod. L, f. Gk *khlamus -udos* cloak+*monos* single]

chlor-¹′². See **chloro-¹′²**.

chlōr′al (kl-) *n.* ~ (**hydrate**), white crystalline trichloroacetaldehyde hydrate, a hypnotic and anaesthetic. [F (*chlore* CHLORINE, *alcool* ALCOHOL)]

chlŏrămphē′nicŏl (kl-) *n.* antibiotic prepared from *Streptomyces venezuelae* or synthetically. [f. CHLORO-²+AMIDE+PHENO-+NITRO-+GLYCOL]

chlōr′āte (kl-) *n.* salt of chloric acid. [f. CHLORIC+-ATE¹ (3)]

chlōrĕ′lla (kl-) *n.* unicellular green alga of genus *Chlorella*. [mod. L, dim. of Gk *khlōros* green]

chlōr′ic (kl-) *a.* ~ **acid**, a strong oxidizing acid $HClO_3$. [f. CHLORO-²+-IC]

chlōr′īde (kl-) *n.* binary compound of chlorine; bleaching agent containing chloride. [f. CHLORO-+-IDE]

chlōr′in|āte (kl-) *v.t.* impregnate or treat with chlorine; hence ~**A′TION** *n.*, treatment with chlorine (esp. in disinfecting water, or in extraction of gold from ores). [f. foll. +-ATE³]

chlōr′ine (klōr′ēn) *n.* non-metallic element, yellowish-green heavy gas with irritant smell. [f. Gk *khlōros* green+-INE⁵]

chlōr′īte (kl-) *n.* salt of chlorous acid. [f. CHLOROUS+-ITE¹ (2)]

chlōro-¹, (esp. bef. vowel) **chlōr-¹**, (kl-) *comb. form* (Bot. & Min.) green. [f. as CHLORINE+-O-]

chlōro-², (esp. bef. vowel) **chlōr-²**, (kl-) *comb. form* (Chem.) chlorine. [f. CHLORINE+-O-]

chlō′rofōrm (kl-) *n.*, & *v.t.* **1.** *n.* anaesthetic, thin colourless liquid whose inhaled vapour produces unconsciousness. **2.** *v.t.* treat (person) with or render unconscious by chloroform. [f. F *chloroforme* f. a CHLORO-²+*formyle* (cf. FORMIC)]

Chlōromy̆cē′tin (kl-) *n.* (P) = CHLORAMPHENICOL. [CHLORO-²+Gk *mukēs -ētos* fungus+-IN]

chlō′rophy̆ll (kl-) *n.* colouring-matter of green parts of plants. [f. F CHLORO¹(*phylle* f. Gk *phullon* leaf)]

chlō′roplăst (kl-) *n.* plastid containing chlorophyll. [f. G *chloroplast(id)* (as CHLORO-¹, PLASTID)]

chlōr|ō′sis (kl-) *n.* (*pl.* ~**oses** *pr.* -ō′sēz). (Hist.) green sickness, anaemic disease of young women, causing greenish complexion; (Bot.) blanching of green parts or turning green of petal etc.; hence ~**o′TIC** *a.* [CHLORO-¹+-OSIS]

chlōr′ous (kl-) *a.* ~ **acid**, an oxidizing acid, $HClO_2$. [f. CHLORO-²+-OUS]

chlōrprō′mazine (kl-) *n.* bitter drug used as sedative and against vomiting. [F (as CHLORO-², PROME-THAZINE)]

Ch.M. *abbr.* Master of Surgery. [f. L *Chirurgiae Magister*]

||chŏc *n.* (colloq.) chocolate; ~-**ice**, bar of ice cream enclosed in thin layer of chocolate. [abbr.]

chŏ′chō *n.* (*pl.* ~**s**). (W. Ind.) = CHOKO.

chŏck¹ *n.* block of wood, esp. wedge for stopping motion of cask or wheel. [prob. f. ONF **choque* etc. OF *ço(u)che*, of unkn. orig.]

chŏck² *v.t.*, & *adv.* **1.** *v.t.* make fast with chocks. **2.** *adv.* closely, tightly, close up; ~-**a-block**, jammed together, crammed *with*; ~-**full**, crammed full (*of*). [prec.]

||chŏ′cker *a.* (sl.) fed up, disgusted. [f. CHOCK²-*a-block*]

chŏ′colate (-kŏl-, -kl-) *n.* & *a.* **1.** *n.* edible paste or solid made from cacao seeds by roasting, grinding, etc. sweetmeat made of or covered with chocolate; drink of chocolate in hot milk or water. **2.** *n.* & *a.* (of) dark -brown colour. **3.** *a.* flavoured with chocolate; ~-**biscuit** (coated with chocolate); ~-**box**, decorated box filled with chocolates, (fig.) stereotyped romantic style of pictures; ~ **soldier**, (fig.) soldier unwilling to fight. [f. F *chocolat* or Sp. *chocolate* f. Aztec *chocolatl*]

Chŏ′ctaw *n.* (Skating). step from either edge of skate to other edge on other foot in opposite direction [name of Amer. Ind. tribe; cf. MOHAWK]

choice¹ *n.* **1.** choosing, selection; **by** or **for** ~ preferably (of (one's) ~, that one chooses; **make** or **take** one's ~, decide between possibilities. **2.** power, right, faculty, of choosing (**from** ~, willingly; **have no** ~, have no alternative; HOBSON'S *choice*). **3.** élite, best, *of*; variety to choose from; thing or person chosen; alternative (*have no choice but*). [ME f. OF *chois* (*choisir* f. Gmc **kausja* CHOOSE)]

choice² *a.* of picked quality; exquisite; carefully

chosen; hence ~'LY² (-slǐ) *adv.*, ~'NESS (-sn-) *n.* [ME, f. prec.]

hoir (kwīr), (arch.) **quīre²**, *n.* **1.** band of singers performing or leading in musical parts of church service; chancel of cathedral, minster, or large church; choral society, company of singers, birds, angels, etc. **2.** ~'**boy**, boy who sings in choir; ~'**master**, conductor of a choir; ~ **organ**, (Mus.) [corruption of *chair organ*] softest of three parts (GREAT, SWELL-, ~, *organ*) making up large compound organ, with lowest of three keyboards; ~ **school**, school maintained by cathedral etc. for choirboys and other pupils; *choir*-STALL¹. [ME, f. OF *quer* f. L CHORUS; cf. BRIER¹, FRIAR]

hōke¹ *v.* & *n.* **1.** *v.t.* stop breath of, suffocate, temporarily or finally, by squeezing throat, blocking it up, or (of water, smoke, etc.) being unbreathable; (fig., of emotion) make speechless; smother, stifle, kill, (plant, fire, etc.) by deprivation of light, air, etc.; suppress (feelings); fill chock-full; block up wholly or partly (tube by narrowing part of it, channel with sand, stones, etc.); (in *p.p.*, colloq.) disgusted, disappointed; ~ **back**, conceal (emotion etc.) with difficulty; ~ **down**, swallow (food) with difficulty; ~ **off**, (colloq.) dissuade, discourage, rebuke, (person, attempt), esp. forcibly. **2.** *v.i.* suffer temporary or permanent stoppage of breath; become speechless from emotion. **3.** *n.* narrowed part of gun bore etc.; valve in petrol engine controlling inflow of air; (Electr.) inductance coil used to smooth variations of alternating current or to alter its phase. **4.** ~'**berry**, (scarlet fruit of) N. Amer. shrub of genus *Aronia*; ~-**cherry**, astringent N. Amer. cherry; ~-**damp**, carbon dioxide in mines, wells, etc. [ME, f. OE *ācēocian* (A- 1, *cēoce*, *cēce* CHEEK)]

hōke² *n.* centre part of artichoke. [prob. confusion of ending of *artichoke* w. prec.]

hō′ker *n.* In vbl senses; clerical or other high collar; close-fitting necklace. [f. CHOKE¹ + -ER¹]

chō′key. See CHOKY¹.

hō′kō *n.* (*pl.* ~s). (Austral. & NZ) succulent vegetable like cucumber. [f. W. Ind. CHOCHO f. Braz. name]

chō′ky¹, ‖**chō′key,** *n.* (sl.) prison. [orig. Anglo-Ind., f. Hindi *cauki* shed]

chō′ký² *a.* tending to choke or cause choking. [f. CHOKE¹ + -Y²]

hŏl(ė)- (k-) *comb. form.* (Med. & Chem.) bile, as: **cholangio′graphy,** X-ray examination of gall--bladder and bile-ducts; **cholecysto′graphy,** X-ray examination of gall-bladder. [f. Gk *kholē* gall, bile]

hŏ′ler (k-) *n.* (Hist.) one of the four HUMOUR¹s, bile; (poet. or arch.) anger, irascibility. [ME, f. OF *colere* bile, anger f. L f. Gk *kholera* diarrhoea, in LL = bile, anger (Gk *kholē* bile)]

hŏ′lera (k-) *n.* infectious often fatal bacterial disease with severe intestinal symptoms; **chicken** or **fowl** ~, infectious disease of fowls; ~ **belt,** flannel or silk waistband worn to prevent intestinal ailments; ~ **morbus,** bilious disorder from over-eating etc.; hence ~IC (-ǎ′ĭk) *a.* [ME f. L f. Gk *kholera*; see prec.]

hŏ′lerĭc (k-) *a.* irascible; angry; *choleric* TEMPERA-MENT; hence **chŏlĕ′rĭcALLY** *adv.* [ME, f. OF *cholerique* f. L f. Gk *kholerikos* (as CHOLER; see -IC)]

hŏlĕ′sterŏl (k-) *n.* (Chem.) steroid alcohol found in body cells and fluids and thought to promote arteriosclerosis. [f. *cholesterin* f. Gk *kholē* bile + *stereos* stiff, + -OL]

hō′li (kō′lē) *n.* Indian woman's short-sleeved bodice. [f. Hindi *colī*]

hō′liămb (k-) *n.* (Pros.) = SCAZON; hence ~IC (-ǎ′-) *a.* [f. LL f. Gk *khōliambos* (*khōlos* lame; see IAMBUS)]

hō′line (k-; -īn, -ēn) *n.* (Chem.) strong base occurring widely in living matter. [f. G *cholin* f. Gk *kholē* bile; see -IN]

hŏmp *v.t.* = CHAMP¹. [imit.]

hŏndrī-, chŏndro-, (k-) *comb. forms.* (Med. &

Physiol.) cartilage. [f. Gk *khondros* grain, cartilage + -I-, -O-]

chŏ′ndrīte (k-) *n.* meteorite containing granules. [f. G *chondrit* f. Gk *khondros* granule; see -ITE¹]

*****chōō′-chōō** *n.* (colloq. or childish). railway train or locomotive. [imit.]

chōōse (-z) *v.* (chose *pr.* chōz; cho′sen *pr.* chō′z-). **1.** *v.t.* select out of greater number; (Theol., esp. in *p.p.*) destine to be saved (**the chosen people** or **race,** Jews); decide (*to* do one thing rather than another); think fit, be determined, *to* do; (w. compl.) select as (*was chosen king*); **nothing** etc. **to** ~ **between them** (they are nearly equal). **2.** *v.i.* ~ **between** or **from,** take one or another of; **cannot** ~ **but,** (arch.) must, have to; PICK² *and* choose. **3.** Hence **chōō′sER¹** (-z-) *n.*, **chōō′s(e)ry** (-zǐ) *a.*, (colloq.) fastidious. [OE *cēosan,* = OS, OHG *kiosan,* ON *kjósa,* Goth. *kiusan* f. Gmc **kiusan*]

chŏp¹ *v.* (-**pp**-). **1.** *v.t.* cut by a blow usu. with axe (*off, away, down,* etc.; ~ **up,** chop into small pieces, mince); (esp. in *p.p.*) cut (meat etc.) small; strike (ball) with short heavy edgewise blow. **2.** *v.i.* make chopping blow (*at*); cut by chopping (*through* etc.). [ME, var. of CHAP¹]

chŏp² *n.* **1.** cutting stroke with axe etc.; (Austral. & NZ, freq. in *pl.*) wood-chopping contest. **2.** thick slice of meat, esp. pork or lamb, usu. including rib; ~-**house,** (esp. cheap) restaurant. **3.** broken motion of water usu. due to action of wind against tide; hence ~'**pY²** *a.* **1.** short heavy edgewise blow in boxing, cricket, tennis, etc.; **the** ~, (sl.) being killed or dismissed. [f. prec.]

chŏp³ *n.* (usu. in *pl.*) jaw of animal etc.; **lick** one's ~s (with relish or anticipation); ~s **of the Channel,** entrance from Atlantic Ocean to Engl. Channel; see also CHAP². [16th c., var. of CHAP²; orig. unkn.]

chŏp⁴ *v.* (-**pp**-). ~ **and change** (emphatic for *change,* usu. as *v.i.*), vacillate, be inconstant; ~ **round,** **about,** (esp. of wind) change direction suddenly; ~ **logic,** engage in pedantically logical arguments. [ME, perh. rel. to *chap* f. OE *cēapian* (as CHEAP)]

‖**chŏp⁵** *n.* trade mark, brand of goods; **first, second,** ~, (colloq.) first, second, -class; **no** ~, **not much** ~, (Austral. & NZ) no good. [orig. in India & China, f. Hindi *chāp* stamp]

chŏp-chŏp′ *adv.* & *int.* (pidgin Engl.) quick, quickly. [f. Chin. dial. *k′wăi-k′wăi*]

chŏ′pper *n.* In vbl senses; large-bladed short axe; butcher's cleaver; device for regularly interrupting light-beam etc.; (colloq.) helicopter; *****(sl.) machine--gun. [f. CHOP¹ + -ER¹]

chŏ′pstick *n.* one of a pair of sticks of wood, ivory, etc., held in one hand, used by Chinese etc. to lift food to mouth. [pidgin Engl. (*chop* = quick; STICK²) equivalent of Chin. dial. *k′wăi-tsze* nimble ones]

chŏp-su′ey (-sōō′-, -sū′-) *n.* Chinese dish of meat or chicken fried in sesame oil with rice, onions, etc. [f. Chin.]

chŏr′al¹ (k-) *a.* **1.** of or sung by choir; ~ **service** (with canticles, anthems, etc. so sung); ~ **society** (of persons interested in choral music). **2.** (read or said) by group of voices; of or with chorus. **3.** Hence ~'LY² *adv.* [f. med. L *choralis* f. L CHORUS; see -AL]

chōrā′le, chōrā′l², (k-; k̄ŏrah′l) *n.* (metrical hymn to) simple tune usu. sung in unison chiefly in Lutheran church; harmonized form of this; group of singers. [f. G *choral(gesang)* f. med. L *cantus choralis*]

chŏrd¹ (k-) *n.* **1.** (poet. or fig.) string of harp etc.; **strike a** ~, recall something to person's memory; **touch the right** ~, appeal skilfully to emotion. **2.** (Anat., arch.) = CORD (*vocal chord; spinal chord*). **3.** (Math., Aeron., etc.) straight line joining ends of arc, wing, etc. [16th-c. refash. of CORD after L *chorda*]

chŏrd² (k-) *n.* (Mus.) group of notes sounded usu. together, combined according to some system (BROKEN *chord*; **common** ~, any note with its major or minor third and perfect fifth). [orig. *cord* f. ACCORD², later confused w. prec.]

chŏr'dal (k-) *a.* of or like a CHORD[1,2]. [f. CHORD[1,2] +-AL]

chŏr'dāte (k-) *a.* & *n.* (Zool.) (member) of the phylum Chordata, with developed notochord. [f. mod. L *Chordata* f. L *chorda* CHORD[1], after *Vertebrata* etc.]

chŏre *n.* odd job; recurrent, routine, or tedious task. [orig. dial. & US form of CHAR[2]]

chore'a (k-) *n.* St. Vitus's DANCE[2]. [L, f. Gk *khoreia* (as CHORUS)]

chŏrĕŏ'graphy̆ (k-) *n.* arranging or designing of ballet or stage-dance; so **chŏrĕŏ'GRAPHER** *n.*, **chŏ'rĕŏgraph** (-ahf) *v.t.* & *i.*, **chŏrĕŏGRA'PHIC** *a.*, (k-). [f. Gk *khoreia* choral dancing to music (see prec.)+-GRAPHY]

chŏriă'mb|us (k-) *n.* (*pl.* ∼i *pr.* -ī). (Pros.) foot consisting of two short syllables between two long; hence ∼IC *a.* [LL, f. Gk *khoriambos* (*khoreios* of the dance; see IAMBUS)]

chŏr'ic (k-) *a.* of or like chorus in Greek play. [f. LL f. Gk *khorikos* (as CHORUS; see -IC)]

***chŏr'ine** (kōr'ēn) *n.* chorus-girl. [f. CHORUS + -INE[3,4]]

chŏr'ion (k-) *n.* outermost membrane enclosing foetus. [f. Gk *khorion*]

chŏ'rister (k-) *n.* member of choir, esp. choirboy (also fig. of angels, birds); *leader of choir. [ME, f. AF *cueristre*, OF *cueriste* (*quer* CHOIR)]

chŏrŏ'graph|y̆ (k-) *n.* description of regions or districts of size between those involved in topography and in geography; hence ∼ER[1] *n.*, **chŏrŏGRA'PHIC** (k-) *a.* [f. F *chorographie* or f. L f. Gk *khōrographia* (*khōra* region; see -O-, -GRAPHY)]

chŏr'oid (k-) *a.* & *n.* like chorion in shape or vascularity; ∼ (**coat** or **membrane**), membrane lining eyeball between retina and iris. [f. Gk *khoroeidēs* for *khorioeidēs* (as CHORION; see -OID)]

chŏrŏ'log|y̆ (k-) *n.* study of geographical distribution of animals and plants; hence **chŏrŏLO'GICAL** (k-) *a.*, ∼IST (3) *n.* [f. Gk *khōra* region + -o- + -LOGY]

chŏr'tle *v.i.*, & *n.* (utter) loud gleeful chuckle. [portmanteau wd (Lewis Carroll) app. f. CHUCKLE + SNORT[1]]

chŏr'us (k-) *n.* & *v.* **1.** *n.* band of singers, choir; thing sung by many at once; any simultaneous utterance by many persons etc. (**in** ∼, in unison, all speaking etc. together); group of singers and dancers in musical comedy etc. **2.** (Mus.) composition in several (usu. four) parts each sung by several voices; refrain or main part of popular song; jazz improvisation on this. **3.** (Gk Ant.) band of dancers and singers in religious ceremonies and dramatic performances; (one of) their utterances. **4.** character speaking prologue etc. in play. **5.** ∼-**girl**, young woman who sings or dances in chorus of musical comedy etc.; ∼-**master**, conductor of chorus or choir. **6.** *v.t.* & *i.* sing, speak, say, in chorus. [L, f. Gk *khoros*]

chose. See CHOOSE.

chose jugée (shōz zhoō'zhā) *n.* thing it is idle to discuss, as already settled. [F]

chosen. See CHOOSE.

chou (shoō) *n.* (*pl.* ∼x *pr.* same). rosette or ornamental knot of ribbon, chiffon, etc., on woman's hat or dress; small round cake of pastry filled with cream etc. [F, f. L *caulis* cabbage]

choucroute (shoōkroō't) *n.* kind of pickled cabbage. [F, f. G dial. *surkrut* SAUERKRAUT]

chough (chŭf) *n.* red-legged crow of genus *Pyrrhocorax*. [ME, prob. orig. imit.]

chou moe'llier (-mŏ-') *n.* (Austral. & NZ) coarse kind of kale grown as fodder. [F, = marrow-filled cabbage]

choux (shoō) *n.* = CHOU (sing. or pl.); ∼ **pastry**, very light pastry enriched with eggs. [F, pl. of CHOU]

chow *n.* (animal of) a Chinese breed of dog; (sl.) food. [shortened f. foll.]

chow-chow *n.* Chinese preserve of orange-peel, ginger, etc.; = prec. [pidgin Engl.]

***chow'der** *n.* stew or soup of fresh fish or clams with bacon, onions, biscuit, etc. [perh. f. F phr. *faire la*

chaudière supply a pot etc. for cooking a stew of fish etc (*chaudière* pot, CAULDRON)]

chow mei'n (-mā'n) *n.* Chinese dish of fried noodle usu. with shredded meat and vegetables. [f. Chir *chao mian* fried flour]

Chr. *abbr.* Chronicles (OT).

chrēmati'st|ic *a.* (k-) of money-making; hence ∼IC *n.*, study of wealth. [f. Gk *khrēmatistikos* (*khrēmatiz* make money f. *khrēma -matos* money; see -IC)]

chrēstŏ'mathy̆ (k-) *n.* collection of choice passage esp. to help in learning a language. [f. F *chrestomathy* or f. Gk *khrēstomatheia* (*khrēstos* useful, *-matheia* learn ing)]

chri'sm (krī'zem) *n.* consecrated oil, unguen anointing, esp. in sacred rites. [OE *crisma* f. eccl. L Gk *khrisma* anointing]

chri'som (k-) *n.* (Hist.) ∼(-**cloth** etc.), child's whit robe at baptism, used as shroud if it died within month; ∼-**child** (less than a month old). [ME, f. pop pronunc. of prec.]

Christ (k-) *n.* Messiah or Lord's anointed of Jewis prophecy; (title, now treated as name, given to) Jesu as fulfilling this prophecy; image or picture of Jesus ∼ !, (vulg.) excl. expr. surprise, impatience, etc.; **th** ∼-**child**, Christ as a child; hence ∼'HOOD (-t-h-) *n* ∼'LESS, ∼'LIKE, *adjs.* [OE *Crīst*, = OS, OHG *Krīst*, L *Christus* f. Gk *khristos* anointed one (*khriō* anoint transl. of Heb. *māšīah* MESSIAH)]

Christadĕ'lphian (k-) *a.* & *n.* (member) of religiou sect rejecting doctrine of Trinity and expectin second coming of Christ. [f. prec. + Gk *adelphc* brother + -IAN]

chri'sten (krī'sen) *v.t.* admit to Christian Church b baptism; give name to (person at baptism, or a nickname; *christen her*, *christen him John*, *Shorty*; als ship, bell, etc., with analogous ceremony); (colloq. use etc. for first time. [OE *crīstnian* make Christia (*crīsten* a. Christian, = OS, OHG *kristīn* f. L *Chris ianus* CHRISTIAN)]

Chri'stendom (krī'sen-) *n.* Christians; Christia countries. [OE *cristendōm* (*crīsten* a.; see prec., -DOM)]

Chri'stian (krī'styan) *a.* & *n.* (person) believing ir professing, or belonging to, the religion of Christ; c Christ or his religion; (person) showing characte consistent with Christ's teaching, of genuine piety Christlike; (sl.) civilized, decent, (person); ∼ buria (with the ceremonies of the church); ∼ **er** (reckoned from birth of Christ); ∼ **name**, nam given (as) at baptism, personal name (cf. SURNAME ∼ **Science, Scientist**, (adherent of) a system c combating disease etc. without medical treatment b mental effect of patient's Christian faith; *Christia* SOCIALISM, YEAR; hence -IZE (2, 3) *v.i.* & *t.*, ∼IZA'TIO *n.* [f. L *Christianus* (*Christus* CHRIST; see -IAN)]

Christia'nia (k-; -ah'n-) *n.* (Skiing). turn in whic the skis are kept in parallel, used for stopping shor [∼ (now Oslo) in Norway]

Christiă'nity (k-) *n.* the Christian faith, doctrines o Christ and his apostles; being a Christian, Christia quality or character; Christendom. [ME *cristianit* earlier *crist(i)ente* f. OF *crestienté* (*crestien* CHRISTIAN see -ITY)]

Chri'stie (k-) *n.* Christiania. [abbr.]

Chri'stmas (krī'sm-) *n.* **1.** festival of Christ's birth celebrated on 25 Dec. (∼ **Day**) and devoted esp. t family reunion and merry-making, (**Father** ∼, ol man dressed in red, personification of family fes tivity, = SANTA CLAUS); ∼(-**tide**), period of som days beginning 24 Dec. (∼ **Eve**). **2.** ||∼-**box**, sma present or gratuity given at Christmas esp. to em ployees of firms providing regular services; ∼ **bush** Austral. shrub with flower-like fruits at Christmas; ∼ **card** (sent with greetings at or just before Christ mas); ∼ **present**, gift given at Christmas; ||∼ **pudding**, plum pudding eaten at Christmas; ∼ **rose**, white-flowered hellebore blooming in winter ∼ **stocking** (hung up by children on Christmas Ev for Father Christmas to fill with presents); ∼ **tree**

evergreen or artificial tree set up in room or in the open and hung with lights, presents, etc., (Austral.) Christmas bush. **3.** Hence ∼**sy²** a. [OE *Crīstes mæsse* (MASS¹)]

Christo- (k-) *comb. form.* Christ, as: ∼LATRY (-ŏ′l-) *n.*; ∼**logy** (-ŏ′l-), branch of theology relating to Christ; ∼**phany** (-ŏ′f-), manifestation of Christ esp. after Resurrection. [f. L *Christus* or Gk *Khristos*+-o-]

Chri′stў (k-) *n.* Christiania. [abbr.]

chrō′ma (k-) *n.* purity or intensity of colour. [f. Gk *khrōma* colour]

chrō′māte (k-) *n.* (Chem.) salt of chromic acid. [f. CHROMIC+-ATE¹ (3)]

chrōmă′tic (k-) *a.* **1.** of, produced by, full of bright, colour; ∼ **aberration,** failure of different colours to come to same focus after refraction. **2.** (Mus.) of or having notes not included in diatonic scale; ∼ **scale** (proceeding by semitones); ∼ **semitone,** interval between note and its flat or sharp. **3.** Hence **chromă′ti**CALLY (k-) *adv.,* ∼**ISM** (3) *n.* [f. F *chromatique* or f. L f. Gk *khrōmatikos* (*khrōma -atos* colour; see -IC)]

chrōmăti′citў (k-) *n.* quality of colour regarded independently of brightness. [f. prec.+-ITY]

chrō′matin (k-) *n.* (Biol.) cell-nucleus constituent that can be readily stained. [G (as CHROMATO-, -IN)]

chrōmato-, chrŏmo-², (k-) *comb. forms.* colour, as: **chromato′psia,** abnormally coloured vision. [f. Gk *khrōma -atos* colour+-o-]

chrōmatŏ′graphў (k-) *n.* (Chem.) separation of substances by slow passage through or over adsorbing etc. material; so **chrōmă′to**GRAM (k-) *n.,* result of this, **chrōmă′to**GRAPH (2, 3) (k-) *n.,* & *v.t.,* **chrōmatogră′ph**IC (k-) *a.* [f. G *chromatographie* (as CHROMATO-, -GRAPHY)]

chrōme (k-) *n.* ∼ (**yellow**), yellow pigment and colour got from lead chromate; = *chromium-plate*; ∼ **leather** (tanned with chromium salts); ∼**nickel** *a.,* stainless (steel) containing chromium and nickel; ∼ **steel,** hard fine-grained steel containing much chromium. [F, = chromium, f. Gk *khrōma* colour]

chrō′mic (k-) *a.* of chromium; ∼ **acid,** H_2CrO_4 forming yellow salts, or its anhydride, CrO_3. [f. prec.+-IC]

chrŏ′minance (k-) *n.* difference in colour quality, measured with respect to a reference colour of equal brightness. [f. Gk *khrōma* colour, after *luminance*]

chrō′mīte (k-) *n.* mineral composed of chromium and iron oxides. [f. CHROME or foll.+-ITE¹]

chrō′mium (k-) *n.* (Chem.) metallic element, forming brilliantly coloured compounds; ∼-**plate,** (*n.*) electrolytically deposited protective coating of chromium, (*v.t.*) coat thus; ∼-**plated,** (fig.) pretentiously decorative. [f. CHROME+-IUM]

chrōmo-¹ (k-) *comb. form.* chromium. [f. prec. +-o-]

chromo-². See CHROMATO-.

chrōmoli′thograph (k-; -ahf) *n.,* & *v.t.* (picture) print(ed) in colours by lithography; so **chrōmolithŏ′**GRAPHER, **chrōmolithŏ′**GRAPHY, *ns.,* **chrōmolitho**GRA′PHIC *a.,* (k-). [f. CHROMO-² +LITHOGRAPH]

chrō′mosōm|e (k-) *n.* (Biol.) rodlike or threadlike structure occurring in pairs in the nucleus of animal and plant cells, carrying genes; hence ∼AL *a.* [f. G *chromosom* (as CHROMO-², -SOME³)]

chrō′mosphēre (k-) *n.* reddish gaseous envelope of sun or other star; hence **chrōmosphě′r**IC (k-) *a.* [f. CHROMO-²+SPHERE]

Chron. *abbr.* Chronicles (OT).

chrŏ′nic (k-) *a.* lingering, lasting, (of disease, cf. ACUTE); (of invalid) with chronic complaint; constant (*chronic doubt, rebellion*); ||(colloq.) bad, intense, severe; hence **chrŏ′nic**ALLY *adv.,* **chroni′city** *n.,* (k-). [f. F *chronique* f. L *chronicus* (in LL of disease) f. Gk *khronikos* (*khronos* time; see -IC)]

chrŏ′nicle (k-) *n.,* & *v.t.* (enter or relate in a) continuous register of events in order of time; **C∼s,**

name of two historical books of OT; narrative, account; (*C∼*) newspaper name; hence **chrŏ′nicleR¹** (k-) *n.* [ME, f. AF *cronicle* var. of OF *cronique* f. LL *chronica* sing. f. L f. Gk *khronika* neut. pl. annals (see prec.)]

chrŏ′nogrăm (k-) *n.* phrase etc. of which the Roman-numeral letters added give a date, as LorD haVe MerCIe Vpon Vs = 50+500+5+1000+100+ 1+5+5 = 1666; hence **chrŏnogrammă′t**IC (k-) *a.* [f. Gk *khronos* time+-o-+-GRAM]

chrŏ′nograph (k-; -ahf) *n.* instrument recording time with extreme accuracy; stop-watch; hence **chrŏnogra′ph**IC (k-) *a.* [f. as prec.+-GRAPH]

chronŏ′log|ў (k-) *n.* science of computing dates; arrangement of events according to dates or times of occurrence, table or treatise displaying this; hence ∼ER¹, ∼IST (3), *ns.,* **chrŏno**LO′GICAL (k-) *a.,* ∼IZE (3) *v.t.* [f. mod. L *chronologia* (as prec.; see -LOGY)]

chronŏ′mēter (k-) *n.* time-measuring instrument, esp. one keeping accurate time at all temperatures etc., used for navigation by astronomical observation at sea. [f. Gk *khronos* time+-o-+-METER]

chronŏ′mětrў (k-) *n.* accurate time-measurement; hence **chrŏnomě′tr**IC(AL) (k-) *adjs.* [f. as prec. +-METRY]

chrŏ′noscōpe (k-) *n.* apparatus measuring velocity of projectiles, or person's reaction times. [f. as prec. +-SCOPE]

chrў′salis (k-) *n.* (*pl.* ∼**es,** or **chrysalides** *pr.* krĭsă′lĭdēz). pupa, esp. quiescent one of butterfly or moth; case enclosing it; (fig.) preparatory or transition state. [L f. Gk *khrusallis -idos* (*khrusos* gold)]

chrўsă′nthemum (k-) *n.* (Bot.) composite plant of genus *Chrysanthemum,* e.g. corn marigold; (pop., colloq. abbr. **chrysa′nth**) one of the autumn-blooming cultivated varieties of this. [L, f. Gk *khrusanthemon* (*khrusos* gold, *anthemon* flower)]

chrўsĕ′lĕphă′ntīne (k-) *a.* overlaid with gold and ivory as by ancient Greek sculptors. [f. Gk *khruselephantinos* (*khrusos* gold, *elephas* elephant, ivory; see -INE²)]

chrўsŏbĕ′rўl (k-) *n.* yellowish-green gem, a compound of beryllium. [f. L *chrysoberyllus* f. Gk *khrusos* gold+*bērullos* beryl]

chrў′solīte (k-) *n.* precious stone, a variety of olivine. [ME f. OF *crisolite* f. med. L *crisolitus* f. L f. Gk *khrusolithos* (*khrusos* gold, *lithos* stone)]

chrў′soprāse (k-; -z) *n.* apple-green variety of chalcedony; (N1 etc.) prob. a golden-green variety of beryl. [ME f. OF *crisopace* f. L *chrysopassus* var. of L f. Gk *khrusoprasos* (*khrusos* gold, *prason* leek)]

chthŏ′nic (kth-) *a.* dwelling in the underworld. [f. Gk *khthōn* earth+-IC]

chŭb *n.* (*pl.* same). thick-bodied coarse-fleshed river fish (*Leuciscus cephalus*) of carp family. [15th c., of unkn. orig.]

Chŭbb *n.* (P) ∼ (**lock**), patent lock with tumblers and device for fixing bolt immovably if attempt is made to pick the lock. [f. name of inventor, a 19th-c. London locksmith]

chŭ′bb|ў *a.* plump-faced; plump; hence ∼**INESS** *n.* [f. CHUB+-Y²]

chŭck¹ *v.t.,* & *n.* **1.** (give) playful touch *under the chin.* **2.** (colloq.) fling or throw (down) with contempt, carelessness, or ease; **the ∼,** (sl.) dismissal (*give person the chuck*). **3.** *v.t.* (colloq.) = THROW¹ *away, out, up,* etc.; throw out, throw up; ∼ **it,** (sl.) stop, desist; ∼ **out,** expel (troublesome person) from meeting, public house, etc., whence ||∼ER¹-**ou′t** *n.* [16th c., perh. f. F *chuquer, choquer* to knock]

chŭck² *n.,* & *v.t.* **1.** contrivance in lathe etc. for holding workpiece; cut of beef from neck to ribs. **2.** *v.t.* fix (wood etc.) to chuck. [var. of CHOCK¹]

***chŭck³** *n.* (colloq.) food; ∼-**wagon,** provision-cart on ranch etc. [19th c., perh. f. prec.]

chŭ′ckle *v.i.,* & *n.* (make) suppressed laugh(s) of glee etc.; exult *over.* [f. *chuck* cluck+-LE 3]

chŭ′ckle-head (-hĕd) *n.*, **chŭ′ckle-headėd** (-hĕd-) *a.* stupid (person). [f. *chuckle* clumsy, prob. rel. to CHUCK[2]]

chŭff *v.i.* (Of engine etc.) work with regular sharp puffing sound. [imit.]

||**chŭffed** (-ft) *a.* (sl.) pleased; displeased. [f. dial. *chuff*]

chŭg *n.*, & *v.i.* (-gg-). (make) muffled sound of slowly--running internal combustion engine or its exhaust; move with this sound. [imit.]

chukär′ *n.* red-legged Indian partridge (*Alectoris chukar*). [f. Hindi *cakor*]

chŭ′kker, chŭ′kka, *n.* each of the periods into which game of polo is divided; ∼ **boot,** ankle-high leather boot as worn for polo. [f. Hindi *cakkar* f. Skr. *cakra* wheel]

chŭm *v.i.* (-mm-), & *n.* (colloq.) **1.** *v.i.* share rooms (*with*); ∼ **up,** form close friendship (*with*). **2.** *n.* familiar friend (esp. among boys); **new** ∼, (Austral. & NZ) recent immigrant, greenhorn; hence ∼′MY[2] *a.* [17th c., prob. short for *chamber-fellow*]

chŭmp *n.* short thick lump of wood; ||thick end, esp. of loin of lamb or mutton (so *chump chop*); ||(colloq.) head, esp. **off** one's ∼, crazy, wild with excitement etc.; (colloq.) foolish person. [18th c., blend of foll. w. LUMP[1] etc.]

chŭnk *n.* thick lump cut or broken off (wood, bread, cheese, etc.); (fig.) (substantial) amount; *small sturdy person or horse; hence ∼′Y[2] *a.*, consisting of chunks, short and thick, small and sturdy. [prob. var. of CHUCK[2]]

||**Chŭ′nnel** *n.* (colloq.) proposed tunnel under the English Channel. [portmanteau wd f. *Channel tunnel*]

chŭ′nter, *chŭ′nner, v.i.* (colloq.) mutter; grumble, complain. [prob. imit.]

chupä′ttў, -i, chapä′t(t)ĭ, *n.* (Ind.) small flat thin cake of coarse unleavened bread. [f. Hindi *capāti*]

chŭrch[1] *n.* **1.** building for public Christian worship, ||esp. according to established religion of country; public worship (*go to church*; *meet after church*). **2.** (C∼). body of all Christians (C∼ **militant,** Christians on earth warring against evil; C∼ **triumphant,** Christians at peace in heaven; *Church* VISIBLE); organized Christian society of any time (*primitive Church*), country (*Church of Scotland*), or distinguishing principle (*Reformed Church*); C∼ **of England,** English branch of Western or Latin Church rejecting Pope's supremacy since Reformation; **Established** C∼ (recognized by State, as Church of England or Scotland). **3.** organization, clergy and other officers, of a religious society or corporation; clerical profession (**go into the** C∼, take holy orders); HIGH, Low[1], BROAD, **Church,** parties with different views of Anglican doctrine and discipline. **4.** C∼ **Army,** Church of England mission to poorer classes; C∼ **Commissioners,** body managing finances of Church of England; ∼**-goer,** ∼**-going,** attender, attendance, at public worship; ∼′**man,** ∼′**man-ship,** member, membership, of clergy or church; ∼ **mouse** (proverbially poverty-stricken); ∼ **parade,** (Mil. etc.) attendance at worship; ∼ **school** (founded by or associated with Church of England etc.); ∼ **service,** public worship; *Church* SLAVONIC; ∼′**warden,** elected lay representative of parish (usu. one of two, elected one by incumbent, one by parishioners), long clay pipe, *church administrator; ∼′**woman,** fem. of churchman; ∼′**yard,** (*n.*) enclosed ground in which church stands, esp. as used for burials, (*a.*, of cough) seeming to herald death; *Church* YEAR. [OE *cir(i)ce* etc., = OS *kirika*, OHG *chirihha* f. WG *kirika* f. med. Gk *kurikon* f. Gk *kuriakon* (sc. *dōma*) Lord's (house) f. *kurios* lord; cf. KIRK]

chŭrch[2] *v.t.* perform church service of thanksgiving for (esp. woman after childbirth). [ME, f. prec.]

Churchi′llian *a.* of or relating to or characteristic of one of the Spencer-Churchill family, esp. Lord Randolph Churchill, Brit. statesman d. 1895, or his son Sir Winston Churchill, Brit. statesman d. 1965. [f. *Churchill* + -IAN]]

chŭrr′ch′lў *a.* obtrusively or intolerantly devoted to the Church or opposed to religious dissent; like a church; hence ∼iNESS *n.* [f. CHURCH[1] + -Y[2]]

chŭri′nga (-ngga) *n.* (*pl.* ∼**s** *or* same). sacred amulet of Australian Aboriginals. [Aboriginal]

chŭrl *n.* **1.** (arch.) peasant; person of low birth. **2.** ill--bred fellow; (arch.) surly or niggardly person; hence ∼′ISH[1] *a.*, ill-bred, surly, niggardly. [OE *ceorl*, = MLG *kerle* f. WG **kerl-* man]

chŭrn *n.* & *v.* **1.** *n.* butter-making machine in which milk or cream is agitated; ||large milk-can (orig. shaped like butter-churn). **2.** *v.t.* agitate (milk or cream) in churn; produce (butter thus); stir (liquid) about, cause to froth; ∼ (**up**), agitate violently; ∼ **out,** (fig.) produce in quantity without quality. **3.** *v.i.* operate butter-churn; (of liquid) wash to and fro, foam, seethe; hence ∼′ING[1] (1, 2) *n.* [OE *cyrin*, **ci(e)rn*, = MDu., MLG *kerne*, ON *kirna* f. Gmc **kernjōn*]

chŭrr *v.i.*, & *n.* (make) deep trill as of nightjar. [imit.; cf. CHIRR]

Chŭrrigueré′sque (-gerĕ′sk) *a.* lavishly ornamented in late Spanish baroque style. [f. J. *Churriguera*, Sp. architect d. 1723 + -ESQUE]

chuse. Var. (arch.) of CHOOSE.

chŭt *int.* expr. impatience. [imit.; cf. F *chut*]

chute (shoōt) *n.* **1.** sloping channel or slide, with or without water, for conveying things to lower level; slope for shooting rubbish down. **2.** (colloq.) para-chute. [F *chute* fall (of water etc.), f. OF *cheoite* fem. p.p. (as *n.*) of *cheoir* fall f. L *cadere*; so with senses of SHOOT[2]; sense 2 abbr.]

chŭ′tney, *chŭ′nner, n.* pungent orig. Indian condiment of fruits, vinegar, spices, etc. [f. Hindi *catnī*]

chu′tzpah (hŏ̄′tspə) *n.* (sl.) shameless audacity. [Yiddish]

chўle (k-) *n.* white milky fluid formed by action of pancreatic juice and bile on chyme. [f. LL f. Gk *khulos* juice]

chўme (k-) *n.* food converted by gastric secretion into acid pulp. [f. LL f. Gk *khumos* juice]

chypre (shē-) *n.* heavy perfume made from sandal-wood. [F, = Cyprus, perh. where first made]

||**CI** *abbr.* Channel Islands; Order of the Crown of India.

Ci *abbr.* curie.

CIA *abbr.* Central Intelligence Agency (US).

ciao (chow) *int.* (colloq.) goodbye; hello. [It.]

cibōr′i|um *n.* (*pl.* ∼**a**). (Archit.) canopy, canopied shrine; receptacle for reservation of Eucharist, shaped like shrine, or cup with arched cover. [med. L, f. Gk *kibōrion* seed-vessel of water-lily, cup made from it]

cica′da, cica′la, ciga′la, (-ah′-), *n.* transparent--winged shrill-sounding insect of genus *Cicada*. [L *cicada*, It. f. L *cicala*, It. *cicala*, fr. L]

ci′catr|ice, cicä′tr|ix (*pl.* ∼**ices** *pr.* sĭkatrī′sēz), *n.* scar of healed wound; scar on tree bark; (Bot.) mark left on stem by fall of leaf etc., hilum of seed; hence **cicatrī′cIAL** (-shəl) *a.* [ME f. OF *cicatrice* or f. L *cicatrix -icis*]

ci′catrīz|e, -īs|e (-īz), *v.t.* & *i.* heal, skin over; mark with scars; hence ∼A′TION *n.* [f. F *cicatriser* (*cicatrice*, see prec.; assim. to -IZE)]

ci′celў *n.* umbelliferous plant of genus *Myrrhis* or *Osmorhiza*; SWEET *cicely*. [app. f. L f. Gk *seselis*, w assim. to the woman's Christian name]

cicerō′n|e (chĭch-, sĭs-) *n.* (*pl.* ∼**i** *pr.* -ē). guide who understands and explains antiquities etc. [It., f. L *Cicero -onis* Roman orator d. 43 BC]

Cicerō′nian *a.* eloquent, classical, or rhythmical, in the style of Cicero. [f. L *Ciceronianus* (as prec.; see -IAN)]

ci′chlid (-k-) *n.* tropical freshwater fish of family Cichlidae, esp. kind kept in aquaria. [f. mod. L *Cichlidae* f. Gk *kikhlē* a kind of fish]

cicisbe|o (chĭchĭzbā′ō) *n.* (*pl.* ∼**i** *pr.* -ē). (esp. Hist.) married Italian woman's male companion or lover [It.]

‖**CID** abbr. Criminal Investigation Department.

-cide suf. forming ns. meaning (1) person or substance that kills (regicide, insecticide), (2) killing of (homicide, suicide). [(1) f. or after F, f. L -cida, (2) f. or after F, f. L -cidium, both f. L caedere kill]

ci′der n. fermented *or unfermented drink made from apple-juice; ∼-press (for squeezing juice from apples). [ME, f. OF sidre f. eccl. L f. Gk sikera f. Heb. šēkār strong drink]

ci-devant (sēdevah′ṅ) a. or adv. former(ly), that has been (w. person's earlier name or status). [F, = heretofore]

‖**CIE** abbr. Companion (of the Order) of the Indian Empire.

c.i.f. abbr. cost, insurance, freight.

cig n. (colloq.) cigarette, cigar, etc. [abbr.]

cigala. See CICADA.

cigâr′ n. roll of tobacco-leaf for smoking; ∼-holder, device holding cigar for smoking; ∼-lighter, device (esp. in motor car) for lighting cigar, cigarette, etc.; ∼-shaped, cylindrical with pointed end(s). [f. F cigare or f. Sp. cigarro]

cigarĕ′tte, *-ĕ′t, n. small cylinder of finely-cut tobacco or of narcotic or medicated substance rolled in paper for smoking; ∼-card, picture card included in packet of cigarettes; ∼-case (for holding cigarettes before use); ∼-end, unsmoked remainder of cigarette; ∼-holder, device holding cigarette for smoking; ∼-lighter, mechanical device for lighting cigarettes; ∼-paper (for rolling tobacco in to make cigarette). [F, dim. of cigare; see prec., -ETTE]

cigarī′llō n. (pl. ∼s). small cigar. [Sp., dim. of cigarro cigar]

ci′ggў (-gĭ) n. (colloq.) cigarette. [abbr.; see -Y³]

CIGS abbr. (Hist.) Chief of Imperial General Staff.

ci′lice n. (garment of) haircloth. [F, f. L f. Gk kilikion (Kilikia Cilicia in Asia Minor)]

ci′li|um n. (pl. ∼a). eyelash; similar fringe on leaf, insect's wing, etc.; (Biol.) hairlike vibrating organ on animal and vegetable tissue, used by many aquatic lower animals for locomotion; hence ∼ARY¹, ∼ATE⁰, ∼ātED¹, adjs., ∼A′TION n. [L, = eyelash]

cill. Var. of SILL.

ci′mbalom n. dulcimer. [Magyar, f. It. cembalo; see CYMBALO]

Cimmēr′ian a. & n. **1.** a. (Of darkness, night, etc.) thick, gloomy. **2.** n. member of nomadic people who overran Asia Minor in 7th c. BC. [f. L f. Gk Kimmerios (of Cimmerii, people fabled to dwell in perpetual night) +-AN]

C.-in-C. abbr. Commander-in-Chief.

cinch n., & v.t. **1.** n. saddle-girth used in Mexico etc., usu. of twisted horsehair; firm hold; (sl.) sure thing, a certainty, easy task. **2.** v.t. put cinch on; tighten as with cinch; secure grip on; (sl.) make certain of. [f. Sp. cincha]

cinchō′na (-ngk-) n. evergreen tree or shrub of genus Cinchona (orig. S. Amer.), with fragrant flowers, which yields cinchona bark and quinine; the bark, drug made from it containing quinine etc. and highly esteemed as tonic and febrifuge; hence **ci′nchon**INE⁵ (-ngk-) n. [mod. L, f. Countess of Chinchón d. 1641, introducer of drug into Spain]

ci′ncture n., & v.t. (surround with or a with) girdle, belt, or border; (Archit.) ring at end of column-shaft. [f. L cinctura (cingere cinct- gird; see -URE)]

ci′nder n. slag; residue of coal, wood, etc., that has ceased to flame (whether cold or not) but has still combustible matter in it (burnt to a ∼, made useless by burning); (in pl.) ashes; ∼-path, ∼-track, foot-path or running-track laid with fine cinders; hence ∼Y² a. [OE sinder, (= OHG sintar, ON sindr), w. assim. to the unconnected F cendre and L cinis ashes]

Cinderĕ′lla n. person or thing of unrecognized or disregarded merit or beauty; neglected or despised member of group. [character in fairy-tale]

ci′né a. cinematographic (cine-camera, film, projector); **ciné-vérité** = CINÉMA-vérité. [abbr.]

ci′néáste, -ăst, n. cinema enthusiast or devotee. [f. F cinéaste (as prec., ENTHUSIAST)]

ci′néma n. cinematography, moving pictures; production of these as an art or industry; theatre where these are shown; ∼-goer, one who frequents such showings; ∼ organ, (Mus.) kind with extra stops and effects; **cinéma-vérité** (-vĕ′rītă) [F], documentary films avoiding artificiality; hence **cinĕmă′t**IC a., relating to or having the qualities characteristic of the cinema. [f. F cinéma, abbr.; see foll.]

cinĕmă′tograph (-ahf) n. apparatus producing illusion of motion by rapid projection on a screen of many photographs taken successively on a long film; hence **cinĕmătō′**GRAPHER n., **cinĕmăto**GRA′PHIC a., **cinĕmătō′**GRAPHY n. [f. F cinématographe f. Gk kinēma -atos movement (kineō move); see -GRAPH]

ciner′ia n. bright-flowered composite plant, variety of Senecio cruentus. [mod. L, fem. of L cinerarius of ashes (cinis -eris ashes) f. ash-coloured down on leaves]

cinerâr′ium n. place where a cinerary urn is deposited. [LL, n. of cinerarius; see prec., -ARIUM]

ci′nerary a. of ashes; ∼ urn (holding ashes of dead after cremation). [f. L cinerarius (see CINERARIA, -ARY¹)]

cinēr′éous a. (Esp. of bird or plumage) ash-grey. [f. L cinereus (cinis -eris ashes) +-OUS]

Cingalē′se (-nggalē′z) a. & n. (arch.) Sinhalese. [f. F cing(h)alais f. as SINHALESE]

ci′ngul|um (-ngg-) n. (pl. ∼a). (Anat.) ridge round base of tooth-crown. [L, = belt]

ci′nnabâr n. red mercuric sulphide; vermilion; moth with reddish-marked wings. [ME, f. L cinnabaris f. Gk kinnabari, of Oriental orig.]

ci′nnamon n. SE Asian tree of genus Cinnamomum; its aromatic inner bark used as spice; ∼ bear, cinnamon-coloured phase of N. Amer. black bear; ∼-colour(ed), yellowish-brown; ∼ toast, buttered toast spread with ground cinnamon and sugar. [ME, f. OF cinnamome f. L f. Gk kinnamōmon, and L f. Gk kinnamon, f. Semitic (Heb. kinnamōn)]

cinque, cinq, (sĭngk) n. the five on dice. [ME, f. OF cinc, cink f. L quinque five]

cinquĕcĕ′nt|ō (chĭngkwĭchĕ′-) n. Italian style of art of the 16th c., with reversion to classical forms; hence ∼IST (2, 3) n. [It., = 500, used w. ref. to years 15—]

ci′nq(ue)foil (sĭ′ngkf-) n. plant of genus Potentilla, with compound leaf of five leaflets; (Archit.) five-cusped ornament in circle or arch. [ME, f. L quinquefolium (quinque five, folium leaf)]

Cinque Pôrts (sĭnk-) n. pl. group of ports (orig. five only) on SE coast of England with ancient privileges. [ME, f. OF cink porz, L quinque portus five ports]

Cinza′nō (chĭnzah′-) n. (pl. ∼s). (P) an Italian vermouth. [f. name of manufacturer]

***CIO** abbr. Congress of Industrial Organizations.

***ci′on** Var. of SCION 1.

ci′pher¹, cy′pher¹, n. **1.** arithmetical symbol (0) denoting no amount but used to occupy vacant place in decimal etc. numeration; person or thing of no importance; any Arabic numeral. **2.** secret or disguised writing, thing so written, key to it; interlaced initials of person, company, etc., monogram. **3.** continuous sounding of organ-pipe owing to mechanical defect. [ME, f. OF cif(f)re f. med. L cif(e)ra f. Arab. ṣifr (ZERO)]

ci′pher², cypher², v. **1.** v.i. (arch.) do arithmetic. **2.** v.t. work (usu. out) by arithmetic, calculate; put into secret writing, encipher. [f. prec.]

ci′polin n. Italian white-and-green marble. [F, or f. It. cipollino (cipolla onion)]

circa (ser′ka) prep. about (w. dates). [L]

circâ′dian a. (Physiol.) occurring or recurring about once per day. [irreg. f. L circa about + dies day +-AN]

Cîrcă′ssian a. & n. (member or language) of tribes of Circassia in N. Caucasus, whose women are noted for their beauty. [f. Circassia (f. Russ. cherkes) +-AN]

Cîrcē′an a. bewitching, dangerously attractive. [f. Circe, enchantress in Gk Myth. +-AN]

cĭr′cĭnate a. (Bot. & Zool.) rolled up with apex in centre. [f. L *circinatus* p.p. of *circinare* make round (*circinus* pair of compasses); see -ATE²]

circiter (sĕr′sĭter) *prep.* about (w. dates). [L]

cĭr′cle¹ n. **1.** (line enclosing) perfectly round plane figure whose circumference is everywhere equidistant from its centre (SQUARE² *the circle*; ANTARCTIC, ARCTIC, POLAR, *Circle*; **great, small,** ~, circle on surface of sphere whose plane passes, does not pass, through sphere's centre). **2.** roundish enclosure; ring; road, railway, etc., without ends, allowing traffic to circulate continuously, esp. (*C*~) London underground line; curved tier of rows of seats at theatre etc. (‖DRESS² *circle*); (Archaeol.) ring of stones; (Hockey) striking-circle; **go round in** ~s, make no progress despite effort; **run round in** ~s, (colloq.) be fussily busy with little result. **3.** period, cycle, (**come full** ~, return to starting-point). **4.** (**vicious**) ~, (1) fallacy of proving proposition from another that rests on it for proof, (2) unbroken sequence of reciprocal cause and effect, (3) action and reaction that intensify each other. **5.** persons grouped round centre of interest; set, coterie, class, (*circle in which* one *moves*; *not done in the best circles*). [ME f. OF *cercle* f. L *circulus* dim. of *circus* ring]

cĭr′cle² v. **1.** v.i. move in a circle (*round, about*); ~ **back,** move in wide loop towards starting-point. **2.** v.t. revolve round; form circle round. [ME, f. prec.]

cĭr′clet n. small circle; circular band, esp. of gold, jewelled, etc., worn on head or elsewhere. [f. CIRCLE¹ + -ET¹]

cĭrcs n. pl. (colloq.) circumstances. [abbr.]

cĭr′cuĭt (-kĭt) n. **1.** line enclosing an area, distance round; area enclosed; roundabout journey; motor--racing road. **2.** sequence of sporting events (*the American golf circuit*); sequence of athletic exercises; chain of theatres, cinemas, etc., under a single management; journey of judge in particular district to hold courts, this district, lawyers making the circuit; group of local Methodist churches forming a minor administrative unit. **3.** (Electr.) path of current (SHORT *circuit*); apparatus through which current passes; ~**-breaker,** device for interrupting circuit; CLOSED-*circuit*; hence ~RY n., circuits collectively, equipment forming circuit(s). [ME f. OF, f. L *circuitus* f. CIRCUM(*ire it-* go)]

circu′itous a. going a long way round, indirect; hence ~LY² adv., ~NESS n. [f. med. L *circuitosus* (*circuitus* CIRCUIT; see -OSE¹)]

cĭr′cular a. & n. **1.** a. having form of circle; taking place along circle; (Logic etc.) of or using a vicious circle; addressed to a circle of persons, customers, etc. **2.** ~ letter, letter, notice, advertisement, etc., of which many copies are made for distribution; ~ saw, toothed disc rotated by machinery for sawing; ‖~ tour, one which brings traveller back to starting--place. **3.** Hence **cĭr′culā′rity** n., ~LY² adv. **4.** n. notice or advertisement distributed as circular letter. [ME f. AF *circuler*, OF *circulier*, *cerclier* f. LL *circularis* (*circulus* CIRCLE¹; see -AR¹)]

cĭr′cularize, -ise (-īz), v.t. send circulars to. [f. prec. + -IZE]

cĭr′culāt|e v.i. & t. go round (*blood circulates through veins, water in pipes, wine on table, newspaper to readers*); cause to go round, give currency to, (book, report, scandal, etc.); circularize; ~**ing library** (with books taken by subscribers in succession); ~**ing medium,** notes, gold, etc., used in exchange; hence or cogn. ~IVE a., ~OR n. [f. L *circulare* (*circulus* CIRCLE¹) + -ATE³]

cĭrculā′tion n. movement of blood from and to heart; similar movement of sap etc.; movement to and fro (of water, atmosphere, currency, etc.; **in, out of,** ~, (fig.) participating, or not, in activities etc.); trans- mission, distribution, (of news, books, etc.); number of copies sold, esp. of newspapers; currency, coin, etc. [F, or f. L *circulatio* (*circulare*; see prec., -ATION)]

cĭrculātory̆ (-lā′-, sĕr′-) a. of circulation of blood or sap. [f. CIRCULATE + -ORY]

cĭrcum- *pref.* round, about, used (1) adverbially, as: **circumfu′se,** pour round or about; (2) preposi- tionally, as: **circumli′ttoral,** bordering the shore; **circumo′cular,** surrounding the eye. [f. or after L, f. *circum* prep. = round, about]

cĭrcumă′mbi|ent a. (Esp. of air or other fluid) surrounding; hence ~ENCY n. [f. CIRCUM- (1) + AMBIENT]

cĭrcumă′mbŭl|āte v.t. & i. walk round or about; hence ~A′TION n., ~atory a. [f. CIRCUM- (1) + *ambu- late* f. L *ambulare* walk + -ATE³]

cĭrcumbe′ndĭbus n. (joc.) roundabout method; cir- cumlocution. [f. CIRCUM- (1) + BEND² + -*ibus* ending of L abl. pl. case]

cĭr′cumcĭrcle n. (Geom.) circle passing through all vertices of triangle or polygon. [f. CIRCUM- (1) + CIRCLE¹]

cĭr′cumcīse (-z) v.t. cut off foreskin or clitoris of (as Jewish or Muslim rite, or surgically); (Bibl.) purify (heart etc.). [ME, f. OF *circonciser*, or *circoncis*- stem of *circoncire*, f. L CIRCUM(*cidere cis-* = *caedere* cut)]

cĭrcumcĭ′sion (-zhon) n. act or rite of circumcising; (Eccl.) feast of Circumcision of Christ, 1 Jan. [ME, f. OF *circoncision* f. LL *circumcisio -onis* (as prec.; see -ION)]

cĭrcŭ′mference n. enclosing boundary, esp. of circle or other figure enclosed by curve; distance round; so **circumfere′ntial** (-shal) a. [ME, f. OF *circonference* f. L CIRCUM(*ferentia* f. *ferre* bear; see -ENCE)]

cĭr′cumflĕx n. & a. **1.** ~ (**accent**), mark (^ or ˜) placed over vowel in some languages to indicate contraction, length, or special quality. **2.** a. (Anat.) curved, bending round something else, (*circumflex artery, nerve,* etc.). [f. L CIRCUM(*flexus* p.p. of *flectere* bend) transl. of Gk *perispōmenos* drawn around]

circŭ′mflu|ent (-lōō-) a. flowing round, surrounding; hence ~ENCE n. [f. L CIRCUM(*fluere* flow); see -ENT]

cĭrcumjā′cent a. situated around. [f. L CIRCUM- (*jacēre* lie); see -ENT]

cĭrcumlocū′tion n. use of many words where a few would do; evasive talk; a roundabout expression; hence ~AL, ~ARY¹, **cĭrcumlŏ′cŭtory,** adjs., ~IST (1) n. [ME f. F, or f. L CIRCUM(*locutio* LOCUTION) transl. of Gk PERIPHRASIS]

circŭmlu′nar (-lōō′-, -lū′-) a. moving or situated around the moon. [f. CIRCUM- (2) + LUNAR]

cĭrcumnă′vig|āte v.t. sail round (esp. the world) hence ~A′TION, ~ātor, ns. [f. L CIRCUM(*navigare* NAVIGATE)]

cĭrcumpō′lar a. (Astron., of star, motion, etc.) above horizon at all times in a given latitude; (Geog.) around or near one of the earth's poles. [f. CIRCUM- (2) + POLAR]

cĭr′cumscrībe v.t. draw line round; (Geom.) draw (figure) round another meeting it at points, but not cutting it (cf. INSCRIBE); lay down limits of, confine, restrict; hence **cĭrcumscrĭ′ption** n. [f. L CIRCUM- (*scribere script-* write)]

cĭrcumsō′lar a. moving or situated around or near the sun. [f. CIRCUM- (2) + SOLAR]

cĭr′cumspĕct a. cautious, wary, taking everything into account; so evasive; hence ~NESS, ns., ~LY² adv. [ME, f. L CIRCUM(*spicere spect-* = *specere* look)]

cĭr′cumstance n. **1.** (in pl.) time, place, manner, cause, occasion, surroundings, etc. that act or event external conditions affecting or that might affect action (in ~ or under the ~s, owing to or making allowance for them; in or under no ~s, not whatever happens, never); state of financial or material welfare (in REDUCED, STRAITENED, circum- stances). **2.** full detail in narrative; ceremony, fuss (*pomp and circumstance*); incident, occurrence, fact (esp. *the circumstance that*). **3.** Hence **cĭr′cumstanced²** (-st) part of stare stand); see -ANCE

For other words in circum- see CIRCUM-.

ĭrcumstă'ntial (-shăl) *a.* depending on circumstances (∼ **evidence,** evidence tending to establish a conclusion by inference from known facts otherwise hard to explain); adventitious, incidental; detailed (*circumstantial story*); hence **cĭrcumstăntiă'lĭTY** (-shĭ-) *n.,* ∼LY² *adv.* [f. L *circumstantia* (see prec.) +-AL]

ĭrcumterrĕ'strial *a.* moving or situated around the earth. [f. CIRCUM- (2) +TERRESTRIAL]

ĭrcumvă'llāte *v.t.* surround (as) with rampart. [f. L CIRCUM(*vallare* f. *vallum* rampart) +-ATE³]

ĭrcum|vĕ'nt *v.t.* entrap by surrounding; evade (difficulty etc.); outwit; occasionally ∼vĕ'ntION *n.* [f. L CIRCUM(*venire vent-* come)]

ĭrcumvolu'tion (-lōō'-) *n.* rotation; winding of one thing round another; sinuous movement. [ME, f. L CIRCUM(*volvere volut-* roll); see -ION]

ĭr'cus *n.* **1.** travelling show of horses, riders, acrobats, clowns, performing animals, etc.; (colloq.) disturbance, scene of lively action; (colloq.) group of persons performing in sports etc. together or in succession. **2.** (Hist.) rounded or oval arena lined with tiers of seats, for equestrian and other exhibitions. **3.** amphitheatre of hills; ‖open space in town, where streets converge (*Piccadilly Circus*). [L, = ring]

ĭré (sē'rā) *n.* & *a.* (fabric) with smooth polished surface, obtained esp. by waxing and heating. [F, = waxed]

ĭre perdue (sēr perdü') *n.* method of bronze-casting by filling space between core and mould after wax coating of core has been melted away. [F, = lost wax]

ĭrl *n.* ∼ **bunting,** brightly-coloured species of bunting (*Emberiza cirlus*). [f. It. *cirlo,* prob. f. *zirlare* to whistle like thrush]

ĭrque (-k) *n.* **1.** (Geog.) bowl-shaped hollow at head of valley or on mountain-side. **2.** (poet.) ring; arena, amphitheatre. [F, f. L CIRCUS]

ĭrrhō's|is (sĭrō'-) *n.* (*pl.* ∼es *pr.* -ēz). chronic disease of liver, esp. suffered by alcoholics. [mod. L, f. Gk *kirrhos* tawny; see -OSIS]

ĭ'rrĭpĕd, -ēde, *n.* marine crustacean in valved shell, immobile when adult; barnacle. [f. mod. L *Cirripedia* f. L *cirrus* curl (from form of legs) +*pes pedis* foot]

ĭ'rr|us *n.* (*pl.* ∼i *pr.* -ī). (Bot.) tendril; (Zool.) slender appendage, as beard of fish, foot of cirriped; (Meteorol.) form of cloud with diverging filaments like lock of hair or wool, whence ∼o- *comb. form;* hence ∼OSE¹, ∼OUS, *adjs.* [L, = curl]

ĭs- *pref.* on this side of, opp. TRANS- or ULTRA-, retaining in some (orig. L) wds the Roman sense (**ci'spadane, cisa'lpine,** S. or Rome-wards of Po, Alps), but usu. w. ref. to user's or majority's position (**cisatla'ntic,** on one's own side of the Atlantic; **cislu'nar,** between earth and moon; **cispo'ntine,** in London, on north orig. better-known side of bridges or Thames); also of time (**cis-Elizabe'than**); (Chem.) having two atoms or groups on same side of plane of symmetry. [L prep.]

ĭ'scō *n.* (*pl.* ∼es). N. Amer. white fish of genus *Leucichthys*. [19th c.; orig. unkn.]

ĭ'ssỹ. See SISSY.

ĭst¹ (s-, k-) *n.* (Archaeol.) prehistoric stone or hollowed-tree coffin or burial-chamber. [W, = CHEST]

ĭst² *n.* (Gk Ant.) box used for sacred utensils. [f. L f. Gk *kistē* box]

ĭstĕr'cian (-shan) *n.* & *a.* (monk or nun) of order founded 1098 as stricter offshoot of Benedictines. [f. F *cistercien,* f. L *Cistercium* Cîteaux near Dijon in France (where founded); see -IAN]

ĭ'stern *n.* reservoir for storing water, esp. one in roofspace supplying taps, or above water-closet; underground reservoir for rain-water. [ME, f. OF *cisterne* f. L *cisterna* (*cista;* see CIST²)]

ĭ'stus *n.* shrub of genus *Cistus,* with large white or red flowers. [mod. L, f. Gk *kistos*]

ĭ'tadel *n.* fortress, esp. one guarding or dominating

city; meeting-hall of Salvation Army. [f. F *citadelle* or f. It. *cittadella* dim. of obs. *cittade* f. L *civitas -tatis* CITY]

cĭtā'tion *n.* citing; mention in official dispatch; descriptive note accompanying announcement of award. [f. as foll. +-ATION]

cīte *v.t.* summon to appear in lawcourt; quote (passage, book, author) in support of a position; mention as example or in official dispatch. [ME, f. F *citer* f. L *citare* (*cière* set moving)]

ci'ther. Var. of foll.

ci'thern, ci'ttern, *n.* (Hist.) wire-stringed lutelike instrument usu. played with plectrum. [f. L *cithara,* Gk *kithara* kind of harp, w. assim. to GITTERN]

ci'tified (-īd) *a.* made city-like or urban in appearance or behaviour. [p.p. of *citify,* f. CITY + -FY]

ci'tizen *n.* inhabitant or freeman of city; townsman; *civilian; member, native or naturalized, of a State or Commonwealth (usu. *of*; ∼ **of the world,** one who is at home everywhere, cosmopolitan); inhabitant *of*; ∼**'s arrest** (by ordinary person without warrant, allowable in certain cases); ∼**s' band** (of radio frequencies for local communication by individuals); hence ∼HOOD, ∼RY (1), ∼SHIP, *ns.* [ME f. AF *citesein,* OF *citeain* f. Rom. **civitatanus* f. L *civitas -tatis* CITY; cf. DENIZEN]

cĭtrŏ'le *n.* small cithern. [ME f. OF, cogn. w. CITHERN +dim. suf.]

ci'tr|ic *a.* (Chem.) ∼**ic acid,** sharp-tasting acid in juice of lemons etc.; hence ∼ATE¹ (3) *n.* [f. F *citrique* f. L *citrus* citron; see -IC]

ci'trine *a.* & *n.* 1. *a.* lemon-coloured. 2. *n.* = *false* TOPAZ. [ME f. OF *citrin* f. LL **citrinus* (*citrus* citron; see -INE¹)]

ci'tron *n.* (tree, *Citrus medica,* bearing) fruit like lemon but larger, less acid, and thicker-skinned. [F, f. L CITRUS, after *limon* lemon]

citronĕ'lla *n.* fragrant S. Asian grass (*Cymbopogon nardus*); oil from it, used for keeping insects away. [mod. L, f. as prec. +dim. suf.]

ci'trous *a.* belonging to genus *Citrus* (see foll.). [f. foll. + -OUS]

ci'trus *n.* tree of genus *Citrus,* including citron, lime, orange, and grapefruit; ∼ (**fruit**), fruit from such a tree. [L, = citron-tree or thuja]

ci'ttern. See CITHERN.

ci'tỹ *n.* **1.** large town; ‖(strictly) town created city by charter, esp. as containing cathedral; *municipal corporation occupying a definite area; **Eternal C∼, C∼ of the Seven Hills,** Rome; **Heavenly C∼, C∼ of God,** Paradise; HOLY *City;* **the C∼,** part of London governed by Lord Mayor and Corporation, business part of this, commercial circles. **2.** (*attrib.*) of a city or the City; ‖**C∼ Company,** corporation representing ancient trade-guild; *∼ **desk,** newspaper department for local news; ‖**C∼ editor,** one who deals with financial news in a daily or weekly journal; *∼ **editor,** one who deals with local news; ∼ **fathers,** persons responsible for administration of a city, *∼ **hall,** municipal offices or officers; ∼ **manager,** official directing administration of a city; ‖∼ **page** (in newspaper, dealing with financial and business news); *city of* REFUGE; ∼**scape,** view of a city, city scenery; ∼ **slicker,** (1) plausible rogue as usu. found in cities, (2) smart and sophisticated city-dweller; ∼**-state,** (Hist.) city that is also an independent state. **3.** Hence ∼WARD(s) *a.* & *adv.* [ME, f. OF *cité* f. L *civitas -tatis* (*civis* citizen; see -TY¹)]

cityfied *a.* Var. of CITIFIED.

ci'vĕt *n.* ∼(-cat), carnivorous quadruped of family Viverridae, esp. *Civettictis civetta* of central Africa; strong musky perfume got from anal glands of this. [f. F *civette* f. It. *zibetto* f. med. L *zibethum* f. Arab. *azzabād* (*al* the, *zabād* this perfume)]

ci'vic *a.* of or proper to citizens (∼ **crown,** ancient-Roman garland of oak-leaves and acorns given to one who saved fellow citizen's life in war); of city, municipal, (∼ **centre,** area where municipal offices and other public buildings are situated); of citizenship, civil, (*civic virtues*); hence **cǐ′vic**ALLY *adv.*, **cǐ′vics** *n.*, study of rights and duties of citizenship. [f. F *civique* or f. L *civicus* (*civis* citizen; see -IC)] **civies.** See CIVVIES. **cǐ′vil** (-ĭl, -ǐl) *a.* **1.** of or proper to citizens. **2.** polite, obliging, not rude. **3.** not naval, military, etc. **4.** not ecclesiastical. **5.** (Law). not criminal or political; pertaining to civil law. **6.** (Of time measurement) fixed by custom or enactment, not natural or astronomical. **7.** ~ aviation (not military etc., and esp. commercial); ~ **commotion,** riot or similar disturbance; ~ **day** (as used for time reckoning in ordinary affairs); ~ **defence,** organization of civilians for dealing esp. with air raids; ~ **disobedience,** refusal to obey laws, pay taxes, etc., as part of political campaign; *civil* ENGINEER[1], so ~ **engineering;** ~ **law,** law concerning private rights only, (Hist.) Roman or non-ecclesiastical law; *civil* LIBERTY; ‖~ **list,** annual allowance by Parliament for sovereign's household expenses; ~ **marriage** (solemnized as civil contract without religious ceremony); ~ **rights,** rights of each citizen, *esp. of Negroes, to liberty, equality, etc.; C~ **Service,** all non-military branches of State administration, whence ~ **servant;** ~ **state** (being single, married, divorced, etc.); ~ **war** (between citizens of same country, esp. in England (17th c.), US (1861–65), or Spain (1936–39)); *civil* YEAR. **8.** Hence ~LY[2] *adv.* [ME f. OF, f. L *civilis* (*civis* citizen; see -IL)] **cǐvǐ′lian** (-yan) *n.* & *a.* (person) not in or of navy or army or air force or police; hence ~IZE (3) *v.t.*, convert (Service post) into a civilian one, ~ĭzA′TION *n.* [f. prec. +-IAN] **cǐvǐ′lǐtў** *n.* politeness; (in *pl.*) acts of politeness. [ME, f. OF *civilité* f. L *civilitas* -*tatis* (as CIVIL; see -ITY)] **cǐvǐlǐzā′tion,** -ǐs- (-ǐz-), *n.* making or becoming civilized; state reached in this process; stage, esp. advanced stage, in social development; civilized States. [f. foll. +-ATION] **cǐ′vǐlīz‖e,** -ǐs‖e (-ǐz), *v.t.* bring out of barbarism, enlighten; refine and educate; hence ~ABLE *a.*, ~ER[1] *n.* [f. F *civiliser* (CIVIL; see -IZE (3))] **cǐ′v(v)ǐes** (-vǐz) *n. pl.* (sl.) civilian clothes. [abbr.] ‖**Cǐ′vvў Street** *n.* (sl.) civilian life. [abbr.] **CJ** *abbr.* Chief Justice. **cl.** *abbr.* centilitre(s); class. **Cl** *symb.* chlorine. **clǎck** *n.* & *v.i.* **1.** *n.* sharp sound as of clogs on stone or of boards struck together; flap-valve in pumps etc.; noise of continual talking. **2.** *v.i.* chatter loudly; make clack, clatter. [ME, = to chatter, prate, prob. f. ON *klaka* chatter, twitter, of imit. orig.] **clǎd**[1]. See CLOTHE and IRON[1]*clad*. **clǎd**[2] *v.t.* (-dd-). provide with cladding. [app. f. prec.] **clǎ′dding** *n.* coating or covering on structure, material, etc. [f. prec. +-ING[1]] **clāde** *n.* (Biol.) group of organisms evolved from a common ancestor. [f. Gk *klados* branch] **clā′dōde** *n.* (Bot.) flattened leaflike stem. [f. Gk *kladōdēs* many-shooted (*klados* shoot)] **claim**[1] *v.t.* demand as one's due or property (recognition etc., *to be, that* one should be, recognized etc.); have as achievement or consequence (*the fire claimed many victims*); represent oneself as having (*claim the victory, accuracy*); profess *to* (*be* the owner, *have* told the truth); demand recognition of the fact *that*; contend, assert; (fig.) deserve (esp. *attention*); hence ~ABLE *a.*, ~ANT *n.* [ME, f. OF *claim*- stressed st. of *clamer* f. L *clamare* call out] **claim**[2] *n.* demand for something as due (*lay claim to*); = PAY[1]-*claim*; right, title, *to* thing; right to make demand *on* person; statement of novel features in patent; contention, assertion; (Mining etc.) piece of land allotted or taken; **stake** (**out**) **a** ~, (fig.) make statement of one's rights; *~-**jumper,** one who appropriates a mining claim already taken by another. [ME, f. OF *claime* (*clamer*; see prec.)]

clairau′dǐ‖ence *n.* faculty of perceiving, as if b⟨ hearing, what is inaudible; so ~ENT *a.* & *n.* [f. F *clai⟩ CLEAR+AUDIENCE, after foll.] **clairvoy′ance** *n.* faculty of perceiving, as if by seeing what is happening or exists out of sight; exceptiona insight. [F, f. *clairvoyant* (*clair* clear, *voyant* part. of *voi⟩ see); cf. -ANCE, -ANT] **clairvoy′ant** *n.* (occas. *fem.* ~e) & *a.* (person) havin⟨ clairvoyance. [F, = clear-sighted; see prec.] **clǎm** *n.*, & *v.i.* (-mm-). **1.** *n.* bivalve mollusc, esp. th N. Amer. hard or round clam (*Mercenaria mercenaria* and soft or long clam (*Mya arenaria*), used for foo⟨ (sl.) taciturn person; *~′bake, social gathering fo⟩ eating (esp. clams and fish) outdoors. **2.** *v.i.* dig fo⟩ clams; *~ **up,** (sl.) become silent, cease talking. [16t⟩ c., app. f. *clam* a clamp] **clā′mant** *a.* (literary). noisy, insistent; urgent; henc ~LY[2] *adv.* [f. L *clamare* cry out; see -ANT] **clǎ′mber** *v.i.*, & *n.* climb with hands and feet; clim⟩ with difficulty or labour. [ME, prob. f. *clamb* (obs past tense of CLIMB) +-ER[5]] **clǎ′mm‖ў** *a.* moist, usu. cold, and sticky or slimy; (⟨ weather) cold and damp; hence ~ĭLY[2] *adv.*, ~ĭNESS ⟨ [ME, f. *clam* to daub+-Y[2]] ‖**clǎ′mour** (-mer), *clǎ′mor, *n.*, & *v.i.* & ⟨ shout(ing); (make) loud appeal, complaint, or d⟨ mand (*for, against, to* do); (make) confused noise; ⟨ clǎ′morous *a.* [ME, f. OF *clamour* f. L *clamor* -or⟨ (*clamare* call out)] **clǎmp**[1] *n.* & *v.* **1.** *n.* brace, clasp, or band, usu. of iron for strengthening other materials or holding thing together; appliance or tool with screw connection c parts for holding or compressing. **2.** *v.t.* strengthen o fasten (as) with clamp(s); place or hold firmly. **3.** *v* ~ **down on,** become stricter regarding, put a sto to; hence ~-**down** *n.* [ME, prob. f. MDu., ML⟨ *klamp(e)*, f. *klamp-, *klam- press together] **clǎmp**[2] *n.* pile (of bricks for burning, ‖potatoes et⟨ under straw and earth, turf, peat, garden rubbisł etc.). [16th c., prob. f. Du. *klamp* heap, rel. to CLUMP -making, rel. to CLUMP] **clǎn** *n.* group of (esp. Highland) Scots with commo ancestor, esp. while under patriarchal contro (~′sman, member, fellow member, of clan); trib⟨ family holding together, whence ~′nish[1] *a.*; part⟩ coterie; genus, species, class; hence ~′ship *a.* clan system or behaviour. [ME, f. Gael. *clann* f. L *plan⟩* sprout] **clǎndě′stǐne** *a.* surreptitious, secret; hence **clǎndě⟩ tǐ′nǐty** *n.*, ~LY[2] (-nlǐ) *adv.* [f. F *clandestin* or f. ⟨ *clandestinus* (*clam* secretly)] **clǎng** *n.* & *v.* **1.** *n.* loud resonant metallic sound (esp. ⟨ trumpet, armour, large bell, some birds). **2.** *v.i.* ⟨ make, cause (thing) to make, clang; hence ~′ER *n.* ⟨ (esp., sl.) blunder (*drop a* ~er, make this). [imit., b⟨ infl. by L *clangere* resound, *clangor* (of trumpe⟨ birds)] ‖**clǎ′ngour,** *clǎ′ngor, (-ngger) *n.* succession ⟨ prevalence of clanging noises; hence **clǎ′ngoro**⟨ (-ngg-) *a.* [f. L *clangor* (see prec., -OR)] **clǎnk** *n.* & *v.* **1.** *n.* sound as of heavy pieces of met⟨ meeting or chain rattling. **2.** *v.i.* & *t.* make, caus⟨ (bucket, chain, etc.) to make, clank. [imit.; cf. CLAN⟨ CLINK, Du. *klank*] **clannish, clanship, clansman.** See CLAN. **clǎp**[1] *n.* explosive noise (of thunder, of hand-palm⟨ against each other, whence slap to applause); slap, pat (*gave him a cl⟩ on the shoulder.* -ANCE], -ANT, f. foll.] **clǎp**[2] *n.* (-pp-). **1.** *v.i.* & *t.* ~ (one's **hands**), sho⟨ approval (of) by striking palms together loudly, (us⟨ w. *hands*) strike them for warmth, as in delig⟨ etc.; flap (wings) audibly; ~ (= SLAP) **on the bacl** **2.** *v.t.* put or place quickly or energetically (perso⟨ *in(to)* prison, duty on goods; *clap on all sail*); ~ped ou⟨ (sl.) exhausted, worn out; ~ **eyes on,** (colloq.) cat⟨ sight of (esp. w. neg.); ~-**net,** fowler's or ent⟨ mologist's net shut by pulling string. [OE *clappi⟨*

throb, beat, = OHG *klapfōn*, ON *klappa*; OE *clæppan*, OHG *klepfen*, of imit. orig.]

lăp³ *n*. (vulg.) venereal disease, esp. gonorrhoea. [f. OF *clapoir* venereal bubo]

clă'pboard (klă'pbōrd, klă'berd) *n*. = WEATHER--*board*. [Anglicized f. LG *klappholt* cask-stave]

:lă'pham (-pam) *n*. **the man on the ~ omnibus,** the average man. [~ in SW London]

lă'pper *n*. In vbl senses; tongue or striker of bell; ~(-**board**), (Cinemat.) device making sharp noise for synchronization of picture and sound; **like the ~s,** (sl.) very fast or very hard. [f. CLAP² + -ER¹]

lă'ptrăp *n*. language used or sentiments expressed only to gain applause; pretentious but empty assertions; nonsense. [f. CLAP¹ + TRAP¹]

laque (-ahk, -ăk) *n*. hired body of applauders; so **claqueur** (klahkēr') *n*., member of claque. [F (*claquer* to clap)]

larabĕlla (-ă'r-, -ar̄'-) *n*. organ stop of flute quality. [f. fem. forms of L *clarus* clear, *bellus* pretty]

lă'rence *n*. (Hist.) four-wheeled closed carriage with seats for four inside and two on box. [f. Duke of C~, afterwards William IV]

Clă'renceux (-sū) *n*. second KING¹ of Arms, with jurisdiction south of the Trent. [ME f. AF, f. Duke of *Clarence* (*Clare* in Suffolk)]

lă'ret *n*. & *a*. red wine from Bordeaux (or elsewhere); (sl.) blood (**tap** person's ~, make his nose bleed with blow of fist); ~-**colour(ed)**, reddish-violet [ME, f. OF (*vin*) *claret* (orig. of light red wines) f. *claré* clarified f. med. L *claratum* (*vinum*) (*clarare* f. L *clarus* clear)]

lă'rĭfy *v*. **1.** *v.t.* make clear (difficult subject, obscure statement, mind, sight); free from impurities, make transparent, (butter, liquid, air, etc.). **2.** *v.i.* become transparent; be made clear or pure (lit., or fig. of literary style etc.). **3.** Hence **clărĭfĭcā'tĬon** *n*. [ME, f. OF *clarifier* f. LL *clarificare* f. L *clarus* clear; see -FY]

lărĭnĕ't *n*. wood-wind instrument with single-reed mouthpiece, holes, and keys, whence **clărĭnĕ'ttĬst** (3), *-ĕ'tĬst, n.*; its player; organ stop of like quality. [f. F *clarinette* dim. of *clarine* kind of bell]

lă'rĭon *n*. & *a*. **1.** *n*. (Hist.) shrill narrow-tubed war trumpet; rousing sound; organ stop of clarion quality. **2.** *a*. clear and loud. [ME, f. med. L *clario -onis* f. L *clarus* clear]

lărĭonĕ't. Var. of CLARINET.

lă'rĭtў *n*. clearness (esp. fig.). [ME, f. L *claritas* (*clarus* clear; see -ITY)]

lar̄'kĭa *n*. annual plant of genus *Clarkia*, with showy white, pink, or purple flowers. [mod. L, f. W. *Clark*, US explorer d. 1838 + -IA¹]

lar̄'ў *n*. aromatic herb of genus *Salvia*. [ME, f. obs. F *clarie* repr. med. L *sclarea*]

lăsh *v.i.* & *t.*, & *n*. (make, cause to make) loud jarring sound as of collision, striking weapons, cymbals, bells rung together; meet(ing) with force, conflict; disagree(ment), be(ing) at variance or incompatible with, (of colours) be(ing) discordant. [imit.; cf. *clack, clang, crack, crash*]

:asp¹ (-ah-) *n*. contrivance of interlocking parts for fastening, buckle, brooch; metal fastening of book-cover; embrace, reach; grasp, handshake; bar of silver on medal-ribbon with name of battle etc. (in campaign commemorated by medal) at which wearer was present; ~-**knife** (folding, usu. with catch fixing blade when open). [ME; etym. unkn.]

:asp² (-ah-) *v*. **1.** *v.t.* & *i*. fasten (clasp); fasten with or as clasp. **2.** *v.t.* encircle, hold closely, embrace; grasp another's hand; ~ **hands,** shake hands with fervour or affection; ~ one's **hands,** interlace fingers). **3.** Hence ~-**ER**¹ *n*., (esp., in *pl.*) appendages of some male fish and insects to hold female in copulation. [f. prec.]

:ass (-ahs) *n.*, & *v.t.* **1.** *n*. rank or order of society (*upper, middle, lower, working, class* or *classes*); ~-**conscious(ness)**, esp. realizing and usu. taking part in the conflict or ~ **war** between one's own and other

classes); (in *pl.*, arch.) *the* rich or educated; caste system; hence ~'LESS *a.*, making no distinction of classes. **2.** set of students taught together, their time of meeting, their course of instruction, *all college or school students of same standing (~ **of** 1970, those graduating then); ~-**fellow, -mate,** present or past member of same class as oneself; ~-**room** (where class is taught). **3.** (In conscripted armies) all the recruits of a year (*the* 1960 *class*). **4.** ||division of candidates by merit in examination; **take a ~,** gain honours; ~-**list** (issued by examiners). **5.** division according to quality (FIRST, SECOND, etc., *class*); **in a** ~ **of** (or **on**) **its** (or one's) **own,** unqualled; **no ~,** (colloq.) quite inferior. **6.** group of persons or things having some characteristic in common. **7.** (Biol.) group of animals or plants usu. next below phylum or division. **8.** distinction, high quality, (also *attrib.*). **9.** *v.t.* place in a class; hence ~'ABLE *a.* [f. L *classis* assembly]

clă'ssĭcal *a.* & *n.* **1.** *a.* of the first class, of acknowledged excellence; remarkably typical, outstandingly important, (*a classic case*). **2.** of the ancient Latin and Greek standard authors, art, or culture; of Roman and Greek antiquity. **3.** (Of style) simple, harmonious, well-proportioned, and finished, in accordance with established forms (cf. ROMANTIC); having literary or historic associations (*classic ground*); (of clothes) made in simple style not much affected by changes of fashion; ||~ **races,** Two and One Thousand Guineas, Derby, Oaks, St. Leger. **4.** *n.* writer, artist, work, example, of acknowledged excellence or value; ancient Latin or Greek writer; (arch.) Latin and Greek scholar; follower of classic models (cf. ROMANTIC); garment in classic style; (in *pl.*) classical studies, ||classic races. [f. F *classique* or f. L *classicus* (*classis* class; see -IC)]

clă'ssĭcal *a.* **1.** standard or first-class, esp. in literature, **2.** of ancient Latin or Greek standard authors or art; learned in these; based on these (*classical education*); (of language) having form used by ancient standard authors (*classical LATIN, Hebrew*). **3.** in or following the restrained style of classical antiquity (as prec.; cf. ROMANTIC); pertaining to a long-established style etc.; (of music) serious or conventional, opp. *romantic*, or *folk, modern, popular*, etc.; (Phys.) relating to concepts preceding relativity, quantum theory, etc. **4.** Hence ~-ISM (3), ~-ITY (-ă'l-), *ns.*, ~-LY² *adv.* [f. L *classicus* (see prec.) + -AL]

clă'ssĭcˌism *n.* following of classic style; classical scholarship; advocacy of classical education; Latin or Greek idiom; hence ~-IST (2, 3) *n.* [f. CLASSIC + -ISM]

clă'ssĭcĭze, -ise (-īz), *v.* **1.** *v.t.* make classic. **2.** *v.i.* imitate the classical style. [f. CLASSIC + -IZE (2, 3)]

clă'ssĬˌfў *v.t.* arrange in classes; assign to a class; designate as officially secret or not for general disclosure; hence or cogn. ~fīABLE, ~fĬcāTORY, *adjs.*, ~fĬcā'TĬON, ~fīER¹, *ns.* [back-form. f. *classification* f. F (as CLASS)]

clă'ssў (-ah'-) *a.* (sl.) superior; stylish. [f. CLASS + -Y²]

clă'stĬc *a.* (Geol.) composed of broken pieces of older rocks; ~ **rocks,** conglomerates etc. [f. F *clastique* f. Gk *klastos* broken in pieces; see -IC]

clă'thrāte *n.* (Chem.) compound in which one component is enclosed in structure of another. [f. L *clathratus* f. *clathri* f. Gk *klēthra* lattice-bars; see -ATE¹]

clă'tter *v.* & *n.* **1.** *v.i.* & *n.* (make) rattling sound as of many plates or wooden objects struck together; (resound with) noisy talk; move, fall, etc., with clatter. **2.** *v.t.* cause (plates etc.) to clatter. [OE *clatrian*, of imit. orig.]

claudĭcā'tĬon *n.* (Med.) limping. [f. L *claudicare* limp (*claudus* lame); see -ATION]

claus|e (-z) *n.* (Gram.) distinct part of a sentence including a subject and predicate; single statement in treaty, law, bill, or contract; hence ~'AL *a.* [ME f. OF, f. L *clausula* conclusion (*claudere claus-* shut; see -ULE)]

clau′stral *a.* of the cloister, monastic; narrow-minded. [ME, f. LL *claustralis* (*claustrum* CLOISTER; see -AL)]

claustrophō′b|ia *n.* (Psych.) morbid dread of confined places; hence ∼IC *a.*, suffering from or inducing claustrophobia. [mod. L, f. L *claustrum* (see CLOISTER) + -O- + -PHOBIA]

clā′vāte *a.* (Bot.) club-shaped. [f. mod. L *clavatus* f. L *clava* club; see -ATE²]

clave¹ (-āv, -ahv) *n.* (Mus.) one of two hardwood sticks used to make a hollow sound. [Amer. Sp. f. Sp., = keystone f. L *clavis* key]

clāve². See CLEAVE².

clǎvice′mbalō (-chĕ′-) *n.* (*pl.* ∼s). (Mus.) harpsichord. [It.]

clǎ′vichŏrd (-k-) *n.* (Hist.) predecessor of piano, first stringed instrument with keyboard. [ME, f. med. L *clavichordium* (L *clavis* key, *chorda* string, CHORD¹)]

clǎ′vicle *n.* collar-bone; so **clavi′cūlAR¹** *a.* [f. L *clavicula* dim. of *clavis* key; from its shape]

clā′vier *n.* (Mus.) (instrument with) keyboard. [F, or f. G *klavier* f. med. L *claviarius*, orig. = key-bearer, f. L *clavis* key; see -ER²]

clǎ′vifŏrm *a.* club-shaped. [f. L *clava* club + -I- + -FORM]

claw¹ *n.* pointed horny nail of animal's or bird's foot; foot so armed; pincers of shellfish; contrivance for grappling, holding, etc.; ∼-and-ball, (of furniture) having feet which represent claw holding ball; ∼-hammer (with bent split end for extracting nails); hence (-)∼ED² (-awd) *a.* [OE *clawu* f. obl. cases of *clēa*, = OS *clāuua*, OHG *klāwa* f. WG **klāwa*]

claw² *v.t. & i.* scratch, tear, seize, or pull towards one, with claws or hands; (Naut.) beat to windward; (Sc.) scratch gently (∼ **me and I′ll** ∼ **thee**, of mutual aid or flattery); ∼ **back**, regain gradually or laboriously, take back (allowance by added taxation etc.), whence ∼-BACK *n.* [OE *clawian* (as prec.)]

clay *n.* stiff tenacious earth, material of bricks, pottery, etc. (*feet of clay*, see FOOT¹; *clay* PIGEON¹); (material of) human body; ∼ (**pipe**), tobacco-pipe made of clay; ∼-**pan,** (Austral.) natural hollow in clay soil retaining water after rain; hence ∼′ey² *a.* [OE *clǣg*, = (M)Du., (M)LG *klei*, f. WG **klaija* (**klai-* etc., cogn. w. CLEAVE²)]

clay′mŏre *n.* (Hist.) Scottish two-edged broadsword; basket-hilted often single-edged broad sword; *type of anti-personnel mine. [f. Gael. *claidheamh mór* great sword]

-cle. See -CULE.

clean¹ *a.* **1.** free from or *of* dirt or contaminating matter, unsoiled; clear, not or no longer having what is regarded as making defective or destroying original state; ∼ **air** (unpolluted); *clean* BILL⁴ *of* health; *clean* BREAST¹; ∼ **fingers,** (fig.) absence of corruption or bribery; ∼ **hands,** (fig.) absence of guilt; **show a** ∼ **pair of heels,** escape by speed; ∼ **sheet** or **slate,** (Austral.) unbranded animal, (sl.) person without police record; **come** ∼, (colloq.) own up, confess everything. **2.** free from ceremonial defilement or from disease; (of food) not prohibited. **3.** (colloq., of nuclear weapon) causing relatively little fall-out. **4.** cleanly; (of children and animals) trained to defecate in proper place. **5.** well-formed, slender and shapely, (of joints, figure; so ∼-**limbed**; (of ship or aircraft) smooth, streamlined. **6.** smart, adroit, not bungling (*clean fielding*). **7.** even, unobstructed, clear-cut, complete; ∼ **break** (quick and final); **make a** ∼ **job of,** (colloq.) do thoroughly; *clean* SWEEP²; ∼ **timber** (without knots). **8.** (colloq.) free from impropriety. **9.** Hence ∼′NESS (-n-n-) *n.* [OE *clǣne*, = OS *klēni*, OHG *kleini* f. WG **klaini*]

clean² *adv.* completely, outright, simply, (*clean bowled*; *cut clean through*; *clean wrong*); in a clean manner (∼-**cut,** sharply outlined; ∼-**living,** of upright character: ∼-**shaven,** without beard or whiskers or moustache). [OE *clǣne*, *clēne* (as prec.)]

clean³ *v. & n.* **1.** *v.t. & i.* make or become clean (*of* dir etc.); eat all the food on (one's plate); (Cookery remove innards of (fish, fowl); make one*self*, mak oneself, clean. **2.** ∼ **down,** clean by brushing o wiping; ∼ **out,** empty, strip, (esp. sl., person of hi money); ∼ **up,** make (oneself) clean, put things tidy put (things) tidy, clear (mess) away, (colloq.) acquir as, or make, gain or profit, (fig.) deal with disorde immorality, crime, etc., in (place), whence ∼-**up** *n.* 3 Hence ∼′ER¹ (1, 2) *n.*, (esp.) person who cleans room or clothes; **take to the** ∼**ers,** (sl.) (1) rob or defrau (person) of all his money, (2) criticize strongly an adversely. **4.** *n.* cleaning (*give it a clean*). [f. CLEAN¹]

clea′nly¹ *adv.* in clean way. [OE *clǣnlīce* (as CLEAN¹ -LY²)]

clea′nl|y̆² (-ĕ′n-) *a.* habitually clean; attentive t cleanliness; hence ∼iLY² *adv.*, ∼iNESS *n.* [OE *clǣnl* (as CLEAN¹, -LY¹)]

cleans|e (-ĕnz) *v.t.* purify (*of* sin etc.); (usu. formal o arch.) make clean; (Bibl.) cure (leper etc.); ∼**in** cream, tissue, (for removing unwanted matte from face, hands, etc.); ∼**ing department,** loca service of refuse collection etc.; hence ∼′ER¹ (1, 2) *n* [OE *clǣnsian* (*clǣne* CLEAN¹)]

clear¹ *a. & adv.* **1.** *a.* unclouded, transparent, n turbid, lustrous, unblemished; *clear* CONSCIENCE; ∼ fire (with little smoke); *clear* SKY; ∼ **soup** (con taining little solid matter); *clear*-**starch,** stiffen wit colourless starch. **2.** distinct, easily perceive unambiguous, intelligible, (*make* thing *clear*; *mak* one*self clear*); not confused or doubtful, manifest; ∼, not in cipher or code. **3.** discerning, penetrating (so ∼-**eyed,** ∼-**headed,** ∼-**sighted,** ∼-**sighted ness,** usu. fig.; *clear thinking*); confident, decide certain, (*on* or *about* point, *of* fact, *that*). **4.** withou deduction, net; free *of* (**in the** ∼, free of suspicion o difficulty); complete (*three clear days*). **5.** open, unob structed, (∼ **of,** not obstructed by; **the coast is** ∼ there is no chance of being hindered or observed ||∼′**way,** road on which vehicles must not stop unengaged, free, unencumbered by debt. **6.** Henc ∼′LY² *adv.*, ∼′NESS *n,* **7.** *adv.* clearly (*speak loud an clear*; ∼-**cut,** well defined); quite (*clear away, through three feet clear*); *all the way *to*; apart, without contac (*keep, hang,* STEER¹, *get, clear; stand clear of the doors* [ME f. OF *cler* f. L *clarus*]

clear² *v.t. & i.* **1.** make or become clear (*of;* ∼ **the ai** lit. of sultriness, fig. of suspicion, tension, etc.; ∼ one throat, by slight coughing; *clear the* WAY 4). **2.** sho or declare to be innocent (*of*); declare (person) fit t have secret information etc.; free from or *of* prohibi tion or obstruction (∼ **the decks** (**for action**), mak ready to fight, lit. or fig.; ∼ **land,** cut down trees etc before cultivating or building; ∼ **room** etc., caus persons to leave it); remove (obstruction, unwante object, etc.; esp. *clear out of the way*); ∼ (**off),** discharg (debt); pass (cheque) through clearing-house; mak or become empty or unobstructed (∼ (**away),** up, (o mist, symptoms, etc.) disappear. **3.** pass over or b without touching (esp. by jumping); pass throug (customs office etc.). **4.** make (sum) as net gain or t balance expenses. **5.** ∼ **away,** remove, remov remains of meal from table; ∼ **off,** get rid of, go away ∼ **out,** empty, make off; ∼ **up,** solve (mystery), mak tidy, (of weather etc.) grow clear; ∼ **thing with,** ge approval or authorization of it from (person). [ME prec.]

clear′ance *n.* **1.** making clear; removal of obstruc tions, old buildings, etc.; removal of persons o objects so as to clear land. **2.** clearing of cheque (certificate of) clearing of ship at customs; permissio (esp. for aircraft to land or take off, or for person t have secret information etc.); clear space allowe for the passing of two objects or parts. **3.** ∼ **order** (for demolition of buildings); ||∼ **sal** (to effect clearance of superfluous stock). [f prec. + -ANCE]

clear'côle *n.*, & *v.t.* (paint with) size and whiting or white lead as first coat in house-painting. [f. F *claire colle* clear glue]

clear'ing *n.* In vbl senses; piece of land in forest cleared for cultivation; ~ **bank,** member of clearing--house; ~-**house,** bankers' institution where cheques and bills are exchanged, so that only the balances need be paid in cash, (fig.) agency for collecting and distributing information etc. [ME, f. CLEAR² + -ING¹]

*****clear'story.** Var. of CLERESTORY.

‖leat *n.* wedge; projecting piece bolted on spar, gangway, boot, etc., to give footing or prevent rope from slipping; piece of wood or iron bolted on for securing ropes to, or to strengthen woodwork etc. [OE *clēat, = OHG klōz lump f. WG *klaut-; cf. CLOT]

lea'vage *n.* way in which mineral, party, opinion, etc., tends to split; (colloq.) hollow between woman's breasts, esp. as exposed by low-cut garment. [f. foll. + -AGE]

leave¹ *v.t.* & *i.* (clove *pr.* klōv *or* cleft *pr.* klĕft *or* cleaved; clo'ven *or* cleft *or* cleaved). 1. (literary). split; chop, break, or come, apart, esp. along grain or line of cleavage; make way through (water, air). 2. break apart (esp. of mineral); **cleft palate,** congenital fissure in roof of mouth; **in a cleft stick,** in tight place allowing neither retreat nor advance (also fig.); **cloven foot** or **hoof** (of ruminant quadrupeds, of god Pan, and so of Devil; *show the cloven hoof,* reveal one's evil nature). 3. Hence **clea'vable** *a.* [OE *clēofan, = OS klioban, OHG kliuban, ON kljúfa f. Gmc *kleubhan]

leave² *v.i.* (*past also* **clave** *pr.* klāv). (arch.) stick fast, adhere, *to.* [OE *cleofian, clifian, = OS klibon, OHG klebēn f. WG *klibhōjan (*klibh-; cf. CLAY)]

lea'ver *n.* In vbl senses; butcher's chopping-tool for carcasses. [f. CLEAVE¹ + -ER¹]

lea'vers, cli'vers, (-z) *n.* (as *sing.* or *pl.*) goose-grass, creeper with prickly stem sticking to clothes etc. [OE *clīfe, = OS, OHG klība f. as CLEAVE²]

lêf *n.* (Mus.) one of the several symbols (ALTO, BASS³ or F, SOPRANO, TENOR, TREBLE or C, *clef*) indicating pitch of staff. [F, f. L *clavis* key]

lêft¹ *n.* space or division made by cleaving; fissure, split. [OE *clyft (OHG, ON kluft), cogn. w. CLEAVE¹; assim. to foll.]

lêft². See CLEAVE¹.

clĕg *n.* gadfly; horse-fly. [15th c., f. ON kleggi]

‖eistogã'mic (klī-) *a.* (Bot., of flower) permanently closed and self-fertilizing. [f. Gk kleistos closed + gamos marriage]

lematis (klĕ'ma-, klemā'-) *n.* climbing or erect plant of genus Clematis, e.g. *C. vitalba* (traveller's joy or old man's beard). [L, f. Gk klēmatis (klema vine branch)]

lê'm|ent *a.* (Of temper or weather) mild; showing mercy; so ~ENCY *n.* [ME, f. L clemens -entis; see -ENT]

lê'mentine (-īn, -ēn) *n.* kind of small orange, hybrid of tangerine and sour orange. [f. F clémentine]

lênch *v.t.*, & *n.* 1. *v.t.* secure (nail, rivet) by driving point sideways when through. 2. close (teeth, fingers) tightly; grasp firmly. 3. *n.* any of the above actions or the resulting state. [OE *clencan, = OHG klenken f. Gmc *klankjan (*klank- etc.; cf. CLING)]

lĕpsȳdra (-ĕ'p-, -sī'-) *n.* ancient time-measuring device worked by flow of water. [L, f. Gk klepsudra (klepto steal, hudōr water)]

lĕr'estory (-ĕr's-) *n.* part of wall of cathedral or large church, with series of windows, above aisle roofs; *raised section of railway-carriage roof with windows or ventilators. [ME, f. CLEAR¹ + STOREY]

lĕr'gy *n.* (usu. treated as *pl.*) the body of all persons ordained for religious duties; clergymen (30 clergy were present); BENEFIT¹ of clergy; ~**man,** ordained minister, |esp. of Established Church (clergyman's sore THROAT). [ME, partly f. OF clergé f. eccl. L clericatus, partly f. OF clergie (clerc CLERK, -ie = -Y¹)]

lĕ'ric *n.* clergyman. [orig. a. f. eccl. L f. Gk klērikos (klēros lot, heritage, as in Acts 1: 17)]

lĕ'rical *a.* of clergy, clergyman, or clergymen

(~ **collar,** upright white collar fastening at back); of or made by clerk(s) (~ **error,** made in copying or writing out); hence ~ISM (3), ~IST (2), *ns.*, ~IZE (3) *v.t.*, ~ITY (-ă'l-) *n.*, ~LY² *adv.* [f. eccl. L clericalis (as prec.; see -AL)]

clĕ'rihew *n.* short witty, comic, or nonsensical verse, usu. in two rhyming couplets with lines of unequal length. [f. E. Clerihew Bentley, Engl. writer d. 1956, its inventor]

clĕ'risȳ *n.* (arch.) learned or literary persons as a class. [app. after G klerisei, ult. f. as CLERIC]

clerk (klärk) *n.*, & *v.i.* 1. *n.* (arch. or Law) ~ **(in holy orders,** clergyman; lay officer of parish church, university college chapel, etc.; *clerk* REGULAR. 2. officer in charge of records etc., secretary, agent, of town council (*town clerk*), corporation, court, etc.; ‖senior official in Parliament; person employed in bank, office, shop, etc., to make entries, copy letters, keep accounts, etc.; *assistant in shop or hotel; ~ **of the course,** judges' secretary etc. in horse or motor racing; ~ **of the weather,** imaginary person supposed to control weather; ~ **of (the) works,** overseer of building works etc.; hence ~'DOM, ~'ESS¹ (Sc.), ~'SHIP (1, 3), *ns.*, ~'LY¹ *a.* 3. *v.i.* work as clerk. [f. OE cleric, clerc, & OF clerc, f. eccl. L clericus CLERIC]

clĕ'ver *a.* skilful, talented; (of doer or thing done) ingenious; adroit, dextrous, neat in movement; BOX⁵ clever; ~ **Dick,** ~-**sticks,** (colloq.) (would-be) smart or knowing person; hence ~LY² *adv.*, ~NESS *n.* [ME, — adroit, perh. rel. to CLEAVE², w. sense 'apt to seize']

clĕ'ver-clĕver *a.* ostentatiously clever; eagerly seeking to appear clever. [redupl. of prec.]

clĕ'vis *n.* U-shaped piece of metal at end of beam for attaching tackle etc.; connection in which bolt holds one part that fits between forked ends of another. [16th c., perh. f. OE *clyfes (*klubisī, rel. to CLEAVE¹)]

clew (-ōō) *n.*, & *v.t.* 1. *n.* (arch.) ball of thread or yarn; this as used in myth to guide through labyrinth; = CLUE. 2. (Naut.) small cords suspending hammock; lower or after corner of sail. 3. *v.t.* (Naut.) ~ **down,** let down (sail) by clews in unfurling; ~ **up,** draw lower ends of (sail) to upper yard or mast ready for furling. [OE cliwen, cleowen, = Du., MLG kluwen, corresp. to OHG kliuwa, kliuwi ball]

cliā'nthus *n.* Australian shrub or vine of genus Clianthus, with handsome drooping clusters of red flowers. [mod. L, app. f. Gk klei-, kleos glory + anthos flower]

clîché (klē'sha) *n.* hackneyed phrase or opinion; metal casting of stereotype or electrotype; hence ~(')d *a.*, hackneyed, full of clichés. [F (clicher to stereotype, perh. imit.)]

click *n.*, & *v.t.* 1. *n.* (make) slight sharp sound (with tongue, heels, etc.) as of dropping latch or of billiard--balls meeting (~ **beetle,** kind that makes such sound in recovering from capsized position); catch in machinery acting with this sound; (of horse) touch(ing of) shoes of fore and hind feet; (make) sharp non-vocal suction, used as speech-sound in some languages; (sl.) secure one's object, come to an agreement, be successful, be understood, become friendly with person of opposite sex; hence ~ER¹ *n.*, foreman shoemaker who cuts out leather and gives out work, (Print.) foreman of companionship of compositors who distributes copy etc. [imit.; cf. Du. klikken, F cliquer]

cli'ent *n.* person using services of professional man (lawyer, architect, social worker, etc.), customer; (Rom. Hist.) plebeian under protection of patrician; (arch.) dependant, hanger-on; hence ~SHIP *n.* [ME, f. L cliens -entis (cluere hear, obey; see -ENT)]

clientè'le (klēon-) *n.* customers (of shop); patrons (of theatre etc.); persons who seek professional advice (of lawyer etc.). [f. L clientela clientship & F clientèle]

cliff *n.* steep rock-face, usu. facing sea; ~-**hanger,** ~-**hanging,** (story etc.) with outcome excitingly uncertain ; hence ~'Y² *a.* [OE clif, = OS, ON klif, OHG klep f. Gmc *klibham]

climacteric (-măkter-, -măktĕ'r-) *a.* & *n.* **1.** *a.* constituting a crisis, critical; (Med.) occurring at period of life (45–60) at which vital force begins to decline. **2.** *n.* supposed critical period in life (esp. occurring at intervals of seven years). [f. F *climatérique* or f. L f. Gk *klimaktērikos* f. *klimaktēr* critical period (*klimax -akos* ladder); see -IC]

climă'ctic. See CLIMAX.

cli'mate *n.* (region with certain) prevailing conditions of temperature, humidity, wind, etc.; (fig.) prevailing trend of opinion or feeling in community or period; hence **climă'tIC** *a.*, **climatŏ'LOGY** *n.*, **climatoLO'GICAL** *a.* [ME, f. OF *climat* or f. LL f. Gk *klima -at-* (*klinō* slope)]

cli'măx *n.* & *v.* **1.** *n.* event or point of greatest intensity or interest, culmination, apex; sexual orgasm; (Rhet.) series arranged in order of increasing importance etc.; last term in such series; (Ecol.) state of equilibrium reached by plant community; hence **climă'ctIC** *a.* **2.** *v.i.* & *t.* come or bring to a climax. [LL, f. Gk *klimax -akos* ladder, climax]

climb (-īm) *v.* (arch. *past* **clomb** *pr.* -ōm) & *n.* **1.** *v.t.* & *i.* ascend, mount, go *up*, (often with help of hands); **∼ down,** descend (cliff etc., or abs.) similarly, retreat from position taken up, give in (so **∼-down** *n.*). **2.** *v.i.* (Of sun, aeroplane, etc.) go upwards; (of plant) grow upwards with support by tendrils or twining from tree, trellis, etc.; slope upwards; rise by effort in social rank, intellectual or moral strength, etc. **3.** **∼'ing-frame,** structure of joined pipes etc. for children to climb on: **∼'ing-iron,** spikes attachable to boot for climbing trees or ice slopes. **4.** Hence **∼'ABLE** (-ma-) *a.* **5.** *n.* ascent by climbing; place (to be) climbed. [OE *climban,* = MDu., MLG *klimmen,* OHG *kliman* f. WG **klimban* f. nasalized var. of **klibhan* CLEAVE²]

cli'mber (-ī'mer) *n.* In vbl senses; climbing plant; one who climbs mountains; person climbing socially. [f. prec. + -ER¹]

clime *n.* (literary). tract, country; climate. [f. LL *clima*; see CLIMATE]

clinch *v.* & *n.* **1.** *v.i.* (Of boxers) come too close for full-arm blow; (colloq.) embrace. **2.** *v.t.* (Naut.) fasten (rope) with special half-hitch. **3.** confirm, settle (argument, bargain, etc.) conclusively; = CLENCH 1. **4.** *n.* any of the above actions or the resulting state. [16th c. var. of CLENCH]

cli'ncher *n.* In vbl senses; remark or argument that clinches a matter; **∼-built,** = CLINKER³-*built.* [f. prec. + -ER¹]

cline *n.* (Biol.) graded sequence of differences within species etc. [f. Gk *klinō* to slope]

cling *v.i.* (**clung**). stick, adhere *to,* (by stickiness, suction, grasping, or embracing; **∼ together,** remain in one body or in contact; resist separation); remain (stubbornly) faithful *to* (friend, habit, idea, etc.); **∼** ('stone), kind of peach or nectarine in which flesh adheres to stone. [OE *clingan,* = MDu. *klingen* stick, MHG *klingen* climb, f. Gmc **kling-, *klang-, *klung-* parallel to **klink-* etc.; cf. CLENCH]

cli'nic *n.* private or specialized hospital; place or occasion for giving medical treatment or advice, esp. in a hospital and devoted to one topic (*fertility clinic, fracture clinic, welfare clinic*); teaching of medicine or surgery at hospital bedside; **conference* or short course on particular subject; hence **clinI'CIAN** *n.* [f. F *clinique* f. Gk *klinikē* CLINICAL art]

cli'nical *a.* **1.** (Med.) of or at the sick-bed (esp. of teaching so given); **∼ death** (judged by observation of person's condition); **∼ medicine** (based on observed symptoms); *clinical* THERMOMETER. **2.** objective, dispassionate; coldly detached. **3.** Hence **∼LY²** *adv.* [f. L f. Gk *klinikos* (*klinē* bed); see -IC, -AL]

clink¹ *n.* & *v.* & *t.* (make, cause (glasses etc.) to make) sharp ringing sound; **∼'stone,** kinds of felspar [f. ringing like iron when struck]; hence **∼'ING²** *a.* & *adv.,* (sl.) exceedingly (good etc.). [ME, prob. f. MDu. *klinken*; cf. CLANG, CLANK]

clink² *n.* (sl.) prison (esp. *in clink*). [16th c.; orig unkn.]

cli'nker¹ *n.* In vbl. senses; (sl.) excellent specimen ***(sl.) error in performance, blunder. [f. CLINK¹ + -ER¹]

cli'nker² *n.* mass of slag or lava; stony residue from burnt coal. [earlier *clincard* etc. f. obs. Du. *klinkaer* (*klinken* CLINK¹)]

cli'nker³ *n.* **∼-built,** (of boat) made with external planks overlapping downwards and fastened with clenched copper nails. [f. *clink* N. Engl. var. of CLINCH + -ER¹]

clinŏ'meter *n.* instrument for measuring slopes. [f Gk *klinō* to slope + -O- + -METER]

cliome'trics *n. pl.* (usu. treated as *sing.*) method of historical research making much use of statistical information and methods. [f. *Clio,* Muse of history + METRIC + -ICS]

clip¹ *v.t.* (-pp-), & *n.* **1.** *v.t.* surround closely, grip tightly; fix with clip; **∼-on** *a.,* attached by clip. **2.** *n.* appliance (usu. worked by spring) for holding thing together or for attachment to object as marker; piece of jewellery fastened by clip; set of attached cartridges for firearm; PAPER¹-*clip*; **∼'board,** small board with sprung clip for holding papers etc. [OE *clyppan* embrace f. WG **kluppjan*]

clip² *v.t.* (-pp-), & *n.* **1.** *v.t.* cut with shears or scissors, trim thus, take away part of (hair, wool) thus; **∼** person's **wings,** prevent him from pursuing his ambition or from acting. **2.** remove hair or wool of (sheep etc.) thus; remove small piece of (railway, bus, etc. ticket) to show that it has been used; **cut from newspaper etc.; (sl.) swindle, rob; pare edge of (coin). **3.** (colloq.) hit smartly. **4.** omit letters or syllables of (words); omit (letter etc.). **5.** *n.* operation of shearing or hair-cutting; quantity of wool clipped from sheep flock, etc.; extract from motion picture; smart blow with hand, cut with whip, etc.; (colloq.) rate of (esp rapid) motion; **∼-joint,** (sl.) club etc. charging exorbitant prices. [ME, f. ON *klippa*; prob. imit.]

cli'p-clŏp *n.* & *v.i.* (-pp-). (make) sound resembling beat of horse's hooves. [imit.]

cli'pper *n.* In vbl senses; (usu. in *pl.*) instrument for clipping hair; fast horse or ship, esp. fast sailing-ship with raking bows and masts. [ME, f. CLIP² + -ER¹]

‖**cli'ppie** *n.* (colloq.) bus conductress. [f. CLIP² + -IE¹]

cli'pping *n.* In vbl senses; piece clipped off; **news paper etc. cutting. [ME, f. CLIP² + -ING¹]

clique (-ēk) *n.* small exclusive group; coterie; hence **cli'quISH¹** (-ē'k-), **cli'que(e)y²** (-ē'kī), *adjs.,* **cli'quism** (2) (-ē'k-) *n.* [F (*cliquer* CLICK)]

‖**C.Lit.** *abbr.* Companion of Literature.

cli'tor|is *n.* small erectile part of female genitals; hence **∼AL,** **clitŏr'IAL,** *adjs.* [mod. L, f. Gk *kleitoris*]

clivers. See CLEAVERS.

‖**Cllr.** *abbr.* Councillor.

clŏā'c|a *n.* (*pl.* **∼ae** *pr.* -sē). sewer; excretory cavity in birds, reptiles, etc.; hence **∼AL** *a.* [L]

cloak, (arch.) **clōke,** *n.* & *v.* **1.** *n.* loose usu. sleeveless outdoor upper garment (**∼-and-dagger,** involving intrigue and espionage); covering (*cloak of snow*); pretence, pretext, (*under the cloak of*); **∼'room,** room for leaving cloaks, coats, hats, etc., or any luggage ‖(euphem.) (also **∼s**), lavatory. **2.** *v.t.* put cloak on (*oneself* or another); conceal, disguise. [ME f. OF *cloke,* dial. var. of *cloche* bell, cloak (from its bell shape) f. med. L *clocca* bell; see CLOCK¹]

clŏ'bber¹ *n.* (sl.) clothing, equipment. [19th c.; orig unkn.]

clŏ'bber² *v.t.* (sl.) hit, thrash; defeat; criticize severely. [20th c.; orig. unkn.]

clŏche (-sh) *n.* **∼** (**hat**), woman's bell-shaped hat (orig. bell-shaped) small translucent esp. glass cover for forcing or protecting outdoor plants. [F, = bell, f. med. L *clocca* (see foll.)]

clŏck¹ *n.* & *v.* **1.** *n.* time-measuring instrument with wheels etc. kept in motion by periodically wound up

springs or weights or by electricity etc., and recording hours, minutes, etc., by hands on a dial or by displayed figures; **o'clock** = of the clock, usu. appended only to the hour itself (*six o'clock*, but *quarter to six, six fifteen, 7.25*; *what o'clock is it?*, what is the time?; also to indicate direction by imaginary dial, e.g. *one o'clock* = 30° to right of straight ahead); **against the** ~, so as to finish a task by a certain time; **beat the** ~, complete a task before a stated time; **hold the** ~ **on**, ascertain time taken by, TIME²; **put the** ~ **back**, (fig.) go back to a past age or outmoded practice; **the** ~ **round, round the** ~, for all 12 or 24 hours; **watch the** ~, be eager to reach end of working day. **2.** clocklike device showing readings on a dial; (colloq.) taximeter, speedometer, or odometer; (colloq.) stop-watch; (sl.) face; downy seed-head of dandelion etc. **3.** ~ **golf**, lawn game of holing ball with putter from successive points in circle; ~'**wise**, **anti-** or **counter-**~'**wise**, *advs.* & *adjs.*, moving in curve from left to right, right to left, as seen from central position; ~'**work**, mechanism on clock principle (**like** ~**work**, smoothly, regularly, automatically), (*attrib.*, fig.) regular, mechanical. **4.** *v.i.* (Of factory workers etc.) ~ **in, on,** ~ **out, off,** register arrival or departure by means of an automatic recording clock. **5.** *v.t.* (colloq.) time (race) with stop-watch; ~ (**up**), (colloq.) attain or register (stated time, distance, or speed in race etc.); ||(sl.) hit. [ME, f. MDu., MLG. *klocke* (= OHG *glocka*, ON *klokka*), Gmc f. med. L. *clocca* bell; perh. f. Celt.]
clock² *n.* pattern used as ornament on side of sock or stocking. [16th c.; orig. unkn.]
clod *n.* lump *of* earth etc.; lump of earth; ~('**hopper**), ~'**poll**, bumpkin, lout, (so ~'**-hopping**, loutish); whence ~'**dish¹** *a.*; meat cut from neck of ox; ~'**hopper**, (also, colloq.) large clumsy shoe. [ME, var. of CLOT]
clog¹ *n.* wooden-soled shoe; block of wood to impede animal's movement; (arch.) impediment, encumbrance; ~-**almanac** (Hist., cut on sides of square wooden block); ~-**dance** (performed in clogs). [ME, of unkn. orig.]
clog² *v.* (**-gg-**). **1.** *v.t.* impede, hamper, impede (animal) with clog; choke *up*, obstruct by stickiness. **2.** *v.t.* & *i.* fill up or *up* with choking matter. [ME, f. prec.]
cloggy (-gǐ) *a.* lumpy, knotty; sticky. [f. CLOG¹ + -Y²]
cloisonné (klwah'zŏnā) *a.* & *n.* ~ (**enamel**), enamel in which colours of pattern are kept apart by thin metal strips etc. [F]
cloister *n.*, & *v.t.* (enclose or shut up in) convent or monastic house; monastic life or seclusion; covered place for walking, often round quadrangle with wall on outer and colonnade or windows on inner side, esp. of convent, college, cathedral buildings; hence ~ED² (-erd) (lit., or fig. secluded, sheltered), **cloi'stral**, *adjs.* [ME f. OF *cloistre* f. L *claustrum*, *clostrum* lock, enclosed place (*claudere claus-* CLOSE³)]
cloke. See CLOAK.
clomb. See CLIMB.
clone *n.*, & *v.t.* **1.** *n.* group of plants produced vegetatively from one original seedling or stock; group of organisms formed asexually from one ancestor; one such organism; hence **clo'nal** *a.* **2.** *v.t.* propagate as clone. [f. Gk *klōn* twig, slip]
clonk *v.* & *n.* (make) abrupt heavy sound of impact; (colloq.) hit. [imit.]
clonus *n.* (Path.) spasm with alternate muscular contractions and relaxations; hence **clo'nic** *a.* [f. Gk *klonos* turmoil]
cloqué (klō'kā) *n.* fabric with irregularly raised surface. [F, = blistered]
close¹ *a.* & *adv.* **1.** *a.* shut; (of vowel) pronounced with relatively narrow opening of mouth; narrow, confined, contracted; (of air etc.) stifling. **2.** covered, concealed, secret, given to secrecy, (**keep, lie,** ~, be in hiding); niggardly. **3.** restricted, limited, (*close corporation* etc.); under prohibition. **4.** ~ (**to**), at

only a short distance (from); in near relation or connection (*close friend, relative*); in intimate friendship or association; in or nearly in contact (*close combat, proximity*); fitting exactly (*close cap, copy, resemblance, translation*); nearly equal (*close contest*). **5.** concentrated, searching, (*close examination, attention*); dense, compact, with no or only slight intervals, (*close texture, thicket, writing*); leaving no gaps or weaknesses (*close reasoning*). **6.** ||~ **borough**, (Hist.) = *pocket* BOROUGH; ~ **call**, (colloq.) = *close shave*; ~-**car'pet** *v.t.*, cover whole floor of (room) with carpet; ~-**cropped**, (of hair) cut very short; ~-**fisted**, niggardly; ~-**grained**, without gaps between fibres etc.; ~ **harmony**, singing of parts within octave or twelfth; ~-**hauled**, (of ship) with sails hauled aft to sail close to wind; ~-**mouthed**, reticent; ~ **quarters**, direct contact or uncomfortable nearness (*at* ~ *quarters*, very near); ~ **scholarship** (open only to restricted group of candidates); ~ **score** (Mus., with more than one part on same staff); ||~ **season** (when something, esp. killing of game etc., is forbidden by law); ~ **shave**, (fig.) narrow escape from accident etc.; ~-**stool**, chamber-pot enclosed in stool with cover; ~ **thing**, = *close shave*; ~-**up**, photograph or film taken at short range and showing subject on large scale, (fig.) intimate description. **7.** Hence ~'I.Y² (-slǐ) *adv.*, ~'NESS (-sn-) *n.* **8.** *adv.* in close manner (*shut close*; *close-*SET³); in near position (SAIL² *close to the wind*; *stand close*; **go** ~, (of racehorse) win or nearly win; ~ **by,** ~ (**up**)**on,** ~ **to,** very near to; ~-**fitting,** (of garment) fitting close to body. [ME f. OF *clos*, f. L *clausus* p.p. of *claudere* shut]
close² *n.* enclosed place; street closed at one end; ||precinct of cathedral; ||school playing-field; (Sc.) entry from street to common stairway or to court at back. [ME f. OF *clos* f. L *clausum* enclosure (as prec.)]
close³ (-z) *v.* & *n.* **1.** *v.t.* & *i.* shut (of lid or box, door or room or house, etc.); (of place of business etc.) declare or be declared no longer open (**clo'sing-time**, time at which public houses, shops, etc., stop business); ~ **on**, (of hand, box, etc.) grasp or imprison; ~ one's **eyes**, (1) die, (2) pay no attention *to*. **2.** conclude, bring or come to an end, complete, settle (bargain etc.); finish speaking (*with* the remark etc.). **3.** bring or come closer or into contact (*close the ranks*); make (electric circuit etc.) continuous; come within striking distance, grapple *with*. **4.** express agreement *with* (offer, terms, or person offering them), **5.** ~ **down**, (of shop, factory, etc.) close permanently, ||(of broadcasting station) end transmission till next day; ~ **in**, enclose, come nearer, (of days) get increasingly shorter; ***~ **on**, discontinue, terminate, dispose of (business); ~ **up**, move closer (*to*), block, coalesce, shut (esp. temporarily). **6.** *n.* conclusion, end; (Mus.) cadence. [ME f. OF *clos-* st. of *clore* f. L *claudere* shut]
closed (-zd) *a.* In vbl senses; (of society, system, etc.) self-contained, not communicating with others; restricted to specified competitors or things; *closed* BOOK¹; ~-**circuit**, (of television) for restricted number of receivers by use of wires not waves for transmission; ~-**end**, having predetermined extent (cf. OPEN¹-*ended*); ***~ **season**, = CLOSE¹ *season*; ~ **shop**, workshop or other establishment where only members of a trade union may be employed, this system; ~ **syllable** (ending in consonant). [p.p. of prec.]
clo'set (-z-) *n.* private or small room, esp. for private interviews (||**Clerk of the C**~, sovereign's principal chaplain) or for study (~ **play**, play to be read not acted); ***cupboard, recess for storage etc.; cupboard for special purpose, e.g. CHINA²-*closet*, = WATER¹-*closet*; hence ~ED¹ *a.*, in private consultation (*with*). [ME f. OF, dim. of *clos*; see CLOSE¹, -ET¹]
clo'sure (-zher) *n.*, & *v.t.* **1.** *n.* closing; closed condition. **2.** (Parl.) decision by vote, or under rules, to put question without further debate. **3.** *v.t.* apply closure to (motion, speakers, etc.). [ME f. OF, f. LL *clausura* (*claudere claus-* CLOSE³; see -URE)]

clot *n.* & *v.* (**-tt-**). **1.** *n.* mass of material stuck together; semi-solid lump of coagulated liquid, esp. of blood exposed to air; (sl.) stupid person. **2.** *v.i.* & *t.* form into clots; ∼**ted cream** (got by scalding milk). [OE *clot(t),* = MHG *kloz* f. WG **klutt-* (**klut-, *klaut-;* cf. CLEAT)]

cloth (-ôth, -awth w. *pl. pr.* -awdhz) *n.* **1.** (piece of) woven or felted material; = TABLE-*cloth.* **2.** woollen woven fabric as used for clothes; duster; ∼ **of gold, of silver,** tissue of gold or silver threads interwoven with silk or wool; **cut** one's **coat according to** one's ∼, adapt expenditure to resources, limit ambition to what is feasible. **3.** profession as shown by clothes, esp. clerical (*respect due to his cloth*; **the** ∼, clergy). **4.** ∼**-binding,** cover of book in linen or cotton cloth over cardboard; ∼**-cap** *a.*, pertaining to the working class; ∼**-eared,** (colloq.) somewhat deaf; ∼**-yard shaft,** (Hist.) arrow a yard long. [OE *clāth,* = MDu. *kleet,* MHG *kleit,* of unkn. orig.]

clothe (-dh) *v.t.* (∼**d** *or,* arch., tech., or formal, **clad**). provide with clothes, put clothes upon; cover as with clothes or a cloth; endue *with* (qualities etc.). [OE **clāthian* (*clāth*; see prec.)]

clothes (-ôdhz, -ôz) *n. pl.* **1.** things worn to cover the body and limbs; = BED[1]*clothes.* **2.** ∼**-bag, -basket,** (for holding or conveying clothes to be washed); *clothes*-HANGER[2]; ∼**-horse,** frame for airing washed clothes, (fig.) affectedly fashionable person; ∼**-line,** rope, wire, etc., for hanging washed clothes etc. to dry; ∼**-moth** (with larva destructive to clothes); ||∼**-peg, *∼-pin,** wooden etc. clip or forked device to hold clothes on clothes-line; ∼**-post,** ∼**-prop,** support for clothes-line. [OE *clāthas* pl. of *clāth* CLOTH]

clo'thier (-dh-) *n.* seller of men's clothes. [ME *clother* f. CLOTH; see -ER[1], -IER]

clo'thing (-dh-) *n.* In vbl senses; clothes collectively. [f. CLOTHE + -ING[1]]

*clo'ture *n.*, & *v.t.* = CLOSURE 2, 3. [f. F *clôture* f. OF CLOSURE]

clou (klōō) *n.* point of greatest interest, chief attraction; central idea. [F, = nail]

cloud *n.* & *v.* **1.** *n.* (mass of) visible, condensed watery vapour floating in air high above general level of ground; *every cloud has* SILVER[1] *lining*; **in the** ∼**s,** mystical, unreal, imaginary, (of person) abstracted, inattentive; **with** one's **head in the** ∼**s,** unrealistic(ally), living in a world of fantasy; **on** ∼ **seven** or **nine,** (colloq.) extremely happy. **2.** unsubstantial or fleeting thing; mass of smoke or dust; local dimness or vague patch of colour in or on liquid or transparent body; great number *of* birds, insects, etc., moving together. **3.** obscurity; state of gloom, trouble, suspicion, frowning or depressed look, (*cloud on brow*; **under a** ∼, out of favour, discredited). **4.** ∼**'berry,** small mountain bramble with white flower and orange-coloured fruit; ∼**'burst,** sudden violent rainstorm; ∼**-castle,** daydream; *cloud* CHAMBER; ∼**-cuckoo-land,** fanciful or ideal realm [transl. of Gk *Nephelokokkugia* (*nephelē* cloud, *kokkux* cuckoo) in Aristophanes' 'Birds']; ∼**-hopping,** (of aircraft) flying from cloud to cloud esp. for concealment; ∼**-land,** utopia, fairyland; ∼**'scape,** picture or picturesque grouping of clouds. **5.** Hence ∼'LESS *a.*, ∼'LET *n.*, ∼'Y[2] *a.*, obscured by clouds, unclear. **6.** *v.t.* overspread or darken with clouds, gloom, or trouble; make unclear; variegate with vague patches of colour (∼**ed leopard,** mottled arboreal S. Asian feline, *Neofelis nebulosa*). **7.** *v.i.* become overcast or gloomy (*cloud up, over*). [OE *clūd* mass of rock or earth, prob. cogn. w. CLOD]

clough (klŭf) *n.* ravine, steep valley usu. with torrent bed. [OE *clôh,* = OHG *klinga,* f. Gmc **klanh-*]

clout *n.*, & *v.t.* **1.** *n.* patch; piece of cloth or clothing (**cast a** ∼, remove a garment); hard hit; (colloq.) influence, power of effective action esp. in politics; (Hist.) canvas on frame as mark at archery; nail with large flat head. **2.** *v.t.* mend with patch; hit hard. [OE

clūt, = MLG, MDu. *klūt(e)*, ON *klútr* kerchief; rel. to CLEAT, CLOT]

clove[1]. See CLEAVE[1].

clove[2] *n.* one of small bulbs making up compound bulb of garlic, shallot, etc. [OE *clufu,* cogn. w. CLEAVE[1]]

clove[3] *n.* (pungent aromatic dried flower-bud of) tropical myrtle (**oil of** ∼**s,** oil extracted from cloves and used in medicine); ∼ (**gillyflower**), ∼ **pink,** clove-scented pink, original of carnation and other double pinks. [ME, f. OF *clou* (*de girofle*) nail (of gillyflower), from its shape, GILLYFLOWER being orig. name of the spice; later applied to the similarly shaped bud of the pink]

clo've hitch *n.* hitch by which rope is secured by passing twice round spar or rope that it crosses at right angles. [old p.p. of CLEAVE[1], as showing parallel separate lines]

clo'ven. See CLEAVE[1].

clo'ver *n.* trefoil plant used for fodder; **in** ∼, in ease and luxury; ∼**-leaf,** junction of roads intersecting at different levels with connecting sections in shape like four-leaved clover. [OE *clāfre,* = MLG *klāver,* f. Gmc **klaibrōn*]

clown *n.* & *v.* **1.** *n.* jester, esp. in pantomime or circus, whence ∼'ERY (4) *n.*; ignorant or ill-bred man, whence ∼'ISH[1] *a.*; (arch.) rustic. **2.** *v.i.* & *t.* play the clown (in). [16th c., perh. of LG orig.]

cloy *v.t.* satiate or weary by richness, sweetness, sameness, excess, of food or pleasure (usu. *with*). [ME, f. obs. *acloy* f. AF *acloyer,* OF *encloyer* f. Rom. **inclavare;* cf. ENCLAVE]

club[1] *n.* **1.** stick with one thick end as weapon etc. (INDIAN *clubs*); stick used in games, esp. golf. **2.** (Bot. etc.) structure or organ with knob at end; ∼**-foot,** congenitally distorted foot; ∼**-moss,** pteridophyte with upright spikes of spore-cases; ∼**-root,** disease of cabbages etc. with swelling at base of stem. **3.** playing-card of suit (∼**s**) denoted by black trefoil. **4.** association of persons united by some common interest, usu. meeting periodically for shared activity (*Alpine, golf, yacht, club*) or socially (**in the** ∼, (sl.) pregnant; **on the** ∼, (colloq.) in benefit society, see below); body of persons combined for social purposes and having premises for resort, meals, temporary residence, etc., (||∼**'land,** St. James's in London, or similar area, where many clubs are; ∼**-man,** member of one or more clubs; ***∼ sandwich,** sandwich with two layers of filling between three slices of toast or bread); ∼ (**'house**), premises used by club; group of persons, nations, etc., having something in common; group of persons in joint arrangement for saving etc. (BENEFIT[1]-*club*). [ME, f. ON *klubba* assim. form of *klumba* club, rel. to CLUMP]

club[2] *v.* (**-bb-**). **1.** *v.t.* beat (as) with club; contribute (money etc.) to a common stock. **2.** *v.i.* combine *together, with,* for joint action, esp. making up a sum of money for a purpose. [f. prec.]

clu'bbable *a.* fit for membership of a club; sociable. [f. CLUB[1] + -ABLE]

cluck *n.*, & *v.i.* (make) guttural cry (as) of hen; = DUMB *cluck;* hence ∼'Y[2] *a.*, (of hen) sitting on eggs. [imit.]

clue (-ōō) *n.*, & *v.t.* **1.** *n.* fact or principle that serves as guide, or suggests line of inquiry, in problem or investigation (**not have a** ∼, (colloq.) be ignorant or incompetent); piece of evidence etc. in detection of crime; word(s) used to indicate word(s) for insertion in crossword; thread of story, train of thought; hence ∼'LESS *a.*, (esp., colloq.) ignorant or stupid. **2.** *v.t.* provide clue to; ∼ **in,** up, (sl.) inform. [var. of CLEW]

Clu'mber *n.* kind of large spaniel. [∼ in Nottinghamshire]

clump *n.* & *v.* **1.** *n.* cluster *of* trees or shrubs; agglutinated mass of blood-cells etc.; thick extra sole on boot or shoe. **2.** *v.i.* tread heavily; form clump. **3.** *v.t.* heap or plant together; (colloq.) hit. [f. MLG *klumpe,* MDu. *klompe;* see CLUB[1]]

clŭ'ms|ў (-zĭ) *a.* awkward in movement or shape, ungainly; ill-contrived; without tact; hence ∼ĬLY² *adv.*, ∼ĬNESS *n.* [f. obs. *clumse* be numb with cold (prob. f. Scand.)+-Y²]

clŭng. See CLING.

clŭnk *n.*, & *v.i.* (make) dull sound as of thick pieces of metal meeting. [imit.]

Clu'n|ў (-ōō'-) *n.* ∼y (lace), kind of bobbin-lace for clothing etc.; so ∼ĬAC *a.* & *n.*, (member) of order of monks separated from Benedictines in 11th c. [∼ in central France]

clŭ'ster *n.* & *v.* **1.** *n.* close group of similar things, esp. such as grow together, bunch (∼ **pine**, Mediterranean pine with clustered cones); swarm, close group, of persons, animals, faint stars, gems, etc. (∼ **bomb**, anti-personnel bomb spraying pellets on impact); group of successive consonants or vowels. **2.** *v.t.* & *i.* bring or come into, be in, cluster(s) (∼ed columns, pillars, shafts, several close together, or disposed round or half detached from pier); gather (*a*)*round*. [OE *clyster*, prob. f. Gmc **klut-*; cf. CLOT]

clŭtch¹ *v.* **1.** *v.t.* seize eagerly, grasp tightly. **2.** *v.i.* snatch *at*. [ME *clucche, clicche* f. OE *clyccan* crook, clench, f. Gmc **klukjan*]

clŭtch² *n.* tight grasp; (in *pl.*) grasping hands, cruel grasp, relentless control; grasping *at*; (Mech.) arrangement for connecting or disconnecting working parts; (in motor vehicle) device for connecting engine to transmission, pedal operating this. [f. prec.]

clŭtch³ *n.* set of eggs; brood of chickens. [18th c.; prob. S. Engl. var. of *cletch* f. *cleck* to hatch f. ON *klekja*, assoc. w. CLUTCH¹]

lŭ'tter *n.*, & *v.t.* **1.** *n.* crowded confusion, confused mass, untidy state, litter. **2.** *v.t.* litter *with*; ∼ up, crowd untidily (*with*). [partly var. of *clotter* (CLOT, -ER⁵) coagulate, partly assoc. w. *cluster, clatter*]

Clў'desdāle (-dzd-) *n.* (one of) a breed of heavy draught-horses; kind of small terrier. [orig. bred near river *Clyde* in Scotland; see DALE]

clў'pě|us *n.* (*pl.* ∼i *pr.* -ī). shieldlike part of insect's head; hence ∼AL, ∼ATE², *adjs.* [L, = round shield]

lў'ster *n.*, & *v.t.* (arch.) (treat with) enema. [ME, f. OF *clystere* or F. L f. Gk *klustēr* syringe (*kluzō* wash out)]

:M *abbr.* Member of the Order of Canada.

:m. *abbr.* centimetre(s).

:m *symb.* curium.

Cmd. *abbr.* COMMAND² Paper (fourth series, 1918-56).

:mdr. *abbr.* Commander.

:mdre. *abbr.* Commodore.

CMG *abbr.* Companion (of the Order) of St. Michael & St. George.

Cmnd. *abbr.* COMMAND² Paper (fifth series, 1956-).

CNAA *abbr.* Council for National Academic Awards.

CND *abbr.* Campaign for Nuclear Disarmament.

nr. *abbr.* corner.

ŏ- *pref.*, orig. form of COM-, used (as in I.) only before vowels, *h*, and *gn*; now before any letter. **1.** prefixed to *vbs.*, = with other subjects (*co-operate*); to *adjs.* & *advs.*, = jointly (*co-belligerent*), mutually (*coequal*, *-ly*), and to *ns.* = joint (*co-author, co-precipitation*), mutual (*coequality*). **2.** (Math.) of the complement (*cosine*); complement of (*co-latitude, coset*). [f. COM-]

:O *abbr.* Colorado; Commanding Officer; conscientious objector.

:o. *abbr.* company; county; **and Co.** (-kō'), (colloq.) and the rest of them, and similar things.

/o *abbr.* care of.

:o *symb.* cobalt.

ŏăcervā'tion *n.* **1.** heaping together; pile. **2.** (Chem.) formation of viscous drops in colloidal solution; so **cŏă'cervATE¹** *n.* [f. L CO(*acervatio* f. *acervare* f. *acervus* heap; see -ATION)]

:oach *n.* & *v.* **1.** *n.* State carriage; privately owned carriage; = STAGE¹-*coach*. **2.** (Official name for) railway carriage; *daytime railway passenger carriage;

chartered or long-distance single-decker bus; *economy-class seating in aircraft. **3.** private tutor; instructor of athletic team etc. **4.** **drive** ∼ **and six** or ∼ **and horses** etc. **through,** render (legislation etc.) useless; ∼**-box,** coachman's seat; ∼**-built,** (of motor-car bodies) built of wood by craftsmen; ∼**-dog,** Dalmatian; ∼**-house,** outhouse for carriages; ∼'**man,** driver of horse-drawn carriage; *coach* STATION; ∼'**whip,** whip used by coachman, (Austral.) whip-bird; ∼'**wood,** (Austral.) tree with close-grained wood suitable for cabinet-making; ∼'**work,** bodywork of road or rail vehicle. **5.** *v.i.* travel in or go by stage-coach (*in the old coaching days*). **6.** *v.t.* tutor, train, (pupil esp. intensively or individually *for* examination, crew *for* race); give hints to, prime with facts. [f. F *coche* f. Magyar *kocsi* a. f. *Kocs* in Hungary]

cŏă'djutor (-ōō-) *n.* assistant esp. to bishop. [ME, f. OF *coadjuteur* f. LL CO(*adjutor* f. adjuvare -jut- help; see -OR)]

cŏă'gūl|āte *v.t.* & *i.* change from fluid to more or less solid stage; clot, curdle; set, solidify; hence or cogn. ∼ABLE *a.*, ∼ANT, ∼A'TION. ∼ātor, *ns.* [ME, cf. L *coagulare* (*coagulum* rennet)+-ATE³]

cŏă'gūl|um *n.* (*pl.* ∼a). coagulated mass. [L; see prec.]

cŏai'ta (kōĭ'-) *n.* small S. Amer. red-faced spider-monkey of genus *Ateles*. [Tupi]

coal *n.* & *v.* **1.** *n.* hard opaque black or blackish mineral, mainly carbonized plant matter, found in seams or strata below earth's surface and used as fuel and in manufacture of gas, tar, etc.; ‖piece of this ready for burning in fire; red-hot piece of coal, wood, etc., in fire; **heap** ∼**s of fire** (**on** person's **head**), cause remorse by returning good for evil, cf. Prov. 25:22; **haul** or **call over the** ∼**s,** reprimand; ∼**s to Newcastle,** thing brought where already plentiful, superfluous action. **2.** ∼**-bed,** stratum of coal; ∼**-black,** completely black; ∼**-box,** receptacle for coal to supply room fire; ∼**-bunker,** place for storing coal in ship etc.; ∼**-cellar,** basement storage place for coal; ∼**-dust,** powdered coal; ∼**-face,** exposed surface of coal in mine; ∼'**field,** district with series of coal strata; ∼**-fired,** heated or driven by coal; ∼**-fish,** saithe; ∼ **gas,** mixed gases extracted from coal and used for lighting and heating; ∼**-heaver,** man employed in moving coal; ‖∼**-hole,** small coal-cellar; ∼**-house,** building etc. for storage of coal; ∼'**man** (who carries or delivers coal), ∼**-master,** (Hist.) owner or lessee of coal-mine; ∼ **measures,** (Geol.) series of rocks formed by seams of coal and intervening strata; ∼**-merchant,** retail seller of coal; ∼**-mine** (in which coal is dug); *∼**-oil,** petroleum or paraffin; ∼**-owner,** (Hist.) = *coal-master*; ∼**-sack,** sack for carrying coal, black patch in Milky Way (esp. one near Southern Cross); ∼**-scuttle,** = *coal-box*; ∼**-seam,** stratum of coal; ∼ **tar,** tar extracted from bituminous coal, source of paraffin, naphtha, benzene, creosote, and aniline dyes; ∼**-tit,** = COAL-MOUSE. **3.** Hence ∼'**ER¹** *n.*, ship transporting coal, ∼'**Y²** *a. v.t.* put coal into (ship etc.). **5.** *v.i.* take in supply of coal. [OE *col*, = MDu. *cole*, MLG *kole*, OHG *kol*(*o*), ON *kol* f. Gmc **kolam*]

cŏălě'sc|e *v.i.* come together and form one whole; combine in coalition; so ∼ENCE *n.*, ∼ENT *a.* [f. L CO(*alescere alit-* grow f. *alere* nourish)]

cŏăli'tion *n.* union, fusion; ‖(Polit.) temporary combination of parties that retain distinctive principles, whence ∼IST (1) *n.* [f. med. L *coalitio* (as prec.; see -ITION)]

coa'lmouse, cŏ'le- (-lm-), *n.* (*pl.* -mice). small greyish bird (*Parus ater*) with dark head. [OE *colmāse* (*col* COAL, *māse* as TITMOUSE)]

coa'ming *n.* raised border round hatches etc. of ship to keep out water. [17th c.; orig. unkn.]

coarse *a.* common, inferior, (∼ **fish,** ‖freshwater fish other than salmon and trout); rough, loose, or large, in texture, grain, or features; not delicate in perception, manner, or taste, unrefined; rude, uncivil, vulgar; (of language) obscene; hence ~LY² (-slī) *adv.*, **coar′sen**⁶ *v.t. & i.*, ~NESS (-sn-) *n.* [ME, of unkn. orig.]

coast¹ *n.* **1. (sea-)~**, border of land near sea, sea-shore, *(the coast is* CLEAR¹); ***the C~**, Pacific coast of US. **2.** ***toboggan slide; (usu. downhill) run on bicycle without pedalling or in motor vehicle without using engine. **3.** ~**′guard**, ~ **guard**, (one of a) body of men employed to keep watch on coasts and thus save life, prevent smuggling, etc.; ~**′line**, the line of the sea-shore esp. with regard to its configuration *(the rugged coastline of the island*); ~**-to-~**, across island or continent. **4.** Hence ~ AL *a.*, ~′WISE *a. & adv.* [ME f. OF *coste* f. L *costa* rib, flank, side]

coast² *v.i.* sail along coast, trade between ports on same coast; *slide down hill on toboggan; ride down hill etc. without use of power (cf. prec. 2); (fig.) make progress without exertion. [ME, f. OF *costeier (coste*; see prec.)]

coa′ster *n.* coasting vessel; silver tray for decanter; small mat for drinking-glass etc.; *sledge for coasting; * = ROLLER-*coaster*. [f. prec. + -ER¹]

coat *n., & v.t.* **1.** *n.* man's or boy's sleeved usu. cloth outer garment (DRESS² *coat*; FROCK-*coat*; GREAT*coat*; OVERCOAT; RAIN¹*coat*; RED*coat*); ~ **of arms**, herald's tabard, person's or corporation's heraldic bearings or shield. **2.** ~ **armour**, blazonry, heraldic arms; ~ **dress**, woman's tailored dress resembling coat; *coat- -HANGER²; cut coat according to* CLOTH; **on** person's ~- **-tails**, undeservedly benefiting from his progress etc.; **trail** one's ~(**-tails**) (for someone to tread on), seek to pick quarrel; **turn** one's ~, change sides, desert. **3.** woman's or girl's outdoor garment, overcoat; (esp. in *coat and skirt*) woman's tailored jacket worn with skirt. **4.** covering comparable to garment; animal's hair, fur, etc.; (Physiol.) membrane etc. enclosing or lining organ; skin, rind, husk; layer of bulb etc.; covering of paint etc. laid on at one time. **5.** Hence (-)~′ED², ~′LESS, *adjs.* **6.** *v.t.* put or be coat of paint, tin, etc., on; (in *p.p.*) covered over with dust, material to give smooth surface, etc.; ~**ed**, covered thus with. [ME f. OF *cote*, f. Rom. **cotta*, f. Frank. **kotta*, of unkn. orig.]

coatee′ *n.* woman's or infant's short coat; (arch.) close-fitting short coat. [f. prec. + -EE]

côa′ti (-ah′-) *n.* Amer. carnivorous mammal of genus *Nasua*, like civet and racoon, with long flexible snout. [Tupi *(cua* belt, *tim* nose)]

côatimu′ndi (kōah-) *n.* = prec. [f. as prec. + Tupi *mondi* solitary]

coa′ting *n.* In vbl senses; layer of paint etc.; material for coats. [f. COAT + -ING¹]

co-au′thor *n., & v.t.* (be) joint author (of). [f. CO- 1 + AUTHOR]

coax *v.t.* persuade gradually or by flattery or by continued trial *(to do, into doing or good temper etc.; coax thing out of person; coax fire to light, key into lock,* etc.). [16th c., f. 'make a *cokes* of', f. obs. *cokes* simpleton, of unkn. orig.]

côā′xial *a.* having a common axis; ~ **cable** (Electr., in which there are several coaxial lines, or = *coaxial line*); ~ **line**, (Electr.) transmission line with two concentric conductors separated by insulator; hence ~LY² *adv.* [CO- 1 + AXIAL]

côb¹ *n.* male swan; sturdy short-legged riding-horse; ~**(-nut)**, large kind of hazel-nut; roundish lump of coal etc.; round-headed loaf; CORN¹-*cob*. [ME; orig. unkn.]

||**côb**² *n.* composition of clay, gravel, and straw, used for building walls. [17th c.; orig. unkn.]

cō′balt (-awlt, -ōlt) *n.* silver-white metallic element similar in many respects to nickel; (also ~ **blue**), (deep-blue colour of) pigment containing it; ~ **bomb**, (1) container of radioactive cobalt for medical use, (2) hydrogen bomb emitting radioactive

cobalt; hence ~IC, ~OUS, (kobaw′-) *adjs.* [f. G *kobalt* etc., prob. = KOBOLD in mines]

cô′bber *n.* (Austral. & NZ colloq.) companion, mate, friend. [19th c.; perh. f. E dial. *cob* take a liking to]

cô′bble¹ *n., & v.t.* **1.** *n.* ~(-stone), water-worn rounded stone of size used for paving; || (in *pl.*) coal in lumps of this size. **2.** *v.t.* pave with cobbles. [ME *cobel*(*-ston*), f. COB¹ + -LE 1]

cô′bble² *v.t.* put together roughly; mend, patch up, (esp. shoes). [back-form. f. foll.]

cô′bbler *n.* mender of shoes; clumsy workman; iced drink of wine, sugar, and lemon, in tall glass (*sherry cobbler*); (in *pl.*, sl.) nonsense [f. rhyming sl. ~′*s awls = balls*]; *fruit pie with rich thick crust; (Austral. & NZ sl.) last sheep to be shorn [w. pun on LAST¹]; ~**'s wax**, resinous substance used for waxing thread. [ME, of unkn. orig.]

Cō′bdenism *n.* (Hist.) policy of free trade, peace, and international collaboration. [f. R. *Cobden*, Engl. statesman d. 1865, its leading advocate, + -ISM]

cō-belli′ger|ent *a. & n.* (nation etc.) jointly waging war; hence ~ENCE, ~ENCY, *ns.* [f. CO- 1 + BELLI-GERENT]

cō′ble *n.* flat-bottomed fishing-boat in Scotland and NE England. [OE, perh. f. Celt.]

Cō′bōl *n.* computer language designed for use in business operations. [f. initial letters of *common business oriented language*]

cō′bra *n.* venomous hooded Indian or African snake of genus *Naja*, with neck dilated like hood when excited. [Port., f. L. *colubra* snake]

cô′bwĕb *n.* spider's network, material of it, thread of this; thing of flimsy texture; (in *pl.*) musty rubbish (esp. fig., *cobwebs of the law, of antiquity*; **blow away the ~s**, remove fustiness); insidious entanglement mesh; hence ~**b**ED² (-bd), ~**b**y², *adjs.* [ME cop(*pe*)*web* f. obs. *coppe* spider + WEB]

cô′ca *n.* S. Amer. shrub *(Erythroxylon coca*); its dried leaves, chewed as stimulant. [Sp., f. Quechua *cuca*]

Cōca-Cō′la *n.* (P) aerated non-alcoholic drink. [f. prec. + COLA]

cocai′n|e *n.* drug from coca, used as local anaesthetic and as stimulant; hence ~ISM (5) *n.* [f. COCA + -INE⁵]

côccĭdiō′s|is *n.* (*pl.* ~es *pr.* -ēz). disease of birds and mammals caused by internal parasite of order Coccidia. [f. *coccidium* (mod. L f. Gk *kokkis* dim. of *kokkos* berry) + -OSIS]

cô′c|us *n.* (*pl.* ~i *pr.* -kī). (roughly) spherical bacterium; hence ~AL, ~OID, *adjs.* [mod. L, f. Gk *kokko* berry]

cô′ccy|x (-ks-) *n.* (*pl.* ~xes, *or* ~ges *pr.* -ksījēz). triangular bone ending spinal column in man and some apes; analogous part in birds etc.; hence **côccy′gēal** (-ks-) *a.* [L, f. Gk *kokkux -ugos* cuckoo (from being shaped like its bill)]

cô′chĭn(-chīna) *n. & a.* (fowl) of Cochin China breed with feathery legs. [place in SE Asia]

cô′chineal *n.* (dried bodies of female of insect reared on cactus in Mexico etc., used for making) a scarlet dye. [f. F *cochenille* or f. Sp. *cochinilla* f. L *coccinus* scarlet (Gk *kokkos* kermes (oak))]

cô′chlèa (-k-) *n.* (*pl.* ~e *pr.* -klīē). spiral cavity of internal ear. [L, = snail-shell, f. Gk *kokhlias*]

cô′ck¹ *n.* male bird, esp. of domestic fowl; woodcock, male lobster or crab or salmon; (**old**) ~ (vulg. form of address to man); || (sl.) nonsense. **2.** ~**-and-bull story**, idle invention, incredible tale; ~**-a-crow** dawn; ~**-a-doodle-doo**, crowing of cock, childish name for cock; ~**-fighting**, setting cocks to fight a sport *(live like fighting* ~s, get best of fare; *that* ~ *won't fight*, that plea or plan will not do); ~**-and-hen**, for both sexes; || ~ **of the north**, brambling; ~ **of the rock**, crested orange S. Amer. bird *(Rupicola rupicola*); ~**′scomb**, (comb of) cock, garden plant of genus *Celosia*, and see COXCOMB; ~**′sfoot**, a pasture grass *(Dactylis glomerata*); ~**-shy**, object set up to be thrown at with sticks, stones, etc., throw at this, (fig.

object of ridicule or criticism; ~ **sparrow**, male sparrow, small lively pugnacious person; ~ **of the walk**, dominant person; ~ **of the wood**, capercaillie, *red-crested woodpecker. **3.** tapped spout, tap, valve controlling flow; (vulg.) penis; lever in gun raised ready to be released by trigger. [f. OE *cocc*, and OF *coq*, prob. f. med. L *coccus* (imit.)]

cŏck² *v.t.*, & *n.* **1.** *v.t.* erect, stick or stand up, jauntily or defiantly (~ **the ears**, raise them in attention; ~ one's **eye**, glance knowingly, wink; *cock a* SNOOK²); bend *knee, wrist*, etc., at an angle; ~ **up**, ||(sl.) bungle; ~**-up**, ||(sl.) mistake, muddle. **2.** ~ one's **hat**, (1) set it on aslant, (2) turn up its brim (opp. *slouch*); ~ed **hat**, (1) hat with brim fixed so, (2) brimless triangular hat pointed at front, back, and top (**knock into a** ~ed **hat**, defeat utterly). **3.** raise cock of (gun) in readiness for firing. **4.** *n.* state of being cocked; **at half** ~, (fig.) when only half-ready. [ME, f. prec.]

cŏck³ *n.*, & *v.t.* **1.** *n.* small conical heap of hay etc. in field. **2.** *v.t.* pile into cocks. [ME, perh. of Scand. orig.]

cŏ′ckabullў (-bŏŏ-) *n.* (NZ) small blunt-nosed freshwater fish. [f. Maori *kokopu*]

cŏcka′d|e *n.* rosette etc. worn in hat as badge of office or party or part of livery; hence ~ED² *a.* [f. F *cocarde* orig. in *bonnet à la coquarde*, f. fem. of obs. *coquard* saucy (*coq* COCK¹; see -ARD)]

cŏck-a-hŏŏ′p *a.* & *adv.* exultant(ly), with boastful crowing. [ME, of unkn. orig.]

Cockai′gne (-ā′n) *n.* imaginary land of idleness and luxury; (punningly w. ref. to COCKNEY) London. [ME, f. OF (*pais de*) *cocaigne* lit. 'land of cakes' f. MLG *kokenje* sweet cake dim. of *koke* CAKE]

cŏck-a-lee′kie *n.* Scottish soup of cock boiled with leeks. [f. COCK¹ + LEEK + -IE]

cŏckalŏr′um *n.* (colloq.) self-important little man; (**hey** or **high**) ~, game like leap-frog. [18th c., arbitrary f. COCK¹]

cŏckatie′l (-tee′l, *n.* (Austral.) small delicately coloured crested parrot. [f. Du. *kaketielje*]

cŏckatōō′ *n.* parrot esp. of genus *Kakatoe*, with erectile crest; (Austral. & NZ colloq.) small farmer. [f. Du. *kaketoe* f. Malay *kakatua*, w. assim. to COCK¹]

cŏ′ckatrĭce *n.* = BASILISK 1; (Her.) fabulous animal, cock with serpent's tail. [ME f. OF *cocatris* f. med. L *calcatrix -cis* L *calcare* tread, track, rendering Gk *ikhneumōn* tracker (see ICHNEUMON)]

cŏ′ckboat *n.* ship's small boat. [f. obs. *cock* small boat (f. OF *coque*) + BOAT¹]

cŏ′ckchāfer *n.* pale-brown nocturnal beetle flying with loud whirring sound. [perh. f. COCK¹ as expr. size or vigour + CHAFER]

cŏ′cker¹ *v.t.* ~ (**up**), indulge, pamper, coddle, (child, invalid, etc.). [ME, of uncert. orig.]

cŏ′cker² *n.* according to ~, exact(ly), correct(ly). [f. E. ~, Engl. writer on arithmetic d. 1675]

cŏ′cker³ *n.* kind of small spaniel. [f. COCK¹ + -ER¹, as rousing woodcocks etc.]

cŏ′ckerel *n.* young cock. [ME, dim. of COCK¹; see -REL]

cŏ′ck-eyed (-īd) *a.* (sl.) squinting, crooked, set aslant, not level; absurd; drunk. [19th c., app. f. COCK² + EYE¹ + -ED²]

cŏ′ck-hŏrse *adv.* (also **a-cock-horse**; see A²) astride, mounted. [16th c., = toy horse]

cŏ′ckle¹ *n.* (corn-)~, purple-flowered plant formerly often growing among corn, esp. wheat; disease of wheat turning grains black. [OE *coccul*, perh. f. med. L *coculus* dim. of LL *coccus*]

cŏ′ckle² *n.* edible bivalve of genus *Cardium*; its shell; ~(-shell), small shallow boat; ~s of one's **heart**, one's feelings (*rejoice, warm*, the cockles etc.). [ME, f. OF *coquille* shell f. med. L *cochilia* f. med. Gk *kokhulia* f. Gk *kogkhulion* f. *kogkhē* (CONCH)]

cŏ′ckle³ *v.* & *n.* **1.** *v.i.* & *t.* (cause to) bulge, curl up, pucker. **2.** *n.* bulge or wrinkle in paper, glass, etc. [f. F *coquiller* blister (bread in cooking) f. *coquille*; see prec.]

cŏ′ck-lŏft *n.* small upper loft. [16th c., orig. uncert.; perh. f. COCK¹ + LOFT]

cŏ′ckney *n.* & *a.* (characteristic of a) native of London, esp. of the East End or speaking its dialect; this dialect; (Austral.) young snapper fish. [ME *cokeney* cock's egg (*cocene* gen. pl., *ey* f. OE *æg*), orig. sense prob. small or ill-shaped egg, later 'pampered child' and 'townsman']

cŏ′ckpĭt *n.* **1.** place made for cock-fights. **2.** arena for any struggle (~ **of Europe**, Belgium); (Aeron.) space for pilot etc. in fuselage of aeroplane or in spacecraft; driver's seat in racing car. [f. COCK¹ + PIT¹]

cŏ′ckroach *n.* insect of order Blattaria, esp. nocturnal voracious dark-brown beetle-like insect infesting kitchens etc. [f. Sp. *cucaracha*, w. assim. to COCK¹, ROACH¹]

cŏcksur′e (-shoor′) *a.* quite convinced *of, about*; self-confident, dogmatic, presumptuous; hence ~NESS *n.* [f. *cock* = God + SURE]

cŏ′cktail *n.* drink of spirits with bitters, sugar, etc.; appetizer containing shellfish etc.; finely-chopped fruit salad; ~ **stick**, small pointed stick for serving onion, small sausage, etc. [earlier senses 'docked horse', 'upstart', f. COCK¹,² + TAIL¹; tail like that of cock, or that cocks up]

cŏ′ck|ў¹ *a.* conceited; saucy; hence ~iLY² *adv.*, ~iNESS *n.* [f. COCK¹ + -Y²]

cŏ′ckў² *n.* (Austral. & NZ colloq.) small farmer. [f. COCKATOO + -Y³]

cŏ′cky-lee′kў. Var. of COCK-A-LEEKIE.

cŏ′cō (*pl.* ~s), **cŏ′coa**¹, *n.* ~(**nut**), tropical palm-tree (*Cocos nucifera*); ~**nut** (-kon-), its large ovate brown hard-shelled seed with edible white lining enclosing whitish liquid (~**nut milk**), (sl.) human head, (**that accounts for the milk in the** ~**nut**, (joc.) now all is explained); ~**nut butter**, solid oil obtained from lining of coconut, used in soap, candles, ointment, etc.; ~**nut ice**, sweet of sugar and desiccated coconut; ~**nut matting** (made from fibre of nut's outer husk); ~**nut shy**, fairground side-show where balls are thrown to dislodge coconuts; **double** ~**nut**, much larger nut of the coco-de-mer. [f. Port. & Sp. *coco* grimace, the base of the shell looking like a face]

cŏ′coaⁿ *n.* powder made from crushed cacao seeds often with other ingredients; drink made from this; ~ **bean**, cacao seed; ~ **butter**, fatty substance got from this; *cocoa* NIBS. [alt. of CACAO]

cŏcō-de-mer′ (-ār′) *n.* tall palm-tree of Seychelles. [F]

cŏ′conŭt. See COCO.

cocŏŏ′n *n.* & *v.* **1.** silky case spun by insect larva to protect it as chrysalis, esp. of silkworm, whence ~ERY (3) *n.*; similar structure made by other animals; protective covering, esp. to prevent corrosion of metal equipment. **2.** *v.t.* & *i.* form, or wrap (as) in, cocoon; spray with protective coating. [f. F *cocon* f. mod. Prov. *coucoun* dim. of *coca* shell]

cocŏ′tte *n.* **1.** small fireproof dish for cooking and serving one portion of food. **2.** (arch.) fashionable prostitute. [F]

cŏd¹ *n.* (*pl.* same). ~(**'fish**), large sea fish of family Gadidae, used as food, esp. *Gadus morrhua*; ~**-bank**, submarine bank frequented by cod; ~**-liver oil** (used as source of vitamins A and D). [ME, of unkn. orig.]

cŏd² *v.t.* & *i.* (-dd-), & *n.* (sl.) hoax; parody; (*attrib.*) = MOCK². [19th c.; orig. unkn.]

cŏd³ *n.* (sl.) nonsense. [abbr. of CODS(WALLOP)]

COD *abbr.* cash on delivery, *collect on delivery; Concise Oxford Dictionary.

cŏ′da *n.* (Mus., or fig.) independent and often elaborate passage introduced after end of main part of a movement; (Ballet) concluding section. [It., f. L *cauda* tail]

cŏ′ddle *v.t.* treat as an invalid, keep from cold and exertion, feed *up*; cook (egg) lightly. [prob. dial. var. of CAUDLE]

cōde *n.*, & *v.t.* **1.** *n.* systematic collection of statutes, body of laws so arranged as to avoid inconsistency and overlapping; set of rules on any subject; prevalent morality of a society or class (esp. *code of* HONOUR[1]); person's standard of moral behaviour. **2.** system of military etc. signals, esp. used to ensure secrecy; system of letter or figure or word groups or symbols with arbitrary meanings for brevity or secrecy, or for machine processing of information; (Biol.) GENETIC *code*. **3.** ～-**book**, list of symbols etc. used in code; ～-**name**, ～-**number**, word or symbol, number, used for secrecy or convenience instead of ordinary name. **4.** *v.t.* put (message etc.) into code; hence **cō′der**[1] *n*. [ME f. OF, f. L CODEX]

cō′deine (-dēn, -dīēn) *n.* alkaloid got from opium, used as hypnotic and analgesic. [f. Gk *kōdeia* poppy-head + -INE[5]]

cō′dex *n.* (*pl.* codices *pr.* kŏ′dīsēz). manuscript volume, esp. of ancient texts; collection of pharmaceutical descriptions of drugs etc. [L, = wood block, tablet, book]

cŏ′dger *n.* (colloq.) fellow, person, esp. strange one. [perh. var. of CADGER]

codices. See CODEX.

cŏ′dicil *n.* supplementary addition, esp. modifying or revoking will; hence **codici′llary**[1] *a.* [f. L *codicillus* (usu. in pl.), dim. of CODEX]

cōdicŏ′logy *n.* study of manuscripts; hence **cōdico-lo′gical** *a.* [f. F *codicologie* f. L CODEX *codicis* + -o- + -LOGY]

cŏ′di|fȳ *v.t.* arrange (laws etc.) as code; hence ～FICA′TION, ～FIER[1], *ns.* [f. CODE + -I- + -FY]

cŏ′dling[1], **cŏ′dlin**, *n.* cooking-apple of long tapering shape; moth whose larva feeds on apples; ～**s-and-cream**, willow-herb. [ME, f. AF *quer de lion* lion-heart]

cŏ′dling[2] *n.* small codfish. [f. COD[1] + -LING[1] 2]

cŏ′dŏn *n.* (Biol.) group of three nucleotides forming unit of genetic code determining amino-acid sequence. [f. CODE + -ON]

cŏ′dpiece *n.* (Hist.) bagged appendage to front of man's breeches. [ME, f. *cod* scrotum + PIECE[1]]

cō-drī′ver *n.* one who takes turns in driving a vehicle esp. in a race etc. [f. CO- 1 + DRIVER]

cŏ′ds(wallop) (-dzwŏ-) *n.* (sl.) nonsense. [20th c.; orig. unkn.]

coecilian. Var. of CAECILIAN.

cŏ′ed *n.* & *a.* (colloq.) **1.** *n.* girl or woman student at coeducational institution. **2.** *a.* coeducational. [abbr.]

cōĕdūcā′tion *n.* education of both sexes together; hence ～AL *a.* [f. CO- 1 + EDUCATION]

cōĕffi′cient (-shent) *n.* (Alg.) quantity placed before and multiplying another quantity; (Phys.) multiplier or factor that measures some property (*coefficient of friction, expansion,* etc.); DIFFERENTIAL *coefficient*. [f. mod. L *coefficiens* (see EFFICIENT)]

coe′lacănth (-sĕ′l-) *n.* fish of family Coelacanthidae orig. thought to have hollow spine, extinct but for one species (*Latimeria chalumnae*). [f. mod. L *Coelacanthus* f. Gk *koilos* hollow + *akantha* spine]

coelĕ′nterāte (sĕl-) *a.* & *n.* (Zool.) (member) of the phylum Coelenterata, incl. jellyfish, sea anemones, and corals. [f. mod. L *Coelenterata* f. Gk *koilos* hollow + *enteron* intestine; see -ATE[2]]

coe′lĭăc (sē′l-), ****cē′lĭăc**, *a.* of the belly; ～ **disease**, intestinal disease with defective digestion of fats. [f. L f. Gk *koiliakos* (*koilia* belly; see -AC)]

coe′lom (sē′l-), ****cē′lom**, *n.* (*pl.* ～**s**, or ～**ata** *pr.* -ō′mata). (Zool.) body cavity or space between intestinal canal and body wall; hence ～ATE[2] *a.* & *n.*, (animal) having coelom. [f. Gk *koilōma* cavity]

coe′lostăt (sĕ′l-) *n.* (Astron.) instrument with rotating mirror to photograph celestial objects without their diurnal motion. [f. L *caelum* sky + -o- + -STAT]

coe′nob|ite (sē′n-), ****cē′n-**, *n.* member of monastic community; hence ～i′tic(AL) *adjs.* [f. OF *cenobite* or eccl. L *coenobita* f. LL f. Gk *koinobion* convent (*koinos* common, *bios* life)]

cōē′qual *a.* & *n.* (arch. or literary). equal; hence **cōēqua′lity** (-kwŏ′l-) *n.*, ～LY[2] *adv.* [ME, f. L or eccl. L *coaequalis* (see CO-, EQUAL[1])]

cōēr′ce *v.t.* forcibly constrain or impel (person) *into* obedience etc.; hence **cōēr′cible** *a.* [ME, f. L CO(*ercēre ercit-* = *arcēre* restrain)]

cōēr′c|ion (-shon) *n.* controlling of voluntary agent or action by force; government by force; hence ～IVE *a.* [f. OF *cohercion*, *-tion* f. L *coer*(*c*)*tio*, *coercitio -onis* (see prec., -ION)]

cōĕsse′ntial (-shal) *a.* of the same substance or essence. [ME, f. eccl. L *coessentialis* transl. Gk *homoousios*; see CO-, ESSENTIAL]

cōĕtā′neous *a.* coeval; hence ～LY[2] *adv.* [f. LL CO(*aetaneus* f. L *aetas* age) + -OUS]

cōētĕr′nal *a.* alike eternal; hence ～LY[2] *adv.* [f. eccl. L CO(*aeternus* ETERNAL) + -AL]

cōē′val *a.* & *n.* (person) having same age, existing at same epoch; (of same duration or date of origin; hence ～ITY (-ā′l-) *n.*, ～LY[2] *adv.* [f. LL CO(*aevus* f. L *aevum* age) + -AL]

cōēxi′st (-gz-) *v.i.* exist together (*with*); so ～ENT *a.*, ～ENCE *n.*; (**peaceful**) ～ence (of peoples with different political and social systems, living in mutual toleration). [f. LL CO(*existere* EXIST)]

cōextĕ′nsive *a.* extending over same space or time. [f. CO- 1 + EXTENSIVE]

C. of E. *abbr.* Church of England.

cŏ′ffee (-fĭ) *n.* **1.** shrub of genus *Coffea*; its seeds raw, or roasted and ground; drink made from the roasted and ground seeds; cupful of, light refreshments with, this drink; light brown colour of white coffee. **2.** *a.* **bar**, café serving coffee and light refreshments; ～**bean**, the seed; *coffee-*BREAK[2]; ～-**cup** (of special shape or size); ～ **essence**, concentrated extract of coffee; ～-**grounds**, sediment after infusion; ～-**house**, (Hist.) refreshment house; ***～-**maker**, device for brewing coffee; ～-**mill** (for grinding roasted seeds); ～ **morning**, morning gathering often in aid of charity, with drinking of coffee; *coffee* NIBS; ～-**pot** (for making or serving coffee in); ***～ **shop**, small restaurant; ～-**spoon** (for stirring coffee in cup); ～ **stall**, movable structure serving as coffee bar; ～-**table**, small low table (～-*table book*, large expensive illustrated book). [ult. f. Turk. *kahveh* f. Arab. *ḳahwa*, the drink]

cŏ′ffer *n.* box, esp. strong-box for valuables; (in *pl.*) treasury, funds; sunk panel in ceiling etc.; ～(-**dam**) watertight case pumped dry in building bridges etc. or for repairing ship. [ME f. OF *coffre* f. L f. Gk *kophinos* basket]

cŏ′ffin, *n.*, & *v.t.* **1.** *n.* box in which corpse is buried or cremated (**nail in** person's ～, thing that slightly hastens his death, by annoyance, over-indulgence, etc.); horse's hoof below coronet (～-**bone**, bone in hoof; ～-**joint**, joint at top of hoof); ***～ **corner** (Footb., between goal-line and sideline); ～-**nail** (sl.) cigarette. **2.** *v.t.* put in coffin. [ME, f. OF *cof*(*f*)*in* little basket etc. f. L *cophinus* (see prec.)]

cŏ′ffle *n.* line of animals, slaves, etc., fastened together. [f. Arab. *ḳāfila* caravan]

cŏg *n.* one of series of projections on edge of wheel or side of bar transferring motion by .engaging with another series; (fig.) unimportant member of organization etc.; ～-**wheel** (with cogs); hence ～GED[2] (-gd) *a.* [ME, prob. of Scand. orig.]

cō′gent *a.* (Of argument, reasons, etc.) forcible, convincing; hence **cō′gency** *n.*, ～LY[2] *adv.* [f. L *cogere* compel (as CO-, *agere* act- drive); see -ENT]

cŏ′gitable *a.* able to be grasped by the mind conceivable. [f. L *cogitabilis* (as foll.; see -ABLE)]

cŏ′git|āte *v.i.* & *t.* ponder, meditate; so ～A′TION *n.*, ～ATIVE *a.*; [f. L *cogitare* = CO(*agitare* AGITATE) think + -ATE[3]]

cogito (kŏ′gĭtō) *n.* (Philos.) principle establishing existence of a being from fact of its thinking or awareness. [L, = I think, in Fr. philosopher Descartes' formula (1641) ～, *ergo sum* I think, therefore I exist]

For other words in co- see CO-.

cŏg'năc (kŏ'nyăk) *n.* French brandy, prop. that distilled from wine of Cognac. [f. *C~* in W. France]

cŏ'gnāte *a.* & *n.* **1.** descended from common ancestor (cf. AGNATE); akin in origin, nature, or quality; a relative. **2.** (Philol.) of same linguistic family; representing same original word or root; of parallel development in different allied languages (as E *father*, G *vater*, L *pater*); cognate word. **3.** (Gram.) ~ **object**, one whose meaning is not distinct from that of its verb (*live a good life* = live virtuously). **4.** Hence **cŏgnā'tic** *a.*, ~LY² (-tlĭ) *adv.*, ~NESS (-tn-) *n.* [f. L CO(*gnatus* born); cf. -ATE²]

cŏgnĭ'tion *n.* (Philos.) action or faculty of knowing, perceiving, conceiving, as opposed to emotion and volition; a perception, sensation, notion, or intuition; hence or cogn. ~AL, **cŏ'gnĭtive**, *adjs.* [f. L *cognitio* f. CO(*gnoscere gnit*- apprehend); see -ITION]

cŏ'gnizab|le (kŏ'gn-, kŏ'n-), **-is-** (-z-), *a.* perceptible; recognizable; within the jurisdiction of a court etc.; hence ~LY² *adv.* [f. foll. + -ABLE]

cŏ'gnizance (kŏ'gn-, kŏ'n-), **-is-** (-z-), *n.* **1.** being aware, notice, sphere of observation or concern; **have ~ of**, know, esp. in a legitimate or official way; **take ~ of**, attend to, not allow to go unobserved. **2.** (right of) dealing with a matter legally or judicially. **3.** distinctive device or mark. [ME, f. OF *conis(s)aunce*, *conois(s)ance*, f. Rom. *connoscentia* f. L *cognoscent*- pres. part. st. of *cognoscere*; see COGNITION, -ANCE]

cŏ'gnizant (kŏ'gn-, kŏ'n-), **-is-** (-z-), *a.* having knowledge, being aware, *of*; (Philos.) having cognition. [f. prec.; see -ANT]

cŏ'gnize, -ise (-īz), *v.t.* (Philos.) have cognition of. [f. COGNIZANCE after *recognize* and other vbs. in -IZE]

ŏgnō'mĕn *n.* nickname; (Rom. Ant.) third personal name (e.g. Marcus Tullius *Cicero*), or fourth name or personal epithet (e.g. Publius Cornelius Scipio *Africanus*); surname. [L]

cognoscent|e (kŏnyŏshĕ'ntĭ) *n.* (*pl.* ~*i pr.* -ē or same). connoisseur. [It., lit., one who knows]

ŏgnō'vĭt *n.* (Law). defendant's acknowledgement, to save expense, that plaintiff's cause is just; acknowledgement of a debt. [L, = he has acknowledged]

ŏhă'bĭt *v.i.* live together, esp. as husband and wife (usu. of persons not married to each other); so ~A'TION *n.* [f. LL *cohabitare* f. L CO(*habitare* dwell frequent. of *habēre* hold)]

ŏhēr'e *v.i.* (Of parts or whole) stick together, remain united; (of argument etc.) be consistent, be well-knit; hence **coher'ER**¹ *n.*, detector of radio waves consisting of glass cylinder containing loose metal filings etc. (which were thought to cohere when struck by a wave). [f. L CO(*haerēre haes*- stick)]

ŏhēr'|ent *a.* cohering (of argument, arguer, etc.) consistent, easily followed; (Phys., of radiation) having constant phase difference from other radiation, and so able to interfere with it; so ~ENCE, ~ENCY, *ns.*, ~entLY² *adv.*; ~**ence theory**, (Philos.) theory that truth should be judged by mutual consistency of propositions. [f. L *cohaerēre* (see prec., -ENT)]

ŏhē'sion (-zhon) *n.* sticking together; force with which molecules cohere; tendency to remain united; so **cŏhē'sive** *a.* [f. L *cohaes*- (see COHERE, -ION), after *adhesion*]

ŏ'hō, cŏ'hōe, *n.* (*pl.* ~s). N. Pacific silver salmon. [19th c., of unkn. orig.]

ŏ'hŏrt *n.* division of ancient-Roman army; band of warriors; persons banded or grouped together; *assistant, colleague. [ME, f. F *cohorte* or f. L *cohors cohort*- enclosure, company]

COHSE *abbr.* Confederation of Health Service Employees.

COI *abbr.* Central Office of Information.

oif *n.* (Hist.) close cap covering top, back, and sides, of head; serjeant-at-law's white cap. [ME, f. OF *coife* f. LL *cofia* helmet]

oiffeur (kwahfēr') *n.* (*fem.* **coiffeuse** *pr.* -ēr'z). hairdresser. [F]

coiffure (kwahfūr') *n.* way hair is arranged. [F]

coign (koin) *n.* projecting corner; ~ **of vantage**, place affording good view of something. [old form of COIN¹; in Shak. *Macbeth* I. vi. 7]

coil¹ *v.t.* & *i.* arrange (rope etc.) in concentric rings; twist (*up*) into circular or spiral shape; move sinuously. [f. OF *coillir* f. L *colligere* COLLECT²]

coil² *n.* length of coiled rope, spring, etc.; arrangement, thing arranged, in concentric circles; single turn of coiled thing, e.g. snake; lock of hair twisted and coiled; wire, piping, etc., wound circularly or helically; flexible loop as contraceptive device in womb; roll of postage stamps; (Electr.) coiled wire for passage of current, esp. for ignition in internal combustion engine. [f. prec.]

coil³ *n.* (arch. or poet.) disturbance, noise; fuss; (esp.) **this mortal ~**, turmoil of life (Shak. *Hamlet* III. i. 67). [16th c.; orig. unkn.]

coin¹ *n.* piece of metal made into money by official stamp; metal money; **false ~**, imitation in base metal etc., (fig.) anything spurious; **other side of the ~**, (fig.) opposite view of a matter; **pay** person in **his own ~**, give tit for tat; ~**box**, (receptacle for coins in) telephone operated by inserting coins; ~**op**, launderette etc. with automatic machines operated by coins. [ME f. OF, = wedge, stamping-die, f. L *cuneus* wedge]

coin² *v.t.* make (money) by stamping metal (~ **money**, (fig.) get money fast); make (metal) into money; invent, fabricate, (esp. new word); **to ~ a phrase** (iron., with banal remark); hence ~ER¹ *n.*, (esp.) ||maker of counterfeit coins. [ME, f. OF *coignier* (*coin*; see prec.)]

coi'nage *n.* coining; coins; system of coins in use (DECIMAL *coinage*); invention, coined word. [ME, OF *coigniage* (*coignier*; see prec., -AGE)]

cŏincī'de *v.i.* occupy same portion of space; occur at or during same time; agree exactly together or *with*; concur in opinion etc. [f. med. L CO(*incidere* fall upon; see INCIDENT²)]

cŏï'ncidence *n.* (instance of) being coincident; notable concurrence of events or circumstances without apparent causal connection; (Phys.) presence of ionizing particles etc. in two or more detectors simultaneously, or of two or more signals simultaneously in a circuit. [f. med. L *coincidentia* f. as prec.; see -ENCE]

cŏï'ncident *a.* coinciding; hence ~LY² *adv.* [f. as COINCIDE; see -ENT]

cŏincidĕ'ntal *a.* of the nature of a coincidence; hence ~LY² *adv.* [f. prec. + -AL]

Coi'ntreau (kwă'ntrō) *n.* (P) colourless orange-flavoured liqueur. [F]

coir (koi'er) *n.* fibre from outer husk of coconut, used for ropes, matting, etc. [f. Malayalam *kāyar* cord (*kāyaru* be twisted)]

cŏï'tion *n.* = foll. [f. L *coitio* f. CO(*ire it*- go); see -ITION]

cŏ'ĭtus *n.* (Med.) sexual intercourse; ~ **interru'ptus** (in which penis is withdrawn before ejaculation); ~ **reserva'tus** (in which orgasm is delayed or avoided); hence **cŏ'ĭtAL** *a.* [L, f. as prec.]

cojones (kŏhō'nās) *n. pl.* (colloq.) testicles; (fig.) courage. [Sp.]

cōke¹ *n.*, & *v.t.* (convert into) solid substance left after heating coal, petrol, etc.; **go and eat ~**, (sl.) go away! [prob. f. N. Engl. dial. *colk* core, of unkn. orig.]

cōke² *n.*, & *v.t.* (sl.) (drug with) cocaine. [abbr.]

Cōke³ *n.* (P) Coca-Cola. [abbr.]

cŏl *n.* **1.** depression in mountain-chain. **2.** (Meteorol.) low-pressure region between anti-cyclones. [F, = neck, f. L *collum*]

col- *pref.*, assim. form of COM- before *l*.

Col. *abbr.* Colonel; Colossians (NT).

col. *abbr.* column.

cō'la, kō'la, *n.* W. Afr. tree of genus *Cola*; its seed, used as condiment and tonic; carbonated drink flavoured with this. [W. Afr.]

co′lander (kŭ′-) *n*. perforated vessel used as strainer in cookery. [ME, perh. f. Prov. **colador* f. Rom. **colator* f. L *colare -at-* strain]

cŏ-lă′tĭtŭde *n*. (Astron.) complement of latitude, difference between it and 90°. [f. CO- 2 + LATITUDE]

‖**cŏlcă′nnon** *n*. Irish & Scottish dish of cabbage and potatoes boiled and pounded. [18th c.; perh. f. COLE]

cŏ′lchic\|um (-chĭ-, -kĭ-) *n*. plant of genus *Colchicum*, esp. meadow saffron; its dried corm or seed, used as drug etc.; hence ∿INE[5] (-ĕn) *n*., poisonous yellow alkaloid present in colchicum, used esp. in plant-breeding. [L, f. Gk *kolkhikon* neut. a. (*Kolkhis* Colchis region E. of Black Sea; see -IC)]

cōld[1] *a*. & *adv*. **1.** *a*. of or at low temperature, esp. when compared with human body or with that usual in things like the one in question (ICE[1]-*cold*, STONE-*cold*; BLOOD[1] *runs cold*). **2.** not heated, or having cooled after heat, (*cold food, water; pour or throw cold* WATER[1] *on*); dead; (sl.) unconscious; (colloq.) at one's mercy (*have person cold*); feeling cold; sexually frigid; (of soil) slow to absorb heat; **unrehearsed*. **3.** without ardour, friendliness (*cold reception*), or affection, undemonstrative, apathetic, (LEAVE[2] person *cold*). **4.** chilling, depressing (*cold facts*); stale (*cold news*). **5.** (Of scent in hunting) weakened by passage of time; (in children's games) far from finding or guessing what is sought. **6.** *cold* BLOOD[1]; ∿**-blooded,** (of fish etc.) having blood temperature varying with that of surroundings, (fig.) sluggish, callous, deliberately cruel; ∿ **cathode** (emitting electrons without being heated); *cold* CHISEL; ∿ **colour,** blue or grey, as of cold or sunless day; ∿ **comfort,** poor consolation; *cold* CREAM[1]; ∿ **cuts,** sliced cold cooked meats; ∿ **feet,** fear or cowardice; ∿ **fish,** (colloq.) emotionless person; ∿ **frame,** unheated frame for growing small plants; ∿ **front** (of advancing mass of cold air); ∿**-hearted,** lacking friendliness or affection; ∿ **meat,** meat cooled after cooking, (sl.) corpse(s); ∿ **shoulder,** (fig.) intentionally unfriendly treatment, so ∿**-shou′lder** *v.t.*; *cold* SNAP, STEEL; ∿ **storage,** storage in refrigerator, (fig.) state of abeyance; *cold* SWEAT; ∿ **table,** dishes of cold food; ∿ **turkey,** ***(sl.) blunt statements, (sl.) abrupt withdrawal of narcotics from addict; *cold* WAR[1], so ∿ **warrior;** ∿ **wave,** (1) kind of permanent hair-wave, (2) see WAVE[2] 4; ∿**-work** *v.t.*, shape (metal) while cold. **7.** Hence ∿′ISH[1] 2 *a.*, ∿′LY[2] *adv.*, ∿′NESS *n*. **8.** *adv*. in cold state; ***(sl.) completely, absolutely. [OE *cald*, = OS *cald*, OHG *kalt*, ON *kaldr*, Goth. *kalds* f. Gmc **kaldaz* cogn. w. L *gelu* frost]

cōld[2] *n*. **1.** prevalence of low temperature esp. in atmosphere, cold weather, (**left out in the** ∿, (fig.) ignored, not looked after); cold condition. **2.** inflamed state of mucous membrane of nose and throat, with hoarseness, running at nose, sore throat, etc., (CATCH[1] *cold*; often *common cold, cold in the head*); **catch a** ∿, (fig.) encounter trouble or difficulties. [OE *cald* neut. adj.; see prec.]

cō′ld-shŏrt *a*. (Of metal) brittle in its cold state. [f. Sw. *kallskör* (*kall* cold, *skör* brittle), w. assim. to SHORT 6]

cōle *n*. cabbage (usu. in *comb.*); ∿**-seed,** rape, plant from which colza oil is got; ∿**-slaw** [cf. SLAW], salad of sliced raw cabbage. [ME, f. ON *kál* (= OE *cāwel*, OHG *chōl(i)*), f. L *caulis* stem, cabbage]

colemouse. See COALMOUSE.

cŏlĕŏ′pter\|ous *a*. of the order Coleoptera (beetles and weevils), with front wings converted to sheaths for hinder wings; so ∿IST *n*., one who studies beetles. [f. mod. L *Coleoptera* f. Gk *koleopteros* (*koleon* sheath, *pteron* wing) + -OUS]

cŏlĕŏ′ptīle *n*. (Bot.) hollow organ containing first leaf of germinating cereal grain. [f. Gk *koleos* sheath + *ptilon* feather]

cō′le-tĭt. Var. of *coal-tit* = COALMOUSE.

cō′leŭs *n*. plant of genus *Coleus*, with variegated coloured leaves. [mod. L, f. Gk *koleos* sheath]

‖**cō′ley** *n*. saithe; rock salmon. [perh. f. *coal-fish*]

cŏ′lic *n*. severe spasmodic griping pain in belly; hence ∿**ky**[2] *a*. [ME, f. F *colique* f. LL *colicus* (COLON[1]; see -IC)]

*cŏlisē′um *n*. large stadium etc. [med. L, f. neut. (as *n*., applied to a Roman amphitheatre) of L *colosseus* gigantic (COLOSSUS)]

coli′tis *n*. inflammation of lining of colon. [f. COLON[1] + -ITIS]

Coll. *abbr*. College.

collă′bor\|āte *v.i.* work jointly (*with*, or abs.) esp. at literary or artistic production; co-operate traitorously with the enemy; hence ∿A′TION, ∿ātor, *ns*. [f. L COL(*laborare* LABOUR[2]) + -ATE[3]]

cŏlla′g\|e (-ah′zh) *n*. abstract form of art, work of art, in which photographs, pieces of paper, string, matchsticks, etc. are placed in juxtaposition and glued to a surface; hence ∿IST (3) *n*. [F, = gluing]

co′llagen *n*. protein found in bone, tendons, etc., yielding gelatin on boiling. [f. F *collagène* f. Gk *kolla* glue + -*gène* = -GEN (1)]

collă′ps\|e *n*. & *v*. **1.** *n.*, & *v.i.* (undergo or experience a) falling in, sudden shrinking together, folding up, giving way, prostration by loss of nervous or muscular power, breakdown of mental energy, loss of courage or value. **2.** *v.t.* cause to collapse; hence ∿IBLE *a*. [v. back-form.] f. *collapsed* f. L *collapsus* p.p. of COL(*labi laps-* slip); n. f. med. L *collapsus* n.]

cŏ′llar[1] *n*. **1.** neckband, upright or turned over, of coat, dress, shirt, etc., (HOT[1] *under the collar*); band of linen, lace, etc., completing upper part of costume; ‖neck-chain of order of knighthood; ‖∿ **of SS** or **esses,** former badge of House of Lancaster, still used in some officials' costume. **2.** leather etc. band round animal's (esp. dog's) neck (DOG[1]-*collar*); (**horse-**) ∿, roll round draught-horse's neck bearing stress (GRIN *through a horse-collar*); restraining or connecting band, ring, pipe, in machines etc. **3.** coloured stripe round animal's or bird's neck; ‖piece of meat, brawn, fish, rolled and tied; ‖∿ **of bacon,** part of flitch nearest neck. **4.** ∿**-beam,** horizontal beam connecting two rafters and forming with them an A-shaped roof-truss; ∿**-bone,** joining breastbone and shoulder-blade; ***∿**-button,** ‖∿**-stud,** (for separate collar to shirt). **5.** Hence (-)∿ED[2] (-*erd*), ∿LESS, *adjs*. [ME f. AF *coler*, OF *colier*, f. L *collare*]

cŏ′llar[2] *v.t.* seize (person) by collar, capture; (Rugby Footb.) lay hold of and stop (opponent holding ball); (sl.) take, esp. illicitly. [f. prec.]

cŏllare′tte *n*. woman's collar of lace, fur, etc. [F *collerette* (*collier* COLLAR[1]; see -ETTE)]

collāt\|e *v.t.* compare in detail (copies of text or document, one copy *with* another); (Bibliog.) verify order (of sheets) by signatures; put together (esp. information); (of Ordinary) appoint (clergyman) *to* benefice; so ∿OR *n.*, one who collates, machine for combining sets of punched cards. [f. L COL(*lat-* p.p. st. of *ferre* bring; see -ATE[3])]

collă′teral *a*. & *n*. **1.** side by side, parallel; subordinate but aside from main subject, course, etc. **2.** *a*. & *n*. (person) of common descent but by different line; ∿ (**security**), property pledged as guarantee for repayment of money. **3.** Hence ∿ITY (-ă′l-) *n.*, ∿LY[2] *adv*. [ME, f. med. L COL(*lateralis* LATERAL)]

collā′tion *n*. **1.** collating or being collated. **2.** (RC Ch.) light meal in evening of fast-day. **3.** light meal, esp. at unusual time. [ME f. OF, f. L *collatio -onis* (as COLLATE + -ION); sense 2 f. Benedictine monastery readings of Cassian's *Lives of the Fathers* (*Collationes Patrum*) followed by light repast]

cŏ′lleague (-ēg) *n*. fellow official or worker, esp. in a profession or business. [f. F *collègue* f. L COL(*lega* f. *legare* depute) partner in office]

cŏ′llect[1] (-ĕkt, -ĭkt) *n*. short prayer of Anglican or RC Church, esp. one assigned to a particular day or season. [ME f. OF *collecte* f. L *collecta* fem. p.p. (as n.) of *colligere* (see foll.)]

For other words in co- see CO-.

colle′ct² *v.* **1.** *v.t.* & *i.* assemble, accumulate, bring or come together; get (taxes, contributions, goods to be serviced, etc.) from a number of people (*∼ **on delivery,** = CASH¹ *on delivery*); (colloq.) receive money; (colloq.) call for, fetch. **2.** *v.t.* obtain (specimens, books, stamps, etc.) for addition to others, esp. as hobby; regain control of, concentrate, recover, (one*self*, one's thoughts, energies, courage), (in *p.p.*) not distracted, cool; keep (horse) well in hand; (arch.) infer, gather, conclude; hence ∼ABLE, ∼IBLE, *adjs.* [f. F *collecter* or f. med. L *collectare*, f. L *collectus* p.p. of COL(*ligere* = *legere* pick)]

colle′ct³ *a.* & *adv.* to be paid for by recipient (of telephone call, telegram, parcel, etc.). [imper. of prec.]

collectanea (kŏlĕktā′nĭa) *n. pl.* collected passages, miscellany. [L, neut. pl. of *collectaneus* a. (as COLLECT²; cf. -ANEOUS)]

colle′ction *n.* collecting or being collected; collecting of money, money collected, at meeting or church service for charitable or religious purpose; regular removal of letters etc. for dispatch by post; accumulation *of* water, dust, etc.; group of things collected and belonging together (literary materials, specimens, fashionable clothes, works of art, etc.); ‖ (in *pl.*) college terminal examination at Oxford etc. [ME f. OF, f. L *collectio -onis* (as COLLECT²; see -ION)]

colle′ctive *a.* & *n.* **1.** *a.* formed by or constituting a collection, taken as a whole, aggregate; ∼ **fruit** (resulting from many flowers, as mulberry). **2.** of or from many individuals, common; ∼ **bargaining,** negotiation of wages etc. by organized body of employees; ∼ **farm,** jointly operated amalgamation of several smallholdings; ∼ **ownership** (of land, means of production, etc., by all for benefit of all, whence **colle′ctiv**ISM (3), **colle′ctiv**IST (2), *ns.*, **colle′ctiv**IZE (3) *v.t.*); ∼ **security,** (Polit.) policy or principle of the alliance of several countries to guarantee the security of each one; ∼ **unconscious,** part of unconscious mind deriving from ancestral experience. **3.** (Gram. & Logic). ∼ **noun,** sing. noun denoting many individuals, e.g. *troop*. **4.** Hence ∼LY² (-vlĭ) *adv.*, **colle′cti′v**ITY *n.* **5.** *n.* collective farm; collective noun. [f. F *collectif* a. f. L *collectivus* (as COLLECT²; see -IVE)]

colle′ctor *n.* one who collects (specimens, books, stamps, railway tickets at station, money due, esp. taxes, rent, and subscriptions; ∼'s **item** or **piece,** thing of sufficient beauty or rarity to be placed in a collection); collecting-apparatus in various machines; region in transistor absorbing carriers of charge; hence ∼SHIP *n.* [ME f. AF *collectour* f. med. L *collector* (as COLLECT²; see -OR)]

collee′n *n.* (Ir.) girl. [Ir. *cailín*, dim. of *caile* countrywoman; cf. -EEN]

co′llège *n.* **1.** organized body of persons with shared functions and privileges (**Sacred C∼,** body of cardinals, (Hist.) the Pope's council of 70; *∼*ELECTORAL *college*; ‖ **C∼ of Arms,** (colloq.) Heralds' **C∼,** corporation recording lineage and granting arms in England and Wales; *College of Physicians, Preceptors,* etc.). **2.** ‖ independent corporation in university, usu. with master, fellows, scholars, and students not on the foundation; small university; one not teaching beyond first degree; place of professional study (military, naval, agricultural, etc.; **C∼ of Education,** place for training schoolteachers); ‖ public school; private school; buildings of any of these (*lives in college*). **3.** ∼ **living,** benefice in gift of a college; ∼ **pudding,** small plum pudding for one person. **4.** Hence or cogn. ‖ **co′llège**ER¹ *n.*, one of 70 pupils on the foundation at Eton, **colle′gi**AL *a.*, **collegiā′lity** *n.*, sharing by bishops in government of RC Church. [ME f. OF, or f. L *collegium* (*collega* COLLEAGUE)]

colle′gian *n.* member of a college. [f. med. L *collegianus* (as prec.; see -IAN)]

colle′giate *a.* constituted as or belonging to a college,

corporate; ∼ **church,** church endowed for chapter but without see, or (Sc. & US) under joint pastorate; hence ∼LY² (-tlĭ) *adv.* [f. LL *collegiatus* (as COLLEGE; see -ATE²)]

colle′nchyma (-ngk-) *n.* (Bot.) thickened tissue strengthening walls of young stems etc. [f. Gk *kolla* glue + *egkhuma* infusion]

Co′llès *n.* ∼ **fracture,** (Med.) fracture of lower end of radius with backward displacement of hand. [f. A. ∼, Ir. surgeon d. 1843]

co′llet *n.* encompassing band or ring on spindle etc.; socket; flange holding gem, bezel. [F, dim. of COL]

colli′de *v.i.* come into collision; be in conflict. [f. L COL(*lidere lis-* = *laedere* strike and hurt)]

co′llie *n.* (orig. Scottish) sheep-dog with long pointed nose and usu. long hair. [perh. f. *coll* COAL (as being orig. black) + -IE]

co′lli|er (-yer) *n.* coal-miner; coal-ship; sailor on this; hence ∼ERY (-yerĭ) *n.*, coal-mine and its buildings. [ME, f. COAL + -IER]

co′llig|āte *v.t.* bring into connection (esp. isolated facts by a generalization); so ∼A′TION *n.* [f. L COL(*ligare* bind) + -ATE³]

co′llim|āte *v.t.* adjust line of sight of (telescope etc.); make (telescopes, rays) parallel; hence ∼A′TION, ∼ātor, *ns.* [f. L *collimare,* false reading in Cicero for COL(*lineare* f. *linea* line) + -ATE³]

colli′near *a.* in same straight line; hence ∼ITY (-ă′r-) *n.*, ∼LY² *adv.* [f. COL- + LINEAR]

‖ **Co′llins¹** (-z) *n.* (colloq.) letter of thanks from guest after visit. [character in Jane Austen's *Pride & Prejudice*]

Co′llins² (-z) *n.* iced drink of gin, whisky, etc., with soda, lemon or lime juice, and sugar (JOHN or TOM *Collins*). [20th c.; orig. unkn.]

colli′sion (-zhon) *n.* striking together, colliding; violent encounter of moving body, esp. ship or vehicle, with another or with fixed object; (fig.) clashing of opposed interests etc. (esp. *in collision, come into collision with*); ∼ **course,** course or action bound to end in collision (lit. or fig.); ∼**-mat** (Naut., ready for putting over hole made by collision; hence ∼AL *a.* [ME, f. LL *collisio* (as COLLIDE; see -ION)]

co′lloc|āte *v.t.* place together; arrange; set in particular place; (Ling.) juxtapose (word) *with* another; so ∼A′TION *n.* [f. L COL(*locare* f. *locus* place) + -ATE³]

collocūtor (kŏ′lo-, kolŏ′-) *n.* partaker in talk (**my ∼,** the person talking to me). [LL, f. COL(*loqui locut-* talk); see -OR]

collo′dion *n.* solution of pyroxylin in ether, used in photography and surgery. [f. Gk *kollōdēs* gluelike (*kolla* glue; cf. -ODE)]

collo′gue (-g) *v.i.* talk confidentially *with.* [prob. alt. of obs. *colleague* conspire; by assoc. w. L COL(*loqui* speak) *converse*]

co′lloid *a.* & *n.* **1.** gluey (substance); (Path.) (substance) of homogeneous gelatinous consistency. **2.** *n.* (Chem.) non-crystalline substance with very large molecules, forming viscous solution with special properties; finely divided substance dispersed in another; hence **colloi′d**AL *a.* [f. Gk *kolla* glue + -OID]

co′llop *n.* slice of meat, escalope. [ME (= fried bacon and eggs), of Scand. orig.]

collo′quial *a.* of or in talk, oral; belonging to familiar speech or writing, not used in formal or elevated language; hence ∼ISM (2, 4) *n.*, ∼LY² *adv.* [f. L *colloquium* COLLOQUY + -AL]

collo′qui|um *n.* (*pl.* ∼a). academic conference or seminar. [L; see foll.]

co′lloqu|y *n.* act of conversing; a conversation; judicial and legislative court in Presbyterian Church; so ∼IZE *v.i.*, converse. [f. L COL(*loquium* f. *loqui* speak); see -Y¹]

co′llotype *n.* thin sheet of gelatin exposed to light, treated with reagents, and then printed from by lithography; print so made. [f. Gk *kolla* glue + -o- + TYPE¹]

collu'de (-ōō'd, -ū'd) *v.i.* (arch.) practise collusion. [f. L COL(*ludere lus-* play)]
collu'sion (-ōō'zhon, -ū'-) *n.* fraudulent secret understanding, esp. between ostensible opponents in lawsuit; hence **collu'sive** (-ōō'-) *a.* [ME f. OF, or f. L *collusio* (as prec.; see -ION)]
collў'ri|um *n.* (*pl.* ~a). eye-lotion. [L, f. Gk *kollurion* poultice (*kollura* coarse bread-roll)]
cŏ'llўwŏbbles (-bɛlz) *n.pl.* (colloq.) rumbling in the intestines; stomach-ache; feeling of apprehension (with intestinal symptoms). [fanciful, f. COLIC + WOBBLE]
Colo. *abbr.* Colorado.
cŏ'lobus *n.* short-thumbed African monkey of genus *Colobus*. [mod. L, f. Gk *kolobos* docked]
cŏ'locўnth *n.* (bitter-apple, gourd plant with bitter-pulped fruit used as) purgative drug. [f. L f. Gk *kolokunthis*]
colŏ'gne (-ŏ'n) *n.* eau-de-Cologne or other lightly-scented toilet water. [abbr.]
cŏ'lon[1] (-on, -ŏn) *n.* (Anat.) greater part of large intestine, from caecum to rectum; hence **cŏlŏ'nic** *a.*, ~I'TIS *n.* [ME, f. OF or f. L f. Gk *kolon*]
cŏ'lon[2] *n.* punctuation-mark (:), used esp. to mark antithesis, illustration, (sometimes with dash:—) quotation or listing, or between numbers in a proportion, Bibl. reference, etc. [f. L f. Gk *kōlon* limb, clause]
colonel (kẽr'nel) *n.* highest regimental officer; *officer of corresponding rank in Air Force; = LIEUTENANT-*colonel*; ||*Colonel* BLIMP; *Colonel-in-*CHIEF[1]; hence ~CY *n.* [f. obs. F *coronel* f. It. *colonnello* (*colonna* COLUMN)]
colŏ'nial *a.* & *n.* (native or inhabitant) of a colony or colonies, esp. of a British Crown Colony; *(house etc.) built or designed in, or in style characteristic of, the period of the British colonies in America before they became the US; ~ **goose**, (Austral. & NZ) stuffed boned mutton; ||C~ **Office**, (Hist.) government department in charge of colonies; hence ~LY[2] *adv.* [F, or f. COLONY + -AL]
colŏ'nial|ism *n.* policy of maintaining colonies, (esp., derog.) alleged policy of exploitation of backward or weak peoples, whence ~IST (2) *n.*; colonial idiom. [f. prec. + -ISM]
cŏ'lonist *n.* settler in or inhabitant of colony. [f. foll. + -IST]
cŏ'loniz|e, -īs|e (-īz), *v.* **1.** *v.t.* establish colony in; *(Polit.) plant voters in (a district) for party purposes. **2.** *v.i.* establish or join a colony. **3.** Hence ~A'TION, ~ER[1], *ns.* [f. COLONY + -IZE]
colŏnnā'd|e *n.* series of columns with entablature; row of trees etc.; hence ~ED[2] *a.* [F (*colonne* COLUMN; see -ADE)]
cŏ'lonў *n.* **1.** settlement or settlers in new country forming community fully or partly subject to mother State; their territory; people of one nationality or occupation in a city, esp. if living more or less in isolation or in a special quarter (so of animals, *colony of sparrows* etc.); segregated group (*leper colony, nudist colony*); (Biol.) aggregate of animals, plants, etc., connected or living close together. **2.** (Gk Hist.) independent city founded by emigrants; (Rom. Hist.) garrison settlement (usu. of veteran soldiers) in conquered territory. [ME, f. L *colonia* (*colonus* farmer f. *colere* cultivate; see -Y[1])]
cŏ'lophon *n.* tailpiece in manuscript or book, often ornamental, giving writer's or printer's name, date, etc. (**from title-page to ~**, from cover to cover); publisher's device esp. on title-page, imprint. [LL f. Gk *kolophōn* summit, finishing touch]
colŏ'phonў *n.* rosin. [f. L *colophonia* (*resina* resin) of *Colophon* in Lydia]
cŏloqui'ntida. Var. of COLOCYNTH.
color[1,2]. See COLOUR[1,2].
Cŏlora'dŏ (-rah'-) *n.* ~ **beetle**, yellow black-striped beetle, destructive to potato plant. [~ in US]

colo(u)rā'tion (kŭler-) *n.* colouring, method of putting on or arranging colour; natural, esp. variegated, colour of living or other things. [F, or f. LL *coloratio* (*colorare* COLOUR[2]; see -ATION)]
cŏloratur'a (-ahtoor*a*, -atūr'*a*) *n.* florid passages in vocal music; singer of these, esp. soprano. [It., f. L *colorare* COLOUR[2]; cf. -URE]
colori'fic (kŏ-, kŭ-) *a.* producing colour(s); highly coloured. [f. F *colorifique* or mod. L *colorificus* (as COLOUR[1]; see -FIC)]
colori'|mēter (kŏ-, kŭ-) *n.* instrument for measuring intensity of colour; hence ~ME'TRIC *a.*, ~METRY *n.* [f. L *color* COLOUR[1] + -I- + -METER]
colŏ'ssal *a.* of or like a colossus; gigantic, huge; (colloq.) remarkable, splendid, delightful; (Archit., of order) more than one storey high; hence ~LY[2] *adv.* [F (*colosse* COLOSSUS; see -AL)]
colŏ'ss|us *n.* (*pl.* ~i *pr.* -ī, or ~uses). statue of much more than life size; gigantic person or personified empire etc., esp. conceived (like Colossus of Rhodes) as standing astride over dominions. [L, f. Gk *kolossos*]
colŏ'stomў *n.* (Surg.) incision in colon to provide artificial anus through abdominal wall in cases of stricture etc. [f. as COLON[1] + -O- + Gk *stoma* mouth + -Y[1]]
colŏ'strum *n.* first milk of mammal after parturition. [L]
colŏ'tomў *n.* (Surg.) incision in colon. [f. as COLON[1] + -O- + -TOMY]
||**co'lour**[1], *co'lor*[1], (kŭ'ler) *n.* **1.** sensation produced on eye by rays of light when resolved by prism, selective reflection, etc. (cf. *black*, effect produced by no light or by surface reflecting no rays, and *white*, effect produced by rays of unresolved light). **2.** particular hue; one, or any mixture, of the constituents into which light can be separated as in spectrum, including (loosely) black and white (**complementary** ~, colour that combined with given colour makes white or black; **primary** ~s, red, green, and violet, or for paints etc. red, blue, and yellow, giving all others by mixture; **secondary** ~, mixture of two primary colours); (Photog. etc.) use of all colours, not only black and white; (dark) skin pigmentation, esp. as reason for prejudice, discrimination, etc.; **see the ~ of** person's **money**, receive some evidence of forthcoming payment from him. **3.** ruddiness of face (*lose, gain, colour*; **change** ~, turn pale or red; OFF *colour*). **4.** (usu. in *pl.*) appearance, aspect, (**paint in bright** ~s, describe optimistically; *see in its true colours*). **5.** colouring, colour-system, -perception, effects as of colour got by light and shade in engraving, whence ~IST (3) *n.*; pigment, paint; blackness of printed type; conventional colour (gules, azure, etc.) used in heraldry. **6.** (in *pl.*) coloured ribbon, dress, etc., worn as symbol of party, membership of club, jockey's employer, etc. (||send in, **give** person **his**, ~s, be include him, in sports team esp. as regular member; *show* (**true**) ~s, one's party or character); (in *sing.*) sportsman awarded colours. **7.** flag of ship, pair of silken flags (**Queen's** or **King's** ~, regimental ~) carried by regiment, (||TROOPING *the colour* or *colours*; **with the** ~s, serving in armed forces; *sail under* FALSE *colours*; **come off** or **through with flying** ~s, win credit; **haul down** one's ~s, admit defeat; **nail** one's ~s **to the mast**, persist, refuse to give in). **8.** show of reason, pretext, false plea, (*lend colour to; under colour of*). **9.** (Mus.) timbre, quality; variety of expression. **10.** character, tone, quality, mood, shade of meaning, (*take one's colour from*). **11.** (In literature) picturesqueness, ornate style, (LOCAL[2] *colour*). **12.** *atlas*, chart exemplifying shades of colour; ~ **bar**, legal or social discrimination between white and non-white persons; ~**-blind**, unable to distinguish certain colours; ~-**box** (of assorted artists'-paints); ~ **code**, use of colours as standard means of identification (so ~-*code v.t.*);

∿-**fast,** dyed in colours that will not fade or be washed out; ∿ **line,** social demarcation between white and non-white persons; ∿-**man,** dealer in paints; ∿ **scheme,** arrangement of colours esp. in design of room decoration or garden planting; ∿-**sergeant,** senior sergeant of infantry company; ∿ **supplement** (with coloured illustrations, to newspaper etc. otherwise printed without colour); ∿-**wash** n., & v.t., (paint with) coloured distemper. **13.** Hence ∿FUL a., full of colour or interest, bright, gay, (lit. or fig.). [ME f. OF color, -our f. L color]

‖**co′lour²,** *co′lor², (kŭ′ler) v. **1.** v.t. give colour to; paint, stain, dye; disguise; misrepresent (highly coloured details); (fig.) imbue with its own colour (emotion colours one's judgement). **2.** v.i. take on colour; ∿ (up), blush. **3.** So ∿ANT n., colouring substance. [ME, f. OF colo(u)rer f. L colorare (color COLOUR¹)]

‖**co′lourab|le,** *-or-, (kŭ′ler-) a. specious, plausible, counterfeit; hence ∿LY² adv. [ME, f. COLOUR¹ + -ABLE]

‖**colouration.** See COLORATION.

‖**co′loured,** *-or-, (kŭ′lerd) a. & n. having colour(s); (person) wholly or partly of non-white descent; (C∿; S. Afr.) (person) of mixed brown and white or black and white descent. [p p. of COLOUR²]

‖**co′louring,** *-or-, (kŭ′ler-) n. In vbl senses; style in which thing is coloured, or in which artist employs colour; facial complexion. [f. COLOUR² + -ING¹]

‖**co′lourist,** *-or-, (kŭ′ler-) n. See COLOUR¹ 5.

‖**co′lourless,** *-or-, (kŭ′ler) a. without colour; pale; dull-hued; lacking character or vividness; neutral, impartial, indifferent; hence ∿LY² adv., ∿NESS n. [f. COLOUR¹ + -LESS]

‖**co′loury,** *-orȳ, (kŭ′lerĭ) a. having colour, esp. indicative of good quality. [f. COLOUR¹ + -Y²]

cŏ′lpo- comb. form. vagina, as: ∿**scope,** instrument for inspection of vagina; ∿TOMY (-ŏ′t-) n. [f. Gk kolpos womb]

cŏlpŏrteur (kŏ′-; -er, -ēr′) n. book-pedlar, esp. employed by a society to distribute Bibles. [F (colporter prob. f. comporter transport f. L comportare)]

cŏlt¹ n. young male horse from when it is taken from dam to age of usu. 4 or 5; (Bibl.) young camel; inexperienced person, esp. young cricketer etc. in junior team; ∿′**sfoot,** common large-leaved yellow-flowered weed; hence ∿′HOOD (-t-h-) n., ∿′ISH¹ a. [OE, = young ass or camel, of unkn. orig.; perh. f. Scand.]

Cŏlt¹ n. (P) type of firearm, esp. repeating pistol. [f. ∿ Co. (S. ∿, US inventor d. 1862)]

*cŏ′lter. See COULTER.

cŏ′lubrine a. snakelike; esp., of or like the Colubrinae, a subfamily of non-poisonous snakes. [f. L colubrinus (coluber snake; see -INE¹)]

cŏlumbār′i|um n. (pl. ∿a). building with niches for reception of cinerary urns. [L, = pigeon-house (columba pigeon; see -ARIUM)]

cŏ′lumbine¹ n. garden plant with flower like five clustered pigeons, aquilegia. [ME, f. OF colombine f. med. L columbina (herba) (columba pigeon; see -INE¹)]

Cŏ′lumbine² n. partner of Harlequin in pantomime. [f. F Colombine f. It. Colombina (colombo dovelike)]

*cŏlu′mb|ium n. (Chem.) niobium; hence ∿ITE¹ n., native ore of iron and niobium. [f. Columbia (poet.) America + -IUM]

cŏ′lumn (-um) n. **1.** (Archit.) long vertical often slightly tapering cylinder usu. supporting entablature or arch, or alone as monument. **2.** column-shaped object (e.g. part of animal body or plant, part of machine, etc.); vertical cylindrical mass of liquid or vapour. **3.** vertical division of page, table, etc., for figures etc., or to reduce length of lines in printed matter (∿-**inch,** quantity of print occupying one inch length of column); part of newspaper, sometimes more or less than one column, devoted to special subject or writer, as advertisement columns, PERSONAL column, 'Cassandra's' column; **our** ∿**s, the** ∿**s** of The Times, etc., contents of newspaper; hence ∿IST (-mnĭ-, -mĭ-) n., journalist who regularly contributes to a newspaper a column esp. of miscellaneous comment on people and events. **4.** narrow-fronted deep arrangement of troops or armoured vehicles in successive lines (**dodge the** ∿, (colloq.) shirk duty, avoid work; FIFTH column); similar arrangement of ships; *party, faction. **5.** Hence or cogn. **cŏlŭ′mn**AR¹, ∿ED² (-md), adjs. [ME, f. OF columpne & f. L columna pillar]

cŏlū′re n. (Astron.) one of two great circles intersecting at right angles at poles and dividing celestial equator and ecliptic into four equal parts, one passing through equinoctial, and one through solstitial, points of ecliptic. [ME, f. LL f. Gk kolouros truncated]

cŏ′lza n. rape plant; ∿-**oil** (made from it and used in lamps etc.). [f. F kolza(t) f. LG kōlsāt (see COLE, SEED)]

com- pref. meaning 'with', 'together', 'jointly', 'altogether'; used before b, m, p, and occas. before vowels and f, becoming co- esp. before vowels, h, and gn, col- before l, cor- before r, and con- before other consonants. [f. L com-, cum with]

cŏ′ma¹ n. unnatural heavy sleep, prolonged unconsciousness; hence ∿TOSE¹ a. [f. med. L f. Gk kōma -atos deep sleep]

cŏ′ma² n. (pl. ∿e). (Bot.) tuft of silky hairs at end of seed; (Astron.) nebulous envelope round nucleus of comet. [L, f. Gk komē hair of head]

cŏmb¹ (-m) n. **1.** toothed strip of bone, metal, plastic, etc., for arranging, cleaning, or confining the hair; = CURRY²-comb. **2.** thing of same shape, look, or purpose, in many machines, esp. for dressing wool, or collecting electricity, or in animal structure; red fleshy crest of fowl esp. cock, analogous growth in other birds; = HONEYCOMB. **3.** Hence (-)∿ED² (-md) a. [OE camb, = OS camb, OHG kamb, ON kambr f. Gmc *kambaz]

cŏmb² (-m) v. **1.** v.t. draw comb through (hair), curry (horse), dress (wool, flax) with comb; (colloq.) search (place) thoroughly; ∿ **out,** arrange (hair) with comb, search or attack systematically, separate for removal, so ∿-**out** n. **2.** v.i. (Of wave) curl over. [ME, f. prec.]

co′mbat (kŏ′mbăt, kŭ′-, -at) n., & v.t. & i. (engage in) battle or contest (**single** ∿, duel); oppose, strive against; ∿ **fatigue,** mental disorder due to stress in wartime combat. [f. F combat f. combattre f. LL (COM-, *battere f. L batuere fight)]

co′mbatant (kŏ′-, kŭ′-) a. & n. (person) that fights. [OF pres. part. (as prec.; see -ANT)]

co′mbative (kŏ-, kŭ′-) a. pugnacious; hence ∿LY² (-vlĭ) adv., ∿NESS (-vn-) n. [f. COMBAT v. + -IVE]

‖**combe.** See COOMB.

cŏ′mber¹ (-mer) n. In vbl senses; machine for combing cotton or wool very fine; long curling wave, breaker. [f. COMB² + -ER¹]

‖**cŏ′mber²** n. fish of sea-perch family, Serranus cabrilla. [18th c.; orig. unkn.]

combinā′tion n. combining, combined state (in combination with); combined set of things or persons; small instrumental band; (Math.) group of things chosen from a larger number without regard to their arrangement. **2.** united action, (Chess) ingenious sequence of moves. **3.** (Chem.) union of substances in compound whose properties differ from theirs. **4.** ‖(in pl.) single undergarment for body and legs. **5.** ‖motor cycle with side-car attached. **6.** sequence of numbers etc. used to open ∿ **lock** (complicated locking arrangement for safes, strong-rooms, etc.). **7.** ‖∿-**room,** (Camb. Univ.) = COMMON¹-room. **8.** Hence **cŏ′mbin**ATIVE a. [obs. V. f or f. LL combinatio (as COMBINE; see -ATION)]

cŏmbinatōr′ial a. (Math.) relating to combinations of items selected from larger groups. [f. prec. + -ORY + -AL]

combi′ne|¹ v.t. & i. join together, unite for common purpose; possess (qualities usu. separate) together; (cause to) coalesce in one substance, form chemical compound; co-operate; ∿**ed operation** (in which fighting services, or others, co-operate); ∿**ing form,** (Gram.) special form of word used in combinations (e.g. *Anglo-* repr. *English*); ∿**ing weight,** (Chem.) equivalent. [ME, f. OF *combiner* or f. LL COM(*binare* f. L *bini* two together)]

cŏ'mbīne² *n.* combination of persons or firms to control prices etc.; ∿ **(harvester),** combined reaping and threshing machine. [f. prec.]

cō'mbing (-mī-) *n.* In vbl senses; (in *pl.*) hairs combed off; ∿**-wool** (long-stapled, suitable for combing and making into worsted). [f. COMB² + -ING¹]

cŏ'mbō *n.* (*pl.* ∿**s**). (sl.) combination (esp. of jazz instruments). [abbr.; see -O]

||**cŏmbs** (-mz) *n. pl.* (colloq.) combinations (undergarments). [abbr.]

combŭ'st *v.t.* subject to combustion. [f. obs. *combust* adj. f. L *combustus* p.p. (as COMBUSTION)]

combŭ'st|ĭble *a.* & *n.* (substance or thing) capable of or used for burning; excitable; hence ∿IBI'LITY *n.* [F, or f. med. L *combustibilis* (as foll.; see -IBLE)]

combŭ'stion (-schon) *n.* **1.** consumption by fire. **2.** (Chem. etc.) development of light and heat with chemical combination (SPONTANEOUS *combustion*); oxidation of organic tissue. [ME f. F, or f. LL *combustio* f. L *comburere* -*ust*- burn up]

come (kŭm) *v.i.* (**came** *pr.* kām; **come**). **1.** start or move towards, or arrive at, a point, time, or result, specified or obvious; EASY *come, easy go*; ∿ **and go,** pass to and fro, pay brief visit(s), be transitory (so ∿-**-and-go** *n.*); **not know whether one is coming or going,** be utterly confused; *come to* HAND¹, *to* LIGHT¹; ∿ **to a point,** taper; *come* SHORT, *into the* WORLD. **2.** (in *subj.*, colloq.) ∿ **Friday,** when Friday comes; *two years* ∿ **Christmas,** including time from now to Christmas. **3.** be brought (*the grocery order came; come to one's attention; came to no harm*); be available (*this dress comes in three sizes*); **as** (*tough* etc.) **as they** ∿, supremely. **4.** become perceivable e.g. by motion of beholder etc. (*church came into sight or view; news came as a surprise*). **5.** reach or extend to specified point (*motorway comes within ten miles of us*). **6.** occur, take or occupy specified position (*comes on page 20, within the scope of the inquiry; one comes before, after, another; ideas come into* one's *head*). **7.** happen (*how comes it that . . .?; how did you come to break your leg?*); **how** ∿**?,** (colloq.) how did that happen?; *to* ∿ *pred. a.,* future (*for a year to come*); ∿ **what may,** whatever happens. **8.** become present instead of future (∿ *to pass,* happen; *the time will come when*); **coming man,** person likely to be important in future; **coming week** etc., next following the present; **have it coming to** one, (colloq.) deserve what one suffers. **9.** be the result or descendant *of,* (*that's what comes of grumbling; nothing came of it; come of noble parents*). **10.** enter or be brought *into* (collision, play, prominence). **11.** amount or be equivalent *to* (*total comes to £2; the idea came to nothing; if it* ∿ *s* **to that,** (colloq.) ∿ to that, in that case). **12.** take form (*the butter will not come*). **13.** reach specified state (*have come to believe; has come to be used wrongly; string came undone, untied; all came right in the end; come expensive, easy, natural to* one); *come of* AGE¹, *to* BLOW⁵*s,* CLEAN¹, *to an* END¹, *to* GRIEF, HOME¹ *to,* TRUE; *come unstuck* (see UNSTICK). **14.** (w. cogn. obj.) traverse, accomplish, (*have come 3 miles, a long way*). **15.** (sl.) play a part (*come the bully over;* ∿ *it over,* try to impress deceptively; *come it* (too) STRONG). **16.** (vulg.) experience sexual orgasm. **17.** (in *imper.* as excl.) now then (encouraging), think again, don't be hasty. **18.** (w. *advs.*): ∿ **about,** happen (and cf. ABOUT 9); ∿ **across,** (sl.) be perceived or effective, part (*with money* etc.); *come* AGAIN; ∿ **along,** move forward, arrive, (colloq., in *imper.*) make haste or an effort; *come* APART; ∿ **away,** become detached, be left *with* (impression etc.); ∿ **back,** return (*to* place, subject), recur to memory, **retaliate or retort*; ∿-*back n.,* return to or reinstatement in one's former position

(*stage a come-back*), (sl.) retaliation or retort, (Austral. & NZ) sheep bred for both wool and meat; ∿ **by,** pass; ∿ **down,** come to place regarded as lower, be handed down by tradition, fall (esp. in price), (of aircraft) land, make decision (*in favour of* etc.), amount basically *to,* be humbled (esp. *in the world,* lose social status); ∿-*down* n., downfall, degradation; ∿ **down on,** pounce on, rebuke, punish, exact reparation from; ∿ **down with,** pay (money), begin to suffer from (disease); *come* FORWARD²; ∿ **-hi'ther** *a.,* enticing, flirtatious; ∿ **in,** enter house or room, (Cricket) begin innings, take specified place in race etc. (*come in third*), be elected, come to power, be received as income, begin radio transmission, become seasonable or fashionable, serve a purpose (esp. *come in handy or useful*), find a place (*where does the joke come in?*; **where do I** ∿ **in?,** what is my role?, how are my interests advanced?); ∿ **in for,** be given; **this is where we came in,** this is the same point as we started from; ∿ **in on,** join (enterprise etc.); *come* NEAR¹ (*to*) do*ing*; ∿ **off,** be detached or detachable, fall from horse or bicycle, extricate oneself from contest etc. (*with flying colours, badly*), be accomplished, fulfilled, or successful, (Cricket) cease bowling, (of play etc.) reach end of run, (vulg.) = *come* (sense 16); ∿ **on,** continue coming, advance esp. to attack, progress, thrive, begin, be heard or seen on television, telephone, etc., (of wind, storm, disease) supervene, arise to be discussed, appear on stage or scene, (Cricket) begin to bowl, (in *imper.*) hurry, follow me, please do what I ask, I defy you; ∿-*on* n., (sl.) lure, swindler; ∿ **out,** go on strike, emerge from examination etc. with specified result, emerge from clouds, be revealed, declare oneself (*for or against*), be satisfactorily visible in or as photograph, be solved, become covered *in* (rash etc.), (of stain etc.) be removed, be published (*comes out on Saturdays*), make début on stage or in society; ∿ **out with,** utter; ∿ **over,** come from some distance or across obstacle (*came over with the* Conqueror, *over from London to see us*), change sides or opinion, (colloq.) undergo a feeling (*come over faint*); ∿ **round,** make informal or casual visit, recover from ill temper or unconsciousness, be converted to other person's opinion, (of date) recur; ∿ **through,** survive, be received by telephone etc.; ∿ **to,** cease moving, regain consciousness, revive; ∿ **up,** come to place regarded as higher, join university, approach person e.g. for talk, get abreast *with,* arise from out of ground, be discussed, present itself, be equal *to* standard etc.; ∿ **up against,** be faced with or opposed by; ∿ **up with,** produce (idea etc.) in response to challenge; **coming up,** (colloq., of food etc.) ready, about to be served. **19.** (w. *preps.*): ∿ **across,** meet or find by chance; ∿ **at,** reach, get access to, (whence ∿-**a't-able** *n.*), attack; ∿ **before,** be dealt with by (judge etc.); ∿ **between,** interfere with relationship of (persons or things); ∿ **by,** obtain; ∿ **into,** receive esp. as heir, and see sense 10; ∿ **off it,** (colloq.) stop talking or acting like that; ∿ **on** = *come upon;* ∿ **over,** gain influence over (*what has come over you to behave like this?*); ∿ **through,** survive; ∿ **to,** inherit, return to (one*self* or one's *senses,* from unconsciousness), (colloq.), equal in total, amount to (see sense 11), be assigned by fate or by another to, arrive at (*what is the world coming to?*); ∿ **under,** be classed as or among, be subjected to (influence or authority); ∿ **upon,** attack by surprise, make demand on, be burden to, meet or find by chance; ∿ **with,** (of things) (normally) accompany or be supplied together with (*this model comes with optional features*) (cf. sense 3). [OE *cuman,* = OS *cuman,* OHG *queman, coman,* ON *koma,* Goth. *qiman* f. Gmc **kweman,* *kuman]

Cŏ'mĕcŏn *n.* economic association of Communist countries esp. in E. Europe. [abbr. of *Council for Mutual Economic Assistance*]

comē'dĭan *n.* actor in comedy; humorous performer on stage, radio, etc. [f. F *comédien* (*comédie* COMEDY]

For other words in *co-* **see** CO-.

comĕ'dic *a.* of comedy. [f. L f. Gk *kōmōidikos* (as COMEDY; see -IC)]
comĕdïe'nne *n.* woman comedian. [F, fem., as COMEDIAN]
cŏ'mĕdist *n.* writer of comedies. [f. COMEDY + -IST]
cŏ'mĕdō *n.* (*pl.* ~nes *pr.* -ō'nēz). (Med.) blackhead. [L, = glutton (*comedere* eat up)]
cŏ'mĕdÿ *n.* stage-play or film or broadcast play of light, amusing, and often satirical character, chiefly representing everyday life, and with happy ending (cf. TRAGEDY; *comedy of* MANNERS; MUSICAL *comedy*); humorous genre of drama etc.; humorous or farcical incident(s) in life; humour. [ME, f. OF *comedie* f. L f. Gk *kōmōidia* (*kōmōidos* comic poet f. *kōmos* revel)]
co'mel|ÿ (kŭ'mlĭ) *a.* pleasant to look at (usu. of personal appearance); hence ~INESS *n.* [ME *cumelich*, *cumli* prob. f. *becumelich* (BECOME, -LY[1])]
co'mer (kŭ'-) *n.* In vbl senses (usu. qualified, as *first comer*; **all** ~**s**, anyone who applies, takes up a challenge, etc.); *(colloq.)* coming man. [f. COME + -ER[1]]
comĕ'stible *n.* (formal or joc.; usu. in *pl.*) thing to eat. [ME f. F, f. med. L *comestibilis* f. L *comedere -est-* eat up]
cŏ'mĕt *n.* (Astron.) hazy object usu. with starlike nucleus and with tail pointing away from sun, moving in elliptical or nearly parabolic path about the sun; hence ~ARY[1] *a.* [ME f. OF *comete* f. L *cometa* f. Gk *kometes* long-haired (star); cf. -ET[2]]
come-ŭ'ppance (kŭm-) *n.* (colloq.) one's deserts (for misbehaviour etc.). [f. COME + UP + -ANCE]
co'mfit (kŭ'-) *n.* (arch.) sweet containing nut, seed, etc., in sugar. [ME, f. OF *confit* f. L CON(*fectum* = *factum* neut. p.p. of *facere* make)]
co'mfort (kŭ'-) *n.*, & *v.t.* **1.** *n.* relief in affliction, consolation, being consoled (COLD[1] *comfort*); person who consoles one or saves one trouble; cause of satisfaction; physical well-being, being comfortable; possession of ~**s**, things that make life easy (**creature** ~**s**, good food, clothes, etc.), *warm* quilt; *~* **station**, public lavatory; hence ~LESS *a.*, (esp.) dreary, cheerless. **2.** *v.t.* soothe in grief, console; make comfortable. [ME, f. OF *confort(er)* f. LL *confortare* strengthen (as CON-, L *fortis* strong)]
co'mfortab|le (kŭ'-) *a.* & *n.* **1.** *a.* such as to obviate hardship, save trouble, and promote content, ministering to comfort; at ease, free from hardship, pain, and trouble; enjoying comfort, having ample money for one's needs; having an easy conscience; hence ~LY[2] *adv.* **2.** C~le **Words**, four scriptural passages following and confirming the Absolution in the Communion Office. **3.** *n.* *warm quilt. [ME, f. AF *confortable* (as prec.; see -ABLE)]
co'mforter (kŭ'-) *n.* one who comforts (**the C~**, Holy Spirit; JOB[4]'s *comforter*); ||baby's dummy teat of rubber etc.; ||woollen scarf; *warm quilt. [ME, f. AF *confortour*, OF -*éor* (as prec.; see -ER[1])]
co'mfrey (kŭ'-) *n.* tall rough-leaved ditch-plant of genus *Symphytum*, with clusters of usu. white or purple bells. [ME, f. AF *cumfrie*, OF *confi(e)re* f. med. L *conferva*, L *conferva* f. CON(*fervēre* boil)]
co'mfy (kŭ'-) *a.* (colloq.) comfortable. [abbr.; see -Y[3]]
cŏ'mic *a.* & *n.* **1.** *a.* of, in the style of, comedy; causing or meant to cause laughter, facetious, burlesque, funny, (*comic paper*, *song*). **2.** *comic* OPERA[1], STRIP[2]. **3.** *n.* theatre etc. comedian; amusing person; comic paper, e.g. (orig. children's) periodical with narrative mainly in pictures. [f. L f. Gk *kōmikos* (*kōmos* revel; see -IC)]
cŏ'mical *a.* causing laughter; hence ~ITY (-ă'l-) *n.*, ~LY[2] *adv.* [f. as prec. + -AL]
coming. See COME.
Co'mintêrn *n.* Third INTERNATIONAL. [f. Russ. *Komintern* (*kommunisticheskiĭ* communist, *internatsional'nyĭ* international)]
cŏmità'djï *n.* member of band of irregular soldiers in Balkans. [common Balkan form, f. Turk. *komitaci*, lit. 'member of a (revolutionary) committee']

cŏ'mitÿ *n.* courtesy (~ **of nations,** friendly recognition as far as practicable of each other's laws and usages); association of nations etc. for mutual benefit. [f. L *comitas* (*comis* courteous; see -ITY)]
cŏ'mma *n.* punctuation-mark (,) of the least separation indicated between parts of sentence, also used to separate (groups of) figures etc., (INVERT[1]*ed comma*); (Mus.) definite minute interval or difference of pitch; ~ **bacillus** (comma-shaped kind causing cholera); ~ (**butterfly**), kind with white comma-shaped mark on under-side of hind wings. [f. L f. Gk *komma* clause]
comma'nd[1] (-ah'-) *v.* **1.** *v.t.* give command(s) to, order, bid, (*what God commands, commands us, commands us to do, commands that we should do, commands to be done*; *let us do as God commands*; *God commands and man obeys*); have authority over or control of; be in command of (ship, forces, etc.). **2.** restrain, master, (passions, one*self*); have at disposal or within reach (money, skill, person; so **yours to** ~, (arch.) yours obediently); deserve and get (sympathy etc.); dominate (strategic position) from superior height, look down over. **3.** *v.i.* be supreme; be in command. [ME, f. AF *comaunder*, OF *comander* f. LL *commandare* COMMEND]
comma'nd[2] (-ah'-) *n.* **1.** authoritative statement that person must do something, order, bidding, (**at or by** person's ~, in pursuance of his bidding; **word of** ~, customary order for movement in drill); description of operation in computer, signal initiating such operation. **2.** exercise or tenure of authority, esp. naval or military (**in** ~ **of,** commanding; **under** ~ **of,** commanded by; HIGH *command*). **3.** control, mastery, possession, (great ~ **of language,** skill in speech; **at** ~, ready to be used at will). **4.** body of troops etc., district, under commander (*Bomber Command, Western Command*). **5.** ~ **module,** control compartment in spacecraft; ~ **performance,** theatrical etc. performance given by royal command; ||C~ **Paper,** paper laid by command of the Crown before Parliament etc.; ~ **post,** headquarters of military unit. [f. prec.]
comma'nda'nt *n.* commanding officer, esp. of particular force, military academy, etc.; *Commandant-in-*-CHIEF[1]; hence ~SHIP (1) *n.* [F, or f. It. or Sp. *commandante* (see COMMAND[1], -ANT)]
cŏmmandeer' *v.t.* seize (men or goods) for military service; take arbitrary possession of. [f. S. Afr. Du. *kommanderen* f. F *commander* COMMAND[1]]
comma'nder (-ah'-) *n.* **1.** one who commands (*Commander-in-*CHIEF[1]; **C~ of the Faithful,** title of Caliph); naval officer just below captain; ||WING *commander*; officer in charge of London police district. **2.** (knight) ~, member of higher class in some orders of knighthood. **3.** Hence ~SHIP (1) *n.* **4.** large wooden mallet. [ME, f. OF *comandere*, -*éor* f. Rom. *commandator* (as COMMAND[1]; see -OR)]
comma'nding (-ah'-) *a.* In vbl senses; (of person, looks, ability, etc.) dignified, exalted, impressive; (of hill, position, etc.) giving wide view. [f. COMMAND[1] + -ING[2]]
comma'ndment (-ah'-) *n.* divine command; **the** Ten C~s, those given by God to Moses on Mt. Sinai (Exod. 20 : 1–17). [ME, f. OF *comandement* (as COMMAND[1]; see -MENT)]
comma'ndō (-ah'-) *n.* (*pl.* ~s). party called out for military service, body of troops; (member of) unit of British amphibious shock troops; (member of) similar troops elsewhere. [Port. (COMMAND[1])]
comme'dia dell'arte (kŏmĕdiă dĕl ār'tā) *n.* improvised popular comedy in Italian theatres of 16th–18th c., with stock characters. [It., = comedy of art]
comme il faut (kŏm ēl fō') *pred. a.*, & *adv.* proper(ly), as it should be, (esp. of behaviour etc.). [F, = as is necessary]
commĕ'mor|āte *v.t.* celebrate in speech or writing; preserve in memory by some celebration; (of thing) be a memorial of; hence ~ATIVE *a.*, ~āTOR *n.* [f. L COM(*memorare* relate f. *memor* mindful) + -ATE[3]]

commĕmŏrā'tion *n.* act of commemorating; service or part of service in memory of saint or sacred event; ||(Oxford Univ.) annual celebration in memory of founders and benefactors (∼ **ball,** dance held at time close to this). [ME f. F, or f. L *commemoratio* (as prec.; see -ATION)]

commĕ'nce *v.t.* begin (work, do*ing, to* do, or abs.); ||take university degree of (MA etc.); (arch.) begin to act or work as (*commence author*). [ME, f. OF *com*(*m*)*encier* f. Rom. *cominitiare (as COM-, L *initiare* INITIATE[1])]

commĕ'ncement (-sm-) *n.* commencing; ceremony of degree conferment. [ME, f. OF (as prec.; see -MENT)]

commĕ'nd *v.t.* entrust, commit, (thing *to* person's care; *dying man commends his soul to God*); praise (**highly** ∼ed competitor, just missing prize-list); recommend (*I commend this method to you*; *method commends itself*); ∼ **me to,** (arch.) remember me kindly to, (often iron.) I prefer. [ME, f. L COM(*mendare* = *mandare* entrust; see MANDATE[1])]

commĕ'nd|able *a.* praiseworthy; hence ∼able**NESS** (-beln-) *n.*, ∼**ABLY** *adv.* [ME f. OF, f. L *commendabilis* (as prec.; see -ABLE)]

cŏmmĕndā'tion *n.* praise; act of commending or recommending (esp. person to another's favour). [ME f. OF, f. L *commendatio* (as COMMEND; see -ATION)]

commĕ'ndatorў *a.* commending, recommending. [f. LL *commendatorius* (as prec.; see -ORY)]

commĕ'nsal *a.* & *n.* (one) who eats at the same table; (animal or plant) living harmlessly with or in another and thus obtaining food; hence ∼**ITY** (-ă'l-), *ns.* [ME f. F, or f. med. L COM(*mensalis* f. *mensa* table); see -AL]

commĕ'nsur|able (-sher-, -syer-) *a.* measurable by the same standard (*with, to*); (of numbers) in ratio equal to ratio of integers; proportionate *to;* hence ∼ABI'LITY, ∼able**NESS** (-beln-), *ns.,* ∼**ABLY** *adv.* [f. LL COM(*mensurabilis,* as MEASURE[1]; see -ABLE)]

commĕ'nsurate (-sher-, -syer-) *a.* coextensive (*with*); proportionate (*to, with*); hence ∼LY[2] (-tlī) *adv.,* ∼**NESS** (-tn-) *n.* [f. LL COM(*mensuratus,* as prec.; see -ATE[2])]

cŏ'mmĕnt[1] *n.* explanatory note; remark; criticism; (fig., of event etc.) illustration (*the play is a comment on present-day values*); **no** ∼, (colloq.) I decline to answer your question. [ME, f. L *commentum* contrivance (in LL also = interpretation), neut. p.p. of *comminisci* devise]

cŏ'mmĕnt[2] *v.i.* write explanatory notes (*up*)*on;* make (esp. unfavourable) remarks (*on, upon, that*). [f. prec., or F *commenter* f. as prec.]

cŏ'mmentarў *n.* expository treatise; series of comments on various points in book or descriptive remarks (esp. broadcast or accompanying film) on event or performance; comment. [f. L *commentarius,* -*ium a.* used as n. (as COMMENT[1]; see -ARY[1])]

cŏ'mmentāte *v.i.* act as commentator. [back-form. f. foll.]

cŏ'mmentātor *n.* writer or speaker of commentary; one who comments on current events. [L (*commentari* frequent. of *comminisci* devise; see -OR)]

cŏ'mmĕrce *n.* exchange of merchandise or services, esp. on a large scale; buying and selling; CHAMBER *of Commerce;* (arch.) intercourse (esp. sexual). [F, or f. L COM(*mercium* f. *merx mercis* merchandise)]

commĕr'cial (-shăl) *a.* & *n.* **1.** *a.* of, engaged in, bearing on, commerce; interested in financial return rather than artistry; (of chemicals) unpurified. **2.** ∼ **art** (used in advertising etc.); ∼ **broadcasting** (in which advertisements are included to gain revenue); ∼ **college** etc. (giving instruction in commercial subjects); ||∼ **traveller,** firm's representative who visits shops etc. to show samples and get orders; ∼ **vehicle** (used for transport of goods or fare-paying passengers). **3.** Hence ∼ISM (2, 3) *n.,* ∼IZE *v.t.,* make (merely) commercial, derive commercial profit from, ∼LY[2] *adv.* **4.** *n.* (broadcast) advertisement or

programme containing it; (arch.) commercial traveller. [f. prec. + -IAL]

||**cŏ'mmère** (-mār) *n.* female compère. [F, fem. of COMPÈRE]

Cŏ'mmĭe *n.* (sl.) Communist. [abbr. + -IE]

cŏmmĭnā'tion *n.* threatening of divine vengeance; recital of divine threats against sinners in Anglican Liturgy for Ash Wednesday, service that includes this. [ME, f. L *comminatio* (*comminari* threaten; see -ATION)]

cŏ'mminatorў *a.* threatening, denunciatory. [f. med. L *comminatorius* (as prec.; see -ORY)]

commi'ngle (-nggel) *v.t.* & *i.* (literary). mingle together. [f. COM- + MINGLE]

cŏ'mminŭte *v.t.* reduce to small fragments (∼d **fracture,** one producing multiple fragments of bone); divide (property) into small portions; so **cŏmminŭ'tion** *n.* [f. L COM(*minuere* -*ut*- lessen)]

cŏ'mmis (-mī) *n.* (*pl.* same *pr.* same or -īz). junior waiter or chef. [orig. = deputy, clerk, f. F, p.p. of *committre* entrust (as COMMIT)]

commi'ser|ate (-z-) *v.t.* (arch.) & *i.* feel or express pity for; condole *with;* hence or cogn. ∼A'TION *n.,* ∼ATIVE *a.* [f. L COM(*miserari* pity f. *miser* wretched) + -ATE[3]]

cŏ'mmissăr *n.* (Hist.) head of government department of USSR. [f. Russ. *kommissar* f. F *commissaire* (as COMMISSARY)]

cŏmmissăr'iat *n.* department (esp. Mil.) for supply of food etc.; food supplied; (Hist.) government department of USSR. [F, & f. med. L *commissariatus* (as foll.; cf. -ATE[1])]

cŏ'mmissarў (kŏ'mĭ-, komī'-) *n.* deputy, delegate; (Cambridge Univ.) assessor in Vice-Chancellor's court; representative of bishop in part of his diocese, or of absent bishop; (Mil.) officer charged with, *store for, supply of food etc. to soldiers; *restaurant in film studio etc.; food supplied; hence **cŏmmisăr'ial.,** ∼**SHIP** (1) *n.* [ME, f. med. L *commissarius* person in charge (as COMMIT; see -ARY[1])]

commi'ssion[1] (-shon) *n.* **1.** command, instruction; authority, body of persons having authority, to perform certain tasks; office or department of Commissioner; ||∼ **of the peace,** (authority given to) Justices of the Peace; HIGH *Commission;* ||**Royal C∼,** commission of inquiry or committee appointed by the Crown at the instance of the Government. **2.** warrant conferring authority, esp. that of officers in the army, navy, and air force, above a certain rank. **3. in** ∼, (of warship etc.) manned, armed, and ready for sea; **out of** ∼, not in service, not in working order. **4.** entrusting of authority etc. to a person; charge or matter entrusted to person to perform. **5.** authority to act as agent for another in trade (*have goods on commission*); pay of such agent, percentage on amount involved; ∼-**agent,** (esp.) bookmaker. **6.** committing (*of* crime, sin, etc.). [ME f. OF, f. L *commissio -onis* (as COMMIT; see -ION)]

commi'ssion[2] (-shon) *v.t.* empower by commission; give (officer) command of ship; prepare (ship) for active service; bring (machine, equipment, etc.) into operation; give (artist etc.) a commission for piece of work, order (work) thus. [f. prec.]

||**commissionair'e** (-shonār') *n.* uniformed door-attendant at theatre, cinema, large shop, office, etc. [F, as foll.]

commi'ssioner (-sho-) *n.* one appointed by commission, e.g. head of London police, delegate to General Assembly of Church of Scotland; member of a commission, esp. of government boards etc. (*Charity, Civil Service, Commissioner*); representative of supreme authority in a district, department, etc. (HIGH *Commissioner;* **Lord (High) C∼,** representative of the Crown at General Assembly of Church of Scotland); **C∼ for Oaths,** solicitor authorized to administer oath to person making affidavit; PARLIA-MENTARY *Commissioner for Administration.* [ME, f. med. L *commissionarius* (as COMMISSION[1], -ARY[1], -ER[2] (2))]

For other words in co- see CO-.

cŏmmissūre n. junction, seam; joint between two bones; line where lips or eyelids meet; band of nerve tissue connecting hemispheres of brain, two sides of spinal cord, etc.; hence **cŏmmissūr'AL** a. [ME, f. L *commissura* junction (as foll.; see -URE)]

commi't v.t. (-tt-). **1.** entrust or consign for treatment or safe keeping (*to* person, his care, *to* writing, MEMORY, the earth, the waves, the flames); refer (bill etc.) to committee; ~ (**to** prison), consign officially to custody, esp. until trial. **2.** be doer of (crime, sin, blunder); expose to risk, involve, (character, honour, one*self*); pledge one*self* by implication, bind (person, one*self*, *to* a course of action). **3.** Hence ~tABLE a., ~tAL n., committing to prison, grave, etc., committing of oneself, ~MENT n., (esp.) engagement or involvement that restricts freedom of action. [ME, f. L COM(*mittere miss-* send) join, entrust]

commi'ttĕd a. In vbl senses; morally dedicated (*to* doctrine or cause); obliged to adhere *to* (course of action); (Polit.) aligned. [p.p. of prec.]

committee n. **1.** (kŏmi'tĭ). body of persons appointed for special function by (and usu. out of) a (usu. larger) body (SELECT *committee*; **standing** ~, one that is permanent during existence of appointing body); (esp.) such body appointed by Parliament etc. to consider details of proposed legislation; (*C*~) whole House of Commons when sitting as committee; ~**-man**, ~**-woman**, member of committee(s). **2.** (kŏmĭte'). (Law). person entrusted with charge of another or his property. [f. COMMIT + -EE]

commi'x v.t. & i. (arch. or poet.) mix; so ~tURE n. [ME, back-form. f. *commixt* p.p. f. L COM*mixtus*; cf. MIX]

commō'de n. chest of drawers; chiffonier; (**night-**)~, chamber-pot enclosed in chair or box with cover. [F, a. (as n.) f. L COM(*modus* measure) convenient]

commō'dious a. roomy and convenient; (arch.) convenient; hence ~LY² adv., ~NESS n. [f. F *commodieux* or f. med. L *commodiosus* f. L *commodus* (see prec.)]

commŏ'dĭtў n. useful thing; article of trade, esp. product as opp. to service. [ME, f. OF *commodité* or f. L *commoditas* (as COMMODE; see -ITY)]

cŏmmodō're n. naval officer above captain and below rear-admiral; (in air force: *Commodore-in--Chief*¹; **||air** ~, officer of air force just above group captain); commander of squadron or other division of fleet; president of yacht-club; senior captain of a shipping line. [prob. f. Du. *komandeur* f. F *commandeur* COMMANDER]

cŏ'mmon¹ a. (~er, ~est). **1.** belonging equally to, coming from, or done by, more than one (*our common humanity; common* CAUSE¹; *common consent*). **2.** belonging to, open to, affecting, the public (*common* CRIER, hangman, *lodging-house, scold*). **3.** of ordinary occurrence (*a common experience*; ~ **or garden**, (colloq.) ordinary); ordinary, of ordinary qualities, (*common honesty; no common mind*); without rank or position (*common* JURY, SOLDIER; *the common people*); of the most familiar type (*common* COLD², *nightshade, snake*). **4.** of inferior quality; low-class, vulgar. **5.** (Math.) belonging to two or more quantities (*common denominator, factor, multiple*); (Gram., of noun) applicable to any one of a class (opp. PROPER), (of gender) indifferently masculine or feminine; (Pros., of syllable) that may be either short or long; (Mus.) (of time, measure) having two or four beats, esp. four crotchets, in bar; *common* CHORD². **6.** ~ carrier, one legally obliged to serve the public; *C*~ Era, Christian era; *common* FORM¹; ~ **ground**, basis for argument etc. accepted by both sides; *common* INFORMER; ~ **knowledge**, thing known to most people; ~ **law**, unwritten law of England, applied by the national courts, purporting to be derived from ancient usage and judges' decisions (~-**law husband** or **wife**, one recognized by common law, usu. after cohabitation without ceremony of marriage); *Common* MARKET¹; ~ **metre**, hymn stanza of four lines with 8, 6, 8, and 6 syllables;

C~ **Prayer**, Church of England liturgy orig. set forth in *Book of Common Prayer* of Edward VI (1549); ~ **property**, (fig.) = *common knowledge*; ||~**-room**, (in some colleges, schools, etc.) room to which members have common access for business or social purposes, members using this; *common* SALT; ~ **seal** (of corporate body); ~ **sense**, normal understanding, good practical sense in everyday affairs, general feeling (of mankind or community); ~se'nsical, possessing or marked by common sense; *Common* SERJEANT; *~ **stock**, ORDINARY shares; ~ **weal**, ~**weal**, (arch.) public welfare; *common* YEAR. **7.** Hence ~LY² adv. (esp., ordinarily), ~NESS (-n-n-) n. [ME f. OF *comun*, f. L *communis*]

cŏ'mmon² n. **1.** (largish piece of) land belonging to a community, esp. unenclosed waste land; (**right of**) ~, a man's right over another's land, e.g. *common of pasturage*. **2.** (sl.) common sense. **3. out of the** ~, unusual; **in** ~, in joint use, shared; **in** ~ **with**, in the same way as. **4.** (in *pl.*) see COMMONS. **5.** (Eccl.) service used for each of a group of occasions. [ME, f. F COMMUNE¹ and L *commune* neut. of *communis* (as prec.)]

cŏ'mmonable a. (Of animal) that may be pastured on common land; (of land) that may be held in common. [f. obs. *common* to exercise right of common + -ABLE]

cŏ'mmonage n. right of common; (condition of) land held in common; commonalty. [f. COMMON² + -AGE]

cŏmmonă'litў n. sharing of an attribute; common occurrence. [var. of foll.]

cŏ'mmonaltў n. the common people; general body (of mankind etc.); corporate body. [ME f. OF *comunalté*, f. med. L *communalitas -tatis* (as COMMON¹; see -AL, -ITY)]

cŏ'mmoner n. one of the common people (below the rank of peer); student without financial support from college, paying for his own commons; one who has right of common. [ME, f. med. L *communarius* (*communa*; see COMMUNE¹, -ER² (2))]

cŏ'mmonplace n. & a. **1.** n. notable passage, entered for use in a ~-**book**; ordinary topic; everyday saying; platitude; anything usual or trite. **2.** a. lacking originality, trite; hence ~NESS (-sn-) n. [transl. of L *locus communis* = Gk *koinos topos* general theme]

cŏ'mmons (-z) n. pl. **1.** the common people; third estate in Britain or other similar constitution, (**House of** *C*~**, the** *C*~, Lower House of Parliament, or its buildings). **2.** provisions shared in common; daily fare (**short** ~, not enough food). [ME, pl. of COMMON²]

cŏ'mmonwealth (-wĕl-) n. independent State or community; republic or democratic State (lit., or fig.: *commonwealth of learning*); (*C*~) republican government in Britain 1649-60; (*C*~) title of federated Australian States; (**British**) *C*~ (**of Nations**), association of UK with various independent States (previously subject to Britain) and dependencies; *State of the US (in titles of some of them); ||*C*~ **Day** (celebrated on Queen's official birthday); ||*C*~ **preference**, taxation system favouring imports from British Commonwealth countries. [f. COMMON¹ + WEALTH]

commō'tion n. physical or mental disturbance; bustle, confusion; tumult, insurrection. [ME f. OF, or f. L *commotio* (see COM-, MOTION¹)]

commo've (-ōō'v) v.t. (arch.) move (lit. or fig.) violently, excite. [ME, f. OF COM*movoir*; see MOVE²]

cŏ'mmūnal a. of or for the or a community, for the common use; of a community, esp. that of Paris; hence ~IZE (3) v.t., ~LY² adv. [F, f. LL *communalis* (as COMMUNE¹; see -AL)]

cŏ'mmūnal|ism n. principle of communal organization of society; so ~IST (3) n., ~ĭ'stIC a. [f. prec. + -ISM]

cŏ'mmūnărd n. member of a commune; adherent of the Paris Commune. [F (as foll.; see -ARD)]

cŏ'mmūne¹ n. communal settlement; group of

persons not all of one family, sharing living accommodation and goods; French territorial division, smallest for administrative purposes; similar division elsewhere; **the C~**, communalistic government in Paris in 1871. [F, f. med. L *communia* neut. pl. of L *communis* common]

commūne² (-mū´n, kŏ´m-) *v.i.* have intimate discussion (*with* friend, one's heart, etc.; *together*); feel in close touch *with* (nature etc.); *receive Holy Communion. [ME, f. OF *comuner* share (*comun* COMMON¹)]

commū´nic|able *a.* that can be imparted (esp. of disease); (arch.) communicative; hence ~ABI´LITY, ~**able**NESS (-beln-), *ns.*, ~ABLY *adv.* [ME f. OF, or f. LL *communicabilis* (as COMMUNICATE; see -ABLE)]

commū´nicant *n.* one who (esp. regularly) receives Holy Communion; one who imparts information. [f. as foll.; see -ANT]

commū´nicāt|e *v.* **1.** *v.t.* impart, transmit, (heat, motion, feeling, illness, news, a discovery, *to*); administer Holy Communion to. **2.** *v.i.* receive Holy Communion; have social dealings *with*; succeed in conveying information or evoking understanding; (of room etc.) have common door (*with*); hence ~OR *n.* [f. L *communicare* (as COMMON¹ + *ic* factitive suf.) + -ATE³]

commūnicā´tion *n.* **1.** act of imparting (esp. news; ||~ **cord**, cord or chain for pulling by passenger to stop train in emergency; ~(**s**) **satellite**, artificial satellite for broadcast communications); information given; paper read to learned society; social dealings; access; common door or passage or road or rail or telephone or other connection between places. **2.** (in *pl.*) science and practice of transmitting information, (Mil.) means of transport between base and front; ~ **theory**, study of language and other means of conveying information. [ME, f. as prec.; see -ATION]

commū´nicative *a.* ready to impart; open, talkative; hence ~LY² (-vlĭ) *adv.*, ~NESS (-vn-) *n.* [f. LL *communicativus* (as COMMUNICATE; see -IVE)]

commū´nion (-yon) *n.* sharing, participation; fellowship (esp. between branches of Catholic Church; *communion of* SAINTs); body professing one branch of Christian faith; social dealings; **(Holy) C~**, (participation in) Eucharist (so ~-**cloth**, -**cup**, -**table**); ~-**rail** (at which Holy Communion is administered). [ME f. OF, or f. L *communio* (*communis* common; see -ION)]

commū´niqué (-kā) *n.* official communication, esp. report. [F, = communicated]

cŏ´mmūn|ism *n.* system of society with vesting of property in the community, each member working for the common benefit according to his capacity and receiving according to his needs; (usu. C~*ism*) movement or political party advocating communism esp. as derived from Marxism, communistic form of society established in 20th c. in USSR and elsewhere; hence ~IST (2) *n.* (often *attrib.*), ~**i´st**IC *a.* [f. F *communisme* (*commun* COMMON¹; see -ISM)]

commūnitā´rian *n. & a.* (member) of a community practising co-operation and some communism. [f. foll. + -ARIAN, after *unitarian* etc.]

commū´nity *n.* **1.** joint ownership (*community of goods*) or liability; state of being shared or held in common; fellowship (*community of interest* etc.). **2.** organized political, municipal, or social body; body of people living in same locality; body of people having religion, profession, etc., in common, (*the immigrant, mercantile, Jewish, community*); *the* public; monastic, socialistic, etc., body practising community of goods; body of nations unified by common interests; (Ecol.) group of plants or animals growing or living together in a given area. **3.** ~ **centre**, place providing social, recreational, and educational facilities for a neighbourhood; *~ **chest**, fund for charity and welfare work in a community; ||~ **home**, centre for housing young offenders, replacing approved school and remand home; ~ **singing** (in chorus by large

gathering of people); ~ **spirit**, feeling of membership of a community. [ME, f. OF *comuneté* f. L *communitas -tatis* (as COMMON¹; see -ITY)]

cŏ´mmūnīz|e (-ĭs|e (-ĭz), *v.t.* make (land etc.) common property; make communistic; hence ~A´TION *n.* [f. L *communis* COMMON¹ + -IZE]

commū´t|able *a.* exchangeable, convertible into money; that can be compounded for; hence ~ABI´LITY *n.* [f. L *commutabilis* (as COMMUTE; see -ABLE)]

cŏ´mmūtāte *v.t.* (Electr.) regulate direction of (current), esp. to make it a direct current. [f. L *commutare* (as COMMUTE) + -ATE³]

cŏmmūtā´tion *n.* commuting; commutating; (Math.) interchange of order of two quantities added etc.; *~ **ticket**, season-ticket. [F, or f. L *commutatio* (as COMMUTE; see -ATION)]

commū´tative (komū´tat-, kŏ´mūtāt-) *a.* relating to or involving substitution; (Math.) unchanged in result by interchange of order of quantities. [f. F *commutatif* or f. med. L *commutativus* (as COMMUTE; see -ATIVE)]

cŏ´mmūtātor *n.* person or thing that commutes; device for commutating electric current. [as foll.; see -OR]

commū´t|e *v.* **1.** *v.t.* interchange (two things); make payment etc. to change (one obligation) *for, into*, another; change (punishment *to* another less severe); change (one kind of payment *into, for*, another); (Electr.) commutate. **2.** *v.i.* *buy and use season (commutation) ticket; travel esp. by train or car to and from one's daily work in city etc., whence ~ER¹ *n.*; (Math.) have commutative relation. [f. L *commutare* (*mutare -tat-* change)]

cŏ´mōse *a.* (Of seeds etc.) hairy, downy. [f. L *comosus* (as COMA²; see -OSE)]

cŏmp *n. & v.* (colloq.) **1.** *n.* accompaniment; competition; compositor. **2.** *v.t. & i.* play accompaniment (to); work as compositor (on). [abbr.]

||**Comp²** *abbr.* (On banknotes) Company.

cŏ´mpăct¹ *n.* agreement or contract between two or more. [f. L *compactum* f. COM(*pacisci pact-* covenant); cf. PACT]

compā´ct² *a.* closely or neatly packed together; made up *of*, (of style) condensed, terse; not wasteful of space; hence ~LY² *adv.*, ~NESS *n.* [ME, f. L COM-(*pingere pact-* = *pangere* fasten)]

cŏ´mpăct³ *n.* small flat case for face-powder etc.; object formed by compacting of powder; *medium-sized motor car. [f. prec.]

compā´ct⁴ *v.t.* join or press firmly together; condense; devise, compose, (*of*); so **compā´ct**ION, ~OR, *ns.* [f. as COMPACT²]

compā´gēs (-z) *n.* (*pl.* same). framework, complex structure (lit. or fig.). [L COM(*pages* f. *pangere* fix)]

compā´nion¹ (-yon) *n. & v.* **1.** *n.* one who associates with or accompanies another; associate *in*, sharer *of*, (~ **in arms**, fellow-soldier); ||member of lowest grade of some orders of distinction (*Companion of the Bath*; ||C~ of Honour, Literature, member of orders founded 1917, 1961); woman paid to live with and accompany another. **2.** handbook or reference-book, thing that matches another; star etc. that accompanies another; (piece of) equipment combining several requisites; ~-**set**, set of fireside implements on stand. **3.** Hence ~ATE², ~LESS, *adjs.* **4.** *v.t.* accompany. **5.** *v.i.* (literary) consort *with*. [ME, f. OF *compaignon* f. Rom. *companio -onis* (as COM-, L *panis* bread)]

compā´nion² (-yon) *n.* (Naut.) raised frame on quarterdeck for lighting cabins etc. below; ~ **hatch**, wooden covering over companion-way; ~-**ladder**-way, opening in deck leading to cabin; ~-**ladder** (from deck to cabin); ~(-**way**), staircase to cabin. [f. obs. Du. *kompanje* quarterdeck f. OF *compagne* f. It. *compagna* pantry, prob. ult. f. prec.]

compa′nionab|le (-nyo-) *a.* sociable, agreeable as companion; hence ∼leNESS (-beln-) *n.*, ∼LY² *adv.* [f. COMPANION¹ + -ABLE]

compa′nionship (-nyo-) *n.* state of being companion(s); ‖(Print. Hist.) company of compositors working together. [f. COMPANION¹ + -SHIP]

co′mpany (kŭ′-) *n.* & *v.* **1.** *n.* state of being companion or fellow; **in** ∼, not alone; **in** ∼ **with**, together with; **keep** or (arch.) **bear** person ∼, accompany him, save him from feeling lonely; **keep** ∼ **(with)**, associate habitually (with); **part** ∼ **(with)**, (lit. or fig.) cease association (with). **2.** number of persons assembled; social party, guests. **3.** one's associate(s) (*addicted to low company*; **good, bad,** ∼, a pleasant, dull, companion; **I err in good** ∼, better people have done the same). **4.** body of persons combined for common (esp. commercial) object (JOINT²-*stock company*, ‖*limited* LIABILITY *company*); partner(s) not named in title of firm (*Smith and Co.*); party of actors etc.; group of Guides; subdivision of infantry battalion usu. commanded by major or captain (∼ **officer**, captain or lower commissioned officer; *company* SERGEANT-*major*); **ship's** ∼, entire crew. **5.** *v.t.* (arch.) accompany. **6.** *v.i.* (literary). consort *with*. [ME, f. AF *compainie*, OF *compai(g)nie* f. Rom. **compania (*companio*; see COMPANION¹, -Y¹)]

co′mpar|able *a.* that can be compared (*with*); fit to be compared (*to*); hence ∼ABI′LITY, ∼ableNESS (-beln-), *ns.*, ∼ABLY *adv.* [ME f. OF, f. L *comparabilis* (as COMPARE¹; see -ABLE)]

compa′ratist *n.* user of comparative methods in study of language or literature. [f. foll. + -IST]

compa′rative *a.* & *n.* **1.** *a.* of or involving comparison (esp. of sciences etc.: *comparative anatomy, philology*); (Gram.) ∼ **adjective, adverb,** one in the ∼ **degree,** expressing a higher degree of a quality (*braver; more absurdly*); estimated by comparison (*the comparative merits of the two proposals*); perceptible by comparison (*in comparative comfort*); hence ∼LY⁸ (-vlĭ) *adv.* **2.** *n.* (Gram.) comparative degree or form. [ME, f. L *comparativus* (as COMPARE¹; see -ATIVE)]

compa′rator *n.* device for comparing product, output, etc., with a standard. [f. as foll. + -OR]

compār′e¹ *v.* **1.** *v.t.* liken, pronounce similar, (*to*; esp. w. neg.: *not to be compared to*); estimate similarity or dissimilarity of (one thing *to* another in quality, *with* another in quantity or detailed nature; two things); observe similarity or relation between (passages of book etc.; ∼ **notes,** exchange ideas or opinions); (Gram.) form comparative and superlative degrees of (adjective, adverb). **2.** *v.i.* bear comparison (*this compares favourably with previous results*), be on terms of equality *with*. [ME, f. OF *comparer* f. L COM(*parare* f. *par* equal)]

ompār′e² *n.* (literary). comparison (*beyond, without, compare*). [app. f. (*without) compare* (obs. var. of COM-PEER), assoc. w. prec.]

compa′rison *n.* act of comparing (**bear** or **stand** ∼, be able to be compared favourably *with*; **beyond** ∼, totally different in quality; **in** ∼ **with,** compared to); simile, illustration; **degrees of** ∼, (Gram.) positive, comparative, superlative, (of adjectives and adverbs). [ME, f. OF *comparesoun* f. L *comparatio -onis* (as COMPARE¹; see -ATION, -ISON)]

compār′tment *n.*, & *v.t.* **1.** *n.* division separated by partitions, esp. of railway carriage; watertight division of ship. **2.** *v.t.* put into compartments (lit. or fig.); hence ∼A′TION *n.* [f. F *compartiment* f. It. *compartimento* f. LL COM(*partiri* share); see -MENT]

compārtme′ntal *a.* consisting of or pertaining to compartment(s); hence ∼IZE (3) *v.t.*, ∼LY² *adv.* [f. prec. + -AL]

co′mpass¹ (kŭ′-) *n.* **1.** (usu. in *pl.*) instrument for taking measurements and describing circles, with two legs connected at one end by movable joint; **beam-**∼(**es**) (with beam connecting sliding sockets, for large circles); BOW¹-*compass(es)*. **2.** circumference,

boundary; area, extent, scope, (lit. or fig.; *beyond my compass*); range of tones of voice or musical instrument; (arch.) roundabout way (*fetch* or *go a compass*). **3.** instrument of navigation or orientation showing magnetic or true north and bearings from it (*mariner's compass,* GYRO-*compass*); BOX³ *the compass;* ∼ **card,** card showing the 32 principal bearings (*points of the compass;* see POINT¹ 19); ∼ **rose,** circle of the principal directions marked on chart; ∼-**saw,** narrow saw for cutting curves; ∼ **window,** bay window with semicircular curve. [ME, f. OF *compas* (*compasser;* see foll.)]

co′mpass² (kŭ′-) *v.t.* (literary). go round; hem in; grasp mentally; contrive, accomplish; hence ∼ABLE *a.* [ME, f. OF *compasser,* f. Rom. **compassare* measure (as COM-, L *passus* PACE¹)]

compa′ssion (-shon) *n.* pity inclining one to be helpful or merciful. [ME f. OF, f. eccl. L *compassio -onis* f. COM(*pati pass-* suffer); see -ION]

compa′ssionate¹ (-sho-) *a.* sympathetic, pitying; granted out of compassion; ‖(∼ **allowance** (granted when an ordinary pension or allowance is not admissible under official rules); ‖(∼ **leave** (granted on grounds of bereavement etc.); hence ∼LY² (-tlĭ) *adv.* [f. obs. F *compassionné* (*compassionner* feel pity f. as prec.) + -ATE²]

compa′ssionāte² (-sho-) *v.t.* (arch.) regard or treat with compassion. [f. prec. or obs. F *compassionner* (see prec.) + -ATE³]

compa′t|ible *a.* consistent, able to coexist, (*with*); mutually tolerant; (of equipment etc.) able to be used in combination; hence or cogn. ∼IBI′LITY *n.*, ∼IBLY *adv.* [F, f. med. L *compatibilis* (see COMPASSION, -IBLE)]

compā′triot *n.* fellow-countryman; hence ∼IC (-ŏ′t-) *a.* [f. F *compatriote* f. LL COM(*patriota* PATRIOT)]

compeer′ *n.* equal, peer; comrade. [ME f. OF *comper* (as COM-, PEER¹)]

compe′l *v.t.* (-**ll**-). constrain, force, (*to do, to a course of action*); bring about (an action) by force (*compel submission*); (arch.) drive forcibly; (in *pres. part.*) rousing strong interest or attention or feeling of admiration; hence ∼LABLE *a.* [ME, f. L COM(*pellere puls-* drive)]

compe′ndious *a.* comprehensive but fairly brief; hence ∼LY² *adv.*, ∼NESS *n.* [ME, f. OF *compendieux* f. L *compendiosus* brief (as foll.; see -OUS)]

compe′ndi|um *n.* (pl. ∼ums or ∼a). abridgement; summary, abstract; collection of table-games etc.; package of letter-stationery. [L, = what is weighed together, f. COM(*pendere* weigh)]

co′mpěnsāt|e *v.* **1.** *v.t.* counterbalance; recompense (person *for* thing); (Mech.) provide (pendulum etc.) with arrangement to neutralize effects of temperature etc. **2.** *v.i.* make amends (*for* thing, *to* person, *for* abs.). (Psych.) offset deficiency or frustration by developing another characteristic. **3.** Hence **compe′nsative** *a.*, ∼OR *n.*, **compe′nsatory** *a.* [f. L COM(*pensare* frequent. of *pendere pens-* weigh) + -ATE³]

cŏmpensā′tion *n.* compensating or being compensated; thing given as recompense; money given for requisitioned property; **salary or wages; (Psych.) act or result of compensating; ∼ **pendulum** (designed so as to neutralize effects of temperature variation); hence ∼AL *a.* [ME f. OF, f. L *compensatio* (as prec.; see -ATION)]

‖cŏ′mpère (-pār) *n.*, & *v.t.* **1.** *n.* person at variety entertainment who introduces the artistes, comments on the turns, etc. **2.** *v.t.* act as compère to. [F, = godfather, f. Rom. **compater* (as COM-, L *pater* father)]

compē′te *v.i.* strive (*with* or *against* another *for* thing, *in* doing, or abs.); strive for superiority *in* a quality. [f. L COM(*petere -tit-* seek), in late sense 'strive after or contend for (something)']

cŏ′mpětence, -cȳ, *ns.* sufficiency of means for living, easy circumstances; ability (*to do, for* a task); (of court, magistrate, etc.) legal capacity, right to take cognizance. [f. foll. + -ENCE, -ENCY]

cŏ′mpĕtent *a.* adequately qualified (*to do, for* a task); legally qualified (judge, court, witness); effective. adequate; (of action etc.) appropriate, legitimate; hence ∼LY² *adv.* [ME f. OF, or f. L competent- (as COMPETE; see -ENT)]

cŏmpĕtĭ′tion *n.* act of competing (*for*), by examination, in trade, etc.; event in which persons compete; those competing with one (*the competition is not very strong*); competition-WALLAH. [f. LL competitio rivalry (as foll.; see -ITION)]

compĕ′tĭtive *a.* of, by, offered for, involving, competition; (of prices etc.) comparable with those of rival sellers etc.; hence ∼LY² (-vlĭ) *adv.*, ∼NESS (-vn-) *n.* [f. p.p. st. of L competere (COMPETE) + -IVE]

compĕ′tĭtor *n.* one who competes, rival, esp. in trade. [f. F compétiteur or f. L competitor (as prec.; see -OR)]

cŏmpĭlā′tion *n.* compiling or being compiled; thing compiled. [ME f. OF, f. L compilatio -onis (as foll.; see -ATION)]

compī′l|e *v.t.* collect (materials) into a list, volume, etc.; make up (volume etc.) of such materials; accumulate (high score at cricket, etc.); hence ∼ER¹ *n.*, (esp.) routine for putting program into form suitable for a particular computer. [ME, f. OF compiler or its app. source, L compilare plunder, plagiarize]

complā′cency, -ce, *ns.* tranquil pleasure, esp. self--satisfaction. [f. med. L complacentia f. L COM(placēre please); see -ENCY]

complā′cent *a.* self-satisfied; hence ∼LY² *adv.* [f. L complacēre; see prec., -ENT]

complai′n *v.i.* express dissatisfaction (*at, that*); emit mournful sound, groan, creak; ∼ **of,** express dissatisfaction with, announce that one is suffering from (headache etc.), state grievance concerning; hence ∼ANT *n.*, plaintiff in certain lawsuits. [ME, f. OF complaindre (st. -aign-) f. Rom. COM(plangere planctlament) bewail]

complai′nt *n.* utterance of grievance; expression of grief; formal accusation; *plaintiff's case in civil action; subject or ground of complaint; bodily ailment. [ME, f. OF complainte (complaint p.p. of complaindre; see prec.)]

complai′s|ance (-z-) *n.* politeness; deference; willingness to please others; acquiescence; so ∼ANT *a.* [F, f. complaire (st. -plais-) acquiesce to please, f. L complacēre (see COMPLACENCY)]

complea′t. See COMPLETE¹.

cŏ′mplĕment¹ *n.* that which completes; (Gram.) word(s) added to verb to complete the predicate; full number required (to man ship, fill conveyance, etc.); (Math.) ∼ **of an angle,** its deficiency from 90° (cf. SUPPLEMENT¹); (Biol.) = ALEXIN; hence ∼AL (-ĕ′n-) *a.* [ME, f. L complementum (as COMPLETE¹; see -MENT)]

cŏ′mplĕmĕnt² *v.t.* complete; form complement to. [f. prec.]

cŏmplĕmĕ′ntar|y *a.* completing, forming a complement; (of two or more things) complementing each other; ∼y angles (making up 90°); complementary COLOUR¹s; hence ∼ĭLY² *adv.*, cŏmplĕmĕntā′rĭty *n.*, (esp., Phys.) explainability of phenomena in terms of waves and particles jointly. [f. COMPLEMENT¹ + -ARY¹]

complē′te¹ *a.* having all its parts, entire; finished; having the maximum extent or degree (*it was a complete surprise; he was a complete stranger*); accomplished (*a complete horseman;* also **compleat,** after Walton's *Compleat Angler*); ∼ **with,** having (as important accompaniment); hence ∼LY² (-tlĭ) *adv.*, ∼NESS (-tn-) *n.* [ME, f. OF complet f. L completus p.p. of COMPLĒre fill up]

complē′te² *v.t.* finish; make whole or perfect; make up the amount of; add what is required to (questionnaire etc.); so **complē′tION** *n.* [f. prec.]

cŏ′mplĕx¹ *n.* complex whole; (Psych.) related group of usu. repressed ideas etc. causing abnormal behaviour or mental state (INFERIORITY complex, OEDIPUS complex), (pop.) obsession; (Chem.) complex substance. [f. L complexus embrace etc. as (as foll.)]

cŏ′mplĕx² *a.* consisting of parts, composite; complicated; (Chem.) formed by combination of compounds; (Math.) containing real and IMAGINARY parts; complex SENTENCE; hence complĕ′xĬTY *n.*, ∼LY² *adv.* [f. F complexe or f. L complexus p.p. of complectere embrace, assoc. w. complexus plaited]

complĕ′xion (-kshon) *n.* natural colour, texture, and appearance, of the skin (esp. of face); (fig.) character, aspect, (*put a different complexion on the matter*); hence (-)∼ED² (-nd) *a.*, ∼LESS *a.*, pale-faced. [ME f. OF, f. L complexio -onis (as prec.; see -ION); orig. = combination of supposed qualities determining nature of a body]

compli′ance *n.* action in accordance with request, command, etc. (**in** ∼ **with,** according to (wish etc.)); unworthy submission; (Mech.) (degree of) yielding under applied force. [f. COMPLY + -ANCE]

compli′ant *a.* disposed to comply, yielding; hence ∼LY² *adv.* [f. COMPLY + -ANT]

cŏ′mplicacy *n.* complexity; complicated structure. [f. foll. + -ACY]

cŏ′mplicāte *v.t.* mix up (*with* other things); (esp. in *p.p.*) make complex or intricate. [f. L COM(plicare fold) + -ATE³]

cŏmplicā′tion *n.* involved condition; entangled state of affairs; complicating circumstance (*here is a further complication*); (Path.) secondary disease or condition aggravating a previous one. [F, or f. LL complicatio (as prec.; see -ATION)]

compli′cĭty *n.* partnership in wrongdoing. [f. complice (see ACCOMPLICE) + -ITY]

cŏ′mplĭmĕnt¹ *n.* polite expression of praise; act implying praise; (in *pl.*) formal greetings (esp. as accompaniment to message, note, present, etc.; often printed on ∼ **slip**); **the** ∼**s of** (greeting appropriate to) **the season; return the** ∼, give compliment in return for another, (fig.) give benefit, or retaliate, in kind; hence ∼ARY¹ (-ĕ′n-) *a.*, expressing compliment(s), given free of charge by way of compliment. [F, f. It. complimento f. Rom. *complimentum f. L (as COMPLEMENT¹)]

cŏ′mplĭmĕnt² *v.t.* pay compliment to (person *on* thing); present (person *with* thing) as mark of courtesy. [f. F complimenter (as prec.)]

co′mpline *n.* (Eccl.) (office of) last of the canonical hours of prayer. [ME, f. OF complie, fem. p.p. (as n.) of obs. complir complete f. Rom. *complire f. L COMplēre fill up]

comply′ *v.i.* act in accordance (*with* wish, command, etc., or abs.). [f. It. complire f. Cat. complir, Sp. cumplir f. L COMplēre fill up]

cŏ′mpō *n.* (*pl.* ∼**s**). composition, esp. = stucco, plaster; composite; ∼ **rations** (in large pack designed to last several days). [abbr.]

compō′nent *a.* & *n.* **1.** *a.* contributing to the composition of a whole. **2.** *n.* component part, esp. of motor vehicle; (Math.) one of two or more vectors equivalent to given vector. [f. L COM(ponere put); see -ENT]

compō′r′t *v.t.* & *i.* (literary). conduct or behave oneself; ∼ **with,** suit, befit; so ∼MENT *n.* [f. L COM(portare carry)]

compos. See COMPOS MENTIS.

compō′s|e (-z) *v.t.* **1.** (Of elements) make up, constitute, (esp. in *pass.*, *be composed of*). **2.** construct in words, produce in literary form (poem etc. or abs.); (Mus.) construct in notes, produce in written form, (song, symphony, etc., or abs.) set (words) to music; (Print.) set up (type) to form words and blocks of words, set up (article etc.) in type; put together to form a whole, arrange artistically. **3.** settle (dispute etc.). **4.** arrange in specified or understood manner, or for specified purpose, (*compose yourself to write, your countenance, your thoughts for action*); calm (oneself, passions, etc.; esp. in *p.p.*, whence ∼ĕdLY² *adv.*). [f. F composer, f. L COM(ponere put); see POSE¹]

compō′ser (-z-) *n.* one who composes (esp. music). [f. prec. + -ER¹]

For other words in *co-* see CO-.

cŏ'mposĭte (-z-) *a.* & *n.* (thing) made up of various parts; (material) made of constituents that remain recognizable; (Archit.) fifth classical (order), Ionic and Corinthian mixed; (Bot.) (plant) of family Compositae, in which the so-called flower is a head of many flowers, e.g. daisy, dandelion; hence ∿LY² (-tlĭ) *adv.*, ∿NESS (-tn-) *n.* [F, f. L *compositus* p.p. of COM(*ponere* posit- put); see -ITE²]

cŏmposĭ'tion (-z-) *n.* **1.** act of putting together; formation, construction; formation of words into a compound word. **2.** construction of sentences, art of literary production; act or art of composing music; setting-up of type. **3.** mental constitution (*a touch of madness in his composition*); constitution of a substance, nature of its ingredients; arrangement (of parts of picture etc.). **4.** thing composed, mixture; piece of music or writing; compound artificial substance, esp. one serving the purpose of a natural one. **5.** compromise; agreement for payment of sum in lieu of larger sum or other obligation (*made a composition with his creditors*); sum thus paid. **6.** Hence ∿AL *a.* [ME f. OF, f. L *compositio* -*onis* (as prec.; see -ITION)]

compŏ'sĭtor (-z-) *n.* one who sets up type for printing. [ME, f. AF *compostour* f. L *compositor* (as COMPOSITE; see -OR)]

compŏs (mentĭs) (kŏ'mpŏs mě'ntĭs) *a.* having control of one's mind, not mad. [L]

compŏ'ssĭble *a.* able to coexist (*with*). [OF, f. med. L *compossibilis* (as COM-, POSSIBLE)]

cŏ'mpŏst *n.*, *a. v.t.* (treat with or make into) mixed manure of organic origin; loam soil or other medium with added organic matter to grow plants in; (fig.) mixture of ingredients; ∿ **heap** or **pile**, structure of alternate layers of garden refuse, soil, etc., for quick production of compost. [ME, f. OF *composte* f. L *compos(i)tum* (as COMPOSITE)]

compŏ'sure (-zher) *n.* tranquil demeanour, calmness. [f. COMPOSE + -URE]

cŏ'mpŏte *n.* fruit preserved or cooked in syrup. [F, f. OF *composte,* f. **compos(i)ta* (as COMPOSITE)]

compoŭnd¹ *v.* **1.** *v.t.* mix (ingredients, lit. or fig.); combine (verbal elements) into a word; make up (a composite whole); increase, complicate, (difficulties etc.). **2.** settle (matter by mutual concession, debt by partial payment, subscription by lump sum, or abs.). **3.** condone (liability, offence) for money etc., forbear prosecution of (felony) from private motives. **4.** Hence ∿ABLE *a.* **5.** *v.i.* come to terms (*with* person) for forgoing claim etc., *for* offence). [ME *compoun(e)* f. OF *compondre* f. L COM(*ponere* put); -*d* as in *expound*]

cŏ'mpoŭnd² *a.* & *n.* **1.** *a.* made up of several ingredients; consisting of several parts or (Zool.) individual organisms or (Biol.) simple parts; combined, collective; ∿ **fracture** (complicated by skin wound); *compound* INTEREST¹; ∿ **interval** (Mus.) exceeding one octave); *compound* SENTENCE; ∿ **time** (Mus., having more than one group of simple-time units in each bar). **2.** *n.* mixture of elements, compound thing, esp. compound word; (Chem.) substance consisting of two or more elements chemically united in fixed proportions by weight. [ME, orig. p.p. of *compoun(e)*; see prec.]

cŏ'mpoŭnd³ *n.* (In India, China, etc.) enclosure in which house or factory stands; (in S. Afr.) enclosure in which miners live; large fenced-in space in prison etc.; = POUND². [f. Port. *campon* or Du. *kampong* f. Malay]

compradŏr'(e) *n.* Chinese chief agent of foreign business-house; (fig.) agent of a foreign power. [Port. *comprador* buyer f. LL *comparator* f. L *comparare* purchase]

cŏmprehĕ'nd *v.t.* grasp mentally, understand, (person, thing); include, take in. [ME, f. OF *comprehender* or f. L COM(*prehendere* -*hens-* grasp)]

cŏmprehĕ'ns|ĭble *a.* ∿ (**to**), that may be understood (by); that may be comprised; hence ∿IBI'LITY *n.*, ∿IBLY *adv.* [f. F *compréhensible* or f. L *comprehensibilis* (as prec.; see -IBLE)]

cŏmprehĕ'nsion (-shon) *n.* act or faculty of understanding, esp. of writing or speech; inclusion; (Eccl. Hist.) inclusion of Nonconformists in Anglican Church. [f. F *compréhension* or f. L *comprehensio* (as prec.; see -ION)]

cŏmprehĕ'nsĭve *a.* & *n.* including much or all (*comprehensive term*; *comprehensive grasp,* fig. or lit.); of understanding (*comprehensive faculty*); ∿ (**school**), large secondary school providing courses for children of all abilities; hence ∿LY² (-vlĭ) *adv.*, ∿NESS (-vn-) *n.* [f. F *compréhensif* -*ive* or f. LL *comprehensivus* (as prec.; see -IVE)]

cŏ'mprĕss¹ *n.* soft pad of lint etc. for compressing artery etc.; (**water**) ∿, piece of wet cloth covered with waterproof bandage, for relief of inflammation. [f. F *compresse* (*compresser*; see foll.)]

comprĕ'ss² *v.t.* squeeze together; bring (air, language, expressed thoughts) into smaller space; ∿ed **air** (at more than atmospheric pressure); hence ∿IBLE, ∿IVE, *adjs.,* ∿ION (-shon) *n.,* (also) (amount of) reduction in volume of fuel mixture in internal combustion engine before ignition. [ME, f. OF *compresser* or f. LL *compressare* frequent. of L COM-(*primere press-* = *premere* press)]

comprĕ'ssor *n.* machine for compressing air or other gasses. [f. prec. + -OR]

comprī's|e (-z) *v.t.* include, comprehend; consist of (*the house comprises three bedrooms etc.*); compose, make up; hence ∿ABLE *a.* [ME. f. F, fem. p.p. of *comprendre* COMPREHEND]

cŏ'mpromĭse¹ (-z) *n.* settlement of dispute by mutual concession; (finding of) intermediate way *between* conflicting opinions, courses, etc., by modification of each. [ME, f. OF *compromis* f. LL *compromissum* neut. p.p. (as n.) of COM(*promittere* PROMISE²)]

cŏ'mpromĭse² (-z) *v.* **1.** *v.t.* settle (dispute) by mutual concession; bring (person, one*self*) under suspicion or into danger by indiscreet action. **2.** *v.i.* make a compromise. [f. prec.]

compte rendu (kawnt rahndü') *n.* (*pl.* -**es** -*us pr.* same). report; review; statement. [F]

Cŏmptŏ'meter (P) type of calculating-machine. [app. f. F *compte* COUNT¹ + -O- + -METER]

comptrŏ'ller (kŏn-) *n.* controller (sp. retained in some titles of financial officers, esp. *Comptroller and Auditor General,* **Comptroller General*). [var. of CON-TROLLER by erron. assoc. w. COUNT¹, L *computus*]

compŭ'lsion (-shon) *n.* constraint, obligation; (**under** ∿, because one is compelled); (Psych.) irresistible urge to a form of behaviour esp. against one's normal wishes. [ME f. F, f. LL *compulsio* -*onis* (as COMPEL; see -ION)]

compŭ'lsĭve *a.* tending to compel; resulting or acting (as if) from compulsion (*compulsive gambler*); *n.* (Psych.) contrary to one's conscious wishes; irresistible (*the book is compulsive reading*); hence ∿LY² (-vlĭ) *adv.* [f. med. L *compulsivus* (as COMPEL; see -IVE)]

compŭ'lsor|y̆ *a.* (of action) enforced; compelling (*compulsory legislation* etc., comp. *permissive*); ∿y **purchase** by authority, of land etc. needed for public purposes; hence ∿ILY² *adv.,* ∿INESS *n.* [f. med. L *compulsorius* (as COMPEL; see -ORY)]

compŭ'nct|ion *n.* pricking of conscience; slight regret, scruple, (*without compunction*); hence ∿IOUS (-shus) *a.* [ME, f. OF *componction* f. eccl. L *compunctio* -*onis* f. L COM(*pungere punct-* prick); see -ION]

cŏmpŭrgā'tion *n.* clearing from charge or accusation by oaths of others; see also **cŏ'mpŭrgātor** *n.,* (Hist.) witness who swore to innocence or good character of accused person, **compŭr'gatory** *a.* [f. med. L *compurgatio* f. COM(*purgare* purify); see -ATION]

compū'te *v.* **1.** *v.t.* reckon (number or amount, *that*). **2.** *v.i.* make reckoning, use computer. **3.** Hence **compūTABLE** (-pū'-, kŏ'-) *a.,* **cŏmpūtA'TION** *n.* [f. F *computer* or f. L COM(*putare* reckon)]

compŭ'ter *n.* automatic electronic apparatus for making calculations or controlling operations that are expressible in numerical or logical terms; reckoner, calculator; hence ∿IZE *v.t.*, equip with, perform by, produce by, computer. [f. prec.+-ER¹]

cŏ'mrade (-rād, -rĭd) *n.* mate or fellow in work or play or (also ∿-in-arms) fighting, an equal with whom one is on familiar terms, (usu. of males); fellow socialist, communist, etc., (also as *voc.*, or title before name); hence ∿LY¹ (-dlĭ) *a.*, ∿SHIP (-dsh-) *n.* [earlier cama-, camerade f. F, f. Sp. camarada room-mate (as CHAMBER; see -ADE)]

cŏ'msăt *n.* satellite used for communication. [abbr.]

Cŏ'mt|ism *n.* = POSITIVISM; so ∿IST (2) *n.* [f. A. Comte, Fr. philosopher d. 1857+-ISM]

cŏn¹ *v.t.* (-nn-) ∿ (over), study, learn by heart. [ME cunn-, con, forms of CAN²]

cŏn², ***cŏnn**, *v.t.* (-nn-). direct steering of (ship, or abs.); **co'nning-tower**, armoured pilot-house of warship, superstructure of submarine from which steering, firing, etc., are directed when it is on or near the surface, and which contains periscope. [app. weakened form of obs. cond, condie, f. F conduire f. L conducere CONDUCT²]

cŏn³ *n.* **1.** (colloq.) confidence (trick etc.). **2.** contra. **3.** (sl.) convict. [abbr.]

cŏn⁴ *v.t.* (-nn-). (sl.) persuade; swindle. [f. prec. = confidence]

con- *pref.*, assim. form of COM- before c, d, f, g, j, n, q, s, t, v, and occas. before vowels (conurbation).

cŏ'năcre (-ker) *n.* (Ir.) letting by tenant of small portions of land prepared for crop or grazing. [f. CORN¹+ACRE]

con amore (kŏn amōr'ā) *adv.* with devotion or zeal; (Mus.) with tenderness. [It., = with love]

conā'tion *n.* (Philos.) desire to perform an action, volition, voluntary action; so **cŏ'natIVE** *a.* [f. L conatio (conari try; see -ATION)]

con brio (kŏn brē'ō) *adv.* (Mus.) with vigour. [It.]

concă'tèn|āte (-n-k-) *v.t.* link together (fig.); so ∿A'TION *n.* [f. LL CON(catenare f. catena chain)+-ATE³]

cŏ'ncāve (-n-k-) *a.* with outline or surface curved like interior of circle or sphere (cf. CONVEX); hence or cogn. ∿LY² (-vlĭ) *adv.*, **concā'vITY** (-n-k-) *n.* [f. L CON(cavus hollow), or thr. F concave]

concea'l *v.t.* keep secret (from); not allow to be seen or noticed; so ∿MENT *n.* [ME, f. OF conceler f. L CON(celare hide)]

concē'de *v.t.* admit to be true (that, defeat, etc.); grant (right, privilege, points or start in game etc.; to person); (Sport) allow opponent(s) to score (goal), to win (match), etc.; admit defeat in (election etc.). [f. F concéder or L CON(cedere cess- yield)]

concei't (-sē't) *n.* personal vanity; fanciful notion, far-fetched comparison, etc. esp. as affectation of style; (arch.) **in one's own ∿** (judgement), **out of ∿**, no longer pleased with. [ME, f. CONCEIVE after deceit, deceive, etc.]

concei'tèd (-sē't-) *a.* having too high an opinion of one's own beauty, ability, etc.; hence ∿LY² *adv.* [f. prec.+-ED²]

concei'v|able (-sē'v-) *a.* that can be (mentally) conceived; hence ∿ABI'LITY, ∿ableNESS (-beln-), *ns.*, ∿ABLY *adv.* [f. foll.+-ABLE]

concei've (-sē'v) *v.t. & i.* become pregnant (with); ∿ (of), form in the mind (conceive a dislike for), imagine; fancy, think, (that); (usu. in pass.) formulate, express, (conceived in plain terms). [ME, f. OF conceiv- stressed st. of concevoir f. L CON(cipere cept- = capere take).]

concē'lèbr|āte *v.i.* (RC Ch., of two or more priests) celebrate mass together, (esp., of newly ordained priest) celebrate mass with ordaining bishop; hence ∿ANT, ∿A'TION, *ns.* [f. L CON(celebrare CELEBRATE)+-ATE³]

cŏ'ncentr|āte *v. & n.* **1.** *v.t.* bring together to one point (troops, power, attention); (Chem.) increase strength

of (liquid etc.) by removing water or other diluent; (fig., in p.p., of hate etc.) intense. **2.** *v.i.* employ all one's power or attention (on, upon). **3.** Hence ∿A'TION *n.* (∿ation camp, for detention of political prisoners, internees, etc., esp. in Nazi Germany), ∿ātIVE *a.*, ∿ātOR *n.* **4.** *n.* concentrated substance; concentrated form of something, esp. animal food. [f. after concentre f. F concentrer (f. as CON-+CENTRE¹)+-ATE³]

∥concē'ntre (-ter), ***-ter**, *v.t. & i.* bring or come to a common centre. [f. F concentrer (see prec.)]

concē'ntr|ic *a.* having a common centre (with, or abs.); hence ∿ICALLY *adv.*, **cŏncentrī'cITY** *n.* [ME, f. OF concentrique or f. med. L CON(centricus, as CENTRE¹; see -IC)]

cŏ'ncĕpt *n.* idea of a class of objects; general notion (the concept of evolution); invention (a new concept in caravans). [f. LL conceptus f. concept- (see CONCEIVE)]

concē'ption *n.* conceiving or being conceived; thing conceived, idea, (**no ∿ of**, inability to imagine); hence ∿AL *a.* [ME f. OF, f. L conceptio -onis (as prec.; see -ION)]

concē'ptIVE *a.* conceiving (mentally); of conception. [f. L conceptivus (as prec.; see -IVE)]

concē'ptŭal *a.* of mental conceptions or concepts; hence ∿IZE (3) *v.t.* [f. med. L conceptualis (conceptus, as prec.; see -AL)]

concē'ptŭal|ism *n.* (Philos.) doctrine that universals exist, but only as mental concepts; so ∿IST (2) *n.* [f. prec.+-ISM]

concē'r'n¹ *v.t.* **1.** relate to, affect; **to whom it may ∿** (introducing testimonial etc.). **2.** interest oneself (with, in, about, matter; to do). [f. F concerner or f. LL CON(cernere sift, discern)]

concē'r'n² *n.* **1.** relation, reference, (with); **have no ∿** (nothing to do) **with; have a ∿** (interest, share) **in. 2.** (feeling of) anxiety or worry (asked with deep concern); (in Quaker use) conviction of divine will; matter that affects one (no concern of mine); (in pl.) affairs (meddling in my concerns); business, firm, (sold as a GOING² concern; see GO¹ 6); (colloq.) thing (smashed the whole concern). [f. prec.]

concē'r'n|ed (-nd) *a.* involved, interested, (spoke to the people concerned; concerned to prove, with proving, his innocence); troubled, anxious, (a concerned air; am concerned that, to hear, at, for person, about); **be ∿ed,** take part (in); **I am not ∿ed,** it is not my business (to); **as or so far as I am ∿ed,** as regards my interests; hence ∿èdLY² *adv.*, ∿èdNESS *n.* [p.p. of CONCERN¹]

concē'r'ning *prep.* about, regarding. [f. CONCERN¹+-ING²]

concē'r'nment *n.* affair, business; importance; being concerned (with); anxiety. [f. CONCERN¹+-MENT]

cŏ'ncert¹ *n.* **1.** agreement, union, (work in concert (with); **C∿ of Europe,** (Hist.) chief European powers acting together); combination of voices or sounds (voices raised in concert). **2.** musical entertainment by two or more performers; ∿-goer, one who frequents concerts; ∿ **grand,** grand piano of largest size for concerts; ∿ **-master,** leading first-violin player in some orchestras; ∿ **overture,** (Mus.) piece like overture but for independent performance; ∿ **performance** (of opera etc., without scenery, costume, or action); ∿ **pitch,** (Mus.) pitch normally used for performances, (fig.) state of unusual efficiency or readiness. [F, f. It. (see foll.)]

concē'r't¹ *v.t.* arrange (by mutual agreement or co-ordination). [f. F concerter, v.t. concertare harmonize, of uncert. orig.]

concē'r'tèd *a.* in vbl senses; (Mus.) arranged in parts for voices or instruments. [p.p.p. of prec.]

cŏncertī'na (-tē'-) *n. & v.* (∿ed or ∿'d, pr. -ad). **1.** *n.* portable musical instrument consisting of a bellows and reeds, with set of finger-studs at each end to

For other words in co- see CO-.

control valves. **2.** *v.t.* & *i.* compress or collapse in folds like those of concertina. [f. CONCERT¹ + -INA]

concerti'no (-nchērtē'-) *n.* (*pl.* ∼s). (Mus.) simple or short concerto; solo instrument(s) in concerto. [It., dim. of foll.]

concer't|o (-nchēr'-, -ār'-) *n.* (*pl.* ∼os, *or* ∼i *pr.* -ē). (Mus.) composition (usu. in three movements) for solo instrument(s) accompanied by orchestra; ∼o **grosso** (grō'sō), composition with small group of solo instruments accompanied by orchestra. [It. (see CONCERT¹); *grosso* big]

conce'ssion (-shon) *n.* act of conceding; thing conceded, esp. right to use land etc. (esp. for specific purpose) or sell goods; land or premises thus used; hence ∼ARY¹ *a.* [F, or f. L *concessio* (as CONCEDE; see -ION)]

concessionair'e, -nnair'e, (-shonār') *n.* holder of concession or grant, esp. of use of land or trading rights. [F (-*nn*-) (as prec.; see -ARY¹)]

conce'ssive *a.* of or tending to concession; (Gram.) expressing concession. [f. LL *concessivus* (as CONCEDE; see -IVE)]

conch (-nch, -ngk) *n.* shellfish, esp. large gastropod; its shell; (Archit.) domed roof of semicircular apse; = foll. [f. L *concha* shell f. Gk *kogkhē* mussel etc.]

co'ncha (-ngka) *n.* (*pl.* ∼e). external ear or its central cavity. [L (see prec.)]

co'nchie, co'nchy, (-nshĭ) *n.* (sl.) conscientious objector. [abbr.]

conchoi'dal (-ngk-) *a.* (Min., of crystal fracture etc.) like the surface of a bivalve shell. [f. CONCH + -OID + -AL]

concho'log|y (-ngk-) *n.* study of shells and shellfish; so **concho**LO'GICAL (-ngk-) *a.*, ∼IST (3) *n.* [f. Gk *kogkhē* shell; see -LOGY]

co'ncierge (kaw'nsĭārzh, kŏ'n-) *n.* (In France etc.) door-keeper, porter, (esp. of flats etc.). [F, f. Rom. *CONservius* fellow slave]

conci'liar *a.* of ecclesiastical councils. [f. med. L *consiliarius* counsellor; see -AR²]

conci'li|ate *v.t.* pacify; win over from hostility; reconcile (disagreeing parties etc., e.g. employer and employees without arbitration); gain (esteem, goodwill); hence ∼ATIVE, **a**tORY (-lya-), *adjs.*, ∼**ātor** *n.* [f. L *conciliare* combine, gain (*concilium* COUNCIL) + -ATE³]

concilia'tion *n.* reconcilement; use of conciliating measures. [f. L *conciliatio* (as prec.; see -ATION)]

conci'nnity *n.* elegance or neatness of literary style. [f. L *concinnitas* (*concinnus* well-adjusted; see -ITY)]

conci'se *a.* (Of speech, writing, style, person) brief but comprehensive in expression; hence ∼LY² (-slĭ) *adv.*, ∼NESS (-sn-) *n.* [f. F *concis* or f. L *concisus* p.p. of CON(*cidere cis-* = *caedere* cut)]

conci'sion (-zhon) *n.* conciseness (esp. of style). [ME, f. L *concisio* (as prec.; see -ION)]

co'nclave (-n-k-) *n.* meeting-place or assembly of cardinals for election of pope; private meeting. [ME f. OF f. L CON*clave* lockable room (*clavis* key)]

conclu'de (-n-klōō'd) *v.t.* & *i.* bring or come to an end, make an end (of), (conclude one's *speech* etc., or *conclude*, *with* remark etc., *by* saying etc.); infer (*from* premisses etc.); settle, arrange, (treaty etc.); decide (*to do*). [ME, f. L CON(*cludere clus-* = *claudere* shut)]

conclu'sion (-n-klōō'zhon) *n.* **1.** termination; final result; decision; **in** ∼, lastly, to conclude. **2.** judgement reached by reasoning; (Logic) proposition reached from previous ones, esp. last of three forming a syllogism; JUMP² *to conclusions*; **try** ∼**s with**, engage in trial of skill etc. with. **3.** settling, arrangement, (*of* peace etc.). [ME f. OF, or f. L *conclusio* (as prec.; see -ION)]

conclu'sive (-n-klōō'-) *a.* decisive, convincing; hence ∼LY² (-vlĭ) *adv.*, ∼NESS (-vn-) *n.* [f. LL *conclusivus* (as prec.; see -IVE)]

conco'ct (-n-k-) *v.t.* make up of mixed ingredients (soup, drink; story, plot); hence or cogn. ∼ION, ∼OR, *ns.* [f. L CON(*coquere coct-* cook)]

conco'mitance, -cy, (kon-k-) *ns.* coexistence, esp. doctrine of coexistence of body and blood of Christ in each of the Eucharistic elements (esp. in the bread). [f. med. L *concomitantia* (as foll.; see -ANCE, -ANCY)]

conco'mitant (-n-k-) *a.* & *n.* **1.** *a.* going together (*concomitant circumstances*); hence ∼LY² *adv.* **2.** *n.* accompanying thing. [f. LL CON(*comitari* f. L *comes -mitis* companion); see -ANT]

co'ncord¹ (-ngk-, -n-k-) *n.* agreement, harmony, between persons or things; treaty; (Mus.) chord pleasing or satisfactory in itself without others to follow; (Gram.) agreement between words in gender, number, etc. [ME f. OF *concorde* f. L *concordia* f. CON(*cors* f. *cor cordis* heart) of one mind]

*****Co'ncord**² (-ngk-, -n-k-) *n.* ∼ **grape** (large dark variety). [∼ in Massachusetts]

conco'rdance (kon-k-) *n.* agreement; alphabetical arrangement of (chief) words occurring in a book (esp. the Bible) or author, usu. with citations of the passages concerned. [ME f. OF, f. med. L *concordantia* (as foll.; see -ANCE)]

conco'rdant (-n-k-) *a.* agreeing, harmonious, (*with*, or abs.); in musical concord; hence ∼LY² *adv.* [ME f. OF, f. L *concordare* (*concors*; see CONCORD¹, -ANT)]

conco'rdat (-n-k-) *n.* agreement, esp. between Church and State. [F, or f. L *concordatum* neut. p.p. (as n.) of *concordare* (see prec.)]

concours d'élégance (kawnkoor dělěgah'ns) *n.* parade of vehicles with prizes for the most elegant-looking. [F, = contest of elegance]

co'ncourse (-ngkōrs, -n-k-) *n.* crowd; coming together of things (*fortuitous concourse of atoms*); open central area in large public building, railway station, etc. [ME, f. OF *concours* f. L *concursus* (as CONCUR)]

concre'sc|ence (kon-k-) *n.* (Biol.) coalescence, growing together; so ∼ENT *a.* [f. CON-, after *excrescence* etc.]

co'ncrete¹ (-n-k-, -ngk-) *a.*, *n.*, & *v.t.* **1.** *a.* existing in material form, real, (**in the** ∼, in sphere of reality or practice); specific, definite (*concrete evidence, proposals*); (Gram., of noun) denoting thing as opposed to quality, state, or action, not abstract; ∼ **music** (constructed by rearrangement of recorded sounds); ∼ **poetry** (using typographical devices to enhance visual effect); hence ∼LY² (-tlĭ) *adv.* **2.** *n.* composition of gravel, cement, etc., for building; ∼**mixer,** machine (usu. with revolving drum) for mixing ingredients of concrete. **3.** *v.t.* cover with concrete; embed in concrete. [f. F *concret* or f. L *concretus* p.p. of CON(*crescere cret-* grow)]

concre'te² (-n-k-) *v.t.* & *i.* form into a mass, solidify; make concrete instead of abstract. [f. prec.]

concre'tion (-n-k-) *n.* coalescence; concreted mass, esp. (Path.) morbid formation in the body, stone; (Geol.) mass formed of solid particles, whence ∼ARY¹ *a.* [f. L *concretio* (as CONCRETE¹; SEE -ION)]

co'ncretiz|e, -īs|e, (-n-k-, -ngk-; -īz) *v.t.* make concrete instead of abstract; hence ∼A'TION *n.* [f. CONCRETE¹ + -IZE]

concu'bin|age (-n-k-) *n.* cohabiting of man and woman not legally married; having or being a concubine; so ∼ARY¹ *a.* [ME f. F (as foll.; see -AGE)]

co'ncubine *n.* woman who cohabits with a man, not being his wife; (among polygamous peoples) secondary wife. [ME f. OF, f. L CON(*cubina* f. *cubare* lie; see -INE⁴)]

concu'pisc|ence (kon-k-) *n.* sexual desire; so ∼ENT *a.* [ME f. OF, f. LL *concupiscentia* f. L CON*cupiscere* begin to desire, incept. f. *cupere* desire; see -ENCE]

concur' (-n-k-) *v.i.* (-**rr**-). happen together, coincide; (of cause etc.) combine in its action (*with*, or abs.); agree in opinion, express agreement, (*with*). [f. L CON(*currere* run)]

concu'rr|ent (-n-k-) *a.* running in same direction, or parallel lines; (of three or more lines) meeting at or tending to one point; existing or acting together or at the same time (*with*); agreeing; hence ∼ENCE *n.*, ∼ent LY² *adv.* [f. as prec.; see -ENT]

concu′ss (-n-k-) *v.t.* subject to concussion; shake violently; (arch.) intimidate. [f. L CON(*cutere cuss-* = *quatere* shake)]

concu′ssion (-n-kŭ′shon) *n.* violent shaking; shock; (Med.) injury to brain etc. caused by heavy blow etc. [f. L *concussio* (as prec.; see -ION)]

condĕ′mn (-m) *v.t.* **1.** censure, blame. **2.** give judgement against; bring about conviction of (*his looks condemn him*); sentence *to* punishment, esp. sentence to death; *condemned* CELL. **3.** pronounce forfeited (smuggled goods etc.), unfit for use, uninhabitable, incurable. **4.** Hence ~ABLE (-mn-) *a.* [ME, f. OF *condem*(*p*)*ner* f. L CON(*demnare* = *damnare* DAMN)]

cŏndĕmnā′tion *n.* censure; judicial conviction; ground for condemning (*his own conduct is his condemnation*). [ME, f. LL *condemnatio* (as prec.; see -ATION)]

condĕ′mnatorў *a.* expressing condemnation. [f. med. L *condemnatorius* (as CONDEMN; see -ORY)]

condensāte (kondĕ′-, kŏ′nde-) *n.* product of condensation. [f. CONDENSE + -ATE¹]

cŏndĕnsā′tion *n.* act of condensing; condensed material (esp. of water on cold windows etc.; ~ **trail**, trail of water from aircraft or rocket at high altitude, seen as white streak against sky); abridgement; (Chem.) combination of molecules with elimination of water etc. [f. LL *condensatio* (as foll.; see -ATION)]

condĕ′nse *v.t.* & *i.* make denser or more compact (~ed **milk**, milk thickened by evaporation and sweetened); reduce or be reduced from gas or vapour to liquid; express in fewer words, make concise; hence ~ABLE *a.*, ~ERY (3) *n.*, factory for making condensed milk. [f. F *condenser* or L CON(*densare* f. *densus* thick)]

condĕ′nser *n.* In vbl senses; chamber in steam-engine in which steam is condensed on leaving cylinder; (Chem) device for condensing vapour leaving flask etc.; (Electr.) = CAPACITOR; lens or system of lenses for concentrating light. [f. prec. + -ER¹]

cŏndĕscĕ′nd *v.i.* be gracious enough (*to* do) though showing one's feeling of dignity or superiority; disregard one's superiority (*to* a person); hence ~ING² *a.*, patronizing, kind to inferiors. [ME, f. OF *condescendre* f. eccl. L (*descendere* DESCEND)]

cŏndĕscĕ′nsion (-shon) *n.* affability to inferiors; patronizing manner. [obs. F, f. eccl. L *condescensio* (as prec.; see -ION)]

condī′gn (-ī′n) *a.* (Usu. of punishment) severe and well-deserved; hence ~LY² *adv.* [ME, f. OF *condigne* f. L CON(*dignus* worthy)]

cŏ′ndiment *n.* substance used to give relish to food, seasoning. [ME, f. L *condimentum* (*condire* pickle; see -MENT)]

condi′tion¹ *n.* **1.** stipulation, thing upon the fulfilment of which depends that of another, (**on** ~ **that**, with the condition that); (Gram.) clause expressing a condition; *subject in which student must pass examination within stated time to maintain provisionally granted status. **2.** (in *pl.*) circumstances, esp. those essential to a thing's existence (*conditions of equilibrium*; *favourable conditions*; *under existing conditions*). **3.** state of being (*eggs arrived, machine is still, in good condition*; *not in a condition to be mended*); social rank (*all sorts and conditions of men*); **in**, **out of**, ~, in good, bad, condition; **in no** ~, certainly not fit enough *to* do; ~ **powder**, medicine to keep animal in condition. **4.** state of being physically or mentally abnormal (*has a heart condition*). [ME, f. OF *condicion* f. L *condicio -onis* f. CON(*dicere* say) agree on; see -ION]

condi′tion² *v.t.* **1.** govern, determine; impose conditions on (*they condition the universe anew*); be essential to (*the two things condition each other*); *subject to re-examination (cf. prec.). **2.** bring into desired state or condition (*for*); make fit (esp. dogs, horses, etc.); teach, accustom, (*conditioned to respond to the stimulus*; ~ed **reflex**, reflex response to non-natural stimulus, established by training); test condition of (textile etc.); AIR¹-*conditioned*. **3.** Hence ~ER¹ *n.* [ME, f. OF *condicionner* or med. L *condicionare*, f. as prec.]

condi′tional *a.* & *n.* **1.** *a.* not absolute, dependent (*on*, or abs.); (Gram.) ~ **clause**, one expressing a condition, ~ **mood** (used in apodosis); hence ~ITY (-ă′l-) *n.*, ~LY² *adv.* **2.** *n.* conditional mood etc. [ME f. OF *condicionel* or f. LL *condicionalis* (as CONDITION¹; see -AL)]

condō′latorў *a.* expressing condolence. [f. foll., after *consolatory* etc.]

condō′l|e *v.i.* express sympathy (*with* person *on* loss etc.); hence ~NCE *n.* [f. LL CON(*dolēre* suffer)]

cŏ′ndom *n.* contraceptive or prophylactic sheath worn on penis in sexual intercourse. [18th c.; orig. unkn.]

cŏndomī′nĭum *n.* joint control of a State's affairs vested in two or more other States; *set of flats, cottages, etc., rented or bought by a group of persons, unit of property so held. [mod. L (as CON-, L *dominium* DOMINION)]

condō′ne *v.t.* forgive, overlook, (offence, esp. husband's or wife's adultery); (of action) atone for (offence); so **cŏndona′tion** *n.* [f. L CON(*donare* give)]

cŏ′ndor *n.* large vulture of S. America or (**California** ~) N. America. [Sp., f. Quechua *cuntur*]

condottier|e (kŏndŏtyā′rĭ) *n.* (*pl.* ~*i pr.* -ē). (Hist.) leader or member of troop of mercenaries in Italy etc. [It. (*condotta* a contract f. *condotto* CONDUCT¹)]

condŭ′c|e *v.i.* (Usu. of event or attribute) lead or contribute *to* (result); hence ~IVE *a.* [f. L CON(*ducere* duct- lead)]

cŏ′nduct¹ *n.* **1.** leading, guidance; SAFE² *conduct*; ~-money (paid for travelling expenses). **2.** manner of conducting (business etc.); (Art) mode of treatment; behaviour (esp. in its moral aspect); ~ **sheet**, record of person's offences and punishments. [ME, f. L *conductus* (as prec.)]

condŭ′ct² *v.t.* & *i.* **1.** lead or guide (*to*); ~ed **tour** (led by guide on fixed itinerary). **2.** *v.t.* be conductor of (orchestra, choir, concert, or eds.); direct, manage, (business etc.); ~ **one**self, behave (*well, with* judgement, etc.); (Phys.) transmit (heat, electricity, etc.) by conduction, hence ~ANCE *n.*, conducting power of specified conductor, ~IBLE *a.* [ME f. OF *conduite* p.p. of *conduire* f. L CON(*ducere duct-* lead); later assim. to L (see prec.)]

condŭ′ction *n.* transmission (of heat or electricity by contact etc.); conducting (of liquid through pipe etc., esp. of natural processes); transmission of impulses along nerves. [F, or f. L *conductio* (as prec.; see -ION)]

condŭ′ctive *a.* having the property of conducting; hence ~LY² (-vlĭ) *adv.*, **cŏnductī′vITY** *n.*, conducting power of specified material. [f. CONDUCT² + -IVE]

condŭ′ctor *n.* leader, guide; manager, director; director of orchestra, choir, etc., who indicates rhythm etc. by gestures; official in charge of bus, tram, or *train; thing that conducts or transmits (esp. heat or electricity; *good, bad, non-, SEMI-, conductor*; ~ **rail** (transmitting current to electric train etc.); LIGHTNING-*conductor*); hence ~SHIP *n.*, **condŭ′ctr**ESS¹ *n.* (esp. in bus etc.). [ME, f. F *conducteur* f. L *conductor* (as CONDUCT²; see -OR)]

condŭ′ct|us (-ŭs) *n.* (*pl.* ~*i pr.* -ī). musical composition of 12th–13th c., with Latin text. [med. L (see foll.)]

cŏ′nduĭt (-dĭt, -dūĭt) *n.* channel or pipe for conveying liquids (lit. or fig.); tube or trough for protecting insulated electric wires, length of this. [ME f. OF *conduit* f. med. L *conductus* CONDUCT¹]

‖Cŏ′ndў *n.* ~'s **fluid,** (colloq.) ~, strong solution of sodium (per)manganate as disinfectant. [f. H. B. ~, 19th-c. Engl. chemical manufacturer]

cŏ′ndўl|e *n.* (Anat.) rounded process at end of bone, forming articulation with another bone; hence ~OID *a.* [F, f. L f. Gk *kondulos* knuckle]

cōne *n.*, & *v.t.* **1.** *n.* solid figure with circular (or other curved) plane base, tapering to a point, so **cō′n**OID *a.* & *n.*; thing of similar shape, solid or hollow; cone--shaped structure in retina etc.; dry fruit of pine or fir; marine gastropod of family Conidae; ice-cream CORNET¹; conical mountain, esp. of volcanic origin. **2.** *v.t.*

For other words in *co-* **see** CO-.

shape like cone; mark *off* with cones. [f. F *cône* f. L f. Gk *kônos* pine-cone etc.]

cŏ'ney. See CONY.

cŏnfă'bŭl|āte *v.i.* converse, chat, (*with*, or abs.); (Psych.) devise imaginary experiences after loss of memory; so ∿AʹTION *n.*, ∿atORY *a.* [f. L CON(*fabulari* f. *fabula* tale) + -ATE³]

cŏnfě'ct *v.t.* (literary). put together ingredients of. [f. L CON(*ficere fect-* = *facere* make) put together]

cŏnfě'ction *n.* mixing, compounding; thing compounded, esp. from sweet things, whence ∿ARY¹ *a.*; fashionable article of women's dress. [ME f. OF, f. L *confectio -onis* (as prec.; see -ION)]

cŏnfě'ction|er *n.* maker or seller of sweetmeats, pastry, etc.; hence ∿ERY (1, 2, 3) *n.* [f. *confection* prepare confections + -ER¹]

cŏnfě'deracy *n.* league, alliance; conspiracy; collusion; body of confederate persons or States. [ME, AF, OF *confederacie* f. as foll.; see -ACY]

cŏnfě'derate¹ *a.* & *n.* **1.** *a.* allied (lit. or fig.); C∿ States (seceding from the US, 1861–5). **2.** *n.* ally, esp. (in bad sense) accomplice; C∿, supporter of the Confederate States. [f. LL *confoederatus* (as CON-; see FEDERATE)]

cŏnfě'der|āte² *v.t.* & *i.* bring (person, State, one*self*) or come into alliance (*with*); so ∿AʹTION *n.*, (csp.) fairly permanent union of States. [prob. f. prec. + -ATE³]

cŏnfěr' *v.* (-rr-). **1.** *v.t.* grant or bestow (title, degree, favour, etc., *on*, *upon*); hence ∿MENT *n.*, ∿TABLE *a.* **2.** *v.i.* converse, take counsel, (*with*, or abs.). **3.** Hence **cŏnferEE'** *n.*, recipient of grant etc., participant in conference. [f. L CON(*ferre* bring)]

cŏ'nference *n.* consultation (**in** ∿, engaged in discussion); (esp. annual) meeting of any organization, association, etc., for consultation etc.; annual assembly of Methodist Church; association in commerce, sport, etc.; PRESS¹ *conference*; hence **cŏnferě'n-tiAL** (-shal) *a.* [f. F *conférence* or f. med. L *conferentia* (as prec.; see -ENCE)]

cŏnfě'ss *v.t.* & *i.* acknowledge (*I confess my fault, that I did it, to doing it, to having done it, to a dread of spiders*); ∿ (one*self*), formally declare one's sins; csp. to a priest, whence ∿ANT *n.*; (of priest) hear confession (of); hence ∿ědLY² *adv.* [ME, f. OF *confesser* f. Rom. **confessare* f. L *confessus* p.p. of *confiteri — fessi* declare, avow)]

cŏnfě'ssion (-shon) *n.* acknowledgement (of offence, fact, etc.; of sins to priest, whence ∿ARY¹ *a.*); thing(s) confessed; body of persons sharing a ∿ of faith, declaration of religious doctrine, creed, statement of one's principles in any matter, whence ∿IST (2) *n.* [ME f. OF, f. L *confessio -onis* (as prec.; see -ION)]

cŏnfě'ssional (-sho-) *a.* & *n.* **1.** *a.* of confession; denominational. **2.** *n.* stall in which priest hears confession; act or practice of confessing to priest. [a. f. prec. + -AL; n. f. F, f. It. f. med. L *confessionale* neut. (as n.) of *confessionalis* (as prec.; see -AL)]

cŏnfě'ssor *n.* one who confesses; one who avows his religion in face of danger, but does not suffer martyrdom (*King Edward the Confessor*); (or kŏ'nfěser) priest who hears confession. [ME, f. AF *confessur*, OF *-our*, f. eccl. L *confessor* (as CONFESS; see -OR)]

cŏnfě'tti *n. pl.* small bits of coloured paper, thrown by wedding guests at bride and bridegroom. [It., = sweetmeats f. L (as COMFIT)]

cŏnfidănt (kŏ'-, -dă'-) *n.* (*fem.* ∿e *pr.* same). person trusted with knowledge of one's private affairs. [18th c. for earlier CONFIDENT 2, prob. for sound of F *confidente* (as foll.)]

cŏnfi'de *v.* **1.** *v.i.* have confidence *in*; be trustful; ∿ **in**, talk confidentially to. **2.** *v.t.* impart (secret *to*); entrust (object of care, task, *to*). [f. L CON(*fidere* trust)]

cŏ'nfidence *n.* firm trust; assured expectation; self-reliance; boldness, impudence; telling of private

matters with mutual trust (**in** ∿, as a secret; **in** person's ∿, allowed to know his private thoughts or affairs; **take into** one's ∿, confide in); thing so told; **∿ **game**, || ∿ **trick**, theft by persuading victim to entrust valuables to one as sign of his confidence; ∿ **man**, one who robs thus. [ME, f. L *confidentia* (as prec.; see -ENCE)]

cŏ'nfident *a.* & *n.* **1.** *a.* trusting, fully assured (*that*, *of*, or abs.); bold, impudent; hence ∿LY² *adv.* **2.** *n.* confidant. [F, f. It. *confidente* (as CONFIDE; see -ENT)]

cŏnfidě'ntial (-shal) *a.* spoken or written in confidence; entrusted with secrets; charged with secret task; inclined to confide; hence ∿ITY (-shiă'l-), ∿NESS, *ns.*, ∿LY² *adv.* [f. prec. + -IAL]

cŏnfigūrā'tion *n.* mode of arrangement, e.g. of equipment etc.; conformation, outline; (Astron.) relative position of planets etc.; (Psych.) = GESTALT; hence ∿AL *a.* [f. LL *configuratio* f. L CON(*figurare* fashion); see -ATION]

cŏ'nfīne¹ *n.* (usu. in *pl.*) borderland, esp. (fig.) between two classes of ideas etc.; boundary, limit. [ME, f. F *confins* pl. f. L CON(*finia* neut. pl. f. *finis* end, limit)]

cŏnfī'ne² *v.t.* keep (person, thing, one*self*) in narrow place, *within* or to limits or defined area; imprison; (in *pass.*) be in childbirth. [f. F *confiner* (*confins*; see prec.)]

cŏnfī'nement (-nm-) *n.* imprisonment; being confined, esp. in childbirth; limitation. [f. prec. + -MENT]

cŏnfīr'm *v.t.* establish more firmly (power, possession, person *in* possession); ratify (treaty, possession, title); make definitely valid (statement, evidence, provisional arrangement), whence ∿atIVE, ∿atORY, *adjs.*; establish, encourage, (person *in* habit, opinion, etc.), whence ∿ED¹ (-md) *a.*, permanent, unlikely to change (*confirmed bachelor, invalid*); administer religious rite of confirmation to, whence **cŏnfi'rmănd** [-ND¹] *n.*, candidate for confirmation. [ME, f. OF *confermer* f. L CON(*firmare* f. *firmus* firm)]

cŏnfirmā'tion *n.* **1.** act of confirming; corroboration; (Sc. Law) grant of probate. **2.** rite of confirming baptized persons esp. at age of discretion in various Christian Churches; ceremony of confirming persons of about this age in Jewish faith. [ME f. OF, f. L *confirmatio -onis* (as prec.; see -ATION)]

cŏ'nfiscāt|e *v.t.* appropriate to the public treasury (by way of penalty); seize as by authority or summarily; so **confi'scABLE, confi'scatORY**, *adjs.*, **cŏnfiscA'TION**, ∿OR, *ns.* [f. L CON(*fiscare* f. *fiscus* treasury) + -ATE³]

cŏnflagrā'tion *n.* great and destructive fire. [f. L *conflagratio -onis* (L *flagrare* blaze); see -ATION]

cŏnflā'te *v.t.* fuse together, blend, esp. (fig.) two variant texts or readings into one; so ∿AʹTION *n.* [f. L CON(*flare* blow) + -ATE³]

cŏ'nflict¹ *n.* fight, struggle, (lit. or fig.); **in** ∿, discrepant (*with*); collision; clashing (of opposed principles etc.); (Psych.) (distress due to) opposition of incompatible wishes etc. in person. [ME, f. L *conflictus* (as foll.)]

cŏnfli'ct² *v.i.* struggle (*with*, or abs., usu. fig.); clash, be incompatible; so ∿ION *n.* [ME, f. L CON(*fligere flict-* strike)]

cŏ'nflu|ent (-ōoent) *a.* & *n.* **1.** *a.* flowing together, uniting, (of streams, roads, or fig.); so ∿ENCE *n.* **2.** *n.* stream joining another (prop. of same size). [f. L CON(*fluere* flow); see -ENT]

cŏ'nflux *n.* confluence. [f. LL *confluxus* (as foll.)]

cŏnfōr'm *v.* **1.** *v.t.* form according to pattern, make similar (*to*). **2.** *v.i.* be conformable (*to*); comply with rules or general custom; ∿ **to** or **with**, whence ∿ANCE, ∿ER¹, *ns.* [ME, f. OF *conformer* f. L *conformare* f. *forma* shape)]

cŏnfōr'm|able *a.* similar (*to*); consistent (*with*), adapted (*to*); tractable; (Geol., of strata in contact) lying in same direction; hence ∿ABI'LITY, ∿ABLY *adv.* [f. med. L *conformabilis* (as prec.; see -ABLE)]

cŏnfōr'mal *a.* (Of map) representing any small area in its correct shape; hence ∿LY² *adv.* [f. LL *conformalis* (as CONFORM; see -AL)]

cŏnformā′tion *n.* manner in which a thing is formed, structure; adaptation (*to*). [f. L *conformatio* (as CONFORM; see -ATION)]

confŏr′m|ist *n.* one who conforms to a practice or usage, esp. ||one who conforms to usages of Church of England; so ∿ISM (3) *n.* [f. CONFORM + -IST]

confŏr′mĭtÿ *n.* likeness (*to, with*); compliance (*with, to*), esp. ||with usages of Church of England. [ME, f. OF *conformité* or f. LL *conformitas* (as CONFORM; see -ITY)]

confou′nd *v.t.* **1.** defeat (plan, hope); (in *subj.*, as mild oath) = DAMN **2**; discomfit; throw into perplexity. **2.** throw (things) into disorder; mix up; confuse (in one's mind). [ME, f. AF *conf(o)undre*, OF *confondre* f. L CON(*fundere fus-* pour) mix up]

confou′ndėd *a.* (colloq.) = DAMNED **2**; hence ∿LY² *adv.* [p.p. of prec.]

cŏnfratĕr′nĭtÿ *n.* brotherhood (esp. religious or charitable). [ME, f. OF *confraternité* f. med. L CON-(*fraternitas* FRATERNITY)]

cŏ′nfrère (-râr) *n.* fellow member of profession, scientific body, etc. [ME f. OF, f. med. L CON(*frater* brother)]

confro′nt (-ŭ′nt) *v.t.* meet and look at, stand facing; be opposite to; face in hostility or defiance; (of difficulties etc.) oppose; bring (person) face to face *with* (accusers etc.); make comparison of; hence **cŏnfrontā′TION** *n.* [f. F *confronter* f. med. L CON-(*frontare* f. *frons -ntis* face)]

Confū′cian (-sh*a*n) *a.* & *n.* (follower) of Confucius; hence ∿ISM (3) *n.* [f. *Confucius*, Chin. philosopher d. 479 BC (Latinization of *Kongfuze* Kong the master) + -AN]

confu′s|e (-z) *v.t.* throw into disorder; make indistinct (*confuse the issue*); mix up in the mind (*confuse Reddish and* or *with Redditch*); (usu. in *pass.*) abash, perplex; (in *p.p.*) mentally decrepit; hence ∿ėdLY² *adv.* [19th c. back-form. f. *confused* (14th c.) f. OF *confus* f. L *confusus*; see CONFOUND]

confu′sion (-zh*o*n) *n.* act of confusing; confused state; tumult; ∿ **of tongues** (cf. Gen. 11: 1–9); ∿ **worse confounded** (made worse than it was). [ME f. OF, or f. L *confusio* (as prec.; see -ION)]

confū′te *v.t.* prove (person) to be in error; prove (argument) to be false; so **confūtā′TION** *n.* [f. L *confutare* restrain]

cŏ′nga (-ngg*a*) *n.*, & *v.i.* (∿ed or ∿'d, *pr.* -ad). (perform) Latin-Amer. dance of Afr. origin, usu. with several persons in single line; ∿ (**drum**), tall, narrow, low-toned drum beaten with hands. [Amer. Sp., f. Sp. *conga* (fem.) of the Congo]

congé (kaw′nzhā) *n.* unceremonious dismissal; leave-taking. [F; earlier *congee*, ME f. OF *congié* f. L *commeatus* leave of absence f. COM(*meare* go) go and come; now usu. treated as mod. F]

congea′l (-nj-) *v.t.* & *i.* freeze, solidify by cooling; (of blood etc., or fig.) coagulate; hence ∿ABLE *a.*, ∿MENT *n.* [ME f. OF *congeler* f. L CON(*gelare* f. *gelu* frost)]

cŏngēlā′tion (-nj-) *n.* congealing; congealed state; congealed substance. [ME f. OF, or f. L *congelatio* (as prec.; see -ATION)]

cŏ′ngėner (-nj-) *n.* one of the same kind as another (*the goldfinch is a congener of the canary*); *by-product giving distinctive character in whisky etc. [L (CON-, GENUS)]

cŏngėnė′ric (-nj-) *a.* of same genus, kind, or race; allied in nature or origin; so **congĕ′nerOUS** (-nj-) *a.* [f. prec. + -IC]

congē′nial (-nj-) *a.* (Of person, character, etc.) of kindred disposition, agreeable, (*with, to*); suited, agreeable, (*to*); hence ∿ITY (-ă′l-) *n.*, ∿LY² *adv.* [f. CON- + GENIAL¹]

congĕ′nital (-nj-) *a.* (Esp. of disease, defect, etc.) existing from birth; that is such from birth (*congenital idiot*); hence ∿LY² *adv.* [f. L CON(*genitus* p.p. of *gigno* beget) + -AL]

cŏ′nger (-ngg-) *n.* ∿ (**eel**), large sea eel of family Congridae. [ME, f. OF *congre* f. L *conger, congrus*, f. Gk *goggros*]

congeries (-njēr′ĕz, -njĕ′rīēz) *n.* (*pl.* same). disorderly collection, mass, heap. [L, f. as foll.]

congĕ′st (-nj-) *v.t.* (esp. in *p.p.*) affect with congestion; hence ∿IVE *a.* [f. L CON(*gerere gest-* bring)]

congĕ′stion (-njĕ′sch*o*n) *n.* abnormal accumulation (of blood in a part of the body; of population, traffic, etc.). [F, f. L *congestio -onis* (as prec.; see -ION)]

conglŏ′merate¹ (-n-g-) *a.* & *n.* gathered into a round mass; (Geol.) (pudding-stone, water-worn fragments of rock) cemented into a mass (cf. AGGLOMERATE²); heterogeneous mixture; group or corporation formed by merging of unrelated firms. [f. L *conglomeratus* p.p. of CON(*glomerare* f. *glomus -eris* ball); see -ATE²]

conglŏ′mer|āte² (-n-g-) *v.t.* & *i.* collect into a coherent mass (lit. or fig.); so ∿A′TION *n.* [f. as prec. + -ATE³]

Cŏngolē′se (-nggol̄ē′z) *a.* & *n.* (native) of Congo region or republic. [f. F *congolais* (*Congo* river and region of central Africa); cf. -ESE]

cŏ′ngou (-nggŏō, -ō) *n.* black China tea. [f. Chin. dial. *kung hu tē* tea laboured for]

congrā′ts, congră′tters (-z), (-n-g-) *int.* (colloq.) congratulations. [abbr.; see -ER¹(5)]

congră′tūl|āte (-n-g-) *v.t.* address (person) with expressions of sympathetic joy (*on* an event or condition); ∿ate oneself, think oneself fortunate; hence ∿ANT *a.* & *n.*, ∿ATIVE, ∿atORY, *adjs.*, ∿ātOR *n.* [f. L CON(*gratulari* show joy f. *gratus* pleasing) + -ATE³]

congrătūlā′tion (-n-g-) *n.* congratulating; (in *pl.*, esp. as *int.*) congratulatory expressions. [f. L congratulatio (as prec.; see -ATION)]

cŏ′ngrĕgant (-ngg-) *n.* member of a (Jewish) congregation. [f. L *congregare* (see foll., -ANT)]

cŏ′ngrĕgāte (-ngg-) *v.i.* & *t.* collect, gather, into a crowd (of persons) or mass (of things). [ME, f. L CON(*gregare* f. *grex gregis* flock) + -ATE³]

cŏngrĕgā′tion (-ngg-) *n.* collection into a crowd or mass; assemblage; ||(Oxford etc.; *C*∿) general assembly of resident senior members of university; body assembled for religious worship or to hear preacher; body of persons regularly attending a particular church etc.; (RC Ch.) body of persons obeying a common religious rule; permanent committee of RC College of Cardinals. [ME f. OF, or f. L *congregatio* (as prec.; see -ATION)]

cŏngrĕgā′tional (-ngg-) *a.* of a congregation; (*C*∿) of or adhering to Congregationalism. [f. prec. + -AL]

Cŏngrĕgā′tional|ism (-ngg-) *n.* system of ecclesiastical organization that leaves legislative, disciplinary, and judicial functions to the individual church and congregation (in England & Wales largely merged in UNITED *Reformed* Church from 1972); hence ∿IST (2) *n.*, ∿IZE (4) *v.t.* [f. prec. + -ISM]

cŏ′ngrĕss (-ngg-) *n.* coming together, meeting; formal meeting of delegates for discussion, esp. of persons belonging to a particular body or engaged in special studies; (*C*∿) national legislative body, esp. of US; C∿ (**Party**), (Ind.) a political party; C∿man, C∿woman, member of Congress. [f. L *congressus* f. CON(*gredi gress-* = *gradi* walk)]

congrĕ′ssional (-n-grĕ′sh*o*-) *a.* of a congress. [f. prec. & L *congressio* (as -ION) + -AL]

cŏ′ngru|ence (-ngg-rŏōens), ∿|ency (-nj-), *ns.* agreement, consistency; (Geom.) state of being congruent. [ME, f. L *congruentia* (as foll.; see -ENCE)]

cŏ′ngruent (-ngg-rŏō-) *a.* suitable, accordant (*with*); (Geom., of figures) coinciding exactly when superimposed; hence ∿LY² *adv.* [ME, f. L *congruere* agree; see -ENT]

cŏ′ngruous (-nggrŏō-) *a.* accordant, conformable, (*with*); fitting; hence or cong. **congru′ITY** (-nggrŏō′-) *n.*, ∿LY² *adv.* [f. L *congruus* (as prec.) + -OUS]

cŏ′nic *a.* & *n.* **1.** *a.* of a cone; ∿ **section**, (Math.) figure formed by intersection of cone and plane. **2.** *n.* conic section; (in *pl.*) study of conic sections. [f. mod. L f. Gk *kōnikos* (as CONE; see -IC)]

For other words in co- see CO-.

cŏ'nǐcal *a.* cone-shaped; *conical* PROJECTION; hence ∿LY² *adv.* [f. as prec.+-AL]

coni'di|um *n.* (*pl.* ∿a). asexual spore of fungus or bacterium, not formed in a sporangium. [mod. L, dim. f. Gk *konis* dust]

cŏ'nifer *n.* cone-bearing tree; hence **coni'**FEROUS *a.* [L (as CONE; see -FEROUS)]

cŏ'nifŏrm *a.* cone-shaped. [f. L *conus* cone+-I-+-FORM]

cŏ'niine (-ïēn) *n.* alkaloid forming poisonous principle of hemlock. [f. L *conium* f. Gk *kōneion* hemlock+-INE⁵]

conjĕ'ctural (-kcher-) *a.* involving or in the habit of conjecture; hence ∿LY² *adv.* [F, f. L *conjecturalis* (as foll.; see -AL)]

conjĕ'cture¹ *n.* formation of opinion on incomplete grounds; guessing, esp. in textual criticism, of a reading not in the text; guess, proposed reading. [ME f. OF, or f. L *conjectura* f. CON(*jicere ject-* = *jacēre* throw); see -URE]

conjĕ'ctur|e² *v.* **1.** *v.t.* guess; propose (conjectural reading). **2.** *v.i.* make guess. **3.** Hence ∿ABLE *a.* [ME, f. OF *conjecturer* f. LL *conjecturare* (as prec.)]

conjoi'n *v.t.* & *i.* join, combine. [ME, f. OF *conjoign-* pres. st. of *conjoindre* f. L CON(*jungere junct-* join)]

conjoi'nt *a.* united; associated; hence ∿LY² *adv.* [ME f. OF, p.p. (as prec.)]

cŏ'njugal (-ōō-) *a.* of marriage (*conjugal* RITES; ∿ **rights**, right of sexual intercourse with spouse); of mutual relation of husband and wife (*conjugal affection*); hence ∿ITY (-ă'l-) *n.*, ∿LY² *adv.* [t. L *conjugalis* f. OF, p.p. (as prec.)]

cŏ'njugāte¹ (-ōō-) *v.* **1.** *v.t.* (Gram.) inflect (verb) in voice, mood, tense, number, person. **2.** *v.i.* unite sexually; (Biol., of gametes) become fused; (Chem., of protein) combine with non-protein. [f. L CON(*jugare* f. *jugum* yoke) yoke together+-ATE³]

cŏ'njugate² (-ōō-) *a.* & *n.* **1.** *a.* joined together, esp. coupled; (Gram.) derived from same root; (Math.) joined in a reciprocal relation, esp. having same real parts, and equal magnitudes but opp. signs of IMAGINARY parts; (Biol.) fused; hence ∿LY² (-tli) *adv.*, ∿NESS (-tn-) *n.* **2.** *n.* conjugate word or thing. [f. as prec.; see -ATE²]

cŏnjugā'tion (-ōō-) *n.* joining together; (Gram.) scheme of verbal inflexion; (Biol.) fusion of two gametes in reproduction; hence ∿AL *a.* [f. L *conjugatio* (as prec.; see -ATION)]

conjŭ'nct *a.* joined together; combined; associated, joint. [ME, f. L *conjunctus*; see CONJOIN]

conjŭ'nction *n.* **1.** union, connection; **in** ∿, together (*with*). **2.** (Astrol. & Astron.) apparent proximity of two heavenly bodies to each other. **3.** combination of events or circumstances; number of associated persons or things. **4.** (Gram.) uninflected word used to connect clauses or sentences, or to co-ordinate words in same clause. **5.** Hence ∿AL *a.* [ME, f. OF *conjonction* f. L *conjunctio -onis* (as prec.; see -ION)]

conjuncti'v|a *n.* mucous membrane connecting eyeball and inner eyelid; hence ∿AL *a.*, **conjŭnctivi'tis** *n.* [med. L (for *tunica* ∿), f. as foll.]

conjŭ'nctive *a.* & *n.* **1.** *a.* serving to join (*conjunctive tissue*). **2.** (Gram.) of the nature of a conjunction. **3.** Hence ∿LY² (-vli) *adv.* **4.** *n.* conjunctive word. [f. LL *conjunctivus* (as CONJOIN; see -IVE)]

conjŭ'ncture *n.* combination of events; state of affairs. [obs. F f. It. *congiuntura* (as CONJOIN; see -URE)]

cŏnjurā'tion (-ōō-) *n.* solemn appeal; incantation. [ME f. OF, f. L *conjuratio -onis* (as foll.; see -ATION)]

conjure *v.* **1.** *v.t.* (konjoor'). appeal solemnly to (person or do). **2.** (kŭ'njer). constrain (spirit) to appear by invocation (∿ **up**, bring into existence as if by magic, cause to appear to the eye or mind, evoke); effect, bring *out*, convey *away*, (as if) by magic. **3.** *v.i.* (kŭ'njer). produce magical effects by natural means (*conjuring trick*); perform marvels (*a name* to ∿ with, of great importance); ***∿ man, woman***, witch(-doctor). [ME, f. OF *conjurer* plot, exorcise, f. L CON(*jurare* swear) band together by oath]

co'njuror, co'njurer, (kŭ'njerer) *n.* one who performs conjuring tricks. [f. prec.+-ER¹ & f. AF *conjurour* (OF -*eor*) f. med. L *conjurator* (as prec.; see -OR)]

cŏnk¹ *n.* (sl.) nose; head; punch on nose etc. [19th c.; perh. = CONCH]

cŏnk² *v.i.* (colloq.) ∿ (**out**), break down, give out (usu. of mechanism etc.), faint or die. [20th c.; orig. unkn.]

cŏ'nker *n.* horse-chestnut fruit; (in *pl.*) children's game played with these on strings, each player seeking to break with his own that held by opponent. [f. dial. *conker* snail-shell (orig. used in the game), assoc. w. CONQUER]

con moto (kŏn mō'tō) *adv.* (Mus.) with spirited movement. [It., = with movement]

****cŏnn.** See CON².*

Conn. *abbr.* Connecticut.

cŏ'nnāte *a.* born with a person, innate; formed at same time; allied; congenial; (Bot. & Zool.) united from the start of life. [f. LL *connatus* p.p. of CON(*nasci* be born); see -ATE²]

connā'tural (-cher-) *a.* innate, belonging naturally (*to*); of like nature; hence ∿LY² *adv.* [f. LL CON(*naturalis* NATURAL)]

connĕ'ct *v.* **1.** *v.t.* join (two things, one *to* another); join in sequence or order; cause to be joined mentally or practically (*with*); (usu. in *pass.* or *refl.*) unite *with* other(s) in having same origin or nature or consequence or purpose; put into communication by telephone. **2.** *v.i* join on (*with*); operate in connection *with* (*train connects with boat*); form logical sequence, be meaningful; (colloq.) hit target with blow etc.; ∿**ing-rod** (between piston and crankpin etc. in engine, or between wheels of locomotive). **3.** Hence ∿ER¹ (2), ∿OR, *ns.*, ∿ABLE, ∿IBLE, *adjs.* [f. L CON(*nectere nex-* bind)]

connĕ'cted *a.* In vbl senses; joined in sequence, coherent, whence ∿LY² *adv.*, ∿NESS *n.*; having relationships (**well** ∿, associated with persons of good social position). [p.p.p. of prec.]

connĕ'ction, ‖**connĕ'xion**, (-kshən) *n.* **1.** act of connecting; state of being connected (**cut the ∿**, separate things, have no more to do with something; **in** ∿ **with**, with reference to, (of train etc.) meeting (another conveyance) for transfer of passengers); relation of ideas (**in this** or **that** ∿, on a related matter); connecting part; connecting train, boat, etc. (*miss the* or *one's connection*). **2.** personal dealings (arch.) sexual relation or intercourse; family relationship; person connected with others by family relationship, marriage, etc.; (sl.) supplier of narcotics; religious body, esp. Methodist, whence ∿AL *a.*; body of customers etc. (*business with a good connection*). [f. L *connexio* (as CONNECT; see -ION); sp. -*ct*- after CONNECT]

connĕ'ctive *a.* & *n.* (word) serving or tending to connect; ∿ **tissue**, (Anat.) fibrous tissue connecting and supporting organs. [f. CONNECT+-IVE]

‖**connexion.** See CONNECTION.

***cŏ'nning-tower.** See CON².*

****conni'ption** *n.* (sl.) ∿ (**fit**), fit of rage or hysteria. [19th c.; orig. unkn.]

conni'vance *n.* conniving (*at, in*); tacit permission (*done with his connivance*). [f. F *connivence* or f. L *conniventia* (as foll.; see -ENCE, -ANCE)]

conni've *v.i.* **1.** ∿ **at**, tolerate, disregard, (misbehaviour). **2.** conspire (*with*). [f. F *conniver* or f. L *connivēre* shut the eyes (to)]

cŏnnoisseur (kŏnəsēr') *n.* expert judge (of or in matters of taste, esp. in the fine arts); hence ∿SHIP *n.* [F, obs. sp. of *connaisseur*; as if *connaître* know+-*eur* -OR; cf. *reconnoitre*]

connō'te *v.t.* (Of words) imply in addition to the primary meaning; (of fact etc.) imply as a consequence or condition; mean, signify; so **cŏnnotA'TION** *n.*, **cŏ'nnot**ATIVE *a.* [f. med. L CON(*notare* f. *nota* mark) mark in addition]

connū'bial *a.* of marriage; of husband and wife; hence ∿ITY (-ă'l-) *n.*, ∿LY² *adv.* [f. L *connubialis* f. CON(*nubium* f. *nubere* marry); see -AL]

cŏ'noid. See CONE.

cŏ'nquer (-ngkₑr) v.t. overcome (opponent, or abs.) by force; overcome (habit, passion, etc.) by effort of will; acquire, subjugate, (country); climb (mountain) successfully; hence ∼ABLE a. [ME, f. OF conquerre f. Rom. *conquerere f. L CON(quirere = quaerere seek, get)]

cŏ'nqueror (-ngkₑror) n. one who conquers (**the C**∼, William I of England); ‖conker. [ME, f. AF conquerour (OF -eor) f. conquerre (see prec., -OR)]

cŏ'nquĕst n. subjugation (of country etc.); the (Norman) C∼, acquisition of English crown by William of Normandy in 1066; conquered territory; person whose affections have been won. [ME, f. OF conquest(e) f. p.p. of Rom. *conquerere; see CONQUER]

conquĭ'stadŏr (-n-kw-) n. (pl. ∼es pr. -ōrĕz, or ∼s). conqueror, esp. one of the Spanish conquerors of Mexico and Peru in 16th c. [Sp.]

cŏ'n-rŏd n. (colloq.) connecting-rod. [abbr.]

Cons. abbr. Conservative.

cŏnsăngui'n|ĕous (-nggw-) a. having the same lineage, akin; so ∼ITY n. [f. L CON(sanguineus f. sanguis -inis blood) +-OUS]

cŏ'nscience (shₑns-) n. moral sense of right and wrong (good or clear, bad or guilty, ∼, consciousness that one's actions are right, wrong; have on one's ∼, feel guilty about; keep person's ∼, ensure that he forms sound moral judgements; in all ∼, (colloq.) by any reasonable standard; for ∼ (or ∼') sake, to satisfy one's conscience); case of ∼, matter in which conscience has to decide conflict of principles; ∼ clause in a law, one ensuring respect for the consciences of those affected; ∼ money (sent to relieve the conscience, esp. in payment of evaded income tax); freedom or liberty of ∼, system allowing all citizens free choice of religion; prisoner of ∼, person in prison for act of social protest; ∼-smitten, -stricken, -struck, made uneasy by bad conscience; hence ∼LESS a. [ME f. OF, f. L conscientia f. CON(scire know) be privy to; see -ENCE]

cŏnsciĕ'ntious (-shĭĕ'nshus) a. (Of person or conduct) obedient to conscience, scrupulous; ∼ objector, person who avails himself of conscience clause, esp. one who for reasons of conscience objects to military service etc.; hence ∼LY² adv., ∼NESS n. [f. F consciencieux f. med. L conscientiosus (as prec.; see -OUS)]

cŏ'nscious (-shus) a. & n. 1. a. aware, knowing, (of fact, of external circumstances, that, or abs.); with mental faculties awake; self-conscious, affected; (of action, emotion, etc.) realized by the doer etc. (with conscious superiority; a hardly conscious movement); (as suf.) aware of, concerned with, (class-conscious; clothes--conscious); hence ∼LY² adv. 2. n. the conscious mind. [f. L conscius knowing with others or in oneself, f. CON(scire know); see -OUS]

cŏ'nsciousnĕss (-shus-) n. state of being conscious; totality of a person's thoughts and feelings, or of a class of these (moral consciousness; STREAM of consciousness); perception (of, that). [f. prec. +-NESS]

conscrī'be v.t. = foll. [f. L conscribere (see CONSCRIP-TION)]

conscrī'pt² v.t. enlist by conscription. [back-form. f. CONSCRIPTION]

cŏ'nscript² n. one enlisted by conscription. [f. F conscrit f. L conscriptus (as foll.)]

conscrī'ption n. compulsory enlistment for State service, esp. military service. [F, f. LL conscriptio levying of troops f. L CON(scribere script- write) enrol]

cŏ'nsĕcrāt|e v.t. set apart as sacred (to); devote to (purpose); sanctify; hence ∼OR n., ∼ORY a. [ME, f. L CON(secrare = sacrare dedicate f. sacer sacred) +-ATE³]

cŏnsĕcrā'tion n. act of consecrating, dedication, esp. of church, churchyard, etc., by bishop; ordination to sacred office, esp. of bishop; devotion to (a purpose). [ME f. OF, or f. L consecratio (as prec.; see -ATION)]

cŏnsĕcū'tion n. logical sequence; sequence of events. [f. L consecutio f. CON(sequi secut- pursue) overtake; see -ION]

consĕ'cūtĭve a. following continuously; proceeding in logical sequence; (Gram.) expressing consequence (consecutive clause); ∼ intervals, (Mus.) intervals of same kind, occurring adjacently between same two parts, esp. fifths or octaves; hence ∼LY² (-vlī) adv., ∼NESS (-vn-) n. [f. F consécutif -ive f. med. L consecutivus (as prec.; see -IVE)]

consĕ'nsual (-sū-, -shōō-) a. of or by consent or consensus; hence ∼LY² adv. [f. L consensus (see foll.) +-AL]

consĕ'nsus n. agreement (of opinion, testimony, etc.); majority view (consensus government). [L, = agreement (as foll.)]

consĕ'nt¹ v.i. express willingness, give permission, agree, (to a thing, to do, that, or abs.); ∼ing adult, (esp.) homosexual. [ME, f. OF consentir f. L CON-(sentire sens- feel) agree]

consĕ'nt² n. voluntary agreement, compliance; permission; age of ∼ (above which consent, esp. of girl to sexual intercourse, is valid in law); with one ∼, (arch.) unanimously. [ME f. OF consente f. consentir (see prec.)]

cŏnsĕntā'nĕous a. accordant, suited, (to, with); unanimous, concurrent. [f. L consentaneus (consentire CONSENT¹) +-OUS]

consĕ'ntient (-shₑnt) a. agreeing; concurrent; consenting (to). [f. L (as CONSENT¹; see -ENT)]

cŏ'nsĕquence n. 1. what comes by causation or follows by logic (from something preceding; in ∼, as a result (of); take the ∼s, accept whatever results from one's choice or act). 2. importance (of no ∼, unimportant); social distinction, rank (persons of consequence). 3. (in pl., usu. treated as sing.) round game in which narrative is made up by players each ignorant of what has already been contributed. [ME f. OF, f. L consequentia (as foll.; see -ENCE)]

cŏ'nsĕquent a. & n. 1. a. following as a result (on, upon); following logically; logically consistent; hence ∼LY² adv. & conj., as a result, therefore. 2. n. event that follows another; (Logic) the second part of a conditional proposition, dependent on the antecedent. [ME f. OF, f. L consequi; see CONSECUTION, -ENT]

cŏnsĕquĕ'ntial (-shₐl) a. following or required as a result or inference; following or resulting indirectly (consequential damage); self-important; hence ∼ITY (-shĭă'l-) n., ∼LY² adv. [f. L consequentia CONSE-QUENCE +-AL]

consĕr'vancy n. ‖commission etc. controlling a port, river, etc., (Thames Conservancy); similar body concerned with other resources (Nature Conservancy); official preservation (of forests etc.). [18th c. alt. of obs. conservacy. AF conservacie f. AL conservatia f. L conservatio (see foll., -ANCY)]

cŏnservā'tion n. preservation, esp. of natural environment, whence ∼IST (3) n.; ‖∼ area (containing noteworthy buildings etc. and specially protected against undesirable changes); ∼ of energy, momentum, etc., (Phys.) principle that total quantity of energy etc. of any system of bodies not subject to external action remains constant. [ME f. OF, or f. L conservatio (as CONSERVE²; see -ATION)]

consĕr'vative a. & n. 1. a. tending to conserve; averse to rapid changes; C∼ Judaism (allowing only minor changes in traditional ritual etc.); ∼ surgery (seeking to preserve parts as far as possible). 2. ‖C∼ Party, (Polit.) that which is disposed to maintain existing institutions and promote individual enterprise. 3. (Of estimate etc.) moderate, cautious, purposely low; (of views, taste, etc.) avoiding extremes. 4. Hence consĕr'vatISM (3) n., ∼LY² (-vlī) adv. 5. n. conservative person or (arch.) thing; (C∼) member of the Conservative Party. [ME, f. LL conservativus (as CONSERVE²; see -IVE)]

conservatoire (konsēr'vatwār) *n.* (Usu. Continental) school of music or other arts. [F, f. It. *conservatorio* (as CONSERVATORY)]

conservator (kŏ'nservā-, konsēr'va-) *n.* preserver; official custodian (of museum etc.); member of conservancy. [ME, f. AF *conservatour*, OF *-ateur* f. L *conservator -oris* (as CONSERVE²; see -OR)]

conser'vatory *n.* **1.** greenhouse for tender plants. **2.** **Conservatoire*; so (Austral.) **consērvator'ium** *n.* [sense 1 f. LL *conservatorium*, neut. (as n.) of *conservatorius* (as CONSERVE²; see -ORY); sense 2 f. It. *conservatorio* f. LL *conservatorium*]

consērve¹ *n.* (-ēr'v, kŏ'-) (also in *pl.*) fruit etc. preserved in sugar; jam, esp. made from fresh fruit. [ME f. OF, = med. L *conserva*, f. as foll.]

consēr've² *v.t.* keep from harm, decay, or loss, esp. with view to later use (*conserve one's energy, resources*); (Phys., esp. in *p.p.*) maintain quantity of (energy etc.) constant. [ME, f. OF *conserver* f. L CON(*servare* keep)]

consi'der *v.t.* contemplate mentally; weigh merits of (*course of action, claim, candidate*, etc.); give mental attention to (*that, whether*, etc., or abs.); reckon with, make allowance for; be of opinion (*that*); regard as (*I consider him to be, as*) *a swindler*; *consider yourself under arrest*); (in *p.p.*) made after careful thought (*considered opinion*); **all things ∿ed**, when all aspects of the matter have been taken into account. [ME, f. OF *considerer* f. L *considerare* examine]

onsi'derable *a.* worth considering; (of person) notable, important; (of immaterial or *material things) much, no little, (trouble, annoyance, pleasure, *liquor); hence ∿LY² *adv.* [f. med. L *considerabilis* (as prec.; see -ABLE)]

onsi'derate *a.* thoughtful for others; (arch.) careful; hence ∿LY² (-tlī) *adv.*, ∿NESS (-tn-) *n.* [f. L *consideratus* p.p. of *considerare* (as CONSIDER; see -ATE²)]

onsidera'tion *n.* **1.** act of considering; meditation; **in ∿ of**, in return for, on account of; **take into, leave out of**, ∿, make, fail to make, allowance for, under ∿, being considered. **2.** fact or thing regarded as a reason (*on no consideration*); compensation, reward, (*for a consideration*); (Law) thing given or done as equivalent by person to whom a promise is made; thoughtfulness for others; (arch.) importance. [ME f. OF, f. L *consideratio -onis* (as prec.; see -ATION)]

onsidera'tion *n.* **1.** act of considering; meditation;

consi'gn (-ī'n) *v.t.* hand over or deliver *to* (misery, watery grave, person, person's care); transmit, send by rail etc., *to* (person), whence ∿EE', ∿OR, *ns.*; deposit (money) in bank etc.). [ME, f. F *consigner* or f. L CON(*signare* SIGN²) mark with seal]

consi'gnment (-ī'n-) *n.* consigning; goods consigned. [f. prec. + -MENT]

onsi'st *v.i.* be composed *of* (esp. material things); have its essential feature(*s*) *in* (virtue consists in being uncomfortable); harmonize *with*. [f. L CON(*sistere* stop) exist]

onsi'stency, -ce, *ns.* degree of density, esp. of thick liquids; firmness, solidity, (lit. or fig.); state of being consistent. [f. F *consistence* or f. LL *consistentia* (as prec.; see -ENCE, -ENCY)]

onsi'stent *a.* compatible, not contradictory, (with); (of person) constant to same principles; hence ∿LY² *adv.* [f. L *consistere* (see CONSIST, -ENT)]

onsi'story (-sī'-, kŏ'n-) *n.* council of pope and cardinals; C∿ (Court), Anglican bishop's court for ecclesiastical causes and offences; Lutheran clerical board; court of presbyters; so **consistōr'ial** *a.* [ME, f. AF *consistorie*, OF *-oire* f. LL *consistorium* (as CONSIST; see -ORY)]

onsō'ciāte (-shī-, -sī-) *v.t. & i.* associate, esp. closely; so **consōcia'tion** *n.*, (esp., Ecol.) part of association with one dominant species. [f. L CON(*sociare* f. *socius* fellow) + -ATE³]

consōlā'tion *n.* act of consoling; consoling circumstance; ∿ **prize** (given to competitor just missing main prizes). [ME f. OF, f. L *consolatio -onis* (as CONSOLE¹; see -ATION)]

consō'latory *a.* tending or intended to console. [ME, f. L *consolatorius* (as foll.; see -ORY)]

consō'le¹ *n.* comfort, esp. in grief or depression; hence ∿ABLE *a.*, ∿ER¹ *n.* [f. F *consoler* f. L *consolari*]

cŏ'nsōle² *n.* (Archit.) slightly-projecting ornamented bracket or corbel; (Mus.) keyboards, stops, pedals, etc., of organ; panel for switches etc.; cabinet for television set etc.; ∿ **table**, one supported by bracket against wall. [F, perh. f. *consoler* (f. as foll.)]

consō'lidāte *v.t. & i.* **1.** solidify. **2.** *v.t.* strengthen (usu. fig., one's power etc.); combine (territories, estates, companies, statutes, debts) into one whole; ∥∿ed **annuities**, = foll.; ∥C∿ed **Fund**, united product of various taxes etc., whence interest of National Debt and other agreed regular charges are paid; hence **consōlida'tion**, ∿OR, *ns.*, ∿ORY *a.* [f. L CON(*solidare* f. *solidus* solid) + -ATE³]

cō'nsōls (-z) *n. pl.* Government etc. securities without maturity date. [abbr. of *consolidated annuities*]

consō'mmé (-mā) *n.* clear meat soup. [F, p.p. (as n.) of *consommer* f. L *consummare* (see CONSUMMATE¹)]

co'nsonance *n.* recurrence of same or similar sounds (esp. consonants) in words, assonance; sounding of two notes in harmony; (Mus.) consonant interval, concord; (fig.) agreement, harmony. [ME f. OF, or f. L *consonantia* (as foll.; see -ANCE)]

cō'nsonant¹ *a.* agreeable *to*, consistent *with*; harmonious; corresponding in sound; (Mus.) making concord; hence ∿LY² *adv.* [ME f. F, f. L CON(*sonare* sound f. *sonus*); see -ANT]

cō'nsonant² *n.* speech sound in which breath is at least partly obstructed, that in forming a syllable is combined with vowel; letter(s) representing it; hence **cŏnsonā'ntAL** *a.* [ME f. OF, f. L *consonans -ntis* (*littera letter*) sounding with another (as prec.)]

con sordino (kŏn sōrdē'nō) *adv.* (Mus.) with use of mute; (fig.) muted. [It.]

cŏ'nsŏrt¹ *n.* **1.** husband or wife; PRINCE *consort*; **queen** ∿, king's wife. **2.** ship sailing with another. [ME f. F, f. L CON(*sors sortis* lot) sharer, comrade]

consōr't² *v.t. & i.* class or bring together, keep company, (with); agree, harmonize, (with). [prob. f. SORT² 2]

cŏ'nsŏrt³ *n.* (Mus.) group of players or instruments. [earlier form of CONCERT¹]

consōr'tium *n.* (*pl.* ∿**a**) association of several States, companies, etc.; (Law) right of association with husband or wife (*loss of consortium*). [L, = partnership (as CONSORT¹)]

cŏnspecī'fic *a.* of same species. [f. CON- + SPECIFIC]

conspē'ctus *n.* general or comprehensive survey; summary, synopsis. [L, f. CON(*spicere spect-* look at)]

conspi'cuous *a.* clearly visible, striking to the eye; attracting notice, remarkable, (*conspicuous by its absence, for his loyalty*); (of expenditure etc.) lavish; hence ∿LY² *adv.*, ∿NESS *n.* [f. L *conspicuus* (as prec.; see -OUS)]

conspi'racy *n.* act of conspiring; combination for unlawful purpose, plot; ∿ **of silence**, agreement to say nothing concerning a matter. [ME, f. AF *conspiracie*, alt. f. OF *-ation* f. L *conspiratio -onis* (as CONSPIRE; see -ATION)]

conspi'rator *n.* one engaged in a conspiracy; hence **conspirator'IAL** *a.* [ME, f. AF *conspiratour*, OF *-teur*, f. as foll.; see -OR]

conspi're *v.i.* combine secretly (with) for unlawful purpose, esp. treason, murder, or sedition; combine, concur, (*to* do); plot, devise. [ME, f. OF *conspirer* f. L CON(*spirare* breathe) agree, plot]

co'nstable (kŭ'-, kŏ'-) *n.* ∥policeman (**Chief C**∿, head of police force of county etc.; **police** ∿, policeman or policewoman of lowest rank; SPECIAL *constable*); governor or warden of royal fortress or

castle; (Hist.) principal officer of household of king or noble, commander-in-chief in king's absence. [ME, f. OF *conestable, cun-*, f. LL *comes stabuli* count of the stable]

constǎ'būlarÿ *a.* & *n.* (organized body) of constables or police. [f. med. L *con(e)stabularius* (as prec.; see -ARY¹)]

cǒ'nstancÿ *n.* firmness, endurance; faithfulness; unchangingness. [f. L *constantia* (as foll.; see -ANCY)]

cǒ'nstant *a.* & *n.* 1. *a.* unmoved; resolute; faithful (*to*); unchanging; unremitting, frequently occurring, (*constant attention, chatter*); hence ∼LY² *adv.* 2. *n.* (Math.) quantity that does not vary; (Phys.) number expressing relation, property, etc., and remaining same in all circumstances (*constant of gravitation*) or for same substance in same conditions (*dielectric constant*). [ME f. OF, f. L CON(*stare* stand); see -ANT]

cǒ'nstantan *n.* copper-nickel alloy used in electrical work. [f. prec.]

cǒnstatā'tion *n.* ascertainment; thing ascertained. [F (*constater* verify f. L *constat* it is certain; see -ATION)]

cǒ'nstellāte *v.t.* form into (group like) constellation; adorn as with stars. [f. as foll. + -ATE³]

cǒnstellā'tion *n.* group of fixed stars within imaginary outline; (fig.) group of associated persons, ideas, etc. [ME f. OF, f. LL *constellatio -onis* (CON-, *stella* star; see -ATION)]

cǒ'nsternāte *v.t.* (usu. in *pass.*) dismay. [f. L CON-(*sternare = sternere* throw down) + -ATE³]

cǒnsternā'tion *n.* amazement or dismay such as to cause mental confusion. [F, or f. L *consternatio* (as prec.; see -ATION)]

cǒ'nstipāte *v.t.* (esp. in *p.p.*) affect (person, bowels) with constipation; (fig.) restrict, hinder. [f. L CON-(*stipare* press) + -ATE³]

cǒnstipā'tion *n.* irregular and difficult defecation; (fig.) restrictedness. [ME f. OF, or f. LL *constipatio* (as prec.; see -ATION)]

constǐ'tüencÿ *n.* body of voters who elect a representative member; area so represented; body of customers, supporters, etc. [f. foll.; see -ENCY]

constǐ'tüent *a.* & *n.* 1. *a.* composing or making up a whole; appointing, electing; able to frame or alter a (political) constitution (*constituent assembly, power*). 2. *n.* component part; member of a constituency; one who appoints another his agent. [f. L *constituent-* (partly thr. F -*ant*), f. as foll.; see -ENT]

cǒ'nstitūte *v.t.* appoint (*constitute him president; constitute oneself a judge*); establish, form, (*this does not constitute a precedent*); give legal form to (assembly etc.); frame, form, (esp. in *pass.* of bodily or mental constitution); make up, be the components of; hence **cǒ'nstitūtor** *n.* [f. L CON(*stituere -ut- = statuere* set up)]

cǒnstitū'tion *n.* act or mode of constituting; character of body as regards health, strength, etc.; mental character; mode in which State is organized; body of fundamental principles according to which a State or other organization is governed (**written** ∼, document embodying these); (Hist.) decree, ordinance. [ME f. OF, or f. L *constitutio* (as prec.; see -ION)]

cǒnstitū'tional *a.* & *n.* 1. *a.* of, inherent in, affecting, bodily or mental constitution; essential. 2. of, in harmony with, authorized by, the political constitution; ∼ **sovereign, monarchy, government,** (limited by constitutional forms); hence ∼ITY (-ǎ'l-) *n.*, ∼IZE (3) *v.t.* 3. Hence ∼LY² *adv.* 4. constitutional walk, taken regularly for health's sake. [f. prec. + -AL]

cǒnstitū'tional|ism *n.* constitutional government; adherence to constitutional principles; so ∼IST (2) *n.* [f. prec. + -ISM]

cǒ'nstitūtive *a.* constructive, formative; essential; component; hence ∼LY² (-vlī) *adv.* [f. LL *constitutivus* (as CONSTITUTE; see -IVE)]

constrai'n *v.t.* urge irresistibly or by necessity (person *to do, to* action or state, or abs.); bring about by compulsion; confine forcibly, imprison (lit. or fig.); (in *p.p.*) forced, embarrassed, (*constrained voice,*

---

manner); hence ∼ědLY² *adv.* [ME, f. OF *constraindre* (st. *constraign-*) f. L CON(*stringere strict-* tie)]

constrai'nt *n.* constraining; being constrained (*under constraint*); confinement; restraint of natural feelings, constrained manner; limitation imposed on motion or action. [ME, f. OF *constreinte*, fem. p.p. (as n.); see prec.]

constrǐ'ct *v.t.* make narrow, compress; cause (organic tissue) to contract; so ∼ION *n.*, ∼IVE *a.* [f. L, as CON-STRAIN]

constrǐ'ctor *n.* muscle that draws together or narrows a part; snake that kills by compressing, esp. BOA constrictor. [mod. L (as prec.; see -OR)]

constrǐ'nge (-nj) *v.t.* (literary). constrict. [f. L *constringere* (see CONSTRAIN)]

constrǔ'ct¹ *v.t.* fit together, frame, build, (lit. or fig.); (Gram.) combine (words) syntactically; draw, delineate, esp. according to given conditions (*construct a triangle*); hence ∼OR *n.* [f. L CON(*struere struct-* pile, build)]

cǒ'nstruct² *n.* thing constructed, esp. by the mind; (Psych.) object of perception or thought constructed by combining sense-impressions; (Ling.) group of words in phrase. [f. prec.]

constrǔ'ction *n.* 1. act or mode of constructing; thing constructed: syntactical connection. 2. construing, explanation, (of words); interpretation (of conduct etc.; *put a good, bad, construction on his refusal*). 3. Hence ∼ISM *n.*, = CONSTRUCTIVISM. [ME f. OF, f. L *constructio -onis* (as CONSTRUCT¹; see -ION)]

constrǔ'ctional *a.* of or involving construction; structural, belonging to the original structure. [f. prec. + -AL]

constrǔ'ctive *a.* of construction; tending to construct; helpful, opp. *destructive* (*constructive criticism*); belonging to the structure of a building; inferred, not directly expressed, virtual, (*constructive denial, permission, blasphemy, treason*); hence ∼LY² (-vlī) *adv.* [f. LL *constructivus* (as CONSTRUCT¹; see -IVE)]

constrǔ'ctiv|ism *n.* kind of art making use of various materials combined into forms that usu. do not depict anything; hence ∼IST (2) *n.* [f. Russ. *konstruktivizm* (as prec.; see -ISM)]

construe' (-ōō') *v.t.* combine (words *with* others) grammatically (*'rely' is construed with 'on'*); analyse (sentence), translate word for word; expound, interpret, (words, actions). [ME, f. L *construere* CON-STRUCT¹]

cǒnsubstǎ'ntial (-shal) *a.* of one substance, esp. of the three Persons of the Trinity; hence ∼ITY (-shiǎ'l-) *n.* [ME, f. eccl. L *consubstantialis* transl. Gk *homoousios*; see CON-, SUBSTANTIAL]

cǒnsubstǎ'ntiāte (-shī-) *v.t.* & *i.* unite as one substance. [f. LL *consubstantiatus* (as prec.; see -ATE²,³)]

cǒnsubstǎntiā'tion (-shī-, -sī-) *n.* (doctrine of) real substantial presence of body and blood of Christ together with bread and wine in Eucharist. [f. mod. L *consubstantiatio*, after *trans(s)ubstantiatio* TRANSUB-STANTIATION]

cǒ'nsuetūde (-sw-) *n.* custom, esp. as having legal force; so **cǒnsuetū'dinarÿ¹** (-sw-) *a.* [ME f. OF, or f. L *consuetudo -dinis* (*consuetus* accustomed; see -TUDE).]

cǒ'nsul *n.* State agent residing in foreign town to protect subjects there and assist commerce; one of two magistrates elected for one year and exercising supreme authority in Roman Republic; holder of corresponding title in Roman Empire; one of three chief magistrates of French Republic 1799-1804 (**First C**∼, Napoleon); hence or cong. **cǒ'nsulAr¹** *a.*, ∼SHIP *n.* [L, f. rel. to *consulere* take counsel]

cǒ'nsulate (-at) *n.* office or establishment of a (modern) consul; (period of) consular government in France; office of (Roman) consul. [ME, f. L *consulatus* (as prec.; see -ATE¹)]

consǔ'lt¹ *v.i.* have deliberations (*with* person, *or* abs.). 2. *v.t.* seek information or advice from (person, book, one's watch, etc.); take into consideration

For other words in *co-* see CO-.

(feelings, interests); ~**ing room** (in which doctor examines patients); hence ~ABLE, ~ative, *adjs*. [f. F *consulter* f. L *consultare* frequent. of *consulere -sult-* take counsel]

consŭ'lt|ant *n*. one who consults; consulting physician etc.; hence ~ANCY *n*., work or position of consultant. [prob. F (as prec.; see -ANT)]

cŏnsultā'tion *n*. act of consulting; deliberation; conference. [ME f. OF, or f. L *consultatio* (as prec.; see -ATION)]

consŭ'lting *a*. In vbl senses; ~ **architect, chemist, engineer,** etc., (whose business is to advise those doing work in his field); ~ **physician** (who is consulted by colleagues or patients in special cases). [f. CONSULT + -ING²]

consŭ'm|e *v*. **1.** *v.t.* destroy; use up; eat or drink; spend, waste, (time, trouble, etc.); (in *p.p.*) entirely preoccupied (*with* envy etc.); hence ~ABLE a. & *n*. (usu. in *pl*.), (article) intended for consumption. **2.** *v.i.* waste away. [ME, f. L CON(*sumere sumpt-* take up); partly thr. F *consumer*]

consŭ'mĕdly *adv*. (arch.) excessively. [f. p.p. of prec. + -LY²]

consŭ'mer *n*. In vbl senses; (Econ.) user of an article (opp. *producer*); purchaser of goods or services (~ **goods,** those used directly (esp. domestically), not in manufacturing etc.; ~ **research,** investigation of such purchasers' needs and opinions; ~ **resistance,** = SALES *resistance*); hence ~ISM (3) *n*., protection of such purchasers' interests, ~IST (?) *n* [f CONSUME + -ER¹]

consŭ'mmate¹ *a*. complete, perfect, (*consummate skill, folly*); fully accomplished (*a consummate general*); hence ~LY² (-tlĭ) *adv*. [f. L CON(*summare* complete f. *summus* utmost); see -ATE²]

cŏ'nsummāt|e² (-sŭm-, -sūm-) *v.t.* accomplish, complete, (esp. marriage, by sexual intercourse); hence ~IVE *a*., ~OR *n*. [f. as prec. + -ATE²]

cŏnsummā'tion *n*. completion (esp. of marriage; see prec.); desired end, goal; perfection; perfected thing. [ME, f. OF *consommation* or f. L *consummatio* (as prec.; see -ATION)]

consŭ'mption *n*. using up; destruction; waste; amount consumed; wasting disease, esp. pulmonary tuberculosis; purchase and use of goods etc. [ME, f. OF *consomption* f. L *consumptio* (as CONSUME, see -ION)]

consŭ'mptive *a*. & *n*. **1.** *a*. tending to consume, tending to or affected with pulmonary tuberculosis; hence ~LY² (vlĭ) *adv*. **2.** *n*. consumptive patient. [f. med. L *consumptivus* (as prec.; see -IVE)]

cont. *abbr*. contents; continued.

cŏ'ntăct *n*., & *v.t.* **1.** *n*. state or condition of touching or communicating (*be in contact with*; **come in(to)** ~ **with,** (fig.) come across, meet); (Electr.) connection for passage of current (*make, break contact*), device for providing this; (Math.) touching of straight line and curve, two curves, or two surfaces; (Med.) person likely to carry contagion through being near infected person; person who is or may be contacted for information, assistance, etc. **2.** ~ **lens,** small lens worn on eyeball or cornea to correct vision; ~ **man,** intermediary; ~ **print,** (Photog.) print made by placing negative directly on sensitized paper etc. and illuminating it. **3.** *v.t.* (*or* kontă'kt) get into touch with (person); begin correspondence or personal dealings with. [f. L *contactus* f. CON(*tingere tact-* = *tangere* touch)]

contadin|o (kŏntadē'nō) *n*. (*pl.* ~**i** pr. -ē; *fem.* ~**a,** *pl.* ~**e** pr. -ā). Italian peasant. [It. (*contado* county)]

contā'gion (-jon) *n*. communication of disease from body to body; contagious disease; moral corruption; (fig.) contagious influence. [ME, f. L CON(*tagio* f. *tangere* touch; see -ION)]

contā'gious (-jus) *a*. communicating disease by contact (lit. or fig.); (of disease) so communicable (~ **abortion,** BRUCELLOSIS of cattle); (fig. of emotions etc.) infectious; hence ~LY² *adv*., ~NESS *n*. [ME, f. LL *contagiosus* (as prec.; see -IOUS)]

contai'n *v.t.* **1.** have or (be able to) hold within itself; comprise, include; (of measure) be equal to (*pound contains 16 ounces*); (in *pass.*) be included (*within a space, between* limits); (Geom.) enclose, form boundary of; (of number) be divisible by (number) without remainder. **2.** restrain (*could not contain himself for joy*; *contain your anger*); prevent from moving or extending. **3.** Hence ~ABLE *a*., ~MENT *n*., (esp.) policy of preventing expansion of hostile nation etc. [ME, f. OF *contenir* f. L CON(*tinēre tent-* = *tenēre* hold)]

contai'ner *n*. In vbl senses; vessel, box, etc., designed to contain some particular thing(s), esp. large boxlike receptacle of standard design for transport of goods; ~ **ship, train,** etc. (carrying goods so packed); hence ~IZE *v.t.*, pack in or transport by container. [f. prec. + -ER¹]

contă'min|āte *v.t.* pollute, esp. with radioactivity; infect; hence ~ANT, ~A'TION, *ns*. [f. L *contaminare* (CON-, *tamen-* rel. to *tangere* touch) + -ATE³]

‖**contă'ngō** (-nggō) *n*. (*pl*. ~**s**). percentage paid by buyer of stock for postponement of transfer (cf. BACKWARDATION); ~ **day,** eighth day before settling day. [19th c.; orig. unkn.]

conte (kawnt) *n*. short story (as a form of literary composition); medieval narrative tale. [F]

contĕ'mn (-m) *v.t.* (literary). despise, treat with disregard; hence ~ER¹ (-mer, -mn-) *n*. [ME, f. OF *contemner tempt-* despise)]

cŏ'ntempl|āte *v*. **1.** *v.t.* gaze upon; view mentally; expect, regard as possible; intend, purpose. **2.** *v.i.* meditate. **3.** So ~A'TION *n*. (**in** ~**ation,** intended), ~**ātor** *n*. [f. L *contemplari* (CON-, *templum* place for observations) + -ATE³]

contempla'tive (kontĕ'mpla-, kŏ'ntemplā-) *a*. & *n*. **1.** *a*. meditative, thoughtful; (of life) given up to religious contemplation, opp. *active*; hence ~LY² (-vlĭ) *adv*., ~NESS (-vn-) *n*. **2.** *n*. person devoted to religious contemplation. [ME, f. OF *contemplatif -ive*, f. L *contemplativus* (as prec.; see -IVE)]

contĕmporā'neous *a*. existing or occurring at the same time (*with*); of the same period; hence **contĕmporā'n**ITY, ~NESS, *ns*., ~LY² *adv*. [f. L CON(*temporaneus* f. *tempus -oris* time; see -ANEOUS)]

contĕ'mpor|arỹ *a*. & *n*. (person, newspaper etc.) belonging to the same time, esp. as oneself; (person) equal in age; modern or ultra-modern in style or design; so ~IZE (3) *v.t.* [f. med. L *contemporarius* (as prec.; see -ARY¹)]

contĕ'mpt *n*. act or mental attitude of despising; condition of being despised (**have** or **hold in** ~, despise; **bring, fall, into** ~, make, become, despised); (Law) disobedience to sovereign's lawful commands or to authority of Parliament or other body, esp. ~ **of court,** disobedience to, or interference with administration of justice by, courts of law. [ME, f. L *contemptus* (as CONTEMN)]

contĕ'mpt|ible *a*. deserving contempt, despicable; hence ~LY² *adv*., ~NESS *n*. [f. med. L *contemptibilis* (as CONTEMN; see -IBLE)]

Old Cŏ'ntempt|ible *n*., (colloq.) British Army in France 1914 [w. ref. to German Emperor's alleged mention of a 'contemptible little army']; hence **contĕmpti**BI'LITY, ~NESS (-beln-), *ns*., ~IBLY *adv*. [ME f. OF, or f. LL *contemptibilis* (as CONTEMN; see -IBLE)]

contĕ'mptuous *a*. showing contempt (*of*); scornful; insolent; hence ~LY² *adv*., ~NESS *n*. [f. med. L *contemptuosus* f. L *contemptus* (see CONTEMPT, -OUS)]

contĕ'nd *v*. **1.** *v.i* strive, fight, (*with person for thing*); struggle *with* or *against* (feelings, natural forces); compete, be in rivalry, (*contending passions*); argue (*with*). **2.** *v.t.* maintain, assert, (*that*). [f. OF *contendre* or f. L CON(*tendere tent-* stretch, strive)]

cŏ'ntĕnt¹ *n*. **1.** (in *pl*.) ~**s of,** what is contained in (vessel etc., book, document); (**table of** ~) ~**s,** summary of subject-matter of book, usu. list of titles of chapters etc. **2.** capacity (of vessel); volume (of solid). **3.** constituent elements of a conception; substance (of cognition, art, etc., opp. *form*; amount (of some particular constituent) contained (*ester content of an* *oil*), or yielded (*sugar content per acre of beet*). [ME, f. med. L *contentum*, pl. -*ta* (as CONTAIN)]

conte͞'nt² *n.* contented state, satisfaction; **to** one's **heart's** ∿, to the full extent of one's desires. [16th c., perh. f. foll.]

conte͞'nt³ *pred. a. & n.* **1.** *a.* willing (*to* do); ∿ **with**, not wishing to have more or other than. **2.** *n.* ||(In House of Lords) affirmative vote(r). [ME f. OF, f. L *contentus* satisfied, p.p. of *continēre* (see CONTAIN)]

conte͞'nt⁴ *v.t.* satisfy; ∿ one**self with,** be content with, accept or do no more than; so ∿MENT *n.*, satisfied state, tranquil happiness. [ME, f. OF *contenter* f. Rom. *contentare* f. L *contentus* (as prec.)]

conte͞'ntèd *a.* satisfied; willing to be content *with*; willing *to* do; hence ∿LY² *adv.*, ∿NESS *n.* [p.p. of prec.]

conte͞'ntion *n.* strife, dispute, rivalry (**in** ∿, competing); point contended for in argument. [ME f. OF, or f. L *contentio* (as CONTEND; see -ION)]

conte͞'ntious (-shus) *a.* quarrelsome; involving contention; hence ∿LY² *adv.*, ∿NESS *n.* [ME, f. OF *contentiosus* (as prec.; see -IOUS)]

conte͞r'minous *a.* having a common boundary (*with, to*); coextensive (in space, time, or meaning); coterminous; hence ∿LY² *adv.* [f. L CON(*terminus* boundary) + -OUS]

conte͞'ssa *n.* Italian countess. [It., f. LL *comitissa*; see COUNTESS]

co͞'ntèst¹ *n.* debate, controversy; strife; (friendly) competition. [f. foll., or f. F *conteste* (*contester*, f. as foll.)]

conte͞'st² *v.* **1.** *v.t.* debate, dispute (point, statement, etc.; *truth* or *accuracy of*); dispute by fighting (field, victory, issue, battle); contend or compete in (||election) or for (seat in Parliament etc.); *dispute result of (election); hence ∿ABLE *a.* **2.** *v.i.* strive in argument (*with, against*). **3.** So ∿ANT *n.* [f. L CON(*testari* f. *testis* witness)]

co͞nte͞sta͞'tion *n.* disputation; assertion contended for. [(partly thr. F) f. L *contestatio* (as prec.; see -ATION)]

co͞'ntèxt *n.* parts that precede or follow a passage or word and fix its meaning (**out of** ∿, without these and hence misleading); ambient conditions; **in this** ∿ (connection); hence **conte͞'xtūal** *a.* [ME, f. L *contextus* f. CON(*texere* text- weave)]

conte͞'xture *n.* (literary) structure; fabric. [F, prob. f. med. L *contextura* (as CON-, TEXTURE)]

co͞ntigū'ity *n.* contact; proximity; (Psych.) proximity of ideas or impressions in place or time, as principle of association. [f. LL *contiguitas* (as foll.; see -ITY)]

conti͞'guous *a.* ∿ (**to**), touching, adjoining, next in order; neighbouring; hence ∿LY² *adv.* [f. L *contiguus* f. CON(*tingere* = *tangere* touch) + -OUS]

co͞'ntin|ent¹ *a.* temperate; chaste; having normal control over one's excretions; hence or cogn. ∿ENCE *n.*, ∿ent LY² *adv.* [ME, f. L CONTAIN; see -ENT)]

co͞'ntinent² *n.* continuous land, mainland; one of the main continuous bodies of land (Europe, Asia, Africa, N. & S. America, Australia, Antarctica); **the C**∿, mainland of Europe as distinct from British Isles. [f. L *terra continens* continuous land (as prec.)]

co͞ntine͞'ntal *a. & n.* **1.** *a.* of a continent; ∿ **climate** (having wide variations of temperature); ∿ **drift**, (Geol.) slow movement of the continents to their present positions, on a deep-lying plastic substratum; ∿ **shelf**, bed of shallow sea area bordering continent. **2.** (*C*∿). belonging to or characteristic of the Continent; **C**∿ **breakfast**, light breakfast of coffee, rolls, etc.; **C**∿ **Sunday**, Sunday as a day of recreation rather than rest and worship; **C**∿ **System**, Napoleon's plan to blockade England in 1806. **3.** Hence ∿IZE (3) *v.t.*, ∿LY² *adv.* **4.** *n.* inhabitant of the Continent; (sl.) currency note of an early US issue that rapidly depreciated, least possible amount (*don't care* or *give a continental*). [f. prec. + -AL]

conti͞'ngency (-nj-) *n.* uncertainty of occurrence; chance occurrence; thing that may happen at later time (∿ **plan**, to take account of such); thing

dependent on an uncertain event; thing incident to another, incidental expense etc. (∿ **fund**, to deal with these). [earlier -*ence* f. LL *contingentia* (as foll.; see -ENCE, -ENCY)]

conti͞'ngent (-nj-) *a. & n.* **1.** *a.* of uncertain occurrence; fortuitous; incidental *to*; true only under existing or specified conditions; non-essential; conditional or dependent (*on, upon*); hence ∿LY² *adv.* **2.** *n.* troops contributed to form part of army etc.; group contributed to larger one. [f. L CON(*tingere* = *tangere* touch); see -ENT]

conti͞'nūal *a.* always happening; very frequent and without cessation; hence ∿LY² *adv.* [ME f. OF *continuel* (*continuer*; see CONTINUE, -AL)]

conti͞'nūance *n.* continuing, duration; remaining, stay, (*in* place, condition, etc.); *(Law) adjournment. [ME f. OF (as CONTINUE; see -ANCE)]

conti͞'nūant *a. & n.* (Phonet.) (consonant) of which sound can be prolonged as desired (e.g. *f, r, s, v*). [F, & f. L *continuare* (as CONTINUE; see -ANT)]

continūā'tion *n.* carrying on or resumption (of an action, course, story, book, etc.); ||(St. Exch.) carrying over an account to next settling day (∿ **day** = CONTANGO *day*); that by which a thing is continued, additional part(s); ∿ **school** (Hist., for additional teaching in spare time of those who had left full-time education). [ME f. OF, f. L *continuatio -onis* (as prec.; see -ATION)]

conti͞'nūative *a.* tending or serving to continue. [f. LL *continuativus* (as prec.; see -IVE)]

conti͞'nūator *n.* one who writes continuation to another's work. [f. as foll.; see -OR]

conti͞'nūe *v.* **1.** *v.t.* maintain, keep up, not stop (action etc.); take up, resume, (narrative, journey, etc., or abs.); prolong, be sequel to; *(Law) adjourn; hence ∿ABLE *a.* **2.** *v.i.* still be in existence; stay (*in, at*, place, in a state); not become other than (*weather continues fine; if you continue obstinate*); not cease (do*ing, to* do). [ME, f. OF *continuer* f. L *continuare* make or be CONTINUOUS]

conti͞'nūity *n.* state of being continuous; unbroken succession; logical sequence; detailed scenario of film (∿ **girl** etc., person who ensures necessary agreement of detail between different filmings); linkage between broadcast items; **law of** ∿ (that all changes in nature are continuous, not abrupt). [F *continuité* f. L *continuitas -tatis* (as CONTINUOUS; see -ITY)]

conti͞'nūō *n.* (*pl.* ∿s). (Mus.) figured BASS³; (usu. keyboard) accompaniment improvised from this; instrument(s) playing it. [f. *basso continuo* (It., = continuous bass)]

conti͞'nūous *a.* (Of material things) connected, unbroken; uninterrupted in time or sequence; (Gram.) progressive; ∿ **creation**, creation of the universe or matter in it regarded as a continuous process; ∿ **stationery** (with sheets joined together and folded alternately); ∿ **wave**, (Phys.) electromagnetic wave of constant amplitude; hence ∿LY² *adv.*, ∿NESS *n.* [f. L *continuus* uninterrupted f. CON(*tinēre = tenēre* hold) + -OUS]

conti͞'nū|um *n.* (*pl.* ∿**a**). thing whose structure is continuous not discrete (*continuum of matter, sensation, events*, etc.; SPACE¹-*time continuum*). [L, neut. of *continuus*; see prec.]

contor͞'t *v.t.* twist out of normal shape, distort. [f. L CON(*torquēre tort*- twist)]

contor͞'tion *n.* twisting; twisted state (esp. of face or body). [f. L *contortio* (as prec.; see -ION)]

contor͞'tionist *n.* acrobat who adopts unusual postures; one who contorts meanings etc. [f. prec. + -IST]

co͞'ntour (-oor) *n. & v.t.* **1.** *n.* outline; line separating differently-coloured parts of design; outline of coast, mountain mass, etc.; ∿ (**line**), one representing horizontal contour of earth's surface at given elevation, as in a ∿ **map**; ∿ **ploughing** (along lines of constant altitude to minimize soil erosion). **2.** *v.t.* mark with contour lines; carry (road) round side of hill. [F, f. It. *contorno* f. *contornare* draw in outline (as CON-, *tornare* turn)]

cŏ'ntra *prep.* & *n.* See PRO[1]. [L, adv. & prep. = against]

cŏntra- *pref.* **1.** against, opposite, etc., (*contradict, contradistinguish*). **2.** (Mus., of instruments and organ- -stops) having a pitch of an octave below (*contra- -bassoo'n*). [f. or after L, as prec.]

cŏ'ntrabănd *n.* & *a.* **1.** *n.* prohibited trade, smuggling; smuggled goods; ∿ **of war,** anything forbidden to be supplied by neutrals to belligerents; hence ∿IST *n.*, smuggler. **2.** *a.* forbidden to be imported or exported (*contraband goods*); concerned with these (*contraband trade, trader*). [f. Sp. *contrabanda* f. It. CONTRA(*bando* proclamation f. as BAN[1])]

cŏ'ntrabăss *n.* = DOUBLE[1]-*bass.* [f. It. CONTRA(*basso* BASS[3])]

cŏntracĕ'ptĭve *a.* & *n.* preventive of pregnancy, or of implantation of ovum; so **cŏntracĕ'ption** *n.*, use of contraceptives. [f. CONTRA- + CONCEPTIVE, CONCEPTION]

cŏ'ntrăct[1] *n.* **1.** agreement between parties, States, etc.; business agreement for supply of goods or performance of work at specified price; agreement enforceable by law (NUDE *contract*). **2.** accepted promise to do or not do; formal agreement for marriage; conveyance of property; (Bridge etc.) commitment to make stated number of tricks; ∿ (**bridge**), form of auction bridge in which only tricks bid and won count towards game. [ME f. OF, f. L *contractus* (as foll.)]

cŏntră'ct[2] *v.t.* & *i.* **1.** enter into business or legal engagement (*to* do, *for* piece of work, or abs.); arrange (work) to be done by contract; ∿ (one**self**) **in**(**to**), **out** (*of*), arrange for one's subjection to, exemption or exclusion from, provisions (*of* law etc.), agree, refuse, to take part (in). **2.** enter into (marriage); form (friendship, habit); become infected with (disease), whence ∿ABLE *a.*; incur (debt). **3.** draw together (muscles, brow, etc.), make smaller, whence ∿IBLE *a.*; (Gram.) shorten (word) by combination or elision (as *do not* to *don't*); shrink, become smaller. **4.** Hence ∿IVE *a.* [f. earlier *contract* adj. (= contracted) f. OF, f. L *contractus* (CON-, *trahere tract-* draw)]

contrà'ctĭle *a.* capable of or producing contraction (*contractile muscles, force*); hence **cŏntractī'lity** *n.* [f. prec.; see -IL]

contrǎ'ction *n.* shrinking, contracting; shortening of word by combination or elision; contracted form of word(s); contracting (*of* debt, disease, habit). [F, f. L *contractio -onis* (as CONTRACT[2]; see -ION)]

contrà'ctor *n.* undertaker of contract, esp. for building to specified plans; contracting muscle. [LL (as CONTRACT[2]; see -OR)]

contrà'ctŭal *a.* of (the nature of) a contract; hence ∿LY[2] *adv.* [f. L *contractus* (CONTRACT[1]) + -AL]

contradĭ'ct *v.t.* deny (statement, or abs.); deny statement made by (person); be contrary to (*these rumours contradict each other*); hence ∿ABLE *a.*, ∿OR *n.* [f. L CONTRA(*dicere dict-* say)]

contradĭ'ction *n.* denial; opposition; statement contradicting another; inconsistency; ∿ **in terms,** self- -contradictory statement or words ('*almost quite ready*' *is a contradiction in terms*). [ME f. OF, f. L *contradictio -onis* (as prec.; see -ION)]

cŏntradĭ'ctious (-shŭs) *a.* inclined to contradict; disputatious; hence ∿LY[2] *adv.*, ∿NESS *n.* [f. CONTRA- DICT + -IOUS]

cŏntradĭ'ctor|ў *a.* making denial; mutually opposed or inconsistent; inclined to contradict; (Logic, of two propositions) so related that one and only one must be true; hence ∿ILY[2] *adv.*, ∿INESS *n.* [ME, f. LL *contradictorius* (as CONTRADICT; see -ORY)]

cŏntradistī'n|guish (-nggw-) *v.t.* distinguish (things, one *from* another) by contrast; so ∿CTION *n.* [f. *contra-* + DISTINGUISH]

cŏ'ntrail *n.* condensation trail. [abbr.]

cŏntra-ĭ'ndĭc|āte *v.t.* (esp. Med.) act as indication against (use of a particular treatment etc.); so ∿A'TION *n.* [f. CONTRA- + INDICATE]

contră'ltō *n.* (*pl.* ∿s). (Mus.) lowest female voice; singer with contralto voice; part written for contralto voice. [It. (CONTRA-, ALTO); cf. COUNTER-TENOR]

cŏntraposĭ'tion (-z-) *n.* opposition, contrast; (Logic) conversion of proposition from *all A is B* to *all not-B is not-A*; so **cŏntrapŏ'sĭtĭve** (-z-) *a.* & *n.* [f. LL *contrapositio* (CONTRA-, *ponere posit-* place; see -ION)]

contră'ption *n.* (colloq.) strange machine; device, contrivance. [19th c.; perh. f. CONTRIVE (cf. *conceive, conception*), assoc. w. TRAP[1]]

cŏntrapŭ'nt|al *a.* of or in counterpoint; so ∿IST *n.*, person skilled in counterpoint, ∿ALLY *adv.* [f. It. *contrappunto* counterpoint + -AL]

contrarī'etў *n.* opposition in nature, quality, or action; disagreement, inconsistency. [ME, f. OF *contrarieté* f. LL *contrarietas -tatis* (as CONTRARY; see -TY[1])]

contrā'rious *a.* (arch.) opposed; perverse; (of things) adverse; hence ∿LY[2] *adv.*, ∿NESS *n.* [ME f. OF, f. med. L *contrariosus* (as CONTRARY; see -OUS)]

contrā'rĭwīse (-z) *adv.* on the other hand; in the opposite way; perversely. [ME, f. foll. + -WISE]

cŏ'ntrarў (sec also sense 2) *a.*, *n.*, & *adv.* **1.** *a.* opposed in nature or tendency (*to*); (of wind) impeding, unfavourable; opposite (of two things); opposite in position or direction; hence **cŏ'ntrarіLY**[2] *adv.* **2.** (kŏntrā'rĭ; colloq.) perverse, self-willed; hence **contrā'rĭNESS** *n.*, **contrā'rĭLY**[2] *adv.* **3.** *n.* the opposite; **by contraries,** taking *Yes* for *No* etc., oppositely to logic or expectation; **on the** ∿ (intensifying a denial expressed or understood: *Have you nearly finished?*—*On the contrary, I have only just begun*); **to the** ∿, to the opposite effect (*there is no evidence to the contrary*). **4.** *adv.* in opposition to (*act contrary to nature*). [ME, f. AF *contrarie*, OF *contraire*, f. L *contrarius* (as CONTRA; see -ARY[1])]

contra'st[1] (-ah'-) *v.* **1.** *v.t.* set (two things, one *with* another) in opposition so as to show their differences. **2.** *v.i.* show striking difference on comparison (*with*). [f. F *contraster* f. It. f. med. L CONTRA(*stare* stand)]

cŏ'ntrast[2] (-ah-) *n.* juxtaposition or comparison (esp. of form, colours, etc.) showing striking differences (*between; in contrast with*); thing or person having noticeably different qualities (*to*); degree of difference between tones in photograph or television picture, whence ∿Y[2] *a.*, showing a high contrast; change of apparent brightness, colour, etc., of an object caused by adjacent objects; hence **contra'stIVE** (-ah'-) *a.* [f. F *contraste* f. It. *contrasto* (as prec.)]

cŏntra-suggĕ'stĭble (-sŭj-) *a.* (Psych.) tending to respond to a suggestion by believing or doing the contrary. [f. CONTRA- + SUGGESTIBLE]

cŏ'ntrāte *a.* ∿ **wheel,** = CROWN[1] wheel. [f. med. L & Rom. *contrata*; see COUNTRY]

cŏntravē'ne *v.t.* infringe (law); (of things) conflict with. [f. LL CONTRA(*venire vent-* come)]

cŏntravē'ntion *n.* infringement (*in* ∿ *of*, violating). [F, f. med. L *contraventio* (as prec.; see -ION)]

cŏntretĕmps (kawn'trĕtahn) *n.* unlucky or embarrassing occurrence; unexpected mishap. [F]

contrĭ'būte *v.t.* & *i.* pay or furnish (*to* common fund etc.), pay or give jointly with others; (literary contribution) help, be instrumental (*to*); write (article) for publication with others); ∿ **to,** tend to bring about. [f. L CON(*tribuere -ut-* bestow)]

cŏntribū'tion *n.* act of contributing; thing, help, literary work, contributed; lay together ∿, exact contributions from. [ME f. OF, or f. LL *contributio* (as prec.; see -ION)]

contrĭ'būtor *n.* one who contributes (esp. literary work). [f. AF *contributour* (as CONTRIBUTE; see -OR)]

contrĭ'būtorў *a.* & *n.* **1.** *a.* that contributes (∿ **negligence,** (Law) by injured person who has failed or omitted to take proper precautions against accident); operated by means of contributions (*contributory* *pension scheme*). **2.** *n.* ‖(Law). person liable to contribute towards payment of wound-up company's debts. [f. med. L *contributorius* (as CONTRIBUTE; see -ORY)]

cŏ'ntrīte *a.* crushed in spirit by sense of sin; completely penitent; (of action) showing a contrite spirit; hence ∼LY² (-tlī) *adv.*, ∼NESS (-tn-) *n.* [ME, f. OF *contrit* f. L *contritus* bruised (as CON-, *terere trit-* rub)]

contri'tion *n.* being contrite; thorough penitence. [ME f. OF, f. LL *contritio -onis* (as prec.; see -ION)]

contri'vance *n.* act of contriving; deceitful practice; invention; mechanical device; inventive capacity. [f. foll. + -ANCE]

contri've *v.t.* devise, plan with skill; bring to pass, manage, (thing, *to* do; *contrive to open the window*; *contrive to make matters worse*); (abs., arch.) manage household affairs etc. resourcefully; hence ∼ABLE *a.*, ∼ER¹ *n.* [ME, f. OF *controver* find, imagine f. med. L *contropare* compare]

contrŏ'l *n.* **1.** power of directing, command, (**in** ∼, directing an activity; **out of** ∼, no longer subject to guidance; **under** ∼, (fig.) in proper order); restraint; means of restraint, check; (usu. in *pl.*) means of regulating prices etc. **2.** standard of comparison for checking inferences deduced from experiment, esp. specimen, patient, etc., like those being investigated, but not specially treated etc. **3.** personality directing actions of spiritualist medium; place where racing-cars etc. must stop for recording, inspection, etc., or where their speed is controlled; (usu. in *pl.*) various devices in aircraft or vehicle used to control direction, speed, etc., devices for operation of machine. **4.** ∼ **board** or **panel,** surface containing switches, dials, etc., for remote control of apparatus; ∼ **rod** (of neutron-absorbing material used to vary power of nuclear reactor); ∼ **room,** room where an operation is controlled; ∼ **tower,** high building at airport etc. from which air traffic is controlled by radio. [f. foll. or f. F *contrôle* (contrôler; see foll.)]

contrŏ'l *v.t.* (-ll-). dominate, command; exert control over (∼**ling interest,** ownership of majority of stock or other means to determine policy of a business etc.); hold in check (one*self*, one's anger); check, verify; regulate (prices etc.); hence ∼LABLE *a.* [ME, f. AF *contreroller* keep copy of roll of accounts, f. med. L *contrarotulare* (as CONTRA-, *rotulus* ROLL¹)]

contrŏ'ller *n.* In vbl senses; one who checks expenditure, steward, COMPTROLLER; hence ∼SHIP *n.* [ME *counterroller* f. AF *contrerollour* (as prec.; see -OR)]

cŏntrovê'rsial (-shal) *a.* of, open to, given to, controversy; hence ∼ISM (3), ∼IST (2), *ns.*, ∼LY² *adv.* [f. LL *controversialis* (as foll.; see -AL)]

contrŏvê'rsȳ (kŏ'ntrŏ-; **D** kŏntrŏ'-) *n.* disputation; (prolonged) debate, esp. conducted in writing; **beyond** ∼, unquestionably. [ME, f. L *controversia* (as foll.; see -Y¹)]

cŏntrovê'rt (kŏ'-, -êr't) *v.t.* dispute about, discuss; dispute, deny; hence ∼IBLE *a.* [orig. p.p. for earlier *controversed* (cf. *converse, convert*) f. F *controvers(e)* f. L *controversus* (CONTRA-, *vertere* turn)]

cŏntūmā'cious (-shus) *a.* insubordinate, stubbornly or wilfully disobedient, esp. to order of court; hence or contemp. ∼LY² *adv.*, ∼NESS, **cŏ'ntūmacy,** *ns.* [f. L *contumax* (perh. rel. to *tumēre* swell); see -ACIOUS] *contumax* (perh. rel. to *tumēre* swell); so -ACIOUS]

cŏntūmē'lious *a.* insolent; reproachful; hence ∼LY² *adv.* [ME, f. OF *contumelieus* f. L *contumeliosus* (as foll.; see -OUS)]

cŏ'ntūmely *n.* insolent or reproachful language or treatment; disgrace. [ME, f. OF *contumelie* f. L CON(*tumelia* f. *tumēre* swell)]

contū'se (-z) *v.t.* injure by blow without breaking skin, bruise; so **contū'sion** (-zhon) *n.* [f. L CON(*tundere tus-* thump)]

conŭ'ndrum *n.* riddle esp. with punning answer; hard question. [16th c.; orig. unkn.]

cŏnŭrbā'tion *n.* aggregation of contiguous towns forming single community in some respects. [f. CON- + L *urbs urbis* city + -ATION]

cŏ'nūre *n.* Amer. parrot of genus *Aratinga* etc., resembling macaw. [f. mod. L *conurus* f. Gk *kōnos* cone + *oura* tail]

cŏnvalē'sce *v.i.* regain health after illness. [ME, f. L CON(*valescere* incept. of *valēre* be well)]

cŏnvalē'sc|ent *a.* & *n.* (person) recovering from illness; ∼ent home or hospital (for convalescents); so ∼ENCE *n.* [f. prec. + -ENT]

convê'ct|ion *n.* transport of heat by movement of heated substance; (Meteorol.) vertical movement of air; hence ∼OR *n.*, heating appliance for circulating warm air, ∼ion**AL**, ∼IVE, *adjs.* [f. LL *convectio* f. L CON(*vehere vect-* carry); see -ION]

convenance (kaw'nvenahns) *n.* (usu. in *pl.*) conventional propriety. [F (*convenir* be fitting, f. as foll.; see -ANCE)]

convē'n|e *v.t.* & *i.* assemble; convoke (assembly); summon (person *before* tribunal); hence ∼ABLE *a.*, ∼ER¹, ∼OR, *ns.*, (esp.) person who arranges meetings of committee etc. [ME, f. L CON(*venire vent-* come) assemble, agree, fit]

convē'nience *n.* **1.** suitableness; material advantage (FLAG⁴ *of convenience*; **marriage of** ∼, one that is not primarily a love-match); freedom from trouble or difficulty (*for convenience*; **at your** ∼, in a way, at a time, convenient to you; **at your earliest** ∼, as soon as you can); advantage (*a great convenience*; **make a** ∼ **of** person, utilize his services without considering his feelings); ∼ **food** etc. (needing very little preparation and used whenever one wishes). **2.** useful thing, esp. equipment or installation; water-closet; public lavatory. [ME, f. L *convenientia* (as prec.; see -ENCE)]

convē'nient *a.* suitable; easily accessible; not troublesome (*if it is convenient to* or *for you*); available or occurring at a suitable moment (*went out and hailed a convenient taxi*); (colloq.) well situated as regards access (*convenient for station and shops*); hence ∼LY² *adv.* [ME, f. as CONVENE; see -ENT]

cŏ'nvent *n.* religious community of women; cf. MONASTERY; living together under discipline; building occupied by this; ∼ **school** (conducted by members of convent). [ME f. AF *covent*, OF *convent* f. L *conventus* assembly (as CONVENE)]

convê'nticle *n.* clandestine religious meeting, esp. ‖(Hist.) of Nonconformists or Dissenters; building used for this. [ME, f. L *conventiculum* (place of) assembly, dim. of *conventus* (as CONVENE)]

convê'ntion *n.* **1.** act of convening; formal assembly, whence *∼EER' n.*; (Hist.) meeting of Parliament without summons from sovereign. **2.** agreement between parties; agreement between States, less formal than treaty; general (often implicit) consent; practice based on this, accepted social behaviour esp. if artificial or formal; (Cards) accepted method of play in leading, bidding, etc.) used to convey information. [ME f. OF, f. L *conventio -onis* (as CONVENE; see -ION)]

convê'ntional *a.* depending on convention(s); not natural, not spontaneous; following tradition; (of bomb, power source, etc.) other than nuclear; hence ∼ISM (3), ∼IST (2), ∼ITY (-ă'l-), *ns.*, ∼IZE (3) *v.t.*, ∼LY² *adv.* [f. F *conventionnel* or f. LL *conventionalis* (as prec.; see -AL)]

convê'ntual *a.* & *n.* (member or inmate) of a convent; (member) of the less strict branch of Franciscans, living in large convents. [ME, f. med. L *conventualis* (as CONVENT; see -AL)]

convê'rge *v.i.* (Of lines) tend to meet in a point; come together as if to meet or join; (Math., of series) approximate in the sum of its terms towards a definite limit. [f. LL CON(*vergere* incline)]

convê'rg|ent *a.* converging; (Biol.) having tendency to become similar in same environment; (Psych., of thought) tending to reach only the most rational result; hence ∼ENCE, ∼ENCY, *ns.* [f. as prec.; see -ENT]

convers|ant (kŏnvê'r-, kŏ'nver-) *a.* having frequent dealings, well acquainted, *with* person, subject, etc.

For other words in *co-* see CO-.

hence ∼ANCE, ∼ANCY, ns. [ME f. OF, part. of *converser* CONVERSE[1]; see -ANT]

cŏnversā′tion n. informal exchange of ideas by spoken words, whence ∼IST (1) n.; instance of this; **make** ∼, converse only as social duty; ∼ **piece**, (1) kind of genre painting of group of figures, (2) thing that serves as topic of conversation owing to its unusualness etc. [ME f. OF, f. L *conversatio -onis* (as CONVERSE[1]; see -ATION)]

cŏnversā′tional a. fond of, good at, pertaining to, conversation; hence ∼IST n., one who is good at conversing, ∼LY[2] adv. [f. prec. + -AL]

cŏnversāziō′n|ē (-ăts-) n. (pl. ∼es, or ∼i pr. -ē). social gathering held by learned or art society. [It., f. L (as CONVERSATION)]

convĕr′se[1] v.i. engage in conversation (*with* person, *on* or *about* subject). [ME, f. OF *converser* f. L *conversari* keep company (with), frequent. of *convertere* (CONVERT[1])]

cŏ′nverse[2] n. (arch.) conversation. [f. prec.]

cŏ′nverse[3] a. & n. **1.** a. opposite, contrary; hence **convĕr′seLY[2]** (-slī) adv. **2.** n. form of words produced by transposition of some terms of another (*he had learning without wealth* is the converse of *he had wealth without learning*); (Math.) proposition whose premiss and conclusion are the conclusion and premiss of another. [f. L *conversus*, p.p. of *convertere* (CONVERT[1])]

convĕr′sion (-shon) n. **1.** converting or being converted (see foll.). **2.** transposition, inversion; (Theol.) change from sinfulness to holiness; (Psych.) change of unconscious conflict into physical disorder or disease; adaptation of building for new purposes, building so modified; transformation of fertile into fissile material in nuclear reactor. [ME f. OF, f. L *conversio -onis* (as foll.; see -ION)]

convĕr′t[1] v. **1.** v.t. change (*into*); change in character or function; (Logic) interchange terms of (proposition); cause to turn, bring over, (*to* opinion, party, faith, etc.), change (moneys, stocks, units in which a quantity is expressed, etc.) into others of different kind; (Rugby Footb.) complete (a try, or abs.) by kicking goal; (Amer. Footb.) complete (a touchdown) by kicking goal or crossing goal-line; make structural alterations in (building; cf. prec.); ∼ **to** one's **own use**, wrongfully make use of (another's property). **2.** v.i. be able to be converted (*sofa converts into double bed*). **3.** Hence ∼ER[1] (1, 2) n. [ME, f. OF *convertir* f. Rom. **convertire* for L CON(*vertere vers-* turn) turn about]

cŏ′nvĕrt[2] n. person converted (*to* opinion etc.), esp. to religious faith or life. [f. prec.]

convĕr′t|ible a. & n. **1.** a. that may be converted; (of terms) synonymous; (of currency etc.) that may be converted into gold or US dollars; (of motor car etc.) with roof that can be folded down or removed; hence ∼IBI′LITY n., ∼IBLY adv. **2.** n. convertible motor car etc. [OF, f. L *convertibilis* (as CONVERT[1]; see -IBLE)]

cŏ′nvĕx a. with outline or surface curved like exterior of circle or sphere (cf. CONCAVE); hence or cogn. **convĕ′xITY** n., ∼LY[2] adv. [f. L *convexus* vaulted]

convey′ (-vā′) v.t. transport, carry; transmit (sound, smell, etc.); impart, communicate, (idea, meaning); (Law) transfer (property *to*, or abs.); hence ∼ABLE a., ∼ER[1], ∼OR, ns., (esp.) endless belt etc. as mechanical contrivance for conveying articles or materials, esp. during manufacture. [ME, f. OF *conveier* f. med. L CON(*viare* f. *via* way)]

convey′ance (-ā′a-) n. carrying; transmission; communication (of ideas etc.); (document effecting) transfer of property; means of transport, vehicle. [f. prec. + -ANCE]

convey′anc|er (-ā′a-) n. lawyer who prepares documents for conveyance of property; so ∼ING[1] n., such work. [f. prec. + -ER[1]]

cŏ′nvict[1] n. condemned criminal undergoing imprisonment. [f. obs. *convict* convicted f. L *convictus* (as foll.)]

convĭ′ct[2] v.t. prove guilty (*of* offence); declare guilty by verdict of jury or decision of judge; cause (person) to admit he is guilty *of* (sin etc.); hence ∼IVE a. [ME, f. L CON(*vincere vict-* conquer)]

convĭ′ction n. **1.** proving or finding guilty; **summary** ∼ (by judge or magistrates without jury). **2.** act of convincing; settled belief (*have the* COURAGE *of* one's *convictions*; **carry** ∼, be convincing); awakened consciousness of sin. [f. L *convictio* (as prec.; see -ION)]

convĭ′nc|e v.t. persuade to believe firmly the truth (*of, that*); hence ∼eMENT (-sm-) n. (esp. of religious conviction), ∼IBLE a. [L (as CONVICT[2])]

convĭ′ncing a. such as to convince; able to convince; hence ∼LY[2] adv., ∼NESS n. [f. prec. + -ING[2]]

convĭ′vial a. of or befitting a feast; festive, jovial; hence ∼ITY (-ă′l-) n., ∼LY[2] adv. [f. L *convivialis* f. *convivium* feast (as CON-, *vivere* live); see -AL]

cŏnvocā′tion n. calling together; assembly; ||synod of Anglican clergy of province of Canterbury or York; ||legislative or deliberative assembly of university; hence ∼AL a. [ME, f. L *convocatio* (as foll.; see -ATION)]

convō′ke v.t. call together; summon to assemble. [f. L CON(*vocare* call)]

cŏ′nvoluted (-ōōt-) a. coiled, twisted; complex. [p.p. of *convolute* f. L *convolutus* (as CON-, *volvere volut-* roll)]

cŏnvolu′tion (-ōō′) n. coiling, twisting; coil, twist; sinuous fold of brain surface; complexity. [f. L *convolutio* f. as prec.; see -ION]

convŏ′lve v.t. & i. (esp. in *p.p.*) roll together; coil up. [f. L *convolvere* (see CONVOLUTED)]

convŏ′lvŭlus n. twining plant of genus *Convolvulus*, with trumpet-shaped flowers. [L]

cŏ′nvoy[1] v.t. (Of warship) escort (merchant or passenger vessel); escort, esp. with armed force. [ME, f. OF *convoyer*, var. of *conveier* CONVEY]

cŏ′nvoy[2] n. act of convoying; company, supply of provisions, etc., under escort; number of merchant ships sailing in company under escort; group of vehicles travelling under escort or together. [f. F *convoi* (*convoier*; see prec.)]

convŭ′lsant a. & n. (Med.) (drug etc.) that produces convulsions. [F, f. *convulser* (as foll.); see -ANT]

convŭ′lse v.t. shake violently (lit. or fig.); (usu. in *pass.*) throw into convulsions; cause to be violently seized with laughter. [f. L CON(*vellere vuls-* pull)]

convŭ′lsion (-shon) n. violent irregular motion of limb or body due to involuntary contraction of muscles (usu. in *pl.*, and esp. as disorder of infants); (in *pl.*) violent fit of laughter; violent social or political agitation; violent natural disturbance, esp. earthquake etc.; hence ∼ARY[1] a. [F, or f. L *convulsio* (as prec.; see -ION)]

convŭ′lsive a. attended or affected with, producing, convulsions (lit. or fig.); hence ∼LY[2] (-vlī) adv., ∼NESS (-vn-) n. [f. CONVULSE + -IVE]

cŏ′nỹ, cŏ′ney, n. rabbit; rabbit fur; (Bibl.) hyrax. [ME *cunin*(*g*) f. AF *coning*, OF *conin*, f. L *cuniculus*]

cōō v., n., & int. **1.** v.i., & n. (make) soft murmuring sound of or as of doves and pigeons; BILL[3] *and coo*. **2.** v.t. say cooingly. **3.** int. (sl.) expr. surprise or incredulity. [imit.]

cōō′ee n., int., & v. int. & v. (esp. Austral. & NZ) (make) sound used to attract attention, esp. at a distance; **within** (a) ∼ (of), (colloq.) very near to. [imit. of signal used by Aboriginals and copied by settlers]

cŏŏk[1] n. **1.** one who cooks food, esp. as profession (**too many** ∼s **spoil the broth**, one director is enough); (Chess) unintended solution to problem. **2.** **∼***book**, cookery book; ||∼**-general**, servant who does both cooking and housework; ∼**house**, camp kitchen, outdoor kitchen in warm countries, ship's galley; ∼**-shop**, eating-house, (NZ) sheep-station's kitchen; **∼***-stove**, cooking-stove. [OE *cōc* f. pop. L *cocus* for L *coquus*]

cŏŏk[2] v. **1.** v.t. prepare (food, or abs.) by heating (∼ person's **goose**, ruin his chances); ∼ (**up**), (fig.) concoct; (colloq.) falsify (accounts etc.), alter to produce desired result; ‖(sl., esp. in *p.p.*) fatigue; (sl.) ruin, spoil; (Chess) find unintended solution to (problem); *∿'**out**, gathering with open-air cooked meal. **2.** *v.i.* undergo cooking; **what's** ∿**ing?**, (colloq.) what is happening or planned? [ME, f. prec.]

Cook³ *n.* ∿'**s tour**, extensive usu. rapid tour. [f. T. ∿, Engl. travel agent d. 1892]

coo'ker *n.* appliance or vessel for cooking food; fruit etc. that is better cooked than eaten raw. [f. COOK² + -ER¹]

coo'kery *n.* art or practice of cooking; *place for cooking; ∿ **book** (containing recipes for preparation of food). [ME, f. COOK¹,² + -ERY]

coo'kie *n.* **1.** (Sc.) plain bun. **2.** *small sweet biscuit; (sl.) person; *the **way the** ∿ **crumbles**, (colloq.) how things turn out, the unalterable situation of affairs. [f. Du. *koekje* dim. of *koek* cake]

coo'king *n.* In vbl senses; (*attrib.*) suitable for or used in cooking (*cooking apple*, *sherry*). [f. COOK² + -ING¹]

cool¹ *a.* & *n.* **1.** *a.* of or at fairly low temperature, fairly cold; unexcited, calm, (*cool and collected*; LEAVE² person *cool*; PLAY¹ it *cool*; ∿-**headed**, not easily excited); (Jazz) restrained, relaxed; unemotional, lacking zeal, lukewarm; lacking cordiality; (colloq.) excellent. **2.** calmly audacious; (colloq., of large sums of money) *it cost me* **a** ∿ (no less than a) **thousand. 3.** Hence ∿'ISH¹ 2 *a.*, ∿'LY² (-l-lī) *adv.*, ∿'NESS *n.* **4.** *n.* coolness; cool air or place; (sl.) composure (*keep*, *lose*, one's *cool*). [OE *cōl* f. Gmc *kōluz* (*kōl-*, *kal-*; cf. COLD¹)]

cool² *v.i.* & *t.* ∿ (**down, off**), become or make cool (lit. or fig.); ∿ **it**, (sl.) relax, calm down; ∿ one's **heels**, be kept waiting; ∿**ing-o'ff period** (to allow change of mind before irrevocable action); ∿'**ing tower**, industrial structure for cooling hot water before reuse. [OE *cōlian*, = OS *cōlon* f. Gmc *kōlōjan* (as prec.)]

coo'labah *n.* (Austral.) one of various gum-trees, esp. *Eucalyptus microtheca*. [Aboriginal]

coo'lant *n.* cooling agent; fluid used to lessen friction of cutting-tool; fluid used to remove heat from internal combustion engine, nuclear reactor, etc. [f. COOL² + -ANT, after *lubricant*]

coo'ler *n.* vessel in which a thing is cooled; *refrigerator; (sl.) prison (cell). [f. COOL² + -ER¹]

coo'libah. Var. of COOLABAH.

coo'lie, coo'ly, *n.* unskilled native labourer in Eastern countries; ∿ **hat**, broad flat hat as worn by coolies. [perh. f. *Kulī*, aboriginal tribe of Gujarat, India]

coolth *n.* (colloq.) coolness. [f. COOL¹ + -TH¹]

‖**coomb,** ‖**combe,** (koōm) *n.* valley on flank of hill; short valley running up from coast. [OE *cumb*; cf. CWM]

coon *n.* *racoon; (sl., derog.; R) Negro; *∿ **dog** (trained to hunt racoons); ∿'**skin,** (cap etc. of) racoon skin. [abbr.]

coon-ca'n *n.* simple card-game like rummy (orig. Mexican). [f. Sp *con quién* with whom?]

coop¹ *n.* cage placed over sitting or fattening fowls; fowl-run (*fly the* ∿, (sl.) depart abruptly); ‖basket used in catching fish; small place of confinement, esp. prison. [ME *cupe* basket f. MDu., MLG *kūpe*, ult. f. L *cupa* cask]

coop² *v.t.* put in coop; ∿ (**in, up**), confine (person). [f. prec.]

co'-öp *n.* (colloq.) ‖co-operative society or store; *co-operation. [abbr.]

coo'per *n.*, & *v.t.* **1.** *n.* maker of casks and similar vessels; (on ship) repairer of casks etc.; hence ∿AGE (2, 4, 5) *n.* **2.** *v.t.* make or repair (cask). [ME, f. MDu., MLG *kūper* (*kūpe* COOP¹; see -ER¹)]

co-ö'per|āte, **coö'p-,** *coöp-, *v.i.* work together (*with* person *in* a work, *to* an end); (things) concur in producing an effect; so ∿ANT (n.), ∿ātor *n.* [f. eccl. L CO(*operari* f. *opus operis* work) + -ATE³]

co-öperā'tion, **coöp-,** *coöp-, *n.* working together to

same end; (Econ.) co-operative combination. [ME, f. L *cooperatio* (as prec.; see -ION); partly thr. F *coopération*]

co-ö'perative, **coö'p-,** *coöp-, *a.* & *n* **1.** *a.* of, tending to, offering, co-operation; (Econ.) ∿ **farm, society**, etc., (for production or distribution of goods, profits being shared by members), ∿ **shop, store,** (belonging to co-operative society); hence ∿LY² (-l-lī) *adv.* **2.** *n.* co-operative farm etc.; *dwelling jointly owned or leased by occupiers. [f. LL *cooperativus* (as prec.; see -IVE)]

co-ö'pt, *coö-, *v.t.* elect to committee etc. by votes of existing members; hence or cogn. ∿A'TION, ∿ION, *ns.*, ∿IVE *a.* [f. L CO(*optare* choose)]

co-ōr'dinate¹, **coōr'-,** *coör-, *a.* & *n.* **1.** *a.* equal in rank or importance, esp. (Gram.) of parts of compound sentence (cf. SUBORDINATE¹); consisting of coordinate things; hence ∿LY² (-l-lī) *adv.* **2.** *n.* co-ordinate thing, esp. (Math., usu. *coor-*) each of a system of magnitudes used to fix position of point, line, or plane; (in *pl.*) women's outer clothes that can be worn together harmoniously. [f. CO- + L *ordinare* (*ordo -inis* order); see -ATE²]

co-ōr'din|āte², **coōr'-,** *coör-, *v.t.* make co-ordinate; bring (parts, movements, etc.) into proper relation, cause to function together or in proper order; so ∿A'TION, ∿ātor, *ns.*, ∿ATIVE *a.* [f. as prec. + -ATE³]

coot *n.* aquatic bird of genus *Fulica*, esp. **bald** ∿ (with base of upper mandible extended to form white plate on forehead, whence **bald as a** ∿, entirely bald); (colloq.) stupid person. [ME, prob. f. LG]

coo'tie *n.* (sl.) body-louse. [perh. f. Malay *kutu* a biting parasite]

cop¹ *n.* (Spinning.) conical ball of thread wound on spindle. [OE *cop* summit]

cop² *n.* (sl.) policeman; ∿-**shop**, police station. [cf. foll. and COPPER²]

cop³ *v.* (-**pp**-) & *n.* (sl.) **1.** *v.t.* catch (∿ **it**, get into trouble, be punished, die); take, get. **2.** *v.i.* ∿ **out,** escape, give up attempt, go back on one's promise; ∿-**out** *n.*, (way of) escape, cowardly evasion, escapist. **3.** *n.* capture (esp. **it's a fair** ∿, the arrest is justifiable); **no** ∿, **not much** ∿, of little or no value or use. [perh. f. obs. *cap* arrest f. OF *caper* seize]

copacé'tic *a.* (sl.) excellent, in good order. [20th c.; orig. unkn.]

copai'ba (-pī'-) *n.* aromatic resin from S. Amer. plants of genus *Copaifera*, used in medicine and perfumery. [Sp. & Port., f. Guarani *cupauba*]

co'pal *n.* resin from various tropical trees, used for varnish. [Sp., f. Aztec *copalli* incense]

copār'cenary, **copār'cener,** *ns.* (Law). = PARCENARY, PARCENER. [see CO-]

copār'tner *n.* partner, sharer, associate; hence ∿SHIP *n.* [f. CO- + PARTNER]

cope¹ *n.*, & *v.t.* **1.** *n.* (Eccl.) long cloak worn in processions etc.; (fig., poet.) vault of heaven; ∿-**stone,** (fig.) finishing touch. **2.** *v.t.* furnish with cope or coping. [ME, repr. OE -*cāp,* *cāpe* (= ON *kápa*), med. L *capa* var. of LL *cappa* CAP¹, CAPE¹]

cope² *v.i.* contend successfully (*with* person, task); (colloq.) deal competently with situation or problem. [ME, f. OF *coper*, *colper*, (*cop*, *colp* blow f. med. L *colpus* f. L f. Gk *kolaphos* blow with fist)]

co'peck *n.* Russian coin (hundredth part of a rouble). [f. Russ. *kopeika* dim. of *kopye* lance (from figure of Ivan IV bearing lance instead of sword 1535)]

co'pepod *n.* small aquatic crustacean of subclass Copepoda, with oarlike feet. Hence f. Gk *kōpē* oar-handle + *pous podos* foot]

co'per *n.* horse-dealer. [f. obs. *cope* buy, f. MDu., MLG *kōpen,* G *kaufen* (rel. to CHEAP) + -ER¹]

Copér'nican *a.* ∿ **system, theory**, (that the planets, including the earth, move round the sun; cf. PTOLEMAIC). [f. *Copernicus* latinized f. N. *Koppernigk*, Polish astronomer d. 1543 + -AN]

co'pier *n.* In vbl senses; person or machine that copies (esp. documents). [f. COPY² + -ER¹]

For other words in *co-* see CO-.

cō'-pīlot, *cō'p-**, *n.* second pilot in aircraft. [f. CO- 1 + PILOT]

cō'ping[1] *n.* top (usu. sloping) course of masonry in wall; ∼-**stone** (used for coping). [f. COPE[1] + -ING[1]]

cō'ping[2] *n.* ∼ **saw** (for cutting wood into curves). [f. cope cut wood f. OF *coper* (see COPE[2]) + -ING[1]]

cō'pious *a.* existing in large amounts; abounding in information; profuse in speech; hence ∼LY[2] *adv.*, ∼NESS *n.* [ME, f. OF *copieux* or f. L *copiosus* (*copia* plenty; see -OUS)]

copi'ta (-pē'-) *n.* tulip-shaped sherry-glass; glass of sherry. [Sp., dim. of *copa* cup]

cōplā'nar *a.* (Math.) in same plane; hence **cō-planǎ'rity** *n.* [f. CO- 1 + PLANAR]

cōpŏ'lÿmer *n.* polymer with units of more than one kind; so ∼IZE (2, 3) *v.i.* & *t.* [f. CO- 1 + POLYMER]

cŏ'pper[1] *n.*, *a.*, & *v.t.* **1.** *n.* reddish malleable ductile metallic element; bronze coin; butterfly with copper--coloured wings; metal boiler, esp. for laundry. **2.** *a.* made of or coloured like copper. ∼ **beech** (kind with copper-coloured leaves); ∼ **belt**, copper--mining area of Central Africa; ∼-**bit**, soldering tool pointed with copper; ∼-**bottom** *v.t.*, sheathe bottom of (ship, pan, etc.) with copper, (in *p.p.*) (financially) reliable; ∼-**head**, venomous Amer. or Austral. snake; ∼-**plate**, polished copper plate for engraving or etching, print from this, (*a*, of writing) careful and neat; *copper* PYRITES, ∼-**smith**, one who works in copper; *copper* VITRIOL. **4.** Hence ∼Y[2] *a.*, (esp.) *copper-coloured.* **5.** *v.t.* cover (ship's bottom, pan, etc.) with copper. [OE *copor, coper, = ON koparr* f. *kupar, MDu. coper* f. LL *cuprum* for L *cyprium aes* Cyprus metal]

||**cŏ'pper**[2] *n.* (sl.) policeman. [f. COP[3] + -ER[1]]

cŏ'pperas *n.* green iron-sulphate crystals. [ME *coperose* f. OF *couperose* f. med. L *cup(e)rosa*, perh. orig. *aqua cuprosa* copper water]

cŏ'ppice *n.* & *v.* **1.** *n.* small wood of undergrowth and small trees, grown for periodical cutting; ∼-**wood**, undergrowth. **2.** *v.t.* & *i.* grow as coppice. [f. OF *copeiz* f. Rom. **colpaticium* (**colpare* cut f. med. L *colpus*; see COPE[2])]

cŏ'pra *n.* dried kernels of coconut. [Port., f. Malayalam *koppara* coconut]

cō-prĕcipitā'tion *n.* (Chem.) simultaneous precipitation of more than one compound from a solution. [f. CO- 1 + PRECIPITATION]

cŏ'pro- *comb. form.* dung, faeces, as: ∼**lite,** (piece of) fossil dung; ∼**logy** (-ŏ'l-), treatment of filthy subjects in literature etc.; ∼**phagous** (-ŏ'f-) *a.*, (of beetles) dung-eating; ∼**phi'lia,** undue interest in faeces and defecation. [f. Gk *kopros* dung + -O-]

coprŏ'sma (-z-) *n.* small Australasian evergreen plant of genus *Coprosma.* [mod. L, f. Gk *kopros* dung + *osmē* smell]

cŏpse *n.*, & *v.t.* = COPPICE; ∼'**wood**, undergrowth; hence **cŏ'psÿ**[2] *a.* [shortened f. COPPICE]

Cŏpt *n.* native Egyptian Christian, member of independent sect of Eastern Church. [f. F *Copte* or mod. L *Coph(th)tus* f. Arab. *al-ḳibṭ, al-ḳubṭ* Copts f. Copt. *Gyptios* f. Gk *Aiguptios* Egyptian]

Cŏ'ptic *a.* & *n.* **1.** *a.* of the Copts. **2.** *n.* medieval language of Egyptians, now used only in Coptic Church. [f. prec. + -IC]

cŏ'pul|a *n.* (Logic & Gram.) verb *be* (as mere sign of predication), or verb with similar function; hence ∼AR[1] *a.* [L (CO-, *apere* fasten); cf. -ULE]

cŏ'pul|āte *v.i.* have physical copulation (*with*); so ∼**atory** *a.* [f. L *copulare* fasten together (as prec.) + -ATE[3]]

cŏpulā'tion *n.* physical union of male and female persons or animals as in act of procreation; grammatical or logical connection. [ME f. OF, or f. L *copulatio* (as prec.; see -ION)]

cŏ'pulative *a.* serving to connect; (Gram.) (1) connecting words or clauses that are joined in sense (cf. DISJUNCTIVE), (2) connecting subject and predicate; (Zool. & Anat.) relating to sexual union; hence ∼LY[2] (-vlĭ) *adv.* [ME, f. OF *copulatif -ive*, or f. LL *copulativus* (as prec.; see -IVE)]

cŏ'pÿ[1] *n.* **1.** thing made to look like another; written or printed specimen (of book etc.). **2.** model to be copied; page written after model (of penmanship); **fair** ∼, written matter transcribed after correction; ROUGH *copy.* **3.** manuscript or matter to be printed (*incident* etc. will make good ∼, lends itself to interesting narration in newspapers etc.); text of advertisement. **4.** ∼-**book**, (*n.*) book containing copies for learners to imitate (BLOT[2] one's *copy-book*), (*a.*) (1) tritely conventional, (2) accurate, exemplary; ***∼ **desk** (where copy is edited for printing); ∼-**editor**, ∼-**reader**, (who reads and edits copy for printing); ∼-**taster**, one who selects copy for printing; ∼-**typist**, one who makes typewritten transcripts of documents; ∼-**writer**, one who writes or prepares copy (esp. of advertisements) for publication. [ME, f. OF *copie* f. L *copia* abundance etc., in med. L = transcript, f. phr. *facere copiam describendi* give permission to transcribe]

cŏ'pÿ[2] *v.t.* & *i.* make copy (of); ∼ (**out**), transcribe; imitate; ∼-**cat**, (colloq.) slavish imitator; ∼**ing-ink**, -**pencil**, (used for indelible writing); hence ∼IST (3) *n.* [ME, f. OF *copier* f. med. L *copiare* f. as prec.]

||**cŏ'pÿhōld** *n.* (Hist.) tenure in accordance with transcript of manorial records; land so held; hence ∼ER[1] *n.*, such tenant. [f. COPY[1] + HOLD[2]]

cŏ'pÿright (-rīt) *n.* & *a.*, & *v.t.* **1.** *n.* exclusive right given by law for term of years to author, designer, etc., or his assignee to make copies or give performances of his original work. **2.** *a.* (of book etc.) protected by copyright; ||∼ **library** (entitled to free copy of each book published in UK). **3.** *v.t.* secure copyright for (book etc.). [f. COPY[1] + RIGHT[3]]

coq au vin (kŏk ō vă'n) *n.* chicken cooked in wine. [F]

cŏ'quĕtrÿ (-kĭ-) *n.* coquettish behaviour or act; (fig.) trifling. [f. F *coquetterie* (*coqueter*, as foll.; see -ERY)]

coquĕ'tte (-kĕ't) *n.*, & *v.i.* **1.** *n.* woman who trifles with men's affections to gain admiration; crested humming-bird of genus *Lophornis.* **2.** Hence ∼ISH[1] *a.* **3.** *v.i.* behave as coquette; flirt (*with*). [F, fem. of *coquet* wanton, dim. of *coq* cock]

*coqui'na (-kē'-) *n.* soft limestone of broken shells, used in road-making. [Sp., = cockle]

coqui'tō (-kē'-) *n.* (*pl.* ∼**s**). Chilean palm-tree yielding palm-honey and fibre. [Sp., dim. of *coco* coconut]

||**côr** *int.* (vulg.) expr. surprise, alarm, etc.; *cor* BLIMEY. [corrupt. of *God*]

cor- *pref.*, assim. form of COM- before *r*.

Cor. *abbr.* Corinthians (NT); *corner.

||**cŏ'racle** *n.* small boat of wickerwork covered with watertight material, used on Welsh and Irish lakes and rivers. [f. W *corwgl* (*corwg* = Ir. *currach* boat; cf. CURRACH)]

cŏ'racoid *a.* & *n.* ∼ (**process**), short projection from shoulder-blade in vertebrates. [f. mod. L *coracoides* f. Gk *korakoeidēs* raven-like (*korax -akos* raven; see -OID)]

cŏ'ral *n.* & *a.* **1.** *n.* calcareous substance (red, pink, white, etc.) secreted by many kinds of marine polyps for support and habitation; unimpregnated roe of lobster. **2.** *a.* like coral, esp. red; made of coral; ∼ **island**, **reef**, (formed by growth of coral); ∼ **rag**, limestone containing beds of petrified corals; ∼-**snake**, small brightly-coloured snake. [ME f. OF, f. L *corallum* f. Gk *korallion*, prob. of Semitic orig.]

cŏ'ralline[1] *n.* seaweed of genus *Corallina*, with calcareous jointed stem; (pop.) name of various plant-like calcareous animals. [f. It. *corallina* dim. of *corallo*, f. as prec.]

cŏ'ralline[2] *a.* coral-red; like or composed of coral. [f. F *corallin -ine* or f. LL *corallinus* (as CORAL; see -INE[1])]

cŏ'ralli̇te *n.* fossil coral; coral skeleton of polyp. [f. L *corallum* CORAL + -ITE[1]]

cŏ'ralloid *a.* & *n.* (organism) like or akin to coral. [f. CORAL + -OID]

coram populo (kōˈram pŏˈpūlō) *adv.* in public. [L, = in the presence of the people]

côr anglais (kôr ahˈńglā, ŏˈngglā) *n.* (Mus.) instrument like oboe but lower in pitch; its player; organ stop of similar quality. [F, = English horn]

côrˈbel *n. & v.* (‖-ll-). (Archit.) **1.** *n.* projection of stone, timber, etc., jutting out from wall to support weight; short timber laid longitudinally under beam to help support it; ∿-**table**, projecting course resting on corbels. **2.** *v.t. & i.* ∿ **out, off,** (cause to) project on corbels. [ME f. OF, dim. of *corp* (see foll., -LE 2)]

côrˈbie *n.* **1.** (Sc.) raven; carrion crow. **2.** ∿-**steps,** steplike projections on sloping sides of gable. [ME, f. OF *corb, corp* f. L *corvus* crow + -IE]

côrd *n.,* & *v.t.* **1.** *n.* (piece of) long thin flexible material made from several twisted strands; (Anat.) similar structure in animal body (SPINAL, UMBILICAL, *cord*; VOCAL *cords*); *electric flex, whence ∿ˈLESS *a.* **2.** cordlike rib on cloth; ribbed cloth, esp. corduroy; (in *pl.*) corduroy breeches or trousers. **3.** measure of cut wood (usu. 128 cubic ft.); ∿ˈwood, wood that is or can easily be so measured. **4.** (fig.) moral or emotional tie (*cords of discipline, affection; fourfold cord of evidence*). **5.** *v.t.* fasten or bind with cord; (in *p.p.*) furnished with cords, (of cloth) ribbed, (of muscles) standing out like taut cords. [ME, f. OF *corde* f. L f. Gk *khordē* gut, string of musical instrument]

côrˈdage *n.* cords or ropes, esp. in rigging of ship. [ME f. F (as prec.; see -AGE)]

côrˈdāte *a.* heart-shaped. [f. mod. L *cordatus* (*cor cordis* heart; see -ATE²)]

côrdélier′ *n.* Franciscan friar of strict rule (wearing knotted cord round waist). [ME f. OF (*cordele* dim. of *corde* CORD; see -IER)]

côrˈdial *a. & n.* **1.** (medicine, food, drink) that stimulates the heart; flavoured and sweetened drink made from fruit. **2.** *a.* hearty, sincere; warm, friendly; hence ∿ITY¹ (-ăˈl-) *n.,* ∿LY² *adv.* [ME, f. med. L *cordialis* (*cor cordis* heart; see -IAL)]

côrdiller′a (-lyārˈa) *n.* mountain ridge (one of parallel series), esp. of the Andes and in Central America and Mexico. [Sp. (*cordilla* dim. of *cuerda* CORD)]

côrˈdīte *n.* smokeless explosive made from gun-cotton, nitroglycerine, and vaseline. [f. CORD (from its appearance) + -ITE¹]

côrˈdon *n.,* & *v.t.* **1.** *n.* chain of military posts; line or circle of police etc.; ∿ (**sanitaire,** *pr.* sănītārˈ), guarded line between infected and uninfected (lit. or fig.) districts. **2.** ornamental cord or braid; ribbon of knightly order; ∿ **bleu** (kôrdawň blêˈr) first-class cook. **3.** fruit-tree trained to grow as single stem; (Archit.) string-course. **4.** *v.t.* ∿ (**off**), enclose with (military, police, etc.) cordon. [f. It. *cordone* augment. of *corda* CORD, & F *cordon* (as CORD; see -OON)]

côrˈdovan *n.* kind of soft leather. [f. Sp. *cordovan* of Cordova, where orig. made]

côrˈduroy (-er-, -ūr-) *n.* coarse ribbed cotton velvet; (in *pl.*) corduroy trousers; ∿ **road** (of tree-trunks laid across swamp). [18th c., prob. f. CORD ribbed fabric + obs. *duroy* coarse woollen fabric]

‖côrˈdwainer *n.* (arch.) shoemaker (now only as guild-name etc.). [f. obs. *cordwain* CORDOVAN + -ER¹]

côre *n.,* & *v.t.* **1.** *n.* horny capsule containing seeds of apple, pear, etc.; central part cut out (esp. of rock etc. in boring); piece of soft iron forming centre of electromagnet or induction coil; internal mould filling space to be left hollow in a casting; (Archaeol.) trimmed flint after removal of flakes; region of fissile material in nuclear reactor; unit of structure in computer, whose magnetization is reversible; central strand of rope, inner strand of electric cable. **2.** central part of different character from what surrounds it; central region of the earth; innermost part (lit., or fig.: *rotten at the core; English to the core*). **3.** *v.t.* remove core from; hence **côrˈER¹** (2) *n.* [ME, of unkn. orig.]

*****CORE** *abbr.* Congress of Racial Equality.

côrêlāˈtion. Var. of CORRELATION.

co-rêliˈgionist, *côrê-, (-jo-) *n.* adherent of same religion. [f. CO- 1 + RELIGION + -IST]

corêˈlla *n.* (Austral.) white long-billed cockatoo that can be taught to talk. [app. Latinized f. Aboriginal *ca-rall*]

côrêôˈpsis *n.* plant with rayed usu. yellow composite flowers. [mod. L, f. Gk *koris* bug + *opsis* appearance, w. ref. to shape of seed]

co-rêspôˈndent, *côrê-, *n.* person (esp. man) charged with adultery with respondent in divorce suit; ‖∿ **shoes,** (joc.) man's two-toned shoes. [f. CO-1 + RESPONDENT]

‖côrf *n.* (*pl.* **corves** *pr.* -vz). large basket formerly used in mining; basket in which fish are kept alive in water. [f. MDu., MLG *korf,* OHG *chorp, korb* f. L *corbis* basket]

côrˈgi (-gĭ) *n.* (**Welsh**) ∿, dog of short-legged breed with foxlike head. [W (*cor* dwarf, *ci* dog)]

côriăˈceous (-shus) *a.* like leather, leathery. [f. LL *coriaceus* (*corium* leather; see -ACEOUS)]

côriăˈnder *n.* annual plant (*Coriandrum sativum*) of S. Europe etc., with aromatic fruit (pop. called ∿ **seed**) used for flavouring. [ME, f. OF *coriandre* f. L *coriandrum* f. Gk *koriannon*]

Coriˈnthian *a. & n.* (native) of Corinth; (arch.) profligate; ∿ **order,** (Archit.) most ornate of the three Greek ORDER¹s, having bell-shaped capital with rows of acanthus leaves. [f. L f. Gk *Korinthios* + -AN]

côrˈium *n.* (Anat.) dermis. [L, = skin]

côrk *n.,* & *v.t.* **1.** *n.* buoyant light-brown bark of cork-oak; piece of cork used as float for fishing-line etc.; bottle-stopper of cork or other material; (Bot.) inner division of the bark in higher plants; (*attrib.*) made of cork. **2.** ∿-**oak,** S. European oak (*Quercus suber*); ∿ˈscrew, steel screw for drawing cork from bottle, thing spirally twisted, (*v.t. & i.*) move spirally; ‖∿-**tipped** *a.,* (of cigarette) having end band or filter of corklike material; ∿ˈwood, (tree yielding) light porous wood. **3.** *v.t.* stop (*up*) as with cork; bottle *up* (feelings etc.). [ME, f. Du. & LG *kork,* f. Sp. *alcorque* cork sole, perh. f. Arab.]

côrˈkage *n.* charge made by hotel or restaurant for serving wine etc. (esp. that brought from elsewhere). [f. prec. + -AGE]

côrked (-kt) *a.* stopped with cork; blackened with burnt cork; (of wine) impaired by defective cork. [f. CORK + -ED¹]

côrˈker *n.* (sl.) astonishing or surpassing good thing or person. [f. CORK + -ER¹]

***côrˈking** *a.* (sl.) unusually large or excellent. [f. prec. + -ING²]

côrˈký *a.* corklike; (of wine) corked. [f. CORK + -Y²]

côrm *n.* (Bot.) bulblike underground stem, solid bulb. [f. mod. L f. Gk *kormos* trunk with boughs lopped off]

côrˈmorant *n.* large lustrous-black voracious sea-bird. [ME, f. OF *cormaran* f. med. L *corvus marinus* sea-raven; for ending -*ant* cf. *peasant, tyrant*]

côrn¹ *n.* **1.** grain or seed, pea of cereal (also of pepper etc.); (collect. *sing.*) cereal(s) before or after harvesting, esp. wheat or oats or *maize; (colloq.) something CORNY², esp. music. **2.** ‖*corn*-CHANDLER; ∿-**cob,** cylindrical part to which grains are attached in ear of maize (∿-**cob pipe,** tobacco-pipe made of this; ∿ **on the cob,** maize cooked and eaten in this form); *corn*-COCKLE¹; ∿ˈcrake, bird (*Crex crex*) with harsh grating voice; ∿ˈdolly, symbolic or decorative figure made of plaited straw; ∿ **exchange** (for trade in corn); ‖∿-**factor,** dealer in corn; ∿ˈfield, field in which corn is grown; ∿ˈflakes, breakfast cereal of toasted flavoured maize flakes; ∿ˈflour, (U.S.) fine-ground maize, (2) flour of rice or other grain; ∿ˈflower, one of various plants growing among corn, esp. *Centaurea cyanus*; ‖C∿ **Laws** (regulating corn-trade, esp. English laws restricting importation, repealed 1846); ∿ **marigold,** daisy-like yellow-flowered cornfield weed; *∿ **pone,** baked or fried maize bread; ∿-salad, lamb's-lettuce; *∿ silk = SILK 4; corn-SPURRY; ∿'starch, = cornflour; *∿--whiskey, whisky distilled from maize. [OE, = OS, OHG, ON korn, Goth. kaurn f. Gmc *kurnam cogn. w. L granum grain]

corn² v.t. (esp. in p.p.) sprinkle or preserve with salt or brine; ∿ed beef (thus preserved and tinned). [f. prec.]

corn³ n. horny usu. tender place esp. on foot, extending into subcutaneous tissue; TREAD on person's corns. [ME f. AF, f. L cornu horn]

cor'nbräsh n. (Geol.) coarse calcareous sandstone. [f. CORN¹ + BRASH¹]

cor'ne|a n. transparent part of anterior covering of eyeball, over iris and pupil; hence ∿AL a. [mod. L, f. med. L cornea (tela) horny tissue, f. L corneus horny (cornu horn)]

cor'nel n. plant of genus Cornus, e.g. cornelian cherry and dogwood. [16th c., thr. G, ult. f. L cornus]

cornē'lian¹, car-, n. dull red or reddish-white chalcedony. [ME, f. OF corneline; car- after L caro carnis flesh]

cornē'lian² n. ∿ cherry, European berry-bearing tree (Cornus mas). [f. CORNEL + -IAN]

cor'nĕous a. hornlike, horny. [f. L corneus (cornu horn) + -OUS]

cor'ner n. & v, 1. n. place where converging sides or edges meet; projecting angle, esp. where two streets meet (cut (off) a ∿, avoid it by a short cut, or pass round it as closely as possible; (fig.) scamp work; just (a)round the ∿, (colloq.) very near, imminent; turn the ∿, pass round it into another street, (fig.) pass critical point (in illness etc.)); triangular piece from ham or gammon. 2. hollow angle enclosed by meeting walls etc.; (Boxing, Wrestling) angle of ring, esp. one where contestant rests between rounds; (fig.) drive into a ∿ (difficult position from which there is no escape), a TIGHT corner; within the four ∿s of, within the scope or extent of. 3. secluded or remote place (done in a corner; HOLE¹-and-corner transactions); region, quarter, esp. remote (from the four corners of Britain, of the earth). 4. buying up of the whole of any stock in the market, so as to compel speculative sellers to buy from one to fulfil their obligations; any combination to raise price by securing monopoly. 5. (Hockey & Assoc. Footb.). ∿(-hit, -kick), free hit or kick from corner of pitch after ball has been hit or kicked over his own goal-line by an opponent. 6. ∿-boy, -man¹, street rough, loafer; ∿ cupboard (fitted into corner of room); ∿-man² (at either end of row of Negro minstrels, playing bones or tambourine and contributing comic effects); ∿ shop (at corner of street, or small local shop esp. as opp. supermarket etc.); ∿-stone, one in projecting angle of wall, foundation stone, (fig.) indispensable part, basis. 7. Hence ∿WAYS, ∿WISE, advs. 8. v.t. drive into corner (esp. fig.); force (dealers) or control (commodity) by means of corner. 9. v.i. (esp. of, or in, vehicle) move round corner. [ME f. AF, f. Rom. *cornarium, f. L cornu horn; see -ER² (2)]

cor'nĕt¹ n. 1. brass musical instrument like trumpet but shorter and wider, whence ∿(t)IST (3) (kor'-, -ĕ't-) n.; its player; organ stop of similar quality; cornetto. 2. conically-rolled piece of paper for groceries etc.; ‖conical wafer containing ice cream. [ME f. OF, dim. of Rom. *corno f. L cornu horn; see -ET¹]

‖cor'nĕt² n. (Hist.) fifth commissioned officer in cavalry troop, who carried the colours; hence ∿CY n. [earlier sense 'pennon, standard', f. F cornette dim. of corne f. Rom. *corna horn f. L cornua horns]

cornĕ'tt|ō (pl. ∿i pr. -ē), cor'nĕtt, n. old wood-wind instrument like flageolet. [It., dim. of corno horn (as CORNET¹)]

cor'nic|e n. 1. (Archit.) horizontal moulded projection crowning a building or structure, esp. uppermost member of entablature of an order, surmounting frieze; ornamental moulding round wall of room just below ceiling. 2. (Mount.) overhanging mass of

hardened snow at edge of precipice. 3. Hence ∿ED² (-st) a. [f. F corniche etc. f. It. cornice, perh. f. L cornix -icis crow]

corniche (kor'nĭsh, -nē'sh) n. ∿ (road), road along edge of cliff etc., coastal road with wide views. [F; see prec.]

Cor'nish a. & n. 1. a. of Cornwall, England; ∿ boiler, cylindrical flue-boiler; ∿ cream, CLOTTED cream; ∿ pasty, seasoned meat and vegetables baked in pastry without dish; Cornish RIVIERA. 2. n. ancient Celtic language of Cornwall. [f. Cornwall + -ISH¹]

‖cor'nstōne n. mottled red and green limestone, subordinate bed in Old Red Sandstone. [f. CORN¹ + STONE]

cornūco'pĭ|a n. goat's horn represented as overflowing with flowers, fruit, and corn, horn of plenty; ornamental vessel shaped like this; overflowing store; hence ∿AN a. [LL, f. L cornu copiae horn of plenty]

cor'nў¹ a. of or abounding in corn. [f. CORN¹ + -Y²]

cor'nў² a. (colloq.) out of date, old-fashioned; trite; sentimental. [f. as prec.; orig. sense 'rustic']

coro'lla n. (Bot.) whorl of modified leaves (petals), separate or combined, forming inner envelope of flower. [L, dim. of corona crown]

coro'llarў n. proposition appended to one already demonstrated; natural consequence, result. [ME, f. L corollarium money paid for garland, gratuity, neut. adj. f. prec.; see -ARY¹]

corō'na¹, n, (pl. ∿e or ∿s). 1. small circle of light round sun or moon; rarefied gaseous envelope of sun, seen as halo of white light around disc of moon in total eclipse of sun. 2. circular chandelier hung from roof. 3. (Archit.) member of cornice, with broad vertical face, usu. of considerable projection. 4. (Anat.) one of various crownlike parts of body. 5. (Bot.) appendage on top of seed or inner side of corolla. 6. (Electr.) glow around conductor at high potential. [L, = crown]

corō'na² n. long straight-sided cigar. [f. Sp. La Corona (P) the crown]

cŏ'ronach (-k, -x) n. funeral-song, dirge, in Scottish Highlands and Ireland. [f. Ir. coranach, Gael. corranach (comh- together; rànach outcry)]

corō'nagraph (-ahf) n. instrument for observing sun's corona, esp. other than during eclipse. [f. CORONA¹ + -GRAPH]

cŏ'ronal¹ n. circlet (esp. of gold or gems) for the head; wreath, garland. [ME, app. f. AF *coronal (corone CROWN¹; see -AL¹)]

coronal² (korō'-, kŏ'ro-) a. (Anat.) ∿ suture, transverse suture of skull separating frontal bone (∿ bone) from parietal bones; of the crown of the head; (Astron. & Bot.) of a corona. [F, or f. L coronalis (as CORONA¹; see -AL)]

cŏ'ronarў a. & n. 1. a. (Med.) resembling, encircling like, a crown; ∿ arteries, those that supply the tissues of the heart with blood; ∿ thrombosis (in coronary artery). 2. n. coronary artery or thrombosis. [f. L coronarius (corona crown; see -ARY¹)]

cŏronā'tion n. ceremony of crowning sovereign or sovereign's consort. [ME f. OF, f. med. L coronatio -onis (coronare to crown f. CORONA¹; see -ATION)]

cŏ'roner n. officer of county, district, or municipality, holding inquest on bodies of persons who may have died by violence or accident; official holding inquiry in cases of treasure trove; (Hist.) officer charged with maintaining rights of private property of Crown; hence ∿SHIP n. [ME, f. AF cor(o)uner (coro(u)ne CROWN¹; see -ER² (2))]

cŏ'ronet (-ĭt, -ĕt) n. small crown as worn, or used as heraldic device, by peer or peeress; band of precious materials, esp. as decorative part of woman's head-dress; garland or wreath for the head; lowest part of horse's pastern; ring of bone at base of deer's antler. [f. OF coronet(t)e dim. of corone CROWN¹]

cŏ'ronĕtĕd a. wearing a coronet (esp. as belonging to peerage). [f. prec. + -ED²]

coro′zō *n.* (*pl.* ∿s). S. Amer. palm-tree, of various species; ∿-**nut**, seed of one kind (*Phytelephas macrocarpa*) from which vegetable ivory is made. [Sp.]

Corp. *abbr.* Corporal; *Corporation.

cŏr′pora. See CORPUS.

cŏr′poral[1] *a.* of the human body; ∿ **oath**, (arch.) one ratified by touching a sacred object; ∿ **punishment** (esp. by flogging); hence ∿LY[2] *adv.* [ME f. OF, f. L *corporalis* (*corpus -oris* body; see -AL)]

cŏr′poral[2] *n.* cloth on which consecrated elements are placed during celebration of Eucharist. [OE f. OF, or f. med. L *corporale* (*pallium*) body cloth (as prec.)]

cŏr′poral[3] *n.* non-commissioned officer ranking just below sergeant (**the little C∿**, Napoleon I); ∥**ship's** ∿, officer attending to police matters under master-at-arms; *fallfish. [obs. F, var. of *caporal* f. It. *caporale* prob. f. L *corporalis* (as prec.), confused w. It. *capo* head]

cŏrporä′lĭtў *n.* material existence; body. [ME, f. LL *corporalitas* (as CORPORAL[1]; see -ITY)]

cŏr′porate *a.* **1.** forming a corporation (*corporate body*, *body corporate*); ∿ **town** (having municipal rights). **2.** forming one body of many individuals; of or belonging to a corporation or group (*corporate responsibility*); corporative. **3.** Hence **cŏr′poratism** *n.*, corporativism, ∿LY[2] (-tlĭ) *adv.* [f. L *corporare* form into a body (*corpus -oris*); see -ATE[2]]

cŏrporä′tion *n.* united body of persons, esp. one authorized to act as an individual; fictitious person created by charter, prescription, or act of the legislature, comprising many persons (∿ **aggregate**) or one (∿ **sole**); (**municipal**) ∿, civic authorities of borough, town, or city; (colloq.) prominent abdomen. [f. LL *corporatio* (as prec.; see -ATION)]

cŏr′porativ|e *a.* of a corporation; governed by or organized in corporations, esp. of employers and employed, whence ∿ISM (3) *n.* [f. CORPORATE + -IVE]

cŏrpŏr′ĕal *a.* bodily; material; (Law) consisting of material objects (*corporeal hereditament*); hence ∿ITY (-ă′l-) *n.*, ∿LY[2] *adv.* [f. LL *corporealis* f. L *corporeus* (*corpus -oris* body); see -AL]

cŏrporē′ĭtў *n.* quality of being or having a material body; bodily substance. [f. F *corporéité* or f. med. L *corporeitas* f. L *corporeus* (see prec., -ITY)]

cŏr′posant (-z-) *n.* luminous electrical discharge sometimes seen on ship or aircraft during storm. [f. OSp., Port., It. *corpo santo* holy body]

cŏrps (kōr) *n.* (*pl.* same *pr.* kōrz). **1.** = ARMY *corps.* **2.** body of troops for special (medical, ordnance, intelligence, etc.) service; body of persons engaged in same activity (DIPLOMATIC *corps,* *press corps*); students' society in German university. **3.** ∿ **de ballet** (kōr də bă′lā), the company of ensemble dancers in a ballet; ∿ **d'élite** (kōr dālē′t), select group; ∿ **diplomatique** (kōr dīplōmătē′k), = DIPLOMATIC *corps.* [F (as foll.)]

cŏrpse *n.* dead (usu. human) body; ∿-**candle**, (1) lambent flame seen in churchyard or over grave, regarded as omen of death, (2) lighted candle placed beside corpse before burial. [ME *corps,* var. sp. of *cors* (CORSE), f. OF *cors* f. L *corpus* body]

cŏr′pŭl|ent *a.* bulky (of body); fat; so ∿ENCE, ∿ENCY, *ns.* [ME, f. L *corpulentus* (*corpus* body; see -ULENT)]

cŏr′pus *n.* (*pl.* **cor′pora**). **1.** body or collection of writings etc. **2.** ∿ **delicti** (dĭlĭ′ktī), all that goes to make a breach of law, (pop.) tangible evidence of crime, esp. corpse; ∿ **vile** (vī′lĭ), thing worthless except as object of experiments. **3.** (Anat.) structure of special character in the animal body; ∿ **lu′teum** (lōō′tĭum), body developed in ovary after discharge of ovum, remaining in existence only if pregnancy has begun. **4.** C∿ **Chri′sti** (krī′stī), Feast of the Body of Christ (Thursday after Trinity Sunday). [ME f. L, = body]

cŏr′puscle (-sel) *n.* minute body esp. forming distinct part of organism, e.g. (in *pl.*) those constituting large parts of blood in vertebrates; so **cŏrpŭ′sculAR**[1] *a.* [f. L *corpusculum* (as prec.; see -CULE)]

corra′l (-ah′l) *n.*, & *v.t.* (-ll-). **1.** defensive enclosure of wagons in encampment; enclosure for capturing wild animals; *pen for horses, cattle, etc. **2.** *v.t.* form (wagons) into corral; confine in corral; *(colloq.) acquire. [Sp. & OPort., f. as KRAAL]

corrā′sion (-zhon) *n.* (Geol.) local wearing away of earth's surface by movement of air, water, ice, etc. [f. L COR(*radere ras-* scrape); see -ION]

corrĕ′ct[1] *v.t.* **1.** set right, amend; substitute right for (wrong); mark errors in (proof-sheet etc.) for amendment. **2.** set right, admonish, (person; **stand** ∿ed, accept correction from another person); (arch.) punish (person, fault). **3.** counteract (harmful quality); bring (reading of barometer etc.) into accordance with standard; eliminate aberration etc. from (lens etc.). [ME, f. L COR(*rigere rect-* = *regere* guide)]

corrĕ′ct[2] *a.* true, accurate; (of conduct, manners, etc.) right, proper; in accordance with a good standard (of taste etc.); hence ∿LY[2] *adv.*, ∿NESS *n.* [F, f. as prec.]

corrĕ′ction *n.* correcting (**I speak under** ∿, I may be wrong; thing substituted for what is wrong; (arch.) punishment (*house of correction*); hence ∿AL *a.* [ME f. OF, f. L *correctio -onis* (as prec.; see -ION)]

corrĕ′ctitūde *n.* correctness, esp. conscious correctness of conduct. [19th c., f. CORRECT[2] + RECTITUDE]

corrĕ′ctive *a.* & *n.* (thing) serving or tending to correct or counteract what is harmful; hence ∿LY[2] (-vlĭ) *adv.* [F *correctif -ive,* or f. LL *correctivus* (as CORRECT[1]; see -IVE)]

corrĕ′ctor *n.* one who corrects; censor, critic; ∥∿ of **the press,** proof-reader. [ME, f. AF *cor(r)ectour* f. L *corrector* (as CORRECT[1]; see -OR)]

cŏ′rrĕlāte[1] *n.* each of two related things (esp. so related that one implies the other). [f. as foll.; see -ATE[1]]

cŏ′rrĕlāte[2] *v.* **1.** *v.i.* have a mutual relation (*with, to*). **2.** *v.t.* bring (thing) into mutual relation (*with* another). [back-form. f. correlation, correlative; see -ATE[3]]

cŏrrĕlā′tion *n.* mutual relation between two or more things; interdependence of variable quantities; quantity measuring extent of this; act of correlating; hence ∿AL *a.* [f. med. L *correlatio;* see foll., -ATION]

corrĕ′lative *a.* & *n.* **1.** having a mutual relation (*with, to*); (Gram., of words) corresponding to each other and regularly used together, e.g. *either* and *or*; hence ∿LY[2] (-vlĭ) *adv.*, **corrĕlati′vity** *n.* correlative word or thing. [f. med. L COR(*relativus* RELATIVE)]

cŏrrespŏ′nd *v.i.* **1.** be in harmony (*with, to*); be similar or analogous (*to*); agree in amount, position, etc. (*to*); hence ∿INGLY *adv.* **2.** communicate by interchange of letters (*with*); ∿**ing member** of (learned society etc.), honorary non-resident member with no voice in the society's affairs. [f. F *correspondre* f. med. L COR(*respondere* RESPOND[1])]

cŏrrespŏ′ndence *n.* agreement, harmony, (*with, to; between* two); communication by letters; letters; ∿ **college, school,** (instructing by post, and conducting ∿ **courses**); ∿ **column,** part of newspaper etc. with letters from its readers; ∿ **theory,** (Philos.) theory that truth should be judged by accordance with external facts. [ME f. OF, f. med. L *correspondentia* (as prec.; see -ENCE)]

cŏrrespŏ′ndent *n.* & *a.* **1.** *n.* one who writes letters (*to* person or newspaper); person employed to contribute matter for publication etc. in newspaper (*our Moscow, chess, correspondent*) or broadcasting; person or firm having regular business relations with another esp. in another country. **2.** *a.* (arch.) corresponding (*to, with,* or abs.); hence ∿LY[2] *adv.* [ME, f. OF *correspondant* f. med. L *correspondens* (see -ENT)]

corri′da (-ē′-) *n.* bullfight(ing). [Sp. *corrida* (*de toros*) running (of bulls)]

cŏ′rridŏr *n.* main passage in large building, esp. one on to which many rooms open (∿**s of power**, (fig.) places where covert influence is exerted in government); outside passage connecting parts of building; (Polit.) strip of a State's territory that runs through that of another and secures access to the sea etc.; passage in railway carriage with door to each compartment (~ **train**, one made up of such carriages); route to which aircraft are restricted. [F, f. It. *corridore* corridor for *corridojo* running-place (*correre* run) by confus. w. *corridore* runner]

ŏ′rrie *n.* (esp. Sc.) circular hollow on mountainside, cirque. [f. Gael. *coire* cauldron]

:ŏrrige′nd|um *n.* (*pl.* ~a). thing to be corrected (esp. error in printed book). [L, neut. gerundive of *corrigere* (see CORRECT[1])]

:ŏ′rrigible *a.* capable of being corrected; (of person) submissive, or open, to correction. [ME f. F, f. med. L *corrigibilis* (as CORRECT[1]; see -IBLE)]

orrŏ′borant *a.* & *n.* (arch.) strengthening (medicine); corroborating (fact). [F, or f. as foll.; see -ANT]

orrŏ′bor|āte *v.t.* confirm formally (law etc.); confirm (person, statement) by evidence etc.; hence or cogn. ~ATIVE, ~atoRY, *adjs.*, ~A′TION, ~ātOR, *ns.* [f. L COR(roborare f. *robur -oris* strength) strengthen + -ATE[3]]

orrŏ′boree *n.* festive or warlike night-dance of Australian Aboriginals; noisy party. [Aboriginal dial.]

orrŏ′de *v.* 1. *n.t.* (Of rust, chemical agent, disease, or fig.) wear away, destroy gradually. 2. *v.i.* be worn away, decay. 3. So **corrō′sion** (-zhon) *n.* [ME, f. L COR(*rodere ros-* gnaw)]

orrŏ′sive *a.* & *n.* (substance) tending to corrode (lit. or fig.); ~ **sublimate**, mercuric chloride, a strong acrid poison, used as fungicide etc.; hence ~LY[2] (-vlĭ) *adv.*, ~NESS (-vn-) *n.* [ME, f. OF *corosif -ive* (as prec.; see -IVE)]

ŏ′rrugate (-ŏŏ-) *v.t.* & *i.* contract into wrinkles or folds; mark with or bend into ridges, esp. to produce stronger material (*corrugated iron, paper*); so **cŏrrugA′TION** (-ŏŏ-) *n.* [f. L COR(*rugare* f. *ruga* wrinkle) + -ATE[3]]

ŏ′rrugātor (-ŏŏ-) *n.* (Anat.) one of two muscles that contract the brow in frowning. [mod. L (as prec.; see -OR)]

orru′pt[1] *a.* rotten; depraved; wicked; influenced by bribery (~ **practices**, forms of bribery esp. at elections; (of language, text, etc.) vitiated by errors or alterations; hence ~LY[2] *adv.*, ~NESS *n.* [ME f. OF, or f. L *corruptus* p.p. of COR(*rumpere rupt-* break)]

orru′pt[2] *v.* 1. *v.t.* infect, taint, (lit. or fig.); deprave; bribe; destroy purity of (language), vitiate (text). 2. *v.i.* become corrupt. 3. So ~IBLE, ~IVE, *adjs.* [ME, f. prec., replacing obs. *corrump*]

orru′ption *n.* decomposition; moral deterioration; use of corrupt practices (bribery etc.); perversion (of language, text, etc.) from its original state; deformation (of word); ~ **of blood**, (Hist.) effect of attainder upon person attainted, depriving him and his heirs of all rank and titles. [ME f. OF, or f. L *corruptio* (as CORRUPT[1]; see -ION)]

ŏr′săc, -ăk, *n.* (Zool.) small fox of Central Asia. [Turki]

ŏrsa′ge (-ah′zh) *n.* bodice of woman's dress; *small bouquet (to be) worn on bodice. [ME f. OF (*cors* body; see CORPSE, -AGE)]

ŏr′sair *n.* (Hist.) privateer, privateering vessel, esp. of Barbary; pirate. [f. F *corsaire* f. med. L *cursarius cursus* inroad, f. *currere* run; see -ARY[1])]

ŏrse. Var. (arch. or poet.) of CORPSE.

ŏr′selet (-sl-). Var. of CORSELETTE, CORSLET.

ŏr′selètte (-sel-, -sl-) *n.* woman's foundation garment combining corset and brassière. [f. CORSLET]

ŏr′sèt *n.*, & *v.t.* 1. *n.* woman's closely-fitting supporting undergarment; man's or woman's similar garment worn because of injury, weakness, or deformity; hence ~ED[2] *a.*, ~RY (1, 2) *n.* 2. *v.t.* provide with corset; (fig.) control closely. [ME f. OF, dim. of *cors* body; see CORPSE, -ET[1]]

cŏr′sètière (-tyār) *n.* woman who makes or fits corsets. [F, fem. of *corsetier* (as prec., -IER)]

Cŏr′sican *a.* & *n.* (native, inhabitant, or Italian dialect) of Corsica; **the** ~ (**ogre** etc.), Napoleon I. [f. *Corsica*, island in the Mediterranean + -AN]

cŏr′slèt *n.* garment (usu. tight-fitting) covering body as distinct from limbs; (Hist.) piece of armour covering body; (Zool.) hard part of fish's or insect's thorax. [f. OF *corselet*, dim. f. as CORSET; see -LET]

cŏrtège (-tā′zh) *n.* train of attendants; (esp. funeral) procession. [F]

Cŏr′tĕs (-s, -z) *n.* legislative assembly of Spain or (Hist.) Portugal. [Sp. & Port., pl. of *corte* COURT[1]]

cŏr′tĕx *n.* (*pl.* cor′tices *pr.* -tĭsēz). bark; outer grey matter of brain; outer part of kidney, adrenal gland, or hair; so **cŏr′ticAL** *a.* [L *cortex, -icis* bark]

Cŏr′tĭ *n.* organ of ~, structure in mammalian ear responsible for perception of sound. [f. A. ~, It. anatomist d. 1876]

cŏr′tĭcāte, -ātĕd, *adjs.* having bark or rind; barklike. [f. L *corticatus* (as CORTEX; see -ATE[2])]

cŏrticōtrŏ′p(h)ic, cŏrticōtrŏ′p(h)in. Vars. of ADRENOCORTICOTROP(H)IC, -IN.

cŏr′tisōne (-z-) *n.* steroid hormone produced by the adrenal cortex or synthetically used medicinally against inflammation and allergy. [f. Chem. name 17-hydroxy-11-dehydro*corticosterone*]

coru′ndum *n.* crystallized alumina of various colours, with great hardness, used as abrasive and as gems. [f. Tamil *kurundam* f. Skr. *kuruvinda* ruby]

cŏ′ruscāte *v.i.* sparkle, flash, (lit., or fig. of wit etc.); so ~A′TION *n.* [f. L *coruscare* glitter + -ATE[3]]

cŏrvée (-vā′) *n.* day's work of unpaid labour due by vassal; labour done in lieu of taxes; onerous task. [ME f. OF, f. Rom. *corrogata* (*opera*) requisitioned (work), f. COR(*rogare* ask)]

‖**corves.** See CORF.

cŏrvĕ′tte *n.* (Naut.) 1. (Hist.) flush-decked warship with one tier of guns. 2. small fast naval escort-vessel. [F, f. MDu. *korf* kind of ship, + dim. -ETTE]

cŏrvī′na (-ē′-) *n.* Amer. or Afr. weakfish. [Sp. & Port., f. L *corvīnus*; perh. f. its black fins]

cŏr′vine *a.* of or akin to the raven or crow. [f. L *corvinus* (*corvus* raven; see -INE[1])]

cŏrybă′ntic *a.* wild, frenzied. [f. *Corybantes* priests of Cybele performing wild dances (L f. Gk *Korubantes*) + -IC]

cŏ′rymb *n.* (Bot.) type of inflorescence, raceme in which lower flower-stalks are proportionally longer, forming flattish top; hence ~OSE[1] *a.* [f. F *corymbe* or f. L f. Gk *korumbos* cluster]

cŏryphae′|us *n.* (*pl.* ~i *pr.* -ē′ī) leader of a chorus (lit. or fig.) [L, f. Gk *koruphaios* (*koruphē* head)]

cŏ′ryphée (-fā) *n.* a leading dancer in a *corps de ballet*. [F, as prec.]

cory′za *n.* nasal catarrh; disease with this as symptom, esp. COLD[2]. [L, f. Gk *koruza* running at nose]

cŏs[1] *n.* kind of long-leaved lettuce. [f. *Cos*, island in the Aegean, where it originated]

cŏs[2], ′cŏs, (-z) *adv.* & *conj.* (colloq.) because. [abbr.]

cŏs[3] (-s, -z) *abbr.* cosine.

*****Cŏsa Nŏ′stra** (-za) *n.* Amer. branch of Mafia. [It., = our thing]

cŏ′sĕc *abbr.* = foll.

cŏsē′cant *n.* (Math.) secant of complement of given angle. [f. mod. L *cosecans* and F *cosécant* (as CO- 2, SECANT)]

cŏsei′smal (-sī′z-) *a.* & *n.* (line or curve connecting points) of simultaneous shock from earthquake centre. [f. CO- 1 + SEISMAL]

cŏ′sĕt *n.* (Math.) set that when added to another forms a given larger set. [f. CO- 2 + SET[3]]

‖**cŏsh[1]** *n.*, & *v.t.* (colloq.) 1. *n.* heavy stick or bludgeon. ~**boy**, youth or man armed with cosh. 2. *v.t.* strike with cosh. [19th c.; orig. unkn.]

cŏsh[2] (kŏsh, kŏsä′ch) *abbr.* hyperbolic cosine.

cŏ′sher *v.t.* pamper. [19th c.; orig. unkn.]

cŏ-sĭ′gnatŏrў, *cōsĭ′-, *a.* & *n.* (person or State) signing jointly with others. [f. CO- 1 +SIGNATORY]

cŏ′sĭne *n.* (Math.) sine of complement of given angle or quantity. [f. mod. L *cosinus* (as CO- 2, SINE)]

cŏ′smĕa (-z-) *n.* = COSMOS². [mod. L, f. as COSMOS²; see -A 1]

cŏsmĕt′|ĭc (-z-) *a.* & *n.* **1.** *a.* intended to beautify hair, skin, or complexion etc.; (of surgery or prosthetic device) imitating or restoring normal appearance; (fig.) intended to improve appearances; hence ∼ICALLY *adv.*, *∼I′CIAN, ∼ŏ′LOGY, *ns.* **2.** *n.* cosmetic substance. [f. F *cosmétique* f. Gk *kosmētikos* (*kosmeō* adorn f. *kosmos* order, adornment; see -ETIC)]

cŏ′smic (-z-) *a.* **1.** of the universe or cosmos (esp. as distinguished from the earth); ∼ **dust,** minute particles of matter in or from outer space; ∼ **radiation,** ∼ **rays,** radiations from outer space etc. that reach earth from all directions, with high energy and penetrative power. **2.** pertaining to space travel (*cosmic rocket* etc.). **3.** Hence ∼AL *a.*, ∼ALLY *adv.* [f. COSMOS¹ + -IC]

cŏsmŏ′gon|ў (-z-) *n.* (theory of) the origin of the universe; hence **cŏsmogŏ′n**IC(AL) (-z-), *adjs.*, ∼IST (3) *n.* [f. Gk *kosmogonia* (*kosmos* world, -*gonia* -begetting)]

cŏsmŏ′graphў (-z-) *n.* description or mapping of general features of universe or earth; hence or cogn. **cŏsmŏ′**GRAPHER *n.*, **cŏsmo**GRA′PHIC(AL) *adjs.*, (-z-). [ME, f. F *cosmographie* or f. LL f. Gk *kosmographia* (as COSMOS¹; see -GRAPHY)]

cŏsmŏ′log|ў (-z-) *n.* science or theory of the universe; hence **cŏsmŏlŏ′g**ICAL (-z-) *a.*, ∼IST (3) *n.* [f. F *cosmologie* or mod. L *cosmologia* (as COSMOS¹; see -LOGY)]

cŏ′smonaut (-z-) *n.* (Esp. Russian) astronaut. [f. COSMOS¹, after *astronaut*]

cŏsmŏ′polis (-z-) *n.* cosmopolitan city. [f. Gk *kosmos* world + *polis* city]

cŏsmopŏ′lĭtan (-z-) *a.* & *n.* (person) belonging, (member) of group of persons belonging, to many or all parts of the world; (person) free from national limitations; hence ∼ISM (3) *n.*, ∼IZE (2, 3) *v.t.* & *i.* [f. foll. + -AN]

cŏsmŏ′polite (-z-) *n.* & *a.* **1.** *n.* citizen of the world. **2.** *a.* free from national attachments or prejudices. [F, f. Gk *kosmopolitēs* (*kosmos* world, *politēs* citizen)]

cŏ′smŏs¹ (-z-) *n.* the universe as an ordered whole; ordered system of ideas, etc., sum-total of experience. [f. Gk *kosmos*]

cŏ′smŏs² (-z-) *n.* plant of genus *Cosmos*, bearing single dahlia-like blossoms of various colours. [mod. L, f. Gk *kosmos* ornament]

COSPAR *abbr.* Committee on Space Research.

Cŏ′ssăck *n.* member of a people of S. Russia, esp. (Hist.) as light horseman in Russian army; ∼ **hat,** brimless hat widening towards top. [f. F *cosaque* f. Russ. *kazak* f. Turki *quzzāq* mod. adventurer]

cŏ′ssĕt *v.t.* pamper. [f. earlier *n.* = pet lamb, f. AF *coscet*, *cozet* f. OE *cotsǣta* cottager (as COT¹, SIT)]

cost¹ (-z-, -kaw-) *n.* **1.** price (to be) paid for thing (*cost of* LIVING¹; **prime** ∼, ∼ **price,** that at which merchant etc. buys); (in *pl.*) law expenses, esp. those allowed in favour of winning party or against losing party; expenditure of time, labour, etc. **2. at** ∼, at the initial cost, at cost price; **at all** ∼**s, at any** ∼, no matter what it may cost [prob. orig. f. obs. cost manner]; **at the** ∼ **of,** at the expense of losing; **count the** ∼, consider the risks before action; **to person's** ∼, with loss or disadvantage to him (**know to one's** ∼, have learnt by bitter experience). **3.** ∼ **accountant, clerk,** one who records costs and (esp. overhead) expenses in a business concern; ∼**-benefit** *analysis* etc., assessing relation of cost of an operation to value of resulting benefits; ∼**-effective** *a.*, effective in relation to its cost; ∼**-plus** *a.*, calculated as basic cost plus profit factor; ∼ **push,** factors other than demand that cause inflation. [ME f. AF, OF *coust* (*couster*; see foll.)]

cost² (kŏ-, kaw-) *v.* (**cost**). **1.** *v.t.* (w. ind. obj.) be acquirable at, involve expenditure of, (*cost him five pounds,* the EARTH¹; *cost the writer infinite labour*); result in the loss of (*cost him his life*); ∼ person **dear**(**ly**) involve a heavy penalty on him. **2.** (∼′ed). fix or estimate price of; ∼**′ing clerk,** = COST¹ *clerk*. **3.** *v.i.* & *t.* be costly (to). [ME, f. OF *coster*, *couster* f. Rom **costare* f. L CON(*stare* stand) stand firm, stand at a price]

cŏ′stal *a.* of the ribs. [F, f. mod. L *costalis* f. L *costa* rib; see -AL]

cŏ′-stăr *n.* & *v.* (**-rr-**). **1.** *n.* cinema or stage star appearing with other star(s) of equal importance. **2.** *v.i.* perform as co-star. **3.** *v.t.* include as co-star. [f. CO 1 + STAR¹ 3]

||**cŏ′stard** *n.* large ribbed kind of apple; (arch., joc.) head. [ME f. AF (*coste* rib f. L *costa*; see -ARD)]

cŏ′stāte *a.* ribbed, having ribs or ridges. [f. L *costatu* (*costa* rib; see -ATE²)]

||**cŏ′ster(monger)** (-ŭngg-) *n.* man who sells fruit, vegetables, etc., from barrow in street. [f. COSTARD + MONGER]

cŏ′stive *a.* constipated; (fig.) niggardly; hence ∼LY *adv.*, ∼NESS (-vn-) *n.* [ME f. AF *costif, OF *costive* f. L *constipatus* CONSTIPATED]

cŏ′stl|ў (kŏ′-, kaw′-) *a.* of great value; expensive; hence ∼INESS *n.* [f. COST¹ + -LY¹]

cŏ′stmārў *n.* aromatic perennial composite plant (*Chrysanthemum balsamita*), formerly used in medicine and for flavouring ale. [OE *cost* f. L f. Gk *kostos* Arab. *ḳust*, + (*St.*) *Mary* (with whom it was associated in medieval times)]

cŏ′stūme *n.*, & *v.t.* **1.** *n.* style or fashion of dress or attire, esp. of a particular nation, class, or period, e.g. as worn by actors; complete set of outer garments, garment(s) for a particular activity (*bathing-costume*); woman's matching jacket and skirt; ∼ **jewellery,** artificial jewellery worn to decorate clothes; ∼ **piece, play,** (in which actors wear historical costume). **2.** *v.t.* provide with costume. [F f. It., f. L *consuetudo* CUSTOM]

cŏstū′mier, **cŏ′stūmer,** *n.* maker of or dealer in costumes. [F *costumier* (as prec.; see -IER)]

cŏ′s|ў, cŏ′z|ў, *cŏ′z′|ў, *a.*, *n.*, & *v.* **1.** *a.* (of person or place) comfortable, snug; warm and friendly; (derog.) complacent; hence ∼ĭLY² *adv.*, ∼ĭNESS *n.* **2.** *n.* canopied corner seat for two [cf. F *causeuse*]; cover to retain heat in boiled egg (**egg-**∼**y**), teapot (**tea-**∼**y** etc. **3.** *v.t.* (colloq.) ∼**y** (**along**), reassure, delude. **4.** *v.i.* *(colloq.) ∼**y up** to, snuggle up to, ingratiate oneself with. [18th c., orig. Sc.; etym. unkn.]

cŏt¹ *n.*, & *v.t.* (**-tt-**). **1.** *n.* small erection for shelter, = COTE (*bell-cot, sheep-cot*); (poet.) cottage. **2.** *v.t.* (sheep) into cot. [OE, = MDu., MLG, ON *kot,* f. Gmc]

cŏt² *n.* ||small tall-sided bed esp. for child; (Ind.) light bedstead; (Naut. Hist.) swinging bed; *camp-bed, hospital bed; ∼**-case,** person too ill to leave bed; ∼**-death,** unexplained death of sleeping baby. [Anglo-Ind., f. Hindi *khāṭ* bedstead, hammock]

cŏt³ *abbr.* cotangent.

cŏt′ngent (-nj-) *n.* (Math.) tangent of complement of given angle. [f. CO- 2 + TANGENT]

cōte *n.* shed, stall, shelter, esp. for birds and animals (DOVE¹*cote, sheep-cote*). [OE, = LG *kote,* f. Gmc *kutō cogn. w. COT¹]

cōtĕ′mporarў etc. Var. of CONTEMPORARY.

cō′terie *n.* circle or set of persons exclusively sharing interests; select circle in society. [F, orig. = association of tenants, f. *cote hut f. MLG *kote* COTE; see -ERY]

cŏtē′rminous *a.* having same boundaries or extent (in space, time, or meaning). [f. CO- 1 + TERMINUS; -OUS]

cŏth *abbr.* hyperbolic cotangent.

cŏthŭ′r|nus *n.* (*pl.* **-n|i** *pr.* **-ī**). buskin, thick-soled boot of Athenian tragic actor. [L f. Gk *kothornos*]

cō-tī′dal *a.* ∼ **line** (on map, connecting places at which high water occurs at same time). [f. CO 1 + TIDAL]

coti'llion (-lyǒn) *n.* one of various French dances with elaborate steps, figures, and ceremonial; *quadrille; *formal ball. [f. F *cotillon* petticoat, dim. of *cotte* f. OF *cote* COAT]

cotōnea'ster *n.* small shrub or tree of genus *Cotoneaster*, resembling hawthorn and bearing red or orange berries. [mod. L, f. L *cotoneum* QUINCE + -ASTER]

Co'tswōld *n.* ~ (sheep), sheep of a long-woolled breed originating in the *Cotswold* Hills, Gloucestershire.

cŏ'tta *n.* short surplice. [It., f. as COAT]

cŏ'ttage *n.* **1.** labourer's or villager's small dwelling; small country or suburban house. **2.** ~ **cheese** (soft white kind, made from curds without pressing); ~ **hospital** (without resident medical staff); ~ **industry** (partly or wholly carried on at home); ~ **loaf** (of two round masses, smaller on top of larger); ~ **piano** (small upright); ~ **pie**, shepherd's pie. **3.** Hence ~Y² (-tĭjĭ) *a.* [ME, f. AF *cotage*, f. as COT¹, COTE; see -AGE]

cŏ'ttager (-tĭ-) *n.* inhabitant of a cottage. [f. prec. + -ER¹]

cŏ'ttar, cŏ'tter¹, *n.* (Hist. & Sc.) peasant occupying cottage and labouring as required; (Ir. Hist.) = COTTIER. [f. COT¹ + -ER¹ (Sc. *-ar*)]

cŏ'tter² *n.* key, wedge, bolt, for securing parts of machinery etc.; (esp.) split pin that opens after passing through hole; ~**-pin**, (1) cotter, (2) pin to keep cotter in place. [17th c., rel. to earlier *cotterel*; orig. unkn.]

cŏ'ttier *n.* cottager; (Hist.) Irish peasant under ~ **tenure** (letting of land in small portions at rent fixed by competition). [ME, f. OF *cotier* (med. L *cotarius*), f. *cote*; see COTERIE, -IER]

cŏ'tton¹ *n.* **1.** white downy fibrous substance clothing seeds of ~**-plant** (*Gossypium*), used for making cloth, thread, etc.; cotton-plant(s); thread spun from cotton yarn, used for sewing etc.; cloth made of cotton; GUN-*cotton*. **2.** ~**-cake**, compressed cotton seed as food for cattle; *~ **candy**, candy-floss; *cotton*--GIN¹; ~**-grass**, sedge of genus *Eriophorum* with long white silky hairs; *~**-picking** *a.*, (sl.) unpleasant, wretched; ~**-spinner**, worker who spins cotton, owner of cotton-mill; ~**tail**, common Amer. rabbit of genus *Sylvilagus*, with white fluffy tail; ~ **waste**, refuse yarn used to clean machinery etc.; ~**wood**, Amer. poplar with cottony seed-hairs, Austral. downy-leaved tree; ~ **wool**, raw cotton as prepared for wadding, *raw cotton. **3.** Hence ~Y² *a.* [ME, f. OF *coton* f. Arab. *kutn*]

cŏ'tton² *v.i.* become attracted *to*; ~ **on to**, form liking for (person, thing); ~ **on** (to), (sl.) understand; ~ **up to**, (arch.) make friendly advances to. [f. prec.]

cotylē'don *n.* primary leaf in embryo of higher plants, seed-leaf; plant of genus *Cotyledon*, e.g. pennywort; hence ~ARY, ~OUS, *adjs.* [L, = pennywort, f. Gk *kotuledōn* cup-shaped cavity (*kotule* cup)]

ou'cal (kōō'-) *n.* tropical bird of genus *Centropus*, allied to cuckoo and resembling pheasant. [F, perh. f. *coucou* cuckoo + *alouette* lark]

ouch¹ *n.* **1.** long bedlike seat with half-back and head-end only; piece of furniture on which doctor's or psychiatrist's patient reclines during examination. **2.** (arch. or literary). bed; thing one sleeps on. [ME f. OF *couche* (*coucher*; see foll.)]

ouch² *v.* **1.** *v.t.* lay (as) on couch; lower (spear etc.) to position of attack; treat (cataract, cataract-patient's eye) by displacement of lens; express (thought etc. *in* words). **2.** *v.i.* (of animal) lie (esp. in lair); lie in ambush. [ME, f. OF *coucher* f. L COL(*locare* place)]

ouch³ (kōō, kow-) *n.* ~(**grass**), grass with long creeping roots, esp. *Agropyron repens*. [var. of QUITCH]

ou'chant *a.* (Her., of animal) lying with body resting on legs and head raised. [F, pres. part. as COUCH²; see -ANT]

ouche'tte (kōōsh-) *n.* (berth in) railway carriage with seats convertible into sleeping-berths. [F, = little bed, dim. of *couche* COUCH¹]

coudé (kōōdā') *a.* & *n.* (of or pertaining to) a telescope in which rays are bent to a focus off the axis. [F, p.p. of *couder* bend at right angles (*coude* elbow f. as CUBIT)]

Couë'ism (kōō'āi-) *n.* system of usu. optimistic auto--suggestion as psychotherapy. [f. E. *Coué*, Fr. psychologist d. 1926 + -ISM]

*****cou'gar** (kōō'-) *n.* puma. [F, repr. Guarani *guaçu ara*]

cough¹ (kǒf, kawf) *v.* **1.** *v.i.* expel air from lungs with violent effort and noise produced by abrupt opening of glottis, to remove obstruction or congestion; (of engine, gun, etc.) make similar noise; (sl.) confess. **2.** *v.t.* ~ **out, up**, eject by, or say with, cough; ~ **up**, (sl.) bring out or produce reluctantly (esp. money), disclose. [ME *coghe, cowhe*, rel. to MDu. *kuchen*, MHG *küchen*, of imit. orig.]

cough² (kǒf, kawf) *n.* act of coughing; tendency to cough; condition of respiratory organs causing coughing; ~**-drop**, medicated lozenge (also ~--sweet, *~ candy) to relieve cough, (fig., sl.) awkward or disagreeable person or thing; ~ **mixture**, medicine to relieve cough. [f. prec.]

could, couldn't, etc. See CAN²

coulée (kōōlā, kōō'lĭ) *n.* **1.** (Geol.) lava-flow. **2.** *deep ravine. [F, fem. p.p. of *couler* flow, f. L *colare* strain, filter]

couli'sse (kōōlē's) *n.* (usu. in *pl.*) wings in theatre; space between two of these; body of unofficial dealers on bourse; corridor; place of informal discussion or negotiation. [F, f. *coulis* sliding (see PORTCULLIS)]

cou'loir (kōō'lwär) *n.* steep gully on mountainside. [F (*couler* glide; see COULÉE, -ORY)]

cou'lomb (kōō'lŏm) *n.* unit of electric charge, quantity of electricity conveyed in one second by current of one ampere. [f. C. A. de *Coulomb*, Fr. physicist d. 1806]

coulo'mĕtry (kōō'-) *n.* (chemical analysis by) measurement of number of coulombs used in electrolysis; hence **coulomĕ'tric** (kōō-) *a.* [f. prec. + -METRY]

cou'lter (kōl') *cō'l-, n.* vertical iron cutting blade fixed in front of ploughshare. [OE f. L *culter*]

cou'marin (kōō'-) *n.* aromatic crystalline substance found in seeds of tonka bean etc. [F *coumarine* f. Tupi *cumarú* tonka bean; see -IN]

cou'marone (kōō'-) *n.* colourless organic liquid obtainable from coal tar or by synthesis; ~ **resin**, thermoplastic resin formed by polymerization of coumarone. [f. prec. + -ONE]

cou'ncil *n.* **1.** ecclesiastical assembly (*ecumenical, diocesan, council*); (NT) Sanhedrin. **2.** advisory or deliberative assembly; body of persons chosen as advisers (Privy Council; Queen etc. in **C~**, Privy Council as issuing *Orders in Council* (ORDER¹ 15) or receiving petitions etc.; ~ **of war**, generals and officers called in special emergency, also fig.). **3.** local administrative body of parish, district, town, city or administrative county. **4.** ~**-chamber**, room in which council meets; ~ **estate, flat, house,** etc., dwelling-place(s) owned and let by local council; ~--house, building in which council meets; ~**man**, member of council in City of London & in US); ~ **school** (supported by town or county council). [ME, f. AF *cuncile* f. L *concilium* convocation, assembly, (as CON-, *calare* summon); cf. COUNSEL¹]

cou'ncillor *n.* member of a (town etc.) council; hence ~SHIP *n.* [ME, alt. of COUNSELLOR, assim. to prec.]

cou'nsel¹ *n.* **1.** consultation (**take ~**, consult (*with*, or abs.)); plan of action; advice (~ **of despair**, action taken when all else fails; ~ **of perfection**, advice guiding towards moral perfection, (fig.) advice that is ideal but impracticable; **keep** one's **own ~**, not confide in others). **2.** (body of) legal adviser(s) in cause. **3.** (*pl.* same); barrister; ||**Queen's, King's, C~**, counsel to the crown, taking precedence of other barristers. [ME, f. OF *c(o)unseil*, f. L *consilium* consultation, advice, rel. to *consulere* (cf. CONSUL, *consultare* consult; cf. COUNCIL]

cou′nsel[2] *v.t.* (||-ll-). advise (person *to* do); give advice to (person) professionally on social problems etc.; recommend (thing, *that*). [ME, f. OF *conseiller* f. L *consiliari* (*consilium*; see prec.)]

cou′nsellor, *-elor, *n.* adviser, *esp. of students; senior officer in diplomatic service; ∿(-at-law), *barrister, (Ir.) advising barrister; ||C∿ of State, temporary regent during sovereign's absence. [ME, f. OF *conseiller* (f. L *consiliarius*), *conseillour, -eur* (f. L *consiliator*); see COUNSEL[1], -OR]

count[1] *n.* counting; one's reckoning (**keep, lose, ∿**, be aware, fail to know, how many there have been); sum total of things (BLOOD[1] *count*, POLLEN *count*); (Law) each charge in an indictment; one of several points under discussion; (Boxing) counting of up to ten seconds by referee when boxer is knocked down (**out for the ∿**, defeated by being unable to rise within ten seconds, also fig.; **take the ∿**, be defeated); measure of fineness of yarn as number of threads per unit length; (Phys.) record of ionization event. [ME, f. OF *co(u)nte* f. LL *computus* (*computare*; see foll.)]

count[2] *v.* **1.** *v.t.* find number of, esp. by assigning successive numerals; *count* one's CHICKENs, the COST[1]; **∿ out**, count while taking from a stock, complete count of ten seconds over (fallen boxer), (in children's games) select (player) for special role or dismissal by counting with words of rhyme etc., (colloq.) exclude from reckoning or plan, ||procure adjournment of (House of Commons) when fewer than 40 members are present; **∿ up**, find sum of; hence ∿′ABLE *a*. **2. ∿ (in)**, include in reckoning or plan; **not ∿ing**, excluding from reckoning. **3.** *v.t. & i.* consider (thing or person) to be (lucky etc.); **∿ on** or **upon**, depend or rely on, expect confidently. **4.** *v.i.* repeat numerals in order; conduct reckoning (∿′ing-house, place where accounts are kept); so ∿′**down** *n*. **5.** be included in reckoning (*that does not count*, *counts double*); **∿ against**, be reckoned to disadvantage of; **∿ for**, be worth (much etc.). [ME, f. OF *co(u)nter* f. L *computare* COMPUTE]

count[3] *n.* foreign noble corresp. to earl; *Count* PALATINE[1]; hence ∿′**SHIP** *n*. [f. OF *conte* f. L *comes comitis* companion]

cou′ntĕnance[1] *n.* **1.** (expression of) face; **change ∿** (from emotion). **2.** composure; **keep** (person) **in ∿** (usu. by show of support); **keep** one's **∿**, maintain composure, esp. refrain from laughing; **lose ∿**, become embarrassed; **out of ∿**, disconcerted. **3.** moral support. [ME, f. AF *c(o)untenance*, OF *contenance* bearing (*contenir*; see CONTAIN, -ANCE)]

cou′ntĕnance[2] *v.t.* give approval to (act); encourage (person, practice, person *in* practice). [f. prec.]

cou′nter[1] *n.* **1.** small disc of metal, ivory, etc., used for keeping account in games, esp. cards; token representing coin; thing used in bargaining. **2.** banker's or money-changer's table; table in shop on which money is counted out and across which goods are delivered (∿-jumper, (derog.) shopman; **over the ∿**, by ordinary purchase in shop; **under the ∿**, surreptitiously, esp. illegally); similar structure for service of goods in library, cafeteria, etc. **3.** apparatus for counting manufactured products, ionization events, etc. [f. AF *count(e)our*, OF *conteo(i)r*, f. med. L *computatorium* (as COMPUTE; see -ORY(2))]

cou′nter[2] *n.* part of horse's breast between shoulders and under neck; curved part of stern of ship; part of printing-type etc. enclosed by outline (e.g. loop of P). [17th c.; orig. unkn.]

cou′nter[3] *n.* back part of shoe or boot round heel. [abbr. of *counterfort* buttress]

cou′nter[4] *a. & n.* opposed; opposite; duplicate; ∿-(-rocking-turn or -rocker), skating figure (see ROCK[3]). [arising f. wds formed w. COUNTER-]

cou′nter[5] *v.* **1.** *v.t.* oppose, contradict; meet by countermove. **2.** *v.i.* make countermove; (Boxing)

give return blow while parrying. [ME, f. COUNTER- and COUNTER[7]]

cou′nter[6] *adv.* in the opposite direction (**go, hunt, run, ∿**, i.e. to direction taken by quarry); contrary; **act, go, ∿, to**, disobey (instructions etc.); **run ∿ to**, act contrary to. [ME, f. OF *countre* f. L *contra* against]

cou′nter[7] *n.* parry; countermove. [f. F *contre* (as prec.)]

counter- *pref. w.* senses (1) reciprocation, opposition, (*counter-threat*), frustration, rivalry (*counter-cheers*), (2) opposite direction (*counter-current*), (3) correspondence, match, (of things having naturally two opposite parts), (4) duplicate, substitute. [f. or after AF *countre-*, OF *contre* f. L *contra* against]

counterȧ′ct *v.t.* hinder, defeat, by contrary action; neutralize; hence ∿ION *n.*, ∿IVE *a*. [f. COUNTER- (1) + ACT[2]]

cou′nter-attȧ′ck *n., & v.t. & i.* attack (lit. or fig.) in reply to attack by enemy or opponent. [f. COUNTER- (1) + ATTACK[1,2]]

cou′nter-attrȧ′ction *n.* attraction of contrary tendency; rival attraction. [f. COUNTER- (1) + ATTRACTION]

cou′nterbȧlance *n., & v.t.* **1.** *n.* weight (lit. or fig.) balancing another. **2.** *v.t.* act as counterbalance to. [f. COUNTER- (1, 3) + BALANCE[1,2]]

cou′nterblast (-ah-) *n.* energetic declaration or action in opposition (*to* something). [f. COUNTER- (1) + BLAST[1]]

cou′nterchange (-nj) *v.* **1.** *v.t.* interchange; chequer, esp. with systematic contrast. **2.** *v.i.* change places or parts. [f. F *contrechanger* (as COUNTER- (1), CHANGE[2])]

cou′ntercharge *n., & v.t.* charge in opposition to another or against accuser. [f. COUNTER- (1) + CHARGE[1,2]]

cou′nterchĕck *n.* restraint that opposes a thing; restraint that operates against another; (arch.) retort (*countercheck* quarrelsome, f. Shak. *As You Like It* v. iv 85). [f. COUNTER- (1) + CHECK[1]]

cou′nter-claim *n., & v.t.* claim against another claim; claim as defendant in suit. [f. COUNTER- (1) + CLAIM[1,2]]

counter-clŏ′ckwīse (-z). See CLOCK[1].

cou′nter-cŭlture *n.* mode of life deliberately departing from established social practices. [f. COUNTER- (1) + CULTURE]

counter-ĕ′spionage (-īj, -ahzh) *n.* action against an enemy's spy system. [f. COUNTER- (1) + ESPIONAGE]

cou′nterfeit[1] (-fīt, -fēt) *a. & n.* (coin, writing, etc.) made in imitation, not genuine; pretended (disman etc.). [ME, f. OF *countrefet, -fait*, p.p.s of *contrefaire* f Rom. *CONTRA(facere* make)]

cou′nterfeit[2] (-fīt, -fēt) *v.t.* imitate fraudulently; forge, (coin, banknote, handwriting); make imitation of; simulate (feelings); (fig.) resemble closely; hence ∿ER[1] *n.* [ME, f. AF *countrefeter* (*countrefet*, f. as prec.)]

cou′nterfoil *n.* complementary part of bank cheque, official receipt, etc., with note of particulars, retained by person issuing such document. [f. COUNTER- (3) + FOIL[1]]

cou′nter-intĕ′lligence *n.* counter-espionage. [f. COUNTER- (1) + INTELLIGENCE 4]

counter-i′rrit|ant *n.* thing used to produce surface irritation and thus counteract symptoms of disease (also fig.); so ∿A′TION *n.* [f. COUNTER- (1) + IRRITANT]

counterma′nd (-ah-) *v.t., & n.* **1.** *v.t.* revoke (command); recall (person, forces, etc.) by contrary order; cancel order for (thing). **2.** *n.* contra revoking previous one. [ME, f. OF *contremander* f. med. L CONTRA(*mandare* order)]

cou′ntermărch *v.i. & t., & n.* **1.** *n.* (cause to) march in contrary direction. [f. COUNTER- (2) + MARCH[4,5]]

cou′ntermeasure (-ĕzher) *n.* action taken to counteract danger, threat, etc. [f. COUNTER- (1) + MEASURE[1]]

cou′ntermīne *n. & v.* **1.** *n.* mine made to intercept that of besiegers; submarine mine sunk to explode

For other words in *co-* see CO-.

enemy's mines by its own explosion; (fig.) counterplot. **2.** *v.t.* & *i.* make countermine (against). [f. COUNTER- (1) + MINE¹]

cou'ntermove (-ōōv) *n.* move or action in opposition to another. [f. COUNTER- (1) + MOVE¹]

cou'nter-offe'nsive *n.* (Mil. etc.) offensive action designed to allow escape from defensive situation. [f. COUNTER- (1) + OFFENSIVE]

cou'nterpane *n.* bedspread. [alt. (w. assim. to *pane* in obs. sense 'cloth') f. obs. *counterpoint* f. OF *contrepointe* alt. f. *cou*(*l*)*tepointe* f. med. L *culcita puncta* quilted mattress]

cou'nterpart *n.* person or thing extremely like another; one of two copies of legal document; person or thing forming natural complement to another (*∼ **funds** etc., in local currency and equivalent to goods etc. received from abroad). [f. COUNTER- (3, 4) + PART¹, after OF *contrepartie*]

cou'nterplot *n.*, & *v.i.* (-**tt**-). (make) plot contrived to defeat another plot. [f. COUNTER- (1) + PLOT]

cou'nterpoint *n.*, & *v.t.* **1.** *n.* (Mus.) melody added as accompaniment to given melody; art or mode of adding melodies as accompaniment according to fixed rules; **strict** ∼ (acc. to code of rules as academic exercise, not as actual composition). **2.** *v.t.* add counterpoint to; (fig.) set in contrast. [f. OF *contrepoint* f. med. L CONTRA*punctum* pricked or marked opposite, i.e. to the original melody (*pungere punct-* prick)]

cou'nterpoise¹ (-z) *n.* counterbalancing weight; thing of equivalent force etc. on opposite side; equilibrium. [ME f. OF *countrepeis*, *-pois*, (*contre* COUNTER- (1), *peis*, *pois* f. L *pensum* weight; cf. POISE¹)]

cou'nterpoise² (-z) *v.t.* counterbalance; compensate; bring into or keep in equilibrium. [ME, f. OF *contrepeser* (as prec.); later assim. to prec.]

counter-produ'ctive *a.* having the opposite of the desired effect. [f. COUNTER- (2) + PRODUCTIVE]

counter-reforma'tion *n.* reformation running counter to another, esp. (Hist.; *C-, R-*) that in Church of Rome following on Protestant Reformation. [f. COUNTER- (1) + REFORMATION²]

counter-revolu'tion (-lōō'-) *n.* revolution opposed to a former one or reversing its results; hence ∼ARY¹ *a.* & *n.* [f. COUNTER- (1) + REVOLUTION 2]

cou'nterscarp *n.* outer wall or slope of ditch in fortification. [f. F *contrescarpe* f. It. *contrascarpa* (as CONTRA-, SCARP)]

cou'ntershaft (-ah-) *n.* intermediate shaft driven by main shaft and transmitting motion to particular machine etc.; * = LAY³*shaft*. [f. COUNTER- (4) + SHAFT]

cou'ntersign¹ (-īn) *n.* watchword, password, spoken to man on guard (cf. PAROLE); mark used for identification etc. [f. F *contresigne* f. It. *contrasegno* (as COUNTER- (3), SIGN¹)]

cou'ntersign² (-īn) *v.t.* add signature to (document already signed by another); ratify; so **countersi'gnature** *n.* [f. F *contresigner* (as prec.)]

cou'ntersink *v.t.* (-**sunk**). bevel off (rim of hole) to receive head of screw or bolt; sink (screw) into such hole. [f. COUNTER- (3) + SINK¹]

cou'nterstroke *n.* stroke given in return. [f. COUNTER- (1) + STROKE¹]

counter-te'nor *n.* (Mus.) male voice higher than tenor, but with quality of tenor; singer with counter-tenor voice; part written for counter-tenor voice. [ME, f. F *contre-teneur* f. obs. It. *contratenore* (as CONTRA-, TENOR)]

cou'ntervail *v.t.* counterbalance (∼**ing duty**, one put on imports to offset subsidy in exporting country or tax on similar goods not from abroad); avail against. [ME, f. AF *countrevaloir* f. L *contra valēre* be of worth against]

cou'ntervalue *n.* equivalent value (esp. in strategy). [f. COUNTER- (3) + VALUE]

cou'nterweight (-wāt) *n.* counterbalancing weight. [f. COUNTER- (1) + WEIGHT¹]

cou'ntess *n.* wife or widow of count or earl; woman holding rank of count or earl in her own right. [ME, f. OF *contesse*, *cuntesse*, f. LL *comitissa* fem. of *comes* COUNT³; see -ESS¹]

cou'ntless *a.* too many to be counted. [f. COUNT¹ + -LESS]

cou'ntrified, -ryfied, (kŭ'ntrĭfīd) *a.* rural, rustic, (in appearance, manners, etc.). [p.p. of *countrify* f. foll. + -FY]

cou'ntry (kŭ'-) *n.* **1.** land of a region; the region associated with a person (*the Hardy country*); territory of a nation; territory (lit. or fig.; person's **line of** ∼, subject with which he is familiar; **unknown** ∼, unfamiliar place or topic); land of a person's birth, citizenship, etc., fatherland. **2.** rural districts as opp. to towns, esp. the rest of a land as opp. to the capital (**across** ∼, not keeping to main roads etc.; **in the** ∼, (Cricket, sl.) far from the wickets; **up** ∼, away from the capital or coast); ‖national population, esp. as electors (*appeal*, GO¹ 24, *to the country*). **3.** ∼(-**and**-**western**, rural or cowboy songs to guitar etc.; ∼ **club**, sporting and social club in a rural district; ∼ **cousin**, relation or person of countrified manners or appearance; ∼ **dance**, English rural, native, or traditional dance, esp. with couples face to face in long lines; ∼ **gentleman,** gentleman with landed property in rural area; ∼ **house,** rural residence, esp. of country gentleman; ∼ **music,** = *country-and-western*; ∼ **party,** political party supporting agricultural against manufacturing interests; *country* SEAT, ∼**side,** (inhabitants of) particular rural district, or rural areas generally; ∼-**wide** *a.*, extending throughout a nation. [ME, f. OF *cuntree*, f. med. L *contrata* (*terra*) (land) lying opposite (CONTRA); see -Y⁴]

countryfied. See COUNTRIFIED.

cou'ntryman (kŭ'n-) *n.* (*pl.* ∼**men;** *fem.* ∼**woman** *pr.* -wŏŏman, *pl.* ∼**women** *pr.* -wĭmĭn). man of one's own (or a specified) country; person living in rural parts. [f. COUNTRY + MAN¹]

cou'nty *n.* & *a.* **1.** *n.* ‖territorial division, chief unit for administrative, judicial, and political purposes; administrative division in Commonwealth; *political and administrative division next below State; people of a country, esp. county families; *County* PALATINE¹. **2.** ∼ **borough,** (Hist.) large borough ranking as county for administrative purposes; ∼ **corporate,** (Hist.) city or town ranking as administrative county; ∼ **council,** representative governing body of administrative county; ∼ **court,** judicial court for civil (*and criminal) cases; ‖∼ **cricket** (between teams representing counties); ∼ **family** (with ancestral seat in a county), ‖∼ **school** (supported by county council); *∼ **seat,** ‖∼ **town,** town in which business of county is or was transacted. **3.** *a.* having social status or characteristics of county families. [ME, f. AF *counté*, OF *conté*, *cunté*, f. L *comitatus* (as COUNT³; see -ATE¹, -Y⁴)]

coup (kōō) *n.* (*pl. pr.* kōōz). **1.** notable or successful stroke or move; (Billiards) direct pocketing of ball. **2.** ∼ (**d'état**) (-dātah'), violent or illegal change in government; ∼ **de foudre** (-de fōō'dr), sudden unforeseen event, love at first sight; ∼ **de grâce** (-de grah's), finishing stroke; ∼ **de main** (-de mă'n), sudden vigorous attack; ∼ **d'œil** (-dŭ'ē), comprehensive glance, general view; ∼ **de théâtre** (-de tāah'tr), dramatically sudden or sensational action or turn of events. [F, f. med. L *colpus* blow (see COPE²)]

coupe¹ (kōōp) *n.* shallow glass or dish; ice cream and fruit etc. served in glass. [F, = goblet]

coupé (kōō'pā), ***coupe²** (kōōp), *n.* enclosed motor car, esp. one with two seats and sloping rear; (Hist.) four-wheeled enclosed carriage for two inside and driver. [F, p.p. (as *n.*) of *couper* cut (f. as COUP)]

cou'pla (kŭ'-) *n.* (colloq.) = couple of. [corrupt.]

cou'ple¹ (kŭ'-) *n.* **1.** (in *pl.*) joined collars for holding two hounds together. **2.** (*pl.* same). pair, brace, esp. of hunting dogs; **a ∼ of,** two, approximately two, a few. **3.** married or engaged pair; pair of partners in dance etc.; pair of rafters; (Mech.) pair of equal and parallel forces acting in opposite directions, and tending to cause rotation about an axis perpendicular to the plane containing them. [ME, f. OF *cople, cuple,* f. L COPULA] **cou'ple**[2] (kŭ'-) *v.* **1.** *v.t.* fasten or link together (esp. dogs in pairs); connect (railway carriages, oscillators, etc.) by a coupling; associate in thought or speech (two things *together,* one *with* another). **2.** *v.i.* copulate. [ME, f. OF *copler, cupler* f. L *copulare* (see COPULATE)] **cou'pler** (kŭ'-) *n.* In vbl senses; (Mus.) device in organ for connecting two manuals, or manual with pedals, or notes with their octaves above or below *(octave coupler).* [f. prec. + -ER[1]] **cou'plet** (kŭ'-) *n.* pair of successive lines of verse, esp. when rhyming and of same length. [F, dim. of *couple* f. as COUPLE[1]; see -ET[1]] **cou'pling** (kŭ'-) *n.* In vbl senses; link connecting railway carriages etc.; device for connecting parts of machinery; (Phys.) connection between two oscillating systems, causing one to oscillate when the other does so; arrangement of items on gramophone record(s), item so arranged. [f. COUPLE[2] + -ING[1]] **cou'pon** (kōō'-) *n.* detachable ticket entitling holder to payment, goods, services, etc., or ration of food, clothes, etc.; form etc. to be completed and sent as application for information, gift, etc.; entry-form for football pool etc.; voucher given with retail purchase, a certain number of which entitle holder to a 'free gift'. [F, = piece cut off (*couper* cut; see COUPÉ, -OON)] **cou'rage** (kŭ'-) *n.* bravery, boldness, (*take, pluck up, lose, courage*); **take** one's **∼ in both hands,** nerve oneself to a venture; **Dutch ∼** (temporary, induced by drinking); **∼ of** one's **convictions,** courage to act up to what one believes. [ME f. OF *corage,* f. Rom. *coraticum f. L *cor* heart; see -AGE] **coura′geous** (kŭrā′jus) *a.* brave, fearless; hence **∼LY**[2] *adv.,* **∼NESS** *n.* [ME f. AF *corageous,* OF *corageus* (as prec.; see -OUS)] **coura′nte** (koorah'-) *n.* running or gliding dance; music for it, e.g. as suite movement. [F, fem. pres. part. (as n.) of *courir* run f. L *currere*] **courgĕ'tte** (koorzhĕ't) *n.* small variety of vegetable marrow. [F, dim. of *courge* gourd] **cou'rier** (kōō'-) *n.* special messenger; person employed to guide and assist group of tourists; (*C∼*) title of some newspapers. [ME f. obs. F, f. It. *corriere,* & f. OF *coreor* f. Rom. **curritor,* both f. L *currere* run; see -ER[2], -OR] **cour'lan** (koor-) *n.* long-billed rail-like wading bird of tropical America, noted for its dismal cry. [F, f. Galibi *kurliri*] **course**[1] (kōrs) *n.* **1.** onward movement; direction taken (*change* one's *course; ship's course; course of events;* **∼ of nature,** ordinary events or procedure); correct or intended direction (*ship was off course*); line of conduct. **2.** pursuit of game (esp. hares) with (grey)hounds by sight rather than scent. **3.** ground on which race is run; channel in which water flows; golf links. **4.** career (**run ∼ take its ∼,** complete its natural development); series (of lectures etc.), book for or like such series; sequence of medical treatment etc. **5.** each of successive divisions of meal (esp. soup, fish, meat, etc.) **6.** continuous horizontal layer of stone etc. in building. **7.** (Naut.) fore, main, ∼, fore, main, -sail. **8. in the ∼ of,** during (*in the ∼ of time,* as time goes by), while do*ing;* **in ∼ of,** in the process of (construction, being constructed, etc.); **in due ∼,** in the natural order, at about the expected time; **of ∼,** naturally, as was to be expected; admittedly; **matter of ∼,** natural or expected thing. [ME f. OF *cours* f. L *cursus* (*currere curs-* run), & f. corresp. fem. form OF *course* f. Rom. *cursa] **course**[2] (kōrs) *v.* **1.** *v.t.* pursue (game, as prec. 2); use (hounds) in coursing. **2.** *v.i.* (Esp. of liquid) run about, run. [f. prec.]

cour'ser (kōr'-) *n.* **1.** (poet.) swift horse. **2.** fast-running African or Asian bird of genus *Cursorius* etc., akin to plover. [sense 1 ME, f. OF *corsier* f. Rom. *cursarius (*cursus* COURSE[1]; see -ARY[1], -ER[2]); sense 2 f. LL *cursorius* adapted for running (see -ORY)] **court**[1] (kōrt) *n.* **1. ∼**('**yard,** space enclosed by walls or buildings; ||(Camb. Univ.) college quadrangle; subdivision of building open to the general roof; ||confined yard opening off street; (in town) yard surrounded by houses and communicating with street by an entry. **2.** enclosed quadrangular area, open or covered, for games, (*tennis, croquet, fives, -court*); plot of ground marked out for lawn tennis; **the ball is in your ∼,** (fig.) you must be next to act. **3.** sovereign's residence; his establishment and retinue; body of courtiers; sovereign and his councillors as ruling power (**C∼ of St. James's,** British sovereign's court); assembly held by sovereign, state reception, (**hold ∼,** (fig.) preside over admirers etc.). **4.** assembly of judges or other persons acting as tribunal, (*court of law, lawcourt; court of justice, of judicature,* LEET[1], *of* RECORD[2]; *Court of* SESSION; *court of* SUMMARY *jurisdiction*); place or hall in which justice is administered; **go to ∼,** take legal action; **in ∼,** appearing as party or advocate; **out of ∼,** (of plaintiff) not entitled to be heard, (of settlement) before hearing or judgement, (fig.) not worthy of consideration. **5.** (meeting of) qualified members of company, corporation, (in some friendly societies) = LODGE[1] 4. **6.** attention paid to one whose favour, affection, interest, is sought (*pay court to*). **7. ∼-card,** playing-card that is king, queen, or jack [orig. *coat-card*]; ||**∼ circular,** daily report of doings of royal court published in newspapers; **∼ cupboard,** 16th–17th c. sideboard usu. with cupboard in top part only; **∼ dress,** formal dress as worn at royal court; **∼-house,** building in which judicial court is held, *building containing administrative offices of county; **∼ martial** (pl. **∼s** *martial*), judicial court of naval, military, or air force officers; **∼-mar'tial** *v.t.* (||-ll-), try by this; **∼ plaster,** sticking-plaster for cuts etc. (formerly used by ladies at court for face-patches); **∼ roll,** (Hist.) manorial-court register of holdings; **∼ shoe,** woman's light shoe with low-cut upper; **∼ tennis,** = TENNIS 1; **∼'yard** (see sense 1). [ME, f. AF *curt,* OF *cort* f. Rom. **curte,* *corte f. L *cohors -ortis* yard, retinue] **court**[2] (kōrt) *v.t.* pay court to; try to win favour or affection of, try to attract sexually, (person, or abs.); seek to win (applause etc.); unwisely invite (inquiry etc.; *you are courting disaster).* [f. OIt. *corteare,* OF *courtoyer* (*cort;* see prec.)] **court bouillon** (koor bōōyaw'n) *n.* stock made from wine, vegetables, etc., in which fish is boiled. [F (*cour* short, BOUILLON)] **cour'téous** (kĕr'-) *a.* polite, kind, considerate, in manner or approach; hence **∼LY**[2] *adv.,* **∼NESS** *n.* [ME, f. OF *corteis, curteis* f. Rom. *cortensis (as COURT[1]; see -ESE); assim. to wds in -OUS] **courtĕsa'n** (kōrtĭză'n) *n.* prostitute, esp. one whose clients are wealthy or upper-class. [f. F *courtisane* f. It. *cortigiana,* fem. of *cortigiano* courtier (*corte* COURT[1])] **cour'tesў** (kĕr'-) *n.* courteous behaviour or disposition or act; (arch.) = CURTSY; **by∼,** by favour, not of right; **by ∼ of,** with the kind permission of (person etc.); **∼ light,** light in motor car switched on by opening door; **∼ title,** one held by courtesy (usu. having no legal validity), ||e.g. of lower peerage given to heir of duke etc. [ME, f. OF *curtesie, co(u)rtesie* (*curteis* etc. COURTEOUS; see -Y[1])] **cour'tier** (kōr'-) *n.* attendant at or frequenter of sovereign's court. [ME, f. AF *courte(i)our,* f. OF *cortoyeur (*cortoyer* be present at court); assim. to -IER] **cour'tlỹ** (kōr'-) *a.* polished, refined, in manners obsequious; **∼y love,** conventional medieval tradition of knightly love and etiquette; hence **∼iNESS** *n.* [f. COURT[1] + LY[1]] **cour'tship** (kōr'-) *n.* period of courting with view to marriage; courting of animals, birds, etc. [f. COURT[1] + -SHIP]

cou′scous (kōō′skōōs) n. N. Afr. dish of crushed wheat or coarse flour steamed over broth, freq. with meat or fruit added. [F, f. Arab. *kuskus* (*kaskasa* to pound)]

cou′sin (kŭ′zin) n. 1. ∼(-german), first ∼, child of one's uncle or aunt; second ∼, one's parent's first cousin's child; first ∼ once (*twice* etc.) removed, (1) one's first cousin's child (grandchild etc.), (2) one's parent's (grandparent's etc.) cousin. 2. title formerly used by sovereign in addressing another sovereign or a nobleman of same country. 3. Hence ∼HOOD, ∼SHIP, ns., ∼LY[1] a. [ME, f. OF *cosin*, *cusin*, f. L *consobrinus* mother's sister's child]

:outh (kōōth) a. cultured; well-mannered. [back-form. as antonym of UNCOUTH]

:outūr′e (kōō-) n. dressmaking; design and making of fashionable garments; HAUTE *couture*. [F, = sewing, dressmaking]

:outūr′|ier (kōōtūr′yā) n. (*fem.* ∼ière *pr.* -yār). fashion designer. [F]

:ouva′de (kōōvah′d) n. primitive people's custom by which husband feigns illness and is put to bed when his wife is giving birth to child. [F (*couver* hatch f. L *cubare* lie down)]

:ouvert (kōōvār′) n. = COVER[2] 3. [F]

:ouvertūr′e (kōō-) n. chocolate for covering sweets, cakes, etc. [F, = covering]

ōva′l|ent a. (Chem.) linking atoms by a bond in which a pair of electrons is shared; so ∼ENCE, ∼ENCY, ns., ∼enti.Y[2] adv. [f. CO- + -valent, after *trivalent* etc.]

ōve[1] n. small bay or creek; sheltered recess; (Archit.) concave arch, curved junction of wall with ceiling or floor. [OE *cofa* chamber, = MLG *cove*, MHG *kobe* stable, ON *kofi* hut f. Gmc **kubon*]

ōve[2] v.t. arch (esp. ceiling at junction with wall); slope (fireplace sides) inwards; hence **cō′VING** (2) n. [f. prec.]

ōve[3] n. (sl.) fellow, chap [16th c. cant, of unkn. orig.]

o′ven (kŭ-) n. assembly of witches. [var. of *covent*; see CONVENT]

o′venant (kŭ-) n. & v. 1. n. agreement, bargain; (Law) contract under seal, clause of this; (Bibl.) compact between God and the Israelites (ARK *of the Covenant*; land of the C∼, Canaan); Day of the C∼, (S. Afr.) 16 Dec.; National C∼ (in defence of Presbyterianism in Scotland, 1638); Solemn **League and C∼** (establishing Presbyterianism in England and Scotland, 1643). 2. v.i. & t. agree, esp. by legal covenant, (*with* person *for* thing, *to* do, *that*); hence ∼OR n. [ME f. OF, pres. part. of *co*(*n*)*venir* f. as CONVENE]

o′venantéd (kŭ-) a. bound by a covenant. [p.p. of prec.]

o′venanter (kŭ-) n. one who covenants, esp. (Sc. Hist., C∼) adherent of the National COVENANT or the Solemn League and COVENANT. [f. COVENANT + -ER[1]]

ó′ventry n. send to ∼, refuse to associate with or speak to (person). [∼ in W. Midlands]

o′ver[1] (kŭ-) v.t. 1. protect or conceal (*with* cloth, lid, etc. put over or in front); put cover on; strew thoroughly (*with*); ∼ in, provide with roof etc. 2. lie over, be a covering to; (of stallion, bull, etc.) copulate with; extend over, occupy the whole surface of (*covered in dirt*, *in bruises*, *with writing*, (fig.) *with disgrace*); protect; clothe; ∼ (up), conceal (traces, face, feelings, crime, etc., or abs.; so ∼-up n.; ∼ for, temporarily deputize for); travel (specified distance etc.); (in .p.) wearing hat, having roof; ∼ing letter, note, explanatory one with enclosure. 3. (Of fortress, guns, etc.) command (territory); aim gun at; (Mil. & Cricket) stand behind (front-rank man, another player to stop balls he misses; ∼-point, fieldsman covering point, his place); play card higher than (one already played to same trick, or abs.). 4. include, comprise; deal with (subject); (Journalism) report occurrences, proceedings of meeting, etc.), in-

vestigate as reporter; suffice to defray (expenses). 5. Hence ∼ING (3) n. [ME, f. OF *covrir*, *cuvrir* f. L CO(*operire opert-* cover)]

co′ver[2] (kŭ′-) n. 1. thing that covers (LOOSE[1] *cover*); lid; binding of book; either board of this (from ∼ to ∼, from beginning to end of a book); wrapper or envelope of letter (UNDER *separate cover*); outer case of pneumatic tyre; (in *pl.*) bedclothes. 2. hiding-place, shelter, (take ∼, use natural or prepared shelter against attack); supporting force protecting from attack; = COVER[1]-*point*; screen, pretence, (*under cover of humility*); spy's pretended identity or activity as concealment; woods or undergrowth sheltering game, COVERT[2], (break ∼, leave such shelter); vegetation covering ground; funds (esp. obtained by insurance) to meet liability or secure against contingent loss; state of being thus protected. 3. plate, napkin, etc., laid for each person at table. 4. ∼ **charge**, service charge usu. per person in restaurant etc.; ∼ **crop** (grown for protection or enrichment of soil); ∼**-drive**, (Cricket) drive past cover-point; ∼ **girl**, girl or woman whose picture illustrates cover of magazine etc.; ∼ **note** (certifying existence of current insurance policy). [f. prec.]

co′verage (kŭ′-) n. area or amount covered; area reached by a particular broadcasting station or advertising medium; risk covered by insurance policy; reporting of events etc. for newspaper etc. [f. COVER[1] + -AGE]

co′verall (kŭ′verawl) a. & n. (thing) covering entirely; (usu. in *pl.*) full-length protective outer garment. [f. COVER[1] + ALL]

co′verlet (kŭ′-) n. bedspread. [ME, f. AF *covrelet*, -*lit* f. OF *covrir* cover + *lit* bed]

co′vert[1] (kŭ′-) a. (Of threat, glance, etc.) secret, disguised; FEME *covert*; hence ∼LY[2] adv. [ME f. OF, p.p. of *covrir* COVER[1]]

co′vert[2] (kŭ′vert, -er) n. shelter, esp. thicket hiding game; feather covering base of bird's wing feather or tail feather; ∼ **coat**, short light overcoat worn for shooting, riding, etc. [ME, f. OF *covert* p.p. (as n.); see prec.]

co′verture (kŭ′-) n. covering, cover; condition of married woman under husband's protection. [ME f. OF (as COVERT[1]; see URE)]

co′vet (kŭ′-) v.t. desire eagerly (usu. what belongs to another); hence ∼ABLE a. [ME, f. OF *cu-*, *coveitier* f. Rom. **cupiditare* f. as CUPIDITY]

co′vetous (kŭ′-) a. eagerly desirous (*of another's property* etc.); grasping, avaricious; hence ∼LY[2] adv., ∼NESS n. [ME, f. OF *coveitous* f. Gallo-Rom. **cupidilosus* (as CUPIDITY; see OUS]

co′vey (kŭ′-) n. brood of partridges; party, group, of persons or things. [ME, f. OF *covee* f. Rom. **cubata* hatching f. L *cubare* lie; see -Y[4]]

co′vin (kŭ′-) n. (arch.) fraud, deception; (Law) conspiracy, collusion. [ME, f. OF *covin*(*e*) f. med. L *convenium -ia* (*connenire*; see CONVENE)]

cō′ving. See COVE[2].

cow[1] (kow) n. (*pl.* ∼s, arch. kine). 1. female of any bovine animal, esp. ∼s of the domestic species (*Bos taurus*) and esp. one that has calved; female elephant, rhinoceros, whale, seal, etc.; (vulg., derog.) woman, esp. coarse or unpleasant one; (Austral. & NZ sl.) unpleasant person, thing, situation, etc.; till the ∼s come home, (sl.) for an indefinitely long time. 2. ∼**′bane**, water hemlock; ∼**′bell** (worn round cow's neck or used as percussion instrument); ∼**′berry**, (dark red fruit of) northern shrub (*Vaccinium vitis-idaea*); ∼**′boy**, (1) boy in charge of cows, (2) *man in charge of grazing cattle on ranch, (3, sl.) one who is boisterous or undisciplined, or recklessly unscrupulous in business; *∼**′catcher**, apparatus fixed in front of locomotive engine to remove cattle and other obstructions; ∼**-fish**, (1) sea-cow, (2) Ind. and Amer. fish with hornlike spines over eyes; ∼**-grass**, wild species of trefoil; ∼**′heel**, foot of cow or ox

stewed to jelly; ∼'herd, one who tends cows at pasture; ∼'hide, (leather, whip, made of) cow's hide; ∼'itch, = COWAGE; ∼-lick, projecting lock of hair; ∼'man, = *cowherd*; ∼-parsley, wild form of chervil; ∼-pat, roundish patch of cow-dung; *∼'poke, = *cowboy* (2); ∼'pox, disease of cows of which the virus is used in vaccination against smallpox; *∼'puncher, = *cowboy* (2); ∼'shed (for cattle when not at pasture); ∼'shot, (Cricket, sl.) pull across ball to leg side; *∼ town, small provincial town with cattle-dealers; ∼-tree, S. Amer. tree with milklike juice used as food; ∼-wheat, cornfield plant of genus *Melampyrum*. [OE *cū*, = OS *kō*, OHG *kuo*, ON *kýr* f. Gmc *kō̆(u)z*, cogn. w. L *bos*, Gk *bous*]
cow² *v.t.* intimidate, dispirit. [prob. f. ON *kúga* oppress]
cow'age *n.* tropical vine with stinging hairs on pod. [f. Hindi *kawāñch*]
cow'ard *n.* & *a.* (person) having little or no bravery; hence ∼LY¹, (colloq.) ∼Y², *adjs.*, ∼LY² *adv.* [ME, f. OF *cuard, couard*, f. Rom. *coda* tail f. L *cauda*; see -ARD]
cow'ardice *n.* lack of bravery; MORAL *cowardice*. [ME, f. OF *couardise* (as prec.; see -ICE)]
cow'er *v.i.* stand or squat in bent position; crouch, esp. from fear. [ME, f. MLG *küren* lie in wait, of unkn. orig.]
cowl *n.* 1. monk's hooded garment; hood of this; hence ∼ED² (-ld) *a.* 2. hood-shaped covering of chimney or ventilating shaft; hence ∼'ING¹ (3) *n.*, removable cover of vehicle or aircraft engine. [OE *cugele, cūle*, = MDu. *cōghel*, OHG *cucula* etc. f. eccl. L *cuculla* f. L *cucullus* hood of cloak]
cō'-worker (-wēr-) *n.* one who works in collaboration with another. [f. CO- 1 + WORKER]
cowr'ie, -ȳ, *n.* small gastropod of Indian Ocean; its shell, used as money in Africa and S. Asia; gastropod of family Cypraeidae, with highly polished shell. [f. Urdu & Hindi *kaurī*]
cow'slip *n.* wild plant (*Primula veris*) growing in pastures, with fragrant yellow flowers (∼ tea, wine, made from these); *marsh marigold. [OE *cūslyppe* (*cū* COW¹, *slyppe* slimy substance, i.e. cow-dung)]
cŏx *n.* & *v.* 1. *n.* = COXSWAIN, esp. of racing-boat. 2. *v.i.* & *t.* act as cox (of). [abbr.]
cŏ'xa|n *n.* (*pl.* ∼ae). (Anat.) hip; (Zool.) first segment of insect's leg; hence ∼AL *a.* [L]
cŏ'xcŏmb (-m) *n.* conceited showy person; hence ∼RY (5) *n.*, ∼ICAL *a.* [= COCK¹'s *comb*; orig. (cap worn by) jester]
cŏ'xswain (-kswān, -ksan) *n.* & *v.* 1. *n.* steersman of (esp. rowing-)boat; senior PO in small ship; hence ∼LESS *a.*, ∼SHIP *n.* 2. *v.i.* & *t.* act as coxswain (of). [ME, f. *cock* (see COCKBOAT) + SWAIN; cf. BOATSWAIN]
coy *a.* (Esp. of girl) modest, shy; affectedly modest; archly reticent; hence ∼'LY² *adv.*, ∼'NESS *n.* [ME, f. OF *coi, quei*, f. Rom. *quetus* f. L *quietus* QUIET²]
Coy. *abbr.* (esp. Mil.) Company.
coyō'te (koyō'tĭ, koi'ōt) *n.* N. Amer. prairie-wolf (*Canis latrans*). [Mex. Sp., f. Aztec *coyotl*]
coy'pu (-ōō) *n.* aquatic beaver-like rodent, orig. from S. America. [Araucan]
coz (kŭz) *n.* (arch.) cousin. [abbr.]
co'zen (kŭ-) *v.* (literary). 1. *v.t.* cheat, defraud, (*of, out of*); beguile (*into* doing). 2. *v.i.* act deceitfully. 3. Hence ∼AGE (3) *n.* [16th c. cant, perh. rel. to COUSIN]
*cō'zy. See COSY.
CP *abbr.* Cape Province; Communist Party; (Austral.) Country Party; Passionist [f. *Congregation of the Passion*].
c.p. *abbr.* candle-power.
cp. *abbr.* compare.
Cpl. *abbr.* Corporal.
CPO *abbr.* Chief Petty Officer.
CPR *abbr.* Canadian Pacific Railway.
∥CPRE *abbr.* Council for the Protection of Rural England.

c.p.s. *abbr.* cycles per second.
CR *abbr.* Community of the Resurrection.
Cr. *abbr.* Councillor; creditor.
cr. *abbr.* crescendo.
Cr *symb.* chromium.
crăb¹ *n.* 1. ten-footed crustacean, esp. of group Brachyura, with first pair of legs modified into pincers; edible form of this found near most sea--coasts; its flesh as food; machine for hoisting heavy weights; (C∼) *the* zodiacal sign Cancer; **catch a ∼,** (Rowing) get oar jammed under water by faulty stroke, or miss the water with one's stroke. 2. *∼-grass, creeping grass infesting lawns; ∼(-louse), parasitical insect infesting human body; ∼-pot, wicker trap for crabs. 3. Hence ∼'LIKE *a.* [OE *crabba,* = MDu. *krabbe,* ON *krabbi,* rel. to MLG *krabben,* ON *krafla* scratch]
crăb² *v.t.* & *i.* (-bb-). (colloq.) criticize adversely or captiously; act so as to spoil. [orig. of hawks fighting, f. MLG *krabben* (cf. prec.)]
crăb³ *n.* ∼(-apple), sour esp. wild apple (∼(-apple), ∼-tree, tree bearing it); sour person. [ME, perh. alt. (after CRAB¹ or foll.) of earlier *scrab,* prob. of Scand. orig.]
crä'bbĕd *a.* 1. cross-grained, perverse; morose, irritable. 2. (Of handwriting) ill-formed and hard to decipher; difficult to understand. 3. Hence ∼LY² *adv.,* ∼NESS *n.* [ME, f. CRAB¹ + -ED², assoc. w. CRAB³]
crä'bbў *a.* = prec. 1. [f. CRAB³ + -Y²]
crä'bwise (-z) *adv.* (moving) sideways or backwards like a crab. [f. CRAB¹ + -WISE]
crăck¹ *n.* & *a.* 1. *n.* sudden sharp or explosive noise (of whip, rifle, thunder); ∼ **of doom,** thunder-peal of Day of Judgement; **fair ∼ of the whip,** (colloq.) fair chance to participate etc. 2. sharp blow (*a crack on the head*); **have a ∼ at,** (colloq.) attempt. 3. ∼ **of dawn,** (colloq.) daybreak. 4. (colloq.) = WISE¹*crack.* 5. narrow opening formed by breaking or by opening door etc.; chink; partial fracture (the parts still cohering); hence ∼'Y² *a.* 6. good player, horse, etc. 3. *a.* (colloq.) first-rate (*crack regiment, shot, train*). [ME f. MDu. *crak,* OHG *krach;* cf. foll.]
crăck² *v.t.* & *i.* 1. (cause to) make sudden sharp or explosive noise (*crack a whip; whips crack*); utter (joke etc.); ∼ **down on,** (colloq.) take severe measures against, whence ∼-down *n.;* ∼ **up,** (colloq.) praise; collapse under strain, whence ∼-up *n.,* (also) crash of vehicle. 2. break (nut, skull, etc.) with sudden sharp report; break into (safe etc.); find solution to (problem, code, etc.); ∼ **a bottle,** open it and drink its contents; ∼ **a crib,** (sl.) break into a house; **get ∼'ing,** (colloq.) begin action. 3. break without complete separation of parts; (of voice, esp. boy's at age of puberty, or old person's) become dissonant; give way, yield, (under torture etc.); decompose (heavy oils) by heat and pressure with or without catalyst to produce lighter hydrocarbons (such as petrol); break (wheat) into coarse pieces. 4. ∼-brained, crazy; ∼'ing *a.* & *adv.,* (sl.) outstanding(ly), very good; ∼-jaw, (colloq.) (word) difficult to pronounce; ∼'pot, (colloq.) eccentric or unpractical (person); ∼-willow, species of willow with brittle branches. [OE *cracian* resound, = MDu. *krāken,* OHG *krahhōn*]
crä'ckĕd (-kt) *a.* In vbl senses; (colloq.) crazy, infatuated. [p.p. of prec.]
crä'cker *n.* in vbl senses; firework exploding with sharp report; small paper toy containing paper hat etc. and made so as to explode when ends are pulled; instrument for cracking, (esp., in *pl.*) nutcrackers thin dry biscuit; *biscuit; *(derog.) POOR-WHITE person; *∼-barrel, a homespun (philosophy etc.) *∼jack, (sl.) exceptionally fine or expert (thing or person); ∼s *pred. a.,* (sl.) crazy, infatuated. [f. CRACK² + -ER¹]
crä'ckl|e *v.i.,* & *n.* 1. *v.i.* emit repeated slight cracking sound. 2. *n.* such sound; (smooth surface of

paintwork, china, or glass with appearance of minute cracks. **3.** Hence ~Y² a. [f. CRACK²+-LE 3]

crä′ckling a. In vbl senses; crisp skin of roast pork; (**bit of**) ~, (colloq.) attractive woman. [f. prec.+-ING¹]

crä′cknel n. light crisp biscuit. [ME, f. F *craquelin* f. MDu. *krākelinc* (*krāken* CRACK²)]

crä′cks|man n. (pl. ~men). burglar. [f. CRACK¹ +MAN¹]

-cracy suf. forming ns., meaning 'rule of, ruling body of, class influential by' (*aristocracy, bureaucracy, democracy, plutocracy, snobocracy*). [f. or after F *-cratie*, med. L *-cratia*, Gk *-kratia* power (*kratos* strength)]

crä′dle n., & v.t. **1.** n. bed or cot for infant, esp. one mounted on rockers (**from the** ~ (**to the grave**), from infancy (till death)); (fig.) place in which thing begins or is nurtured in earliest stage (*cradle of an art, of a nation*); framework resembling cradle, esp. that on which ship or boat rests during construction or repairs, or on which person is supported to work on vertical face of building, ship, etc.; part of telephone supporting receiver when not in use; CAT¹'s-*cradle*; ~ Catholic, person belonging to RC Church from infancy; ~-**snatcher**, (sl.) person amorously attracted to a much younger person; ~-**song**, lullaby. **2.** v.t. place in cradle; contain or shelter (as) in cradle (*cradle in one's arms*). [OE *cradol*, perh. rel. to OHG *kratto* basket]

crä′dling n. In vbl senses; (Archit.) wooden or iron framework esp. in ceiling. [f. prec. +-ING¹]

craft (-ah-) n., & v.t. **1.** n. skill; cunning, deceit; art, trade, (esp. in comb., as *handicraft, priestcraft, statecraft*); the GENTLE *craft*. **2.** members of a craft; **the C**~, brotherhood of Freemasons. **3.** (pl. same). boat, vessel; aircraft or spacecraft. **4.** ~-**brother, -guild**, workman, guild of workmen, of same trade. **5.** v.t. *make in skilful manner (*handcrafted jewelry; a superbly crafted novel*). [OE *cræft,* = OS, OHG *kraft*, ON *kraptr* strength]

crä′fts|man (-ah′-) n. (pl. ~men). one who practises a handicraft; skilled person; private soldier in REME; hence ~man*ship* (3) n. [ME, orig. *craft's man*]

crä′ft|y (-ah-) a. cunning, artful, wily; hence ~ĭLY² adv., ~ĭNESS n. [OE *cræftig,* = OS *kraftag, -ig,* OHG *kreftig,* ON *kroptugr*; see -Y¹]

cräg¹ n. steep or rugged rock; ~'s**man** (-z-), skilled climber of crags; hence ~**gy**² (-gǐ) a., (csp., of person, face, etc.) rugged. [ME, of Celt. orig.]

cräg² n. (Geol.) deposits of shelly sand found in E. Anglia; strata containing them. [18th c.; perh. f. prec.]

cräke n. bird of family Rallidae, e.g. CORN*crake*; cry of corncrake. [ME, f. ON *krāka* (imit.); cf. CROAK]

cräm v. (-mm-). **1.** v.t. fill overfull; force (thing in, into, down); ~-**full**, as full as cramming can make it. **2.** feed to excess (poultry etc. *with* food). **3.** v.t. & i. prepare for examination by intensive study; eat greedily. [OE *crammian* (= ON *kremja*, MLG *kremmen* squeeze); cogn. w. *crimman* cram, f. Gmc **kram-, *krem-*]

crä′mbō n. (pl. ~es). game in which player gives word or verse-line to which each of the others must find rhyme; **dumb** ~, game in which one side must guess word, a rhyme to which is given, by miming various possible answers. [earlier *crambe*, app. allus. L *crambe repetita* cabbage served up again]

crä′mmer n. In vbl senses; one who crams pupils for examinations. [f. CRAM+-ER¹]

crämp¹ n., & v.t. **1.** n. painful involuntary contraction of muscle(s) from cold etc. (*often suffers from cramp*); WRITER's *cramp*; ~-**fish**, electric ray, torpedo. **2.** v.t. affect with cramp. [ME, f. OF *crampe* f. MDu., MLG *krampe*, OHG *krampfo* f. adj. meaning 'bent'; cf. foll. and CRIMP¹]

crämp² n. ~(-**iron**), metal bar with bent ends for holding masonry etc. together; portable tool for pressing two planks etc. together; restraint. [ME, f. MDu. *krampe*, as prec.]

crämp³ v.t. **1.** ~ (**up**), confine narrowly; restrict (energies etc.); ~ person's **style**, prevent him from acting freely; (in *p.p.,* of handwriting) small and difficult to read. **2.** fasten with cramp. [f. prec.]

crä′mpon, *crämpōō′n, n. metal hook, grappling- -iron; iron plate with spikes fixed to boot for walking on ice etc. [ME f. F, f. Frank. **krampo*, as CRAMP²; see -OON]

crän n. (Sc.) measure for fresh herrings (37½ gal.). [= Gael. *crann*, of uncert. orig.]

crä′nage n. use of crane(s); money paid for this. [ME, f. CRANE¹+-AGE]

crä′nberry n. (small red acid berry of) European or American shrub of genus *Vaccinium*. [17th c., named by Amer. colonists f. G *kranbeere,* LG *kranebere* crane- -berry]

crāne¹ n. **1.** large wading bird of family Gruidae, with long legs, neck, and bill. **2.** machine for moving heavy weights, which are usu. suspended by rope or chain from JIB¹; moving platform for camera; (**water-**)~, tube for supplying water to locomotive. **3.** ~-**fly**, long-legged two-winged fly of family Tipulidae; ~'s- -**bill**, plant of genus *Geranium*. [OE *cran,* = OS, OHG *krano,* rel. to L *grus,* Gk *geranos*]

crāne² v.t. & i. stretch (neck), stretch neck, like crane; move with crane; (of camera) change position etc. on crane. [f. prec.]

crä′niate a. & n. (Zool.) (animal) having a skull. [f. mod. L *craniatus* f. CRANIUM; see -ATE²]

crānio- comb. form. = full., as. ~LO′GICAL a., ~LOGIST, ~LOGY, (-ŏ′l-) ns., ~METRY (-ŏ′m-) n. [f. foll.+-o-]

crä′ni|um n. (pl. ~a or ~ums). bones enclosing the brain; bones of the whole head, skull; hence ~AL a. (~al index, ratio of width and length of skull). [ME f. med. L, f. Gk *kranion* skull]

cränk¹ n., & v.t. **1.** n. part of axle or shaft bent at right angles for converting reciprocal into circular motion, or vice versa; elbow-shaped connection in bell- -hanging. **2.** ~'**case**, case enclosing crankshaft; ~'**pin**, pin by which connecting-rod is attached to crank; ~'**shaft**, shaft driven by crank. **3.** v.t. turn into crank shape, furnish or fasten with crank; turn (engine, or abs.) with crank; ~ **up**, start (engine of motor car) by turning a crank, (sl.) increase (speed etc.) by intensive effort. [OE *cranc*, app. f. *crincan* by- -form of *cringan* fall in battle, orig. 'curl up']

cränk² n. & a. eccentric (person); fanciful turn of speech (*quips and cranks*). [back-form. f. CRANKY]

cränk³ a. (Naut.) liable to capsize. [perh. f. *crank* weak, shaky or CRANK¹]

crä′nk|y a. shaky; crotchety, eccentric; ill-tempered; hence ~ĭLY² adv., ~ĭNESS n. [perh. f. obs. *crank* rogue feigning sickness+-Y²]

crä′nnog n. lake dwelling in Scotland or Ireland. [Ir. (*crann* tree, beam)]

crä′nn|y n. chink, crevice, crack; hence ~ĭED² (-ĭd) a. [ME, f. OF *crané* p.p. of **craner* (*cran* f. pop. L *crena* notch)]

cräp¹ n., & v.i. (-pp-). (vulg.) **1.** n. faeces; nonsense, rubbish. **2.** v.i. defecate; (fig.) be unsuccessful, withdraw from game etc. [earlier senses 'chaff, refuse from fat-boiling', ME f. Du. *krappe*]

*cräp² n. losing throw of 2, 3, or 12 in craps; ~ **game**, game of craps. [f. as CRAPS]

crāpe n., & v.t. **1.** n. crêpe, usu. of black silk or imitation silk, esp. for mourning dress; band of this round hat etc. as sign of mourning; ~ **fern**, NZ fern with tall dark-green plumes; ~ **hair**, artificial hair for actor's false beard etc.; hence crā′pY² a. **2.** v.t. cover, clothe, drape, with crape. [earlier *crispe, crespe* f. F *crespe* CRÊPE]

crä′ppie n. Amer. freshwater sunfish of genus *Pomoxis*. [19th c.; orig. uncert.]

crä′pp|y a. (vulg.) rubbishy; disgusting. [f. CRAP¹ +-Y²]

*cräps n. pl. game of chance played with dice; **shoot** ~, play this. [19th c.; perh. f. *crab* lowest throw at dice]

crä′pūl|ent a. given to or suffering from effects of, resulting from, intemperance; hence or cogn. ∼ENCE n., ∼OUS a. [f. LL crapulentus very drunk f. L crapula inebriation f. Gk kraipalē drunken headache; see -ULENT]

crä′quelūre (-ă′kl-) n. network of small cracks in a painting or its varnish. [F]

cräsh[1] v., adv., & n. **1.** v.i. make a crash; move or go with a crash, collide violently with obstacle etc., run violently into, (of aircraft or airman) fall violently on to land or sea; undergo financial ruin; (colloq.) be heavily defeated. **2.** v.t. throw or drive with a crash; cause (vehicle etc.) to crash; pass (red traffic-light etc.); (colloq.) enter without permission. **3.** adv. with a crash (go, fall, crash). **4.** n. noise as of broken crockery, thunder, loud music, etc.; violent percussion or breakage; (fig.) ruin, esp. financial; violent impact or fall, esp. collision of vehicle or aircraft with another or with fixed object; (attrib.) done rapidly or urgently (crash course, programme). **5.** ∼ **barrier,** barrier against car leaving road, etc.; ∼-**dive,** (of submarine) dive hastily and steeply in an emergency, (of aircraft) dive and crash; so ∼-dive n.; ∼-**halt,** sudden stop by vehicle; ∼-**helmet** (worn to protect head in case of crash); ∼-**land,** (of aircraft or airman) land hurriedly with a crash, usu. without lowering undercarriage; ∼ **pad,** (sl.) place to sleep, esp. in emergency; ∼-**stop,** = crash-halt; ∼-**tackle,** (Footb.) vigorous tackle. [ME; imit.]

cräsh[2] n. coarse plain linen, cotton, etc., fabric for towels etc. [f. Russ. krashenina coloured linen]

crä′shing a. In vbl senses; (colloq.) overwhelming (a crashing bore). [f. CRASH[1] + -ING[2]]

crä′s|is n. (pl. ∼es pr. -ēz). (Gk Gram.) contraction of two adjacent vowels into one long vowel or diphthong. [f. Gk krasis mixture]

cräss a. thick, gross; (fig.) gross (crass stupidity); grossly stupid; hence ∼′ITUDE n., ∼′LY[2] adv., ∼′NESS n. [f. L crassus solid, thick]

-crăt suf. forming ns., meaning supporter or member of a -CRACY; hence -crä′TIC(AL) adj. sufs. [f. or after F -crate f. adjs. in -cratique (as -CRACY, -IC)]

crätch n. rack for feeding animals out of doors. [ME, f. OF creche f. Rom. *creppja f. Gmc *krippja CRIB[1]]

crāte n., & v.t. **1.** n. open-work or wood-framed or partitioned case or basket for carrying fragile goods; (sl.) (old) aeroplane or other vehicle; hence ∼′FUL 2 (-tf-) n. **2.** v.t. pack in crate. [ME, perh. f. Du. krat basket etc.]

crä′ter n., & v.t. **1.** n. mouth of volcano; bowl-shaped cavity, esp. that made by explosion of shell or bomb; (Astron.) raised bowl-shaped hollow on surface of moon etc.; (Gk Ant.) large bowl. **2.** v.t. form crater in. [L, f. Gk kratēr mixing-bowl]

-crä′tic(al). See -CRAT.

cravă′t n. short strip of material worn round neck; necktie; hence ∼TED[2] a. [f. F cravate f. G Krawat, Kroat f. Serbo-Croatian Hrvat Croat]

crāve v. **1.** v.t. beg for; long for. **2.** v.i. beg for, long for. **3.** Hence **crä′VING**[1] n., strong desire, intense longing, (for). [OE crafian, rel. to ON krefja]

crä′ven a. & n. **1.** a. cowardly, abject, (person, behaviour, etc.); hence ∼LY[2] adv. **2.** n. craven person. [ME cravand etc. perh. f. OF cravanté defeated, p.p. of cravanter f. Rom. *crepantare f. L crepare burst; assim. to -EN[1]]

craw n. crop of bird or insect; **stick in** one's ∼, be unacceptable. [ME, cogn. w. MDu. crāghe, MLG krage, MHG krage neck, throat]

craw′fish n. (pl. same), & v.i. **1.** n. large marine spiny lobster. **2.** v.i. *retreat, back out. [var. of CRAYFISH]

crawl v.i., & n. **1.** v.i. move slowly, dragging body along close to ground etc., or on hands and knees; walk or move slowly; (colloq.) behave abjectly or ingratiatingly to; (of ground etc.) be covered with crawling things; be filled with; feel creepy sensation, whence ∼′Y 2 a.; swim with crawl stroke. **2.** n.

crawling; slow rate of movement; high-speed swimming stroke with alternate overhand arm-movements and rapid kicks with legs; PUB-crawl. [ME, of unkn. orig.; cf. Sw. kravla, Da. kravle]

craw′ler n. In vbl senses; (usu. in pl.) baby's overall for crawling in; crawling insect; tractor moving on endless chain. [f. prec. + -ER[1]]

cray′fish (pl. same), (Austral. & NZ) **cray,** n. small lobster-like freshwater crustacean; crawfish. [ME, f. OF crevice, crevis, Frank. *krabitja = OHG krebiz CRAB[1]; assim. to FISH[1]]

cray′on n., & v.t. **1.** n. stick or pencil of coloured chalk or other material for drawing; drawing made with this. **2.** v.t. draw with crayons, (fig.) sketch. [F, f. craie f. L creta chalk; see -OON]

crāze v. & n. **1.** v.t. make insane (usu. in p.p.); produce small cracks on (pottery glaze etc.). **2.** v.i. develop such cracks. **3.** n. insane fancy, mania, crazy condition; (object of) temporary enthusiasm. [ME, orig. = break, shatter, perh. f. ON *krasa (Sw. krasa crunch)]

crä′z|ỹ a. (Of person, action, etc.) insane, mad; (colloq.) extremely enthusiastic (about; **like** ∼, like MAD[1]); (sl.) unrestrained, exciting, excellent; (of paving, quilt, etc.) made of irregular pieces fitted together; (of ship, building, etc.) unsound, shaky; *∼y **bone,** funny bone; hence ∼iLY[2] adv., ∼iNESS n. [f. prec. + -Y[2]]

creak n., & v.i. **1.** n. harsh strident noise, as of unoiled hinge, new boots, etc. **2.** v.i. make creak; move (as) with creaks. **3.** Hence ∼′Y[2] a. [ME, imit.; cf. CRAKE, CROAK]

cream [1] n. **1.** n. part of milk with high content of fat, which gathers on the top, and by churning is made into butter; CLOTTed cream; DAIRY cream. **2.** the best or choicest part of anything, esp. point of an anecdote, or group of persons outstanding in some way among a larger group. **3.** part of a liquid that gathers at the top; ∼ **of tartar,** purified and crystallized potassium bitartrate, used in medicine etc. **4.** preparation, esp. cosmetic (**cold** ∼, cooling skin-unguent); dish or sweet like or made with cream; soup or sauce containing cream or milk; full-bodied mellow sherry; sweet or biscuit with creamy filling. **5.** ∼ **bun, cake,** (filled with cream); ∼ **cheese,** soft rich kind made of unskimmed milk and cream; ∼ **cracker,** crisp unsweetened biscuit; ∼(-**coloured),** yellowish white; ||∼ **ice,** ice cream; ∼-**laid,** -**wove,** laid, wove, cream-coloured (paper); ∼ **puff,** puff pastry filled with cream, (fig.) unimportant person or thing; ∼ **tea,** afternoon tea with jam and clotted cream. **6.** Hence ∼′Y[2] a. [ME, f. OF cre(s)me f. LL cramum (perh. f. Gaulish) & eccl. L chrisma CHRISM]

cream [2] v. **1.** v.i. (Of milk or other liquid) form cream or scum. **2.** v.t. take cream from (milk); ∼ (**off**), take the best part (of any specified) part of (anything); add cream to (tea etc.); treat (skin) with cosmetic cream; work (butter etc.) to creamy consistency. [ME, f. prec.]

crea′mer n. flat dish for skimming cream off milk; machine for separating cream; *jug for cream. [f. prec. + -ER[1]]

crea′merỹ n. butter-factory; shop where milk, cream, etc., are sold. [f. CREAM[1] + -ERY, after F crèmerie]

crease[1] n. & v. **1.** n. line caused by folding, fold, wrinkle, (Cricket) line defining position of bowler and batsman, as BOWLING-crease, POPPING-crease; (Ice Hockey, Lacrosse) area near goal into which puck or ball must precede players. **2.** v.t. make crease; move (as) with creases. **3.** Hence ∼′Y[2] a. [ME, imit.; prob. var. of CREST ridge in material]

crease[2]. See KRIS.

creā′te v. **1.** v.t. bring into existence, give rise to; make by one's actions (create a diversion, a good impression); originate (actor creates a part); invest (person) with rank (create him a peer; create a peer). **2.** v.i. (sl.) make a fuss, grumble, (about). **3.** Hence **creā′tABLE** a. [ME, f. L creare + -ATE[3]]

cre'atine n. amino-acid found in muscles etc. of vertebrates. [f. Gk *kreas* meat + -INE⁵]

crea'tion n. act of creating (esp. the world); investing with title, rank, etc.; all created things; product of human (esp. designer's or actor's) intelligence, esp. of imaginative thought. [ME f. OF, f. L *creatio -onis* (as CREATE; see -ATION)]

crea'tion|ism n. theory attributing origin of matter and biological species to special creation (not to evolution); so ~IST (2) n. [f. prec. + -ISM]

crea'tive a. creating; able to create; inventive, imaginative; showing imagination as well as routine skill; hence ~LY² (-vli) adv., ~NESS (-vn-), **creati'v-ITY**, ns. [f. CREATE + -IVE]

crea'tor n. one who creates; **the C~,** God; hence **crea'trESS¹, crea'TRIX,** ns. [ME, f. OF *creat(o)ur* f. L *creator -oris* (as CREATE; see -OR)]

crea'ture n. created thing; animate being; animal (often as distinct from man); human being, person, (esp. w. term of admiration, contempt, patronage, etc.); one who owes his fortune to, and remains subservient to, another; *creature* COMFORTS; *creature of* HABIT¹. [ME f. OF, f. LL *creatura* (as prec.; see -URE)]

crèche (krāsh) n. day nursery for infants; model of the manger-scene at Bethlehem. [F (as CRATCH)]

cre'dal. See CREED.

cre'dence n. belief (**give** ~ **to,** believe); **letter of** ~ (INTRODUCTION, esp. of ambassador); ~ (**table**), small side-table, shelf, or niche for Eucharistic elements before consecration. [ME f. OF, f. med. L *credentia* (*credere* believe; see -ENCE)]

crede'ntial (-shal) n. (usu. in pl.) letter(s) of INTRO-DUCTION; evidence of achievement or trustworthiness. [f. med. L *credentialis* (as prec.; see -AL)]

crede'nza n. sideboard or cupboard. [It., f. med. L (as CREDENCE)]

cre'd|ible a. (Of person or statement) believable, worthy of belief; (of threat etc.) convincing; hence or cogn. ~IBI'LITY n. (~**ibility gap,** seeming difference between official statements and the facts), ~IBLY adv. ME, f. L *credibilis* (*credere* believe; see -IBLE)]

cre'dit n. **1.** belief, trust; **give** ~ **to,** believe (story). **2.** good reputation (**do** ~ **to,** enhance reputation of); power derived from this; acknowledgement of merit (*get, give, have, take, the credit for*); grade above 'pass' in examination; (usu. in pl.) acknowledgement of contributor's services to film, book, etc., (~ **title,** this at beginning or end of cinema or television film); source of honour (*a credit to the school*). **3.** trust in person's ability and intention to pay at a later time for goods etc. supplied (*give credit; deal on credit; long credit*), reputation of solvency and honesty; ~ **account,** ~ **sale,** (for later payment by agreement); ~ **card** (authorizing obtaining of goods on credit); ~ **rating,** estimate of person's ability and intention to pay his debts in due course. **4.** sum at person's disposal in books of a bank etc. (**letter of** ~, (authorizing person to draw money from writer's correspondent in another place)); (Bookk.) acknow-ledgement of payment by entry in account, (sum entered on) credit side of account; *certificate of completion of course by student; ~ **note** (acknow-ledging sum credited, e.g. for goods returned); ~ **transfer** (from one person's bank account to another's); **get** ~ **for,** be given credit for; **give** person ~ **for,** enter (sum) to his credit, (fig.) ascribe (usu. good quality) to him; **to** one's ~, in one's favour. [f. F *crédit* f. It. *credito* f. L *creditum* (*credere -it-* believe, trust)]

cre'dit v.t. believe; enter on credit side of account (*credit amount* to person, *person with* amount); ~ person **with,** ascribe (usu. good quality) to him. [f. prec. or f. L *credere* (see prec.)]

cre'ditab|le a. that brings credit or honour (*to*); hence ~LY² adv. [f. CREDIT¹ + -ABLE]

cre'ditor n. one to whom a debt is owing; one who gives credit for money or goods. [ME f. AF *creditour* (OF -*eur*) f. L *creditor -oris* (as CREDIT¹; see -OR)]

cre'dō (-ē'-, -ā'-) n. (pl. ~**s**). creed (esp. Apostles' and Nicene, beginning in Latin with *credo*); musical setting of Nicene Creed. [ME f. L, = I believe]

cre'dulous a. too ready to believe; (of behaviour) showing such readiness; hence or cogn. **credu'lITY,** ~NESS, ns., ~LY² adv. [f. L *credulus* (*credere* believe; see -ULOUS)]

creed n. brief formal summary of Christian doctrine, esp. APOSTLES' (also *the Creed*), NICENE, ATHANASIAN, *Creed*; this as part of Mass; system of religious belief; set of opinions or principles on any subject; hence ~'AL, **cre'dAL,** adjs. [OE *crēda* f. L CREDO]

creek n. |inlet on sea-coast; small harbour; short arm of river; (Austral. & NZ) stream, brook; (US etc.) tributary of river; **up the** ~, (sl.) (1) in difficulties or trouble, (2) crazy. [ME *crike* f. ON *kriki* nook (or partly f. OF *crique,* f. ON), & ME *crēke* f. MDu. *krēke* (or f. *crike* by lengthening); ult. orig. unkn.]

creel n. large wicker basket for fish; angler's fishing-basket. [ME, orig. Sc.; ult. orig. unkn.]

creep v.i. (**crept**), & n. **1.** v.i. move with body prone and close to ground; move timidly, slowly, or stealthily. **2.** insinuate oneself *into,* come *in, up,* unobserved, proceed or exist abjectly; (of plant) grow along ground, wall, etc.; develop gradually (*creeping inflation*); (Metallurgy) undergo creep; (of flesh) feel as if things were creeping over it (result of fear, repugnance, etc.). **3.** n. creeping; shrinking horror, as (colloq. in pl.) *gave me the creeps,* low arch under railway embankment, road, etc.; (sl.) disliked person; (Geol.) gradual movement of disintegrated rock due to atmospheric changes etc., or of strata by ex-pansion, compression, etc.; (Metallurgy) gradual change of shape under stress. [OE *crēopan,* = OS *criopan,* ON *krjúpa* f. Gmc *kreupan etc.]

cree'per n. In vbl senses; plant that creeps along ground or up wall; bird that climbs up trees, over bushes, etc., esp. TREE-*creeper*; (sl.) soft-soled shoe. [f. prec. + -ER¹]

cree'ping a. In vbl senses; ~ **barrage** (moving ahead of advancing troops); ~ **Jenny,** one of various creeping plants, esp. moneywort; ~ **Jesus,** (sl.) abject or hypocritical person. [f. CREEP + -ING²]

cree'py̆ a. having a creeping of the flesh; producing this; given to creeping; ~**crawly** a. & n., creeping and crawling (insect etc.). [f. CREEP + -Y²]

creese. See KRIS.

crem|ā'te v.t. consume (corpse) by fire; so ~A'TION n. [f. L *cremare* burn + -ATE³]

cremator'i|um n. (pl. ~**a** or ~**ums**). place for cremating corpses. [mod. L, f. as CREMATE; see -ORY]

cre'matory̆ a. & n. **1.** a. of or pertaining to cremation. **2.** n. * = prec. [f. CREMATE + -ORY]

crème (krām) n. = CREAM¹ 4; ~ **brûlée** (brōō'lā), cream or custard topped with caramelized sugar; ~ *de la* ~ (-dlah-), the very pick, élite; ~ *de menthe* (demah'nt), peppermint liqueur. [F, ~ CREAM]

cre'n|āte a. (Bot. & Zool.) with notched edge or rounded teeth; so ~**āted**¹ a., ~A'TION, ~**atURE,** ns. [f. mod. L *crenatus* f. pop. L *crena* notch; see -ATE³]

cre'nel, crène'lle n. open space or indentation in embattled parapet, for shooting through etc. [ME, f. OF *crenel,* f. Gallo-Rom. *crenellum dim. of pop. L *crena* notch]

cre'nell|āte v.t. furnish with battlements or loopholes; hence ~A'TION n. [f. F *créneler* (as prec.) + -ATE³]

Crē'ōle n. **1.** n. descendant of European settlers in W. Indies or Central or S. Amer.; white descendant of French settlers in southern US; person of mixed European and Negro descent; creolized language. **2.** a. that is a Creole; of Creole(s); (~) of local origin or production. [f. F *créole, criole* f. Sp. *criollo,* prob. f. Port. *crioulo* home-born slave (*criar* breed f. L *creare* CREATE)]

cre'olīze, -īse (-īz) v.t. make (language of dominant

group, in modified form) into sole language of dominated group. [f. prec. + -IZE]

crě′osōte *n.*, & *v.t.* **1.** *n.* colourless oily fluid distilled from wood tar, a strong antiseptic; ∼ (**oil**), dark-brown oil distilled from coal tar, used as wood-preservative. **2.** *v.t.* treat with creosote. [f. G *kreosote* f. Gk *kreas* flesh + *sōtēr* preserver, w. ref. to its antiseptic properties]

crêpe (-āp) *n.* **1.** gauzelike fabric with wrinkled surface; ∼ **de Chine** (*de* shē′n), **China** ∼, fine silk crêpe; ∼ **paper**, thin crinkled crêpelike paper; ∼ (**rubber**), very durable wrinkled sheet rubber used for shoe-soles etc. **2.** thin pancake; ∼ **Suzette**, small dessert pancake served heated in sauce. [F, f. OF *crespe* curled f. L *crispus*]

crě′pit|āte *v.i.* make crackling sound; (of beetle) eject pungent fluid with sharp report; so ∼ANT *a.*, ∼A′TION *n.*, (esp., Med.) crepitus. [f. L *crepitare* frequent. of *crepare* creak + -ATE³]

crě′pitus *n.* (Med.) grating noise of ends of fractured bone; rattle of breath in pneumonia etc. [L (*crepare* rattle)]

crěpt. See CREEP.

crěpǔ′scūlar *a.* of twilight; (Zool.) appearing or active in twilight; dim, not yet fully enlightened. [f. L *crepusculum* twilight + -AR¹]

||**Cres.** *abbr.* Crescent.

crěscě′ndō (krǐsh-) *adv.*, *a.*, & *n.* (*pl.* ∼s). (Mus.) (passage performed) with gradual increase of loudness; (fig.) progress towards a climax. [It., part. of *crescere* grow (as foll.)]

crě′scent *n.* & *a.* **1.** *n.* waxing moon; figure of moon in first or last quarter; this as emblem of Turkey or Islam; **the C**∼, the Muslim religion. **2.** anything of crescent shape, esp. ||street of houses. **3.** *a.* increasing; crescent-shaped. [ME f. AF *cressaunt*, OF *croissant*, f. L *crescere* grow; see -ENT]

crě′sŏl *n.* one of three isomeric phenols present in creosote and used as disinfectants. [f. CREOSOTE + -OL]

crěss *n.* cruciferous plant usu. with pungent edible leaves; **garden** ∼, *Lepidium sativum*; **INDIAN** *cress*; **WATER**¹*cress*. [OE *cresse* etc., = MLG *kerse*, OHG *kressa*, -*o*, f. WG **krasjō*-]

crě′ssèt *n.* (Hist.) metal vessel for holding oil, coal, etc., for light, usu. mounted on pole. [ME f. OF *cresset, craisset*, f. *craisse* = *graisse* GREASE¹]

crěst *n.* & *v.* **1.** *n.* comb or tuft on bird′s or animal′s head (∼′**fallen**, with drooping crest, (fig.) dejected, abashed). **2.** plume or tuft of feathers; (apex of) helmet. **3.** head, top, esp. of mountain, roof, or wave; surface line of neck in animals; mane; **on the** ∼ **of the** or **a wave**, (fig.) at most favourable moment in one′s progress. **4.** (Anat.) ridge along surface of bone, as **frontal, occipital,** ∼ of skull. **5.** (Her.) device above shield and helmet on coat of arms, or separately, as on seal, notepaper, etc. **6.** *v.t.* furnish with crest; serve as crest to; reach crest of (hill, wave). **7.** *v.i.* (Of wave) form into a crest. [ME, f. OF *creste* f. L *crista* tuft]

crětā′ceous (-shus) *a.* & *n.* of (the nature of) chalk; (C∼, Geol.) (of the) latest Mesozoic period or system, above Jurassic, containing chalk. [f. L *cretaceus* (*creta* chalk; see -ACEOUS)]

Crē′tan *a.* & *n.* (native) of Crete (at one time supposed to contain many liars). [f. L *Cretanus* (*Creta* f. Gk *Krētē* Crete, island in E. Mediterranean; see -AN)]

crē′tic *n.* (Pros.) foot consisting of one short syllable between two long. [f. L f. Gk *Krētikos* (as prec.; see -IC)]

crē′tin *n.* person with deformity and mental retardation caused by thyroid deficiency; (colloq.) stupid person; hence ∼ISM (2) *n.*, ∼IZE (3) *v.t.*, ∼OUS *a.* [f. F *crétin* f. Swiss F *crestin, crestin* f. L *Christianus* CHRISTIAN]

crētŏnne (-ŏ′n, -ĕ′-) *n.* cotton cloth with pattern printed on one or both sides. [F, f. *Creton* in Normandy]

crěvä′sse *n.* deep fissure in ice of glacier; *breach in river levee. [F, f. OF *crevace* (see foll.)]

crě′vice *n.* narrow opening, fissure, esp. in rock, building, etc. [ME f. OF *crevace* (*crever* burst f. L *crepare*)]

crew¹ (-ōō) *n.* & *v.* **1.** *n.* body of persons manning ship, boat, aircraft, train, etc.; such persons other than officers; associated body, company, of persons; set, gang, mob; ∼ **cut**, man′s hair cut short all over; ∼′**man**, member of crew; ∼ **neck**, round close-fitting neckline. **2.** *v.i.* & *t.* supply, act as, (member of) crew (for). [ME, f. OF *creüe* increase, fem. p.p. (as n.) of *croistre* grow f. L *crescere*]

crew². See CROW³.

crew′el (-ōō′-) *n.* thin worsted yarn for tapestry and embroidery; ∼**-work**, design in worsted on linen or cloth ground. [ME *crule* etc.; orig. unkn.]

crib¹ *n.* **1.** barred receptacle for fodder etc.; ∼**-biting**, horse′s habit of seizing manger in teeth and at same time noisily drawing in breath. **2.** small bed for child, with barred or latticed sides; model of the manger-scene at Bethlehem; framework lining shaft of mine; ∼(′**work**), heavy crossed timbers used in foundations in loose soil etc. **3.** set of cards given to dealer at cribbage by himself and other player(s); (colloq.) cribbage. **4.** (colloq.) plagiarism; translation for (esp. illegitimate) use of students. **5.** small house; (sl.) brothel; CRACK² *a crib.* **6.** (Austral. & NZ) food; light meal. [OE *crib(b)*, = OS *kribbia*, OHG *krippa*]

crib² *v.t.* (**-bb-**). confine in small space; pilfer; copy (work, or abs.) unfairly or without acknowledgement; (colloq.) grumble. [f. prec.]

cri′bbage *n.* card-game for two, three, or four persons, in which dealer scores also from cards in CRIB¹ 3; ∼**-board** (with pegs and holes for scoring at cribbage). [17th c.; orig. unkn.]

cri′bŏ *n.* (*pl.* ∼s). large harmless snake of tropical America. [19th c.; orig. unkn.]

cri′brifŏrm *a.* (Anat. & Bot.) having numerous small holes. [f. L *cribrum* sieve + -I- + -FORM]

crick *n.*, & *v.t.* **1.** *n.* sudden painful stiffness of muscles of neck, back, etc. **2.** *v.t.* produce crick in (neck etc.). [ME, of unkn. orig.]

cri′ckèt¹ *n.* jumping chirping insect living in hearths etc.; MOLE²-*cricket*. [ME, f. OF *criquet* (*criquer* creak etc.; imit.)]

cri′ckèt² *n.* & *v.i.* **1.** *n.* open-air summer game played with ball, bats, and wickets, between two sides of 11 players each; ||**not** ∼, (colloq.) infringing the codes of fair play between honourable opponents or any sphere; ∼**-bag**, long bag for carrying cricketer′s bat etc. **2.** *v.i.* play cricket; hence ∼ER¹ *n.* [16th c.; orig. uncert.]

cri′coid *a.* & *n.* ring-shaped (cartilage of larynx). [f. mod. L *cricoides* f. Gk *krikoeidēs* (*krikos* ring; see -OID)]

||**cri de cœur** (krē de kĕr′) *n.* (*pl.* **cris** *pr.* same). passionate appeal, complaint, or protest. [F, = cry from the heart]

cri′er *n.* one who cries; officer who makes public announcements in court of justice or (**town** or **common** ∼) in a town. [ME f. AF *criour*, OF *criere* (*crier* CRY²; see -OR)]

cri′key *int.* (sl.) expr. astonishment. [euphem. for CHRIST]

crīme *n.*, & *v.t.* **1.** *n.* act (usu. grave offence) punishable by law; evil act; such acts collectively; (colloq.) shameful act; soldier′s offence against regulations (∼**-sheet**, record of offences); ∼ **wave**, sudden brief increase in number of crimes committed; ∼**-writer**, author who writes about fictional crimes. **2.** *v.t.* (Mil. etc.) charge with or convict of offence. [ME f. OF, f. L *crimen -minis* judgement, offence]

crime passionnel (krēm pǎsyŏně′l) *n.* (*pl.* **-es -ls** *pr.* same). crime, esp. murder, due to sexual jealousy. [F, = crime of passion]

cri'minal *a.* & *n.* **1.** *a.* of (the nature of) crime; guilty of crime; ∼ **law** (concerned with punishment of offenders), opp. CIVIL *law*; so ∼ **code, court, lawyer**); *criminal* LIBEL; hence ∼ITY (-ă'l-) *n.*, ∼LY² *adv.* **2.** *n.* person guilty of crime. [ME, f. LL *criminalis* (as CRIME; see -AL)]

criminali'st|ic *a.* pertaining to (the habits of) criminals; so ∼ICS *n.*, use of physical sciences in investigating crimes. [f. prec. + -IST + -IC]

cri'min|āte *v.t.* charge with crime; prove guilty of crime; censure; hence or cogn. ∼A'TION *n.*, ∼ātIVE, ∼ātORY, *adjs.* [f. L *criminari* (as CRIME) + -ATE³]

criminŏ'log|ў *n.* scientific study of crime; hence **criminŏLO'GICAL** *a.*, ∼IST (3) *n.* [f. L *crimen -minis* CRIME + -O- + -LOGY]

cri'mĭnous *a.* (arch.) ∼ **clerk,** clergyman guilty of crime. [AF; OF *crimineux* f. L *criminosus* (as prec.; see -OUS)]

crimp¹ *v.t.*, & *n.* **1.** *v.t.* compress into pleats or folds, frill; make narrow wrinkles or flutings in, corrugate; make waves or curls in (hair) with hot iron. **2.** *n.* crimped thing or form; *put a ∼ in, (sl.) thwart, interfere with; hence ∼'Y² *a.* [ME, prob. f. MDu., MLG *krimpen*, OHG *krimphan*]

crimp² *n.*, & *v.t.* (agent whose business is to) entrap for service in army or navy. [17th c.; orig. unkn.]

cri'mson (-z-) *a.*, *n.*, & *v.* **1.** *a.* & *n.* rich deep-red (colour) inclining to purple; *crimson* RAMBLER. **2.** *v.t.* & *i.* turn crimson. [ME *cremesin, crimesin,* ult. f. Arab. *ḳirmizī* KERMES]

cringe (-nj) *v.i.*, & *n.* **1.** *v.i.* cower; bow servilely; behave obsequiously (*to*). **2.** *n.* (arch.) fawning obeisance, cringing. [ME *crenge, crenche,* OE *cringan, crincan;* see CRANK¹]

cri'ngle (-nggl) *n.* (Naut.) eye of rope containing thimble for another rope to pass through. [f. LG *kringel* dim. of *kring* ring f. root of CRANK¹]

cri'nkl|e *v.t.* & *i.*, & *n.* (form) wrinkle or bend esp. in line or surface; hence ∼Y² *a.* [ME, frequent. f. st. of OE *crincan* yield; see CRINGE, CRANK¹, -LE 3]

crinkum-crä'nkum *n.* & *a.* (thing) full of twists and turns (lit. or fig.). [18th c., playful f. CRANK¹]

cri'noid *a.* & *n.* (Zool.) lily-shaped (echinoderm); hence **crinoi'dAL** *a.* [f. Gk *krinoeidēs* (*krinon* lily; see OID)]

cri'noline (-ĭn, -ēn) *n.* stiff fabric of horsehair etc. for linings, hats, etc.; (Hist.) hooped petticoat. [F, f. L *crinis* hair + *linum* thread]

criŏ'llō *n.* (*pl.* ∼s). high-quality kind of cocoa. [Sp., = local; see CREOLE]

cri'pes (-ps) *int.* (vulg.) expr. astonishment. [perversion of CHRIST]

cri'pple *n.*, & *v.t.* **1.** *n.* (permanently) lame person, hence ∼DOM (-peld-), ∼HOOD (-pelh-), *ns.* **2.** *v.t.* lame; (fig.) disable, impair, have severe adverse effect on. [OE *crypel,* = OLG *krupil,* & OE *crēopel,* = MLG, MDu. *krēpel,* cogn. w. CREEP]

cris. Var. of KRIS.

crise de nerfs (krēz de nāir') *n.* (*pl.* *crises* pr. same). fit of hysterics. [F]

cri's|is *n.* (*pl.* ∼es pr. -ēz). turning-point, esp. of disease; time of danger or suspense in politics, commerce, etc. [L, f. Gk *krisis* decision (*krinō* decide)]

crisp *a.*, *n.*, & *v.* **1.** *a.* hard but fragile, brittle, (∼'bread, thin crisp biscuit of crushed rye etc. grains); bracing (*crisp air*); brisk, decisive, (*crisp manner, style,* etc.); (of hair etc.) curly; neat, clearly defined; hence ∼'LY² *adv.*, ∼'NESS *n.* **2.** *n.* thing overdone in roasting etc.; (usu. in *pl.*) ||thin fried slice of potato (marketed in packets etc.). **3.** *v.t.* & *i.* curl in short stiff folds or waves; make or become crisp. [OE *crisp, crips,* f. L *crispus* curled]

cri'spāte *a.* crisped; (Bot. & Zool.) having wavy margin. [f. L *crispare* curl; see -ATE²]

cri'spý *a.* curly; brittle; brisk; crisp. [ME, f. CRISP + -Y²]

cri'ss-cross (-ŏs, -aws) *n.*, *a.*, *adv.*, & *v.* **1.** *n.* crossing of lines, currents, etc.; network of crossing lines. **2.** *a.* in cross lines (*criss-cross pattern, traffic*). **3.** *adv.* crosswise, at cross purposes (*everything went criss-cross*). **4.** *v.i.* & *t.* move crosswise; work or mark with criss-cross pattern; intersect repeatedly. [orig. (15th c.) f. *Christ's cross;* later treated as redupl. of *cross*]

cri'sta *n.* (*pl.* ∼e). (Anat. & Zool.) ridge, crest; so **cri'stATE²** *a.* [L]

cristŏ'balite *n.* (Min.) a principal form of silica, occurring in massive form as opals. [f. G *cristobalit* (Cerro San *Cristóbal* in Mexico; see -ITE¹ (2))]

crit *n.* (colloq.) criticism; critique; critical mass. [abbr.]

critēr'i|on *n.* (*pl.* ∼a). principle or standard that a thing is judged by; hence ∼AL *a.* [f. Gk *kritērion* (as foll.)]

cri'tic *n.* one who pronounces judgement; censurer; judge of literary or artistic works, esp. professional reviewer of books etc.; one skilled in textual criticism. [f. L f. Gk *kritikos* (*kritēs* judge f. *krinō* decide; see -IC)]

cri'tical *a.* **1.** censorious, fault-finding, (*was critical of me, my efforts*); skilful at or engaged in criticism; providing textual criticism (*a critical edition of Ibsen*); belonging to criticism; ∼ **apparatus,** apparatus criticus. **2.** pertaining to a crisis, involving risk or suspense, (*critical condition, operation*); decisive, crucial, (*arrive at the critical moment; matter of critical importance*). **3.** (Math. & Phys.) marking transition from one state etc. to another (*critical angle*), (of nuclear reactor) maintaining a self-sustaining chain reaction, whence ∼ITY (-ă'l-) *n.*; ∼ **mass,** amount of fissile material needed to maintain nuclear chain reaction; ∼ **path,** sequence of stages determining minimum time needed for an operation; ∼ **temperature** (above which a gas cannot be liquefied). **4.** Hence ∼LY² *adv.* [f. L *criticus* (as prec.) + -AL]

criticäster (-kă'-, krĭ'-) *n.* petty or inferior critic. [f. CRITIC + -ASTER]

cri'ticism *n.* **1.** work of a critic; critical article, essay, or remark; **textual** ∼ (dealing with and seeking correct reading of esp. MS text of an author); the **higher** ∼ (dealing with origin, character, etc., of texts, esp. of Biblical writings); the **lower** ∼, textual criticism of Bible. **2.** censure. [f. CRITIC or L *criticus* + -ISM]

cri'ticīze, -īse (-īz), *v.t.* discuss critically (work, or abs.); censure. [f. as prec. + -IZE]

critl'quu (-ē'k) *n.*, & *v.t.* **1.** *n.* critical essay or analysis; art of criticism. **2.** *v.t.* discuss critically. [t. obs. *critic* criticism, after its source F *critique* f. Gk *kritikē* (*tekhnē*) critical art]

cri'tter *n.* (dial. or joc.) creature; (derog.) person [var. of CREATURE]

croak *n.* & *v.* **1.** *n.* deep hoarse sound uttered by frog or raven; sound resembling this; hence ∼'Y² *a.* **2.** *v.i.* utter croak; (sl.) die. **3.** *v.t.* utter with croak or dismally; (sl.) kill. **4.** Hence ∼'ER¹ *n.*, (esp.) prophet of evil. [ME, imit.]

Crō'ăt *n.* native or inhabitant of Croatia in Yugoslavia; language of Croats; so **Crōā'tIAN** (-shan) *a.* & *n.* [f. mod. L *Croatae* pl. f. Serbo-Croatian *Hrvat*]

crŏc *n.* (colloq.) crocodile. [abbr.]

crō'cēăte *a.* saffron, saffron-coloured. [f. L *croceus* (CROCUS); see -ATE²]

crō'chet (-shă, -shī) *n.*, & *v.t.* **1.** *n.* knitting (material or work) done with hooked needle forming intertwined loops. **2.** *v.t.* make (shawl etc., or abs.) in crochet. [F, dim. of *croc* hook]

crŏci'dolite *n.* fibrous blue or green silicate of iron and sodium, blue asbestos. [f. Gk *krokis -idos* nap of cloth + -O- + -LITE]

crŏck¹ *n.* earthenware pot or jar; broken piece of earthenware used for covering hole in flowerpot. [OE *croc*(*ca*), rel. to Icel. *krukka* & prob. to OE *crōg, crūce*]

crŏck² *n.* & *v.* **1.** *n.* (colloq. or dial.) inefficient or broken-down or worn-out person; (sl.) worn-out vehicle, ship, etc. **2.** *v.i.* ~ **up,** (colloq.) break down, collapse. **3.** *v.t.* ~ (**up**), (colloq.) disable, cause to collapse. [orig. Sc., perh. f. Flem.]

crŏ′ckerў *n.* earthenware vessels, esp. for household use. [f. obs. *crocker* potter (CROCK[1]); see -ERY]

crŏ′ckėt *n.* small ornament (usu. bud or curled leaf) on inclined side of pinnacle etc. [ME, f. ONF var. of OF CROCHET]

Crŏ′ckford *n.* (colloq.) (Used for) 'Crockford's Clerical Directory' of Anglican clergy. [f. J. ~ d. 1865, nominal first publisher]

crŏ′codīle *n.* large thick-skinned long-tailed amphibious tropical loricate of genus *Crocodilus* etc. (~ **tears,** hypocritical grief [from belief that crocodile wept while devouring, or to allure, its victim]); its skin; ‖(colloq.) line of schoolchildren etc. walking in pairs; hence **crŏcodī′lIAN** *a.* [ME f. OF *cocodrille* f. med. L *cocodrillus* f. L f. Gk *krokodilos*]

crŏ′cus *n.* dwarf plant of genus *Crocus*, with corm and brilliant (often yellow or purple) flowers; AUTUMN *crocus.* [ME, = saffron, f. L, f. Gk *krokos* crocus, of Semitic orig.]

Croe′sus (krē′s-) *n.* wealthy person. [f. ~, king of Lydia in 6th c. BC]

‖**croft** (-ŏ-, -aw-) *n.,* & *v.i.* **1.** *n.* enclosed piece of (usu. arable) land; smallholding of crofter. **2.** *v.i.* farm croft; live as crofter. [OE, of unkn. orig.]

‖**cro′fter** (-ŏ′-, -aw′-) *n.* one who rents a smallholding, esp. joint tenant of divided farm in parts of Scotland. [f. prec. + -ER[1]]

croi′ssant (krwah′sahn) *n.* crescent-shaped bread roll. [F, f. as CRESCENT]

Crŏ-Mă′gnon (-nyon, -gnon) *a.* of a tall broad-faced European race of late palaeolithic times. [name of hill in Dordogne, France, where remains were found in 1868]

crŏ′mbĕc *n.* Afr. warbler of genus *Sylvietta.* [F, f. Du. *krom* crooked + *bek* beak]

crŏ′mlĕch (-k) *n.* megalithic tomb, dolmen; circle of upright prehistoric stones. [W (*crom* fem. of *crwm* bent, *llech* flat stone)]

cromŏr′ne. Var. of KRUMMHORN.

crône *n.* withered old woman; old ewe. [ME, prob. f. MDu. *c(a)roonje* carcass f. ONF *carogne* CARRION]

crŏnk *a.* (Austral. colloq.) unfit; unsound; fraudulent. [19th c.; cf. CRANK[3]]

crŏ′nў *n.* intimate friend. [17th c. *chrony,* univ. sl. f. Gk *khronios* of long standing, chronic, (*khronos* time)]

crŏŏk *n., a.,* & *v.* **1.** *n.* hooked staff of shepherd or bishop; anything hooked; hook; bend, curve; act of bending. **2.** (colloq.) rogue, swindler; professional criminal, whence ~′ERY (5) *n.;* by HOOK[1] *or by crook;* **on the** ~, dishonestly. **3.** *a.* crooked; (Austral. & NZ colloq.) unsatisfactory, unpleasant, dishonest, bad-tempered (**go** ~, become angry, lose one's temper; **go** ~ **at** or **on,** become angry with, rebuke), unwell, injured; ~-**back**(**ed**), hunchback(ed); *~′**neck,** kind of SQUASH[2] with curved neck. **4.** *v.t.* & *i.* bend, curve; ~ one's **elbow,** one's **little finger,** (sl.) drink alcohol (esp. to excess). [ME, f. ON *krókr* hook etc.]

crooked *a.* **1.** (krŏŏ′kĭd; ~er, ~est). not straight, bent, twisted; deformed; bent with age; (fig.) not straightforward, dishonest; hence ~LY[2] *adv.,* ~NESS *n.* **2.** (krŏŏkt). (of stick) having a transverse handle; (Austral. & NZ sl.) = CROOK 3. [ME, f. prec. + -ED[2], prob. after ON *krókóttr*]

Crŏŏkes (-ks) *n.* ~ **glass,** type of glass protecting eyes from bright sunlight etc.; ~ **tube,** vacuum tube for observation of stratified electric discharges. [f. Sir W. ~, Engl. scientist d. 1919]

crŏŏn *v.t.* & *i.,* & *n.* (hum, sing, etc., in) low subdued voice; hence ~′ER[1] *n.,* esp. one who sings popular sentimental songs in low smooth voice. [ME, orig. Sc. and N. Engl., f. MDu., MLG *krönen* groan, lament]

crŏp[1] *n.* **1.** pouchlike enlargement of gullet in birds, where food is prepared for digestion (~-**full,** having

a full crop or stomach, lit. or fig.). **2.** stock or handle of whip; (**hunting-**)~, short whipstock with loop and (or instead of) lash. **3.** produce of cultivated plants, esp. cereals (*crop*-DUSTING; ~-**over,** W. Ind. celebration of end of sugar-cane harvest); season's total yield (of cereal etc.); group or amount appearing or produced at one time (*this year's crop of students*); entire hide of animal tanned. **4.** cropping of hair; style of wearing hair cut short; NECK[1] *and crop;* ~-**eared,** with ears (or hair) cut short. **5.** piece cut off. [OE *crop*(*p*), = MDu., MLG *kropp,* OHG *kropf,* ON *kroppr*]

crŏp[2] *v.* (-**pp-**). **1.** *v.t.* cut off; (of animals) bite off (tops of plants); cut short (ears, tail, hair, nap of cloth, edges of book). **2.** gather, reap; sow, plant, (land *with* barley etc.). **3.** *v.i.* bear a crop; turn *up* unexpectedly; ~ **up** or **out,** (Geol.) appear at surface. [ME, f. prec.]

crŏ′pper *n.* In vbl senses; **good, heavy, light,** ~, plant yielding good etc. crop; (sl.) heavy fall (lit. or fig.; *come a cropper*). [f. CROP[2] + -ER[1]]

crŏ′quet[1] (-kā, -kǐ) *n.* game, played on lawn, in which wooden balls are driven with mallets through hoops; act of croqueting a ball. [perh. NF dial. form of F CROCHET hook]

crŏ′quet[2] (-kā, -kǐ) *v.t.* (Croquet). drive away (opponent's ball, or abs.) with one's own by placing the two together and striking one's own (cf. ROQUET). [f. prec.]

croquĕ′tte (-kě′t) *n.* fried breaded ball or roll of potato, meat, etc. [F (*croquer* crunch; see -ETTE)]

crŏre *n.* (Ind.) ten million; one hundred lakhs (of rupees, units of measurement, persons, etc.). [f. Hindi *k*(*a*)*rōr* f. Prakrit *kroḍi,* Skr. *koṭi* apex]

crŏ′sier, -zier, *n.* hooked staff symbolizing pastoral office of bishop etc., crook. [orig. = bearer of a crook, f. OF *crocier, crossier* (*croce, crosse* f. Rom. **croccia* f. *croccus* CROOK), & f. OF *croisier* cross-bearer (*crois* CROSS[1]; see -IER)]

cross[1] (-ŏs, -aws) *n.* **1.** stake (usu. with transverse bar) used for crucifixion of criminals, esp. (*C*~) that on which Christ was crucified; model of this as religious emblem; = SIGN[1] *of the cross;* staff surmounted by cross and borne before archbishop or in procession; monument in form of cross, esp. one in centre of town; **the C**~, the Christian religion. **2.** trial, affliction, (*bear one's cross*); cause of trouble or vexation. **3.** cross--shaped thing or mark esp. as symbol (see X); (**Southern**) **C**~, a southern constellation whose stars form a cross; CELTIC, FIERY, GREEK, LATIN, MALTESE, SAINT *Andrew's, Anthony's*), TAU, *cross; cross or* PILE[4]. **4.** cross-shaped decoration in orders of knighthood (**Grand C**~, highest degree of this); decoration for personal valour (VICTORIA, GEORGE, *Distinguished Service, Military, Distinguished Flying, Cross*). **5.** intermixture of breeds; animal resulting from this; mixture or compromise *between* two things; crosswise movement of actor, football, boxer's fist, etc. (**on the** ~, diagonally); (sl.) fraud, swindle, (**on the** ~, dishonestly). **6.** Hence ~′LET *n.,* ~′WAYS *adv.,* ~′WISE *a.* & *adv.* [OE *cros* f. ON *kross* f. OIr. *cros* f. L *crux crucis*]

cross[2] (-ŏs, -aws) *v.* **1.** *v.t.* cross transverse (*cross one's legs*); ~ one's **fingers, keep** one's **fingers** ~**ed,** crook one finger over another to bring good luck; ~ **swords,** (fig.) have fight or controversy or overt rivalry (*with*); ~ **wires,** make accidental telephone connection, (fig.) have misunderstanding. **2.** make sign of cross on or over (esp. one**self,** as sign of awe, to invoke divine protection, etc.); ~ one's **heart** (in attestation of sincerity); **3.** draw line across; ~ **out** or **off,** make invalid thus; ‖~ **a cheque** (with two parallel lines, usu. adding '& Co.' or name of bank through which or person with whom cheque must be paid); ~ **fortune-teller's hand** or **palm with,** give her (coin); *cross the t's* (see T). **4.** ~ (**over**), go across (road, river, sea, etc., or abs.); *cross a* BRIDGE[1] *when one comes to it;* ~ person's **mind,** occur to him; ~ **the path of,** meet with, thwart; **would not** ~ **the road to** do, (colloq.) is completely uninterested in doing.

5. thwart (person, plans, etc.; *crossed in love*); (sl.) cheat. **6.** cause to interbreed; cross-fertilize (plants). **7.** *v.i.* meet and pass; **letters** ~ (each being dispatched to the other's sender before receipt of the other). [ME, f. prec.]

cross[3] (-ŏs, -aws) *a.* **1.** passing from side to side, transverse; (Cricket, of bat) held aslant. **2.** intersecting. **3.** contrary, opposed, (*to* a purpose etc., or abs.; **at** ~ **purposes**, misunderstanding or conflicting with each other); (colloq.) peevish, out of humour, (*be cross with* person; *as cross as two sticks*); hence ~**LY**[2] *adv.*, ~**NESS** *n.* [f. CROSS[1] & f. obs. *cross* adv.]

cross- (-ŏs, -aws) *comb. form.* (1) f. CROSS[1], objectively (*cross-bearer*), or *attrib.* = having a transverse part (*crossbow*); (2) f. CROSS[3], = crossing, transverse, (*crossbar, cross-beam, -current, -piece*), opposing (*cross--petition*); (3) f. *cross* adv. (*cross-breed, -examine, -fertilize, -fire*); (4) = ACROSS (*cross-Channel, -country, *-town*): ~**bar** (2), horizontal bar, esp. of bicycle or football goal; ||~**bench** (2) (in Parliament for members not belonging to Government or official Opposition party), whence ~**be'ncher**[1] (4) *n.*; ~**bill** (2), bird of genus *Loxia*, with mandibles crossing when bill is closed; ~**bones** (2), representation of two thigh-bones (see SKULL), ~**bow** (1), bow fixed across wooden stock, with groove for arrow etc. and mechanism for drawing and releasing string; ~**breed** (3), (*n.*) breed of animals or plants produced by crossing, individual of such breed, (*v.t.*) produce by such breeding; ~**buttock** (4), throw over hip in wrestling; ~**check** (3) *n.* & *v.*, check by alternative method of verification; ~**country** (4) *a.* & *adv.*, across fields etc., not following (main) roads; ~**cultural** (4), (of (comparison between) different cultures; ~**cut** (2), diagonal cut, path, etc. (~*cut saw*, for cutting across grain of wood); ~**dating** (3), (Archaeol.) dating by correlation with another site or level; ~**examine** (3), examine (esp. witness in lawcourt) minutely to check or extend previous testimony; hence ~**examin**ATION *n.*; ~**eyed** (2), having one or both eyes turned permanently towards nose in squint; ~**fade** (3) *v.t.*, (Radio etc.) fade in one sound as another is faded out; ~**fertilize** (3), fertilize (animal or plant) from one of a different species, (fig.) help by interchange of ideas etc.; ~**fire** (3), firing in two crossing directions, (fig.) (danger due to) attacks from several quarters; ~**grain** (2), grain of timber running across regular grain (~**grained** *a.*, having such grain, (fig.) perverse, intractable); ~**hair** (2), fine wire at focus of optical instrument for use in measurement; ~**hatch** (3) *v.t.*, shade with intersecting sets of parallel lines; ~**head** (2), bar between piston rod and connecting-rod in steam engine; ~**head**(**ing**) (2), heading printed across column before section of article in newspaper etc.; ~**keys** (2), two keys depicted in form of X; ~**legged** (3), squatting with legs crossed or sitting in chair with one leg laid across the other; ~**link**(**age**) (2), (Chem.) bond between chains of atoms in polymer etc.; ~**over** *n.* & *a.*, (having) point or place of crossing from one side to the other; ~**patch** (2), ill-tempered person; ~**piece** (2), transverse component of structure etc.; ~**ply** (2) *a.*, (of tyre) having fabric layers with cords lying crosswise; ~**pollinate** (3), pollinate (plant) from another; ~**question** (3) *v.t.*, = *cross-examine*; ~**reference** (2), (*n.*) reference from one part of book to another for further information, (*v.t.*) provide with this; ~**road**(**s**) (2), intersection of two roads (*at the* ~*roads*, (fig.) at critical turning-point in life etc.); ~**ruff** (3) *n.*, & *v.t.*, (Bridge etc.) (play by) alternate trumping of partners' leads; ~**section** (2), (drawing etc. of a) transverse SECTION, (fig.) representative sample, (Phys.) quantity expressing probability of interaction between particles, whence ~**section**AL *a.*; ~**stitch** (2), (needlework made with) stitch formed of two stitches crossing; ~**talk** (3), unwanted transfer of signals between communication channels, repartee; *~**-tie** (2), railway sleeper; ~**trees** (2), pair of horizontal timbers to support mast; ~**voting** (3), voting for a party not one's own or for more than one party; ~**wind** (2), wind blowing at right angles (or not parallel) to one's direction of travel; ~**wire** (2) = *cross-hair*.

crosse *n.* netted crook used in lacrosse. [F, f. OF *croce, croc*, hook; see CROSIER]

cro'ssing (-ŏ'-, -aw'-) *n.* In vbl senses; intersection of two roads, railways, etc. (*GRADE *crossing*; ||LEVEL *crossing*); intersection of church nave and transepts; place where street is crossed (PEDESTRIAN *crossing*; ZEBRA *crossing*); ~**over**, exchange of genes between homologous chromosomes; ~**sweeper**, (Hist.) one who sweeps this. [f. CROSS[2] + -ING[1]]

cro'ssword (-ŏ'swerd, -aw'-) *n.* puzzle in which words crossing (usu. vertically and horizontally according to a chequered pattern) have to be filled in from clues. [f. CROSS- (2) + WORD[1]]

crotch *n.* bifurcation, fork (esp. of human body or garment). [perh. = ME & OF *croc(he)* hook f. as CROOK]

cro'tchet *n.* ||(Mus.) black-headed note with stem, = two quavers, or half of minim; whimsical fancy, whence ~**EER'** *n.*, ~**Y**[2] *a.*, whimsical, peevish; hook. [ME, f. OF *crochet* dim. of *croc* hook (see prec.)]

cro'ton *n.* plant of genus *Croton* or *Codiaeum*, akin to spurge; ~ **oil**, drastic purgative obtained from one species of this. [mod. L, f. Gk *krotōn* sheep-tick, croton (from shape of seeds)]

crouch *v.i.*, & *n.* **1.** *v.i.* stand or lie with legs bent close to body, e.g. for concealment or timidly or servilely. **2.** *n.* crouching. [ME, perh. f. OF *crochir* be bent (*croc* hook f. ON *krókr*; cf. CROOK)]

croup[1] (-ōōp) *n.* rump, hindquarters, (esp. of horse). [ME f. OF *coupe* f. Rom. **croppa* f. Gmc **kruppō*, rel. to CROP[1]]

croup[2] (-ōōp) *n.* inflammation of larynx and trachea of children, marked by hard cough and difficult breathing; hence ~**Y**[2] *a.* [f. *croup* to croak (imit.)]

crou'pier (-ōō'pier, -iā) *n.* raker-in and payer-out of money at gaming-table; assistant chairman at foot of table at public dinner. [F, orig. = rider on the CROUP[1]]

crou'ton (krōō'tawn) *n.* small piece of fried or toasted bread served with soup or used as garnish. [F (*croûte* CRUST)]

crow[1] (-ō) *n.* **1.** bird of genus *Corvus* or family Corvidae, esp. ROOK[1], CARRION *crow*; **as the ~ flies**, in a straight line; ~ **to pick** or **pluck**, (fig.) fault to find; *eat ~, submit to humiliation; **white** ~, a rarity. **2.** ~(**'bar**), bar of iron (usu. with beaklike end) used as lever; ~**'berry**, black flavourless edible fruit of a small heathlike shrub, *cranberry; ~**bill**, forceps for extracting bullets etc.; ~**'foot**, name of various plants, esp. of genus *Ranunculus*, (Naut.) arrangement of small ropes for suspending awning; ~**'s-foot**, (1, usu. in *pl.*) wrinkle at outer corner of person's eye, (2) caltrop; ~**'s-nest**, barrel fixed at mast-head of sailing vessel as shelter for look-out man; ~ **steps**, corbie-steps; ~**toe**, (arch. or dial.) bluebell (or other flower, e.g. buttercup). [OE *crāwe*, = OS *krāia*, OHG *krāja* etc., f. as CROW[3]]

crow[2] (-ō) *n.* crowing of cock; joyful cry of infant. [ME, f. foll.]

crow[3] (-ō) *v.i.* (||*past* in sense 1 also **crew** *pr.* krōō). **1.** utter loud cry of cock. **2.** (of infant) utter joyful cry. **3.** exult loudly (*over*). [OE *crāwan* = OHG *krāen*, WG of imit. orig.]

crowd[1] *n.* large number of persons gathered together without orderly arrangement (**follow the** ~, conform with the majority; **would pass in a** ~, is not conspicuously defective); mass of spectators, audience; *the* multitude; (colloq.) company, set, lot; (in *sing.* or *pl.*) large number of (things); actors representing a crowd. [f. foll.]

crowd² v. **1.** v.i. & t. collect in a crowd. **2.** v.t. fill, occupy, cram, (space etc. *with*); fill (place etc.) as a crowd does (lit. or fig.); come aggressively close to; *(colloq.) approach (specified age); force (thing, person) *into* etc.; ~ **out,** exclude by crowding; ~ (**on**) **sail,** hoist large number of sails. **3.** v.i. force one's way *into, through,* etc. (confined space etc., or abs.). [OE *crūdan* press, drive, corresp. to MDu., MLG *kruden* press, push]

crown¹ n. **1.** wreath of flowers etc. worn on head, esp. as emblem of victory, (also fig., as *martyr's crown, world heavyweight crown*). **2.** monarch's head-covering of gold etc. and jewels; (C~, fig.) king or queen, regal power, supreme governing power in a monarchy. **3.** crown-shaped thing, esp. device or ornament; bird's high crest. **4.** British coin worth 25p, formerly 5s.; foreign coin, esp. = KRONE, KRONA. **5.** top part, esp. of head, tree, etc.; part of plant just above and below ground; upper part of cut gem above girdle; highest or central part of arch or arched structure (*crown of the road*); thing that completes or forms the summit; top of hat; part of tooth projecting from gum, artificial replacement for (outer part of) this (cf. coll. 3). **6.** size of paper, 504 × 384 mm. **7.** ~ **and anchor,** gambling game played with dice marked with crowns, anchors, etc., and a corresponding board; ~ **cap,** cork-lined metal cap for bottle-top; **C~ Colony,** British colony controlled by the Crown; **C~ Court,** court of criminal jurisdiction in England and Wales; **C~ Derby,** kind of china made at Derby and often marked with crown; ~ **glass** (without lead or iron, used formerly in windows, now as optical glass of low refractive index; orig. made in circular sheet); ~ **green,** bowling-green with middle higher than sides; ~ **imperial,** tall fritillary with flower-cluster at top of stalk; ~ **jewels** (forming part of sovereign's regalia; also fig.); ||C~ **Office** (transacting common--law business of Chancery); **C~ prince,** male heir to sovereign throne, (fig.) likely successor in any office; **C~ princess,** Crown prince's wife, female heir to sovereign throne; ~-**roast,** roast of rib-pieces of pork or lamb in crownlike arrangement; ~ **saw,** cylinder with toothed edge for making circular hole; ~ **of thorns,** poisonous starfish of genus *Acanthaster* [cf. John 19]; ~ **wheel** (with teeth at right angles to its plane). **8.** Hence (-)~ED² (-nd), ~LESS, *adjs.* [ME, f. AF *corune,* OF *corone* f. L *corona*]

crown² v.t. **1.** place crown on (person, head); invest (person) with regal crown or dignity (*crown him, crown him king*); ~**ed heads,** kings and queens); put head of, form chief ornament to, (lit. or fig.); put finishing touch to (**to ~ all,** often iron. = to complete one's bad luck); bring (efforts) to happy issue; (sl.) hit on the head. **2.** (Draughts). make (piece) a king. **3.** (Dent.) protect remains of (tooth) with gold etc. cap cemented on. [ME, f. AF *coruner,* OF *coroner* f. L *coronare* (*corona* crown)]

crow'ner n. (joc., arch., or dial.) = CORONER. [pop. by-form of *coroner,* assim. to *crown*]

crozier. See CROSIER.

CRT abbr. cathode-ray tube.

cru (kröö) n. (grade of wine from) French vineyard or wine-producing region. [F (*crû* grown)]

cruces. See CRUX.

cru'cial (kröö'shal) a. decisive, critical, (case, point, test, etc.); (colloq.) very important; hence ~LY² adv. [F, f. L *crux crucis* cross + -AL]

cru'cian (kröö'shan) n. yellow fish (*Carassius carassius*) allied to carp. [f. LG *karusse* etc. + -AN]

cru'ciate (-öö'sh-) a. (Zool. etc.) cross-shaped. [f. mod. L *cruciatus* f. L (as foll.; see -ATE²)]

cru'cible (-öö'-) n. melting-pot (usu. of earthenware) for metals etc.; (fig.) severe trial. [ME, f. med. L *crucibulum* night-lamp, crucible, f. L *crux crucis* cross]

cruci'ferous (-öö-) a. (Bot.) of the family Cruciferae, having flowers with four equal petals arranged crosswise. [f. LL *crucifer* (as CRUCIAL; see -FEROUS)]

cru'cifix (-öö'-) n. model of (Christ on) the Cross. [ME f. OF, f. eccl. L *crucifixus* f. L *cruci fixus* fixed to a cross; see CROSS¹, FIX¹]

crucifi'xion (-öösīfĭ'kshon) n. crucifying, esp. (C~) of Christ; picture of this. [f. eccl. L *crucifixio* (as prec.; see -ION)]

cru'ciform (-öö'-) a. cross-shaped (esp. of church with transepts). [f. L *crux crucis* cross; see -FORM]

cru'cify (-öö'-) v.t. put to death by fastening to a cross; (fig.) mortify (passions, sins, flesh); cause extreme mental pain to; torment, persecute. [ME, f. OF *crucifier* f. Rom. *crucificare (see -FY) for LL *crucifigere* (as CRUCIFIX)]

||**crŭck** n. one of paired curved timbers extending to ground in framework of house-roof. [var. of CROOK]

crŭd n. (sl.) unpleasant person; unwanted impurity etc.; illness; nonsense; hence ~'dy² a. [var. of CURD]

crude (-ööd) a. & n. **1.** a. in the natural or raw state; (fig.) ill-digested, rough, unpolished, lacking finish; (of action, statement, manners) rude, blunt; (Statistics) not adjusted or corrected (*crude death rate*); hence or cogn. ~LY² (-dlĭ) adv., ~NESS (-dn-), **cru'dITY** (-öö'-), ns. **2.** n. natural mineral oil. [ME, f. L *crudus* raw, rough]

cru'el (-öö'-) a. (~er, ~est; ||-ll-). having or showing indifference to or pleasure in another's suffering; causing pain or suffering; hence or cogn. ~LY² adv., ~TY¹ n. [ME f. OF, f. L *crudelis,* rel. to *crudus* (see prec.)]

cru'et (-öö'-) n. small stoppered glass bottle etc. for condiments at table; small vessel for wine or water in celebration of Eucharist; ~(-**stand**) (for cruets, mustard-pot, etc.). [ME, f. AF **cruet(e)* dim. of OF *crue* pot f. OS *krūka,* rel. to CROCK¹]

cruise (-ööz) v.i., & n. **1.** v.i. sail to and fro for protection of shipping etc.; sail about for pleasure, making for no particular place or calling at series of places. **2.** (Of motor vehicle or aircraft) travel at **cruising speed** (economical travelling speed, less than top speed); (of vehicle or driver) travel at random, esp. slowly when patrolling, looking for passengers, etc. **3.** n. cruising voyage; ~ **missile** (low-flying and guided continuously to target); ||~'**way,** canal assigned for recreational use. [prob. f. Du. *kruisen* (*kruis* CROSS¹)]

crui'ser (-öö'z-) n. warship of high speed and medium armament; BATTLE¹-*cruiser;* = CABIN *cruiser;* *police patrol-car; ~**weight,** (Boxing) see BOX⁵*ing-weights.* [f. Du. *kruiser* (as prec.; see -ER¹)]

***crŭ'ller** n. small cake made of dough containing eggs, butter, sugar, etc., twisted or curled and fried in fat. [prob. f. Du. *krullen* curl]

crŭmb (-m) n., & v.t. **1.** n. small fragment, esp. of bread; (fig.) small particle, atom, (*of* comfort etc.); soft inner part of bread; (sl.) objectionable person; hence ~'Y² a. (also = CRUMMY). **2.** v.t. cover or thicken with crumbs; break into crumbs. [OE *cruma,* = MDu. *crūme,* MDu., MLG *crōme,* MHG *krume,* Icel. *kr(a)umr*]

crŭ'mble v. & n. **1.** v.t. & i. break or fall into crumbs or fragments (lit. or fig.). **2.** n. crumbly or crumbled substance; dish, esp. of cooked fruit, with crumbly topping (*apple crumble*). [ME, f. OE *crymelan f. as prec.]

crŭ'mbly a. apt to fall into crumbs or fragments. [f. prec. + -Y²]

||**crŭmbs** (-mz) int. expr. dismay or surprise. [euphem. for *Christ*]

crŭ'mhorn. Var. of KRUMMHORN.

crŭ'mm|y a. (sl.) dirty, unpleasant; inferior, worthless; hence ~iNESS n. [var. of CRUMBY]

crŭmp v.i., & n. (Army sl.) (sound of, make sound of) bursting bomb or shell. [imit.]

crŭ'mpet n. soft cake of yeast mixture, cooked on griddle etc. and eaten toasted with butter; (sl.) head; (sl.) sexually desirable woman, women collectively. [17th c., of uncert. orig.]

crŭ'mple v. **1.** v.t. crush together or *up* into creased state; ruffle, wrinkle. **2.** *v.i.* become creased; ∼ (**up**), (fig.) collapse, give way. [f. obs. *crump* v. & a. (make or become) curved + -LE 3]

crŭnch v. & n. **1.** *v.t.* crush with teeth, esp. noisily, whence ∼'y² *a.*; grind under foot (gravel etc.). **2.** *v.i.* go (*up, through,* etc.) thus. **3.** *n.* crunching (noise); decisive event (**when it comes to the** ∼, **when the** ∼ **comes,** in a show-down). [earlier *cra(u)nch,* imit.; assim. to *munch*]

crŭ'pper n. strap buckled to back of saddle and looped under horse's tail; hindquarters of horse. [ME, f. AF *cropere,* OF *-iere,* f. Rom. **cropparia, -eria* (**croppa;* see CROUP¹, -ER²)]

crur'al (-oor'-) *a.* (Anat.) of the leg. [F, or f. L *cruralis* (*crus cruris* leg; see -AL)]

crusā'd|e (-ōo-) *n.,* & *v.i.* **1.** *n.* (Hist.) one of several Christian expeditions to recover Jerusalem etc. from Muslims; war instigated by Church for alleged religious ends; (fig.) vigorous movement against poverty etc. **2.** *v.i.* engage in crusade; hence ∼ER¹ *n.* [earlier *croisade* (F, f. *croix* CROSS¹), *crusado, -ada* (Sp., f. *cruz* CROSS¹); see -ADE]

cruse (-ōoz) *n.* (arch.) earthenware pot or jar; WIDOW's *cruse.* [OE *crūse* of unkn. orig.]

crŭsh¹ *v.t.* compress with violence, so as to break, bruise, etc.; reduce to powder by pressure; crumple, crease (dress etc.) by rough handling; (fig.) subdue, overwhelm, (*a crushing defeat, reply*); *crushed* STRAW-BERRY. [ME, f. AF *crussir, corussier,* OF *croissir, cruissir,* gnash (teeth), crack, f. Rom. **cruscire,* of unkn. orig.]

crŭsh² *n.* act of crushing; crowded mass (esp. of persons); (colloq.) crowded social gathering; fenced passage with one narrow end for handling cattle etc.; drink made from juice of crushed fruit; (sl.) group of persons; (sl.) (object of) infatuation (**have a** ∼ **on,** be infatuated with); ∼ **bar,** place for theatre audience to buy drinks in the intervals; ∼**-barrier,** (temporary) barrier for restraining a crowd; ∼ **hat,** opera-hat. [ME, f. prec.]

crŭst n. & *v.* **1.** *n.* hard outer part of bread; similar casing of anything, e.g. harder layer over soft snow; UPPER *crust.* **2.** hard dry scrap of bread; pastry covering pie; hard dry formation on skin, scab. **3.** (Geol.) outer rocky portion of earth; hence ∼'AL *a.* **4.** coating or deposit on surface of anything; deposit on sides of winebottle; (fig.) superficial hardness of demeanour etc.; (sl.) impudence. **5.** *v.t.* cover with or form into crust. **6.** *v.i.* become covered with crust. [ME, f. OF *crouste* f. L *crusta* rind, shell]

rŭstā'cean (-shan) *a.* & *n.* (member) of the Crustacea, a large class of arthropods with hard shells, mainly aquatic, e.g. crab, lobster, shrimp, wood-louse; hence **crŭstācēo'LOGY** *n.,* **crŭstā'ceous** (-shus) *a.* [f. mod. L *crustaceus* (*crusta;* see prec., -ACEOUS) + -AN]

rŭ'stĕd *a.* having a crust; (of wine) having deposited a crust; (fig.) antiquated, venerable, (*crusted prejudice, theory*). [f. CRUST + -ED¹,²]

rŭ'st|ÿ *a.* crustlike, hard; having a crisp crust; irritable; curt; hence ∼ILY² *adv.,* ∼INESS *n.* [ME, f. CRUST + -Y²]

rŭtch n. support (usu. with cross-piece at top) for lame person (usu. *pair of crutches*); support, prop, (lit. or fig.); fork of the human body, corresp. part of garment, (cf. CROTCH). [OE *cryc(e),* = OS *krukka,* OHG *krucka,* ON *krykkja* f. Gmc **krukjō(n)* bend]

rŭx n. (*pl.* ∼**es,** or **cruces** *pr.* krōō'sēz). difficult matter, puzzle; decisive point at issue; ∼ ansata (ănsā'ta), ankh (lit. = handled cross). [L, = cross]

ruzeir'ō (krōozār'ō) *n.* (*pl.* ∼**s**). monetary unit of Brazil. [Port., dim. of *cruz* cross]

rȳ¹ n. **1.** loud inarticulate utterance of grief, pain, fear, joy, etc. (∼ **from the heart,** *cri de cœur*); loud excited utterance of words; loud natural utterance of animal, esp. of excited hounds (**in full** ∼, hotly pursuing); creaking of bent tin etc. **2.** appeal, entreaty; proclamation of goods or business in streets;

public demand (*for*); watchword (BATTLE¹-*cry,* WAR¹- -*cry*). **3.** fit or spell of weeping (∼-**baby,** person who weeps easily or without good reason). **4. a far** ∼, (fig.) a long way. [ME f. OF *cri* (*crier* CRY²)]

crȳ² *v.* **1.** *v.t.* utter loudly, exclaim, (*that*); announce for sale (*cry* one's *wares,* STINKING *fish*). **2.** weep (tears etc., or abs.); ∼ one's **heart** or **eyes out,** weep bitterly; *cry over spilt* MILK¹; ∼ one**self to sleep,** weep till one falls asleep exhausted. **3.** *v.i.* make loud utterance (*cry out; cry to* person; **for** ∼ing **out loud** *int.,* (colloq.) expr. surprise or impatience); (of animal, esp. bird) make loud call. **4.** ∼ **down,** disparage; ∼ (**out**) **for,** demand, ask for, (lit. or fig.; ∼ **for the moon,** ask for what is unattainable); ∼ **off,** withdraw from agreement, decline to keep promise; ∼ **up,** praise, extol; *cry* QUARTER¹, QUITS. [ME, f. OF *crier* f. L *quiritare* wail]

crȳ'er. Var. of CRIER.

crȳ'ing *a.* In vbl senses; (of evil) calling for notice, flagrant. [f. CRY² + -ING²]

crȳ'ō- *comb. form.* (extreme) cold, as: ∼**bio'logy,** biology of materials below their normal operating temperature; ∼**gen,** freezing-mixture; ∼**ge'nic,** relating to very low temperatures; ∼**ge'nics,** branch of physics dealing with these and their effects; ∼**pump,** vacuum-pump using liquefied gases; ∼**stat,** apparatus for maintaining low temperature; ∼**sur'gery** (using local application of intense cold for anaesthesia or therapy). [f. Gk *kruos* frost + -o-]

crȳ'olīte n. lustrous mineral found in Greenland, consisting mainly of sodium-aluminium fluoride and used as source of aluminium. [f. as prec. + -LITE]

crȳpt n. underground cell, vault, esp. one beneath church, used as burial-place etc. [ME, f. L f. Gk *kruptē* (*kruptos* hidden)]

crȳpt|anā'lysis n. art of deciphering cryptograms by analysis; hence ∼**ā'nalȳst** n. [-IST (3)], ∼**ānalȳ'ti-**c(AL) *adjs.* [f. CRYPTO- + ANALYSIS]

crȳ'pt|ic *a.* secret, mystical; mysterious, enigmatic; obscure in meaning; (Zool., of coloration etc.) serving for concealment; hence ∼ICALLY *adv.* [f. LL f. Gk *kruptikos* (as CRYPTO-; see -IC)]

crȳ'ptō n. (*pl.* ∼**s**). (colloq.) person owing secret allegiance to a political creed etc.; (esp.) = crypto- -Communist. [as foll.]

crȳ'ptō- *comb. form.* concealed, secret; as: ∼**bra'n-chiate,** having concealed gills; ∼**-Co'mmunist,** secret sympathizer with Communism; ∼**cry'stal-line,** having crystalline structure visible only when magnified; ∼**zo'ic,** (Geol.) pre-Cambrian. [f. Gk *kruptos* hidden + -o-]

crȳ'ptogăm n. (Bot.) plant that has no stamens or pistils, and therefore no true flowers or seeds, e.g. fern, moss, fungus; hence ∼IC (-ă'm-), **crȳptō'gamous,** *adjs.* [f. F *cryptogame* f. mod. L *cryptogamae* (*plantae*) f. as CRYPTO- + Gk *gamos* marriage]

crȳ'ptogram n. thing written in cipher; so **crȳptō'-**GRAPHER, **crȳptō'GRAPHY,** *ns.,* **crȳptoGRA'PHIC** *a.* [f. CRYPTO- + -GRAM]

crȳptomēr'ia n. evergreen tree (*Cryptomeria japonica*) of the cypress type, Japanese cedar. [f. CRYPTO- + Gk *meros* part (because the seeds are enclosed by scales)]

crȳ'stal n. & *a.* **1.** *n.* clear transparent icelike mineral; ROCK¹-*crystal.* **2.** piece of this. **3.** ∼ **ball,** globe-shaped crystal used for forecasting the future by ∼-**gazing,** concentrating one's gaze on a crystal to obtain a picture by hallucination etc.; ∼ **set,** simple form of receiving apparatus in early days of broadcasting using a crystal touching a metal wire as the rectifier. **4.** ∼ (**glass**), highly transparent glass, flint glass; vessel etc. of this; glass over face of watch. **5.** (Chem. & Min.) aggregation of molecules with definite internal structure and external form of solid enclosed by symmetrically arranged plane faces, solid with regular arrangement of atoms etc. **6.** *a.* made of, like, clear as, crystal. [OE, f. OF *cristal* f. L f. Gk *krustallos* ice, crystal]

crȳ'stallīne *a.* made of, clear as, like, crystal; (Chem. & Min.) having the structure and form of a crystal; ∼ **lens**, transparent body in membranous capsule behind iris of eye; hence **crȳstalli'nɪᴛʏ** *n.* [ME, f. OF *cristallin* f. L f. Gk *krustallinos* (as prec.; see -ɪɴᴇ²)]

crȳ'stallīte *n.* small crystal of no definite mineral; individual crystal or grain in metal etc.; region of cellulose etc. with crystal-like structure. [f. ᴄʀʏsᴛᴀʟ + -ɪᴛᴇ¹]

crȳ'stallīz|e, -īs|e (-īz), *v.t. & i.* form into crystals or (fig., often ∼e out) definite or permanent shape; ∼ed **fruit** (preserved by impregnation with sugar, and coated with sugar crystals); hence ∼ᴀʙʟᴇ *a.*, ∼ᴀ'ᴛɪᴏɴ *n.* (**water of** ∼**ation**, water forming essential part of structure of some crystals). [f. ᴄʀʏsᴛᴀʟ + -ɪᴢᴇ]

crȳstallo'graphȳ *n.* science of crystal structure; hence **crȳstallo'ɢʀᴀᴘʜᴇʀ** *n.*, **crȳstalloɢʀᴀ'ᴘʜɪᴄ** *a.* [f. Gk *krustallos* crystal + -o- + -ɢʀᴀᴘʜʏ]

crȳ'stalloid *a. & n.* crystal-like; (body) with crystalline structure (cf. ᴄᴏʟʟᴏɪᴅ). [f. ᴄʀʏsᴛᴀʟ + -ᴏɪᴅ]

CS (sēē's) *n.* ∼ **gas**, irritant substance used as finely divided solid for riot-control etc. [f. B. B. Corson & R. W. Stoughton, Amer. chemists]

CS *abbr.* ||chartered surveyor; Civil Service; Court of Session.

c/s *abbr.* cycles per second.

Cs *symb.* caesium.

csȧr'das, czȧr'das, (chȧr'dahsh) *n.* (*pl.* same). Hungarian dance with slow start and quick wild finish. [f. Magyar *csárdás* (*csárda* inn)]

CSC *abbr.* Civil Service Commission; ||Conspicuous Service Cross.

||CSE *abbr.* Certificate of Secondary Education.

||CSI *abbr.* Companion (of the Order) of the Star of India.

CSIRO *abbr.* (Austral.) Commonwealth Scientific and Industrial Research Organization.

||CSM *abbr.* Company Sergeant-Major.

***CST** *abbr.* Central Standard Time.

CT *abbr.* Connecticut.

ct. *abbr.* carat; cent.

||CTC *abbr.* Cyclists' Touring Club.

ctē'noid (t-) *a. & n.* (fish with scales or teeth) like a comb. [f. Gk *kleis ktenos* comb + -ᴏɪᴅ]

ctē'nophȯre (t-) *n.* marine animal of phylum Ctenophora, like jellyfish with ciliate swimming-organs. [f. mod. L *ctenophorus* (as prec., -ᴘʜᴏʀᴇ)]

CU *abbr.* Cambridge University.

cu. *abbr.* cubic.

Cu *symb.* copper. [f. LL *cuprum*]

cŭb *n. & v.* (-**bb**-). 1. *n.* young fox, bear, lion, tiger, etc.; young man lacking good manners etc.; *apprentice; ∼ (**reporter**), (colloq.) young or inexperienced newspaper reporter; **C**∼ (**Scout**), member of junior branch of Scout Association; hence ∼ʜᴏᴏᴅ *n.* 2. *v.t.* bring forth (cubs, or abs.). 3. *v.i.* hunt fox-cubs. [16th c., of unkn. orig.]

Cūba li'bre (lē'brả) *n.* drink of lime-juice and rum. [Amer. Sp., = free Cuba]

Cū'ban *n. & a.* (native or inhabitant) of Cuba; ∼ **heel,** moderately high straight heel of shoe. [f. *Cuba* + -ᴀɴ]

cŭ'bbȳ *n.* ∼(-**hole**), snug or confined place. [f. dial. *cub* stall, pen, of LG orig.]

cūbe *n., & v.t.* 1. *n.* solid contained by six equal squares; block of anything so or similarly shaped; product of a number multiplied by its square (∼ **root,** number which produces a given number when cubed). 2. *v.t.* find cube of (number); cut (food for cooking etc.) into small cubes. [F, or f. L f. Gk *kubos*]

cŭ'bĕb *n.* pungent berry of a Javan shrub, *Piper cubeba,* crushed for use in medicated cigarettes. [ME, f. OF *cubebe, quibibe,* f. Rom. **cubeba* f. Arab. *kobāba, kubāba*]

cū'bic *a.* cube-shaped; of three dimensions (∼ **content** of solid, its volume expressed in cubic metres etc.; ∼ **metre** etc., volume of a cube whose edge is

one metre etc.); involving third and no higher power of unknown quantity or variable (*cubic equation*); (Cryst.) having three equal axes at right angles. [f. F *cubique* or f. L f. Gk *kubikos* (as ᴄᴜʙᴇ; see -ɪᴄ)]

cū'bical *a.* cube-shaped; hence ∼ʟʏ² *adv.* [f. prec. + -ᴀʟ]

cū'bicle *n.* small separate sleeping-compartment; small partitioned space for dressing, private discussion, etc. [f. L *cubiculum* (*cubare* lie down; see -ᴄᴜʟᴇ)]

cū'bifȯrm *a.* cube-shaped. [f. ᴄᴜʙᴇ + -ɪ- + -ꜰᴏʀᴍ]

cū'bism *n.* style of art (esp. painting) in which objects are so presented as to give the effect of an assemblage of geometrical figures; so **cū'bɪsᴛ** (3) *n.* [f. F *cubisme* (as ᴄᴜʙᴇ, -ɪsᴍ)]

cū'bit *n.* ancient measure of length, approximately equal to length of forearm. [ME, f. L *cubitum* elbow, cubit]

cū'bital *a.* of the forearm; of the corresponding part in animals. [ME, f. L *cubitalis* (as prec.; see -ᴀʟ)]

cū'boid *a.* & *n.* 1. *a.* cube-shaped, like a cube; ∼ **bone** (of the tarsus). 2. *n.* cuboid bone; rectangular parallelepiped; hence **cūboi'dᴀʟ** *a.* [f. mod. L *cuboides* f. Gk *kuboeidēs* (as ᴄᴜʙᴇ; see -ᴏɪᴅ)]

cŭ'cking-stōōl *n.* (Hist.) chair in which disorderly women etc. were ducked as punishment. [ME, f. obs. *cuck* defecate f. ON **kúka*]

cŭ'ckold *n.,* & *v.t.* 1. *n.* husband of adulteress; hence ∼ʀʏ (2) *n.* 2. *v.t.* make cuckold of. [ME *cukeweld, cokewold,* f. AF **cucuald,* OF *cucuault,* pejorative form of *cucu* cuckoo]

cu'ckōō (kōō'-) *n. & pred. a.* 1. *n.* migratory bird with characteristic cry, depositing its eggs in nests of small birds (∼ **in the nest,** unwanted intruder); bird of family Cuculidae, with or without this habit; simpleton. 2. *n.* ∼ **clock** (striking with sound like cuckoo's note); ∼ **flower,** (1) meadow plant with pale lilac spring flower, lady-smock, (2) ragged robin; ∼**-pint,** wild arum; ∼**-spit,** froth exuded by larvae of insects of family Cercopidae as a protection. 3. *a.* (sl.) crazy. [ME, f. OF *cucu,* imit.]

cū'cŭmber *n.* (creeping plant with) long green fleshy fruit eaten in thin slices in salad, or as pickle; **cool as a** ∼, quite cool, self-possessed; *∼**-tree,** magnolia with fruit like small cucumber. [ME, f. OF *co(u)combre* f. L *cucumer*]

cūcūr'bit *n.* = ɢᴏᴜʀᴅ 1; hence ∼ᴀ'ᴄᴇᴏᴜs *a.* [f. L *cucurbita*]

cŭd *n.* food that ruminating animal brings back from its stomach into mouth and chews at leisure; **chew the** ∼, (fig.) reflect, ruminate. [OE *cwidu, cudu* what is chewed, corresp. to OHG *kuti, quiti* glue]

cŭ'dbear (-bār) *n.* purple or violet dyeing-powder prepared from various lichens. [var. of *Cuthber* Gordon, 18th-c. Sc. chemist, who patented it]

cŭ'ddl|e *v. & n.* 1. *v.t.* hug, embrace, fondle. 2. *v.i.* close and snug; nestle together. 3. *n.* hug, embrace. 4. Hence ∼ᴇsᴏᴍᴇ¹ (-dels-), ∼ʏ², *adjs.,* given to cuddling, tempting to cuddle. [16th c., perh. f. dial. *couth* snug -ʟᴇ 3]

cŭ'ddȳ *n.* (Sc.) donkey; stupid person. [perh. pet-form of man's Christian name *Cuthbert*]

cŭ'dgel *n.,* & *v.t.* (||-ll-). *n.* short thick stick used as weapon; **take up the** ∼**s (for),** (fig.) defend vigorously. 2. *v.t.* beat with cudgel; ∼ **one's brains,** think hard about a problem. [OE *cycgel,* of unkn. orig.]

cŭ'dweed *n.* composite plant of genus *Gnaphalium,* with chaffy scales round flower-heads, given to cattle that have lost their cud. [f. ᴄᴜᴅ + ᴡᴇᴇᴅ]

cūe¹ *n., & v.t.* (∼'**ing** *pr.* kū'ĭ-). 1. *n.* last words of speech in play, serving as signal to another actor to enter or speak; similar guide to other performer, e.g. singer or player; **on** ∼, at the correct moment. 2. stimulus to perception etc.; signal for action; hint how to behave (**take one's** ∼ **from,** follow the example or advice of); ∼**-bid,** (Bridge) artificial bid to show particular card in bidder's hand. 3. *v.t.* label so as to show proper choice; give cue to; ∼ **in,** insert cue for, (fig.) give information to. [16th c., of unkn. orig.]

cūe² n. & v. 1. n. long straight tapering leather-tipped rod for striking ball in billiards etc.; ∿-ball (that is to be struck with cue); hence ∿ist (3) (kū′ĭ-) n. 2. v.i. & t. use cue (on). [var. of QUEUE]

cuě′sta (kwě′-) n. (Geog.) gentle slope, esp. ending in steep drop. [Sp., = slope, f. L costa; see COAST¹]

cŭff¹ n. end part of sleeve (off the ∿, extempore, without preparation; separate band of linen worn round wrist; *trouser turn-up; (in pl., colloq.) handcuffs; ∿-link, device of two joined buttons etc. to fasten sides of cuff together; hence (-)∿ED² (-ft) a. [ME, of unkn. orig.]

cŭff² v.t., & n. 1. v.t. strike with open hand. 2. n. such blow. [16th c., perh. imit.]

Cū′fic, Kū′fic, a. & n. (of) early angular form of the Arabic alphabet found chiefly in decorative inscriptions. [f. Čufa, city S. of Baghdad + -IC]

cui bono? (kwē bō′nō) n. question of who stood to gain (and therefore was likely to be responsible). [L, = to whom (is it) a benefit?]

cuirǎ′ss (kwĭ-) n. body armour, breastplate and back-plate fastened together; device for artificial respiration. [ME, f. OF cuirace, *coirace f. Rom. *coriacea f. LL coriaceus (corium leather; see -ACEOUS)]

cuirassier′ (kwĭ-) n. cavalry soldier wearing cuirass. [F (as prec.; see -IER)]

culsh. See CUISSE.

cuisi′ne (kwĭzē′n) n. (country's or establishment's style of) cooking. [F, f. L coquina (coquere cook)]

cuisse (kwĭs), cuish (kwĭ-), n. (Hist., usu. in pl.) thigh armour. [ME, f. OF cuisseaux pl. of cuissel f. LL coxale (coxa hip)]

cŭ′l-de-sǎc n. (pl. culs- pr. same). street, passage, etc., closed at one end; (Anat.) tube etc. open at one end only. [F, = sack-bottom]

-cūle, -cle, suf. forming (orig. dim.) ns. (molecule, particle, article). [f. F -cule or f. L. -culus -cula -culum]

cu′linarў a. pertaining to a kitchen or cooking; fit for cooking (culinary plants). [f. L culinarius (culina kitchen; see -ARY¹)]

cŭll v.t., & n. 1. v.t. pick (flower etc.); select; select from flock etc. and kill (surplus animals etc.). 2. n. act of culling; culled animal. [ME, f. OF coillier etc., f. Rom. *colgere f. L. colligere COLLECT²]

cŭ′llět n. refuse glass added to new material in glass-making; broken glass. [var. of COLLET]

cŭ′llў n. (sl.) mate, pal. [17th c.; orig. unkn.]

cŭlm¹ n. coal-dust (esp. of anthracite); (Geol.) strata under coal measures in Europe. [ME, prob. rel. to COAL]

cŭlm² n. (Bot.) stem of plant (esp. of grasses; so ∿i′FEROUS a. [f. L culmus stalk]

cŭ′lminant a. at or forming the top; (Astron.) on the meridian. [f. as foll. + -ANT]

cŭ′lmin|āte v.i. reach its highest point (in; lit. or fig.); (Astron.) be on the meridian; hence ∿A′TION n [f. LL culminare (culmen summit) + -ATE³]

cŭlŏ′tte n. (usu. in pl., pr. same). women's trousers cut to resemble skirt. [F, = knee-breeches]

cŭ′lpab|le a. blameworthy (culpable negligence; hold him culpable); hence cŭlpABI′LITY, ∿leNESS (-beln-), ns., ∿LY² adv. [ME f. OF coupable f. L culpabilis (culpare f. culpa blame; see -ABLE)]

cŭ′lprit n. person accused of or guilty of offence. [17th c.; orig. in formula Culprit, how will you be tried?, said by Clerk of Crown to prisoner pleading Not Guilty; perh. abbr. of AF Culpable: prest d'averrer etc. (You are) guilty: (I am) ready to prove etc.]

cŭlt n. system of religious worship esp. as expressed in ceremonies; devotion or homage to person or thing (esp. derog. of transient fad); hence ∿IC a., ∿′ISM (3), ∿′IST (2), ns. [f. F culte or f. L cultus worship (colere cult-inhabit, till, worship)]

cŭ′ltivar n. (Bot.) variety produced by cultivation. [f. foll. + VARIETY]

cŭ′ltĭv|āte v.t. prepare and use (soil) for crops; produce (crops) by tillage; culture (bacteria etc.); prepare (ground) with cultivator; (fig., esp. in p.p.) improve, develop, (person, mind, manners); pay attention to, cherish, (faculty, art, person, his acquaintance); so ∿A′TION n. [f. med. L cultivare f. cultiva (terra) arable (land); see CULT, -IVE, -ATE³]

cŭ′ltĭvātor n. one who cultivates; implement or machine for breaking up ground and uprooting weeds. [f. prec. + -OR]

cŭ′lture n., & v.t. 1. n. tillage of the soil; rearing, production, (of bees, oysters, fish, silk, bacteria); quantity of bacteria thus produced. 2. improvement by (mental or physical) training; intellectual development; particular form, stage, or type of intellectual development or civilization (the two ∿s, literature and science), group of products or achievements resulting from this; ∿ vulture, (joc.) person eager to acquire culture. 3. Hence cŭ′lturAL (-cher-) a., (esp.) relating to culture of mind or manners. 4. v.t. maintain (bacteria etc.) in conditions suitable for growth; (fig.) cultivate, esp. in p.p. pr. -cherd; ∿d pearl (formed by oyster after insertion of suitable foreign body). [ME f. F, or f. L cultura (as CULT; see -URE); v. f. obs. F culturer or f. med. L culturare]

cŭ′ltus n. system of religious worship; cult. [L; see CULT]

cŭ′lverin n. (Hist.) long cannon; small firearm. [ME, f. OF coulevrine (couleuvre snake f. Rom. *colobra f L. colubra; see -INE¹)]

cŭ′lvert n. channel or conduit carrying water across under road, canal, etc.; channel for electric cable. [18th c., of unkn. orig.]

cŭm prep. with; ∿ dividend, including dividend about to be paid; (indicating combined nature or function) laboratory-cum-workshop, religious-cum-philosophical; ||(in names of combined parishes) Chorlton-cum-Hardy. [L]

Cumb. abbr. Cumberland (former county in England).

cŭ′mber v.t., & n. (literary) 1. v.t. hamper, hinder; burden (with). 2. n. hindrance, obstruction, burden. [ME, prob. f. ENCUMBER]

cŭ′mbersome a. inconvenient in size or weight or shape; hence ∿LY² (-mlī) adv., ∿NESS (-mn-) n. [ME, f. prec. + -SOME¹.]

Cŭ′mbrian a. & n. (native) of Cumberland or of the ancient British kingdom or modern county of Cumbria [f. med. L Cumbria f. W Cymry Welshmen + -AN]

cŭ′mbrous a. = CUMBERSOME; hence ∿LY² adv., ∿NESS n. [f. CUMBER + -OUS]

cum grano salis (kŭm grahnō sā′lĭs) adv. = with a grain of SALT. [L]

cŭ′min, cŭ′mmin, n. umbelliferous plant (Cuminum cyminum) like fennel, with aromatic seeds. [ME, f. OF cumin, comin f. L f. Gk kuminon, prob. of Semitic orig.]

cŭ′mmerbŭnd n. waist sash. [f. Hind. & Pers. kamar-band loin-band]

cŭ′mmin. See CUMIN.

cŭ′mquat, kŭ′mquat, (-ŏt) n. plum-sized orange-like fruit with sweet rind and acid pulp, used in preserves. [Cantonese dial. form of Chin. jinju golden orange]

cŭ′mulate¹ a. heaped up, massed. [as foll.; see -ATE²]

cŭ′mul|āte² v.t. & i. accumulate; combine (catalogue entries etc.); so ∿A′TION n. [f. L cumulare (cumulus heap) + -ATE³]

cŭ′mulative a. tending to accumulate; increasing in force etc. by successive additions (cumulative evidence, poison); formed by successive additions; (of shares) entitling holders to arrears of interest before any other distribution is made; ∿ voting, system in which each voter has as many votes as there are representatives, and may give all to one candidate; hence ∿LY² (-vlī) adv., ∿NESS (-vn-) n. [f. as prec. + -IVE]

cu'mul|us *n.* (*pl.* ~**i** *pr.* -ī). heap; set of rounded masses of cloud heaped on each other and having horizontal base; hence ~**o-** *comb. form,* ~**ous** *a.* [L]

cu'neate *a.* wedge-shaped. [f. L *cuneus* wedge + -ATE²]

cu'neifōrm (-nīif-, -nif-) *a.* & *n.* **1.** *a.* wedge-shaped. **2.** *n.* writing in cuneiform impressed strokes usu. in clay in ancient inscriptions of Assyria, Persia, etc. [f. F *cunéiforme* or mod. L *cuneiformis* f. L *cuneus* wedge; see -FORM]

cu'njèvoi *n.* (Austral.) green arum; sea-squirt. [Aboriginal]

cŭnnili'ngus (-ngg-), **-li'nctus,** *n.* stimulation of vulva or clitoris by licking. [L (*cunnus* vulva, *lingere* lick)]

cu'nning¹ *n.* selfish cleverness or insight; skill in deceit or evasion; (arch.) ability, dexterity. [ME, perh. f. ON *kunnandi* knowledge (*kunna* know; cf. CAN²)]

cu'nning² *a.* (~**er,** ~**est**). artful, crafty; (arch.) skilful, ingenious; *attractively quaint, small, etc.; hence ~**LY²** *adv.* [ME, f. ON *kunnandi* knowing (as prec.)]

cŭnt *n.* (vulg.) female genitals; (derog.) unpleasant or stupid person. [ME, = ON *kunta,* MLG, MDu. *kunte* f. Gmc *kuntōn*]

cŭp¹ *n.* **1.** drinking-vessel, with or without handle and stem (*teacup, coffee-cup*); ornamental vessel as prize for race etc. (**C**~ **Final,** (Footb. etc.) final match in competition for cup; *cup*-TIE²); small rounded open container; part of brassière to contain or support one breast. **2.** cupful (~ **of tea,** (colloq., fig.) person or thing of specified kind; one's ~ **of tea,** (colloq.) what interests or suits one; wine, cider, etc., with various flavourings, usu. chilled; chalice used, wine taken, at Eucharist; fate, experience, (*a bitter cup; his* ~ **was full,** his happiness or misery was complete). **3.** **between** ~ **and lip,** just before attainment; **in** one's ~**s,** while (getting) drunk. **4.** rounded cavity, esp. calyx of flower, socket of bone, etc. **5.** ~'**bearer,** one who serves wine, esp. officer of royal or noble household; ~-**cake** (baked in small open container or from ingredients measured in cupfuls); ~-**moss,** lichen with cup-shaped processes arising from thallus. **6.** Hence ~'FUL (2) *n.,* (*esp.) half-pint or 8-ounce measure in cookery. [OE *cuppe* f. med. L *cuppa* cup, prob. different. f. L *cupa* tub]

cŭp² *v.t.* (-**pp-**). take or hold as in a cup; make cup-shaped; (Hist.) bleed (person) by means of a ~'**ping-glass,** in which partial vacuum is formed by heating. [ME, f. prec.]

CUP *abbr.* Cambridge University Press.

cŭ'pboard (kŭ'berd) *n.* (usu. shelved) recess or piece of furniture, with door, for crockery, provisions, etc.; ~ **love** (simulated for sake of what one can get by it); SKELETON *in the cupboard.* [ME, f. CUP¹ + BOARD¹]

cū'pel *n.,* & *v.t.* (||-ll-). **1.** *n.* small flat circular vessel used in assaying gold or silver in the presence of lead. **2.** *v.t.* assay or refine in cupel; hence ~**la'tion** *n.* [f. F *coupelle* f. LL *cupella* dim. of *cupa;* see CUP¹]

Cū'pid *n.* Roman god of love; representation of him as beautiful naked winged boy with bow and arrows; ~'**s bow,** (upper edge of) upper lip etc., shaped like double-curved bow carried by Cupid. [ME, f. L *Cupido* (*cupere* desire)]

cūpi'dity *n.* greed for gain. [ME, f. OF *cupidité* or f. L *cupiditas* (*cupidus* desirous; see -ITY)]

cū'pola *n.* small rounded dome forming or adorning roof; ceiling of dome; ~(-**furnace**), furnace for melting metals; revolving dome protecting mounted guns on warship or in fort. [It., f. LL *cupula* dim. of *cupa* cask]

||**cŭ'ppa,** ||**cŭ'pper,** *n.* (colloq.) cup of; cup of tea. [corrupt.]

cūprammō'nium *n.* complex ion of copper and ammonia, solutions of which dissolve cellulose. [f. LL *cuprum* copper + AMMONIUM]

cū'prèous *a.* of or like copper. [f. LL *cupreus* (*cuprum* copper) + -OUS]

cū'pric *a.* of copper; so **cūpri'**FEROUS, **cū'prous,** *adjs.* [f. LL *cuprum* + -IC 1]

cū'prō- *comb. form.* copper, as: ~-**ni'ckel,** alloy of copper and nickel, esp. in proportions 3:1 as used in 'silver' coins. [f. as prec. + -O-]

cū'pūle *n.* (Bot. & Zool.) cup-shaped organ, receptacle, etc. [f. LL *cupula* (see CUPOLA)]

cŭr *n.* worthless, low-bred, or snappish dog; surly, ill-bred, or cowardly fellow. [ME, prob. orig. in *cur-dog,* perh. f. ON *kurr* grumbling]

cūr'able. See CURE².

cūr'açao, cūr'açoa, (-sō) *n.* (*pl.* ~**s**). liqueur of spirits flavoured with peel of bitter oranges. [f. F *Curaçao,* name of Caribbean island producing these oranges]

cūr'acy *n.* curate's office; (Hist.) benefice of PERPETUAL curate. [f. CURATE; see -ACY]

cūrā'r̤e *n.* resinous bitter substance from S. Amer. plants of genus *Strychnos,* paralysing the motor nerves, used by Indians to poison arrows. [f. Carib]

cūr'ar|ine (-ēn) *n.* alkaloid derived from curare and used to relax muscles; hence ~**IZE** (5) *v.t.* [f. prec. + -INE⁵]

cūr'assow (-ō) *n.* turkey-like bird of Central and S. America, of family Cracidae. [Anglicized f. *Curaçao;* see CURAÇAO]

cūr'ate *n.* assistant to parish priest; (arch.) ecclesiastical pastor; ~-**in-char'ge,** clergyman appointed to take charge of parish during incapacity or suspension of incumbent; ~'**s egg,** thing partly good and partly bad; PERPETUAL *curate.* [ME, f. med. L *curatus* f. L *cura* CURE¹]

cūr'ative *a.* & *n.* (thing) tending to cure (esp. disease). [F *curatif -ive,* f. med. L *curativus* f. L *curare* CURE²; see -ATIVE]

cūrā'tor *n.* person in charge, manager; keeper or custodian of museum; ||member of board managing property or having general superintendence in University; (Sc. Law) guardian of minor etc.; hence **cūrā'tor**IAL *a.,* ~**SHIP** *n.* [ME, f. AF *curatour* (OF *-eur*) or f. L *curator* (as prec.; see -OR)]

cŭrb *n.,* & *v.t.* **1.** *n.* chain or strap passing under lower jaw of horse, used as a check; (fig.) check, restraint; hard swelling on back of horse's leg. **2.** frame round top of well; timber or iron plate round edge of circular structure; fender round hearth; = KERB; ~ **roof** (of which each face has two slopes, the lower one steeper). **3.** *v.t.* put curb on (horse); (fig.) restrain. [ME, f. OF *courber* f. L *curvare* bend, CURVE¹]

cūr'cūma *n.* turmeric, substance used in curry-powder, as test for alkalis (*curcuma paper*), etc.; tuberous plant of genus *Curcuma,* yielding this and other commercial substances. [med. or mod. L, f. Arab. *kurkum* saffron, f. Skr. *kuṅkuma*ᵐ]

cŭrd *n.* coagulated substance formed (naturally or artificially) by action of acids on milk, and made into cheese or eaten as food (often in *pl.;* ~**s and whey,** milk thus treated); fatty substance found between flakes of boiled salmon flesh; edible head of cauliflower etc.; LEMON¹ *curd;* ~**-soap** (white, of tallow and soda); hence ~'Y² *a.* [ME *crud(de), crod(de),* of unkn. orig.]

cūr'dle *v.t.* & *i.* congeal, form into curd; (fig.) ~ **the blood** (with horror). [frequent. f. *curd* v. (f. prec.) + -LE 3]

cūre¹ *n.* thing that cures (*no cure for this disease*); restoration to health; course of medical or other treatment (REST²-*cure*), success with this; spiritual charge (*cure of souls*); (degree of) vulcanization of rubber or curing of plastic. [ME f. OF, f. L *cura* care]

cūre² *v.* **1.** *v.t.* restore to health, relieve (person *of* disease), (lit. or fig.); ~-**all,** panacea); eliminate (an evil); preserve (meat, fruit, tobacco) by salting, drying, etc.; harden (concrete or plastic); vulcanize (rubber); hence **cūr'**ABLE *a.* **2.** *v.i.* effect a cure; undergo process of curing. [ME, f. OF *curer* f. L *curare* take care of (*cura* care)]

curé (kūr'ā) *n.* parish priest in France etc. [F, f. med. L *curatus;* see CURATE]

curettage (-ĕ'tij, -ah'zh) *n.* use of or operation with curette. [F (as foll.; see -AGE)]

curẽ'tte *n.* & *v.* **1.** *n.* surgeon's small scraping-instrument. **2.** *v.t.* & *i.* clean or scrape with curette. [F, f. *curer* cleanse (CURE²)]

cur'few *n.* **1.** (Hist.) medieval regulation for extinction of fires at fixed hour in evening; hour for this; bell announcing it; ringing of bell at fixed evening hour. **2.** signal or time after which persons must remain indoors until next day. [ME, f. AF *coeverfu*, OF *cuevrefeu*, f. st. of *couvrir* COVER¹ + *feu* fire]

Cur'i|a *n.* Papal court, government departments of Vatican; hence ∿AL *a.* [L, orig. division of ancient Roman tribe, senate-house at Rome, feudal court of justice]

-ur'ie *n.* unit of radioactivity, corresp. to 3.7×10^{10} disintegrations per second; quantity of radioactive substance having this activity. [f. P. *Curie*, Fr. scientist d. 1906]

ur'io *n.* (*pl.* ∿s). rare or unusual object or person. [19th-c. abbr. of CURIOSITY]

urio'sa *n. pl.* curiosities; erotic or pornographic books. [neut. pl. of L *curiosus*; see CURIOUS]

urio'sity *n.* desire to know; inquisitiveness; strangeness; strange or rare object. [ME, f. OF *curiouseté* f. L *curiositas -tatis* (as foll.; see -ITY)]

ur'ious *a.* **1.** eager to learn; inquisitive. **2.** strange, surprising, odd; (euphem. of books etc.) erotic, pornographic. **3.** Hence ∿LY² *adv.*, ∿NESS *n.* [ME, f. OF *curios* f. L *curiosus* careful (*cura* care; see -IOUS)]

ur'ium *n.* (Chem.) artificially made transuranic radioactive metallic element. [f. M. *Curie* d. 1934 and P. *Curie* d. 1906, Fr. scientists + -IUM]

ûrl¹ *n.* **1.** coiled lock of hair; ∿-paper (used for twisting hair into curls). **2.** anything spiral or curved inwards. **3.** act of curling (∿ of the lip, expressing scorn); state of being curled (*keep the hair in curl*; out of ∿, (fig.) lacking energy; disease of plants in which leaves are curled up. [f. foll.]

ûrl² *v.* **1.** *v.t.* & *i.* bend or coil (*up*) into spiral shape; (cause to) form curls; ∿ person's hair or make his hair ∿, (fig.) horrify him. **2.** *v.i.* (of smoke etc.) move in spiral form; play at curling; ∿ up, (fig.) writhe with horror, shame, etc., (colloq.) lie or sit with knees drawn up, (sl.) collapse. [ME; earliest form *crolled, crulled*, f. obs. adj. *crolle, crulle* curly, f. MDu. *krul*]

ur'ler *n.* In vbl senses; pin, clip, etc., for curling the hair. [f. prec. + -ER¹]

ûr'lew *n.* wading bird of genus *Numenius*, with long slender curved bill. [ME, f. OF *courlieu, courlis* orig. imit., but assim. to OF *courliu* courier (*courre* run, *lieu* place)]

ûr'licue *n.* decorative curl or twist. [f. CURLY + CUE² (= pigtail) or Q]

ûr'ling *n.* In vbl senses; game played on ice, esp. in Scotland and elsewhere with large flat round stones; ∿-iron, ∿-pins, ∿-tongs, (for use in curling the hair). [f. CURL² + -ING¹]

ûr'l|y *a.* having, or arranged in, curls; *curly* KALE; hence ∿iNESS *n.* [f. CURL¹ + -Y²]

ûrmu'dgeon (-ŭ'jon) *n.* churlish or miserly fellow; hence ∿LY¹ *a.* [16th c.; orig. unkn.]

u'rrach, cu'rragh, (-ra) *n.* (Ir.) coracle. [Ir.; cf. CORACLE]

u'rrajông. Var. of KURRAJONG.

u'rrant *n.* dried fruit of seedless variety of grape grown in the Levant, much used in cookery; (fruit of) plant of genus *Ribes* (**red, white, black,** ∿; **flower-ing** ∿, N. Amer. species grown for ornament); *currant* TOMATO. [ME, *raysons of coraunce* f. AF, = grapes of Corinth (orig. source)]

u'rrawông *n.* (Austral.) small crowlike bird of genus *Strepera*, with resonant call. [Aboriginal]

u'rrency *n.* time during which a thing is current; (of money) circulation; money in actual use in a country (**HARD** currency, **SOFT** currency); other commodity used

as medium of exchange; prevalence (of words, ideas, reports). [f. foll.; see -ENCY]

cu'rrent¹ *a.* (Of money, opinion, rumour, word) in general circulation or use (*current* ACCOUNT²; **pass** ∿, be generally accepted as true or genuine); (of time) now passing (*current week, month*); belonging to the current time (*current events; the current issue of this journal*); hence ∿LY² *adv.*, (esp.) at the present time. [ME, f. OF *corant*, pres. part. of *courre* f. L *currere* run; see -ENT]

cu'rrent² *n.* running stream; water, air, etc., moving in given direction; course, tendency, (of events, opinions, etc.); movement of electrically charged particles, quantity representing intensity of such movement. [ME, f. OF *corant* n. (as prec.)]

cu'rricle *n.* (Hist.) light open two-wheeled carriage (usu. with two horses abreast). [f. L *curriculum* (see foll.)]

curri'cul|um *n.* (*pl.* ∿a). course (of study); ∿um **vitae** (-vē'tī), brief account of one's previous career; hence ∿AR¹ *a.* [L, = course, race-chariot (*currere* run); *vitae* of life]

cu'rrier *n.* one who dresses and colours tanned leather. [ME f. OF *corier*, f. L *coriarius* (*corium* leather; see -ARY¹, -ER²)]

cur'rish *a.* like a cur; snappish; ignoble; hence ∿LY² *adv.*, ∿NESS *n.* [f. CUR + -ISH¹]

cu'rry¹ *n.*, & *v.t.* **1.** *n.* dish of meat, fish, eggs, etc., cooked with crushed spices and turmeric; ∿-powder etc., preparation of spices etc. for making curry. **2.** *v.t.* prepare or flavour with curry-powder. [f. Tamil *kari* sauce]

cu'rry² *v.t.* clean and tidy (horse etc.) with ∿-comb (held in hand, with several serrated projections); treat (tanned leather) to improve its properties; thrash; ∿ **favour** [orig. *favel* f. OF *fauvel* chestnut horse], ingratiate oneself (*with* person) by flattery etc. [ME, f. OF *correier* f. Rom. **conredare* f. Gmc **garǣdhjan* (as Y-, READY)]

curse¹ *n.* utterance of deity or of person invoking deity, consigning person or thing to destruction; divine vengeance, etc. (*curses come home to* ROOST¹; **under a** ∿, feeling or liable to its effects); sentence of excommunication; profane oath, imprecation; accursed object; evil inflicted in response to a curse, great evil, bane; **the** ∿, (colloq.) menstruation. [OE *curs*, of unkn. orig.]

curse² *v.* **1.** *v.t.* utter curse against; (as oath) ∿ **it, you,** (= *may God curse*); excommunicate; (esp. in *pass.*) afflict *with* ∿. *v.i.* utter curses. [OE *cursian* (as prec.)]

cur'sed, (arch.) **curst,** *a.* In vbl senses; damnable, abominable; hence ∿LY² *adv.*, ∿NESS *n.* [ME, p.p. of prec.]

cur'sive *a.* & *n.* (writing) done with joined characters, opp. *block* or *uncial*. [f. med. L (*scriptura*) *cursiva* f. L *currere* curs- run; see -IVE]

cur'sor *n.* transparent slide engraved with hair-line and forming part of slide-rule. [L, = runner (as prec.; see -OR)]

cursôr'ial *a.* having limbs adapted for running (*cursorial birds* etc.). [f. as prec. + -IAL]

cur'sor|y *a.* hasty, hurried, (*cursory reader, inspection*); hence ∿iLY² *adv.*, ∿iNESS *n.* [f. L *cursorius* of a runner (as CURSOR; see -ORY)]

curt *a.* discourteously brief; terse, concise; hence ∿'LY² *adv.*, ∿'NESS *n.* [f. L *curtus* cut short, abridged]

curtail' *v.t.* cut short (lit. or fig.); deprive *of*; hence ∿MENT *n.* [f. obs. *curtal* horse with docked tail f. F *courtault* (*court* short f. L *curtus*); assim. to *tail*]

cur'tain (-tan) *n.*, & *v.t.* **1.** *n.* suspended cloth used as screen, usu. movable sideways or upwards; = IRON¹ *curtain* or similar barrier to passage of information etc.; screen separating stage of theatre from auditorium, raised at start of action and lowered at end (SAFETY *curtain*); rise of curtain at start of play etc.; fall of curtain at end of scene; = *curtain-call*; (in *pl.*, sl.) the end. **2.** ∿(-wall), plain wall of fortified place, connecting two towers etc., piece of plain wall not supporting a roof; partition of cover. **3.** ∼-**call**, audience's summons to actor(s) to take bow after fall of curtain; ∼-**fire**, (Mil.) barrage; ∼ **lecture**, wife's private reproof to husband, orig. behind bed-curtains; ∼-**raiser**, short opening theatre-piece, (fig.) preliminary event. **4.** *v.t.* furnish, cover, shut *off*, with curtain(s). [ME f. OF *cortine*, f. LL *cortina* transl. Gk *aulaia* (*aulē* court)]

cŭrta'na (-ā'-, -ah'-) *n.* unpointed sword borne before English sovereign at Coronation, as emblem of mercy. [ME, f. AL *curtana* (*spatha* sword), f. AF *curtain*, OF *cortain* name of Roland's similar sword (*cort* short f. as CURT)]

cŭr'tilage *n.* area attached to dwelling-house as part of its enclosure. [ME f. AF; OF *co*(*u*)*rtillage* (*co*(*u*)*rtil* small court f. *cort* COURT¹; see -AGE)]

cŭr'tsy̆, cŭr'tsey, *n.,* & *v.i.* **1.** *n.* woman's or girl's salutation made by bending knees and lowering body (*make* or *drop a curtsy*). **2.** *v.i.* make curtsy (*to* person). [var. of COURTESY]

cŭr'ule (-ōōl) *a.* (Rom. Ant.) ∼ **chair,** one shaped like camp-stool, inlaid with ivory; ∼ **magistrate,** one entitled to this. [f. L *curulis* f. *currus* chariot (*currere* run)]

cûrvă'ceous (-shus) *a.* (colloq.) having many curves (esp. of shapely female figure). [f. CURVE² + -ACEOUS]

cûr'vature *n.* curving; curved form; (Geom.) deviation of curve from straight line, or of curved surface from plane, quantity expressing this. [OF, f. L *curvatura* (as foll.; see -URE)]

cûrve¹ *v.t.* & *i.* bend or shape so as to form a curve. [f. L *curvare* (as foll.)]

cûrv|e² *n.* line of which no part is straight; surface of which no part is plane; curved form or thing; line showing diagrammatically a continuous variation of quantity, force, etc., graph; (Baseball) ball caused to deviate by pitcher's spin; hence ∼'y² *a.* [orig. *curve line; curve* a. f. L *curvus* bent]

cûrve't *n.,* & *v.i.* (-tt- or -t-). **1.** *n.* horse's leap with forelegs raised together and hind legs raised with spring before forelegs reach ground. **2.** *v.i.* (Of horse or rider) make curvet. [f. It. *corvetta* dim. of *corva* curve, f. as prec.]

cûr'vĭ- *comb. form.* curved, as: ∼**cau'date,** ∼**co'state,** ∼**de'ntate,** ∼**ro'stral,** with curved tail, ribs, teeth, beak; ∼**fo'liate,** with leaves bent back; ∼**form,** of curved shape. [f. L *curvus* curved + -I-]

cûrvĭli'near *a.* contained by or consisting of curved line(s); hence ∼**LY²** *adv.* [f. prec. after *rectilinear*]

cŭ'scus¹ *n.* aromatic fibrous root of Indian grass of genus *Vetiveria,* used for fans etc. [f. Pers. *ḵaṣḵaṣ* poppy]

cŭ'scus² *n.* spotted phalanger of New Guinea and N. Australia. [f. native name]

cŭ'sĕc *n.* (flow of) one cubic foot (esp. of water) per second. [abbr.]

cush (kŏosh) *n.* (colloq.) cushion (esp. Bill.). [abbr.]

cŭ'shat *n.* (Sc.) wood-pigeon, ring-dove. [OE *cúscute* etc., of unkn. orig.]

cu'sh-cush (kŏo'shkŏosh) *n.* S. Amer. species of yam (*Dioscorea trifida*). [native name]

cu'shion¹ (kŏo'shon) *n.* **1.** mass of soft or elastic material, esp. stuffed into bag of cloth, silk, etc., for sitting, kneeling, reclining, on; PIN¹*cushion.* **2.** means of protection against shock; elastic lining of sides of billiard table, from which ball rebounds; body of air supporting hovercraft etc.; steam left in cylinders as buffer to piston; fleshy part of buttock (of pig etc.); frog of horse's hoof. **3.** Hence ∼**y²** *a.* [ME, f. OF *co*(*i*)*ssin, cu*(*i*)*ssin,* f. Gallo-Rom. f. L *culcita* mattress, cushion]

cu'shion² (kŏo'shon) *v.t.* furnish or protect with cushions (lit. or fig.); mitigate effects of (as) with cushion (*cushion the blow*); quietly suppress; (Bill.) place, leave, rebound, (ball) against cushion. [f. prec.]

Cŭshi'tic *a.* & *n.* (of) group of E. Afr. languages of Hamitic type. [f. *Cush* ancient country in Nile valley + -ITE¹ (1) + -IC]

cu'shy̆ (kŏo'-) *a.* (colloq.) (Of a post, task, etc.) easy, pleasant, comfortable. [Anglo-Ind., f. Hind. *ḵhūsh* pleasant]

cŭsp *n.* apex, peak; horn of crescent moon etc.; (Geom.) point at which two parts of a curve meet from same direction with common tangent and terminate; (Archit.) projecting point between small arcs in Gothic tracery; (Bot.) pointed end, esp. of leaf (Astrol.) initial point of house; hence ∼**ED²** (-pt) *a.* [f. L *cuspis -idis* point, apex]

cŭ'spāte *a.* cusp-shaped. [f. prec. + -ATE²]

cŭ'spĭd|al *a.* of (the nature of) a cusp; so ∼**ATE²** *a.* [f. as CUSP + -AL]

***cŭ'spidŏr** *n.* spittoon. [Port., = spitter (*cuspir* spit f. L *conspuere;* see -OR)]

cŭss *n.* & *v.* (colloq.) curse (TINKER'*s cuss;* *∼-word,* swear-word); (usu. derog.) person, creature. [vulg. pr. of CURSE¹,²]

cŭ'ssĕd *a.* (colloq.) cursed; perverse, obstinate; hence ∼**LY²** *adv.,* ∼**NESS** *n.* [as prec. f. CURSED]

cŭ'stard *n.* **1.** baked usu. sweetened mixture of eggs and milk. **2.** sauce made of cooked sweetened mixture of milk with eggs or cornflour etc.; ∼ **powder,** preparation of cornflour etc. for making this. **3.** ∼-**apple,** W. Ind. fruit with custard-like pulp ∼-**pie,** (pie containing custard freq. thrown in) slapstick comedy acting. [ME, earlier *crusta*(*r*)*de* f. AF *crustade* (*cruste,* OF *crouste* CRUST; see -ADE)]

cŭstŏ'dial *a.* relating to custody. [f. L *custodia* CUSTODY + -AL]

cŭstŏ'dian *n.* guardian, keeper, esp. of public building etc. [f. foll. + -AN, after *guardian*]

cŭ'stody̆ *n.* guardianship, care, (*parent has custody of child; child is in the custody of the father*); imprisonment (*take into* ∼, arrest). [f. L *custodia* (*custos -odis,* guardian; see -Y¹)]

cŭ'stom *n.* **1.** usual way of behaving or acting; (Law) established usage having the force of law. **2.** (in *pl.* duty levied upon imports from foreign countries, area at port etc. where goods are examined for this purpose, (C∼s) government department dealing with this; ∼-**house,** office (esp. in seaport) at which customs are collected; ∼**s union,** group of States with agreed common tariff, and usu. free trade with each other. **3.** business patronage, regular dealings of regular customers; ∼ **car** (built or modified to owner's design); *∼* **clothes** etc. (made to customer's order; so ∼-**built, -made,** etc. [ME and OF *custume* f. Rom. *costume* for *costudne* f. L *consuetudo -dinis;* see CONSUETUDE]

cŭ'stomar|y̆ *a.* & *n.* **1.** *a.* usual; (Law) subject to or held by custom (of the manor etc.); hence ∼**iLY²** *adv.* ∼**iNESS** *n.* **2.** *n.* book etc. listing customs of a community. [f. med. L *custumarius* (*custuma* f. AF *custume* f. as prec.; see -ARY¹)]

cŭ'stomer *n.* one who buys, esp. regularly from one seller; account-holder of bank; person with whom one is concerned; (colloq.) **cool, queer, awkward,** etc. ∼ (person to deal with). [ME, f. AF *custumer* f. as prec., or f. CUSTOM + -ER¹]

cŭ'stomīze, -ĭse (-īz), *v.t.* make to order or according to individual requirements. [f. CUSTOM + -IZE]

cŭt¹ *n.* **1.** act of cutting; stroke or blow with knife, sword, whip etc.; ∼ **and thrust,** use of both edge and point of sword, (fig.) lively interchange of argument etc. **2.** act or utterance that wounds the feelings; (Cricket, Lawn Tennis, Croquet, etc.) stroke made by cutting **3.** refusal to recognize a person. **4.** way thing is cut fashion, style, (of clothes, hair, etc.; *the cut of his* JIB¹); **a ∼ above,** (colloq.) markedly superior to. **5.** wound made by cutting; railway cutting; new channel made for river; excision of part of play, film, book, etc.; **short ∼,** crossing that shortens the distance (lit. or fig.); engraved block for printing; = WOODcut; piece (esp. of meat) cut off; reduction in wages, prices, time services, etc.; cessation (of power supply etc.); (sl. commission, share of profits. [ME, f. foll.]

cŭt² v. (-tt-; cut). **1.** v.t. & i. penetrate, wound, with sharp-edged thing (lit. or fig.; *the knife cut his finger, he cut his finger with a knife; knife will not ∿*, is blunt; *action ∿s both ways*, has good and bad effects, *argument ∿s both ways*, supports both sides; *a cutting wind, retort; it cut him to the heart*). **2.** v.t. divide with knife, axe, etc. *in two, in* or *into* or *to pieces* (∿ **no ice**, (sl.) have no influence or importance, achieve little or nothing; ∿ **the knot,** (fig.) solve problem in irregular but efficient way; cf. GORDIAN); meet and cross *(line cuts circle at two points)*; (fig.) renounce (a connection), refuse to recognize (a person); detach by cutting, harvest (wheat etc.), divide stalk for removal of (flower); castrate; carve (meat); divide (pack of cards, or abs.) to select dealer etc., select (card) thus; hit (ball, or abs.) with chopping motion; (Golf) slice. **3.** v.i. cross, intersect, *(two lines cut)*; pass through, across, etc., esp. as shorter way (∿ **across,** (fig.) transcend (normal limitations); *cut* LOOSE¹); (sl.) run (∿ **and run,** run away); (Cricket, of ball) turn sharply on pitching. **4.** v.t. reduce by cutting (hair, nails, corns, hedge, etc.); reduce (wages, prices, time, services, etc.), cease (services, talk, etc.); switch off (engine etc.); absent oneself from (lecture etc.); *dilute, adulterate; (in p.p., sl.) drunk; cut a CORNER, it FINE²; ∿ **a loss**, or one's *losses*, abandon a losing speculation in good time; ∿ **short,** shorten by cutting (lit. or fig.), interrupt, terminate before the natural time; *cut down to* SIZE¹. **5.** shape or fashion by cutting (coat, gem, glass, key, record, etc.); make (coat, open, etc. by cutting; perform, execute, make, *(cut a caper, dash, sorry figure); cut coat according to* CLOTH; ∿ **a tooth,** have it appear through gum (∿ one's **teeth on,** (fig.) acquire experience from; *cut one's* EYE¹-*teeth*). **6.** v.t. & i. (Cinemat.) edit (film); stop the cameras; go quickly to another shot. **7.** ∿ **back,** reduce (expenditure etc.), prune, (Cinemat.) repeat, for dramatic effect, part of previous scene; so ∿-*back* n.; ∿ **dead,** completely refuse to recognize (person); ∿ **down,** bring or throw down by cutting, kill by sword or disease, (fig.) reduce (expenses); ∿ **in,** come in abruptly, interpose (in conversation), join in card-game by taking place of player who cuts out, take dance-partner from another, obstruct path of vehicle one has just overtaken by returning to one's own side of the road too soon, connect (source of electricity), give share of profits etc. to (person); ∿ **off,** remove by cutting, bring to abrupt end or (esp. early) death, intercept (supplies, communications), shut off (flow), exclude *(from* access etc.); ∿ **off with a shilling,** disinherit (bequeathing only a shilling); ∿-*off* n., action of cutting off, device for stopping flow; ∿ **out,** remove by cutting, omit, stop doing or using (something), (fig.) outdo or supplant (rival), fashion or shape (lit. or fig.; *have* one's WORK¹ *cut out*), *detach (animal) from the herd, be excluded from card-game as result of cutting, (usu. in *pass.*) make suitable for *(was not cut out to be a teacher)*, (cause to) cease functioning; ∿-*out* n., device for automatic disconnection, release of exhaust gases, etc., figure cut out of paper etc.; *∿-out box*, = FUSE³-*box*; ∿ **up,** cut in pieces, destroy utterly, (fig.) criticize severely, (usu. in *pass.*) distress greatly, *behave in comical or unruly manner; ∿ **up rough,** show resentment; ∿ **up well,** (sl.) bequeath large fortune. **8.** ∿'**away** a., (of diagram etc.) with some parts of object absent to reveal interior, (of coat) with skirt cut back from waist; ∿-**and-come-again,** abundance; ∿ **and dried,** completely decided, prearranged, (of opinions etc.) ready-made, lacking freshness; ∿-**line,** caption to illustration, (Rackets) line above which served ball must strike wall; ∿-**price** a., selling or sold at reduced price; ∿'**purse,** (arch.) pickpocket, thief; ∿-**rate** a., = *cut-price*; ∿'**throat,** (n.) murderer, *species of trout with red mark under jaw, (a.) (of competition) intense, merciless, (of card-game) three-handed, (of razor) having long blade set in

handle; ∿'**water,** forward edge of ship's prow, wedge-shaped projection from pier or bridge; ∿'**worm,** caterpillar that cuts off young plants level with the ground. [ME *cutte, kitte, kette,* perh. f. OE **cyttan*]

cūtā'néous a. of the skin. [f. mod. L *cutaneus* f. L *cutis* skin; see -ANEOUS]

cŭtch. Var. of COUCH³.

cūte a. (colloq.) clever, shrewd; ingenious; *attractive, quaint; hence ∿'LY² (-tlĭ) adv., ∿'NESS (-tn-̦) n. [f. ACUTE]

cū'ticle n. epidermis or other superficial skin; dead skin at base of finger-nail or toe-nail; (Bot.) thin surface film on plants; hence **cūtĭ'cŭlAR**¹ a. [f. L *cuticula* dim. of *cutis* skin]

cū'tie n. (sl.) attractive young woman. [f. CUTE + -IE]

cū'tĭs n. (Anat.) true skin or dermis, underlying the epidermis. [L, = skin]

cŭ'tlass n. short sword with slightly curved blade, esp. (Hist.) that used by sailors; machete. [f. F *coutelas* f. Rom. **cultellaceum* augment. of L *cultellus* (see foll.)]

cŭ'tler n. one who makes or deals in knives and similar utensils; so ∿ERY (1, 2) n., (esp.) knives, forks, and spoons for use at table. [ME, f. AF *cotillere,* OF *coutelier* f. *coutel* (f. L *cultellus* dim. of *culter* COULTER); see -ER² (2)]

cŭ'tlět n. neck-chop of mutton or lamb; small piece of veal etc. for frying; minced meat etc. in shape of cutlet. [f. F *côtelette,* OF *costelet* dim. of *coste* rib f. L *costa*]

cŭ'tter n. In vbl senses; tailor etc. who takes measurements and cuts cloth; boat belonging to ship of war, fitted for rowing and sailing; small one-masted vessel rigged like sloop, but with running bowsprit; *light horse-drawn sleigh; (Cricket) ball turning sharply on pitching. [ME, f. CUT² + -ER¹]

cŭ'tting n. In vbl senses; ||excavation of high ground for railway, road, etc.; ||(press) ∿, paragraph etc. cut from newspaper or magazine; piece cut from plant for propagation. [ME, f. CUT² + -ING¹]

cŭ'ttle n. ∿(**fish**) mollusc of genus *Sepia,* ejecting black fluid when pursued; ∿-**bone,** its internal shell, crushed and used for polishing teeth etc. or as addition to diet of cage-bird. [OE *cudele,* corresp. to OFrank. *cudele,* Norw. dial. *kaule,* rel. to E cod f. bag, w. ref. to the ink-bag]

cŭ'ttÿ a. & n. (Sc. & N. Engl.) **1.** a. cut short, abnormally short; ∿-**stool,** (Hist.) stool of repentance. **2.** n. short tobacco-pipe. [f. CUT² + -Y²]

cuvée (kūvā') n. blend or batch of wine. [F, = vatful *(cuve;* see foll.)]

cŭvě'tte n. shallow vessel for liquid. [F, dim. of *cuve* cask f. L *cupa*]

c.v. abbr. curriculum vitae.

||**CVO** abbr. Commander of the Royal Victorian Order.

Cwlth. abbr. Commonwealth.

cwm (kōōm) n. **1.** Welsh var. of COOMB. **2.** cirque. [W]

c.w.o. abbr. cash with order.

cwt. abbr. hundredweight.

-cÿ suf., form of -Y¹ (esp. & orig. -ACY, -ANCY, -CRACY, -ENCY, -MANCY) *(bankruptcy, captaincy, chaplaincy, colonelcy, idiocy).* [f. after L *-cia, -tia,* Gk *-k(e)ia, -t(e)ia*]

cÿ'an a. & n. greenish-blue (colour). [f. Gk *kuan(e)os* dark blue]

cÿă'namide n. (Chem.) (salt of) cyanogen amide, esp. its calcium salt used as fertilizer. [f. CYANOGEN + AMIDE]

cÿă'nic a. (Chem.) of or containing cyanogen; ∿ **acid,** colourless pungent unstable strong acid (HCNO). [f. CYANOGEN + -IC]

cÿ'anĭde n. salt or ester of hydrocyanic acid; highly poisonous such substance used e.g. in extraction of gold and silver. [f. CYANOGEN + -IDE]

cÿanōcōba'lamin (-baw'-) n. (Chem.) vitamin B₁₂. [f. CYANOGEN + *cobalamin* f. COBALT + VITAMIN]

cy̆ă'nogen n. (Chem.) colourless inflammable highly poisonous gas, a compound of carbon and nitrogen. [f. F *cyanogène* f. Gk *kuanos* dark-blue mineral + -O- + -GEN, as being constituent of Prussian blue]

cy̆anŏ's|is n. (pl. ∾es pr. -ēz). (Path.) blue discoloration of skin due to presence of de-oxygenated blood. [mod. L f. Gk *kuanōsis* blueness (f. as prec.; see -OSIS)]

cy̆berna�text'tion n. control by machines. [f. foll. + -ATION]

cy̆berně'tics n. pl. (usu. treated as *sing.*) science of systems of control and communications in animals and machines; hence **cy̆berně'tic** a. [f. Gk *kubernētēs* steersman + -ICS]

cy̆'cad n. (Bot.) palmlike plant of family Cycadaceae (esp. of genus *Cycas*, yielding sago). [f. mod. L *cycas cycad-* f. supposed Gk *kukas*, scribal error for *koikas*, pl. of *koix* Egyptian palm]

Cy̆clă'dĭc a. of the Cyclades, esp. of the prehistoric civilization there. [f. *Cyclades*, circular group of islands in Aegean Sea (L, f. Gk *Kuklades* f. *kuklos* circle) + -IC]

cy̆'clamăte n. a sulphamate used as artificial sweetening agent. [f. Chem. name *cyclohexylsulphamate*]

cy̆'clamen n. European plant of genus *Cyclamen* with reflexed petals, often grown in pots. [med. L, f. L f. Gk *kuklaminos*, perh. f. *kuklos* circle, w. ref. to bulbous roots]

cy̆'cle n., & v.i. **1.** n. recurrent period (of events, phenomena, etc.); period of a thing's completion; (Electr.) = cycle per second, hertz. **2.** recurring series of operations or states; complete set or series; series of poems, of songs (**song-**∾), composed round central event or idea. **3.** bicycle, tricycle, or similar machine; ∾-**track,** ∾**way,** road or path for cycles. **4.** v.i. move in cycles; ride cycle. [ME f. OF, or f. LL f. Gk *kuklos* circle]

cy̆'clic a. **1.** recurring in cycles; belonging to a chronological cycle. **2.** of a cycle of poems etc.; (Bot., of flower) with its parts arranged in whorls; (Math.) of a circle or cycle; (Chem.) with constituent atoms forming ring. [f. F *cyclique* or f. L f. Gk *kuklikos* (as prec.; see -IC)]

cy̆'clical a. = prec. 1; hence ∾LY[2] adv. [f. as prec. + -AL]

cy̆'clist n. rider of a cycle. [f. CYCLE 3 + -IST]

cy̆'clo- comb. form. circle, cycle, cyclic, as: ∾**graph,** instrument for tracing circular arcs; ∾**meter** (-ŏ'm-), instrument for measuring (1) circular arcs, (2) distance traversed by bicycle etc.; ∾**pa'raffin,** (Chem.) saturated cyclic hydrocarbon; ∾**ra'ma** (-ah'-), circular panorama, curved wall or cloth at rear of stage (esp. to represent sky). [f. Gk *kuklos* circle + -O-]

cy̆'clŏ-crŏss n. cross-country racing on bicycles. [f. CYCLE + CROSS- (4)]

cy̆'cloid n. (Math.) curve traced by point on circle rolling along straight line; hence **cy̆cloi'dAL** a. [f. Gk *kukloeidēs* (as CYCLE; see -OID)]

cy̆'clōne n. system of winds rotating inwards to area of low barometric pressure; violent hurricane of limited diameter; centrifugal machine for separating solids; hence **cy̆clŏ'nIC** a. [prob. repr. Gk *kuklōma* wheel, coil of snake, f. *kuklos* circle]

cy̆clopae'd|ia, -pē'd|ia, n. encyclopaedia; hence ∾IC a. [abbr. of ENCYCLOPAEDIA]

Cy̆'clŏps n. **1.** (pl. same or ∾es, or **Cyclopes** pr. -ō'pēz). (Gk Myth.) one-eyed giant; so **Cy̆clopE'AN,** **Cy̆clŏ'piAN,** adjs., (esp., of ancient masonry) made with large irregular blocks. **2.** (c∾; pl. same or -pes). copepod of genus *Cyclops* with single central eye. [L, f. Gk *Kuklōps* (*kuklos* circle, *ōps* eye)]

cy̆'clostōme n. primitive vertebrate with large sucking mouth, e.g. lamprey. [f. CYCLO- + Gk *stoma* mouth]

cy̆'clostyle n., & v.t. **1.** n. apparatus printing copies of writing from stencil-plate, orig. of kind cut by pen with small toothed wheel. **2.** v.t. print or reproduce with this. [f. CYCLO- + STYLE]

cy̆clothy̆'m|ia n. (Psych.) condition with cyclic change from exhilaration to depression; hence ∾IC a. [f. CYCLO- + Gk *thumos* temper + -IA[1]]

cy̆'clotrŏn n. (Phys.) apparatus for acceleration of charged atomic particles revolving in magnetic field. [f. CYCLO- + -TRON]

cy̆'der. Var. of CIDER.

cy̆'gnět n. young swan. [ME, f. AF *cignet* dim. of OF *cigne* swan f. med. L *cicinus* f. L f. Gk *kuknos*; see -ET[1]]

cy̆'linder n. **1.** (Geom.) solid shaped like rolling-pin, pencil, tree-trunk, etc., generated by straight line moving without change of direction and describing with one of its points any fixed curve, esp. circle. **2.** roller-shaped body, hollow or solid; container for liquefied gas etc.; barrel-shaped object of baked clay covered with cuneiform writing and buried under Babylonian or Assyrian temple; small stone of similar shape used in antiquity as seal; ∾ **saw,** crown saw. **3.** cylinder-shaped part of various machines, esp. chamber in which liquid or gas exerts pressure on piston etc.; metal roller used in printing; revolving roller in lock. [f. L f. Gk *kulindros* (*kulindō* to roll)]

cy̆li'ndrical a. cylinder-shaped; *cylindrical* PROJECTION; hence ∾LY[2] adv. [f. mod. L f. Gk *kulindrikos* (as prec.; see -IC) + -AL]

cy̆'ma n. **1.** ogee moulding of cornice (∾ **recta** with concave, ∾ **reversa** with convex, curve uppermost). **2.** = CYME. [mod. L, f. Gk *kuma* wave, wavy moulding]

cy̆'mbal n. concave brass or bronze plate, struck with another or with stick etc. to make ringing sound; hence ∾IST (3) n. [ME, f. L f. Gk *kumbalon* (*kumbē* cup)]

cy̆'mbalō n. (pl. ∾s). dulcimer. [f. It. *cembalo, cimbalo*, f. L *cymbalum* (see prec.)]

cy̆mbi'dium n. tropical orchid of genus *Cymbidium*, with recess in flower-lip. [mod. L, f. Gk *kumbē* cup]

cy̆'mbifŏrm a. (Anat. & Bot.) boat-shaped. [f. L f. Gk *kumbē* boat; see -FORM]

cy̆me n. (Bot.) inflorescence in which primary axis bears single terminal flower that develops first, system being continued by axes of secondary and higher orders each with flower (cf. RACEME); hence **cy̆'mOSE**[1] a. [F, var. of *cime* summit, f. pop. L *cima*, f. Gk *kuma* wave]

Cy̆'mric (k-) a. Welsh. [f. W *Cymru* Wales + -IC]

cyngha'nedd (kunghah'nědh) n. intricate system of alliteration and rhyme in Welsh poetry. [W]

cy̆'nic a. & n. **1.** a. of or characteristic of the Cynic philosophers; cynical. **2.** n. (C∾) ancient-Greek philosopher of sect founded by Antisthenes, marked by ostentatious contempt for ease and pleasure; one who sarcastically doubts or despises human sincerity and merit; hence ∾ISM (2) n. [f. L f. Gk *kunikos* (*kuōn kunos* dog, nickname for Cynic; see -IC)]

cy̆'nical a. like a cynic, incredulous of human goodness; sneering; hence ∾LY[2] adv. [f. prec. + -AL]

cy̆nocě'phalus n. fabled dog-headed man; (Zool.) baboon. [ME f. L, f. Gk *kunokephalos* (*kuōn kunos* dog, *kephalē* head)]

cy̆noglŏ'ssum n. tall plant of genus *Cynoglossum*, with tongue-shaped leaves. [mod. L, f. Gk *kunoglōsson* (as prec., *glōssa* tongue)]

cy̆'nosure (-z-) n. guiding star; centre of attraction or admiration. [F, or f. L f. Gk *kunosoura* dog's tail, Ursa Minor (as prec., *oura* tail)]

cy̆'pher[1,2]. See CIPHER[1,2].

cy̆ pres (sē prā') adv. & a. (Law). as near as possible (to testator's or donor's intentions these cannot be precisely followed). [AF, = F *si près* so near (as etc.)]

cy̆'prèss n. coniferous tree of genus *Cupressus*, with hard wood and dark foliage, taken as symbol of mourning. [ME f. OF *cipres* f. LL *cypressus* f. Gk *kuparissos*]

Cy̆'prian, Cy̆'priot, Cy̆'priōte, adjs. & ns. (native or inhabitant) of Cyprus. [f. L *Cyprius* + -AN, Gk *Kupriōtēs*, f. *Cyprus* (Gk *Kupros*) in E. Mediterranean]

cy̆'prinoid *a.* & *n.* (fish) like or akin to carp. [f. L f. Gk *kuprinos* carp + -OID]

cy̆pripē'dium *n.* orchid of genus *Cypripedium*, esp. lady's slipper. [mod. L, f. Gk *Kupris* Aphrodite + *pedilon* slipper]

cy̆'psèla *n.* (*pl.* ~e). (Bot.) achene with attached calyx, as in dandelion. [mod. L, f. Gk *kupselē* hollow vessel]

Cy̆rēnā'ic *a.* & *n.* (philosopher) of the hedonistic school of Aristippus of Cyrene. [f. L f. Gk *Kurēnaikos* (*Kurēnē* Cyrene in N. Africa)]

Cy̆ri'llic *a.* of alphabet used by Slavonic peoples of the Orthodox Church. [f. St. *Cyril* d. 869, reputed author, + -IC]

cy̆st *n.* (Biol.) hollow organ, bladder, etc., in animal or plant, containing liquid secretion; (Path.) sac containing morbid matter, parasitic larva, etc.; (Biol.) cell containing embryo etc. [f. LL *cystis* f. Gk *kustis* bladder]

cy̆'stic *a.* of the urinary bladder; of the gall-bladder;

of the nature of a cyst. [f. F *cystique* or mod. L *cysticus* (as prec.; see -IC)]

cy̆'sto- *comb. form.* bladder, esp. urinary bladder, as: **cy̆sti'TIS**, ~SCOPE, ~TOMY (-ŏ't-), *ns.* [f. Gk *kustē*, *kustis* bladder + -O-]

-cy̆te *suf.* (Biol.) mature cell (*leucocyte*); cf. -BLAST. [f. Gk *kutos* vessel]

cy̆'tidine (-ēn) *n.* crystalline nucleoside obtained from RNA by hydrolysis. [f. G *cytidin* (as prec.)]

cy̆'to- *comb. form.* (Biol.) cell, as: ~logy (-ŏ'l-), study of cells; ~plasm, protoplasmic content of cell other than the nucleus; ~sine, crystalline base occurring as constituent of DNA. [f. as -CYTE + -O-]

czar etc. See TSAR etc.

czardas. See CSARDAS.

Czěch (chěk) *n.* & *a.* (native or language) of Bohemia; = foll. [Pol. sp. of Bohemian *Čech*]

Czěchŏslō'văk, Czěchŏslŏvá'kïan, (chěk-) *adjs.* & *ns.* (native) of Czechoslovakia. [f. prec. + -O- + SLOVAK; see -IAN]

D

D, d, (dē) *n.* (*pl.* **Ds** *or* **D's**). fourth letter of alphabet; = DEE; (Mus.) second note in diatonic scale of C major; fourth highest class (of academic marks, population as regards affluence, etc.); (as Roman numeral) 500 (**dc** 600).

D. *abbr.* *Democrat; dimension (*3-D*).

d. *abbr.* daughter; deci-; delete; departs; died; ‖(former) penny [f. L DENARIUS].

D *symb.* deuterium.

'd[1] *v.* (colloq., chiefly after pronouns). = *had, would.* [abbr.]

-d, -'d[2], *suf.* (*heard, subpoena'd, toga'd,* etc.): see -ED[1,2].

DA *abbr.* deposit account; *District Attorney.

da *abbr.* deca-.

dăb[1] *v.* (-bb-). **1.** *v.t.* & *i.* strike lightly or undecidedly, hit feebly (*at*), tap, peck. **2.** *v.t.* press briefly but not rub (surface) with sponge etc., press (brush, sponge, colour etc.) on surface thus. [ME, imit.]

dăb[2] *n.* slight or undecided blow, tap, peck; brief application of sponge, handkerchief, etc., to surface without rubbing; moisture, colour, etc., so applied; (in *pl.*, sl.) fingerprints. [ME, f. prec.]

dăb[3] *n.* flat-fish of genus *Limanda*. [16th c., of unkn. orig.]

dăb[4] *n.* & *a.* (colloq.) adept (*at* games etc., *doing*; ~ **hand**, expert). [17th c., of unkn. orig.]

dă'bbl|**e** *v.* **1.** *v.t.* wet intermittently, slightly, or partly; soil, moisten, splash. **2.** *v.i.* move feet, hands, bill, about in shallow water; engage *in* or *at* pursuit etc. as desultory hobby; hence ~ER[1] *n.* [16th c., f. Du. *dabbelen* or DAB[1]+-LE 3]

dă'bchick *n.* water-bird of grebe family, esp. little grebe. [16th c. *dap-, dop-,* later *dip-*; perh. cogn. w. OE *dūfedoppa,* DEEP[1], DIP[1]]

dă'bster *n.* = DAB[4]; = DAUB*ster;* *one who dabbles. [f. DAB[4]+-STER]

da ca'pō (dah kah'-) *adv.* (Mus.) repeated from the beginning. [It.]

dāce *n.* (*pl.* same). small freshwater fish allied to carp, esp. of genus *Leuciscus.* [ME, f. OF *dars;* see DART]

dă'cha *n.* small country villa in Russia. [Russ. = act of payment]

dă'chshund (-ks-hoŏ-) *n.* short-legged long-bodied breed of dog. [G, = badger-dog]

dacoi't *n.* member of Indian or Burmese armed robber band. [f. Hindi *ḍakait* (*ḍākā* gang-robbery)]

dacoi'tÿ *n.* (act of) gang-robbery. [f. Hindi *ḍakaitī* (as prec.)]

dă'ctÿl *n.* (Pros.) foot consisting of one long syllable followed by two short. [ME, f. L f. Gk *daktulos* finger (w. its 3 bones), dactyl]

dăctÿ'lic *a.* & *n.* (Pros.) **1.** *a.* of or using dactyls (*dactylic* HEXAMETER). **2.** *n.* (usu. in *pl.*) dactylic verse. [f. L f. Gk *daktulikos* (as prec.; see -IC)]

***dăd**[1] *n.* (colloq., in oaths etc.) God. [corrupt.]

dăd[2] *n.* (colloq.) = DADDY 1. [perh. imit. of child's *da, da*]

Da'da (dah'dah) *n.* international movement in art and literature about 1915-20, repudiating conventions and intended to shock; hence ~ISM (3), ~IST (2), *ns.* [F, title of review (1916-), f. *dada* hobby-horse]

dă'ddÿ *n.* (colloq.) **1.** (esp. as *voc.*) father; man. **2.** oldest or most important person or thing. **3.** ~-lo'ng-legs, crane-fly, *harvestman. [f. DAD[2]+-Y[3]]

dā'dō *n.* (*pl.* ~s). cube of pedestal between base and cornice; plinth of column; lower part of room-wall when faced or coloured differently from upper part. [It., = DIE[1]]

dae'dal *a.* (literary). skilful, inventive; complex, mysterious; (of the earth etc.) adorned with natural wonders. [f. L. f. Gk *daidalos* skilful, variegated]

Daedā'lian, -ėan, *a.* in the manner of Daedalus; intricate; labyrinthine. [f. L. *Daedaleus,* Gk *daidaleos* (*Daidalos* Daedalus, who built the Cretan labyrinth; cf. prec.)+-IAN, -EAN]

daemon(ic). See DEMON(IC).

daff[1] (dahf) *v.t.* (arch.) put aside, waive, (esp. *daff the world aside,* Shak. *1 Henry IV* IV. i. 96). [var. of DOFF]

dăff[2] *n.* (colloq.) = foll. [abbr.]

dă'ffodil *n.* yellow-flowered narcissus; this as Welsh national emblem; pale-yellow colour. [f. earlier *affodill* (*d-* unexplained) f. med. L *affodilus* f. L f. Gk *asphodelos* asphodel]

dă'ffÿ *a.* (sl.) = foll. [f. *daff* simpleton+-Y[2]]

daft (dah-) *a.* foolish, reckless, wild; crazy. [ME *daffte* = OE *gedæfte* mild, meek f. Gmc *gadhaftjaz* (*gadhafti* fitting, suitable)]

dă'geraad (-gerahd, -t) *n.* (S. Afr.) brilliantly coloured sea-fish. [Afrik. f. Du., = daybreak]

dă'gga *n.* (S. Afr.) hemp used as narcotic; similarly used plant of genus *Leonotis.* [Afrik., f. Hottentot *dachab*]

dă'gger (-g-) *n.* **1.** stabbing-weapon with short pointed and edged blade (**at** ~**s drawn**, on the point of fighting, in bitter enmity, *with* person, or abs.; **look** ~**s**, stare angrily *at* person, or abs.). **2.** (Print.) (**double**) ~, = (*double*) OBELISK. [ME, perh. f. obs. *dag* pierce+-ER[1], infl. by OF *dague* long dagger]

dā'gō *n.* (*pl.* ~s *or* ~es). (sl., derog.; **R**) Spaniard, Portuguese, Italian; any foreigner. [f. Sp. *Diego* = James]

daguě'rreotype (-gě'ro-) *n.* (photograph taken by) early photographic process using iodine-sensitized silver(ed) plate and mercury vapour. [f. L. *Daguerre,* Fr. inventor d. 1851, +-o-+TYPE[1]]

dahabee'yah (dah-ha-), **-bi'ah** (-bě'-), *n.* Nile sailing-boat. [f. Arab. *ḍahabīya* = the golden, orig. used of gilded barge of Muslim rulers of Egypt]

dah'lia (dā'l-) *n.* Mexican composite plant of genus *Dahlia* cultivated for its many-coloured single or double flowers; **blue** ~, something impossible. [f. A. *Dahl,* Sw. botanist d. 1789+-IA[1]]

Dáil (Éireann) (doil (ā'ran)) *n.* lower house of Parliament in the Republic of Ireland. [Ir., = assembly (of Ireland)]

dai'lÿ *a., adv.,* & *n.* **1.** *a.* & *adv.* (produced or occurring) on every day or weekday; from day to day, constant(ly), often; *daily* BREAD; *daily* DOZEN. **2.** *n.* daily newspaper; ‖(colloq.) charwoman coming daily. [ME, f. DAY+-LY[1,2]]

dai'miō (dī'-) *n.* (*pl.* ~s). (Hist.) Japanese feudal vassal of the emperor. [Jap. (*dai* great, *myō* name)]

dai'm|ŏn (dī'-) *n.* = DEMON 2; hence ~ŏ'nic *a.* [Gk, = deity]

dai'ntÿ[1] *n.* choice morsel, delicacy, (lit. or fig.). [f. AF *dainté,* OF *daintié, deintié* f. L *dignitas -tatis* (*dignus* worthy; see -ITY)]

dai'nt|ÿ[2] *a.* delicate, choice; tasteful, pretty, of delicate beauty; having delicate tastes and sensitivity, fastidious; hence ~ILY[2] *adv.,* ~INESS *n.* [ME, f. prec.]

dai'quiri (dī'k-, dā'k-) *n.* cocktail of rum, lime-juice, etc. [f. D~ in Cuba]

dair'ÿ *n.* **1.** room or building for keeping milk and cream and making butter, cheese, etc.; shop for milk etc.; department of farm or farming concerned with dairy products. **2.** ~ **cattle** (kept for milk production); ~ **cream**, real cream (not synthetic); ~ **factory**, (NZ) factory making butter and cheese; ~ **farm**, one chiefly concerned with dairy products;

∼**maid,** woman employed in dairy; ∼**man,** dealer in milk etc.; ∼ **products,** milk and its derivatives, e.g. cream, butter, cheese. [ME *deierie* (*deie* maidservant f. OE *dǣge* kneader of dough; see -ERY)]

dair′ȳing *n.* dairy operations; production of milk, butter, etc. [f. *dairy* v. keep COWS + -ING¹]

dais (dā′is, dās) *n.* low platform, esp. at end of hall for high table, throne, etc. [ME f. OF *deis* f. L *discus* disc, dish, in med. L = table]

dai′sȳ (-zī) *n.* **1.** small European wild and garden flower (*Bellis perennis*), with yellow disc and white rays; other plant resembling it, esp. the larger ox-eye daisy, MICHAELMAS *daisy*, SHASTA *daisy*; (sl.) first-rate specimen of anything; **pushing up the daisies,** (sl.) dead and buried. **2.** ∼**-chain,** string of daisies threaded together; ∼**-cutter,** horse lifting feet very little, (Cricket) ball travelling along ground. [OE *dæges ēage* day's eye, the disc being revealed in the morning]

dak. See DAWK.

Dak. *abbr.* Dakota.

dal. See DHAL.

Dalai. See LAMA¹.

dāle *n.* valley (esp. in N. Engl.); HILL *and dale;* ∼′**sman** (-z-), inhabitant of dales in northern England. [OE *dæl,* = OS *dal,* OHG *tal,* ON *dalr,* Goth. *dal(s)* f. Gmc **dalam, *dalaʒ*]

dā′llȳ *v.* **1.** *v.i.* amuse oneself, sport or flirt or trifle (*with,* or abs.). **2.** idle, loiter, delay. **3.** *v.t.* ∼ *away,* consume (time, opportunity) to no purpose. **4.** Hence **dā′llIANCE** *n.* [ME, f. OF *dalier* chat]

Dălmā′tian (-shan) *n.* large short-haired white dog with dark spots. [f. *Dalmatia* in Yugoslavia + -AN]

dălmă′tic *n.* wide-sleeved loose long vestment with slit sides worn by deacons and bishops on some occasions, and by kings and emperors esp. at coronation. [ME, f. OF *dalmatique* or LL *dalmatica* (*vestis* robe) of Dalmatia]

dăl se′gnō (ă′nyō) *adv.* (Mus.) repeated from point indicated. [It., = from the sign]

Da′lton (daw′-) *n.* ∼ **plan,** system of education in which pupils are made responsible for completion of assignments over fairly long periods at a time; hence ∼IZE (3) *v.t.* [∼ in Massachusetts, location of first school to use the plan]

da′ltonism (daw′l-) *n.* colour-blindness, esp. congenital inability to distinguish green from red. [f. F *daltonisme* f. J. *Dalton,* Engl. chemist d. 1844, who suffered from it, + -ISM (5)]

dăm¹ *n.,* & *v.t.* (-mm-). **1.** *n.* barrier constructed to hold back water and raise its level, to form a reservoir, or to prevent flooding; barrier constructed in stream by beavers; *(Dent.) rubber sheet to keep saliva from teeth during operation; causeway. **2.** *v.t.* furnish or confine with dam; block *up,* hold *back,* obstruct, (lit. or fig.). [ME f. MLG, MDu.; MHG *tam,* of doubtful orig.]

dăm² *n.* mother (esp. of animal). [ME, var. of DAME]

dăm³. Var. of DAMN 4, 5.

dă′mage *n.,* & *v.t.* **1.** *n.* loss of what is desirable (*to one's great damage*); injury impairing value or usefulness; (Law, in *pl.*) sum of money claimed or adjudged in compensation for loss or injury; (sl.) cost (*what's the damage?*). **2.** *v.t.* injure (usu. thing) so as to diminish value; detract from reputation of (person etc.); *trying to damage the Government; a damaging admission*); hence ∼ABLE (-īja-) *a.* [ME f. OF *damage* n., *damagier* v., f. *dam(me)* loss f. L *damnum*]

damascene (dă′m-, -ē′n) *v.t.* ornament (metal) with inlaid gold or silver; ornament (steel) with watered pattern produced in welding. [f. *Damascene* adj. of Damascus, f. L f. Gk *Damaskēnos*]

dă′mask *n.* & *a.,* & *v.t.* **1.** *n.* figured woven material (orig. of silk) with pattern visible on either side; twilled table-linen with woven designs shown by reflection of light. **2.** (Hist.) steel of or as of Damascus, with wavy surface-pattern due to special welding of

iron and steel together. **3.** ∼ **rose,** old sweet-scented variety grown esp. to make attar. **4.** *a.* coloured like damask rose, velvety pink or light red; made of or resembling damask silk, linen, or steel. **5.** *v.t.* weave with figured designs; = DAMASCENE; ornament with pattern. [ME, f. AF *Damasc f. L *Damascus*]

dāme *n.* **1.** (arch., poet., joc., or *sl.) woman; (arch.) mistress of household. **2.** (*D*∼). title of woman of rank, or of thing personified as woman (*Dame Nature*); ||(title of) woman Knight Commander or holder of Grand Cross in Order of the Bath, Order of the British Empire, Royal Victorian Order, or Order of St. Michael and St. George. **3.** comic middle-aged woman in modern pantomine, usu. played by man; woman with administrative duties in Eton boarding-house. **4.** ∼**-school,** (Hist.) primary school of kind kept by elderly women; ∼′**s violet,** cruciferous plant with pale lilac flowers that have no scent until evening. [ME f. OF, f. L *domina* mistress]

dă′mfōōl *a.* & *n.* (colloq.) foolish, stupid, (person). [f. DAMN 4 + FOOL¹]

dă′mmar *n.* (resin used in varnish-making, obtained from) E. Asian tree esp. of genus *Agathis* or *Shorea.* [f. Malay *damar*]

dă′mmit *int. etc.* = DAMN *int.*

dămn (-m) *v.t., n., a.,* & *adv.* **1.** *v.t.* condemn, censure, (*damn a person's character;* ∼ **with faint praise,** commend so frigidly as to suggest disapproval); bring condemnation upon, be the ruin of. **2.** doom to hell, cause damnation of, curse (person or thing, or abs.; often in *subj.,* = *may God damn* person or thing, or without object); ||∼ **all,** (sl.) nothing at all; I'll be ∼ed, (colloq.) I am astonished; (**I'm, I'll be**) ∼ed **if** I (*know, will agree,* etc.), (colloq.) I certainly do not. **3.** *n.* uttered curse; negligible amount (*don't care or give, not worth, a damn;* TINKER's *damn*). **4.** *a.* (colloq.) = DAMNED 2. **5.** *adv.* (colloq.) = DAMNED 3. [ME, f. OF *dam(p)ner* f. L *damnare* inflict loss on (*damnum* loss)]

dă′mnab|le *a.* subject to or deserving damnation; hateful, annoying; hence ∼LY² *adv.* [ME, f. OF *dam(p)nable* f. LL *dam(p)nabilis* (as prec.; see -ABLE)]

dămnā′tion *n.* & *int.* **1.** *n.* (condemnation to) eternal punishment in hell. **2.** *int.* = may damnation take a person or thing. [ME, f. OF *dam(p)nation* f. L *damnatio -onis* (as DAMN, see -ATION)]

dă′mnatorȳ *a.* conveying or causing censure or damnation. [f. L *damnatorius* (as DAMN; see -ORY)]

dămned (-md) *a.* & *adv.* **1.** *a.* In vbl senses; **the** ∼, souls in hell. **2.** damnable; infernal, unwelcome; **do** one's ∼**est,** do one's utmost. **3.** *adv.* damnably, extremely, (*damned hot, funny*); ∼ **well,** simply (*you can be damned well do without it*). [p. p. of DAMN]

dă′mni|fȳ *v.t.* (Law). cause injury to; hence ∼FICA′TION *n.* [f. OF *damnifier* etc. f. LL *damnificare* injure f. L *damnificus* hurtful (*damnum* loss; see -FY)]

dă′mning (-mī-) *a.* In vbl senses; (of evidence etc.) that proves guilt; hence ∼LY² *adv.* [f. DAMN + -ING²]

damnosa hereditas (dămnōsa hĭrē′dĭtăs) *n.* inheritance that brings more burden than profit. [L, = insolvent inheritance]

dă′mnum *n.* (Law). loss or wrong. [L, = hurt, harm]

Dă′moclēs (-z) *n.* **sword of** ∼, imminent danger esp. in midst of prosperity. [L f. Gk, name of flatterer whom Dionysius of Syracuse (4th c. BC) feasted while sword hung by a hair over him]

dă′mosĕl (-z-), **dă′mozĕl,** *n.* (arch.) Var. of DAMSEL.

dămp *n., a., & v.* **1.** *n.* moisture in air, liquid vapour, or diffused through solid; dejection, chill, discouragement, (*cast* or *strike a damp over* or *into*); *damp*-PROOF²; ∼(**-proof**) **course,** layer of damp-proof felt etc. in wall near ground to keep damp from rising. **2.** = CHOKE¹ *-damp;* = FIRE¹*damp.* **3.** *a.* slightly or fairly wet (*damp* SQUIB); hence *∼′**en** vb & *t.,* ∼′LY² *adv.;* ∼′**NESS** *n.* **4.** *v.t.* stifle, choke, dull, extinguish, (∼ **down,** heap (fire) with ashes etc. to retard combustion); (Mus. & Phys.) stop vibration of (string), reduce amplitude of (sound waves etc.); discourage, depress, (zeal, hopes); moisten. **5.** *v.i.* ∼ **off,** (of plant) die from fungus attack in damp conditions. [ME f. MLG, = vapour etc., OHG *dampf* steam f. WG **thamp-*] **dä′mper** *n.* In vbl senses; (Mus.) pad silencing piano--string except when removed by pedal or by note's being struck; shock-absorber in vehicle; metal plate in flue to control draught and combustion; device for moistening anything; (Austral., NZ, etc.) unleavened bread or cake of flour and water baked in wood ashes. [f. prec. + -ER¹] **dä′msel** (-z-) *n.* **1.** (arch. or literary). young unmarried woman. **2.** ∼**fish,** small brightly-coloured fish of coral reefs; ∼**fly,** slender insect of order Odonata, like dragonfly but with wings folded over body when resting. [ME, f. OF *dam(e)isele,* earlier *danzele, donsele* f. Gallo-Rom. **dominicella* dim. of L *domina* mistress] **dä′mson** (-z-) *n.* & *a.* **1.** *n.* small dark-purple plum (∼ **plum,** larger similar plum); tree (*Prunus insititia*) bearing it; ∼ **cheese,** solid preserve of damsons and sugar. **2.** *a.* damson-coloured. [ME *dama(s)cene, damesene,* f. L *damascenum* (*prunum* plum) of *Damascus*; see DAMASCENE] **dăn¹** *n.* ∼ (**buoy**), small buoy used as marker in deep--sea fishing, or showing limits of area cleared by minesweepers. [17th c.; orig. unkn.] **dăn²** *n.* (holder of) degree of proficiency in judo etc. [Jap.] **Dăn³** *n.* **from** ∼ **to Beersheba,** over the whole extent. [∼ in Palestine, f. name of a tribe of Israel] **Dan.** *abbr.* Daniel (OT). **dance¹** (dah-) *v.* **1.** *v.i.* move with rhythmical steps, glides, leaps, revolutions, gestures, etc., usu. to music, alone or with partner or set, (∼ **to** person's **tune,** do as he demands; **dancing-girl,** female professional dancer, esp. member of a group); jump about, skip, (*dancing with rage, with joy*), (of heart, blood, etc.) move in lively way; bob up and down on water etc. **2.** *v.t.* perform (minuet, waltz, polka, a ballet, etc.; ∼ **attendance** (*on*), be deliberately kept waiting (by), follow about obsequiously); move up and down, dandle, (child). [ME, f. OF *dancer, danser* f. Rom. **dansare,* of unkn. orig.] **dance²** (dah-) *n.* **1.** dancing motion; special form of this; single round or turn of one (**lead** person **a** ∼, cause him much trouble); tune for dancing to, or in dance rhythm; dancing-party. **2.** **D**∼ **of Death,** medieval representation of Death leading all to grave; ∼**-drama,** expression of dramatic situation by dance; ∼**-hall,** public hall for dancing; **St. Vitus's** ∼, disorder chiefly in children, with convulsive involuntary movements. [ME, f. OF *dance, danse,* f. as prec.] **da′ncer** (dah′-) *n.* In vbl senses; one who dances in public for money; ||**merry** ∼**s,** aurora borealis. [f. DANCE¹ + -ER¹] **dăncĕ′tty** *a.* (Her., of line) drawn with broad indentations. [alt. f. F *danché* etc. f. LL **denticatus* f. L *dens dentis* tooth] **d. and c.** *abbr.* (Med.) dilatation and curettage. **dä′ndèlion** *n.* yellow-flowered composite plant (*Taraxacum officinale*) with widely toothed leaves; ∼ **coffee,** (drink made from) dried dandelion roots. [f. F *dent-de-lion* f. med. L *dens leonis* lion's tooth] **dä′nder** *n.* (colloq.) temper, anger, indignation, (person's ∼ **is up,** he is angry). [19th c.; orig. uncert.] **Dăndie Dï′nmont** *n.* (breed of) short-legged rough--coated terrier from Scottish Border. [character in Scott's *Guy Mannering*] **dä′ndle** *v.t.* dance (child) on one's knees or in one's arms; pamper, pet. [16th c., of unkn. orig.] **dä′ndrŭff** *n.* dead skin in small scales among the hair; condition of having this. [16th c.; -*ruff* perh. akin to ME *rove* scurfiness f. ON *hrufa* or MLG, MDu. *rōve*] **dä′ndÿ** *n.* & *a.* **1.** *n.* man unduly devoted to smartness

esp. of clothes, whence **dăndï′ACAL** *a.,* **dä′ndïFY** *v.t.,* ∼ISH¹ *a.,* ∼ISM (2) *n.*; (colloq.) excellent thing. **2.** *a.* (colloq.) very good of its kind, splendid, first-rate. **3.** ∼**-brush** (for cleaning horse); ∼**-roll**(**er**), device for solidifying, and impressing watermark in, paper during manufacture. [18th c., perh. orig. = *Andrew,* in *Jack-a-dandy*] **Dāne** *n.* native or inhabitant of Denmark; (Hist.) Northman invader of England in 9th-11th c.; (**Great**) ∼, powerful short-haired breed of dog; ∼**s′-blood,** **d**∼**′weed, d**∼**′wort,** herb of ELDER² genus said to have sprung where Danes were wounded in battle. [ME, f. ON *Danir* pl., LL *Dani*] **Dā′negĕld** (-n-g-) *n.* (Hist.) annual tax prob. imposed orig. in 10th c. to provide funds to protect England against the Danes; tax; appeasement by bribery. [OE, f. as prec. + ON *gjald* payment] **Dā′nelaw** (-nl-) *n.* (Hist.) part of N. & E. England occupied by Danes in 9th-11th c. [OE *Dena lagu* Danes' law] **dăng.** Var. of DAMN 2, 3. **dā′nger** (-nj-) *n.* **1.** liability or exposure to harm, risk, peril, (*of* one's *life, of death* or other evil; **in** ∼ **of,** likely to incur etc.; **out of** ∼, not likely to die from present illness etc.). **2.** position of railway signal directing stoppage or caution (*signal is at danger*); thing that causes peril (*a danger to peace, to navigation*). **3.** ∼ **list,** list of dangerously ill hospital patients; ∼ **money,** payment above basic wages when dangerous work is done. [earlier sense 'jurisdiction, power', ME f. OF *dangier* f. Rom. **domniarium* f. L *dominus* lord] **dā′ngerous** (-nj-) *a.* causing danger, unsafe; ∼ **drug** (esp. that can cause addiction); hence ∼LY² *adv.* [ME, f. AF *da(u)ngerous,* OF *dangereus* (as prec.; see -OUS)] **dä′ngle** (-nggl) *v.* **1.** *v.i.* be suspended and sway to and fro; (arch.) hover *after, round, about,* person as follower, lover, etc.; ***lack proper grammatical connection (*dangling participle*). **2.** *v.t.* hold or carry (thing) swaying loosely; hold (hopes etc.) as temptation *before* person. [16th c., imit.; cf. Sw. *dangla,* Da. *dangle,* and -LE 3] **Dä′niel** (-yel) *n.* upright judge, person of infallible wisdom. [Sus. 45-64, and Shak. *Merchant of Venice* iv. i. 223, 333] **Dä′nish** *a.* & *n.* (language) of Denmark or the Danes; ∼ **blue,** soft white cheese with blue veins; ∼ **modern,** simple plain and light style of furniture; ∼ **pastry,** (cake of) yeast pastry topped with icing, nuts, etc. [ME, f. AF *danes,* OF *daneis* f. med. L *Danensis* (as DANE), assim. to -ISH¹] **dănk** *a.* oozy; (of air, weather, etc.) unpleasantly or unwholesomely cold and damp. [ME, prob. f. Scand.; cf. Sw. *dank* marshy spot] **danse du ventre** (dahṅs dū vah′ṅtr) *n.* belly-dance. [F] **danse macabre** (dahṅs makah′br) *n.* DANCE² of Death. [F; see DANCE², MACABRE] **danseur** (dahṅsēr′) *n.* (fem. **danseuse** (-sẽr′z) male ballet-dancer. [F, = dancer] **Dantean** (dä′ntïan, -ē′an) *a.* & *n.* (student) of Dante; in style of or reminiscent of Dante's writings; so **DăntE′SQUE** (-ĕsk) *a.;* (*Dante* Alighieri, It. poet d. 1321 + -EAN] **dănthō′nia** *n.* (Austral. & NZ) tufted pasture grass of genus *Danthonia.* [mod. L, f. É. *Danthoine,* 19th-c. Fr. botanist + -IA¹] **dăp** *v.i.* & *t.* (-**pp**-). fish by letting bait bob on water; dip lightly; make (ball) bounce, (of ball) bounce, on ground. [cf. DAB¹] **dä′phne** *n.* flowering shrub of genus *Daphne,* e.g. spurge laurel. [ME, = laurel, f. Gk *daphnē*] **dä′pper** *a.* (Of person) neat, smart, in appearance or movement; sprightly. [ME, f. MLG, MDu. *dapper* strong, stout, = OHG *tapfar* weighty, ON *dapr* sad] **dä′pple** *v.* & *n.* **1.** *v.t.* & *i.* variegate or become variegated with rounded spots or patches of colour or shade. **2.** *n.* dappled effect; dappled horse etc.; ∼-**grey**, (horse) of grey with darker spots. [ME *dappled, dappled,* adj., of unkn. orig.]

||**dar'bies** (-bĭz) *n. pl.* (sl.) handcuffs. [allus. use of *Father Darby's bands,* some rigid form of bond for debtors (16th c.)]

Dar'by *n.* ∼ **and Joan,** devoted old married couple; ||∼ **and Joan club,** club for elderly people. [18th c.; perh. f. poem 1735 in *Gentleman's Magazine*]

dare *v.t.* (3 *sing. pres.* usu. **dare** before expressed or implied inf. without *to*; *past* in this position (arch.) **durst;** *neg.* **dare not** or **do(es) not dare** or (colloq.) **daren't** *pr.* dărnt), & *n.* **1.** *v.t.* venture (to), have the courage or impudence (to), (**I** ∼ **say,** I am prepared to believe, I do not deny, it is very likely; **I** ∼ **swear,** I feel sure that; *dare he do it?*; *he dares to insult me; I would if I dared; they dared not come, did not dare to come;* (abs.) *how dare you?*).**2.** attempt, take the risks of, (*dare all things,* person's *anger*); defy (person); challenge (person) *to* do, *to a fight,* etc.; ∼'**devil,** reckless (person). **3.** *n.* act of daring; challenge. [OE *durran,* = OS *gidurran,* OHG *giturran,* Goth. *gadaursan,* preterite--present vbs. f. Gmc **ders-,* **dars-,* **durs-,* f. IE **dhers-* etc.; cf. Skr. *dhṛsh,* Gk *tharseō* be bold]

darg *n.* (Sc., N. Engl., & Austral.) day's work; definite amount of work, task. [ME, f. *daywerk* or *daywark* day-work]

dar'ing[1] *n.* In vbl senses; adventurous courage. [f. DARE + -ING[1]]

dar'ing[2] *a.* In vbl senses; adventurous, bold; fearless; whence ∼LY[2] *adv.* [f. DARE + -ING[2]]

dă'riôle *n.* savoury or sweet dish cooked and served in a small mould called a ∼ (**mould**). [ME f. OF]

dark[1] *a.* **1.** with no or relatively little light, unilluminated; gloomy, sombre. **2.** (Of colour) more or less near black (esp. as pref. to adjs. of colour: *dark-brown* etc.); with brown or black hair or skin, not blond. **3.** evil, atrocious; cheerless (*dark side of things*); sad, sullen (*dark thoughts*); frowning. **4.** obscure (*dark saying, oblivion*); secret, mysterious, (*keep* thing *dark*); **keep** ∼, remain in hiding; little known of; unenlightened (*in the darkest ignorance*; **in** ∼**est Africa,** with ref. to paucity of knowledge of Africa or to its relative lack of enlightenment, hence joc. of other places regarded as remote or uncivilized). **5.** **D**∼ **Ages,** Middle Ages, esp. 5th–10th c., (fig.) period of relative lack of enlightenment; **D**∼ **Age(s),** time between end of Bronze Age and beginning of archaic period in Greece etc.; *dark* BLUE[2]; **D**∼ **Continent,** Africa; ∼ **current,** (Electr.) current in a photoelectric device when no radiation is incident; ∼ **days** (of adversity); ∼ **glasses,** spectacles with dark-tinted lenses; ∼ **horse,** racehorse whose form is little known, (fig.) person who is little known yet successful in contest; ∼ **lantern,** one with means for covering its light; ∼-**room** (with actinic rays such as daylight excluded for photographic work). **6.** Hence or cogn. ∼'ISH[1] 2 *a.,* ∼'LY[2] *adv.,* ∼'NESS *n.,* (esp.) wickedness (*the powers of darkness;* PRINCE *of Darkness*). [OE *deorc,* prob. f. Gmc **derk-,* **dark-*]

dark[2] *n.* absence of light (esp. *in the dark;* ∼-**adapted,** (of eye) adjusted to low intensity of light); nightfall (*after dark*); dark colour (esp. in Art, *the lights and darks of a picture*); lack of knowledge (*am in the dark about it*; **leap in the** ∼, rash step or enterprise; SHOT[1] *in the dark*); hence ∼'SOME[1] *a.* (arch. or poet.). [ME, f. prec.]

dar'ken *v.t.* & *i.* make or become dark (lit. or fig.); ∼ person's **door,** visit him (usu. w. neg.). [ME, f. DARK[1] + -EN[6]]

dar'kie. Var. of DARKY.

dar'kle *v.t.* be seen darkly; become dark. [back-form. f. foll.; cf. -ING[2]]

dar'kling *adv.* & *a.* in the dark. [ME, f. DARK[1] + -LING[2]]

dar'ky *n.* (colloq.; R.) a Black. [f. DARK[1] + -Y[3]]

dar'ling *n.* & *a.* loved, best loved, lovable, especially

favoured, (colloq.) pretty, (person or thing). [OE *dēorling* (as DEAR, -LING[1])]

darn[1] *v.t.,* & *n.* **1.** *v.t.* mend (esp. knitted material, or hole in it) by interweaving yarn with needle across hole, whence ∼'ING (5) *n.*; embroider with ∼'ing--**stitch** (large running stitch as used in darning material); ∼'ing-**egg** etc., curved piece of wood etc. to support material being darned. **2.** *n.* place so mended. [16th c., perh. f. obs. *dern* hide; cf. MDu. *dernen* stop holes in (a dike)]

darn[2] *v.t., n., a.,* & *adv.* (sl.) (Mild form of) DAMN 2, 3, 4, 5. [corrupt. of DAMN]

darned (-nd) *a.* & *adv.* (sl.) (Mild form of) DAMNED 2, 3. [corrupt. of DAMNED]

dar'nel *n.* grass of genus *Lolium,* growing as weed among corn, or cultivated as ornament. [ME; cf. Walloon *darnelle*]

darshan (dar'shahn) *n.* (Ind.) seeing an august or holy personage. [f. Hindi *darśan* f. Skr. *darśana* view (*drś* see)]

dart *n.* & *v.* **1.** *n.* small pointed missile used as weapon; (in *pl.,* usu. treated as *sing.*) indoor game with light usu. feathered darts and target (∼'**board**); sting of insect etc.; sudden rapid motion; tapering stitched tuck in garment. **2.** *v.t.* throw (missile); direct suddenly (glance, flash). **3.** *v.i.* throw missile; start rapidly in some direction. [ME, f. OF *darz, dars,* f. Frank. *daroth spear, lance]

dar'ter *n.* In vbl senses; tropical web-footed bird of genus *Anhinga,* snake-bird; small Amer. perchlike fish. [f. prec. + -ER[1]]

Dar'tmoor (-moor, -mōr) *n.* ∼ **pony** (small and shaggy); ∼ **sheep,** hardy moorland sheep bred on Dartmoor. [∼ in Devon]

dar'tre (-ter) *n.* Generic name for various skin diseases, esp. herpes; hence **dar'trous** *a.* [F, f. med. L *derbita* f. Gaulish]

Darwi'nian *a.* & *n.* (adherent) of Darwin's doctrine of evolution of species; so **Dar'win**ISM (3), **Dar'win**IST (2), *ns.* [f.C. *Darwin,* Engl. naturalist d. 1882 + -IAN]

dash[1] *v.* **1.** *v.t.* strike with violence so as to shatter; knock, drive, throw, or thrust, *away, off, out, down,* etc.; fling, drive, splash, (thing or person) *against* etc., bespatter *with* mud etc. (∼'**board,** board of wood or leather in front of carriage to keep out mud, board beneath motor-vehicle windscreen, in aircraft, etc., containing instruments and controls; ∼'**pot,** device for damping shock or vibration); frustrate (*dash* one's *hopes*), daunt, discourage, confound; dilute, MIX. **2.** write *down* or throw *off* rapidly (letter, composition, sketch). **3.** (sl.) (Mild form of) DAMN 2. **4.** *v.i.* fall, move, throw oneself, with violence; come into collision *against* etc.; ride, run, or drive *up,* move about, behave, with spirit or display, whence ∼'ING[2] *a.* [ME, prob. imit.]

dash[2] *n.* **1.** sound of water striking or struck; splash of colour; slight admixture of liquid etc. (*dash of brandy, of good blood*); = DASH[1]*board.* **2.** hasty pen-stroke; horizontal stroke in writing or printing to mark a break in sense, (in pairs) a parenthesis, omitted letters or words, etc.; (Mus.) short vertical stroke indicating 'extremely staccato'; longer signal of the two used in Morse code. **3.** rush, onset, sudden advance (**make a** ∼ **for,** try to reach by quickness); *sprinting-race; (capacity for) vigorous action; showy appearance or behaviour (**cut a** ∼, make a brilliant show). [ME, f. prec.]

dash[3] *n., v.t.* (sl.) bribe; (W. Afr.) (provide with) gift or commission. [f. Guinean *dashee*]

da'shiki (dah'-) *n.* loose brightly-coloured shirt worn by Amer. Blacks. [W. Afr.]

da'ssie (dă'-, dah'-) *n.* (S. Afr.) Cape rock-badger; small coastal fish with black tail-spot. [Afrik., f. Du. *dasje* dim. of *das* badger]

dă'stard *n.* mean, base, or despicable coward; hence ∼LY[1] *a.* [ME, prob. f. *dazed* p.p. + -ARD, or obs. *dasart* dullard and *dotard*]

da'syure *n.* (Austral.) small ferocious arboreal catlike

carnivorous marsupial of genus *Dasyurus*. [F, f. mod.
L *dasyurus* f. Gk *dasus* rough + *oura* tail]
data. See DATUM.
dāte¹ *n.* ∿(-**palm**), W. Asian and N. Afr. tree (*Phoenix
dactylifera*); its oblong brown sweet fruit. [ME f. OF, f.
L f. Gk *daktulos* finger, from its leaf-shape]
dāte² *n.* **1.** statement in document, letter, book, or
inscription, of the time (and often place) of execution,
writing, publication, etc.; time at which thing happens or is to happen; (colloq.) engagement, appointment; * (colloq.) person of opposite sex with whom one
has a social engagement. **2.** period to which antiquities etc. belong; duration, term of life. **3.** out of ∿, old-
-fashioned, obsolete; **to** ∿, until now; **up to** ∿, meeting, according to, the latest requirements or knowledge, whence **up-to-**∿ *attrib. a.* **4.** ∿-**line,** (1) line
from north to south pole partly along meridian 180°
from Greenwich, east and west of which the date
differs, (2) line in newspaper at head of dispatch,
special article, etc., giving date and place of writing;
∿-**stamp,** (1) adjustable rubber stamp etc. used to
record date of delivery, receipt, etc., (2) impression
made by this. [ME f. OF, f. med. L *data*, fem. p.p. of
dare, = (letter) given (at specified time and place)]
dāte³ *v.* **1.** *v.t.* mark (letter etc.) with date; refer (event,
thing) *to* a time (*pottery dated to 1500* BC); (colloq.)
make evidently belonging to a past time (*dated
fashions*); ∿ (**up**), *(colloq.)* make social engagement
with; hence **dā′tАBLE** *a.* **2.** *v.i.* count time, reckon;
bear date, be dated; ∿ **back to,** ∿ **from,** have existed since (*church dates from the 14th c.*). **3.** be recognizable as belonging to a past or particular period;
(colloq.) be or become out of date. [ME, f. prec.]
dā′teless (-tl-) *a.* having no date; of immemorial age;
not likely to become out of date; hence ∿NESS *n.* [f.
DATE² +-LESS]
dā′tive *a.* & *n.* **1.** (Gram.) ∿ (**case**), case of nouns etc.
expressing indirect object or recipient, = *to* or *for* w.
the noun etc.; hence **datī′vAL** *a.*, ∿LY² (-vlī) *adv.* **2.**
a. (Sc. Law, of executor) named by court, not by
testator. [ME, f. L (*casus*) *dativus* (*dare dat-* give; see
-IVE), in sense 1 transl. Gk (*ptōsis*) *dotikē*]
dā′tum (dā′-, dah′-) *n.* (*pl.* ∿**a**). **1.** thing known or
granted, assumption or premiss from which infer-
ences may be drawn (SENSE-*datum*); fixed starting-
-point of scale etc. (*datum-line*; ORDNANCE *datum*). **2.**
(in *pl.*, also (**D**) treated as *sing.*) facts or information,
esp. as basis for inference; quantities or characters
operated on by computers etc. and stored or transmitted on punched cards etc.; ∿**a bank,** place where
data are stored in large amounts; ∿**a base,** quantity
of data available for use; ∿**a processing,** automatic
performance of operations on data; ∿**a processor,**
machine for this; ∿**a sheet,** leaflet summarizing
information on a subject. [L, neut. p.p. of *dare* give]
datū′r′a *n.* poisonous plant of genus *Datura*. [mod. L, f.
Hindi *dhatura*]
daub *v.* & *n.* **1.** *v.t.* coat (wall etc.) with plaster, clay,
etc.; smear (surface), lay on (greasy or sticky stuff);
soil, stain. **2.** *v.t.* & *i.* paint crudely and inartistically,
lay (colours) on crudely and clumsily; hence ∿′ER¹,
∿′STER, *ns.* **3.** *n.* plaster, clay, etc., for surface-coating
esp. mixed with straw etc. and applied to laths or
wattles to form wall; crude painting; smear of paint
etc.; hence ∿′Y² *a.* [ME, f. OF *dauber* f. L DE(*albare* f.
albus white) whitewash]
daube (dōb) *n.* braised meat (usu. beef) stew with
wine etc. [F]
dau′ghter (daw′t-) *n.* female child in relation to her
parents; female descendant, female member of family,
nation, etc.; woman who is the spiritual or intellectual product *of* person or thing; product personified as female (*Carthage, daughter of Tyre; Fortune and
its daughter Confidence*); (Phys.) nuclide formed by disintegration of another; (Biol.) cell etc. formed by
division etc. of another; ∿**-in-law,** son's wife; **D**∿**s
of the American Revolution,** patriotic Amer.

women's society; hence ∿HOOD *n.*, ∿LY¹ *a.* [OE
dohtor, = OS *dohtar*, OHG *tohter*, ON *dóttir*, Goth.
dauhtar f. Gmc *dohtēr*, *dhuktēr* f. IE *dhughetēr*]
daunt *v.t.* discourage, intimidate. [ME, f. AF *daunter*,
OF *danter*, *donter* f. L *domitare* frequent. of *domare* tame]
dau′ntless *a.* intrepid, persevering; hence ∿LY² *adv.*,
∿NESS *n.* [f. prec. +-LESS]
dau′phin *n.* (Hist.) King of France's eldest son; hence
∿ESS¹ *n.*, wife of dauphin. [ME, f. F, f. Prov. *dalfin* f.
med. L *dalphinus*, L *delphinus* DOLPHIN, as name of
lords of Viennois or Dauphiné]
dă′venpốrt *n.* ||escritoire with drawers and hinged
writing-slab; *large sofa. [19th c.; f. maker's name]
Dā′vis *n.* ∿ **apparatus,** means of escaping from submarine. [f. Sir R. H. ∿, Engl. inventor d. 1965]
dă′vĭt *n.* crane on board ship, used for hoisting
anchor, torpedo, etc. inboard or outboard; one of
pair of cranes for suspending or lowering ship's boat.
[f. AF & OF *daviot* dim. of *Davi* David]
Dā′vy *n.* ∿ (**lamp**), miner's safety lamp with wire
gauze to prevent explosion of gas. [f. Sir H. ∿, Engl.
chemist d. 1829, who invented it]
Dāvy̆ Jō′nes (-nz) *n.* (Naut. sl.) evil spirit of the sea;
∿'s **locker,** the deep, a watery grave (in the sea).
[18th c., f. unkn. orig.]
daw *n.* = JACK¹*daw*. [ME, corresp. to OE *dāwe*, OHG
tāha]
daw′dle *v.* & *n.* **1.** *v.i.* idle, dally. **2.** *v.t.* ∿ **away,** waste
(time etc.). **3.** *n.* act of dawdling; dawdling person.
[cf. dial. *daddle*, *doddle*, sense 1]
dawg. Var. (colloq.) of DOG¹.
dawk, dak (dawk), *n.* (Ind. Hist.) (post or transport
by) relay of men or horses; ∿ **bungalow,** house for
travellers at place on route of dawk. [f. Hindi &
Marathi *dāk*]
dawn *v.i.*, & *n.* **1.** *v.i.* (of day, daylight, morning,
country shone upon, thing becoming evident to
mind, intelligence, civilization, etc.) begin to appear
or grow light; ∿ (**up**)**on,** begin to be perceptible to;
hence ∿′ING¹ *n.*, daybreak, (fig.) first beginning of
something. **2.** *n.* first light of day, daybreak, rise or
incipient gleam of anything; ∿ **chorus,** early-
-morning bird-song. [n. f. v., back-form. f. *dawning*,
ME f. earlier *dawing* after Scand., as DAY]
day *n.* **1.** time during which sun is above horizon,
interval of light between two nights (*during the day; a
foggy day*); daylight (*by day; was broad day; clear as day*);
time during which work is customarily done (*works an
8-hour day*); day of notable eventfulness etc. **2.** time for
one rotation of earth, period of 24 hours as unit of
time (CIVIL, SIDEREAL, SOLAR, *day*), esp. from midnight to midnight. **3.** civil day as point of time, date,
etc. **4.** date of specified festival etc. (BIRTH*day*,
CHRISTMAS *Day*, LAST³ *Day*) **5.** date agreed upon; day
for regular event (always at home to guests, etc.). **6.**
victory (*carry, lose, save,* WIN, *the day*). **7.** (*in sing.* or *pl.*)
period (*in the days of Queen Victoria; in the days of old; in
days to come; men of other days; in this, that day*); the current
period (*questions of the day*). **8.** (*in sing.* or *pl.*) one's
lifetime, period of prosperity, activity, or power; **has
had its** ∿, is no longer useful. **9. all** (**the**) ∿'s **work,**
part of normal routine; **any** ∿, at any time, under
any conditions; **better** ∿**s,** time when one was or
will be better off; **call it a** ∿, consider that one has
done a day's work and cease working, (fig.) rest
content, cease one's action; (**in**) **this** ∿ **and age,** (at)
the present time; *day* IN², *day out*; ∿ **off** (away from
work etc.); ∿ **out** (away from home or lodgings); *days
of* GRACE; *day of* RECKONING; ∿ **and night,** throughout day or in both alike; ∿ **of rest,** the Sabbath; *day
of the* WEEK; *day* BY¹ *day*; ∿ **to** ∿, continuous(ly),
routine(ly); **every dog has his** ∿, no one is always
unlucky; **at the end of the** ∿, in the final reckoning;
end one's ∿**s,** die, pass last part of one's life; EVIL
day(*s*); **if he's** ∿, (of time, age, etc.) at least;
late in the ∿, (fig.) too late to be useful; SEE¹ *the light*

of day; MAKE[1] one's *day*; MAKE[1] *a day of it*; **not** one's $\sim$, time when things go badly for one; **on** one's $\sim$, at time of one's best achievement etc.; ONE *day*; **one of these** (**fine**) $\sim$s, before long; ORDER[1] *of the day*; *the* OTHER *day*; **some** $\sim$, *so'meday, adv.*, in the future; **that will be the** $\sim$, it will be worth waiting for, (iron.) it will never happen; (**in**) **these** $\sim$s *adv.*, nowadays; **those were the** $\sim$s, past times were better or (iron.) worse; **one of those** $\sim$s, a day of misfortune; TIME[1] *of day*; *a good day's* WORK[1]. **10.** $\sim$**-bed**, bed for daytime sleep or rest; $\sim$**-book**, account-book in which esp. sale transactions are entered at once for later transfer to ledger; $\|\sim$**-boy**, schoolboy in boarding-school but living at home; $\sim$'**break,** dawn, first light of day; $\sim$ **care**, supervision of young children during the day, esp. while mothers are out at work; $\sim$ **centre**, place providing care for elderly or handicapped persons during the day; $\sim$**-dream** *n.*, & *v.i.*, (indulge in) fancy or reverie while awake; $\sim$**-fly**, insect living only a few hours or days; $\|\sim$**-girl**, schoolgirl in boarding-school but living at home; $\sim$**-labourer** (hired by the day); *$\sim$ letter, -priority telegram sent by day; $\sim$ **lily**, plant of genus *Hemerocallis*, with flowers lasting only a day; $\sim$**-long** *a.* & *adv.*, (lasting) (for whole day; $\sim$ **nursery**, (1) room for children in daytime, (2) place where children are looked after while mothers work; $\sim$**-owl**, hawk-owl hunting by day; $\sim$ **release,** system of allowing employees days off work for education; $\sim$**-return,** (ticket) at reduced rate for journey both ways in one day; $\sim$**-room** (used by day only, esp. common living-room at boarding-schools); $\sim$**-school**, opp. Sunday, evening, or boarding--school; $\sim$ **shift,** opp. *night shift*; $\sim$**-spring,** (arch. or poet.) dawn; $\sim$**-star**, sun or morning star; $\sim$'**time,** not night, esp. *in the daytime*; $\sim$'**work** (paid for according to time worked). [OE *dæg,* = OS *dag,* OHG *tac,* ON *dagr,* Goth. *dags* f. Gmc **dagaz*]

Dayak. Var. of DYAK.

day'light (-līt) *n.* light of day; openness, publicity; dawn (*before, at, daylight*); (in *pl., sl.*) internal organs (esp. *beat, scare,* etc. *the daylights out of*); visible interval, e.g. between boats in race, wine and glass-rim, or rider and saddle; **burn** $\sim$, (arch.) use artificial light in daytime; **see** $\sim$, (fig.) understand what was previously puzzling; $\sim$ **robbery,** unashamed swindling; $\sim$ **saving,** use of modified time to give longer evening daylight esp. in summer, by making clocks show later time. [ME, f. DAY + LIGHT[1]]

däze *v.t.,* & *n.* **1.** *v.t.* stupefy, bewilder. **2.** *n.* (state of) stupefaction or bewilderment. [ME *dased* p.p., f. ON *dasathr* weary]

dä'zzle *v.* & *n.* **1.** *v.t.* confuse or dim (sight, eye, person) with excess of light, intricate motion, incalculable number, etc.; delude or surprise (mind, person) by brilliant display or prospect; confuse or impress *by* or *with* brilliance etc., hence $\sim$MENT (-zəlm-) *n.* **2.** *v.i.* (arch.) (Of eyes) be dazzled. **3.** *n.* bright confusing light; $\sim$ **paint** (patterned on ship to deceive enemy about her type or course). [ME, f. prec. + -LE 3]

dB abbr. decibel(s).

$\|$**DBE** *abbr.* Dame Commander (of the Order) of the British Empire.

DC *abbr.* da capo; (*or* **d.c.**) direct current; District of Columbia; District Commissioner.

$\|$**DCB** *abbr.* Dame Commander (of the Order) of the Bath.

DCL *abbr.* Doctor of Civil Law.

DCM *abbr.* Distinguished Conduct Medal.

$\|$**DCMG** *abbr.* Dame Commander (of the Order) of St. Michael & St. George.

$\|$**DCVO** *abbr.* Dame Commander of the Royal Victorian Order.

DD *abbr.* Doctor of Divinity.

D-Day (dē'dā) *n.* day (6 June 1944) on which British and American forces invaded N. France; day (in Britain 15 Feb. 1971) on which decimal currency

came into use; day on which any operation is scheduled to begin. [f. *D* for *day* + DAY]

DDT (dēdētē') *n.* white chlorinated hydrocarbon used as insecticide. [f. Chem. name *dichlorodiphenyltri-chloroethane*]

de- *pref.* meaning (1) down (*depend, descend*), away (*defend, deduct*), removal (*decapitate*), completely (*declare, denude*), in a bad sense (*deceive, defame, deride*); (2) [thr. OF *des-* f. L *dis-*] removal or reversal, forming compd. vbs. (w. derivs.) from vbs. (*de-acidify, decentralize, decentralization, de-escalate, demoralize, demoralization, depressurize, desegregate*) and ns. (*defuse, dehorn, de-ice, delouse, detrain*). [f. or after L *de adv.* & prep. = off, from]

DE *abbr.* Delaware.

*****dea'con** *v.t.* read aloud each line of (hymn etc.) before it is sung; deceive to slight extent. [f. foll.]

dea'con[2] *n.* **1.** (In Episcopal churches) member of third order of ministry, below bishop and priest. **2.** (In Nonconformist churches) lay officer attending to congregation's secular affairs. **3.** (In early Church) appointed minister of charity. **4.** Hence $\sim$ATE[1], $\sim$SHIP, *ns.*[OE *diacon* f. eccl. L f. Gk *diakonos* servant]

dea'coness *n.* woman in early and some modern Churches with functions analogous to deacon's. [f. prec., after LL *diaconissa* (see -ESS[1])]

dēa'ctiv|āte *v.t.* render inactive or less reactive; hence $\sim$A'TION, $\sim$**ātor**, *ns.* [f. DE- + ACTIVATE]

dead (dĕd) *a., adv.,* & *n.* **1.** *a.* that has ceased to live (**the** $\sim$, dead person or persons, all who have ever died; **from the** $\sim$, from among these); $\sim$ **as a doornail,** $\sim$ **as mutton,** quite dead; FLOG *a dead horse*; $\sim$ **from the neck up,** (colloq.) brainless; **wouldn't be seen** $\sim$ **in** etc., (colloq.) shall have nothing to do with, refuse to wear etc.; *dead* BODY[1]; *dead men's* SHOE[1]*s*. **2.** benumbed, insensible, (hands etc.; $\sim$ **to,** unconscious or unappreciative of, hardened against: $\sim$ **to the world,** unconscious or fast asleep); extremely tired or ill; without spiritual life. **3.** obsolete, past, not effective, ($\sim$ **as the** or **a dodo,** entirely obsolete). **4.** inanimate; extinct, dull, lustreless, without force, muffled, (of champagne etc.) no longer effervescent; (of coal) no longer red-hot; (of match) already struck and burnt out; (of sound) not resonant. **5.** inactive (*the dead season*), motionless, idle; (of microphone, telephone, etc.) not transmitting sounds; (of ball in games) out of play. **6.** abrupt, complete, unrelieved, *exact, (come to a dead stop; a dead loss; a dead faint; on a dead level; a dead calm; in dead silence;* (colloq.) *in dead trouble; be in dead earnest; a dead certainty;* **a** $\sim$ **shot,** unerring). **7.** (Golf, of ball) very close to hole, within sure holing distance **8.** $\sim$**-(and-)alive,** (of place, work, etc.) dull, monotonous, (of person) spiritless; $\sim$ **bat,** (Cricket) bat held loosely so that ball strikes it and immediately falls to the ground; $\sim$ **centre,** exact centre, position of crank etc. in line with connecting--rod and not exerting torque; $\sim$ **duck,** (sl.) unsuccessful or useless person or thing; $\sim$ **end,** closed end of passage etc.; $\sim$**-end** *a.,* (fig., of job, policy, etc.) having no prospects of advancement ($\sim$**-end kid,** young slum-dwelling tough); $\sim$**-eye,** (Naut.) round flat three-holed block for extending shrouds; *$\sim$'-**fall,** trap with falling weight to kill animal (also fig.); $\sim$**-fire,** corposant as presaging death; $\sim$ **hand,** post-humous control (esp. fig., of undesirable persisting influence); $\sim$'**head,** faded flower-head (*v.t.,* remove these from (plant)), non-paying theatre-goer etc. or passenger, useless or unenterprising person; $\sim$ **heat,** race in which two or more competitors finish exactly level (so $\sim$*-heat* v.i.); $\sim$ **language,** one no longer ordinarily spoken, e.g. Latin; $\sim$ **letter,** law no longer observed, disused practice, unclaimed or undelivered letter; $\sim$ **lift,** exertion of utmost strength to lift something; $\sim$'**light,** (Naut.) shutter inside porthole; $\sim$'**line,** line beyond which it is not permitted or possible to go, time-limit; $\sim$'**lock,** (1) lock that opens and shuts only with key, (2) complete standstill or lack of progress (so as *v.t.*, bring to standstill); ~ **loss**, complete loss, (colloq.) worthless person or thing; ~ **man's fingers**, (1) kind of orchis, (2) soft coral of genus *Alcyonium*, (3) finger-like divisions of lobster's or crab's gills; ~ **man's handle, pedal**, etc., controlling-device on electric and other trains, disconnecting power supply if released; ~ **march**, marchlike funeral music; ~ **men**, (colloq.) emptied bottles; ~ **nettle**, plant of genus *Lamium*, with nettle-like leaves but not stinging; ~ **pan**, expressionless (face); ~ **reckoning** (Naut., of ship's position by log, compass, etc., when observations are impossible); dead SET²; ~'s **part**, (Sc. Law) part of estate whose disposal is decidable by testator; ~'**stock**, farm machinery; ~ **time**, (Phys.) period after recording of pulse etc. when detector is unable to record another; ~ **weight**, inert mass, (fig.) debt not covered by assets, weight of cargo, fuel, crew, and passengers carried by ship; ~ **wood**, wood no longer alive, (fig.) useless person(s) or thing(s). **9.** Hence ~**NESS** *n.* **10.** *adv.* profoundly, absolutely, exactly, completely,(*dead asleep, drunk, easy, level, on the target* etc., *slow, straight, tired*); CUT² person *dead*; STOP¹ *dead*; ~ **against**, directly opposed or opposite to; ~**-beat**, (person) completely exhausted or without money or *(sl.)* continually in debt, (Phys., of instrument) without recoil; ~**-on** *a.*, exactly right. **11.** *n.* inactive or silent time (*the dead of night, winter*). [OE *dēad* = OS *dōd*, OHG *tōt*, ON *dauthr*, Goth. *dauths* f. Gmc *dhaudhaz* f. *dhautós* p.p. of *dhau*- DIE²]

dea'den (dĕ'd-) *v.t.* & *i.* deprive of or lose vitality, force, brightness, feeling, etc.; make insensitive *to*. [f. prec.+-EN⁶]

dea'dl|ў¹ (dĕ'd-) *a.* causing fatal injury or serious damage; (of aim etc.) accurate; of poisonous nature (*deadly* NIGHTSHADE); entailing damnation (*deadly* SIN¹); implacable, internecine; deathlike (*deadly paleness, faintness, gloom*); intense (*deadly dullness*); (colloq.) dreary; hence ~**íNESS** *n.* [OE *dēadlic* (as DEAD, -LY¹)] **dea'dlỹ²** (dĕ'd-) *adv.* as if dead (*deadly pale, faint*); extremely (*deadly tired, dull*). [OE *dēadlīce* (as DEAD, -LY²)]

dē-aer'|āte (-āɪ'-) *v.t.* remove air from; hence ~**A'TION** *n.* [f. DE-+AERATE]

deaf (dĕf) *a.* **1.** wholly or partly without hearing (**the** ~, deaf people; *deaf in one ear*). **2.** insensitive to harmony, rhythm, etc. (TONE¹-*deaf*); not giving ear *to*, uncompliant; **turn a** ~ **ear**, be unresponsive (*to* appeal etc.); **fall on** ~ **ears**, be ignored. **3.** ~**-aid**, hearing aid; ~**-and-dumb alphabet, language**, etc., manual signs for communication with the deaf; ~ **mute**, deaf and dumb person; ~ **nut**, one with no kernel. **4.** Hence ~'**LY²** *adv.*, ~'**NESS** *n.* [OE *dēaf*, = OS *dōf*, OHG *toup*, ON *daufr* f. Gmc *daubhaz*]

dea'fen (dĕ'f-) *v.t.* deprive of hearing by noise, temporarily or permanently. [f. prec.+-EN⁶]

deal¹ *n.* **a great, good**, ~, (colloq.) **a** ~, a large or considerable amount, (*adv.*) to a large or considerable extent, (esp. w. compar. or superl.) by much, considerably. [OE *dǣl*, = OS *dēl*, OHG *teil*, Goth. *dails* f. Gmc *dailiz*; cf. DOLE¹]

deal² *v.* (~t *pr.* dĕlt) & *n.* **1.** *v.t.* distribute, give *out*, (gifts etc.) among several; (esp. of Providence etc.) deliver as share or deserts to person (*dealt him happiness, good measure*); cause to be received, administer, (esp. ~ **a blow**, lit. or fig.). **2.** *v.t.* & *i.* distribute (cards) to players for a game or round. **3.** *v.i.* associate *with* (esp. w. neg.; *refuse to deal with*); do business *with* person, *in* goods (lit. or fig.). **4.** occupy oneself *with* (esp. with view to discussion or refutation), take (esp. corrective or punitive) measures *with*; (w. *adv.*) behave (*deal honourably, cruelly*, etc., esp. *with* or *by* person). **5.** Hence ~'**ING²** (1) *n.* (**have** ~**ings with**, associate with). **6.** *n.* distribution of cards by dealing, player's turn for this (*it is my deal*), round of play following this; set of hands dealt to players; (colloq.)

bargain, transaction (BIG *deal*); **it's a** ~, (colloq.) I agree to the terms you propose; **new** ~, new and improved arrangement, esp. (*New Deal*) of US reforms 1932–; **raw** or **rough** ~, harsh or unfair treatment; **fair** or SQUARE² *deal*); *secret or dishonest bargain. [OE *dǣlan*, = OS *dēljan*, OHG *teilen*, ON *deila*, Goth. *dailjan* f. Gmc (as prec.)]

deal³ *n.* piece of sawn fir or pine wood of standard size; a quantity of these; fir or pine timber. [ME, f. MLG, MDu. *dele* plank, OHG *dil* etc., ON *thilja* f. Gmc *thelaz* etc.]

dea'ler *n.* In vbl senses; player dealing at cards; trader, usu. in comb., as *horse-dealer*; jobber on Stock Exchange. [f. DEAL²+-ER¹]

dealt. See DEAL².

dĕămbŭlā'tion *n.*, **dĕă'mbūlatorў** *a.* walking about. [f. L *deambulatio, deambulatorius*, f. DE(*ambulare* walk); see -ATION, -ORY]

dean¹ *n.* head of cathedral or collegiate-church chapter; ||(**rural**) ~, clergyman exercising supervision over group of parochial clergy within division of archdeaconry; (in college or university) resident fellow, or one of several, with disciplinary and advisory functions; head of university faculty or department or of medical school; = DOYEN; **D**~ **of Faculty**, president of the Faculty of Advocates in Scotland. [ME, f. AF *de(e)n*, OF *d(e)ien* f. LL *decanus* (*decem* ten); orig. = chief of group of 10]

||**dean².** See DENE².

dea'nerў *n.* office or house of dean; ||group of parishes presided over by rural dean. [f. DEAN¹+-ERY]

dear *a., n., adv.,* & *int.* **1.** *a.* beloved (often as merely polite or even iron. form in talk, esp. **my** ~ **sir, my** ~ **Jones**; now used as part of polite formula at beginning of most letters: *Dear Sir; Dear Mr Jones; Dear Jones* or — ||less formally, *more formally — My dear Jones; Dear Jane; Dear Father*). **2.** precious *to*; cherished (**for** ~ **life**, as though life itself were at stake); earnest (*his dearest desire is for your happiness*). **3.** high-priced relative to its value; having high prices; (of money) available as loan only at high rate of interest. **4.** Hence ~'**LY²** *adv.* (*love* ~**ly** or ~**ly love**, love very much), ~'**NESS** *n.* **5.** *n.* (esp. in *voc.*; also ~'**est**). dear person. **6.** *adv.* at high price relative to value (*buy*, COST² person, *pay, sell, dear*). **7.** *int.* (usu. ~, ~! or ~ **me!** or **oh** ~!) expr. surprise, distress, sympathy, etc.; ~ **knows**, = GOD knows. [OE *dēore*, = OS *diuri*, OHG *tiuri*, ON *dýrr* f. Gmc *deurjaz*]

dear'ie *n.* (usu. in *voc.*) darling; ~ **me!**, = prec. **7.** [f. prec.+-IE]

dearth (dēr-) *n.* scarcity and dearness of food; scanty supply *of*. [ME, f. as DEAR; see -TH¹]

dea'sil (dĕ's-) *adv.* (esp. Sc.) in the direction of sun's apparent course (considered as lucky), clockwise. [f. Gael. *deiseil*]

death (dĕth) *n.* **1.** dying, final cessation of vital functions; DIE² *the death*; **as sure as** ~, quite certain. **2.** event that terminates life; **civil** ~, ceasing to have citizen's privileges through outlawry, banishment, etc.; **catch one's** ~, (colloq.) catch fatal chill etc. **3.** being killed or killing (**be the** ~ **of**, cause death of; *bleed, drink* oneself, *put, stone, work*, etc., *to death; war to the death*); **be in at the** ~, see fox killed, or (fig.) any enterprise ended; **be** ~ **on**, (sl.) be skilful at killing game, prey, etc., or (fig.) at doing anything; **do to** ~, kill, (fig.) overdo; **fate worse than** ~, (joc.) being raped; **scared to**, sick, **tickled to, tired to,** ~ (to utmost limit); **worked to.** ~, (fig.) hackneyed. **4.** ceasing to be, annihilation (*death of one's hopes*); (**D**~) personified power that annihilates; at ~'**s door**, close to death; **like** ~ **warmed up**, (sl.) very tired or ill; *hold on* **like grim** ~, with all one's force. **5.** being dead (*eyes closed in death*, LIVING² DEATH). **6.** lack of spiritual life (**everlasting** ~, damnation). **7. Black D**~, (mod. name, transl. f. G, for) great epidemic of plague in Europe in 14th c. **8.** Hence or cogn. ~'**LESS**, ~'**LIKE**, *adjs.*, ~**LY¹** *a.* & *adv.* **9.**

∼ **adder,** venomous Austral. snake; ∼**'bed,** bed on which person dies (∼*bed repentance* etc., last-minute change of conduct or policy); ∼**-blow,** blow that causes death (lit. or fig.); ∼ **cap,** a poisonous toadstool (*Amanita phalloides*); ∼ **cell** (for person condemned to death); ∼ **certificate,** official statement of cause and date and place of person's death; ∼**-dealing,** lethal; ||∼ **duty,** (Hist.) tax levied on property after owner's death; *∼ **house,** group of death cells; ∼**-knell,** tolling of bell to mark person's death, (fig.) event that heralds the end of something; ∼**-mask,** cast taken of dead person's face; ∼ **penalty,** capital punishment; ∼ **rate,** number of deaths per thousand of population per year; ∼**-rattle,** sound in dying person's throat; ∼**-ray,** (imaginary) ray that causes death; ∼**-roll,** list or number of those killed in accident, battle, etc.; ∼**'s head,** skull as emblem of mortality (∼**'s head moth,** large dark hawk-moth with skull-like markings on back of thorax); *∼ **tax,** = *death duty*; ∼**-toll,** = *death-roll*; ∼**-trap,** unsuspectedly unwholesome or dangerous place or structure; ∼**-warrant** (for execution of criminal or (fig.) abolition of custom, etc.); ∼**-watch (beetle),** small beetle whose larva bores in old wood and which makes sound like watch ticking, once supposed to portend death; ∼**-wish,** (Psych.) (usu. unconscious) wish for death of oneself or another. [OE *dēath,* – OS *dōth,* OHG *tōd,* ON *dauthr,* Goth. *dauthus* f. Gmc **dauthuz* (**dau-* DIE[2]; see -TH[1])]
dĕb *n.* (colloq.) débutante. [abbr.]
débâcle (dābah'kl) *n.* **1.** break-up of ice in river; sudden rush of water carrying along blocks of stone and other debris. **2.** sudden collapse; downfall, e.g. of a government; confused rush or rout, stampede. [F (*débâcler* unbar)]
dĕbă'g *v.t.* (-gg-). (sl.) remove the trousers of (person) as punishment or joke. [f. DE-+BAG[1]]
dĕbar' *v.t.* (-rr-). exclude *from* admission or right; prohibit *from* doing. [ME, f. F *débarrer,* OF *desbarrer* (*des-* DE-, *barrer* BAR[2])]
dĕbâr'k[1] *v.t. & i.* = DISEMBARK; hence **dĕbărkā'TION** *n.* [f. F *débarquer* (as DE-, BARK[3])]
dĕbâr'k[2] *v.t.* remove bark from (tree). [f. DE-+BARK[1]]
dĕbâr'k[3] *v.t.* operate on (dog) to prevent it from barking. [f. DE-+BARK[4]]
dĕbă'se *v.t.* lower in quality, value, or character; deprociate (coin) by alloying etc.; hence ∼MENT (-sm-) *n.* [f. DE-+obs. *base* for ABASE]
dĕbă'tab|le *a.* questionable, subject to dispute; capable of being debated; ∼**le ground,** borderland (lit. or fig.) claimed by both sides; hence ∼LY[2] *adv.* [OF, or f. AL *debatabilis* (as foll.; see ABLE)]
dĕbā't|e *v. & n.* **1.** *v.t. & i.* dispute about, discuss, (a question); hold formal argument, esp. in legislature or public meeting; consider, ponder; (arch.) contest; hence ∼ER[1] *n.* **2.** *n.* debating, discussion; public argument. [ME; (n. f. OF *debat*) f. OF *debatre* f. Rom. **desbattere* (as DE-, BATTLE[1])]
dĕbā'ting *n.* In vbl senses; ∼ **club, society,** (for practice in debating); ∼ **point,** inessential matter used to gain advantage in debate. [f. prec.+-ING[1]]
dĕbau'ch *v.t., & n.* (literary). **1.** *v.t.* pervert from virtue or morality; make intemperate or sensual; seduce (woman); vitiate (taste, judgement); (in *p.p.*) dissolute. **2.** *n.* bout or habit of sensual indulgence; hence ∼ERY (4) *n.* [f. F *débauche(r),* OF *desbaucher,* of unkn. orig.]
dĕbauchee' *n.* excessively sensual person; person addicted to sensual indulgence. [f. F *débauché* p.p.; see prec., -EE]
dĕbea'k *v.t.* remove upper part of beak of (bird) to prevent fighting etc. [f. DE-+BEAK[1]]
dĕbĕ'nture *n.* **1.** ||sealed bond of corporation or company acknowledging sum on which interest is due, esp. as prior charge on assets (∼ **stock,** stock comprising debentures, with only interest secured);

*∼ **(bond),** fixed-interest bond of corporation or company; (arch.) voucher for payment from government department. [ME, f. L *debentur* are owing (*debēre* owe); assim. to -URE]
dĕbi'lităte *v.t.* enfeeble (constitution etc.). [f. L *debilitare* (as foll.)+-ATE[3]]
dĕbi'lity *n.* feebleness (of health, purpose, etc.). [ME, f. OF *debilité* f. L *debilitas -tatis* (*debilis* weak; see -ITY)]
dĕ'bit *n., & v.t.* **1.** *n.* (Bookk.) record of sum owing by entry in account; (sum entered on) debit side of account. **2.** *v.t.* enter on debit side of account (amount *against* or to person, person *with* amount). [f. F *débit* f. L *debitum* DEBT]
dĕbonair' *a.* having pleasant manners; cheerful, carefree, unembarrassed. [ME, f. OF *debonaire* = *de bon aire* of good disposition]
dĕbou'ch (-ow'ch, -ōō'sh) *v.i.* (Of troops, stream) issue from ravine, wood, etc., into open ground; (of river, road, etc.) emerge *into* larger body or area (sea, square, etc.); hence ∼MENT *n.* [f. F *déboucher* (dé- DE-, *bouche* mouth)]
||**Dĕbrè'tt** *n.* (colloq.) (Used for) 'Debrett's Peerage etc.' [f.J. ∼, compiler d. 1822]
dĕbrie'f *v.t.* (colloq.) interrogate (person) after completion of mission etc. [f. DE-+BRIEF[2]]
dĕ'bris (dĕ'brē, dā'-) *n.* scattered fragments, wreckage, drifted accumulation. [f. F *débris* f. obs. *débriser* break down (as DE-, *briser* break)]
dĕbt (dĕt) *n.* **1.** money, goods, or service, owing; BAD *debt,* ∼**-collector,** one whose business it is to collect debts for creditors; ∼ **of honour** (not legally recoverable, esp. of sum lost in gambling); ∼ **of nature,** necessity of death; **floating** ∼ (repayable on demand, or at stated time); **National D∼,** money owed by State because of loans to it. **2.** being under obligation to pay something (*in, out of, get into, debt*); **in** person's ∼, under obligation to him. [ME *det(te)* f. OF *dette* (later *debte*) f. Rom. **debita* f. L *debitum* p.p. of *debēre* owe]
dĕ'btor (dĕ't-) *n.* one who owes money or an obligation or duty. [ME f. OF *det(t)o(u)r* f. L *debitor* (as prec.; see -OR)]
dĕbŭ'g *v.t.* (-gg-). remove bugs (lit., or fig. = defects or microphones) from. [f. DE-+BUG]
dĕbŭ'nk *v.t.* (colloq.) remove falsely good reputation from (person, institution, cult, etc.); expose falseness of (claim etc.). [f. DE-+BUNK[1]]
dĕbŭ's *v.t. & i.* (-ss-). (esp. Mil.) unload (men, stores) or alight from motor vehicles. [f. DE-+BUS]
dĕbut, *debut, (dā'bōō, bū) *n.* first appearance in society, or on stage, in sport, etc. as performer. [F (*débuter* lead off)]
dĕbutante, *deb-, (dĕ'būtahnt, dā'-) *n.* woman performer making début; young woman making social début. [F, fem. part. of *débuter* (see prec.)]
Dec. *abbr.* December.
dec. *abbr.* deceased; declared.
dĕ'ca- *comb. form.* **1.** tenfold, having ten, as: **deca'gynous** (-ă'j-), having ten pistils; ∼HE'DRAL, having ten faces (∼HE'DRON, such solid); **deca'ndrous,** having ten stamens; ∼**style,** ten-columned (portico). **2.** ten, esp. of a unit in the metric system (*decagram, decalitre, decametre*). [f. Gk *deka* ten]
decade (dĕ'kād, D dīkā'd) *n.* set or series of ten; ten years; so **dĕ'cadAL, dĕcā'dIC,** *adjs.* [ME, f. F *décade* f. LL *decas -adis* f. Gk (*deka* ten); see -AD, -ADE]
dĕ'cadence *n.* falling away, decline, deterioration, (esp. of a period of art or literature after culmination). [f. F *décadence* f. med. L *decadentia* (*decadere* DECAY); see -ENCE)]
dĕ'cadent *a. & n.* **1.** *a.* declining, decaying, self-indulgent; of a period of decadence. **2.** *n.* decadent person; 19th-c. writer or artist with artificial and obscure style, whence ∼ISM (3) *n.* [f. F *décadent* (as prec.; see -ENT)]
dĕcă'ffeinate (-fĭn-) *v.t.* remove caffeine from or

reduce quantity of caffeine in (coffee). [f. DE- + CAFFEINE + -ATE³]

dě′cagon n. plane figure with ten sides and angles; hence **děcă′gon**AL a. [f. med. L f. Gk dekagōnon (as DECA-, -GON)]

*****dě′căl** n. picture transferred to and permanently fixed on china or other material. [abbr. of decalcomania such process f. F décalcomanie (décalquer transfer; see -MANIA)]

děcă′lci‌fy̆ v.t. deprive (bone etc.) of lime or calcareous matter; hence ∼FICA′TION n. [f. DE- + CALCIFY]

Dě′calŏgue (-ŏg) n. the Ten COMMANDMENTS collectively. [ME f. OF, or f. eccl. L f. Gk dekalogos (after hoi deka logoi the ten commandments)]

děcă′mp v.i. break up or leave camp; go away suddenly, take oneself off, abscond; hence ∼MENT n. [f. F décamper (as DE-, CAMP¹)]

decanal (dǐkā′-, dě′ka-) a. of dean or deanery; of S. side (on which dean sits) of choir (cf. CANTORIAL). [f. med. L decanalis f. LL decanus DEAN¹; see -AL]

děcā′nī a. (Mus.) to be sung by decanal side in antiphonal singing (cf. CANTORIS). [L, gen. of decanus DEAN¹]

děcă′nt v.t. pour off (liquid or solution) by gradual inclination of vessel without disturbing sediment; pour (wine) similarly from bottle into decanter; (fig.) move or transfer as if by pouring. [f. med. L DE(canthare f. L f. Gk kanthos canthus, used of lip of beaker)]

děcă′nter n. stoppered glass bottle in which wine or spirit is brought to table. [f. prec. + -ER¹]

děcă′pĭt‌āte v.t. behead (esp. as legal punishment); cut the head or end from; *dismiss abruptly from office; so ∼A′TION n. [f. LL DE(capitare f. caput -itis head)]

dě′capŏd n. ten-footed crustacean (crab, lobster, etc.). [f. F décapode f. mod. L decapoda f. Gk deka ten + pous podos foot]

děcā′r′bonīz‌e, -īs‌e (-īz) v.t. remove carbon from (internal combustion engine etc.); hence ∼A′TION n. [f. DE- + CARBON + -IZE]

děcă′sualīz‌e (-zhyōō-, -zyōō-), **-īs‌e** (-īz) v.t. do away with casual employment of (labour) by introducing permanent jobs; hence ∼A′TION n. [f. DE- + CASUAL + -IZE]

děcasy̆lla′bic a. & n., **dě′casy̆llable** n. (metrical line) of ten syllables. [f. DECA- + SYLLABIC, SYLLABLE]

děc‌|ă′thlon n. athletic contest comprising ten different events for competitor; hence ∼ A′THLETE n. [f. DECA- + Gk athlon contest]

děcay′¹ v.i. & t. (cause to) become rotten; (cause to) deteriorate, lose quality, decline in power, wealth, energy, beauty, etc.; (Phys.) decrease in amplitude or intensity of radioactivity, (of substance etc.) change by radioactivity into another. [ME, f. OF decair f. Rom. *DE(cadere fall)]

děcay′² n. decline in health, loss of quality; rotten or ruinous state, wasting away; decayed tissue; (Phys.) loss of amplitude or intensity of radioactivity, change into another substance etc. by radioactivity. [ME, f. prec.]

děcea′s‌e n., & v.i. (Esp. formal and Law). death, die; hence ∼ED¹ (2) (-ē′st) a. & n. (with or without the), (person) who has died (esp. recently). [ME, f. OF deces f. L DE(cessus n. f. cedere cess- go)]

*****děcē′dent** n. deceased person. [f. L decedere (as prec., -ENT]

děcei′t (-sē′t) n. misrepresentation, deceiving; trick, stratagem; willingness to deceive; hence ∼FUL a. [ME f. OF, f. p.p. of deceveir f. L DE(cipere cept- = capere take) deceive]

děcei′ve (-sē′v) v. 1. v.t. persuade of what is false, mislead purposely, (∼ oneself, be ∼d, be mistaken or deluded); disappoint (esp. hopes). 2. v.i. use deceit. 3. Hence or cogn. **děcei′vable** a., **děcei′ver¹** n., (-sē′-). [ME, f. OF deceivre or deceiv- stressed st. of deceveir (as prec.)]

děcē′ler‌āte v. 1. v.t. make slower (decelerated motion);

cause to move more slowly. 2. v.i. begin to move more slowly. 3. Hence ∼A′TION, ∼ātor, ∼ŏ′meter, ns. [f. DE-, after ACCELERATE]

Děcē′mber n. twelfth month of year. [ME, f. OF decembre f. L December (decem ten; orig. tenth month of Roman year)]

dě′cency̆ n. propriety of behaviour; what is accepted as being required by good taste or delicacy; avoidance of obscene language and gestures and of undue exposure of person; respectability; (in pl.) requirements of respectable behaviour. [f. L decentia (decēre be fitting; see -ENCY)]

děcě′nnial a. lasting, recurring every, ten years; hence ∼LY² adv. [f. L (as foll.) + -AL]

děcě′nni‌um n. (pl. ∼ums or ∼a). period of ten years. [L, f. decennis of ten years (decem ten, annus year)]

dē′cent a. seemly, not immodest or obscene or indelicate; respectable; passable, good enough, tolerable; ‖(colloq.) kind, generous, obliging; hence ∼LY² adv. [f. F décent or f. L decēre be fitting; see -ENT]

děcě′ntralīz‌|e, -īs‌|e (-īz), v.t. do away with centralization of; confer local government on; distribute (administrative powers etc.) among local centres; hence ∼A′TION n. [f. DE- + CENTRALIZE]

děcě′ption n. deceiving or being deceived; thing that deceives, trick, sham. [ME f. OF, or f. LL deceptio (decipere; see DECEIT, -ION)]

děcě′ptive a. apt to deceive, easily mistaken for something else; hence ∼LY² (-vlĭ) adv., ∼NESS (-vn-) n. [f. OF deceptif -ive or f. LL deceptivus (as prec.; see -IVE)]

děcě′rebrate a. having had the cerebrum removed. [f. DE- + CEREBRUM + -ATE²]

dě′ci- comb. form. one-tenth, esp. of a unit in the metric system (DECIBEL, decigram, decilitre, decimetre). [f. L decimus tenth]

dě′cibĕl n. unit (= one-tenth of a bel) used in comparison of power levels in electrical communication or intensities of sound, one of the compared values often being an understood standard. [f. prec. + BEL]

děci′d‌|e v.t. & i. settle (question, issue, dispute) by giving victory to one side; give judgement (between, for, in favour of, against, that, or abs.); bring or come to a resolution (that decides me; decide to do, on, for or against thing or doing, that); hence ∼ABLE a. [ME, f. F décider or f. L DE(cidere cis- = caedere cut)]

děci′dĕd a. In vbl senses; definite, unquestionable, (a decided difference); (of person) having clear opinions or vigorous initiative, not vacillating; hence ∼LY² adv. [p.p. of prec.]

děci′der n. in vbl senses; game, race, etc., to decide between competitors with equal scores. [f. DECIDE + -ER¹]

děci′dŭous a. (Of leaves, teeth, horns etc.) shed periodically or normally; (of tree) shedding its leaves annually; (of ant etc.) shedding its wings after copulation; (fig.) fleeting, transitory. [f. L deciduus f. DE(cidere = cadere fall) + -OUS]

dě′cimal a. & n. 1. a. of tenths or ten, reckoning or proceeding by tens; ∼ arithmetic (counting in tens); ∼ coinage, currency, (in which units are decimal multiples or fractions of each other); ∼ fraction, one whose denominator is a power of ten esp. when expressed by figures written to right of the ∼ point or dot placed after the unit figure; decimal SCALE³; ∼ system (in which each denomination (weight, measure) is ten times the value of the one before it, or in which each class is divided into ten subclasses). 2. of decimal coinage; go ∼, adopt decimal coinage. 3. Hence ∼IZE v.t., express as decimal, convert to decimal system, ∼LY² adv. 4. n. decimal fraction (RECURRING decimal). [f. mod. L decimalis f. decimus tenth (decem ten; see -AL)]

dě′cim‌|āte v.t. 1. (Hist.) put to death one in ten of (mutinous or cowardly soldiers). 2. (Of epidemic

etc.) destroy tenth or large proportion or (**D**) nine-
-tenths of. **3.** So ∿ᴀ′ᴛɪᴏɴ *n.* [f. L *decimare* take the
tenth man (*decimus*; see prec.) + -ᴀᴛᴇ³]
dĕcī′pher *v.t.* turn into ordinary writing or make out
by means of key (text written in cipher); make out
meaning of (bad writing, hieroglyphics, anything
perplexing); hence ∿ᴀʙʟᴇ *a.*, ∿ᴍᴇɴᴛ *n.* [f. ᴅᴇ-+
ᴄɪᴘʜᴇʀ²]
dĕcī′sion (-zhon) *n.* settlement (*of* question etc.),
conclusion, formal judgement; making up one's
mind, resolve, (*come to, make, take, a decision*); resoluteness, decided character. [ME f. OF, or f. L *decisio* (as
ᴅᴇᴄɪᴅᴇ; see -ɪᴏɴ)]
dĕcī′sive *a.* deciding, conclusive, (esp. *decisive battle*);
= ᴅᴇᴄɪᴅᴇᴅ (*decisive character, decisive preference*); hence
∿ʟʏ² (-vlĭ) *adv.*, ∿ɴᴇss (-vn-) *n.* [f. F *décisif -ive* f.
med. L *decisivus* (as ᴅᴇᴄɪᴅᴇ; see -ɪᴠᴇ)]
dĕck¹ *n.* **1.** platform of planks or wood-covered iron
extending from side to side of ship or part of it; **below**
∿(**s**), in or into space under main deck; ᴄʟᴇᴀʀ² *the
decks*; ʟᴏᴡᴇʀ³ *deck*; **on** ∿, not below deck, (fig.)
available for work etc. **2.** floor of pier; floor or
compartment of bus etc.; platform for sunbathing
etc.; device for carrying and moving (and playing
etc., or transferring information to or from) magnetic
tape in recorder; similar arrangement in record-
-player; (sl.) ground. **3.** ∿-**chair**, folding chair of
wood and canvas, used in passenger ships and
elsewhere; ∿-**hand**, man employed on vessel's deck
in cleaning and odd jobs; ∿-**house**, room erected on
deck; ∿ **passenger** (having no cabin); ∿ **quoits**
(played with rope quoit and peg); ∿ **tennis**, game of
tossing quoit etc. to and fro over net. **4.** *pack of
cards; *packet of narcotics. [ME = 'covering', f.
MDu. *dec* roof, cloak]
dĕck² *v.t.* **1.** ∿ (**out**), array, adorn. **2.** furnish with or
cover as a deck. [f. MDu. *dekken* cover; cf. ᴛʜᴀᴛᴄʜ]
decker *comb. form.* having (so many, such) decks or
layers (*double-decker bus*); **three**-∿ (= three-volume)
novel. [f. ᴅᴇᴄᴋ¹ + ᴇʀ¹]
dĕ′ckle *n.* frame in paper-making machine for limiting size of sheet (∿-**edge**, rough uncut edge formed
by deckle). [f. G *deckel* dim. of *decke* cover; cf. -ʟᴇ l]
dĕclai′m *v.i.* & *t.* speak or utter rhetorically; inveigh
against; practise speaking or recitation; deliver impassioned (rather than reasoned) speech; hence
∿ᴇʀ¹ *n.* [ME, f. F *déclamer* or f. L *declamare*; see ᴅᴇ-l,
ᴄʟᴀɪᴍ¹]
dĕclamā′tion *n.* act or art of declaiming; rhetorical
exercise, set speech; impassioned speech, harangue;
so **dĕclā′matory** *a.* [f. F *déclamation* or f. L *declamatio*
(as prec.; see -ᴀᴛɪᴏɴ)]
dĕclā′rant *n.* one who makes legal declaration. [f. F
déclarant part. of *déclarer,* f. as ᴅᴇᴄʟᴀʀᴇ]
dĕclarā′tion *n.* stating or announcing openly or
formally; emphatic, solemn, or legal assertion, announcement, or proclamation (∿ **of the poll,**
public official announcement of vote-totals of
election-candidates; ∿ **of war,** announcement before beginning hostilities); written public announcement of intentions, terms of agreement, etc.; (Cricket)
act of declaring (see foll.); (Law) plaintiff's statement
of claim, affirmation in lieu of oath; (Cards) naming
of trumps by player in turn or by winning bid,
announcement of combination held. [ME, f. L
declaratio (as foll.; see -ᴀᴛɪᴏɴ)]
dĕclā′re *v.* **1.** *v.t.* make known, announce openly or
formally, (*declare* ᴡᴀʀ¹, *a dividend*); state explicitly; (of
things) make evident, prove, (*the heavens declare the
glory of God*); (abs.) **well, I** (**do**) ∿ (excl. of incredu-
ity, surprise, or vexation). **2.** *v.t.* & *i.* pronounce
(*person* etc.) to be something (*declare him to be*) *a
villain*); ∿ one**self,** avow intentions, reveal character; ∿ **for** or **against,** openly side with or against; ∿
innings closed), (Cricket) elect to cease team's
batting before all wickets have fallen; (in *p.p.*) who is
such by his own admission (*a declared atheist*). **3.** *v.t.*

acknowledge possession of (dutiable goods, income,
etc.). **4.** (Cards). name the trump suit (see prec.);
announce that one holds (certain combinations of
cards etc.). **5.** Hence or cogn. **dĕclă′rative, dĕ-
clă′ratory** *adjs.,* **dĕclar′ᴇʀ¹** *n.* (esp. at cards; in
Bridge, player in pair making highest bid who first
made bid in same suit or no-trumps). [ME, f. L
ᴅᴇ(*clarare* f. *clarus* clear)]
déclassé (dāklă′sā) *a.* (*fem.*∿**e** *pr.* same). that has
fallen in social status. [F]
dĕclă′ssify *v.t.* cease to designate (information etc.)
as secret. [f. ᴅᴇ-+ᴄʟᴀssɪꜰʏ]
dĕclĕ′nsion (-shon) *n.* **1.** declining, deterioration. **2.**
(Gram.) variation of form of noun etc. to give its
cases; class in which noun etc. is put according to this
variation. [f. OF *declinaison* (*decliner* ᴅᴇᴄʟɪɴᴇ¹), after
L *declinatio,* assim. to *ascension* etc.]
dĕclinā′tion *n.* downward bend or turn; *declining,
refusal; (Astron.) angular distance of star etc. north
or south of celestial equator; (Phys.) angular deviation of compass needle, E. or W. from true north;
hence ∿ᴀʟ *a.* [ME, f. L *declinatio* (as foll.; see -ᴀᴛɪᴏɴ)]
dĕclī′ne¹ *v.* **1.** *v.i.* slope downwards; bend down,
droop; (of day, life, etc.) draw to close (**declining
years,** old age); fall off, decay, deteriorate; decrease
in price etc. **2.** *v.t.* bend down, how; turn away from,
refuse, (discussion, challenge, battle; *decline* to do,
doing, *to be made use of* etc.); say politely that one
cannot accept (invitation etc., or abs., ∿ **with
thanks,** freq. iron., reject scornfully). **3.** (Gram.)
inflect, state the case-forms of; so **dĕclī′nable** *a.*
[ME, f. OF *decliner* f. L ᴅᴇ(*clinare* bend)]
dĕclī′ne² *n.* sinking, gradual loss of vigour or excellence (*on the decline*); decay, deterioration; (arch.)
tuberculosis or similar disease; fall in price; setting,
last part of course, (of sun, life, etc.). [ME, f. prec.]
dĕclĭnŏ′meter *n.* instrument for measuring astronomical or magnetic declination. [irreg. f. L *declinare*
(see ᴅᴇᴄʟɪɴᴇ¹) + -ᴏ- + -ᴍᴇᴛᴇʀ]
dĕclī′vĭt|**ў** *n.* downward slope; sloping ground; hence
∿ᴏᴜs *a.* [f. L *declivitas* f. ᴅᴇ(*clivis* f. *clivus* slope); see
-ɪᴛʏ]
dĕclŭ′tch *v.i.* disengage clutch of motor vehicle;
double-∿, release and re-engage clutch twice when
changing gear. [f. ᴅᴇ-+ᴄʟᴜᴛᴄʜ²]
dĕcŏ′ct *v.t.* make decoction of. [ME, f. L *decoquere* boil
down; see foll.]
dĕcŏ′ction *n.* boiling down so as to extract essence;
liquor resulting from this. [ME f. OF, or f. LL
ᴅᴇ(*coctio* f. *coquere coct-* boil; see -ɪᴏɴ)]
dĕcŏ′de *v.t.* decipher (coded message); hence ∿ᴇʀ¹ *n.*,
(esp.) device for analysing stereophonic signals and
feeding separate amplifier-channels. [f. ᴅᴇ-+ᴄᴏᴅᴇ]
||**dĕcŏ′ke** *v.t.,* & *n.* (colloq.) **1.** *v.t.* remove carbon from
(internal combustion engine). **2.** *n.* process of de-
coking. [f. ᴅᴇ-+ᴄᴏᴋᴇ¹]
dĕcŏ′llate *v.t.* behead; truncate; so ∿ᴀ′ᴛɪᴏɴ *n.* [f. L
ᴅᴇ(*collare* f. *collum* neck) + -ᴀᴛᴇ³]
décolletage (dākŏ′ltahzh) *n.* (exposure of neck and
shoulders by) low-cut neck of woman's garment. [F
(ᴅᴇ-, *collet* collar of dress; see -ᴀɢᴇ)]
décolleté (dākŏ′ltā) *a.* (*fem.* ∿**e** *pr.* same). (Of garment) low-necked; (of woman) wearing low-necked
garment. [F, as prec.]
dĕcŏlonizā′tion *n.* withdrawal of a State from its
former colonies, leaving them independent; acquisition of such independence. [f. ᴅᴇ-+ᴄᴏʟᴏɴɪᴢᴀᴛɪᴏɴ]
dĕcŏ′loriz|**e,** ||**-our-,** (-kŭ′ler-), **-ĭs**|**e** (-īz), *v.t.* & *i.*
remove colour from; bleach; hence ∿ᴀ′ᴛɪᴏɴ *n.* [f.
ᴅᴇ-+ᴄᴏʟᴏᴜʀ¹+-ɪᴢᴇ]
dĕcŏmpŏ′s|**e** (-z) *v.t.* & *i.* separate (substance, light,
etc.) into its elements or simpler constituents; disintegrate, break up; rot; decay; hence ∿ᴀʙʟᴇ *a.,*
dĕcŏmposi′tion (-z-) *n.* [f. F *décomposer* (as ᴅᴇ-,
ᴄᴏᴍᴘᴏsᴇ)]
dĕcŏ′mposite (-z-) *a.* & *n.* = foll. [f. LL *decompositus*
(transl. Gk *parasunthetos*; as ᴅᴇ-, ᴄᴏᴍᴘᴏsɪᴛᴇ)]

dē'compound *a.* & *n.* (substance, word, etc.) that is a compound of something itself a compound (e.g. *gentlemanly* from *gentleman*). [f. DE- (as prec.) + compound²]

dēcomprĕ'ss *v.t.* relieve or reduce pressure on (e.g. underwater or other worker by means of an air-lock); hence **dēcomprĕ'ssION** (-ĕ'shon) *n.* ∿**ion sickness,** caisson disease), ∿OR *n.*, device for reducing pressure in motor-vehicle engine. [f. DE- + COMPRESS²]

dēcongĕ'stant (-nj-) *a.* & *n.* (drug etc.) that relieves congestion. [f. DE- + CONGEST + -ANT]

dēcŏ'nsēcr|āte *v.t.* transfer from sacred to secular use; hence ∿A'TION *n.* [f. DE- + CONSECRATE]

dēcontă'min|āte *v.t.* remove (risk of) contamination from (esp. area, clothes, person, etc., affected by poison gas or by radioactivity); hence ∿A'TION *n.* [f. DE- + CONTAMINATE]

dēcontrō'l *v.t.* (-ll-), & *n.* **1.** *v.t.* release (commodity, etc.) from (esp. Government) control. **2.** *n.* act of decontrolling. [f. DE- + CONTROL¹,²]

décor (dā'kōr) *n.* furnishing and decoration of room or stage. [F (*décorer,* as foll.)]

dē'cor|āte *v.t.* furnish with adornments (esp. church with flowers, street with flags, house or room with new paint, etc.); serve as adornment to; invest with order, medal, etc.; hence ∿ativE *a.* [f. L *decorare* (*decus -oris* beauty) + -ATE³]

dē'corātĕd *a.* In vbl senses; **D**∿ **style,** (Archit.) second stage of English Gothic (14th c.), with increasing decoration and geometrical tracery. [p.p. of prec.]

dēcorā'tion *n.* In vbl senses; medal, cross, etc., conferred and worn as honour (*D∿ Day,** Memorial Day); (in *pl.*) flags etc. put up on occasion of public rejoicing. [f. F *décoration* or f. LL *decoratio* (as DECOR-ATE; see -ATION)]

dē'corātor *n.* In vbl senses; tradesman who papers, paints, etc., houses. [f. DECORATE + -OR]

dē'corous *a.* not violating good taste or propriety; dignified and decent; hence ∿LY² *adv.*, ∿NESS *n.* [f. L *decorus* seemly + -OUS]

dēcŏr'tic|āte *v.t.* remove bark, rind, or husk from; remove cerebral cortex from; hence ∿A'TION *n.* [f. L DE(*corticare* f. *cortex -icis* bark) + -ATE³]

dēcŏr'um *n.* seemliness, propriety, etiquette; particular usage required by politeness or decency. [L, neut. (as n.) of *decorus* seemly]

découpage (dākōōpah'zh) *n.* decoration of surfaces with paper cut-outs. [F, = action of cutting out]

décou'ple (-kŭ'-) *v.t.* (Electr.) make coupling between (oscillators etc.) so weak that there is little transfer of energy between them. [f. DE- + COUPLE²]

décoy' *n.*, & *v.t.* **1.** *n.* (or dē'-). pond with narrow netted arms into which wild duck may be tempted and caught; bird etc. trained to entice others; swindler's confederate, tempter; bait, enticement. **2.** *v.t.* entice into decoy; allure *into, out of,* etc., ensnare. [17th c., perh. f. Du. *de kooi* the decoy (*de* THE, *kooi* f. L *cavea* cage)]

dēcrea'se¹ *v.i.* & *t.* lessen, diminish. [ME, f. OF *de(s)creiss-,* pres. st. of *de(s)creistre* f. Rom. **discrescere* f. L DE(*crescere cret-* grow)]

dē'crease² *n.* diminution, lessening. [ME, f. OF *de(s)creis* f. st. of *de(s)creistre* (see prec.)]

dēcree' *n.*, & *v.t.* **1.** *n.* ordinance or edict set forth by authority; judgement in court of equity, admiralty, probate, or divorce (∿ **nisi** *pr.* nī'sī, provisional order for divorce, made absolute unless cause to the contrary is shown within fixed period); will, as shown by result, of God, Providence, Nature, etc. **2.** *v.t.* ordain by decree. [ME, f. OF *decré* f. L DE(*cretum* neut. p.p. of *cernere* sift) thing decided]

dē'crĕment *n.* decrease, amount lost by diminution or waste; (Phys.) ratio of amplitudes in successive cycles of damped oscillation. [f. L *decrementum* (as DECREASE¹; see -MENT)]

dēcrĕ'pi|t *a.* wasted, worn out, enfeebled with age

and infirmities; dilapidated; so ∿TUDE *n.* [ME, f. L DE(*crepitus* p.p. of *crepare* creak)]

dēcrĕ'pit|āte *v.t.* & *i.* calcine (mineral or salt) till it ceases to crackle in fire; crackle under heat; hence ∿A'TION *n.* [prob. f. mod. L *decrepitare* f. DE- + L *crepitare* crackle; see -ATE³]

dēcrĕscĕ'ndō (dākrĕsh-) *adv.*, *a.*, & *n.* (*pl.* ∿s). = DIMINUENDO. [It., part. of *decrescere* DECREASE¹]

dēcrĕ'scent *a.* (Usu. of moon) waning, decreasing. [f. L *decrescere* (see DECREASE¹, -ENT)]

dēcrē'tal *n.* papal decree; (in *pl.*) collection of these, forming part of canon law. [ME, f. med. L *decretale* f. LL (*epistola*) *decretalis* (letter) of decree f. L *decernere* (see DECREE, -AL)]

dēcrī'minaliz|e, -īs|e (-īz), *v.t.* treat (action etc.) as no longer criminal; hence ∿A'TION *n.* [f. DE- + CRIMINAL + -IZE]

dēcry' *v.t.* disparage, depreciate; hence **dēcrī'ER¹** *n.* [f. DE- + CRY², after F *décrier;* cf. *cry down*]

dēcry'pt *v.t.* decipher (cryptogram), with or without knowledge of its key; hence ∿ION *n.* [f. DE- + CRYPTO-GRAM]

dē'cūman *a.* **1.** (Esp. of wave) very large. **2.** (Rom. Ant.) of tenth cohort; ∿ **gate,** main gate of camp, where this cohort was quartered. [f. L *decumanus,* *decimanus* of the tenth (*decimus*), large; see -AN]

dēcū'mbent *a.* (Bot. & Zool.) (Of plant, shoot, bristles) lying along ground or surface of body. [f. L DE(*cumbere* lie); see -ENT]

dē'cūple *a.*, *n.*, & *v.* **1.** *a.* & *n.* tenfold (amount). **2.** *v.t.* & *i.* multiply by ten. [ME, f. LL *decuplus* f. L *decem* ten]

dē'cūplet *n.* set of ten things of same kind. [f. prec., after *triplet*]

dēcŭ'ssate¹ *a.* X-shaped; (Bot.) with pairs of opposite leaves etc. each at right angles to pair below. [f. L *decussatus* p.p. of *decussare* divide in cross shape (*decussis* numeral ten or shape X f. *decem* ten); see -ATE²]

dēcŭ'ssāte² *v.t.* & *i.* arrange or be arranged in decussate form; intersect; so **dēcŭssA'TION** *n.* [f. as prec. + -ATE³]

deda'ns (-ah'n) *n.* (Tennis). open gallery at end of service-side of a court; spectators watching a tennis match. [F, = inside]

dē'dicāt|e *v.t.* devote with solemn rites (*to* God or saint or to sacred use; of church etc. esp. without certain forms necessary for legally consecrating ground or buildings); give up (*to* special purpose); put words in (book etc.) as compliment *to* friend, patron, etc.; hence *or* cogn. ∿EE', ∿OR, *ns.*, ∿IVE, ∿ORY, *adjs.* [f. L DE(*dicare* declare) + -ATE³]

dē'dicātĕd *a.* In vbl senses; (of person) devoted to aims or vocation, having single-minded loyalty or integrity. [p.p. of prec.]

dēdicā'tion *n.* In vbl senses; dedicatory inscription or building etc. or in book etc. [ME, f. OF *dedicacion* or f. L *dedicatio* (as DEDICATE; see -ATION)]

dēdŭ'c|e *v.t.* infer, draw as logical conclusion, (*from*) (arch.) trace course or derivation of; hence ∿IBLE *a.* [f. L DE(*ducere duct-* lead)]

dēdŭ'ct *v.t.* take away, put aside, (amount, portion etc., *from,* or abs.); hence ∿IBLE *a.,* (esp.) that may be deducted from one's tax or taxable income. [f. L, as prec.]

dēdŭ'ction *n.* **1.** deducting; amount deducted. **2.** deducing, inference from general to particular (cf. *induction*); thing deduced. [ME f. OF, or f. L *deducti*... (as DEDUCE; see -ION)]

dēdŭ'ctive *a.* of, or reasoning by, deduction; hence ∿LY² (-vlī) *adv.* [f. med. L *deductivus* (as DEDUCE; see -IVE)]

dee *n.* thing shaped like) letter D; (Phys.) hollow semicircular electrode in cyclotron; (euphem.) damn. [name of the letter]

deed *n.*, & *v.t.* **1.** *n.* thing done intentionally or responsibly; brave, skilful, or conspicuous act; actual fact, performance, (*in word and deed; in deed and not in name,* whence INDEED; (arch.) *in very deed*); (Law written or printed instrument effecting legal disposition and bearing disposer's signature and seal; ∿-**box**, strong box for keeping deeds and other documents; ∿ **poll**, deed made and executed by one party only (paper polled or cut even, not indented). **2.** *v.t.* *convey or transfer by legal deed. [OE *dǣd*, = OS *dād*, OHG *tāt*, ON *dath*, Goth. *-dēths* f. Gmc **dǣdiz* (**dhētis* f. IE **dhē-*, **dho-*; cf. DO¹)]

dee'dȳ *a.* active, industrious; earnest. [f. prec.+-Y²]

deejay' *n.* (sl.) disc jockey. [f. abbr. *DJ*]

deem *v.t.* believe, consider, judge, or count, to be (*deem it one's duty; was deemed sufficient; shall be deemed to have given his assent*; abs. in parenth.: *it was, I deemed, time to go*). [OE *dēman*, = OS *dōmian*, OHG *tuomen*, ON *dœma*, Goth. *domjan* f. Gmc **dōmaʒ* DOOM¹]

dē-ē'mphasīze, -īse (-īz), *v.t.* remove emphasis from; reduce emphasis on. [f. DE-+EMPHASIZE]

dee'mster *n.* one of two justices of Isle of Man. [f. DEEM+-STER]

deep¹ *a.* **1.** extending far down from top (lit. or fig.; *deep breath, hole, water, draught, drink, drinker; go* (*in*) *off the deep* END¹; *in deep* WATER¹(*s*)); going far in from surface or edge (*deep wound, plunge, shelf, border*; (fig.) *deep insight, thinker*); ∿ **breathing** (esp. as form of physical exercise); ∿-**freeze** [*P], refrigerator etc. in which food can be quickly frozen and kept for long periods at very low temperature, (fig.) suspension of activity; so ∿-*freeze* v.t., ∿ **kiss** (with contact between partners' tongues); ∿ **mourning** (expressed by wearing only black clothes); ∿ **therapy**, curative treatment with short-wave X-rays of high penetrating power. **2.** lying far down, back, or inwards; (Cricket) distant from batsman; (Football) distant from front line of one's team; difficult to understand, profound, not superficial, penetrating, (*the deeper causes; deep learning, study*); **a** ∿ **one**, (sl.) cunning or secretive person; ∿ **sea**, deeper parts of ocean; *Deep* SOUTH; ∿ **space**, regions beyond solar system or earth's atmosphere. **3.** heartfelt, absorbing, absorbed (*deep affection, feelings, interest*); ∿ **in**, giving all one's attention to (a pursuit etc.). **4.** intense, vivid, extreme, (*deep disgrace, sleep, night, sin, colour; deep-red* etc.). **5.** (*pred.*) going or placed (so) far down, back, or inwards (*water 8 ft. deep; ankle-deep in mud; ship deep in the water; hands deep in pockets; deep in debt, in thought*); in (so many) ranks one behind another (*soldiers drawn up six deep*). **6.** brought from far down (*deep sigh*); low-pitched, full-toned, not shrill, (*deep note, bell, voice*); ∿-**mouthed**, (esp. of dog) having deep voice. **7.** Hence ∿'**NESS** *n.*, ∿'**LY²** *adv.* & *i.*, ∿'**LY²** ∿'**NESS** *n.* [OE *dēop*, = OS *diup, diop*, OHG *tiuf*, ON *djúpr*, Goth. *diups* f. Gmc **deupaz*; cogn. w. DIP¹]

deep² *n.* deep part(s) of the sea; abyss, pit, cavity; (poet. or rhet.) mysterious region of thought or feeling; (poet.) *the* sea; **the ∿**, (Cricket) deep position of fieldsmen. [f. as prec. (neut. a. in OE)]

deep³ *adv.* **1.** deeply, far down or in, (*read deep into the night*; **still waters run ∿**, quiet manner covers depths of feeling or knowledge or cunning). **2.** ∿-**drawn**, (of metal etc.) shaped by forcing through die while cold; ∿-**fried**, (of food) fried in fat etc. covering it; ∿-**laid**, (of scheme) secret and elaborate; ∿-**rooted** (esp. of convictions); ∿-**seated** (of disease, emotion, etc.). [OE *dīope, dēope*, (as DEEP¹)]

|**dee'ping** *n.* section, one fathom deep, of fishing-net. [f. DEEP¹+-ING³]

deer *n.* (*pl.* same). **1.** ruminant quadruped of family Cervidae, the male usu. with deciduous branching horns; **small ∿**, (arch.) insignificant animals or things collectively. **2.** ∿-**forest**, wild land reserved for stalking of deer; ∿-**hound**, large rough-haired greyhound; ∿-**lick**, spring or damp spot impregnated with salt etc. where deer come to lick; ∿'**skin**, (made of) deer's skin; ∿'**stalker**, sportsman stalking deer, cloth cap peaked fore and behind. [OE *dēor* animal, deer, = OS *dior*, OHG *tior*, ON *dýr*, Goth.

*dius f. Gmc **deuzam* f. IE **dheusóm* creature that breathes]

dē-ĕscal|āte *v.t.* reduce level or intensity of; so ∿A'TION *n.* [f. DE-+ESCALATE]

dēfā'ce *v.t.* spoil appearance or beauty of, disfigure; make illegible; hence ∿ABLE (-sa-) *a.*, ∿MENT (-sm-) *n.* [ME, f. F *défacer* f. OF *desfacier* (as DE-, FACE¹)]

de facto (dē fǎ'ktō, dā f-) *a.* & *adv.* (existing) in fact, whether by right or not. [L]

dē'faecāte etc. Var. of DEFECATE etc.

dē'falcāt|e *v.i.* commit defalcations, misappropriate property in one's charge; so ∿OR *n.* [f. med. L DE(*falcare* lop f. L *falx -cis* sickle)+-ATE³]

dēfalcā'tion *n.* defection, shortcoming; misappropriation of money; amount misappropriated. [ME, f. med. L *defalcatio* (as prec.; see -ATION)]

dēfā'me *v.t.* attack the good reputation of, speak ill of; so **dēfamā'TION** *n.*, **dēfā'matORY** *a.* [ME, f. OF *diffamer* etc. f. L *diffamare* spread evil report (as DIS-, *fama* report); see DE-]

dēfā't *v.t.* (**-tt-**). remove fat(s) from. [f. DE-+FAT]

dēfau'lt (-aw'lt, -ŏ'lt) *n.* **1.** lack, absence; **in ∿ of**, if or since thing is lacking. **2.** failure to act or appear, neglect, (*make default*); **go by ∿**, be absent, be ignored because of absence; **judgement by ∿** (given for plaintiff on defendant's failure to plead). **3.** failure to pay, defaulting. [ME, f. OF *defaut(e)* f. *defaillir* fail f. Rom. **DE*(*fallire*); see FAIL²]

dēfau'lt² (-aw'lt, -ŏ'lt) *v.* **1.** *v.i.* fall to act or appear, esp. in lawcourt; fail to meet pecuniary or other obligation; hence ∿ER¹ *n.*, (esp., ||Mil.) soldier guilty of military offence. **2.** *v.t.* declare (party) in default and give judgement against him. [ME, f. prec. & f. OF *defaillir* (3 sing. *defaut*); see prec.]

dēfea'sance (-z-) *n.* rendering null and void. [ME, f. OF *defesance* f. de(*s*)*faire* undo (as DE-, *faire* make f. L *facere*; see -ANCE)]

dēfea's|ible (-z-) *a.* capable of annulment, liable to forfeiture; hence ∿IBI'LITY *n.*, ∿IBLY *adv.* [AF, f. as prec.; see -IBLE]

dēfea't *v.t.*, & *n.* **1.** *v.t.* reduce to submission in battle or other contest, matter decided by voting, etc.; frustrate, baffle; (Law) annul. **2.** *n.* defeating; being defeated. [ME, f. AF *defeter* f. *defet* f. OF *deffait, desfait* p.p. of *desfaire* f. med. L *disfacere* (as DIS-, L *facere* do)]

dēfea'tism *n.* conduct or thinking that tends to bring about acceptance of defeat; so ∿IST (2) *n.* [f. F *défaitisme* (*défaite* defeat, as prec.; see -ISM)]

dē'fēc|āte *v.* **1.** *v.i.* discharge faeces from body. **2.** *v.t.* clear of dregs, refine, purify, (lit. or fig.). **3.** Hence ∿A'TION *n.*, ∿ātOR *n.* [f. obs. *defecate* purified f. L DE(*faecare* f. *faex faecis* dregs); see -ATE²]

dēfē'ct *n.*, & *v.i.* *n.* (or *de'fĕkt*). lack of something essential to completeness; shortcoming, failing, (*has the ∿s of his qualities*, the particular ones that often accompany his particular virtues); blemish; amount by which thing falls short. **2.** *v.i.* desert, esp. to another country etc.; hence ∿OR *n.* [f. L *defectus* n. f. DE(*ficere* fect- = *facere* do) desert, fail]

dēfe'ction *n.* falling away from allegiance to leader, party, religion, or duty; desertion, esp. to another country etc. [f. L *defectio* (as prec.; see -ION)]

dēfe'ctive *a.* & *n.* **1.** *a.* having defect(s), (in some respect) incomplete, faulty; lacking or deficient (*in*); mentally DEFICIENT (Gram.) not having all the usual inflexions; hence ∿LY² (-vlĭ) *adv.*, ∿NESS (-vn-) *n.* **2.** *n.* mentally defective person. [ME, f. OF *defectif -ive* or f. LL *defectivus* (as prec.; see -IVE)]

||**dēfe'nce**, **dēfē'nse*, (-ns) *n.* **1.** defending from or resistance against attack (cf. OFFENCE; **best ∿ is offence**, advantage goes with the initiative); (Cricket) guarding one's wicket, batting as opposed to bowling; ∿ **mechanism**, body's reaction against disease organisms, (Psych.) usu. unconscious mental process avoiding conscious conflict or anxiety. **2.** military resources of a country; (in *pl.*) fortifications; *defence in* DEPTH. **3.** thing that protects; means of resisting

attack; justification, vindication, speech or writing used to this end; (Law) accused party's denial, pleading, and proceedings, counsel for the accused party; player(s) in defending position. **4.** Hence ∼LESS (-sl-) *a*. [ME f. OF *defens(e)*, f. LL *defensum, -a*, p.p. of *defendere* (see foll.)]

defe′nd *v*. **1.** *v.t.* ward off attack made on, keep safe, protect (*against, from*; person, thing, or abs. for *refl.*); uphold by argument, vindicate, speak or write in favour of; (Law) make defence of in court (∼ oneself, conduct one's own defence). **2.** *v.i.* make defence; (arch.) forbid, avert (*God* or *heaven defend*). [ME, f. OF *defendre* f. L DE(*fendere fens-*; cf. OFFEND)]

defe′ndant *n*. person etc. sued or accused in court of law. [ME f. OF, part. of *defendre* (see prec., -ANT)]

defe′nder *n*. one who defends (**D∼ of the Faith,** title of Engl. sovereigns from Henry VIII, who received it from Pope Leo X in 1521 for writing against Luther); (Sport) holder of championship etc. defending the title (opp. *challenger*). [ME f. AF *defendour*, OF *-eor* (as DEFEND; see -OR)]

defe′nestra′tion *n*. action of throwing (esp. person) out of a window; so **defe′nestrate**[3] *v.t.* [f. mod. L *defenestratio* f. as DE- + L *fenestra* window + -ATION]

*defe′nse. See DEFENCE.

defe′ns|ible *a*. easily defended (in war or argument); justifiable; hence ∼IBI′LITY *n*., ∼IBLY *adv*. [ME, f. LL *defensibilis* (as DEFEND; see -IBLE)]

defe′nsive *a*. & *n*. **1.** *a*. serving, used, done, for defence, protective, not aggressive; hence ∼LY² (-vlī) *adv*. **2.** *n*. state or position of defence (esp. *be, stand, act, on the defensive*). [ME, f. F *défensif -ive* f. med. L *defensivus* (as DEFEND; see -IVE)]

defer′[1] *v.t.* (-rr-). put off to later time, postpone, (∼red annuity, one not beginning immediately; ∼red payment (by instalments); ∼red shares, stock, (on which smaller dividend may be paid than on ordinary shares); *postpone date of call-up of (person); hence ∼MENT, ∼RAL, *ns*., ∼RABLE *a*. [ME, orig. same as DIFFER]

defer′[2] *v.t.* (-rr-). submit or make concessions in opinion or action *to* (person). [ME, f. F *déférer* f. L DE(*ferre* bring)]

de′ference *n*. compliance with advice etc. of one superior in wisdom or position (*pay* etc. *deference to*); respect, manifestation of desire to comply, courteous regard, (**in** ∼ **to,** out of respect for authority of). [f. F *déférence* (as prec.; see -ENCE)]

defere′ntial (-shal) *a*. showing deference, respectful; hence ∼LY² *adv*. [f. prec., after *prudential* etc.]

defi′ance *n*. challenge to fight or maintain cause, assertion, etc.; open disobedience, bold resistance, (*bid defiance to, set at defiance*); **in** ∼ **of,** disregarding, in conflict with. [ME f. OF (as DEFY; see -ANCE)]

defi′ant *a*. openly disobedient; showing defiance; hence ∼LY² *adv*. [f. prec. + -ANT]

defi′ciency (-i′shen-) *n*. being deficient; lack; thing lacking; amount by which thing, esp. revenue, falls short; ∼ disease (caused by lack of some essential or important element in the diet); ∼ payment (by Government to farmers to ensure guaranteed minimum price). [f. foll. + -ENCY]

defi′cient (-i′shent) *a*. incomplete, lacking (*in*) a specified quality; insufficient in quantity, force, etc.; (mentally) ∼, incapable of adequate social or intellectual behaviour through imperfect mental development; hence ∼LY² *adv*. [f. L *deficiens* part. of *deficere*; see DEFECT, -ENT]

de′ficit *n*. amount by which thing (esp. sum of money) is too small (opp. *surplus*); excess of liabilities over assets; ∼ spending (of funds raised by borrowing, not by taxation). [f. F *déficit* f. L *deficit* 3 sing. pres. of *deficere* (see DEFECT)]

defi′er. See DEFY.

defila′de *v.t.*, & *n*. **1.** *v.t.* secure (fortification) against enfilading fire. **2.** *n*. this precaution or arrangement. [f. foll. + -ADE]

defi′le[1] *v.i.*, & *n*. **1.** *v.i.* march in file(s). **2.** *n*. (*or* dē′fīl). narrow way through which troops can only march in file; gorge. [f. F *défiler* and *défilé* p.p. (as DE-, FILE³)]

defi′le[2] *v.t.* make dirty, befoul; pollute, corrupt; desecrate, profane; deprive of virginity; make ceremonially unclean; hence ∼MENT (-lm-) *n*. [ME *defoul* f. OF *def(o)uler* trample down, outrage (as DE-, *fouler* see FOIL²), altered after obs. *befile* f. OE *befȳlan* (BE-, *fūl* FOUL²)]

defi′n|e *v.t.* mark out limits of; make clear, esp. in outline (*well-defined image*; ∼e one's **position,** state it precisely); set forth essence of, declare exact meaning or scope of, (abs.) frame definitions; (of properties) make up total character of; hence ∼ABLE *a*. [ME, f. OF *definer* f. Rom. *definare for L DE(*finire* finish f. *finis* end)]

de′finite *a*. having exact limits; determinate, distinct, precise, not vague; *definite* ARTICLE¹; *definite* INTEGRAL; PAST¹ *definite*; hence ∼LY² (-tlī) *adv*. & *int.* (colloq.) yes, certainly, ∼NESS (-tn-) *n*. [f. L *definitus* p.p. of *definire* (see prec.)]

defini′tion *n*. stating precise nature of thing or meaning of word; form of words in which this is done; making or being distinct, degree of distinctness, in outline (esp. of image given by lens or shown in photograph or on cinema or television screen). [ME f. OF, f. L DE(*finitio* f. as DEFINE; see -ITION)]

defi′nitive *a*. (Of answer, treaty, verdict, etc.) decisive, unconditional, final; (of edition of book etc.) most authoritative, final; not commemorative etc.; hence ∼LY² (-vlī) *adv*. [ME, f. OF *definitif -ive* f. L *definitivus* (as prec.; see -IVE)]

de′flagr āte *v.t.* & *i.* burn away with sudden flame; hence or cogn. ∼A′TION, ∼ātor, *ns*. [f. L DE(*flagrare* blaze) + -ATE³]

defla′te *v.* **1.** *v.t.* let inflating air or gas out of (tyre, balloon, etc.); (Econ.) subject (currency) to deflation; reduce importance of, depreciate; cause to lose one's conceitedness or confidence. **2.** *v.i.* be deflated; lose confidence; pursue policy of deflation. [f. DE- + INFLATE]

defla′tion *n*. deflating; (esp., Econ.) reverse or reversal of INFLATION (of currency etc.); (Geol.) removal of particles of rock etc. by wind; hence ∼ARY¹ *a*., ∼IST (2) *n*. [f. prec. + -ATION]

defle′ct *v.t.* & *i.* bend or turn aside from straight course; (cause to) deviate (*from*); hence ∼OR *n*., (esp.) device for deflecting flow of air etc. [f. L DE(*flectere flex-* bend)]

defle′xion (-kshon), **-ĕ′ction,** *n*. lateral bend or turn, deviation, (lit. or fig.); (Phys.) movement of instrument's pointer from its zero position. [f. LL *deflexio* (as prec.; see -ION)]

deflora′tion *n*. deflowering. [ME f. OF, or f. LL *defloratio* (as foll.; see -ATION)]

deflow′er *v.t.* deprive (woman) of virginity, ravish; ravage, spoil; strip of flowers. [ME, f. OF *de(s)flo(u)rer* f. Rom. *disflorare for LL DEflorare (*flos floris* flower)]

defo′cus *v.t.* & *i.* (-s- *or* -ss-). (cause to) go out of focus. [f. DE- + FOCUS]

defo′li āte *v.t.* remove leaves from, esp. as military tactic; hence ∼ANT *a.* & *n.*, ∼A′TION *n*. [f. LL DEfoliare (*folium* leaf) + -ATE³]

defo′rest *v.t.* remove forest(s) from; hence ∼A′TION *n*. [f. DE- + FOREST]

defor′m *v.* **1.** *v.t.* make ugly, deface; put out of shape, misshape, (*in p.p.*, of person with misshapen body or limb). *v.i.* undergo deformation. [ME, f. OF *deformer* f. L *difformare*, Rom. *disformare f. L DE(*formare* f. *forma* shape)]

deforma′tion *n*. disfigurement; perverted form of word (*dang* for *damn*, etc.); (Phys.) change in shape of quantity representing amount of this, whence ∼AL *a*. [ME f. OF, or f. L *deformatio* (as prec.; see -ATION)]

defor′mity *n*. being deformed, ugliness, disfigurement, (physical or moral); malformation, esp. of

For other words in **de-** see **DE-**.

body or limb. [ME, f. OF *deformité* etc. f. L *deformitas -tatis* f. DE(*formis* f. *forma* shape); see -ITY]

defrau'd *v.t.* cheat (person, person *of*, or abs.) by fraud. [ME, f. OF *defrauder* or f. L DE*fraudare* (*fraus* FRAUD)]

defray' *v.t.* provide money to pay (cost, expense); hence ∿ABLE *a.*, ∿AL 2 *n.* [f. F *défrayer* f. as DE- + obs. *frai(t)* cost, f. med. L *fredum, -us* fine for breach of peace]

defrò'ck *v.t.* = UNFROCK. [f. F *défroquer* (as DE-, FROCK)]

defro'st (-ŏ'-, -aw'-) *v.t.* remove frost from, unfreeze, (esp. frozen food, interior of refrigerator, or windscreen); hence ∿ER¹ (2) *n.* [f. DE- + FROST]

deft *a.* dextrous, (esp. manually) skilful, handling things neatly; hence ∿'LY² *adv.*, ∿'NESS *n.* [ME, var. of DAFT in obs. sense 'meek']

defü'nct *a.* dead; no longer existing; no longer used or in fashion. [f. L DE(*functus* p.p. of *fungi* perform) dead]

defü'se *v.t.* remove fuse from (explosive); (fig.) reduce likelihood of trouble arising from (crisis etc.). [f. DE- + FUSE²]

defy' *v.t.* challenge *to* do or prove something; resist openly, refuse to obey; (of thing) present insuperable obstacles to (*defies definition, capture*, etc.); (arch.) challenge to combat; hence **defï'ER¹** *n.* [ME, f. OF *defier* f. Rom. *DIS(fidare f. fidus faithful, fides faith)]

deg. *abbr.* degree.

dégagé (dāgah'zhā) *a.* (*fem.* ∿e *pr.* same). easy, unconstrained. [F, p.p. of *dégager* set free]

dēgà's *v.t.* (-ss-). remove unwanted gas from. [f. DE- + GAS¹œ]

dēgau'ss (-gow's) *v.t.* demagnetize (television receiver, ship esp. as precaution against magnetic mines, etc.) with encircling current-carrying conductor. [f. DE- + GAUSS]

dēgĕ'nerate¹ *a.* & *n.* **1.** *a.* having lost the qualities that are normal and desirable or proper to its kind, fallen from former excellence; (Biol.) having reverted to lower type; hence **dēgĕ'ner**ACY *n.* **2.** *n.* degenerate person or animal. [f. L *degeneratus* p.p. (as foll.; see -ATE²)]

dēgĕ'nerate² *v.i.* become degenerate. [f. L *degenerare* f. DE(*gener* f. *genus -eris* race) ignoble + -ATE³]

dēgĕnerā'tion *n.* becoming degenerate; (Path.) morbid deterioration of tissue or change in its structure. [ME, f. F *dégénération* or f. LL *degeneratio* (as prec.; see -ATION)]

dēglutì'tion (-glōō-) *n.* (arch.) swallowing. [f. F *déglutition* or mod. L *deglutitio* f. L DE(*glutire* swallow); see -ITION]

dégrà'd|e *n.* **1.** *v.t.* reduce to lower rank, esp. as punishment; bring into dishonour or contempt, whence ∿ING² *a.*; (Biol.) reduce to lower organic type; (Chem.) reduce to simpler molecular structure; (Phys.) reduce (energy) to less convertible form; (Geol.) wear down (rocks etc.) by disintegration. **2.** *v.i.* degenerate; (Chem.) disintegrate. **3.** Hence or cogn. ∿ABLE *a.*, **dēgrad**A'TION *n.*, *a.* [ME, f. OF *degrader* f. eccl. L DE*gradare* f. L *gradus* step]

dēgrea'se *v.t.* remove grease or fat from. [f. DE- + GREASE¹]

dēgree' *n.* **1.** thing placed like step in series, tier, row; stage in ascending or descending scale or process (**by** ∿s, a little at a time; SONG *of* Degrees); step in direct genealogical descent (**forbidden or prohibited** ∿s, number of these too few to allow of marriage between two related persons). **2.** social or official rank; relative condition (*each good in its degree*); stage in intensity or amount (*in some degree; to a high or the last degree*; **to a** ∿, colloq.) considerably; (Law) grade of crime or criminality (*murder, principal, in the first* etc. *degree*); (Gram.) *degrees of* COMPARISON; *degree of* FREEDOM; (Math.) highest power of unknowns or variables (*of equation* etc.); **third** ∿, (1) rank of master freemason, (2) *severe and protracted interrogation by police to extract confession etc., (3) extent of burns character-

ized by much destruction of skin. **3.** academic rank conferred as mark of proficiency, or (**honorary** ∿) on distinguished person, (∿ **day**, when these are formally awarded); masonic rank (**third** ∿; see above). **4.** (Math.) unit of angular or circular-arc measurement, 1/90 of right angle or 1/360 of circumference (symbol °, as 45°; *degree of* LATITUDE, LONGITUDE, etc.); (Phys.) unit in scale of temperature, hardness, etc., (symbol ° or deg, or omitted where letter indicating scale used serves as symbol). [ME, f. OF *degré* f. Rom. *DE(gradus step)]

dēgrĕ'ssive *a.* descending; (of taxation) at successively lower rates on low amounts. [f. L DE(*gredi gress-* = *gradi* walk); see -IVE]

dégringolade (dāgrǎngōlah'd) *n.* rapid fall or deterioration. [F (*dégringoler* fall rapidly; see -ADE)]

de haut en bas (de ōt ahn bah') *adv.* in a condescending or superior manner. [F, = from above to below]

dēhi'sc|e *v.i.* gape, burst open, (esp. in Bot. of seed-vessel, and in Physiol.); so ∿ENCE *n.*, ∿ENT *a.* [f. L DE(*hiscere* incept. of *hiare* gape)]

dēhö'r'n *v.t.* remove horns from (animal). [f. DE- + HORN¹]

dēhü'manïze, -ïse (-īz), *v.t.* divest of human characteristics; make impersonal or machine-like. [f. DE- + HUMAN + -IZE]

dēhy'dr|āte *v.* **1.** *v.t.* remove water from (esp. foods for preservation and reduction of bulk); make dry (lit. or fig.). **2.** *v.i.* lose water. **3.** Hence ∿A'TION *n.* [f. DE- + Gk *hudōr* water + -ATE³]

dē-ï'c|e *v.t.* remove, or prevent formation of, ice on aircraft, windscreen, etc.; so ∿ER¹ (2) *n.* [f. DE- + ICE¹]

dē'ïcide *n.* killer or killing of a god. [f. eccl. L *deicida* f. L *deus* god; see -CIDE]

dei'ctic (dī'k-) *a.* & *n.* (Philol. & Gram.) pointing, demonstrative, (word). [f. Gk *deiktikos* (*deiktos* capable of proof f. *deiknumi* show; see -IC)]

dē'ïförm *a.* godlike in form or nature. [f. med. L *deiformis* (*deus* god; see -FORM)]

dē'ïfy *v.t.* make a god of; treat as a god, worship; so **dēïfica'TION** *n.* [ME, f. OF *deifier* f. eccl. L *deificare* (*deus* god; see -FY)]

deign (dān) *v.i.* & *t.* think fit, condescend, *to* do; (arch., usu. neg.) condescend to give (answer etc.). [ME, f. OF *degnier, deigner, daigner* f. L *dignare*, *-ari* deem worthy (*dignus*)]

Dei gratia (dāi grah'tia, -shïa) *adv.* by God's grace. [L]

dē'ïonïz|e, -ïs|e (-īz), *v.t.* remove ions or ionic constituents from (water etc.); hence ∿A'TION, ∿ER¹ (2), *ns.* [f. DE- + IONIZE]

deipnŏ'sophist (dī-) *n.* person skilled in dining and table-talk. [f. Gk *deipnosophistēs* (in pl. as title of work by Athenaeus (3rd c.) describing long discussions at a banquet; *deipnon* dinner, *sophistēs* wise man; see SOPHIST)]

dē'|ism *n.* belief in the existence of a god without accepting revelation (cf. THEISM), natural religion; so ∿IST (2) *n.*, ∿i'STIC(AL) *adjs.* [f. L *deus* god + -ISM]

dē'ïty (dē'-, **D** dā'-) *n.* divine status, quality, or nature; god; **the D**∿, the Creator, God. [ME, f. OF *deité* f. eccl. L *deitas -tatis* transl. Gk *theotēs* (*theos* god); see -ITY]

déjà vu (dāzhah vü') *n.* **1.** (Psych.) illusory feeling of having already experienced a present situation. **2.** something tediously familiar. [F, = already seen]

dējĕ'ct *v.t.* (esp. in *p.p.*) make sad or gloomy. [ME, f. L DE(*jicere ject-* = *jacĕre* throw)]

dējĕ'ction *n.* dejected state, low spirits. [ME, f. L *dejectio* (as prec.; see -ION)]

de jure (dē joor'ī, dā yoor'ā) *a.* & *adv.* rightful(ly), by right. [L]

dĕ'kkō *n.* (*pl.* ∿s). (sl.) a look (*let's have a dekko*). [f. Hindi *dekho* imper. of *dekhnā* look]

Del. *abbr.* Delaware.

dĕlai'ne *n.* light woollen dress-fabric. [f. F (*mousseline*) *de laine* woollen (MUSLIN) f. *de* of + *laine* f. L *lana* wool]

dēlā'te v.t. (arch.) inform against, impeach, (person); report (offence); so **dēlā'tion**, **dēlā'tor**, ns. [f. L DE(lat- p.p. st. of ferre carry)]

dēlay' v. & n. 1. v.t. postpone, defer; make late; hinder; ∼ed-action a., operating after an interval of time. 2. v.i. loiter, be late; wait. 3. n. act or process of delaying; hindrance; time lost by inaction or inability to proceed; ∼ line, (Electr.) device producing desired delay in transmission of signal. [ME, f. OF delayer v., delai n., prob. f. des- DIS- + laier leave; see RELAY²]

dēl cre'derè (-ā'd-) a., adv., & n. (Commerc.) subject to, charge made for, selling-agent's guarantee that buyer is solvent. [It., = of trust]

dē'lè v.t. (Print.) delete (letter, word, etc., struck out or otherwise indicated). [L, imper. of delēre (see DELETE)]

dēlĕ'ctab|le a. (literary or iron.) delightful, pleasant; hence ∼LY² adv. [ME f. OF, f. L delectabilis (delectare DELIGHT; see -ABLE)]

dēlĕctā'tion n. enjoyment (usu. for one's delectation). [ME f. OF (as prec.; see -ATION)]

dē'lègacў n. system of delegating; appointment as delegate; body of delegates. [f. foll. + -ACY]

dē'lègate¹ n. deputy; member of committee: elected representative sent to conference; member of deputation. [ME, f. L delegatus (as foll.; see -ATE²)]

dē'lègate² v.t. depute (person), send as representative(s); commit (authority, powers, etc.) to or to agent. [f. L DE(legare depute) + -ATE³]

dēlègā'tion n. entrusting of authority to deputy; body of delegates; deputation. [f. L delegatio (as prec.; see -ATION)]

dēlē'te v.t. make no longer effective by crossing out or obliterating or removing (letter, word, passage); so **dēlē'tion** n. [f. L delēre -let- efface]

dēlētēr'ious a. harmful (to mind or body); hence ∼LY² adv. [f. med. L deleterius f. Gk dēlētērios noxious + -OUS]

dēlft n. ∼('ware), glazed earthenware made at Delft in Holland.

*dē'li n. (colloq.) delicatessen shop. [abbr.]

dēli'berate¹ a. intentional; fully considered, not impulsive; slow in deciding, cautious; (of movement etc.) leisurely, not hurried; hence ∼LY² (-tlǐ) adv., ∼NESS (-tn-) n. [f. L deliberatus p.p. (as foll.; see -ATE²)]

dēli'berāte² v. 1. v.i. think carefully; take counsel, consult, hold debate. 2. v.t. consider (question, what to do, etc.). [f. L DE(liberare = librare weigh f. libra balance) + -ATE³]

dēlibera'tion n. weighing in mind, careful consideration; discussion of reasons for and against, debate; care, avoidance of precipitancy; unhurriedness of movement. [ME f. OF, f. L deliberatio -onis (as prec.; see -ATION)]

dēli'berative a. of, appointed for purpose of, deliberation or debate (deliberative assembly or functions); hence ∼LY² (-vlǐ) adv. [f. F délibératif -ive or f. L deliberativus (as DELIBERATE²; see -IVE)]

dē'licacў n. 1. fineness of texture, graceful slightness, tender beauty. 2. weakliness, susceptibility to disease or injury, need of care, discretion, or skill; (of person, sense, or instrument) accuracy of perception, sensitiveness. 3. consideration for others' feelings; avoidance of what is immodest or offensive. 4. choice kind of food, dainty. [ME, f. foll. + -ACY]

dē'licate a. 1. fine in texture, soft, slender, slight; (of exquisite quality or workmanship; (of food) dainty and palatable; (of colour) subdued; subtle, hard to appreciate. 2. easily injured, liable to illness (in a ∼ condition, (arch.) pregnant); requiring careful handling (lit. or fig.), critical, ticklish; (of person or instrument) highly sensitive. 3. deft (a delicate touch); avoiding the offensive or immodest; (esp. of actions) considerate. 4. Hence ∼LY² (-tlǐ) adv. [ME, f. OF delicat or f. L delicatus, of unkn. orig.; see -ATE²]

dēlicatě'ssen n. (shop selling) prepared delicacies or

relishes for the table. [f. G delikatessen or Du. delicatessen f. F. délicatesse (délicat, as prec.)]

dēli'cious (-shŭs) a. highly delightful, esp. to taste, smell, or sense of humour; hence ∼LY² adv., ∼NESS n. [ME f. OF, f. LL deliciosus f. L deliciae delight; see -OUS]

dēli'ct n. (arch.) violation of law, offence. [f. L delictum neut. p.p. (as n.) of DE(linquere leave) offend]

dēli'ght (-ī't) v. & n. 1. v.t. please greatly (shall be delighted to accept the invitation; was delighted that you won, with or at the result); hence ∼EDLY adv. 2. v.i. take or find great pleasure in; be highly pleased to do. 3. n. great pleasure; thing that causes it; hence ∼FUL a., ∼FULLY adv., ∼SOME¹ a. (literary). [ME, f. OF delitier, delit, f. L delectare frequent. of delicere; alt. after light etc.]

Dēli'lah (-la) n. temptress, seductive and wily woman. [f. ∼, betrayer of Samson (Judges 16)]

dēli'mit v.t. determine limits or territorial boundary of; so ∼ATE³ v.t., ∼A'TION n. [f. F délimiter f. L DE(limitare f. limes -itis boundary)]

dēli'nè|āte v.t. show by drawing or description, portray; hence or cogn. ∼A'TION, ∼ātor, ns. [f. L DE(lineare f. linea line) + -ATE³]

dēli'nquencў n. neglect of duty; guilt (esp. juvenile delinquency); misdeed. [f. eccl. L delinquentia (L delinquens part. of delinquere; see DELICT, -ENCY)]

dēli'nquent a. & n. 1. a. defaulting, guilty, *in arrears. 2. n. offender (esp. juvenile delinquent). [f. L delinquens (as prec.; see -ENT)]

dēliquĕ'sc|e v.i. become liquid, melt, (fig.) melt away; (Chem.) dissolve in water absorbed from the air; so ∼ENT a., ∼ENCE n. [f. L DE(liquescere incept. of liquēre be liquid); see -ESCE]

dēli'rious a. affected with delirium, temporarily or apparently mad, raving; wildly excited, ecstasy; betraying delirium or ecstasy; hence ∼LY² adv. [f. as foll. + -OUS]

dēli'rium n. disordered state of mind with incoherent speech, hallucinations, and frenzied excitement; great excitement, ecstasy; ∼ tremens (trē'mĕnz), special form of delirium with tremors and terrifying delusions due to excessive consumption of alcohol. [L, f. DElirare be deranged (lira ridge between furrows)]

dēli'ver v.t. 1. save, rescue, set free, (from). 2. assist at birth of or in giving birth; give birth to; (in pass.) give birth (lit. or fig.; was delivered of a child, a sonnet); unburden oneself (of opinion etc.) in discourse. 3. give up or over, abandon, resign, hand on to another; distribute (letters, parcels, ordered goods) to addressee or purchaser (∼ the goods or ∼, (fig.) carry out one's part of agreement); present, render, (account); (Law) hand over formally (esp. sealed deed to grantee). 4. launch, aim, (blow, ball, attack); (of judge) pronounce (judgement); utter, recite, (well-delivered sermon). 5. Hence ∼ABLE a., ∼ER¹ n. [ME, f. OF delivrer f. Gallo-Rom. *deliberare (as DE-, L liberare LIBERATE)]

dēli'verance n. rescue; formally expressed opinion, (in jurors' oath) verdict. [ME, f. OF delivrance (as prec.; see -ANCE)]

dēli'verў n. 1. childbirth. 2. surrender of. 3. delivering of letters etc., a periodical performance of this; take ∼ of, receive (thing purchased). 4. (Law). formal handing over of property, transfer of deed to grantee or third party. 5. sending forth of missile, esp. of cricket-ball or baseball; action shown in doing this (a good, high, delivery); uttering of speech etc. (its delivery took two hours); manner of doing this (a telling delivery). [ME, f. AF delivree p.p. (as prec.) of delivrer (see DELIVER, -Y⁴)]

dēll n. small secluded vale. wooded hollow or valley. [OE, ∼ MLG, MDu. delle, MHG telle f. Gmc *daljō (*dal-; cf. DALE)]

Dĕlla Crŭ'scan a. & n. (member) of academy in Florence concerned with purity of Italian; (member) of school of English poets with artificial style in late 18th c. [f. It. (Accademia) della Crusca (Academy) of the bran w. ref. to sifting) + -AN]

For other words in de- see DE-.

dělou'se *v.t.* rid of lice, or (fig.) of undesirable things. [f. DE-+LOUSE]

Dě'lphian, Dě'lphic, *adjs.* (as) of the ancient Greek oracle of Delphi; obscure, ambiguous, enigmatic. [f. *Delphi*+-AN, -IC]

dělphi'nium *n.* ranunculaceous usu. blue-flowered plant of genus *Delphinium,* e.g. larkspur. [mod. L, f. Gk *delphinion* larkspur (*delphin* dolphin)]

dě'lphinoid *n.* & *a.* (animal) like dolphin; (member) of the family including dolphins, porpoises, grampuses, etc. [f. Gk *delphinoeidēs* (*delphin* dolphin; see -OID)]

dě'lta *n.* fourth Greek letter (Δ, δ) = d; (Astron.) fourth star in a constellation; fourth-class mark in examination; triangular alluvial tract at mouth of river enclosed or traversed by its diverging branches, whence **děltā'ic** *a.*; ∼ **connection,** (Electr.) triangular arrangement of three-phase windings with circuit wire from each angle; ∼ **rays,** rays of low penetrative power consisting of slow electrons knocked from an atom by other particles, esp. alpha rays; ∼ **wing,** triangular swept-back wing of aircraft. [ME f. Gk, f. Phoen. *daleth*]

děltiǒ'|logy *n.* hobby of collecting postcards; hence ∼LOGIST *n.* [f. Gk *deltion* dim. of *deltos* writing-tablet +-O-+-LOGY]

dě'ltoid *a.* & *n.* triangular; ∼ (**muscle**), muscle of shoulder lifting upper arm; like a river delta. [f. F *deltoïde* or f. mod. L *deltoides* f. Gk *deltoeidēs* (DELTA; see -OID)]

dělu'de (-ū'd, -ōō'd) *v.t.* impose on, deceive. [ME, f. L DE(*ludere lus-* play) mock]

dě'lŭge *n.,* & *v.t.* **1.** *n.* great flood, inundation (**the** D∼), Noah's flood, Gen. 6–8); heavy fall of rain; flood of words etc. **2.** *v.t.* flood, inundate, (lit. or fig.). [ME f. OF, f. L *diluvium,* rel. to *lavare* wash]

dělu'sion (-ū'zhon, -ōō'-) *n.* imposing or being imposed on; false impression (*was under the delusion that*) *or opinion, esp.* as symptom or form of madness (∼*s* **of grandeur,** hallucinatory exaggeration of one's own personality or status), whence ∼AL *a.* [ME, f. LL *delusio* (as DELUDE; see -ION)]

dělu'sive (-lū'-, -lōō'-) *a.* deceptive, disappointing, unreal; hence ∼LY[2] (-vlĭ) *adv.,* ∼NESS (-vn-) *n.* [f. as DELUDE+-IVE]

|dělū'stre, *-ster,* *v.t.* remove lustre from (textile). [f. DE-+LUSTRE[1]]

de lu'xe (lŭ'ks, lōō'ks) *a.* luxurious, sumptuous; of superior kind. [F, = of luxury]

dělve *v.* **1.** *v.t.* & *i.* (poet.) dig. **2.** *v.i.* make laborious research in documents etc. [OE *delfan,* = OS *-delban,* OHG *-telban* f. WG **delbh-* etc.]

Dem. *abbr.* Democrat.

děmā'gnětiz|e, -ĭs|e (-ĭz), *v.t.* remove magnetization of; hence ∼A'TION *n.* [f. DE-+MAGNETIZE]

dě'magŏgue (-g), **-gŏg, n.* leader of the populace; political agitator appealing to desires or prejudices of the mob; hence or cogn. **děmagŏ'gic** (-gĭk) *a.,* **dě'magŏguERY** (4) (-gerĭ), **dě'magŏgY**[1] (-gĭ), *ns.* [f. Gk *dēmagōgos* (*dēmos* the people, *agōgos* leading)]

děma'nd[1] (-ah'-) *n.* **1.** request made as of right or peremptorily (∼ **note,** ‖request for payment, **bill payable at sight; payable* etc. **on** ∼, as soon as the demand is made). **2.** desire of would-be purchasers or users for commodity (∼ **pull,** available money as factor causing economic inflation; **in** ∼, sought after; SUPPLY[1] *and demand*); urgent claim (*many demands on me, on my time*). [ME, f. OF *demande* (*demander;* see foll.)]

děma'nd[2] (-ah'-) *v.t.* ask for (thing) as of right or peremptorily or urgently (*of* or *from* person; *demand an answer, to know, that one be told*); require, need (*piety demands it; task demands skill*); ask to be, insist on being, told (*demand person's business, what he wants*); (in *pres. part.,* abs.) making demands, requiring skill, effort, etc.; hence ∼ABLE *a.,* ∼ANT *n.* [ME, f. OF *demander* f. L DE(*mandare* order; cf. MANDATE) entrust]

děmā'ntoid *n.* lustrous green garnet. [G]

děmārcā'tion *n.* marking of boundary or limits, esp. between work considered by trade unions to belong to different trades (*demarcation dispute*); hence (as back-form.) **dě'mārc**ATE[3] *v.t.* [f. Sp. *demarcación* (*demarcar* mark bounds of; as DE-, MARK[2]; see -ATION]

démarche (dā'mârsh) *n.* (Diplom.) political step or proceeding, esp. in initiating fresh policy. [F (*démarcher* take steps; as DE-, MARCH[5])]

děmatēr'ializ|e, -ĭs|e (-ĭz), *v.t.* & *i.* make or become non-material or spiritual; hence ∼A'TION *n.* [f. DE-+MATERIALIZE]

děme *n.* township of ancient Attica; administrative division in modern Greece; (Ecol.) local population of closely related plants and animals. [f. Gk *dēmos* the people]

děmea'n[1] *v. refl.* (w. *adv.*) behave, conduct one*self.* [ME, f. OF *demener* f. Rom. **deminare* (as DE-, L *minare* drive animals f. *minari* threaten)]

děmea'n[2] *v.t.* (usu. *refl.*) lower the dignity of; ∼ one*self,* be so undignified as *to do.* [f. DE-+MEAN[3], after *debase*]

‖děmea'nour (-ner), ***-or,** *n.* bearing, outward behaviour. [f. DEMEAN[1], prob. after obs. *havour* behaviour]

děmě'nt *n.* demented person. [orig. a. f. F *dément* or f. L *demens* (see foll.)]

děmě'ntěd *a.* driven mad, crazy; hence ∼LY[2] *adv.* [p.p. of *dement* v. f. OF *dementer* or f. LL *dementare* f. L *demens* out of one's mind (*mens mentis*)]

démenti (dāmah'ntē) *n.* official denial of rumour etc. [F (*démentir* accuse of lying)]

děmě'ntia (-sha) *n.* (Med.) insanity consisting in loss of intellectual power, due to brain disease or injury; ∼ **praecox** (prē'kŏks), schizophrenia. [L (*demens;* see DEMENTED)]

děmerār'a *n.* light-brown raw cane sugar brought orig. and chiefly from *Demerara* in Guyana.

děmě'rĭt *n.* quality or action deserving blame; fault, defect; *mark awarded to offender; hence ∼*ōr'ious* [-ORY, -OUS] *a.* [ME, f. OF *de(s)merite* or f. L *demeritum* neut. p.p. of *demerēri* deserve; orig. sense DESERT[1] (good or bad)]

děmēr'sal *a.* being or living near sea-bottom. [f. L *demersus* p.p. of DE(*mergere* plunge)+-AL]

děme'sne (-ē'n, -ā'n) *n.* **1.** (Law). possession (of real property) as one's own (*estate* held **in** ∼, occupied by owner by his tenants). **2.** Sovereign's or State's territory, domain; landed property, estate; land attached to mansion etc.; region, sphere, (*of*-). [ME, f. AF, OF *demeine* (later AF *demesne*) belonging to a lord, f. L *dominicus* (see DOMINICAL)]

dě'mi- *pref.* half-size, half, imperfect, partial(ly), semi-. [ME f. F, f. med. L *dimedius* half, for L *dimidius*]

dě'migŏd *n.* (*fem.* ∼**dess**). partly divine being, offspring of god(dess) and mortal; person who seems to have godlike powers. [f. DEMI-+GOD]

dě'mijŏhn (-jŏn) *n.* bulging narrow-necked bottle of 3–10 gal., usu. cased in wicker and with wicker handles. [prob. corrupt. of F *dame-jeanne* Lady Jane, assim. to DEMI-, JOHN]

děmī'litarĭz|e, -ĭs|e (-ĭz), *v.t.* remove military organization or forces from (frontier, zone, etc.); hence ∼A'TION *n.* [f. DE-+MILITARY+-IZE]

demi-monde (dě'mĭmawnd) *n.* class of women of doubtful reputation and social standing; group behaving with doubtful legality or propriety; so ∼*aine* (-ān) *n.,* woman of the demi-monde. [F, = half-world]

děmī'neralĭz|e, -ĭs|e (-ĭz), *v.t.* remove salts from (sea-water etc.); hence ∼A'TION *n.* [f. DE-+MINERALIZE]

demi-pension (demĭpah'nsyawn) *n.* accommodation at hotel etc. with bed, breakfast, and one main meal per day. [F (as DEMI-, PENSION 2)]

dě'mi-rěp *n.* (arch.) woman of doubtful reputation esp. as regards chastity. [abbr. of *demi-reputable* (DEMI-, REPUTABLE)]

děmī'se (-z) *v.t.,* & *n.* **1.** *v.t.* convey or grant (estate) by will or lease; transmit (title etc.) by death or abdication. **2.** *n.* conveyance or transfer by demising; death (lit. or fig.). [v. f. n., AF use of p.p. of *de(s)mettre* DIMISS, in refl. abdicate]

‖**dĕmisĕmiquāver** (-sĕ'-, dĕ'-) *n.* (Mus.) note, with three-hooked symbol, equal to half a semiquaver. [f. DEMI- + SEMI*quaver*]

dēmi'st *v.t.* clear mist from (windscreen etc.); so ∼ER[1] (2) *n.* [f. DE- + MIST]

dĕmi't *v.t.* (-tt-). resign, abdicate, (office, or abs.); so **dĕmi'ssion** (-shon) *n.* [f. F *démettre* f. L DE(*mittere* misssend)]

dĕ'mităsse *n.* small coffee-cup; its contents. [F, = half-cup]

dĕ'miŭrge *n.* (In Platonic philosophy) creator of world; (in Gnosticism etc.) a being subordinate to Supreme being; hence **dĕmiŭr'gic** *a.* [f. eccl. L f. Gk *dēmiourgos* craftsman (*dēmios* public f. *dēmos* people, *-ergos* working)]

demi-vierge (dĕmivyār'zh) *n.* woman who behaves licentiously but retains her physiological virginity. [F, = half-virgin]

dĕ'mō *n.* (*pl.* ∼s). (colloq.) = DEMONSTRATION **4.** [abbr.]

dēmō'b *v.t.* (-bb-), & *n.* (colloq.) demobilize, demobilization. [abbr.]

dēmō'bilīz|e, -īs|e (-īz) *v.t.* release from mobilized state, disband, (troops, ships); hence ∼A'TION *n.* [f. F *démobiliser* (as DE-, MOBILIZE)]

dĕmŏ'cracy *n.* (State having) government by all the people, direct or representative; form of society ignoring hereditary class distinctions and tolerating minority views; *principles or members of Democratic Party. [f. F *démocratie* f. LL f. Gk *dēmokratia* (*dēmos* the people; see -CRACY)]

dĕ'mocrăt *n.* advocate of democracy; *(D∼) member of Democratic Party; hence **dĕmŏ'cratISM** (3) *n.* [f. F *démocrate* f. as prec., after *aristocrate*)]

dĕmocră'tic *a.* of, like, practising, advocating, constituting, (a) democracy; favouring social equality; *D∼ Party (opposed to Republican Party and supporting social reform and international commitment); so **dĕmocră'tICALLY** *adv.*, **dĕmŏ'cratIZE** (3) *v.t.* & *i.* [f. F *démocratique* f. med. L f. Gk *dēmokratia* (*dēmokratia* DEMOCRACY; *see* -IC)]

démodé (dāmō'dā) *a.* out of fashion. [F, p.p. of *démoder* (as DE-, *mode* fashion)]

dēmŏdūlā'tion *n.* (Radio etc.) process of extracting modulating signal from modulated wave etc. [f. DE- + MODULATION]

dĕmŏ'graphy *n.* study of statistics of births, deaths, disease, etc., as illustrating conditions of life in communities; hence **dĕmŏ'GRAPHER** *n.*, **dĕmo-GRA'PHIC(AL)** *adjs.* [f. Gk *dēmos* the people + -o- + -GRAPHY]

dĕmoisĕ'lle (-mwaz-) *n.* (Zool.) small crane of Asia & N. Africa; damselfish; damselfly; (arch.) young lady. [F, = DAMSEL]

dĕmŏ'lish *v.t.* pull or throw down (building), destroy; overthrow (institution), refute (theory); (joc.) eat up; so **dĕmoli'tION** *n.* [f. F *démolir* (-ISH[2]) f. L DE(*moliri* -*it*- construct f. *moles* mass)]

dē'mon *n.* **1.** evil spirit or devil (esp. possessing a person); malignant supernatural being; cruel, malignant, destructive, forceful, or fierce, person (∼ bowler, (Cricket) very fast bowler; **is a** ∼ **for work**, works strenuously); personified evil passion. **2.** (Also **dae'mon**). supernatural being in Gk Myth.; attendant or indwelling spirit. **3.** Hence ∼ŏ'LATRY, ∼ŏ'LOGY, *ns.* [ME f. med. L, f. Gk *daimōn* deity]

dēmo'nĕtiz|e (-mŭ'n-), -**īs|e** (-īz), *v.t.* withdraw (coin etc.) from use as money; hence ∼A'TION *n.* [f. F *démonétiser* (as DE-, L *moneta* MONEY, -IZE)]

dĕmŏ'niăc *a.* & *n.* (person) possessed by an evil spirit; of such possession; of or like demons; fiercely energetic, frenzied; so **dĕmonī'acAL** *a.* [ME, f. OF

demoniaque f. eccl. L *daemoniacus* (*daemonium* f. Gk *daimonion* dim. of *daimōn*; cf. DEMON)]

dēmŏ'nic, dae-, *a.* demoniac; having supernatural genius or power. [f. LL f. Gk *daimonikos* (as DEMON; see -IC)]

dē'monism *n.* belief in the power of demons. [f. DEMON + -ISM]

dēmonīze, -īse (-īz), *v.t.* make into or like, represent as, demon. [f. DEMON + -IZE]

demonstr|able (dē'mon-, dǐmŏ'n-) *a.* capable of being shown or logically proved; hence ∼ABI'LITY *n.*, ∼ABLY *adv.* [ME, f. L *demonstrabilis* (as foll.; see -ABLE)]

dē'monstrāte *v.1. v.t.* show evidence of (feelings etc.); describe and explain by help of specimens or experiments; logically prove the truth of; be proof of the existence of. **2.** *v.i.* act as demonstrator; make, take part in, a demonstration by public meeting etc. [f. L DE(*monstrare* show) + -ATE[3]]

dēmonstrā'tion *n.* **1.** outward exhibition *of* feeling etc. **2.** logical proving, clear proof, argument etc. serving as proof. **3.** exhibition and explanation of specimens or experiments as way of teaching. **4.** exhibition of opinion on political or other question; public meeting or procession for such purpose; show of military force. **5.** Hence ∼AL *a.* [ME f. OF, or f. L *demonstratio* (as prec.; see -ATION)]

dēmŏ'nstrative *a.* & *n.* **1.** *a.* serving to point out or exhibit; (Gram.) indicating person or thing referred to (*demonstrative* PRONOUN). **2.** giving proof *of*; logically conclusive; concerned with proof. **3.** given to or marked by open expression of feelings (*demonstrative person, behaviour, affection,* etc.). **4.** Hence ∼LY[2] (-vlǐ) *adv.*, ∼NESS (-vn-) *n.* **5.** *n.* (Gram.) demonstrative word. [ME, f. OF *demonstratif -ive* f. L *demonstrativus* (as prec.; see -IVE)]

dē'monstrātor *n.* one who demonstrates; one who teaches by demonstration, esp. in laboratory etc.; person who explains working of machine etc. to prospective customers; one who takes part in demonstration by public meeting etc. [L (as DEMONSTRATE; see -OR)]

dēmŏ'ralīz|e, -īs|e (-īz), *v.t.* destroy morale of; (arch.) corrupt morals of; hence ∼A'TION *n.* [f. F *démoraliser* (as DE-, MORAL, -IZE)]

Dē'mŏs *n.* personification of the populace, esp. in a democracy. [Gk, = the people]

dēmŏ'te *v.t.* reduce to lower rank or class; hence **dēmŏ'tION** *n.* [f. DE- + PROMOTE]

dēmŏ'tic *a.* & *n.* popular, vulgar, (language etc.); (of) the popular simplified form (opp. *hieratic*) of ancient Egyptian writing; (of) the popular form of modern Greek. [f. Gk *dēmotikos* f. *dēmotēs* one of the people (*dēmos*); see -IC]

dēmou'nt *v.t.* take (apparatus etc.) from its mounting; dismantle for later reassembly. [f. F *démonter*; cf. DISMOUNT]

dēmŭ'lcent *a.* & *n.* soothing (medicine). [f. L DE-(*mulcēre* sooth); see -ENT]

dēmŭr' *v.i.* (-rr-), & *n.* **1.** *v.i.* raise scruples or objections *to* or *at*; (Law) put in a demurrer, whence **dēmŭ'rrANT** *n.* **2.** *n.* objecting, objection, (usu. *without, no, demur*). [ME, f. OF *demeure(r)* f. Rom. *DE(morare* f. L *morari* delay)]

dēmŭr'e *a.* (∼r, ∼st). sober, grave, composed; affectedly or artificially quiet and serious; decorous; hence ∼LY[2] (-ūr'lǐ) *adv.*, ∼NESS (-ūr'n-) *n.* [ME; perh. f. AF *demuré* f. OF of *demorer* remain f. as prec. (cf. STAID), infl. by OF *meür* f. L *maturus* ripe]

dēmŭ'rrable *a.* (esp. Law). that may be demurred to; open to objection. [f. DEMUR + -ABLE]

dēmŭ'rrage *n.* rate or amount payable to shipowner by charterer for failure to load or discharge ship within time allowed; similar charge on railway trucks or goods; such detention, delay. [f. OF *demo(u)rage* (*demorer*, as DEMUR; see -AGE)]

dēmŭ'rrer *n.* legal objection to relevance of opponent's point even if granted, which stays action till

For other words in *de-* see DE-.

relevance is settled; exception taken. [AF, inf. as n., = DEMUR; see -ER⁴]

demy′ *n.* size of paper, 564 × 444 mm.; ||scholar of Magdalen College, Oxford (orig. with half Fellow's allowance), whence ∼SHIP *n.* [ME, var. of DEMI-]

demy′sti|fy *v.t.* clarify (obscure beliefs etc.); reduce or remove irrationality etc. of (person); hence ∼FICA′TION *n.* [f. DE- + MYSTIFY]

demythŏ′logize, -īse (-īz), *v.t.* remove mythical elements from (legend etc.); reinterpret mythological elements in (Bible). [f. DE- + MYTHOLOGIZE]

den *n.* wild beast's lair; resort of criminals etc. (*opium den; den of vice*); small room in which person secludes himself to work etc. [OE *denn,* = MLG, MDu. *denne,* OHG *tenni,* f. Gmc **danjam, danjō;* cogn. w. DEAN²]

denāri|us *n.,(pl. ∼i pr. -ī).* ancient-Roman silver coin. [L, = (coin) of ten asses (as foll.; see AS²)]

de′narÿ *a.* of ten, decimal; *denary* SCALE³. [f. L *denarius* containing ten (*deni* by tens, distrib. of *decem* ten; see -ARY¹)]

denā′tionaliz|e, -īs|e (-īz), *v.t.* deprive (nation) of its status or characteristics, (person) of membership or characteristics of his nation; transfer (institution, industry, etc.) from national to private ownership; hence ∼A′TION *n.* [f. F *dénationaliser* (as DE-, NATIONAL, -IZE)]

denā′turaliz|e, -īs|e, (-cheralīz) *v.t.* change nature or properties of, make unnatural; deprive (esp. one*self*) of citizenship; make (alcohol etc.) unfit for drinking; hence ∼A′TION *n.* [f. DE- + NATURAL + -IZE, or f. DE- + NATURALIZE]

denā′tur|e *v.t.* denaturalize; change properties of (protein) by heat etc.; so ∼ANT, ∼A′TION, (-cher-) *ns.* [f. F *dénaturer* (as DE-, NATURE)]

denă′zi|fy (-ah′tsi-, -ah′zi-) *v.t.* remove (Nazis or their supporters) from Nazi allegiance; remove Nazis from (official positions etc.); hence ∼FICA′TION *n.* [f. DE- + NAZI + -FY]

de′ndrīte *n.* (stone or mineral with) natural treelike or mosslike marking; (Zool.) branching process conducting signals to nerve-cell. [F, f. Gk *dendrītēs* a. (*dendron* tree); see -ITE¹]

dendri′t|ic *a.* of or like a dendrite; treelike in shape or branching; so ∼ICALLY *adv.* [f. prec. + -IC]

dendrŏchronŏ′log|ÿ (-k-) *n.* study of chronology by means of annual growth rings in timber; hence ∼IST (3) *n.* [f. Gk *dendron* tree + -o- + CHRONOLOGY]

de′ndroid *a.* tree-shaped. [f. Gk *dendrōdēs* treelike + -OID]

dendrŏ′logÿ *n.* study of trees. [f. Gk *dendron* tree + -o- + -LOGY]

||dēne¹ *n.* bare sandy tract, low sand-hill, by sea. [perh. rel. to LG *düne,* Du. *duin;* cf. DUNE]

||dēne², ||dean², *n.* vale (esp. as ending of place--names); narrow wooded valley of stream. [f. OE *denu,* cogn. w. DEN]

denēgā′tion *n.* (arch.) denial. [f. LL DE(*negatio* f. L *negare* deny); see -ATION]

||dēne-hōle *n.* (Archaeol.) artificial cave in chalk entered by vertical shaft. [18th c.; orig. uncert., perh. f. DANE + HOLE¹]

de′nguē (-nggi) *n.* infectious eruptive tropical fever causing acute pains in joints. [W. Ind. Sp., f. Swahili *denga, dinga,* w. assim. to Sp. *dengue* fastidiousness, w. ref. to stiffness of patient's neck and shoulders]

denī′able. See DENY.

denī′al *n.* refusal of request or wish (SELF-*denial*); statement that thing is not true (*meet charge with flat denial*) or existent, contradiction; disavowal of person as one's leader etc. [f. DENY + -AL 2]

de′nier (-nyer) *n.* unit of weight by which fineness of silk, rayon, or nylon yarn is estimated. [orig. name of a small coin; ME f. OF, f. L *denarius* (see DENARY)]

de′nigr|āte *v.t.* blacken (fig.), defame; hence ∼ātor, ∼A′TION, *ns.,* ∼ātorÿ *a.* [f. L DE(*nigrare* f. *niger* black) + -ATE³]

de′nim *n.* twilled hard-wearing cotton fabric used for overalls, jeans, etc.; (in *pl.*) garment made of this. [for *serge de Nim* (*Nîmes* in S. France)]

denī′tri|fỹ *v.t.* remove nitrates or nitrites from (soil etc.); so ∼FICA′TION *n.* [f. DE- + NITRIFY]

de′nīzen *n.* inhabitant or occupant (*of* place); foreigner admitted to residence and certain rights; naturalized foreign word, animal, or plant; hence ∼SHIP *n.* [ME, f. AF *deinzein* f. OF *deinz* within (L *de* from, *intus* within) + -*ein* (L -*aneus;* see -ANEOUS)]

denŏ′mināte *v.t.* give name to; call or describe (person or thing) as. [f. L DE(*nominare* NOMINATE) + -ATE³]

denŏminā′tion *n.* name, designation, esp. characteristic or class name; class of units in numbers, weights, money, etc., (*reduce to the same denomination; money of small denominations*); class or kind having specific name; rank of playing-card within suit, or of suit relative to others; Church or religious sect, whence ∼AL *a.* (∼al education, according to principles of a Church or sect). [ME f. OF, or f. L *denominatio* (as prec.; see -ATION)]

denŏ′minative *a.* serving as or giving a name. [f. LL *denominativus* (as prec.; see -ATIVE)]

denŏ′minātor *n.* number below line in vulgar fraction, divisor; (*least, lowest*) **common ∼,** (least) common multiple of denominators of several fractions, (fig.) common feature of members of a group. [f. F *dénominateur* or f. med. L *denominator* (as DE-NOMINATE; see -OR)]

de nos jours (de nō zhoor′) *a.* (placed after *n.*) of the present time. [F, = of our days]

denŏ′t|e *v.t.* distinguish, be the sign of; indicate; give to understand, (esp. *that*); stand as name for, designate; signify; so **denot**A′TION *n.,* ∼ATIVE *a.* [f. F *dénoter* or f. L DE(*notare* mark f. *nota* NOTE¹)]

dénouement, de-, (dānōō′mahn) *n.* unravelling of plot or complications; final resolution in play, novel, etc. [f. F *dénouement* (*dénouer* unknot, f. as DE-, L *nodare* f. *nodus* knot; see -MENT)]

denou′nce *v.t.* inform against, accuse publicly, openly inveigh against; give notice of termination of (armistice, treaty); hence ∼MENT (-sm-) *n.* [ME, f. OF *denoncier* f. L DE(*nuntiare* make known f. *nuntius* messenger)]

de nouveau (de nōōvō′) *adv.* afresh, starting again. [F]

de novo (dē nō′vō, dā-) *adv.* − prec. [L]

dĕnse *a.* closely compacted in substance (*dense fog, forest*); crowded together; crass, stupid; hence ∼LY² (-slī) *adv.,* ∼′NESS (-sn-) *n.* [F, or f. L *densus*]

densito′meter *n.* instrument for measuring photographic density. [f. foll. + -o- + -METER]

de′nsitÿ *n.* closeness of substance; (Phys.) degree of consistency measured by quantity of mass in unit volume; (Photog.) opaqueness of image; crowded state; stupidity. [f. F *densité* or f. L *densitas* (as DENSE, see -ITY)]

dĕnt *n.,* & *v.t.* **1.** *n.* surface impression (as) from blow of blunt-edged instrument. **2.** *v.t.* mark with dent; (fig.) have (esp. adverse) effect on. [ME, prob. f. INDENT¹]

de′ntal *a.* of tooth, teeth, or dentistry; (Phonet.) of consonant) pronounced with tongue-tip against upper front teeth (as *th*) or ridge of teeth (as *n, s, t*), whence ∼IZE (3) *v.t.;* ∼ **floss,** threads of floss silk etc. used to clean between teeth; ∼ **mechanic,** person who makes and repairs artificial teeth; ∼ **surgeon,** dentist. [f. LL *dentalis* f. L *dens dentis* tooth; see -AL]

dentā′li|um *n.* (*pl.* ∼a). tooth-shell of genus *Dentalium,* used as ornament or currency. [mod. L, f. LL *dentalis* (see prec.)]

de′ntāte *a.* (Bot. & Zool.) toothed, with toothlike notches. [f. L *dentatus* (*dens dentis* tooth; see -ATE²)]

de′nti- *comb. form.* tooth, teeth, as: ∼li′ngual, formed by teeth and tongue. [f. L *dens dentis* tooth; see -I-]

de′nticle *n.* (Zool.) small tooth or toothlike projection; so **denti′cūl**ATE² *a.* [ME, f. L *denticulus* dim. of *dens dentis* tooth; see -CULE]

děn'tǐfrǐce *n.* powder, paste, etc., for tooth-cleaning. [F, f. L *dentifricium* (*dens dentis* tooth, *fricare* rub)]

děn'tǐl *n.* one of series of small rectangular blocks under bed-moulding of cornice in classical architecture. [f. obs. F *dentille* dim. of *dent* tooth f. L *dens dentis*]

děn'tǐne (-ēn), ***děn'tǐn,** *n.* hard dense tissue forming main part of teeth. [f. L (as prec.)+-INE⁴]

děn'tǐst *n.* one whose profession is to treat diseases and malformations of the teeth, extract them, insert artificial ones, etc.; hence ∼RY (5) *n.* [f. F *dentiste* (*dent* tooth; see DENTIL, -IST)]

děntǐ'tǐon *n.* cutting of teeth, teething; characteristic arrangement of teeth in species etc. [f. L *dentitio* (*dentire* to teethe; see -ITION)]

děn'ture *n.* set of (esp. artificial) teeth. [F (*dent* tooth; see DENTIL, -URE)]

děnū'clěarīz│e, -īs│e (-īz), *v.t.* remove nuclear armaments from; hence ∼A'TION *n.* [f. DE-+NUCLEAR+-IZE]

děnū'd│e *v.t.* make naked; strip *of* clothing, covering, possession, attribute; (Geol.) lay (rock, formation) bare by removal of what lies above; so **děnūdA'TION** *n.*, ∼ATIVE *a.* [f. L DE(*nudare* f. *nudus* naked)]

děnū'mer│able *a.* (Math.) able to be counted by correspondence with infinite set of integers; hence ∼ABI'LITY *n.* [f. LL DE(*numerare* NUMBER²)+-ABLE]

děnū'nciātion *n.* denouncing; invective; so **dě-nū'nciative**, **děnū'nciatORY**, (-sha-) *adjs.*, **dě-nū'nciātor** (-shī-) *n.* [f. F *dénonciation* or f. L *denunciatio* (as DENOUNCE; see -ATION)]

děnȳ' *v.t.* declare untrue or non-existent (*deny the charge, the possibility, having lied, that it is so, this to be the case*); disavow, repudiate, (*deny one's word, signature, faith, leader*); refuse (person, thing, person a thing, thing *to* person; *I was denied this, this was denied me* or *to me*); refuse access to (person sought); ∼ one**self**, be abstinent; hence **děnī'ABLE** *a.* [ME, f. OF *denier* f. L DE(*negare* say no)]

deoch an doris (dǒχ an dǒ'rǐs, dǒk-) *n.* (Sc. & Ir.) drink taken at parting, stirrup-cup. [f. Gael. *deoch an doruis* drink at the door]

‖**dē'odǎnd** *n.* (Hist.) thing forfeited to Crown for religious or charitable use, as having caused a human death. [f. AF *deodande* f. AL *deodanda* f. L *Deo dandum* thing to be given to God (*Deus* God, *dare* give)]

dē'odār *n.* Himalayan cedar. [f. Hindi *dē'* *odār* f. Skr. *deva-dāru* divine tree]

děō'dorant *a.* & *n.* (substance) that removes or conceals unwanted odours. [f. as foll.+-ANT]

děō'dorīz│e, -īs│e (-īz), *v.t.* destroy odour of; hence ∼A'TION *n.* [f. DE-+L ODOR smell+-IZE]

Deo gratias (dāō grah'tǐas, -shǐas) *int.* thanks be to God. [L, = (we give) thanks to God]

děǒ'ntǐc *a.* of or relating to duty or obligation. [f. as foll.+-IC]

děǒntŏ'logȳ *n.* science of duty, ethics; hence **děǒnto-LO'GICAL** *a.*, **děǒntŏ'LOGIST** *n.* [f. Gk *deont-* part. st. of *dei* it is right+-o-+-LOGY]

Deo volente (dāō volě'ntā) *adv.* God being willing; if nothing prevents it. [L]

dē-ǒ'xȳgenāte *v.t.* remove (the free) oxygen from. [f. DE-+OXYGENATE]

děǒxȳrǐbonūclě'ǐc *a.* ∼ **acid,** substance in chromosomes of higher organisms, storing genetic information. [f. DE-+OXYGEN+RIBONUCLEIC]

dep. *abbr.* departs; deputy.

depār't *v.i.* & *t.* (formal or literary). go away (*from*), take one's leave; set out, start, leave, (*for* place; esp. of public transport); die, leave by death, (*depart from life, depart this life*); diverge, deviate, (*depart from accepted view, custom*). [ME, f. OF *departir* f. Rom. *departire*, *dispartire* for L *dispertire* divide]

depār'těd *a.* & *n.* bygone (*departed greatness*); deceased (person(s); esp. *the departed*). [p.p. of prec.; hence -ED¹ (2)]

depār'tment *n.* separate part of complex whole,

branch, esp. of municipal or State administration, university, shop; administrative district in France etc.; area of activity; ∼ **store,** large shop supplying many kinds of goods from various departments. [f. F *département* (as DEPART; see -MENT)]

depār'tmě'ntal *a.* of or belonging to a department; ∼ **store,** = *department store*; hence ∼ISM (3) *n.*, ∼IZE (3) *v.t.*, ∼LY² *adv.* [f. prec.+-AL]

depār'ture *n.* going away; deviation *from* (truth, standard); starting of train, aircraft, etc., (*the departure platform, lounge*); setting out on course of action or thought (esp. *new departure*); (Naut.) amount of ship's change of longitude. [f. OF *departeüre* (as DEPART; see -URE)]

děpa'stur│e (-ah'-) *v.t.* & *i.* (Of cattle) graze upon, graze; put (cattle) to graze; (of land) give pasturage to (cattle); hence ∼AGE *n.* [f. DE- + PASTURE]

dépaysé (dāpā'zā) *a.* (*fem.* ∼e *pr.* same). removed from one's habitual surroundings. [F, = removed from one's own country]

děpě'nd *v.i.* 1. be contingent (**that** ∼**s,** the question can only be answered conditionally); ∼ (**up**)**on,** be controlled or determined by (**it** ∼**s upon himself,** i.e. upon his efforts, skill, wisdom, etc.); be grammatically dependent (*up*)*on.* 2. ∼ (**up**)**on,** be obliged to use, be unable to do without, (*she depends upon her own efforts, her pen, her mother, my help*), rely on (esp. in *imper.*: ∼ **upon it,** you may be sure). 3. (poet., arch., etc.) hang down (*from*). [ME, f. OF *dependre* f. Rom. *dependere* for L DE(*pendēre* hang)]

děpě'nd│able *a.* that may be relied on; hence ∼ABI'LITY, ∼ableNESS (-beln-), *ns.*, ∼ABLY *adv.* [f. prec.+-ABLE]

děpě'ndant, *-ent¹, *n.* one who depends on another for support; retainer, servant. [f. F *dépendant* part. of *dépendre* (see DEPEND, -ANT, -ENT)]

děpě'ndence *n.* depending; being dependent; reliance, confident trust. [f. F *dépendance* (as prec.; see -ANCE, -ENCE)]

děpě'ndencȳ *n.* subordinate or dependent thing, esp. country or province controlled by another. [f. as prec.; see -ENCY]

děpě'ndent¹. See DEPENDANT.

děpě'ndent² *a.* depending (*on*), contingent, subordinate, subject; unable to do without something (esp. a drug); maintained at another's cost; (Gram., of clause, phrase, or word) in subordinate relation to a sentence or word; (Math., of variable) having value determined by that of another quantity. [ME, earlier *-ant* = dependANT]

děpēr'sonalīz│e, -īs│e (-īz), *v.t.* deprive of personality; make impersonal; hence ∼A'TION *n.* (esp., Psych.) morbid loss of sense of identity. [f. DE-+PERSONAL+-IZE]

děpǐ'ct *v.t.* represent in drawing or colours; portray in words, describe; hence ∼ER¹, ∼ION, ∼OR, *ns.*, ∼IVE *a.* [f. L DE(*pingere pict-* paint)]

dē'pǐl│āte *v.t.* remove hair from; hence ∼A'TION *n.*, **dépǐ'latORY** *a.* & *n.* [f. L DE(*pilare* f. *pilus* hair)+-ATE³]

děplā'ne *v.i.* & *t.* descend or remove from aeroplane. [f. DE-+PLANE³]

děplē'te *v.t.* empty out, exhaust; reduce numbers or quantity of (*depleted forces, stores*); so **děplē'**TION *n.* [f. L DE(*plēre plet-* fill)]

děplōr'│e *v.t.* bewail, grieve over, regret; be scandalized by; hence ∼ABLE *a.*, (esp.) exceedingly bad, ∼ABLY *adv.* [f. F *déplorer* or It. f. L DE(*plorare* bewail)]

děplo'y *v.* 1. *v.t.* & *i.* (Mil.) spread (troops) out, (of troops) spread out, from column into line. 2. *v.t.* bring (forces, arguments, etc.) into effective action. 3. So ∼MENT *n.* [f. F *déployer* f. L DIS(*plicare* fold) & LL DEplicare explain]

děplu'me (-ōō'm) *v.t.* strip of feathers or (fig.) honour etc. [ME, f. F *déplumer* f. med. L DE(*plumare* f. L *pluma* feather)]

děpŏ'larīz│e, -īs│e (-īz), *v.t.* (Phys.) reduce or remove polarization of; hence ∼A'TION *n.* [f. DE-+POLARIZE]

For other words in *de-* see DE-.

dĕpŏli'tĭcĭz|e, -ĭs|e (-īz), *v.t.* make non-political; remove from political activity or influence; hence ∾A'TION *n*. [f. DE- + POLITICIZE]

dĕpŏ'lўmerĭz|e, -ĭs|e (-īz), *v.t.* & *i*. (Chem.) (cause to) break down into monomers or other smaller units; hence ∾A'TION *n*. [f. DE- + POLYMERIZE]

dĕpō'nent *a*. & *n*. **1.** *a*. (L & Gk Gram., of verb) passive (or, in Gk, middle) in form but active in sense [named from notion that it had laid aside the passive sense]. **2.** *n*. deponent verb; person making deposition under oath or giving written testimony for use in court etc. [f. L DE(*ponere posit-* place); see -ENT]

dĕpō'pŭl|āte *v.t.* & *i*. reduce population of; decline in population; hence ∾A'TION *n*. [f. L DE(*populari* lay waste f. *populus* people) + -ATE³]

dĕpŏr't *v.t.* **1.** bear or conduct one*self* (in specified manner). **2.** remove, esp. to another country, banish; hence **dĕpŏrtA'TION** *n*., **dĕpŏrtEE'** *n*., person who is or has been deported. [sense 1 f. OF *deporter* (as DE-, *porter* carry f. L *portare*); sense 2 f. F *déporter* f. L DE(*portare* carry)]

dĕpŏr'tment *n*. bearing, demeanour, manners, esp. of cultivated kind. [f. F *déportement* (as prec. 1; see -MENT)]

dĕpō's|e (-z), *v*. **1.** *v.t.* remove from office, esp. dethrone; hence ∾ABLE *a*. **2.** *v.i.* bear witness *that*, testify *to*, esp. on oath in court. [ME, f. OF *deposer* after L *deponere* (see DEPONENT, POSE¹)]

dĕpŏ'sĭt¹ (-z-) *n*. thing stored or entrusted for safe keeping; sum placed in bank, ||usu. at interest and not to be withdrawn without notice (**on** ∾, so placed; *has a current and a* ∾ **account**); sum required and paid as pledge or first instalment; layer of precipitated matter, natural accumulation. [f. L DE(*positum* neut. p.p. (as *n*.) of *ponere* place)]

dĕpŏ'sĭt² (-z-) *v.t.* lay down in a (usu. specified) place; (of water or natural agency) leave (matter) lying; store or entrust for keeping (esp. sum in bank ||at interest); pay as pledge for fulfilment of contract or further payment. [f. obs. F *déposter* or f. med. L *depositare* frequent. of L *deponere*; see prec.]

dĕpŏ'sĭtarў (-z-) *n*. person to whom thing is entrusted, trustee. [f. LL *depositarius* (as DEPOSIT¹; see -ARY¹)]

dĕposĭ'tion (-z-) *n*. deposing from office, esp. dethronement; (giving of) sworn evidence, allegation; depositing; (picture of) taking down of Christ from the Cross. [ME f. OF, f. L *positio -onis* (*deponere*; see DEPOSIT¹, -ION)]

dĕpŏ'sĭtor (-z-) *n*. person who deposits money, property, etc. [f. DEPOSIT² + -OR]

dĕpŏ'sĭtorў (-z-) *n*. storehouse (lit. or fig.); = DEPOSIT-ARY. [f. LL *depositorium* (as DEPOSIT¹; see -ORY)]

dĕ'pŏt (-ō) *n*. **1.** (Mil.) place for stores; headquarters of regiment. **2.** storehouse, emporium; place from which goods or vehicles are dispatched; *railway or bus station. [f. F *dépôt*, OF *depost* f. L (as DEPOSIT¹)]

dĕprā've *v.t.* make bad, deteriorate; pervert, corrupt, esp. in moral character or habits; so **dĕpravA'TION** *n*. [ME, f. OF *depraver* or f. L DE(*pravare* f. *pravus* crooked)]

dĕprä'vĭtў *n*. moral corruption, wickedness; (Theol.) innate corruptness of human nature. [f. DE- + obs. *pravity* f. L *pravitas* (as prec.; see -ITY), after prec.]

dĕ'prĕc|āte *v.t.* plead against (∾ person's **anger**, entreat him not to be angry); express wish against or disapproval of (*deprecate war, hasty action, panic*); so ∾A'TION *n*., ∾ATIVE, ∾ātorУ *adjs*. [f. L DE(*precari* pray) + -ATE³]

dĕprē'cĭāt|e (-shĭ-, -sĭ-) *v*. **1.** *v.t.* & *i*. diminish in value. **2.** *v.t.* lower market price of; reduce purchasing power of (money); disparage, belittle. **3.** Hence ∾ORY (-sha-) *a*. [f. LL DE(*pretiare* f. *pretium* price) + -ATE³]

dĕprēcĭā'tion (-shĭ-, -sĭ-) *n*. depreciating or being depreciated; (allowance made in valuations, estimates, and balance sheets for) wear and tear. [f. prec. + -ATION]

dĕprĕdā'tion *n*. (usu. in *pl*.) despoiling, ravages. [f. F *déprédation* f. LL DE(*praedatio -onis* f. L *praedari* plunder; see -ATION)]

dĕ'prĕdātor *n*. despoiler, pillager. [f. LL *depraedator* (as prec.; see -OR)]

dĕprĕ'ss *v.t.* push or pull down, lower; reduce activity of (esp. trade); dispirit, deject; ∾ed **area**, area of economic depression; ∾ed **classes**, (Ind.) persons of the lowest castes, 'untouchables'; hence ∾IBLE *a*. [ME, f. OF *depresser* f. LL DE(*pressare* frequent. of *premere* press)]

dĕprĕ'ssant *a*. & *n*. (influence) that depresses; (Med.) sedative (drug etc.). [f. prec. + -ANT]

dĕprĕ'ssion (-shon) *n*. lowering, sinking; (Astron. etc.) angular distance of object below horizon or horizontal plane; sunk place, hollow, on surface; reduction in vigour (esp. of trade; **the D**∾, the slump of 1929-), vitality, or spirits; (Meteorol.) lowering of barometer level or atmospheric pressure, esp. centre of minimum pressure or system of winds round it; (Psych.) state of morbidly excessive melancholy, mood of hopelessness and feelings of inadequacy, often with physical symptoms. [ME f. OF, or f. L DE(*pressio* f. *premere* press- press; see -ION)]

dĕprĕ'ssĭve *a*. & *n*. **1.** *a*. tending to depress (lit. or fig.); (Psych.) involving or characterized by depression. **2.** *n*. (Psych.) person suffering from depression. [f. F *dépressif -ive* or f. med. L *depressivus* (as prec.; see -IVE)]

dĕprĕ'ssor *n*. (Anat.) ∾ (**muscle**), one pulling down some organ etc.; (Surg.) instrument for pressing down some organ etc. [L (as prec.; see -OR)]

dĕprĕ'ssurĭze, -ĭse, (-sherĭz) *v.t.* cause appreciable drop of pressure in (enclosed gas, esp. to natural level). [f. DE- + PRESSURIZE]

dĕprĭvā'tion (dĕprĭ-, dēprī-) *n*. loss, being deprived, *of*; deposition from office. ecclesiastical office; loss of desired thing (*that is a great deprivation*). [f. med. L *deprivatio* (as foll.; see ATION)]

dĕprī'v|e *v.t.* strip, bereave, debar from enjoyment, *of*; depose (as clergyman) from office (esp. in *p.p.*); prevent (child etc.) from having normal home life; hence ∾ABLE *a*., ∾AL 2 *n*. [ME, f. OF *depriver* f. med. L *deprivare* (as DE- + L *privare* deprive)]

de profundis (dā profoo'ndĭs) *n*. & *adv*. (cry) from the depths (of sorrow etc.). [initial L wds of Ps. 130]

Dept. *abbr*. Department.

dĕpth *n*. **1.** being deep; measurement from top down, from surface inwards, or from front to back. **2.** abstruseness; sagacity; intensity of colour, darkness, etc. **3.** (in *pl*.) deep water, deep place, abyss; low moral condition; lowest or inmost part (*lives in the depths of the country*). **4.** middle (*in the depth of winter*); deep or mysterious region of thought, feeling, etc. **5.** **in** ∾ *adv*. & *a*., comprehensive(ly), profound(ly), thorough(ly) (**defence in** ∾, system of defence with successive areas of resistance); **out of** one's ∾, in water too deep to stand in, (fig.) engaged on task or subject beyond one's powers. **6.** ∾-**bomb**, ∾-**charge**, bomb exploding under water, for dropping on submerged submarine etc.; ∾ **psychology**, psychoanalysis to reveal hidden motives etc. [ME, f. as DEEP¹ + -TH¹]

dĕ'pūr|āte *v.t.* & *i*. make or become free from impurities; so ∾A'TION, ∾ātOR, *ns*., **dĕpūr'**ATIVE *a*. & *n*. [f. med. L DE(*purare* f. L *purus* pure)]

dĕpūtā'tion *n*. body of persons appointed to represent others. [ME, f. LL *deputatio* (as foll.; see -ATION)]

dĕpū'te *v.t.* commit (task, authority) to or *to* substitute; appoint as deputy. [ME, f. OF *deputer* f. L DE(*putare* think) regard as, allot]

dĕ'pūte² (-ū) (Sc.) deputy. [ME, f. OF *député*, p.p. of *deputer* (see prec.)]

dĕ'pūtĭze, -ise (-īz), *v.i.* act as deputy or understudy (*for*). [f. foll. + -IZE]

dĕ'pūtў *n*. person appointed or delegated to act for another or others (**by** ∾, by proxy); parliamentary representative (**Chamber of Deputies,** lower house in some parliaments); coal-mine overseer responsible for safety; (*attrib.*) deputed, acting (||∼ **lieutenant,** deputy of Lord Lieutenant of county); hence ∼**ship** (1) *n.* [ME, var. of DEPUTE²; see -Y⁴]

děră'cǐn|ăte *v.t.* (literary). tear up by the roots (lit. or fig.); hence ∼A'TION *n.* [f. F *déraciner* (as DE-, *racine* f. LL *radicina* dim. of *radix* root) + -ATE³]

déraciné (dārā'sǐnā) *a.* & *n.* (*fem.* ∼e *pr.* same). (person) 'uprooted' from natural environment. [F, p.p. (as prec.)]

derai'l (dǐ-, dē-) *v.t.* (usu. in *pass.*) cause (train etc.) to leave the rails; hence ∼MENT *n.* [f. F *dérailler* (as DE-, RAIL¹)]

děrā'nge (-nj) *v.t.* throw into confusion, put out of order, disorganize, cause to act irregularly; (esp. in *p.p.*) make insane; disturb, interrupt; so ∼MENT (-jm-) *n.* [f. F *déranger* (as DE-, *rang* RANK¹)]

děrā'te *v.t.* & *ı.* remove part or all of burden of rates (RATE¹ 2) (from). [f. DE- + RATE¹]

děrā'tion *v.t.* remove (food etc.) from rationing. [f. DE- + RATION]

Der'by (där'-) *n.* **1.** annual horse-race at Epsom (∼ **Day,** that of the race); similar race elsewhere. **2.** any important sporting contest; *local* ∼ (between two teams from same district). **3.** (*d∼*). low-heeled shoe; *bowler hat. [f. 12th Earl of∼ d. 1834, founder of the horse-race]

děrě'gister *v.t.* remove from register; hence **dē-rēgistrA'TION** *n.* [f. DE- + REGISTER¹]

de régle (de rā'gl) *pred. a.* customary, proper. [F, = of rule]

dě'rělict *a.* & *n.* **1.** *a.* abandoned, ownerless, (esp. of ship at sea or decrepit property); *negligent. **2.** *n.* abandoned property, esp. ship; socially forsaken person, one not established in society. [f. L *derelictus* p.p. of DE(*relinquere* leave)]

děrěli'ction *n.* abandoning, being abandoned; neglect *of duty*; failure in duty, shortcoming; retreat of sea exposing new land. [f. L *derelictio* (as prec.; see -ION)]

děrěquisi'tion (-z-) *v.t.* return (requisitioned property) to its former owner. [f. DE- + REQUISITION]

děrěstri'ct *v.t.* remove restrictions from, (esp.) remove or not impose speed limit on traffic in a specified road etc.; so ∼ION *n.* [f. DE- + RESTRICT]

děrī'de *v.t.* laugh scornfully at; treat with scorn. [f. L DE(*ridēre ris-* laugh)]

de rigueur (de rĭgēr') *pred. a.* required by custom or etiquette (*evening dress is de rigueur*). [F, = of strictness]

děri'sion (-zhon) *n.* ridicule, mockery, (*bring into derision*); **hold, have, in** ∼, (arch.) mock at. [ME f. OF, f. LL *derisio -onis* (as DERIDE; see -ION)]

děrī'sive *a.* = foll. 1 (*derisive cheers*); hence ∼LY² (-lǐ) *adv.* [f. prec. + -IVE]

děrī'sory (-s-, -z-) *a.* **1.** scoffing; ironical. **2.** so small or unimportant as to be ridiculous (*derisory offer, result*). [f. LL *derisorius* (as DERISION; see -ORY)]

děrivā'tion *n.* obtaining from a source; extraction, descent; formation of word from word or root, tracing or statement of this; hence ∼AL *a.* [f. F *dérivation* or f. L *derivatio* (as DERIVE; see -ATION)]

děri'vatǐve *a.* & *n.* **1.** (thing, word, chemical substance) derived from a source, not primitive or original; hence ∼LY² (-vlǐ) *adv.* **2.** *n.* (Math.) quantity measuring rate of change of another. [f. F *dérivatif -ive* f. L *derivativus* (as foll.; see -IVE)]

děrīv|e *v.* **1.** *v.t.* get or obtain or form (*from* a source); have *origin* etc. *from*; gather, deduce, (knowledge, truth, ideas, etc.) *from*; trace descent of (person), show origin of (thing), assert formation of (word), *from*; hence ∼ABLE *a.* **2.** *v.i.* be descended, originate, *from*. [ME, f. OF *deriver* or f. L *derivare* (as DE-, *rivus* stream)]

děrm, děr'ma. Vars. of DERMIS.

děrmati'tis *n.* inflammation of the skin. [f. Gk *derma -atos* skin + -ITIS]

děrmat|ŏ'logy *n.* study of skin and its diseases; hence ∼OLO'GICAL *a.,* ∼ŏ'LOGIST *n.* [f. as prec. + -O- + -LOGY]

děr'm|is *n.* (Anat.) skin; true skin or layer of tissue below epidermis; so ∼AL, ∼IC, *adjs.* [mod. L, after *epidermis*]

*dern, *děrned (-nd). Var. of DARN², DARNED.

dernier cri (dārnyā krē') *n.* the very latest fashion. [F, lit. 'last cry']

dě'rogāte *v.i.* detract, take away *from*, *from* (a merit, right, etc.); deviate *from* (correct behaviour etc.). [f. L DE(*rogare* ask) + -ATE³]

děrogā'tion *n.* lessening or impairment *of* law, authority, position, dignity, etc.; deterioration, debasement. [ME, f. F *dérogation* or f. L *derogatio* (as prec.; see -ATION)]

děrŏ'gator|ў *a.* tending to detract *from*, involving impairment, disparagement, or discredit, *to*; lowering, unsuited to one's dignity or position; depreciatory; hence ∼ILY² *adv.* [f. LL *derogatorius* (as DEROGATE; see -ORY)]

dě'rrick *n.* contrivance for moving or hoisting heavy weights, kind of crane with adjustable arm pivoted at foot to central post, deck, or floor; framework over oil-well or similar boring. [obs. senses *hangman, gallows,* f. name of London hangman *c.* 1600]

derrière (derĭār') *n.* (colloq.) buttocks. [F]

děrring-do' (-dōō') *n.* (literary). heroic courage or action. [ME, = *daring to do,* misinterpreted by Spenser and by Scott]

dě'rringer (-nj-) *n.* small large-bore pistol. [f. H. *Deringer,* Amer. inventor d. 1868]

dě'rris *n.* tall woody tropical climbing plant of genus *Derris*; insecticide made from powdered tuberous root of some kinds of derris. [mod. L f. Gk, = leather covering (w. ref. to its pod)]

dě'rrý *n.* (Austral. & NZ). dislike, prejudice, (*have a derry on a person*). [app. f. song-refrain *derry down*]

děrv *n.* fuel oil used in heavy road-vehicles. [f. *d*iesel-*e*ngined *r*oad *v*ehicle]

děr'vish *n.* Muslim religious man vowed to poverty and austerity; **dancing** or **whirling** ∼, **howling** ∼, (according to the practice of his order). [f. Turk. *derviş* f. Pers. *darvēsh* poor, a mendicant]

děsä'lin|āte *v.t.* remove salt from (esp. sea-water); hence ∼A'TION *n.* [f. DE- + SALINE + -ATE³]

děsa'lt (-sŏ'lt, -saw'lt) *v.t.* = prec. [f. DE- + SALT]

děscā'le *v.t.* remove scale from. [f. DE- + SCALE¹ 3]

dě'scǎnt¹ *n.* **1.** (poet.) melody, song. **2.** (Mus.) melodic independent treble accompaniment; ∼ **recorder** (highest-pitched of standard kinds). [ME, f. OF *deschant* f. med. L DIS(*cantus* song, CHANT)]

děscǎ'nt² *v.i.* talk lengthily, dwell freely, *upon* (esp. in praise, *descant upon the beauties of*); sing descant. [f. prec.]

děscē'nd *v.* **1.** *v.i.* go or come down; (of thing) sink, fall; (Print., of letter) have tail below line, whence ∼ER¹ *n.,* such letter or tail; slope downwards, (of ∼ing slope) be along descending slope. **2.** make sudden attack or (fig.) unexpected visit (*on*); sink in thought, rank, or degree of quality; (of sound) become lower in pitch; go forward in point of time; go from greater to less or from particular to particular; degrade oneself morally *to* (unworthy act); (of qualities, property, privileges) be transmitted by inheritance *from*, pass (*to* heir). **3.** *v.t.* go down (hill, stairs); go along (river) towards sea etc. [ME, f. OF *descendre* f. L DE(*scendere* = *scandere* climb)]

děscē'ndant *n.* ∼ (of), person or thing descended (from). [F, part. of *descendre* (as prec.; see -ANT)]

děscē'ndǎd *a.* sprung, having origin, *from* (ancestor or stock). [p.p. of DESCEND; see -ED¹ (2)]

děscē'ndǐble *a.* that may be descended; that may descend by inheritance. [f. OF *descendable* (as DESCEND; see -ABLE, -IBLE)]

děscē'nt *n.* **1.** act of descending; downward motion; way by which one may descend; downward slope; sudden attack. **2.** decline, sinking in scale, fall; being descended, lineage; transmission (of qualities, property, privileges) by inheritance. [ME, f. OF *descente* (*descendre* (DESCEND)]

descri′be *v.t.* set forth in words, recite the characteristics of, (∼ **as**, assert to be, call); mark out, draw, (esp. figure in Geom.); move in (specified line, curve); hence **descri′bABLE** *a.* [f. L DE(*scribere* scriptwrite)]

descri′ption *n.* describing, verbal portrait(ure), of person, object, or event, (**answers** (**to**) or **fits the** ∼, has the qualities specified); more or less complete definition; sort, kind, class, (*no food of any description*; *tyrant of the worst description*). [ME f. OF, f. L *descriptio -onis* (as prec.; see -ION)]

descri′ptive *a.* serving or seeking to describe (*descriptive touches, writer*); not expressing feelings or judgements; (Ling.) describing a language factually as it is, without drawing comparisons; hence ∼LY² (-vlĭ) *adv.* [f. LL *descriptivus* (as DESCRIBE; see -IVE)]

descri′ptor *n.* expression, word, etc., used to describe or identify. [L, = describer (as DESCRIBE; see -OR)]

descry′ *v.t.* catch sight of, succeed in discerning (lit. or fig.). [ME, earlier senses 'proclaim, DECRY', f. OF *descrier*; prob. confused w. var. of obs. *descrive* f. OF *descrivre* DESCRIBE]

dĕ′secr|āte *v.t.* deprive of sacred character; outrage, profane, (sacred thing); hence ∼A′TION, ∼āTOR, *ns.* [f. DE-+CONSECRATE]

dĕsĕ′grĕg|āte *v.t.* abolish racial segregation in (schools etc.) or of (persons etc.); hence ∼A′TION *n.* [f. DE-+SEGREGATE¹]

dĕsĕ′nsĭtĭz|e, -īs|e (-īz), *v.t.* reduce or destroy the sensitiveness of (photographic materials, allergic person, etc.); hence ∼A′TION *n.* [f. DE-+SENSITIZE]

dĕsĕr′t¹ (-z-) *n.* deserving, being worthy of reward or punishment; (in *pl.*) acts or qualities deserving good or bad recompense, recompense, (*reward him according to, give him, he has got, his deserts*). [ME f. OF (*deservir* DESERVE)]

dĕ′sert² (-z-) *a.* & *n.* **1.** *a.* uninhabited, desolate; uncultivated, barren. **2.** *n.* waterless and treeless region, (fig.) uninteresting or barren subject, period, etc.; ∼ **boot**, suède etc. boot reaching to or just above ankle; ∼ **island**, remote and presumably uninhabited island; ‖∼ **rat**, (colloq.) soldier of 7th British armoured division (with jerboa as badge) in N. Afr. desert campaign 1941-2. [ME f. OF, f. L *desertus* (eccl. L *desertum* n.) p.p. of *deserere* leave, forsake]

dĕsĕr′t³ (-z-) *v.* **1.** *v.t.* abandon, give up, (thing); depart from (place, haunt), leave (place) empty; forsake (person or thing having claims on one; *desert one's wife, husband, post, ship*); fail (*his presence of mind deserted him*). **2.** *v.i.* run away (esp. from service in armed forces), whence ∼ER¹ *n.* **3.** So **dĕsĕr′tION** (-z-) *n.* [f. F *deserter* f. LL *desertare* f. L *desertus* (see prec.)]

dĕsĕrtĭfĭcā′tion (-z-) *n.* making or becoming a desert; so **dĕsĕrtĭz|A′TION** (dez-) *n.* [f. DESERT² + -I- + -FICATION]

dĕsĕr′v|e (-z-) *v.* **1.** *v.t.* show conduct or qualities worthy of (reward or treatment; *to* be so do); hence ∼edLY² *adv.* **2.** *v.i.* have established a claim to be *well* or *ill* treated at the hands of. [ME, f. OF *deservir* f. L DE(*servire* serve)]

dĕsĕr′ving (-z-) *a.* meritorious; ∼ **of**, showing conduct or qualities that ought to be given (praise, censure, help, etc.); hence ∼LY² *adv.* [f. prec.+-ING²]

dĕ-sĕ′x *v.t.* castrate or spay; deprive of sexual qualities or attractions. [f. DE-+SEX]

dĕsĕ′xūalĭze, -īse (-īz), *v.t.* deprive of sex or sexual characters or qualities. [f. DE-+SEXUAL+-IZE]

déshabillé (dāzăbē′ā) *n.* (state of) being only partly or not carefully dressed. [F, = undressed]

dĕ′sĭcc|āte *v.t.* remove moisture from, dry up, (esp. foodstuffs for preservation); hence or cogn. ∼ANT, ∼A′TION, *ns.*, ∼ATIVE *a.* [f. L DE(*siccare* f. *siccus* dry) + -ATE³]

dĕ′sĭccātor *n.* apparatus for desiccating. (Chem.)

apparatus containing drying agent for removing moisture from specimens. [f. prec.+-OR]

dĕsī′derāte (-z-, -s-) *v.t.* (arch.) feel to be missing, regret absence of, wish to have. [f. L DE(*siderare*; see CONSIDER)+-ATE³]

dĕsī′derative (-z-, -s-) *a.* & *n.* (Gram.) verb, conjugation, etc.) formed from another verb etc. and denoting desire to perform the action of that verb etc. [f. LL *desiderativus* (as prec.; see -IVE)]

dĕsīderā′t|um (-z-, -s-) *n.* (*pl.* ∼a). thing lacking but needed or desired. [L, neut. p.p. (as n.); see DESIDERATE]

dĕsī′gn¹ (-zī′n) *n.* **1.** mental plan; scheme of attack (**have** ∼s **on**, plan to harm or appropriate). **2.** purpose (**by** ∼, on purpose; *whether by accident or design*); end in view; adaptation of means to ends (**argument from** ∼, deducing existence of a God from evidence of such adaptation in the universe). **3.** preliminary sketch for picture, plan of building, machine, etc.; arrangement of lines, drawing, etc., decorating or distinguishing a thing; art of making these. **4.** established form of a product; general idea, construction from parts. [f. obs. F *desseing* (*desseigner* f. L *designare* DESIGNATE²)]

dĕsī′gn² (-zī′n) *v.* **1.** *v.t.* set (thing) apart for person; destine (person, thing) *for* a service. **2.** contrive, plan; purpose, intend, (*designs an attack, to do, doing, that*; *design* thing or person *to* be or do something). **3.** make preliminary sketch of (picture); draw plan of (future building etc.). **4.** *v.i.* be a designer. [f. F *désigner* appoint & f. L *designare* DESIGNATE²]

dĕ′sĭgnate¹ (-z-) *a.* (placed after *n.*) appointed to office but not yet installed (*bishop designate* etc.). [f. L *designatus* p.p. (as foll.; see -ATE²)]

dĕ′sĭgnāte² (-z-) *v.t.* specify, particularize; serve as name or distinctive mark of; style, describe *as*; appoint to office (*as, to, for*). [f. L DE(*signare* f. *signum* mark)+-ATE³]

dĕsĭgnā′tion (-z-) *n.* appointing to office; name, description, title. [ME f. OF, or f. L *designatio* (as prec.; see -ATION)]

dĕsī′gnĕdly (-zī′n-) *adv.* by design, on purpose. [f. p.p. of DESIGN²+-LY²]

dĕsī′gner (-zī′n-) *n.* in vbl senses; draughtsman who makes plans for manufacturers; person who prepares designs for clothing, stage-productions, etc. [f. DESIGN²+-ER¹]

dĕsī′gning (-zī′n-) *a.* in vbl senses; crafty, artful, scheming; hence ∼LY² *adv.* [f. DESIGN²+-ING²]

dĕsīr′|able (-z-) *a.* worth having or wishing for; causing desire; hence ∼ABI′LITY, ∼ableNESS (-beln-), *ns.*, ∼ABLY *adv.* [ME f. OF (as DESIRE²; see -ABLE)]

dĕsīr′e¹ (-z-) *n.* unsatisfied longing, feeling that one would derive pleasure or satisfaction from attaining or possessing something; expression of this, request; thing desired; lust. [ME, f. OF *desir* (*desirer* as foll.)]

dĕsīr′e² (-z-) *v.t.* long for, want earnestly (thing, *to do, that*); ask for (**leaves much to be** ∼d, is very imperfect); (arch.) pray, entreat, command, (*desire him to wait*; *she desired they would wait*). [ME, f. OF *desirer* f. L *desiderare* DESIDERATE]

dĕsīr′ous (-z-) *pred. a.* wishful to do, *that*; ambitious of (success etc.); having the desire *of* doing. [ME f. AF, OF *desireus* f. Rom. *desiderosus (as prec.; see -OUS)]

dĕsī′st (-zĭ′-, -sĭ′-) *v.i.* (literary) abstain *from* continuing (action etc.). [f. OF *desister* f. L DE(*sistere* stop, redupl. f. *stare* stand)]

dĕsk *n.* fixed or movable piece of furniture or box having flat or sloped surface serving as rest for writing or reading at; compartment for cashier, accountant, etc.; music-stand; section of newspaper office etc. dealing with specified topics or *editorial work; ∼-**bound**, obliged to remain working at a desk. [ME, f. med. L *desca* f. L DISCUS disc]

dĕ′sman *n.* aquatic insectivorous shrewlike mammal of two species, one in Russia and one in Pyrenees. [F & G, f. Sw. *desman-råtta* musk-rat]

dĕ'solate[1] *a.* left alone, solitary; uninhabited; ruinous, neglected, barren, dreary; forlorn, wretched; hence ∼LY[2] (-tlĭ) *adv.*, ∼NESS (-tn-) *n.* [ME, f. L *desolatus* p.p. of DE(*solare* f. *solus* alone); see -ATE[2]]

dĕ'solāt|e[2] *v.t* depopulate; devastate; make (person) wretched; hence ∼OR *n.* [ME, f. as prec. + -ATE[3]]

dĕsolā'tion *n.* desolating; neglected, ruined, solitary, or barren state; being forsaken, loneliness; grief, wretchedness. [ME, f. LL *desolatio* (as prec.; see -ATION)]

dĕsōr'ption *n.* release of substance from surface on which it is adsorbed; hence (as back-form.) **dĕsōr'b** *v.t.* & *i.*, **dĕsōr'bENT** *a.* & *n.* [f. DE- + ADSORPTION]

dĕspair' *n.*, & *v.i.* **1.** *n.* complete loss or absence of hope; thing that causes this, whether by badness or unapproachable excellence. **2.** *v.i.* lose hope, be without hope, (*of*); ∼ **of,** lose hope that person or thing will succeed, be maintained, etc. (*his life is despaired of*). [ME, f. OF *desespeir, desperer* f. L DE(*sperare* hope)]

∥dĕspä'tch[1,2]. See DISPATCH[1,2].

dĕspera'dō (-ah'dō) *n.* (*pl.* ∼es *or* *∼s*). desperate or reckless person, esp. criminal. [after foll. (as obs. n.) & wds in -ADO]

dĕ'sperate *a.* **1.** leaving no or little room for hope, extremely dangerous or serious (*desperate situation*). **2.** reckless from despair, violent, lawless; staking all on a small chance (*desperate remedy*); so **dĕsperA'TION** *n.* **3.** extremely bad (*a desperate night, storm,* etc.). **4.** Hence ∼LY[2] (-tlĭ) *adv.*, ∼NESS (-tn-) *n.* [ME, f. L *desperatus* p.p. of DE(*sperare* hope); see -ATE[2]]

despicab|le (dĕ'-, D dĭspĭ'-) *a.* vile, morally contemptible; hence ∼LY[2] *adv.* [f. LL *despicabilis* f. DE(*spicari* cogn. w. *specere* look at); see -ABLE]

dĕspi'se (-z) *v.t.* regard as inferior or worthless; feel contempt for. [ME, f. *despis-* pres. st. of OF *despire* f. L DE(*spicere = specere* look at)]

dĕspi'te *n.* & *prep.* **1.** *n.* (arch.) outrage, injury; malice, hatred, (*died of mere despite*); (**in**) ∼ **of,** in spite of; hence ∼FUL (-tf-) *a.* **2.** *prep.* in spite of or (arch.) *of.* [ME, f. OF *despit* f. L *despectus* n. f. *despicere* (see prec.)]

dĕspoi'l *v.t.* (literary). plunder, rob, deprive (person or place *of*); hence or cogn. ∼ER[1], ∼MENT, **dĕspōliA'TION,** *ns.* [ME, f. OF *despoill(i)er* f. L DE(*spoliare* SPOIL[2])]

dĕspŏ'nd *v.i.*, & *n.* **1.** *v.i.* lose heart or hope, be dejected; hence ∼ENCY *n.*, ∼ENT *a.*, ∼entLY[2] *adv.* **2.** *n.* (arch.) **Slough of D∼,** state of despondency (f. name of bog in Bunyan's *Pilgrim's Progress*). [f. L DE(*spondēre* promise) give up, abandon]

dĕ'spot *n.* absolute ruler; tyrant, oppressor; so **dĕspŏ'**TIC *a.*, **dĕspŏ'**TICALLY *adv.*, ∼ISM (3) *n.* [f. F *despote* f. med. L *despota* f. Gk *despotēs* master, lord]

dĕ'squam|āte *v.i.* come off in scales; hence ∼A'TION *n.*, **dĕsquä'mat**IVE, **dĕsquä'mat**ORY, *adjs.* [f. L DE(*squamare* f. *squama* scale) + -ATE[3]]

dĕssẽr't (-z-) *n.* sweet (course of meal); ∥course of fruit, nuts, etc., at end of dinner; *dessert-*SPOON[1]; ∼ **wine** (for drinking with dessert or after meal). [F, p.p. of *desservir* (as DIS-, *servir* SERVE) clear the table]

dĕstinā'tion *n.* place to which person or thing is going. [OF, or f. L *destinatio* (as foll.; see -ATION)]

dĕ'stīne *v.t.* appoint, foreordain, devote, set apart, (person or thing *to* do, *to* or *for* a service, achievement, etc.); **was ∼d to,** later (as we now know) did. [ME, f. F *destiner* f. L DE(*stinare = *stanare* settle f. *stare* stand)]

dĕ'stĭnў *n.* predetermined events; what is destined to happen to person, country, etc.; power that foreordains, invincible necessity. [ME, f. OF *destinee* f. Rom. *destinata* fem. p.p. (as n.) of *destinare*; see prec., -Y[4]]

dĕ'stĭtūte *a.* without resources, in great need of food, shelter, etc.; devoid *of*; so **dĕstĭtū'**TION *n.* [ME, f. L *destitutus* p.p. of DE(*stituere -tut- = statuere* place) forsake]

dĕ'strier *n.* (Hist.) war-horse. [ME, f. AF *destrer,* OF *destrier* f. Rom. *destrarius* (*caballus* horse) f. L DEXTER[1] (as knight's horse was led by squire with right hand)]

dĕstroy' *v.t.* pull or break down, demolish; make useless; kill (esp. animal that is seriously ill or injured, or unwanted); cause to cease to exist; nullify, neutralize effect of; hence ∼ABLE *a.* [ME, f. OF *destruire* f. Rom. *destrugere* for L DE(*struere struct-* build)]

dĕstroy'er *n.* In vbl senses; fast warship designed to protect other ships by attacking submarines etc. with guns and torpedoes. [f. prec. + -ER[1]]

*****dĕstrū'ct** *v.t.*, & *n.* **1.** *v.t.* bring about deliberate destruction of (one's own rocket etc.). **2.** *n.* action of destructing. [f. L *destruere* (see DESTROY), or as back-form. f. DESTRUCTION]

dĕstrū'ct|ĭble *a.* able to be destroyed; hence ∼IBI'LITY *n.* [F, or f. LL *destructibilis* (as DESTROY; see -IBLE)]

dĕstrū'ction *n.* destroying or being destroyed; what destroys, cause of ruin, (*is our destruction*). [ME f. OF, f. L *destructio -onis* (as DESTROY; see -ION)]

dĕstrū'ctĭve *a.* destroying; tending to destroy; deadly *to,* causing destruction *of*; merely negative, refuting etc. without amending, opp. *constructive* (*destructive criticism*); hence ∼LY[2] (-vlĭ) *adv.*, ∼NESS (-vn-) *n.* [ME, f. OF *destructif -ive,* f. LL *destructivus* (as DESTROY; see -IVE)]

∥dĕstrū'ctor *n.* refuse-burning furnace. [f. as prec. + -OR]

desuĕtūde (dĭsū'ĭ-, dĕ'swĭ-) *n.* (passing into) state of disuse. [f. F *désuétude* or f. L DE(*suetudo* f. *suescere suet-* be accustomed; see -TUDE)]

dĕ'sultor|ў *a.* going constantly from one subject to another; disconnected, unmethodical; hence ∼ĭLY[2] *adv.*, ∼iNESS *n.* [f. L *desultorius* superficial f. *desultor* vaulter f. DE(*sult- = salt-* p.p. st. of *salire* leap)]

dĕtā'ch *v.t.* unfasten and remove (*from*) (lit. or fig.; ∼ed mind, view, etc., regarding things impartially, unemotional; ∼ed house, one not joined to another on either side); send (ship, regiment, officer, etc.) on separate mission; hence ∼ABLE *a.*, ∼ẽdLY[2] *adv.* [f. F *détacher* (as DE-, ATTACH)]

dĕtā'chment *n.* detaching or being detached; portion of army etc., or large body, separately employed; being aloof from or unaffected by surroundings, public opinion, etc.; independence of judgement. [f. F *détachement* (as prec.; see -MENT)]

dē'tail[1] *n.* dealing with things item by item (*in detail; in great or much detail*; **go into** ∼, give the items separately); account of separate small items, number of particulars; item, small or subordinate particular, (**but that is a** ∼, often iron. to call special attention); minor decoration in building, picture, etc., way of treating this; part of picture etc. shown alone; (Mil.) distribution of orders of the day; small detachment for special duty. [f. F *détail* (*détailler*; as foll.)]

dē'tail[2] *v.t.* **1.** give particulars of, relate circumstantially; (in *p.p.*) described item by item. **2.** (Mil.) assign for special duty. [f. F *détailler* (as DE-, *tailler* cut f. as TAIL[2])]

dĕtai'n *v.t.* keep in confinement or under restraint; keep waiting, delay; hence ∼EE' *n.*, person detained in custody, usu. on political grounds. [ME, f. OF *detenir* f. L *detenēre **detenēre* for L DE(*tinēre tent- = tenēre* hold)]

dĕtai'ner *n.* (Law). wrongful detaining of goods taken from owner for distraint etc.; keeping of person in confinement. [f. AF *detener* f. OF *detenir*; see prec., -ER[4]]

dĕtĕ'ct *v.t.* reveal guilt of, discover, (person, person in doing); discover existence or presence of; (Phys.) use instrument to observe (signal, radiation, etc.); hence ∼ABLE *a.* [f. L DE(*tegere tect-* cover)]

dĕtĕ'ction *n.* detecting; work of a detective; (Electr.) extraction of desired signal, demodulation. [f. LL *detectio* (as prec.; see -ION)]

dĕtĕ'ctĭve *a.* & *n.* **1.** *a.* serving to detect. **2.** *n.* policeman or other person employed to investigate crimes e.g. by eliciting evidence or information (**private** ∼, person undertaking special inquiries for

---

For other words in *de-* see DE-.

private employer); ～ **story** etc. (describing crime and detection of criminals). [f. DETECT+-IVE]

dĕtĕ'ctor *n.* In vbl senses; (Electr.) device for detection or demodulation of signals. [f. DETECT+-OR]

dĕtĕ'nt *n.* catch by removal of which machinery is allowed to move; (in clock etc.) catch that regulates striking. [f. F *détente* f. OF *destente* f. *destendre* slacken (as DE-, *tendre* stretch f. L *tendere*)]

détente (dātah'ṅt) *n.* easing of strained relations esp. between States. [F, = relaxation]

dĕtĕ'ntion *n.* detaining or being detained; military imprisonment; confinement of aliens etc.; compulsory delay; (at schools) keeping in as punishment; ||～ **centre**, institution for brief detention of young offenders. [f. F *détention* or f. LL *detentio* (as DETAIN; see -ION)]

détenu (dātĕnoō') *n.* person detained in custody. [F, p.p. of *détenir* DETAIN]

dĕtĕr' *v.t.* (-rr-). discourage or hinder (*from*) by fear, dislike of trouble, etc.; hence ～MENT *n.* [f. L DE(*terrēre* frighten)]

dĕtĕr'gent *a.* & *n.* cleansing (agent), esp. substance used with water for removing dirt etc. (usu. a synthetic substance other than soap). [f. L DE(*tergēre* *ters*- wipe); see -ENT]

dĕtĕr'ior|āte *v.t.* & *i.* make or become worse; hence or cogn. ～A'TION *n.*, ～ATIVE *a.* [f. LL *deteriorare* f. L *deterior* worse, +ATE[3]]

dĕtĕr'minant *a.* & *n.* determining; decisive, conditioning, defining, (agent, factor, element, word); (Math.) quantity obtained by adding products of elements of a square matrix according to a certain rule. [f. L *determinare* (see DETERMINE, -ANT)]

dĕtĕr'min|ate *a.* limited; definite, distinct; finite; definitive; hence ～ACY *n.*, ～ateLY[2] (-tlĭ) *adv.*, ～ateNESS (-tn-) *n.* [ME, f. L *determinatus* p.p. (as DETERMINE; see -ATE[2])]

dĕtĕrminā'tion *n.* **1.** delimitation, definition; exact ascertainment *of* amount etc. **2.** fixing of purpose, fixed intention; resoluteness. **3.** (Law). cessation of estate or interest. **4.** conclusion of debate; judicial decision or sentence; fixing of date etc. **5.** (arch.) tendency to move in fixed direction. [ME (in sense 3) f. OF, f. L *determinatio* -*onis* (as DETERMINE; see -ATION)]

dĕtĕr'minative *a.* & *n.* (thing) that serves to define, qualify, or direct. [f. F *déterminatif* (as foll.; see -IVE)]

dĕtĕr'mine *v.* **1.** *v.t.* & *i.* settle, decide, (dispute); person's fate, *what is to be done, that, whether*, etc.), come to a conclusion, give decision; be the decisive factor in regard to (*demand determines supply*); ascertain precisely, (arch.) direct, impel *to*. **2.** decide (person) *to do*; resolve (*to do, that, on* doing, *on* a course of action); **be ～d**, have resolved. **3.** *v.t.* & *i.* (esp. Law). bring or come to an end. **4.** *v.t.* limit in scope, define; fix (date) beforehand. **5.** Hence **dĕtĕr'min**ABLE *a.* [ME, f. OF *determiner* f. L DE(*terminare* f. *terminus* end)]

dĕtĕr'mined (-nd) *a.* In vbl senses; resolute, unflinching; hence ～LY[2] *adv.*, ～NESS *n.* [p.p. of prec.]

dĕtĕr'min|ism *n.* doctrine that human action is not free but determined by motives regarded as external forces acting on the will; so ～IST (2) *n.*, ～ī'STIC *a.* [f. DETERMINE+-ISM]

dĕtĕr'r|ent *a.* & *n.* **1.** *a.* that deters; hence ～ENCE *n.* **2.** *n.* thing that deters, esp. nuclear weapon of a State or alliance as deterring attack by another. [f. as DETER; see -ENT]

dĕtĕ'st *v.t.* abhor, dislike intensely; so ～ABLE *a.*, intensely hateful, abominable, ～ABLY *adv.* [f. L DE(*testari* call to witness f. *testis* witness)]

dĕtĕstā'tion *n.* abhorrence, intense dislike; detested person or thing. [ME f. OF, f. L *detestatio* -*onis* (as prec.; see -ATION)]

dĕthrō'ne *v.t.* remove from throne (lit. or fig.); ruler, dominant influence); hence ～MENT (-nm-) *n.* [f. DE-+THRONE]

dĕ'tinue *n.* (Law). (suit against) wrongful detention

of personal chattel. [f. OF *detenue* fem. p.p. (as *n.*) of *detenir* DETAIN]

dĕ'ton|āte *v.i.* & *t.* (cause to) explode with loud report; hence ～ATIVE *a.* [f. L DE(*tonare* thunder)+-ATE[3]]

dĕtonā'tion *n.* detonating; premature combustion of fuel in internal combustion engine, causing it to PINK[6]. [f. F *détonation* (*détoner* f. as prec.; see -ATION)]

dĕ'tonātor *n.* detonating contrivance, esp. as part of bomb or shell; railway fog-signal that detonates. [f. DETONATE+-OR]

de'tour (dē'toor, dā'-) *n.* & *v.* **1.** *n.* deviation, roundabout way, digression, (esp. *make a detour*). **2.** *v.t.* & *i.* (cause to) make a detour. [f. F *détour* change of direction (*détourner* turn away f. as DE-, TURN[1])]

dĕtŏ'xic|āte *v.t.* remove poison from; hence ～A'TION *n.* [f. DE-+L *toxicum* poison, after *intoxicate*]

dĕtŏ'xi|fȳ *v.t.* = prec.; hence ～FICA'TION *n.* [f. as prec.+-FY]

dĕtră'ct *v.t.* & *i.* take away (*much, something*, etc., or abs.) *from* a whole; ～ **from**, reduce credit due to, depreciate; so ～ION, ～OR, *ns.*, ～IVE *a.* [f. L DE(*trahere tract*- draw)]

dĕtrai'n *v.t.* & *i.* discharge or alight from railway train; hence ～MENT *n.* [f. DE-+TRAIN]

détraqué (dātrah'kā) *a.* & *n.* (*fem.* ～e *pr.* same). deranged or psychopathic (person). [F, p.p. of *détraquer* derange]

dĕtrī'bal|e, -is|e (-īz), *v.t.* make (person) no longer member of tribe; destroy tribal habits of; hence ～A'TION *n.* [f. DE-+TRIBAL+-IZE]

dĕ'triment *n.* harm, damage, (esp. *without detriment to*); thing that causes harm or damage. [ME f. OF or f. L DE(*trimentum* f. *terere trit*- rub, wear; see -MENT]

dĕtrimĕ'ntal *a.* harmful, causing loss; hence ～LY[2] *adv.* [f. prec.+-AL]

dĕtrī'tĕd *a.* worn down; (Geol.) disintegrated, formed as detritus. [f. L *detritus* p.p. of *deterere* (see DETRIMENT)+-ED[1]]

dĕtrī'tion *n.* wearing away by rubbing. [f. med. L *detritio* f. as DETRIMENT; see -ITION]

dĕtrī't|us *n.* matter produced by detrition, as gravel, sand, silt; debris; hence ～AL *a.* [after F *détritus* f. L *detritus* n. = wearing down, f. as DETRIMENT]

de trop (de trō') *pred. a.* not wanted, unwelcome, in the way. [F, = excessive]

dĕtūmĕ'scence *n.* subsidence from swollen state. [f. L DE(*tumescere* swell); see -ENCE]

deuce[1] *n.* the two on dice or (arch.) cards, (Tennis) state of score (40 all, or five or more games all) at which either side must gain two consecutive points or games to win. [f. OF *deus* f. L *duo* (acc. *duos*) two]

deuce[2] *n.* misfortune, mischief; the Devil (*deuce take it*), **who, where, what**, etc., **the ～?** (imprecations expr. annoyance or complete ignorance); **the ～!** (excl. of annoyance or surprise); **the ～ to pay**, trouble to be expected; **a** (or **the**) ～ **of a**, a very bad or very remarkable (mess, fellow, etc.). [f. LG *duus*, = G *daus*, f. as prec., two aces at dice being the worst throw]

deuced (dū'sĭd, dūst) *a.* & *adv.* (arch.) = DAMNED 2, 3; hence ～LY[2] (-ĭdlĭ) *adv.* [f. prec.+-ED[2]]

deus ex machina (dāōs ĕks mă'kĭna, dēus) *n.* power or event that comes in the nick of time to solve difficulty; providential intervention, esp. in novel or play. [mod. L transl. Gk *theos ek mēkhanēs*, = god from the machinery (by which in Gk theatre the gods were shown in the air)]

Deus misereatur (dēus mĭzĕrĭā'ter) *n.* canticle 'God be merciful', Ps. 67. [L]

Deut. *abbr.* Deuteronomy (OT).

deuterā'gonist *n.* person of next importance to PROTAGONIST in drama. [f. Gk *deuteragōnistēs* (as DEUTERO-, *agōnistēs* actor)]

deu'ter|āte *v.t.* replace ordinary hydrogen in (substance) by deuterium; hence ～A'TION *n.* [f. DEUTERIUM+-ATE[3]]

deutĕr'ium *n.* (Chem.) heavy isotope of hydrogen

with mass about double that of ordinary hydrogen; so **deu′ter**ON *n.*, nucleus of deuterium atom, consisting of proton and neutron. [mod. L, f. as foll. + -IUM]

deu′terō- *comb. form.* second, as: **D∿-Isaiah,** supposed later author of Isaiah 40-55. [f. Gk *deuteros* second + -o-]

Deuterŏ′nom|ў *n.* fifth book of Pentateuch; hence **Deuteronŏ′mi**C(AL) *adjs.*, ∿IST *n.*, (joint) writer of Deuteronomy. [ME, f. eccl. L f. Gk DEUTERO(*nomion* f. *nomos* law) second law (Deut. 17:18), mistranslation f. Heb.]

Deu′tschmărk (doi′ch-) *n.* currency unit in Federal Republic of Germany. [G, = German MARK³]

deu′tzia (dū′ts-, doi′ts-) *n.* ornamental shrub of genus *Deutzia,* with usu. white flowers. [mod. L, f. J. *Deutz* 18th-c. Du. patron of botany + -IA¹]

dĕvă′lū|e *v.t.* reduce value of; (Econ.) reduce value of (currency) relative to that of other currencies or gold; hence ∿A′TION *n.* [f. DE- + VALUE]

Devana′gari (dăvanah′-) *n.* alphabet used for Sanskrit, Hindi, and other Indian languages. [Skr., = divine town script]

dĕ′vast|āte *v.t.* lay waste, ravage; ∿ātING² *a.*, (fig.) very effective, overwhelming, (criticism, handicap, loveliness); hence or cogn. ∿A′TION, ∿ātOR, *ns.* [f. L DE(*vastare* lay waste) + -ATE³]

dĕvĕ′lop *v.* **1.** *v.t.* & *i.* unfold, reveal or be revealed, bring or come from latent to active or visible state; *make or become known; make or become fuller, more elaborate or systematic, or bigger. **2.** *v.t.* construct buildings etc. on (land), convert (land) to new use, so as to realize its potentialities; treat (photographic material) so as to make picture visible; (Mus.) elaborate (theme) by modification of melody, harmony, rhythm, etc.; (Chess) bring (piece) into position for effective use. **3.** *v.t.* & *i.* make progress; begin to exhibit or suffer from (*develop a habit, measles, a squeak*); come or bring to maturity; ∿ing **country,** poor or primitive country that is developing better economic and social conditions. **4.** Hence ∿ABLE *a.* (∿able **surface,** one that can be flattened into a plane without overlap or separation, e.g. cylinder), ∿ER¹ (1, 2) *n.* [f. F *développer* f. Rom. v. f. as DIS- + *volup-, *velup-,* of unkn. orig.]

dĕvĕ′lopment *n.* **1.** gradual unfolding, fuller working out; developing of land etc. (||∿ **area,** one where new industries are encouraged in order to counteract severe unemployment there); growth; evolution (of animal and plant races); full-grown state; stage of advancement; developing of photograph, (Mus.) elaboration of theme, esp. in second part of sonata movement; (Chess) developing of pieces from original position **2.** product; more elaborate form; developed land. [f. prec. + -MENT]

dĕvĕlopmĕ′ntal *a.* incidental to growth (*developmental diseases*); evolutionary; hence∿LY² *adv.* [f. prec. + -AL]

dĕ′vi|ant *a.* & *n.* (thing or person) that deviates from normal behaviour; hence ∿ANCE, ∿ANCY, *ns.* [ME, f. as foll.; see -ANT]

dĕ′viāte¹ *v.i.* turn aside, diverge, (*from* course of action, rule, truth, etc.); digress. [f. LL DE(*viare* f. *via* way) + -ATE³]

dĕ′viate² *n.* = DEVIANT, esp. sexual pervert. [f. prec.]

dĕviā′tion *n.* deviating; deflexion of compass-needle by iron in ship etc.; (Statistics) amount by which single measurement differs from mean (**standard** ∿, quantity calculated to indicate extent of this difference for group as a whole); (Polit.) departure from (esp. Communist) party doctrine, whence ∿AL *a.*, ∿ISM (3), ∿IST (2), *ns.* [f. F *déviation* f. med. L *deviatio -onis* (as DEVIATE¹; see -ION)]

dĕvī′ce *n.* **1.** plan, scheme, trick; contrivance, invention, thing adapted for a purpose or designed for a particular function. **2.** drawing, design, figure; emblematic or heraldic design; motto. **3.** (in *pl.*) fancy, will; left to one's own ∿s, allowed to do whatever one is able or wishes without assistance or

advice. **4.** (arch.) make, look, (*things of rare device*). [ME f. OF *devis* f. Rom., f. L as DIVIDE¹]

dĕ′vil¹ *n.* **1.** the D∿, (Jewish & Christian Theol.) supreme spirit of evil, tempter of mankind, enemy of God. **2.** heathen god; demon, evil spirit supposed to be in a demoniac; one of Satan's followers, superhuman malignant being. **3.** wicked or cruel person; mischievously energetic, clever, baffling, or self-willed person; luckless or wretched person (usu. *poor devil*); vicious animal; awkward problem etc. **4.** junior legal counsel working for a principal. **5.** literary hack doing what his employer takes the credit and pay for; **printer's** ∿, (Hist.) errand-boy in printing office. **6.** personified evil quality (*the devil of greed* etc.); fighting-spirit, energy or dash in attack. **7.** = TASMANIAN *devil;* instrument or machine for tearing etc.; (dust) ∿, (S. Afr.) violent dust-storm. **8.** (or D∿). = DEUCE² (q.v. for phrases); **the** (**very**) ∿, a great difficulty or nuisance; **go to the** ∿, be damned, (in *imper.*) depart at once; **like the** ∿, with great energy etc.; ∿ **a bit,** not at all; ∿ **a one,** not even one. **9.** (or D∿). **between the** ∿ **and the deep** (**blue**) **sea,** in a dilemma; ∿ **take the hindmost** (motto of selfish competition); *give the Devil his* DUE²; **play the** ∿ **with,** cause severe damage to; RAISE *the devil*; **speak** or **talk of the** ∿ (**and he will appear**) (said when person comes just after being mentioned). **10.** ∿'s **advocate,** official who puts the case against beatification or canonization by RC Church, (transf.) one who indicates shortcomings so as to cause discussion; ∿'s **bit,** plant whose root looks bitten off, esp. species of scabious or blazing-star; ||∿'s **coach-horse,** large rove-beetle; ∿'s **darning-needle,** dragonfly or damselfly; *devil's* DOZEN; ∿'s **own,** very difficult or unusual (*devil's own problem, luck,* etc.); *devil's* PATERNOSTER, TATTOO¹. **11.** ∿-**fish,** angler-fish, *manta;* ∿-**may-care,** reckless, rollicking; ∿**s-on-horseback,** (1) (see ANGEL 3), (2) similar dish of prune or plum in bacon; *∿**wood,** small hard-wood tree. **12.** Hence ∿DOM, ∿ISM (2), *ns.* [OE *dēofol,* = OS *diubul, -al,* OHG *tiufal,* ON *djöfull,* f. LL f. Gk *diabolos* accuser, slanderer (*dia* across, *ballō* to throw), in Septuagint rendering Heb. *śātān* SATAN]

dĕ′vil² *v.* (||-ll-). **1.** *v.i.* work as lawyer's or author's devil (usu. *for* principal). **2.** *v.t.* cook with peppery condiments; *(colloq.) worry, harass. [f. prec.]

dĕ′vilish *a.* & *adv.* **1.** *a* like or worthy of the Devil; damnable; hence ∿LY² *adv.* **2.** *adv.* (arch. colloq.) very. [f. DEVIL¹ + -ISH¹]

dĕ′vilment *n.* mischief, wild spirits; devilish or strange phenomenon. [f. DEVIL¹ + -MENT]

dĕ′vilrý, dĕ′viltrý, *n.* diabolical art, black magic; the Devil and his works; wickedness, cruelty; reckless mischief, daring, or hilarity. [f. DEVIL¹ + -RY; *-try* wrongly after *harlotry* etc.]

dĕ′vious *a.* remote, sequestered; winding, circuitous, erratic; erring; unscrupulous, insincere; hence ∿LY² *adv.*, ∿NESS *n.* [f. L DE(*vius* f. *via* way) + -OUS]

dĕvī′s|e (-z) *v.t.*, & *n.* **1.** *v.t.* (Law) assign, give (realty *to* person; cf. BEQUEATH) by will, whence ∿EE′, ∿OR, *ns.* **2.** plan, invent, plot, scheme, (thing, how, to do). **3.** Hence or cogn. ∿ABLE *a.*, ∿ER² (4) *n.* **4.** *n.* (Law.) devising act or clause. [ME, f. OF *deviser* f. Rom. *divisare* frequent. of L *divider -vis-* DIVIDE; n. f. OF *devise* f. med. L *divisa* fem. p.p. of *dividere*]

dĕvī′tal|iz|e, -īs|e (-īz) *v.t.* make lifeless or effete; make more languid. [f. DE- + VITALIZE]

dĕvī′tri|fy *v.t.* deprive of vitreous quality, make (glass or vitreous rock) opaque and crystalline; hence ∿FICA′TION *n.* [f. DE- + VITRIFY]

dĕvoi′d *pred. a.* ∿ **of,** quite lacking or free from. [ME, p.p. of obs. *devoid* f. OF DE(*voidier* f. *voider* VOID)]

dĕ′voir (-vwär) *n.* (arch.) duty, one's best, (*do one's devoir*), (in *pl.*) courteous or formal attentions (*pay one's devoirs to*). [ME f. AF *dever* = OF *deveir* f. L *debēre* owe]

dĕ′volute (-ōot, -ūt) *v.t.* transfer by devolution. [f. as DEVOLVE]

dĕvolu'tion (-loo'-) *n.* **1.** descent through a series of changes; descent of property by due succession; lapse of unexercised right to ultimate owner; (Biol.) degeneration. **2.** deputing, delegation, of work or power (esp. by House of Parliament to bodies appointed by and responsible to it, or by central government to local or regional administration esp. in Scotland and Wales, whence ∼IST (2) *n.* [f. LL *devolutio* (as foll.; see -ION)]

dĕvŏ'lve *v.t.* & *i.* throw (duty, work), (of duties) be thrown, fall, descend, *upon* (deputy, or one who must act for want of others); descend, fall by succession, (*to, upon*). [ME, f. L DE(*volvere volut-* roll)]

Dĕvŏ'nian *a.* & *n.* (native) of Devon(shire); (Geol.) (of) Palaeozoic period or system, above Silurian and below Carboniferous. [f. med. L *Devonia* Devonshire + -AN]

Dĕ'vonshire (*-er, -ēr*) *n.* ∼ **cream**, CLOTted cream. [∼ (now Devon) in England]

dévot (dāvō') *n.* (*fem.* ∼ *e pr.* -ō't). devotee. [F, f. OF as DEVOUT]

dĕvŏ'te *v.t.* consecrate, give up exclusively, (one*self*, person, thing, esp. one's life, abilities, etc.) *to* (God, person, pursuit, purpose); (arch.) doom to destruction; hence ∼MENT (tm) *n.* [f. L DE(*vovēre not-* vow)]

dĕvŏ'tĕd *a.* In vbl senses; zealously loyal or loving (*devoted friend*), whence ∼LY² *adv.* [p.p. of prec.]

dĕvotee' *n.* votary *of*, one devoted *to*; zealously or fanatically pious person; enthusiast *of* sport etc. [f. DEVOTE + -EE]

dĕvŏ'tion *n.* devoutness; devoting; divine worship, (in *pl.*) prayers (and meditation), worship, (*was at his devotions*), whence ∼AL *a.*; enthusiastic addiction or loyalty (*to*). [ME f. OF, or f. L *devotio* (as DEVOTE; see -ION)]

dĕvour' *v.t.* (Of animal) eat; eat like a beast or ravenously; (of fire etc.) engulf; take in greedily with ears or eyes (book, story, beauty or beautiful person); (esp. in *pass.*) absorb the attention of (*devoured by anxiety*); hence ∼ER¹ *n.* [ME, f. OF *devorer* f. L DE(*vorare* swallow)]

dĕvou't *a.* (Of person, act, etc.) reverential, earnestly religious, pious, whence ∼NESS *n.*; earnest, hearty, genuine (*devout hope*); hence ∼LY² *adv.* [ME f. OF *devot* f. L *devotus* p.p. (as DEVOTE)]

dew¹ *n.* **1.** atmospheric vapour condensing in small drops on cool surfaces between evening and morning; freshness, refreshing quality; beaded or glistening moisture, esp. tears or sweat; MOUNTAIN dew. **2.** ∼'berry, bluish fruit like blackberry; ∼-claw, rudimentary inner toe of some dogs, false hoof of deer etc.; ∼-fall, time when dew begins to form, evening; ∼-point, temperature at which dew forms; ||∼-pond, shallow, usu. artificial, pond once supposed fed by atmospheric condensation. [OE *dēaw, =* OS *dau,* OHG *tou,* ON *dögg* f. Gmc **dauwaz, -am*]

dew² *v.* **1.** *v.t.* wet (as) with dew. **2.** *v.i.* (arch., impers.) form or fall as or like dew (*it is beginning to dew*). [ME, f. OE **dēawian, =* OS **daujan,* OHG *touwōn,* ON *döggva* f. Gmc **dauwōjan* (as prec.)]

DEW³ *abbr.* distant early warning.

dēwa'n (-wah'n) *n.* prime minister or finance minister of Indian state. [f. Arab. & Pers. *diwān* fiscal register]

Dew'ar *n.* double-walled flask with evacuated interspace to reduce transfer of heat. [f. Sir J. *Dewar,* Brit. physicist d. 1923]

Dew'ey *n.* ∼ **system,** decimal system of library classification. [f. M. ∼, Amer. librarian d. 1931, its deviser]

dew'lăp *n.* fold of loose skin hanging from throat of cattle (transf., of other animals, birds, or men). [ME, f. DEW¹ + LAP¹, perh. after ON **döggleppr*]

dew'|ÿ *a.* wet with or affected by dew; ∼y(-eyed), innocently trusting, naïvely sentimental; hence ∼ILY² *adv.,* iNESS *n.* [OE *dēawig* (as DEW¹, -Y²)]

lĕ'xter¹ *a.* (Her.) of or on right-hand side of shield etc. (i.e. to the spectator's left). [L, = on the right]

dĕ'xter² *n.* (animal of) small hardy breed of Irish cattle. [19th c., perh. f. name of breeder]

dĕxtĕ'ritÿ *n.* manual or mental adroitness, skill, neatness of handling; right-handedness, using of right hand. [f. F *dextérité* f. L DEXTER¹(*itas* -ITY)]

dĕ'xterous. See DEXTROUS.

dĕ'xtral *a.* & *n.* **1.** right-handed (person). **2.** *a.* of or on the right; (of flat-fish) with right side uppermost; (of spiral shell) with whorls rising to right. **3.** Hence ∼ITY (-ă'l-) *n.,* ∼LY² *adv.* [f. med. L *dextralis* f. L *dextra* right hand; see -AL]

dĕ'xtrăn *n.* (Chem.) amorphous gum formed by fermentation of sucrose etc.; degraded form of this used as substitute for blood-plasma. [G, f. as DEXTRO- + *-an* as in various Chem. names]

dĕ'xtrin *n.* (Chem.) soluble gummy substance obtained from starch and used as adhesive. [f. F *dextrine* f. L *dextra* on the right; see foll., -IN]

dĕ'xtrō- *comb. form.* (Chem.) having the property of causing plane of polarized light ray to rotate to right (opp. LAEVO-, which see for compounds). [f. L *dexter, dextra* on or to the right + -o-]

dĕ'xtrōrse *a.* rising towards the right (esp. Bot. of spiral stem). [f. L *dextrorsus* (as prec.)]

dĕ'xtrōse *n.* (Chem.) dextro-rotatory form of glucose. [f. as DEXTRO- + -OSE²]

dĕ'xtrous, dĕ'xterous, *a.* handling things neatly; skilful; mentally adroit, clever; using right hand by preference; hence ∼LY² *adv.* [f. L DEXTER¹ + -OUS]

dey (dā) *n.* (Hist.) ruler of Algiers 1710–1830; governor of Tunis or Tripoli. [F, f. Turk. *dayi* mother's brother, used as friendly title of older people by janizaries]

DF *abbr.* Defender of the Faith [f. L *Defensor Fidei*]; direction-finder.

||**DFC** *abbr.* Distinguished Flying Cross.

||**DFM** *abbr.* Distinguished Flying Medal.

DG *abbr. Dei gratia; Deo gratias;* director-general.

dhal, dal, (dahl) *n.* split pulse, a common foodstuff in India. [Hindi]

dhar'ma (dā̆r', dĕr'-) *n.* (Ind.) social custom; right behaviour, virtue, justice; the Buddhist truth; the Hindu moral law. [Skr., = decree, custom]

dhō'bi (dō'-) *n.* (Ind. etc.) washerman or washerwoman; ∼('s) **itch,** troublesome tropical dermatitis. [f. Hindi *dhōbī* (*dhōb* washing)]

dhō'ti (dō'-) *n.* (Ind. etc.) loincloth worn by male Hindus. [f. Hindi *dhōtī*]

dhow (dow) *n.* lateen-rigged Arabian-Sea ship. [19th c.; orig. unkn.]

dhurra. See DURRA.

di-¹ *pref.* Form of DIS-, occurring before *l, m, n, r, s* + cons., *v,* usu. *g,* and sometimes *j.* [L var. of *dis-*]

di-² *comb. form.* twice, two-, double-; (Chem., forming names of compounds) containing two atoms or groups of a specified kind (*dichromate, dioxide*). [Gk (*dis* twice)]

di-³ *pref.* = DIA- before vowel (*dioptric*).

||**DI** *abbr.* Defence Intelligence.

dia- *pref. w.* sense 'through' (*diaphanous*), 'apart' (*diacritical*), 'across' (*diameter*). [Gk (*dia* through)]

dia. abbr. diameter.

diăbē'tēs (-z) *n.* ∼ **insipidus,** disorder of pituitary with excessive thirst and urination; ∼ (**mellitus**), disease in which sugar and starch are not properly absorbed, with thirst, emaciation, and excessive urine containing glucose. [orig. = siphon, L f. Gk (*diabainō* go through)]

diabĕ'tic *a.* & *n.* of diabetes; (person) suffering from diabetes; (of food) made especially for diabetes patients. [f. prec. + -IC]

dia'blerie (-ah'-) *n.* devil's work; sorcery; wild recklessness. [F *diable* f. L *diabolus* DEVIL¹; see -ERY]

diăbŏ'lic(al) *adjs.* of, having to do with, proceeding from, externally like, the Devil; devilish, inhumanly cruel or wicked or clever or cunning or annoying;

hence **diăbŏ′licalⅬY²** *adv.* [ME, f. OF *diabolique* or LL *diabolicus* f. L *diabolus* (as DEVIL¹; see -IC)]

diă′bol|ism *n.* sorcery; devilish conduct or nature; belief in or worship of the Devil; hence ∾IST (2) *n.* [f. Gk *diabolos* DEVIL¹ + -ISM]

diă′bolize, īse (-īz), *v.t.* make into or represent as a devil. [f. as prec. + -IZE]

diă′bolō *n.* (*pl.* ∾s). game with two-headed top thrown up and caught with string stretched between two sticks; the top itself. [It., = DEVIL¹; formerly called *devil on two sticks*]

diachrŏ′n|ic (-k-) *a.* (Ling. etc.) concerned with historical development of a subject (esp. a language; opp. *synchronic*); hence ∾ICALLY *adv.*, **diă′chron**ISM (3), **diă′chron**Y¹ (1), (-k-) *ns.*, **diăchronī′st**IC, **diă′chron**OUS, (-k-) *adjs.* [f. F *diachronique* (as DIA-, Gk *khronos* time, -IC)]

diă′conal *a.* of a deacon. [f. eccl. L *diaconalis* (*diaconus* DEACON²; see -AL)]

diă′conate (-āt, -at) *n.* office of, one's time as, deacon; body of deacons. [f. eccl. L *diaconatus* (as prec.; see -ATE¹)]

diacri′tic *a.* & *n.* = foll. [as foll.]

diacri′tical *a.* & *n.* distinguishing, distinctive; ∾ (**mark** or **sign**), sign used to indicate different sounds or values of a letter (accent, diaeresis, cedilla, etc.). [f. Gk DIA(*kritikos*; see CRITIC) + -AL]

diădĕ′lphous *a.* (Bot.) with stamens united in two bundles (cf. *monadelphous, polyadelphous*). [f. DI-² + Gk *adelphos* brother + -OUS]

di′adĕm *n.*, & *v.t.* 1. *n.* crown, or plain or jewelled head-band, as badge of sovereignty; wreath of leaves or flowers worn round head; sovereignty; crowning distinction or glory. 2. *v.t.* (esp. in *p.p.*) adorn (as) with diadem. [ME, f. OF *diademe* f. L f. Gk DIA(*dēma* f. *deō* bind)]

diaer′ĕs|is (-ēr′-), **dīēr′ĕs|is**, *n.* (*pl.* ∾es *pr.* -ēz). mark (as in *Brontë, naïve*) over vowel indicating that it is separately sounded; (Pros.) break where foot ends at end of word. [LL, f. Gk DI³(*airesis* f. *haireō* take) separation]

dīagnō′se (-z) *v.t.* make diagnosis of (disease, mechanical fault, etc.); infer presence of (specified disease etc.) from symptoms. [f. foll.]

dīagnō′s|is *n.* (*pl.* ∾es *pr.* -ēz). identification of disease by means of patient's symptoms etc., formal statement of this; ascertainment of cause of mechanical fault etc.; distinctive characterization of species etc. [mod. L f. Gk (DIA-, *gignōskō* recognize)]

diagnŏ′st|ic *a.* & *n.* 1. *a.* of or assisting diagnosis. 2. *n.* symptom. 3. Hence ∾ICALLY *adv.*, ∾I′CIAN, ∾ICS, *ns.* [f. Gk DIA(*gnōstikos* as prec.; see -IC)]

diă′gonal *a.* & *n.* (straight line) joining two non-adjacent angles of rectilinear figure or solid contained by planes, or opposite corners of a thing; (line) obliquely placed like the diagonal of a parallelogram; inclined at other than a right angle, having some part so inclined; hence ∾LY² *adv.* [f. L *diagonalis* f. Gk DIA(*gōnios* f. *gōnia* angle); see -AL]

di′agr|ăm *n.*, & *v.t.* (‖-mm-). 1. *n.* sketch showing the features of an object needed for exposition; graphical or symbolic representation, by lines, of process, force, etc.; (Geom.) figure made of lines used in proving theorem etc.; hence or cogn. ∾amm∧′TIC *a.*, **dīagră′mmat**IZE (1) *v.t.* 2. *v.t.* represent in diagram. [f. L f. Gk DIA-(*gramma -atos* f. *graphō* write; cf. -GRAM)]

di′agrid *n.* supporting structure of diagonally intersecting ribs of metal etc. [f. DIAGONAL + GRID]

di′al *n.* & *v.* (‖-ll-). 1. *n.* face of clock or watch, marked to show hours etc.; plate in steam-gauge, gas-meter, etc., on which pressure, consumption, etc., are indicated by pointer; = SUN*dial*; circular plate on telephone with numbers etc. and movable disc with finger-holes for effecting connection with other telephones; (illuminated) plate etc. showing wavelength selected on radio receiver or channel selected on television set; (sl.) person's face. 2. *v.t.* measure or indicate (as) with dial. 3. *v.i.* & *t.* make telephone call by using dial; ring up (number etc.) thus; ∾ling **code,** sequence of numbers dialled to connect telephone to exchange of telephone being called; ∾ (**ling**) **tone,** sound given by automatic-exchange telephone to show that caller may start to dial. [ME, = sundial, f. med. L *diale* clock-dial f. **dialis* f. L *dies* day; see -AL]

di′alĕct *n.* form of speech peculiar to a district or class; subordinate variety of a language with non-standard vocabulary, pronunciation, or idioms; hence **diălĕ′ct**AL *a.*, ∾ŏ′LOGY, ∾ŏ′LOGIST, *ns.* [f. F *dialecte* or f. L f. Gk *dialektos* discourse (DIA*legomai* converse)]

dialĕ′ctic¹ *n.* 1. (also in *pl.*, occas. treated as *sing.*) art of investigating the truth of opinions, testing of truth by discussion, logical disputation. 2. criticism dealing with metaphysical contradictions and their solutions; existence or action of opposing social forces etc. 3. So **diălĕct**I′CIAN *n.* [ME, f. OF *dialectique* or f. L f. Gk *dialektikē* (*tekhnē* art) of debate (as prec.; see -IC)]

dialĕ′ctic² *a.* & *n.* logical, of disputation; (person) skilled in critical inquiry by discussion; dialectal. [f. L or Gk *dialektikos* (see prec.)]

diălĕ′ctical *a.* = prec.; belonging to DIALECTIC¹ (sense 2); ∾ **materialism,** Marxist theory of political and historical events as due to conflict of social forces caused by man's material needs; hence ∾LY² *adv.* [f. prec. + -AL]

dialŏ′gic *a.* in or of dialogue. [f. LL f. Gk *dialogikos* (as DIALOGUE; see -IC)]

diă′logist *n.* speaker in or writer of dialogue. [f. LL f. Gk *dialogistēs* (as foll.; see -IST)]

di′alŏgue (-ŏg), **di′alŏg, n.* conversation; piece of written work in conversational form, this kind of composition (*written in dialogue; plays contain much dialogue*); conversational part in a novel; discussion of proposals. [ME, f. OF *dialoge* f. L f. Gk *dialogos* (DIA*legomai* converse)]

diă′lÿs|is *n.* (*pl.* ∾es *pr.* -ēz). 1. (Chem.) separation of particles in liquid by differences in their ability to pass through membrane into another liquid. 2. (Med.) purification of blood by flow past suitable membrane. 3. Hence or cogn. **di′alÿse** (-z) *v.t.* separate thus, **dialÿ′t**IC *a.* [f. L f. Gk DIA(*lusis* f. *luō* set free)]

diămăgnĕ′t|ic *a.* & *n.* (body or substance) tending to become magnetized so as to lie transversely to a magnetic field force; hence **diămă′gnĕt**ISM (2) *n.* [f. DIA- + MAGNETIC]

diamanté (dēamah′ńtā) *a.* & *n.* (material) scintillating with powdered crystal etc. [F, p.p. of *diamanter* set with diamonds (*diamant* DIAMOND)]

diămăntī′ferous *a.* diamond-yielding. [f. F *diamantifère* (*diamant* DIAMOND; as -I-, -FEROUS)]

diămă′ntine *a.* of or like diamonds. [f. F *diamantin* (as prec.; see -INE¹)]

diă′mĕt|er *n.* straight line passing from side to side of any body or figure through its centre; transverse measurement, width, thickness; unit of linear measurement of magnifying-power (*lens magnifying 2000 diameters*); so ∾ral *a.* [ME, f. OF *diametre* f. L f. Gk DIA*metros* (*grammē* line) measuring across f. *metron* measure]

diamĕ′trical *a.* of or along a diameter, diametral; (of opposition, difference, etc.) complete, like that between opposite ends of diameter; hence ∾LY² *adv.* [f. Gk *diametrikos* (as prec.; see -IC) + -AL]

di′amond *n.* & *v.t.* 1. *n.* colourless or tinted brilliant precious stone of pure carbon crystallized in octahedrons and allied forms, hardest naturally-occurring substance; **black** ∾, (1) dark-coloured diamond, (2, in *pl.*) coal; **rough** ∾, diamond not yet cut, (fig.) person of intrinsic worth but rough manners; ∾ **cut** ∾, wit or cunning is met by its like. 2. glittering particle or point (of frost etc.). 3. tool with small diamond for glass-cutting. **4.** figure shaped like cross-section of diamond, rhombus, (∼ **panes,** small panes so shaped set in lead); playing-card of suit (∼s) denoted by red rhombus. **5.** (Baseball). space enclosed by bases; entire field. **6.** ∼**-back,** moth, *snake, or terrapin with diamond-shaped markings; ∼**-bird,** (Austral.) pardalote; ∼**-cement** (for setting diamonds); ∼**-drill** (set with diamonds for boring hard substance); ∼**-field,** tract yielding diamonds; ∼ **jubilee,** 60th (or 75th) anniversary of sovereign's accession or other event; ∼**-point,** (1) diamond--tipped stylus for engraving, (2) place where two railway lines intersect obliquely; ∼**-snake,** (Austral.) greenish-black carpet-snake with diamond--shaped markings; ∼ **wedding,** 60th (or 75th) anniversary of wedding. **7.** Hence ∼**ı̄'ferous** *a.* **8.** *a.* made of or set with diamond or diamonds; rhombus--shaped. **9.** *v.t.* adorn (as) with diamonds. [ME f. OF *diamant* f. med. L *diamas -mant-* var. of L f. Gk *adamas* ADAMANT]

)ı̄'na *n.* horsewoman, huntress. [ME f. L, name of goddess of hunting]

ı̄ä'ndrous *a.* having two stamens. [f. DI-² after *monandrous*]

ı̄ä'nthus *n.* flowering plant of genus *Dianthus,* e.g. carnation or pink. [f. Gk *Dios* of *Zeus* + *anthos* flower]

ı̄apā'son (-s-, -z-) *n.* **1.** compass of voice or instrument; range, scope; fixed standard of musical pitch; **open, stopped,** ∼, two chief foundation stops in organ, extending through its whole compass. **2.** combination of notes or parts in harmonious whole; melody, strain, esp. grand swelling burst of harmony. [ME in sense 'octave' f. L, f. Gk *dia pasōn* (*khordōn*) through all (notes)]

ı̄'apause (-z) *n.* period of retarded or suspended development in some insects. [f. DIA- + PAUSE]

ı̄'aper *n.,* & *v.t.* **1.** *n.* linen or cotton fabric with small diamond pattern; baby's nappy (orig. of this material); ornamental design of diamonds etc. for panels, walls, etc. **2.** *v.t.* decorate with diaper design. [ME, f. OF *diapre* f. med. L *diasprum* f. med. Gk *diaspros* adj. (DIA-, *aspros* white)]

ı̄ä'phanous *a.* (Of fabric etc.) light and delicate, and so almost transparent; hence ∼**ly²** *adv.* [f. med. L *diaphanus* f. Gk DIA(*phanēs* -showing f. *phainō* show) + -OUS]

ı̄aphorĕ'tic *a.* & *n.* (drug) inducing perspiration. [f. LL f. Gk *diaphoretikos* (*diaphorein* perspiration f. DIA*phoreō* carry through; see -ETIC)]

ı̄'aphrăgm (-ăm) *n.* **1.** muscular partition separating thorax from abdomen in mammals; partition in shellfish and plant tissues. **2.** thin sheet used as partition etc. (∼ **pump,** pump in which flexible diaphragm replaces piston); disc pierced by one or more holes in optical and acoustic systems etc.; device for varying effective aperture of lens in camera etc.; thin contraceptive cap fitting over cervix. **3.** Hence **diaphrăgmă'tic** *a.* [ME, f. LL f. Gk DIA(*phragma* -atos f. *phrassō* fence in)]

ı̄apŏ'sı̄tive (-z-) *n.* positive photographic slide or transparency. [f. DIA- + POSITIVE]

ı̄'archy (-kı̄) *n.* government by two independent authorities (esp. in India 1921-37); hence **diǎr'chaL, diǎr'chIC,** (-k-) *adjs.* [f. DI-² + Gk -*arkhia* rule, after *monarchy*]

ı̄'arist *n.* one who keeps a diary; hence **diarı̄'stIC** *a.* [f. DIARY + -IST]

ı̄'arı̄ze, -ı̄se (-ı̄z), *v.i.* & *t.* keep, enter in, a diary. [f. DIARY + -IZE]

ı̄arrhoe'|a, *diarrhē'|a, (-rē'a) *n.* excessive evacuation of too fluid faeces; (fig.) excessive flow of words etc.; hence ∼**AL,** ∼**IC,** *adjs.* [ME f. LL f. Gk DIA(*rrhoia* f. *rheō* flow)]

ı̄'ary *n.* daily record of events or thoughts; journal; book prepared for keeping this in; book etc. with daily memoranda esp. for persons of a particular profession. [f. L *diarium* (*dies* day; see -ARY¹)]

dı̄'ascōpe *n.* optical projector giving images of transparent objects. [f. DIA- + -SCOPE]

Dı̄ä'spora *n.* the Dispersion (of the Jews); Jews so dispersed; (situation of) any group of people similarly dispersed. [Gk, f. DIA(*speirō* scatter)]

dı̄'astāse *n.* (Chem.) enzyme converting starch to sugar, important in digestion; hence or cogn. **dı̄astă'sIC, dı̄astă'tIC,** *adjs.* [F, f. Gk *diastasis* separation (DIA-, *stasis* placing)]

dı̄ä'stolĕ *n.* (Physiol.) dilatation of heart rhythmically alternating with systole to form pulse; hence **dı̄astŏ'lIC** *a.* [LL f. Gk, f. DIA- (*stellō* place)]

dı̄atĕ'ssarŏn *n.* arrangement of the four Gospels as one narrative. [ME, f. LL f. Gk *dia tessarōn* composed of four]

dı̄athĕr'mancy *n.* quality of transmitting radiant heat; so **dı̄athĕr'manous, dı̄athĕr'mIC,** *adjs.* [f. F *diathermansie,* f. Gk DIA- through + *thermansis* heating, assim. to -ANCY]

dı̄'athĕrmy *n.* application of high-frequency electric currents to produce heat in deeper tissues of body. [f. G. *diathermie* f. Gk *dia* through + *thermon* heat + -Y¹]

dı̄ä'thĕs|ıs *n.* (*pl.* ∼**es** *pr.* -ēz). **1.** (Med.) constitutional predisposition to disease etc. **2.** (Gram.) voice of verb. [mod. L f. Gk (DIA*tithēmi* arrange)]

dı̄'atŏm *n.* microscopic unicellular alga with silicified cell-wall, found as plankton and forming fossil deposits; hence **dı̄atoma'ceous** *a.* [f. mod. L *Diatoma* (genus-name) f. Gk DIA(*tomos* f. *temnō* cut)]

dı̄atŏ'mic *a.* (Chem.) consisting of two atoms; having two replaceable atoms or radicals. [f. DI-² + ATOM + -IC]

dı̄ä'tomite *n.* substance composed of siliceous skeletons of diatoms. [f. DIATOM + -ITE¹]

dı̄atŏ'nic *a.* (Mus.) (Of scale or interval) involving only notes proper to key without chromatic alteration; (of melody or harmony) constructed from such a scale. [f. F *diatonique* or f. LL f. Gk DIA(*tonikos* TONIC) at intervals of a tone]

dı̄'atrı̄be *n.* piece of bitter criticism; invective; denunciation. [F, f. L f. Gk *diatribē* spending of time, discourse, f. DIA(*tribō* rub)]

dı̄ä'zō *n.* **1.** (Chem.) ∼ **compound,** one containing two nitrogen atoms joined by usu. double bond. **2.** ∼**(type),** copying or colouring process using diazo compound decomposed by light. [f. DI-² + AZO-]

dib *v.i.* (-bb-) = DAP [var. of DAB¹]

dı̄bā'sic *a.* (Chem.) having two replaceable hydrogen atoms. [f. DI-² + BASE¹ 5 + -IC]

dı̄'bber *n.* instrument for dibbling, dibble. [f. DIB in sense of foll. + -ER¹]

dı̄'bble *n.* & *v.* **1.** *n.* pointed instrument for making holes in ground for bulbs etc. **2.** *v.t.* prepare (soil) with this; sow or plant thus. **3.** *v.i.* use dibble. [ME, perh. rel. to DIB]

dı̄bs (-z) *n.pl.* (sl.) money. [earlier sense 'pebbles for tossing-game'; also *dib-stones,* perh. f. DIB]

dı̄ce¹. See DIE¹.

dı̄ce² *v.* **1.** *v.i.* & *t.* play dice (see DIE¹); gamble *away* or dice; take great risks (*dicing with death*); hence **dı̄'cer** *n.* **2.** *v.t.* chequer, mark with squares; (Cookery) cut into small cubes. [ME, f. prec.]

dı̄'cey *a.* (di'cier, di'ciest). (sl.) risky, unreliable. [f. DICE¹ + -Y²]

dı̄chŏ'tom|y (-k-) *n.* division (esp. sharply defined) into two; result of such division; binary classification; (Bot. & Zool.) repeated bifurcation; hence **dı̄chotŏ'mIC** (-k-), ∼**OUS,** *adjs.,* ∼**IZE** (1, 3) *v.t.* & *i.* [f. mod. L f. Gk *dikhotomia* (dikho- apart; see -TOMY)]

dı̄chrŏ'|ic (-k-) *a.* (Esp. of doubly refracting crystals) showing two colours; so ∼**ISM** (2) *n.* [f. Gk DI²(*khroos* f. *khrōs* colour) + -IC]

dı̄chromă'tic (-k-) *a.* two-coloured; (of animal species) having individuals that show different colorations; having vision sensitive to only two of three primary colours, whence **dı̄chrŏ'matISM** (5)

dick (-k-) *n.* [f. DI-² + Gk *khrōmatikos* (*khrōma* -*atos* colour; see -IC)]

||**dick¹** *n.* (sl.) take one's ∼, swear, affirm, (*that*). [abbr. of *declaration*]

dick² *n.* (sl.) detective. [perh. abbr.]

dick³ *n.* **1.** CLEVER *Dick*; TOM, *Dick, and Harry*. **2.** (vulg.) penis. [pet form of man's Christian name *Richard*]

di'ckĕns (-z) *n.* (colloq., in imprecations etc.) devil, deuce. [16th c.; prob. use of surname *Dickens*]

Dickĕ'nsian (-z-) *a.* & *n.* **1.** *a.* of Dickens or his works; having similarities to the situations described by Dickens (*Dickensian squalor*). **2.** *n.* admirer or student of Dickens('s works). [f. C. *Dickens*, Engl. novelist d. 1870 + -IAN]

di'cker *v.i.* trade by barter; haggle; dither, hesitate. [perh. f. *dicker* set of ten (hides), as unit of trade]

di'ckў¹, di'ckey, *n.* (colloq.) ∼(-bird), small bird; false shirt-front; ||driver's seat in carriage; ||extra folding seat at back of vehicle. [some senses f. *Dicky* (as DICK³)]

di'ckў² *a.* (sl.) unsound, shaky. [19th c., perh. f. 'as queer as Dick's hatband']

di'cŏt *n.* = foll. [abbr.]

dicŏtўlē'don *n.* flowering plant having two cotyledons; hence ∼OUS *a.* [f. mod. L *dicotyledones* (as DI-², COTYLEDON)]

dicrŏ'tic *a.* (Of pulse) with double beat. [f. Gk *dikrotos* + -IC]

di'cta. See DICTUM.

Di'ctaphōne, d-, *n.* (P) machine that records and later reproduces for transcription or rehearing what is spoken into it. [f. DICTATE² + -PHONE]

di'ctāte¹ *n.* (usu. in *pl.*) authoritative instruction (esp. *of* reason, conscience, nature, etc.). [f. L *dictatum* neut. p.p. (as n.) of *dictare*; see foll.]

dictā'te² *v.t.* & *i.* **1.** say or read aloud (matter to be written down, *to* writer or recording-machine). **2.** (Of person, motive, etc.) prescribe, lay down authoritatively, (terms, thing to be done); lay down the law, give orders, (*will not be dictated to*). **3.** So **dicta'TION** *n.*; **dictation speed,** rate of speech used by person dictating (sense 1). [f. L *dictare* frequent. of *dicere* dict-say + -ATE³]

dictā'tor *n.* absolute ruler, usu. temporary or irregular, of a State, esp. one who suppresses or succeeds a democratic government; (Rom. Ant.) chief magistrate with absolute power, appointed in emergencies; person with absolute authority in any sphere; domineering person; hence ∼SHIP *n.*, (esp.) State ruled by a dictator. **2.** one who dictates for transcription. [ME f. L (as prec.; see -OR)]

dictatŏr'ial *a.* of a dictator; imperious, overbearing; hence ∼LY² *adv.* [f. L *dictatorius* (as prec.) + -AL]

di'ction *n.* **1.** choice of words and phrases in speech or writing. **2.** manner of enunciation in speaking or singing. [F, or f. L *dictio* (*dicere* dict- say; see -ION)]

di'ctionary *n.* book explaining, usu. in alphabetical order, the words of a language or words and topics of some special subject, author, etc., wordbook, lexicon, (**French-English** etc. ∼, list of French etc. words with English etc. translation or explanation; *dictionary of Americanisms, of architecture, of the Bible, of proverbs, Dictionary of National Biography, Shakespeare dictionary,* etc.). [f. med. L *dictionarium* (*manuale* manual) & *dictionarius* (*liber* book) f. L *dictio* (see prec., -ARY¹)]

di'ctum *n.* (*pl.* ∼**a** *or* -**ums**). formal saying, pronouncement; (Law) = OBITER DICTUM; maxim, current saying. [L, neut. p.p. of *dicere* say]

***di'ctў** *a.* (sl.) conceited; stylish. [20th c.; orig. unkn.]

did. See DO¹.

di'dachē (-kē) *n.* instructional element in early Christian theology (opp. *kerygma*). [Gk *didakhē* teaching; cf. foll.]

dīdă'ct|ic *a.* meant to instruct; having the manner of an authoritarian teacher; hence ∼ICALLY *adv.* ∼**īcISM** (2) *n.* [f. Gk *didaktikos* (*didaskō* teach; see -IC)

didakai, diddicoy, etc. Vars. of DIDICOI.

di'dăpper *n.* dabchick. [for *dive-dapper* f. earlier *divedap* f. OE *dūfedoppa* (*dūfan* dive, *doppa* cf. DIP)]

di'ddle *v.t.* & *i.* (sl.) cheat, swindle; *waste time [prob. back-form. f. Jeremy *Diddler* in Kenney's 'Raising the Wind' (1803)]

didgeridoo', -dj-, *n.* Australian Aboriginal musical instrument of long tubular shape. [imit.]

di'dicoi *n.* (sl.) gypsy; itinerant tinker. [Romany]

didn't. See DO¹.

***di'dō** *n.* (colloq.) (*pl.* ∼**es** *or* ∼**s**). antic, caper, prank (esp. *cut* (*up*) *didoes*). [19th c.; orig. unkn.]

didst. See DO¹.

didў'mium *n.* mixture of praseodymium and neodymium, orig. regarded as element. [mod. L, f. Gk *didumos* twin (from being closely associated with lanthanum) + -IUM]

dīe¹ *n.* **1.** (*pl.* **dice,** also colloq. as *sing.*) small cube with faces bearing usu. 1–6 spots used in games of chance (in *pl.*) game played with these; (in *pl.*) small cubes of meat etc. for cooking; **the ∼ is cast,** irrevocable step is taken; **no dice,** (colloq.) no success or prospect of it; **as straight** or **true as a ∼,** (fig.) entirely honest or loyal. **2.** (*pl.* ∼**s**). (Archit.) cube of pedestal between base and cornice; plinth of column. **3.** engraved stamp for coining, striking medal, embossing paper etc.; hollow mould for shaping extruded metal cutting screw-thread, etc. **4.** ∼**-casting,** process of product of casting from metal moulds; ∼**-sinker,** engraver of dies; ∼**-stamping,** embossing paper etc with die. [ME f. OF *de* f. L *datum* neut. p.p. (as n.) of *dare* give, play]

dīe² *v.i.* (*part.* **dy'ing** *pr.* dī'ī-). **1.** (Of person or animal) cease to live, expire, (*of* illness, hunger, etc. *by* violence, the sword, one's own hand, *from* wound etc., *through* neglect, *on* scaffold, *at* the stake, *in* battle *for* friend, cause, etc., *in* poverty; *die a beggar, a martyr die a glorious, a dog's, death*). **2.** ∼ **the death,** (arch. or joc.) be put to death; ∼ **game** (fighting, not tamely); ∼ **hard** (not without struggle); ∼**hard** *n.,* conservative or stubborn person; ∼ **in** one's **bed** (of age or illness, not by violence), ∼ **in** one's **boots** or **shoes** (by violence), in **harness** (while still at work), **in the last ditch** (desperately defending something), *like a* DOG¹; *never* say ∼, not give in, keep up courage. **3. be dying** *for* to do, have great desire; **be dying** *of* boredom etc., fin it exceedingly vexatious; ∼ (*of*) **laughing,** laugh to exhaustion. **4.** (Of plant etc.) lose vital force, deca (∼ **back,** from tip towards root); come to an end cease to exist or function; (of flame, fame, sound, etc. go out, disappear, be forgotten, fade away, (*away down*); ∼**-away** *a.,* languishing; ∼ **off,** (of group) b gradually removed by death; ∼ **out,** become extinct *secret* etc. ∼**s with** person, he dies without revealin it. [ME, prob. f. ON *deyja* = DEAD, DEATH; f. Gmc *dawjan;* cf. DEAD, DEATH]

die'ldrin *n.* crystalline insecticide got by oxidation c aldrin. [f. O. *Diels*, Ger. chemist d. 1954 + ALDRIN]

dīēlĕ'ctric *a.* & *n.* (Electr.) insulating (medium c substance); ∼ **constant,** permittivity. [f. DI-³ + ELECTRIC = through which electricity is transmitte (without conduction)]

dī'ēne *n.* (Chem.) organic compound with two doubl bonds between carbon atoms. [f. DI-² + -ENE]

***diĕr'esis.** See DIAERESIS.

die'sel (-z-) *n.* **1.** ∼ (**engine**), internal combustio engine in which ignition of fuel is produced by heat o air highly compressed; vehicle driven by, fuel fo diesel engine; hence ∼IZE (4) *v.t.* **2.** ∼**-electri** driven by electric current from generator driven b diesel engine; ∼ **oil,** heavy petroleum fraction used i diesel engines. [f. R. *Diesel,* Ger. engineer d. 1913]

Dies irae (dēaz ēr'ī) *n.* Latin hymn sung in Mass fo the dead. [L (its first words), = day of wrath]

dies non (dī'ēz nŏ'n) *n*. (Law) day on which no legal business is done; day that does not count or cannot be used. [L, short for *dies non juridicus* non-judicial day]

di'et¹ *n*. & *v*. **1.** *n*. way of feeding; prescribed course of food; one's habitual food. **2.** *v.i.* restrict oneself to special food, esp. in order to control one's weight; hence ∼ER¹ *n*. **3.** *v.t.* feed, esp. on special food as treatment or punishment. [ME, f. OF *diete*(*r*) f. L f. Gk *diaita* way of life]

di'et² *n*. conference, congress, on national or international business; meeting of the estates of the realm or confederation (esp. as English name for some foreign parliamentary assemblies); (Sc.) session of court. [ME, f. med. L *dieta* day's work, wages, etc.]

di'etary *n*. & *a*. **1.** *n*. (course of) diet; allowance or nature of food in hospital, prison, etc. **2.** *a*. of diet(ary). [ME, f. med. L *dietarium* (as DIET¹; see -ARY¹)]

dietē't|ic *a*. of diet; hence ∼ICALLY *adv*., ∼ICS *n*. [f. L f. Gk *diaitētikos* (as DIET¹; see -ETIC)]

dieti'tian, -i'cian, (-shan) *n*. one versed in or practising dietetics. [f. DIET¹ + -ICIAN; *-itian* irreg.]

dif- *pref*. Form of DIS-, occurring before *f*. [L var. of DIS-]

di'ffer *v.i.* be unlike; be distinguishable *from*; disagree, be at variance, (*from*, *with*); AGREE to *differ*. [ME, f. OF *differer* f. L DIF(*ferre* bear, tend), all used in senses (a) *differ*, (b) DEFER¹]

di'fference *n*., & *v.t.* **1.** *n*. being different, dissimilarity, non-identity (DISTINCTION *without difference*). **2.** point in which things differ (**make all the** ∼, be very important or significant; **make a** ∼ **between**, treat differently; *make a great difference, make no difference*; **with a** ∼, in a special way); characteristic mark distinguishing individual or species; quantity by which amounts differ, remainder after subtraction, (**split the** ∼, take average of two proposed amounts). **3.** disagreement in opinion, dispute, quarrel. **4.** *n*., & *v.t.* (Her.) (make) alteration in (coat of arms) to distinguish members of same family. [ME f. OF, f. L *differentia* (as foll.; see -ENCE)]

di'fferent *a*. able to be distinguished, unlike, of other nature, form, or quality, (*from*, **D** *to*, ∗*than*); distinct, separate, (*several different people, colours*); unusual; hence ∼LY² *adv*. [ME f. OF, f. L (as DIFFER; see -ENT)]

differe'ntia (-shǐa) *n*. (*pl*. ∼e). distinguishing mark, esp. of species within a genus. [L; see DIFFERENCE]

differe'ntial (-shal) *a*. & *n*. **1.** *a*. of, exhibiting, depending on, a difference; varying according to circumstances. **2.** constituting a specific difference, distinctive, relating to specific differences (*differential diagnosis*); (Math.) relating to infinitesimal differences (∼ **calculus**, for finding rates of change, maximum and minimum values, etc.; cf. INTEGRAL). **3.** (Phys. & Mech.) concerning the difference of two or more motions, pressures, etc.; ∼ (**gear**), gear enabling motor vehicle's rear wheels to revolve at different speeds in rounding corners. **4.** Hence ∼LY² *adv*. **5.** *n*. (Math.) infinitesimal difference between successive values of a variable (∼ **coefficient**, = DERIVATIVE; ∼ **equation**, one involving derivatives); difference between rates of interest etc.; difference in wage between industries or between different classes of workers in same industry. [f. med. & mod. L *differentialis* (as DIFFERENCE; see -AL)]

differe'nti|ate (-shǐ-) *v.t.* & *i*. constitute difference between, of, or in; make or become different in process of growth or development (species, word-forms, functions, synonyms); discriminate, discriminate between; (Math.) calculate derivative of; hence ∼A'TION (-shǐ-, -sǐ-) *n*. [f. med. L *differentiare* (as DIFFERENCE) + -ATE³]

di'fficult *a*. needing much labour to do or practise; troublesome, perplexing, (*difficult of access, to answer*, etc.); unaccommodating, stubborn. [ME, back-form. f. foll.]

di'fficult|y *n*. being difficult (**with** ∼**y**, not easily) or

obscure; difficult thing or problem (**make** ∼**ies**, be unaccommodating); hindrance; (often in *pl*.) trouble, esp. shortage of money. [ME, f. L DIF(*ficultas* = *facultas* FACULTY)]

diffïd|ent *a*. lacking self-confidence, excessively modest; hence or cogn. ∼ENCE *n*., ∼ent**ly²** *adv*. [f. L DIF(*fidere* trust); see -ENT]

diffrä'ct *v.t.* (Phys.) (Of edge of opaque body, narrow slit, etc.) break up (beam of light) into series of dark and light bands or coloured spectra, or (beam of radiation or particles) into series of alternately high and low intensities; so ∼ION *n*., ∼IVE *a*., ∼ŏ'METER *n*., instrument for measuring diffraction esp. in crystallographic work. [f. L DIF(*fringere fract-* = *frangere* break)]

diff ū'se¹ *a*. (Of light, inflammation, etc.) spread out, diffused, not concentrated; not concise, long-winded, verbose; hence ∼LY² (-slǐ) *adv*., ∼NESS (-sn-) *n*. [ME, f. F *diffus* or L DIF(*fusus* p.p. of *fundere* pour) extensive]

diffūs'|e² (-z) *v.t.* & *i*. **1.** disperse or be dispersed from a centre; (be) spread widely (light, lighting to avoid glare, particles, heat, geniality, knowledge, rumour). **2.** (Phys., esp. of fluids) intermingle by diffusion. **3.** So ∼IBLE, ∼IVE, *adjs*. [f. L, as prec.]

diffū'sion (-zhon) *n*. diffusing or being diffused; (Phys.) interpenetration of substances by natural movement of their particles; (Anthrop.) spread of elements of culture etc. to another region or people, whence ∼OIST (2) *n*. [ME, f. L *diffusio* (as DIFFUSE¹, see -ION)]

dig *v*. (-gg-; dug, arch. ∼ged *pr*. -gd), & *n*. **1.** *v.i.* use spade or pick, claws, hands, or snout, in excavating or turning over ground; excavate archaeologically; make search (*for* information, *into* book etc.); make way by digging *into*, *through*, *under*. **2.** *v.t.* excavate or turn up (ground) with spade etc. or for archaeological purposes; make (hole, grave, etc.) by digging (∼ **a pit for**, fig., try to entrap); obtain by digging (potatoes etc.); (sl.) understand, experience, or admire. **3.** thrust (spurs, one's nails, feet, point of weapon) *into* something or *in* (∼ one's **feet, heels,** or **toes in**, be obstinate); poke (person *in the ribs*). **4.** ∼ (oneself) **in**, prepare defensive trench or pit, establish one's position; ∼ **in** or **into**, mix (thing) with the soil by digging (colloq.) begin eating; ∼ **out** or **up**, get or find by digging (lit. or fig.); ∼ **up**, break up soil of (fallow land). **5.** *n*. piece of digging (colloq.) archaeological excavation; thrust, poke, (esp. *in the ribs*, ∼ **at**, (fig.) remark directed against); || (in *pl*., colloq.) lodgings. [ME, perh. f. OE ∗*dīcigian* (*dīc* DITCH)]

digä'mma *n*. sixth letter (*F*, *ϝ*) of original Greek alphabet (prob. pronounced w), later disused but philologically important. [L f. Gk DI-², GAMMA]

di'gam|ў *n*. second marriage, after divorce or death of first spouse; hence or cogn. ∼IST (1) *n*., ∼OUS *a*. [f. LL f. Gk DI²(*gamia* f. *gamos* marriage)]

digä'stric *a*. (Anat.) (Of muscle) having two wide parts with tendon between. **2.** *n*. muscle that opens the jaw. [f. mod. L DI²(*gastricus* f. Gk *gastēr* belly)]

di'gest¹ *n*. methodical compendium or summary esp. of a body of laws (**the D**∼, that of Roman laws compiled by order of Justinian); periodical synopsis of current literature or news. [ME, f. L *digesta* things methodically arranged, neut. pl. p.p.; see foll.]

digě'st² *v.t.* **1.** reduce to a systematic or convenient form, classify; summarize; think over, arrange in the mind. **2.** assimilate (food) in stomach and bowels; treat (substance) with heat or solvent in order to decompose it, extract essence, etc., whence ∼ER¹ (2) *n*.; endure (insults etc.); understand and assimilate mentally. **3.** So ∼IBI'LITY *n*., ∼IBLE *a*. [ME, f. L DI¹(*gerere gest-* carry) distribute, dissolve, digest]

digě'stion (-schon) *n*. digesting of physical or mental food; power of digesting (*a good, weak, digestion*);

digesting of substance by heat or solvent. [ME f. OF, f. L *digestio -onis* (as prec.; see -ION)]

dĭge'stive *a.* & *n.* of or promoting digestion; substance aiding digestion; ||kind of wholemeal (biscuit); hence ∿LY² (-vlĭ) *adv.* [ME, f. OF *digestif -ive* or f. L *digestivus* (as DIGEST²; see -IVE)]

dĭ'gger (-g-) *n.* In vbl senses; (colloq.) Australian or New Zealander, esp. private soldier; (Austral. colloq. form of address) = MATE² 1; member of 17th-c. Engl. religious group cultivating commons; hippie believing in free sharing of property and food; ∿'s delight, (Austral.) kind of speedwell thought to indicate presence of gold; ∿(-wasp), burrowing wasp of family Sphecidae. [f. DIG + -ER¹]

dĭ'gging (-g-) *n.* In vbl senses; (in *pl.*) mine or goldfield, ||(colloq.) lodgings; ∿-stick, pointed stick as primitive digging implement. [f. DIG + -ING¹]

dĭght (dīt) *a.* (arch.) clothed, arrayed. [p.p. of *dight* v. f. OE *dihtan* f. L *dictare* DICTATE²]

dĭ'gĭt *n.* 1. (Zool. & Anat., or joc.) finger or toe. 2. any numeral from 0 to 9, esp. when forming part of number; hence ∿IZE (3) *v.t.* 3. finger's breadth as unit of length, ¾ inch. [ME, f. L *digitus*]

dĭ'gĭtal *a.* of digit(s); ∿ clock (showing time by displayed digits, not by hands); ∿ computer (making calculations with data represented by digits or in similar discrete form); ∿ recording (of sound represented by digits or in similar discrete form, to improve quality); hence ∿IZE (3) *v.t.* [f. L *digitalis* (as prec.; see -AL)]

dĭgĭtā'lĭis *n.* drug prepared from dried foxglove leaves, used as heart-stimulant; hence ∿IN *n.*, steroid poison extracted from foxglove leaves. [mod. L, genus-name of foxglove after G *fingerhut* thimble; see prec.]

dĭ'gĭtate *a.* (Zool. & Bot.) having separate fingers or toes; having deep radiating divisions; hence **digĭt**A'-TION *n.* [f. L *digitatus* (as DIGIT; see -ATE²)]

dĭ'gĭtigrāde *a.* & *n.* (animal) that walks on its toes not touching ground with heels, e.g. dog, cat, lion (cf. PLANTIGRADE). [F, f. L *digitus* + -I- + -*gradus* -walking]

dĭ'gnĭfied (-ĭd) *a.* having or showing dignity; self--respecting, stately. [p.p. of foll.]

dĭ'gnĭfy *v.t.* make worthy or illustrious; confer dignity on, ennoble; make stately; give high-sounding title to (*school dignified with name of college*). [f. obs. F *dignifier* f. OF *dignefier* f. LL *dignificare* (*dignus* worthy; see -FY)]

dĭ'gnĭtary *n.* person holding high rank or office, esp. ecclesiastical. [f. foll. + -ARY¹, after *proprietary*]

dĭ'gnĭty *n.* true worth, excellence, (*the dignity of labour*); high rank or estimation (**beneath** one's ∿, unfitting for one to do); honourable office, rank, or title; elevated manner, proper stateliness (**stand on** one's ∿, insist on respectful treatment). [ME f. OF *digneté*, *dignité* f. L *dignitas -tatis* (*dignus* worthy; see -ITY)]

dĭ'graph (-ahf) *n.* group of two letters representing one sound (*ph, ea*). [f. DI-² + -GRAPH]

dĭgrĕ'ss *v.i.* diverge from the track, stray; depart from the main subject temporarily in speech or writing (*to digress for a moment; must not digress from the point at issue*); so ∿ION (-shǒn) *n.*, ∿IVE *a.* [f. L DI¹(*gredi gress- = gradi* walk)]

dĭhē'dral *a.* & *n.* 1. *a.* having or contained by two plane faces; ∿ angle, (esp.) angle formed by aircraft wing with horizontal. 2. *n.* dihedral angle. [f. *dihedron* (DI-², -HEDRON) + -AL]

dĭhy'drĭc *a.* (Chem.) containing two hydroxyl groups. [f. DI-² + HYDRIC]

dĭ'k-dĭk *n.* small Afr. antelope of genus *Madoqua* or *Rhynchotragus*. [name in E. Africa & in Afrik.]

dĭke¹, dȳke¹, *n.,* & *v.t.* 1. *n.* ditch; ||natural watercourse; low wall esp. of turf. 2. *n.* embankment, long ridge, dam, against flooding, esp. one of those in Holland against sea; causeway; (fig.) barrier, obstacle, defence; (Mining & Geol.) intrusion of igneous rock across strata; (sl.) lavatory. 3. *v.t.* provide or defend with dike(s). [ME, f. ON *dík* or f. MLG *dīk* dam, MDu. *dijc* ditch, dam; cf. DITCH]

dīke², dȳke², *n.* (sl.) masculine Lesbian. [20th c.; orig unkn.]

dĭ'kköp *n.* (S. Afr.) stone-curlew. [Afrik. (*dik* thick *kop* head)]

dĭ'ktät *n.* imposition of severe terms by victor; dictate categorical statement. [G, = DICTATE¹]

dĭlă'pĭdātĕd *a.* (Of building, furniture, clothing) in disrepair or decay. [p.p. of *dilapidate* f. L DI¹(*lapidare* f *lapis* stone) squander + -ATE³]

dĭlăpĭdā'tion *n.* bringing or coming into, being in disrepair; ||(Eccl.) sum charged against incumben for wear and tear during his tenancy. [ME, f. LL *dilapidatio* (as prec.; see -ATION)]

dĭlā't|e *v.* 1. *v.t.* & *i.* make or become wider or larger expand, widen, enlarge, (*with dilated eyes*); hence o cogn. ∿ABLE *a.*, **dĭlat**A'TION *n.*, (esp., Med.) widen ing of cervix e.g. for curettage, **dĭlA**'TION *n.* 2 expatiate, speak or write at length (*upon*). [ME, f. O *dilater* f. L DI¹(*latare* f. *latus* wide) spread out]

dĭlā'tor *n.* (Anat.) muscle that dilates an organ (Surg.) instrument for dilating tube or cavity i body. [f. prec. + -OR]

dĭ'lator|ý *a.* tending to, designed to cause, given to delay; hence ∿ĭLY² *adv.*, ∿ĭNESS *n.* [f. LL *dilatoriu* (DI¹*lat-* p.p. st. of *differre* DEFER¹; see -ORY)]

dĭ'ldō *n.* (*pl.* ∿s). artificial penis used by women fo sexual pleasure. [17th c.; orig. unkn.]

dĭlĕ'mma *n.* argument forcing opponent to choos one of two alternatives (**horns of the** ∿) bot unfavourable to him; position that leaves only choice between equally unwelcome possibilities; [th difficult situation. [L, f. Gk DI²(*lēmma* assumption premiss)]

dĭlĕtta'nt|è *n.* (*pl.* ∿i *pr.* -ē, *or* ∿es) & *a.* 1. *n.* lover c the fine arts; amateur; one who toys with subject o studies it without seriousness; hence ∿ISH¹ *a.*, ∿ISI (1) *n.* 2. *a.* trifling, not thorough; amateur. [It., part. of *dilettare* f. L *delectare* DELIGHT; see -ANT]

dĭ'lĭgence¹ *n.* persistent effort or work; industriou character. [ME f. OF, f. L *diligentia* (as DILIGENT; se -ENCE)]

dĭlĭgence² (dĭ'lĭjens, dēlēzhah'ns) *n.* (Hist.) publi stage-coach, esp. in France. [F, for *carrosse de diligenc* coach of speed]

dĭ'lĭgent *a.* steady in application, industrious, atten tive to duties; hence ∿LY² *adv.* [ME f. OF, f. L *diligen* assiduous, part. of DI¹(*ligere lect- = legere* choose) tak take delight in; see -ENT]

dill *n.* umbelliferous annual yellow-flowered her (*Anethum graveolens*) with scented seeds; ∿ pickl pickled cucumber etc. flavoured with dill; ∿-wate distillate of dill as carminative. [OE *dile*, = OS *dill* OHG *tilli*, ON *dylla*, of unkn. orig.]

dĭ'llý *n.* (sl.) remarkable or excellent person or thing [f. *dilly* a. f. DELIGHTFUL or DELICIOUS; see -Y³]

dĭ'llý-dăllý *v.i.* (colloq.) vacillate; dawdle, loite [redupl. of DALLY]

dĭ'lŭent *a.* & *n.* diluting (agent). [f. L *diluere* DILUTE see -ENT]

dĭlūte¹ (-ū't, dī'-) *a.* weakened by addition of wate or other solvent; (of colour) washed-out, faded; (fig watery, watered down. [f. L *dilutus* p.p. of *diluere* (se foll.)]

dĭlū'te² *v.t.* reduce strength of (fluid) by adding wate or other solvent; diminish brilliance of (colour); mak (doctrine, zeal) less strict or forceful; substitute proportion of unskilled for skilled (workers); hence ∿ **dĭlū**TEE' *n.*, unskilled person thus substituted. **dĭlu** TION (-ū'-, -ōō'-) *n.* [f. L DI¹(*luere lut-* wash)]

dĭlu'vĭal (-ū'-, -ōō'-) *a.* 1. of a flood, esp. of the Floo in Genesis. 2. (Geol.) of the drift formation now calle Glacial Drift; ∿ theory etc. (postulating genera deluge or catastrophic water-action, whence ∿IST (-2 *n.*). [f. LL *diluvialis* (*diluvium* DELUGE; see -AL)]

dĭlu'vĭum (-ū'-, -ōō'-) *n.* (Geol.) = DRIFT¹. [L (se prec.)]

dĭm *a.* & *v.* (-mm-). 1. *a.* faintly luminous or visibl not bright (lit. or fig.), clear, or well-defined; (colloq.) stupid; obscure; seeing or seen, hearing or heard, apprehending or apprehended, indistinctly; **take a ~ view of**, (colloq.) regard with disfavour or pessimism; **~-wit(ted)**, (colloq.) stupid (person); hence **~'ly²** *adv.*, **~'mish¹** 2 *a.*, **~'ness** *n.* **2.** *v.i.* & *t.* become or make dim, becloud, outshine; ***dip** (headlights); **~ out**, reduce brightness of (lights on stage, or street lights etc. esp. in wartime); so **~-out** *n.* [OE *dim(m)*, = ON *dimmr*, cogn. w. OHG *timbar*, of unkn. orig.]

dim. *abbr.* diminuendo.

*dime *n.* (US & Can.) 10 cents, 1/10 of dollar, as amount or coin; **a ~ a dozen**, commonplace; **~ novel**, cheap sensational novel. [ME, orig. = tithe, f. OF *disme* f. L *decima* (*pars* part) fem. of *decimus* tenth]

dime'nsion (-shon) *n.* **1.** measurable extent of any kind, as length, breadth, thickness, area, volume, (often in *pl.*; **of great ~s**, very large); **the three ~s**, length, breadth, and thickness (point has no dimensions, line one, surface two, solid body three); **fourth ~**, property of bodies that would make them be to solids as solids are to surfaces, (Phys.) time viewed as lengthlike quantity. **2.** (Alg.) number of unknown or variable quantities contained as factors in a product (x^n, x^2y, *xyz*, are all of three dimensions); (Phys.) power of length, time, mass, etc., contained in a quantity. **3.** extent in a particular aspect (*gave the problem a new dimension*). **4.** Hence (-)**~AL** *a.* (TWO-*dimensional* etc.), **~LESS** *a.* **5.** *v.t.* give dimensions or measurements to. [ME f. OF, f. L DI¹(*mensio -onis* f. *metiri mensus* measure; see -ION)]

di'mer *n.* (Chem.) compound whose molecule contains twice the numbers of atoms in another compound (the *monomer*); hence **dime'ric** *a.* [f. DI-² + -*mer* after POLYMER]

di'merous *a.* (Bot. & Entom.) having two parts in whorl, tarsus, etc. [f. mod. L *dimerus* f. Gk *dimerēs* bipartite; see -MEROUS]

di'meter *n.* (Pros.) line of two measures. [f. LL f. Gk *dimetros* (as DI-², -METER)]

dimi'diate *a.* halved, split in two. [f. L *dimidiatus* p.p. of *dimidiare* f. L *dimidium* f. *medius* mid) half; see -ATE²]

dimi'nish *v.t.* & *i.* make or become smaller or less (in fact or in appearance); lessen the reputation of (person); **law of ~ing returns**, (Econ.) fact that expenditure, taxation, etc., beyond a certain point does not produce proportionate yield; hence **~ABLE** *a.* [ME, blending of earlier *minish* f. OF *menusier* f. L a3 MINCE², and *diminue* f. OF *diminuer* f. L DI¹*minuere* -*minut*- break up small]

dimi'nished (-sht) *a.* In vbl senses; (Mus., of interval) less by a semitone than corresp. minor or perfect interval; **~ responsibility**, (Law) limitation of criminal responsibility on ground of mental weakness or abnormality. [p.p. of prec.]

diminue'ndo *adv.*, *a.*, & *n.* (*pl.* **~s**) (Mus.) (passage performed) with gradual decrease of loudness. [It., part. of *diminuire* DIMINISH]

diminu'tion *n.* diminishing, amount of it; (Mus.) repetition of passage in notes shorter than those previously used. [ME f. OF, f. L *diminutio -onis* (as DIMINISH; see -ION)]

dimi'nutive *a.* & *n.* remarkably small, tiny; (Gram.) (word) describing small or liked or despised specimen of the thing denoted by corresponding radical word (*ringlet*, *duckling*; *wifie*; *princeling*), whence **diminuti'val** *a.*; hence **~LY²** (-vli) *adv.*, **~NESS** (-vn-) *n.* [ME f. OF (-*if*-*ive*) f. LL *diminutivus* (as DIMINISH; see -IVE)]

di'missory *a.* sending away; permitting to depart; **letters ~**, (Eccl.) bishop's authorization of candidate's ordination outside the bishop's own see. [ME, f. LL *dimissorius* (DI¹*mittere -miss-* send away; see -ORY)]

di'mity *n.* cotton fabric woven with raised stripes or checks. [ME, f. It. *dimito* or f. med. L *dimitum* f. Gk DI²(*mitos* warp-thread)]

di'mmer *n.* In vbl senses; device for dimming lights in theatre etc. [f. DIM + -ER¹]

dimor'phic, dimor'phous, *adjs.* (Biol., Chem., & Min.) exhibiting, or occurring in, two distinct forms; hence **dimor'ph**ISM (2) *n.* [f. Gk DI²(*morphos* f. *morphē* form) + -IC, -OUS]

di'mple *n.* & *v.* **1.** *n.* small hollow or dent, esp. in cheek or chin; ripple in water; hence **di'mply²** *a.* **2.** *v.t.* produce dimples in. **3.** *v.i.* show dimples. [ME, prob. f. OE *dympel, = OHG *tumphilo* deep place in water, perh. nasalized form f. as DEEP¹]

din *n.* & *v.* (-**nn**-). **1.** *n.* continued confused stunning or distracting noise. **2.** *v.t.* get (thing to be learnt) *into* person or person's *ears* by incessant repetition; assail with din. **3.** *v.i.* make a din. [OE *dyne, dynn, dynian* v., = OHG *tuni*, ON *dynr, dynja* rumble down f. Gmc *dunjaz, *dunjan v.]

DIN *abbr.* German standard. [G (*Deutsche Industrie-Norm*)]

di'nar (dē'-) *n.* unit of currency in Yugoslavia and in several countries of Middle East and N. Africa. [f. Arab. & Pers. *dīnār* f. Gk *dēnarion* f. L *denarius* (see DENIER)]

dine *v.i.* & *t.* eat dinner; entertain (persons) at dinner; **~ out** (away from home); **~ out on**, be invited to dinner mainly because of one's knowledge of (interesting event etc.). [ME, f. OF *di(s)ner* f. Rom. **dis(je)-junare* break one's fast f. DIS- + LL *jejunare* (*jejunus* fasting)]

di'ner *n.* In vbl senses; railway dining-car; *restaurant; (small) dining-room; **~-out**, one who often dines away from home, esp. one much invited for his social qualities. [f. prec. + -ER¹]

dine'tte (dī'-, -ē't) *n.* small room or part of room used for meals; compactly designed set of furniture for dining. [f. DINE + -ETTE]

Ding an sich (dīng ahn zī'χ) *n.* (Philos.) thing in itself. [G]

di'ngbat *n.* **1.** *piece of money; *tramp; *thing-ummy'. **2.** (Austral. & NZ, in *pl.*) discomfort; madness. [19th c., perh. f. *ding* to beat + BAT²]

ding-dong (-ŏ'-, -ī'-) *adv.*, *n.*, & *a.* (with) alternating strokes as of two bells; with great energy (*hammer away at it* ding-dong); **~ race** etc. (in which each has the better of it alternately); sound of bell(s); (colloq.) riotous party, heated argument. [16th c.; imit.]

dinge¹ (-nj) *n.* dinginess. [f. DINGY f. dial. or rare *dinge* make dingy]

*dinge² (-nj) *n.* (sl., derog.) a Black (der. of Black jazz style). [f. DINGY]

di'nghy (-nggī, -ngī) *n.* small boat of ship; small pleasure-boat; (esp. aircraft's) small inflatable rubber boat for emergency use. [orig. native rowing-boat on Indian rivers, f. Hindi *dīngī, dēngī*]

di'ngle (-nggel) *n.* deep dell, esp. shaded with trees. [ME; orig. unkn.]

di'ngo (-nggō) *n.* (*pl.* **~es**). wild or half-domesticated Australian dog (Austral. sl.) cheat, traitor, coward. [Aboriginal]

di'ngus (-ngg-) *n.* (colloq.) gadget, what's-its-name. [f. Du. *ding* thing]

di'ng|y (-njī) *a.* dull-coloured or drab; grimy, dirty-looking; hence **~ILY²** *adv.*, **~iNESS** *n.* [perh. rel. to DUNG; see -Y²]

di'ning *n.* In vbl senses; **~-car**, railway carriage in which meals are served; **~-room**, room in house where meals are eaten; **~-table** (on which meals are served in dining-room etc.). [f. DINE + -ING¹]

di'nkel *n.* = SPELT². [G]

di'nkum *a.* & *n.* (Austral. & NZ colloq.) **1.** *a.* genuine, real; **~ oil**, the honest truth, reliable information. **2.** *n.* hard work. [19th c.; orig. unkn.]

di'nky *a.* (colloq.). ||pretty, neat, dainty; *trifling. [f. Sc. *dink* neat (of unkn. orig.) + -Y²]

di'nner *n.* chief meal of day, whether at midday or evening (formal meal with several courses); public banquet in honour of person or event; **~-dance**, dinner followed by dancing; ||**~-jacket**, man's short usu. black coat for evening dress; **~-SERVICE¹** or

-*set*; ∼-**table** (at which dinner is eaten); ∼-**wagon,** trolley with tiers for holding dishes etc.; hence ∼LESS *a.* [ME, f. *di(s)ner*; see DINE, -ER⁴]

dinŏr'nis *n.* ostrich-sized New Zealand flightless bird of genus *Dinornis* now extinct, moa. [f. Gk *deinos* terrible + *ornis* bird]

di'nosaur *n.* reptile (freq. huge) of Mesozoic era; hence **dinosaur'**IAN *a.* & *n.* [f. mod. L *dinosaurus* f. Gk *deinos* terrible + *sauros* lizard]

di'nothēre *n.* huge elephant-like animal of extinct genus *Deinotherium*. [f. mod. L *dinotherium* f. Gk *deinos* terrible + *thērion* wild beast]

dint *n.*, & *v.t.* **1.** *n.* (arch.) blow, stroke. **2.** **by** ∼ **of,** by force or means of. **3.** mark made by blow or pressure, dent. **4.** *v.t.* mark with dints, dent. [ME, f. OE *dynt*, and partly f. cogn. ON *dyntr*; ult. orig. unkn.]

diŏ'cĕsan *a.* & *n.* **1.** *a.* of a diocese. **2.** *n.* bishop in relation to diocese or its clergy; ||member of diocese in relation to bishop. [ME, f. F *diocésain* f. LL. *diocesanus* (as foll.; see -AN)]

di'ocèse *n.* district under pastoral care of bishop. [ME f. OF *diocise* f. LL *diocesis* f. L f. Gk DI³(*oikēsis* f. *oikeō* inhabit) administration]

di'ōde *n.* thermionic valve having two electrodes; semiconductor rectifier having two terminals. [f. DI-² + ELECTRODE]

dioe'cious (-ē'shus) *a.* **1.** (Bot.) with male and female organs on separate plants. **2.** (Zool.) having the two sexes in separate individuals. [f. DI-² + Gk -*oikos* -housed + -OUS]

Diony'siăc, -ian, *adjs.* of Dionysus, the Greek god of wine, or his worship; sensual, unrestrained. [f. L *Dionysius* a. f. L f. Gk *Dionusos*, + -AN]

Diŏphă'ntīne *a.* (Math.) ∼ **equations** (containing more unknowns than there are equations, but usu. to be solved for rational numbers). [f. *Diophantus*, Alexandrian mathematician of 3rd c. + -INE¹]

||**diŏ'ptre** (-ter), *****diŏ'pter,** *n.* refractive power of lens having focal length of one metre; unit of refractive power when this is expressed as reciprocal of focal length in metres. [F *dioptre* f. L f. Gk *dioptra* (see foll.)]

diŏ'ptr|ic *a.* serving as medium for sight, assisting sight by refraction, (*dioptric glass, lens, system*); of refraction, refractive; hence ∼ICS *n.*, part of optics dealing with refraction. [f. Gk *dioptrikos* (DI³*optra* kind of theodolite; see -IC)]

diora'ma (-rah'-) *n.* scenic painting in which changes in colour and direction of illumination simulate sunrise etc.; small representation of scene with three--dimensional figures, viewed through window etc.; small-scale model or film-set; hence **diorā'm**IC *a.* [f. DI-³ + Gk *horama* -*atos* (*dioraō* see)]

di'or|īte *n.* variety of GREEN¹*stone* (1); hence ∼i'tIC *a.* [F, irreg. f. Gk *diorizō* distinguish + -ITE¹]

diŏ'xīde *n.* (Chem.) oxide containing two atoms of oxygen (*carbon dioxide*). [f. DI-² + OXIDE]

dip¹ *v.* (-pp-). **1.** *v.t.* put or let down into liquid, immerse; dye thus; make (candle) by immersing wick in hot tallow; wash (sheep) in vermin-killing liquid; take *up* (liquid, grain, etc.) in scoop, pan, etc., take *out of* (liquid etc.) thus. **2.** lower (esp. flag, sail, aircraft's wing in flight) for a moment esp. as salute; ||lower (beam of vehicle's headlight) to reduce its brightness; ||(colloq.) involve in debt, mortgage. **3.** *v.i.* go under water and emerge quickly; put hand, ladle, etc., *into* to take something out (∼ **into,** spend from one's *pocket, purse, reserves,* etc.); go below any surface or level (*sun dips below horizon; bird dips and rises in flight; balance-scale dips*). **4.** extend downwards; have downward slope (esp. of magnetic needle, and of strata; ∼'**ping-needle,** one so mounted as to measure magnetic dip). **5.** look cursorily *into* (book etc.). [OE *dyppan* f. Gmc **dupjan*, cogn. w. DEEP¹]

dip² *n.* **1.** dipping (LUCKY¹ *dip*); quantity dipped up; (colloq.) bathe in sea etc.; (sl.) pickpocket. **2.** (Astron. & Surv.) apparent depression of horizon seen by observer's elevation; (Phys.) angle made by magnetic

needle with horizon. **3.** downward slope of stratum, road, etc.; depression in skyline etc. **4.** tallow candle. **5.** washing-preparation for SHEEP etc. **6.** sauce or dressing into which food is dipped before eating. **7.** ∼-**circle,** dipping-needle with graduated vertical circle; ∼-**needle,** = *dipping-needle* (see prec.); ∼-**net,** small fishing-net with long handle; ∼ **pen,** pen that has to be dipped in ink, not fountain-pen; ∼-**stick,** rod for measuring depth of liquid; ||∼-**switch,** switch for dipping vehicle's headlight beams. [f. prec.]

Dip. *abbr.* Diploma.

||**Dip. A. D.** *abbr.* Diploma in Art and Design.

Dip. Ed. *abbr.* Diploma in Education.

dīpĕ'ptīde *n.* (Chem.) peptide formed by combination of two amino-acids. [f. DI-² + PEPTIDE]

||**Dip. H.E.** *abbr.* Diploma of Higher Education.

diphthēr'ia *n.* acute infectious bacterial disease with inflammation of a mucous membrane esp. of throat, and formation of false membrane; hence **diphthēr'i**AL, **diphthĕ'r**IC, **diphtheri'ti**C, **di'phther**IOID, *adjs.* [mod. L, f. F *diphthérie*, earlier *diphthérite* f. Gk *diphthera* skin, hide; see -IA¹, -ITIS]

di'phthŏng *n.* union of two vowels (letters or sounds) pronounced in one syllable (as in *coin, loud, side*); two vowel characters representing sound of single vowel (as in *feat*); compound vowel character, ligature, (as *æ*); hence **diphthŏ'ng**AL *a.*, ∼IZE (3) *v.t. & i.*, (-ngg-). [f. F *diphtongue* f. LL f. Gk DI² (*phthoggos* -sounded f. *phthoggos* voice)]

diplo- *comb. form.* double, as: ∼**co'ccus,** coccus occurring mainly in pairs; **diplo'docus** (-ŏ'd-) [Gk *dokos* wooden beam], giant herbivorous dinosaur. [f. Gk *diplous* double + -o-]

di'ploid *a.* & *n.* (Biol.) (organism or cell) having chromosomes in homologous pairs; hence ∼Y¹ *n.*, condition of being diploid. [G, f. as DIPLO- + -OID]

diplō'ma *n.* **1.** State paper, official document, charter. **2.** document conferring honour or privilege; (certificate of) university or college (**or school) degree or qualification, whence ∼'D², ∼ED² (-mad), *a.* [L, f. Gk *diplōma -atos* folded paper (*diploō* to fold f. *diplous* double)]

diplō'macy *n.* management of, skill in managing, international relations; adroitness in personal relations, tact. [f. F *diplomatie* (*diplomatique* DIPLOMATIC after *aristocratie*; see -ACY)]

di'plomăt *n.* one engaged in diplomacy, esp. accredited to court or seat of government; adroit negotiator. [f. F *diplomate*, back-form. f. *diplomatique* (see DIPLOMATIC)]

di'plomāte *n.* holder of diploma. [f. DIPLOMA + -ATE¹]

diploma'tic *a.* & *n.* **1.** *a.* of diplomas (sense 1); of diplomacy (∼ **bag,** bag containing official mail from embassy etc.; ∼ **corps,** ambassadors and their staff at a court or seat of government; ∼ **immunity,** exemption of diplomatic staff etc. abroad from arrest, taxation, etc.; ∼ **service,** branch of public service concerned with representation of country abroad); skilled in diplomacy, tactful; proceeding by negotiation; (of statement etc.) uncandid, subtle; (of edition etc.) exactly reproducing the original; hence **diplomă'tic**ALLY *adv.* **2.** *n.* (in *sing.* or *pl.*) palaeographic and critical study of diplomas (sense 1). [f. mod. L *diplomaticus* and F *-ique* f. L DIPLOMA; see -IC]

diplō'matist *n.* = DIPLOMAT. [f. as DIPLOMAT + -IST]

diplō'matīze, -īse (-īz), *v.i.* act as diplomat; use diplomatic skill. [f. DIPLOMAT + -IZE]

di'pōle *n.* (Phys.) object oppositely charged or magnetized at two points or poles; (Chem.) molecule in which positive and negative charges are separated (Radio etc.) aerial of two equal rods in line, meta strip serving as reflector for a certain wavelength; hence **dipō'l**AR¹ *a.*, having two poles, as a magnet. [f DI-² + POLE²]

di'pper *n.* in vbl senses; Anabaptist or Baptist; diving bird, esp. water OUZEL; ladle; BIG *dipper*, LITTLE *dipper* [ME, f. DIP¹ + -ER¹]

di'ppy *a.* (sl.) crazy. [20th c.; orig. uncert.]

di'psō *n.* (*pl.* ~s). (colloq.) =DIPSOMANIAC. [abbr.]

dipsomā'nia *n.* morbid craving for alcoholic liquor; hence **dipsoma'niac** *n.* [f. Gk *dipso-* (*dipsa* thirst; see -O-) + -MANIA]

di'pteral *a.* (Archit.) with double peristyle. [f. L f. Gk DI²(*pteros* -winged f. *pteron* wing) + -AL]

di'pteran *a.* & *n.* (member) of the order Diptera (see foll.). [f. mod. L f. Gk *diptera* neut. pl. of *dipteros* two-winged (as DI-², *pteron* wing) + -AN]

di'pterous *a.* (Entom.) two-winged, belonging to the order Diptera (insects with one pair of membranous wings, e.g. fly, gnat, mosquito); (Bot.) having two winglike appendages. [f. mod. L f. Gk *dipteros* (see prec.) + -OUS]

di'ptych (-ĭk) *n.* ancient hinged two-leaved writing-tablet with inner sides waxed; painting, esp. altar-piece, on two leaves closing like book. [f. LL *diptycha* f. Gk DI²(*ptukha* neut. pl. of -*ptukhos* f. *ptukhē* fold)]

dīre *a.* dreadful, calamitous; ominous; urgent (*in dire need*); hence ~LY² (dīr'lĭ) *adv.* [f. L *dīrus*]

dīre'ct¹ *v.t.* **1.** give indications for delivery of (letter etc. *to* person or place); utter or write *to* or to be conveyed *to* (*I direct my remarks to you*); send (remark, blow, etc., *at, towards*); turn (thing, person, eyes, efforts, attention) straight *to* or *towards* or *at* something, tell (person) the way (*to*); assign (worker) to particular industry etc. **2.** control, govern movements of; guide as adviser, principle (*duty directs my actions*), etc.; order (person) *to* do, thing *to be* done; supervise acting etc. of (film, play, etc.); give orders (*that*, or abs.). [ME, prob. f. foll.]

dīre'ct² *a.* & *adv.* **1.** straight, not crooked(ly) or oblique(ly) or round about (*the direct road; went direct to heaven*); (of descent) lineal(ly), not collateral(ly); (of argument) following uninterrupted chain of cause and effect etc.; without intermediaries (*prefer every direct dealings, to deal with him direct; as a direct result of his action*). **2.** straightforward, frank(ly), going straight to the point, not ambiguous(ly). **3.** *a.* diametrical (*direct contradiction, contrary, opposite*). **4.** (Astron.) proceeding from west to east, not retrograde. **5.** (Mus., of interval or chord) not inverted. **6.** ~ **action**, exertion of pressure on the community by action (e.g. strike or sabotage) seeking immediate effect, rather than by Parliamentary means; ~ **current**, (Electr.) current flowing in one direction only; ~ **debit** (of bank account at request of creditor); ~ **dye** (not needing mordant), ||~ **grant** (of money given to certain schools by Government not local authority); ~ **hit** (without ricochet, or exactly on target); ~ **labour** (by employees without intervention of contractor); ~ **method**, teaching foreign language without use of native language or study of formal grammar; ~ **object** (Gram., expressing primary object of action of verb); ~ **proportion**, relation between quantities whose ratio is constant; ~ **ray** (not reflected or refracted); ~ **rule** (without devolution); ~ **speech**, words quoted as actually spoken, not as modified in reporting; ~ **tax** (levied on person who bears the ultimate burden of the tax, e.g. income tax, but not value added tax). **7.** Hence ~NESS *n.* [ME, f. L *directus* p.p. of DI¹(*rigere rect-* = *regere* put straight)]

dīre'ction *n.* **1.** directing, aiming, guiding, managing; (usu. in *pl.*) instruction what to do, order. **2.** course pursued by moving body, point to or from which, line along which, person or thing moves or looks, (*in the direction of London*; **sense of** ~, ability to know without guidance the places towards which one is walking, etc.; ~-**finder**, receiver of radio waves that determines the direction from which they come; ~-**indicator**, device showing direction in which driver is about to take motor vehicle); scope, sphere, subject (*new directions of inquiry; improvement in many directions*); hence ~AL *a.* (esp. of radio transmission within a narrow angle). [ME f. F, or f. L *directio* (as prec.; see -ION)]

dīre'ctive *a.* & *n.* **1.** *a.* serving to direct. **2.** *n.* general instruction for procedure or action. [ME, f. med. L *directivus* (as DIRECT²; see -IVE)]

dīre'ctly *adv.* & *conj.* **1.** *adv.* in a direct manner; exactly (*directly in front of*); at once, without delay; presently, in no long time. **2.** *conj.* ||(colloq.) as soon as (*went directly I knew*). [ME, f. DIRECT² + -LY²]

Dīre'ctoire (-twär) *a.* (Dressmaking & Art). in imitation of styles prevalent during the French Directory (~ **knickers**, straight knee-length kind). [F, as DIRECTORY]

dīre'ctor *n.* superintendent, manager, esp. member of managing-board of commercial company, (~-**general**, chief administrator); person who directs film, play, etc.; (Eccl.) priest acting as spiritual adviser; (Fr. Hist.) member of Directory; hence **dīrectōr'IAL** *a.*, ~SHIP *n.* [f. AF *directour* f. LL *director* governor (as DIRECT²; see -OR)]

dīre'ctorate *n.* office of director; board of directors. [f. prec. + -ATE¹]

dīre'ctory *n.* book with list of telephone subscribers, inhabitants of district, members of profession etc., with various details; (Fr. Hist., *D*~) revolutionary executive of five persons in power 1795–9; book of rules, esp. for order of public or private worship. [f. LL *directorium* neut. (as n.) of *directorius* adj. (as DIRECT²; see -ORY)]

dīre'ctress, dīre'ctrice (-ēs), *ns.* woman director. [f. DIRECTOR + -ESS¹, F *directrice* f. as foll.]

dīre'ctr|ix *n.* (*pl.* ~ices *pr.* -isēz). (Geom.) fixed line used in describing curve or surface. [med. L, f. LL DIRECTOR; see -TRIX]

dīr'eful (dīr'f-) *a.* (literary). terrible, dreadful; hence ~LY² *adv.* [f. DIRE + -FUL]

dīrge *n.* song of mourning sung at burial, or in commemoration of the dead; slow mournful song; lament. [ME, f. L *dirige* imper. of *dirigere* DIRECT¹, first wd in Latin antiphon (from Ps. 5: 8) in Matins part of Office of the Dead]

dīr'ham *n.* coin of Morocco etc. [Arab., f. L DRACHMA]

diri'gible (dĭ'-, -rĭ'-) *a.* & *n.* **1.** *a.* (Esp. of balloon) capable of being guided. **2.** *n.* dirigible balloon or airship. [f. as DIRECT²; see -IBLE]

dirig|isme (dērēzhē'zm) *n.* policy of State direction and control in economic and social matters; hence ~i'ste (-ē'st) *a.*, pertaining to such policy. [F (*diriger* DIRECT¹; see -ISM)]

di'riment *a.* nullifying; ~ **impediment** (making marriage null and void from the first). [f. L *dirimere* (*dir-* = DIS-, *emere* take); see -ENT]

dirk *n.* kind of long dagger (esp. of Sc. Highlander). [17th c. *durk*, of unkn. orig.]

dīr'ndl (-del) *n.* woman's dress imitating Alpine peasant costume with bodice and full skirt; ~ (**skirt**), full skirt with tight waistband. [G dial., dim. of *dirne* girl]

dirt *n.* **1.** unclean matter that soils; wet mud; excrement; dirtiness, foul or scurrilous talk; anything worthless; **treat** person **like** ~ (entirely without respect); ~ **cheap**, very cheap. **2.** earth, soil; ***~ **farmer** (raising crops on his own land); ***~ **road**, road without made surface; **do** person ~, (sl.) harm or injure him maliciously; **eat** ~, put up with insult etc., ***make humiliating confession; ***PAY¹ DIRT. **3.** ~-**eating**, disease with morbid craving to eat earth; ~-**track**, course made of rolled cinders, brick-dust, etc., for motor-cycle racing, or of earth for flat races; ***~-**wagon**, dust-cart. [ME, f. ON *drit* excrement]

dīr'ty *a.*, *adv.*, & *v.* **1.** *a.* soiled, foul, like or connected with dirt; (colloq., of nuclear weapon) causing considerable fall-out; obscene, lewd; sordid, mean, despicable; ill-gotten; (of weather) rough, squally; (of colour) not pure or clear, tinged with black or brown. **2.** Hence **dīr'tiLY²** *adv.*, **dīr'tiNESS** *n.* **3.** ~ **dog**, (sl.) despicable or untrustworthy person; ~ **end of the stick**, (colloq.) difficult or unpleasant part in a situation; ~ **look**, (colloq.) look of disapproval or disgust); ~ **money** (paid to those who must handle dirty materials); ~ **trick**, despicable act; ~ **word**, (1) obscene word, (2) word denoting concept regarded as discreditable; ~ **work**, dishonourable or illicit behaviour; **do the** ~, play a mean trick *on*. **4.** *adv.* (sl.) very (*big, great*, etc.). **5.** *v.t.* & *i.* make or become dirty. [f. prec.+-Y²]

dis- *pref.* forming *ns.*, *adjs.*, and *vbs.*, meaning: apart (*distinguish*), away (*dispose*), utterly (*disannul, disembowel, disgruntled*), not (*dishonest*), reverse of action (*disabuse*), absence of action (*disbelieve*) or state (*disaccord*), removal of thing (*disarm*) or quality (*disable*), expulsion from (*disbar*). [f. or after OF *des-*, or LL *dis-* (L DE-), or L *dis-*, cogn. w. *bis* twice; cf. DI-¹, DIF-]

disabi'lity *n.* thing or lack that prevents one's doing something; legal disqualification; physical incapacity caused by injury or disease. [f. DIS-+ABILITY]

disa'ble *v.t.* make unable, incapacitate *from doing* or *for* work etc.; (esp. in *p.p.*) cripple, deprive of or reduce power of acting, walking, etc.; disqualify legally; hence ~MENT (-bel-m-) *n.* [ME, f. DIS-+ABLE]

disabū'se (-z) *v.t.* undeceive, disillusion, (person, mind); relieve *of* illusion etc. [f. DIS-+ABUSE²]

disaccō'rd *n.*, & *v.i.* disagree(ment), (be at) variance. [ME, f. F *désaccorder* v. (as DIS-, ACCORD¹)]

disadva'ntage (-vah'-) *n.* unfavourable condition (*taken at a disadvantage*); loss or injury to reputation etc. [ME, f. OF *desavantage* (as DIS-, ADVANTAGE¹)]

disadva'ntaged (-vah'ntijd) *a.* placed in unfavourable conditions (esp. of person lacking normal social opportunities etc.). [p.p. of *disadvantage* v., f. prec.]

disàdvantā'geous (-jŭs) *a.* involving disadvantage or discredit; derogatory; hence ~LY² *adv.* [f. DIS-+ADVANTAGEOUS]

disaffe'ctèd *a.* estranged, unfriendly; disloyal, esp. to one's superiors. [p.p. of *disaffect* v., orig. = dislike, disorder (DIS-, AFFECT¹,²)]

disaffe'ction *n.* political discontent, disloyalty. [f. DIS- or prec., after AFFECTION]

disaffi'li|āte *v.t.* & *i.* cease affiliation (of); detach; hence ~A'TION *n.* [f. DIS-+AFFILIATE]

disaffi'rm *v.t.* (Law). reverse (previous decision); repudiate (settlement); hence **disàffirm**A'TION *n.* [f. DIS-+AFFIRM]

||**disaffō'rest** *v.t.* reduce from legal status of forest to that of ordinary land; clear of forests; hence ~A'TION *n.* [ME, f. AL DIS(*afforestare* AFFOREST)]

disagree' *v.i.* ~ (**with**), differ in nature (from), be unlike, not correspond (to); ~ (**with**), differ in opinion (from), dissent (from), quarrel (with); ~ **with**, (of food, climate, etc.) prove unsuitable for, have bad effects on, (person, his health, digestion, etc.); hence ~MENT *n.* [ME, f. OF *desagreer* (as DIS-, AGREE)]

disagree'ab|le (-grī'a-) *a.* & *n.* **1.** *a.* not to one's taste, unpleasant; unamiable, bad-tempered; hence ~leNESS (-beln-) *n.*, ~LY² *adv.* **2.** *n.* (in *pl.*) disagreeable things or experiences. [ME, f. OF *desagreable* (as DIS-, AGREEABLE)]

disallow' *v.t.* refuse to sanction or accept as reasonable or admit, prohibit. [ME, f. OF *desalouer* (as DIS-, ALLOW)]

disàmbi'gū|āte *v.t.* remove ambiguity from; so ~A'TION *n.* [f. DIS-+AMBIGUOUS+-ATE³]

disame'nitў *n.* disadvantage, unpleasant feature of place etc.). [f. DIS-+AMENITY]

disannu'l *v.t.* (-ll-). cancel, annul. [f. DIS-+ANNUL]

disappear' *v.* **1.** *v.i.* cease to be visible, vanish, pass from sight or existence. **2.** *v.t.* cause to disappear. **3.** Hence ~ANCE *n.* [ME, f. DIS-+APPEAR]

disappoi'nt *v.t.* fail to fulfil desire or expectation of, break appointment with, (person, or abs.; *disappointed at* failure, *in* thing, *of* one's expected gain, *that, to find* etc., *in* or *with* person; **agreeably** etc. ~**ed**, glad to find one's fears groundless); frustrate (hope, purpose, etc.; person *in love*); hence ~MENT *n.*, event etc. that disappoints, resulting distress. [ME, f. F *désappointer* (as DIS-, APPOINT)]

disàpprobā'tion *n.* disapproval; so **disà'pprobā**tIVE, **disà'pprobāt**ORY, *adjs.* [f. DIS-+APPROBATION]

disappro'v|e (-ōō'v) *v.t.* & *i.* have or express unfavourable opinion (of or *of*); hence ~AL 2 *n.* [f. DIS-+APPROVE]

disā'r'm *v.* **1.** *v.t.* deprive of or *of* weapons; deprive of weapon (esp. in Fencing); deprive (city, ship) of means of defence; reduce (army) to peace footing; deprive of power to injure; remove fuse of (bomb etc.); pacify hostility or suspicions of, whence ~ING² *a.* **2.** *v.i.* (Of nation etc.) disband or reduce its armed forces, whence **disar'mament** *n.* [ME, f. OF *desarmer* (as DIS-, ARM³)]

disarra'nge (-nj) *v.t.* bring into disorder, disorganize; hence ~MENT (-jm-) *n.* [f. DIS-+ARRANGE]

disarray' *n.*, & *v.t.* (throw into) disorder. [ME, f. or after DIS-+ARRAY¹,²]

disàrti'cūl|āte *v.t.* & *i.* separate or be separated at the joints; hence ~A'TION *n.* [f. DIS-+ARTICULATE²]

disàsse'mble *v.t.* take (machine etc.) to pieces; so **disàsse'MB|LY** *n.* [f. DIS-+ASSEMBLE]

disàssō'ci|āte (-shī-, -sĭ-) *v.t.* & *i.* = DISSOCIATE; hence ~A'TION *n.* (esp. Psych.). [f. DIS-+ASSOCIATE²]

disa'st|er (-zah'-) *n.* sudden or great misfortune, calamity; complete failure (*a record of disaster*); ~**er area** (in which major disaster has recently occurred); so ~ROUS *a.* [orig. 'unfavourable aspect of star', f. F *désastre* or f. It. *disastro* (as DIS-, *astro* f. L *astrum* star)]

disavow' *v.t.* say one does not know or have responsibility for or approve of; disclaim, repudiate; hence ~AL 2 *n.* [ME, f. OF *desavouer* (as DIS-, AVOW)]

disbà'nd *v.t.* & *i.* discontinue organized state (of), disperse, (troops etc.); hence ~MENT *n.* [f. obs. F *desbander* (as DIS-, BAND¹ 4)]

disbā'r *v.t.* (-rr-). expel from membership of the bar, deprive of status of barrister; hence ~MENT *n.* [f. DIS-+BAR¹ 5]

disbelie've *v.* **1.** *v.t.* refuse to believe (person, statement, etc.). **2.** *v.i.* be a sceptic; have no faith *in*. **3.** So **disBELIE'F**, ~ER¹, *ns.* [f. DIS-+BELIEVE]

||**disbe'nch** *v.t.* deprive of status of bencher. [f. DIS-+BENCH]

disbou'nd *a.* (Of pamphlet etc.) removed from bound volume. [f. DIS-+p.p. of BIND¹]

disbū'd *v.t.* (-dd-). remove (esp. superfluous) buds of. [f. DIS-+BUD¹]

disbū'r'den *v.t.* relieve of or *of* a burden; get rid of, discharge, (load, anxieties, etc.). [f. DIS-+BURDEN¹]

disbū'r'se *v.* **1.** *v.t.* expend (money); defray (cost). **2.** *v.i.* pay money. **3.** Hence **disbū'r'SAL**, ~MENT (-sm-), *ns.* [f. OF *desbourser* (as DIS-, BOURSE)]

disc, disk, *n.* **1.** thin circular plate of any material (e.g. medal, coin); round flat or apparently flat surface (*sun's disc*) or mark; round flattened part in body, plant, etc., e.g. layer of cartilage between vertebrae (**slipped** ~, one that has become displaced and causes lumbar pain by pressure on nerves); gramophone record. **2.** ~ **brake** (using disc--shaped friction surfaces); ~ **harrow** (with row(s) of concave discs at oblique angle); ~ **jockey**, (colloq.) compère of broadcast programme of gramophone records; ~ **parking**, system in which parked vehicles must display disc showing time of arrival or latest permitted time of departure. [f. F *disque* or f. L DISCUS]

discā'lced (-st) *a.* (Of friar or nun) barefooted or only sandalled. [var. of *discalceated* (after F *déchaux*) f. L DIS(*calceatus* f. *calceus* shoe); see -ATE², -ED¹]

discā'r'd¹ *v.t.* cast aside, give up, (clothes, unwanted material, habit, belief, friend, etc.); throw out or reject from hand at cards (specified card, or abs. of playing non-trump that does not follow suit). [f. DIS-+CARD²]

discā'r'd² *n.* discarded card(s) or thing(s). [f. prec.]

discā'r'nate *a.* disembodied, separated from the flesh. [f. DIS-+L *caro carnis* flesh +-ATE²]

discēr'n *v.t.* **1.** perceive clearly with mind or senses, make out by thought or by gazing, listening, etc.;

hence ∿IBLE *a.*, ∿ING² *a.*, (esp.) having quick or true insight; ∿MENT *n.*, (esp.) insight, keen perception. **2.** (arch.) distinguish (good *and* or *from* bad, *between* good and bad). [ME, f. OF *discerner* f. L DIS(*cernere cret-* separate)]

discĕr'pt|ible *a.* (literary). that can be plucked apart, not indestructibly one; hence ∿IBI'LITY *n.* [f. L DIS(*cerpere cerpt-* = *carpere* pluck) + -IBLE]

discĕr'ption *n.* (arch.) pulling apart, severance; severed piece. [f. LL *discerptio* (as prec.; see -ION)]

dischằr'g|e¹ *v.* **1.** *v.t.* relieve (ship etc.) of load; fire (gun). **2.** release electric charge from; hence ∿ER¹ (2) *n.* **3.** dismiss, cashier, (*was discharged from the service*); release (prisoner), relieve (bankrupt) of residual liability, let go (patient, jury). **4.** put forth, get rid of, send out, emit, (missile, liquid, purulent matter, abuse); unload from ship; carry out, pay, perform, (duty, debt, vow); (Law) cancel (order of court). **5.** *v.i.* undergo discharge of contents; (of river) flow *into* sea etc. [ME, f. OF *descharger* (as DIS-, CHARGE²)]

dischằrge² (-ắr'j, dĭ'-) *n.* discharging or being discharged; unloading (of ship or cargo); firing of gun etc.; emission (of liquid, purulent matter), substance emitted; release of electric charge esp. with emission of light; release, exoneration, exemption, acquittal, written certificate of these; dismissal; liberation; payment (*of* debt); performance (*of* obligation). [ME, f. prec.]

discī'ple *n.* **1.** one of Christ's personal followers, esp. one of the twelve Apostles; any early believer in Christ. **2.** follower or adherent of any leader of thought, art, conduct, etc. **3.** Hence ∿SHIP (-pelsh-) *n.*, **discī'pūl**AR¹ *a.* [OE *discipul* f. L *discipulus* (*discere* learn)]

disciplinằr'ian *n.* maintainer of discipline (sense 2) (*strict, good, poor, no, disciplinarian*). [f. as foll. + -AN]

disciplīnằry (dĭ'-, -lĭ'n-) *a.* of or promoting discipline (sense 2). [f. med. L *disciplinarius* (as foll.; see -ARY¹)]

dĭ'sciplin|e¹ *n.* **1.** branch of instruction or learning; mental and moral training, adversity as effecting this; system of rules for conduct; behaviour according to established rules. **2.** order maintained among school-children, soldiers, prisoners, etc.; control exercised over members of church or other organization. **3.** chastisement; (Eccl.) mortification by penance. **4.** Hence ∿AL *a.* [ME f. OF, f. L *disciplina* (*discipulus* DISCIPLE; see -INE⁴)]

dĭ'sciplin|e⁸ *v.t.* bring under control, train to obedience and order, drill; punish; chastise; hence ∿ABLE *a.* [ME, f. OF *discipliner* or f. LL & med. L *disciplinare*, f. as prec.]

disclaï'm *v.t.* renounce legal claim to (thing or abs.); disown, disavow, deny one's connection with, (*responsibility* etc.). [ME, f. AF *desclaim-* stressed st. of *desclamer* (as DIS-, CLAIM¹)]

disclaï'mer *n.* act of disclaiming, renunciation, disavowal. [ME f. AF (= prec. as n.; see -ER⁴)]

disclō'se (-z) *v.t.* remove cover from, expose to view; make known, reveal. [ME, f. OF *desclos-* st. of *desclore* f. Gallo-Rom. **disclaudere* (as DIS-, CLOSE³)]

disclō'sure (-zher) *n.* disclosing; thing disclosed. [f. prec. + -URE, after *closure*]

dĭ'scō *n.* (*pl.* ∿s). (colloq.) discothèque; party at, equipment on, which records are played for dancing. [abbr.]

discŏ'bol|us *n.* (*pl.* ∿i *pr.* ∿-ī). ancient discus--thrower; statue of one in act of throwing. [L, f. Gk *diskobolos* (*diskos* DISCUS, *-bolos* -throwing f. *ballō* to throw)]

discŏ'graphy *n.* catalogue raisonné or study of gramophone records. [f. DISC + -O- + -GRAPHY]

dĭ'scoid *a.* disc-shaped. [f. Gk *diskoeidēs* (*diskos* DISCUS; see -OID)]

‖**disco'lour**, **disco'lor*, (-ŭ'ler) *v.t.* & *i.* change or spoil colour of, stain, tarnish; become stained etc.; so **discolorA'TION**, ‖**-our-**, (-ūler-) *n.* [ME, f. OF *descolorer* or med. L *discolorare*, as DIS- + L *colorare* COLOUR²]

*discombŏ'būlāte *v.t.* (joc.) disturb, disconcert. [prob. based on *discompose* or *discomfit*]

disco'mfit (-ŭ'm-) *v.t.* baffle, thwart, disconcert; (arch.) defeat in battle; so ∿URE *n.* [ME, f. *disconfit* f. OF p.p. of *desconfire* f. Rom. **disconficere* (as DIS-, L *conficere* put together; see CONFECTION)]

disco'mfort (-ŭ'm-) *n.*, & *v.t.* **1.** *n.* uneasiness of body or mind; lack of comfort. **2.** *v.t.* make uneasy. [ME, f. OF *desconfort(er)* (as DIS-, COMFORT)]

discommō'd|e *v.t.* put to inconvenience; so ∿IOUS *a.* [f. obs. F *discommoder* var. of *incommoder*; see DIS-, INCOMMODE]

discompō'se (-z) *v.t.* disturb composure of, ruffle, agitate; hence **discompō's**URE (-zher) *n.* [f. DIS- + COMPOSE]

disconcĕr't *v.t.* spoil, upset, (plan, concerted measures); disturb self-possession of, ruffle, fluster; hence ∿ION, ∿MENT, *ns.* [f. obs. F *desconcerter* (as DIS-, *concerter* CONCERT²)]

disconfïr'm *v.t.* (tend to) disprove (hypothesis etc.); so **disconfirm**A'TION *n.* [f. DIS- + CONFIRM]

disconnĕ'ct *v.t.* break the connection of (things, one *from* another); (Electr.) put (apparatus) out of action by disconnecting parts. [f. DIS- + CONNECT]

disconnĕ'cted *a.* in vbl senses; (of speech or writing) incoherent, with bad connection; hence ∿LY⁸ *adv.*, ∿NESS *n.* [p.p. of prec.]

disconnĕ'ction, ‖**disconnĕ'xion**, (-kshon) *n.* disconnecting; lack of connection, disconnectedness. [f. DISCONNECT after *connection*]

disconsŏ'nsolate *a.* forlorn, inconsolable; unhappy, disappointed; hence ∿LY² (-tli) *adv.*, ∿NESS (-tn-) *n.* [ME, f. med. L DIS(*consolatus* p.p. of L *consolari* console)]

disconte'nt *n.*, & *v.t.* **1.** *n.* dissatisfaction of contentment; grievance. **2.** *v.t.* (esp. in *p.p.*) make dissatisfied; hence ∿MENT *n.* [f. DIS- + CONTENT², ⁴]

disconti'nū|e *v.t.* & *i.* (cause to) cease (to exist or be done or made); cease from, give up, (doing, habit, etc.); cease taking, paying, (newspaper, subscription); so ∿ANCE *n.* [ME, f. OF *discontinuer* f. med. L DIS(*continuare* CONTINUE)]

disconti'nūous *a.* lacking continuity in space or time, having interstices or breaks, intermittent; hence cogn. **discontinū'ity** *n.*, ∿LY² *adv.* [f. med. L DIS(*continuus* CONTINUOUS) + -OUS]

di'scŏrd¹ *n.* **1.** disagreement, opposition of wills, strife; harsh noise, clashing sounds. **2.** (Mus.) lack of harmony between notes sounding together; chord unpleasing or unsatisfactory in itself and requiring to be resolved by another; any interval except unison, octave, perfect fifth and fourth, major and minor third and sixth, and their octaves; single note dissonant with another. [ME, f. OF *descord*, *discord*, f. as foll.]

discŏr'd² *v.i.* disagree, quarrel, be different or inconsistent, (*with*); be dissonant, jar, clash. [ME, f. OF *descorder*, *discorder* f. L DIS(*cors* *-cord-* hearted f. *cor cordis* heart) discordant]

discŏr'd|ant *a.* not in harmony, dissonant, disagreeing, (*of, from, with*); hence *or* cogn. ∿ANCE, ∿ANCY, *ns.*, ∿ant LY² *adv.* [ME f. OF, part. of *discorder* (see prec., -ANT)]

di'scothèque (-těk) *n.* club, baffé, etc., where records are played for dancing. [F, = record-library]

di'scount¹ *n.* deduction from amount due or price of goods in consideration of its being paid promptly or in advance, or for special class of buyers; deduction from amount of bill of exchange etc. by one who gives value for it before it falls due (cf. PREMIUM), (fig.) depreciated, not in demand; (*at* **a** ∿, below nominal or usual price; ‖∿ **house**, firm discounting bills; **∿ **rate**, minimum lending rate; ∿ **shop** etc., one that regularly sells goods at less than normal retail price. [f. obs. F *descompte*, *-conte* (as foll.)]

discou'nt² *v.t.* give or get present worth of (bill not yet due); disregard or disbelieve partly or wholly; lessen, detract from; reduce effect of (event etc.) by previous action; hence ∼ABLE *a*. [f. obs. F *descompter* or f. It. (*di*)*scontare* (as DIS-, COUNT²)]

discou'ntĕnance *v.t.* refuse to countenance; discourage, show disapproval of; disconcert (person). [f. DIS-+COUNTENANCE¹]

discou'rage (-kŭ'-) *v.t.* deprive of courage, confidence, or energy; dissuade *from*; show disapproval of; so ∼MENT (-rīm-) *n*. [ME, f. OF *descouragier* (as DIS-, COURAGE)]

di'scourse¹ (-ôrs) *n*. **1**. (literary). talk, conversation; dissertation, treatise, sermon. **2**. (Ling.) connected series of utterances. [ME, f. L DIS(*cursus* COURSE¹)]

discour'se² (-ôr's) *v.i.* talk, converse; speak or write at length on a subject (*of*, (*up*)*on*, or abs.); (arch.) give forth (music etc.). [f. prec., partly after F *discourir*]

discour'tĕous *a*., **discour'tĕsy̆** *n*., (-kêr'-). impoliteness), rude(ness); hence **discour'tĕous**LY² (-kêr'-) *adv*. [f. DIS-+COURTEOUS, COURTESY]

disco'ver (-kŭ'-) *v.t.* **1**. find out (fact etc., *that* etc., unknown country); become aware *that*. **2**. expose to view, reveal; (arch.) make known; (arch.) exhibit, manifest; (arch.) disclose, betray; (Chess) give (check) by removing one's own obstructing man. **3**. Hence ∼ABLE *a*., ∼ER¹ *n*. [ME, f. OF *descovrir* f. LL DIS(*cooperire* COVER¹)]

disco'verẙ (-kŭ'-) *n*. revealing, disclosure; (Law) compulsory disclosure, by party to action, of facts or documents on which he relies; finding out, making known; thing found out. [f. prec., after *recover*, *recovery*]

discrĕ'dit¹ *n*. loss of repute (*bring discredit on*; *bring into discredit*); person or thing causing loss of repute; doubt, lack of credibility, (*throws discredit on*); loss of commercial credit. [f. DIS-+CREDIT¹]

discrĕ'dit² *v.t.* refuse to believe; bring disrepute to; cause to be disbelieved. [f. DIS-+CREDIT²]

discrĕ'ditab|le *a*. bringing discredit, shameful; hence ∼LY² *adv*. [f. DIS-+CREDITABLE]

discree't *a*. (∼er, ∼est). judicious, prudent; circumspect in speech or action; unobtrusive; hence ∼LY² *adv*. [ME, f. OF *discret -ete* f. L DIS(*cretus* p.p. of *cernere* sift) separate, w. LL sense f. its derivative *discretio* discernment]

discrĕ'p|ant *a*. differing, inconsistent; so ∼ANCY *n*. [f. L DIS(*crepare* creak) be discordant; see -ANT]

discrĕ'te *a*. separate, individually distinct, discontinuous; hence ∼LY² (-tlī) *adv*., ∼NESS (-tn-) *n*. [ME, f. L *discretus*; see DISCREET]

discrĕ'tion *n*. **1**. liberty of deciding as one thinks fit, absolutely or within limits, (**use** one's ∼, make such decision; *it is within* one's *discretion to*; **at the** ∼ **of**, to be settled or disposed of according to the judgement or choice of; **at** ∼, as one pleases); (Law) court's degree of freedom to decide sentence etc.; hence ∼ARY¹ *a*. **2**. being discreet; discernment, prudence, judgement, (**years** or **age of** ∼, age at which one is fit to manage one's own affairs). [ME f. OF, f. L *discretio -onis* (as DISCREET; see -ION)]

discri'min|āte *v.t. & i.* be, set up, or act on the basis of, a difference between or *between*, distinguish *from* another; make a distinction, esp. unjustly on grounds of race or colour or sex, (∼ate **against**, select for unfavourable treatment by taxation etc.); observe distinctions carefully, have good judgement; so ∼A'TION, ∼ātOR, *ns.*, ∼ATIVE, ∼atORY, *adjs*. [f. L *discriminare* (*discrimen -minis* distinction f. *discernere* DISCERN) +-ATE³]

discri'minating *a*. In vbl senses; discerning, acute; hence ∼LY² *adv*. [f. prec.+-ING²]

discrow'n *v.t.* take crown from, depose (sovereign; lit. or fig.). [f. DIS-+CROWN¹, ²]

discū'rsive *a*. rambling, digressive, expatiating; proceeding by argument or reasoning, not intuitive; hence ∼LY² (-vlī) *adv*., ∼NESS (-vn-) *n*. [f. med. L *discursivus* f. L DIS(*currere curs-* run); see -IVE]

di'scus *n*. heavy thick-centred disc thrown in ancient and modern athletic sports. [L, f. Gk *diskos*]

discū'ss *v.t.* examine by argument, debate, whence ∼ANT *n*.; hold conversation about; (arch.) consume (food, wine, meal) with leisurely enjoyment; hence ∼ABLE, ∼IBLE, *adjs*. [ME, f. L DIS(*cutere cuss-* = *quatere* shake) disperse]

discū'ssion (-shon) *n*. examination by argument; a debate; a conversation; (arch.) consumption *of* food etc. with leisurely enjoyment. [ME f. OF, f. LL *discussio -onis* (as prec.; see -ION)]

disdai'n *n*., & *v.t.* **1**. *n*. scorn, contempt. **2**. *v.t.* regard with disdain; think beneath oneself or one's notice (thing, to do, doing). [ME, f. OF *desdeign(ier*) f. Rom. **disdignare* f. L DE(*dignari* f. *dignus* worthy)]

disdai'nful *a*. showing disdain, scornful, contemptuous; hence ∼LY² *adv*., ∼NESS *n*. [f. prec.+-FUL]

disea'se (-zē'z) *n*. unhealthy condition of body, mind, plant, or some part thereof, illness, sickness; particular kind of this with special symptoms or location. [ME, f. OF *desaise* (as DIS-, EASE¹)]

disea'sed (-zē'zd) *a*. affected with disease; abnormal, disordered. [ME, p.p. of *disease* v. f. OF *desaaisier* (as prec.)]

disĕco'nomy̆ *n*. absence or reverse of economy, increase of costs, esp. in large-scale operation. [f. DIS-+ECONOMY]

disĕmbâr'k *v.t. & i.* put or go ashore from ship or on land from aircraft; hence **disĕmbârk**A'TION *n*. [f. F *désembarquer* (as DIS-, EMBARK)]

disĕmbā'rrass *v.t.* free from embarrassment, rid or relieve (*of*); hence ∼MENT *n*. [f. DIS-+EMBARRASS]

disĕmbŏ'd|y̆ *v.t.* separate, free, (soul, idea, etc.) from body or the concrete form; (arch.) disband (troops); hence ∼MENT *n*. [f. DIS-+EMBODY]

disĕmbŏ'gue (-g) *v.i. & t.* (Of river etc.) pour (*itself*) forth at mouth; (fig.) discharge, pour forth. [f. Sp. *desembocar* (as DIS-, *en* in, *boca* mouth)]

disĕmbow'el *v.t.* (||-ll-). remove entrails of; rip up so as to cause bowels to protrude; hence ∼MENT *n*. [f. DIS-'utterly'+EMBOWEL]

disĕmbroi'l *v.t.* extricate from confusion or entanglement. [f. DIS-+EMBROIL]

disĕncha'nt (-ah'-) *v.t.* free from enchantment or illusion; hence ∼MENT *n*. [f. F *désenchanter* (as DIS-, ENCHANT)]

disĕncū'mber (-n-k-) *v.t.* free from encumbrance. [f. DIS-+ENCUMBER]

disĕndow' *v.t.* strip (esp. Church) of endowments; hence ∼MENT *n*. [f. DIS-+ENDOW]

disĕnfrâ'nchīse (-z) *v.t.* disfranchise. [f. DIS-+EN-FRANCHISE]

disĕngā'ge (-n-g-) *v. & n.* **1**. *v.t.* detach, liberate, loosen; separate (engaged parts); remove (troops) from (area of) fighting. **2**. *v.i.* become detached; (Fencing) pass point of sword to other side of opponent's. **3**. *n*. fencer's movement to disengage. [f. DIS-+ENGAGE]

disĕngā'ged (-n-gā'jd) *a*. in vbl senses; at leisure to attend to any visitor or business that comes; vacant, not bespoken; uncommitted. [p.p. of prec.]

disĕngā'gement (-n-gā'jm-) *n*. disengaging; freedom from ties, detachment; ease of manner or behaviour; dissolution of engagement to marry; (Fencing) = DIS-ENGAGE. [f. DISENGAGE+-MENT]

disĕntai'l *v.t.* (Law). free from entail, break the entail of. [f. DIS-+ENTAIL²]

disĕntā'ngle (-nggel) *v*. **1**. *v.t.* extricate, free from complications; unravel, untwist; hence ∼MENT *n*. **2**. *v.i.* become disentangled. [f. DIS-+ENTANGLE]

disĕnthra'l, *-ll, (-aw'l) *v.t.* (-ll-). free from enthralment; hence **disĕnthra'l(l)**MENT (-aw'l-) *n*. [f. DIS-+ENTHRAL]

disĕntī'tle *v.t.* deprive of any rightful claim (*to*). [f. DIS-+ENTITLE]

disĕnto'mb (-ōō'm) *v.t.* remove from tomb, disinter; unearth; hence ∼MENT (-m-m-) *n*. [f. DIS-+ENTOMB]

disĕquili'brium *n*. lack or loss of equilibrium, instability. [f. DIS-+EQUILIBRIUM]

For other words in *dis-* **see** DIS-.

disèstà´blish *v.t.* terminate establishment of; deprive (Church) of State connection; depose from official position; hence ∼MENT *n.* [f. DIS-+ESTABLISH]

diseur´ (dēzȫr´) *n.* (*fem.* **diseuse** *pr.* dēzȫz´). artiste entertaining with spoken monologue. [F, = talker (*dire dis-* say)]

‖**disfā´vour** (-ver), ***disfā´vor**, *n.*, & *v.t.* **1.** *n.* dislike, disapproval; being disliked (*fall into, be in, disfavour*). **2.** *v.t.* regard or treat with disfavour. [f. DIS-+FAVOUR[1, 2]]

disfi´gure (-ger) *v.t.* spoil beauty of, deform, deface; hence ∼MENT *n.* [ME, f. OF *desfigurer* f. Rom. *DIS figurare* (L *figura* FIGURE[1])]

disfo´rèst *v.t.* = DISAFFOREST; clear of forests. [f. AL *disforestare* (as DIS-, *foresta* FOREST)]

disfrä´nchīse (-z) *v.t.* deprive of rights as citizen or of franchise held; deprive (place) of right of sending, (person) of right of voting for, parliamentary representative; hence ∼MENT (-zm-) *n.* [ME, f. DIS-+obs. *franchise* = enfranchise]

disfrŏ´ck *v.t.* unfrock. [f. DIS-+FROCK]

disgŏr´ge *v.t.* eject (as) from throat (what has been swallowed, lit. or fig., esp. wrongfully taken, or abs.); (of river etc.) discharge (waters, or abs.). [ME, f. OF *desgorger* (as DIS-, GORGE[1])]

disgrä´ce[1] *n.* loss of favour or respect, downfall from position of honour, ignominy, shame, (*is in disgrace*); thing or person involving dishonour, cause of reproach. [f. F *disgrâce* f. It. *disgrazia* (as DIS-, GRACE)]

disgrä´ce[2] *v.t.* dismiss from favour, degrade from position of honour; bring shame or discredit on, be a disgrace to. [f. F *disgracier* f. It. *disgraziare* (as prec.)]

disgrä´ceful (-sf-) *a.* shameful, dishonourable; degrading; hence ∼LY[2] *adv.*, ∼NESS *n.* [f. DISGRACE[1]+-FUL]

disgrŭ´ntle|d (-teld) *a.* discontented, moody, sulky; hence ∼MENT *n.* [f. DIS-+*gruntle* obs. frequent. of GRUNT]

disguī´se[1] (-gī´z) *v.t.* conceal identity of (*disguise oneself*, person or thing, *as someone or something else*, *with false beard* etc.), misrepresent, show in false colours; conceal, cover up, (*disguise* one's *intentions*, *opinion*); hence ∼MENT *n.* [ME, f. OF *desguis(i)er* (as DIS-, Rom. *guisa* GUISE)]

disguī´se[2] (-gī´z) *n.* (use of) changed dress or appearance for concealment or deception; disguised condition (BLESSING *in disguise*). [ME, f. prec.]

disgŭ´st[1] *n.* repugnance, strong aversion, indignation, (*at, for*); in ∼, as a result of such feeling (*I left in disgust*). [f. OF *desgoust* f. *desgouster*, or f. It. *disgusto* f. *disgustare* (as DIS-, GUSTO)]

disgŭ´st[2] *v.t.* cause disgust in (*disgusted with, at, by, that, to find* etc.). [f. OF *desgouster* or It. *disgustare* (see prec.)]

disgŭ´stful *a.* disgusting, repulsive; (of curiosity etc.) caused by disgust. [f. DISGUST[1]+-FUL]

dish[1] *n.* **1.** shallow usu. flat-bottomed vessel of earthenware, glass, metal, etc., for holding food at meals or for cooking; (in *pl.*) all utensils after use at meal (*wash the dishes*). **2.** food so held, particular kind of food (MADE *dish*, SIDE[1]-*dish*); (colloq.) attractive person, esp. woman; (sl.) thing that suits one's taste etc. **3.** ‖(arch.) cup, esp. ∼ **of** tea, cup of tea, tea-drinking. **4.** dish-shaped receptacle, object, or cavity; concave aerial for microwaves. **5.** ∼´**cloth**, ∼´**rag**, (for washing dishes); ∼**cloth gourd**, loofah; ∼**-cover** of metal etc. for keeping food in dish hot; ∼´**washer**, (1) water wagtail, (Austral.) restless flycatcher, (2) machine for automatically washing dishes; ∼**-water** (in which dishes have been washed). [OE *disc* plate, bowl, = OS *disk*, OHG *tisc*, ON *tiskr* f. L *discus* DISC]

dish[2] *v.t.* **1.** put (food) into dish ready for serving; (colloq.) circumvent, outmanœuvre; (colloq.) put an end to (hopes etc.); ∼ **out**, (sl.) distribute, esp. carelessly or indiscriminately; ∼ **up**, dish (food), prepare to serve (meal, or abs.), (fig.) seek to present (facts, argument) attractively. **2.** make concave or dish-shaped. [f. prec.]

dishabi´lle (-sabē´l). Var. of DÉSHABILLÉ.

dishär´mon|ȳ (-s-h-) *n.* lack of harmony; discord; so **dishärmŏ´nious** (-s-h-) *a.*, ∼IZE (1) *v.t.* [f. DIS-+HARMONY]

dishear´ten (-s-här´-) *v.t.* make despondent, cause to lose courage or confidence; hence ∼MENT *n.* [f. DIS-+HEARTEN]

‖**dishě´velled**, ***-veled**, (-ld) *a.* (Of hair) loose, disordered; (of person) untidy, ruffled; hence **dishě´vel**MENT *n.* [ME *dischevelee*, f. OF *deschevelé* p.p. (as DIS-, *chevel* hair f. L *capillus*)+-ED[1]]

dishŏ´nèst (-sŏ´-) *a.* (Of person, act, statement) fraudulent, insincere; hence ∼LY[2] *adv.* [ME, f. OF *deshoneste* (as DIS-, HONEST)]

dishŏ´nèsty (-sŏ´-) *n.* lack of honesty; deceitfulness, fraud. [ME, f. OF *deshon(n)esté* (as prec.; see -Y[1])]

‖**dishŏ´nour**[1], ***dishŏ´nor**[1], (-sŏ´ner) *n.* state of shame or disgrace, discredit; thing that causes such state. [ME, f. OF *deshonor* f. Rom. *DIS*-(*honor* HONOUR[1])]

‖**dishŏ´nour**[2], ***dishŏ´nor**[2], (-sŏ´ner) *v.t.* treat without honour or respect; (arch.) violate chastity of; disgrace; refuse to accept or pay (cheque, bill of exchange). [ME, f. OF *deshonorer* f. med. L DIS-(*honorare* HONOUR[2])]

‖**dishŏ´nourab|le**, ***-nor-**, (-sŏ´ner-) *a.* causing disgrace, ignominious; unprincipled, base, against dictates of honour; hence ∼leNESS (-beln-) *n.*, ∼LY[2] *adv.* [f. prec.+-ABLE or DIS-+HONOURABLE]

dishŏr´n (-s-h-) *v.t.* dehorn. [f. DIS-+HORN[1]]

di´shȳ *a.* (sl.) very attractive. [f. DISH[1] 2 'attractive person'+-Y[2]]

disillu´sion (-lū´zhon, -lŏŏ´-) *n.*, & *v.t.* disenchant(ment), free(dom) from illusions; hence ∼IZE (3) *v.t.*, ∼MENT *n.* [f. DIS-+ILLUSION]

disince´ntive *a.* & *n.* (thing) that tends to discourage a particular (esp. economic) action etc. [f. DIS-+INCENTIVE]

disinclīnā´tion (-n-k-) *n.* absence of liking or willingness (*for* course of action, *to do*). [f. DIS-+INCLINATION]

disinclīne´ (-n-k-) *v.t.* make unwilling (*to do, for* course of action). [f. DIS-+INCLINE[1]]

disincŏr´porāte (-n-k-) *v.t.* dissolve (corporate body). [f. DIS-+INCORPORATE]

disinfe´ct *v.t.* cleanse (room, clothes, etc.) of infection; hence or cogn. **disinfe´ct**ANT *a.* & *n.*, **disinfe´ct**ion *n.* [f. F *désinfecter* (as DIS-, INFECT)]

disinfe´st *v.t.* rid (person, building, etc.) of infesting insects, vermin, etc.; so ∼A´TION *n.* [f. DIS-+INFEST]

disinflā´tion *n.* (Econ.) policy designed to counteract inflation without producing disadvantages of deflation; hence ∼ARY[1] *a.* [f. DIS-+INFLATION]

disinformā´tion *n.* deliberately false information. [f. DIS-+INFORMATION]

disingě´nuous (-nj-) *a.* insincere, having secret motives, not candid; hence ∼LY[2] *adv.*, ∼NESS *n.* [f. DIS-+INGENUOUS]

disinhě´rit *v.t.* reject as one's heir, deprive of right of inheritance; hence ∼ANCE *n.* [ME, f. DIS-+INHERIT in obs. sense 'make heir']

disi´ntegr|āte *v.t.* & *i.* separate into component parts or fragments; deprive of or lose cohesion; (Phys.) (cause to) undergo disintegration; hence ∼A´TION *n.*, (e.g., Phys.) process in which nucleus emits particle(s) or divides into smaller nuclei, ∼ātor *n.* [f. DIS-+INTEGRATE[2]]

disinter´ *v.t.* (-rr-). remove (buried object, corpse, etc.) from ground; unearth (lit. or fig.); hence ∼MENT *n.* [f. F *désenterrer* (as DIS-, INTER[1])]

disi´nterèst (-tr-, -ter-) *n.* impartiality; (D) unconcern. [f. DIS-+INTEREST[1]]

disi´nterèsted (-tr-, -ter-) *a.* not influenced by one's own advantage, impartial; (D) uninterested; hence ∼LY[2] *adv.*, ∼NESS *n.* [p.p. of *disinterest* v. divest of interest]

disinvě´stment *n.* realization of invested assets of a person, institution, etc. [f. DIS-+INVESTMENT]

disjecta membra (dĭsjĕktă mĕ'mbră) *n. pl.* fragments, scattered remains. [L, alt. of Horace's *disjecti membra poetae* limbs of a dismembered poet]

disjoi'n *v.t.* separate, disunite, part. [ME, f. OF *desjoindre* f. L DIS(*jungere junct-* join)]

disjoi'nt *v.t.* dislocate, disturb working or connection of; (in *p.p.*, esp. of talk) incoherent, desultory; take to pieces at the joints. [ME, f. obs. *disjoint* adj. f. p.p. of OF *desjoindre*, as prec.]

disju'nction *n.* disjoining, separation. [ME f. OF, or f. L *disjunctio* (as DISJOIN; *see* -ION)]

disju'nctive *a.* disjoining, involving separation; (Logic, of proposition) expressing an alternative; (Gram.) expressing choice between two words etc. (cf. COPULATIVE); hence ~LY² (-vlĭ) *adv.* [ME, f. L *disjunctivus* (as DISJOIN; see -IVE)]

disk. See DISC.

disli'k|e *v.t.*, & *n*. **1.** *v.t.* not like, have aversion or objection to, (doing, person, thing); hence ~ABLE *a.* **2.** *n.* feeling that thing etc. is unattractive, unpleasant, etc.; object of this. [f. DIS- + LIKE²]

di'slocate *v.t.* disturb normal connection of (esp. joint in the body); put (machinery, affairs) out of order or normal course; (Geol.) make (strata) discontinuous; displace. [prob. back-form. f. foll.]

disloca'tion *n.* act or result of dislocating; (Phys.) displacement of crystal lattice structure. [ME f. OF, or f. med. L *dislocatio* f. DIS(*locare* place); see -ATION]

dislo'dge *v.t.* remove from established or fixed position; hence ~MENT, **dislo'dg**MENT, (-jm-) *n.* [ME, f. OF *dislog(i)er* (as DIS-, LODGE²)]

disloy'al *a.* unfaithful to or *to* friend(ship) etc.; untrue to allegiance, disaffected to government, whence ~IST (2) *n.*; hence or cogn. ~LY² *adv.*, ~TY¹ *n.* [ME, f. OF *desloial* (as DIS-, LOYAL)]

di'smal (-z-) *a.* causing or showing gloom, miserable, sombre, dreary; (colloq.) feeble, inept; ||~ **Jimmy**, (colloq.) gloomy person; ~ **science**, (arch.) economics; **the** ~**s**, melancholy; hence ~LY² *adv.*, ~NESS *n.* [orig. n. = unlucky days, ME f. AF *dis mal* f. med. L *dies mali* two days in each month held to be unpropitious]

dismă'ntle *v.t.* strip *of* covering, protection, etc.; pull down, take to pieces; deprive of defences, equipment, etc.; hence ~MENT (-tĕlm-) *n.* [f. OF *desmanteler* (as DIS-, MANTLE¹)]

disma'st (-ah'-) *v.t.* remove mast(s) from (ship). [f. DIS- + MAST¹]

dismay' *v.t.*, & *n.* (fill with) consternation, discourage(ment), (reduce to) despair. [ME, f. OF *de(s)maiier* f. Rom. **dismagare* make powerless f. as DIS- + Gmc **mag-* be able; cf. MAY¹]

disme'mber *v.t.* tear or cut limbs from; partition (empire, country), divide up; hence ~MENT *n.* [ME, f. OF *desmembrer* f. Rom. **desmembrare* f. as DIS- + L *membrum* limb]

dismi'ss *v.* **1.** *v.t.* & *i.* send away, disperse, disband, (assembly, army); allow to go; (Mil. in *imper.*) word of command at end of drilling. **2.** *v.t.* send away (esp. dishonourably) from service or office (*was dismissed the,* or *from the, army*); send away from one's presence. **3.** put out of one's thoughts, cease to feel or discuss; treat (subject) summarily; (Law) send out of court, refuse further hearing to, (case); (Cricket) put (batsman, side) out (usu. *for* score). **4.** Hence ~AL 2 *n.*, ~IBLE, ~IVE, *adjs.*, ~ION (-shon) *n.* [ME, orig. as p.p. after OF *desmis* f. med. L *dismissus* (DIS-, L *mittere* miss-send)]

dismou'nt *v.i.* & *t.* (cause to) alight or fall from or *from* horseback etc.; remove (thing) from its mount (esp. gun from carriage). [f. DIS- + MOUNT²]

Disneyě'sque (dĭznĭĕ'sk) *a.* like the animated cartoons of Disney. [f. W. E. *Disney*, Amer. cartoonist d. 1966 + -ESQUE]

disobě'di|ent *a.* disobeying (~**ent to** orders, master, etc.); rebellious, rule-breaking; so ~ENCE *n.* (CIVIL

disobedience), ~ent**LY²** *adv.* [ME, f. OF *desobedient* (as DIS-, OBEDIENT)]

disobey' (-bā') *v.t.* disregard (orders), break (rules); fail or refuse to obey (person, law, etc., or abs.). [ME, f. OF *desobeir* f. Rom. **desobedire* (as DIS-, OBEY)]

disobli'ge *v.t.* refuse to consider convenience or wishes of. [f. F *désobliger* f. Rom. **desobligare* (as DIS-, OBLIGE)]

disŏr'der¹ *n.* lack of order, confusion; tumult, riot, commotion; disturbance of normal state of body, organ, etc., ailment, disease. [f. foll.]

disŏr'der² *v.t.* disarrange, throw into confusion; put out of good health, upset. [ME assim. to ORDER² of earlier *disordain* f. OF *desordener* (as DIS-, ORDAIN)]

disŏr'derl|ў *a.* **1.** untidy, confused; irregular, unruly, riotous; hence ~iNESS *n.* **2.** contrary to public order or morality (~**ly house**, brothel). [f. DISORDER¹ + -LY¹]

disŏr'ganiz|e, -īs|e (-īz), *v.t.* destroy system, order, etc. of; throw into confusion; (in *p.p.*) lacking organization or system; so ~A'TION *n.* [f. F *désorganiser* (as DIS-, ORGANIZE)]

disorient (-ŏr'-, -ŏ'r-) *v.t.* = foll. [f. F *désorienter* (as DIS-, ORIENT²)]

disorient|āte (-ŏ'r-, -ōr'-) *v.t.* confuse (person) as to his bearings or (fig.) sense of what is correct; hence ~A'TION *n.* [f. DIS- + ORIENTATE]

disow'n (-ō'n) *v.t.* refuse to recognize, repudiate, disclaim; renounce connection with or allegiance to; hence ~ER⁴ *n.* [f. DIS- + OWN²]

dispa'rage *v.t.* bring discredit on; speak slightingly of, depreciate; so ~MENT (-ijm-) *n.* [ME, f. OF *desparagier* marry unequally (as DIS-, *parage* equality of rank f. Rom. **paraticum* f. L *par* equal; see -AGE)]

di'sparate *a.* & *n.* **1.** *a.* essentially different, diverse in kind, incommensurable, without comparison or relation; hence ~LY² (-tlĭ) *adv.*, ~NESS (-tn-) *n.* **2.** *n.* (in *pl.*) things so unlike that there is no basis for their comparison. [f. L DIS(*paratus* p.p. of *parare* prepare) separated, infl. in sense by L *dispar* unequal]

dispa'rity *n.* inequality, difference, incongruity. [f. F *disparité* f. LL *disparitas -tatis* (as DIS-, PARITY)]

dispa'rk *v.t.* convert (parkland) to other uses. [f. DIS- + PARK¹]

dispa'rt *v.t.* & *i.* (arch.) separate, divide. [f. It. or f. L *dispartire* (as DIS-, PART²)]

dispa'ssionate (-sho-) *a.* free from emotion, calm, impartial; hence ~LY² (-tlĭ) *adv.*, ~NESS (-tn-) *n.* [f. DIS- + PASSIONATE]

dispă'tch¹, dèspă'tch¹, *v.t.* send off to a destination or for a purpose; give the death-blow to, kill; get (task, business) promptly done, settle, finish off; eat (food, meal) quickly; hence ~ER¹ *n.*, (esp.) one who gives orders for departure of goods, vehicles, etc. [f. It. *dispacciare* or Sp. *despachar* expedite (as DIS-, It. *impacciare* and Sp. *empachar* hinder, of uncert. orig.)]

dispă'tch², dèspă'tch², *n.* **1.** sending off (of messenger, letter, etc.); putting to death (**happy** ~, hara-kiri); prompt settlement of business, promptitude, efficiency, rapidity. **2.** written message, esp. official communication on State or military affairs (**mention in** ~**es**, distinction given by having one's actions etc. commended in these; ~ **box**, ~**case**, container for carrying these or other documents; ~**rider**, esp. motor-cyclist or horseman carrying military messages), or sent in by newspaper's correspondent. [f. prec., or It. *dispaccio*, Sp. *despacho*, as prec.]

dispe'l *v.t.* (-ll-) dissipate, disperse, scatter, (suspicions, fears, darkness). [f. L DIS(*pellere* drive)]

dispe'nsable *a.* not necessary, that can be done without; (of law etc.) that can be relaxed in special cases. [f. med. L *dispensabilis* (as DISPENSE; see -ABLE)]

dispe'nsarў *n.* place where medicines etc. are dispensed; public or charitable institution for medical advice and dispensing. [f. med. L *dispensarius* (as DISPENSE; see -ARY¹)]

dispénsa'tion *n.* 1. distributing, dealing out. **2.** ordering, management, esp. of the world by Providence;

arrangement made by Nature or Providence; special dealing of Providence with community or person; religious system regarded as divinely ordained for a nation or period (*Mosaic, Christian, dispensation*). **3.** exemption *from* penalty or duty; ∼ **with**, doing without. [ME f. OF, or f. L *dispensatio* (as foll.; see -ATION)]

dispĕ'ns|**e** *v.* **1.** *v.t.* distribute, deal out; administer (sacrament, justice); make up (and give out) (medicine etc.) according to prescription (∼**ing chemist**, one qualified to do this); hence ∼ER[1] *n.*, (esp.) person who dispenses something, device that dispenses a selected quantity at a time. **2.** grant dispensation to (person *from* obligation). **3.** *v.i.* ∼**e with**, relax, give exemption from, (rule), render needless (usu. *the need of* or *for* etc.), do without. [ME, f. OF *despenser* f. L *dispensare* frequent. of DIS(*pendĕre pens-* weigh) weigh or pay out]

dispeo'ple (-pē'p-) *v.t.* depopulate. [ME, f. OF *despeupler* (as DIS-, PEOPLE)]

dispĕr's|**e** *v.* **1.** *v.t.* & *i.* scatter; drive, go, throw or send, in different directions. **2.** *v.t.* send to or station at separate points; put in circulation, disseminate; (Phys.) distribute (small particles) uniformly in fluid (whence ∼ANT *n.*), divide (white light) into its coloured constituents. **3.** Hence ∼AL 2 *n.*, ∼IVE *a.* [ME, f. L DI[1](*spergere spers-* = *spargere* scatter)]

dispĕr'sion (-shon) *n.* dispersing; the D∼, the Jews dispersed among Gentiles after Captivity; (Phys.) mixture of one substance dispersed in another, separation of white light into colours or of any radiation according to wavelength etc.; (Statistics) extent to which values of a variable differ from the mean. [ME, f. LL *dispersio* (as prec.; see -ION) transl. Gk DIASPORA]

dispi'rit *v.t.* (esp. in *p.p.*) make despondent, deject. [f. DIS-+SPIRIT[1]]

displä'ce *v.t.* **1.** shift from its place (∼**d person**, one who has had to leave his home country as a result of war, persecution, etc.); remove from office. **2.** oust, take the place of, put something else in the place of. [f. DIS-+PLACE[1, 2] or obs. F *desplacer*]

displä'cement (-sm-) *n.* **1.** displacing or being displaced; amount by which thing is shifted from its place. **2.** ousting, replacement by something else; (Psych.) substitution of one idea or impulse for another, unconscious transfer of strong unacceptable emotions. **3.** amount or weight of fluid displaced by solid floating or immersed in it (*a ship with a displacement of 11,000 TON's*). [f. prec.+-MENT]

display'[1] *v.t.* exhibit, expose to view; show ostentatiously; reveal, betray, allow to appear; present as a display (see foll.). [ME, f. OF *despleier* f. L DIS(*plicare* fold); cf. DEPLOY]

display'[2] *n.* displaying; exhibition, show, (*is on display*); ostentation; (Print.) arrangement and choice of type with a view to calling attention; presentation of signals or data on screen of cathode-ray tube etc.; bird's special pattern of behaviour as means of visual communication. [f. prec.]

displea's|**e** *v.t.* offend, annoy, make indignant or angry, be unpleasing to; **be ∼ed** (*at, with,* or abs.), disapprove, be indignant or dissatisfied; hence ∼ING[2] *a.* (*to*). [ME, f. OF *desplaisir* (as DIS-, L *placēre* please)]

displea'sure (-lĕ'zher) *n.*, & *v.t.* **1.** *n.* displeased feeling, dissatisfaction, disapproval, anger. **2.** *v.t.* (arch.) cause displeasure to, annoy. [ME, f. OF as prec., assim. to PLEASURE]

dispŏ'rt *v.* & *n.* (literary). **1.** *v.i.* & *refl.* frolic, gambol, enjoy oneself. **2.** *n.* relaxation, pastime. [ME, f. AF *desporter* v., OF *desport* n. f. *desporter* (as DIS-, *porter* carry f. L *portare*)]

dispŏ's|**able** (-za-) *a.* & *n.* **1.** *a.* that can be disposed of, got rid of, made over, or used; at one's disposal; that is designed to be thrown away after one use, not to be laundered or refilled; hence ∼ABI'LITY *n.* **2.** *n.* article that is disposable (esp. in last sense). [f. DISPOSE+-ABLE]

dispō'sal (-zal) *n.* disposing *of*, getting rid *of*; settling, dealing with; bestowal, assignment; sale; control, management, (at one's ∼, available for one's use, subject to one's orders or decisions); placing, disposition, arrangement. [f. foll.+-AL 2]

dispō'se (-z) *v.* **1.** *v.t.* place suitably, at intervals, or in order; bring (person, mind) into certain state (esp. in *pass.*, have a specified tendency of mind: *be* WELL- or *ill disposed*); incline, make willing or desirous, to something or *to* do; give (thing) tendency *to*. **2.** *v.i.* determine course of events (*man proposes, God disposes*); ∼ **of**, do what one will with, get rid of, sell, settle, finish, kill, prove (claim, argument, opponent) to be incorrect, consume (food). [ME, f. OF DIS(*poser*; see POSE[1]), confused with L *disponere* thr. such derivs. as foll.]

disposi'tion (-zĭ'-) *n.* setting in order, arrangement, relative position of parts; (usu. in *pl.*) plan, preparations, stationing of troops ready for attack etc.; ordinance, dispensation, (*a disposition of Providence*); bestowal by deed or will; control, disposal; bent, temperament, natural tendency; inclination *to*. [ME f. OF, f. L DIS(*positio -onis* f. *ponere posit-* place)]

disposse'ss (-oz-) *v.t.* oust, dislodge, (person); deprive *of*; hence **disposse'ssion** (-zĕ'shon) *n.* [f. OF *despossesser* (as DIS-, POSSESS)]

disprai'se (-z) *v.t.*, & *n.* disparage(ment), censure. [ME; n. f. DIS-+PRAISE or v., f. OF *despreisier* f. Rom. *despretiare* f. LL *depretiare* DEPRECIATE]

disproo'f *n.* refutation; thing that disproves. [f. DIS-+PROOF[1]]

dispropŏr'tion *n.* lack of proportion; being out of proportion. [f. DIS-+PROPORTION]

dispropŏr'tionate *a.* lacking proportion; relatively too large or small; hence ∼LY[2] (-tlĭ) *adv.* [f. DIS-+PROPORTIONATE]

dispro've (-ōō'v) *v.t.* prove false, show fallacy of, refute. [ME, f. OF *desprover* (as DIS-, PROVE)]

dispūtab'le (-ū'-, dĭ'-) *a.* open to question, uncertain; hence ∼LY[2] *adv.* [F, or f. L *disputabilis* (as DISPUTE[1]; see -ABLE)]

dispūtä't|**ion** *n.* argument, controversy; debate; formal attack on and defence of set question or thesis; hence ∼IOUS (-shus) *a.*, fond of argument. [ME f. F, or f. L *disputatio* (as foll.; see -ATION)]

dispū'te[1] *v.* **1.** *v.i.* argue, hold disputation, (*with, against,* person; *on, about,* subject); whence **dispū't**ANT *n.*; quarrel, have altercation. **2.** *v.t.* discuss esp. heatedly (*whether, how,* etc.; point, question; question correctness of (statement, alleged fact); resist (landing, advance, etc.); contend for, strive to win, (pre-eminence, possession, victory, ground fought over). [ME, f. OF *desputer* f. L DIS(*putare* reckon estimate]

dispū'te[2] (-ū't; D dĭ'-) *n.* controversy, debate, (in ∼, being argued about; *beyond,* past, without, ∼, certainly, indisputably); heated contention, quarrel, difference of opinion. [f. prec.]

disqualifică'tion (-ŏl-) *n.* In vbl senses; thing that disqualifies. [f. foll.+-FICATION]

disqua'lify (-ŏ'l-) *v.t.* make unfit, disable, (*for* some purpose or office, *from* doing); incapacitate legally, pronounce unqualified; debar from competition because of infringement of rules. [f. DIS-+QUALIFY]

disquī'et *v.t.*, & *n.* **1.** *v.t.* deprive of peace; worry. **2.** *n.* anxiety, unrest. [f. DIS-+QUIET[1, 3]]

disquī'etude *n.* state of uneasiness, anxiety. [f. *disquiet*]

disquisi'tion (-zĭ'-) *n.* long or elaborate treatise or discourse on subject; hence ∼AL *a.* [F, f. L DIS(*quisitio* f. *-quirere -quisit-* = *quaerere* seek; see -ION)]

disrä'te *v.t.* reduce (sailor) to lower rating or rank. [f. DIS-+RATE[1]]

disregär'd *v.t.* & *n.* **1.** *v.t.* pay no attention to, ignore, treat as of no importance. **2.** *n.* indifference, neglect (*of, for*); hence ∼FUL *a.* [f. DIS-+REGARD[1, 2]]

disrĕ'lish *v.t.* dislike, (regard with) distaste. [f. DIS-+RELISH[1, 2]]

disrĕmĕ'mber *v.t. & i.* (esp. dial.) fail to remember. [f. DIS- + REMEMBER]

disrepair' *n.* bad condition due to lack of repairs (*is in disrepair, in a state of disrepair*). [f. DIS- + REPAIR³]

disrĕ'pŭtab|le *a.* discreditable; of bad repute, not respectable in character or appearance; hence ~leNESS (-beln-) *n.*, ~LY² *adv.* [*f.* DIS- + REPUTABLE, after foll.]

disrepū'te *n.* lack of good repute, discredit. [f. DIS- + REPUTE]

disrĕspĕ'ct *n.* lack of respect; discourtesy; so ~FUL *a.* [f. DIS- + RESPECT¹]

disrō'be *v.t. & i.* divest (oneself) of robe or garment (lit. or fig.); undress (oneself).[f. DIS- + ROBE]

disrŭ'pt *v.t.* shatter, separate forcibly; interrupt flow or continuity of; hence ~ION *n.* (**the D~ion**, split in Church of Scotland 1843), ~IVE *a.* [f. L DIS(*rumpere rupt-* break)]

dĭssă'tisfȳ *v.t.* fail to satisfy, make discontented (*dissatisfied with, at, that, to find* etc.); so **dĭs**SATISFA'C-TION *n.* [f. DIS- + SATISFY]

dĭssă've *v.i.* spend more than one's income, by drawing on savings or capital. [f. DIS- + SAVE¹]

dĭssĕ'ct *v.t.* cut into pieces; cut up (animal, plant) to show its parts, structure, etc.; examine part by part, analyse, criticize in detail; hence or cogn. ~ION, ~OR, *ns.* [f. L DIS(*secare sect-* cut)]

dĭssei'se, -ze, (-sē'z) *v.t.* (Law). dispossess (esp. wrongfully) *of.* [ME, f. AF *disseisir,* OF *dessaisir dispossess* (as DIS-, SEIZE)]

dĭssei'sin (-ē'z) *n.* (Law). wrongful dispossession of estates etc. [ME, f. AF *disseisine,* OF *dessaisine* (as DIS-, SEISIN)]

dĭssĕ'mbl|e *v.* **1.** *v.t.* cloak, disguise, conceal, (character, feeling, intention, act). **2.** *v.i.* conceal one's motives etc.; talk or act hypocritically. **3.** Hence ~ER¹ *n.* [ME, alt. after *semblance* of obs. *dissimule* f. OF *dissimuler* f. L DIS(*simulare* SIMULATE)]

dĭssĕ'min|āte *v.t.* scatter about, sow in various places, (esp. fig. of doctrines, sedition, disease, etc.); *disseminated* SCLEROSIS; hence or cogn. ~A'TION, ~ātOR, *ns.* [f. L DIS(*seminare* f. *semen -inis* seed) + -ATE³]

dĭssĕ'nsion (-shon) *n.* discord arising from difference in opinion. [ME f. OF, f. L DIS(*sensio -onis* f. *sentire sens-* feel; see -ION)]

dĭssĕ'nt¹ *v.i.* refuse to assent; disagree, think differently or express such difference (*from*), esp. in religious doctrine from an established, national, or orthodox church. [ME, f. L DIS(*sentire* feel)]

dĭssĕ'nt² *n.* (expression of) difference of opinion; refusal to accept doctrines of established, national, or orthodox church, nonconformity. [f. prec.]

dĭssĕ'nter *n.* In vbl senses; ||(D~) member of a sect that has separated itself from the Church of England, Nonconformist. [f. DISSENT¹ + -ER¹]

dĭssĕ'ntient (-shĭent, -shent) *a. & n.* (person) disagreeing with a majority or official view. [f. DIS(*sentire* feel); see -ENT]

dĭssĕ'piment *n.* (Bot. & Zool.) partition, septum. [f. L DIS(*saepimentum* f. *saepire* to shut in f. *saepes* hedge; see -MENT)]

dĭssertā'tion *n.* detailed discourse on a subject, esp. as submitted for higher degree in university. [f. L *dissertatio* (*dissertare* discuss, frequent. of *disserere -sert-* examine (as DIS-, *serere* join))]

dĭssĕr've *v.t.* do an ill turn to, esp. when intending to help; serve (person) badly or imperfectly; so **dĭs**SER'VICE¹ *n.* [f. DIS- + SERVE]

dĭssĕ'ver *v.t. & i.* sever, divide; hence or cogn. ~ANCE, ~MENT, *ns.* [ME, f. AF *des(c)everer,* OF *dessevrer* f. LL *disseparare* (as DIS-, SEPARATE²)]

dĭ'ssidence *n.* disagreement, dissent. [F, or f. L *dissidentia* (as foll.; see -ENCE)]

dĭ'ssident *a. & n.* (person) disagreeing, at variance, esp. with established doctrine etc.; dissentient. [F, or f. L DIS(*sidēre = sedēre* sit) disagree; see -ENT]

dĭssĭ'milar *a.* unlike (*to*); hence **dĭssĭmilā'r**ITY *n.*, ~LY² *adv.* [f. DIS- + SIMILAR]

dĭssĭ'mil|āte *v.t.* (Philol.) make (sounds in a word) unlike each other, as in *cinnamon,* orig. *cinnamom;* hence ~A'TION *n.*, ~atORY *a.* [f. L DIS(*similis* like), after *assimilate*]

dĭssĭmĭ'lĭtūde *n.* unlikeness. [f. L *dissimilitudo* (as prec.; see -TUDE)]

dĭssĭ'mŭl|āte *v.t. & i.* dissemble; hence or cogn. ~A'TION, ~ātOR, *ns.* [f. L DIS(*simulare* SIMULATE) + -ATE³]

dĭ'ssĭpāt|e *v.t. & i.* disperse, dispel, (cause to) disappear, (cloud, vapour, care, fear, darkness); break up entirely, bring or come to nothing; squander (money); fritter away (energy, attention); hence ~IVE *a.* [f. L DIS(**sipare* throw) + -ATE³]

dĭ'ssĭpātĕd *a.* In vbl senses; given to dissipation, dissolute. [p.p. of prec.]

dĭssĭpā'tion *n.* scattering, dispersion, disintegration; wasteful expenditure *of;* frivolous amusement; intemperate or dissolute living. [F, or f. L *dissipatio* (as DISSIPATE; see -ATION)]

dĭssō'cĭ|āte (-shĭ-, -sĭ-) *v.* **1.** *v.t.* disconnect, separate, in thought or in fact (*from;* ~**ate** oneself **from,** declare oneself unconnected with); (Chem.) decompose, esp. reversibly, e.g. by heat; (Psych.) cause (person's mind) to develop more than one centre of consciousness (~**ated personality,** pathological coexistence of two or more distinct personalities in the same person). **2.** *v.i.* become dissociated. **3.** Hence or cogn. ~A'TION (-sĭ-) *n.*, ~ATIVE *a.* [f. L DIS(*sociare* f. *socius* companion) + -ATE³]

dĭssŏ'l|ūble *a.* that can be disintegrated, loosened, or disconnected; hence ~UBI'LITY *n.*, ~UBLY *adv.* [F, or f. L DIS(*solubilis* SOLUBLE)]

dĭ'ssolute (-ōōt, -ūt) *a.* lax in morals, licentious; hence ~LY² (-tlĭ) *adv.*, ~NESS (-tn-) *n.* [ME, f. L *dissolutus* p.p. of *dissolvere* DISSOLVE]

dĭssolu'tion (-lōō'-, -lū'-) *n.* disintegration, decomposition; undoing or relaxing of bond, partnership, marriage, or alliance; dismissal or dispersal of assembly, esp. of parliament for new election; death; coming or being brought to an end, fading away, disappearance. [ME f. OF, or f. L *dissolutio* (as foll.; see -ION)]

dĭssŏ'lv|e (-z-) *v. & n.* **1.** *v.t. & i.* make or become liquid, esp. by immersion or dispersion in liquid (~**e into tears,** begin to weep copiously); (cause to) vanish; (Cinemat.) change gradually (*into* a different picture); dismiss or disperse (assembly, esp. parliament; cf. prec.); put an end to (partnership etc.), annul; hence ~ABLE *a.* **2.** *n.* act or process of dissolving a picture. [ME, f. L DIS(*solvere solut-* loosen)]

dĭssŏ'lvent (-z-) *a. & n.* (thing) that dissolves or tends to dissipate. [f. L *dissolvere* (as prec., -ENT)]

dĭ'sson|ant *a.* not in harmony, harsh-toned, incongruous; so ~ANCE *n.*, ~antLY² *adv.* [ME f. OF, f. L DIS(*sonare* sound); see -ANT]

dĭssuā'de *v.t.* give advice or exercise influence to discourage or divert (person *from*); so **dĭssuā'**SION (-wā'zhon) *n.*, **dĭssuā'**SIVE (-swā'-) *a.* [f. L DIS(*suadēre suas-* persuade)]

dĭssȳ'llable etc. See DISYLLABLE etc.

dĭssȳ'mmĕ'trical *a.*, **dĭssȳmmĕtrȳ** *n.* (having) no symmetry; (having) symmetry of mirror images or the two hands (esp. of crystals with two corresponding forms). [f. DIS- + SYMMETRICAL, SYMMETRY]

dĭ'staff (-ahf) *n.* cleft stick holding wool or flax wound for spinning by hand; corresp. part of spinning-wheel; woman's work; ~ **side,** female branch of family. [OE *distæf,* f. as STAFF¹, the first element being app. = LG *diesse,* MLG *dise(ne)* bunch of flax]

dĭ'stal *a.* (Anat. or Bot.) situated away from centre of body or point of attachment, terminal; hence ~LY² *adv.* [f. DISTANT + -AL]

dĭ'stance *n. & v.t.* **1.** *n.* being far off, remoteness; avoidance of familiarity, aloofness, reserve, (esp. *keep*

For other words in *dis-* **see** DIS-.

one's, or *at a, distance*). **2.** extent of space between, interval, (**within hailing, walking,** etc., ∼, near enough to reach easily by that means); distant point (*to, from, a distance*; **at a** ∼, far off, not very near); remoter field of vision (*in the distance*; **middle** ∼, in painted or actual landscape, part between foreground and far part); space of time (*at this distance of time*); (Racing) length of 240 yds. or thereabouts (orig. between winning-post and ∼-**post**, used to disqualify slower runners in heats); (Boxing) scheduled duration of fight (**go the** ∼, complete this without previous knock-out etc.). **3.** *v.t.* place or make seem far off; leave far behind in race or competition. [ME f. OF *distance, destance* f. L *distantia* (DI¹*stare* stand apart; see -ANCE)]

di′stant *a.* far, or at a specified distance, away or *from* (*three miles distant*); remote, far apart, in position, time, resemblance, etc., (*a distant prospect, relation, connection, likeness*; *distant ages*; ∼ **early warning,** N. Amer. radar system for detection of missile attack; ∼ **signal** on railway, one in advance of home signal to give warning of latter's setting); not intimate, reserved, cool; hence ∼LY² *adv.* [ME f. OF, or f. L *distant-* part. st. of *distare* (see prec., -ANT)]

distä′ste *n.* dislike, repugnance, (slight) aversion, (*for*); hence ∼FUL (-tf-) *a.* (*to*). [f. DIS- + TASTE²]

diste′mper¹ *v.t.* (arch., usu. in *p.p.*) upset, derange, in health or sanity (*a distempered fancy*). [ME, f. LL DIS(*temperare* mingle correctly)]

distě′mper² *n.* derangement or ailment of body or mind; dog-disease with catarrh, cough, and weakness; similar disease of other animals; (arch.) political disorder. [f. prec.]

distě′mper³ *n.,* & *v.t.* **1.** *n.* method of painting on plaster or chalk with powder colours mixed with yolk or white of egg, size, etc., instead of oil, used for scene-painting and internal walls (*paint in distemper*); paint so used. **2.** *v.t.* paint (wall etc., or abs.) thus. [n. f. v., f. OF *destremper* or f. LL *distemperare* soak, macerate (see DISTEMPER¹)]

distě′nd *v.t.* & *i.* swell out (balloon, vein, nostril, etc.) by pressure from within; so **distě′nsIBLE** *a.,* **distěnsIBI′LITY, distě′nsION** (-shon), *ns.* [ME, f. L DIS(*tendere tens-* stretch)]

di′stich (-k) *n.* (Pros.) pair of verse lines, couplet. [f. L f. Gk DI²(*stikhon* f. *stikhos* line) neut. a. (as n.)]

dï′stichous (-k-) *a.* (Bot.) arranged in two vertical rows. [f. L *distichus* (as prec.) + -OUS]

disti′l, *disti′l|l, *v.i.* & *t.* (-ll-). trickle down; come or give forth in drops, exude; turn to vapour by heat, condense by cold, and re-collect (liquid, esp. to remove dissolved impurities or to separate mixed liquids boiling at different temperatures); extract essence of (plant etc., or (fig.) doctrine etc.); drive (volatile constituent) *off* or *out* by heat; make (whisky, essence) by distilling raw materials; undergo distillation; so ∼LA′TION *n.,* ∼latORY *a.* [ME, f. L *distillare* f. DE(*stillare* f. *stilla* drop)]

di′stillāte *n.* product of distillation. [f. prec.; see -ATE¹]

disti′ll|er *n.* In vbl senses; one who manufactures alcoholic liquor by distilling, whence ∼ERY (3) *n.* [f. DISTIL + -ER¹]

disti′nct *a.* not identical, separate, individual, different in quality or kind, unlike, (*from*, or abs.); clearly perceptible, plain, definite, unmistakable, decided, positive; hence ∼LY² *adv.,* ∼NESS *n.* [ME, f. L *distinctus* p.p. of *distinguere* DISTINGUISH]

disti′nction *n.* making of a difference, discrimination; the difference made (∼ **without a difference,** a merely nominal or artificial one); being different; thing that differentiates, mark, name, title; showing of special consideration, mark of honour; distinguished character, excellence, eminence. [ME f. OF, f. L *distinctio -onis* (as DISTINGUISH; see -ION)]

disti′nctive *a.* distinguishing, characteristic; hence ∼LY² (-vlĭ) *adv.,* ∼NESS (-vn-) *n.* [f. as prec. + -IVE]

distingué (dĭstă′nggā) *a.* (*fem.* ∼*e pr.* same). having a distinguished air, features, manners, etc. [F, p.p. of *distinguer* (see foll.)]

disti′nguish (-nggw-) *v.* **1.** *v.t.* divide *into* classes etc.; be, see, or point out, the difference of (thing, thing *from* another); make out by listening, looking, etc.; differentiate, draw distinctions between. **2.** characterize, be a mark or property of; make one*self* prominent or noteworthy (*by* gallantry etc.). **3.** Hence ∼ABLE *a.* **4.** *v.i.* make distinction *between*. [f. F *distinguer* or f. L DI¹(*stinguere stinct-* extinguish) w. irreg. use of -ISH²; cf. *extinguish*]

disti′nguished (-nggwisht) *a.* In vbl senses; remarkable (*for* or *by* quality of excellence etc.), eminent, famous, of high standing; *distingué.* [p.p. of prec.]

distôr′t *v.t.* put out of shape, make crooked or unshapely, (actually or, as by curved mirror etc., apparently); misrepresent (motives, facts, statements). [f. L DIS(*torquēre tort-* twist)]

distôr′tion *n.* distorting or being distorted; (Electr.) change in form of signal during transmission etc., usu. with impairment of quality; hence ∼AL, ∼LESS, *adjs.* [f. L *distortio* (as prec.; see -ION)]

distrā′ct *v.t.* draw (attention, the mind, etc.) away *from* or in different directions; divide or confuse the attention of, bewilder, perplex; (usu. in *p.p.*) make mad or angry (*distracted with, by, at*). [ME, f. L DIS(*trahere tract-* draw)]

distrā′ction *n.* **1.** diversion of, thing that diverts, the mind; interruption, lack of concentration; amusement, relaxation from work. **2.** confusion, perplexity, internal conflict, dissension; frenzy, madness, (**to** ∼, almost to a state of madness). [ME f. OF, or f. L *distractio* (as prec.; see -ION)]

distrai′n *v.i.* (Law). impose distraint (*upon* person, his goods, or abs.); hence ∼EE′, ∼ER¹, ∼MENT, ∼OR, *ns.* [ME, f. OF *destreindre* f. L DI¹(*stringere strict-* draw tight)]

distrai′nt *n.* (Law). seizure of chattels to make person pay rent etc. or meet obligation, or to obtain satisfaction by their sale. [f. prec., after *constraint*]

distrait (dĭstrā′) *a.* (*fem.* ∼*e pr.*-ā′t). absent-minded, not paying attention; distraught. [ME, f. OF *destrait* p.p. of *destraire* f. as DISTRACT]

distrau′ght (-aw′t) *a.* much agitated in mind; nearly crazy with worry etc. [ME, alt. of obs. *distract* adj. (f. as DISTRACT) after *straught* obs. p.p. of STRETCH]

distre′ss¹ *n.* severe pressure of pain, sorrow, etc., anguish; lack of money or necessaries, damage or danger to ship etc. (*in distress*); exhaustion, being tired out, breathlessness; misfortune, calamity; (Law) distraint; ∼-**signal** (from ship in danger); ∼-**warrant** (authorizing distraint); hence ∼FUL *a.* (literary). [ME, f. OF *destresse* etc. f. Gallo-Rom. **districtia* f. as DISTRAIN]

distre′ss² *v.t.* subject to distress; exhaust; afflict; cause anxiety to, vex, make unhappy. [ME, f. AF *destresser,* OF *-ecier,* f. as prec.]

distre′ssed (-ě′st) *a.* In vbl senses; impoverished (*distressed gentlefolk*); (of furniture) with simulated marks of age and wear; (∼ **area,** region of high unemployment). [p.p. of prec.]

distri′butary *n.* river or glacier branch that does not return to main stream after leaving it (as in a delta). [f. foll. + -ARY¹]

distri′but|e *v.t.* deal out, give share out to each of a number; spread about, scatter, put at different points; divide into parts, arrange, classify; (Print.) separate (type that has been set up) and return each letter to its proper box in the case; (Logic) use (term) in its full extension so that it includes every individual of the class; hence ∼ABLE *a.* [ME, f. L DIS(*tribuere tribut-* assign)]

distribū′tion *n.* distributing, apportionment; (esp., Econ.) dispersal among consumers effected by commerce, extent to which individuals or classes share in aggregate products of community; (Statistics) way

in which a characteristic is spread over members of a class; hence ∿AL *a*. [ME f. OF, or f. L *distributio* (as prec.; see -ION)]
distri′bŭtive *a*. & *n*. **1.** *a*. of, concerned with, produced by, distribution; (Logic & Gram.) referring to each individual of a class, not to the class collectively (*distributive* PRONOUN); hence ∿LY² (-vlĭ) *adv*. **2.** *n*. (Gram.) distributive word (*each, neither, every*). [ME, f. F (-*if* -*ive*), or f. LL -*ivus* (as DISTRIBUTE; see -IVE)]
distri′bŭtor *n*. person or thing that distributes; agent who markets goods; electric cable from which lines run to individual premises; device in internal combustion engine for passing current to each sparking-plug in turn. [f. DISTRIBUTE + -OR]
di′strict *n*., & *v.t*. **1.** *n*. territory marked off for special administrative purpose; ‖division of county; tract of country with common characteristics, region. **2.** *∿ attorney, prosecuting officer of a district; *∿ court, Federal court of first instance; ∿ heating, supply of heat or hot water from one source to a district or group of buildings; ‖∿ nurse, nurse serving rural or urban area; ‖∿ visitor, person working under clergyman's direction in section of parish. **3.** *v.t*. *divide into districts. [F, f. med. L *districtus* (territory of) jurisdiction f. as DISTRAIN]
distri′ngăs (-ngg-) *n*. (Law). = STOP²-*order*; (Hist.) writ ordering distraint by sheriff etc. [L (first word of writ) = you shall distrain]
distrŭ′st¹ *n*. lack of trust; doubt, suspicion; hence ∿FUL *a*. (*of*). [f. DIS-+ TRUST 1]
distrŭ′st² *v.t*. have no confidence in; doubt, not rely on. [ME, f. DIS-+ TRUST 10]
distûr′b *v.t*. break the rest or quiet or calm of; agitate, worry; move from settled position (*nothing has been disturbed*; *don't let me disturb you, don't disturb yourself*); (Psych., in *p.p*.) emotionally or mentally unstable or abnormal. [ME, f. OF *desto*(u)*rber* f. L DIS(*turbare* f. *turba* tumult)]
distûr′bance *n*. interruption of tranquillity; agitation; tumult, uproar; (Law) molestation, interference with rights or property. [ME, f. OF *desto*(u)*rbance* (as prec.; see -ANCE)]
dīsŭ′lphīde, *-sŭ′lf-, *n*. (Chem.) sulphide formed from two atoms of sulphur and one of metal or non-metal (*carbon disulphide*). [f. DI-² + SULPHIDE]
dīsū′nion (-ĭon, -yon) *n*. separation, lack of union; dissension; so **dīsuni′te** *v.t*. & *i*., **dīsu′nity** *n*. [f. DIS-+ UNION]
dīsū′se¹ *n*. discontinuance, lack of use or practice; disused state (*fall into disuse*). [f. DIS-+ USE¹]
dīsū′se² (-z) *v.t*. cease to use. [ME, f. OF *desuser* (as DIS-, USE²)]
dīsy′ll|able, diss-, *n*. word or metrical foot of two syllables; so ∿ă′bIC *a*. [f. F *disyllabe* f. L f. Gk *disullabos* (as DI-², SYLLABLE)]
ditch *n*. & *v*. **1.** *n*. long narrow excavation, esp. to hold or conduct water or serve as boundary; watercourse; last ∿, place of final desperate defence (DIE² *in last ditch*); ∿-water (stagnant in ditch; esp. *dull as ditch-water*). **2.** *v.i*. & *t*. make or repair ditches (esp. *hedging and ditching*), whence ∿ *ER¹* (1, 2) *n.*; provide with ditches, drain; (sl.) abandon, discard, leave in the lurch; (sl.) defeat, frustrate; (sl.) make forced landing on sea, bring (aircraft) down thus; drive (vehicle) into ditch, *derail (train). [OE *dīc*, = OS *dīk*, MHG *tīch*, ON *dīki*, of unkn. orig.; cf. DIKE]
dīthē′|ism *n*. religious dualism, belief in independent principles of good and evil; hence ∿IST (2) *n*. [f. DI-² + THEISM]
di′ther (-dh-) *v.i*., & *n*. **1.** *v.i*. tremble, quiver; vacillate, hesitate. **2.** *n*. state of dithering; (colloq.) state of tremulous excitement or apprehension (*all of a dither*); hence ∿Y² *a*. [var. of *didder*, DODDER²]
di′thÿrămb (-ăm) *n*. Greek choric hymn, wild in character; Bacchanalian song; passionate or inflated poem, speech, or writing; so **dithÿră′mbIC** *a*. [L f. Gk *dithurambos*]

di′ttany *n*. herb of genus *Dictamnus*, formerly of medicinal repute. [ME, f. OF *dita*(i)*n* f. med. L *dictamus* f. L f. Gk *diktamnon* perh. f. *Diktē* in Crete]
di′ttō *n*. (*pl*. ∿s), & *v.t*. **1.** *n*. the aforesaid, the same, (in accounts, inventories, etc., or colloq.); duplicate, similar thing; ‖(in *pl*., arch.) clothes all of same material and colour; ∿ marks, inverted commas etc. representing the word 'ditto'; say ∿ to, agree with, endorse opinion of. **2.** *v.t*. repeat (another's action or words). [It. dial., f. L *dictus* p.p. of *dicere* say]
ditto′graphy *n*. copyist's mistaken repetition of letter, word, or phrase; hence **dittogra′phIC** *a*. [f. Gk *dittos* double + -GRAPHY]
di′tty *n*. short simple song. [ME, f. OF *dité* composition f. L *dictatum* neut. p.p. (as n.) of *dictare* DICTATE²]
di′tty-băg, -bŏx, *ns*. sailor's or fisherman's receptacle for odds and ends. [19th c.; orig. unkn.]
dīūrē′s|is *n*. (*pl*. ∿es *pr*. -ēz). (Med.) increased excretion of urine. [mod. L f. Gk (as DI-³, *ourēsis* urination)]
dīūrĕ′tic *a*. & *n*. (drug) causing increased excretion of urine. [ME, f. OF *diuretique*, or f. LL f. Gk *diourētikos* f. DI³(*oureō* urinate); see -ETIC]
dīūr′nal *a*. of the day, not nocturnal; (Astron.) occupying one day; daily, of each day; (Zool.) active in daytime; hence ∿LY² *adv*. [ME, f. LL *diurnalis* f. L *diurnus* (*dies* day); see -AL]
Div. *abbr*. Division.
dī′va (dē′-) *n*. great woman singer, prima donna. [It. f. L, = goddess]
dī′vag|āte *v.i*. (literary). stray, digress; hence ∿A′TION *n*. [f. L DI¹(*vagari* wander) + -ATE³]
divalent (dī′va-, dīvā′-) *a*. (Chem.) having a valence of two. [f. DI-² + *valent-* part. st. f. as VALENCE²]
divan (dīvă′n, dī′văn) *n*. long low seat against room-wall; couch or bed without head- or foot-board; oriental council of State; oriental council-chamber, court of justice; (arch.) (smoking-room attached to) cigar-shop. [f. F *divan* or It. *divano* f. Turk. *dīvān* f. Arab. *dīwān* f. Pers. *dīwān* anthology, register, court, bench]
dīvă′ric|āte *v.i*. (literary & Biol.) diverge, branch, separate widely; hence or cogn. ∿A′TION *n*., ∿ATE² *a*. [f. L DI¹(*varicare* f. *varicus* straddling) + -ATE³]
dīve *v*. (∿d, or *dove *pr*. dōv), & *n*. **1.** *v.i*. plunge, esp. head foremost, into water etc., esp. as sport; (of aircraft) plunge steeply downwards at increasing speed, (of submarine) submerge; go (esp. down or out of sight) suddenly; put one's hand *into* water, vessel, pocket, handbag, etc.; penetrate or search mentally *into*; di′ving-bell, open-bottomed box or bell with air supplied by tube, in which person can be let down into deep water; di′ving-board, elevated board for diving from; di′ving-suit, watertight suit usu. with helmet and air-supply for work under water. **2.** *v.t*. plunge (hand etc.) *into*. **3.** *n*. act of diving, plunge, header; submerging of submarine, aircraft's steep descent; sudden darting movement; (colloq.) drinking-den, disreputable place of resort; (Boxing, sl.) pretended knock-out. **4.** ∿-bomber, aircraft designed to aim and release bombs while diving towards target; so ∿-bomb *v.t*. [OE *dūfan* v.i. dive, sink, and *dȳfan* v.t. immerse, f. Gmc *dubh-* etc. cogn. w. DEEP¹, DIP¹]
dī′ver *n*. in vbl senses; person who dives (esp. in diving-suit) to examine sunken ships, etc.; pearl-diver; diving bird, esp. loon. [f. prec. + -ER¹]
dīvēr′ge *v*. **1.** *v.i*. proceed in different directions from point; take different courses from each other; go aside *from* track (lit. or fig.); differ; (Math., of series) become indefinitely large in the sum of a sufficient number of its terms. **2.** *v.t*. cause to diverge, deflect. [f. med. L *divergere* f. as DI-¹ + L *vergere* incline]
dīvēr′g|ent *a*. diverging; (Psych., of thought) tending towards a variety of possible solutions when analysing a problem; so ∿ENCE, ∿ENCY, *ns*., ∿entLY² *adv*. [f. prec. + -ENT]

di'vers (-z) *a.* (arch.) sundry, several, more than one. [ME f. OF, f. L DI¹(*versus* p.p. of *vertere* turn) = foll.]

diverse (dīvē̆r's, dī'-) *a.* unlike in nature or qualities; varied, changeful; hence ∼LY² (-slĭ) *adv.* [ME, as prec.]

divē̆r'si|fȳ *v.t.* make diverse, vary, modify, variegate; spread (investment) over several enterprises or products, esp. to guard against loss; so ∼FICA'TION *n.* [ME, f. OF *diversifier* f. med. L *diversificare* (as DIVERS; see -FY)]

divē̆r'sion (-shon) *n.* deflecting, deviation; diverting of attention, manœuvre to secure this, feint; recreation, pleasant mental distraction, pastime; ∥alternative route when road is temporarily closed to traffic; hence ∼ARY¹ *a.*, ∼IST (2) *n.*, (esp., in Communist use) saboteur, conspirator against State. [f. LL *diversio* (as DIVERT; see -ION)]

divē̆r'sitȳ *n.* being diverse, unlikeness; different kind; variety. [ME, f. OF *diversité* f. L *diversitas -tatis* (as DIVERS; see -ITY)]

divē̆r't *v.t.* turn aside, deflect, (stream etc., *from, to,* or abs.); ∥cause (traffic) to take different route; turn elsewhere, get rid of, ward off; draw attention of (away *from* one thing *to* another), distract; entertain, amuse, whence ∼·ING² *a.* [ME, f. F *divertir* f. L DI¹(*vertere* turn)]

diverti'cūl|um *n.* (*pl.* ∼a). (Anat.) blind tube forming side branch of cavity or passage; hence or cogn. ∼ı'TIS, ∼O'SIS, *ns.* [med. L, var. of L *doverticulum* byway f. DE(*vertere* turn); see -CULE]

divertime̊'nt|ō (-vār-) *n.* (*pl.* ∼i *or* ∼os). (Mus.) composition primarily for entertainment, esp. suite for chamber orchestra. [It., = diversion]

divertissement (dēvē̆rtē̆'smahn) *n.* short ballet etc. between acts or longer pieces; diversion, entertainment. [F, f. *divertiss-* st. of *divertir* DIVERT; see -MENT]

Di'vĕs (-z) *n.* rich man. [L, in Vulgate transl. of Luke 16]

divĕ'st *v.t.* unclothe; strip *of* garment etc.; deprive or rid *of* (∼ oneself of, abandon); hence ∼īTURE, ∼MENT, *ns.* [f. earlier *devest* f. OF *desvestir* etc. (as DIS-, L *vestire* f. *vestis* garment)]

di'vi. See DIVVY.

divi'de¹ *v.t. & i.* 1. separate into or in(*to*) parts, split or break up (*∼d highway*, dual carriageway; ∼d skirt, culotte); separate, part, cut off or *off*, (things, thing *from*); mark out into parts, specify different kinds of; cause to disagree, set at variance (*opinion is divided*; ∼d against itself, formed into factions). 2. distribute, deal *out*, (*among, between*); share *with* others; find how many times number contains another (*divide 20 by 9*), do DIVISION, (of number) be contained in (number) without remainder; part (legislative assembly etc.) into two sets in voting, be thus parted. [ME, f. L DI¹(*videre* vis-)]

divi'de² *n.* watershed; (fig.) dividing line; **the Great D∼** (between life and death). [f. prec.]

di'vidĕnd *n.* 1. (Math.) number to be divided by divisor. 2. sum payable as profit of joint-stock company or to creditors of insolvent estate; individual's share of it (EX² *dividend*, CUM *dividend*; ∼ stripping, evasion of tax on dividends by arrangement between company liable to pay tax and another able to claim repayment of tax; ∥∼-warrant, authority for shareholder to receive dividend). 3. benefit from any action (*his long training paid dividends*). [f. AF *dividende* f. L *dividendum* (as DIVIDE¹; see -ND¹)]

divi'der *n.* In vbl senses; screen, piece of furniture, etc., to divide room into two parts; (in *pl.*) measuring-compasses, esp. with screw for setting to small intervals. [f. DIVIDE¹ + -ER¹]

di'vi-divi *n.* curved pods of a small tropical-Amer. tree (*Caesalpinia coriaria*), used in tanning; this tree. [Carib]

divinā'tion *n.* insight into or discovery of the unknown or future by supernatural means; skilful forecast, good guess; hence **divī'natORY** *a.* [ME f. OF, or f. L *divinatio* (as DIVINE²; see -ATION)]

divī'ne¹ *a.* (∼r, ∼st) & *n.* 1. *a.* of, from, like, God or a god (∼ right of kings, doctrine that kings have authority independently of their subjects' will); devoted to God, sacred, (*divine* OFFICE; ∼ service, meeting for worship); superhumanly excellent, gifted, or beautiful; (colloq.) excellent, delightful; hence or cogn. **di'vinIZE** (3) *v.t.*, ∼LY² (-nlĭ) *adv.*, ∼NESS (-n-n-) *n.* 2. *n.* person (usu. cleric) skilled in theology. [ME, f. OF *devin -ine* f. L *divinus* (*divus* godlike; see -INE¹)]

divī'n|e² *v.* 1. *v.t.* discover by inspiration, magic, intuition, or guessing; foresee, predict, conjecture. 2. *v.i.* practise divination; ∼ing-rod (see DOWSE²). 3. Hence ∼ER² (1) *n.* (water-∼er, dowser). [ME, f. F *deviner* f. OF *devin* (see prec.)]

divī'nitȳ *n.* being divine, godhood; a god, godhead; theology, university theological faculty; ∼ calf, dark brown bookbinding style with blind tooling. [ME, f. OF *divinité* f. L *divinitas -tatis* (as DIVINE¹; see -ITY)]

divi's|ible (-z-) *a.* capable of being divided actually or in thought; ∼ible by, (Math.) containing (a number) some number of times without remainder; hence ∼IBI'LITY *n.* [f., or f. LL *divisibilis* (as DIVIDE¹; see -IBLE)]

divi'sion (-zhon) *n.* 1. dividing or being divided, severance; distribution, sharing, (∼ of labour, improvement of efficiency by giving different parts of manufacturing process etc. to different persons). 2. disagreement, discord, (*division of opinion*). 3. (Math.) process of dividing number by another; ∼ sign, ÷; long ∼ (writing down details of calculation); short ∼ (writing quotient directly). 4. separation of legislative assembly etc. into two sets for counting votes; ∼-bell (announcing this). 5. dividing line, boundary; part, section. 6. one of several large parts into which an organization is divided, e.g. group of Army regiments, number of teams playing each other within a league; group of three or two Army brigades, district defined for administrative purposes; ∥part of county or borough returning a Member of Parliament. 7. (Bot.) major taxonomic grouping equivalent to phylum; (Zool.) subsidiary category between major levels of classification; (Logic) classification of kinds, parts, or senses. 8. Hence ∼AL *a.* [ME, f. OF *divisiun* f. L *divisio -onis* (as DIVIDE¹; see -ION)]

divi'sive *a.* tending to cause division, esp. in opinion etc.; hence ∼LY² (-vlĭ) *adv.*, ∼NESS (-vn-) *n.* [f. LL *divisivus* (as DIVIDE¹; see -IVE)]

divi'sor (-z-) *n.* (Math.) number by which dividend is to be divided; number that divides another without remainder. [ME, f. F *diviseur* or f. L *divisor* (as DIVIDE¹; see -OR)]

divôr'ce¹ *n.* legal dissolution of marriage; decree of nullity of marriage; (fig.) severance, separation. [ME f. OF, f. L *divortium* f. *divortere = vertere* turn)]

divôr'ce² *v.t.* legally dissolve marriage between; separate (spouse) by divorce *from*; obtain divorce from (spouse); detach, separate, (things, one *from* another); (fig.); (arch.) dissolve (union); hence **divôrcEE'** *n.* (also **divorcé** *masc.*, **divorcée** *fem.*, (divōr'sā) [F]), ∼MENT (-sm-) *n.* [ME, f. OF *divorcer* f. LL *divortiare* (as prec.)]

di'vot *n.* 1. (Sc.) piece of turf, sod. 2. (Golf) piece of turf cut out by club-head in making a stroke. [16th c.; orig. unkn.]

divŭ'lg|e *v.t.* disclose, reveal, (secret etc.); hence or cogn. **divŭlgA'TION**, ∼EMENT (-jm-), ∼ENCE, *ns.* [f. L DI¹(*vulgare* publish f. *vulgus* common people)]

di'vvȳ, dī'vi, *n.*, & *v.t.* (colloq.) 1. *n.* dividend, share; distribution. 2. *v.t.* ∼ (up), divide, share out. [abbr. of DIVIDEND]

Diwa'li (-ah'lē) *n.* Hindu festival with illuminations, held in October. [f. Hind. *dīwālī* f. Skr. *dīpāvalī* row of lights (*dīpa* lamp)]

Di'xie[1] *n.* Southern States of US; *∼crat*, (colloq.) member of seceding group of Democrats in Dixie; *∼land*, (1) Dixie, (2) kind of jazz with strong two--beat rhythm and collective improvisation. [19th c.; orig. uncert.]

‖**di'xie**[2] *n.* large iron pot in which stew, tea, etc., are made or carried by soldiers etc. [f. Hind. *degchī* cooking-pot f. Pers. *degcha* dim. of *deg* pot]

DIY *abbr.* do-it-yourself.

dizz|**y̆** *a.*, & *v.t.* **1.** *a.* giddy, dazed, unsteady, tottering, confused; making giddy (*dizzy heights, speed*); (of mountain, tower, etc.) very high; whirling rapidly; hence *∼ĭLY*[2] *adv.*, *∼ĭNESS n.* **2.** *v.t.* make dizzy, bewilder. [OE *dysig*, = MDu. *dosech*, LG *dusig, dösig*, OHG *tusic* weak f. WG **dus-*; see -Y[2]]

DJ *abbr.* ‖dinner-jacket; disc jockey.

djě'llaba. Var. of JELLABA.

djibba(h). Var. of JIBBA(H).

djinn. Var. of JINN.

‖**DL** *abbr.* Deputy Lieutenant.

dl. *abbr.* decilitre(s).

D-layer (dē'lāer) *n.* lowest stratum of ionosphere. [f. *D* (arbitrary) + LAYER]

D.Litt. *abbr.* Doctor of Letters. [f. L *Doctor Litterarum*]

dm. *abbr.* decimetre(s).

DM, D-mark, *abbr.* Deutschmark.

D.Mus. *abbr.* Doctor of Music.

*DMZ *abbr.* demilitarized zone.

DNA *abbr.* deoxyribonucleic acid.

DNB *abbr.* Dictionary of National Biography.

‖**D-notice** (dē'nōtĭs) *n.* official request to news editors not to publish items on specified subjects, for reasons of security. [f. *defence* + NOTICE]

do[1] (doō, *when unstressed* do) *v.t., i.*, & *aux.* (*sing. pres.* 2(arch.) **doest** *pr.* doō'ĭst as *t.* & *i.*, **dost** *pr.* dŭst as *aux.*, 3 **does** *pr.* dŭz or doz, (colloq.) **'s,** (arch.) **doth** *pr.* dŭth, (arch.) **doeth** *pr.* doō'ĭth; *past* **did,** (2 *sing.* arch.) **didst**; *part.* DOING; *p.p.* DONE; *neg.* **do not** *or* (colloq.) **don't** *pr.* dōnt, **does not** *or* (colloq.) **doesn't** *pr.* dŭ'zent *or* (vulg.) **don't, did not** *or* (colloq.) **didn't** *pr.* dī'dent). **1.** *v.t.* bestow, impart, grant, give, (*does him* CREDIT[1], does credit to his intelligence; *do me a favour; does me good, harm; do justice to; did a service to his country*). **2.** perform, carry out, effect, complete, bring to pass, (thing, work, good, right, wrong, duty, bidding, penance; *do one's* BEST[1]; *easier said than done*); *do* BATTLE[1], one's BIT[2]; **do a degree,** study for and obtain it; DO-GOODER; *do the* HONOUR[1]*s*; **do a play,** give performance(s) of it; **do something for** *or* **to,** (colloq.) enhance appearance or quality of; *do the* TRICK; *do 30 miles to the gallon, do 100 m.p.h.*; **do it,** achieve success (*he's done it at last*), incur disaster (*now you've done it*); **that's done it,** excl. of achievement or dismay; **do a,** (colloq.) act like (*Garbo* etc.); **do-it--yourself** *a.*, (to be) made etc. by amateur handyman. **3.** produce, make, (*copies, omelette, painting, translation*); provide (*we do bed and breakfast*). **4.** operate on, deal with, repair, set in order, (*do to* DEATH; **do the dishes,** wash up; **do the flowers,** arrange them; **do one's hair,** comb or arrange it; **do one's head** *or* **nut,** (sl.) be very worried or angry; **do a room,** clean it or paint it etc.); cook, esp. to right degree (*do it in the oven, done to a* TURN[2], *overdone*; *do* BROWN[1]); solve (problem); translate or transform (*into* English, book *into* film, etc.); work at (lesson, subject); play the part of, act like, (*did Lear, do the cicerone,* hence *do the affable* etc.); (sl.) rob (*did a shop in Soho*); (sl.) prosecute, convict; (sl.) have sexual intercourse with. **5.** exhaust, tire out; *∼* (**in the eye**), (sl.) swindle, cheat, (*out of*); (sl.) defeat, ruin, kill. **6.** traverse (distance); (colloq.) visit, see sights of, (place, entertainment, etc.); (sl.) undergo (term of punishment). **7.** (colloq.) ‖provide food etc. for (*they do one very well here*; **do** oneself **well,** make liberal provision for one's own comfort); ‖satisfy (*that will do me nicely*); *do* PROUD. **8.** *v.i.* (w. adv. etc.) act, proceed, (*do as they do in Rome; would do wisely to withdraw*); perform deeds (**do or die,** be undeterred

by danger); make an end (*have* DONE *with*); (of person or thing) fare, get on, (well, badly, etc.; **do well for** one**self,** prosper; WELL[3]-*to-do*; **do well out of,** of, profit by; *mother and child doing well*; **how do you do?,** conventional greeting on being introduced); be suitable or acceptable, serve purpose, suffice (**that will do!,** stop it; *it doesn't do to worry*; MAKE[1] *do*); be in progress (**nothing doing,** nothing happening, (colloq.) no prospect of success; **what is to do,** what is happening, what is the matter; TO-DO). **9.** *v.* *substitute.* (*a*) replacing v. and taking its construction (*I treat him as he does me*), (*b*) replacing v. and obj. etc. (*if you knew him as well as I do*), (*c*) as ellipt. aux. (*did you see him?—yes, I did; why don't you answer?—but I did!*), (*d*) with *so, it, which,* etc. (*I wanted to see him, and I did so* or *and so I did*; *when visiting London, which I seldom do; if you want to tell him, do it now*), (*e*) in emphatic repetition (*tell me, do!; you don't know me, do you?*). **10.** *v. aux.* w. inf. as pres. or past (*a*) for special emphasis (*I do so wish I could*), esp. in contrast with what precedes or follows (*but I did see him; I did go, but she wasn't in*), (*b*) for inversion (*rarely does it happen that; little did I imagine that; did he but know it*), (*c*) in questions and negations exc. with *be,* CAN[2], DARE, *have* v. aux. & ‖sometimes v.t., *may, must,* sometimes NEED[2], *ought, shall, will*; in neg. commands also with *be, have* (**don't-care** *n.,* person who is careless or indifferent; **don't-know** *n.,* person who does not answer definitely to questionnaire item etc.); w. inf. as imper. for emphasis, urgency, etc., (*do tell me*). **11.** (w. preps.) **do by,** treat, deal with, in specified way; **do for,** be satisfactory or sufficient for; (colloq.) ruin, destroy, kill, ‖(colloq.) act as housekeeper etc. for; **do to** or (arch.) **unto,** = *do by*; **do with,** accept, find useful or sufficient; *could do with,* (colloq.) would be glad to have, would be improved by having; *to do with,* concerned with, related to; *have to do with,* be concerned with, have dealings with; *not know what to do with* oneself, be embarrassed or bored; *what did you do with it?,* where did you put it; **do without,** manage without, complete one's task in the absence of, (thing expressed or implied). **12.** (w. *advs.*) **do away with,** abolish, kill; **do down,** (colloq.) overcome, cheat, swindle; **do in,** (sl.) ruin, kill, (colloq.) exhaust, tire out; **do out,** clean or redecorate (room); **do over,** (sl.) attack, beat, *(colloq.) do again; **do up,** fasten, make into parcel or bundle, refurbish, adorn (one*self*), (sl.) ruin, beat. [OE *dōn* = OS *dōn,* OHG *tuon,* f. WG **do-* f. IE **dhō-* etc. (Skr. *dádhāmi* put, Gk *tithēmi* place, L *facere* do)]

do[2] (doō) *n.* (*pl.* **dos** *or* **do's**). **1.** (sl.) swindle, imposture, hoax. **2.** ‖(colloq.) entertainment, jollification, elaborate operation etc.; (in *pl.*) share (**fair dos!,** share fairly). **3.** **dos and don'ts,** rules of behaviour. [f. prec.]

do[3]. See DOH.

do. *abbr.* ditto.

DOA *abbr.* dead on arrival (at hospital etc.).

do'able (doō'-) *a.* that can be done. [ME, f. DO[1] + -ABLE]

doat. Var. of DOTE.

do'bbin *n.* draught-horse; farm horse. [pet-form of man's Christian name *Robert*]

*do'bĕ *n.* adobe. [abbr.]

Do'bermänn *n.* *∼* (**pinscher** *pr.* pĭ'nsher) (breed of) German hound with smooth coat and docked tail. [f. L. *∼,* 19th-c. Ger. dog-breeder; G *pinscher* terrier]

dŏc *n.* (colloq.) doctor. [abbr.]

Docĕ't'ism *n.* heresy that Christ's body was only apparently human; so *∼ĭC a., ∼ĭST* (2) *n.* [f. med. L f. Gk *Dokētai* adherents of the heresy (*dokeō* seem) + -ISM]

doch an dorris. Var. of DEOCH AN DORIS.

do'cĭle *a.* teachable; submissive; easily managed; hence or comp. *∼LY*[2] *adv.,* **docĭ'lĭTY** *n.* [ME, f. L *docilis* (*docēre* teach; see -IL).]

dŏck[1] *n.* coarse weed of genus *Rumex*, with leaves used to cure nettle-stings. [OE *docce*; cf. MDu. *docke-blaederen*]

dŏck[2] *n.* solid fleshy part of animal's tail; crupper of saddle or harness. [ME, perh. f. OE **docca*, MLG *dokke* bundle of straw, OHG *tocka* doll]

dŏck[3] *v.t.* cut short (tail of animal), cut short tail of (animal); lessen; deprive (person) *of*, put limits on or deduct (part) *from* wages, supplies etc.); (colloq.) make deduction from (wages) or from wages of (person); ~**-tailed,** with tail docked. [ME, f. prec.]

dŏck[4] *n.* & *v.* **1.** *n.* artificial enclosed body of water in which ships may be loaded, unloaded, or repaired (**dry** or **graving** ~, dry enclosure for repairing or building, water being pumped out; **floating** ~, floating structure usable as dry dock; **in** ~, (colloq.) in hospital or repair-shop); (usu. in *pl.*) range of dock basins with wharves and offices, dockyard; *ship's berth, wharf; (Theatr.) = SCENE-*dock*; hence ~'AGE (4) *n.* **2.** ~**-glass,** large glass for wine-tasting; ~'**land,** district near docks; ~'**yard,** area with docks and all shipbuilding and repairing appliances, esp. for naval use. **3.** *v.t.* & *i.* bring (ship), (of ship) come, into dock; furnish with dock(s); join (spacecraft) together in space, be thus joined. [f. MDu. *docke*, of unkn. orig.]

dŏck[5] *n.* enclosure in criminal court for prisoner, **in the** ~, on (judicial) trial (lit. or fig.); ||~ **brief** (handed direct in court to barrister selected by prisoner in dock). [16th c., prob. orig. cant = Flem. *dok* cage, of unkn. orig]

dŏck'er *n.* labourer in docks. [f. DOCK[4] + -ER[1]]

dŏck'ket *n.,* & *v.t.* **1.** *n.* ||document recording payment of customs duties, nature of goods delivered, jobs done, etc.; voucher, order form; endorsement of document to indicate its contents; label attached to goods etc. **2.** *list of causes for trial or persons having causes pending; *list of things to be done. **3.** *v.t.* label with docket. [15th c., of unkn. orig.]

dŏc'tor *n.* **1.** physician; *dentist or veterinary surgeon; (colloq.) one who carries out repairs (lit. or fig.; *company doctor*; *tree doctor*); (sl.) cook on board ship or in camp; **what the** ~ **ordered,** (colloq.) something beneficial or desirable; **you're the** ~, (colloq.) the decision is up to you; ~**-bird,** W. Ind. humming -bird; ~**s' stuff,** (derog.) medicines. **2.** holder of the highest university degree in any faculty (often honorary; used as prefix to surname); **D**~**s' Commons,** (Hist.) London building in which various legal business was done. **3.** (arch.) teacher, learned man, (*who shall decide when doctors disagree?*) **4.** **D**~**s of the Church,** certain, esp. four Eastern and four Western, early Fathers of the Church. **5.** mechanical appliance for regulating, adjusting, etc.; artificial fishing-fly. **6.** Hence or cogn. ~AL, **dŏctŏr'IAL** *adjs.,* ~ATE[1], ~HOOD, ~SHIP (1, 3), *ns.* [ME, f. OF *doctour* f. L *doctor* (*docēre doct-* teach; see -OR)]

dŏc'tor[2] *v.* (colloq.) **1.** *v.t.* confer degree of doctor on; treat (patient, one*self*) medically; castrate or spay; patch up (machinery etc.); adulterate; falsify. **2.** *v.i.* practise as physician (esp. ~ING[1] (1) *n.*). [f. prec.]

dŏctrinair'|**e** *n.* & *a.* **1.** *n.* pedantic theorist, person who applies principle without allowance for circumstances; hence ~ISM (2) *n.* **2.** *a.* theoretical and unpractical. [F, f. *doctrine* DOCTRINE + -*aire* -ARY[1]]

doctrinal (dŏktrī'-, dŏ'ktrī-) *a.* of or inculcating doctrine(s); hence ~LY[2] *adv.* [f. LL *doctrinalis* (as foll.; see -AL)]

dŏc'trin|e *n.* what is taught, body of instruction; religious, political, scientific, etc., belief, dogma, or tenet; hence ~ISM (2), ~IST (1), *ns.* [ME f. OF, f. L *doctrina* teaching (as DOCTOR[1]; see -INE[4])]

dŏc'ūment[1] *n.* thing, esp. title-deed, writing, or inscription, that furnishes evidence (esp. in law and commerce); hence ~AL (-č'n-) *a.,* **dŏcūmē'ntal**IST *n.,* person engaged in documentation. [ME f. OF, f. L *documentum* proof (*docēre* teach; see -MENT)]

dŏc'ūment[2] *v.t.* prove by or provide with documents

or evidence; hence ~A'TION *n.,* (esp.) accumulation, classification, and dissemination of information, material thus collected. [f. prec.]

dŏcūmē'ntary *a.* & *n.* **1.** *a.* pertaining to or consisting of documents; factual, based on real events. **2.** *n.* documentary film etc. [f. DOCUMENT[1] + -ARY[1]]

*DOD *abbr.* Department of Defense.

dŏ'dder[1] *n.* slender leafless threadlike twining parasitic plant of genus *Cuscuta*. [ME, = MLG *dod(d)er*, MHG *toter*]

dŏ'dder[2] *v.i.* tremble or nod owing to frailty, palsy, etc. (~**-grass,** quaking-grass); totter, be feeble; hence ~ER[1] *n.,* infirm, feeble, or inept person, ~Y[2] *a.* [17th c., var. of obs. dial. *dadder*]

dŏ'ddered (-erd) *a.* (Of oak or other tree) having lost top or branches. [prob. f. obs. *dod* poll, lop]

dŏ'ddle *n.* (colloq.) easy task. [perh. f. *doddle* = toddle]

dōdē'ca- *comb. form.* twelve, as: ~**gon,** plane figure with twelve sides and angles; ~**he**'DRON, solid figure with twelve faces; ~**pho'nic,** = TWELVE-*note*; ~**sy'l-lable,** metrical line of twelve syllables. [f. Gk *dōdeka*]

dŏdge[1] *v.* **1.** *v.i.* move to and fro, change position, shuffle; move quickly *round, about,* or *behind,* obstacle so as to elude pursuer, blow, etc.; quibble, prevaricate; (of bell in change-ringing) move one place contrary to the normal sequence. **2.** *v.t.* baffle by artfulness, trifle with; elude (pursuer, opponent, blow) by sideward deviation etc.; evade by trickery (*dodge paying one's fare*; *dodge the* COLUMN). [16th c.; orig. unkn.]

dŏdge[2] *n.* piece of dodging, quick side-movement; trick, artifice, clever expedient; dodging of bell in change-ringing. [f. prec.]

dŏ'dgem *n.* small electrically-powered car at fun-fair, in which driver bumps into similar cars in enclosure. [f. DODGE[1] + 'EM]

dŏ'dger *n.* In vbl senses; artful or elusive person; screen on ship's bridge etc. as protection from spray etc., *small handbill; *maize-flour cake (*corn dodger*); (sl.) sandwich, bread, food. [f. DODGE[1] + -ER[1]]

dŏ'dgy *a.* cunning, artful; (colloq.) awkward, unreliable, tricky. [f. DODGE[1] + -Y[2]]

dō'dō *n.* (*pl.* ~s *or* ~es). large extinct bird of Mauritius etc.; old-fashioned, stupid, or inactive person; **as dead as the** *or* **a** ~, entirely obsolete. [f. Port. *doudo* simpleton]

dōe *n.* female fallow deer, reindeer, hare, or rabbit; ~**'skin** (dō's-), skin of doe fallow deer, leather of this, fine cloth resembling it. [OE *dā*, of unkn. orig.]

||DOE *abbr.* Department of the Environment.

doek (dook) *n.* (S. Afr.) cloth, esp. head-cloth. [Afrik.]

do'er (dōō'-) *n.* In vbl senses; one who acts rather than merely talking or thinking; (Austral.) eccentric person. [ME, f. DO[1] + -ER[1]]

does, doest, doeth. See DO[1].

dŏff *v.t.* (literary). take off (hat, clothing). [ME, = *do off*]

dŏg[1] *n.* **1.** carnivorous quadruped of genus *Canis*, of many breeds wild and domesticated; one used for hunting (*dogs of* WAR[1]); male of dog, wolf (also ~**-wolf**), or fox (also ~**-fox**). **2.** despicable person (esp. *dirty dog*); (colloq.) fellow (*sly, lucky, gay, dull, dog*; SEA-*dog*);*(sl.) something poor, a failure; (in *pl.,* sl.) feet [f. rhyming sl. *dog's feet*]. **3.** mechanical device for gripping etc.; = FIRE[1]*dog*. **4.** BOTTOM[1] *dog*; **not a** ~**'s chance,** not even the least chance; *every dog has his* DAY; **die like a** ~ (miserably or shamefully); **like a** ~**'s dinner,** (colloq.) smartly or flashily (dressed, arranged, etc.); **give a** ~ **a bad name and hang him,** nicknaming or slander is effective; **go to the** ~**s,** be ruined; **hair of the** ~ **that bit one,** further drink to cure effects of drink; **help a lame** ~ **over a stile,** be friend in time of need; HOT[1] *dog*; **keep a** ~ **and bark** oneself, do work for which one employs others; **love me, love my** ~, accept my friends as yours; ~ **in the manger,** one who prevents others from enjoying what is useless to him; **put on** ~, (colloq.) behave pretentiously; *rain* CAT[1]s *and dogs; let* SLEEP[2]*ing dogs lie;* **like a ∼ with two tails,** delighted; ||**the ∼s,** (colloq.) greyhound racing; TOP[1] *dog;* **try it on the ∼,** experiment so that only inferior or unimportant person or thing may be harmed. **5.** ∼'**berry,** fruit of dogwood; ∼-**biscuit** (for feeding dogs); ∼'**cart,** two-wheeled driving-cart with cross seats back to back (orig. with compartment for dogs); ∼-**clutch** (with teeth of one part engaging in slots in other part); ∼-**collar,** lit., and fig. of person's straight high collar divided at back, (colloq.) clerical collar; ∼ **days,** hottest period of year [reckoned in antiquity from heliacal rising of dog-star]; ∼-**ear,** corner of book-page turned down through use; so ∼-*eared* a. (of book); ∼-**eat**-∼, ruthlessly competitive; ∼-**end,** (sl.) cigarette-end; ∼-**faced,** epithet of kind of baboon (*Cynocephalus*); ∼-**fall** (in which wrestlers touch ground together); ∼-**fennel,** stinking camomile; ∼'**fight,** fight (as) between dogs, general uproar, (colloq.) fight between aircraft; ∼'**fish,** small shark; ∼'**house,** *dog's kennel; *in the ∼house,* (sl.) in disgrace; ∼ **Latin,** incorrect or mongrel Latin; ∼-**leg(ged),** bent like dog's hind leg; ∼-**paddle** *n.,* & *v.i.,* (use) an elementary swimming-stroke; ∼'**rose,** wild hedge-rose; ∼**sbody,** (Naut. sl.) junior officer, (colloq.) drudge; ∼'**s breakfast,** (sl.) mess; ∼'**shore,** temporary wooden support for ship just before launching; ∼'**skin,** leather of or imitating dog's skin used for gloves; ∼'**s life,** life of misery or wretched servitude; ∼'**s meat,** horse's or other flesh as food for dogs, carrion; ∼'**s nose,** drink of beer mixed with gin or rum; ∼('**s)-tail,** grass of genus *Cynosurus;* ∼-**star,** chief star of constellation Canis Major or Minor, esp. Sirius; ∼'**s-tongue,** cynoglossum; ∼'**s-tooth,** violet of genus *Erythronium,* esp. one with speckled leaves, purple flowers, and toothed perianth; ∼-**tag,** dog's or *(sl.) soldier's metal identity-disc; ∼-**tired,** tired out; ∼-**tooth,** small pointed ornament or moulding esp. in Norman and Early English architecture; ∼-**violet,** scentless wild kind; ∼-**watch,** (Naut.) short watch of two hours (4–6 or 6–8 p.m.); ∼'**wood,** wild cornel or its wood, one of various similar trees. **6.** Hence ∼'**g**ISH[1] (-g-), ∼'LIKE, *adjs.,* ∼'HOOD *n.* [OE *docga,* of unkn. orig.]

dŏg[2] *v.t.* (-gg-). follow closely, pursue, track, (person, his *steps*); (Mech.) grip with dog. [f. prec.]

dŏ'gāte *n.* office of doge. [f. F *dogat* f. It. *dogato* (as foll.; see -ATE[1])]

dōge *n.* (Hist.) chief magistrate of Venice or Genoa. [F f. It., f. Venetian *doze* f. L *dux ducis* leader]

dŏ'gged (-g-) *a.* obstinate, tenacious, persistent, unyielding; **it's ∼ as does it,** (colloq.) persistence succeeds; hence ∼LY[2] *adv.,* ∼NESS *n.* [ME, f. DOG[1] + -ED[2]]

dŏ'gger[1] (-g-) *n.* two-masted bluff-bowed Dutch fishing-boat. [ME f. MDu., = fishing-boat]

dŏ'gger[2] (-g-) *n.* (Austral.) dingo-hunter. [f. DOG[1] + -ER[1]]

Dŏ'gger[3] *n.* (Geol.) middle section of European Jurassic strata. [dial., = kind of iron-stone, perh. f. DOG[1]]

dŏ'ggerel (-g-) *a.* & *n.* trivial, worthless, or irregular, (verse). [ME, app. f. DOG[1] (as in *dog Latin* etc.); cf. -REL]

dŏ'ggie (-gī) *n.* little dog; (pet-name for) dog. [f. DOG[1] + -IE]

dŏ'ggŏ *adv.* (sl.) **lie ∼** (motionless or hidden, making no sign). [prob. f. DOG[1]; cf. -o]

dŏ'ggŏne *a., adv.,* & *v.t.* (sl.) **1.** *a.* & *adv.* = DAMNED 2, 3. **2.** *v.t.* = DAMN 2. [prob. f. *dog on it = God damn it*]

doggy[1]. Var of DOGGIE.

dŏ'gg|ў[2] (-gī) *a.* of dogs; devoted to dogs; hence ∼iNESS *n.* [f. DOG[1] + -Y[2]]

*****dŏ'gie** (-gī) *n.* motherless or neglected calf. [19th c.; orig. unkn.]

dŏ'gma *n.* principle, tenet, doctrinal system, esp. as laid down by authority of Church; arrogant declara-

tion of opinion. [L f. Gk *dogma -matos* opinion (*dokeō* seem)]

dŏgmă't|ic *a.* of dogma(s), doctrinal, (*dogmatic theology*); based on a priori principles, not on induction; asserting dogmas or opinions (*about*), authoritative, arrogant; hence ∼ICS *n.,* ∼ICALLY *adv.* [f. LL f. Gk *dogmatikos* (as prec.; see -IC)]

dŏ'gmat|īze, -t|īse (-īz), *v.* **1.** *v.i.* make positive unsupported assertions, speak authoritatively. **2.** *v.t.* express (principle etc.) as a dogma. **3.** So ∼ISM (1), ∼IST (1), *ns.* [f. F *dogmatiser* or f. LL f. Gk *dogmatizō* (as DOGMA; see -IZE)]

do-goŏ'd|er (dōō-) *n.* well-meaning but unrealistic philanthropist or reformer; so **do'-goŏd** (dōō'-) *a.* & *n.,* ∼ISM (2), ∼Y[2] *a.* [f. DO[1] + GOOD + -ER[1]]

doh (dō), **dō**[3], *n.* (Mus.) keynote of scale (*movable doh*), or the note C (*fixed doh*), in systems of SOLMIZATION. [18th c., f. It. *do*]

doi'lȳ, doy'ley, *n.* small ornamental mat of paper, linen, etc., on plate for cakes etc. [orig. name of a fabric, f. surname]

do'ing (dōō'-) *n.* In vbl senses; activity, effort; (colloq.) scolding, beating; (in *pl.,* sl.) adjuncts, things needed. [f. DO[1] + -ING[1]]

doit *n.* (arch.) very small amount of money. [f. MLG *doyt,* MDu. *duit,* of unkn. orig.]

dō'jŏ *n.* (*pl.* ∼s). room or hall, mat, for practising judo and other martial arts. [Jap.]

dol. *abbr.* dollar(s).

dolce far niente (dŏlchă fär nĭe'ntĭ) *n.* pleasant idleness. [It., = sweet doing nothing]

dolce vita (dŏlchă vē'ta) *n.* life of pleasure and luxury. [It., = sweet life]

dŏ'ldrums (-z) *n. pl.* **the ∼,** dullness, low spirits; becalmed state of ship; (fig.) state of stagnation; region of calms, sudden storms, and light unpredictable winds near equator. [prob. after *dull* and *tantrum*]

dōle[1] *n.,* & *v.t.* **1.** *n.* charitable distribution; charitable (esp. sparing, niggardly) gift of food, clothes, or money; ||**the ∼,** (colloq.) benefit claimable by the unemployed from State (*on the ∼,* receiving this). **2.** (arch.) lot, destiny. **3.** *v.t.* deal out sparingly, esp. as alms. [OE *dāl* f. Gmc **dailaz;* cf. DEAL[1]]

dōle[2] *n.* (poet.) grief, woe; lamentation. [ME, f. OF *do(e)l* etc. f. pop. L *dolus* f. L *dolēre* grieve]

dō'leful (-lf-) *a.* dreary, dismal; sad, discontented, melancholy; hence ∼LY[2] *adv.,* ∼NESS *n.* [ME, f. prec. + -FUL]

dō'lerīte *n.* coarse basaltic rock. [f. F *dolérite* f. Gk *doleros* deceptive (because its constituents are difficult to distinguish); see -ITE[1]]

dŏlichocĕphă'lic, -cĕ'phalous, (-ko-) *adjs.* having a long or narrow head. [f. Gk *dolikhos* long + -CEPHALIC, -CEPHALOUS]

doli'na, doli'ne, (-ē'-) *n.* (usu. large) sink-hole. [Russ. *dolina* valley]

dŏll *n.* & *v.* **1.** *n.* small model of human figure, esp. of child as toy (∼'**s house,** *∼'house,** miniature toy house for dolls, diminutive dwelling-house); ventriloquist's dummy; pretty but silly woman; (sl.) young woman; (sl.) attractive person. **2.** *v.t.* & *i.* (colloq.) esp. in *p.p.) dress up* smartly. [pet-form of woman's Christian name *Dorothy*]

dŏ'llar *n.* unit of US currency (∼ **mark** or ∼ **sign,** $); unit of currency in other countries; (Hist.) German thaler, piece of eight; ∼ **area** (in which currency is linked to US dollar); ∼-**bird,** (Austral.) roller with round white patch on wing; ∼-**diplomacy** (seeking to advance country's financial and commercial interests abroad, and hence its international influence); ∼ **gap,** excess of country's import trade with dollar area over corresp. export trade; ∼ **spot,** (discoloured patch caused by) fungal disease of lawns etc. [f. LG *daler* f. G *taler* (*Joachimstaler,* coin from silver-mine of *Joachimstal* in Bohemia)]

dŏ'llop *n.,* & *v.t.* (colloq.) **1.** *n.* clumsy or shapeless lump of food etc. **2.** *v.t.* serve *out* in large quantities. [perh. f. Scand.]

dŏ'llÿ *n., a., & v.* **1.** *n.* (pet-name, esp. in *voc.*, for) doll; stick for stirring in clothes-washing; movable platform fur cine camera; (colloq.) easily hit or caught ball at cricket; CORN[1] *dolly*; ∼(-**bird**), (colloq.) attractive and stylish young woman; ∼ **mixture** (of tiny variously shaped and coloured sweets). **2.** *a.* (colloq.) attractive, stylish, (girl, etc.); (Cricket) easily hit or caught. **3.** *v.t.* dress *up* smartly. **4.** *v.i.* move cine camera (*in* or *up* to subject, *out* from it). [f. DOLL + -Y[3]]

Dŏllÿ Vâr'den *n.* CHAR[1] (*Salvelinus malma*) of western N. America; woman's large hat with one side drooping and with floral trimming. [character in Dickens's *Barnaby Rudge*]

dŏ'lman *n.* long Turkish robe open in front; hussar's jacket worn with sleeves hanging loose; woman's mantle with capelike or dolman sleeves; ∼ **sleeve**, loose sleeve cut in one piece with body of coat etc. [ult. f. Turk. *dolama*]

dŏ'lmĕn *n.* megalithic tomb with large flat stone laid on upright ones. [F, perh. f. Cornish *tolmēn* hole of stone]

dŏ'lomīte *n.* mineral or rock of calcium magnesium carbonate; hence **dŏlomī'tic** *a.* [F, f. S. G. de *Dolomieu*, Fr. geologist d. 1802; see -ITE[1]]

*dŏ'lor. See DOLOUR.

dŏ'lorous *a.* (literary or joc.) distressing, painful; dismal, doleful; distressed; hence ∼LY[2] *adv.* [ME, f. OF *doleros* f. LL *dolorosus* (as DOLOUR; see -OUS)]

‖**dŏ'lour** (-ler), ***dŏ'lor,** *n.* (literary). sorrow, distress. [ME f. OF, f. L *dolor -oris* pain, grief]

dŏ'lphin *n.* small whale (*Delphinus delphis*), resembling porpoise but larger and with beaklike snout, whence ∼AR'IUM *n.*, aquarium for dolphins; (pop.) dorado; curved fish in heraldry, sculpture, etc.; bollard, pile, or buoy, for mooring; structure for protecting pier of bridge. [ME, also *delphin* f. L *delphinus* f. Gk *delphis -inos*]

dŏlt *n.* stupid person; hence ∼'ISH[1] *a.* [app. related to *dol*, *dold*, obs. vars. of DULL, DULLED]

Dŏm *n.* Title prefixed to names of some RC dignitaries, and Benedictine and Carthusian monks; Portuguese equivalent of DON[1]. [f. L *dominus* master, in second sense thr. Port.]

DOM *abbr.* to God, the best and greatest. [f. L *Deo optimo maximo*]

-dom *suf.* forming **1.** denoting (1) rank, condition, domain, f. *ns.* or *adjs.* (*earldom, freedom, kingdom*), (2) collective pl. or the ways of—s, f. *ns.* (*officialdom*). [OE -*dōm*, — OS *dōm*, OHG -*tuom* orig. an independent n. = DOOM[1]]

domai'n *n.* estate, lands, dominions; district under rule, realm, sphere of influence; scope, field, province, of thought or action; (Math.) set of possible values of an independent variable; (Phys.) elementary region of magnetism in ferromagnetic material; **eminent** ∼, lordship of the sovereign power over all property in a State, with right of expropriation; hence **domā'nial** *a.* [ME, f. F *domaine*, OF *demeine* DEMESNE, assoc. w. L *dominus* lord]

domai'ne *n.* vineyard. [F; see prec.]

dōme *n., & v.t.* **1.** *n.* rounded vault as roof, with circular, elliptical, or polygonal base, large cupola; revolving openable hemispherical roof of observatory; (Geol.) dome-shaped structure; natural vault, canopy, (of sky, trees, etc.); rounded summit of hill etc.; (sl.) head; (poet.) stately building; hence **dōmED**[2] (-md), having or shaped like dome(s), **dō'mIC**(AL), ∼'LIKE (-ml-), **dō'mY**[2], *adjs.* **2.** *v.t.* cover with or shape as dome. [f. F *dôme* f. It. *duomo* cathedral, dome, f. L *domus* house]

Do'mesday (dŏŏ'mzdā) *n.* ∼ (Book), record of lands in England made in 1086 by order of William I. [ME var. of DOOM[1]*sday*, as being book of final authority]

domě'stic *a. & n.* **1.** *a.* of the home, household, or family affairs, (∼ **science**, study of household

management); of one's own country, not foreign or international (*domestic* TRADE); native, home-made; (of animal) kept by or living with man; fond of home life; hence **domě'stiCALLY** *adv.* **2.** *n.* household servant. [f. F *domestique* f. L *domesticus* (*domus* home)]

domě'stic|āte *v.t.* naturalize (plant, animal); make fond of home life; bring (animal) under human control, tame; hence ∼ABLE *a.*, ∼A'TION *n.* [f. med. L *domesticare* (as prec.) + -ATE[3]]

dŏmĕsti'cïtÿ *n.* being domestic; home life or privacy. [f. DOMESTIC + -ITY]

dŏ'micile, dŏ'micil, *n., & v.t.* **1.** dwelling-place, home; (Law) place of permanent residence, fact of residing. **2.** *v.t.* establish, settle, in a place; make (bill of exchange) payable *at* place. [ME f. OF, f. L *domicilium* (*domus* home)]

dŏmicī'liary (-lyeri) *a.* of a dwelling-place (∼ **visit**, visit of doctor, officials, etc., to person's home). [f. F *domiciliaire* f. med. L *domiciliarius* (as prec.; see -ARY[1])]

dŏ'min|ant *a. & n.* **1.** *a.* ruling, prevailing, most influential; (of high place) outstanding, overlooking others. **2.** *n.* (Mus.) fifth note of diatonic scale of any key; reciting note in church mode, usu. fifth from final. **3.** *a. & n.* (Genetics). (characteristic) appearing in offspring even when a corresponding opposite characteristic is also inherited. **4.** Hence ∼ANCE *n*, ∼antLY[2] *adv.* [F, f. L *dominari* (as foll.; see -ANT)]

dŏ'minäte *v.t. & i.* have commanding influence over or over, (of person, power, sound, feature of scene) be the most influential or conspicuous; (of high place) overlook, hold commanding position *over*. [f. L *dominari* (*dominus* lord) + -ATE[3]]

dŏminā'tion *n.* **1.** ascendancy, sway, control. **2.** (in *pl.*) fourth ORDER[1] of ninefold celestial hierarchy. [ME f. OF, f. L *dominatio -onis* (as prec.; see -ATION)]

dŏminee'r *v.i.* act imperiously, tyrannize, be overbearing. [f. Du. *domineren* f. F *dominer* (as DOMINATE; see -EER)]

domi'nical *a.* of the Lord's day, Sunday-, (∼ **letter**, the one of the seven A-G indicating dates of Sundays in a year); of the Lord (Christ). [F, or f. LL *dominicalis* f. L *dominicus* (*dominus* lord; see -IC) + -alis -AL]

Domi'nican *a. & n.* **1.** *a.* of St. Dominic or his order of preaching friars, founded 1215, and nuns. **2.** *n.* Black or Dominican friar or nun. [f. med. L *Dominicanus* (*Dominicus* I, name of *Domingo* de Guzmán (St. Dominic) + -AN)]

dŏ'minie *n.* (Sc.) schoolmaster. [later sp. of *domine* sir, voc. of L *dominus* lord]

domi'nion (-yon) *n.* lordship, sovereignty, control; domains of feudal lord, territory of sovereign or government; (Hist.) title of self-governing territories of British Commonwealth. [ME f. OF, f. med. L *dominio -onis* f. L *dominium* (*dominus* lord)]

dŏ'minō *n.* (*pl.* ∼-es). **1.** loose cloak with mask for upper part of face, worn to conceal identity esp. at masquerade; hence ∼ED[2] (-ōd) *a.* **2.** one of usu. 28 small oblong pieces marked with usu. 0-6 pips in each half, used in game of ∼es (usu. treated as *sing.*); ∼ **theory** (that political event etc. in one place will cause similar events in others, like row of falling dominoes). [F, prob. f. L *dominus* lord, but unexplained]

dŏn *n.* **1.** (*D*∼) Spanish title prefixed to Christian name (**Don Juan**, rake, libertine; **Don Quixote**, Spanish gentleman, Spaniard. **2.** head, fellow, or tutor, of college, esp. at Oxford or Cambridge; (arch.) person of distinction. [Sp., f. L *dominus* lord]

dŏn *v.t.* (-**nn**-). put on (clothing). [= *do on*]

dŏ'na(h) *n.* (sl.) woman, sweetheart. [f. Sp. *doña* or Port. *dona* f. L (as DONNA)]

donā'te *v.t.* make donation of. [back-form. f. foll.]

donā'tion *n.* bestowal, presenting; thing presented, gift (esp. of money) given to institution). [ME f. OF, f. L *donatio -onis* (*donare* give f. *donum* gift: see -ATION)]

dŏ'native *a. & n.* (given as) donation or bounty; (Hist., of benefice) given directly, not presentative.

[ME, f. L *donativum* gift, largess (*donare*; see prec., -IVE)]
done (dŭn) *a.* In vbl senses; (colloq.) socially acceptable (*the done thing; it isn't done*); ~ (**in, up**), (colloq.) tired out; (esp. as *int.* in reply to offer etc.) accepted; **be ~ with**, have (been) finished with; **have ~**, cease; **have ~ with**, finish dealing with. [p.p. of DO¹]
dōnee' *n.* recipient of gift. [f. DONOR + -EE]
dŏng *v.i.*, & *n.* (make) deep sound of large bell; (Austral. & NZ colloq.) heavy blow. [imit.]
dŏ'nga (-ngga) *n.* (S. Afr. etc.) gully, ravine. [Bantu]
do'njon (dŏ'-, dŭ'-) *n.* great tower of castle, keep. [arch. sp. of DUNGEON]
dŏ'nkey *n.* = ASS¹ (**talk the hind leg off a ~**, talk incessantly); stupid person; ~**-drop**, (colloq.) ball moving slowly in high curve; ~ **engine**, small auxiliary engine; ~ **jacket**, workman's thick weatherproof jacket; ~**'s years**, (colloq.) a very long time; ~**-work**, drudgery, laborious part of an enterprise. [18th c., perh. f. DUN¹, or man's Christian name *Duncan* (cf. *dicky, neddy*)]
dŏ'nna *n.* (*D*~, title of) Italian or Spanish or Portuguese lady. [It., f. L *domina* mistress fem. of *dominus*; cf. DON¹]
donnée, donné (dŏ'nā) *n.* subject or theme of story etc.; basic fact or assumption. [F, fem. or masc. p.p. of *donner* give]
dŏ'nnish *a.* like a college don; pedantic; hence ~LY² *adv.*, ~NESS *n.* [f. DON¹ + -ISH¹]
Dŏ'nnýbrŏŏk *n.* scene of uproar, free fight. [~ near Dublin, Ireland, formerly site of annual fair]
dŏ'nor *n.* giver of gift; person or animal providing blood for transfusion, semen for insemination, organ for transplantation, etc.; (Chem. & Phys.) atom or molecule that gives an electron to another or to a crystal. [ME, f. AF *donour*, OF *doneur* f. L *donator -oris* (*donare* give; see -OR)]
dŏn't¹. See DO¹.
dŏn't² *n.* prohibition (DO²*s and don'ts*). [f. prec.]
***dōŏ'dăd** *n.* fancy article; trivial ornament; gadget. [20th c.; orig. unkn.]
dōŏ'dah *n.* (sl.) = prec.; **all of a ~**, excited, dithering. [f. refrain of song *Camptown Races*]
dōŏ'dle *v.i.*, & *n.* **1.** *v.i.* scrawl or draw, absent-mindedly; hence **dōŏ'dl**ER¹ *n.* **2.** *n.* scrawl or drawing so made; ~**-bug**, *(larva of) tiger-beetle, *unscientific device for locating minerals, (colloq.) flying bomb. [orig. = foolish person; cf. LG *dudelkopf*]
***dōŏ'hickey** *n.* (colloq.) small object, esp. mechanical. [f. DOODAD + HICKEY]
dōŏm¹ *n.* **1.** fate, destiny, (usu. evil); ruin, death; ~**'watch**, observation to prevent destruction of the environment. **2.** (Hist.) statute, law, decree. **3.** (arch.) decision, sentence, condemnation. **4.** the Last Judgement (*crack, day, of doom; doo'msday*; ~**sday machine**, hypothetical weapon able to annihilate mankind; **till ~sday**, for ever; cf. DOMESDAY). [OE *dōm* statute, judgement, = OS *dōm*, OHG *tuom*, ON *dómr*, Goth. *dōms* f. Gmc *dōmaz* that which is set, f. as DO¹]
dōŏm² *v.t.* pronounce sentence against, condemn *to* some fate, *to* do; (esp. in *p.p.*) consign to misfortune or destruction. [ME, f. prec.]
door (dŏr) *n.* **1.** hinged or sliding barrier usu. of wood or metal for closing entrance to building, room, safe, vehicle, etc. (FRONT *door; lives* etc. **next ~**, in next house or room; so **three ~s away** etc.; **next ~ to**, (fig.) nearly, almost, near to; *at* DEATH'*s door*); ~**-to-~** *a.*, (of selling etc.) done at each house in turn, (of journey) from start to finish. **2.** entrance, access, exit, (**close the ~ to**, make impossible; **foot in the ~**, chance of ultimate success; **leave the ~ open**, preserve possibility; **open the ~ to**, create opportunity for; **packed to the ~s**, entirely full; **show person the ~**, dismiss him); doorway. **3.** out of ~s, in or into the open air; DARKEN person's *door*; **lay, lie, at the ~ of**, impute, be imputable, to. **4.** ~**'bell**, bell

in house rung by handle or button outside door; ~**-case, -frame**, structure in which door is fitted; ~**-head**, upper part of door-case; ~**-keeper**, person who guards door, janitor, porter; ~**'knob** (for turning to release latch of door); ~**'man**, = *door-keeper*; ~**'mat**, mat for wiping mud from shoes, (fig.) despised passive person; ~**'nail** (with which doors were studded for strength or ornament; DEAD *as a doornail*); ~**-plate** (usu. of brass, bearing occupant's name); ~**'post**, upright of door-case; ~**'step**, step leading up to usu. outer door (*on one's or the ~step*, (fig.) very near), (sl.) thick slice of bread; ~**'stop**, device for keeping door open or to prevent it from striking wall etc.; ~**'way**, opening filled by door; *~**'way**, yard or garden near house-door. **5.** Hence (-)~ED² (dŏrd), ~'LESS, *adjs.* [OE *duru, dor*, = OS *duru, dor*, OHG *tor*, Goth. *daur* f. Gmc *dur-*]
dŏp *n.* (S. Afr.) cheap brandy; tot of liquor. [Afrik.]
dŏ'pa *n.* crystalline amino-acid used in treatment of Parkinsonism. [G, f. *dioxyphenylalanine*]
dōpe *n.* & *v.* **1.** *n.* thick liquid used as food or lubricant; varnish used esp. in aeroplane manufacture; (sl.) narcotic, stupefying drug (~**-fiend**, drug addict); drug etc. given to horse or greyhound to affect its performance or to athlete as stimulus; (sl.) information about a subject, esp. if not generally known; (sl.) misleading information; (colloq.) stupid person. **2.** *v.t.* administer dope to, drug; add impurity to (semiconductor etc.), whence **dŏ'p**ANT *n.*; ~ **out**, (sl.) discover. **3.** *v.i.* indulge in narcotics etc. [f. Du. *doop* sauce (*doopen* to dip)]
dŏ'pey *a.* (sl.) stupefied (as) by a drug; stupid. [f. prec. + -Y²]
doppelgänger (dŏ'pelgĕng+r) *n.* wraith of living person. [G, = double-goer]
Dŏ'pper *n.* (S. Afr.) member of the Gereformeerde Kerk, usu. regarded as old-fashioned in ideas, etc. [Afrik.]
Dŏ'ppler *n.* ~ **effect** or **shift**, apparent increase (decrease) in frequency of sound, light, or other waves when source and observer become closer (more distant). [f. C. J. ~, Austrian physicist d. 1853]
dŏr *n.* insect flying with loud humming noise. [OE *dora*; prob. imit.]
dora'dō (-ah'-) *n.* (*pl.* ~s). blue and silver sea-fish of genus *Coryphaena*, showing brilliant colours when dying out of water; S. Amer. carplike fish of genus *Salminus*. [Sp., f. L DE(*auratus* gilt f. *aurum* gold; see -ADO)]
Dŏr'ian *a.* & *n.* **1.** (inhabitant) of or from Doris in ancient Greece. **2.** *a.* ~ **mode**, (Mus.) (1) ancient Greek MODE, reputedly simple and solemn in character, (2) first of church modes (with D as final and A as dominant). [f. L f. Gk *Dōrios* (*Dōris*; cf. foll.) + -AN]
Dŏ'ric *a.* & *n.* **1.** *a.* (Of dialect) broad, rustic; ~ **order**, (Archit.) oldest, sturdiest, and simplest of the five ORDER¹s. **2.** *n.* dialect of Dorians in ancient Greece; rustic English or esp. Scots; Doric order. [f. L f. Gk *Dōrikos* (as prec.; see -IC)]
Dŏr'king *n.* (bird of) breed of large white fowl with five toes. [~ in Surrey]
dŏrm *n.* (colloq.) dormitory. [abbr.]
dŏr'm|ant *a.* lying inactive as in sleep (of some animals throughout winter, undeveloped buds, volcano, potential faculties); (Her., of beast) lying with head on paws; not acting or in use, in abeyance, (*lie dormant*); hence ~ANCY *n.* [ME f. OF, part. of *dormir* f. L *dormire* sleep; see -ANT]
dŏr'mer *n.* ~ (**window**), projecting upright window in sloping roof. [f. OF *dormeor* (as prec.; see -ER² (3))]
dŏr'mitorý *n.* sleeping-room with several beds and sometimes cubicles; suburban or country district of city workers' residences; *university or college hall of residence or hostel. [ME, f. L *dormitorium* (*dormire -it-* sleep; see ORY)]
dŏr'mouse *n.* (*pl.* -mice *pr.* -mīs). small hibernating

rodent of family Gliridae, resembling mouse and squirrel. [ME; orig. unkn.]

dôr'mÿ a. (Golf). (Of player or side) as many holes ahead in score as there are holes left to play (*dormy one*, *five*, etc.). [19th c.; orig. unkn.]

||**Dô'rothÿ** n. ~ **bag**, woman's open-topped handbag closed by draw-string and slung by loops from wrist. [woman's Christian name]

dôrp n. (S. Afr.) village, small township. [Du., as THORP]

dôr'sal a. (Anat., Zool., & Bot.) of, on, near, the back; ridge-shaped; hence ~LY² adv. [F, or f. LL *dorsalis* f. L *dorsum* back; see -AL]

dôr'ter, dôr'tour (-ter), n. (Hist.) bedroom, dormitory, esp. in monastery. [ME, f. OF *dortour* f. L *dormitorium* DORMITORY]

dôr'ÿ¹ n. (Also **John D~**) yellow European marine food-fish (*Zeus faber*). [ME, f. F *dorée* fem. p.p. of *dorer* gild (as DORADO)]

dôr'ÿ² n. flat-bottomed skiff, esp. *fishing-vessel's boat. [18th c.; orig. unkn.]

dos-à-dos (dōzahdō') adv., n. (pl. same), & a. **1.** adv. (arch.) back to back. **2.** n. seat, carriage, etc., in which occupants sit back to back. **3.** a (Of two books) bound together with shared central board and pages in opposite directions. [F]

dô'sage n. giving of medicine in doses; size of dose. [f. foll. + -AGE]

dôse n., & v.t. **1.** n. amount of medicine to be taken at one time (lit., or fig. of flattery, punishment, etc.; **like a ~ of salts**, (sl.) very fast); amount of radiation received by person or thing exposed to it, whence **dôsi'**METER, **dôsi'**METRY, ns., **dôsimĕ'**tric a.; (sl.) venereal infection. **2.** v.t. give medicine to (person); adulterate, blend, (esp. wine with spirit). [F, f. LL f. Gk *dosis* gift (*didōmi* give)]

||**döss** n., & v.i. (sl.) **1.** n. bed, esp. in ~**-house** = cheap lodging-house. **2.** v.i. sleep, esp. in doss-house; ~ **down**, sleep on makeshift bed; hence ~ER¹ n. [prob. = *doss* ornamental covering for seat-back etc., f. OF *dos* t. pop. L *dossum* f. L *dorsum* back]

dô'ssal n. hanging cloth behind altar or round a chancel. [f. med. L *dossale* f. LL *dorsalis* DORSAL]

do'ssier (dô'sier, dŏ'syā) n. set of documents, esp. record of information about a person or event. [F, so called f. label on back (*dos* f. L *dorsum*; see -ER² (2))]

dost. See DO¹.

dŏt¹ n. small spot, speck, roundish pen-mark; such mark written or printed as part of *i* or *j*, or as diacritical mark; (Mus.) such mark used to denote lengthening of note or rest, or to indicate staccato; decimal point; tiny object; shorter signal of the two used in Morse code; **on the ~**, exactly on time; ||**the year ~**, (colloq.) very long ago. [16th c., perh. repr. OE *dott* head of boil]

dŏt² v.t. (-tt-). mark with dot(s); place dot over (letter); ~ **the i's and cross the t's**, (fig.) be minutely accurate, emphasize details; (Mus.) mark (note or rest) to show time value increased by half; partly cover as with dots (*sea dotted with ships*; *dot with butter*); scatter (*about, all over*) like dots; (sl.) hit (*dotted him one in the eye*); ~ **and carry** (**one**), child's formula for remembering to carry in addition sum, (joc., also ~ **and go one**, n., a., & adv.) limp, limping(ly); ~**ted line**, (esp.) line of dots on document to show place left for signature (*sign on the ~ted line*, give formal agreement). [f. prec.]

dot³ (dŏt) n. woman's dowry. [F, f. L *dos dotis* (*dowgive*)]

dô'tage. See DOTE.

dô'tard n. one in his dotage. [ME, f. foll. + -ARD]

dôte v.i. be silly, deranged, infatuated, or feeble-minded, esp. from age, whence **dô'tAGE** (2) n.; ~ **on**, be excessively fond of. [ME, corresp. to MDu. *doten* be silly]

doth. See DO¹.

dô'tterel n. small plover, *Eudromias morinellus*. [ME, f.

DOTE + -REL, named from the ease with which it is caught, taken to indicate stupidity]

dô'ttle n. remnant of unburnt tobacco in pipe. [f. DOT¹ + -LE 1]

dô'tt|ÿ a. (colloq.) feeble-minded; silly; absurd; hence ~iNESS n. [f. DOT¹ + -Y²]

Dou'ai, Dou'ay, (dōo'ā, dow'ā) n. ~ **version, Bible**, English translation of the Bible used in RC Church, completed at ~ in France early in 17th c.

doua'ne (dōoah'n) n. foreign custom-house. [F, f. It. *do(g)ana* f. Turk. *duwan*, Arab. *dīwān*; cf. DIVAN]

dou'ble¹ (dŭ'-) a. & adv. **1.** a. consisting of two members, things, layers, sets, etc., forming a pair, twofold; folded, bent, stooping. **2.** having some part double; (of flower) with petals multiplied by conversion of stamens etc.; (of domino) with same number of pips on each half. **3.** having twofold relation, dual, ambiguous; twice as much or as many (*double the amount*); of twofold or extra size, strength, value, etc., (*a double whisky*); (Mus.) lower in pitch by an octave (*double bassoon*); deceitful, hypocritical (*playing a double game*). **4.** Hence ~NESS (-beln-) n., dou'bLY¹ (dŭ'-) adv. **5.** adv. to twice the amount etc. (**see ~**, seem to see two things when there is only one; esp. of drunken person); two together (*sleep double*). **6.** *double* ACROSTIC; ~**-acting** (in two ways, directions, etc., esp. of engine in which steam acts on both sides of piston); ~ **agent**, one who spies for two rival countries etc.; ~ **axe** (with two blades); ~**-banking**, (1) = *double-parking*, (2) (Austral. & NZ) riding two on a horse etc.; ~**-barrel**, double-barrelled (gun); ~**-barrelled**, (of gun) having two barrels, (fig.) twofold, (of surname) having two parts; ~**-bass**, (n.) lowest-pitched instrument of violin family, (a.) lowest-pitched (member of a group of similar instruments); ~ **bed** (for two persons); ~ **bill**, programme with two principal items; ~ **bind**, dilemma; ~**-bitt** v.t. (Naut.) pass (cable) twice round bitts or round two pairs of bitts; ~**-blind** a. & n., (test etc.) in which neither tester nor subject has knowledge of identities etc. that might lead to bias; ~ **boiler**, saucepan with detachable upper compartment heated by boiling water in lower; ~ **bond**, (Chem.) pair of bonds between two atoms; ~**-breasted**, (of coat etc.) having two fronts overlapping across body; ~**-check**, v.t., verify twice or in two ways; ~ **chin**, chin with fold of flesh under it; ~ **concerto** (for two solo instruments); ~ **cream**, thick cream with high fat-content; ~**-cross** n., & v.t., (subject to) act of treachery or cheating; *double* DAGGER; ~**-dealer**, deceiver; ~**-dealing** n. & a., deceit(ful); *double*-DECKER; *double*-DECLUTCH; ~ **decomposition**, (Chem.) simultaneous decomposition of two compounds in reaction; ~ **drummer**, (Austral.) noisy kind of cicada; *double* DUMMY, DUTCH¹; ~**-dyed**, dyed twice (usu. fig., deeply stained with guilt); *double* EAGLE; ~**-edged**, having two cutting edges, (fig.) damaging to user as well as his opponent; *double* ENTRY; ~ **exposure**, (Photog.) accidentally or deliberately repeated exposure of film etc.; ~**-faced**, insincere; *double* FAULT; ~ **feature**, cinema programme with two full-length films; *double figures* (FIGURE¹ 5); ||~ **first**, (person winning) first-class honours in two subjects or examinations at university; ~ **fleece**, (Austral. & NZ) from sheep that has missed a shearing; ~**-fronted**, (of house) with principal windows on either side of front door; ~**-ganger**, = DOPPELGÄNGER; ~ **glazing**, (provision of) two sheets of glass in a window to reduce heat loss etc.; ~ **harness**, harness for two horses, (fig.) matrimony or close partnership; *~ **header**, two games etc. in succession between same opponents; ~ **helix**, pair of parallel helices with common axis, esp. in structure of DNA molecule; ~**-jointed**, having joints that allow unusual bending of fingers, limbs, etc.; ~ **life**, sustaining of two different characters in one's life, one virtuous and the other not;

∼-**lock** *v.t.*, lock by double turn of key; ∼ **meaning,** = DOUBLE ENTENDRE; *double* OBELISK, PADDLE[1]; ∼- -**parking,** parking of vehicle alongside one that is already parked at roadside; ∼ **play,** (Baseball) putting out two runners; ∼ **pneumonia** (of both lungs); ∼-**quick** *a.* & *adv.*, at running pace (lit. or fig.); ∼-**reef** *v.t.*, (Naut.) reduce spread of (sail) by two reefs; *double* REFRACTION, RHYME[1]; ∼ **room,** bedroom for two persons; ∼ **salt,** (Chem.) salt composed of two simple salts and having different crystal properties from either; ∼ **saucepan,** = *double boiler*; *double* SHUFFLE; ∼ **standard,** (1) rule etc. applied more strictly to some persons than to others, (2) bimetallism; ∼ **star,** two stars actually or apparently very close together; ∼-**stopping,** (Mus.) sounding of two notes at once on stringed instrument; ∼ **take,** delayed reaction to situation etc. immediately after one's first reaction; ∼-**talk,** verbal expression that is (usu. deliberately) ambiguous; ∼-**think,** mental capacity to accept contrary opinions etc. at same time; *double* TIDE[1]s; ∼ **time,** payment of employee at twice normal rate, (Mil.) regulation running- -pace; *double* TRACK[1]; ∼ **wedding** (of two couples at same time). [ME, f. OF *doble, duble* f. L *duplus* DUPLE]

dou′ble² (dŭ′-) *n.* **1.** double quantity or thing, double measure of spirits etc., twice as much or many (∼ or **quits,** game, throw, toss, deciding whether person shall pay either twice his loss or debt, or nothing); counterpart of thing or person, understudy, wraith; **at the** ∼, running, hastening. **2.** pair of victories over same team, pair of championships at same game, etc.; (Bridge) doubling of a bid; (Tennis etc., in *pl.*) game between two pairs; (Darts) throw on narrow ring enclosed by two outer circles of dartboard, scoring double; (Racing) bet on two horses etc. in different races, winnings, and stake from one race being bet on the second; sharp turn of hunted animal, or of river. [f. prec. and foll.]

dou′ble³ (dŭ′-) *v.* **1.** *v.t.* make double, increase twofold, multiply by two; (of actor) play (two parts) in same piece; amount to twice as much as; (Bridge) make call increasing value of points to be won or lost on (opponent's bid); (Mus.) add same note in higher or lower octave to; (of musician) play as second (instrument) besides one's main instrument. **2.** ∼ (**up**), put (passenger etc.) in same quarters as another, bet twofold (stake). **3.** bend or turn (paper, cloth) over upon itself; clench (fist). **4.** (Naut.) get round (headland). **5.** *v.t.* & *i.* ∼ **up,** bend one's body into stooping or curled-up position (fig., be convulsed with laughter or pain), cause (another) to do this by blow, fold (paper, leaf, etc.) or become folded. **6.** (Bill.) (cause to) rebound. **7.** *v.i.* move at double pace, run. **8.** turn sharply in flight or pursuit, take tortuous course (∼ **back,** take direction opposite to previous one). **9.** play twofold part (*as*). [ME, f. OF *dobler, dubler* f. LL *duplare* (L *duplus* DOUBLE[1])]

double entendre (dōōbl ahṅtah′ṅdr) *n.* ambiguous expression, phrase with two meanings, one usu. indecent; use of such phrases. [obs. F, = double understanding]

double entente (dōōbl ahṅtah′ṅt) *n.* = prec. [F]

dou′blèt (dŭ′-) *n.* **1.** (Hist.) man's close-fitting body- -garment with or without sleeves and short skirts; ∼ **and hose,** masculine attire, light attire without cloak. **2.** one of a pair, esp. one of two words of same derivation but different sense (*fashion* and *faction, cloak* and *clock*). **3.** (in *pl.*) same number on two dice thrown at once. **4.** pair of associated lines close together in spectrum. **5.** combination of two simple lenses. [ME f. OF *dublet*; see DOUBLE[1], -ET)]

dou′bleton (dŭ′belton) *n.* two cards only of a suit (dealt to a player). [f. DOUBLE[1], after *singleton*]

doublōō′n (dŭ-, du-) *n.* (Hist.) Spanish gold coin, double pistole; (sl., in *pl.*) money. [f. F *doublon* or f. Sp. *doblón* (as DOUBLE[1]; see -OON)]

doublure (dōōblūr′) *n.* ornamental usu. leather lining inside book-cover. [F, = lining (*doubler* to line; see -URE)]

doubt¹ (dowt) *n.* **1.** feeling of uncertainty (*about*), undecided frame of mind, inclination to disbelieve (*of, about*), hesitation, (*be in no doubt about*; *have* or *make no doubt that*; *have* one's *doubts about*; **no** ∼, certainly, probably, admittedly). **2.** uncertain state of things, lack of full proof (BENEFIT[1] *of the doubt*) or of clear signs of the future; **beyond** ∼, **without** (**a**) ∼, certainly. [ME, f. OF *d(o)ute (douter*; see foll.)]

doubt² (dowt) *v.i.* & *t.* feel undecided or uncertain (*about*); be undecided about or *about*, hesitate to believe or trust, call in question, (person, thing, *whether, if,* (neg. or interrog.) *that, but, but that*); have doubts *of* (esp. w. neg.; *never doubted of success*); ‖(arch. or dial.) be afraid, rather think, suspect, that (*I doubt we are late*); ∼**ing Thomas,** incredulous or sceptical person (after John 20: 24–29); hence ∼′ER¹ *n.* [ME f. OF *doter, duter, douter,* f. L *dubitare* hesitate; mod. sp. after L]

dou′btful (dow′t-) *a.* feeling or causing doubt; uncertain in meaning, character, truth, or result; undecided, ambiguous, questionable; unreliable (*doubtful ally*); giving reason to suspect evil; unsettled in opinion, uncertain, hesitating; hence ∼LY² *adv.,* ∼NESS *n.* [ME, f. DOUBT¹ + -FUL]

dou′btless (dow′t-) *adv.* certainly, no doubt; probably; admittedly. [f. DOUBT¹ + -LESS]

douce (dōōs) *a.* (Sc.) sober, gentle, sedate. [ME, f. OF *dous douce* f. L *dulcis* sweet]

douceur (dōō′sēr) *n.* gratuity; bribe. [F, f. Rom. **dulçōre* f. LL *dulcor* sweetness]

douche (dōōsh) *n.* & *v.* **1.** *n.* jet of liquid applied to body as form of bathing or for medicinal purpose; device for producing such jet. **2.** *v.t.* administer douche to. **3.** *v.i.* take douche. [F, f. It. *doccia* pipe (*docciare* pour by drops f. Rom. **ductiare* f. L *ductus*; see DUCT)]

dough (dō) *n.* kneaded moistened flour, bread-paste; (sl.) money; ∼′**boy,** boiled dumpling, (colloq.) US infantryman; hence ∼Y² (dō′i) *a.* [OE *dāg,* = OHG *teic,* ON *deig,* Goth. *daigs* f. Gmc **daigaz* (**daig-* f. IE **dhoigh-* etc. knead)]

dou′ghnut (dō′n-) *n.* sweetened and fried cake of dough, often ring-shaped; ring-shaped object, esp. (Phys.) vacuum chamber for acceleration of particles in betatron etc. [f. prec. + NUT]

dou′ght|ў (dow′tĭ) *a.* (arch. or joc.) valiant, stout, formidable; hence ∼ĭLY² *adv.,* ∼ĭNESS *n.* [OE *dohtig* var. of *dyhtig* = MLG, MDu. *duchtich,* MHG *tühtic* f. Gmc **dug-* be strong]

Dou′glas (dŭ′-) *n.* ∼ **fir, pine,** or **spruce,** large conifer of genus *Pseudotsuga,* orig. of western N. America. [f. D. ∼, Sc. botanist d. 1834]

Dou′khobŏr (dōō′ko-) *n.* member of Russian religious sect, with some likeness in doctrines to Quakers, of which large numbers migrated from Russia to Canada in 1899 after persecutions for refusing military service. [f. Russ. *dukhobor* spirit-wrestler]

doum (dowm, dōōm) *n.* ∼(-**palm**), Egyptian palm- -tree (*Hyphaene thebaica*) with edible fruit. [f. Arab. *dawm, dūm*]

dour (door) *a.* severe, stern, obstinate; hence ∼′LY² *adv.,* ∼′NESS *n.* [ME, orig. Sc., prob. f. Gael. *dúr* dull, obstinate, perh. f. L *durus* hard]

douroucou′li (dooroōkoō′-) *n.* nocturnal Amer. monkey of genus *Aotus,* with large staring eyes. [f. Indian name]

douse, dowse¹, *v.t.* **1.** (Naut.) lower (sail), close (porthole). **2.** extinguish (light); throw water over, drench. [16th c., perh. rel. to MDu., LG *dossen* strike]

dove¹ (dŭv) *n.* bird of family Columbidae, pigeon, (esp. RING¹-*dove,* STOCK*dove,* TURTLE¹-*dove*); Holy Spirit; gentle or innocent person, beloved person; (Polit.) person advocating negotiation rather than violence; ∼-**colour**(**ed**), (of) warm grey; ∼′**cot**(**e**), pigeon-house (*flutter the ~cots*, alarm quiet people); ~-**hawk**, hen-harrier (from its colour); ~'s-**foot**, kind of crane's-bill; ~-**tree**, Chinese tree (*Davidia involucrata*) with dovelike flowers. [ME, f. ON *dúfa*, = OS *dūba*, OHG *tūba*, Goth. *dūbo* f. Gmc *dūbhōn, perh. imit.]

dōve². See DIVE.

do'vekie (dŭ'vkĭ) *n*. little AUK. [Sc. dim of DOVE¹]

Dō'ver *n*. ~'s **powder**, medicine of opium and ipecacuanha. [f. T. ~, Engl. physician d. 1742]

do'vetail (dŭ'vt-) *n*. & *v*. **1.** *n*. tenon shaped like dove's spread tail or reversed wedge, fitting into corresponding mortise and forming joint; such a joint. **2.** *v.t.* & *i*. put together with dovetails; (fig.) fit together compactly or neatly (*into, with*). [f. DOVE¹ + TAIL¹]

dow'ager *n*. woman with title or property derived from her late husband (often in comb., *Queen dowager*, *dowager countess* or *countess dowager, dowager duchess*); (colloq.) dignified elderly lady. [f. OF *douag(i)ere* (*douage*, as DOWER; see -ER² (2))]

dow'dĭy *n*. & *a*. (woman) shabbily, badly, or unfashionably dressed; (of dress etc.) unattractively dull, unfashionable; hence ~ĭLY² *adv.*, ~ĭNESS *n*. [f. ME *dowd* slut, of unkn. orig]

dow'el *n*., & *v.t.* (||-ll-). **1.** *n*. headless pin of wood, metal, etc., for keeping two pieces of wood, stone, etc., in proper relative position; hence ~(l)ING¹ (3) *n*. **2.** *v.t.* fasten with dowel. [ME, f. MLG *dovel*, = OHG *tubili*; cf. THOLE²]

dow'er *n*., & *v.t.* **1.** *n*. widow's share for life of husband's estate; (arch. or poet.) dowry; endowment, gift of nature, talent; ||~ **house**, smaller house near big one, forming part of widow's dower; hence ~LESS *a*. **2.** *v.t.* give dowry to; endow *with* talent etc. [ME, f. OF *douaire* f. med. L *dotarium* f. L *dos dotis*; see -ARY¹]

Dow-Jō'nes (-nz) *n*. ~ **index** etc., figure indicating relative price of shares on NY Stock Exchange. [f. C. H. *Dow* d. 1902 & E. D. *Jones* d. 1920, Amer. economists]

dow'las *n*. strong coarse calico or (Hist.) linen. [f. *D(a)oulas* in Brittany]

down¹ *n*. open high land, esp. (in *pl*.) treeless undulating chalk uplands of S England and elsewhere, used for pasture; the **D~s**, part of sea (opposite North Downs) off E. Kent. [OE *dūn*, = OS *dūna*, perh. f. OCelt. *dunom]

down² *n*. first covering of young birds; bird's under-plumage, used in cushions etc.; fine short hair, esp. first hair on youth's face; similar substance on plant, fruit, etc., fluffy substance (THISTLE*down*). [ME, f. ON *dúnn*]

down³ *adv.* (*superl.* ~'**most**). **1.** denoting motion: from above, to lower place, to ground, from bedroom etc., (*knock, fall, down*; BRING down, COME down, GET¹ *down*, GO¹ *down*, PUT¹ *down*, SET¹ *down*, TURN¹ *down*; brought down by river; *cash* ~, *pay* ~, (at once, as though on counter); WRITE, *copy*, ~, (on paper); *meeting is* ~ *for next week, he is* ~ *to speak at the meeting*, (on programme)); to place regarded as lower, into helpless position, with current or wind, southwards, ||from capital or university, (of ship's helm) with rudder to windward, (BEAR³ *down*; SEND¹ *down*; UP *and down*; *run, ride, hunt,* ~, overtake and trap; *howl, shout,* ~ (into silence); *down to Norfolk from Scotland, to Scotland* or *the country from London*); (as *int*.) lie, get, put, bring, etc., down (*down, Bonzo!*; and w. *with, down with the aristocrats!*). **2.** denoting position: in lower place (*blinds were down; is not ~ yet*, i.e. out of bedroom etc.); in place regarded as lower, ||not in capital or university (*down in Devon, in the country, in the south*; ~ **south**, ~ **east**, *in southern, eastern, States); in fallen posture, prostrate, at low level, swallowed, in depression, humiliation, restraint, etc., (*hit a man who is down; many down with colds; river, sun, temperature, tide, is down; could not get the pill down; down to one's last penny, one's underwear*; KEEP¹ *down*; *bread is* ~, now cheaper);

(of ball in Amer. & Can. Footb.) out of play. **3.** denoting order, time, quality: inclusively of lower limit in series (*from King down to cobbler*); from earlier to later time (*custom handed down*); to finer particles (*grind down*) or smaller bulk (*boil down*) or thinner consistency (WATER² *down*); into quiescence (*calm down*); ||in position of lagging or loss (*team was three goals down; £5 down on the transaction*). **4.** be ~ **on**, disapprove of; DO¹ *down*; ~ **to the ground**, (colloq.) completely; ~-**hearted**, dejected; *down at* HEEL¹; *down on* one's LUCK; ~ **in the mouth**, down-hearted; ~ **and out**, unable to resume fight in boxing, (fig.) beaten in the struggle of life, completely without resources or means of livelihood (so ~-**and-out** *n*.); ~-**to-earth**, practical, realistic; ~ **under**, at the antipodes, in Australia etc. [OE *dūn(e)* (*adūne* ADOWN)]

down⁴ *prep.* downwards along, through, or into; from top to bottom of; at or in a lower part of (*situated down the river*); UP *and down*; along (*walk down the road; cut down the middle*); *down*-MARKET¹; ~ **stage**, at or to front of theatre stage; ~ **town**, into town from higher or outlying part, *to or in business part of city; ~ (**the**) **wind**, in direction in which it is blowing (*let go* ~ *the wind*, abandon, discard). [f. prec.]

down⁵ *a*. (*superl.* ~'**most**). directed downwards; ~ **beat**, (Mus.) accented beat; ~ **draught**, downward draught, esp. one down chimney into room; ~ **grade**, descending slope of road or railway, (fig.) deterioration; ~ **payment** (made in cash, esp. initially and to be followed by instalments); ~-**stroke** (made or written downwards); ~ **time** (during which machine is prevented from working); ~ **train**, train going or coming from capital or place regarded as higher (~ **platform**, for such train's departure or arrival). [f. DOWN³]

down⁶ *v.t.* (colloq.) knock, bring, swallow, (person, aeroplane, drink) down; ~ **tools**, cease work for the day etc., go on strike. [f. DOWN³]

down⁷ *n*. act of putting down (esp. opponent in Wrestling, ball in Amer. & Can. Footb.); reverse of fortune (usu. **ups and** ~**s**, UP 10); (Dominoes) play of first piece; **have a** ~ **on**, (colloq.) dislike, have grudge against. [f. DOWN³]

Down⁸ *n*. ~'s **syndrome**, mongolism. [f. J. L. H. ~, Engl. physician d. 1896]

dow'nbeat *a*. pessimistic, gloomy; relaxed, unemphatic. [f. DOWN³ *beat*]

dow'ncast¹ (-n-kah-) *n*. shaft for introducing fresh air into mine. [f. DOWN³ + CAST³]

dow'ncast² (-n-kah-) *a*. (Of look) directed downwards; dejected. [f. DOWN³ + p.p. of CAST¹]

dow'ncomer (-n-kŭ-) *n*. pipe for downward transport of water or gas. [f. DOWN³ + COMER]

dow'ner *n*. (sl.) depressant drug, a depressing experience. [f. DOWN⁶ + -ER¹]

dow'nfall (-awl) *n*. great fall of rain etc.; (cause of) fall from prosperity, ruin. [ME, f. DOWN³ + FALL²]

dow'nfōld *n*. (Geol.) syncline. [f. DOWN³ + FOLD²]

dow'ngrāde (-n-g-) *v.t.* lower in rank etc. [f. DOWN⁵ *grade*]

downhill *n*., *a*., & *adv*. **1.** *n*. (dow'-). downward slope, decline. (~ **of life**, later half); downhill race in skiing. **2.** *a*. (dow'-). sloping down, descending, declining. **3.** *adv.* (-ĭ'l). in descending direction, on a decline. [f. DOWN³·⁴ + HILL]

Dow'ning Street *n*. British Government, Prime Minister, or Foreign (etc.) Office. [street in London containing Foreign & Commonwealth Office and (No. 10; cf. NUMBER¹) official residence of Prime Minister, f. Sir G. *Downing*, Brit. diplomat d. 1684 + STREET]

dow'nland *n*. = DOWN¹. [f. DOWN¹ + LAND¹]

dow'nmōst. See DOWN³·⁵.

dow'npīpe *n*. pipe to carry rain-water from roof to drain. [f. DOWN³ + PIPE¹]

dow'npour (-pōr) *n*. heavy fall of rain etc. [f. DOWN³ + POUR]

dow'nright (-rīt; downrī't as *a.* after *n.*) *a.* & *adv.* **1.** *a.* plain, definite, straightforward, blunt, whence ∼NESS *n.*; not short of being, out-and-out, (*a downright lie, atheist; downright nonsense*). **2.** *adv.* thoroughly, positively, quite, (*downright scared, insolent*). [ME, f. *adownright* (ADOWN, RIGHT[1,4])]

***dow'nspout** *n.* downpipe. [f. DOWN[5]+SPOUT]

downstair's *adv.* & *n.*, **dow'nstair(s)** *a.*, (-z). down the stairs; (to, on, of) lower floor of house etc. [f. DOWN[3]+STAIR]

***dow'nstāte** *a.*, *adv.*, & *n.* (pertaining to, in) part of state remote from large cities, esp. southern part. [f. DOWN[4]+STATE[1]]

dow'nstream *a.* & *adv.* in the direction in which a stream or river flows. [f. DOWN[4]+STREAM]

dow'nthrow (-ō) *n.* (Geol.) downward dislocation of strata. [f. DOWN[3]+THROW[2]]

***dow'ntown** *a.*, *adv.*, & *n.* (pertaining to, in, into) lower or more central part or business part of town or city. [f. DOWN[4] *town*]

dow'ntrŏdden *a.* oppressed, kept under. [f. DOWN[3]+TRODDEN]

dow'ntŭrn *n.* decline, esp. in economic or business activity. [f. DOWN[3]+TURN[2]]

dow'nward *a.* & *adv.*, **dow'nward|s** (-z) *adv.* (moving, extending, pointing, leading) towards what is lower, inferior, less important, or later; hence ∼LY[2] *adv.* [ME, f. ADOWN+-WARD(S)]

dow'nwarp (-ôrp) *n.* (Geol.) broad surface depression, syncline. [f. DOWN[3]+WARP[2]]

dow'nwĭnd *a.* & *adv.* in the direction in which the wind is blowing. [f. DOWN[4]+WIND[1]]

dow'ny̆[1] *a.* of or like downs. [f. DOWN[1]+-Y[2]]

dow'n|y̆[2] *a.* of, like, covered with, down; (sl.) aware, knowing; hence ∼ĭLY[2] *adv.*, ∼ĭNESS *n.* [f. DOWN[2]+-Y[2]]

dow'ry̆ (dow'erĭ) *n.* property or money brought by bride to her husband; talent, natural gift. [ME, f. AF *dowarie*, OF *douaire* DOWER]

dowse[1]. See DOUSE.

dows|e[2] (-z) *v.i.* search for hidden water or minerals with forked twig (∼**'ing-rod**, or *divining-rod*) which dips suddenly when held over the right spot; hence ∼'ER[1] *n.* [17th c.; orig. unkn.]

dŏxŏ'|grapher *n.* writer who collected and recorded the opinions of the ancient Greek philosophers; hence **dŏxo**GRA'PHIC *a.*, ∼GRAPHY *n.* [f. mod. L *doxographus* f. Gk (*doxa* opinion, -GRAPHER)]

dŏxŏ'logy̆ *n.* liturgical formula of praise to God. [f. med. L f. Gk *doxologia* (*doxa* glory; see -LOGY)]

dŏ'xy̆[1] *n.* (arch.) beggar's wench; paramour. [16th c. cant, of unkn. orig.]

dŏ'xy̆[2] *n.* (arch. joc.) opinion, esp. on theological matters. [f. *orthodoxy, heterodoxy*]

doyen (doi'en, dwah'yăn) *n.* (*fem.* **doyenne** *pr.* dwahy̆ĕ'n). senior member *of* a body of colleagues, esp. senior ambassador at a court. [F, f. as DEAN[1]]

doy'ley. See DOILY.

doz. *abbr.* dozen.

dōze *v.i.*, & *n.* **1.** *v.i.* sleep lightly, be half asleep; ∼ **off**, fall slightly asleep. **2.** *n.* short light sleep. [17th c.; cf. Da. *döse* make drowsy]

do'zen (dŭ'-) *n.* (*pl.* ∼ *or* ∼**s**; for pl. usage see HUNDRED). twelve; set of twelve (*pack them in dozens*); (colloq.) about twelve, fairly large indefinite number, whence ∼TH[2] *a.* & *n.*; ∼**s of**, (colloq.) very many; **by the** ∼, in large quantities; **daily** ∼, (colloq.) physical exercises done daily on rising; BAKER's, **devil's, long,** ∼, thirteen; **half a** ∼, (about) six; ‖**talk nineteen to the** ∼ (incessantly). [ME, f. OF *dozeine*, ult. f. L *duodecim* twelve]

dō'zer *n.* (colloq.) bulldozer. [abbr.]

dō'zy̆ *a.* drowsy; (colloq.) stupid, lazy. [f. DOZE+-Y[2]]

DP *abbr.* displaced person.

DPH *abbr.* Diploma in Public Health.

D.Phil. *abbr.* Doctor of Philosophy.

DPM *abbr.* Diploma in Psychological Medicine.

‖**DPP** *abbr.* Director of Public Prosecutions.

Dr *abbr.* debtor; Doctor; Drive.

dr. *abbr.* drachm(s); drachma(s); dram(s).

drăb[1] *n.* slut, slattern; prostitute. [perh. rel. to LG *drabbe* mire, Du. *drab* dregs]

drăb[2] *a.* & *n.* (of) dull light-brown colour; dull, monotonous; monotony; hence ∼'LY[2] *a.*, ∼'NESS *n.* [prob. f. obs. *drap* cloth f. OF, f. LL *drappus*, perh. of Celt. orig.]

drăb[3] *n.* See DRIB.

dră'bble *v.i.* & *t.* become or make dirty and wet with water or mud. [ME, f. LG *drabbelen* paddle in water or mire; cf. DRAB[1]]

drăchm (-ăm) *n.* apothecaries' weight (‖Hist.) of 60 grains, ⅛ ounce; (**fluid**) ∼, apothecaries' measure of 60 minims, ⅛ fluid ounce; avoirdupois weight, one-sixteenth ounce; (arch.) small quantity. [ME *dragme* f. OF, or f. LL *dragma* f. L f. Gk *drakhmē* Attic weight and coin]

dră'chma (-k-) *n.* (*pl.* ∼**s** *or* ∼**e**). ancient-Greek silver coin; modern-Greek monetary unit and coin. [L, f. Gk *drakhmē*]

dră'cŏne *n.* large flexible container for liquids, towed on surface of sea. [f. L, as DRAGON]

Dracŏ'nian, Dracŏ'nic, (dra-, drā-) *adjs.* (Of laws) rigorous, harsh, cruel. [f. *Drakōn*, Athenian legislator *c.* 620 BC+-IAN, -IC]

draff (-ăf, -ahf) *n.* dregs, lees; refuse. [ME, perh. f. OE ***dræf** = MLG *draf*, MDu. *draf*, OHG ***trab**, ON ***draf*]

draft[1] (-ah-) *n.* **1.** (selection of) detachment from larger body for special duty or purpose; contingent, reinforcement; *(Mil.) conscription. **2.** drawing of money by written order, (fig.) demand made *on* person's confidence, friendship, etc.; bill or cheque drawn, esp. by one branch of bank on another. **3.** sketch of work to be executed; preliminary version of document. **4.*** = DRAUGHT[1]. [phonetic sp. of DRAUGHT[1]]

draft[2] (-ah-) *v.t.* **1.** draw off (part of larger body) for special duty or purpose; *conscript (lit. or fig.), whence ∼EE' *n.* **2.** prepare, make preliminary version of, (document, e.g. Parliamentary Bill), whence ∼'ER[1] *n.* [f. prec.]

dra'fts|man (-ah'f-) *n.* (*pl.* ∼**men**). one who drafts documents; = DRAUGHTSMAN 1. [phonetic sp. of DRAUGHTSMAN]

***dra'fty̆** (-ah'-) *a.* = DRAUGHTY. [f. DRAFT[1]+-Y[2]]

drăg[1] *v.* (**-gg-**). **1.** *v.t.* pull along with force, difficulty, or friction; allow (feet, tail, etc.) to trail; (colloq.) take (person *to* place etc., esp. against his will); **ship** ∼**s her anchor,** anchor fails to hold; search bottom of (river etc.) with grapnels or drags. **2.** *v.i.* trail, go or pass heavily or slowly or laboriously; use grapnel or drag (*for* drowned person or lost object); (colloq.) suck on or at (cigarette). **3.** ∼ one's **feet** or **heels,** (fig.) be deliberately slow or reluctant; ∼ **in,** introduce (subject) needlessly; ∼ **on,** continue tediously; ∼ **out,** protract; ∼ **up,** (colloq.) rear (child) roughly and without proper training, deliberately mention an event (usu. unpleasant) that is previously forgotten. [ME, f. OE *dragan* or ON *draga* DRAW[1]]

drăg[2] *n.* **1.** (Hist.) four-horsed private vehicle like stage-coach. **2.** = *drag-net*; apparatus for dredging or recovering drowned persons etc. from under water; strong-smelling lure for hounds in lieu of fox (so ∼-**hounds**), club for pursuing this sport. **3.** obstruction to progress; slow motion, impeded progress; iron shoe for retarding coach etc. downhill; boring or dreary performance, person, etc.; (Aeron.) longitudinal retarding force exerted by air. **4.** act of dragging; (sl.) suck at cigarette; *(sl.) influence, pull. **5.** (sl.) motor car; acceleration race between cars usu. over quarter-mile distance (∼**ster,** car modified to take part effectively in this). **6.** *(sl.) street, road, (esp. *main drag*). **7.** (sl.) women's clothes worn by men; party at which clothes are so worn; clothes in general. **8.** ∼-**anchor,** = SEA anchor; ∼-**line,** excavator with bucket pulled in by wire rope; **∿-net**, net drawn through river or across ground to trap fish or game, (fig.) means of systematically discovering criminals, etc. [ME, f. prec.]

dragée (drah'zhā) n. sugar-coated almond etc.; small silver ball for decorating cake; chocolate-coated sweet. [F; see DREDGE²]

drä'ggle v. **1.** v.t. make wet, limp, and dirty, by trailing. **2.** v.i. hang trailing; lag, straggle in rear; ∿--tail(ed), (woman) with draggled or untidily trailing skirts. [f. DRAG¹+-LE 3]

drä'ggy (-gǐ) a. (colloq.) tedious; unpleasant. [f. DRAG¹+-Y²]

drä'gom|an n. (pl. ∿ans or ∿en). interpreter or guide, esp. in countries using Arabic, Turkish, or Persian. [F, f. It. dragomano f. med. Gk dragomanus f. Arab. tarjumān (tarjama interpret, f. Aram. targēm f. Assyr. targumânu interpreter)]

drä'gon n. **1.** mythical monster like reptile, usu. with wings and claws and often breathing fire; (w. allus. to legends) watchful guardian of treasure etc.; fierce person; **the (old) D∿**, Satan; lizard of genus Draco with winglike structures; KOMODO dragon. **2.** ∿**-fly**, neuropterous insect with long slender body and two pairs of large wings usu. spread while resting; ∿**'s blood**, red gum that exudes from fruit of some palms, esp. ∿**-tree** (Dracaena draco); ∿**'s teeth**, (colloq.) anti--tank etc. obstacles resembling teeth pointed upwards. [ME f. OF, f. L draco -onis f. Gk drakōn serpent]

drä'gonet n. brightly-coloured spiny fish of family Callionymidae. [ME f. F, dim. of prec.]

dragonnä'de n., & v.t. **1.** n. persecution by use of troops, esp. (in pl.) of French Protestants under Louis XIV by quartering dragoons on them. **2.** v.t. subject to dragonnade. [F (dragon; see foll., -ADE)]

dragoo'n n., & v.t. **1.** n. cavalryman (orig. mounted infantryman armed with carbine); rough fierce fellow; variety of pigeon. **2.** v.t. set dragoons upon, persecute; force into a course of action by persecution. [orig. = carbine, f. F dragon DRAGON, so named as breathing fire; see -OON]

drail n. fish-hook and line weighted with lead for dragging at depth through water. [app. var. of TRAIL]

drain¹ v. **1.** v.t. draw (liquid) off or away by pipe etc (lit. or fig.; drain the wealth of England); drink (liquid), empty (vessel), to the dregs; make (land etc.) dry by providing outflow for moisture; (of river) carry off superfluous water of (district); remove purulent matter from (abscess); deprive (person, thing) of property, strength, etc. **2.** v.i. trickle through, flow off or away; (of wet cloth, vessel, etc.) get rid of moisture by its flowing away (set it there to drain). **3.** ∿**'ing--board, *∿'board**, sloping usu. grooved board on which washed dishes etc. are put to drain. [OE drē(a)hnian, prob. f. *drēag- f. Gmc *draug-; cf. DRY¹]

drain² n. channel carrying off liquid, artificial conduit for water, sewage, etc., (down the ∿, (colloq.) lost, wasted; laugh like a ∿, (colloq.) guffaw); tube for drawing off discharge from abscess etc.; constant outlet, withdrawal, demand, or expenditure (a great drain on my resources; BRAIN drain); (sl.) a drink; ∿--pipe, pipe for carrying off surplus water or liquid sewage from a building, (attrib., colloq., of trousers etc.) very narrow; ∿**-pipes**, (colloq.) such trousers. [f. prec.]

drai'nage n. draining; system of drains, artificial or natural; what is drained off, sewage. [f. DRAIN¹+-AGE]

drai'ner n. In vbl senses; thing in or on which things are put to drain, e.g. DRAIN¹ing-board. [f. DRAIN¹+-ER¹]

dräke¹ n. mayfly, esp. as used in fishing. [OE draca dragon, = MLG, MDu. drake, OHG trahho, WG *drako f. L draco; see DRAGON]

dräke² n. male duck (play DUCK¹s and drakes). [ME, corresp. to LG drake, drache, WG *drako, corresp. to second element in OHG antrehho]

dräm n. = DRACHM; small drink of spirit etc. (∿--drinker, tippler); *∿-shop, (arch.) = BAR¹ 7. [ME, f. OF drame or med. L drama, dragma; cf. DRACHM]

dra'ma (-ah-) n. play for acting on stage, radio, etc.; dramatic quality or series of events; (the) ∿, dramatic art, composition and presentation of plays. [LL, f. Gk drama -atos (draō do)]

dramä't|ic a. of (the study of) drama; as of a play--actor, theatrical; fit for theatrical representation, sudden, striking, impressive; ∿**ic irony**, = TRAGIC irony; hence ∿ICALLY adv., ∿ICS n., dramatic performance or behaviour. [f. LL f. Gk dramatikos (as prec.; see -IC)]

dramatis persō'nae (-nē, -nī) n. pl. (often treated as sing.) (list of) characters in a play. [L, = persons of the drama]

dra'matist n. writer of dramas. [f. Gk DRAMA+-IST]

dra'matiz|e, -īs|e (-īz), v.t. & i. convert (novel etc.) into a play, admit of such conversion; make a drama or dramatic scene of, behave dramatically; hence ∿A'TION n. [f. as prec.+-IZE]

dra'matûrg|e n. dramatist; so **dramatûr'gic**(AL) adjs., ∿Y¹ n. [F, f. Gk dramatourgos (as DRAMA, -ergos worker)]

Drämbu'ie (-boo'ĭ, -bū'ĭ) n. (P) Scotch whisky liqueur. [f. Gael. dram buidheach satisfying drink]

dränk. See DRINK¹.

dräpe v.t., & n **1.** v.t. cover, hang, adorn, with cloth etc.; arrange (clothes, hangings) in graceful folds. **2.** n. piece of drapery,* curtain; ∿ **suit**, (sl.) man's suit of long jacket and narrow trousers. [ME, f. OF draper (drap f. LL drappus cloth)]

||dra'per n. retailer of textile fabrics. [ME f. AF, OF drapier (as prec.; see -ER²(2))]

dra'perý n. [|cloth, textile fabrics; ||draper's trade; arrangement of clothing in sculpture etc.; clothing or hangings disposed in folds; *curtain. [ME, f. OF draperie (drap f. LL drappus; see -ERY)]

dra'st|ic (-ă'-, -ah'-) a. acting strongly or severely; vigorous, violent, (esp. of purgative); hence ∿ICALLY adv. [f. Gk drastikos (draō do; see -IC)]

drät v.t. (-tt-; esp. in 3 sing. subj.) (As mild imprecation) confound, curse, bother; hence ∿'tED¹ a. [for 'od (= God) rot]

draught¹ (-ahft) n. **1.** drawing, traction; ∿**-horse** etc. (for drawing cart, plough, etc.). **2.** drawing of net for fish etc.; fish taken at one drawing. **3.** drawing of liquor from cask etc.; ∿ **beer** (not bottled) **4.** single act of drinking, amount so drunk; dose of liquid medicine. **5.** (Naut.) depth of water ship draws or requires to float her. **6.** (in pl., usu. treated as sing.) ||game for two, with initially 24 pieces of equal value on ∿**-board** (same as chess-board). **7.** current of air in confined space (room, chimney, etc.); **feel the ∿**, (sl.) suffer from adverse (usu. financial) conditions; **forced** ∿ (provided by blower etc.); hence ∿'Y² a. **8.** = DRAFT 1, 2, 3. [ME draht, perh. f. ON drahtr, dráttr, = MDu. dragt, OHG traht f. Gmc *dragan DRAW¹]

draught² (-ahft) v.t. = DRAFT². [f. prec.]

drau'ghtsman (-ah'ft-) n. (pl. -men). **1.** one who makes drawings, plans, or sketches (good, bad, no, ∿, one who draws well etc.), whence ∿SHIP (3) n. **2.** = DRAFTSMAN. **3.** piece in game of draughts. [f. draught's+MAN¹]

dräve. See DRIVE¹.

Draví'dian n. (member or language) of a dark--skinned people of S. India and Sri Lanka (including Tamils and Kanarese). [f. Skr. Dravida, a province of S. India+-IAN]

draw¹ v. (drew pr. drōō; DRAWN). **1.** v.t. pull (boat up from water, hat over face, belt tighter, pen across paper, friend aside for private talk); pull (plough, cart, cart-load, etc.); (Hist.) drag (criminal) on hurdle etc. to execution. **2.** haul in (net); bend (bow; draw a BEAD¹ on); draw in one's HORN¹s; pull at (∿ **bit, bridle, rein**, check horse, or (fig.) oneself);

pull (curtain, veil) open or shut; (of ship) need (specified depth of water) for floating; (Bowls) cause (bowl) to travel in curve to desired point; (Cricket) divert (ball) to on-side with bat; (Golf) drive (ball) purposely to left (of right-handed player). **3.** attract, bring to oneself or to something, take in, (*drew a deep breath*; *I felt drawn to him*; *drew my attention to the matter*; *draw him into conversation*; *display draws customers*), (abs.) *chimney, pipe,* ~s **well,** promotes or allows draught; induce *to* do; bring about, entail, (*drew after it great consequences*; *draw criticism, ruin, upon* oneself; ~ person's **fire,** deflect it from more important target). **4.** take out (cork, tooth, gun-charge, nail, cricket- -stumps from ground (at close of play), card from pack; pistol, sword from sheath); (abs.) = draw one's sword or pistol; ~ one's **sword against,** attack; *draw* LOTS; (abs.) = draw lots; obtain by lot (*drew the winner*; *draw* (*a*) BLANK²); drag (badger, fox) from hole; haul up (water) from well; bring out (liquid from vessel, blood from body; ~ it mild, [orig. of beer] = be moderate, not exaggerate); extract liquid essence of; leave (game, or abs.; battle) undecided. **5.** take or get from a source (*draw inspiration*, one's *salary, money from bank*); elicit, evoke; (Cards) cause to be played (*draw all the trumps*); cause (person) to reveal information, talent, irritation, etc.; deduce, infer, (conclusion). **6.** disembowel (criminal is hanged, ~n, **and quartered;** ~ **fowl** before cooking); remove coals of (a fire). **7.** (Hunt.) search (cover) for game (~ **blank,** find none; cf. sense 4 and BLANK²). **8.** protract, stretch, elongate, (*long drawn agony*); make (wire) by pulling piece of metal through successively smaller holes. **9.** trace (furrow, figure, line; ~ **the line at,** refuse to go as far as or beyond); delineate, make (picture), represent (object), by drawing lines, (abs.) practise this; frame (document) in due form, compose; formulate, institute, (comparisons, distinctions); write out (bill, cheque, draft, *on* banker etc.), (abs.) make call *on* person or his faith, memory, one's imagination, etc., for money or service. **10.** *v.i.* make one's way, move, *towards, round, into, near, off, back,* etc. (*draw to an end* or *close*; (Racing) get farther *away* to the front, come *level,* gain *on*; (of tea) infuse; (of sail) swell tightly in wind; ~ **at,** suck some smoke from (pipe). **11.** (w. *advs.*): ~ **back,** withdraw from undertaking; ~ **in,** entice, persuade to join, (of day) approach its end, (of successive days) become shorter, (of train etc.) enter station etc.; ~ **off,** withdraw (troops); ~ **on,** lead to, bring about, allure, come nearer, put (gloves, boots, etc.) on; ~ **out,** lead out, detach, or array (troops), prolong, elicit, induce to talk, write out in proper form, (of days) become longer, (of train etc.) leave station etc.; ~ **up,** come up *with* or *to* = overtake, come to a halt, bring or come into regular order, compose (document etc.), make oneself stiffly erect. **12.** ~**-hoe** (used with pulling action); ~**-sheet** (that can be taken from under patient without remaking bed); ~**-string** (that can be pulled to tighten mouth of bag, waist of garment, etc.); ~**-well,** deep well with rope and bucket. [OE *dragan,* = OS *dragan,* OHG *tragan,* ON *draga,* Goth. *gadragan* f. Gmc **dragan*]

draw² *n.* act of drawing; strain, pull; *pull at cigarette etc.; attractive effect, person or thing that draws custom, attention, etc.; drawing of lots, raffle; drawn game; act of whipping out revolver in order to shoot (*quick on the draw,* lit. or fig.); *movable part of drawbridge. [f. prec.]

draw'back *n.* amount of excise or import duty paid back or remitted on goods exported; deduction *from*; thing that impairs satisfaction, disadvantage; ~ **lock** (with spring bolt that can be drawn back by inside knob). [f. DRAW¹ + BACK³]

draw'bridge *n.* bridge hinged at one end for drawing up to prevent passage or to open channel. [ME, f. DRAW¹ + BRIDGE¹]

Drawcǎ'nsir *n.* person formidable to both friend and

foe; fierce swashbuckler. [name of character in Villiers's 'The Rehearsal' (1672), perh. intended to suggest *draw can* (of liquor)]

drawee' *n.* person on whom draft or bill is drawn. [f. DRAW¹ + -EE]

draw'er *n.* In vbl senses; (arch.) tapster; (*pr. also* draw) receptacle sliding in and out of frame (~s or **chest of** ~s) or of table etc., for holding clothes, papers, etc. (BOTTOM¹ *drawer*; TOP¹ *drawer*), whence ~FUL 2 *n.*; (in *pl.*) knickers or other garment worn next to body below waist. [f. DRAW¹ + -ER¹]

draw'ing *n.* In vbl senses; art of representing by line, delineation without colour or with single colour (**out of** ~, incorrectly depicted); product of this, black- -and-white or monochrome sketch; ~ **account,** account from which money can be drawn, esp. against credited future earnings; ~**-board,** board for spreading drawing-paper on (*back* to the ~*-board,* (colloq.) the enterprise has failed, we must begin afresh); ~**-paper** (stout, for drawing pictures etc. on); ||~**-pin** (for fastening paper to drawing-board etc.). [f. DRAW¹ + -ING¹]

draw'ing-room (-o͞om, -o͞om) *n.* room for formal reception of company, to which ladies retire after dinner, (*attrib.*) restrained, observing social proprieties; (Hist.) levee, formal reception esp. at court; *private compartment in train. [f. earlier WITH-DRAWing-*room*]

drawl *v.* & *n.* **1.** *v.i.* & *t.* speak or utter with indolent or affected slowness. **2.** *n.* drawling utterance. [16th c., prob. orig. cant, f. LG, Du. *dralen* delay, linger]

drawn *a.* In vbl senses; (of face etc.) distorted with pain or fear; (of butter) melted; (of position in chess etc.) resulting in draw if both players make best moves; ~-(**thread-)work,** ornamental work on linen etc. done by drawing out threads, usu. with additional needlework. [p.p. of DRAW¹]

dray¹ *n.* **1.** low esp. brewer's cart without sides for heavy loads; ~**-horse** (large and powerful); ~'**man,** brewer's driver. **2.** (Austral. & NZ) two-wheeled cart. [ME, f. OE *dræge* drag-net, *dragan* DRAW¹]

dray². Var. of DREY.

dread¹ (-ĕd) *v.t.,* & *n.* **1.** *v.t.* be in great fear of; shrink from, look forward to with terror; fear greatly (*that, to* learn etc.), be afraid (*to* do). **2.** *n.* great fear, awe, apprehension; object of fear or awe. [OE *ādrǣdan, ondrǣdan,* = OS *antdrādan,* OHG *intrātan,* f. and- (cf. ANSWER¹) + WG base of uncert. orig.]

dread² (-ĕd) *a.* dreaded, dreadful; (arch.) awful, revered. [ME, p.p. of prec.]

drea'dful (-ĕ'd-) *a.* terrible, awe-inspiring (||**penny** ~, cheap story-book full of horrors); (colloq.) troublesome, disagreeable, boring, very bad or long, horrid; hence ~LY² *adv.,* ~NESS *n.* [ME, f. DREAD¹ + -FUL]

drea'dnought (-ĕ'dnawt) *n.* **1.** (arch.) (cloth used for) thick coat for stormy weather; fearless person. **2.** (Hist.; D~). type of battleship greatly superior in armament to all predecessors (f. name of first, launched 1906). [f. DREAD¹ + NOUGHT]

dream¹ *n.* series of pictures or events in mind of sleeping person (**like a** ~, (colloq.) easily, effortlessly; WET *dream*); act or time of seeing such vision; (**waking**)~, similar experience of one awake; = DAY-*dream*; state of mind without proper perception of reality (*goes about in a dream*); ideal, (esp. national) aspiration or ambition; person, dress, dish, etc. of dreamlike goodness, beauty, or refinement; ~**-boat,** (colloq.) very attractive person or thing; ~**-land,** ideal or imaginary land; ~**-time,** (Austral.) alcheringa; hence ~'FUL, ~'LESS, ~'LIKE, adjs. [ME, corresp. to OE **drēam,* OS *drōm,* OHG *troum,* ON *draumr*]

dream² *v.* (~t *pr.* -ĕmt, or ~ed *pr.* -ēmd or -ĕmt). **1.** *v.i.* have visions etc. (as) in sleep; (w. neg. etc.) think *of* even in a dream, so much as contemplate possibility *of,* (*would not dream of upsetting them*), have any conception *of*; fall into reverie; be inactive or unpractical. **2.** *v.t.* see, hear, etc., in sleep; (w. neg. etc.) imagine as in a dream, believe possible (*never dreamt that he would behave so badly*); spend (time) *away* unpractically; ∼ **up**, imagine, invent. **3.** Hence ∼'ER¹ *n.*, (esp.) unpractical person. [ME, as prec.]

drea'm|ў *a.* given to reverie, fanciful, unpractical; dreamlike, vague, misty; (poet.) full of dreams; (colloq.) delightful; hence ∼ïLY² *adv.*, ∼ïNESS *n.* [f. DREAM¹ + -Y²]

drear *a.* (esp. poet.) = foll. [abbr.]

drear'|ў *a.* dismal, gloomy, dull; hence ∼ïLY² *adv.*, ∼ïNESS *n.* [OE *drēorig* (*drēor* gore), cogn. w. *drēosan* to drop, f. Gmc *dreuzaz*]

drĕdge¹ *n.* & *v.* **1.** *n.* apparatus for bringing up oysters, specimens, etc., or clearing out mud etc., from river or sea bottom. **2.** *v.t.* bring *up*, clear *away* or *out*, (as) with dredge; clean out (harbour, river) with dredge. **3.** *v.i.* use dredge. [15th c. Sc. *dreg*, perh. rel. to MDu. *dregghe*]

drĕdge² *v.t.* sprinkle with flour or other powder; sprinkle (flour etc.) *over*. [f. obs. *dredge* sweetmeat, f. OF *dragie, dragee*, perh. f. L f. Gk *tragēmata* spices]

dre'dger¹ *n.* In vbl senses; (boat with) machine used for dredging rivers etc. [f. DREDGE¹ + -ER¹]

dre'dger² *n.* container with perforated lid for sprinkling flour etc. [f. DREDGE² + -ER¹]

dree *v.t.* (arch. or Sc.) endure; ∼ one's **weird**, submit to one's destiny. [OE *drēogan* f. Gmc *dreug-* etc. |

dreep *n.* (colloq.) ineffective or lugubrious person. [f. obs. v. *dreep* drip]

drĕg *n.* (usu. in *pl.*) sediment, grounds, lees, (*drink, drain*, **to the** ∼**s**, leaving nothing); worthless part, refuse; (in *sing.*) small remnant (esp. *not a dreg*); hence ∼'**gy**¹ (-gi) *a.* [ME, prob. f. ON *dreggjar*]

drĕnch¹ *n.* draught or dose administered to animal; (arch.) medicinal or poisonous draught; a soaking or downpour. [OE *drenc* f. Gmc *drank-* (*drink-* DRINK¹)]

drĕnch² *v.t.* force (animal) to take draught of medicine; wet thoroughly (by immersion or by falling liquid); saturate, steep, as if in liquid; (arch.) cause to drink. [OE *drencan*, = OS *drenkian*, OHG *trenchen*, ON *drekkja*, Goth *dragkjan* f. Gmc *drankjan* (as prec.)]

Dre'sden (-z-) *n.* ∼ **china, porcelain**, kind made at Meissen near Dresden, with elaborate decoration and delicate colourings; (*attrib.*, fig.) delicately pretty. [∼ in Germany]

drĕss¹ *v.t.* & *i.* **1.** array, clothe (*dressed in black, in rags*); provide oneself with and wear clothes (*dress well*); put on one's clothes; put on evening dress (esp. *dress for dinner*); ∼ **out**, attire conspicuously; ∼ **up**, attire oneself, attire (another), elaborately or in masquerade, (fig.) disguise by embellishment. **2.** deck, adorn, (ship with flags, shop-window with attractive goods). **3.** treat (wound) with remedies; apply dressing to. **4.** subject to cleansing, trimming, smoothing, etc.; prepare (bird, crab, etc.) for cooking or eating; brush, comb, do up, (hair); curry (horse, leather); manure; ∼ **down**, (fig.) thrash or scold. **5.** finish surface of (textile fabrics, building-stone). **6.** (Mil.) correct the alignment of (companies etc. in relation to each other, or men in line), come into correct place in line etc. [ME, f. OF *dresser* f. Rom. *directiare* f. L *directus* DIRECT²]

drĕss² *n.* **1.** clothing, esp. the visible part of it, formal or ceremonial costume (EVENING, FULL¹, MORNING, *dress*); woman's or girl's garment of bodice and skirt. **2.** external covering, outward form, (*birds in their winter dress; French book appearing in English dress*). **3.** ||∼ **circle**, first gallery in theatres, in which evening dress was at one time required; ∼ **coat** (swallow-tailed for evening dress); ∼**-improver**, (Hist.) = BUSTLE³; ∼ **length**, piece of material sufficient to make a dress; ∼'**maker**, ∼'**making**, (woman) making women's dresses; ∼ **parade**, (1) display of clothes by mannequins, (2) military parade in full dress uniforms; ∼**-preserver**, = *dress-shield*; ∼ **rehearsal**, (esp. final) rehearsal in costume; ∼**-shield**, piece of

waterproof material fastened under armpit of dress to protect it from perspiration; ∼**-shirt** (to wear with evening dress). [f. prec.]

dre'ssage (-ahzh) *n.* training of horse in obedience and deportment. [F (*dresser* train)]

dre'sser¹ *n.* kitchen sideboard with shelves for dishes etc.; *dressing-table. [ME, f. OF *dresseur* (*dresser* prepare; see -ER²); cf. med. L *directorium*]

dre'sser² *n.* In vbl senses; surgeon's assistant in hospital operations; one who helps to dress actors or actresses, looks after costumes, etc. [f. DRESS¹ + -ER¹]

dre'ssing *n.* In vbl senses; seasoning, sauce, stuffing, etc. for food; manure etc. spread over land; bandage, ointment, etc., for wound; size or stiffening used in finishing textile fabrics; ∼**-case** (of toilet necessaries); ∼ **down**, scolding or thrashing; ∼**-gown**, loose robe worn while one is resting, not fully dressed, etc.; ∼**-room**, place for dressing or changing clothes, esp. in theatre, sports-ground, etc., or attached to bedroom; ∼**-station**, place for giving emergency treatment to wounded; ∼**-table**, table with mirror etc. for use while dressing. [ME, f. DRESS¹ + -ING¹]

dre'ss|ў *a.* fond of or smart in dress; (of clothes) stylish; (fig.) over-elaborate; hence ∼ïNESS *n.* [f. DRESS² + -Y²]

drew. See DRAW¹.

drey (drā) *n.* squirrel's nest. [17th c.; orig. unkn.]

drĭb *n.* ∼**s and drabs**, small scattered amounts. [*drib* f. v. (see foll.) *drab* redupl.]

drĭ'bble *v.* & *n.* **1.** *v.i.* & *t.* (let) flow in drops or trickling stream; (of child etc.) run at the mouth. **2.** (Footb., Hockey, etc.) move (ball) forward with slight touches of feet or of stick. **3.** *n.* act or process of dribbling; small trickling stream. **4.** Hence **drĭ'bbly** *a.* [frequent. of obs. *drib*, var. of DRIP¹; see -LE 3]

drĭ'blĕt *n.* small quantity, petty sum; **in** or **by** ∼**s**, a little at a time. [f. *drib* (see prec.) + -LET]

dried (drīd). See DRY².

drĭ'er¹, drĭ'est. See DRY¹.

drĭ'er², drỹ'er. *n.* In vbl senses; machine for drying hair, laundry, etc.; substance mixed with oil-paint or ink to promote drying. [f. DRY² + -ER¹]

drift¹ *n.* **1.** state of being driven by current; slow movement or variation; ship's deviation from course, due to currents; projectile's deviation due to its rotation; aircraft's deviation due to side-wind; controlled slide of racing car etc. **2.** ||driving of cattle in forest, esp. to one place on appointed day to determine ownership etc. **3.** awaiting events, inaction, (esp. derog.; *the policy of drift*). **4.** intention, meaning, tenor, or scope, of person or his words. **5.** shower, driving mass; snow, sand, etc., accumulated by wind; ∼(-**ice**, '**wood**, etc.), material driven by water; (Geol.) material deposited by wind, current of water, etc. (**D**∼, Pleistocene ice detritus, boulder clay); large mass of flowering plants. **6.** ∼(-**net**), large net for herrings etc., allowed to drift with tide. **7.** (Mining.) horizontal passage following mineral vein. **8.** (S. Afr.) ford. **9.** tool for enlarging or shaping hole in metal. [ME f. ON & MDu., MHG *trift* movement of cattle etc. w. DRIVE¹]

drift² *v.i.* & *t.* be carried (as) by current of air or water, (of current) carry; move passively, casually, or aimlessly; pile or be piled by wind into drifts; cover (field, road) with drifts; form or enlarge (hole) with drift; hence ∼'AGE *n.*, ∼'ER¹ *n.*, (esp.) aimless person, and esp. hand in drift-net fishing. [f. prec.]

drill¹ *n.* & *v.* **1.** *n.* pointed steel tool, or tool (fig. revolving tool, or with socket, for boring holes in securing wells; shellfish that bores into shells of young oysters. **2.** instruction or training in military exercises; (fig.) rigorous discipline, (exact) routine, (colloq.) recognized procedure. **3.** *v.t.* & *i.* (Of person or troop) make hole with drill through (metal etc.), make (hole) with drill; subject to or undergo disciplining etc.; impart (knowledge etc.) by strict method. [n. f. v., f. MDu. *drillen* bore, of unkn. orig.]

drill² *n.*, & *v.t.* **1.** *n.* small furrow for sowing seed in; ridge with such furrow on top; row of plants so sown. **2.** machine for furrowing, sowing, and covering seed. **3.** *v.t.* sow (seed) thus, plant (ground) in drills. [perh. f. obs. *drill* rill, 17th c., of unkn. orig.]

drill³ *n.* W. Afr. baboon (*Mandrillus leucophaeus*) akin to mandrill. [prob. native name; cf. MANDRILL]

drill⁴ *n.* coarse twilled linen or cotton fabric. [earlier *drilling* f. G *drillich* f. L *trilix -licis* (*tri-* three-, *licium* thread)]

dri´lỹ. See DRY¹.

drink¹ *v.* (**drank; drunk**). **1.** *v.t.* swallow (liquid); swallow contents of (vessel); ~ **off**, drink the whole (contents) of at once; ~ **up**, drink the whole or remainder of. **2.** (Of plant, porous material, etc.) absorb (moisture; ~ **in**, (fig.) contemplate or listen to with delight or eagerness); bring (one*self* to death etc.) by drinking (~ **under the table**, outlast (person) in ability to continue drinking liquor etc.); wish good health etc. to by drinking (*drink* person's *health*); spend (wages etc. *away*) on drink. **3.** *v.i.* swallow liquid, take draught, (*of* or *from* a source; ~ **deep**, take large draught(s); ~ **up**, empty one's glass etc.; ~´**ing-song**, song about (and usu. sung at time of) drinking; ~**ing-u´p** time, short period legally allowed for consumption of drinks bought before closing-time in public house; ~´**ing-water**, water reserved, or pure enough, for drinking); take alcoholic liquor esp. to excess, tipple, be a drunkard, (*drink hard, heavily, like a* FISH¹; *drinking-bout*); ~ **to**, pledge, toast, wish success to. **4.** Hence ~´ABLE *a.*, (-)~ER¹ *n.* [OE *drincan*, = OS *drinkan*, OHG *trinkan*, ON *drekka*, Goth. *drigkan* f. Gmc **drenkan*]

drink² *n.* liquid swallowed or absorbed; liquid for drinking; (**strong**) ~, intoxicating liquor, excessive indulgence in it, intemperance (**in** ~, drunk); glass etc. or portion of liquid for drinking (*have* or *take a drink*), esp. alcoholic; **the** ~, (colloq.) the sea; hence ~´LESS *a.* [OE *drinc(a)* (*drincan*; see prec.)]

drip¹ *v.i.* & *t.* (**-pp-**). fall or let fall in drops; let drops fall, be so wet (*with* blood etc.) as to shed drops (~´**ping wet**, very wet); ~**dry**, (*v.i.* of fabric etc.) dry when hung up to drip, without wringing or ironing, (*a.*) that will drip-dry. [f. MDa. *drippe* f. Gmc **drupp-* (cf. DROP¹)]

drip² *n.* act of dripping; dripping liquid; (Archit.) projection keeping rain from parts below (so ~**-moulding**, ~´**stone**); (sl.) stupid or dull person; (sl.) grumble; (sl.) flattery, drivel; ~**-feed**, feeding (esp. intravenously) by liquid a drop at a time; ~**-mat**, small mat under a glass etc.; hence ~´pY² *a.* [f. prec.]

dri´pping *n.* In vbl senses; fat melted from roasted meat, and used for cooking or as food; (in *pl.*) water, grease, etc., dripping from anything. [ME, f. DRIP¹ + -ING¹]

drive¹ *v.t.* & *i.* (**drove** *pr.* drōv, arch. **drave** *pr.* -āv; **driven** *pr.* dri´ven). **1.** urge in some direction by blows, threats, violence, etc., (usu. w. adv. or prep.: *away*, *back*, *in*, *out*, *from*, *to*, *through*, etc.; ~ **out**, oust, take place of). **2.** chase or frighten (game, wild beasts, enemy esp. in guerilla warfare) from large area into small in order to kill or capture; ||hold DRIFT¹ (sense 2). **3.** (urge and) direct course of (animal drawing vehicle or plough); operate and direct course of (vehicle etc., or locomotive); convey in vehicle; direct course of vehicle; be competent to direct course of motor vehicle etc. (**driving-licence, driving test,** etc., concerned with such competence); travel or go in private car or carriage (cf. RIDE 1); ~**-in** *a.* & *n.*, (bank, cinema, etc.) that can be used without getting out of one's car; ~**-on** *a.*, (of ship) on to which motor vehicle can be driven. **4.** impel forcibly, constrain, compel, (*to, into, to* do); force into state of being (*mad* etc.); overwork (*was very hard driven*; *tends to drive himself*). **5.** impel, (of wind, water) carry along; throw, propel, send, cause to go in some direction,

(inanimate thing); (Cricket) return (ball) from freely swung bat to or past bowler; (Golf) strike (ball, or abs.) with driver from tee (**driving-range,** area for practising this); (Tennis) hit (ball) with freely swung racket. **6.** force (stake, nail, etc.) *into* ground etc. by blows; bore (tunnel, horizontal cavity); (**let**) ~, aim blow or missile (*at*) **7.** (Of steam or other power) set or keep (machinery) going (**driving-wheel,** wheel communicating motive power in machinery, large wheel of locomotive); (of person) ~ **a quill, a pen,** be author or clerk. **8.** carry on, effect, conclude, (*drove a roaring trade, a good bargain*). **9.** postpone (*drive it to the last minute*). **10.** dash, rush, hasten; work hard *at*. **11.** float along, drift, tend; be moved by wind etc., esp. rapidly (*driving rain*); ~ **at**, seek, intend, mean (*what is he driving at?*). **12.** Hence **dri´vABLE** *a.* [OE *drīfan*, = OS *drīban*, OHG *trīban*, ON *drífa*, Goth. *dreiban* f. Gmc **drīban*]

drive² *n.* **1.** excursion or journey in vehicle; driving of game or enemy; stroke made by driving at cricket, golf, etc. **2.** transmission of power to machinery, wheels of motor vehicle, etc., (*belt drive*; *front-wheel drive*); position of steering-wheel of motor vehicle (*left-hand drive*). **3.** energy, capacity to achieve things; (Psych.) inner urge to attain a goal or satisfy a need. **4.** organized effort to achieve a special purpose; game of whist, bingo, etc., with many players. **5.** street or road, esp. scenic one; ~(´**way**), road for vehicles, esp. private one leading to house. [f. prec.]

dri´vel *v.* (||**-ll-**) & *n.* **1.** *v.i.* run at mouth or nose like child; talk childishly or idiotically. **2.** *v.t.* fritter *away*. **3.** Hence ~LER¹ *n.* **4.** *n.* silly nonsense, twaddle. [OE *dreflian*; cf. DRAFF]

dri´ven. See DRIVE¹.

dri´ver *n.* In vbl senses; person who drives vehicle (*bus-driver, cab-driver, engine-driver, taxi-driver*; **in the** ~**'s seat**, in charge); (Golf) straight-faced wooden-headed club for driving from tee; (Electr.) device or part of circuit providing power for output; (Mech.) wheel etc. receiving power directly and transmitting motion to other parts; hence ~LESS *a.* [f. DRIVE¹ + -ER¹]

dri´zzle *n.*, & *v.i.* **1.** *n.* rain in very small drops. **2.** *v.i.* (Of rain, *it*) fall in drizzle. **3.** Hence **dri´zzlY²** *a.* [prob. f. ME *drēse*, OE *drēosan* fall + -LE 3]

dro´gue (-ōg) *n.* buoy at end of harpoon line; sea anchor; (Aeron.) truncated cone of fabric used as brake, target for gunnery, wind-sock, etc. [18th c., of unkn. orig.]

droit *n.* right, due, legal perquisite; ~**s of Admiralty,** proceeds of enemy's ships, wrecks, etc.; ~ **de** or **du seigneur** (drwah de-, dūsānyêr´), alleged right of feudal lord to copulate with vassal's bride on her wedding-night. [ME f. OF, f. L *directum* n. f. *directus* DIRECT²]

dröll *a.* & *n.* **1.** *a.* amusing (esp. through quaintness); queer, odd, surprising; hence or cogn. **drō´llY²** (-ō´l-lĭ) *adv.*, ~´ERY (4), ~´NESS, *ns.* **2.** *n.* (arch.) jester, wag; droll person. [f. F *drôle*, perh. f. MDu. *drolle* little man]

dröme *n.* (colloq.) aerodrome. [abbr.]

-drome *suf.* forming *ns.* denoting (1) place for running etc. (*aerodrome, hippodrome*), (2) thing that runs (*palindrome, syndrome*). [f. or after Gk *dromos* course, running]

dro´medarỹ (-ŏ´m-, -ŭ´m-) *n.* light fast-moving (esp. Arabian or one-humped) camel bred for riding. [ME, f. AF **dromedarie*, OF *dromedaire*, or f. LL *dromedarius* f. L f. Gk *dromas -ados* runner; see -ARY¹]

drŏ´mond *n.* (Hist.) large medieval ship for war or commerce. [ME f. AF; OF *dromon(t)* f. LL *dromo -onis* f. late Gk *dromōn* light vessel]

drōne *n.* & *v.* **1.** *n.* male of honey-bee, which does not work in hive but may impregnate queen; idler; remotely-controlled pilotless aircraft or missile. **2.** deep humming sound; monotonous speech or speaker; low-pitched pipe (as of bagpipe) or string;

fixed continuous note emitted by this. **3.** *v.i. & t.* buzz like bee or bagpipe; talk or utter monotonously; be idle; idle *away* (life etc.). [OE *drān, drǣn*, = OS *drān, dreno*, OHG *treno*, prob. f. WG **dran-*, **dren-*, *drunboom]

drŏ′ngō (-nggō) *n.* (*pl.* ∼**s** *or* ∼**es**). black bird of India, Africa, or Australia, of family Dicruridae; (Austral. sl.) simpleton. [Malagasy]

drŏōl *v.i., & n.* drivel, slobber; show much pleasure *over.* [contr. of *drivel*]

drŏōp *v. & n.* **1.** *v.i.* hang down, slope, incline, as in weariness; (of eyes) look downwards; (poet., of sun etc.) sink; languish, decline, flag, lose heart; hence ∼′y² *a.* **2.** *v.t.* let (head, face, eyes) fall forward or down. **3.** *n.* drooping attitude, loss of spirit; ∼**-snoot**, (colloq.) (aircraft with) adjustable nose or leading-edge flap. [ME, f. ON *drúpa* hang the head f. Gmc **drūp-* (cf. foll.)]

drŏp¹ *n.* **1.** round, pear-shaped, or hemispherical portion of liquid (water, tears, sweat, dew, rain, blood) such as hangs or falls separately or adheres to surface; (Med.) smallest separable quantity of a liquid, (in *pl.*) liquid medicine to be measured by drops; minute quantity (∼**in a bucket** or **the ocean**, infinitesimal factor); glass etc. of intoxicating liquor (*take a drop*; **has had a** ∼ **too much**, is drunk); pendant, hanging ornament, (of glass chandelier etc.; **ear-**∼**s**, ear-rings); sweet, lozenge, (ACID¹, COUGH²-, PEAR-, etc., *drops*); hence ∼′LET *n.* **2.** act of dropping, fall, social come-down, descent in prices, temperature, etc., (*at the drop of a* HAT; **get** or **have the** ∼ **on**, (colloq.) have the advantage over); thing that drops or is dropped; ∼(**-curtain** or **-scene**), (Theatr.) painted curtain or scenery let down on to stage; (in gallows) platform or trapdoor withdrawn from under feet of condemned person; distance dropped; abrupt fall or steep slope of surface, amount of this; ∼(**-kick**), kick at football made by dropping ball and kicking it as it bounces; (sl.) hiding-place for stolen or illicit goods, secret letters, etc.; (sl.) bribe; *box for letters etc. **3.** ∼**-forging**, system of forcing piece of white-hot metal by heavy weight through open-ended die of required shape; ∼**-hammer**, forging-machine using power of dropped weight; ||∼**-head**, adjustable canvas roof of car; ∼**-leaf**, (of table etc.) having hinged flap; ||∼ **scone** (made by dropping spoonful of batter on hot cooking surface); ∼**-shot**, (Lawn Tennis) shot dropping abruptly after clearing net; ∼**-test** *n., & v.t.*, test by dropping under standard conditions; ∼′**wort**, plant (*Filipendula hexapetala*) with tuberous root fibres. [OE *dropa*, = OS *dropo*, ON *dropi* f. Gmc *dropon*, & OE *droppa f. Gmc *droppon f. **drup-*; cf. DRIP¹, DROOP]

drŏp² *v.* (**-pp-**). **1.** *v.i.* fall in drops; give off moisture in drops. **2.** fall by force of gravity from not being held etc., (fig.) be uttered casually (*the remark dropped from him; he let drop a remark*); (of card) be played in same trick as higher card. **3.** sink to ground esp. because exhausted, wounded, etc., (∼ **dead!**, sl. excl. of intense scorn; ∼ **on** one's **knee**(**s**), kneel; **fit** or **ready to** ∼, (colloq.) tired out). **4.** fall naturally *asleep*, (*back*) *into* habit etc.; die; cease, lapse, (*affair was allowed to drop*; *the correspondence dropped*). **5.** fall in direction, condition, amount, degree, pitch, (*price, voice, wind, drops*); go *down* stream, hillside, etc.; fall *behind, to the rear*, etc. **6.** come or go casually *by* or *in* as visitor, *into* place, *across* person. **7.** *v.t.* let fall (liquid, tears, words) in drops, shed; let go, relinquish, cease to hold, (∼ **anchor**, anchor ship; *drop a* BRICK¹, *a* STITCH); give birth to (esp. lamb). **8.** utter casually as if unconsciously (esp. *drop a hint*); send casually (*drop me a postcard, line, note*). **9.** lose (money, esp. in gambling). **10.** fell with axe, blow of fist, or bullet; cause (card) to drop (sense 2). **11.** set down (passenger, parcel); allow (supplies etc.) to fall by parachute. **12.** omit (letter, one's AITCHes, *syllable*) in speech. **13.** let (eyes) droop; lower (voice); *drop* CURTSY; place in lower than

usual position (*dropped handlebars* of bicycle, *dropped waist* of garment). **14.** (Footb.) send (ball), make (goal), by DROP¹-kick. **15.** cease to associate with, have done with, abandon, (∼ **it!**, stop that). **16.** ∼ **away**, decrease or depart gradually; ∼ **in**, come in gradually or casually; ∼ **off**, (1) = *drop away*, (2) fall asleep, (3) = sense 11; ∼ **on**, reprimand or punish; ∼ **out**, cease to appear or participate, esp. in course of study or in conventional society; ∼**-out** *n.*, (colloq.) one who drops out, (Rugby Footb.) restarting of game by drop-kick after defender's touch-down etc.; ∼ **to**, (sl.) become aware of. [OE *drop(p)ian* (as prec.)]

drŏ′pper *n.* In vbl senses; device for administering liquid in drops; (Austral., NZ, & S. Afr.) light vertical member of fence etc. [f. prec.+-ER¹]

drŏ′ppings (-z) *n. pl.* what falls or has fallen in drops, e.g. wax from candles; dung of animals or birds. [f. DROP²+-ING¹+-s¹]

drŏ′ps│ў *n.* **1.** disease in which watery fluid collects in cavities or tissue of the body; hence ∼ICAL *a.* **2.** (sl.) tip or bribe. [ME, f. HYDROPSY]

drŏ′shkў *n.* Russian low four-wheeled open carriage. [f. Russ. *drozhki* dim. of *drogi* wagon (*droga* shaft)]

drosŏ′phila *n.* fruit-fly of genus *Drosophila*, used extensively in genetic research. [mod. L, f. Gk *drosos* dew, moisture+*philos* loving]

drŏss *n.* scum separated from metals in melting; foreign matter mixed with anything, impurities; refuse, rubbish; hence ∼′Y² *a.* [OE *drōs*, = MDu. *droese* dregs; cf. MLG *drōsem*, OHG *truosana*]

drought (-owt) (poet., Sc., Ir., & US) **drouth**, *n.* continuous dry weather, absence of rain; (fig.) prolonged lack of something; (arch.) dryness, lack of moisture, thirst; hence **drou′ghty²** (-ow′ti), **drou′thy²**, *a.* [OE *drūgath* (*drȳge* DRY¹; see -TH¹)]

drŏve¹ *n.* herd or flock being driven or moving together; crowd, multitude, shoal, large number, esp. as moving together; ∼**-road**, ancient unmetalled track for cattle. [OE *drāf* (*drīfan* DRIVE¹)]

drŏve². See DRIVE¹.

drŏ′ver *n.* driver of droves to market, cattle-dealer; hence (by back-form.) **drŏve³** *v.t.*, **drŏ′ving¹** *n.* [ME, f. DROVE¹+-ER¹]

drown *v.* **1.** *v.t.* (Of person, liquid, etc.) suffocate (person, animal) by submersion; submerge, flood, drench, (*esp.* fig ; *like a drowned* RAT¹; ∼**ed valley** etc., one partly or wholly submerged by change in land-levels; ∼ **out**, drive out by flood). **3.** deaden (grief etc.) with or in drink; overpower (esp. of louder sound making voice etc. inaudible). [ME (orig. north.) *drun*(*e*), *droun*(*e*), perh. f. OE *drŭnian, rel. to ON *drukna* be drowned; cogn. w. DRINK¹]

drowse (-z) *v. & n.* **1.** *v.i.* be dull and sleepy or half asleep; (arch.) be sluggish. **2.** *v.t.* make drowsy; pass *away* (time) in drowsing. **3.** *n.* half-asleep condition. [back-form. f. foll.]

drow′s│ў (-zĭ) *a.* sleepy, half asleep, dozing; lulling, soporific; sluggish; ∼**y-head**, sleepy person; hence ∼ĭHEAD (arch.), ∼ĭNESS *n.s.*, ∼ĭLY² *adv.* [prob. rel. to OE *drūsian* be languid or slow, cogn. w. *drēosan* fall; cf. DREARY]

drŭb *v.t.* (**-bb-**) cudgel, thump, belabour; beat in fight; beat (notion) *into, out of*, person; hence ∼′bING¹ *n.* [ult. f. Arab. *ḍaraba* beat]

drŭdg│e *n., & v.i.* **1.** *n.* servile worker, slave, toiler; hence ∼′ERY (2, 5) *n.* **2.** *v.i.* work slavishly *at* laborious, dull, or distasteful work. [15th c., perh. rel. to DRAG¹]

drŭg *n. & v.* (**-gg-**). **1.** *n.* medicinal substance, used alone or as ingredient; (esp.) narcotic, hallucinogen, or stimulant, (*drug addict, habit, traffic*; DANGEROUS *drug*); unsaleable commodity, thing no longer in demand (usu. ∼ **on the market**); *∼′**store**, chemist's shop also selling miscellaneous articles, light refreshments, etc.; hence ∼′gY² (-gĭ) *a.* **2.** *v.t.* add drug, esp.

narcotic or poison, to (food or drink); administer drugs, esp. narcotics, to; (arch.) nauseate, cloy. **3.** *v.i.* indulge in narcotics etc. [ME *drogges, drouges,* f. OF *drogue,* of unkn. orig.]

drŭg'gėt (-g-) *n.* (floor-covering etc. of) coarse woven fabric used for floor or table covering. [f. F *droguet,* of unkn. orig.]

drŭg'gist (-g-) *n.* dealer in drugs, pharmaceutical chemist. [f. F *droguiste* (as DRUG; see -IST)]

Dru'id (-ōō'-) *n.* **1.** priest, magician, soothsayer, among Celts of ancient Gaul, Britain, and Ireland. **2.** officer of Welsh etc. Gorsedd. **3.** Hence ~ESS[1], ~ISM (3), *ns.*, **Druï'dic**(AL) (-ōō-) *adjs.* [f. F *druide* or f. L pl. *druidae, -des,* Gk *druidai* f. Gaulish *druides*]

drŭm[1] *n.* **1.** musical instrument or toy sounded by striking and made of hollow cylinder or hemisphere with skin or parchment stretched over opening(s) (*bass, tenor, big,* SIDE[1]-, KETTLE-, *drum*); its player; (in *pl.*) percussion section of jazz band etc. **2.** (Zool. & Anat.) natural organ giving resonance, e.g. howler monkey's hyoid bone; membrane of middle ear. **3.** sound (as) of drum. **4.** cylindrical structure or object; cylinder or barrel in machinery on which something is wound or for other purposes; solid part of Corinthian or composite capital; stone block forming section of shaft; cylindrical receptacle for packing dried fruit, holding oil, etc. **5.** (Hist.) evening or afternoon-tea party. **6.** ~(-**fish**), Amer. fish able to make drumming noise. **7.** (sl.) house, night-club, brothel. **8.** ~ **brake,** one in which shoes on vehicle press against drum on wheel; ~'**fire,** heavy continuous rapid artillery fire usu. heralding infantry attack, (fig.) barrage of criticism etc.; ~'**head,** skin or membrane of drum (~*head court martial, service,* etc., improvised or summary), ear-drum, circular top of capstan; ~ **major,** leader of marching band, (arch.) NCO commanding drummers of regiment; ~ **majorette,** female drum major [see -ETTE]; ~'**stick,** stick with knob or pad for beating drum, lower joint of cooked fowl's leg. [f. obs. *drombslade, drombyllsclad,* f. LG *trommelslag* drum-beat (*trommel* drum, *slag* beat)]

drŭm[2] *v.* (-**mm**-). **1.** *v.i.* play the drum; beat, tap, or thump, continuously on something (*on* piano, *at* door; *feet drum on floor; a drumming in the ears*); (of bird, insect) make loud hollow noise with quivering wings; ~ **up,** (sl.) make tea in billycan etc. **2.** *v.t.* summon, call *up,* (as) by drumming (~ **out,** cashier by beat of drum, dismiss with ignominy); drive (lesson) *into* person by persistence; strike (hands etc.) repeatedly (*up*)*on* something; play (tune etc.) (as) on drum. [f. prec.]

drŭm[3], **drŭ'mlin,** *ns.* (Geol.) long oval mound of drift or diluvial formation; hence **drŭ'mlin**OID *n.* [f. Gael. & Ir. *druim* ridge; -*lin* perh. for -LING[1]]

drŭ'mmer *n.* In vbl senses; commercial traveller; (sl.) thief. [f. DRUM[2] + -ER[1]]

drŭnk *a.* & *n.* **1.** *a.* deprived of proper control of oneself by alcoholic liquor, (*blind, dead, half, drunk; drunk as a fiddler* or *lord; Philip drunk to Philip* SOBER); (fig.) overcome *with* joy, success, etc.; hence ~'ARD *n.,* *~ŏ'*METER *n.,* breathalyser. **2.** *n.* drunken person; (sl.) drinking-bout, period of drunkenness. [p.p. of DRINK[1]]

drŭ'nken *a.* (usu. *attrib.*) = prec.; fond of drinking, often drunk; caused by or exhibiting drunkenness (*drunken frolic, brawl*); hence ~LY[2] *adv.,* ~NESS (-n-n-) *n.* [as prec.; see -EN[1]]

drup|e (-ōōp) *n.* fleshy or pulpy fruit enclosing stone or nut with kernel, e.g. olive, plum, peach, cherry; hence ~A'CEOUS *a.* [f. L f. Gk *druppa* olive]

dru'pel (-ōō'-), **dru'pelėt** (-ōō'pl-), *ns.* small drupe in aggregate fruit, e.g. blackberry. [f. prec. + -EL, -LET]

druse[1] (-ōōz) *n.* crust of crystals lining rock-cavity; cavity so lined. [F f. G, = weathered ore]

Druse[2] (-ōōz) *n.* member of political and religious sect of Muslim origin living near Mt. Lebanon. [F, f. Arab. *durūz* pl., prob. f. their founder *al-Darazī* (11th c.)]

drȳ[1] *a.* (**dri'er, dri'est,** *pr.* -ī'-). **1.** without moisture; (of eyes) free from tears; (of shampoo) for use without water; (of shave) with electric etc. razor; not rainy, with deficient rainfall, (*dry spell, climate,* SEASON); *dry* STEAM[1]; HIGH *and dry.* **2.** parched, dried up, (colloq.) thirsty; (of liquid) having disappeared by evaporation, draining, wiping, etc.; (of country, state, legislation, etc.) teetotal, prohibiting sale of alcoholic liquor at some or all times (**go** ~, enact such legislation). **3.** not yielding water, milk, etc., (*well, cow, is dry*). **4.** without butter etc. (*dry bread, toast*). **5.** solid, not liquid, (*dry provisions*). **6.** (Of wine etc.) free from sweetness; *dry* MARTINI. **7.** unconnected with liquid (*dry distillation*; **die a** ~ **death,** not by drowning or bloodshed; ~ **cough,** without phlegm). **8.** impassive, unsympathetic, stiff, hard, cold; (of jest, sarcasm, humour) expressed in matter-of-fact tone with pretended unawareness. **9.** meagre, plain, bare, not enlarged upon, (*dry facts, thanks*); uninteresting, dull, unprofitable, (*dry as dust*); unprejudiced. **10.** ~ **battery,** ~ **cell,** (Electr.) battery or cell in which electrolyte is absorbed in a solid and cannot be spilt; ||*dry*-BOB[5]; ~-**clean,** clean (clothes etc.) by means of organic solvents without using water; ~-**cure,** cure (meat etc.) without pickling in liquid; *dry* DOCK[4]; ~-**fly** *a.,* & *v.i.,* (fish) with artificial fly floating lightly on water; ~ **goods,** non-liquid goods, e.g. corn, *drapery and haberdashery; dry* ICE[1]; ~ **land,** land as opp. sea, river, etc.; ~ **measure,** measure of capacity for dry goods; *~* **milk,** dried milk; *dry*-NURSE[1] 2; ~-**plate,** photographic plate with sensitized film hard and dry for convenience of keeping, developing at leisure, etc.; ~-**point,** needle for engraving without acid on bare copper plate, engraving so produced; ~ **rot,** decayed state of wood when not well ventilated, caused by certain fungi, these fungi, (fig.) unsuspected moral or social decay; ~ **run,** (colloq.) rehearsal; ~-**salt** *v.t.,* = *dry-cure;* ~-**salter,** dealer in drugs, dyes, gums, oils, pickles, tinned meats, etc.; ~-**shod** *a.* & *adv.,* without wetting the shoes; ~'**stone,** ~-**walling,** (without mortar). **11.** Hence ~'ISH[1] 2 *a.,* **drȳ'LY**[2], ~'LY[2], *adv.* (esp. in fig. senses), ~'NESS *n.* [OE *drȳge,* rel. to MLG *drōge,* MDu. *drōghe,* f. Gmc *draug- etc.]

drȳ[2] *v.t.* & *i.* make or become dry by wiping, evaporation, draining, etc.; preserve food by removal of moisture (*dried egg, fruit, milk*); ~ (**off**), (cause to) cease yielding milk; ~ **out,** become fully dry, (of drug addict etc.) undergo treatment to cure addiction; ~ **up,** make utterly dry, dry washed dishes, (of moisture) disappear utterly, (of well etc.) cease to yield water, (colloq., esp. in *imper.*) cease talking or doing something; ~ (**up**), (Theatr., colloq.) forget one's lines. [OE *drygan* (as prec.)]

drȳ'ăd *n.* (Myth.) nymph inhabiting tree, wood--nymph. [ME, f. OF *dryade* f. L f. Gk *druas -ados* (*drus* tree)]

Drȳ'asdŭst (-az-) *n.* & *a.* **1.** *n.* dull laborious antiquary or historian. **2.** *a.* (*d~*). very dry, uninteresting. [Dr ~, fictitious person (*dry as dust*) to whom Scott dedicated novels]

drȳ'er. See DRIER[2].

DS *abbr.* dal segno; disseminated sclerosis.

DSC *abbr.* Distinguished Service Cross.

D.Sc. *abbr.* Doctor of Science.

DSM *abbr.* Distinguished Service Medal.

||**DSO** *abbr.* (Companion of the) Distinguished Service Order.

DT(s) *abbr.* delirium tremens.

dū'al *a., n.,* & *v.t.* (||-**ll**-). **1.** *a.* of two, twofold, divided in two, double, (*dual ownership;* || ~ **carriageway,** road with dividing strip between traffic in opposite directions; ~ **control** (esp. of vehicle or aircraft controlled by instructor as well as by learner); ~- -**purpose** *a.,* (of vehicle) suitable for passengers or goods; shared by two, joint. **2.** *a.* & *n.* (Gram.) ~ (**number**), (form of noun, verb, etc.) denoting two

persons or things (additional to singular and plural).
3. *v.t.* ||convert (road) into dual carriageway. **4.** So
dŭä′ITY *n.*, ∼IZE (3) *v.t.*, ∼LY² *adv.* [f. L *dualis* (*duo*
two; see -AL)]
dŭ′alism *n.* duality; theory recognizing two independent principles (mind and matter, cf. *idealism* and
materialism; good and evil in the universe; two personalities in Christ; so ∼IST (2) *n.*, ∼i′stIC *a.* [f. DUAL
+ -ISM]
dŭb¹ *n.* (sl.) inexperienced or unskilful person. [perh. f.
foll. in sense 'beat flat']
dŭb² *v.t.* (-bb-). **1.** make (person) a knight by touching
his shoulders with sword; give title of, name, nickname, (person or thing, with complement: *dubbed me
Doctor, a crank*). **2.** ||dress (artificial fishing-fly). **3.**
smear (leather) with grease. [OE **dubbian*, f. AF
duber, aduber, OF *adober* equip with armour, repair, of
unkn. orig.]
dŭb³ *v.t.* (-bb-). make another sound-track of (film)
esp. in a different language; add (sound effects or
music) to a film or broadcast; combine (sound-tracks) into one. [abbr. of DOUBLE³]
dŭb⁴ *v.i.* (-bb-). (sl.) ∼ **in, up,** pay up, contribute
money. [19th c.; orig. uncert.]
dŭ′bbin *n.*, & *v.t.* **1.** *n.* prepared grease for softening
and waterproofing leather. **2.** *v.t.* apply dubbin to. [f.
foll.]
dŭ′bbing *n.* In vbl senses; = prec [f. DUB²,³ + -ING¹]
dūbī′etý *n.* feeling of doubt, doubtful matter. [f. LL
dubietas (*dubium* doubt; see -TY¹)]
dū′bious *a.* hesitating, doubting; unreliable (*dubious
friend*); of questionable value or truth (*a dubious claim,
compliment*); of doubtful result (*dubious undertaking*); of
suspected character (*dubious gains, company*); hence
∼LY² *adv.*, ∼NESS *n.* [f. L *dubiosus* (*dubium* doubt; see
-OUS)]
dūbĭtā′tion *n.* doubt, hesitation. [ME f. OF, or f. L
dubitatio (*dubitare* DOUBT²; see -ATION)]
dū′bitative *a.* of, expressing, inclined to, doubt or
hesitation; hence ∼LY² (-vli) *adv.* [f. F *dubitatif -ive* or
f. LL *dubitativus* (as prec.; see -IVE)]
Dū′blin *n.* ∼ (**Bay**) **prawn,** Norway lobster, (in *pl.*)
scampi; hence ∼ER¹ (4) *n.* [∼ in Ireland)]
dúcal *a.* of, like, bearing title of, duke. [F (*duc* DUKE;
see -AL)]
dŭ′cat *n.* (Hist.) gold coin, current in most European
countries; coin, (in *pl.*) money. [ME, f. It. *ducato* or f.
med. L *ducatus* DUCHY]
dŭ′chess *n.* **1.** duke's wife or widow; woman holding
rank of duke in her own right; imposing woman. **2.**
||(sl.) costermonger's wife; (sl.) mother, wife, woman.
[ME, f. OF *duchesse*, f. med. L *ducissa* (as DUKE, see
-ESS¹)]
duchesse (dū′chĭs, doōshĕ′s) *n.* soft heavy kind
of satin; ∼ **lace,** kind of Brussels pillow-lace; ∼
potatoes, mashed potatoes mixed with egg, baked or
fried, and served as small cakes; ∼ **set,** cover or set of
covers for dressing-table. [F, = prec.]
dŭ′chỹ *n.* territory of duke or duchess; royal dukedom
of Cornwall or Lancaster, each with certain estates,
revenues, and jurisdiction of its own. [ME, f. OF
duché(e) f. med. L *ducatus* & Rom. **ducitas* f. L *dux* (see
DUKE)]
dŭck¹ *n.* (*pl.* ∼s *or* collect. ∼). **1.** swimming-bird of
family Anatidae, esp. the domesticated form of the
mallard or wild duck; female of this; its flesh as food.
2. like a (dying) ∼ **in a thunderstorm,** with
upturned eyes, looking flabbergasted, distressed, etc.;
LAME duck; **like water off a** ∼**'s back,** producing
no effect; **take to thing like a** ∼ **to water** (very
readily). **3.** ||('y³), ∼s, (colloq.) darling (esp. in *voc.*),
attractive thing. **4.** (Cricket). ∼('s egg), batsman's
score of 0; **break** one's ∼, score one's first run in the
innings. **5.** BOMBAY DUCK; ∼(s) **and drake(s),** game
of making flat stone skip along water (*make* ∼*s and
drakes of, play* ∼*s and drakes with,* squander); ||∼('s)-
-arse, *-ass, (sl.) haircut with back hair shaped like

duck's tail; ∼**'bill,** = *duck-billed* PLATY*pus*; ∼-
-boards, path of wooden slats in trench or over mud;
∼-hawk, ||marsh harrier, *peregrine; *∼'pin, short
squat bowling pin; ∼'s disease, (joc.) short legs; *∼
soup, (sl.) easy task; ∼'weed, plant that carpets
surface of still water. **6.** Hence ∼'LING¹ 2 *n.* (UGLY
duckling). [OE *duce, dūce* (*dūcan dive; see foll.)]
dŭck² *v.* & *n.* **1.** *v.i.* plunge, dive, dip head, into
water and emerge; bend quickly, bob, to avoid blow
or being seen or by way of bow or curtsy; (colloq.)
withdraw, abscond; (Bridge) lose trick deliberately
by playing low card. **2.** *v.t.* plunge (person etc.)
momentarily in or *in* water, whence ∼'ING¹ (1) *n.*
(∼ing-stool, chair at end of rising and falling pole,
formerly used for ducking scolds and other objectionable persons); lower (head) suddenly; (colloq.)
avoid, dodge. **3.** *n.* quick dip below water in bathing,
or lowering of head. [f. OE *dūcan (= MLG, MDu.
dūken, OHG *tūhhan*)]
dŭck³ *n.* strong untwilled linen or cotton fabric for
small sails and coarse clothing esp. of sailors; (in *pl.*)
trousers of this. [f. MDu. *doek,* = OS *dōk,* OHG *tuoh,* of
unkn. orig.]
dŭck⁴ *n.* (colloq.) amphibious landing-craft. [f.
DUKW, official designation]
dŭ′ckling. See DUCK¹ 6.
dŭ′ckỹ¹. See DUCK¹ 3.
dŭ′ckỹ² *a.* (colloq.) sweet, pretty; splendid. [f. DUCK¹
+ -Y³]
dŭct *n.*, & *v.t.* **1.** *n.* channel or tube for conveying
liquid, gas, cable, etc.; tube in body conveying
secretions etc. (∼'less gland, one secreting directly
into bloodstream); vessel of plant's vascular tissue
holding air, water, etc.; hence ∼'ING¹ (6) *n.* **2.** *v.t.*
convey through duct. [f. L *ductus* leading, aqueduct
(*ducere duct-* lead)]
dŭ′ctile *a.* capable of being drawn out into wire,
tough; (of clay etc., or of person or character) pliable,
tractable, docile; hence **dŭctī′lItỹ** *n.* [ME f. OF, or f.
L *ductilis* (*ducere duct-* lead; see -IL)]
dŭd *n.* & *a.* (sl.) **1.** *n.* counterfeit article; shell etc. that
fails to explode; futile thing or person; (in *pl.*) clothes,
rags. **2.** *a.* counterfeit; useless, worthless, unsatisfactory, futile. [ME; orig. unkn.]
***dude** (dūd, doōd) *n.* (sl.) fastidious aesthetic person;
foppish person; holiday-maker in western US, esp. on
ranch; ∼ **ranch,** cattle ranch converted to holiday
centre for tourists etc.; hence **dŭ′dISH¹** (dū′-, doō′-) *a.*
[19th c., prob. f. G dial. *dude* fōōl]
dudee′n, dudhee′n, (doōdĕ′n) *n.* (Ir.) short clay pipe.
[f. Ir. *dúidín,* dim. of *dúd* pipe; cf. -EEN]
dŭ′dgeon (dŭ′jon) *n.* resentment, feeling of offence; in
(**high**) ∼, (very) angr(il)y. [16th c.; orig. unkn.]
dūe¹ *a.* & *adv.* **1.** *a.* owing, payable, as a debt or
obligation; **fall, become,** ∼, (e.g. of bill reaching
maturity). **2.** that ought to be given *to* person (*first
place is due to Milton; it is due to him to admire his skill*);
merited, appropriate, (*has his due reward*); rightful,
proper, adequate, (*after due consideration*); to be looked
for, calculated or foreseen (*in due time*); in due COURSE¹.
3. to be ascribed to cause, agent, etc., (*the difficulty is due
to our ignorance; the discovery is due to Newton*); under
engagement to do something (*is due to speak tonight*);
intended to arrive at certain time (*train due at 7.30*). **4.**
adv. (Of point of compass) exactly, directly, (*went due
east; a due north wind*); ∼ **to,** (**D**) because of (*was late due
to an accident*). [ME, f. OF *dëu* f. Rom. *debutus f. L
debitus p.p. of *debēre* owe]
dūe² *n.* person's right, what is owed him, (**give** person,
esp. the Devil, **his** ∼, not be unjust to him, however
undeserving; what one owes (*pay* one's *dues*); (usu. in
pl.) toll, fee, legally demandable (*harbour, light, tonnage, university, dues*). [ME, f. F *du* p.p. (as n.) of *devoir*
owe f. L *debēre*]
dū′el *n.*, & *v.i.* (||-ll-). **1.** *n.* fight with deadly weapons
between two persons, in presence of two seconds, to
settle quarrel; any contest between two persons,

animals, parties, causes; hence ∼list (1), *∼ist (1), *n*. **2.** *v.i.* fight duel(s). [f. It. *duello* or L *duellum* (arch. form of *bellum* war), in med. L = single combat]

duĕ'ndė (dōō-) *n*. evil spirit; inspiration. [Sp.]

dŭĕ'nna *n*. older woman acting as governess and companion in charge of girls (orig. and esp. in Spanish family); chaperon. [f. Sp. *dueña* f. L *domina* mistress]

dŭĕ't *n*. (Mus.) (composition for) two voices or performers; (fig.) dialogue; hence ∼tist (1) *n*. [f. G *duett* or f. It. *duetto* dim. of *duo* duet f. L *duo* two]

dŭff[1] *n*. boiled pudding (PLUM *duff*). [N. Engl. form of DOUGH]

dŭff[2] *v.t.* (sl.) (Austral.) steal and alter brands on (cattle); ||(Golf) mishit (shot, ball); bungle; ∼ up, (sl.) beat, thrash. [perh. back-form. f. DUFFER]

dŭff[3] *n*. & *a*. (sl.) worthless, counterfeit, useless, (thing). [perh. = DUFF[1]]

dŭ'ffer *n*. inefficient, useless, or stupid person; (Austral.) one who duffs cattle. [perh. f. Sc. *doofart* stupid person (*douf* spiritless)]

dŭ'ffle, dŭ'ffel, *n*. coarse woollen cloth with thick nap; *sportsman's or camper's kit; ∼ **bag,** cylindrical canvas bag closed by draw-string; ∼**-coat,** hooded overcoat of duffle with toggle fastenings instead of buttons. [f. *Duffel* in Belgium]

dŭg[1] *n*. udder or breast, teat, nipple, (of female mammal, or derog. of woman). [16th c., of unkn. orig.]

dŭg[2]. See DIG.

du'gŏng (dōō'-, dū'-) *n*. (*pl*. ∼s or ∼). sirenian (*Dugong dugon*) of Asian seas and coasts. [ult. f. Malay *dūyong*]

dŭ'g-out *n*. canoe made by hollowing tree-trunk; roofed shelter esp. for troops in trenches; (sl.) retired officer etc. recalled to service. [f. DUG[2]+OUT]

dui'ker[1], **duy'ker,** (dī'k-) *n*. small Afr. antelope of genus *Cephalophus*. [f. Du. *duiker* diver, from plunging through bushes when pursued]

duiker[2] (dī'k-) *n*. (S. Afr.) cormorant of genus *Phalacrocorax*. [Afrik., f. as prec.]

dūke *n*. **1.** (*fem.* **duchess**). person holding highest hereditary title of nobility (**royal** ∼, one who is also royal prince); sovereign prince ruling duchy or small State. **2.** (sl., usu. in *pl*.) hand, fist. **3.** cherry intermediate between sweet and sour kinds. [ME, f. OF *duc* f. L *dux ducis* leader]

dū'kedom (-kd-) *n*. territory ruled by, rank of, duke. [f. prec. + -DOM]

DUKW *n*. = DUCK[4].

dŭ'lcėt *a*. (Esp. of sound) sweet, soothing. [ME, earlier *doucet* f. OF dim. of *doux* f. L *dulcis* sweet]

dŭ'lci|fy *v.t.* sweeten, make gentle; hence ∼FICA'TION *n*. [f. L *dulcificare* (*dulcis* sweet; see -FY)]

dŭ'lcimer *n*. musical instrument with strings of graduated length over sounding-board or box struck with hammers, prototype of piano. [f. OF *doulcemer*, said to repr. L *dulce melos* sweet song]

Dŭlcinea (-sĭnē'a, -sĭ'nĭa) *n*. idolized and idealized lady. [f. ∼ del Toboso, object of Don Quixote's devotion in Cervantes' romance]

dŭ'lcitône *n*. (Mus.) keyboard instrument with steel tuning-forks struck by hammers. [f. L *dulcis* sweet + TONE[1]]

dŭ'lia *n*. (RC Ch.) reverence paid to saints and angels. [med. L, f. Gk *douleia* servitude (*doulos* slave)]

dŭll *a*. & *v*. **1.** *a*. slow of understanding, obtuse, stupid, whence ∼'ARD *n*.; (of ears, eyes, etc.) without keen perception. **2.** (Of pain etc.) indistinctly felt, not acute; (of person, animal, trade) sluggish, slow--moving, stagnant; (of goods, stocks) not easily saleable, not in demand; listless, depressed. **3.** tedious, monotonous; (esp. of edge) blunt; (of colour, light, sound, taste) not bright, vivid, or keen; (of weather) overcast, gloomy. **4.** Hence ∼'ISH[1] *a*., ∼'NESS, **dŭ'lNESS** *n*., **dŭ'lLY**[2] (-l-lĭ) *adv*. **5.** *v.t.* make dull (∼ **the edge of,** blunt, make less sensitive, interest-

ing, or effective). **6.** *v.i.* lose force, intensity, clearness, or keenness. [ME, f. MLG, MDu. *dul*, = OE, OS *dol* stupid, OHG *tol*]

dŭlse *n*. edible kind of red seaweed. [f. Ir. & Gael. *duileasg*]

dū'ly *adv*. rightly, properly, fitly; sufficiently; punctually. [ME, f. DUE[1]+-LY[2]]

du'ma (dōō'-) *n*. (Hist.) Russian council of state. [Russ., orig. elective municipal council]

dŭmb (-m) *a*. (∼'er *pr*. -mer, ∼'est *pr*. -mĭst). **1.** unable to speak, either abnormally (of human beings; *the dumb, the deaf and dumb,* as *ns*.) or normally (∼ **animals, our** ∼ **friends,** term of pity or contempt; ∼ **chum,** ∼ **friend,** a domestic animal); inarticulate, having no voice in government etc., (*the dumb millions*); silenced by surprise, shyness, etc., (esp. *strike dumb*); taciturn, reticent. **2.** (colloq.) stupid, ignorant, [G *dumm*]; ∼ **blonde,** pretty but stupid blonde woman. **3.** (Of action) performed without speech (*dumb* CRAMBO; ∼ **show,** significant gestures, part of play given in early drama without words). **4.** unheard, giving no sound; without voice, sound, or other property, usual in things of the name; ∼ **piano,** set of keys for exercising fingers; ∼ **waiter,** movable table esp. with revolving shelves making waiter unnecessary in dining-room, lift for food etc. **5.** ∼**-bell,** short bar with weight at each end used in pairs for exercising muscles, (sl.) stupid person; ∼ **cluck,** *∼'**head,** (sl.) stupid person; ∼**-iron,** curved side--piece of motor-vehicle chassis, joining it to front springs. **6.** Hence ∼'LY[2] (-mlĭ) *adv*., ∼'NESS (-mn-) *n*. [OE, = OS *dumb*, OHG *tumb* stupid, ON *dumbr*, Goth. *dumbs* mute, of unkn. orig.]

dŭm(b)fou'nd (-mf-) *v.t.* strike dumb; confound, nonplus. [f. DUMB + CONFOUND]

dŭ'mdŭm *a*. & *n*. ∼ (**bullet**), kind of soft-nosed bullet that expands on impact and inflicts laceration. [f. *Dum-Dum* in India, where first produced]

dŭ'mmy *n*., *a*., & *v.i.* **1.** *n*. (Whist) imaginary fourth player whose hand is turned up and played by partner; (Bridge) partner of declarer, whose cards are exposed after first lead, this player's hand (**double** ∼, play with two hands exposed, allowing every card to be located). **2.** person taking no real part, or present only for show, figure-head; stupid person. **3.** counterfeit object, sham package etc., object serving to replace real or normal one; tailor's model of body to hang clothes on; ventriloquist's model of person, or animal, which he can make seem to talk etc.; baby's indiarubber teat; **sell the** or **a** ∼, (Rugby Footb. colloq.) deceive opponent by feigning to pass ball. **4** *a*. sham; ∼ **run,** practice attack etc., trial run rehearsal. **5.** *v.i.* (Footb., colloq.) use feigned pass or swerve etc.; *∼ **up,** (sl.) keep quiet, give no information. [f. DUMB + -Y[3]]

dŭmp[1] *n*. heap of refuse; place for depositing refuse accumulated pile of ore, earth, etc.; temporary deposit of ammunition, provisions, etc.; (colloq.) unpleasant or dreary place; ∼ **truck** etc. (with body that tilts or opens at back for unloading). [f. foll.]

dŭmp[2] *v*. **1.** *v.t.* shoot, deposit, (rubbish); let fall with bump; leave (ammunition etc.) in dump; send (goods unsaleable at high price in home market) to foreign market for sale at low price, to avoid lowering home price and capture new market; (colloq.) abandon **2.** *v.i.* fall with thud. **3.** Hence ∼'ER[1] (1, 2) *n*. [ME perh. f. Norse; cf. Da. *dumpe*, Norw. *dumpa* fall suddenly]

dŭ'mpling *n*. mass of dough boiled or baked either plain or enclosing apple etc.; small fat person. [app. dim. (-LING[1]) of *dump* small round object, but recorded very much earlier]

dŭmps *n. pl*. (colloq.) depression, melancholy, (*in the dumps*). [prob. f. LG or Du., fig. use of MDu. *domp* exhalation, haze, mist, rel. to DAMP]

dŭ'mp|ў *a*. short and stout; hence ∼iLY[2] *adv*., ∼iNES *n*. [f. *dump* (cf. DUMPLING) + -Y[2]]

dŭn[1] *a. & n.* **1.** (of) dull greyish-brown colour as of ass or mouse; ∼**-bird,** pochard; ∼ **diver,** female or young male of goosander. **2.** *a.* (poet.) dark, dusky. **3.** *n.* dun horse; dark fishing-fly. [OE *dun(n)*, = OS *dun* nut-brown]

dŭn[2] *n.*, & *v.t.* (**-nn-**). **1.** *n.* importunate creditor; debt--collector; demand for payment. **2.** *v.t.* importune for payment of debt; pester. [abbr. of obs. *dunkirk* privateer, f. *Dunkirk* in France]

dŭnce *n.* one slow at learning, dullard; ∼**'s cap,** paper cone formerly put on head of dunce at school as mark of disgrace. [f. John *Duns* Scotus, schoolman d. 1308, whose followers were ridiculed by 16th-c. humanists and reformers as enemies of learning]

Dŭndee' *n.* ∼ **cake,** rich fruit-cake usu. decorated with almonds; ∼ **marmalade,** special kind orig. made in Dundee. [∼ in Scotland]

dŭ'nderhead (-ĕd) *n.*, **dŭ'nder-headĕd** (-ĕd-) *a.* stupid (person). [17th c., perh. rel. to dial. *dunner* resounding noise]

Dŭndrear'y̆ *n.* ∼ **whiskers,** (arch.) long side--whiskers worn without beard. [f. Lord ∼, character in T. Taylor's *Our American Cousin* (1858)]

dūne *n.* mound or ridge of loose sand etc. formed by wind; *dune* BUGGY[2]. [F, f. MDu. *dūne*; cf. DOWN[1]]

dŭng *n. & v.* **1.** *n.* faeces of animal, occas. of person; manure; ∼**-beetle** (whose larvae develop in dung); ∼**-cart, -fork,** (for conveying, loading, and spreading, manure); ∼**-fly** (feeding in dung); ∼**'hill,** heap of dung or refuse in farmyard; ∼**-worm** (found in cow-dung and used as bait). **2.** *v.t.* apply dung to (land). **3.** *v.i.* excrete dung. [OE, = OHG *tunga*, Icel. *dyngja*, of unkn. orig.]

dŭngaree' (-ngg-) *n.* coarse Indian calico; (in *pl.*) overalls etc. of dungaree or similar material. [f. Hindi *dungrī*]

dŭ'ngeon (-njon) *n.*, & *v.t.* **1.** *n.* strong subterranean cell for prisoners; (arch.) donjon. **2.** *v.t.* (arch.) shut up, imprison in dungeon. [orig. = *donjon*; ME, f. OF *donjon* f. Gallo-Rom. *domnio -onis f. L *dominus* lord]

du'niwăssal (dōō'-) *n.* (Sc.) Highland gentleman of secondary rank. [f. Gael. *duine* man, *uasal* noble]

dŭnk *v.t.* dip (bread, cake, etc.) into soup or beverage while eating; immerse (lit. or fig.). [f. Pennsylvanian G *dunke* to dip (G *tunken*)]

Dŭnkir'k (-n-k-) *n.* scene of crisis or withdrawal; ∼ **spirit,** refusal to surrender or despair in time of crisis. [∼ in France, whence British forces were evacuated in 1940]

dŭ'nlin *n.* red-backed sandpiper. [prob. f. *dunling f. DUN[1] + -LING[1]]

dŭ'nnage *n.* mats, brushwood, gratings, etc., stowed under or among cargo to prevent wetting and chafing; (colloq.) miscellaneous baggage. [= AL *dennagium*, of unkn. orig.]

dŭnnō (-ō', dŭ'-) *v.i. & t.* (colloq.) (I) do not know. [corrupt.]

dŭ'nnock *n.* HEDGE[1]-sparrow. [app. f. DUN[1] + -OCK, f. its brown and grey plumage]

dŭ'nny *n.* (Sc.) underground passage or cellar esp. in tenement; (esp. Austral. & NZ) earth-closet, outdoor privy. [20th c.; orig. uncert.]

dū'ō *n.* (*pl.* ∼s). pair of artistes (*comedy duo*); (Mus.) duet. [It. f. L, = two]

dŭode'cimal *a.* of twelfths or twelve; reckoning or reckoned by twelves; hence ∼LY[2] *adv.* [f. L *duodecimus* twelfth (*duodecim* twelve) + -AL]

dŭode'cimō *n.* (*pl.* ∼s). book-size in which each leaf is 1/12 of printing-sheet; book of this size. [f. L (*in*) *duodecimo* in a twelfth (as prec.)]

dŭode'nary̆ *a.* proceeding by twelves, in sets of twelve. [f. L *duodenarius* (*duodeni* distrib. of *duodecim* twelve; see -ARY[1])]

dŭode'n|um *n.* (Anat.) first portion of small intestine immediately below stomach; hence ∼AL *a.*, ∼l'TIS *n.* [ME f. med. L (*duodeni*; see prec.) from its length of 12 fingers' breadth)]

dū'olŏgue (-ŏg) *n.* conversation between two persons; dramatic piece with two actors. [irreg. f. L or Gk *duo* two, after *monologue*]

duŏ'mō (dw-) *n.* (*pl.* ∼s). Italian cathedral. [It., = DOME]

dŭŏ'poly̆ *n.* possession of trade in a commodity etc. by only two sellers. [f. Gk *duo* two + *pōleō* sell, after *monopoly*]

dū'otōne *n. & a.* **1.** *n.* (process of making) half-tone illustration in two colours from same original with different screen angles. **2.** *a.* in two colours. [f. L *duo* two + TONE[1]]

dŭp|e *n.*, & *v.t.* **1.** *n.* victim of deception; hence ∼'ERY (2) *n.* **2.** *v.t.* cheat, make a fool of; hence ∼'ABLE *a.*, ∼'ER[1] *n.* [F, f. dial. F *dupe* hoopoe, from the bird's stupid appearance]

dūpion *n.* rough silk fabric from threads of double cocoons; imitation of this with other fibres. [f. F *doupion* f. It. *doppione* (*doppio* double)]

dū'ple *a.* ∼ **ratio,** (Math.) that of 2 to 1; ∼ **time** (Mus., with two beats to the bar). [f. L *duplus* (*duo* two)]

dū'plĕx *a. & n.* **1.** *a.* having two elements, twofold; two-storey (set of rooms), two-family (house). **2.** *n.* duplex house etc.; dwelling forming part of this. [L *duplex duplicis* (*duo* two, *plic-* fold)]

dū'plicate[1] *a. & n.* **1.** *a.* having two corresponding parts, existing in two examples; doubled, twice as large or many (∼ **ratio,** proportion of squares of two numbers); exactly like a thing already existing (with any number of copies or specimens); ∼ **bridge** or whist, form where same hands are played successively by different players. **2.** *n.* one of two things exactly alike, esp. that made after the other; second copy, with equal legal force, of letter or document; (arch.) pawnbroker's ticket; one of two or more specimens of thing exactly or virtually alike; exact correspondence between two things (*made in duplicate*); = *duplicate bridge* etc. [ME, f. L *duplicatus* p.p. of *duplicare* (see foll., -ATE[2])]

dū'plic|āte[2] *v.t.* double, multiply by two; make in duplicate, make or be exact copy of, produce or supply copies of; repeat (action etc.), esp. unnecessarily; hence ∼A'TION *n.*, ∼ātOR *n.*, (esp.) machine for making copies of documents etc. [f. L *duplicare* (as DUPLEX) + -ATE[3]]

dŭpli'cit|y̆ *n.* double-dealing, deceitfulness, (arch.) doubleness; hence ∼OUS *a.* [ME, f. OF *duplicité* or f. LL *duplicitas* (as DUPLEX, see -ITY)]

dŭ'ppy̆ *n.* (W. Ind.) malevolent ghost or spirit. [perh. of Afr. orig.]

dura. See DURRA.

dur'ab|le *a. & n.* **1.** *a.* capable of lasting, not transitory; (of goods) remaining useful for a period, not immediately consumed; resisting wear, decay, etc.; hence **dūr**ABI'LITY, ∼leNESS (-beln-), *ns.*, ∼LY[2] *adv.* **2.** *n.* (in *pl.*) durable goods. [ME f. OF, f. L *durabilis* (*durare* endure f. *durus* hard; see ABLE)]

Dūră'lūmin *n.* (P) aluminium alloy with copper etc., remarkable for its strength and hardness combined with lightness. [perh. f. *Düren* in the Rhineland or L *durus* hard + ALUMINIUM]

dūra mā'ter *n.* (Anat.) tough outer membrane enveloping brain and spinal cord. [med. L = hard mother, transl. of Arab. *al-'umm al-jāfiya* ('mother' in Arab. indicating relationship of things)]

dūrā'mĕn *n.* heartwood of exogenous tree. [L (*durare* harden)]

dūr'ance *n.* (arch.) imprisonment (esp. *in durance vile*). [ME f. F *durer* last f. L *durare* (see DURABLE, -ANCE)]

dūrā'tion *n.* continuance in, length of, time; time for which thing, esp. war, continues (**for the** ∼, until end of war, (fig.) for a very long time). [ME f. OF, f. med. L *duratio -onis* (as prec.; see -ATION)]

dūr'ative *a.* (Gram.) denoting continuing action. [f. prec. + -IVE]

dŭr'bar *n.* (Hist.) court of Indian ruler; public levee of Indian prince or Anglo-Ind. governor or viceroy. [Urdu, f. Pers. *darbār* court]

dur'chkömpōniert (door'χ-) a. (Mus., of song) having different music for each verse. [G (*durch* through, *komponiert* composed)]

dŭrĕss (-ĕ's, dūr'ĕs) n. forcible restraint, imprisonment; compulsion, esp. imprisonment, threats, or violence, illegally used to force person to do something (*under duress*). [ME, f. OF *duresse* f. L *duritia* (*durus* hard; see -ESS²)]

dur'ian (door'-) n. (SE Asian tree, *Durio zibethinus*, bearing) large oval fruit containing pulp notable for its fetid smell and agreeable taste. [f. Malay *durian* (*dūrī* thorn)]

dūr'ing *prep.* throughout the continuance of; at some point in the duration of. [ME, part. of obs. *dure* continue, after OF *durant* and L abl. abs. constr., as *durante vita* (or *vita durante*) while life continues]

dūr'mast (-ah-) n. sessile-flowered species of oak, *Quercus petraea*. [f. dur- (perh. erron. for DUN¹) + MAST²]

***dūrn, *dūrned** (-nd). Var. of DARN², DARNED.

du'rra, du'ra, dhu'rra, (dōō'-) n. kind of sorghum (esp. *Sorghum vulgare*) grown in Asia, Africa, and US. [f. Arab. *ḏur(r)a*]

dūrst. See DARE.

dūr'um n. species of wheat with hard seeds. [L, neut. of *durus* hard]

dūr'zi (-zē) n. Indian tailor. [f. Hindi f. Pers. *darzī* (*darz* sewing)]

dŭsk n., a., & v. **1.** n. shade, gloom; darker stage of twilight. **2.** a. (poet.) shadowy, dim, dark-coloured. **3.** v.t. & i. (poet.) make or become shadowy or dim. [ME *dosk, dusk,* f. OE *dox* dark, swarthy, *doxian* darken in colour]

dŭ'sk|ў a. shadowy, dim; dark-coloured; hence ~iLY² adv., ~iNESS n. [f. prec. + -Y²]

dŭst¹ n. **1.** finely powdered earth or other matter lying on ground or on surfaces or carried about by wind (BITE¹ *the dust;* ~ **and ashes,** something very disappointing; **in the ~,** humiliated; **shake the ~ off** one's **feet,** depart indignantly or disdainfully; **throw ~ in** person's **eyes,** mislead him by misrepresentation or diverting attention from point). **2.** ||household refuse. **3.** pollen; fine powder of any material (*gold dust; pyrethrum dust*). **4.** cloud of dust (RAISE a dust); (fig.) confusion, turmoil. **5.** dead person's remains (*honoured dust;* **in the ~,** dead); (arch.) the human body, man. **6.** ~**-bath,** bird's rolling in or sprinkling itself with dust to freshen its feathers; ||~'**bin,** container for household refuse; ~ **bowl,** area denuded of vegetation by drought and erosion and so reduced to desert; ||~-**cart,** vehicle for collecting household refuse; ~-**coat, -cloth,** (worn or put over objects to keep off dust); ~-**colour,** dull light brown; ~-**cover,** removable cloth to keep dust off furniture etc., = JACKET 3; *dust* DEVIL¹ 7; ~-**jacket,** = JACKET 3; ||~'**man,** (1) man who removes refuse from dustbins, (2) = SANDman; ~'**pan** (into which dust is brushed from floor); ~-**sheet,** dust-cover for furniture; ~-**shot,** smallest-sized shot; ~-**trap,** something on or in or under which dust readily collects; ~-**up,** (colloq.) fight, disturbance; ~-**wrapper,** book's dust-cover. **7.** Hence ~'LESS a. [OE *dūst,* = MDu. *donst, dūst,* ON *dust;* cf. LG *dunst* vapour]

dŭst² v. **1.** v.t. sprinkle with dust or powder; make dusty; sprinkle (dust, powder). **2.** clear of dust by brushing, wiping, or beating (~ person's *jacket,* (colloq.) thrash him); clear away as dust. **3.** v.i. clear furniture etc. of dust; (of bird) take dust-bath. [ME, f. prec.]

dŭ'ster n. cloth for dusting furniture etc.; person who does this; woman's light loose casual full-length coat; ||RED duster. [f. prec. + -ER¹]

dŭ'sting n. In vbl senses; **crop-~,** sprinkling of powdered insecticide or fertilizer on crops, esp. from the air; ~-**powder,** (esp.) talcum powder. [f. DUST² + -ING¹]

dŭ'st|ў a. full of, strewn with, finely powdered like, dust; dry as dust, uninteresting; (of colour) dull; vague, indefinite, unsatisfactory, (*dusty answer*); || **not so ~y,** (sl.) fairly good; ~**y miller,** auricula plant [from white dust on leaves and flowers], artificial fishing-fly, *speckled moth; hence ~iLY² adv., ~iNESS n. [OE *dūstig* (as DUST¹, -Y²)]

Dŭtch¹ a. & n. **1.** a. (of the language or people) of the Netherlands. **2.** originating in the Netherlands, made or invented by the Dutch, (*Dutch chair, cheese*). **3.** characteristic of or attributed to the Dutch; *Dutch* AUCTION; ~ **bargain** (concluded by drinking together); ~ **barn,** roof on poles over hay etc.; ~ **cap,** (1) woman's lace cap with triangular piece turned back on each side, (2) contraceptive diaphragm; *Dutch* COURAGE; ~ **doll,** jointed wooden doll; ~ **elm disease,** fungous disease of elms, first found in the Netherlands; *Dutch* HOE; ~ **interior,** painting of interior of Dutch room or house, esp. by P. de Hooch (d. 1683); ~ **metal,** copper-zinc alloy imitating gold leaf; *Dutch* OVEN; ~ **treat** etc., party where each person pays for his own share (**go ~,** share expenses thus); **talk to** person **like a ~ uncle,** lecture him with kindly severity; ~ **wife,** frame of cane etc. for resting the limbs in bed, long bolster similarly used. **4.** (arch.) of Germany incl. Netherlands (**High ~,** of S Germany; **Low ~,** of N. Germany and Netherlands). **5.** *(sl.) German; (S. Afr.) of Dutch descent. **6.** n (**High ~,** language of the Netherlands (**double ~** gibberish); (S. Afr.) Afrikaans; **the ~,** (*pl.*) people of the Netherlands (*beat the ~,* (colloq.) do something remarkable), (S. Afr.) Afrikaans-speakers; in ~, (sl.) in disgrace. **7.** (arch.) language of Germany incl. Netherlands (**High ~,** German). **8. Low ~** Low German or language of the Netherlands. [f MDu. *dutsch* etc. Hollandish, Netherlandish, German, OHG *diutisc* national]

||**dŭtch²** n. = DUCHESS 2. [abbr.]

Dŭ'tchman n. (*pl.* -men; *fem.* -woman). native of the Netherlands (**or I'm a ~, I'm a ~ if,** forms of asseveration); Dutch ship (**Flying ~,** spectral ship of its captain); *(sl.) a German; *~'s breeches,** (*Dicentra cucullaria*) with white flowers and finely divided leaves. [f. DUTCH¹ + MAN¹]

dū'tèous a. (literary). (Of person or conduct) dutiful obedient; hence ~LY² adv., ~NESS n. [f. DUTY + -OUS (cf. *beauteous*)]

dū'tiable a. liable to customs or other duties. [f. DUTY + -ABLE]

dū'tiful a. regular or willing in obedience and service hence ~LY² adv., ~NESS n. [f. foll. + -FUL]

dū'tў n. **1.** behaviour due to superior, deference expression of respect. **2.** payment to public revenue levied on import, export, manufacture, or sale, of goods (CUSTOMs, EXCISE¹, *duty*), transfer of property (DEATH, PROBATE, *duty*), licences, legal recognition of documents, etc. **3.** moral or legal obligation, what one is bound or ought to do (~**-bound,** obliged by duty; ~ **visit** etc., thing that one would rather not but feels bound to, do); binding force of what is right **4.** business, office, function, performance of or engagement in these (HEAVY-*duty;* **on, off, ~,** actually so engaged or not); (Eccl.) performance of church services; ~ **officer** etc., the one currently on duty; **~ for,** serve as or pass for (something else). **5.** measure of engine's effectiveness in units of work done per unit of fuel. **6.** ~-**paid, -free,** (of goods) on which customs or excise duty has been paid, is no leviable; ~-**free shop,** one at which duty-free good can be bought. [f. AF *deweté, dueté* (as DUE¹; see -TY¹)]

dūū'mvir n. (Rom. Hist.) one of two coequal magistrates or officials; hence ~ATE¹ n. [L, f. *duum virum* of the two men]

du'vet (dōō'vā) n. thick soft quilt used instead of bedclothes. [F]

dŭx n. (Sc., NZ, S. Afr., etc.) top pupil in class or school. [L, = leader]

duyker. See DUIKER[1].

DV abbr. Deo volente.

Dvr. abbr. Driver.

dwāle n. = BELLADONNA 1. [prob. f. Scand.]

dwarf (-ôrf) n. (pl. ~s, or **dwarves** pr. -vz), a., & v.t. **1.** n. person, animal, or plant, much below ordinary size of species, whence ~'ISH[1] a.; small dense star. **2.** small supernatural being in Gmc (esp. Scand.) mythology, skilled in metal-working. **3.** a. undersized (esp. in plant-names); puny, stunted, (naturally or deliberately). **4.** v.t. stunt in growth, or in intellect etc.; make look small by contrast or distance. [OE dweorg, dweorh, = MDu. dwerch, OHG twerg, ON dvergr f. Gmc *dwergaz]

dwar'fism (-ôr'-) n. condition or character of being a dwarf. [f. prec. + -ISM (5)]

dwell v.i. (dwelt), & n. **1.** v.i. keep one's attention fixed, write or speak at length, (up)on subject; ~ **upon,** prolong (note, syllable, etc.). **2.** (literary). make one's abode, spend one's time, live, in, at, near, on, etc. **3.** (Of horse) be slow in raising feet, pause before taking fence. **4.** Hence (-)~ER[1] n., (esp.) inhabitant. **5.** n. slight regular pause in motion of machine. [OE dwellan lead astray, = MDu. dwellen stun, OHG twellan, ON dvelja delay, etc., f. Gmc *dwel- etc.]

dwe'lling n. In vbl senses; ~(-place), place of residence, house; ~-house (used as residence, not as office, warehouse, etc.). [ME, f. prec. + -ING[1]]

dwelt. See DWELL.

dwi'ndle v.i. become gradually smaller, shrink, waste away; lose importance, decline, degenerate. [f. dwine fade away f. OE dwīnan, ON dvina, + -LE 3]

dwt. abbr. pennyweight.

d.w.t. abbr. dead-weight tonnage.

dȳ n. sediment rich in organic matter, deposited in unproductive lakes. [Sw., = mire]

Dy symb. dysprosium.

dȳ'ăd n. the number two; group of two, couple; hence **dyă'dIC** a. [f. LL f. Gk duas duados (duo two; see -AD 1)]

Dȳ'ăk n. aboriginal of Borneo or Sarawak. [f. Malay dayak up-country]

dyarchy. Var. of DIARCHY.

dȳ'bbuk (-ŏŏk) n. (pl. ~im or ~s). malevolent spirit in Jewish folklore. [f. Heb. dibbūḳ (dābaḳ cling)]

dye[1] n. **1.** colour produced as by dyeing, tinge, hue, (lit., or fig.: crime, scoundrel, of (the) blackest, deepest, dye), **2.** ~('stuff), substance used for dyeing, colouring-matter in solution. **3.** ~-line, (print made by) diazo process; ~'wood, wood yielding dye. [f. foll.]

dye[2] v.t. (part. ~ing pr. dī'i-). colour, stain, tinge; impregnate with colouring-matter (~d in the wool, in grain, while material is in raw state, giving more permanent result, (fig.) unchangeable), make (thing) a specified colour esp. thus (dye cloth red etc.). [OE deagian, of unkn. orig.]

dȳ'er n. one who dyes cloth etc.; ~'s broom, bugloss, oak, weed, etc., names of plants yielding dyes. [f. prec. + -ER[1]]

dȳ'ing n. In vbl senses; connected with, at time of, death (dying words, declaration, wish; **to** one's ~ **day,** for the rest of one's life; ~ **oath,** made at, or with solemnity proper to, death). [f. DIE[2] + -ING[1]]

dyke[1],[2]. See DIKE[1],[2].

dyn abbr. dyne.

dynă'mic a. & n. **1.** a. of motive force (opp. static); of force in actual operation (opp. potential); active, potent, energetic; of dynamics; (Med.) affecting function (opp. organic); (Philos.) relating to dynamism; (Mus.) relating to volume of sound; dynamic VISCOSITY. **2.** n. energizing or motive force; (Mus.) = DYNAMICS. **3.** [f. F dynamique f. Gk dunamikos (dunamis power; see -IC)]

dynă'mical a. of dynamics; of force or mechanical power actively operative; (Theol., of inspiration) divine with divine power, not impelling mechani-

cally; of dynamism; hence ~LY[2] adv. [f. as prec. + -ICAL]

dȳnă'mics n. pl. (usu. treated as sing.) **1.** branch of mechanics that treats of motion in itself, and of the motion of bodies or matter under the influence of forces (including kinematics and kinetics; opp. statics), whence **dȳnă'micIST** (3) n.; branch (of any science) in which forces or changes are considered (now often with a specific prefix: aerodynamics, population dynamics). **2.** motive forces, physical or moral, in any sphere. **3.** (Mus.) variation or amount of volume of sound. [f. DYNAMIC + -ICS]

dȳ'nam|ism n. energizing or dynamic action or power; (Philos.) theory that phenomena of matter and mind are due merely to the action of forces, whence ~IST (2) n. [f. Gk dunamis power + -ISM]

dȳ'namite n., & v.t. **1.** n. high explosive of nitro-glycerine mixed with inert absorbent; potentially dangerous person or thing; (sl.) heroin or similar narcotic. **2.** v.t. charge or shatter with dynamite. [f. prec. + -ITE[1]]

dȳ'namo n. (pl. ~s). machine converting mechanical into electric energy by electric induction, e.g. by rotating conductor in magnetic field; (fig.) energetic person. [abbr. of dynamo-electric machine, f. Gk dunamis power + -o-]

dȳnamo'meter n. instrument measuring energy expended by animal, engine, or mechanical force. [f. F dynamomètre f. Gk dunamis force; cf. -METER]

dȳ'nast n. ruler; member of a dynasty. [f. L f. Gk dunastēs (dunamai be able)]

dȳ'nasty n. line of hereditary rulers; succession of leaders in any field; hence **dynă'stIC** a., **dynă'sti**-CALLY adv. [f. F dynastie or f. LL f. Gk dunasteia lordship (as prec.)]

dȳ'natrŏn n. (Electr.) thermionic valve with four electrodes, used to generate continuous oscillations. [f. Gk dunamis power + -TRON]

dȳne n. (Phys.) unit of force, the force that, acting for one second on one-gram mass, gives it velocity of one centimetre per second. [F, f. Gk dunamis force]

dȳs- comb. form. (esp. Med. etc.) bad, difficult, as: **dysgra'phia,** inability to write coherently; **dysmenorrhoe'a,** painful menstruation. [f. Gk dus-bad]

dȳ'sentery n. disease with inflamed intestinal mucous membrane and glands, griping pains, diarrhoea, and evacuation of mucus and blood; so **dysentě'rIC** a. [f. OF dissenterie or f. L f. Gk DYS(enteria f. entera bowels); see -Y[1]]

dysfu'nction n. abnormality or impairment of function; hence ~AL a. [f. DYS- + FUNCTION]

dȳsge'nic a. exerting a detrimental effect on later generations. [f. DYS- + -GENIC]

dȳslě'x|ia n. word-blindness; hence **dȳslě'ctIC,** adjs. & ns. [f. Gk dyslexie (as DYS-, Gk lexis speech, -IA[1]]

dȳslogi'st|ic a. (Of sense in which term is used) disapproving, opprobrious; hence ~ICALLY adv. [f. DYS- + EULOGISTIC]

dȳspě'psia n. indigestion; so **dȳspě'ptIC** a. & n., (person) subject to dyspepsia or the resulting depression. [L, f. Gk DYS(pepsia f. peptos cooked, digested)]

dȳ'sphèmism n. (substitution of) unpleasant or derogatory word etc. for pleasant or inoffensive one. [f. DYS- + EUPHEMISM]

dȳsphŏr'ia n. state of unease or mental discomfort; hence **dȳsphŏ'rIC** a. [f. Gk dysphoria (dusphoros hard to bear, f. as DYS- + pherō bear; see -IA[1]]

dȳsplā'sia (-zĭa) n. (Path.) abnormal growth of tissues etc.; so **dȳsplă'stIC** a. [mod. L, f. as DYS- + Gk plasis formation; see -IA[1]]

dȳspnoe'|a (-nē'a), *dȳspnĕ'|a,** n. (Path.) difficult or laboured breathing; hence ~IC a. [L, f. Gk DYS(pnoia f. pneō breathe)]

dȳsprŏ'sium (-zĭ-) n. (Chem.) metallic element of lanthanide series. [mod. L, f. Gk dusprositos hard to get at + -IUM]

dystopia　　　　　　　302　　　　　　　**dziggeta**

dỹ'stōpia *n.* imaginary place where everything is as bad as possible. [mod. L, f. DYS- + UTOPIA]

dỹ'strophỹ *n.* defective nutrition; **muscular** ～, hereditary progressive weakening and wasting of muscles. [f. mod. L *dystrophia* f. as DYS- + Gk *-trophia* nourishment; see -Y¹]

dỹsūr'ia *n.* painful urination. [LL, f. Gk DYS(*ouria* f. *ouron* urine)]

dzhō, dzō, *n.* (*pl.* ～s *or* ～). hybrid of cow and yak. [f. Tibetan *mdso*]

dzi'ggetai (ji'getī) *n.* = KIANG. [Mongolian (*tchikk* ear)]

E

E, e, (ē) *n.* (*pl.* **Es** *or* **E's**). fifth letter of alphabet; (Mus.) third note in diatonic scale of C major.

E. *abbr.* east(ern); Egyptian (*£E*); Engineering (*M.I. Mech.E.,* etc.).

e- *pref.*, form of EX-¹ 1 bef. consonants exc. *c, f, h, p, q, s, t,* and in *adjs.* w. sense 'not having' (*ecaudate* tailless).

ea. *abbr.* each.

each *a.* & *pron.* (Of two or more) every (one), taken separately (*each man has two votes, each of us has two votes, we have two votes each; they cost a penny each; each is worse than the one before*; **sides of two triangles are equal ∼ to ∼,** each side of one equals the corresponding side of the other); **∼ and every,** every single; **∼ other** (used as compound reciprocal pron.; **they hate ∼ other,** each hates the other(s); **they wore ∼ other's hats,** each wore the hat of the (*or* an) other); ||**∼ way,** (of bet) backing horse etc. to win and to be placed. (OE *ǣlc,* = MLG, MDu. *elk,* OHG *eogilīh* f. WG *aiwō galīkaz ever alike (as AYE, ALIKE)]

ea'ger (-g-) *a.* full of keen desire (*eager* BEAVER¹); strongly desirous (*to do, for,* etc.); keen, impatient; (arch., of air) cold; hence **∼LY²** *adv.*, **∼NE33** *n.* [ME, f. AF *egre,* OF *aigre* keen, f. Rom. *acrum f. L *acer acris*]

ea'gle *n.* **1.** large bird of prey of family Accipitridae, with keen vision and powerful flight; figure of this, esp. as (Hist.) ensign of Roman or French army, as symbol of State (esp. US), or as lectern in church; *coin worth ten dollars. **2.** (Golf) hole played in two strokes under par or bogey. **3. double ∼,** figure of eagle with two heads, *(Golf) = ALBATROSS, *coin worth twenty dollars; **∼ eye,** keen sight, watchfulness; **∼-owl,** large horned owl, or other owl of genus *Bubo.* [ME, f. AF *egle,* OF *aigle* f. L *aquila*]

ea'glet *n.* young eagle. [f. prec. + -ET¹]

ea'gre (ā'ger, ē'ger) *n.* = BORE⁵. [17th c.; orig. unkn.]

-ean (-ē'an, -ian) *suf.* forming *adjs.* and *ns.,* orig. = -AN + end of stem (*Achaean, antipodean, empyrean, Epicurean, European, Herculean, Jacobean*). [f. or after L *-aeus, -eus,* Gk *-aios, -eios* + -AN]

E. & O. E. *abbr.* errors and omissions excepted.

ear¹ *n.* **1.** organ of hearing in man and animals, esp. external part of this; faculty of discriminating sound (*an ear for music*); listening, attention (**give ∼,** listen *to*); ear-shaped thing, esp. handle of jug. **2. bring** (storm, hornets' nest, etc.) **about** one's **∼s,** down upon oneself; **all ∼s,** listening attentively; *not* BE-LIEVE one's *ears*; one's *ears* BURN²; *turn a* DEAF *ear*; *with a* FLEA *in* one's *ear*; **give** one's **∼s,** make any sacrifice (*for* a thing, *to* do, *if*); **∼ to the ground,** alertness regarding rumours or trend of opinion; **have** person's **∼,** have his favourable attention; **over head and ∼s, head over ∼s,** deeply immersed (lit. or fig.); **in** (at) **one ∼ and out** (at) **the other,** heard but leaving no impression; **out on** one's **∼,** dismissed ignominiously; *play by ear* (PLAY¹ 6); PRICK² *up* one's *ears*; **set by the ∼s,** cause to quarrel; **up to the ∼s,** (colloq.) very deeply involved *in*; **wet behind the ∼s,** immature, inexperienced; **a word in your ∼** (in private). **3. ∼'ache,** pain in ear-drum; **∼-drops,** (1) medicinal drops for the ear, (2) hanging ear-rings; **∼-drum,** DRUM¹ 2 of ear, tympanum; **∼'mark,** (*n.*) mark on ear of sheep etc. as sign of ownership, (fig.) mark of ownership, (*v.t.*) mark (sheep etc.) thus, (fig.) assign (money etc.) to definite purpose; **∼-muff** (protecting ears against cold, noise, etc.); **∼'phone,** device worn on ear to aid hearing or to listen to radio or telephone communication; **∼-piece,** apparatus to be applied to ear as part of

telephone etc.; **∼-piercing,** shrill; **∼-plug,** piece of wax etc. placed in ear to protect against cold air, water, or noise; **∼-ring** (worn in or on lobe of ear for ornament); **∼-shot,** distance over which something can be heard (*within, out of, earshot*); **∼-splitting,** excessively loud; **∼-trumpet,** tube used by partly deaf person; **∼-wax,** yellow waxy secretion in ear. **4.** Hence (-)**∼ED²** (ērd) *a.* (*eared* SEAL¹), **∼'FUL** 2 *n.,* (colloq.) large amount of talk etc., strong reprimand, **∼'LESS** *a.* [OE *ēare,* = OS, OHG *ōra,* ON *eyra,* Goth. *ausō* f. Gmc *auson etc. cogn. w. L *auris,* Gk *ous*]

ear² *n.* spike or head of corn, containing its flowers or seeds. [OE *ēar,* = OS *ahar,* OHG *ahir,* ON *ax,* Goth. *ahs* f. Gmc **ahuz,* *ahiz]

ear'ing *n.* (Naut.) small rope (one of several) fastening upper corner of sail to yard. [f. EAR¹ + -ING¹ or RING¹]

earl (ērl) *n.* (*fem.* **countess**). British nobleman ranking between marquis and viscount (cf. COUNT³); ||**E∼ Marshal,** officer presiding over College of Arms, with ceremonial duties on various royal occasions; hence **∼'DOM** *n.* [OE *eorl,* = OS, OHG *erl,* ON *jarl,* of unkn. orig.]

ear'ly (ēr'-) *a.* & *adv.* **1.** before the due or usual time (*was early for his appointment; it is too early to look for blackberries;* **∼ riser,** one who gets up unusually early from bed); forward in flowering, ripening, etc., (*early peaches*); not far on in day or night, or in time (*seek an early opportunity for discussion; on Wednesday* **at earliest,** not before then); not far on in a period, development, etc., (*the early part of the century; the early spring; the early morning, chapters, Christians*); of the distant past (*early man*). **2. ∼ bird,** (joc.) person who arrives, rises, etc., early; **∼ closing,** shutting of business premises on the afternoon of one particular day of the week; **∼ days,** early in time for something (to happen, etc.); **E∼ English style,** (Archit.) first stage of English Gothic (13th c.), with pointed arches, lancet windows, and simple tracery; **keep ∼ hours,** rise and go to bed early; **∼ night** (when one goes to bed earlier than usual); **∼ on,** at an early stage [f. *earlier on,* formed by anal. w. *later on*]; **∼ warning** (esp. of aerial etc. attacks). **3.** Hence **ear'liNESS** (ēr'-) *n.* [orig. adv., f. OE *ǣrlīce, ārlīce* (ǣr ERE; see -LY²)]

earn (ērn) *v.t.* (Of person, action, conduct, etc.) obtain or be entitled to as reward of labour or merit; incur (reproach etc.); bring in as income or interest; (Baseball) score (run) without help from opponent. [OE *earnian,* = OHG *arnōn* reap f. WG *aznōjan (*aznu,* rel. to OE *esne,* Goth. *asneis* labourer]

ear'nest¹ (ēr'-) *a.* & *n.* **1.** *a.* serious, zealous, not trifling; ardent (desire etc.); hence **∼LY²** *adv.,* **∼NESS** *n.* **2.** *n.* seriousness; **in** (real) **∼,** serious(ly), not joking(ly). [OE *eornust, eornost,* = OHG *ernust* f. **ern-* (cf. ON *ern* vigorous)]

ear'nest² *n.* money paid as instalment, esp. to confirm contract etc.; foretaste, presage, token, (*is an, in, earnest of what is to come*). [ME *ernes,* prob. var. of *erles, arles* prob. f. med. L *arrhula dim. of L *arr(h)a* pledge]

ear'ning (ēr'-) *n.* In vbl senses; (in *pl.*) money earned. [f. EARN + -ING¹]

earth¹ (ēr-) *n.* **1.** dry land; soil, mould; ground (*it fell to earth*); **come back to ∼,** return to realities; DOWN³-*-to-earth.* **2.** hole of badger, fox, etc.; **gone to ∼,** (fig.) in hiding; **run to ∼,** (fig.) find after long searching. **3.** land and sea, opp. sky; (or **E∼**) the planet on which we live; present abode of man, opp. heaven or hell as places of future existence; **on ∼,** existing anywhere (*happiest man on earth; looked like nothing on earth; what on earth do you mean?*); (colloq.) huge sum etc. (*cost the earth*). **4.** (Chem.) one of several naturally occurring metallic oxides; RARE[1] *earth*. **5.** ||(Electr.) connection to earth as completion of circuit. **6.** ∿**-born,** of mortal race, (Myth.) emerging from earth at birth; ∿**-bound,** (1) attached (lit. or fig.) to the earth, (2) moving towards the earth; ||∿- **-closet** (like water-closet, but with dry earth used to cover excreta); ∿**-light,** partial illumination of dark part of moon by light reflected from earth; ∿ **mother,** (Myth.) spirit symbolizing earth, (fig.) sensual and maternal woman; ∿**-moving,** excavation of large quantities of soil; ∿**-nut,** (edible roundish tuber of) one of various plants, esp. (1) an umbelliferous woodland plant (*Conopodium denudatum*), (2) PEA*nut*; ∿′**quake,** convulsion of earth's surface due to geol. faults or volcanic action, (fig.) social etc. disturbance; ∿ **sciences,** those dealing with the earth or part of it (e.g. geology, oceanography); ∿**-shaking** *a.*, (fig.) having a violent effect; ∿**-shine,** = *earth-light; earth* TREMOR; ∿′**work,** (raising of) bank of earth in fortification or construction of road etc.; ∿′**worm,** annelid worm living in ground. **7.** Hence ∿′**WARD**(s) *a.* & *adv.* [OE *eorthe,* = OS *ertha,* OHG *erda,* ON *jörth,* Goth. *airtha* f. Gmc **erthō*]

earth[2] (ēr-) *v.* **1.** *v.t.* cover (roots of plants *up*) with heaped-up earth; drive (fox) to earth; ||(Electr.) connect to earth. **2.** *v.i.* (Of fox etc.) run to its earth. [ME, f. prec.]

ear'then (ēr'-) *a.* made of earth; made of baked clay. [ME, f. EARTH[1] +-EN[5]]

ear'thenware (ēr'-) *n.* & *a.* (vessels etc.) made of baked clay, esp. coarser kind (opp. porcelain); baked clay. [f. prec. +WARE[1]]

ear'thling (ēr'-) *n.* inhabitant of the earth. [f. EARTH[1] +-LING[1]]

ear'thl|y (ēr'-) *a.* of the earth, terrestrial, (opp. *celestial*); **no** ∿**y** *use, reason, chance,* (colloq.) no use etc. at all; **not an** ∿**y,** (sl.) no chance whatever; hence ∿**iNESS** *n.* [OE *eorthlic* (as EARTH[1], -LY[1])]

ear'th|y (ēr'-) *a.* like or of earth or soil; (fig.) grossly material, coarse (*earthy jokes*); hence ∿**iNESS** *n.* [f. EARTH[1] +-Y[2]]

ear'wig *n.,* & *v.t.* (**-gg-**). **1.** *n.* insect of order Dermaptera, with large terminal forceps; *small centipede. **2.** *v.t.* (arch.) influence (person) by secret communications. [OE *ēarwicga* (*ēare* EAR[1], *wicga* earwig, prob. rel. to *wiggle*; once thought to enter head through ear)]

ease[1] (ēz) *n.* **1.** freedom from pain or trouble (**set** person **at** ∿, relieve his anxiety). **2.** freedom from constraint (*at one's ease;* ILL *at ease;* **put** or **set** person **at his** ∿, avoid undue formality); relief from pain; **at** ∿, (Mil.) in relaxed attitude, with feet apart; CHAPEL *of ease.* **3.** facility (**with** ∿, without difficulty). **4.** Hence ∿′LESS (-zl-) *a.* [ME, f. AF *ese,* OF *eise, aise* f. Rom. **adjaces* f. L *adjacens* ADJACENT]

ease[2] (ēz) *v.* **1.** *v.t.* relieve from pain etc. or *of* burden; give mental ease to (person, one*self,* one's mind); ∿ **nature,** = one**self,** urinate or defecate; (joc.) rob (person *of* his purse etc.); relax, adjust, (what is too tight); (Naut.) slacken (rope, sail, *away, down, off*); cause to move by gentle force. **2.** *v.i.* ∿(**off, up**), become less burdensome (*pain, rain, is easing*), begin to take it easy; (of shares etc.) descend in price. [ME, f. OF (*a*)*aisier* (*a aise* at ease), & f. prec.]

ea'seful (ē'zf-) *a.* (arch.) comfortable, soothing; at rest; slothful; hence ∿LY[2] *adv.,* ∿NESS *n.* [ME, f. EASE[1] +-FUL]

ea'sel (ē'z-) *n.* wooden frame to support picture, blackboard, etc. [f. Du. *ezel* = G *esel* ASS[1]]

ea'sement (ē'zm-) *n.* **1.** (Law) right of way or similar right over another's ground or property. **2.** (arch.) supplementary building, shed, etc.; (arch.) relief from pain or burden. [ME, f. OF *aisement* (as EASE[2]; see -MENT)]

ea'sily (-z-) *adv.* In adj. senses; without doubt (*easily the best*). [f. EASY +-LY[2]]

east *adv., n.,* & *a.* **1.** (towards, at, near) point of

horizon where sun rises at the equinoxes (cardina point 90° to right of North); (**to the**) ∿ (**of**), in an eastward direction (from); *lie* ∿ **and west,** length wise along line from east to west; ∿ **wind,** wind blowing from the east. **2.** *n.* (usu. *E*∿). part of the world lying east of Europe; part of country or town lying to the east; Communist States of eastern Europe; eastern part of late-Roman world; altar-end of church (whether truly oriented or not); card-playe occupying position designated 'east'; ***the E**∿, (esp. north-east region of the US; **Far E**∿, China, Japan etc.; **Middle E**∿, (esp.) countries from Egypt to Iran inclusive; **Near E**∿, (1) = *Middle East,* (2) (arch. Turkey and Balkan countries. **3.** ∿′**about,** east wards; ∿′**bound,** travelling eastwards; *east* BY[1] *north or south;* ||**E**∿ **End,** eastern part of London including docks (*E*∿*-Ender,* inhabitant thereof); **E**∿ **India man,** (Hist.) large ship engaged in trade with Eas Indies; *East* INDIAN; ∿**-north**∿, compass poin midway between east and north-east (so ∿**-south** -∿); **E*∿ **Side,** eastern part of Manhattan. **4.** Hence ∿′WARD *a.* & *n.,* ∿′WARD(s) *adv.* [OE *ēast-,* = OS OHG *ōst,* ON *aust-* f. Gmc **austo-, *austro-* f. IE **aus-*]

Ea'ster *n.* Christian festival commemorating Christ' resurrection, corresponding to Passover, and ob served on a variable Sunday (∿ **Day,** ∿ **Sunday**) in March or April; ∿ (**week**), week commencing with Easter Day; ∿ **egg,** edible artificial (esp. chocolate or hard-boiled egg as gift at Easter; ∿ **offering**(s) customary payments made to the incumbent or Easter Day (now usu. the collection-proceeds) ∿**tide,** Easter and following days or weeks. [O] *ēastre,* pl. *ēastron,* = OHG *ōstarūn* app. f. Ēostre goddes with festival in spring, f. Gmc **Austrōn* (see prec.)]

ea'sterly *a., adv.,* & *n.* in an eastern position o: direction; (wind) blowing (nearly) from the east [prob. f. obs. *easter* (perh. compar. of EAST) +-LY[1]]

ea'stern *a.* of or (dwelling) in the east; lying o: directed towards the east; (*E*∿) of the (*Far, Middle Near*) East; **E**∿ **Church,** Orthodox Church; **E**∿ **Empire** (cf. ROMAN[2] *Empire*); *Eastern* HEMISPHERE **E**∿ **Time,** standard time used in eastern Canada and US or in eastern Australia; hence ∿ER[1] (4) *n.* ∿MOST *a.* [OE *ēasterne* (as EAST, -ERN)]

ea'sting *n.* (Naut. etc.) distance travelled or measured eastward; easterly direction. [f. EAST +-ING[1]]

ea'sy (ē'zǐ) *a.* & *adv.* **1.** *a.* free from pain, discomfort annoyance, anxiety, etc. (∿ **circumstances,** (col loq.) **E**∿ **Street,** affluence). **2.** free from embarrass ment, constraint, strictness, etc., (*easy manners;* FREE *and easy*). **3.** not difficult (*to* do, or abs.; ∿ **of access** easily got at; ∿ **on the eye** etc., (colloq.) pleasant to look at). **4.** easily persuaded, compliant; **of** ∿ **virtue,** (of woman) sexually promiscuous; **I'm** ∿ (colloq.) I have no preference. **5.** *adv.* in easy manner; with ease; *come easy to* (COME 13); ∿ **come** ∿ **go,** what is easily got is soon lost or spent; ∿ **does it** go carefully; **go** ∿, be sparing or cautious (*with*) **take it** ∿, proceed comfortably or carefully, do only what is necessary. **6.** (As command) ∿**!,** move gently, ∿ **all!,** stop (prop. rowing); ||**stand** ∿! (Mil.) permission to squad standing at ease to relax attitude further. **7.** ∿ **chair,** one designed for comfort, usu. with arms; ∿**going,** (of horse) having an easy gait, (of person) fond of comfort, not strict, indolent, taking things as they are; ∿ **mark, meat,** TOUCH[2], (colloq.) person or thing easily overcome, persuaded, etc.; ∿ **money,** money got without effort (esp. illicitly). **8.** Hence **ea'siNESS** (-z-) *n.* [ME, f. AF *aisé,* OF *aisié* p.p. of *aisier* (as EASE[2]; see -Y[4]]

eat *v.* (**ate** *pr.* ět *or* āt; **ea'ten**). **1.** *v.t.* & *i.* take into mouth, chew and swallow (solid food); swallow (soup etc.); *eat the* BREAD *of; eat* DIRT; ∿ **out of** person's hand, be entirely submissive to him; *eat* one's HAT; ∿ **its head off,** (of animal) cost more to feed than it is worth; ∿ person **out of house and home,** ruin him by eating (lit. or fig.) all he has; *eat* HUMBLE *pie;* ||∿ **one's**

terms, be studying for the Bar (and so have to dine a certain number of times at Inn of Court); **what's ∼ing you?,** (colloq.) why are you vexed?; **∼** one's **words,** retract them in humiliating manner. **2.** destroy, consume, (*eat* one's HEART *out*); make (hole) by corrosion etc.; **∼ away,** destroy gradually (lit. or fig.); **∼ into,** begin to consume (fig.); **∼ up,** consume completely, finish eating, waste, (lit. or fig.), absorb (*eaten up with pride*), traverse (distance) rapidly. **3.** *v.i.* consume food, take a meal; **∼ of,** (arch.) eat (some of); **∼ out,** take a meal other than at home. **4.** Hence **ea′**TABLE *a.* & *n.* (usu. in *pl.*), **∼′ERY** (3) *n.* (colloq.). [OE *etan,* = OS *etan,* OHG *ezzan,* ON *eta,* Goth. *itan* f. Gmc *etan f. IE **ed-*]

:a′ter *n.* In vbl senses (**big ∼,** one who eats much food); ∥fruit suitable for eating raw. [f. prec. + -ER¹]

:a′ting *n.* In vbl senses; **∼ apple** etc. (suitable for eating raw); **∼-house,** restaurant. [ME, f. EAT + -ING¹]

:ats *n. pl.* (colloq.) food. [pl. of obs. *eat,* something edible (OE *ǣt*), or f. EAT]

:au (ō) *n.* **∼-de-Cologne** (ōdekolō′n), perfume made orig. at Cologne; **∼ de Javelle** (ō de zhavě′l), JAVELLE water; **∼-de-Nil** (ōdenē′l), greenish colour (supposed to resemble Nile water); **∼-de-vie** (ȯdeve′), brandy; **∼ sucrée** (ō sŏō′krā), water and sugar. [F, = water]

:aves (ēvz) *n. pl.* overhanging edge of roof or thatch; **∼′drop** *v.i.,* (orig.) stand under this to listen to secrets, (fig.) listen secretly to private conversation; **∼′dropper,** one who does this (usu. fig.). [orig. sing., f. OE *efes;* cf. OHG *obasa,* ON *ups,* Goth. *ubizwa* porch, f. Gmc *obhaswa etc., prob. rel. to OVER]

:bb *n.,* & *v.i.* **1.** *n.* outward movement of tide (*ebb and flow;* ebb-TIDE¹); decline, decay, (*at a low ebb*). **2.** *v.i.* flow back; recede, decline, decay. [OE (*ebbian* v. f.) *ebba* n. f. WG *abhigo (**abh-* OFF)]

:-boat (ē′-) *n.* (Hist.) fast boat of 1939-45) German torpedo-boat. [f. *enemy* + BOAT¹]

′bon *a.* (poet.) made of or black as ebony. [ME f. OF *eban,* f. med. L *ebanus* f. L f. Gk *ebenos* ebony tree, of Semitic origin]

′bonite *n.* = VULCANITE. [f. foll. + -ITE¹]

′bony *n.* & *a.* **1.** *n.* hard heavy black wood from tropical tree esp. of genus *Diospyros.* **2.** *a.* made of or black as ebony. [earlier *hebeny* f.(*h*)*eben*(*e*) = EBON, perh. after *ivory*]

bu′lli‖ent (-ŭ′-, -ōŏ′-) *a.* boiling; exuberant; hence **∼ENCE, ∼ENCY,** *ns.,* **∼entLY²** *adv.* [f. L E(*bullire -it-* boil); see -ENT]

bulli′tion *n.* boiling; (fig.) sudden outburst (*of passion, war, etc.*). [f. LL *ebullitio* (as prec.; see -ITION)]

:C *abbr.* East Central.

′căd *n.* (Ecol.) organism modified by its environment. [f. Gk *oikos* house + -AD]

carté (ākār′tā) *n.* card-game for two persons in which cards may be exchanged for others; (Ballet) position with one arm and leg extended. [F, p.p. of *écarter* discard]

:cce Hŏ′mō (ĕksĭ-, ĕkĭ-, ĕchā-) *n.* picture of Christ wearing crown of thorns. [L, = behold the man (John 19:5)]

:cc′ntr‖ic (ĭks-) *a.* & *n.* **1.** *a.* (Of circle etc.) not concentric (*to* another); not placed, not having its axis etc. placed, centrally; (of orbit) not circular; irregular. **2.** odd, whimsical; differing from the usual in behaviour etc. **3.** Hence **∼ICALLY** *adv.,* **∼centri′**CITY (ĕks-) *n.* **4.** *n.* eccentric person; (Mech.) eccentric contrivance for changing rotatory into backward-and-forward motion, esp. for slide-valve of steam-engine. [f. LL *eccentricus* f. Gk *ekkentros* (*ek* out of, *kentron* CENTRE¹; see -IC]

E′ccles (ě′kelz) *n.* **∼ cake,** round cake of pastry filled with currants etc. [**∼** in Greater Manchester]

:ccles. *abbr.* Ecclesiastes (OT).

:cclē′sia (-z-) *n.* (Gk Ant.) general assembly of citizens; assembly at Athens. [f. Gk *ekklēsia* (see ECCLESIASTES)]

ecclē′sial (-z-) *a.* pertaining to the Church. [f. Gk *ekklēsia* (see foll.) + -AL]

Ecclēsia′stēs (ĭklēzĭā′stēz) *n.* OT book, traditionally ascribed to Solomon. [ME, f. Gk *ekklēsiastēs* public speaker, preacher (*ekklēsia* assembly, church f. *ekklētos* summoned out f. *ek* out + *kaleō* call)]

ecclēsiă′stic (-zĭ-) *n.* clergyman, priest. [f. F *ecclésiastique* or f. LL f. Gk *ekklēsiastikos* f. as prec.]

ecclēsiă′stic‖al (-zĭ-) *a.* of the Church or the clergy; *ecclesiastical* YEAR; hence or cogn. **∼ALLY** *adv.,* **∼ISM** (3) *n.* [f. prec. + -AL]

Ecclēsiā′sticus (ĭklēzĭ-) *n.* book of the Apocrypha, containing moral and practical maxims. [LL, containing moral and practical maxims. [LL, ECCLESIASTIC, = of (i.e. to be read in) church]

ecclēsiŏ′log‖y (-zĭ-) *n.* science of churches, esp. of church building and decoration; hence **ecclēsio-lŏ′g**IC(AL) (-zĭ-) *adjs.,* **∼**IST (3) *n.* [f. Gk *ekklēsia* (see ECCLESIASTES) + -O- + -LOGY]

Ecclus. *abbr.* Ecclesiasticus (Apocrypha).

ě′ccrīne *a.* (Of gland) secreting without loss of cell material. [f. Gk *ek* out of + *krinō* sift]

ě′cdys‖is *n.* (*pl.* **∼es** *pr.* -ēz.) casting off (of shell or outer skin). [mod. L, f. Gk *ekdusis* (*ekduō* put off)]

ECG *abbr.* electrocardiogram.

e′chelon (ě′sh-, ā′sh) *n.,* & *v.t.* **1.** *n.* arrangement of troops in parallel groups each with its end clear of those ahead and behind; similar arrangement of things (e.g. ships); **in ∼,** so drawn up. **2.** division of main supply service in warfare; group of persons at a particular level in an organization. **3.** *v.t.* arrange in echelon. [(v. f. n. or f. F *échelonner*) f. F *échelon* (*échelle* ladder f. L *scala;* see -OON)]

ěchěvě′r′ia *n.* tropical Amer. succulent plant of genus *Echeveria.* [f. M. *Echeveri,* 19th-c. Mex. botanical draughtsman + -IA¹]

ěchǐ′dna (ĭk-) *n.* Australian toothless burrowing egg-laying animal like hedgehog, spiny ant-eater. [mod. L, f. Gk *ekhidna* viper]

e′chinıte (ě′k-) *n.* fossil echinoderm. [f. *echinus* + -ITE¹]

echinodě′rm (ĭkĭ′n-, ě′kĭn-) *n.* animal of phylum Echinodermata, incl. starfish and sea-urchins, some having spiny skins. [f. as foll. + Gk *derma* -*atos* skin]

ěchǐ′noīd (ĭk-) *n.* sea-urchin. [f as foll + -OID]

ěchī′nus (ĭk-) *n.* sea-urchin of genus *Echinus,* incl. common European kind; (Archit.) rounded moulding below abacus. [ME f. L, f. Gk *ekhinos* hedgehog, sea-urchin]

ě′chō¹ (ě′kō) *n.* (*pl.* **∼es**). **1.** repetition of sound by reflection of sound-waves, secondary sound so produced, (*cheer* person etc. **to the ∼,** loudly); (*E∼*) cause of this personified; newspaper (used in titles, as *Daily Echo*); reflected radio or radar wave. **2.** close imitation or imitator; (Bridge etc.) conventional mode of play to show number of cards held in suit led etc. **3. ∼gram,** record of **∼-sounder** (apparatus for determining depth of sea beneath ship from time taken to receive echo from bed); **∼graph,** device for automatic recording of echograms; **∼loca′tion,** location of objects by reflected sound; **∼ verse** (3) *n.* in which a line is made to repeat the last syllables of the previous line). **4.** Hence **∼LESS** *a.* [ME, f. OF or f. L f. Gk *ēkhō,* conn. w. *ēkhē* a sound]

ě′chō²(ě′kō) *v.* **1.** *v.i.* (Of place) resound with echo; (of sound) be repeated, resound; (Bridge etc.) play an echo (see prec.). **2.** *v.t.* repeat (sound) by echo; repeat (another's words), imitate words or opinions of (person). [f. prec.]

ě′choīsm (ě′k-) *n.* = ONOMATOPOEIA; so **ěchō′**IC (ěk-) *a.* [f. ECHO¹ + -ISM]

ěchōlā′lia (ě-k-) *n.* (Path.) meaningless repetition of speech; repetition of speech by child learning to talk. [mod. L, f. Gk *ēkhō* echo + *lalia* talk]

e′chovīrus (ě′k-) *n.* type of enterovirus sometimes causing mild meningitis. [f. enteric cytopathogenic *human* orphan (because not originally assignable to any known disease) + VIRUS]

echt (ěχt) *a.* authentic, genuine, typical. [G]

éclair (ā'klār, āklār') *n.* small finger-shaped cake of choux pastry filled with cream and iced, esp. with chocolate icing. [F, = lightning]

éclaircissement (āklārse'smahň) *n.* (arch.) explanation (of conduct etc.). [F (*éclaircir* clear up; see -MENT)]

éclă'mp|sĭa *n.* kind of convulsion caused by toxaemia to which pregnant women are especially liable; so ∼TIC *a.* [mod. L, f. F *eclampsie* f. Gk *eklampsis* sudden development (*eklampō* shine forth)]

éclat (ĕklah', ā'klah) *n.* conspicuous success, general applause, (*with great éclat*); social distinction; brilliant display. [F (*éclater* burst out)]

éclĕ'ct|ic *a.* & *n.* (ancient philosopher) selecting from each school of thought such doctrines as pleased him; (person, doctrine) borrowing freely from various sources; not exclusive in opinion, taste, etc.; hence ∼ICALLY *adv.*, ∼ICISM (3) *n.* [f. Gk *eklektikos* (*eklegō* pick out; see -IC)]

éclī'pse¹ *n.* interception of the light of a luminous body (sun, moon, etc.), by intervention of another body between it and the eye or between the luminous body and what illuminates it (ANNULAR, PARTIAL, TOTAL, *eclipse*); deprivation of light; loss of brilliance or splendour(**in** ∼, (of bird) having lost the courting plumage); periodical obscuration of lighthouse light. [ME f. OF, f. L f. Gk *ekleipsis* vbl n. f. *ekleipō* fail to appear, be eclipsed (*leipō* leave)]

éclī'pse² *v.t.* (Of heavenly body) obscure (another) by passing between it and spectator or between it and the source of its light; intercept (light, esp. of lighthouse); (fig.) deprive of lustre, outshine, surpass. [ME, f. prec.]

éclī'ptic *n.* & *a.* 1. *n.* sun's apparent path among stars during year. 2. *a.* of eclipse or ecliptic. [ME, f. L f. Gk *ekleiptikos* (as ECLIPSE¹; see -IC)]

é'clŏgue (-g) *n.* short poem, esp. pastoral dialogue, such as those of Virgil. [f. L f. Gk *eklogē* selection (*eklegō* pick out)]

éclŏ'sion (-zhon) *n.* emergence of insect from pupa--case or of larva from egg. [f. F *éclosion* (*éclore* hatch f. as EX-¹ + L *claudere* to close)]

ē'co- *pref.* ecology, ecological, as: ∼**climate**, climate as an ecological factor; ∼**sphere**, region of space where living things can exist; ∼**system**, system of interacting organisms in a particular habitat. [f. ECOLOGY]

ēcŏ'log|ÿ *n.* branch of biology dealing with organisms' relations to one another and to their surroundings; (**human**) ∼**y**, study of interaction of persons with their environment; hence **ēcoLO'GICAL** *a.*, ∼IST (3) *n.* [f. G *ökologie* f. Gk *oikos* house; see -LOGY]

Econ. *abbr.* Economics.

ĕcŏnomĕ'tr|ics *n.* branch of economics concerned with application of mathematical economics by use of statistics; hence or cogn. ∼IC(AL) *adjs.*, ∼I'CIAN *n.* [f. ECONOMY + METRIC + -ICS]

ĕconŏ'mic *a.* & *n.* 1. *a.* of economics; maintained for profit, on a business footing; paying (at least) the expenses, (of rent) high enough to compensate builder, owner, etc.; ∼ **botany, geography,** etc., botany etc. studied from the utilitarian standpoint. 2. *n.* (in *pl.*, treated as *sing.*) practical and theoretical science of the production and distribution of wealth; application of this to a particular thing (*the economics of publishing*); condition of a country as regards material prosperity. [ME, f. OF *economique* or f. L f. Gk *oikonomikos* (as ECONOMY; see -IC)]

ĕconŏ'mical *a.* saving, thrifty, avoiding waste (*of*). [f. as prec. + -AL]

ĕconŏ'micallÿ *adv.* In adj. senses. [f. ECONOMIC or prec.; see -ICALLY]

ĕcŏ'nomist *n.* manager (*of* money etc.); thrifty person; student of or writer on economics. [f. Gk *oikonomos* (see ECONOMY) + -IST]

ĕcŏ'nomīz|e, -īs|e (-īz), *v.* 1. *v.t.* use sparingly. 2. *v.i.* practise economy, reduce expenses, ∼**e on,** use

sparingly. 3. Hence ∼A'TION *n.*, ∼ER¹ *n.* (esp., device to save heat). [f. as prec. + -IZE]

ĕcŏ'nomÿ *n.* 1. (administration or condition of) concerns and resources of a community; **political** ∼, study of economic problems of government, (arch.) economics. 2. careful use of resources, frugality; instance of this; cheapest class of air travel; ∼**-size** (of goods etc.) so large as to be economically advantageous to the customer. 3. (arch.) organized system. [f. F *économie* or f. L f. Gk *oikonomia* f. *oikonomo* steward (*oikos* house, *-nomos* f. *nemō* manage)]

écossai'se (ĕkōsā'z) *n.* (dance to) lively tune in duple time. [F, fem. of *écossais* Scotch]

ecru (ā'krōō) *n.* colour of unbleached linen, light fawn. [f. F *écru* unbleached]

ĕ'cstasīze, -īse (-īz), *v.t.* & *i.* throw or go into ecstasies. [f. foll. + -IZE]

ĕ'cstas|ÿ *n.* exalted state of feeling, rapture, (esp. of delight; **in** ∼**ies**, extremely delighted etc.); trance, poetic frenzy. [ME, f. OF *extasie* f. LL f. Gk *ekstasi* vbl n. f. *existēmi* put (person) out of (his senses) (EX-² *histēmi* place)]

ĕcstă't|ic *a.* & *n.* 1. *a.* of, subject to, producing, ecstasy (esp. of joy); hence ∼ICALLY *adv.* 2. *n.* person subject to (religious) ecstasy. [f. F *extatique* f. Gk *ekstatikos* (as prec.; see -IC)]

ECT *abbr.* electroconvulsive therapy.

ĕ'ctŏ- *comb. form.* outside, as: ∼**blast,** (Biol.) outer membrane of cell; ∼**derm,** (Biol.) outermost layer of embryo in early development; ∼**plasm,** (1) = EXOplasm, (2) supposed viscous substance exuding from body of spiritualistic medium during trance; ∼**zoon,** external parasite. [f. Gk *ekto-* st. of *ektos* outside]

ĕctogĕ'nĕsis *n.* (Biol.) production of structures outside the organism; hence **ĕctogĕnĕ'tic, ĕctogĕ'nic** **ĕctŏ'gĕnous,** *adjs.* [mod. L, f. as prec. + GENESIS]

ĕ'ctomŏrph *n.* lean-bodied person (with predominance of structures formed from ectoderm of embryo); hence ∼IC *a.* [f. ECTO- + Gk *morphē* form]

-ĕ'ctomÿ *suf.* forming *ns.*, denoting surgical operation in which some part is removed, as: **appendice'c tomy,** removal of the appendix; **hystere'ctomy** removal of the womb. [f. Gk *ektomē* excision (*ek* out *temnō* cut)]

ĕctŏ'pic *a.* (Path.) in abnormal place or position. [f *ectopia* (mod. L f. Gk *ektopos* out of place) pathological displacement + -IC]

ECU *abbr.* European Currency Unit.

ĕcūmĕ'nical *a.* of or representing the whole Christian world; seeking world-wide Christian unity; world -wide; hence ∼ISM (3), **ēcūmeni'cITY, ē'cūmenISM** (3), *ns.* [f. LL f. Gk *oikoumenikos* of the inhabited earth (*oikoumenē*) + -AL]

ĕ'czĕma (ĕ'kz-, ĕ'ks-) *n.* inflammation of the skin, with itching and discharge from vesicles; hence **ĕczĕ'ma** tous *a.* [mod. L f. Gk *ekzema -atos* (*ek* out, *zeō* boil)]

-ed¹ *suf.* (1) forming *past* and *p.p.* of weak vbs. (also -*d* -'*d*, -*t* as in cold, subpoena'd, bought*; see notes on Verl forms, p. xvii); (2) forming *adjs.* f. such *p.p.* (also occas f. *v.i.*) meaning: (*a*) that has been subject to vbl action (*b*) (f. *v.i.*) that has performed vbl action (*fallen idol escaped prisoner, am finished with it*), (*c*) that habituall performs vbl action in stated manner (*outspoken, well -behaved*), (*d*) that expresses having been subject to vb action (*pained look*). [OE *-ed, -ad, -od;* -*d* f. Gmc *-dha* f. IE *-tos*]

-ed² *suf.* forming *adjs.* f. *ns.*, meaning 'having, wearing affected with, etc.' (*diseased, moneyed, tuxedoed, talentee wooded*), having the habits of (*bigoted, dogged*); esp used to form *adj.* f. phr. of adj. & *n.* (*quick-witted, good -humoured, stout-hearted, three-cornered*); see notes on Verb forms, p. xvii. [OE *-ede,* = OS *-ōdi* f. Gmc *-ōdhje*

‖ED *abbr.* Efficiency Decoration.

Ed. *abbr.* Edward.

ed. *abbr.* edited (by); edition; editor; educated.

ĕdā'cious (-shus) *a.* (literary or joc.) of eating; greedy so **ĕdā'cITY** *n.* [f. L *edax -acis* (*edere* eat; see -ACIOUS)]

E'dăm (ē'-) *n.* spherical Dutch cheese, usu. yellow with red rind. [~ in Holland, where orig. made]

ĕdă'phĭc *a.* (Bot.) of the soil; (Ecol.) produced or influenced by the soil. [f. G *edaphisch* f. Gk *edaphos* floor; see -IC]

E'dda (ĕ'-) *n.* Elder, Poetic, ~, collection of ancient Icelandic poems; Younger, Prose, ~, miscellaneous handbook (*c.* 1230) to Icelandic poetry. [perh. f. a name in ON poem or f. ON *óthr* poetry]

ĕ'ddy̆ *n.* & *v.* **1.** *n.* small whirlpool; wind, fog, smoke, moving like this; ~ **current,** (Electr.) circulating current induced in conductor by varying magnetic field. **2.** *v.t.* & *i.* whirl round in eddies. [prob. f. OE *ed*-again, back]

e'delweiss (ā'delvīs) *n.* Alpine plant with woolly leaves and white flowers, growing in rocky places. [G (*edel* noble, *weiss* white)]

*ēdē'ma. See OEDEMA.

E'den (ē'-) *n.* abode of Adam and Eve at their creation; delightful abode; state of supreme happiness; hence ~IC (ēdĕ'-) *a.* [ME, f. LL f. Gk *Ēdēn* f. Heb. *ēden,* orig. = delight]

-dĕ'ntāte *a.* & *n.* (animal, esp. mammal of order Edentata) having few or no teeth. [f. L E(*dentatus* f. *dens dentis* tooth; see -ATE²)]

:dge¹ *n.* **1.** sharpened side of blade of cutting instrument or weapon; sharpness of this (*the knife has no edge*), (fig.) effectiveness; **be on** ~, be excited or irritable; **take the** ~ **off,** blunt, weaken, dull, (appetite, argument, etc.); **have the** ~ **on,** (colloq.) have an advantage over; **set** person's **teeth on** ~, cause him revulsion as from eating sour fruit; **rough** or **sharp** ~ **of** one's **tongue,** reviling. **2.** edge--shaped thing, esp. crest of a ridge; meeting-line of two surfaces of a solid; narrow surface of thin object. **3.** boundary line of region or surface; area close to steep drop (of precipice); **on the** ~ **of,** (fig.) almost involved in or affected by. **4.** ~**-tool,** cutting-tool (in fig. sense also *edged tool*). **5.** Hence ~'LESS (-jl-) *a.* [OE *ecg*, = OS *eggia*, OHG *ekka*, ON *egg* f. Gmc **agjō* (**ag*- f. IE **ak*- be sharp)]

:dge² *v.* **1.** *v.t.* sharpen (tool etc., also fig.); ~ **on,** = EGG² *on*; furnish with or *with* border, form border to; insinuate, push, (thing, one*self*) *into, in, out, off,* etc.; (Cricket) strike (ball) with edge of bat. **2.** *v.i.* advance, esp. gradually and obliquely. [ME, f. prec.]

:'dgeways (-jwāz), **ĕ'dgewīse** (-jwīz), *advs.* with edge uppermost or foremost; (fig.) **get a word in** ~ (in talkative person's silent interval); (of two things) edge to edge. [f. EDGE¹ + -WAYS, -WISE]

:'dging *n.* In vbl senses; border, fringe; ~**-shears** (for trimming edges of lawn). [f. EDGE² + -ING¹]

:'dg|y̆ *a.* sharp-edged; having one's nerves on edge, irritable; hence ~ĭLY² *adv.* [f. EDGE¹ + -Y²]

:dh, ĕth, *n.* name of OE & Icel. letter, = th. [Icel. *eth*]

:'dible *a.* & *n.* (thing) fit to be eaten; hence **ĕdIBI'LITY** *n.* [f. LL *edtbĭlis* (*edere* eat; see -IBLE)]

'dict *n.* order proclaimed by authority; so **ĕdĬ'ctAL** *a.* [ME, f. L *edictum* f. E(*dicere dict*- say) proclaim]

:'dĭfice *n.* building (esp. large stately one; also fig.). [ME f. OF f. L *aedificium* (*aedis* dwelling + -*ficium* f. *facere* make)]

:'dĭfy *v.t.* benefit spiritually; improve morally; so **ĕdIFICA'TION** *n.* [ME, f. OF *edifier* f. L *aedificare* (as prec.; see -FY)]

:'dĭt *v.t.* prepare an edition of (another's work); set in order for publication (material chiefly provided by others); take extracts from and collate (films, tape--recordings, etc.) to form a unified sequence; act as editor of (newspaper etc.); reword for a purpose. [f. F *éditer* f. as foll.; partly back form. f. EDITOR]

:di'tion *n.* form in which a literary work is published (*first, paperback, pocket, edition*); one copy in such form (*this is a first edition*); whole number of copies of book, newspaper, etc., issued from same types, or = IMPRESSION; whole number of any product issued at one time; (fig.) product of the same kind, person etc. resembling

another (*a more charming edition of her sister*). [f. F *édition* f. L *editio -onis* f. E(*dere dit*- = *dare* give) put out]

editio princeps (ĭdĭshĭō prī'nsĕps) *n.* (*pl.* **editiones principes** *pr.* -ōnēz -sĭpēz). first printed edition of a book. [L]

ĕ'ditor *n.* one who prepares the work of others for publication, broadcasting, etc.; one who conducts a newspaper or periodical, or a section of one (*financial editor*); head of department of publishing house; one who edits films etc.; hence ~SHIP, **ĕ'dĭtRESS¹,** *ns.* [L (as EDIT; see -OR)]

ĕdĭtō̆'rial *a.* & *n.* **1.** *a.* of an editor; written by or as by the editor, opp. news and advertising matter; hence ~LY² *adv.* **2.** *n.* newspaper article written by or under responsibility of the editor; hence ~IST (3) *n.,* ~IZE *v.i.,* writer of, write, editorials. [f. prec. + -IAL]

-edly (usu. *pr.* -ĭdlĭ) *suf.* forming *advs.* f. *vbs.,* meaning 'in manner characterized by performance of or undergoing of vbl action' (*allegedly, discontentedly, disgustedly, heatedly, hurriedly*). [f. -ED¹ + -LY²]

EDP *abbr.* electronic data processing.

*EDT *abbr.* Eastern Daylight Time.

ĕ'dŭc|āte *v.t.* give intellectual and moral training to; provide schooling for; train (person, one*self,* a physical or mental faculty, *to* do); ~**ated guess** (based on experience); hence ~'ABI'LITY, ~ātOR, *ns.,* ~ABLE, ~ATIVE, *adjs.* [f. L *educare* conn. w. EDUCE + -ATE²]

ĕdŭcā'tion *n.* educating, being educated; systematic (course of) instruction (*classical, commercial,* FURTHER, *education*); development of character or mental powers; COLLEGE *of Education;* hence ~AL *a.,* ~(**al**)IST (3) *ns.* [f. F *éducation* or f. L *educatio* (as prec.; see -ATION)]

ĕdŭ'c|e *v.t.* bring out, develop, from latent or potential existence; elicit, evoke; infer (number, principle, *from* data); hence ~IBLE *a.,* **ĕdŭ'ctION** *n.* [ME, f. L E(*ducere duct*- lead)]

ĕdŭ'lcorāte *v.t.* free from acid properties or from soluble particles, purify; hence ~A'TION *n.* [f. med. L *edulcorare,* f. as E- + LL *dulcor* sweetness (*dulcis* sweet); see -ATE³]

Edw. *abbr.* Edward.

Edwar'dian (ĕ-; -ōr'-, -ār'-) *a.* & *n.* **1.** *a.* of the time of any of the Kings Edward. **2.** (esp.) characteristic of Edward VII's reign (1901–10). **3.** *n.* person belonging to this period. [f. *Edward* + -IAN]

-ee¹ *suf.* forming *ns.* expr. (1) person affected by vbl action, corresp. to agent *ns.* in *-or,* orig. in legal terms after AF (*appellw, appellee*), extended to indirect obj (*lessee, vendee*) and non-tech. wds without corresp. *-or* (*employee, payee*), (2) person concerned with or described as (*absentee, bargee, dilutee, escapee, refugee*), (3) object of smaller size (*bootee, coatee*) [f. or after AF *-ee* f. L *-atus*]

EE *abbr.* Early English.

EEC *abbr.* European Economic Community.

EEG *abbr.* electroencephalogram.

eel *n.* snakelike fish of order Apodes; (fig.) slippery or evasive person or thing; ~**-grass,** marine plant with long narrow leaves; ~**-pout,** burbot or blenny; ~'**worm,** nematode worm infesting plants; hence ~'Y² *a.* [OE *ǣl,* = OS, OHG *āl,* ON *áll* f. Gmc **ǣlaz,* of unkn. orig.]

e'en¹·²·. See EVEN¹·³.

-ee'n *suf.* (Ir.) forming dim. *ns.* (*colleen, dudeen, poteen, spalpeen*). [f. Ir. -*ín* dim. suf.]

e'er. See EVER.

-eer *suf.* forming (1) *ns.* denoting 'person concerned with' (*auctioneer, mountaineer;* often derog., *profiteer, sonneteer*), (2) *vbs.* denoting 'be concerned with' (*electioneer*), so back-form. f. *electioneering* etc. [f. or after F *-ier* f. L *-arius;* cf. -IER, -ARY¹]

eer'|ie *a.* (~ier, ~iest). gloomy; strange, weird; hence ~ĭLY² *adv.,* ~INESS *n.* [Icel. orig. 'timid', f. OE *earg*]

ef- *pref.,* assim. form of EX-¹ 1 before f.

ĕff *v.* (sl.) **1.** *v.t.* & *i.* = FUCK (*eff off*). **2.** *v.i.* say *fuck* or similar taboo word; ~ **and blind,** use strong expletives. [name of letter *F,* as euphem. abbr.]

efface *v.t.* rub out; (fig.) obliterate, wipe out; utterly surpass, eclipse; treat or regard one*self* as unimportant; hence ∿**ABLE** (-sa-) *a.*, ∿**MENT** (-sm-) *n.* [f. F *effacer* (es- EX-¹, *face* FACE¹)]

effect *n.* **1.** result, consequence, (**in** ∿, for practical purposes; **to that** ∿, having that result or implication); efficacy (*of no effect*); combination of colour or form in picture etc. (*a pretty effect*). **2.** (in *pl.*) property (*personal effects*; '**no** ∿**s**', written by banker on dishonoured cheque); lighting, sounds, etc., used to accompany play, film, or broadcast. **3.** impression produced on spectator, hearer, etc., (*did it only* **for** ∿, to impress hearers etc.); (Phys.) phenomenon, usu. named after discoverer (*Doppler effect*). **4.** operativeness (**bring** or **carry into** ∿, accomplish; **give** ∿ **to**, make operative; **take** ∿, become operative; **with** ∿ **from**, coming into operation at (stated time)). **5.** Hence ∿**LESS** *a.* [ME f. OF, or f. L *effectus* f. EF(*ficere* *fect-* = *facere* make)]

effect² *v.t.* bring about, accomplish; cause to exist or occur. [f. prec.]

effective *a.* & *n.* **1.** *a.* having an effect; powerful in effect; striking, remarkable; coming into operation (*effective as from 1 September*); actual, existing; actually usable, equivalent in its effect; hence ∿**LY²** (-vlĭ) *adv.*, ∿**NESS** (-vn-) *n.* **2.** *a.* & *n.* (soldier etc.) fit for work or service. [ME, f. L *effectivus* (as EFFECT¹; see -IVE)]

effector *n.* & *a.* (Biol.) (organ) acting in response to stimulus. [f. EFFECT² + -OR]

effectual *a.* answering its purpose, sufficient to produce an effect; valid; hence ∿**LY²** *adv.*, ∿**NESS** *n.* [ME, f. med. L *effectualis* (as EFFECT¹; see -AL)]

effectuate *v.t.* cause to happen; accomplish; hence ∿**A'TION** *n.* [f. med. L *effectuare* (as EFFECT¹) + -ATE³]

effeminate *a.* womanish, unmanly; hence ∿**ACY** *n.*, ∿**ateLY²** (-tlĭ) *adv.* [ME, f. L *effeminatus* p.p. of EF(*feminare* f. *femina* woman); see -ATE²]

effendi *n.* man of education or standing in E. Mediterranean or Arab country; (Hist.) title of respect or courtesy in Turkey. [f. Turk. *efendi* f. mod. Gk *afentēs* f. Gk *authentēs* lord, master (as AUTHENTIC)]

efferent *a.* (Physiol.) conducting outwards (*efferent nerves, vessels*) (opp. *afferent*). [f. L EF(*ferre* carry); see -ENT]

effervesce *v.i.* give off bubbles of gas, bubble, (lit., or fig. of persons); hence ∿**ENCE**, ∿**ENCY**, *ns.*, ∿**ENT** *a.* [f. L EF(*fervescere* incept. of *fervēre* be hot); see -ESCE]

effete *a.* exhausted, worn out; feeble, incapable; hence ∿**NESS** (-tn-) *n.* [f.L EF*fetus* worn out by bearing young (cf. FOETUS)]

efficacious (-shŭs) *a.* (Of thing) producing, sure to produce, desired effect; hence or cogn. ∿**LY²** *adv.*, ∿**NESS**, **efficACY**, *ns.* [f. L *efficax* (as EFFICIENT; see -ACIOUS)]

efficiency (-shensĭ) *n.* state or quality of being efficient; (Mech. & Phys.) ratio of useful work done to total energy expended or heat taken in; *∿ (**apartment**), one with limited facilities for washing and cooking; ∿ **bar**, restriction of salary until there is proof of efficiency; ∿ **expert**, one who advises on efficiency of an organization or production process. [f. L *efficientia* (as foll.; see -ENCY)]

efficient (-shent) *a.* productive of effect; (of person) competent, capable; ∿ **cause**, that which makes a thing what it is; hence ∿**LY²** *adv.* [ME, f. L EF(*ficere* = *facere* make) accomplish; see -ENT]

effigy *n.* portrait, image; **burn** etc. (person) **in** ∿, burn etc. a figure representing him. [f. L *effigies* (EF*fingere* to fashion)]

effloresce *v.i.* burst out into flower (lit. or fig.); (Chem., of crystalline substance) turn to fine powder on exposure to air, (of salts) come to the surface and there crystallize, (of ground or wall) become covered with salt particles; so ∿**ENCE** *n.*, ∿**ENT** *a.* [f. L EF(*florescere* incept. of *florēre* bloom f. *flos floris* flower); see -ESCE]

effluence (-lōō-) *n.* flowing out (of light, electricity, etc., or fig.); that which flows out. [F, or f. med. L *effluentia* (as foll.; see -ENCE)]

effluent (-lōō-) *a.* & *n.* **1.** *a.* flowing forth or out. **2.** *n.* stream flowing from larger stream, lake, sewage tank, industrial process, etc. [f. L EF(*fluere flux-* flow); see -ENT]

effluvium (-lōō-) *n.* (*pl.* ∿**ia**). exhaled substance (esp. unpleasant) affecting lungs or sense of smell etc. [L, f. as prec.]

efflux *n.* flowing out (of liquid or gas, or fig.); that which flows out; hence **efflu'xion** (-kshon) *n.* [f. med. L *effluxus* f. as EFFLUENT]

effort *n.* strenuous exertion; vigorous attempt (*at, to* do); force exerted; special activity; (colloq.) something accomplished involving concentration or special activity (*that's a pretty good effort*); hence ∿**FUL** *a.* [F, f. OF *esforcier* f. Rom. *EX¹(fortiare* f. L *fortis* strong)]

effortless *a.* (Of skill etc.) without effort, easy; (arch.) making no effort, passive; hence ∿**LY²** *adv.*, ∿**NESS** *n.* [f. prec. + -LESS]

effrontery (-ŭ'-) *n.* shameless insolence. [f. F *effronterie* f. *effronté* f. Rom. *EX(frontatus* f. LL EF(*frons -ntis* forehead) shameless; see -ERY]

effulgent *a.* radiant (lit. or fig.); hence or cogn. ∿**ENCE** *n.*, ∿**entLY²** *adv.* [f. L EF(*fulgēre* shine); see -ENT]

effuse¹ *a.* (Bot., of inflorescence etc.) spreading loosely; (of shell) with lips separated by groove. [f. L *effusus* p.p. of EF(*fundere fus-* pour)]

effuse² (-z) *v.t.* pour forth (liquid, air, light, smell; or fig.). [ME, f. L (as prec.)]

effusion (-zhon) *n.* pouring forth (lit. or fig.; *∿ of* **blood**, bloodshed); unrestrained utterance (often derog. of literary work). [ME f. OF, or f. L *effusio* (as EFFUSE¹; see -ION)]

effusive *a.* (Of speech or emotion) exuberant, demonstrative; (Geol., of igneous rock) poured out when molten and later solidified; hence ∿**LY²** (-vlĭ) *adv.*, ∿**NESS** (-vn-) *n.* [f. as EFFUSE¹; see -IVE]

eft *n.* newt. [OE *efeta*, of unkn. orig.]

EFTA (ĕ'-), **EFTA**, *n.* European Free Trade Association. [abbr.]

eftsoons (-z) *adv.* (arch. or joc.) soon afterwards; occasionally. [OE *eftsōna* (*eft* again, *sōna* SOON) + -s³]

e.g. *abbr.* for example. [L *exempli gratia*]

egad *int.* (arch.) by God. [prob. orig. *a* ah + GOD]

egalitarian *a.* & *n.* of, relating to, (person) holding the principle of equal rights etc. for all persons; hence ∿**ISM** (3) *n.* [f. F *égalitaire* (*égal* EQUAL¹) + -IAN]

Egeria (ĭ-) *n.* patroness and adviser. [L, name of Roman goddess said to have instructed Numa Pompilius]

egg¹ *n.* **1.** spheroidal body produced by female of birds etc., containing germ of a new individual; (esp.) that of domestic fowl, for eating; **bad** ∿, person or scheme that comes to no good; **with** ∿ **on** one's **face**, (colloq.) made to look foolish; **have all** one's ∿**s in one basket**, risk all on a single venture; **teach** one's **grandmother to suck** ∿**s**, presume to advise those who are more experienced; **as sure as** ∿ **is** or **are** ∿**s**, undoubtedly. **2.** (Zool.) ovum; (pop.) pupa or ant etc.; (sl.) person or thing (*good, tough*, etc., *egg*) (sl.) bomb, mine. **3.** ∿ **and anchor, dart, tongue**, (Archit.) kinds of moulding with egg-shaped and triangular figures; ∿**-and-spoon race** (in which runners carry egg in spoon); ∿**-beater**, device for beating eggs, *(sl.) helicopter*; **egg**-COSY; ∿**-cup** (for holding egg boiled in shell); ∿ **custard**, = CUSTARD 1; ∿**-flip**, hot or cold beer, cider, wine, etc., with eggs and usu. milk stirred in; ∿**'head**, (colloq.) intellectual person; ∿**-nog**, = *egg-flip*; ∿**-plant**, (fruit of) purple- or white-fruited *Solanum melongena*, aubergine; ∿**-plum**, small egg-shaped yellow plum; **egg** SAUCE; ∿**'shell**, shell of egg, fragile thing (∿*shell china*, very thin kind), (of paint etc.) slightly glossy; ∿**-slice**, utensil for taking omelette from pan; ∿**-spoon**, small spoon for eating boiled egg; ∿-**timer,** device for timing cooking of egg; ∿-**tooth,** protuberance on bill-sheath of embryo bird or reptile for cracking shell; ∿-**whisk,** utensil for beating eggs; ∿-**white,** WHITE² of egg. **4.** Hence ∿'LESS, ∿'Y², adjs. [ME, f. ON; OS, OHG ei, Goth. *addi- f. Gmc *ajjaz]

ĕgg² v.t. urge (person) on (to an act, to do). [ME, f. ON eggja = EDGE²]

ĕ'gger, ĕ'ggar, n. kind of large moth with egg-shaped cocoon. [prob. f. EGG¹+-ER¹]

ĕ'glantīne n. sweet-BRIER¹. [ME, f. F églantine f. OF aiglent f. Rom. *aculentus f. L acus needle; see -LENT]

ĕ'gō n. (pl. ∿s). (Metaphys.) conscious thinking subject; (Psych.) part of the mind that reacts to reality and has sense of individuality; self-esteem; ∿-**ideal,** (Psych.) part of mind developed from ego by awareness of social standards, (pop.) idealization of oneself; ∿-**trip,** (colloq.) activity etc. devoted entirely to one's own interests or feelings. [L, = I]

ĕgocĕ'ntric a. centred in the ego; self-centred, egoistic; hence **ĕgocĕntrī'cITY** n. [f. EGO+CENTRIC, after geocentric etc.]

ĕ'gōism n. ethical theory that treats self-interest as foundation of morality; systematic selfishness; self--opinionatedness; = EGOTISM; hence ∿IST (2) n., ∿i'stIC(AL) adjs. [f. F égoïsme f. mod. L egoismus (as EGO; see -ISM)]

ĕgōmā'ni|a n. morbid egotism; hence ∿AC n. [f. EGO+-MANIA]

ĕ'got|ism n. too frequent use of 'I' and 'me'; practice of talking about oneself; self-conceit; selfishness; hence ∿IST (2) n., ∿i'stIC(AL) adjs., ∿IZE (2) v.i. [f. EGO+-ISM, w. intrusive -t-]

ĕgrē'gious (-jŭs) a. shocking (egregious folly, blunder, ass); (arch.) remarkable; hence ∿LY² adv., ∿NESS n. [f. L E(gregius f. grex gregis flock) illustrious, lit. 'standing out from the flock']

ĕ'grĕss n. (right of) going out; (Astron.) end of eclipse or transit; way out (lit. or fig.). [f. L egressus f. L E(gredi gress- = gradi step)]

ĕgrē'ssion (-shŏn) n. going out or forth. [f. egress v. (f. prec.)+ION]

ĕ'grĕt n. lesser white heron. [ME; var. of AIGRETTE]

Egy'ptian (ijĭ'pshan) a. & n. (native or inhabitant) of Egypt; Hamitic language used in Egypt until 3rd c.; ∿ lily, calla lily; hence ∿IZE (3) v.t. [ME, f. Egypt+-IAN]

Egyptŏ'|logy (ē-) n. study of Egyptian antiquities; so ∿LOGIST n. [f. Egypt+-O-+-LOGY]

eh (ā) int. (colloq.) expr. inquiry or surprise, or inviting assent, or asking for something to be repeated or explained. [ME ey, instinctive excl.]

-eian suf. — -ey or -y | -AN (Bodleian, Rugbeian).

ei'der (ī'-) n. ∿ (**duck**), large northern duck, esp. of genus Somateria, yielding ∿(-**down**), small soft feathers from its breast; ∿-**down,** quilt stuffed with eider-down or other soft material. [f. Icel. aethr]

oidŏ'tic (ī-) a. & n **1.** a. (Psych., of mental image) having unusual vividness and detail, as if actually visible. **2.** n. person able to have eidetic images. [f. G eidetisch f. Gk eidētikos (eidos form; see -ETIC)]

eidŏ'l|on (ī-) n. (pl. ∿ons or ∿a). spectre, phantom; idealized figure. [f. Gk eidōlon (see IDOL)]

ei'gen- (ī'g-) comb. form. (Math. & Phys.) proper, characteristic; ∿**frequency,** one of the frequencies causing resonance of a system; ∿**value,** value of a parameter for which a differential equation has a non-zero solution satisfying given conditions. [f. G eigen OWN¹]

eight (āt) a. & n. one more than seven; symbol for this (8, viii, VIII); (**figure of**) ∿, 8-shaped figure; card with eight pips; time of eight o'clock; size etc. denoted by eight; set of eight, esp. crew of eight in rowing-boat (∿**s,** boat-races at Oxford etc. between such crews); eight-oared boat; **have one over the** ∿, (sl.) get slightly drunk; *****behind the** ∿ **ball,** baffled, at a disadvantage [f. high-valued ball in game of pool]; hence ∿'FOLD a. & adv., **eigh**TH² (ātth) a. &

(*****∿**h-note,** (Mus.) quaver), ∿**h**LY² (ā'tth-) adv. [OE e(a)hta, = OS, OHG ahto, ON átta, Goth. ahtau f. Gmc *ahtō f. IE *oktō]

eighteen (ātē'n, ā'tēn) a. & n. one more than seventeen; symbol for this (18, xviii, XVIII); set of eighteen, esp. persons forming side at Australian Rules football; ∿**mo,** OCTODECIMO; hence ∿TH² a. & n. [OE e(a)htatēne, = OS ahtotian, OHG ahtozehan, ON áttján (as prec., -TEEN)]

ei'ghtsome (ā't-) n. & a. ∿ (**reel**), lively Scottish reel for eight dancers. [f. EIGHT+-SOME²]

8vo abbr. octavo.

ei'ghty (ā'tĭ) a. & n. **1.** eight times ten; symbol for this (80, lxxx, LXXX); (in pl.) numbers etc., esp. years of a century or a life, from 80 to 89; hence ∿FOLD a. & adv., **eighti**ETH¹ (āt-) a. & n. **2.** ∿-**one** etc., (arch.) **one-and-**∿ etc., eighty plus one etc., w. corresp. ordinals ∿-**first** etc. [OE -eahtatig (as EIGHT, -TY²)]

ei'nkŏrn (ī'n-k-) n. species of wheat (Triticum monococcum). [G (ein one, korn seed)]

einstei'nium (īnstī'-) n. (Chem.) artificially made transuranic radioactive metallic element. [mod. L, f. A. Einstein, Ger.-Amer. physicist d. 1955+-IUM]

eire'nic. Var. of IRENIC.

eire'nicŏn (īr-) n. proposal tending to make peace. [Gk, neut. of eirēnikos adj. (eirēnē peace; see -IC)]

eisteddfod (īstĕ'dhvod) n. (pl. ∿s, or ∿au pr. -ī). congress of Welsh bards; national or local gathering for musical competitions etc.; hence ∿IC (-ŏ'd-) a. [W, lit. — session (eisteddfod sit)]

ei'ther (ī'dh-, ē'dh-) a., pron., & adv. or conj. **1.** a. & pron. each of two (at either end was a lamp; either view is tenable; either is tenable); one or other of two (put the lamp at either end; there is no lamp at either end; either of you can go); either WAY 12. **2.** adv. or conj. on one or other supposition, which way you will, (he is either drunk or mad; either come in or go out); (w. neg. or interrog.) any more than the other (if you do not go, I shall not either); moreover (there is no time to lose, either); ∿-**or,** (involving) unavoidable choice between alternatives. [OE ægther, æg(e)hwæther, = OHG eogihwedar f. Gmc *aiwo gihwatharo every each of two; cf. AYE², EACH, WHETHER)]

ejā'cŭl|āte¹ v.t. utter suddenly (words esp. of prayer or other emotion, or abs.); eject (fluid etc., esp. semen) from the body; hence ∿A'TION n., ∿āTORY a. [f. L E(jaculari f. jaculum javelin) to dart+-ATE³]

ejā'cŭlate² n. ejaculated semen. [f. prec.]

ejĕ'ct v.t. expel (from place, office, property; spent cartridge from gun, pilot from aircraft or spacecraft esp. in emergency); dispossess (tenant) by legal process; dart forth, emit; hence or cogn. ∿ION, ∿MENT, ∿OR, ns., ∿IVE a; ∿ion or ∿or seat (for ejection of pilot). [f. L E(jicere ject- = jacĕre throw)]

ēke¹ v.t. ∿ **out,** supplement, make best use of, (defective means etc. with, by), contrive to make (livelihood) or support (existence). [OE *ēacan, = OS ōkian, ON auka, Goth. aukan, cogn. w. L augēre increase]

ēke² adv. (arch.) also. [OE ē(a)c, = OS ōk, OHG ouh, ON, Goth. auk, perh. f. IE *au again, or as prec.]

ēkĭ'st|ics n. study of human settlements and their development; hence ∿IC a., ∿I'CIAN n. [f. mod. Gr. oikistikē f. Gk oikistikos (oikizō settle a colony f. oikos house); see -ICS]

ĕ'kka n. (Ind.) small one-horse vehicle. [f. Hindi ekkā unit]

*****ĕl** n. (colloq.) elevated railway. [abbr.]

-el. See -LE 1, 2.

ĕlă'borate¹ a. carefully or minutely worked out; highly developed or complicated; hence ∿LY² (-tlĭ) adv., ∿NESS (-tn-) n. [f. L elaboratus p.p. of E(laborare f. labor work); see -ATE²]

ĕlă'bor|āte² v. **1.** v.t. produce by labour; work out (invention, theory, etc.) in detail; (of natural agency) produce (substance etc.) from its elements or sources. **2.** v.i. explain something in detail (I need not elaborate in

3. Hence or cogn. ∼A'TION *n.*, ∼ATIVE *a.* [f. as prec. +-ATE³]

élan (ā'lahń) *n.* vivacity; impetuous rush; ∼ **vital** (-vētah'l), life-force in Bergson's philosophy, mysterious vital principle. [F (*élancer* launch)]

ē'land *n.* large Afr. antelope of genus *Taurotragus.* [Du., = elk]

ĕlä'pse *v.i.* (Of time) pass away. [f. L E (*labi laps-* glide)]

ĕlä'smobränch (-z-; -ngk) *n.* fish of class Chondrichthyes (shark, skate, etc.). [f. mod. L *elasmobranchii* f. Gk *elasmos* beaten metal + *bragkhia* gills]

ĕlä'smosaur'us (-zm-) *n.* large extinct marine reptile. [mod. L, f. as prec. + Gk *sauros* lizard]

ĕla'st|ic (-ä'-, -ah'-) *a.* & *n.* **1.** *a.* spontaneously resuming its normal bulk or shape after contraction, dilatation, or distortion, (*elastic* STOCKING; ∼ic **band,** = RUBBER² *band*); springy; (of feelings or person) buoyant; flexible, adaptable (*elastic conscience*); (Econ., of demand) variable according to price; (Phys., of collision) involving no decrease of kinetic energy; hence ∼ICALLY *adv.*, **ĕlästĭ'cITY** *n.*, ∼ĭcIZE (3) *v.t.* **2.** *n.* elastic cord or fabric, usu. woven with strips of rubber. [f. mod. L *elasticus*, f. Gk *elastikos* propulsive (*elaunō* drive)]

ĕla'sticātĕd (īlä'-, īlah'-) *a.* (Of fabric) made elastic by weaving with rubber thread. [f. prec. +-ATE³ +-ED¹]

ĕlä'sto|mēr *n.* natural or synthetic rubber or rubber-like plastic; hence ∼mĕ'rIC *a.* [f. ELASTIC, after *isomer*]

ĕlä'te *v.t.*, & *a.* **1.** *v.t.* inspirit, stimulate, (esp. in *p.p.*); make proud. **2.** *a.* (arch.) in high spirits, exultant, proud. **3.** So **ĕlā'tION** *n.* [ME, f. L E*ferre* E*lat-* raise]

ē'later *n.* click beetle. [mod. L, f. Gk *elatēr* driver (*elaunō* drive)]

E-layer (ē'lāer) *n.* = HEAVISIDE *layer.* [f. E (arbitrary) +LAYER]

ĕ'lbow¹ (-ō) *n.* **1.** joint between forearm and upper arm, corresponding part in animal; elbow-shaped bend or corner, short piece of piping bent through right angle; part of garment covering elbow. **2. at** one's ∼, close at hand; **bend** or **lift** one's ∼, drink too much liquor; **out at** ∼**s,** (of coat) worn-out, (of person) ragged, poor; RUB¹ *elbows with*; **up to the** ∼**s,** busily engaged *in.* **3.** *∼**-chair,** armchair; ∼**-grease,** (joc.) vigorous polishing, hard work; ∼**-room,** plenty of room to move or work in. [OE *el(n)boga,* = OHG *elinbogo,* ON *öllnbogi* f. Gmc *alinobogon (as ELL, BOW¹)]

ĕ'lbow² (-ō) *v.t.* & *i.* thrust, jostle, (as) with elbows (person *aside,* one*self into, in,* one's *way,* etc.). [f. prec.]

ĕld *n.* (arch. or poet.) old age; olden time. [OE · (*i*)*eldu,* = OS *eldi,* OHG *elti,* ON *elli* f. Gmc **aldh-*; cf. OLD]

ĕ'lder¹ *a.* (attrib.) & *n.* **1.** (the) earlier-born (of two related or indicated persons; *his elder brother*; *which is the elder?; he is my elder by ten years*); ||∼ **brother** (pl. ∼ **brethren**), one of thirteen senior members of Trinity House; ∼ **hand,** (Cards) first player; elder STATES-MAN. **2.** *n.* (in *pl.*) persons of greater age (*respect your elders*) or venerable because of age. **3.** person advanced in life; (Hist.) member of a senate or governing body; official in early-Christian, Presbyterian, or Mormon Church, whence ∼SHIP *n.* [OE *eldra,* = OS *aldira,* OHG *altiro, eltiro,* ON *ellri,* Goth. *althiza* (as OLD, -ER³)]

ĕ'lder² *n.* low white-flowered dark-fruited tree, or shrub or herb, of genus *Sambucus*; ∼(-berry) **wine** (made from fruit of the tree). [OE *ellærn,* = MLG *ellern, elderne,* etc., prob. orig. adj.]

ĕ'lderl|ў *a.* somewhat old; (of person) past middle age; hence ∼iNESS *n.* [f. ELDER¹ +-LY¹]

ĕ'ldĕst *a.* first-born or eldest surviving (member of family, son, daughter, etc.); ∼ **hand,** (Cards) first player. [OE = OHG *altist,* ON *ellztr,* Goth. *altista* (as ELDER¹, -EST¹)]

ĕldora'dō (-ah'-) *n.* (pl. ∼s) fictitious country or city abounding in gold; place of great abundance. [f. Sp. *el dorado* the gilded]

ĕ'ldrĭtch *a.* (Sc.) weird; hideous. [16th c., perh. f. OE *elfrīce fairy realm]

Eleä'tic (ĕl-) *a.* & *n.* **1.** *a.* relating to Elea, an ancient Greek city in SW Italy, or the school of philosophers who were born or lived there about the 6th c. BC, esp. Xenophanes, Parmenides, and Zeno. **2.** *n.* an Eleatic philosopher. [f. L *Eleaticus* (*Elea*; see -ATIC)]

ĕlĕcămpā'ne *n.* perennial plant (*Inula helenium*), with bitter aromatic leaves and root; sweetmeat flavoured with this. [corrupt. of med. L *enula* (for L *inula* f. Gk *helenion*) *campana* (prob. = of the fields)]

ĕlĕ'ct¹ *a.* chosen; select, choice; (Theol.) chosen by God; (after *n.*) chosen to office etc. (*president elect*). [ME, f. L *electus* p.p. of E (*ligere lect-* = *legere* pick)]

ĕlĕ'ct² *v.t.* choose (thing, *to* do); choose (person) by vote, (elect a chairman, *elect him to the chair, elect him* (*to be*) *chairman*); (Theol., of God) choose (persons) in preference to others for salvation. [f. as prec.]

ĕlĕ'ction *n.* electing or being elected; **general** ∼ (of representatives, esp. members of House of Commons, throughout the country etc.); **by-**∼ (of MP etc. to fill casual vacancy). [ME f. OF, f. L *electio -onis* (as prec.); see -ION)]

ĕlĕctioneer' *v.i.*, & *n.* **1.** *v.i.* busy oneself in political elections. **2.** *n.* one who electioneers. [f. prec. +-EER]

ĕlĕ'ctive *a.* & *n.* **1.** *a.* (Of official, office, authority) appointed by, filled up by, derived from, election; having power to elect; (of course of study) chosen by student, optional; having tendency to act on or be concerned with some things rather than others (*elective affinity*); (of surgical operation etc.) optional, not urgently necessary; hence ∼LY² (-vlĭ) *adv.* **2.** *n.* *elective course of study. [f. F *électif -ive* f. LL *electivus* (as ELECT¹; see -IVE)]

ĕlĕ'ctor *n.* one who has right of voting to elect MP etc.; (Hist.; *E*∼) German prince entitled to share in election of Emperor; *member of electoral college; hence ∼SHIP *n.* [ME, f. F *électeur* f. L *elector* (as ELECT¹; see -OR)]

ĕlĕ'ctoral *a.* relating to or ranking as electors; *∼ **college,** body of persons representing states of US who cast votes for election of President. [f. prec. +-AL]

ĕlĕ'ctorate *n.* body of electors; (Hist.) dignity or dominions of German Elector. [f. ELECTOR +-ATE¹]

Elĕ'ctra (ĭ-) *n.* ∼ **complex,** (Psych.) daughter's feelings of attraction to father and hostility to mother; cf. OEDIPUS. [f. ∼ in Gk tragedy, who caused her mother to be killed for having murdered ∼'s father]

Elĕ'ctrĕss (ĭ-) *n.* (Hist.) wife of German Elector. [f. ELECTOR +-ESS¹]

ĕlĕ'ctrĕt *n.* permanently polarized piece of dielectric material, analogous to permanent magnet. [f. ELEC-TRICITY +MAGNET]

ĕlĕ'ctric *a.* & *n.* **1.** *a.* of, charged with, capable of generating, operated or produced by, electricity; suddenly exciting, as if caused by electricity (*had an electric effect*). **2.** *electric* BLANKET¹; ∼ **blue,** steely or brilliant light blue; ∼ **chair** (used in electrocution of criminals); *∼ **cord,** = FLEX²; ∼ **eel,** eel-like fish able to give electric shock; ∼ **eye,** photoelectric cell operating relay when beam of light is obstructed; ∼ **fence** (charged with electricity; often of one strand); *electric* FIELD 6; ∼ **fire,** electrically operated incandescent (esp. domestic) heater; *electric* GUITAR; ∼ **organ,** (1) organ giving electric shock in some fishes, (2) (Mus.) electrically-operated organ; ∼ **ray,** RAY³ that can give electric shock; ∼ **shock,** effect of sudden discharge of electricity on person or animal, usu. with stimulation of nerves and contraction of muscles; ∼ **storm,** violent disturbance of electrical condition of atmosphere; *electric* TORCH. **3.** Hence **ĕlĕ'ctricALLY** *adv.*, **electrĭ'cIAN** (īlĕ-, ĕlĭ-) *n.* **4.** *n.* electric circuit, light, motor car, etc.; (in *pl.*) electrical equipment. [f. mod. L *electricus* f. L f. Gk *ēlektron* amber, rubbing of which causes electrostatic phenomena; see -IC]

ĕlĕc′trical *a.* relating to, connected with, of the nature of, electricity; *electrical* ENGINEER[1] 4; suddenly exciting, as if produced by electricity (*the effect was electrical*). [f. prec. + -AL]

ĕlĕctrĭ′cĭtў (ĭ-, ĕ-) *n.* 1. form of energy occurring as two types (see NEGATIVE[1] 4, POSITIVE 9) in elementary particles (cf. ELECTRON, PROTON) and hence in macroscopic bodies, either statically (see CHARGE[1]) or dynamically (see CURRENT[2]). 2. branch of science concerned with this. 3. supply of electric current for lighting, heating, etc. [f. ELECTRIC + -ITY]

ĕlĕ′ctri∥fў *v.t.* charge (body) with electricity; convert (railway, factory, farm, etc.) to electric working; (fig.) startle, excite, as if by electric shock; hence ∼FICA′TION *n.* [f. ELECTRIC + -FY]

ĕlĕ′ctrō *n.* (*pl.* ∼s), & *v.t.* (colloq.) = ELECTRO-PLATE, ELECTROTYPE. [abbr.]

ĕlĕctrō- *comb. form.* of, pertaining to, caused by, electricity, as: ∼bio′logy, science of the electrical phenomena of living beings; ∼che′mical, ∼che′mistry, (study) of electricity as applied to chemistry; ∼dyna′mic, ∼dyna′mics, (study) of electricity in motion; ∼mecha′nical, pertaining to application of electricity to mechanical process, device, etc.; ∼ne′gative, ∼po′sitive, of negative, positive, electricity, (of element) tending to acquire, lose, electrons; ∼the′rapy, treatment of diseases by use of electricity, whence ∼the′rapist; ∼ther′mal, relating to heat electrically derived. [f Gk ēlektron amber (see ELECTRIC) + -O-]

ĕlĕctrōcăr′dĭŏ∥grăm *n.* record of electric currents generated by person's heartbeats; so ∼GRAPH (2), **ĕlĕctrōcărdĭŏ′**GRAPHY, *ns.* [f. G elektrocardiogramm (as ELECTRO-, CARDIO-, -GRAM)]

ĕlĕctrōconvŭ′lsĭve *a.* (Esp. of therapy) making use of convulsive response to application of electric shocks. [f. ELECTRO- + CONVULSIVE]

ĕlĕ′ctrocūte *v.t.* kill by electricity (as capital punishment); cause death of (person etc.) by electric shock; hence **ĕlĕctrocū′**TION *n.* [f. ELECTRO-, after *execute*]

ĕlĕ′ctrōde *n.* conductor through which electricity enters or leaves an electrolyte, gas, vacuum, or other medium. [f. ELECTRO + Gk *hodos* way]

ĕlĕctrōĕncĕ′phalo∥grăm *n.* record of electrical activity of brain; so ∼GRAPH (2), **ĕlĕctrōĕncĕphalŏ′**GRAPHY, *ns.* [f. G elektrenkephalogramm (as ELECTRO-, ENCEPHALO-, -GRAM)]

ĕlĕctrolier′ *n.* cluster of electric lamps. [f. ELECTRO-, after *chandelier*]

ĕlĕ′ctrolyse (-z), *-yze, v.t.* subject to or treat by electrolysis. [f. foll. after *analyse* etc.]

ĕlĕctrŏ′lys∥ĭs (ĭ-, ĕ-) *n.* (*pl.* ∼es pr. -ēz). chemical decomposition by electric action; (Surg.) breaking up of tumours, hair-roots, etc., by electric action; hence **ĕlĕctrolý′**TIC *a.* [f. ELECTRO- + -LYSIS]

ĕlĕ′ctrolyte *n.* (substance that can dissolve to give a) solution able to conduct electric current, esp in electric cell or battery. [f. ELECTRO- + Gk *lutos* released (*luō* loosen)]

ĕlĕctrōmă′gnĕt *n.* magnet consisting of material surrounded by coil etc. carrying electric current. [f. ELECTRO- + MAGNET]

ĕlĕctrōmăgnĕ′tic *a.* having both electrical and magnetic character; ∼ radiation etc., kind of radiation including visible light, radio waves, gamma rays, etc., in which electric and magnetic fields vary simultaneously; ∼ units (based primarily on magnetic properties of electric currents). [f. prec. + -IC]

ĕlĕctrōmă′gnĕtĭsm *n.* (study of) magnetic forces produced by electricity. [f. as prec. + -ISM]

ĕlĕctrŏ′mĕter (ĭ-, ĕ-) *n.* instrument for measuring electrical potential by means of forces between charges; hence **ĕlĕctromĕ′**TRIC *a.* [f. ELECTRO- + -METER]

ĕlĕctromō′tĭve *a.* producing or tending to produce electric current; ∼ force (set up by difference of potential in electric circuit). [f. ELECTRO- + MOTIVE[1]]

ĕlĕ′ctrŏn *n.* 1. stable elementary particle with indivisible charge of negative electricity, found in all atoms and acting as carrier of electricity in solids. 2. (**positive**) ∼, positron. 3. ∼ **beam,** stream of electrons; ∼ **gun,** device for producing narrow stream of electrons from heated cathode; ∼ **lens,** device for focusing stream of electrons by electric and magnetic fields; ∼ **microscope,** microscope with high magnification and resolution using electron lenses; *electron* OPTICS; ∼ **pair,** electron and positron; ∼**-volt,** unit of energy, amount gained by electron when accelerated through potential difference of one volt. [f. ELECTRIC + -ON]

ĕlĕctrŏ′n∥ĭc (ĭ-, ĕ-) *a.* pertaining to electrons or to electronics; (of music) produced electronically or electrically without pipes, strings, etc., (of musical instrument) operating thus; ∼**ic brain** (colloq.), ∼**ic computer,** computer operated by electronic means; ∼**ic flash** (from gas-discharge tube, used in high-speed photography); hence ∼ICALLY *adv.* [f. prec. + -IC]

ĕlĕctrŏ′nĭcs (ĭ-, ĕ-) *n. pl.* (treated as *sing.*) branch of physics and technology concerned with phenomena associated with movement of electrons in vacuum, gas, semiconductor, etc.; circuits etc. used in this. [f. prec.; see -ICS]

ĕlĕctrophŏ′nĭc *a.* (Of music etc.) = ELECTRONIC. [f. ELECTRO- + -PHONE + IC]

ĕlĕctrŏphor∥ē′sĭs *n.* (*pl.* ∼eses pr. -ē′sēz). (Phys.) movement of colloidal particles in a fluid under the influence of an electric field; hence ∼E′TIC *a.* [f. ELECTRO- + Gk *phorēsis* being carried]

ĕlĕctrŏ′phorus (ĭ-, ĕ-) *n.* device for repeatedly generating static electricity by induction. [mod. L, f. ELECTRO- + Gk *-phoros* bearing]

ĕlĕ′ctrōplāte *v.t.*, & *n.* 1. *v.t.* coat (utensil etc.) with chromium, silver, etc., by electrolysis. 2. *n.* objects thus produced. [f. ELECTRO- + PLATE[2]]

∥**ĕlĕ′ctroplĕxў** *n.* electroconvulsive therapy. [f. ELECTRO- + APOPLEXY]

ĕlĕ′ctroscōpe *n.* instrument for detecting and measuring electricity, esp. as indication of ionization of air by radioactivity. [f. ELECTRO- + -SCOPE]

ĕlĕctrō-shŏ′ck *n.* electric shock; ∼ **treatment,** medical treatment by means of electric shocks. [f. ELECTRO- + SHOCK[1]]

ĕlĕctrōstă′t∥ĭc *a.* of electrical charges at rest; ∼**ic unit** (based primarily on forces between electric charges); hence ∼ICS *n.*, study of electricity at rest. [f. ELECTRO- + STATIC, after *hydrostatic*]

ĕlĕctrōtĕchn∥ŏ′logў (-tĕk-) *n.* science of the application of electricity in technology; so ∼IC(AL) *adjs.*, ∼ICS *n.*, (-tĕk′-). [f. ELECTRO- + TECHNOLOGY]

ĕlĕ′ctrotype *n.*, & *v.t.* copy (formed) by electrolytic deposition of copper on mould, esp. for printing. [f. ELECTRO- + TYPE[1]]

ĕlĕctrōvā′l∥ent *a.* (Chem.) linking ions by a bond resulting from electrostatic attraction; so ∼ENCE, ∼ENCY, *ns.* [f. ELECTRO- + -valent after *trivalent* etc.]

ĕlĕ′ctrum *n.* alloy of silver and gold used by the ancients; (Min.) native argentiferous gold ore. [ME f. L, f. Gk *ēlektron* amber, electrum]

ĕlĕ′ctuarў *n.* medicinal powder etc. mixed with honey or other sweet substance. [ME, f. LL *electuarium*, prob. f. Gk *ekleikton* (*ekleikhō* lick up)]

ĕlĕēmŏ′sўnarў (-s-, -z-) *a.* of or dependent on alms; charitable; gratuitous. [f. med. L *eleemosynarius* f. LL *eleemosyna* (see ALMS, -ARY[1])]

ĕ′lĕg∥ant *a.* (Of movements, style, author, manners) graceful; tasteful; refined; (of mode of life etc.) of refined luxury; ingeniously simple and effective; *excellent; hence or cogn. ∼ANCE *n.*, ∼antLY[2] *adv.* [f. F *élégant* or L *elegant-* f. *elegare* rel. to *eligere* (cf. ELECT[1])]

ĕlĕ′gĭ′ac *a.* & *n.* 1. *a.* (Of metre) used for elegies, esp. ∼ **couplet,** (usu. *pl.*) dactylic hexameter and pentameter; ∼ **stanza,** four iambic pentameters rhyming *abab*; mournful. 2. *n.* (in *pl.*) elegiac verses. [f. F *élégiaque* or f. LL f. Gk *elegeiakos* (as ELEGY; see -AC)]

ĕ'lĕgīze, -īse (-īz), *v.* **1.** *v.i.* write an elegy (*upon*); write in mournful strain. **2.** *v.t.* write an elegy upon. **3.** So **ĕ'lĕgIST** (1) *n.* [f. foll. +-IZE]

ĕ'lĕgy̆ *n.* song of lamentation, esp. for the dead (sometimes vaguely used of other poems); poem in elegiac metre. [f. F *élégie* or f. L f. Gk *elegeia* (*elegos* mournful poem; see -Y[1])]

ĕ'lĕment *n.* **1.** component part (**reduced to its** ∼**s,** analysed; *the elements of national wealth*; *there was an element of cant, cant was a notable element, in his style*). **2.** (Chem.) any of the (about 100) substances that cannot be resolved by chemical means into simpler substances. **3.** any of **the four** ∼**s** (earth, water, air, fire) in ancient and medieval philosophy; one of these as a being's natural abode or sphere, (usu. fig.: **in** one's ∼, in one's accustomed or preferred surroundings).**4.** (in *pl.*) atmospheric agencies, esp. wind and storm. **5.** (Electr.) resistance wire in an electric heater, cooker, etc.; electrode. **6.** (in *pl.*) rudiments of learning (i.e. the ABC) or of an art or science; **Euclid's E**∼**s** (of Geometry). **7.** (in *pl.*) bread and wine used in Eucharist. **8.** (Math. and Logic). entity that is a member of a set. [ME f. OF, f. L *elementum*]

ĕlĕmĕ'ntal *a.* & *n.* **1.** *a.* of the four elements; of the powers of nature (*elemental worship*), whence ∼ISM (3) *n.*; comparable to these (*elemental grandeur, tumult*); uncompounded (*elemental oxygen*); essential. **2.** *n.* entity or force thought to be physically manifested by occult means. [f. med. L *elementalis* (as prec.; see -AL)]

ĕlĕmĕ'ntar|**y̆** *a.* rudimentary, introductory, simple; (Chem.) not decomposable; ∼**y particle,** (Phys.) one of several subatomic particles not known to be composed of simpler particles; ∼**y school** (in which elementary subjects are taught to young children); hence ∼**ĭLy̆**[2] *adv.*, ∼**ĭNESS** *n.* [ME, f. L *elementarius* (as ELEMENT; see -ARY[1])]

ĕ'lĕmī *n.* fragrant resin of tropical tree, used in ointments, varnish, etc. [prob. f. Arab. *al-lami*]

ĕlĕ'nch|**us** (-ngk-) *n.* (*pl.* ∼**i** *pr.* -ī). logical refutation; **Socratic** ∼**us,** mode of eliciting truth by short question and answer; so **ĕlĕ'nctIC** *a.* [L, f. Gk *elegkhos*]

ĕ'lĕphant *n.* **1.** largest living land animal, of which two species survive, with trunk and long curved ivory tusks; **pink** ∼**s,** hallucinations due to excessive indulgence in alcohol etc.; **white** ∼, (fig.) burdensome or unwanted possession [from cost of maintenance]. **2.** ∼ **bird,** aepyornis; ∼ **seal,** = SEA *elephant*; ∼**'s-ear,** begonia or taro. **3.** size of paper, 711 × 584 mm. **4.** Hence **ĕlĕphă'ntOID** *a.* [ME, orig. *olifaunt* etc. f. OF *oli-, elefant,* f. Rom. **olifantus* f. elephantus, elephans f. Gk *elephas -antos* ivory, elephant]

ĕlĕphantī'asis *n.* skin disease due to nematode parasite, causing gross enlargement of limb etc.; (fig.) undue expansion or enlargement. [L f. Gk (as prec.; see -ASIS)]

ĕlĕphă'ntīne *a.* of elephants; huge; clumsy, unwieldy, (*elephantine movements, humour*). [f. L f. Gk *elephantinos* (as ELEPHANT; see -INE[2])]

Eleusī'nian (ē-) *a.* of Eleusis in Attica; ∼ **mysteries,** (Gk Ant.) annual celebrations there in honour of Demeter. [f. L f. Gk *Eleusinios* + -AN]

ĕ'lĕvāt|**e** *v.t.* **1.** bring to higher position; (Eccl.) hold up (the Host) for adoration; raise (one's eyes, voice, hopes); raise axis of (gun); raise (railway etc.) above ground level. **2.** exalt in rank etc.; (esp. in *p.p.*) raise morally or intellectually (aims, style); (in *p.p.*, colloq.) slightly drunk. **3.** Hence ∼**ORY** *a.* [f. L E(*levare* lift f. *levis* light) + -ATE[3]]

ĕlĕvā'tion *n.* elevating or being elevated; angle (esp. of gun or direction of heavenly body) with the horizontal; height above given (esp. sea) level; high place; drawing or diagram made by projection on vertical plane (cf. PLAN), flat drawing of front, side, or back, of house etc., whence ∼AL *a.*; grandeur, dignity; (Ballet) leap from ground, action of tightening muscles and uplifting the body. [ME f. OF, or f. L *elevatio* (as prec.; see -ATION)]

ĕ'lĕvātor *n.* person, thing that elevates; muscle that raises limb etc.; machine for hoisting, place for storing grain etc.; * = LIFT 4; (Aeron.) movable part of tailplane, used to change aircraft's attitude. [mod. L (as prec.; see -OR)]

ĕlĕ'ven *a.* & *n.* one more than ten; symbol for this (11, xi, XI); time of eleven o'clock; size etc. denoted by eleven; set of eleven, esp. eleven persons forming side at cricket, football, etc.; **the E**∼ (Apostles, without Judas); ||∼**s**(**es**) *n.*, light refreshment about 11 a.m.; ||∼**-plus,** examination taken at age 11-12 before entering secondary school; hence ∼TH[2] *a.* & *n.* (**the** ∼**th hour,** latest possible time). [OE *endleofon* etc., = OS *elleban*, OHG *einlif*, ON *ellifu*, Goth. *ainlif* f. Gmc **ainaz* ONE + **lif-*, perh. = one *left* over (ten)]

ĕ'lĕvŏn *n.* (Aeronaut.) movable part of trailing edge of delta wing. [f. ELEVATOR + AILERON]

ĕlf *n.* (*pl.* **elves** *pr.* -vz). (Gmc Myth.) a supernatural being; mischievous creature; dwarf, little creature; ∼**-arrow,** ∼**-bolt,** ∼**-dart,** (arch.) flint arrowhead; ∼**-land,** Fairyland; ∼**-lock,** tangled mass of hair; hence **ĕ'lfISH**[1], **ĕ'lvISH**[1], *adjs.* [OE, = MDu. *elf* f. Gmc **albhiz*]

ĕ'lfĭn *a.* & *n.* **1.** *a.* of elves, elfish. **2.** *n.* (arch.) dwarf, child. [f. prec., perh. infl. by ME *elvene* gen. pl. of *elf*, and *Elphin* in Arthurian romance]

ĕli'cĭt *v.t.* draw forth (what is latent; usu. fig.); draw out, evoke, (admission, answer *from* person). [f. L E(*licere licit-* = *lacere* deceive)]

ĕli'de *v.t.* omit (vowel, syllable) by ELISION. [f. L E(*lidere lis-* = *laedere* knock) crush out]

ĕ'lig|**ible** *a.* fit or entitled to be chosen (*for* award etc.); desirable, suitable, esp. as partner in marriage (*eligible bachelor*); hence ∼IBI'LITY *n.*, ∼IBLY *adv.* [f. F *éligible* f. LL *eligibilis* (as ELECT[1]; see -IBLE)]

ĕli'mĭn|**āte** *v.t.* remove, get rid of; (Physiol.) discharge (waste matter *from* body); (Chem.) remove (simpler substance *from* a compound); ignore as irrelevant; exclude from competition etc. by defeat; (Alg.) get rid of (quantity) by combining equations; hence ∼ABLE *a.*, ∼A'TION, ∼ātOR, *ns.* [f. L E(*liminare* f. *limen liminis* threshold) + -ATE[3]]

ĕli'sion (-zhon) *n.* omission of vowel or syllable in pronouncing, (*I'm; let's; e'en*), or of passage in book etc. [f. LL *elisio* (as ELIDE; see -ION)]

ĕlīt|**e** (ālē't) *n.* **1.** *the* choice part, (*the best*, (of a group); select of letters in typewriting (12 per inch); select group or class. **2.** Hence ∼ISM *n.*, advocacy of or reliance on leadership or dominance by a select group; so ∼IST (2) *n.* [F, f. p.p. of *élire* f. Rom. **exlegere* ELECT[2]]

ĕli'xir *n.* alchemist's preparation designed to change metals into gold or (∼ **of life**) to prolong life indefinitely; sovereign remedy; (Pharm.) aromatic solution used as medicine or flavouring. [ME f. med. L, f. Arab. *al-iksīr* (*al* the, *iksīr* prob. f. Gk *xērion* desiccative powder for wounds f. *xēros* dry)]

Elizabē'than (ī-) *a.* & *n.* (person, writer) of the time of Queen Elizabeth I or II. [f. *Elizabeth* + -AN]

ĕlk *n.* (*pl.* ∼**s** *or* ∼). large species of deer (*Alces alces*) in N. Europe and Asia; moose; **wapiti*; IRISH *elk*; **(E*∼) member of a social and charitable organization; ∼**-hound,** large Scandinavian shaggy-coated hunting dog. [ME, prob. repr. OE *e*(*o*)*lh*]

ĕll *n.* (Hist.) measure of length (**English** ∼, = 45 in.); **give him an inch** (a little) **and he'll take an** ∼ (much). [OE *eln*, = OS, OHG *elina*, ON *öln*, Goth. *aleina* orig. 'forearm'; cogn. w. L ULNA]

ĕlli'pse[1] *n.* regular oval, traced by point moving in plane so that the sum of its distances from two other points is constant, or produced when a cone is cut by a plane making smaller angle with base than side of cone makes (cf. HYPERBOLA). [F, f. L f. Gk *elleipsis* f. *elleipō* come short (*ein*, *leipō* leave)]

ĕlli'psĭs, ĕlli'pse[2], *n.* (*pl.* **elli'pses** *pr.* -ēz). omission from sentence of words needed to complete construction or sense; omission of sentence at end of paragraph; set of three dots etc. indicating such omission. [f. as prec.]

ĕlli'psoid *n.* solid of which all plane sections through one axis are ellipses and all other plane sections are ellipses or circles; hence **ĕllipsoi'd**AL *a.* [f. ELLIPSE¹ + -OID]

ĕlli'ptic(al) *adjs.* of or relating to an ellipse or ellipsis; hence **ĕlli'ptic**ALLY *adv.*, **ĕllipti'ci**TY *n.* [f. Gk *elleiptikos* defective f. *elleipō* (see ELLIPSE¹)]

ĕlm *n.* tree of genus *Ulmus*, esp. *U. procera* with rough doubly serrated leaves; ∼('wood), its wood; hence ∼'Y² *a.* [OE, = OHG *elm*, cogn. w. ON *álmr*, L *ulmus*]

ĕ'locŭte *v.i.* (joc.) practise elocution; declaim. [back-form. f. foll., after *execute* etc.]

ĕlocŭ'tion *n.* art of expressive speech; style of speaking; hence ∼ARY¹ *a.*, ∼IST (3) *n.* [f. L *elocutio* f. E(*loqui* locutspeak); see -ION]

éloge (ĕlŏ'zh) *n.* discourse in honour of deceased person (esp. member of French Academy, pronounced by his successor). [F, f. L *elogium* epitaph]

Elō'hist (ĕ-) *n.* author(s) of parts of Hexateuch where God is called 'Elohim' (cf. JEHOVIST). [f. *Elohim* (Heb., pl. of *'elōah* god) + -IST]

ĕ'lŏngāte (-ngg-) *v.* & *a.* **1.** *v.t.* lengthen, prolong. **2.** *v.i.* (Bot.) be of slender or tapering form. **3.** *a.* (Bot. & Zool.) long in proportion to its width. [f. LL E(*longare* f. L *longus* long) + -ATE³,²]

ĕlŏngā'tion (-ngg-) *n.* lengthening; part (of line etc.) formed by lengthening; (Astron.) angular distance of planet from sun or of satellite from planet; (Mech.) amount of extension under stress. [ME, f. LL *elongatio* (as prec.; see -ATION)]

ĕlō'pe *v.i.* (Of woman) run away from husband, or from home for secret marriage, (*with* her lover); (of couple) run away together to get married; abscond; hence ∼MENT (-pm-) *n.* [f. AF *aloper* perh. f. ME *alope* p.p of *alepe* run away (A- 1, LEAP¹)]

ĕ'loquence *n.* fluent, forcible, and apt use of language; rhetoric. [ME f. OF, f. L *eloquentia* f. E(*loqui* speak); see -ENCE]

ĕ'loquent *a.* possessing or showing eloquence; (fig.) clearly indicative (*of*); hence ∼LY² *adv.* [ME f. OF, f. L *eloqui* (as prec.; see -ENT)]

∥E'lsăn (ĕ'-) *n.* (P) type of lavatory in which chemicals are used for deodorization etc. [app. f. E. L. Jackson (manufacturer) + SANITATION]

ĕlse *adv.* **1.** (following indef. or interrog. pron.) besides, in addition, (*someone, anybody, nowhere, else; who else?; who else's?, whose else?*); instead (*what else could I say?*). **2.** otherwise, if not, (*run, (or) else you will be late*); or ∼ (colloq., expr. warning or threat; *hand over the money or else*); ∼'**where**, in or to some other place. [OE *elles*, = OHG *elles*, OSw. *äljes* gen. sing. cogn. w. Goth. *aljis* other, L *alius*, Gk *allos*]

ĕ'lŭant. See ELUENT.

ĕ'lŭāte *n.* (Chem.) solution obtained by elution. [f. as ELUENT + -ATE¹]

ĕlu'cid|āte (-ū'-, -ōō'-) *v.t.* throw light on, explain; hence ∼A'TION, ∼ātor, *ns.*, ∼ative, ∼ātory, *adjs.* [f. LL E(*lucidare* f. *lucidus* bright, LUCID) + -ATE³]

ĕlu'de (-ū'd, -ōō'd) *v.t.* escape adroitly from (blow, danger, difficulty, person's grasp, person, inquiry, observation); avoid compliance with (law, request) or fulfilment of (obligation); escape from, baffle, (person's memory, understanding); so **ĕlu'sion** (-zhon), **ĕlu'siveness** (-vn-), *ns.*, **ĕlu'sive**, **ĕlu'sory**, (-ū'-, -ōō'-) *adjs.* [f. L E(*ludere* lus- play)]

ĕ'lŭent, ĕ'lŭant, *n.* (Chem.) fluid used for elution. [f. L E(*luere* lut- wash); see -ENT, -ANT]

elusion etc. See ELUDE.

ĕlū'tion *n.* (Chem.) removal of adsorbed substance by washing; so **ĕlū'te** *v.t.* [G, f. LL *elutio* (as ELUENT; see -ION)]

ĕlū'tri|āte *v.t.* (Chem.) separate lighter and heavier particles in a mixture by washing or gas flow; hence ∼A'TION *n.* [f. L E(*lutriare* wash) + -ATE³]

ĕ'lver *n.* young eel. [var. of *eel*-FARE¹ = brood of young eels]

elves, ĕ'lvish. See ELF.

Ely'si|um (ĭlĭ'z-) *n.* (Gk Myth.) abode of the blessed after death; place or state of ideal happiness; hence ∼AN *a.* (∼an **fields**, Elysium). [f. L f. Gk *Elusion* (*pedion* plain)]

ĕ'lytr|ŏn *n.* (*pl.* ∼a). outer hard wing-case of coleopterous insect. [f. Gk *elutron* sheath]

E'lzėvir (ĕ-) *a.* & *n.* (book) printed by Elzevier family at Amsterdam etc. in 17th c.

ĕm *n.* (Print.) unit for measuring amount of printed matter in line, equal to space occupied by m; measure-unit of 12 points; em QUADRAT, RULE. [name of letter M]

'em *pron.* (colloq.) them (*let 'em all come*). [orig. a form of ME *hem*, dat. & acc. 3rd pers. pl. pron.; now regarded as abbr. of THEM]

em-¹,² *pref.*, assim. form of EN-¹,² bef. *b*, *p*.

ĕmā'ci|āte (-shī-, -sī-) *v.t.* (esp. in *p.p.*) make (person, face, etc.) thin; make feeble; hence ∼A'TION *n.* [f. L E(*maciare* f. *macies* leanness) + -ATE³]

ĕ'manāte *v.* **1.** *v.i.* issue, originate, (*from* source, person, etc.); (of gas, light, etc.) proceed, issue, (*from*). **2.** *v.t.* cause to emanate, send forth. [f. L E(*manare* flow) + -ATE³]

ĕmanā'tion *n.* issuing (*from*); thing proceeding from a source (esp. fig., of virtues, qualities, moral powers); (Chem.) radioactive gas formed by radioactive decay of solid; hence **ĕ'manātive** *a.* [f. LL *emanatio* (as prec.; see -ATION)]

ĕmă'ncipāt|e *v.t.* free from legal, social, political, intellectual, or moral restraint (*emancipate from slavery; emancipated people ignoring social conventions*); (Rom. Law) release (child, wife) from power of paterfamilias; hence ∼OR *n.*, ∼ORY *a.* [f. L E(*mancipare* transfer property f. *manus* hand + *capere* take) + -ATE³]

ĕmă'ncipā'tion *n.* emancipating; setting free, esp. from slavery or from legal disabilities; whence ∼IST (2) *n.*; setting free, freedom, from intellectual or moral restraint. [f. L *emancipatio* (as prec.; see -ATION)]

ĕmă'ncipist *n.* (Austral. Hist.) ex-convict who had served his term. [f. EMANCIPATE + -IST]

ĕmă'sculate¹ *a.* castrated; effeminate. [f. L *emasculatus* p.p. of E(*masculare* f. *masculus* dim. of *mas* male); see -ATE²]

ĕmă'scul|āte² *v.t.* castrate; weaken, make effeminate; impoverish (language); weaken (literary composition) by excisions, (legislation) by amendments etc.; hence ∼A'TION *n.*, ∼ATORY *a.* [f. as prec. + -ATE³]

ĕmba'lm (-ah'm) *v.t.* preserve (corpse) from decay orig. with spices, now by means of arterial injection; preserve from oblivion; endue with balmy fragrance; hence ∼MENT (-m-m-) *n.* [ME, f. OF EM¹(*baumer*, as BALM)]

ĕmbă'nk *v.t.* shut in or confine (river etc.) by banks, raised stone structure, etc. [f. EM-¹ + BANK²]

ĕmbă'nkment *n* bank etc. for confining a river etc.; long bank or mound of earth etc. carrying road or railway. [f. prec. + -MENT]

ĕmbă'r|gō (ĕ-, ĭ-) *n.* (*pl.* ∼es), & *v.t.* **1.** *n.* order forbidding ships of a foreign power to enter, or any ships to leave, the country's ports; suspension of (a branch of) commerce or other activity (*be under an embargo*); impediment. **2.** *v.t.* place (ships, trade, etc.) under embargo; seize (ship, goods) for State service. [Sp., f. *embargar* arrest f. Rom. *imbarricare* as IM-¹, *barra* BAR¹)]

ĕmbă'rk *v.t.* & *i.* put or go on board ship or aircraft (*for* destination), whence **ĕmbărk**A'TION *n.*; engage (*in*, *on*, *upon*, undertaking, war, etc.). [f. F EM¹(*barquer* f. *barque* BARK³)]

embarras de choix, de richesse(s), (ahn̄bahrah' de shwah', de rēshĕ's) *n.* more alternatives, wealth, than one knows how to deal with. [F, = embarrassment of choice, of riches]

ĕmbă'rrass *v.t.* encumber, impede; make (person) feel awkward or ashamed; complicate (question etc.);

perplex; (in *p.p.*) encumbered with debts; hence ∾MENT *n.* [f. F *embarrasser* f. Sp. *embarazar* f. It. *imbarrazzare* (*imbarrare* bar in, f. as IM-¹, BAR²)]

e̓'mbassy̆ *n.* ambassador's function, office, or residence; deputation to a sovereign etc. [earlier *ambassy* f. OF *ambassée* etc. f. med. L *ambasciata* f. Rom. *ambactiare; see AMBASSADOR]

e̓mbă'ttle¹ *v.t.* set (army etc.) in battle array; fortify against attack. [ME, f. OF EM¹(*bataillier* f. *bataille* BATTLE¹)]

e̓mbă'ttle² *v.t.* furnish (building, wall) with battlements; (in *p.p.*, Her.) like battlements in form. [ME, f. EM-¹+OF *bataillier*; see BATTLEMENT]

e̓mbay' *v.t.* enclose (as) in a bay, shut in; form (coast) into bays; hence ∾MENT *n.* [f. EM-¹+BAY²]

e̓mbe̓'d, imbe̓'d, *v.t.* (-dd-; esp. in *p.p.*) fix firmly in surrounding mass; (of mass) surround thus; place (as) in a bed. [f. EM-¹, IM-¹+BED¹]

e̓mbe̓'llish *v.t.* beautify, adorn; heighten (narrative) with fictitious additions; hence ∾MENT *n.* [ME, f. OF EM¹(*bellir* f. *bel* f. L *bellus* handsome); see -ISH²]

e̓'mber¹ *n.* (usu. in *pl.*) small piece of live coal or wood in dying fire; (fig.) almost extinct residue of activity etc. [OE *ǣmyrge*, = OHG *eimuria* pyre, ON *eimyrje* embers f. Gmc *aimuzjōn; for -*b*- cf. SLUMBER]

e̓'mber² *a.* ∾ **days,** days of fasting and prayer (esp. in Anglican & RC Ch.), the Wed., Fri., and Sat., after (1) 1st Sun. in Lent, (2) Whit Sunday, (3) Holy Cross Day (14 Sept.), and (4) St. Lucy's day (13 Dec.). [OE *ymbren* n., perh. f. *ymbryne* period (*ymb* about, *ryne* course)]

e̓'mber³ *n.* ∾(**-goose**), a sea-bird, species of LOON² (*Gavia immer*). [f. Norw. *emmer*]

e̓mbe̓'zzle *v.t.* divert (money etc., or abs.) fraudulently to one's own use; hence ∾MENT (-zelm-) *n.* [f. AF *embesiler* (as EM-¹, *besiler* = OF *besillier* maltreat, ravage, of unkn. orig.]

e̓mbi̓'tter *v.t.* make bitter (fig.); aggravate (evil); exasperate (person, feeling); hence ∾MENT *n.* [f. EM-¹+BITTER]

e̓mblā'zon *v.t.* portray conspicuously, as on heraldic shield; adorn (shield) with heraldic devices; adorn; celebrate, extol; hence ∾MENT *n.* [f. EM-¹+BLAZON²]

e̓mblā'zonry̆ *n.* blazonry. [f. prec.+-RY]

e̓'mblem *n.* symbol, typical representation (∾ **book,** of drawings with allegorical explanations); (of person) type (*of* a quality); heraldic device or symbolic object as distinctive badge; so **e̓mblem-a'tic(al)** (*of*), *adjs.* [ME, f. L f. Gk *emblēma -matos* insertion f. EM²(*ballō* throw)]

e̓mble̓'matize, -ise (-īz), *v.t.* serve as emblem of; represent by an emblem. [f. as prec.+-IZE]

e̓'mblement *n.* (Law, usu. in *pl.*) profits of sown land; natural products of soil. [ME, f. OF *emblaement* (EM¹*bla(i)er* f. *blé* corn; see -MENT)]

e̓mbo̓'dy̆ *v.t.* clothe (spirit) with body; give concrete form to (ideas etc.); express tangibly (principles *in* actions etc.); (of thing or person) be an expression of (ideas etc.); form into a body; include, comprise; hence ∾ĭMENT *n.* [f. EM-¹+BODY¹]

e̓mbo̓'lden *v.t.* make bold, encourage (*to* do). [f. EM-¹+*bolden* (BOLD, -EN⁶)]

e̓'mbolism *n.* obstruction of artery etc. by clot of blood, air-bubble, etc., esp. as cause of paralysis; embolus. [ME, = 'intercalation' f. LL f. Gk *embolismos* (EM²*ballō* throw in; see -ISM)]

e̓mboli̓'smic (-z-) *a.* (Of year, in Jewish calendar) containing an intercalated month. [f. prec.+-IC]

e̓'mbol|us *n.* (*pl.* ∾**i** *pr.* -ī). object causing embolism of artery etc. [L, = piston, f. Gk *embolos* peg, stopper]

embonpoint (ah̐bawn̐pwă'n̐) *n.* plumpness (of person). [f. F phr. *en bon point* in good condition]

e̓mbo̓'som (-ŏ͞o'z-) *v.t.* (literary) embrace; enclose, surround. [f. EM-¹+BOSOM]

e̓mbo̓'ss *v.t.* carve or mould in relief; cause figures etc. to stand out on (surface); make protuberant; hence ∾MENT *n.* [ME, f. OF *embocer (as EM-¹, BOSS¹)]

embouchure (ah̐bŏ͞oshoor') *n.* mouth of river; opening of valley; (Mus.) part of musical instrument applied to mouth, mode of applying mouth to this. [F, f. *s'emboucher* discharge itself by mouth (as EM-¹, *bouche* mouth); see -URE]

e̓mbow'el *v.t.* (∥-ll-). (arch.) disembowel. [f. OF *emboweler* f. *esboueler* (*es*- EX-¹, *bouel* BOWEL)]

e̓mbow'er *v.t.* enclose as in bower. [f. EM-¹+BOWER¹]

e̓mbrā'ce *v.t.*, & *n.* **1.** *v.t.* hold (person etc.; in *pl.* abs. = embrace one another) closely in the arms, usu. as sign of affection; clasp, enclose; accept eagerly (offer, opportunity, etc.); adopt (course of action, doctrine, party, cause); include, comprise, (thing *in* another); take in with eye or mind; hence ∾ABLE *a.* (-sa-), ∾MENT (-sm-) *n.* **2.** *n.* folding in the arms; (euphem.) sexual intercourse. [ME, f. OF *embracer* f. Rom. *imbracchiare f. L *in*- IN-¹ + *bracchium* arm]

e̓mbra̓'nchment (-ah'-) *n.* branching-out (of arm of river etc.). [f. F *embranchement* (as EM-¹, BRANCH¹, -MENT)]

e̓mbră'ngle (-ngg*e*l) *v.t.* entangle, confuse; hence ∾MENT (-gelm-) *n.* [f. EM-¹+obs. *brangle* wrangle]

e̓mbrā'sure (-zh*e*r) *n.* bevelling of wall at sides of door or window, splaying; opening in parapet, widening from within, for gun. [F (*embraser* splay, of unkn. orig.; see -URE)]

e̓mbri̓'ttle *v.t.* make brittle; hence ∾MENT (-telm-) *n.* [f. EM-¹+BRITTLE]

e̓mbroca'tion *n.* liquid used for rubbing on body to relieve muscular pain etc. [F, or f. med. L *embrocatio* (*embrocare* f. LL f. Gk *embrokhē* lotion; see -ATION)]

e̓mbroi'der *v.t.* ornament (cloth etc., or abs.) with needlework; heighten (narrative) with fictitious additions; hence ∾ER¹ *n.* [ME, f AF *enbrouder* (as EN-¹, OF *brouder, broisder* f. Gmc *brusdan)]

e̓mbroi'dery̆ *n.* embroidering; embroidered work; inessential ornament. [ME, f. AF *enbrouderie* (as prec.; see -ERY]

e̓mbroi'l *v.t.* bring (affairs, narrative, etc.) into state of confusion; involve (person) in hostility (*with* another); hence ∾MENT *n.* [f. F EM¹(*brouiller* f. Rom. *brodiculare)]

e̓mbrow'n *v.t.* make brown or dark. [f. EM-¹+BROWN¹]

e̓'mbryŏ *n.* (*pl.* ∾**s**) & *a.* **1.** *n.* offspring of animal before birth (or emergence from egg); human offspring in first eight weeks from conception; rudimentary plant contained in seed; thing in rudimentary stage (**in** ∾, undeveloped); hence **embryŏ'nic** *a.* **2.** *a.* undeveloped; immature. [LL *embryo -onis* erron. f. Gk EM²(*bruon* f. *bruō* swell, grow)]

e̓'mbryŏ- *comb. form.* = prec., as: ∾**ge'nesis,** formation of embryo; ∾**logy** (-ŏ'l-), science of the embryo. [f. Gk *embruon* (see prec.)+-o-]

e̓mbū's *v.t.* & *i.* (-ss-). (esp. Mil.) put (men, stores) or get into motor vehicle. [f. EM-¹+BUS, after *embark*]

embusqué (ah̐bŏ͞o'skă) *n.* one who avoids military service by obtaining government work etc. [F, p.p. of *embusquer* ambush]

e̓mcee' *n.* & *v.* (sl.) **1.** *n.* master of ceremonies; compère of show etc. **2.** *v.t.* & *i.* act as emcee (of). [f. letters *MC*]

-ēme *suf.* (Ling.) forming *ns.* denoting units of structure etc. (*grapheme, morpheme*). [F *-ème* unit f. Gk *-ēma*]

e̓mē'nd *v.t.* (seek to) remove errors from (text of book etc.); so **e̓mendā'tion, ē'mendātor,** *ns.*, ∾**atory** *a.* [ME, f. L E(*mendare* f. *menda* fault)]

e̓'merald *n.* bright-green precious stone, variety of beryl; ∾ (**green**), colour of this; **E**∾ **Isle,** Ireland; hence ∾INE¹ (-ĭn) *a.* [ME, f. OF *e(s)meraude* f. Rom. *smaralda f. L f. Gk *smaragdos*]

e̓mēr'g|e *v.i.* come up out of a liquid; come into view (*from* enclosed space etc.); come out (*from* state of suffering etc.); (of facts etc.) become known as result of inquiry or trial; (of question, difficulty, etc.) crop up; so ∾ENCE *n.,* ∾ENT *a.,* (esp., of nation) newly independent. [f. L E(*mergere* mers- dip)]

e̓mēr'gency̆ *n.* & *a.* **1.** *n.* sudden state of danger etc., (patient with) condition needing immediate treatment; (Polit.) condition approximating to that of war. **2.** *a.* used or arising in an emergency. [f. med. L *emergentia* (as prec.; see -ENCY)]

ĕmĕ′ritus *a.* honourably discharged from service; retired and holding honorary title (*emeritus professor, professor emeritus*). [L, p.p. of E(*merēri* earn)]

ĕmĕr′sion (-shon) *n.* emerging; (Astron.) reappearance of celestial body after eclipse or occultation. [f. LL *emersio* (as EMERGE; see -ION)]

ĕ′merÿ *n.* coarse corundum used for polishing metal, stones, etc.; **~-board**, emery-coated nail-file; **~-cloth**, **-paper**, **-wheel**, (covered with emery powder). [f. F *émeri*(*l*) f. It. *smeriglio* f. Rom. *smericulum* f. Gk *smiris*, *smēris* polishing powder]

ĕmĕ′tic *a.* & *n.* (medicine) that causes vomiting. [f. Gk *emetikos* (*emeō* vomit; see -ETIC)]

émeute (īmū′t) *n.* popular uprising. [F, f. Rom. *exmovita* (*exmovēre*; cf. EMOTION)]

EMF *abbr.* electromotive force.

*-ē′mia. See -AEMIA.

ĕ′migrāte *v.* **1.** *v.i.* leave one country to settle in another. **2.** *v.t.* assist (person) to emigrate. **3.** Hence or cogn. **~ANT** *a.* & *n.*, **~A′TION** *n.*, **~ātory** *a.* [f. L E(*migrare* MIGRATE) | -ATE³]

émigré (ĕ′mǐgrā) *n.* emigrant, esp. political exile. [F, p.p. of *émigrer*, = prec.]

ĕ′minence *n.* **1.** piece of rising ground. **2.** distinguished superiority (social, intellectual, etc.); important person; (*E~*) cardinal's title. [f. L *eminentia* (as EMINENT; see -ENCE)]

éminence grise (āmēnahṅs grē′z) *n.* confidential agent, esp. one who exercises power unofficially. [F, = grey cardinal (see prec. **2**; orig. applied to Cardinal Richelieu's private secretary, Père Joseph d. 1638)]

ĕ′minent *a.* exalted, distinguished, (*eminent* DOMAIN); (of qualities) remarkable in degree, whence **~LY²** *adv.* [ME, f. L *eminēre* jut; see -ENT]

ĕmīr′ (-ēī′) *n.* Title of various Muslim rulers; (arch.) male descendant of Muhammad; hence **~ATE¹** (1) (ĕmēr′at, ĕ′mīrat) *n.* [f. F *émir* f. Sp. *emir* f. Arab. 'amīr (cf. AMIR)]

ĕ′missarÿ *n.* person sent on special (occas. odious or underhand) mission. [f. L *emissarius* scout, spy (as EMIT; see -ARY¹)]

ĕmi′ssion (-shon) *n.* emitting (*of* radiation, heat, smell, noise, fluid from body, etc.); thing emitted; so **ĕmi′ssIVE** *a.*; **ĕmissi′vITY** *n.*, power of radiating light, heat, etc. [f. L *emissio* (as foll.; see -ION)]

ĕmi′t *v.t.* (**-tt-**). send out or forth (stream, smoke, smell, light, heat, sound; (arch.) opinion, paper currency, etc.); hence **~tER¹** *n.*, (e.g.) region in transistor producing carriers of current. [f. L E(*mittere miss-* send)]

E′mment(h)al (ĕ′mentahl) *n.* kind of Swiss cheese with many holes. [f. G *Emmentaler* f. **~** in Switzerland]

ĕ′mmer *n.* species of wheat (*Triticum dicoccum*). [G dial.]

ĕ′mmĕt *n.* (arch. or dial.) ant. [OE *ǣmete*; see ANT]

*E′mmÿ (ĕ′-) *n.* statuette awarded to outstanding television programme or performer. [perh. f. *Immy* f. *image* (*orthicon tube*) + -Y³]

ĕmŏ′llient (-lye-) *a.* & *n.* (substance) that softens skin etc.; soothing (agent). [f. L E(*mollire* f. *mollis* soft); see -ENT]

ĕmŏ′lŭment *n.* profit from office or employment, salary. [ME f. OF, or f. L *emolumentum*, orig. prob. 'payment for corn-grinding', f. E(*molere* grind); see -MENT]

ĕmŏ′te *v.i.* act emotionally. [back-form. f. foll.]

ĕmŏ′tion *n.* disturbance of mind; mental sensation or state; instinctive feeling as opposed to reason; hence **~LESS** *a.* [f. F *émotion* (*émouvoir* excite, after *mouvoir* MOVE², *motion* MOTION¹)]

ĕmŏ′tional *a.* of or relating to the emotions; expressing emotion; liable to excessive emotion, whence

~ISM (1), **~IST** (2), **~ITY** (-ă′l-), *ns.*, **~IZE** (3) *v.t.*, **~LY²** *adv.* [f. prec. + -AL]

ĕmŏ′tive *a.* of emotion; tending to excite emotion; arousing feeling, not purely descriptive; hence **~LY²** (-vlǐ) *adv.*, **ĕmŏti′vITY** *n.* [f. L E(*movēre mot-* MOVE²); see -IVE]

ĕmpā′nel, **im-**, *v.t.* (||-ll-). enter on panel, enrol, (jury). [f. AF EM¹(*paneller* f. as PANEL¹)]

ĕmpā′radise. Var. of IMPARADISE.

ĕ′mpath|ÿ *n.* (Psych.) power of projecting one's personality into (and so fully comprehending) object of contemplation; hence **~E′TIC**, **ĕmpā′thIC**, *adjs.*, **~IST** (2) *n.*, **~IZE** (1, 2) *v.t.* & *i.* (*with*). (Psych.) einfühlung (*ein* in, *fühlung* feeling), after Gk *empatheia* (as EM-²; see SYMPATHY)]

ĕmpĕ′nnage *n.* (Aeron.) arrangement of stabilizing surfaces at tail of aircraft. [F (*empenner* feather (an arrow); cf. -AGE)]

ĕ′mperor *n.* (*fem.* EMPRESS). sovereign of higher rank than king; sovereign of an empire; **~ penguin**, largest known species of penguin, confined to Antarctic; PURPLE *emperor*; hence **~SHIP** *n.* [ME, f. OF *emperere*, *empereor*, f. L *imperator -oris* f. IM¹(*perare* = *parare* prepare, order) command; see -OR]

ĕ′mperÿ *n.* (poet.) dominion(s). [ME f. OF *emperie*, f. L (as EMPIRE)]

ĕ′mphas|ĭs *n.* (*pl.* **~es** *pr.* -ēz). stress laid on word(s) to indicate special meaning or importance; vigour or intensity of expression, feeling, action, etc.; importance assigned to fact, idea, etc.; prominence, sharpness of contour. [L f. Gk f. EM²(*phainō* show) exhibit]

ĕ′mphasīze, **-īse** (-īz), *v.t.* lay stress on (word in speaking); bring (fact etc.) into special prominence. [f. prec. + -IZE]

ĕmphā′t|ic *a.* (Of language, tone, gesture) forcibly expressive; (of word) bearing the stress; (of person) expressing himself with emphasis; (of action or process) forcible, significant; hence **~ICALLY** *adv.* [f. LL f. Gk *emphatikos* (as EMPHASIS; see -IC)]

ĕmphÿsē′ma *n.* (Path.) enlargement of air vesicles of the lungs; swelling caused by presence of air in connective tissues of body. [LL, f. Gk *emphusēma* (*emphusaō* puff up)]

ĕ′mpīre *n.* supreme and extensive (political) dominion; (arch.) absolute control (*over*); (period of) government in which sovereign is called emperor; territory of an emperor; (Hist.) the **E~**, (usu.) British Empire or Holy Roman Empire; large commercial organization etc. owned or directed by one person or group; **~-builder**, one who deliberately acquires extra territory, authority, etc., esp. unnecessarily; **E~** Day, former name of COMMONWEALTH Day, orig. 24 May; ***E~** **City, State,** (of New York); (*attrib.*, *E~*) denoting a style of furniture or dress fashionable during the first (1804–14) or second (1852–70) French Empire, or ||wine etc. from the Commonwealth. [ME f. OF, f. L *imperium* conn. w. *imperare*; see EMPEROR]

ĕmpī′ric *a.* & *n.* **1.** *a.* = foll.; hence **~ISM** (3), **~IST** (2), *ns.*; LOGICAL *empiricism*. **2.** *n.* (arch.) person relying solely on experiment; quack doctor. [f. L f. Gk *empeirikos* (*empeiria* experience f. *empeiros* skilled; see -IC)]

ĕmpī′rical *a.* based on or acting on observation or experiment, not on theory; regarding sense-data as valid information; deriving knowledge from experience alone; **~ formula**, (Chem.) formula showing constituents of a compound but not their configuration; hence **~LY²** *adv.* [f. prec. + -AL]

ĕmplā′cement (-sm-) *n.* situation; placing; platform for gun(s). [F (as EM-¹, PLACE¹, -MENT)]

ĕmplā′ne *v.i.* & *t.* go or put on board aeroplane. [f. EM-¹ + PLANE³]

ĕmploy′ *v.t.*, & *n.* **1.** *v.t.* use (thing, one's power, time, etc., *for*, *in*, *on*, a purpose); use services of (person); keep (person) in one's service; busy, keep occupied, (one*self*, others, doing, *in*, etc.); hence **~ABLE** *a.*,

∼ER¹ *n.* **2.** *n.* being employed, esp. for wages; **in the** ∼ **of,** employed by. [ME, f. OF *employer* f. Rom. *implicare* f. L *implicari* be involved (*implicare* enfold; see IMPLICATE¹)]

employé (ŏmploi'ā) *n.* (*fem.* -*ée pr.* same). (*arch.*) = foll. [F, p.p. of *employer* (as prec.)]

employee, *employé, (-oiē', -oi'ē) *n.* person employed for wages. [f. EMPLOY + -EE]

employ'ment *n.* In vbl senses; one's regular trade or profession; ∼ **agency,** business that finds employers or employees for those seeking them; ∼ **exchange,** State office performing similar function; **full** ∼, condition in which there is no idle capital or labour of kind that is in demand. [f. EMPLOY + -MENT]

empoi'son (-z-) *v.t.* (arch. or literary). put poison into; taint; (fig.) corrupt; embitter (feelings). [ME, f. OF EM¹(*poisonner* POISON)]

empō'lder. Var. of IMPOLDER.

empōr'i|um *n.* (*pl.* ∼**ums** or ∼**a**). centre of commerce, market; large shop. [f. L f. Gk *emporion* (*emporos* merchant)]

empow'er *v.t.* authorize, license, (person *to* do); give power to, make able, (person *to* do). [f. EM-¹ + POWER]

e'mprèss *n.* wife of emperor; woman emperor. [ME, f. OF *emperesse* fem. of *emperere* EMPEROR; see -ESS¹]

empresse'ment (ahṅprě'smahṅ) *n.* display of cordiality or eagerness. [F]

emprī'se (-z) *n.* (arch.) (chivalrous) enterprise. [ME f. OF, f. Rom. *imprensa,* fem. p.p. (as n.) of *IM¹(pre(he)ndere* take)]

e'mpt|y¹ *a. & n.* **1.** containing nothing (*on an empty* STOMACH); devoid *of* (qualities); (colloq.) hungry; (of house etc.) devoid of furniture or occupants; (of van, ship, etc.) without load; foolish, unsatisfactory; meaningless. **2.** *n.* empty truck, bottle, box, etc., after removal of contents. **3.** ∼**y-handed,** bringing no gift, carrying nothing away; ∼**y-headed,** lacking common sense. **4.** Hence ∼**iLY²** *adv.,* ∼**iNESS** *n.* [OE *ǣm(e)tig* (*ǣmetta* leisure; see -Y²)]

e'mpt|y² *v.* **1.** *v.t.* remove contents of (vessel etc.), deprive (vessel etc.) *of* its contents; transfer (contents of one thing *into* etc. another). **2.** *v.i.* (Of river) discharge itself (*into*); become empty. [f. prec.]

empur'ple *v.t.* make purple, redden. [f. EM-¹ + PURPLE]

empyē'ma *n.* (Path.) collection of pus in cavity, esp. in pleura. [LL, f. Gk *empuēma* (EM²*pueō* suppurate f. *puon* pus)]

empyrē'an *a. & n.* (of) the highest heaven, as the sphere of fire in ancient cosmology or as the abode of God; (of) the visible heavens; so **empyreAL** (-ĭ'rĭ-, -īrē'-) *a.* [f. med. L *empyreus* f. Gk EM²(*purios* f. *pur* fire) + -EAN]

EMS *abbr.* European Monetary System.

e'mū *n.* large flightless fast-running Australian bird allied to the cassowary. [earlier *emia, eme,* f. Port. *ema*]

e.m.u. *abbr.* electromagnetic unit(s).

e'mūl|āte *v.t.* try to equal or excel; rival; imitate zealously; hence or cogn. ∼**A'TION,** ∼**ātOR,** *ns.,* ∼**ATIVE** *a.* [f. L *aemulari* (as foll.) + -ATE³]

e'mūlous *a.* eagerly or jealously imitative (*of*); actuated by spirit of rivalry; hence ∼**LY²** *adv.* [ME, f. L *aemulus* rival + -OUS]

emū'lsi|fy *v.t.* convert into an emulsion; hence ∼**FIABLE** *a.,* ∼**FICA'TION,** ∼**fIER¹** (1, 2), *ns.* [f. as foll. + -FY]

emū'lsion (-shon) *n.* fine dispersion of one liquid in another, esp. as paint, medicine, etc.; (Photog.) mixture of silver compound suspended in gelatin etc. for coating plates or films; hence or cogn. ∼**IZE** (3) *v.t.,* **emū'lsIVE** *a.* [f. F *émulsion* f. mod. L *emulsio* f. E(*mulgēre muls-* to milk); see -ION]

e'n *n.* (Print.) unit of width, half an EM; *en* QUADRAT, RULE. [name of letter *N*]

en-¹ *pref.* = IN-¹, forming vbs. (1) f. *ns.,* w. sense 'put into or on' (*enamour, embed, engulf, entrust*), (2) f. *ns.* or *adjs.,* w. sense 'bring into condition of' (*enslave*), often w. *suf.* -EN⁶ (*embolden, enlighten*), (3) f. *vbs.,* w. sense 'in, into, on' (*enfold*) or intensively (*entangle*). [f. or after F *en-* f. L *in-*]

en-² *pref.* in, inside, (*energy, enthusiasm*). [Gk]

-en¹, -n¹, *suf.* forming *p.p.* of strong vbs. (*spoken, sworn*), sometimes w. only restricted use (*drunken, gotten*); cf. -ED¹ (2). [OE, = OS, OHG -*an,* ON -*inn,* -*enn,* Goth. -*ans*]

-en² *suf.* forming dims. of *ns.* (*chicken, maiden*). [f. Gmc *-īnam,* neut. of *-īnaz* -EN⁵]

-en³ *suf.* forming *fem. ns.* (*vixen*), or abstract *ns.* (*burden*). [f. WG *-innja* f. Gmc *-inī*]

-en⁴ *suf.* forming *pl. ns.* (*children, oxen*). [orig. part of stem in weak-decl. nouns, but retained only in *pl.,* and added to other plurals (*children* earlier *childer*). [ME, f. OE -*an*]

-en⁵, -n², *suf.* forming *adjs.* f. *ns.,* usu. expr. material (*wooden*); often arch. (*silvern*) or metaph. (*golden*). [f. Gmc *īnaz*]

-en⁶ *suf.* forming *vbs.* f. *adjs.,* w. sense 'make or become' (*deepen, fasten, moisten*), or f. *ns.* (*happen, heighten, hearten, listen*). [f. or after OE -*an*]

enā'bl|e *v.t.* authorize, empower, (person *to* do); supply (person etc.) with means *to* (do); make possible; ∼**ing act,** statute empowering person or body to take certain action, *statute legalizing something otherwise unlawful. [ME, f. EN-¹ + ABLE]

enā'ct *v.t.* **1.** ordain, decree, (thing, *that*); make (bill etc.) a law; hence ∼**ION,** ∼**MENT,** *ns.,* ∼**IVE,** ∼**ORY,** *adjs.* **2.** play (scene, part, on stage or in life). [ME, f. EN-¹ + ACT¹,²]

enā'mel¹ *n.* glasslike opaque or semi-transparent coating on metallic or other hard surfaces for ornament or as preservative lining (also fig.); smooth hard coating (e.g. of ∼ **paint**), cosmetic simulating this; hard glossy natural coating of teeth; painting done in enamel; (poet.) smooth bright surface colouring, verdure, etc. [ME, f. foll.]

enā'mel² *v.t.* (||-ll-). inlay, encrust, (metal etc.) with enamel; portray (figures etc.) with enamel; (arch.) adorn with varied colours. [ME, f. AF EN¹*ameler* -*amailler,* f. OF *esmail* f. Gmc *smalt-*]

||**enā'mour** (-mer), *enā'mor,** *v.t.* (esp. in *p.p.*) inspire with love or liking (*of*); charm, delight. [ME, f. OF EN¹(*amourer* f. AMOUR love)]

enanthē'ma *n.* (Path.) disease with eruptions on mucosa. [mod. L, f. Gk EN²*anthēma* eruption (as EXANTHEMA)]

enā'ntiomörph *n.* mirror image, form (esp. crystal) related to another as an object is to its image in a mirror; hence ∼**IC, -OUS,** (-ōr'-) *adjs.,* ∼**ISM** (2) (-ōr'-) *n.* [Gk, f. EN²(*enantios* opposite + *morphē* form]

enā'rthrō's|is *n.* (*pl.* ∼**es** *pr.* -ēz). (Anat.) ball-and-socket joint. [Gk, f. EN²(*arthros* f. *arthron* joint); see -OSIS]

en attendant (ahṅ attahṅ'ndahṅ) *adv.* while waiting. [F]

en bloc (ahṅ blŏ'k) *adv.* in a block, wholesale, all at the same time. [F]

en brosse (ahṅ brŏ's) *a.* (Of hair) cut short and bristly. [F]

encae'nia (-sē'n-) *n.* dedication festival; ||(Oxf. Univ.) = COMMEMORATION. [L, f. Gk *egkainia* (EN-², *kainos* new)]

encā'ge (ĭn-k-) *v.t.* confine (as) in cage. [f. EN-¹ + CAGE]

encā'mp (ĭn-k-) *v.t. & i.* settle in military camp; lodge in the open in tents. [f. EN-¹ + CAMP¹]

encā'mpment (ĭn-k-) *n.* In vbl senses; place where troops etc. are encamped. [f. prec. + -MENT]

encā'psūl|āte (ĭn-k-) *v.t.* enclose (as) in a capsule; (fig.) summarize or isolate as if in capsule; hence ∼**A'TION** *n.* [f. EN-¹ + L *capsula* CAPSULE + -ATE³]

encā'se (ĭn-k-) *v.t.* put into a case; surround as with a case; hence ∼**MENT** (-sm-) *n.* [f. EN-¹ + CASE²]

||**encā'sh** (ĭn-k-) *v.t.* convert (bills etc.) into cash; receive in form of cash, realize; hence ∼**ABLE** *a.,* ∼**MENT** *n.* [f. EN-¹ + CASH¹]

encau′stic (ĭn-k-) *a.* & *n.* (painting, art of painting) by burning-in wax paint etc.; ∿ **brick, tile,** (inlaid with differently coloured clays burnt in). [f. L f. Gk *egkaustikos* (as EN-², CAUSTIC)]

-ence *suf.* forming *ns.* of quality (or instance of it) (*congruence, sapience; an impertinence*) or action (*reference, reminiscence*). [f. or after F *-ence* f. L *-entia, -antia* (cf. -ANCE) f. pres. part. st. *-ent-, -ant-*]

enceinte (ahňsǎ′ňt) *a.* & *n.* **1.** *a.* (arch.) (Of woman) pregnant. **2.** *n.* enclosure (in fortification). [F, 1 f. med. L IN²*cincta* ungirded, 2 f. L IN¹*cincta* girded in; cf. CINCTURE]

encephă′lic (ĕn-k-, ĕns-) *a.* of the brain. [f. Gk *egkephalos* brain (as EN-², *kephalē* head) + -IC]

encephali′tis (ĕn-k-, ĕns-) *n.* inflammation of the brain; ∿ **lethargica,** infectious encephalitis caused by virus, usu. with extreme drowsiness, sleepy sickness. [f. as prec. + -ITIS]

encě′phalo- (ĕn-k-, ĕns-) *comb. form.* brain, as: ∿**gram,** X-ray photograph of the brain; ∿**graph,** instrument for recording electrical activity of brain. [f. Gk *egkephalos* brain (see ENCEPHALIC) + -o-]

enchai′n *v.t.* chain up, fetter; hold fast (attention, emotions); hence ∿MENT *n.* [ME, f. F *enchaîner* f. Gallo-Rom. *IN¹(catenare* f. L *catena* chain)]

encha′nt (-ah′-) *v.t.* bewitch (lit. or fig.); charm, delight, (*with, by*); hence or cogn. ∿ER¹, ∿MENT, ∿RESS¹, *ns.; enchanter's* NIGHTSHADE. [ME, f. F *enchanter* f. L IN¹(*cantare* frequent. of *canere* cant- sing)]

enchă′se *v.t.* place (jewel) *in* setting; set (gold etc.) *with* gems; inlay with gold etc.; adorn with figures in relief; engrave; enclose. [ME, f. F *enchâsser* (as EN-¹, CHASE⁵)]

enchila′da (-ah′-) *n.* tortilla with meat etc. and chilli sauce. [Amer. Sp., fem. p.p. (as n.) of *enchilar* season with chilli]

enchiri′dion (ĕn-k-) *n.* handbook. [f. LL f. Gk *egkheiridion* (as EN-², *kheir* hand, *-idion* dim. suf.)]

enci′pher *v.t.* write (message etc.) in cipher. [f EN-¹ + CIPHER¹]

enci′rcle *v.t.* surround, encompass, (*with*); form a circle round; hence ∿MENT (-kĕlm-) *n.* (esp. by supposedly hostile nations). [ME, f. EN-¹ + CIRCLE¹]

encl. *abbr.* enclosed; enclosure.

en clair (ahn klār′) *a.* & *adv.* (Of telegram, official message, etc.) in ordinary language (not in code or cipher). [F, lit. 'in clear']

encla′sp (ĭn-klah′-) *v.t.* hold in clasp or embrace. [f. EN-¹ + CLASP¹,²]

e′nclāve (ĕ′n-k-) *n.* foreign territory surrounded by one's own territory. [F, f. *enclaver* f. Rom. *IN¹(clavare* f. *clavis* key)]

encli′t|ic (ĕn-k-) *a.* & *n.* (Gram.) (word) so unemphatic as to be pronounced as if part of preceding word, e.g. *not* in *cannot, -que* in L *virginibus puerisque;* hence ∿ICALLY *adv.* [f. LL f. Gk *egklitikos* (EN-², *klinō* lean; see -IC)]

enclo′se, inclo′se, (ĭn-klō′z) *v.t.* surround, fence in, (land etc. *with*, in walls etc.; esp. of common land, see foll.); shut up in receptacle (esp. something besides letter in envelope); bound on all sides, contain, (esp. Math.); hem in on all sides; seclude (religious community) from the outside world. [ME, f. OF *enclos* p.p. of *enclore* f. Rom. *includere* f. L (as INCLUDE)]

enclo′sure (ĭn-klō′zher) *n.* enclosing (esp. of common land, to make it private property); enclosing fence etc.; enclosed place, esp. for special class of persons at sporting event; paper etc. enclosed with letter in envelope. [AF & OF (as prec.; see -URE)]

enco′d|e (ĭn-k-) *v.t.* write (message etc.) in code or cipher; hence ∿ER¹ (1, 2) *n.* [f. EN-¹ + CODE²]

enco′miast (ĕn-k-) *n.* composer of an encomium; flatterer; so ∿IC (-ă′-) *a.* [f. Gk *egkōmiastēs* f. as foll.]

enco′mi|um (ĕn-k-) *n.* (*pl.* ∿ums or ∿a.) formal or high-flown praise. [L, f. Gk *egkōmion* (EN-², *kōmos* revelry)]

enco′mpass (ĭn-kŭ′m-) *v.t.* surround, form circle about, esp. to protect or attack; contain; hence ∿MENT *n.* [f. EN-¹ + COMPASS¹]

encore (ŏngkōr′, ŏ′-) *int., n.,* & *v.t.* **1.** *int.* & *n.* (spectators' or audience's demand for song etc. to be sung etc.) again, once more; further item given in response to such demand. **2.** *v.t.* call for repetition of (song etc.); summon (performer) for this. [F, = once again]

encou′nter (ĭn-k-) *v.t.,* & *n.* **1.** *v.t.* meet as adversary; meet, esp. by chance or unexpectedly. **2.** *n.* meeting in combat or by chance; ∿ **group** (of persons seeking psychological benefit through close contact with one another). [ME; (n. f. OF *encontre*) f. OF *encontrer* f. Rom. *IN¹(contrare* f. L *contra* against)]

encou′rage (ĭn-kŭ′-) *v.t.* give courage to; urge, advise, (*person to* do); stimulate by help, reward, etc.; promote, assist, (commerce, opinion, etc.); hence or cogn. ∿MENT (-kŭ′rĭjm-) *n.* [ME, f. F *encourager* (as EN-¹, COURAGE)]

e′ncrinīte (ĕ′n-k-) *n.* fossil crinoid. [f. mod. L *encrinus* f. Gk *en* EN-² + *krinon* lily + -ITE¹]

encroa′ch (ĭn-k-) *v.i.* intrude usurpingly (*on* others' territory, rights, etc., or abs.); (fig.) make gradual inroads *on*; hence ∿MENT *n.* [MF, f. OF EN¹(*crochier* f. *croc* hook, see CROOK)]

encrū′st, incrū′st, (ĭn-k-) *v.* **1.** *v.t.* cover with crust; overlay (surface) with ornamental crust of precious material. **2.** *v.i.* form into a crust. **3.** Hence ∿ MENT *n.* [f. F *incruster* f. L IN¹(*crustare* f. *crusta* CRUST)]

encrustation. Var. of INCRUSTATION.

encu′mber (ĭn-k-) *v.t.* hamper (person, movement, action, *with* burden, difficulty, etc.); burden (person, estate, *with* debts, esp. mortgages); fill, block, (place *with* lumber etc., lit. or fig.); hence ∿MENT *n.* [ME, f. OF *encombrer* block up f. Rom. *INcombrare*]

encu′mbrance (ĭn-k-) *n.* burden; annoyance; impediment (**without** ∿, having no children); claim, mortgage, etc., on property. [ME, f. OF *encombrance* (as prec.; see -ANCE)]

-ency *suf.* forming *ns.* denoting quality (*efficiency, fluency*) or state (*presidency*), but not action (cf. -ENCE). [f. L *-entia* (cf. -ANCY)]

ency′clic(al) *adj.* & *ns.* (Pope's letter) for extensive circulation. [f. LL *encyclicus* f. Gk *egkuklios* (EN-², *kuklos* circle)]

encyclopae′d|ia, -pē′d|ia, (ĕ-, ĭ-) *n.* literary work giving information on all branches of knowledge or of one subject, usu. arranged alphabetically, (*E∿,* Hist.) *the* French encyclopaedia of Diderot, D'Alembert, and others; WALKING² *encyclopaedia;* hence ∿IC *a.,* ∿ISM (3), ∿IST (3), *ns.* [mod. L f. spurious Gk *egkuklopaideia* for *egkuklios paideia* all-round education (cf. *encyc.*)]

ency′st *v.t.* & *i.* enclose (itself) in a cyst; hence ∿A′TION, ∿MENT, *ns.* [f. EN-¹ + CYST]

end¹ *n.* **1.** extreme limit, point beyond which a thing does not continue; extremity of line, or of greatest dimension of object; farthest point (*to the ends of the earth*); **the** ∿, (colloq.) the limit of endurability; ||EAST End, WEST End; at one's wits' end (WIT²); WRONG end of the stick. **2.** surface bounding a thing at either extremity, head of cask etc.; remnant (*candle ends, cigarette end;* ODDS *and ends;* ROPE*'s end*); portion, part, side (*no problem at my end*); BIG end; LITTLE end; at a LOOSE¹ end. **3.** half of sports pitch or court occupied by one team or player; (US & Can.) football player at extremity of line or team; (Bowls) unit of play from one side of green towards the other; **deep** ∿, end of swimming-pool where water is deeper; **go** (**in**) **off the deep** ∿, (colloq.) give way to emotion or anger. **4.** conclusion (of period, action, state, book, etc.; *end of the* WORLD; WORLD *without end*); latter or final part; result; destruction, downfall, death; ultimate state or condition. **5.** thing one seeks to attain, purpose, (*to achieve his ends; to what end?*); object for which a thing exists. **6. all** ∿**s up,** completely; **at an** ∿, exhausted or completed; **come to an** ∿, become exhausted, be completed or finished; **come to a bad** ∿, meet with ruin or disgrace; ∿ **for** ∿, so as to interchange position of ends; *end of* one's TETHER; ∿ **on**, with end facing one, or with end adjoining end of next object etc.; ∿ **to** ∿, lengthwise continuously; **in the** ∿, finally, after all; **keep** one's ∿ **up**, sustain one's part in undertaking or performance; **make an** ∿ **of**, put a stop to; **make (both)** ∿**s meet**, live within one's income; **no** ∿, (colloq.) very much; **no** ∿ **of**, (colloq.) much or many of; **on** ∿, (1) (place, stand) upright, (2) continuously (*for three weeks on end*); **put an** ∿ **to**, stop, abolish, destroy; ∿ **of the road**, (fig.) point at which survival etc. becomes impossible; WITHOUT *end*. **7.** ∿**-game**, final stage of game in chess, bridge, etc., when few men or cards remain; ∿**-man**, CORNER-*man*[2]; ∿**-note**, note put at end of book, chapter, etc.; ∿'**paper**, blank leaf at beginning or end of book; ∿**-play**, (Bridge) method of play in last few tricks to force opponent to make disadvantageous lead; ∿**-point**, final stage of process, esp. point at which effect is observed in titration, dilution, etc.; ∿**-product**, final product of manufacture, radioactive decay, etc.; ∿**-stopped**, (of verse) having pause at end of each line. [OE *ende*, = OS *endi*, OHG *enti*, ON *endi(r)*, Goth. *andeis* f. Gmc **andja-* f. IE **antjó*]

ĕnd[2] *v.* **1.** *v.t.* bring (action, speech, life, etc.) to an end; put an end to, destroy; ∿ **it (all)**, (colloq.) commit suicide. **2.** *v.i.* come to an end; ∿ **by** doing, eventually do (*will end by marrying a millionaire*); result *in*; ∿ **up**, conclude, finish, arrive finally. [OE *endian*, = OS *endion*, OHG *entōn*, ON *enda*, f. as prec.] **-ĕnd** *suf.* See -ND[1].

ĕndă'mage *v.t.* = DAMAGE. [ME, f. EN-[1] + DAMAGE, or f. OF **endamagier*]

ĕndā'nger (-nj-) *v.t.* cause danger to; hence ∿MENT *n.* [ME, f. EN-[1] + DANGER]

ĕndear' *v.t.* render (person, thing, one*self*) dear (*to*); hence ∿ING[2] *a.*, inspiring affection, ∿MENT *n.*, (esp.) action or utterance expressing affection. [f. EN-[1] + DEAR]

‖**ĕndea'vour, *-vor**, (-dĕ'ver) *v.* & *n.* **1.** *v.t.* & *i.* try (*to* do); (arch.) strive *after*. **2.** *n.* attempt (*to* do, *at* doing). [ME, f. *put oneself in* DEVOIR]

ĕndĕ'm|ĭc *a.* & *n.* **1.** *a.* regularly or only found among (specified) people or in (specified) country; hence ∿ICALLY *adv.*, **ĕndĕmĭ'cĭTY** *n.* = foll. **2.** *n.* endemic disease or plant. [f. F *endémique* or mod. L *endemicus* f. Gk *endēmos* native (as EN-[2], *dēmos* the people); see -IC] **ĕ'ndēmĭsm** *n.* character or quality of being endemic. [f. prec. + -ISM]

ĕndĕr'mĭc *a.* acting on or through the skin. [f. EN-[2] + Gk *derma* skin + -IC]

ĕ'nding *n.* In vbl senses; latter or final part (of word, story, etc.). [OE (as END[1], -ING[1])]

ĕndi'stance *v.t.* (Theatr. etc.) produce alienation of (audience). [f. EN-[1] + DISTANCE]

ĕ'ndīve *n.* salad plant (*Cichorium endivia*); *chicory crown. [ME f. OF, f. LL *endivia* f. med. Gk *indibi* f. L *intibum* f. Gk *entubon*]

ĕ'ndlĕss *a.* infinite; eternal; incessant; (colloq.) innumerable; ∿ **band, belt, cable, chain**, etc., (with ends joined for continuous action over wheels etc.); ∿ **screw**, short length of screw revolving to turn cog-wheel; hence ∿LY[2] *adv.*, ∿NESS *n.* [OE *endelēas* (as END[1], -LESS)]

ĕ'ndmōst *a.* nearest the end. [f. END[1], after *hindmost*]

ĕ'ndō- *comb. form.* internal, as; ∿**car'dĭum**, lining membrane of heart; ∿**cardi'tĭs**, inflammation of this; ∿**carp**, innermost layer of pericarp; ∿**crine** (-krīn), (of gland) secreting directly into the blood, ductless [Gk *krinō* sift]; ∿**derm**, (Biol.) innermost layer of embryo in early development; ∿**gamous**, ∿**gamy**, (-ŏ'g-), (of) marrying within the tribe, (Bot.) (of) pollination from same plant; ∿**gen**, plant that develops wood in interior of stem; ∿**genous** (-ŏ'j-), growing or originating from within; ∿**lymph**,

fluid in membranous labyrinth of ear; ∿**me'trium**, ∿**metri'tis**, (inflammation of) lining membrane of womb; ∿**morph**, mineral enclosed in another, person of pyknic build; ∿**pa'rasite**, internal parasite; ∿**plasm**, inner fluid layer of cytoplasm; ∿**scope**, instrument for viewing internal parts of body; ∿**skeleton**, internal skeleton, as of vertebrates etc.; ∿**sperm**, albumen enclosed with germ in seeds; ∿**spore**, inner coat of spore, spore formed in a case; ∿**the'lium**, layer of cells lining blood-vessels etc.; ∿**ther'mic**, occurring or formed with absorption of heat. [f. Gk *endon* within + -o-]

ĕndôr'se, indôr'se, *v.t.* **1.** write on back of (document), esp. sign one's name on back of (bill, cheque, etc.); write (explanation, comment, *on* back of document); transfer one's rights in (bill, etc. *to* another person). **2.** confirm (statement, opinion); declare one's approval of. **3.** ‖make official entry regarding offence on (motorist's, publican's, licence). **4.** Hence ∿MENT (-sm-) *n.* [f. med. L IN[1](*dorsare* f. *dorsum* back)]

ĕndow' *v.t.* bequeath or give permanent income to (person, institution); invest (person) *with* (privileges etc.); (esp. in *p.p.*) furnish (person) *with* (ability etc.). [ME, f. AF *endouer* f. *en* EN-[1] + OF *douer* f. L *dotare* (*dos dotis* DOWER)]

ĕndow'ment *n.* act of endowing; property etc. with which person or body is endowed; talent etc. with which person is endowed; ∿ **assurance** or **insurance**, form of life insurance with payment of fixed sum to insured person on specified date, or to his estate on earlier death. [f. prec. + -MENT]

ĕndūe', indūe', *v.t.* put on (clothes etc., lit. or fig.); clothe (person) *with*; (usu. in *pass.*) furnish (person *with* powers, qualities, etc.). [ME, f. OF *enduire* f. L IN[1](*ducere* lead, draw), assoc. in sense w. L *induere* put on (clothes)]

ĕndūr'ance *n.* habit or power of enduring (*beyond endurance*); act of enduring; ability to withstand prolonged strain (*endurance test*). [OF (*endurer*; see foll.; -ANCE)]

ĕndūr'|e *v.* **1.** *v.t.* undergo (pain etc.); tolerate (*cannot endure that fellow*); submit to; (esp. w. neg.) bear *to* do; hence ∿ABLE *a.* **2.** *v.i.* remain in existence, last. [ME, f. OF *endurer* f. L IN[1](*durare* harden f. *durus* hard)]

ĕ'ndways, ĕ'ndwīse, (-z) *adv.* with its end turned towards the spectator or uppermost or foremost; end to end. [f. END[1] + -WAYS, -WISE]

-ēne *suf.* **1.** (Chem.) forming names of unsaturated hydrocarbons (*benzene, ethylene* or *ethene*). **2.** forming names of natives or inhabitants of places (*Cairene, Gadarene, Nazarene*). [f. or after Gk *-ēnos*]

ENE *abbr.* east-north-east.

enema (ĕ'nĭ-, ĭnē'-) *n.* (*pl.* ∿**s**, or ∿**ta** *pr.* ĭnĕ'mata), injection of liquid or gas into rectum esp. to expel its contents; fluid or syringe so used. [LL, f. Gk *enema* (EN[2]*iēmi* inject f. *hiēmi* send)]

ĕ'nemў *n.* & *a.* **1.** *n.* person who hates one and eagerly seeks one's defeat etc.; opponent (*of, to*, another; the E∿, the Devil); member of hostile army or nation, hostile force or ship or aircraft; thing that harms or injures; **how goes the** ∿?, (colloq.) what is the time?; be one's **own worst** ∿, be nobody's ∿ **but** one's **own**, be responsible for one's own misfortunes. **2.** *a.* of or belonging to the enemy (*enemy ships, aircraft*); *destroyed by enemy action*). [ME, f. OF *enemi* f. L IN[2](*imicus = amicus* friend)]

ĕnergĕ't|ĭc *a.* & *n.* strenuously active; forcible, vigorous; powerfully operative; hence ∿ICS *n.*, science of energy, ∿ICALLY *adv.* [f. Gk *energētikos* f. EN[2](*ergeō* f. *ergon* work); see -IC]

ĕ'nergīze, -īse (īz), *v.* **1.** *v.t.* infuse energy into (person, work); provide energy for operation of (device). **2.** *v.i.* (arch.) be in active operation. [f. ENERGY + -IZE]

ĕnêrgū'mĕn *n.* demoniac; enthusiast, fanatic. [f. LL f. Gk *energoumenos* p.p. of *energeō* (see ENERGETIC)]

ĕ'nergў *n.* **1.** force, vigour, (of speech, action, person etc.); active operation; (in *pl.*) individual powers in use (*devote your energies to this*);(arch.) (latent) ability. **2.** (Phys.) ability of matter or radiation to do work; CONSERVATION *of energy*; **kinetic** ∼, body's ability to do work by virtue of its motion; **mass** or **rest** ∼, body's ability to do work by virtue of its mass, released in nuclear fission etc.; **potential** ∼, body's ability to do work by virtue of its position relative to others, stresses within itself, electric charge, etc. **3.** means of doing work by utilizing matter or radiation (*the country's energy requirements*). [f. F *énergie* or f. LL f. Gk EN²*ergeia* (*ergon* work; see -Y¹)]

ėnêr'vateª *a.* lacking (physical, moral, literary, artistic) vigour. [f. L *enervatus* p.p. of E(*nervare* f. *nervus* sinew); see -ATE²]

ě'nerv|āteª *v.t.* weaken (physically etc., as prec.); so ∼A'TION *n.* [f. as prec. + -ATE³]

en face (ahn fah's) *a.* facing forwards; on facing page of book etc. [F, = opposite]

en famille (ahn fămē'ye) *adv.* at home; in or with one's family. [F, = in family]

enfant gâté (ahnfahn gah'tā) *n.* person given undue flattery or indulgence. [F, = spoilt child]

enfant terrible (ahnfahn těrē'bl) *n.* child who asks awkward questions, embarrassingly repeats what he has heard, etc.; (fig.) person or thing causing embarrassment by unruliness. [F, = terrible child]

ėnfee'ble *v.t.* make feeble; hence ∼MENT (-belm-) *n.* [ME, f. OF EN¹(*feblir* f. *feble* FEEBLE)]

ėnfeo'ff (-fě'f) *v.t.* invest (person) with FEUD²; (arch., fig.) surrender; hence ∼MENT *n.* [ME, f. AF *enfeoffer*, OF *enfeffer* (as EN-¹, FIEF)]

en fête (ahn fā't) *adv. & pred. a.* engaged in, attired etc. for, holiday-making. [F, = in festival]

ėnfe'tter *v.t.* bind in fetters (lit. or fig.); enslave (person *to*). [f. EN-¹ + FETTER]

ėnfilā'de *n., & v.t.* **1.** *n.* fire from guns etc. sweeping line from end to end. **2.** *v.t.* subject (troops, road, etc.) to enfilade. [F, f. EN¹(*filer* f. *fil* thread); see -ADE]

ėnfo'ld *v.t.* wrap up (person etc. *in, with*); clasp, embrace; shape into folds. [f. EN-¹ + FOLD¹,²]

ėnfor'ce *v.t.* urge, press home, (argument, demand); impose (action, conduct, (*up*)*on* person etc.); compel observance of (law etc.), hence or cogn. ∼ABLE (-sa-) *a.*, ∼MENT (-sm-) *n.* [ME, f. OF *enforci(e)r* f. Rom. *IN¹(forti(a)re* f. L *fortis* strong)]

ėnfra'nch|ise (-z) *v.t.* invest (town) with municipal rights, esp. that of representation in parliament; admit (person) to electoral franchise; release (slave, villein, etc.) from bondage; hence ∼isEMENT (-zm-) *n.* [f. OF EN¹(*franchir* f. *franc franche* FRANK²); see -ISH²]

ėngā'ge (ĭn-g-) *v.* **1.** *v.t.* bind by contract (*to* perform, lecture, etc.). **2.** bind by promise (esp. of marriage). **3.** hire (servant, employee); arrange beforehand to occupy (seat, cab, etc.). **4.** (Archit.) fasten (pillar) into wall; (Mech.) interlock (thing *with* another), cause (part) to interlock thus; (of fencers etc.) interlock (weapons, or abs.). **5.** hold fast (attention); (usu. in *pass.*) employ busily. **6.** bring (troops) into conflict; enter into conflict with (enemy etc.). **7.** *v.i.* take part *in* (politics etc.). **8.** pledge oneself (*to do, that*); ∼ **for,** (arch.) guarantee, promise. **9.** (Of mechanical part) interlock *with* another; (of troops etc.) come into conflict *with* enemy etc. [f. F *engager* f. Rom. *IN¹(wadiare* f. *wadium* GAGE¹)]

engagé (ahngah'zhā) *a.* (Of writer etc.) morally committed. [F, p.p. of *engager* (see prec.)]

ėngā'ged (ĭn-gā'jd) *a.* In vbl senses; under promise to marry; occupied by person, with business, etc.; (of telephone line) unavailable because already in use (∼ **signal** etc., indicating this condition); = prec. [p.p. of ENGAGE]

ėngā'gement (ĭn-gā'jm-) *n.* action of engaging; state of being engaged; appointment made with another person; moral commitment; battle; ∼ **ring,** finger--ring given by man to woman when they promise to marry. [F (*engager*; see ENGAGE)]

ėngā'ging (ĭn-g-) *a.* In vbl senses; attractive, charming; hence ∼LY² *adv.* [f. ENGAGE + -ING²]

en garçon (ahn gär'sawn) *adv. & pred. a.* as a bachelor. [F]

ėngâr'land (ĭn-g-) *v.t.* put a garland on; wreathe *with* (flowers etc.). [f. EN-¹ + GARLAND]

ėngě'nder (ĭnj-) *v.t.* give rise to, bring about; (arch.) beget (lit. or fig.). [ME, f. OF *engendrer* f. L IN¹(*generare* GENERATE)]

ě'ngĭne (ě'nj-) *n.,* & *v.t.* **1.** *n.* mechanical contrivance consisting of several parts working together, esp. as source of power; =STEAM¹-*engine*, locomotive; FIRE¹--*engine.* **2.** (arch.) machine or instrument used in war; instrument, means. **3.** ∼-**driver** (of engine, esp. railway locomotive); ∼-**room,** room containing engines (esp. of ship); ∼-**turning,** engraving of symmetrical patterns on metals by machine. **4.** *v.t.* fit (ship etc.) with engine(s). [f. OF *engin* f. L *ingenium* talent, device (cf. INGENIOUS)]

ėngineer'¹ (ěnj-) *n.* **1.** one who designs and constructs military works; soldier trained for this purpose (ROYAL *Engineers*). **2.** (civil) ∼, one who designs or maintains works of public utility (roads, bridges, canals, gasworks, etc.). **3.** maker of engines. **4.** one who works in a branch of engineering (*chemical, electrical, mechanical, engineer*), esp. as qualified professional. **5.** one who has charge of engine; *engine*--*driver.* **6.** person with special skill in treatment of human problems (*human engineer*); skilful or artful contriver (*of* plan etc.). **7.** Hence ∼SHIP (1) *n.* [ME f. OF *engineor* f. med. L *ingeniator -oris* (*ingeniare* as ENGINE; see -OR); ending later assim. to -EER]

ėngineer'² (ěnj-) *v.* **1.** *v.i.* act as engineer. **2.** *v.t.* construct, manage, (bridge, work, etc.) as engineer; (colloq.) arrange, contrive, bring about, esp. artfully. [f. prec.]

ėngineer'ing (ěnj-) *n.* application of science for the control and use of power, esp. by means of machines; ∼ **science,** engineering as a field of study. [f. prec. + -ING¹]

ě'ngĭnery (ě'njĭnrĭ) *n.* engines; machinery (lit. or fig.). [f. ENGINE + -RY]

ėngĭr'd(le) (ĭn-g-) *vbs. t.* surround (as) with girdle. [f. EN-¹ | GIRD¹, GIRDLE¹]

E'nglander (ĭ'ngg-) *n.* Little ∼, (Hist.) one opposed to British imperial policy. [f. *England* | -ER¹]

E'nglish¹ (ĭ'ngg-) *a. & n.* **1.** *a.* of England; ∼**man,** ∼**woman,** one who is English by birth, descent, or naturalization; EARLY *English.* **2.** of, written or spoken in, the English language. **3.** *n.* the language of England (now used in UK, US and in most Commonwealth countries, and often internationally); **the King's, Queen's,** ∼, the English language as correctly written or spoken; **Middle** ∼ (*c.* 1150-1500); **Old** ∼ (before about 1150); **in plain** ∼, in plain words. **4.** *(Bill.)* = SIDE¹ 12; the ∼, (*pl.*) people of England. **5.** *English* BOND¹ 5, FLUTE; ∼ **horn,** cor anglais; *English* MUSTARD. [OE *englisc, ænglisc* (as ANGLE⁴, -ISH¹)]

english² (ĭ'ngg-) *v.t.* (arch. or pedantic) render into English. [ME, f. prec.]

ėngor'ge (ĭn-g-) *v.t.* devour greedily; (in *pass.*) be crammed, (Path.) be congested with blood; hence, ∼MENT (-jm-) *n.* [f. F EN¹(*gorger* GORGE²)]

ėngra'ft, ėngra'ft, (ĭn-grah'-) *v.t.* insert (scion of one tree *into, upon,* another); implant (principles etc. *in* the mind etc.); incorporate (thing *into* another). [f. EN-¹, IN-¹ + GRAFT¹]

ėngrai'l (ĭn-g-) *v.t.* indent the edge of, give serrated appearance to, (esp. Her.). [ME, f. OF EN¹(*gresler* f. *gresle* HAIL¹)]

ėngrai'n (ĭn-g-) *v.t.* (usu. fig.) cause (dye etc.) to sink deeply into a thing; (in *p.p.*; cf. INGRAINED) inveterate (*an engrained rogue*). [ME, f. OF *engrainer* dye in grain (*en graine*); see GRAIN 4]

ě'ngrăm (ě'n-g-) *n.* memory-trace, supposed permanent change in brain accounting for existence of memory; hence ∼**ma**′tic *a*. [f. G *engramm* f. Gk *en* in + *gramma* letter of alphabet]

en grande tenue (ahṅ grahṅd tenū′) *adv*. in full dress. [F]

engra′v|**e** (ĭn-g-) *v.t.* inscribe, ornament, (hard surface *with* incised marks); carve (figures etc. *on* surface); (fig.) impress deeply (*on* memory etc.); cut (figures etc.) as lines on metal plate for printing; hence ∼**er**[1] *n*. [f. **en**-[1] + **grave**[2]]

engra′ving (ĭn-g-) *n*. In vbl senses; copy of picture etc. from engraved plate. [f. prec. + -**ing**[1]]

engrō′ss (ĭn-g-) *v.t.* **1.** write (document) in large letters; express in legal form. **2.** (arch.) monopolize (conversation etc.). **3.** fully occupy (person, his attention, time, etc.; esp. in *p.p.*, *engrossed in subject* etc.); hence ∼**ing**[2] *a*. **4.** Hence ∼**ment** *n*. [ME, f. AF *engrosser*; l f. *en* in, *grosse* large writing; 2, 3 f. *en gros* wholesale]

engŭ′lf (ĭn-g-) *v.t.* plunge into, swallow up (as) in, a gulf; hence ∼**ment** *n*. [f. **en**-[1] + **gulf**]

enha′nce (-hah′-) *v.t.* heighten, intensify, (qualities, powers, value, etc.); (arch.) exaggerate; hence ∼**ment** (-sm-) *n*. [ME, f. AF *enhauncer*, prob. alt. f. OF *enhaucier* f. Rom. **in*[1](*altiare* f. L *altus* high)]

enharmŏ′n|**ic** *a*. (Mus.) of or having intervals smaller than semitone (esp. such intervals as that between G sharp and A flat, these notes being made the same in a scale of equal temperament); hence ∼**ically** *adv*. [f. LL f. Gk **en**[2]*armonikos* (*harmonia* **harmony**; see -**ic**)]

eni′gma *n*. riddle; puzzling person or thing; hence or cogn. **enigmă′tic**(**al**) *adjs*., ∼**tize** (3) *v.t.* [f. L f. Gk *ainigma -matos* f. *ainissomai* speak allusively (*ainos* fable)]

eni′sle (-ī′l) *v.t.* (literary). make into or place on island. [f. **en**-[1] + **isle**]

enjă′mbment, -bem-, (-m-m-) *n*. (Pros.) continuation of sentence without pause beyond end of line, couplet, or stanza. [f. F *enjambement* f. **en**[1](*jamber* f. *jambe* leg; see -**ment**]

enjoi′n *v.t.* prescribe, impose, (action, conduct, *on* person); command (person *to* do); issue instructions (*that*); (Law) prohibit by injunction (*from* doing). [ME, f. OF *enjoindre* (st. -*joi*(*g*)*n*-) f. L **in**[1](*jungere* join)]

enjoy′ *v.t.* take delight or pleasure in, whence ∼**able** *a*., ∼**ably** *adv*.; have use of (advantages etc.); (arch.) copulate with (woman); experience (*enjoy poor health*); ∼ one**self**, experience pleasure; hence ∼**ment** *n*. [ME, f. OF **en**[1](*joier* f. *joie* **joy**[1]) give joy to, (refl.) enjoy, or f. OF **en**[1](*joïr* f. L *gaudēre* rejoice)]

enki′ndle (ĭn-k-) *v.t.* cause (flame, passions, war, etc.) to blaze up; inflame with passion. [f. **en**-[1] + **kindle**]

enlā′ce *v.t.* encircle tightly; enfold; entwine; hence ∼**ment** (-sm-) *n*. [ME, f. OF *enlacier* f. Rom. **in*[1]-(*laciare* f. **lacium* f. L *laqueus* noose)]

enlâr′ge *v*. **1.** *v.t.* make larger or wider (lit. or fig.); (Photog.) reproduce on larger scale; (arch.) liberate; hence ∼**able** (-ja-) *a*. **2.** *v.i.* grow larger; expatiate *upon*. **3.** Hence ∼**ment** (-jm-) *n*., (esp.) photographic reproduction on larger scale, **enlâr′ger**[1] *n*., apparatus for enlarging or reducing photographic negatives or positives. [ME, f. OF **en**[1](*larger* f. *large* **large**)]

enli′ghten (-ī′t-) *v.t.* instruct, inform, (person *on* subject); (rhet. or poet.) shed light on (object), give light to (person); (esp. in *p.p.*) free (person) from prejudice or superstition; hence ∼**ment** *n*. (**the** E∼**ment**, 18th-c. philosophy allegedly placing too much emphasis on reason and individualism against tradition). [ME, f. **en**-[1] + **lighten**[2]]

enli′st *v*. **1.** *v.t.* & *i.* engage for military service (*∼**ed man**, soldier or sailor below rank of officer). **2.** *v.t.* secure as means of help or support. **3.** Hence ∼**ment** *n*. [f. **en**-[1] + **list**[1]]

enli′ven *v.t.* animate, inspirit, (persons, feelings, trade, etc.); brighten (picture, scene); hence ∼**ment** *n*. [f. **en**-[1] + **life** + -**en**[6]]

en masse (ahṅ mă′s) *adv*. in a mass; all together. [F]

enmě′sh *v.t.* entangle (as) in a net; hence ∼**ment** *n*. [f. **en**-[1] + **mesh**[1]]

e′nmĭty *n*. hatred; state of being an enemy. [ME, f. OF *enemi*(*s*)*tié* f. Rom. *inimicitas-tatis (as **enemy**; see -**ty**[1])]

e′nneăd *n*. group of nine. [f. Gk *enneas enneados* (*ennea* nine; see -**ad**)]

ennō′ble *v.t.* make (person) a noble; make noble, elevate; hence ∼**ment** (-belm-) *n*. [f. F **en**[1](*noblir*, as **noble**)]

ennui (ŏ′nwē) *n*. mental weariness from lack of occupation or interest; so **ennuyé** (ŏnwē′yä; *fem. -ée*, *pl. -és, -ées, pr.* same) *a*. [F, f. L *in odio*; cf. **odium**]

*ēnō′logў. See **oenology**.

enŏr′mĭty *n*. monstrous wickedness; dreadful crime; serious error; (**D**) enormousness. [ME, f. F *énormité* f. L *enormitas -tatis* (*enormis*; see foll., -**ity**)]

enŏr′mous *a*. very large, huge, (*enormous animal, difference*); hence ∼**ly** [2] *adv*., ∼**ness** *n*. [f. L **e**(*normis* f. *norma* pattern, standard) + -**ous**]

ēnō′sis *n*. proposed political union of Cyprus and Greece. [f. mod. Gk *henōsis* (*heis hen-* one)]

enou′gh (ĭnŭ′f) *a., n., & adv*. not less than the required number, quantity, degree, as: (a.) *we have apples enough, enough apples, beer enough, enough beer, he made enough noise* (to justify supposition etc.), *enough noise to wake the dead, for his purpose;* (n.) *we have enough of everything except beer, enough of* (stop) *this folly, enough!* (say no more), *enough* said (no more need be said), *enough is as good as a feast, cry 'enough'* (acknowledge defeat), *I have had enough* (am tired) *of him, I had enough to do* (no easy task) *to catch the train, you have done more than enough or enough and to spare;* (pred. a. or n.) *five men are enough, five metres is not enough;* (adv.) *it is boiled* (just) *enough, he does not advertise enough, are you warm enough? he is willing enough* (but incapable), *she sings well enough* (tolerably well but not excellently), *you know well enough* (very well) *what I mean;* **oddly** etc. ∼ (to justify the term *oddly* etc.); **sure** ∼, undeniably, as was (or might have been) expected. [OE *genog*, = OS *ginōg*, OHG *ginuog*, ON *gnógr*, Goth. *ganōhs* f. Gmc *ganŏgaz]

enou′nce *v.t.* enunciate; pronounce (words); hence ∼**ment** (-sm-) *n*. [f. F *énoncer* (as **enunciate**), after *announce, pronounce*]

enow′. Var. (poet.) of **enough** *a*. & *adv*.

en pantoufles (ahṅ pahṅtōō′fl) *adv*. in a free and easy manner; in relaxed atmosphere. [F, lit. 'in slippers']

en passant (ahṅ pă′sahṅ) *adv*. by the way; **take** ∼ (Chess) take (opponent's pawn that advances two squares at once) with one's own pawn that could have taken it if it had advanced only one. [F, = in passing]

en pension. See **pension** 2.

enplā′ne. Var. of **emplane**.

en plein (ahṅ plă′ṅ) *a*. (Of gambling bet) placed wholly on one number etc. [F, = in full]

en poste (ahṅ pŏ′st) *a*. (Of diplomat) occupying official position (at specified place). [F]

en prise (ahṅ prē′z) *a*. (Chess) in a position to be taken. [F]

||**enquire, enquiry.** See **inquire, inquiry**.

enrā′ge *v.t.* make furious (*enraged at, by, with*). [f. **en**[1](*rager* f. as **rage**[1])]

en rapport (ahṅ răpōr′) *adv*. in harmony or rapport (*with*). [F; see **rapport**]

enrā′pture *v.t.* delight intensely. [f. **en**-[1] + **rapture**]

en règle (ahṅ rä′gl) *adv*. in due form. [F, = in rule]

enri′ch *v.t.* make rich; add to contents of (collection, museum, book); make richer in quality, flavour, nutritive value, etc.; increase content of an isotope in (material); hence ∼**ment** *n*. [ME, f. OF **en**[1](*richir* f. *riche* **rich**)]

enrō′be *v.t.* put a robe on. [f. **en**-[1] + **robe**]

enrō′l, *-ll, *v*. (-**ll**-). **1.** *v.t.* write name of (person or list, esp. of army); incorporate (person) as member (*in* society etc.); (Hist.) enter (deed etc.) among rolls of court of justice; record, celebrate. **2.** *v.i.* enter one′ name on list etc. **3.** Hence **enrō′lment, *-ll-,** *n*. (esp.

*number of students in a school etc.). [ME, f. OF EN¹(*roller* f. *rolle* ROLL¹)]

en route (ahṅ rōō't) *adv.* on the way (*to, for*, place etc., or abs.). [F]

ens (-z) *n.* (*pl.* **entia** *pr.* ĕ'nshĭa). entity (esp. as abstract notion). [LL *ens ent-* part. of *esse* be (after *absens*), transl. Gk *on* being]

ensa'mple (-ah'-) *n.* (arch.) example. [ME, f. AF *ensa*(*u*)*mple*, OF *essemple* f. L (as EXAMPLE)]

ensa'nguined (-nggwĭnd) *a.* (literary). bloodstained, bloody, (lit. or fig.). [f. EN-¹ + L *sanguis -inis* blood + -ED¹]

enscŏ'nce *v.t.* establish (one*self* etc. in secret, safe, snug, etc., place). [f. EN-¹ + SCONCE³]

en secondes noces (ahṅ zegawṅd nŏ's) *adv.* by a second marriage. [F]

ensemble (ahṅsah'ṅbl) *n.* **1.** (*or* TOUT ENSEMBLE). thing viewed as a whole; general effect. **2.** (Mus.) concerted passage in which all performers unite (**good** ~, accurate and balanced performance of such passage); group of musicians performing thus. **3.** group of subsidiary dancers in ballet, musical comedy, etc. **4.** (Math.) group of systems with same constitution but possibly in different states. **5.** woman's outfit of harmonizing items. [F, f. Rom. *insemul* f. L *insimul* (*in* IN-¹, *simul* at same time)]

enshri'ne *v.t.* enclose (relic etc.) in shrine; serve as shrine for (precious thing; lit. or fig.); hence ~MENT (-nm-) *n.* [f. EN-¹ + SHRINE]

enshrou'd *v.t.* cover completely, hide from view. [f. EN-¹ + SHROUD]

e'nsiform *a.* sword-shaped; = XIPHOID. [f. L *ensis* sword + -FORM]

e'nsign (-īn, -in) *n.* **1.** banner, flag, (esp. Naut.); ||flag with union in corner (**blue** ~ of government departments and formerly of naval reserve etc., **red** ~ of merchant service, **white** ~ of Royal Navy and Royal Yacht Squadron). **2.** standard-bearer; *lowest commissioned officer in navy; (Hist.) lowest commissioned infantry officer, whence ~CY *n.* **3.** (arch.) badge (of office etc.). [ME, f. OF *enseigne* f. L INSIGNIA]

e'nsilage *n.*, & *v.t.* **1.** *n.* preservation of green fodder in silo or pit without drying; fodder thus preserved. **2.** *v.t.* treat (fodder) by ensilage. [F (as foll.; see -AGE)]

ensi'le *v.t.* put (fodder) into silo; preserve (fodder) in silo. [f. F *ensiler* f. Sp. *ensilar* (as EN-¹, SILO)]

ensla've *v.t.* make (person etc.) a slave (lit., or fig. *to* habit, superstition, etc.), hence ~MENT (-vm-) *n.* [f. EN-¹ + SLAVE]

ensnar'e *v.t.* entrap (lit. or fig.). [f. EN-¹ + SNARE]

ensou'l (-sŏ'l) *v.t.* infuse a soul into. [f. EN-¹ + SOUL]

enspher'e *v.t.* (literary). encircle or enclose (as) in a sphere [f. EN-¹ + SPHERE]

ensue *v.* **1.** *v.i.* happen afterwards; result (*from, on*). **2.** *v.t.* (arch.) seek after. [ME, f. OF *ensuivre* f. Rom. *IN¹(*sequere* = L *sequi* follow)]

en suite (ahṅ swē't) *adv.* forming a single unit (*bedroom with bathroom en suite*. [F, = in sequence]

ensur'e (-shoor') *v.t.* make (person, thing) safe (*against* risks); make certain (thing, *that*); secure (thing *to, for*, person etc.). [ME, f. AF EN¹*seürer* f. OF *aseürer* ASSURE]

enswa'the (-dh) *v.t.* bind or wrap in bandage (lit. or fig.); hence ~MENT (-dhm-) *n.* [f. EN-¹ + SWATHE²]

-ent *suf.* forming *adjs.* denoting existence of action or state (*consequent, effluent*), and *ns.* denoting agent (*coefficient, president*), usu. f. *vbs.* (cf. -ANT)] [= or after F *-ent* or f. L *-ent-* pres. part. st. of *vbs.* (cf. -ANT)]

ENT *abbr.* ear, nose, and throat.

enta'blature *n.* (Archit.) the part of an order above the column, including architrave, frieze, and cornice. [f. It. *intavolatura* f. IN¹(*tavolare* f. *tavola* table) board up; see -URE]

enta'blement (-belm-) *n.* horizontal platform(s) supporting statue, above dado and base. [F, f. EN¹(*tabler* f. TABLE); see -MENT]

entai'l¹ *n.* settlement of succession of landed estate so that it cannot be bequeathed at pleasure or sold;

estate so secured; (fig.) inalienable inheritance (of qualities, beliefs, etc.). [ME, f. foll.]

entai'l² *v.t.* **1.** settle (land etc.) by entail; bestow (thing) as inalienable possession (*on* person). **2.** impose (expense, labour, *on* person); necessitate. **3.** Hence ~MENT *n.* [ME, f. EN-¹ + AF *taile* TAIL²]

enta'ngle (-nggel) *v.t.* catch in snare or among obstacles; involve (person etc.) in difficulties or illicit activities; make (thing) tangled or intricate (lit. or fig.). [f. EN-¹ + TANGLE¹]

enta'nglement (-nggelm-) *n.* In vbl senses; compromising (esp. amorous) relationship; thing that entangles, (Mil.) extensive barrier erected to obstruct enemy's movements (esp. one made of stakes and interlaced barbed wire). [f. prec. + -MENT]

e'ntasis *n.* (Archit.) slight convexity of column shaft (introduced to correct visual illusion of concavity). [mod. L f. Gk (*enteinō* to stretch)]

ente'lechy (-kĭ) *n.* (Philos.) realization, the becoming or being actual of what was potential. [f. LL f. Gk *entelekheia* (*en telei ekhō* be in perfection; see -Y¹)]

ente'llus *n.* = HANUMAN. [name of person in Virgil's *Aeneid*]

ente'nte (ahṅtah'ṅt) *n.* friendly understanding, esp. between States; group of States in such relation; ~ **cordiale**, = entente, esp. of Britain and France 1904, or of these with Russia 1908. [F, = understanding (as INTENT¹)]

e'nter *v.* **1.** *v.i.* go or come in (*into* place, room, etc., or abs.); (3rd pers. subjunctive as stage direction) come on stage (*Enter Macbeth*); announce oneself as competitor in race etc. **2.** ~ **into**, engage in (conversation, relations, agreement, inquiry, etc.), sympathize with (person's feelings etc.), form part of (calculations, plans, etc.), bind oneself by (recognizances, treaty, contract). **3.** ~ (**up**)**on**, assume possession of (property) or functions of (office), begin (process etc.), begin to deal with (subject). **4.** *v.t.* go or come into (place etc.); penetrate (flesh etc.); become member of (a society, army, church, etc.); admit, procure admission for, (pupil, person as member of a society); ~ (**up**), write (name, details etc.) in list, book, etc.; record in due form before court of law or in minutes of debate etc.; make known (a protest etc.); record name of (person etc.) as competitor *for* (contest, race, etc.); ~ **up**, complete series of entries in (account-books etc.); hence ~ABLE *a.* [ME, f. OF *entrer* f. L *intrare* (*intra* within)]

ente'ric *a.* & *n.* of the intestines; ~ (**fever**), typhoid; so **enteri'tis** *n.* [f. Gk *enterikos* (as foll.; see -IC)]

e'ntero- *comb. form.* intestine, as: ~**stomy** (-ŏ'3-), making of permanent opening in intestine; ~**tomy** (-ŏ't-), cutting open the intestine; ~**vir'us**, virus infecting intestine and sometimes other organs. [f. Gk *enteron* intestine + -o-]

e'nterprise (-z) *n.* undertaking, esp. bold or difficult one, (FREE¹ *enterprise*, PRIVATE *enterprise*); business firm; courage, readiness, to engage in enterprises (*he has no enterprise*). [ME, f. OF *entreprise* fem. p.p. (as *n.*) of *entreprendre* var. of *emprendre* f. L IM¹(*pre*(*he*)*ndere* take)]

e'nterprising (-z-) *a.* ready to engage in enterprises; showing courage or imaginativeness; hence ~LY² *adv.* [part. of arch. v. *enterprise* (f. prec.)]

entertai'n *v.t.* amuse, occupy agreeably, (person etc.; often iron.), whence ~ING² *a.*; receive with hospitality (guest, or abs.; *entertained me at* or ||*to lunch; they entertain a great deal*); harbour, cherish, welcome or consider, (idea, feeling, proposal). [ME, f. F *entretenir* f. Rom. *INTER-* (*tenēre* hold)]

entertai'ner *n.* In vbl senses; professional provider of amusement. [f. prec. + -ER¹]

entertai'nment *n.* In vbl senses; hospitality; amusement (*much to my entertainment*); diversions or amusements for guests etc.; public performance or show. [f. ENTERTAIN + -MENT]

enthalpy (ĕ'-, -ă'-) *n.* (Phys.) total heat content of a system. [f. Gk EN²(*thalpō* make hot); see -Y¹]

ènthra'l, *-ll, (-aw'l) *v.t.* (-ll-). enslave (usu. fig.); please greatly; hence **ènthra'lMENT, *-ll-,** (-aw'l-) *n.* [f. EN-¹ + THRALL]

ènthrŏ'ne *v.t.* place (king, bishop, etc.) on throne, esp. with ceremony; exalt; hence ∼MENT (-nm-) *n.* [f. EN-¹ + THRONE]

ènthrŏnīzā'tion, in-, -īs- (-z-), *n.* enthronement (lit. or fig.). [f. obs. *enthronize* f. OF *introniser* f. LL *inthronizare* f. Gk EN²(*thronizō* as THRONE; see -IZE) + -ATION]

ènthu'se (-ū'z, -ōō'z) *v.i.* & *t.* (colloq.) show, or fill with, enthusiasm. [back-form. f. foll.]

ènthu'sĭăsm (-ū'z-, -ōō'z-) *n.* strong interest or admiration (*for, about,* a person, purpose, cause, etc.); great eagerness; object of enthusiasm; (arch.) extravagant religious emotion. [f. F *enthousiasme* or f. LL f. Gk *enthousiasmos* (*enthousiazō* f. EN²(*theos* god) possessed by a god, inspired)]

ènthu'sĭăst (-ū'z-, -ōō'z-) *n.* one who is full of enthusiasm (*for* cause etc.); visionary, self-deluded person; hence ∼IC (-ă'-) *a.* [f. F *enthousiaste* or f. eccl. L f. Gk *enthousiastēs* (as prec.)]

ĕ'nthȳmēme *n.* (Logic). syllogism in which one premiss is not explicitly stated. [f. L f. Gk *enthumēma* f. EN²(*thumeomai* f. *thumos* mind) consider]

entia. See ENS.

ènti'ce *v.t.* persuade by offer of pleasure etc. (person etc. *from* place, course of action, etc., *into* another; *to* do); so ∼MENT (-sm-) *n.* [ME, f. OF *enticier* prob. f. Rom. *IN¹(*titiare* f. *titius firebrand)]

èntī're *a.* & *n.* **1.** *a.* whole, complete; not broken or decayed; not castrated; unqualified (*an entire delusion, success*); all in one piece, continuous; (Bot.) without indentation; pure, unmixed; hence ∼NESS (-īr'n-) *n.* **2.** *n.* uncastrated animal; ||(arch.) kind of mixed beer. [ME, f. AF *enter,* OF *entier* f. Rom. *integro f. L IN²(*teger* f. **tag-, tangere* touch)]

ènti̇̄r'elÿ (-īr'lĭ) *adv.* wholly (*stock is entirely exhausted*); solely (*did it entirely for my benefit*). [f. prec. + -LY²]

ènti̇̄r'etÿ (-īr'tĭ, -īr'etĭ) *n.* completeness (**in its** ∼, in its complete form); sum total (*of*). [ME, f. OF *entiereté* f. L *integritas -tatis* f. *integer* (see ENTIRE, -TY¹)]

ènti̇̄'tle *v.t.* give (book etc.) the title of (*War and Peace* etc.); (arch.) give (person) the title of (sultan etc.); (of circumstances, qualities, ticket, etc.) give (person etc.) a rightful claim (*to* a thing, *to* do); hence ∼MENT (-telm-) *n.* [ME, f. AF *entitler,* OF *entiteler* f. LL IN¹(*titulare* f. *titulus* TITLE)]

ĕ'ntitÿ *n.* thing's existence, as opp. to its qualities or relations; thing that has real existence; so **ĕ'ntitATIVE** *a.* [f. F *entité* or f. med. L *entitas,* f. LL ENS; see -ITY]

ĕ'ntŏ- *comb. form.* within, as: ∼**pa'rasite,** = ENDO-*parasite;* ∼**phyte,** plant growing inside a plant or animal. [f. Gk *entos* within + -o-]

ènto'mb (-ōō'm) *v.t.* place in tomb (lit. or fig.); serve as tomb for, hence ∼MENT (-m-m-) *n.* [f. OF EN¹(*tomber* f. *tombe* TOMB)]

èntŏ'mic *a.* of insects. [f. as foll. + -IC]

èntŏmo- *comb. form.* insect, as: ∼**phagous** (-ŏ'f-), insect-eating; ∼**philous** (-ŏ'f-), (Bot.) pollinated by insects. [f. Gk EN²(*tomos* f. *temnō* cut) cut up, in neut. = INSECT]

èntŏmŏ'log|ÿ *n.* study of insects; hence **èntomoLO'G-ICAL** *a.,* ∼IST (3) *n.,* ∼IZE (2) *v.i.* [f. F *entomologie* or mod. L *entomologia* (as prec.; see -LOGY)]

entourage (ŏntoorah'zh) *n.* surroundings; attendant persons. [F (*entourer* surround; see -AGE)]

en-tout-cas (ahǹtōōkah') *n.* (*pl.* same). umbrella--sunshade; (*En-Tout-Cas,* **P**) all-weather hard lawn--tennis court. [F, = in any case]

entr'acte (ŏ'ntrăkt) *n.* (performance in) interval between acts of play. [F (*entre* between, *acte* act)]

ĕ'ntrails (-z) *n. pl.* bowels, intestines; (fig.) inner parts (*of* the earth etc.). [ME, f. OF *entrailles* f. med. L *intralia* alt. f. L *interanea* neut. pl. of *interaneus* internal (*inter* among)]

èntrai'n¹ *v.t.* drag along; (of fluid) carry (particles

etc.) along in its flow, whence ∼MENT *n.* [f. F EN¹(*traîner* drag f. as TRAIN)]

èntrai'n² *v.t.* & *i.* put (esp. troops) or get into a train. [f. EN-¹ + TRAIN 12]

entrain³ (ahǹtră'n) *n.* enthusiasm, animation. [F]

èntră'mmel *v.t.* (||-ll-). entangle, hamper. [f. EN-¹ + TRAMMEL]

ĕ'ntrance¹ *n.* going or coming in; coming of actor on stage; entering *into* or *upon* (office etc.); right of admission; ∼ (**fee**), fee paid for admission to society, club, exhibition, etc.; door, passage, etc., one enters by. [OF (as ENTER, -ANCE)]

èntra'nc|e|² (-ah'-) *v.t.* throw into a trance; overwhelm (*with* joy, fear); carry away as in trance, whence ∼ING² *a.,* (esp.) delightful; hence ∼eMENT (-sm-) *n.* [f. EN-¹ + TRANCE]

ĕ'ntrant *n.* one who enters room, profession, etc., or *for* race etc. [F, part. of *entrer* (see ENTER, -ANT)]

èntră'p *v.t.* (-pp-). catch (as) in trap; beguile (person *to* destruction etc., *into* doing); hence ∼MENT *n.* [f. OF EN¹(*traper* f. *trappe* TRAP¹)]

èntrea't *v.t.* ask (person) earnestly (*to* do, *that*); ask earnestly for; (arch.) treat, act towards, (person). [ME, f. OF EN¹(*traitier* TREAT)]

èntrea'tÿ *n.* earnest request. [f. prec., after *treaty*]

entrechat (ŏ'ntreshah) *n.* dancer's leap with one or more crossings of legs while in air. [F, f. It. (*capriola*) *intrecciata* complicated (caper)]

e'ntrecôte (ŏ'ntrekŏt) *n.* boned steak cut off sirloin. [F (*entre* between, *côte* rib)]

entrée (ŏ'ntrā, ahǹtrā) *n.* right or privilege of admission, esp. at Court; ||dish served between fish and meat courses; *main dish of meal. [F, = ENTRY]

entremets (ŏ'ntremă) *n.* side dish; sweet dish. [F (*entre* between, *mets* dish)]

èntrĕ'nch, intrĕ'nch, *v.* **1.** *v.t.* surround (post, army, town) with trench as fortification; establish firmly in defensible position; apply extra safeguards to (rights etc. guaranteed by legislation); ∼ one**self,** adopt well-defended position (lit. or fig.). **2.** *v.i.* entrench oneself; encroach, trespass, *upon.* **3.** Hence ∼MENT *n.* [f. EN-¹, IN-¹ + TRENCH]

entre nous (ŏntre nōō') *adv.* between you and me; in private. [F, = between ourselves]

entrepôt (ŏ'ntrepō) *n.* storehouse for deposit; commercial centre for import and export, and collection and distribution. [F, f. *entreposer* store (*entre-* INTER-*poser* place)]

entrepreneur (ŏntreprenĕr') *n.* person in effective control of commercial undertaking; one who undertakes a business or enterprise, with chance of profit or loss; contractor acting as intermediary; hence ∼IAL (-ĕr'-, -ūr'-) *a.,* ∼SHIP *n.* [F (*entreprendre* undertake; see ENTERPRISE)]

entresol (ŏ'ntresŏl) *n.* low storey between first and ground floor. [F (*entre* between, *sol* ground)]

ĕ'ntropÿ *n.* **1.** (Phys.) measure of the unavailability of a system's thermal energy for conversion into mechanical work; measure of the degradation or disorganization of the universe. **2.** (Math.) measure of the rate of transfer of information in a message etc. [f. G *entropie* as EN-² + Gk *tropē* transformation; see -Y¹]

èntrŭ'st, intrŭ'st, *v.t.* give responsibility for (duty person, thing, its safety) *to* (person in whom one has confidence); ∼ (such person) **with,** make him responsible for (duty, object of care). [f. EN-¹, IN-¹ + TRUST]

ĕ'ntrÿ *n.* **1.** going or coming in; liberty to do this (∼ **permit,** etc., authorization to enter a particular country); ceremonial entrance; (Law) taking possession; coming of actor on stage; place of entrance, door, gate, lobby, mouth of river; passage between buildings; start or resumption of performer's part in concerted music; (Bridge) (card providing) transfer of lead to partner's hand. **2.** registration in records, account-books, diary, etc.; item so entered; **double,** **single,** ∼ (in which each item is entered twice, once in ledger); list of competitors for race etc.; person or thing competing in race, contest, etc. [ME f. OF *entree* f. Rom. **intrata* fem. p.p. (as n.) of L *intrare* ENTER]

entwī′ne v.t. interweave (lit. or fig.); wreathe (thing, *with, about, round,* another); (arch.) embrace like twining plant. [f. EN-¹+TWINE]

entwī′st v.t. (arch.) clasp with or form into a twist; twist (thing) in *with* (another). [f. EN-¹+TWIST]

enū′clĕ|āte v.t. (Surg.) extract (tumour etc.) from shell, (eye) from socket, etc.; (arch.) explain; hence ~A′TION n. [f. L E(*nucleare* f. NUCLEUS kernel) +-ATE³]

enū′mer|āte v.t. count; specify, mention one by one, (items); hence or cogn. ~ABLE a., ~A′TION n., ~ātor n. (esp. person employed in census-taking), ~ATIVE a. [f. L E(*numerare* NUMBER²) +-ATE³]

enū′nci|āte v.t. express (proposition, theory) in definite terms; proclaim; pronounce (words); hence or cogn. ~A′TION n., ~ātOR, ns., ~ATIVE (-sĭa-, -sha-) a. [f. L E(*nuntiare* announce f. *nuntius* messenger) +-ATE³]

enūr′e v.i. = INURE 2. [var. of INURE]

enūr|ē′sis n. (Path.) involuntary urination; hence ~E′TIC a. & n. [mod. L, f. Gk *enoureō* urinate in (as EN-², *ouron* urine)]

envĕ′lop v.t. wrap up (person, thing, subject, etc., *in* garment, flames, clouds, mystery); (of garment etc.) cover closely on all sides; (Mil.) effect the surrounding of (enemy); hence ~MENT n. [ME, f. OF *envoluper* (as EN-¹; cf. DEVELOP)]

e′nvelōpe (ĕ′-, ŏ′-) n. wrapper, covering, (lit. or fig.); folded and usu. gummed cover for letter; gas container of balloon or airship; outer vessel of vacuum-tube; (Electr.) curve joining successive peaks of modulated wave; (Bot.) calyx or corolla or both; (Math.) line or curve tangent to each line or curve of a given family. [f. F *enveloppe* (as prec.)]

envĕ′nom v.t. put poison on or into (weapon, air, etc.); infuse venom or bitterness into (feelings, words, actions). [ME, f. OF EN-¹- (*venimer* f. *venim* VENOM)]

′nviab|le a. such as to excite envy (of desirable thing or its possessor); hence ~LY² adv. [f. ENVY²+-ABLE]

′nvious a. full of envy; feeling envy of (person, thing); hence ~LY² adv. [ME f. AF; OF *envieus* (*envie* ENVY¹; see -OUS)]

envī′r′on v.t. (Of persons or things) form a ring, be stationed, round; surround (person, place, etc.) hostilely, protectively, etc.; surround (person or thing *with* others). [ME, f. OF *environer* (*environ* surroundings; see ENVIRONS)]

envī′r′onment n. surrounding; surrounding objects, region, or conditions, esp. circumstances of life of person or society, whence ~AL (-mĕ′n-) a. [f. prec. +-MENT]

nvī′r′onmĕ′ntalist n. one who is concerned with protection of the environment; one who considers that environment has primary influence on person's or group's development. [f. ENVIRONMENTAL+-IST]

environs (invīr′onz, ĕ′nvironz) n. pl. district surrounding (*of*) town etc. [F, f. OF *environ* n. f. adv. (*en* in, *viron* circuit, neighbourhood, f. *virer* turn, VEER²)]

envi′sage (-z-) v.t. **1.** contemplate, esp. under particular aspect; imagine (thing or conditions not yet existing). **2.** (arch.) look in the face of; face (danger, etc.). Hence ~MENT (-jm-) n. [f. F EN¹(*visager* f. as VISAGE)]

envi′sion (-zhon) v.t. = prec. 1. [f. EN-¹+VISION]

e′nvoy¹, ĕ′nvoi, n. short stanza concluding ballade etc.; (arch.) author's concluding words etc. [ME, f. OF *envoi* f. *envoyer* send (*en voie* on the way f. L *via*)]

′nvoy² n. messenger, representative, esp. on diplomatic mission; ~ (**extraordinary**), minister plenipotentiary, ranking below ambassador and above chargé d'affaires; hence ~SHIP n. [f. F *envoyé* p.p. (as prec.)]

′nvy̆¹ n. resentful or admiring contemplation (*of* more fortunate person, *of, at,* his advantages, or abs.); object or ground of this (*his car is the envy of the neighbourhood*). [ME f. OF *envie* f. L *invidia* f. IN¹(*videre* see) envy]

ĕ′nvy² v.t. feel envy of (*I envy him, envy his impudence, envy him his impudence*). [ME, f. OF *envier* (*envie*; see prec.)]

ěnwea′ve. See INWEAVE.

ěnwī′nd v.t. (**enwou′nd**). (Of thing) wind itself or be wound round (another). [f. EN-¹+WIND³]

ěnwo′mb (-ōō′m) v.t. (arch.) enclose (as) in womb. [f. EN-¹+WOMB]

ěnwrā′p (īnr-) v.t. (-**pp**-). wrap, enfold, (*in;* lit. or fig.). [ME, f. EN-¹+WRAP]

ěnwrea′the (īnrē′dh) v.t. surround (as) with wreath. [f. EN-¹+WREATHE]

Enzĕ′d (ĕ-) n. (Austral. & NZ colloq.) New Zealand(er); hence ~dER¹ n., New Zealander. [pr. of *NZ*]

ěnzōō′tic a. & n. (disease) regularly affecting animals in a particular district or at a particular season (cf. ENDEMIC). [f. Gk *en* in+*zōion* animal+-IC]

e′nzym|e n. (Chem.) protein catalyst of a specific biochemical reaction; hence ~A′TIC, **ěnzy̆′m**IC, adjs., ~ŏ′LOGY n. [f. G *enzym* f. mod. Gk *enzumos* leavened f. Gk *en* in+*zumē* leaven)]

E′ocēne (ē′-) a. & n. (Geol.) (of) second lowest division of Tertiary period or system. [f. Gk *ēōs* dawn+*kainos* new]

***ĕ′ōllian.** See AEOLIAN.

ē′olith n. (Archaeol.) flint object found in Tertiary strata, possibly an early artefact. [f. Gk *ēōs* dawn+*lithos* stone]

ēoli′thic a. (Archaeol.) of the period preceding the palaeolithic age, possibly with earliest use of worked flint implements. [f. F *éolithique* (as prec.; see -IC)]

E′on. See AEON.

E′onism (ē′-) n. transvestism, esp. by a man. [f. C. d'*Éon,* Fr. adventurer d. 1810+-ISM]

ē′osin n. red fluorescent dyestuff used (esp.) as stain in microscopy; hence **ēosī′no**PHIL a. & n., (cell) readily stained by eosin. [f. Gk *ēōs* dawn+-IN]

-ēous suf. forming adjs. meaning 'of the nature of' (*ligneous* like wood, *vitreous* like glass). [f. or after L *-eus*+-OUS; cf -ACEOUS, -ANEOUS]

ep- *pref.* See EPI-.

EP *abbr.* electroplate; extended play (record).

e.p. *abbr.* (Chess) en passant.

Ep. *abbr.* Epistle.

ē′pǎct n. age of moon on 1 Jan. [f. F *épacte* f. LL f. Gk *epaktai* (*hēmerai*) intercalated (days) f. EP(*agō* bring) intercalate]

ē′parch (-k) n. governor or bishop of diocese in Orthodox Church; so ~Y¹ n., his diocese. [f. Gk EP(*arkhos* ruler)]

éparant (āpahtah′n) a. shockingly unconventional. [F, part. of *épater* (see foll.)]

épater les bourgeois (apahta la boor′zhwah) v.i. startle or shock those bound by conventional beliefs. [F, = flabbergast the ordinary citizens]

ěpaulĕtte, *ěpaulĕt, (ĕ′pawl-, ĕ′pŏl-, ĕpelĕ′t) n. ornamental shoulder piece of uniform or coat. [f. F *épaulette* dim. of *épaule* shoulder f. L SPATULA; see -ETTE]

épée (āpā′) n. sharp-pointed duelling-sword, used (blunted) in fencing; hence ~IST (3) n. [F, = sword, f. OF *espee* (see SPAY)]

ěpeirogĕ′nēsis, ěpeirŏ′gĕny̆ (ěpīr-) n. (Geol.) process of making continents. [f. Gk *ēpeiros* mainland+GENESIS, GENY]

ěpĕ′nthes|is n. (*pl.* ~es *pr.* -ēz) insertion of a letter or sound within a word, e.g. *b* in THIMBLE; so **ěpĕn-thě′t**IC a. [LL f. Gk (*epentithēmi* insert f. as EPI-+EN-²+*tithēmi* place)]

ěpĕr′gne (īpĕr′n) n. centre ornament (esp. in branched form) for dinner-table, holding flowers or fruit. [18th c.; orig. unkn.]

ěpěxěg|ē′sis n. (*pl.* ~eses *pr.* -ē′sēz) additional, addition of, words to make meaning clear (e.g. 'difficult *to do*'); hence ~ě′tic(AL) adjs. [Gk *epexēgēsis* (as EP-, EXEGESIS)]

Eph. *abbr.* Ephesians (NT).

ĕphē′be n. (Gk Ant.) young man of 18–20 undergoing military training. [f. L f. Gk *ephēbos* (as EPI-, *hēbē* early manhood)]

ĕphe′dra n. evergreen trailing shrub of genus *Ephedra*. [mod. L f. Gk *ephedra* sitting upon]

ĕ′phedrine (-ēn, -īn) n. alkaloid drug found in some ephedras, used to relieve asthma, hay fever, etc. [f. prec. +-INE⁵]

ĕphĕ′mera n. (pl. ∿s or ∿e). insect living only a day or a few days; insect of order Ephemeroptera, e.g. mayfly; short-lived thing; thing of short-lived usefulness. [mod. L, f. LL f. Gk *ephēmeros* lasting only a day (*epi* on, *hēmera* day)]

ĕphĕ′meral a. lasting only a day; (of insect, flower, etc.) lasting a day or a few days; short-lived, transitory; hence ∿ITY (-ă′l-) n. [f. Gk *ephēmeros* (see prec.) +-AL]

ĕphĕ′mer|is n. (pl. ∿ides pr. ĕfĭmĕ′rĭdēz). astronomical almanac or table of predicted positions. [L, f. Gk *ephēmeris* diary (as prec.)]

ĕphĕ′mer|on n. (pl. ∿ons or ∿a). = EPHEMERA. [f. as EPHEMERA]

ĕ′phod n. Jewish priestly vestment. [ME, f. Heb. *'ēp̄ōd̄*]

ĕ′phor n. (Gk Ant.) one of five magistrates controlling kings of Sparta; hence ∿ATE¹, ∿SHIP, ns. [f. Gk EP(*horos* f. *horaō* see) overseer]

ĕpi- pref. (usu. **ep-** bef. vowel or *h*) w. sense 'upon' (*epicycle*), 'above' (*epicotyl*), 'in addition' (*epiphenomenon*). [f. Gk *epi* prep.]

ĕ′piblăst n. (Biol.) outermost layer of gastrula etc.; ectoderm. [f. EPI-+-BLAST]

ĕ′pic a. & n. (poem) narrating continuously achievements of one or more heroes, e.g. the *Iliad*, *Paradise Lost*; (subject) fit for recital in an epic; (book, film, etc.) of heroic type or scale; **folk** ∿, **national** ∿, poem of any form, embodying nation's conception of its past history; hence ∿AL a., ∿ALLY adv. [f. L f. Gk *epikos* (as EPOS; see -IC)]

ĕ′picărp n. (Bot.) outermost layer of pericarp. [f. EPI-+Gk *karpos* fruit]

ĕpicĕ′di|um n. (pl. ∿a). funeral ode; hence ∿AN a. [L, f. Gk EPI(*kēdeion* f. *kēdos* care)]

ĕ′picēne a. & n. for or used by both sexes; (person) with characteristics of both sexes; (person) without sexual characteristics; effete, effeminate, (person); (Gram.) denoting either sex without change of gender. [ME, f. LL f. Gk EPI(*koinos* common)]

||ĕ′picĕntre (-ter), ***-ter**, n. point at which earthquake reaches earth's surface (also fig.). [f. Gk EPI(*kentros* a. f. as CENTRE¹)]

ĕpiclē′s|is n. (pl. ∿es pr. -ēz). (Eccl.) invocation of Holy Spirit to consecrate and transubstantiate Eucharistic elements. [f. Gk EPI(*klēsis* f. *kaleō* to call)]

ĕpicŏntinĕ′ntal a. (Of sea) over continental shelf. [f. EPI-+CONTINENTAL]

ĕpicŏ′tyl n. (Bot.) part of embryo or seedling above cotyledon(s). [f. EPI-+COTYLEDON]

ĕ′picūr|e n. person with refined tastes in food, literature, etc.; hence ∿ISM (2) n. [f. med. L *epicurus* one preferring sensual pleasures, appellative use of L f. Gk *Epikouros* Epicurus, Athenian philosopher d. 270 BC]

ĕpicūrē′an a. & n. **1.** (E∿). (follower) of Epicurus (cf. prec.), who taught that highest good was calmness of mind. **2.** (person) devoted to pleasure, esp. refined sensuous enjoyment. **3.** Hence ∿ISM (3) n. [f. F *épicurien* or f. L *epicureus* f. Gk *epikoureios* (as prec.; see -EAN)]

ĕ′picycle n. (Geom.) small circle moving round circumference of a larger one; hence **ĕpicy′cl**IC a. [ME f. OF, or f. LL f. Gk EPI(*kuklos* circle)]

ĕpicy′cloid n. (Math.) curve traced by point on circumference of circle rolling on exterior of another circle; hence ∿AL (-oi′d-) a. [f. prec.+-OID]

ĕpidei′ctic (-dī′-) a. meant for effect or display. [f. Gk EPI(*deiktikos* f. *deiknumi* show; see -IC)]

ĕpidĕ′mic a. & n. (disease, lit. or fig.) prevalent among community at special time (cf. ENDEMIC);

outbreak of this; hence ∿AL a., ∿ALLY adv. [f. F *épidémique* (*épidémie* f. LL f. Gk *epidēmia* prevalence of disease f. *epidēmios* a. f. as EPI-+ *dēmos* the people)]

ĕpidēmiŏ′logў n. science of epidemics. [f. Gk *epidēmio.* (see prec.) +-LOGY]

ĕpidĕr′m|is n. outer layer of skin of animals, cuticle; outer chitinous integument of shell; true skin of (esp young) plant below cuticle; hence ∿AL, ∿IC, ∿OID adjs. [LL f. Gk (as EPI-, DERMIS)]

ĕpidi′ascōpe n. optical projector giving images of both opaque and transparent objects. [f. EPI- + DIA-+-SCOPE]

ĕpidi′dўmis n. (Anat.) coil of efferent duct behind testis. [f. Gk EPI(*didumis* f. *didumoi* testicles)]

ĕpidūr′al a. (Anat.) on or affecting the dura mater. [f EPI-+DURA MATER +-AL]

ĕ′pifauna n. animals living on a marine deposit or on aquatic animal or plant. [Da. (as EPI-, FAUNA)]

ĕpigă′str|ium n. part of abdomen immediately over stomach; hence ∿IC a. [LL, f. Gk EPIgastrion neut adj. (*gastēr* belly)]

ĕpigē′al a. (Bot.) having cotyledon(s) above ground growing above ground. [f. Gk EPI(*geios* f. *gē* earth) +-AL]

ĕ′pigēne a. (Geol.) produced on surface of earth; (o crystal) chemically altered since its formation. [f. *épigène* f. Gk EPI(*genēs* born)]

ĕpiglŏ′tt|is n. erect cartilage at root of tongue depressed during swallowing to cover glottis; henc ∿AL, ∿IC, adjs. [Gk EPI(*glōttis* f. *glōtta* tongue)]

ĕ′pigŏne n. (pl. ∿s, or **epigoni** pr. ĕpī′gonī). one of later (and less distinguished) generation. [pl. f. *épigones* f. L f. Gk *epigonoi* those born afterwards (a EPI-, root of *gignomai* be born)]

ĕ′pigrăm n. short poem ending in witty turn o thought; pointed saying or mode of expression; s **ĕpigrammă′t**IC a., **ĕpigră′mmat**IST (3) n., **ĕpi gră′mmat**IZE (1, 2) v.t. & i. [f. F *épigramme* or f. L f Gk EPI(*gramma -atos*); cf. -GRAM]

ĕ′pigraph (-ahf) n. inscription on stone, statue, coin at head of chapter, etc.; hence **ĕpigră′ph**IC a **ĕpi′graph**IST (3), **ĕpī′graph**Y (1, 2), ns. [f. Gk EPI(*graphē* f. *graphō* write)]

ĕ′pil|āte v.t. remove hair from; hence ∿A′TION n. [f. *épiler*, after DEPILATE, +-ATE³]

ĕ′pilĕpsў n. nervous disorder in which patient suffer mild or severe convulsions with or without loss c consciousness. [f. F *épilepsie* or f. LL f. Gk *epilēpsia* EPI(*lambanō* take) attack]

ĕpilĕ′ptic a. & n. of epilepsy; (person) subject t epilepsy. [f. F *épileptique* f. LL f. Gk *epilēptikos* (as prec see -IC)]

ĕpili′mni|on n. (pl. ∿a). upper layer of water i stratified lake. [f. EPI- + Gk *limnion* dim. of *limnē* lake

ĕpi′logist n. writer or speaker of epilogue. [f. foll. -IST]

ĕ′pilŏgue (-g) n. concluding part, appendix, of literar work; speech or short poem addressed to spectator by actor at end of play (cf. PROLOGUE). [ME, f. *épilogue* f. L f. Gk EPI(*logos* speech)]

ĕ′pimer n. (Chem.) one of two isomers with differer configurations of atoms about one of several asyn metric carbon atoms present; hence **ĕpimĕ′r**IC a **ĕpi′mer**ISM (3) n., **ĕpi′mer**IZE (3) v.t., convert (or epimer) into the other. [Gk, f. as EPI-+-MER]

ĕpi′năstў n. (Bot.) tendency in plant-organs to gro more rapidly on upper side. [f. EPI- + Gk *nast* pressed +-Y¹]

ĕpinĕ′phrine n. (Chem.) = ADRENALIN. [f. Gk *e* upon +*nephros* kidney +-INE³]

ĕpi′phanў n. **1.** (E∿). manifestation of Christ to th Magi; festival of this (6 Jan.). **2.** manifestation of superhuman being. **3.** Hence **ĕpiphă′n**IC a. [M] sense 1 f. OF *epiphanie* f. eccl. L f. Gk *epiphania* neut. f adj. f. EPI(*phainō* show), sense 2 f. Gk *epiphane* manifestation (*epiphanēs* manifest)]

ĕpiphĕnŏ′mĕn|on n. (pl. ∿a). **1.** (Med. & Philos

secondary symptom, mere concomitant of something else not regarded as its cause or result. **2.** (Psychol.) consciousness regarded as a by-product of brain activity. **3.** Hence ∼AL *a.*, ∼AL**ISM** (3) *n.* [f. EPI- +PHENOMENON]

ĕpĭ′phy̆s|is *n.* (*pl.* ∼**es** *pr.* -ēz). (Anat.) end part of long bone during growth; pineal gland. [mod. L, f. Gk EPI(*phusis* growth)]

ĕ′piphy̆te *n.* plant growing on (usu. not fed by) another; vegetable parasite on animal body; hence **ĕpĭphy̆′t**AL, **ĕpĭphy̆′t**IC, *adjs.* [f. EPI- + Gk *phuton* plant]

Epīr′ot, -ōte, (ī-) *n.* native or inhabitant of Epirus. [f. Gk *ēpeirōtēs* (*ēpeiros* mainland; see -OT[2])]

ĕpĭ′scopacy̆ *n.* government of church by bishops; **the** ∼, the bishops. [f. as EPISCOPATE + -ACY, after *prelacy*]

ĕpĭ′scopal *a.* of bishop(s); ∼ **church** (constituted on principle of prec., esp. *Episcopal Church*, Church of England in US and Scotland); hence ∼ISM (3) *n.*, ∼LY[2] *adv.* [ME, f. F *épiscopal* or f. eccl. L *episcopalis* (*episcopus* BISHOP; see -AL)]

ĕpĭscopā′lian *a.* & *n.* (adherent) of episcopacy; (E∼) (member) of episcopal church; hence ∼ISM (3) *n.* [f. prec. + -IAN]

ĕpĭ′scopate *n.* office, position, tenure, of bishop; **the** ∼, the bishops. [f. eccl. L *episcopatus* (*episcopus* BISHOP; see -ATE[1])]

ĕ′piscōpe *n.* optical projector giving images of opaque objects. [f. EPI- + -SCOPE]

ĕpĭsēmā′tic *a.* (Zool.) (Of coloration, markings, etc.) serving to help recognition by other members of same species. [f. EPI- + Gk *sēma sēmatos* sign + -IC]

ĕ′pĭsōde *n.* incidental narrative or series of events forming digression in poem etc.; incident in narrative, part of serial story; incident, event, viewed as part of sequence; (Mus.) passage introducing new subject; part between two choric songs in Gk tragedy (orig. interpolated); hence **ĕpĭsŏ′d**IC(AL) *adjs.*, (also) sporadic, irregularly occurring. [f. Gk *epeisodion* f. as EPI- + *eisodos* entry (*eis* into, *hodos* way)]

ĕpĭstā′xis *n.* nose-bleeding. [mod. L. f. Gk (as EPI-, *staxo* drip)]

ĕpĭstĕ′m|ic *a.* (Philos.) relating to knowledge or degree of acceptance; hence ∼ICALLY *adv.* [f. Gk *epistēmē* knowledge + -IC]

ĕpĭstĕmŏ′log|y̆ *n.* theory of the method or grounds of knowledge; hence **ĕpĭstĕmolŏ′gic**AL *a.*, ∼IST (3) *n.* [f. as prec. + -O- + -LOGY]

ĕpĭ′stle (-sel) *n.* letter in NT, written by apostle; (E∼) extract from this read in church service (**E**∼ **side,** S. side of altar, at which Epistle is read); (usu. joc.) = LETTER 2; literary work, usu. verse, in form of letter. [ME f. OF, f. L f. Gk *epistolē* f. EPI(*stellō* send)]

ĕpĭ′stolary̆ *a.* of, carried on by, suited to, letters. [f. F *épistolaire* or f. L *epistolaris* (as prec.; see -ARY[2])]

ĕpĭ′stoler *n.* (Eccl.) reader of the Epistle. [f. OF *epistelier* or f. med. L *epistolari(u)s* (as EPISTLE; see ER[2] (1, 2))]

ĕpĭ′strophe *n.* repetition of word at end of successive clauses. [Gk EPI(*strophē* turning; see STROPHE)]

ĕ′pistỹle *n.* (Archit.) = ARCHITRAVE. [f. F *épistyle* or f. L f. Gk *epistulion* f. EPI(*stulos* pillar)]

ĕ′pitaph (-ahf) *n.* words (composed as if to be) inscribed on tomb. [ME, f. OF *epitaphe* f. L f. Gk EPI(*taphion* f. *taphos* tomb) funeral oration]

ĕpĭtaxy̆ (ĕ′-, -ă′-) *n.* growth of crystals on an underlying crystal that determines their orientation; hence **ĕpĭtă′xi**AL *a.* [f. F *épitaxie* f. as EPI- + Gk *taxis* arrangement; see -Y[1]]

ĕpĭthala′mi|um *n.* (*pl.* ∼**ums** *or* ∼**a**). nuptial song or poem; hence ∼AL, **ĕpĭthală′m**IC, *adjs.* [f. L f. Gk EPI(*thalamion* f. *thalamos* bridal chamber)]

ĕpĭthē′li|um *n.* (*pl.* ∼**ums** *or* ∼**a**). tissue forming outer layer of body surface or lining of cavity that opens to body surface; (Bot.) epidermis formed of young cells; hence ∼AL *a.* [mod. L, f. EPI- + Gk *thēlē* teat; see -IUM]

ĕ′pĭthĕt *n.* adjective expressing quality or attribute; this as term of abuse or profanity; title, significant appellation; hence ∼IC(AL) (-ĕ′t-) *adjs.* [f. F *épithète* or L f. Gk *epitheton* f. EPI(*tithēmi* place)]

ĕpĭ′tom|ē *n.* summary or abstract of book; condensed account; (fig.) thing that represents another in miniature, person who embodies a quality etc.; hence ∼IST (1) *n.*, ∼IZE (3) *v.t.* [f. L f. Gk *epitomē* f. EPI(*temnō* cut) abridge]

ĕpĭzŏ′|ŏn *n.* (*pl.* ∼**a**). external parasite or commensal. [mod. L f. as EPI- + Gk *zōion* animal]

ĕpĭzŏŏ′tic *a.* & *n.* (disease) temporarily prevalent among animals (cf. ENZOOTIC, EPIDEMIC); outbreak of this. [f. F *épizootique* (*épizootie* f. as EPI- + Gk *zōion* animal); see -IC]

EPNS *abbr.* electroplated nickel silver.

ĕ′pŏch (-k) *n.* beginning of era in history, science, life, etc., (∼-**making,** marking the beginning of a new era, remarkable); date; period in history or life marked by special events; (Geol.) division of a PERIOD, corresp. to a SERIES in rocks; hence ∼AL *a.* [f. mod. L f. Gk *epokhē* stoppage f. EP(*ekhō* hold)]

ĕ′pŏde *n.* **1.** form of lyric poem with long line followed by shorter one. **2.** See STROPHE. [f. F *épode* or f. L *epodos* f. Gk *epōidos* (as EPI-, ODE)]

ĕ′ponym *n.* one who gives his name to a people, place, or institution; so **epŏ′nym**OUS *a.* [f. Gk EP(*ōnumos* f. *onoma* name)]

ĕ′popee *n.* epic (poem or poetry). [f. F *épopée* f. Gk *epopoiia* (as foll., *poieō* make)]

ĕ′pŏs *n.* early unwritten epic poetry; epic poem. [L, f. Gk *epos* word, song]

ĕpŏ′xĭde *n.* (Chem.) compound in which oxygen atom and two carbon atoms form ring. [f. EPI- + OXIDE]

ĕpŏ′xy̆ *a.* & *n.* pertaining to or derived from an epoxide; ∼ (**resin**), synthetic thermosetting resin containing epoxide rings. [f. EPI- + OXY- (2)]

ĕpris (apre′) *a.* (fem. **ĕprise** *pr.* ăprē′z). enamoured (*of*, *with*). [F]

ĕpsī′lon *n.* fifth Greek letter (E, ε) = ĕ (cf. ETA[1]). [ME f. Gk, = bare E (*psilos* bare)]

E′psom (ĕ′-) *n.* ∼ **salt(s)**, magnesium sulphate used as purgative etc. [∼ in Surrey]

ĕpy̆′lli|on *n.* (*pl.* ∼**a**). miniature epic poem. [f. Gk *epullion* dim. of EPOS]

ĕ′qu|able *a.* uniform, even, not easily disturbed; uniform and moderate (*equable climate*), hence *or* cogn. ∼ABI′LITY *n.*, ∼ABLY *adv.* [f. L *aequabilis* (as EQUATE; see -ABLE)]

ĕ′qual[1] *a.* & *n.* **1.** *a.* the same in number, size, value, degree, rank, musical pitch, etc., (*to*, *with*, or abs.; *twice three is equal to six*; *the totals are equal*; speaks French and Dutch with equal ease; came equal second with Jones in the race*; *the two are equal in ability*; *met his rival on equal terms*); ∼(**s**) **sign,** = . **2.** having strength, courage, ability, etc., adequate *to* (*the occasion, a ten-mile walk, doing*, etc.). **3.** uniform in operation etc. (*equal laws*); evenly balanced (fight etc.); ∼ **pay** (for same work done, esp. by either sex); ∼ **rights** (esp. for the two sexes; *equal* TEMPERAMENT. **4.** Hence ∼LY[2] *adv.* **5.** *n.* person equal to another in rank etc. (*mix with one's equals* or in power etc. (*he has no equal*; *in pl.*) equal things (*if equals be added to equals*). [ME, f. L *aequalis* (*aequus* even; see -AL)]

ĕ′qual[2] *v.t.* (||-ll-) *a.* be equal to (person, thing, in quality, number, etc.; *twice three equals six*); do something equal to (feat etc.). [f. prec.]

ĕqualitār′ian (-ŏl-) etc. Var. of EGALITARIAN etc.

ĕqua′lity̆ (-ŏ′l-) *n.* condition of being equal (*between* two or more; *with* person etc. *in or of* quality etc.; or abs.); **E∼ **State**, Wyoming (first to let women vote). [ME, f. OF *equalité* f. L *aequalitas* -*tatis* (as EQUAL[1]; see -ITY)]

ĕ′qualiz|e, -īs|e (-īz), *v.* **1.** *v.t.* make (thing etc.) equal (*to*, *with*). **2.** *v.i.* become equal; (Footb. etc.) bring score to equality with opponent's. **3.** Hence ∼A′TION *n.*, ∼ER¹ *n.*, (esp.) goal that equalizes, (sl.) revolver or other weapon. [f. EQUAL¹+-IZE]

ĕquani'mĭtў *n.* evenness of mind or temper; composure; resignation, acceptance of fate; so **ĕquã'nimous** *a.* [f. L *aequanimitas* (*aequanimis* f. *aequus* even + *animus* mind; see -ITY)]

ĕquã't|e *v.* **1.** *v.t.* state equality of (thing *to*, *with*, another); treat or regard as equivalent (*with*); hence ∼ABLE *a.* **2.** *v.i.* ∼ **with**, be equivalent to. [ME, f. L *aequare* (*aequus* equal) +-ATE³]

ĕquã'tion (-ā'zhon) *n.* **1.** making equal, equating, balancing, (of demand and supply etc.). **2.** (amount or process of) correction for inaccuracy; **personal** ∼, (Astron.) allowance for person's time of reaction in making observations, (fig.) bias or prejudice. **3.** (Math.) formula affirming equivalence of two expressions connected by the sign = . **4.** (Chem.) formula indicating reaction by use of symbols. **5.** Hence ∼AL *a.* [ME f. OF, or f. L *aequatio* (as prec.; see -ATION)]

ĕquã'tor *n.* great circle of the earth, sun, etc., equidistant from the poles; great circle of sky in plane perpendicular to earth's axis; **magnetic** ∼, aclinic line. [ME, f. OF *equateur* or f. med. L *aequator* (as prec.; see -OR)]

ĕquatôr'ial *a.* of or near the equator; ∼ **telescope** (attached to axis perpendicular to plane of equator); hence ∼LY² *adv.* [f. prec.+-IAL]

equerrў (ĕ'kwerĭ, ĭkwĕ'rĭ) *n.* (Hist.) officer of prince or noble, charged with care of horses; officer of British royal household, attending sovereign etc. [earlier *esquiry* etc. f. obs. F *escu(i)rie* stable, of unkn. orig.; in E wrongly assoc. w. L *equus* horse]

ĕquĕ'strian *a.* & *n.* **1.** *a.* of horse-riding (∼ **statue**, of person on horse); of knights. **2.** *n.* (*fem.* **equestrie'nne**). rider or performer on horseback; hence ∼ISM (2) *n.* [f. L *equestris* (*eques* horseman, knight, f. *equus* horse)+-AN]

ĕqui- *comb. form.* equal, as: ∼**a'ngular**, having equal angles; ∼**di'stant**, separated by equal distances; ∼**la'teral**, having all sides equal, (of hyperbola) rectangular. [f. L *aequi-* (*aequus* equal; see -I-)]

equilibr|āte (ĭkwĭ'lĭ-, ĕkwĭlī'-) *v.t.* & *i.* cause (two things) to balance; balance; so ∼A'TION *n.* [f. LL *aequilibrare* (*aequi-* EQUI-, *libra* balance) +-ATE³]

ĕqui'librĭst *n.* rope-dancer, acrobat. [f. foll.+-IST]

ēquĭli'brĭ|um *n.* (*pl.* ∼**a** *or* ∼**ums**). state of balance (lit. or fig.); mental state of uncertainty or equanimity; **stable, unstable, neutral,** ∼**um** (in which body when disturbed tends to return to equilibrium, to move farther from equilibrium, or has neither tendency). [L (*aequi-* EQUI-, *libra* balance)]

ĕ'quīne *a.* of or like a horse. [f. L *equinus* (*equus* horse; see -INE¹)]

ĕquinŏ'ctial (-shal) *a.* & *n.* **1.** *a.* of equal day and night; ∼ **line**, celestial EQUATOR; ∼ **point** (at which ecliptic crosses equator); *equinoctial* YEAR. **2.** happening at or near time of equinox (*equinoctial gales*). **3.** at or near the (terrestrial) equator. **4.** *n.* equinoctial line. [ME f. OF, or f. L *aequinoctialis* (as foll.; see -AL)]

ĕ'quinŏx *n.* time or date at which sun crosses equator, and day and night are equal (**spring** or **vernal** ∼, about 20 Mar.; **autumn** or **autumnal** ∼, about 22 Sept.); equinoctial point; PRECESSION *of equinoxes.* [ME, f. OF *equinoxe* or f. med. L *equinoxium* for L *aequinoctium* (as EQUI-, *nox noctis* night)]

ĕqui'p *v.t.* (-**pp**-). furnish (ship, army, person, *with* requisites); furnish (one*self* etc.) with what is needed for journey etc. [f. F *équiper*, prob. f. ON *skipa* to man (ship) f. *skip* SHIP¹]

ĕ'quipage *n.* requisites for an undertaking; outfit for journey etc.; carriage and horses with attendants. [f. F *équipage* (as prec.; see -AGE)]

ēquipärtĭ'tion *n.* (Phys.) equal division of energy between degrees of FREEDOM of a system in thermal equilibrium. [f. EQUI-+PARTITION]

ĕqui'pment *n.* equipping or being equipped; manner in which person or thing is equipped; outfit, tools,

apparatus, necessary for expedition, job, warfare, etc.; intellectual resources. [f. F *équipement* (as EQUIP; see -MENT)]

ĕ'quipoise (-z) *n.*, & *v.t.* **1.** *n.* equilibrium (usu. fig.); counterbalancing thing. **2.** *v.t.* counterbalance. [f. EQUI-+POISE¹]

ĕquipŏ'll|ent *a.* & *n.* **1.** *a.* equal in power, force, etc., practically equivalent; so ∼ENCE, ∼ENCY, *ns.* **2.** *n.* equipollent thing. [ME, f. OF *equipolent* f. L *aequipollens -entis* of equal value (as EQUI-, *pollēre* be strong)]

ēquĭpŏ'nder|āte *v.t.* counterbalance; so ∼ANT *a.* & *n.* [f. med. L *ΑΕQUI(ponderare* weigh f. L *pondus -eris* weight)+-ATE³]

ĕquipotĕ'ntial (-shal) *a.* & *n.* (Phys.) (surface, line, etc.) such that the potential of a force is the same or constant at all its points. [f. EQUI-+POTENTIAL]

ēquiprŏ'b|able *a.* (Logic). equally probable; hence ∼ABI'LITY *n.* [f. EQUI-+PROBABLE]

ĕ'quitab|le *a.* fair, just, whence ∼**leNESS** (-beln-) *n.*, ∼LY² *adv.*; (of claim etc.) valid in equity as opposed to law. [f. F *équitable* (as EQUITY; see -ABLE)]

ĕquĭtā'tion *n.* riding on horseback; horsemanship. [f. F *équitation* or f. L *equitatio* (*equitare* ride horse f. *eques -itis* horseman f. *equus* horse; see -ATION)]

ĕ'quitў *n.* **1.** fairness; recourse to principles of justice to correct or supplement law; system of justice supplementing or prevailing over common and statute law. **2.** ||(*E*∼). actors' trade union. **3.** (in *pl.*) stocks and shares not bearing fixed interest. **4.** value of shares issued by a company; net value of mortgaged property after deduction of charges. [ME, f. OF *equité* f. L *aequitas -tatis* (*aequus* fair; see -ITY)]

ĕqui'val|ent *a.* & *n.* **1.** *a.* equal in value, amount, or importance, (*to*); (of words) meaning the same; (Chem.) equal in combining value (*to*); having same result; corresponding. **2.** *n.* equivalent thing, amount, word, etc.; (Chem.) amount that is equivalent esp. to three grams (or other units) of carbon. **3.** So ∼ENCE, ∼ENCY, *ns.* [ME f. OF, f. LL *aequi(valēre* be worth); see EQUI-, -ENT]

ĕqui'vocal *a.* **1.** of double meaning, ambiguous; of uncertain nature. **2.** (Of person, character, etc.) questionable, suspicious. **3.** Hence ∼ITY (-ă'l-), ∼NESS, *ns.*, ∼LY² *adv.* [f. LL *aequivocus* (as EQUI-, *vocare* call)+-AL]

ĕqui'voc|āte *v.i.* use ambiguous words to conceal the truth, prevaricate; hence or cogn. ∼A'TION, ∼ātOR, *ns.* [ME, f. LL *aequivocare* (as prec.)+-ATE³]

ĕ'quivŏque (-k), **-vōke,** *n.* pun; ambiguity. [ME in sense 'equivocal', f. OF *equivoque* or f. LL *aequivocus* EQUIVOCAL]

ēr *int.* expr. hesitation. [imit.]

-er¹ *suf.* forming *ns.* f. *ns.*, *adjs.*, and almost all *vbs.*, meaning (1) person or animal that does (*lover, maker, pointer, executioner, probationer*), person or thing that has or is (*foreigner, fiver, four-wheeler, three-decker, second-rater*), (2) instrument, machine, occurrence, action, etc., (*poker, computer, deodorizer, eye-opener, header*), (3) person concerned with thing (*hatter, geographer*), (4) person belonging to place etc. (*Londoner, Merseysider, Britisher, Hamburger, villager, sixth-former,* *fourth--grader), (5) sl. distortion of word with other ending (*rugger, soccer*). [orig. 'one who has to do with', f. OE *-ere* f. Gmc *-*arjaz*]

-er² *suf.* forming *ns.* and *adjs.* (1) ME f. OF, f. L *-aris*, now usu. -AR¹ (SAMPLER²); (2) ME f. AF (OF *-ier*) f. L *-arius, -arium* (*butler, carpenter, danger*); (3) f. OF *-eüre* f. L *-atura* or OF *-eör* f. L *-atorium* (COUNTER¹, FRITTER¹); (4) = -OR.

-er³ *suf.* forming *compar.* of *adjs.* and *advs.* esp. of one or sometimes two syllables (*wider, narrower*); see notes on *-iz(on)-, -ŏz(on)-*). [OE *-ra* adj., *-or* adv. f. Gmc *-iz(on)-, -ŏz(on)-*]

-er⁴ *suf.* forming *ns.* (esp. Law) meaning (single instance of) the vbl action, document effecting this, (*cesser, disclaimer, misnomer, dinner, supper*). [AF inf. ending of vbs.]

-er⁵ *suf.* forming frequent. *vbs.* f. *vbs.* (*wander* f. *wend*) or on sound-imitations (*twitter*); clamber, mutter, shudder, slumber. [OE -(*e*)*rian*, = OS, OHG -*arōn*, ON -*ra* f. Gmc *-*rōjan*]

ER *abbr.* East RIDING²; King Edward [f. L *Edwardus Rex*]; Queen Elizabeth [f. L *Elizabetha Regina*].

Er *symb.* erbium.

ēr'a *n.* system of chronology starting from some particular point of time (*Christian era*); historical or other period; date forming commencement of this; (Geol.) major division of time. [f. LL *aera* number expressed in figures (pl. of *aes aeris* money, treated as fem. sing.)]

***ERA** *abbr.* Equal Rights Amendment.

ėrä'dic|āte *v.t.* tear up by roots; extirpate, remove, get rid of; hence ~ABLE *a.*, ~A'TION, ~ātOR, *ns.* [ME, f. L E(*radicare* f. *radix* -*icis* root) +-ATE³]

ėra's|e (-z) *v.t.* rub out; obliterate, remove all traces of (*from* memory etc.); remove recorded signal from (magnetic tape etc.); hence **ėrā'sABLE** (-z-) *a.*, ~ER¹ (2), ~URE (-zher), *ns.* [f. L E(*radere ras-* scrape)]

Era'stian (ĭ-) *a.* & *n.* (Hist.) (adherent) of the supposed doctrines of Erastus, subordinating ecclesiastical to secular power; hence ~ISM (3) *n.*, ~IZE (3) *v.t.* & *i.* [f. *Erastus*, Swiss physician d. 1583 +-IAN]

ēr'bium *n.* (Chem.) metallic element of lanthanide series. [mod. L, f. *Ytterby* in Sweden +-IUM]

***ERDA** *abbr.* Energy Research & Development Administration.

ere (āҽ̄r) *prep.* & *conj.* (poet. or arch.) before (of time; *ere noon, ere he went*); ~whi'le, (poet. or arch.) formerly. [OE ǣr, = OS, OHG ēr, Goth. *airis* f. Gmc *airiz* compar. of *air* adv. early]

ėrė'ct¹ *a.* upright, not stooping, (lit. or fig.); vertical; (of hair etc.) set up, bristling; (of part of the body) enlarged and rigid, esp. from sexual excitement; hence ~LY² *adv.*, ~NESS *n.* [ME, f. L E(*rigere rect-* = *regere* direct) set up]

ėrė'ct² *v.t.* raise, set upright, (one*self*, body, etc.); build, establish, (lit. or fig.); form or elevate *into* (principle, system, etc.); hence ~OR *n.* [ME, f. as prec.]

ėrė'ctile *a.* that can be erected or become erect; ~ tissue in animals (capable of being distended and becoming rigid upon excitement). [f. F *érectile* (as ERECT¹; see -IL)]

ėrė'ction *n.* erecting, building, structure, (lit. or fig.); (occurrence of) erect state of part of body, esp. of penis. [f. F *érection* or f. L *erectio* (as prec.; see -ION)]

ė'rėmīte *n.* hermit (esp. Christian recluse); hence **ėrėmi'tic**(AL) *adjs.* [ME f. OF, var. of (*h*)*ermite* HERMIT]

ė'rėthism *n.* (Path.) abnormal excitement (of organ or tissue, fig. of mind). [f. F *éréthisme* f. Gk *erethismos* (*erethizō* irritate; see -ISM)]

ėrg¹ *n.* (Phys.) unit of work or energy, work done by force of one dyne when its point of application moves one centimetre in the direction of action of the force. [f. Gk *ergon* work]

ėrg² *n.* (pl. ~s or **areg**). area of shifting sand dunes in the Sahara. [F, f. Arab. '*irj*]

ēr'gō *adv.* therefore. [L]

ėrgonō'm|ics *n.* study of efficiency of persons in their working environment; hence ~IC *a.*, **ėrgō'nomIST** (3) *n.* [f. Gk *ergon* work; cf. ECONOMICS]

ėrgō'sterōl *n.* steroid present in ergot etc., a source of vitamin D₂. [f. foll., after CHOLESTEROL]

ėr'got *n.* (disease of rye etc. caused by) fungus of genus *Claviceps*; dried mycelium of the fungus, used in medicine. [F, f. OF *argot* cock's spur, f. appearance produced]

ēr'gotism *n.* disease produced by bread made from flour affected by ergot. [f. prec. +-ISM]

erica (ė'rīka, ėrī'ka) *n.* heath of genus *Erica*. [L, f. Gk *ereikē* heath]

ėri'gerōn *n.* hardy composite herb of genus *Erigeron*, with daisy-like flowers. [f. Gk *ērigerōn* (*ēri* early, *gerōn* old man), some species bearing grey down]

Erin (ė'rĭn, ēr'ĭn) *n.* (Ancient or poet. name of) Ireland. [Ir.]

Eri'nÿ|s (ė-) *n.* (*pl.* ~es *pr.* ėrī'nīēz). (Gk Myth.) a Fury. [Gk]

ėri'stic *a.* & *n.* (art or exponent) of disputation; (of argument or arguer) aimed or aiming at victory rather than truth. [f. Gk *eristikos* (*erizō* wrangle f. *eris* strife; see -IC)]

||ērk *n.* (sl.) naval rating; aircraftman; disliked person. [20th c.; orig. unkn.]

Er'lang (ēr'-) *n.* ~ unit, measure of intensity of traffic flow, corresponding to full occupation of capacity. [f. A. K. ~, Da. mathematician d. 1929]

ēr'l-king *n.* (Gmc Myth.) bearded golden-crowned giant who lures little children to land of death. [f. G *erlkönig* alder-king, a mistransl. of Da. *ellerkonge* king of the elves]

ēr'min|e *n.* 1. carnivorous animal (*Mustela erminea*) of weasel family, whose fur is brown in summer and white (except black tail-tip) in winter. 2. its winter fur, used in robes of judges, peers, etc.; emblem of honour and purity; hence ~ED² (-nd) *a.* 3. (Her.) white fur marked with black spots; ~ **moth** (having white wings with black spots). [ME, f. OF (*h*)*ermine*, prob. f. med. L (*mus*) *Armenius* Armenian (mouse)]

-ern *suf.* forming *adjs.* (*northern* etc.). [OE *erne*, = OS, OHG -*roni*, ON -*rœnn*, f. Gmc * *rōnja*]

ērne, *ērn, *n.* sea eagle. [OE *earn*, = OHG *arn*, ON *örn* f. Gmc **arnuz*]

||Er'nie (ēr'-) *n.* device for drawing prize-winning numbers of Premium Bonds. [f. initial letters of **e**lectronic **r**andom **n**umber **i**ndicator **e**quipment]

ėrō'd|e *v.* 1. *v.t.* (Of acid, current, course of events, etc.) eat away, destroy gradually, wear out; (Geol.) wear away (earth's surface) by action of water etc. 2. *v.i.* become eroded. So ~IBLE *a.*, **ėrō'sION** (-zhon) *n.*, **ėrō'sIVE** *a.* [f. F *éroder* or f. L E(*rodere ros-* gnaw)]

ėrō'gėnous *a.* giving rise to sexual desire or excitement. [irreg. f. as foll. +-GENOUS]

Er'ōs (ēr'-) *n.* earthly or sexual love; god of love, Cupid. [L, f. Gk *Erōs*, as EROTIC]

erosion etc. See ERODE.

ėrō'tic *a.* of sexual love, amatory, esp. tending to arouse sexual desire or excitement; hence or cogn. ~A *n.* pl., erotic literature or art, **ėrō'tICALLY** *adv.*, ~ISM *n.*, erotic spirit or character. [f. F *érotique* f. Gk *erōtikos* (*erōs erōtos* sexual love; see -IC)]

ė'rotism *n.* sexual desire or excitement; eroticism. [f. F *érotisme* f. Gk *erōs* (see prec.) +-ISM]

ėrōtogė'nĭa, **ėrotō'gėnous**, *adjs.* = EROGENOUS [f. as foll. +-GENIC, -GENOUS]

ėrotō'logy *n.* description of methods of love-making. [f. Gk *erōs erōtos* sexual love + o +-LOGY]

ėrōto|mā'nia *n.* excessive or morbid erotic desire; preoccupation with sexual passion; hence ~MA'NIAC *n.* [f. as prec. +-MANIA]

ėrr *v.i.* make mistake(s); (of statement etc.) be incorrect; sin; ~ **on the right side**, avoid the more dangerous of possible errors. [ME, f. OF *errer* f. L *errare* stray, rel. to Goth. *airzei* error, *airzjan* lead astray]

ė'rrand *n.* 1. short journey on which person goes or is sent to carry message, deliver goods, etc. (*run, go, (on) errands; errand-boy, errand-girl*; ~ **of mercy**, journey to relieve distress etc.). 2. object of journey; purpose. [OE ǣrende = OS ārundi, OHG ārunti f. Gmc **ǣrundjam*]

ė'rrant *a.* 1. roaming in quest of adventure, esp. KNIGHT errant; (of official) itinerant. 2. erring, deviating from correct standard of behaviour, esp. **ė'rrANCY** *n.* [ME; sense 1 f. OF *errer* f. Rom. **iterare* f. L *itinerare* (*iter* journey), sense 2 f. as ERR; see -ANT]

ė'rrantrÿ *n.* (condition, conduct, fortunes, of) knight errant. [f. prec. +-RY]

ėrrā't|ic *a.* uncertain in movement; irregular in conduct, habit, opinion; ~**ic block**, (Geol.) large rock brought from a distance by glacier; hence ~ICALLY *adv.* [ME, f. OF *erratique* f. L *erraticus* (as ERR; see -ATIC)]

erra′t|um (-ā′-, -ah′-) *n.* (*pl.* ∼**a**). error in printing or writing, esp. (in *pl.*) errors shown in list attached to book etc. [L, neut. p.p., f. as ERR]

errō′neous *a.* mistaken, incorrect; hence ∼LY² *adv.*, ∼NESS *n.* [ME, f. OF or L *erroneus* (*erro -onis* vagabond, f. as ERR) +-OUS]

e′rror *n.* **1.** mistake (*make, commit, an error*; CLERICAL *error*); condition of erring in opinion or conduct (*error of judgement*; *realize the error of* one's *ways*); wrong opinion; **in** ∼, mistaken(ly), by mistake. **2.** (Math. etc.) amount of deviation from correct or accurate result. **3.** Hence ∼LESS *a.* [ME f. OF *errour* f. L *error -oris* (as ERR; see -OR)]

er′satz (ĕr′zăts, ār′zahts) *n.* & *a.* substitute, imitation, (esp. of inferior kind). [G, = replacement]

Erse (ērs) *a.* & *n.* Irish Gaelic or Highland Gaelic (language). [early Sc. form of IRISH]

ērst *adv.* (arch.) formerly, of old. [OE *ǣrest* superl. of *ǣr*; see ERE]

ēr′stwhīle *a.* & *adv.* **1.** *a.* former, previous. **2.** *adv.* (arch.) = prec. [f. prec. +WHILE¹]

ĕrubĕ′scent (ĕrōō-) *a.* reddening, blushing. [f. L E(*rubescere* incept. of *rubēre* be red); see -ESCENT]

ērŭctā′tion *n.* belching (lit. or fig., esp. of volcano). [f. L *eructatio* f. E(*ructare* belch); see -ATION]

e′rud|īte (-rōō-) *a.* (Of person or writings) remarkably learned; hence or cogn. ∼**īte**LY² (-tlĭ) *adv.*, ∼I′TION *n.* [ME, f. L *eruditus* p.p. of E*rudire* instruct, train (*rudis* untrained); see -ITE²]

ĕrŭ′pt *v.i.* break out or through (lit., or fig. of anger etc.); (of volcano) emit rocks, lava, etc.; (of geyser) spurt water; (of rash etc.) appear on skin; (of teeth) break through gums. [f. L E(*rumpere rupt-* break)]

ĕrŭ′ption *n.* erupting, outbreak, (of volcano, geyser, disease, war, passion, mirth, wit); (Path.) breaking out (of rash etc.); (of teeth) breaking through gums. [OF, or f. L *eruptio* (as prec.; see -ION)]

ĕrŭ′ptīve *a.* bursting forth; tending to burst forth; of, formed by, forced up by, (esp. volcanic) eruption; hence ∼LY² (-vlĭ) *adv.*, ∼NESS (-vn-), **ērupti′vITY**, *ns.* [f. ERUPT +-IVE]

-erў, -rў, *suf.* forming *ns.* meaning (1) class of goods (*drapery*) or things (*greenery, machinery*), body of persons (*citizenry*), (2) employment or condition (*archery, slavery*), (3) place of work or cultivation or breeding or *obtaining (*brewery, orangery, piggery, eatery*), (4) conduct (*mimicry*), (5) (often derog.) all that has to do with (*popery*), thing of the nature of. [ME, f. or after F *-erie* (a) f. Rom. *-aria* f. L *-ario-*, (b) f. OF *-ere* (f. L *-ator*) +*-ie* -Y¹]

ĕrў′ngō (-nggō) *n.* (*pl.* ∼**s**). sea holly. [f. It. or Sp. *eringio* f. L f. Gk *ēruggion* dim. of *ēruggos* sea holly]

ĕrўsi′pèlas *n.* local inflammation caused by streptococcus, producing deep red colour on skin. [ME f. L, f. Gk *erusipelas*]

ĕrўthē′ma *n.* superficial inflammation of the skin in patches; hence **ĕrў′thēm**AL *a.* [mod. L, f. Gk *eruthēma* f. *eruthainō* be red (*eruthros*)]

ĕrў′throblăst *n.* immature erythrocyte. [G, f. as foll. +-BLAST]

ĕrў′throcўte *n.* red blood-corpuscle. [f. Gk *erythros* red +-o-+-CYTE]

-es¹ *suf.* Var. of -s¹; see notes on Plurals, p. xvi.

-es² *suf.* Var. of -s²; see notes on Verb forms, p. xvii.

Es *symb.* einsteinium.

ESA *abbr.* European Space Agency.

ĕscadrī′lle *n.* French squadron of aeroplanes. [F]

ĕscalā′de *n.* scaling of walls with ladders. [F, f. Sp. *escalada, -ado*, f. med. L *scalare* (*scala* ladder); see -ADE]

e′scal|āte *v.t.* & *i.* increase or develop by successive stages; hence ∼A′TION *n.* [back-form. f. foll.]

e′scalātor *n.* staircase with endless chain of steps moving continuously up or down; ∼ **clause** etc. (providing for change in price etc. under stated conditions). [f. *escalade* v. 'climb wall by ladder' + ELEVATOR]

ĕscallō′nia *n.* flowering shrub of genus *Escallonia*, orig. S. Amer. [f. *Escallon*, 18th-c. Sp. traveller +-IA¹]

ĕscā′llop *n.* = SCALLOP 1, 2; (Her.) scallop-shell as device; = foll.; (in *pl.*) = SCALLOP 4. [f. as foll.]

e′scalōpe *n.* slice of boneless meat, esp. from leg of veal. [F; in OF = shell; see SCALLOP]

ĕscapā′de *n.* breaking loose from restraint; piece of irresponsible or unorthodox conduct. [F, f. Prov. or Sp. *escapada* (as ESCAPE²; see -ADE)]

ĕscā′pe¹ *n.* **1.** act of escaping; fact of having escaped (*a narrow escape*). **2.** means of escaping (FIRE¹-*escape*); distraction or relief from reality, esp. given by literature etc. **3.** leakage (of gas etc.); garden plant growing wild. **4.** ∼ **clause** (specifying conditions under which contracting party is free from an obligation); ∼**-hatch,** means of emergency exit (from ship etc., or fig.); ∼**-pipe** (for escape of steam or water); ∼ **road** (for vehicle unable to make turn on race-track, hill, etc.); ∼**-shaft** (for escape of miners when other shaft is blocked); ∼ **velocity,** minimum velocity needed to escape from gravitational field of a body; ∼ **wheel,** toothed wheel in escapement of watch or clock. [f. foll.]

ĕscā′pe² *v.* **1.** *v.i.* get free of restriction or control by fleeing or exertion (*from* prison, person, etc.); (of gas or liquid or granular solid) get out of container etc.; get off safely, go unpunished. **2.** *v.t.* get clear away from (person, his grasp, etc.), avoid (unpleasant thing, do*ing*); not be noticed or recollected by (*his name escapes, had escaped, me*); not be recalled or detected by (person's memory, attention, etc.); (of words, sigh, etc.) issue unawares from (person, his lips); hence **ĕscā′p**ABLE *a.* **3.** Hence **escape**EE (ĭskāpē′, ĕskā′pē), **ĕscā′p**ER¹ *ns.*, one who has escaped. [ME, f. AF, ONF *escaper* f. Rom. *EX(*cappare* f. med. L *cappa* cloak; see CAP¹)]

ĕscā′pement (-pm-) *n.* (In watch or clock) mechanism connecting motive power and regulator; (in piano) space between strings and raised hammer; (arch.) means of escape. [f. F *échappement* (*échapper* escape f. as prec.; see -MENT]

ĕscā′p|ism *n.* tendency to seek distraction or relief from reality; so ∼IST (2) *n.* & *a.* [f. ESCAPE¹ +-ISM]

ĕscapō′|logў *n.* methods and technique of escaping, esp. from captivity, confinement in box, etc.; so ∼LOGIST *n.*, performer skilled in these. [f. ESCAPE¹ + -O-+-LOGY]

ĕscā′rgŏt (-gō) *n.* edible snail. [F]

ĕscā′rp(ment) *n.* (Geog.) long steep face of plateau etc. [f. F *escarpement* (*escarpe* SCARP; see -MENT)]

-ĕsce *suf.* forming usu. incept. *vbs.* (*deliquesce, effervesce, fluoresce*). [f. or after L *-escere*]

-ĕ′scence *suf.* forming *ns.* corresp. to *adjs.* f. foll. (*deliquescence, effervescence, fluorescence, iridescence*). [f. or after F *-escence* or L *-escentia* (as foll.; see -ENCE)]

-ĕ′scent *suf.* forming *adjs.* denoting onset of a state or variation of colour etc. (*deliquescent, effervescent, fluorescent, iridescent*). [f. or after F *-escent* or L *-escent-* pres. part. st. of (usu. incept.) *vbs.* in *-escere*]

ĕschato′|logў (ĕsk-) *n.* (Theol.) doctrine of death, judgement, heaven, and hell; (**realized**) ∼logў, present significance of this in Christian life; hence **ĕschato**LO′GICAL (ĕsk-) *a.*, ∼LOGIST *n.* [f. Gk *eskhatos* last +-o-+-LOGY]

ĕschea′t¹ *n.* (Hist.) lapsing of property to government or lord of manor on owner's dying intestate without heirs; property so lapsing. [ME f. OF *eschete*, f. Rom. *excadecta* p.p. (as n.) of *excadēre* f. L EX(*cidere* = *cadere* fall)]

ĕschea′t² *v.* (Hist.) **1.** *v.t.* confiscate; hand over (property) as an escheat (*to* person, *into* his hands). **2.** *v.i.* revert by escheat (*to, or* abs.). [ME, f. prec.]

ĕschew′ (-ōō′) *v.t.* avoid, abstain from, (action, conduct, kind of food, etc.); hence ∼AL *n.* [ME, f. OF *eschiver* f. Rom. *skivare* f. Gmc *skeuh(w)an* (*skeuh-(w)az* SHY¹)]

eschschŏ′ltzia (ĭskŏ′lsha, ĕshŏ′ltsĭa) *n.* herb of genus

Eschscholtzia, esp. yellow-flowered Californian poppy. [f. J. F. von *Eschscholtz*, Ger. botanist d. 1831 + -IA¹]

ĕ'scŏrt¹ *n.* body of armed men acting as guard to persons, baggage, etc.; person(s), ship(s), etc., accompanying another on journey for protection or guidance, or for courtesy's sake; person accompanying another socially. [f. F *escorte* f. It. *scorta* fem. p.p. (as n.) of *scorgere* conduct]

ĕscŏr't² *v.t.* act as escort to. [f. F *escorter* f. It. *scortare* (*scorta*; see prec.)]

ĕscrī'be *v.t.* (Math.) describe (circle) so as to touch one side of triangle exteriorly and the other two sides produced. [f. E- + L *scribere* write]

ĕ'scritoire (-twär) *n.* writing-desk with drawers etc. [F, f. L SCRIPTORIUM]

ĕscrōw' (-ō') *n.*, & *v.t.* **1.** *n.* written legal engagement to do something, kept in third person's custody until some condition has been fulfilled; *money or goods so kept; *in ~, so kept. **2.** *v.t.* *place in escrow. [f. AF *escrowe*, OF *escroe* scrap, scroll, f. med. L *scroda* f. Gmc *skraudh-*; cf. SHRED]

ĕscū'dō *n.* (*pl.* ~s). monetary unit of Portugal, Portuguese territories, and Chile. [Sp. and Port., f. L *scutum* shield]

ĕ'scŭlent *a.* & *n.* (thing) fit for food. [f. L *esculentus* (*esca* food; see -ULENT)]

ĕscŭ'tcheon (-chŏn) *n.* shield with armorial bearings (blot on one's ~, stain on one's reputation); middle of ship's stern where name is placed; pivoted keyhole cover. [f. AF & ONF *escuchon* f. Rom. *scutio -onis* f. L *scutum* shield]

Esd. *abbr.* Esdras (Apocrypha).

-ēse (ēz) *suf.* forming *adjs.* and *ns.* (1) (*pl.* same) f. names of foreign countries and towns (*Japanese*, *Milanese*, *Viennese*), meaning '(inhabitant or language) of', (2) f. *ns.* or names of writers (*officialese*, *Carlylese*), denoting 'style of written language'. [f. OF *-eis* f. Rom. *-ese* f. L *-ensis*]

ESE *abbr.* east-south-east.

e'sker, ĕ'skar, *n.* (Geol.) long ridge of post-glacial gravel in river valleys. [f. Ir. *eiscir*]

E'skimō (ĕ'-) *n.* (*pl.* ~s or same) & *a.* (member or language) of people inhabiting Arctic coast of America and of E. Siberia; ~ (**dog**), breed of powerful dog used by Eskimos to pull sledges etc. [Da., f. F *Esquimaux* pl., f. Algonquian]

ESN *abbr.* educationally SUBNORMAL.

ĕsŏ'phagus. See OESOPHAGUS.

ĕsotĕ'ric *a.* (Of philosophical doctrine etc.) meant only for the initiated, not generally intelligible; private, confidential; hence ~AL *a.*, ~ALLY *adv.*, ~ISM (2, 3), ~IST (2), *ns.* [f. Gk *esōterikos* (*esōterō* compar. of *esō* within; see -IC)]

ĕspadri'lle *n.* light canvas shoe with plaited fibre sole, alpargata. [F, f. Prov. *espardillo* (*espart* ESPARTO)]

ĕspā'lier *n.* lattice-work on which fruit-trees or ornamental shrubs are trained; tree etc. so trained. [F, f. It. *spalliera* (*spalla* shoulder)]

ĕspar'tō *n.* (*pl.* ~s). ~ (**grass**), species of grass (*Stipa tenacissima*) growing in Spain and N. Africa, used in paper-making. [Sp., f. L f. Gk *sparton* rope]

ĕspe'cial (-shǎl) *a.* pre-eminent, exceptional, (*my especial friend*; *thing of especial importance*); belonging chiefly to one person or thing (*for your especial benefit*); hence ~LY² *adv.*, chiefly, more than in other cases. [ME f. OF, f. L *specialis* SPECIAL]

Ĕsperā'ntŏ (ĕ-) *n.* artificial language designed in 1887 as medium for persons of all nations; hence ~IST (3) *n.* [pen-name (f. L *sperare* hope) of its inventor, L. L. Zamenhof, Pol. physician d. 1917]

ĕspī'al *n.* espying; being espied; (arch.) spying. [ME, f. OF *espiaille* (*espier*; see ESPY, -AL 2)]

ĕs'piŏnage (-ĭj, -ahzh) *n.* practice of spying or using spies, esp. to obtain secret information. [f. F *espionnage* (*espionner* f. *espion* SPY; see -AGE)]

ĕsplanā'de (-ā'd, -ah'd) *n.* level piece of ground, esp. one used for public promenade; level space separating citadel or fortress from town. [F, f. Sp. *esplanada* f. *esplanar* f. L EXPLANARE make level (*planus*); see -ADE]

ĕspou'sal (-zal) *n.* **1.** (arch.; usu. in *pl.*) marriage or betrothal. **2.** (fig.) espousing *of* (cause etc.). [ME, f. OF *espousailles* f. L *sponsalia* neut. pl. of *sponsalis* (*sponsus* p.p., as foll.; see -AL)]

ĕspou'se (-z) *v.t.* (Usu. of man) marry; give (woman) in marriage (*to*); (fig.) adopt, support, (doctrine, cause, etc.). [ME, f. OF *espouser* f. L *sponsare* (*sponsus* p.p. of *spondēre* betroth)]

ĕsprĕ'ssō *n.* (*pl.* ~s). apparatus for making coffee under steam pressure; coffee so made; place where such coffee is sold. [It., = pressed out]

esprit (ĕ'sprē, ĕsprē') *n.* sprightliness, wit; ~ **de corps** (-de kōr'), regard for honour and interests of body one belongs to; ~ **de l'escalier** (-de lěskah'lyā), clever remark that occurs to one after opportunity to make it is lost. [F, f. L *spiritus* SPIRIT¹; *corps* body, *escalier* stairs]

ĕspy' *v.t.* catch sight of; detect (flaw etc.). [ME, f. OF *espier*; see SPY]

Esq. *abbr.* Esquire.

-ĕ'sque (ĕ'sk) *suf.* forming *adjs.* meaning 'in the style of' (*arabesque*, *burlesque*, *Daliesque*, *romanesque*). [F, f. It. *-esco* f. med. L *-iscus*]

E'squimau (ĕ'skīmō) *n.* (*pl.* ~x *pr.* -z). = ESKIMO. [F]

ĕsquīr'e *n.* ||Title appended to name of one regarded as gentleman by birth, position, or education, or to name of any man in formal use or in address of letter where there is no prefixed title; *title of law officer etc.; (arch.) = SQUIRE. [ME, f. OF *esquier* f. L *scutarius* shield-bearer (*scutum* shield; see -ARY¹)]

-ĕss¹ *suf.* forming *ns.* denoting females (*actress*, *adulteress*, *authoress*, *countess*, *goddess*, *lioness*; sometimes w. sense 'wife of', as *mayoress*). [f. or after F *-esse* f. Rom. *-essa* f. LL f. Gk *-issa*]

-ĕss² *suf.* forming abstract *ns.* f. *adjs.* (*duress*). [ME f. F *-esse* f. L *-itia*, cf. -ICE]

ĕ'ssay *n.* **1.** attempt (*at*, *in*). **2.** literary composition (usu. in prose and short) on any subject; hence ~IST (3) *n.* [f. F *essai* (*essayer*; see foll.)]

ĕssay'² *v.t.* attempt (task, to do, or abs.); (arch.) try, test, (person, thing). [ME, f. ASSAY², assim. to F *essayer* f. Rom. *exagiare* weigh, f. LL *exagium* weighing (*exigere* weigh; see EXACT²)]

ĕ'ssence *n.* **1.** all that makes a thing what it is; intrinsic nature (*in ~*, fundamentally); indispensable quality or element (**of the ~**, indispensable). **2.** extract obtained by distillation etc. (lit. or fig.); perfume, scent, etc., esp. as alcoholic solution of volatile substances. **3.** abstract entity; reality underlying phenomena. [ME f. OF, f. L *essentia* f. *essens -ntis* fictitious part. of *esse* be, repr. Gk *ousia*]

Essène (ĕsē'n, ĕ'-) *n.* member of ancient-Jewish ascetic sect, living communally. [f. L f. Gk pl. *Essēnoi*]

ĕssĕ'ntial (-shǎl) *a.* & *n.* **1.** *a.* of or constituting a thing's essence; fundamental; indispensable (*to*); exceedingly important; (of disease) idiopathic; that is or resembles an essence (~ **oil**, volatile OIL with characteristic odour etc.); hence ~ITY (-shiā'l-) *n.*, ~LY² *adv.* **2.** *n.* (esp. in *pl.*) indispensable or fundamental element or thing. [ME, f. LL *essentialis* (as ESSENCE; see -IAL)]

-ĕst¹ *suf.* forming superl. of *adjs.* and *advs.* esp. of one or sometimes two syllables (*widest*, *narrowest*); see notes on Superlatives, p. xvi. [OE *-ost*, *-ust-*, *-ast-* f. Gmc *-ōstaz*, & OE *-est-*, *-st-* f. Gmc *-istaz*]

-ĕst², **-st**, *suf.* (arch.) forming 2nd pers. sing. of *vbs.* (*canst*, *doest*, *dost*, *findest*, *gavest*); see notes on Verb forms, p. xvii. [OE *-est*, *-ast*, *-st*, = OHG *-ist* etc., Goth. *-is* etc.]

EST *abbr.* Eastern Standard Time; electro-shock treatment.

ĕstā'blish *v.t.* set up (government, business, etc.) on permanent basis; settle (person, oneself, *in* office, status, etc.); appoint (civil servant etc.) to permanent (opp. temporary) post; secure permanent acceptance for (custom, precedent, belief, etc.); place beyond dispute (fact, *that*); make (church, religion) officially national. [ME, f. OF *establir* (st. *-iss-*; see *-ISH²*) f. L *stabilire* (*stabilis* STABLE¹)]

èstā′blishment *n.* establishing; church system established by law; organized body of men maintained for a purpose, (*army, navy, civil service, establishment*; **peace, war,** ∿, reduced, increased, army etc. in time of peace, war); household, staff of servants etc.; public institution, house of business; ||(esp. **the E**∿) social group exercising authority or influence, and generally seeking to resist changes. [ME, f. prec. + -MENT]

èstǎblǐshmentār′ian *a.* & *n.* (person) adhering to, or advocating the principle of, an established Church. [f. prec. + -ARIAN]

estaminet (ĕstǎ′mǐnā) *n.* small French café etc. selling alcoholic liquor. [F, f. Walloon *staminé* byre (*stamo* pole for tethering cow, prob. f. G *stamm* stem)]

èstā′te *n.* **1.** order or class forming part of body politic and sharing in government; **the Three E**∿**s** (**of the Realm**) (in England, Lords Spiritual, Lords Temporal, Commons); **third** ∿, (usu.) French bourgeoisie before Revolution; **fourth** ∿, (joc.) the PRESS¹ 6; **E**∿**s General,** = STATE¹*s General.* **2.** person's holdings in landed property (**real** ∿) or movables (**personal** ∿); person's collective assets and liabilities; ||∿ **duty** (Hist.), *∿ tax,* = DEATH *duty.* **3.** landed property; ||∿ **agent,** (1) steward of estate, (2) one who conducts business in sale or lease of houses and land; ||∿ (**car**), light saloon motor car constructed or adapted to carry both passengers and goods in one compartment, usu. with rear door. **4.** property where rubber, tea, grapes, etc., are cultivated. **5.** residential, industrial, etc., district planned by one owner or local council. **6.** (arch.) condition (*come to man's estate; holy estate of matrimony*). [ME, f. OF *estat* f. L STATUS]

èstee′m *v.t.,* & *n.* **1.** *v.t.* think favourably of, regard as valuable; consider (*I shall esteem it* (*as*) *a favour*). **2.** *n.* favourable opinion, regard, respect. [ME, f. OF *estimer* f. L *aestimare* fix price of]

ĕ′ster *n.* (Chem.) compound formed by replacing the hydrogen of an acid by an alkyl, aryl, etc., radical; hence **ĕstĕ′rǐFY** *v.t.* [G, prob. f. *essig* vinegar + *äther* ether]

Esth. *abbr.* Esther (OT & Apocrypha).

ĕ′sthēte etc. Var. of AESTHETE etc.

ĕ′stimable *a.* worthy of esteem. [F, f. L *aestimabilis* (as ESTEEM; see -ABLE)]

ĕ′stimate¹ *n.* approximate judgement (of number, amount, etc.); quantity assigned by this (||**the E**∿**s,** forecasts of national expenditure, presented annually to Parliament); contractor's statement of sum for which he will undertake specified work; judgement of character or qualities. [f. foll., or f. L *aestimatus* f. *aestimare* fix price of; see -ATE¹]

ĕ′stim|āte² *v.t.* form an estimate of or *that*; fix (number etc.) by estimate *at* (so much); form an opinion of or *that*; hence or cogn. ∿ATIVE *a.,* ∿ātOR *n.* [f. L *aestimare* fix price of + -ATE³]

èstimā′tion *n.* judgement of worth (*in my estimation*; (arch.) esteem (*hold in estimation; be in estimation*). [ME f. OF, or f. L *aestimatio* (as prec.; see -ATION)]

estival etc. See AESTIVAL etc.

Estō′nian (ĕ-) *n.* & *a.* (native, Finno-Ugric language) of Estonia. [f. *Estonia,* republic of USSR + -AN]

èstŏ′p *v.t.* (-pp-). (Law). bar or preclude esp. by estoppel (*from thing, from doing*); hence ∿PAGE *n.* [ME, f. AF, OF *estoper* f. LL *stuppare* stop up f. L *stuppa* tow (cf. STOP¹, STUFF)]

èstŏ′ppel *n.* (Law). being precluded from a course of action by one's own previous behaviour. [f. OF *estoup*(*p*)*ail* bung (*estoper,* as prec.; see -AL 2)]

èstŏ′vers (-z) *n. pl.* necessaries allowed by law (as wood for repairs or fuel taken by a tenant from his holding); right of common whereby wood etc. may be

taken from another's property. [f. AF *estover,* OF *-eir* be necessary, f. L *est opus*; see -ER⁴]

èstra′de (-ah′d) *n.* raised platform, dais. [F, f. Sp. *estrado* carpeted floor f. L *stratum* neut. p.p. (as n.) of *sternere* spread]

èstrā′nge (-nj) *v.t.* cause (person) to turn away in feeling or affection (*from* another); hence ∿MENT (-jm-) *n.* [ME, f. AF *estraunger,* OF *estranger* f. L *estran- -eare* treat as a stranger (*extraneus*; cf. EXTRANEOUS)]

èstrea′t *v.t.,* & *n.* (Law). (make) copy of court record of (fine etc.) for use in prosecution; enforcement of fine or forfeiture of recognizance. [ME, f. AF *estrete,* OF *estraite* fem. p.p. (as n.) of *estraire* f. L *extrahere* EXTRACT²]

ĕ′strogen. See OESTROGEN.

ĕ′strum, -us. See OESTRUS.

ĕ′stūar|ў *n.* tidal mouth of large river; hence ∿INE¹ *a.* [f. L *aestuarium* tidal channel, neut. a. (as n.) f. *aestus* tide; see -ARY¹]

e.s.u. *abbr.* electrostatic unit(s).

èsūr′i|ent *a.* (joc. or arch.) hungry; impecunious and greedy; hence ∿ENCE, ∿ENCY, *ns.* [f. L *esurire,* desiderative f. *edere es-* eat; see -ENT]

-**ĕt¹** *suf.* forming *ns.* (orig. dim.) (*bullet, fillet, hatchet, pullet, sonnet*). [f. OF *-et -ete* f. Rom. *-itto -itta*]

-**èt²,** -**ēte,** *suf.* forming *ns.* usu. denoting persons (*athlete, comet, poet*). [f. Gk *-ētēs*]

ē′ta¹ *n.* seventh Greek letter (H, η) = ē (cf. EPSILON). [Gk]

e′ta² (ā′-) *n.* member of outcast class in Japan. [Jap.]

ETA *abbr.* estimated time of arrival.

ètaer′iŏ (-ēr′-) *n.* (*pl.* ∿s). (Bot.) aggregate fruit (e.g. strawberry, raspberry). [f. F *etairion, -ium,* f. Gk *hetaireia* association]

ĕt ăl. *abbr.* and others. [f. L *et alii, et alia,* etc.]

e′talŏn *n.* (Phys.) device of two reflecting plates producing interfering light-beams. [f. F *étalon* standard]

étatisme (ātahtē′zm) *n.* extreme authority of State over individual citizens. [F (*état* STATE¹, *-isme* -ISM)]

etc. *abbr.* = foll.

ĕt cĕ′tera, ètcĕ′tera, *phr.* & *n.* **1.** *phr.* and the rest, and so on; and the customary continuation (*I remain yours etc.*); and similar things; or similar things. **2.** *n.* (in *pl.*) (the usual) extras, sundries. [ME f. L]

ĕtch *v.* & *n.* **1.** *v.t.* reproduce (picture etc.) by engraving metal plate etc. with acids or corrosives, esp. for purpose of printing copies; engrave (plate) thus; (fig.) impress deeply *on.* **2.** *v.i.* practise this craft. **3.** Hence ∿′ANT *n.,* corrosive used in etching, ∿′ER¹ *n.* **4.** *n.* action or process of etching. [f. Du *etsen* f. G *ätzen* etch f. OHG *azzen* cause to eat or be eaten f. Gmc *atjan* causative of *etan* EAT]

ĕ′tching *n.* In vbl senses; copy from etched plate. [f. ETCH + -ING¹]

-**ēte.** See -ET².

etĕr′nal (-l, ē-) *a.* that always (has existed and) will exist (*eternal* LIFE, *punishment*; **the E**∿, God; *Eternal* CITY); unchanging; (colloq.) incessant, too frequent, (*these eternal arguments*); ∿ **triangle,** two men and a woman or two women and a man, with problems resulting from conflict of sexual attractions; hence or cogn. **ĕtĕrn(al)IZE** (3) *vbs. t.,* ∿LY² *adv.* [ME f. OF, f. LL *aeternalis* f. L *aeternus* (= *aeviternus* f. *aevum* age); see -AL]

etĕr′nitў (ĭ-, ē-) *n.* being eternal; (in *pl.*) eternal truths; infinite time, past or future; the future life; (colloq.) very long time; ∿ **ring,** finger-ring with gems set all round it, symbolizing eternity. [ME, f. OF *eternité* f. L *aeternitas -tatis* (*aeternus,* as prec., -ITY)]

Etē′sian (ĭtē′zhan) *a.* ∿ **winds** (blowing annually in Mediterranean from N. for about 40 days in summer). [f. L f. Gk *etēsios* (*etos* year) + -AN]

ĕth. See EDH.

-**ĕth¹.** See -TH².

-**ĕth²,** -**th³,** *suf.* (arch.) forming 3rd pers. pres. sing. of *vbs.* (*doeth, doth, findeth, saith*); see notes on p. xvii. [OE *-eth, -ath, -th,* = OHG *-it* etc., Goth. *-ith* etc.]

ě'thāne *n.* (Chem.) hydrocarbon of the paraffin series, C_2H_6. [f. ETHER + -ANE]

ě'thanŏl *n.* (Chem.) ethyl ALCOHOL. [f. prec. + ALCOHOL]

ē'ther *n.* **1.** clear sky, upper regions beyond clouds. **2.** (Phys.) medium formerly assumed to permeate space and fill interstices between particles of matter; medium in which electromagnetic waves were formerly thought to be transmitted; (colloq.) radio; hence ∼IC *a.* **3.** (Chem.) colourless volatile liquid produced by action of acids on alcohol, used as solvent or anaesthetic; compound with structure similar to this, having oxygen atom joined to two alkyl etc. groups. [ME f. OF, or f. L f. Gk *aithēr* f. root of *aithō* burn, shine]

ěthēr'ěal, -ial, *a.* **1.** light, airy; heavenly; of unearthly delicacy of substance, character, or appearance; whence ∼ITY (-ă'l-) *n.*, ∼IZE (3) *v.t.*, ∼LY² *adv.* **2.** (Phys. & Chem.) of or like ether; ∼ **oil,** essential or volatile oil. [f. L *aethereus, -ius* f. Gk *aitherios* (as prec.) + -AL]

ē'therīz|e, -īs|e (-īz), *v.t.* put (patient) under influence of ether; hence ∼A'TION *n.* [f. ETHER 3 + -IZE]

ě'thic *a.* & *n.* **1.** *a.* relating to morals, treating of moral questions; morally correct, honourable; ∼ **dative,** (Gram.) dative of person indirectly interested (*answer me the telephone*); hence ∼IZE (3) *v.t.* **2.** *n.* set of principles of morals (*the Quaker ethic*); (in *pl.*, also treated as *sing.*) science of morals, moral principles, rules of conduct, whole field of moral science. [ME, f. OF *éthique* or f. L f. Gk *ēthikos* (as ETHOS; see -IC)]

ě'thical *a.* = prec. 1, whence ∼ITY (-ă'l-) *n.*; (of medicine or drug) not advertised to the general public, and usu. available only on doctor's prescription. [f. prec. + -AL]

ě'thically *adv.* In adj. senses. [f. ETHIC or prec.; see -ICALLY]

Ethiō'pian (ē-) *a.* & *n.* (native or inhabitant) of Ethiopia; (arch.) Negro. [f. *Ethiopia* f. L *Aethiops* (as foll.) + -AN]

Ethiō'pic (ē-) *a.* & *n.* (of the) Christian liturgical language of Ethiopia. [f. L f. Gk *aithiopikos* (*Aithiops* Ethiopian f. *aithō* burn + *ōps* face; see -IC)]

ě'thmoid *a.* sievelike; ∼ **bone,** square bone at root of nose, with many perforations through which olfactory nerves pass to nose; hence **ěthmoi'dAL** *a.* [f. Gk *ēthmoeidēs* (*ēthmos* sieve; see -OID)]

ě'thnarch (-k) *n.* governor of a people or province; so ∼Y¹ *n.* [f. Gk *ethnarkhēs* (*ethnos* nation, *arkhēs* ruler)]

ě'thnic *a.* & *n.* **1.** *a.* pertaining to race, ethnological, whence **ěthni'cITY** *n.*; (arch.) gentile, heathen; of a specified racial, linguistic, etc., group (usu. a minority); hence **ě'thnICALLY** *adv.* **2.** *n.* *member of ethnic group; (in *pl.*, usu. treated as *sing.*) ethnology. [ME, f. eccl. L f. Gk *ethnikos* heathen (*ethnos* nation; see -IC)]

ě'thnical *a.* ethnological. [f. prec. + -AL]

ěthnocě'ntr|ic *a.* regarding one's own race as the most important; so ∼i'cITY, ∼ISM (2), *ns.* [f. Gk *ethnos* nation + -CENTRIC]

ěthnŏ'graphy *n.* scientific description of races of men; hence **ěthnŏ'GRAPHER** *n.*, **ěthnŏgră'phIC**(AL) *adjs.* [f. Gk *ethnos* nation + -GRAPHY]

ěthnŏ'logў *n.* science of human races and their relations to one another and their characteristics; hence **ěthnŏlŏ'gIC**(AL) *adjs.*, **ěthnŏ'LOGIST** *n.* [f. as prec. + -LOGY]

ěthnomūsicŏ'log|ў (-z-) *n.* study of music of one or more cultures; so ∼IST (3) *n.* [f. Gk *ethnos* nation + MUSICOLOGY]

ěthŏ'log|ў *n.* science of character-formation; science of animal behaviour; hence **ěthoLO'GICAL** *a.*, ∼IST (3) *n.* [f. L f. Gk *ēthologia* (as ETHOS; see -LOGY)]

ē'thŏs *n.* characteristic spirit and beliefs of community, people, system, literary work, or person. [mod. L, f. Gk *ēthos* nature, disposition]

e'thyl (ě'thĭl, ē'thīl) *n.* (Chem.) radical, C_2H_5, derived from ethane, present in (*ethyl*) ALCOHOL and in ether. [G, f. as ETHER + -YL]

ě'thỹlēne *n.* hydrocarbon of olefin series, C_2H_4; ∼ **glycol,** colourless liquid used as antifreeze etc.; hence **ěthỹlē'nIC** *a.* [f. prec. + -ENE]

-ě'tic *suf.* forming *adjs.* and *ns.* (*ascetic, emetic, genetic, synthetic*). [f. or after Gk *-ētikos* or *-ētikos*; cf. -IC]

ē'tiol|āte *v.t.* make (plant) pale by excluding light; give sickly hue to (person); hence ∼A'TION *n.* [f. F *étioler* f. Norm. *étieuler* make into haulm (*éteule* f. pop. L *stupila* f. L *stipula* straw), + -ATE³]

*ētiŏ'logy. See AETIOLOGY.

ětiquětte (-kě't, ě'tĭk-) *n.* conventional rules of personal behaviour in polite society; ceremonial court; unwritten code restricting professional persons in what concerns interests of their colleagues or dignity of their profession (esp. *medical, legal, etiquette*). [f. F *étiquette* TICKET, etiquette]

E'ton (ē'-) *n.* ∼ **blue,** = CAMBRIDGE *blue*; ∼ **collar** (broad and stiff, worn outside coat-collar); ∼ **crop,** cutting of woman's hair short all over; *Eton* FIVES; ∼ **jacket,** short coat reaching only to waist; hence **Etō'nIAN** (ē-) *a.* & *n.*, (past or present member) of Eton College. [f. ∼ College, school in Berkshire]

étrier (ā'trĭā) *n.* (Mount.) short rope ladder with a few rungs of wood or metal. [F, = stirrup]

Etru'scan (ĭ) *a.* & *n.* (native or language) of ancient Etruria; so **Etrŭscŏ'LOGY** (ĭ-) *n.* [f. L *Etruscus* + -AN]

et seq(q)., et sq(q)., *abbrs.* and the following (pages, matter, etc.). [f. L *et sequentia*]

-ě'tte *suf.* forming *ns.*, meaning (1) small (*cigarette, kitchenette, roomette*), (2) imitation or substitute (*flannelette, leatherette*), (3) female (*suffragette, usherette*). [f. or after OF *-ette* fem. (as -ET¹)]

étude (ā'tūd, ātū'd) *n.* short musical composition or exercise. [F, = study]

étui (ětwē') *n.* small case for needles etc. [f. F *étui* f. OF *estui* prison (*estuier* shut up)]

-ě'tum *suf.* forming *ns.* denoting collection of trees or other plants (*arboretum, pinetum*). [L]

ětỹmŏ'log|īze, -īse (-īz), *v.* **1.** *v.t.* give or trace the etymology of. **2.** *v.i.* study etymology. [f. med. L *etymologizare* f. L *etymologia* (see foll., -IZE)]

ětỹmŏ'logў *n.* account of or facts relating to formation of word and development of its meaning; branch of linguistic science concerned with this; FOLK *etymology*; hence or cogn. **ětỹmŏ'LOGER, ětỹmŏ'LOGIST,** *ns.*, **ětỹmŏlŏ'gIC**(AL) *adjs.* [f. OF *ethimologie* f. L f. Gk *etumologia* (as foll.; see -LOGY)]

ě'tỹm|on *n.* (*pl.* ∼a), word that gives rise to a derivative or borrowed or later form. [L, f. Gk *etumon* (neut. of *etumos* true) literal sense or original form of a word]

eu- *comb. form.* well, easily. [Gk]

Eu *symb.* europium.

eucalŷ'ptus, eu'calỹpt, *n.* Austral. etc. evergreen tree of genus *Eucalyptus*; **eucalyptus (oil),** essential oil from leaves of this used as antiseptic etc. [mod. L, f. EU- + Gk *kaluptos* covered (*kaluptō* cover), unopened flower being protected by cap]

eu'charis (ū'k-) *n.* S. Amer. bulbous plant of genus *Eucharis*, with white umbellate flowers. [Gk EU(*kharis* grace) pleasing]

Eu'charist (ū'k-) *n.* Christian sacrament in which bread and wine are consecrated and consumed; consecrated elements, esp. the bread, (*give, receive, take Eucharist*); hence ∼IC(AL) (-ĭ's-) *adjs.* [ME, f. OF *eucariste* f. eccl. L f. eccl. Gk *eukharistia* thanksgiving f. Gk EU(*kharistos* f. *kharizomai* offer willingly) grateful]

eu'chre (-ker) *n.*, & *v.t.* **1.** *n.* Amer. card-game for 2, 3, or 4 persons. **2.** *v.t.* gain advantage over (opponent) by his failure to take three tricks at euchre; (fig.) deceive, outwit. [19th c.; orig. unkn.]

Eucli'dean *a.* ∼ **geometry,** that of ordinary experience, based on postulates used by Euclid; ∼ **space** (for which Euclidean geometry is valid). [f. L *Euclideus* f. Gk *Eukleideios* (*Eukleidēs* Euclid, Alexandrian geometrician *c.* 300 BC) + -AN]

eudēmŏ'nic, -daem-, (-dīm-) *a.* conducive to happiness. [f. Gk *eudaimonikos* (as foll.; see -IC)]

eudē′mon|ism, -dae′m-, *n.* system of ethics basing moral obligation on likelihood that actions will produce happiness; so ∿IST (2) *n.*, ∿i′stIC *a.* [f. Gk *eudaimonismos* f. *eudaimonia* happiness f. EU(*daimōn* guardian spirit) happy; see -ISM]

eudiŏ′mēter *n.* graduated glass tube in which gases may be chemically combined by electric spark, used in chemical experiments; hence **eudiomē′tr**IC(AL) *adjs.*, **eudiŏ′METRY** *n.* [f. Gk *eudios* clear (weather) + -METER; orig. used to measure amount of oxygen, thought to be greater in clear air]

eugē′n|ic *a.* of the production of fine (esp. human) offspring by improvement of inherited qualities; hence ∿ICALLY *adv.*, ∿ICS, **eu′gēn**IST (2), *ns.* [f. EU- +Gk *gen-* produce + -IC]

euhē′mer|ism *n.* explanation of myths on historical basis; so ∿IST (2) *n.*, ∿i′stIC *a.*, ∿IZE (4) *v.t.* & *i.* [f. *Euhemerus*, Sicilian author of 4th c. BC + -ISM]

eulō′gi|um *n.* (*pl.* ∿a *or* ∿ums). = EULOGY. [med. L; see EULOGY]

eu′log|ize, ∿ise (īz), *v.t.* extol, praise, in speech or writing; so ∿IST (1) *n.*, ∿i′stIC *a.* [f. foll. + -IZE]

eu′logy *n.* speech or writing in praise of person etc., *esp. funeral oration; (expression of) praise. [f. med. L *eulogium* f. (app. by confus. w. L *elogium* epitaph) LL f. Gk *eulogia* praise (as EU-, -LOGY)]

Eumē′nidēs (-ēz) *n. pl.* (Euphemistic name for) the Furies. [Gk, = kindly ones]

eu′nuch (-k) *n.* castrated man, esp. one employed in harem, or as court official (esp. in the Orient or under Roman Empire); (fig.) person lacking effectiveness (*political eunuch*); hence ∿OID *a.* & *n.* [ME, f. L f. Gk *eunoukhos* lit. bedchamber attendant (*eunē* bed, *okh-* cogn. w. *ekhō* hold)]

euŏ′nymus *n.* plant of genus *Euonymus*, e.g. spindle--tree. [L, f. Gk EU(*ōnumos* f. *onoma* name) of lucky name]

eupē′ptic *a.* of or having good digestion. [f. Gk EU(*peptos* f. *peptō* digest) + -IC]

eu′phem|ism *n.* substitution of mild or vague or roundabout expression for harsh or blunt or direct one; expression thus substituted ('*intimacy*' *is a euphemism for* '*sexual intercourse*'); so ∿i′stIC *a.*, ∿IZE (1, 2) *v.t.* & *i.* [f. Gk *euphēmismos* f. EU(*phēmos* f. *phēmē* speaking); see -ISM]

euphō′nium *n.* (Mus.) wind instrument of saxhorn family, tenor tuba. [mod. L, f. Gk *euphōnos*; see foll.]

eu′phony *n.* pleasing sound; (usu. of word, phrase, etc.) quality of having this; tendency to phonetic change for ease of pronunciation; hence **euphŏ′n**IC, **euphŏ′n**IOUS, *adjs.*, **eu′phon**IZE (3) *v.t.* [f. F *euphonie* f. LL f. Gk *euphōnia* f. EU(*phōnos* f. *phōnē* sound)]

euphō′r′bia *n.* herb or shrub of genus *Euphorbia*, spurge. [ME, f. L *euphorbea* f. *Euphorbus* physician to Juba II of Mauritania (1st c. AD) + -IA[1]]

euphō′r′ia *n.* feeling of well-being, esp. one based on over-confidence or over-optimism; hence **euphŏ′r**IC *a.* [Gk, f. EU(*phoros* f. *pherō* bear) well-bearing; see -IA[1]]

euphō′r′iant *a.* & *n.* (drug) inducing euphoria. [f. prec. + -ANT]

eu′phrasy *n.* plant of genus *Euphrasia*, eyebright. [f. med. L f. Gk *euphrasia* cheerfulness f. EU(*phrainō* ō f. *phrēn* mind) gladden]

eu′phrōe. Var. of UPHROE.

eu′phū|ism *n.* artificial or affected style of writing; high-flown style; so ∿IST (2) *n.*, ∿i′stIC *a.* [orig. of writing in imit. of Lyly's *Euphues* (16th c.; Gk, = well endowed by nature); see -ISM]

Eurā′sian (ūrā′zhan) *a.* & *n.* **1.** (person) of mixed European and Asian parentage. **2.** *a.* of Europe and Asia. [f. *Europe + Asia + -AN*]

Eurā′tom (ūr-) *n.* European Atomic Energy Community. [abbr.]

eurē′ka (ūr-) *int.* & *n.* (the exulting exclamation) 'I have (found) it!' [Gk *heurēka* 1st pers. sing. perf. of *heuriskō* find; orig. of ARCHIMEDES]

eurhȳ′thm|ic (ūrĭ′-) *a.* in or of harmonious proportion (esp. in architecture); hence ∿ICS *n. pl.*, harmony of bodily movement, esp. as developed with music and dance into a system of education. [f. *eurhythmy* harmony of proportions etc. f. L f. Gk *euruthmia* (as EU-, *rhuthmos* proportion, rhythm) + -IC]

eur′ō (ūr′ō) *n.* (*pl.* ∿s). (Austral.) large reddish kangaroo. [Aboriginal]

Eur′ō- (ūr′ō) *comb. form.* Europe, European, as: ∿**communism,** form of Communism in European countries, seeking to be independent of the Soviet Communist Party; ∿**crat,** bureaucrat of European Communities; ∿**dollar,** dollar held in bank in Europe etc., not in US; ∿**vision,** television of European range. [abbr.]

Europē′an (ūr-) *a.* & *n.* (native or inhabitant) of Europe; (person) descended from natives of Europe, white (person); happening in or extending over Europe (*a European reputation*); (person) concerned with Europe as a whole rather than its individual countries; *∿ **plan** (charging for hotel-room without meals); hence ∿ISM (2, 3, 4), ∿IZA′TION, *ns.*, ∿IZE (3) *v.t.* [f. F *européen* f. L *europaeus* (L f. Gk *Eurōpē* Europe) + -EAN]

eurō′pium (ūr-) *n.* (Chem.) metallic element of lanthanide series. [mod. L, f. *Europe + -IUM*]

Eustā′chian (-shan) *a.* ∿ **tube,** canal leading from pharynx to cavity of middle ear. [f. L *Eustachius* = B. *Eustachi*, It. anatomist d. 1574 + -AN]

eu′stasy *n.* uniform change of sea level throughout the world; so **eustā′t**IC *a.* [back-form. f. G *eustatisch a.* (as EU-, STATIC)]

eutē′ctic *a.* & *n.* (Phys.) ∿ (**mixture**), mixture whose constituents are in such proportions as to melt and solidify at one temperature (∿ **temperature** or **point**) like a pure substance. [f. Gk EU(*tēktos* f. *tēkō* melt) + -IC]

euthanā′sia (-z-) *n.* gentle and easy death; bringing about of this, esp. in case of incurable and painful disease. [Gk (as EU-, *thanatos* death)]

eutrŏ′phic *a.* (Of lake etc.) rich in nutrients and hence having excessive plant growth, which kills animal life by deprivation of oxygen; hence ∿ATE[3] *v.t.*, make eutrophic, ∿A′TION *n.* [f. foll. + -IC]

eu′trophy *n.* state of being eutrophic. [f. Gk EU(*trophia* f. *trephō* nourish) + -Y[1]]

eV *abbr.* electron-volt.

EVA *abbr.* extra-vehicular activity.

ēvă′cū|āte *v.t.* **1.** empty (esp. bowel or other bodily organ of contents, whence ∿ANT *a.* & *n.*; vessel *of* air etc.); discharge (faeces etc., or abs.; lit. or fig.). **2.** withdraw from, remove occupants of, (place; esp. of troops; remove (person) esp. from place considered to be dangerous *to* safer place, whence ∿EE′ *n.*, person so removed. **3.** So ∿A′TION *n.* [f. L E(*vacuare* f. *vacuus* empty) + -ATE[3]]

ēvā′de *v.t.* escape from, avoid, (attack, pursuit, designs, adversary, blow, obstacle, etc.); avoid doing (duty etc.), answering (question), paying (tax due), yielding to (argument etc.); defeat intention of (law etc., esp. while complying with its letter); (of thing) elude, baffle; hence **ēvā′d**ABLE *a.* [f. F *évader* f. L E(*vadere vas-* go)]

ēvă′gin|āte *v.t.* (Physiol.) turn (tubular organ) inside out; hence ∿A′TION *n.* [f. L E(*vaginare* f. VAGINA) + -ATE[3]]

ēvă′lū|āte *v.t.* ascertain amount of; find numerical expression for; appraise, assess; hence or cogn. ∿A′TION *n.*, ∿ATIVE *a.* [back-form. f. *evaluation* f. F *évaluation* (*évaluer* f. as E-, VALUE)]

ēvane′sce *v.i.* fade out of sight; become effaced; disappear. [f. L E(*vanescere* f. *vanus* empty); see -ESCE]

ēvane′sc|ent *a.* (Of impression, appearance, etc.) quickly fading; hence ∿ENCE *n.*, ∿entLY[2] *adv.* [f. as prec.; see -ENT]

ēvă′ngel (-nj-) *n.* (arch.) the gospel; any of the four Gospels; doctrine, principle, (of politics etc.). [ME, f. OF *evangile* f. eccl. L f. Gk EU(*aggelion*; cf. ANGEL) good news]

evangelic. Var. (arch.) of foll.
ēvăngĕ′lical (-nj-) *a.* & *n.* of or according to the teaching of the gospel or the Christian religion; (member) of the Protestant school maintaining that the essence of the gospel consists in doctrine of salvation by faith in Atonement, whence ∿ISM (3) *n.*; hence ∿LY² *adv.* [f. eccl. L f. eccl. Gk *euaggelikos* (as EVANGEL; see -IC, -AL)]
ĕvă′ngelism (-nj-) *n.* preaching or promulgation of the gospel; = EVANGELICALISM. [f. EVANGEL + -ISM]
ĕvă′ngelist (-nj-) *n.* writer of one of the four Gospels; preacher of the gospel; layman doing missionary work. [ME, f. OF *evangeliste* f. eccl. L *evangelista* f. Gk *euaggelistēs* (as EVANGELIZE; see -IST)]
ĕvăngeli′stic (-nj-) *a.* of the four evangelists; of preachers of the gospel; = EVANGELICAL. [f. prec. + -IC]
ĕvă′ngelīz|e (-nj-), **īs|e** (-īz), *v.t.* preach the gospel to (persons, or area.); win over (person) to Christianity; hence ∿A′TION *n.* [ME, f. eccl. L *evangelizare* f. eccl. Gk *euaggelizomai* (as EVANGEL; see -IZE)]
ĕvă′nish *v.i.* (literary). vanish; die away; hence ∿MENT *n.* [ME, f. OF *evanir* (st. *-iss-*; see *-ISH²*) f. Rom. **exvanire* = L *evanescere* EVANESCE]
ĕvă′por|āte *v.t.* & *i.* turn from solid or liquid into vapour; (cause to) lose moisture as vapour; (fig.) (cause to) be lost or disappear; ∿ated milk, unsweetened milk concentrated by partial evaporation of its liquid content; hence or cogn. ∿ABLE, ∿ATIVE, *adjs.*, ∿A′TION, ∿ator, *ns.* [f. L E(*vaporare* f. as VAPOUR) + -ATE³]
ĕvā′sion (-zhon) *n.* act or means of evading; subterfuge, prevaricating excuse. [ME f. OF, f. L *evasio -onis* (as EVADE; see -ION)]
ĕvā′sive *a.* seeking to evade, addicted to evasion; tending to evasion; ∿ action (to avoid trouble etc.); hence ∿LY² (-vlī) *adv.*, ∿NESS (-vn-) *n.* [f. as prec. + -IVE]
Eve¹ (ēv) *n.* first woman, in Hebrew tradition; daughter of ∿, woman (often w. allus. to feminine curiosity etc.). [OE *Ēfe* f. LL *Eva* f. Heb. *Ḥavvāh*, orig. = life, living]
ēve² *n.* evening or day before (*of*) church festival or any date or event; time just before anything (*on the eve of an election*); (arch.) evening. [ME, − EVEN¹; for loss of -*n* cf. MAID]
ĕvĕ′ction *n.* perturbation of moon's motion by sun's attraction. [f. L E(*vectio* f. *vehere vect-* carry), see -ION]
ē′ven¹, e′en¹ (Sc.; ēn), *n.* 1. (poet.) evening. 2. ∿song, evening prayer in Church of England. [OE *ǣfen*, = OS, OHG *āband*]
ē′ven² *a.* (∿er, ∿est). 1. level (**on an ∿ keel**, of ship or aircraft, or fig.); smooth; uniform in quality; (of temper etc.) equable, unruffled; in same plane or line (*with*; **be or get ∿ with**, have one's revenge on). 2. equally balanced (*even-handed justice*); ∿ **break**, (colloq.) equal chance; ∿ **money**, ∥∿s, equal stakes by both parties in betting, so ∿ **chance** etc. (of success as likely as not). 3. equal in number or amount; (Law & Commerc.) **of ∿** (same) **date**. 4. (Of number) divisible by two, opp. *odd*; (of money, time, etc.) not involving fractions, exact (*dozen* etc.). 5. Hence ∿LY² *adv.*, ∿NESS (-n-n-) *n.* [OE *efen*, = OS, OHG *eban*, ON *jafn*, Goth. *ibns* f. Gmc **ebhnaz*]
ē′ven³, (arch. or poet.) **e′en²** (ēn), *adv.* 1. (Inviting comparison of the assertion, negation, etc., with a less strong one that might have been made:) *he disputes even the facts* (not merely the inferences from them); *I never even opened* (and certainly did not read) *the letter*; *does he even suspect* (not to say realize) *the danger?*: *even if my watch is right we shall be late* (later if it is slow); **∿ now** (as well as previously); **∿ so** (in that case as well as in others); *this applies even more* (not merely equally) *to French* (*than to English*). 2. (arch. or rhet.) neither more nor less than, just, simply, (*even as I was deploring his absence, he came in*; **∿ now**, at this very moment; **∿** (quite) **so**); (emphasizing identity) that

is (*God, even our own God*). [OE *efne*, = OS *efno*, OHG *ebano* f. WG **ebhnō*]
ē′ven⁴ *v.t.* & *i.* make or become even; (arch.) treat as equal or comparable (*to*); ∿ **up**, make or become equal or uniform. [OE *efnan, efnian* (as EVEN²)]
ē′vening (ē′vn-) *n.* close of day, esp. from about 6 p.m. (or earlier sunset) to bedtime (*in or during the evening*; *on Wednesday evening*); this time spent in a particular way (*musical evenings*); (colloq.) = GOOD *evening*; (fig.) decline of life, closing period; ∿ **dress**, that prescribed by fashion to be worn in the evening, esp. at dinner or theatre; ∿ **paper**, newspaper published after (usu.) midday; *evening* PRAYER¹; ∿ **primrose**, plant of genus *Oenothera* with pale yellow flowers that open in the evening; ∿**-school**, night-school; ∿ **star**, planet, esp. Venus, when seen in west after sunset. [OE *ǣfnung* vbl n. (cf. -ING¹) f. *ǣfnian* (as EVEN¹)]
ĕvě′nt *n.* 1. fact of a thing's happening (**in the ∿ of** his death, of his coming, **that he dies, comes*, if he dies, comes); thing that happens, esp. important thing (*quite an event*), whence ∿FUL, ∿LESS, *adjs.*; any of several possible but mutually exclusive occurrences (**double ∿**, combined occurrence of two events, esp. as subject of bet); something on the result of which money is staked; (Sport) item of programme; (Phys.) single occurrence of process, e.g. ionization of one atom. 2. result, outcome; **in any or either ∿, at all ∿s**, in any case; **in the ∿**, as things turn(ed) out; WISE¹ *after the event*. [f. L *eventus* f. E(*venire vent-* come)]
ĕ′ventīde *n.* 1. (arch.) evening. 2. ∥∿ **home** (for old people, orig. run by Salvation Army). [OE EVEN¹, TIDE¹)]
ĕvĕ′ntūal *a.* ultimately resulting, whence ∿LY² *adv.*; (arch.) that will happen under certain circumstances. [f. as EVENT + -AL, after *actual*]
ĕvĕntūā′litў *n.* possible event. [f. as prec. + -ITY]
ĕvĕ′ntūāte *v.i.* turn out (*well, ill*, etc.) as the result; result (*in*, or abs.). [f. as EVENT + -ATE³, after *actuate*]
ĕ′ver, (poet.) **e′er** (ār), *adv.* 1. (usu. arch.) always, at all times; **∿ and again**, **∿ and anon**, occasionally. 2. **for ∿** (**and ∿, and a day**), **fore′ver*(*mor′e*), for all future time, incessantly, (colloq.) for a very long time, (*the Stars and Stripes* etc. **for ∿!**, as expression of support); (**for**) ∿**more**, always; *ever after, ever since*; ∿ **yours** or **yours ∿** (in ending letter to close friend etc.); (in comb. w. participles etc.) constantly (*ever-recurring, ever-present*). 3. (With negative, question, condition, comparison). at any time (*nothing ever happens in this town*; *did you ever hear such nonsense?*; (colloq.) **did you ∿?** (i.e. see or hear the like); *if I ever catch him*; *the best thing I ever heard*; *his best performance ever*; *as good as ever*; *better than ever*; ***(sl.) **is he ∿** (he is very) *conceited* etc.; (strengthening *as*) *as quick as ever you can*). 4. (Emphasizing question, colloq.) *what ever* (or *whatever*) *does he want?*; *who ever can he be?*; *which ever Brown do you mean?*; *when, where, how, ever did I drop it?*; *why ever didn't you say so?*; ∿ **so** [f. earlier *never so*] to any possible extent, (colloq.) very (*it is ever so easy, so much easier*; (vulg.) *very much* (*thanks ever so*); ∿ **such a**, (vulg.) a very (*he is ever such a nice man*). [OE *ǣfre*, of unkn. orig.]
ĕver-dū′ring *a.* (arch.) everlasting. [f. EVER + as DURING]
E′verĕst (ĕ′-) *n.* highest peak of attainment etc. [Mount ∿ in Nepal and Tibet, world's highest mountain, f. Sir G. ∿, Surveyor-General of India d. 1866]
*ĕ′vergläde *n.* marshy tract of land, esp. (in *pl.*) swamp in S. Florida. [prob. f. EVER + GLADE]
ĕ′vergreen *a.* & *n.* 1. *a.* always green or fresh (lit. or fig.). 2. *a. & n.* (tree or shrub) having leaves all the year round (cf. DECIDUOUS). [f. EVER + GREEN¹]
ĕverla′sting (-ah′-) *a.* & *n.* 1. *a.* lasting for ever; lasting too long, repeated too often; (of plant) keeping shape and colour when dried;

everlasting LIFE; ~ **pea,** plant of genus *Lathyrus* with ornamental coloured flowers; hence ~LY² *adv.*, ~NESS *n.* **2.** *n.* eternity *(from everlasting)*; strong twilled woollen stuff; immortelle. [ME, f. EVER + LASTING]

ēvēr't *v.t.* (Physiol.) turn (organ etc.) outwards or inside out; so **ēvēr'sion** *n.* [f. L E(*vertere vers-* turn)]

e'verӯ (ĕ'vrī) *a.* **1.** each single *(every word of it is false; it engaged his every thought)*; (of succession or alternation) *he comes* ~ **day,** ~ **other** *or* **second day** (with one day between each two days of coming, (fig.) in a high proportion of days), ~ **three days,** ~ **third day,** (with two days between each two days of coming); ~ **now and again,** ~ **now and then,** ~ **so often,** from time to time (cf. NOW). **2.** *every* BIT² *as*; ~**body** (else), every (other) person; ~**day** *a.,* occurring daily, worn or used on ordinary days, commonplace; ~ **last,** (sl.) each without any exception; ~ **one,** each one *(every one of them is wrong)*; ~**one** (or ~ **one**), everybody *(everyone likes to have his way)*; **~***place,** everywhere; ~**thing,** all things *(everything depends on that;* **have** ~**thing,** (colloq.), possess every attraction etc.), thing of first importance *(speed is everything)*; ~ **time,** (colloq.) without exception, without any hesitation; ~**way,** in every way, in every respect; ~**where,** in every place, (colloq.) in many places; **~***which way,** in every direction. [OE *ǣfre ǣlc* ever each]

E'verӯmăn (ĕ'vr-) *n.* the ordinary or typical human being, the 'man in the street'. [character in 15th-c. morality play, f. prec. + MAN¹]

ēvǐ'ct *v.t.* expel (person; esp. tenant *from* land etc.); recover (property, title to it, *of, from,* person) by legal process; hence or cogn. ~ION, ~OR, *ns.* [f. L E(*vincere vict-* conquer)]

e'vidence *n.,* & *v.t.* **1.** *n.* clearness, obviousness; **in** ~, conspicuous. **2.** indication, sign, (of quality, treatment, etc.); testimony, facts, in support of (or *for*) a conclusion; INTERNAL, EXTERNAL, *evidence.* **3.** (Law). information (given personally or drawn from documents etc.) tending to establish fact; statements or proofs admissible as testimony in court; *call* (person) **in** ~, as a witness; CIRCUMSTANTIAL, PRESUMPTIVE, *verbal, evidence; turn* ||**King's** or ||**Queen's** or *****State's** ~ (of accomplice in crime testifying for prosecution). **4.** So **ēvǐdĕ'ntIAL** (-shal), **ēvidĕ'ntiARY** (-sherī), *adjs.* **5.** *v.t.* serve to indicate, attest. [ME f. OF, f. L *evidentia* (as foll.; see -ENCE)]

e'vident *a.* obvious (to eye or mind); hence ~LY² *adv.* [ME f. OF, or f. L E(*vidēre* see); see -ENT]

e'vil (-ǐl, -ĭl) *a.* & *n.* **1.** *a.* bad, harmful, (**the E**~ **One,** the Devil); *of evil* (bad) *repute, an evil* (slanderous) *tongue, an evil* (disagreeable) *smell;* ~ **days,** time when one suffers misfortune; ~ **day** or **hour,** time of ill luck, disaster, etc.; ~ **eye,** malicious look (superstitiously believed to do material harm), ability to cast such looks; hence ~LY² *adv.* **2.** *n.* evil thing, sin, harm, *(the lesser of two evils; evil-doer);* KING¹*'s evil;* **speak** ~ **of,** slander. [OE *yfel,* = OS, OHG *ubil,* Goth. *ubils* f. Gmc **ubhilaz*]

ēvǐ'nc|e *v.t.* show, indicate, (quality etc., *that* etc.); show that one has (quality); hence ~IVE *a.* [f. as EVICT]

ēvǐ'scer|āte *v.t.* disembowel; (fig.) empty (thing) of vital contents; hence ~A'TION *n.* [f. L EVISCERARE (VISCERA) + -ATE³]

ēvō'ke *v.t.* call up (spirit from the dead, response, feelings, memories, energies); so **ēvoca'TION** *n.,* **ēvō'catIVE, ēvō'catORY,** *adjs.* [f. L E(*vocare* call)]

évolué (āvō'lūā) *n.* & *a.* (African) with European education or modes of thought. [F, p.p. of *évoluer* EVOLVE]

ē'volute¹ (-ūt, -ŏŏt) *a.* & *n.* (Math.) ~ (**curve**), locus of centres of curvature of another curve that is its involute. [f. L *evolutus* p.p. (as EVOLVE)]

ē'volute² (-ūt, -ŏŏt) *v.i.* & *t.* develop by evolution. [back-form. f. foll.]

ēvolu'tion (-lŏŏ'-) *n.* **1.** opening out (of roll, bud, etc.;

usu. fig.); appearance (of events etc.) in due succession; evolving, giving off, (of gas, heat, etc.). **2.** unfolding of curve; (Math.) extraction of root from any given power (cf. INVOLUTION). **3.** development (of organism, human society, the universe, design, argument, etc.); origination of species by development from earlier forms, not by special creation; hence ~ISM (3), ~IST (2), *ns.,* ~i'stIC *a.* **4.** change in disposition of troops or ships; wheeling about, movement, in dancing etc. **5.** Hence ~AL, ~ARY¹, *adjs.* [f. L *evolutio* unrolling (as EVOLVE; see -ION)]

ē'volutive (-lŏŏ-) *a.* tending to evolution. [f. prec. + -IVE]

ēvŏ'lve *v.t.* & *i.* unfold, open out; give off (gas, heat, etc.); develop, deduce, (theory, facts, etc.); develop by natural process; hence ~MENT (-vm-) *n.* [f. L E(*volvere volut-* roll)]

ēvŭ'lsion (-shon) *n.* forcible extraction. [f. L *evulsio* f. E(*vellere vuls-* pluck); see -ION]

ē'vzōne *n.* member of select Greek infantry regiment. [f. mod. Gk *euzōnos* f. Gk EU(*zōnos* a. f. *zōnē* girdle) dressed for exercise]

ewe (ū) *n.* female (esp. adult) sheep; ~ **lamb,** one's most cherished possession [2 Sam. 12]; ~**-necked,** (of horse) having thin concave neck. [OE *ēowu,* = OS *ewwi,* OHG *ouwi,* ON *ær* f. Gmc **awi* f. IE **owi*]

ew'er *n.* pitcher; water-jug with wide mouth. [ME, f. AF **ewer,* ONF *eviere,* OF *aiguiere* f. Rom. **aquaria,* fem. adj. as n. (L *aqua* water; see -ARY¹)]

ewigkeit (ā'vigkīt) *n.* (joc.) **into, in, the** ~, into thin air, in the unknown. [G, = eternity]

ĕx¹ *a.* & *n.* (colloq.) **1.** *a.* former; outdated. **2.** *n.* former occupant of specified position etc., esp. former husband or wife. [f. EX-¹ 2]

ĕx² *prep.* (Commerc.) (Of goods) out of, sold from, *(ship, store, works,* etc.); (of stocks or shares) without, excluding, (**ex dividend,** not including next dividend). [L, = out of]

ex-¹ *pref.* **1.** forming *vbs.* w. sense 'out', 'forth', *(exclude, exit),* 'upward' *(extol),* 'thoroughly' *(excruciate),* 'bring into a state' *(exasperate),* 'remove, expel, or free, from' *(expatriate, exonerate, excoriate),* and *adjs.* w. sense 'not having', usu. in form *e-* *(ecaudate* tailless). **2.** forming *ns.* f. titles of office, status, etc., in sense 'formerly' *(ex--convict, ex-president, ex-Prime-Minister, ex-wife);* ||**ex--ser'vice** *a.,* having belonged to one of the fighting services, pertaining to former servicemen and -women; so ||**ex-ser'viceman, -woman.** [L *(ex* out of)]

ex-² *pref.* meaning 'out' *(exodus).* [Gk *(ex* out of)]

ē'xa- *pref.* denoting factor of 10¹⁸. [perh. f. HEXA-]

ĕxǎ'cerb|āte *v.t.* aggravate (pain, disease, anger); irritate (person etc.); so A'TION *n.* [f. L EX¹(*acerbare* f. *acerbus* bitter) + -ATE³]

ĕxǎ'ct¹ (ĭgz-) *a.* precise, rigorous, (rules, order, etc.); (of person, judgement, description, report, answer, etc.) accurate, strictly correct; ~ **science** (admitting of absolute or quantitative precision); hence or cogn. ~ITUDE, ~NESS, *ns.* [f. L *exactus* p.p. (as foll.)]

ĕxǎ'ct² (ĭgz-) *v.t.* demand and enforce payment of (money, fees, etc.; *from* or *of* person); demand, insist on, (act, conduct, *from, of*), (of circumstances) require urgently, whence ~ING² *a.;* hence or cogn. ~ABLE *a.,* ~OR *n.* [f. L EX¹(*igere act-* = *agere* drive)]

ĕxǎ'ction (ĭgz-) *n.* exacting (of money etc.); illegal or exorbitant demand, extortion; sum or thing thus exacted. [ME, f. L *exactio* (as prec.; see -ION)]

ĕxǎ'ctlӯ (ĭgz-) *adv.* In adj. senses *(exactly when, when exactly, did it happen?);* (as answer or confirmation) quite so, just as you say; **not** ~, (colloq., iron.) by no means. [f. EXACT¹ + -LY²]

ĕxǎ'gger|āte (ĭgzǎ'j-) *v.t.* enlarge (thing described, or abs.) beyond limits of truth; intensify, aggravate; (arch.) make (physical features etc.) of abnormal size; hence or cogn. ~A'TION *n.,* ~ātOR, *ns.,* ~ATIVE *a.* [f. L EX¹(*aggerare* heap up f. *agger* heap) + -ATE³]

ĕxa'lt (ĭgzaw'lt) *v.t.* raise, place high in rank, power,

For other words in *ex-* see EX-¹, EX-².

etc.; praise, extol, (*exalt to the skies*); dignify, ennoble. [ME, f. L EX¹(*altare* f. *altus* high)]

ĕxaltā′tion (ĕgzawl-, ĕksawl-) *n.* raising, lifting up, (usu. fig.); elation, rapturous emotion; **E**∼ **of the Cross**, (festival on 14 Sept. commemorating) reputed apparition of Cross to Constantine and later recovery of Cross from Persians. [ME f. OF, or f. LL *exaltatio* (as prec.; see -ATION)]

exalté (ĕgzah′ltā) *a.* & *n.* (*fem.* ∼e *pr.* same). excited or elated (person). [F, p.p. of *exalter* EXALT]

ĕxä′m (ĭgz-) *n.* (colloq.) = foll. 2. [abbr.]

ĕxāminā′tion (ĭgz-) *n.* **1.** detailed inspection (*of, into*). **2.** testing of knowledge or ability (of pupils, candidates) by oral or written questions or exercises; ∼**-paper**, series of such questions or of examinee's answers to them. **3.** (Law). formal questioning of witness or accused; ∼**-in-chief** (by party calling witness). **4.** Hence ∼AL *a.* [ME f. OF, f. L *examinatio* -*onis* (as foll.; see -ATION)]

ĕxä′min|e (ĭgz-) *v.* **1.** *v.t.* inquire into nature, condition, etc., of, test (accounts, person *in* or *on* subject, bodily organ, by examination, theory, statement, one's own conscience, *whether*); (Law) formally question (witness or accused). **2.** *v.i.* inquire *into*. **3.** Hence ∼atōr′ial *a.*, ∼ēr′, ∼ĕr¹, *ns.* [ME, f. OF *examiner* f. L *examinare* (*examen -minis* for *exagmen* tongue of balance, examination, as EXACT³)]

ĕxa′mple (ĭgzah′-) *n.* fact or thing illustrating general rule (for ∼), by way of such illustration, problem or exercise designed to do this; specimen of workmanship, quality, etc.; instance of punishment etc. as warning to others (*make an example of him*); precedent (*beyond, without example*); conduct as object of imitation (*give, set, a good example*; cf. EXEMPLARY). [ME f. OF, f. L *exemplum* (as EXEMPT¹)]

ĕxä′nimate (ĭgz-) *a.* dead; lacking animation, spiritless. [f. L *exanimatus* p.p. of EX¹*animare* deprive of life (*anima*); see -ATE²]

ĕxanthē′ma (ĕgz-) *n.* (Path.) disease (esp. feverish) with eruptions on skin. |LL, f. Gk *exanthēma* cruption (EX²*antheō* f. *anthos* blossom)]

ĕ′xärch (-k) *n.* head of autocephalous Orthodox Church; bishop ranking between patriarch and metropolitan; patriarch's representative; (Hist.) governor of Byzantine province; so ∼ATE¹ *n.* [f. eccl. L, f. Gk *exarkhos* (as EX-², *-arkhos* ruler)]

ĕxa′sper|āte (ĭgzā′-, -ah′-) *v.t.* make worse (ill feeling, disease, pain); irritate (person) to annoyance or anger (*exasperated at* or *by*); provoke (person *to* anger etc., *to* do); so ∼A′TION *n.* [f. L EX¹(*asperare* f. *asper* rough) + -ATE³]

ex cathedra (ĕks kathē′dra, kă′thĭdra) *adv.* & *a.* authoritative(ly), (of papal pronouncement) given as infallible judgement. [L, = from the (teacher's) chair]

ĕ′xcav|āte *v.t.* make hollow; make (hole, channel) by digging; dig out (soil) leaving a hole; reveal or extract by digging; hence or cogn. ∼A′TION, ∼ātOR, *ns.* [f. L EX¹(*cavare* f. *cavus* hollow) + -ATE³]

excee′d *v.t.* do more than is warranted by, go beyond the limit set by, (one's instructions; rights, etc.); be greater or more numerous than (quantity, thing, *by* so much); surpass (person etc. *in*). [ME, f. OF *exceder* f. L EX¹(*cedere cess-* go)]

excee′ding *a.* & (arch.) *adv.* surpassing(ly) in amount or degree; pre-eminent(ly); hence ∼LY² *adv.* [f. prec. + -ING²]

ĕxcĕ′l *v.* (-ll-). **1.** *v.t.* be superior to (others or one*self* previously in quality, *in* doing). **2.** *v.i.* be pre-eminent (*in, at*, thing, *in* quality, *in* doing). [ME, f. L EX¹(*cellere*; cf. *celsus* lofty)]

ĕ′xcellence *n.* surpassing merit; thing in which person etc. excels. [ME f. OF, or f. L *excellentia* (as prec.; see -ENCE)]

ĕ′xcellency *n.* Title of ambassadors, governors, and their spouses, and some other officers. [ME, f. L *excellentia* (as EXCEL; see -ENCY)]

ĕ′xcellent *a.* pre-eminent; very good; hence ∼LY² *adv.* [ME f. OF (as EXCEL; see -ENT)]

ĕxcĕ′lsior *int.* & *n.* **1.** *int.* higher (as motto, trade mark, etc.). **2.** *n.* shavings of soft wood for stuffing. [L, compar. of EX¹*celsus* lofty]

ĕxcĕ′ntric *a.* = ECCENTRIC (esp. in sense 1). [f. as ECCENTRIC; see EX-¹]

ĕxcĕ′pt¹ *v.t.* exclude (thing) from enumeration, statement, etc., (*present company excepted*; *except him from the general amnesty*); so ∼IVE *a.* [ME, f. L EX¹(*cipere cept-* = *capere* take)]

ĕxcĕ′pt² *prep.* & *conj.* **1.** *prep.* not including, but, (*we all failed except him*; *he is everywhere except in the right place*; *never to be found except in the wrong place*; *it is right except that the accents are omitted, except for the omission of accents*). **2.** *conj.* (esp. arch.) unless (*except he be born again*). [ME, orig. p.p. f. L *exceptus* (as prec.)]

ĕxcĕ′pting *prep.* & *conj.* = prec., esp. after *not* or *always*. [f. EXCEPT¹ + -ING²]

ĕxcĕ′ption *n.* excepting; thing excepted, thing that does not follow the rule; **the** ∼ **proves the rule,** the excepting of some cases shows that the rule exists, or that it applies to those not excepted; **with the** ∼ **of,** except; **take** ∼, object *to*, whence ∼ABLE *a.*, open to objection. [ME f. OF, f. L *exceptio onis* (as EXCEPT¹; see -ION)]

ĕxcĕ′ptional *a.* forming an exception; unusual (*exceptional advantages*); unusually good; hence ∼ITY (-ă′l-) *n.*, ∼LY² *adv.* [f. prec. + -AL]

exceptis excipiendis (ĕkseptis ĕksĭpiĕ′ndĭs) *adv.* with appropriate exceptions. [LL, f. abl. pl. of *exceptus* p.p., *excipiendus* gerundive, of *excipere* (see EXCEPT¹)]

ĕ′xcerpt *n.* extract from book, manuscript, musical work, etc. [f. L *excerptum* neut. p.p. (as n.) of *excerpere* (see foll.)]

ĕxcĕr′pt *v.t.* extract, quote, (passage *from* book etc., or abs.); hence ∼IBLE *a.*, ∼ION *n.* [f. L EX¹(*cerpere cerpt-* = *carpere* pluck)]

ĕxcĕ′ss *n.* **1.** overstepping of due limits; intemperance in eating or drinking. **2.** fact of exceeding (**in** ∼ **of,** more than). **3.** amount by which one number or quantity exceeds another; agreed amount subtracted by insurer from insured person's claim in determining payment to be made; ∼ **fare,** payment due for travelling farther on or in higher class than ticket allows; ∼ **baggage** or **luggage** (over the weight for free carriage); ∼ **postage,** payment due when stamps on letter etc. are insufficient. **4.** superabundance, extreme degree, (*of* cruelty etc.); exceeding of the proper amount or degree. esp. *in* or *to* excess. **5.** So ∼IVE *a.*, ∼ively² (-vlĭ) *adv.* [ME, f. OF *exces* f. L *excessus* (as EXCEED)]

ĕxchā′nge (-nj) *n.* **1.** act or process of exchanging (*of* goods, prisoners of war, blows, words, etc.); (**fair**) ∼ **is no robbery,** lit., or joc. excuse for unfair exchange; HEAT¹-, ION, *exchange*; **in** ∼, as thing exchanged (*for*); so ∼ **student,** one who is given free tuition etc. at another school etc. in consideration of reciprocal treatment of a student from that school; similarly ∼ **teacher. 2.** exchanging of money for its equivalent in money of same or another country; money-changer's trade; PAR¹ *of exchange*; (**rate of**) ∼, price at which (bills drawn in a) foreign currency may be bought, or difference between this and par; foreign currency, sale by exchange; system of settling debts between persons (esp. in different countries) without use of money, by bills of exchange (see BILL⁴). **3.** (Chess). possession of superior piece (esp. rook) against inferior one. **4.** building where merchants, brokers, etc., assemble to transact business (*corn exchange, stock exchange*); place where potential employers and employees are made known (EMPLOYMENT *exchange*, LABOUR¹ *Exchange*). **5.** central telephone office of a district where connections are made between lines concerned in calls. [ME f. AF *eschaunge*, OF *eschange* (*eschangier*; see foll.)]

ĕxchā′nge² (-nj) *v.* **1.** *v.t.* give (thing) in place of (*for*)

another; give and receive (blows, words, glances, positions, prisoners, etc.); hence ∼e**ABLE** (-nja-) *a*. **2.** *v.i.* take part in exchange of positions etc. (*with* another). **3.** Hence ∼ER[1] (1, 2) *n*. [ME, f. OF *eschangier* f. Rom. *excambiare (as EX-[1], CHANGE[2])]
exchĕ′quer (-ker) *n*. ‖department of public service charged with receipt and custody of revenue (‖**Chancellor of the E**∼, finance minister of United Kingdom); royal or national treasury; money of private person etc.; ‖(**Court of**) **E**∼, (Hist.) court of law now merged in Queen's Bench Division or Court of Session. [orig. = 'chess-board', then w. ref. to keeping of accounts on chequered table-cloth; ME, f. AF *escheker*, OF *eschequier*, *eschaquier*, f. med. L *scaccarium* chess-board, CHEQUER[1]; *ex*- by erron. assoc. w. EX-[1] in *exchange* etc.]
e′xcīse[1] (-z) *n*., & *v.t.* **1.** *n*. duty or tax levied on goods and commodities produced or sold within the country, and on various licences etc.; ‖(Hist.) government office collecting excise (now *Board of Customs and Excise*); ‖∼**man,** (Hist.) officer collecting excise and preventing infringement of excise laws. **2.** *v.t.* force (person) to pay excise; charge excise on (goods); (arch.) overcharge (lit. or fig.); hence **exci′s**ABLE (-z-) *a*. [f. MDu. *excijs, accijs*, perh. f. Rom. *accensum f. *Accensare tax (CENSUS)]
exci′se[2] (-z) *v.t.* cut out or away (passage of book, limb, organ, etc.); so **exci′sion** (-zhon) *n*. [f. L EX[1](*cidere cis-* = *caedere* cut)]
exci′t|**e** *v.t.* **1.** bring into play, rouse up, (feelings, faculties, etc.); provoke, bring about, (action, active condition); promote activity of (bodily organ etc.) by stimulus; move (person) to strong emotion. **2.** (Electr. & Magn.) induce activity in (substance), cause (current) to flow; (Phys.) cause emission of (spectrum), cause (substance) to emit radiation, put (atom etc.) into state of higher energy; hence **excita′tion,** ∼ER[1] (2), *ns*. **3.** Hence or cogn. ∼**abi′**lity, ∼**ement** (-tm-), *ns.*, **e′xcit**ant *a*. & *n*., ∼**able** (esp., of person, easily excited, unmanageable), ∼**ative,** ∼**atory,** *adjs.*, ∼**ēd**LY[2] *adv*. [ME, f. OF *exciter* or f. L *excitare* frequent. of EX[1](*ciēre* set in motion)]
exci′ting *a*. In vbl senses; causing great interest or eagerness; hence ∼LY[2] *adv*., ∼NESS *n*. [f. prec. + -ING[2]]
excitŏn (ĕ′ksī-, ĕksī′-) *n*. (Phys.) combination of excited electron and hole, having some properties of a particle. [f. EXCITATION + -ON]
exclai′m *v*. **1.** *v.i.* cry out, esp. from pain, anger, surprise, etc.; ∼ **against,** (arch.) accuse loudly. **2.** *v.t.* utter (words, *that*) thus. [f. F *exclamer* or f. L EX[1]-(*clamare* cf. CLAIM[1])]
exclama′tion *n*. exclaiming; words exclaimed; ∼ **mark, *point,** punctuation mark (!) indicating exclamation; so **exclă′mat**ORY *a*. [ME f. OF, or f. L *exclamatio* (as prec.; see -ATION)]
e′xclāve *n*. territory surrounded by foreign territory. [f. EX-[1] + ENCLAVE]
exclō′sure (-zher) *n*. (Forestry etc.) area from which unwanted animals are excluded. [f. EX-[1] + ENCLOSURE]
exclu′d|**e** (-lōō′d) *v.t.* shut out (person, thing, *from* place, society, privilege, etc.); prevent the occurrence of, make impossible, (doubt, etc.); ignore as irrelevant; expel and shut out; ∼**ed middle,** (Logic) principle that either a proposition or its negative must be true; hence ∼ER[1] (1, 2) *n*. [ME, f. L EX[1]-(*cludere clus-* = *claudere* shut)]
exclu′sion (-lōō′zhon) *n*. excluding, shutting out; **to the** ∼ **of,** so as to exclude; ∼ **principle,** (Phys.) assertion that no two fermions of same kind can be in same quantum state; hence ∼ARY[1] *a*. [f. L *exclusio* (as prec.; see -ION)]
exclu′sïve (-lōō′-) *a*. & *n*. **1.** *a*. shutting out; not admitting of; desirous of excluding others, (of social circles etc.) chary of admitting members, select, (**E**∼ **Brethren,** more exclusive section of Plymouth Brethren; (of article in shop or newspaper, etc.) not

to be had, not published, elsewhere; high-class, expensive; (of terms etc.) excluding all but what is specified; employed or followed or held to the exclusion of all else (*his exclusive occupation*; *exclusive rights*); ∼ **of,** not including (*20 men, exclusive of our own*); hence ∼LY[2] (-vlĭ) *adv.*, ∼NESS (-vn-), **exclusï′v**ITY (-lōō-), *ns*. **2.** *n*. article etc. published by only one newspaper or periodical. [f. med. L *exclusivus* (as EXCLUDE; see -IVE)]
excŏ′git|**āte** *v.t.* think out, contrive; hence ∼ABLE *a.*, ∼A′TION *n*., ∼ATIVE *a*. [f. L EX[1](*cogitare* COGITATE) + -ATE[3]]
excommū′nicāt|**e**[1] *v.t.* (Eccl.) cut off (person) from participation in sacraments, or from all communication with the Church; hence or cogn. **excommūnic**A′TION, ∼OR, *ns.*, ∼IVE, ∼ORY, *adjs*. [f. eccl. L EX[1](*communicare* f. *communis* COMMON[1]) + -ATE[3]]
excommū′nicate[2] *a*. & *n*. (arch.) excommunicated (person). [f. L *excommunicatus* p.p. (as prec.); see -ATE[2]]
excŏr′i|**āte** *v.t.* remove part of skin of (person etc.) by abrasion etc.; strip, peel off, (skin); (fig.) censure severely; so ∼A′TION *n*. [f. L EX[1](*coriare* f. *corium* hide) + -ATE[3]]
e′xcrèment *n*. (in *sing.* or *pl.*) faeces; hence ∼AL (-ĕ′n-), ∼I′TIOUS[1], *adjs*. [f. F *excrément* or f. L *excrementum* (as EXCRETE; see -MENT)]
excrĕ′scence *n*. abnormal or morbid outgrowth (on animal or vegetable body, or fig.); so **excrĕscĕ′nt**IAL (-shal) *a*. [f. L *excrescentia* (as foll.; see -ENCE)]
excrĕ′scent *a*. growing abnormally; redundant; (Gram., of sound or letter in word) due merely to euphony, not to derivation. [f. L EX[1](*crescere* grow); see -ENT]
excrē′ta *n. pl.* waste discharged from body, esp. faeces and urine. [L, neut. pl. (as *n.*) of p.p. (as foll.)]
excrē′t|**e** *v.t.* (Of animal or plant) separate and expel (waste matter, prop. after metabolism; or abs.) from system; hence or cogn. **excrē′t**ION *n*., ∼IVE, ∼ORY, *adjs*. [f. L EX[1](*cernere cret-* sift)]
excru′ci|**āte** (-krōō′shĭ-) *v.t.* torment acutely (person's senses; esp. in *part.* as *a.*, also joc. of pun, comedy, etc.); torture mentally; hence ∼**āt**INGLY *adv.*, ∼A′TION *n*. [f. L EX[1](*cruciare* torment f. *crux crucis* cross) + -ATE[3]]
e′xculpāte *v.t.* free from blame; clear (person *from* charge etc.); hence **exculp**A′TION *n.*, **excŭ′lpat**ORY *a*. [f. med. L EX[1](*culpare* f. *culpa* blame) + -ATE[3]]
excûr′sion (-shon) *n*. journey or ramble with intention of returning to starting-point (lit. or fig.); pleasure-trip of number of persons, whence ∼IST (3) *n.*, ∼ **train** for excursionists, usu. at reduced rates); digression; (arch.) sortie (ALARUMs *and excursions*); (Astron.) deviation from regular path; hence ∼AL, ∼ARY[1], *adjs*. [f. L *excursio* f. EX[1](*currere curs-* run); see -ION]
excûr′sïve *a*. making or tending to make excursions; diverse; digressive; hence ∼LY[2] (-vlĭ) *adv.*, ∼NESS (-vn-) *n*. [f. as prec. + -IVE]
excûr′sus (ĭ-, ĕ-) *n*. detailed discussion of special point in book, usu. in appendix at end; digression in narrative. [L, vbl n. f. as EXCURSION]
excū′s|**e**[1] (-z) *v.t.* attempt to lessen the blame attaching to (person, act, fault); obtain exemption for (person, one*self, from* duty etc.; ∼**e** one**self,** ask permission or apologize before leaving); (of thing) serve as exculpation of (person, act, person *for* act); release (person (*from*) duty etc.; **be** ∼**ed,** (colloq.) be allowed to leave room etc., e.g. to go to lavatory); forgive (fault or offence, person *for* this); not insist upon (what is due); ∼**e me** (as apology for lack of ceremony, interruption, etc., or as form of dissent); ∼**e-me dance** (in which one may take another dancer's partner); so ∼ABLE, ∼at**ORY,** *adjs.*, ∼ABLY *adv*. [ME, f. OF *escuser* f. L EX[1]*cusare* (*causa* CAUSE[1], accusation)]

For other words in *ex-* **see** EX-[1], EX-[2].

excu'se² *n.* apology offered, exculpation; ground of this; ~ **for**, poor or scanty specimen of. [ME, f. OF (as prec.)]

ex-dire'ctory *a.* (Of telephone number or subscriber) deliberately not listed in the directory. [f. EX²+ DIRECTORY]

ex div. *abbr.* EX² dividend.

e'xeăt *n.* ||permission for temporary absence from college etc.; bishop's permission to priest to move to another diocese. [L, 3rd sing. pres. subj. of EX¹(*ire* go)]

e'xecrab|le *a.* abominable, detestable; hence ~LY² *adv.* [ME f. OF, f. L *execrabilis* (as foll.; see -ABLE)]

e'xecrāt|e *v.t.* & *i.* express or feel abhorrence for; utter curses; hence or cogn. **exècrA'TION** *n.*, ~IVE, ~ORY, *adjs.* [f. L EX¹(*s*)*ecrari* (*sacrare* devote f. *sacer* sacred, accursed) +-ATE³]

exe'cūtant (ĭgz-) *n.* one who executes (sense 1), performer (esp. *of* music etc.). [f. F *éxécutant*, pres. part. f. as foll.]

e'xecūt|e *v.t.* **1.** carry (plan, command, law, judicial sentence, order for goods etc., a will) into effect; carry out design for (product of art or skill); perform (action, operation, etc.); make (legal instrument) valid by signing, sealing, etc.; perform (duty, function, musical composition). **2.** inflict capital punishment on. **3.** Hence ~ABLE *a.* [ME, f. OF *executer* f. med. L *executare* f. L EX¹(*sequi secut*- follow)]

execū'tion *n.* **1.** carrying out, performance; dexterity in performing music; **do** ~, (of weapon, or fig. of argument etc.) have destructive effect. **2.** seizure of property or person of debtor in default of payment. **3.** infliction of capital punishment; hence ~ARY¹ *a.*, ~ER¹ *n.* [ME f. OF, f. L *executio -onis* (as prec.; see -ION)]

exe'cūtive (ĭgz-) *a.* & *n.* **1.** *a.* pertaining to or having the function of executing. **2.** *a.* & *n.* (branch of government or organization) concerned with executing laws, agreements, etc., or with other administration or management; **~* **session**, private meeting (orig. of Senate for executive business). **3.** *n.* person having executive authority; person in executive position in business organization etc.; executive body [f. med. L *executivus* (as EXECUTE; see -IVE)]

execūtor *n.* **1.** (arch.; ě'ksī-). one who carries out or performs. **2.** (ĭgzě'k-). person appointed by testator to execute his will; literary ex, person entrusted with writer's unpublished works etc.; hence **exècūtōr'IAL** (ĭgz-) *a.*, ~SHIP, **exè'cūTRIX** (ĭgz-), *ns.* [ME, f. AF *execut(o)ur* f. L *executor -oris* (as EXECUTE; see -OR)]

exèg|ē'sis *n.* (*pl.* ~eses *pr.* -ē'sēz). exposition esp. of Scripture; hence or cogn. **e'xègete** *n.*, ~è'tIC(AL) *adjs.*, ~ē'tIST (3) *n.* [f. Gk *exēgēsis* f. EX²*ēgeomai* interpret (*hēgeomai* lead)]

exe'mplar (ĭgz-) *n.* model, pattern; typical member (of a class); parallel instance. [ME f. OF *exemplaire*, f. LL *exemplarium* (as EXAMPLE; see -AR²)]

exe'mplar|ў (ĭgz-) *a.* fit to be imitated; (arch.) typical; illustrative; serving as a warning (~y **damages** in Law, exceeding amount needed for simple compensation); hence ~ĭLY² *adv.*, ~ĭNESS *n.* [f. LL *exemplaris* (as EXAMPLE; see -ARY²)]

exe'mpli|fȳ (ĭgz-) *v.t.* illustrate by example; be an example of; make attested copy of (document) under official seal; so ~FICA'TION *n.* [ME, f. med. L *exemplificare* (as EXAMPLE; see -FY)]

exempli gratia (ĕgzĕmplī grā'sha) *adv.* for the sake of example. [L]

exe'mpl|um (ĕgz-) *n.* (*pl.* ~a). example or model, esp. moralizing or illustrative story. [L (see EXAMPLE)]

exe'mpt¹ (ĭgz-) *a.* & *n.* **1.** *a.* freed (*from* taxation, liability, risk, duty, control, failings, etc.); not subject to risk etc. *from.* **2.** *n.* person exempted, person free from tax; || = EXON. [ME, f. L *exemptus* p.p. of EX¹(*imere empt-* = *emere* take)]

exĕ'mpt² (ĭgz-) *v.t.* free *from* (as prec.); so ~ION *n.* [f. as prec.]

exèquā'tur *n.* recognition of a country's consul by a foreign government; temporal sovereign's authorization of bishop under papal authority, or of publication of papal bulls. [L, = let him perform, 3rd sing. pres. subj. of *exequi* = *exsequi* (see EXECUTE)]

e'xèquies (-kwĭz) *n. pl.* funeral rites. [ME f. OF, f. L *exsequiae* f. EX¹(*sequi* follow)]

e'xercīse¹ (-z) *n.* **1.** employment, application, (*of* organ, faculty, power, right); practice (*of* virtue, profession, function, religious rite); act of worship. **2.** exertion of muscles, limbs, etc., esp. for health's sake; bodily, mental, or spiritual training. **3.** task set for such training (**object of the** ~, essential purpose of action etc.); problem, piece of music, etc., used as such task; (in *pl.*) military drill, athletics, etc., academical declamation etc. required for degree, **(in *pl.*) ceremony of conferment of degree etc. [ME, f. OF *exercice* f. L *exercitium* f. EX¹(*ercēre -cit-* = *arcēre* restrain) keep at work; see -ISE²]

e'xercīs|e² (-z) *v.* **1.** *v.t.* employ or apply (faculty, right, influence, restraint, etc.); train (person etc.); tax the powers of; perplex, worry; perform (functions); give (horse etc.) exercise, hence ~ABLE *a.* **2.** *v.i.* take exercise (sense 2). [ME, f. prec.]

exèrcita'tion (ĭgz-) *n.* (arch.) practice, training; literary or oratorical exercise. [ME, f. L *exercitatio* (*exercitare* frequent. of *exercēre*; see EXERCISE¹, -ATION)]

exèrgue (ě'ksērg, ĕgzēr'g) *n.* small space usu. on reverse of coin or medal, below principal device; inscription there; hence **exēr'guAL** (ĕksēr'gal, ĕgz-) *a.* [F, f. med. L *exergum* f. Gk EX-²+*ergon* work]

exēr't (ĭgz-) *v.t.* exercise, bring to bear, (quality, force, influence); ~ one**self**, use efforts or endeavours, strive, (*to do, for* object); hence ~ION *n.* [f. L EX¹(*serere sert-* bind) put forth]

e'xès (-z) *n. pl.* (colloq.) expenses. [abbr.]

exeunt (e'ksiunt) *v.i.* (Stage direction): (actors) leave the stage; ~ *omnes* (ŏ'mnēz), all leave the stage. [L, = they (all) go out, f. as EXIT²]

exfo'li|ăte *v.i.* (Of bone, skin, mineral, etc.) come off in scales or layers; (of tree) throw off layers of bark; hence ~A'TION *n.* [L LL EX¹(*foliare* f. *folium* leaf) +-ATE²]

ex gratia (ĕks grā'sha) *adv.* & *a.* (done etc.) as an act of grace, not under (esp. legal) compulsion. [L, = from favour]

exhalā'tion (ĕksa-) *n.* expiration of air; puff of breath; mist, vapour; emanation, effluvium. [ME, f. L *exhalatio* (as foll.; see -ATION)]

exhā'le *v.* **1.** *v.t.* give off (as) in vapour; breathe out (air, life, soul, words, etc.); (arch.) get rid of (anger etc.) as if by blowing. **2.** *v.i.* be given off in vapour (*from, out of*). [ME, f. OF *exhaler* f. L EX¹(*halare* breathe)]

exhau'st¹ (ĭgzaw'-) *n.* (expulsion or exit of) motive fluid, steam, or gaseous products of combustion from engine cylinder after completion of power stroke by piston; (similar exit of) spent fluid or gas from turbine; ~(-**pipe** etc.) (for this); (apparatus for) production of outward current of air by creating partial vacuum. [f. foll.]

exhau'st² (ĭgzaw'-) *v.t.* **1.** draw off (air, or fig.); empty (vessel) of contents. **2.** consume entirely; account for or use the whole of; find out or say all that is worth knowing of (subject); (esp. in *p.p.*) drain (person, kingdom, etc.) of strength, resources, etc.; tire out; hence ~IBI'LITY *n.*, ~IBLE *a.* [f. L EX¹(*haurire haust*- draw (water), drain)]

exhau'stion (ĭgzaw'schŏn) *n.* exhausting or being exhausted; total loss of strength; process of establishing conclusion by eliminating alternatives. [f. LL *exhaustio* (as prec.; see -ION)]

exhau'stive (ĭgzaw'-) *a.* tending to exhaust, esp. a subject; thorough, comprehensive; hence ~LY² (-vlĭ) *adv.*, ~NESS (-vn-) *n.* [f. EXHAUST²+-IVE]

exhibit 338 **expand**

exhi′bit[1] (ĭgzĭ′-) *n.* **1.** document or thing produced in lawcourt and referred to in written evidence; ∼ **A,** first such document etc., (fig.) thing or person regarded as (important) piece of evidence. **2.** thing or collection of things sent by person, firm, etc., to an exhibition. [f. L *exhibitum,* neut. p.p. (as foll.)]

exhi′bit[2] (ĭgzĭ′-) *v.t.* show, display; submit for consideration; manifest (quality); show publicly (for amusement, in competition, etc.); hence or cogn. ∼OR *n.,* ∼ORY *a.* [f. L EX[1](*hibēre hibit-* = *habēre* hold)]

exhibi′tion (ĕksĭ-) *n.* **1.** showing, display, (of thing); **make an** ∼ **of** oneself, behave so as to appear ridiculous or contemptible. **2.** public display of works of art, industrial products, etc. **3.** ‖scholarship (SCHOLAR 5), esp. from funds of school, college, etc.; hence ∼ER[1] *n.* [ME f. OF, f. LL *exhibitio -onis* (as prec.; see -ION)]

exhibi′tion‖ism (ĕksĭ-) *n.* tendency towards display or extravagant behaviour; (Path.) perverted mental condition characterized by indecent exposure of one's genitals; so ∼IST *n.,* one who behaves thus, ∼ĭ′stIC *a.* [f. prec. + -ISM]

exhi′lar‖āte (ĭgzĭ′-) *v.t.* enliven, gladden, (person, spirits); hence or cogn. ∼ANT *a.* & *n.,* ∼A′TION *n.,* ∼ATIVE *a.* [f. L EX[1](*hilarare* f. *hilaris* cheerful) + -ATE[3]]

exhor′t (ĭgzôr′t) *v.t.* admonish earnestly; urge (person *to* do, *to* a course of action); hence ∼atIVE, ∼atORY, *adjs.* [ME, f. OF *exhorter* or f. L EX[1](*hortari* exhort)]

exhŏrtā′tion (ĕksôr-, ĕgzôr-) *n.* exhorting; formal or liturgical address. [ME f. OF, or f. L *exhortatio* (as prec.; see -ATION)]

exhū′m‖e (ĭgzū′m) *v.t.* dig out, unearth, (esp. buried corpse; lit. or fig.); so ∼A′TION (ĕksū-) *n.* [f. F *exhumer* f. med. L EX[1](*humare* f. *humus* ground)]

ex hypothesi (ĕks hĭpō′thĭsī) *adv.* according to the hypothesis (made). [mod. L]

e′xigence, e′xigency, (ĕ′ks-, ĕ′gz-) *ns.* urgent need or demand; emergency. [f. F *exigence* & f. LL *exigentia* (as foll.; see -ENCE, -ENCY)]

e′xigent (ĕ′ks-, ĕ′gz-) *a.* urgent, pressing; requiring much, exacting. [ME, f. L *exigere* EXACT[2]; see -ENT]

e′xigīble *a.* that may be demanded or exacted (*against* or *from* person). [F (*exiger* f. as EXACT[2]; see -IBLE)]

exi′gūous (ĕgz-, ĭgz-) *a.* scanty, small; hence or cogn. **exigū′ITY,** ∼NESS, *ns.* [f. L *exiguus* scanty (*exigere* weigh exactly; see EXACT[2]) + -OUS]

e′xile[1] (ĕ′ks-, ĕ′gz-) *n.* (state of) being expelled or long absence from one's native land (lit. or fig.); **the E**∼, captivity of Jews in Babylon (6th c. BC). [ME, f. OF *exil, essil* f. L *exilium* banishment (*exul* = foll.)]

e′xīle[2] (ĕ′ks-, ĕ′gz-) *n.* exiled person (lit. or fig.). [ME, prob. f. OF *exilé* p.p. of *exiler* (see foll.), infl. by L *exul*]

e′xīle[3] (ĕ′ks-, ĕ′gz-) *v.t.* condemn to exile (person *from;* lit. or fig.). [ME, f. OF *exil (i)er, essilier* f. LL *exiliare* (as EXILE[1])]

exi′lic (ĕks-, ĕgz-) *a.* of exile, esp. the Exile in Babylon. [f. EXILE[1] + -IC]

exi′st (ĭgz-) *v.i.* have place as a part of objective reality; have being under specified conditions (∼ **as** (in the form of)); (of circumstances etc.) occur, be found; live, esp. under adverse conditions; continue in being. [prob. back-form. f. foll.; cf. LL *existere*]

exi′stence (ĭgz-) *n.* being, existing, (esp. *in existence*); life, esp. under adverse conditions (*a wretched, precarious, existence*); mode of existing; existing thing; all that exists. [ME f. OF, or f. L *existentia* f. L EX[1]- (*sistere* redupl. of *stare* stand); see -ENCE]

exi′stent (ĭgz-) *a.* existing, actual, current. [f. as prec. + -ENT]

existe′ntial (ĕgz-; -shal) *a.* of or relating to existence; (Logic, of a proposition) predicating existence; (Philos.) concerned with existence, esp. with human existence as viewed by existentialism; hence ∼LY[2] *adv.* [f. LL *existentialis* (as EXISTENCE; see -AL)]

existe′ntialism (ĕgz-; -shal-) *n.* philosophical theory

emphasizing existence of the individual person as free and responsible agent determining his own development; hence ∼IST (2) *n.* [f. G *existentialismus* (as prec.; see -ISM)]

e′xit[1] (ĕ′ks-, ĕ′gz-) *n.* departure of actor from stage (lit. or fig.); death; going out or forth; liberty to do this (∼ **permit** etc., authorization to leave a particular country); (Cards) (means of) deliberately losing the lead; passage or door to go out by; *place where vehicles can leave motorway etc. [partly f. L *exitus* going out (as foll.), partly f. foll.]

exit[2] (ĕ′ksĭt) *v.i.* (Stage direction): (actor) leaves the stage (lit. or fig.); *Exit Macbeth*). [L, 3rd sing. pres. ind. of EX(*ire* go)]

e′xit[3] (ĕ′ks-, ĕ′gz-) *v.i.* make one's exit; die; (Cards) deliberately lose lead. [f. EXIT[1]]

ex-lī′bris *n.* (*pl.* same). book-plate, label with arms, design, etc., and owner's name, pasted into front of book. [f. L *ex libris* out of the books of (+ owner's name)]

ex nihilo (ĕks nĭ′hĭlō) *adv.* out of nothing (*creation ex nihilo*). [L]

e′xō- *comb. form.* external, as: ∼**bio′logy,** study of life outside the earth; ∼**crine** (-krĭn), (of gland) secreting through a duct [Gk *krinō* sift]; ∼**derm,** ectoderm; ∼**gamous,** ∼**gamy,** (-ŏ′g-), (of, following) custom compelling man to marry outside his own tribe; ∼**gen,** plant that develops by external growth of stem; ∼**genous** (-ŏ′j-), growing or originating from outside; ∼**plasm,** outermost layer of cytoplasm; ∼**skeleton,** external integument, bony or leathery; ∼**sphere,** layer of atmosphere farthest from the earth; ∼**ther′mal,** ∼**ther′mic,** occurring or formed with evolution of heat. [f. Gk *exō* outside]

Exod. *abbr.* Exodus (OT).

e′xodus *n.* departure, going forth, of many persons (esp. of emigrants); (Bibl.) departure of Israelites from Egypt, (E∼) book of OT relating this. [eccl. L, f. Gk EX[2]*odos* (*hodos* way)]

ex officio (ĕks ofĭ′shĭō) *adv.* & *a.* by virtue of one's office (*ex officio members of committee*). [L]

‖**e′xŏn** *n.* one of four officers acting as commanders of Yeomen of the Guard. [repr. F pr. of EXEMPT[1]]

exŏ′ner‖āte (ĭgz-) *v.t.* free (person *from* blame etc.); release (person *from* duty etc.); hence ∼A′TION *n.,* ∼ATIVE *a.* [f. L EX[1](*onerare* f. *onus oneris* burden) + -ATE[3]]

exŏphthā′lm‖us, ∼**os,** ∼**ĭa,** *n.* protrusion of eyeball; hence -IC *a.* [mod. L, f. Gk EX[2](*ophthalmos* eye) having prominent eyes]

exor. *abbr.* executor (sense 2).

exŏr′bit‖ant (ĭgz-) *a.* (Of price, demand, ambition, person) grossly excessive; hence ∼ANCE *n.,* ∼antLY[2] *adv.* [f. LL EX[1](*orbitare* f. *orbita* ORBIT); see -ANT]

e′xŏrc‖īze, -īse (-īz), *v.t.* expel (evil spirit *from, out of,* person or place) by invocation or use of holy name; free (person, place, *of* evil spirits thus); so ∼ĭzA′TION, ∼ISM (1), ∼IST (1), *ns.* [f. F *exorciser* or f. eccl. L *exorcizare* f. Gk EX[2]*orkizō* (*horkos* oath)]

exŏr′di‖um *n.* (*pl.* ∼**ums** *or* ∼**a**). beginning, introductory part, esp. of discourse or treatise; hence ∼AL *a.* [L, f. EX[1](*ordiri* begin)]

exotē′ric *a.* (Of philosophical doctrine, mode of speech, etc.) intelligible to outsiders (cf. ESOTERIC); (of disciple) not admitted to esoteric teaching; commonplace, ordinary, popular; hence ∼AL *a.,* ∼ALLY *adv.,* ∼ISM (3), ∼IST (2), *ns.* [f. LL f. Gk *exōterikos* (*exōterō* compar. of *exō* outside; see -IC)]

exŏ′tic (ĭgz-) *a.* & *n.* **1.** (Of plant, word, fashion) introduced from abroad; strange, bizarre; attractively strange or unusual; (of fuel, metal, etc.) of kind newly brought into use; ∼ **dancer,** strip-tease dancer. **2.** *n.* exotic plant, word, dancer, etc. [f. L f. Gk *exōtikos* (as EXO-; see -IC)]

exŏ′tica (ĭgz-) *n. pl.* exotic objects. [L, neut. pl. of *exoticus* (see prec.)]

expa′nd *v.* **1.** *v.t.* & *i.* spread out flat; develop (*into*;

swell, dilate, increase in bulk or importance. **2.** *v.t.* set forth, write out, in full (what is condensed or abbreviated, algebraical expression, etc.). **3.** *v.i.* become genial, throw off reserve; expatiate *on*. **4.** ∼ed metal, sheet metal slit and stretched into a lattice, used (esp.) to reinforce concrete; ∼ing universe, the universe regarded as continually expanding and carrying the galaxies farther apart. **5.** Hence or cogn. ∼ABLE *a.*, **expän**SIBI′LITY *n.*, **expä′n-**SIBLE *a.* [ME, f. L EX¹(*pandere pans-* spread)]

expä′nse *n.* wide area or extent; amount of expansion. [f. mod. L *expansum* neut. p.p. (as prec.)]

expä′nsile *a.* (capable) of expansion. [f. as EXPAND; see -IL]

expä′nsion (-shon) *n.* expanding; enlargement of scale of operations in commerce etc.; increase of amount of territory etc., whence ∼ISM (3), ∼IST (2), *ns.*; increase in bulk of steam etc. in cylinder of engine; hence ∼ARY¹ *a.* [f. LL *expansio* (as EXPAND; see -ION)]

expä′nsive *a.* able or tending to expand; extensive, wide-ranging; (of person, feelings, speech) effusive, open; hence ∼LY² (-vlī) *adv.*, ∼NESS (-vn-), **expän-sī′**VITY, *ns.* [f. as EXPAND + -IVE]

ex parte (ĕks pär′tĭ) *adv.* & *a.* (Law or transf.) (made or said) on, or in the interests of, one side only, or by person having interest in proceedings but not being a party to them. [L]

expä′ti|äte (-shī-) *v.i.* speak or write copiously (*on* subject); (usu. fig.) wander unrestrained; hence ∼A′TION *n.*, ∼atORY (-sha-) *a.* [f. L EX¹(*spatiari* walk about, f. *spatium* SPACE¹) + -ATE³]

expä′tri|äte¹ *v.t.* expel, remove one*self*, from home-land; withdraw one*self* from citizenship or allegiance; hence ∼A′TION *n.* [f. med. L EX¹(*patriare* f. *patria* native land) + -ATE³]

expä′triäte² *a.* & *n.* expatriated (person); (person) living abroad. [as prec.; see -ATE¹,²]

expe′ct *v.t.* **1.** look forward to, regard as likely, assume as future event, (*I expect a storm, expect to see him, expect him to come, expect (that) he will come, expect him next week, don't expect me (to come), expect payment today, not so bad as I expected (it to be), just what I expected of him*); **shall not ∼ you till I etc. see you**, allow you to arrive when you please; ∼ **me when you see me**, (colloq.) I do not know when I shall return. **2.** look for as due (*I expect you to be punctual, that you will be punctual; do you expect payment for this?*); (colloq.) think, suppose, (*that*); **be** ∼**ing a baby, a child**, etc. or abs., be pregnant. [f. L EX¹(*spectare* look, frequent. of *specere* see)]

expe′ctancy *n.* state of expectation; prospect, esp. of future possession; prospective chance (*of*). [f. L *ex*(*s*)*pectantia* (as prec.; see -ANCY)]

expe′ctant *a.* & *n.* **1.** *a.* expecting (*of*, or abs.; ∼ **mother**, pregnant woman); having the prospect, in normal course, of possession, office, etc.; character-ized by waiting for events, esp. (Med.) *expectant method*; hence ∼LY² *adv.* **2.** *n.* one who expects; candidate for office etc. [ME, f. as EXPECT; see -ANT]

expectā′tion *n.* awaiting; anticipation (*beyond, contrary to, expectation*); (in *pl.*) prospects of inheritance; thing expected; *expectation of LIFE* 4; probability of a thing's happening. [f. L *expectatio* (as EXPECT; see -ATION)]

expe′ctorant *a.* & *n.* (medicine) that promotes expectoration. [f. as foll.; see -ANT]

expe′ctor|äte *v.t.* eject (phlegm etc.) from throat or lungs by coughing or spitting; (abs.) spit; hence ∼A′TION *n.* [f. L EX¹*pectorare* (*pectus -oris* breast) + -ATE³]

expe′di|ent *a.* & *n.* **1.** *a.* (usu. *pred.*) advantageous, suitable, (*do whatever is expedient; it is expedient that he should go*); politic rather than just; hence or cogn. ∼ENCE, ∼ENCY, *ns.*, ∼entLY² *adv.* **2.** *n.* resource, means of attaining one's end. [ME, f. L *expedire* (see foll., -ENT)]

expe′dīte *v.t.* assist progress of, hasten, (action, process, etc.); accomplish (business) quickly. [f. L

EX¹*pedire -dit-* (*pes pedis* foot) extricate, put in order + -ITE²]

expedi′tion *n.* **1.** warlike enterprise; journey, voyage, for definite purpose; persons or fleet sent on this; hence ∼ARY¹ *a.*, ∼IST (3) *n.* **2.** promptness, speed. [ME f. OF, f. L *expeditio -onis* (as prec.; see -ION)]

expedi′tious (-shŭs) *a.* doing or done speedily; suited for speedy performance; hence ∼LY² *adv.*, ∼NESS *n.* [f. prec.; see -IOUS]

expe′l *v.t.* (-ll-). cause to depart or emerge (person *from* place, bullet *from* gun, etc.) by use of force; compel departure of (person; *from* a country, community, school, etc.); hence ∼LEE′ *n.*, ∼LENT *a.* [ME, f. L EX¹(*pellere puls-* drive)]

expe′nd *v.t.* spend (money, care, time, *on* object, *in* doing); use up (Naut.) wind (spare rope) round spar etc. [ME, f. L EX¹(*pendere pens-* weigh)]

expe′ndable *a.* that may be expended; not regarded as worth preserving or saving; not normally reused; unimportant, that may be sacrificed to gain one's ends. [f. prec. + -ABLE]

expe′nditure *n.* spending (*of* money etc.); using up, consuming; amount expended. [f. EXPEND, after *expenditor*, med. L f. *expenditus* irreg. p.p. of L *expendere*; see -URE]

expe′nse *n.* **1.** spending of money (**go to the** ∼ **of**, spend money on; **put to** ∼, cause to spend money); **at** person's ∼, causing him to spend money or (fig.) suffer injury, ridicule, etc.; **at the** ∼ **of**, so as to cause loss, damage, or discredit to. **2.** amount of money spent; (usu. in *pl.*) amount spent in executing com-mission etc., amount paid to reimburse this, (*he paid my expenses, offered me £10 and expenses*); ∼ **account**, list of employee's expenses payable by employer. [ME f. AF; OF *espense* f. LL *expensa* (*pecunia* money), fem. p.p. of L *expendere* EXPEND]

expe′nsive *a.* of high price, dear; making a high charge; causing much expense; hence ∼LY² (-vlī) *adv.*, ∼NESS (-vn-) *n.* [f. as EXPEND + -IVE]

exper′ienc|e¹ *n.* actual observation of or practical acquaintance with facts or events; knowledge or skill resulting from this, whence ∼ED² (-st) *a.*; event that affects one (*an unpleasant experience*); fact or process of being so affected (*I learnt by experience*); state or phase of religious emotion. [ME f. OF, f. L *experientia* f. EX¹*periri -peri-* try; see -ENCE]

exper′ience² *v.t.* meet with, feel, undergo, (pleasure, treatment, loss, etc.); hence ∼ABLE (-sa-) *a.* [f. prec.]

experie′ntial (-shal) *a.* of experience; ∼ **philosophy** (treating all knowledge as based on experience), whence ∼ISM (3), ∼IST (2), *ns.*; hence ∼LY² *adv.* [f. EXPERIENCE¹ + -IAL, after *inferential* etc.]

expe′rimĕnt¹ *n.* test or trial (*of*); procedure adopted on chance of its succeeding, for testing hypothesis etc., or to demonstrate known fact. [ME f. OF, or f. L *experimentum* (as EXPERIENCE¹; see -MENT)]

expe′rimĕnt² *v.i.* make experiment (*on, with*); hence ∼A′TION *n.*, ∼ER¹, *ns.* [f. prec.]

experimĕ′ntal *a.* based on experience, not on authority or conjecture; based on or making use of experiment (*experimental philosophy, physicist, physics, psychologist, psychology*), whence ∼ISM (3), ∼IST (2), *ns.*; tentative; used in experiments; hence ∼IZE (2), ∼LY² *adv.* [ME, f. med. L *experimentalis* (as EXPERI-MENT¹; see -AL)]

e′xpĕrt¹ *a.* trained by practice, skilful, (*at, in*); hence ∼LY² *adv.*, ∼NESS *n.* [ME f. OF, f. L *expertus* p.p. of *experiri* (as EXPERIENCE¹)]

e′xpĕrt² *n.* person having special skill or knowledge (*at, in*; *mining expert*); (*attrib.*) of or being an expert (*expert evidence, expert witness*). [F, f. adj. f. as prec.]

expĕrti′se¹ (-ē′z) *n.* expert opinion or skill or know-ledge. [F]

e′xpertīze, -īse² (-īz) *v.i.* & *t.* give expert opinion (concerning). [f. EXPERT² + -IZE]

e′xpi|āte *v.t.* pay the penalty of, make amends for, (sin); hence or cogn. ∼ABLE, ∼ātORY, *adjs.*, ∼A′TION,

∽**ātor**, ns. [f. L EX¹(*piare* seek to appease f. *pius* devout) + -ATE³]

expirā′tion n. breathing out (*of* air etc.); expiry. [f. L *expiratio* (as foll.; see -ATION)]

expīr′e v. 1. v.t. breathe out (air *from* lungs, or abs.), whence **expīr′atory** a. 2. v.i. die; (of period) come to an end; (of law, patent, truce, etc., or of right granted for a certain period) become void, complete its term; (of entitlement etc.) cease, become extinct. [ME, f. OF *expirer* f. L EX¹(*spirare* breathe)]

expīr′ÿ n. termination (*of* period, truce, temporary right, etc.). [f. prec. + -Y¹]

explai′n v.t. make known in detail (thing, *that, how,* etc.); make intelligible (meaning, difficulty, etc., or abs.); say (*that*) as explanation; account for (conduct etc.); ∽ **away,** modify, remove force of, (esp. offensive language, awkward facts) by explanation; ∽ one**self,** (1) make one's meaning clear, (2) give an account of one's motives or conduct; hence ∽ABLE a. [f. L EX¹(*planare* f. *planus* flat); assim. to PLAIN¹]

explanā′tion n. explaining; declaration made with view to mutual understanding or reconciliation; statement or circumstance that explains. [ME, f. L *explanatio* (as prec.; see -ATION)]

explä′nator∣ÿ a. serving, or intended to serve, to explain; hence ∽ILY² adv. [f. LL *explanatorius* (as EXPLAIN; see -ORY)]

expla′nt v.t. (Biol.) transfer (living tissue) from body, esp. to nutrient medium; hence ∽A′TION n. [f. mod. L EX¹(*plantare* PLANT²)]

e′xplant² (-ah-) n. (Biol.) explanted tissue, organ, etc. [f. prec.]

explē′tive (ĭ-, ĕ-) a. & n. 1. a. serving to fill out (esp. sentence, line of verse, etc.). 2. n. expletive thing, word, etc., esp. oath or meaningless exclamation. [f. LL *expletivus* f. EX¹(*plēre plet-* fill); see -IVE]

e′xplic∣āte v.t. develop meaning or implication of (notion, principle, etc.); make clear, explain, whence ∽ABLE (ĕ′-, -ĭ′-), ∽ATIVE, ∽ātory, adjs.; hence ∽A′TION n. [f. L EX¹(*plicare plicat-* or *plicit-* fold) unfold + -ATE³]

e′xplicit¹ n. last words (of book etc., or fig.). [LL, = 'here ends', formerly used by scribes to mark end of book or section]

expli′cit² a. stated in detail, leaving nothing merely implied; definite; (of person, book, etc.) outspoken; ∽ **faith,** acceptance of doctrine with clear understanding of all it involves (cf. IMPLICIT); hence ∽LY² adv., ∽NESS n. [f. F *explicite* or f. L *explicitus* (as EXPLICATE)]

explō′de v. 1. v.i. & t. (Of gas, gunpowder, bomb, boiler, etc.) expand suddenly with loud noise owing to release of internal energy, cause (gas etc.) to do this; give vent suddenly to emotion; (of population etc.) increase suddenly or rapidly; ∽**d view** etc. (showing components of machine etc. as if separated by explosion but in same relative positions). 2. v.t. bring (theory, fallacy, etc.) into disrepute by showing it to be baseless. [orig. sense 2, f. L EX¹(*plodere plos-* = *plaudere* clap) hiss off the stage]

e′xploit¹ n. brilliant or daring achievement. [ME, f. OF *esplait, esploit(e)* f. Gallo-Rom. **explictum, *explicta* f. L neut. and fem. p.p. (as EXPLICATE)]

exploi′t² v.t. work, turn to account, (mine etc.); utilize (person etc.) for one's own ends, esp. (derog.) thus utilize workers, colonial possessions, etc., hence or cogn. ∽ABLE a., **exploitā′tion** n., ∽(at)IVE adjs. (esp. derog.). [ME, f. OF *exploiter* f. Gallo-Rom. **explicitare* frequent. of L *explicare* (see EXPLICATE)]

explōr′∣e v.t. inquire into, investigate; examine (wound etc.) by touch; examine (country etc.) by going through it; hence or cogn. **explorA′TION,** ∽ER¹, ns., ∽atIVE, atORY, (-ōr′-, -ŏ′r-) adjs. [f. F *explorer* f. L *explorare*]

explō′sion (-zhon) n. exploding; loud noise due to this; sudden outbreak (of anger etc.); rapid or sudden increase (of population etc.); (Phonet.) plosion. [f. L *explosio* scornful rejection (as EXPLODE; see -ION)]

explō′sive (-s-, -z-) a. & n. 1. a. tending to expand suddenly with loud noise; (of consonant sound) plosive; tending to cause explosion (lit. or fig.); hence ∽LY² (-vlī) adv., ∽NESS (-vn-) n. 2. n. explosive substance (**high** ∽, explosive substance with very violent shattering effect and used in shells, bombs, etc.); plosive consonant, STOP² 5. [f. prec. + -IVE]

expō′nent a. & n. (person or thing) that sets forth or interprets; executant (of music etc.); person who favours or advocates the use *of*; type, representative; (Math.) symbol indicating what power of a factor is to be taken, usu. written at upper right of factor symbol. [f. L EX¹(*ponere posit-* put); see -ENT]

exponĕ′ntial (-shal) a. (Math.) pertaining to an exponent, indicated by an exponent (∽ **function,** one which increases as a quantity raised to a power determined by the variable on which the function depends); (of increase etc.) more and more rapid. [f. F *exponentiel* (as prec.; see -IAL)]

expōr′t¹ (ĭkspōr′t, ĕ′kspōrt) v.t. send out (goods) esp. to another country; hence or cogn. ∽ABLE a., ∽A′TION (ĕ-), ∽ER¹, ns. [f. L EX¹(*portare* carry)]

e′xport² n. exported article; (usu. in *pl.*) amount exported; exportation (∽ **reject,** article sold in its country of manufacture, as being below standard for export); (*attrib.*) suitable for export, esp. of better quality. [f. prec.]

expō′se (-z) v.t. 1. leave (person, thing) unprotected (esp. from weather); subject *to* (risk etc.); (Photog.) subject (film etc.) to light; (Hist.) leave (child) out of doors to perish; (in *p.p.*) open *to* (the east etc.); exhibit, display; put up for sale; ∽ one**self,** display one's body indecently. 3. disclose (secret, project, etc.); reveal (villain, villlainy). [ME, f. OF *exposer,* after L *exponere* (see EXPONENT, POSE¹)]

exposé (ĕkspō′zā) n. orderly statement of facts; revealing (of discreditable thing). [F, p.p. of *exposer* (see prec.)]

exposi′tion (-z-) n. setting forth, description; (Mus.) presentation of principal theme(s); explanation; commentary; (arch.) exposure; exhibition of goods etc. [ME f. OF, or f. L *expositio* (as EXPONENT; see -ION)]

expō′sit∣ive (-z-) a. descriptive; explanatory; so ∽OR n., ∽ORY a. [f. prec. + -IVE]

ex post facto (ĕks pŏst fă′ktō) a. & adv. (acting) retrospectively (*ex post facto law*). [f. LL *ex postfacto* from what is done afterwards]

expō′stul∣āte v.i. make protest, remonstrate earnestly (*with* person *about, on*); hence or cogn. ∽A′TION n., ∽ātORY a. [f. L EX¹(*postulare* demand) + -ATE³]

expō′sure (-zher) n. exposing or being exposed (*to* air, cold, danger, etc.; **indecent** ∽, intentional act of publicly and indecently exposing one's body); unmasking of imposture etc.; aspect (*southern exposure*); (Photog.) action of exposing plate or film to the light, duration of this action, area of film etc. affected by it, (∽ **meter,** device to measure illumination and indicate correct duration of exposure). [f. EXPOSE, after *enclosure* etc.; see -URE]

expou′nd v.t. set forth in detail (doctrine etc.); explain, interpret, (esp. Scripture). [ME, f. OF *espondre* f. as EXPONENT]

exprĕ′ss¹ (a-), adv., & n. 1. a. definitely stated, not merely implied; (arch.) of likeness) exact; hence ∽LY² adv. 2. done, made, sent, for special purpose; (of messages or goods) delivered by special messenger or service. 3. operating at high speed; ∽ **lift** (not stopping at every floor); ∽ **rifle** (discharging bullet at high speed); ∽ **train** (fast, stopping at few intermediate stations); ∽**way,** urban motorway. 4. adv. at high speed; by express messenger or train. 5. n. express train, messenger, rifle, etc.; *company undertaking transport of parcels etc.; newspaper (used in titles, as *Daily Express*). [ME, f. OF *expres* f. L *expressus* distinctly shown, p.p. of EX¹(*primere press-* = *premere* press)]

For other words in *ex-* **see** EX-¹, EX-².

èxprĕ'ss² *v.t.* **1.** squeeze out (juice, air, *from, out of*; milk etc. from breast). **2.** represent by symbols, as (Math.) *express* (quantity) *in terms of* (another). **3.** reveal, betoken, (feelings, qualities); put (thought) into words; ∾ one**self**, say what one means (*strongly* etc. *on* subject, *well, aptly*, etc.). **4.** Hence ∾IBLE *a.* [ME, f. OF *expresser* f. Rom. EX¹(*pressare*; see PRESS²)]

èxprĕ'ss³ *v.t.* send by express (messenger or delivery). [f. EXPRESS¹]

èxprĕ'ssion (-shon) *n.* **1.** expressing; wording, diction, word, phrase; (Math.) collection of symbols expressing a quantity. **2.** aspect (of face), intonation (of voice), esp. as indicating emotion, whence ∾LESS *a.*; (Art) mode of expressing action etc.; (Mus.) execution that expresses the feeling of a passage (∾-mark, sign or word indicating expression required; ∾-stop in harmonium, stop allowing expression by varied air-pressure). **3.** Hence ∾AL *a.* [ME f. OF, or f. L *expressio* f. *exprimere* (see EXPRESS¹, -ION)]

èxprĕ'ssion|ism (-shon-) *n.* style of painting, drama, music, etc., subordinating realism to expression of artist's etc. inner experience; so ∾IST (2) *n.*, **i'stic** *a.* [f. prec. + -ISM]

èxprĕ'ssive *a.* serving to express (*expressive of* motion etc.); (of word, gesture, etc.) significant; hence ∾LY² (-vlĭ) *adv.*, ∾NESS (-vn-), **èxprĕssī'vity**, *ns.* [ME, f. F *expressif -ive* or f. med. L *expressivus* (as EXPRESSION, see -IVE)]

èxprĕ'ssō. Var. of ESPRESSO.

èxprŏ'pri|āte *v.t.* dispossess (*from* estate etc.); (esp. of State) take away (property); so ∾A'TION *n.* [f. med. L EX¹(*propriare* f. *proprium* property); see PROPER, -ATE³]

èxpŭ'ls|ion (-shon) *n.* expelling, being expelled; so ∾IVE *a.* [ME, f. L *expulsio* (as EXPEL; see -ION)]

èxpŭ'nge (-nj) *v.t.* erase, omit, (name *from* list, passage *from* book, etc.); so **èxpŭ'nction** *n.* [f. L EX¹(*pungere punct*- prick)]

è'xpurg|āte *v.t.* purify (book etc.) by removing matter thought objectionable; remove (such matter); hence or cogn. ∾A'TION, ∾ātor, *ns.*, **èxpŭ'rgat-ŏr'IAL, èxpŭr'gatory**, *adjs.* [f. L EX¹(*purgare* cleanse) + -ATE³]

èxquisite (ĕ'kskwĭz-, **D** ĕkskwī'z-) *a.* & *n.* **1.** *a.* of great delicacy or beauty; acute, keenly felt, (*exquisite pain, pleasure*); keen (*exquisite sensibility* etc.); hence ∾LY² (-tlĭ) *adv.*, ∾NESS (-tn-) *n.* **2.** *n.* coxcomb, dandy. [ME, f. L EX¹(*quirere quisit- = quaerere* seek)]

xrx. *abbr.* executrix.

xsä'nguināte (-nggwĭn-) *v.t.* drain of blood. [f. L EX¹(*sanguinatus* f. *sanguis -inis* blood) + -ATE³]

xsci'nd *v.t.* cut out, excise, (lit. or fig.). [f. L EX¹(*scindere* cut)]

xsĕr't *v.t.* (Biol.) put forth. [f. L *exserere*; see EXERT]

x-sĕr'vice. See EX-¹ 2.

'xsiccāte *v.t.* dry up; drain dry. [f. L EX¹(*siccare* f. *siccus* dry) + -ATE³]

èx silentio (ĕks sĭlĕ'nshĭō) *adv.* by absence of contrary evidence. [L, = from silence]

xt. *abbr.* exterior; external.

xtant (ĕkstä'nt, ĕ'kstant) *a.* (Esp. of document etc.) still existing. [f. L EX¹(*stare* stand); see -ANT]

xtĕ'mpor|è *adv.* & *a.* (spoken or done) without preparation; offhand; **speak** ∾e (without notes or preparation); hence or cogn. ∾A'NEOUS, ∾ARY¹, *adjs.* [L *ex tempore* on the spur of the moment, lit. out of the time (*tempus* time)]

xtĕ'mporīz|e, -īs|e (-īz) *v.* **1.** *v.t.* compose or produce extempore. **2.** *v.i.* speak extempore. **3.** Hence ∾A'TION *n.* [f. prec. + -IZE]

xtĕ'nd *v.* **1.** *v.t.* lay out (esp. body, limbs, etc.) at full length; write out at full length. **2.** cause to be continuous *over* space, *to* point, etc.; prolong (period, line; ∾ed-play *a.*, containing a recording longer than that of a gramophone record etc. that is taken as 'normal'); enlarge (scope, meaning of word, etc.; ∾ed family, that includes relatives living near); (usu. in *pass.* or *refl.*) tax powers of (horse, athlete,

etc.) to the utmost. **3.** stretch forth (hand, arm); accord (kindness, patronage, *to*); offer (invitation, welcome, *to*). **4.** *v.i.* stretch (*to* point; *over, across*, etc., space). **5.** Hence or cogn. ∾IBI'LITY, **èxtĕnsIBI'LITY, èxtĕ'nsIBLE, èxtĕ'nsIBLE**, *adjs.* [ME, f. L EX¹-(*tendere tens*- or *tent*- stretch)]

èxtĕ'nsīle *a.* capable of being stretched out or protruded. [f. as prec.; see -IL]

èxtĕ'nsion (-shon) *n.* **1.** extending or being extended; extent, range; (Logic) group of things denoted by a term; prolongation; enlargement. **2.** additional part (of railway, plan, theory, etc.); (number of a) subsidiary telephone distant from main instrument; extramural instruction by university or college (*extension course*). **3.** Hence ∾AL *a.* [ME, f. LL *extensio* f. as EXTEND; see -ION]

èxtĕ'nsive *a.* (Of space, purchase, operation, etc.) large; far-reaching, comprehensive; (of agricultural production etc.) depending on extension of area (cf. INTENSIVE); hence ∾LY² (-vlĭ) *adv.*, ∾NESS (-vn-) *n.* [f. F *extensif -ive* or f. LL *extensivus* (as prec.; see -IVE)]

èxtĕnsŏ'mĕter *n.* instrument for measuring deformation of metal under stress; instrument using such deformation to record elastic strains in other materials. [f. L *extensus* p.p. of *extendere* (see EXTEND) + -O- + -METER]

èxtĕ'nsor *n.* ∾ (muscle), muscle that extends or straightens out part of the body. [mod. L (as EXTEND; see -OR)]

èxtĕ'nt *n.* space over which a thing extends; width or limits of application; scope (*to a great extent; to the full extent of his power*); large space (*a vast extent of marsh*). [ME, f. AF *extente* f. med. L *extenta* fem. p.p. (as n.) of L *extendere* (see EXTEND)]

èxtĕ'nuāte *v.t.* lessen seeming seriousness of (guilt, offence) by partial excuse (*we must not extenuate, nothing can extenuate, his behaviour; there were extenuating circumstances*), whence **èxtĕ'nuātory** *a.*; (arch.) make thin or weak; hence ∾A'TION *n.* [f. L EX¹(*tenuare* f. *tenuis* thin) + -ATE³]

èxtĕr'ior *a.* & *n.* **1.** *a.* outer (opp. *interior*); situated on the outside (relative *to*); coming from outside; (Cinemat.) outdoor; ∾ angle (between side of rectilineal figure and adjacent side produced); hence ∾ITY (-ŏ'r-) *n.*, ∾IZE (3) *v.t.*, ∾LY² *adv.* **2.** *n.* outward aspect or surface or demeanour; (Cinemat.) outdoor scene. [L, compar. of *exterus* outside]

èxtĕr'min|āte *v.t.* destroy utterly (species, race, sect, opinion); hence or cogn. ∾A'TION, ∾ātor, *ns.*, ∾ātory *a.* [f. L EX¹(*terminare* f. *terminus* boundary) + -ATE³]

èxtĕr'nal *a.* & *n.* **1.** *a.* of, or situated on, the outside or visible part (opp. *internal*); (of remedy etc.) applied to the outside of the body; (of the foreign affairs of a State; pertaining to students taking examinations of, but not attending, a university; belonging to the ∾ world of phenomena, outside the conscious subject; ∾ evidence (derived from source independent of the thing discussed); hence **èxtĕrnä'lITY** ∾IZE *v.t.*, give or attribute external existence to, ∾LY² *adv.* **2.** *n.* (in *pl.*) outward features or aspect; external circumstances; inessentials. [f. med. L *externalis* f. L *externus* (*exterus* outside); see -AL]

èxteroce'ptive *a.* (Biol.) relating to stimuli produced outside an organism. [irreg. f. L *externus* exterior + -O- + -RECEPTIVE]

èxtĕrritŏr'ial *a.* = EXTRATERRITORIAL; so ∾ITY (-ă'l-) *n.* [f. EX-¹ + TERRITORIAL]

èxti'nct *a.* (Of fire etc.) no longer burning; (of volcano) that not longer erupts (∾ volcano, (fig.) person no longer having remarkable energy etc.); (of life, hope, etc.) terminated, quenched; (of family, class, species) that has died out; (of office etc.) obsolete; (of title of nobility) having no qualified claimant. [ME, f. L EX¹(*stinguere stinct*- quench)]

èxti'nct|ion *n.* extinguishing, being extinguished; making, being, becoming, extinct; abolition, wiping

out (of debt), annihilation; (Phys.) reduction in intensity of radiation by absorption, scattering etc.; hence ~IVE *a*. [f. L *extinctio* (as prec.; see -ION)]
exti′nguish (-nggw-) *v.t.* make extinct, terminate (light, hope, life, faculties); (arch.) eclipse, obscure, (person) by superior brilliancy, reduce (opponent) to silence; destroy; abolish, wipe out (debt), annihilate; hence ~ABLE *a.*, ~MENT *n.* [irreg. f. L *extinguere* (as EXTINCT) + -ISH²; cf. *distinguish*]
exti′nguisher (-nggw-) *n.* In vbl senses; hollow conical cap for extinguishing flame of candle etc.; (**fire**) ~, apparatus with jet for discharging liquid chemicals or foam to extinguish fire. [f. prec. + -ER¹]
e′xtirp|āte *v.t.* destroy, root out, (tree, weed, species, nation, tumour, heresy, etc.); hence or cogn. ~A′TION, ~ātOR, *ns.* [f. L EX¹(*stirpare* f. *stirps* stem) + -ATE³]
extŏ′l *v.t.* (-ll-). praise enthusiastically (*extol him to the skies*). [f. L EX¹(*tollere* raise)]
extŏr′t *v.t.* obtain (money, promise, etc.) by violence, intimidation, persistent demands, etc. (*from*); extract forcibly (meaning, inference, *from* words, data); hence ~IVE *a.* [f. L EX¹(*torquēre tort-* twist)]
extŏr′tion *n.* extorting, esp. of money; illegal exaction; hence ~ER¹ *n.* [ME, f. LL *extortio* (as prec.; see -ION)]
extŏr′tionate *a.* using or given to extortion; (of price etc.) exorbitant. [f. prec. + -ATE²]
e′xtra *a.*, *adv.*, & *n.* **1.** *a.* additional; more than is usual or necessary; ~ **cover**, (Cricket) fieldsman on line between cover-point and mid-off but beyond these, his place; ~ **time**, further period of play at end of football etc. match when scores are equal. **2.** *adv.* more than usually (*extra strong*); additionally; ~ **dry** or **sec,** (of champagne) very slightly sweetened. **3.** *n.* extra thing; thing for which extra charge is made (*dancing is an extra*); (Cricket) run not scored from hit with bat; special issue of newspaper etc.; (Theatr., Cinemat.) person engaged temporarily for minor part or to be one of a crowd. [prob. for EXTRA-ORDINARY, after sim. forms in F and G]
extra- *pref.* forming *adjs.* usu. f. *adjs.*, w. senses 'situated outside', not coming within the scope of', as: ~-**at-mosphe′ric,** of the space beyond the atmosphere; ~-**corpor′eal,** outside the body; ~**cra′nial,** outside the skull; ~-**curri′cular,** not coming within the normal curriculum; ~**gala′ctic,** situated outside the Galaxy; ~-**i′llustrate,** add pictures to (book) from another source; ~**judi′cial,** not belonging to the case before the court, not legally authorized, (of confession) not made in court; ~-**ma′rital,** of sexual relationships outside marriage; ~**mu′ndane,** outside our world or the universe; ~**phy′sical,** not subject to physical laws; ~-**se′nsory,** derived by means other than the known senses (e.g. telepathy); ~**terre′strial,** outside the earth or its atmosphere; ~-**vehi′cular,** outside a vehicle, esp. a spacecraft. [med. L, f. L *extra* outside]
e′xtract¹ *n.* substance got by treating another with solvents and then evaporating them; preparation containing active principle of a substance in concentrated form; passage from book, music, etc. [f. L *extractum,* neut. p.p. (as n.) of *extrahere* (see foll.)]
extră′ct² *v.t.* **1.** copy out (passage in book etc.); take passages from (book etc.). **2.** take out by force (tooth, anything firmly fixed); draw forth (money, admission, etc.) against person's will; obtain (juice etc.) by suction, pressure, distillation, etc.; obtain extract from (substance); derive (pleasure etc. *from*); (arch.) deduce (principle etc. *from*); (Math.) find (root of a number). **3.** Hence ~ABLE *a.*, ~OR *n.* (~or fan, ventilating fan in window etc. to remove stale air). [f. L EX¹(*trahere tract-* draw)]
extră′ction *n.* extracting; lineage, descent, (*of Indian extraction*). [ME f. F, f. LL *extractio -onis* (as prec.; see -ION)]
extră′ctive *a.* & *n.* (thing) of the nature of an extract;

~ **industries** (obtaining coal, ore, oil, etc.). [f. EXTRACT² + -IVE]
extradi′table *a.* liable to, (of crime) warranting, extradition. [f. foll. + -ABLE]
e′xtradīte *v.t.* give up (fugitive foreign criminal or accused person) to another State; obtain the extradition of. [back-form. f. foll.]
extradi′tion *n.* delivery of fugitive foreign criminal or accused person to another State; (Psych.) localizing of sensation at distance from the centre of sensation. [F (as EX¹, TRADITION)]
extră′dŏs *n.* upper or outer curve of arch. [f. EXTRA- (*dos* back f. L *dorsum*)]
extramūr′al *a.* outside walls or boundaries (of town or city); additional to ordinary university teaching or studies, esp. for non-resident students. [f. L *extra muros* outside the walls + -AL]
extră′neous *a.* of external origin; foreign *to* (object to which it is attached etc.); not belonging (*to* matter in hand, class); hence ~LY² *adv.*, ~NESS *n.* [f. L *extraneus* (*extra* outside) + -OUS]
extraŏr′dinar|y (īkstrŏr′-, ĕkstraŏr′-) *a.* **1.** out of the usual course; (of official etc.) additional, specially employed (ENVOY² *extraordinary*). **2.** exceptional, surprising; unusually great. **3.** Hence ~iLY² *adv.*, ~iNESS *n.* [f. L *extraordinarius* (*extra ordinem* outside the usual order; see -ARY¹)]
extră′pol|āte *v.t.* & *i.* (Math. etc.) calculate approximately *from* known values, data, etc., (others which lie outside the range of those known); so ~A′TION *n.* [f. EXTRA- + INTERPOLATE]
extratěrritŏr′ial *a.* (Of ambassador etc.) free from jurisdiction of the territory in which one resides; so ~ITY (-ă′l-) *n.* [f. L *extra territorium* outside the territory + -AL]
extră′vag|ance (-vag-, -vĭg-) *n.* being extravagant; extravagant thing; absurd statement or action; so ~ANCY *n.* [F (as foll.; see -ANCE)]
extră′vagant (-vag-, -vĭg-) *a.* immoderate; exceeding the bounds of reason; profuse, wasteful; (of price etc.) exorbitant; hence ~LY² *adv.* [ME, f. med. L EXTRA-(*vagari* wander); see -ANT; infl. in sense by F *extravagant*]
extrăvagă′nza *n.* fanciful composition (literary, musical, or dramatic); extravagant language or behaviour. [f. It. *estravaganza*, after EXTRA-]
extră′vag|āte *v.i.* (arch.) wander away (*from* right course, *into* error etc.); exceed due bounds; hence ~A′TION *n.* [f. as EXTRAVAGANT + -ATE³]
extră′vasāte *v.* **1.** *v.t.* force out (fluid, esp. blood) from its proper vessel. **2.** *v.i.* (Of blood, lava, etc.) flow out. **3.** Hence **extră′vasA′TION** *n.* [f. L *extra* outside + *vessel* + -ATE³]
e′xtravĕrt etc. Var. of EXTROVERT.
extrē′me *a.* & *n.* **1.** *a.* outermost, farthest from centre, situated at either end (*extreme and mean ratio,* see GOLDEN *section*); utmost; last; ~ **unction,** (RC & Orthodox Ch.) anointing of dying person by priest. **2.** reaching a high or the highest degree (*extreme old age; in extreme danger*); **an** ~ **case** (having some characteristic in the utmost degree). **3.** (Of action, measure) severe, stringent; (of opinion, person, etc.) going to great lengths, advocating severe measures, not moderate, whence **extrē′m**ISM (3), **extrē′m**IST (2), *ns.* **4.** Hence ~LY² (-mlī) *adv.*, in extreme degree, very, ~NESS (-mn-) *n.* **5.** *n.* thing at either end of anything, esp. (in *pl.*) things as remote or as different as possible (*extremes meet*); (Logic) subject or predicate in proposition, major or minor term in syllogism; (Math.) first or last term of ratio or series; **go to** ~**s,** take an extreme course of action; **go to the other** ~, take a diametrically opposite course of action; **in the** ~, in the extreme degree. [ME f. OF, f. L *extremu.* superl. of *exterus* outward]
extrĕ′mity *n.* extreme point, very end; (in *pl.*) hands and feet; extreme adversity, embarrassment, etc. (*driven to extremity; what can we do in this extremity?*)

For other words in *ex-* **see** EX-¹, EX-².

(arch., usu. in *pl.*) extreme measure(s). [ME, f. OF *extremité* or f. L *extremitas* (as prec.; see -ITY)]

extre'm|um *n.* (*pl.* ~a *or* ~ums). (Math.) maximum or minimum value of a function; hence ~AL *a.* [L, neut. of *extremus* EXTREME]

e'xtric|āte *v.t.* disentangle, release, (person, thing, *from* confinement, difficulty); hence ~ABLE *a.*, ~A'TION *n.* [f. L EX¹(*tricare* f. *tricae* perplexities) + -ATE³]

extri'ns|ic *a.* lying outside, not belonging, (*to*); originating or operating from without; not inherent or essential; hence ~ICALLY *adv.* [f. LL *extrinsicus* f. L *extrinsecus* adv. (*exter* outside + -*im* (as *interim*) + *secus* beside)]

extrover'sion *n.* (Psych.) direction of thoughts and interests to things outside oneself (opp. INTROVERSION); so **e'xtrovert** *n.* & *a.*, **e'xtrovert|ed¹** *a.*, (person) characterized by extroversion, sociable or unreserved (person). [f. as EXTRA- (after *intro*-) + VERSION]

extru'|de (-rōō'd) *v.t.* thrust out (person, thing, *from*); shape (metal, plastics, etc.) by forcing through die; hence or cogn. ~SION (-zhon) *n.*, ~SILE, ~SIVE, *adjs.* [f. L EX¹(*trudere trus*- thrust)]

exŭ'ber|ant (igz-) *a.* luxuriantly prolific (lit. or fig.); growing luxuriantly; (of health, emotion, etc.) overflowing, abounding; (of person, action, etc.) effusive, overflowing with high spirits; (of language) copious, lavish in ornament; abundant; hence or cogn. ~ANCE *n.*, ~antLY² *adv.* [f. F *exubérant*. f. L EX¹(*uberare* f. fruitful f. *uber* fertile); see -ANT]

exŭ'berāte (igz-) *v.i.* be exuberant; (arch.) abound, overflow, indulge freely *in*. [f. L (as prec.) + -ATE³]

exŭ'd|e (igz-) *v.i.* & *t.* ooze out, give off (moisture etc.), emit (smell), (fig.) show (pleasure etc.) abundantly; so **e'xŭdate¹** (5); **exŭda'tion**, *ns.*, ~ATIVE (īgz-) *a.* [f. L EX¹(*sudare* sweat)]

exŭ'lt (igz-) *v.i.* rejoice exceedingly (*at, in,* thing, *to* find etc.); triumph (*over* person); hence or cogn. ~ANCY, **exŭlta'tion** (ĕgz-, ĕks-), *ns.*, ~ANT *a.* [f. L EX¹(*sultare* = *saltare* frequent. of *salire salt*- leap)]

e'xŭrb *n.* district outside city or town, esp. prosperous area beyond suburbs; so **exŭr'ban** *a.*, **exŭr'ban|ite¹** (1) *n.* [f. L *ex* out of l *urbs* city, or back-form. f. *exurban* f. EX-¹ + URBAN, after *suburban*]

exŭr'bia *n.* exurbs collectively, region beyond suburbs. [f. EX-¹, after *Suburbia*]

exŭ'vi|ae *n. pl.* animal's cast skin, shell, or covering, (recent or fossil, or fig.); hence ~AL *a.* [L, = animal's skins, spoils of enemy, f. EX¹*uere* divest oneself of]

exŭ'vi|āte *v.t.* & *i.* shed (exuviae, or fig.), slough; hence ~A'TION *n.* [f. prec. + -ATE³]

ex voto (ĕks vō'tō) *adv.* & *n.* (offering made) in pursuance of a vow. [L, = out of a vow]

-ey. See -Y³.

ey'as (ī'as) *n.* young hawk in nest, or taken from nest for training, or not yet completely trained. [orig. *nyas* f. F *niais* f. Rom. **nid(i)ax -acis* f. L *nidus* nest; for loss of *n*- cf. ADDER]

eye¹ (ī) *n.* **1.** organ of sight in man and animals; iris of this (*blue, brown, eyes*); region of the eyes (BLACK¹ *eye*). **2.** all ~s, watching intently; all my ~, (sl.) nonsense; *turn a* BLIND¹ *eye*; CATCH¹ *the eye*; CLAP² *eyes on*; CRY² *one's eyes out*; ~ *of day*, sun; do (person) in the ~, defraud or thwart; *throw* DUST¹ *in person's eyes*; EASY *on the eye*; EVIL *eye*; ~ for an ~, retaliation in kind (Exod. 21:24); ~s and no ~s (said of or to one who is unobservant); ~s down, (colloq.) start of play at bingo; ~s front, left, right, (Mil.) turn head in direction stated; ~s on stalks (colloq., protruding in amazement etc.); GLAD *eye*; have ~s for, be interested in; have an ~ to, have as one's object, prudently consider; hit person in the ~, (fig.) be very obvious; in or through the ~s of, from the point of view of, in the judgement of; keep an ~ on, direct one's attention (lit. or fig.) to; keep an ~ open or out, keep one's ~s open or skinned etc., watch

carefully (*for*); *keep* one's *eye on the* BALL¹; look person in the ~ (directly or unashamedly at him); make (sheep's) ~s, look amorously (*at*); MEET² *the eye*; *in the* MIND¹'s *eye*; my ~, (sl.) nonsense; NAKED *eye*; one in the ~, disappointment or discomfiture *for* (person); OPEN² one's, person's, *eyes*; with one ~ on, directing one's attention partly to; with one's ~s open, (fig.) deliberately, with full awareness; pore etc. one's ~s out, tire them; cast or run an or one's ~ over, examine cursorily; PIPE² one's *eye*; PRIVATE *eye*; *in the* PUBLIC *eye*; see ~ to ~, be in full agreement *with* (person); SET¹ *eyes on*; SHUT¹ one's *eyes to*; with one's ~s shut, (fig.) (1) without full awareness, (2) with great ease; SMACK² *in the eye*; up to the ~s, deeply (engaged, involved, etc.); *in the* WIND¹'s *eye*; WIPE one's or person's *eye(s)*; *view* with a *friendly, jealous,* etc., ~, with feeling of friendship, jealousy, etc.; with an ~ to, with a VIEW to, prudently considering. **3.** faculty of seeing, sight; (in *sing.* or *pl.*) look, gaze, glance; have an ~ for, be capable of perceiving or appreciating; a good ~ for, sound appreciation of; half an ~, the slightest degree of perceptiveness; get one's ~ in, become accustomed to conditions of batting etc., so as to judge speed etc.; lose an ~, become unable to see with it; *a* STRAIGHT *eye*. **4.** thing like an eye, e.g. spot on peacock's tail or insect's wing, ~ of needle etc. (hole for thread etc.); hole in head of axe etc. for insertion of handle; calm region in centre of hurricane etc., centre of flower, loop of cord or rope, leaf bud of potato; APPLE *of the eye*; BULL¹'s-*eye*; ELECTRIC *eye*; glass ~ (artificial, of glass etc.); HOOK¹ *and eye*; MAGIC *eye*. **5.** ~'ball, eye within lids and socket (~*ball to* ~*ball*, (colloq.) confronting closely); ~'bath, small glass etc. for applying lotion etc. to eye; ~'black, mascara; ~'bolt, bolt or bar with eye at end for hook etc.; ~'bright, plant of genus *Euphrasia*, formerly used as remedy for weak eyes; ~'brow, hair growing on ridge over eye (*raise an* ~*brow* or one's ~*brows*, show surprise; *up to the* ~*brows*, deeply engaged), moulding etc. so shaped; ~-cup, − *eye-bath*, ~'glass, salts for correcting or assisting defective sight, (in *pl.*) pair of these held in position by hand or frame or by spring on nose; ~'hole, hole containing eye, hole to look through; ~'lash, hair or row of hairs on edge of eyelid, (fig.) hairbreadth; ~-level, level seen by eyes looking horizontally; ~'lid, upper or lower fold of skin that can cover eye (*hang on by the* ~*lids*, (fig.) have only slight hold); ~-liner, cosmetic applied as line round eye; ~-opener, enlightening or surprising circumstance etc., *drink taken on awakening; ~'piece, lens(es) at eye-end of telescope etc.; ~-rhyme, correspondence of words in spelling but not in pronunciation (*love, move*); ~-service, (arch.) service performed only when one is watched by employer; ~-shade, device to protect eyes from strong light; ~-shadow, cosmetic applied to skin round eyes, ~'shot, seeing-distance (*beyond, in, out of, eyeshot*); ~'sight, power or faculty of seeing; ~-sore, ugly object, thing that offends the sight; ~-stalk, (Zool.) movable stalk carrying eye; ~-strain, weariness of eyes from excessive or incorrect use; ~-tooth, canine tooth just under or next to eye, esp. in upper jaw (*cut one's* ~-*teeth*, attain wordly wisdom); ~'wash, lotion for eye, (sl.) bunkum, mere pretentious concealment; ~-water, tears, lotion for eye, aqueous or vitreous humour of eye; ~-witness, one who can bear witness from his own observation. **6.** Hence (-)eyED² (īd), ~'LESS (ī'l-), *adjs.*, ~'FUL 2 (ī'f-) *n.*, (esp., colloq.) thorough look, remarkable or attractive thing or person. [OE *ēage*, = OS *ōga*, OHG *ouga*, ON *auga*, Goth. *augo* f. Gmc **augon*]

eye² (ī) *v.t.* (~ing or eying, *pr.* ī'ing). observe, watch, (*jealously, narrowly, with disgust, askance,* etc.). [f. prec.]

eye'lět (ī'l-) *n.* small eye; small hole in leather, cloth, sail, etc., for lace, ring, rope, etc., or as ornament; loophole; ~-hole, small hole to look or shoot through. [ME, f. OF *oillet* dim. of *oil* eye f. L *oculus*]

Eyetä′lian (ītă′lyan), **Eye′tie** (ī′tī), *ns.* & *adjs.* (sl., derog.; **R**) Italian. [repr. vulg. or joc. pr.]

eyot. See AIT.

eyr′a (āī′a) *n.* red form of jaguarundi. [f. Tupi (*e*)*irara*]

eyre (āī) *n.* (Hist.) circuit, circuit court, (*Justices in Eyre*). [ME, f. OF *eire* f. L *iter* journey]

eyr′ie, aer′ie, (āī′ī, ēī′ī, īr′ī) *n.* nest of bird of prey, esp. eagle, or of other bird that builds high up; human residence perched high on mountain. [f. med. L *aeria, aerea*, etc., prob. f. OF *aire* lair f. Rom. f. L *agrum* piece of ground]

Ezek. *abbr.* Ezekiel (OT).

F

F, f, (ĕf) *n.* (*pl.* **Fs** *or* **F's**). sixth letter of alphabet; (Mus.) fourth note in diatonic scale of C major.

F. *abbr.* Fahrenheit; farad(s); Fellow of; (Biol.) filial generation; fine (pencil-lead).

f. *abbr.* female; feminine; femto-; filly; focal length (cf. F-NUMBER); folio; following page etc.; FORTE².

F *symb.* fluorine.

fa. See FAH.

FA *abbr.* FANNY ADAMS 2; ||Football Association.

făb *a.* (colloq.) marvellous. [abbr. of FABULOUS]

Fā′bian *a.* & *n.* **1.** *a.* employing cautious and dilatory strategy to wear out an enemy (esp. *Fabian policy*); ∼ **Society** (of socialists aiming at gradual social change; so ∼ISM (3), ∼IST (2), *ns.*). **2.** *n.* member of or sympathizer with Fabian Society. [f. L *Fabianus* (Q. *Fabius* Cunctator (= delayer), Roman general d. 203 BC; see -AN)]

fā′ble¹ *n* (esp. supernatural) story not founded on fact; (collect.) myths, legendary tales; false statement, lie; thing only supposed to exist; short story, esp. with animals as characters, conveying a moral; (arch.) plot of play etc. [ME f. OF, f. L *fabula* discourse (*fari* speak)]

fā′ble² *v.* (arch. or poet.) **1.** *v.i.* tell fictitious tales, whence **fā′bler¹** *n.* **2.** *v.t.* describe fictitiously; (in *p.p.*) celebrated in fable, legendary, fictitious. [ME, f. OF *fabler* f. L *fabulari* (*fabula*; see prec.)]

fā′bliau (-lō) *n.* (*pl.* ∼x *pr.* -z). metrical tale in early French poetry, often coarsely humorous. [F, f. OF dial. *fablia(u)x* pl. of *fablel* dim. as FABLE¹]

fā′bric *n.* thing put together; frame, structure, (lit. or fig.); walls, floor, and roof of building; woven, knitted, or felted material; other material resembling this; construction, texture, tissue; (arch.) edifice, building. [ME, f. F *fabrique* f. L *fabrica* (*faber* metal-worker etc.)]

fā′bric|āte *v.t.* **1.** construct, manufacture, (esp. product in final shape from semi-finished metal stock etc.). **2.** invent (story), forge (document). **3.** Hence or cogn. ∼A′TION, ∼ātor, *ns.* [f. L *fabricare* (as prec.) + -ATE³]

fā′būlist *n.* composer of fables; liar. [f. F *fabuliste* f. L *fabula* (see FABLE¹, -IST)]

fā′būlous *a.* celebrated in fable; unhistorical, legendary; incredible, absurd, exaggerated; (colloq.) marvellous; hence or cogn. **făbūlo′sity**, ∼NESS, ns., ∼LY² *adv.* [f. F *fabuleux* or f. L *fabulosus* (as FABLE¹; see -OUS)]

faça′de (-sah′d) *n.* face of building (esp. principal front) towards street or open space; frontal or outward appearance, esp. deceptive one. [F (as foll.; see -ADE)]

făce¹ *n.* **1.** front of head from forehead to chin; corresponding part of animal's head; ∼ **to** ∼, confronted; ∼ **to** ∼ **with,** confronting; **fly in the** ∼ **of,** openly disobey; **in (the)** ∼ **of,** despite; **in one's** ∼, straight against one, as one approaches; **look** person **in the** ∼, confront him steadily; **put** one's ∼ **on,** (colloq.) apply make-up to one's face; **set** one's ∼ **against,** steadfastly oppose; **show** one's ∼, let oneself be seen; SMACK² *in the face;* **to** person's ∼, openly in his presence. **2.** what is shown by one's face, expression of countenance; grimace (*make* or *pull a face* or *faces*); LONG¹ *face* **3.** composure, coolness, effrontery; **have the** ∼, be shameless enough; **save** person's or one's ∼, forbear from or evade shaming him or oneself openly. **4.** outward show, aspect, (**on the** ∼ **of it,** to judge by appearances; **put a new** ∼ **on,** alter aspect of; **put a good** or **bold** ∼ **on** (a matter), make it look well, show courage in facing it); **lose** ∼, be humiliated,

lose one's credit or good name [transl. of Chin. *diu lian*]. **5.** surface (*from the face of the earth*); front, façade, right side, obverse, dial-plate of clock etc., distinctive side of playing-card, working surface of implement etc.; (Geom.) each surface of a solid; = TYPE¹-*face*; = COAL-*face*. **6.** ∼**-ache,** neuralgia, (sl.) mournful-looking person; ∼ **card,** = COURT¹-*card*; ∼**-cloth,** (1) cloth for washing face, (2) smooth-surfaced woollen cloth; ∼**-cream,** cream applied to face to improve complexion; ||∼**-flannel,** = *face-cloth* (1); ∼**-fungus,** (colloq.) beard; ∼**-lift,** face-lifting, (fig.) improvement in appearance; ∼**-lifting,** operation for removing wrinkles by tightening skin of face; ∼**-saving,** that saves one's face (see sense 3); ∼ **value,** nominal value as stated on coin, note, etc., (fig.) apparent nature (esp. if taken as genuine); ∼**-worker,** miner who works at coal-face. **7.** Hence -fāceD² (‖st) *a.* [ME f. OF, f. Rom. **facia* f. L *facies*]

făce² *v.* **1.** *v.t.* meet confidently or defiantly (∼ *matter* **out,** carry it through by effrontery; ∼ *opponent* **down,** overcome him by show of determination or browbeating); not shrink from (*face the facts;* **let's** ∼ **it,** (colloq.) we must recognize unwelcome fact); stand fronting (∼ **the music,** be resolute in face of difficulty or unpleasant consequences); meet in contest; present itself to (*the problem that faces us, that we are faced with*). **2.** turn (card) face upwards. **3.** *v.i.* (Of person etc.) look, (of thing) be situated with front, in a certain direction (*on, to,* or *north, eastwards,* etc.); ∼ **up to,** confront. **4.** *v.t.* front towards, be opposite to, (*to face page 20*). **5.** *v.t.* & *i.* (Lacrosse, Ice Hockey, etc.) place (ball, puck, etc.) between crosses, sticks, etc., of two opposing players as preliminary to commencement of play, start or restart play thus, (also ∼ **off**); so ∼**-off** *n.,* act of doing this. **6.** *(Mil.) (cause to) turn in certain direction while remaining in same place (*left, about, face; he faced his men about*). **7.** *v.t.* supply (garment) with facings; cover (surface) with layer of other material; dress surface of. [ME, f. prec.]

fā′celèss (-sl-) *a.* without a face; without identity; purposely not identifiable, hence ∼NESS *n.* [f. FACE¹ + -LESS]

fā′cer *n.* blow in the face; great and sudden difficulty. [f. FACE¹ + ER¹]

făc′ĕt *n.* one side of many-sided body, esp. of cut gem, one segment of compound eye; particular aspect of thing (*another facet of his genius*); hence ∼ED² *a.* [f. F *facette* dim. f. as FACE¹; see -ETTE]

facē′tiae (-shiē) *n. pl.* pleasantries, witticisms; (in bookselling) pornography [L, pl. of *facetia* jest (*facetus* witty)]

facē′tious (-shŭs) *a.* addicted to or marked by pleasantry or joking; hence ∼LY² *adv.,* ∼NESS *n.* [f. F *facétieux* (*facétie* f. L *facetia*; see prec.)]

fā′cia (-sha) *n.* plate over shop-front with occupier's name etc.; instrument panel of motor vehicle. [var. of FASCIA]

fā′cial (-shal) *a.* & *n.* **1.** *a.* of the face; ∼ **angle,** that formed by two lines from nostril to ear and to forehead. **2.** *n.* beauty treatment for the face. [f. med. L *facialis* (as FACE¹; see -AL)]

-fā′cient (-shent) *suf.* forming *adjs.* & *ns.* w. sense '(substance etc.) producing an action or state' (*abortifacient, liquefacient, rubefacient*). [f. or after L *-faciens -entis* part. (*facere* make; see -ENT)]

fā′cies (-shēz) *n.* (*pl.* same). (Med.) appearance or expression of face; (Geol.) character of rock etc. expressed by composition, fossil content, etc. [L, = FACE¹]

fā′cile *a.* **1.** (often derog.) easily done or won, working easily, ready, fluent. **2.** (arch.) of easy temper, gentle, flexible, yielding. **3.** Hence ∿LY² (-l-lĭ) *adv*. [F, or f. L *facilis* (*facere* do; see -IL)]

facile princeps (făsĭlĭ prĭ′nsĕps) *a.* & *n.* (one who is) easily first; the acknowledged leader or chief. [L]

faci′lit|āte *v.t.* make easy, promote, help forward, (action or result); hence ∿A′TION *n*. [f. F *faciliter* f. It. *facilitare* (*facile* easy f. L *facilis*) + -ATE³]

faci′litȳ *n.* being easy, absence of difficulty, unimpeded opportunity (*give facilities for* action or doing, *of* doing); (esp. in *pl*.) equipment or physical means for doing something (*washing, conference, facilities*); ease or readiness of speech etc., aptitude, dexterity, fluency; (arch.) pliancy. [f. F *facilité* or f. L *facilitas* (as FACILE; see -ITY)]

fā′cing *n.* In vbl senses; material covering part of garment etc. for contrast or strength; (in *pl*.) cuffs, collar, etc., of military(-style) jacket, differently coloured from rest; coating of different material, esp. of stone etc. on wall. [f. FACE² + -ING¹]

façon de parler (fahsawn de pär′lā) *n.* manner of speaking; mere formula. [F]

facsi′milè *n.* & *v.* **1.** *n.* exact copy, esp. of writing, printing, picture, etc., (*reproduced in* ∿, exactly); system of producing this by radio etc. transmission of signal from scanning of writing etc. **2.** *v.t.* & *i.* make or be facsimile (of). [mod. L, f. L *fac* imper. of *facere* make + *simile* neut. of *similis* like]

fäct *n.* **1.** thing certainly known to have occurred or be true, datum of experience, (often with explanatory clause or phrase: *the fact that fire burns, the fact of my having seen him*); ∿**s and figures,** precise information; ∿ **of life,** something whose existence cannot be ignored; **the** ∿**s of life,** (colloq., euphem.) knowledge of human sexual functions. **2.** thing assumed as basis for inference (*his facts are disputable*). **3.** what is true or existent, reality; **in** ∿, in reality, (in summarizing) in short; MATTER¹ *of fact* **4.** perpetration of wrongful act (*before* or *after the fact; confess the fact*). **5.** ∿**-finding** *a.*, engaged in finding out facts. [f. L *factum* neut. p.p.(as n.) of *facere* do]

fä′ctice *n.* rubber-like substance got by vulcanizing unsaturated vegetable oils. [f. G *faktis* f. L *facticius* FACTITIOUS]

fä′ction *n.* self-interested, turbulent, or unscrupulous party or group, esp. in politics; prevalence of partisan spirit; hence ∿AL *a.* [F, f. L *factio -onis* (*facere fact-* do ; see -ION); cf. FASHION]

-fä′ction *suf.* forming *ns.* of action f. *vbs.* in -FY (*petrifaction, satisfaction*). [f. or after L *-factio -onis* (*-facere* make)]

fä′ctious (-shus) *a.* characterized by or pertaining to faction(s); hence ∿LY² *adv*., ∿NESS *n*. [f. F *factieux* or f. L *factiosus* (as FACTION; see -OUS)]

fäcti′tious (-shus) *a.* made for a special purpose, not genuine; not natural, artificial; hence ∿LY² *adv*., ∿NESS *n*. [f. L *facticius* (*facere fact-* make) + -OUS; see -ITIOUS¹]

fä′ctitive *a.* (Gram.) ∿ **verb,** one with sense of making, calling, or thinking, that takes obj. and compl. (*appointed him captain, called it a swindle, thought her mad*). [f. mod. L *factitivus*, irreg. f. L *factitare* frequent. of *facere fact-* make; see -IVE]

fä′ctor *n.* & *v.* **1.** *n.* merchant buying and selling on commission, whence ∿AGE (4) *n*.; (Sc.) land-agent, steward; agent, deputy. **2.** (Math.) one of the numbers etc. that make up a number or expression by multiplication; (Biol.) gene etc. determining hereditary character; *factor of* SAFETY. **3.** circumstance, fact, or influence, contributing to a result. **4.** ∿ **cost,** cost of product to producer. **5.** *v.t.* resolve into factors or components. **6.** *v.i.* buy at discount the debts owed to another, in order to profit by collecting them. [f. F *facteur* or f. L *factor* (as prec.; see -OR)]

fäctō′r|ial *n.* & *a.* (Math.) **1.** *n.* product of series of factors in arithmetical progression; product of an integer and all lower integers. **2.** *a.* of factor(s) or factorial(s); ∿ **4,** = product of 4, 3, 2, and 1 (denoted by '4!'). [f. prec. + -IAL]

fä′ctorīz|e, -īs|e (-īz), *v.* (Math.) **1.** *v.t.* resolve into factors. **2.** *v.i.* be capable of resolution into factors. **3.** Hence ∿A′TION *n*. [f. FACTOR + -IZE]

fä′ctorȳ *n.* building(s) and equipment for manufacturing, workshop; (Hist.) merchant company's foreign trading station; ‖**F**∿ **Acts** (regulating operation of factories for benefit of employees); ∿ **farm** (organized on industrial lines); ‖∿ **ship,** base-ship of whaling fleet. [f. Port. *feitoria* & f. LL *factorium*]

fäctō′tum *n.* one who does all kinds of work; servant managing his master's affairs. [med. L, f. L *fac* imper. of *facere* make + *totum* neut. of *totus* whole]

fä′ctüal *a.* concerned with or of the nature of fact(s); hence ∿ITY (-ă′l-), ∿NESS, *ns*., ∿LY² *adv*. [f. FACT, after *actual*]

fä′ctüal|ism *n.* (Philos.) theory maintaining that facts are pre-eminent and fundamental; so ∿IST (2) *n*. [f. prec. + -ISM]

fä′ct|um *n.* (*pl.* ∿**ums** or ∿**a**). (Law). act, deed; statement of facts. [F, f. L (see FACT)]

fä′cture *n.* quality of execution of (esp. surface of) a painting. [ME f. OF, f. L *factura* (*facere fact-* make; see -URE)]

fä′cül|a *n.* (*pl.* ∿**ae**). (Astron.) bright spot or streak on sun; hence ∿AR¹, ∿OUS, *adjs*. [L, dim. of *fax facis* torch]

fä′cultăt̆ive *a.* permissive; optional; contingent; (Biol.) not restricted to a particular function, mode of life, etc.; of a faculty. [f. F *facultatif -ive* f. as foll.; see -IVE]

fä′cultȳ *n.* **1.** aptitude or competence for any special kind of action; power inherent in the body or in an organ; a mental power (e.g. the will, reason). **2.** branch of art or science, those qualified to teach it, department of University teaching, *staff of university or college; members of a particular profession, esp. medicine. **3.** (esp. Eccl.) liberty to do something given by law or a superior, authorization, licence. [ME, f. OF *faculté* f. L *facultas -tatis* (*facilis* easy; see -TY¹)]

fäd *n.* peculiar notion or rule of action; craze; hence ∿′dISH¹, ∿′dY², *adjs.*, ∿′dISM (3), ∿′dIST (2), *ns*. [19th c., orig. dial., prob. f. *fidfad* f. FIDDLE-FADDLE]

fāde *v.* & *n.* **1.** *v.i.* ∿ (**away, out**), droop, wither, lose freshness and vigour, disappear gradually, depart, (of colour, light, etc.) grow pale or dim, (of sound) grow faint; (of brake) gradually lose power; (of radio signal) vary irregularly in intensity; (of golf-ball etc.) deviate from straight course, esp. in deliberate slice. **2.** *v.t.* cause to lose freshness or colour; (Cinemat.) cause (picture) to come gradually *in* or *out* (of view on the screen); bring (sound) *up* or *in*, *away* or *out* (of audibility); cause (golf-ball etc.) to fade. **3.** So ∿**-away,** ∿**-in,** ∿**-out,** *ns.* **4.** *n.* action or process of fading; **do a** ∿, (sl.) depart; hence ∿′LESS (-dl-) *a.* [ME, f. OF *fader* (*fade* dull, insipid f. Rom. *fatidus*, prob. f. L *fatuus* silly + *vapidus* VAPID)]

fädo (fah′dō) *n.* (*pl.* ∿**s**). melancholy Portuguese folk-song. [Port., = fate]

fae′cēs, *fē′cēs, (-z) *n. pl.* waste matter discharged from bowels; hence **fae′CAL, *fē′CAL,** *a.* [L, pl. of *faex dregs*]

fā′erie, fā′erȳ, *n.* (arch.) Fairyland, the fairies, esp. as represented by Spenser; (*attrib.*) visionary, fancied. [var. of FAIRY]

Faeroese. Var. of FAROESE.

‖**fäff** *v.i.,* & *n.* (colloq.) fuss, dither. [imit.]

fäg¹ *v.* (-**gg**-) & *n.* **1.** *v.i.* & *t.* toil; (of occupation) tire (*out*), make weary; ‖(at schools, of senior) use the service of (junior), (of junior) do service for senior; fray (end of rope). **2.** *n.* ‖drudgery, unwelcome task (*what a fag!*); ‖exhaustion (*brain-fag*); ‖(at schools) junior who has to fag; (sl.) cigarette; ∿**-end,** inferior or useless remnant, (sl.) cigarette-end. [orig. unkn.; cf. FLAG⁵]

*făg² *n.* (sl.) homosexual (usu. male). [abbr. of foll.]

fă'ggot, *fă'got, *n.* & *v.* **1.** *n.* bundle of sticks or twigs bound together as fuel; bundle of iron rods for heat treatment; bunch of herbs; (usu. in *pl.*) dish of liver etc. chopped, seasoned, and baked as ball or roll; unpleasant woman; *(sl.) homosexual (usu. male), whence ~y² *a.*; ~-**stitch** (used in FAGGOTING); ~-**vote,** (Hist.) vote manufactured by transferring sufficient property to unqualified person. **2.** *v.t.* & *i.* bind in faggots, make faggot(s); use, join by, FAG-GOTING. [ME, f. OF *fagot* f. It. *fagotto,* dim. of Rom. *facus]

fă'ggoting *n.* embroidery in which threads are fastened together like faggot; joining of materials in similar manner. [f. prec. + -ING¹]

Fă'gin (-g-) *n.* person who receives stolen goods or trains thieves. [character in Dickens's *Oliver Twist*]

*fă'got. See FAGGOT.

fah, fa, (fah), *n.* (Mus.) fourth note of scale in movable-doh system; the note F in fixed-doh system. [ME *fa* f. L. *famuli*; see GAMUT]

Fahr. *abbr.* = foll.

Fah'renheit (fă'rĕnhīt) *a.* pertaining to the ~ **scale** of temperature, on which water freezes at 32° and boils at 212° under standard conditions. [f. G. ~, Ger. physicist d. 1736]

faïence (fah'yahns, fiah'ns) *n.* decorated earthenware and porcelain, e.g. delf or majolica. [f. F *faïence* f. *Faenza* in Italy]

fail¹ *n.* failure in an examination; **without** ~, for certain, irrespective of hindrances, (emphasizing injunction or promise). [ME, f. OF *fail(l)e* (*faillir* FAIL²)]

fail² *v.* **1.** *v.i.* & *t.* be absent, be or become insufficient, not suffice for needs of (person), run short. **2.** *v.t.* neglect, not remember or not choose or not be able, *to* (*he failed to appear; don't fail to let me know; I fail to see the reason*). **3.** *v.i.* become extinct, die away; flag, break down, (*engine, health, fails;* ~ **safe,** revert to danger--free condition in event of breakdown etc.); become weaker or less efficient. **4.** *v.i.* & *t.* prove misleading, disappoint hopes of, not serve when needed, (*the prophecy failed; the wind failed us; his heart failed him;* **words** ~ **me,** I cannot adequately describe etc.), be insufficiently equipped *in,* not succeed in the attainment *of;* not succeed (*in doing* or *to* do; hence ~ED¹ (2) (-ld) *a.,* unsuccessful); miscarry, come to nothing; become bankrupt. **5.** be rejected as candidate, reject (candidate), be unsuccessful in (examination). [ME, f. OF *faillir* f. Rom. *fallire = L *fallere* deceive]

fai'ling¹ *n.* In vbl senses; foible, shortcoming, weakness in character. [f. prec. + -ING¹]

fai'ling² *prep.* in default of (~ **this,** if this does not happen; **whom** ~ or ~ **whom,** or in his absence for proxy appointments). [f. FAIL² + -ING²]

fai'lure (-lyer) *n.* failing; non-occurrence, non--performance; running short, breaking down; (Med.) cessation or impairment of vital function (*heart failure; renal failure*); lack of success; unsuccessful person, thing, or attempt; bankruptcy. [earlier *failer* f. AF, = OF *faillir* FAIL²; cf. -ER⁴, -URE]

fain¹ *pred. a.,* & *adv.* (arch.) **1.** *a.* willing under the circumstances *to;* left with no alternative but *to.* **2.** *adv.* would ~, would be glad to. [OE *fægen,* = OS *fagan,* ON *feginn* f. Gmc **fagin-*]

‖fain², fains (-z), **fen²(s)** (-z), *v.t.* forbid, not want, (usu. in child's formulae **fains I** etc. claiming exemption from unwelcome duty etc.). [f. FEND in obs. sense 'forbid']

fainéant (fă'nāahn) *n.* & *a.* idle(r), inactive (official etc.); hence ~**ism(e)** (fă'nāahntizm) *n.* [F (*fait* does, *néant* nothing)]

faint¹ *a.* **1.** timid (~ **heart,** cowardly spirit; ~-**heart,** coward); feeble (*a faint show of resistance; faint praise*). **2.** dim, indistinct, pale (~ or **feint lines, ruled** ~ or **feint,** of paper with inconspicuous lines to guide writing); (of idea etc.) inadequate; giddy or languid

through fear, hunger, etc., inclined to faint; (arch., of air, scent, etc.) sickly, oppressive. **3.** Hence ~'NESS *n.* [ME f. OF, p.p. of *faindre* FEIGN]

faint² *v.i.,* & *n.* **1.** *v.i.* lose consciousness (esp. through syncope); (arch.) lose courage, give way. **2.** *n.* act or state of fainting (**in a dead** ~, completely uncon-scious). [ME, f. prec.]

fai'ntly *adv.* feebly; indistinctly; very slightly. [f. FAINT¹ + -LY²]

fair¹ *n.* periodical gathering for sale of goods, often with shows and entertainments, at place and time fixed by charter, statute, or custom, (~**ground,** outdoor area on which fair is held; **a day after the** ~, too late); exhibition, esp. to publicize specified product(s); = FUN-*fair.* [ME, f. OF *feire* f. LL *feria* sing. f. L *feriae* holiday]

fair² *a., n.,* & *v.* **1.** *a.* beautiful (**the** ~ **sex,** women); (arch.) kind (*fair sir* etc., in courteous address). **2.** considerable, satisfactory, (*a fair heritage*); specious (*fair speeches*); complimentary (*fair words*). **3.** blond, not dark, (*a fair man, complexion; fair hair*); hence ~-**haired** *a.,* blond, (fig.) favourite (person). **4.** clean, clear, unblemished, (*fair water; fair COPY¹*); ~-**faced** *a.,* (of brickwork etc.) not plastered. **5.** just, unbiased, equitable, legitimate, in accordance with rules; ~ **and square** *a.* & *adv.,* (1) without finesse, above-board, (2) exactly (*in the middle* etc.); *fair COP²; fair or SQUARE² deal; fair DO²s!;* ~ **enough!,** (colloq.) that is a reasonable or satisfactory proposition; *a fair* FIELD *and no favour; fair* GAME¹ 8; *all's fair in love and war; by fair means or foul;* ~ **play,** equal conditions for all. **6.** of (only) moderate quality, not bad, pretty good, whence ~'ISH¹ 2 *a.;* ~-**to-middling,** slightly above average. **7.** favourable, promising, gentle, unobstructed, (*fair* WIND¹; *fair or foul weather*); ~-**weather friend** (not good in a crisis); **in a** ~ **way** (likely) *to* succeed; **by** ~ **means,** without violence or fraud; ~**lead,** (Naut. etc.) device to guide rope etc., e.g. to prevent cutting or chafing; ~**way,** navigable channel, regular course or track of ship, prepared part of golf-links free from rough grass between tee and green. **8.** (Austral., NZ, & sl.) complete, unquestionable; **a** ~ **treat,** (colloq.) very enjoyable or attractive thing or person. **9.** Hence ~'NESS *n.* **10.** *n.* fair thing; (arch.) beautiful woman; **for** ~, *(sl.) completely; ~'**s** ~, (colloq.) (reciprocal) fairness is desirable. **11.** *v.i.* (Of weather) become fair. **12.** *v.t.* make (surface of ship etc.) smooth and regular (~'**water,** structure on ship etc. assisting its passage through water). [OE *fæger,* = OS, OHG *fagar,* ON *fagr,* Goth. *fagrs* f. Gmc *fagraz]

fair³ *adv.* **1.** in a fair manner; **speak** person ~, address him courteously; ~-**spoken,** (of person) courteous, bland; **write out** ~ (as fair COPY¹); **fight** ~ (according to the rules); BID¹ *fair.* **2.** exactly, completely; ~ **and square** (see FAIR² 5). [OE *fægre* (as prec.)]

‖fair'ing¹ *n.* present bought at a fair. [f. FAIR¹ + -ING¹]

fair'ing² *n.* making surface of ship, aircraft, motor vehicle, etc., smooth and streamlined; structure added for this purpose. [f. FAIR² 12 + -ING¹]

Fair' Isle (-īl) *n.* & *a.* (jersey etc.) knitted in charac-teristic particoloured design. [~ in the Shetlands]

fair'ly *adv.* In adj. senses; utterly, completely, (*fairly beside himself*); considerably (*fairly narrow*); accept-ably (*fairly good*); actually (*fairly jumped for joy*); ~ **and squarely,** = FAIR² 5 *and* square. [ME, f. FAIR² + -LY²]

fair'y *n.* & *a.* **1.** *n.* mythical small being with magical powers; (sl.) male homosexual. **2.** ~-**cycle,** low small-wheeled bicycle for children; ~ **godmother,** (fig.) benefactress; F~**land,** home of fairies, enchan-ted region; ~ **lights,** small coloured lights for esp. outdoor decoration; ~ **ring,** circular band of darker grass caused by fungi and attributed to dancing of fairies; ~ **story,** ~-**tale,** tale about fairies, of strange incident, coincidence, marvellous progress, etc., fabrication, fib. **3.** Hence ∼ISM (2) *n.* **4.** *a.* of fairies; fairy-like, beautiful and delicate or small. [ME, f. OF *faerie* f. *fae* FAY; see -ERY]

faisandé (fā′zahṅdā) *a.* affected, theatrical. [F, p.p. of *faisander* hang (game) till high]

fait accompli (f ā t ahkaw′ṅplē, -kŏ′mplī) *n.* thing done and no longer worth arguing against. [F]

faith *n.* **1.** reliance or trust *in*; belief founded on authority (**pin** one's ∼ **on**, **put** one's ∼ **in**, believe implicitly). **2.** (Theol). belief in religious doctrines, esp. such as affects character and conduct, spiritual apprehension of divine truth apart from proof; system of religious belief (*the Christian, Jewish, faith*; DEFENDER *of the Faith*; **the** ∼, the true religion); things (to be) believed; (arch.) **in** ∼, **by my** ∼, etc. (in asseveration). **3.** promise, engagement, (*give, keep,* one's *faith*; *break faith with*); (observance of) duty to fulfil trust, promise, etc., (**good** ∼, honesty of intention; **bad** ∼, intent to deceive; **Punic** ∼, treachery). **4.** ∼**-cure, -curer, -healing, -healer,** (acting by prayer, not drugs etc.). [ME, f. AF *fed,* f. OF *feid* (pr. fāth) f. L *fides*]

fai′thful *a.* showing faith; loyal, constant, (*to* person, one's word), conscientious; trustworthy; true to fact, the original, etc., accurate; **the** ∼, (*pl.*) true believers, esp. Muslims (COMMANDER *of the Faithful*); hence ∼NESS *n.* [ME, f. prec. +-FUL]

fai′thfully *adv.* In adj. senses; **yours** ∼, customary formula for closing business or formal letter; (colloq.) emphatically (*promise faithfully*). [f. prec. +-LY²]

fai′thless *a.* unbelieving; perfidious, false to promises; unreliable; hence ∼LY² *adv.*, ∼NESS *n.* [ME, f. FAITH +-LESS]

fāke¹ *v.t.*, & *n.* (Naut.) **1.** *v.t.* coil (rope). **2.** *n.* one round of a coil of rope. [ME; cf. Sc. *faik* fold]

fāk|e² *v.t., n.,* & *a.* **1.** *v.t.* ∼**e** (**up**), make presentable or plausible; alter so as to deceive; contrive out of poor or sham material; feign; hence ∼′ER¹, ∼′ERY (5), *ns.* **2.** *n.* piece of faking, thing faked up (esp. sham antique); trick; spurious person or thing. **3.** *a.* spurious, counterfeit. [f. obs. *feak, feague* thrash, f. G *fegen* sweep, thrash]

fä′kir (-ēr, fakēr′) *n.* Muslim (or Hindu) religious mendicant or ascetic. [f. Arab. *faḳīr* poor man]

Fala′ng|e (-lah′nj, -lä′nj) *n.* Spanish Fascist and right-wing political party; Christian political party in Lebanon; hence ∼ISM (3), ∼IST (2), *ns.* [Sp., = PHALANX]

fä′lbala *n.* flounce or trimming on dress. [F, 17th c., of unkn. orig.; cf. FURBELOW]

fä′lcāte *a.* (Anat. etc.) curved like a sickle. [f. L *falcatus* (*falx falcis* sickle; see -ATE²)]

fa′lchion (faw′lchon) *n.* (Hist.) broad curved convex-edged sword. [ME *fauchoun* f. OF *fauchon* f. Rom. *falcio -onis f. L *falx falcis* sickle]

fä′lciförm *a.* (Anat.) curved like a sickle. [f. L *falx falcis* sickle +-I- +-FORM]

fa′lcon (faw′-, fö′-) *n.* small long-winged diurnal bird of prey, esp. as trained to hunt game-birds for sport; (in falconry) female of this (cf. TERCEL). [ME f. OF *faucon* f. LL *falco -onis,* perh. f. L *falx* scythe or Gmc *falkon]

fa′lconer (faw′-, fö′-) *n.* keeper and trainer of hawks; one who hunts with hawks. [ME f. AF *fauconer,* OF *fauconier* (as prec.; see -ER² (2))]

fa′lconet (faw′-, fö′-) *n.* **1.** (Hist.) light cannon. **2.** pygmy falcon. [sense 1 f. It. *falconetto* dim. of *falcone* FALCON; sense 2 f. FALCON +-ET¹]

fa′lconry (faw′-, fö′-) *n.* breeding and training of hawks. [f. F *fauconnerie* (as FALCON; see -ERY)]

fä′lderäl *n.* gewgaw, trifle; *nonsense. [cf. FAL-LAL]

fa′ldstool (faw′l-) *n.* bishop's backless folding chair; ‖movable desk for kneeling at; small desk for litany to be said from. [OE *fældestōl,* f. med. L *faldistolium* f. WG *faldistōl (as FOLD², STOOL)]

Faler′nian *a.* & *n.* (famous wine) of Falernus in ancient Campania, Italy. [f. L *Falernus* +-IAN]

fall¹ (fawl) *v.i.* (**fell**, ∼′**en,** conjugated with *have* or *be,* see -ED¹ (2), or used as *a.*). **1.** go or come down freely (∼**ing star,** meteor) or (as) from previously fixed place (*he let fall a remark*; **hair** ∼**s** (is lost from head to cause baldness); **lambs** ∼ (are born); *rain, darkness, falls*); come down, lose high position (*statesman falls*; *fall from* GRACE, *into error*; ∼**en angel,** one of those cast out of heaven; ∼**en arch** (of foot); swoop (*vengeance fell*). **2.** become detached, hang down; sink to lower level (*demand, price, falls*); (of barometer etc.) show lower atmospheric pressure; decline, slope down; (of river) discharge *into*; subside, ebb, abate; show dismay (*face falls*); (of eyes, glance) look downwards. **3.** cease to stand (∼**ing sickness,** (arch.) epilepsy), become prostrate, come to the ground, be overthrown, sin, perish esp. by violence (*fell in battle*; *fall a prey* or *sacrifice to*); (of fortress) be captured; (of woman) (1) lose chastity, (2) become pregnant; (of house) tumble in ruins; (of card) = DROP² 2; ∼ **apart, in two, to pieces,** disintegrate; ∼ **on evil times,** suffer misfortune; ∼ **to the ground,** (of plan etc.) be abandoned, fail; **wicket** ∼**s,** (Cricket) batsman is out. **4.** take specified direction (*his eye fell upon me*), have specified place (*accent falls on first syllable*), alight, come by chance, duty, etc., (*the lot fell upon me*; *it fell to my lot, to me, to*; *it fell in my way*; *fall amongst thieves*; *subject falls into three divisions*). **5.** pass into specified state (*fell into a rage,* in LOVE¹), become (*fall asleep, dumb, due, ill*); lapse, revert, (*revenues fall to the Crown*). **6.** occur, have date, (*Easter falls early*), find place (*what now falls to be described*). **7.** (w. preps.): ∼ **-doing,** (arch.) begin to do (*fell a-sighing and a-sobbing*); ∼ **behind,** be outstripped by; ∼ **for,** (colloq.) be captivated or deceived by, admire, yield to the charms or merits of; ∼ **from,** (of words) be spoken by; ∼ **into,** (line) take one's place in the ranks, collaborate with others, (*conversation with*) begin talking to, (*habit* etc.) adopt it; *fall into* PLACE¹; ∼ **on,** assault, come across; ∼ *on* one's *face,* ridiculously; ∼ *on* one's *feet,* get well out of difficulty; ∼ *on* one's *sword,* kill oneself with sword; ∼ **over,** stumble at; ∼ **over** oneself, (colloq.) be very awkward or hasty or eager; ∼ **to,** be killed etc. by; ∼ **to doing,** (arch.) begin to do (*fell to quarrelling among themselves*); ∼ **under,** be classed among, be subjected to (observation etc.); ∼ **within,** be included in. **8.** (w. advs.): ∼ **about,** be helpless esp. with mirth; ∼ **astern,** (of ship) drop behind; ∼ **away,** desert, revolt, apostatize, decay, become few or thin, vanish; ∼ **back,** retreat (∼ *back on,* have recourse to); ∼ *-back a.,* emergency, esp. minimum (wage) paid when no work is available; ∼ **behind,** lag; ∼ **down** (on), (colloq.) fail (*in*); *fall* FLAT² 1; ∼ **foul of,** come into collision with, quarrel with; ∼ **in,** (Mil.) take place in line, (of building etc.) collapse inwards, (of debt etc.) become due, (of land etc.) become available, (of lease) run out; ∼ **in with,** happen to meet, accede to (views, plans), agree with (person), coincide with, humour; ∼ **off,** withdraw, decrease in size or number, deteriorate, (of ship) deviate to leeward, so ∼*-off* n.; ∼ **out,** quarrel, come to pass, result *well* etc., (Mil.) leave the ranks; ∼*-out* n., airborne radioactive debris from nuclear explosion, (fig.) side-effects; *fall over* BACKWARDS; ∼ **short,** be or become insufficient or inadequate, (of missile) not go far enough; ∼ **short of,** fail to obtain or reach; ∼ **through,** miscarry, fail; ∼ **to,** begin working, eating, fighting, etc.; ∼ **together,** (Phonet., of sounds) become identical. [OE *f(e)allan,* = OS, OHG *fallan,* ON *falla* f. Gmc *fallan]

fall² (fawl) *n.* **1.** act or manner of falling (RIDE *for a fall*); overthrow; succumbing to temptation; **the F**∼ (**of Man**), Adam's sin and its results; ∼ **guy,** (sl.) (1) easy victim, (2) scapegoat; ∼**-pipe,** downpipe. **2.** amount of rain etc. that falls; downward trend, amount of descent. **3.** *autumn; *∼**′fish,** N. Amer.

freshwater fish like chub. **4.** cataract, cascade, (esp. in *pl.*; *Niagara Falls*). **5.** wrestling-bout, throw in this which keeps opponent on ground for specified time; **try a** ∼, contend *with* (lit. or fig.). **6.** rope of hoisting- -tackle; loosely hanging attachment to garment. **7.** (number at a) birth of lambs etc. [ME, partly f. ON, partly f. prec.]

fa'llacy *n.* misleading argument, sophism; (Logic) flaw that vitiates syllogism, one of the types of such flaws; delusion, error, (PATHETIC *fallacy*); unsoundness, delusiveness, disappointing character, (of arguments, or beliefs); so **falla**'cious *a.* [f. L *fallacia* (*fallax -acis* deceiving f. *fallere* deceive); see -ACY]

fäl-lä'l *n.* (arch.) piece of finery; hence **fällä'l(l)**ery (5) *n.* [perh. f. FALBALA]

fallen. See FALL[1].

fa'll|ible *a.* liable to err or be erroneous; hence ∼IBI'LITY *n.* [f. med. L *fallibilis* (*fallere* deceive; see -IBLE)]

Fallō'pian *a.* ∼ **tube,** oviduct in female mammals. [f. G. *Fallopius,* Latinized name of *Fallopio,* It. anatomist d. 1562 + -AN]

fa'llow[1] (-ō) *n. a.,* & *v.t.* **1.** *n.* & *a.* (ground) ploughed and harrowed but left uncropped for a year; uncultivated (land). **2.** *a.* (Of sow) not pregnant; potentially useful but not yet in use (*ideas lying fallow*); inactive. **3.** *v.t.* break up (land) for sowing or to destroy weeds. [ME, f. OE *fealh* n., *fealgian* v.]

fa'llow[2] (-ō) *a.* of pale brownish or reddish yellow; ∼ **deer,** species (*Dama dama*) of deer smaller than red deer, white-spotted in summer. [OE *f(e)alu,* = OS *falu,* OHG *falo,* ON *fölr* f. Gmc **falwaz*]

false (fawls, fŏls) *a.* & *adv.* **1.** *a.* wrong, incorrect, (*false idea, verdict, weights*); illegal (*false imprisonment*); ∼ **concord,** breach of agreement rules in grammar; ∼ **note** (in music); ∼ **position,** one in which person must seem to act against his principles; ∼ **pride, shame,** (based on wrong notions); ∼ **quantity,** incorrect length of vowel in verse or pronunciation; ∼ **start,** incorrect start (in racing, or fig.); ∼ **step,** stumble, transgression; *false* SYLLOGISM. **2.** lying, deceitful, treacherous, unfaithful *to*; deceptive; spurious, sham, artificial, (*false* COIN[1], *god, hair, prophet,* SCENT, *teeth,* WINDOW); illusory (*a false economy*); improperly so called, pseudo-, (*false acacia,* RIB, TOPAZ); ∼ **alarm** (given without valid cause, either to deceive or under misapprehension of danger); ∼ **bottom,** (disguised) horizontal partition in vessel, drawer, suitcase, etc.; ∼ **card,** one played contrary to usual custom, in order to mislead opponents (so ∼-*card* v.i.); ∼ **ceiling,** dummy ceiling below real one; ∼ **colours,** flag one has no right to (lit., or fig. of hypocrite or impostor); ∼ **dawn,** transient light in east before dawn; *false* KEEL[1]; ∼ **pretences,** misrepresentations made with intent to deceive; ∼'**work,** temporary framework used during building. **3.** Hence or cogn. ∼'LY[2] (-slī) *adv.,* ∼'NESS (-sn-), **fa'ls**ITY (fawl-, fŏl-), *ns.* **4.** *adv.* **play** person ∼, cheat or betray him; RING[2] *false.* [f. OE *fals* and OF *fals, faus,* f. L *falsus* p.p. of *fallere* deceive]

fa'lsehood (faw'ls-h-, fŏ'l-) *n.* falseness; untrue thing; lying, lie(s). [ME, f. prec. + -HOOD]

falsě'ttō (fawl-, fŏl-) *n.* (*pl.* ∼s). high-pitched artificial voice esp. when used by male singers; singer using falsetto. [It., dim. of *falso* FALSE]

fa'lsies (faw'lsĭz, fŏ'lsĭz) *n. pl.* (colloq.) padded brassière; shaped padding etc. to increase apparent size of breasts. [f. FALSE + -IE + -s[1]]

fa'lsi|**fý** (faw'l-, fŏ'l-) *v.t.* fraudulently alter (document); misrepresent; make wrong, pervert; show to be false; disappoint (hope, fear, etc.); so ∼FICA'TION *n.* [ME, f. F *falsifier* or f. med. L *falsificus* f. L *falsificus* (*falsus*); see -FY]

Falstä'ffian (fawl-, fŏl-) *a.* like or characteristic of Falstaff; fat, jovial, and humorous. [f. Sir John *Falstaff* in Shakespeare's 'Henry IV' etc. + -IAN]

fa'lter (faw'l-, fŏ'l-) *v.* **1.** *v.i.* stumble, stagger, go unsteadily; waver, lose courage, flinch. **2.** *v.t.* & *i.* stammer, speak hesitatingly; ∼ **out,** utter or say thus. [ME, perh. f. *falde* (FOLD[2]) in obs. sense 'falter', after *totter* etc.]

fāme[1] *n.* **1.** renown, celebrity. **2.** (arch.) public report, rumour. **3.** reputation (**ill** ∼, disrepute; **house of ill** ∼, (arch.) brothel); good reputation. [ME f. OF, f. L *fama*]

fāme[2] *v.t.* (In *p.p.*) famous, much spoken of, (*for* valour etc.); (arch., in *pass.*) be currently reported *as, for,* to be or do. [ME, f. OF *famer* (*fame*; see prec.)]

fami'lial (-lyəl) *a.* of, occurring in, characteristic of, (members of) a family. [F, f. L *familia* FAMILY; see -AL]

fami'liar (-lyer) *a.* & *n.* **1.** *a.* well acquainted or intimate (*with*), in close friendship, (∼ **spirit,** demon attending and obeying witch etc.); closely acquainted *with* (subject); well known, no longer novel, (*to*); common, current, usual; unceremonious, informal; excessively informal, impertinent; sexually intimate (*with*); hence ∼LY[2] *adv.* **2.** *n.* intimate friend or associate; (RC Ch.) person rendering certain services in pope's or bishop's household; = *familiar spirit.* [ME, f. OF *familier* f. L *familiaris* (as FAMILY; see -AR[1])]

familiä'rity *n.* close relationship; close acquaintance with person or subject; sexual intimacy, (in *pl.*) caresses etc.; unceremonious action or behaviour, treating of inferiors or superiors as equals, (*familiarity breeds contempt*). [ME, f. OF *familiarité* f. L *familiaritas -tatis* (as prec.); see -ITY]

fami'liariz|e, -īs|e, (-lyerīz), *v.t.* make (thing) well known; make (person, person's *mind* etc., one*self*) well acquainted *with*; hence ∼A'TION *n.* [f. F *familiariser* (*familiaire,* as FAMILIAR; see -IZE)]

famille (fämē'y) *n.* ∼ **jaune** (zhōn), **noire** (nwär), **rose** (rōz), **verte** (vārt), Chinese enamelled porcelain with predominant colour yellow, black, red, green. [F, = family]

fa'mily *n.* **1.** members of a household, parents, children, servants, etc.; set of parents and children, or of relations, living together or not (HOLY *Family*; ROYAL *family*); person's children. **2.** all descendants of common ancestor, house, lineage, (**of good** ∼, descended from noble or worthy persons); race or group of peoples from common stock; group of all languages ultimately derived from one early language. **3.** brotherhood of persons or nations united by political or religious ties. **4.** group of objects distinguished by common features; (Math.) group of curves etc. obtained by varying one quantity. **5.** (Biol.) group of allied genera of animals or plants, usu. subdivision of order. **6.** ∼ **allowance** (paid by State or employer to parent of family); ∼ **Bible,** large Bible with pages for recording births etc.; ∼ **butcher** etc. (supplying meat to families as opp. to institutions etc.); ||F∼ **Division** (of High Court, dealing with adoption, divorce, etc.); ∼ **doctor,** general practitioner normally consulted by a family; ∼ **hotel** (with special terms for families); ∼ **likeness,** that between relations, vague resemblance; ∼ **man,** one with family, domestic person; ∼ **name,** surname (also when used as Christian name); ∼ **planning,** birth control; ∼ **tree,** genealogical chart; **in a** ∼ **way,** without ceremony; **in the** or **a** ∼ **way,** (colloq.) pregnant. [ME, f. L *familia* household (*famulus* servant; see -Y[1])]

fä'mine *n.* extreme scarcity of food in a district etc.; dearth of something specified (*water famine*; ∼ **prices,** prices raised by scarcity); (arch.) hunger, starvation (*die of famine*). [ME f. OF (*faim* f. L *fames* hunger)]

fä'mish *v.t.* & *i.* reduce or be reduced to extreme hunger; **be** ∼**ing** or ∼**ed,** (colloq.) feel very hungry. [ME, f. obs. *fame* (f. OF *afamer* f. Rom. *AFFamare f. L *fames* hunger) + -ISH[2]]

fä'mous *a.* celebrated (*for* quality etc.), well known; (colloq.) excellent; hence ∼LY[2] *adv.* [ME f. AF, OF *fameus* f. L *famosus* (*fama* fame; see -OSE[1])]

fă′mŭl|us *n.* (*pl.* ∼**i** *pr.* -ī). attendant on magician or scholar. [L, = servant]

făn¹ *n.* **1.** device (usu. folding, and sector-shaped when spread out) for moving air to cool one's face etc.; anything so spread out, as bird's tail, wing, leaf, kind of ornamental vaulting (*fan tracery*). **2.** rotating apparatus giving current of air for ventilation etc.; small sail for keeping head of windmill towards wind. **3.** device for winnowing grain. **4.** fan-shaped deposit of alluvium esp. where stream begins to descend gentler slope. **5.** ∼ **belt** (transmitting torque from engine of motor vehicle to fan that cools radiator); ∼ **dance** (in which dancer is nude but partly concealed by fans); ∼ **heater** (in which electric fan drives air over electric heater into room etc.); ∼**-jet,** jet engine with additional thrust from cold air drawn in by fan; ∼**′light,** (fan-shaped) window over door or other window; ∼ **palm,** palm-tree with fan-shaped leaves; ∼**′tail,** fan-shaped tail or end, fan of windmill, projecting part of boat's stern, broad-tailed pigeon, flycatcher of genus *Rhipidura*. [OE *fann* (in sense 3) f. L *vannus* winnowing-fan]

făn² *v.* (-**nn**-). **1.** *v.t.* move (air) with fan; drive current of air (as) with fan upon, to cool (face etc.) or to kindle (flame etc.; ∼ **the flame,** (fig.) increase excitement etc.); (of breeze) blow gently on, cool. **2.** winnow (grain), whence ∼′ɴᴇʀ¹ (2) *n.*; winnow away (chaff), sweep away (as) by wind from fan; (sl.) search (person) for weapons etc.; (Baseball) strike out (batter). **3.** *v.t.* & *i.* spread *out* in fan shape. [f. OE *fannian* (as prec.)]

făn³ *n.* devotee of a specified amusement, performer, etc., (*film fans*; *football fans*); ∼ **club,** organized group of person's devotees; ∼ **mail,** letters from fans; hence ∼′ᴅᴏᴍ *n.* [abbr. of foll.]

fană′tic *a.* & *n.* (person) filled with excessive and mistaken enthusiasm, esp. in religion; hence ∼ᴀʟ *a.,* ∼ᴀʟʟʏ *adv.,* ∼ɪsᴍ (1) *n.,* ∼ɪᴢᴇ (2, 3) *v.i.* & *t.* [f. F *fanatique* or f. L *fanaticus* (*fanum* temple; see -ᴀᴛɪᴄ)]

fă′ncier *n.* In vbl senses; connoisseur or follower or amateur breeder of some article or activity or animal (*rose-fancier, dog-fancier*). [f. ғᴀɴᴄʏ² + -ᴇʀ¹]

fă′nciful *a.* indulging in fancies, whimsical, capricious; fantastically designed, ornamented, etc., odd-looking; imaginary, unreal; hence ∼ʟʏ² *adv.,* ∼ɴᴇss *n.* [f. foll. + -ғᴜʟ]

fă′ncy¹ *n.* & *attrib. a.* **1.** *n.* delusion, unfounded belief. **2.** faculty of calling up things not present, of inventing imagery; mental image. **3.** arbitrary supposition; caprice, whim; individual taste, inclination, (*take a fancy to* or *for*; **catch** or **take the** ∼ **of,** please; ∼**-free,** not in love); fancy cake. **4.** those who have a certain hobby, fanciers, esp. patrons of boxing; art of breeding fancy animals. **5.** *a.* ornamental, not plain, (*fancy bread, cake*; ∼ **dress,** fanciful costume esp. representing animal, character in history or fiction, etc.; ∼ **goods,** ornamental novelties etc.; ∼**-work,** ornamental sewing etc.); *(of foods etc.) above average quality; (of flowers etc.) particoloured. **6.** capricious, whimsical, extravagant, (*at a fancy price*; ∼ **franchise,** (Hist.) based on complicated or arbitrary qualifications; (of animal) bred for particular points of beauty etc. **7.** based on imagination, not fact. **8.** ∼ **man,** (sl., derog.) (1) woman's lover, (2) man living on earnings of prostitute, pimp; ∼ **woman,** (sl., derog.) = ᴍɪsᴛʀᴇss 4. [contraction of ғᴀɴᴛᴀsʏ]

fă′ncy² *v.t.* **1.** picture to oneself, conceive, imagine, (*fancy oneself dead*; *fancy a blue dahlia*; *fancy him to be here, that he is here*); (in *imper.* as excl. of surprise) *fancy!, fancy that!, fancy his believing it!.* **2.** be inclined to suppose, rather think. **3.** take a fancy to, like; (colloq.) have unduly high opinion of (one*self*, one's ability, etc.). **4.** breed, grow, (animals, plants) with attention to certain points. [f. prec.]

făndă′ngle (-ă′nggel) *n.* fantastic ornament; nonsense, tomfoolery. [perh. f. foll., after *newfangle*]

făndă′ngō (-nggō) *n.* (*pl.* ∼**es** *or* ∼**s**). lively Spanish

dance for two; music for it; nonsense, tomfoolery. [Sp., perh. of Negro orig.]

fāne *n.* (poet.) = ᴛᴇᴍᴘʟᴇ¹. [ME, f. L *fanum*]

fă′nfāre *n.* short showy or ceremonious sounding of trumpets, bugles, etc. [F, imit.]

fănfăronă′de *n.,* arrogant talk, brag; fanfare. [f. F *fanfaronnade* (*fanfaron* braggart f. as prec., -ᴏᴏɴ; see -ᴀᴅᴇ)]

făng¹ *n.* canine tooth, esp. of dog or wolf; serpent's venom-tooth; (colloq.) tooth; tang of tool; (prong of) root of tooth; hence (-)∼ᴇᴅ² (-ngd), ∼′ʟᴇss, *adjs.* [OE f. ON (= OS, OHG) *fang* f. Gmc **fang-, *fanh-* to catch]

făng² *v.t.* strike with fang; prime (pump) by pouring in water to start it. [f. prec.]

fă′nnȳ¹ *n.* (Naut.) tin container for drink. [20th c., perh. f. woman's Christian name *Fanny*]

fă′nnȳ² *n.* **1.** *(sl.) buttocks. **2.** ||(vulg.) female genitals. [20th c.; orig. unkn.]

fă′nnȳ³ *n.,* & *v.t.* (sl.) (deceive or persuade by) glib talk. [20th c.; orig. unkn.]

Fănnȳ A′dams (-ă′damz) *n.* (sl.) **1.** (Naut.) tinned meat; stew. **2.** (**sweet**) ∼, nothing at all. [f. name of murder victim *c.* 1870]

făntă′bulous *a.* (sl.) of almost incredible excellence. [f. ғᴀɴᴛᴀsᴛɪᴄ + ғᴀʙᴜʟᴏᴜs]

fă′n-tăn *n.* Chinese gambling game in which players try to guess remainder after division by four of number of coins etc. hidden under bowl; card-game with play of sevens and sequences on them. [Chin., = repeated divisions]

făntā′sia (-tä′zía, -tazē′a) *n.* musical or other composition in which form is of minor importance, or which is based on several familiar tunes. [It., = ғᴀɴᴛᴀsʏ]

fă′ntas|ize, -|īse (-īz), *v.t.* & *i.* have fantasy or fanciful vision (of); so ∼ɪsᴛ (1) *n.* [f. ғᴀɴᴛᴀsʏ + -ɪᴢᴇ]

fă′ntăst *n.* visionary, dreamer. [f. med. L f. Gk *phantastēs* boaster (*phantazomai* make a show f. *phainō* to show)]

făntă′stic *a.* extravagantly fanciful, capricious, eccentric, (*light fantastic* ᴛᴏᴇ); grotesque or quaint in design etc.; (colloq.) excellent, extraordinary; hence ∼ɪsᴍ (2) *n.,* [f. obs. *fantastical*) ∼ ă′ʟɪᴛʏ, ∼ᴀʟɴᴇss, *ns.,* ∼ᴀʟʟʏ² *adv.* [ME, f. OF *fantastique* f. med. L *fantasticus* f. LL f. Gk *phantastikos* (as prec.; see -ɪᴄ)]

făntă′stic|āte *v.t.* make fantastic; hence ∼ᴀ′ᴛɪᴏɴ *n.* [f. prec. + -ᴀᴛᴇ³]

fă′ntasȳ, phă′ntasȳ, *n.,* & *v.t.* **1.** *n.* image-inventing faculty, esp. when extravagant or visionary; mental image, day-dream; fantastic invention or composition, fantasia; whimsical speculation. **2.** *v.t.* imagine in visionary manner. [ME, f. OF *fantasie* f. L f. Gk *phantasia* appearance (see ғᴀɴᴛᴀsᴛ, -ʏ¹)]

Fă′nti, Fă′ntē, Fă′ntee, *n.* member or language of a Black tribe inhabiting Ghana; **go** ∼, (of European) conform to native habits. [native name]

fantoccini (făntōchē′nē) *n. pl.* mechanically worked puppets; marionette show. [It., pl. of dim. of *fantoccio* puppet (*fante* boy)]

fă′ntŏd *n.* crotchety behaviour; state of alarm or worry; (in *pl.*) state of restlessness, fidgets. [19th c.; orig. uncert.]

||FANY *abbr.* First Aid Nursing Yeomanry.

fă′nzine (-ēn) *n.* magazine for (esp. science-fiction) fans. [f. ғᴀɴ³ + ᴍᴀɢᴀᴢɪɴᴇ]

FAO *abbr.* Food and Agriculture Organization.

FAQ *abbr.* fair average quality.

faquir. Var. of ғᴀᴋɪʀ.

fär¹ *adv.* (ғᴀʀᴛʜᴇʀ, ғᴜʀᴛʜᴇʀ; ғᴀʀᴛʜᴇsᴛ, ғᴜʀᴛʜᴇsᴛ). **1.** at, to, by, a great distance, a long way (off), in space or time, or fig., (*far away, off, out,* etc.); *driven far into the ground, talked far into the night; far different, better,* the *best*). **2. as** ∼ **as,** (1) right to, not short of, (place), (2) to whatever extent (*travel as far as you like*); ∼ **and away,** by a very large amount (*better* etc.); ∼ **and near,** everywhere; ∼ **and wide,** over a large area; ∼

be it from me to, I would on no account; **by ~,** by a great amount; **~ from,** more nearly the opposite of than the same as (*problem is far from easy*; (*so*) *far from seeking help he offered it*); **from ~,** from a considerable distance; **go ~,** (fig.) achieve much, contribute greatly *to*(*wards*); **not go ~,** be soon spent or used; **go too ~,** (fig.) go beyond limits of what is reasonable, polite, etc.; **how ~,** to what extent; (**in**) **so ~ as,** to the extent that; **so ~,** to such an extent or distance, until now; **so ~ so good,** progress has been satisfactory. **3. ~-away,** remote, long-past, (of look etc.) absent, dreamy, (of voice) sounding as if from a distance; **~ between,** infrequent; *Far* EAST(ERN); **~- -famed,** widely known; **~-fetched,** (of simile, illustration etc.) carefully but unnaturally sought out, not obvious, strained; **~-flung,** (rhet.) widely extended; **~ gone,** advanced in time, very ill or mad or drunk or much in debt; **~-off,** remote; **~-out,** distant, (fig.) avant-garde or unconventional or excellent; **~- -reaching,** widely applicable, carrying many consequences; **~-seeing,** prescient, prudent; **~-sighted,** (1) far-seeing, (2) seeing distant things more clearly than near ones; *Far WEST(ERN). [OE. *feor*(*r*), = OS, OHG *fer*, ON *fjarri*, Goth. *fairra* f. Gmc **ferrō* compar. of *fer- f. IE *per-]

fär² *a.* (compar. & superl. as prec.). situated at or extending over a great distance in space or time, remote, (*a far* CRY¹); more distant (*the far end of the hall*); hence **~'NESS** *n.* [OE. *feorr*, = OS, OHG *fer* f. WG *ferro-]

fä'rad *n.* (Electr.) unit of capacitance, such that one coulomb of charge causes a potential difference of one volt. [f. M. *Faraday*, Engl. physicist d. 1867]

färadä'ic, **farä'dic,** *adjs.* (Electr.) inductive, induced. [f. as prec. + -IC]

fä'raday *n.* (Electr.) quantity of charge needed to form one gram-equivalent of an element in electrolysis; **F~ cage,** earthed metal screen excluding electrostatic influence; **F~'s constant,** = *faraday*; **F~ effect,** rotation of plane of polarization of electromagnetic waves in certain substances in a magnetic field. [f. as FARAD]

färandô'le *n.* lively Provençal dance; music for it. [F, f. mod. Prov. *farandoulo*]

färce *n.* dramatic work meant merely to cause laughter, often by presenting ludicrously improbable events; this branch of drama; absurdly futile proceedings, pretence, mockery. [F, orig. = stuffing, f. OF *farsir* f. L *farcire* to stuff, used metaph. of interludes etc.]

farceur (farsör') *n.* joker, wag; actor or writer of farces. [F (*farcer* act farces)]

fär'cical *a.* of or like farce; extremely ludicrous or futile; hence **~ITY** (-ă'l-) *n.*, **~LY²** *adv.* [f. FARCE + -ICAL]

fär'cy *n.* glanders (**~ bud, button,** small lymphatic tumour in this); bacterial disease of cattle. [ME, f. earlier & OF *farcin* f. LL *farciminum* (*farcire* stuff)]

fär'dĕd *a.* (Of face etc.) painted with cosmetics. [p.p. of obs. *fard* f. OF *farder*]

fär'del *n.* (arch.) bundle, burden. [ME f. OF, dim. of Rom. *fardum f. Arab. *fard*(*a*) camel-load; see -LE 2]

färe¹ *n.* **1.** price of passenger's conveyance, passage- -money; passenger paying to travel in public vehicle; *fare-*STAGE¹. **2.** food provided (*good, bad, plentiful,* etc., *fare*; BILL¹ *of fare*). [OE *fær* and *faru* journeying, both f. same root as foll.]

färe² *v.i.* **1.** (poet. or literary). journey, go, travel; **~ forth,** start. **2.** (arch.) happen, turn out, (*how fares it?*). **3.** get on *well, ill,* etc., have good, bad, etc., luck; (arch.) be entertained, be fed or feed oneself, *well* etc. [OE *faran,* = OS, OHG, Goth. *faran* f. Gmc *faran (*far- f. IE *por-)]

*fär'e-thee-wĕll (far'dh-), ***fär'e-you-wĕll** (fär'ū-), *ns.* (colloq.) **to a ~,** to the utmost degree, to perfection. [f. *fare* (impers.) *thee* or *you well* = foll. (FARE² 3)]

färewĕ'll (farw-) *int.* & *n.* **1.** *int.* goodbye!, adieu!, (**~ to,** there will be no more of). **2.** *n.* leave-taking, departure; parting good wishes. [ME, f. imper. of FARE² + WELL³]

fari'na (-ī'-, -ē'-) *n.* flour or meal of cereal, nuts, or starchy roots; powdery substance; (Bot.) pollen; ||(Chem.) starch; so **färinA'ceous** *a.* [L (*far* corn; see -INE⁴)]

färl *n.* (Sc.) thin cake, orig. quadrant-shaped, of oatmeal or flour. [f. obs. *fardel* quarter (as FOURTH, DEAL¹)]

färm¹ *n.* **1.** tract of land used under one management for cultivation (||**home ~,** reserved and worked by owner of estate containing other farms; SEWAGE- *-farm*); **~** (**'house**), dwelling-place attached to farm; tract of water used as a preserve (*fish-farm; oyster- -farm*); place for storage of oil etc.; place where animals are bred for fur etc. (*mink farm*); place where children are farmed (see foll.). **2. ~-hand,** worker on farm; **~'stead,** farm with buildings on it; **~'yard,** yard or enclosure attached to farmhouse. [ME f. OF *ferme* f. med. L *firma* fixed payment (L *firmare* f. *firmus* FIRM²; orig. applied only to leased land)]

färm² *v.* **1.** *v.t.* & *i.* cultivate, till; till the soil, be farmer; **~ the bowling,** (Cricket) contrive to receive most of balls bowled. **2.** *v.t.* take proceeds of (tax, office, etc.) on payment of fixed sum; (**~ out**), let out proceeds of (tax etc.) to person for fixed sum, delegate (work) to sub-contractor etc., arrange for (person) to be farmed (see next sense). **3.** let the labour of (person) for hire; contract to maintain and care for (person, esp. child) for fixed sum. **4.** Hence **~'ING** (1) *n.* [ME in sense 'rent land', f. prec.]

fär'mer *n.* one who cultivates a farm; one who undertakes collection of taxes after paying fixed fee (**~-general,** of districts in France before the Revolution); one who farms children etc. [ME, f. AF *fermer,* OF *fermier* f. med. L *firmarius, firmator,* (*firma* FIRM¹)]

fär'ō *n.* gambling card-game, with bets on order of appearance of cards. [F *pharaon* PHARAOH (said to have been name of king of hearts)]

Faröe'se (fär-, fär-; -z) *a.* & *n.* (*pl.* same). (native, inhabitant, or Norse language) of Faröe Islands. [f. *Faröe* + -ESE]

farou'che (-ōō'sh) *a.* sullen, shy; hence **~LY²** (-shlĭ) *adv.* [F, f. OF *faroche, forache* f. med. L *forasticus* f. L *foras* out of doors]

farra'gō (-rah'-) *n.* (*pl.* **~s** or ***~es**). medley, hotchpotch; hence **farrä'ginous** *a.* [L *farrago farraginis* mixed fodder (*far* corn)]

||fä'rrier *n.* smith who shoes horses; horse-doctor; hence **fä'rriĕry** (2) *n.* [f. OF *ferrier* f. L *ferrarius* (*ferrum* iron, horseshoe; see -ER² (2))]

fä'rrow (-ō) *n.* & *v.* **1.** *n.* giving birth to, litter of, pigs (*20 at one farrow*). **2.** *v.t.* & *i.* (Of sow) produce (pigs). [OE *fearh, færh* pig, = OS **farh,* OHG *farah* f. WG *farha f. IE *porkos]

farru'ca (-ōō'-) *n.* type of flamenco dance. [Sp.]

Fär'si *n.* Persian language. [Pers.; cf. PARSEE]

färt *v.i.* & *n.* (vulg.) **1.** *v.i.* emit wind from anus; fool *about* or *around.* **2.** *n.* emission of wind from anus; contemptible person. [OE **feortan,* = OHG *ferzan,* ON *freta* f. Gmc *fertan etc.]

fär'ther (-dh-) *adv.* & *a.* (used as compar. of FAR¹·²). **1.** *adv.* to or at a more advanced point or greater extent or distance; = FURTHER 1. **2.** *a.* more extended, additional, more; more distant or advanced; = FURTHER 2; hence **~MOST** *a.* [ME *ferther* var. of FURTHER]

fär'thĕst (-dh-) *a.* & *adv.* (used as superl. of FAR¹·²). **1.** *a.* most distant; = FURTHEST 1. **2.** *adv.* to or at the greatest distance; = FURTHEST 2. [ME, var. of FURTHEST]

färthing (-dh-) *n.* **1.** (Hist.) quarter of a penny, lowest-valued coin recently current in Britain. **2.** least possible amount (*doesn't matter a farthing*; BRASS *farthing*). [OE *fēorthing* (*fēortha* fourth; see -ING³)]

fär'thingāle (-dhĭngg-) *n.* (Hist.) hooped petticoat or stiff curved roll to extend woman's skirt. [earlier *vard-*, *verd-*, f. F *verdugale* f. Sp. *verdugado* (*verdugo* rod; see -ADO)]

fär'tlĕk *n.* (Athl.) method of training for middle- and long-distance running, in which athlete runs over country, mixing fast with slow work. [Sw. (*fart* speed, *lek* play)]

f.a.s. *abbr.* free alongside ship.

fä′scēs (-z) *n. pl.* (Rom. Hist.) bundle of rods with projecting axe-blade, carried by lictor before high magistrate; emblems of authority. [L, pl. of *fascis* bundle]

fa′scia (fā′shĭa, fā′sha) *n.* (Archit.) long flat surface of wood or stone under eaves or cornice; (Anat.) thin sheath of fibrous tissue; stripe, band, fillet, belt; = FACIA. [L, = band, door-frame, etc.]

fä′sciāte, fä′sciātèd, (-shī-) *a.* **1.** (Bot.) (of contiguous parts) compressed or growing into one; so **fäscīA′TION** *n.* **2.** striped or banded. [f. L *fasciatus*, p.p. of *fasciare* swathe (as prec.); see -ATE², -ED¹]

fä′scicle, fä′scicūle, fascī′cūlus (*pl.* -**li** *pr.* -lī), *ns.* (Bot. etc.) bunch, bundle, whence **fä′sciclED²** (-keld), **fascī′cūlAR¹, fascī′cūlATE²,** *adjs.,* **fascicūlA′TION** *n.*; one part of book published in instalments. [f. L *fasciculus* dim. of *fascis* (see FASCES, -CULE)]

fä′scin|āte *v.t.* (Esp. of serpent) deprive (victim) of power of escape or resistance by look or presence; attract irresistibly, enchant, charm, whence **∿ātED¹** *a.* (*with* or *by*), **∿ātING²** *a.*; hence or cogn. **∿A′TION, ∿ātOR** (esp. woman's head-scarf of light material), *ns.* [f. L *fascinare* (*fascinum* spell) + -ATE³]

fäsci′ne (-sē′n) *n.* long faggot used for engineering purposes and (esp. in war) for lining trenches, filling ditches, etc. [F, f. L *fascina* (*fascis* bundle; see -INE¹)]

Fä′sc|ism (-shī-) *n.* principles and organization of Italian nationalist and anti-communist dictatorship (1922–43); similar nationalist and authoritarian movement in other countries; system of extreme right-wing or authoritarian views; so **∿IST** (2) *n.* (often *attrib.*), **∿i′stIC** *a.* [f. It. *fascismo* (*fascio* bundle, (politically organized) group, f. L *fascis* bundle)]

fäsh *v.t.* (or *refl.*), & *n.* (Sc.) bother, trouble, inconvenience. [f. obs. F *fascher* f. Rom. **fastidicare* f. L *fastus* disdain]

fä′shion (-shon) *n.,* & *v.t.* **1.** *n.* make, shape, style, pattern, manner; **after the ∿ of,** like; **after** or **in a ∿,** not satisfactorily, but somehow or other; (as *suf.*) = -WISE (*walk crab-fashion*). **2.** prevailing (usu. transient) custom, esp. in dress; **∿-plate,** picture showing style of dress, (fig.) person who dresses in the current fashion. **3.** conventional usages of society; *man* etc. **of ∿,** of high social standing esp. as shown by dress and behaviour; OLD-*fashioned*; **the ∿,** whatever is in accord with these usages for the time being; **in, out of,** (**the**) **∿,** agreeing or not with current usages; **set the ∿,** give the example in changing them. **4.** *v.t.* give shape to, form, mould, (*into*); shape (stocking) to fit contour of leg. [ME, f. AF *fasun*, OF *façon*, f. L *factio -onis* (*facere fact-* make; see -ION)]

fä′shionab|le (-shon-) *a.* & *n.* **1.** *a.* following or suited to the fashion; characteristic of, treating of, or patronized by, those who are in the fashion; hence **∿leNESS** (-bəln-) *n.,* **∿LY²** *adv.* **2.** *n.* fashionable person. [f. prec. + -ABLE]

fast¹ (fah-) *v.i.* **1.** abstain from all or some kinds of food as religious observance or in sign of mourning. **2.** go without food. [OE *fæstan*, = OHG *fastēn*, ON *fasta*, Goth. *fastan* f. Gmc **fastējan* (as FAST³)]

fast² (fah-) *n.* act of, season or day appointed for, fasting (see prec. 1); going without food (**break** one's ∿, end this, esp. = BREAKFAST *v.*). [ME, f. ON *fasta* (OS, OHG *fasta*) f. as prec.]

fast³ (fah-) *a.* **1.** firmly fixed or attached (BED¹*fast*); ∿ **colour** (unfading, not affected by washing etc.); ∿ **friend** or **friendship** (steady, close); HARD *and fast*; **make ∿,** fasten; **play ∿ and loose,** ignore obligations, be unreliable, trifle; **take ∿ hold of,**

hold tightly. **2.** rapid, quick-moving, producing or allowing quick motion (*fast and* FURIOUS); (of cricket--pitch, tennis-court, putting-green, etc.) on which ball bounces or runs quickly; (of clock etc.) showing too advanced time; (of person) immoral, dissipated; (of photographic film) needing only short exposure, (of lens) having large aperture; **∿'back,** (motor car with) rear sloping continuously down to bumper; ∿ **bowler** (imparting high speed to ball); ∿ **breeder** (**reactor**) (using mainly fast neutrons); *fast* BUCK⁸; ∿ **lane** (on road, for overtaking by fast-moving vehicles); ∿ **neutron** (with high kinetic energy, esp. not slowed by moderator etc.); ∿ **one,** (sl.) unfair action to gain advantage (*pull a fast one*); ∿ **reactor,** nuclear reactor using mainly fast neutrons; ∿ **worker,** one who makes rapid progress (esp. in amatory activities). [OE *fæst,* = OS *fast,* OHG *festi,* ON *fastr,* prob. f. Gmc **fastuz*]

fast⁴ (fah-) *adv.* firmly, fixedly, tightly, securely, (*stand, sit, stick, fast*; ∿ **bind** ∿ **find,** lock up what you would not lose; *eyes fast shut*); soundly *asleep*; (arch. or poet) close *beside, by,* etc.; quickly, in quick succession; **∿-talk,* (colloq.) persuade by rapid or deceitful talk. [OE *fæste,* = OS, OHG *fasto,* ON *fast* f. Gmc **fastō* (as prec.)]

fa′sten (fah′sen) *v.* **1.** *v.t.* attach, fix, secure by some tie or bond, (*to, on* adv. or prep., *together, up, in* adv. or prep., or abs.: *fasten parcel, garment, door,* etc., or *string, button, bolt,* etc.; *fasten off thread* etc., secure with knot or otherwise); hence **∿ING¹** (4) *n.* **2.** direct (look, thoughts, etc.) keenly (*up*)*on*; fix (nickname, imputation, etc.) (*up*)*on*. **3.** *v.i.* become fast (*door will not fasten*); ∿ (**up**)**on,** lay hold of, single out for attack, seize upon (pretext). **4.** Hence **∿ER¹** (2) (fah′sner) *n.* [OE *fæstnian,* = OS *fastnon,* OHG *fastinōn* f. Gmc **fastinōjan* (**fastuz* FAST³; see -EN⁶)]

fästi′dious *a.* easily disgusted, carefully selective, hard to please; hence **∿LY²** *adv.,* **∿NESS** *n.* [ME, f. L *fastidiosus* (*fastidium* loathing; see -OUS)]

fästi′giate *a.* (Bot.) with conical or tapering outline. [f. L *fastigium* gable-top + -ATE²]

fa′stnèss (fah′-) *n.* in adj. senses; stronghold, fortress. [OE *fæstnes* (as FAST³, -NESS)]

fät *a., n.,* & *v.* (-tt-). **1.** *a.* well-fed, plump, corpulent; (of animal) made plump for slaughter, fatted; **∿* **cat,** (sl.) wealthy person, esp. as contributor of funds; ∿ **hen,** = GOOD *King Henry*; **∿'stock,** livestock made fat for slaughter. **2.** thick, substantial, (esp. of printing-type); containing much fat; greasy, oily, unctuous, (Theatr., of actor's part) giving opportunity for skill or display, (of coal) bituminous, (of clay etc.) sticky. **3.** fertile, rich, yielding abundantly, (*fat lands, benefice, job*); ∿ **lime,** nearly pure lime, slaking easily; **a ∿ lot,** (sl.) a great deal (usu. iron. = very little, so *a fat chance* etc.). **4.** slow-witted, indolent; **∿-head(ed),** stupid (person). **5.** Hence **∿'tIsH¹,²** *a.,* **∿'NESS** *n.* **6.** *n.* the fat part of anything (**live off** or **on the ∿ of the land,** have the best of everything). **7.** oily or greasy substance esp. composing fat parts of animal bodies; **a bit of ∿,** (colloq.) piece of good luck; CHEW *the fat;* **the ∿ is in the fire,** (usu. fig.) there will be an explosion of anger. **8.** (Chem.) natural ester of glycerol and acid. **9.** Hence **∿'LESS** *a.* **10.** *v.t. & i.* fatten; **kill the fatted calf,** celebrate, receive returned prodigal with joy (Luke 15). [OE *fæt*(*t*) *a., fǣttian* v., = MDu., MLG *vett,* OHG *feizzit* f. WG **faitidha* p.p., f. Gmc **faitjan* fatten (*faitaz* fat)]

fä′tal *a.* like fate, inevitable, necessary; of or appointed by destiny (F∿ **Sisters,** the Fates; ∿ **thread,** allotted length of life); fateful, important, decisive. **2.** destructive, ruinous, ending in death, (*to*); deadly, sure to kill; disastrous, ill-advised, (*made the fatal mistake of being over-confident*). **3.** Hence **∿LY²** *adv.,* **∿NESS** *n.* [ME f. OF, or f. L *fatalis* (as FATE; see -AL)]

fä′tal|ism *n.* belief that all events are predetermined by arbitrary decree; submission to all that happens as inevitable; so **∿IST** (2) *n.,* **∿i′stIC** *a.* [f prec. + -ISM]

fatá'litỹ *n.* subjection to or supremacy of fate, predestined liability to disaster; fatal influence; misfortune, calamity; death by accident, in war, etc. [f. F *fatalité* or f. LL *fatalitas* (*fatalis* FATAL; see -ITY)]

fata mŏr̄ga'na (fah-; -gah'-) *n.* kind of mirage seen esp. in S. Italy; illusion. [It. (*fata* FAY, *Morgana* sister of King Arthur)]

fāte *n.,* & *v.t.* **1.** *n.* power predetermining events unalterably from eternity; (Myth., usu. *F*~) goddess, esp. one of the three Greek or Scandinavian goddesses, of destiny. **2.** what is destined to happen (**as sure as** ~, quite certain); appointed lot of person etc.; person's or thing's ultimate condition (*decide, fix, seal,* person's *fate; fate worse than* DEATH 3); death, destruction. **3.** *v.t.* (usu. in *pass.*) preordain (*he was fated to do* or *be; it was fated that*); (in *p.p.*) doomed to destruction. [ME, f. It. *fato* & f. L *fatum* that which is spoken, neut. p.p. (as n.) of *fari* speak]

fā'teful (-tf-) *a.* fraught with destiny, important, decisive; controlled by or showing power of fate; prophetic; hence ~LY² *adv.* [f. prec. + -FUL]

fa'ther¹ (fah'dh-) *n.* **1.** male parent (lit., or fig.: **the wish is ~ to the thought,** one believes because one wishes to; **the child is ~ of the man,** tendencies in childhood foreshadow adult development); (**adoptive**) ~, man who has adopted a child; **the ~ and mother of a,** (colloq.) an extremely large, severe, etc. **2.** progenitor, forefather; originator, designer, early leader, (~ **of English poetry,** Chaucer; **F~ of History,** Herodotus; **F~ of lies,** the Devil; **F~s (of the Church),** Christian writers esp. of first five centuries); FOUND¹*ing father;* PILGRIM *Fathers.* **3.** one who deserves filial reverence (*father of his country*); religious teacher. **4.** (*F*~). God; First Person of the Trinity. **5.** confessor; priest belonging to religious order, superior of monastic house; **Right, Most, Reverend F~ in God,** titles of CE bishop, archbishop; **Holy F~,** the Pope; (*F*~, as prefixed title) priest; venerable person, god, (*Father* CHRISTMAS, *Thames,* TIME¹, etc., as personifications). **6.** oldest member, doyen, (*father of the* CHAPEL; **F~ of the House of Commons,** member with longest continuous service; ***F~ of Waters,** the Mississippi); (in *pl.*) leading men, elders, (CITY *fathers*); (**Conscript**) **F~s,** Roman senators. **7.** ~**-figure,** older person regarded as a trusted leader; ~**-in-law,** father of one's wife or husband; ~**land,** one's native land (esp. of Germany); **F~'s Day,** day (usu. third Sunday in June) established for special tribute to fathers. **8.** Hence ~HOOD, ~SHIP, ns., with dead or unknown father, ~LIKE, ~LY¹,², *adjs.* & *advs.* [OE *fæder,* = OS *fadar,* OHG *fater,* ON *fathir,* Goth. *fadar* f. Gmc *fuder f. IE **p'ter*]

fa'ther² (fah'dh-) *v.t.* beget, be father of; produce by education etc.; originate (statement etc.); appear as or confess oneself father or author of (child, book); (arch.) govern paternally; fix paternity of (child, book) *on.* [ME, f. prec.]

fā'thom¹ (-dh-) *n.* (*pl.* often same when used with number). measure of six feet, chiefly used in soundings; ||quantity of wood 6 ft. square in cross-section, whatever the length. [OE *fæðm* the outstretched arms, cogn. w. OS *fathmos,* OHG *fadum* cubit, ON *fathmr* embrace f. Gmc *fathmaz]

fā'thom² (-dh-) *v.t.* measure (depth of water) with sounding-line; (fig.) get to the bottom of, comprehend, whence ~LESS *a.*; (arch.) encircle with arms as in measuring. [OE *fæthmian* (as prec.)]

Făthŏ'mĕter (-dh-) *n.* (*P) type of ECHO¹-sounder. [f. FATHOM¹ + -METER]

fati'dical *a.* gifted with prophetic power. [f. L *fatidicus* (*fatum* FATE, *-dicus* -saying) + -AL]

fati'gue (-ē'g) *n.,* & *v.t.* **1.** *n.* weariness after exertion; weakness in metals etc. after repeated variations of stress; reduction of efficiency of muscle, organ, etc., after prolonged activity; task etc. that wearies; soldier's non-military duty (~**-party** or ~, party ordered to do this; ~**-dress** or ~**s,** garments worn for it). **2.** *v.t.* tire, exhaust, cause fatigue in. [f. F *fatigue*(*r*) f. L *fatigare* exhaust as by riding or working]

Fa'tiha(h) (fah'tihah) *n.* short first sura of Koran, used as Muslim prayer. [f. Arab. *fātiḥa* opening (*fataḥa* to open)]

Fā'timid, Fā'timīte, *ns.* descendent of Fatima; member of dynasty ruling in N. Africa in 10th–12th c. [f. *Fatima,* daughter of Muhammad d. 632 + -ID³, -ITE¹]

fā'tling *n.* young fatted animal. [f. FAT 10 + -LING¹]

Fă'tsō *n.* (*pl.* ~**es**). (sl. joc. or derog.) fat person. [prob. f. FAT = fat person + -s¹ + -o]

fă'tten *v.* **1.** *v.t.* make fat (esp. animals for slaughter); enrich (soil). **2.** *v.i.* become fat. [f. FAT + -EN⁶]

fă'ttỹ *a.* & *n.* **1.** *a.* like fat, unctuous, greasy; consisting of fat, adipose; with morbid deposition of fat (~ **degeneration** of heart or kidney); ~ **acid,** (Chem.) member of a series of acids occurring in or derived from natural fats, waxes, etc. **2.** *n.* fat person (esp. as nickname). [ME, f. FAT + -Y²]

fā'tūous *a.* vacantly silly, purposeless, idiotic; hence or cogn. fatū'ITY *n.,* ~LY² *adv.,* ~NESS *n.* [f. L *fatuus* foolish + -OUS]

faubourg (fō'boorg) *n.* suburb, esp. of Paris. [F; cf. med. L *falsus burgus* not the city proper]

fau'cēs (-z) *n. pl.* (Anat.) cavity at back of mouth. [L, = throat]

fau'cet *n.* tap for barrel etc.; *any kind of tap. [ME, f. OF *fausset* vent-peg f. Prov. *falset* (*falsar* to bore)]

faugh (faw) *int.* expr. disgust. [spontaneous utterance]

fault (fawlt, fŏlt) *n.* & *v.* **1.** *n.* defect, imperfection, blemish, of character or of structure, appearance, etc. (*generous* etc. **to a** ~, excessively so; **with all** ~**s,** at buyer's risk); break or other defect in electric circuit. **2.** transgression, offence, thing wrongly done, (Tennis etc.) ball wrongly served (**double** ~, two consecutive faults losing point); **find** ~ (**with**), make adverse criticism (of), complain (of); ~'**finder** *n.,* ~'**finding** *n.* & *a.,* (esp. of captious criticism). **3.** responsibility for something wrong (*the fault was mine; it will be our own fault*); defect that causes something undesirable; **at** ~, (arch.) **in** ~, guilty, to blame. **4.** (Hunt.) loss of scent, check so caused, (**be at** ~, lit., or fig. = be puzzled, not know what to do). **5.** (Geol.) break in continuity of strata or vein. **6.** *v.t.* find fault with, blame; declare to be faulty; (Geol.) break continuity of (strata or vein). **7.** *v.i.* commit fault; (Geol.) show fault. **8.** Hence ~LESS *a.,* ~'Y² *a.,* ~'iLY² *adv.,* ~iNESS *n.* [ME f. OF *faut*(*e*) f. Rom. *fallita fem. p.p. (as n.) of L *fallere* FAIL²]

faun *n.* Latin rural deity with horns and tail. [ME, f. OF *faune* or f. L *Faunus* Latin god identified w. Gk Pan]

fau'n|a *n.* (*pl.* ~**ae** or ~**as**). animals of a region or epoch; treatise on or list of these; hence ~AL *a.,* ~IST (3) *n.,* ~**i'stic**(AL) *adjs.* [mod. L, f. name of rural goddess, sister of Faunus (see prec.)]

faute de mieux (fōt de myẽr') *adv.* & *a.* (used) for want of any better alternative. [F]

fauteuil (fōtŭ'ē) *n.* theatre stall, seat in bus, etc., resembling armchair; seat or rank of member of French Academy; (arch.) armchair. [F, f. OF *faudestuel, faldestoel* FALDSTOOL]

fau'vism (fō'-) *n.* style of painting with vivid use of colour; so ~IST (2) *n.* [f. F *fauve* wild beast, applied to painters of Matisse's school; see -ISM]

faux bonhomme (fō bŏnŏ'm) *n.* seemingly good-natured but actually sly person. [F, = false good-natured man]

faux-naïf (fōnahē'f) *a.* & *n.* (person) pretending to be ingenuous; self-consciously unaffected (person). [F (*faux* false, *naïf* NAÏVE)]

faux pas (fō pah') *n.* (*pl.* same *pr.* -ah'z). act that compromises one's, esp. a woman's, reputation; offence against social convention, indiscreet speech or action. [F, = false step]

favela (fahvā'la) *n*. Brazilian shack or slum. [Port.]

‖**fā'vour**[1] (-ver), ***fā'vor**[1], *n*. **1.** friendly regard, goodwill, (**find ~ in the eyes of,** be liked by; CURRY *favour*); approval (*look with favour on*); esteem, liking, (*be* or *stand high* etc. in person's *favour*); kindness beyond what is due or usual (*should esteem it a favour*; *do me the favour of accepting*; *woman* **bestows her ~s,** allows sexual intercourse); (arch., Commerc.) letter (*your favour of yesterday*). **2.** (arch.) leave, pardon, (*by your favour*; **under ~,** if one may venture to say so). **3.** partiality, too lenient or generous treatment (FEAR[1] *or favour*). **4.** aid, support, furtherance, (*under favour of night*); **in ~ of,** on behalf or in support of, on the side of, to the advantage or account of, (*am in favour of a five-day week*; *cheques to be drawn in favour of the treasurer*). **5.** thing given or worn as mark of favour, knot of ribbons, rosette, cockade, badge. **6.** (arch.) looks, countenance; hence WELL-, *ill, hard,* etc., **~**ED[2] (-erd) *a*. [ME f. OF, f. L *favor -oris* (*favēre* show kindness to; see -OR)]

‖**fā'vour**[2] (-ver), ***fā'vor**[2], *v.t.* **1.** look kindly upon, approve; treat kindly, countenance; oblige *with*. **2.** treat with partiality, be unjust on behalf of. **3.** aid, support; tend to confirm (theory etc.); prove advantageous to (person), facilitate (process etc.), whence **~**ING[2] *a*. **4.** (colloq.) resemble in features (*favour one's father*). **5.** (in *p.p.*) having unusual advantages (*most favoured* NATION). [ME, f. OF *favorer* f. med. L *favorare* f. L *favor* (see prec.)]

‖**fā'vourab**‖**le** (-ver-), ***fā'vorab**‖**le,** *a*. well-disposed, propitious; commendatory, approving; giving consent (*favourable answer*); promising, auspicious, satisfactory, (*favourable aspect*); helpful, suitable, (*to*); hence **~le**NESS (-beln-) *n*., **~**LY[2] *adv*. [ME, f. OF *favorable* f. L *favorabilis* (as FAVOUR[1]; see -ABLE)]

‖**fā'vourite** (-ver-), ***fā'vorite,** *n*. & *a*. (person or thing) preferred above others (*the favourite of*; *a favourite with* or *of*); (Sport) competitor generally expected to win, horse etc. at shortest odds; person chosen as intimate by king or superior and unduly favoured; *** **~ son,** person preferred as presidential candidate by delegates from his own state. [f. obs. F *favorit* f. It. *favorito,* p.p. of *favorire* FAVOUR[2]; see -ITE[2]]

‖**fā'vouritism** (-ver-), ***fā'voritism,** *n*. unfair favouring of one person or group at expense of another. [f. prec. + -ISM]

fawn[1] *n*., *a*., & *v.t*. **1.** young fallow etc. deer; buck or doe of first year; **in ~,** (of deer) pregnant. **2.** *n*. & *a*. **~** or **~-colour(ed),** (of) light yellowish brown. **3.** *v.t*. (Of deer) bring forth (young, or abs.). [ME, f. OF *faon* etc. f. Rom. ***feto** *-onis* f. L *fetus* offspring (cf. FOETUS)]

fawn[2] *v.i*. (Of animal, esp. dog) show affection by tail--wagging, grovelling, etc. (**~ on, upon,** lavish caresses on); (of person) behave servilely, cringe (*on* or *upon,* or abs.), whence **~**ING[2] *a*. [OE *fagnian, fægnian,* f. as FAIN[1]]

fay *n*. (literary). fairy. [ME, f. OF *fa(i)e* f. L *fata* pl. the FATES]

fāze *v.t*. (usu. w. neg.) disconcert, perturb. [var. of *feeze* drive off, f. OE *fēsian,* of unkn. orig.]

FBA *abbr*. Fellow of the British Academy.

***FBI** *abbr*. Federal Bureau of Investigation.

FC *abbr*. Football Club.

***FCC** *abbr*. Federal Communications Commission.

‖**FCO** *abbr*. Foreign & Commonwealth Office.

fcp. *abbr*. foolscap.

FD *abbr*. Defender of the Faith. [f. L *Fidei Defensor*]

***FDA** *abbr*. Food & Drugs Administration.

FDC *abbr*. first-day cover; *fleur de coin.*

Fe *symb*. iron. [f. L *ferrum*]

fē'alty *n*. feudal tenant's or vassal's (acknowledgement of obligation of) fidelity to his lord (*do, make, receive, swear, fealty*); allegiance. [ME, f. OF *feau(l)té* f. L *fidelitas -tatis* (*fidelis* faithful f. *fides* faith; see -TY[1])]

fear[1] *n*. **1.** painful emotion caused by impending danger or evil, state of alarm (*was in fear*), dread *of,*

that, or *lest*; **for ~ of,** (*that*), **lest,** to avoid the risk of or that; **without ~** or **favour,** impartially; hence **~**LESS *a*. (*fearless of danger*). **2.** dread and reverence (*the fear of God*; **put the ~ of God into,** terrify); anxiety for the safety of (*in fear of his life*); **no ~,** (colloq.) it is not likely. [OE *fǣr* sudden calamity, danger, = OS *vār* ambush, OHG *fāra,* ON *fár* misfortune f. Gmc ***fǣraz**]

fear[2] *v*. **1.** *v.i.* be afraid; (*refl.,* arch.) *I fear me* (used in parenthesis); **never ~,** there is no danger of that. **2.** *v.t.* be afraid of; hesitate *to* do, shrink from do*ing*; revere (God); apprehend, have uneasy expectation of; be afraid (*that*) (*need not* etc. *fear but* or *that*). [OE *fǣran,* = OS *fāron* lie in wait, OHG *fārēn,* ON *færa* taunt; cf. prec.]

fear'ful *a*. terrible, awful; (colloq.) annoying, extreme, etc. (*in a fearful mess*); frightened, timid, apprehensive *of, lest,* (*that*); lacking resolution *to*; reverential; hence **~**LY[2] *adv.,* **~**NESS *n*. [ME, f. prec. + -FUL]

fear'some *a*. appalling, awe-inspiring, esp. in appearance; hence **~**LY[2] (-mlī) *adv.,* **~**NESS (-mn-) *n*. [f. FEAR[1,2] + -SOME[1]]

fea's‖**ible** (-z-) *a*. practicable, possible; (colloq.) manageable, convenient, serviceable, plausible; hence **~**IBI'LITY *n*., **~**IBLY *adv*. [ME, f. OF *faisable, -ible* f. *fais-* st. of *faire* f. L *facere* do; see -IBLE]

feast *n*. & *v*. **1.** *n*. joyful religious anniversary (**movable, immovable, ~,** one that recurs on different, same, date; **movable ~,** (joc.) meal taken at no regular time); annual village festival; sumptuous meal, esp. public one given to many guests; (fig.) gratification to the senses or mind (**~ of reason,** intellectual talk); **~-day** (on which feast is held). **2.** *v.i.* partake of feast, eat and drink sumptuously; hence **~**ER[1] *n*. **3.** *v.t.* pass (night etc.) *away* in feasting; regale (guests, one's *eyes* on beauty etc.). [ME, f. OF *feste*(r) f. pop. L *festa* neut. pl. of *festus* joyous]

feat[1] *n*. noteworthy act, esp. deed of valour (esp. *feat of arms*); action showing dexterity or strength, surprising trick. [ME, f. OF *fait, fet* f. as FACT]

‖**feat**[2] *a*. (arch. or dial.) adroit, smart, dextrous, neat; hence **~**LY[2] *adv*. [ME, f. OF *fet* (as prec.)]

fea'ther[1] (fě'dh-) *n*. **1.** one of the appendages growing from bird's skin, consisting of quill, shaft, and two vanes of barbs, (**show the white ~,** betray cowardice, white feather in game-bird's tail being mark of bad breeding); (collect.) plumage (**in high** or **full ~,** in good spirits etc.; BIRDS *of a feather*); game-birds (**fur and ~,** game animals and birds). **2.** piece(s) of feather attached to arrow; plume worn in hat etc. (**~ in one's cap,** achievement one may be proud of); very light object (**you could have knocked me down with a ~,** I was astonished); fringe of long hair on dog's leg etc. **3.** (Rowing). action of feathering (see foll.). **4.** **~ bed,** mattress stuffed with feathers; **~-bed** *v.t.* (*-dd-*), make things easy for (esp. in economic or financial respects); pamper; **~-brain(ed),** = *feather-head(ed)*; **~ duster,** dusting-brush made of feathers; **~-edge,** fine edge of wedge--shaped board; **~-head(ed), ~-pate(d),** silly (person); **~-stitch,** ornamental zigzag sewing; **~weight,** very light thing or person, esp. boxer (see BOX[5]*ing-weights*). **5.** Hence (-)**~**ED[2] (-erd), **~**LESS, **~**Y[2] *adjs.,* **~**INESS, **~**LET, *ns*. [OE *fether,* = OS *fethara,* OHG *fedara,* ON *fjöthr* f. Gmc ***fethrō** f. IE ***petra**]

fea'ther[2] (fě'dh-) *v*. **1.** *v.t.* furnish, adorn, line, coat, (as) with feathers (*feather an arrow*; **~** one's **nest,** enrich oneself when opportunity occurs; TAR *and feather*). **2.** *v.t.* & *i.* turn (oar) so as to pass through air edgeways; (Aeron. & Naut.) make (propeller blades) rotate in such a way as to lessen air or water resistance; vary angle of incidence of (helicopter blades). **3.** *v.i.* float, move, or wave, like feathers. **4.** (Hunt., of hound) make quivering motion of body and tail while seeking scent. [f. OE *gefithrian* & f. prec.]

fea'thering (fě'dh-) *n*. In vbl senses; plumage; feathers of an arrow; feather-like structure in animal's coat; (Archit.) cusps in tracery. [f. prec. + -ING¹]

fea′ture *n.* & *v.* **1.** *n.* (usu. in *pl.*) part of face, esp. with regard to shape and visible effect. **2.** distinctive or characteristic part of a thing, part that arrests attention; distinctive or prominent article etc. in newspaper etc.; ∼ (**film**), one of some length forming main item in cinema programme, whence **featur-**ε′τΤΕ (-cher-) *n.*; ∼ (**programme**), broadcast based on one specific theme. **3.** *v.t.* be feature of; (arch.) portray, sketch the prominent points of; make special display or attraction of, give special prominence to, (esp. in film etc.). **4.** *v.i.* be feature; be (important) participant *in.* **5.** Hence **-feature**ED² (-cherd), ∼LESS (-cherl-), *adjs.* [ME, f. OF *feture, faiture* form f. L *factura* formation (see FACTURE)]

Feb. *abbr.* February.

fĕ′brĭfūge *n.* medicine to reduce fever, cooling drink; hence **fĕbrĭ′fūg**AL *a.* [f. F *fébrifuge* f. L *febris* fever; see -FUGE]

fĕ′brĭle *a.* of fever, feverish; hence **fĕbrĭ′lĭTY** *n.* [f. F *fébrile* or f. med. L *febrilis* f. L *febris* fever; see -IL]

Fĕ′bruarў (-rŏŏ-) *n.* second month of year; ∼ **fill--dike** (name referring to its rain and snow). [ME, f. OF *feverier* f. Rom. *febrarius* f. L *februarius* (*februa* purification feast held in this month)]

***fĕ′cal,** ***feces.** See FAECAL, FAECES.

fĕ′ckless *a.* feeble, futile, inefficient, aimless; hence ∼∙LY² *adv.*, ∼∙NESS *n.* [f. Sc. *feck* (*effeck* var. of EFFECT¹) + -LESS]

fĕ′cŭl∣ent *a.* turbid; fetid; containing sediments or dregs; hence ∼ENCE *n.* [f. F *féculent* or f. L *faeculentus* (as FAECES; see -ULENT)]

fĕ′cund *a.* prolific, fertile; fertilizing; so **fĕcŭ′nd**ITY *n.* [ME, f. F *fécond* or f. L *fecundus*]

fĕ′cund∣āte *v.t.* make fruitful; = FERTILIZE 2; so ∼A′TION *n.* [f. L *fecundare* (*fecundus* fruitful) + -ATE³]

fĕd¹. See FEED¹.

***Fĕd²** *n.* (sl.) Federal official, esp. member of Federal Bureau of Investigation; Federal Reserve Board [abbr. of FEDERAL]

fĕdayee′n (-a-y-) *n. pl.* Arab guerrillas operating esp. against Israel. [f. colloq. Arab. *fidā′iyīn* pl. f. Arab. *fidā′ī* adventurer]

fĕ′deral *a.* **1.** of a system of government in which several States form a unity but remain independent in internal affairs; concerning this whole and not the separate parts. **2.** relating to or favouring central government, as dist. from government by separate provinces etc.; *of the Northern States in the Civil War; ∼ **district, territory,** etc., region used as seat of federal government; *∼ **reserve,** national system of reserve cash available to banks. **3.** (Theol.) based on doctrine of God's covenants with Adam and Christ. **4.** comprising an association of largely independent units (∥*federal university*). **5.** Hence or cogn. ∼ISM (3), ∼IST (2), *ns.,* ∼IZE (3) *v.t.,* ∼LY² *adv.* [f. mod. L *foederalis* f. L *foedus -eris* covenant + -AL; in sense 1 orig. of dispositions by treaty]

fĕ′der∣āte *v.t.* & *i.* band together in league for some common object; organize (States) on federal basis; so ∼ATE², ∼ATIVE, *adjs.* [f. LL *foederare* (as prec.) + -ATE³]

fĕderā′tion *n.* federating, whence ∼IST (2) *n.*; federated society; federal group of States etc. [f. F *fédération* f. LL *foederatio* (as prec.; see -ATION)]

fĕdŏr′a *n.* low soft felt hat with crown creased lengthways. [f. *Fédora,* drama by V. Sardou (1882)]

fee *n.,* & *v.t.* (∼′d *or* ∼d). **1.** *n.* sum payable to public officer for performing his function; remuneration of lawyer, physician, or any professional person, for consultation etc. (RETAINING *fee*); money paid to another employer for transfer of footballer etc.; entrance money for examination, society, etc.; (in *pl.*) regular payment for instruction at school, university, etc.; gratuity. **2.** inherited estate; ∼ **simple** (without limitation to particular class of heirs); ∼-**tail** (with

such limitation [TAIL²]); **hold in** ∼ (**simple**) as absolute property. **3.** (Hist.) fief, feudal benefice. **4.** *v.t.* pay fee to; engage for a fee. [ME f. AF, = OF *feu, fieu,* etc. f. med. L *feodum, feudum,* Rom. *feudum,* perh. f. Frank. *fehu-ōd* cattle-property; cf. FEUD², FIEF]

***feeb** *n.* (sl.) feeble-minded or stupid person. [abbr. of foll.]

fee′b∣le *a.* weak, infirm; deficient in character or intelligence (∼le-minded, mentally deficient, esp. with mental age of 8 or 9); lacking energy, force, or effect; dim, indistinct; hence ∼leNESS (-beln-) *n.,* ∼lISH¹ 2 *a.,* ∼LY² *adv.* [ME, f. AF & OF *feble, fieble, fleible* f. L *flebilis* lamentable (*flēre* weep)]

feed¹ *v.* (**fed**). **1.** *v.t.* supply with food; put food into mouth of (*cannot feed himself*); graze (cattle). **2.** gratify (vanity etc.); comfort (person) with food etc. **3.** serve as food for; nourish, make grow; ∼ (**up**), (1) fatten, (2) satiate, whence **fed up** (colloq.), **fed to death, to the** (**back**) **teeth,** etc., (sl.), having had too much of something, discontented, bored *with.* **4.** keep (reservoir, fire, etc.) supplied; supply (machine) with material; give out (fodder) to animals; use (land) as pasture; supply (material) (*in*)*to* machine; (Theatr. sl.) supply (actor etc.) with cues; (Footb. etc.) give passes to; ∼′ing-bottle (with teat, for hand-fed infants); ∼′ing-cup (with spout, for invalids); ∼′ing-time (at which captive animals etc. are fed). **5.** *v.i.* take food, eat, (esp. of animal, or colloq.); ∼ **on,** consume, be nourished by. **6.** *v.t.* & *i.* ∼ **back,** return by or as FEEDBACK. [OE *fēdan,* = OS *fōdean,* OHG *fuoten,* ON *fœtha,* Goth. *fōdjan* f. Gmc *fōdjan* (*fōdhon* FOOD)]

feed² *n.* **1.** act or instance of feeding, giving of food; **off** one's ∼, with no appetite; **on the** ∼, (of fish) feeding or looking out for food; **out at** ∼, turned out to graze. **2.** pasturage, green crops; horse's allowance of oats etc.; fodder; (colloq.) meal, feast; feeding of machine, material supplied, charge of gun, (*feed-cock, -pipe, -shaft,* etc.). **3.** (Theatr. sl.) actor who supplies another with cues. **4.** ∼′lot, area of land where animals are fed; ∼′stock, raw material supplied to machine etc.; ∼-tank, holding water for conductive or for drinking. [f. prec.]

feed³. See FEE.

fee′dbăck *n.* **1.** (Electr.) return of fraction of output signal from one stage of circuit, amplifier, etc., to input of same or a preceding stage (**positive, negative,** ∼, tending to increase, decrease, the amplification etc.); signal so returned. **2.** (Biol., Psych., etc.) modification or control of a process or system by its results or effects, esp. by difference between desired and actual result. **3.** information about result of experiment etc.; response. [f. FEED¹ + BACK³]

fee′der *n.* in vbl senses; one who eats in specified manner; child's feeding-bottle; ∥child's bib; tributary stream (fig.); hopper or feeding apparatus in machine; branch road, railway line, etc., linking outlying districts with main communications system; main carrying electricity to distribution point; (Theatr. sl.) = FEED² 3. [ME, f. FEED² + -ER¹²]

feel *v.* (**felt**) & *n.* **1.** *v.t.* explore by touch ∼ **the pulse of,** lit. to ascertain state of health, or fig. = cautiously ascertain intentions or sentiments of; ∼ one's **way,** find it by groping, or fig. = proceed carefully); try to ascertain *whether, if, how;* perceive by touch, have sensation of, (*feel a hard substance, heat, pain, a blow; I felt him move, moving, that he was cold; feel* one's OATS); ∼ **out,** investigate (cautiously); ∼ (**up**), (sl.) caress genitals of. **2.** be conscious of, have sense, emotion, conviction, *feel* the DRAUGHT 7; ∼ **no pain,** (sl.) be very drunk; **make** one's **presence felt,** have effect on others). **3.** experience, undergo, (*he shall feel my vengeance; felt the storm severely*); be affected by. **4.** behave as if conscious of (*ship feels her helm*); be emotionally affected by (*feel the censure keenly*); have vague or emotional impression (*that;* esp. *feel in* one's BONE′s); consider, think, (*I feel it necessary to make a correction*). **5.** *v.i.* search (*about*) with hand etc. *after* or

for; have sensation of touch (*can you feel in your fingers?*).
6. be consciously (*well, warm, angry,* CHEAP 1, GOOD 12); ~ **like,** (colloq.) desire (thing), have inclination towards doing; ~ (**quite**) one**self,** be fit, self--possessed, etc.; ~ **up to,** be ready to face (*work* etc.).
7. be emotionally affected (*feel strongly about it*); have sympathy *with* or compassion *for*. **8.** be consciously perceived as, produce impression of being, (*air feels chilly; this feels like velvet*). **9.** *n.* sense of touch (*firm to the feel*); act of feeling, testing by touch; sensation characterizing a material, a situation, etc. [OE *fēlan,* = OS *-fōlian,* OHG *fuolen* f. WG *fōljan]*
fee'ler *n.* In vbl senses; organ in certain animals for testing things by touch or for searching for food; tentative proposal or hint, *ballon d'essai;* ~ **gauge** (equipped with blades for measuring gaps etc.). [f. prec. + -ER¹]
fee'ling¹ *n.* **1.** In vbl senses; sense of touch; physical sensation. **2.** emotion (*of hope, fear,* etc.); (in *pl.*) susceptibilities, sympathies, (*strong feelings on the matter;* **hurts my** ~**s,** offends me); readiness to feel, tenderness for others' sufferings, (**good** ~, avoidance of unkindness etc.); consciousness of (*had a feeling of safety*); belief not based solely on reason; sentiment (*the general feeling was against it*); general emotional effect produced by work of art. [ME, f. FEEL² + -ING¹]
fee'ling² *a.* In vbl senses; sensitive; sympathetic; showing emotion; hence ~LY² *adv.* [ME, f. FEEL² + -ING²]
fee'lthy *a.* (sl.) obscene. [joc. imit. of foreigners' pr. of FILTHY]
feet. See FOOT¹.
feign (fān) *v.t. & i.* **1.** simulate, pretend, (*feign that one is mad, to be mad,* one*self mad, madness; feign innocence, ignorance*); practise simulation. **2.** (arch.) invent (excuse, story, accusation), forge (document); represent in fiction, imagine. [ME, f. *feign-* st. of OF *feindre* f. L *fingere* mould, contrive]
feijo'a (fā-, fī-) *n.* evergreen shrub or tree of genus *Feijoa;* its guava-like fruit. [mod. L, f. J. da Silva *Feijo,* 19th-c. Sp. naturalist + -A 1]
feint¹ (fā-) *n., & v.i.* **1.** *n.* sham attack (blow, cut, thrust, or military assault) to divert attention or deceive opponent; pretence (*make a feint of doing*). **2.** *v.i.* make feint (*at, upon, against*). [f. F *feinte,* fem. p.p. (as *n.*) of *feindre* FEIGN]
feint² (fā-) *a.* (Commerc.) = FAINT¹ (*feint lines; ruled feint*). [ME f. OF, p.p. of *feindre* FEIGN]
feis (fēsh, fāsh) *n.* (*pl.* ~*'eanna pr. -ana*). early Celtic parliament of kings etc.; Irish or Scottish arts festival like eisteddfod. [Ir., = assembly]
***fei'st|ў** (fī'-) *a.* (sl.) aggressive, exuberant; touchy; hence ~iNESS *n.* [f. *feist* (= FIST) small dog + -Y²]
fěla'fel (-ah'-) *n.* (Israel etc.) flat bread roll stuffed with seasoned vegetables. [f. Arab. *falāfil*]
fě'ldscher (-sher) *n.* Russian medical auxiliary without professional qualifications. [f. Russ. *fel'dsher* f. G *feldscher* field surgeon (*feld* FIELD)]
fě'ldspăr, fě'lspăr, *n.* widely distributed white or flesh-red mineral containing aluminium and other silicates in various proportions; hence **fěldspǎ'thic** *a.,* **fě'ldspathoid** *n.* [f. G *feldspat(h)* (*feld* FIELD, *spat(h)* SPAR²); *feldspar* by false deriv. f. G *fels* rock]
***Félibre** (fālē'br) *n.* member of the Félibrige, society of Provençal poets and writers founded 1854; so **Fe'librism** (3) (fā'-') *n.* [F, f. Prov. *felibre* teacher in the temple (Luke 2:46), prob. f. LL *fellibris* nursling (of the Muses) f. L *fellare* suck]
felici'fic *a.* (Eth.) tending to produce happiness. [f. L *felix -icis* happy + -I- + -FIC]
feli'cit|āte *v.t.* congratulate (usu. *on*); hence ~A'TION *n.* (usu. in *pl.*). [f. LL *felicitare* make very happy f. L *felix* happy, + -ATE³]
feli'citous *a.* (Of expression, quotation, civilities, or person in these connections) strikingly apt, pleasantly ingenious; hence ~LY² *adv.* [f. foll. + -OUS]
feli'citў *n.* **1.** being happy; intense happiness; thing causing happiness. **2.** fortunate trait; happy faculty in

expression, appropriateness; well chosen phrase. [ME, f. OF *felicité* f. L *felicitas -tatis* (*felix felicis* happy; see -ITY)]
fe'line *a. & n.* **1.** *a.* of cats; catlike esp. in beauty or slyness; hence **fěli'nity** *n.* **2.** *n.* animal of cat family Felidae. [f. L *felinus* (*feles* cat; see -INE¹)]
fěll¹ *n.* animal's hide or skin with hair; human skin (FLESH¹ *and fell*); thick or matted hair or wool, fleece; ~'**monger,** one who prepares skins for leather--making, (arch.) dealer in hides and skins. [OE *fel(l),* = OS, OHG *fel,* ON *-fjall,* Goth. *-fill* f. Gmc *fellam* f. IE *pello-]*
||**fěll²** *n.* hill, mountain, (in names, as *Scafell*); stretch of high moorland. [ME, f. ON *fjall, fell* hill, prob. cogn. w. OS, OHG *felis* rock]
fěll³ *a.* (poet. or rhet.) fierce, ruthless, terrible, destructive; **at one** ~ **swoop,** in a single (deadly) action. [ME, f. OF *fel* f. Rom. *fel(l)o* FELON¹]
fěll⁴ *v.t., & n.* **1.** *v.t.* strike (person, animal) down by blow or cut; cut down (tree); stitch down (edge of seam) to lie flat. **2.** *n.* amount of timber cut. [OE *fellan,* = OS *fellian,* OHG *fellen,* ON *fella* f. Gmc *falljan* causative of *fallan* FALL¹]
fěll⁵. See FALL¹.
fě'lla, fě'llah¹, *n.* = FELLOW 5. [repr. affected or vulg. pronunc.]
fě'llah² (-a) *n.* (*pl.* ~**in** *pr.* -a-hēn). Egyptian peasant. [f. Arab. *fallāḥ* husbandsman (*falaḥa* till the soil)]
fělla'tiö (-ah'tiō, -shiō) *n.* (*pl.* ~**s**). sucking or licking of penis; hence **fěllā'te** *v.t.,* perform fellatio on (person), **fěllā'tor, fěllā'trix,** *ns.* [mod. L, f. L *fellare* suck; cf. -ATION]
fě'ller¹ *n.* In vbl senses. [f. FELL⁴ + -ER¹]
fě'ller² *n.* = FELLOW 5; **young** ~**-me-lad,** frivolous young man. [repr. affected or vulg. pronunc.]
fě'llöe, fě'llў, *n.* outer circle (or one piece of it) of wheel, attached by spokes. [OE *felg,* = MLG, MDu. *velge,* OHG *felga,* of unkn. orig.]
fě'llow (-ō) *n. & a.* **1.** *n.* one associated with another, comrade, (usu. in *pl.*; *separated from his fellows*); ~**-feeling,** sympathy; **good** ~, congenial companion; HAIL³.*-fellow-well-met.* **2.** counterpart, match, other of pair; equal, one of same class; contemporary. **3.** incorporated senior member of college (~ **commoner,** (Hist.) undergraduate with privilege of dining at fellows' table); elected graduate receiving stipend for period of research. **4.** member of governing body in some universities; member of learned society. **5.** (colloq.) man, boy, (*poor fellow!; my dear* or *good fellow, old fellow;* STOUT *fellow*); (derog.) despised person; **young** ~**-my-lad** (cf. FELLER²). **6.** *attrib.* or *a.* belonging to same class (~ **creature,** person or animal also created by God), associated in joint action (*fellow soldier*), in same relation to same object (*fellow-countryman*); ~**-traveller,** (1) one who travels with another, (2) non-Communist who sympathizes with aims and general policy of Communist Party. [OE *fēolaga* f. ON *félagi* (*fé* cattle, property, money; see LAY³)]
fě'llowship (-lō-) *n.* participation, sharing, community of interest; companionship, intercourse, friendliness; body of associates, company, (**right hand of** ~, sign of admission); guild, corporation; brotherhood, fraternity; status or emoluments of fellow of college or society. [ME, f. prec. + -SHIP]
fě'llў. See FELLOE.
fělōdēsē' *n.* (*pl.* **felones** *pr.* fĭlōnēz-, or **felos, de se**). self-murderer; self-murder. [AL (*felo* FELON¹, *de se* of himself)]
fě'lon¹ *n. & a.* **1.** *a.* (arch.) cruel, wicked, murderous. **2.** *n.* one who has committed felony; hence ~RY (1) *n.* [ME f. OF, f. med. L *fel(l)o -onis,* of unkn. orig.]
fě'lon² *n.* whitlow. [ME, perh. as prec.; cf. med. L *fel(l)o* in same sense]
felō'nious *a.* criminal; (Law) of or involving felony; who has committed felony; hence ~LY² *adv.* [f. foll. + -OUS]

fe'lony n. crime regarded by the law as grave, and usu. involving violence. [ME, f. OF *felonie* (as FELON[1]; see -Y[1])]

fe'lspar. See FELDSPAR.

felt[1] n. & v. **1.** n. kind of cloth made by rolling and pressing, or by weaving and shrinking, wool etc.; similar material made from other fibres; ~(-**tipped**) **pen,** pen with point made of felt; hence ~'Y[2] a. **2.** v.t. make into felt, mat together; cover with felt. **3.** v.i. become matted. [OE, = OS *filt*, OHG *filz* f. WG **felta, *felti*]

felt[2]. See FEEL.

felü'cca n. small Mediterranean coasting vessel with oars or lateen sails or both. [f. It. *feluc(c)a* f. obs. Sp. *faluca* f. Arab. *fulk*, perh. f. Gk *efolkion* sloop]

fe'lwort (-ert) n. purple-flowered gentian (*Gentianella amarella*). [f. OE *feldwyrt* (as FIELD, WORT 1)]

fe'māle a. & n. **1.** a. of the sex that can bear offspring or produce eggs (*female child, slave, dog, ostrich, salmon, wasp*); (of plants or their parts) fruit-bearing, having pistil and no stamens, or thought of as female because of colour etc., (~ **fern,** tall slender kind; *female bamboo, myrtle*); of women (*female sex, education,* SUFFRAGE; ~ **impersonator,** male performer dressed and acting as woman) or female animals; *female* RHYME[1]. **2.** (In instruments etc.) designed to receive corresponding male part; ~ **screw** (as in nut). **3.** n. female person or animal; (derog. or joc.) woman, girl. [ME, f. OF *femelle* n. f. L *femella* dim. of *femina* woman, w. assim. to *male*]

fēme n. (Law). woman, wife; ~ **covert** (kŭ'-), married woman; ~ **sole,** woman without husband (esp. if divorced). [ME f. AF & OF, f. L *femina* woman]

fe'minal a. womanly; hence ~ITY (-ă'l-) n. [f. med. L *feminalis* f. L *femina* woman; see -AL]

femine'itỹ n. womanliness; womanishness. [f. L *femineus* womanish (*femina* woman) + -ITY]

fe'minine a. & n. **1.** a. of women; womanly (*feminine intuition*). **2.** (Gram.) having gender proper to women's names. **3.** (Pros.) ~ **caesura** (not immediately following stress); ~ **rhyme** (of two syllables, the second being unstressed; orig. in F verse, of feminine wds ending in mute -*e*). **4.** ~ **ending** (of verse line or phrase of music with unaccented syllable or note after final stress). Hence ~LY[2] (-nlĭ) adv., ~NESS (-n-n-), **fĕminī'nITY,** ns. **6.** n. feminine gender or word. [ME, f. OF *feminin -ine* or f. L *femininus* (*femina* woman; see -INE[1])]

fe'min|ism n. advocacy of women's rights on ground of equality of the sexes, whence ~IST (2) n.; (Path.) development of female characteristics in male person. [f. F *féminisme*, or f. L *femina* woman + -ISM]

femi'nity n. = FEMININITY. [ME, f. OF *feminité* f. med. L *feminitas -tatis* f. L *femina* woman; see -ITY]

fe'miniz|e, -is|e (-īz), v.t. & i. make or become feminine or female; hence ~A'TION n. [f. L *femina* woman + -IZE]

femme fatale (făm fătah'l) n. dangerously attractive woman. [F]

fe'mto- pref. denoting factor of 10⁻¹⁵ (*femtometre*). [f. Da. or Norw. *femten* fifteen + -O-]

fe'mur n. (pl. ~s, or femora pr. fě'-). thigh-bone; corresponding part of insect; so **fe'mor**AL a. [L *femur femoris* thigh]

fĕn[1] n. **1.** low marshy or flooded tract of land (**the** F~s, low-lying districts in Cambs. etc.). **2.** ~**-berry,** cranberry; ~**-fire,** will-o'-the-wisp; ~'**man,** inhabitant of Fens. **3.** Hence ~'nY[2] a. [OE *fen(n)*, = OS *fen(n)i*, OHG *fenna, fenni*, ON *fen*, Goth. *fani* f. Gmc **fanjam*]

fĕn[2]**, fens.** See FAIN[2].

fĕnce[1] n. **1.** hedge, railing, bank, etc., preventing entry to or exit from field etc.; ~ JUMP[1] 5; **sunk ~** (placed along bottom of ditch, or formed by ditch); **mend** one's ~**s,** make peace with person; **sit on the ~,** remain neutral in contest, not take sides, not commit oneself. **2.** guard, guide, gauge, in various machines. **3.** receiver, receiving-house, of stolen goods. **4.** (arch.) art of fencing; means of defence. [ME, f. DEFENCE]

fĕnce[2] v. **1.** v.i. practise sword-play, use the sword scientifically; (fig.) ~ **with** *question* or *questioner*, parry, evade answering. **2.** v.t. screen, shield, protect, (*from, against*); repel, keep *off* or *out*. **3.** surround (as) with fence, enclose, fortify, (*about, in, round, up*). **4.** v.i. (Of horse etc.) leap fences. **5.** v.i. & t. deal in (stolen goods). **6.** Hence **fě'nc**ER[1] n. (esp. of swordsman or horse). [f. prec.]

fe'nceless (-sl-) a. unenclosed; (poet. or arch.) unfortified, defenceless. [f. FENCE[1] + -LESS]

fe'ncible n. (Hist.) soldier liable only for home service. [ME, f. DEFENSIBLE]

fe'ncing n. In vbl senses; enclosure, railing; fences; material for fences. [f. FENCE[2] + -ING[1]]

fĕnd v. **1.** v.t. ward *off*, keep *away*, repel *from*. **2.** v.i. provide *for* (usu. one*self*). [ME, f. DEFEND]

fe'nder n. thing used to keep something off, prevent collision, etc.; (Naut.) piece of old cable, matting, etc., hung over vessel's side to protect it against impact; **bumper* or mudguard of motor car etc.; guard, esp. metal frame for fire to keep coals from rolling into room; ~**-stool,** long footstool before fender. [ME, f. prec. + -ER[1]]

fĕnĕstĕ'lla n. (Archit.) niche in wall S. of altar holding piscina and often credence. [L, dim. of *fenestra* window]

fenĕ'stra n. (pl. ~e). small hole or opening in bone etc., esp. one of two (~ **ovalis** and ~ **rotunda**) in inner ear; perforation in surgical instrument; (Surg.) hole made by fenestration. [L, = window]

fenĕ'strate a. (Bot. & Zool.) having small window-like perforations or transparent areas. [f. L *fenestratus* p.p. of *fenestrare* (*fenestra* window); see -ATE[2]]

fenĕ'strāted a. having windows; perforated; = prec. (Surg.) having fenestrae. [f. as prec. 1 -ED[1]]

fĕnĕstrā'tion n. (Archit.) arrangement of windows in a building; (Bot. & Zool.) being fenestrate; (Surg.) (operation of making) artificial 'window' in labyrinth of ear, used in some cases of deafness. [f. as prec. + -ATION]

Fē'nian n. & a. (Hist.) **1.** n. member of 19th-c. league among Irish in US & Ireland for promoting revolution and overthrowing British government in Ireland; hence ~ISM (3) n. **2.** a. of Fenians or Fenianism. [f. OIr. *féne* name of ancient Irish race, confused w. *fiann* guard of legendary kings]

fĕnks n. pl. fibrous parts of whale's blubber, refuse of blubber when melted. [19th c.; orig. unkn.]

fe'nnĕc n. small N. Afr. fox notable for its huge pointed ears. [f. Arab. *fanak*]

fe'nnel n. yellow-flowered fragrant umbelliferous herb used in salads and sauces; plant related or similar to this. [f. OE *finugl* etc. & f. OF *fenoil* f. L *feniculum* (*fenum* hay; see -CULE)]

Fĕnnōscā'ndi|a n. region of Scandinavia and Finland as political unit or (Geol.) ancient land-mass; hence ~AN a. [f. G *fennoskandisch* a., f. L *Fenni* Finns + *Scandia* Scandinavia]

fe'nŭgreek n. leguminous plant (*Trigonella foenumgraecum*) with aromatic seeds. [ME, f. OF *fenugrec* f. L *fenugraecum* (*fenum* hay, *Graecus* Greek); used by Romans as fodder]

feoff (fĕf) n. = FEUD[2]. [AF var. of FIEF]

feoffee (fĕfē') n. (Hist.) person to whom freehold estate in land is conveyed by feoffment; ~ **in** or **of trust,** trustee invested with such estate. [ME, f. AF *feoffé* p.p. of *feoffer* f. OF *fie(u)ffer* (as FIEF)]

feo'ffment (fĕ'f-) n. (Hist.) mode of conveying freehold estate by formal transfer of possession. [ME, f. AF *feoffement* (as prec.; see -MENT)]

feo'ffor, feo'ffer, (fĕ'f-) n. (Hist.) one who makes feoffment to another. [ME, f. AF *feoffour* (as FEOFFEE; see -OR)]

ferae naturae (fērē natūr′ē) *a.* (*pred.* or placed after *n.*) not domesticated, living in a wild state, (*hares are, the hare is, ferae naturae; animals ferae naturae*). [L, = of wild nature]

fer′al *a.* wild, untamed, uncultivated; in wild state after escape from captivity; brutal. [f. L *ferus* wild + -AL]

fer de lance (fär de lah′ns) *n.* large and very venomous snake of tropical S. America. [F, = iron (head) of lance]

fe′retory *n.* shrine for saint's relics; chapel in which this was deposited. [ME, f. OF *fiertre* f. L *feretrum* f. Gk *pheretron* (*pherō* bear), w. assim. to wds in *-tory*]

fer′ial *a.* (Eccl.) (Of day) ordinary, not appointed for festival or fast; (of service etc.) for use on ferial day. [ME f. OF, or f. med. L *ferialis* (*feriae*; see FAIR[1], -AL)]

ferma′t|a (-mah′-) *n.* (*pl.* ~as, *or* ~e *pr.* -ä). (Mus.) (sign indicating) unspecified prolongation of note or rest. [It.]

fer′ment[1] *n.* leaven, fermenting-agent; (arch.) enzyme; fermenting, fermentation; agitation, excitement, tumult. [ME f. OF, or f. L *fermentum* (*fervēre* boil; see -MENT)]

ferme′nt[2] *v.i.* & *t.* undergo or subject to fermentation; (cause to) effervesce; excite, stir up, foment; hence ~ABLE *a.* [ME, f. OF *fermenter* f. L *fermentare* (as prec.)]

fermẽntā′tion *n.* process like that induced by leaven in dough, with effervescence, evolution of heat, and change of properties; agitation, excitement; so **fermẽ′ntᴀTIVE** *a.* [ME, f. LL *fermentatio* (as prec.; see -ATION)]

fer′mi *n.* (Phys.) unit of length equal to 10⁻¹⁵ metre. [f. E. *Fermi*, Ital.-Amer. physicist d. 1954]

fer′miŏn *n.* (Phys.) particle obeying relations stated by Fermi and Dirac, with half-integral spin. [f. as prec. + -ON]

fer′mium *n.* (Chem.) artificially made transuranic radioactive metallic element. [f. as FERMI + -IUM]

fern *n.* vascular cryptogam of order Filicales, usu. with feathery fronds; (collect.) quantity of ferns; ~owl, nightjar; hence ~′LESS, ~′Y², *adjs.*, ~′ERY (3) *n.* [OE *fearn*, = MDu. *væren*, OHG *farn* f. WG **farno*]

fero′cious (-shus) *a.* fierce, savage, cruel; hence ~LY² *adv.*, ~NESS *n.* [f. L *ferox -ocis* + -OUS]

fero′city *n.* ferocious character or act. [f. F *férocité* or f. L *ferocitas* (as prec.; see -ITY)]

-ferous *suf.* forming *adjs.* (usu. w. intermediate -I-) w. sense 'bearing, having' (*auriferous, odoriferous*); hence ~LY² *adv. suf.*, ~NESS *n. suf.* [f. or after F *-fère* or L *-fer* producing (*ferre* bear) + -OUS]

fe′rrate *n.* (Chem.) salt of (hypothetical) ferric acid, H_2FeO_4. [f. L *ferrum* iron + -ATE[1] (3)]

fe′rrel. See FERRULE.

fe′rret *n.* half-tamed variety or species of polecat kept for driving rabbits from burrows, killing rats, etc.; searcher, detective; hence ~Y² *a.* [ME, f. OF *fu(i)ret* alt. f. *fu(i)ron* f. LL *furo -onis* f. L *fur* thief]

fe′rret[2] *v.* 1. *v.i.* hunt with ferrets (*go ferreting*); rummage, search about, (*for*). 2. *v.t.* clear out (holes, ground), take or drive away (rabbits etc.), with ferrets (*about, away, out,* etc.); search out (secrets, criminals, etc.). [f. prec.]

fe′rret[3] *n.* (arch.) stout cotton or silk tape. [f. It. *fioretti* floss silk pl. of *fioretto* dim. of *fiore* f. L *flos floris* flower]

ferri- *comb. form.* containing iron, esp. in ferric compounds. [f. L *ferrum* iron + -I-]

fe′rriage *n.* conveyance by or charge for using ferry. [f. FERRY + -AGE]

fe′rric *a.* of iron; (Chem.) containing iron in trivalent form (cf. FERROUS). [f. L *ferrum* iron + -IC]

ferrimā′gnĕtism *n.* form of ferromagnetism with non-parallel alignment of neighbouring atoms or ions; hence **ferrimāgnĕ′tɪc** *a.* [f. F *ferrimagnétisme* (as FERRI-, MAGNETISM)]

Fe′rris *n.* ~ **wheel**, giant revolving vertical wheel with passenger cars on its periphery used at amusement parks etc. [f. G. W. G. *Ferris*, Amer. engineer d. 1896]

fe′rrite *n.* 1. (Chem.) salt of (hypothetical) acid, $H_2Fe_2O_4$, often with magnetic and insulating properties. 2. allotrope of pure iron occurring as solvent in low-carbon steel; hence **ferri′tɪc** *a.* [f. L *ferrum* iron + -ITE[1]]

ferrŏ- *comb. form.* containing iron, esp. in ferrous compounds; (of alloys) containing iron and (*chromium, manganese,* etc.). [f. L *ferrum* iron + -o-]

ferrŏcŏ′ncrēte (-n-k-, -ngk-) *n.* & *a.* (made of) reinforced concrete. [f. FERRO- + CONCRETE[1] 2]

ferrŏélĕ′ctric *a.* & *n.* (Phys.) exhibiting permanent electric polarization and hysteresis when subjected to electric field; hence **ferrŏélĕctri′cɪTY** *n.* [f. ELECTRIC after *ferromagnetic*]

ferrŏmā′gnĕtism *n.* form of magnetism with high variable permeability and with hysteresis, as found in iron etc.; hence **ferrŏmāgnĕ′tɪc** *a.* [f. FERRO- + MAGNETISM]

fe′rrous *a.* containing iron (*ferrous and non-ferrous metals*); (Chem.) containing iron in divalent form (cf. FERRIC). [f. L *ferrum* iron + -OUS]

ferru′ginous (-rōō′-) *a.* of or containing iron-rust, or iron as a chemical constituent; rust-coloured, reddish-brown. [f. L *ferrugo -ginis* rust (*ferrum* iron) + -OUS]

fe′rrule (-ōol, -ul), **fe′rrel,** *n.* metal ring or cap strengthening end of stick or tube; band strengthening or forming joint. [earlier *verrel* etc. f. OF *virelle, virol(e),* f. L *viriola* dim. of *viriae* bracelet; assim. to L *ferrum* iron]

fe′rry *v.* & *n.* 1. *v.t.* & *i.* convey or pass in boat or aircraft, work (craft), (of craft) pass to and fro, over stretch of water; transport (persons or things) from one place to another, esp. as regular service. 2. *n.* place for or means of or service of ferrying; right to operate ferry service; means of transporting astronaut from surface of planet etc. to spacecraft. [ME, f. ON *ferja* n. & v. f. Gmc **farjōn, *farjan (*far-* go)]

fe′rtile *a.* bearing abundantly, fruitful, (lit. or fig.); (of seed, egg, etc.) capable of developing into new individual; able to become a parent; (of nuclear material) able to become fissile by capture of neutrons; F~ **Crescent,** semicircular region from E. Mediterranean to Persian Gulf; so **fe′rtɪ′lɪTY** *n.* [ME f. F, f. L *fertilis*]

fe′rtiliz|e, -is|e (-īz), *v.t.* 1. make (esp. soil) fertile or productive. 2. make (egg etc., female individual or organ, plant) develop new individual by introduction of male reproductive material. 3. Hence ~ABLE *a.*, ~A′TION, ~ER[1] (1, 2), *ns.* [f. prec. + -IZE]

fe′rula (-ōō-) *n.* giant fennel or other plant of genus *Ferula*; = foll. [ME f. L, = giant fennel, rod]

fe′rule (-ōol) *n.,* & *v.t.* (strike with) flat ruler with widened end for punishing boys. [ME, f. as prec.]

fer′vent *a.* hot, glowing; ardent, intense, (*fervent soul, lover, hatred*); hence or cogn. **fer′vency** *n.*, ~LY² *adv.* [ME f. OF, f. L *fervēre* boil; see -ENT]

fer′vid *a.* 1. ardent, intense. 2. (poet.) hot, glowing. 3. Hence ~LY² *adv.* [f. L *fervidus* (as prec.; see -ID[1])]

||fer′vour (-er), ***fer′vor,** *n.* glowing condition, intense heat; vehemence, passion, zeal. [ME f. OF, f. L *fervor -oris* (as FERVENT; see -OR)]

Fe′scĕnnine *a.* obscene or scurrilous (songs, remarks, etc.). [f. L *Fescenninus* (*Fescennia* in Etruria, famous for scurrilous verse; see -INE[1])]

fe′scue *n.* small stick, teacher's pointer; grass of genus *Festuca*, valuable for pasture and fodder. [ME *festu(e)* f. OF *festu* f. Rom. **festucum* f. L *festuca* stalk, straw]

fess[1] *v.i.* ~ (up), (colloq.) = CONFESS. [abbr.]

fess[2], fĕsse, *n.* (Her.) horizontal stripe across middle of shield; ~ **point** (at centre of shield); **in** ~, arranged horizontally. [ME f. OF, f. L *fascia* band]

*fest *n.* festival or special occasion (*filmfest, shooting fest*). [G, = festival]

fe′stal *a.* of a feast; engaging in holiday activities; gay; hence ~LY² *adv.* [OF, f. LL *festalis* (as FEAST; see -AL)]

fe'ster v. **1.** v.i. (Of wound or sore) become purulent or ulcerated; (of poison, disease, grief) cause suppuration, rankle; putrefy, rot. **2.** v.t. cause festering in. [ME, f. obs. *fester* n. or OF *festrir*, f. OF *festre* f. L FISTULA]

fe'stival n. & attrib. a. **1.** n. feast day, celebration, merry-making; periodic musical etc. performance(s) of special importance. **2.** a. of a feast(-day). [n. f. a., ME f. OF, f. med. L *festivalis* (as foll.; see -AL)]

fe'stive a. of a feast; joyous; fond of feasting, jovial; hence ∼LY² (-vlĭ) adv. [f. L *festivus* (*festum*, as FEAST; see -IVE)]

festi'vity n. gaiety, rejoicing; festive celebration, (in pl.) festive proceedings. [ME, f. OF *festivité* or f. L *festivitas* (as prec.; see -ITY)]

festoo'n n., & n.t. **1.** n. chain of flowers or leaves, or ribbons etc., hung in curve between two points; carved or moulded ornament representing this. **2.** v.t. adorn (as) with or form into festoons. **3.** Hence ∼ERY (5) n. [f. F *feston* f. It. *festone* (*festa* FEAST; see -OON)]

Fe'stschrift (-shr-) n. (pl. ∼en or ∼s). collection of writings presented to scholar to mark an occasion in his life. [G, = festival-writing]

***fe'tal**. See FOETAL.

fetch¹ v. & n. **1.** v.t. & i. (go for and) bring back (person or thing; *go and*) *fetch a doctor*); FAR¹-*fetched*; ∼ **and carry**, run backwards and forwards with things, be a mere servant; *fetch a* COMPASS¹; ∼ **up**, come to rest. **2.** v.t. cause to come, draw forth, (blood, tears; ∼ **up**, vomit); bring in, realize, be sold for, (a price); heave (sigh), draw (breath); deal (blow; usu. w. ind. obj., *fetch him a box on the ears*). **3.** move feelings of, delight, whence ∼'ING² a.; irritate. **4.** n. act of fetching; dodge, trick; (Naut.) line of continuous extent of water from point to point, e.g. of a bay or of open sea, or traversed by wind or waves. [OE *fecc(e)an* var. of *fetian*, prob. cogn. w. *fatian*, OHG *fazzōn* grasp]

fetch² n. person's wraith or double. [18th c.; orig. unkn.]

fête (fāt) n., & v.t. **1.** n. festival, great entertainment, (∼-day, appointed for fête); saint's day; bazaar-like function to raise money for charity. **2.** v.t. entertain, make much of, (person). [f. F *fête* (as FEAST)]

fête champêtre (fāt shahñpā'tr) n. outdoor entertainment, rural festival. [F (as prec., *champêtre* rural)]

fe'tid, foe'tid (fē'-), a. stinking; hence ∼LY² adv., ∼NESS n. [f. L *fetidus* (*fetēre* stink; see -ID¹)]

fe'tish n. inanimate object worshipped by primitive peoples for its supposed inherent magical powers or as being inhabited by a spirit; principle etc. irrationally reverenced; (Psych.) abnormal stimulus, or object, of sexual desire; hence ∼ISM (3), ∼IST (2), ns., ∼i'stIC a. [f. F *fétiche* f. Port. *feitiço* charm, orig. adj. = made by art, f. L *factitius* FACTITIOUS]

fe'tlock n. part of horse's leg where tuft of hair grows behind pastern-joint. [ME *fet(e)lak* etc. corresp. to MHG *vizzeloch*; rel. to G *fessel* & Gmc *fet-* f. IE *ped-*; cf. FOOT¹]

fe'tor n. stench. [L (as FETID; see -OR)]

fe'tter n., & v.t. **1.** n. shackle for the feet; bond, (in pl.) captivity; check, restraint; ∼lock, (heraldic representation of) D-shaped fetter for tethering horse by leg. **2.** v.t. bind (as) with fetters; impede, restrain. [OE *feter*, = OS *feteros*, OHG *fezzera*, ON *fjǫturr* f. Gmc *feterō*, *feteraz* (*fet-*; cf. FOOT¹)]

fe'ttle n., & v.t. **1.** n. condition, trim, (*in good*, *fine*, etc. *fettle*). **2.** v.t. trim, clean, (rough edge of metal casting, pottery before firing, etc.); hence ∼ER¹ n., (|)esp.) railway maintenance worker. [n. f. v., f. dial. n. = girdle, f. OE *fetel*, OHG *fezzil* chain, ON *fetill* bandage f. Gmc *fatilaz* (*fat*hold)]

***fe'tus**. See FOETUS.

eu n., & v.t. (Sc.) **1.** n. perpetual lease at fixed rent; piece of land so held. **2.** v.t. grant (land) on feu. [OF (see FEE)]

eud¹ n., & v.i. **1.** n. lasting mutual hostility (*be at feud with*), esp. between two tribes, families, etc., with

murderous assaults in revenge for previous injury. **2.** v.i. conduct feud, whence *∼'IST (1) n. [ME *fede*, f. OF *feide*, *fede* f. MDu., MLG *vēde* = OHG *fēhida*, OE *fǣhthu* enmity f. Gmc *faihithō* (*faih-*; cf. FOE)]

feud² n. land held under feudal system or in fee, fief. [f. med. L *feudum* (see FEE)]

feu'dal a. of a feud or fief; ∼ **system**, medieval European form of government based on relation of vassal and superior arising from holding of lands on condition of homage and service; of, resembling, according to, this system; hence ∼ISM (3), ∼IST (2), ns., ∼i'stIC a., ∼IZE (3) v.t., ∼LY² adv. [f. med. L *feudalis*, *feodalis* (*feudum*, *feodum* FEE 1, perh. f. Gmc; see -AL)]

feudà'lity n. feudal system or principles; feudal holding, fief. [f. F *féodalité* (*féodal* f. as prec.; see -ITY)]

feu'datory a. & n. **1.** a. feudally subject *to*, under overlordship. **2.** n. feudal vassal. [f. med. L *feudatorius* f. *feudare* enfeoff (as FEUD²; see -ATE³, -ORY)]

feu de joie (fẽr də zhwah') n. (pl. **feux** pr. same). salute by firing rifles etc. on ceremonial occasion. [F, = fire of joy]

feuilleton (fẽr'yetawñ) n. (part of newspaper etc. devoted to) fiction, criticism, light literature, etc. [F, = leaflet]

fe'ver n., & v.t. **1.** n. (Path.) abnormally high temperature with excessive change and destruction of tissues; disease so characterized (*scarlet*, *typhoid*, *fever*); nervous excitement, agitation; ∼ **heat**, high temperature of body in fever, (fig.) fever pitch; ∼ **pitch**, state of abnormal excitement; ∼ **therapy**, treatment of disease by artificially causing fever. **2.** v.t. throw into fever; affect with fever (*fevered brow*). [f. OE *fēfor* & f. AF *fevre*, OF *fievre* f. L *febris*]

fe'verfew n. feathery-leaved herb (*Chrysanthemum parthenium*) formerly used as febrifuge. [f. OE *feferfuge* f. L *febrifuga* (as FEBRIFUGE)]

fe'verish a. having symptoms of fever; excited, fitful, restless; (of place) infested by fever, feverous; hence ∼LY² adv., ∼NESS n. [ME, f. FEVER + -ISH¹]

fe'verous a. infested with or apt to cause fever; (arch.) feverish. [ME, f. FEVER + -OUS]

few a. & n. **1.** not many (*few words*, *only a few words*; *man of few* WORD¹*s*; *many are called but few are chosen*; *visitors are few*); **every** ∼ *days* etc., once in every small group of days etc.; **in** ∼, (arch.) in few words, briefly; **no** ∼**er than**, as many as (specified number); **not a** ∼, a considerable number; **the** ∼, the minority, the elect, etc.; hence ∼'NESS n ?. **a** ∼, some, not none, (*a few words should be added*; *a few of his friends were there*); **a good** ∼, **quite a** ∼, (colloq.) a fairly large number; **have a** ∼, (colloq.) take several alcoholic drinks; **some** ∼, some but not at all many. [OE *fēawe*, *fēawa*, – OS, OHG *fao*, ON *fár*, Goth. pl. *fawai* f. Gmc *faw-* f. IE *pau-*]

fey (fā) a. **1.** (Sc.) fated to die, at point of death. **2.** disordered in mind (often with over-confidence etc.) like person about to die; clairvoyant, other-worldly; elfin; whimsical. **3.** Hence ∼'NESS n. [OE *fǣge*, = OS *fēgi*, OHG *feigi*, ON *feigr* f. Gmc *faigjaz*]

fez n. (pl. ∼'zes). (esp. Muslim) man's flat-topped conical red cap with tassel; hence ∼ZED² (-zd) a. [Turk., perh. f. *Fez* (now *Fès*) in Morocco]

ff. abbr. folios; following pages etc.; fortissimo.

fia'cre (fēah'kr) n. small four-wheeled cab. [f. the Hôtel de St. F∼, Paris]

fiancé (fēah'ñsā) n. (fem. ∼e pr. same). person who is betrothed to another (esp. *my*, *your*, etc., *fiancé*). [F, p.p. of *fiancer* betroth f. OF *fiance* a promise]

fianchè'tto n. (pl. ∼es), & v.t. (Chess). develop(ment of) bishop on longest diagonal of board. [It., dim. of *fianco* FLANK]

fiä'scō n. (pl. ∼s). failure or breakdown (orig. in dramatic etc. performance); ignominious result. [It., = bottle (w. unexplained allusion); see FLASK]

fi'at (-ăt, -at) n. authorization; decree, order; ***∼ money**, inconvertible paper-money made legal tender by Government decree. [L, = let it be done]

fib *n.*, & *v.i.* (**-bb-**). (tell) trivial or venial lie; hence ~'ber[1], ~'ster, *ns.* [perh. f. obs. *fible-fable* nonsense, redupl. of FABLE[1]]

***fi'ber**. See FIBRE.

Fibona'cci (fēbonah'chĭ) *n.* ~ **numbers, series,** (in which each is the sum of the two preceding, esp. 1, 1, 2, 3, 5, 8, etc.). [f. L. ~, Tuscan mathematician *c.* 1200]

||**fi'bre** (-ber), ***fi'ber**, *n.* **1.** threadlike cell or filament forming with others animal or vegetable tissue or textile substance; threadlike piece of glass etc. (~ **optics,** transmission of images through glass etc. fibres by total internal reflection). **2.** substance consisting of fibres; substance that can be spun, woven, or felted. **3.** fibrous structure; structure, grain, character, (*lacks moral fibre; man of coarse fibre*). **4.** ~**board,** building material made of wood or other plant fibres compressed into boards; ~**glass,** (1) fibrous glass woven as fabric or used as insulator etc., (2) plastic containing this. **5.** Hence (**-**)**fi'br**ED[2], ***(-)fi'ber**ED[2], (-berd), ~**LESS** (-erl-), **fi'bri**FORM, **fi'br**OUS, *adjs.* [ME f. F, f. L *fibra*]

fi'bril *n.* small fibre; subdivision of fibre; ultimate subdivision of root; hence ~lAR, ~lARY[1], *adjs.* [f. mod. L *fibrilla* dim. of L *fibra* fibre]

fi'brill|ate *v.* **1.** *v.i.* (Of fibre) split up into fibrils; (of muscle, esp. in heart) undergo quivering movement in fibrils. **2.** *v.t.* break (fibre) into fibrils. **3.** Hence ~A'TION *n.* [f. as prec.+-ATE[3]]

fi'brin *n.* insoluble protein formed in blood-clotting from the soluble blood-plasma protein **fibri'no**GEN *n.*; hence ~OID *n.*, substance with same staining--behaviour as fibrin. [f. FIBRE+-IN]

fi'brō *n.* (*pl.* ~s). (Austral.) (house constructed mainly of) fibro-cement. [abbr.]

fi'brō- *comb. form.* fibre (||~**-cement,** mixture of asbestos and cement used in sheets for building etc.); fibrous tissue. [f. FIBRE+-O-]

fi'broid *a.* & *n.* **1.** *a.* (esp. Path.) of or characterized by fibrous structure or appearance. **2.** *n.* fibroid uterine tumour. [f. FIBRE+-OID]

fi'brōin *n.* chemical substance of which silk (etc.) mainly consists. [f. FIBRO-+-IN]

fibrō'ma *n.* (*pl.* ~s or ~ta). fibrous tumour. [mod. L, f. L *fibra* fibre+-OMA (2)]

fibrō's|is *n.* (*pl.* ~es *pr.* -ēz). (Path.) development of excessive fibrous tissue; hence **fibro'**TIC *a.* [mod. L, f. L *fibra* fibre+-OSIS]

fibrosi'tis *n.* rheumatic painful inflammation or disorder of fibrous tissue; hence **fibrosi'**TIC *a.* [mod. L (*fibrosus* FIBROUS; see -ITIS)]

fi'brous. See FIBRE.

fi'bul|a *n.* (*pl.* ~ae or ~as). (Anat.) outer and usu. smaller of two bones from knee to ankle; (Ant.) brooch or clasp; hence ~AR[1] *a.* [L, perh. cogn. w. *figere* fix]

-fic *suf.* forming (usu. w. intermediate -i-) *adjs.* w. sense 'producing, making' (*beatific, horrific, malefic, pacific, scientific*); hence ~fiCALLY *adv. suf.* [f. or after F -*fique* or L -*ficus* (*facere* make)]

-fica'tion *suf.* forming (usu. w. intermediate -i-) *ns.* of action etc. (cf. -ATION) f. *vbs.* in -FY (*acidification, beautification, purification*). [f. or after F, or L -*ficatio -onis* (-*ficare*; see -FY)]

fiche (fēsh) *n.* (*pl.* same). = MICRO*fiche*. [F, = slip of paper]

fi'chu (-shōō) *n.* woman's small triangular shawl for lace etc. for shoulders and neck. [F]

fi'ckle *a.* inconstant, changeable; hence ~NESS (-keln-) *n.*, **fi'ck**LY[2] *adv.* [OE *ficol*; cf. *befician* deceive, *fǽcne* deceitful, -LE 1]

fi'ctile *a.* made of earth or clay by potter; of pottery. [f. L *fictilis* (*fingere fict-* fashion; see -IL)]

fi'ction *n.* feigning, invention; thing feigned or imagined, invented statement or narrative; literature consisting of such narrative, esp. novels, whence ~EER', ~IST (3), *ns.*; conventionally accepted false-

hood (esp. LEGAL, *polite, fiction*); hence ~AL *a.*, ~al**IZE** (3) *v.t.* [ME f. OF, f. L *fictio -onis* (as prec.; see -ION)]

ficti'tious (-shus) *a.* counterfeit, not genuine; (of name or character) assumed; imaginary, unreal; of or in novels; regarded as what it is called by legal or conventional fiction; hence ~LY[2] *adv.*, ~NESS *n.* [f. L *ficticius* (as FICTILE; see -ITIOUS[1])]

fi'ctive *a.* creating or created by imagination; not genuine. [f. F *fictif -ive* or f. med. L *fictivus* (as FICTILE; see -IVE)]

fid *n.* **1.** (Naut.) conical wooden pin used in splicing; square wooden or iron bar to support topmast. **2.** small thick piece or wedge or heap of anything. [17th c.; orig. unkn.]

||**Fid. Def.** *abbr.* Defender of the Faith. [f. L *Fidei Defensor*]

fi'ddle *n.* & *v.* **1.** *n.* (colloq. or derog.) violin; **fit as a** ~, in good condition and spirits; **face as long as a** ~, dismal face; **play first, second,** ~, take leading, subordinate, position. **2.** other instrument of viol family; (Naut.) contrivance for stopping things from rolling or sliding off table in bad weather. **3.** (sl.) piece of cheating, swindle. **4.** ~**-back,** fiddle-shaped back of chair or front of chasuble; ~**-de-dee'** *int.* & *n.* nonsense; ~**-head,** scroll-like carving at ship's bows; ~ **pattern** (of spoons and forks with fiddle-shaped handles); ~**stick,** bow for fiddle, (usu. in *pl.*, as *int.*) nonsense! **5.** *v.i.* & *t.* play the fiddle, play (tune etc.) on fiddle; be idle or frivolous, make aimless movements, (*about, at, with,* etc.); (sl.) cheat, swindle falsify, get by cheating. [OE *fithele*, = OHG *fidula*, ON *fithla* f. Gmc **fithula* f. Rom. **vitula* VIOL]

fi'ddle-fāddle *n.*, *a.*, *v.i.*, & *int.* **1.** *n.* trifling or trivia matter(s). **2.** *a.* (Of person or thing) petty, fussy. **3.** *v.i.* fuss, trifle. **4.** *int.* nonsense!. [redupl. of prec.]

fi'ddler *n.* player on fiddle (F~'s Green, sailor' Elysium); (sl.) swindler, cheat; small crab of genu *Uca,* the male having one large claw held in positior like violinist's arm. [OE *fithelere* as prec.; see -ER[1]]

fi'ddling *a.* In vbl senses; petty; futile, contemptible inconsiderable; (colloq.) = foll. [f. FIDDLE+-ING[2]]

fi'ddly *a.* (colloq.) awkward or tiresome to do or use [f. FIDDLE+-Y[2]]

fi'de|ism *n.* doctrine that knowledge depends on faith or revelation; so ~IST (2) *n.*, ~i'st**IC** *a.* [f. L *fide* faith+-ISM]

Fidě'l|ism *n.* = CASTROISM; hence ~IST (2) *n.* [f. Sp *Fidelismo* (*Fidel Castro Ruz*; see -ISM)]

fidě'lity *n.* faithfulness, loyalty, (*to*); strict conformity to truth or fact; exact correspondence to the original (Radio etc.) precision of reproduction (HIGH *fidelity*). ~ **insurance** (by employer against losses by em ployees' fault). [f. F *fidélité* or f. L *fidelitas* (see FEALTY)]

fi'dget[1] *n.* **1.** (in *sing.* or *pl.*) bodily uneasiness seekin relief in spasmodic movements; restless mood. **2.** *n* who fidgets or causes others to; act of bustling etc. **3** Hence ~Y[2] *a.* [sense 1 f. obs. or dial. *fidge* to twitch sense 2 f. foll.]

fi'dget[2] *v.* **1.** *v.i.* move restlessly (*about*); be uneasy worry. **2.** *v.t.* make uncomfortable, worry, (*person* [f. prec.]

Fi'dō *n.* device for enabling aircraft to land b dispersing fog by means of petrol-burners on ground [f. initials of *Fog Intensive Dispersal Operation*]

fidū'cial (-shal) *a.* ~ **line, point,** etc., (Surv Astron., etc.) one assumed as fixed basis of com parison. [f. LL *fiducialis* (*fiducia* trust f. *fidere* to trus see -AL)]

fidū'ciar|y (-sherĭ) *a.* & *n.* **1.** *a.* of trust or trustee(ship held or given in trust; (of paper currency) dependin for its value on public confidence or securities. **2.** *n* trustee. [f. L *fiduciarius* (as prec.; see -ARY[1])]

fidus Achates (fīdus akā'tēz) *n.* faithful friend, de voted follower. [L, = faithful Achates (companio of Aeneas in Virgil's *Aeneid*)]

fie *int.* expr. disgust or pretence of outraged propriety [ME, f. OF f. L *fi* excl. of disgust at stench]

fief (fēf) *n.* = FEUD²; one's sphere of operation or control; hence ∼'DOM *n.* [F, f. as FEE]

field *n.* & *v.* **1.** *n.* (piece of) ground, esp. one used for pasture or tillage, and usu. bounded by hedges etc.; tract abounding in some natural product (*coalfield, diamond field, gas field, oilfield*); = AIR¹*field*, PLAYING--*field*, etc. **2.** ground on which battle is fought, battlefield (lit., or fig., *left his rival in possession of the field*; **a fair** ∼ **and no favour,** equal conditions in contest; ∼ **of honour** (where duel or battle is fought); **hold the** ∼, not be superseded); scene of campaign (**in the** ∼, campaigning, (fig.) working etc. outside headquarters, laboratory, etc.; **take, keep, the** ∼, begin, continue, campaign); battle. **3.** ground for playing cricket, football, etc.; part of this as area of attack or defence; player(s) stationed in such area; players or partakers in outdoor contest or sport; all competitors or all except specified one(s) (**a good** ∼, many and good competitors; *∼play the ∼, (colloq.) avoid exclusive commitment to one person etc.); (Cricket) side not batting, one of this side (LONG¹*field*). **4.** large stretch, expanse, of sea, sky, ice, snow, etc., (lit., or fig., *the whole field of history*). **5.** (Her.) surface of escutcheon or of one of its divisions; groundwork of picture, coin, flag, etc. **6.** area or sphere of operation, observation, intellectual activities, etc., (*each supreme in his own field; filled the field of the telescope; field of view; wide field of vision*); region of electric, gravitational, magnetic, etc., influence; presence of such influence, force exerted by it on standard object. **7.** *attrib.* (Of animal etc.) found in the open country (*field-mouse*); carried out in the natural environment (*field test*); (of artillery etc.) light and mobile for use with armies in the field. **8.** ∼**-book** (used in field by surveyor for technical notes); ∼ **boot** (knee-length and close-fitting); ∼**-cornet,** magistrate of township in Cape Province etc.; ∼**-day,** (Mil.) manœuvring--exercise or review, (fig.) great occasion, important debate, great triumph; ∼ **events,** athletic sports such as weight putting, jumping, discus-throwing, etc. (i.e. other than races); ∼**-glasses,** binoculars for outdoor use; ∼ **goal,** (Amer. Footb., Basketball) goal scored when ball is in normal play; *∼ **hockey,** = HOCKEY; ∼ **hospital,** temporary hospital near battlefield; ||F∼ **Marshal,** army officer of highest rank; ∼ **mustard,** charlock; ∼ **officer,** ∼ **rank,** (rank of) army officer above captain and below general; ∼**'sman** (-z-), (Cricket & Baseball) member of side not batting; ∼ **sports,** outdoor sports, esp. hunting, shooting, fishing; ∼**'stone** (used in its natural form); ∼ **telegraph** (movable kind for use on campaign); ∼ **work,** (1) temporary fortification, (2) outdoor work of surveyor, collector of scientific data, sociologist, etc.; so ∼**-worker. 9.** *v.i.* act as fieldsman in cricket, baseball, etc. **10.** *v.t.* stop (and return) (ball); put (football team etc.) into the field; (fig.) deal with (succession of questions etc.) **11.** Hence ∼'ER¹ *n.,* ∼'WARD(s) *adv.* [OE *feld,* = OS, OHG *feld* f. WG *felthu*]

fie'ldfāre *n.* species of thrush (*Turdus pilaris*) spending winter, not summer, in Britain etc. [ME *feldefare,* perh. f. as FIELD + FARE²]

fiend *n.* the Devil; evil spirit, demon; person of superhuman wickedness, esp. cruelty; person causing mischief or annoyance; (w. qualifying wd) devotee or addict (*fresh-air fiend, dope fiend, camera fiend*); hence ∼'ISH¹, ∼'LIKE, adjs. [OE *fēond,* = OS *fiond,* OHG *fiant,* ON *fjándi,* Goth. *fijands* pres. part. of Gmc *fijējan* hate; cf. FRIEND]

fierce *a.* violent in hostility, angrily combative; raging, vehement; (of mechanism) violent, not smooth or easy in action; ardent, eager; unpleasantly strong or intense; hence ∼'LY² (-slī) *adv.,* ∼'NESS (-sn-) *n.* [ME, f. AF *fers,* OF *fiers/fier* proud f. L *ferus* savage]

ieri fā'ciăs (-shī-) *n.* (Law). writ to sheriff for executing judgement. [L, = cause to be made]

fier'|y (fīr'ī) *a.* consisting of or flaming with fire (∼y

cross, wooden cross charred or set on fire as rallying--signal in Scotland or *intimidating symbol); (of arrow etc.) fire-bearing; looking like fire, blazing-red; (of eyes) flashing, ardent; hot as fire; acting like fire, producing burning sensation, inflaming, (*fiery taste, condiment,* etc.); eager, pugnacious, spirited, irritable (*fiery temper*); (of horse) mettlesome; (of gas, mine, etc.) inflammable, liable to explosions; (of cricket--pitch) making ball rise dangerously; hence ∼iLY² *adv.,* ∼iNESS *n.* [ME, f. FIRE¹ + -Y¹]

fie'sta (fēē'-) *n.* religious festival in Spanish-speaking countries; festivity, holiday. [Sp., = feast]

FIFA (fē'fa) *abbr.* International Football Federation. [f. F *Fédération Internationale de Football Associations*]

fi. fa. *abbr.* fieri facias.

fife *n.* & *v.* **1.** *n.* kind of small shrill flute used with drum in military music; its player. **2.** *v.i.* & *t.* play the fife; play (air etc.) on the fife; hence **fi'fER¹** *n.* [f. G *pfeife* PIPE¹, or F *fifre* f. Swiss G *pfifre* piper]

fi'fe-rail (-fr-) *n.* (Naut.) rail round mainmast with belaying-pins. [18th c., of unkn. orig.]

fifteen (-ē'n, fī'f-) *a.* & *n.* one more than fourteen; symbol for this (15, xv, XV); size etc. denoted by fifteen; (Rugby Footb.) team of fifteen players; **the F∼,** Jacobite rebellion of 1715; hence ∼TH² *a.* & *n.* [OE *fiftēne,* = OS *fiftein,* OHG *fimfzehan,* ON *fimtán,* Goth. *fimftaihun* (as FIVE, -TEEN)]

fifth *a.* & *n.* **1.** *a.* next after fourth; ∼ **part,** one of five equal parts into which thing is or might be divided. **2.** *n.* fifth part, thing, etc.; (Mus.) (note at) interval of which the span involves five alphabetical notes, harmonic combination of notes thus separated; *(colloq.) (bottle containing) fifth of a gallon of liquor. **3.** ∼ **column,** organized body sympathizing with and working for the enemy within a country at war etc. [f. Gen. Mola's ref. to such support in besieged Madrid 1936]; ∼**-co'lumnist,** member of fifth column, traitor, spy; ∼ **day,** Thursday; F∼ **Monarchy,** last of the five great empires (Dan. 2: 44); F∼**-monarchy-man,** 17th-c. zealot expecting immediate second coming of Christ and repudiating all other government; **smite under the** ∼ **rib,** (arch.) kill; ∼ **wheel,** (1) extra wheel of coach, (2) superfluous person or thing, (3) horizontal turntable over front axle of carriage as extra support to prevent its tipping. **4.** Hence ∼'LY² *adv.,* in the fifth place. [earlier & dial. *fift* f. OE *fīfta,* OS *fīfto,* OHG *fimfto,* ON *fimti* f. Gmc *fimfton* f. IE *penqto-*; assim. to *fourth*]

fi'ftў *a.* & *n.* **1.** five times ten; symbol for this (50, l, L); set of fifty persons or things; (in *pl.*) numbers etc., esp. years of a century or life, from 50 to 59; large indefinite number (*have fifty things to tell you*); ∼-∼ *adv.* & *a.,* (colloq.) half and half, with equal shares (*go fifty--fifty; on a fifty-fifty basis*) or chances; hence **fi'ftiETH¹** *a.* & *n.,* ∼FOLD *a.* & *adv.* **2.** ∼**-one** etc., (arch.) **one--and-**∼ etc., fifty plus one etc., w. corresp. ordinals ∼**-first** etc. [OE *fiftig,* = OS *fīftich,* OHG *fimzug,* ON *fimmtigr,* Goth. *fimftigjus* (as FIVE, -TY²)]

fig¹ *n.* **1.** ∼(-tree), broad-leaved tree, esp. *Ficus carica,* bearing soft pear-shaped many-seeded fruit eaten fresh or dried; fruit of this tree. **2.** valueless thing (*don't care a fig for; a fig for—!,* as excl.). **3.** ∼**-bird,** Austral. oriole feeding on figs etc.; ∼**-leaf,** device for concealing something, esp. genitals (Gen. 3:7); ∼**'wort,** brown-flowered herb of genus *Scrophularia,* formerly thought useful against scrofula. [ME, f. OF *figue* f. Prov. *fig(u)a* f. Rom. *fica* f. L *ficus*]

fig² *n.* dress, equipment, (*in full fig*); condition, form, (*in fine or good fig*). [f. foll.]

fig³ *v.t.* (-gg-). ∼ **out** or **up,** make (horse) lively; ∼ **out,** dress up (person). [var. of obs. *feague* f. G *fegen*; see FAKE²]

fig. *abbr.* figure.

fight (fīt) *v.* (**fought** *pr.* fawt). **1.** *v.i.* contend in war or battle or single combat (*against, with*; ∼ **for,** fight on behalf of (person) or to secure (thing)); ∼ **back,** resist; ∼ **shy of,** be unwilling to approach (person, task, etc.); *that* COCK[1] *won't fight.* **2.** *v.t.* maintain (cause, suit at law, quarrel) against opponent, contend over (question, election), make one's *way* by fighting; contend with in war or battle or duel, or with the fists; strive to overcome (disease, fire, fear, etc.); cause (cocks, dogs) to fight; handle (troops, ship) in battle; ∼ **back** or **down,** suppress (one's feelings); ∼ **off,** repel with effort; ∼ (dispute etc., or *it*) **out,** settle by fighting. [OE *feohtan,* = OS, OHG *fehtan* f. WG **fehtan*]

fight[2] (fīt) *n.* act of fighting; battle (**make a** ∼ **of it, put up a** ∼, offer resistance); combat, esp. unpremeditated, between two or more persons, animals, or parties (**running** ∼, fight kept up while one party flees and one pursues; SHAM *fight*; STAND[1]-*up fight*); boxing-match; (fig.) strife, conflict; appetite or ability for fighting (*has fight in him yet*; **show** ∼, not yield tamely). [OE *feoht(e)* (as prec.)]

fi'ghter (fī't-) *n.* In vbl senses; fast military aircraft designed mainly for aerial combat; ∼**-bomber,** aircraft serving as both fighter and bomber. [ME, f. FIGHT[1] + -ER[1]]

fi'ghting (fī't-) *a.* & *n.* In vbl senses; ***∼ **chair,** fixed chair on boat for person catching large fish; ∼ **chance,** opportunity of succeeding by great effort; *fighting* COCK[1]; ∼ **drunk,** (colloq.) drunk and quarrelsome; ∼ **fish,** Siamese fish of genus *Betta*; ∼ **fit,** fit enough to fight, at peak of fitness; ∼ **fund,** money raised to support campaign etc.; ∼ **mad,** furiously angry; ∼**-top,** (Naut.) circular gun-platform high on warship's mast; *in fighting* TRIM; ∼ **words,** (colloq.) words indicating willingness to fight. [f. FIGHT[1] + -ING[1,2]]

fi'gment *n.* invented statement; thing that has no existence except in imagination. [ME, f. L *figmentum* (*fig*- see FIGURE[1], -MENT)]

figura (figūr′a) *n.* person or thing representing or symbolizing fact etc.; (Theol.) type of a person etc. [mod. L, f. L, = FIGURE[1]]

fi'gural *a.* figurative; pertaining to figures or shapes; (Mus.) florid, with rapid repetitive accompaniment. [OF, or f. LL *figuralis* (*figura* FIGURE[1]; see -AL)]

figurant (fī′gŭrant) *n.* (*fem.* **figurante**[1] *pr.* same). ballet-dancer appearing only in a group. [F, pres. part. of *figurer* FIGURE[2]]

figurant|e[2] (figŭrä′ntĭ) *n.* (*pl.* ∼**i** *pr.* -ē). = prec. [It., pres. part. of *figurare* FIGURE[2]]

figura'tion *n.* assignment to a certain form; the resulting form; shape, outline; allegorical representation; ornamentation by designs; (Mus.) use of florid counterpoint. [ME f. F, or f. L *figuratio* (as FIGURE[2]; see -ATION)]

fi'gurative (-gūr-, -ger-) *a.* emblematic, typical; of pictorial or sculptural representation; metaphorical, not literal; metaphorically so called; abounding in or addicted to figures of speech; hence ∼LY[2] (-vlī) *adv.*, ∼NESS (-vn-) *n.* [ME, f. LL *figurativus* (as prec.; see -ATIVE)]

fi'gure[1] (-ger) *n.* **1.** external form, shape; (Geom.) two-dimensional space enclosed by line(s) or three--dimensional space enclosed by surface(s), or any of the classes of these, as triangle, sphere; bodily shape (*has a well-developed figure*; **keep** one's ∼, not grow stout). **2.** person as seen (*saw a figure leaning against the door*; ∼ **of fun,** grotesque person); person as contemplated mentally (*the most terrible figure in our history*; FATHER[1]-*figure*; **public** ∼, person known to many); conspicuous appearance (**make** or **cut a brilliant, poor,** etc., ∼, produce such impression). **3.** image, likeness; representation of human form, statue, person in picture, emblem, type, simile. **4.** diagram, illustrative drawing; horoscope; decorative pattern (*figure in the* CARPET); evolution in dancing, division of set dance; (Skating) movement, series of movements, beginning and ending at centre. **5.** numerical symbol, esp. one of the ten in Arabic notation (**double** ∼**s,** number from 10 to 99; **three, four,** etc., ∼**s,** number

from 100 to 999, from 1,000 to 9,999, etc., whence **three** etc. **-figure** *a.*; *figure of* EIGHT); number so expressed, amount of money, value; (in *pl.*) arithmetical calculations. **6.** ∼ (**of speech**), recognized form of rhetorical expression giving variety, force, etc., esp. hyperbole or metaphor. **7.** (Gram.) permitted deviation from rules of construction, e.g. ellipsis. **8.** (Logic). particular form of syllogism according to position of middle term. **9.** (Mus.) short succession of notes producing single impression, brief melodic or rhythmic formula out of which longer passages are developed. **10.** ∼**-head,** (1) carving, usu. bust or full--length figure, over ship's cutwater, (2) nominal leader or president without real authority. **11.** Hence ∼LESS (-gerl-) *a.* [ME f. OF, f. L *figura* (**fig*- st. of *fingere* fashion; see -URE)]

fi'gure[2] (-ger) *v.* **1.** *v.t.* represent in diagram or picture; picture mentally, imagine; be symbol of, represent typically; embellish with pattern (*figured satin*) or (Mus.) figures; mark with numbers (*figured* BASS[3]) or prices; calculate; ***understand, ***ascertain; ∼ **out,** work out by arithmetic or logic, ***estimate, ***understand. **2.** *v.i.* do arithmetic; make appearance, appear, be conspicuous; ***(colloq.) be likely or understandable (*that figures*); ***∼ **on,** count on, expect. [ME, f. OF *figurer* f. L *figurare* (as prec.)]

fi'gurine (-ēn) *n.* statuette. [F, f. It. *figurina* dim. of *figura* FIGURE[1]]

fi'lagree. Var. of FILIGREE.

fi'lament *n.* slender threadlike body, fibre, (esp. in animal or vegetable structure); not easily fusible conducting wire or thread in electric bulb or therm-ionic valve, heated or made incandescent by current; (arch., of air, light, etc.) imaginary portion of stream, row of particles following each other; (Bot.) part of stamen that supports anther; hence ∼ARY[1] (-ĕ′n-), ∼ED[2], ∼OUS (-ĕ′n-), *adjs.* [F, or f. mod. L *filamentum,* f. LL *filare* spin f. L *filum* thread; see -MENT]

fi'lar|i'a *n.* (*pl.* ∼**ae**). parasitic nematode worm introduced into the blood by certain flies and mosquitoes; hence ∼AL *a.*, **filari′**ASIS *n.* [mod. L, f. L *filum* thread (see -AR[1], -IA[1])]

fi'lature *n.* (establishment for) reeling silk from cocoons. [F, f. It *filatura* (*filare* spin; see -URE)]

fi'lbert *n.* (nut of) cultivated hazel. [ME *philliberd* f. AF *philbert,* dial. F *noix de filbert,* nut ripe about St Philibert's day (20 Aug.)]

filch *v.t.* steal, pilfer. [16th-c. thieves' sl., of unkn orig.]

file[1] *n.,* & *v.t.* **1.** *n.* instrument usu. of steel with roughened surface(s) for shaping or smoothing objects; (sl.) (esp. artful) person; ∼**-fish** (with skin like surface of file). **2.** *v.t.* smooth or shape with file, elaborate to perfection (esp. literary work); ∼ **away,** remove (roughness etc.) with file. [OE *fīl* = OS OHG *fīla* f. WG **fīhalā*]

file[2] *n.,* & *v.t.* **1.** *n.* stiff pointed wire on which documents etc. are run for keeping; folder etc. for holding papers arranged for reference; set of papers so kept, esp. in office, or in lawcourt referring to a cause; series of issues of a newspaper etc. in order; collection of records stored for use by computer. **2.** *v.t.* place (papers) on file or among public records; submit (application for patent, petition for divorce, etc.) to appropriate authority; (of reporter) send (information, story, etc.) to newspaper. [f. F *fil* f. L *filum* thread]

file[3] *n.,* & *v.i.* **1.** *n.* (Mil. etc.) line of persons one behind another (**single, Indian,** ∼, arrangement o marchers etc. in file, with no two abreast); smal detachment *of* men (now usu. two); row of persons or things one behind another; (Chess) line of squares from player to player (cf. RANK[1]). **2.** *v.i.* march in file ∼ **off, away,** go off by files. [f. F *file* f. LL *filare* spin or f. L *filum* thread]

fi'lemot *a.* & *n.* (arch.) dead-leaf colour(ed), brownish yellow. [f. F *feuille morte* dead leaf]

fi'lèt n. kind of net or lace with square mesh; fillet of meat (~ **mignon** pr. me͂'nyawṅ, small tender piece from end of undercut). [F, = thread]

fi'lial a. of or due from son or daughter; (Biol.) resulting from cross-breeding; hence ~LY² adv. [ME f. OF, or f. LL filialis (filius son, filia daughter; see -AL)]

filia'tion n. being child of specified parent(s); descent, transmission, (from); formation of offshoots; branch of a society or language; genealogical relation or arrangement. [F, f. LL filiatio -onis f. L filius son; see -ATION]

fi'libĕg n. (Sc.) kilt. [f. Gael. feileadh-beag little fold]

fi'libŭster n. & v. 1. n. one who engages in unauthorized warfare against foreign State; obstruction(ist) in legislative assembly, esp. by prolonged speaking. 2. v.i. & t. act as filibuster (against); hence ~ER¹ n. [ult. f. Du. vrijbuiter FREEBOOTER infl. by F flibustier, Sp. filibustero]

fi'ligree n. ornamental work of gold or silver or copper as fine wire formed into delicate tracery, fine metal open-work; anything delicate resembling this; hence **fi'ligreED²** a. [earlier filigreen, filigrane f. F filigrane f. It. filigrana (L filum thread, granum seed)]

fi'ling n. In vbl senses; (usu. in pl.) particle(s) rubbed off by file; ~ **cabinet**, case with drawers for storing documents. [f. FILE¹ + -ING¹]

Fillpi'n|ŏ (-pē'-) n. (pl. ~os, fem. ~a) & a. (native or inhabitant) of the Philippine Islands. [Sp., = Philippine]

fill v. & n. 1. v.t. & i. make or become full (with); (of sail) be distended by wind. 2. v.t. stock abundantly; occupy whole capacity or extent of, spread over, pervade, (~ **the bill**, do all that is required, suffice); (of dentist) block up (hollow tooth, cavity) with cement, amalgam, gold, etc.; satisfy, satiate, (esp. in pres. part., of food); (Poker etc.) complete (holding) by drawing necessary cards. 3. hold (position), discharge duties of (office); execute (order, commission, etc.); occupy (vacant time); appoint person to occupy (vacant post). 4. ~ **in**, add material to occupy space within (cavity, outline), add what is wanted to complete (unfinished document, blank cheque, etc.), (sl.) thrash, find occupation during (time of inactivity), *(colloq.) inform (person) more fully, act as substitute; ~ **out**, enlarge, become enlarged, or plumper, to the proper limit, * = fill in (document etc.); ~ **up**, fill completely, provide what is needed to occupy vacant parts or places or deal with deficiencies in, fill in (document etc.), do away with (pond etc.) by filling, fill tank of motor car with petrol, become full; ~-**up** n., thing that fills up. 5. n. as much as one wants of food etc. (drink, have, etc., one's fill; weep her fill); enough to fill something (a fill of ink, tobacco); earth etc. used to fill cavity. [OE fyllan, = OS fullian, OHG fullen, ON fylla, Goth. fulljan f. Gmc *fulljan (*fullaz FULL¹)]

fille fē'ye) n. ~ **de chambre** (de shah'ṅbr), (arch.) chamber-maid; ~ **de joie** (de zhwah'), prostitute. [F, = daughter]

fi'ller n. In vbl senses; object or material used to fill cavity or increase bulk; ~ **cap** (closing filling-pipe leading to petrol tank of motor vehicle). [f. FILL + -ER¹]

fi'llèt n., & v.t. 1. n. fleshy boneless piece of meat from near loins or ribs; ~ (**steak**), undercut of sirloin; thick boneless half or quarter of fish. 2. headband, ribbon, string, or narrow band, for binding the hair or worn round head; band, bandage; thin narrow strip of anything. 3. (Archit.) narrow flat band separating two mouldings; small band between flutes of column. 4. (Her.) horizontal division of shield, quarter of CHIEF¹ in depth. 5. raised rim or ridge on any surface; plain line impressed on cover of book; added structure to round off interior angle. 6. v.t. bind (hair), provide (person for hair), with fillet; encircle with ornamental band; divide (meat, fish) into fillets; remove bones from (fish etc.). [ME f. OF filet f. Rom. dim. of L filum thread; see -ET¹]

fi'lling n. In vbl senses; material used to fill tooth-cavity, sandwich, etc.; *weft; ~-**station**, establishment selling petrol etc. to motorists. [f. FILL + -ING¹]

fi'lip n. & v. 1. n. sudden release of finger or thumb when it has been bent and checked by thumb or finger; slight smart stroke thus given; stimulus, incentive. 2. v.t. propel (coin, marble, etc.) with a fillip; stimulate (fillip one's memory or wits); strike slightly and smartly. 3. v.i. make a fillip. [imit.]

fi'llis n. (Hort.) loosely-twisted string. [f. F filasse tow]

fi'llister n. rabbet(ing-plane) for window-sashes etc. [19th c.; perh. f. F feuilleret]

fi'lly n. young female horse (cf. COLT¹); (sl.) young woman, esp. lively one. [ME, prob. f. ON fylja f. Gmc *fuljōn- (as FOAL).]

film n. & v. 1. n. thin skin, sheet, coating, or layer. 2. (Photog.) coating of emulsion on plastic or other support in form of sheet or rolled strip, single roll of this; ~'**setting**, (Print.) photographic composing; ~-**strip**, series of transparencies for projection, esp. in teaching. 3. story, drama, episode, etc., recorded on cinematographic film and shown in cinemas etc.; (in pl.) the cinema industry; ~-**goer**, one who frequents the cinema; ~-**star**, star actor or actress in films; hence ~ŏ'GRAPHY n., list of films by one director etc. or on one subject, ~IC a. 4. dimness or morbid growth affecting eyes; slight veil of haze etc.; fine thread or filament. 5. Hence ~'Y² a. 6. v.t. & i. cover or become covered (as) with film; photograph (scene, person, etc., or abs.) for the cinema; make cinema film of (book etc., or abs.); be (well or ill) suited for reproduction on film. [OE filmen membrane = OFris. filmene skin, f. WG *filminja ult. f. *fellam FELL¹]

fi'losèlle n. floss silk. [F]

fils (fēs) n. the son, junior, (appended to name to distinguish between father and son of same names; cf. PÈRE). [F, = son]

fi'lter n. & v. 1. n. device for freeing liquids from suspended matter, esp. by passing them through unsized paper or stratum of sand, charcoal, etc.; screen for absorbing light of some or all colours, or X-rays etc.; (Electr.) circuit that attenuates signals outside specified frequency range; arrangement for filtering of traffic. 2. ~-**bed**, (tank or pond containing) layer of sand etc. for filtering large quantities of liquid; ~-**paper**, porous paper for filtering; ~-**tip**, (cigarette) having filter at mouth end to purify the smoke. 3. v.t. & i. pass (liquid, electrical signal, etc.) or flow through filter; make way gradually through, into, etc., percolate, (of news etc.) leak out or come through; (of road traffic) join traffic coming from another direction at junction, esp. when other traffic from one's own direction has to stop; ~ **out**, separate or hold back (as) by filtering. 4. Hence ~ABLE a., (esp., of virus) able to pass through a filter that retains bacteria. [f. F filtre f. med. L filtrum f. WG *filtir FELT¹ (earliest filters being of felt)]

filth n. loathsome dirt; corruption, vileness, pollution, obscenity; foul language. [OE fylth, = OS fūlitha, OHG fūlida (as FOUL, -TH¹)]

fi'lth|y a. & adv. 1. a. loathsomely dirty; obscene; (of weather) very unpleasant; ~y lucre, dishonourable gain (Tit. 1:11); (joc.) money; hence ~iLY² adv., ~iNESS n. 2. adv. filthily (filthy dirty, rich). [ME, f. prec. + -Y²]

fi'ltrable a. Var. of FILTERABLE.

fi'ltrāte¹ n. filtered liquid. [f. as foll. + -ATE² (5)]

fi'ltr|āte² v.t. & i. = FILTER 3; so ~A'TION n. [f. mod. L filtrare (f. as FILTER) + -ATE¹]

fi'mbriate, fi'mbriātĕd, adjs. 1. (Bot. & Zool.) fringed, bordered with hairs etc. 2. (Her.) having a narrow border. [f. L fimbriatus (fimbriae fringe); see -ATE², -ED¹]

fin n. & v. (-nn-). 1. n. organ for propelling and

steering, growing on fish and cetaceans at various parts of body (*anal, caudal, dorsal, pectoral, ventral*, etc., *fin*); underwater swimmer's flipper. **2.** sharp lateral projection on share or coulter of plough; small projecting surface on aircraft or rocket for ensuring stability; similar projection on other devices to improve heat transfer etc.; projecting attachment on motor car (esp. *tail-fin*). **3.** ~-**back**, ~ **whale**, rorqual. **4.** *v.t.* provide with fins. **5.** *v.i.* swim under water. **6.** Hence (-)~ᴍᴇᴅ² (-nd), ~′ʟᴇss, *adjs*. [OE *fin(n)*, = MLG *finne*, MDu. *vinne*]

fi′nable. See FINE¹.

fină′gle *v.i.* & *t.* (colloq.) act or obtain dishonestly or by trickery. [f. dial. *fainaigue* cheat]

fi′nal *a.* & *n.* **1.** *a.* at the end, coming last, ultimate (~ **drive,** last part of transmission system in motor vehicle); putting an end to doubt, conclusive, definitive, unalterable; ~ **solution,** German policy (1941-5) of exterminating Eur. Jews. **2.** concerned with the purpose or end aimed at (~ **cause,** ultimate purpose of a thing; ~ **clause,** (Gram.) one expressing purpose, introduced by *in order that, lest,* etc.). **3.** Hence ~ʟʏ² *adv.* **4.** last or deciding heat or game in sports or competition (Cᴜᴘ¹ *Final*), whence ~ɪsт *n.*, competitor in this; (in *sing.* or *pl.*) last of a series of examinations; edition of newspaper published latest in the day; (Mus.) principal note in any mode. [ME f. OF, or f. L *finalis* (*finis* end; see -ᴀʟ)]

fina′lè (-nah′-) *n.* last movement of instrumental composition, piece of music closing act in opera; close of drama etc.; conclusion. [It., f. as prec.]

fi′nalism *n.* doctrine that natural evolution etc. is directed towards some goal; so **finali′st**ɪᴄ *a.* [f. FINAL + -ISM]

fină′lity *n.* quality or fact of being final; belief that something is final; final act, state, or utterance; principle of final cause viewed as operative in the universe. [f. F *finalité* f. LL *finalitas -tatis* (as FINAL; see -ɪᴛʏ)]

fi′nalīz|e, -īs|e (-īz), *v.t.* complete, bring to an end; put in final form; approve final form or details of; hence ~ᴀ′ᴛɪᴏɴ *n.* [f. FINAL + -IZE]

fină′nce (fĭnă′-, fī′-) *n.*, & *v.t.* **1.** *n.* (in *pl.*) money resources of State, company, or person. **2.** management of (esp. public) money, science of revenue; money support for an undertaking; ~ **company, house,** company mainly concerned with providing money for hire-purchase transactions. **3.** *v.t.* provide with money, esp. capital. [ME f. OF (*finer* settle debt f. *fin* end; see FINE¹, -ANCE)]

fină′ncial (-shǎl) *a.* of revenue or money matters (*financial* YEAR); (Austral. & NZ sl.) possessing money; hence ~ʟʏ² *adv.* [f. prec. + -IAL]

fină′ncier¹ (-shǎl) *n.* one skilled in establishing and managing public funds; capitalist. [F (as FINANCE; see -IER)]

finănci′er′² *v.i.* (usu. derog.) conduct financial operations. [f. prec.]

finch *n.* small passerine bird esp. of genus *Fringilla* (usu. w. defining wd: BULL¹*finch,* GOLD*finch*). [OE *finc,* = OHG *finc(h)o* f. WG **finki,* **finkjo(n)*]

find *v.t.* (**found**), & *n.* **1.** *v.t.* become aware of or get possession of by chance (*was found dead; we find St. John saying; found a treasure*); (sl.) steal. **2.** obtain, receive; ~ **favour,** prove acceptable; ~ one's **feet,** get the use of them, develop one's powers. **3.** recognize as present, acknowledge or discover to be so-and-so, (*I find no sense in it, find the terms reasonable; woke to find myself in hospital; found herself agreeing to this absurd idea; word is not found in the Bible*); **take us as you ~ us,** put up with us as we are; **how do you ~ yourself?,** how are you? **4.** discover by trial to be or do or (*that*) or to (*has been found inadequate; finds rest agreeable; is found to pay; I find it pays, pay, or to pay, or that it pays; find it impossible or necessary to reply* etc.); discover by search; discover (game, or abs.) in hunting; reach by natural or normal process (*water finds its own level*). **5.** succeed in obtaining (money, bail, sureties; *can't find time to read;*

found courage to protest; find it in one's HEART (*to* do); *find expression, place, vent*); (arch.) reach the conscience of; ascertain by study or calculation or inquiry (~ one's **way to,** contrive to reach, arrive at; ~ **its way,** be brought or get *into* etc.). **6.** (Law, of jury etc.) determine and declare (*it,* i.e. the offence, *murder*; person *guilty* etc.; *that* or abs.); ~ **against, for,** decide against, in favour of, (person), judge to be guilty, innocent. **7.** supply, provide, furnish, ~ **in,** provide with (*they found him in clothes*); **all found,** (of servants' wages) with board and lodging provided free. **8.** ~ one**self,** (1) provide for one's own needs, (2) discover one's vocation; ~ **out,** discover, devise, solve, detect in offence. **9.** Hence ~′ᴀʙʟᴇ *a.* **10.** *n.* finding of discovery of treasure, minerals, etc.; thing found; person who comes usefully to notice; ~-**spot,** (Archaeol.) place where object is found. [OE *findan,* = OS, OHG *findan,* ON *finna,* Goth. *finthan* f. Gmc *finthan]

fi′nder *n.* In vbl senses; small telescope attached to large one to locate object for observation; viewfinder of camera; ~s **keepers,** (colloq.) whoever finds a thing is entitled to keep it. [f. prec. + -ᴇʀ¹]

fin de siècle (făn de syā′kl) *a.* characteristic of end of nineteenth century; decadent. [F, = end of century]

fi′nding *n.* In vbl senses; conclusion reached by judicial or other inquiry; *(in *pl.*) small parts or tools used by workmen. [f. FIND + -ɪɴɢ¹]

fine¹ *n.*, & *v.t.* **1.** *n.* sum of money fixed as penalty for offence; (Hist.) sum of money paid by incoming tenant in consideration of only small rent. **2. in** ~, to sum up, finally, in short. **3.** *v.t.* punish by a fine (*fined him £5*); hence **fi′n**ᴀʙʟᴇ *a.* [ME, f. OF *fin* f. med. L *finis* sum paid on settling lawsuit (L *finis* end)]

fine² *a.*, *n.*, *adv.*, & *v.* **1.** *a.* of high quality; clear, pure refined, (of gold or silver) containing specified proportion of pure metal; delicate, subtle, exquisitely fashioned, (of feelings) refined, elevated. **2.** of slender thread, in small particles, thin, sharp (*not to put too fine a* POINT¹ *on it*), (of pen) narrow-pointed; (Cricket behind wicket and near ball's line of flight; (of print, small-sized (cf. SMALL *print*); **cut** or **run it** ~, allow only minimum margin, time, amount, etc. **3.** capable of delicate perception or discrimination; perceptible only with difficulty (*a fine distinction*). **4.** excellent, of striking merit, good, satisfactory, fortunate, of good effect, (*had fine sport; has been a fine thing for him;* (iron.) *a fine friend you have been!, all very fine, but . . .*); well conceived or expressed; of handsome appearance or size, dignified, (*fine potatoes; a man of fine presence*); in good health. **5.** (Of weather etc.) bright and clear free from precipitation or thick fog and with some sunshine, (**one** ~ **day,** once upon a time; **one of these** ~ **days,** some day in the future). **6.** ornate showy, smart, (~ **feathers,** gaudy plumage, lit. or fig.: *fine feathers make fine birds*). **7.** fastidious, dainty pretending refinement, (of speech or writing) affectedly ornate. **8.** complimentary, euphemistic, (*say fine things about person; call things by fine names*). **9.** ~ **arts** those appealing to mind or to sense of beauty, a poetry, music, and esp. painting, sculpture, architecture; *fine* CHEMICALS; ~-**draw,** sew together (tw pieces of cloth, edges of rent, parts of garment) so tha join is imperceptible; ~-**drawn,** subtle, extremely thin; ~ **gentleman, lady,** person of fashion, perso who thinks himself or herself above working; ~-**spun,** delicate, flimsy, (of theory, etc.) excessively subtle, unpractical; ~-**tooth comb,** comb with narrow close-set teeth, (fig.) detailed search. **10** Hence ~′ʟʏ² (-nlī) *adv.*, ~′ɴᴇss (-n-n-) *n.* **11.** *n.* fine weather (*in rain or fine*); (in *pl.*) very small particles in mining, milling, etc. **12.** *adv.* finely; (colloq.) very we (*that will suit me fine*). **13.** *v.t.* & *i.* ~ (**down**), mak (beer) clear; (of liquid) become clear; ~ **away down, off,** make or become finer, thinner, less coarse, (make) dwindle, taper. [ME, f. OF *fin* f. Rom **finus,* f. L *finire* finish, after *grossus, grossire* (GROSS²)]

fine[3] (fēn) *n.* = foll. [abbr.]

fine champagne (fēn shahn̄pah'ny*e*) *n.* old liqueur brandy. [F, = fine (brandy from) Champagne (vineyards in Charente)]

fī'nerў[1] *n.* showy dress or decoration. [f. FINE[2] 6 + -ERY, after *bravery*]

fī'nerў[2] *n.* hearth where cast iron is made malleable or steel made from pig-iron. [f. F *finerie* (*finer* refine, FINE[2] 13; see -ERY)]

fines herbes (fēnz ārʹb) *n. pl.* mixed herbs used in cooking, esp. chopped as omelette-flavouring. [F, = fine herbs]

fĭnĕ'sse *n.* & *v.* **1.** *n.* delicate manipulation, subtle discrimination; artfulness, cunning strategy; (Cards) attempt to take trick with card that is not the highest and might lose to an opponent's card. **2.** *v.i.* use finesse; (Cards) make a finesse. **3.** *v.t.* play (card) by way of finesse; achieve by finesse; evade or trick by finesse. [F, f. Rom. **finitia* (**finus* FINE[2]; see -ESS[2])]

fĭ'nger (-ngg-) *n.*, & *v.t.* **1.** *n.* one of five terminal members of hand (*thumb*, *fore-* or *index finger*, *middle finger*, *ring finger*, *little finger*), or four excluding thumb; **little ~**, (fig.) smallest part of body (*more wit in his little finger than you in your whole body*). **2.** BURN[2] one's *fingers*; CROSS[2] one's *fingers*; one's **~s itch,** one is longing or impatient (*to* do); **lay a ~ on,** touch however slightly; **lift, move, raise, a ~**, make the least effort; **get, pull, take,** one's **~ out,** (sl.) hurry up, begin work in earnest; *finger in* PIE[2]; **point ~ at** (esp. in scorn); **put the ~ on,** (sl.) inform against, identify as victim; **put** one's **~ on,** point with precision to (cause of trouble etc.); **shake** or **wag** one's **~ at** (in reproof etc.); **let slip through** one's **~s,** lose hold of, (fig.) miss opportunity of having; one's **~s are** (**all**) **thumbs,** one is clumsy; **twist** or **wind round** one's (**little**) **~**, persuade (person) without difficulty, dominate (person) completely; *work* one's *fingers to the* BONE[1]. **3.** part of glove etc. that holds finger; finger-like object (FISH[1] *finger*); long narrow structure; (sl.) amount of liquor one finger-breadth deep in glass; (sl.) policeman, informer, pickpocket, etc. **4. ~ alphabet,** deaf-and-dumb alphabet; **~-board,** part of neck of violin etc. where strings are pressed by fingers; **~-bowl, -glass,** (for rinsing fingers esp. after dessert); *finger* LANGUAGE; **~-mark,** mark left on surface by (dirty) finger; *finger*-NAIL[1]; **~-paint** *n.*, & *v.i.*, (use) paint that can be applied with the fingers; **~-plate** (fastened on door to prevent finger-marks); **~-post,** signpost at junction of roads; **~print,** (*n.*) impression made on surface by person's finger, esp. as used for identifying criminals etc., (fig.) distinctive characteristic, (*v.t.*) record fingerprint(s) of (person); **~-stall,** cover of leather or rubber to protect finger in handicraft etc. or when injured; **~-tight,** as tight as it can be made by the hand; **~tip,** tip of finger (**have at** one's **~tips,** be fully conversant with; **to the** or one's **~tips,** completely). **5.** Hence (-)~ED[2] (-ngg*e*rd), ~LESS, *adjs.* **6.** *v.t.* touch with, turn about in, the fingers; play upon (instrument) with the fingers, play (passage) with fingers used in particular way, mark (music) with signs showing which fingers are to be used; *(sl.) indicate (victim, or criminal to police). [OE, = OS, OHG *fingar*, ON *fingr*, Goth. *figgrs* f. Gmc **fingraz*]

fĭ'ngerĭng[1] (-ngg-) *n.* In vbl senses; (Mus.) action or method of using fingers to play an instrument, indication of this by numerals etc. [f. prec. 6 + -ING[1]]

fĭ'ngerĭng[2] (-ngg-) *n.* fine wool for knitting. [earlier *fingram*, perh. f. F *fin grain*, as GROGRAM f. *gros grain*]

||**fĭ'ngerlĭng** (-ngg-) *n.* parr. [f. FINGER + -LING[1]]

fĭ'nĭal *n.* (Archit.) ornament finishing off apex of roof, pediment, gable, tower-corner, canopy, etc.; topmost part of pinnacle. [ME, f. AF **finial* or AL **finialis* f. OF *fin* f. L *finis* end; see -AL]

fĭ'nĭcal *a.* over-particular, precise, fastidious; (arch.) too much elaborated in details; hence ~LY[2] *adv.*, ~ITY (-ăʹl-), ~NESS, *ns.* [16th c., prob. orig. univ. sl. f. FINE[2] + -ICAL]

fĭ'nĭcking *a.* = prec. [f. prec. + -ING[2]]

fĭ'nĭckў *a.* finical; needing much attention to detail. [var. of prec.; see -Y[2]]

fī'nĭs *n.* (At end of book) the end; end of anything, esp. of life. [L]

fĭ'nĭsh *v.* & *n.* **1.** *v.t.* bring to an end, come to the end of, (thing, or do*ing*; **~ off,** provide with an ending), complete; consume, get through, the whole or remainder of (food, book); **~** (**off**), kill, dispatch, overcome completely; make perfect or highly accomplished, put final touches to, (*finished manners*, *gentleman*; *finishing* STROKE[1] 1, 5); complete education of (girl); complete manufacture of (woodwork, cloth, etc.) by surface treatment. **2.** *v.i.* reach the end, cease; come to end of horse-race etc. (*finishing*-POST[1]); **~** (**up**), end *in* something or *by* doing; **~ with,** complete one's use of or association with (*be ~ed with*, have or have been finished with). **3.** *n.* last stage, termination, esp. of a fox-hunt (*be in at the finish*, lit. or fig.); point at which race etc. ends (**fight to a ~**, till one party is completely beaten); what serves to give completeness; accomplished or completed state; mode of finishing (esp. furniture, as *mahogany finish*). [ME, f. OF *fenir* f. L *finire* (*finis* end); see -ISH[2]]

fĭ'nĭsher *n.* In vbl senses; workman or machine doing last operation in manufacture; (colloq.) discomfiting thing, crushing blow, etc. [f. prec. + ER[1]]

fī'nīte *a.* bounded, limited, not infinite or infinitesimal; (Gram., of verb part) limited by person and number; hence ~LY[2] (-tlĭ) *adv.*, ~NESS (-tn-) *n.* [f. L *finitus* p.p. of *finire* FINISH]

fī'nīt|ism *n.* belief in finiteness of world, God, etc.; so ~IST (2) *n.* [f. prec. + -ISM]

fĭnk[1] *n.* (S. Afr.) weaver-bird. [f. Afrik. *vink* FINCH]

***fĭnk**[2] *n.*, & *v.i.* (sl.) **1.** *n.* unpleasant person; informer; detective; strike-breaker. **2.** *v.i.* inform *on*. [20th c.; orig. unkn.]

Fĭnn *n.* native or inhabitant of Finland. [OE *Finnas* pl., = ON *Finnr*]

fĭ'nnan *n.* **~** (**haddock**), haddock cured with smoke of green wood, turf, or peat. [f. *Findhorn* or *Findon*, Scotland]

fĭ'nner *n.* rorqual, fin whale. [f. FIN + -ER[1]]

fĭ'nneskō *n.* (*pl.* same). boot of tanned reindeer-skin with hair on outside. [f. Norw. *finnsko* (as FINN, *sko* SHOE[1])]

Fĭ'nnĭc *a.* of the group of peoples allied to the Finns; of the group of languages allied to Finnish. [f. FINN + -IC]

Fĭ'nnĭsh *a.* & *n.* (language) of the Finns. [f. FINN + -ISH[1]]

Fĭnnō-U'grĭc (-ōōʹg-) *a.* & *n.* (belonging to) group of Ural-Altaic languages including Finnish, Estonian, Lapp, and Magyar; so **Fĭnnō-U'grĭan** (-ōōʹg-) *a.* & *n.* [f. FINN + -O- + UGRIAN, UGRIC]

fĭ'nnў *a.* having fins; like a fin; of or teeming with fish. [f. FIN + -Y[2]]

fī'nō (fēʹ-) *n.* (*pl.* **~s**). light-coloured dry sherry. [Sp., = fine]

fiŏrd, fjŏrd, (fy-) *n.* long narrow arm of sea between high cliffs as in Norway. [Norw., f. ON *fjörthr* f. Gmc **ferthuz*; cf. FIRTH, FORD]

fiŏrĭtur'a (-oorʹ*a*) *n.* (Mus.) decoration of melody. [It., = flowering (*fiorire* to flower; see -URE)]

fĭ'pple *n.* plug at end of whistle etc.; **~ flute,** flute played by blowing endwise. [17th c.; cf. Icel. *flipi* horse's lip]

fĭr *n.* **~** (**-tree**), evergreen coniferous tree esp. of genus *Abies*, with needles placed singly on the shoots (cf. PINE[1]; SCOTCH[1], SILVER[1], SPRUCE[2], *fir*); its wood; **~-cone,** its fruit; hence **~'rў**[2] *a.* [ME, prob. f. ON *fyri-* f. Gmc **furhjōn*]

fīre[1] *n.* **1.** active principle operative in combustion, in which substances join chemically with oxygen in air and usu. give out bright light and heat; flame,

incandescence; **set ∼ to,** cause to start burning, kindle; **strike ∼,** elicit sparks by friction or blow; **(there is) no smoke without ∼,** rumour is never entirely baseless. **2.** state of combustion; **on ∼,** burning, (fig.) excited; **catch ∼, take ∼,** (Sc. & Ir.) **go on ∼,** begin to burn; **set on ∼,** ignite, kindle; ||**set the Thames on ∼,** set the world on ∼, (usu. w. neg.) do something remarkable. **3.** burning fuel in grate, furnace, etc.; = ELECTRIC *fire,* GAS[1] *fire,* etc.; *heap* COALS *of fire; the* FAT *is in the fire;* ∼ **in** one's **belly,** ambition, enthusiasm; *out of the frying-pan into the fire* (see FRY[2]); **play with ∼,** trifle with dangerous matters. **4.** conflagration, destructive burning; ∼!, warning call at a fire; ∼ **and brimstone,** torment in hell; ∼ **and sword,** burning and slaughter esp. by invading army; **go through ∼ and water,** face all perils; **Greek ∼,** (Hist.) combustible composition for igniting enemy's ships etc. **5.** luminosity, glow, (SAINT *Elmo's fire*); burning heat, fever, (SAINT *Anthony's fire*). **6.** vehement emotion, fervour, spirit, lively imagination, vivacity, poetic inspiration. **7.** firing of guns (lit. or fig.); CEASE[1] *fire,* HANG[1] *fire;* **line of ∼,** path of bullet etc. about to be shot; MISS[2] *fire,* OPEN[2] *fire;* **running ∼,** successive shots from line of troops etc. (esp. fig., of criticism, objections, etc.); **between two ∼s,** shot at from two directions; **under ∼,** being shot at, adversely criticized, etc. **8.** ∼**-alarm,** device for giving warning of fire; ∼'**arm,** (usu. in *pl.*) rifle, gun, pistol, etc.; ∼'**back,** (1) (iron sheet for) back wall of fireplace, (2) SE Asian pheasant of genus *Lophura;* ∼**-ball,** large meteor, ball of flame from nuclear explosion, ball lightning, energetic person, (Mil. Hist.) ball filled with combustibles; ∼**-balloon** (made buoyant by heat of fire burning at its mouth); ∼**-bird,** small orange or red bird; ∼**-blast,** ∼**-blight,** diseases of plants causing scorched appearance; ∼**-bomb,** incendiary bomb; ∼**-box,** fuel--chamber of steam-boiler; ∼'**brand,** piece of burning wood, person or thing kindling strife; ∼**-break,** open space as obstacle to spread of fire in forest etc.; ∼**-brick** (proof against fire, used in grates etc.); ∼ **brigade,** organized body of men trained and employed to extinguish fires; ∼**-bug,** (colloq.) incendiary, pyromaniac; ∼**-clay** (kind used for fire-bricks); ∼ **company,** (1) fire brigade, (2) fire-insurance company; ∼**-control,** system of regulating fire of ship's or fort's guns; *∗*∼'**cracker,** explosive firework; ∼'**crest,** warbler very similar to goldcrest; ∼'**damp,** miners' name for methane, which is explosive when mixed in certain proportion with air; *∗*∼**department,** fire brigade; ∼'**dog,** metal support for burning wood or for grate or fire-irons; ∼**-drake,** (Gmc Myth.) fiery dragon [cf. DRAKE[1]]; ∼**-drill,** (1) primitive device for kindling fire with stick and wood, (2) rehearsal of procedure to be used in case of fire; ∼**-eater,** conjurer who (allegedly) eats fire, person fond of fighting or quarrelling; ∼**-engine,** vehicle carrying equipment used to extinguish large fires; ∼**-escape,** apparatus or emergency staircase for saving people in burning building; *fire* EXTINGUISHER; ∼**-eyed,** (poet.) with glowing eyes; ∼**-fighter,** one whose task is to extinguish fires; ∼'**fly,** beetle emitting phosphorescent light; ∼**-guard,** (1) protective frame or grating in front of fire in room, (2) *∗* = *fire--watcher,* (3) *∗* = *fire-break;* ∼**-hose,** hose-pipe for extinguishing fires; *∗*∼'**house,** fire station; ∼ **insurance** (against losses by fire); ∼**-irons,** tongs, poker, and shovel, for tending domestic fire; ∼'**light,** light from fireplace; ||∼**-lighter,** piece of inflammable material to help start fire in grate; ∼'**lock,** (Hist.) musket in which priming was ignited by sparks; ∼'**man,** one who tends furnace or steam-engine fire or steamship fire, man employed to extinguish fires, member of fire brigade; ∼**-new,** (arch.) brand-new; ∼**-office** (insuring against fire); ∼**-opal,** girasol; ∼'**place,** place for domestic fire (esp. at base of chimney), structure surrounding or area before this;

∼**-plug,** connection in water-main for fire-hose, hydrant; ∼**-policy,** fire-office's certificate guaranteeing compensation in case of fire; ∼**-power,** ability of guns etc. to inflict destruction; ∼**-practice,** = *fire--drill* (2); ∼'**proof** *a.,* & *v.t.,* (make) able to resist fire or great heat; ||∼**-raising,** arson; ∼**-screen,** (1) screen to keep off direct heat of fire, (2) *∗* = *fire-guard* (1), (3) ornamental screen for fireplace; ∼**-ship,** (Hist.) ship freighted with combustibles and sent adrift to ignite enemy's ships etc.; ∼'**side,** space round fireplace, home (esp. as place of informal talk etc.); ∼ **station,** headquarters of fire brigade; ∼**-step,** = FIRING-*step;* ∼**-stone,** kind that resists fire, used for furnaces etc.; ∼**-storm,** high wind or storm following fire caused by bombs; *fire*-TONGS; ∼**-trap,** building without proper exits in case of fire; ∼**-tree,** pohutukawa; ∼**-walking,** (religious) ceremony of walking barefoot over white-hot stones, wood-ashes, etc.; ∼ **wall,** fireproof wall to prevent spread of fire; *∗*∼ **warden,** person employed to prevent or extinguish fires; ∼**-watcher,** person keeping watch for fires esp. those caused by bombs; ∼**-water,** (colloq.) strong alcoholic liquor; ∼'**wood,** wood prepared for fuel; ∼'**work,** device giving spectacular effects by use of combustibles etc., squib, rocket, etc., (fig., in *pl.*) display of wit, passion, etc.; ∼**-worship,** treatment of fire as a deity, (pop.) Zoroastrianism. **9.** Hence ∼'LESS (fīr'l-) *a.* [OE *fȳr,* = OS, OHG *fiur,* f. WG **fũir*]

fire[2] *v.* **1.** *v.t.* set fire to with intention of destroying; kindle (explosives); (fig.) stimulate (the imagination), fill (person) with enthusiasm; cause to glow or redden. **2.** bake (pottery, bricks), cure (tea, tobacco) by artificial heat; (Farriery) cauterize. **3.** supply (furnace, engine, boiler, power-station) with fuel. **4.** cause (explosive) to explode; discharge (gun); produce (broadside, salute, etc.) by discharge of guns; propel (missile) from gun etc. (lit. or fig.); ∼ (*∗***out**), expel, dismiss, reject, (person). **5.** *v.i.* (Of explosive etc.) catch fire; (of cylinder in internal combustion engine) undergo ignition of its fuel; become heated or excited; ∼ **up,** show sudden anger. **6.** shoot, discharge gun etc. (*at, into, on,* etc.); (of gun etc.) be discharged; ∼ **away,** (fig.) begin, go ahead. **7.** Hence fīr'ER[1] *n.* [OE *fȳrian* (as prec.)]

fīr'ing *n.* In vbl senses; material for a fire, fuel; discharge of guns; (fig.) stimulate (the imagination), fill (person) with enthusiasm; ∼**-line,** front line of battle (lit. or fig.); ∼**-party,** ∼**-squad,** group detailed to fire salute at military funeral or perform military execution; ∼**-step,** step on which soldier in trench stands to fire. [f. prec.+-ING[1]]

fīr'kin *n.* small cask for liquids, butter, fish, etc.; (as measure) half of kilderkin. [ME *ferdekyn,* prob. f. MDu. **vierdekijn* dim. of *vierde* fourth; see -KIN]

fĭrm[1] *n.* partners carrying on business; group of persons working together, esp. of hospital doctors and assistants. [earlier = signature, style, f. Sp. and It. f. med. L *firma* (L *firmare* confirm f. *firmus* FIRM[2]); cf. FARM[1]]

fĭrm[2] *a., adv.,* & *v.* **1.** *a.* of solid or compact structure; fixed, stable; steady, not shaking; established, immutable, (of offer etc.) not liable to cancellation after acceptance; steadfast, unflinching, resolute; constant *to;* (Commerc., of prices, goods) maintaining their level or value; hence ∼'LY[2] *adv.,* ∼'NESS *n.* **2.** *adv.* firmly (*stand firm; hold firm to*). **3.** *v.t.* & *i.* solidify, make or become firm or compact; fix firmly (plants in soil). [ME, f. OF *ferme* f. L *firmus*]

fĭr'mament *n.* (literary) vault of HEAVEN with its clouds and stars; hence ∼AL (-ĕ'n-) *a.* [ME f. OF, f. L *firmamentum* (*firmare,* as FIRM[1]; see -MENT)]

fĭr'man *n.* oriental sovereign's edict; grant, permit. [f. Pers. *fermān,* Skr. *pramāṇam* right measure]

fĭr'ry. See FIR.

fĭrst *a., n.,* & *adv.* **1.** *a.* earliest or earlier in time or order (**come in ∼,** win race; **in the ∼ place,** to begin with; *shall do it* etc. ∼ **thing,** (colloq.) before anything else; **the two** etc. ∼, **the ∼ two** etc., (1) the two etc. equally first, (2) the first and second etc.); basic or evident (*first principles*). **2.** foremost in position, rank, or importance (*head, feet,* etc., *first,* with the head etc. in front); most willing, likely, etc., (*should be the first to admit the difficulty*); (Mus.) performing highest or chief of two or more parts for same instrument or voice; F∼ Lord, F∼ Secretary, etc., (titles of chief officers); ∼ things ∼, the most important things before any others. **3.** coming next after a specified or implied time (*shall take the first train; the first cuckoo*). **4.** the ∼, even one elementary (*he doesn't know the first thing about it*). **5.** ∼ aid, help given to injured person until medical treatment is available; *first* BASE¹ 9, BLOOD¹; First CAUSE¹; *first*-CHOP⁵; ∼ class, set of persons or things grouped together as better than others, best accommodation in train, ship, etc., mail given preferential treatment, (place in) highest division in examination-list; ∼-class, (*a.*) belonging to or travelling by the first class, of best quality, very good, (*adv.*; -ah´s) by the first class (*travels first-class*); ∼´ coat, first layer of paint; ‖∼ cost, = *prime* COST¹; *first* COUSIN; ∼ day, Sunday; ∼-day cover, envelope with stamps postmarked on first day of issue; *first* EDITION, FLOOR; ∼-foot *n.*, & *v.i.* (Sc.) (be) first person to cross threshold in the New Year; ∼-fruit, (usu. in *pl.*) first products of agriculture for the season esp. as offered to God, (fig.) first results of work etc., (Hist.) payment to a superior by new holder of office; *first* GEAR; ∼´hand, direct, without intermediate agency (*at first hand,* directly from the original source); *first* INTENTION; *F∼ Lady,* wife of US President; *first* LESSON, LIEUTENANT; ∼ light, time when light first appears in the morning; ∼ name, personal or Christian name; ∼ night, ∼-ni´ghter, (habitual attender of) first public performance of plays etc.; ∼ offender (against whom no previous conviction is recorded); ∼ officer, mate on merchant ship; ∼ past the post, (of election-candidate) winning because receiving the most votes though perhaps not having absolute majority; *first* PERSON 5, 6, ‖POST⁴; ∼-rate, of the highest class, excellent(ly), (colloq.) very well, (*a first-rate machine; feeling first-rate*); *first* READING; ‖∼ school (for children from 5 to 9 years old); *∼ sergeant,* highest-ranking NCO in company; *first* STRING, WATER¹ 5. **6.** *n.* the ∼, person or thing first mentioned or occurring (*at ∼, at* the beginning; from the ∼, from the beginning; from ∼ to last, throughout); first day of month; first gear; (person having) place in first class in examination; (winner of) first place in race; (in *pl.*) best quality of goods. **7.** *adv.* before anyone or anything else (*first of all, first and foremost; first come first served;* ∼ and last, taking one thing with another, on the whole; ∼ or last, sooner or later; *∼* off, (colloq.) at first, first of all); before some specified or implied event, time, etc., (*must get this done first*); in preference, rather, (*will see him damned first*); for the first time (*when did you first see her?*); hrst-class (*I usually travel first*); ∼-born *a.* & *n.,* eldest (child). [OE *fyrst,* = OS, OHG *furist,* ON *fyrstr* f. Gmc **furistaz,* superl. f. **fur-, *for-* f. IE **pr-*]

fir´stling *n.* (usu. in *pl.*) first result of anything, first-fruits; first offspring, first born in a season. [f. prec. + -LING¹]

fir´stly *adv.* in the first place, first, (in enumerating topics, arguments, etc.). [f. FIRST + -LY²]

firth, frith, *n.* arm of sea; estuary. [ME, orig. Sc., f. ON *fjörthr* FIORD]

fisc *n.* public treasury of ancient Rome, Roman emperor's privy purse. [F, or f. L *fiscus* rush-basket, purse, treasury]

fi´scal *a.* & *n.* **1.** *a.* of public revenue; *fiscal* YEAR; hence ∼LY² *adv.* **2.** *n.* legal official in some countries; (Sc.) = PROCURATOR *fiscal.* [F, or f. L *fiscalis* (as prec.; see -AL)]

fisca´lity *n.* (excessive regard for) fiscal matters. [f. prec. + -ITY]

fish¹ *n.* (*pl.* usu. same). **1.** vertebrate cold-blooded animal having gills throughout life and limbs (if any) modified into fins (FLAT²-*fish,* FLYING *fish,* GOLD*fish,* SUN*fish,* SWORD*fish,* etc.); any animal living in water (CUTTLE*fish,* JELLY*fish,* SHELL¹*fish*). **2.** cry stinking ∼, disparage one's own efforts; drink like a ∼ (excessively); feed the ∼es, (1) be drowned, (2) be seasick; ∼ out of water, person not in accustomed or preferred surroundings; there's as good ∼ in the sea as ever came out of it, no fear of scarcity; pretty KETTLE *of fish.* **3.** (colloq.) person (*cool, queer,* etc., *fish*). **4.** flesh of fish (*fish, flesh, and fowl*); neither ∼, flesh, nor good red herring, of indefinite character; other ∼ to fry, more important business to attend to. **5.** (in *pl.*; F∼(*es*)). *the* zodiacal sign Pisces. **6.** ∼ and chips, fried fish and fried chipped potatoes; *fish* BALL¹ 5; ∼-bowl, glass bowl for keeping fish in; ∼ cake, small cake of shredded fish and mashed potato; ∼-carver, knife for serving fish; ∼ eagle, osprey; ‖∼-eaters, knife and fork for eating fish; ∼-eye, (of lens) wide-angled with curved front; ∼-farm, place where fish are bred for food; ∼ finger, small oblong piece of fish in batter or bread-crumbs; ∼-fork (for eating or serving fish); ∼-glue, isinglass; ∼-hawk, osprey; *fish*-HOOK¹; ∼-kettle, oval pan for boiling fish; ∼-knife (for eating or serving fish); ∼ louse, small crustacean parasitic on fish; ∼-meal, ground dried fish as fertilizer etc.; ‖∼-monger, dealer in fish; ∼-net, (of fabric) open-meshed; ∼-pond, ∼-pool, pond in which fish are kept; ∼-pot, wicker trap for eels, lobsters, etc.; ∼-slice, carving-knife for fish, cook's implement for turning or taking out fish; ∼-sound, fish's swimming-bladder; ∼-tail, (*n.*) thing shaped like fish's tail (*fish-tail burner,* with jet of gas so shaped), (*v.i.*) move tail of vehicle etc. from side to side; ∼´wife, woman selling fish. [OE *fisc,* = OS, OHG *fisk,* ON *fiskr,* Goth. *fisks* f. Gmc **fiskaz* f. IE **piskos*]

fish² *v.* **1.** *n.i* try to catch fish (∼ in troubled waters, make one's profit out of disturbances, whence ∼´ERY (2, 3) *n.* **2.** search *for* something in or under water or in concealed place; seek by indirect means *for* (secrets, compliments, etc.). **3.** *v.t.* try to catch (fish) or get (coral etc.) from below water; (colloq.) draw *out* (*of* water, pocket, etc.) or *up* (from these); draw flukes of (anchor) up to gunwale; try to catch fish in (pool etc.; ∼ out, exhaust the fish in); get (fact, opinion, secret) *out.* **4.** Hence ∼´ING¹ (1) *n.;* ∼´ing expedition, (fig.) search etc. made in hope of coming across incriminating evidence; ∼´ing frog, angler-fish; ∼´ing-rod, long tapering usu. jointed rod to which fishing-line is attached; ∼´ing story, exaggerated account of an incident. [OE *fiscian,* — OS *fiskon,* OHG *fiskōn,* ON *fiska,* Goth. *fiskōn* f. Gmc **fiskōjan* (as prec.)]

fish³ *n.,* & *v.t.* **1.** *n.* (Naut.) piece of wood, convex and concave, used to strengthen mast etc. **2.** flat plate of iron, wood, etc. to strengthen beam or joint (∼-plate, one of two holding rails together and fastened with ∼-bolt). **3.** *v.t.* mend or strengthen (spar etc.), join (rails), with fish. [n. f. v., f. F *ficher* fix f. Rom. **figicare* f. L *figere*]

fish⁴ *n.* piece of ivory etc. used as counter in games. [f. F *fiche* (*ficher;* see prec.)]

fi´sher *n.* fishing animal, esp. pekan; (arch.) fisherman (∼ of men, evangelist, Matt. 4: 19); ∼man, man who lives by fishing, angler, fishing-boat; ∼man('s knit), kind of thick ribbed knitting. [OE *fiscere,* = ON, OS *fiskari,* OHG *fiskāri* f. Gmc **fiskarjaz* (as FISH¹; see -ER¹)]

fi´shery *n.* see FISH² fish.

fi´sh|y *a.* like that of fish; (of eye) dull, vacant-looking; smelling or tasting like fish; (joc. or poet.) abounding in fish; consisting of fish (*a fishy repast*); (colloq.) of dubious character, questionable; hence ∼ILY² *adv.,* ∼INESS *n.* [f. FISH¹ + -Y²]

fisk *n.* (Sc.) state treasury, exchequer. [var. of FISC]

fi´ssile *a.* cleavable, tending to split; capable of

undergoing nuclear fission; hence **fissi′l**ITY *n*. [f. L *fissilis* (as FISSURE; see -IL)]

fi′ssion (-shon) *n*. & *v*. **1.** *n*. (Biol.) division of cell etc. into new cells etc. as mode of reproduction. **2.** (Phys.) splitting of heavy atomic nucleus spontaneously or on impact of another particle, with release of energy; ∼ **bomb**, atomic bomb. **3.** *v.t.* & *i*. (cause to) undergo fission. **4.** Hence ∼ABLE *a*. [f. L *fissio* (as FISSURE; see -ION)]

fissi′parous *a*. (Biol. or fig.) reproducing by fission; hence **fissipä′r**ITY, ∼NESS, *ns*. [f. L *fissus* p.p. (as foll.) after *viviparous*]

fi′ssure (-sher) *n*. & *v*. **1.** *n*. opening, usu. long and narrow, made esp. by cracking, splitting, or separation of parts; (Bot. & Anat.) narrow opening in organ etc., esp. depression between convolutions of brain; cleavage. **2.** *v.t.* & *i*. split, crack. [ME f. OF, or f. L *fissura* (*findere fiss-* cleave; see -URE)]

fist *n*., & *v.t.* **1.** *n*. clenched hand, esp. as used in boxing; (joc.) hand (**give us your** ∼, shake hands), handwriting (*writes a good fist*; *I know his fist*); HAND¹ *over fist*; **make a** (*good, poor*) ∼ **at** or **of**, (colloq.) make a (good, poor) attempt at; hence -∼′ED² *a*. **2.** *v.t.* strike with fist; (Naut.) handle (sail, oar, etc.). [OE *fȳst*, = MLG, OHG *fūst* f. WG *fūsti*]

fi′stic(al) *adjs*. (joc.) pugilistic. [f. prec. + -IC, -ICAL]

fi′sticuffs *n*. *pl*. fighting with the fists. [prob. f. obs. *fisty* a. = prec., + CUFF²]

fi′stül|a *n*. long pipelike ulcer etc. with narrow mouth; surgically made body-passage; natural pipe or spout in whales, insects, etc.; hence ∼AR¹, ∼OUS, *adjs*. [L, = pipe, flute]

fit¹, fÿtte, *n*. (arch.) section of a poem. [OE *fitt*, = OS *fittia*, perh. = OHG *fizza* edge of cloth, ON *fit* hem]

fit² *n*. **1.** sudden transitory or recurring attack of an illness; sudden seizure (with loss of consciousness or convulsions) of hysteria, apoplexy, fainting, paralysis, or epilepsy; (fig.) attack of strong feeling (**give** person **a** ∼, surprise or outrage him; **have a** ∼, be greatly surprised or outraged). **2.** sudden transitory state (*a fit of energy, idleness, devotion, indifference, pique*, etc.); **by** or **in** ∼s (**and starts**), spasmodically. **3.** capricious impulse, mood, (*when the fit was on him*). [ME, = position of danger, perh. = OE *fitt* conflict (?); orig. unkn.]

fit³ *a*. & *adv*. **1.** *a*. well adapted or suited (*for* some purpose or status, *to* do or be; SURVIVAL *of the fittest*); good enough *for* (*a dinner fit for a king*); becoming, proper, right, (*it is fit that*); **see** or **think** ∼, decide or choose (*to* do esp. arbitrary or foolish thing). **2.** qualified, competent, worthy, *to* do (*not fit to hold a* CANDLE *to*); in suitable condition, ready, *to* do or *for*; angry, troubled, or exhausted enough *to* (do something violent, sink to the ground, etc.). **3.** in good athletic condition or health (*fit as a* FIDDLE). **4.** Hence ∼′LY² *adv*., ∼′NESS *n*. **5.** *adv*. (vulg.) in a suitable manner *to* (*was laughing fit to bust*). [ME, of unkn. orig.]

fit⁴ *v.t*. (-tt-), & *n*. **1.** *v.t*. be in harmony with, become, befit; (esp. of dress) be of right measure, shape, and size for (person, or abs.: *the* CAP¹ *fits*). **2.** fill up, exactly correspond to, be in accordance with, (receptacle, counterpart, etc.; or abs., often *in, into, in with*); cause to do this; ∼ (= FILL) **the bill**; ∼**ted carpet** (cut to fit floor exactly); ∼**ted coat** etc. (shaped to fit a person's figure). **3.** make suitable, adapt, *for*, *to* thing or person, *to* do; make competent *for* or *to*; ∼ **on**, try on (garment). **4.** supply, furnish, (ship etc. *with*); fix in place (*fit a lock on* or *to the door*); ∼ **out, up,** equip; ∼-**up**, (Theatr. sl.) temporary stage etc., travelling company. **5.** Hence ∼′TER¹ *n*., one who supervises cutting, fitting, altering, etc., of garments, mechanic who fits (up) all kinds of machinery. **6.** *n*. adaptation, adjustment, style in which garment or machine-part fits (*a tight, bad, excellent, fit*). [ME, perh. f. prec.]

fitch *n*. polecat; (brush made of) polecat's or similar hair. [f. MDu. *fisse* etc.; cf. foll.]

fi′tchew (-ōō) *n*. polecat. [14th c., f. OF *ficheau, fissel*, dim. of MDu. *fisse*]

fi′tful *a*. having irregular periods of activity or strength; spasmodic, capricious; hence ∼LY² *adv*., ∼NESS *n*. [f. FIT² + -FUL]

fi′tment *n*. (usu. in *pl*.) piece of fixed furniture. [f. FIT⁴ + -MENT]

fi′tting¹ *n*. In vbl senses; action of having a garment fitted; (usu. in *pl*.) fixture(s), apparatus, furniture; ∼-**shop**, place where machine-parts are put together. [f. FIT⁴ + -ING¹]

fi′tting² *a*. In vbl senses; becoming, proper, right, whence ∼LY² *adv*. [f. FIT⁴ + -ING²]

FitzGë′rald (-ts-) *n*. ∼(-**Lorentz**) **contraction** or **effect**, (Phys.) shortening of moving body in direction of its motion, small except at speeds comparable with that of light. [G. F. ∼, Ir. physicist d. 1901]

five *a*. & *n*. **1.** one more than four; symbol for this (5, v, V); card etc. with five pips; time of five o'clock; size etc. denoted by five; set of five; hit at cricket scoring five runs; (in *pl*.) gloves, shoes, etc., of fifth size; ∥**bunch of** ∼**s**, (sl.) hand. **2.** ∼-**corner**(s), (Austral.) (pentagonal fruit of) shrub of genus *Styphelia*; *five-day* WEEK; ∼-**eighth,** (Austral. & NZ Rugby Footb.) player between half-back and three-quarter; ∼-**finger exercise,** exercise on piano for exercising all fingers, (fig.) easy task; ∼ **hundred,** form of euchre in which 500 points make a game; ∼ **o′clock shadow,** beard-growth visible on man's face after about 5 p.m.; *five* ORDER¹s; ∼-**star,** of highest class; ∥∼-**stones,** jacks played with five stones; ∼-**year plan** (for the economic development of USSR in 5 years, inaugurated in 1928, later of other countries and repeated in USSR). **3.** Hence ∼′FOLD (-vf-) *a*. & *adv*. [OE *fīf*, = OS *fīf*, OHG *fimf, finf*, ON *fimm*, Goth. *fimf* f. Gmc *fimfi* f. IE *pempe, *penqwe*]

fi′ver *n*. £5 or $5 note. [f. prec. + -ER¹]

fives (-vz) *n*. ball-game played with gloved hands or with bat in court with three (**Eton** ∼) or four (**Rugby** ∼) walls. [*pl*. of FIVE used as *sing*.; significance unkn.]

fix¹ *v*. **1.** *v.t.* make firm or stable, fasten, secure, implant (principles, memory, etc.), (*in, on, to*, etc.); attach (bayonet) to muzzle of rifle etc. **2.** direct steadily, set, (eyes, gaze, affection, attention) *on* or *upon*; (of object) attract and hold (attention, eyes, etc.). **3.** make (eyes, features) rigid; deprive of volatility or fluidity; congeal; (of plant etc.) assimilate (nitrogen or carbon dioxide) by formation of non-gaseous compound; make (colour, microscope-specimen, photographic image) fast or permanent; single out (person) *with* one's eyes etc. **4.** place definitely or permanently, station, establish; assign precise position of; refer (thing, person) to definite place or time. **5.** determine incidence of (liability etc.); settle, determine, specify, (price, date, place). **6.** arrest changes or development in (language, literature). **7.** mend, repair; ∼ (**up**), arrange, organize, prepare; (sl.) deal with, silence, kill, (person); obtain support of (person) esp. by bribery etc.; arrange (result of match etc.) fraudulently; castrate or spay (animal); (sl.) inject oneself with narcotic. **8.** *v.i.* become rigid or congealed, lose volatility or fluidity; (arch.) take up one's position; settle one's choice, decide, *on* or *upon*; (sl.) take injection of narcotic. [ME, partly f. obs. *fix* fixed f. OF *fix* or f. L *fixus* p.p. of *figere* fix, fasten, partly f. med. L *fixare* f. *fixus*]

fix² *n*. **1.** (colloq.) predicament, position hard to escape from. **2.** finding position, position found, by bearings or astronomical observations (**radio** ∼, position of aircraft, ship, etc., found by radio). **3.** (sl.) dose of narcotic drug; *(sl.) bribery. [f. prec.]

fixä′te *v.t.* direct one's gaze on; (Psych.) arrest (part of libido) at immature stage, causing abnormal attachment to persons or things, cause (person) to undergo this process. [f. L *fixus* (see FIX¹) + -ATE³]

fixä′tion *n*. fixing, being fixed; process of rendering solid, coagulation; process of combining a gas with a solid; act or process of being fixated; (pop.) obsession, concentration on one idea. [ME, f. med. L *fixatio* (*fixare*; see FIX¹, -ATION)]

fi′xative *a.* & *n.* **1.** *a.* tending to fix. **2.** *n.* substance used to fix colours or drawings, hair, microscope--specimens, volatile components of perfumes, etc. [f. FIX¹ + -ATIVE]

fixed (-kst) *a.* In vbl senses; (*pred.*, colloq.) situated as regards money etc.; ~ **capital,** machinery etc. that remains in owner's use; ~ **focus,** camera focus at distance from lens that is not adjustable; ~ **idea,** *idée fixe*; ~ **income** (from pension, investment at fixed interest, etc.); ~ **odds** (predetermined, in betting); ~ **oil** (non-volatile); ~ **point,** (Phys.) well-defined reproducible temperature; *fixed* STAR¹; hence **fi′x-ėdLY²** *adv.*, **fi′xėdNESS** *n.* [p.p. of FIX¹]

fi′xer *n.* In vbl senses; substance for fixing photographic image etc.; one who makes (esp. illicit) arrangements. [f. FIX¹ + -ER¹]

***fi′xings** (-z) *n. pl.* apparatus, equipment; trimmings of dress or dish, adjuncts. [f. FIX¹ + -ING¹ + -s¹]

fi′xity *n.* fixed state; stability, permanence. [f. obs. *fix* fixed (see FIX¹) + -ITY]

fi′xture *n.* thing fixed or fastened in position; (Law, in *pl.*) accessory articles annexed to house or land and regarded as legally part of it; person or thing confined to or established in one place (chiefly in pred.; *seems to be a fixture*); (Sport) (date appointed for) match, race, etc. [alt. of obs. *fixure* f. LL *fixura* f. L *figere fix-* fix; see -URE]

fi′zgig (-g-) *n.* & *a.* (arch.) **1.** *n.* giddy flirtatious young woman; kind of small firework, cracker. **2.** *a.* flighty. [prob. f. foll. + obs. *gig* flighty girl]

fizz *v.i.,* & *n.* (make) hissing or spluttering sound, whence ~Y² *a.*; effervescence; (colloq.) effervescent drink, esp. champagne. [imit.]

fi′zzle *v.i.,* & *n.* (make) feeble hissing or spluttering sound; ~ **out,** come to lame conclusion. [f. as prec. + -LE 3]

FJI *abbr.* Fellow of the Institute of Journalists.

fjord. See FIORD.

FL *abbr.* Florida.

fl. *abbr.* floor; floruit; fluid.

Fla. *abbr.* Florida.

fláb *n.* (sl.) fat, flabbiness. [imit., or back-form.] FLABBY

flā′bbergast (-gah-) *v.t.* (colloq.) dumbfound, overwhelm with astonishment. [18th c., perh. f. foll. + AGHAST]

flā′bby *a.* (Of flesh etc.) hanging down, flaccid, limp; (of language or character) feeble; hence ~iNESS *n.* [alt. f. earlier *flappy* f. FLAP + -Y²]

flā′ccid (-ks-) *a.* (Of flesh etc.) hanging loose or wrinkled, limp, flabby; relaxed, drooping; lacking vigour, feeble; hence ~ITY (-ĭ′d-) *n.* [f. F *flaccide* or f. L *flaccidus* (*flaccus* flabby)]

***flắck** *n.* (sl.) publicity agent. [20th c.; orig. unkn.]

flăg¹ *n.* plant with bladed leaf esp. of genus *Iris* growing on moist ground; long slender leaf of a plant; hence ~'gY² (-gĭ) *a.* [ME; cf. MDu. *flag*, Da. *flæg*]

flăg² *n.,* & *v.t.* (-gg-). **1.** *n.* ~('stone), flat slab of rock for paving, (in *pl.*) pavement made of these. **2.** *v.t.* pave with flags. [ME, = sod; cf. Icel. *flag* spot whence sod has been cut out, ON *flaga* slab of stone, and FLAKE²]

flăg³ *n.* ~(-feather), quill-feather of bird's wing. [perh. rel. to obs. *fag* loose flap; cf. FLAG⁵]

flăg⁴ *n.,* & *v.t.* (-gg-). **1.** *n.* piece of bunting or other material, usu. oblong or square, attachable by one edge to staff or halyard and used as standard, ensign, or signal; **black** ~, (1) pirate's ensign, (2) flag formerly hoisted outside prison to announce execution of criminal; **red** ~, (1) symbol of revolution, (2) danger-signal on shooting-range, railway, etc.; **white** ~, flag of truce, flag disclaiming hostile intention; **yellow** ~, flag displayed by ship with infectious disease on board, hospital ship, or ship in quarantine. **2.** ~ **of convenience,** foreign flag under which a ship is registered to avoid financial charges etc.; ~ **of truce,** white flag indicating desire to parley; **hoist the** ~ (as claim to discovered territory); **keep the** ~ **flying,** (usu. fig.) continue the fight; **put the** ~ **out,** celebrate victory etc.; **show the** ~, make official visit to foreign port etc., (fig.) ensure that notice is taken of oneself, one's own country, etc. **3.** (Naut.) flag carried by flagship as emblem of admiral's rank afloat. **4.** oblong strip of metal etc. used as signal that taxi is for hire; small paper etc. device resembling flag. **5.** ~-**boat** (serving as mark in sailing-matches); ~-**captain,** captain of flagship; ||~-**day** (on which money is raised for a cause by sale to passers-by etc. of small paper etc. flags to be worn as evidence of having given); *F~ **Day,** 14 June, anniversary of the adoption of the Stars and Stripes in 1777; ~-**lieutenant,** admiral's ADC; ||~-**list,** roll of flag-officers; ~′**man,** signaller at races etc.; ~-**officer,** admiral, vice-admiral, or rear-admiral, or commodore of yacht club; ~-**pole,** = *flagstaff;* ~-**rank** (of flag-officers); ~′**ship,** ship having admiral on board; ~′**staff,** pole on which flag is hoisted; ~-**station** (where trains stop only if signalled); ~-**wagging,** (sl.) signalling with hand-held flags; ~-**waver,** chauvinist, political agitator. **6.** *v.t.* flag on or over; mark out (as) with flag(s); inform (person), communicate (information, *that*), by flag -signals; ~ (**down**), signal to (vehicle or driver) to stop. [16th c., perh. f. obs. *flag* drooping]

flăg⁵ *v.i.* (-gg-). hang down, flap loosely; droop, fade, become limp; lag, lose vigour, grow languid; become uninteresting. [16th c., as prec.]

flagellant (flă′je-, flăjĕ′-) *n.* & *a.* (one) who scourges himself, (one) who engages in flogging, esp. as religious discipline or sexual stimulus. [f. L *flagellare* whip (FLAGELLUM); see -ANT]

flă′gellāte *v.t.* scourge, flog, (cf. prec.); hence or cogn. ~A′TION, ~ător, *ns.,* ~ătory *a.* [f. as prec. + ATE³]

flā′gellate² *a.* & *n.* (protozoan) having flagella (see foll.). [f. foll. + -ATE²]

flage′ll|um *n.* (*pl.* ~a). (Bot.) runner, creeping shoot; (Biol.) lashlike appendage; hence ~AR, ~iFORM, *adjs.* [L, = whip, dim. of *flagrum* scourge]

flăgeolĕt¹ (flăjōlĕ′t, flā′j-) *n.* small flute blown at end, like recorder but with two thumb-holes; organ stop of like quality. [F, dim. of OF *flag(e)ol* f. Prov. *flajol,* of unkn. orig.; see FT¹]

flăgeole′t² (-jōlĕ′t, -lā′) *n.* French kidney-bean. [F]

flagi′tious (-shŭs) *a.* deeply criminal; utterly villainous; hence ~LY² *adv.,* ~NESS *n.* [ME, f. L *flagitiosus* (*flagitium* shameful crime; see -OUS)]

flā′gon *n.* large vessel esp. with handle, spout, and lid, to hold liquor for table; similar vessel for Eucharist; flattened globular glass wine- or cider-bottle holding nearly twice as much as ordinary bottle. [ME *flakon* f. AF *flagon,* OF *flacon,* *flascon* f. LL *flasco -onis* FLASK]

flā′grant *a.* (Of offence or offender) glaring, notorious, scandalous; hence or cogn. **flā′grANCY** *n.,* ~LY² *adv.* [F, or f. L *flagrare* blaze; see -ANT]

flail *n.* & *v.* **1.** *n.* hand threshing-implement, wooden staff at end of which a short heavy stick hangs swinging. **2.** *v.t.* beat or strike (as) with flail. **3.** *v.i.* wave or swing wildly or erratically. [OE *flegil,* = OS *flegil,* OHG *flegel,* WG *flagil-* prob. f. L FLAGELLUM]

flair *n.* instinct for selecting or performing what is excellent, useful, etc. [F (*flairer* to smell f. Rom. *flagrare* = L *fragrare;* see FRAGRANT)]

flăk *n.* anti-aircraft fire; (fig.) barrage of criticism; ~ **jacket,** protective jacket of heavy fabric reinforced with metal. [abbr. of G *fliegerabwehrkanone,* lit. aviator-defence-gun]

flāke¹ *n.* rack for storing oatcake etc.; stage for drying fish etc. [ME, perh. f. ON *flaki, fleki* wicker shield]

flāke² *n.* & *v.* **1.** *n.* small light thin piece, esp. of snow; portion of ignited matter thrown off; thin broad piece peeled off, chiplike piece (CORN¹flakes, *soap flakes*);

(Archaeol.) piece of hard stone chipped off and used as tool; natural division of fish's flesh; dogfish or other shark as food. **2.** *v.i.* & *t.* fall like, sprinkle as with, snow; take or come away or off in flakes; ∼ **out,** (colloq.) faint, fall asleep from exhaustion etc. [ME; orig. unkn.; cf. ON *flakna* flake off]

flā′kў *a.* of or like flakes; (of pastry) consisting of thin flakes after baking. [f. prec. + -Y²]

flăm *n.* sham story; trick, deception. [perh. f. FLIM-FLAM]

flambé (flah′nbā) *a.* (Of food) covered with spirit and served alight. [F, p.p. of *flamber* singe (as foll.)]

flă′mbeau (-bō) *n.* (*pl.* ∼s *or* ∼x, *pr.* -z). flaming torch, esp. of several thick waxed wicks. [F (*flambe* f. L *flammula* dim. of *flamma* flame)]

flămboy′|ant *a.* floridly decorated; gorgeously coloured; ostentatious, showy; (Archit.) marked by wavy flamelike lines; hence ∼ANCE, ∼ANCY, *ns.*, ∼antLY² *adv.* [F, in Archit. sense, pres. part. of *flamboyer* (*flambe*; see prec.)]

flāme¹ *n.* **1.** (portion of) ignited gas (**the** ∼**s,** fire, esp. as consuming; visible combustion (*in flames; burst into flame* or *flames*). **2.** bright light, brilliant colouring; red colour of flame. **3.** passion, esp. of love, (FAN² *the flame*); (joc.) sweetheart (*an old flame of mine*). **4.** ∼ **gun** (throwing flames to destroy weeds etc.); *flame-*PROOF²; ∼**-projector, -thrower,** weapon for throwing spray of flame; ∼**-tree,** one of several trees with brilliant red or yellow flowers. **5.** Hence ∼′LESS (-ml-), **flā′mY²,** *adjs.* [ME, f. AF **flaume*, OF *flame* f. L *flamma*]

flāme¹ *v.* **1.** *v.i.* emit flames, blaze, (*away, forth, out, up*); (of passion) burst out; (of person) break *out*, blaze *up*, into anger; shine or glow like flame; (poet.) move like flame; ∼ **out,** (of jet aircraft engine) lose power through extinction of flame in combustion chamber. **2.** *v.t.* subject to action of flame; send (signal) by means of flame. [ME, f. OF *flam(m)er* (as prec.)]

flā′měn *n.* (Rom. Ant.) priest serving a particular deity. [ME f. L]

flamě′ncō *n.* (*pl.* ∼s). Spanish gypsy style of song or dance. [Sp., = Flemish]

flā′ming *a.* In vbl senses; very hot (*flaming June; a flaming sun*); bright-coloured; (arch.) exaggerated, over-laudatory, (*a flaming description*); (colloq.) passionate (*had a flaming row about it*); (colloq.) = DAMNED 2, 3, (*that flaming dog*). [f. FLAME² + -ING²]

flami′ngō (-nggō) *n.* (*pl.* ∼s *or* ∼es). tall long--necked web-footed (sub)tropical bird with pink, scarlet, and black plumage. [f. Port. *flamengo* f. Prov. *flamenc* (*flama* flame, *-enc* = -ING³)]

flă′mm|able *a.* inflammable; hence ∼ABI′LITY *n.* [f. L *flammare* (*flamma* flame) + -ABLE]

flăn *n.* pastry or sponge cake filled or spread with jam, fruit, cheese, etc.; disc of metal from which coin etc. is made. [F, orig. = round cake, f. OF *flaon* f. med. L *flado -onis* f. Frank. **flado* flat cake]

flanch (-ah-) *v.i.* & *t.* (cause to) slope inwards towards the top (esp. of chimney); hence ∼′ING¹ (2) *n.* [perh. f. OF *flanchir* (*flanche, flanc* FLANK)]

flânerie (flah′nrē) *n.* idling; so **flâneur** (flahnẽr′) *n.*, idler. [F (*flâner* lounge)]

flănge (-nj) *n.*, & *v.t.* **1.** *n.* projecting flat rim, collar, or rib, used for strengthening or attachment. **2.** *v.t.* provide with flange. [17th c., perh. f. *flange* widen out f. OF *flangir* (as FLANCH)]

flănk *n.*, & *v.t.* **1.** *n.* fleshy part of side of body between ribs and hip; side of building, mountain, etc.; right or left side of army or other body of persons (**in** ∼, at the side; TURN¹ *flank of*); ∼ **forward,** (Rugby Footb.) wing forward. **2.** *v.t.* guard or strengthen on the flank; menace flank of; enfilade, rake; be posted or situated at flank of. [ME, f. OF *flanc* f. Frank. **hlanca* side]

flā′nker *n.* fortification guarding or menacing flank; thing that flanks anything; (Rugby Footb.) flank forward; (sl.) trick, swindle. [f. prec. + -ER¹]

flă′nnel¹ *n.* **1.** woven woollen stuff, usu. without nap;

(in *pl.*) garments (esp. trousers) of flannel, whence ‖∼IED², *∼ED², (-ld) *a.*; hence ∼′ETTE (2) *n.*, napped cotton fabric imitating texture of flannel, ∼lY² *a.* **2.** ‖piece of flannel etc. used in washing hands, face, etc., or cleaning floor. **3.** (sl.) nonsense; flattery; bragging. **4.** Hence ∼**board,** ∼**graph,** sheet of flannel for attachment of paper or cloth cut-outs esp. in teaching; *∼**-mouth,** flatterer, braggart. [perh. f. W *gwlanen* (*gwlân* wool)]

flă′nnel² *v.t.* & *i.* (‖-ll-). use flannel to wash or clean; (sl.) use flattery (on). [f. prec.]

flăp *v.* (-**pp-**) & *n.* **1.** *v.t.* strike with something broad, drive (flies etc.) *away* or *off* thus; move (wings) up and down. **2.** *v.i.* swing or sway about, flutter, oscillate; (of wings) move up and down; beat the wings; (colloq., of ears) be listening intently; (colloq.) be agitated or panicky; hence ∼′pY² *a.* **3.** *n.* light blow with something broad; up-and-down motion of wing etc.; (colloq.) state of agitation or fuss (*be in, get into, a flap*). **4.** broad piece hinged or attached by one side only, e.g. trapdoor, pocket-cover, envelope-seal, table-leaf, valve, fish's gill-cover; open mushroom-top; (Aeronaut.) aileron, hinged or sliding section used to control lift. [ME, prob. imit.]

flăpdoō′dle *n.* (colloq.) nonsense. [19th c.; orig. unkn.]

flă′pjăck *n.* pancake; sweet oatcake; vanity case for face-powder. [f. FLAP + JACK¹]

flă′pper *n.* **1.** instrument that is flapped to kill flies, scare birds, etc.; young wild-duck or partridge; (arch. sl.) (esp. unconventional) young woman. **2.** hinged or hanging piece, flap; broad fin; crustacean's tail. [f. FLAP + -ER¹]

flāre *v.* & *n.* **1.** *v.i.* (Of ship's sides, wineglass, trousers, skirt, etc.) widen gradually in upward or downward direction. **2.** blaze with bright spreading unsteady flame, glow as with flame, (*away, out*); ∼ (**up**), burst into sudden blaze or anger or activity, whence ∼**-up** *n.* **3.** *v.t.* cause to flare. **4.** *n.* dazzling irregular light, unshaded flame in open air; sudden outburst of flame; (Astron.) sudden outburst of radiation from sun or star; signal light used at sea; bright light used as signal; container of combustible material, dropped from aircraft to illuminate target etc. (∼**-path,** area illuminated to enable aircraft to land or take off); (Photog.) extraneous illumination caused by internal reflection etc. **5.** upward bulge in ship's sides; gradual widening (esp. of skirt). [16th c., of unkn. orig. (perh. Scand.)]

flăsh *v.* **1.** *v.i.* break suddenly into flame, give out flame or sparks, (∼ **in the pan,** cf. foll.); ∼′**ing-point,** = FLASH²*-point*; ∼ **over,** make electrical circuit by sparking across gap, whence ∼**-over** *n.*); emit or reflect light briefly or intermittently, gleam, (*lighthouse flashes once a minute*); ∼ **out** or **up,** show sudden passion. **2.** burst suddenly into view or perception (*idea flashed upon me*); move swiftly; (of water) rush along, rise and flow; (sl.) briefly display oneself indecently; ∼′**back,** (Cinemat. etc.) scene returning to or changing to earlier time; ∼**-board** (for sending more water from mill-dam into mill-race); ∼**-flood,** sudden local flood due to heavy rain etc. **3.** *v.t.* send or reflect like a flash or in flashes (*eyes flash fire, flash back defiance*); cause to gleam or shine briefly (*flashed his sword; had a torch flashed in my face; flash headlights of car*); signal to (person) by causing (head)lights to shine briefly; show suddenly or ostentatiously; send (news etc.) by radio, telegraph, etc. [ME, orig. app. imit. of sea etc.; cf. *splash*]

flăsh² *n.* **1.** sudden transitory blaze, esp. of lightning or (fig.) of wit, (∼ **in the pan,** promising start followed by failure [from priming of old guns]); (Photog.) = *flashlight* (2). **2.** very brief time, instant, (*in a flash*); brief news dispatch by radio, telegraph, etc.; sudden short access of feeling (*a flash of hope*). **3.** (Cinemat.) momentary exposure of a scene. **4.** rush of water, esp. down weir to take boat over shallows, contrivance for producing this. **5.** ‖(Mil.) coloured patch of cloth on uniform etc. as distinguishing emblem of unit etc. **6.** ∼ **bulb** (giving light for flashlight photograph); ∼ **burn** (caused by sudden intense heat esp. from nuclear explosion); ∼ **card** (with words etc. for brief inspection during learning); ∼**-cube**, set of four flash bulbs arranged as cube and operated in turn; ∼**-gun**, device to operate camera flashlight; ∼**-lamp**, portable flashing electric lamp; ∼**'light**, (1) flashing light used for signals and in lighthouses, (2) illuminating device for photographing by night etc., picture so taken, (3) *electric TORCH; ∼**-point**, temperature at which vapour from oil etc. will ignite, (fig.) point at which indignation etc. begins. [f. prec.]

flash[3] *a.* gaudy, showy; counterfeit (*flash notes, money*); cant, slang; connected with thieves, tramps, etc. [f. prec.]

flä'sher *n.* In vbl senses; automatic device for switching lights rapidly on and off; sign or signal using this. [f. FLASH[1] + -ER[1]]

flä'shing *n.* strip of metal to prevent flooding or leakage at joint of roofing etc. [f. dial. *flash* flashing with lead sheets or obs. *flash* flashing, + -ING[1]]

flä'sh|y *a.* brilliant but shallow or transitory, cheaply attractive; showy, gaudy; given to display; hence ∼iLY[2] *adv.*, ∼iNESS *n.* [f. FLASH[1,2] + -Y[2]]

flask (-ah-) *n.* narrow-necked bottle for wine or oil, or for use in chemistry; traveller's pocket bottle of metal or (usu. leather-covered) glass for wine, spirits, etc.; = VACUUM *flask*, (Hist.) – POWDER-*flask*. [f. F *flasque* & (prob.) It.*fiasco* f. med. L *flasca, flasco*; cf. FLAGON]

flät[1] *n.* rooms on one floor as residence; hence ∼'LET *n.* [alt. f. obs. *flet* = OE & ON *flet* floor, dwelling f. Gmc *flatjam* (as foll.)]

flät[2] *a., adv., n.,* & *v.t.* (-tt-). **1.** *a.* horizontal, level; spread out, lying at full length, (*fell flat*; *flat against the wall*; *with the flat hand*). **2.** even, smooth, unbroken, without projection, (of tint) uniform; with broad level surface and little depth (*flat cap, heel, nose*). **3.** unqualified, plain, downright, (*flat denial, refusal*; *flat nonsense, blasphemy*; *that's* ∼, let there be no doubt about it); dull, lifeless, monotonous, (*fall* ∼, prove a failure, not win applause); (of market, prices, etc.) inactive, sluggish; (Photog.) lacking contrast; (of paint etc.) not glossy; dejected, without energy, (of drink) that has lost its effervescence; (of accumulator etc.) unable to generate any more electric current until recharged. **4.** (Mus.) below true pitch (**B, E,** etc., ∼, a semitone lower than B, E, etc.); (of key) having flat(s) in signature. **5.** ∼ **arch** (with flat intrados); ∼**(-bottomed) boat** (with flat bottom for transport in shallow water); *∼**'car**, railway wagon without raised sides or ends; ∼**-fish**, fish of order Heterosomata, including sole, turbot, plaice, etc.; ∼ **foot**, foot with less than normal arch; ∼**'foot**, (sl.) policeman; ∼**-footed**, having flat feet, (colloq.) downright, resolute, uninspired, unprepared; ∼**-foot** *a.*, (of engine) having four cylinders all horizontal, two on each side of crankshaft; ∼**-head**, snake with flat head of genus *Heterodon*, (sl.) foolish person; ∼**-iron** (for ironing clothes etc., usu. triangular and heated by external means); ∼ **race** (over level ground, opp. hurdle-race or steeplechase); ∼ **rate** (same in all cases, not proportional etc.); ∼ **spin**, (Aeron.) nearly horizontal spin, (colloq.) agitation or panic; *∼**-top**, (sl.) aircraft-carrier; ∼ **tyre** (deflated or punctured); ∼**'ware**, plates, saucers, etc. (opp. hollow-ware), *domestic cutlery; ∼**'worm**, worm of phylum Platyhelminthes (tapeworm, fluke, etc.). **6.** Hence ∼LY[2] *adv.*, ∼'NESS *n.*, ∼'tISH[1] 2 *a.*, ∼'WAYS, ∼'WISE, *advs.* **7.** *adv.* in a flat manner (*lies flat*; *turned it down flat*; *sings flat*); (colloq.) completely (*flat broke*), exactly or not exceeding (*ten seconds flat*); ∼ **out**, at top speed, using all one's strength or resources. **8.** *n.* what is flat; flat part of anything (*the flat of the hand*; *with the flat of his sword*); level ground, plain, low land, swamp; flat tyre; (*the* season of flat races for horses; (Theatr.)

section of scenery mounted on frame (**join the** ∼**s**, (fig.) make a thing into a coherent whole, preserve appearance of a consistent attitude); (sl.) foolish person. **9.** (Mus.) note lowered a semitone below natural pitch; sign indicating this lowering; **sharps and** ∼**s**, black keys on piano. **10.** *v.t.* make flat (esp. tech. & *Mus.). [ME, f. ON *flatr*, OHG *flaz* f. Gmc *flataz*]

flä'tten *v.t.* & *i.* make or become flat; humiliate; ∼ **out**, (Aeronaut.) bring aircraft parallel to ground. [f. prec. + -EN[6]]

flä'tter *v.t.* pay obsequious attention to; compliment unduly, overpraise; gratify vanity of, make feel honoured; inspire (person, or abs.) with (esp. unfounded) hope; please or delude one*self* with the belief (*that*); gratify (eye, ear, etc.; ∼**ing unction**, salve one administers to one's own conscience or self-esteem [Shak. *Hamlet* III. iv. 145]); (of portrait, painter, etc.) exaggerate good looks of, represent too favourably; hence or cogn. ∼ER[1], **flä'ttERY** (4, 5), *ns.* [ME, perh. rel. to OF *flater* to smooth]

flä'ttie, flä'ttý, *n.* (colloq.) flat-heeled shoe; flat-bottomed boat; policeman. [f. FLAT[2] + -IE, -Y[3]]

flä'tül|ent *a.* causing formation of gas in the alimentary canal; caused by, accompanied by, troubled with, accumulation of such gas; inflated, puffed up, windy, pretentious; hence or cogn. ∼ENCE, ∼ENCY, *ns.*, ∼ent|LY[2] *adv.* [F, f. mod. L *flatulentus* (as foll.; see -ULENT)]

flä'tus *n.* wind in or from stomach or bowels. [L, – blowing (*flare* blow)]

flaunch. Var. of FLANCH.

flaunt *v.i.* & *t.* wave proudly; display oneself or one's finery; show off, parade, (one*self*, finery, etc.); hence ∼'y[2] *a.* [16th c.; orig. unkn.]

flau'tist *n.* flute-player. [f. It. *flautista* (*flauto* FLUTE)]

flave'scent *a.* turning yellow, yellowish. [f. L *flavescere* (*flavus* yellow; see -ESCENT)]

flä'vine (-ēn) *n.* yellow dye got from dyer's oak; antiseptic derived from acridine. [f. L *flavus* yellow + -INE[5]]

flävöprö'tein (-tēn) *n.* (Biol.) one of group of conjugated proteins concerned in oxidation and reduction reactions in cells. [f. as prec. + -o- + PROTEIN]

‖**flä'vour** (-ver), *flä'vor, n.,* & *v.t.* **1.** *n.* aroma, mingled sensation of smell and taste; distinctive taste; undefinable characteristic quality; slight admixture of (usu. undesirable) quality; hence **flä'vorous, ∼**FUL, ∼LESS, ∼SOME[1], *adjs.* **2.** *v.t.* give flavour to, season; hence ∼ING[1] (3) *n.* [ME, f. OF *flaor*, perh. f. Rom. *flator* f. L *flatus* blowing & *foetor* stench; assim. to *savour*]

flaw[1] & *v.* **1.** *n.* crack, breach, rent; imperfection, blemish; (Law) invalidating defect in document, procedure, evidence, etc.; hence ∼'LESS *a.* **2.** *v.t.* & *i.* crack; damage; spoil. [ME, perh. f. ON *flaga* slab f. Gmc *flah-, *flag-; cf. FLAKE[2], FLAG[2]]

flaw[2] *n.* squall of wind; short storm. [prob. f. MDu. *vlāghe*, MLG *vlāge*, perh. = stroke]

flax *n.* blue-flowered plant (*Linum usitatissimum*) cultivated for its textile fibre and its seeds (LINSEED); similar plant (*toadflax*; **New Zealand** ∼, = *flax-lily*); fibres of flax, dressed or not; (arch.) cloth of flax, linen; ∼**-lily**, NZ plant of genus *Phormium* yielding valuable fibre; ∼**-seed**, linseed. [OE *flæx*, = OHG *flahs* f. WG *flahsa*]

flä'xen *a.* flax; of (hair) coloured like dressed flax, pale yellow. [f. prec. + -EN[5]]

flay *v.t.* strip off skin or hide of; peel off (skin, bark, peel); (fig.) criticize severely; (arch.) pillage, plunder, (person); ∼**-flint**, (arch.) extortioner, miser. [OE *flēan*, = MDu. *vlae(gh)en*, ON *flā* f. Gmc *flahan*]

F-layer (ě'flāer) *n.* highest and most strongly ionized region of ionosphere. [f. F (arbitrary) + LAYER]

flea *n.* **1.** small wingless jumping insect of order Siphonaptera, feeding on human and other blood (*send person away* **with a** ∼ **in his ear,** discomfited by reproof or repulse); small jumping crustacean; = *flea-beetle*. **2.** ∿-**bag,** (sl.) sleeping-bag, unattractive place (esp. lodgings); ∿'**bane,** one of various composite plants supposed to drive away fleas; ∿-**beetle,** jumping beetle infesting hops, cabbages, etc.; ∿-**bite,** (1) bite of flea, (2) (fig.) slight inconvenience or expense, mere trifle, (3) small reddish or brown or black spot in animal's coloration (so ∿-**bitten,** sprinkled with these on lighter ground); *∿-**bug,** = *flea-beetle*; ∿-**circus,** show of performing fleas; ∿-**dock,** butterbur; ∿-**louse,** jumping plant-louse of family Psyllidae; ∿ **market,** (joc.) street market; ∿-**pit,** (sl.) allegedly verminous place of public assembly, e.g. cinema; ∿-**wort,** one of various plants supposed to drive away fleas. [OE *flēa(h)*, = MLG, MDu. *vlō*, OHG *flōh*, ON *fló* f. Gmc **flauh-* or **thlauh-*; cf. FLEE]

fleam *n.* lancet for bleeding of horses. [f. OF *flieme* f. Rom. **fleutomum* f. LL *phlebotomus* f. Gk *phlebotomon* (see PHLEBOTOMY)]

flèche (flāsh) *n.* slender spire perforated with windows, esp. at intersection of nave and transept. [F, orig. = arrow]

flĕck *n.,* & *v.t.* **1.** *n.* spot in the skin, freckle; patch of colour or light; small particle, speck; hence ∿'LESS *a.* **2.** *v.t.* mark with flecks, dapple, variegate. [perh. f. ON *flekkr* n., *flekka* v., or MLG, MDu. *vlecke,* OHG *flec, fleccho*]

flĕ'cker *v.t.* dapple, variegate; scatter in patches. [f. prec. + -ER⁵]

***flĕ'ction.** See FLEXION.

flĕd. See FLEE.

flĕdge *v.t.* **1.** provide (bird, arrow) with feathers or plumage; wing for flight; deck with feathers or down. **2.** bring up (young bird) till it can fly; (in *p.p.*) able to fly, (fig.) mature, independent. [f. obs. *fledge a.* 'fit to fly', f. OE **flecge, *flycge*, MDu. *vlugghe,* OHG *flucchi* f. WG *fluggja* (**flug-* FLY²)]

flĕ'dgling, flĕ'dgeling, (-jl-) *n.* young bird; inexperienced person. [f. as prec. + -LING¹]

flee *v.* (**fled**). **1.** *v.i.* run away, seek safety thus, (*from, before*); vanish, cease, pass away. **2.** *v.t.* run away from, leave abruptly; eschew, shun. [OE *flēon*, = OS, OHG *fliohan,* ON *flý(j)a,* Goth. *thliuhan* f. Gmc **thleuhan*]

fleece *n.,* & *v.t.* **1.** *n.* woolly covering of sheep or similar animal (**Golden F**∿, (Gk Myth.) fleece of gold sought and won by Jason); (Her.) representation of this suspended from ring; quantity of wool shorn from a sheep at one time; rough, abundant, or woolly head of hair; thing like fleece (white cloud, falling snow, etc.); soft silky textile fabric used for lining etc.; hence (-)**fleeceD²** (-ĕst), **flee'cY²,** *adjs.* **2.** *v.t.* remove fleece from (sheep etc.); strip (person) of or of money, property, etc., whence ∿'ABLE (-sa-) *a.*; overspread as with fleece (*sky fleeced with clouds*). [OE *flēos,* = Du. & MHG *vlies* f. WG **fleusa,* & OE *flēs* f. WG **fleusi*]

fleer *v.i.,* & *n.* **1.** *v.i.* laugh impudently or mockingly, gibe, jeer, sneer. **2.** *n.* mocking look or speech. [ME, prob. f. Scand.; cf. Norw. & Sw. dial. *flira* to grin]

fleet¹ *n.* **1.** naval force, number of warships under one commander-in-chief, *the* navy; number of ships or boats sailing in company; similar force of aircraft; ∿ **of buses, lorries, taxis,** etc., (owned by one proprietor). **2.** **Fleet* ADMIRAL; **F**∿ **Air Arm,** (Hist.) aviation service of Royal Navy. [OE *flēot* ship, shipping (*flēotan* float, FLEET⁵)]

fleet² *n.* **1.** ‖(dial.) creek, inlet. **2. the F**∿, (1) stream (now covered) running into Thames E. of Fleet Street in London, (2) (Hist.) prison that stood near it; **F**∿ **marriage,** (Hist.) wedding performed by disreputable clergyman (**F**∿ **parson**) in or near the Fleet Prison ready to conduct weddings clandestinely; **F**∿ **Street,** the London press, London journalism. [OE *flēot,* = MDu. *vliet,* MHG *vliez,* ON *fljót* f. Gmc **fleut-* FLEET⁵]

fleet³ *a.* (poet. or literary). swift, nimble; hence ∿'LY² *adv.,* ∿'NESS *n.* [prob. f. ON *fljótr* f. Gmc **fleut-* FLEET⁵]

‖**fleet⁴** *a.* & *adv.* (dial.) **1.** *a.* (Of water) shallow. **2.** *adv.* at or to a small depth (*plough* or *sow fleet*). [perh. f. OE **flēat*; cf. Du. *vloot* shallow, f. as foll.]

fleet⁵ *v.i.* **1.** (arch.) glide away, vanish, be transitory; pass rapidly, slip *away*; move swiftly, fly. **2.** Hence ∿'ING² *a.,* transitory, brief, ∿'INGLY *adv.* [OE *flēotan* float, swim, = OS *fliotan,* OHG *fliozan,* ON *fljóta* f. Gmc **fleutan*]

Flē'ming *n.* native of Flanders. [OE f. ON *Flǣmingi* & MDu. *Vlāming,* f. root of *Vlaanderen* Flanders; see -ING³]

Flē'mish *a.* & *n.* (language) of Flanders; *Flemish* BOND¹ **5.** [f. MDu. *Vlāmisch* (as prec.; see -ISH¹)]

flĕnch, flĕnse, flinch¹, *v.t.* cut up (whale or seal); flay (seal). [f. Da *flense*; cf. Norw. *flinsa, flunsa* flay]

flĕsh¹ *n.* **1.** soft substance between skin and bones, esp. muscular part of animal bodies. **2.** body as opp. to mind or soul; **all** ∿, whatever has bodily life (*the way of all flesh,* experience common to all men); ∿ **and blood,** (*n.*) the body or its material, mankind, human nature with its emotions and infirmities, (*a.*) actually living, not supernatural or imaginary; one's **own** ∿ **and blood,** near relatives, descendants; ∿ **and fell,** (*n.*) the whole body, (*adv.*) entirely; **in the** ∿, in bodily form, in life; **make** person's ∿ **creep,** frighten or horrify him esp. with dread of the supernatural; **one** ∿, united as one personality [Gen. 2:24]; PROUD *flesh*; **sins of the** ∿, unchastity. **3.** pulpy substance of fruit or plant. **4.** plumpness, fat, (**lose, put on,** ∿, grow thinner, fatter). **5.** tissue of animal bodies (excluding fish and sometimes fowl) as food, meat, esp. muscle with or without fat (*flesh-eater* etc.; *neither* FISH¹, *flesh, nor* etc.). **6.** visible surface of human body, w. ref. to its colour or appearance; ∿-**colour**(ed), yellowish pink. **7.** ∿-**brush** (for stimulating circulation by rubbing); ∿-**fly** (depositing eggs or larvae in dead flesh); ∿-**pots,** luxurious living [Exod. 16:3]; ∿ (side), side of a hide that adjoined the flesh; ∿-**tints,** (esp.) painter's rendering of flesh-colours; ∿-**wound,** one not reaching bone or vital organ. **8.** Hence ∿'LESS *a.* [OE *flǣsc* = OS *flēsk,* OHG *fleisc,* ON *flesk* pork f. Gmc **flaiskaz, -iz*]

flĕsh² *v.* **1.** *v.t.* incite (hound etc.) by taste of blood; initiate in bloodshed; inflame by foretaste of success; use (sword etc.) for first time on flesh (or fig. of pen, wit, etc.); embody in flesh. **2.** *v.t.* & *i.* ∿ **out,** make or become substantial. [f. prec.]

flĕ'sher *n.* (Sc.) butcher. [ME, f. FLESH¹ + -ER¹]

flĕ'shings (-z) *n. pl.* actor's flesh-coloured tights. [f. FLESH¹ + -ING¹ + -s¹]

flĕ'shlȳ *a.* (Of desire etc.) bodily, lascivious, sensual; mortal, material, not divine or spiritual; worldly; hence ∿INESS *n.* [OE *flǣsclic* (as FLESH¹, -LY¹)]

flĕ'shȳ *a.* plump, fat; of flesh, without bone; (of plant or fruit tissue) pulpy; like flesh; hence ∿INESS *n.* [ME, f. FLESH¹ + -Y²]

flĕ'tcher *n.* (arch.) maker or seller of arrows. [ME, f. OF *flech(i)er* (*fleche* arrow)]

Flĕ'ton *n.* type of brick made by semi-dry process. [∿ in Cambs., near where clay was orig. taken for this process]

fleur de coin (flĕr de kwā'n) *n.* mint or perfect condition of a coin. [F, = bloom of the minting-die]

fleur-de-lis, -lys, (flĕrdelē') *n.* (*pl.* **fleurs-** *pr.* same). iris flower; heraldic lily composed of three petals bound together near their bases; (in *sing.* or *pl.*) former royal arms of France. [ME f. OF *flour de lys* flower of lily]

fleur'ĕt (-oor'-) *n.* ornament like small flower. [f. F *fleurette* (*fleur* flower; see -ET¹)]

fleuron (flĕraw'n) *n.* flower-shaped ornament in architecture or printing, on coin, etc. [ME, f. OF *floron* (*flour* FLOWER)]

fleur'ȳ (-oor'ĭ), **flŏ'r'ȳ,** *a.* (Her.) decorated with fleurs-de-lis. [ME, f. OF *flo(u)ré* (as prec.; see -Y⁴)]

flew. See FLY².

flews (-ōoz) *n. pl.* hanging lips of bloodhound etc. [16th c.; orig. unkn.]

flěx[1] *v.t.* (Anat.) bend (joint, limb); move (muscle) to bend joint; (Geol.) distort (strata); (Archaeol.) place (corpse) with legs drawn up under chin. [f. L *flectere flex-* bend]

||**flěx**[2] *n.* flexible insulated wire used for carrying electric current to lamp, iron, etc. [abbr. of foll.]

flě′x|ible *a.* that will bend without breaking, pliable, pliant; easily led, manageable; adaptable; versatile; supple, complaisant; hence or cogn. ∼IBI′LITY *n.*, ∼IBLY *adv.* [ME f. OF or f. L *flexibilis* (as FLEX[1]; see -IBLE)]

flě′xile *a.* (arch.) supple, mobile; tractable; versatile; hence **flěxi′LITY** *n.* [f. L *flexilis* (as FLEX[1]; see -IL)]

flě′xion (-kshon), ***flě′ction**, *n.* bending, curvature, bent state, (esp. of limb or joint); bent part, curve; (Gram.) inflexion, whence ∼AL, ∼LESS, *adjs.*; (Math.) = FLEXURE. [f. L *flexio* (as FLEX[1]; see -ION)]

flě′xitime *n.* (system of) working-hours with set total but times partly as chosen by employee. [f. FLEXIBLE + TIME[1]]

flě′xor *n,* ∼ (**muscle**), muscle that bends part of the body. [mod. L (as FLEX[1]; see -OR)]

flě′xŭous *a.* full of bends, winding; hence or cogn. **flěxŭo′SITY** *n.*, ∼LY[2] *adv.* [f. L *flexuosus* (*flexus* bending f. as FLEX[1]) + -OUS]

flě′xur|e (-ksher) *n.* bending, curvature, bent state; bend, curve, turn; (Math.) curving of line or surface or solid (esp. from straight line, plane, etc.); (Geol.) bending of strata under pressure; hence ∼AL *a.* [f. L *flexura* (as FLEX[1]; see -URE)]

flĭbbertigĭ′bbět *n.* gossiping, flighty, frivolous, or restless person. [imit. of chatter]

flick *n. & v.* **1.** *n.* light sharp blow with whiplash etc. shot out and withdrawn, or with finger-nail; sudden movement, jerk; quick turn of wrist in playing games; slight sharp sound; (colloq.) cinema film, (in *pl.*) cinema performance; ∼-**knife,** weapon with blade springing out when button is pressed. **2.** *v.t.* strike or move with a flick; dash or jerk (*dust etc.*) *away, off;* give a flick with (whip, towel, etc.). **3.** *v.i.* make flicking movement; ∼ **through,** turn over (cards, pages, etc.), turn over pages etc. of, by rapid movement of fingers. [ME, imit.]

flĭ′cker[1] *v.i., & n.* **1.** *v.i.* (Of flag, leaf, serpent's tongue, wind, etc.) quiver, vibrate, or wave or move to and fro, blow lightly and unsteadily; (of flame, or fig. of hope, etc.) burn up and die away by turns; (of light) undergo transient increase or decrease of brightness; ∼ **out,** die away after final flicker. **2.** *n.* flickering movement or light. [OE *flicorian, flycerian*]

flĭ′cker[2] *n.* N. Amer. woodpecker of genus *Colaptes.* [imit. of its note]

flĭ′er. See FLYER.

flight[1] (-īt) *n., & v.t.* **1.** act or manner of flying through air (**take** or **wing** one's ∼, fly); pursuit of game by hawk; migration, migrating body, flock, of birds or insects. **2.** swift movement of projectiles etc.; passage of projectile from gun to target; trajectory and pace of ball in games; (of time) swift passage; soaring, excursion, sally, (*of* wit, fancy, ambition, etc.); distance that bird, aircraft, or missile, can fly. **3.** series (*of* stairs in straight line or between two landings, or *of* hurdles or rails for racing over); volley (*of* arrows etc.); tail of dart; **in the first** or **top** ∼, taking a leading place. **4.** act or technique of travelling in aircraft, spacecraft, etc.; movement of such craft; regular journey by airline; RAF unit of about six aircraft. **5.** ∼ **bag,** small zipped bag with shoulder--strap, as carried by air travellers; ∼ **control,** system (internal or external) directing movement of aircraft; ∼-**deck,** (1) deck of aircraft-carrier for take-off and landing, (2) accommodation for pilot, navigator, etc., in aircraft; ∼-**feather** (supporting bird in flight); ∼ **lieutenant, sergeant,** ranks in RAF; ∼ **officer,** rank in WRAF, corresp. to *flight lieutenant;* ∼ **path,** planned course of aircraft or spacecraft; ∼-**recorder,** device in aircraft to record technical details during flight for use in case of accident; ∼-**test** *v.t.,* test (aircraft, rocket, etc.) during flight. **6.** *v.t.* shoot (wildfowl, or abs.) in flight; vary trajectory and pace of (cricket-ball etc.); provide (arrow) with feathers. [OE *flyht,* = OS *fluht* f. WG **flūhti* (*fleugan* FLY[2])]

flight[2] (-īt) *n.* act or manner of fleeing, hasty retreat, (**take, take to,** ∼, run away; **put to** ∼, rout); (Econ.) selling of currency, investments, etc., in anticipation of fall in value, (*flight from sterling*). [OE **flyht,* = OS, OHG *fluht,* ON *flótti* f. Gmc **thluhtiz* (**thleuhan* FLEE)]

flĭ′ghtlėss (-ī′t-) *a.* (Of bird etc.) unable to fly. [f. FLIGHT[1] + -LESS]

flĭ′ght|y̆ (-ī′tĭ) *a.* guided by whim or fancy, fickle; crazy; hence ∼iLY[2] *adv.,* ∼iNESS *n.* [f. FLIGHT[1] + -Y[2]]

flĭ′mflăm *n., & v.t.* (-mm-). **1.** *n.* trifle, nonsense, idle talk; piece of humbug, deception. **2.** *v.t.* cheat, deceive; hence ∼MER[1], ∼MERY (4), *ns.* [imit. redupl.]

flĭ′ms|y̆ (-zĭ) *a. & n.* **1.** *a.* easily destroyed, frail, lightly put together; paltry, trivial; frivolous, superficial; hence ∼iLY[2] *adv.,* ∼iNESS *n.* **2.** *n.* flimsy thing or material; (document on) thin paper. [17th c., prob. f. prec.; cf. TIPSY]

flinch[1]. See FLENCH.

flinch[2] *v.i.* give way, draw back, (*from* duty, course, etc.); wince. [f. OF *flenchir, flainchir* f. WG **hlankjan*]

flĭ′nders (-z) *n. pl.* fragments, splinters. [ME, prob. f. Scand.]

fling *v.* (**flung**) *& n.* **1.** *v.t.* throw, hurl, (*about, aside, away, out, up, at*; rejected thing, missile, foam, dice); throw one*self into* person's arms, a boat, etc., *on* person's compassion etc., or *into* an enterprise (i.e. take it up with all one's might); utter (words) forcefully; suddenly spread *out* (arms), kick *up* (heels); put *on,* take *off,* (clothes) carelessly; (arch.) send, emit, (sound, smell, light). **2.** put (person) suddenly or violently *into* prison; launch (troops etc.) *on* enemy or *against* fortress or enemy; *fling* thing *in* person's *tooth* (see TOOTH). **3.** *v.i.* rush, go angrily or violently (*fling out of the room; flung away in a rage*); (of horse etc.) kick and plunge (*out*). **4.** *n.* throw, cast, (**have a** ∼ **at,** make an attempt at, jeer at); impetuous dance (esp. **Highland** ∼); violent movement, plunge; spell of indulgence in pleasure (*have one's fling*). [ME, perh. f. ON **flinga,* rel. to *flengja* flog]

flint *n.* **1.** hard stone of nearly pure silica found in pebbly lumps steel-grey within and encrusted with white; piece of flint, esp. as flaked or chipped by prehistoric man to form tool or weapon, (**set** one's **face like a** ∼, be steadfast; SKIN[2] *a flint*); anything hard and unyielding. **2.** piece of flint used with steel to produce fire (*flint and steel*) esp. in flintlock gun; piece of hard alloy of rare-earth metals used to give igniting spark in cigarette-lighter etc. **3.** ∼ **corn,** variety of maize having very hard kernels; ∼ **glass** (pure lustrous kind orig. made with flint); ∼-**lock,** (Hist.) (lock of) gun discharged by spark from flint. **4.** Hence ∼′Y[2] *a.* [OE, = MDu. *vlint,* OHG *flins*]

flip[1] *v.* (-pp-) *& n.* **1.** *v.t.* put (pellet, coin, etc.) in motion with a fillip or flick; fillip or flick (person's ear, cheek, etc.), strike lightly; turn over (∼ one's **lid** or **wig,** (sl.) lose self-control, go mad). **2.** *v.i.* make a fillip with fingers; move (fan, whip, etc.) about with sudden jerk(s); strike smartly *at* with whip etc.; (sl.) become excited or enthusiastic; ∼ **through,** = FLICK *through;* hence ∼′PING[2] *a. & adv.,* (sl.) = DAMNED 2, 3. **3.** *n.* smart light blow, fillip, flick; (colloq.) (short) flight in aeroplane; quick tour etc.; turning over (∼ **side,** reverse, less important, side of gramophone record). [prob. f. FILLIP]

flip[2] *n.* beer and spirit mixed, sweetened, and heated with hot iron; EGG[1]-*flip.* [perh. f. prec. in sense *whip up*]

flip[3] *a.* (colloq.) glib, flippant. [f. FLIP[1]]

flĭ′p-flŏp *n., & v.i.* (-pp-). **1.** *n.* electronic switching circuit changed from stable state to another, or via an unstable state back to its stable state, by triggering pulse; plastic or rubber sandal of sole and straps; *backward somersault. **2.** *v.i.* go or act in way suggested by 'flip-flop'. [imit.]

fli'ppant *a.* lacking in seriousness, treating serious things lightly, disrespectful; hence **fli'pp**ANCY *n.*, ∼LY² *adv.* [f. FLIP¹+-ANT]

fli'pper *n.* limb used to swim with, as in turtle and penguin; rubber etc. attachment to foot for underwater swimming; (sl.) hand. [f. FLIP¹+-ER¹]

flirt *v. & n.* **1.** *v.t.* fillip, send with a jerk; wave or move briskly (fan, bird's tail). **2.** *v.i.* pretend courtship or love-making (*with*); toy *with* (idea etc.); move with a jerk; hence ∼A'TION *n.*, ∼ä'tious (-shŭs) *a.* **3.** *n.* sudden jerk, quick motion quickly checked; woman who invites or accepts man's attentions merely for amusement, whence ∼'y² *a.* [imit.]

flit *v.i.* (-tt-), & *n.* **1.** *v.i.* migrate, depart; (esp. Sc. & N. Engl.) change one's abode, move; pass lightly, softly, or rapidly, (*about, by, to and fro*); (of bat or bird) fly lightly, make short flights. **2.** *n.* change of abode, esp. to evade creditor etc. [ME, f. ON *flytja*, cogn. w. FLEET⁵]

flitch *n.* side of pork salted and cured (**Dunmow** ∼, flitch given periodically at Dunmow in Essex to any couple proving conjugal harmony for year and day); slab (usu. outside one) of timber from tree-trunk; ∼-beam, compound beam, esp. of iron plate between two slabs of wood; ∼(-plate), strengthening plate in beam etc. [OE *flicce*, = MLG *vli(c)ke*, ON *flikki* f. Gmc *flikkjam (*flik- rag)]

fli'tter *v.i.* flit about, flutter; ∼-mouse, BAT¹. [f. FLIT+-ER⁵]

***fli'vver** *n.* (sl.) cheap motor car or aeroplane; failure. [20th c.; orig. uncert.]

fli'xweed *n.* cruciferous plant formerly thought to cure dysentery. [earlier *fluxweed* f. FLUX+WEED]

float¹ *n.* **1.** raft; cork or quill used on fishing-line as indicator of bite; cork supporting edge of fishing-net; hollow or inflated part or organ supporting fish etc. in water; structure to enable aircraft to float on water; floating device to control flow of water, petrol, etc. **2.** (Theatr., in *sing.* or *pl.*) footlights; ∼(-**board**), one of the boards of water-wheel or paddle-wheel; low-bodied cart, esp. ‖MILK¹-*float*; platform on wheels with display in processions; tool for smoothing plaster; sum of money made available for minor expenditures or change-giving. **3.** ∼ **process**, making ∼ **glass** by drawing it continuously on to surface of molten metal for hardening from the molten state. [partly f. OE & ON *flot* floating state, OE *flota* ship, ON *floti*; partly f. foll.]

float² *v.* **1.** *v.i.* rest or move on surface of liquid without sinking; (of stranded ship) get afloat; move with moving liquid, drift; move or be suspended freely *in* liquid or gas; (sl.) move in leisurely or casual way; hover *before* eye or mind; (Commerc., of acceptance) be in circulation; (Finance, of currency) be allowed to have fluctuating exchange rate. **2.** *v.t.* (Commerc.) bring (company, scheme) into favour, launch. **3.** (arch.) cover with liquid, inundate. **4.** (Of water etc.) support, bear along, (buoyant object); set afloat; cause (currency) to float; circulate (rumour); waft through air. **5.** ∼-stone, light porous stone that floats. [OE *flotian*, = OS *floton*, ON *flota* cogn. w. FLEET⁵; in ME infl. by OF *floter* f. Rom. *flottare, prob. also f. Gmc]

floa'tage *n.* floating; ‖(right of appropriating) flotsam; ships etc. afloat on river; floating masses; buoyancy; part of ship above water-line. [f. FLOAT¹+-AGE]

floatä'tion. Var. of FLOTATION.

floa'ter *n.* in vbl senses; ‖(St. Exch.) government stock certificate etc. recognized as security; floating voter; one who frequently changes his job; (sl.) mistake, gaffe. [f. FLOAT²+-ER¹]

floa'ting *a.* In vbl senses² (*floating* DEBT, DOCK⁴, RIB);

fluctuating, variable, not settled in a definite place, (*the floating population*); ∼ **anchor,** sea-anchor; ∼ **bridge,** (1) bridge on pontoons etc., (2) ferry working on chains; ∼ **kidney,** abnormal condition in which the kidneys are movable, such kidney; ∼ **light,** lightship, lifebuoy with lantern; ∼ **point,** (in computer) decimal etc. point that does not occupy fixed position in numbers processed; ∼ **voter** (not attached to any political party). [f. FLOAT²+-ING²]

flŏc *n.* flocculent mass of fine particles. [abbr. of FLOCCULUS]

flŏccinaucinihilipilificā'tion (flŏksī-) *n.* (joc.) act or habit of estimating as worthless. [f. L *flocci, nauci, nihili, pili,* wds denoting 'at little value'+-FICATION]

flŏ'ccŭl|āte *v.t. & i.* form into flocculent masses; hence ∼A'TION *n.* [f. FLOCCULUS+-ATE³]

flŏ'ccŭle *n.* small portion of matter like flock of wool. [f. FLOCCULUS; see -ULE]

flŏ'ccŭl|ent *a.* like tufts of wool; in or showing tufts; hence ∼ENCE *n.* [f. L *floccus* FLOCK¹+-ULENT]

flŏ'ccŭl|us *n.* (*pl.* ∼**i** *pr.* -ī). floccule; (Anat.) small lobe in under-surface of cerebellum; (Astron.) small cloudy wisp on sun's surface. [mod. L, dim. of foll.]

flŏ'cc|us *n.* (*pl.* ∼**i** *pr.* -ŏ'ksī). tuft of woolly hairs or filaments. [L, = foll.]

flŏck¹ *n.* lock or tuft of wool, cotton, etc.; (in *pl.*) material for quilting and stuffing made of wool-refuse or torn-up cloth; powdered wool or cloth; (Chem., in *pl.*) light loose masses precipitated; ∼-**bed,** ∼-**mattress,** (stuffed with flocks); ∼-**paper,** wallpaper sized and then sprinkled with powdered wool; hence ∼'y² *a.* [ME, f. OF *floc* f. L *floccus*]

flŏck² *n., & v.i.* **1.** *n.* number of animals of one kind, esp. birds, feeding or travelling together; number of domestic animals, usu. sheep, goats, or geese, kept together (∼-**master,** sheep-farmer; ∼s **and herds,** sheep and cattle); large crowd of people. **2.** Christian body, congregation esp. in relation to its pastor; family of children, number of pupils, etc. **3.** *v.i.* congregate, go in great numbers, troop, (*about, after, into, to, in, out, together*). [OE *flocc,* = MLG *vlocke,* ON *flokkr*]

flŏe *n.* sheet of floating ice. [prob. f. Norw. *flo* f. ON *fló*]

flŏg *v.* (-gg-). **1.** *v.t.* beat with birch, cane, whip, etc. (∼ **to death,** (colloq.) talk about, promote, etc., *ad nauseam*); drive (learning etc.) *into* or (laziness etc.) *out of* person; urge (horse etc.) on with whip (∼ **a dead horse,** waste energy on something unalterable); (sl.) defeat, excel; (sl.) sell; (sl.) steal. **2.** *v.i* (sl.) proceed by violent or painful effort. [17th-c. cant; prob. imit., or f. L *flagellare* to whip]

flŏng *n.* prepared paper for making stereotype moulds. [f. F *flan* FLAN]

flood (-ŭd) *n. & v.* **1.** *n.* inflow of tide; (poet.) river, stream, sea (∼ **and field,** sea and land). **2.** irruption of water over land, inundation, (**the F**∼, that described in Genesis); outpouring (as) of water, torrent, downpour, (*flood of rain*; *a flood of abuse* or *light* or *tears* or *words*); (colloq.) = *floodlight*. **3.** ∼'**gate,** gate opened and closed to admit or exclude water, esp. lower gate of lock, (fig.) what holds back rain, tears, etc.; ∼'**light** *n., & v.t.,* (illuminate with, lamp used for) copious artificial light projected from many directions, eliminating all shadows on surface illuminated; *flood*-TIDE¹. **4.** *v.t.* overflow in or cover with a flood (lit. or fig.; *market was flooded with foreign goods*; *I was flooded with letters*); irrigate; deluge (burning house, mine) with water; overfill (carburettor) with petrol; (of rain) fill (river) to overflowing; drive *out* (of home etc.) because of flood. **5.** *v.i.* come (in) in great quantities; become flooded; have uterine haemorrhage. [OE *flōd,* = OS *flōd,* OHG *fluot,* ON *flóth,* Goth. *flōdus* f. Gmc *flōdhuz,* *flōdham *flō- f. IE *plō-]

floor (-ōr) *n., & v.t.* **1.** *n.* lower surface of room, boards etc. of which it is made, (*mop* or WIPE *the floor with*); bottom of sea, cave, cavity, etc.; level area; part of legislative assembly which members sit in and speak from; right to speak next in debate (*have* or *be given the floor*); (Cricket colloq.) *the* ground; minimum of prices, wages, etc.; **cross the** ∿, join opposing side in debating-assembly; **from the** ∿, given by individual member at meeting, not by those on platform etc.; **take the** ∿, (1) begin to dance on dance-floor etc., (2) *speak in debate. **2.** set of rooms etc. on same level in building (GROUND¹ *floor*, *first** ∿, on ground level; ||**first** ∿, *second** ∿, next above this), storey. **3.** ∿-board (used for floors); ∿-cloth (for washing floors); *∿-lamp, standard lamp; *∿-leader, leader of party in legislative assembly; ∿ manager, stage manager of a television production, shop-walker; ∿ plan, diagram of rooms etc. on one storey of building; ∿-polish, manufactured substance for making floors glossy; ∿ show, entertainment presented not on stage but on floor of night-club etc.; *∿-walker, shopwalker. **4.** Hence ∿'ING¹ (3) *n.*, ∿'LESS *a*. **5.** *v.t.* furnish with floor, pave; serve as floor of; bring to the floor or ground, knock down; confound, nonplus, baffle; overcome, get the better of. [OE *flōr*, = MDu. *vloer*, MHG *vluor*, ON *flór* f. Gmc **floruz*]

floo'zie, floo'sie, (-zĭ) *n.* (colloq.) girl or woman, esp. disreputable one. [20th c.; cf. FLOSSY and dial. *floosy* fluffy]

flŏp *v.i.* (-**pp**-), *n.*, & *adv.* **1.** *v.i.* sway about heavily and loosely; move in ungainly way; sit, kneel, lie, fall, *down* awkwardly or suddenly; change one's behaviour etc. suddenly; make dull sound of soft body falling or of flat thing slapping water; (sl.) sleep; (sl.) fail, collapse; hence ∿'PY² *a*. (∿**py disc**, flexible disc bearing machine-readable data). **2.** *n.* flopping motion, sound made by it; (sl.) thing or person that fails; *(sl.) bed; ∿-house, (sl.) doss-house. **3.** *adv.* with a flop. [var. of FLAP]

flor. abbr. floruit.

flōr'a *n.* (*pl.* ∿e *or* ∿s). plants of a region, epoch, or environment; treatise on or list of these. [mod. L, f. name of goddess of flowers (*flos floris* flower)]

floral (-ŏr'-, -ŏ'r-) *a.* of flowers; decorated with or depicting flowers; of flora(e). [f. L *floralis* or *flos floris* flower; see -AL]

flō'rĕăt *v.i.* may (he etc.) flourish. [L, 3rd sing. pres. subj. of *florēre* flourish]

Flō'rentine *a*. & *n*. (native or inhabitant) of Florence in Italy. [f. F *Florentin -ine* or f. L *Florentinus* (*Florentia* Florence; see -INE¹)]

flore'scence (-ŏr-, -ŏr-) *n.* flowering time or state (lit. or fig.). [f. mod. L *florescentia* f. L *florescere* (*florēre* bloom; see -ESCENCE)]

flŏr'ĕt *n*. (Bot.) one of small flowers making up a composite flower (∿ **of the disc, of the ray,** of the flower's centre or circumference); small flower, floweret. [f. L *flos floris* flower + -ET¹]

flŏr'ĭāte *v.t.* decorate with flower-designs etc. [f. as prec. + -ATE³]

floribu'nda (-ŏr-, -ŏr-) *n.* plant, esp. rose, bearing dense clusters of flowers. [mod. L (*floribundus* freely flowering f. L *flos floris* flower + -*bundus*; cf. MORIBUND; infl. by L *abundus* copious)]

floricu'ltur|e (-ŏr'-, -ŏ'r-) *n.* cultivation of flowers; hence ∿AL *a*., ∿IST (3) *n*., (-ŭ'lcher-). [f. L *flos floris* flower + CULTURE, after *horticulture*]

flō'rĭd *a*. profusely adorned as with flowers, (of literary, artistic, or musical style) elaborately ornate; ostentatious, showy; ruddy, flushed, high-coloured; hence **flori'd**ITY, ∿NESS, *ns.*, ∿LY² *adv*. [f. F *floride* or f. L *floridus* (*flos floris* flower; see -ID¹)]

Flō'rida *n*. ∿ **water,** perfume like eau-de-Cologne; hence **Flori'd**IAN *a*. & *n*. [∿ in US]

flori'ferous (-ŏr-, -ŏr-) *a*. (Of seed or plant) producing many flowers. [f. L *florifer* (*flos floris* flower) + -OUS; see -FEROUS]

flōrile'gi|um *n*. (*pl.* ∿a *or* ∿ums). anthology. [mod. L (L *flos floris* flower, *legere* gather), transl. of Gk *anthologion* ANTHOLOGY]

flō'rĭn *n*. foreign coin of gold or silver, esp. Dutch guilder; (Hist.) English gold coin (6s. 8d.) of 14th c. and silver coin (2s.) of 19th–20th c. [ME f. OF, f. It. *fiorino* dim. of *fiore* flower f. L *flos floris*, orig. coin having figure of lily on it]

flō'rist *n*. one who deals in or grows flowers; hence ∿RY (5) *n*. [f. L *flos floris* flower + -IST]

flŏri'st|ic *a*. relating to study of distribution of plants; hence ∿ICALLY *adv*., ∿ICS *n*. [f. FLORA + -IST + -IC]

floruit (-ŏr'ōō-, -ŏ'r-) *n*., & *v.i.* (period or date at which person) was alive or working. [L, = he or she flourished]

flŏr'ў. See FLEURY.

flō'scŭlar, flō'scŭlous, *adjs.* having florets, composite-flowered. [f. L *flosculus* dim. of *flos* flower (see -CULE) + -AR¹, -OUS]

flŏss *n*. rough silk enveloping silkworm's cocoon; untwisted silk thread for embroidery; CANDY-*floss*; DENTAL *floss*; ∿ **silk,** rough silk used in cheap goods. [f. F (*soie*) *floche* floss(-silk) f. OF *flosche* down, nap of velvet]

flŏ'ssy *a*. of or like floss; (colloq.) fancy, showy. [f. prec. + -Y²]

flŏtā'tion *n*. floating (**centre of** ∿, centre of gravity in floating body; starting of company or enterprise; separation of components of crushed ore etc. by their different capacities to float. [alt. of *floatation* (FLOAT², -ATION) after *rotation* etc.]

floti'lla *n*. small fleet; fleet of boats or small ships. [Sp., dim. of *flota* fleet, OF *flote* multitude]

flŏ'tsam *n*. wreckage found floating; ∿ **and jetsam,** (fig.) odds and ends, vagrants etc. [f. AF *floteson* (*floter* FLOAT²)]

flounce¹ *v.i.*, & *n*. **1.** *v.i.* go with agitated or violent motion, flop, plunge, throw the body about, (*away*, *out*, *about*, *down*, *up*). **2.** *n*. fling or jerk of body or limb(s). [16th c., of unkn. orig.; perh. imit., as *bounce*, *pounce*]

flounce² *n*., & *v.t.* **1.** *n*. ornamental wide strip gathered and sewn by upper edge esp. round woman's skirt, and with lower edge hanging. **2.** *v.t.* trim with flounce(s). [alt. of earlier *frounce* fold, pleat, f. OF *fronce* (*froncir* wrinkle f. Frank. **hrunkjan*)]

floun'der¹ *n*. flat-fish, type of small edible species. [ME, f. AF *floundre*, OF *flondre*, prob. of Scand. orig.]

floun'der² *v.i.*, & *n*. **1.** *v.i.* struggle and plunge (as) in mud or when wading; make mistakes, manage business badly or with difficulty. **2.** *n*. act of floundering. [imit., perh. assoc. w. *founder*, *blunder*]

flour *n*., & *v.t.* **1.** *n*. finer part of meal of grain, obtained by bolting; wheat meal; CORN¹*flour*; fine soft powder, esp. from seeds, farinaceous roots, etc.; hence ∿'Y² *a*. **2.** *v.t.* sprinkle with flour; *grind into flour. [ME, different. sp. of FLOWER in sense 'finest part']

flou'rish¹ (flŭ'-) *v*. **1.** *v.i.* grow vigorously; thrive, prosper, be successful; be in one's prime; be in good health; spend one's life, be active, *in*, *at*, *about*, etc., a certain time (cf. FLORUIT). **2.** *v.t.* show ostentatiously; wave (weapon); move (limbs) about vigorously. [ME, f. OF *florir* (-ISH²) f. Rom. **florire* f. L *florēre* (*flos floris* flower)]

flou'rish² (flŭ'-) *n*. ornament of flowing curves about letter or word in handwriting; rhetorical embellishment, florid expression; ostentatious waving of weapon, hand, etc. (*removed his hat with a flourish*); (Mus.) fanfare of brass instruments, florid passage, extemporized addition or prelude; prosperity, flourishing; hence ∿Y² *a*. [f. prec.]

flout *v*. & *n*. **1.** *v.t.* mock, insult, express contempt for by word or act. **2.** *v.i.* mock or scoff *at*. **3.** *n*. flouting speech or act. [perh. f. Du. *fluiten* whistle, hiss (cf. FLUTE)]

flow (-ō) *v.i.*, & *n*. **1.** *v.i.* glide along as a stream; (of blood, money, electric current) circulate; (of persons or things) come or go in large numbers or smoothly; (of talk, literary style, etc.) proceed smoothly; (of garment, hair, etc.) hang easily, undulate; (of solid) undergo permanent change of shape under stress. **2.** gush out, spring; (of blood) be spilt; result *from*; run full, be in flood (*ebb and flow*; **swim with the** ~**ing tide,** be on the winning side); (of wine) be poured out without stint; (arch.) be plentifully supplied *with* (*land flowing with milk and honey*). **3.** *n.* flowing movement in stream; gradual deformation of solid under stress; amount that flows; manner in which a thing flows; flowing liquid; outpouring, stream, copious supply; rise of tide (*ebb and flow*) or river; ~ **chart,** ~ **diagram,** ~**-sheet,** diagram of movement or action of things or persons in a complex activity; ~ **of soul,** genial conversation (as complement to FEAST *of reason*); ~ **of spirits,** habitual cheerfulness; ~'**stone,** (Geol.) rock deposited by flow of water in thin sheet. [OE *flōwan,* cogn. w. ON *flóa,* Du. *vloeien,* f. Gmc **flō-* (FLOOD)]

flow'er *n.* & *v.* **1.** *n.* coloured (usu. not green) part of plant, from which fruit or seed is later developed; (Bot.) reproductive organ in plant containing one or more pistils or stamens or both, and usu. a corolla and calyx; a blossom apart from the plant, esp. as used in groups for decoration or as mark of honour or respect (**No** ~**s,** intimation that wreaths etc. are not desired at funeral); state of blooming (*in flower*); plant cultivated or esteemed for its flowers. **2.** (In *pl.*) ornamental phrases (*flowers of speech*). **3.** *the* pick or choice *of*; *the* best part, essence; *the* choicest embodiment *of*; prime (*in the flower of his age*). **4.** (In *pl.*) powder obtained by sublimation (*flowers of sulphur*); scum formed by fermentation; ~**s of tan,** a mould (*Fuligo septica*) found on dead wood, bark, etc.; *flowers of* ZINC. **5.** ~**-bed,** garden bed in which flowers are grown; ~ **-de-luce,** (arch.) fleur-de-lis, *iris flower; ~**-girl,** woman who sells flowers esp. in street; ~**-pecker,** Austral. etc. bird of family Dicaeidae; ~ **children,** ~ **people,** young people carrying flowers as symbols of peace and love; ~**pot,** pot of red earthenware, plastic, etc., holding soil in which plant may be set; ~**-show,** competitive or other exhibition of flowers. **6.** Hence (-)~ED² (*-erd*), ~LESS (esp. of cryptogam), *adjs.,* ~ET¹ *n.* **7.** *v.i.* produce flowers, bloom or blossom (lit. or fig.), whence ~ER¹ *n.,* plant that flowers at specified time etc., ~ING² *a.* (~**ing cherry, currant,** etc., tree grown mainly for its flowers; ~**ing fern,** osmund). **8.** *v.t.* cause or allow (plant) to flower; decorate with worked flowers or floral design. [ME f. AF *flur,* OF *flour, flor,* f. L *flos floris*]

flow'er|ỹ *a.* abounding in flowers; full of fine words, compliments, figures of speech, etc., whence ~iNESS *n.* [ME, f. prec. + -Y²]

flow'ing (-ō'ĭ-) *a.* (in vbl senses; (of style) fluent, easy; (of line, curve, contour) smoothly continuous, not abrupt; (of hair, garment, sail, etc.) unconfined; *flowing* SHEET³; hence ~LY² *adv.* [f. FLOW + -ING²]

flown¹ (-ōn) *a.* (arch.) swollen, puffed up, (*flown with insolence and wine*). [obs. p.p. of FLOW, used by Milton (*Paradise Lost* I. 502)]

flown². See FLY².

FLQ *abbr.* Front de Libération du Québec.

Flt. Lt., Flt. Off., Flt. Sgt., *abbrs.* Flight Lieutenant, Officer, Sergeant.

flu (flōō) *n.* (colloq.) influenza. [abbr.]

*flŭb *v.* (-bb-) & *n.* **1.** *v.t.* & *i.* botch, bungle. **2.** *n.* thing badly or clumsily done. [20th c.; orig. unkn.]

*flŭ'bdŭb *n.* bombastic or inept language. [19th c., prob. fanciful formation]

flŭ'ctŭ|āte *v.i.* vary irregularly, rise and fall, move to and fro, be unstable; vacillate, waver; so ~A'TION *n.* [f. L *fluctuare* (*fluctus* flow, wave f. *fluere fluct-* flow) + -ATE³]

flue (flōō) *n.* smoke-duct in chimney; channel for conveying heat, esp. hot-air passage in wall, tube for heating water in some kinds of boiler; ~**-cure,** cure (tobacco) by artificial heat from flues; ~**-pipes,** (Mus.) organ-pipes other than reed-pipes. [16th c.; orig. unkn.]

flu'ence (flōō'-) *n.* influence; **put the** ~ **on,** apply hypnotic etc. power to (person). [f. INFLUENCE]

flu'encỹ (flōō'-) *n.* smooth easy flow, esp. in speech; ready utterance. [f. foll. + -ENCY]

flu'ent (flōō'-) *a.* flowing easily; (arch.) not settled, liable to change; (of motion, curve, etc.) graceful, easy; (of speech or style) copious, coming easily, ready; expressing oneself quickly and easily; hence ~LY² *adv.* [f. L *fluere* flow; see -ENT]

flŭff *n.,* & *v.t.* **1.** *n.* light feathery stuff given off by blankets etc.; soft fur; soft downy mass or bunch (**bit of** ~, (arch. colloq.) young woman); (sl.) theatrical part imperfectly known, mistake in speaking, playing game, playing music, etc.; hence ~'Y² *a.* **2.** *v.t.* put soft surface on (flesh side of leather); make into fluff; shake (*oneself,* its feathers etc.) up or out into fluffy mass; (sl.) blunder in (theatrical part), mispronounce, misplay, etc. **3.** *v.i.* become fluffy; (sl.) make mistake in speaking, playing game, playing music, etc. [prob. dial. alt. of *flue* fluff]

flu'gelhŏrn (flōō'g-) *n.* brass wind instrument of bugle family. [f. G *flügelhorn* (*flügel* wing, *horn* horn)]

flu'id (flōō'-) *a.* & *n.* **1.** *a.* consisting of particles that move freely among themselves and yield to the slightest pressure; moving or changing readily, not solid or rigid or stable, (*situation is fluid*); hence **flui'dĭfý** *v.t.,* **flui'dĭTY** *n.,* (flōō-). **2.** *n.* fluid substance (including gases and liquids); liquid constituent or secretion; ~ **clutch, coupling, flywheel,** etc., (using liquid to transmit power); *fluid* DRACHM, OUNCE¹. [f. F *fluide* or f. L *fluidus* (*fluere* flow; see -ID¹)]

flui'd|ics (flōō-) *n. pl.* (usu. treated as *sing.*) technique of using small interacting flows and fluid jets for amplification, switching, etc.; hence ~IC *a.* [f. prec. + -ICS]

flu'idĭz|e, -ĭs|e, (flōō'ĭdīz) *v.t.* cause (finely divided solid) to acquire characteristics of fluid by upward passage of gas etc.; hence ~A'TION *n.* [f. FLUID + -IZE]

*flu'idounce (flōō'-) *n.* fluid OUNCE¹. [contr.]

*flu'idrăm (flōō'-) *n.* fluid DRACHM. [contr.]

fluke¹ (flōōk) *n.* flat-fish, flounder; trematode worm found in sheep's liver. [OE *flōc,* = ON *flóki;* cf. MLG, MDu. *flac* flat, OHG *flah*]

fluke² (flōōk) *n.* broad triangular plate on arm of anchor; barbed head of lance, harpoon, etc.; lobe of whale's tail. [16th c., perh. f. prec.]

fluk|e³ (flōōk) *n.* & *v.* **1.** *n.* lucky accidental stroke; chance breeze; hence ~'Y² *a.* **2.** *v.i.* make fluke. **3.** *v.t.* get, hit, etc., by fluke. [19th c., perh. f. dial. *fluke* guess]

flume (flōōm) *n.* & *v.* **1.** *n.* artificial channel conveying water etc. for industrial use; ravine with stream. **2.** *v.i.* build flumes. **3.** *v.t.* convey down a flume. [ME f. OF *flum, flun,* f. L *flumen* river (*fluere* flow)]

flŭ'mmerỹ *n.* sweet dish made with flour, milk, eggs, honey, etc.; empty compliments, trifles, nonsense. [f. W *llymru,* of unkn. orig.]

flŭ'mmox *v.t.* (colloq.) confound, bewilder, disconcert. [19th c.; prob. dial., imit.]

flŭmp *v.* & *n.* (colloq.) **1.** *v.i.* & *t.* fall or move heavily, set or throw *down,* with dull noise. **2.** *n.* action or sound of flumping. [imit.]

flŭng. See FLING.

*flŭnk *v.* (colloq.) **1.** *v.i.* fail, esp. in examination, ~ **out,** be dismissed from school etc. because of flunking. **2.** *v.t.* fail (examination); reject (examination candidate). [cf. FUNK and obs. *flink* be coward]

flŭ'nkey, flŭ'nkỹ, *n.* (usu. derog.) liveried servant, footman; toady, snob; *cook, waiter, etc.; whence ~DOM, ~ISM (-3), (-kĭ-) *ns.* [18th c., orig. Sc.; perh. f. FLANK, w. sense 'sidesman, flanker']

fluō- (flōōō) *comb. form.* fluorine, as: ~**boric acid** (containing fluorine and boron). [f. FLUORINE + -O-]

fluor|ĕ'scence (floo-) *n.* visible or invisible radiation produced from certain substances by incident radiation of shorter wavelength, electrons, etc., as that given by violet and ultraviolet light and X-rays; property of absorbing light of short (invisible) wavelength and emitting light of longer (visible) wavelength; hence ⌣E′SCE *v.i.*, exhibit fluorescence, ⌣E′SCENT *a.* (⌣escent lamp, lamp radiating largely by fluorescence, esp. tubular lamp in which phosphor on inside surface of tube is made to fluoresce by ultraviolet radiation from mercury vapour; ⌣escent screen, screen coated with fluorescent material to show images from X-rays etc.). [f. FLUORSPAR (which fluoresces) after *opalescence*]

fluorid|a′tion (floo-) *n.* addition of traces of fluoride to drinking-water in order to prevent or reduce tooth-decay, whence ⌣ā′tionIST (2) *n.*; application of fluoride to teeth for similar purpose; hence ⌣ATE³ (-oo′-) *v.t.* [f. foll. + -ATION]

flu′oride (floo-) *n.* binary compound of fluorine. [f. FLUORINE + -IDE]

fluoridiza′tion (floo-). Var. of FLUORIDATION.

flu′orin|āte (floo′-) *v.t.* = FLUORIDATE; (Chem.) introduce fluorine into (compound; *fluorinated hydrocarbons*); hence ⌣A′TION *n.* [f. foll. + -ATE³]

flu′orine (floo′erēn) *n.* non-metallic element, a pale yellow highly reactive gas. [F (as FLUORSPAR; see -INE⁵)]

flu′orite (floo′-) *n.* = FLUORSPAR. [It. (as FLUORSPAR; see -ITE¹ (2))]

flu′oro- (floo′-) *comb. form.* 1. (Chem.) Fluorine, as: ⌣car′bon, synthetic compound of carbon and fluorine; ⌣form, compound analogous to chloroform but with fluorine in place of chlorine. 2. fluorescence, as: ⌣scope, instrument with fluorescent screen used instead of dark room to show X-ray effects. [f. FLUORINE & FLUORESCENCE + -O-]

fluorō′sis (floo-) *n.* poisoning by fluorine or its compounds. [f. F *fluorose* (as FLUORO- 1; see -OSIS)]

flu′orspar (floo′-) *n.* calcium fluoride as mineral. [f. *fluor* flow, mineral used as flux (sense 4), fluorspar, f. L *fluor* (*fluere* flow) + SPAR²]

flu′rry *n.*, & *v.t.* 1. *n.* gust, squall; commotion, excitement; nervous hurry, agitation; sudden burst of activity. 2. *v.t.* confuse by haste or noise, agitate. [imit.; cf. obs. *flurr* ruffle, *hurry*]

flush¹ *v.* 1. *v.i.* (Of bird) fly up and away. 2. *v.t.* cause to do this, put up, (birds); reveal, drive *out*. [ME, imit.; cf. *fly*, *rush*]

flush² *v.* 1. *v.i.* spurt, rush out; (of plant) throw out fresh shoots; glow with warm colour; (of blood) rush into and redden face; (of face) become red or hot, blush. 2. *v.t.* cleanse (drain, lavatory, etc.) by flow of water; dispose of thing thus (*away*, *down*); flood (meadow); (usu. in *p.p.*) cause to glow or blush, suffuse with warm colour, inflame with pride or passion, encourage, (*flushed with exercise, joy, victory, insolence*, etc.). [perh. = prec., infl. by *flash* and *blush*]

flush³ *n.* 1. rush of water; sudden abundance; cleansing of drain, lavatory, etc., by flushing. 2. rush of emotion, elation produced by it or by victory etc. 3. freshness, vigour; fresh growth of grass etc. 4. glow of light or colour; rush of blood to face, reddening caused by it; hot fit in fever, menopause, etc. [ME, f. prec.]

flush⁴ *a.*, & *v.t.* 1. *a.* full to overflowing, in flood; (usu. *pred.*) having plentiful supply of or *of* money etc., (of money) abundant. 2. even, in same plane, level *with*, without projections or raised edges. 3. *v.t.* make level; fill in (joint) level with surface. [prob. f. FLUSH²]

flush⁵ *n.* hand of cards all of one suit; straight ⌣, flush that is also a sequence; royal ⌣, (Poker) straight flush headed by ace. [f. OF *flus*, *flux* f. L *fluxus* FLUX]

flu′ster *v.* & *n.* 1. *v.t.* confuse with drink, half-intoxicate; flurry, make nervous. 2. *v.i.* be agitated, bustle. 3. *n.* flurry, flutter, agitation. [ME, orig. unkn.; cf. Icel. *flaustr(a)* hurry, bustle]

flute (floot) *n.* & *v.* 1. *n.* wood-wind instrument without reed, having holes along it stopped by fingers or keys, and blow-hole in side near end, whence

flu′tER¹ (1) (arch.), *flu′tIST (3), (floo′-) *ns.*; its player; organ stop of like quality; English ⌣, recorder. 2. semicylindrical vertical groove in pillar, similar groove elsewhere, e.g. in frills, whence flu′t-ING¹ (6) (floo′-) *n.*; tall wineglass. 3. *v.i.* play flute, whistle, sing, or speak, in flutelike tones. 4. *v.t.* play (tune etc.) on flute; make flutes or grooves in. [ME, f. OF *fleute*, *flaute*, *flahute*, prob. f. Prov. *flaüt*]

flu′tter *v.* & *n.* 1. *v.i.* flap wings without flying or in short flights; come or go with quivering motion (usu. to the ground); go about restlessly, flit, hover; quiver, vibrate, (of pulse) beat feebly and irregularly; tremble with excitement, be agitated. 2. *v.t.* flap (wings) without flying or in short flights; move (flag etc.) irregularly, agitate, ruffle; throw (person) into confusion or agitation (*flutter the* DOVE′*cots*). 3. *n.* fluttering; tremulous excitement (*be* or *put in a flutter*); vibration, esp. undesired oscillation in part of aircraft etc. under stress; (Med.) abnormal rapid but regular contractions of muscle; (Mus.) rapid movement of tongue by player of wind instrument (esp. *flutter-tonguing* etc.); rapid variation of pitch or loudness of sound; ∥(sl.) small bet or speculation. [OE *floterian*, *flotorian*, frequent. form cogn. w. FLEET⁵; see -ER⁵]

flu′ty (floo′-) *a.* like flute in tone, soft and clear. [f. FLUTE + -Y²]

flu′vial (floo′-) *a.* of or found in river(s). [ME, f. L *fluvialis* (*fluvius* river f. *fluere* flow; see -AL)]

flu′viatile (floo′-) *a.* of, found in, produced by, river(s). [F, f. L *fluviatilis* (*fluviatus* moistened f. *fluvius*; see prec., -IL)]

flu′vio- (floo′-) *comb. form.* river, as: ⌣gla′cial, of or caused by streams from glacial ice, or combined action of rivers and glaciers; ⌣METER (-ŏ′m-) *n.*, instrument for measuring rise and fall of rivers. [f. L *fluvius* river (*fluere* flow) + -O-]

flux *n.* & *v.* 1. *n.* flowing out, issue; flowing; inflow of tide (*flux and reflux*; usu. fig.); (arch.) morbid or excessive discharge of blood, excrement, etc., (**bloody** ⌣, dysentery). 2. flood *of* talk etc.; continuous succession of changes (*in a state of flux*). 3. (Phys.) rate of flow of any fluid across given area, amount crossing area in given time, (⌣-line, line representing direction and rate of flow at each point); amount of radiation or particles incident on area in given time; total electric or magnetic field passing through a surface. 4. substance mixed with metal etc. to promote fusion. 5. *v.i.* issue in a flux, flow copiously. 6. *v.t.* make fluid, fuse; treat with a fusing flux. [ME f. OF, or f. L *fluxus* (*fluere* flux- flow)]

flu′xion (-kshon) *n.* (arch.) flowing, (Math.) rate at which a variable quantity increases, derivative, (**method of** ⌣s, the Newtonian calculus); hence ⌣AL, ⌣ARY¹, *adjs.* [F, or f. L *fluxio* (as prec.; see -ION)]

fly¹ *n.* 1. two-winged insect; ⌣ in amber, curious relic; ⌣ in the ointment, trifling circumstance that spoils enjoyment; ⌣ on the wall, unperceived observer; ⌣ on the wheel, person who overestimates his own influence; *die* etc. like flies (in large numbers); (**there are**) **no flies on him**, (sl.) he is very astute. 2. winged insect (BUTTERFLY, FIRE¹*fly*, MAY²*fly*). 3. disease of plants or animals, caused by one of various flies. 4. natural or artificial fly used as fishing-bait; DRY¹*-fly*. 5. ⌣ agaric, poisonous mushroom (*Amanita muscaria*); ⌣-blow, fly's egg in meat etc.; ⌣-blown, tainted (lit. or fig.); ⌣-book, case for keeping fishing-flies in; ⌣′catcher, (1) trap for flies, (2) bird that catches insects in the air; ⌣-fish *v.i.*, fish with fly; ⌣-flap (for driving away flies); ⌣-net, net or fringe protecting horse from flies; ⌣-paper (for catching or poisoning flies); ⌣-specked, marked with flies' excrement; ⌣-spray, liquid for killing flies, to be sprayed from canister etc.; ⌣-strip, impregnated plastic strip for poisoning flies; ⌣-swatter, device for killing flies by hitting them; ⌣-trap, (1) trap for catching flies, (2) plant able to catch flies, esp. VENUS's *fly-trap*; ⌣′weight (see

BOX⁵*ing-weights*); ∼-**whisk** (for driving away flies). [OE *flȳge, flēoge,* = OS, OHG *flioga* f. WG **fleug(j)ō* f. Gmc **fleugan* (cf. foll.)]

flȳ² *v.* (**flew** *pr.* flōō; **flown** *pr.* flōn). **1.** *v.i.* move through air with wings (*about, away, off, out;* **bird is** or **has flown,** person wanted has escaped; *as the* CROW¹ *flies;* ∼ **high,** (1) be ambitious, (2) prosper; HIGH- -*flown*); move through air or space in or as aircraft or spacecraft; ∼ **in,** ∼ **out,** arrive, depart, by aircraft; ∼ **past,** make ceremonial flight of aircraft past some person or place; so ∼-*past* n. **2.** (Hawk.) soar by way of attack *at;* ∼ **at higher game,** (fig.) have nobler ambitions. **3.** pass or rise quickly through air; jump clear over or *over* fence etc. **4.** (Of flag, hair, garment, etc.) wave. **5.** travel swiftly, rush along, pass rapidly (*time flies*); spring, start, hasten, (∼ **to arms,** take up arms eagerly; *fly in the* FACE¹ *of;* ∼ **at, upon,** attack violently; ∼ **into** a passion, raptures, etc.); be driven or forced off suddenly (*made sparks* or *feathers* or FUR *fly; send flying;* **make the money** ∼, spend it quickly; *door flew open;* **glass** etc. **flies,** breaks in pieces; *fly off the* HANDLE¹); **let** ∼, discharge (missile), (abs.) shoot, hit, or use strong language, *at* (person etc. *with* missile etc.). **6.** run away, flee; (colloq.) depart hastily. **7.** *v.t.* control flight of (aircraft); transport (passengers etc.) in aircraft; traverse (distance, region) in or as aircraft. **8.** make (pigeon, hawk) fly; make (kite) rise and stay aloft; ∼ **a kite,** (1) raise money by accommodation bill, (2) make announcement or take step so as to test public opinion; **go* ∼ **a kite,** (colloq.) go away. **9.** set or keep (flag) flying. **10.** flee from (*must fly the country*); **∼* **the coop,** (colloq.) depart suddenly. **11.** ∼-**away,** (of garment) streaming, loose, (of person) flighty; ∼-**by,** (1) = *fly-past* (see sense 1), (2) close approach of spacecraft to planet etc.; ∼-**by-night,** (*n.*) one who makes night excursions or decamps by night, (a.) unreliable, dishonest; ∼'**over,** (1) = *fly-past* (see sense 1), (2) bridge for carrying railway or road over another; ∼'**under,** passage of road or railway under another; ∼'**way,** birds' customary migration-route. [OE *flēogan,* = OS, OHG *fliogan,* ON *fljúga* f. Gmc **fleugan*]

flȳ³ *n.* **1.** flying; **on the** ∼, on the wing, while in motion in the air. **2.** (*pl.* usu. ∼**s**). ‖(Hist.) one-horse hackney carriage. **3.** lap on garment (esp. trousers) to contain or cover fastening; flap at entrance of tent; TENT¹-*fly;* part of flag farthest from staff; breadth of flag from staff to end. **4.** (Theatr., in *pl.*) space over proscenium. **5.** speed-regulating device in clockwork and machinery. **6.** ∼ **ash** (from burning of powdered coal); ∼ **ball,** baseball hit so as to be catchable; ∼-**half,** (Rugby Footb.) stand-off half; ∼'**leaf,** blank leaf at beginning or end of book, blank leaf of circular etc.; ∼-**post** *v.t.,* display (handbills etc.) rapidly in unauthorized places; ∼'**sheet,** 2 or 4 page circular etc.; ∼'**wheel,** heavy-rimmed wheel on revolving shaft to regulate machinery or accumulate power. [f. prec.]

flȳ⁴ *a.* (sl.) knowing, wide awake; hence ∼'NESS *n.* [19th c.; orig. unkn.]

flȳ'er, flī'er, *n.* In vbl senses; bird etc. that flies (HIGH, *poor,* etc., *flyer*); (colloq.) ambitious or outstanding person; animal, vehicle, etc., going with exceptional speed; airman or airwoman; aircraft; **small hand-bill; *speculative investment; flying jump. [ME, f. FLY² + -ER¹]

flȳ'ing¹ *n.* In vbl senses; ∼ **field,** airfield; ∼ **machine**¹ (esp. heavier-than-air) machine able to fly in the air; ‖∼ **officer,** rank in RAF; ∼ **school,** place for learning to fly aircraft. [f. FLY² + -ING¹]

flȳ'ing² *a.* In vbl senses; hanging loose, fluttering, passing, hasty (*flying visit*); temporary (*flying bridge*); designed for rapid movement; ∼ **bedstead,** experimental aircraft shaped like bedstead for tests of vertical take-off; ∼ **boat,** seaplane with boatlike fuselage; ∼ **bomb,** pilotless aircraft with explosive warhead; ∼ **buttress** (slanting from column etc. up

to wall, usu. on arch.); *with flying* COLOUR¹*s;* ∼ **column,** military force capable of rapid movement and independent operation; ∼ **doctor** (using aeroplane to visit distant patients); *Flying* DUTCHMAN; ∼ **fish,** tropical fish able to rise into air by winglike pectoral fins; ∼ **fox,** fruit-eating bat of genus *Pteropus;* ∼ **jib,** light sail set on extension of jib-boom; ∼ **jump, leap,** (with running start); ∼ **lemur,** nocturnal animal of genus *Cynocephalus* able to make long leaps by means of folds of skin from neck to tail; ∼ **lizard,** lizard of genus *Draco* able to make long leaps by means of membranes on extended ribs; ∼ **mare,** a throw in wrestling; ∼ **phalanger,** small phalanger able to make long leaps by means of skin joining fore and hind legs; ∼ **saucer,** unidentified saucer-shaped object reported as seen in the sky; ∼ **squad,** police detachment or other body organized for rapid movement; ∼ **squadron,** military detachment or other body organized for rapid movement; ∼ **squirrel,** (1) squirrel esp. of genus *Pteromys* able to make long leaps by means of skin joining fore and hind legs, (2) = *flying phalanger;* ∼ **start,** start in which starting-point is passed at full speed, (fig.) initial advantage; ∼ **tackle** (Footb. etc., made while running or jumping); ∼ **trapeze** (on or from which acrobats swing to and fro); ∼ **wing,** aircraft without fuselage or tailplane. [f. FLY² + -ING²]

flȳ'ting *n.* (Hist.) contest of invective between two persons. [f. *flyte* wrangle f. OE *flītan* contend + -ING¹]

FM *abbr.* Field Marshal; frequency modulation.

fm. *abbr.* fathom(s).

Fm *symb.* fermium.

f-number (ĕf'-) *n.* (Photog.) quantity giving ratio of focal length and effective diameter of lens. [f. *f.* (denoting focal length) + NUMBER¹]

FO *abbr.* Flying Officer; ‖(Hist.) Foreign Office.

fo. *abbr.* folio.

foal *n.,* & *v.t.* **1.** *n.* young horse, ass, etc., colt or filly; **in** or **with** ∼, (of mare etc.) pregnant. **2.** *v.t.* (Of mare etc.) bring forth (young, or abs.). [OE *fola,* = OS, OHG *folo,* ON *foli,* Goth. *fula* f. Gmc **folon;* cf. FILLY]

foam *n.* & *v.* **1.** *n.* collection of small bubbles formed in liquid by agitation, fermentation, etc.; froth of saliva or perspiration; (poet.) the sea; rubber or plastic in cellular mass (∼'**back,** thin layer of synthetic foam on fabric); ∼ **extinguisher,** fire-extinguisher generating mass of foam; hence ∼'LESS, ∼'Y², adjs. **2.** *v.i.* emit foam, froth at the mouth, (colloq.) be very angry; (of water etc.) froth, gather foam, run foaming *along, down, over,* etc., pass off or away in foam; (of cup etc.) be filled with foaming liquor. **3.** *v.t.* (in *p.p.*) having or given cellular structure like that of foam (*foamed slag*). [OE *fām,* = OHG *feim* f. WG **faim-* f. IE **poimo-*]

fob¹ *n.,* & *v.t.* (-**bb**-). **1.** *n.* small pocket for watch etc. in waistband of trousers; ∼(-**chain**), chain attached to watch carried in fob; ornamental attachment to fob-chain, tab on key-ring. **2.** *v.t.* put in one's fob, pocket. [orig. cant, prob. f. G]

fob² *v.t.* (-**bb**-). cheat; palm (something inferior) *off on* (person); put (person) *off with* (something inferior). [16th c.; cf. obs. *fop* to dupe, G *foppen* to banter]

f.o.b. *abbr.* free on board.

fō'cal *a.* of, situated or collected at, a focus; ∼ **distance** or **length,** distance between centre of mirror or lens and its focus; ∼ **plane,** plane through focus perpendicular to axis of mirror or lens. [f. mod. L *focalis* (as FOCUS; see -AL)]

fō'caliz|e, -is|e (-īz), *v.t.* = FOCUS 4; hence ∼A'TION *n.* [f. prec. + -IZE]

fo'c's'le. See FORECASTLE.

fō'cus *n.* (*pl.* foci *pr.* -sī, or ∼**es**), & *v.* (-**s**- *or* -**ss**-). **1.** *n.* (Geom.) one of points such that their distances from any point of given curve or solid have constant sum, difference, etc., or are in constant ratio to distance of directrix from that point. **2.** (Phys.) point at which rays or waves meet after reflection or refraction, point from which rays etc. appear to proceed, point at which object must be situated for image given by lens or mirror to be well defined (*in, out of, bring into, focus*); focal length of lens; adjustment of eye or lens necessary to produce clear image; (fig.) state of clear definition (*in* or *into focus*). **3.** principal seat (of disease, activity, etc.); place of origin of earthquake. **4.** *v.t.* & *i.* converge or make converge to a focus; adjust focus of (lens, eye); bring into focus; concentrate or be concentrated *on*. [L, = hearth]

fŏ′dder *n.*, & *v.t.* **1.** *n.* dried food, hay, straw, etc., for stall-feeding cattle; CANNON¹-*fodder*. **2.** *v.t.* give fodder to. [OE *fōdor*, = OHG *fuotar*, ON *fóthr* f. Gmc **fōdhram* (**fōdh-*; cf. FOOD)]

fŏe *n.* (poet. or rhet.) enemy, adversary, opponent, ill-wisher; ~′**man**, (arch. or literary) enemy in war (lit. or fig.). [OE *fāh* adj. f. WG **faiha* and OE *gefā* n. (*gefāh* a. at feud, OHG *gifēh* f. WG **gafaiha*); cf. FEUD¹]

foehn. Var. of FÖHN.

foetid. See FETID.

foe′t|us (fē′t-), **fē′t|us, n.* unborn or unhatched offspring, esp. human one more than 8 weeks after conception; hence ~AL *a.*, ~ĭCIDE (2) *n.* [ME, f. L *fetus* offspring]

fŏg¹ *n.*, & *v.t.* (-gg-). **1.** *n.* aftermath; long grass left standing in winter; a fodder-grass (*Holcus lanatus*). **2.** *v.t.* leave (land) under fog; feed (cattle) on fog. [ME, of unkn. orig.]

fŏg² *n.* & *v.* (-gg-). **1.** *n.* thick cloud of water droplets or smoke suspended in atmosphere at or near earth's surface; obscurity caused by this (**in a** ~, puzzled, at a loss); (Photog.) cloud on developed negative etc. obscuring image. **2.** ~-**bank**, mass of fog at sea; ~-**bound**, unable to proceed because of fog; ~-**bow** (like rainbow, produced by light in fog); ~-**horn**, sounding instrument for warning ships in fog, (fig.) loud penetrating voice; ~-**lamp** (used to improve visibility in fog); ~-**signal**, detonator placed on railway line in fog to warn driver. **3.** *v.t.* envelop (as) with fog; bewilder, perplex; (Photog.) make (negative etc.) obscure or cloudy. **4.** *v.i.* become covered with fog or condensed vapour. [perh. back-form. f. FOGGY]

fogey. See FOGY.

fŏ′gg|y̆ (-gĭ) *a.* (Of air) thick, murky; of, like, having much, FOG²; obscure, dull, confused, (*has only a foggy idea of it*; *have* **not** the ~**iest**, (colloq.) no idea at all); beclouded, indistinct; hence ~ĭLY², *adv.*, ~ĭNESS *n.* [f. FOG¹ + -Y²; earlier senses 'covered with coarse grass, boggy, flabby (of flesh)']

fŏ′gle *n.* (arch. sl.) silk handkerchief. [19th c., of unkn. orig.]

fŏ′gy̆, fŏ′gey, (-gĭ) *n.* (old) ~, old-fashioned person, person with antiquated ideas; hence ~DOM, **fŏ′gy̆ISM** (2), *ns.*, **fŏ′gy̆ISH¹** *a.*, (-g-). [18th c., rel. to sl. *fogram*, of unkn. orig.]

föhn (fērn) *n.* hot southerly wind on N. slope of the Alps; warm dry wind on lee side of mountains. [G, ult. f. L *Favonius* mild west wind]

foi′ble *n.* weak point, weakness of character, quality on which one mistakenly prides oneself; (Fenc.) part of sword-blade from middle to point (cf. FORTE¹). [F, obs. form of *faible* (as FEEBLE)]

foie gras (fwah grah′) *n.* (colloq.) = PÂTÉ *de foie gras*. [abbr.]

foil¹ *n.* **1.** (Archit.) arc or space between cusps of window. **2.** metal hammered or rolled into thin sheet (*gold, silver, tin,* etc., *foil*); sheet of this, or of tin amalgam, placed behind mirror-glass as reflector; sheet of it used to wrap or cover food; leaf of it placed under precious stone etc. to brighten or colour it or enhance its brightness by contrast. **3.** thing or person that sets another off by contrast. [ME f. OF, f. L *folium* leaf, and f. OF *foille* f. L *folia* pl.]

foil² *v.t.*, & *n.* **1.** *v.t.* (Hunt.) run over or cross (scent, ground) so as to baffle hounds; (abs., of deer etc.) spoil the scent thus. **2.** beat off, repulse; frustrate,

parry, baffle. **3.** *n.* track of hunted animal; (arch.) repulse, defeat, check. [ME, = trample down, perh. f. AF **fuler,* OF *fouler* to full cloth, trample f. Rom. **fullare* f. L *fullo* FULLER¹]

foil³ *n.* blunt-edged sword with button on point used in fencing; hence ~′IST (3) *n.* [16th c., of unkn. orig.]

foil⁴ *n.* hydrofoil. [abbr.]

foi′son (-z-) *n.* (arch.) plenty, abundance. [ME f. OF, f. Rom. **fusio -onis* f. L *fusio* (*fundere fus-* pour; see -ION)]

foist *v.t.* introduce surreptitiously or unwarrantably *into* (thing) or *in*; palm (*off*) *on* or *upon,* falsely fix authorship (of composition) *upon.* [orig. of palming false die, f. Du. dial. *vuisten* take in the hand (*vuist* FIST)]

fol. *abbr.* folio.

fōld¹ *n.,* & *v.t.* **1.** *n.* = SHEEP-*fold*; (fig.) church, body of believers. **2.** *v.t.* enclose (sheep etc.) in fold; place sheep in fold or folds on (land) to manure it. [OE *fald,* = MLG *valt*]

fōld² *v.* & *n.* **1.** *v.t.* double (flexible thing) over upon itself (*in, over, together*; ~ **away, up,** make more compact by folding); bend portion of (thing) *back, down.* **2.** wind, clasp, (arms etc.) *about, round*; embrace in arms or to breast; lay (one's arms) together across chest, clasp (one's hands); swathe, envelop, (*fold it in paper*; *hills folded in mist*); ~ in, (Cookery) add (ingredient) gently with spoon etc. so as to mix it in without stirring or beating. **3.** *v.i.* become folded; be able to be folded (*folding stool*, ~**ing door**(**s**), pair of doors with jambs on each side of opening, the doors themselves often able to be folded; (colloq.) paper money); ~ **out,** be able to be unfolded; ~ (up), collapse (lit. or fig.), cease to function, go bankrupt; ~**away,** adapted to be folded away; ~**out,** oversize page in book etc. to be unfolded by reader; ~**up,** adapted to be folded up. **4.** *n.* doubling of folded object; hollow between two thicknesses (*carried it in a fold of her dress*), hollow or nook in mountain etc.; coil of serpent, string, etc.; act of folding; line made by folding, (Geol.) folding or curvature of strata; ~′**boat,** collapsible boat. [OE *f(e)aldan,* = OHG *faltan,* ON *falda,* Goth. *falthan* f. Gmc **falthan*]

-fōld *suf.* forming *adjs.* and *advs.* f. cardinal numerals, w. sense 'multiplied by', 'in an amount multiplied by', 'having so many parts', (*a twofold charm*; *repaid tenfold*; *a threefold cord*; MANIFOLD), & sim. *ns.* f. numerals used with *a* (*repaid a hundredfold*) [OE *-f(e)ald* = OS *-fald,* OHG *-falt,* ON *-faldr,* Goth. *-falths,* cogn. w. prec.; orig. sense 'folded in so many layers etc.']

fō′lder *n.* in vbl senses; folded circular etc.; folding cover or holder for loose papers. [f. FOLD² + -ER¹]

fō′lderŏl. Var. of FALDERAL.

foli′aceous (-shus) *a.* leaflike; having organs like leaves; of leaves; laminated. [f. L *foliaceus* leafy (*folium* leaf; see -ACEOUS)]

fō′liage *n.* leaves, leafage, (lit., or as represented in art); ~ **leaf** (opp. petals etc.); ~ **plant** (cultivated for foliage, not for flowers). [ME, f. F *feuillage* (*feuille* leaf. OF *foille*; see FOIL¹, -AGE)]

fō′liar *a.* of leaves; ~ **feed** (supplied to leaves of plant). [f. mod. L *foliaris* f. L *folium* leaf; see -AR¹]

fō′liate¹ *a.* leaflike; having leaves; having specified number of leaflets (*1, 5,* etc., *-foliate*). [f. L *foliatus* (*folium* leaf; see -ATE²)]

fō′li|āte² *v.* **1.** *v.i.* split into laminae. **2.** *v.t.* decorate (arch, door-head) with foils; number leaves (not pages) of (volume) consecutively. **3.** Hence ~A′TION *n.* [f. L *foliatus* leaf + -ATE³]

fō′lic *a.* ~ **acid,** B-group vitamin, deficiency of which causes human anaemia. [f. L *folium* leaf (because found especially in green leaves) + -IC]

folie (fŏ′lē) *n.* madness, insanity; ~ **à deux** (ah dĕr′), delusion shared by two emotionally associated persons; ~ **de grandeur** (de grahňdĕr′), DELUSIONS of grandeur. [F, = FOLLY]

fō'liŏ *n.* (*pl.* ~s) & *a.* **1.** *n.* leaf of paper, parchment, etc., esp. if not numbered as two separate pages; leaf--number or page-number of printed book. **2.** number of words (72 or 90 or 100) taken as unit in reckoning length of document. **3.** sheet of paper folded once; **in** ~, (of book) on such paper. **4.** *n.* & *a.* (book) made of such sheets, largest-sized (volume). [L, abl. of *folium* leaf, f. use in refs. = *on leaf 50* etc.]

fō'liŏle *n.* division of compound leaf, leaflet. [F, f. LL *foliolum* dim. of L *folium* leaf]

folk (fōk) *n.* (*pl.* ~ *or* ~s). **1.** a people, nation, race (BEAKER *Folk*); = *folk-music.* **2.** (in *pl.* exc. arch. or dial.) people in general; people of specified class; one's relatives. **3.** (*attrib.*) of the people; traditional; ~-**dance,** (music for) dance of popular origin; ~ **etymology,** popular modifying of word's form to make it seem to be derived from familiar words (*sparrowgrass* for *asparagus*); ~'**lore,** traditional beliefs etc., study of these, whence ~'**lōric** *a.*, ~'**lōrist** (3) *n.*; ~-**memory,** recollection of past persisting among a people; ~-**music,** music of popular origin or style; ~'**nik,** devotee of folk-music [after *beatnik*]; ~-**singer,** singer of folk-songs; ~-**song,** ~-**tale,** song, tale, of popular or traditional origin or style; ~'-**ways,** traditional behaviour of a people; ~'**weave,** rough loosely woven fabric. **4.** Hence ~'**SY²,** ~'**Y²,** *adjs.,* friendly, sociable, informal, having characteristics of folk art. [OE *folc,* = OS, OHG *folc,* ON *folk* f. Gmc *folkam]

fō'llicle *n.* small sac or vesicle; small sac-shaped secretory gland or cavity containing hair-root; (Bot.) single-carpelled fruit opening on one side only; hence **fŏlli'cŭlAR¹, fŏlli'cŭlATE², fŏlli'cŭlātED²,** *adjs.* [f. L *folliculus* dim. of *follis* bellows; see -CULE]

fō'llow (-ō) *v.* **1.** *v.t.* & *i.* go or come after or *after* (moving thing or person); ~ **the hounds,** go hunting; ~-**my-leader,** *~-the-leader,** game in which each player must do as leader does; *follow* one's NOSE, ~ **the plough,** be ploughman. **2.** *v.t.* go along (path); come after in order or time; accompany, serve; provide (thing, or abs.) *with* sequel or successor; go after as admirer or suitor; attend (funeral, corpse to grave). **3.** result from, be the necessary consequence of, be involved in. **4.** strive after, aim at. **5.** treat or take as guide or leader, obey, espouse opinions or cause of; conform to, act upon, (*follow advice, the fashion,* SUIT); practise (profession etc.; ~ **the sea,** be sailor). **6.** keep up with mentally, grasp the meaning of, (argument, speaker); be aware of the present state or progress of (events, football team, etc.). **7.** *v.i.* go or come after person or thing (*follow in his steps, in the wake of*); come next in order (*his arguments are as follows*); happen after something else, ensue; result, be deducible, (*from*). **8.** ~ **on,** provide continuation, (Cricket, of side) bat a second time immediately after making score less than that·of opponents by certain number (so ~-*on* n. & a.); ~ **out,** pursue to the end, carry out (instructions etc.) precisely; ~ **through,** continue to completion, (Golf etc.) carry stroke through to fullest extent possible after striking ball (so ~-*through* n.); ~ **up,** pursue steadily, add another blow, action, etc., to (previous blow etc.), make further investigation of, (Footb. etc.) keep near (player with) ball to support; ~-**up,** continuation of an action, esp. second advertisement, letter, etc., referring to earlier one. [OE *folgian,* = OS *folgon,* OHG *folgēn* & OE *fylgan* = ON *fylgja* f. Gmc **fulg-*]

fō'llower (-ōer) *n.* In vbl senses; adherent, disciple; part moved by cam etc.; (arch.) man courting maid-servant. [f. prec. + -ER¹]

fō'llowing¹ (-ō-) *n.* In vbl senses; body of adherents, followers. [f. FOLLOW + -ING¹]

fō'llowing² (-ō-) *a.* & *prep.* **1.** *a.* In vbl senses; now to be mentioned (thing, or abs.: *the following is* or *are* noteworthy); (of wind) blowing in one's direction of travel. **2.** *prep.* as a sequel to, coming after in time. [f. FOLLOW + -ING²]

fō'lly *n.* being foolish, lack of good sense, unwise conduct; foolish act, idea, or practice, ridiculous thing; costly structure that is (considered) useless; (Theatr., in *pl.*) (revue with) glamorous female performers. [ME, f. OF *folie* (*fol* mad, FOOL¹; see -Y¹)]

fomě'nt (fo-, fō-) *v.t.* bathe with warm or medicated lotions, apply warmth to; foster, stimulate, or instigate (sentiment, conduct, sedition, etc.), whence ~ER¹ *n.* [ME, f. F *fomenter* f. LL *fomentare* f. L *fomentum* poultice, lotion (*fovēre* heat, cherish; see -MENT)]

fomĕntā'tion *n.* In vbl senses; (application of) warm cloths etc. for fomenting. [ME f. OF, or f. LL *fomentatio* (as prec.; see -ATION)]

fŏnd *a.* foolishly credulous or optimistic (*fond hopes of success*); over-affectionate, doting; tender, loving; ~ **of,** having much love for, much inclined to; hence ~'LY² *adv.,* ~'NESS *n.* [ME, p.p. of obs. *fon* be foolish, or f. obs. *fon* fool + -ED² (cf. *wretched*)]

fo'ndant *n.* soft sweetmeat of flavoured sugar. [F, pres. part. of *fondre* melt f. L *fundere* pour; see -ANT]

fō'ndle *v.* **1.** *v.t.* touch or stroke lovingly. **2.** *v.i.* dally amorously (*with, together*). [back-form. f. *fondling* fondled person (FOND, -LING¹)]

fō'ndue (-dū, -doō) *n.* dish of flavoured melted cheese. [F, fem. p.p. of *fondre* melt f. L *fundere* pour]

fons et orīgo (fŏnz ět ŏrī'gō) *n.* source and origin (*of*). [L]

fŏnt¹ *n.* receptacle for baptismal water (~-**name,** baptismal name); receptacle for holy water; oil--reservoir of lamp. [OE *font, fant* f. OIr. *fant, font* f. L *fons fontis* fountain, baptismal water]

*fŏnt². See FOUNT².

fo'ntal *a.* primary, original, of the fountain-head; baptismal. [OF, or f. med. L *fontalis* as prec.; see -AL]

fŏntaně'lle, *fŏntaně'l, *n.* membranous space in infant's skull at angles of parietal bones. [f. F *fontanelle* f. mod. L *fontanella* f. OF *fontenelle* dim. of *fontaine* FOUNTAIN; see -LE 2]

food *n.* **1.** substance(s) (to be) taken into the body to maintain life and growth; **be ~ for fishes** (drowned); ~ **for powder,** soldiers; **be ~ for worms** (dead). **2.** solid food (*food and drink*). particular kind of food; nutriment for plants, skin, etc.; material for mental work (*food for thought* etc.). **4.** ~-**chain,** (Ecol.) series of organisms dependent on one another for supply of food; ~-**cycle,** ~-**web,** group of food-chains in a community; ~ **poisoning,** illness due to bacteria or toxins in food; ~ **processor,** machine for chopping, mixing, etc., food materials; *~ **stamps** (issued cheaply to the poor and usable to buy food); ~'**stuff,** substance used as food; ~ **value,** relative nourishing power of a food. [OE *fōda* f. Gmc **fōdhon;* cf. FEED¹]

fool¹ *n., a.,* & *v.* **1.** *n.* person who acts or thinks unwisely or imprudently; **be a ~ to,** (arch.) be nothing in comparison with; **a ~'s bolt is soon shot,** his stock of argument is soon exhausted; **no ~, nobody's ~,** prudent person. **2.** jester or clown in medieval great household; **act** or **play the ~,** indulge in buffoonery, act foolishly. **3.** dupe (*make a fool of*); **be a ~ for,** be unable to resist attractions of. **4.** ALL *Fools' Day,* APRIL *fool;* ~'**s errand** (fruitless); ~'**s gold,** pyrite; *fool's* MATE¹; ~'**s paradise,** illusory happiness; ~'**s parsley,** species of hemlock resembling parsley. **5.** Hence ~'**ERY** (4, 5) *n.,* ~'**PROOF²** *a.* (of rules etc. so plain or simple as to be incapable of misuse or misinterpretation), (of machinery etc.) that cannot break down. **6.** *a.* *(colloq.) foolish, silly. **7.** *v.i.* play the fool, idle, trifle, (*about, around*); *~ **along,** proceed at leisure. **8.** *v.t.* cheat (person) *out of* money etc. or *into* doing; throw (time, money) *away* foolishly; make a fool of, dupe, play tricks on. [ME f. OF *fol* f. L *follis* bellows, empty-headed person]

fool² *n.* creamy liquid of fruit stewed, crushed, and mixed with milk, cream, custard, etc. (esp. *gooseberry fool*). [16th c., perh. f. prec.]

foo′lhard|y *a.* foolishly venturesome, delighting in needless risks; hence ∼**iness** *n.* [ME, f. OF *folhardi* (*fol* foolish, cf. FOOL¹; *hardi* HARDY¹)]

foo′lish *a.* lacking good sense or judgement; indicative of folly; ridiculous; hence ∼**ly²** *adv.*, ∼**ness** *n.* [ME, f. FOOL¹+-ISH]

foo′lscăp (-s-, -z-) *n.* size of paper, about 330 × 200 (or 400) mm. [f. use as watermark of *fool's cap* = jester's cap with bells (FOOL¹ 2)]

foot¹ *n.* (*pl.* **feet;** cf. senses 6 and 11). **1.** terminal part of leg beyond ankle. **2.** step, pace, tread, (*swift of foot; has a light foot*). **3.** ||(Hist.) infantry (*the 4th Foot; regiment of foot; a captain of foot*). **4.** lower end of table, bed, grave, couch, etc. (opp. HEAD¹ 12); part of stocking etc. covering foot. **5.** (Pros.) metrical unit with varying number of syllables one of which is stressed; similar unit of speech etc. **6.** (*pl.* also **foot**). linear measure of 12 in., 30.48 cm (*10 feet long; a ten--foot pole; six foot or feet three; six feet three inches*; SQUARE² *foot*, CUBIC *foot*). **7.** lower (usu. projecting) part, base; part of sewing-machine that holds material steady. **8.** (Zool.) locomotive or adhesive organ of invertebrates. **9.** (Bot.) part by which petal is attached; root of hair. **10.** lowest part, bottom, of hill, ladder, staircase, wall, list, page, class, etc. **11.** (*pl.* ∼**s**). dregs, oil refuse; coarse sugar. **12. at** ∼, (of foal) accompanying its mother; **at** person's **feet**, as his disciple, subject, or suppliant; BALL¹ *at* one's *feet*; BEST¹ *foot forward*; **have a** ∼ **in both camps**, belong to each of two opposing factions etc.; CHANGE² one's *feet*; **feet of clay**, fundamental weakness [cf. Dan. 2:33]; DRAG¹ one's *feet*; FALL¹ *on* one's *feet*; FIND one's *feet*; **feet first** or **foremost**, being carried to burial; *foot in the* DOOR; **have one** ∼ **in the grave**, be near death; **have** one's **feet on the ground**, be practical; **keep** one's **feet**, not fall; **my** ∼**!**, colloq. excl. of contemptuous contradiction; **with** one's ∼ **on the neck of**, completely dominating; OFF one's *feet*; **on** ∼, (1) walking not riding etc., (2) afoot; **set on** ∼, start (action etc.); **on** one's **feet**, = *on* one's LEGS; **put** one's ∼ **down**, (1) be firmly insistent or repressive, (2) accelerate motor vehicle; **put** one's ∼ **in it**, (colloq.) blunder; **put** one's **feet up**, take a rest; **on the right** ∼, in an advantageous position; **set** ∼ **in** or **on**, enter, go to, (place etc.); **stand on** one's **own feet**, be self-reliant or independent; **to** one's **feet**, to a standing position; **under** ∼, on the ground (*wet under foot*); **tread under** ∼, (fig.) oppress; **under** one's **feet**, obstructing one's progress; **get** one's **feet wet**, (fig.) begin to participate; **on the wrong** ∼, in a disadvantageous position; **not put a** ∼ **wrong**, make no mistakes. **13.** ∼**-and-mouth (disease)**, contagious virus disease of cattle etc. with ulceration of mouth, around hooves, etc.; ∼**-bath**, washing of feet, small bath used for this; ∼**′board** (in or on vehicle, for resting or placing feet); ∼**-brake**, foot--operated brake on vehicle; ∼**-bridge**, bridge for foot passengers only; ∼ **candle**, illumination given by source of one candela at distance of one foot; ∼**′fall**, sound of footstep; ∼**-fault**, (Lawn Tennis) (make) fault consisting in overstepping baseline or running etc. while serving; ∼**-gear**, = *footwear*; ||F∼ **Guards**, Grenadier, Coldstream, Scots, Irish, and Welsh Guards; ∼**′hill** (lying at base of mountain or range); ∼**′hold**, place giving support for feet, surface for standing on, (lit. or fig.); ∼**′lights**, screened lights in front of stage at level of actors' feet; ∼**′loose**, free to act as one pleases; ∼**′man**, (1) infantry-man, (2) liveried servant for carriage, door, and table, (3) trivet to hang on grate bars; ∼**′mark**, footprint; ∼**-muff** (for keeping feet warm); ∼**′note** (inserted at foot of page); ∼**-pace**, ∼**′s pace**, walking pace; ∼**′pad**, (Hist.) unmounted highway-man; ∼**-passenger**, one who walks, not rides or drives; ∼**′path** (for walkers, esp. ||pavement at side of road); ∼**′plate**, driver's and fireman's platform in locomotive; ∼**-pound**, quantity of energy that will

raise 1 lb. to height of 1 foot; ∼**-pound-second system** (using these as basic units of length, mass, and time); ∼**′print**, impression left by foot; ∼**-race**, race between persons on foot; ∼**-rope** (below yard, for sailors to stand on when furling or reefing); ∼**-rot**, disease of foot in sheep and cattle, or of base of plant--stems; ∼**-rule**, rigid measure 1 foot long; ∼**-slog** *v.i.* (-*gg*-), & *n.*, (colloq.) walk, march; ∼**-soldier**, infantryman; ∼**′sore**, having sore feet, esp. from walking; ∼**′stalk**, (Bot.) stalk of leaf or peduncle of flower, (Zool.) attachment of barnacle etc.; ∼**′step**, tread, footprint, (*follow* or *tread in* person's *footsteps*, (fig.) do as he did); ∼**′stool** (for resting feet on when sitting); ∼**′sure**, sure-footed; ∼**′warmer**, thing to warm feet; ∼**′way**, path for foot-passengers; ∼**′wear**, shoes, socks, etc.; ∼**′work**, use of feet in sports, dancing, etc., agility. **14.** Hence (-)∼**ED²**, ∼**LESS**, *adjs.*; (sense 6) ∼**AGE** (1) *n.* (esp. of cinema or television film), -∼**ER¹** (1) *n.* (*six-footer*). [OE *fōt*, = OS *fōt*, OHG *fuoz*, ON *fōtr*, Goth. *fōtus* f. Gmc **fōt-* f. IE **pōd-* etc.]

foot² *v.* **1.** *v.t.* walk etc. on; ∼ **it**, dance, walk not ride. **2.** put new foot to (stocking). **3.** add up or *up* (account); pay (bill). **4.** *v.i.* (Of bill, items, etc.) mount *up to.* [ME, f. prec.]

foo′tball (-awl) *n.*, & *v.i.* **1.** *n.* large round or elliptical inflated usu. leather ball; (fig.) person or thing continually kicked or tossed or bandied about. **2.** open-air game played with such ball by two sides each seeking to move it across opponents' goal-line by kicking or other permitted means; *football* POOL². **3.** *v.i.* play football; hence ∼**ER¹** *n.* [ME, f. FOOT¹ + BALL¹]

||**foo′ter** *n.* (sl.) = prec. **2.** [f. FOOT¹ + -ER¹ (5)]

foo′ting *n.* placing of feet, foothold; surface for standing on, secure position, (lit. or fig.); conditions, relations, position, status, in which person or organization stands towards others, degree of intimacy etc.; entrance on new position, admittance to trade, society, etc., (**pay** for) one's ∼, pay customary fee for it); projecting course at foot of wall etc. [ME, f. FOOT² | -ING¹]

foo′tl|e *v.i.* **1.** (sl.) trifle (*about*), play the fool. **2.** Hence ∼**ING²** *a.*, trivial, silly. [19th c., perh. f. dial. *footer* idle, bungle, assoc. w. -LE 3]

foo′tsie *n.* (colloq.) amorous play with the feet. [joc. dim. of FOOT¹; see -IE]

foo′ty *n.* **1.** (colloq.) = FOOTSIE. **2.** (Austral. & NZ colloq.) = FOOTBALL **2.** [joc. dim. of FOOT¹; see -Y³]

foo′zle *v.t.*, & *n.* (sl., esp. in Golf). **1.** *v.t.* do clumsily, bungle, make a mess of. **2.** *n.* clumsy failure. [f. G dial. *fuseln* work badly; cf. FUSEL]

fŏp *n.* = DANDY; hence ∼**LING²** 2, ∼**PERY** (4, 5), *ns.*, ∼**PISH¹** *a.* [17th c., perh. f. earlier *fop* fool]

for (or, when stressed, *för*; occas. *för*) *prep.* & *conj.* **1.** *prep.* representing, in place of, in exchange against; as price or penalty of, in requital of, (*sits for, member for, Oxford*; ONCE *for all; A for Andrew*; substituted *for*; agent *for*; got it *for £1; thrashed for his pains; fined for speeding; do you take me for a fool?*); in defence or support or favour of, on side of, (*take* etc. *my* WORD¹ *for it*; hurrah for person or thing; *am for* abandoning the attempt; *arguments for and against*); with a view to, in order to be, conducive(ly) to, (*go for a walk*; (arch.) *went for a soldier; is, did it, for her good; for* SALE¹); to obtain, win, or save, (*send, go, for a doctor; would not do it for the world; would not; paid for; play for penny points; fishing for salmon; was tried for his life; cannot do it for the life of me; run for* IT¹); to reach, arrive at, be received by, or belong to, (*left, sailed, for India; made for shelter; meeting is at 7.30 for* (so as to start promptly at) *8; getting on for two o'clock; bought shoes for the children; won a name for himself*); **there's** or **that's** (*courage, gratitude*, etc.) ∼ **you!** (expr. enthusiasm or resignation). **2.** (after *vbs., adjs., ns.*, & *ints.* of emotion, faculty, or fitness, after *adjs.* & *advs.* with *too, enough*, after expressions implying fitness etc.) as regards, in the direction of, (*don't care for games*; *a longing for praise*; *an eye for colour*; *fit for nothing*; *ready for dinner*; O² *for wings!*; NOW *for it!*; *too beautiful for* WORD¹*s*; *good enough for me*; *time for school*; **is not long** ~ **this world,** will soon die; **there is nothing** ~ **it but to submit,** submission is the only course open; **be** ~′ **it,** (sl.) be involved in punishment or trouble; *is the man for the job*; *is is for you to make the move*; *the motive for retreating*). **3.** with the result of, at the cost of, to the amount of, (*all out for 44*; *150 for 5 wickets*; *a bill for £100*; *drew on him for £100*); to affect or as affecting, beneficially or the reverse, (*they live for each other*; *can shift for myself*; *wish to see it for myself*, not rely on others' descriptions; *things look bad for you*; *it is bad for him to smoke*); hence *for* with *n.* or *pron.* & *inf.* as noun-phrase: **it is wicked** ~ **him to smoke** (his smoking is wicked), **it is usual** ~ **hats to be worn** (that hats should be worn). **4.** in the character of, as, as being, (*hold it for certain*; *was often mistaken for Churchill*; *be hanged for a pirate*; *was beaten up and left for dead*; *take for* GRANTed; *I for one do not believe it*; *did it for the second time*; *for FREE¹ 6; *for one* THING; *for* GOOD); by reason of, under influence of, because of, on account of, (*did it for pure wantonness*; *avoid it for fear of accidents*; *I* TREMBLE *for him*; *famous for cider*; *notorious for parsimony*; *do it for my sake*; *alas for him!*); in spite of (*for all his bragging*, *for all that*, *for all* (*that*) *you say*, *for all* (*that*) *he seems to dislike me*, *I still like him*); on account of the hindrance of (*can't see* WOOD *for trees*; *could not speak for laughing*; *were it not for*, but for, except for, one thing I might be happy). **5.** corresponding to, in contrast with, (*for one enemy he has a hundred friends*; *bulk for bulk*, taking equal bulk of each; WORD¹ *for word*); so far as concerns, regarding, (*for the rest*; *for all the* WORLD; *for my part*; *for all or aught I know*; *hard up for money*; *wants for nothing*); considering, or making the allowance required by, the usual nature of (*quite active for a man of 80*; *very bright for a winter day*). **6.** during, over, to the extent of, (*has been so for months*; *walk for two miles*, *for two hours*; *made comfortable for life*, *for the present*; *left him alone for once*, *for* EVER). **7.** *conj.* (Introducing new clause or series of clauses containing proof of or reason for believing what has been previously stated) seeing that, since, (*something fell in*, *for I heard a splash*); in order to be convinced of this observe or remember that . . . (*the angles are equal*; *for ABC is isosceles*). [OE, = OS *for*, Goth. *faur*, prob. shortened f. Gmc *fora FORE²]

for- *pref.* forming *vbs.* etc., meaning (1) away, off, apart, (*forbye, forget, forgive*), (2) prohibition (*forbid, forfend*), (3) abstention, neglect, (*forbear, forgo, forsake, forswear*), (4) bad effect (*fordo*), (5) excess, intensity, (*forlorn*). [OE *for-, fær-*, = OS *for-, far-*, OHG *fir-, far-*, Goth. *fair-, faur-, fra-* f. IE pref. with many senses]

f.o.r. *abbr.* free on rail.

fo′rage *n.* & *v.* **1.** *n.* food for horses and cattle, esp. for horses in army; foraging (*on the forage* etc.); ~**-cap,** infantry undress cap. **2.** *v.t.* collect forage from, ravage; supply with forage; get by foraging. **3.** *v.i.* search for forage; search *for* (thing), rummage. **4.** So **fo′rager**² (-ĭj-) *n.*, one who forages. [ME, f. OF *fourrage*(*r*) (*fuerre* f. Frank. *fōder FODDER)]

fora′m|en *n.* (*pl.* ~**ina**). (Anat. etc.) orifice, hole, passage; so **fora′min**ATE² *a.* [f. L *foramen -minis* (*forare* bore a hole)]

foramini′ferous *a.* of the order Foraminifera of protozoans, usu. marine organisms with perforated shells. [f. as prec. + -I- + -FEROUS]

forasmu′ch (-z-) *adv.* (arch.) ~ **as,** (*conj.*) seeing that, since. [= *for as much*]

fo′ray *n.*, & *v.i.* (make, go on) incursion, raid, inroad. [ME, prob. n. f. v. back-form. f. *forayer* f. OF *forrier* forager f. Rom. *fodrarius (*fodro FODDER)]

forbad(e). See FORBID.

for′bear¹, for′ebear, (fōr′bār) *n.* (usu. in *pl.*) ancestor. [f. FORE- + obs. *bear, beer* (BE, -ER¹)]

forbear′² (-bār′) *v.t.* & *i.* (**forbor′e; forbor′ne).**

abstain or refrain from or *from*; not use or mention; be patient; hence ~ANCE *n.* [OE *forberan*, = OHG *farberan*, Goth. *frabairan* (as FOR- (3), BEAR³)]

forbi′d *v.t.* (-**dd-**; **forba′de** *pr.* -ăd, *or* **forba′d** *pr.* -ăd; FORBIDDEN). **1.** command (person etc.) not *to* do, (person etc.) not to go to (place), (*forbid him to go*, *in the court*); not allow (person etc. something; person or thing to exist or happen; *forbid him wine*; *forbid duels*; *was forbidden wine*; *wine was forbidden him*). **2.** (of circumstances, hindrance, etc.) exclude, prevent, make undesirable, (God ~!, may it not happen!). [OE *forbēodan*, = OHG *farbiotan*, Goth. *faurbiudan* (as FOR- (2), BID¹)]

forbi′dden *a.* In vbl senses; *forbidden* DEGREES; ~ **fruit,** thing desired because not allowed; ~ **line,** (Phys.) spectral line occurring with low probability but observable in certain conditions. [f. prec. + -EN¹]

forbi′dding *a.* repellent, of uninviting appearance; stern; hence ~LY² *adv.*, ~NESS *n.* [f. FORBID + -ING²]

forbŏr′(n)e. See FORBEAR².

forby′e, *prep.* & *adv.* (arch. or Sc.) **1.** *prep.* besides. **2.** *adv.* in addition. [ME, f. FOR- (1) + BY¹]

fŏrce¹ *n.* **1.** strength, power, impetus, violence, intense effort; military strength. **2.** body of armed men, army, (in *pl.*) troops, fighting strength of a nation or commander; body of police (**the** ~, the police); body of workers etc. (*labour force*); **join** ~**s,** combine efforts. **3.** strength exerted on an object, coercion, (**by** ~, by compulsion). **4.** mental or moral strength; influence, controlling power, efficacy, power to convince, vividness of effect, (*the force of circumstances*, *force of* HABIT¹, *brought it about*; *there is force in what you say*; *described with much force*). **5.** binding power, validity, (*has the force of law*; *comes into force*; **put in** ~, enforce). **6.** real import, precise meaning (*what is the force of 'but' here?*). **7.** (Phys.) measurable and determinable influence tending to cause motion of a body, intensity of this; (fig.) agency likened to this (*considers himself a force in the world*); (Bridge) forcing bid. **8. by** ~ **of,** by means of, (1) in large numbers, (2) (of law etc.) valid, effective. **9.** ~ **cup,** rubber cup on handle, clearing blocked drain by vacuum; ~**-feed,** feed (prisoner etc.) by force; ~ **field,** (esp.) invisible barrier of force (in science fiction etc.); ~**-out,** (Baseball) putting-out of runner displaced from base by next runner; ~**-pump** (that forces water beyond range of atmospheric pressure). [ME f. OF, f. Rom. *fortia f. L *fortis* strong]

fŏrce² *v.* **1.** *v.t.* constrain, compel; ~ person's **hand,** compel him to act prematurely or adopt policy unwillingly; ~**d-choice** *a.*, (of question) in which choice must be made between two alternatives; *force the* ISSUE¹; ~**d labour,** compulsory labour usu. under rigorous conditions; ~**d landing,** unavoidable landing of aircraft in an emergency (so ~**-land** *v.t.* & *i.*). **2.** compel (person) *to* do, *into* doing, or *into* course of action; (Phys.) modify by external action; put strained sense upon (words); compel (card-player) to trump etc., compel play of (card); rape (woman); ~ **down,** compel (aircraft) to land. **3.** strain to the utmost, urge; overstrain (analogy etc.); ~ **the bidding** (at auction), raise price rapidly; ~ **the game,** run risks to score quickly; ~ **the pace,** adopt high speed in race to tire adversary out quickly; ~ one's **voice,** strain to get notes beyond usual compass or degree of loudness beyond what is easy or natural; *forced* DRAUGHT¹; ~**d march** (by troops etc., requiring special effort). **4.** overpower, capture, make way through, break open, (stronghold, defences, pass, lock, door) by force. **5.** drive or propel violently or against resistance. **6.** impose, press, (thing) (*up*)*on* person (~ **a card,** in conjuring, make person choose a particular card unconsciously). **7.** cause or produce by effort (~ **a smile,** make oneself smile; ~ one's **way,** make a passage); take by force, extort, wring, (*force it out of his hands*; *forced loan*; *forced tears from his eyes*, *the facts out of him*). **8.** artificially hasten the growth or maturity of (plant, scholar, child); **for′cing-house**, place where this is done. **9.** *v.i.* (Of card-player or his action) compel particular (type of) bid or play by another player. [ME, f. OF *forcer* (as prec.)]

force³ *n.* (N. Engl.) waterfall. [f. ON *fors*]

for′ceful (-sf-) *a.* powerful, vigorous; (of speech etc.) impressive, effective; hence ∼**LY²** *adv.*, ∼**NESS** *n.* [f. FORCE¹ + -FUL]

force majeure (fōrs mahzhěr′) *n.* irresistible compulsion or coercion, unforeseeable course of events excusing from fulfilment of contract. [F, = superior strength]

for′cemeat (-sm-) *n.* meat etc. chopped, spiced, and seasoned for stuffing or garnish. [f. obs. *force, farce* stuff f. OF *farsir* (see FARCE)]

for′ceps *n.* (*pl.* same). surgical pincers (also **pair of** ∼); (Anat. & Zool.) organ resembling forceps, whence **for′cipATE²** *a.* [L *forceps forcipis*]

for′cible *a.* done by or involving force; forceful; ∼**-feeble**, disguising feebleness under show of force; hence ∼**NESS** (-beln-) *n.*, **for′cibLY²** *adv.* [ME f. AF & OF (as FORCE²; see -IBLE)]

ford *n.* & *v.* **1.** *n.* shallow place where river etc. may be crossed by wading or with vehicle. **2.** *v.t.* & *i.* cross (water), cross water, by wading or with vehicle. **3.** Hence ∼**ABLE**, ∼**LESS**, *adjs.* [OE, = OS *-ford*, OHG *furt* f. WG **furdu* f. Gmc **fer-* etc.; cf. FARE²]

fordo′ (-ōō′) *v.t.* (**fordi′d; fordo′ne** *pr.* -dū′n; cf. DO¹). (arch.) kill, destroy; spoil; (in *p.p.*) exhausted, tired out. [OE *fordōn* = OS *fardōn*, OHG *fartuon* (as FOR- (4), DO¹)]

fore¹ *a.* & *n.* **1.** *a.* situated in front (opp. *hind, back, aft*); *fore* COURSE¹. **2.** *n.* fore part, bow of ship; **to the** ∼, conspicuous (*come to the* ∼, take leading part), available. [ME; developed f. compounds w. FORE-]

fore² *adv.* & *prep.* **1.** *adv.* ∼ **and aft**, at bow and stern, all over ship, backwards and forwards or lengthwise in ship etc.; ∼**-and-aft cap** (with peak at each end); ∼**-and-aft rigged**, having mainly fore-and-aft sails (i.e. sails set lengthwise, not on yards), opp. to *square--rigged*. **2.** *prep.* in presence of (in adjurations; *fore* God). [OE, = OS, OHG *fora*, Goth. *faura* f. Gmc **for-*; *prep.* often regarded as *'fore* abbr. of *before*]

fore³ *int.* (Golf). (To person in probable line of flight of ball) look out! [prob. for *before* or *afore*]

fore- *pref.* **1.** To *vbs.* and their derivatives, meaning (1) in front (*foreshorten*), (2) beforehand, in advance, (*foreordain*). **2.** To *ns.*, meaning (3) in front, front-, (*forecourt, forelimb, fore-paw*), (4) front part of (*forearm*), (5) of, near, or towards bow of ship or connected with foremast (*forecastle, forehold*), (6) anticipatory, precedent, (*forefather*). [f. FORE²]

fore′arm¹ (fōr′ärm) *n.* arm from elbow to wrist or finger-tips; corresponding part in foreleg or wing. [f. FORE- (4) + ARM¹]

forear′m² (fōrär′m) *v.t.* arm beforehand (usu. fig.). [f. FORE- (2) + ARM³]

forebear. See FORBEAR¹.

forebo′de (fōrb-) *v.t.* betoken, portend; have presentiment of (usu. evil) or *that*. [f. FORE- (2) + BODE]

forebo′ding (fōrb-) *n.* presage or omen, presentiment, (esp. of evil). [ME, f. prec. + -ING²]

fore′cast¹ (fōr′kahst) *v.t.* (∼ *or* ∼**ed**). estimate or conjecture beforehand, predict. [ME, f. FORE- (2) + CAST¹]

fore′cast² (fōr′kahst) *n.* conjectural estimate of something future, esp. of coming weather; prediction. [f. prec.]

forecastle, fo′c′s′le (fō′ksel) *n.* (Naut.) forward part of ship where sailors live; (Hist.) short raised deck at bow, forward part of upper deck. [ME in second sense, f. FORE- (5) + CASTLE¹]

foreclo′s|e (fōrklō′z) *v.t.* bar, preclude, prevent, shut out from enjoyment (*of*); bar (person entitled to redeem mortgage) upon non-payment of money due, bar (right of redemption), take away power of

redeeming (mortgage), whence ∼**URE** (fōrklō′zher) *n.*; settle (arguable point etc.) by anticipation. [ME, f. OF *forclos* p.p. of *forclore* (*for-* out f. L *foras*; see CLOSE³)]

foreco′nscious (fōrkŏ′nshus) *a.* & *n.* (Psych.) (of) part of mind below threshold of immediate conscious attention, from which memories etc. can easily become consciously recalled. [after G *vorbewusst* (*vor-* FORE-, *bewusst* conscious)]

fore′court (fōr′kŏrt) *n.* enclosed space in front of building, outer court; part of filling-station where petrol is supplied; part of lawn-tennis court between service-line and net. [f. FORE- (3) + COURT¹]

foredoo′m (fōrd-) *v.t.* doom or condemn beforehand (*to*). [f. FORE- (2) + DOOM²]

fore′-edge (fōr′ej) *n.* front or outer edge (esp. of pages of book); ∼ **painting**, decoration of spread fore-edges with coloured design. [f. FORE- (3) + EDGE¹]

fore′father (fōr′fahdher) *n.* (usu. in *pl.*) person from whom one's father or mother is descended, ancestor; member of past generations of a family or race; ***F∼s' Day**, 21 Dec., anniversary of first settlers' landing at Plymouth, Massachusetts. [ME, f. FORE- (6) + FATHER¹]

foreefee′l (fōrf-) *v.t.* (**forefe′lt**). feel beforehand, have presentiment of. [f. FORE- (2) + FEEL]

for′efinger (fōr′fingger) *n.* finger next to thumb. [ME, f. FORE- (3) + FINGER]

for′efoot (fōr′f‏-) *n.* (*pl.* **for′efeet**). front foot of animal; (Naut.) foremost piece of keel. [ME, f. FORE- (3, 5) + FOOT¹]

for′efront (fōr′frunt) *n.* very front, foremost part, van, (*in the forefront of the battle*). [ME, f. FORE- (3) + FRONT].

foregather. Var. of FORGATHER.

forego′¹ (fōrgō′) *v.t.* & *i.* (**forewe′nt; forego′ne** *pr.* -gŏ′n *or* -gaw′n *or attrib.* fōr′-; cf. GO¹). precede in place or time; ∼**ne conclusion**, (1) decision or opinion come to in advance of the evidence or necessary facts, (2) result that can be or could have been foreseen; so ∼**ER¹** *n.*, predecessor. [OE *foregān* (as FORE², GO¹)]

forego′². Var. of FORGO.

fore′egoing (fōr′g-, -gō′-) *a.* In vbl senses; previously mentioned (thing, or abs.). [f. FOREGO¹ + -ING²]

fore′ground (fōr′g-) *n.* part of view, esp. in picture, nearest observer; (fig.) most conspicuous position. [f. Du. *voorgrond* (as FORE- (3), GROUND¹)]

fore′ehand (fōr′h-) *n.* & *a.* **1.** *n.* part of horse in front of rider. **2.** *n.* & *a.* (Tennis etc.) (stroke) played with palm of hand towards opponent; (of part of court) where forehand stroke is used. [f. FORE- (3) + HAND¹]

fore′ehanded (fōr′h-) *a.* = prec. **2**; ***thrifty.** [f. as prec. + -ED²]

forehead (fŏ′rid, fōr′hĕd) *n.* part of face above eyebrows and between temples. [OE *forhēafod* (as FORE- (4), HEAD¹)]

fore′ehock (fōr′h-) *n.* foreleg cut of pork or bacon. [f. FORE- (3) + HOCK²]

fore′ehold (fōr′h-) *n.* (Naut.) hold in fore part of ship. [f. FORE- (5) + HOLD³]

fo′reign (-rin) *a.* **1.** belonging to or proceeding from other persons or things; alien, irrelevant, dissimilar, or inappropriate, *to*; introduced from outside (esp. ∼ **body** or **substance** in the tissues etc.). **2.** situated outside, coming from another district, society, etc.; outside the country, not of one's own land; of, in, characteristic of, coming from, dealing with, some country or language other than one's own (*foreign correspondent; foreign and home* TRADE). **3.** ∼ **aid**, money or goods given by one State to another; ∼ **devil**, (Chinese derog.) foreigner, esp. European; ∼ **exchange**, (dealings in) currency of other countries; ∼**-going**, (of ship) going to foreign countries; *foreign* LEGION; **F∼ Minister**, equivalent of ||*Foreign Secretary* in most countries other than UK; ||**F∼ and Commonwealth Office**, ||**F∼ Office** (Hist.), government department dealing with matters concerning other countries (F∼ **Secretary,** head of this). **4.** Hence ∼ISM (2, 4) *n.,* ∼IZE (3) *v.t.* & *i.* [ME, f. OF *forein, forain* f. Rom. **foranus* f. L *foras, -is* outside; for *-g-* cf. *sovereign*]

fŏ′reigner (-rĭn-) *n.* person born or dwelling in foreign country or place or habitually speaking foreign language; foreign ship, imported animal or article. [ME, f. prec. +-ER¹]

fŏreju̇′dge (fŏrj-) *v.t.* judge or determine before hearing the evidence. [f. FORE- (2) +JUDGE²]

fŏreknow′ (fŏrnō′) *v.t.* (**foreknew′** *pr.* fŏrnū′; **foreknow′n** *pr.* fŏrnō′n). know beforehand, have prescience of; so **fŏre**KNOW′LEDGE (fŏrnŏ′lǐj) *n.* [f. FORE- (2) +KNOW¹]

*fŏr′elȧdy̆ (fŏr′l-) *n.* = FOREWOMAN 2. [f. FORE- (3) + LADY]

fŏr′eland (fŏr′l-) *n.* cape, promontory; piece of land in front of something. [ME, f. FORE- (3) +LAND¹]

fŏr′elĕg (fŏr′l-) *n.* front leg of animal. [ME, f. FORE- (3) +LEG]

fŏr′elŏck (fŏr′l-) *n.* lock of hair growing just above forehead (**take time** etc. **by the** ∼, not let chance slip). [ME, f. FORE- (3) +LOCK¹]

fŏr′e|man (fŏr′m-) *n.* (*pl.* ∼**men**). **1.** president and spokesman of jury. **2.** principal workman superintending others. [ME, f. FORE- (3) +MAN¹]

fŏr′emast (fŏr′mahst) *n.* forward (lower) mast of ship (∼ **man** etc., sailor below rank of petty officer). [f. FORE- (5) +MAST¹]

fŏr′emost (fŏr′mōst, -ŏst) *a.* & *adv.* **1.** *a.* most advanced in position, front, (**head, end,** etc., ∼, with head etc. in front); most notable, best, chief, (*foremost authority on Dickens*). **2.** *adv.* before anything else in position, in the first place, (*first and foremost*). [earlier *formost, formest* superl. of OE *forma* first, assim. to FORE¹ and -MOST; cf. FORMER¹]

fŏr′enāme (fŏr′n-) *n.* first or Christian name. [f. FORE- (3) +NAME¹]

fŏr′eno͞on (fŏr′n-) *n.* (Naut., Law, or arch.) the day till noon, morning. [f. FORE² +NOON]

forĕ′ns|ic *a.* of or used in courts of law (*forensic science*) or in forensic science etc. (*forensic laboratory*); ∼**ic medicine,** application of medical knowledge to legal problems; hence ∼ICALLY *adv.* [f. L *forensis* (FORUM) +-IC]

fŏreŏrdai′n (fŏrŏr-) *v.t.* predestinate, ordain beforehand; hence **fŏre**ORDINA′TION (fŏrŏr-) *n.* [ME, f. FORE- (2) +ORDAIN]

fŏr′epeak (fŏr′p-) *n.* (Naut.) end of forehold in angle of bows. [f. FORE- (5) +PEAK¹]

fŏr′eplay (fŏr′p-) *n.* stimulation preceding sexual intercourse. [f. FORE- (6) +PLAY²]

fŏrerŭ′n (fŏr-r-) *v.t.* (**-nn-;** forera′n; foreru′n). go before; indicate the coming of, foreshadow; hence **fŏr′erŭn**NER¹ (1, 2) (fŏr-r-) *n.* [ME, f. FORE- (1) + RUN¹]

fŏr′esail (fŏr′sāl, -sal) *n.* principal sail on foremast (lowest square sail, or fore-and-aft bent on mast, or triangular before mast). [ME, f. FORE- (5) +SAIL¹]

fŏresee′ (fŏrsē′) *v.t.* (**foresaw′; foresee′n**). see or be aware of beforehand (thing, or *that*); ∼**able future,** period during which general course of events can reasonably be predicted. [OE *foresēon* (as FORE- (2), SEE¹)]

fŏreshȧ′dow (fŏrshȧ′dō) *v.t.* prefigure, serve as type or presage of, indicate (future event). [f. FORE- (2) + SHADOW²]

fŏr′e-sheets (fŏr′sh-) *n. pl.* inner part of bows of boat with gratings for bowman to stand on. [f. FORE- (5) +SHEET¹ +-s¹]

fŏr′eshȯre (fŏr′sh-) *n.* part of shore between high- and low-water marks, or between water and land cultivated or built on. [f. FORE- (4) +SHORE¹]

fŏreshŏr′ten (fŏrsh-) *v.t.* show or portray (object) with the apparent shortening due to visual perspective. [f. FORE- (1) +SHORTEN, prob. after Du. *verkorten*]

fŏreshow′ (fŏrshō′) *v.t.* (*p.p.* ∼**n**). foretell; foreshadow, portend, prefigure. [f. FORE- (2) +SHOW¹]

fŏr′esı̆ght (fŏr′sīt) *n.* foreseeing; care for the future; front sight of gun; (Surv.) sight taken forwards. [ME, prob. after ON *forsjá, forsjó* (as FORE-, SIGHT¹)]

fŏr′eskin (fŏr′s-) *n.* loose skin covering end of penis. [f. FORE- (3) +SKIN¹, after G *vorhaut*]

fŏr′rĕst *n.,* & *v.t.* **1.** *n.* large tract covered with trees and undergrowth sometimes mixed with pasture; trees growing in it (lit. or fig.; *a forest of masts*); DEER-*forest;* district formerly forest but now cultivated (*Sherwood Forest*); ||(Hist.) unenclosed woodland district kept for hunting and usu. owned by sovereign; ∼**tree** (of large growth suitable for forest). **2.** *v.t.* plant with trees; convert into forest. [ME f. OF, f. LL *forestis* (*silva* wood) outside (walls of park) f. L *foris* outside]

fŏresta′l|l (fŏrstaw′l) *v.t.* anticipate the action of; anticipate and so baffle, deal with before the regular time, anticipate (action of another, or event); (Hist.) buy up (goods) in order to profit by enhanced price; hence ∼MENT *n.* [ME in last sense; cf. AL *for(e)stallare* f. OE *for(e)steall* an ambush (as FORE- (6), STALL¹)]

fŏr′estay (fŏr′s-) *n.* stay from head of foremast to ship's deck to support foremast. [ME, f. FORE- (5) + STAY²]

fŏ′rĕster *n.* officer in charge of forest, or of growing timber; dweller in forest; (F∼) member of the Ancient Order of Foresters (friendly society); bird or animal of forest, e.g. New Forest pony, forest-dwelling moth, great kangaroo. [ME, f. OF *forestier* (as FOREST, -IER)]

fŏ′rĕstry̆ *n.* wooded country, forests; science or art of managing forests. [f. FOREST +-RY]

fŏr′etāste¹ (fŏr′t-) *n.* partial enjoyment or suffering (*of*) in advance, anticipation. [ME, f. FORE- (2) + TASTE²]

fŏretā′ste² (fŏrt-) *v.t.* taste beforehand, anticipate enjoyment etc. of. [ME, f. FORE- (2) +TASTE¹]

fŏretĕ′ll (fŏrt-) *v.t.* (**foreto′ld**). tell of (event etc.) before it takes place, predict, prophesy; presage, be precursor of. [ME, f. FORE- (2) +TELL¹]

fŏr′ethought (fŏr′thawt) *n.* previous thinking or devising; deliberate intention; care for the future. [ME, f. FORE- (6) +THOUGHT¹]

fŏr′etı̆me (fŏr′t-) *n.* (arch.) the past, early days, old times. [f. FORE- (6) +TIME¹]

fŏretŏ′ken (fŏr′t-) *n.* sign of something to come. [OE *foretācn* (as FORE- (6), TOKEN)]

fŏretŏ′ken² (fŏrt-) *v.t.* portend, indicate beforehand. [f. prec.]

fŏr′etŏp (fŏr′t-) *n.* top of foremast (TOP¹ 7); **foretop-gallant mast,** mast above fore-topmast (mast above foremast); **foretop-gallant-sail,** sail above fore-topsail (sail above foresail). [ME, f. FORE- (5) +TOP¹]

*forĕ′ver, *forĕvermŏr′e. See *for ever* (EVER 2).

fŏrewar′n (fŏrwŏr′n) *v.t.* warn beforehand (*fore-warned is forearmed*). [ME, f. FORE- (2) +WARN]

forewent. See FOREGO¹,².

fŏr′e|woman (fŏr′wȯ͞oman) *n.* (*pl.* ∼**women** *pr.* -wı̆mı̆n). **1.** woman foreman of jury. **2.** chief workwoman supervising others. [f. FORE- (3) +WOMAN]

fŏr′eword (fŏr′wĕrd) *n.* preface; introductory remarks, esp. by person other than the author of the book etc. [f. FORE- (3) +WORD¹, after G *vorwort*]

fŏr′eyȧrd (fŏr′yȧrd) *n.* lowest yard on foremast. [f. FORE- (5) +YARD¹]

fŏr′feit (-fı̆t) *n., a.,* & *v.t.* **1.** *n.* & *a.* (thing) lost owing to crime or fault. **2.** *n.* penalty for breach of contract or neglect, fine; trivial fine for breach of rules in clubs etc. or in games; article surrendered by player in game of ∼s to be redeemed by performing ludicrous task; forfeiting. **3.** *v.t.* lose right to, be deprived of, have to pay, as penalty of crime, neglect, etc., or as necessary consequence of something; hence ∼ABLE *a.,* ∼URE *n.* [ME, = crime, f. OF *forfet, forfait* p.p. of *forfaire* transgress (*for(s)* beyond (what is right)) f. L *foris* outside, *faire* f. L *facere* do)]

fŏrfĕ′nd *v.t.* (arch.) avert, keep off, (*God, Heaven,*

For other words in *fore-* see FORE-.

forfend!); *protect by precautions. [ME, f. FOR- (2) +FEND]

forga'ther (-dh-) *v.i.* assemble, meet together, associate. [16th c. Sc., f. Du. *vergaderen*, assim. to FOR- (5), GATHER]

forga've. See FORGIVE.

forge¹ *n.* smithy; blacksmith's hearth or fireplace, with bellows; furnace or hearth for melting or refining metal, workshop containing it. [ME f. OF, f. Rom. *faurga* f. L *fabrica* trade, workshop, FABRIC]

forge² *v.t.* shape by heating in fire and hammering (lit. or fig.); fabricate, invent, (tale, lie); make (money etc.) in fraudulent imitation, esp. write (document, signature) in order to pass it off as written by another, whence **for'ger**¹ *n.*; hence ~ABLE (-'ja-) *a.* [ME, f. OF *forger* f. L *fabricare* FABRICATE]

forge³ *v.t.* make one's way, advance, gradually or steadily; ~ (**ahead**), take lead in race, move forward rapidly. [18th c., perh. alt. f. FORCE²]

for'gery *n.* forging, counterfeiting, or falsifying, of document etc.; spurious thing, esp. document or signature. [f. FORGE²+-ERY]

forge't (-g-) *v.* (-**tt-**; forgo't; forgo'tten, US or arch. or poet. also forgo't). **1.** *v.t. & i.* lose remembrance of or about (thing, person, *that, how to, where,* etc., or abs.); neglect (*to* do), inadvertently omit to bring or mention or attend to; put out of mind, cease to think of, (*forgive and forget*); ~ (**about**) it!, (colloq.) take no more notice of it, there is no need for apology or thanks. **2.** *v.t.* disregard, slight. **3.** ~ one**self**, (1) neglect one's own interests, (2) act unbecomingly or unworthily, (3) (arch.) lose consciousness. **4.** ~**-me- -not**, plant of genus *Myosotis*, esp. of species with small yellow-eyed bright blue flowers. **5.** Hence ~tABLE *a.* [OE *forgietan*, = OS *fargetan*, OHG *firgezzan* f. WG (as FOR- (1), GET¹)]

forge'tful (-g-) *a.* ~ (**of**), apt to forget, forgetting, neglectful (of); (poet.) causing one to forget; hence ~LY² *adv.*, ~NESS *n.* [ME, f. prec.+-FUL]

forgi've (-g-) *v.t.* (forga've; forgi'ven). remit, let off, (debt, person debt); cease to resent, pardon, (offence, offender, offender offence, or abs.; *forgive us our trespasses*); hence ~ABLE, ~ING², *adjs.* [OE *forgiefan*, = OS, OHG *fargeban*, ON *fyrirgefa*, Goth. *fragiban* grant; as FOR- (1), GIVE¹]

forgi'veness (-gĭ'vn-) *n.* act of forgiving; state of being forgiven. [OE *forgief(e)nes* (as prec., -NESS)]

forgo' *v.t.* (forwe'nt; forgo'ne *pr.* -gŏ'n *or* -gaw'n; cf. GO¹). abstain from, go without, let go; omit or decline to take or use (pleasure, advantage, etc.); relinquish. [OE *forgān* (as FOR- (3), GO¹)]

forgo't(ten). See FORGET.

fo'rint *n.* principal monetary unit of Hungary. [Magyar, f. It. *fiorino* (see FLORIN)]

fork *n. & v.* **1.** *n.* pronged agricultural implement used for digging, lifting, carrying, or throwing; two, three, or four, -pronged instrument used in eating at table or cooking; TUNING-*fork*, pronged device pushed under load to be lifted; forked support for bicycle wheel; stick with forked end used as support for vines etc. **2.** forking bifurcation, e.g. that of human legs, of diverging roads, or of branches; one such branch; flash of forked lightning; (Chess) simultaneous attack on two men by one. **3.** ~-**lift** (*truck* etc.), vehicle with fork in front for lifting and carrying loads; ~ **lunch, supper,** etc., (eaten with fork at buffet etc.). **4.** *v.i.* form fork, have or develop branches; take one or other road etc. at fork (*fork left for Banbury*). **5.** *v.t.* dig, lift, carry, or throw with fork; (Chess) attack (two men) at once. **6.** *v.i. & t.* (sl.) ~ **out** or **over** or **up,** hand over, pay. [OE *forca, force,* = OS *furka,* OHG *furcha,* ON *forkr* f. L *furca*]

forked (-kt) *a.* having fork or forklike end or branches; divergent, cleft, (**three-**~ etc., having three etc. prongs). [ME, f. prec.+-ED²]

forlor'n *a.* desperate, hopeless; abandoned, forsaken, (poet.) deprived *of*; in pitiful condition, of wretched appearance; ~ **hope,** desperate enterprise, faint hope. [p.p. of obs. *forlese* f. OE *forlēosan* (as FOR- (5), LOSE); *forlorn hope* f. Du. *verloren hoop* lost troop (*hoop* company, HEAP¹), orig. of storming-party etc.]

form¹ *n.* **1.** shape, arrangement of parts, visible aspect (esp. apart from colour), shape of body. **2.** person or animal as visible or tangible (*saw a form, the form of my son, before me*). **3.** (Philos.) essential nature of a species or thing. **4.** mode in which thing exists or manifests itself (*in, under, take, the form of*); species, kind, variety; cf. CONTENT¹. **5.** (Gram.) one of the ways in which a word may be spelt or pronounced or inflected; external characteristics of words apart from meaning. **6.** class in schools (usu. numbered from sixth downwards). **7.** arrangement and style in literary or musical composition. **8.** customary method (*in due form; that is* **common** ~, what is usually done and of no special significance; **matter of** ~, mere routine); set order of words, formula; regularly drawn document; document with blanks to be filled up. **9.** formality, mere piece of ceremony. **10.** behaviour according to rule or custom (**good, bad,** ~, complying with or offending against current social conventions); correct procedure (*he knows the form*). **11.** (Of horse, athlete, etc.) condition of health and training (**in, out of,** ~, fit or not for racing etc.; **in good** or **top** ~, **on** ~, playing, performing, etc., well; **off** ~, not playing etc. well); details of previous performances in racing etc.; (sl.) criminal record; good spirits (*was in great form*). **12.** long seat without back, bench. **13.** (Print.) = FORME. **14.** hare's lair. **15.** ~('**work**), temporary structure to hold concrete during setting. **16.** ~ **criticism,** textual analysis of Bible etc. by tracing history of its content of proverbs, myths, and other forms; ~ **letter,** standardized letter to deal with frequently occurring matters. [ME, f. OF *forme* f. L *forma* mould, shape, beauty]

form² *v.* **1.** *v.t.* fashion, mould, (*into* certain shape; *after, by, from, on,* pattern; or abs.). **2.** mould by discipline, train, instruct, (person, or faculty etc.); embody, organize, *into* a company etc. **3.** frame, make, produce; articulate (word); conceive (idea, judgement); develop (habit); enter into (alliance); be material of, make up, be *one of* or *part of*. **4.** (Gram.) construct (new word) by derivation, inflexion, etc. **5.** *v.i.* take shape, be formed. **6.** *v.t. & i.* (Mil. etc.). draw up or *up* in order, assume specified formation (*form line, column*), take up arrangement in a formation (*right, left, form*). [ME, f. OF *fo(u)rmer* f. L *formare* (as prec.)]

-form *suf.* forming adjs. (usu. w. intermediate -I-) (1) w. sense 'having the form of' (*cruciform, cuneiform*), (2) referring to number of (*uniform, multiform*). [f. or after F *-forme* f. L *-formis* (*forma* FORM¹)]

for'mal *a. & n.* **1.** *a.* of the outward form, shape, appearance, arrangement, or external qualities; (Philos.) of the essence of a thing, essential not material; (Logic) concerned with the form, not the matter, of reasoning. **2.** valid or correctly so called in virtue of its form, explicit and definite, not merely tacit or accepted as equivalent; in accordance with recognized forms or rules of art etc. **3.** ceremonial, required by convention (*a formal call*); perfunctory, having the form without the spirit; observant of forms or rules, precise, regular, (*formal garden*); prim, excessively regular or symmetrical, stiff, methodical. **4.** Hence ~LY² *adv.* **5.** *n.* evening dress; occasion on which evening dress is worn. [ME, f. L *formalis* (as FORM¹; see -AL)]

forma'ldehyde *n.* aldehyde of formic acid, HCHO, used as disinfectant and preservative and in manufacture of synthetic resins. [f. FORMIC+ALDEHYDE]

for'malin *n.* aqueous solution of formaldehyde. [f. prec.+-IN]

for'mal|ism *n.* **1.** excessive adherence to prescribed forms; use of forms without regard to inner significance. **2.** treatment of mathematics as manipulation of meaningless symbols; (Theatr.) symbolic and stylized manner of production; (derog.) artist's concentration on form at expense of content. **3.** Hence ~IST (2) *n.*, **i'stic** *a.* **4.** (Phys.) mathematical description of physical situation etc. [f. FORMAL + -ISM]

formä'lity *n.* conformity to rules, propriety; ceremony, elaborate procedure; formal or ceremonial act, requirement of etiquette, regulation, or custom, (often with implied lack of real significance); being formal, precision of manners, stiffness of design. [f. F *formalité* or f. med. L *formalitas* (as FORMAL; see -ITY)]

fŏr'mǎliz|e, -īs|e (-īz), *v.t.* give definite shape or legal formality to; make ceremonious, precise, or rigid, imbue with formalism; hence ~A'TION *n.* [f. FORMAL + -IZE]

fŏr'mant *n.* characteristic pitch-constituent of vowel; morpheme occurring only in combination in word or word-stem. [G, f. L *formare*; see FORM², -ANT]

fŏr'mǎt *n.*, & *v.t.* (-tt-). **1.** *n.* shape and size (of book etc.); style or manner of arrangement or procedure; arrangement of data etc. for processing or storage by computer. **2.** *v.t.* arrange in format, esp. for computer. [F f. G, f. L *formatus* (*liber*) shaped (book), p.p. of *formare* FORM²]

fŏr'mäte. See FORMIC.

fŏrmä'tion *n.* forming, being formed; thing formed; arrangement of parts, structure, (Mil.) arrangement of troops; a number of aircraft flying in company; (Geol.) assemblage of rocks or series of strata having some common characteristic; hence ~AL *a.* [ME f. OF, or f. L *formatio* (as FORM²; see -ATION)]

fŏr'mative *a.* & *v.t.* **1.** *a.* serving to fashion, of formation; (Gram., of flexional or derivative suffix or prefix) used in forming words. **2.** *n.* formative element. [ME, f. OF *formatif -ive* or f. med. L *formativus* (as FORM²; see -ATIVE)]

||**fŏrme** *n.* (Print.) body of type secured in chase for printing at one impression; quantity of film arranged for making plate etc. [var. of FORM¹]

fŏr'mer¹ *attrib. a.* of the past or an earlier period (*in former times; more like her former self; our former haunts*), whence ~LY² *adv.*; * = EX-¹ 2; **the** ~ (w. noun, or abs.), the first or first mentioned of two (opp. *latter*). [ME, f. *forme* first + -ER³, after FOREMOST]

fŏr'mer² *n.* In vbl senses; (Electr.) frame or core for winding coil; (Aeron.) transverse strengthening member in wing or fuselage. [f. FORM² + -ER¹]

fŏr'm|ic *a.* (Chem.) ~ic **acid**, colourless irritant volatile acid (HCOOH) contained in fluid emitted by ants; hence ~ATE¹ (3) *n.* [f. L *formica* ant + -IC]

Fŏrmi'ca *n.* (P) hard durable plastic laminate used on surfaces. [20th c.; orig. uncert.]

fŏrmicä'tion *n.* sensation as of ants crawling over the skin. [f. L *formicatio* (*formica* ant; see -ATION)]

fŏr'midab|le (fŏr'-; D -mī'-) *a.* to be dreaded or viewed with respect; likely to be hard to overcome, resist, or deal with; hence ~leNESS (-beln-) *n.*, ~LY² *adv.* [F, or f. L *formidabilis* (*formidare* fear; see -ABLE)]

fŏr'mless *a.* shapeless, without determinate or regular form; hence ~LY² *adv.*, ~NESS *n.* [f. FORM¹ + -LESS]

fŏr'mūla *n.* (*pl.* ~e or ~s). **1.** fixed form of words as definition or enunciation of principle or as occurring in literary composition; statement prescribed or accepted for use on ceremonial or social occasion etc.; rule unintelligently followed, conventional usage or belief; list of ingredients, recipe; *infant's food made up from recipe; principle serving to reconcile difference of aim or opinion (*diplomats seeking a formula*). **2.** (Math.) rule or statement in algebraic symbols; (Chem.) expression by symbols of substance's constituents; tabulation of certain facts by symbols and figures; classification of racing car esp. by engine capacity. **3.** Hence **fŏrmūlā'IC** *a.*, **fŏr'mūl(ar)IZE** (3) *v.t.* [L, dim. of *forma* FORM¹; see -ULE]

fŏr'mūlary *n.* & *a.* **1.** *n.* collection of formulae; document or book of set forms esp. for religious use. **2.** *a.* using formulae; in or of formulae. [n. f. F *formulaire*

or f. med. L *formularius* (*liber* book) f. L (as prec.); a. f. prec. + -ARY¹]

fŏr'mūl|āte *v.t.* reduce to or express in a formula; set forth systematically; hence ~A'TION *n.* [f. FORMULA + -ATE²]

fŏr'mūl|ism *n.* adherence to or dependence on conventional formulas; so ~IST (2) *n.* [f. FORMULA + -ISM]

fŏr'nicǎt|e *v.i.* commit fornication; so ~OR *n.* [f. eccl. L *fornicari* (L *fornix -icis* brothel) + -ATE³]

fŏrnicä'tion *n.* voluntary sexual intercourse between unmarried persons or (esp. Bibl.) other than between husband and wife. [ME f. OF, f. eccl. L *fornicatio -onis* (as prec.; see -ATION)]

fo'rrader. See FORWARD².

forsä'ke *v.t.* (forsoo'k *pr.* -ŏŏ'k; ~n). give up, break off from, renounce; withdraw one's help, friendship, or companionship from, desert, abandon. [OE *forsacan* deny, renounce, refuse, = OS *forsakan*, OHG *firsahhan* f. WG (as FOR- (3); cf. OE *sacan* quarrel)]

forsoō'th *adv.* (arch., iron., or derog.) truly, in truth, no doubt. [OE *forsōth* (as FOR, SOOTH)]

forspě'nt *a.* (arch.) tired out. [p.p. of obs. *forspend* f. OE *forspendan* (as FOR- (5), SPEND)]

forswear' (-wār') *v.t.* (forswor'e; forswor'n). abjure, renounce on oath; (in *p.p.*) perjured; ~ oneself, swear falsely, perjure oneself. [OE *forswerian* (as FOR- (3, 1), SWEAR)]

forsy̆'thia *n.* spring-flowering ornamental shrub of genus *Forsythia* bearing bright-yellow flowers. [mod. L, f. W. *Forsyth*, Engl. botanist d. 1804 + -IA¹]

fŏrt *n.* fortified building or position; (Hist.) trading-station, orig. fortified; **hold the** ~, act as temporary substitute, cope with emergency. [F, or f. It. *forte*, abs. uses of adj. = strong f. L *fortis*]

fŏr'talice *n.* (arch.) fortress; small outwork of fortification, small fort. [ME, f. med. L *fortalitia* f. L *fortis* strong]

fŏrte¹ (-'tā, -t) *n.* person's strong point, thing in which one excels; (Fenc.) part of sword-blade from hilt to middle (cf. FOIBLE). [f. F *fort* abs. use of adj. = strong; for substitution of fem. form cf. *morale, locale*]

fŏr'te² *a.*, *adv.*, & *n.* (Mus.) (passage to be) performed loudly; ~ **piano**, loud(ly) and then immediately soft(ly). [It., = strong, loud]

fŏrth *adv.* & *prep.* (arch. exc. in set phrs.) **1.** forwards (**back and** ~, to and fro); onwards in time (*from this time forth; henceforth* etc.); forward, into view, (*bring, come,* HOLD¹, SET¹, *show,* etc., *forth*); out from home etc. (*set* etc. *forth*); **and so** ~, and so on, and the like. **2.** *prep.* from out of. [OE, = OS *forth*, MHG *vort* f. Gmc *furtha* f. IE *prto*]

fŏr'thcoming (-kŭ-, -kŭ'-). *a.* about or likely to come forth or appear; approaching; produced when wanted (*no reply was forthcoming*); (of person) informative, responsive, whence ~NESS *n.* [f. prec. + COME + -ING²]

fŏr'thright (-rīt) *adv.*, *a.*, & *n.* **1.** *adv.* (-rī't). straight forward, in a direct manner; (arch.) immediately. **2.** *a.* (fŏr'-). going straight; outspoken; unswerving; decisive, unhesitating. **3.** *n.* (fŏr'-; arch.) straight course (*forthrights and meanders*). [OE *forthriht(e)* (as FORTH, RIGHT¹,⁴)]

fŏrthwi'th (-th, -dh) *adv.* immediately, without delay. [f. earlier *forthwithal* (FORTH, WITH, ALL)]

fŏr'tieth. See FORTY.

fŏrtificä'tion *n.* fortifying; strengthening of wine with alcohol; (Mil.) (art or science of) providing with defensive works, (usu. in *pl.*) defensive work(s), wall(s), earthwork(s), tower(s), etc. [ME f. F, f. LL *fortificatio -onis* act of strengthening (as foll.; see -ATION)]

fŏr'tif|y *v.* **1.** *v.t.* strengthen structure of; impart vigour or physical strength or endurance to, strengthen mentally or morally, encourage; increase nutritive value of (food, esp. with vitamins); strengthen (wine) with alcohol; (arch.) corroborate, confirm, (statement); provide (town, army, etc.)

with defensive works; hence ∼IABLE *a*. **2.** *v.i.* erect fortifications. [ME, f. OF *fortifier* f. LL *fortificare* f. L *fortis* strong; see -FY]

for·tis'sim|o *a., adv.,* & *n.* (*pl.* ∼**os,** *or* ∼**i** *pr.* -ē). (Mus.) (passage to be) performed very loudly. [It., superl. of FORTE²]

for'titūde *n.* courage in pain or adversity. [ME f. F, f. L *fortitudo -dinis* (*fortis* strong; see -TUDE)]

for'tnight (ĭt) *n.* period of two weeks; **today, this day,** Monday, etc., ∼, **a** ∼**(from) today, a** ∼ **on** Monday, etc., a fortnight before or esp. after today etc. [OE *fēowertēne niht* fourteen nights]

for'tnightly (-ĭt-) *a., adv.,* & *n.* **1.** *a.* & *adv.* (produced or occurring) once every fortnight. **2.** *n.* fortnightly magazine etc. [f. prec. + -LY¹·²]

For'trän *n.* computer language used esp. for scientific calculations. [f. FORMULA + TRANSLATION]

for'tress *n.,* & *v.t.* **1.** *n.* military stronghold, esp. strongly fortified town fit for large garrison. **2.** *v.t.* (arch.) serve as fortress to; protect. [ME, f. OF *forteresse* f. Rom. *fortaritia f. L *fortis* strong]

fortū'it|ism *n.* belief that adaptation in nature is due to mere chance; so ∼IST (2) *n.* [f. foll. + -ISM]

fortū'itous *a.* due to or characterized by chance, accidental, casual; hence ∼LY² *adv.,* ∼NESS *n.* [f. L *fortuitus* (*forte* by chance) + -OUS]

fortū'ity *n.* fortuitousness; a chance occurrence, accident. [irreg. f. as prec. + -ITY]

for'tunate (-chŏŏ-) *a.* favoured by fortune, lucky, prosperous; auspicious, favourable. [ME, f. L *fortunatus* (as FORTUNE¹; see -ATE²)]

for'tunately (-chŏŏnatlǐ) *adv.* luckily, successfully, (qualifying whole sentence) it is fortunate that. [f. prec. + -LY²]

for'tune¹ (-chun, -chŏŏn) *n.* **1.** chance or luck as a power in human affairs (**F**∼, this power personified as goddess; *Fortune's* WHEEL¹; SOLDIER *of fortune*). **2.** (in *sing.* or *pl.*) luck good or bad that falls to anyone or to an enterprise etc. **3.** person's destiny; (of gypsies etc. claiming to foretell the future) *tell person his fortune, tell fortunes,* ∼**-teller,** ∼**-telling;** *∼ **cookie,** baked dough cake enclosing prediction etc. on slip of paper. **4.** good luck; prosperity; prosperous condition, wealth, (**make** one's ∼, prosper; **make a** ∼, become rich; (**small**) ∼, large sum of money; **marry a** ∼, (arch.) marry rich heiress; ∼**-hunter,** man seeking rich wife for himself. [ME f. OF, f. L *fortuna* luck, chance]

for'tune² (-chun, -chŏŏn) *v.i.* (arch. or poet.) chance, occur, (esp. impers., *it fortuned that*); come by chance upon. [ME, f. OF *fortuner* f. L *fortunare* make fortunate (as prec.)]

for'ty *a.* & *n.* **1.** four times ten; symbol for this (40, xl, XL); (in *pl.*) numbers etc., esp. years of a century or life, from 40 to 49; ∼ **winks,** short sleep esp. after dinner; HUNGRY *Forties;* **roaring forties,** stormy ocean tracts between lat. 40° and 50° S.; ‖**the Forties,** sea area between NE coast of Scotland and SW coast of Norway [f. its depth of forty fathoms or more]; hence ∼FOLD *a.* & *adv.,* ∼**for'tiETH**¹ *a.* & *n.* **2.** ∼**-one** etc., (arch.) **one-and-**∼, forty plus one etc., w. corresp. ordinals ∼**-first** etc.; **the F**∼**-fi've,** Jacobite rebellion of 1745; *∼**-ni'ner,** seeker for gold etc., esp. in California (1849). [OE *fēowertig,* = OS *fiwartig,* OHG *fiorzug,* ON *fjórir tigir,* Goth. *fidwor tigjus* (as FOUR, -TY²)]

for'um *n.* **1.** (Rom. Ant.) public place, market-place, place of assembly for judicial and other business, esp. at Rome. **2.** place of or meeting for public discussion; periodical etc. giving opportunity for debate etc.; court, tribunal, (lit. or fig., *the forum of conscience* etc.). [L]

for'ward¹ *a.* & *n.* **1.** *a.* lying in one's line of motion (*the forward horizon*), onward or towards the front (*the forward path*); (Naut.) belonging to fore part of ship; (Cricket) of playing FORWARD²; (Rugby Footb. etc., of pass) towards opponents' goal-line; (of opinions

etc.) advanced or extreme. **2.** (Commerc.) relating to future produce, delivery, etc., (*forward contract*). **3.** advanced, progressing to maturity or completion; (of plant, crop, season) well advanced or early; (arch.) ready, prompt, eager, (*to* do); precocious; presumptuous, pert. **4.** Hence ∼LY² *adv.,* ∼NESS *n.* **5.** *n.* (position of) an attacking player in football, hockey, etc. [f. foll.]

for'ward² *adv.* **1.** towards the future, continuously onwards, (*from this time forward;* CARRIAGE *forward;* **date** ∼, post-date). **2.** towards the front in the direction one is facing; in normal direction of motion or traversal; BACKWARD(s) *and forward(s);* with continuous forward motion (*rushing forward*). **3.** (Cricket). **play** ∼, reach forward to play short-pitched ball. **4.** in advance, ahead, (*send him forward;* BRING *forward;* CARRY¹ *forward;* ∼**-looking,** progressive); to the front, into prominence, (BRING *forward;* **come** ∼, offer oneself for task, post, etc.; PUT¹ *forward;* SET¹ *forward*). **5.** (Naut. & Aeron.) in or near or to or towards bow or nose. **6.** onward so as to make progress; **go** ∼, be going on, progress; **can't get any forwarder** or (colloq.) **forrader,** can make no progress. [OE *forweard,* var. of *forthweard* (as FORTH; see -WARD)]

for'ward⁰ *v.t.* help forward, promote; accelerate growth of, send (letter etc.) on to further destination; dispatch (goods etc.; *forwarding agent*). [f. prec.]

for'wards (-dz) *adv.* = FORWARD² **2.** [ME, f. FORWARD²; *sēε* -S², -WARD(s)]

forwear'ied (-ĭd), **forwōr'n,** *adjs.* (arch.) tired out. [f. FOR- (4); see WEARY, WEAR¹]

forwĕ'nt. See FORGO.

fŏ'ssa *n.* (*pl.* ∼**e.** (Anat.) shallow depression or cavity. [L, = ditch, fem. p.p. of *fodere* dig]

fŏsse *n.* long narrow excavation, canal, ditch, trench, esp. in fortification; (Anat.) = prec.; **F**∼ **Way,** Roman road in Britain with fosse on each side. [ME f. OF, f. L FOSSA]

fŏ'ssick *v.i.* (Austral. & NZ sl.) rummage, search *about;* search for gold etc. in abandoned workings. [19th c. ; cf. dial. *fossick* bustle about]

fŏ'ssil *a.* & *n.* **1.** *a.* found buried, dug up, (∼ **fuel,** coal etc. formed in geological past, esp. opp. *nuclear fuel*). **2.** *a.* & *n.* (thing) preserved in strata of earth and recognizable as remains or vestiges of plant or animal of past (usu. prehistoric) ages (*fossil bones, shells,* IVORY; *hunting for fossils*); (person or thing) belonging to the past, antiquated, incapable of further development; (word etc.) that has become obsolete except in set phrases or forms, e.g. *hue* in *hue and cry;* hence ∼**i'FEROUS** *a.,* ∼IZE (3) *v.t.* & *i.,* ∼IZA'TION *n.* [f. F *fossile* f. L *fossilis* (*fodere foss*- dig; see -IL).]

fŏssōr'ial *a.* (Zool.) burrowing; used in burrowing. [f. med. L *fossorius* (*fossor* digger f. as prec.; see -OR) + -AL]

fŏ'ster¹ *v.t.* having a specified relationship not by blood, but in virtue of nursing or bringing up (*foster--brother, -child, -daughter, -father, -mother, -parent, -sister, -son*); concerning care of orphans etc. (*foster care; foster home*); ‖∼**-mother,** apparatus for rearing chickens hatched in incubator. [orig. 'food', f. OE *fōster* (as FOOD)]

fŏ'ster² *v.t.* promote growth of; encourage or harbour (feeling); (of circumstances) be favourable to; nurse or bring up as foster-child; (arch.) tend affectionately, cherish, keep warm (in bosom). [OE *fōstrian* (as prec.)]

fŏ'sterage *n.* fostering; custom of employing foster--mothers. [f. prec. + -AGE]

fŏ'sterling *n.* foster-child, nursling, protégé. [f. OE *fōsterling* (as FOSTER¹, -LING¹)]

Fou'cault (fōō'kō) *n.* ∼ **current,** (Electr.) eddy current; ∼**('s) pendulum** (showing rotation of earth by turning of its plane of motion relative to floor etc.). [f. J.B.L. ∼, Fr. physicist d. 1868]

fouetté (fwĕtā') *n.* (Ballet). quick whipping movement of raised leg. [F, p.p. of *fouetter* whip]

fouga'sse (fōogah's) n. improvised mortar excavated in the ground, charged with stones, bits of iron, etc., and fired by gunpowder. [F, alt. of *fougade* f. It. *fogata*]

fought. See FIGHT¹.

foul a., n., adv., & v. **1.** a. offensive to the senses, loathsome, stinking; dirty, soiled, (*foul linen*), filthy; (sl.) revolting, disgusting; defaced with corrections (*foul copy*). **2.** containing noxious matter (*foul air, water*); clogged, choked, (*foul gun-barrel*); (of ship's bottom) overgrown with weed, barnacles, etc.; morally polluted, obscene, disgustingly abusive, (*foul deed, motive, talk*; *foul-mouthed, -tongued*); ugly (*fair or foul*). **3.** unfair, against rules of game etc., (*foul blow, stroke*); (of weather) wet, rough, stormy; in collision (FALL¹ or *run foul of*, lit. or fig.); entangled (*foul anchor*; *rope is foul*). **4.** ~ **brood,** bacterial disease of larval bees; ~ **fiend,** the Devil; ~ **line** (marking boundary of playing area etc.); ~ **play,** unfair play in games, (fig.) treachery or murder or violence. **5.** Hence ~'LY² (-l-lī) adv., ~'NESS n. **6.** n. foul thing; collision, entanglement, esp. in riding, rowing, or running; foul stroke or piece of play. **7.** adv. in foul way (*hit him foul*; **play** person ~, deal treacherously with him). **8.** v.i. become foul, get clogged or entangled. **9.** v.t. make foul or dirty (*foul one's own NEST*; *dog fouls pavement*, esp. with excrement); pollute with guilt, dishonour; ~ (**up**), cause (anchor, cable, etc.) to become entangled or muddled, jam or block (crossing, railway line, traffic), (colloq.) spoil or bungle; commit foul against (player); run foul of, collide with; ~**-up** n., state of muddle or confusion. [OE *fūl*, = OS, OHG *fūl*, ON *fúll*, Goth. *fuls* stinking f. Gmc *fūlaz* (*fū*- f. IE *pū*-)]

foulâr'd (fōol-) n. (handkerchief etc. of) thin soft material of silk or silk and cotton. [F]

fou'mart (fōo'-) n. polecat. [ME *fulmert* etc. (as FOUL, *mart* MARTEN)]

found¹ v. **1.** v.t. lay base of (building etc.); be original builder, begin building, of (town, edifice); set up, establish (esp. with endowment), originate, initiate, (institution). **2.** construct, base, (tale, one's fortunes, classification, rule, etc.) (*up*)*on* or in some ground, support, principle, etc., (WELL, **ill,** etc., -~**ed,** reasonable or justified, baseless, etc.). **3.** v.i. rely, base oneself, (of argument etc.) be based, (*up*)*on*. **4.** ~**ing father,** person associated with a founding, esp. Amer. statesman at time of Revolution. [ME, f. OF *fonder* f. L *fundare* (*fundus* bottom)]

found² v.t. melt and mould (metal), fuse (materials for glass); make (thing of metal, glass) thus; hence ~'RY (3) n. [ME, f. OF *fondre* f. L *fundere fus-* pour]

found³. See FIND.

founda'tion n. **1.** establishing, constituting on permanent basis, esp. of an endowed institution; such institution, e.g. monastery, college, or hospital, (**on the** ~, entitled to benefit by its funds, whence ||~ER¹ n.), or its revenues; NEW¹, OLD, *foundation*. **2.** solid ground or base, natural or artificial, on which building rests, (usu. in *pl.*) lowest part of building usu. below ground-level; basis, groundwork, underlying principle, (*report has no foundation*; *base religion on a moral foundation*); body or ground on which other parts are overlaid. **3.** ~(**cream**) (used as base for applying cosmetics); ~ (**garment**), woman's supporting undergarment, e.g. corset; ~**-school** (endowed); ~**-stone,** (esp.) stone laid with ceremony to celebrate founding of edifice, (fig.) basis; ~ **stop,** (Mus.) organ stop sounding only a note and its octaves. [ME, f. OF *fondation* f. L *fundatio -onis* (as FOUND¹; see -ATION)]

fou'nder¹ n. In vbl senses; one who founds an institution (*founder-member*; ~'**s kin,** relatives of founder entitled to election or preference); hence ~SHIP, **fou'ndr**ESS¹, ns. [f. FOUND¹ + -ER¹]

fou'nder² n. In vbl senses. [f. FOUND² + -ER¹]

fou'nder³ v. & n. **1.** v.i. (Of earth, building, etc.) fall down or in, give way; (of horse or its rider) fall to the ground, fall from lameness, stick fast in bog etc.; (of ship) fill with water and sink; (of plan etc.) fail. **2.** v.t. cause (horse) to break down, esp. with founder; cause (ship) to founder. **3.** n. inflammation of horse's foot from overwork; rheumatism of chest-muscles in horses. [ME, f. OF *fondrer*, *esfondrer* submerge, collapse, f. Rom. *(EX¹)fundorare* f. L *fundus* bottom]

fou'ndling n. deserted infant of unknown parents. [ME, perh. f. obs. *funding* (as FIND, -ING³), assim. to -LING¹]

fou'ndry̆. See FOUND².

fount¹ n. reservoir of oil in lamp or of ink in pen; (poet. or rhet.) spring, source, fountain. [back-form. f. FOUNTAIN¹, after MOUNT¹]

||**fount²** (fow-, fō-), ****fônt²***, n. (Print.) set of type of same face and size. [f. F *fonte* (*fondre* FOUND²)]

fou'ntain¹ (-tĭn) n. water-spring; source of river etc. (lit., or fig., *the Crown is the fountain of honour*; *poison the fountains of trust*); jet(s) of water made to spout, structure provided for this; structure for constant public supply of drinking-water; = SODA-*fountain*; reservoir in lamp, printing-press, etc., for oil, ink, etc., (~**-pen,** pen with ink drawn into this); ~**-head,** original source; hence (-)~ED² (-ĭnd) a. [ME, f. OF *fontaine* f. LL *fontana* (*aqua* water) fem. of L *fontanus* a. (*fons fontis* a spring; see -AN)]

fou'ntain² (-tĭn) v.i. & t. (cause to) rise like waters of fountain. [f. prec.]

four (fôr) a. & n. **1.** one more than three; symbol for this (4, iv, IV, rarely iiii, IIII); card etc. with four pips; time of four o'clock; size etc. denoted by four; set of four, esp. horses, card-players, or crew of four in rowing-boat(~**s,** boat-races between such crews); hit at cricket scoring four runs; (in *pl.*) gloves, shoes, etc., of fourth size, candles weighing four to the pound; **on all** ~**s,** (1) on all four feet (of quadruped), (2) crawling on hands and knees, (3) completely analogous or corresponding (*the examples are not on all fours*). **2.** ||~**-ale,** (Hist.) ale sold at 4d. a quart; ~**-ball,** golf match between two pairs with each person using a separate ball; ~**-colour problem** (to prove that any plane map can be coloured with only four different colours so that no two same-coloured regions have a common boundary); ~**-cycle,** = four-stroke; *four-*DIMENSIONAL; ~**-eyes,** (sl.) bespectacled person; ****~-flush,** almost worthless poker hand having four (not five) cards of same suit; ****~-flusher,** bluffer, humbug; ~**-footed,** having four feet (esp. opp. biped); ****~-H,** of clubs etc. for instruction of young people in agriculture and citizenship [improving head, heart, hands, and health]; ~**-handed,** (of monkey) quadrumanous, (of game) for four persons, (of piece of keyboard music) for two players; ****~ hundred,** highest social group of a locality; ~**-in-hand,** (1) vehicle with four horses driven by one person on the box, (2) **necktie worn with knot and two hanging ends superposed; ~**-leaf or ~-leaved clover,** clover leaf with four leaflets thought to bring good luck; ~**-letter word,** vulgar monosyllable referring to sexual or excretory functions; ~ **o'clock,** the plant MARVEL¹ of Peru; ~**-part,** arranged for four voices to sing; ||~'**pence,** sum of 4p or 4d.; ||~'**penny,** costing 4p or 4d. (*fourpenny one*, (colloq.) hit, blow); ~**-post,** (of bed) having four posts to support canopy (~**-poster,** such bed); ~**-pounder,** gun throwing 4-lb. shot; ~**-rowed barley** (with four rows of awns); ~'**score,** (arch.) eighty; ~**-square,** square-shaped, solidly based or steady, resolute(ly); ~**-stroke,** (of internal combustion engine) having a cycle of four strokes (intake, compression, combustion, and exhaust); ~**-wheel,** having four wheels, acting on all four wheels of a vehicle (*four-wheel drive*); ~**-whee'ler,** (Hist.) four-wheeled hackney carriage. **3.** Hence ~'FOLD a. & adv. [OE *fēower*, = OS *fiwar* etc., OHG *fior, fier*, ON *fjórir*, Goth. *fidwōr* f. Gmc *petwor*- f. IE *quetwōr*-]

fourchĕ'tte (foorshĕ't) *n.* (Anat.) membrane at posterior junction of labia minora. [F, dim. of *fourche* (as FORK); see -ETTE]

Fourdri'nier (foor-; -ĭer, -ĭā) *n.* ∼ **(machine)**, machine for making paper as continuous sheet by drainage on wire mesh belt. [f. H. & S. ∼, Brit. printers d. 1854, 1847]

fourgon (foor'gawn) *n.* luggage-van. [F]

Four'ier (foor'ĭā) *n.* (Math.) ∼ **analysis, series**, etc., (relating to resolution of vibrations etc. into combinations of simple harmonic functions). [f.J.B.J. ∼, Fr. mathematician d. 1830]

Four'ierism (foor'-) *n.* system for reorganization of society (cf. PHALANX 2). [f. C. *Fourier*, Fr. socialist d. 1837 +-ISM]

four'some (fōr'-) *n.* golf match between two pairs with partners playing same ball; a company, party, or dance of four persons. [f. FOUR +-SOME²]

fourteen (fôrtē'n, fōr'-) *a.* & *n.* one more than thirteen; symbol for this (14, xiv, XIV); size etc. denoted by fourteen; hence ∼ER¹ *n.*, (Pros.) line of fourteen syllables, ∼TH² *a.* & *n.* [OE *fēowertīene*, = OS *fiertein*, OHG *fiorzehan*, ON *fjórtán*, Goth. *fidwōrtaihun* (as FOUR, -TEEN)]

fourth (fōr-) *a.* & *n.* **1.** *a.* next after third; ∼ **part**, quarter. **2.** *n.* quarter, fourth part; fourth thing etc.; player who completes a group of four; (person having) place in fourth class in examination; fourth gear; (Mus.) (note at) interval of which the span involves four alphabetical notes, harmonic combination of notes thus separated; ||F∼ **of June**, principal annual celebration at Eton College; *F∼ **of July**, anniversary of Declaration of Independence (1776). **3.** ∼ **day**, Wednesday; *fourth* DIMENSION, ESTATE; ∼ **wall**, (Theatr.) proscenium opening through which audience sees performance. **4.** Hence ∼LY² *adv.*, in the fourth place. [OE *fēo(we)rtha*, = OS *fiortho*, OHG *fiordo*, ON *fjórthi* f. Gmc *fi̯(dh)worthon* f. IE *qweturto-]

-to *abbr.* quarto.

fō'vė|a *n.* (*pl.* ∼ae). (Anat.) small depression or pit; hence ∼AI, ∼ATE², *adjs.* [L]

-ovė'ola *n.* (*pl.* ∼e). (Anat.) small fovea; hence **fō'vėolATE²** *a.* [L, dim. of prec.]

owl *n.* (pl. ∼s or ∼), & *v.i.* **1.** *n.* domestic cock or hen of genus *Gallus* (*fowl* CHOLERA; ∼ **pest,** ∼ **plague,** ∼ **pox**, infectious virus diseases of fowls; ∼**-run**, place where fowls may run, breeding establishment for fowls); its flesh as food. **2.** bird (arch. exc. in comb.: GAME¹*fowl*, GUINEA-*fowl*, WILD*fowl*); flesh of birds as food (*fish, flesh, and fowl*). **3.** *v.i.* catch, hunt, shoot, or snare, wildfowl; hence ∼ **ER¹**, ∼'**ING¹**, *ns.* (∼**ing piece**, light gun used in fowling) [OE *fugol*, = OS *fugal*, OHG *fogal*, ON *fugl*, Goth. *fugls* f. Gmc *foglaz*, *fuglaz*, f. *flug-* FLY²]

öx¹ *n.* **1.** red-furred sharp-snouted bushy-tailed carnivorous quadruped preserved in England etc. as beast of chase and proverbial for cunning; its fur; (fig.) crafty person, *(sl.)* attractive woman. **2.** animal of species related to this; FLYING² *fox.* **3.** ∼'**glove**, tall plant with purple or white flowers like glove-fingers; ∼'**hole**, (Mil.) hole in ground used as shelter against missiles or as firing-point, (fig.) place of refuge or concealment; ∼'**hound**, kind of hound bred and trained to hunt foxes; ∼**-hunt** *n.*, & *v.i.*, chasing of, chase, fox with hounds, whence ∼**-hunter** *n.*, ∼**-hunting** *a.* & *n.*, (fond of) this sport; ∼**-mark**, brown spot or stain caused by damp in book etc.; ∼ **shark**, thresher; ∼'**tail**, (1) fox's tail, (2) grass with brushlike spikes; ∼**-terrier** (short-haired for unearthing fox, but kept chiefly as pet); ∼'**trot** *n.*, & *v.i.* (-*tt*-), (perform) ballroom dance with slow and quick steps, music for it. [OE, = OS *vuhs*, OHG *fuhs* f. WG *fuhs*]

öx² *v.* **1.** *v.i.* act craftily, dissemble. **2.** *v.t.* deceive, puzzle, trick; (esp. in *p.p.*) discolour (leaves of book, engraving, etc.) with fox-marks, whence ∼'**ING¹** (2) *n.* [f. prec.]

fö'x|ў *a.* foxlike, crafty(-looking); reddish-brown; damaged by mildew etc.; hence ∼**iNESS** *n.* [f. FOX¹ + -Y²]

foyer (foi'ā, fwah'yā) *n.* large room in theatre etc. for audience's use during interval; entrance hall of hotel etc. [F, = hearth, home, f. Gallo-Rom. **focarium** f. L *focus* fire]

FP *abbr.* former pupil; freezing point.

fp *abbr.* forte piano.

||**FPA** *abbr.* Family Planning Association.

FPS *abbr.* Fellow of the Pharmaceutical Society; foot-pound-second.

f.p.s. *abbr.* feet per second.

Fr. *abbr.* Father; French.

fr. *abbr.* franc(s).

Fr *symb.* francium.

Fra (-ah) *n.* = FRATE (as prefixed title.) [It.]

frā'bjous *a.* delightful, joyous; hence ∼LY² *adv.* [made by Lewis Carroll perh. on FAIR², JOYOUS]

frā'cas (-kah) *n.* (*pl.* same *pr.* -kahz). noisy quarrel, row. [F (*fracasser* f. It. *fracassare* make uproar)]

frā'ction *n.* **1.** numerical quantity that is not a whole number, one or more aliquot parts, (DECIMAL, IMPROPER, PROPER, VULGAR, *fraction*). **2.** small part, piece, or amount. **3.** portion of mixture obtainable by physical separation, e.g. by distillation. **4.** dividing of Eucharistic bread. **5.** Hence ∼ARY² *a.*, ∼IZE (3) *v.t.* [ME f. OF, f. LL *fractio -onis* f. L *frangere fract-* break; see -ION]

frā'ctional *a.* of fraction(s); being a fraction; very slight; ∼ **crystallization, distillation**, etc., separation of parts of a mixture by making use of their different physical properties; hence ∼IZE (3) *v.t.*, ∼LY² *adv.* [f. prec. +-AL]

frā'ction|āte *v.t.* break up into parts; separate (mixture) by fractional distillation etc.; hence ∼A'TION *n.* [f. FRACTION +-ATE³]

frā'ctious (-shus) *a.* unruly; peevish; hence ∼LY² *adv.*, ∼NESS *n.* [f. FRACTION in obs. sense 'brawling' + -OUS; prob. after *factious* etc.]

frā'ctō- *comb. form* (Meteorol., of cloud form) broken, fragmentary, (*fracto-cumulus; fracto-nimbus*). [f. L *fractus* broken (see FRACTION) +-O-]

frā'cture *n.* & *v.* **1.** *n.* breaking, breakage, esp. of bone or cartilage (COMMINUTED, COMPOUND², *fracture*); surface shown by mineral when broken with hammer. **2.** substitution of diphthong, diphthong substituted, for simple vowel owing to influence esp. of following consonant. **3.** *v.t.* cause fracture in, break continuity of; *(sl.)* impress, amuse greatly. **4.** *v.i.* undergo fracture. [ME f. F, or f. L *fractura* (as FRACTION; see -URE)]

frac'nūl|um, frē'nūl|um, *n.* (*pl.* ∼a). small fraenum. [mod. L, dim. of foll.]

frae'n|um, frē'n|um, *n.* (*pl.* ∼a). small ligament checking motion of organ. [L, = bridle]

frā'gile *a.* easily snapped or shattered, weak, perishable, of delicate frame or constitution; hence or cogn. ∼LY² (-l-lĭ) *adv.*, **fragi'lITY** *n.* [F, or f. L *fragilis* (*frag-* root of *frangere* break; see -IL.)]

frā'gment *n.* & *v.* **1.** *n.* part broken off, detached piece; isolated or incomplete part, remainder of otherwise lost or destroyed whole, esp. extant remains or unfinished portion of writing or work of art; hence ∼IZE (3) *v.t.* **2.** *v.t.* & *i.* (or -ĕ'nt). break or separate into fragments. [ME f. F, or f. L *fragmentum* (as prec.; see -MENT]

frā'gmentar|ў *a.* consisting of fragments; disconnected; (Geol). composed of fragments of previously existing rocks; hence ∼iLY² *adv.* [f. prec. +-ARY¹]

frāgmenta'tion *n.* breaking into fragments; ∼ **bomb** etc. (designed to break up into small rapidly-moving fragments when exploded). [f. FRAGMENT +-ATION]

frā'grance *n.* sweetness of smell; sweet scent. [F, or f. L *fragrantia* (as foll.; see -ANCE)]

frā'grant *a.* sweet-smelling (lit. or fig.). [ME f. F, or f. L *fragrare* smell sweet; see -ANT] '**fraid** a. (colloq.) afraid; ∼('y) **cat**, timorous person. [f. AFRAID]

frail[1] n. rush basket for packing figs, raisins, etc.; quantity (e.g. 32 lb.) contained in this. [ME f. OF *fraiel*, of unkn. orig.]

frail[2] a. & n. **1.** a. fragile; transient (*frail life, bliss*, etc.); in weak health; morally weak, unable to resist temptation, (arch. euphem., of woman) unchaste; hence ∼NESS n. **2.** n. *(sl.) woman. [ME, f. OF *fraile*, *frele* f. L *fragilis* FRAGILE]

frail'ty n. liability to err or yield to temptation; fault, weakness, foible. [ME, f. OF *frailete* f. L *fragilitas -tatis* (as FRAGILE; see -ITY)]

fraise (-z) n. tool for enlarging circular hole, or cutting teeth in watch-wheels. [F (*fraiser* enlarge hole)]

Frä'ktur (-oor) n. German style of black-letter type. [G]

framboe'sia, *frambe'sia**, (-bē'z-) n. = YAWS. [mod. L, f. F *framboise* raspberry f. L *fraga ambrosia* ambrosial strawberry + -IA[1]]

fram|e[1] v.t. **1.** shape, direct, dispose, (thoughts, acts, (arch.) person) to a purpose (*for, to, to* do, or w. *adv.*); adapt, fit, *to* or *into*; construct by combination of parts or adaptation to design, contrive, devise, invent, compose, express, (complex article, plot, rule, story, theory); articulate (words); (arch.) conceive, imagine. **2.** [f. foll.] set in or provide with a frame, serve as frame for (*landscape framed in an archway*), whence ∼ING[1] (3) n.; (sl.) concoct false charge or evidence against, devise plot with regard to; *∼e up, (sl.) prearrange (event) with sinister intent, fake result of (race, election, etc.); hence ∼e-up n., (colloq.) conspiracy, esp. to make innocent person appear guilty. **3.** Hence ∼ABLE a., ∼ER[1] n. [OE *framian* be helpful (*fram* forward; see FROM)]

frame[2] n. **1.** construction, constitution, build; established order, plan, system, (*the frame of society* or *government*; ∼ **of reference**, system of geometrical axes for showing position, set of standards etc. governing behaviour); temporary state (*of mind*). **2.** framed work or structure (*the frame of heaven* or *earth*) human or animal body (*sobs shook her frame; man of gigantic frame*); skeleton of building, underlying or surrounding support or essential substructure of anything; rigid part of bicycle, spectacles, umbrella, etc.; supporting skeleton of motor vehicle, aircraft, etc. **3.** case or border enclosing picture, pane of glass, door, etc., whence ∼LESS (-ml-) a.; single complete image or picture on cinema film or transmitted in series of lines by television; single picture in comic strip; (Hort.) glazed portable boxlike structure protecting plants from cold; removable box of slats for building of honeycomb in beehive; triangular frame for setting up snooker etc. balls or skittles, balls so set up, round of play during which skittles are thrown at or balls are pocketed; *(sl.) = FRAME[1]-*up*. **4.** ∼ **aerial**, revolving aerial composed of rectangle or loop or wire, adapted for directional reception; ∼-**house** (of wooden skeleton covered with boards etc.); ∼-**saw** (stretched in frame to make it rigid); ∼'**work**, frame, structure, upon or into which casing or contents can be put (lit. or fig.). [f. prec.]

franc n. monetary unit of France, Belgium, Switzerland, and other countries. [ME, f. OF, f. *Francorum Rex* king of the FRANK[1]s, legend on earliest gold coins so called (14th c.)]

fra'nchise (-z) n., & v.t. **1.** n. right of voting at public elections esp. for Parliament etc.; principle of qualification for this (FANCY[1] *franchise*). **2.** full membership of corporation or State, citizenship. **3.** authorization to sell company's goods or services in a particular area. **4.** (Hist.) legal immunity or exemption from burden or jurisdiction. **5.** right or privilege granted to person or corporation. **6.** v.t. grant franchise to. [ME f. OF (*franc, franche* free, FRANK[2]; see -ISE[2])]

Franci'scan a. & n. (friar or nun) of order founded

1209 by St. Francis of Assisi; of the Franciscans. [f. F *franciscain* f. mod. L *Franciscanus* (*Franciscus* Francis; see -AN)]

frä'ncium n. (Chem.) radioactive metallic element, heaviest alkali metal. [mod. L, f. *France* (discoverer's country) + -IUM]

Frä'nco- comb. form. French (and), as: ∼-**Ger'man**, French and German; ∼MA'NIA n., ∼PHIL(E), ∼PHOBE, ns. & adjs., ∼PHO'BIA n. [f. med. L *Francus* FRANK[1] + -o-]

frä'ncolin n. partridge of genus *Francolinus*. [F, f. It. *francolino*]

frä'ncophone n. & a. French-speaking (person). [f. FRANCO- + Gk *phōnē* voice]

franc tireur (frahn tērēr') n. (*pl.* -*cs* -*rs pr.* same). guerrilla fighter; (Hist.) member of irregular light-infantry corps. [F, = free shooter]

frä'ngible (-nj-) a. breakable, fragile. [OF, or f. med. L *frangibilis* f. L *frangere* to break; see -IBLE]

frä'ngipane (-nj-) n. = foll.; flavoured almond cream or paste. [F, prob. f. *Frangipani*, Italian inventor of the perfume]

frängipa'ni (-njĭpă'-, -pah'-) n. (perfume of) fragrant shrub or tree of genus *Plumeria*. [var. of prec.]

franglais (frah'nglā) n. corrupt version of French with indiscriminate use of words etc. borrowed from English. [F (*français* French, *anglais* English)]

Fränk[1] n. member of the Germanic nation or coalition that conquered Gaul in 6th c.; (in Levant) person of Western nationality; hence ∼ISH[1] a. [f. OE *Franca*, OHG *Franko*, perh. f. weapon (cf. OE *franca* javelin)]

fränk[2] a. ingenuous, open, (*a frank face*); candid, outspoken, (*a frank opinion*); undisguised, avowed, (*frank admiration*; (Med.) unmistakable; hence ∼LY[2] adv. (also ellipt., = 'to speak frankly': *frankly, you haven't a chance*), ∼'NESS n. [ME, f. OF *franc* f. med. L *francus* free, f. prec. (since only Franks had full freedom in Frankish Gaul)]

fränk[3] v.t., & n. **1.** v.t. put stamp on or mark (letter) to record payment of postage; ||∼'**ing-machine** (for so marking letters etc. and recording cost of postage incurred). **2.** (Hist.) superscribe (letter etc.) with signature ensuring conveyance without charge, send without charge; (arch.) facilitate coming and going of (person), give social passport to; (Hist.) exempt from future payment of charges (*a franking duty, imposition*). **3.** n. franking signature or mark; franked cover. [f. prec. in obs. sense 'free of charge']

***fränk**[4] n. (colloq.) frankfurter. [abbr.]

Frä'nkenstein (-tīn) n. ∼('s **monster**), thing that becomes terrifying to the person who has created it. [character in & title of novel (1818) by M. W. Shelley]

frä'nkfürter, *frä'nkfurt**, n. seasoned smoked beef-and-pork sausage. [f. G *Frankfurter wurst* Frankfurt sausage]

frä'nkincěnse n. aromatic gum resin from trees of genus *Boswellia* used for burning as incense; turpentine from conifers. [ME, f. OF *franc encens* (as FRANK[2] in obs. sense 'high-quality', INCENSE[1])]

frä'nklin[1] n. (Hist.) landowner of free but not noble birth in 14th-15th c. [ME *francoleyn* etc., f. AL *francalanus* (*francalis* held without dues f. *francus* free, FRANK[2])]

***Frä'nklin**[2] n. ∼ **stove**, free-standing stove for heating room. [f. B. ∼, Amer. inventor etc. d. 1790]

frä'nk-plědge n. (Hist.) system by which each member of tithing was responsible for good behaviour of every other. [f. med. L *franciplegium* f. AF *fraunceplege* (as FRANK[2], PLEDGE[1]), mistransl. of OE *frithborh* peace-pledge (see free-pledge)]

frä'nt|ic a. wildly excited, distraught with rage, pain, grief, joy, haste, etc.; showing frenzy, uncontrolled, violent, (*frantic effort*); (colloq.) extreme, very great hence ∼ICALLY, ∼ICLY[2], advs. [ME *frentik, frantik* f. OF *frenetique* f. L *phreneticus* (see PHRENETIC)]

frä'p v.t. (-pp-). (Naut.) bind tightly. [f. F *frapper* bind strike]

frappé (frä'pā) *a.* & *n.* **1.** *a.* (Esp. of wine) iced, cooled. **2.** *n.* iced drink; soft water-ice. [F, p.p. of *frapper* strike, ice (drinks)]

fräss *n.* excrement of larvae; refuse left by boring insects. [G (*fressen* devour f. as FRET²)]

***frät¹** *n.* (sl.) (member of) students' fraternity. [abbr.]

frät² *n.*, & *v.i.* (-tt-). (sl.) **1.** *n.* fraternization by troops; woman with whom soldier fraternizes. **2.** *v.i.* (Of troops) fraternize. [abbr.]

frä'tchy *a.* (colloq.) irritable, quarrelsome. [imit.]

frat|e (frah'tā) *n.* (*pl.* ~i *pr.* -ē). friar. [It., = brother]

frä'ter *n.* (Hist.) refectory. [ME, f. OF *fraitur* (*refreitor* f. med. L *refectorium* REFECTORY)]

fratêr'nal *a.* (as) of brother(s), brotherly; *~ order*, = FRATERNITY 3; **~ twins** (developed from separate ova and not necessarily closely similar). [f. med. L *fraternalis* f. L *fraternus* (*frater* brother; see -AL)]

fratêr'nity *n.* **1.** being fraternal, brotherliness. **2.** religious brotherhood. **3.** guild, company with common interests, set of men of same class etc. **4.** *male students' society in university or college. [ME, f. OF *fraternité* f. L *fraternitas -tatis* (as prec.; see -ITY)]

frä'terniz|e, -is|e (-īz), *v.i.* associate, make friends, behave as intimates, (*with, together,* or abs.); (of troops) enter into friendly relations *with* (enemy troops, or inhabitants of an occupied country); so **~A'TION** *n.* [f. F *fraterniser* & med. L *fraternizare* f. L *fraternus* (see FRATERNAL, -IZE)]

frä'tricid|e *n.* killing of one's brother or sister; one who kills his brother or sister; hence **~AL** *a.* [F, or f. LL *fratricidium*, L *fratricida*, (*frater fratris* brother; see -CIDE)]

Frau (frow) *n.* (*pl.* ~'en) Title of German wife or widow = Mrs.; German woman. [G]

fraud *n.* criminal deception, use of false representations to gain unjust advantage; dishonest artifice or trick (**pious ~**, deception intended to benefit those deceived, and esp. to strengthen religious belief); impostor, person or thing not fulfilling expectation or description; (arch.) deceitfulness. [ME, f. OF *fraude* f. L *fraus fraudis*]

frau'dul|ent *a.* guilty of, of the nature of, characterized or effected by, fraud; hence or cogn. **~ENCE** *n.*, **~ently²** *adv.* [ME f. OF, or f. L *fraudulentus* (as prec.; see -ULENT)]

fraught (frawt) *a.* **1.** **~ with,** involving, attended with, full of (meaning etc.), threatening or promising, destined to produce, (sorrow, danger, etc.). **2.** (colloq.) causing or suffering anxiety or distress. **3.** (poet.) stored or equipped *with.* [ME, p.p. of obs. v. *fraught* load with cargo, f. MDu. *vrachten* (*vracht* FREIGHT)]

Fräulein (froi'līn) *n.* Title of German spinster = Miss (also as *voc.*); German spinster; German governess. [G, dim. of FRAU]

Frau'nhöfer (frow'n-) *n.* **~ lines,** dark lines in solar and stellar spectra. [f. J. von ~, Bavarian physicist d. 1826]

fräxinĕ'lla *n.* perennial herb (*Dictamnus albus*), species of dittany. [mod. L, dim. of L *fraxinus* ash-tree]

fray¹ *n.* noisy quarrel, brawl; fight, conflict, (lit. or fig.; *eager* or *ready for the fray*). [ME, f. *fray* to quarrel f. *affray* v. f. as AFFRAY]

fray² *v.t.* & *i.* wear through by rubbing, ravel out edge or end of, (usu. woven material); become ragged at edge (lit., or fig. of nerves, temper, etc.); **~ (its head,** (of deer) rub velvet off new horns. [f. F *frayer,* *freiier* f. L *fricare* rub]

frä'zil *n.* (Can. & US). ice crystals in a stream or on its bed. [f. Can. F *frasil* snow floating in the water; cf. F *fraisil* cinders]

frä'zzle *n.* (colloq.) worn or exhausted state (esp. *worn, beaten,* etc. *to a frazzle*). [perh. f. FRAY² + dial. *fazzle* tangle]

freak¹ *n.* **1.** caprice, vagary; capriciousness. **2.** product of sportive fancy; **~ (of nature),** monstrosity, abnormally developed individual, abnormal or

irregular thing (often *attrib.*: *a freak storm*). **3.** one who freaks out; drug addict; unconventional person, whence **~'y²** *a.* **4.** Hence **~'ish¹** *a.* [16th c., prob. f. dial.]

freak² *v.i.* & *t.* (sl.) **~ (out),** (cause to) undergo narcotic etc. hallucinations or strong emotional experience, adopt unconventional life-style; hence **~-out** *n.,* such experience. [f. prec.]

freaked (-kt) *a.* oddly flecked or streaked. [f. FREAK¹ + -ED²]

frĕ'ckle *n.* & *v.* **1.** *n.* light brown spot on skin, usu. from exposure to sun. **2.** *v.t.* & *i.* spot or be spotted with freckles. [ME *fracel* etc. f. dial. *freken* f. ON *freknur* pl.]

free¹ *a.* (**freer** *pr.* frē'er; **freest** *pr.* frē'ĭst) & *adv.* **1.** *a.* not in bondage to another, having personal rights and social and political liberty; (of State, its citizens or institutions) subject neither to foreign domination nor to despotic government, having national and civil liberty, (*free press, society*; **it's a ~ country,** (colloq.) the action proposed is not illegal). **2.** loose, unrestricted; at liberty, not confined, released from ties or duties, unimpeded; unfettered in action (*go free; set free*); permitted *to* do, independent; unconstrained (*free step, gestures*); (of literary style) not observing strict laws of form; (of translation) not literal; (arch.) allowable (*for* or *to* person *to* do). **3.** open to all comers; clear of obstructions, clear *of* or *from* something undesirable, clear of engagements etc. (*are you free on Monday?*), not occupied or in use (*the bathroom is free now*). **4.** not fixed, not in contact; (Chem.) not combined (*free radical*); (Phys.) not bound in an atom or molecule; (of power or energy) disengaged or available. **5.** spontaneous, unforced; (Phys.) not modified by external force; unearned; gratuitous; willing; lavish, profuse, unstinted, copious, (*free of* or *with his money, free flow of water*); frank, unreserved; forward, familiar, impudent, (**make** or **be ~,** take liberties *with*); (of talk, stories, etc.) slightly indecent. **6.** released or exempt *from* (*free from the ordinary rules, from disease, difficulty,* etc.); not subject to tax, duty, trade-restrictions, or fees; (***for) ~,** provided without payment; **~ of,** having right to enter and use, having freedom of company or city. **7.** *free* AGENT; **~ association,** (Psych.) association of ideas by person under test without suggestion or control by tester; **~'board,** part of ship's side between water-line and deck; **~-born,** inheriting citizen's rights and liberty; **F~ Church,** (1) Church free from State control, (2) nonconformist Church; **F~ Church of Scotland** (seceding from Presbyterian establishment 1843-1929); **~ and easy,** unceremonious; **~ enterprise,** freedom of private business from State control; **~ fall,** movement under force of gravity only, esp. (1) part of parachute descent before parachute opens, (2) movement of spacecraft in space without thrust from engines; **~ fight** (in which all present may join); **~-for-all** *n.* & *a.,* free (fight), unrestricted (discussion), etc.; **~ gift** (not in return for anything; esp. object given away to promote sales); **~ hand,** right of acting at discretion; **~-hand,** (of drawing) done without artificial aid to the hand; **~-ha'nded,** generous; **~'hold,** (*n.*) (land or property held by) tenure in fee simple or fee-tail or for life, (office held by) similar tenure, (*a.*) held by freehold; **~'holder,** possessor of freehold; ||**~ house,** inn or public house that may sell any brewer's liquor; **~ kick,** (Footb.) kick allowed to be taken without interference by opponents, as minor penalty against them; **~ labour,** (1) labour of freemen not slaves, (2) labour of workmen not in trade unions; **~ lance,** (1) medieval mercenary, (2) person working for no fixed employer (so **~lance** *v.i.*; cf. free LIBRARY; **~ list,** list of persons or things to be admitted free of payment, duty, etc.; **~-li'ver,** one who indulges in pleasures esp. of eating; **~-loader,** (sl.) one who eats or drinks at others' expense, sponger; **~ love,** (doctrine permitting) sexual relations irrespective of marriage;

~'man, (1) person not slave or serf, (2) one who has freedom of city, company, etc.; ~ market (in which prices are determined by unrestricted competition); F~'mason, member of a fraternity for mutual help called *Free and Accepted Masons* and having elaborate secret rituals; F~'masonry, system and institutions of Freemasons, (fig.; *f-*) instinctive sympathy or understanding; ~ on board, rail, etc., without charge for delivery to ship, railway wagon, etc.; ~ pass, authority to travel on railway etc. or enter place of entertainment etc. without payment; ~ port, (1) port open to all traders, (2) port area where goods are exempt from customs duty during loading and unloading; ~-range, (of hens etc.) given freedom of movement in seeking food; *free* REIN; ~ school (with no fees charged); ~ speech, right to express opinions of any kind; ~-spoken, not concealing one's opinions; ~-standing, not supported by a structural framework; ~ state, State not subject to another, *State of US in which slavery did not exist; ~-stone, (1) fine-grained easily sawn sandstone or limestone, (2) kind of peach with stone loose when fruit is ripe; ~-style, (of swimming-race) in which any stroke may be used, (of wrestling) all-in; ~ thinker, rejector of authority in religious belief, rationalist etc. (so free-thinking *n.* & *a.*, free thought); ~ trade (left to its natural course without restriction on imports etc.); ~ verse, = VERS LIBRE; ~ vote, Parliamentary vote not subject to party discipline; ~'way, express highway esp. with limited access; ~ wheel, driving-wheel of bicycle able to revolve with pedals at rest; ~-wheel *v.i.*, ride bicycle without pedalling, coast, (fig.) move or act without constraint or effort; *free* WILL² 1, 3; ~-will *attrib. a.*, voluntary; ~ world, non-Communist countries' collective name for themselves. 8. Hence ~'LY *adv.* 9. *adv.* freely; without cost or payment; (Naut.) not close-hauled. [OE *frēo*, = OS, OHG *frī*, ON **frīr*, Goth. *freis* f. Gmc **frijaz* f. IE **prijos* dear]

free² *v.t.* make free, set at liberty, (~'dman, emancipated slave); relieve *from*, rid or ease *of*; clear, disengage, disentangle. [OE *frēon, freog(e)an*, = ON *fría frið* f. Gmc **frijējan* (as prec.)]

-free *comb. form.* free of or from (*disease-free*; POST²-*free*). [f. FREE¹]

*free'bie *n.* & *a.* (colloq.) (thing provided) free of charge. [arbitr. f. FREE¹]

free'booter *n.* pirate, piratical adventurer (lit. or fig.); hence [by back-form.] free'boot *v.i.* [f. Du. *vrijbuiter* (as FREE¹, BOOTY, -ER¹); cf. FILIBUSTER]

free'dom *n.* 1. personal liberty, non-slavery, (*freedom of* CONSCIENCE); civil liberty, independence, (*freedom of the* PRESS¹); liberty of action, right *to* do, (the four ~s, freedom of speech and religion, freedom from fear and want; *freedom of the* WILL²); power of self-determination, independence of fate or necessity. 2. frankness, outspokenness, undue familiarity; facility or ease in action; boldness of conception; degree of ~, (Phys.) independent direction etc. in which motion can occur, (Chem. etc.) independent manner in which a system can vary without fundamental change of constituents. 3. exemption *from* defect, disadvantage, burden, duty, etc.; privilege possessed by city or corporation; participation in privileges of membership *of* company etc. or citizenship *of* city (often given as honour to distinguished persons); unrestricted use *of* (*has the freedom of the library*). 4. ~ fighter, one who takes part in resistance to established political system etc.; *~ ride, organized ride in buses etc. as demonstration against racial segregation. [OE *frēodōm* (as FREE¹, -DOM)]

free'martin *n.* hermaphrodite or imperfect female calf etc. [17th c., of unkn. orig.]

freer, freest, See FREE¹.

free'sia (-z-) *n.* bulbous Afr. plant of genus *Freesia*, with fragrant coloured flowers. [mod. L, f. F. H. T. *Freese*, Ger. physician d. 1876 + -IA¹]

freeze *v.* (froze; fro'zen; *pr.* frō-), & *n.* 1. *v.i.* (impers.) it ~s, it is freezing, etc., there is etc. frost. 2. be converted into or covered (*over, up*) with ice; become rigid or solid as result of cold (~ to death, die by extreme cold); become fastened *to* or *together* by frost (~ on to, (sl.) take or keep tight hold of); be or feel very cold (lit. or fig.); be chilled by fear; make oneself suddenly motionless. 3. *v.t.* cause to congeal, form ice in or on (fluid or thing containing it); make solid by cold; preserve (food) by refrigeration below freezing-point; ~-dry, freeze and dry by evaporation of ice in high vacuum; ~ up, obstruct by formation of ice; so ~-up *n.* 4. make (credits, assets, etc.) temporarily or permanently unrealizable; fix or stabilize (prices, wages, etc.); determine (details), arrest (action) at a certain stage of development; arrest (movement in film) by repeating a frame. 5. render (person) powerless, chill (feelings), paralyse (powers); stiffen, harden, injure, kill, by chilling (*frozen to death*); ~ person's blood, terrify him; *~ out, (sl.) exclude from business, society, etc., by competition or boycotting etc. 6. freezing-mixture, salt and snow or other mixture used to freeze liquids; freezing--point, temperature at which liquid, esp. water, freezes; freezing works, (Austral. & NZ) place where animals are slaughtered and carcasses frozen for export; frozen limit, (colloq.) the extreme of what is objectionable or unendurable; *frozen* MITT(EN). 7. *n.* state, coming, or period, of frost; fixing or stabilization of prices, wages, etc.; film-shot in which movement is arrested by repetition of a frame. [OE *frēosan*, = OHG *friosan*, ON *frjósa*, Goth. **friusan* f. Gmc **freusan* (**freus-* etc. f. IE **preus-* etc.)]

free'zer *n.* In vbl senses; refrigerated room or compartment esp. for keeping food frozen, deep-freeze. [f. prec.+-ER¹]

freight (frāt) *n.*, & *v.t.* 1. *n.* hire of ship or aircraft for transporting goods; transport of goods in containers or by water or air (or *by* land), charge for this; goods thus carried, cargo, shipload, (*freight* TON¹); load, burden; ~ liner, train carrying goods in containers; ~ (train), container train, *goods train. 2. *v.t* load (ship) with cargo; transport as freight; hire or let out (ship) for carriage of goods and passengers. [f. MDu., MLG *vrecht* var. of *vracht*; cf. FRAUGHT]

frei'ghtage (-ā't-) *n.* hire of ship for, or cost of, conveyance of goods; freighting or hiring of ship; cargo. [f. prec.+-AGE]

frei'ghter (-ā't-) *n.* 1. one who (charters and) loads ship; one who consigns goods for carriage inland; one whose business is to receive and forward freight. 2. cargo ship, freight-carrying aircraft; *freight-wagon. [f. FREIGHT+-ER¹]

Frênch *a.* & *n.* 1. *a.* of France or its language or people; having the qualities attributed to French people, esp. culturedness or slight impropriety. 2. ‖~ bean, kidney or haricot bean (*Phaseolus vulgaris*) used as vegetable both in unripe sliced pods and as ripe seeds; ~ bread, bread in long crisp loaf; ~ Canadian *a.* & *n.*, (native or inhabitant) of French-speaking area of Canada; ~ chalk, kind of steatite used for marking cloth and removing grease and as dry lubricant; ~ cricket, informal type of cricket using batsman's legs as stumps; ~ cuff (of double thickness); ~ curve, template used for drawing curved lines; ~ drain (of rubble, letting water soak away); ~ dressing, salad dressing of vinegar and oil, usu. seasoned; ~ fried potatoes, *~ fries, potato chips; ~ grey, grey with lavender tint; *French* HORN¹, ~ kiss, = DEEP¹ *kiss*; ~ knickers (wide-legged); take ~ leave, depart or act without having permission or giving notice; ~ letter, (colloq.) condom; ~'man, man of French birth or nationality, French ship, ‖red-legged partridge; *French* MOROCCO, ‖MUSTARD; ~ polish, shellac polish for wood (~-polish *v.t.* polish with this); ~ roof, mansard; ~ seam (with raw edges enclosed); ~ toast, bread (1) buttered on one side and toasted on the other, (2) dipped in egg and milk and fried; ~ **vermouth** (dry); ~ **window,** glazed door in outside wall, serving as window and door; ~'**woman,** woman of French birth or nationality. **3.** Hence ~'NESS *n.*, ~'Y² *a.*, ~'Y³ *n.*, (colloq.) French person. **4.** *n.* the French language; (euphem.) bad language (*excuse my French*); dry vermouth (*gin and French*); (sl.) fellatio; **the** ~, (*pl.*) the French people. [OE *frencisc* f. Gmc **frankiskaz* (**Frankon* FRANK¹; see -ISH¹)]

Frě'nchi|fȳ, f-, *v.t.* (usu. in *p.p.*) make French in form, character, or manners; hence ~FICA'TION *n.* [f. prec. +-I-+-FY]

frěně'tic *a.* frantic; fanatic. [ME, f. OF *frenetique* f. L *phreneticus* f. Gk *phrenitikos* (*phrenitis* delirium f. *phrēn* mind); see -ITIS, -IC]

frě'nūlum, frě'num. See FRAENULUM, FRAENUM.

frě'nz|ȳ *n.*, & *v.t.* **1.** *n.* mental derangement, temporary insanity, paroxysm of mania; delirious fury or agitation, wild folly. **2.** *v.t.* (usu. in *p.p.*) drive to frenzy, infuriate, (~**ied rage,** that of a frenzied person). [ME, f. OF *frenesie* f. med. L *phrenesia* f. L *phrenesis* f. Gk *phrēn* mind]

frě'quency *n.* **1.** being frequent, frequent occurrence; commonness of occurrence (*word frequency*); being repeated at short intervals. **2.** (Of pulse) number of beats per minute, (Phys.) rate of recurrence (of vibration etc.), number of repetitions in given time esp. per second, number of cycles of carrier wave per second, band or group of frequency values; (Statistics) ratio of number of actual to possible occurrences of an event; ~ **modulation** (in which frequency of carrier wave is varied); ~ **response,** dependence on signal-frequency of output-input ratio of amplifier etc. [f. L *frequentia* (as foll.; see -ENCY)]

frě'quent¹ *a.* **1.** found near together, numerous, abundant; often occurring, common, (*it is a frequent practice to*); happening in close succession, (of pulse) rapid; hence ~LY² *adv.* **2.** habitual, constant, (*a frequent caller*). [f. F *fréquent* or f. L *frequens -entis* crowded; see -ENT]

frěquě'nt² *v.t.* go often or habitually to (place, meetings, company, house); hence **frěquěnta'TION,** ~ER¹, *ns.* [f. F *fréquenter* or f. L *frequentare* (as prec.)]

frěquě'ntative *a.* & *n.* (Gram.) (verb or verbal form or conjugation) expressing frequent repetition of intensity of action (*chatter, dribble, twinkle*). [f. F *fréquentatif -ive* or f. L *frequentativus* (as prec.; see -ATIVE)]

frě'scō *n.* (*pl.* ~**s** or ~**es**), & *v.t.* **1.** *n.* method of painting (esp. *in fresco*), or picture done, in water--colour laid on wall or ceiling before plaster is dry; ~ **secco, =** SECCO. **2.** *v.t.* paint (wall etc., picture or subject) in fresco. [It., = cool, fresh]

rěsh *a., adv.,* & *n.* **1.** *a.* new, novel, not previously known, used, met with, or introduced, (*break fresh* GROUND¹ 7); additional, other, different, further, (*begin a fresh chapter*). **2.** recent, lately made or arrived, just come from; raw, inexperienced, (~'**man,** first--year student at university or *high school). **3.** not preserved by salting, pickling, smoking, tinning, freezing, etc., (*fresh herrings, butter, meat, fruit*; see also 4 and 6). **4.** not salt or bitter (*fresh butter, water*); ~'**water** *a.*, of fresh water, not of the sea, (*freshwater fish, fishing, sailor*; *~**water college,** rustic or provincial college). **5.** (Of air, wind, water) pure, untainted, invigorating, refreshing, cool. **6.** not stale, musty, or vapid (*fresh eggs, fish, meat, fruit*; see also 3); newly made (*fresh tea*); not faded (*fresh flowers, memories*). **7.** unsullied, bright and pure in colour (*a fresh complexion*), looking healthy or young. **8.** not weary, brisk, vigorous, fit, (*never felt fresher*; **as** ~ **as a daisy, as paint,** very brisk); **a** ~ **wind** (of fair strength). **9.** presumptuous, forward, cheeky, amorously impudent, [perh. infl. by G *frech* saucy]. **10.** Hence ~'EN⁶ *v.t.* & *i.*, ~'LY² *adv.*, ~'NESS *n.* **11.** *adv.* newly, just in comb. (*fresh-caught, -coined*); ~-**run,** (of salmon) lately come up from the sea. **12.**

n. fresh part of the day, year, etc. (*in the fresh of the morning*); rush of water in river, flood. [ME, f. OF *freis fresche* f. Rom. **friscus* f. Gmc **friskaz*]

||**frě'sher** *n.* (sl.) = FRESHman. [f. prec. +-ER¹]

frě'shět *n.* rush of fresh water flowing into sea; flood of river from heavy rain or melted snow. [prob. f. OF *freschete* f. *frais* FRESH]

frět¹ *n.*, & *v.t.* (-**tt**-). **1.** *n.* (Greek) ~, ornamental pattern made of continuous combinations of straight lines joined usu. at right angles. **2.** (Her.) device of narrow bands and diamond interlaced. **3.** *v.t.* variegate, chequer; adorn (esp. ceiling) with carved or embossed work; ~'**saw,** very narrow saw stretched on frame for cutting thin wood in ornamental patterns; ~'**work,** (1) carved work in decorative patterns esp. of straight lines, (2) wood cut with fretsaw. [ME, f. OF *frete* trellis-work and *freter* v.]

frět² *v.* (-**tt**-) & *n.* **1.** *v.t.* gnaw, wear or consume or torment by gnawing, (lit. of moth etc., horse champing bit, action of frost, rust, corrosives, friction, etc., or fig. of emotions); make (passage etc.) by wearing away; chafe, irritate, annoy; worry, distress, (person, *oneself*); ruffle (water). **2.** *v.i.* distress oneself with regret or discontent (*at*; ~ **and fume,** show angry impatience); (of stream etc.) flow or rise in little waves, chafe. **3.** Hence ~'FUL *a.* **4.** *n.* irritation, vexation, querulousness, (*in a fret; fret and fume; on the fret*). [OE *fretan, =* OHG *frezzan,* Goth. *fraitan* f. Gmc **fra-* FOR- (5) + **etan* EAT]

frět³ *n.* bar or ridge on finger-board of some stringed instruments fixing positions of fingers to produce required notes. [15th c.; orig. unkn.]

Freu'dian (froi'd-) *a.* & *n.* (disciple) of Freud or his methods of psychoanalysis; ~ **slip,** unintentional error that seems to reveal subconscious feelings. [f. S. Freud, Austrian psychologist d. 1939 +-IAN]

Fri. *abbr.* Friday.

frī'able *a.* easily crumbled; hence **frīABI'LITY,** ~NESS (-bełn-), *ns.* [F, or f. L *friabilis* (*friare* crumble; see -ABLE]

frī'ar *n.* member of one of certain religious orders of men, esp. the four mendicant orders of Franciscans (*Grey Friars, Friars Minor*), Augustinians (*Austin Friars*), Dominicans (*Black Friars, Friars Major*), and Carmelites (*White Friars*); ~(-**bird**), (Austral.) honey-eater of genus *Philemon* etc.; ~'**s** or ~**s'** **balsam,** tincture of benzoin etc. used esp. as inhalant; hence ~LY¹ *a.* [ME & OF *frere* f. L *frater fratris* brother]

frī'ary *n.* convent of friars. [f. prec. +-Y¹]

frī'bble *v.i., a.,* & *n.* **1.** *v.i.* trifle, be frivolous, **2.** *n.* trifler. [earlier senses 'stammer, totter'; imit.]

frī'candeau (-dō) *n.* (*pl.* ~**x** *pr.* -z), & *v.t.* **1.** *n.* (slice of) fried or stewed meat, esp. veal, served with sauce. **2.** *v.t.* make into fricandeaux. [F]

fricassee (-ĭ'-, -ē') *n.*, & *v.t.* **1.** *n.* meat cut up, fried or stewed, and served with sauce, esp. ragout of birds or small animals cut up. **2.** *v.t.* make fricassee of. [F, fem. p.p. (as n.) of *fricasser* cut up and stew in sauce]

frī'cative *a.* & *n.* (Phonet.) (consonant) made by friction of breath in narrow opening, as *f, th,* Scots *ch.* [f. mod. L *fricativus* f. L *fricare* rub; see -ATIVE]

frī'ction *n.* rubbing of two bodies; (Phys. & Mech.) resistance body encounters in moving over another (**angle of** ~, maximum angle at which one will remain on another without sliding); rubbing the body for therapeutic purposes; massage of scalp; (fig.) clash of wills, temperaments, opinions, etc., (usu. between two persons); ~-**ball** (used in bearings to lessen friction); ~-**clutch, -cone, -coupling, -disc, -gear**(ing), contrivances for transmitting motion by frictional contact; hence ~AL, ~LESS, *adjs.* [F, f. L *frictio -onis* (*fricare frict-* rub; see -ION)]

Frī'day (-dā, -dĭ) *n.* & *adv.* **1.** *n.* day of week, following Thursday; **Good** ~, Friday before Easter day, commemorating Crucifixion; **girl** ~, **man** ~. [f. Man ~ in Defoe's *Robinson Crusoe*], assistant doing general duties in office etc. **2.** *adv.* (colloq.) on Friday (*see you Friday*); ~**s**, on Fridays, each Friday. [OE *frīgedæg,* = OHG *frīatag,* day of *Frigg* (wife of Odin) cogn. w. FREE¹; WG transl. of LL *Veneris dies* day of planet Venus]

‖**fridge** *n.* (colloq.) refrigerator. [abbr.]

friend (frĕnd) *n.,* & *v.t.* **1.** *n.* one joined to another in intimacy and mutual benevolence independently of sexual or family love (**be** or **keep, make,** ~**s**, be, become, friendly (*with*); BOY-*friend,* GIRL-*friend*; hence ~′ED² *a.*); person who acts for one, e.g. as second in duel; acquaintance, stranger that one comes across or has occasion to mention again, (*my friend in the brown hat now left me*; used in *voc.* as polite form or in irony, and (Hist.) by Quakers as ordinary address; preceding a name, *friend Jones, friend Dick*; ‖**my honourable** ~, **my noble** ~, used of another member of same party in House of Commons, House of Lords; **my learned** ~, of another lawyer in court); (in *pl.*) one's near relatives, those responsible for one; (*F*~) member of the Society of Friends, Quaker. **2.** sympathizer, helper, patron, (*no friend of* or *to order, virtue,* etc.; **a** ~ **at court,** one whose influence may be made use of); helpful thing (*my shyness was here my best friend*); one who is not an enemy, one who is on the same side; (usu. in *pl.*) regular contributor of help, money, etc., to support an institution. **3.** Hence ~′LESS *a.* **4.** *v.t.* (arch. or poet.) befriend, help. [OE *frēond,* = OS *friund,* OHG *friunt,* ON *frǣndi,* Goth. *frijonds,* part. of Gmc **frijōjan* love (**frijaz* beloved; cf. FREE¹)]

frie′ndly (frĕ′-) *a., n.,* & *adv.* **1.** *a.* acting or disposed to act as friend; characteristic of friends, expressing, showing, or prompted by, kindness; not hostile, on amicable terms (*with*), (*a friendly nation;* ~ **action,** (Law) action brought merely to get a point decided; ~ **match,** match played for pleasure merely, not in competition for cup etc.); favourably disposed, ready to approve or help, (of thing) serviceable, convenient, opportune; ‖F~ **Society,** = BENEFIT¹ society; hence **frie′ndli**NESS *n.,* (frĕ′-). **2.** *n.* friendly match etc. **3.** *adv.* in friendly manner. [f. prec.+-LY¹,²]

frie′ndship (frĕ′-) *n.* being friends, relation between friends; friendly disposition felt or shown. [f. OE *frēondscipe* (as FRIEND, -SHIP)]

fri′er. See FRYER.

Frie′sian (-zĭan, -zhan) *a.* & *n.* (of, one of) a breed of usu. black and white large dairy cattle orig. from Friesland. [var. of FRISIAN]

frieze¹ *n.* coarse woollen cloth with nap usu. on one side only. [ME, f. F *frise* f. med. L **(lana) frisia* Frisian (wool)]

frieze² *n.* part of entablature coming between architrave and cornice; horizontal broad band of sculpture filling this; band of decoration elsewhere, esp. along wall near ceiling. [f. F *frise* f. med. L *frisium, frigium* f. L *Phrygium* (*opus* work) of Phrygia]

‖**frig²** (-j) *n.* (colloq.) refrigerator. [abbr.]

frig² *v.* (-gg-) & *n.* (vulg.) **1.** *v.i.* & *t.* copulate (with); masturbate; = DAMN 2; mess, fool, *about* or *around*; make *off.* **2.** *n.* act of frigging. [perh. imit.; orig. senses 'move about, rub']

fri′gate *n.* ‖large corvette or small destroyer; **large destroyer or small cruiser; (Hist.) warship next in size and equipment to ships of the line; ~(**-bird**), large swift tropical marine bird of prey. [f. F *frégate* f. It. *fregata,* of unkn. orig.]

fright (frīt) *n.,* & *v.t.* **1.** *n.* sudden fear, violent terror, (**take** ~, become frightened); instance of this (*gave me a fright*); grotesque or ridiculous-looking person or thing. **2.** *v.t.* (poet.) frighten. [OE *fryhto,* metathetic form of *fyrhto* = Goth. *faurhtei* (OS, OHG *foraht*) f. Gmc **furhtīn* (**furhtaz* afraid)]

fri′ghten (-ī′t-) *v.t.* throw into a fright, terrify, (*out of* or *into doing*); drive *away, out of* (place etc.), or *into* (submission etc.), by fright; *frightened at* or *of* (*at* usu. w. ref. to a particular occasion); hence ~ER¹ *n.* (**put the** ~**ers on,** (sl.) intimidate). [f. prec.+-EN⁶]

fri′ghtful (-ī′t-) *a.* **1.** dreadful, shocking, revolting; ugly, hideous; hence ~NESS *n.* (esp. to render G *schrecklichkeit* terrorizing of civilian population as military resource). **2.** (colloq.) very great, extreme. **3.** Hence ~LY² *adv.* [ME, f. FRIGHT+-FUL]

fri′gid *a.* cold (esp. of climate or air; *frigid* ZONE); without ardour, apathetic, formal, forced; (of woman) sexually unresponsive; chilling, depressing; dull, flat, insipid; hence or cogn. **frigi′d**ITY, ~NESS, *ns.,* ~LY² *adv.* [f. L *frigidus* (*frigēre* be cold f. *frigus* n. cold)]

frijoles (frēhō′lās) *n. pl.* beans. [Sp., pl. of *frijol* bean ult. f. L *phaseolus*]

frill *n.,* & *v.t.* **1.** *n.* ornamental edging of woven material, one side of strip being gathered and the other left loose with fluted appearance; similar paper ornament on ham-knuckle etc.; natural fringe of feathers, hair, etc., on bird, animal, or plant; ~(**ed**) **lizard,** large N. Austral. lizard with erectile membrane round neck. **2.** (in *pl.*) airs, affectation, (*put on frills*); useless embellishments, showy accomplishments. **3.** Hence ~ED² (-ld) *a.,* ~′ERY (5), ~′ING⁸ (3, 6), *ns.* **4.** *v.t.* decorate with a frill. [16th c.; orig. unkn.]

fri′ll|**y** *a.* & *n.* **1.** *a.* having frill(s); resembling a frill; hence ~ĭNESS *n.* **2.** *n.* (in *pl.*, colloq.) frilled underwear. [f. prec.+-Y²]

fringe (-nj) *n.,* & *v.t.* **1.** *n.* ornamental bordering of threads left loose or formed into tassels or twists; such bordering made separately; border, edging; fron hair allowed to hang over forehead; natural border o hair etc. in animal or plant. **2.** outer edge or margin; outer limit of area, population, etc. (~ **benefit** perquisite or benefit supplementing money wage o salary; **lunatic** ~, fanatical or eccentric or visionary minority of polit. party etc.); thing of secondary o minor importance; band of contrasting brightness o darkness produced by diffraction or interference o light; strip of false colour in optical image; ** = fring benefit.* **3.** Hence ~′LESS (-njl-), **fri′ng**Y² (-njī), *adjs.* **4** *v.t.* adorn or encircle with fringe, serve as fringe to whence **fri′ng**ING¹ (3) (-nj-) *n.*; **fringing reef,** cora reef that fringes shore. [ME & OF *frenge* f. Rom **frimbia* f. LL *fimbria* fibres, fringe]

fri′ppery *n.* & *a.* **1.** *n.* finery, needless or tawdr adornment esp. in dress; empty display esp. i literary style; knick-knack(s), trifle(s). **2.** *a.* frivolous contemptible. [f. F *friperie* f. OF *freperie* (*frepe* rag; s -ERY)]

fri′ppet *n.* (sl.) frivolous or showy young woma [20th c.; orig. unkn.]

Fri′sbee (-zbĭ) *n.* (**P**) concave plastic disc thrown i air as game. [perh. f. *Frisbie* bakery (Bridgepor Conn.), whose pie-tins could be used similarly]

*****Fri′sco** *n.* (sl.) San Francisco. [abbr.]

Fri′sian (-z-) *a.* & *n.* (native or language) of Fries land. [f. L *Frisii* pl. f. OFris. *Frīsa, Frēsa*+-AN]

frisk *v.* & *n.* **1.** *v.i.* leap or skip playfully. **2.** *v.t.* feel ove or search (person) for weapon etc. (usu. rapidly **3.** *n.* playful leap or skip, whence ~′Y² *a.*; frisking o person. [f. obs. *frisk a.* f. OF *frisque* lively, of unkr orig.]

fri′sket *n.* (Print.) thin iron frame keeping sheet i position while printing on hand-press. [f. F *frisquette* Prov. *frisqueto* f. Sp. *frasqueta*]

frisson (frē′sawn) *n.* emotional thrill. [F, = shiver]

frit *n.,* & *v.t.* (-tt-). **1.** *n.* calcined mixture of sand an fluxes as material for glass-making; vitreous compos tion from which soft porcelain, enamel, etc., an made. **2.** *v.t.* make into frit, partially fuse, calcine. [It. *fritta* fem. p.p. of *friggere* FRY²]

fri′t-fly *n.* small fly destructive to wheat. [19th c.; orig unkn.]

frith. See FIRTH.

fritillary (-tī′-, -ī′t-) *n.* plant of genus *Fritillaria,* wild snake's-head; spotted butterfly, esp. of genu *Argynnis.* [f. mod. L *fritillaria* f. L *fritillus* dice-box; s -ARY¹]

fri'tter[1] n. piece of fried batter often containing (a slice of) fruit, meat, etc., (*apple, oyster*, etc., *fritter*). [ME, f. OF *friture* f. Rom. **frictura* f. L *frigere* frict-FRY[2]; see -URE, -ER[2] (3)]

fri'tter[2] v.t. throw (time, money, energy, etc.) *away* triflingly and wastefully on divided aims; (arch.) subdivide. [f. obs. n. *fritter*(*s*) = obs. *fitters* n. pl., perh. rel. to MHG *vetze* rag]

fritto misto (frītō mǐ'stō) n. mixed grill. [It., = mixed fry]

*fritz (-ts) n. (sl.) **on the ~,** out of order, unsatisfactory. [20th c.; orig. unkn.]

fri'vol v. (||-ll-). **1.** v.i. be a trifler, trifle. **2.** v.t. throw (money, time) *away* foolishly. [back-form. f. foll.]

fri'volous a. paltry, trumpery, trifling, futile; given to trifling, not serious, silly; hence *or* cogn. **frivŏ'lity,** ~NESS, ns., ~LY[2] adv. [f. L *frivolus* silly, trifling + -OUS]

frizz v.t., & n. **1.** v.t. **1.** n. curl, crisp, form into mass of small curls, (hair); frizz hair of (person); dress (wash-leather etc.) with pumice or scraping-knife. **2.** n. frizzed state, frizzed hair, row of curls; hence ~'Y[2] a. [f. F *friser*, perh. f. st. of *frire* FRY[2]]

fri'zzle[1] v. & n. **1.** v.t. & i. curl (*up*, of hair etc.) in small crisp curls. **2.** n. frizzled hair; hence **fri'zzly**[2] a. [16th c.; orig. unkn.; earlier than FRIZZ]

fri'zzle[2] v.i. & t. fry, toast, or grill, with sputtering noise; burn, shrivel, (*up*). [f. *frizz* v. in same sense (FRY[2], w. imit. ending) + -LE 3]

Frl. abbr. *Fräulein.*

frō adv. See TO[2] [ME, f. ON *frá* FROM]

frŏck n., & v. **1.** n. woman's or girl's dress; monk's or priest's long gown with loose sleeves, (fig.) priestly character; sailor's woollen jersey; = SMOCK-*frock*; ~(*-coat*), man's long-skirted coat not cut away in front; military coat of like shape. **2.** v.t. invest with priestly office (cf. UNFROCK). [ME, f. OF *froc* f. Frank. **hrok*]

*frōe, *frow, (frō) n. cleaving tool with handle at right angles to blade. [abbr. of *frower* f. FROWARD 'turned away']

Froebel (-ō'b-, -ēr'b-) n. ~ **system** etc., education of children by use of kindergarten; hence ~IAN (-bē'-) a., ~ISM (3) n. [f. F. W. A. *Fröbel*, Ger. teacher d. 1852]

frŏg[1] n. tailless smooth-skinned leaping amphibian of order Anura, developing from tadpole; hollow in face of brick; nut of violin-bow; ~**-bit,** a floating aquatic plant (||*Hydrocharis morsus-ranae*, **Limnobium spongia*); ~(*-eater*), (derog.) Frenchman; ~**-fish,** angler-fish; ~ **in the** or one's **throat,** (colloq.) hoarseness; ~**'man,** person equipped with rubber suit and flippers etc. and oxygen supply for underwater operations orig. against enemy shipping; ~('s)- **-march,** (n.) carrying of prisoner face downwards by four persons each holding a limb, (v.t.) carry thus or hustle forward after seizing from behind and pinning arms; ~**-spawn,** spawn of frog, (fig.) alga or pudding resembling it. [OE *frogga*, pet name for *forsc, frosc, frox* = OHG *frosc*, ON *froskr* f. Gmc **froskaz*]

frŏg[2] n. elastic horny substance in middle of sole of horse's foot. [perh. f. prec.]

frŏg[3] n. attachment to waist-belt to support sword, bayonet, etc.; ornamental coat-fastening of spindle-shaped button and loop, whence ~GED[2] (-gd) a., ~'GING[1] (6) (-g-) n. [18th c.; orig. unkn.]

frŏg[4] n. grooved piece of iron at place in railway where tracks cross. [19th c.; orig. unkn.]

fro'ggy (-gĭ) a. & n. **1.** a. of or like frog(s); cold as a frog; abounding in frogs; (derog.) French. **2.** n. (F~). (derog.) Frenchman. [f. FROG[1] + -Y[2]]

frŏ'lic a., v.i. (-ck-), & n. **1.** a. (arch.) joyous, mirthful, sportive, full of pranks. **2.** v.i. play pranks, gambol. **3.** n. outburst of gaiety, prank, merriment, merry-making, merry party; hence ~SOME[1] a. [f. Du. *vrolijk* adj. (*vro* glad, *-lijk* -LY[1])]

from (or, when stressed, frŏm) prep. expr. separation or origin, followed by: **1.** Person, place, etc., that is the starting-point of motion (*comes from the clouds; repeated from mouth to mouth*). **2.** Starting-point of extent in space or time (*from title-page to colophon; from 2 July*; ~ **now on,** henceforward; ~ **day to day,** daily; ~ **time to time,** occasionally; ~ **year to year,** each year, as years pass; ~ **a child,** since childhood). **3.** Lower limit (*saw from 10 to 20 boats; tickets from £5*). **4.** Object etc. whose distance or remoteness is reckoned or stated (*ten miles from Rome; am far from saying*; ~ **home,** out, away; *absent, away, from home; apart from its moral aspect*). **5.** Thing or person got rid of, escaped, avoided, of which one is deprived etc., person or thing deprived, (*took his sword from him; released him from prison; cannot refrain from laughing; appeal from lower court; dissuade from folly*). **6.** State changed for another (*from being attacked he became the aggressor; raise penalty from banishment to death*). **7.** Thing distinguished (*doesn't know black from white*). **8.** Source (*dig gravel from pit; a man from Italy; draw conclusion from premisses; quotations from the Fathers*). **9.** Place of one who observes etc. (*saw it from the roof*; ~ **his point of view,** as he sees things). **10.** Giver, sender, etc., (*gifts from Providence; clothes from Selfridges; have had no news from him*). **11.** Model (*painted from* NATURE). **12.** Reason, cause, motive, (*died from fatigue; suffering from shingles; from his looks you might suppose*). **13.** Advs. or adv. phrs. of place or time (*from long ago, of old, above, abroad, within,* etc.), or prepositions (*from behind her spectacles; from among the nettles; took a live coal from off the altar*). [OE *fram, from* = OS, OHG, Goth. *fram,* ON *frá* f. Gmc **fra-* forward]

frŏnd n. (Bot.) leaflike organ formed by union of stem and foliage in certain flowerless plants, esp. ferns, and differing from leaf in usu. bearing fructification; (Zool.) leaflike expansion; hence ~AGE (1) n., ~'OSE[1] a. [f. L *frons frondis* leaf]

frŏndeur' (-ēr') n. political rebel. [F, = slinger, applied to party (the Fronde) rebelling during minority of Louis XIV of France]

front (-ŭnt) n., a., & v. **1.** n. side or part normally nearer or towards spectator or direction of motion (*front of car, chair, door, house, mouth*). **2.** (Archit.) any face of building, esp. that of main entrance. **3.** (Mil.) foremost line or part of army etc., line of battle, part of ground towards real or imaginary enemy, scene of actual fighting (**go to the ~,** join troops on campaign), direction in which formed line faces (*change front*); (fig.) sector of activity regarded as resembling military front, organized political group. **4.** outward appearance; bluff; pretext; person etc. serving to cover subversive or illegal activities. **5.** (Meteor.) forward edge of advancing mass of cold or warm air. **6.** *the* promenade of a seaside resort; *the* auditorium of a theatre. **7.** breast of man's shirt; false shirt-front. **8.** (poet. or rhet.) forehead. **9.** face; bearing, demeanour, (*show a bold front*). **10.** forward position; **come to the ~,** become conspicuous; **in ~,** advanced or facing spectator; **in ~ of,** (1) ahead of, in advance of, (2) confronting, in the presence of. **11.** Hence ~'WARD a. & adv., ~'WARDS adv. **12.** a. of the front; situated in front; (Phonet.) formed at front of mouth; ||~ **bench,** foremost seats of Government and Opposition parties in Parliament (so ~-be'ncher, occupant of such seat); ~ **door,** chief entrance of house or (fig.) of country, situation, etc.; ~ **line,** = sense 3 (~ *line States,* group of countries in Southern Africa); ~ **man,** person acting as front (sense 4); ~ **matter,** (Print.) title-page, preface, etc., preceding the text; ~ **office,** main office, esp. police headquarters; ~ **page,** first page of newspaper, esp. as containing important or remarkable news; *front* PASSAGE[1]; ~ **runner,** leading contestant. **13.** v.i. turn one's or its front directed *to, towards,* (*up*)*on*; (sl.) act as front (sense 4) *for*. **14.** v.t. stand opposite to, front towards; have front on side of (street etc.); lead (band); (arch.) confront, meet, oppose; furnish with front (*fronted with stone*). [ME, f. OF *front* n., *fronter* v. f. L *frons frontis*]

fro'ntag|e (-ŭ'n-) *n.* land abutting on street or water, land between front of building and road, whence ⁓ER¹ (4) *n.*; extent of front; front of building; facing a certain way, exposure, outlook; *⁓e road, service road. [f. prec. + -AGE]

fro'ntal¹ (-ŭ'n-) *n.* covering for front of altar; façade. [ME, f. OF *frontel* f. L *frontale* (as FRONT; see -AL)]

fro'ntal² (-ŭ'n-) *a.* of forehead (*frontal bone, artery*); of or on front (⁓ **attack,** delivered direct, not on flank or rear); of person facing spectator (*frontal picture*); hence ⁓LY² *adv.* [f. mod. L *frontalis* (as FRONT; see -AL)]

fro'ntier (-ŭ'n-) *n.* part of a country that borders on another country; *borders of civilization; limits of attainment in science etc.; ⁓**sman** (-z-), one living on or beyond the borders of civilization. [ME, f. AF *frounter,* OF *frontiere,* f. Rom. deriv. of L *frons frontis* FRONT]

fro'ntispiece (-u'n-) *n.* **1.** illustration facing title-page of book or one of its divisions. **2.** (Archit.) principal face of building, decorated entrance, pediment over door etc. [f. F *frontispice* or f. LL *frontispicium* façade f. L *frons frontis* FRONT + -*spicium* f. *specere* look; assim. to PIECE¹]

fro'ntlet (-ŭ'n-) *n.* band worn on forehead; = PHYLACTERY; animal's forehead; cloth hanging over upper part of altar frontal. [f. OF *frontelet* (as FRONTAL¹; see -LET)]

frontōgě'nĕsis (frŭ-) *n.* (Meteorol.) formation or development of fronts; hence **frontōgěnĕ'tic** (frŭ-) *a.* [f. G *frontogenese* (as FRONT, -O-, GENESIS)]

fro'nton (frŭ'-) *n.* pediment. [F, f. It. *frontone,* augment. of *fronte* forehead (see FRONT, -OON)]

frōre *a.* (poet.) frozen, frosty. [arch. p.p. of FREEZE]

frost (-ŏ-, -aw-) *n.* & *v.* **1.** *n.* freezing, prevalence of temperature below freezing-point of water (||**ten degrees of** ⁓, 22° Fahrenheit; **hard, sharp,** ⁓ (severe); **white, black,** ⁓, with, without, hoar-frost; **Jack F**⁓, frost personified; frozen state of consistency (*there is still frost in the ground*); frozen dew or vapour (*windows covered with frost*); hence ⁓'LESS *a.* **2.** influence that chills, makes grey, etc.; (sl.) failure. **3.** ⁓**-bite,** inflammation or gangrene of and below skin from severe cold (⁓**-bitten,** affected with this); ⁓**-fish,** (NZ) scabbard-fish; ⁓**-flower,** flower-like ice crystal; ⁓**-work,** tracery made by frost on glass etc. **4.** *v.t.* injure (plant etc.) with frost; cover (as) with rime, powder (cake etc.) with frostlike coating of sugar etc., whence ⁓'ING (3) *n.*; give roughened or finely granulated surface to (glass, metal). **5.** *v.i.* become covered (*over, up*) with frost. [OE, = OS, OHG, ON *frost* f. Gmc *frustaz,* *frustam (*fruesan FREEZE)]

fro'st|ỹ (-ŏ'-, -aw'-) *a.* cold with frost; cold, chilling, frigid, lacking in warmth of feeling; (seeming to be) covered with hoar-frost; hence ⁓iLY² *adv.,* ⁓iNESS *n.* [f. prec. + -Y²]

froth (-ŏ-, -aw-) *n.* & *v.* **1.** *n.* collection of small bubbles in liquid, caused by shaking, fermenting, etc., foam; impure matter on liquid, scum; worthless matter, idle talk, light substance, etc.; ||⁓**-blower,** (joc.) beer-drinker (esp. as designation of member of a charitable organization); hence ⁓'Y² *a.* **2.** *v.i.* emit or gather froth (*frothing at the mouth*). **3.** *v.t.* cause (beer etc.) to foam. [ME, f. ON *frotha, frauth* f. Gmc *freuth-* etc.]

frŏtta'ge (-ah'zh) *n.* **1.** (Psych.) abnormal desire for contact between clothed bodies of oneself and another. **2.** (Art) technique or process of taking rubbing from uneven surface to form basis of work of art. [F, = rubbing (*frotter* rub f. OF *froter*; see -AGE)]

frou'-frou (frōō'frōō) *n.* rustling, esp. of dresses. [F, imit.]

frow¹ *n.* Dutchwoman; housewife. [ME, f. Du. *vrouw* woman]

*****frow².** See FROE.

frō'ward (-ōerd) *a.* (arch.) perverse, refractory; hence ⁓LY² *adv.,* ⁓NESS *n.* [ME, f. FRO + -WARD]

frown *v.* & *n.* **1.** *v.i.* knit brows esp. to express displeasure or concentrate one's attention; (of thing) present gloomy aspect; express disapprobation (*at, on, upon*). **2.** *v.t.* drive *away, into* silence, etc., with frown; express (defiance etc.) with frown. **3.** *n.* vertically furrowed or wrinkled state of brow; look expressing severity, disapproval, or deep thought. [ME, f. OF *frongnier, froignier* (*froigne* surly look f. Celt.)]

frowst *n.,* & *v.i.* (colloq.) **1.** *n.* fusty warmth in room. **2.** *v.i.* stay in or enjoy frowst. [back-form. f. foll.]

frow'st|ỹ *a.* fusty, stuffy; hence ⁓iNESS *n.* [var. of foll.]

frow'z|ỹ *a.* ill-smelling, fusty, musty, close; slatternly, unkempt, dingy; hence ⁓iNESS *n.* [17th c., of unkn. orig.; cf. earlier *frowy*]

frō'ze(n). See FREEZE.

FRS *abbr.* Fellow of the Royal Society.

FRSE *abbr.* Fellow of the Royal Society of Edinburgh.

frŭcti'ferous *a.* bearing fruit. [f. L *fructifer* (*fructus* FRUIT; see -FEROUS)]

frŭctificā'tion *n.* (Bot.) fructifying; reproductive parts of plant, esp. of ferns and mosses. [f. LL *fructificatio* (as foll.; see -FICATION)]

frŭ'ctify *v.* **1.** *v.i.* bear fruit (lit. or fig.). **2.** *v.t.* make fruitful, impregnate. [ME, f. OF *fructifier* f. L *fructificare* (*fructus* FRUIT; see -FY)]

frŭ'ctōse *n.* (Chem.) sugar found in fruit juice, honey, etc. [f. L *fructus* FRUIT + -OSE²]

frŭ'ctŭous *a.* full of or producing fruit (lit. or fig.). [ME f. OF, or f. L *fructuosus* (as FRUIT; see -OUS)]

fru'gal (frōō'-) *a.* careful, sparing (*of*), economical, esp. as regards food; sparingly used or supplied, costing little; hence or cogn. **frugä'lITY** *n.* (frōō-), ⁓LY² *adv.* [f. L *frugalis* (*frugi* economical; see -AL)]

frugi'vorous (frōō-) *a.* feeding on fruit. [f. L *frux frugis* fruit + -VOROUS]

fruit (frōōt) *n.* & *v.* **1.** *n.* plant's or tree's edible product of seed with its envelope, quantity of these (*feeds on fruit*); vegetable with seed with envelope as means of reproduction; (usu. in *pl.*) vegetable products fit for food (*fruits of the earth*), so ⁓'AGE (1) *n.*; (sl.) male homosexual. **2.** produce of action, (in *pl.*) revenues produced (*the fruits of industry*); (Bibl.) offspring (usu. *fruit of the body, loins, womb*); result, issue, consequence BEAR³ *fruit.* **3.** ⁓**-bat,** fruit-eating bat, esp. flying fox; ⁓**-body,** spore-bearing part of fungus; ⁓**-cake** (containing currants etc.); ⁓ **cocktail,** finely-chopped fruit salad; ⁓**-fly** (whose larvae feed on fruit; esp. DROSOPHILA); ⁓**-knife** (with silver etc. blade unaffected by acid); ||⁓ **machine,** gaming machine operated by coins etc., in which a player is successful who gets a certain combination of different symbols often representing fruit; ⁓ **salad,** various fruits cut up and mixed in bowl and often eaten with cream etc., (sl.) display of military decorations; ⁓ **salts,** effervescent health salts (SALT 4); ⁓ **sugar** fructose; ⁓**-tree** (grown for its fruit); ⁓**-wood** fruit-tree, esp. when used in furniture. **4.** Hence (-)⁓'ING (3) *n.* & **5.** *v.i.* & *t.* bear or make bear fruit. [ME f OF, f. L *fructus* enjoyment (*frui* enjoy)]

fruitar'ian (frōō-) *n.* one who eats only fruit. [f. prec. + -ARIAN]

frui'ter (frōō'-) *n.* tree producing fruit (*good, poor fruiter*); ||fruit-grower; ship carrying fruit. [ME, f. OF *fruitier* (as FRUIT, -ER²); later f. FRUIT + -ER¹]

frui'terer (frōō'-) *n.* dealer in fruit. [ME, f. prec. + -ER¹]

frui'tful (frōō'-) *a.* productive, fertile, causing fertility productive of offspring, prolific, (lit., or fig., *a long and fruitful career*); beneficial, remunerative; hence ⁓LY *adv.,* ⁓NESS *n.* [ME, f. FRUIT + -FUL]

frui'tion (frōō-) *n.* enjoyment, attainment of thing desired, realization of hopes etc.; bearing of fruit (lit or fig.). [ME f. OF, f. LL *fruitio -onis* (*frui* enjoy; see -ION) erron. assoc. w. FRUIT]

frui'tless (frōō'-) *a.* not bearing fruit; yielding no profit, ineffectual, useless, empty, vain; hence ⁓LY *adv.,* ⁓NESS *n.* [ME, f. FRUIT + -LESS]

frui′tlĕt (frōō′-) *n.* (Bot.) = DRUPEL. [f. FRUIT + -LET]

frui′t|ў (frōō′-) *a.* of fruit; (of wine) tasting of the grape; (colloq.) full of rich quality, suggestive, full of rough humour or (usu. scandalous) interest; hence ∼ĭNESS *n.* [f. FRUIT + -Y²]

fru′mentў (frōō-), **fŭr′mĕtў,** *n.* hulled wheat boiled in milk and seasoned with cinnamon, sugar, etc. [ME f. OF *frumentee* (*frument* f. L *frumentum* corn); see -Y⁴]

frŭmp *n.* old-fashioned dowdily-dressed woman; hence ∼′ISH¹, ∼′Y², *adjs.* [16th c., perh. f. dial. v. *frumple* wrinkle f. MDu. *verrompelen* (as FOR-, RUMPLE)]

frŭ′strāte¹ *a.* (arch.) frustrated. [ME, f. L *frustratus* p.p. of *frustrari* (see foll., -ATE²)]

frŭstr|āte² (-ā′t, -ŭ′s-) *v.t.* balk, baffle, neutralize, counteract, disappoint; (in *p.p.*) discontented through inability to achieve one's desires; so ∼A′TION *n.* [ME, f. L *frustrari* (*frustra* in vain) + -ATE³]

frŭ′stūle *n.* two-valved shell of diatom. [F, f. L *frustulum* (as foll.; see -ULE)]

frŭ′st|um *n.* (*pl.* ∼a *or* ∼ums). remainder of cone or pyramid whose upper part has been cut off by plane parallel to base; part of cone or pyramid intercepted between two planes. [L, = piece cut off]

frutĕ′scent (frōō-) *a.* (Bot.) of the nature of a shrub. [irreg. f. L *frutex* bush + -ESCENT]

fru′t|ĕx (frōō′) *n.* (*pl.* ∼ices *pr.* -īsēz). (Bot.) woody-stemmed plant smaller than tree, shrub. [L *frutex fruticis*]

fru′ticōse (frōō′-) *a.* (Bot. etc.) resembling a shrub. [f. L *fruticosus* (as prec.; see -OSE¹)]

frȳ¹ *n.* young fishes fresh from the spawn; young of other creatures produced in large numbers, e.g. bees or frogs; **small** ∼, young or insignificant beings, children etc. [ME, f. ON *frjó* = Goth. *fraiw* seed]

frȳ² *v.* & *n.* **1.** *v.t.* & *i.* cook in hot fat (*other* FISH¹ *to fry*; ∼′**ing-pan,** shallow pan used in frying; **out of the** ∼**ing-pan into the fire,** from bad situation to worse); (in *p.p.,* sl.) drunk. **2.** *v.i.* ∼ **up,** heat or reheat (food) in frying-pan (hence ∼-**up** *n.*); (sl.) electro-cute. **3.** *v.i.* (sl.) be electrocuted. **4.** *n.* fried meat etc.; various internal parts of animals usu. fried, esp. LAMB'*s fry*; *social gathering to eat fried food; *∼-**pan,** frying-pan. [ME, f. OF *frire* f. L *frigĕre*]

frȳ′er, frī′er, *n.* vessel for frying fish; one who fries (fish); *chicken suitable for frying. [f. prec. | -ER¹]

FSA *abbr.* Fellow of the Society of Antiquaries.

FSSU *abbr.* Federated Superannuation Scheme for Universities.

Ft. *abbr.* Fort.

ft. *abbr.* feet; foot.

***FTC** *abbr.* Federal Trade Commission.

‖**fŭ′bsў** (-zĭ) *a.* fat or squat. [f. obs. *fubs* small fat person + -Y²]

fu′chsia (fū′sha) *n.* drooping-flowered shrub of genus Fuchsia. [mod. L, f. L *Fuchs*, Ger. botanist d. 1566 + -IA¹]

fu′chsine (fōō′k-) *n.* deep red aniline dye. [f. prec. (f. resemblance to colour of flower) + -INE⁵]

fŭck *v.* & *n.* (vulg.) **1.** *v.t.* copulate with; = DAMN 2; mess *up.* **2.** *v.i.* copulate; mess, fool, about or around; make *off.* **3.** Hence ∼′ER¹ *n.* (often as general term of abuse), ∼′ING² *a.* & *adv.* (often as mere intensive). **4.** *n.* act of copulation; person as partner in copulation; slightest amount (*not care* or *give a fuck*). [16th c.; orig. unkn.]

fū′c|us *n.* (*pl.* ∼i *pr.* -sī). seaweed of genus Fucus, with flat leathery fronds; hence ∼OID *a.* [L, = rock-lichen, f. Gk *phukos,* of Semitic orig.]

fŭ′ddle *v.* & *n.* **1.** *v.i.* tipple, booze. **2.** *v.t.* intoxicate; stupefy, confuse. **3.** *n.* spell of drinking (*on the fuddle*), intoxication; confusion. [16th c.; orig. unkn.]

fŭ′ddy-dŭddў *n.* & *a.* (sl.) old-fashioned (person), ineffectual (old fogy). [20th c.; orig. unkn.]

fŭdge¹ *int.* & *n.* **1.** *int.* expr. disbelief or annoyance. **2.** *n.* nonsense; piece of late news inserted in newspaper page; soft-grained toffee-like sweetmeat made with milk, sugar, butter, etc. [f. foll.]

fŭdge² *v.* & *n.* **1.** *v.t.* fit together, patch, make up, in a makeshift or dishonest way; deal with incompetently. **2.** *v.i.* practise such methods. **3.** *n.* piece of fudging. [perh. f. obs. *fadge* v.i. fit]

fuehr′er, führ′er, (fūr′er) *n.* leader, esp. tyrannical one. [f. G *führer* leader; part of title assumed 1934 by HITLER]

fū′el *n.* & *v.* (‖-ll-). **1.** *n.* material for burning as fire or source of heat or power; food as source of energy; material used as source of nuclear energy; thing that sustains or inflames passion etc. **2.** ∼ **cell,** primary cell producing electric current direct from chemical reaction; ∼ **element,** assemblage of nuclear fuel etc. for use in reactor; ∼ **injection,** direct introduction of fuel under pressure into combustion unit of internal combustion engine; ∼-**value,** amount of energy available from a fuel. **3.** *v.t.* supply (fire, engine, controversy, etc.) with fuel (lit. or fig.). **4.** *v.i.* get fuel. [ME, f. AF *fuaille, fewaile,* OF *fouaille* f. Rom. *focalia f. L *focus* hearth]

fŭg *n.,* & *v.i.* (-**gg**-). (colloq.) **1.** *n.* fustiness of air in room; hence ∼′**gy** (-gĭ) *a.* **2.** *v.i.* stay in or enjoy fug. [19th c.; orig. unkn.]

fūgā′cious (-shus) *a.* fleeting, evanescent, hard to capture or keep; so **fūgA′CITY** *n.* [f. L *fugax fugacis* (*fugere* flee; see -ACIOUS)]

fū′gal *a.* of the nature of a fugue; hence ∼LY² *adv.* [f. FUGUE + -AL]

-fūge *suf.* forming *adjs.* & *ns.* w. sense '(agent) dispelling or expelling' (*febrifuge, vermifuge*). [f. or after mod. L *-fugus* f. L *fugare* put to flight]

fū′gitive *a.* & *n.* **1.** *a.* fleeing, running away, that has taken flight; flitting, shifting; transient, evanescent, of short duration, quickly fading; (of literature) of passing interest, ephemeral, occasional. **2.** *n.* one who flees, esp. *from* danger, enemy, justice, or master, exile, refugee. [ME, f. OF *fugitif -ive,* f. L *fugitivus* (*fugere fugit-* flee; see -IVE)]

fū′gle|man (-gelm-) *n.* (*pl.* ∼**men**). **1.** (Hist.) soldier placed in front of regiment etc. while drilling to show the motions and time. **2.** leader, organizer, spokesman; hence [by back-form.] **fū′gle** *v.i.* [G *flügelmann* (*flügel* wing, *mann* man)]

fūgue (fūg) *n.,* & *v.i.* **1.** *n.* (Mus.) polyphonic composition in which short melodic theme ('subject') is introduced by one part and successively taken up by others and developed by interweaving the parts; hence **fū′guist** (l) (-gī-) *n.* **2.** (Psych.) loss of awareness of one's identity, often coupled with disappearance from one's usual environment. **3.** *v.i.* (Mus.) compose or perform fugue (**fuguing** or ∼**d,** in the form of a fugue). [F, or f. It. f. L *fuga* flight]

führer. See FUEHRER.

-ful *suf.* **1.** Forming *adjs.* f. *ns.,* w. sense 'full of' (*beautiful*), 'having qualities of' (*masterful*), or f. *adjs.* or L adj. stems (*direful, grateful*). w. little change of sense (perh. after diton synonyms in *-ful*), or f. *vbs.* w. sense 'apt to, able to, accustomed to' (*forgetful, mournful*), occas. w. passive force (*bashful*). **2.** (fōōl). Forming *ns.* (*pl.* **-fuls,** occas. **-sful**). w. sense 'amount needed to fill' (*handful, houseful, mouthful, spoonful*). [f. FULL¹]

fu′lcr|um (fŭ′-, fŏŏ′-) *n.* (*pl.* ∼a). (Mech.) point against which lever is placed to get purchase or on which it turns or is supported. **2.** means by which influence etc. is brought to bear. [L, = post of couch (*fulcire* to prop)]

fulfi′l, *fulfi′ll, (fŏŏl-) *v.t.* (-**ll**-). bring to consummation, carry out (prophecy, promise); satisfy (desire, prayer); perform, execute, do, (command, duty); answer (purpose), comply with (conditions); bring to an end, finish, complete, (period, work); ∼ oneself, develop one's gifts and character to the full; hence ∼MENT *n.* [OE *fullfyllan* (as FULL¹, FILL)]

fŭ′lgent *a.* (poet. or rhet.) shining, brilliant. [ME, f. L *fulgēre* shine; see -ENT]

fulgūrā′tion *n.* (Med.) destruction of tumours etc. by

means of electric sparks. [f. L *fulguratio* sheet lightning (*fulgurare* f. *fulgur* lightning; see -ATION)]

fŭ'lgŭrite *n.* (Geol.) rocky substance of sand fused or vitrified by lightning. [f. L *fulgur* lightning + -ITE¹ (2)]

fŭli'ginous *a.* sooty, dusky. [f. LL *fuliginosus* (*fuligo -ginis* soot; see -OUS)]

full¹ (fŏŏl) *a., n., adv., & v.* **1.** *a.* holding all (*of*, or abs.) its limits will allow, replete, (*full to the brim*; *full of water*; (colloq.) *full up*); (of heart etc.) overcharged with emotion; (sl.) drunk. **2.** holding or having abundance *of*, crowded, showing marked signs *of* (*full of vitality*). **3.** engrossed with the thought *of* (*full of himself, of his subject*; ~ **of the news** etc., unable to keep from talking of it). **4.** replete with food (*full stomach*; arch. or vulg. of persons; (chiefly Bibl.) having had plenty *of* (*full of years and honours*). **5.** abundant, sufficient, copious, satisfying, (*a full meal*; *turned it to full account*; *give full details*; *he is very full on this point*). **6.** complete, entire, perfect, answering in every way to its name or description, reaching the specified or usual limit, entirely visible, (*full daylight, membership, orchestra*; *waited a full hour*; *it was full summer*; *in full bloom*); used for entire cover in bookbinding (*full leather*). **7.** (Of light) intense, (of colour or tone) deep, mellow, (of motion etc.) vigorous (*a full pulse*; *full gallop, speed*, etc., used as *advs.* with *come* etc.). **8.** swelling, plump, protuberant; (of garment) containing much material arranged in folds etc. **9.** ~ **age**, adult status (esp. w. ref. to legal rights and duties); ~ **back,** (position of) player behind half--backs in football etc.; ~ **blood,** pure descent; ~**-blooded,** (1) not hybrid, (2) vigorous, hearty, sensual; ~ **board,** provision of bed and all meals at hotel etc.; ~**-bodied,** rich in quality, tone, etc.; ~**-bottomed,** (of wig) long at back; ~ **brother** (born of same father and same mother); ~ **and by,** close-hauled but with sails filling; *full* CIRCLE¹; ~**-cream** *a.* or made from unskimmed milk; ~ **dress,** dress worn on great occasions; ~**-dress** *a.*, (of debate etc.) of major importance; *full* EMPLOYMENT; ~ **face** (entirely visible to spectator); *in full* FEATHER¹; ~ **hand,** (Poker) hand with three of a kind and a pair; ~**-hearted,** zealous, confident, courageous; ~ **house,** (1) = *full hand*, (2) maximum or large attendance in Parliament, at theatre, etc.; ~**-length,** not shortened or abbreviated, (of mirror, portrait, etc.) showing whole height of human figure; **at** ~ **length,** (1) lying stretched out, (2) without abridgement; *full* LOCK² 6; ~ **marks,** maximum award in examination, in assessment of person, etc.; *full* MEASURE¹; ~ **moon,** moon with whole disc illuminated, time when this occurs; ~**-mouthed,** (of cattle) having full set of teeth, (of dog) baying loudly, (of oratory etc.) sonorous, vigorous; ~ **page,** entire page of newspaper etc.; ~ **pay** (amount allowed on active service); ~ **pitch,** (Cricket) ball pitched right up to batsman, (*adv.*) without ball's having touched ground; ~ **point,** = *full stop* (1); ~ **professor,** professor of highest grade in university etc.; ~**-scale,** not reduced in size, complete; ~ **score,** (Mus.) score giving parts for all performers on separate staves; *full* SERVICE¹ 6; ~ **sister** (born of same father and same mother); ~ **speed** or STEAM¹ **ahead!** (order to proceed at maximum speed or pursue course of action energetically); *full* STOMACH; ~ **stop,** (1) punctuation-mark (.) for pause at end of sentence or to show end of abbreviation, (2) complete cessation; *in full* SWING; *full* TERM¹, TILT¹; ~ **time,** (1) total normal duration of work etc. (so ~**-*time*** *a.*, occupying or using all one's working time, ~**-*time*R¹** (1) *n.*), (2) end of football etc. match; ~ **toss,** = *full pitch*; *full* TREATMENT; **in** ~ **view,** entirely visible. **10.** *n.* whole (*cannot tell you the full of it*; **in** ~, without abridgement, to or for the full amount (*paid in full*); **to the** ~, to the utmost extent, quite); height, acme, (*season is past the full*); state or time of full moon. **11.** *adv.* very (*know it*

full well); quite, fully, (*full six miles*; *full ripe*; esp. in comb., as ~**-blown,** (of flowers) quite open, (fig.) fully developed, complete, (*full-blown dignity* etc.); ~**-fashioned,** = FULLY-*fashioned*; ~**-fledged,** mature; ~**-grown,** having reached maturity); exactly (*hit him full on the nose*); more than sufficiently (*full early*); ~ **out,** complete, at full power, (Print.) flush with margin. **12.** *v.i. & t.* be or become or make (esp. dress) full. [OE, = OS *ful*, OHG *foll*, ON *fullr*, Goth. *fulls* f. Gmc **fullaz* f. IE **pļnōs*]

full² (fŏŏl) *v.t.* cleanse and thicken (cloth). [ME, back--form. f. foll.; cf. OF *fouler* (FOIL²)]

fu'ller¹ (fŏŏ'-) *n.* one who fulls cloth; ~'s **earth,** type of clay used in fulling cloth and as adsorbent. [OE *fullere,* f. L *fullo* + -ER¹]

fu'ller² (fŏŏ'-) *n., & v.t.* **1.** *n.* grooved or rounded tool on which iron is shaped; groove made by this esp. in horseshoe. **2.** *v.t.* stamp with fuller. [19th c.; orig. unkn.]

fu'l(l)nèss (fŏŏ'l-) *n.* **1.** being full; **the** ~ **of the heart,** (Bibl.) emotion, genuine feelings; **the** ~ **of time,** the destined time. **2.** (Of sound, colour, etc.) richness, volume, body; all that is contained (in the world etc.). [ME, f. FULL¹ + -NESS]

fu'lly (fŏŏ'-) *adv.* completely, without deficiency; quite as many as (esp. w. numbers); ~**-fashioned,** (of women's stockings etc.) seamed and shaped to fit the body; ~**-fledged,** mature. [OE *fullīce* (as FULL¹, -LY²)]

-fully *suf.* forming *advs.* corresp. to *adjs.* in -FUL (*beautifully, dutifully, gratefully, masterfully, mournfully*). [f. -FUL + -LY²]

fu'lmar (fŏŏ'-) *n.* northern herring-gull-sized sea-bird related to petrels. [orig. Hebridean dial., perh. f. ON *fúll* FOUL (w. ref. to its smell) + *már* gull (cf. MEW¹)]

fu'lminant *a.* fulminating; (Path., of disease) developing suddenly. [f. or f. L (as foll.; see -ANT)]

fu'lmināt|**e¹** *v.* **1.** *v.i.* flash like lightning, explode, detonate, (~**ing gold, mercury,** etc., various explosive fulminates; see foll.); (Path., of disease) develop suddenly; issue censures *against*. **2.** *v.t.* thunder forth, utter or publish, (censure). **3.** Hence or cogn. **fulmin**A'TION *n.,* ~ORY *a.* [f. L *fulminare* (*fulmen -minis* lighting) + -ATE³]

fu'lmināte² *n.* (Chem.) salt of hypothetical *fulminic acid,* an isomer of cyanic acid. [f. L *fulmen* (see prec.) + -ATE² (3), many fulminates being explosive]

fulness. See FULLNESS.

-fulness *suf.* forming *ns.* corresp. to *adjs.* in -FUL (*distrustfulness, forgetfulness, hopefulness*). [f. -FUL + -NESS]

fu'lsome (fŏŏ'-) *a.* cloying, excessive, disgusting by excess (of flattery, servility, exaggerated affection); hence ~LY² (-mlĭ) *adv.,* ~NESS (-mn-) *n.* [ME, f. FULL¹ + -SOME¹]

fu'lvous *a.* reddish-yellow, tawny; so **fŭlve'scent** *a.* [f. L *fulvus* + -OUS]

fŭ'marŏle *n.* crevice in or near volcano, through which hot vapour issues; hence **fŭmarŏ'lic** *a.* [f. F *fumarolle*]

fŭ'mbl|**e** *v. & n.* **1.** *v.i.* use the hands awkwardly, grope about (*at* or *with* fastening etc.; *for* or *after* thing sought). **2.** *v.t.* handle or deal with awkwardly or nervously; (Games) not stop (ball) cleanly. **3.** Hence ~ER¹ *n.* **4.** *n.* bungling attempt. [f. LG *fummeln, fommeln,* Du. *fommelen*]

fūme *n. & v.* **1.** *n.* (usu. in *pl.*) (esp. malodorous or harmful) smoke, vapour, or exhalation; noxious vapour supposed to rise from stomach to brain (*the fumes of wine* etc., or (fig.) of excitement, enthusiasm, etc.); ||~**-chamber** etc., laboratory structure with ventilator for removal of noxious gases; hence **fū'my** *a.* **2.** fit of anger (*in a fume*). **3.** *v.t.* fumigate; perfume with incense; subject to chemical fumes esp. those of ammonia (photographic film, oak, to darken tints). **4.** *v.i.* emit fumes; (of vapour etc.) rise, be emitted; be angry or irritated (*at*). [ME, f. OF *fum* f. L *fumus* smoke & OF *fume* (*fumer* f. L *fumare* to smoke)]

fū′mig|āte *v.t.* apply fumes to; disinfect or purify with fumes; hence or cogn. ∼ANT, ∼A′TION, ∼ātor, *ns.* [f. L *fumigare* (*fumus* smoke) + -ATE³]

fū′mitorў *n.* herb of genus *Fumaria*, formerly used against scurvy. [ME, f. OF *fumeterre* f. med. L *fumus terrae* earth-smoke; assim. to -ORY]

fŭn *n.* & *a.* **1.** *n.* sport, amusement, jocularity, drollery, (**make** ∼ **of, poke** ∼ **at**, tease, ridicule; **for** or **in** ∼, as a joke, not seriously; **for** ∼, **for the** ∼ **of it**, not for a serious purpose; FIGURE¹ *of fun*; **have** ∼, (1) enjoy oneself, (2) engage in sexual intercourse; **like** ∼, vigorously, quickly, much, (iron.) not at all; **what** ∼!, how amusing!). **2.** source of amusement (**is good** or **great** ∼, is very amusing). **3.** ∼ (**and games**), (colloq.) exciting or amusing goings-on. **4.** ||∼**-fair**, (part of) fair devoted to amusements and side-shows. **5.** *a.* amusing, entertaining, enjoyable. [f. obs. v. *fun* var. of *fon* befool; cf. FOND]

fūnā′mbūlist *n.* rope-dancer. [f. F *funambule* or f. L *funambulus* (*funis* rope, *ambulare* walk) + -IST]

fŭ′nction *n.*, & *v.i.* **1.** *n.* activity proper to person or institution; mode of action or activity by which thing fulfils its purpose; office-holder's duty, employment, profession, calling; religious or other public ceremony or occasion, social meeting of formal or important kind; (Math.) variable quantity in relation to other(s) in terms of which it may be expressed or on which its value depends (*x is a function of y and z*); basic operation in computer; hence ∼LESS *a.* **2.** *v.i.* fulfil a function, operate, act. [f. F *fonction* f. L *functio -onis* (*fungi funct-* perform; see -ION)]

fŭ′nctional *a.* of function(s); (Physiol., esp. of disease) of or affecting the functions of an organ etc. only, not structural or organic, (of mental disorder) having no discernible organic cause, (of organ) having a function, not functionless or rudimentary; (Math.) of a function; (of building etc.) shaped or constructed with regard mainly to its function rather than to aesthetic considerations, whence ∼ISM (3), ∼IST (2), *ns.*; practical, utilitarian; hence ∼LY² *adv.* [f. prec. + -AL]

fŭ′nctionarў *n.* person who has to perform functions or duties; official. [f. FUNCTION + -ARY¹]

fŭ′nctionāte *v.i.* = FUNCTION 2. [f. FUNCTION + -ATE²]

fŭnd *n.*, & *v.t.* **1.** *n.* permanent stock of something ready to be drawn upon (*a fund of common sense, tenderness, labour, knowledge*); stock of money, esp. one set apart for a purpose (SINKING-*fund*); (in *pl.*) pecuniary resources (**in** ∼**s**, having money to spend); ||**the** ∼**s**, stock of National Debt (as mode of investment). **2.** *v.t.* convert (floating debt) into more or less permanent debt at fixed interest; provide with money; put into a fund. [f. L *fundus* bottom, piece of land]

fŭ′ndament *n.* buttocks; anus. [ME, f. OF *fondement* f. L *fundamentum* (as FOUND¹; see -MENT)]

fŭndame′ntal *a.* & *n.* **1.** *a.* of the groundwork, going to the root of the matter, serving as base or foundation, essential, primary, original, from which others are derived, (*a fundamental change; the fundamental rules; the fundamental form*); ∼ **particle**, = ELEMENTARY *particle*. **2.** (Mus.) ∼ **note**, lowest note of chord in its original (uninverted) form; ∼ **tone** (produced by vibration of whole sonorous body, opp. *harmonics* produced by that of its parts). **3.** Hence ∼ITY (-ă′l-) *n.*, ∼LY² *adv.* **4.** *n.* (usu. in *pl.*) principle, rule, article, serving as groundwork of system. **5.** (Mus.) fundamental note or tone. [ME, f. F *fondamental* or f. LL *fundamentalis* (as prec.; see -AL)]

fŭndame′ntal|ism *n.* strict maintenance of traditional orthodox religious beliefs such as the inerrancy of Scripture and literal acceptance of the creeds as fundamentals of Protestant Christianity; so ∼IST (2) *n.* [f. prec. + -ISM]

fŭ′nd|us *n.* (*pl.* ∼**i** *pr.* -ī). (Anat.) lowest or farthest part of stomach or other hollow organ. [L, = bottom]

fūnē′brial *a.* of funeral(s) (*custom is funebrial in origin*); melancholy. [f. L *funebris* (*funus*; see foll.) + -AL]

fū′neral *attrib. a.*, & *n.* **1.** *a.* of, or used etc. at, burial or cremation of the dead (*funeral oration*); *funeral* HONOUR¹*s*; ∼ **pile, pyre**, pile of wood etc. on which corpse is burnt; ∼ **urn** (holding ashes of cremated body). **2.** *n.* burial or cremation of the dead with its ceremonies, obsequies; burial or cremation procession or *service; (sl.) one's (unpleasant) concern (*that's your funeral*). [ME; a. OF, f. LL *funeralis* (L *funus -eris* funeral + -AL); n. f. OF *funeraille* f. med. L *funeralia* neut. pl. of *funeralis*; see -AL 2]

fū′nerarў *a.* of funeral(s). [f. LL *funerarius* (as prec.; see -ARY¹)]

fūnēr′eal *a.* appropriate to a funeral; gloomy, dismal, dark; hence ∼LY² *adv.* [f. L *funereus* (as FUNERAL) + -AL]

fū′ngible (-nj-) *a.* (Law). that can serve for, or be replaced by, another answering to the same definition (of goods etc. contracted for, when an individual specimen is not meant). [f. med. L *fungibilis* f. *fungi* (*vice*) serve (in place of); see -IBLE]

fū′ngicīde (-nj-) *n.* fungus-destroying substance; hence **fŭngicī′d**AL (-nj-) *a.* [f. FUNGUS + -I- + -CIDE]

fŭngistā′tic (-nj-) *a.* inhibiting growth of fungi. [f. FUNGUS + -I- + -STATIC]

fū′ngoid (-ngg-) *a.* & *n.* **1.** *a.* resembling a fungus in texture or in rapid growth; ||of a fungus or fungi. **2.** *n.* fungoid plant. [f. FUNGUS + -OID]

fū′ngous (-ngg-) *a.* of fungi, having nature of a fungus; springing up like a mushroom, transitory. [ME, f. L *fungosus* (as foll.; see OUS)]

fŭ′ng|us (-ngg-) *n.* (*pl.* ∼**i** *pr.* -njī or -njī, *or* ∼**uses**) mushroom, toadstool, or allied plant including moulds; (Bot.) cryptogamous plant without chlorophyll feeding on organic matter; thing of sudden growth; (Path.) spongy morbid growth or excrescence; skin-disease of fish; (sl.) beard; hence ∼AL, ∼**iform** (-nj-), ∼**i′vorous** (-nj-), *adjs.* [L, perh. f. Gk *sp(h)oggos* SPONGE¹]

fūni′cular *a.* & *n.* **1.** *a.* of a rope or its tension; ∼ **railway**, cable railway with ascending and descending cars counterbalanced. **2.** *n.* funicular railway. [f. L *funiculus* (*funis* rope; see -CULE) + -AR¹]

fŭnk¹ *n.* & *v.* (sl.) **1.** *n.* fear, panic, (**blue** ∼, terror); coward; ||∼**-hole**, (1) trench dug-out, (2) employment used as pretext for evading military service. **2.** *v.i.* flinch, shrink, show cowardice. **3.** *v.t.* (try to) evade (undertaking), shirk; be afraid of. [18th c. Oxford sl.; perh. f. sl. FUNK² = tobacco-smoke]

fŭnk² *n.* (sl.) funky music; *strong smell. [f. *funk* blow smoke on, perh. f. F dial. *funkier* f. L (as FUMIGATE)]

fū′nkia *n.* = HOSTA. [mod. L, f. H. C. *Funck*, Prussian botanist d. 1839 + -IA¹]

fŭ′nkў¹ *a.* (sl.) terrified, cowardly. [f. FUNK¹ + -Y²]

fŭ′nkў² *a.* (sl.) (Of jazz etc.) uncomplicated, emotional; fashionable; *strong-smelling. [f. FUNK² + -Y²]

fŭ′nnel *n.* & *v.* (||-ll-). **1.** *n.* narrowing tube, or truncated cone and tube, for guiding liquid, powder, etc., into small opening; metal chimney of steam-engine or ship; hence (-)**fŭ′nnel**(1)ED² (-ld) *a.* **2.** *v.t.* & *i.* (cause to) move (as) through funnel. [ME, f. Prov. *fonilh* f. LL *fundibulum* f. L *infundibulum* f. IN¹(*fundere* pour)]

fŭ′nniment *n.* joke, drollery. [f. FUNNY + -MENT]

fŭnniŏ′sitў *n.* (joc.) comicality; comical thing. [f. foll. + -OSITY]

fŭ′nnў *a.* & *n.* **1.** *a.* affording fun, comical. **2.** curious, perplexing, hard to account for; (colloq.) slightly unwell, insane, etc. **3.** ∼**-bone**, part of elbow over which ulnar nerve passes; ∼ **business**, comic behaviour, jesting, (sl.) misbehaviour or deception; ∼**-face** (joc. & colloq., as form of address); ∼ **farm**, (sl.) mental hospital; ∼**-ha-ha′**, (colloq.) = sense 1; ∼ **man**, (esp. professional) clown or jester; ∼ **paper**, newspaper etc. containing humorous matter; ∼**-pecu′liar**, (colloq.) = sense 2. **4.** Hence **fŭ′nni**LY² *adv.*, **fŭ′nni**NESS *n.* **5.** *n.* (usu. in *pl.*) comic strip in newspaper; joke. [f. FUN + -Y²]

fūr *n.* & *v.* (-rr-). **1.** *n.* short fine soft hair of certain animals distinguished from the longer hair, (in *pl.*) skins of such animals with the fur; (Her.) representation of tufts on plain ground; (collect.) furred animals (esp. *fur and* FEATHER[1]); **make the ∼ fly,** make a disturbance, stir up trouble; **∼-seal,** eared seal with valuable undercoat. **2.** trimming or lining made of dressed coat of certain animals, e.g. ermine, beaver, or of material imitating this; coat of such animals, as material for trimming etc.; garment of or trimmed or lined with fur. **3.** crust adhering to surface, e.g. deposit from wine; coating formed on tongue in sickness; coating formed by hard water in kettle etc. **4.** *v.t.* (esp. in *p.p.*) provide (garment, animal), clothe (person), coat (tongue, inside of kettle), with fur; (Carpent.) level (floor-timbers) by inserting strips of wood. **5.** *v.i.* ∼ (**up**), (of kettle etc.) become coated with fur. [ME; n. f. v. f. AF **furrer,* OF *forrer (forre, fuerre* sheath f. Gmc **fōdhram*)]

fur. *abbr.* furlong(s).

fūr′bèlow (-ō) *n.,* & *v.t.* **1.** *n.* gathered strip or pleated border of skirt or petticoat; (in *pl.,* derog.) showy ornaments. **2.** *v.t.* adorn with furbelow(s). [18th c. var. of FALBALA]

fūr′bish *v.t.* remove rust from, polish *up,* burnish; ∼ (**up**), give new look to, renovate, revive, (something antiquated). [ME, f. OF *forbir* (-ISH[2]) f. Gmc **furbjan*]

fūr′cate[1] (-āt, -at) *a.* forked, branched. [f. LL *furcatus* f. L *furca* fork; see -ATE[2]]

fūr′c|āte[2] *v.i.* form a fork, divide; so ∼A′TION *n.* [f. L *furca* fork + -ATE[3]]

fūrfurā′ceous (-shus) *a.* scurfy; (Bot.) covered with branlike scales. [f. *furfur* scurf f. L *furfur* bran + -ACEOUS]

fūr′ious *a.* full of fury; very angry (constr. as ANGRY); raging, frantic, violent, intense; **fast and ∼,** rapidly, (of mirth etc.) eager(ly), uproarious(ly); hence ∼LY[2] *adv.* [ME, f. OF *furieus* f. L *furiosus* (as FURY; see -OUS)]

fūrl *v.* **1.** *v.t.* roll up and bind (sail on yard or boom; umbrella, flag); close (fan), fold up (wings), draw away (curtain), relinquish (hopes). **2.** *v.i.* become furled. [f. F *ferler* f. OF *fer(m)* FIRM[2] + *lier* bind f. L *ligare*]

fūr′lŏng *n.* eighth of mile, 220 yds. [OE *furlang (furh* FURROW, *lang* LONG[1]; orig. = length of furrow in common field)]

fūr′lough (-lō) *n.* & *v.* **1.** *n.* leave of absence, esp. granted to soldier or missionary. **2.** *v.t.* *grant furlough to. **3.** *v.i.* *spend furlough. [f. Du. *verlof* (after G *verlaub*; as FOR-, LEAVE[1])]

fūr′mĕtȳ. See FRUMENTY.

fūr′nace (-ĭs) *n.* & *v.t.* **1.** *n.* apparatus including combustion chamber in which minerals, metals, etc., may be subjected to continuous intense heat (BLAST[1]-*-furnace*); very hot place; (fig.) severe test (*tried in the furnace*); closed fireplace for heating water to warm building etc. by hot pipes. **2.** *v.t.* heat in furnace. [ME, f. OF *fornais* f. L *fornax -acis (fornus* oven)]

fūr′nish *v.t.* **1.** ∼ **with,** cause to have possession or use of. **2.** fit up (house, room) with all necessary appliances, esp. movable furniture (**∼ed house, rooms,** etc., esp. premises let with furniture); hence ∼ER[1] *n.,* (esp.) one who sells furniture, ∼ING[1] (3) *n.* (esp. in *pl.*). **3.** provide, afford, yield. [f. OF *furnir* (-ISH[2]) f. Rom. **fornire* ult. f. WG **frumjan* supply, promote, (**frum-;* cf. FRAME[1], FROM)]

fūr′niture *n.* **1.** movable contents of building or room (tables, chairs, etc.); ∼ **beetle,** *Anobium punctatum,* boring in furniture; ∼ **van,** large van used to move furniture from one house to another; **part of the ∼,** (colloq.) person or thing taken for granted. **2.** (Print.) pieces of wood or metal placed round or between type to make blank spaces and fasten the matter in the chase. **3.** (Naut.) ship's equipment, esp. tackle etc. **4.** (arch.) contents of receptacle; things occupying a place. **5.** accessory equipment, e.g. handles and lock of door. [f. F *fourniture (fournir,* f. as prec.; see -URE)]

furŏr′è, *fūr′ŏr, *n.* enthusiastic admiration; rage, craze; uproar, fury. [It., f. L *furor -oris (furere* be mad; see -OR)]

fūr′phȳ *n.* (Austral. sl.) false report or rumour; absurd story. [f. water and sanitary F∼ *carts* of 1914–18 war, made at foundry set up by F∼ family]

fŭ′rri|er *n.* dealer in or dresser of furs; hence ∼ERY (2) *n.* [ME *furrour* f. OF *forreor (forrer* trim with fur), assim. to -IER]

fŭ′rrin(er). Var. (joc. or dial.) of FOREIGN(ER).

fŭ′rrow (-ō) *n.,* & *v.t.* **1.** *n.* narrow trench made by plough (PLOUGH[2] *a lonely furrow*); ship's track; rut, track, groove, long indentation, deep wrinkle, hollow between ridges; ∼-**slice,** slice of earth turned up by mould-board of plough; hence ∼LESS, ∼Y[2], *adjs.* **2.** *v.t.* plough; make furrows, grooves, etc., in; mark with wrinkles. [OE *furh,* = OHG *furuh,* ON *for* trench f. Gmc **furh-* f. IE **prk-*]

fŭr′rȳ *a.* of or like fur; covered with or wearing fur. [f. FUR + -Y[2]]

fŭr′ther (-dh-) *adv.* & *a.* (used as *compar.* of FAR[1,2]), & *v.t.* **1.** *adv.* to or at more advanced point in space or time (*unsafe to proceed further; and then to lapse unless further continued*); to greater extent, more, (*inquire further*); ∼(**more**), in addition (esp. introducing fresh consideration in argument); at greater distance (*nothing was further from his thoughts*); (euphem.) in hell (**I'll see you ∼ first,** as strong refusal of request). **2.** *a.* going beyond what exists or has been dealt with, additional, (*threats of further punishment;* ‖∼ **education** (provided for persons above school age; usu. excl. university); **till ∼ notice** or **orders,** to continue until explicitly changed); more distant (*on the further side*); hence ∼MOST *a.* **3.** *v.t.* help on, promote, favour, (undertaking, movement, cause); hence ∼ANCE *n.,* (arch.) ∼SOME[1] *a.* [OE *furthor adv., furthra* adj., *fyrthrian* v., f. as FORTH, -ER[3]]

fŭr′thěst (-dh-) *a.* & *adv.* (used as *superl.* of FAR[1,2]). **1.** *a.* most distant; **at (the)** ∼, at the greatest distance, at the latest, at most. **2.** *adv.* to or at the greatest distance. [ME, *superl.* formed f. prec.; see -EST[1]]

fŭr′tive *a.* done by stealth, clandestine, meant to escape notice; sly, stealthy; stolen, taken secretly; thievish, pilfering; hence ∼LY[2] (-vlĭ) *adv.,* ∼NESS (-vn-) *n.* [f. F *furtif -ive* or f. L *furtivus (furtum* theft; see -IVE)]

fŭr′ŭnc|le *n.* = BOIL[1]; hence ∼ūlAR, ∼ūlOUS, (-ŭ′ngk-) *adjs.* [f. L *furunculus (fur* thief; see -UNCLE)]

fŭrŭnculō′s|is *n.* (*pl.* ∼es *pr.* -ēz). **1.** diseased condition in which boils appear. **2.** bacterial disease of salmon and trout. [mod. L, f. as prec. + -OSIS]

fŭr′ȳ *n.* **1.** fierce passion, wild anger, rage, (**in a ∼,** in a fit of rage); impetuosity in battle etc.; violence of weather, disease, etc.; **like ∼,** (colloq.) with great force or effort. **2.** (usu. in *pl.;* F∼) goddess of Gk myth (esp. Alecto, Tisiphone, or Megaera) sent from Tartarus to punish crime; (fig.) avenging spirit, remorseful pang, (*haunted by the furies of her father's blood*). **3.** virago, angry or malignant woman. [ME, f. OF *furie* f. L *furia (furere* be mad; see -Y[1])]

‖**fŭrze** *n.* spiny yellow-flowered evergreen shrub growing esp. on European waste lands, gorse, whin; hence *fŭr′zy[2] a.* [OE *fyrs,* of unkn. orig.]

fŭ′scous *a.* sombre, dark-coloured. [f. L *fuscus* dusky + -OUS]

fūse[1] (-z) *v.t.* & *i.* melt with intense heat; blend or amalgamate into one whole (as) by melting (of metals, living bones, institutions, motives, etc.); hence fū′sIBLE *a.,* fūsIBI′LITY *n.,* (-z-). [f. L *fundere fus-* pour, melt]

fūse[2] (-z), **fūze,** *n.,* & *v.t.* **1.** *n.* tube, casing, cord, etc., filled or saturated with combustible matter for igniting bomb, blasting-charge, etc., component in shell, mine, etc., designed to detonate explosive charge after an interval (*time-fuse*) or on impact or when subjected to magnetic or vibratory stimulation. **2.** *v.t.* fit fuse to. [f. It. *fuso* f. L *fusus* spindle]

fūse³ (-z) *n. & v.* (Electr.) **1.** *n.* (device containing) strip or wire of easily melted metal placed in circuit so as to interrupt current by melting when current exceeds safe value; ~**-box,** small cupboard or box containing fuses for circuits in house etc. **2.** *v.t.* provide (circuit etc.) with fuse(s); cause (appliance etc.) to fuse. **3.** *v.i.* (Of appliance etc.) cease to function, owing to melting of fuse. [f. FUSE¹]

fūsee' (-z-), ***fūzee',*** *n.* conical pulley or wheel esp. in watch or clock; large-headed match for lighting cigar or pipe in wind; *railway signal-flare. [f. F *fusée* spindle f. LL *fusata* f. L *fusus*]

fū'sel (-z-) *n.* ~ **oil,** mixture of several alcohols, chiefly amyl alcohol, produced, usu. in small amounts, during alcoholic fermentation and making alcoholic liquors harmful or poisonous. [f. G *fusel* bad brandy etc.; cf. *fuseln* FOOZLE]

fū'selage (-zəlahzh, -lij) *n.* body of aeroplane. [F (*fuseler* cut in spindle form f. *fuseau* spindle f. OF *fusel* f. Rom. **fusellus* dim. of L *fusus*; see -AGE)]

fusible. See FUSE¹.

fū'sifôrm (-z-) *a.* (Bot. & Zool.) shaped like spindle or cigar, tapering at both ends. [f. L *fusus* spindle + -I- + -FORM]

fū'sil (-z-) *n.* (Hist.) light musket. [F, f. LL **focile* f. L *focus* hearth, fire; see -IL]

fusilier', ***fūsileer',*** (-zĭ-, -zɪ-) *n.* (usu. in *pl.*) **1.** (Hist.) soldier armed with fusil. **2.** (member of) one of several British regiments formerly armed with fusils [F (as prec.; see -IER)]

fūsillā'de (-z-) *n., & v.t.* **1.** *n.* (wholesale execution by) continuous discharge of firearms; sustained outburst of criticism etc. **2.** *v.t.* assault (place), shoot down (persons), by fusillade. [F (*fusiller* shoot; see -ADE)]

fū'sion (-zhən) *n.* **1.** fusing, melting; fused mass; blending of different things into one; coalition, whence ~IST (2) *n.* **2.** (Phys.) union of atomic nuclei to form heavier one, usu. with release of energy; this process as source of energy; ~ **bomb** (using this process, esp. hydrogen bomb). [F, or f. L *fusio* (as FUSE¹; scc -ION)]

füss *n. & v.* **1.** *n.* bustle, excessive commotion, ostentatious or nervous activity; **make a** ~, complain vigorously; **make a** ~ **of** or **over,** treat (person) with display of affection or attention. **2.** treatment of trifles as important; abundance of petty detail. **3.** ~(-**pot**), -'**budget,** (colloq.) person who continually makes a fuss. **4.** *v.i.* make fuss; busy oneself restlessly with trifles; move fussily *about, up and down,* etc. **5.** *v.t.* agitate, worry, (person). [18th c., perh. Anglo-Ir.]

fu'ss|y *a.* fond of fussing; full of unnecessary detail or decoration; fastidious; hence ~iLY² *adv.,* ~iNESS *n.* [f. prec.+ -Y²]

fûstanĕ'lla *n.* man's stiff white kilt worn in Albania and Greece. [It. dim. of mod. Gk *phoustani* prob. f. It. *fustagno* FUSTIAN]

fū'stian *n. & a.* **1.** *n.* thick twilled short-napped cotton cloth usu. dyed dark; turgid speech or writing, bombast. **2.** *a.* made of fustian, (fig.) bombastic, worthless. [ME, f. OF *fustaigne* (med. L *fustaneus* adj. ref. to cloth from *Fostat* suburb of Cairo)]

fū'stic *n.* one of two kinds of wood yielding yellow dye (**young** ~, from Venetian sumac; ~ or **old** ~, from tropical Amer. tree *Chlorophora tinctoria*); dye from these. [f. F. Sp. *fustoc* f. Arab. *fustuķ* f. Gk *pistakē* pistachio]

fū'stig|āte *v.t.* (joc.) cudgel; hence ~A'TION *n.* [f. LL *fustigare* (*fustis* cudgel) + -ATE³]

fū'st|y *a.* stale-smelling, musty, mouldy; close, stuffy; antiquated, old-fashioned; hence ~iLY² *adv.,* ~iNESS

n. [ME, f. OF *fusté* smelling of the cask (*fust* cask, tree--trunk, f. L *fustis* cudgel)]

fu'thôrc (fŏŏ'-) *n.* Scandinavian runic alphabet. [f. its first six letters *f, u, th, ö, r, k*]

fū'tile *a.* useless, ineffectual, vain, frivolous; hence or cogn. **fūti'l**ITY *n.,* ~LY² (-l-lĭ) *adv.* [f. L *futilis* leaky, futile, (**fud*- st. of *fundere* pour; see -IL)]

fūtilitā'r|ian *a. & n.* (person) devoted to futile pursuits. [joc. f. prec. after *utilitarian*]

fū'ttock *n.* one of ship's middle timbers between floor and top timbers; ~ **plates,** iron plates in a ship's top to which the ~ **shrouds** (lower ends of which are fastened to ring on mast below) are fixed, as well as the dead-eyes of the topmast rigging. [ME *votekes* etc. pl. f. MLG (*fŏt* FOOT¹, *-ken* -KIN)]

fū'ture *a. & n.* **1.** *a.* about to happen or be become; that will be hereafter (~ **life, state,** existence after death); that will be something specified (*my future wife*); of time to come, (Gram., of participle or tense) describing event yet to happen (*future* PERFECT¹). **2.** *n.* time to come (**for the** ~, **in** ~, from now onwards; *past, present, and future*); what will happen in the future; person's, country's, etc., prospective condition; prospective condition of success etc. (*that idea has no future*); (Gram.) future tense; (Commerc., in *pl.*) goods and stocks sold for future delivery, contracts for these; hence ~LESS (-cherl-) *a.* [ME f. OF *futur-ure* f. L *futurus* fut. part. of *esse* be f. st. *fu-* be]

fū'turism (-cher-) *n.* movement in art, literature, music, etc., with violent departure from traditional forms so as to express movement and growth. [f. FUTURE + -ISM, after It. *futurismo,* F. *futurisme*]

fū'turist (-cher-) *n.* **1.** (Theol.) one who believes that the prophecies of the Apocalypse etc. are still to be fulfilled. **2.** (Art etc.) adherent of futurism. **3.** student of the future, believer in human progress. [f. FUTURE + -IST]

fūturi'stic (-cher-) *a.* **1.** having characteristics of futurism, ultra-modern. **2.** pertaining to the future. [f. prec.+ -IC]

fūtūr'ity *n.* future time; (in *sing.* or *pl.*) future events; future condition, existence after death, *~ **stakes,** stakes raced for long after entries or nominations are made. [f. FUTURE + -ITY]

fūturo'logy (-cher-) *n.* systematic forecasting of future esp. from present trends in society; hence ~LOGIST *n.* [f. FUTURE + -o- + -LOGY]

fūze, ***fūzee'.*** See FUSE², FUSEE.

fuzz *n.* loose volatile matter, fluff; fluffy or frizzed hair; (sl.) police(man) [perh. diff. wd]; ~**-ball,** puff-ball fungus. [17th c., prob. f. LG or Du.]

fu'zz|y *a.* like fuzz; frayed, fluffy; blurred, indistinct; frizzy; ~**-y-wuzzy,** (colloq.) Sudanese soldier, (sl.) coloured native of other countries; hence ~iLY² *adv.,* ~iNESS *n.* [f. prec.+ -Y²]

f.w.d. *abbr.* four-wheel drive; front-wheel drive.

fwd. *abbr.* forward.

-fy *suf.* forming (usu. w. intermediate -I-) *vbs.* (1) f. *ns.* w. sense 'make, produce' (*pacify, satisfy*), 'make into' (*deify, petrify*), 'make like' (*countrify*), (2) f. *adjs.* w. sense 'bring or come into state' (*Frenchify, sanctify, solidify*), (3) f. L *vbs.* w. causative sense (*horrify, stupefy*). [f. or after F *-fier* f. L *-ficare* (cf. -FICATION) and *-facere* (cf. -FACTION)]

f.y. *abbr.* fiscal year.

fy'lfot *n.* swastika. [perh. f. *fill-foot,* pattern to fill the foot of a painted window]

fŷrd *n.* (duty to serve in) English militia before 1066. [OE, = OS *fard,* OHG *fart,* ON *ferth* f. Gmc (as FARE²)]

fytte. See FIT¹.

G

G, g, (jē) *n.* (*pl.* **Gs** *or* **G's**). seventh letter of alphabet; (Mus.) fifth note in diatonic scale of C major.

G *abbr.* gauss; giga-.

g. *abbr.* gelding; gram(s); (acceleration due to) gravity.

GA, Ga., *abbrs.* Georgia (US).

Ga *symb.* gallium.

gäb *n.* (colloq.) talk, prattle, twaddle; **gift of the ~,** (1) talent for speaking, (2) loquacity; **stop your ~,** be silent. [17th-c. var. of GOB³]

gä′bardine (-ēn) *n.* smooth durable twill-woven cloth esp. of worsted or cotton; garment of this. [var. of GABERDINE]

gä′bble *v.* & *n.* **1.** *v.i.* talk volubly or inarticulately; read aloud too fast. **2.** *v.t.* utter too fast esp. in reading aloud. **3.** *n.* voluble confused unintelligible talk. [f. MDu. *gabbelen*; imit.]

gä′bbrō *n.* (*pl.* **~s**). dark granular igneous rock of crystalline texture resembling dolerite and granite; hence **gä′bbro**ID *a.* [It., f. L *glaber* smooth]

gä′bbў *a.* (colloq.) talkative. [f. GAB + -Y²]

gabe′lle *n.* (Hist.) tax (usu. foreign tax, esp. the French pre-Revolution salt-tax). [ME f. F, f. It. *gabella* f. Arab. *al-ḳabāla* the tribute]

ga′berdine (-ēn) *n.* (Hist.) loose long upper garment esp. of Jews and almsmen; gabardine. [f. OF *gauvardine* perh. f. MHG *wallevart* pilgrimage]

***gä′bfèst** *n.* (sl.) gathering for conversation; prolonged spell of talking. [f. GAB + FEST]

gä′bion *n.* cylinder of wicker or woven metal bands to be filled with earth or stones for use in engineering or (Hist.) fortification; hence **~A′DE** *n.*, line of gabions. [F, f. It. *gabbione* (*gabbia* CAGE; see -OON)]

gä′ble *n.* triangular upper part of wall at end of ridged roof; **~(-end)**, gable-topped wall; gable-shaped canopy over window or door, whence **gä′bl**ET¹ *n.*; hence **(-)gä′bl**ED² (-beld) *a.* [ME *gavel* f. ON *gafl*; ME *gable* f. OF f. ON *gafl*]

gä′bў *n.* (arch. or dial.) simpleton. [18th c.; orig. unkn.]

gäd¹ *int.* (*or by* **~**) expr. surprise, asseveration, etc. [= *God*]

gäd² *v.i.* (-dd-), & *n.* **1.** *v.i.* go about idly or in search of pleasure, rove, wander, (*about, abroad, out*); (of plant, esp. in *pres. part.*) straggle; **~′about** *n.* & *a.*, (person) given to gadding. **2.** *n.* **(up)on the ~,** going about, on the move. [back-form. f. obs. *gadling* companion f. OE *gædeling* (*gæd* fellowship; see -LING¹)]

Gä′darēne *a.* of Gadara in ancient Palestine; involving or engaged in headlong rush or flight. [f. LL f. Gk *Gadarēnos* (cf. -ENE 2), w. ref. to Matt. 8:28 ff.]

ga′ddī (gŭ′-) *n.* (Hist.) cushioned throne of Indian ruler; power as sovereign. [f. Hind. *gaddī*, lit. cushion]

gä′dflў *n.* cattle-biting fly, esp. horse-fly or bot-fly; irritating or harassing person. [f. obs. *gad* spike f. ON *gaddr*, cogn. w. YARD¹]

gä′dgèt *n.* small fitting or contrivance in machinery etc.; adjunct; (mere) knick-knack; hence **~EER′, ~RY** (5), *ns.*, **~Y²** *a.* [19th c. Naut.; orig. unkn.]

Gadhĕ′lic (-dĕ′-) *a.* & *n.* = GAELIC 2. [f. Ir. *Gaedheal* Gael + -IC]

gä′doid *a.* & *n.* (fish) of the cod family Gadidae. [f. mod. L *gadus* f. Gk *gados* cod + -OID]

gä′dolinite *n.* dark mineral containing silicates of rare-earth elements. [f. J. *Gadolin*, Finnish mineralogist d. 1852 + -ITE¹ (2)]

gädoli′nium *n.* metallic element of lanthanide series, found in gadolinite. [mod. L, f. prec. + -IUM]

gadrōō′n *n.* convex curves in series forming ornamental edge like inverted fluting on silverware etc. [f. F *godron*; cf. *goder* pucker, -OON]

gä′dwall (-awl) *n.* brownish-grey freshwater duck (*Anas strepera*). [17th c.; orig. unkn.]

gädzŏŏ′ks *int.* (arch.) expr. asseveration etc. [f. GAD¹ + *zooks* of unkn. orig.]

Gael (gāl) *n.* Scottish Celt; Gaelic-speaking Celt; hence **~′DOM** *n.* [f. Gael. *Gaidheal*]

Gae′lic (gā′l-) *a.* & *n.* **1.** (language) of Scottish Celts. **2.** (language) of Scottish and Irish and Manx Celts. **3. ~ coffee** (with cream and Irish whisky). [f. prec. + -IC]

Gaeltacht (gā′ltaχt) *n.* region in Ireland where vernacular language is Irish. [Ir.]

gäff¹ *n.*, & *v.t.* **1.** *n.* barbed fishing-spear; stick with iron hook for landing large fish; spar extending top of fore-and-aft sail not set on stays, or carrying ensign; **~-rigged,** having gaff on mainsail; **~ topsail,** small sail having foot on gaff. **2.** *v.t.* seize (fish) with gaff. [ME, f. Prov. *gaf* hook]

gäff² *n.* (sl.) **blow the ~,** let out plot or secret; ***stand the ~,** endure difficulties. [19th c.; orig. unkn.]

||gäff³ *n.* (arch.sl.) public place of amusement; (**penny**) **~,** low theatre or music-hall. [18th c.; orig. unkn.]

gäffe *n.* blunder, indiscreet act or remark, *faux pas*. [F]

gä′ffer *n.* elderly rustic, old fellow, (also as title or in *voc.*); ||foreman of gang of workmen. [prob. contr. of GODfather; *ga-* by assoc. w. *grandfather*; cf. GAMMER, GOSSIP]

gäg *n.* & *v.* (-gg-). **1.** *n.* thing thrust into or held over mouth to prevent speech or outcry or (Surg.) hold it open for operation; (Parl.) closure or guillotine. **2.** actor's interpolations in dramatic dialogue; (Theatr.) carefully prepared comic effect or business introduced into music-hall sketch, stage-play, etc.; **~-man,** **~′STER,** professional deviser of gags. **3. ~-bit,** specially powerful bit for horse-breaking; **~-rein** (arranged to make the bit more powerful). **4.** joke, hoax; humorous action or situation; imposture, deception. **5.** *v.t.* apply gag to; silence, deprive of free speech; apply gag-bit to (horse); cause to choke or retch. **6.** *v.i.* (Theatr.) make gags; choke, retch. [n. f. v., ME, perh. imit. of choking]

ga′ga (gah′gah) *a.* (sl.) fatuous, senile; slightly crazy. [F, = senile (person)]

gäge¹ *n.*, & *v.t.* **1.** *n.* pledge, thing deposited as security; (glove thrown down as, any symbol of) challenge to fight. **2.** *v.t.* (arch.) stake, pledge, offer as guarantee. [ME; n. f. OF *gage* f. Rom. *gwadjo* f. Gmc *wadhjam* (cf. WED); v. f. F *gager* (*gage*) or f. ENGAGE]

gäge²,³. See GAUGE¹,².

gäge⁴ *n.* greengage. [abbr.]

gä′ggle *n.*, & *v.i.* **1.** *n.* flock (of geese); (derog.) company (of women); (disorderly) group. **2.** *v.i.* (O geese) cackle. [ME, n. f. v., imit.; cf. *gabble, cackle*]

gai′etў, *gay′etў, *n.* being gay, mirth (**~ of nations,** cheerfulness or pleasure of numerous people); merry-making, amusement; bright appearance. [f. F *gaiete* (as GAY, -TY¹)]

gaillar′dia *n.* showy-flowered composite plant of genus *Gaillardia*. [mod. L, f. *Gaillard de Marentonneau*, 18th-c. Fr. botanist + -IA¹]

gai′lў. See GAY.

gain¹ *n.* increase of possessions etc., profit, advance, improvement; acquisition of wealth; (in *pl.*) sums acquired by trade etc., emoluments, winnings; increase in amount; (Electr.) (logarithm of) factor by which power etc. is increased. [OF *gaaignier* GAIN²]

gain³ *v.* **1.** *v.t.* obtain or secure (usu. desired or desirable thing; *gain advantage, recognition,* one's *ends*; **~ time,** obtain delay by pretexts or slow methods); win (sum) as profits or as result of changed conditions etc., whence **~′ings** (-z) *n. pl.* [-ING¹ (2)]; obtain as increment or addition (*gain momentum, weight*). **2.** wir (land from sea, battle, victory; *gain* GROUND¹, *the* UPPER *hand*); bring over or *over* to one's interest or views; reach, arrive at, (desired place); (of clock etc.) become fast by (amount of time). **3.** *v.i.* make a profit, be benefited, improve or advance *in* some respect; be enhanced *by* comparison or contrast; (of clock etc.) become fast, indicate time ahead of correct time; ∼ (**up**)**on**, come closer to (what is pursued). **4.** Hence ∼′ABLE *a.*, ∼′ER¹ *n.* [f. OF *gaigner*, *gaaignier* to till, acquire, f. Rom. **gwadanjare* f. Gmc **waithanjan* (**waithō* pasture)]

gai′nful *a.* lucrative, remunerative; bent on gain; paid (employment); hence ∼LY² *adv.* [f. GAIN¹ + -FUL]

gainsay′ *v.t.* (**gainsai′d** *pr.* -ā′d *or* -ē′d). (arch. or literary). deny, contradict; hence ∼ER¹ *n.* [ME, f. obs. *gain-* pref. against, f. ON *gegn* straight, f. Gmc **gagan-*, **gagin-* + SAY²]

'gainst *prep.* (poet.) = AGAINST. [abbr.]

gait *n.* manner of walking, bearing or carriage as one walks (**go** one's (**own**) ∼, pursue one's own course); manner of forward motion of runner, horse, vehicle, etc. [var. of GATE²]

gai′ter *n.* covering of cloth, leather, etc., for leg below knee, for ankle, for part of machine, etc.; hence ∼ED² (-erd) *a.* [f. F *guêtre*, perh. cogn. w. WRIST]

găl¹ *n.* (vulg.) girl. [repr. variant pr.]

găl² *n.* (Phys.) unit of acceleration due to gravity, one centimetre per second per second. [f. *Galileo* (see GALILEAN¹)]

Gal. *abbr.* Galatians (NT).

gal. *abbr.* gallon(s).

ga′la (gah′-, gā′-) *n.* festive occasion, fête; ‖festive gathering for sports. [F, or f. It. f. Sp., f. Arab. *ḵil'a* presentation garment]

gală′ctic *a.* of the Galaxy; of a galaxy or galaxies. [f. Gk *galaktias*, var. of *galaxias* (see GALAXY) + -IC]

gală′ct∣o- *comb. form.* (Med. etc.) milk, as: ∼**agogue** (-ŏg), (substance) inducing a flow of milk. [f. Gk *gala galaktos* milk; *agōgos* leading]

gală′gō *n.* (*pl.* ∼s). small African tree-climbing lemur of genus *Galago*. [mod. L]

galah′ *n.* (Austral.) rose-breasted grey backed cockatoo; (sl.) fool, simpleton. [Aboriginal]

Gă′lahăd (-*a*-h-) *n.* person characterized by nobility, integrity, courtesy, etc. [f. noblest knight of Round Table in Arthurian legend]

ga′lantine (-ēn) *n.* white meat boned, cooked, pressed, and served cold in aspic etc. [ME f. OF, alt. f. *galatine* jellied meat f. med. L *galatina*]

gală′ntý *n.* ∼ **show**, (Hist.) pantomime made by shadows of puppets on screen. [perh. f. It. *galanti* pl. of *galante* GALLANT]

gă′laxý *n.* **1.** (G∼) the irregular luminous band of stars indistinguishable to naked eye encircling the heavens, Milky Way; one of many independent systems of stars, gas, dust, etc., existing in space, esp. (G∼) the one which contains the earth. **2.** brilliant company (*of* beauties, talent, etc.). [ME, f. OF *galaxie* f. med. L *galaxia*, LL f. Gk *galaxias* (*gala galaktos* milk)]

gă′lbanum *n.* gum resin from kinds of ferula. [ME f. L, f. Gk *khalbanē*, prob. of Semitic orig.]

gāle¹ *n.* (sweet-)∼, bog myrtle. [OE *gagel(le)*, = MDu. *gaghel*]

gāle² *n.* very strong wind, esp. (on Beaufort scale) of 32-54 m.p.h.; (Naut.) storm; outburst, esp. of laughter; (poet.) gentle breeze. [16th c.; orig. unkn.]

gā′lé∣a *n.* (Bot. & Zool.) structure like helmet in shape, function, or position; so ∼ATE², ∼āteD¹, *adjs.* [L, = helmet]

galē′na *n.* commonest lead ore, lead sulphide. [L, = lead ore (in partly purified state)]

galē′nic *a.*, **galē′nical** *a.* & *n.* of or according to Galen; (remedy) made of vegetable, not synthetic, components. [f. *Galen*, Gk physician of 2nd c. AD + -IC(AL)]

galère (galār′) *n.* coterie, (usu. undesirable). group of people; unexpected situation. [F, = galley, used fig. in Molière's *Scapin*]

Gălǐlē′an¹ *a.* of Galileo; ∼ **satellite**, one of Jupiter's four largest moons; ∼ **telescope** (with bi-convex objective and bi-concave eyepiece). [f. *Galileo* Galilei, It. astronomer d. 1642 + -AN]

Gălǐlē′an² *a.* & *n.* **1.** *a.* of Galilee; Christian. **2.** *n.* native or inhabitant of Galilee; Christian; (derog.) Christ. [f. *Galilee* in Palestine + -AN]

gă′lilee *n.* porch or chapel at entrance of church. [f. OF *galilée* f. med. L *galilea*, w. some ref. to *Galilee* in Palestine]

gălima′tias (-ă′tĭas, -ā′shas) *n.* confused or meaningless talk, rigmarole. [F, of unkn. orig.]

gă′lingāle (-ngg-) *n.* aromatic rhizome of E. Asian plant of genus *Alpinia* or *Kaempferia*, formerly used in cookery and medicine; (**English**) ∼, sedge (*Cyperus longus*) having root with similar properties. [OF *galengar*, & f. OF *galingal* f. Arab. *kalanjān* f. Chin. *ge-liang-jiang* mild ginger from Ge in Canton]

gă′liot *n.* see GALLIOT.

gă′lipŏt *n.* hardened turpentine formed on stem of cluster pine. [F, of unkn. orig.]

gall¹ (gawl) *n.* **1.** bile of animals; gall-bladder and its contents. **2.** (fig.) anything bitter, bitterness, (*gall and wormwood*); asperity, rancour, (**dip** one's **pen in** ∼, write virulently); (sl.) impudence. **3.** ∼**-bladder**, vessel containing bile after secretion by liver; ∼′**stone**, calculous formation in gall-bladder. [ON, = OE *gealla*, OS, OHG *galla* f. Gmc **gallam* etc.]

gall² (gawl) *n.* sore produced by chafing; mental soreness, exasperation or its cause; place rubbed bare, flaw; bare spot in field or coppice. [ME, f. MLG, MDu. *galle* (OE *gealla* sore on horse, ON *galli* fault)]

gall³ (gawl) *v.t.* rub sore, injure by rubbing; vex, annoy, harass, humiliate, whence ∼′ING² *a.* [ME, f. prec., orig. as back-form. f. *gall*ED²]

gall⁴ (gawl) *n.* ∼(′**nut**), excrescence produced by insect, fungus, or bacterium, on plant, esp. on oak; ∼**-fly**, ∼**-mite**, ∼**-wasp**, (producing galls). [ME, f. OF *galle* f. L *galla*]

gall. *abbr.* gallon(s).

Gă′lla *n.* & *a.* (member or language) of group of Hamitic peoples in equatorial Africa. [perh. f. Arab. *galīẓ* wild]

gă′llant (*or* in senses 3, 5, 6, 7, galā′nt) *a.*, *n.*, & *n* **1.** *a.* (Of ship, horse, etc.) grand, fine, stately; (arch.) finely dressed. **2.** brave, chivalrous; (used as conventional epithet of Member of Parliament who was in the Services: *the honourable and gallant member*). **3.** markedly attentive to women; associated with sexual love, amatory. **4.** Hence ∼LY² *adv.* **5.** *n.* (arch.) man of fashion, fine gentleman; ladies' man, lover, paramour. **6.** *v.t.* flirt with; escort, act as cavalier to, (lady). **7.** *n i* play the gallant; flirt *with*. [ME, f. OF *galant* past. of *galer* make merry (see *gale* rejoicing); see -ANT]

gă′llantrý *n.* bravery, dashing courage; courtliness, devotion to women; polite act or speech; conduct of a gallant, sexual intrigue, immorality. [f. F *galanterie* (as prec.; see -ERY)]

gă′llěon *n.* (Hist.) vessel shorter and higher than galley; ship of war (usu. Spanish); large Spanish ship used in American trade. [f. MDu. *galjoen* f. F *galion* (*galie* galley), or f. Sp. *galeón* (see -OON)]

gă′llery *n.*, & *v.t.* **1.** *n.* covered space for walking in partly open at side, portico, colonnade; balcony; long narrow passage in thickness of wall or supported on corbels, open towards interior of building. **2.** platform projecting from inner wall of church, hall, etc., providing extra room for spectators etc. or reserved for musicians etc. (*minstrels' gallery*); (Theatr.) highest balcony thus constructed, persons there seated, least refined part of audience (**play to the** ∼, appeal to unrefined tastes); group of spectators at golf-match etc. **3.** long narrow room (e.g. SHOOTING-*gallery*), passage, corridor; room or building used for showing works of art; (Mil. & Mining) horizontal underground passage; ∼ **tray**, silver tray with raised rim, used to carry glasses etc. **4.** *v.t.* provide, pierce, etc., with gallery or galleries. [f. F *galerie* f. It. *galleria* f. med. L *galeria*, perh. alt. of *galilea* GALILEE]

gä'lley *n.* **1.** (Hist.) low flat single-decked vessel using sails and oars, and usu. rowed by slaves or criminals; ancient Greek or Roman warship with one or more banks of oars; large open rowing-boat, e.g. that used by captain of man-of-war; **in this** etc. ~ (unexpected situation; after Molière, see GALÈRE). **2.** ship's or aircraft's kitchen. **3.** (Print.) oblong tray for set type; corresponding part of composing-machine; ~ (**proof**), proof in form of long single-column strips from type in galley, not in sheets or pages. **4.** ~-slave, person condemned to row in galley, (fig.) drudge. [ME, f. OF *galie* f. med. L *galea*, med. Gk *galaia*]

***gä'lley-wëst** *adv.* (colloq.) **knock** ~, knock askew, confuse, defeat. [f. E dial. *colly-west*(*on*), perh. f. village in Northamptonshire]

gälliä'mbic *a.* & *n.* (verse) in metre formed of two iambic dimeters, as in Tennyson's *Boadicea*. [f. L *galliambus* song of *Galli* or priests of Cybele; see IAMBUS, -IC]

gä'lliard *n.* (Hist.) quick and lively dance in triple time for two persons; music for it. [ME, f. OF *gaillard* valiant, perh. f. Rom. *gallia* strength, of Celt. orig.]

gä'llic¹ *a.* (Chem.) ~ **acid** (obtained from gallnuts etc. and used in making ink). [f. F *gallique* (*galle* GALL⁴; see -IC)]

Gä'llic² *a.* of the Gauls, Gaulish; (often joc.) (typically) French, whence **Gä'llicISM** (4) *n.*, **Gä'llicIZE** (2, 3) *v.t.* & *i.* [f. L *Gallicus* (*Gallus* a Gaul; see -IC)]

Gä'llican *a.* & *n.* **1.** (adherent) of the school of Roman Catholics (orig. in France) claiming partial autonomy with regard to Pope (opp. ULTRAMONTANE); hence ~ISM (3), ~IST (2), *ns.* **2.** *a.* of the ancient church of Gaul or France. [F, or f. L *Gallicanus* (as prec.; see -AN)]

gä'llicè *adv.* in French. [L, = in Gaulish]

gälligä'skins (-z) *n. pl.* (joc.) breeches, trousers. [orig. wide hose of 16th–17th c., f. obs. F *garguesque* for *greguesque* f. It. *grechesca* fem. of *grechesco* Greek (see -ESQUE)]

gällimau'frÿ *n.* heterogeneous mixture, jumble, medley. [f. F *galimafrée*, of unkn. orig.]

gällinä'ceous (-shŭs) *a.* of the order Galliformes, incl. domestic poultry, pheasants, partridges, etc. [f. L *gallinaceus* (*gallina* hen f. *gallus* cock; see -ACEOUS)]

gä'llinüle *n.* small aquatic bird of genus *Gallinula*. [f. mod. L *gallinula*, dim. of L *gallina* hen (see prec., -ULE)]

Gä'lliō *n.* (*pl.* ~s). indifferent easy-going person. [name of Roman proconsul (Acts 18:17)]

gä'l(l)iot *n.* Dutch cargo-boat or fishing-vessel; small (usu. Mediterranean) galley. [ME, f. OF *galiote* f. It. *galeotta* f. med. L *galea* galley]

gä'llipöt *n.* small pot of earthenware, metal, etc., used for ointments etc. [prob. f. GALLEY, as being brought in galleys from the Mediterranean, + POT¹]

gä'llium *n.* soft bluish-white metallic element. [mod. L, perh. f. L *gallus* cock, transl. of *Lecoq* de Boisbaudran, name of its discoverer (1875) + -IUM]

gällivä'nt *v.i.* (colloq.) gad about; flirt. [perh. corrupt. of GALLANT 7]

gä'lliwasp (-ŏsp) *n.* W. Ind. lizard (*Diploglossus monotropis*). [18th c., of unkn. orig.]

Gällo- *comb. form.* **1.** French, as: ~MA'NIA *n.*, ~MA'NIAC *a.* & *n.*, ~PHIL(E), ~PHOBE, *ns.* & *adjs.*, ~PHO'BIA *n.* **2.** Gaul, as: ~-Ro'man *n.* & *a.*, (inhabitant or language) of Gaul when under Roman rule. [L *Gallus* a Gaul + -o-]

gä'llon *n.* measure of capacity, = 8 pints (||**imperial** ~, ||~, 4546 c.c.; ||**wine** ~, *~, 3785 c.c.) for liquids, ||corn, etc., whence ~AGE (1) *n.*; (colloq., usu. in *pl.*) large amount. [ME, f. ONF *galon*, OF *jalon*, f. Rom. *gallone*; cf. med. L *galletum*, *galleta*, OF *jaloie* liquid measure]

gallöo'n *n.* narrow close-woven braid of gold, silver, silk, cotton, nylon, etc., for binding dresses etc. [f. F *galon* (*galonner* trim with braid, of unkn. orig.)]

gä'llop *n.* & *v.* **1.** *n.* horse's or other quadruped's fastest pace, with all feet off ground together in each stride (**full** ~, **at a** ~, going thus); ride at this pace; track or ground for such riding. **2.** *v.i.* (Of horse or its rider, or of other quadruped) go at a gallop; read, recite, or talk, fast (*through, over*); move or progress rapidly (*galloping consumption, inflation*). **3.** *v.t.* make (horse etc.) gallop. **4.** Hence ~ER¹ *n.* [f. OF *galop*(*er*); see WALLOP]

Gä'llophil etc. See GALLO-.

gä'lloway (-o-) *n.* horse of small strong breed from Galloway; small horse; one of a breed of cattle from Galloway. [f. *G*~, area in SW Scotland]

gä'llows (-ŏz) *n. pl.* (usu. treated as *sing.*) structure, usu. of two uprights and cross-piece, for the hanging of criminals; punishment by hanging; ~-**bird**, person fit to be hanged; ~ **humour** (grim and ironical); ~-**tree**, gallows. [ME, f. OE *gealga* = OE *gealga*, OS, OHG *galgo*, Goth. *galga* f. Gmc *galgon*]

Gä'llup *n.* ~ **poll**, assessment of public opinion by questioning representative sample, esp. as basis of forecasts of voting etc. [f. G. H. ~, Amer. statistician b. 1901]

gä'llusès (-z) *n. pl.* (dial. & US) trouser-braces. [pl. of *gallus* var. of GALLOWS]

galöo't *n.* (colloq.) (strange or clumsy) person. [19th c. Naut. sl.; orig. unkn.]

gä'lop *n.*, & *v.i.* **1.** *n.* lively dance in duple time; music for it. **2.** *v.i.* perform this dance. [F; see GALLOP]

galō're *adv.* in abundance (*whisky galore*). [f. Ir. *go leór* to sufficiency]

galō'sh, ||**golō'sh**, *n.* overshoe usu. of rubber to keep shoe clean or dry. [ME, f. OF *galoche* f. LL *gallicula* small Gallic shoe]

galŭ'mph *v.i.* (colloq.) go prancing in triumph; move noisily or clumsily. [made by Lewis Carroll perh. on GALLOP, TRIUMPHANT]

gälvä'n|ic *a.* **1.** of, produced by, as of, galvanism (~**ic battery, pile,** former names for types of primary battery; ~**ic electricity,** electricity from a primary battery). **2.** (fig.) sudden and remarkable (*had a galvanic effect*); stimulating; full of energy (*a galvanic performance*). **3.** Hence ~ICALLY *adv.* [f. foll. + -IC]

gä'lvan|ism *n.* (Hist.) electricity from a primary battery; use of this or other direct-current electricity for medical purposes; hence ~IST (3) *n.* [f. F *galvanisme* (L. *Galvani*, It. physiologist d. 1798); see -ISM]

gä'lvaniz|e, -is|e (-īz), *v.t.* **1.** stimulate by or as if by electricity; (fig.) rouse (*into* action etc.) by shock or excitement. **2.** coat (iron) with zinc (usu. without the use of electricity) to protect it from rust; hence ~A'TION *n.* [f. F *galvaniser* (as prec.; see -IZE)]

gälvanö'meter *n.* instrument for detecting and measuring small electric currents. [f. GALVANISM + -o- + -METER]

gä'lvō *n.* (*pl.* ~s). (colloq.) = prec. [abbr.]

gä'mba *n.* (stop), organ stop with string tone. [abbr. f. (earlier sense) VIOLA¹ *da gamba*]

gambä'de, gambä'dō (*pl.* -os *or* -oes), *n.* horse's leap or bound; fantastic movement; escapade. [-*ade* F f. It. *gambata* (*gamba* leg; see -ADE 1); -*ado* f. Sp. *gambada* (*gamba* leg; see -ADO)]

gä'mbier *n.* astringent extract of Eastern plant used in tanning etc. [f. Malay *gambir* name of the plant]

gä'mbit *n.* **1.** chess opening in which player sacrifices pawn or piece to secure advantage. **2.** (fig.) opening move in discussion etc.; trick, device. [earlier *gambett* f. It. *gambetto* tripping up (*gamba* leg), -*it* = F *gambit*, Sp. -*ito*]

gä'mbl|e *v.* & *n.* **1.** *v.i.* play games of chance for money, esp. for high stakes; take great risks to secure great results in war, finance, etc.; ~**e on,** act in hope of (*gamble on its being fine tomorrow*); hence ~ER¹ *n.* **2.** *v.t.* ~**e away,** lose by gambling. **3.** *n.* gambling; risky undertaking or attempt. [f. obs. *gamel* to sport, *gamene* GAME³]

gämbo'ge (-ōō'zh, -ō'zh) *n.* gum resin from various

E. Asian trees used as yellow pigment and as purgative. [f. mod. L *gambaugium* f. *Cambodia* in SE Asia]
gă'mbol *n.*, & *v.i.* (||-ll-). caper, frisk. [f. GAMBADE]
gă'mbrel *n.* ~ (roof), roof like mansard but with gable-like ends. [f. ONF *gamberel* (*gambier* forked stick f. *gambe* leg), f. resemblance to shape of horse's hind leg]
găme¹ *n.* **1.** (form of) contest played according to rules and decided by skill, strength, or luck; ROUND¹ game; SQUARE² game; **be on, off,** one's ~, be playing well, badly; **beat** person **at his own** ~, outdo him in his chosen procedure; *the* NAME¹ *of the game*; **not in the** ~, unlikely to succeed; **play the** ~, (lit. or fig.) observe the rules, behave honourably; ~ **that two can play,** behaviour that can be copied to its originator's disadvantage; **play a good, poor,** ~ be skilful or not. **2.** (in *pl.*) (In antiquity) athletic, dramatic, and musical contests, gladiatorial etc. shows; athletic contests (*Highland Games*, OLYMPIC *Games*); athletics or sports as organized in school etc. **3.** scheme, undertaking, etc., followed up like a game (*was playing a deep, double, winning, losing*, etc., *game; so that's your* LITTLE *game; spoilt my game*); **the** ~ **is up,** success is now impossible; **play** person's ~, advance his schemes unintentionally; *game not worth the* CANDLE; **give the** ~ **away,** reveal intentions. **4.** policy, line of action, the ~, (sl.) prostitution or thieving (esp. *on the game*). **5.** (in *pl.*) dodges, tricks, (*none of your games!*). **6.** single portion of play forming a scoring unit in some contests, e.g. bridge or tennis, (~ **all,** one game scored to each side); equipment for a game; winning score in game (~ **and,** short for *game and set* in tennis); state of score in game (*the game is four all, love three,* etc.). **7.** jest (**make** ~ **of,** ridicule); diversion, spell of play (*a game of ball*); piece of fun (*was only playing a game with you*). **8.** hunted animal, quarry, object of pursuit or attack (**fair** ~, legitimately to be pursued or attacked); (collect.) wild animals, birds, fish, etc., hunted for sport or food, flesh of these, (**big** ~, lions, elephants, etc.). **9.** kept flock (of swans). **10.** ~ **act,** **law,** (usu. in *pl.*), enactment regulating killing and preservation of game; ~'**bag,** ~'**book,** (for holding, recording, game killed by sportsman); ~ **ball,** state of game in fives etc. at which one point may win; ~ **chips,** thin round potato chips served with game; ~'**cock,** ~'**fowl,** (of kind bred for cock-fighting); ~'**keeper,** man employed to breed and take care of game, prevent poaching, etc.; ~ **law,** = *game act*; ~ **licence** (to kill, or deal in, game); ~ **point,** state of game when one side needs only one more point to win it; ~**preserver,** landowner etc. who breeds game and applies game laws strictly; ~**tenant,** lessee of shooting or fishing rights; ~(**s**) **theory,** mathematical analysis of conflicts in war, economics, games of skill, etc.; ~**warden,** person locally supervising game and hunting. [OE *gamen*, = OS, OHG, ON *gaman*]
găme² *a.* like a gamecock, spirited (DIE² *game*; **as** ~ **as** *Ned Kelly,* (Austral. colloq.) very brave); having the spirit or energy *to* do; valiantly ready *for;* hence ~'**LY²** (-mlĭ) *adv.,* ~'**NESS** (-mn-) *n.* [f. GAME¹ in obs. sense 'fighting spirit']
găme³ *v.i.* play at games of chance for money, gamble; **gaming-house, -table,** (frequented for gambling); hence ~'**STER** (-tə-) *n.* [ME, f. GAME¹]
găme⁴ *a.* (Of leg, arm, etc.) lame, crippled. [18th c. dial., of unkn. orig.]
ă'melän *n.* E. Ind. orchestra, mainly of percussion instruments; kind of xylophone used in this. [Jav.]
ă'mes|man (-mzm-) *n.* (*pl.* ~**men**). exponent of gamesmanship; hence ~**manSHIP** *n.,* art or practice of winning games or other contests by psychological means rather than skill. [f. GAME¹+-*sman* as in SPORTSMAN]
ă'mesome (-ms-) *a.* merry, sportive; hence ~**LY²** (-mlĭ) *adv.,* ~**NESS** (-mn-) *n.* [ME, f. GAME¹+-SOME¹]
ămĕtă'ngi|um (-nj-) *n.* (*pl.* ~**a**). organ in which gametes are formed. [f. as foll.+Gk *aggeion* vessel]

gamēte (gamē't, gă'-) *n.* (Biol.) mature germ-cell, which unites with another in sexual reproduction; hence **gamē'tic** *a.* [f. mod. L f. Gk *gametē* wife (*gamos* marriage)]
gamē'to|phyte *n.* gamete-producing form of plant with alternation of generations; hence ~**phy'tic** *a.* [f. prec.+-o-+-PHYTE]
gă'min (-mĭn, -măn) *n.* (street) urchin; impudent child. [F]
gami'ne (-ē'n) *n.* girl gamin; small attractively informal, mischievous or elfish young woman. [F]
gă'mma *n.* third Greek letter (Γ, γ) = g; (Astron.) third brightest star in a constellation; third-class mark in examination (~ **plus,** ~ **minus,** rather better, worse, than average third-class); species of Y-moth with γ-shaped markings; ~ **radiation,** ~ **rays,** X-rays of very short wavelength emitted by radioactive substances. [ME, f. Gk]
gammā'dion *n.* arrangement of shapes of capital gamma (Γ), esp. of four as swastika or as hollow Greek cross. [late Gk (as prec.)]
gă'mmer *n.* (arch.) (Rustic name for) old woman. [prob. contr. of GODmother; *ga*- by assoc. w. *grandmother;* cf. GAFFER, GOSSIP]
gă'mmon¹ *n.,* & *v.t.* **1.** *n.* bottom piece of flitch of bacon including hind leg; ham of pig cured like bacon. **2.** *v.t.* cure (bacon). [f. ONF *gambon* (*gambe* leg; cf. JAMB)]
gă'mmon² *n.,* & *v.t.* **1.** *n.* kind of victory scoring two games at backgammon. **2.** *v.t.* defeat thus. [app. – ME *gamen* GAME¹]
gă'mmon³ *n.* & *v.i.* **1.** *n.* humbug, deception. **2.** *v.i.* talk speciously; pretend. **3.** *v.t.* hoax, deceive. [perh. as prec.]
gă'mmon⁴ *v.t.,* & *n.* (Naut.) **1.** *v.t.* lash (bowsprit) to stem. **2.** *n.* ~(**ing**), rope etc. used in such lashing. [perh. f. GAMMON¹, w. ref. to tying-up of ham]
gă'mmy *a.* (sl.) = GAME⁴. [f. dial. form of GAME⁴]
||**gămp** *n.* (colloq.) umbrella, esp. large untidy one. [f. Mrs. *Gamp* in Dickens's 'Martin Chuzzlewit']
gă'mut *n.* **1.** (Mus.) lowest note in medieval sequence of hexachords = modern G on lowest line of bass staff; whole series of notes used in medieval or modern music; major diatonic scale; people's or period's recognized scale; voice's or instrument's compass. **2.** whole series or range or scope of anything (*the whole gamut of crime; run up and down the gamut*). [f. med. L *gamma ut* (GAMMA taken as name for note one tone lower than A of classical scale, *ut* first of six arbitrary names of notes forming hexachord, being the italicized syllables of a 7th-c. Latin hymn: *Ut queant laxis resonare fibris Mira gestorum famuli tuorum, Solve polluti labii reatum, Sancte Iohannes*)]
gă'm|ў *a.* = GAME²; having flavour or scent of game kept till it is high; *scandalous, sensational; hence ~**iLY¹** *adv.,* ~**iNESS** *n.* [f. GAME¹,²+-Y²]
gă'nder *n.,* & *v.i.* **1.** *n.* male goose (**sauce for the goose is sauce for the** ~, what is permissible in one case should be so in other comparable ones); fool, simpleton. **2.** *n.,* & *v.i.* (sl.) look, glance. [OE *gan(d)ra* = MLG *ganre,* LG, Du. *gander;* cogn. w. GANNET]
gă'ndў *a.* ~ **dancer,** (sl.) railway maintenance worker. [20th c. orig. uncert.]
găng¹ *n.* & *v.* **1.** *n.* company of workmen, of slaves or prisoners; band of persons acting or going about together, esp. for criminal purpose or (colloq.) other purpose causing disapproval; set of tools etc. arranged to work simultaneously; ~**bang,** ~**shag,** (sl.) successive copulation of group of men with one woman on same occasion; ~'**board,** ~'**plank,** movable plank usu. with cleats nailed on it for walking into or out of boat etc.; ~'**land,** domain of gangsters; ~ **rape,** successive rape by group of persons on same occasion; *gang* WAR¹. **2.** *v.i.* join *up with,* act in concert *with;* ~ **up on,** (colloq.) combine against; ~**up** *n.,* (colloq.) act of ganging up. **3.** *v.t.*

arrange (tools etc.) to work in co-ordination. [f. ON *gangr, ganga* GOING[1], = OE, OS, OHG *gang*, Goth. *gaggs*, Gmc f. *gangan GO[1]]

gäng[2] *v.i.* (Sc.) go; ∼ **agley,** (of plan etc.) go wrong. [OE *gangan*; cf. GANG[1], GO[1]]

‖**gä′nger** *n.* foreman of gang of workmen. [f. GANG[1] + -ER[1]]

Gänge′tic (-nj-) *a.* of the river Ganges. [f. L *Gangeticus* f. Gk *Gangēs*; see -IC]

gä′ng-gäng *n.* (Austral.) small grey cockatoo, the male being red-crested. [Aboriginal]

gä′ngle (-nggel) *v.i.* move ungracefully. [back-form. f. foll.]

gä′ngling, gä′nglў, (-ngg-) *a.* (Of person) loosely built, lanky. [f. *gangle frequent. of GANG[2]]

gä′ngli|on (-ngg-) *n.* (*pl.* ∼**a** *or* ∼**ons**). enlargement or knot on nerve, containing assemblage of nerve--cells; mass of grey matter in central nervous system forming a nerve-nucleus; (Path.) cyst esp. on tendon--sheath; (fig.) centre of force, activity, or interest; hence ∼**onāt**ED[1], **gängliŏ′n**IC (-ngg-), ∼**FORM**, *adjs.* [f. Gk *gagglion*]

gä′ngrēne (-ngg-) *n.* & *v.* **1.** *n.* necrosis, usu. with decomposition, of part of the body, usu. caused by obstructed circulation; (fig.) moral corruption; hence **gä′ngrēn**OUS (-ngg-) *a.* **2.** *v.i.* & *t.* become affected, affect, with gangrene. [f. F *gangrène* f. L f. Gk *gaggraina*]

gä′ngster *n.* member of a gang of violent criminals; hence ∼ISM (1) *n.* [f. GANG[1] + -STER]

gängue (-ng) *n.* valueless earth etc. in which ore is found. [F, f. G *gang* lode = GANG[1]]

gä′ngway *n.* & *int.* **1.** *n.* ‖passage esp. between rows of seats (in House of Commons, cross-passage half-way down giving access to back benches; members **above, below,** ∼ are more, less, closely associated with official policy of their party); passage etc. on ship, esp. platform connecting quarterdeck and forecastle; opening in bulwarks by which ship is entered or left; bridge laid from ship to shore, on building site, etc. **2.** *int.* make way! [17th c., f. GANG[1] + WAY]

gä′nister *n.* close-grained hard siliceous stone found in the lower coal-measures of South Yorkshire, and used for furnace-linings. [19th c.; orig. unkn.]

gä′nja *n.* marijuana. [f. Hindi *gānjhā*]

gä′nnet *n.* sea-bird of genus *Sula*, esp. solan goose, *Sula bassana*, whence ∼RY (3) *n.*; (sl.) greedy person. [OE *ganot*, = MHG *ganiz, genz,* OHG *ganazzo* f. Gmc *ganitaz, *ganoton; cogn. w. GANDER]

gä′noid *a.* & *n.* **1.** *a.* (Of fish-scale) enamelled, smooth and bright; having ganoid scales. **2.** *n.* ganoid fish. [f. F *ganoïde* f. Gk *ganos* brightness; see -OID]

***gä′ntlet.** See GAUNTLET[2].

gä′ntrў *n.* structure supporting travelling crane, railway or road signals, equipment to prepare rocket for launching, etc.; (also **gau′ntry**) wooden stand for barrels. [prob. f. dial. form of GALLON + TREE]

‖**gaol** (jāl), **jail,** *n.,* & *v.t.* (g- in official use, g- and j- in literary use, j- in US). **1.** *n.* public prison for detention of persons committed by process of law; confinement in this; ∼**′bird,** prisoner, habitual criminal, rogue; ∼**′break,** escape from gaol; ∼ **delivery,** clearing of gaol esp. formerly at assizes by trying all prisoners awaiting trial; ∼ **fever,** virulent typhus formerly endemic in gaols. **2.** *v.t.* put in gaol. [ME, f. ONF *ga(i)ole* & OF *jaiole, jeole* f. Rom. dim. of L *cavea* CAGE]

‖**gao′ler** (jā′l-), **jai′ler, jai′lor,** *n.* (see prec.) person in charge of gaol or prisoners in it. [f. as prec. + -ER[2] (2)]

gäp *n.* breach in hedge or fence or wall; gorge, pass; unfilled space or interval, blank, break in continuity (**bridge, close, fill, stop, a** ∼, make up deficiency; ∼**-toothed** *a.*, having gaps between teeth); wide (usu. undesirable) divergence in views, sympathies, development, etc., (CREDIBILITY *gap,* GENERATION *gap*); hence ∼**p**ED[2] (-pt), ∼**′p**Y[2], *adjs.* [ME, f. ON, = chasm, cogn. w. foll.]

gäpe *v.i.,* & *n.* **1.** *v.i.* open mouth wide, (of mouth, oyster, wound, chasm, etc.) open or be open wide; split, part asunder; stare, gaze curiously, *at*; yawn. **2.** *n.* yawn; open-mouthed stare; **the** ∼**s,** disease of birds with gaping as symptom, caused by nematode ∼**′worm** in windpipe, (joc.) fit of yawning. **3.** expanse of open mouth or beak; part of beak that opens; rent, opening. [ME, f. ON *gapa* cogn. w. MHG *gaffen*]

gä′per *n.* In vbl senses; the comber fish, which gapes when dead; bivalve mollusc of genus *Mya,* with shell open at one or both ends; (colloq.) easy catch at cricket. [f. GAPE + -ER[1]]

gär. See GARFISH.

gä′rage (-ahzh, -ij) *n.,* & *v.t.* **1.** *n.* building or shed for storage of motor vehicle(s); establishment selling petrol etc., or repairing and selling motor vehicles. **2.** *v.t.* put or keep (motor vehicle) in garage. [F (*garer* shelter; see -AGE)]

gärb *n.,* & *v.t.* **1.** *n.* dress, costume, esp. of distinctive kind; way one is dressed. **2.** *v.t.* attire; (usu. in *pass.* or *refl.*) dress. [obs. F *garbe* f. It. *garbo* grace, f. Gmc, cogn. w. GEAR]

F *garbe* f. It. *garbo* f. Gmc, cogn. w. GEAR]

gär′bage *n.* refuse, filth; domestic waste (*∼ **can,** dustbin); foul or rubbishy literature etc. [AF; orig. unkn.]

gär′ble *v.t.* make (usu. unfair or malicious) selections from (facts, statements, etc.); mutilate in order to misrepresent; unintentionally distort or confuse (facts, statement, message, etc.). [f. It. *garbellare* f. Arab. *ġarbala* sift (cf. *ġirbāl* sieve), perh. f. LL *cribellare* to sieve f. L *cribrum* sieve]

gär′board (-berd) *n.* ∼ (**strake**), first range of planks laid on ship's bottom next to keel; corresponding plates in iron ship. [f. Du. *gaarboord* (perh. as GATHER, BOARD[1])]

garçon (gär′sawn) *n.* waiter in French restaurant, hotel, etc. [F, lit. 'boy']

gär′den *n.,* & *v.i.* **1.** *n.* piece of ground devoted to growing flowers, fruit, or vegetables (KITCHEN *garden*; ‖MARKET[1] *garden*; **everything in the** ∼ **is lovely,** (colloq.) all is well; **lead up the** ∼ (**path**), (colloq.) entice, mislead. **2.** ornamental grounds for public resort (*botanical, zoological,* etc., *garden* or *gardens*); similar place with service of refreshments (*beer, tea, garden*); *large public hall; especially fertile region (**the** ∼ **of England,** Kent, Vale of Evesham, etc.); ‖(usu. in *pl.* w. name prefixed, as *Onslow, Spring, Gardens*) street, square, etc.; **the G**∼, philosophy or school of Epicurus (cf. ACADEMY, LYCEUM, PORCH). **3.** (*attrib.,* with or without hyphen) cultivated, not wild (*garden plants*; *garden-cress*); **common or** ∼, (colloq.) ordinary; ∼ **centre,** establishment where gardening tools, plants, etc., are sold; ∼ **chair,** ∼ **roller,** ∼ **seat,** (for use in a garden); ∼ **city,** industrial or other town laid out systematically with spacious and garden-like surroundings; so ‖∼ **suburb,** ‖∼ **village;** ∼ **party,** social event on lawn or in garden. ***G**∼ **State,** New Jersey; ∼ **stuff,** vegetables etc. from garden; hence ∼ **warbler,** a woodland bird (*Sylvia borin*). **4.** Hence ∼E′SQUE *a.* **5.** *v.i.* cultivate, work in, a garden; hence ∼ING[1] (1) (-dn-) *n.* [ME, f. ONF *gardin* (OF *jardin*) f. Rom. *gardino f. Gmc *gardon; cf. YARD[2]]

gär′dener (-dn-) *n.* person who gardens; person employed to tend a garden; (**jobbing**) ∼, employee working in garden at intervals; ∼**-bird,** bower-bird making 'garden' of moss etc. in front of bower; ∼′s **garters,** ribbon-grass. [ME, f. ONF *gardinier (OF *jard-*), f. as prec. + -ER[2] (2)]

gärdē′nia *n.* tree or shrub of genus *Gardenia,* with large white or yellow flowers and usu. fragrant scent, flower of this. [mod. L, f. name of Dr A. *Garden,* Sc naturalist d. 1791 + IA[1]]

gär′efowl (gār′f-) *n.* the great AUK. [f. Icel. *geirfugl* (*geir* of doubtful meaning; see FOWL]

gär′fish *n.* (*pl.* same). fish with long spearlike snout, o genus *Belone* (needlefish), **Lepisosteus* (gar), or (Austral. & NZ) *Hyporhynchus* (halfbeak). [app. f. OE *gār* spear + *fisc* FISH[1]]

gār′ganey *n.* a duck (*Anas querquedula*). [f. It., dial. var. of *garganello*]

gārgă′ntūan *a.* enormous, gigantic. [f. *Gargantua*, giant in Rabelais's book so named + -AN]

gār′gĕt (-g-) *n.* inflammation of cow's or ewe's udder; *pokeweed. [perh. f. obs. *garget* throat f. OF *gargate*, *-guete*]

gār′gle *v.* & *n.* **1.** *v.t.* & *i.* wash (mouth and throat), esp. for medicinal purposes, with liquid kept in motion by breath; make sound as when doing this. **2.** *n.* liquid used thus. [f. F *gargouiller* (*gargouille*; see foll.)]

gār′goyle *n.* grotesque spout usu. in form of human or animal mouth, head, or body, projecting from gutter of (esp. Gothic) building to carry water clear of wall. [f. OF *gargouille* throat, gargoyle]

gārība′ldi (-baw′l-) *n.* kind of woman's or child's loose blouse, orig. of bright red material; ‖biscuit containing layer of currants; *small Californian fish (*Hypsypops rubicundus*). [f. (red shirts of) G. *Garibaldi* (It. patriot d. 1882) and his followers]

gār′ish *a.* obtrusively bright, showy; gaudy, over-decorated; hence ∼LY[2] *adv.*, ∼NESS *n.* [16th c. *gaurish* app. irreg. f. obs. *gaure* stare + -ISH[1]]

gār′land *n.*, & *v.t.* **1.** *n.* wreath of flowers, leaves, etc., worn on head or hung on something as decoration; distinction, palm, prize, for victory etc.; anthology, miscellany; metal etc. object resembling garland. **2.** *v.t.* crown with garland; deck with garlands; serve as garland to. [ME, f. OF *ger-*, *garlande*, of unkn. orig.]

gār′lic *n.* (plant of genus *Allium* with) bulbous strong-smelling pungent-tasting root used as flavouring in cookery; hence ∼KY[2] *a.* (esp. of smell). [OE *gārleac* (*gār* spear; see LEEK)]

gār′ment *n.*, & *v.t.* **1.** *n.* article of dress; (in *pl.*) clothes; outward and visible covering of anything. **2.** *v.t.* (rhet., usu. in *p.p.*) attire. [ME f. OF *garnement* (as GARNISH; see -MENT)]

gārn *int.* (colloq.) expr. disbelief or ridicule. [repr. cockney pronunc. of *go on*]

gār′ner *v.t.*, & *n.* **1.** *v.t.* store, deposit; collect. **2.** *n.* (literary) storehouse, granary, (lit. or fig.). [ME, v. f. n. f. OF *gernier* f. L *granarium* GRANARY]

gār′nĕt[1] *n.* vitreous silicate mineral, of which transparent deep-red kind is used as gem. [ME, f. OF *grenat* f. med. L *granatum* POMEGRANATE, f. resemblance to the pulp of the fruit]

Gār′nĕt[2] *n.* (all) **Sir** ∼, (sl.) satisfactory. [f. Sir ∼ Wolseley, Brit. mil. commander d. 1913]

gār′nish *v.t.*, & *n.* **1.** *v.t.* decorate, embellish, (esp. dish for table); (Law) serve notice on (person) for purpose of legally seizing money belonging to debtor or defendant; summon (person) as party to litigation started between others; hence ∼MENT *n.* **2.** *n.* ∼(ing), decorative or savoury addition, esp. to dish for table, or (fig.) of literary embellishments. [ME, f. OF *garnir* (-ISH[2]) f. Gmc *warnjan* guard]

gār′nishee′ *n.*, & *v.t.* (Law). **1.** *n.* person garnished. **2.** *v.t.* garnish (person); attach (money etc.) by way of garnishment. [f. prec. + -EE]

gār′niture *n.* appurtenances, accessories; adornment, trimmings esp. of dish. [F (as GARNISH; see -URE)]

garŏ′tte. See GARROTTE.

gār′pike *n.* needlefish or gar (see GARFISH). [f. *gar* + PIKE[3]]

gă′rrĕt *n.* room (esp. wretched) on top floor or partly or entirely in roof; attic; hence ∼EER′ *n.*, dweller in garret, esp. literary hack. [ME, f. OF *garite* watch-tower (*garir* f. Gmc *warjan* defend)]

gă′rrison *n.*, & *v.t.* **1.** *n.* troops stationed in fortress, town, etc., to defend it; building they occupy; ∼ **town** (having permanent garrison). **2.** *v.t.* furnish with or occupy as garrison; place (troops, soldier) on garrison duty. [ME, f. OF *garison* (*garir*; see GARRET, -ISON) defence, w. sense of F & obs. E *garnison* (GARNISH)]

gar(r)ŏ′tt\|e, ***garrŏ′t\|e**, *n.*, & *v.t.* **1.** *n.* Spanish method of capital punishment by strangulation; apparatus used in it; highway robbery in which victim is throttled. **2.** *v.t.* execute or kill by strangulation; throttle in order to rob. [f. F *garrotter* or Sp. *garrotear* (*garrote* a cudgel, of unkn. orig.)]

gă′rrulous (-rōō-) *a.* given to talk, esp. on unimportant matters; loquacious, wordy; (of bird, stream, etc.) chattering, babbling; hence or cogn. ∼LITY (-rōō′-), ∼NESS, *ns.*, ∼LY[2] *adv.* [f. L *garrulus* (*garrire* chatter) + -OUS]

Gă′rrў *n.* ∼ **oak**, a N. Amer. oak (*Quercus garryana*). [f. N. ∼, Hudson's Bay Co. officer d. 1856]

gă′rrўa *n.* ornamental catkin-bearing evergreen shrub of genus *Garrya*. [mod. L, f. as prec. + -A 1]

gār′ter *n.*, & *v.t.* **1.** *n.* band worn to keep a sock or stocking up (‖**the G**∼, (badge of) highest order in English knighthood, membership of this); ‖(**G**∼) = *Garter King of Arms* (KING[1] 7); *suspender for sock or stocking; *∼**belt**, suspender belt; ∼**snake**, striped snake of N. Amer. (*Thamnophis*) or S. Afr. (*Elaps*); ∼ **stitch**, plain knitting stitch or pattern, forming ridges in alternate rows. **2.** *v.t.* fasten (stocking), encircle (leg), with garter. [ME, f. OF *gartier* (*garet* bend of knee, perh. f. Celt.)]

‖gārth *n.* **1.** (arch. or prov.) close, yard; garden, paddock. **2.** open space within cloisters. [ME, f. ON *garthr* = OE *geard* YARD[2]]

gar′uda (gār′ōōdah) *n.* fabulous partly human bird of Indian myth; national emblem of Indonesia. [f. Skr. *garudá*]

gās[1] *n.* (*pl.* ∼es *pr.* gă′sĭz). **1.** any airlike or completely elastic fluid (esp. one that does not become liquid or solid at ordinary temperatures, other gases being usu. called 'vapours'); such fluid, esp. COAL *gas*, or **natural** ∼ (found in earth's crust, not manufactured), used for lighting, heating, or cooking. **2.** *(colloq.) petrol, gasoline [abbr.]; **step on the** ∼, accelerate motor vehicle by pressing down accelerator pedal with foot, (fig.) hurry. **3.** explosive mixture of firedamp with air; hydrogen, helium, etc., used to fill balloon or airship; nitrous oxide or other gas as (esp. dental) anaesthetic; (**poison**) ∼, gas or vapour used to disable enemy in war. **4.** jet of gas used for lighting. **5.** (colloq.) pointless talk, boasting, humbug, windbag eloquence. **6.** (sl.) very attractive or impressive person or thing. **7.** Hence **gā′seous** *a.*, ∼′ify *v.t.*, ∼′ifica′tion *n.* **8.** ∼′**bag**, bag for holding gas, balloon's or airship's gas-container, (derog.) empty talker; ∼ **bracket**, pipe with gas-burner(s) projecting from wall; ∼ **chamber** (used to kill animals or prisoners by gas poisoning); ∼ **chromatography** (using carrier gas as moving medium); ∼ **cooker** (heated by gas); ∼**cooled**, (of engine etc.) cooled by current of gas; ∼ **engine, motor**, internal combustion engine using mixture of gas and air as fuel; ∼ **fire**, domestic heater (usu. fixed) burning gas; ∼**fired**, using gas as fuel; ∼**fitter**, workman providing house with ∼**fittings**, apparatus for heating etc. with gas; ∼ **gangrene** (rapidly spreading, with evolution of gas); ∼ **helmet**, ∼ **mask**, kinds of appliance including respirator worn as defence against poison gas; ∼′**holder**, large receptacle for storing gas, gasometer; ∼′**light**, light given by (esp. coal) gas, jet of burning gas; ∼ **lighter**, (1) device for igniting gas, (2) lighter for cigarettes etc. with gaseous fuel; ∼ **main**, main pipe supplying gas; ∼′**man**, man employed in manufacture of gas, collector of sums due for gas-supply, gas-fitter; ∼ **mask** (as *gas helmet*); ∼ **meter**, apparatus registering amount of gas consumed; ∼ **motor** (as *gas engine*); ∼ **oil**, kind of fuel-oil distilled from petroleum, heavier than paraffin oil; ∼ **oven**, = *Quercus cooker* or *gas chamber*; ∼ **poker**, hollow poker through which gas flows to be ignited and kindle fire; *gas*-PROOF[2]; *∼ **range**, = *gas cooker*; ∼ **ring** (perforated, hollow, and fed with gas for cooking etc.); *∼ **station**, filling-station; ∼ **stove** (heated by gas); *gas-TIGHT*; ∼ **turbine** (driven by gas flow or by gas from combustion); ∼'**works**, place where gas is manufactured. [wd invented by J. B. van Helmont, Belgian chemist d. 1644, after Gk *khaos* chaos]

găs² *v.* (-ss-). **1.** *v.t.* expose to gas; *∼ (**up**), (colloq.) fill (motor-vehicle tank) with petrol; (in *p.p.*) killed or disabled by gas, (sl.) drunk. **2.** *v.i.* (colloq.) talk idly or pointlessly or boastfully; hence ∼'SER¹ *n.*, empty talker, (sl.) very attractive or impressive person or thing. [f. prec.]

Gă'scon *n.* native of Gascony; braggart; so **gǎsconA'DE** *n.*, boasting. [F, f. L *Vasco -onis*]

gă'sèous. See GAS¹ 7.

găsh¹ *n.*, & *v.t.* **1.** *n.* long and deep slash, cut, or wound; cleft such as might be made by slashing cut; act of making such cut. **2.** *v.t.* make gash in, cut. [16th c., var. of ME *garse* v. & n., f. OF **garce* (*garcer* scarify, wound)]

∥**găsh²** *a.* (sl.) spare, extra. [20th c. Naut. sl.; orig. unkn.]

gă'sify etc. See GAS¹ 7.

gă'skét *n.* small cord for securing furled sail to yard; strip of tow etc. for packing piston or caulking joint; flat sheet or ring of rubber, asbestos, etc., to seal junction of metal surfaces. [perh. alt. of obs. *gassit* f. F *garcette* little girl, thin rope]

gă'skin *n.* hinder part of horse's thigh. [perh. erron. f. GALLIGASKINS]

****gă'sohŏl** *n.* mixture of petrol and alcohol as fuel. [f. GAS¹ 2 + ALCOHOL]

gă'soline (-ēn), **gă'solēne**, *n.* **1.** volatile inflammable liquid got by distilling petroleum and used for heating and lighting. **2.** *petrol. [f. GAS¹ + -OL + -INE⁵, -ENE]

gǎsŏ'mĕter *n.* large reservoir in which gas is stored for distribution by pipes; (Chem.) vessel for holding gas. [f. F *gazomètre* (*gaz* GAS¹, *-mètre* -METER)]

gasp (gah-) *v.* & *n.* **1.** *v.i.* catch breath, strain *for* air or breath, with open mouth as in exhaustion or astonishment. **2.** *v.t.* ∼ **life** etc. **away** or **out**, expire; ∼ (**out**), utter with gasps. **3.** Hence ∼'ER¹ *n.*, (∥esp., sl.) (cheap) cigarette. **4.** *n.* convulsive catching of breath; **at one's last** ∼, at point of death, (fig.) exhausted. [ME, f. ON *geispa*; cf. *geip* idle talk]

găspereau (gǎ'sperō, -rŏ') *n.* (*pl.* **-s** *or* **-x**, *pr.* -z). (Can.) the alewife fish. [f. Can. F *gaspareau, gasparot*]

gă'ssý *a.* of, full of, like, gas; (colloq., of talk etc.) pointless, verbose. [f. GAS¹ + -Y²]

gă'steropŏd. Var. of GASTROPOD.

ga'sthaus (gah'st-hows) *n.* small German inn or hotel. [G (*gast* GUEST, *haus* HOUSE¹)]

gă'stric *a.* of the stomach; *gastric* INFLUENZA; ∼ **juice**, thin clear nearly colourless acid fluid secreted by stomach glands and used in digestion. [f. mod. L *gastricus* f. Gk (as foll.; see -IC)]

gǎstrō- *comb. form.* stomach, as: ∼-**ente'ric**, of stomach and intestines; *gastro-enteri'*TIS, *gastrE'*CTOMY, *gastri'*TIS, *ga'stros*COPE, *ns.* [f. Gk *gastēr -(e)ros* stomach + -o-]

gǎ'stronōme *n.* judge of good eating and drinking. [F, back-form. f. *gastronomie*; see foll.]

gǎstrŏ'nomý *n.* art and science of good eating and drinking; hence or cogn. **gǎstronŏ'mIC** *a.* [f. F *gastronomie* f. Gk *gastronomia* (GASTRO-, *-nomia* f. *nomos* law)]

gă'stropŏd *n.* mollusc (e.g. snail, limpet) of class Gastropoda, with locomotive organ placed ventrally; hence **gǎstrŏ'podOUS** *a.* [f. F *gastéropode* f. mod. L *gasteropoda* f. as GASTRO- + Gk *pous podos* foot]

gă'stroscōpe. See GASTRO-.

gă'strula (-rŏŏ-) *n.* (*pl.* ∼e). (Zool.) embryonic stage developing from blastula. [mod. L, f. Gk *gastēr* belly; see -ULE]

găt¹ *n.* (sl.) revolver or other firearm. [abbr. of GATLING]

găt². See GET¹.

gāte¹ *n.*, & *v.t.* **1.** *n.* opening in wall of city, enclosure, or large building, made for entrance and exit and capable of being closed with barrier; mountain pass; means of entrance or exit; numbered place of access to aircraft at airport; (sl.) mouth; **(sl.) dismissal; ∼ **of ivory, horn,** by which false, true, dreams come. **2.** barrier closing the opening of a wall, road, or passage; wooden or iron framework, solid or of bars or gratings, hung on hinges, turning on pivots, or sliding, single or double; arrangement of slots into which motor-vehicle gear lever moves to engage different gears; device for holding frame of cine film momentarily in position behind lens of camera or projector; electrical signal that causes or controls passage of other signals; electrical circuit with one output that depends on combination of several input signals; contrivance regulating passage of water in lock etc.; number entering by payment at gates to see football match etc.; ∼(-**money**), amount of money thus taken. **3.** ∼'**crasher**, uninvited intruder at party etc.; so ∼'**crash** *v.*; ∼'**fold**, folded oversize page in magazine etc.; ∼'**house**, lodge of park etc., entrance building of castle, (Hist.) room over city gate often used as prison; ∼'**keeper**, (1) attendant at gate, (2) large brown species of butterfly; ∼'**leg**(**ged**), (of table) having legs in gatelike frame swinging back to allow top to fold down; ∼'**man**, = *gate-keeper* (1); ∼'**post** (on which gate is hung or against which it shuts; *between you and me and the* ∼*post*, in strict confidence); ∼'**way**, = gate (first sense), frame of or structure built over gate, means of entrance or exit (lit. or fig.). **4.** *v.t.* ∥confine to college or school entirely or after certain hours. [OE *gæt, geat*, pl. *gatu*, = OS, ON *gat* f. Gmc **gatam*]

gāte² *n.* (With prefixed name in N. England etc.) street. [ME, f. ON *gata*, = OHG *gazza*, Goth. *gatwō* f. Gmc **gatwōn*]

gǎ'teau (-tō) *n.* (*pl.* **-s** *or* **-x**, *pr.* -z). large rich cream-cake. [F *gâteau* cake]

gǎ'ther (-dh-) *v.* **1.** *v.t.* bring together, cause to assemble; **be** ∼**ed to** one's **fathers,** die. **2.** acquire by gradually collecting, amass; pluck (flowers etc.); collect (grain etc.) as harvest; pick *up* from ground; infer, deduce, (*that*); receive addition of (*rolling stone gathers no* MOSS; *unread books gathering dust*; *train gathered speed*; *invalid gathers strength*; ∼ **way,** (of ship) begin to move). **3.** summon up (energy); gain or recover (breath); draw (garment, fabric, brow) together in folds or wrinkles, esp. pucker (part of dress) by running thread through, (∼**ed skirt,** with gathers at waist); draw *up* (limbs, one*self*) into smaller compass; sum *up* (scattered facts); summon *up* (thoughts, strength, etc.) for an effort. **4.** Hence (-)∼ER¹ *n.* **5.** *v.i.* come together, congregate, form a mass; receive additions; come to a head, develop purulent swelling. [OE *gaderian*, = MLG *gadern*, f. WG **gadurōjan* (**gaduri* together)]

gă'thering (-dh-) *n.* in vbl senses; assembly, meeting, e.g. in Scottish Highlands, cf. Highland GAME¹s; purulent swelling; group of leaves taken together in bookbinding. [f. GATHER + -ING¹]

gă'thers (-dherz) *n. pl.* part of garment that is gathered or drawn in. [f. GATHER + -s¹]

Gǎ'tling *n.* ∼ (**gun**), machine-gun with clustered barrels. [f. R.J. ∼, Amer. inventor d. 1903]

'gǎ'tor** *n.* (colloq.) alligator. [abbr.]

GATT (gǎt) *abbr.* General Agreement on Tariffs and Trade.

gauche (gōsh) *a.* tactless; without ease or grace, socially awkward; hence ∼'NESS *n.* [F, = left(-handed), awkward]

gau'cherie (gō'sherē) *n.* gauche manners; a gauche action. [F]

gau'chō (gow'-, gaw'-) *n.* (*pl.* ∼**s**). one of a mixed European and Amer. Ind. people of mounted herdsmen in S. America. [Sp., f. Quechua]

gaud *n.* gaudy thing, showy ornament; (in *pl.*) showy

ceremonies. [perh. thr. AF f. OF *gaudir* rejoice f. L *gaudēre*]

||**gau'dy**[1] *n.* annual feast or entertainment, esp. college dinner for old members etc. [f. L *gaudium* joy or *gaude* imper. of *gaudēre* rejoice]

gau'dy[2] *a.* tastelessly or inappropriately fine, showy, or brilliant (of dress, decoration, literary style, etc.); hence ~ɪʟʏ[2] *adv.*, ~ɪɴᴇss *n.* [prob. f. GAUD + -ʏ[2]]

gauge[1] (gāj), *****gāge**[2] (also || in sense 2), *n.* **1.** standard measure to which things must conform, esp. measure of capacity or contents of barrel, fineness of textile, diameter of bullet, or thickness of sheet metal; capacity, extent, scope (**take the ~ of,** estimate); distance between pair of rails or opposite wheels. **2.** (Naut.; usu. *gage.*) relative position with respect to wind; **have the weather ~ of,** be to windward of, (fig.) have advantage of. **3.** graduated instrument measuring force or quantity of rainfall, stream, tide, wind, etc. (**~ pressure,** amount by which pressure exceeds that of atmosphere); contrivance attached to vessel to show height of its contents; instrument for testing and verifying dimensions of tools, wire, etc.; carpenter's adjustable tool for marking parallel lines; (Print.) strip regulating depth of margin etc.; means of estimating, criterion, test. [ME, f. ONF *gauge* (OF *jauge*), of unkn. orig.]

gauge[2] (gāj), *****gāge**[3], *v.t.* measure exactly (esp. objects of standard size, as wire, bolts; fluctuating quantities or forces, as rainfall, wind; depth of liquid content); find capacity or content of (cask etc.) by measurement and calculation; estimate, take measure of, (person, character); make uniform, bring to standard size or shape; hence ~'ABLE (-ja-) *a.*, **gau'gER**[1] (1, 2) (gā'j-) *n.*, (esp.) exciseman. [ME, f. ONF *gauger* (prec.)]

Gaul *n.* inhabitant of ancient Gaul. [f. *Gaul* the country f. F *Gaule* f. Gmc *walhoz* foreigners]

gau'leiter (gow'līter) *n.* Nazi district political leader; (fig.) local or petty tyrant. [G (*gau* administrative district, *leiter* leader)]

Gau'lish *a.* & *n.* (language) of ancient Gauls. [f. GAUL + -ɪsʜ[1]]

Gau'll|ism (gō'-) *n.* (adherence to) principles and policies of Charles de Gaulle, Fr. military and political leader (d. 1970); so ~ɪsᴛ (2) *n.* [f. F *Gaullisme*; see -ɪsᴍ]

Gau'loise (gō'lwahz) *n.* (P) brand of French cigarettes. [F (*gaulois* Gallic)]

gault *n.* (Geol.) series of clay and marl beds between upper and lower greensand in S. England; clay obtained from these. [16th c., of unkn. orig.]

gaulthēr'ia *n.* evergreen aromatic plant of genus *Gaultheria,* some species of which yield medicinal oil. [f. J.-F. *Gaultier,* Can. botanist d. 1756 + -ɪA[1]]

gaunt *a.* lean, haggard; grim or desolate looking; so ~'ɴᴇss *n.* [ME, of unkn. orig.]

gau'ntlet[1] *n.* stout glove with long loose wrist for driving, fencing, wicket-keeping, etc.; wide wrist-part of glove; (Hist.) armoured glove; (fig.) **fling, throw, down the ~,** issue challenge; **pick, take, up the ~,** accept challenge. [ME, f. OF *gantelet* (*gant* glove f. Gmc *want-*; see -ʟᴇᴛ)]

gau'ntlet[2], *****gä'ntlet,** *n.* **run the ~,** pass between rows of persons who strike one with sticks, cords, etc., as military, naval, or school punishment (also fig., of being subjected to criticism). [earlier *gantlope* f. Sw. *gatlopp* (*gata* lane, *lopp* course), w. assim. to prec.]

gau'ntry *see* GANTRY.

gaur (gowr) *n.* wild ox (*Bibos gaurus*) of E. Asia. [Hind.]

gauss (gows) *n.* (*pl.* same or ~'es). electromagnetic unit of magnetic induction. [f. K. *Gauss,* Ger. mathematician d. 1855]

gauz|e *n.* thin transparent fabric of silk, cotton, etc.; fine mesh of wire, etc.; slight haze; hence ~'ʏ[2] *a.* [f. F *gaze* f. *Gaza* in Palestine]

gāve. *See* GIVE[1].

gă'vel *n.*, & *v.i.* (||-ll-). **1.** *n.* auctioneer's hammer; chairman's or judge's hammer for calling attention etc. **2.** *v.i.* use gavel. [19th c., of unkn. orig.]

||**gă'velkind** *n.* (Hist.) form of land-tenure (esp. in Kent) with equal division of intestate's property among sons. [ME, f. OE *gafolgecynd (*gafol* tribute, *gecynd* KIND[1])]

gä'vial *n.* long-snouted Asian crocodile. [F, f. Hind.]

gavŏ'tte *n.* medium-paced dance of 18th c.; music for it; piece of music in common time, each phrase beginning on third beat of bar. [F, f. Prov. *gavoto* (*Gavot* native of region in Alps)]

Gawd *n.* (vulg. or sl. pr. of) God.

gawk[1] *n.* awkward or bashful person. [rel. to obs. *gaw* gaze (f. ON *gá* heed) and GAWK[2]]

gawk[2] *v.t.* (colloq.) stare stupidly. [rel. to obs. *gaw* (see prec.) and GAWK[1]]

gaw'k|y *a.* & *n.* awkward, ungainly, bashful, (person); hence ~ɪʟʏ[2] *adv.*, ~ɪɴᴇss *n.* [f. GAWK[1] or GAWK[2] + -ʏ[2]]

gawp *v.i.* = GAWK[2]. [earlier *gaup, galp* f. ME *galpen* yawn, cogn. w. YELP]

gay *a.* & *n.* **1.** *a.* full of or disposed to or indicating mirth; light-hearted, carefree, sportive; airy, offhand. **2.** (euphem.) dissolute, immoral; (sl.) homosexual, frequented by homosexuals. **3.** showy, brilliant, bright-coloured; finely dressed or decorated *with.* **4.** Hence **gai'**ʟʏ[2] *adv.* ~'ɴᴇss *n.* **5.** *n.* (sl.) homosexual. [ME, f. OF *gai,* of unkn. orig.]

*****gay'ety.** *See* GAIETY.

*****gazā'bō, *****gazē'bō**[2], *n.* (*pl.* ~s). (sl., often derog.) person. [19th c.; orig. unkn.]

gazā'nia *n.* S. Afr. herb of genus *Gazania,* with showy yellow or orange flowers. [18th c., f. Theodore of *Gaza,* Greek scholar d. 1478 + -ɪA[1]]

gāze *v.i.,* & *n.* **1.** *v.i.* look fixedly (*at, on, upon*). **2.** *n.* intent look; **at ~,** gazing in wonder etc. [ME, orig. unkn., but cf. obs. *gaw* (GAWK[1])]

gazē'bō[1] *n.* (*pl.* ~s or ~es). structure whence a view may be had; belvedere, turret, balcony, etc. [perh. joc. formation f. prec. on L future (cf. LAVABO)]

*****gazē'bō**[2]. *See* GAZABO.

gazĕ'lle *n.* small graceful soft-eyed Asian or African antelope, esp. of genus *Gazella.* [F, prob. f. Sp. *gacela* f. Arab. *ğazāl*]

gazĕ'tte *n.,* & *v.t.* **1.** *n.* (Hist.) news-sheet, periodical publication giving current events. **2.** ||**London G~,** **Edinburgh G~, Belfast G~,** official journals with lists of government appointments, bankruptcies, and other public notices. **3.** newspaper (used in titles, as *Isle of Thanet Gazette, Oxford University Gazette*). **4.** *v.t.* ||publish in official gazette (esp. in *pass.,* of official etc. with status so announced). [F, f. It. *gazzetta* (*gazeta,* a Venetian small coin)]

găzetteer' *n.* geographical index. [so called as first provided for 'gazetteers' in earlier sense 'journalists', f. F *gazettier* f. It. *gazzettiere* (as prec.; see -EER)]

gazpa'cho (gahspah'-) *n.* (*pl.* ~s). Spanish cold vegetable soup. [Sp.]

gazŭ'mp *v.t.* (sl.) swindle; raise price of house etc. after accepting offer from (intending buyer, or abs.). [20th c.; orig. uncert.]

GB *abbr.* Great Britain.

||**GBE** *abbr.* Knight (or Dame) Grand Cross (of the Order) of the British Empire.

||**GC** *abbr.* George Cross.

||**GCB** *abbr.* Knight (or Dame) Grand Cross (of the Order) of the Bath.

||**GCE** *abbr.* General Certificate of Education.

||**GCIE** *abbr.* Knight Grand Commander (of the Order) of the Indian Empire.

||**GCMG** *abbr.* Knight (or Dame) Grand Cross (of the Order) of St. Michael & St. George.

||**GCSI** *abbr.* Knight Grand Commander (of the Order) of the Star of India.

||**GCVO** *abbr.* Knight (or Dame) Grand Cross (of the Order) of the Royal Victorian Order.

Gd *symb.* gadolinium.

Gdn(s). *abbr.* Garden(s).

GDP *abbr.* gross domestic product.

GDR *abbr.* German Democratic Republic.

Ge *symb.* germanium.

||**gean** (g-) *n.* mazard cherry. [f. F *guine*, of unkn. orig.]

gear (g-) *n.* & *v.* **1.** *n.* equipment; apparel, esp. (colloq.) for young people, and cf. HEAD¹ 23; harness of draught animals. **2.** apparatus, appliances (*aircraft's landing gear*); tackle, tools. **3.** combination of wheels, levers, etc., usu. for special purpose (*winding-gear*); wheels working on one another by teeth etc.; arrangements connecting motor or engine with its work (**in** ∿, connected or working; **out of** ∿, with connection interrupted or not working, (fig.) out of order); particular state of adjustment of such connection (**high, low,** ∿, by which driven part of bicycle, motor car, etc., revolves faster, slower, relatively to driving part; similarly ||**top,** ||**bottom** or ||**first,** ∿, the available extremes; CHANGE² *gear*). **4.** rigging. **5.** goods, household utensils. **6.** ∿'**box,** ∿'**case,** (enclosing gearing of motor car, bicycle, etc.); ∿--**lever,** *∿-**shift,** (used to engage or change gear); ∿'**wheel,** cog-wheel, esp. that in bicycles which is driven directly by pedals. **7.** *v.t.* harness (draught animal; often *up*); put (machinery) in gear, provide with gear (∿ **up, down,** provide with high, low, gear); make (industry or factory) subservient or ancillary *to* another, or *to* a programme; adjust or adapt *to*. **8.** *v.i.* be in gear, work smoothly *with*. [ME, f. ON *gervi*, OS *gerwi*, OHG *garawī* f. Gmc **garwīn-* prepare]

gear'ing (g-) *n.* set or arrangement of gears in machine; ||(fig., Finance) allocation of part of dividend to preferred recipients, amount of this part. [f. prec. + -ING¹]

gĕ'ckō (g-) *n.* (*pl.* ∿s *or* ∿es). house lizard found in warm climates, able to climb walls by its adhesive toes. [f. Malay *gēkoq*, imit. of its cry]

||**gee¹, gee'-gee,** *n.* (colloq.) horse. [orig. child's wd, f. foll.]

gee², gee'-hō, gee'-ŭp, *ints.* of command to horse etc.: go on, go faster; (occas.) turn to right. [17th c., of unkn. orig.]

gee³, gee whi'llikins (-nz), **gee whi'z,** *ints.* expr. asseveration, discovery, etc. [perh. abbr. of JESUS]

****gee⁴** *n.* (sl.) person, fellow. [f. first letter of GUY²]

geese. See GOOSE.

gee'-string. Var. of G-STRING 2.

gee'zer (g-) *n.* (sl.) old man; person. [dial. pronunc. of GUISER]

Gěhě'nna (g-) *n.* hell; place of burning, torment, or misery. [eccl. L, f. Hellenistic Gk *geenna* f. Heb. *gē' hinnōm* hell, orig. valley of Hinnom near Jerusalem where children were sacrificed]

Gei'ger (gī'ger) *n.* ∿ **counter,** cylindrical device for detecting and counting ionizing particles in order to measure radioactivity etc. [f. H. ∿, Ger. physicist d. 1945]

gei'sha (gā'-) *n.* (*pl.* ∿s *or* same). trained Japanese hostess entertaining men with dance and song; Japanese prostitute. [Jap.]

Gei'ssler (gī'-) *n.* ∿ **tube,** sealed glass or quartz tube with central constriction, filled with vapour for production of luminous electrical discharge. [f. H. ∿, Ger. mechanic d. 1879]

geist (gīst) *n.* (individual) spirit; intellectuality, intelligence. [G (cf. GHOST)]

gěl *n.,* & *v.i.* (-ll-). (form) semi-solid colloidal solution or jelly, of solid dispersed in liquid. [abbr. of foll.]

gě'latin, ||**gě'latine** (-ēn) *n.* almost colourless transparent tasteless water-soluble substance derived from animal skin, tendons, ligaments, etc., and used in food preparation, photography, etc.; **blasting** ∿, an explosive nitro-glycerine solution of collodion cotton; ∿ **paper** (coated with sensitized gelatin for photography); hence *or* cogn. **gělă'tin**IZE (3) *v.t.* & *i.*, **gělă'tin**OUS *a.*, (esp.) of jelly-like

consistency. [f. F *gélatine* f. It. *gelatina* (*gelata* JELLY; see -IN, -INE⁵)]

gělă'tion¹ *n.* solidification by freezing. [f. L *gelatio* (*gelare* freeze; see -ATION)]

gělă'tion² *n.* formation of a gel. [f. GEL + -ATION]

gěld (g-) *v.t.* deprive (usu. male animal) of ability to reproduce; castrate or spay, excise testicles or ovaries of. [ME, f. ON *gelda* (*geldr* barren, OHG *galt*, f. Gmc **galduz*)]

gě'lding (g-) *n.* gelded animal, esp. male horse. [ME, f. ON *geldingr* (as prec.; see -ING³)]

gě'lid *a.* icy, ice-cold; chilly, cool. [f. L *gelidus* (*gelu* frost; see -ID¹)]

gě'lignīte *n.* explosive based on blasting GELATIN. [f. GELATIN + L *ignis* fire + -ITE¹ (2)]

gě'llÿ *n.* (sl.) gelignite. [abbr.]

gěm *n.,* & *v.t.* (-mm-). **1.** *n.* precious stone, esp. when cut and polished; object of great beauty or worth; choicest part *of*; prized thing; precious or semi-precious stone with engraved design; hence ∿'LIKE, ∿'MY², *adjs.* **2.** *v.t.* adorn (as with gems). [ME, f. OF *gemme* f. L *gemma* bud, jewel]

Gě'mǎr'a (g-) *n.* rabbinical commentary on Mishnah, forming second part of Talmud. [f. Aram. *gᵉmārā* completion]

gě'mināte¹ *a.* combined in pairs. [f. L *geminatus* p.p. of *geminare* (*geminus* twin); see -ATE²]

gě'min|āte² *v.t.* double, repeat; arrange in pairs; so ∿A'TION *n.* [f. as prec. + -ATE³]

Gě'min|ī *n.* (person born under) sign of the ZODIAC, the Twins; hence ∿E'AN *a.* & *n.*, (person) born under Gemini. [L, = twins]

gě'mma *n.* (*pl.* ∿e). (In cryptogams) small cellular body that separates from mother-plant and starts a new one. [L; see GEM]

gěmmǎ'tion *n.* reproduction by gemmae. [F (*gemmer* to bud, *gemme* bud; see -ATION)]

gě'mmi'ferous *a.* producing precious stones; bearing buds. [f. L *gemmifer* (as GEMMA, -I-, -FEROUS)]

gě'mmi'parous *a.* of, or propagating by, gemmation. [f. mod. L *gemmiparus* (*gemma* bud, *parĕre* bring forth) + -OUS]

gěmmŏ'|logÿ *n.* science of gems; hence ∿LOGIST *n.* [L *gemma* GEM + -O- + -LOGY]

gě'mmūle *n.* encysted embryonic cell-cluster in sponges. [F, or f. L *gemmula* little bud (as GEM; see -ULE)]

gě'mmÿ. See GEM.

gemü'tlich (gemōō'tlĭk, -mū'-) *a.* cheerful; cosy; genial; so ∿keit (-kīt) *n.*, cheerfulness, cosiness, geniality. [G]

||**gěn** *n.* & *v.* (-nn-). (sl.) **1.** *n.* information. **2.** *v.t.* & *i.* ∿ **up,** provide (oneself) with information. [perh. f. first syl. of *general information*]

-gen *suf.* forming *ns.* (1) (Chem.) in *oxygen* and later formations *-gen* has the sense 'that which produces' (*hydrogen, nitrogen, cyanogen, antigen*); (2) (Bot.) in *endogen, exogen,* etc., *-gen* = 'growth' (*acrogen, thallogen*). [f. F *-gène* f. Gk *-genēs* -born, of a specified kind, (*-gen-,* root of *gi-gn-omai* be born, become)]

Gen. *abbr.* General; Genesis (OT).

ge'ndǎrme (zhŏ'n-) *n.* **1.** soldier, mounted or on foot, employed in police duties esp. in France; so ∿rie (zhŏndār'merē) *n.*, force of gendarmes, gendarmes' headquarters. **2.** rock-tower on mountain, occupying and blocking arête. [F, f. *gens d'armes* men of arms]

gě'nder *n.* grammatical classification (or one of the classes) of objects roughly corresponding to the two sexes and sexlessness (see MASCULINE, FEMININE, NEUTER, COMMON¹); (of nouns and pronouns) property of belonging to such class, (of adjectives) appropriate form for accompanying a noun of one such class; (colloq.) one's sex. [ME, f. OF *gendre* f. Rom. **genero* f. L GENUS]

gēne *n.* (Biol.) unit of heredity in chromosome, controlling a particular inherited characteristic of an individual. [mod. formation in G (*gen*); cf. -GEN]

gĕnĕălŏ'gical *a.* of genealogy; tracing family descent; ∼ **tree**, chart like inverted branching tree showing descent of family or of animal species; hence ∼LY² *adv.* [f. F *généalogique* f. Gk *genealogikos* (as GENEALOGY; see -IC) + -AL]

gĕnĕă'logĭ/y *n.* account of descent from ancestor by enumeration of intermediate persons, pedigree; investigation of pedigrees; plant's or animal's line of development from earlier forms; hence ∼IST (3) *n.*, ∼IZE (1, 2) *v.t.* & *i.* [ME, f. OF *genealogie* f. LL f. Gk *genealogia* (*genea* race; see -LOGY)]

gĕ'nera. See GENUS.

gĕ'neral *a.* & *n.* **1.** *a.* completely or almost universal; including or affecting all or nearly all parts or cases or things; not partial, particular, local, or sectional; **G**∼ **American,** US speech not markedly dialectal or regional; *general* AVERAGE¹; **G**∼ **Certificate of Education,** examination set esp. for secondary-school pupils in England and Wales, certificate gained by passing it; ∼ **confession** (to be made by whole congregation); *∼ **delivery** (of letters to callers at post office); *general* ELECTION; ∼ **headquarters** (of Commander-in-Chief); ∼ **meeting** (open to all members of a society etc.); ∼ **post,** (1) first morning delivery, (2) an indoor game, (3) (fig.) general and rapid exchange of positions etc.; ||**G**∼ **Post Office,** chief post office in city or town; ∼ **staff** (assisting military commander in planning and administration); ∼ **strike** (of workers in all or most trades, esp. in Britain in 1926); *general* SYNOD. **2.** prevalent, widespread, usual; **in a** ∼ **way,** ordinarily. **3.** not limited in application; relating to whole class of objects, occasions, etc.; true of all or (opp. *universal*) nearly all cases (**as a** ∼ **rule,** in most cases); including points common to individuals of a class and neglecting differences (*general word, term, notion*). **4.** not restricted to one department, not specialized; ∼ **dealer,** trader in many kinds of article; ∼ **hospital,** (1) hospital not specializing in any particular disease or age or sex, (2) large military hospital receiving sick and wounded from field hospitals; ∼ **knowledge** (of miscellaneous facts); ∼ **practice,** work of ∼ **practitioner,** doctor treating cases of all kinds (opp. *consultant* or *specialist*); ∼ **reader** (of miscellaneous literature). **5.** roughly corresponding or adequate; sufficient for practical purposes; not detailed (*general resemblance, idea*). **6.** vague, indefinite, (*spoke only in general terms*). **7.** (Mil., of officer) above rank of colonel. **8.** chief, head, having unrestricted authority, (*general manager, secretary*; often appended to titles: ATTORNEY-*General*, SECRETARY-*General*, SOLICITOR-*General*). **9. in** ∼, generally, in all ordinary cases, barring special exceptions, for the most part. **10.** *n.* chief of religious order, e.g. of Jesuits, Dominicans, Salvation Army; (Mil.) officer next below Field Marshal or *general of the army or air force (see below) (also, by courtesy, of lieutenant-general and major-general; *∼ **of the army** or **air force,** officer of highest rank); commander of army; tactician or strategist of specified merit (*a good, bad, great, general*; *no general*); ||(colloq.) General Post Office; ||(colloq.) servant for general work; (arch.) *the* public. [ME f. OF, f. L *generalis* (as GENUS; see -AL)]

gĕnĕralĭ'ssĭmö *n.* (*pl.* ∼s). commander of combined military and naval and air force, or of several armies. [It., superl. of *generale* GENERAL]

gĕ'neralist *n.* person competent in several different fields (opp. *specialist*). [f. GENERAL + -IST]

gĕnĕra'litý *n.* being general; applicability to whole class of instances; vagueness, lack of detail; general point, principle, law, or statement; main body, bulk, majority, *of*. [f. F *généralité* f. LL *generalitas -tatis* (as GENERAL; see -ITY)]

gĕnĕralĭzā'tion, -isā'tion (-z-), *n.* (forming of) general notion or proposition obtained by induction (often derog., esp. **hasty** ∼, one based on too few instances). [f. F *généralisation* (as foll.; see -ATION)]

gĕ'neralĭz/e, -ĭs/e (-īz), *v.* **1.** *v.t.* reduce to general laws; form into a general notion; give a general character to; call by a general name. **2.** infer (law, conclusion) by induction; base general statement on (facts etc.). **3.** (Math. & Philos.) express in general form, extend application of. **4.** form general notions by abstraction; make vague; (Paint.) render only the typical characteristics of. **5.** bring into general use. **6.** *v.i.* use generalities, speak vaguely. **7.** Hence ∼ER¹ *n.* [f. F *généraliser* (as GENERAL; see -IZE)]

gĕ'nerallý *adv.* for the most part, extensively; in a general sense, without regard to particulars, not specially, (∼ **speaking,** in general); as a general rule, usually. [f. GENERAL + -LY²]

gĕ'neralship *n.* office of a general; strategy, military skill; skilful management, tact, diplomacy. [f. GENERAL + -SHIP]

gĕ'nerāte *v.t.* bring into existence, produce, evolve, (heat, force, light, friction, electricity, etc.; result, state of things, state of mind, etc.); (Math., of point, line, surface, conceived as moving) make (line, surface, solid). [f. L *generare* beget (as GENUS; see -ATE³)]

gĕnĕrā'tion *n.* **1.** procreation, propagation of species, begetting or being begotten. **2.** production by natural or artificial process, esp. production of electricity. **3.** single step in descent or pedigree (*have known them for three generations, his descendant in the tenth generation*); whole body of persons born about the same time (*my generation; the rising generation;* ∼ **gap,** differences of opinion between those of different generations; **first** ∼ *Americans, university students,* etc., whose parents were not so); average time in which children are ready to take place of parents (usu. reckoned at about 30 years); stage in development (*third-generation computers*). **4.** Hence ∼AL *a.* [ME f. OF, f. L *generatio -onis* (as prec.; see -ATION)]

gĕ'nerative (-āt-, -āt-) *a.* of procreation; able to produce, productive; ∼ **grammar,** set of rules whereby permissible sentences may be generated from elements of a language. [ME, f. OF (-*tĭf*) or f. LL *generativus* (as prec.; see -ATIVE)]

gĕ'nerātor *n.* apparatus for producing gases, steam, etc.; machine for converting mechanical into electrical energy, e.g. dynamo; originator. [f. GENERATE + -OR]

gĕnĕ'r/ic *a.* characteristic of a genus or class; applied to (any individual of) a large group or class; general, not specific or special; hence ∼ICALLY *adv.* [f. F *générique* f. L GENUS, see -IC]

gĕ'ner/ous *a.* **1.** magnanimous, noble-minded; not mean or prejudiced; free in giving, munificent; so ∼O'SITY *n.* **2.** ample, abundant, copious; (of wine) rich and full. **3.** Hence ∼OUSLY² *adv.* [f. OF *genereus* f. L *generosus* (as GENUS; see -OUS) noble, magnanimous]

gĕ'nĕsĭs *n.* **1.** (G∼). first book of OT, with account of the creation of the world. **2.** origin, mode of formation or generation. [L, f. Gk (*gen-* be produced)]

gĕ'nĕt, gĕnĕ'ttĕ, *n.* (fur of) civet-cat of genus *Genetta*. [ME, f. OF *genete* f. Arab. *jarnayt*]

gĕnĕ'tic *a.* **1.** of, in concerning, origin; causal. **2.** of genetics or genes; ∼ **code,** system of storage of genetic information in chromosomes; ∼ **engineering,** deliberate modification of hereditary features by treatment of DNA to transfer certain genes. **3.** Hence **gĕnĕ'tICALLY** *adv.* [f. GENESIS after *antithesis* -*etic*]

gĕnĕ'tic/s *n.* study of heredity and variation in animals and plants; hence ∼IST (3) *n.* [pl. of prec. used as n.; see -ICS]

gĕ'nĕva¹ *n.* Hollands gin. [f. Du. *genever* f. OF *genevre* f. L *juniperus* juniper; w. assim. to foll.]

Gĕnĕ'va² *n.* ∼ **bands,** clerical BAND¹s like those of Swiss Calvinists; ∼ **Conventions** (of 1864 and later, governing status of wounded, hospitals, ambulances, etc., in war); ∼ **cross,** red Greek cross on white ground distinguishing hospitals, ambulances, etc., in war; ∼ **gown,** black gown worn by Calvinists and other clergy in pulpit; ∼ **Proctocol** (of 1925, against

use of poison gas and bacteria in war); hence **Gĕnĕve′se** *a*. & *n*. [∼ in Switzerland]
gĕ′nial¹ *a*. **1.** (Of air, climate, etc.) conducive to growth, mild, pleasantly warm; cheering, enlivening; jovial, kindly, sociable, whence ∼ITY (-ă′l-) *n*., ∼IZE (3) *v.t.* **2.** of or showing genius. **3.** Hence ∼LY² *adv.* [f. L *genialis* (as GENIUS; see -AL)]
gĕni′al² *a*. (Anat.) of the chin. [f. Gk *geneion* chin (*genus* jaw) + -AL]
gĕ′nic *a*. pertaining to genes. [f. GENE + -IC]
-gĕ′nic *suf.* forming *adjs.* meaning (1) producing (*carcinogenic, pathogenic*); (2) well suited to (*photogenic, radiogenic*); (3) produced by (*iatrogenic*); hence **-gĕ′ni**CALLY *adv. suf.* [f. -GEN + -IC]
gĕ′nie *n*. (*pl.* usu. **genii** *pr.* jĕ′nī-ī). jinnee, sprite or goblin of Arabian tales. [f. F *génie* f. L GENIUS; cf. JINNEE]
gĕ′nii. See GENIE, GENIUS.
gĕni′sta *n*. flowering shrub of genus *Genista*, e.g. dyer's broom. [L]
gĕ′nital *a*. & *n*. **1.** *a*. of animal reproduction. **2.** *n*. (in *pl.*) external organs of reproduction. [OF, or f. L *genitalis* (*gignere genit-* beget; see -AL)]
gĕnitā′lia *n*. *pl.* = prec. **2.** [L, neut. pl. (as n.) of *genitalis* (see prec., -IA²)]
gĕ′nitive *a*. & *n*. (Gram.) ∼ (**case**), case of nouns etc. in inflected languages, corresponding to *of*, *from*, and other prepositions with noun representing source, possessor, etc.; *genitive* ABSOLUTE; hence **gĕnitī′val** *a*., **gĕnitī′val**LY² *adv.* [ME, f. OF *genetif* or *-ive* or f. L *genitivus* (*casus* case), transl. Gk *genikē* (*ptōsis* case), as GENITAL; see -IVE]
gĕ′nitŏ- *comb. form.* = GENITAL, as: ∼**urinary**, of the genital and urinary organs. [f. GENITAL + -O-]
gĕ′nius *n*. (*pl.* ∼**es**, or **ge′nii** *pr.* -ī). **1.** tutelary spirit of person, place, or institution; **good, evil,** ∼, one of two opposed spirits or angels supposed to attend each person, person who powerfully influences one for good or ill. **2.** nation's, age's, etc., prevalent feeling, opinions, or taste; character, spirit, drift, method, of a language, law, etc.; associations or inspirations of a place. **3.** natural ability or tendency; special mental endowments; exalted intellectual power; instinctive and extraordinary imaginative, creative, or inventive capacity; (∼ ∼**es**) person having this. **4.** ∼ **loci** (lō′sī; *pl.* **genii loci**), presiding deity, associations, etc., of a place. [L, in sense 1, f. root of *gignere* beget]
geni′zah (gĕnē′za) *n*. room attached to synagogue, housing damaged, discarded, or heretical books etc. and sacred relics. [Heb. *gĕnīzāh*, lit. hiding-place (*gānaz* hide, set aside)]
Gĕ′nŏa *n*. ∼ **cake**, rich fruit-cake with almonds on top; ∼ (**jib**), large jib on racing-yacht; hence **Gĕnōe′se** *a*. & *n*. [∼ in Italy]
gĕ′nocīd|e *n*. deliberate extermination of a race, nation, etc.; hence ∼AL (jĕ′-, -sī′-) *a*. [f. Gk *genos* race + -CIDE (2)]
gĕ′no|type *n*. (Biol.) genetic constitution of an individual; hence ∼tў′p*ic* *a*. [f. G *genotypus* (as GENE, -O-, TYPE¹)]
-genous *suf.* forming *adjs.* w. sense 'produced' (*endogenous*). [f. -GEN + -OUS]
genre (zhahnr) *n*. kind or style, esp. of art or literature; ∼(-**painting**), portrayal of scenes etc. from ordinary life. [F, = kind; see GENDER]
gĕns (-z) *n*. (*pl.* **ge′ntes** *pr.* -ēz). **1.** (Rom. & Gk Ant.) group of families with supposed common origin, sharing name and religious rites; clan. **2.** (Biol.) group of related organisms. **3.** line of descent through father. [L, f. **gen-* root of *gignere* beget]
gĕnt *n*. gentleman (vulg. or joc.); ∼**s**, (in shops) men (*gents' hairdresser*); ||**the G**∼**s**, (colloq.) men's public lavatory. [abbr. of GENTLEMAN]
gĕntee′l *a*. **1.** (arch., iron., or vulg.) appropriate to, characteristic of, belonging to, the upper classes. **2.** (genuinely or affectedly) stylish, fashionable, well--dressed, or elegant; SHABBY-*genteel*. **3.** Hence ∼ISM (4)

n., word used because thought to be more elegant than the usual one (e.g. *perspire* for *sweat*), ∼LY² (-l-lĭ) *adv.* [earlier *gentile*, readoption of F *gentil* GENTLE]
gĕ′ntian (-shan, -shĭan) *n*. plant of genus *Gentiana* or *Gentianella* (usu. blue-flowered), found esp. in mountain regions; ∼ (**bitter**), liquor extracted from its root; ∼ **violet**, a dye, used as antiseptic, esp. in treatment of burns. [OE f. L *gentiana* (*Gentius* king of Illyria; see -AN)]
gĕ′ntile *a*. & *n*. **1.** (person) not Jewish; hence ∼DOM (-ld-) *n*. **2.** of a nation or tribe; (Gram.) (word) indicating nationality; heathen, pagan. [ME, f. L *gentilis* (GENS *gentis* family; see -IL)]
gĕntili′tial (-shal) *a*. of a nation or family; of the gentry. [f. L *gentilicius* national (GENS) + -AL]
gĕntī′lity *n*. social superiority, good manners, upper--class habits; SHABBY-*gentility*; (arch.) gentle birth, gentlefolk. [ME, f. OF *gentilité* (as foll.; see -ITY)]
gĕ′ntle *a*., *n*., & *v.t.* **1.** *a*. (Of birth, family, pursuits, etc.) honourable, belonging to or fit for the class of gentlemen; (in *comb.*, as GENTLEMAN) well-born; ∼**folk**(**s**), ∼**people**, people of good position and family. **2.** (arch.) generous, noble, courteous, (∼ **reader**, author's formula of address). **3.** tame, quiet, (**the** ∼ **art** or **craft**, angling or other activity requiring patience or (iron.) force); easily managed; not stormy, rough, or violent, (*a gentle breeze*; *has a gentle nature*); (of medicine) mild, not drastic; (of rule etc.) not severe; moderate (*a gentle heat*); gradual (*a gentle slope*); kind, tender, mild, (*a gentle hint* (also iron.); **the** ∼ **sex**, women). **4.** *n*. maggot, larva of meat-fly or bluebottle, used as fishing-bait [f. obs. sense 'soft' of adj.]. **5.** *v.t.* make gentle; break in (horse), handle (horse etc.) firmly but gently. [ME, f. OF *gentil* f. L *gentilis* GENTILE]
gĕ′ntleman (-telm-) *n*. (*pl.* -**men**). **1.** man of chivalrous manners and good breeding; man of good social position, man of wealth and leisure (*country gentleman*); (Hist.) non-professional cricketer; (euphem.) smuggler; *gentleman at* LARGE; ∼'s ∼, valet. **2.** (courteous synonym for) man, esp. in Parliament, Congress, etc.; **old** ∼, the Devil (OLD 5); (in *pl.* as *voc.*) male members of audience, (also as *pl.* of SIR 1, and in letter = *Dear* SIR*s*); ||**the Gentle-men**('**s**), (as *sing. n.*) men's public lavatory. **3.** man of gentle birth attached to household of sovereign or great person (*gentleman in waiting* etc.). **4.** ∼**-at--arms**, one of sovereign's bodyguard; ∼ **farmer**, country gentleman who farms; ∼ **usher**, gentleman acting as usher to great person; ∼'s or gentlemen's agree-**ment** (binding in honour, but not enforceable at law). **5.** Hence ∼LY¹ *a.*, feeling, behaving, or looking, like a gentleman, befitting a gentleman. [f. GENTLE + MAN¹, after OF *gentilz hom*]
gĕ′ntleness (-teln-) *n*. kindliness, mildness; freedom from severity, sudddenness, violence, steepness, etc. [f. GENTLE + -NESS]
gĕ′ntle|woman (-telwŏŏman) *n*. (*pl.* ∼**women** *pr.* -wĭmĭn). (arch.) woman of good birth or breeding; lady. [f. GENTLE + WOMAN]
gĕ′ntlỹ *adv.* quietly, moderately, softly, slowly; (as *int.* expr. remonstration) do not go so fast etc.; mildly, tenderly, kindly; ∼ **born**, of gentle birth. [f. GENTLE + -LY²]
gĕ′ntōo *n*. kind of penguin (*Pygoscelis papua*). [perh. f. Anglo-Ind. *Gentoo* = Hindu, f. Port. *gentio* GENTILE]
gĕ′ntrỹ *n. pl.* people next below the nobility in position and birth; (derog., esp. *these gentry*) people. [prob. f. obs. *gentrice* f. OF *genterise* var. of *gentelise* nobility (*gentil* GENTLE)]
gĕ′nŭflĕct *v.i.* bend the knee, esp. in worship; hence or cogn. ∼OR, **gĕnŭflĕ′x**ION, ∼ION (-kshon), *ns.*, ∼ORY *a.* [f. eccl. L *genuflectere* *-flex-* f. L *genu* knee + *flectere* bend]
gĕ′nŭine *a*. of the original stock, pure-bred; really proceeding from its reputed source or author; having the supposed character, not sham or feigned; properly

so called; hence ∿LY² (-nlĭ) adv., ∿NESS (-n-n-) n. [f. L genuinus (genu knee, w. ref. to father's acknowledging new-born child by placing on knee; see -INE¹); later assoc. w. GENUS]

gē′nus n. (pl. ge′nera pr. jĕ′-). 1. (Logic) kinds of things including subordinate kinds or species. 2. (Biol.) group of animals or plants having common structural characteristics distinct from those of all other groups, and usu. containing several species. 3. (pop.) kind, class, order, tribe. [f. L genus -eris birth, race, stock] -gény suf. forming ns. w. sense 'mode of production or development of' (anthropogeny, ontogeny, pathogeny). [f. F -génie (as -GEN, -Y¹)]

gēo- comb. form. earth, as: geobo′tany, study of geographical distribution of plants; ge′omancy, divination from configuration of handful of thrown earth or random dots, whence geoma′ntic a. [f. Gk geō- (gē earth)] Geo. abbr. George.

gēoce′ntric a. considered as viewed from the earth's centre (∿ latitude, that at which planet would appear to observer at earth's centre); having or representing the earth as centre, not heliocentric. [f. GEO-+-CENTRIC]

gēoche′m|istrȳ (-k-) n. the chemistry of the earth; hence ∿ICAL a., ∿IST (3) n. [f. GEO-+CHEMISTRY] gēochrono′log|ȳ (-k-) n. measurement of geological time; ordering of geological events; hence gēochrōnolo′gICAL (-kr-) a., ∿IST (3) n. [f. GEO-+CHRONOLOGY]

gē′ode n. (rock containing) cavity lined with crystals or other mineral matter; hence gēo′dIC a. [f. L f. Gk geōdēs earthy (gē earth; see -ODE)]

gēo′d|esȳ n. branch of mathematics dealing with figure and area of the earth or large portions of it; so gēode′sIC, gēode′tIC adjs.; ∿esic (or ∿etic) dome (built of short struts along geodesic lines); ∿esic (or ∿etic) line, shortest possible line on surface between two points; ∿esIST (3) n. [f. mod. L f. Gk GEO(daisia f. daiō divide)]

gēogra′phic, -ic|al, adjs. of geography; ∿(al) latitude, angle made with plane of equator by perpendicular to earth's surface at any point; ∿al mile = 1′ of longitude on equator, or of latitude, about 1850 metres; hence ∿ALLY adv. [f. F géographique or f. LL f. Gk GEO(graphikos -GRAPHIC)+-AL]

gēo′graphȳ n. science of the earth's surface, form, physical features, natural and political divisions, climate, productions, population, etc. (mathematical, physical, political, ∿, the science in these aspects); subject-matter of geography; features, arrangement, of place, esp. (colloq.) location of w.c. or other rooms in house; so gēo′GRAPHER n. [f. F géographie or f. L f. Gk GEO(graphia -GRAPHY)]

gē′oid n. the earth's figure; shape formed by mean sea-level and its imagined extension under land areas. [f. Gk geoidēs (as GEO-; see -OID)]

gēo′logȳ n. science of the earth's crust, its strata, and their relations and changes; geological features of district; corresponding study of moon etc.; hence gēolo′gIC(AL) adjs., gēolo′gICALLY adv., gēo′LOGIST n., gēo′logIZE (1, 2) v.t. & i. [f. mod. L geologia (as GEO-; see -LOGY)]

gēomā′gnetism n. study of the earth's magnetic properties; hence gēomāgne′tIC a. [f. GEO-+MAGNETISM]

gēo′mēter n. person skilled in geometry; moth esp. of family Geometridae (from its caterpillar's seeming to measure ground by its mode of walking). [ME, f. LL geometra f. L f. Gk GEO(metrēs measurer)]

gēome′tric, -ic|al, adjs. of, according to, like, geometry; ∿al architecture (with figures of geometric form, as circles, trefoils, etc.); geometric MEAN¹; G∿ pottery (of ancient Greece, using geometric forms in decoration); ∿al progression (with constant ratio between successive quantities, as

1:3:9:27:81); ∿ spider (constructing web of geometric pattern); geometric TRACERY; hence ∿ALLY adv. [f. F géometrique f. L f. Gk geōmetrikos (as prec.; see -IC)+-AL]

gēo′mētr|ȳ n. science of properties and relations of magnitudes (as lines, surfaces, solids) in space; relative arrangement of objects or parts; hence or cogn. gēomētrī′CIAN n., ∿IZE (1) v.t. [ME, f. OF geometrie f. L f. Gk (as GEO-; see -METRY)]

gēomŏ̄rpho′log|ȳ n. study of the physical features of the earth's surface and their relation to its geological structures; hence gēomŏ̄rpholŏ′gICAL a., ∿IST (3) n. [f. GEO-+MORPHOLOGY]

gē′ophōne n. device for detecting vibrations in ground. [f. GEO-+-PHONE]

gēophȳ′sic|s (-z-) n. the physics of the earth; hence ∿AL a., ∿IST (3) n. [f. GEO-+PHYSICS]

gēopŏ′litics n. politics of a country as determined by its geographical features; hence gēopoli′tICAL a. [f. GEO-+POLITICS]

‖Geor′die (jŏr′-) n. native of Tyneside. [f. foll.+-IE]

George (jŏrj) n. 1. ‖(sl.) automatic pilot of aircraft. 2. by ∿, oath or exclamation of surprise or approval; ‖∿ Cross, Medal, decorations (esp. for esp. civilian) gallantry, instituted 1940 by King George VI. [man's Christian name]

george′tte (jŏrj-) n. a thin silk or other crêpe dress-material. [f. dressmaker's name]

Geor′gian¹ (jŏr′-) a. of the time of the first four Kings George (1714-1830); of the time of Kings George V and VI (1910-52), esp. of literature of 1910-20. [f. GEORGE+-IAN]

Geor′gian² (jŏr′-) a. & n. (native, inhabitant, or language) of Georgia in the Caucasus; (native or inhabitant) of Georgia in US. [f. Georgia+-AN]

gē′osphēre n. solid surface of the earth; any of the almost spherical concentric regions of the earth and its atmosphere. [f. GEO-+-SPHERE]

gēostā′tionarȳ a. (Of artificial satellite of earth) moving so as to remain always above same point on earth's surface. [f. GEO-+STATIONARY]

gēostrŏ′phic a. (Meteorol.) depending on the rotation of the earth. [f. GEO-+Gk strophē a turning (strephō to turn)+-IC]

gēother′mal a. pertaining to the earth's internal heat. [f. GEO-+THERMAL]

gēo′tropism n. plant-growth in relation to gravity; positive ∿, tendency of roots etc. to grow towards, negative ∿, tendency of stems etc. to grow away from, centre of earth; so gēotrŏ′pIC a. [f. GEO-+Gk tropikos (tropē a turning f. trepō to turn; see -IC)+-ISM]

Ger. abbr. German.

gerā′nium n. herb or shrub of genus Geranium bearing fruit shaped like bill of crane; (pop.) cultivated pelargonium; colour of the scarlet geranium. [L, f. Gk geranion (geranos crane)]

ger′bera (j-, g-) n. African or Asian herb of genus Gerbera, esp. Transvaal daisy. [f. T. Gerber, Ger. naturalist d. 1743+-A1]

ger′bil, jer′bil, n. mouselike desert rodent of subfamily Gerbillinae, with long hind legs. [f. F gerbille f. mod. L gerbillus dim. of gerbo JERBOA]

ge′renuk (gĕ′renōōk) n. long-necked E. African antelope. [f. Somali]

gerfalcon. Var. of GYRFALCON.

gēriă′tr|ic a. relating to ∿ICS n. pl., branch of medical or social science dealing with health and welfare of old people; so gēriātrī′CIAN, ∿IST (3), ns. [f. Gk gēras old age+iatros physician+-IC]

germ n., & v.i. 1. portion of organism capable of developing into a new one, rudiment of animal or plant; embryo of seed (wheat germ). 2. micro-organism or microbe, esp. one of those supposed to cause disease, whence ∿′Y² a. 3. (fig.) that from which something may spring, elementary principle (in ∿, not yet developed). 4. ∿-cell, cell in body of an organism, specialized for reproductive purposes and able to unite with one of the opposite sex to form new individual; ~-**plasm**, nuclear part of germ-cell by which, according to Weismann's theory, hereditary characteristics are transmitted; ~ **warfare** (using germs to spread disease). **5.** *v.i.* (fig.) germinate, sprout. [f. F *germe* f. L *germen germinis* sprout]

gẽr′man[1] *a.* **1.** (placed after *brother, sister, cousin*). in the fullest sense of relationship, not half-brother etc. **2.** (arch.) = GERMANE. [ME, f. OF *germain* f. L *germanus* genuine, of same parents]

Gẽr′man[2] *a.* & *n.* **1.** *a.* of or characterizing Germany or its people or language. **2.** ~ **band** (of street musicians); ~ **measles**, contagious disease like mild measles, rubella; ~ **Ocean**, (arch.) North Sea; ~ **sausage**, large sausage stuffed with spiced partly cooked meat; ~ **shepherd (dog)**, Alsatian; ~ **silver**, silver-like white alloy of nickel, zinc, and copper. **3.** *n.* native or language of Germany (**High** ~, form of German orig. spoken in South, but now in literary and cultured use throughout Germany; **Low** ~, (1) dialects of Germany that are not High German, (2) all forms of West Germanic, including English and Dutch, except High German). **4.** Hence ~ISH[1] *a.*, ~ISM (2, 3, 4), ~IST (1, 3), *ns.*, ~IZE (2, 3, 4) *v.t.* & *i.*, ~IZA′TION, ~IZER[1], *ns.*, **Gẽr′mäno**- *comb. form*, **Gẽrmäno**MA′NIA *n.*, **Gẽrmä′no**PHIL(E), **Gẽrmä′no**PHOBE, *ns.* & *adjs.*, **Gẽrmä′no**PHO′BIA *n.* [f. L *Germanus* a. & n. of related peoples of central and N. Europe, name perh. given by Celts to their neighbours (cf. OIr. *gair* neighbour)]

gẽrmä′nder *n.* plant of genus *Teucrium*; ~ **speedwell**, blue-flowered speedwell with germander-like leaves. [ME, f. med. L *germandra* ult. f. Gk *khamaidrus* (*khamai* on the ground, *drus* oak)]

gẽrmä′ne *a.* relevant or pertinent *to* the matter or subject. [var. of GERMAN[1]]

Gẽrmä′nic[1] *a.* & *n.* **1.** *a.* (Hist.) of the Germans (*Germanic Confederation, Empire*). **2.** of the Scandinavians, Anglo-Saxons, or Germans. **3.** *a.* & *n.* (of) the primitive language of the Germanic peoples; **East** ~, Gothic and some almost lost languages, as Burgundian and Vandal; **INDO**-*Germanic*; **North** ~, Scandinavian; **West** ~, High and Low German, English, Frisian, Dutch, etc. **4.** having German characteristics; hence ~ISM (2, 4) *n.* [f. L *Germanicus* (as GERMAN[2]; see -IC)]

gẽrmä′nic[2] *a.* (Chem.) of or containing germanium, esp. in quadrivalent state. [f. foll. + -IC]

gẽrmä′nium *n.* brittle greyish-white semi-metallic element. [mod. L, f. *Germanus* GERMAN[2] + -IUM]

gẽrmä′nous *a.* (Chem.) containing germanium in the bivalent state. [f. prec. + -OUS]

gẽr′men *n.* (Bot.) rudiment of seed-vessel. [L, = sprout]

gẽr′micīd|e *n.* substance having power to destroy (esp. disease-)germs; hence ~AL *a.* [f. GERM + -I- + -CIDE (1)]

gẽr′minal *a.* of germs, of the nature of a germ, (GERM 1); in the earliest stage of development; productive of new ideas etc.; hence ~LY[2] *adv.* [f. as GERM + -AL]

gẽr′min|āte *v.* **1.** *v.i.* sprout, bud, put forth shoots, (lit. or fig.); so ~ANT *a.* (fig.). **2.** *v.t.* cause to shoot or sprout, develop, produce. **3.** Hence or cogn. ~A′TION, ~ātOR, *ns.*, ~ATIVE *a.* [f. L *germinare* (as GERM) + -ATE[3]]

gẽr′mon *n.* = ALBACORE 1. [F]

gẽrönt|ŏ′cracy *n.* government by, governing body of, old men; hence ~OCRA′TIC *a.* [f. Gk *gerōn -ontos* old man + -o- + -CRACY]

gẽröntŏ′|logỹ *n.* scientific study of old age and process of ageing, and of old people's special problems; hence **gẽrönt**OLO′GICAL *a.*, ~LOGIST *n.* [f. as prec. + -O- + -LOGY]

gẽröntophi′lia, gẽröntŏ′philỹ, *n.* desire for sexual relations with old people; so **gẽrŏ′nto**PHIL(E) *n.* & *a.*, **gẽröntophi′l**IC *a.* [f. as GERONTOCRACY + -PHIL + -IA[1], -Y[1]]

-**gerous** *suf.* forming *adjs.* (usu. w. intermediate -I-), w. sense 'bearing' (*lanigerous, setigerous*). [f. or after L -*ger* bearing (*gerere* bear) + -OUS]

gẽrrỹmä′nder *v.t.*, & *n.* **1.** *v.t.* manipulate boundaries of (constituency etc.) unfairly so as to secure disproportionate influence at election for some party or class; hence ~ER[1] *n.* **2.** *n.* such manipulation. [v. f. n., orig. US, by substitution of name of governor *Gerry* of Massachusetts (1812) for *sala-* in *salamander*]

gẽr′tcha (g-) *int.* (vulg.) get away with you! (expr. disbelief). [corrupt.]

gẽ′rund *n.* **1.** form of Latin verb (-*ndum -ndi -ndo*) serving as cases of infinitive used as noun, construed as noun but able to govern object etc. like the verb; ~-**grinder**, (arch.) teacher of Latin. **2.** English verbal noun in ~ING[1] when used distinctly as part of verb (*what is the use of my scolding him?*). **3.** Hence **gerŭ′nd**IAL *a.* [f. LL *gerundium* f. *gerundum* var. of *gerendum* gerund of L *gerere* do]

gerŭ′ndĭve *a.* & *n.* **1.** *a.* of or like the gerund. **2.** *n.* Latin verbal adjective (-*ndus*) from gerund stem having sense 'that should be done' etc.; hence **gẽrundī′**VAL *a.*, ~LY[2] (-vlĭ) *adv.* [f. LL *gerundivus* (*modus* mood) f. *gerundium* (see prec.)]

gẽ′ssō *n.* (*pl.* ~es). plaster of Paris or gypsum prepared for use in painting or sculpture. [It., f. L GYPSUM]

gẽ′stagen *n.* (Med.) substance having hormonal effects similar to those of ovulation; hence **gestagẽ′n**IC *a.* [f. GESTATION + -GEN]

Gesta′lt, **g-**, (geshtah′lt) *n.* (Psych.) perceived organized whole that is more than sum of its parts, e.g. a melody as distinct from the separate notes of it; ~ **psychology** (holding that perceptions, reactions, etc., are Gestalts); hence ~ISM (3), ~IST (2), *ns.* [G, = form, shape]

Gesta′pō (gestah′-, gĕ-) *n.* German secret state police of Nazi regime; organization comparable to this. [G, f. *Geheime Staatspolizei*]

gẽstä′te *v.t.* carry (as) in gestation. [f. as foll. + -ATE[3]]

gẽstä′tion *n.* carrying or being carried in the womb between conception and birth; this period; (fig.) private development of plan etc. [f. L *gestatio* (*gestare* frequent. of *gerere* carry; see -ATION)]

gẽstatŏ′rial *a.* ~ **chair** (for carrying Pope on certain occasions). [f. L *gestatorius* (*gestator* carrier f. as prec. + -OR; see -ORY) + -AL]

gẽstǐ′cŭl|āte *v.* **1.** *v.i.* use expressive motion of limbs or body with or instead of speech. **2.** *v.t.* express thus. **3.** Hence or cogn. ~A′TION, ~ātOR, *ns.*, ~ATIVE, ~ātORY, *adjs.* [f. L *gesticulari* (*gesticulus* dim. of *gestus* GESTURE) + -ATE[3]]

gẽ′stur|e *n.* & *v.* **1.** *n.* significant movement of limb or body; use of such movements as expression of feeling or as rhetorical device; (fig.) step or move calculated to evoke response from another or to convey (esp. friendly) intention; hence ~AL *a.* **2.** *v.i.* & *t.* = prec. [ME, f. med. L *gestura* (L *gerere gest-* wield; see -URE)]

gesundheit (gezoō′nt-hīt) *int.* expr. wish of good health, esp. to person who sneezes. [G, = health]

gět[1] (g-) *v.* (-**tt-**; *past* got, arch. gat; *p.p.* got, in comb. abbr. of *has got* or *have got*). **1.** *v.t.* come into possession of, obtain, procure, by effort or contrivance, extract (coal from mine), prepare (meal etc.), earn (*cannot get a living*), gain (*got little by it*), win (*get the UPPER hand, the advantage*, the BETTER[1], *of* person; *get the* BEST[1] *of it*; *get fame, credit, glory*, etc.; *get a* KICK[1] *out of*, WIND[1] *of*; *get runs* or *wickets* at cricket, *tricks* at cards etc.). **2.** learn *by heart* or *by rote*. **3.** obtain as result of calculation (*we get 9.5 as the average*). **4.** receive as gift, wages, etc.; extract by prayer, demand, inquiry, etc., (*from, out of*; *could not get leave, any supper*); come to have (desired thing, as *rest*, one's *way*, a *sight of*, *possession of*; *get* RELIGION); contract (idea etc.; *get it* into one's **head**, be convinced *that*; *get measles, the giggles*; *get* person or thing *on the* BRAIN; **have got it bad(ly)**, (sl.) be

infatuated); have inflicted on one, suffer, receive as
one's lot or penalty, (*fall, blow, the worst of it, six months
in prison*; **get his, theirs,** etc., (sl.) be killed; **get it,** be
punished, scolded, etc.; *get it in the* NECK[1]; *get the* BOOT[1],
the SACK[1]). **5.** (with *for* or ind. obj.) procure, provide,
(*got him a place, some dinner*; *we can get it for you*). **6.** catch
(fish, train, etc.); (deliberately) kill or injure; bring
in, carry home, (crop); pick up (broadcast signal);
communicate with (person or place) by telephone;
(esp. in *perf.* and *past*, colloq.) corner, puzzle, catch in
argument; (colloq.) understand (person or thing);
(colloq.) annoy; (colloq.) attract, obsess; (colloq.)
take, cat, (dinner etc.). **7.** (in *perf.*, colloq.) have (*have
not got a penny*; *I've got it!*; **have got to** = *have to*, see
HAVE[1] 13). **8.** (Usu. of animals) beget. **9.** (w. compl.)
succeed in bringing, placing, etc., (*got it over or across,
through door, into room*, etc., (fig.) *flattery will get you
nowhere*); bring into some state (**get with child,** make
pregnant; *get them ready*; *get your hair cut*; *get ship* etc.
under WAY; *get it done*; *got himself elected, arrested*);
suffer injury etc. to some part of one (*got my elbow
dislocated*; *shall get my feet wet*); induce, prevail upon,
(person) *to do*. **10.** *v.i.* succeed in coming or going *to,
from, into, out of, through, over, here, nowhere* (lit. or fig.),
as far as, etc. (*where has it got to?*, what has become of
it?; ***get to** do, succeed in doing); (sl.) be off, clear
out; (w. *inf.*) acquire habit (*one soon gets to like it*);
come to be doing or to do (*they got talking, got to know her
quite well*; *get* CRACK[2]*ing*); become (*get tired, hot, excited,
drunk*; **get well, better,** recover from illness; *get clear,
rid, or quit, of*; **get-rich-quick,** attempting to acquire
wealth rapidly, *get* ROUND[3] *to*; *get under* WAY; *get WISE[1]
to; *get in a panic, married, used to it, caught in the rain,
shelved*). **11.** (w. *preps.*): ∼ **across,** (sl.) annoy;
*∼ **around,** = *get round*; ∼ **at,** reach (whence ∼**-a't-
-able** *a.*), get hold of, ascertain, (colloq.) imply (*what
are you getting at?*), (sl.) tamper with, bribe, etc., (sl.)
attack, taunt, (*who are you getting at?*); ∼ **into,**
(colloq.) put on (boots, clothes), become interested
in, take possession of (*what's got into you tonight?*), (of
liquor) affect, confuse, (one's head); ∼ **off,** dismount
from, obtain release from (engagement etc.), not
remain on (the grass etc.); ∼ **on,** place oneself on,
climb on to, (horse, bicycle, etc.; *get on* person's
NERVES), rise on one's *feet* or *legs* to speak in public,
(colloq.) discover *something* else; *∼* **outside (of),** (sl.) eat; ∼ **over,** surmount
(difficulty), show (evidence, argument) to be un-
convincing, recover from (illness) or from surprise at,
accomplish (distance, task, etc.); ∼ **round,** (1)
cajole, (2) evade; ∼ **through,** bring to an end, (of
Bill etc.) be passed by (Lords, Commons, etc.), spend
(money), while away (time etc.); ∼ **to,** arrive at,
begin (business etc.). **12.** (w. *advs.*): ∼ **about,** go from
place to place, begin walking after illness etc., (of
news) be circulated, esp. orally; ∼ **across,** (colloq.)
be or make effective or acceptable; ∼ **along,** advance,
meet with success, fare *ill* or *well* etc., manage *without*
something, live harmoniously (*together* or *with*); ∼
along with you!, (colloq.) be off!, nonsense!; *∼
around, visit many places; ∼ **away,** escape (*from*),
start, (colloq., in *imper.*) be off! nonsense!, (usu. w.
neg.) escape *from* (fact etc.); ∼**-away** *n.*, escape esp.
after committing crime; ∼ *away with* action, MURDER[1],
or *it*, (colloq.) succeed in what one tries to do, escape
retribution, act with impunity; ∼ **back,** come home
etc., recover (lost thing); ∼ *back at*, (colloq.) retaliate
on; ∼ (*some of*) one's *own back*, (sl.) have revenge; ∼
by, (colloq.) be (just) adequate, manage *without* etc.;
∼ **down,** alight, swallow, record in writing, (colloq.)
depress, weary; ∼ *down to*, begin work on; ∼ **in,** be
elected as MP etc., obtain place at college etc., enter
vehicle, arrive at destination, bring home (crop),
collect (money owed etc.), fit (work etc.) into given
time, become friendly *with*, succeed in placing (blow);
get a word in EDGEWAYS; ∼ **off,** escape (from), alight
from public vehicle (*tell* person *where he gets off*, (colloq.)

rebuke his presumption etc.), start, (cause to) go to
sleep, be acquitted or pardoned, be let off *with* or *for*
specified penalty, procure acquittal or slight penalty
for (person), dispatch (letter etc.); ∼ *off with*, (colloq.)
become on friendly or amorous terms with member of
opposite sex; ∼ **on,** display (pace; *get a* MOVE[1] *on*),
advance, make progress, prosper, fare, enter public
vehicle, manage *without* something, agree or live
sociably (*with*); *getting on*, becoming old or (of time)
late; *getting on for*, approaching (an age, time, etc.); ∼
on to, (colloq.) succeed in understanding, become
aware of (fact), communicate with (person); ∼ **out,**
transpire, elicit, succeed in uttering, publishing, etc.,
finish (puzzle etc.), dismiss or be dismissed at cricket,
leave one's house, alight from vehicle, (colloq., in
imper.) be off!, nonsense!; ∼ *out of*, issue or escape from
(*got out of* BED[1] *on wrong side*; *get out of sight*, disappear;
get out of one's DEPTH; *get out of* HAND[1] 13), abandon
(habit) gradually, evade doing, elicit (information) or
obtain (money) from (person); ∼**-out** *n.*, (colloq.)
means of evasion (*for* or *like all get-out*, (sl.) with
utmost vigour etc.); ∼ **over,** = *get across* adv.; ∼
over (with), bring (troublesome task) to an end; ∼
round, (of news) = *get about*; ∼ *round to*, find time etc.
to deal with; ∼ **there,** (sl.) succeed, understand what
is meant; ∼ **through,** bring to or reach destination,
(of Bill) be passed in Parliament, succeed in an
examination, make contact by radio or telephone; ∼
through to, (colloq.) reach attention or understanding
of; ∼ *through with*, succeed in doing or enduring; ∼ **together,** collect (*t.* & *i.*), unite in discussion, promotion
of plan, etc., (sl.) put in order; ∼**-together** *n.*, (colloq.)
(social) assembly; ∼ **under,** subdue (fire); ∼ **up,** rise
esp. from bed, mount esp. on horseback, (of fire,
wind, sea) begin to be violent, (of game) rise from
cover, (of cricket-ball) rise sharply from pitch,
organize, set on foot, make presentable, arrange the
appearance of (hair, one*self*, mounting of play,
binding and print of book), make rise (*get* person's
BACK[1] *up*), produce (*get up speed*, STEAM[1]; *get the* WIND[1]
up), work up (factitious emotion, subject for examination etc.; *got-up*, artificially produced or adorned to
impress or deceive); ∼*-up* *n.*, style of equipment,
costume, production of book, etc.; ∼ *up to*, indulge in
(prank etc.). **13.** Hence ∼'**TABLE** *a.* [ME, f. ON *geta*
obtain, beget, guess, = OE *-gietan* (cf. BEGET, FORGET)
f. Gmc *getan etc. f. IE **ghed-* seize]

gĕt[2] (g-) *n.* begetting, offspring, (of animals); (sl.) fool,
idiot. [ME, f. prec.]

ge'ta (gā'-) *n. pl.* Japanese wooden shoes with thong
between big toe and other toes. [Jap. (*ge* under, *ta*
footwear)]

get-at-able, gettable. See GET[1] 11, 13.

gĕ'tter (g-) *n.*, & *v.t.* **1.** *n.* In vbl senses; (Phys.)
substance used to remove residual gas from evacuated
vessel. **2.** *v.t.* remove (gas), evacuate (vessel), by
means of getter. [ME, f. GET[1] + -ER]

gĕ'um *n.* rosaceous plant of genus *Geum*, incl. herb
bennet. [mod. L, var. of L *gaeum*]

GeV *abbr.* gigaelectron-volt.

gew'gaw (g-) *n.* gaudy plaything or ornament, bauble;
paltry showy trifle. [ME, of unkn. orig.]

gey (gā) *a.* & *adv.* (Sc.) **1.** *a.* considerable; ∼ **and,**
= sense 2. **2.** *adv.* very, considerably. [var. of GAY]

gey'ser *n.* **1.** (gī'z-, gā'z-). intermittent hot spring
throwing up column of water. **2.** ||(gē'z-). apparatus
for quickly heating water for washing etc. [f. Icel. *Geysir*
name of a particular spring in Iceland (*geysa* to gush)]

GG *abbr.* Governor-General.

Ghanai'an (gah-) *a.* & *n.* (native or inhabitant) of
Ghana. [f. *Ghana* in W. Africa + -IAN]

ghâr'ial (gâr'-). Var. of GAVIAL.

ghâ'rry (gă'-) *n.* Indian carriage (usu. horse-drawn
and plying for hire). [f. Hindi *gāṛī*]

gha'stl|ÿ (gah'-) *a.* & *adv.* **1.** *a.* horrible, frightful,
shocking; (colloq.) objectionable, unpleasant; death-
like, pale, wan, lurid; (of smile etc.) painfully forced;

hence ~ĭLY² *adv.*, ~ĭNESS *n.* **2.** *adv.* ghastlily (*pale* etc.). [ME *gastlich* f. obs. *gast* terrify + -LY¹; *gh-* after *ghost*]

ghat, ghaut, (gawt) *n.* (Ind.) **1.** flight of steps leading to river; landing-place; **burning-~,** level area at top of river ghat on which Hindus burn their dead. **2.** mountain pass, defile; **Eastern, Western, G~s,** mountain chains parallel to east and west coasts of S. India. [f. Hindi *ghāṭ*]

Gha'zi (gah'-) *n.* Muslim fighter against non--Muslims. [f. Arab. *al-ġāzī* part. of *ġazā* raid]

ghee, ghi, (gē) *n.* Indian clarified butter from milk of buffalo or cow. [f. Hindi *ghī* f. Skr. *ghṛitá-* sprinkled]

gherao' (gĕrow') *n.* (*pl.* ~s). (India & Pakistan). harassment of employers etc. by workers' preventing them from leaving premises until claims are granted. [f. Hind. *gherna* besiege]

ghĕr'kin (gĕr'-) *n.* young green, or small kind of, cucumber used for pickling. [f. Du. *gurkkijn* dim. of (*a*)*gurk* f. Slavonic, ult. f. med. Gk *aggourion*]

ghĕ'ttō (gĕ'-) *n.* (*pl.* ~s), & *v.t.* **1.** *n.* (Hist.) Jews' quarter in city. **2.** part of city, esp. slum area, occupied by minority group(s); isolated or segregated group or area. **3.** *v.t.* put or keep (people) in ghetto. [perh. f. It. *getto* foundry (applied to site of first ghetto in Venice 1516)]

ghi. See GHEE.

Ghi'bellin|e (gĭ'-) *n.* & *a.* **1.** *n.* member of emperor's faction (opp. GUELPH) in medieval Italian States; hence ~ISM (3) *n.* **2.** *a.* adhering to Ghibellines. [f. It. *Ghibellino* supposed to be f. G *Waiblingen* estate belonging to Hohenstaufen emperors]

ghillie. Var. of GILLIE.

ghōst (gō-) *n.* & *v.* **1.** *n.* soul of dead person in Hades etc.; spectre esp. of dead person appearing to the living (**raise, lay, ~,** cause it to appear or to cease appearing); emaciated person; shadowy outline or semblance (**not the ~ of a chance,** no chance at all). **2. give** or (arch.) **yield up the ~,** die, (fig.) give up hope; HOLY *Ghost.* **3.** bright spot or secondary image in field of telescope due to defect of lens; faint duplicated image in television picture. **4.** ~ (**writer**), artistic or literary hack doing the work for which his employer takes credit. **5.** ~ **moth,** hovering white nocturnal moth; ~ **town,** town with few or no remaining inhabitants; ~**-word,** word originating from writer's or printer's error or popular etymology, e.g. *tweed*; **the ~ walks,** (Theatr. sl.) salaries are, or will soon be, paid. **6.** Hence ~'HOOD (-t-h-) *n.*, ~'LIKE *a.* **7.** *v.t.* & *i.* haunt, prowl, act, as a ghost; act or write as a ghost writer etc. (*for*). [OE *gāst*, = OS *gēst*, OHG *geist* f. WG *gaista; orig. *gh-* first in Caxton, prob. due to Flem. *gheest;* sense 2 f. obs. meanings 'principle of life, spirit']

ghō'stl|ў (gō'-) *a.* **1.** as of a ghost, spectral. **2.** (arch.) spiritual, incorporeal, concerned with sacred or ecclesiastical matters. **3.** Hence ~ĭNESS *n.* [OE *gāstlic* (as prec., -LY¹)]

ghoul (gōōl, gowl) *n.* spirit preying on corpses in Muslim superstition; (fig.) person unnaturally interested in death etc.; hence ~'ĬSH¹ *a.* [f. Arab. *ġūl* protean desert demon]

GHQ *abbr.* General Headquarters.

‖**ghyll.** Var. of GILL².

GI (jē'ī, jēī') *a.* & *n.* **1.** *a.* for or pertaining to US armed forces or servicemen; ~ **bride,** foreign woman married to US serviceman on duty abroad; ~ **Joe,** (colloq.) US private soldier. **2.** *n.* US private soldier. [abbr. of *government* (or *general) issue*]

giallo antico (jahlō ahntē'kō) *n.* rich-yellow marble found in Italian ruins. [It., = ancient yellow]

gī'ant *n.* & *a.* **1.** *n.* legendary being of human form but superhuman stature; (Gk Myth.) one of such beings who fought against the gods; abnormally tall person, animal, or plant; large diffuse star. **2.** agency of enormous power; person of extraordinary ability, courage, strength, etc., (**there were ~s in those ·**

days, our forefathers were superior to us). **3.** ~--**killer,** one who defeats a seemingly much more powerful opponent; ~-**powder,** kind of dynamite; ~('s)-**stride,** gymnastic apparatus of pole with revolving head and hanging ropes enabling user to take huge strides round pole. **4.** Hence ~ESS¹ *n.*, ~ISM *n.* = GIGANTISM, ~-LIKE *a.* **5.** *a.* of extraordinary size or force, gigantic, monstrous; (of plant) unusually large (*the giant fennel*); *giant* PANDA, SLALOM. [ME *geant* (later infl. by L) f. OF, f. Rom. **gagante* f. L f. Gk *gigas gigantos*]

giaour (jowr) *n.* (Turkish derog. name for) non--Muslim, esp. Christian. [f. Pers. *gaur, gōr*]

gĭb (j-, g-) *n.* piece of wood or metal used to keep some part of machine etc. in place; bolt, pin, or wedge. [18th c.; orig. unkn.]

Gib. *n.* (colloq.) Gibraltar. [abbr.]

gĭ'bber¹ (g-) *n.* (Austral.) boulder, (large) stone. [Aboriginal]

gĭ'bber² (j-, g-) *v.i.* & *n.* **1.** *v.i.* speak fast and inarticulately, chatter like an ape. **2.** *n.* such speech or sound. [imit.]

gibberĕ'llin *n.* one of a group of compounds acting as growth-regulators in many plants. [f. *Gibberella* genus of fungi, dim. of genus-name *Gibbera* f. L *gibber* hump + -IN]

gĭ'bberish (j-, g-) *n.* unintelligible speech, meaning-less sounds; blundering or ungrammatical talk. [perh. f. GIBBER² (but found earlier) + -ISH¹ as used in *Spanish, Swedish,* etc.]

gĭ'bbĕt *n.*, & *v.t.* **1.** *n.* (Hist.) gallows; upright post with arm on which bodies of executed criminals were hung up. **2.** death by hanging. **3.** *v.t.* put to death by hanging; expose on gibbet; hang up as on gibbet; hold up to infamy or contempt. [ME, f. OF *gibet* gallows dim. of *gibe* club, prob. f. Gmc]

gĭ'bbon (g-) *n.* long-armed SE Asian ape of genus *Hylobates.* [F, f. aboriginal name]

gĭ'bbous (g-) *a.* convex, protuberant; (of moon or planet) having bright part greater than semicircle and less than circle; humped, humpbacked; hence or cogn. **gibbō'sity** (g-) *n.*, ~-LY² *adv.* [ME, f. LL *gibbosus* (*gibbus* hump; see -OUS)]

gibe, jibe², *v.* & *n.* **1.** *v.i.* & *t.* flout, jeer, mock, (at or *at*); hence **gī'bER¹** *n.* **2.** *n.* act of gibing, taunt. [perh. f. OF *giber* handle roughly]

gĭ'blĕt|s *n. pl.* edible parts of bird taken out or cut off before cooking, as liver, gizzard; ~ **soup** (made with these). [f. OF *gibelet* game stew, perh. f. **giberet* (*gibier* game)]

giddăp (gĭ'dăp, -ă'p) *int.* (colloq.) of command to horse etc.: go on, go faster. [f. *get up*]

gĭ'ddȳ (g-) *a.* & *v.* **1.** *a.* having sensation of whirling and tendency to fall, stagger, or spin round (*with sickness, success,* etc.); making dizzy (*a giddy precipice, maze, success*); circling with bewildering speed; mentally intoxicated, incapable of attention, excit-able, frivolous (**play the ~ goat** or **ox,** fool about); inconstant, flighty, (also as intensive, esp. iron.); **my ~ aunt,** sl. excl. of surprise; hence **gĭ'ddĭLY²** *adv.,* ~'ddĬNESS *n.,* (g-). **2.** *v.t.* & *i.* make or become giddy. [OE *gidig* insane (as GOD, -Y²), lit. 'possessed by a god']

Gĭ'dĕon (g-) *n.* member of organization placing Bibles in hotel rooms etc. [f. ~ in Judges 6:11 ff.]

gift (g-) *n.*, & *v.t.* **1.** *n.* giving (*the living* is in the ~ of *the Bishop,* is his to bestow; *came to me by free gift*); (Law) voluntary transference of property without compensation. **2.** thing given, present, donation, (FREE¹ *gift*; *would not have it as a ~,* (arch.) **at a ~,** even gratis); faculty miraculously bestowed, virtue looked upon as emanation from heaven etc., (*gift of* TONGUE¹s); natural endowment (*gift of the* GAB), talent, whence ~'ED²*a.;* easy task etc. **3.** ~-**book,** book given or suitable for giving as present; ~ **coupon,** voucher issued with certain commodities, a quantity of which entitles holder to a gift; ~-**horse,** horse given as present (*look a ~-horse in the mouth,* find fault with a gift); ∼ **shop,** shop selling articles suitable for gifts; ∼ **token** or **voucher,** voucher for money to buy something, used as gift; ∼**-wrap** *v.t.*, wrap attractively (as gift). **4.** Hence ∼'IE *n.* (Sc.; *the giftie gie us to see oursels as others see us*). **5.** *v.t.* endow with gifts, present *with* as gift; bestow as gift (*to* person; *away*). [ME, f. ON *gipt* = OE, OS, OHG *gift*, Goth. *-gifts* f. Gmc **geftiz (*gebh-* GIVE[1])]

gig[1] (g-) *n.* **1.** light two-wheeled one-horse carriage. **2.** light narrow clinker-built ship's-boat for rowing or sailing; rowing-boat chiefly used for racing. [ME in var. senses; prob. imit.]

gig[2] (g-) *n.* kind of fish-spear. [short for *fizgig, fishgig*; cf. Sp. *fisga* harpoon]

gig[3] (g-) *n.*, & *v.i.* **(-gg-).** (colloq.) **1.** *n.* engagement of musician(s) to play jazz etc., esp. for one night only; place of such performance. **2.** *v.i.* perform gig. [20th c.; orig. unkn.]

gī'ga- (j-, g-) *pref.* denoting factor of 10[9] (*gigametre*). [f. Gk *gigas* giant]

gīgǎ'nt|ic *a.* giant-like in size, stature, etc., abnormally large, huge; hence or cogn. ∼E'SQUE *a.*, ∼ICALLY *adv.* [f. L *gigas gigantis* GIANT + -IC]

gi'gantism *n.* abnormal largeness, esp. (Path.) excessive growth due to hormonal imbalance, or to polyploidy in plants. [f. as prec. + -ISM]

gi'ggle (g) *v.* & *n.* **1.** *v.i.* laugh in affected or silly manner, titter, have small bursts of half-suppressed laughter. **2.** *v.t.* utter thus. **3.** *n.* such laugh, freq. in *pl.* (*fit of*) the giggles; (colloq.) amusing person or thing, a joke (*did it for a giggle*); hence **gi'ggly**[2] *a.* [imit.; cf. Du. *gi(e)chelen*, G *gickeln*]

gi'glet, gi'glot, (g-) *n.* giggling girl. [ME, perh. f. obs. *gig* flighty girl (GIG[1]), later assoc. w. prec.]

gigmǎ'nity (g-) *n.* respectable unimaginative middle classes, Philistines. [made by Carlyle 1831, f. *gigman* (GIG[1], MAN[1]) + -ITY]

gi'golō (jĭ'-, zhĭ'-) *n.* (*pl.* ∼s). professional male dancing-partner or escort; young man paid by older woman for his attentions. [F, formed as masc. of *gigole* dance-hall woman]

gi'got *n.* leg of mutton etc.; ∼ **sleeve** = LEG-*of*-mutton sleeve. [F, dim. of dial. *gigue* leg]

gigue (zhēg) *n.* = JIG[1]; (Mus.) lively dance with two sections each repeated. [F, see JIG[1]]

Gi'la (hē'la) *n.* ∼ **(monster),** large venomous lizard of SW United States. [River ∼ in New Mexico & Arizona]

gi'lbert (g-) *n.* electromagnetic unit of magnetomotive force. [f. W. *Gilbert,* Engl. physician d. 1603]

Gilbēr'tian (g-; -tĭan, -shan) *a.* (Of situation etc.) ludicrous or paradoxical, as in Gilbert and Sullivan opera. [f. W. S. *Gilbert,* Engl. librettist d. 1911 + -IAN]

gild[1] (g-) *v.t.* (*p.p.* sometimes **gilt** as *adj.* in lit. sense, otherwise ∼'ed). cover with thin layer of gold laid on as gold leaf or otherwise (*gild the LILY*; ∼ **the pill,** soften down unpleasant necessity), whence ∼'ER[1], ∼'ING[1] (2, 4), *ns.*; tinge or adorn with golden colour or light; give specious brilliance to by fair words; ∼ed **cage,** luxurious but restrictive surroundings; ∼ed or **gilt spurs,** (arch.) emblem of knighthood; ∼ed **youth,** young people of fashion and wealth; **gi'ltwood** *a.*, made of wood and gilded. [OE *gyldan,* = ON *gylla* f. Gmc **gulthjan (*gultham* GOLD)]

gild[2]. See GUILD.

*Gi'lderoy (g-) *n.* (colloq.) **higher than** ∼'**s kite,** very high, out of sight. [name of Scottish robber]

gi'lgai (gĭ'lgī) *n.* (Austral.) saucer-like natural reservoir for rain-water. [Aboriginal]

gill[1] (g-) *n.* (usu. in *pl.*), & *v.t.* **1.** *n.* respiratory organ in fishes and other water-breathing animals; wattles or dewlap of fowls; vertical radial plate on under side of mushroom etc.; flesh below person's jaws and ears (**rosy, green, about the** ∼**s,** healthy-looking, sickly-looking). **2.** ∼**-cover,** bony case protecting fish's gills; ∼**-net,** (for entangling fishes by the gills). **3.** Hence (-)∼ED[2] (-ld) *a.* **4.** *v.t.* gut (fish); cut off gills of

(mushroom); catch in gill-net. [ME, f. ON **gil* f. Gmc **geliz*]

||**gill**[2] (g-) *n.* deep usu. wooded ravine; narrow mountain torrent. [ME, f. ON *gil* glen]

gill[3] *n.* quarter-pint liquid measure; ||(dial.) half-pint. [ME, f. OF *gille,* med. L *gillo* f. LL *gello, gillo* water-pot]

gill[4] *n.* **1.** (derog.) young woman. **2.** (colloq.) female ferret. [ME, abbr. of *Gillian* f. OF *Juliane* f. L *Juliana* (*Julius*)]

gillaroo' (g-) *n.* Irish species of trout. [f. Ir. *giolla* fellow, *ruadh* red]

gi'llie (g-) *n.* **1.** man or boy attending person hunting or fishing in Scotland. **2.** (Hist.) Highland chief's attendant. [f. Gael. *gille* lad, servant]

gi'llion (-yon) *n.* a thousand million; large number. [f. GIGA- + MILLION]

gi'llyflower *n.* **1.** (clove) ∼, clove-scented pink (CLOVE[3]). **2.** other similarly scented flower, as wall-flower or white stock. [ME *gilofre, gerofle,* f. OF *gilofre, girofle* f. med. L f. Gk *karuophullon* (*karuon* nut, *phullon* leaf) clove-tree; assim. to FLOWER]

gilt[1] (g-). See GILD[1].

gilt[2] (g-) *n.* **1.** gilding (**take the** ∼ **off the gingerbread,** strip thing of adventitious attractions); ∼**-edged,** (of securities, stocks, etc.) having high degree of reliability as investment. **2.** gilt-edged security. [f. prec.]

gilt[3] (g-) *n.* young sow. [ME, f. ON *gyltr*]

gi'mbals (j-, g-; -z) *n. pl.* contrivance (usu. of rings and pivots) for keeping articles (esp. compass and chronometer) horizontal at sea; ∼**-ring,** (ring in) gimbals. [var. of earlier *gimmal* f. OF *gemel* double finger-ring, f. L *gemellus* dim. of *geminus* twin]

gi'mcrack *n.* & *a.* **1.** *n.* trumpery article, knick-knack, useless ornament; hence ∼ERY (5) *n.*, ∼Y[2] *a.* **2.** *a.* showy and flimsy, worthless, trumpery. [ME *gibecrake* (? inlaid work), of unkn. orig.]

gi'mlet (g-) *n.* kind of small boring-tool (usu. with wooden crosspiece as handle and screw at pointed end); cocktail usu. of gin and lime-juice; ∼**-eye,** eye with sharp or piercing glance. [ME, f. OF *gumbelet,* dim. of *guimble*]

gi'mme (g-) *v.t.* (colloq.) = *give me.* [contr.]

gi'mmick (g-) *n.* (colloq.) tricky device, esp. one adopted for the purpose of attracting attention or publicity; hence ∼RY (5) *n.*, ∼Y[2] *a.* [20th c. US; orig. unkn.]

gimp[1], **gymp,** (g-) *n.* silk, worsted, or cotton twist with cord or wire running through it, used esp. as trimming; fishing-line of silk etc. bound with wire; coarser thread outlining design of lace. [Du., of unkn. orig.]

gimp[2] (g-) *n.* (sl.) courage. [20th c.; orig. uncert.]

gin[1] *n.*, & *v.t.* **(-nn-). 1.** snare, net, trap. **2.** *n.* hoisting apparatus, kind of crane or windlass. **3.** machine for separating cotton from its seeds. **4.** *v.t.* remove seeds of (cotton) with gin. [ME, f. OF *engin* ENGINE]

gin[2] *n.* **1.** spirit distilled from grain or malt and flavoured with juniper berries, GENEVA[1]; *gin and* IT[2]; **pink** ∼, gin flavoured with angostura bitters. **2.** *∼**-mill,** (sl.) drinking-saloon; ∼**-palace,** gaudily decorated public house; ∼ **rummy,** form of RUMMY[2] where player with cards totalling less than ten may terminate play; *gin SLING[2]. [abbr. of GENEVA[1]]

gin[3] (g-) *conj.* (Sc. & dial.) if. [app. rel. to *gif* (as IF, perh. after GIVE[1])]

gin[4] *n.* (Austral.) Aboriginal woman. [Aboriginal]

gi'nger (-nj-) *n.*, *a.*, & *v.t.* **1.** *n.* (plant esp. of genus *Zingiber* with) hot spicy root used in cooking and medicine and preserved in syrup or candied as sweet (**black** ∼, unscraped, **white** ∼, scraped, ginger). **2.** mettle, spirit; stimulation; ||∼ **group,** group that urges party or movement to more decided action. **3.** *n.* & *a.* (of) light reddish-yellow colour. **4.** ∼**-ale, -beer,** kinds of aerated ginger-flavoured drink (∼*-beer plant,* mixture of yeast and bacteria to ferment sugar solution in making ginger-beer); ∼**bread,** (*n.*) a cake made with treacle and flavoured with ginger (∼*bread nut,* small button-like biscuit of it; *take the* GILT[2] *off the* *gingerbread*, (*a.* & *n.*, w. allus. to fancy and often gilded shapes in which it was made) gaudy, showy, tawdry, (ornaments, e.g. Archit.); ∼**-nut**, gingerbread nut; ∼**-pop**, (colloq.) = *ginger-ale*; ∼**-race**, a root of ginger; ∼**-snap**, thin brittle biscuit flavoured with ginger; ∼ **wine**, drink of fermented sugar, water, and bruised ginger. **5.** Hence ∼Y² *a*. **6.** *v.t.* flavour with ginger; (fig., from treatment of horses) rouse *up* (person). [ME f. OE *gingiber* & OF *gingi-*(*m*)*bre*, both f. med. L *gingiber* f. L *zingiber* f. Gk *ziggiberis* f. Skr. *śṛṅgaveram* (*śṛṅgam* horn, *-vera* body, f. antler-shape of root)]

‖**gingerá'de** (-nj-) *n*. = GINGER-*beer*. [f. prec., after *lemonade*]

gi'ngerlȳ (-nj-) *adv.* & *a*. with or showing extreme caution so as to avoid making a noise or injuring oneself or what is touched or trodden on. [perh. f. OF *gensor* delicate, compar. of *gent* graceful f. L *genitus* (well-)born + -LY¹,²]

gi'ngham (gĭ'ngam) *n*. plain-woven cotton cloth of dyed yarn often in stripes or checks. [f. Du. *gingang* f. Malay *ginggang* (orig. adj. = striped)]

gi'ngili (-nj-) *n*. sesame (oil). [f. Hindi *jinjali* f. Arab. *juljulān*]

gingī'val (-nj-) *a*. of the gums; so **gingivi'tis** (-nj-) *n*. [f. mod. L *gingivalis* f. L *gingiva* GUM¹; see -AL]

gi'ngkō (g-). Var. of GINKGO.

gi'nglȳm|us (-nggl-) *n*. (*pl.* ∼**i** *pr.* -ī). (Anat.) hingelike joint in body with motion only in one plane (e.g. elbow). [mod. L, f. Gk *gigglumos* hinge]

gink (g-) *n*. (sl., usu. derog.) fellow, man. [20th c. US; orig. unkn.]

gi'nkgō (g-;-ngkgō,-ngkō) *n*. (*pl.*∼s *or*∼es). tree with fan-shaped leaves and yellow flowers, orig. from China and Japan. [f. Jap. *ginkyo* f. Chin. *yinxing* silver apricot]

gi'nsĕng *n*. (root of) medicinal plant of genus *Panax* found in E. Asia and N. America. [f. Chin. *renshen* perh. = man-image, w. allus. to forked root]

Giocǒ'nda (jo-). *a*. (Of smile etc.) enigmatic. [f. painting *La Gioconda* by L. da Vinci of wife of F. del *Giocondo*]

gi'ppȳ *n*. (sl.) Egyptian soldier; Egyptian cigarette; gypsy; ∼ **tummy**, diarrhoea of visitors to hot countries. [f. foll. & *Egyptian* + -Y³]

gi'psȳ. See GYPSY.

gira'ffe (-ah'f, -ă'f) *n*. African ruminant quadruped, tallest living animal, with spotted skin and long neck and forelegs. [f. F *girafe*, ult. f. Arab. *zarāfa*]

gi'randōle *n*. revolving firework, discharge of rockets from revolving wheel; revolving jet of water; branched candle-bracket or candlestick; ear-ring or pendant with large central stone surrounded by small ones. [F, f. It. *girandola* (*girare* GYRATE²)]

gi'rasŏl, -sōle, *n*. kind of opal reflecting reddish glow, fire-opal. [orig. = sunflower, f. F *girasol* or f. It. *girasole* (*girare* as prec., *sole* sun)]

gĭrd¹ (g-) *v.t.* (∼'**ed** *or* **girt**). (literary). **1.** ∼ (**up**), encircle (waist), encircle waist of (person), with belt esp. to confine clothes (∼ one**self**, (**up**) one's **loins**, prepare for action); (arch.) invest *with* strength, power, etc. **2.** equip *with* sword in belt; fasten (sword etc.) on *or* *on* with belt (*to* or *upon* or *on*); secure (clothes) on body with girdle or belt; put (cord etc.) *round*; encircle (town etc.) *with* besiegers or siege-works; (of belt, fence, sea, etc.) encircle. [OE *gyrdan*, = OS *gurdian*, OHG *gurten*, ON *gyrtha* f. Gmc *gurdhjan* (as GIRTH)]

gĭrd² (g-) *v.i.* & *n*. jeer or gibe *at*. [ME = 'strike' etc.; orig. unkn.]

gĭr'der (g-) *n*. beam supporting joists of floor; iron or steel beam for like use; latticed or other compound structure of steel etc. forming span of bridge, roof, etc. [f. GIRD¹ + -ER¹]

gĭr'dle¹ (g-) *n*., & *v.t.* **1.** *n*. belt, cord, etc. used to gird waist; corset, esp. elasticated and not extending above waist; thing that surrounds like a girdle; part of cut gem dividing crown from base and embraced by

the setting; (Anat.) bony support for upper or lower limb (*shoulder* or *pectoral, pelvic* or *hip, girdle*); ring round tree made by removal of bark. **2.** *v.t.* surround with girdle (*about, in, round*); kill (tree) or make it more fruitful by removing ring of bark round trunk. [OE *gyrdel*, = OHG *gurtil*, ON *gyrthill* (as GIRD¹, -LE 1)]

gĭr'dle² (g-) *n*. (Sc. & N. Engl.) circular iron plate placed over fire or otherwise heated for baking, toasting, etc.; ∼**-cake** (made on girdle). [var. of GRIDDLE]

gĭr'dler (g-) *n*. (arch.) maker of girdles (now only as guild-name). [ME, f. GIRDLE¹ + -ER¹]

gĭrl (g-) *n*. **1.** female child; young woman; *old girl* (see OLD 7); woman working in office, shop, factory, etc., woman secretary or other assistant; female servant; man's sweetheart. **2.** *girl* FRIDAY; ∼**-friend**, female friend, esp. boy's or man's usual or preferred female companion; ∼ **guide,** = GUIDE¹ 4; **les** ∼**s** (lā-; after F *les* than), girls collectively, esp. chorus-girls; **the** ∼**s,** group of women esp. with similar interests, grown-up daughters of a family; *∼ **scout,** = GUIDE¹ 4. **3.** Hence ∼'DOM, ∼'HOOD, *ns.*, ∼'ISH¹ *a*. [ME *gurle, girle, gerle,* perh. cogn. w. LG *gör* child]

gĭr'lie (g-) *n.* & *a*. **1.** *n*. little girl (as term of endearment). **2.** *a*. (Of publication etc.) containing many erotic pictures of young women usu. with little or no clothing. [f. prec. + -IE]

gĭr'lȳ-gĭr'lȳ (g-; -g-) *a*. exaggeratedly or affectedly girlish. [redupl. f. *girly* (GIRL, -Y²)]

gĭr'ō *n*. (*pl.* ∼s). system of credit transfer between banks, post offices, etc. [G f. It., = circulation (of money)]

gĭrt¹ (g-). See GIRD¹.

gĭrth, gĭrt², (g-) *n*. & *v*. **1.** *n*. leather or cloth band tightened round body of horse etc. to secure saddle etc.; measurement round any more or less cylindrical thing. **2.** *v.t.* surround; encircle (horse etc.), secure (saddle etc.), with girth. **3.** *v.i.* measure (so much) in girth. [ME, f. ON *gjörth*, Goth. *gairda* f. Gmc **gerðō,* cogn. w. GARTH, GIRD¹, GIRDLE¹]

***gi'smō,** ***gi'zmō,** (gĭ'z-) *n*. (*pl.* ∼s). (sl.) gadget, gimmick. [20th c.; orig. unkn.]

gist *n*. **1.** substance or essence of a matter. **2.** (Law) real ground of action etc. [OF, 3rd sing. pres. of *gesir* lie f. L *jacēre*]

git (g-) *n*. (sl., derog.) worthless person. [var. of GET¹.]

gi'ttern (g-) *n*. gut-stringed instrument, kind of early guitar. [ME, f. OF *guiterne*; cf. CITHERN, GUITAR]

give¹ (g-) *v.t.* & *i*. (**gave** *pr*. gāv; GIVEN). **1.** *v.t.* transfer possession of gratuitously, hand over as present, (*to* recipient); confer ownership of with or without actual delivery, render (benefit etc.) without payment; (abs.) bestow alms or donations (*to*); confer, grant, (favour, honour, etc.); accord (one's heart, affection, confidence); (of God etc.) grant (faculty etc., or *to* be or do; ∼ **me,** (in *imper*.) I prefer or admire: *give me the good old times*); bequeath; sanction marriage of (daughter etc.; usu. *in marriage*); ∼ one**self,** (of woman) yield sexually. **2.** deliver, hand over, (without reference to ownership), put (food etc.) for person to consume, administer (medicine, *the* BOOT¹, *the* SACK¹; ∼ **it him** etc. (**hot**), administer punishment; ∼ *child* etc. **something to cry for,** chastise for causeless crying; ∼ person **what for,** (sl.) punish or scold him severely); deliver (message, LOVE¹, compliments, etc.); commit, consign, entrust, (*give into custody* or ‖*in* CHARGE¹); pledge, assign as guarantee, (one's WORD¹, honour, etc.). **3.** make over in exchange or payment, pay, sell *for* price, (∼ **as good as** *one* **gets,** retort adequately in words or blows; *give a* ROLAND *for an* Oliver; *not give a* DAMN etc.; *give* person *his* DUE²; *would give the* WORLD or one's EAR¹.5.). **4.** devote, dedicate, addict, (*gave his life to it*; *give* one's *mind to a matter*; *much given to these pursuits*). **5.** exert (some action or effort) esp. to affect another person (*give him a kick, a kiss, a sly look*; *give a jump, cry,* etc.; *give orders*; *give person one's blessing*; *give*

BIRTH, CHASE[1], RISE[2], TONGUE[1]; *give you joy, good day,* [prob. orig. w. ellipsis of *God*, now taken as = *wish* with *I* expressed or omitted]); (colloq.) tell, offer, (esp. something unacceptable), (abs.) tell what one knows; deliver (judgement etc.) authoritatively (*give the case,* or *it, for* or *against* person; of umpire in cricket, *give batsman out* or *not out*); (in *p.p.,* of document) dated; provide (party, meal) as host. **6.** present, offer, expose, hold out, show, (*give* person one's *hand* or *arm,* a BACK[1], EAR[1]; '*The Times*' *gives the facts; gives no sign of life; thermometer gives 80° in the shade*); read, recite, sing, act, perform, (play, lecture, etc.). **7.** make partaker of, impart, be source of, (*gave me his sore throat; gave its name to the battle; she gave him four sons; give a piece of* one's MIND[1]; *give to the* WORLD; ∼ person *to understand, know,* etc., inform or assure him). **8.** allot, assign, ascribe, grant, assume, (*he was given the contract, the name of John, quarters; under the given conditions; given health, given that I remain healthy, the thing can be done*). **9.** yield as product or result (*lamp gives a bad light; analysis gives the following figures*). **10.** cause or allow to have (*solitude gives it its only charm; gave me much pain; this gives him a right to complain; give* oneself AIR[1]s; *give* person BEST[1]; *give* GROUND[1], PLACE[1] 12, WAY; *can give you five minutes before I must go; gave myself an hour to get there; give him thirty seconds start; was given a rest*); ∼ **and take,** (*v.i.*) exchange words, blows, or concessions, (*n.*) exchange of words etc., compromise; ∼ **or take,** (colloq.) add or subtract in estimating. **11.** *v.i.* collapse, lose firmness, yield to pressure, become relaxed, make room, shrink. **12.** (Of window, passage, etc.) look, lead, (*up*)*on, on to, into.* **13.** (colloq.) be happening (*what gives?*). **14.** (w. advs.): ∼ **away,** transfer by gift, hand over (bride) ceremonially to bridegroom, betray or expose to ridicule or detection (*give the* GAME[1] or SHOW[2] *away*), distribute (prizes), ∼*-away* n., (colloq.) act of giving away, free gift, low price, inadvertent betrayal; ∼ **back,** give (thing) to previous owner or in exchange; ∼ **down,** (of cow) let (milk, or abs.) flow; ∼ **forth,** emit, publish, report; ∼ **in,** yield, cease fighting or arguing, hand in (document) to proper official; ∼ **off,** emit (vapour etc.); ∼ **out,** announce, emit, distribute, cease or break down from exhaustion etc., run short; ∼ **over,** cease from doing, abandon (habit etc.), desist, hand over, devote; ∼ **up,** resign, surrender, part with (*give up the* GHOST), deliver (fugitive etc.) into hands of pursuers etc., abandon one*self to* a feeling etc., cease to have to do with, cease from effort of doing, (in *refl.* or *p.p.*) devote or addict *to,* divulge (names of accomplices etc.), pronounce incurable or insoluble, renounce hope (of). **15.** Hence ∼'ABLE (-və-) a., gi'VER[1] (g-) n. [OE g(*i*)*efan,* = OS, OHG *geban,* ON *gefa,* Goth. *giban* f. Gmc **gebhan*]

give[2] (g-) n. yielding to pressure, elasticity, (*there is no give in a stone floor*). [f. prec.]

gi'ven (g-) a. & n. **1.** a. In vbl senses; *∼ **name,** name given (as) at baptism. **2.** n. known fact or situation. [p.p. of GIVE[1]]

*****gizmo.** See GISMO.

gi'zzard (g-) n. bird's second stomach for grinding food mixed in the first with gastric juice; specially muscular stomach of some fish, insects, molluscs, etc.; **stick in** one's ∼, be distasteful. [ME *giser* f. OF *giser, gesier* etc. f. Rom. **gicerium* f. L *gigeria* cooked entrails of fowl]

glabe'lla n. (*pl.* ∼e). (Anat.) smooth part of forehead above line of eyebrows. [mod. L, f. L *glabellus* a. dim. of *glaber* smooth]

glā'brous a. (Anat. & Bot.) free from hair or down, smooth-skinned. [f. L *glaber glabri* hairless + -OUS]

glacé (glǎ'sā) a. (Of cloth, leather, etc.) smooth, polished; (of fruit) iced, sugared; ∼ **icing** (made with icing sugar and water). [F, p.p. of *glacer* to ice, gloss (*glace* ice; see GLACIER)]

glā'cial (-sĭəl, -shəl) a. **1.** of ice, icy, (lit. or fig.); (Chem.) forming icelike crystals on freezing. **2.** (Geol.) characterized or produced by the presence or agency of ice; ∼ **epoch** or **period** (when unusually

large area was covered with ice-sheet). **3.** Hence ∼LY[2] adv. [F, or f. L *glacialis* icy (*glacies* ice; see -AL)]

glā'ciāted a. marked or polished by ice-action; covered with glaciers or ice-sheet; so **glāciA'TION** n. [p.p. of *glaciate* f. L *glaciare* freeze (*glacies* ice) + -ATE[3]]

glā'cier n. slowly moving river or mass of ice formed by accumulation of snow on higher ground. [F (*glace* ice f. Rom. **glacia* f. L *glacies*)]

glăciŏ'log|ȳ n. science of geological action of ice; hence **glăciolŏ'g**ICAL a., ∼IST (3) n. [f. L *glacies* ice + -o- + -LOGY]

glā'cis (-sĭs, -sē) n. (*pl.* same *pr.* -siz or -sēz). bank sloping down from fort, on which attackers are exposed to defenders' missiles etc. [F, f. OF *glacier* to slip (*glace* ice; see GLACIER)]

glăd[1] a., & v.t. (**-dd-**). **1.** *pred. a.* pleased (*I am glad, glad about* or *of* it, glad *to hear* it, glad (*that*) *it is so, shall be glad to come* etc., (iron.) *should be glad to know*). **2.** a. (Of looks, feelings, etc.) marked by, filled with, expressing, joy; (of news or event) giving joy; (of natural objects) bright, beautiful. **3. the** ∼ **eye,** (sl.) amorous glance; ∼ **hand,** the hand of welcome; ∼**-ha'nd** v.t., greet cordially; ∼ **rags,** (colloq.) best clothes, evening dress. **4.** Hence ∼'dEN[6] v.t., ∼'LY[2] adv., ∼'NESS n., (poet.) ∼'SOME[1] a. **5.** v.t. (arch.) make glad. [OE *glæd,* = OS *glad,* ON *glathr,* OHG *glat* smooth f. Gmc **gladhaz*]

glăd[2] n. (colloq., usu. in *pl.*) gladiolus. [abbr.]

glāde n. clear open space or passage between forest trees. [16th. c.; orig. unkn.]

glā'diātor n. man trained to fight with sword or other weapon at ancient Roman shows; political etc. champion in argument, controversialist; hence **glădiātōr'**IAL a. [L (*gladius* sword)]

glădiō'l|us n. (*pl.* ∼i *pr.* -ī, or ∼uses). iridaceous plant with sword-shaped leaves and (often bright-coloured) flower-spikes. [L, dim. of *gladius* sword]

Glā'dstone n. & a. ∼ (**bag**), light portmanteau opening into two equal compartments. [f. W. E. ∼, Engl. statesman d. 1898]

Glăgoli'tic n. of alphabet ascribed to St. Cyril and formerly used in writing some Slavonic languages. [f. mod. L *glagoliticus* f. Serbo-Croatian *glagolica* Glagolitic alphabet f. OSlav. *glagol* word]

glair, glair|e, n. white of egg; adhesive preparation made from it; any similar viscous substance; hence ∼'EOUS, ∼'Y[2], adjs. [ME, f. OF *glaire,* ult. f. L *clara* fem. of *clarus* clear]

glaive n. (arch. or poet.) broadsword, sword. [ME f. OF, app. f. L *gladius* sword]

glăm n., a., & v.t. (**-mm-**). (colloq.) **1.** n. glamour. **2.** a. glamorous. **3.** v.t. glamorize. [abbr.]

Glam. abbr. Glamorgan(shire).

glā'moriz|e, -is|e (-īz), ||**-our-** (-er-), v.t. make glamorous or attractive; hence ∼A'TION n. [f. foll. + -IZE]

||**glā'mour** (-er), *****glā'mor,** n., & v.t. **1.** n. magic, enchantment, (**cast a** ∼ **over,** enchant); delusive or alluring or exciting beauty or charm; (esp. feminine) physical attractiveness (∼ **girl,** young woman possessing this; so ∼ **boy**); hence **glă'mor**OUS a. **2.** v.t. affect with glamour, bewitch, enchant; (colloq.) make glamorous. [18th c., var. of GRAMMAR in sense GRAMARYE]

glance[1] (-ah-) v. & n. **1.** v.i. & t. (Of weapon) glide off or *off* object instead of striking it full; (Cricket) deflect (ball) with glance-stroke; (of talk or talker) pass quickly *over,* glide *off* or *from,* subject; ∼ **at,** make passing and usu. sarcastic allusion to. **2.** v.i. (Of bright object or light) flash, dart, gleam; (of eye) cast momentary look (*down, up,* etc.); ∼ **at,** give brief look at; ∼ **over,** read cursorily. **3.** v.t. ∼ one's **eye,** direct it *at, over,* etc. **4.** n. swift oblique movement or impact; (Cricket) stroke with bat's face turned slantwise to deflect ball; (sudden glance producing) flash or gleam; brief look (*at, into, over,* etc.); **at a** ∼, immediately upon looking. [ME *glence* etc., prob. a nasalized form of obs. *glace* in same sense, f. OF *glacier* to slip (see GLACIS)]

glance² (-ah-) *n.* lustrous sulphide ore (*copper glance, lead glance*). [f. G *glanz* lustre]

gländ¹ *n.* organ in animal body secreting substances for use in the body or for ejection; (Bot.) secreting cell or group of cells on surface of plant-structure; so ~ULE *n.* [f. F *glande* f. OF *glandre* f. L *glandulae* throat-glands]

gländ² *n.* (Mech.) sleeve used to press a packing tight on a piston. [19th c., perh. var. of earlier *glam, glan* a vice, rel. to CLAMP¹]

glä'nder|s (-z) *n. pl.* (sometimes treated as *sing.*) contagious horse-disease with swellings below jaw and mucous discharge from nostrils; this disease communicated to man or to other animals; hence ~ED² (-erd), ~OUS, *adjs.* [f. OF *glandre* (see GLAND¹)]

glä'ndŭlar *a.* of or pertaining to gland(s) or glandule(s); ~ **fever,** infectious disease with swelling of lymph-glands. [f. F *glandulaire* (as GLAND¹*ule*; see -AR)]

gläns (-z) *n.* (*pl.* ~*des pr.* -dēz). (Anat.) conical part forming end of penis or clitoris. [L, = acorn]

glär|e¹ *v. & n.* **1.** *v.i.* shine dazzlingly or disagreeably; be over-conspicuous or obtrusive, whence ~ING² (2) *n.*; look fixedly or fiercely (*at, upon*). **2.** *v.t.* express (hate, defiance) by look. **3.** *n.* strong fierce light, oppressive unrelieved sunshine; tawdry brilliance; fierce or fixed look; hence ~'Y² *a.* [ME, = MDu. and MLG *glaren* gleam, glare]

*****gläre²** *a.* (Esp. of ice) smooth and glassy. [perh. f. *glare* frost (16th c., of uncert. orig.)]

glass¹ (-ahs) *n.* **1.** substance, usu. transparent, lustrous, hard, and brittle, made by fusing sand with soda or potash or both and other ingredients (CROWN¹, FLINT, PLATE¹, *glass*); substance of similar properties or composition (WATER¹-*glass*). **2.** glass utensils, ornaments, windows, greenhouse(s); glass vessel esp. for drinking from; ~('FUL), amount of liquid contained in this, drink (*a friendly glass; fond of his glass*; **has had a ~ too much,** is rather drunk); = HOUR-*glass*, SAND-*glass*; plate of glass covering picture; glass disc covering watch-face; glazed frame for plants. **3.** = LOOKING-*glass*; (esp. in *pl.*) = EYE¹*glass*; lens, esp. one that magnifies; telescope; (esp. in *pl.*) = FIELD--*glasses*, OPERA¹-*glass*; microscope; barometer. **4.** ~--**blower,** one who blows and shapes semi-molten glass; ~ **case** (chiefly of glass, for exhibiting or protecting objects); ~-**cloth,** (1) linen cloth for drying glasses, (2) cloth covered with powdered glass like glass-paper; ~ **cloth,** woven fabric of fine-spun glass; ~-**cutter,** workman or tool cutting glass; *glass* EYE¹ 4; ~ **fibre,** filament(s) of glass esp. as made into fabric or embedded as reinforcement in plastic; ~--**gall,** sandiver; ~'**house,** building where glass is made, greenhouse, (sl.) military prison; ~-**making,** manufacture of glass; ~-**paper** (covered with glass--dust, used for polishing); ~ **snake,** snakelike lizard of Southern US etc., with very brittle tail; ~'**ware,** articles made of glass; ~ **wool,** glass in form of fine fibres for packing and insulation; ~'**wort,** plant of genus *Salicornia* or *Salsola* formerly burnt for use in glass-making. [OE *glæs*, = OS, OHG *glas* f. WG var. of Gmc *glazam*]

glass² (-ahs) *v.t.* **1.** (usu. in *p.p.*) fit with glass, glaze. **2.** reflect as in mirror. **3.** look at or for with field-glasses. [f. prec.; cf. GLAZE]

gla'ssine (-ah'sēn) *n.* glossy transparent paper. [f. GLASS¹ + -INE⁵]

gla'ss|ў (-ah'-) *a.* having properties of or resembling glass; (of eye etc.) lacking fire, dull, fixed; (of water) lustrous and transparent, or smooth, as glass (so *glassy calm, surface,* etc.); hence ~ĭLY² *adv.,* ~ĭNESS *n.* [ME, f. GLASS¹ + -Y²]

Glaswē'gian (-ă-, -ah-; -s-, -z-; -jĭan, -jan) *a. & n.* (native or inhabitant) of Glasgow. [f. *Glasgow* after *Norwegian* etc.]

Glau'ber (-aw'-, -ow'-) *n.* ~'s **salt(s),** crystalline (hydrated) sodium sulphate used esp. as laxative. [f. J. R. ~, Ger. chemist d. 1668]

glaucō'ma *n.* eye-condition with increased pressure within eyeball and gradual loss of sight; hence ~tous *a.* [L, f. Gk *glaukōma -atos* (*glaukos*; see foll.)]

glau'cous *a.* (esp. Bot.) of dull greyish green or blue; covered with powdery bloom as of grapes. [f. L f. Gk *glaukos* + -OUS]

glāze *v. & n.* **1.** *v.t.* fit (window, picture) with glass, furnish (building) with glass windows (~ **in,** enclose thus). **2.** cover (pottery etc.) with glaze; fix (paint) on pottery thus; overlay (cloth, paper, leather, pastry, meat, etc.) with glaze. **3.** cover (eye) with film. **4.** cover (painted surface) with glaze. **5.** give glassy surface to, e.g. by rubbing. **6.** *v.i.* (Esp. of eye) become glassy; ~**d frost,** = SILVER¹ *thaw.* **7.** Hence **glā'zer¹** (1, 2) *n.*, **glā'zY²** *a.* **8.** *n.* vitreous substance used to glaze pottery; smooth lustrous coating on materials, e.g. edible coating of gelatin etc. on food; thin top-coat of transparent paint to modify tone of underlying colour; smooth surface formed by glazing; *thin coating of ice. [ME, f. obl. form of GLASS¹]

glā'zi|er (-zĭer, -zher) *n.* one whose trade is to glaze windows etc.; hence ~ERY (2) *n.* [ME, f. prec.; see -IER]

glā'zing *n.* In vbl senses; windows (DOUBLE *glazing*); material used to produce glaze. [ME, f. GLAZE + -ING¹]

||GLC *abbr.* Greater London Council.

gleam *n.,* & *v.i.* **1.** *n.* subdued or transient light; faint, temporary, or intermittent show of some quality etc. (*an occasional gleam of humour; not a gleam of hope*); hence ~'Y² *a.* **2.** *v.i.* emit gleams; shine with subdued or interrupted brightness. [OE *glǽm*, cogn. w. OS *glīmo*, MHG *glīmen* shine, OHG *gleimo* glow-worm, WG **glaimiz*; cf. GLIMMER]

glean *v.* **1.** *v.i.* gather ears of corn left by reapers. **2.** *v.t.* gather (such remains); strip (field etc.) thus; collect in small quantities, scrape together, (news, facts, etc.); hence ~'ER¹, ~'ING¹ (1, 2), *ns.* [ME, f. OF *glener* f. LL *glennare*, prob. f. Gaulish **glenn-* f. Celt. **glendn-*]

glēbe *n.* **1.** portion of land going with clergyman's benefice and providing revenue. **2.** (poet.) earth, land; a field. [ME, f. L *gl(a)eba* clod, soil]

glēde *n.* (arch. or dial.) = KITE 1. [OE *glida*, = ON *gletha* f. Gmc **glidhon* (as GLIDE)]

glee *n.* **1.** musical composition for three or more (prop. adult male) voices, one to each part, set to words grave or gay, often with contrasted movements and prop. without accompaniment; ~ **club,** society for singing glees and other part-songs; ~'**man,** (Hist.) travelling minstrel etc. **2.** mirth, lively and manifest delight; hence ~'FUL, ~'SOME¹, *adjs.* [OE *glīo*, *glēo* minstrelsy, jest, = ON *glý* f. Gmc **gliujam*]

Gleichschaltung (glī'kshahltŏong) *n.* standardization of political etc. institutions among authoritarian States. [G]

glĕn *n.* narrow valley. [f. Gael. & Ir. *gleann*]

glĕnga'rry (-n-g-) *n.* Highland cap with pointed front and usu. pair of ribbons attached at back. [f. G~ in Highland, Scotland]

glē'noid *a.* (Anat.) ~ **cavity** etc., shallow cavity on bone (esp. scapula and temporal bone) receiving projection of other bone to form joint. [f. F *glénoïde* f. Gk *glēnoeidēs* (*glēnē* socket; see -OID)]

gley (-ā) *n.* blue-grey waterlogged soil. [Ukrainian, = sticky blue clay, cogn. w. CLAY]

glī'|a *n.* = NEUROglia; hence ~AL *a.* [Gk, = glue]

glib *a.* (Of speaker, speech, etc.) fluent, ready, more voluble than sincere or thoughtful; (arch.) smooth, unimpeded; hence ~'LY² *adv.,* ~'NESS *n.* [rel. to obs. *glibbery* slippery = MLG *glibberich,* Du. *glibberig* f. Gmc **glibh-,* perh. imit.]

glīde *v. & n.* **1.** *v.i.* (Of liquid, ship, bird, train, snake, skater, etc.) pass, change position, by smooth continuous movement; (of aircraft) fly without engine-power; go quietly or stealthily; (of time etc.) pass gently and imperceptibly; pass gradually, shade off insensibly, *into*. **2.** *v.t.* cause to glide (*light airs glided the ship on her course*); traverse in glider. **3.** *n.* act of gliding; (Phonet.) gradually changing sound made in passing from one position of speech-organs to another; (Cricket) = GLANCE[1]; gliding dance or dance-step; flight in glider; ∼ **path,** aircraft's line of descent to land, esp. as indicated by ground radar. [OE *glīdan*, = OS *glīdan*, OHG *glītan* f. WG **glīdhan*]

gli′der *n.* In vbl senses; engineless aeroplane; (expert) user of this. [f. prec. + -ER[1]]

glim *n.* faint light; (arch. sl.) candle, lantern, (*douse the glim*). [17th c., perh. abbr. of GLIMMER or GLIMPSE]

gli′mmer *v.i.*, & *n.* **1.** *v.i.* shine faintly or intermittently. **2.** *n.* feeble or wavering light; faint gleam *of* hope or understanding; glimpse, half-view. [ME, prob. f. Scand. f. WG **glim-*, **glaim-* (see GLEAM)]

gli′mmering *n.* In vbl senses; = prec. 2. [ME, f. prec. + -ING[1]]

glimpse *n.* & *v.* **1.** *n.* faint and transient appearance, momentary or imperfect view *of*. **2.** *v.t.* catch glimpse of, see faintly or partly. **3.** *v.i.* shine faintly or intermittently; (poet.) appear faintly, dawn. [ME *glimse*, corresp. to MHG *glimsen* f. WG **glimisōjan* (as prec.)]

glint *v.* & *n.* **1.** *v.i.*, & *n.* flash, glitter, sparkle. **2.** *v.t.* make flash, reflect, (light). [alt. of ME *glent*, prob. of Scand. orig.]

glissa′de (-ä′d, -ā′d) *n.*, & *v.i.* **1.** (Mountaineering). slide down steep slope esp. of snow usu. on the feet with support of ice-axe etc. **2.** (Dancing). (make) gliding step. [F (*glisser* slip, slide; see -ADE)]

glissa′nd|**ō** *n.* (*pl.* ∼**i** *pr.* -e, *or* ∼**os**). (Mus.) succession of sounds made in passing from one note to another without silence of voice or instrument. [It., f. F *glissant* sliding (as prec.)]

glissé (glīsā′) *n.* (Ballet). (**pas**) ∼, sliding step in which flat of foot is often used. [F, p.p. of *glisser* (see GLISSADE)]

gli′sten (-ĭ′sen) *v.i.*, & *n.* **1.** glitter, sparkle. **2.** *v.i.* shine fitfully. [OE *glisnian* (*glisian* shine; see -EN[6])]

gli′ster *v.i.*, & *n.* (arch.) sparkle, glitter. [ME, f. MLG *glistern*, MDu. *glisteren*, cogn. w. prec.]

glitch *n.* (sl.) sudden irregularity or malfunction of equipment etc. [20th c.; orig. unkn.]

gli′tter *v.i.*, & *n.* **1.** (shine with) brilliant tremulous light, gleam, sparkle. **2.** *v.i.* be showy or splendid (*with* jewels etc., or fig., *glittering rhetoric, prospects*). [ME, f. ON *glitra* f. Gmc **glit-*]

gloa′ming *n.* evening twilight. [OE *glomung* (*glom* twilight cogn. w. GLOW; see -ING[1])]

gloat *v.i.*, & *n.* **1.** *v.i.* feast eyes or mind lustfully, avariciously, malignantly, triumphantly, etc., (*up*)*on* or *over*. **2.** *n.* act of gloating; look or expression of triumphant satisfaction. [16th c.; orig. unkn., but perh. cogn. w. ON *glotta* grin, MHG *glotzen* stare]

glo′bal *a.* world-wide; pertaining to or embracing the whole of a group of items etc.; total; hence ∼LY[2] *adv.* [F, f. as foll. + -AL]

globe *n.* & *v.* **1.** *n.* spherical body; *the* earth; planet, star, sun. **2.** spherical representation of the earth or the constellations; **use of the** ∼**s**, (arch.) teaching of geography and astronomy by these. **3.** golden orb as emblem of sovereignty; (Anat.) eyeball; approximately spherical glass vessel, esp. lampshade, fish-bowl, or electric-light bulb. **4.** *globe* ARTICHOKE; ∼-**fish,** tropical fish of family Tetraodontidae, able to inflate itself into globular form; ∼-**flower,** ranunculaceous plant of genus *Trollius* with globular usu. yellow flowers; ∼ (= BALL[1]) **lightning;** ∼-**trotter, -trotting,** hurried traveller, hurried travelling, through foreign countries esp. for sightseeing. **5.** Hence or cogn. **glo′boid** *a.* & *n.*, **glo′bose**[1] *a.* **6.** *v.t.* & *i.* make (usu. in *pass.*) or become globular. [F, or f. L *globus*]

globigeri′na (-ĭ′na, -ē′na) *n.* foraminiferous organism of genus *Globigerina*, living near surface of sea. [mod. L, f. as prec. + *-ger* carrying + -INA]

glo′bular *a.* globe-shaped, spherical; composed of globules; hence ∼ITY (-ă′r-) *n.*, ∼LY[2] *adv.* [f. as foll. + -AR[1]]

glo′bule *n.* small globe or round particle, drop, pill. [F, or f. L *globulus* (as GLOBE; see -ULE)]

glo′bulin *n.* protein found usu. associated with albumin in animal and plant tissues. [f. prec. + -IN]

glo′ckenspiel (-nsp-, -nshp-) *n.* musical instrument consisting of a series of bells or metal bars or tubes struck by hammers. [G, = bell-play]

*glöm *v.t.* & *i.* (-mm-). (sl.) ∼ (**on** to), steal, grab. [var. of Sc. *glaum* (18th c., of unkn. orig.)]

glo′merate *a.* (Bot. & Anat.) compactly clustered. [f. L *glomeratus* p.p. of *glomerare* (*glomus -eris* ball); see -ATE[2]]

glo′merule (-ōōl) *n.* clustered flower-head; = foll. [f. as foll.; see -ULE]

glomě′rul|**us** *n.* (*pl.* ∼**i** *pr.* -ī). cluster of small organisms, tissues, blood-vessels, etc., esp. of capillaries in kidney; hence ∼AR *a.* [mod. L, dim. of L *glomus -eris* ball]

gloom[1] *n.* darkness, obscurity; melancholy, despondency; (poet.) dark place. [perh. back-form. f. GLOOMY]

gloom[2] *v.* **1.** *v.i.* look sullen, frown, be gloomy or melancholy; (of sky etc.) lour, be dull or threatening; appear darkly or obscurely. **2.** *v.t.* cover with gloom, make dark or dismal. [ME *gloum(b)e*, of unkn. orig.; cf. GLUM]

gloo′m|y *a.* dark, unlighted; depressed, sullen; dismal, depressing; hence ∼ILY[2] *adv.*, ∼INESS *n.* [f. obs. *gloom* a frown f. prec. + -Y[2]]

*glŏp *n.* (sl.) liquid or viscous substance, esp. unattractive food. [imit.; cf. obs. *glop* swallow greedily]

glor′ia *n.* **1.** G∼ (**Patri**), doxology *Glory be to the Father* etc.; G∼ (**tibi**), response *Glory be to thee* etc.; G∼ (**in excelsis**), hymn *Glory be to God on high*, as part of Mass etc. **2.** aureole. [L, = glory]

glor′ify *v.t.* make glorious, exalt to the glory of heaven; invest with radiance; transform into something more splendid; (try to) make (common or inferior thing) seem more splendid than it really is; extol, praise; so ∼FICA′TION *n.* [ME, f. OF *glorifier* f. eccl. L *glorificare* f. LL *glorificus* f. L *gloria* glory; see -FY]

glor′iole *n.* aureole, halo. [F, f. L *gloriola* dim. of *gloria* glory]

glor′ious *a.* possessing glory, illustrious; conferring glory, honourable; splendid, magnificent, intensely delightful, (*a glorious view, day; glorious fun*; (iron.) *the glorious uncertainty of cricket, a glorious muddle*); (colloq.) ecstatically happy with drink; hence ∼LY[2] *adv.* [ME f. AF; OF *glorios, -eus* f. L *gloriosus* (as foll.; see -OUS)]

glor′y[1] *n.* **1.** exalted renown, honourable fame; adoring praise and thanksgiving; ∼ (**be**)!, devout ejaculation or (vulg.) excl. of surprise or delight. **2.** resplendent majesty, beauty, or magnificence; effulgence of heavenly light, imagined unearthly beauty; bliss and splendour of heaven (**go to** ∼, (sl.) die, be destroyed); state of exaltation, prosperity, etc., (*is in his glory*). **3.** thing that brings renown, special distinction, (*OLD *Glory*); circle of light round head or figure of deity or saint, aureole, halo; anthelion; ∼-**box,** (Austral. & NZ) box for woman's clothes etc. stored in preparation for marriage; ∼-**hole,** *open quarry, (sl.) untidy room, drawer, or receptacle; ∼-**of-the-snow,** chionodoxa. [ME, f. AF & OF *glorie* f. L *gloria*; see -Y[1]]

glor′y[2] *v.i.* exult, pride oneself, *in* thing or do*ing, to* do. [ME, f. L *gloriari* boast (*gloria* glory)]

Glos. *abbr.* Gloucestershire.

gloss[1] *n.* & *v.* **1.** *n.* word inserted between lines or in margin to explain word in text; comment, explanation, interpretation, paraphrase; misrepresentation of another's words; glossary, interlinear translation, or annotations. **2.** *v.t.* insert glosses in (text etc.) or concerning (word etc.); read different sense into, explain away. **3.** *v.i.* write glosses; make (esp.

unfavourable) comments *on*. [alt. of GLOZE after med. L *glossa*]

glöss[2] *n.*, & *v.t.* **1.** *n.* superficial lustre; deceptive external appearance; ∼ **paint** etc. (containing varnish to give glossy finish). **2.** *v.t.* make glossy; ∼ (over), give specious appearance to, seek to conceal. [16th c., of unkn. orig.]

glŏ′ssal *a.* (Anat.) of the tongue, lingual. [f. Gk *glōssa* tongue + -AL]

glŏ′ssar|y̆ *n.* collection of glosses; list and explanations of abstruse, obsolete, dialectal, or technical terms, partial dictionary; hence **glössār′IAL** *a.*, ∼IST (1) *n.* [f. L *glossarium* (*glossa* GLOSS[1]; see -ARY[1])]

glŏssā′tor *n.* writer of glosses, commentator, esp. on medieval law-texts. [ME f. med. L (*glossare* f. *glossa* GLOSS[1]; see -OR)]

glŏ′ssēme *n.* feature of a language that carries meaning and does not consist of smaller meaningful units. [f. Gk *glōssēma* (*glōssa* GLOSS[1]; see -EME)]

glössī′tis *n.* inflammation of the tongue. [f. Gk *glōssa* tongue + -ITIS]

glössō- *comb. form.* **1.** tongue, as: ∼-**lary′ngeal**, of tongue and larynx. **2.** = GLOSS[1], as: **glössŏ′GRAPHER** *n.*, commentator, **glössŏ′LOGY** *n.*, terminology. [sense 1 f. Gk *glōssa* tongue, sense 2 f. GLOSS[1], + -O-]

glŏ′ssolā′lia *n.* gift of TONGUE[1]s. [mod. L, f. as prec. l +Gk -*lalia* speaking]

glŏ′ss|y̆ *a.* & *n.* **1.** *a.* having a gloss; (of paper etc.) smooth and shiny; (of magazine etc.) printed on such paper; hence ∼ILY[2] *adv.*, ∼INESS *n.* **2.** *n.* (colloq.) photograph with glossy surface; glossy magazine. [f. GLOSS[2] + -Y[2]]

glŏ′ttal *a.* of or produced by the glottis; ∼ **stop**, sound produced by sudden opening or shutting of glottis; hence ∼IZE *v.t.*, articulate with glottis wholly or partly closed. [f. foll. + -AL]

glŏ′tt|is *n.* opening at upper end of windpipe and between vocal cords, affecting modulation of voice by contracting or dilating; hence ∼IC *a.* [mod. L, f. Gk *glōttis* (*glōtta* var. of *glōssa* tongue)]

Glou′cester (glŏ′ster) *n.* kind of hard cheese made in Gloucestershire (now usu. **double** ∼, orig. a richer kind). [∼ in England]

glove (-ŭv) *n.*, & *v.t.* **1.** *n.* covering to protect hand or keep it warm or clean or cool, usu. with separated fingers; **fit like a** ∼ (exactly); HAND[1] *and* or *in glove*; **throw down**, **take up**, **the** ∼, issue, accept, challenge. **2.** = BOX[5]*ing-glove*; **with the** ∼**s off** etc. (of arguing or contending in earnest, mercilessly, etc.). **3.** ∼ **box**, (1) box for gloves, (2) = *glove compartment*, (3) closed chamber with sealed-in gloves for handling radioactive material etc.; ∼ **compartment**, recess for small articles in motor-car dashboard; ∼ **puppet** (made to fit on hand like a glove, the fingers then working its arms and head). **4.** Hence ∼′LESS (-vl-) *a.*, **glŏ′vER**[1] (3) (-ŭ′v-) *n.* **5.** *v.t.* cover with glove; provide with gloves. [OE *glōf*, = ON *glófi*, perh. f. Gmc *galōfō* (*ga-* Y-; cf. ON *lófi*, Goth. *lofa* hand)]

glow (-ō) *v.i.*, & *n.* **1.** *v.i.* be heated to incandescence, throw out light and heat without flame; shine like thing intensely heated; show warm colour; burn *with* or be indicative of bodily heat, emotional fervour, etc., (*glowing cheeks*; *gave me a glowing account of the achievement*). **2.** *n.* glowing state (**in a** ∼, hot or flushed); brightness and warmth of colour, e.g. red of cheeks; ardour; passion. **3.** ∼-**discharge**, luminous sparkless electrical discharge from pointed conductor or in gas; ∼-**worm**, beetle whose wingless female emits light from end of abdomen. [OE *glōwan* = OS *glōjan*, OHG *gluoen*, ON *glóa* f. Gmc *glō̆-*]

glow′er *v.i.* stare or scowl (*at*). [orig. uncert.; perh. Sc. var. of ME *glore* f. LG or Scand., or f. obs. (ME) *glow* stare + -ER[5]]

glŏxi′nia *n.* American tropical plant of genus *Gloxinia*, with large bell flowers of various colours. [mod. L, f. B. P. *Gloxin*, 18th-c. Ger. botanist + -IA[1]]

glōze *v.* **1.** *v.i.* (arch.) comment (*up*)*on*; talk speciously, fawn. **2.** *v.t.* ∼ (**over**), palliate, explain away, extenuate. [ME, f. OF *gloser* (*glose* f. med. L *glosa*, *gloza* f. L *glossa* tongue, GLOSS[1])]

glu′cagon (glōō′-) *n.* polypeptide hormone formed in pancreas, which aids breakdown of glycogen. [f. Gk *glukus* sweet + *agōn* leading]

glu′cōse (glōō′kōs, -z) *n.* **1.** (Chem.) sugar found widely in its dextro-rotatory form (*dextrose*) in fruit juice, blood, etc., and obtainable from carbohydrates by hydrolysis. **2.** syrup containing glucose etc. from incomplete hydrolysis of starch. [F, f. Gk *gleukos* sweet wine, rel. to *glukus* sweet; see -OSE[2]]

glu′coside (glōō′-) *n.* (Chem.) compound giving glucose and other product(s) on hydrolysis. [f. prec. + -IDE]

glue (glōō) *n.*, & *v.t.* **1.** *n.* hard brittle brownish gelatin made by boiling hides and bones and used warm for uniting substances; adhesive or viscous substance got from other sources (*fish, vegetable, casein, resin, glue*). **2.** ∼-**pot**, pot with outer vessel holding water to heat glue, (colloq.) area of ground sticky because of wet or mud; ∼-**sniffer**, person who inhales fumes of plastic cement as narcotic. **3.** Hence ∼′Y[2] (glōō′ĭ) *a.* (**glu′ier**, **glu′iest**). **4.** *v.t.* fasten or join (as) with glue; apply or attach tightly or closely (*eye, ear, glued to the keyhole*). [ME, f. OF *glu* n., *gluer* v. f. LL *glus glutis* f. L *gluten*]

glŭm *a.* sullen, looking or feeling dejected or displeased; hence ∼′LY[2] *adv.*, ∼′NESS *n.* [rel. to dial. *glum* v. frown, var. of *gloume* GLOOM[2]]

glum|e (glōōm) *n.* (Bot.) chafflike bract in spikelet of grasses and sedges; husk of grain; hence or cogn. ∼A′CEOUS, ∼′OSE[1] *a.*, *adjs.* [f. L *gluma* husk]

glŭt *v.t.* (-tt-), & *n.* **1.** *v.t.* feed (person, stomach) or indulge (appetite, desire) to the full, overload with food (lit. or fig.), satiate, cloy; choke up, fill to excess; overstock (market) with goods. **2.** *n.* full indulgence; one's fill, surfeit; supply exceeding demand (*a glut in the market*). [n. f. v., ME prob. f. OF *gloutir* swallow f. L *gluttire*; cf. GLUTTON]

glu′tamāte (glōō′-) *n.* (Chem.) salt or ester of glutamic acid, esp. the sodium salt used to flavour food. [f. foll. + -ATE[1] (3)]

glută′mic (glōō-) *a.* (Chem.) ∼ **acid**, amino-acid normally found in proteins. [f. foll. + AMINE + -IC]

glu′ten (glōō′-) *n.* **1.** viscous animal-secretion; nitrogenous part of flour remaining as viscid substance when starch is washed out; ∼ **bread** (with high gluten content). **2.** (arch.) sticky substance. [F, f. L *gluten glutinis* glue]

glu′tě|us (glōō′-) *n.* (*pl.* ∼**i** *pr.* -ī). one of three muscles of each buttock; hence ∼AL *a.* [mod. L, f. Gk *gloutos* buttock]

glu′tinous (glōō′-) *a.* sticky, gluelike, viscid; hence ∼LY[2] *adv.*, ∼NESS *n.* [f. F *glutineux* or f. L *glutinosus* (as GLUTEN; see -OUS)]

glŭ′tton *n.* **1.** excessive eater, gormandizer; greedy reader (*of books*), person insatiably eager (*for work*). **2.** voracious animal (*Gulo gulo*) of weasel family. **3.** Hence or cogn. ∼IZE (2) *v.i.*, ∼OUS *a.*, ∼Y[1] *n.* [ME, f. OF *gluton*, *gloton* f. L *glutto -onis* (*gluttire* swallow, *gluttus* greedy)]

gly̆′cer|ine (-ēn), *glȳ′cer|in, n.* colourless sweet viscous liquid formed as by-product in saponification of fats, used as ointment, as vehicle for drugs, in explosives, etc.; hence ∼INE *n.* [f. F *glycerin* f. Gk *glukeros* sweet; see -INE[5], -IN]

glỹ′cerŏl *n.* (Chem.) glycerine. [f. GLYCERINE + -OL 1]

gly̆′cine (-ēn) *n.* simplest amino-acid, a general constituent of proteins. [f. G *glycin* f. Gk *glukus* sweet; see -INE[5]]

glỹco- *comb. form.* sugar, as: ∼**pro′tein**, protein with short side-chain(s) of carbohydrates. [irreg. f. Gk *glukus* sweet + -O-]

glỹ′co|gen *n.* polysaccharide serving to store carbohydrates in animal tissues and yielding glucose on hydrolysis; so ∼GE′NIC (1) *a.*, ∼ge′nesis, formation of glycogen from sugar. [f. prec. + -GEN]

glȳ′cŏl *n.* aliphatic dihydric alcohol, esp. ethylene glycol; hence **glȳcŏ′l(l)**ɪᴄ *a.* [f. GLYCERINE + -OL l, orig. as being intermediate between glycerine and alcohol]

glȳcŏ′lȳs|is *n.* (*pl.* ∼es *pr.* -ēz). breakdown of sugars etc. by enzymes to release energy in animal tissues or in fermentation etc. [f. GLYCO- + -LYSIS]

glȳ′cosĭde *n.* (Chem.) compound giving sugar and other product(s) on hydrolysis. [f. GLYCO-, after GLUCOSIDE]

glȳ′cosūr′|ĭa *n.* (Path.) diseased condition with sugar present in the urine; hence ∼ɪᴄ *a.* [f. F *glycose* glucose + -URIA]

glȳph *n.* sculptured character or symbol; hence ∼′ɪᴄ *a.* [f. F *glyphe* f. Gk *gluphē* carving (*gluphō* carve)]

glȳ′ptäl *n.* alkyd resin, esp. one formed from glycerine and phthalic acid or anhydride. [perh. f. *glycerol* + *phthalic*]

glȳ′ptic *a.* of carving esp. on precious stones. [f. F *glyptique* or f. Gk *gluptikos* (*gluptēs* carver f. *gluphō* carve; see -ɪᴄ)]

glȳ′ptodŏn *n.* extinct S. Amer. quadruped allied to armadillos, with fluted teeth. [mod. L, f. Gk *gluptos* carved (as prec.) + *odous odontos* tooth]

glȳptŏ′graphȳ *n.* art and science of gem-engraving. [f. as prec. + O- | -GRAPHY]

||**GM** *abbr.* George Medal.

gm. *abbr.* gram(s).

*****G-man** (jē′măn) *n.* (*pl.* **G-men**). (sl.) federal criminal-investigation officer. [f. Government + MAN¹]

GMT *abbr.* Greenwich mean time.

||**GMWU** *abbr.* General & Municipal Workers' Union.

gnärled (närld), **gnär′lȳ** (n-), *adjs.* (Of tree, hands, etc.) covered with protuberances, twisted, rugged. [var. of *knurled* (KNURL; see -ED², -Y²)]

gnäsh (n-) *v.* **1.** *v.i.* (Of teeth) strike together; grind the teeth. **2.** grind (the teeth). [var. of obs. *gnacche* or *gnast* rel. to ON *gnastan* a gnashing (imit.)]

gnät (n-) *n.* small two-winged biting fly of genus *Culex*, *****esp. mosquito; insignificant annoyance, tiny thing; STRAIN¹ *at a gnat.* [OE *gnætt*, cogn. w. LG *gnatte*, G dial. *gnatze*]

gnä′thic (n-) *a.* of the jaws. [f. Gk *gnathos* jaw + -ɪᴄ]

gnaw (n-) *v.t.* & *i.* (*p.p.* ∼ed or ∼n). bite persistently, wear away thus, (*away, off, in two,* etc.; *at, into*); (of destructive agent, pain, etc.) corrode, waste away, consume, torture. [OE *gnagan*, = OS, OHG *gnagan*, ON *gnaga*; ult. imit.]

gneiss (gnīs, nīs) *n.* (Geol.) coarse-grained metamorphic rock of quartz, felspar, and mica; hence ∼′ɪᴄ, ∼′OID, ∼′OSE¹, *adjs.* [G]

gnŏ′cchi (nŏ′kī, nyŏ′kī) *n. pl.* small dumplings cooked and served with cheese etc. [It., pl. of *gnocco* (*nocchio* knot in wood)]

gnōme¹ (nō′mē, nōm) *n.* maxim, aphorism. [f. Gk *gnōmē* opinion (*gignōskō* know)]

gnōme² (nōm) *n.* legendary dwarfish spirit of subterranean race guarding treasures of earth; goblin, dwarf; figure of gnome esp. in garden; (colloq., esp. in *pl.*) person with sinister influence, esp. in international finance; hence **gnŏ′mɪSH**¹ (n-) *a.* [F, f. mod. L *gnomus* (wd invented by Paracelsus)]

gnŏ′m|ic (n-) *a.* of, consisting of, using, gnomes (GNOME¹), sententious; (Gram., of tense) used without implication of time to express a general truth, e.g. *men were deceivers ever*; hence ∼ɪᴄᴀʟʟʏ *adv.* [f. Gk *gnōmikos* (as GNOME¹; see -ɪᴄ)]

gnŏ′mon (n-) *n.* pillar, rod, pin, or plate, of sundial, showing time by its shadow on marked surface; column etc. used in observing sun's meridian altitude; (Geom.) part of parallelogram left when similar one has been taken from its corner; hence **gnŏmŏ′nɪᴄ** (n-) *a.* [F, or f. L f. Gk *gnōmōn* indicator etc. (*gignōskō* know)]

gnŏ′s|is (n-) *n.* (*pl.* ∼es *pr.* -ēz). knowledge of spiritual mysteries. [f. Gk *gnōsis* knowledge (as prec.)]

gnŏ′stic (n-) *a.* & *n.* **1.** *a.* relating to knowledge, cognitive; having esoteric spiritual knowledge; (*G*∼) of the Gnostics, occult, mystic. **2.** *n.* (*G*∼; usu. in *pl.*) Christian heretic of 1st-3rd c. claiming gnosis; hence ∼ɪSM (3) *n.*, ∼ɪZE (2, 3, 4) *v.i.* & *t.* [f. eccl. L f. Gk *gnōstikos* (as prec.; see -ɪᴄ)]

GNP *abbr.* gross national product.

||**Gnr.** *abbr.* Gunner.

||**gns.** *abbr.* guineas.

gnu (nōō, nū) *n.* oxlike antelope of genus *Connochaetes*. [ult. f. Kaffir *ngu*]

gō¹ *v.* (**went**; **gone**; *part.* GOING²; *sing. pres.* 2 (arch.) **goest** *pr.* gō′ist, 3 **goes** *pr.* gōz, (arch.) **goeth** *pr.* gō′ith). **1.** *v.i.* start, depart, move, continue moving, with self-originated or imparted motion, from some place, position, time, etc., specified or obvious; *****to go,** (of refreshments etc.) for taking away from place of supply before consumption. **2.** journey, travel, proceed, progress, (*go* FAR¹, *the* PACE¹, WEST; *go easy, straight; go by car, by train, by air; went miles round; go (for) a walk, (on) a journey, the same way, the shortest way*); **go slow,** (esp.) work at deliberately slow pace; **go-slow** *n.,* such action as industrial protest. **3.** (Of line etc.) lie, point, in certain direction. **4.** be guided *by,* act in harmony *with,* judge or act (*up*)*on,* (*a good rule to go by; have nothing to go upon; always goes with his party; promotion goes by favour*); **go with the tide** or **times,** do as others do. **5.** be habitually or for a time in specified state (*go hungry,* SHORT 3, *armed, in rags, in fear of one's life; plea went unheeded*); *six months* etc. **gone with child,** (colloq.) **gone,** having spent that time in gestation. **6.** be moving, acting, working, etc., (**who goes there?** (sentry's challenge); *clock does not go, goes well; tongue goes nineteen to the* DOZEN). **7.** make specified motion (*go like this with your left foot*). **8.** (Of bell, striking clock, gun, or other source of sound) emit sound; make sound of specified kind (*go bang, go crack*). **9.** (Of time) pass, elapse, (*ten days to go before Easter*); (of distance etc.) be traversed or accom plished (*ten miles to go*). **10.** be current or accepted (*the gold sovereign went anywhere; the* STORY¹ *goes*); be known *by,* or *under, the name of; be on the average (is a good actor as actors go nowadays*). **11.** (Of document, verse, tune, etc.) run, have specified content or wording. **12.** (Of verse, song) be rhythmical, be adaptable *to* a tune. **13.** (Of events) turn out *well, ill,* HARD, etc., (of decision, election, etc.) result *for* or against, (of constituency, politician, voter) take certain course or views, (*Liverpool went Labour; go* DRY¹; *case goes by* DEFAULT¹; *goes without* SAYING; **how goes it, how is it going, how are things going?,** what progress is being made?); be successful (*make the party go*); (colloq.) be acceptable or permitted (*anything goes*), be accepted without question (*what he says goes*). **14.** begin motion; **go!** (starter's word in race); **from the word go,** (colloq.) from the very beginning; LET² *go*; HERE *goes!.* **15.** get away *free, unpunished,* etc. **16.** be sold (*go cheap, for £1,* etc.); **going!, gone!** (auctioneer's announcement that bidding is almost, quite, closed). **17.** (Of money) be spent (*in* or *on* thing). **18.** be relinquished, dismissed, abolished, or lost (*the car, the cook, must go; my sight, our trade, is going; my headache has gone; next wicket goes for nothing*). **19.** die (esp. in *p.p.,* and in many phrs.: *go the way of all the earth* or *of all flesh, to a better world, to* one's *account* or *reward,* (sl.) *aloft,* etc.). **20.** fail, give way, succumb, break down, crack; LET² *oneself go.* **21.** make one's way *to, towards, into,* etc., (*go to* BLAZE¹s, HELL, JERICHO, *the* DEVIL¹; *go* HANG¹ 5; *go* PLACE¹s; *which road goes to Bristol?*; **go to** *church, market, a ball,* etc., attend it; *go to* SCHOOL¹; **go to the bar, to sea,** become barrister, sailor; **go on the stage, the streets,** become actor, prostitute; *go to* STOOL¹). **22.** proceed to do (*went to find him*), and do (esp. colloq. = be so foolish as to do; **have been and gone and done it,** (vulg.) have made a blunder etc.), on *pilgrimage, on an errand, on the spree,* etc.; (colloq. or US) proceed to (do) (*go jump in the lake*); be about to do; **go**

doing, (arch.) **a-doing**, make an expedition to do (*went shopping, fishing*), (colloq.) be so foolish as to do (*don't go making him angry*). **23.** act as (BAIL¹ *for* person). **24.** have recourse, refer, appeal, *to* (||**go to the country**, test opinion by general election; *go to war, work*). **25.** carry action to certain point (*went to any or all lengths*; *will go so far as to say*; *will go as high as £100* (in bidding or offering price); **go halves** (see HALF 2) or SHARE¹s; *went to great expense, trouble*, etc.; *go the whole* HOG¹; *go one* BETTER¹; *go* NEAR¹ *doing or to do*). **26.** penetrate, sink, (*ship went to the bottom*; *goes to* one's HEART); find room, (of number) be capable of being contained in another either without remainder or at all, (*will not go into* or *in the basket*; *6 into 12 goes twice, into 5 will not go, into 13 goes twice and one over*; *thread is too thick to go through needle*). **27.** belong in receptacle, *on* shelf, etc. **28.** (Of prize, victory, inheritance, office, etc.) pass, be allotted, etc., *to* person; be applied *to* purpose, contribute *to or towards* result, amount together *to* (*12 inches go to the foot*), tend *to show* etc. **29.** reach, extend, (*the difference goes deep*); **as** (or **so**) **far as it goes** (caution against taking statement too widely); **goes a long** etc. **way**, *goes* FAR¹, (1) has great etc. effect *towards*, (2) (of food, money, etc.) lasts long etc., buys much etc. **30.** pass into specified condition (*go absent, blind, brown, mad, to seed, to sleep*; *go* HOT¹ *and cold*; *go* NATIVE²; *go to* PIECE¹s; *go* SICK¹). **31.** *v.t.* bid, declare, (*go* NAP³, *two spades*). **32. go it**, (sl.) act vigorously, furiously, etc., indulge in dissipation; *go it* ALONE; **go it strong**, (sl.) go to great lengths, use exaggeration. **33.** (w. *preps.*): **go about**, set to work at; **go at**, attack, take in hand energetically; **go for**, go to fetch, pass or be accounted as or achieve *nothing, little*, etc., be applicable to, strive to attain, prefer, choose, (sl.) attack; **go into**, enter (profession, Parliament), frequent (society), take part in, be a part of, allow oneself to pass into (hysterics etc.), dress oneself in (mourning etc.), investigate; **go off**, begin to dislike; **go on**, become chargeable to (parish, relief fund, etc.), (colloq.) use as evidence, (colloq., esp. neg.) concern oneself (*much* etc.) about; **go over**, inspect details of, rehearse, retouch; **go through**, discuss in detail, scrutinize (successively), perform, (ceremony, recitation, etc.), undergo, (of book) be successively published in (so many editions), make holes in, use up, spend (money); **go to it**, (colloq., esp. in *imper.*) begin work; **go with**, be concomitant of, take same view as, agree to, match, be harmonious with, follow the drift of; **go without**, not have, put up with lack of, (thing expressed or implied). **34.** (w. *advs.*): **go about**, move from place to place, endeavour *to do*, be in the habit of *doing*, (Naut.) change to opposite tack; **go ahead**, proceed without hesitation; **go along with**, = *go with*; **go around**, be regularly in company *with*, be in the habit of *doing*; **go away**, depart esp. from home for holiday etc.; **go back on** one's *word* etc., fail to keep it; **go by**, pass; **go down**, (of ship) sink, (of sun) set, be continued *to* specified point, fall *before* conqueror, deteriorate, fail, be recorded in writing, be swallowed, find acceptance *with*, leave university, (sl.) be sent to prison; **go down with**, begin to suffer from (disease); **go in**, enter as competitor (*go in and win!*), excl. of encouragement, (Cricket) take or begin innings, (of sun etc.) become obscured by cloud; **go in for**, take as one's object, pursuit, style, principle, etc.; **go off**, leave the stage, begin, explode, die, gradually cease to be felt, deteriorate, become unconscious in sleep, faint, etc., be got rid of by sale, result *well, badly*, etc.; **go on**, continue, persevere, (*doing, with, in*, or abs.), talk at undue length, make it one's next step *to* do, happen, conduct oneself (*shamefully* etc.), (colloq.) rail *at*, appear on stage, (Cricket) begin bowling, (of garment etc.) be large enough for wearer, take one's turn to do something, (colloq., in *imper.*) don't talk nonsense!; **go out**, leave room or house, fight duel, be broadcast, be extinguished, (of Government) leave office, cease

to be fashionable, depart *to* colony etc., (colloq.) lose consciousness, mix in society, (of workmen) strike, (of heart etc.) expand with love etc. *to* person, play first 9 holes in round of golf, (Cards) be first to dispose of one's hand; **go over**, change one's allegiance or religion, (of play etc.) be successful; **go round**, pay informal visit *to*, be long enough to encompass, (of food etc.) suffice for the whole party, = *go around*; **go slow** (see sense 2); **go through**, be dealt with or completed; **go through with**, complete, not leave unfinished; **go to**, (*imper.*, arch.) excl. of remonstrance, incredulity, impatience, etc.; **go together**, be concomitant, match, be courting; **go under**, sink, fail, succumb; **go up**, enter university, increase in price, explode, be consumed *in flames* or *in smoke*. **35.** **go-ahead**, (*a.*) enterprising, (*n.*) permission to proceed; **go-as-you-please**, unfettered by regulations; **go-between**, intermediary, negotiator; **go-by**, passing (usu. in *give the go-by to*, outstrip, leave behind, elude, disregard, cut, slight); **go-cart**, handcart, push-chair, (arch.) baby-walker; ***go-devil**, movable contrivance used to clean interior of pipes etc.; **go-getter**, (colloq.) enterprising person; **go-go**, (colloq.) unrestrained, energetic, (of investment) speculative, (of dancer, music, etc.) full of verve, movement, and excitement; **go-kart**, miniature racing car with skeleton body; [after *go-cart*]; **go-off**, start (usu. *at the first go-off*); **go-to-mee'ting**, (of hat, clothes, etc.) fit or kept for going to church in. [OE *gān*, = OS, OHG *gan* f. Gmc **gai-, *gǣ-*; *went* orig. past of WEND¹]

gō² *n.* (*pl.* **goes** *pr.* gōz). **1.** act of going; mettle, spirit, dash, animation; (colloq.) vigorous activity (*it's all go*); (colloq.) unforeseen turn of affairs (*here's, what, a go!*; *a rum go*); (colloq.) success (*make a go of it*); (colloq.) turn or attempt at doing something (*have a go at*; *scored seven at one go*); (colloq.) quantity of liquor etc. served at one time; attack of an illness. **2. all the go**, (colloq.) in fashion; **it's a go**, (colloq.) the bargain is agreed; **it's no go**, (colloq.) the task is impossible, the situation is hopeless; **near go**, (colloq.) narrow escape; **no-go'**, impossible to achieve, impossible to enter (because of barricade, prohibition, etc.); **on the go**, (colloq.) in constant motion. [f. prec.]

gō³ *a.* (colloq.) functioning properly; fashionable, progressive. [f. GO¹]

gō⁴ *n.* Japanese board game of territorial possession and capture. [Jap.]

goad *n.*, & *v.t.* **1.** *n.* spiked stick used for urging cattle; thing that torments, incites, or stimulates. **2.** *v.t.* urge with goad; irritate; ∼ (**on**), instigate, drive, by annoyance (*to do, into doing, to or into fury* etc.). [OE *gād*, cogn. w. Lombard *gaida* arrowhead f. Gmc **gaidō*]

goal *n.* **1.** point marking end of race; object of effort or ambition; destination. **2.** pair of posts between which ball is to be driven in football etc., cage or basket used similarly in other games, point(s) so won (DROP², *kick, make, score, a goal*). **3.** ∼ *average*, ratio of numbers of goals scored by and against a team in a series of matches; ∼ **difference**, difference of such numbers; ∼'**keeper**, player stationed to protect goal; ∼**-kick**, (Assoc. Footb.) kick by defending side after attackers send ball over goal-line, (Rugby Footb.) attempt to kick a goal; ∼**-line**, line between each pair of goal-posts, extended to form end-boundary of field of play (cf. TOUCH²-*line*); ∼**-mouth**, space between or near goal-posts; ***∼-minder**, ***∼-tender**, goalkeeper at ice hockey. **4.** Hence ∼'IE *n.*, (colloq.) goalkeeper, ∼'LESS (-l-l-) *a.* [16th c., of unkn. orig., perh. identical with ME *gol* boundary]

gōä'nna *n.* (Austral.) large monitor lizard of genus *Varanus*. [corrupt. of IGUANA]

goat *n.* **1.** hardy lively frisky usu. horned and (in the male) bearded ruminant of genus *Capra* (SHEEP *and goats*); related animal (MOUNTAIN *goat*). **2.** (G∼) the zodiacal sign Capricorn. **3.** licentious person; (colloq.) foolish person; ***scapegoat**; **get** person's ∼, (sl.)

irritate him; *play the* GIDDY *goat*. **4.** ∼**-antelope,** antelope-like member of goat family; ∼**-god,** Pan; ∼**'herd** (-t-h-), one who tends goats; ∼**'s-beard,** (1) meadowsweet, (2) meadow plant of genus *Tragopogon*, (3) fungus of genus *Clavaria*; ∼ **moth,** large moth of family Cossidae; ∼**'skin,** (garment or bottle made of) skin of goat; ∼**'sucker,** = NIGHT*jar*. **5.** Hence ∼'ISH[1], ∼'Y[2], *adjs.*, ∼'LING[1] *n*. [OE *gāt* she-goat, = OS *gēt*, OHG *geiz*, ON *geit*, Goth. *gaits* f. Gmc **gaitaz* f. IE **ghaidos*]

goatee' *n*. chin-tuft like goat's beard. [f. prec. +-EE]

gŏb[1] *n*., & *v.i.* (-bb-). (vulg.) **1.** *n*. clot of slimy substance etc. **2.** *v.i.* spit. [ME, f. OF *go(u)be* mouthful]

gŏb[2] *n*. (sl.) US sailor. [20th c.; cf. GOBBY]

gŏb[3] *n*. (sl.) mouth; ∼**-stopper,** large hard sweet for sucking. [perh. f. Gael. & Ir., = beak, mouth]

gŏbă'ng *n*. game played on board marked with squares, each player seeking to place five counters in line. [f. Jap. *goban* perh. f. Chin. *qiban* GO[4]-board]

gŏ'bbĕt *n*. **1.** (arch.) piece, lump, esp. of raw flesh or food. **2.** extract from a text esp. set for translation or comment in examination. [ME, f. OF *gobet* (as GOB[1]; see -ET[1])]

gŏ'bble[1] *v.t.* & *i.* eat hurriedly and noisily. [prob. dial., f. GOB[1]+-LE 3]

gŏ'bble[2] *n*. (Golf). rapid straight putt into the hole. [prob. f. prec.]

gŏ'bble[3] *v.i.* (Of turkey-cock) make characteristic sound in throat; make such sound when speaking, from rage etc. [Imit.; perh. based on GOBBLE[1]]

gŏ'bbledĕgook, -dўg, (-beldigook, -ook) *n*. pompous or unintelligible official, or professional, jargon. [prob. imit. of turkey-cock]

gŏ'bbler *n*. In vbl senses; turkey-cock. [f. GOBBLE[1,3] + -ER[1]]

gŏ'bbў *n*. (sl.) coastguard; American sailor. [perh. f. GOB[1]+-Y[2]]

Gŏ'belin *n*. ∼ tapestry (made, or imitated from that made, at the Gobelins. [f. name of State factory in Paris, called *Gobelins* after its orig. owners]

gŏ'bemouche (gŏ'bmoosh) *n*. (*pl.* ∼s *pr.* same). credulous hearer of news. [f. F *gobe-mouches*, = fly--catcher (*gober* swallow, *mouches* flies)]

gŏ'blĕt *n*. glass or other drinking-vessel having foot and stem; (arch.) metal or glass drinking-cup, bowl--shaped and without handles, sometimes with foot and cover; (poet.) drinking-cup. [ME, f. OF *gobelet*, dim. of *gobel* cup, of unkn. orig.; see -ET[1]]

gŏ'blin *n*. mischievous ugly demon. [ME, prob. f. AF **gobelin*, med. L *gobelinus*, prob. f. name dim. of *Gobel*, rel. to *Kobold* (see COBALT)]

gŏ'bў *n*. small fish with ventral fins joined into a disc or sucker. [f. L *gobius*, *cobius* f. Gk *kōbios* GUDGEON[1]]

GOC *abbr.* General Officer Commanding.

gŏd *n*. **1.** superhuman being worshipped as having power over nature and human fortunes, deity; ∼ **from machine,** *deus ex machina*; **ye** ∼**s (and little fishes)**!, mock-heroic excl.; **feast or sight for the** ∼**s,** something exquisite etc.; **on the knees** or **in the lap of the** ∼**s,** beyond human control. **2.** image, animal, or other object, worshipped as symbolizing, being the visible habitation of, or itself possessing, divine power; an idol (TIN *god*). **3.** adored, admired, or influential person. **4.** (Theatr., in *pl.*) (occupants of) gallery. **5.** (**God**). supreme being, Creator and Ruler of universe; **God the Father, Son, Holy Ghost,** Persons of Trinity. **6. act of God,** operation of uncontrollable natural forces; **God knows,** (1) it is beyond mortal or my knowledge, (2) I call God to witness that; *God save the* MARK[1]; **God's Acre,** church-yard; **God's book,** Bible; **God's earth,** the whole earth; **God's gift,** a godsend; **God's (own) country,** earthly paradise, esp. the United States regarded as such; **God's plenty, quantity,** (colloq.) abundance; **God's truth,** the absolute truth; **God willing,** if Providence allows; **God wot,** (arch.) God knows; MAN[1] *of God*; **play God,** seek to be all-powerful;

under God (qualifying attribution of full agency to man); **with God,** dead and in heaven. **7.** (In excl.:) (of asseveration) **by God,** *so* HELP[1] *me God*, (of astonishment etc.) *God* BLESS *me, my soul,* etc., (of imprecation) **God damn** (*you, him,* etc.), (of pain, grief, or anger) **God in Heaven, good God, my God, oh God,** (of pleasure or relief) **thank God,** (of prayer) **God bless** (*you, him,* etc.), **God** FORBID, **God grant** (*that* etc.), **God help** *you, him,* etc., (of urgent supplication) **for God's sake,** *in God's* NAME[1]; **THANK** God. **8. God-awful,** (sl.) extremely unpleasant; ∼**'child,** child sponsored at baptism; ∼**-dam**(n), ∼**-damned,** accursed, damnable; ∼**-daughter,** female godchild; ∼**'father,** male godparent, (fig.) person after whom person or thing is named*, person directing illegal organization; *my* ∼*fathers!*, (euphem.) *my* God!; **God-fearing,** sincerely religious; **God-forsaken,** devoid of all merit, dismal; **Go'dman,** Christ; ∼**'mother,** female godparent; ∼**'parent,** sponsor at baptism; ∼**'send,** unexpected welcome event or acquisition; ∼**'son,** male godchild; **Godspee'd,** wish of 'God speed you!' to departing person. **9.** Hence ∼**'HOOD** (-d-h-), ∼**'SHIP,** *ns*., ∼**'WARD** *adv.* & *a.*, ∼**'WARDS** *adv.* [OE, = OS, ON *god*, OHG *got*, Goth. *guth* f. Gmc **gudh*- f. IE **ghut*-]

gŏ'ddĕss *n*. female deity in polytheism; woman one adores. [ME, f. prec. +-ESS[1]]

gŏ'dĕt (-dā) *n*. triangular piece of material inserted in a dress, glove, etc. [F]

godē'tia (-sha) *n*. showy-flowered hardy annual plant of genus *Godetia*. [mod. L, f. C. H. *Godet*, Swiss botanist d. 1879+-IA[1]]

gŏ'dhead (-d-hĕd) *n*. being God or a god, divine nature; deity; the **G**∼, God. [ME, f. GOD+-HEAD]

gŏ'dlĕss *a*. without a god; not recognizing God; impious, wicked; hence ∼NESS *n*. [f. GOD+-LESS]

gŏ'dlīke *a*. resembling God or a god in some quality; fit for, or like that of, a god. [f. GOD+-LIKE]

gŏ'dlǐў *a*. religious, pious, devout; hence ∼iNESS *n*. [ME, f. GOD+-LY[1]]

godow'n *n*. warehouse in parts of E. Asia, esp. in India. [f. Port. *gudão* f. Malay *godong, gadong,* perh. f. Telugu *giḍaṅgi* place where goods lie (*kiḍu* lie)]

gŏ'dwit *n*. wading bird like curlew but with bill straight or slightly curved upwards. [16th c.; orig. unkn.]

Gŏdwŏ'tterў *n*. affected or over-elaborate treatment esp. of gardens. [f. *God wot* (in poem in gardens, by T. E. Brown 1876)+-ERY]

gŏ'er *n*. person or thing that goes (*good, slow,* etc., *goer*; *comers and goers*); person who goes to (*church-goer,* *theatre-goer*); lively or persevering person. [ME, f. GO[1]+-ER[1]]

goes, goest, goeth. See GO[1].

Goe'thian, -ean, (gĕr'tĭ-) *a.* & *n.* (admirer or follower) of Goethe. [f. J. W. von *Goethe*, Ger. writer d. 1832+ -IAN, -EAN]

gŏ'ffer *v.t.*, & *n.* *v.t.* make wavy, flute, crimp, (lace edge, trimming, etc.) with heated irons; (in *p.p.*) embossed (edges of book). **2.** *n.* iron used for goffering; ornamental plaiting used for frills etc. [f. F *gaufrer* f. *gaufre* honeycomb, cogn. w. WAFER, WAFFLE[1]]

gŏ'ggle *v.i.*, *a.*, & *n.* **1.** *v.i.* squint, roll eyes about with wide-open eyes; (of eyes) be rolled or project. **2.** *v.t.* turn (eyes) sideways or from side to side. **3.** *a.* (Of eyes) protuberant, full and rolling; so ∼**-eyED**[2] (-gelĭd) *a.* **4.** *n.* (in *pl.*) spectacles for protecting eyes from glare, dust, etc., often with side shields and coloured glass, wire gauze, etc.; a sheep disease, staggers. **5.** ∼**-box,** (sl.) television set; ∼**-dive,** underwater dive by person wearing goggles. [ME, prob. frequent. f. imit. base **gog* (cf. JOG)+-LE 3]

gŏ'glĕt *n.* (Ind.) long-necked vessel esp. of porous ware for keeping water cool. [f. Port. *gorgoleta*]

Goi'del *n.* member of GAELIC (sense 2) peoples; hence **Goidĕ'lic** *a.* & *n.* [f. OIr. *Góidel*]

gō'ing[1] *n.* In vbl senses; condition of ground for walking, riding, etc. (esp. for horse-racing); progress as helped or hindered by this, lit. or fig. (heavy ~, slow or difficult progress; **while the ~ is good,** while conditions are favourable); **~ away,** (esp.) departure for honeymoon; **~s-o'n,** (usu. *strange, such,* etc.) behaviour; **~-over,** (colloq.) inspection or overhaul, (sl.) thrashing, *(colloq.) scolding. [f. GO[1] + -ING[1]]

gō'ing[2] *a.* In vbl senses; in or into action (*set the clock going*); existing, to be had, (*one of the best fellows going*; *there is cold beef going*); currently valid (*the going rate*); ~ **concern,** business already in operation; **get ~** *v.t.* & *i.,* start steadily talking, working, etc.; ~ **(on) fifteen,** etc., approaching one's fifteenth etc. birthday; ~ **for** one, (colloq.) acting in one's favour; *going great* GUNs; ~ **on for,** approaching (a time, age, etc.); **to be ~ on with,** to start with, for the time being; *going* STRONG; ~ **to,** about to, intending or intended to, likely to. [f. GO[1] + -ING[2]; in some senses f. earlier *a-going* (A[3], prec.)]

‖**goi'tre** (-ter), *goi'ter,** *n.* morbid enlargement of thyroid gland, often showing as large pendulous swelling in neck; hence or cogn. **goi'tr**ED[2], *goi'ter**ED[2], (-terd), **goi'tr**OUS, *adjs.* [F, back-form. f. *goitreux,* or f. Prov. *goitron,* ult. f. L *guttur* throat]

Gōlcŏ'nda *n.* mine of wealth (lit. or fig.). [city near Hyderabad, India]

gōld *n.* & *a.* **1.** *n.* precious yellow non-rusting malleable ductile metallic element of high density, used as a fundamental monetary medium (*as* GOOD *as gold*); **go off ~,** abandon the gold STANDARD; **worth** one's **weight in ~,** exceedingly helpful etc.); coins made of this, money in large sums, wealth; the metal as used for coating surface or as pigment, gilding; the colour of the metal; bull's-eye of archery target (usu. gilt); = *gold medal.* **2.** (fig.) brilliant, beautiful, or precious things, material, etc. (*all that glisters* or *glitters is not gold; a heart, voice,* etc., *of gold; she is pure gold*); **age of ~,** = GOLDEN *age.* **3.** *a.* made wholly or chiefly of gold; coloured like gold; (of money) reckoned at undepreciated value according to gold standard. **4.** ~ **amalgam,** plastic combination of gold with mercury; **~-beater,** one who beats gold out into gold leaf; **~-beater's skin,** membrane used to separate leaves of gold during beating, or as covering for slight wounds; ~ **bloc** (of countries having gold STANDARD); ~ **brick,** (sl.) thing with only a surface appearance of value, sham, fraud, *(sl.) lazy person; ~'crest,** very small bird with golden crest; **~-digger,** one who digs for gold, (sl.) coquette who wheedles money out of men; **~-dust,** (1) gold in fine particles as found naturally, (2) plant (*Alyssum saxatile*) with many small yellow flowers; **~-fever,** rage for going in search of gold; **~-field,** district in which gold is found as mineral; **~'finch,** bright-coloured songbird with patch of yellow on wings; ~'**fish,** small reddish-golden Chinese carp kept for ornament; ~*fish bowl,* (fig.) situation lacking privacy; ~ **foil,** ~ **leaf,** gold beaten into thin sheet, *gold foil* being the thicker; ~ **medal,** medal of gold (usu. awarded as first prize); **~-mine,** source of wealth (lit. or fig.); ~ **of pleasure,** annual yellow-flowered plant (*Camelina sativa*); ~ **plate,** (1) vessels made of gold, (2) material plated with gold; ~*plate* v.t., plate with gold; ~ **reserve** (of gold coins or bullion held by central bank etc.); **~-rush,** a rush to some new gold-field; ~'**smith,** worker in gold, manufacturer of gold articles, (~*smith beetle,* beetle with gold-coloured wing-covers); *gold* STANDARD; ‖**Gold Stick,** (bearer of) gilt rod borne on State occasions by colonel of Life Guards or captain of gentlemen-at-arms; *gold* THREAD[1]. [OE, = OS, OHG *gold,* ON *gull,* Goth. *gulth* f. Gmc *gultham* f. IE *ghltom* (*ghel-* yellow)]

*gōldă'r'n** *v.t., a.,* & *adv.* (sl.) = DAMN 2, DAMNED 2, 3. [euphem. corrupt. of *God damn*]

gō'lden *a.* **1.** made or consisting of gold; abounding in or yielding gold; coloured or shining like gold (*golden hair*); precious, excellent, important, (*a golden opportunity, remedy*). **2.** ~ **age,** (1) past time when men were happy and innocent, (2) period of nation's greatest prosperity or literary etc. merit; *~-a'ger,* old person; ~ **balls,** pawnbroker's sign; ~ **boy,** popular or successful boy or man; *golden* CALF[1]; ~ **chain,** laburnum; ~ **disc,** award to artiste after sale of half a million copies of gramophone record made by him or her; ~ **eagle,** large eagle with yellow-tipped head-feathers; **~-eye,** duck of genus *Bucephala;* *Golden* FLEECE; ~ **girl,** popular or successful girl or woman; *golden* HAMSTER; ~ **handshake,** gratuity as compensation for dismissal or compulsory retirement; **G~ Horde,** Tartar horde that overran E. Europe in 13th c. [f. richness of leader's tent]; **G~ Horn,** harbour of Istanbul; ~ **jubilee,** 50th anniversary of sovereign's accession or other event; *Golden* LEGEND; ~ **mean,** (1) neither too much nor too little, principle of moderation, (2) = *golden section;* **~-mouthed** eloquent; ~ **number,** (of year in Metonic lunar cycle, from its importance in fixing Easter); ~ **opinions,** high regard; ~ **perch,** (Austral.) edible freshwater fish (*Plectroplites ambiguus*); ~ **retriever,** retriever dog with thick golden-coloured coat; ~ **rod,** plant of genus *Solidago* with rodlike stem and spike of small bright-yellow flowers; *golden* ROSE[1]; ~ **rule,** (1) 'do as you would be done by', (2) basic principle of action; ~ **section,** division of line so tha whole is to one part as that part to other part; *G~ State,* California; ‖*golden* SYRUP; ~ **wedding,** 50th anniversary of wedding. [ME, f. GOLD + -EN[5]]

gō'ldilŏcks *n.* person with golden hair; kind of buttercup (*Ranunculus auricomus*); composite plant (*Linosyris vulgaris*) like golden rod. [f. *goldy* (GOLD, -Y[2]) + LOCK[1]s]

gō'lĕm *n.* clay figure supernaturally brought to life (in Jewish legend); automaton, robot. [f. Yiddish *goylem* f. Heb. *gōlem* shapeless mass]

gōlf *n.,* & *v.i.* **1.** *n.* game in which small hard ball is struck in fewest possible strokes with clubs having wooden or metal heads into each of a series of (usu. 18 or 9) holes on smooth greens at varying distances apart and separated by fairways, rough ground, hazards, etc. **2.** **~-bag** (for carrying clubs and balls); ~ **ball,** (1) ball used in golf, (2) (colloq.) small ball used in some electric typewriters to carry the type; ~ **cart,** (1) trolley for carrying clubs in golf, (2) motorized cart for golfers and equipment; **~-club** (1) club used in golf, (2) (premises of) association for playing golf; **~-course, ~-links,** area of land on which golf is played; ~ **widow,** woman whose husband spends much leisure time at golf. **3.** *v.i.* play golf. [15th c. Sc., of unkn. orig.]

gō'lfer *n.* golf-player; cardigan. [f. prec. + -ER[1]]

Goli'ath *n.* giant; ~ **beetle,** very large African black white-striped beetle; ~ **(crane),** powerful travelling crane; ~ **(heron),** African giant heron. [LL, f. Heb *golyat* giant slain by David (1 Sam. 17)]

gō'liwŏg *n.* black-faced brightly-dressed soft doll with fuzzy hair. [19th c., perh. f. GOLLY[1] + POLLIWOG]

gō'llop *v.t.,* & *n.* (colloq.) (swallow with) greedy or hasty gulp. [perh. f. GULP, infl. by GOBBLE[1]]

gō'lly[1] *int.* = (*by*) *God.* [euphem. for GOD]

gō'lly[2] *n.* = GOLLIWOG. [abbr.]

‖**golō'sh.** See GALOSH.

golŭ'ptious (-shus) *a.* (joc.) luscious, delightful. [perh f. *voluptuous*]

GOM *abbr.* Grand Old Man.

gŏmbee'n *n.* (Ir.) usury (**~-man,** money-lender). [Ir. *gaimbín* perh. f. same OCelt. source as med. cambire CHANGE[2]]

-gon *suf.* forming *ns.* denoting plane figures with specified number of angles (*hexagon, polygon, n-gon*). [Gk -*gōnos* -angled]

gō'nad *n.* animal organ producing gametes, e.g. testis or ovary; hence **gōnā'd**AL *a.* [f. mod. L *gonas -adis* Gk *gonē, gonos,* generation, seed; see -AD]

gŏnadotrō′phic, -trŏ′pic, *a.* (Physiol.) regulating activity of gonads. [f. prec. + -o- + -TROPHIC, -TROPIC]

gŏ′ndola *n.* light flat-bottomed boat with cabin amidships and high point at each end, worked by one oar at stern, used on Venetian canals; car suspended from airship; *~* (**car**), flat-bottomed open railway goods wagon; car attached to ski-lift; island shelves to display goods in self-service shop. [It., f. Rhaeto--Rom., = rock, roll]

gŏndolier′ *n.* rower of gondola. [F, f. It. *gondoliere* as prec.; see -IER)]

gone (gŏn, gawn) *a.* In vbl senses; lost, hopeless; dead; (of time) past (*not until gone nine*); **be ~**, depart (cf. BEGONE), (colloq.) be temporarily absent; FAR[1] *gone*; **~ away!** (huntsman's indication that fox has been started); *~* **goose** or **gosling,** (colloq.) person or thing beyond hope; **~ on,** (sl.) infatuated with. [p.p. of GO[1]]

gŏ′ner *n.* (sl.) person or thing that is doomed, ended, irrevocably lost, etc. [f. prec. + -ER[1]]

gŏ′nfalon *n.* banner, often with streamers, hung from crossbar, esp. (Hist.) as standard of some Italian republics; so *~*IER′ *n.* [f. It. *gonfalone* f. Frank. **gundfano* f. Gmc **gund-* war + Frank. **fano* banner (cf. VANE)]

gŏng *n.,* & *v.t.* **1.** *n.* metal disc with turned rim giving resonant note when struck, saucer-shaped bell; (sl.) medal or decoration. **2.** *v.t.* summon with gong; (of traffic police) sound gong etc. to direct (motorist) to stop. |f. Malay *gong, gung,* of imit. orig.]

gŏ′ngorism (-ngg-) *n.* Spanish literary style marked by inversion, antithesis, and classical allusion, corresponding to euphuism in England. [f. L. de *Góngora* y Argote, Sp. poet d. 1627 + -ISM]

gŏniŏ′meter *n.* instrument for measuring angles; hence or cogn. **gŏniŏ′METRY** *n.,* **gŏniŏmě′tric**(AL) *adj.* [f. F *goniomètre* f. Gk *gōnia* angle; see -METER]

gŏ′nna (vulg., or US colloq.) = GOING[2] *to.* [corrupt.]

gŏnocŏ′cc|us *n.* (*pl. ~i pr.* -kī). micro-organism causing gonorrhoea. [f. Gk *gonos* generation, semen + COCCUS]

‖**gŏnorrhoe′|a, *gŏnorrhē′|a,** (-orē′a) *n.* venereal disease with inflammatory discharge of mucus from urethra or vagina; hence ~AL *a.* [LL, f. Gk *gonorrhoia* (*gonos* semen, *rhoia* flux)]

goo *n.* (sl.) viscous or sticky substance; (fig.) sickly sentiment. [20th c.; perh. f. BURGOO]

good *a.* & *adv.* (BETTER[1], BEST[1]), & *n.* **1.** *a.* having the right qualities, satisfactory, adequate; *a good fire* (not too small or dull); *good health,* freedom from illness; *meat keeps good* (untainted); *good soil* (fertile); *good theatre* etc., entertainment suited to specified medium; **not ~ enough,** (colloq.) not worth doing, accepting, etc.; **in ~ time,** with no risk of being late; **all in ~ time,** in due course but without haste; (used as conventional epithet in) *the good ship* —, *the good town of* —; *good law* (valid, sound); *is good eating* etc. (pleasant to eat etc.). **2.** commendable (*good and true*); *a good dog* (well shaped); *~* **for you** etc., *~* **man,** *~* **old** —, (Austral. & NZ) *~* **o′n you** etc., (colloq. forms of approval); **a ~ one,** (sl.) incredible lie or exaggeration, excellent joke etc.; (used in courteous, patronizing, ironically polite, or indignant address, as) *my good friend, man, sir*; (used in polite or indulgently contemptuous description, as) *your good lady, the good man.* **3.** right, proper, expedient, (*it is good that you came; I thought, it seemed, good to* do something; or abs. as excl. of approval or consent). **4.** morally excellent, virtuous, (*do one's good deed for the day*). **5.** kind, benevolent, (so of God etc.; in excl. of surprise etc.: *good God!, good gracious!, good heavens!*); *how good of you!*; *did me a good turn; has always been good to me*; **be so ~ as, be ~ enough, to** do, please do; **put in** or **say a ~ word for,** commend, defend. **6.** (Esp. of child) well behaved, not giving trouble, (*as good as gold*). **7.** gratifying, agreeable, favourable, advantageous, beneficial, wholesome, (*good NEWS; it's good to be alive; for BETTER[1]*

for worse; (used in forms of greeting or parting, as) *good afternoon, day, evening, morning, night*; *have a good* NIGHT; *a good saying* or *story, as good as a play,* (amusing); *oil is good for burns; beer is not good for him* or *for his health; are acorns good to eat?*); **take in ~ part,** not be offended at; *~* **times,** period of prosperity; **have a ~ time,** enjoy oneself. **8.** adapted to a purpose, efficient, suitable, competent, (*a good actor, correspondent, driver; good English; good at describing* etc.; *has been a good wife to him*). **9.** reliable, safe, sure; financially sound, able to meet liabilities; *good debts* (sure to be paid); *~* **for** an amount, safely to be trusted to pay it, (of draft etc.) drawn for so much; *~* **for,** able to perform, inclined for, (*good for a ten-mile walk*). **10.** valid, sound, thorough, ample, considerable, (*gave her a good beating*; *did it for good reasons; rule holds good; a good excuse*; (colloq.) *is a good bit better*); *a good* DEAL[1], FEW, MANY; *have a good* MIND[1]; *a good* WHILE[1]; (as intensive before adj., as) *went a good round pace, will take a good long time.* **11.** not less than (*played for a good hour; it is a good three miles from the station*). **12. as ~ as,** practically (*he as good as told me so; as good as dead; it is as good as done*); **feel ~,** be in good spirits; **make ~,** compensate for, pay (expense), fulfil (promise), effect (purpose, intended action), demonstrate (statement), substantiate (charge), gain and hold (position), replace or restore (thing lost or damaged), (abs.) accomplish what one has attempted. **13.** *good* BOOK[1](*s*); *~* **breeding,** correct or courteous manners; *good* BUY, CAUSE[1], FAITH; **of ~ family,** well-born; *~* **fellow,** virtuous man, sociable person, agreeable companion; *~***-fe′llow-ship,** conviviality, sociability; *good* FORM[1]; *~***-for--nothing,** *~***-for-nought,** *adjs.* & *ns.,* worthless (person); *Good* FRIDAY; *with a good* GRACE; *~***-hearted,** kindly or well-meaning; *~* **humour,** cheerful mood or disposition, amiability; *~***-humoured,** cheerful, amiable; *good* JOB[1]; G*~* **King Henry,** kind of goose--foot used in cooking; *good* LIVER[2] (1, 2), LIVING[1]; *~***-loo′ker,** handsome person; *~***-loo′king,** handsome; *~′***-looking,** of virtuous appearance; *~* **looks,** personal beauty; *~* **luck,** being fortunate, happy chance; *good luck to you!* (as wish); ‖*~***′man,** (arch.) head of household, husband, father, etc.; *~* **money,** genuine money, money that might have been spent usefully elsewhere (*throw good money after bad*), (colloq.) high wages; ‖*~* **morrow,** (arch.) = *good morning* (see sense 7); *~* **nature,** kindly disposition, willingness to subordinate one's own interests; *~***-natured,** kindly, willing to please; *~* **neighbour,** one who acts in friendly manner; *good* OFFICES; *~* **oil,** (Austral. sl.) reliable information; **the ~ people,** fairies; *~* **question** (not answerable immediately or easily); *~* **sense,** soundness of judgement, practical wisdom; **in ~ spirits,** not depressed; *~***-tempered,** having good TEMPER[2]; *~* **thing,** anything one approves of, advantageous bargain or speculation, witty saying, (in *pl.*) dainties or luxuries; *~* **time** (see senses 1 and 7); *~***-time,** recklessly pursuing pleasure; *~′***wife,** (Sc.) mistress of house; *~* **will,** virtuous intent (cf. GOODWILL); *~* **works,** charitable acts. **14.** Hence *~*ISH[1] *a.* **15.** *adv.* (colloq.) *well, properly, (*doing pretty good*); *~* **and,** (colloq., as intensive: *raining good and hard, *I was good and angry*). **16.** *n.* what is good or beneficial, well-being, profit, benefit, advantage, (*is a power for good; deceive him for his (own) good; what good is it, what is the good of it, what good will it do?; much good may it do you!* (often iron.)); **be any, much, no, some, ~,** be of any etc. use; **come to (no) ~,** yield (no) good result; **do ~,** show kindness to, act philanthropically, be beneficial to; **for ~ (and all),** permanently or finally; **in ~,** (colloq.) in favour *with*; **no~** *n.* & *a.,* useless (thing, person); (be £1 etc.) **to the ~,** (have) as net profit, advantage, something extra, etc. **17.** desirable end or object, thing worth attaining; **no ~,** some mischief (*is up to, after, no good*). **18.** (as *pl.*) virtuous persons (*the good and the bad alike respect him*). **19.** (in *pl.*) movable property; merchandise, wares, (**piece** of ~**s**, (joc.) person); ||things for transmission by rail etc. (opp. *passengers*; so *goods agent, station, train,* etc.; **by** ~**s**, by goods train). **20.** (in *pl.*, colloq.) objects etc. one has undertaken to supply (*deliver the goods*, lit. or fig.); *the* real thing, *the* genuine article; information etc. **to** one's own advantage (*have the goods on a person*). [OE *gōd*, = OS *gōd*, OHG *guot*, ON *góthr*, Goth. *gōths* f. Gmc *gōdhaz cogn. w. **gadh-* in GATHER]

goodbye', ***goodbÿ'**, *int.* & *n.* (*pl.* **goodbyes** or ***goodbys**). (saying of) farewell (expressing good wishes on parting, ending telephone conversation, etc., or fig. w. ref. to thing got rid of or irrevocably lost). [contr. of *God be with you!*, w. good substituted after *good night* etc.]

goo'dlÿ *a.* comely, handsome; of considerable size etc.; hence ~**iNESS** *n.* [OE *gōdlic* (as GOOD, -LY[1])]

goo'dnēss *n.* **1.** virtue; positive or comparative excellence; benevolence, kindness, generosity, (**have the** ~, be kind enough *to*); what is good in thing, its essence or strength. **2.** (In excl., substituted for) God (*goodness knows*; *for goodness' sake*; THANK *goodness!*; *I wish to goodness*; ~ **gracious!,** ~ **me!,** excl. of surprise or indignation). [OE *gōdnes* (as GOOD, -NESS)]

goo'dō *a.* (Austral. & NZ) = GOOD 3. [f. GOOD + -O]

goodwi'll *n.* kindly feeling to person, favour; cheerful acquiescence, heartiness, zeal; established custom or popularity of business etc.; privilege granted by seller of established business, of trading as recognized successor; amount paid for this. [f. GOOD + WILL[2]]

goo'dÿ[1] *n.* (arch.) elderly woman of humble station; (as prefix to surname) *Goody Blake* etc. [for GOODwife; cf. HUSSY]

goo'dÿ[2] *n.* something good or attractive, esp. to eat; (colloq.) hero etc., opp. *baddy* (BAD 3). [f. GOOD + -Y[3]]

goo'dÿ[3], **goo'dÿ-goo'dÿ**, *a.* & *n.* (person who is) primly, affectedly, obtrusively, weakly, or sentimentally virtuous; hence (**goodÿ-)goo'diNESS** *n.* [f. GOOD + -Y[3]]

goo'dÿ[4] *int.* expr. childish delight or surprise. [f. GOOD + -Y[3]]

goo'ey *a.* (goo'ier, goo'iest). (sl.) viscous or sticky; (fig.) sentimental. [f. GOO + -Y[2]]

goof[1] *n.* (sl.) foolish or stupid person; mistake; ~**'ball,** (1) marijuana or other drug tablet, (2) foolish or stupid person; hence ~**'y**[2] *a.*, (sl.) silly. [var. of dial. *goff* f. F *goffe* f. It. *goffo* f. med. L *gufus* coarse]

goof[2] *v.* (sl.) **1.** *v.i.* idle; blunder. **2.** *v.t.* bungle, mess up; (in *p.p.*) stupefy with drug. [f. prec.]

goo'glÿ *n.* (Cricket). off-break ball bowled with apparent leg-break action. [20th c.; orig. unkn.]

***gook** (goōk, goŏk) *n.* (sl., derog.) foreigner, esp. coloured person from E. Asia etc. [20th c.; orig. unkn.]

goōn *n.* (sl.) stupid person; person hired by racketeers etc. to terrorize workers. [perh. f. dial. *gooney* booby; infl. by subhuman cartoon character 'Alice the *Goon*']

goōp *n.* (sl.) stupid or fatuous person; hence ~**'y**[2] *a.* [20th c.; cf. GOOF[1]]

goōsä'nder *n.* duck (*Mergus merganser*) with sharp serrated bill. [app. f. foll.; cf. *bergander* sheldrake]

goōse *n.* (*pl.* geese pr. gēs, exc. in sense 3), & *v.t.* **1.** *n.* large web-footed bird of genus *Anser* etc., between duck and swan in size; female of this (opp. *gander*); flesh of goose as food; **all his geese are swans,** he overestimates the merits of his own schemes, friends, etc.; **kill the ~ that lays the golden eggs,** sacrifice future profit to greed of the moment; COOK[2] person's *goose*; GONE *goose*; *say* BOO *to goose*; *sauce for goose is sauce for* GANDER. **2.** simpleton. **3.** (*pl.* ~**s**). tailor's smoothing-iron (with handle like goose's neck). **4.** *~ **bumps,** = *goose-flesh*; *~**-egg,** zero score in game; ~**-flesh,** rough bristling state of skin produced by cold or fright; ~**-foot** (*pl.* ~**-foots**), plant esp. of genus *Chenopodium*, named from shape of leaves; ~**-grass** (employed to tend geese); ~**-grass,** cleavers; ~**'herd,** one who tends geese; ~**-neck,** thing shaped like neck of goose; ~**-pimples,** ~**-skin,** = *goose-flesh*;

~ **step,** (1) balancing-drill taught to army recruits, (2) balance step of marching soldiers with knees kept stiff. **5.** *v.t.* (sl.) poke person in sensitive (esp. genital or anal) region. [OE *gōs*, = OHG *gans*, ON *gás* f. Gmc **gans-* f. IE **ghans-*]

goo'seberry (-zb-) *n.* **1.** (edible berry of) any thorny species of *Ribes*; (arch.) wine made of gooseberries; **play** ~, act as chaperon, or be unwelcome companion, for pair of lovers. **2.** ~ **bush** (w. ref. to source of babies in explanation sometimes given to children); *gooseberry* FOOL[2]. [perh. f. prec., but cf. dial. *groser* (F *groseille*)]

||**goo'segog** (-zg-) *n.* (colloq.) gooseberry. [joc. corrupt.]

***GOP** *abbr.* Grand Old Party (the Republican Party).

go'pher[1] *n.* (Bibl.) tree from wood of which Noah's ark was made; ~ (**-wood**), tree (*Cladrastis lutea*) yielding yellowish timber. [f. Heb. *gōper*]

go'pher[2] *n.* **1.** American burrowing rodent of family Geomyidae. **2.** N. Amer. ground-squirrel of genus *Citellus*. **3.** nocturnal burrowing tortoise of Southern US. **4.** ~ **snake,** cribo; ***G~ State,** Minnesota. [18th c.; said to be f. Can. F *gaufre* honeycomb, w. ref. to burrowing]

gō'ral *n.* Indian antelope of genus *Naemorhedus*. [native name]

||**go'rblī'mey** *int.* (vulg.) expr. surprise, indignation, etc. [corrupt. of *God blind me*]

go'r'cŏck *n.* (Sc. & N. Engl.) male of the red grouse. [f. *gor-* (of unkn. orig.) + COCK[1]]

Go'r'dian *a.* ~ **knot,** intricate knot, difficult problem or task; **cut the ~ knot,** solve problem by force or by evading the conditions. [f. *Gordius* king in Phrygia, who tied a knot later cut by Alexander the Great, + -AN]

Go'r'don *n.* ~ (**setter**), black and tan setter used as gun dog. [f. 4th Duke of ~ d. 1827, promoter of the breed]

gore[1] *n.* blood shed and thickened or clotted; hence **go'r'y**[2] *a.*, **go'r'iLY**[2] *adv.* [OE *gor* dung, dirt, = OHG, ON *gor* slimy matter]

gore[2] *n.* & *v.t.* **1.** wedge-shaped piece of cloth inserted to adjust width of a garment; triangular or lune--shaped piece in umbrella, balloon, dome, globe, etc. **2.** *v.t.* shape or narrow with gore. [OE *gāra* triangular piece of land, = OHG *gēro*, ON *geiri*, cogn. w. OE *gār* spear, w. ref. to shape of spearhead]

gore[3] *v.t.* pierce with horn, tusk, etc. [ME, of unkn. orig.]

gorge[1] *n.* **1.** what has been swallowed, contents of stomach, (**cast the ~ at,** reject with loathing; one's ~ **rises at,** one is sickened or disgusted by); (rhet.) internal throat. **2.** (Fortif.) neck of bastion or other outwork, rear entrance to a work. **3.** narrow opening, usu. with stream, between hills; *mass of ice etc. blocking narrow passage. [ME f. OF = throat, f. Rom. *gurga for L *gurges* whirlpool]

gorge[2] *v.* & *n.* **1.** *v.i.* feed greedily. **2.** *v.t.* satiate, glut; swallow, devour greedily; fill full, distend, choke up. **3.** *n.* act of gorging, surfeit. [ME, f. OF *gorger* (as prec.)]

gor'geous (-jus) *a.* richly coloured, sumptuous, magnificent; (colloq.) very pleasant, splendid, (*had a gorgeous time*); hence ~**LY**[2] *adv.*, ~**NESS** *n.* [earlier *gorgayse, -yas* f. OF *gorgias* fine, elegant, of unkn. orig.]

gor'gėt *n.* (Hist.) piece of armour for throat; woman's wimple. **2.** patch of colour on throat of bird etc. [f. OF *gorgete* (as GORGE[1]; see -ET[1])]

Gor'giō *n.* (*pl.* ~**s**). (gypsy name for) non-gypsy. [Romany]

Gor'gon *n.* **1.** (Gk Myth.) one of three sisters (esp. Medusa) whose looks turned any beholder to stone. **2.** terrible or ugly person, repellent woman. **3.** hence **gorgō'nian** *a.* [f. L *Gorgo -onis* f. Gk *Gorgō* (*gorgos* terrible)]

gorgō'nia *n.* polyp of genus *Gorgonia*, e.g. sea-fan; hence ~**AN** *a.* & *n.* [mod. L, f. as prec. + -IA[1], w. ref. to its petrifaction]

gŏr′gonize, -ise (-īz), *v.t.* stare at like gorgon; paralyse with terror etc. [f. GORGON + -IZE]

Gŏrgonzō′la *n.* type of rich blue-veined cheese. [~ in Italy]

gori′lla *n.* large powerful forest-dwelling anthropoid ape, with reputation for fierceness. [perh. Afr. for 'wild man', in Gk account of Hanno's voyage 5th or 6th c. BC, adopted as specific name 1847]

gŏr′mandīz|e, -ĭs|e (-īz), *n.* & *v.* l. *n.* = GOURMANDISE. **2.** *v.i.* & *t.* eat or devour voraciously; hence ~ER[1] *n.* [f. as GOURMANDISE]

gŏr′mléss *a.* (colloq.) foolish, lacking sense; hence ~NESS *n.* [orig. *gaumless* f. dial. *gaum* understanding + -LESS]

gŏrse *n.* = FURZE; hence **gŏr′sY**[2] *a.* [OE *gors(t)* cogn. w. OHG *gersta*, L *hordeum*, barley]

Gŏr′sĕdd (-ĕdh) *n.* meeting of Welsh etc. bards and druids (esp. as daily preliminary to the eisteddfod). [W, lit. 'throne']

gŏr′ў. See GORE[1].

gŏsh *n.* (In excl. etc., substituted for) God (*gosh, my gosh, gosh-awful*, etc.). [euphem.]

gŏ′shawk (-s-h-) *n.* large short-winged hawk. [OE *gōs-hafoc* (as GOOSE, HAWK[1])]

gŏ′sling (-z-) *n.* young goose; GONE *gosling*. [ME, orig. *gesling* f. ON *gǽslingr* (as GOOSE, -LING[1])]

gŏ′spel *n.* **1.** glad tidings preached by Christ; religious doctrine of Christ and his apostles, Christian revelation. **2.** (G~.) record of Christ's life and teaching in first four books of NT (Matthew, Mark, Luke, John); one of these books; portion from one of them read at Communion service. **3.** thing that may safely be believed (*takes his dreams for gospel*); principle that one acts upon, believes in, or preaches, (*the gospel of efficiency, laissez-faire, soap and water*). **4.** ~ **oath** (sworn on the Gospels); G~ **side**, N. side of altar, at which Gospel is read; ~ (**song**), fervent or evangelical singing esp. as style of jazz; ~ **truth**, truths contained in Gospel, something as true as Gospel. [OE *gōdspel* (gŏd GOOD, *spel* news, SPELL[1]), rendering eccl. L *bona annuntiatio, bonus nuntius = evangelium* EVANGEL; assoc. w. GOD]

gŏ′speller *n.* reader of Gospel in Communion service; **hot** ~, zealous puritan, rabid propagandist. [f. prec. + -ER[1]]

gŏ′ssamer *n.* & *a.* **1.** *n.* light filmy substance, the webs of small spiders, floating in calm air or spread over grass; a thread of this; something flimsy; delicate gauze; hence ~ED[2] (-erd), ~Y[2], *adjs.* **2.** *a.* light and flimsy as gossamer. [ME *gos(e)somer(e)*, app. f. GOOSE + SUMMER[1] (*goose summer* = St. Martin's summer, i.e. early November when geese were eaten, gossamer being most seen then)]

gŏ′ssip *n.*, & *v.i.* **1.** *n.* ‖(arch., esp. of woman). familiar acquaintance, friend. **2.** idle talker, newsmonger, tattler. **3.** idle talk, groundless rumours, tittle-tattle, whence ~-MONGER *n.*; easy unconstrained talk or writing esp. about persons or social incidents (~ **column**, section of newspaper etc. containing this); hence ~RY (4, 5) *n.*, ~Y[2] *a.* **4.** *v.i.* talk idly or lightly, tattle; write in gossipy style; hence ~ER[1] *n.* [earlier sense 'godparent', f. OE *godsibb* person related to one in GOD; see SIB]

gŏssoō′n *n.* (Ir.) lad. [earlier *garsoon* f. F *garçon* boy]

gŏt. See GET[1].

Gŏth *n.* uncivilized or ignorant person. [f. name of Gmc tribe invading Eastern & Western Empires in 3rd-5th c.; f. LL *Gothi* pl. f. Gk *Go(t)thoi* f. Goth. *Gutos* or *Gutans*]

Gŏ′tham (-tam) *n.* **1.** town proverbial for folly (**wise man of** ~, fool). **2.** (or gō′tham). *(colloq.)* New York City. **3.** Hence ~ITE[1] (1) *n.* [ME, perh. f. the village in Notts.]

Gŏ′thic *a.* & *n.* **1.** *a.* of the Goths or their language. **2.** (Archit.) in the pointed-arch style prevalent in churches etc. of Western Europe in 12th-16th c., including in England the Early English, Decorated,

and Perpendicular; ~ **Revival,** reversion to this in 19th c. **3.** (arch.) barbarous, rude, uncouth. **4.** (Print.) old-fashioned German, black letter, or sanserif, (type). **5.** (Of novel etc.) in style popular in 18th-19th c., with supernatural or horrifying events. **6.** Hence **Gŏ′thi**CALLY *adv.*, ~ISM (2, 3, 4) *n.*, ~IZE (2, 3) *v.i.* & *t.* **7.** *n.* Gothic language, architecture, or type. [f. F *gothique* or f. LL *gothicus* (*Gothi*; see GOTH, -IC)]

gŏ′tta (colloq. or vulg.) = (*have*) *got a* or (*have*) *got to.* [corrupt.]

gŏ′tten. See GET[1].

Götterdä′mmerung (gĕrterdĕ′merŏŏng) *n.* twilight of the gods; (fig.) complete downfall of regime etc. [G, esp. as title of opera by Wagner]

gouache (gŏōah′sh) *n.* (way of painting in) opaque colours ground in water and thickened with gum and honey; picture thus painted. [F, f. It. *guazzo*]

Gou′da *n.* flat round cheese. [~ in Holland, where orig. made]

gouge (gowj, gōōj) *n.* & *v.* **1.** *n.* concave-bladed chisel used in carpentry, sculpture, and surgery; *(colloq.)* swindle. **2.** *v.t.* cut with gouge; cut *out* (a cork, a channel) (as) with gouge; force (*out*, esp. person's eye with thumb) (as) with gouge; force out eye of; *(colloq.)* swindle, extort money from. **3.** *v.i.* (Austral.) dig for opal. [F, f. LL *gubia*, perh. of Celt. orig.]

gou′lash (gŏō′lăsh, -ălsh) *n.* **1.** highly seasoned stew of meat and vegetables. **2.** (Contract Bridge). re-deal, several cards at a time, of the four hands (unshuffled, but with each hand arranged in suits and order of value) when no player has bid. [f. Magyar *gulyás-hús* (*gulyás* herdsman, *hús* meat)]

gourami (goor′amī, -ah′-) *n.* large SE Asian freshwater food-fish (*Osphronemus goramy*); smaller fish of same family, freq. kept in aquaria. [f. Malay *gurāmi*]

gourd (goord) *n.* **1.** (fleshy usu. large fruit of) trailing or climbing plant of family Cucurbitaceae. **2.** rind of gourd-fruit emptied, dried, and used as bottle etc.; hence ~FUL 2 *n.* [ME, f. AF *gurde*, OF *gourde* ult. f. L *cucurbita*]

gour′mand (goor′-) *a.* & *n.* **1.** *a.* gluttonous, fond of eating. **2.** *n.* greedy feeder, glutton; gourmet; hence ~ISM (2) *n.* [ME, f. OF, of unkn. orig.]

gourmandise (goor′mahndēz) *n.* habits of a gourmand, indulgence in good eating, gluttony. [F (as prec.; cf. -ISE[2])]

gour′met (goor′mā) *n.* connoisseur of table delicacies; judge of good food. [F, = wine-taster; sense infl. by GOURMAND]

gout *n* **1.** paroxysmal disease with inflammation of smaller joints, esp. that of big toe, and chalky deposits; ~**weed**, herb Gerard; hence ~Y[2] *a.* **2.** wheat-disease caused by ~**fly** (*Chlorops*). **3.** drop, esp. of blood; splash, spot. [ME, f. OF *goute* f. L *gutta* drop, w. ref. to medieval theory of flowing down of humours]

gov. Var. of GUV.

Gov. *abbr.* Government; Governor.

gŏ′vern (gŭ′-) *v.* **1.** *v.t.* rule with authority, conduct the policy, actions, and affairs, of (State, subjects) either despotically or constitutionally; regulate proceedings of (corporation etc.); ~**ing body,** managers of hospital, school, etc.); be in military command of (fort, town). **2.** sway, rule, influence, regulate, determine, (person, his acts, course or issue of events). **3.** conduct one*self* in some way; curb, bridle, (one's passions, one*self*). **4.** constitute a law, rule, standard, or principle, for; serve to decide (case). **5.** (Gram., esp. of *v.* or *prep.*) have (noun or pronoun, case) depending on it, require (case) in certain case of dependent word). **6.** Hence ~ABLE *a.* **7.** *v.i.* exercise function of government in person; *king reigns but does not govern* (merely selects those who are to govern). **8.** be predominating influence. [ME, f. OF *governer* f. L *gubernare* steer, rule f. Gk *kubernaō* steer]

gŏ′vernance (gŭ′-) *n.* act, manner, fact, or function,

of governing; sway, control. [ME f. OF (as prec.; see -ANCE)]

go'verness (gŭ'-) *n.* **1.** female teacher, usu. of children in private household; hence ~v² *a.* (esp., prim). **2.** ||~-car(t), (Hist.) light two-wheeled tub-shaped cart with rear entrance, and side seats face to face. [earlier *governeress* f. OF *governeresse* (as GOVERNOR; see -ESS¹)]

go'vernment (gŭ'-) *n.* **1.** system of governing, form of organization of State. **2.** body or successive bodies of persons governing a State; the State as an agent; an administration or ministry; **form a G**~ (of Prime Minister selecting colleagues); **G**~ **House,** official residence of governor; *~ **issue,** (equipment) provided by the government; **G**~ **paper, securities,** bonds etc. issued by the government; ~ **surplus,** unused equipment sold by the government. **3.** (Gram.) relation between governing and governed word. **4.** act, manner, or fact, of governing. **5.** Hence ~AL (-ĕ'n-) *a.* [ME, f. OF *governement* (as GOVERN; see -MENT)]

go'vernor (gŭ'-) *n.* **1.** one who governs, ruler; official appointed to govern province, town, etc., representative of Crown in Commonwealth country that regards Queen as Head of State (*Governor-Ge'neral*) or in colony; executive head of each State of US; officer commanding fortress or garrison; head, or one of governing body, of institution; official in charge of prison. **2.** (sl.) one's employer, one's father; (as *voc.*) sir. **3.** (Mech.) automatic regulator of supply of gas, steam, water, etc., to machine, ensuring uniform motion. **4.** Hence ~ATE¹ (1), ~SHIP (1, 2), *ns.* [ME, f. AF *governour*, OF *governëo(u)r* f. L *gubernator -oris* (as GOVERN; see -OR)]

Govt. *abbr.* Government.

gow'an *n.* (Sc.) daisy; white or yellow field-flower. [prob. var. of dial. *gollan* ranunculus etc., and cogn. w. mari*gold*]

gowk *n.* (dial.) cuckoo; awkward or half-witted person, fool. [ME, f. ON *gaukr* = OE *gēac*, OHG *gouh* f. Gmc **gaukaz*]

gown *n.,* & *v.t.* **1.** *n.* loose flowing outer garment, esp. woman's dress (now usu. of dress with some pretension to elegance), frock; ancient Roman toga; surgeon's overall; official or uniform robe of various shapes worn by alderman, judge, lawyer, clergyman, member of university, college, or school, etc., (**town and** ~, non-members and members of university esp. at Oxf. and Camb.); ~'**sman** (-z-), wearer of gown, member of university. **2.** *v.t.* (usu. in *p.p.*) attire in gown. [ME, f. OF *goune, gon(n)e* f. LL *gunna* fur garment (cf. med. Gk *gouna* fur)]

goy *n.* (*pl.* ~s *or* ~'im). (Jewish derog. name for) GENTILE 1. [f. Heb. *gōy* people, nation]

GP *abbr.* general practitioner; Grand Prix.

Gp. Capt. *abbr.* Group Captain.

GPI *abbr.* general paralysis of the insane.

GPO *abbr.* General Post Office; *Government Printing Office.

GR *abbr.* King George. [f. L *Georgius Rex*]

gr. *abbr.* grain(s); gram(s); grey; gross.

Graa'fian (grah'f-) *a.* ~ **follicle** or **vesicle,** one of small sacs in mammal ovary in which ova are matured. [f. R. de *Graaf*, Du. anatomist d. 1673 + -IAN]

gräb *v.* (-bb-) & *n.* **1.** *v.t.* seize suddenly; appropriate rapaciously; capture, arrest; (sl.) attract attention of, impress. **2.** *v.i.* make sudden snatch *at*; (of brakes of motor vehicle) act harshly or jerkily. **3.** Hence (-)~'bER¹ *n.* **4.** *n.* sudden clutch, grasp, seizure, or attempt to seize (***up for** ~s, (sl.) easily obtainable, inviting capture); practice of grabbing, rapacious proceedings esp. in politics or commerce; (Mech.) device or implement for clutching; children's card-game in which certain cards may be snatched from the table; *~-**bag,** lucky dip; ~ **handle,** ~ **rail,** etc., (to steady passengers in moving vehicle). [f. MLG, MDu. *grabben*; cf. GRIP², GRIPE, GROPE]

gra'bble *v.i.* grope about, feel for something; sprawl on all fours, scramble (*for* something). [f. Du. & LG *grabbeln* scramble for a thing (as prec.; see -LE 3)]

gra'bby *a.* (colloq.) having tendency to grab; greedy. [f. GRAB + -Y²]

gra'ben (-ah'-) *n.* (*pl.* ~s *or* ~). (Geol.) depression of earth's surface between faults. [G, orig. = ditch]

grāce *n.,* & *v.t.* **1.** *n.* pleasing quality, attractiveness, charm, esp. that belonging to elegant proportions or ease and refinement of movement, action, expression, or manner. **2.** becomingness (*cannot with any grace ask him*; **have the** ~ **to,** be sufficiently conscious of duty or decency to); air with which thing is done (**with a good** ~, as if willingly; **with a bad** *or* **an ill** ~, reluctantly, ungraciously). **3.** attractive feature, accomplishment, ornament, (*social graces*); **airs and** ~**s,** behaviour adopted with a view to effect or attraction. **4.** (Mus.) ~(-note), -notes, extra note(s) as embellishments not essential to harmony or melody. **5.** (Gk Myth.; *G*~). one of three beautiful goddess sisters, bestowers of beauty and charm. **6.** favour, benignant regard or its manifestation, on part of superior; **be in** person's **good** ~**s,** enjoy his favour or liking; ~ **and favour** *house* etc., occupied by permission of sovereign etc. **7.** unconstrained goodwill as ground of concession; **act of** ~, privilege or concession that cannot be claimed as right (and see 11); **by the** ~ **of God,** (esp. in royal titles) through God's favour. **8.** ||permission to take university degree; dispensation from university statutes; (Camb. Univ.) decree of Senate or Regent House. **9.** (Theol.) unmerited favour of God, divine regenerating, inspiring, and strengthening influence; (**state of**) ~, condition of being so influenced (**fall from** ~, lapse into sin or disgrace from good behaviour etc.); divinely given talent etc.; SAVING¹ *grace*; **year of** ~, date AD. **10.** favour shown by granting delay (*give a day's, year's, grace*); **days of** ~, time allowed by law for payment of bill of exchange or insurance premium after it falls due. **11.** mercy, clemency; **Act of** ~, formal, esp. general, pardon by Act of Parliament (and see 7). **12.** short thanksgiving before or after meal (~-**cup,** cup of wine etc. passed round after grace, parting drink). **13.** His, Her, Your, G~ (forms of description or address for duke, duchess, or archbishop). **14.** *v.t.* lend grace to, adorn, enhance *with*; confer honour or dignity on, honour *with* title etc.; do credit to. [ME f. OF, f. L *gratia* (*gratus* pleasing; cf. GRATEFUL)]

grā'ceful (-sf-) *a.* pleasing, attractive, esp. in form, movement, or action; hence ~LY² *adv.,* ~NESS *n.* [ME, f. prec. + -FUL]

grā'celèss (-sl-) *a.* **1.** (arch. or joc.) unregenerate, depraved; ~ **florin** (of 1849, from which the letters *D.G.* were omitted). **2.** lacking sense of decency, unabashed. **3.** lacking charm or elegance. **4.** Hence ~LY² *adv.,* ~NESS *n.* [ME, f. GRACE + -LESS]

grā'cile *a.* slender; gracefully slender; hence **graci'lity** *n.,* slenderness, (of literary style) unornamented simplicity. [f. L *gracilis* slender]

grā'cious (-shŭs) *a.* & *int.* **1.** *a.* (Of exalted person, or iron. or joc.) kind, indulgent and beneficent to inferiors; (esp. as polite epithet of royal persons or their acts: *the gracious speech from the throne*); ~ **living,** elegant way of life with observance of proprieties etc. **2.** (Of God) dispensing grace, merciful, benignant; (arch.) agreeable, pleasing; (poet.) kindly, courteous. **3.** Hence or cogn. ~LY² *adv.,* ~NESS, **grāciò'sity,** *ns.* **4.** *int.* (orig. ellipt. for *gracious God* in excl. of indignation or surprise) *gracious!, good gracious!, gracious me!* [ME f. OF, f. L *gratiosus* (as GRACE; see -OUS)]

grā'ckle *n.* **1.** Asian bird of mina family, esp. of genus *Gracula.* **2.** Amer. oriole, esp. of genus *Quiscalus.* [f. mod. L *Gracula* f. L *graculus* jackdaw]

gräd *n.* (colloq.) = GRADUATE¹ 1. [abbr.]

gradā'te *v.i.* & *t.* (cause to) pass by imperceptible degrees from one shade of colour to another; arrange in steps or grades of size etc. [back-form. f. foll.]

gradā'tion *n.* **1.** (usu. in *pl.*) stage of transition or advance; degree in rank, merit, intensity, divergence, etc. **2.** such degree; arrangement in such degrees. **3.** (Paint. etc.) gradual passing from one shade, tone, etc., to another. **4.** (Philol.) ablaut. **5.** Hence ∿AL *a.* [f. L *gradatio* (*gradus* step; see -ATION)]

grāde *n.* & *v.* **1.** *n.* degree in rank, proficiency, quality, value, etc., class of persons or things alike in these; *class or form in school, usu. numbered from first up to twelfth (*∿ school, elementary school); mark indicating quality of student's work. **2.** variety of cattle produced by crossing native stock with superior breed. **3.** group of animals at similar level of development. **4.** (Philol.) relative position in ablaut-series. **5.** gradient, slope, rate of ascent or descent; *at ∿, on same level; *∿ crossing, LEVEL crossing; on the up or down ∿, rising or falling (lit. or fig.); make the ∿, reach desired standard. **6.** *v.t.* arrange in grades, class, sort; give grade to (student); blend so as to affect grade of colour with tints passing into each other. **7.** reduce (road, canal, etc.) to easy gradients. **8.** cross (cattle) with better breed (∿ up, improve thus). **9.** Hence **grā'der**[1] (1, 2) *n.* **10.** *v.i.* pass gradually (*down*, *up*, etc.) from one grade into or *into* another. [F, or f. L *gradus* step]

‖**grā'delý** (-dĭl) *a.* (dial.) excellent, thorough; handsome, comely, real, true, proper. [ME *grayihly* f. ON *greithligr* (*greithr* = OE *gerǣde* ready; see -LY[1])]

Grä'dgrĭnd *n.* person without warm feelings, interested only in facts. [character in Dickens's *Hard Times*]

grā'dĭent *n.* **1.** amount of slope, inclination to the horizontal, in road, railway, etc.; inclined part of road etc. **2.** (rate of) rise or fall of temperature, pressure, etc. in passing from one region to another. [prob. formed on GRADE after *salient*]

gradi'ne (-ē'n), **grā'dĭn,** *n.* one of series of low steps or tier of seats; ledge at back of altar. [f. It. *gradino* dim. of *grado* GRADE]

grā'duăl[1] *n.* response sung between Epistle and Gospel in the service of the Mass; book of music for Mass service. [so called as being sung at steps of altar or while deacon mounted ambo; f. med. L *graduale* neut. adj. (as n.), see foll.]

grā'duăl[2] *a.* **1.** taking place by degrees, slowly progressing, not rapid, steep, or abrupt; hence ∿ISM (3), ∿IST (2), *ns.*, (advocate of) policy of gradual not sudden change, ∿LY[2] *adv.*, ∿NESS *n.* **2.** ∿ psalm, = SONG *of Degrees.* [f. med. L *gradualis* (L *gradus* step; see -AL)]

‖**grā'duănd** *n.* one about to receive an academic degree. [f. med. L *graduandus* gerundive of *graduare* GRADUATE[2]; see -ND[1]]

grā'duate[1] *n.* **1.** one who holds academic degree; *one who has completed a school course; *∿ nurse, trained nurse; *∿ school, department of university for advanced work by graduates. **2.** chemist's graduated measuring-glass. [f. med. L *graduatus* p.p. of *graduari* (see foll., -ATE[2])]

grā'dū|āte[2] *v.i.* & *t.* **1.** take or *admit to academic degree or *certificate of completion of school studies; *send out or come as graduate *from* (university etc.); move up *to* (higher grade of activity etc.); gain qualifications *as.* **2.** *v.t.* mark out in degrees or portions; arrange in gradations, apportion incidence of (tax) according to a scale. **3.** *v.i.* pass by degrees (*into* or *away*). **4.** Hence ∿A'TION, ∿ātOR, *ns.* [f. med. L *graduari* f. L *gradus* step, + -ATE[3]]

grā'dus *n.* (Hist.) dictionary of Latin prosody used in schools to help in writing Latin verse. [abbr. of its title '*Gradus ad Parnassum*' steps to Parnassus]

Grae'cĭsm *n.* a Greek idiom, esp. as imitated in another language; Greek spirit, style, mode of expression, etc.; imitation of these. [f. F *grécisme* or f. med. L *Graecismus* (*Graecus* GREEK; see -ISM)]

Grae'cīze, -īse (-īz), *v.t.* give a Greek character or form to. [f. L *Graecizare* (as prec.; see -IZE)]

Grae'cŏ-, Grē'cŏ-, *comb. form.* Greek (and), as:

∿MA'NIA(C) *ns.*, ∿PHIL(E) *n.* & *a.*; ∿**-Roman,** of the Greeks and Romans (esp. of wrestling style attacking only upper part of body). [f. L *Graecus* GREEK + -O-]

graffi'to (-fē'-) *n.* (*pl.* ∿i *pr.* -ē). **1.** (usu. in *pl.*) drawing or writing scratched or scribbled on wall etc. **2.** decoration by scratches through plaster showing different-coloured under-surface. [It. (*graffio* scratching)]

graft[1] (-ah-) *n.* & *v.* **1.** *n.* shoot or scion inserted in slit of stock, from which it receives sap; (Surg.) piece of transplanted living tissue; process of grafting; place where graft is inserted; (sl.) hard work. **2.** *v.t.* insert (scion) as graft (*in*, *into*, *on*, *upon*, *together*); (fig.) insert or fix *in* or *on* so as to produce vital or indissoluble union; insert graft(s) on (stock); sew together (two pieces of knitted material not cast off); (Surg.) transplant (living tissue). **3.** *v.i.* insert graft(s); (sl.) work hard. **4.** ∿**ing-clay, -wax,** composition for covering united parts of graft and stock. [ME, earlier *graff* n. & v. f. OF *grafe*, *grefe* f. L f. Gk *graphion* stylus (*graphō* write)]

graft[2] (-ah-) *n.*, & *v.i.* (colloq.) **1.** *n.* illicit gain esp. in connection with politics or business; practices intended to secure this, esp. bribery. **2.** *v.i.* seek or make graft; hence ∿'ER[1] *n.* [19th c.; orig. unkn.]

*****gra'ham** (-a'am) *n.* ∿ **bread** etc. (made from ∿ **flour,** unbolted wheat flour). [f. S. *Graham*, Amer. dietitian d. 1851]

grail[1] *n.* (arch.) = GRADUAL[1]. [ME f. OF *grael*, f. med. L *gradale* var. of *graduale* GRADUAL[1]]

Grail[2] *n.* (Holy) ∿, cup or platter used (according to legend) by Christ at Last Supper, and in which Joseph of Arimathea received Christ's blood at the Cross; this as object of prolonged quest (by medieval knights, or fig.). [ME, f. OF *graal* etc. f. med. L *gradalis* dish, of unkn. orig.]

grain *n.* & *v.* **1.** *n.* fruit or seed of a cereal; (collect.) wheat or the allied food-grasses and their fruit, corn; a particular species of corn; grain ELEVATOR; ∿s of **Paradise,** capsules of W. Afr. plant (*Aframomum meleguet*a*) used as spice and drug. **2.** small hard particle of sand, gold, SALT, gunpowder, incense, etc.; (usu. small) discrete particle or crystal in rock or metal; piece of solid propellant used in rocket engine. **3.** smallest unit of weight in some systems, 1/480 of oz. troy, 1/437.5 of oz. avoirdupois; smallest possible quantity (*without a grain of vanity, of love*). **4.** (Hist.) kermes or cochineal, or dye made from either of these (**dye in** ∿, dye in kermes, dye in any fast colour, dye in the fibre or thoroughly; **in** ∿, thorough, genuine, by nature, downright, indelible); (poet.) dye, colour. **5.** granular texture, roughness of surface, mottling; texture, arrangement and size, of constituent particles, in flesh, skin, wood, stone, etc.; lines of fibre in wood or paper giving a pattern; lamination or planes of cleavage in coal, slate, etc.; (fig.) nature, temper, tendency, (**against the** ∿, contrary to inclination). **6.** ∿**-leather** (dressed with the grain-side out); ∿**-side** (of hide, on which the hair was). **7.** Hence (-)∿ED[2] (-nd), ∿'LESS, ∿'Y[2], *adjs.* **8.** *v.t.* & *i.* form into grains. **9.** *v.t.* dye in grain; dye granular surface to; remove hair from (hides); paint in imitation of grain of wood or marble; hence ∿'ER[1] (1, 2) *n.* [ME f. OF, f. L *granum*, and (sense 4) f. OF *graine* f. Rom. *grana* collect. fem., orig. neut. pl. of L *granum*]

graip *n.* (Sc.) three- or four-pronged fork used for lifting dung or digging potatoes etc. [f. ON *greip* corresp. to OE *grāp* grasp; cf. GRIP[1], GROPE]

grăllatōr'ĭal *a.* (Zool.) of the long-legged wading birds. [f. mod. L *grallatorius* f. L *grallator* stilt-walker (*grallae* stilts) + -AL]

grā'lloch (-ok) *n.*, & *v.t.* **1.** *n.* dead deer's viscera. **2.** *v.t.* disembowel (deer etc.). [f. Gael. *grealach* intestines]

grăm[1] *n.* chick-pea; any pulse used as horse-fodder. [f. Port. *grão* f. L *granum* grain]

grăm[2], **grămme,** *n.* unit of mass or weight in metric system, now defined as thousandth part of the

KILOGRAM; ∼**-atom,** quantity of chemical element whose mass in grams numerically equals its atomic weight; ∼**-equivalent,** (Chem.) equivalent with gram as unit; ∼**-force,** unit of force, equal to weight of one gram under standard attraction of gravity; ∼**-molecule,** quantity of substance whose mass in grams numerically equals its molecular weight. [f. F *gramme* f. Gk *gramma* small weight]

Gräm³ *n.* ∼ **method** (of staining bacteria with iodine solution); ∼**-positive,** ∼**-negative,** that can, cannot, be stained by this method. [f. H. C. J. ∼, Da. physician d. 1938]

-gräm *suf.* forming *ns.*: (1) prepositional compds. f. Gk w. ref. to writing (*anagram, diagram, epigram*), (2) denoting thing written or recorded (*chromatogram, chronogram, logogram, telegram*), (3) compds. w. Gk numerals (*monogram, pentagram*). [f. or after Gk *gramma -atos* thing written, letter of alphabet (*graphō* write)]

grä′ma, grä′mma, *n.* ∼ (**grass**), pasture grass of genus *Bouteloua* in W. and SW parts of US. [f. Sp. *grama*]

grä′marye *n.* (arch.) magic, necromancy. [ME, f. AF *gramarie,* OF *gramaire* learning, GRAMMAR]

gramēr′cy̆ *int.* (arch.) thank you. [ME, f. OF *grant merci* (God give you) great reward (as GRAND, MERCY)]

grāminā′ceous (-shŭs), **grami′néous,** *adjs.* of or like grass, grassy. [f. L *gramen -inis* grass + -ACEOUS, and L *gramineus* (see -EOUS)]

grāmini′vorous *a.* feeding on grass, cereals, etc. [f. as prec. + -I- + -VOROUS]

grä′mmalŏgue (-ŏg) *n.* word represented by single shorthand sign; logogram. [irreg. f. Gk *gramma* letter of alphabet + *logos* word]

grä′mmar *n.* **1.** art and science dealing with a language's inflexions or other means of showing relation between words as used in speech or writing, and its phonetic system, and the established rules for using these, (**historical** ∼, study of the development of a language's inflexions and syntax). **2.** treatise or book on grammar. **3.** person's manner of using grammatical forms; speech or writing regarded as good or bad by the rules of grammar; what is correct according to those rules. **4.** body of forms and usages in a language (*Latin grammar*). **5.** elements or rudiments of an art or science. **6.** ||(colloq.) = *grammar school*. **7.** ∼ **school,** (1) ||school founded in or before 16th c. for teaching Latin, later becoming secondary school teaching languages, history, science, etc., (2) ||secondary school with similar curriculum, (3) *school intermediate between primary school and high school. **8.** Hence ∼LESS *a.* [ME, f. AF *gramere,* OF *gramaire* f. *gramadie* f. L f. Gk *grammatikē* (*tekhnē* art) of letters (*gramma -atos* letter of alphabet)]

grammār′ian *n.* one versed in grammar or linguistics, philologist. [ME, f. OF *gramarien* (as prec.; see -IAN)]

-grammă′tic *suf.* forming *adjs.* corresp. to *ns.* in -GRAM (1, 3). [f. as -GRAM + -ATIC]

grammă′tical *a.* **1.** of grammar; ∼ **gender** (determined by form etc. of word, not by sex of what it denotes); ∼ **sense** (literal, irrespective of considerations other than the rules of grammar). **2.** conforming to the rules of grammar, or to the formal principles of an art. **3.** Hence ∼IZE (3) *v.t.,* express by or adorn in grammar, ∼LY² *adv.* [F, or f. LL *grammaticalis* f. L f. Gk *grammatikos* (as GRAMMAR, -IC); see -AL]

grammă′ticīze, -īse (-īz), *v.t.* = GRAMMATICALIZE. [f. *grammatic* earlier form of prec. + -IZE]

grämme. See GRAM².

grä′mophōne *n.* instrument for reproduction of recorded sound by vibrations of stylus resting in irregular spiral groove on rotating disc (cf. RECORD²-*player*); hence **grämophŏ′n**IC *a.* [formed by inversion of PHONOGRAM]

grä′mpus *n.* blowing blunt-headed dolphin-like cetacean, esp. *Grampus griseus*; person breathing heavily and loudly. [earlier *graundepose, grapeys* f. OF *grapois* etc. f. med. L *craspiscis* f. L *crassus piscis* fat fish]

grăn *n.* (colloq. or childish). granny, grandmother. [abbr.]

gränadi′lla, grĕ-, *n.* passion-fruit. [Sp., dim. of *granada* pomegranate]

grä′nary̆ *n.* storehouse for threshed grain; region producing, and esp. exporting, much corn. [f. L *granarium* (*granum* grain; see -ARY¹)]

grănd *a.* & *n.* **1.** *a.* (In official titles) chief over others, of highest rank, (*Grand* CROSS¹; *grand* LODGE¹, VIZIER). **2.** (Law). great, principal, (opp. *petit* or *petty* or *common*; *grand* LARCENY). **3.** of most or great importance (*that is the grand question*; *made a grand mistake*; *grand* SLAM²); final, summing up minor constituents, (*grand total*; *grand finale*; *the grand sum* or *result of his achievements*). **4.** (Distinguishing parts of large building) main (*the grand staircase, entrance,* etc.). **5.** (In F phrases or imitations) great (*grand army, Grand Hotel*; G∼ **Monarch,** Louis XIV). **6.** conducted with solemnity, splendour, etc.; fine, splendid, gorgeous. **7.** belonging to high society, distinguished, (**do the** ∼, put on airs); imposing, impressive, great and handsome. **8.** dignified or lofty in conception, treatment, or expression; morally imposing, noble, admirable. **9.** (colloq.) very enjoyable, excellent, (*had a grand run*; *ground was in grand condition*). **10.** (In names of relationships) in the second degree of ascent or descent; ∼**′parent,** person's parent's parent; so ∼**′father,** ∼**′mother,** (∼*father clock,* clock worked by weights in tall wooden case; ∼*mother clock,* similar clock in smaller case; *teach* one's *grandmother to suck* EGG¹*s*); (colloq. or childish) ∼**-dad**(dy), ∼**′ma**(ma), ∼**′pa**(**pa**); ∼**′child,** person's child's child; so ∼**′daughter,** ∼**′son;** ∼**′aunt,** ∼**′uncle,** person's parent's aunt, uncle; ∼**′nephew,** ∼**′niece,** person's nephew's or niece's son or daughter. **11.** ∼ **air,** distinguished appearance; ∼ **duke** or **duchess,** (1) ruler of State called ∼ **duchy,** (2) (Hist.) (grand) child of Russian Emperor; *grand* INQUEST; *Grand* INQUISITOR; ∼ **jury,** (Hist. or US) group of persons selected to examine validity of accusation prior to trial; ∼ **manner,** style suited to noble subjects; ∼ **master,** (1) head of military order of knighthood, of Freemasons, etc., (2) chess-player of highest class; ||G∼ **National,** annual steeplechase at Liverpool; ∼ **old man,** venerated person, esp. Gladstone or Churchill or W. G. Grace; **G∼ **Old Party,** the Republican Party; ∼ **opera,** serious opera without spoken dialogue; ∼ **passion,** = GRANDE *passion*; ∼ **piano,** (usu. large full-toned) piano with horizontal strings; ∼**′sire,** (1) animal's sire's sire, (2) (arch.) grandfather, ancestor, old man, (3) a method of change-ringing; ∼**′stand,** principal stand for spectators at races etc. (∼*stand finish,* close and exciting finish in sport; **∼stand play,* way of playing with view to gaining applause); ∼ **style,** = *grand manner*; ∼ **tour,** (Hist.) tour of chief towns etc. of Europe completing education, (fig.) extensive tour, flight to several planets, etc. **12.** Hence ∼LY² *adv.,* ∼′NESS *n.* **13.** *n.* grand piano. **14.** (sl.; *pl.* usu. same). thousand pounds, **dollars, etc. [ME f. AF *graunt,* OF *grant* f. L *grandis* full-grown]

grä′ndăd. Var. of *grand-dad* (GRAND 10).

grä′ndăm *n.* **1.** (arch.) grandmother; ancestress; old woman. **2.** animal's dam's dam. [ME, f. AF *graund dame* (as GRAND, DAME)]

grä′ndăme. Var. of prec. **1.**

grande (grahñd) *a.* ∼ **amoureuse** (ahmoorĕr′z), passionate or amorous woman; ∼ *dame* (dahm), dignified lady of high rank; ∼ *passion* (pá′syawñ), overwhelming love affair; ∼ *tenue* (tenū′), full dress. [F, fem. of *grand* great (see GRAND)]

grandee′ *n.* Spanish or Portuguese nobleman of highest rank; person of high rank or eminence. [f. Sp. & Port. *grande* (*grande* a. GRAND), assim. to -EE]

grä′ndeur (-njer, -ndyer) *n.* great power, rank, or eminence, great nobility of character; sublimity or majesty of appearance or effect; conscious dignity, splendour of living, surroundings, etc. (DELUSIONS *of grandeur*). [F (*grand* great, GRAND)]

Grand Guignŏ'l (grahṅ gēnyŏ'l) *n*. dramatic entertainment in which short sensational or horrific pieces are played successively. [name (= Great PUNCH⁴) of theatre in Paris]

grăndiflŏr'a *a*. bearing large flowers. [mod. L (often used in specific names of large-flowered plants) f. L *grandis* great + FLORA]

grăndi'loqu|ent *a*. pompous in language; given to boastful talk; hence ∼ENCE *n*., ∼entLY² *adv*. [f. L *grandiloquus* (as GRAND, -*loquus* -speaking f. *loqui* speak), after *eloquent* etc.]

gra'ndiōse *a*. producing, intended or trying to produce, an impression of greatness; planned on a magnificent scale; pompous; hence **grăndio'sITY** *n*., ∼LY² (-slĭ) *adv*. [F, f. It. *grandioso* (as GRAND; see -OSE¹)]

Grăndisŏ'nian *a*. marked by stately courtesy and chivalric magnanimity. [f. Sir C. *Grandison* in Richardson's novel + -IAN]

grand mal (grahṅ mah'l) *n*. serious form of epilepsy with loss of consciousness. [F, = great sickness]

Grand Prix (grahṅ prē') *n*. motor(-cycle) racing championship event held in various countries under international rules. [F, = great or chief prize]

grand siècle (grahn syĕ'kl) *n*. classical or golden age, esp. 17th c. in France. [F, = great century or age]

grănge (-nj) *n*. country house with farm-buildings; (arch.) barn. [ME, f. AF *graunge*, OF *grange* f. med. L *granica* (*villa*) (*granicus* f. L *granum* GRAIN)]

gra'nger|ize (-nj-), **-|ise** (-īz), *v.t.* illustrate (book) by inserting prints etc. often cut from other books; hence ∼IZA'TION, ∼īzER¹, ∼ISM (1), ∼ITE¹ (1), *ns*. [f. J. Granger, Engl. biographer d. 1776, whose *History of England* (1769) had blank pages for this purpose, + -IZE]

grani'ferous *a*. producing grain or grainlike seed; so **gră'niFORM** *a*. [f. L *granum* GRAIN + -I- + -FEROUS]

grăni't|a (-ē'-) *n*. (*pl.* ∼e *pr.* -ā). coarse Italian water-ice. [It., fem. of *granito* (see foll.)]

grä'nite *n*. granular crystalline rock of quartz, orthoclase felspar, and mica or hornblende, used for building; (fig.) unyieldingness; **bite on** ∼, waste pains, persist in vain; **the** ∼ **city**, Aberdeen; ∼-**ware**, (1) speckled pottery imitating appearance of granite, (2) kind of enamelled ironware; hence **grani'tIC** *a*., **grä'nitOID** *a*. & *n*. [f. It. *granito*, lit. grained (*grano* f. L *granum* GRAIN)]

grani'vorous *a*. feeding on grain. [f. L *granum* GRAIN + -I- + -VOROUS]

grä'nnў, grä'nnie, *n*. **1**. (colloq. or childish). grandmother. **2**. ∼ **flat**, part of house, made into self-contained accommodation for a relative; ∼ (**knot**), reef-knot crossed the wrong way and therefore insecure; **G**∼ **Smith**, Australian green variety of apple [f. Maria Ann ('Granny') Smith d. 1870]. [f. *grannum* for GRANDAM + -Y⁰]

grănoli'thic *a*. & *n*. (of) concrete made with crushed granite. [f. L *granum* grain + Gk *lithos* stone + -IC]

grant (-ah-) *v.t.*, & *n*. **1**. *v.t.* consent to fulfil (request etc.). **2**. concede as indulgence, allow (person) to have (thing or *that*). **3**. give (possession, right) formally, transfer (property) legally, whence ∼EE', ∼OR', *ns*. **4**. concede (proposition) as basis for argument (**I** ∼ **you**, I admit; **take for** ∼**ed**, regard as necessarily true or certain to happen, cease to appreciate through familiarity). **5**. Hence ∼'ABLE *a*., ∼'ER¹ *n*. **6**. *n*. granting (*the grant or refusal of*); formal conferment, legal assignment; thing, esp. sum of money, granted (∼-**in-aid**, sum granted esp. by government to school etc.); conveyance by written instrument; ||∼-**aided school**, school receiving some financial assistance from public funds. [ME, f. OF *gr(e)anter* var. of *creanter* f. Rom. *credentare f. part. of L *credere* entrust]

Granth (grŭnt) *n*. sacred scriptures of the Sikhs.

[Hindi, = book, code f. Skr. *grantha* tying, literary composition]

gran turismo (grăn toorĭ'zmō) *n*. (*pl.* ∼s). touring-car. [It., = great touring]

grä'nŭlar *a*. of or like grains or granules; having granulated surface or structure; hence ∼ITY (-ă'r-) *n*., ∼LY² *adv*. [f. LL *granulum* GRANULE + -AR¹]

grä'nŭl|āte *v*. **1**. *v.t.* & *i*. form into grains (*granulated sugar*). **2**. *v.t.* roughen surface of. **3**. *v.i.* (Of wound etc.) form small prominences as beginning of healing or junction; heal, join. **4**. Hence ∼A'TION, ∼ātOR, *ns*. [f. as prec. + -ATE³]

grä'nŭle *n*. small grain. [f. LL *granulum*, dim. of L *granum* grain; see -ULE]

grä'nŭlo|cȳte *n*. (Med.) cell having conspicuous granules in its cytoplasm; hence ∼cȳ'tIC *a*. [f. GRANULE + -O- + -CYTE]

grănŭlomě'tric *a*. pertaining to distribution of grain sizes in sand etc. [f. F *granulométrique* (as GRANULE, -O-, METRIC)]

grāpe *n*. **1**. berry (usu. green, purple, or black) growing in clusters on vine, eaten as fruit or used in making wine; (**the juice of**) **the** ∼, wine; **sour** ∼**s** (said when person disparages what he desires but cannot attain). **2**. ∼ *grape-shot*; (in *pl*.) diseased growth like bunch of grapes on pastern of horse etc., or on pleura in cattle. **3**. ∼ **brandy** (distilled from grapes, or wine, alone); ∼'**fruit** (*pl*. same), large round yellow citrus fruit growing in clusters, with acid juicy pulp; ∼ **hyacinth**, small herb of genus *Muscari* with raceme of usu. blue flowers; ∼-**scissors** (for thinning grape-bunches at early stage of growth, or for dividing bunches at table); ∼-**shot**, (Hist.) small balls put several together in bag etc. to make scattering charge for cannon; ∼-**sugar**, dextrose; ∼-**vine**, (1) vine, (2) skating figure in which both feet are on ice together and form interlacing lines, (3) means of transmission of rumour or (secret) information. **4**. Hence **grā'pERY** (3) *n*., **grä'pEY², grä'pY²**, *adjs*. [ME, f. OF, bunch of grapes, prob. f. *graper* gather (grapes) f. *grap*(*p*)*e* hook f. Rom. *grap(*p*)*o* f. Gmc *krappon]

graph¹ (-ăf, -ahf) *n*., & *v.t.* **1**. *n*. diagram showing relation between two variable quantities each measured along one of a pair of axes usu. at right angles; ∼ **paper** (printed with network of lines to assist in drawing graphs). **2**. *v.t.* plot or trace on a graph. [abbr. of *graphic formula*]

graph² (-ăf, -ahf) *n*. (Philol.) visual symbol, esp. letter(s), representing phoneme or other feature of speech. [f. Gk *graphē* writing]

-graph (-ahf) *suf*. forming *ns. & vbs.* denoting: (1) thing written, drawn, etc., in specified way (*autograph, photograph, pictograph*), (2) instrument that records something or by some means (*heliograph, seismograph, telegraph*), (3) write in specified way (*hectograph*). [f. or after F -*graphe* f. L f. Gk -*graphos* written, writing]

grä'phēm|e *n*. (Ling.) class of letters etc. representing a phoneme; feature of written expression that cannot be analysed into smaller meaningful units; hence ∼A'TIC, graphē'mIC, *adjs*. [f. GRAPH² + -EME]

-grapher *suf*. forming *ns*. denoting person skilled in -GRAPHY (*geographer, radiographer*). [f. or after Gk -*graphos* writer + -ER¹]

grä'phic *a*. **1**. of or l. of drawing, painting, engraving, etching, etc.; vividly descriptive, lifelike; of writing; (of minerals) showing marks like writing on surface or in fracture; graphical; ∼ **arts**, arts of writing, printing, decorating, etc., on flat media. **2**. *n*. product of graphic art; *pl*. GRAPHICS. [f. L f. Gk *graphikos* (*graphē* writing; see -IC)]

-grä'phic(al) *sufs*. forming *adjs*. denoting (of or by) -GRAPH or -GRAPHY (*geographical, photographic*); hence **-grä'phICALLY** *adv*. *suf*. [f. or after Gk -*graphikos* prec.) + -IC]

grä'phical *a*. of GRAPH¹s; graphic. [f. as GRAPHIC + -ICAL]

grā′phĭcallў adv. In adj. senses. [f. GRAPHIC or GRAPHICAL; see -ICALLY]

grā′phĭcs n. pl. (usu. treated as sing.) use of diagrams in calculation and design; production of diagrams etc. by computer; design and decoration involving or accompanying typographic work. [f. GRAPHIC; see -ICS]

grā′phīte n. crystalline allotropic form of carbon used in pencils, as lubricant, etc.; hence **graphī′tic** a., **grā′phītīze** (3) v.t. & i. [f. G graphit f. Gk graphō write; cf. -ITE[1]]

graphŏ′|logў n. study of, or art of inferring character from, handwriting; system of graphic formulae, notation for GRAPH[1]s; (Ling.) study of systems of writing; hence **grăpholo′gical** a., **∿logist** n. [f. Gk graphē writing + -o- + -LOGY]

grā′phў n. (Philol.) = GRAPH[2]. [f. F graphie writing--system]

-graphў suf. forming ns. denoting: (1) style or method of writing, drawing, etc., (calligraphy, lithography, stenography), (2) descriptive science (bibliography, geography). [f. or after F or G -graphie f. L f. Gk -graphia writing]

grā′pnel n. iron-clawed instrument thrown with rope attached to seize object, esp. enemy's ship or when dragging river etc.; small anchor with several flukes used for boats and balloons. [ME, f. AF *grapenel f. OF grapon f. Gmc *krǎppon; cf. GRAPE]

grā′ppa n. brandy distilled from refuse of grapes after wine-making. [It.]

grā′ppl|e n. & v. 1. n. clutching-instrument, grapnel. 2. hold or grip (as) of wrestlers, contest at close quarters. 3. v.t. seize or fasten (as) with grapnel; take hold of or grip with the hands, come to close quarters with. 4. v.i. contend (with, together, or abs.) in close fight, battle with; **∿e with**, (fig.) try to overcome, accomplish, or deal with. 5. **∿ing-hook** or **-iron**, grapnel. [f. OF grapil f. Prov., dim. of grapa hook f. as GRAPNEL]

grā′ppling n. In vbl senses; **∿-iron**, grapnel. [f. prec. + -ING[1]]

grā′ptolīte n. extinct marine animal found as fossil leaving marks on lower Palaeozoic rocks. [f. Gk graptos marked with letters + -LITE]

grasp (-ah-) v. & n. 1. v.i. **∿ at**, try to seize, accept with avidity; grasp at a STRAW[1]. 2. v.t. clutch at, seize greedily; hold firmly (∿ **the nettle**, tackle difficulty or danger boldly), grip; get mental hold of, comprehend; hence **∿′ABLE** a. 3. n. firm hold, grip; control, mastery; mental hold, comprehensiveness of mind; **within, beyond**, one's ∿, close, not close, enough to be grasped (lit. or fig.). [ME graspe, grapse perh. f. OE *grǣpsan f. Gmc *graip- GROPE; but cf. LG grapsen]

grā′sping (-ah′-) a. In vbl senses; avaricious, miserly, whence **∿LY[2]** adv., **∿NESS** n. [f. prec. + -ING[2]]

grass (-ahs) n. & v. 1. n. herbage of which blades or leaves and stalks are eaten by cattle, horses, sheep, etc. (**not let the ∿ grow under** one's **feet**, be quick to act or seize opportunity; any species of this; (Bot.) plant of family Gramineae, incl. also cereals, reeds, and bamboos; (sl.) marijuana; (sl.) asparagus. 2. grazing, pasture, (be at grass; go, turn out, to grass; **at** ∿, (fig.) out of work, on holiday, etc.); pasture land; grass-covered ground, lawn, (keep off the grass); (Mining) earth's surface, pit-head; (sl.) police informer. 3. **∿-box**, receptacle for cut grass on lawn--mower; **∿-cloth**, linen-like cloth woven from ramie etc.; **∿ court**, grass-covered lawn-tennis court; **∿′hopper**, jumping and chirping insect of sub-order Saltatoria; **∿′land**, area of land covered with grass, esp. if used for grazing; **∿ parakeet**, (Austral.) parakeet frequenting grassland; **∿ of Parnassus**, saxifrage of genus Parnassia; **∿ roots**, fundamental level or source, esp. (Polit.) the voters themselves; **∿ skirt** (made of long grass and leaves fastened to waistband); **∿ snake**, ‖common ringed snake (Natrix natrix), *common green snake (Ophiodrys vernalis); **∿ widow(er)**, person whose husband or wife is absent

for a period; **∿-wrack**, eel-grass; **∿ wren**, (Austral.) small bird of genus Amytornis. 4. Hence **∿′LESS**, **∿′Y[2]**, adjs. 5. v.t. cover with turf; *provide with pasture; knock down, fell, (opponent); bring (fish) to bank, (bird by shot) to ground; (sl.) betray. 6. v.i. (sl.) inform police. [OE grǣs, = OS, OHG, ON, Goth. gras f. Gmc *grasam, cogn. w. GREEN[1], GROW]

grāte[1] n. (frame of metal bars for confining fuel in) recess of fireplace or furnace; hence **∿′LESS** (-tl-) a. [ME = grating, f. OF, f. Rom. *grata, *crata f. L cratis hurdle]

grāt|e[2] v. 1. v.t. reduce to small particles by rubbing on rough surface, whence (-)∿′ER[1] (2) n.; utter in harsh tone; grind (teeth). 2. v.t. & i. rub with harsh scraping noise against or (up)on something else. 3. v.i. have irritating effect (up)on; sound harshly or discordantly (a grating laugh, voice); (of hinge etc.) creak. [ME, f. OF grater f. Rom. *grattare f. WG *krattōn scratch]

grā′teful (-tf-) a. 1. acceptable, comforting, refreshing. 2. feeling or showing gratitude (to person, for thing; that, to do). 3. Hence **∿LY[2]** adv., **∿NESS** n. [f. obs. grate a. f. L gratus + -FUL]

grā′tĭcūle n. 1. fine lines or fibres incorporated in telescope or other optical instrument as measuring scale or as aid in locating objects. 2. (Surv.) network of lines on paper representing meridians and parallels. [F, f. med. L graticula for craticula gridiron (L cratis hurdle; see -ULE)]

grā′tĭfў v.t. 1. please, satisfy, oblige, delight, whence **∿ING[2]** a. (to); please by compliance, assent to wish of, give free scope to or indulge (desire, feeling, impulse). 2. (arch.) remunerate, make present usu. of money to; bribe. 3. So **grātĭFICA′TION** n. [f. F gratifier or f. L gratificari do a favour to, make a present of (gratus pleasing; see -FY)]

gratin (grā′tǎn) n. way of cooking, dish cooked, with crisp brown crust usu. of bread crumbs or grated cheese; **au ∿** (ō-), (dish) so prepared. [F (gratter GRATE[2])]

grā′ting n. framework of parallel or crossed wooden or metal bars; (Opt.) set of parallel wires, or surface of glass etc. ruled with parallel lines, for producing spectra by diffraction. [f. GRATE[1] + -ING[1]]

grā′tis (-ā′-, -ah′-) adv. & a. gratuitous(ly); (given, done) for nothing, without charge, free. [L, contr. abl. pl. of gratia favour]

grā′tĭtūde n. being thankful, appreciation of and inclination to return kindness. [f. F, or f. med. L gratitudo (gratus thankful; see -TUDE)]

gratū′ĭtous a. got or given free, not earned or paid for; uncalled for, unwarranted, motiveless, done or acting without good or assignable reason (a gratuitous lie or liar); hence **∿LY[2]** adv., **∿NESS** n. [f. L gratuitus spontaneous; cf. fortuitous]

gratū′ĭtў n. money present of amount fixed by giver in recognition of an inferior's good offices, tip; ‖bounty to soldier etc. on demobilization or retirement or some other occasions. [f. OF gratuité or f. med. L gratuitas gift (L gratus grateful; see -ITY)]

grā′tŭl|āte v.t. (arch.) = CONGRATULATE; so **∿A′TION** n. [f. L gratulari (gratus pleasing) + -ATE[3]]

grā′tŭlātorў a. expressing joy at another's success etc., complimentary, congratulatory. [f. LL gratulatorius (as prec.; see -ORY)]

graunch v.t. & i. (cause to) make crunching or grinding sound; damage (mechanism). [imit.]

gravā′měn n. (pl. ∿s or **grava′mina**). 1. grievance; memorial from Lower House of Convocation to Upper on disorders or grievances of Church. 2. essence, worst part, of accusation. [LL, = inconvenience, f. L gravare to load (gravis heavy)]

grāve[1] n. 1. excavation to receive corpse, mound or monument over it; **dig** ∿ of, cause downfall of; one FOOT[1] in the grave; **make** person **turn in his** ∿ (of act etc. that would have shocked him while alive); someone walking on my ∿ (said when one shivers unaccountably); hence **∿′LESS** (-vl-) a. 2. being dead death, (carry the scar to one's grave); hence ∿WARD (-vw-) adv. & a. **3.** receptacle of or for what is dead (∿ **of reputations,** place where many reputations have been lost). **4.** ∿-**clothes,** wrappings in which corpse is buried; ∿-**digger,** (1) person who digs graves, (2) beetle that buries bodies of insects etc. as food for its larvae; ∿-**goods,** objects found with corpses in ancient graves; ∿'**stone,** stone over grave, inscribed stone at head or foot of grave; ∿'**yard,** (1) burial-ground (∿yard cough, = CHURCH¹yard cough), (2) = sense 3. [OE græf, = OS graf, OHG grap f. WG *grabha]

grāve² v.t. (p.p. **gra'ven** or ∿d). **1.** (arch.) carve, sculpture, engrave, (material, representation; ∿n **image,** idol). **2.** (fig.) fix indelibly (on or in mind etc.). [OE grafan dig, engrave, = OHG graban, ON grafa, Goth. graban dig f. Gmc *grabhan (as prec.; cf. GROOVE)]

grāve³ a. **1.** important, weighty, needing serious thought; (of faults, difficulties, responsibilities, symptoms) formidable, threatening, serious; dignified, solemn, slow-moving, not gay; sombre, plain, not showy; hence ∿LY² (-vlĭ) adv. **2.** (Of sound) low-pitched, not acute. [F, or f. L gravis heavy, serious]

grāve⁴ v.t. (Hist.) clean (ship's bottom) by burning off accretions and tarring while aground or in graving DOCK⁴. [perh. f. F dial. grave = OF greve shore f. Celt. *gravo- gravel, pebbles]

grave⁶ (-ahv, -āv) a. & n. ∿ (**accent,** mark (`) placed over vowels in some languages to show quality etc., orig. indicating low or falling pitch. [f. GRAVE³]

grā'vel n., & v.t. (∥-ll-). **1.** n. coarse sand and small water-worn or pounded stones, used for paths and roads; (Geol. & Mining) stratum of this, esp. one containing gold; (Path.) (disease with) aggregations of visible urinary crystals; ∿-**blind,** almost completely blind (orig. joc. = more than sand-blind, Shak. Merchant of Venice II. ii. 38); hence ∿**ly²** a. (of voice, deep and rough-sounding). **2.** v.t. lay or strew with gravel; perplex, puzzle, nonplus, (f. obs. sense run aground). [ME, f. OF gravel(e) dim. of grave (as GRAVE⁴)]

grā'ver n. In vbl senses; burin. [ME, f. GRAVE² + -ER¹]

Graves¹ (grahv) n. (pl. same pr. ∾z). light white or occas. red wine produced in the Graves district. [∿ in SW France]

Grāves² (-vz) n. ∿' **disease,** exophthalmic goitre. [f. R J ∿, Ir physician d. 1853]

Gravě'ttian a. & n. (culture) of a palaeolithic period in Europe, upper Aurignacian. [f. La Gravette in SW France + -IAN]

grā'vid a. (literary or Zool.) pregnant. [f. L gravidus (gravis heavy)]

gravi'mēter n. instrument measuring difference in force of gravity between two places. [f. F gravimètre f. L gravis heavy; cf. -METER]

grāvimĕ'tric a. pertaining to gravimeters or gravimetry. [f. prec.]

gravi'mĕtrỹ n. measurement of weight. [f. as GRAVIMETER + -METRY]

gravitas (grā'vĭtahs) n. solemn demeanour, seriousness. [L (as GRAVE³; see -ITY)]

grā'vitāte v. **1.** v.t. & i. move or tend by force of gravity towards a body; sink (as) by gravity, tend to low level, settle down. **2.** v.i. move because, or be, strongly attracted to(wards) some centre of influence. [f. mod. L gravitare (after GRAVITAS) + -ATE³]

grāvitā'tion n. falling of bodies to earth; (movement or tendency towards centre of) attraction exercised by every particle of matter on every other; **law of** ∿ (specifying force of this attraction in terms of masses concerned and their distance apart); hence ∿AL a. [f. mod. L gravitatio (as prec.; see -ATION)]

grā'vitỹ n. **1.** being serious, solemnity; importance, seriousness; staidness, sobriety, serious demeanour. **2.** weight (**centre of** ∿, centre of MASS² of rigid body,

(fig.) point of chief importance; **specific** ∿, relative weight of any kind of matter, expressed by ratio of given volume to same volume of a standard—usu. water for liquid or solid, and air for gas). **3.** attractive force by which bodies tend to centre of earth etc.; degree of intensity of this measured by acceleration; gravitational force. **4.** ∿ **feed,** supply of material by its fall under gravity; ∿ **wave,** (1) wave on liquid surface caused mainly by gravity, (2) hypothetical periodic variation of gravitational field, propagated as wave. [f. F gravité or f. L GRAVITAS]

gravūr'e n. photogravure. [abbr.]

grā'vỹ n. **1.** juices that exude from meat during and after cooking; dressing for food, made from these with other materials; (sl.) unearned or unexpected money. **2.** ∿-**boat,** boat-shaped vessel for serving gravy; ∿ **train,** source of easy financial benefit. [ME, perh. f. misreading as gravé of OF grané, prob. f. grain spice, GRAIN]

gray¹ n. (Phys.) unit of absorbed radiation dose, corresp. to one joule per kilogram. [f. L. H. Gray, Engl. radiobiologist d. 1965]

***gray².** See GREY.

gray'ling n. silver-grey freshwater fish with long high dorsal fin; butterfly with grey under-side to wings. [f. prec. + -LING¹]

***graywacke.** See GREYWACKE.

grāz|e¹ v. **1.** v.t. feed (sheep or cattle) on growing grass; feed on (grass). **2.** v.i. (Of sheep or cattle) eat growing grass; tend grazing cattle; pasture cattle. **3.** Hence ∿'ING¹ (3) n. [OE grasian (græs GRASS)]

grāze² v. & n. **1.** v.t. touch lightly in passing; abrade (skin etc.) in rubbing past; suffer slight abrasion of (part of body). **2.** v.i. go with passing contact against, along, through, by, past, etc. **3.** n. grazing abrasion. [perh. by transf. f. prec. 'take off the grass close to the ground' (of a bullet etc.)]

grā'zi|er (-zīer, -zher) n. one who feeds cattle for market; (Austral.) sheep-farmer; hence ∿ERY (2) n. [f. GRASS + -IER]

grease¹ n. **1.** oily or fatty matter, esp. semi-solid as lubricant; oily matter in wool, uncleansed wool, (**wool in the** ∿, wool in fleeces). **2.** fat of deer or other game (**in** ∿, **in pride** or **prime of** ∿, fit for killing, fat); melted fat of dead animals, esp. when soft. **3.** ∿-**box** (attached to train-wheel for lubrication); ∿-**gun,** small pump for applying grease as lubricant to bearings etc.; ∿ **monkey,** (sl.) a mechanic; ∿-**paint,** composition for painting actors' faces; grease-PROOF² (esp. of paper); ∿-**trap,** appliance for catching grease in drains. [ME, f. AF grece, gresse, OF graisse f. Rom. *crassia (L crassus a. fat)]

grease⁸ (-z, -s) v.t. anoint, soil, or lubricate, with grease; smear (e.g. cooking-pan) with fat; **like** ∿d **lightning,** (sl.) very fast; ∿ **palm of,** bribe; ∿ **the wheels,** make affairs go smoothly, esp. by use of money. [ME, f. prec..]

grea'ser (z, -s-) n. In vbl senses, engineer on ship; *(sl., derog.) native Mexican or Spanish-American; (sl.) objectionable person; (sl.) member of gang of young motor-cyclists. [f. prec. + -ER¹]

grea'sỹ (-zĭ, -sĭ) a. smeared or covered with, containing, made of, like, with too much, grease; (of wool) uncleansed; slimy with mud or moisture; (of manners or expression) disagreeably unctuous; ∿y **pole** (greased for difficult climbing or walking on in sports); ∿y **spoon,** (sl.) cheap inferior eating-house; hence ∿iLY² adv., ∿iNESS n. [f. GREASE¹ + -Y²]

great (grāt) a. & n. **1.** a. occupying much space, extending far, large, big, (usu. with implied surprise, admiration, contempt, indignation, etc.; made a great blot, look at that great wasp, colloq.) a great big loaf or thick stick); ∿('er) n. as distinctive epithet of the larger species or individual: great St. John's wort, greater celandine etc., great titmouse, Great BEAR¹, DANE, LAKE¹s, Great Malvern etc., Great Portland Street etc.); capital (A etc.); a great DEAL¹, many; **Greater London** etc.

(including adjacent urban areas); **the ~ majority,** much the larger part; *greatest common* MEASURE[1]; *a great* MIND[1]; *lived a great* WHILE[1] *ago*; **~ with child,** (arch.) advanced in pregnancy. **2.** beyond the ordinary (*take great care; lived to a great age; shows great ignorance; are great friends*). **3.** important, worthy of consideration, elevated, distinguished, critical, *the chief*, pre- -eminent, (*it is a great thing to have courage; to a great extent; a great occasion; the great attraction; in great* SPIRIT[1]*s*); (in excl.) *Great God!, Caesar!, Scott!* ; **the** G~ (appended in sense *historically important and most distinguished of the name*, as *Alexander the Great*, or prefixed in titles, *the Great Mogul*, etc., and burlesqued in *the great* ‖UNPAID, UNWASHED). **4.** of remarkable ability, genius, intellectual or practical qualities, or loftiness or integrity of character, (*a great judge, painter,* etc.; *the truly great man; great thoughts*). **5.** *pred.* having much skill *at* or information *on*. **6.** (colloq.) highly satisfactory (*wouldn't it be great if we won?*; *had a great time in Monte Carlo*). **7.** fully deserving the name of, (with agent-nouns) doing a thing much or on a large scale, (*a great scoundrel, fiasco; is not a great one for travelling; is a great believer in fresh air, reader, landowner*). **8.** (Prefixed once or more to *uncle, aunt, nephew, niece,* and kinship words compounded with GRAND) one degree further removed upwards or downwards. **9.** G~ **Assize,** Judgement Day; **G~ Bible** (Coverdale's version 1539); **G~ Britain,** England, Wales, and Scotland; *Great* CHARTER[1]; *great* CIRCLE[1]; **~'coat,** heavy overcoat; *Great* DIVIDE[2]; **~ game,** (1) golf, (2) spying; **~ gross,** twelve gross; **~-hearted,** having noble or generous mind; **~ house,** chief house in village etc.; *great* HUNDRED, INQUEST; **~ organ,** chief manual with its related pipes and mechanism in an organ having two or more manuals; **G~ Power,** State having military or political influence and great international importance; *Great* REBELLION; **G~ Russian,** (member or language) of principal ethnic group of USSR; ‖*Great* SEAL[2]; **~ toe,** big toe; *great* VASSAL; **G~ War** (of 1914–18); **G~ White Way,* theatre area of Broadway in New York. **10.** Hence **~'EN[6]** *v.t.* & *i.* (arch.), **~'NESS** *n.* **11.** *n.* great (sense 3) person or thing; **the ~,** (as *pl.*) great persons; **the ~est,** (sl.) extremely remarkable person. **12. Greats,** Oxford BA course or final examination esp. in classics and philosophy. [OE *grēat*, = OS *grōt*, OHG *grōz* f. WG **grauta*]

grea'tly (grā't-) *adv.* much, by much, (usu. w. verbs, participles, or comparatives; *greatly esteemed, superior*; *should greatly prefer*); nobly, loftily. [ME, f. prec. + -LY[2]]

greave *n.* (usu. in *pl.*) piece of armour for shin. [ME, f. OF *greve* shin, greave, of unkn. orig.]

greaves (-vz) *n. pl.* fibrous refuse of tallow as dog-food etc. [f. LG *greven*, = OHG *griubo*]

grēbe *n.* short-bodied lobe-footed almost tailless diving bird esp. of genus *Podiceps*. [f. F *grèbe*, of unkn. orig.]

Grē'cian (-shan) *a.* & *n.* **1.** *a.* (Of architecture or facial outline, or arch.) Greek; ‖**~ bend,** affected attitude in walking prevalent *c.* 1870; **~ gift,** = GREEK *gift*; ‖**~ knot,** way of dressing woman's hair at back of head as ancient Greeks did; **~ nose** (straight, and continuing forehead line without dip); ‖**~ slipper,** soft slipper with low sides. **2.** *n.* person skilled in Greek; ‖boy in highest class at Christ's Hospital. [f. OF *grecien* or f. med. L **graecianus* f. L *Graecia* Greece; see -IAN]

Grē'cism, Grē'cīze. Vars. of GRAECISM etc.

Grē'cō-. See GRAECO-.

greed *n.* insatiate longing esp. for wealth or food. [back-form. f. foll.]

gree'd‖**y** *a.* having inordinate appetite for food or drink, gluttonous, (*of*); avaricious, covetous, (*of* or *for*); eager, keen, intensely desirous, (*to* do); **~-y-guts,** (vulg.) gluttonous person; hence **~iLY[2]** *adv.*, **~iNESS** *n.* [OE *grǣdig*, = OS *grādag*, OHG *grātac*, ON *gráthugr*, Goth. *grēdags*, f. Gmc **grēdhagaz* (**grēdhuz* hunger)]

gree'gree *n.* African charm or fetish. [17th c., of native orig.]

Greek *n.* & *a.* **1.** *n.* native or inhabitant of Greece; **~ meets ~** (said of encounter between equals). **2.** member of Orthodox Church. **3.** (arch.) cunning person, sharper. **4.** the Greek language (**~ to me,** beyond my comprehension), whence **~'LESS** *a.* **5.** *a.* of Greece or its people, Hellenic; of, according to, written or spoken in, Greek (*Greek alphabet, letter, philology*). **6.** *Greek* CALENDS; **~ Church,** ORTHODOX Church; **~ cross** (with four equal arms); **~ Fathers,** Fathers of the Church who wrote in Greek; *Greek* FIRE[1], FRET[1] or *key*; **~ gift,** one given with intent to harm (Virgil's *Aeneid* ii. 49); **~ god,** (fig.) paragon of male beauty. **7.** Hence **~'NESS** *n.* [OE *Grēcas* (pl.), = ON *Grikkir* (pl.), OHG *Chrēch*, Goth. *Krēks* f. Gmc **Krēkaz* f. L *Graecus* Greek f. Gk *Graikoi* prehistoric name of Hellenes (in Aristotle)]

green[1] *a.* & *n.* **1.** *a.* of the colour between blue and yellow in the spectrum, coloured like grass, sea- -water, emerald, olive, etc. **2.** covered with herbage, verdant, in leaf; **a ~ Christmas, winter, Yule,** (mild, without snow). **3.** (Of complexion) pale, sickly-hued; (fig.) jealous, envious. **4.** vegetable (*green food, green salad*). **5.** (Of fruit etc.) unripe, young and tender, flourishing, not dried. **6.** full of vitality, not withered or worn out, (*a green old age*). **7.** immature, undeveloped, inexperienced, naïve, gullible. **8.** not dried, seasoned, smoked, or tanned. **9.** (arch.) fresh, not healed, (*a green wound*). **10.** **~'back,* (1) US legal-tender note, (2) green-backed animal; **~ belt,** area of open land round city, designated for preservation; **G~ Beret,** (colloq.) British or American commando; **~-blind,** having retina insensitive to green rays; **~ card,** international insurance document for motorists; **~ cheese,** (1) whey cheese, (2) cheese coloured green with sage, (3) unripened cheese; ‖(*Board of*) **G~ Cloth,** Lord Steward's department of Royal Household; **~ crop** (used as food in green state, opp. *hay* etc.); **~ drake,** common mayfly; **~ earth,** hydrous silicate of potassium, iron, and other metals; **~ eye, ~-eyed monster,** jealousy; **~-eyed,** (fig.) jealous; **~ fat** (of turtle, esteemed by epicures); **~'finch,** finch with yellow and green plumage; **~ fingers,** (colloq.) skill in making plants grow; ‖**~'fly,** green aphid; **~'gage,** roundish green fine-flavoured plum [Sir W. *Gage c.* 1725]; **~ goose** (killed under four months old and eaten without stuffing); ‖**~'grocer(y),** (business of, things sold by) retail dealer in fruit and vegetables; **~'head,** (1) biting fly of family Tabanidae, (2) Austral. ant with painful sting; **~'heart,** (hard greenish wood of) one of several tropical Amer. trees; **~'horn,** ignoramus, raw recruit, simpleton; **~'house** (of glass for rearing delicate plants or hastening growth of plants); **~'keeper,** keeper of golf course; **~ leek,** green-faced Austral. parakeet; **~ light,** signal to proceed on road, railway, etc., (colloq.) permission to go ahead with some project; **~ linnet,** = *greenfinch*; **~ manure,** growing plants ploughed into soil as fertilizer; *green* MEAT; **G~* **Mountain State,** Vermont; ‖**G~ Paper,** tentative report of Government proposals, without commitment; **~ plover,** lapwing; **~'pound,** currency exchange unit for payments to agricultural producers in EEC; **~ revolution,** greatly increased crop production in developing countries; **~-room** (in theatre, accommodating actors and actresses when off stage); **~'sand,** (1) = *green earth*, (2) kind of sandstone largely composed of this earth, (3) stratum largely formed of this sandstone; **~'shank,** large sandpiper (*Tringa nebularia*); **~'sick(ness),** (affected with) chlorosis; **~'stick,** (of bone-fracture, esp. in children) in which one side of bone is broken and one only bent; **~'stone,** (1) green igneous rock containing felspar and hornblende, (2) variety of jade found in NZ, used for tools, ornaments, etc.; **~'stuff,** vegetation, green vegetables; **~'sward,** grassy turf;

~ **tea** (made from steam-dried, not fermented, leaves); ~ **thumb**, (colloq.) = *green fingers*; ~ **turtle**, green-shelled species of turtle esteemed as food; *green* VITRIOL; ~'**weed**, dyer's broom; ~'**wood**, woodlands in summer, esp. as scene of outlaw life; ||~'**yard**, enclosure for stray animals, pound. **11.** Hence ~'ISH¹ 2, ~'Y² (in comb.: *greeny-yellow*), *adjs.*, ~'LY² *adv.*, ~'NESS (-n-n-) *n.* **12.** *n.* green colour (**do you see any** ~, i.e. sign of gullibility, **in my eye?**); green pigment; green clothes or material (*dressed in green*); green ball in snooker etc.; colour symbolizing Ireland; green light; *the* LONG¹ *green*. **13.** vigour, youth, virility, (*in the green*). **14.** verdure, vegetation. **15.** (in *pl.*) green vegetable leaves before or after cooking. **16.** piece of public or common grassy land (*village green*); grass-plot used for special purpose (*bleaching*, *bowling*, PUTT*ing*, -*green*); (Golf) (1) putting-green, (2) fairway (~-**fee**, charge for playing one round on a course; **through the green**, between tee and putting-green). **17.** (sl.) money; low-grade marijuana; (in *pl.*) sexual intercourse. [OE *grēne*, = OS *grōni*, OHG *gruoni*, ON *grœnn* f. Gmc **grōnjaz* (**grō*-; see GROW)]
green² *v.* **1.** *v.i.* become green, esp. with verdure. **2.** *v.t.* make green, soil etc. with green; (sl.) hoax, take in. [OE *grēnian* (as prec.)]
gree'nery *n.* verdure, vegetation; ~-**ya'llery**, (colloq.) (affectedly) favouring green and yellow colours. [f. GREEN¹ + -ERY]
gree'ning *n.* kind of apple, green when ripe. [prob. f. MDu. *groeninc* (as GREEN¹; see -ING³)]
Gree'nland *n.* ~ **whale**, Arctic species of whale (*Balaena mysticetus*); hence ~ER¹ (4) *n.* [~, large island in Arctic Ocean]
Greenlä'ndic *a.* & *n.* (dialect or language) of Greenland. [f. prec. + -IC]
gree'nlet *n.* = VIREO. [f. GREEN¹ + -LET]
greenth *n.* (literary). verdure. [f. GREEN¹ + -TH¹]
Gree'nwich (grĭ'nĭj, grĕ'n-, -ĭch) *n.* ~ (**mean**) **time**, (mean) time on the meridian of Greenwich, used as international basis of time-reckoning. [~ in London, former site of Royal Observatory]
greet¹ *v.t.* accost with salutation; salute *with* words or gestures, receive on meeting or arrival *with* speech or action (friendly or not); (of cheers etc.) hail; (of sight, sound, etc.) meet (eye, ear); hence ~'ING¹ (1, and, often in *pl.*, 2) *n.* [OE *grētan* handle, attack, salute, = OS *grōtian* call on, OHG *gruozzen* address, attack, f. WG **grōtjan* cry out etc.]
greet² *v.i.* (Sc.) weep. [OE *grētan*, = OS *grātan*, ON *gráta*, Goth. *grētan* f. Gmc **grētan* cogn. w. prec., & OE *grēotan*, = OS *griotan*, of uncert. orig.]
grĕ'ffier *n.* registrar, notary, (in Channel Islands etc.). [F, f. med. L *graphiarius* f. *graphium* register; see GRAFT¹]
grĕgā'rious *a.* living in flocks or communities; fond of company; (Bot.) growing in clusters; of flocks, of crowds; hence ~LY² *adv.*, ~NESS *n.* [f. L *gregarius* (*grex gregis* flock; see -ARY¹) + OUS]
grège (gräzh) *a.* & *n.* (of) colour between beige and grey. [F, = raw (silk)]
Grĕgŏ'rian *a.* & *n.* **1.** *a.* of or according to the plainsong ritual music named after Pope Gregory I; ~ **tones**, eight plainsong melodies prescribed for psalms in RC Ch. **2.** ~ **calendar**, correction of the Julian calendar, established by Pope Gregory XIII in 1582. **3.** ~ **telescope**, reflecting telescope in which light reflected from secondary mirror passes through hole in primary mirror, devised by J. Gregory, Sc. mathematician d. 1675. **4.** *n.* Gregorian chant. [f. med. L *Gregorianus* f. LL f. Gk *Grēgorios* Gregory + -AN]
grĕ'gory-powder *n.* compound powder of rhubarb, magnesia, and ginger, used as aperient. [f. J. *Gregory*, Sc. physician d. 1822 + POWDER]
greige. Var. of GRÈGE.
grĕ'mial *n.* silk apron placed on bishop's lap at Mass etc. [f. med. L *gremiale* f. L *gremium* lap; see -AL]

grĕ'mlin *n.* (sl.) mischievous sprite alleged to cause mishaps to machinery etc. [20th c.; orig. unkn., but prob. after *goblin*]
grĕnā'de *n.* small explosive shell thrown by hand (**hand**-~) or shot from rifle-barrel (**rifle**-~); glass receptacle thrown to disperse chemicals for testing drains, extinguishing fires, etc. [F, f. OF *grenate* & Sp. *granada* POMEGRANATE]
grĕnadier' *n.* **1.** (Hist.) soldier who threw grenades. **2.** ||G~s or G~ **Guards**, first regiment of household infantry. **3.** S. Afr. weaver-bird with red and black plumage. **4.** deep-sea fish of family Macrouridae, with long tapering body and pointed tail. [F (as prec.; see -IER)]
grĕnadi'lla. See GRANADILLA.
grĕ'nadine¹ *n.* dish of veal or poultry fillets, trimmed, larded, and glazed. [f. F *grenadin*]
grĕ'nadine² *n.* dress-fabric of loosely woven silk or silk and wool. [F, earlier *grenade* grained silk (*grenu* grained f. *grain*; see GRAIN, -INE⁴)]
grĕ'nadine³ (-ēn) *n.* French cordial syrup of pomegranates etc. [F, f. *grenade* (see GRENADE)]
Grĕ'sham *n.* ~'**s law**, (Econ.) tendency for money of lower intrinsic value to circulate more freely than money of higher intrinsic and equal nominal value. [f. Sir T. ~, Engl. financier d. 1579]
grĕssō'rial *a.* (Zool.) walking; adapted for walking. [f. mod. L *gressorius* f. L *gradi gress-* walk; see -OR, -IAL]
Grĕtna Gree'n *n.* (Hist.) ~ **marriage** etc. (contracted by runaway couples from England immediately after entering Scotland, where parental consent was not necessary). [~ in Scotland, close to the border with England]
grew. See GROW.
grey (grā), **gray²*, *a.*, *n.*, & *v.* **1.** *a.* intermediate between black and white, coloured like ashes or lead. **2.** between light and dark, dull, clouded, depressing, dismal; (of hair) turning white with age etc., (of person) having grey hair; ancient, immemorial; belonging to old age, experienced, mature; (of person) anonymous, unidentifiable; less extreme than 'black' (*grey market*, *grey-out*). **3.** ~ **area**, borderline topic not clearly dealt with by rules etc.; ~-**back**, grey-backed animal or bird; ***(Hist.) Confederate soldier; ~'**beard**, old man, large stoneware jug for spirits, ||clematis; ~ **cells**, = *grey matter*; ~ **crow**, hooded crow; ||~ **drake**, species of mayfly; ~ **eminence**, = ÉMINENCE GRISE; ~ **eye** (with grey iris); G~ **Friar**, Franciscan [f. their grey cloaks]; ~ **goose**, greylag; ~-**headed**, old, of long service *in*, ancient, time-worn; ~-**hen**, female of black grouse (cf. BLACK¹*cock*); ~ **mare**, (fig.) wife who dominates husband; ~ **matter**, material of active part of brain and spinal cord; ~ **monk**, Cistercian [f. their grey habits]; *grey* NURSE³; ~ **squirrel**, Amer. squirrel (*Sciurus carolinensis*) brought to Europe in 19th c.; ~'**stone**, grey volcanic rock. **4.** Hence ~'ISH¹ 2 *a.*, ~'LY² *adv.*, ~'NESS *n.* **5.** *n.* grey clothes or material (*dressed in grey*); cold sunless light; grey colour; grey pigment; grey horse (||**the Greys** or **Scots Greys**, 2nd Dragoons); ***(Negro sl.) white person. **6.** *v.i.* & *t.* become or make grey. [OE *grǣg*, = OHG *grāo*, ON *grár* f. Gmc **grǣwaz*]
grey'hound (grā'-) *n.* slender long-legged keen-sighted swift dog used in coursing hares etc.; ~-**racing**, sport in which mechanical hare is coursed by greyhounds on track as opportunity for betting; OCEAN *greyhound*. [OE *grīghund* (corresp. to ON *greyhundr*) f. **grīeg* bitch (Gmc **graujam*) + *hund* dog, HOUND¹]
grey'läg (grā'-) *n.* ~ (**goose**), common European wild goose. [f. GREY + LAG¹ (f. its staying long in England for a migrant)]
grey'wäcke, **gray'wäcke*, (grā'wăke, -ăk) *n.* (Geol.) conglomerate rock consisting of rounded pebbles and sand cemented together. [Anglicized f. G *grauwacke* (*grau* grey; see WACKE)]
grid *n.* **1.** frame of spaced parallel bars, grating;

perforated or ridged plate carrying active substance in accumulator; wire network between filament and anode of thermionic valve, or other perforated electrode with same function of controlling flow of electrons. **2.** system of numbered squares printed on map and forming basis of map references. **3.** network of lines, electric-power connections, gas-supply lines, etc. **4.** = GRIDIRON 1, 2, 3. **5.** pattern of lines marking starting-places on car-racing track. **6.** arrangement of town streets in rectangular pattern. **7.** Hence ∼'dED² *a.* [back-form. f. GRIDIRON]

gri'ddle *n.*, & *v.t.* **1.** *n.* = GIRDLE². **2.** miner's wire--bottomed sieve. **3.** *v.t.* sieve with griddle. [ME, f. OF *gredil, gridil* gridiron f. Rom. *graticulum, *craticulum f. L *craticula* dim. of *cratis* hurdle; cf. GRATE¹, GRILL²]

gride *v.i.*, & *n.* **1.** *v.i.* cut or scrape *along, through*, etc., with strident or grating sound. **2.** *n.* grating sound. [orig. sense *pierce*, by metath. f. GIRD²]

gri'diron (-īern) *n.* **1.** cooking utensil of metal bars for broiling or grilling. **2.** frame of parallel beams for supporting ship in dock. **3.** *football field (with parallel lines marking out area of play). **4.** (Theatr.) plank structure over stage supporting mechanism for drop-scenes etc. **5.** ∼(-**pendulum**), compensation pendulum with parallel rods of different metals. **6.** = GRID 6. [ME *gredire*, var. of *gredil* GRIDDLE, later assoc. w. IRON¹]

grief *n.* **1.** deep or violent sorrow, keen regret; cause of this; **come to** ∼, meet with disaster, fail, fall. **2. good** or **great** ∼ (excl. of surprise, alarm, etc.). [ME f. AF *gref*, OF *grief* (*grever* GRIEVE¹)]

grie'vance *n.* real or fancied ground of complaint. [ME, = injury, f. OF *grevance* (as prec.; see -ANCE)]

grieve¹ *v.* **1.** *v.t.* give deep sorrow to. **2.** *v.i.* feel grief (*at, for, about, over*). [ME, f. OF *grever* f. Rom. *grevare f. L *gravare* (*gravis* heavy)]

grieve² *n.* (Sc.) farm-bailiff, overseer. [OE *grǣfa*; cf. REEVE¹]

grie'vous *a.* bringing serious trouble, injurious, (∼ **bodily harm**, (Law) serious injury); (of pain etc.) severe; flagrant, heinous; causing grief; hence ∼LY² *adv.* [ME, f. OF *grevos* (as GRIEVE¹; see -OUS)]

‖**griff** *n.* (sl.) news; reliable information. [abbr. of foll.]

‖**gri'ffin**¹ *n.* (sl.) betting tip; hint. [19th c.; orig. unkn.]

gri'ffin², **grȳ'phon**, *n.* fabulous creature with eagle's head and wings and lion's body. [ME, f. OF *grifoun* f. Rom. *grypho -onis augment. of LL *gryphus* f. L f. Gk *grups*]

gri'ffon¹ *n.* = prec.; ∼ (**vulture**), large vulture of genus *Gyps*. [var. of prec.]

gri'ffon² *n.* European coarse-haired terrier-like (breed of) dog. [F, = GRIFFIN²]

***grift** *n.*, & *v.i.* (sl.) = GRAFT²; hence ∼'ER¹ *n.* [perh. corrupt.]

grig *n.* small eel; grasshopper or cricket; **merry** or **lively as a** ∼, full of fun, extravagantly lively. [ME, orig. = 'dwarf', of unkn. orig.]

gri-gri. Var. of GREEGREE.

grill¹ *v.* & *n.* **1.** *v.t.* & *i.* cook on gridiron or under grill; (fig.) subject to or undergo torture or great heat; hence ∼'ER¹ (1, 2) *n.* **2.** *v.t.* subject to severe questioning (esp. by police). **3.** *n.* (dish of) grilled food; ∼(-**room**), informal restaurant. [f. F *griller* (as foll.)]

grill² *n.* gridiron (sense 1); device on cooker for downward emission of radiant heat. [f. F *gril* = OF *grail, greil* masc. form of *grille* (see GRILLE)]

grill³. See GRILLE.

gri'llage *n.* heavy framework of cross-timbering as foundation for building in treacherous soil. [F (as foll.; see -AGE)]

grill|e, grill³, *n.* grating, latticed screen, esp. in door for observing callers, in convent separating nuns from visitors, (Hist.) in front of Ladies' Gallery in House of

Commons, etc.; (Tennis) square opening in wall; metal grid to protect radiator of motor vehicle; hence ∼ED² (-ld) *a.* [F, f. OF *graille* f. med. L *graticula, craticula*; see GRIDDLE]

grilse *n.* young salmon that has been only once to the sea. [ME; orig. unkn.]

grim *a.* **1.** stern, unrelenting, merciless, severe; of forbidding or harsh aspect; **hold on like** ∼ **death** (with great determination). **2.** sinister, ghastly, mirthless, (*has a grim truth in it; a grim smile*); unpleasant, unattractive. **3.** Hence ∼'LY² *adv.*, ∼'NESS *n.* [OE, = OS, OHG *grim*, ON *grimmr* f. Gmc *grimmaz]

grimā'c|e *n.*, & *v.i.* **1.** *n.* distortion of face expressing annoyance etc. or meant to cause laughter; affected look; use of such looks, affectation. **2.** *v.i.* make grimace; hence ∼ER¹ *n.* [F, f. Sp. *grimazo* (*grima* fright)]

grima'lkin (-ă'l-, -aw'l-) *n.* old she-cat; spiteful old woman. [f. GREY + *Malkin* dim. of woman's Christian name *Matilda* (see -KIN)]

grime *n.*, & *v.t.* **1.** *n.* soot or dirt ingrained in some surface, esp. walls or the skin; hence **grī'm**Y² *a.* **2.** *v.t.* blacken with grime, befoul. [n. f. v., f. MLG, MDu. *grīmen]

Grimm *n.* ∼'s **law** (specifying regular consonantal differences between related words in different Indo--European languages). [f. J. L. C. ∼, Ger. philologist d. 1863]

grin *v.* (-nn-) & *n.* **1.** *v.i.* show teeth esp. in amusement or pain or in forced or unrestrained or vacant smile (*at*); ∼ **and bear it**, take pain etc. stoically; *grin like a* CHESHIRE *cat*; ∼ **through a horse-collar** (in grimacing-match at rustic sports). **2.** *v.t.* express (contempt, satisfaction) by grinning. **3.** *n.* act or action of grinning. [OE *grennian*, rel. to OHG *grennan* mutter, *granōn* grunt, ON *grenja* howl. f. Gmc *gran-; cogn. w. GROAN]

grind *v.* (**ground**) & *n.* **1.** *v.t.* reduce to small particles or powder by crushing between millstones, teeth, etc., (*down, small, to pieces, into dust*, etc.). **2.** oppress, harass with exactions, (*grinding poverty, tyranny; grind the faces of the poor* etc.). **3.** produce (flour) by grinding; sharpen or smooth by friction (*has an* AXE *to grind*; *grind lenses, diamonds*, etc.; *grind engine-valve in*, or *into its seat*; **ground glass**, glass made non-transparent by grinding etc.); work (hand-mill); turn handle of (barrel-organ etc.); produce or bring *out* with effort. **4.** *v.i.* toil monotonously, study hard. **5.** *v.t.* & *i.* rub gratingly *on, into, against*, etc., (*ground his heel into it*; *ground to a halt*; *ship was grinding on rocks*); rub (teeth) hard together. **6.** ∼'**stone**, thick revolving stone disc for grinding, sharpening, and polishing (**hold** or **keep** person's **nose to the** ∼**stone**, make him work incessantly), kind of stone used for these. **7.** *n.* grinding; size of ground particles; hard monotonous work or task (**the daily** ∼, (colloq.) one's usual day's work); *student who works hard; (sl.) (act of) sexual intercourse; (sl.) dancer's rotatory movement of hips. [OE *grindan*, of unkn. orig.]

grī'nder *n.* molar tooth; grinding-machine; upper millstone; person who grinds (esp. in comb., as *organ, knife, -grinder*); *student who works hard. [ME, f. prec. + -ER¹]

gri'ngo (-nggō) *n.* (*pl.* ∼s) foreigner (esp. Briton or American) in Spanish-speaking country. [Sp., = gibberish]

grip¹ *n.* **1.** firm hold, tight grasp or clasp; **at** ∼**s, come** or **get to** ∼**s with,** (of close combat, or purposeful approach to a subject). **2.** grasping power; way of clasping hands; way of grasping or holding (*overlapping grip*; **shorten, lengthen,** one's grip, hold bat, club, etc., nearer, farther from, point of impact). **3.** control, mastery, intellectual hold, (*get a grip on* ONEself; *lose one's grip*); power of arresting attention. **4.** part in machinery etc. that clips, part of weapon etc. that is held; hair-grip; = GRIP²*sack*. [OE *gripe* grasp & *gripa* handful, both f. as GRIPE]

grip² *v.* (-**pp**-). **1.** *v.t.* seize, grasp, or hold, tightly; compel attention of; *∼'**sack**, suitcase or travelling--bag; hence ∼'**per¹** (2) *n.* **2.** *v.i.* take firm hold esp. by friction. [OE *grippa*, = MHG *gripfen*, f. as GRIPE]

gripe *v. & n.* **1.** *v.t. & i.* clutch, grip. **2.** *v.t.* oppress, pinch; affect with colic; (Naut.) secure with gripes. **3.** *v.i.* (Naut., of ship) turn to face wind in spite of helm; (sl.) complain. **4.** *n.* act of griping, clutch; (arch.) hold, control; (in *pl.*) colic; handle of implement or weapon; (Naut., in *pl.*) lashings securing boat in its place; (sl.) complaint; ∼-**water**, carminative esp. for babies. [OE *grīpan*, = OS *grīpan*, OHG *grīfan*, ON *grípa*, Goth. *greipan* f. Gmc *grīp*-; cf. GROPE]

grippe *n.* influenza. [F (*gripper* seize)]

grisaille (-zā'l, -zī') *n.* method of decorative painting in grey monochrome representing figures and objects in relief; stained-glass window of this kind. [F (*gris* grey)]

griseofu'lvin (-z-) *n.* antibiotic used esp. against ringworm. [f. mod. L *griseofulvum* f. med. L *griseus* grey + L *fulvus* reddish yellow, + -IN]

grise'tte (-z-) *n.* young Frenchwoman of working class. [F, orig. = grey dress-material (*gris* grey; see -ETTE)]

gris-gris. Var. of GREEGREE.

||**gri'skin** *n.* lean part of loin of bacon pig. [app. f. obs. *gris, grice* young pig f. ON *gríss*, + -KIN]

gri'sly (z) *a.* causing horror, terror, or superstitious dread; hence ∼**iness** *n.* [OE *grislic* (*grīsan* terrify; sec -LY¹)]

gri'son (-z-) *n.* S. Amer. carnivore of weasel family, resembling glutton. [F, app. f. adj. = grey (*gris* grey)]

grissi'ni (-ē'nē) *n. pl.* crisp bread in long thin sticks. [It.]

grist¹ *n.* corn for grinding (**brings ∼ to the mill,** is profitable; **all is ∼ that comes to his mill,** he utilizes everything); malt crushed for brewing. [OE, f. Gmc *grinst*- (*grindan* GRIND)]

grist² *n.* size or thickness of yarn or rope. [perh. cogn. w. GIRD¹]

gri'stle (-sel) *n.* whitish tough flexible tissue in vertebrates, cartilage; hence **gri'stly²** (-slī) *a.* [OE, = OFris. & MLG *gristel*; cf. OHG *chrustila*, of unkn. orig.]

grit¹ *n.* small particles of stone or sand, esp. as causing discomfort or clogging machinery etc.; ∼-(**'stone**), coarse sandstone; gain or texture of stone; (colloq.) strength of character, pluck, endurance; hence ∼'**ty²** *a.* [OE *grēot*, = OS *griot*, OHG *grioz*, ON *grjót* f Gmc *greutam*; cf. GRITS, GROATS]

grit² *v.i. & t.* (-**tt**-). produce, or move with, grating sound; grind or clench (teeth); spread grit on (icy roads etc.). [f. prec.]

grits *n. pl.* husked but unground oats; coarse oatmeal. [OE *grytt(e)*, = OHG *gruzzi* f. WG *grutjō*; cf. GRIT¹, GROATS]

||**gri'zzle** *v.i.* (colloq.) (Esp. of child) whimper, cry fretfully. [19th c.; orig. unkn.]

gri'zzled (-zeld) *a.* grey(-haired) or partly so. [f. *grizzle* grey f. OF *grisel* (*gris* grey; see -LE 2) + -ED²]

gri'zzly *a. & n.* **1.** *a.* grey, greyish, grey-haired; ∼ **bear,** large fierce N. Amer. bear. **2.** *n.* grizzly bear. [f. as prec. + -Y²]

groan *v. & n.* **1.** *v.i., & n.* (make) deep inarticulate sound expressing pain, grief, or disapproval, (∼ inwardly, be distressed). **2.** *v.t.* utter with groans. **3.** *v.i.* be oppressed or loaded *under, beneath, with,* (*groan under injustice; shelf groans with books;* ∼**ing board,** well-loaded dining-table); (arch.) long *for.* [OE *grānian* f. Gmc *grain*-, cogn. w. GRIN]

groat *n.* **1.** (Hist.) silver coin issued 1351–1662, equal in value to four pennies; fourpenny piece 1836–56. **2.** (arch.) small sum (*don't care a groat*). [ME, f. MDu. *groot*, orig. = great, in sense thick (penny); cf. GROSCHEN]

groats *n. pl.* hulled (sometimes also crushed) grain, esp. oats. [OE *grotan* pl.; cf. *grot* fragment, *grēot* GRIT¹, *grytt* bran]

Grō'bian *n.* coarse slovenly person. [G, or f. med. L *Grobianus* imaginary typical German boor f. G *grob* coarse (as GRUFF)]

grō'c|er *n.* dealer in tea, butter, flour, sugar, spices, tinned foods, and miscellaneous household stores; hence ∼**ery** (2, and, usu. in *pl.*, 1) *n.* [ME & AF *grosser*, orig. one who sells in the gross, f. OF *grossier* f. med. L *grossarius* (as GROSS², -ARY¹)]

***grōcetēr'ia** *n.* self-service grocery shop. [f. GROCERY after *cafeteria*]

grŏg *n. & v.* (-**gg**-). **1.** *n.* drink of spirit and water; (Austral. & NZ colloq.) alcoholic liquor; ∼-**blossom,** pimple or redness on nose from intemperance. **2.** *v.t.* drink grog. **3.** *v.t.* extract spirit from (empty cask) by pouring in hot water. [reputedly from GROGRAM, nickname (from his cloak) of Adm. Vernon, who in 1740 first had grog served out to sailors instead of neat rum]

grō'gg|y (-gī) *a.* unsteady, tottering; (of horse) weak in forelegs; (arch.) drunk; hence ∼**ily²** *adv.,* ∼**iness** *n.* [f. prec. + -Y²]

grō'gram *n.* coarse fabric of silk, mohair, and wool, or these mixed, often stiffened with gum. [f. F *gros grain* coarse grain (as GROSS², GRAIN)]

groin¹ *n., & v.t.* **1.** *n.* depression between belly and thigh. **2.** (Archit.) edge formed by intersecting vaults, arch supporting vault; hence ∼'**ing¹** (6) *n.* **3.** *v.t.* build with groins. [ME *grynde*, perh. f. OE *grynde* depression]

***groin².** See GROYNE.

grō'mmet *n.* See GRUMMET.

grō'mwell *n.* plant of genus *Lithospermum*, with hard seeds formerly used in medicine. [ME f. OF *gromil*, prob. f. med. L *gruinum milium* crane's millet (*grus* CRANE¹ (1)]

groom (-ōōm, -ŏŏm) *n., & v.t.* **1.** *n.* ||one of certain officers of Royal Household. **2.** person employed to take care of horses. **3.** bridegroom; ∼'**sman** (-z-), best man or other unmarried male friend officially attending bridegroom at wedding. **4.** *v.t.* curry, tend, etc., (horse); give neat appearance to (person etc.); prepare (person) as political candidate, for career, etc. [ME, orig. = 'boy', of unkn. orig.]

grōōve *n. & v.* **1.** *n.* channel or hollow, esp. one made to direct motion or receive corresponding ridge; spiral cut in gramophone record for needle; **in the ∼,** (sl.) performing excellently, appreciative of such performance, excellent. **2.** piece of routine, undeviating course. **3.** (sl.) well played jazz; something excellent or very satisfying. **4.** *v.t.* make groove(s) in, (sl.) give pleasure to (person). **5.** *v.i.* settle into (routine etc.). **6.** (sl.) be 'in the groove'; enjoy well-played jazz; make progress; get on well *with* (person). [ME, = mine-shaft, f. obs. Du. *groeve* furrow, OHG *gruoba*, ON *gróf*, Goth. *gröha* f. Gmc *gröbh*-; cf. GRAVE¹]

grōō'v|y *a.* of or resembling a groove; (sl.) = *in the* GROOVE; hence ∼**ily²** *adv.,* ∼**iness** *n.* [f. prec. + -Y²]

grōpe *v.* **1.** *v.i.* feel about as in dark (*for, after,* or abs.), search blindly (lit. or fig.). **2.** *v.t.* find one's *way* by feeling or tentatively; (sl.) caress genitals of. [OE *grāpian*, = OHG *greifōn* f. WG *graipōjan* f. Gmc *graip*-; cogn. w. GRIP², GRIPE]

grō'per *n.* (esp. Austral. & NZ) = GROUPER. [var. of GROUPER]

grō'sbeak *n.* = HAW¹*finch.* [f. F *grosbec* (as GROSS², BEAK¹)]

grō'schen (-shen) *n.* **1.** (Hist.) small German silver coin. **2.** smallest Austrian coin, 1/100 of schilling. **3.** (colloq.) German 10-pfennig piece. [G, f. MHG *grosse* f. med. L (*denarius*) *grossus* thick (penny); cf. GROAT]

grō'sgrain (-ō'gr-) *n.* corded silk etc. fabric. [F, = coarse grain (as GROSS², GRAIN)]

***gros point** (grō' pwǎn) *n.* embroidery on canvas using cross-stitches. [F (as GROSS², POINT¹)]

grŏss¹ *n.* (*pl.* same). twelve dozen; **by the** ∼, in large quantities, wholesale. [ME, f. F *grosse* (*douzaine* dozen) fem. of *gros* great, GROSS²]

grŏss² *a.* **1.** luxuriant, rank; overfed, bloated, repulsively fat. **2.** flagrant, glaring, (*gross negligence*). **3.** total, without deductions, not net, (*gross* TON¹, *tonnage*, *weight*; ∼ **national product,** annual total value of goods produced and services provided in a country; ∼ **domestic product,** this excluding transactions with other countries). **4.** dense, thick, solid; not ethereal, transparent, or impalpable; (of food) coarse, greasy, uncleanly, repulsive, (∼ **feeder,** one who likes such food); (of senses etc.) not delicate, dull. **5.** coarse in manners or morals, unrefined, indecent. **6.** Hence ∼LY² *adv.,* ∼NESS *n.* [ME, f. OF *gros grosse* big, f. LL *grossus*]

grŏss³ *v.t.* produce or earn as gross profit; ∼ **up,** increase (net amount) to its value before deduction of tax etc. [f. prec.]

grosso modo (grŏsō mō'dō) *adv.* roughly, approximately. [It.]

grŏt *n.* (poet.) grotto. [f. F *grotte* f. It. *grotta* GROTTO]

grŏtě'sque (-sk) *n.* & *a.* **1.** *n.* decoration with fantastic interweaving of human and animal forms with foliage; comically distorted figure or design; sanserif type. **2.** *a.* in the style of a grotesque; distorted, bizarre; ludicrous from incongruity, absurd. **3.** Hence ∼LY² *adv.,* ∼NESS, **grŏtě'squerie** (-skerĭ) [-ERY (5)], *ns.* [earlier *crot-* f. F *crotesque* f. (w. assim. to OF *crote* grotto), It. *grottesca* grotto-like (painting etc.) fem. of *grottesco* (as foll.; see -ESQUE)]

grŏ'ttō *n.* (*pl.* ∼es or ∼s). picturesque cave; artificial ornamental cave, room etc. adorned with shells etc. in imitation of cave, as pleasant retreat; hence ∼ED² (-ōd) *a.* [f. It. *grotta* f. Rom. **grupta,* **crupta* f. L f. Gk *kruptē* CRYPT]

||**grŏ'ttÿ** *a.* (sl.) unpleasant, dirty, ugly, etc. [f. GROTESQUE + -Y²]

grouch *v.i.,* & *n.* (colloq.) **1.** *v.i.* grumble. **2.** *n.* discontented person; cause of discontent; fit of grumbling or bad temper or the sulks; hence ∼'Y² *a.* [var. of *grutch*; see GRUDGE]

ground¹ *n.* & *a.* **1.** *n.* bottom of sea; **touch** ∼, (fig.) come to something solid after vague talk etc.; (in *pl.*) dregs, esp. of coffee. **2.** (Electr.) = EARTH¹ 5. **3.** base, foundation, motive, valid reason, (**on the** ∼ **of,** by reason or under pretext of; *on public* etc. *grounds*). **4.** substratum, underlying part, surface worked upon in embroidery, painting, etc., undecorated part, prevailing colour or tone. **5.** surface of earth (esp. Aeron., opp. *air: ground-based, ground crew,* etc.); **above** ∼, (fig.) alive; **below** ∼, (fig.) dead and buried; **cut** ∼ **from under** person's **feet,** anticipate and defeat his arguments or plans; **down to the** ∼, (colloq.) completely; **fall** etc. **to the** ∼, (of scheme, hope, etc.) be abandoned, fail; *feet on the ground* (see FOOT¹ 12); **from the** ∼ **up,** (colloq.) completely; **get off the** ∼, (fig., colloq.) start successfully; **go to** ∼, (of dog, fox, etc.) enter burrow, (of person) withdraw from public notice; **into the** ∼, (colloq.) to exhaustion etc.; **on the** ∼, on the spot, in practical conditions; **on firm, solid,** etc., ∼, using soundly-based reasoning; **run to** ∼, (fig.) = *run to* EARTH¹; **thin on the** ∼, not numerous; **to the** ∼, completely. **6.** (in *pl.*) enclosed land for ornament or recreation attached to house. **7.** position, area, or distance, on earth's surface; **break** (**fresh** or **new**) ∼, begin work on previously untouched ground (lit. or fig.); **cover much** ∼, (of inquiry, report, etc.) be wide-ranging; **cover the** ∼, deal adequately with subject; **gain** or **make** ∼, advance, catch up *on* (person pursued); **give** or **lose** ∼, retreat, decline; **hold** one's ∼, = *hold* one's OWN¹; **meet** person on his own ∼, (in his own territory or on his own terms); SHIFT¹, STAND¹, one's *ground*. **8.** area of special kind or use (*camping-ground, cricket-ground, fishing-grounds*); COMMON¹ *ground*; **forbidden** ∼, subject that must be avoided. **9.** ||floor of room etc.

10. (Cricket). area where player may lawfully stand, esp. that of batsman behind popping-crease (*in, out of, his ground*); = *ground-staff* (2). **11.** *a.* (In names of birds) terrestrial, (of animals) burrowing or living on ground, (of plants) dwarfish or trailing. **12.** ∼**-ash,** ash sapling, walking-stick of this; ∼**-bait** *n.,* & *v.t.,* (prepare with) bait thrown to bottom of intended fishing-ground to attract fish, (lit. or fig.); ∼ **ball,** grounder at cricket or baseball; ∼ **bass,** (Mus.) short passage in bass of composition, repeated many times with upper part of music varied; ∼**-box,** small BOX¹ used to edge garden beds; ∼**-cherry,** (1) dwarf cherry, (2) plant of genus *Physalis*; ∼**-colour,** first coat of paint, prevailing colour on which design is done; ∼ **control,** directing of aircraft-landing from ground; ∼**-fish** (living at bottom of water); ∼**-fishing** (with bait near bottom); *ground* FLOOR (**get in on the** ∼ **floor,** be admitted to project, company, etc., as one of the initiators); ∼ **frost** (on surface of ground or in top layer of soil); ||∼ **game,** hares, rabbits, etc.; ∼**'hog,** (1) aardvark, (2) Amer. marmot, woodchuck, (**G∼hog Day,* usu. 2 Feb., when sunny weather is supposed to foretell continuing cold); ∼**-ice** (formed at bottom of water); ∼ **ivy,** creeping herb with bluish-purple flower and kidney-shaped leaf; ***∼**'keeper,** = *groundsman*; ||∼ **landlord,** owner of ground leased for building; ∼ **level,** also (Phys.) lowest energy state of atom etc.; ∼**'man,** = *groundsman*; ∼**-note** (on which a common chord is built, fundamental bass); ∼**-nut,** (1) (edible tuber of) N. Amer. wild bean, (2) ||peanut; ∼**-pine,** (1) yellow-flowered herb with resinous smell, (2) club-moss; ∼**-plan,** plane drawing of divisions of building at ground level, outline or general design of anything; ∼**-rent,** rent paid to ground landlord; ∼ **rule,** basic principle; ∼ **sea,** heavy sea without apparent cause; ∼**'sheet,** waterproof sheet for spreading on ground; ∼**'sman** (-z-), man keeping cricket-ground etc. in order; ∼ **speed,** (Aeron.) aircraft's speed relative to ground; ∼**-squirrel,** terrestrial squirrel-like rodent, e.g. chipmunk, gopher, etc.; ∼ **staff,** (1) non-flying members of aerodrome staff, (2) ||paid staff of players employed by cricket-club; ∼ **state,** (Phys.) = *ground level*; ∼ **stroke,** (Lawn Tennis) stroke played near ground after ball has bounced; ∼ **swell,** heavy sea caused by distant or past storm or earthquake; ∼ **water** (in surface soil); ∼**'work,** foundation or basis (usu. fig.), chief ingredient, general surface of thing showing where not overlaid with embroidery or other ornament; ∼ **zero,** point on ground under exploding bomb. [OE *grund,* = OS *grund,* OHG *grunt,* Goth. **grundus* f. Gmc **grunduz*]

ground² *v.* **1.** *v.t.* & *i.* run ashore, strand. **2.** *v.t.* base, establish, (institution, principle, belief) *on* some fact or authority (in *pass.* also *in*; in *p.p., well, ill,* etc., founded, or abs. = well founded); instruct thoroughly (*in* elements of subject), whence ∼'ING¹ (1) *n.*; place or lay (esp. Mil. arms) on ground; (Electr.) connect with earth as conductor; prevent (aircraft, aviator) from flying. **3.** *v.i.* alight on ground. [ME, f. prec.]

ground³. See GRIND.

||**grou'ndage** *n.* duty levied on ship entering a port or lying on a shore. [f. GROUND¹ + -AGE]

grou'nder *n.* In vbl senses; (Cricket etc.) ball hit along ground. [ME, f. GROUND² + -ER¹]

grou'ndless *a.* without basis, authority, or support; unfounded; hence ∼LY² *adv.,* ∼NESS *n.* [OE *grundléas* (as GROUND¹, -LESS)]

grou'ndling *n.* **1.** = GROUND¹-*fish*; creeping or dwarf plant. **2.** (literary). spectator or reader of inferior taste (w. ref. to Shak. *Hamlet* III. ii. 12). **3.** person on the ground, opp. one in aircraft. [f. GROUND¹ + -LING¹]

grou'ndsel¹ *n.* plant of genus *Senecio,* of which the commonest species is used as food for cage-birds. [OE *grundeswylige, gundæswelgiæ* (perh. f. *gund* pus, **swulg-* SWALLOW¹, = pus-absorber, as being used for poultices)]

grou′ndsel[2] *n.* (arch.) timber serving as foundation, lowest part of wooden framework; threshold. [ME, app. f. GROUND[1]+SILL]

group (-ōōp) *n.*, & *v.t.* **1.** *n.* number of persons or things standing near together; number of persons or things belonging or classed together or forming a whole; number of commercial companies under one owner; (Polit.) smaller unit than a party; division of air force or air-fleet; = POP[3] *group*. **2.** (Math.) set of elements with operation for combining any pair to give another element in the set. **3.** (Chem.) set of ions or radicals giving characteristic qualitative reaction; set of elements having similar properties; combination of atoms having recognizable identity in a number of compounds. **4.** ∼ **captain,** rank in RAF; ∼ **practice,** medical practice in which several doctors are associated; ∼ **sex,** sexual activity in which more than two persons take part simultaneously; ∼ **therapy,** therapy in which patients with similar condition are brought together to assist one another psychologically; ∼ **velocity,** speed of travel of energy of wave-(-group). **5.** *v.t.* form into a group; place in a group (*with*); form (colours, figures, etc.) into well-arranged and harmonious whole; classify; hence ∼′AGE (3), ∼′ING (1, 2), *ns.* [f. F *groupe* f. It. *gruppo* f. Gmc **kruppaz* round mass, cogn. w. CROP[1]]

grou′per (-ōō′-) *n.* marine food-fish of family Serranidae. [f. Port. *garupa*, prob. f. native name in S. Amer.]

grou′pie (-ōō′-) *n.* (sl.) **1.** group captain. **2.** girl who follows touring pop groups. [f. GROUP+-IE]

grouse[1] *n.* (*pl.* same). wild bird of family Tetraonidae with feathered feet, esp. ‖(**red**) ∼, reddish European game-bird (*Lagopus scoticus*); its flesh as food. [16th c., perh. pl. of **grue* f. med. L *gruta* or W *grugiar* (*grug* heath, *iar* hen)]

grous|e[2] *v.i.*, & *n.* (sl.) grumble; hence ∼′ER[1] *n.* [19th c.; orig. unkn.]

grout[1] *n.*, & *v.t.* **1.** *n.* thin fluid mortar for filling interstices. **2.** *v.t.* fill up or finish with grout. [perh. f. foll., but cf. F dial. *grouter* grout a wall]

grout[2] *n.* sediment, dregs. [OE *grūt*, cogn. w. GRITS, GROATS]

grout[3] *v.i.* & *t.* (Of pig, or fig.) turn up earth, turn up (carth etc.), with snout. [var. of *groot* f. ME *groot* mud, rel. to OE *grēot* GRIT]

grōve *n.* small wood, group of trees; hence **gro′vy**[2] *a.* [OE *grāf*, rel. to *græfa* brushwood]

gro′vel *v.i.* (‖-ll-). lie prone in abject humility, humble oneself; hence ‖∼lER[1], **∼ER[1], n.* [back-form. f. foll.]

‖**gro′velling, *gro′veling,** *a.* abject, base, sordid; prone; hence ∼LY[2] *adv.* [f. obs. *grovelling(s)* adv. (*gruf* face down f. *on grufe* f. ON *á grúfu*; see -LING[2]); later taken as pres. part. (-ING[2])]

grow (-ō) *v.* (**grew** *pr.* grōō; ∼**n** *p.p.* w. *have* or *be*, cf. -ED[1] (2), or as *a.*). **1.** *v.i.* develop or exist as living plant (∼ **into one, together,** etc., coalesce); germinate, sprout, spring up; be produced, come naturally into existence, arise, (*grow on* TREES); ∼ **out of,** be result or development of (see also senses 2, 3). **2.** increase in or in size, height, quantity, degree, power, etc.; ∼ **downwards,** extend downwards, (fig.) diminish; *habit, person, picture,* etc., ∼**s on** person, becomes more influential with or admired by him; ∼ **out of,** become too large to wear (garment; see also senses 1, 3); ∼′**ing pains,** neuralgic pain in children's legs due to fatigue etc., (fig.) early difficulties in development of an enterprise etc.; ∼**ing season,** time of year when weather promotes growth of plants; ∼**n man** etc., adult. **3.** become gradually (*grow rich, less*); come by degrees *to* do; ∼ **out of,** become too mature to retain (childish habit etc.; see also senses 1, 2); ∼ **up,** advance to maturity, (esp. in *imper.*) begin to behave sensibly, (of custom) arise, become common; ∼**n-up** *a.* & *n.,* adult. **4.** *v.t.* produce (plants, fruit, wool, etc.) by cultivation, bring forth, let (beard etc.) develop,

whence ∼′ABLE *a.* **5.** (in *pass.*) be covered (*up* or *over*) with some growth. [OE *grōwan,* = OHG *gruoan,* ON *gróa* f. Gmc **grō-* cogn. w. GRASS, GREEN[1]]

grow′er (-ō′er) *n.* plant that grows in specified way (*fast, free, grower*); person growing produce (often in comb., as *fruit-grower*). [f. prec.+-ER[1]]

growl *v.i.* & *t.,* & *n.* (make) guttural sound of anger (*at*); rumble; murmur angrily, angry murmur, complain(t); utter with a growl (*out*). [prob. imit.]

grow′ler *n.* In vbl senses; ‖(Hist.) four-wheeled cab; small iceberg. [f. prec.+-ER[1]]

grown. See GROW.

growth (-ōth) *n.* growing, development, increase in size or value, (**of foreign** etc. ∼, grown abroad etc.; **full** ∼, size ultimately attained); cultivation of produce; what has grown or is growing; crop or yield of grapes; (Path.) morbid formation; ∼ **industry,** one developing faster than most other industries; ∼ **stock** etc. (tending to increase in capital value rather than yield high income). [f. GROW+-TH[1]]

groyne, *groin[2], *n.,* & *v.t.* **1.** *n.* timber framework or low broad wall run out to check drifting of beach and so stop encroachment of sea. **2.** *v.t.* supply (beach) with groynes. [f. (dial.) *groin* snout f. OF *groign* f. LL *grunium* pig's snout f. L *grunnire* grunt]

grub[1] *n.* larva of insect, caterpillar, maggot; (arch.) dull drudge, literary hack, sloven; (sl.) food, a feed; ∼**-screw** (headless); **∼***-stake** *v.t.,* & *n.,* (sl.) (supply with) outfit, provisions, etc., given in return for share in profits (orig. in prospecting for ore). [ME, prob. f. foll.]

grub[2] *v.* (**-bb-**). **1.** *v.t.* & *i.* dig superficially. **2.** *v.t.* clear (ground) of roots and stumps, clear away (roots etc.), fetch *up* or *out* by digging (lit., or fig. in books etc.). **3.** *v.i.* search, rummage; plod, toil, *on, along, away;* (sl.) feed [perh. f. prec.]. **4.** ∼**-axe, -hoe, -hook,** (for grubbing up stumps). **5.** Hence (-)∼**′bER**[1] (1, 2) *n.* [ME, perh. repr. OE **grybban* f. Gmc **grubh-, *grabh-* GRAVE[2]]

gru′bb|y̆ *a.* of or infested with grubs; dirty, grimy, slovenly, whence ∼iLY[2] *adv.,* ∼iNESS *n.* [f. GRUB[1]+-Y[2]]

Gru′b Street *n.* & *a.* (typical of) the tribe of needy authors and literary hacks. [name of a London street (later Milton St., Moorgate), inhabited by such in 17th c.]

grudge *v.t.,* & *n.* **1.** *v.t.* be unwilling to give, grant, or allow (thing; *to* person); show reluctance in doing or to do. **2.** *n.* feeling of resentment or ill will (*have a* or **hold a grudge against*; *bear* or *owe* person *a grudge*). [f. ME *grutch* f. OF *grouc(h)ier* murmur, of unkn. orig.]

gru′dging *a.* reluctant, not willing; hence ∼LY[2] *adv.* [f. prec.+-ING[2]]

gru′el (-ōō′-) *n.,* & *v.t.* (‖-ll-). **1.** *n.* liquid food of oatmeal etc. boiled in milk or water chiefly for invalids; ‖(arch.) punishment, defeat. **2.** *v.t.* ‖exhaust, punish, (esp. ∼(1)ING[1,2] *n.* & *a.*). [ME f. OF, f. Gallo-Rom. **grutellum* f. Frank. **grūt;* cf. GROUT[2], -LE 2]

grue′some (-ōō′s-) *a.* horrible, grisly, disgusting; hence ∼LY[2] (-mlĭ) *adv.,* ∼NESS (-mn-) *n.* [f. Sc. *grue* to shudder (f. Scand.)+-SOME[1]]

grüff *a.* surly, laconic, rough-mannered, rough-voiced; hence ∼′LY[2] *adv.,* ∼′NESS *n.* [f. Du., MLG *grof* coarse, = OHG *grob* f. WG **gahrubha* (as Y-, ROUGH)]

gru′mbl|e *v.i.* & *t.,* & *n.* (utter) dull inarticulate sound, murmur, growl faintly; rumble; complain(t) (*at, about, over*); be discontented; utter complainingly (*out*); hence ∼ER[1] *n.,* ∼ING[2] *a.* (∼**ing appendix,** (colloq.) one that causes intermittent discomfort without developing appendicitis). [f. obs. *grumme*+-LE 3; cf. MDu. *grommen,* MLG *grommelen,* f. imit. Gmc **grum-*]

grum|e (-ōōm) *n.* thick or viscous fluid, esp. clotted blood; hence ∼′OUS *a.* [f. L *grumus* small heap]

gru′mmĕt, grŏ′mmĕt, *n.* **1.** (Naut.) ring usu. of twisted rope as fastening, rowlock, wad, etc. **2.**

insulating washer placed round electric conductor passing through hole in metal etc. **3.** stiffening ring in serviceman's cap. [f. obs. F *grom*(*m*)*ette* (*gourmer* to curb, of unkn. orig.)]

grŭmp *n.* (colloq.) grumpy person; (in *pl.*) fit of sulks; hence ∼'ɪsʜ¹ *a.* [imit.]

grŭ'mp|ў *a.* morosely irritable, surly; hence ∼ɪʟʏ² *adv.*, ∼ɪɴᴇss *n.* [f. prec. in sense 'ill humour' + -ʏ²]

Grŭ'ndў *n.* (**Mrs**) ∼, person embodying conventional propriety and prudery; hence ∼ɪsм (2) *n.* [person repeatedly mentioned in T. Morton's *Speed the Plough* 1798]

grŭ'nion (-nyon) *n.* small Californian sea-fish coming ashore to spawn. [prob. f. Sp. *gruñón* grunter]

grŭnt *v.i.* & *t.*, & *n.* **1.** (utter) low guttural sound characteristic of pigs; express discontent, dissent, fatigue, etc., by this; utter with grunt (*out*). **2.** *n.* Amer. fish of family Pomadasidae, grunting when caught. [OE *grunnettan*, = OHG *grunnizōn*, intensive f. imit. *grun*-]

grŭ'nter *n.* In vbl senses; pig; grunting fish, esp. = prec. 2 [ME, f. prec. + -ᴇʀ¹]

Grunth. Var. of GRANTH.

grŭ'ntled (-teld) *a.* (colloq.) pleased, satisfied. [back-form. f. DISGRUNTLED]

gruyère (grōō'yār) *n.* (orig. Swiss) pale cows'-milk cheese with many cavities. [f. *G*∼ district in Switzerland]

grŷ'phon. See GRIFFIN².

grŷ'sbŏk *n.* small grey S. Afr. antelope. [S. Afr. Du., f. Du. *grijs* grey + *bok* BUCK¹]

‖**gs.** *abbr.* guineas.

G-string (jē'-) *n.* **1.** (Mus.) string on violin etc. sounding note G. **2.** narrow strip of cloth etc. covering genitals, attached to string round waist, as worn by American Indian, chorus-girl, etc. [f. G + STRING]

G-suit (jē'sōōt, -ūt) *n.* garment to enable wearer to withstand high acceleration. [f. *g* (= *gravity*) + SUIT]

GT *abbr. gran turismo.*

Gt. *abbr.* Great.

gua'charŏ (gwah'ch-) *n.* (*pl.* ∼s). the oil-bird of S. America. [S. Amer. Sp.]

guai'ăc (gwī'-) *n.* = foll. 2, 3. [anglicized form of foll.]

guai'acum (gwī'-) *n.* **1.** tropical Amer. tree of genus *Guaiacum* **2.** brownish-green wood of two species of this used in medicine, lignum vitae. **3.** resin from these; drug made from it. [mod. L, f. Sp. *guayaco* of Haitian orig.]

guan (gwahn) *n.* tropical Amer. bird of family Cracidae, allied to curassow. [prob. f. native name]

gua'na (gwah'-) *n.* iguana; iguana. [var. of IGUANA]

guana'cŏ (gwanah'-) *n.* (*pl.* **-s**). wild llama with reddish-brown wool. [f. Quechua *huanaco*]

gua'nine (gwah'nēn) *n.* (Chem.) white base obtained from guano and found as constituent of DNA. [f. foll. + -INE⁵]

gua'nŏ (gwah'-) *n.* (*pl.* ∼s), & *v.t.* **1.** *n.* excrement of sea-fowl, found esp. in islands off Peru and used as manure; artificial manure esp. that made from fish. **2.** *v.t.* fertilize with guano. [Sp., f. Quechua *huanu* dung]

guăr'ani (gw-) *n.* **1.** (*G*∼) language or member of a S. Amer. Indian ethnic group. **2.** monetary unit of Paraguay. [Sp.]

guărantee' (gă-) *n.*, & *v.t.* **1.** *n.* person making guaranty or giving security; guaranty; thing (esp. document) given or existing as security for fulfilment of conditions or permanence etc. of something; ∼ **fund,** sum pledged as contingent indemnity for loss. **2.** *v.t.* be guarantee for, answer for due fulfilment of (contract etc.) or genuineness etc. of (article), assure permanence etc. of; give one's word *that* something has happened or will happen or *to* do; secure possession *of to* person; secure *against* or *from* (risk etc.), or *in* (possession etc.); hence **guăr'rantor** (gă'ranter, -ōr) *n.* [earlier *garante,* perh. f. Sp. *garante* = F *garant* WARRANT¹; later infl. by F *garantie* guaranty]

guă'rantў (gă'-) *n.* written or other undertaking to answer for payment of debt or performance of obligation by another person liable in first instance; ground or basis of security. [f. AF *guarantie,* var. of *warantie* WARRANTY]

guărd¹ (gärd) *n.* **1.** defensive posture or motion in fencing, boxing, etc.; (Cricket) position of bat to defend wicket (**take, give,** ∼, (of batsman, umpire) ascertain correct spot on ground for this). **2.** watch, vigilant state, (**keep** ∼, **be on** ∼, **stand** ∼, act as sentry etc.; **on, off,** one's ∼, prepared, unprepared, against attack, surprise, or one's own impulses etc.). **3.** protector, defender, sentry; ‖official in general charge of train or (Hist.) stage-coach; *prison warder; protective player in basketball or Amer. football. **4.** (in *pl.*) ‖household troops (including FOOT¹ *Guards,* HORSE¹ *Guards,* LIFE *Guards,* and by extension some (orig. seven) regiments of *Dragoon Guards*). **5.** body of soldiers etc. serving as protectors of place or person, escort, separate portion of army, etc., (*advance, rear, -guard; guard of honour;* HOME¹ *Guard;* OLD *guard;* **mount, relieve,** ∼, take up, take others' place on, sentry duty). **6.** thing that protects or defends; contrivance to prevent injury or accident (often in comb.: *fire-guard, mudguard*); part of sword-hilt that protects user's hand. **7.** ∼**-boat,** (1) boat going rounds of fleet in harbour to see that good watch is kept, (2) official harbour boat enforcing quarantine or customs regulations; ∼**-book** (arranged for the reception of additional leaves, letters, etc.); ∼**-chain** (securing watch, brooch, etc.); ∼'**house** (accommodating military guard or securing prisoners); ∼**-rail,** hand or other rail to prevent falling, derailment, etc.; ∼**-ring** (preventing other ring from slipping off finger); ∼'**room** (as *guardhouse*); ∼**-ship,** warship protecting harbour and receiving seamen till they can join their ships; ∼'**sman** (-z-), soldier belonging to guard or Guards; ∼**-tent** (as *guardhouse*). **8.** Hence ∼'LESS *a.* [ME, f. OF *garde* (*garder* f. Rom. *wardare* f. WG *wardho* WARD¹)]

guărd² (gärd) *v.* **1.** *v.t.* keep safe, stand guard over, keep (door etc.) so as to control entry or exit; protect, defend, (*from, against*); secure by explanations or stipulations etc. from misunderstanding or abuse. **2.** keep (thoughts, speech) in check. **3.** *v.i.* use a fencing guard; take precautions *against*; (Curling, Bowling) protect (stone, bowl) by placing one's own between it and later player; (Chess, Cards) protect (man, card) with another. **4.** So ∼'ANT *a.*, (Her.) depicted with body sideways but face towards spectator. [f. prec., or f. OF *garder* (see prec.)]

guăr'dĕd (gär'-) *a.* In vbl senses; (of remarks etc.) cautious; hence ∼ʟʏ² *adv.*, ∼ɴᴇss *n.* [p.p. of prec.]

‖**guărdee'** (gär-) *n.* (colloq.) guardsman, esp. as representing smartness and elegance. [f. GUARD¹ + -ᴇᴇ (2)]

guăr'dian (gär'-) *n.* keeper, defender, protector; ‖(Hist.) member of board elected to administer poor-laws in parish or district; (*G*∼) title of newspaper; (Law) one having custody of person or property (or both) of WARD¹ (minor, lunatic, etc.); superior of Franciscan convent; ∼ **angel,** spirit conceived as watching over person or place; hence ∼sʜɪᴘ *n.* [ME f. AF *gardein,* OF *garden* f. Frank. *warding* (as WARD¹, -ɪɴɢ³); cf. WARDEN¹]

Guărnēr'ius (gw-) *n.* violin or violoncello made by member of *Guarnerius* family of Cremona in 17th–18th c.

gua'va (gwah'-) *n.* (tropical Amer. tree yielding) edible orange-coloured fruit. [f. Sp. *guayaba* prob. f. S. Amer. name]

guayu'lĕ (gwiōō'li) *n.* (silver-leaved Mexican plant furnishing) the sap of which furnishes) a rubber substitute. [Amer. Sp., f. Nahuatl *cuauhuli*]

gŭ'bbins (-z) *n.* trash; valueless thing; gadget; ‖(colloq.) foolish person. [orig. = 'fragments', f. obs. *gobbon,* perh. rel. to GOBBET]

*gūbernatōr′ial *a.* of a governor. [f. L *gubernator* governor + -IAL]

gŭ′ddl∥e *v.* (Sc.) **1.** *v.t.* catch (fish) with the hands, by groping under the stones or banks of a stream. **2.** *v.i.* grope for fish thus. **3.** Hence ∼ER¹ *n.* [19th c.; orig. unkn.]

gŭ′dgeon¹ (-jon) *n.* small freshwater fish used as bait; credulous person. [ME, f. OF *goujon* f. L *gobio -onis* GOBY]

gŭ′dgeon² (-jon) *n.* pivot at end of beam, axle, etc., on which bell, wheel, etc., works; ring of gate fitting on hook of post; socket in which rudder works; pin holding two blocks of stone etc. together; ∼-pin, (esp.) pin holding piston-rod and connecting-rod together. [ME, f. OF *goujon* dim. of *gouge* GOUGE]

guĕ′lder (gĕ′-) *n.* ∼ rose, deciduous shrub with round bunches of creamy-white flowers, snowball-tree. [f. Du. *geldersch* (*Gelderland* province in Holland)]

Guĕlph, Guĕlf, (gwĕ-) *n.* member of medieval Italian party supporting Pope against Emperor (opp. GHIBELLINE); hence ∼IC *a.*, ∼ISM (3) *n.* [f. It. *Guelfo* f. MHG *Welf* name of founder of princely family of Guelphs]

gueno′n (genaw′n) *n.* long-tailed Afr. monkey of various *Cercopithecus* etc. [F, of unkn. orig.]

guĕr′don (gĕr′-) *n.*, & *v.t.* (poet.) reward, recompense. [ME, f. OF *guer(e)don* f. med. L *widerdonum* f. WG *widarlōn* (as WITH, LOAN¹) w. assim. to L *donum* gift]

guéridon (gē′rĭdon) *n.* small ornamental table or stand. [F]

Guĕr′nsey (gĕr′nzĭ) *n.* (animal of) breed of dairy cattle from Guernsey; (*g*∼) thick knitted woollen usu. blue outer tunic or jersey, (Austral.) football shirt; ∼ lily, kind of amaryllis orig. from S. Africa, with large red lily-like flowers. [∼ in Channel Islands]

guerri′lla, guerĭ′lla, (ger-) *n.* person taking part in irregular fighting (∼ war, warfare) by small independently acting groups, URBAN *guerrilla*. [f. Sp. *guerrilla*, dim. of *guerra* war]

guĕss (gĕs) *v.* & *n.* **1.** *v.t.* & *i.* (make) estimate without measurement or detailed calculation. **2.** *v.t.* think likely, think one divines nature of, form hypothesis as to, conjecture, hazard opinion about, (thing, *that, how, when, whether*, etc., thing *to be*, or abs.); conjecture (answer to riddle, solution of problem, or abs.) rightly. **3.** *v.i.* ∼ at, make guess concerning; **I* ∼, I think it likely, I suppose; **keep** person ∼**'ing,** (colloq.) let him remain uncertain. **4.** *n.* rough estimate, conjecture, hypothesis, (**by** ∼, haphazard, also *by guess and by God*(*frey*); ANYBODY'S or *anyone's guess*; **my** ∼ **is,** I am fairly sure; ****miss** one's ∼, make wrong assumption; **have another** ∼ **coming,** be mistaken); ∼'**work,** (procedure based on) guessing; OTHERguess. [ME *gesse*, of uncert. orig.; cf. OSw. *gissa*, MLG, MDu. *gissen*; f. root of GET¹]

guĕ′s(s)timate (gĕ′-) *n.* (colloq.) estimate based on guesswork combined with reasoning. [f. prec. + ESTIMATE¹]

guĕst (gĕst) *n.* **1.** person invited to visit another's house or have meal etc. at his expense (∼ **of honour,** one given especial honours; **paying** ∼, boarder); person lodging at hotel, boarding-house, etc.; occasional performer from outside regular company etc. **2.** ∼-**chamber** (kept for guests); ∼-**house,** superior boarding-house; ∼-**night** (on which guests are entertained at club, college, mess, etc.); ∼-**room** (kept for guests). **3.** Hence ∼'ship *n.* [ME, f. ON *gestr*, = OS, OHG *gast*, Goth. *gasts* f. Gmc **gastiz* f. IE **ghostis*]

guĕ′st-rōpe, guĕss-, (gĕ′s-) *n.* second rope fastened to boat in tow to steady it; rope slung outside ship to give hold for boats coming alongside. [17th c.; orig. uncert.]

gŭff *n.* (sl.) empty talk, nonsense. [19th c., orig. = 'puff'; imit.]

gŭffaw (-aw′, gŭ′-) *n.* & *v.* **1.** *n.* coarse or boisterous laugh. **2.** *v.i.* & *t.* make, say with, guffaw. [orig. Sc.; imit.]

gŭ′ggle. Var. of GURGLE.

gui′chet (gē′shā) *n.* grating, hatch; ticket-office window. [F]

guidance. See GUIDE².

guide¹ (gīd) *n.* **1.** one who shows the way; hired conductor of traveller or tourist; (esp. in Switzerland etc.) professional mountain-climber. **2.** soldier, vehicle, or ship enabling others to regulate their movements. **3.** adviser; directing principle or standard (*the feelings are a bad guide; Scripture is our guide*). **4.** (G∼). ∥member of girls' organization similar to Scouts; **King's** or **Queen's G**∼ (who has reached highest rank of proficiency). **5.** book of rudiments, manual; ∼('**book**), book of information for tourists (*to* cathedral, city, district, etc.). **6.** (Mech.) bar, rod, etc., directing motion of something, gauge etc. controlling tool. **7.** thing marking a position or guiding the eye. **8.** ∼'**book** (see sense 5); ∼-**dog** (trained to guide blind person); ∼-**line,** (fig.) directing principle; ∼-**post,** signpost; ∼-**rope,** (1) small rope attached to load of crane to guide it, (2) rope trailed along ground by balloon or small airship to assist in preserving altitude by drag of rope, (3) one of several ropes steadying an airship before flight; ∼'**way,** groove, track. [ME f. OF (*guie* f. *guider*; see foll.)]

guide² (gīd) *v.t.* **1.** act as guide to, go before, lead, direct course of; arrange course of (events); be the principle, motive, or ground, of (action, judgement, etc.); conduct affairs of (State etc.); ∼**d missile** (under remote control or directed by equipment within itself); ∼**d tour** (accompanied by guide). **2.** Hence **gui′dABLE** *a.,* **gui′d**ANCE *n.,* (gī′-); **Gui′d**ER¹ (gī′-) *n.,* adult leader of Guides (sense 4). [ME, f. OF *guider,* earlier *guier* f. Rom. **wīdare* f. Gmc **wītan,* cogn. w. WIT¹]

gui′don (gī′-) *n.* pennant narrowing to point or fork at free end (used as standard of dragoons or ***cavalry). [F, f. It. *gudone* (*guida* GUIDE¹)]

Guignō′l (gēnyo′l) *n.* = GRAND GUIGNOL; Punch and Judy show; hence ∼E′SQUE *a.* [see GRAND GUIGNOL]

guild, gild², (gĭ-) *n.* society for mutual aid or prosecution of common object; medieval association of craftsmen or merchants; G∼-**hall,** (1) hall in which a medieval guild met, (2) (from being used as meeting-place of Corporation) town hall; ∥(*the*) **Gui′ldhall,** hall of the Corporation of the City of London, used for State banquets, municipal meetings, etc.; ∼ **socialism,** system by which the resources, methods, and profits, of each industry should be controlled by a council of its members. [ME, prob. f. MLG, MDu. *gilde* f. Gmc **geldhjōn;* rel. to OE *gi(e)ld* payment, sacrifice, guild, OS *geld,* OHG *gelt,* ON *gjald,* Goth. *gild* tribute f. Gmc **geldham,* & ON *gildi* f. Gmc **geldhjam*]

gui′lder (gī′-) *n.* monetary unit of Netherlands; (Hist.) gold coin of Netherlands and Germany. [ME, alt. of Du. GULDEN]

guile (gīl) *n.* treachery, deceit, cunning devices; hence ∼'**FUL,** ∼'**LESS** (-l-l-), *adjs.* [ME f. OF, f. Scand. **wihl*WILE]

gui′llemot (gī′-) *n.* auk of genus *Uria* or *Cepphus.* [F, f. *Guillaume* William]

guillō′che (gīlō′sh) *n.* architectural or metalwork ornament imitating braided ribbons. [f. F *guillochis,* or f. F *guilloche* the tool used]

gui′llotine (gī′lotēn, -tē′n) *n.,* & *v.t.* **1.** machine with knife-blade sliding in grooves for beheading; surgical instrument for excising uvula etc.; machine for cutting paper, metal, etc.; ∥(Parl.) method of preventing obstruction, by fixing times at which parts of Bill must be voted on. **2.** *v.t.* use the guillotine upon. [F, f. J.-I. *Guillotin,* Fr. physician d. 1814, who recommended its use for executions in 1789]

guilt (gī-) *n.* fact of having committed a specified or implied offence; (feeling of) culpability; ∼ **complex,** (Psych.) mental obsession with idea of having done wrong. [OE *gylt,* of unkn. orig.]

gui'ltless (gĭ'-) *a.* innocent (*of* offence); not having knowledge or possession *of* (*guiltless of Greek, soap,* etc.); hence ∼LY² *adv.,* ∼NESS *n.* [OE *gyltlēas* (as prec., -LESS)]

gui'lty (gĭ'-) *a.* criminal, culpable; conscious of or promoted by guilt (*guilty conscience, behaviour, look*); having committed a particular offence (*of*); ∼y, **not** ∼y, (verdicts in criminal trials); hence ∼iLY² *adv.,* ∼iNESS *n.* [OE *gyltig* (as GUILT, -Y²)]

guimp. Var. of GIMP¹.

gui'nea (gĭ'nĭ) *n.* **1.** (Hist.) former British gold coin first coined for African trade. **2.** ‖money of account (£1.05) used in stating professional fees, amount of subscriptions, and prices of pictures, horses, estates, etc. **3.** ∼-**corn,** durra; ∼-**fowl, -hen,** gallinaceous bird of genus *Numida,* esp. *Numida meleagris,* with slate-coloured white-spotted plumage; G∼ **grains,** = GRAINS *of Paradise;* ∼-**pig,** S. Amer. rodent of genus *Cavia* kept as pet or for research in biology, person or thing used as subject for experiment, ‖(arch.) person receiving guinea fees, esp. company director or deputy clergyman; G∼ **worm,** tropical nematode infecting human and animal skin. [f. *G∼* in W. Africa]

gui'pure (gē'poor) *n.* heavy lace of linen pieces joined by embroidery. [F (*guiper* cover with silk etc. f. Gmc *wīpan wind round)]

guise (gīz) *n.* external appearance; semblance, assumed appearance, pretence, (*under* or *in the guise of*); (arch.) style of attire, garb. [ME f. OF, f. Rom. *guisa f. Frank. *wīsa f. Gmc *wīsō* (WISE²)]

gui'ser (gĭ'z-) *n.* (Sc. & N. Engl.) mummer, esp. at Hallowe'en. [f. *guise* v. masquerade (f. prec.) + -ER¹]

guitar' (gĭ-) *n.,* & *v.i.* (-**rr**-). **1.** *n.* six-stringed musical instrument played with fingers or plectrum; **electric** ∼ (with built-in microphone); hence ∼IST (3) *n.* **2.** *v.i.* play guitar. [f. (F *guitare* f.) Sp. *guitarra* f. Gk *kithara;* cf. CITHERN, GITTERN]

Gujara'ti (gŏŏjerah'-) *n.* & *a.* (inhabitant or language) of state of Gujarat in W. India. [Hind. (see -I)]

*gulch *n.* ravine, esp. one with torrent. [perh. f. dial. *gulch* to swallow]

gu'lden (gŏŏ-, gŏŏ'-) *n.* = GUILDER. [Du. & G, = GOLDEN]

gules (-lz) *n.,* & *a.* (usu. placed after *n.*) (esp. Her.) red. [ME, f. OF *go(u)les* (pl. of *gole* throat) red-dyed for neck-ornaments]

gulf *n.,* & *v.t.* **1.** *n.* (Geog.) portion of sea, proportionally narrower at mouth than bay, partly surrounded by coast. **2.** deep hollow, chasm, abyss, (poet.) profound depth of the sea; (arch.) whirlpool, what swallows up anything; impassable gap (Luke 16: 26); wide difference of feelings, opinion, etc.; G∼ **Stream,** oceanic warm current flowing from Gulf of Mexico to Europe; ∼-**weed,** sargasso. **3.** *v.t.* engulf, swallow up. [ME, f. OF *golfe* f. It. *golfo* f. Rom. **colp(h)us* f. Gk *kolpos* bosom, gulf]

gull¹ *n.* long-winged web-footed aquatic bird of family Laridae, usu. white with mantle varying from pearly-grey to black, and bright bill; ∼-**wing,** (of door of motor car) opening upwards, (of aeroplane wing) with upward-sloping short inner part and horizontal long outer part; hence ∼ERY (3) *n.* [ME, prob. f. W *gwylan,* Corn. *guilan* f. OCelt. **voilenno-*]

gull² *n.,* & *v.t.* (arch. or dial.) dupe, fool. [perh. f. obs. *gull* yellow f. ON *gulr*]

gu'llet *n.* food-passage from mouth to stomach, oesophagus; throat. [ME, f. OF dim. of *go(u)le* throat f. L *gula;* see -ET¹]

gu'll‖ible *a.* easily cheated or duped; hence ∼IBI'LITY *n.* [f. GULL² + -IBLE]

gu'lly¹ *n.,* & *v.t.* **1.** *n.* water-worn ravine; deep artificial channel, gutter, drain, sink; (Austral. & NZ) river valley. **2.** (Cricket). (position of) fieldsman between point and slips. **3.** ∼-**hole,** opening in street to drain or sewer. **4.** *v.t.* make gullies in, form (channels) by water action. [f. F *goulet* bottle-neck, f. as GULLET]

‖**gu'lly²** *n.* large knife. [16th c.; orig. unkn.]

gulo'sity *n.* (literary). gluttony. [f. LL *gulositas* f. L *gulosus* gluttonous (*gula* throat)]

gulp *v.* & *n.* **1.** *v.t.* swallow (*down*) hastily, greedily, or with effort; ∼ **back** or **down** sobs, tears, suppress. **2.** *v.i.* perform act of swallowing only with difficulty, gasp, choke. **3.** *n.* act of gulping (*drained it at one gulp*); effort to swallow; large mouthful of a drink; hence ∼'Y² *a.* [ME, prob. f. MDu. *gulpen* (imit.)]

gum¹ *n.* (usu. in *pl.*) firm flesh around roots of teeth; ∼'**boil,** small abscess on gum; ∼-**shield,** pad protecting boxer's teeth and gums. [OE *gōma,* = OHG *guomo,* ON *gómr* roof or floor of mouth]

gum² *n.* & *v.* (-**mm**-). **1.** *n.* viscous secretion of some trees and shrubs that hardens on drying but is soluble in water (cf. RESIN), used to stick paper etc. together and stiffen linen etc. **2.** secretion collecting in corner of eye; hard transparent sweet made of gelatin etc.; * = CHEWing-gum; waxy substance round raw-silk filaments; solid deposit in petroleum etc.; = *gum-tree;* * = gumboot. **3.** gum ARABIC; ∼'**boot,** rubber boot; ∼ **dragon,** tragacanth; ∼ **juniper,** sandarac; ∼ **resin,** vegetable secretion of resin mixed with gum, e.g. gamboge; *∼'**shoe,** (1) galosh, (2) (colloq.) stealthy action, (3) (colloq.) detective or policeman; ∼-**tree,** tree exuding gum, esp. eucalyptus (*up a* ∼-*tree,* in great difficulties). **4.** *v.t.* stiffen, smear, or cover with gum; fasten *down, together, up, in,* etc., with gum; ∼ **up,** interfere with smooth running of, spoil, (esp. *gum up the works*). **5.** *v.i.* exude gum. [ME, f. OF *gomme* f. Rom. *gumma f. L *gummi, cummi* f. Gk *kommi* f. Egypt. *kemai*]

gum³ *n.* (vulg.) God (in oaths, as *by gum!*). [corrupt. of *God*]

*gu'mbo *n.* (*pl.* ∼**s**). = OKRA; soup thickened with okra pods; (*G∼*) patois of Blacks and Creoles esp. in Louisiana. [Negro wd]

gu'mma *n.* (Path.) morbid growth of gummy tissue in late stage of syphilis; hence ∼tous *a.* [mod. L, f. L *gummi* GUM²]

gu'mm‖y¹ *a.* viscous, sticky; abounding in or exuding gum; (of ankle or leg) puffy, swollen; hence ∼iNESS *n.* [ME, f. GUM² + -Y²]

gu'mm‖y² *a.* & *n.* **1.** *a.* toothless; hence ∼iLY² *adv.* **2.** *n.* (Austral.) small shark (*Mustelus antarcticus*); (Austral. & NZ) toothless sheep. [f. GUM¹ + -Y²]

gump *n.* (colloq.) = foll. [abbr.]

gu'mption *n.* (colloq.) resource, initiative, enterprising spirit; ready practical sense. [18th c.; Sc., of unkn. orig.]

gun *n.* & *v.* (-**nn**-). **1.** *n.* metal tube for throwing missiles with gunpowder or other propellant; piece of ordnance, cannon, rifle, carbine, pistol; **big** ∼, (sl.) important person; **blow great** ∼**s,** (of wind) blow violently; **give** (engine, motor vehicle) **the** ∼, (colloq.) cause acceleration of; **going great** ∼**s,** proceeding vigorously towards success; **son of a** ∼, (colloq.) contemptible person (also joc.); SPIKE¹ person's *guns;* **stick to** one's ∼**s,** maintain one's position under attack (lit. or fig.). **2.** starting-pistol; **beat** or **jump the** ∼, start before the signal is given, (fig.) act before permitted or agreed or proper time. **3.** device for discharging insecticide, grease, electrons, etc., in desired direction. **4.** member of shooting-party; *gunman; (in *pl.;* Naval sl.) gunnery officer. ∼'**boat,** small vessel of shallow draught and with relatively heavy guns (∼*boat diplomacy,* diplomacy supported by use or threat of military force); *gun*-CARRIAGE, ∼-**cotton,** explosive used for blasting, made by steeping cotton in nitric and sulphuric acids; ∼ **crew,** team manning gun; ∼ **dog,** dog trained to follow sportsmen who use guns; *∼-**fight,** (colloq.) fight with firearms; ∼-**fire,** firing of gun(s), esp. (Mil. & Naut.) of morning or evening gun to show time, or independent firing by each gun of a battery; ∼-**harpoon** (propelled from gun, not by hand); ∼-**layer,** one whose task is to aim large gun; ∼-**lock,**

mechanism by which charge of gun is exploded; ∼'**man,** man armed with gun, assassin using gun; ∼-**metal,** alloy of copper and tin or zinc (formerly used for guns), dull bluish-grey colour; ∼ **moll,** (sl.) gangster's mistress, woman criminal with gun; ∼-**pit,** excavation to protect guns and gun crews; ∼-**play,** use of, a fight with, firearms; **at** ∼'**point,** under threat of injury by a gun; ∼'**powder,** (1) explosive of saltpetre, sulphur, and charcoal, (*Gunpowder Plot,* 5 Nov. 1605 to blow up Parliament), (2) fine green tea of granular appearance; ∼'**power,** quantity of guns available; ||∼'**room,** (1) room for sporting-guns etc. in house, (2) compartment in warship fitted up for junior officers or as lieutenants' mess-room [orig. for gunner and his mates]; ∼-**runner, -running,** (person engaged in) illegal introduction of firearms into country; ∼'**ship,** armed helicopter; ∼'**shot,** (1) shot fired from gun, (2) range of gun (*out of, within, gunshot*); ∼-**shy,** (esp. of sporting dog) frightened at report of gun; ∼-**site,** (usu. fortified) emplacement for gun; ∼-**slinger,** gunman; ∼'**smith,** maker and repairer of small firearms; ∼-**stock,** wooden mounting of gun-barrel. **6.** Hence (*heavily* etc.) ∼ᴍᴇᴅ² (-nd), ∼'ʟᴇss, *adjs.* **7.** *v.t.* shoot at; shoot (*down*); (colloq.) accelerate (engine etc.). **8.** *v.i.* go shooting; ∼ **for,** seek with gun, (fig.) seek to attack, harm, or destroy. [ME *gunne, gonne,* perh. f. *Gunna pet-form of Scand. *Gunnhildr* woman's name]

gŭnge (-nj) *n.* = GUNK. [imit.]

gŭng-hō' *a.* enthusiastic, eager. [f. Chin. *gonghe* work together, slogan adopted by US Marines 1942]

gŭnk *n.* (sl.) viscous or liquid material. [20th c.; orig. P as name of detergent]

gŭ'nnel¹ *n.* small eel-shaped sea-fish (*Pholis gunnellus*). [17th c.; orig. unkn.]

gŭ'nnel². See GUNWALE.

gŭ'nner *n.* artillery soldier (esp. as official term for private; **Master G∼,** RA warrant officer in charge of equipment etc. in a fort, or similarly employed); (Naut.) warrant-officer in charge of battery, magazine, etc. (∼'s **daughter,** (joc.) gun to which sailors were lashed for flogging); member of aircraft crews who operates gun; game-shooter. [ME, f. GUN; see -ᴇʀ² (2)]

gŭ'nnera *n.* ornamental foliage plant of genus *Gunnera,* with large leaves. [f. J. E. *Gunnerus,* Norw. botanist d. 1773 + -ᴀ 1]

gŭ'nnerȳ *n.* construction and management of large guns; firing of guns. [f. GUN + -ᴇʀʏ]

gŭ'nnȳ *n.* coarse sacking, sack, usu. of jute fibre. [f. Hindi & Marathi *gōnī* f. Skr. *gōṇi* sack]

gŭ'nter *n.* **1.** flat 2-ft. rule with scales, logarithmic lines, etc., used for solving mechanically problems in surveying and navigation. **2.** topmast, or its sail, sliding up and down lower mast on rings [from resemblance to sliding gunter]. **3.** G∼'s **chain,** 66-ft. surveying chain; **G∼'s scale,** = sense 1. [f. E. *Gunter,* Engl. mathematician d. 1626]

gŭ'nwale (-nal), **gŭ'nnel²,** *n.* upper edge of (esp. small) ship's or boat's side (∼ **to, under,** level with, below surface of water). [f. GUN + WALE (because formerly used to support guns)]

gŭ'nyah *n.* (Austral.) Aboriginal hut, bush hut. [Aboriginal]

gŭp *n.* (colloq.) silly talk, nonsense. [orig. Anglo-Ind., f. Hindi, = gossip]

gŭ'ppy¹ *n.* small W. Ind. fish freq. kept in aquaria. [f. R. J. L. *Guppy,* 19th-c. Trinidad clergyman who sent first specimen to British Museum]

gŭ'ppy² *n.* streamlined submarine with snorkel. [f. *greater underwater propulsive power* + -ʏ³]

gŭrgitā'tion *n.* surging, bubbling motion or sound. [f. mod. L *gurgitatio f. LL *gurgitare* to surge f. L *gurges gurgitis* whirlpool; see -ᴀᴛɪᴏɴ]

gŭr'gle *v.i.* & *t.,* & *n.* (make) bubbling sound as of water from bottle or among stones; utter with such

sound. [imit., or f. Du. *gorgelen,* G *gurgeln,* or med. L *gurgulare* f. L *gurgulio* gullet]

gŭr'jun *n.* E. Ind. tree of genus *Dipterocarpus* yielding an oleo-resin (∼ **balsam**) used medicinally or as varnish. [f. Bengali *garjan*]

gŭrk *n.,* & *v.i.* & *t.* (colloq.) belch. [imit.]

Gur'kha (gĕrka, goor'-) *n.* member of dominant Hindu race in Nepal, forming regiments in British army. [native name, f. Skr. *gāus* cow + *raksh* protect]

gŭr'nard, gŭr'nĕt, *n.* sea-fish of family Triglidae, having large spiny head with mailed sides, and three finger-like pectoral rays. [ME, f. OF *gornart,* *gronart (*gron(d)ir* to grunt f. L *grunnire*)]

gu'ru (gŏo'rŏo) *n.* Hindu spiritual teacher or head of religious sect; influential teacher; revered mentor. [f. Hindi *gurū* teacher f. Skr. *gurús* grave, dignified]

gŭsh *v.i.* & *t.,* & *n.* **1.** (issue in, send forth) sudden or copious stream (lit., or fig. of speech, tenderness, etc.); emit (water) copiously; (speak or behave with) effusiveness or sentimental affectation. **2.** Hence ∼ᴇʀ¹ *n.,* (esp.) oil-well from which oil flows without being pumped, ∼ɪɴɢ², ∼'ʏ², *adjs.* [ME *gosshe, gusche,* prob. imit.]

gŭ'ssĕt *n.* piece let into garment etc. to strengthen or enlarge some part; iron bracket strengthening angle of structure; hence ∼ᴇᴅ² *a.* [ME, f. OF *gousset (gousse* pod, shell) flexible piece filling up joint in armour]

gŭ'ssȳ *v.t.* (sl.) smarten *up.* [perh. f. pet-form of man's Christian name *Augustus*; see -ʏ³]

gŭst¹ *n.,* & *v.i.* **1.** *n.* sudden violent rush of wind; burst of rain, fire, smoke, sound, or passion. **2.** *v.i.* blow in gusts. [f. ON *gust,* cogn. w. *gjósa* to gush]

gŭst² *n.* (arch. or poet.) sense of taste; keen relish (**have a** ∼ **of,** appreciate); flavour. [ME, f. L *gustus* taste]

gŭstā'tion *n.* tasting; so **gŭ'stᴀᴛɪᴠᴇ, gŭ'statᴏʀʏ,** *adjs.* [F, or f. L *gustatio (gustare* f. *gustus* taste; see -ᴀᴛɪᴏɴ)]

gŭ'stō *n.* (*pl.* ∼**es**). **1.** zest, enjoyment with which something is done. **2.** (arch.) relish or liking *for;* style of artistic execution. [It., f. as GUST¹]

gŭ'st|ȳ *a.* characterized by, blown by, gusts. **2.** characterized by gusto. **3.** Hence ∼ɪʟʏ² *adv.,* ∼ɪɴᴇss *n.* [f. GUST¹ + -ʏ²]

gŭt *n., a.,* & *v.t.* (-tt-). **1.** *n.* (in *pl.*) bowels or entrails (esp. of animals); contents of anything (**has no** ∼**s in it,** is of no real value or force; **hate** person's ∼**s,** (colloq.) dislike him intensely; **sweat** or **work** one's ∼**s out,** (colloq.) work extremely hard). **2.** (particular part of) lower alimentary canal, intestine; ∼-**rot,** (colloq.) = ʀᴏᴛ²-*gut.* **3.** (in *pl.,* vulg.) belly as seat of appetite. **4.** (in *pl.,* colloq.) pluck, force of character, staying power. **5.** material for violin or racket strings or surgical use made from intestines of animals; material for fishing-lines made from intestines of silkworm. **6.** narrow water-passage, sound, straits; defile, narrow passage. **7.** Hence ∼'ʟᴇss *a.,* (colloq.) lacking energy or determination. **8.** *a.* fundamental (*a gut issue*); instinctive (*a gut reaction*). **9.** *v.t.* take out guts of (fish); remove or destroy (esp. by fire) internal fittings of (house etc.); extract essence of (book etc.). [OE *guttas* pl., prob. cogn. w. *gēotan* pour]

gŭts *v.i.* (colloq.) eat greedily. [f. prec.]

gŭ'tser *n.* (Austral., NZ, & colloq.) heavy fall. [f. GUTS + -ᴇʀ¹]

gŭ'ts|ȳ *a.* (colloq.) **1.** greedy. **2.** courageous. **3.** Hence ∼ɪʟʏ² *adv.,* ∼ɪɴᴇss *n.* [f. GUTS + -ʏ²]

gŭtta-pĕr'cha (-cha, -ka) *n.* tough greyish-black plastic substance got from latex of various Malayan trees. [f. Malay *getah* gum + *percha* name of tree]

gŭ'ttāte *a.* (Biol.) having droplike markings. [f. L *guttatus* speckled (*gutta* drop; see -ᴀᴛᴇ²)]

gŭ'tter *n.* & *v.* **1.** *n.* track made by flow of water. **2.** shallow trough below eaves, or channel at side of street, carrying off rain-water; **the** ∼, place of low breeding or vulgar behaviour. **3.** open conduit for outflow of fluid; groove; hence ∼ɪɴɢ¹ (3) *n.* **4.** ∼ **press,** journalism catering for depraved or vulgar tastes; ∼**snipe,** street urchin. **5.** *v.t.* furrow, channel.

6. *v.i.* flow in streams; (of candle) melt away by becoming channelled so that wax etc. runs down. [ME f. AF *gotere*, OF *gotiere* f. Rom. **guttaria* f. L *gutta* drop; see -ER²]

gŭ'ttle *v.t.* & *i.* eat gluttonously. [f. GUT, after *guzzle*]

gŭ'ttural *a.* & *n.* **1.** *a.* of the throat; (of sound) coming from the throat. **2.** *n.* & *a.* (Phonet.) (consonant) produced in throat or by back of tongue and palate (as *k*, *g*). **3.** Hence ∼ISM (1) *n.*, ∼IZE (3) *v.t.*, ∼LY² *adv.* [F, or f. med. L *gutturalis*, f. L *guttur* throat; see -AL]

‖**gŭv,** ‖**gŭ'v'nor,** *ns.* (vulg. or colloq.) = GOVERNOR 2. [abbr.]

guy¹ (gī) *n.*, & *v.t.* **1.** *n.* rope, chain, etc., to steady load of crane etc. or hold tent etc. in place. **2.** *v.t.* secure with guy(s). [prob. of LG orig.; cf. LG, Du. *gei* brail etc.]

guy² (gī) *n.*, & *v.t.* **1.** *n.* ‖effigy of Guy Fawkes in ragged clothing, burnt on 5 Nov.; ‖grotesquely dressed person; (sl.) man, fellow; ‖(sl.) act of decamping (**give the** ∼ **to,** escape from; **do a** ∼, disappear). **2.** *v.t.* exhibit in effigy; ridicule. [f. *Guy* Fawkes, conspirator in GUNpowder Plot]

gŭ'zzle *v.* **1.** *v.i.* & *t.* drink or eat greedily. **2.** *v.t.* consume (money etc.; *away*) in guzzling. **3.** Hence **gŭ'zzlER¹** *n.* [perh. f. OF *gosiller* chatter, vomit (*gosier* throat)]

gwŷ'niad *n.* white-fleshed fish found in Lake Bala, Wales. [W (*gwyn* white)]

Gy *abbr.* GRAY¹.

gŷbe, ***jībe²,** *v.i.* & *t.,* & *n.* (Of fore-and-aft sail or boom) swing across, make (sail) do this, in wearing or running before wind; (of ship, crew, etc.) change (of) course so that this happens. [f. obs. Du. *gijben*]

gŷm *n.* (colloq.) gymnasium, gymnastics; ∼-**slip,** ∼'**tunic,** schoolgirl's sleeveless usu. belted garment reaching from shoulder to knee. [abbr.]

gŷmkha'na (-kah'-) *n.* (orig. Anglo-Ind.) public place with facilities for athletics; athletic-sports display; meeting for competition between horse--riders, vehicle-drivers, etc. [f. Hind. *gendkhāna* ball--house, racket-court, assim. to foll.]

gŷmnä'si¦um (-z-) *n.* (*pl.* ∼**ums** *or* ∼**a**). **1.** place, room, or building, with appliances for practice in gymnastics. **2.** (*or* gĭmnah'zĭoŏm). Continental, esp. German, school of highest grade, preparing pupils for universities; hence ∼AL *a.* [L, f. Gk *gumnasion* (*gumnazō* exercise f. *gumnos* naked)]

gŷ'mnäst *n.* expert in gymnastics. [f. F *gymnaste* or f. Gk *gumnastēs* athlete-trainer (*gumnazō*; see prec.)]

gŷmnä'st¦ic *a.* & *n.* **1.** *a.* of gymnastics, involving bodily or mental exercise, discipline, effort, or activity; hence ∼ICALLY *adv.* **2.** *n.* course of instruction regarded as discipline; gymnastic feat. **3.** Hence ∼ICS *n. pl.* (occas. treated as *sing.*), exercises developing the muscles (esp. such as are performed in gymnasium) or the mind. [f. L f. Gk *gumnastikos* (as GYMNASIUM; see -IC)]

gŷ'mno- *comb. form.* (Biol.) bare, as: ∼**sperm,** ∼**sper'mous,** (plant) having seeds unprotected by seed-vessels, opp. *angiosperm(ous)*. [f. Gk *gumnos* naked +-O-]

gŷmnŏ'soph¦ĭst *n.* one of ancient Hindu philosophic sect going nearly naked and given up to contemplation; so ∼Y¹ *n.* [ME, f. F *gymnosophiste* f. L f. Gk *gumnosophistai* pl. (as prec., SOPHIST)]

gymp. See GIMP¹.

gŷnaecē'um (j-, g-; -nēs-, -nīs-) *n.* **1.** (Gk & Rom. Ant.) women's apartments in house. **2.** (Bot.) = GYNOECIUM. [L, f. Gk *gunaikeion* (*gunē gunaikos* woman)]

gŷnaeco- (g-) *comb. form.* woman, women, as: **gynaecŏ'CRACY** (gīnī-) *n.*, ∼**ma'stia,** condition of man's breasts when they resemble woman's in size and function. [f. Gk *gunē gunaikos* woman +-O-]

gŷnaecŏ'¦logy (gīnī-) *n.* science of physiological functions and diseases of women; hence *∼LO'GIC, ∼LO'GICAL, (-*olŏ'*-) *adjs.*, ∼LOGIST *n.* [f. prec.+ -LOGY]

gŷnä'ndromôrph (g-) *n.* (Biol.) individual (esp. insect) having some parts male and others female;

hence ∼IC *a.*, ∼ISM (2) *n.*, (-ōr'-). [f. as foll.+ Gk *morphē* form]

gŷnä'ndrous (g-) *a.* (Bot.) with stamens and pistil united in one column as in orchids. [f. Gk *gunandrous* (*gunē* woman, *anēr andros* man) of doubtful sex +-OUS]

gŷ'no- (g-) *comb. form.* **1.** = GYNAECO- (*gyno'*CRACY, *gyno*PHO'BIA). **2.** (Bot.) of pistils or ovaries, as: ∼**base,** enlarged part of receptacle supporting gynoecium. [abbr. of GYNAECO-]

gŷnoe'ci¦um (gīnē'-) *n.* (*pl.* ∼**a**). (Bot.) carpels taken collectively. [orig. GYNAECEUM, infl. by Gk *oikion* house; cf. ANDROECIUM]

-gŷnous (g-, j-) *suf.* (Bot.) forming *adjs.* = having specified female organs or pistils (*monogynous, androgynous*). [f. mod. L f. Gk *-gunos* (*gunē* woman) +-OUS]

‖**gŷp¹** *n.* college servant at Cambridge and Durham (cf. SCOUT¹ 5). [perh. for obs. *gippo* scullion, orig. man's short tunic, f. obs. F *jupeau*]

gŷp² *n.* (colloq.) **give** person ∼, scold him or treat him unmercifully, pain him. [19th c., perh. f. GEE-UP]

gŷp³ *v.t.* (-**pp**-), & *n.* cheat, swindle. [19th c.; perh. f. GYP¹]

gŷ'ppÿ. Var. of GIPPY.

gŷpsŏ'phïla *n.* garden plant of genus *Gypsophila*, with profusion of small usu. white composite flowers. [mod. L, f. Gk *gupsos* chalk +*philos* loving]

gŷ'ps¦um *n.* hydrated calcium sulphate, mineral used to make plaster of Paris or as dressing for crop-land; hence ∼EOUS, ∼I'FEROUS, *adjs.* [L, f. Gk *gupsos*]

gŷ'psÿ, gĭ'psÿ, G-, *n.* **1.** member of a wandering people of Hindu origin with dark skin and hair, living often by basket-making, horse-dealing, fortune--telling, etc., and speaking a language related to Hindi; person resembling or living like a gypsy. **2.** ∼ **bonnet** (with large side flaps); ∼ **moth,** kind of tussock-moth very destructive to foliage; ∼ **rose,** scabious; ∼'s **warning,** cryptic or sinister warning; ∼ **table,** light round table on three crossed sticks. **3.** Hence ∼DOM, ∼HOOD, ∼ISM (2), *ns.*, ∼ISH¹ *a.*, ∼FY *v.t.* (usu. in *p.p.*). [earlier *gipcyan, gipsen*, f. EGYPTIAN, f. supposed orig. of gypsies when they appeared in England in early 16th c.]

gÿr'äte¹ *a.* (Bot.) arranged in rings or convolutions. [f. L *gyratus* (as GYRE; see -ATE²)]

gÿr¦ä'te² *v.i.* go in circle or spiral, revolve, whirl; hence or cogn. ∼A'TION *n.*, **gÿr'atORY** *a.* [f. LL *gyrare* (as foll.) +-ATE³]

gÿr'e *v.i.*, & *n.* (esp. poet.) gyrate; gyration. [(v. f. LL *gyrare*) f. L f. Gk *guros* ring]

gyr'falcon (jēr'faw-, -fō-) *n.* large northern falcon of subgenus *Hierofalco*. [ME, f. OF *gerfaucon* f. Frank. *gêrfalco* f. ON *geirfâlki*; see FALCON]

gÿr'ō *n.* (*pl.* ∼**s**). **1.** (colloq.) = GYROSCOPE or *gyro--compass*. **2.** ∼**-compass,** compass giving true north and bearings from it by means of gyroscope; ∼**-pilot,** gyro-compass used for automatic steering; ∼**-stabilizer,** gyroscopic device for keeping ship in equilibrium position. [abbr.]

gÿr'o- *comb. form.* rotation, as: ∼**graph,** instrument recording revolutions; ∼**magne'tic,** of the magnetic and mechanical properties of a rotating charged particle, (of compass) combining gyroscope and normal magnetic compass; ∼**plane,** form of aircraft deriving its lift mainly from freely rotating overhead vanes. [f. Gk *guros* ring +-O-]

gÿr'oscōpe *n.* rotating wheel whose axis is free to turn but maintains fixed direction in absence of perturbing forces, esp. as used for stabilization or to replace compass in ship etc.; hence **gÿroscŏ'pIC** *a.* [F (as prec., -SCOPE)]

gÿr'¦us *n.* (*pl.* ∼**i** *pr.* -ī). fold or convolution, esp. of brain. [L, *pl.* ∼*i*, f. Gk *guros* ring]

gŷ'ttja (yĭ'cha) *n.* (Geol.) lake deposit of usu. black sediment containing much organic material. [Sw., = mud, ooze]

gÿve *n.* (usu. in *pl.*), & *v.t.* (poet.) shackle, fetter. [ME *give*, of unkn. orig.]

H

H, h, (āch) *n.* (*pl.* **Hs** *or* **H's,** *pr.* ā′chĭz). eighth letter of alphabet; *drop* one's *h's* (see AITCH); **H-iron,** girder of H-shaped section.

H. *abbr.* hardness; hard (pencil-lead); henry(s).

h. *abbr.* hecto-; horse; hot; hour(s); husband.

H *symb.* hydrogen.

ha¹ (hah) *int.* expr. surprise, joy, suspicion, hesitation, triumph, etc.; cf. HA HA. [ME]

ha² (hah) *v.i.,* & *n.* (*pl.* **ha's**). See HUM¹,² [f. prec.]

ha. *abbr.* hectare(s).

haar (här) *n.* cold sea-fog on E. coast of England or Scotland. [perh. f. ON *hárr* hoar(y)]

Hab. *abbr.* Habakkuk (OT).

habaner′a (ahbanär′a) *n.* Cuban dance in slow duple time. [Sp., fem. of *habanero* of Havana in Cuba]

hābéas cŏr′pus *n.* writ requiring person to be brought before judge or into court, esp. to investigate lawfulness of his restraint; **Habeas Corpus Act** (of Charles II, 1679, facilitating use of this). [L, = you must have the body]

hă′berdăsh|er *n.* ||dealer in small articles of dress; *dealer in men's wear; hence ∼ERY (1, 3) *n.* [ME, prob. f. AF *haberdasser,* *hapertasser* (*hapertas* perh. name of fabric, of unkn. orig.)]

hă′bergeon (-jon) *n.* (Hist.) sleeveless coat of mail. [ME, f. OF *haubergeon* (as HAUBERK; see -OON)]

hă′bile *a.* (literary). skilful, dextrous. [ME, var. of ABLE]

habĭ′liment *n.* **1.** (in *pl.*) dress suited to any office or occasion (joc. of ordinary clothes). **2.** (arch.) equipment, attire. [ME, f. OF (*h*)*abillement* (*habiller* fit out f. *habile* ABLE; see -MENT)]

habĭ′lit|āte *v.i.* qualify for office (esp. as teacher in German univ.); hence ∼A′TION *n.* [f. med. L *habilitare* (as ABILITY) +-ATE³]

hă′bĭt¹ *n.* **1.** settled tendency or practice (*he is in, has (fallen into), the* or *a (bad) habit of contradiction*); *creature of* ∼, one whose behaviour is guided by his habits; **from (force of)** ∼, **out of** ∼, because it has been one's custom; **make a** ∼ **of,** do regularly; **get out of the** ∼ **of,** cease to do regularly. **2.** mental constitution, esp. *habit of mind;* bodily constitution (*a man of corpulent habit*); (Biol. & Cryst.) mode of growth. **3.** dress of particular class etc., esp. religious order; (**riding-**)∼, woman's riding-dress; (arch.) dress. **4.** (Psych.) automatic reaction to a specific situation. **5.** (colloq.) the practice of taking drugs as addict; hence ∼**-forming** *a.* [ME f. OF *abit,* f. L *habitus* (*habēre* habit- have, (refl.) be constituted)]

hă′bĭt² *v.t.* **1.** (usu. in *p.p.*) clothe. **2.** (arch.) inhabit. [f. OF *habiter* f. L *habitare* inhabit (as prec.)]

hă′bĭt|able *a.* that can be inhabited; hence ∼ABI′LITY, ∼able**NESS** (-beln-), *ns.,* ∼ABLY *adv.* [ME f. OF, f. L *habitabilis* (as prec.; see -ABLE)]

hă′bĭtant *n.* **1.** inhabitant. **2.** (*pr.* ăbētah′ń). (descendant of) early French settler in Canada etc. [F (as HABIT²; see -ANT)]

hă′bĭtăt *n.* natural home of plant or animal; habitation. [L, 3rd sing. pres. (as HABIT²)]

hăbĭtā′tion *n.* inhabiting (*fit for human habitation*); place of abode, house or home. [ME f. OF, f. L *habitatio -onis* (as HABIT²; see -ATION)]

habĭ′tūal *a.* customary; constant, continual; given to (specified) habit (*habitual drunkard*); hence ∼LY² *adv.,* ∼NESS *n.* [f. med. L *habitualis* (as HABIT¹; see -AL)]

habĭ′tū|āte *v.t.* accustom (*to* thing, *to* doing); so ∼A′TION *n.* [f. LL *habituare* (as HABIT¹) +-ATE³]

hă′bĭtūde *n.* mental or bodily disposition; custom, tendency. [ME f. OF, f. L *habitudo -dinis* (*habēre* habit-have; see -TUDE)]

habitué (habĭ′tūā) *n.* habitual visitor or resident (*of*). [F, p.p. of *habituer* (as HABITUATE)]

habutai′ (hahbōōtī′) *n.* soft Japanese silk fabric. [f. Jap. *habutae*]

||**HAC** *abbr.* Honourable Artillery Company.

hăchūr′es (-shūr′) *n. pl.* lines used in hill-shading on maps to indicate steepness of slope by their closeness. [F (*hacher* HATCH³; see -URE)]

hăcĭe′nda *n.* estate or plantation with dwelling-house, or factory, in Spanish-speaking country. [Sp., f. L *facienda* things to be done]

hăck¹ *n.* mattock; miner's pick; (gash, wound, esp. from) kick with toe of boot. [ME, partly f. MLG *hakke* (as foll.), partly f. foll.]

hăck² *v.* **1.** *v.t.* cut with rough blows, notch, mangle; kick shin of (opponent at football). **2.** *v.i.* deal cutting blows (*at*); **a** ∼**ing** (short dry frequent) **cough;** ∼**-saw** (for metal cutting). [OE *haccian* cut in pieces, = MLG, MDu., MHG *hacken* f. WG **hakkon* (**hak-,* imit.)]

hăck³ *n.* board on which hawk's meat is laid; (of eyas hawk) **at** ∼, not allowed to prey for itself. [var. of HATCH¹, perh. assoc. w. NECK¹]

hăck⁴ *n.* & *a.* **1.** *n.* horse let out for hire; = JADE¹ 1; horse for ordinary riding; common drudge, uninspired writer or other worker; *taxi. **2.** *a.* used as a hack; typical of a hack, commonplace. [abbr. of HACKNEY]

hăck⁵ *v.* **1.** *v.t.* make common, hackney. **2.** *v.t.* & *i.* ride (horse) as hack, ride on horseback on road at ordinary pace; ∼**ing coat** or **jacket** (with slits at sides or back and slanting pockets). [f. prec.]

****hă′ckberry** *n.* (purple edible berry of) N. Amer. tree of genus *Celtis.* [var. of *hagberry,* of Norse orig.]

hă′ckerў *n.* (Ind.) bullock-cart. [f. Hindi *chhakrā* two-wheeled cart]

hă′ckle¹ *n.,* & *v.t.* **1.** *n.* steel flax-comb. **2.** long feather(s) on neck or saddle of domestic cock and other birds; **with his** ∼**s rising** or **up,** (lit. of cock, fig. of dog, person) angry, ready to fight. **3.** artificial fly dressed with hackle. **4.** feather in Highland soldier's bonnet. **5.** *v.t.* dress (flax, fly) with hackle. [ME *hechele, hakele,* f. OE **hæcel* f. WG **hakila* (**hak* HOOK¹)]

hă′ckle² *v.t.* hack, mangle. [f. HACK² + -LE 3]

hă′cklў *a.* rough, jagged. [f. prec. + -Y²]

hă′ckmatăck *n.* Amer. larch; its wood. [Amer. Ind.]

hă′ckney *n.* & *v.t.* **1.** *n.* horse of middle size and quality for ordinary riding; ∼ **cab, carriage, coach,** (kept for hire). **2.** *v.t.* (esp. in *p.p.*) make common or trite by indiscriminate use. [ME, perh. f. pastures at *Hackenei* (Hackney) in London, whence horses may have been taken to Smithfield market]

had. See HAVE¹.

hă′ddock (*pl.* same), (esp. Sc.) **hă′ddĭe,** *n.* food-fish (*Melanogrammus aeglefinus*) of N. Atlantic, allied to cod but smaller. [ME, prob. f. AF *hadoc,* OF (*h*)*adot,* of unkn. orig.]

hāde *n.,* & *v.i.* (Geol. & Mining). incline from the vertical. [17th c., perh. dial. form of *head*]

Hā′dēs (-z) *n.* (Gk Myth.) lower world, abode of departed spirits; (euphem.) = HELL 2. [f. Gk *haidēs* (orig. a name of Pluto), transl. Heb. *ŝe′ôl*]

Hă′dĭth *n.* body of traditions relating to Muhammad. [f. Arab. *ḥadīṯ* tradition]

hădj, hăjj, *n.* pilgrimage to Mecca. [f. Arab. *ḥājj* pilgrimage]

hă′dji, hă′jji, *n.* Muslim who has been to Mecca as pilgrim; (*H*∼) title of such person. [f. Pers. & Turk. *ḥāj*(*j*)*ī* pilgrim (as prec.)]

hadn't. See HAVE¹.

hă′drŏn *n.* (Phys.) strongly interacting elementary particle; hence **hădrŏ′n**IC *a.* [f. Gk *hadros* bulky + -ON]

hădst. See HAVE¹.

haeccē′itў (heks-) *n.* (Philos.) quality of being describable as 'this'; individuality. [f. med. L *haecceitas* (*haec* fem. of *hic* this; see -ITY)]

haem, hēme, *n.* red compound containing iron and forming non-protein part of haemoglobin. [f. Gk *haima* blood or f. HAEMOGLOBIN]

hae′mal, *hē′mal, *a.* (Anat.) of the blood; situated on same side of body as the heart and great blood--vessels, ventral. [f. Gk *haima* blood + -AL]

haemä′tĭc, *hĕm-, *a.* (Med.) of or containing blood. [f. Gk *haimatikos* (as foll.; see -IC)]

hae′matĭn, *hĕ′m-, *n.* bluish-black amorphous substance, constituent of haemoglobin. [f. Gk *haima -matos* blood + -IN]

hae′matīte, *hĕ′m-, *n.* ferric oxide as ore. [f. L f. Gk *haimatitēs* (*lithos*) bloodlike stone (as prec.; see -ITE¹)]

hae′mato-, *hē′mato-, *comb. form.* blood, as: ∼cele, **h**(**a**)**emato′ma**, tumour containing extravasated blood; ∼crit [f. Gk *kritēs* judge], (instrument for determining) ratio of volume of red cells to total volume of blood sample; ∼logy (-ŏ′l-), study of physiology of blood; **h**(**a**)**ematur′ia**, (Path.) presence of blood in urine. [f. Gk *haimat-* (*haima* blood)]
-hae′mia. Var. of -AEMIA.

hae′mo-, *hē′mo-, *comb. form.* = HAEMATO-. [abbr.]

haemocў′anin, *hĕm-, *n.* oxygen-carrying substance containing copper, present in blood plasma of arthropods and molluscs. [f. prec. + *cyanin* blue pigment (as CYAN; see -IN)]

haemoglō′bin, *hĕm-, *n.* oxygen-carrying substance containing iron, present in red blood-cells of vertebrates. [f. *haematoglobulin*, compound of HAEMATIN and GLOBULIN]

haemŏ′lў|sĭs, *hĕm-, *n.* (*pl.* ∼ses *pr.* -sēz). loss of haemoglobin from red blood-cells; so ∼tIC (-ĭ′tĭk) *a.* [f. HAEMO- + -LYSIS]

haemophī′l|ia, *hĕm-, *n.* (Med.) (hereditary) tendency to prolonged bleeding from even a slight injury, through failure of blood to clot normally; hence ∼IAC *n.*, sufferer from haemophilia, ∼IC *a.* [mod. L, f. as HAEMO- + -PHILIA]

hae′morrhage, *hĕ′m-, *n.* (hĕ′merĭj) *n.*, & *v.i.* (undergo) escape (esp. profuse) of blood from blood-vessels, bleed(ing). [earlier *haemorrhagy* f. F *hémorr*(*h*)*agie* f. L f. Gk *haimorrhagia* (*haima* blood, st. of *rhēgnumi* burst)]

hae′morrhoid, *hĕ′m-, *n.* (hĕ′meroid) *n.* (usu. in *pl.*) swollen venous tissue near anus. [ME *emeroudis* (Bibl. *emerods*) f. OF *emeroyde*, & f. L f. Gk *haimorrhoides* (*phlebes*) bleeding (veins) (*haima* blood, *-rhoos* -flowing)]

haemŏ′sta|sĭs, *hĕm-, *n.* (*pl.* ∼ses *pr.* -sēz). stoppage of flow of blood; so ∼tIC (hĕmŏstă′tĭk) *a.* [f. HAEMO- + -STASIS]

haer′emai (hīr′ĭmī) *int.* (NZ) welcome. [Maori, lit. 'come hither']

ha′fĭz (hah′-) *n.* Muslim who knows Koran by heart. [Pers., f. Arab. *ḥāfiz* guardian]

hă′fnium *n.* (Chem.) metallic element resembling and usu. accompanying zirconium. [mod. L, f. *Hafnia*, Da. (*København*)*havn*, Copenhagen + -IUM]

haft (hah-) *n.*, & *v.t.* **1.** *n.* handle (of dagger, knife, etc.). **2.** *v.t.* furnish (knife etc.) with haft. [OE *hæft*(*e*), = OHG *hefti*, ON *hepti* f. Gmc *haftjam* (*haf-HEAVE¹*)]

hăg¹ *n.* ugly old woman; witch; ∼('fish), parasite fish allied to lamprey; ∼′ridden, afflicted by nightmare, mentally harassed; hence ∼′gIsH¹ (-g-) *a.* [ME *hegge*, *hagge*, perh. f. OE *hægtesse*, OHG *hagazissa* f. unkn. orig.]

hăg² *n.* (Sc. & N. Engl.) soft place in moor; firm place in bog. [cf. ON *högg* gap, cogn. w. HEW]

Hag. *abbr.* Haggai (OT).

Hagga′dah (-gah′da) *n.* legendary illustrative part of the Talmud; book recited at Seder. [Heb., = tale (*higgīd* tell)]

hă′ggard *a.* & *n.* **1.** *a.* wild-looking (esp. as result of fatigue, privation, worry, etc.). **2.** (of hawk) caught when in the adult plumage, untamed. **3.** Hence ∼LY² *adv.*, ∼NESS *n.* **4.** *n.* haggard hawk. [f. F *hagard*, perh. cogn. w. HEDGE¹]

‖**hă′ggis** (-g-) *n.* minced heart, lungs, and liver, of sheep etc., boiled in maw or artificial bag with suet, oatmeal, etc. [ME; orig. unkn.]

hă′ggle *v.i.*, & *n.* dispute, wrangle, (*about* or *over* price etc.). [earlier sense 'hack' f. ON *höggva* HEW + -LE 3]

hă′gio- (-g-) *comb. form.* saint(ly), as: ∼cracy (-ŏ′k-), government by holy persons; H∼grapha (-ŏ′g-), 12 books of the Hebrew Scriptures not included under Law and Prophets; ∼grapher (-ŏ′g-), ∼gra′phic, (writer) of any of these, or of saints' lives; ∼graphy (-ŏ′g-), writing of saints' lives; ∼latry (-ŏ′l-), worship of saints; ∼logy (-ŏ′l-), literature treating of lives and legends of saints; ∼scope, = SQUINT 4. [f. Gk *hagios* holy + -o-]

hah. Var. of HA¹,².

ha ha (hah hah′) *int.* repr. laughter. [OE; cf. HA¹]

ha-ha (hah′hah) *n.* sunk fence bounding park or garden. [F, perh. from cry of surprise at discovering the obstacle]

hai(**c**)**k** (hāk, hah′īk) *n.* Arab's outer wrapper for head and body. [f. Moroccan Arab. *ḥā′ik*]

hai′ku (hī′kōō) *n.* (*pl.* same). (English imitation of) Japanese three-part poem of usu. 17 syllables. [Jap.]

hail¹ *n.* pellets of frozen rain falling in shower or ∼′-storm; shower *of* missiles, curses, questions, etc.; ∼′-stone, pellet of hail; hence ∼′Y² *a.* [OE *hagol*, *hægl*, = OS, OHG *hagal*, ON *hagl* f. Gmc *hag*(*a*)*laz*, *-am*]

hail² *v.* **1.** *v.i. impers.* it ∼s or is ∼ing, hail falls. **2.** *v.t.* & *i.* (fig.) pour down (blows, words, etc.), come down violently. [OE *hagalian* (as prec.)]

hail³ *int.* of greeting (*to*); ALL hail; ∼-fellow, ∼-fellow-well-met, (too) intimate *with* (person); H∼ Mary, = AVE *Maria*. [ellipt. use of obs. hail a. f. ON *heill* sound, HALE¹, WHOLE]

hail⁴ *v.* & *n.* **1.** *v.t.* salute; greet (person etc. (*as*) king etc.; **hail him king**. **2.** call to (ship, person) to attract attention (**within ∼ing distance**, close enough to do this, lit. or fig.); signal to (bus, taxi) to stop and take one as passenger; LOUD *hailer*. **3.** *v.i.* (Of ship, person) have come originally *from* (place). **4.** *n.* salutation (**within ∼**, close enough to be hailed). [ME, f. prec.]

hair *n.* **1.** one of the fine filaments growing from skin of animals, esp. from human head; (collect. *sing.* or arch. *pl.*) all such filaments on person's head etc.; mass of hairs used in manufacture etc.; elongated cell growing from epidermis of plant; hairlike thing; very small quantity. **2. against the ∼**, (fig.) against the grain; *hair of the* DOG¹ *that bit* one; ∼ **on end** (standing erect with fear or horror); **in** person's ∼, (colloq.) encumbering or annoying him; **keep** one's ∼ **on**, (sl.) remain calm; **let** one's ∼ **down**, (of woman) release it from chignon etc., (fig., colloq.) cease to be formal, behave unconventionally or unrestrainedly; *make* person's *hair* CURL²; **not turn a ∼**, show no sign of exhaustion or discomposure; **put up** one's ∼, (of woman) arrange it in dressed state, not loose or in ringlets etc.; *get* or *have by the* SHORT *hairs*; SPLIT¹ *hairs*; TEAR¹ one's *hair*; **to a ∼**, exactly. **3.** ∼′breadth or ∼′s **breadth**, minute distance (∼*breadth escape*, very narrow); ∼′brush [for smoothing the hair); ∼′cloth (made of hair, for various purposes); ∼ **crack**, short narrow crack in metal; ∼′cut, (style of) cutting of the hair; ∼-do, (colloq.) style or process of woman's hairdressing; ∼′dresser, one whose business is to dress and cut (*women's*) hair; ∼-grass (of genus *Aira* etc., with slender stems); ‖∼-grip, flat hairpin with ends close together; ∼-line, (1) line or rope made of hair, (2) thin up-stroke in writing, thin stroke in printed letter, (3) edge of person's hair on forehead etc., (4) very narrow line, crack, stripe, etc.; ∼-piece, quantity of false hair augmenting person's natural hair; ∼'**pin** (U-shaped, for fastening the hair; ∼*pin bend*, very sharp doubling-back of road); ∼**-raising,** enough to make hair stand on end through fear or horror or excitement; ∼**-restorer,** substance used to promote growth of hair; ∼ **shirt** (of haircloth, for penitents or ascetics); ||∼**-slide,** (usu. ornamental) clip for keeping hair in position; ∼**-space,** (Typogr.) very thin space between words or letters; ∼**-splitting** *a.* & *n.,* over-subtle(ty); ∼'**spring,** fine spring regulating balance-wheel in watch; ∼**-streak,** butterfly of genus *Strymon* etc. with fine streaks on wings; ∼**-stroke,** thin up-stroke in writing; ∼**-style,** particular way of dressing the hair; ∼**-stylist,** one who chooses (and constructs) hair-styles for individual persons; ∼**-trigger,** secondary trigger releasing main one by slight pressure. **4.** Hence (-)∼ED² (hārd), ∼'LESS, ∼'LIKE, *adjs.* [OE *hǣr, hěr,* = OS, OHG *hār,* ON *hár* f. Gmc **hǣram*]

hair'|ў *a.* having much hair; made of hair; (sl.) difficult, unpleasant, crude, clumsy; ∼**y-heeled,** (sl.) uncouth, ill-bred; hence ∼iNESS *n.* [ME, f. prec. + -y²]

hă'jj(ĭ). See HADJ(I).

hāke¹ *n.* edible fish of genus *Merluccius* like cod. [ME, perh. f. **hakefish* f. dial. *hake* hook + FISH¹]

hāke² *n.* wooden frame for drying cheeses, bricks, etc. [cogn. w. or var. of HECK¹]

hakenkreuz (hah'ken-kroits) *n.* swastika, esp. as Nazi symbol. [G (*haken* hook, *kreuz* CROSS¹)]

hakīm'¹ (-ē'm) *n.* (In India and Muslim countries) physician. [f. Arab. *ḥakīm* wise man, physician]

ha'kīm² (hah'-) *n.* (In India and Muslim countries) judge, ruler, governor. [f. Arab. *ḥākim* governor]

Hă'kka *n.* & *a.* (people or dialect) of SE China, esp. Canton. [Cantonese]

Hala'chah (-ah'ʜ̣α) *n.* body of Jewish law in Mishnah. [f. Aram. *hᵃlākāh* law]

hal(l)al (hahlah'l) *v.t.,* & *n.* **1.** *v.t.* kill (meat) as prescribed by Muslim law. **2.** *n.* meat thus prepared. [f. Arab. *ḥalāl* lawful]

hala'tion *n.* (Photog.) spreading of light beyond its proper boundary in a developed image, caused by internal reflection in the support of the emulsion. [irreg. f. HALO + -ATION]

hă'lberd, -rt, *n.* (Hist.) combined spear and battle-axe. [ME, f. F *halleharde* f. It *alabarda* f. MHG *helmbarde* (*helm* handle, *barde* hatchet)]

hălberdier' *n.* man armed with halberd. [f. F *hallebardier* (as prec.; see -IER)]

hă'lcyon *n.* & *a.* **1.** *n.* bird said by the ancients to breed in floating nest on sea at winter solstice, and to charm wind and waves into calm for the purpose; (Zool.) Australasian kingfisher. **2.** *a.* calm, peaceful, esp. ∼ **days** (orig. 14 days about winter solstice); (of period) happy, prosperous. [ME, f. L (*h*)*alcyon* f. Gk (*h*)*alkuōn* kingfisher]

hāle¹ *a.* (Esp. of old person) robust, vigorous, (*hale and hearty*); hence ∼'NESS (-ln-) *n.* [north. repr. of OE *hāl* WHOLE]

hāle² *v.t.* drag or draw forcibly (lit. or fig.). [ME, f. OF *haler* f. ON *hala* = OS *halon,* OHG *halōn*]

half (hahf) *n.* (*pl.* **halves** *pr.* hahvz), *a.,* & *adv.* **1.** *n.* one of two equal or corresponding parts or groups into which a thing is or might be divided (*half of 10 is 5*; *cut it in half* or *into halves*; *your half is bigger than mine*; *two hours and a half* (*hour*) or *two and a half hours*; *half of it is, half of them are, rotten*; see also sense 2); (colloq.) = *half-back, half-pint*; one of two equal periods constituting football etc. match; ||school term (the school year being formerly divided into two portions); (Golf) halved hole; half-price ticket. **2. and a** ∼, (fig., colloq.) of unusual excellence etc. (*that was a game and a half*); BETTER¹ *half*; **by halves,** imperfectly or incompletely (*never does things by halves*); **too** clever etc. **by** ∼ (far more than would be satisfactory; **cry halves,** claim equal share; **go halves, go** ∼ **and** ∼, share equally (*with* person *in* thing); **how the other** ∼ **lives,** other people's mode of life; **the** ∼ **of it, the**

more important part (usu. w. neg.). **3.** *a.* forming a half (*a half length*; *a half share*); of amount or quantity equal to a half (*half the men*; *half your time*; *stays at home half the time*; *half the batch is rotten*; *half a pint*); used in half-binding (*half calf* etc.); *half the* BATTLE¹; **a** ∼**-dozen,** ∼ **a dozen,** six; *half an* EYE¹; ∼**-inch, -pint,** etc., (unit half as large); *half a* LOAF¹; *half a* MIND¹. **4.** *adv.* to the extent of half, (loosely) to a considerable extent, (*it is only half cooked*; *a half-cooked potato*; *half-buried*; *half dead*; *I half wish*; *am half inclined to agree*); **not** ∼, not nearly (*not half long enough*), (colloq.) not at all (*not half bad*; *not half a bad fellow*), (sl.) to the greatest possible extent (*he didn't half get angry*). **5.** by the amount of half (an hour etc.); ∼ **after** or **past two,** thirty minutes after two o'clock; **east** ∼**-south,** half a point south of east. **6.** ∼**-and-**∼, (what is) half one thing and half another, esp. (arch.) mixture of ale and porter; *half as much* or *many* AGAIN; ∼**-arse(d),** (sl.) incompetent, inadequate; ∼**-back,** (Footb. & Hockey) (position of) player immediately behind forwards, (Amer. Footb.) flank back; ∼**-baked,** (fig.) not thorough(ly planned), not earnest, half-witted; ∼**-ball,** (Bill. etc.) with moving ball directed at edge of object-ball; ∼**-beak,** fish with lower jaw projecting beyond upper; ∼**-binding** (of book, with leather back and corners, cloth or paper sides); ∼**-blood,** (1) person having one parent in common with another, (2) this relationship, (3) person of mixed race; ∼**-blooded,** born from parents of different races; ||∼**-blue,** (holder of) award (see BLUE²) made to second string or to representative in minor sports; ∼**-boot** (reaching up to the calf); ∼**-breed,** half-blooded person; *half*-BROTHER; ∼**-butt,** (Bill.) cue of length between ordinary cue and long butt; ∼**-caste** *a.* & *n.,* (that is a) half-breed, esp. (child) of European father and Indian mother; *half* COCK² 4; ***∼**-co'cked,** = *at half cock*; ||∼**-crow'n,** ||∼ **a crown,** (Hist.) coin or amount of 2s. 6d.; ∼**-deck,** (esp.) quarters of cadets and apprentices on merchant vessel; ∼**-hardy,** (plant) able to grow in the open air at all times except in severe frost; ∼**-hearted,** lacking enthusiasm; *half* HITCH²; ∼ **holiday,** day of which (usu. the latter) half is taken as holiday; *half*-HOSE; ∼**-hour,** thirty minutes, point of time 30 minutes after any hour o'clock; ∼**-hourly,** at intervals of thirty minutes; *half*-HUNTER; ∼**-inch,** (sl.) steal [rhyming sl. for *pinch*]; ∼**-integral,** equal to half an odd integer; ∼**-landing** (half-way up flight of stairs); *half*-LAP³; ∼**-length,** portrait of upper half of person; ∼**-life,** (Phys.) time during which radioactivity or other property of substance falls to half of its original value; ∼ **light,** dim imperfect light; **at** ∼**-ma'st,** ∼**-mast high,** (of flag) lowered to half height of mast as mark of respect for the dead; ∼ **measures,** compromise, policy etc. lacking thoroughness; ∼**-miler,** runner whose distance is half a mile; ∼ **moon,** moon when only half disc is illuminated, time when this occurs, semicircular object; ∼ **mourning,** black relieved by grey etc.; ∼**(-)nelson,** a hold in wrestling with arm under opponent's arm and behind his back (*get a* ∼ *nelson on,* hold in a crippling position, gain complete mastery over); ***∼**-note,** (Mus.) minim; ∼ **pay,** reduced allowance to army etc. officer when retired or not in actual service; ∼**-plate,** photographic plate 16·5 by 10·8 cm, photograph reproduced from it; ∼**-price,** reduced price (of admission etc.); ∼**-seas-over,** (sl.) half drunken; ∼**-shell** (of oyster, esp. for serving food on); ∼ **shot,** (Golf) shot played with about half full swing; *half*-SISTER; ∼**-sole,** sole of boot or shoe from shank to toe; ||∼**-so'vereign,** (Hist.) British gold coin worth ten shillings; ***∼**-staff,** = *half-mast*; ***∼**-step,** (Mus.) semitone; ||∼**-ter'm,** period about half-way through school term, esp. as occasion of short holiday; ∼**-timbered,** having walls with timber frame and brick or plaster filling; ∼**-ti'me,** time at which half of a game or contest is completed, interval then occurring; ∼**-title,** (1) title or short title of a book, printed on recto of leaf preceding the title-leaf or at head of first page, (2) title of section of a book printed on recto of leaf preceding it; ∼-**tone**, illustration printed from a block (produced by photographic means) in which lights and shades of original are represented by small and large dots, *(Mus.) semitone; ∼-**track,** (vehicle having) propulsion system with wheels at front and endless driven belt at back; ∼-**truth,** statement that (esp. deliberately) conveys only part of the truth; *half*-VOLLEY; ∼-**way,** *a.* & *adv.*, at point equidistant between two others (MEET² person *half-way*), to the extent of half; ∼-*way house,* inn midway between two towns etc., (fig.) compromise; ∼-*way line* (midway between football goals); ∼-**wit**(**ted**), stupid or foolish (person); ∼-**year'ly,** at intervals of six months. [OE *h(e)alf,* = OS *half, halbha,* OHG *halb(a),* ON *hálfr, hálfa,* Goth. *halbs, halba,* f. Gmc **halbhaz*; orig. = 'side']

hā'lfpennȳ (hā'pnĭ) *n.* (*pl.* usu. **halfpennies** *pr.* hā'pnĭz for separate coins, **halfpence** *pr.* hā'pens for sum of money). British bronze coin worth half a penny; **three halfpence,** a penny and a halfpenny; ∼**worth** (usu. *pr.* hā'perth), **hā'p'orth,** as much as can be bought for a halfpenny, a very small amount. [ME, f. HALF + PENNY]

hā'libut *n.* (*pl.* same). large flat-fish (*Hippoglossus vulgaris*) used for food. [ME, f. *haly* HOLY + BUTT² flat- -fish, perh. because eaten on holy days]

hā'lide *n.* (Chem.) binary compound of a HALOGEN. [f. HALOGEN + -IDE]

hā'lidom *n.* (arch.) holy thing, esp. (as oath) **by my** ∼. [OE *hāligdom* (as HOLY, -DOM)]

hālieu'tic *a.* & *n.* 1. *a.* of fishing. 2. *n.* (in *pl.,* usu. treated as *sing.*). art of fishing. [f. L f. Gk *halieutikos* (*halieutēs* fisherman; see -IC)]

hāliō'tis *n.* gastropod of genus *Haliotis,* with ear- -shaped shell lined with mother-of-pearl. [f. Gk *hals hali-* sea + *ous ōt-* ear]

hā'līte *n.* rock-salt. [f. mod. L *halites* f. Gk *hals* salt; see -ITE¹]

hālitō's|is *n.* (*pl.* ∼es *pr.* -ēz). (Med.) foul breath. [mod. L, f. L *halitus* breath + -OSIS]

hall (hawl) *n.* 1. large public room in palace etc.; principal living-room of medieval house; SERVANTS' *hall.* 2. mansion, large residence esp. of landed proprietor; university building set apart for residence or instruction of students, (in Engl. colleges etc.) common dining-room, dinner in this; building of guild (*Fishmongers' Hall*). 3. large room or building for public gathering; (in *pl.*) music-halls. 4. entrance- -passage or -room of house; *corridor or passage in a building. 5. LIBERTY *Hall;* *H∼ of Fame,* building with memorials of celebrated persons; ∼'**mark,** (*n.*) mark used at Goldsmiths' Hall (and by UK assay offices) for marking standard of gold, silver, and platinum, (fig.) distinctive feature esp. of excellence, (*v.t.*) stamp with this; ||∼ **porter** (esp. carrying luggage etc. in hotel); ∼-**stand** (in hall of house, with mirror, hat-pegs, etc.); ∼'**way,** entrance-hall or corridor. [OE *h(e)all,* = OS, OHG *halla,* ON *höll* f. Gmc **hallō* (**hal-* cover, cogn. W. HELL)]

hallal. See HALAL.

hallelujah. See ALLELUIA.

halliard. See HALYARD.

hallo' *int., n.* (*pl.* ∼s), & *v.i.* 1. *int.* calling attention or || = HELLO. 2. *n.,* & *v.i.* (the) cry 'hallo'. [var. of earlier HOLLO]

halloo'¹ *int.* & *n.* 1. *int.* inciting dogs to the chase, calling attention, or expr. surprise. 2. *n.* the cry 'halloo'; VIEW *halloo.* [as foll.]

halloo'² *v.i.* & *t.* cry 'halloo!', esp. to dogs; urge on (dogs etc.) with shouts; shout to attract attention (*don't halloo till you are out of the* WOOD). [perh. f. *hallow* pursue with shouts f. OF *halloer* (imit.)]

hā'llow¹ (-ō) *n.* 1. (arch.) holy person, saint. 2. All H∼s, H∼mas, = ALL *Saints' Day;* H∼e'en, (esp. Sc. & US) eve of this. [OE *hālga,* form of *hālig* HOLY]

hā'llow² (-ō) *v.t.* make holy; honour as holy. [OE *hālgian,* = OS *hēlagon,* OHG *heilagōn,* ON *helga* f. Gmc (**hailag-* HOLY)]

Ha'llstatt (hah'lshtaht) *a.* relating to the civilization of a phase of the early Iron Age. [∼ in Upper Austria, where remains of this period were discovered]

hallu'cin|āte (-lōō'-) *v.t.* produce illusions in the mind of (person); hence ∼ANT *a.* & *n.* [f. L (*h*)*al(l)ucinari* wander in mind f. Gk *alussō* be uneasy, + -ATE³]

hallucinā'tion (-lōō-) *n.* illusion; apparent percep- tion of external object not actually present; so **hallu'cinatory** (-lōō'-) *a.* [f. L *hallucinatio* (as prec.; see -ATION)]

hallu'cinogēn (-lōō'-) *n.* drug causing hallucinations; hence ∼IC (-ĕ'n-) *a.* [f. prec. + -o- + -GEN]

hā'll|ux *n.* (*pl.* ∼**uces** *pr.* -ūsēz). big toe; innermost digit of hind foot. [mod. L, f. L *allex*]

halm. See HAULM.

hā'lma *n.* game played by two or four persons on board of 256 squares, with men moved by leaping over other men into vacant squares beyond, from one corner to the opposite corner. [Gk, = leap]

hā'lō *n.* (*pl.* ∼es), & *v.t.* 1. *n.* circle of white or coloured light round luminous body, esp. sun or moon; circle, ring; disc of light shown surrounding head of sacred person; (fig.) glory around idealized person etc.; ∼**hat,** woman's hat worn at back of head with brim framing face. 2. *v.t.* surround with halo. [med. L, f. L f. Gk *halōs* threshing-floor, disc of sun or moon]

hā'logen *n.* (Chem.) any of the group of non-metallic elements fluorine, chlorine, bromine, iodine, and astatine, which form halides (e.g. sodium chloride or common salt) by simple union with a metal etc.; hence ∼A'TION *n.,* introduction of halogen atom into molecule. [f. Gk *hals halos* salt + -o- + -GEN]

halt¹ (hawlt, hŏlt) *n.* & *v.* 1. *n.* temporary stoppage on march or journey; interruption of progress (*call a halt to; come, grind, to a halt*); ||railway stopping-place used for local services only and without regular station buildings etc. 2. *v.i.* make a halt. 3. *v.t.* cause (troops etc.) to halt. [orig. in phr. *make halt* f. G *halt machen* (*halt* hold)]

halt² (hawlt, hŏlt) *a.* (arch.) lame; crippled. [OE *h(e)alt,* = OS *halt,* OHG *halz,* ON *haltr,* Goth. *halts* f. Gmc **haltaz*]

halt³ (hawlt, hŏlt) *v.i.* walk hesitatingly; hesitate (*halt between two opinions*); (of argument, verse, etc., esp. in part.) lack smooth progress; (arch.) be lame. [OE *healtian* (as prec.)]

ha'lter (hawl'-, hŏ'l-) *n.,* & *v.t.* 1. *n.* rope, strap, with noose or headstall for horses or cattle; rope with noose for hanging a person; death by hanging; (woman's dress-top held by) strap round back of neck leaving shoulders bare; ∼-**break** *v.t.,* accustom (horse) to halter. 2. *v.t.* fasten (*up*) with halter; hang (person) with halter. [OE *hælftre,* = OLG *heliftra,* WG **halftra-* f. root **halbh-*; cf. HELVE]

hä'ltēr'ēs (-z) *n. pl.* balancing-organs of dipterous insects. [Gk, = weights used to aid leaping (*hallomai* to leap)]

halva(h) (hahlvah') *n.* sweetmeat of sesame flour and honey. [Yiddish, f. Turk. *helva* f. Arab. *ḥalwa*]

halve (hahv) *v.t.* divide into halves; share equally; reduce to half; (Golf) play (hole) in same number of strokes as other player, win same number of holes in (match); fit (crossing timbers) together by cutting out half thickness of each. [ME *halfen,* f. HALF 1]

halves. See HALF.

hā'lyard, hā'liard, hau'lyard, *n.* (Naut.) rope or tackle for raising or lowering sail, yard, etc. [ME *halier* f. HALE² + -IER, assoc. W. YARD¹]

hăm¹ *n.* 1. back of thigh, thigh and buttock; (arch.) bend of the knee. 2. thigh of pig salted and dried in smoke or otherwise for food; meat from this. 3. (sl.) amateur (**radio** ∼, operator of an amateur radio station), inexpert performer, inexperienced or in- effective acting or actor, one who rants and overacts; ∼-**fisted, -handed,** (sl.) heavy-handed, clumsy.

[OE *ham, hom,* = OHG *ham(m)a,* ON *höm* f. Gmc **ham(m)-* be crooked]

hăm² *v.i.* & *t.* (-**mm**-). (sl.) overact. [f. prec.]

hămadrȳ'ăd *n.* **1.** (Gk & Rom. Myth.) nymph living and dying with the tree she inhabited. **2.** king cobra; large Arabian baboon, held sacred in ancient Egypt. [ME f. L, f. Gk *hamadruas (hama* with, *drus* tree)]

hămamē'lis *n.* shrub of genus *Hamamelis,* e.g. wych-hazel. [mod. L, f. Gk *hamamēlis* medlar]

Hă'mbŭrg *n.* ‖small variety of domestic fowl; ∼ **parsley,** variety of parsley with edible parsnip-like root. [∼ in N. Germany]

hă'mbŭrger (-*ger*) *n.* **1.** (*II*∼). native or inhabitant of Hamburg. **2.** cake of minced beef usu. fried and eaten with onions, often in soft bread roll. [G (*Hamburg* in N. Germany; see -ER¹)]

hămes (-mz) *n. pl.* two curved pieces of iron or wood forming (part of) collar of draught-horse, to which traces are attached. [ME, f. MDu. *hame*]

Hă'mīte *n.* (supposed) descendant of Ham, second son of Noah (Gen. 10:6 ff.); member of Egyptian or other N. African people; hence **Hami'tic** *a.,* (esp.) of group of African languages incl. ancient Egyptian, Berber, and Cushitic. [f. *Ham* + -ITE¹]

hă'mlet *n.* small village, esp. one without church. [ME, f. AF *hamelet(t)e,* OF *hamelet* dim. of *hamel* dim. of *ham* f. MLG *hamm;* see -LE 2, -ET¹]

hammam (hă'măm, hŭmah'm, hŭ'mŭm) *n.* Turkish bath(s). [f. Arab. *ḥammām* bath]

hă'mmer¹ *n.* **1.** instrument for beating, breaking, driving nails, etc., with hard solid (usu. steel) head at right angles to handle; machine with metal block serving same purpose; similar contrivance, as for exploding charge in gun (whence ∼LESS *a.*), striking string of piano, etc.; (Anat.) a bone of the ear, the malleus; auctioneer's mallet indicating by rap that article is sold (**come under the** ∼, be sold by auction); metal ball of about 7 kg., attached to wire in athletic contest of **throwing the** ∼; ∼ **and sickle,** symbols of industrial worker and peasant, esp. as emblem on national flag of USSR, or as repr. international communism; ∼ **and tongs,** with great energy (and noise). **2.** ∼**-beam** (projecting from wall at foot of principal rafter); ∼**-blow,** stroke (as) with hammer; ∼ **cloth** (covering driver's seat in coach, orig. unexpl.); ∼**-head,** (1) head of hammer, (2) shark with lateral extensions of head bearing the eyes, (3) Afr. bird with thick bill and occipital crest, (4) *stupid person; ∼**-lock,** hold in which wrestler's arm is bent behind his back; ∼**man,** ∼**-smith,** smith who works with hammer; ∼**-toe** (permanently bent downwards). [OE *hamor, hamer,* = OS *hamur,* OHG *hamar,* ON *hamarr* hammer, back of axe, crag]

hă'mmer² *v.* **1.** *v.t.* strike, beat, drive, (as) with hammer (*hammer home the nail,* one's *advantage; hammer idea into* person's *head*); (colloq.) inflict heavy defeat(s) on in war or games; ∼ **out,** (fig.) devise laboriously, work hard at. **2.** (St. Exch.) declare (person or firm) a defaulter with three taps of hammer on rostrum. **3.** *v.i.* beat (as) with hammer, (fig.) work hard, (*at*). [ME, f. prec.]

hă'mmock *n.* hanging bed of canvas or netting suspended by cords at ends, used esp. on board ship. [earlier *hamaca* f. Sp., of Carib orig.]

Hă'mmond *n.* ∼ **organ,** (Mus.) type of electronic organ. [f. ∼ Electric Co. of Chicago]

hă'mmy *a.* **1.** containing or resembling ham. **2.** (sl.) of or like ham actors. [f. HAM¹ + -Y²]

hă'mper¹ *n.* basketwork packing-case; consignment of eatables, wines, etc., however packed (usu. as a present: *Christmas hamper*). [ME, f. obs. *hanaper,* AF f. OF *hanapier* case for goblet (*hanap* f. Frank. **hnap*)]

hă'mper² *v.t.,* & *n.* **1.** *v.t.* obstruct movement of (person etc.) with material obstacles, (fig.) impede, hinder. **2.** *n.* (Naut.) necessary but cumbersome part of equipment of vessel (TOP¹-*hamper*). [ME, of unkn. orig.]

hă'mster *n.* ratlike hibernating rodent of genus *Cricetus* etc., with short tail, and cheek-pouches for carrying grain to its winter store; **golden** ∼, usu. tawny species (*Mesocricetus auratus*) like large mouse, much kept as pet or laboratory animal. [G, f. OHG *hamustro* corn-weevil]

hă'mstring *n.,* & *v.t.* (**ha'mstrung** *or* ∼**ed**). **1.** (in man) one of five tendons at back of knee; (in quadruped) great tendon at back of hock. **2.** *v.t.* cripple (person, animal) by cutting the hamstrings; (fig.) destroy activity or efficiency of. [f. HAM¹ + STRING]

hă'mŭl|us *n.* (*pl.* ∼**i** *pr.* -ī). (Anat., Zool., & Bot.) hooklike process. [L, dim. of *hamus* hook]

hănd¹ *n.* **1.** terminal part of human arm beyond wrist; similar member of all four limbs of monkey; forefoot of quadruped; forehock of pork. **2.** authority, custody, disposal, (*child is in good hands*); agency (*by the hands of; pass through many hands; the hand of God*); share in action (*have a hand in it*; **bear, give, lend, take, a** ∼, take part in action). **3.** pledge of marriage (*ask for or seek woman's hand; give* one's *hand to*). **4.** manual worker in factory, farm, etc. **5.** person who does something (*a picture by the same hand*; **all** ∼**s,** the whole crew; **a good** ∼, person skilful *at;* OLD *hand*); person or source from which thing comes (FIRST, SECOND, etc., *hand*). **6.** skill (*a hand for pastry*); style of workmanship; TRY one's *hand.* **7.** style of handwriting (*a legible hand*); signature (*witness the hand of A.B.*). **8.** handlike thing, esp. pointer of clock or watch; *hand of* BANANAS. **9.** RIGHT¹ or LEFT¹ side relative to thing or person; side or direction. **10.** linear measure of horse's height, = 4 in. **11.** playing-cards dealt to a player; player holding these (*first, third, hand*); set of such hands dealt to players; round of play with these; FORCE² person's *hand;* PLAY¹ *into* person's *hands;* SHOW¹ one's *hand.* **12.** (colloq.) applause (*got a big hand*). **13. at** ∼, close by, about to happen soon; **at the** ∼(**s**) **of,** through the action of, from; **by** ∼, by manual labour, in handwriting (not typed etc.), by messenger (not by post etc.); *brought up by* ∼, (of child etc.) fed from bottle; **for** one's **own** ∼, on one's own account; *live* **from** ∼ **to mouth,** improvidently; **in** ∼, held in the hand, at one's disposal, still unused, under control, receiving attention; **in** person's ∼**s,** to be dealt with by him, subject to his control (so **fall into the** ∼**s of**); **man of his** ∼**s,** practical person; OFFHAND; **off** one's ∼**s,** no longer on one's hands, no longer one's responsibility etc.; **on** ∼, in one's possession, in attendance; **on** one's ∼**s,** resting on one as a responsibility; **on every** ∼, **on all** ∼**s,** to or from all quarters; **on the one** ∼, **on the other** ∼, (of contrasted points of view etc.); **out of** ∼, (1) without delay, (2) out of control; **to** ∼, within reach; **to** one's ∼, ready for one without exertion on one's own part. **14. change** ∼**s,** (1) pass to different owner, (2) use opposite hands for a task; CLEAN¹ *hands;* **come to** ∼, turn up, be received; **do a** ∼**'s turn,** make the slightest effort (usu. w. neg.); ∼ **and foot,** (bind) completely, (serve) assiduously; ∼ **and** or **in glove,** on intimate terms (*with*); ∼ **in** ∼, with hands mutually clasped, (fig.) in close association; ∼ **over** ∼ or **fist,** with each hand successively passing above the other as in climbing rope etc., (fig.) with steady or rapid progress; ∼ **to** ∼, (of fighting etc.) at close quarters; **get** or **have** or **keep** one's ∼ **in,** become or be in PRACTICE¹ (2); ∼**s down,** (win etc.) easily; ∼**s off!,** do not touch (lit. or fig.); one's ∼**s are tied,** (fig.) one is powerless to act; ∼**s up!** (ordering persons to raise their hands to signify assent or surrender); **have** one's ∼**s full,** be fully occupied; **hold** one's ∼, refrain from action, esp. punishment; **hold** person's ∼, (fig.) give him close guidance or moral support; **hold** or **join** ∼**s,** be hand in hand; LAY³ *hands on;* **lay** or **put** one's ∼ *on,* find; LEAD² *by the hand;* **put** or SET¹ one's *hand to;* SHAKE¹ *hands;* SIT *on* one's *hands;* TAKE¹ *in hand;* **turn** one's ∼ **to,**

undertake (task of new kind); UPPER *hand*; WASH¹ one's *hands* (*of*); **with a heavy ∼,** oppressively; **with a high ∼,** arrogantly; **15.** *attrib.* operated by hand (*hand-brake, hand-mill, hand-press, hand-pump, hand-wheel*); held or carried in the hand (*hand-baggage, -mirror*); done by hand not by machine (*hand-knitted, -sewn, -painted*). **16.** ∼'**bag,** (1) small bag carried by woman to hold purse and other personal articles, (2) travelling-bag; ∼'**ball,** ball for throwing with hand, game played with this in walled court or between two goals; ∼-**barrow,** frame for loads etc. carried by two persons; ∼'**bell,** bell rung by hand, esp. one of a set for musical performance; ∼'**bill,** printed notice circulated by hand; ∼'**book,** (usu. short) treatise, manual, guidebook; ∼('s)-**breadth,** width of average adult hand as measure of distance; ∼'**cart** (pushed or drawn by hand); ∼'**clap,** clapping of hands (SLOW *handclap*); ∼'**craft,** (make by) handicraft; ∼ **cream,** emollient for the hands; ∼'**cuff** *v.t.,* secure with ∼'**cuffs** (pair of metal rings joined by short chain, lockable for securing prisoner's hands); ∼-**gallop,** easy gallop; ∼'**glass,** (1) magnifying glass held in hand, (2) small mirror with handle; *hand--*GRENADE; ∼'**grip** *n.,* grasp, seizure with the hand (friendly or hostile), handle; ∼'**guard** (on sword); ∼-**gun** (held and fired with one hand); ∼'**hold,** something for the hands to grip on (in climbing etc.); ∼'**line,** fishing-line worked without rod; ∼'**list** (of books etc., for reference); ∼'**made,** (of paper etc.) made by hand (esp. opp. to *machine-made*); ∼'**maid(en),** (arch. or fig.) female servant; ∼ **of glory,** charm made from mandrake root or dried hand of executed felon [transl. of F *main de gloire,* corrupted f. *mandragore* mandrake]; ∼-**organ,** barrel--organ with crank turned by hand; ∼-**picked,** (of supporters etc.) carefully chosen; ∼'**rail,** railing along edge of stairs etc.; ∼'**saw,** saw held with one hand (cf. HAWK¹); ∼'**set,** telephone mouthpiece and ear-piece as one unit; ∼'**shake,** shake of person's hand with one's own (see SHAKE¹ 1; GOLDEN *hand-shake*); ∼'**spike,** wooden lever shod with iron, used on shipboard and by artillery; ∼'**spring,** somersault in which one lands first on hands and then on feet; ∼'**stand,** feat of supporting body on hands only; ∼-**towel,** small towel for wiping hands after washing; ∼'**writing,** writing by hand with pen or pencil, esp. as done by particular person. **17.** Hence (-)∼'ED², ∼'LESS, *adjs.* [OE *hand, hond,* = OS *hand,* OHG *hant,* ON *hönd,* Goth. *handus*]

hănd² *v.t.* help (person) with the hand (*into, out of,* carriage etc.); (Naut.) furl (sail); deliver, transfer by hand or otherwise (*over to* person, *down* or *on to* succeeding generations, *in* at office, *on, up,* etc.); offer (food) at meal; ∼ **down,** transmit (decision) from superior court etc.; ∼-**me-down,** ready-made or second-.) hand (clothing, or fig.); ∼ **off,** (Rugby Footb.) push off (tackling opponent) with hand (so ∼-*off* n.); ∼-**out,** information given to the press etc., food or clothes or money given to beggar; ∼ **it to,** (colloq.) acknowledge merit of (person). [f. prec.]

h. & c. *abbr.* hot and cold (water).

hă'ndĕdnĕss *n.* tendency to, or preference for, use of right, or left, hand. [f. HAND¹*ed*+-NESS]

hă'ndful (-ool) *n.* quantity that fills the hand; small number (*of* men etc.); (colloq.) troublesome person or task. [OE *handfull* (as HAND¹, -FUL)]

hă'ndĭcăp *n.,* & *v.t.* (-pp-). **1.** *n.* race or competition in which chances of competitors are made more nearly equal by conceding start, difference in weight to be carried (in horse-race), etc.; extra weight or other condition imposed or advantage conferred on competitor, number of strokes by which golfer normally exceeds par for course; (fig.) hindrance, thing that prevents one from doing something. **2.** *v.t.* impose handicap on (competitor); (fig., of circumstances) place (person) at disadvantage; (in *p.p.*) suffering from physical or mental disability; hence

∼**PER¹** *n.* [app. f. phr. *hand i'* (= in) *cap* describing a kind of sporting lottery]

hă'ndĭcraft (-ahft) *n.* manual skill; manual art or trade or occupation; ∼**sman,** man skilled in a handicraft. [ME, alt. of older (f. OE) *handcraft,* after foll.]

hă'ndĭwork (-wērk) *n.* work done, thing made, by the hands or by anyone's personal agency. [OE *handgeweorc* (as HAND¹+collect. form (see Y-) of *weorc* WORK¹)]

hă'ndkerchief (hăngkerchĭf, -ēf) *n.* (*pl.* ∼s, or -ieves *pr.* -ēvz). square of linen, cotton, silk, etc., carried in pocket (**pocket-∼**) for wiping nose etc., or worn round neck (**neck ∼,** NECK¹*erchief*). [f. HAND¹+ KERCHIEF]

hă'ndle¹ *n.* part of a thing by which it is to be held; fact that may be taken advantage of (*gave a handle to his critics*); ∼**bar,** (1) steering-bar of bicycle etc., with handle at each end, (2) long heavy moustache with curved ends; **fly off the ∼,** (colloq.) lose self-control; ∼ **to** one's **name,** (colloq.) title of nobility etc. [OE (as HAND¹; see -LE 1)]

hă'ndle² *v.t.* touch or feel with the hands; take hold of in or with the hands; manipulate; manage (thing, person); put (thing, person) through stated process; treat (person *roughly, kindly,* etc.); discuss (subject); deal in (goods); hence **hă'ndlER¹** *n.,* (esp.) person in charge of trained police-dog etc. [OE *handlian* (as prec.)]

hă'ndle³ *n.* feel of goods, esp. textiles, when handled. [f. prec.]

hă'n(d)sel (-ns-) *n.,* & *v.t.* (||-ll-). **1.** *n.* gift at beginning of new year, or on coming into new circumstances; earnest-money; foretaste. **2.** *v.t.* ||give handsel to, inaugurate, be the first to try. [ME, corresp. to OE *handselen* giving into a person's hands, ON *handsal* giving of the hand (esp. in promise), f. as HAND¹+OE *sellan* SELL]

hă'ndsome (-ns-) *a.* (∼**r,** ∼**st**). of fine form or figure; (of conduct etc.) generous (*a handsome present; handsome treatment;* ∼ **is as** ∼ **does,** one is judged by behaviour not appearance); (of price, fortune, etc.) considerable; hence ∼LY² (-mlĭ) *adv.* (also, Naut., carefully), ∼NESS (-mn-) *n.* [ME, = 'easily handled', f. HAND¹+SOME¹]

hă'ndȳ *a.* ready to hand, conveniently placed; convenient to handle or use (*the legacy will come in handy*); clever with the hands; ||∼**y-dandy,** child's game in which one player guesses which of other player's hands conceals some object; ∼**yman,** person able to do various odd jobs esp. in house maintenance; hence ∼ĭLY² *adv.,* ∼ĭNESS *n.* [f. HAND¹+-Y²]

hăng¹ *v.* (**hung,** exc. sense 5 or arch. **hanged**). **1.** *v.t.* support from above and otherwise allow to take form determined by action of gravity etc., attach loosely, (*from, on, to,* hook, etc.); place (meat, game) thus to dry (**hung beef,** so cured) or become tender or high. **2.** place (picture) on wall (*hung on the LINE*²). **3.** attach (wallpaper) to wall; fit up (bells in belfry). **4.** rest (door on hinges, coach on springs) in free swinging position. **5.** *v.t.* & *i.* suspend or be suspended by neck as capital punishment; kill one*self* thus; (as imprecation) = DAMN, be damned, (*I'll be hanged if I can see it; well, I'm hanged!; do it and hang the expense; let everything go hang*). **6.** *v.t.* & *i.* (cause to) lean or droop (*hang one's head in shame*). **7.** *v.i.* remain, or be, hung (lit. or fig.; *sword, punishment, hangs over his head or him; dress hangs badly; curtain hangs loose, in folds,* etc.); ∼ **in the balance,** remain uncertain; THERE*by hangs a tale; hang by a* THREAD¹ *or a hair.* **8.** *v.t.* decorate *with* (things hung on). **9.** *prevent (jury, by disagreement) from reaching decision. **10.** ∼ **about** or **around,** loiter about, not move away or disperse; ∼ **back,** show reluctance to act or move, keep rearward position; ∼ **fire,** (of firearm) be slow in going off, (fig.) be delayed in action; ∼ **heavily** or **heavy,** (of time) pass slowly; ∼ **on,** depend or rely on, attend closely to, stick or hold closely (*to*), remain in office, stick to duty etc., (sl.) attach blame for (thing) to, (sl.) wait for a short time, (colloq., in telephoning) not ring off; ∼ *on to*, (colloq.) retain; ∼ **out**, hang from window, clothes-line, etc., (cause to) protrude downwards, (sl.) reside or be often present; *let it all* ∼ *out*, (sl.) be uninhibited; ∼-*out* n., (sl.) place of residence; HANGOVER; **hung-over**, (sl.) having hangover; ∼ **together**, be coherent, be or remain associated; ∼ **up**, hang from hook etc., put aside, postpone indefinitely, end telephone conversation, cause delay or difficulty or (sl.) obsession to; ∼-*up* n., (sl.) difficulty, obsession, inhibition. **11.** ∼'**dog** n. & a., sneaking shamefaced (person); ∼-**glider** (controlled and stabilized by movements of operator suspended in it); ∼'**man**, executioner esp. by hanging; ∼'**nail**, = AGNAIL. [f. ON *hanga* v.t., OE *hōn*, = OS, OHG, Goth. *hāhan*, & f. OE *hangian* v.i., = OS *hangon*, OHG *hangēn*, f. Gmc **hang-*]

häng[2] n. downward droop or bend; way a thing hangs; **get the** ∼ **of**, (colloq.) get the knack of, understand; **not** (*care* etc.) **a** ∼, (colloq.) not at all. [f. prec.]

hä'ngar (-ng-, -ngg-) n. shed for housing aircraft etc.; hence ∼AGE (4) n. [F]

hä'nger[1] n. wood on side of steep hill. [OE *hangra* (*hangian* HANG[1])]

hä'nger[2] n. In vbl senses; loop etc. by which thing is hung; chain, rod, to which pot is hung in fireplace by pot-hook, (**clothes-, coat-**)∼, shaped piece of wood etc. from which clothes may be hung in normal shape; short sword, orig. hung from belt; ∼-**o'n**, follower, dependant. [ME, f. HANG[1] + -ER[1]]

hä'nging[1] n. In vbl senses; (usu. in *pl.*) drapery with which walls etc. are hung; ∼ **committee** (deciding on hanging of pictures in exhibition); **a** ∼ **judge, matter** (likely to bring about capital punishment); ∼ **wardrobe** (for clothes to hang in at full length). [ME, f. HANG[1] + -ING[1]]

hä'nging[2] a. In vbl senses; ∼ **gardens** (placed on steep slope); ∼ **lie**, (Golf) position of ball on ground sloping downhill in direction of play; ∼ **paragraph** (with all lines except first indented); ∼ **valley** (ending in abrupt descent to another valley). [ME, f. HANG[1] + -ING[2]]

hä'ngover n. **1.** unpleasant after-effects of (esp. alcoholic) dissipation. **2.** remainder, surviving part. [f. HANG[1] + OVER]

hänk n. (circular) loop or coil, skein; definite length of cotton yarn (840 yds.), worsted (560 yds.), etc.; (Naut.) ring of rope, iron, etc., for securing staysails to stays. [ME, f. ON *hönk*, **hanku*; cf. Sw. *hank* string, Da. *hank* handle]

hä'nker v.i. ∼ **after, for,** crave or long for; hence ∼-ING[1] n. [rel. to syn. obs. *hank* (-ER[5]), prob. cogn. w. HANG[1]]

hä'nky n. (colloq.) handkerchief. [abbr.; see -Y[3]]

hä'nky-pänky n. (sl.) trickery; underhand dealing; questionable behaviour. [arbitr., perh. after *hocus-pocus*]

Hä'növer n. House of ∼, British sovereigns from George I to Victoria; whence **Hänovēr'IAN** a. & n. [∼ in Germany, whose Elector became George I in 1714]

Hä'nsärd n. official report of proceedings in British and other Parliaments. [f. L. ∼, Engl. printer d. 1828, whose firm orig. compiled it]

Hänse n. (Hist.) guild of merchants; political and commercial league of Germanic towns, whence **Hänseä'TIC** a.; entrance-fee of guild. [f. MHG *hanse*, OHG, Goth. *hansa* company]

hä'nsel. See HANDSEL.

hä'nsom n. ∼ (**cab**), (Hist.) two-wheeled cabriolet for two inside, with driver mounted behind and reins going over roof. [f. J. A. *Hansom*, Engl. architect d. 1882, who designed such a cab]

Hänts. abbr. Hampshire. [f. OE *Hantescire*]

Ha'nukkah (hah'nuka, χ-) n. Jewish festival of lights,

commemorating purification of the Temple in 165 BC. [f. Heb. *ḥānukkāh* consecration]

hanuma'n (-ōōmah'n) n. Indian langur venerated by Hindus; (Hindu Myth., *H*∼) semi-divine monkey-like creature. [Hindi]

häp[1] n. (arch.) chance, luck, lot; chance occurrence. [ME, f. ON *happ*]

häp[2] v.t. (-pp-). (arch.) come about by chance; happen (*to* do). [ME, f. prec.]

hapax legomen|on (häpäks līgŏ'mīnŏn) n. (*pl.* ∼**a**). word of which only one instance is recorded ('*hugger-mugger*' *is hapax legomenon in Shakespeare*). [Gk, = thing said once]

ha'penny. Var. of HALFPENNY.

häphä'zard (-p-h-) n., a., & adv. **1.** n. mere chance (*at* or *by haphazard*). **2.** a. & adv. casual(ly), (at) random. [f. HAP[1] + HAZARD]

hä'pless a. unlucky; hence ∼LY[2] adv. [f. HAP[1] + -LESS]

häplŏ'graphy n. mistake of writing once what should be written twice (e.g. *philogy* for *philology*). [f. Gk *haplous* single + -o- + -GRAPHY]

hä'ploid a. & n. (Biol.) (cell) having a single set of unpaired chromosomes; (organism) having this in somatic cells. [G, f. Gk *haplous* single + *eidos* form]

häplŏ'logy n. mistake of uttering once what should be spoken twice (e.g. *Feb'ry* for *February*). [f. as HAPLOGRAPHY + -LOGY]

hä'plÿ adv. (arch.) by chance; perhaps. [ME, f. HAP[1] + -LY[2]]

||**ha'p'orth.** See HALFPENNY.

hä'ppen v.i. **1.** occur, come to pass, (by chance or otherwise). **2.** chance, have the (good or bad) fortune, *to* (do). **3.** come by chance (*up*)*on* (person, thing), *by*, *in*, etc.; ∼ **to**, be experienced by (*something* etc.). ∼*s to* person, he dies etc.). [ME, f. HAP[1] + -EN[6]]

hä'ppening (-pn-) n. In vbl senses; (usu. in *pl.*) occurrence, event; improvised or spontaneous theatrical etc. performance. [f. prec. + -ING[1]]

*hä'ppenstance n. thing that happens by chance. [f. HAPPEN + CIRCUMSTANCE]

hä'ppi n. loose informal Japanese coat. [Jap.]

hä'ppÿ a. **1.** (Of person or circumstance) lucky, fortunate; contented with one's lot; glad or pleased (*about*, *with*, *that*, to help another etc.); (of language or conduct) apt, felicitous; (colloq.) slightly drunk. **2.** ∼ **birthday, Christmas,** etc., greetings at these times; *happy* DISPATCH[2]; ∼ **event**, birth of child; ∼-**go-lucky**, taking things cheerfully as they happen; *happy* HUNTING-*ground*(s); ∼ **land**, (esp.) heaven; ∼ **medium**, something that achieves satisfactory avoidance of extremes, golden mean; ∼ **pill**, (colloq.) tranquillizer; ∼ **release**, (esp.) death; *happy* RETURN[2]s; ∼ **ship**, ship whose crew work together in harmony, (fig.) organization whose members do likewise; *happy* THOUGHT[1]. **3.** (as *suf.*) excited or dazed or nervous from, behaving irresponsibly over, inclined to use excessively, (*bomb-happy*, TRIGGER-*happy*). **4.** Hence **hä'ppiLY**[2] adv., **hä'ppiNESS** n. [ME, f. HAP[1] + -Y[2]]

hä'ptic a. pertaining to the sense of touch. [f. Gk *haptikos* able to touch (*haptō* fasten; see -IC)]

hära-ki'ri n. suicide by disembowelment, as practised by samurai in Japan when in disgrace or sentenced to death. [colloq. Jap. (*hara* belly, *kiri* cutting)]

hará'ngue (-ng) n. & v. **1.** n. speech to an assembly; loud or vehement address. **2.** v.i. & t. make harangue (to). [ME f. F, f. OF *arenge* f. med. L *harenga*, perh. f. Gmc **harihring-* assembly (**harjaz* crowd, **hringaz* RING[1])]

hä'rass v.t. vex by repeated attacks; trouble, worry; hence ∼MENT n. [f. F *harasser*, pej. f. OF *harer* set a dog on]

här'binger (-nj-) n., & v.t. **1.** n. one who announces another's approach, forerunner; (Hist.) one sent to purvey or of lodgings for army, royal party, etc. **2.** v.t. announce approach of. [ME, f. AF & OF *herbergere* -geour f. *herbergier* to lodge f. *herberge* lodging f. OS *heriberga* (*heri* army, **berg-* protect); *-n-* as in *messenger* etc.]

‖**har′bour** (-ber), ***har′bor**, *n.* & *v.* **1.** *n.* place of shelter for ships; shelter; ∼-**master**, officer in charge of harbour; *∼ **seal**, small Atlantic seal (*Phoca vitulina*); hence ∼LESS *a.* **2.** *v.t.* give shelter to (esp. vermin, criminal, evil thoughts). **3.** *v.i.* come to anchor in harbour. [OE *hereborg(ian)*, (perh. f.) ON *herbergi*, cogn. w. prec.]

‖**har′bourage** (-ber-), ***har′borage**, *n.* (place of) shelter. [f. prec. + -AGE]

hard *a.*, *n.*, & *adv.* **1.** *a.* firm, unyielding to pressure, solid, not easily cut; (of data etc.) reliable; (of radiation) highly penetrating; ∼ **facts** (not disputable like opinions etc.). **2.** difficult (*to* do), not easily allowing one *to* do (*she is hard to please*; *this is hard to believe*; ∼ **nut to crack,** difficult problem, person or thing not easily understood or overcome or influenced; ∼ **of hearing,** somewhat deaf); difficult to understand or explain (*hard question*); (of person or conduct) unfeeling, harsh, (*hard as* NAIL[1]*s*); involving undue or unfair suffering (*hard luck*; *hard cases make bad law*); stingy. **3.** difficult to bear (*hard life*, *times*, LINE[2]*s*); (of season or weather) severe, esp. frosty; (of bargain) without concession; harsh or unpleasant to eye or ear (*hard colours*, *voice*). **4.** (Of liquor) strongly alcoholic; (of drug) potent and addictive; (of water) difficult to use soap with, owing to its mineral salts; (of markets and prices) high, unyielding; (of pornography) highly obscene. **5.** (Phonet.) voiceless (k, t, *and* p, *are hard as opposed to* g, d, *and* b); guttural (*c is hard in* '*cat*', *and* g *in* '*go*'). **6.** strenuous (*a hard drinker*, *fight*, *worker*; *try* one's *hardest*); ∼ **row to hoe,** difficult task; do thing **the** ∼ **way,** by one's unaided efforts or bitter experience. **7.** *n.* ‖sloping roadway across foreshore; (sl.) = *hard labour* (*got 2 years hard*). **8.** *adv.* strenuously, severely, with effort, (Naut.) to full extent, (*try hard*; *raining hard*; *freezing hard*; *look hard at*; *hard a- -port!*); ∼ **pressed,** closely pursued (lit. or fig.). **9.** with difficulty (*hard-earned*). **10.** so as to be hard (*hard- -baked*); ∼-**boiled,** (of egg) boiled to solidify white and yolk, (fig.) tough, callous, shrewd. **11.** ∼ **at** it, working hard; **be** ∼ **put to it,** be in difficulties; **die** ∼ (only after hard struggle; cf. DIE[2]-*hard*); **go** ∼ **with** person, turn out to his disadvantage; **it shall go** ∼ **but** (unless there are overpowering difficulties) *I will find them*; ∼ **by,** close by; ∼ (**up**)**on,** too severe in criticism or treatment of (*don't be too hard on him*), (of circumstances) bearing with undue severity on, close to (*was hard on my* HEEL[1]*s*); ∼ **up,** lacking money etc., at a loss *for*; **run** person ∼, pursue him closely. **12.** ∼ **and fast,** (of distinction made, or rule of behaviour etc.) strict; ∼′**back** *n.* & *a.*, (book) bound in stiff cover; ∼′**bake,** almond toffee; ∼′**bitten,** tough in fight etc.; ∼′**board,** stiff board of compressed and processed wood-pulp fibre used in place of wood; *hard-boiled* (see sense 10); ∼ **case,** (1) instance of hardship, (2) intractable person, (3, Austral. & NZ) amusing person; ∼ **cash,** (1) coins as opp. paper money, (2) money as opp. mere promises of payment; *hard* CHEESE[1]; ∼ **coal,** anthracite; ∼ **copy,** legible permanent record of matter stored on microfilm etc.; ∼ **core,** irreducible nucleus of resistance etc., ‖heavy material forming foundation of road etc., (*attrib.*, w. hyphen) blatant, uncompromising; (∼-*core pornography*, highly obscene); ∼ **court,** lawn-tennis court made of asphalt, concrete, etc., (opp. *grass court*); ∼ **cover,** stiff durable binding-case of book; ∼ **currency** (not likely to depreciate suddenly or fluctuate greatly in value; cf. SOFT *currency*); ∼-**favoured,** -**featured,** having harsh or ugly features; ∼ **feeling**(**s**) resentment; ∼- -**fisted,** stingy; ∼ **hat,** (1) bowler hat, (2) protective headgear used on building-sites etc., (3) reactionary person; ∼-**head,** knapweed; ∼-**headed,** practical, not sentimental; ∼-**hearted,** unfeeling; ∼ **hit,** severely troubled; ∼-**hitting,** vigorous, not sparing

feelings; ∼ **labour,** (orig.) stone-breaking etc. by prisoners, (until 1948 in UK) compulsory labour by prisoners, without privileges during first few weeks of sentence; ∼-**laid,** (of string, fabric, etc.) tightly twisted or woven; ∼ **landing** (in which spacecraft etc. is destroyed on impact); ∼ **line,** unyielding adherence to firm policy (∼-*liner*, one who behaves thus); ∼-**lying money,** extra pay to naval men serving in small craft; *∼ **money,** coins; ∼- -**mouthed,** (of horse) not easily controlled by bit; ∼- -**nose**(**d**), (colloq.) obdurate, realistic, uncompromising; ∼-**on,** (sl.) erection of penis; ∼ **pad,** form of distemper of dogs etc.; ∼ **palate,** front part of palate; ∼ **pan,** firm subsoil of clay etc., hard unbroken ground; ∼ **roe** (of female fish); ∼ **rubber,** ebonite; ∼ **sauce** (of butter and sugar, often with brandy etc. added); *∼-**scrabble** *a.* & *n.*, (land) yielding subsistence only with difficulty; ∼ **sell,** aggressive salesmanship; ∼ **set,** set so as to be hard, (of egg) that has been subjected to incubation, (of person) hungry; ∼′**shell,** having a hard shell, (fig.) rigid, uncompromising; (esp. **Hardshell Baptists*); ∼ **shoulder,** hardened land beside motorway for vehicles to leave road in emergency; ∼ **soap** (made with sodium compounds); *hard* SOLDER; ∼**sta′nding,** area of hard material for vehicle to stand on when not in use; ∼ **swearing,** (euphem.) unabashed perjury; ∼ **tack,** ship biscuit; ∼-**top,** motor car with metal roof; ∼′**ware,** (1) ironmonger's goods, (2) weapons, machinery, (3) physical components of computer etc., opp. SOFT*ware*; ∼-**wearing,** able to stand much wear; ∼ **wheat** (with hard grain rich in gluten); ∼′**wood** (of deciduous tree, not easily sawn); ∼ **words,** (1) words difficult to understand, (2) angry talk; ∼- -**working,** diligent. **13.** Hence ∼′ISH[1] 2 *a.*, ∼′NESS *n.* [OE *h*(*e*)*ard*, = OS *hard*, OHG *hart*, ON *harthr*, Goth. *hardus* f. Gmc *hardhuz f. IE *kratus]

har′den *v.t.* & *i.* make or become hard, callous (esp. in *p.p.*), or robust; ∼ **off,** inure (plant) to cold by gradual increase of exposure; hence ∼ER[1] (1, 2) *n.* [ME, f. prec. + -EN[6]]

har′die. Var. of HARDY[2].

har′dihood *n.* boldness, audacity. [f. HARDY[1] + -HOOD]

har′dly *adv.* **1.** in a hard manner; (only) with difficulty; harshly. **2.** scarcely, only just. [ME, f. HARD + -LY[2]]

har′dship *n.* hardness of fate or circumstance; severe suffering or privation. [ME, f. HARD + -SHIP]

har′d[**y**]**[1]** *a.* **1.** bold, audacious; hence ∼iLY[2] *adv.* **2.** robust, capable of endurance, (Hort., of plant) able to grow in the open air all the year; HALF-*hardy*; ∼y **annual,** annual plant that may be sown, or sows itself, in the open, (fig., joc.) subject that comes up at regular intervals. **3.** Hence ∼iNESS *n.* [ME, f. OF *hardi* p.p. of *hardir* become bold, f. Gmc *hardjan make hard (*hardhuz HARD)]

har′dy[2] *n.* blacksmith's edged blade of hard iron for shaping metal on. [prob. f. prec. or f. HARD]

hare *n.*, & *v.i.* **1.** *n.* mammal of genus *Lepus* like large rabbit, with tawny fur, long ears, short tail, and hind legs longer than foreleys, inhabiting fields, hills, etc.; BELGIAN *hare*; = ELECTRIC *hare*. **2. mad as a March** ∼ (hare in breeding season); **first catch your** ∼ (before trying to cook it; usu. fig.); **hold** (or **run**) **with the** ∼ **and run** (or **hunt**) **with the hounds,** try to remain on good terms with both sides; **start a** ∼, raise topic of discussion. **3.** ∼ **and hounds,** paper- -chase; ∼ **and tortoise,** defeat of ability by persistence; ∼′**bell,** bell-flower with rounded basal leaves (Scottish bluebell), (orig.) wild hyacinth (English bluebell); ∼-**brained,** rash, wild; ∼′**lip,** congenital fissure of upper lip; ∼′**s-ear,** thoroughwax; ∼′**s-foot,** (1) species of clover (*Trifolium arvense*) with soft hair about flowers, (2) corkwood tree, (3) hare's foot formerly used for applying rouge etc. to face. **4.** *v.i.* run with great speed. [OE *hara* = OHG *haso*, ON *heri* f. Gmc *hason, *hazon]

harem (hār'em, hahrē'm) *n.* women's part of Muslim dwelling-house; its occupants; Muslim sacred place. [f. Arab. *ḥarām, ḥarīm* prohibited, sanctuary, women's apartment (*ḥarama* prohibit)]

har'ewood (hār'w-) *n.* stained sycamore-wood used in cabinet-making. [f. G. dial. *ehre* f. Rom. **acre* f. L *acer* maple, + WOOD]

hä'ricot (-kō) *n.* ragout (usu. of mutton or lamb); ∼ (**bean**), (white dried seed of) bean of genus *Phaseolus.* [F]

hä'rijăn *n.* Indian Untouchable. [Skr., = person dedicated to Vishnu (*Hari* Vishnu, *jana* person)]

härk *v.* **1.** *v.i.* listen (*to* or *at* or abs. in *imper.*); ||(as call to hounds) go *forward, away, off,* etc. **2.** *v.i. & t.* ∼ **back,** (of hounds) retrace course to find scent, (fig.) revert (*to* subject), recall (hounds). [ME *herkien* f. OE **he(o)rcian,* = MLG, MDu. *horken,* OHG *hōrechen*; cf. HEARKEN]

här'ken. Var. of HEARKEN.

härl[1] *v. & n.* (Sc.) **1.** *v.t.* drag along the ground. **2.** *v.i.* drag oneself along. **3.** *v.t., & n.* roughcast with lime and small gravel. [ME, of unkn. orig.]

härl[2], **härle,** *n.* barb or fibre of feather; fibre of flax or hemp. [app. f. MLG *herle, harle* fibre of flax or hemp]

här'lĕquin *n. & a.* **1.** *n.* (*H*∼). stock character of witty servant in Italian comedy; mute character in English pantomime, invisible to clown and pantaloon, usu. wearing mask and particoloured tights; buffoon. **2.** ∼(**duck**), northern duck with variegated plumage. **3.** *a.* gaily coloured; variegated. [Γ, f. earlier *Herlequin* leader of legendary nocturnal troop of demon horsemen]

härlĕquinä'de *n.* part of pantomime in which harlequin plays chief part; piece of buffoonery. [f. F *arlequinade* (as prec.; see -ADE)]

||**Här'ley Street** *n.* medical specialists. [∼ in London, associated with eminent physicians and surgeons]

här'lot *n., & v.i.* (arch. or derog.) prostitute (oneself); hence ∼RY (4) *n.* [ME f. OF *harlot, herlot* lad, knave, vagabond, of unkn. orig.]

härm *n., & v.t.* damage, hurt, (**out of** ∼**'s way,** in safety); hence ∼'FUL *a.* [OE *hearm(ian),* = OS, OHG *harm,* ON *harmr* grief, f. Gmc **harmaz*]

härmä'ttan *n.* parching dusty land-wind on W. Afr. coast from Dec. to Feb. [f. Fanti or Twi *haramata*]

här'mlĕss *a.* doing no harm; suffering no harm or loss (**save** or **hold** ∼, indemnify); hence ∼LY[2] *adv.,* ∼NESS *n.* [ME, f. HARM + -LESS]

härmō'nic *a. & n.* **1.** *a.* harmonious, concordant. **2.** (Mus.) relating to harmony; ∼ **minor,** scale with minor 6th and major 7th both ascending and descending; ∼ **tones** (produced by vibration of aliquot parts of strings etc.) **3.** (Math.) in the relation of quantities whose reciprocals are in arithmetical progression (*harmonic series*); (**simple**) ∼ **motion,** oscillatory motion under a retarding force proportional to amount of displacement from equilibrium position; ∼ **function** (representing harmonic motion). **4.** Hence **härmō'nICALLY** *adv.* **5.** *n.* harmonic tone, usu. accompanying the fundamental; component frequency of wave motion. [f. L f. Gk *harmonikos* (as HARMONY; see -IC)]

härmō'nica *n.* musical glasses; mouth-organ. [L, fem. sing. or neut. pl. (as *n.*) of *harmonicus* (see prec.)]

härmō'nious *a.* forming a consistent or orderly or pleasing or agreeable whole, concordant; free from dissent or ill-feeling; sweet-sounding; singing or playing tunefully; hence ∼LY[2] *adv.* [f. HARMONY + -OUS]

här'mon|ist *n.* person skilled in harmony, (arch.) musician; collator of parallel narratives, whence ∼i'stIC *a.*; harmonizer. [f. HARMONY + -IST]

härmō'nium *n.* keyboard instrument in which notes are produced by air blown through reeds. [F, f. L (as HARMONY)]

här'moniz|e, -īs|e (-īz), *v.t. & i.* bring into or be in harmony (*with*); make or be agreeable in artistic effect; add notes to (melody) to form chords; hence ∼A'TION *n.* [f. F *harmoniser* (as foll.; see -ZE)]

här'monў *n.* state of being harmonious; agreeable effect of apt arrangement of parts; (Mus.) (study of) combination of simultaneous notes to form chords (cf. MELODY); sweet or melodious sound (*harmony of the* SPHERES); collation of parallel narratives etc., esp. of the four Gospels. [ME, f. OF *harmonie* f. L f. Gk *harmonia* joining, concord (*harmos* joint)]

här'nĕss *n., & v.t.* **1.** *n.* equipment of draught-horse or other animal, by which it is fastened to cart etc. and controlled; (fig.) working equipment; DOUBLE[1] *harness*; **in** ∼, in the routine of daily work; DIE[2] *in harness*; ∼**-racing** (in which horse pulls two-wheeled vehicle and driver). **2.** arrangement for fastening thing to person, resembling horse's harness; arrangement of straps fitted to dog in place of a collar; apparatus in loom for shifting warp-threads; (Hist.) defensive armour; ∼**-cask,** (Naut.) tub of salt meat for current consumption. **3.** *v.t.* put harness on (horse etc. *to* cart etc.); (fig.) utilize (river, waterfall, natural forces) for motive power. [ME; (v. f. OF *harneschier*) f. OF *harneis* military equipment f. ON **hernest (herr* army, *nest* provisions)]

härp[1] *n.* stringed musical instrument, roughly triangular, played by plucking with the fingers, esp. traditionally by those in heaven, or as large vertical orchestral instrument resting on floor and equipped with pedals to alter pitch of strings; ∼(**-seal**), Greenland seal with harp-shaped dark mark on back. [OE *hearpe,* = OS, ON *harpa,* OHG *hurfa* f. Gmc **harpōn*]

härp[2] *v.i.* play on harp, whence ∼'ER[1], ∼'IST (3), *ns.*; dwell tediously *on* (subject). [OE *hearpian* (as prec.)]

härpōo'n *n., & v.t.* **1.** *n.* spearlike missile with rope attached, for catching whales etc.; ∼**-gun** (for firing this). **2.** *v.t.* strike or spear with harpoon; hence ∼ER[1] *n.,* one who discharges harpoons. [f. F *harpon* (*harpe* clamp f. L f. Gk *harpē* sickle)]

här'psichórd (-k-) *n.* keyboard instrument shaped like grand piano with strings in line with direction of keys and plucked by quill or leather points, used cap. in 16th-18th c. [f. obs. F *harpechorde* f. LL *harpa* harp + *chorda* string; -*s*- of uncert. orig.]

här'pў *n.* (Gk & Rom. Myth.) rapacious monster with woman's face and body and bird's wings and claws; rapacious person; ∼(**-eagle**), S. Amer. crested bird of prey. [f. F *harpie* or f. L f. Gk *harpuiai* snatchers (cf. *harpazō* snatch)]

(**h)är'quĕbus** *n.* (Hist.) early type of portable gun, supported on tripod by hook or on forked rest; so ∼IER' *n.* [f. F (*h)arquebuse,* ult. f. MLG *hakebusse* or MHG *hakenbühse* (*haken* hook, *busse* gun)]

hä'rridan *n.* haggard or ill-tempered old woman. [17th c. cant; perh. f. F *haridelle* old horse]

hä'rrier[1] *n.* one who harries. [f. HARRY + -ER[1]]

hä'rrier[2] *n.* hound used for hunting hares; (in *pl.*) pack of these with huntsmen, group of cross-country runners. [f. HARE + -IER, assim. to prec.]

hä'rrier[3] *n.* falcon of genus *Circus.* [f. *harrower* (HARROW[3], -ER[1]), assim. to HARRIER[1]]

Hä'rris *n.* ∼ **tweed** (hand-woven kind made in Harris). [∼ in Outer Hebrides]

Harrō'vian *n. & a.* (past or present member) of Harrow School; (inhabitant) of Harrow. [f. mod. L *Harrovia* Harrow near London + -AN]

hä'rrow[1] (-ō) *n.* heavy frame with iron teeth for breaking clods or removing weeds on ploughed land, covering seed, etc.; **under the** ∼, in distress. [ME, f. ON *hervi, *harwjan*; cf. MLG & MDu. *harke* rake]

hä'rrow[2] (-ō) *v.t.* draw harrow over (land); lacerate, wound, (lit., or fig. the feelings etc.); distress greatly, whence ∼ING[2] *a.* [ME, f. prec.]

hä'rrow[3] (-ō) *v.t.* harry, rob, esp. (of Christ rescuing righteous souls) *harrow hell.* [ME, var. of HARRY]

*harrŭ'mph *n., & v.i.* (speak with) guttural rasping sound. [imit.]

hä'rrў *v.* ravage, lay waste, (land, or abs.); despoil (person); harass, worry. [OE *her(g)ian* = OS *herion,*

OHG *heriōn*, ON *herja* f. Gmc **harjō(ja)n* (**harjaz* army)]

harsh *a.* rough to the touch, taste, eye, or ear; repugnant to feelings or judgement; cruel, unfeeling; unpleasing, severe; hence ∼'EN⁶ *v.t.* & *i.*, ∼'LY² *adv.*, ∼'NESS *n.* [f. MLG *harsch* (as HAIR; see -ISH¹)]

hart *n.* male of (esp. red) deer, esp. after fifth year; ∼ of ten (branches on horns); ∼'s-tongue, fern with narrow undivided fronds. [OE *heor(o)t,* = OS *hirot,* OHG.*hir(u)z,* ON *hjörtr* f. Gmc **herutaz*]

har'tal *n.* closing of Indian shops and offices as mark of protest or sorrow. [f. Hind. *hartāl, haṭṭāl* f. Skr. *haṭṭa* shop + *tālaka* lock]

har'tebeest *n.* large Afr. antelope of genus *Alcelaphus,* with ringed horns bent back at tips. [Afrik. f. Du. *hert* HART, *beest* BEAST]

har'tshorn (-s-h-) *n.* substance got from horns of hart, formerly chief source of ammonia; (spirit of) ∼, (arch.) aqueous solution of ammonia. [OE (as HART, 's l, HORN¹)]

har'um-scarum *a.* & *n.* (colloq.) reckless (person, conduct). [rhyming form. on HARE, SCARE]

harŭ'sp|ĕx *n.* (*pl.* ∼ices *pr.* -īsēz). (Rom. Ant.) soothsayer divining from inspection of entrails etc. [L]

har'vĕst *n.,* & *v.t.* **1.** *n.* (season for) reaping and gathering-in of grain or other products; corn-crop; season's yield of any natural product; (fig.) product of any action. **2.** ∼-bug, larval mite troublesome during harvest; ∼ festival, thanksgiving service for completion of harvest, in church usu. decorated with grain, fruit, etc.; ∼ home, (festival to mark) close of harvesting; ∼man, arachnid with very long thin legs; ∼ moon (full within fortnight of 22 or 23 Sept., and rising at almost same time for several nights); ∼ mouse, very small mouse species nesting in stalks of growing grain. **3.** *v.t.* reap and collect (crop, or abs.) as harvest; take (wild animals) for food, sport, etc.; lay up, husband. [OE *hærfest,* = OHG *herbist,* ON *haust* f. Gmc **harbhistaz* (**harbh-* reap f. IE **karp-*)]

har'vĕster *n.* reaper; reaping-machine (esp. with sheaf-binding). [f. prec. + -ER¹]

has. See HAVE¹.

hä's-been (-z-) *n.* (colloq.) person who, thing which, has lost a quality or proficiency formerly possessed, out-of-date person or thing. [f. prec. + BEEN]

häsh¹ *v.t.* ∼ (up), cut (meat, or fig.) into small pieces, make into hash, mutilate, mangle, (lit. or fig.). [f. F *hacher* (*hache* HATCHET)]

häsh² *n.* dish of hashed (esp. previously cooked) meat; old matter served up in new form; medley; make a ∼ of, spoil in dealing with; settle person's ∼, (colloq.) make an end of or subdue him; **∼-slinger,* (sl.) waiter or waitress. [f. prec.]

häsh³ *n.* (colloq.) hashish. [abbr.]

Hä'shemīte, Hä'shimīte, *a.* & *n.* (member) of Arab princely family related to Muhammad. [f. *Hāšim,* great-grandfather of Muhammad + ITE¹]

hä'shish *n.* top leaves and tender parts of HEMP 1, dried for smoking or chewing as narcotic. [f. Arab. *ḥašīš* dry herb, powdered hemp-leaves]

Hä'sid *n.* (*pl.* ∼im). member of any of several mystical Jewish sects (esp. one founded in 18th c.); hence **Hasī'dıc** *a.* [f. Heb. *ḥasīd* pious]

hä'slĕt *n.* piece of meat to be roasted, esp. pig's pluck. [ME f. OF *hastelet* dim. of *haste* roast meat, spit, f. OLG, OHG *harst* roast; see -LET]

hasn't. See HAVE¹.

hasp (hah-) *n.,* & *v.t.* **1.** *n.* fastening contrivance, esp. hinged clasp passing over staple and secured by pin or padlock. **2.** *v.t.* fasten with hasp. [OE *hæpse, hæsp,* = MLG *haspe,* OHG *haspa,* ON *hespa*]

Hä'ssid etc. Var. of HASID etc.

hä'ssle *n.,* & *v.i.* (colloq.) quarrel, struggle, wrangle; (have) problem or difficulty. [20th c.; orig. dial.]

hä'ssock *n.* thick firm cushion for kneeling on esp. in church; tuft of matted grass etc. [OE *hassuc,* of unkn. orig.]

häst. See HAVE¹.

hä'stāte *a.* (esp. Bot.) triangular like spearhead. [f. L *hastatus* (*hasta* spear; see -ATE²)]

hāste *n.,* & *v.i.* **1.** *n.* urgency of movement; hurry, precipitancy, (more ∼, less speed, best results are obtained by proceeding with deliberation); in ∼, (1) quickly, (2) hurriedly; make ∼, act quickly (to do, and do). **2.** *v.i.* (arch.) make haste (to do, or abs.); go or come quickly. [ME; (v. f. OF *haster*) f. OF *haste* f. WG **haisti-* violence]

hä'sten (-sen) *v.* **1.** *v.t.* cause (person) to make haste; accelerate (work etc.). **2.** *v.i.* = prec. [f. prec. + -EN⁶]

hä'st|ў *a.* hurried; speedy; rash, inconsiderate; quick-tempered; eat one's ∼y pudding (of ||wheat flour or **maize flour stirred to thick batter in boiling milk or water); hence ∼ILY² *adv.,* ∼iNESS *n.* [ME, f. OF *hasti(f)* (as HASTE; see -IVE)]

hăt *n.,* & *v.t.* (-tt-). **1.** *n.* man's, woman's, or child's esp. outdoor head-covering, often with brim; ||bad ∼, (sl.) immoral or dishonest person; black as one's ∼, completely black; at the drop of a ∼, promptly, immediately; eat one's ∼, perform repulsive task (if expr. one's conviction that condition will not be fulfilled); hang up one's ∼, take up one's quarters; ∼ in hand, (fig.) servilely or humbly; ∼s in the ring, indications of persons' willingness to be contestants; my ∼!, excl. of astonishment; old ∼, (colloq.) something tediously familiar; out of a ∼, by random selection or as if by magic; pass or send the ∼ round, solicit contributions; take off one's ∼ to, applaud as admirable; talk through one's ∼, (sl.) exaggerate, bluff, talk wildly or nonsensically; under one's ∼, in secrecy; wear one's ... ∼, wear two ∼s, present oneself in one specified, or two, capacities at a particular time. **2.** ∼'band, ribbon etc. put round hat; ∼-peg (for hanging hat on); ∼-pin (used to fasten hat in position); ∼ trick, (Cricket) taking 3 wickets by successive balls from same bowler, (Footb. etc.) scoring of 3 goals by same player in same match, winning of 3 races at one meeting etc. **3.** *v.t.* cover, furnish, with hat. **4.** Hence ∼'FUL 2 *n.,* (fig. considerable number), ∼'LESS *a.,* wearing no hat, ∼'tER¹ (3) *n.* [OE *hætt,* = ON *höttr* hood f. Gmc **hattuz* (**hadnús;* cf. HOOD¹)]

hä'table. See HATE².

hätch¹ *n.* lower half of divided door; aperture in door, wall, ceiling, floor, or deck; (Naut.) hatchway, trapdoor covering this (down the ∼, (sl.) down the throat in drinking); under ∼es, below deck, (fig.) down out of sight, brought low, dead); floodgate; opening or door in aircraft or spacecraft; ∼'back, (vehicle with) large sloping rear door hinged at top; ∼'way, opening in ship's deck for lowering cargo. [OE *hæcc,* = MLG *heck,* f. Gmc **hak-*]

hätch² *v.* & *n.* **1.** *v.t.* bring forth or out (young bird etc., or abs.) from egg; incubate (egg); ∼ (up), contrive and develop (plot etc.). **2.** *v.i.* ∼ (out), emerge from egg; (of egg) produce young. **3.** *n.* hatching; brood hatched; hence ∼'LING¹ *n.,* bird or fish just hatched. [ME *hacche,* perh. f. OE **hæccan,* rel. to MHG *hecken,* Sw. *häcka,* Da. *hække,* of unkn. orig.]

hätch³ *v.t.,* & *n.* **1.** *v.t.* mark (surface etc.) with close parallel lines; ∼ed moulding (Archit., with two crossing sets of parallel lines); hence ∼'ING¹ (2) *n.* **2.** *n.* hatched line. [ME, f. F *hacher* (*hache* HATCHET)]

hä'tcherў *n.* place for hatching eggs esp. of fish or poultry. [f. HATCH² + -ERY]

hä'tchĕt *n.* light short-handled axe; ∼ face (narrow, sharp-featured); ∼ man, one who makes a business of killing, maliciously attacking (so ∼ job), etc.; BURY the hatchet; throw the helve after the ∼, add new loss to that already incurred. [ME, f. OF *hachette* dim. of *hache* axe f. med. L *hapia* f. Gmc **hapja;* see -ET¹]

hä'tchment *n.* large (usu. diamond-shaped) tablet with deceased person's armorial bearings, affixed to his house or elsewhere. [contr. of ACHIEVEMENT]

hate¹ *n.* hatred; (colloq.) hated person or thing. [ME, partly f. foll., partly f. ON *hatr*]

hate² *v.t.* have strong dislike of or strong aversion to; dislike greatly or (colloq.) be reluctant *to* do or do*ing*; hence **hā′table** *a.*, **hā′ter¹** *n.* [OE *hatian*, = OS *haton*, OHG *hazzōn*, ON *hata*, Goth. *hatan* f. Gmc **hatōjan*]

hā′teful (-tf-) *a.* exciting hatred; hence ∿**ly²** *adv.*, ∿**ness** *n.* [ME, f. HATE¹ + -FUL]

hăth. See HAVE¹.

hatha yō′ga (hătha, hŭta) *n.* system of physical exercises and breathing-control used in yoga. [f. Skr. *hatha* force; see YOGA]

hā′trĕd *n.* intense dislike; enmity; rejection and ill will. [ME, f. HATE¹ + *-red* f. OE *rǣden* condition]

hā′tter. See HAT.

hau′berk *n.* coat of mail. [ME, f. OF *hau(s)berc* f. Frank. **halsberg* (*hals* neck, **berg-* protect)]

haugh (haw, (Sc. & N. Engl.) hahχ) *n.* piece of flat alluvial land by river. [ME, prob. f. OE *healh* corner, rel. to HOLLOW²]

hau′ght|y̆ (haw′tĭ) *a.* valuing oneself too highly; lofty and disdainful; dignified; hence ∿**ily²** *adv.*, ∿**iness** *n.* [extension of *haught* a., earlier *haut* f. OF *haut* f. L *altus* high; see -Y²]

haul *v.* & *n.* **1.** *v.t.* pull, drag, forcibly; transport by cart or other conveyance, (colloq.) bring *up* for reprimand or trial; *haul down* one's COLOUR¹*s*; *haul over the* COAL*s*. **2.** *v.i.* pull *at* or *on* (rope etc.); (Naut.) turn ship's course (∿ **to** or **upon the wind**, bring ship round to sail closer to wind); (of wind) shift. **3.** *n.* act of hauling; quantity of fish hauled up; (fig.) amount gained; distance to be traversed; hence ∿′AGE (3, 4) *n.* [var. of HALE²]

hau′ler, ‖**hau′lier**, *n.* one who hauls (e.g. tubs in coal-mine to bottom of shaft); jobbing carter; firm or person engaged in road transport of goods. [f. prec. + -ER¹, -IER]

‖**ha(u)lm** (hawm, hahm) *n.* stalk, stem; (collect.) stems, stalks, of peas, beans, potatoes, etc., without the pods etc. [OE *h(e)alm*, – OS, OHG *halm*, ON *hálmr* f. Gmc **halmaz* f. IE **kolmos*]

hau′lyard. See HALYARD.

haunch *n.* part of body (esp. of sheep or deer) on side of spine between last ribs and thigh; fleshy part of buttock and thigh; leg and loin of deer etc. as food; side of arch between crown and pier. [ME, f. OF *hanche*, of Gmc orig.; cf. LG *hanke* hind leg of horse]

haunt *v.* & *n.* **1.** *v.t.* frequent (place); frequent company of (person); (of thoughts, memories, etc.) visit (person) persistently or frequently; (in *p.p.*) visited or frequented by ghosts. **2.** *v.i.* stay habitually (*in* or *about* place; *with* person). **3.** *n.* place of frequent resort; usual feeding-place of animals; place frequented by criminals. [ME, f. OF *hanter* f. Gmc **haimatjan* (**haimaz* HOME¹)]

Hau′sa (how′-) *n.* (*pl.* same or ∿**s**) (member) of Negroid people in Sudan etc.; their Hamitic language, widely used in W. Africa. [native name]

hausfrau (how′sfrow) *n.* (German) housewife. [G (*haus* house, *frau* woman)]

hautboy. See OBOE.

haute couture (ōt kōōtūr′) *n.* high-class dressmaking; leading dressmakers collectively, or their products. [F]

haute cuisine (ōt kwēze′n) *n.* high-class (traditional French) cooking. [F]

haute école (ōt ākō′l) *n.* the more difficult feats of dressage. [F, = high school]

hauteur (ōtēr′) *n.* haughtiness of manner. [F (*haut* high)]

haute vulgarisation (ōt vōōlgárĭzah′syawn) *n.* popularization of abstruse or complex matters. [F, = high vulgarization]

haut monde (ō maw′nd) *n.* fashionable society. [F, = high world]

‖**Havă′na** *n.* cigar made at Havana or elsewhere in Cuba. [∿ in Cuba]

hăve¹ (*or, when unstressed,* hav *or* av) *v.t.*, *i.*, & *aux.* (*sing. pres.* 2 (arch.) **hast**, 3 **has** *pr.* hăz *or* haz *or* az, (colloq.) ′**s**, (arch.) **hath**; colloq. ′VE; *past* **had** *pr.* hăd *or* had *or* ad, (colloq.) ′D, (2 *sing.* arch.) **hadst**; *p.p.* **had**; *neg.* **have not** *or* (colloq.) **haven′t** *pr.* hă′vent, **has not** *or* (colloq.) **hasn′t** *pr.* hă′zn't, (vulg.) **ain′t, had not** *or* (colloq.) **hadn′t** *pr.* hă′dent). **1.** *v.t.* hold in possession as one's property or at one's disposal (*all the money that I had*; *have no* TIME¹ *for*); know (a language; *he has no Latin*; *she has the Gaelic*). **2.** experience the possession of (persons etc. in various relations; *I have two sons, no uncle, no equals*); give birth to (baby); gain advantage over (*I had him there*); ‖(sl.) cheat, deceive, (*you were had*); have sexual intercourse with. **3.** possess or contain as appendage, part, quality, etc., (*June has 30 days*; *has blue eyes*; *trees have leaves*; *it has its advantages*); have an EYE¹ *to*, EYE¹*s for*; *have it in* MIND², *have a good etc.* MIND², *to*; *have what it* TAKE¹*s*. **4.** experience (*I had that pleasure*; *have a good time!*), suffer (*had a toothache, an accident, a shock, my leg broken*); be subjected to specified state (*had my car stolen*; *book has a page missing*); have it coming to one (see COME 8); have a TIME¹ (*of it*). **5.** permit (to), accept, (*am not having any of that behaviour here*; *I won′t have it*; *I will not have you say such things, treated like that*); *is not having* ANY. **6.** be under burden or obligation of (*I had my work to do*; *I had to do my work*); be provided with (*have nothing to do, say, wear*). **7.** let (feeling etc.) be present in the mind (*have no doubt*; *have no fear!*; *has a grudge against me*; *have nothing against drink in moderation*). **8.** show by action that one is influenced by (quality etc.; *have the impudence to disobey*; *have mercy on us*; *have the goodness or kindness to*); have a CARE¹. **9.** engage in, carry on, (*had some conversation, breakfast, sex, a game, a* TRY, *a wash*; *she had an affair with him*; *have a look at this*); have to DO¹ *with*. **10.** obtain, receive, (*we had news*; *there is not a loaf to be had*); eat, drink, etc., (*have an egg, a cup of tea, a cigarette*). **11.** cause, instruct, invite, (person or thing to do, be, etc.; *have her make a copy*; *had me guessing*; *have him dismissed*; *have them to stay with us, to dinner*; *have one's hair cut, one's shoes mended*). **12.** ∿ **it**, express or be aware of the view that, win decision in vote etc. (*the ayes have it*), (colloq.) possess advantage on or over, receive punishment etc. (*let him have it*); ∿ **had it**, (colloq.) have missed one's chance, passed one's prime, been killed, etc.; ∿ **it** (**away** or **off**), (sl.) copulate; *have it in*¹ one; *have it* BOTH *ways*; *have it* (*all*) one's own WAY; **I** ∿ **it**, (colloq.) I have found the answer etc.; *have it in*¹² *for*; *as* LUCK *would have it*; *have* NOTHING *on*; ∿ **it so good**, (colloq.) possess so many advantages. **13.** ∿ **at**, make attack on; ∿ **on**, wear (clothes), be committed to (engagement), (colloq.) play trick on or tease (person); ∿ **out**, settle (dispute) by discussion (*with* person), get (tooth) extracted, complete full duration of (one's sleep etc.); ∿ **to**, (colloq.) ∿ **got to**, be obliged to, MUST¹; ‖∿ **up**, bring (person) before court of justice, interviewer(s), etc. **14.** *v. aux. w. p.p.* of *vbs.*, forming past tenses (*I have, had, shall have, seen*; *had I known I would have gone*); HAS-BEEN; *have* DONE; *have got to* (see sense 13); **had** = would (*had* BETTER¹, RATHER, *as soon*). [OE *habban*, = OS *hebbian*, OHG *habēn*, ON *hafa*, Goth. *haban* f. Gmc **habhēn*, prob. cogn. w. HEAVE¹]

hăve² *n.* one who has (esp. wealth or resources; ∿**s** and ∿**-nots**, rich and poor); (sl.) swindle. [f. prec.]

*****hă′velock** (-vl-) *n.* cloth cap-cover with neck-flap to protect wearer against sun etc. [f. Sir H. *Havelock*, Brit. commander in India d. 1857]

hā′ven *n.* harbour, port; (fig.) refuge. [OE *hæfen* f. ON *höfn*, corresp. to MLG, MDu. *havene*]

have-not. See HAVE².

haven′t. See HAVE¹.

‖**hā′ver** *v.i.*, & *n.* **1.** *v.i.* talk foolishly, babble; vacillate, hesitate. **2.** *n.* (usu. in *pl.*) (Sc.) foolish talk, nonsense. [18th c.; orig. unkn.]

hā′versăck *n.* stout bag for provisions, carried on back or over shoulder by soldier etc. [f. F *havresac* f. G *habersack* (*haber* oats, *sack* SACK¹)]

hä'versīn(e) *n.* (Math.) half of versed SINE. [contr.]
hä'vildär *n.* Indian NCO corresponding to sergeant. [f. Hind. *havildār* f. Pers. *hawāldār* trust-holder]
hä'ving *n.* In vbl senses; (usu. in *pl.*) property, belongings. [ME, f. HAVE¹ + -ING¹]
hä'voc *n.* & *v.t.* (-ck-). **1.** *n.* devastation, destruction, confusion, disorder, (*make havoc of*; *play havoc among* or *with*); **cry** ～, predict imminent disaster, (orig.) give signal to army to seize spoil. **2.** *v.t.* devastate (land etc., or abs.). [ME, f. AF *havok* f. OF *havo(t)*, of unkn. orig.]
haw¹ *n.* (fruit of) hawthorn; (Hist.) hedge, enclosure; ～**finch**, thick-beaked species of finch. [OE *haga*, = OS *hago*, ON *hagi* f. Gmc *hagon-* (*hag-*; cf. HEDGE¹)]
haw² *n.* nictitating membrane of horse, dog, etc., esp. when inflamed. [16th c.; orig. unkn.]
haw³ *v.i.*, & *n.* See HUM¹,². [f. foll.]
haw⁴ *int.* expr. hesitation. [imit.; cf. HA¹]
haw'-haw¹ *int.* & *n.* (expr.) boisterous laugh or sound of repeated hesitation or affected pausing in speech. [imit.]
haw-haw². Var. of HA-HA.
hawk¹ *n.* & *v.* **1.** *n.* diurnal bird of prey once much used in falconry, with rounded wings shorter than falcon's; **know a ～ from a handsaw** [perh. corrupt. of *hernshaw* heron f. OF *heronceau* dim.], have ordinary discernment (Shak. *Hamlet* II. ii. 397). **2.** rapacious or aggressive person, (Polit.) person advocating warlike action. **3.** ～'**bit**, dandelion-like plant of genus *Leontodon*; *H~'eye State*, Iowa; ～**-eyed**, keen-sighted; ～ **monitor**, ～**-moth**, large hovering and darting moth; ～**-nosed**, with aquiline nose; ～**-owl**, diurnal owl somewhat like hawk; ～'**s-bill**, kind of turtle; ～'**weed**, plant of genus *Hieracium*, with yellow flowers. **4.** Hence ～'ISH¹, ～'LIKE, *adjs.* **5.** *v.i.* hunt game with hawk. **6.** *v.i.* & *t.* ～ (**at**), attack as hawk does, (of swallows etc.) hunt on the wing for insects. [OE *h(e)afoc*, *hæbuc*, = OS *habuk*, OHG *habuh*, ON *haukr* f. Gmc *habhukaz*]
hawk² *v.t.* carry (goods) about for sale (lit. or fig.). [back-form. f. HAWKER¹]
hawk³ *v.* **1.** *v.i.* clear the throat noisily. **2.** *v.t.* bring (phlegm etc.) *up* from throat. [prob. imit.]
hawk⁴ *n.* plasterer's square board with handle underneath. [17th c.; orig. unkn.]
haw'ker¹ *n.* one who hawks goods about. [16th c., prob. f. LDu.; cf. MLG *hoker*, LG *höker*, Du. *heuker*; cf. HUCKSTER]
haw'ker² *n.* falconer. [OE *hafocere* (as HAWK¹, -ER¹)]
hawse (-z) *n.* (Naut.) part of ship's bows in which ～**-holes** or ～**-pipes** are placed for cables to run through; space between head of anchored vessel and anchors; arrangement of cables when ship is moored with port and starboard forward anchors; ATHWART**-hawse**. [ME *halse*, prob. f. ON *hāls* neck, ship's bow]
haw'ser (-z-) *n.* (Naut.) large rope or small cable; ～**-laid** (= CABLE¹-laid. [ME, f. AF *haucer*, -*eour* f. OF *haucier* hoist f. Rom. *altiare* f. L *altus* high; see -ER²]
haw'thŏrn *n.* thorny shrub or tree of genus *Crataegus*, with white, red, or pink blossom and small dark red berry or haw; ～ **china** (oriental, with pattern of plum-blossom on dark background). [OE *hagathorn* (as HAW¹, THORN)]
hay¹ *n.* & *v.* **1.** *n.* grass mown and dried for fodder; **hit the ～**, (sl.) go to bed; *look for a* NEEDLE *in a bottle of hay* (= *haystack*); **make ～**, mow grass and turn it over for exposure to sun; **make ～ of**, throw into confusion, overthrow; **make ～ (while the sun shines)**, seize opportunities for profit; *not ～*, (colloq.) a large amount of money; **roll in the ～**, (colloq.) make love. **2.** ～'**box** (stuffed with hay, in which heated food is left to continue cooking); ～'**cock**, conical heap of hay in field; ～ **fever**, summer disorder with catarrhal and freq. asthmatic symptoms, caused by allergy to pollen or dust; ～'**field** (where hay is being or is to be made); ～'**-fork** (for turning over or loading hay); ～'**maker**, one who lifts, tosses, and spreads

hay after mowing, apparatus for shaking and drying hay, (sl.) swinging blow or punch; ～**-mow**, hay in stack or barn; ～'**-rick**, ～'**stack**, regular pile of hay with pointed or ridged top (NEEDLE *in haystack*); ～'**seed**, grass seed from hay, *(colloq.) a rustic; ～'**wire**, poorly or roughly contrived [f. use of hay-baling wire in makeshift repairs], (colloq.) tangled, in disorder, distracted. **3.** *v.t.* put (land) under grass for hay; make into hay. **4.** *v.i.* make hay. [OE *hēg*, *hīeg*, *hīg*, = OS *hōi*, OHG *hewi*, *houwi*, ON *hey*, Goth. *hawi* f. Gmc *haujam* (*hauwan* HEW)]
hay², **hey²**, (hā) *n.* (figure in) country dance with interweaving steps. [f. obs. F *haie*]
hay'ward (-ōrd) *n.* officer of parish etc. in charge of fences and enclosures. [ME, f. obs. *hay* hedge f. OE *hege* (as HAW¹) + WARD¹]
hä'zard *n.*, & *v.t.* **1.** *n.* dice game with complicated chances; chance; (source of) danger; **at ～**, (arch.) at random; **at all ～s**, despite all risks. **2.** each of winning openings in real-tennis court; (Bill.) **winning ～**, striking object-ball into pocket, **losing ～**, pocketing own ball off another; (Golf) obstruction in playing a shot, e.g. bunker, water, road, etc. **3.** *v.t.* expose to hazard; run the risk of; venture on (action, statement, guess). [n. ME, v. f. F *hasarder*, f. OF *hasard* f. Sp. *azar* f. Arab. *az-zahr* chance, luck]
hä'zardous *a.* risky; dependent on chance; hence ～LY² *adv.*, ～NESS *n.* [f. F *hasardeux* (as prec.; see -OUS)]
häze¹ *n.* obscuration of atmosphere near earth by fine particles of water, smoke, or fine dust; (fig.) mental obscurity or confusion [prob. back-form. f. HAZY]
häze² *v.t.* **1.** (Naut.) harass with overwork. **2.** *bully, seek to disconcert. [cf. obs. F *haser* tease, insult]
hä'zel *n.* bush of genus *Corylus* whose fruit is the ～**-nut**, (stick of) its wood; reddish-brown or greenish-brown or light brown colour (esp. of eyes); ～**-grouse, -hen**, species of grouse (*Tetrastes bonasia*); *witch-* or WYCH-*hazel*. [OE *hæsel*, = OHG *hasal*, ON *hasl* f. Gmc *hasalaz* f. IE *kosolos*]
hä'z(l)ȳ *a.* misty; vague, indistinct; (arch.) slightly drunk; hence ～ILY² *adv.*, ～INESS *n.* [17th c., Naut., also *hawsey*, *heysey*, of unkn. orig.]
HB *abbr.* hard black (pencil-lead).
Hb *symb.* haemoglobin.
HBM *abbr.* Her or His Britannic Majesty('s).
H-bomb (ā'chbŏm) *n.* hydrogen bomb. [f. H (for HYDROGEN) + BOMB]
HC *abbr.* Holy Communion; House of Commons.
h.c. *abbr.* honoris causa.
HCF *abbr.* highest common factor; ||Honorary Chaplain to the Forces.
hē¹ (or, *when unstressed*, hǐ) *pron.* (*obj.* him *pr.* ǐm *or*, *when stressed*, hǐm; *refl.* HIMSELF *or* arch. him, *poss.* HIS, *pl.* THEY etc.), *n.*, & *a.* **1.** *pron.* the male (or thing personified as male, e.g. tree, sun, or person of unknown or unspecified sex) previously mentioned or implied or easily identified; (he or any male person *who*; = ? IT¹8; **2.** *pron.* male, man, (cf. SHE). **3.** *a.* (usu. w. hyphen). male (*he-goat*); ～**-man**, masterful or virile man. [OE *he*, *hē*, dat. *him*, = OS *hi(e)*, *he* f. Gmc dem. st. *hi-*]
hē²(-hē') *int.* expr. amusement or derision. [OE; natural excl.]
HE *abbr.* high explosive; His Eminence; His or Her Excellency.
He *symb.* helium.
head¹ (hĕd) *n.* **1.** foremost part of body of animal, upper part of human body, containing mouth, sense-organs, and brain; (as measure) length of head (*taller by a head*; *horse won by a* (SHORT) *head*); *cannot* **make ～ or tail of**, understand at all; **count ～s**, (merely) determine number present, voting, etc. **2.** seat of intellect or imagination; natural mental aptitude or talent (*a good head for business*); ～ **for heights**, ability to be close to edge of high cliff, roof, etc., without giddiness. **3.** (colloq.) headache, esp. as result of blow or intoxication. **4.** life (*it cost him his head*; *a* PRICE *on his*

head). **5.** image of head on one side of coin; (usu. in *pl.*) this side turned upwards after toss (cf. TAIL¹); ∼**s I win, tails you lose,** I win in any event. **6.** antlers of deer; **deer of the first** ∼ (when antlers are first developed). **7.** person with . . . head (*crowned heads*; HOT¹*head*); individual (*£1 a* or *per head*); individual animal of cattle or game, (collect.) cattle or game (*twenty head*), whence ∼'AGE (1) *n.*; ∥number of animals (*large head of game*); (sl.) drug-addict, one who takes drugs. **8.** thing like head in form or position, e.g. cutting or striking part of tool, golf-club, etc., knobbed end of NAIL¹, pin, screw, etc., rounded part of musical note; *(plant)* compact mass of leaves or flowers at top of stem; ∥roof of motor car; flat surface of cask, drum, etc.; closed end of cylinder in pump or engine; device for converting electrical signals into record on magnetic tape etc. or vice versa. **9.** foam on top of liquor; cream on top of milk. **10.** top (of mast, staircase, list, page, etc.); source (of river); ∥∼ **of the river,** leading position in bumping-races. **11.** fully developed part of boil etc., where it tends to break; **come to a** ∼, (fig.) reach a climax or crisis. **12.** upper end; end of table occupied by host; end of lake at which river enters it; end of bed, couch, grave, etc., at which one's head rests. **13.** body of water kept at height for mill etc.; pressure exerted by this; pressure of confined body of steam etc. **14** front (of procession, army, etc.); front part of plough, holding the share; bows of ship (RV¹ *the head*); (colloq.) headlight. **15.** promontory (in names, as *Beachy Head*). **16.** underground passage for working in coal-mine. **17.** ruler, chief; master etc. of college; headmaster of school; (*attrib.*) occupying leading position with regard to others (*head boy, clerk, girl, office, waiter*); hence ∼'SHIP *n.* **18.** position of command (*at the head of*). **19.** main division in discourse; category. **20.** culmination, crisis, (*bring to a head*; cf. sense 11). **21.** (Naut.; in *sing.* or *pl.*) seamen's latrine in ship's bows. **22.** above one's ∼, = *over one's head* (1, 2); **come into** or **enter** person's ∼, (of idea) be thought of; **from** ∼ **to toe** or **foot,** all over a person; **get** one's ∼ **down,** (sl.) go to bed; GET¹ *it into one's head that*; **give** (**horse,** or fig. person) **his** ∼, **let him have his** ∼, allow him to go freely; **go out of** person's ∼, (of idea) be forgotten; **go to** person's ∼, (of liquor, success, etc.) impair his mental acuteness or his modesty; HANG¹ one's *head*; ∼ **and front,** (arch.) essence *of* offence or leader *of* action, (Shak.) highest extent; ∼ **and shoulders,** (*taller* etc.) by measure of the head and shoulders or (fig.) considerably; **drag in** (irrelevant topic) **by the** ∼ **and shoulders;** ∼ **first** or **foremost,** (of plunge etc.) with the head foremost, (fig.) precipitately; *head in the air* or CLOUDS, *in the* SAND; ∼ **of hair,** the hair on person's head, esp. as noticeable feature; one's or person's ∼ **off,** (fig.) into a state of exhaustion (*beat* or *talk* person's *head off*; BITE¹ person's *head off*; EAT *its head off*; *laugh* one's *head off*); ∼ **over ears** or **heels,** = *over head and* EAR¹*s;* ∼ **over heels,** topsy-turvy, so as to turn completely over in somersault etc.; ∼**s will roll,** (fig.) there will be some persons dismissed or disgraced; HOLD¹ one's *head high;* **hold up** one's ∼, not be ashamed; **in** one's ∼, by thought, mental calculation, etc.; **keep** one's ∼, remain calm; **keep** one's ∼ **above water,** (fig.) keep out of debt; **keep** one's ∼ **down,** avoid distraction or danger; ∥KNOCK¹ *on the head;* **lay** or **put** ∼**s together,** consult one another; **lose** one's ∼, (1) be beheaded, (2) become agitated or confused; **make** ∼, make progress or resistance; **off** one's ∼, CRAZY; **off the top of** one's ∼, (sl.) impromptu; *old head on young* SHOULDERS; **on** one's ∼, supported by head and arms with feet off ground, (sl.) with great ease (*could do it on my head*); **on** person's (**own**) ∼, (of vengeance, guilt, responsibility, etc.) falling on one; **out of** one's ∼, (1) from one's own invention, (2) forgotten by one, (3) *crazy; over head and* EAR¹*s;* **over** person's ∼, (1) above him, esp. fig. of impending danger etc., (2) beyond his comprehension, (3) (of another's

promotion, involvement, etc.) when he has prior or stronger claim; **put into** person's ∼, suggest (idea etc.) to him; **put** ∼**s together,** = *lay heads together; head* SCREWed *on the right way;* SWELLed or *swollen head;* **take it into** one's ∼, conceive notion (*that* or *to*); TURN¹ person's *head;* **two** ∼**s are better than one,** combination of two persons' ideas is superior to those of either separately. **23.** ∼'**ache,** continuous pain in head, (colloq.) troublesome or annoying thing; ∼'**achy,** suffering from or causing headache; ∼'**band,** band worn round head; ∼'**board** (forming head of bed etc.); ∼'**borough,** (Hist.) petty constable; **∼* **cheese,** brawn made from pig's head etc.; ∼**-cloth,** cloth or covering for head; ∼**-dress,** covering (esp. ornamental attire) for the head; ∼'**fast,** rope or chain securing head of vessel to quay etc.; ∼'**gear,** (1) hat, cap, head-dress, (2) machinery etc. at top of mine-shaft; ∼**-hunter,** savage who collects heads of his enemies as trophies; ∼'**lamp,** (1) lamp carried on front of bicycle, (2) = *headlight;* ∼'**land,** (1) promontory, (2) strip left (at first) unploughed at end of field; ∼'**light,** (beam from) powerful lamp carried on front of locomotive, motor vehicle, etc.; ∼'**line,** line at top of page containing title etc., title or sub-title in large type in newspaper, (in *pl.*) summary (at beginning of) broadcast news bulletin, (*hit* or *make the* ∼*lines,* be very important news); **∼***liner,** star performer; ∼'**lock,** wrestling hold with arm round opponent's head; ∼'**man,** chief man, chief of tribe etc.; ∼**ma'ster,** ∼**mi'stress,** principal master, mistress, of school; ∼**-money** (paid for or by each person); ∼**-note** (inserted at head of page or document); ∼**-on** *a.,* involving the meeting of two vehicles head to head (*a head-on collision*), or of the head of a vehicle with a stationary object, (fig.) with direct opposition; ∼**-o'n** *adv.,* with the head pointed directly towards some object; ∼'**phone,** radio or telephone earphone held by band fitting over head; ∼'**piece,** (1) helmet, (2) intellect, man of intellect, (3) ornamental engraving at head of chapter etc.; ∼**quar'ters,** (as *pl.* or *sing.*), central or chief place of business etc., (Mil.) quarters of officer commanding army, corps, division, etc.; ∼**-race,** part of mill-race bringing water to wheel; ∼**-rest,** support for head of person sitting in vehicle etc.; ∼**-room,** overhead space; ∼**-sail** (on foremast or bowsprit); ∼'**scarf** (worn instead of hat); ∼ **sea,** waves from forward direction; ∼**-set,** attachment for fixing earphones and microphone to head; ∼**-shrinker,** head-hunter who shrinks enemies' heads, (sl.) psychiatrist; ∼'**spring,** main source of stream (lit. or fig.); ∼'**square,** scarf for head; ∼'**stall,** part of bridle or halter that fits round horse's head; ∼ **start,** = START² 3 (in race, or fig.); ∼'**stock,** bearings of revolving parts in machine; ∼'**stone,** (1) gravestone, (2) chief stone in foundation (lit. or fig.); **∼* **tax,** poll-tax; ∼**-up,** (of instrument-readings in aircraft, vehicle, etc.) shown so as to be visible without lowering one's eyes from view ahead; ∼**-voice,** high register of voice in speaking or singing; ∼**-water(s),** streams from sources of river; ∼'**way,** (1) progress, (of ship) rate of progress, (2) headroom, (3) interval between successive buses etc. on route; ∼ **wind** (blowing from directly in front); ∼'**word,** word forming a heading (of entry in dictionary etc.), (Ling.) word qualified in phrase; ∼**-work,** mental work. **24.** Hence (-)∼'ED, ∼'LESS, *adjs.,* ∼'WARD *a.* & *adv.* [OE *hēafod,* = OS *hōbid,* OHG *houbit,* ON *haufuth,* Gmc f. Gmc **haubhudham*]

head² (hĕd) *v.* **1.** *v.t.* furnish with head or heading; ∼ (**down**), lop off head of (plant, tree); be or form the head of; place inscription, (of name etc.) be placed, at head of (chapter, list, etc.); lead; precede; surpass; ∼ (***up), be, put oneself, at the head of (a company etc.); (Footb.) strike (ball) with head; direct course of *towards* etc.; ∼ **back, off,** get ahead of so as to force to turn back, aside. **2.** *v.i.* form head; face or proceed (in

specified direction); ∼ **for,** (of ship etc.) be moving towards (place, point, or fig. disaster etc.). [ME, f. prec.]
-head (hĕd) *suf.* Var. of -HOOD (*godhead, maidenhead*). [f. ME *-hed(e)* -HOOD]
hea′der (hĕ′d-) *n.* In vbl senses; one who puts heads on casks etc.; brick or stone laid at right angles to face of wall (cf. STRETCHER); (colloq.) dive or plunge head first; (Footb.) act of heading the ball. [ME, f. HEAD[1,2] + -ER[1]]
hea′ding (hĕ′d-) *n.* In vbl senses; (Footb.) striking ball with head; material for making cask-heads; title etc. at head of page etc.; horizontal passage in preparation for tunnel; = DRIFT[1] 7. [ME, f. HEAD[2] + -ING[1]]
hea′dlŏng (hĕ′d-) *adv.* & *a.* head foremost (in falling etc.); precipitate(ly); impetuous(ly). [ME *headling* (HEAD[1], -LING[2]), assim. to -LONG]
hea′dmost (hĕ′dmŏst, -ō-) *a.* (Esp. of ship) foremost. [f. HEAD[1] + -MOST]
hea′ds|man (hĕ′dz-) *n.* (*pl.* ∼**men**). executioner who beheads; man in command of whaling boat. [ME, f. HEAD[1] + -'s l + MAN[1]]
hea′dstrŏng (hĕ′d-) *a.* violently self-willed; obstinate; hence ∼NESS *n.* [ME, f. HEAD[1] + STRONG, = strong in head]
hea′d|ў (hĕ′dĭ) *a.* (Of person, thing, action) impetuous, violent; (of liquor etc., or fig. of triumph etc.) apt to intoxicate; headachy; hence ∼iLY[2] *adv.*, ∼iNESS *n.* [ME, f. HEAD[1] + -Y[2]]
heal[1] *v.* **1.** *v.t.* restore (person, injured part) to health (lit. or fig.); cure (wound; arch. person *of* disease); ∼**-all,** (1) universal remedy, (2) (pop. name of various medicinal plants). **2.** *v.i.* ∼ (**over, up**), (of wound or part) become healed. **3.** Hence ∼′ER[1] *n.* (*time is a great healer*). [OE *hǣlan* = OS *hēlian,* OHG *heilen,* ON *heila,* Goth. *hailjan* f. Gmc **hailjan* (**hailaz* WHOLE)]
heal[2]. See HELE.
heald *n.* = HEDDLE. [app. f. OE *hefel(d)*, = OS *hevild,* ON *hafald* f. Gmc **hafjan* raise]
health (hĕl-) *n.* **1.** soundness of body or mind (lit. or fig.; **for** one's ∼, in order to attain or maintain good health; **not for** one's ∼, for one's material advantage); condition of body (*good, poor, bad, ill, health;* BILL[4] *of health*); toast drunk in person's honour. **2.** ∼ **centre,** local headquarters of medical services; ∼ **certificate** (stating person's fitness for work etc.); ∼ **farm,** establishment where improved health is sought by dieting etc.; ∼ **food** (chosen for its dietary or health-giving or unmodified natural qualities); ∼ **officer** (charged with administering health laws etc.); ∼ **physics,** study of health of persons exposed to radiation from radioactive materials; ∼ **resort,** place visited for benefit of one's health; ∼ **salts,** mild aperient; ∼ **service,** public medical services collectively; ||∼ **visitor,** trained person visiting sick or old people etc. at their homes. [OE *hǣlth,* = OHG *heilida* f. WG **hailitha* f. Gmc **hailaz* WHOLE; see -TH[1]]
hea′lthful (hĕ′l-) *a.* health-giving; conducive to moral or spiritual welfare; hence ∼LY[2] *adv.,* ∼NESS *n.* [ME, f. prec. + -FUL]
hea′lth|ў (hĕ′l-) *a.* having or showing good health (lit. or fig.); conducive to good health (*healthy climate*); beneficial (*a healthy interest in, respect for*); hence ∼iLY[2] *adv.,* ∼iNESS *n.* [f. HEALTH + -Y[2]]
heap[1] *n.* group of things lying one on another; mass of material so shaped; (in *sing.* or *pl.,* colloq.) large number or quantity (*a heap of people; there is heaps of time; have seen it heaps of times; he is heaps better*); (colloq.) slovenly woman, battered old motor vehicle; *knock* or STRIKE *all of a heap;* **top, bottom, of the** ∼, (colloq., fig.) winner, loser. [OE *hēap,* = OS *hōp,* OHG *houf, hūfo,* f. Gmc **haup-, *hūp-*]
heap[2] *v.t.* put (things *up, together,* etc.) in a heap; load (cart, person, etc. esp. above normal level *with* goods, benefits, etc.); place large quantities of (insults etc. *(up)on*). [OE *hēapian* (as prec.)]
*hea′ping *a.* (Of spoonful etc.) heaped; (fig.) mounting up. [f. prec. + -ING[2]]

hear *v.* (**heard** *pr.* hĕrd). **1.** *v.t.* perceive (sound etc., or abs.) with the ear (*I heard a groan, him groaning, him groan; he was heard groaning* or *to groan*). **2.** listen to (*hear him, his lesson, a sermon*); listen judicially to (case, plaintiff, etc.); grant (prayer), obey (order); ∼ **out,** listen to whole of (what is said by). **3.** learn by being told (*that*); ∼ **say,** ∼ **tell** (**of**), be told (about). **4.** *v.i.* be told (*about*); ∼ **from,** receive letter or message from; ∼ **of,** be told about, get knowledge of, (w. neg.) be willing to consider (*will not hear of my paying for it*); ∼ (**more**) **of,** (fig.) be reprimanded etc. for. **5.** ∼!, ∼!, (as form of cheering a speaker or iron. derision etc.); ∼′say, what one hears (but does not certainly know to be true), gossip, (often *attrib.; hearsay evidence*). **6.** Hence ∼′ABLE *a.,* ∼′ER[1] *n.* [OE *hīeran,* = OS *hōrian,* OHG *hōrren,* ON *heyra,* Goth. *hausjan* f. Gmc **hauzjan*]
heard. See prec.
hear′ing *n.* In vbl senses; faculty of perception by response of brain to action of sound on ear (**hard of** ∼, somewhat deaf); trial esp. without jury, chance to state one's case; **come to** person's ∼, become known to him by being told; **within, out of,** ∼, near enough, too far off, to be heard; **in** one's ∼, so that one can hear; **a fair** ∼, impartial listening to statement of case; ∼**-aid,** small sound-amplifier worn by deaf person to improve hearing. [f. HEAR + -ING[1]]
hear′ken (här′-) *v.i.* (arch. or literary). listen (*to*). [OE *he(o)rcnian* (as HARK, -EN[6])]
hearse (hers) *n.* vehicle for carrying coffin at funeral; (arch.) framework supporting pall at great person's funeral and carrying tapers and other decorations. [ME, f. OF *herse* harrow f. med. L *erpica* f. Rom. **herpica* f. L (*h*)*irpex -picis* large rake f. Samnite (*h*)*irpus* wolf, w. ref. to its teeth]
heart (härt) *n.,* & *v.i.* **1.** *n.* hollow muscular organ keeping up circulation of blood by contracting and dilating; disease of this (*I believe he has a heart*). **2.** breast, bosom, (*pressed her to his heart*); mind, intellect; seat of inmost thoughts, = SOUL 2 (∼ **to** ∼, with candour); **after** one's **own** ∼, just such as one likes or desires; one's ∼ **is not in it,** one is not really interested in succeeding etc. **3.** seat of the emotions, esp. of love, opp. *head* as seat of intellect, (**give** or **lose** one's ∼ **to,** fall in love with; *win the heart of*). **4.** susceptibility to emotion (*he has no heart*); courage (*pluck up* or *take, lose, heart*). **5.** (As term of endearment to person: *dear, sweet, heart*); (Naut. etc.) brave fellow. **6.** central or innermost part, e.g. of tree (∼ **of oak,** courageous man); close compact head of cabbage, lettuce, etc.; vital part, essence, (*the heart of the matter*). **7.** ||(Of land) fertility (**in good** ∼, in prime condition; **out of** ∼, in poor condition). **8.** heart-shaped thing; conventional symmetrical figure of a heart with two equal curves meeting in point and cusp; playing-card of suit (∼**s**) denoted by red figure of this kind; (in *pl.*) card-game in which players try not to take tricks containing card of this suit. **9. at** ∼, in one's inmost feelings; **have at** ∼, be deeply interested in; **bless his** etc. ∼ (excl. of pleasure); **bless my** ∼ (excl. of surprise); **from** or **to the bottom of** one's ∼, genuinely, profoundly; **break** one's ∼, be reduced to despair; **break** person's ∼, overwhelm him with sorrow; **by** ∼, in or from memory (*learn* or *say by heart*); **change of** ∼, conversion to different frame of mind; **close to** (= *near,* see below) person's **heart;** **find it in** one's ∼, (esp. w. neg.) prevail upon oneself (*to* do); **from** one's or the ∼, sincere(ly); **go to** one's or **the** ∼, deeply touch or grieve one; **do** one's ∼ **good,** cheer or rejoice one; **have a** ∼, (colloq.) be merciful; **have the** ∼, (esp. w. neg.) be hard-hearted enough (*to* do); *heart* BLEEDS; *to* one's *heart's* CONTENT[2]; one's ∼ **goes out to,** one feels strong affection or sympathy for; one's ∼ **is in** one's **boots,** one is terrified or dejected; *heart of* GOLD; **take** ∼ **of grace,** pluck up one's courage; one's ∼ **is in** one's **mouth,** one is violently alarmed or startled; one's ∼ **is in the**

right place, one has good intentions; **wear** one's ∼ **on** one's **sleeve,** let one's feelings be quite obvious; ∼ **and soul,** with all one's energy or devotion; one's ∼ **stands still,** one is momentarily paralysed with fright; **in** ∼, in good spirits; **in** one's ∼, secretly, in one's inmost feelings; **in** one's ∼ **of** ∼**s,** in one's inmost feelings; **lay to** ∼, think over seriously; **near**(est) person's ∼, dear(est) to him, affecting him (most) deeply; **out of** ∼, in low spirits (and see sense 7); *cry, play,* etc., one's ∼ **out,** to exhaustion, with utmost effort; **eat** one's ∼ **out,** pine away with vexation or longing; SET[1] one's *heart on;* **take to** ∼, be much affected in one's feelings by; **with all** one's ∼, sincerely, with the utmost goodwill. **10.** ∼'**ache,** mental anguish; ∼ **attack,** = *heart failure;* ∼'**beat,** pulsation of heart, (fig.) emotion; ∼**-block,** failure of parts of heart to beat together, caused by muscular defect; ∼('**s**)**-blood,** life-blood, life; ∼**-break,** overwhelming distress (∼**-breaking, -broken,** causing, crushed by, this); ∼'**burn,** pyrosis; ∼**-burn**(**ing**), jealousy, grudge; ∼**-cherry,** heart-shaped cultivated sweet cherry; ∼**-disease** (of heart); ∼ **failure,** deranged action of heart, esp. if fatal; ∼'**felt,** sincere (emotion etc.); ∼'**land,** central or most important part of an area; ∼**-lu'ng machine** (providing means to bypass these organs in blood circulation during an operation); ∼**-rending,** distressing; ∼**s-and--flowers,** undue sentimentality; ∼**-searching,** examination of one's own feelings; ∼'**s-ease,** pansy; ∼'**sick,** despondent; ∼'**sore,** grieved at heart; ∼**-strings,** (fig.) deepest affections; ∼**-throb,** beating of heart, (sl.) object of one's infatuation; ∼**-warming,** emotionally moving and encouraging; ∼**-whole,** (1) undismayed, (2) not in love, (3) sincere; ∼'**wood,** dense inner part of tree-trunk yielding hardest timber. **11.** Hence ∼'ED² *a.* **12.** *v.i.* (of cabbage etc.) form a heart. [OE *heorte,* = OS *herta,* OHG *herza,* ON *hjarta,* Goth. *hairtō* f. Gmc *herton* f. IE *k(e)rd-*]

hear'ten (här'-) *v.* **1.** *v.t.* inspirit, cheer (*up* or *on*). **2.** *v.i.* cheer *up.* [f. prec. v.t. in same sense + -EN⁶]

hearth (härth-) *n.* **1.** floor of fireplace; area in front of this; ∼ **and home,** home and its comforts; ∼**-money,** 17th-c. tax on hearths in England & Wales; ∼'**rug** (laid before fireplace); ∼'**stone,** (1) flat stone forming hearth, (2) stone etc. for whitening hearths etc. **2.** bottom of blast-furnace where molten metal collects. [OE *heorth,* = OS *herth,* OHG *hert* f. WG *herthu*]

hear'tily (här'-) *adv.* In adj. senses; with goodwill, courage, or appetite; very (*am heartily sick of it*). [ME, f. HEARTY + -LY²]

hear'tless (härt'-) *a.* unfeeling, pitiless, cruel; hence ∼LY² *adv.,* ∼NESS *n.* [ME, f. HEART + -LESS]

hear'ty (här'-) *a. & n.* **1.** *a.* cordial, genial; (of feelings) sincere; vigorous (*hearty laugh, appetite*); (of meal) abundant; hence ∼iNESS *n.* **2.** *n.* hearty person (as *voc.* to sailors: *my hearties*), ‖(at university) sportsman, athlete (opp. AESTHETE). [ME, f. HEART + -Y²]

heat¹ *n.* **1.** being hot; sensation or perception of this; (high) temperature; RED, WHITE¹, *heat.* **2.** (Phys.) form of energy arising from random motion of molecules of bodies, capable of transmission by conduction, convection, or radiation, (formerly thought to be an elastic material fluid); amount of this needed to cause a specified process, or evolved in a process, (*heat of formation; heat of solution*); latent ∼, heat required to convert a solid into liquid or vapour, or a liquid into vapour, without change of temperature; RADIANT *heat;* specific ∼, heat required to raise temperature of unit mass of a given substance by given amount (usu. one degree), usu. calculated relatively to water. **3.** hot weather. **4.** (normal or abnormal) high temperature of body. **5.** pungency of flavour. **6.** redness of skin with sensation of heat; PRICKLY *heat.* **7.** single run in race etc.; (**trial**) ∼**s,** races or contests the winners of which compete in

FINAL (*heat*). **8.** warmth of feeling, anger; most vigorous stage (of debate etc.); (sl.) pursuit by police etc.; **in the** ∼ **of the moment,** without pause for thought, as a result of the vigorous action etc. then in progress. **9.** sexual excitement of (esp. female) animals during breeding season (‖**on, in,** or **at** ∼, undergoing this). **10.** ∼ **barrier,** limitation of speed of aircraft etc. by heat resulting from air friction; ∼ **bump,** skin-protuberance thought to be due to heat; ∼ **capacity,** thermal capacity; ∼ **death,** (Phys.) state of uniform distribution of energy to which universe seems to be tending; ∼**-engine** (producing motive power from heat); ∼**-exchange**(**r**), (device for) transfer of heat from one medium to another; ∼ **pump,** reversed heat-engine, using mechanical energy to transfer heat to hotter place; ∼**-resistant,** = *heat-*PROOF²; ∼ **shield,** device to protect from excessive heat (esp. on spacecraft during re-entry); ∼ **sink,** device for removing unwanted heat; ∼**-stroke,** prostration from excessive heat; ∼ **treatment,** use of heat to modify properties of metal etc.; *heat* WAVE². [OE *hætu,* = MDu. *hēte,* OHG *heiz* f. WG *haitī*(*n*) f. Gmc *haitaz* HOT¹]

heat² *v.* **1.** *v.t.* make hot or warm; inflame (blood etc.); (esp. in *p.p.*) inflame with rage or passion, excite, whence ∼EDLY *adv.* **2.** *v.i.* become hot or warm (lit or fig.). [OE *hātan,* = OHG *heizen,* ON *heita* f. Gmc *haitjan* (*haitaz* HOT¹)]

hea'ter *n.* In vbl senses; stove; warming device, (sl.) firearm. [f. prec. + -ER¹]

heath *n.* open flat waste tract of land, esp. if covered with shrubs; shrub growing on such land, esp. of genus *Erica* or *Calluna;* butterfly frequenting heath; ∼**-bell,** bell-shaped flower of heath; ∼**-cock,** blackcock; ∼**-hen,** grey-hen; hence ∼'Y² *a.* [OE *hæth,* = OS *hētha,* OHG *heida,* ON *heithr,* Goth. *haithi* f. Gmc *haithiz*]

hea'then (-dh-) *a. & n.* **1.** (one who is) not an adherent of any of the world's chief religions, esp. (one who is) neither Christian, Jew, nor Muslim; (OT) Gentile; **the** ∼, (collect.) heathen people. **2.** *n.* unenlightened person; person regarded as lacking culture or moral principles. **3.** ∼**-dom,** ∼**ism,** ∼**ry** (2) *ns.,* ∼**ish¹** *a.,* ∼**ize** (3) *v.t. & i.* [OE *hæthen,* = OS *hēthin,* OHG *heidan,* ON *heithinn,* Goth. *haithnō* Gentile, f. Gmc *haithanaz* savage (*haith-* HEATH, perh. rendering L *paganus* PAGAN; see -EN⁵)]

hea'ther (hĕ'dh-) *n.* plant or shrub of genus *Erica, Calluna,* or *Daboecia,* esp. *Calluna vulgaris;* **take to the** ∼, (Sc. Hist.) become outlaw; ∼**-bell,** (flower of) *Erica tetralix* or *E. cinerea;* ∼ **honey** (from nectar of heather); ∼ **mixture,** (fabric) of mixed hues supposed to resemble heather; hence ∼Y² *a.* [ME, Sc. & N. Engl. *hathir* etc., of unkn. orig.; assim. to *heath*]

Heath Rŏ'binson *a.* absurdly ingenious and impracticable in construction. [f. W. ∼, Engl. cartoonist d. 1944, who drew many such contrivances]

heave¹ *v.* (∼**d** or, esp. Naut., **hove** *pr.* hōv). **1.** *v.t.* lift (heavy thing); utter (groan, sigh) with effort; (Naut. or colloq.) throw (*heave the* LEAD¹); (Naut.) haul up, haul, by rope. **2.** *v.i.* rise, swell up; rise with alternate falls, as waves; pant; retch; pull (*at* rope etc.). **3.** ∼ **down,** turn (ship) over on one side for cleaning etc.; ∼ **to,** bring (vessel, or abs.), be brought, to standstill without anchoring; ∼ **in sight,** (Naut. or colloq.) become visible; ∼ **ho** (*int.,* cry of sailors in heaving anchor up), ∼, *n.,* sl.) snub, dismissal. [OE *hebban,* = OS *hebbian,* OHG *heffen,* ON *hefja,* Goth. *hafjan* f. Gmc *habhjan* cogn. w. L *capere* take]

heave² *n.* heaving; (Geol.) sideways displacement in fault; ∼ **of the sea,** force exerted by swell of sea on ship's course; (in *pl.*) disease of horses with laboured breathing, broken wind. [f. prec.]

hea'ven (hĕ'-) *n.* **1.** (usu. in *pl.* exc. poet.) apparent vault over the earth, in which sun, moon, and stars are seen (*the spangled heavens*); region of the atmosphere in which clouds float, winds blow, and birds

fly, (**the ∿s opened,** there was a downpour). **2.**
(Hist.) = SPHERE 3. **3.** abode of immortals; habitation of God and his angels and the beatified spirits,
usually regarded as beyond sky (opp. *hell*); **seventh
∿, ∿ of ∿s,** highest of seven heavens recognized by
Muslims and some Jews, abode of God; **in the
seventh ∿,** in a state of extreme delight or exaltation; **move ∿ and earth,** make every possible effort
(*to* do). **4.** (usu. *H∿*). God, Providence, (*it is Heaven's
will*); (in asseverations and exclamations: **by H∿!,**
GOOD *heavens!,* **H∿s above!, H∿ forbid** or
FORFEND!, **H∿ (only) knows,** *in Heaven's* NAME[1], *for
Heaven's* SAKE[1], THANK *heaven*(*s*)*!,* (cf. phrs. at GOD). **5.**
place or state of supreme bliss or great delight. **6. ∿-
-born,** of divine origin; **∿-sent,** providential. **7.**
Hence **∿WARD** *a.,* **∿WARD**(s) *adv.* [OE *heofon, hefen,
heben,* = OS *heban,* ON *himinn hifn-,* Goth. *himins*]
hea′venly (hĕ′) *a.* of heaven, divine, (**the H∿ City,**
Paradise; **the heavenly** HOST[1]); of the sky (*heavenly*
BODY[1]); of more than earthly or human excellence;
(colloq.) attractive, excellent, (*what a heavenly day!*);
∿-minded, holy, devout; hence **hea′venli**NESS
(hĕ′-) *n.* [OE *heofonlic* (as prec., -LY[1])]
hea′ver *n.* In vbl senses; COAL-*heaver.* [f. HEAVE[1] +
-ER[1]]
Hea′viside (hĕ′-) *n.* **∿ layer,** layer of ionosphere able
to reflect long radio waves. [f. O. ∿, Engl. physicist d.
1925]
hea′vy̌ (hĕ′-) *a.,n.,* & *adv.* **1.** *a.* of great weight; of great
density; weighty because abundant (*a heavy crop*);
laden *with*; (of ordnance) of the larger kind (*heavy
guns, artillery*); (Mil.) carrying heavy arms (*the heavy
brigade*). **2.** (Phys.) having a greater than the usual
mass (esp. of isotopes and compounds containing
them; **∿ hydrogen,** DEUTERIUM; **∿ water,** substance composed entirely or mainly of deuterium
oxide). **3.** severe, intense, extensive, (*heavy fighting,
frost, losses*); acting in this manner (*heavy drinker, loser*);
needing much physical effort (*heavy work*); (of jazz
etc.) serious, forceful. **4.** striking or falling with force
(*heavy blows, rain, sea, storm*); causing strong impact
(*heavy fall*); (colloq.) using brutal methods. **5.** (Of
ground) clinging, difficult to travel over; (of mist or
fog) dense; (of bread etc.) dense from not having
risen; (of food or fig. of writings) hard to digest. **6.** (Of
sky) overcast, gloomy. **7.** clumsy or ungraceful in
appearance or effect (*heavy features*); (of person)
intellectually slow; unwieldy; (of artistic or literary
production) dull, tedious; (of newspaper etc.) serious
in tone; (Theatr.) serious, sombre, (*heavy villain*);
ponderously dignified, sternly repressive, (*heavy
father*). **8.** oppressive, grievous, (*a heavy fate*); sad (*heavy
news*); despondent; doleful; drowsy; LIE[3] *heavy; time
HANG's heavy.* **9. heavier-than-air′,** (of aircraft)
weighing more than the air it displaces; **∿-armed,**
bearing heavy weapons or armour; *heavy* CHEMICALs;
∿-duty, intended to be unusually resistant to stresses
in use; **∿-footed,** ponderous; **∿-handed,** ungraceful, oppressive; **∿-hearted,** melancholy, doleful; ∿
industry (concerned with production of metal,
machines, etc.); **∿ metal,** (1) heavy guns, (fig.)
formidable opponent(s), (2) metal of high density; **∿
oil,** a heavier-than-water oil obtained from coal tar
by distillation at high temperature; **sleeper** (difficult
to rouse); **∿ spar,** barytes; **∿ swell,** strong swell of
sea, (arch. colloq.) man who emphasizes his real or
imagined importance by overdressing etc.; **∿ traffic,**
(1) lorries and other large vehicles, (2) large quantity
of vehicles; **∿ type,** printed characters with unusually thick strokes; *heavy* WEATHER[1]; **∿weight,**
jockey, boxer (see BOX[5]), etc., of more than average
weight, (fig.) person of unusual ability or importance. **10.** Hence **∿**ISH[1] 2 *a.,* **hea′vi**LY[1] *adv.,*
hea′viNESS *n.,* (hĕ′-). **11.** *n.* (Theatr.) heavy character
(see sense 7); (usu. in *pl.*) heavy vehicle, serious
newspaper (in *pl.*) heavy artillery. **12.** *adv.* heavily
(esp. in *comb.*: *heavy-laden*). [OE *hefig,* = OS *hebig,*

OHG *hebīg,* ON *höfugr, höfigr* f. Gmc **habhuza-*
(*habhiz weight, cogn. w. HEAVE)]
Heb. *abbr.* Hebrew; Hebrews (NT).
hĕ′bdomǎd *n.* week (esp. in reference to Dan. 9: 27).
[f. LL f. Gk *hebdomas -ados* (*hepta* seven; see -AD)]
hĕbdŏ′madal *a.* weekly; H∿ **Council,** (Oxf. Univ.)
representative board meeting weekly. [f. LL *heb-
domadalis* (as prec.; see -AL)]
hĕ′bĕtāte *v.t.* & *i.* (literary). make or become dull. [f.
L *hebetare* (*hebes -etis* blunt) + -ATE[3]]
hĕ′bĕtŭde *n.* (literary). dullness, lethargy. [f. LL
hebetudo (as prec.; see -TUDE)]
Hĕbrā′|ic *a.* of Hebrew or the Hebrews; hence **∿-
ICALLY** *adv.* [f. LL f. Gk *Hebraikos* (as HEBREW; see -IC)]
Hē′brā|ism *n.* attribute of the Hebrews; Hebrew
system of thought or religion; Hebrew idiom or
expression esp. in the Greek of the Bible; so **∿IZE** (3)
v.t. & *i.,* **∿i′st**IC *a.* [f. F *hébraïsme* or f. mod. L f. late
Gk. Hebraïsmos; see HEBREW, -ISM]
Hē′brāist *n.* person skilled in Hebrew. [f. HEBRAIC +
-IST]
Hē′brew (-ōō) *n.* & *a.* **1.** *n.* member of Semitic people
in ancient Palestine; Israelite, Jew. **2.** Semitic language of the ancient Jews; modern form of this used
esp. in Israel; (colloq.) unintelligible speech (cf.
GREEK). **3.** *a.* of or in Hebrew; of the Hebrews or the
Jews. [ME, f. OF *Ebreu* f. med. L *Ebreus* f. L f. Gk
Hebraios f. Aram. *'ibray* f. Heb. *'ibrī* one from the other
side (of the river)]
Hebrĭdean (hĕbrĭdē′an, hĭbrī′dĭan) *a.* & *n.* (native or
inhabitant) of the Hebrides. [f. *Hebrides* islands off
W. Scotland + -AN]
hĕ′catomb (-ōōm) *n.* (Gk & Rom. Ant.) great public
sacrifice (prop. of 100 oxen); (fig.) sacrifice of many
victims. [f. L f. Gk *hekatombē* (*hekaton* hundred, *bous*
ox)]
hĕck[1] *n.* (Sc. & N. Engl.) frame obstructing passage of
fish in river. [ME; northern form of HATCH[1]]
hĕck[2] *n.* (colloq., euphem.) = HELL 2. [alt. f. HELL]
hĕ′ckelphŏne *n.* (Mus.) baritone oboe. [f. G *heckelphon*
(W. *Heckel,* 20th-c. Ger. instrument-maker); see
-PHONE]
hĕ′ckl|e *v.t.,* & *n.* **1.** (dress flax or hemp with)
HACKLE[1]. **2.** *v.t.* interrupt (public speaker, or abs.)
with aggressive questions or abuse. **3.** Hence **∿**ER[1] *n.*
[ME, northern and eastern form of HACKLE[1]]
hĕ′ctare (-är, -ār) *n.* metric unit of square measure,
100 ares (2.471 acres). [F (as HECTO-, ARE[1])]
hĕ′ct|ic *a.* & *n.* **1.** *a.* **∿ic fever,** that which accom-
panies consumption and similar diseases, with
flushed cheeks and hot dry skin. **2.** having hectic
fever; morbidly flushed (lit. or fig.); (colloq.) exciting, feverishly active; hence **∿**ICALLY *adv.* **3.** *n.* hectic
fever, patient, or flush. [ME *etik* f. OF *etique* f. LL f. Gk
hektikos habitual (*hexis* habit), assim. to F *hectique* or
LL]
hĕ′cto- *comb. form.* hundred, esp. of a unit in the metric
system (hectoGRAM[2], hectoLITRE, hectoMETRE[2]). [F,
irreg. f. Gk *hekaton* hundred]
hĕ′ctograph (-ahf) *n.,* & *v.t.* **1.** *n.* apparatus for
copying documents by use of gelatin plate. **2.** *v.t.* copy
with hectograph. [f. prec. + -GRAPH]
hĕ′ctor *n.,* & *v.t.* & *i.* bluster(er), bully. [f. *Hector,* L f.
Gk *Hektōr,* son of Priam and Hecuba, Trojan hero in
Homer's 'Iliad' (*hektōr* holding fast)]
hĕ′ddle *n.* one of sets of small cords or wires between
which warp is passed in loom before going through
the reed. [app. f. OE **hefdl, hefeld* (see HEALD)]
hĕdge[1] *n.* **1.** closely planted row of bushes or low trees,
esp. forming boundary of field, garden, or road;
similar boundary of turf, stone, etc. **2.** line of things or
persons forming barrier; (fig.) barrier; act or means of
hedging bet or speculation. **3.** (in *comb.*) living,
working, done, etc., by the wayside, inferior. **4. ∿-
-hop** (-*pp*-), fly at low altitude; **∿-priest,** (Hist.,
derog.) illiterate priest of low status; **∿′row,** row of
bushes forming hedge; **∿-school,** (Hist.) low-class

school, (orig.) open-air school esp. in Ireland; ~-**sparrow**, common British and European thrushlike bird (*Prunella modularis*). [OE **hecg, hegg*, = MDu. *hegghe*, OHG *hegga, hecka* f. Gmc **hagja*; cf. HAW¹]

hĕdg|e² *v.* **1.** *v.t.* surround with hedge (lit. or fig.); fence *off*; hem *in*. **2.** *v.i.* make or trim hedges; hence ~ER¹ *n.* **3.** *v.t.* reduce one's risk of loss on (bet, speculation, or abs.) by similar transactions on the other side. **4.** *v.i.* avoid committing oneself. [ME, f. prec.]

hĕ'dgehŏg (-jh-) *n.* small spiny nocturnal pig-snouted insectivorous mammal of genus *Erinaceus*, rolling itself up into ball for defence; porcupine, sea-urchin, or other animal similarly armed with spines; (Mil.) small self-contained defensive position bristling with fortifications on all sides; prickly seed-vessel of some plants, e.g. corn crowfoot; person hard to get on with, whence ~GY² (-gǐ) *a.* [ME, f. HEDGE¹ (from its habitat) + HOG¹ (from its snout)]

hĕdŏ'n|ic *a.* of pleasure; (Psych.) of pleasant or unpleasant sensations; hence ~ICS *n.*, doctrine of pleasure. [f. Gk *hēdonikos* (as foll.; see -IC)]

hĕ'don|ism *n.* doctrine that pleasure is the chief good or the proper aim; behaviour based on this; so ~IST (2) *n.*, ~i'stic *a.* [f. Gk *hēdonē* pleasure + -ISM]

-hē'dr|on *suf.* (*pl.* ~**a**) forming *ns.* naming geometrical solids with various numbers or shapes of faces (*dodecahedron, rhombohedron*); hence ~AL *adj. suf.* [f. Gk *hedra* seat]

hee'bie-jeebies (-ǐz) *n. pl.* (sl.) **the** ~, state of nervous depression or apprehension. [20th c., of unkn. orig.]

heed *v.t.*, & *v.i.* **1.** *v.t.* concern oneself about, take notice of. **2.** *n.* careful attention (*take heed* (*of*); *pay* or *give heed to*); hence ~'FUL, ~'LESS, *adjs.* [OE *hēdan*, = OS *hōdian*, OHG *huoten* f. WG **hōdjan* (**hōda* care)]

hee'-haw *n.*, & *v.i.* **1.** *n.* ass's bray; loud coarse laugh. **2.** *v.i.* give hee-haw. [imit.]

heel¹ *n.* **1.** hinder part of human foot below ankle (**Achilles'** ~, only vulnerable spot, weak point); (Zool.) corresponding part of hind limb in quadruped, often raised above ground; (of quadruped) hinder part of hoof, (in *pl.*) hind feet. **2.** part of stocking that covers heel; part of boot or shoe that supports heel. **3.** thing like heel in shape or position, e.g. handle end of violin bow, inner end of head of golf-club, part of palm next to wrist; rear end of ski; bottom or end crust of loaf; (Hort.) irregularly shaped piece of plant attached to a cutting. **4.** (sl.) untrustworthy or despicable person. **5. at** ~ = *to heel*; **at the** ~**s of**, close behind (person, event, etc.); **back on** one's ~**s**, into state of discomfiture or astonishment; **show a clean pair of** ~**s**, run away; COOL² one's *heels*; DIG one's *heels in*; **down at** (**the*) ~, (of shoe) with heel worn down, (of person) wearing such shoes, slovenly, shabby; DRAG¹ one's *heels*; *heel-and-toe* WALK-ING¹; ~**s over head**, (arch.) = HEAD¹ *over heels*; **his** ~**s**, (Cribbage) score of two points by dealer turning up a jack; **kick** one's ~**s**, be kept waiting; **lay by the** ~**s**, arrest, overthrow; **on** (= *at*) **the** ~**s of**, close to one's ~**s**, run away; **to** ~, (of dog, or fig.) close behind, under control (*bring* or *come to heel*; as command to dog, *heel!*); **turn on** one's ~, turn sharply round; **under the** ~ **of**, dominated by; **upon** (= *at*) **the** ~**s of.** **6.** ~'**ball**, (1) shoemaker's polishing mixture of hard wax and lampblack, (2) this or similar composition for taking rubbings of monumental brasses etc.; ~**plate**, metal plate protecting heel of shoe; ~'**tap**, (1) a thickness of leather in heel, (2) liquor left at bottom of glass after drinking. **7.** Hence ~'LESS (-l-l-) *a.* [OE *hēla, hǣla*, = OFris. *hēla*, MDu. *hiele*, ON *hæll* f. Gmc **hāhil-*, cogn. w. HOUGH]

heel² *v.* **1.** *v.i.* touch ground with heel, e.g. in dancing. **2.** *v.t.* & *i.* furnish (boot etc.) with heel; (Rugby Footb.) pass ball *out* at back of scrummage with the heels; (Golf) strike (ball) with heel of club; (in *p.p.*, colloq.), armed with revolver, supplied with money (WELL-*heeled*); hence ***(*ward-*)~'ER¹ *n.*, local worker for professional politician. [f. prec.]

heel³ *v.* **1.** *v.i.* (Of ship etc.) lean over owing to pressure of wind or uneven load (cf. LIST³). **2.** *v.t.* cause (ship etc.) to do this. [prob. f. obs. *heeld, hield* incline, f. OE *hieldan*, OS *-heldian* f. *halthjan* (**haltha* inclined)]

heel⁴ *n.* (Naut.) inclination of heeling ship. [f. prec.]

heel⁵. See HELE.

hĕft *n.*, & *v.t.* **1.** *n.* (dial. or US) weight. **2.** *v.t.* lift, esp. to judge weight. [prob. f. HEAVE, after *cleft, weft*]

hĕ'ft|y *a.* sturdy, stalwart, (*a battalion of hefty fellows*); bulky, heavy, powerful; hence ~iLY² *adv.*, ~iNESS *n.* [f. prec. + -Y²]

Hegē'lian (hē-, hā-; -j-, -g-) *a.* & *n.* (adherent) of Hegel or his philosophy of objective idealism; hence ~ISM (3) *n.* [f. G. W. F. *Hegel*, Ger. philosopher d. 1831 + -IAN]

hĕgĕmŏ'nic (-g-, -j-) *a.* ruling, supreme. [f. Gk *hēgemonikos* (as foll.; see -IC)]

hegemony (hǐgĕ'-, hǐjĕ'-, hĕ'jǐ-) *n.* leadership esp. by one State of a confederacy. [f. Gk *hēgemonia* (*hēgemōn* leader f. *hēgeomai* lead); cf. -MONY]

hĕ'gira, hĕ'jira, *n.* **1.** (*H*~). Muhammad's flight from Mecca to Medina (AD 622); Muslim era reckoned from this. **2.** general exodus or departure. [med. L *hegira* f. Arab. *hijra* departure from one's country (*hajara* separate)]

heh (hā) *int.* expr. inquiry or surprise. [imit.]

hē-hē'. See HE².

hei'fer (hĕ'f-) *n.* young cow, esp. one that has not had more than one calf, female calf; (sl., derog.) woman. [OE *heahfore*, of unkn. orig.]

heigh (hā) *int.* expr. encouragement or inquiry; ~-**ho**, *int.* expr. boredom, disappointment, etc. [var. of HEH]

height (hīt) *n.* measurement from base to top, or (of standing person) from head to foot; (Print.) distance from foot to face of type; elevation above ground or recognized (esp. sea) level; considerable elevation (*situated at a height*); high point; top; rising ground; ***~ **of land**, watershed; **the** ~, utmost degree (*of* folly, fashion, luxury, etc.); **at its** ~ (highest degree). [OE *hēhthu*, = OHG *hōhida*, Goth. *hauhitha* f. Gmc **hauhthō* as HIGH, -TH¹)]

hei'ghten (hī't-) *v.* **1.** *v.t.* make high(er); intensify; strengthen details of (description, story). **2.** *v.i.* rise (usu. fig.), become more intense. [f. prec. + -EN⁶]

heil (hīl) *int.* hail! (as used in Nazi greeting *Heil Hitler!*). [G]

hei'nous (hā'n-) *a.* (Of crime or criminal) utterly odious, atrocious; hence ~·LY² *adv.*, ~·NESS *n.* [ME, f. OF *haineus* (*haïne* hatred f. *haïr* to hate f. Frank. **hatjan*; see -OUS)]

heir (ār) *n.* person receiving or entitled to receive property or rank as legal successor of its former owner; (fig.) one to whom something (joy, punishment, etc.) is morally due; *heir* APPARENT; ~-**at-law**, ~-**general**, (by right of blood, esp. to intestate's real property); ~ **in tail** (to entailed estate); ~ **of the** or one's **body** (direct descendant); *heir* PRESUMPTIVE; hence ~'DOM, ~'SHIP, *ns.*, ~'LESS *a.* [ME f. OF *eir* f. LL *herem* f. L *heres -edis*]

heir'ĕss (ār'-) *n.* female heir, esp. to great wealth. [f. prec. + -ESS¹]

heir'loōm (ār'-) *n.* chattel that follows devolution of real estate; piece of personal property or (fig.) quality that has been in family for generations. [f. HEIR + LOOM¹ in sense 'tool']

*****heist** (hī-) *n.*, & *v.t.* (sl.) rob(bery). [repr. local pr. of HOIST¹]

hei-tǐ'ki (hā-) *n.* (NZ) greenstone neck-ornament worn by Maoris. [Maori (*hei* hang, TIKI)]

hĕ'jira. See HEGIRA.

Hē'La *a.* of a strain of human epithelial cells maintained in culture. [f. *Henrietta Lacks*, whose cervical carcinoma provided the original cells]

hĕld. See HOLD¹.

Heldentenor (hĕ'ldntĕnŏr *n.* (singer with) powerful tenor voice suitable for heroic operatic roles. [G (*held* hero)]

hēle, heal², heel⁵, *v.t.* set (plant) in the ground and cover its roots *in*. [OE *helian*, = OS *-hellian*, OHG *-hellen* f. WG **haljan* causative of Gmc **helan* (**helconceal*; cf. HELL)]

hĕ′li- *comb. form.* helicopter (*heliborne, heliport*). [abbr.]

hĕli′acal *a.* (Astron.) relating to or near the sun; ~ **rising, setting**, first rising of a star after, last setting before, a period of invisibility due to conjunction with the sun. [f. LL f. Gk *hēliakos* (*hēlios* sun; see -AC) + -AL]

hēliă′nthus *n.* plant of genus *Helianthus*, e.g. common sunflower. [mod. L, f. Gk *hēlios* sun + *anthos* flower]

hĕ′lic|al *a.* having form of helix; hence or cogn. ~al_LY² *adv.*, ~OID *a.* & *n.* [f. as HELIX + -AL]

hĕlichrȳ′sum (-k-) *n.* composite Afr. or Austral. plant of genus *Helichrysum*, with flowers retaining their appearance when dried. [L, f. Gk *helikhrusos* (*helix* spiral, *khrusos* gold)]

Hĕ′licon *n.* **1.** source of poetic inspiration; so **Hĕlicō′nian** *a.* **2.** (*h~*). large spiral saxhorn encircling body of player. [L, f. Gk *Helikōn* Boeotian mountain sacred to Muses]

hĕ′licŏpter *n.* aircraft deriving both lift and propulsive power from horizontally revolving usu. engine-driven blades or rotors, and capable of ascending and descending vertically. [f. F *hélicoptère* f. Gk HELIX + *pteron* wing]

hĕ′lio- *comb. form.* sun, as: ~ce′ntric, as viewed from centre of sun, taking sun as centre; ~gram, message by heliograph (3); ~-graph, (*n.*) (1) engraving obtained chemically by exposure to light, (2) apparatus for photographing sun, (3) signalling apparatus reflecting sunlight in flashes from movable mirror, (4) message thus sent, (*v.t.*) send (message) by heliograph; ~graphy (-ŏ′g-), (1) description of the sun, (2) process of engraving heliographs, (3) signalling by heliograph; ~gravure, photogravure; ~li′thic, (of civilization) characterized by sun-worship and megaliths; ~meter (-ŏ′m-), instrument for finding angular distance between two stars (orig. for measuring diameter of sun); ~stat, apparatus with mirror driven by clockwork to reflect sunlight in fixed direction; ~the′rapy, use of sun-baths in treating disease; ~tro′pic, ~tropism (-ŏ′t-), (of plant etc.) turning, property of turning, towards or away from (esp. sun)light; ~type, picture obtained from sensitized gelatin film exposed to light. [f. Gk *hēlios* sun + -O-]

hēliŏ′s|is *n.* (*pl.* ~es *pr.* -ēz). sunstroke. [mod. L, f. Gk *hēliōsis* (*hēlios* sun; see -OSIS)]

hĕ′liotrōpe *n.* herb or shrub of genus *Heliotropium*, with fragrant purple flowers; colour or scent of these; bloodstone. [f. L f. Gk *hēliotropion* plant turning flowers to the sun (*hēlios* sun, -*tropos* f. *trepō* turn)]

hĕ′lipŏrt *n.* place for helicopters to take off and land. [f. HELI-, AFTER *airport*]

hē′lium *n.* colourless odourless light inert gaseous element, inferred as existing in sun's atmosphere in 1868, first obtained in 1895; ~ **II**, form of liquid helium with very low viscosity. [f. Gk *hēlios* sun + -IUM]

hē′l|ix *n.* (*pl.* ~ices *pr.* -īsēz). spiral (like corkscrew, or in one plane like watch-spring); (Archit.) spiral ornament; rim of external ear. [L *helix -icis* f. Gk *helix -ikos*]

hĕll *n.* **1.** abode of the dead; abode of devils and of condemned spirits in torment; place or state of wickedness or misery; den for captives in prisoners' base and other games; gaming-house. **2.** (in colloq. imprecations etc.) = *the* DEUCE², *the* DEVIL¹, (*a* or *one or ||*the hell of a* or *helluva*; *go to hell*; *hell take it*; *hell to pay*; *play* (*merry*) *hell with*; RAISE *hell*; *who* etc. *in or the hell?*); **all ~ let loose**, utter pandemonium; (*tired* etc.) **as ~**, exceedingly; **beat or knock ~ out of**, pound heavily; **come ~ or high water**, no matter what the obstacles; **for the ~ of it**, solely for amusement; **get ~**, be severely reprimanded; **give person ~**, make him very uncomfortable; **like ~**, recklessly, exceed-

ingly, (iron.) not at all; **not a hope in ~**, no chance at all; **the ~ you say**, that is very surprising; **to or the ~**, away to perdition (*to hell with it*; *get the hell out of here*); **what the ~** (dismissing a difficulty; *what the hell, I can go tomorrow instead*). **3.** *~′**bender**, large salamander; ~-**bent**, recklessly determined (*for* or *on*); ~-**cat**, spiteful or furious person (esp. woman); ~-**fire**, fire(s) of hell; ~ **for leather**, at full speed (usu. of rider); ~-**hole**, oppressive place; ~-**hound**, fiend; ~**'s angel**, violent lawless young motor--cyclist; ~**'s bells** (excl. of anger or annoyance); ~--weed, dodder or corn crowfoot. **4.** Hence ~′WARD *adv.* & *a.* [OE *hel*(*l*), = OS *hell*(*j*)*a*, OHG *hella*, ON *hel*, Goth. *halja* f. Gmc **haljō* (**hal-*, **hel-* cover, conceal)]

Hĕllă′dĭc *a.* of Bronze Age culture of mainland Greece. [f. Gk *Helladikos* (*Hellas -ados* Greece; see -IC)]

hĕ′llĕbŏre *n.* **1.** ancient name of various plants supposed to cure madness. **2.** plant of genus *Helleborus*, e.g. Christmas rose. [ME, f. OF *ellebore, elebore* or f. med. L *eleborus* f. L f. Gk *helleboros*]

hĕ′llĕborīne *n.* orchid of genus *Epipactis* or *Cephalanthera*. [F, or f. L f. Gk *helleborinē* plant like hellebore (as prec.; see -INE¹)]

Hĕ′llēne *n.* ancient Greek of genuine Grecian descent; subject of modern nation of Greece; so **Hĕllē′nic** *a.* [f. Gk *Hellēn* a Greek]

Hĕ′llĕn|ism *n.* Greek idiom or construction; imitation of the Greeks; Greek character or culture; Greek nationality; so ~IZE (3) *v.t.* & *i.* [f. Gk *Hellēnismos* (*Hellēnizō* speak Greek, make Greek, f. as prec.; see -ISM)]

Hĕ′llĕn|ist *n.* one who used the Greek language but was not a Greek; person skilled in Greek; hence ~i′stIC *a.* (of Greek history etc. after Alexander). [f. Gk *Hellēnistēs* (as prec.; see -IST)]

***hĕ′llgrammīte** *n.* aquatic larva of an Amer. fly, much used as bait. [19th c., of unkn. orig.]

***hĕ′llion** *n.* (colloq.) mischievous or troublesome person, esp. child. [perh. f. dial. *hallion* worthless fellow, assim. to HELL]

hĕ′llĭsh *a.* & *adv.* **1.** *a.* of or like hell; infernal; hence ~LY² *adv.*, ~NESS *n.* **2.** *adv.* infernally (esp. as mere intensive: *hellish expensive*). [f. HELL + -ISH¹]

hĕllō′ (he-, hĕ-) *int.*, *n.* (*pl.* ~s), & *v.i.* **1.** *int.* expr. surprise or informal greeting or beginning telephone conversation. **2.** *n.*, & *v.i.* (the) cry 'hello'. [var. of HALLO]

hĕ′lluva *See* HELL.

hĕlm¹ *n.* (arch.) helmet; hence ~ED² (-md) *a.* [OE, = OS, OHG *helm*, ON *hjálmr*, Goth. *hilms* f. Gmc **helmaz* f. IE **kelmos* (**kel-* cover)]

hĕlm² *n.* & *v.t.* **1.** *n.* tiller or wheel by which rudder is controlled; space through which helm is turned (*more, little, helm*); **down** (**with the**) ~, **up** (**with the**) ~, place helm so as to bring rudder to windward, to leeward; **weather, lee,** ~, helm put up, down. **2.** (fig.) government, guidance; **take the** ~, assume control. **3.** ~′sman (-z-), steersman. **4.** *v.t.* steer (usu. fig.). [OE *helma*, corresp. to ON *hjalm*; prob. rel. to HELVE]

hĕ′lmĕt *n.* defensive or protective head-cover of soldier, policeman, fireman, diver, fencer, motor--cyclist, Amer. footballer, etc.; felt or pith hat for hot climates; (Bot.) arched upper part of corolla in some flowers; shell of mollusc of genus *Cassis*; hence ~ED² *a.* [ME f. OF, dim. of *helme* f. WG (as HELM¹); see -ET¹]

hĕ′lmĭnth *n.* worm (esp. intestinal); hence ~i′ASIS *n.*, disease characterized by presence of worms in the body, **hĕlmi′nthIC**, **hĕlmi′nthOID**, *adjs.*, ~ŏ′LOGY *n.* [f. Gk *helmins -inthos* intestinal worm]

hĕ′lot *n.* **1.** (*H~*). one of a class of serfs in ancient Sparta; **drunken H~**, (made drunk as warning to young Spartans) serf or slave. **2.** serf. **3.** Hence ~ISM (2), ~RY (1, 2), *ns.*, ~IZE (3) *v.t.* [f. L *Helotes* pl. f. Gk *Heilōtes, -ōtai* (*pl.* of *Heilōs, -ōtēs* taken as = inhabitants of *Helos*, Laconian town)]

hĕlp¹ *v.t.* (∼ed or arch. *past* holp and *p.p.* ho'lpen).
1. provide (person etc.) with means towards what is
needed or sought, be of use or service to (person, or
abs.), (*help me*; *help me* (*to*) *lift it*; *help me in lifting it*; *help
me with my work, to an answer*; *help the work on* or *forward*;
help me over the stile; *help! I'm stuck*); enable to come or
go more easily *down, up*, etc.; ∼ person **on, off,** *with
coat* etc., help him put it on, take it off; ∼ person **out**
(of a difficulty); ∼ (person) **to,** serve him with (food
at meal). **2.** distribute (food at meal). **3.** remedy,
prevent, (*it can't be helped*; *I can't help that*); **more than**
one **can** ∼, more than is unavoidable. **4.** (w. neg.)
refrain from or avoid (*cannot help but admire her*; *cannot
help laughing*). **5.** (In invocation or oath) **so** ∼ **me**
(God) (as I keep my word, as I speak the truth, etc.).
6. ∼ oneself, (w. neg.) avoid an undesired action; ∼
oneself (**to,** or abs.), take without seeking assistance
or permission of another; ∼-yourself, (of restaurant
etc.) self-service. **7.** Hence ∼'ER¹ *n.,* ∼'ING² *a.* (a
∼ing hand, (fig.) assistance). [OE *helpan,* = OS
helpan, OHG *helfan,* ON *hjalpa,* Goth. *hilpan* f. Gmc
**help-,* **halp-,* **hulp-*]

hĕlp² *n.* action of helping (*we need your help*) or being
helped (*come to our help*); person or thing that helps;
domestic servant(s) or employee(s) (‖‖**home** ∼, one
who helps in household work; ‖**lady** ∼, (arch.)
assistant and companion to mistress of house;
‖**mother's** ∼, one who gives help in house with
children); remedy or escape (*there is no help for it*);
helping (of food). [OE f. as prec.]

hĕ'lpful *a.* (Of person or thing) useful, serviceable;
hence ∼LY² *adv.,* ∼NESS *n.* [ME, f. prec. + -FUL]

hĕ'lping *n.* In vbl senses; portion of food served. [ME,
f. HELP¹ + -ING¹]

hĕ'lplĕss *a.* lacking help; having or showing inability
to act without help; hence ∼LY² *adv.,* ∼NESS *n.* [ME, f.
HELP² + -LESS]

hĕ'lpmāte *n.* helpful companion or partner (usu. husband or wife). [f. HELP¹,² + MATE², prob. infl. by foll.]

hĕ'lpmeet *n.* = prec. [formed by misunderstanding
of Gen. 2: 18, 20, *help meet* (i.e. suitable helper) being
taken as one word]

hĕ'lter-skĕlter *adv., a., & n.* **1.** (in) disordered haste.
2. *n.* tower-shaped structure in fun-fair etc. with
external spiral track down which persons may slide
on mat. [imit., perh. f. ME *skelte* hasten; cf. HARUM-
-SCARUM]

hĕlve *n.* handle of weapon or tool; *throw the helve after
the* HATCHET. [OE *h(i)elfe,* – OS *helfi,* OHG *halp* f.
WG **halbh-*; cf. HALTER, HELM²]

Hĕlvē'tian (-shan) *a. & n.* Swiss. [f. L *Helvetia*
Switzerland + -AN]

hĕm¹ *n.* border or edge of cloth etc., esp. border made
by turning edge in and sewing it down; ∼-line, lower
edge of skirt etc.; ∼-stitch *n., & v.t.* (to hem with)
ornamental stitch like drawn-work. [OE, perh. rel. to
dial. *ham* enclosure]

hĕm² *v.t.* (-mm-). turn down and sew in edge of (cloth
etc., or abs.); ∼ **in, up,** etc., enclose, confine. [ME, f.
prec.]

hem³ (hĕm, hem) *int., n., & v.i.* (-mm-). **1.** *int.* calling
attention or expressing hesitation by slight cough or
clearing of throat. **2.** *n.* utterance of this. **3.** *v.i.* utter
sound of *hem,* clear throat, hesitate in speech; ∼ **and
ha(w)** (cf. HUM¹). [imit.]

*hē'mal, *hē'mato-, etc. See HAEMAL, HAEMATO-, etc.

hēme. See HAEM.

hēmerocā'llis *n.* = DAY lily. [mod. L, f. L f. Gk
hēmerokalles a kind of lily (*hēmera* day, *kallos* beauty)]

hĕ'mi- *pref.* half-, affecting one half, etc., as:
∼ano'p(s)ia, blindness over half of field of vision;
∼cycle, semicircular figure; ‖∼demisemiquaver,
half a demisemiquaver; ∼HE'DRAL, (Cryst.) having
half number of planes given by complete symmetry;
∼pterous (-ĭ'p-), of the insect order with front wings
thickened. [Gk *hēmi-* = L SEMI-]

*-**hē'mĭa.** Var. of -AEMIA.

hĕmiplē'g|ĭa *n.* (Path.) paralysis of one side of the
body; hence ∼IC *a. & n.* [mod. L, f. Gk HEMI(*plēgia* f.
plēgē stroke) paralysis; see -IA¹]

hē'misphēre *n.* half sphere; half the celestial sphere,
esp. as divided by the equator or by the ecliptic; half
the earth, containing (**Eastern** ∼) Europe, Asia,
and Africa, or (**Western** ∼) America, or as divided
by equator (**Northern, Southern,** ∼); (Anat.) each
half of cerebrum; **Magdeburg** ∼s, pair of brass
hemispheres exhausted of air to show atmospheric
pressure by their cohesion; hence **hĕmisphē'r**IC(AL)
adjs. [f. OF *emisp(h)ere* & f. L *hemisphaerium* f. Gk
HEMI(*sphaira* SPHERE)]

hē'mistich (-k) *n.* half of line of verse. [f. LL f. Gk
HEMI(*stikhion* f. *stikhos* line)]

hē'mlŏck *n.* **1.** poisonous umbelliferous plant (*Conium
maculatum*) whose juice or dried fruit or leaves are used
as powerful sedative; poisonous potion got from this.
2. *∼ (fir or **spruce**), conifer of genus *Tsuga.* [OE
hymlic(e), of unkn. orig.]

*hē'mo- etc. See HAEMO- etc.

hĕmp *n.* **1.** (**Indian**) ∼, herbaceous plant, *Cannabis
sativa,* native of Asia. **2.** its cortical fibre used for rope
and stout fabrics; (joc.) rope for hanging a person. **3.**
narcotic drug made from hemp plant. **4.** other plant
yielding similar fibre (**MANILA** hemp). **5.** ∼
agrimony, perennial composite plant with pale-
-purple flowers and hairy leaves; ∼-nettle, nettle-
-like plant of genus *Galeopsis.* **6.** Hence ∼'EN² *a.* [OE
henep, hænep, = OS *hanap,* OHG *hanaf,* ON *hampr* f.
Gmc *hanipiz cogn. w. Gk *kannabis*]

hĕn *n.* **1.** female bird, esp. of domestic fowl; (in *pl.*)
domestic fowls of either sex; **as scarce as** ∼**'s teeth,**
very scarce; **like a** ∼ **with one chicken,** absurdly
fussy; ∼ **and chickens,** name of a cultivated compound daisy, and other plants. **2.** female lobster or
crab or salmon. **3.** ∼'bane, (drug got from) narcotic
and poisonous plant (*Hyoscyamus niger*); ∼-coop for
keeping fowls in; ∼-harrier, European falcon
(*Circus cyaneus*); *∼-hawk, large hawk attacking
poultry; ∼-hearted, lacking courage; ∼-house,
small building for fowls to roost in; ∼-party (colloq.,
of women only); ∼'pecked, domineered over by
one's wife; ∼-roost, place where fowls roost at night;
∼-run, enclosure for fowls; ∼'wife, (arch.) woman
who keeps fowls. [OE *henn,* = OHG *henna* f. WG
*hannja dim. of *hanon cock]

hĕnce *adv.* **1.** (arch.) (**from**) ∼, from here, from this
place; ∼!, (poet. or rhet.) go away; **go** ∼, die; ∼
with, away with, take away. **2.** from this time (**five
years** ∼, in five years' time from now); ∼'or'th,
∼'for'ward, from this time onwards. **3.** as a result
from this; from this source; as an inference from this
(*hence it appears that*), therefore. [ME *hens, hennes,*
(*henne* adv. f. OE *heonan* f. root of HE¹) + -s³]

hĕ'nch|man *n.* (*pl.* ∼men). **1.** (Hist.) squire, page of
honour. **2.** chief attendant of Highland chief. **3.** trusty
follower; political supporter. [ME *henxman, hengest-
man,* f. OE *heng(e)st* male horse + MAN¹]

hĕndĕ'ca- *comb. form.* eleven, as: ∼gon, plane figure
with eleven sides and angles; ∼sylla'bic *a. & n.,*
(metrical line) of eleven syllables; ∼sy'llable, such a
line. [f. Gk *hendeka* eleven]

hĕndi'adys *n.* expression of a complex idea by two
words connected with *and* (e.g. *in goblets and gold* for *in
golden goblets*; *nice and warm* for *nicely warm*). [med. L, f.
Gk *hen dia duoin* one thing by two]

hĕ'néquen (-k-) *n.* (sisal-like fibre from) species of
agave grown in Mexico etc. [f. Sp. *jeniquen*]

hĕnge (-nj) *n.* monument of wood or stone resembling
the circle of stones at Stonehenge. [f. *Stonehenge* in
Wiltshire]

hĕ'nna *n.* tropical shrub (*Lawsonia inermis*); its shoots
and leaves used as reddish dye esp. for the hair; hence
∼ED² (-ad) *a.,* treated with henna. [f. Arab. *hinnā'*]

hĕ'nothēism *n.* belief in god (of one's tribe etc.)

without asserting that he is the only God. [f. Gk *heis henos* one + *theos* god + -ISM]

hĕ'nr|y̆ *n.* (*pl.* ∼ies *or* ∼ys). (Electr.) unit of inductance which gives an e.m.f. of one volt in a closed circuit with rate of change of current one ampere per second. [f. J. *Henry*, Amer. physicist d. 1878]

hĕŏrtŏ'logy̆ *n.* study of church festivals. [f. G *heortologie*, F *héortologie* f. Gk *heortē* feast; see -LOGY]

hĕp[1]. See HIP[2]

hĕp[2] *a.* (sl.) well-informed; stylish; ∼ **to**, aware of; ∼-**cat**, hep person, jazz or swing addict, HIPSTER[1]. [20th c., of unkn. orig.]

hĕ'parin *n.* substance extracted from animal livers and used to prevent blood-clotting; hence ∼IZE (1) *v.t.* [f. L *hepar* liver + -IN]

hĕpă'tic *a.* of, good for, the liver; liver-coloured, dark brownish-red. [ME, f. L f. Gk *hēpatikos* (*hēpar -atos* LIVER[1]; see -IC)]

hĕpă'tica *n.* plant of genus *Hepatica*, closely related to anemone, with lobed leaves resembling the liver. [med. L, fem. (as n.) of *hepaticus* (see prec.)]

hĕpatī'tis *n.* inflammation of the liver. [mod. L, f. as HEPATIC; SEE -ITIS]

hĕpato- *comb. form.* liver, as: ∼me'galy̆, abnormal enlargement of the liver. [f. Gk *hēpato-* (as HEPATIC; see -o-)]

Hĕ'pplewhīte (-pelwīt) *n.* light and graceful style of furniture. [f. G. ∼, Engl. cabinet-maker d. 1786)

hĕ'pta- *comb. form.* seven, as: ∼**chord** (-k-), 7-stringed musical instrument, 7-note scale; ∼**glot** *a.* & *n.*, (book) in seven languages; ∼**gon**, plane figure with seven sides and angles; so ∼**gonal** (-ă'g-) *a.*; ∼HE'DRON, solid figure with seven faces; ∼**merous** (-ă'm-), having seven parts; ∼**meter** (-ă'mǐ-), verse of seven measures; ∼**sylla'bic** *a.* & *n.*, (metrical line) of seven syllables; H∼**teuch** (-k), first seven books of OT; ∼**va'lent**, (Chem.) having a valence of seven. [f. Gk *hepta* seven]

hĕ'ptăd *n.* group of seven. [f. Gk *heptas -ados* set of seven (*hepta*); see -AD 1]

hĕ'ptāne *n.* (Chem.) hydrocarbon of the paraffin series, C₇H₁₆. [f. HEPTA- + -ANE]

hĕ'ptărchy̆ (-kǐ) *n.* government by seven rulers; supposed seven kingdoms of Angles and Saxons in Britain in 7th–8th c.; so **hĕptăr'chic**(AL) (-k-) *adjs.* [f. HEPTA-, after *tetrarchy*]

hĕr[1] (*or, when unstressed, her*) *pron.* **1.** Obj. case of SHE; (arch.) = HERSELF 2. **2.** (colloq.) = SHE (*it's her all right*; *am older than her*); **not quite** ∼, garment etc. that does not suit her. [OE *hire* dat. of *hīo*, *hēo* fem. of HE[1]]

hĕr[2] (*or, when unstressed, her*) *poss. pron. attrib.* of HER[1] or herself (*it is her hat*; *shook her head*; *her father and mine, her and my father*); (in titles) that she is (*Her Majesty*). [OE *hi(e)re* gen. of *hīo* (see prec.)]

hĕ'rald[1] *n.* **1.** (Hist.) officer who made State proclamations, and bore messages between princes, or officiated in the TOURNAMENT 1, or arranged various State ceremonials, or settled questions of precedence, or recorded names and pedigrees of those entitled to armorial bearings; ||official of *Heralds'* COLLEGE. **2.** messenger (often as title of newspaper); forerunner. **3.** Hence ∼IST *n.*, expert in heraldry. [ME, f. OF *herau(l)t* f. Gmc *hariwald- (*harjaz army, *wald-rule)]

hĕ'rald[2] *v.t.* proclaim the approach (lit. or fig.) of; usher in. [ME, f. OF *herauder* (as prec.)]

hĕrā'ldic *a.* of heraldry. [f. HERALD[1] + -IC]

hĕ'raldry̆ *n.* science or art of a herald, esp. in dealings with armorial bearings; armorial bearings; heraldic pomp. [f. HERALD[1] + -RY]

hĕrb *n.* **1.** plant of which the stem is not woody or persistent and which dies down to ground after flowering; plant of which leaves etc. are used for food, medicine, scent, flavour, etc. **2.** ∼ **beer**, drink made

from herbs; ∼ **bennet**, common yellow-flowered avens (*Geum urbanum*) [prob. f. med. L *herba benedicta* blessed herb, as having expelled the Devil]; ∼ **Christopher**, white-flowered baneberry; ∼ **Gerard**, white-flowered plant (*Aegopodium podagraria*); ∼-**grace**, ∼ of grace, (arch.) RUE[2]; ∼ **Paris**, plant with single flower and four leaves in cross shape; ∼ **Robert**, common wild crane's-bill; ∼-**tea**, -**water**, medicinal infusion of herbs; ∼ **tobacco**, mixture of herbs smoked as substitute for tobacco or as medicine. **3.** Hence or cogn. ∼'ICIDE *n.*, substance toxic to plants and used to destroy unwanted vegetation, ∼ı'FEROUS, ∼'LESS, *adjs.* [ME, f. OF *erbe* f. L *herba* grass, green crops, herb]

hĕrbā'ceous (-shus) *a.* of the nature of herbs; ∼ **border** (in garden, containing esp. perennial flowering plants); ∼ **perennial**, plant whose growth dies down annually but whose roots etc. survive. [f. L *herbaceus* grassy (as prec.; see -ACEOUS)]

hĕr'bage *n.* herbs collectively; succulent parts of herbs; (Law) right of pasture on another's land. [ME, f. OF *erbage* f. med. L *herbaticum, herbagium* right of pasture, f. L *herba* herb; see -AGE]

hĕr'bal *a.* & *n.* (book with descriptions and account of properties) of herbs. [f. med. L *herbalis* (as prec.; see -AL)]

hĕr'balist *n.* one skilled in herbs, esp. early botanical writer; dealer in medicinal herbs. [f. prec. + -IST]

hĕrbā'r'i|um *n.* (*pl.* ∼a). (book, case, room, for) systematically arranged collection of dried plants. [LL (as HERB; see -ARIUM)]

hĕr'bivŏre *n.* animal of group Herbivora, feeding on plants; so **hĕrbĭ'vorous** *a.* [f. L *herba* herb + -I- + -VORE]

hĕr'by̆ *a.* abounding in herbs; of the nature of a herb. [f. HERB + -Y[2]]

Hĕrcūlean (-ū'lĭan, -ē'an) *a.* of Hercules; strong as Hercules; difficult as his labours. [f. L *Herculeus* (as foll.) + -AN]

Hĕr'cūlēs (-z) *n.* **1.** (Gk & Rom. Myth.) hero of prodigious strength, who performed 12 immense tasks (LABOUR[1] *of Hercules*); **Pillars of** ∼, rocks on either side of Strait of Gibraltar, (fig.) ultimate limit. **2.** very strong man; ∼ **beetle** (S. Amer., 5 in. long). [ME f. L, f. Gk *Hēraklēs* (*Hēra* wife of Zeus, *kleos* glory)]

Hĕrcy̆'nian *a.* (Geol.) of an episode of mountain-formation in E. hemisphere in late Palaeozoic era. [f. L *Hercynia silva* forested mountains of central Germany]

hĕrd[1] *n.* **1.** company of animals, esp. cattle, feeding or travelling together; ***ride** ∼, (fig.) keep watch *on*. **2.** (derog.) large number of people (*the herd*; *the common herd*). **3. the** ∼ **instinct**, gregariousness and mutual influence as a psychological factor; ∼-**book**, pedigree-book of cattle or pigs; ∼'**sman** (-z-), owner or keeper of herds. [OE *heord*, = OHG *herta*, ON *hjörth*, Goth. *hairda* f. Gmc *herdhō]

hĕrd[2] *n.* keeper of herds, herdsman, (esp. in comb.: *cowherd, swine-herd*). [OE *hirdi*, = OS *hirdi*, OHG *hirti*, ON *hirthir*, Goth. *hairdeis* f. Gmc *herdhjaz (as prec.)]

hĕrd[3] *v.i.* & *t.* go or cause to go in a herd (*together, with* others; esp. fig., persons); tend (sheep, cattle). [ME, f. HERD[1,2]]

Hĕr'dwick *n.* (animal of) hardy breed of mountain sheep from N. England. [f. obs. *herdwick* pasture-ground (HERD[2], WICK[2]), perh. because breed originated in Furness Abbey pastures]

hēre *adv., n., a.* & *int.* **1.** *adv.* in or at this place or position (*put it here*; *put it down, in, out, over, under, up, here*; *what is this or that dog doing here?*; *has lived here for some years*; (calling attention to person's presence or thing offered) *my son here will show you, here is your coat*); at this point in argument, progress of affairs, situation, etc., (*here I have a question*); ∼ (**below**), in this life; ∼ **goes!** (colloq. expr. commencement of bold act); *here's*

HOW!; ~'s to, I drink to the health of; ~ and there, in various places; ~, there, and everywhere, in many different places; neither ~ nor there, of no importance or relevance; ~ today, gone tomorrow, short-lived, merely transient; ~ we or you are, (colloq.) this is what we or you wanted, the expected place of arrival, etc.; ~ we go again, (colloq.) the same undesirable events are recurring. 2. to this place or position (comes here every day; I don't belong here); LOOK or see here! 3. n. this place (get out of here; lives somewhere near here; fill it up to here; shall leave here tomorrow). 4. int. calling attention or introducing command or remonstration; = I am present (in answer to roll-call). 5. ~abou't(s), near this place; ~a'fter, (adv.) in future, later on, in the world to come, (n.) the future, the world to come; ~a't, (arch.) as a result of this; ~by', by this means, as a result of this; ~i'n, (formal) in this matter, book, etc.; ~ina'fter, (formal) below (in this document etc.); ~inbefor'e, (formal) in a preceding part (of this document etc.); ~o'f, (formal) of this; ~to', (formal) to this matter; ~tofor'e, (formal) before this time; ~u'nder, (formal) below (in book etc.); ~un'to, (arch.) to this; ~upo'n, after this, in consequence of this; ~wi'th, with this (esp. of enclosure in letter etc.). [OE hēr, = OS, Goth. hēr, ON hér, OHG hiar, app. f. Gmc *hi- (IIE¹)]

here'ditable a. that may be inherited. [f. obs. F héréditable or f. med. L hereditabilis f. eccl. L hereditare f. L heres -edis heir; see -ABLE]

hereditament (hĕridĭ'-, hĭrē'dĭ-) n. property that can be inherited; real property; inheritance. [f. med. L hereditamentum (as prec.; see -MENT)]

here'ditar|y a. descending by inheritance; (of disease, instinct, etc.) transmitted from one generation to another; the same as or like what one's parents had (hereditary creed, hatred); of, holding position by, inheritance; hence ~iLY² adv., ~iNESS n. [f. L hereditarius (as foll.; see ARY¹)]

here'dity n. tendency of like to beget like, property of organic beings by which offspring have nature and characteristics of parents or ancestors; genetic constitution of an individual. [f. F hérédité or f. L hereditas heirship (as HEIR; see -ITY)]

He'reford n. (one of a) breed of red and white beef cattle. [~ in England, where it originated]

here'siarch (-ziärk) n. leader or founder of a heresy. [f. eccl. L f. Gk hairesiarkhēs f. as foll. + -arkhēs ruler]

he'res|y n. opinion contrary to the orthodox doctrine of the Christian Church, or to the accepted doctrine on any subject; hence ~iò'LOGY n. [ME f. OF (h)eresie, f. Rom. *heresia f. eccl. L haeresis, in L = school of thought, f. Gk hairesis choice, sect (haireomai choose)]

he'retic n. holder of an unorthodox opinion (orig. in the matter of religion); so **here'tical** a. [ME, f. OF heretique f. eccl. L f. Gk hairetikos able to choose (as prec.; see -IC)]

||he'riot n. (Hist.) tribute of best live beast or dead chattel, or money payment, or (orig.) return of lent equipment, to lord on decease of tenant. [OE heregeatwa (here army, geatwa trappings)]

he'ritab|le a. that passes to heirs-at-law (opp. to movable property); transmissible from parent to offspring; capable of inheriting; hence ~LY² adv. [ME f. OF (heriter f. eccl. L hereditare; see HEREDITABLE)]

he'ritage n. what is or may be inherited; inherited circumstances or benefits; (fig.) portion allotted to anybody; (Bibl.) the ancient Israelites, the Church. [ME f. OF (as prec.; see -AGE)]

he'ritor n. one who inherits. [ME f. AF heriter, OF heritier f. as HEREDITARY, assim. to wds in -OR]

herl. Var. of HARL².

herm n. (Gk Ant.) squared pillar with head (esp. of Hermes) on top, used as boundary-marker etc. (cf. TERMINUS 4). [f. L Herma f. Gk Hermēs messenger of the gods]

hermä'phrod|īte n. & a. 1. n. human being or animal combining characteristics of both sexes; (Zool.) animal having normally both male and female sexual organs, e.g. earthworm; (Bot.) plant in which same flower has stamens and pistils; (fig.) person or thing combining opposite qualities; ship having characters of two kinds of craft. 2. a. combining both sexes, or opposite qualities. 3. Hence ~i'tic(al) adjs., ~itism (2) n. [f. L f. Gk hermaphroditos, orig. the name of son of Hermes and Aphrodite in Gk Myth., who became joined in one body with the nymph Salmacis]

herme'neu't|ic a. of interpretation; so ~ical a., ~ics n. pl. or sing., interpretation, esp. of Scripture. [f. Gk hermēneutikos (hermēneuō interpret; see -IC)]

herme't|ic a. 1. of alchemy or other occult science (hermetic art); esoteric; hence **her'metism** (3) n. 2. ~ic seal, airtight closure by fusion etc. (orig. as used by alchemists). 3. with hermetic seal; (fig.) protected from outside agencies; esoteric, recondite; hence ~iCALLY adv. [f. med. L hermeticus irreg. f. Hermes Trismegistus thrice-greatest Hermes (as founder of alchemy etc.)]

her'mit n. early Christian recluse; person living in solitude; ~-crab, crab of family Paguridae that lives in mollusc's cast-off shell to protect its shell-less hinder parts, ~ thrush, migratory N. Amer. thrush noted for song. [ME f. OF (h)ermite or f. LL eremita f. Gk erēmitēs (erēmia desert f. erēmos solitary; see -ITE¹)]

her'mitage n. hermit's abode; monastery; solitary abode. [ME, f. OF (h)ermitage (as prec.; see -AGE)]

||hern(e). See HERON.

her'ni|a n. (pl. ~as or ~ae). (Path.) displacement and protrusion of part of organ through aperture in wall of cavity containing it, esp. of abdomen; hence ~AL, ~ARY¹, ~āted¹, adjs. [L]

her'nshaw. See HAWK¹.

her'o n. (pl. ~es). 1. (Gk Ant.) man of superhuman qualities, favoured by the gods; demigod. 2. illustrious warrior; ~'s welcome (such as is given to hero returning from battle). 3. man admired for achievements and noble qualities. 4. chief male character in poem, play, or story. 5. ~-worship(per), worship(per) of the ancient heroes, of some great man or men, or of a personal hero (sense 3). [ME, f. L f. Gk hērōs]

hero'ic a. & n. 1. a. (Of act or quality) of or fit for a hero; (of person) having the qualities of a hero; the ~ age (of Greece, before return from Troy). 2. (Of poetry) dealing with heroes; ~ couplet (of rhyming iambic pentameters); ~ verse, that used in heroic poetry (Gk & L hexameter, E iambic pentameter, F alexandrine). 3. (Of language) grand, high-flown; bold, attempting great things. 4. Hence **hero'ically** adv. 5. n. (in pl.) heroic verse; high-flown language or sentiments; unduly bold behaviour. [f. F héroïque or f. L f. Gk hērōikos (as prec.; see -IC)]

heroi-co'mic(al) adjs. combining the heroic with the comic [f. F héroï-comique (as prec., COMIC)]

he'roin n. sedative addictive drug prepared from and acting like morphine, illicitly used to produce intense euphoria. [G, f. as HERO (from its effects on user's opinion of himself) + -IN]

he'roïne n. demigoddess; heroic woman; chief female character in poem, play, or story. [f. F héroïne or f. L f. Gk hērōīnē, fem. of hērōs HERO; see -INE³]

he'roïsm n. heroic conduct or qualities. [f. F héroïsme (héros HERO; see -ISM)]

he'roïze, -ise (-īz), v. 1. v.t. make a hero of; make heroic. 2. v.i. play the hero. [f. HERO + -IZE]

he'ron, ||hern(e) (poet. etc.), n. long-legged long-necked wading bird of genus Ardea; hence ~RY (3) n. [ME, f. OF hairon f. Gmc *haigaron]

her'pes (-z) n. virus disease of skin with outbreaks of blisters; ~ si'mplex (painless form); ~ zo'ster (zō'-), SHINGLES; hence **herpe'tic** a. [ME f. L f. Gk herpēs -ētos shingles (herpō creep)]

herpetö'log|y n. study of reptiles; hence ~IST (3) n. [f. Gk herpeton reptile (herpō creep) + -o- + -LOGY]

Herr (hār) n. (pl. **Herr'en**). Title of German man = Mr; German man. [G, f. OHG *hĕrro* compar. of *hĕr* exalted]

Herrenvolk (hĕ'renfŏlk, -fōk) n. German nation viewed by Nazis as born to mastery; group regarding itself as innately superior. [G, = master-race (as prec., FOLK)]

hĕ'rring n. N. Atlantic fish (*Clupea harengus*) much used for food, coming near coast in large shoals to spawn; RED *herring*; ∼-**bone**, (n.) stitch resembling bones of herring, cloth woven in zigzag pattern, (Archit.) zigzag arrangement of stones, bricks, or tiles, (v.t.) work with herring-bone stitch, mark with herring-bone pattern, (v.i., Skiing) ascend slope by pointing skis outwards; ∼-**gull**, large N. Atlantic gull (*Larus argentatus*) with dark wing-tips; ∼-**pond**, (joc.) sea, esp. North Atlantic. [OE *hǣring, hēring*, = OHG *hāring* f. WG **hēringa*; cf. -ING³]

Herr'nhuter (hār'nhōō-) n. member of MORAVIAN sect. [G, f. *Herrnhut* (= the Lord's keeping), name of their first German settlement; see -ER¹]

hêrs (-z) poss. pron. pred. (& abs.) = HER² (*it is hers; hers is best; I like hers better; gave me one of hers; don't like that smile OF hers; my father and hers; some friends of hers*); **his and** ∼, respectively for husband and wife, or men and women; cf. GET¹ 4. [ME, f. HER² + -s³]

hersĕ'lf pron. **1.** Emphat. form corresp. to SHE OR HER¹ (*she herself will see to it, she will see to it herself; it was good for the others, if not for herself; let her do it herself*); in her normal state of body or mind (*is quite herself again*); **be** ∼, act in her normal or unconstrained manner; **by** ∼, without assistance or companions; *a* LAW¹ *unto herself*. **2.** Refl. form corresp. to HER¹ (*she has hurt herself; she seems pleased with herself; she killed a snake as big as herself*). [OE *hire self* (as HER¹, SELF)]

Herts. abbr. Hertfordshire.

hêrtz (-ts) n. (pl. same). unit of frequency, equal to one cycle per second. [f. H. R. *Hertz*, Ger. physicist d. 1894]

Hĕr'tzian (-ts-) a. ∼ **wave**, electromagnetic wave of length suitable for use in radio. [f. as prec. + -IAN]

hĕ'sit|ant (-z-) a. hesitating; irresolute; so ∼ANCE, ∼ANCY, ns., ∼antLY² adv. [f. as foll.; see -ANT]

hĕ'sit|āte (-z-) v.i. show, speak with, indecision (*about, over*); be deterred by scruples, be reluctant *to* (do); hence or cogn. ∼A'TION n., ∼ātIVE a. [f. L *haesitare* frequent. of *haerēre haes*- stick fast + -ATE³]

Hĕspĕr'ian a. (poet.) western; (Gk Myth.) of the Hesperides. [f. L f. Gk *Hesperios* (as HESPERUS) + -AN]

hĕsperī'di|um n. (pl. ∼**a**). fruit with sectioned pulp inside separable rind, e.g. orange. [f. Gk *Hesperides* nymphs believed to guard golden apples + -IUM]

Hĕ'sperus n. evening star. [ME f. L, f. Gk *hesperos* a. & n., western, evening (star)]

Hĕ'ssian a. & n. **1.** a. of Hesse in Germany; ∼ (**boot**), tasselled high boot first worn by Hessian troops; ∼ **fly**, Amer. midge whose larva destroys wheat [wrongly thought to have been brought to America by Hessian troops]. **2.** n. (h∼). strong coarse cloth of hemp or jute. [f. *Hesse* + -IAN]

hĕst n. (arch.) behest. [OE *hǣs* f. **haitan* call (see HIGHT), assim. to ME ns. in -t]

hĕt a. ∼ **up**, (sl.) excited. [dial. p.p. of HEAT²]

hĕtaer'a (-tēr'a), **hĕtair'a** (-īr'a), n. (pl. ∼**s** or hetaerae, or **hetairai** pr. -ī). courtesan, mistress, esp. in ancient Greece. [Gk *hetaira*, fem. of *hetairos* companion]

hĕtaer'ism (-ēr'-), **hĕtair'ism** (-īr'-), n. recognized system of concubinage; communal marriage in a tribe. [f. Gk *hetairismos* prostitution (as HETAERA; see -ISM)]

hĕ'tero- comb. form. other, different, (freq. opp. to HOMO-, occas. to AUTO-, ISO-, ORTHO-, etc.), as: ∼**chroma'tic**, of several colours; ∼**cy'clic**, (Chem.) with molecular ring composed of atoms of more than one kind; ∼**gamous** (-ŏ'g-), (1) irregular as regards stamens and pistils, (2) characterized by ∼**gamy**

(-ŏ'g-) or ∼**geny** (-ŏ'j-) or ∼**gony** (-ŏ'g-), alternation of generations; ∼**graft** (from individual of another species); ∼**logous** (-ŏ'l-), not homologous; ∼**merous** (-ŏ'm-), (Bot.) not isomerous; ∼**mor'phic**, of dissimilar forms; ∼**mor'phism**, existence in various forms; ∼**nomous** (-ŏ'n-), subject to different laws (of growth etc.), subject to an external law (cf. *autonomous*); ∼**nomy** (-ŏ'n-), presence of a different law, subjection to external law; ∼**pa'thic**, (1) allopathic, (2) differing in effect; ∼**phony** (-ŏ'f-), (Mus.) performing of same melody differently by different voices etc.; ∼**phy'llous**, bearing leaves of different forms on same plant; ∼**pla'stic**, of a heterograft; ∼**ploid**, not haploid or diploid; ∼**po'lar**, having dissimilar poles, (Electr.) with armature passing north and south magnet poles alternately; ∼**se'xual** a. & n., (person) characterized by (the normal) attraction to the opposite sex; ∼**taxy**, abnormal disposition of organs or parts; ∼**tra'nsplant**, = *heterograft*; ∼**tro'phic**, deriving its nourishment from outside, not autotrophic. [f. Gk *heteros* other + -o-]

hĕ'teroclīte a. & n. abnormal (thing or person); (Gram.) irregularly declined (noun). [f. LL f. Gk HETERO(*klitos* f. *klinō* bend, inflect)]

hĕ'terodŏx a. (Of person or opinion) not orthodox; so ∼Y¹ n. [f. LL f. Gk HETERO(*doxos* f. *doxa* opinion)]

hĕ'terodȳne a., & v.i. (Radio). relating to production of, produce, a lower (audible) frequency from the combination of two almost equal high frequencies. [f. as HETERO-, DYNE]

hĕterogĕ'néous a. diverse in character; composed of diverse elements; (Math.) incommensurable through being of different kinds or degrees; hence or cogn. **hĕterogĕnē'ITY**, ∼NESS, ns., ∼LY² adv. f. med. L *heterogeneus* f. Gk HETERO(*genēs* f. *genos* kind) + -OUS]

hĕterogĕ'nĕsis n. birth of a living being otherwise than from parent of same kind, esp. spontaneous generation from inorganic matter; hence **hĕterogĕnĕ'tic** a. [f. HETERO- + GENESIS]

hĕterŏ's|is n. (pl. ∼**es** pr. -ēz). tendency of cross-bred individual to show qualities superior to those of both parents. [Gk (*heteros* different)]

hĕterozȳ'g|ōte n. zygote resulting from fusion of unlike gametes; Mendelian hybrid containing dominant and recessive characters and therefore not breeding true; so ∼OUS a. [f. HETERO- + ZYGOTE]

hĕ'tman n. Polish or Cossack military commander. [Pol., prob. f. G *hauptmann* captain]

heu'chera (hū'k-, hoi'k-) n. N. Amer. perennial plant of genus *Heuchera*, of saxifrage family. [mod. L, f. J. H. von *Heucher*, Ger. botanist d. 1747 + -A 1]

heuri'st|ic (hūr-) a. & n. **1.** a. serving to discover; (of computer problem-solving) proceeding by trial and error; ∼**ic method**, system of education under which the pupil is trained to find out things for himself; hence ∼ICS n. pl. **2.** n. (science of) heuristic procedure. [f. Gk *heuriskō* find; see -IC]

hĕ'vĕa n. S. Amer. tree of genus *Hevea*, whose milky sap yields rubber. [mod. L, f. native *hevé*; see -A]

hew v. (p.p. ∼n or ∼**ed**). **1.** v.t. chop, cut, (thing *down, away, off*, etc.) with axe, sword, etc.; cut into shape; ∼ one's **way**, make a way for oneself by hewing. **2.** v.i. deal cutting blows *at, among*, etc.; **conform to*. [OE *hēawan*, = OS *hauwan*, OHG *houwan*, ON *höggva* f. Gmc **hauwan*]

***HEW** abbr. Department of Health, Education, and Welfare.

hew'er n. one who hews; man who cuts coal from seam; ∼**s of wood and drawers of water**, drudges (Josh. 9: 21). [ME, f. HEW + -ER¹]

***hĕx** v. & n. **1.** v.i. & t. practise witchcraft (on), bewitch. **2.** n. witch; magic spell. [f. Pennsylvanian G *hexe* v., *hex* n., f. G *hexe*(n)]

hĕ'xa- comb. form. six, as: ∼**chord** (-k-), diatonic series of six notes with semitone between third and fourth, used at three different pitches in medieval music;

∼**de′cimal,** using 16 as basis of counting; ∼**gon,** plane figure with six sides and angles; so ∼**gonal** (-ă′g-) *a*.; ∼**gram,** figure formed by two intersecting equilateral triangles (the angular points coinciding with those of a hexagon), figure of six lines; ∼HE′DRAL *a*., ∼HE′DRON *n*., (solid) with six faces; ∼**merous**(-ă′m-), having six parts; ∼**pod** *n*. & *a*., (insect) with six feet; ∼**pody** (-ă′p-), line of verse with six feet; ∼**style** *a*. & *n*., (portico) of six columns; ∼**sylla′bic,** of six syllables; H∼**teuch** (-k), first six books of OT; ∼**va′lent,** (Chem.) having a valence of six. [Gk (*hex* six)]

hĕ′xăd *n*. group of six. [f. Gk hexas -ados (*hex* six); see -AD 1]

hĕxă′mĕter *n*. line of six metrical feet, esp. **dactylic** ∼ (five dactyls and trochee or spondee, any of first four feet, and rarely the fifth, being replaceable by spondee); hence **hĕxamĕ′tric** *a*., **hĕxă′mĕtrIST** (3) *n*. [ME f. L, f. Gk HEXA(*metros* f. *metron* measure)]

hĕ′xāne *n*. (Chem.) hydrocarbon of the paraffin series, C_6H_{14}. [f. HEXA-+-ANE]

hĕ′xapla *n*. sixfold text in parallel columns, esp. of OT or NT. [Gk, neut. pl. of HEXA(*ploos* -fold), orig. of Origen's OT text]

hĕ′xōde *n*. thermionic valve having six electrodes. [G, f. Gk *hex* six +*hodos* way]

hĕ′xōse *n*. (Chem.) monosaccharide with six carbon atoms in each molecule. [f. HEXA-+-OSE[2]]

hey[1] (hā) *int*. calling attention or expr. joy, surprise, or inquiry, or enthusiastic approval *for*; ∼ **presto** (conjuror's phrase of command, hence used to announce surprising transformation etc.). [ME; cf. OF *hay*, Du., G *hei*]

hey[2]. See HAY[2].

hey′-day[1] (hā′-) *int*. (arch.) expr. joy, surprise, etc. [cf. LG *heidi*, *heida*, excl. denoting gaiety]

hey′day[2] (hā′-) *n*. full bloom, flush, (of youth, vigour, prosperity, etc.). [f. prec.]

HF *abbr*. high frequency.

hf. *abbr*. half.

Hf *symb*. hafnium.

HG *abbr*. Her or His Grace; Home Guard.

hg. *abbr*. hectogram(s).

Hg *symb*. mercury. [f. mod. L *hydrargyrum*]

||**HGV** *abbr*. heavy goods vehicle.

HH *abbr*. Her or His Highness; His Holiness; double--hard (pencil-lead).

hh. *abbr*. hands (see HAND[1] 10)

hhd. *abbr*. hogshead(s).

H-hour (ā′chowr) *n*. hour at which an operation is scheduled to begin. [f. *H* for *hour*+HOUR]

hi *int*. calling attention or *(colloq.)* expr. greeting. [parallel form to HEY[1]]

*****HI** *abbr*. Hawaii(an Islands).

hiā′tus *n*. break or gap, esp. in a series, account, or chain of proof; break between two vowels coming together not in the same syllable, as in *though oft the ear*. [L, = gaping (*hiare* gape)]

hī′bern|āte *v.i.* spend the winter (of animal) in torpid state, (of person) in mild climate; (fig.) remain inactive; hence ∼A′TION *n*. [f. L *hibernare* (*hibernus* wintry)+-ATE[3]]

Hibĕr′nian *a*. & *n*. (native) of Ireland. [f. L *Hibernia*, *Iverna* f. Gk *Iernē* f. OCelt. **Iveriu*+-AN]

Hibĕr′nicism *n*. Irish idiom, expression, or BULL[4]. [f. as prec. after *Anglicism* etc.]

hibi′scus *n*. cultivated herb or shrub of genus *Hibiscus*, rose-mallow. [L, f. Gk *hibiskos* marsh mallow]

hic *int*. expr. sound of (esp. drunken) hiccup. [imit.]

hiccough. Var. of foll. (by assim. to COUGH[1,2]).

hĭ′ccup *n*. & *v*. **1.** *n*. involuntary spasm of respiratory organs, with sudden closure of glottis and characteristic sound ((the) ∼s, attack of such spasms); (fig.) temporary minor stoppage; hence ∼Y[2] *a*. **2.** *v.i.* make hiccup. **3.** *v.t.* say, bring out, with hiccup(s). [imit.]

hic ja′cĕt (hĭk jā′sĕt, hēk yă′kĕt) *n*. epitaph. [L, = here lies]

*****hĭck** *n*. (colloq.) countryman, farmer, provincial. [pet-form of man's Christian name *Richard*; cf. *Dick*]

*****hĭ′ckey** *n*. gadget. [20th c., of unkn. orig.]

hĭ′ckory *n*. N. Amer. tree of genus *Carya*, allied to walnut, with tough heavy wood; (stick of) its wood. [f. native Virginian *pohickery*]

hid, hĭ′dden. See HIDE[2].

hĭdă′lgō *n*. (*pl.* ∼s). Spanish gentleman. [Sp. (*hijo dalgo* son of something)]

hīde[1] *n*., & *v.t.* **1.** *n*. animal's skin, raw or dressed; (joc.) human skin (*to save his own hide; will tan your hide*); ∼**′bound,** (of cattle) with skin clinging close as result of bad feeding, (fig.) narrow-minded, bigoted; hence (-)**hī′dED**[2] *a*. **2.** *v.t.* (colloq.) flog. [OE *hȳd*, = OS *hūd*, OHG *hūt*, ON *húth* f. Gmc *hūdhiz* f. IE **kūtis*]

hīde[2] *v*. (*past* **hid,** *p.p.* **hidden** *or* arch. **hid**) & *n*. **1.** *v.t.* put, keep, out of sight (*hide* one's *light under a* BUSHEL[1]); keep (fact) secret (*from*); keep (thing) from view without intention of secrecy; ∼ one's **head,** keep out of sight from shame etc.; **hidden reserves,** extra profits etc. kept concealed in reserve. **2.** *v.i.* conceal oneself; ∼ **out** or **up,** remain in concealment; ∼-**-and-(*go-)seek,** children's game in which players seek one or more hiding from them, (fig.) action involving evasive person or thing; *****∼′away,** ∼**-out, hi′d(e)y-hole,** (colloq.) hiding-place. **3.** *n*. ||place of concealment used in observing or hunting wild animals. [OE *hȳdan*, = MDu. *hüden* f. WG **hūdjan*]

hīde[0] *n*. (Hist.) measure of land, as much as would support one free family and dependants (from 60 to 120 acres according to locality). [OE *hī*(*gi*)*d* (*hīw-*, *hīg-* household)]

hī′dĕous *a*. frightful, repulsive, revolting, to senses or mind (*hideous crime, noise, pattern, scar*); (colloq.) unpleasant; hence ∼LY[2] *adv*., ∼NESS *n*. [ME f. AF *hidous*, = OF *hidos*, *-eus*, earlier *hisdos* (*hisde* horror, of unkn. orig.); assim. to -EOUS]

hī′ding[1] *n*. (colloq.) thrashing; **on a** ∼ **to nothing,** with prospect of loss but none of gain. [f. HIDE[1]+-ING[1]]

hī′ding[2] *n*. In vbl senses; state of remaining hidden (*be in, go into, hiding*); ∼**-place,** place of concealment. [ME, f. HIDE[2]+-ING[1]]

hĭdr|ŏ′sis *n*. (*pl.* ∼**sēs** -ō′sēz). (Med.) perspiration; so ∼o′TIC *a*. [mod. L f. Gk (*hidrōs* sweat)]

hīe *v.i.* & *refl*. (*part.* ∼**′ing** *or* **hy′ing,** *pr.* hī′ī-). (arch. or poet.) go quickly (*to* etc.; *hie to your chamber; hied him to the show*). [OE *hīgian* strive, pant, of unkn. orig.]

hier′arch (hīr′ärk) *n*. chief priest; archbishop. [f. med. L f. Gk *hierarkhēs* (*hieros* sacred, *-arkhēs* ruler)]

hier′arch|y (hīr′ärkī) *n*. **1.** each of three divisions of angels; the angels. **2.** priestly government; organized priesthood in successive grades. **3.** organization with grades or classes ranked one above another. **4.** Hence ∼IC(AL) (-är′-) *adjs*., ∼ISM (3) *n*., ∼IZE (3) *v.t.* [ME f. OF *ierarchie* f. med. L (*h*)*ierarchia* f. Gk *hierarkhia* (as prec.; see -Y[1])]

hierǎ′tic (hīr-) *a*. of the priests (esp. of ancient Egyptian writing of abridged hieroglyphics opp. *demotic*, and of Egyptian and Greek traditional styles of art); priestly. [f. L f. Gk *hieratikos* (*hieraomai* be a priest f. *hiereus* priest; see -IC)]

hier′o- (hīr′o) *comb. form*. sacred, holy, as: ∼**cracy** (-ŏ′k-), priestly rule; ∼**gram,** ∼**graph,** sacred inscription or symbol; ∼**latry** (-ŏ′l-), worship of saints; ∼**logy** (-ŏ′l-), sacred literature or lore. [f. Gk *hieros* sacred+-o-]

hier′oglȳph (hīr′-) *n*. figure of an object standing for a word, syllable, or sound, as used in ancient Egyptian and other writing; writing of this kind; secret or enigmatic symbol; (in *pl.*, joc.) writing difficult to make out. [back-form. f. foll.]

hieroglȳ′phic (hīr-) *a*. & *n*. **1.** *a*. of or written in hieroglyphs; symbolical. **2.** *n*. (in *pl.*) hieroglyphs. **3.** Hence ∼AL *a*., ∼ALLY *adv*. [f. F *hiéroglyphique* or f. LL f. Gk HIERO(*gluphikos* f. *gluphē* carving; see -IC)]

hier′ophănt (hīr′-) *n*. (Gk Ant.) initiating priest;

expounder of sacred mysteries; hence ~IC (-ă'-) a. [f. LL f. Gk HIERO(*phantēs* f. *phainō* show)]

hi'-fī a. & n. (colloq.) **1.** a. = HIGH-*fidelity*. **2.** n. equipment for high-fidelity sound-reproduction; use of this as hobby etc. [abbr.]

hi'ggle v.i. dispute about terms; haggle. [var. of HAGGLE]

hi'ggledy-pi'ggledy (-geldĭ) adv., a., & n. (in) utter confusion and disorder. [rhyming jingle, prob. w. ref. to irregular herding together of pigs]

high (hī) a., n., & adv. **1.** a. of great or (*pred.*) specified upward extent (*high heels*; *a high hill*; *one inch high*; *water was waist-high*); situated far above ground, sea level, etc., (*high altitude*); upper, inland, (*High Asia*); coming above the normal or average level (*jersey with high neck*; *high boots*). **2.** of exalted rank (*in high society*); **the Most H~**, God; **H~ Admiral** etc., chief officer; ~ **card** (that can outrank others, esp. ace or court--card; HOW *is that for high?*; **ace** etc. ~, having this as highest-ranking card); ~**er court** (that can overrule decision of another); ~**er mammal, plant,** etc., (evolved to a greater degree). **3.** of exalted quality (*high art, minds, principles*); luxurious (*high living*); (colloq.) intoxicated by or *on* alcohol or drugs; ~ **opinion of** (very favourable). **4.** (Of meat) beginning to go bad; (of game) hung until slightly decomposed and ready to cook. **5.** great, intense, extreme, powerful, (*high favour, fever, polish, praise, temperature, vacuum, wind*); extreme in opinion (*a high Tory*). **6.** (Of physical action) extending to or from, or performed at, a considerable distance above ground (*high diving, flying*); (of quantity, value, etc.) greater than what is regarded as normal (*high prices*); (of latitude) near N. or S. pole; (of time) far advanced, fully reached (*high noon, high summer*; *it is high time we left*); (of period) at its peak of development (*High Renaissance*) or long since passed (*high antiquity*); (of sound) having rapid vibrations, shrill; (of vowel) = CLOSE¹. **7.** ~ **altar**, chief altar of church; ~ **and dry,** (of ship) out of the water, (fig.) out of the current of events, stranded; ~ **and low,** (people) of all conditions (cf. sense 9); ~ **and mighty,** (colloq.) arrogant, (arch.) of exalted rank; *~'**ball,** (1) drink of spirits and soda etc. served usu. with ice in tall glass, (2) railway signal to proceed; *~'**binder,** ruffian, swindler, assassin; ~-**born,** of noble birth; *~'**boy,** tall chest of drawers on legs; ~'**brow** a. & n., (colloq.) (person) with detached or (consciously) superior intellectual or cultural interests; ~ **camp,** sophisticated CAMP³; ~ **chair,** infant's chair with long legs and usu. tray, for use at meals; H~ **Church,** party or principles revering ritual, authority of bishops and priests, saving grace of sacraments, etc.; H~-**Chur'chman,** holder of such principles; ~-**class,** of high quality; ~ **colour,** flushed complexion; ~ **command,** army commander-in-chief and staff; H~ **Commission(er),** (head of) embassy from one Commonwealth country to another; ||H~ **Court** (of Justice), supreme court of justice for civil cases; ~ **day,** festal day; *High* DUTCH¹; ~ **enema** (delivered into colon); *higher* CRITICISM; ~**er education** (at university etc.); ~**er mathematics** (beyond what is ordinarily taught in schools); ~'**er--ups,** (colloq.) persons of higher rank; *high* EXPLOSIVE; ~**-falu'tin(g)** (-ōō'-) a. & n., (colloq.) absurdly pompous or pretentious (writing etc.) [perh. f. *fluting*]; ~ **fashion,** *haute couture*; *in high* FEATHER¹; ~ **fidelity,** property of reproducing sound with little distortion of signal, giving result very similar to the original; ~ **finance** (dealing with large sums of money); ~**-flown,** extravagant, bombastic; ~**-fly'er, -fli'er,** person with ambition or extravagant notions, person or thing with (capacity for) great achievements; ~**-fly'ing,** reaching a great height, ambitious; ~ **frequency** (esp. in Radio, 3 to 30 megahertz); *high* GEAR; *High* GERMAN²; ~**-grade,** of high quality; ~**-handed,** overbearing, disregarding

the feelings of others; ~ **hat,** tall hat, foot-operated cymbals, (fig.) person affecting superiority; ~**-hat,** (a.) supercilious, *(v.t.)* treat superciliously, *(v.i.)* assume superior attitude; ~ **holiday,** Jewish New Year or Day of Atonement; *on* one's *high* HORSE¹; *high* JINKS; ~ **jump,** athletic contest of jumping as high as possible, (fig.) drastic punishment; ~**-key,** (Photog.) consisting of light tones; ~ **kick,** dancer's kick high in the air; ~**-level,** (of negotiations etc.) conducted by persons of high rank; ~ **life,** luxurious existence ascribed to the upper classes; ~'**light,** (n.) (in painting etc.) any of brightest parts of subject or representation, moment or detail of vivid interest, outstanding feature, (v.t.) bring into prominence, draw attention to; ~**-lows,** (arch.) boots reaching over ankles; *high* MASS¹; ~**-mi'nded,** morally lofty, (arch.) proud; *high-*OCTANE; ~ **old,** (colloq.) most enjoyable (*time* etc.); ~**-pitched,** (of sound) high, (of roof) steep, (of style etc.) lofty; ~ **places,** upper ranks of an organization; ~ **point,** maximum or best state reached; ~ **polymer** (of high molecular weight); ~**-powered,** having great power or energy, forceful; *high* PRESSURE; ~ **priest,** chief priest (esp. of Jews), (fig.) head of any cult; ~**-ranking,** of high rank, senior; *high* RELIEF²; ~**-rise,** (of building) having many storeys; ~ **road,** main road, (fig.) direct route (*to*); ~ **school,** secondary (esp. ||grammar) school; ~ **sea(s),** open seas not within any country's jurisdiction; ~ **season,** period of greatest number of visitors at resort etc.; ||*high* SHERIFF; *~ **sign,** (colloq.) warning or reassuring gesture; ~**-sounding,** pretentious in sound; ~**-speed,** operating at great speed, (of steel) suitable for cutting-tools even when red-hot; *high* SPIRIT¹(*s*); *high-*spirited; ~ **spot,** (sl.) important place or feature; ~**-ste'pper,** horse that lifts its feet high in walking and trotting, (fig.) stately person; ||*High* STEWARD; ~ **street,** main road, esp. principal street of town with shops etc.; ~**-strung,** very sensitive or nervous; ~ **table,** elevated table (1) at public dinner, (2) for fellows of college; *~'**tail** v.i., (sl.) move at high speed; ||*high* TEA; ~**-tensile,** (of metal) having great tensile strength; ~ **tension,** = *high voltage*; *high* TIDE¹; ~**-toned,** stylish, dignified, superior in manner; *high* TREASON; ~**-up,** (colloq.) person of high rank; ~ **voltage,** electrical potential causing some danger of injury or damage; ~ **water,** state of tide when water is highest, time when tide is at the full; ~**-wa'ter mark,** level reached at high water, (fig.) maximum recorded value, highest point of excellence etc.; ~, **wide, and handsome,** in carefree or stylish manner; ~ **wire,** high tightrope; ~ **words,** angry talk; *~ **yellow,** half-caste with light yellow skin. *n.* a high or the highest level or figure; the highest card dealt or drawn; area of high barometric pressure; = TOP¹ 9 (gear); *(colloq.)* high school; (sl.) euphoric state caused by drug; **from on** ~, from heaven or a high place; **on** ~, in or to heaven or a high place; ||**the H~,** (colloq.) High Street, esp. at Oxford. **9.** adv. far up, aloft; in or to a high degree; at a high price; (of sound) at or to a high pitch; **play** ~, play for high stakes, play card of high value; **run** ~, (of sea) have strong current with high tide, (fig., of feelings) be strong; *search* ~ **and low,** everywhere (cf. sense 7). [OE *hēah,* = OS, OHG *hōh,* ON *hár,* Goth. *hauhs* f. Gmc **hauhaz*]

hi'ghland (hī'l-) n. & a. **1.** n. high land (usu. in *pl.,* esp. (*H~s*) of mountainous part of Scotland). **2.** a. of or in highland or (*H~*) the Scottish Highlands; H~ **cattle** (of breed with shaggy hair and long curved widely-spaced horns); H~ **dress,** kilt etc.; *Highland* FLING. **3.** Hence ~ER¹ (4), ~**man,** ns. [OE *hēahland* promontory (as prec., LAND¹)]

hi'ghly (hī'lǐ) adv. in a high degree (*highly amusing, polished, probable*; *commend, esteem, highly*); honourably, favourably, (*think, speak, highly of*); ~**-strung,** = HIGH-*strung*. [OE *hēalīce* (as HIGH, -LY²)]

*hi′gh-mŭck-a-mŭck (hī′m-) *n.* person of (esp. conceitedly) great self-importance. [perh. f. Chinook *hiu* plenty + *muckamuck* food]

hi′ghnĕss (hī′n-) *n.* **1.** Title of various British and other princes etc. (*His* or *Her Highness* or *Royal*, SERENE, *Imperial*, *Highness*). **2.** state of being figuratively high (*the highness of his character, of taxation; fell from sheer highness of ambition*; cf. *the* HEIGHT *of*). [OE *hēanes* (as HIGH, -NESS)]

hĭght (hīt) *a.* (arch., poet., or joc.) called, named. [f. p.p. (from 14th c.) of OE *hātan* command, call, OS *hētan*, OHG *heizzan*, ON *heita*, Goth. *haitan*]

hi′ghway (hī′w-) *n.* public road (**King's** or **Queen's** ∼, regarded as protected by monarch's power); main route; (fig.) ordinary direct course of action; ||**H**∼ **Code**, official book of guidance for road-users; ∼**man**, (Hist.) (usu. mounted) man who robs passengers on highway. [f. HIGH + WAY]

HIH *abbr.* Her or His Imperial Highness.

hi′jăck *v.t.*, & *n.* **1.** *v.t.* seize control of (means of transport, e.g. lorry with goods, aircraft in flight) by (threat of) violence; force (aircraft etc.) *to* new destination thus; steal (contraband etc.) in transit; so ∼ER[1] *n.* **2.** *n.* hijacking. [20th c.; orig. unkn.]

hi′jra. Var. of HEGIRA.

hīke *n.* & *v.* (colloq.) **1.** *n.* long walk in the country undertaken for pleasure or exercise; *increase (of prices etc.). **2.** *v.i.* walk vigorously or laboriously; go for long walk; (transit) *hike*; be hitched *up*. **3.** *v.t.* hoist, shove, force to move, *increase. **4.** Hence **hi′kER**[1] *n.* [19th c. dial.; orig. unkn.]

hilar′ious *a.* mirthful, joyous; causing merriment; boisterously merry; hence or cogn. ∼LY[2] *adv.*, ∼NESS, **hilā′rITY**, *ns.* [f. L *hilaris* f. Gk *hilaros* cheerful + -OUS]

||**Hi′larỹ** *n.* ∼ **term**, (in university etc., beginning in Jan.). [f. *Hilarius* bishop of Poitiers d. 367, w. Anglican festival 13 Jan.]

hĭll *n.*, & *v.t.* **1.** *n.* natural elevation of earth's surface, small mountain; ***over the** ∼, (colloq.) past the crisis or acme; UP *hill and down dale*; **the** ∼**s**, (Anglo-Ind.) a hill-station as health-resort etc.; ∼ **and dale**, (of gramophone record) with groove-undulations in vertical plane; **old as the** ∼**s**, very ancient. **2.** heap, mound, (ant-, dung-, mole-, *hill*). **3.** sloping piece of road. **4.** *∼**-billy**, rustic person from mountains etc., folk music (as) of southern US; ∼ **climb**, race for vehicles over hilly ground; ∼**-fort**, fortified place built on hill; ∼**-man**, inhabitant of hilly country; ∼**side**, lateral slope of hill; ∼**-station**, government settlement in low mountains of N. India; ∼**′top**, summit of hill. **5.** Hence ∼′Y[2] *a.* **6.** *v.t.* form into hill; bank *up* (plants) with soil. [OE *hyll*, = LG *hull*, WG *hulni f. IE *k(*o*)*l*-]

hillō′ *int.* (arch.) = HALLO. [var. of HOLLO]

hi′llock *n.* small hill or mound. [ME, f. HILL + -OCK]

hĭlt *n.*, & *v.t.* **1.** *n.* handle of sword or dagger, or of other weapon or tool; *prove* etc. **up to the** ∼, completely. **2.** *v.t.* furnish with hilt. [OE *hilt*(*e*), = OS *hilte*, ON *hjalt*, OHG *helza* f. Gmc *heltaz]

hi′l|um *n.* (*pl.* ∼**a**). (Bot.) point of attachment of seed to seed-vessel; (Anat.) notch etc. where vessel enters organ. [L., = little thing, trifle]

him. See HE[1].

HIM *abbr.* Her or His Imperial Majesty.

Himalay′an *a.* of the Himalayas. [f. *Himalaya* Mountains in Nepal etc. (Skr., f. *hima* snow + *ālaya* abode) + -AN]

himă′tion *n.* outer garment of ancient Greeks, worn over the left shoulder and under the right. [Gk]

himsĕlf *pron.* Emphat. & refl. form corresp. to HE[1] or HIM (for uses cf. HERSELF). [OE (HIM, SELF)]

Hinaya′na (hēnayah′na) *n.* more conservative form of Buddhism, practised in Burma, Thailand, etc. [Skr. (*hīna* lesser, *yāna* vehicle)]

hĭnd[1] *n.* female (esp. red) deer, esp. in and after third year. [OE, = OS, ON *hind*, OHG *hinta* f. Gmc *hinthjō f. IE *kemti- (*kem- hornless)]

||**hĭnd**[2] *n.* farm servant, esp. (Sc. etc.) married and skilled farm-workman, formerly having charge of two horses, and provided with cottage on the farm; steward; rustic, boor. [ME *hine* f. OE *hīne* pl., app. f. *hī*(*g*)*na* gen. pl. of *hīgan, hīwan* 'members of a family'; cf. HIDE[3]; for -*d* cf. SOUND[2]]

hĭnd[3] *a.* situated at the back, posterior, (esp. opp. *fore*: *hind legs*); ∼**quar′ters**, hind legs and adjoining parts of quadruped; **on** one's ∼ **legs**, (joc.) = *on* one's LEGS (1). [ME, perh. shortened f. OE *bihindan* BEHIND]

hi′nder[1] *a.* situated at the BACK[1] (sense 5). [ME, perh. f. OE *hinderweard* backward; cf. prec.]

hi′nder[2] *v.t.* impede, delay, prevent, (*you will hinder him, his work, its completion, him from working*, or abs.). [OE *hindrian*, = ON *hindra*, OHG *hintarōn* f. Gmc *hindarōjan (*hindar HIND[3])]

Hi′ndi (-ē) *a.* & *n.* (of) a group of spoken dialects of N. India; (of) a literary form of Hindustani with Sanskrit-based vocabulary and Devanagari script, an official language of India. [f. Urdu *hindī* (*Hind* India)]

hi′ndmost (-mōst, -o-) *a.* furthest behind; most remote. [ME, f. HIND[3] + -MOST]

hi′ndrance *n.* obstruction, prevention, obstacle. [ME, f. HINDER[2] + -ANCE]

hi′ndsight (-sīt) *n.* backsight of gun; wisdom after the event (opp. *foresight*). [f. HIND[3] + SIGHT[1]]

Hĭndu, (arch.) **Hindoo′,** (hindŏŏ′, hī′-) *n.* & *a.* **1.** adherent of Hinduism; Indian. **2.** *a.* of the Hindus; that is a Hindu; (arch.) Indian. [Urdu, f. Pers. (*Hind* India)]

Hi′ndu|ism (-ōō-) *n.* religious and social system with adherents esp. in India, with belief in reincarnation, worship of several gods, and caste as basis of society; so ∼IZE (3) *v.t.* [f. prec. + -ISM]

Hindusta′ni (-ah′nē) *a.* & *n.* **1.** *a.* of Hindustan or its people; (of) Hindustani. **2.** *n.* language based on Western Hindi, with admixture of Arabic, Persian, etc., current as standard language and lingua franca in much of N. India and Pakistan; (arch.) Urdu. [Urdu, f. Pers. *hindūstānī* (as HINDU, *-stān* country, -I 2)]

hinge (-nj) *n.* & *v.* **1.** *n.* movable joint or mechanism like that by which door is hung on side post; natural joint doing similar work, e.g. that of bivalve shell; (stamp-)∼, small piece of gummed transparent paper for fixing postage stamp in album etc.; (fig.) central principle, critical point, on which all turns; hence **hing**ED[2] (-njd), ∼′LESS (-jl-), *adjs.*, ∼′WISE (-jw-) *adv.* **2.** *v.t.* attach (as) with hinge. **3.** *v.i.* (Of door etc. or fig.) hang and turn *on* (post, principle, etc.). [ME *heng* etc., rel. to HANG[1]]

hi′nnỹ[1] *n.* offspring of she-ass and stallion. [f. L *hinnus* f. Gk *hinnos, ginnos*]

hi′nnỹ[2], **hi′nnie,** *n.* (Sc. & N. Engl.) = HONEY 2; **singing** ∼, currant-cake baked on griddle. [var. of HONEY]

hint *n.* & *v.* **1.** *n.* slight indication, covert or indirect suggestion (BROAD *hint*; DROP[2], TAKE[1] 9, *a hint*); small piece of practical information. **2.** *v.t.* suggest slightly (*thing, that*). **3.** *v.i.* ∼ **at,** give a hint of, refer indirectly to. [app. f. obs. *hent* grasp, lay hold of, f. OE *hentan* f. Gmc **hent-,* cogn. w. HUNT[1]]

hi′nterländ *n.* district behind coast or river's banks, occas. with suggestion of sparse population or inferior civilization; area served by port or other centre; remote or fringe area. [G (*hinter* behind, *land* LAND[1])]

hip[1] *n.* **1.** projection of pelvis and upper part of thigh-bone on each side of body in men and quadrupeds; (in *sing.* or *pl.*) circumference of body at buttocks; *have* (*person*) **on the** ∼, (arch.) at a disadvantage; **smite** ∼ **and thigh** (unsparingly). **2.** (Archit.) arris of roof from ridge to eaves. **3.** ∼**-bath** (portable, in which one sits immersed to the hips); ∼**-bone,** bone forming hip, esp. ilium; ∼**-disease** (of hip-joint, with fungous growth, inflammation, and caries); ∼**-flask**

(for spirits etc., carried in hip-pocket); ∼-**joint**, articulation of head of thigh-bone with ilium; ∼-**length** *a.*, (of garment) reaching down to the hips; ∼-**pocket** (in trousers, just behind hip); ∼-**roof** (with ends as well as sides inclined). **4.** Hence **(-)∼**PED² (-pt) *a.* (∼**ped roof,** = *hip-roof*). [OE *hype*, = OHG *huf*, Goth. *hups* f. Gmc **hupiz*, rel. to HOP²]

hip², hĕp¹, *n.* fruit of (esp. wild) rose. [OE *hēope*, *hīope*, = OS *hiopo*, OHG *hiufa* f. WG **heup-*]

hip³, hўp, *n.* (arch.) morbid depression of spirits. [abbr. of HYPOCHONDRIA]

hip⁴ *v.t.* (-pp-). (arch.) make low-spirited. [f. prec.]

hip⁵ *int.* introducing united cheer (*hip, hip, hurrah*). [19th c., of unkn. orig.]

hip⁶ *a.* (sl.) = HEP²; ∼-**cat,** = HEP²-*cat*; hence ∼*'*NESS *n.* [20th c., of unkn. orig.]

hippeà'strum *n.* S. Amer. bulbous plant of genus *Hippeastrum* with showy white or red flowers. [mod. L, f. Gk *hippeus* horseman (the leaves appearing to ride on one another) + *astron* star (from the flower-shape)]

hipped (-pt) *a.* (sl.) ∼ **on,** obsessed with. [p.p. of *hip* v. = make HIP⁶]

hi'ppie, hi'ppȳ¹, *n.* (sl.) = HIPSTER¹; unconventionally behaving person who is (thought to be) using hallucinogenic drugs and rebelling against organized society. [f. HIP⁶ + -IE, -Y³]

hi'ppō *n.* (*pl.* ∼s). (colloq.) hippopotamus. [abbr.]

hi'ppo- *comb. form.* horse, as: ∼**ce'ntaur,** centaur; ∼**phagy** (-ŏ'f-), practice of eating horse-flesh; ∼PHIL(E) *n.* & *a.*, ∼PHO'BIA *n.* [f. Gk *hippos* horse + -o-]

hippocà'mp|us *n.* (*pl.* ∼i *pr.* -ī). fish of genus *Hippocampus*, with head suggestive of horse; ∼ **major, minor,** (Anat.) elongated ridges on floor of each lateral ventricle of brain. [L, f. Gk HIPPO(*kampos* sea-monster)]

hi'ppocrās *n.* (Hist.) wine flavoured with spices. [ME, f. OF *ipocras* Hippocrates (see foll.), prob. because strained through filter called 'Hippocrates' sleeve']

Hippocră'tic *a.* ∼ **oath** (stating obligations and proper conduct of physicians, taken by those beginning medical practice). [f. med. L *Hippocraticus* f. *Hippocrates,* Gk physician of 5th c. BC + -IC]

Hi'ppocrēne *n.* poetic or literary inspiration. [name of fountain on Mount Helicon sacred to the Muses, L f. Gk (*hippos* horse, *krēnē* fountain, as having been produced by stroke of Pegasus' hoof)]

hi'ppodrōme *n.* (Gk & Rom. Ant.) course for chariot races etc.; circus; (*H*∼; used as name of) theatre for various stage entertainments. [F, or f. L f. Gk HIPPO(*dromos* race, course)]

hi'ppogriff, -grȳph, *n.* fabulous griffin-like creature with body of horse. [f. F *hippogriffe* f. It. *ippogrifo* (as HIPPO-, *grifo* GRIFFIN²)]

hippopŏ'tam|us *n.* (*pl.* ∼uses, or ∼i *pr.* -ī). large African pachydermatous tusked hairless short-legged quadruped inhabiting rivers etc. [ME f. L, f. Gk HIPPO(*potamos* river)]

hi'ppȳ¹. See HIPPIE.

hi'ppȳ² *a.* having large hips. [f. HIP¹ + -Y²]

hi'pster¹ *n.* (sl.) one who is hep; hep-cat; hence ∼ISM (3) *n.* [f. HIP⁶ + -STER]

hi'pster² *a.* (Of garment) hanging from the hips rather than from the waist. [f. HIP¹ + -STER]

hiraga'na (-ah'-) *n.* cursive form of kana. [Jap., = plain kana]

hīr'cīne *a.* goatlike. [f. L (*hircinus* (*hircus* he-goat; see -INE¹)]

hīre¹ *n.* payment under contract for use of thing for personal service; engagement on these terms; (fig.) reward; ∼-**car** (available for hire); ||∼-**pur'chase (system)** (by which hired thing becomes hirer's after certain number of payments); **for** or **on** ∼, ready to be hired. [OE *hȳr*, = OS *hūria* f. WG **hūrja*]

hīre² *v.t.* employ (person) for wages or **fee*; procure (*from* person), grant (*out*; to person), temporary use of (thing) for stipulated payment; **borrow (money)*;

∼d girl** or **man,** domestic servant esp. on farm; hence ∼ABLE (-ra-), ****hīr'**ABLE, *a.* [OE *hȳrian* (as prec.)]

hīr'eling (hīr'l-) *n.* (usu. derog.) one who serves for hire. [OE *hȳrling* (as HIRE¹, -LING¹)]

hīr'sūte *a.* hairy, shaggy; untrimmed; hence ∼NESS (-tn-) *n.* [f. L *hirsutus*]

hīr'sūtism *n.* excessive growth of hair. [f. prec. + -ISM]

his (ïz *or, when stressed,* hïz) *poss. pron.* of him(self); (arch.) its; for phrs. see HER², HERS. [OE, gen. of HE¹ and IT¹]

Hispă'nic *a.* of Spain (and Portugal); of Spain and other Spanish-speaking countries; hence ∼IST (3) *n.*, ∼IZE (3) *v.t.* [f. L *Hispanicus* (*Hispania* Spain; see -IC)]

Hi'spanist *n.* Hispanicist. [f. as prec. + -IST]

Hispă'nō- *comb. form.* Spanish (and). [f. L *Hispanus* Spanish + -o-]

hi'spïd *a.* (Bot. & Zool.) shaggy; bristly. [f. L *hispidus*; see -ID¹]

hiss *v.* & *n.* **1.** *v.i.,* & *n.* (Of person, snake, goose, liquid poured on fire, etc.) (make) sharp sibilant sound of *s*, esp. as sign of disapproval or derision. **2.** *v.t.* express disapproval of (person etc.) thus; ∼ **off** (*the stage*), **away, down,** etc., drive off etc. by hisses; utter (words) with angry hiss. [ME; imit.]

hist *int.* used to call attention, enjoin silence, or incite dog etc. [16th c.; natural excl.]

hi'stamine (-ïn, -ēn) *n.* (Chem.) simple base present in all body tissues and causing some allergic reactions. [f. as foll. + AMINE]

hi'sto- *comb. form.* (Biol.) tissue, as: ∼**ge'nesis,** ∼**geny** (-ŏ'j-), production of organic tissues; ∼**gene'tic** *a.*; ∼**logy** (-ŏ'l-), science of organic tissues; ∼**lysis** (-ŏ'l-), breaking down of organic tissues; ∼**patho'logy,** (study of) changes in tissues caused by disease. [f. Gk *histos* web + -o-]

hi'stogrăm *n.* diagram in which columns represent frequencies of various ranges of values of a quantity. [f. Gk *histos* mast + -GRAM]

histŏr'ian *n.* writer of history (esp. critical analyst, as opp. to mere annalist or compiler); person learned in history; **English, ancient,** ∼, writer or student of English, ancient, history. [f. F *historien* f. L (as HISTORY; see -AN)]

histŏr'iātĕd *a.* = STORIATED. [f. med. L *historiare* (as HISTORY); see -ATE³, -ED¹]

histŏ'ric *a.* famous in history; (Gram., of tense) normally used of past events (esp. L & Gk imperfect and pluperfect; cf. PRIMARY; ∼ **present** (used for past), ∼ **infinitive** (used for indicative)); (arch.) = foll. [f. L f. Gk *historikos* (as HISTORY; see -IC)]

histŏ'rical *a.* of history (*historical evidence, principles*); belonging to history, not to prehistory or legend; (of study of a subject) based on history or an analysis of development in course of time; in connection with history, from the historian's point of view (*of purely historical interest*); belonging to the past, not of the present; (of novel, picture, etc.) dealing with historical events; hence ∼LY *adv.* [f. as prec. + -AL]

histŏ'ric|ism *n.* theory that social and cultural phenomena are determined by history; belief that historical events are governed by laws; tendency to regard historical development as most basic aspect of human existence; excessive regard for past styles etc.; hence ∼IST (2) *n.* [f. HISTORIC + -ISM, after G *historismus*]

histori'cïtȳ *n.* historical genuineness of alleged event etc. [f. HISTORIC + -ITY]

histŏriŏ'grapher *n.* writer of history, esp. official historian of a court etc. [ME, f. F *historiographe* or f. LL f. Gk *historiographos* (as HISTORY; see -GRAPHER)]

histŏriŏ'graphȳ *n.* writing of history; study of history-writing; hence **histŏriogră'phic**(AL) *adjs.* [f. med. L f. Gk *historiographia* (as foll.; see -GRAPHY)]

hi'storȳ *n.* continuous methodical record of important or public events; study of past events, esp. human affairs; aggregate of past events, course of human affairs; whole train of events connected with nation, person, thing, etc.; eventful past career (*this knife has a history*); systematic account of natural phenomena etc. (NATURAL *history*); historical play; ANCIENT[1] *history*; CASE[1] *history*; **make** ∼, influence the course of history, do something memorable. [ME, f. L L f. Gk *historia* finding out, narrative, history (*histōr* learned, wise man, cogn. w. WIT[1])]

histriŏ′n∣ic *a.* & *n.* **1.** *a.* of actors or acting; stagy, hypocritical, whence **hi′strionism** (2), ∼**icism** (2), *ns.*; hence ∼ICALLY *adv.* **2.** *n.* actor. **3.** (in *pl.*) theatricals, theatrical art, pretence; insincere actions done merely to impress others. [f. LL *histrionicus* f. L *histrio* *-onis* actor; see -IC]

hit[1] *v.* (-tt-; hit). **1.** *v.t.* strike with blow or missile; (of moving body) strike; knock (part of the body) *against* or *on*; deliver (blow, person etc. a blow). **2.** (fig.) cause to suffer, wound, (HARD *hit*); have (esp. adverse) effect on; light upon, get at, (thing aimed at); = *hit upon* (see sense 6); ∼ (**off**), represent exactly; fall in with, suit; (colloq.) encounter (*hit a snag*), arrive at (*hit an all-time low*), indulge in (liquor etc.; *hit the bottle*). **3.** (Cricket) score (runs), strike (ball) or strike ball bowled by (bowler) esp. *for* so many runs, (∥∼ **for six**, (fig.) defeat in argument etc.); ∼ **wicket**, be out by striking wicket with bat etc. **4.** *v.i.* direct blow (lit. or fig.) *at*; (of moving body) strike *against* or *upon*. **5.** ∼ **and run**, (of attackers, vehicle-driver, etc.) do damage and retreat or make off immediately (cf. TIP[2] 2), (Baseball, *a.*) with departure of runner from his base as soon as pitcher begins to throw; ∼ **below the belt**, give foul blow (in Boxing, or fig.); ∼ **the hay**, (sl.) go to bed; *hit the* HEAD[1]*lines*; ∼**-or-miss**, (colloq.) casual, careless; *hit the* (*right*) NAIL[1] *on the head*; *∼ **the trail**, (sl.) depart. **6.** ∼ **back**, retaliate; ∼ **it off**, agree or be congenial (*with*, *together*); ∼ **out**, deal vigorous blows (lit. or fig.); ∼ **up**, (Cricket) score (runs) energetically; ∼ (**up**)**on**, find (what is sought), esp. by chance. [OE *hittan* f. ON *hitta* meet with, of unkn. orig.]

hit[2] *n.* blow, stroke; stroke of sarcasm etc. (*at*); stroke of good luck; shot etc. that hits target; successful attempt; popular success in public entertainment; **make a** ∼, be successful or popular (*with*); *∼ **man**, hired assassin; ∼ **parade**, programme of popular tunes etc. [ME, f. prec.]

hitch[1] *v.* **1.** *v.t.* move (thing) with jerk; shift slightly; ∼ **up**, lift with jerk. **2.** fasten with loop, hook, etc.; *hitch one's* WAGON *to a star*; **get** ∼**ed**, (sl.) marry. **3.** *v.i.* become so fastened (*in*, *on to*, etc.). **4.** ∼**-hike** *v.* & *n.*, ∼ *v.i.*, & *n.*, travel, obtain (transport), by begging free rides in passing motor vehicles; ∼**'ing post**, fixed post for tethering a horse. [ME, of uncert. orig.]

hitch[2] *n.* jerk, abrupt pull or push; (Naut.) noose or knot of various kinds (**half** ∼, formed by passing end of rope round its standing part and then through the bight; CLOVE HITCH); temporary stoppage (TECHNICAL *hitch*); impediment; *(sl.) period of service. [f. prec.]

hi′ther (-dh-) *adv.* & *a.* (literary). **1.** to or towards this place; ∼ **and thither**, ∼ **and yon**, in various directions, here and there. **2.** *a.* situated on this side; the nearer (of two). **3.** ∼**to** (-too, -tōō′), up to this time; ∼**ward**, (arch.) in this direction. [OE *hider*, corresp. to ON *hethra* here, hither, Goth. *hidrē*, f. root *hi-* (HE[1]) + suf. *-ther* (as THITHER)]

Hi′tler *n.* one who embodies characteristics of Hitler; hence ∼ISM *n.*, political principles or policy of Nazi party in Germany, ∼ITE[1] (1) *n.* [f. A. ∼, Ger. dictator d. 1945]

Hi′ttite *n.* & *a.* (member or language) of a powerful ancient people of Asia Minor and Syria, or their subjects. [f. Heb. *Ḥittīm*]

hive *n.* & *v.* **1.** *n.* beehive; (fig.) busy swarming place; hiveful of bees; swarming multitude; hive-shaped thing. **2.** *v.t.* place (bees) in hive, house (persons etc.) snugly, hoard *up*. **3.** *v.i.* enter hive; live together like

bees. **4.** ∼ **off**, swarm off separately like bees, (fig.) form into or assign (work) to subsidiary department or company. [OE *hȳf* f. Gmc **hūf-*]

hives (-vz) *n. pl.* nettle-rash; inflammation of larynx etc. [16th c., orig. Sc., of unkn. orig.]

hi′ya *int.* (colloq.) of greeting. [corrupt. of *how are you?*]

HK *abbr.* Hong Kong; House of Keys.

HL *abbr.* House of Lords.

hl. *abbr.* hectolitre(s).

h′m, hmm. Vars. of HEM[3] 1, 2, HUM[2].

HM *abbr.* headmaster; headmistress; Her or His Majesty('s).

hm. *abbr.* hectometre(s).

HMAS *abbr.* Her Majesty's Australian Ship.

HMCS *abbr.* Her Majesty's Canadian Ship.

HMG *abbr.* Her Majesty's Government.

HMI *abbr.* Her Majesty's Inspector (of Schools).

HMNZS *abbr.* Her Majesty's New Zealand Ship.

HMS *abbr.* Her Majesty's Ship.

HMSO *abbr.* Her Majesty's Stationery Office.

∥**HMV** *abbr.* His Master's Voice.

∥**HNC** *abbr.* Higher National Certificate.

∥**HND** *abbr.* Higher National Diploma.

hō *int.* expr. surprise, admiration, triumph, derision, or calling attention; added to other *ints.* (HEIGH-ho, WHAT *ho*) or (Naut.) to name of destination etc. (*westward ho*). [ME, imit.; cf. ON *hó*]

ho. *abbr.* house.

Ho *symb.* holmium.

hoar *a.* & *n.* **1.** *a.* grey-haired with age; greyish white; (of thing) grey with age; ∼**-frost**, frozen water vapour deposited in clear still weather on lawns etc.; ∥∼**'stone**, ancient boundary stone. **2.** *n.* hoariness; hoar-frost. [OE *hār*, = OS, OHG *hēr* old, ON *hárr* f. Gmc **hairaz* (**hai-* f. IE **koi-* shine)]

hoard *n.* & *v.* **1.** *n.* stock, store, (esp. of money) laid by; amassed stock of facts etc.; (Archaeol.) ancient cache of treasure etc. **2.** *v.t.* amass (money etc., or abs.) and put away, store *up*; store in the mind. **3.** *v.i.* overstock oneself with food etc. in time of scarcity. [OE *hord*, = OS *hord*, *horth*, OHG *hort*, ON *hodd*, Goth. *huzd* f. Gmc **huzdam*]

hoar′ding[1] *n.* In vbl senses. [f. prec. + -ING[1]]

hoar′ding[2] *n.* fence of boards round building during erection or repairs, often used for posting bills; ∥structure erected to carry advertisements etc. [f. obs. *hoard* (1 -ING[1]) f. AF *h(o)urdis* f. OF *hourd*, *hort*, cogn. w. HURDLE]

hoar′hound. Var. of HOREHOUND.

hoarse *a.* (Of voice) rough and deep sounding, husky, croaking; having such a voice; hence ∼**'LY**[2] (-slī) *adv.*, **hoar′seness**[6] *v.t.* & *i.*, ∼**'NESS** (-sn-) *n.* [ME *hors* f. ON **hars* f. Gmc **hairsaz*; earlier ME *hos*, OE *hās*, OHG *heis(i)* f. Gmc **haisaz*]

hoar′∣y *a.* (Of hair) grey, white, with age; having such hair, venerable; old and trite; (Bot. & Entom.) covered with short white hairs; hence ∼INESS *n.* [f. HOAR + -Y[2]]

hoatzin (hwătsē′n) *n.* tropical Amer. strong-smelling bird whose young climb by means of wing-claws. [native name, imit.]

hoax *v.t.*, & *n.* **1.** *v.t.* deceive (person) by way of joke. **2.** *n.* humorous or mischievous deception. [18th c., prob. contr. f. HOCUS]

hob[1] *n.* male ferret; hobgoblin; *play or *raise ∼, cause mischief. [ME, familiar form of *Rob*, short for *Robin* or *Robert*]

hob[2] *n.* side casing of fireplace, having surface level with top of grate; flat support for pan on stove; tool for cutting gear-teeth etc.; peg or pin as mark in quoits etc.; = HOBNAIL. [perh. var. of HUB, orig. = lump]

hŏ′bbit *n.* one of an imaginary race of half-sized persons in stories by Tolkien; hence ∼RY (5) *n.* [invented by J. R. R. Tolkien, Engl. writer d. 1973, and said by him to mean 'hole-builder']

hŏb′ble[1] *v.* **1.** *v.i.* walk lamely, limp; (fig.) proceed haltingly in action or speech. **2.** *v.t.* Cause to hobble; tie together legs of (horse etc.) to prevent it from straying etc.; tie (legs) thus. [ME, prob. f. LG; cf. HOPPLE, and Du. *hobbelen* rock from side to side]

hŏb′ble[2] *n.* **1.** uneven or infirm gait; (arch.) awkward situation. **2.** rope, clog, etc., for hobbling a horse etc.; ∼ **skirt** (so narrow at foot as to impede wearer in walking). [f. prec.]

hŏb′blĕdĕhoy (-bĕld-) *n.* (colloq.) clumsy or awkward youth between boyhood and manhood; hence ∼HOOD *n.*, ∼ISH[1] *a.*, (-oĭ′-). [16th c., of unkn. orig.]

hŏb′bȳ[1] *n.* favourite subject or occupation that is not one's main business; (arch.) small horse; (Hist.) early type of velocipede. [ME *hobyn, hoby*, f. pet-forms of *Robin*; cf. DOBBIN]

hŏb′bȳ[2] *n.* small species of falcon, *Falco subbuteo*. [ME, f. OF *hobé, hobet* dim. of *hobe* small bird of prey]

hŏb′bȳ-hôrse *n.* wicker horse used in morris dance etc.; child's stick with horse's head; rocking-horse; horse on merry-go-round; topic to which one constantly recurs. [f. HOBBY[1] + HORSE[1]]

hŏb′bgŏblin *n.* mischievous imp; bogy, bugbear. [f. HOB[1] + GOBLIN]

hŏb′nail *n.* **1.** heavy-headed nail for boot-soles; hence ∼ED[2] (-ld) *a.* **2.** ∼(ed) **liver** (with many small projections due to cirrhosis). [f. HOB[2] + NAIL[1]]

hŏb′-nŏb *v.i.* (-bb-). drink together; talk informally (*with*). [f. *hob or nob* = give or take, of alternate drinking; earlier *hab nab*, = have or not have]

***hō′bō** *n.* (*pl.* ∼es). wandering workman or tramp. [19th c.; orig. unkn.]

Hŏ′bson *n.* ∼'s **choice**, option of taking the one offered or nothing. [f. T. ∼, Cambridge carrier d. 1631, who let out horses on this basis]

hŏck[1] *n.* joint of quadruped's hind leg between true knee and fetlock, pointing backwards; knuckle of pork. [f. obs. *hockshin* f. OE *hōhsinu* (see HOUGH)]

∥hŏck[2] *n.* German white wine (prop. that of Hochheim on the river Main). [abbr. of obs. *hockamore* f. G *Hochheimer*]

***hŏck**[3] *v.t.*, & *n.* (sl.) pawn, pledge; **in** ∼, in pawn, in prison, or in debt. [f. Du. *hok* hutch, prison, debt]

hŏ′ckey *n.* game played with ball on field (or PUCK[2] on ICE[1]) and curved sticks between goals; (Can.) ice hockey, whence ∼IST (3) *n.* [16th c.; orig. unkn.]

Hŏ′cktĭde *n.* (Hist.) old festival kept on second Monday and Tuesday after Easter, orig. with collection of money for church etc. [ME, of unkn. orig.]

hŏ′cus *v.t.* (∥-ss-). take in, hoax; stupefy (person) with drugs; drug (liquor). [f. obs. *n. hocus* = foll.]

hŏcus-pō′cus *n.* & *v.* (-ss-). **1.** *n.* conjuring deception; typical conjuring formula. **2.** *v.i.* & *t.* play tricks *with* or on. [17th-c. sham L]

hŏd *n.* builder's light open trough on staff for carrying bricks etc.; receptacle for coal; ∼′**man**, labourer who carries hod, (fig.) mechanical worker, literary hack. [prob. = dial. *hot* f. OF *hotte* pannier, of Gmc orig.]

hŏ′dden *n.* (Sc.) coarse woollen cloth; ∼ **grey**, grey hodden, typical rustic garb. [16th c.; orig. unkn.]

∥Hŏdge *n.* typical English agricultural labourer. [pet-form of man's Christian name *Roger*]

hŏ′dgepŏdge (-jp-) *n.* = HOTCHPOTCH 1, 3. [ME; assim. to prec.]

Hŏ′dgkĭn (-jk-) *n.* ∼'s **disease** (of unknown origin, with progressive anaemia and enlargement of liver etc.). [f. T. ∼, Engl. physician d. 1866]

hŏdiĕr′nal *a.* of the present day. [f. L *hodiernus* (*hodie* today) + -AL]

hŏ′dograph (-ahf) *n.* curve in which radius vector represents velocity of moving particle. [f. Gk *hodos* way + -GRAPH]

hŏdŏ′mĕter. Var. of ODOMETER.

hōe *n.* & *v.* (*part.* ∼′ing *pr.* hō′ĭ-). **1.** *n.* tool for loosening soil, scraping up weeds, etc., with thin metal transverse blade on long handle; DRAW[1]-*hoe*; Dutch ∼,

kind pushed forward by user; *∼-**cake**, coarse cake of maize flour orig. baked on blade of hoe; *∼-**down**, lively dance(-party). **2.** *v.t.* weed (crops), loosen (ground), dig up, cut down, with hoe; HARD *row to hoe*. **3.** *v.i.* use hoe. [ME *howe* f. OF *houe* f. OFrank. **hauwa* f. Gmc **hauwan* HEW]

hŏg[1] *n.* **1.** domesticated pig, esp. castrated male reared for slaughter; animal of family Suidae (*wart-hog*); ∥(dial.) young sheep before first shearing (also **hogg**); (fig.) coarse, gluttonous, inconsiderate, or filthy person; **go the whole** ∼, (sl.) do the thing thoroughly; ***live high off** (or **on**) **the** ∼ (luxuriously); ∼ **in armour**, person ill at ease; *∼ **on ice**, (colloq.) insecure person. **2.** ∼('s)-**back**, crested hill-ridge; *∼ **cholera**, swine-fever; ∼-**fish**, fish of genus *Scorpaena* with bristly head; *∼-**pen**, pigsty; ∼'s **fennel**, weed of genus *Peucedanum* with fennel-like leaves; *∼-**tie**, secure by fastening hands and feet or all four feet together, (fig.) restrain, impede; ∼-**wash**, kitchen swill etc. for pigs, (fig.) worthless stuff; ∼'**weed**, coarse weed of which animals are fond. **3.** Hence ∼′GERY (3) (-g-) *n.*, ∼′GISH[1] (-g-), ∼′LIKE, *adjs.* [OE *hogg, hocg*, perh. of Celt. orig.]

hŏg[2] *v.* (-gg-). **1.** *v.t.* & *i.* raise (back etc.), rise, archwise in the centre. **2.** *v.t.* (colloq.) appropriate selfishly, take unduly large share for oneself. [f. prec.]

hŏ′gan *n.* Amer. Indian hut of logs etc. [Navajo]

∥hŏ′ggĕt (-g-) *n.* yearling sheep. [f. HOG[1] + -ET[1]]

hŏ′ggin (-g-) *n.* mixture of sand and gravel; sifted gravel. [19th c., of unkn. orig.]

hŏ′gmanay *n.* (Sc.) (celebration of) last day of year; gift of cake etc. demanded by children on that day. [17th c., corresp. in sense and use to OF *aguillanneuf*, of unkn. orig.; the Norman form *hoguinané* may have been the immediate source]

hŏ′gshead (-z-hĕd) *n.* large cask; liquid or dry measure, usu. about 50 imperial gallons. [ME, f. HOG[1] + -'s l + HEAD[1]; orig. unexpl.]

hō-hō′ *int.* expr. surprise, triumph, or derision. [redupl. of HO]

hō′-hŭm *a.* dull, uninteresting. [imit. of yawn]

hoick *v.t.* (sl.) lift or bring (*out* etc.) esp. with jerk. [perh. var. of HIKE]

hoicks. Var. of YOICKS.

hoi polloi (hoi pŏ′loi, -oi′) *n.* the majority, the masses, the rabble. [Gk, = the many]

hoist[1] *v.t.*, & *n.* **1.** *v.t.* raise (esp. flag) aloft; raise by means of tackle etc.; ∼ one's **flag**, signify that one takes command. **2.** *n.* hoisting; part of flag nearest staff; group of flags raised as signal; goods elevator, lift. [16th c., alt. of *hoise* f. (15th c.) *hysse*, prob. of LG orig.; cf. LG *hissen*]

hoist[2] *a.* ∼ **with his own petard**, blown up by his own bomb, ruined by his own devices against others. [p.p. of *hoise* (see prec.)]

hoitȳ-toi′tȳ *n., a.,* & *int.* **1.** *n.* (arch.) riotous or giddy conduct. **2.** *a.* haughty, petulant; (arch.) frolicsome. **3.** *int.* expr. surprised protest at undue presumption etc. [f. obs. *hoit* indulge in riotous mirth; orig. unkn.]

***hō′key** *a.* (sl.) involving hokum. [f. HOKUM + -Y[2]]

hōkey-pō′key *n.* (colloq.) = HOCUS-POCUS; cheap ice cream sold by street vendors. [f. HOCUS-POCUS; second sense of unkn. orig.]

hŏ′kku (-ōō) *n.* (*pl.* same). = HAIKU. [Jap.]

hō′kum *n.* (sl.) theatrical plot or business, film scenario, designed to appeal to the uncritical; bunkum. [20th c.; orig. unkn.]

holăr′ctic *a.* (Zool.) pertaining to the whole northern or arctic region. [f. as HOLO- + ARCTIC]

hōld[1] *v.* (**held**; also arch. *p.p.* ∼'**en** esp. w. ref. to formal meetings etc.). **1.** *v.t.* keep fast, grasp; keep (thing) in particular position (*hold it to the light*); ∼ thing **over** person, threaten him constantly with it); grasp so as to control (*hold the reins*); keep (one*self*, one's head, etc.) in particular attitude or condition. **2.** (Of vessel etc.) contain or be able to do so (*jug holds* *two pints*; *hall holds 900 people*); not be unduly intoxicated by (liquor etc.). **3.** possess, be the owner or holder or tenant of, (property, stocks, land, or abs.: *holds from the king*); have (specified playing-card or cards) in one's hand; have gained (*holds a law degree*, *the long-jump record*); (Mil. or fig.) keep possession of (place etc.) against attack; occupy (place, person's thoughts, etc.); engross (person, his attention); dominate (*holds the stage*). **4.** keep (person etc.) in specified place, condition, etc., (*hold him at bay*, *prisoner*, *in suspense*); detain in custody; make (person) adhere *to* (terms, promise; ∼ **to bail**, bind by BAIL¹); (Sport) restrict (opponents) *to* (draw etc.). **5.** observe, celebrate, conduct, (festival, meeting, conversation); use (insolent etc.) language. **6.** restrain, (*hold your fire*, *noise*, TONGUE¹); (colloq.) withhold, cease, (∼ **everything!**, ∼ **it!**, cease action or movement); *hold your* HORSE¹*s!*; **there is no** ∼**ing** *him* etc., he etc. is restive or in high spirits or determined. **7.** think, believe, (thing, opinion, *that*, person etc. *to* be; ∼ **it against** person, regard it as to his discredit *that*; ∼ **it good**, think it advisable *to* do); (of judge or court) lay down, decide, (*that*); have specified feeling towards (*hold him in esteem*, *contempt*); ∼ thing **cheap**, not value it; ∼ **dear**, regard with affection. **8.** *v.i.* remain unbroken, not give way; (of weather) continue fine; ∼ **by**, **to**, adhere to (choice, purpose, etc.); ∼ **with**, (sl., usu. w. neg.) approve of. **9.** ∼ (**good**, **true**), (of law etc.) be valid, apply. **10.** keep going (*hold on one's way*). **11.** (arch.) restrain oneself; ∼ (**hard**)!, stop, wait. **12.** *hold the* BABY, one's BREATH, *the* CLOCK¹ *on*, COURT¹, *the* FORT, one's GROUND¹, one's or person's HAND¹, HAND¹*s*; ∼ one's **head high**, behave proudly and confidently; ∼ **the line**, (1) not yield, (2) maintain telephone connection; *hold* one's NOSE; *hold to* RANSOM; ∼ **water**, (fig.) be sound, bear examination. **13.** ∼ **aloof**, avoid communication with persons etc.; ∼ **back**, restrain, impede progress of, keep (thing) to or for oneself, hesitate, refrain *from*; ∼ *back* n., hindrance; ∼ **down**, repress, (colloq.) be competent enough to keep (one's job); ∼ **forth**, offer (inducement etc.), (usu. derog.) speak at length or publicly; *hold* HARMLESS; ∼ **in**, confine, keep in check; ∼ **off**, delay, keep one's distance, not begin action; ∼ **on**, keep one's grasp on something, not ring off, (colloq., in *imper.*) stop or wait; ∼ **out**, stretch forth (hand etc.), offer (inducement etc.), maintain resistance, persist or last, continue to make demand *for*; ∼ **out on**, (colloq.) refuse something to (person); ∼ **over**, postpone; *∼*-over* n., relic; ∼ **together**, (cause to) cohere; ∼ **up**, support, sustain (lit. or fig.), maintain (head etc.) erect (∼ *up* one's *head*, (fig.) not be downcast), exhibit, display, (esp. *to* derision etc.), arrest progress of, obstruct, (stop and) rob by (threat of) violence; ∼*-up* n., robbery of this kind, stoppage or delay by traffic, fog, etc. **14.** ∼**'all**, portable case for miscellaneous articles; ∼**'fast**, firm grasp, staple or clamp securing object to wall etc., attachment-organ of alga. [OE *h(e)aldan*, = OS *haldan*, OHG *haltan*, ON *halda*, Goth. *haldan*]

hold² n. grasp (lit. or fig.: *catch*, *get*, *grab*, *keep*, LAY³, *take*, *hold of*); manner of holding in wrestling etc.; opportunity of holding, thing to hold by; ∼ (**on**, **over**), (fig.) influence (over); (arch.) fortress; **get** ∼ **of**, (fig.) acquire, make contact with (person); **with no** ∼**s barred**, all methods being permitted; **take** ∼, become established. [OE *heald*, and f. ON *hald* (as prec.)]

hold³ n. cavity in ship below deck, where cargo is stowed. [f. obs. *holl* f. OE *hol* f. adj. = OS, OHG *hol*, ON *holr* hollow f. Gmc *hulaz f. IE **kel-* cover; cogn. w. HELL, HELM¹, HOLLOW²; assim. to HOLD¹]

hol'der n. In vbl senses; occupant of office etc.; possessor of title etc.; contrivance for holding something (*cigarette-*, *pen-*, *holder*); SMALLholder. [ME, f. HOLD¹ + -ER¹]

hol'ding n. In vbl senses; tenure of land; land held

(‖SMALL *holding*); cards, stocks, etc., held; ∼ **company**, one created to hold the shares of other companies; ∼ **operation** (to maintain *status quo*). [ME, f. HOLD¹ + -ING¹]

hole¹ n. **1.** empty place in solid body; deep place in stream etc.; animal's burrow; small mean or dingy abode; (sl.) awkward situation; ∼**-and-corner**, secret, underhand. **2.** cavity into which ball etc. must be got in various games; (Golf) point scored by player who gets ball from tee to hole with fewest strokes, terrain or distance from tee to hole. **3.** aperture through something; **in** ∼**s**, worn so much that holes have formed; ∼ **in the heart**, congenital defect in heart membrane; ∼ **in the wall**, small dingy place (esp. of business); **pick** ∼**s in**, find fault with; **make a** ∼ **in**, use large amount of; **round** (or **square**) **peg in square** (or **round**) ∼, person not fitted for his place. **4.** (Phys.) position from which electron is absent, esp. acting as mobile positive particle in semiconductor. **5.** Hence ∼*-*PROOF², **hŏ'le**y², *adjs*. [OE *hol*, = ON *hol* f. as HOLD³]

hole² v. **1.** *v.t.* make holes in; (Naut.) pierce side of (ship); put into hole; ∼ (**out**), send (golf-ball, or abs.) into hole. **2.** *v.i.* *∼ **up**, (sl.) hide oneself. [OE *holian* (as prec.)]

hŏ'libut. Var. of HALIBUT.

hŏ'liday (-dā, -dĭ) n., & *v.i.* **1.** n. day of festivity or recreation, when no work is done; ‖(in *sing.* or *pl.*) period of this, vacation; BANK³, BLIND¹ man's, BUSman's, *holiday*; **make** ∼, **take a** ∼, have break from work; ‖**on** ∼, **on** one's ∼**s**, in course of one's vacation; (*attrib.*, of clothes etc.) festive; ∼ **camp**, ∼ **centre**, place with organized amusements for people on holiday; ∼**-maker**, person on holiday. **2.** *v.i.* spend a holiday. [OE *hāligdæg* (HOLY, DAY)]

hŏ'lily adv. in a holy manner. [OE *hāliglīce* (as HOLY, -LY²)]

hŏ'liness n. sanctity; **His H**∼, title of Pope. [OE *hālignes* (as HOLY, -NESS)]

hŏ'lism n. (Philos.) tendency in nature to form wholes that are more than the sum of the parts by ordered grouping; so ∼**i'stic** a. [f. as HOLO- + -ISM]

hŏ'lla int., n., & v. (∼ **ed** or ∼**'d**, *pr.* -ad). HOLLO¹,². [f. F *holà* (ho, *là* there)]

hŏ'lland n. smooth hard-wearing linen fabric; **brown** ∼, this unbleached. [f. *H*∼ = Netherlands (Du., earlier *Holtland* f. *holt* wood + -*lant* land, describing Dordrecht district)]

hŏ'llandaise (-z) n. ∼ (**sauce**), creamy sauce of butter, egg-yolks, vinegar, etc., served with fish etc. [F, fem. of *hollandais* Dutch (*Hollande* Holland)]

Hŏ'llander n. Dutchman; Dutch ship; engine (invented in Holland) for making paper-pulp from rags. [f. as HOLLAND + -ER¹]

Hŏ'llands (-z) n. gin made in Holland. [f. Du. *hollandsch genever* Dutch gin]

***hŏ'ller** *v.i.* & *t.*, & n. (make, express with) loud cry or noise. [var. of HOLLO²]

hŏ'llō¹ n., & int. (pl. ∼s). **1.** int. calling attention. **2.** n. cry of 'hollo'. [cogn. w. HOLLA]

hŏ'llō², **hŏ'llow¹** (-ō), *v.i.* & *t.* shout; call to (hounds). [as prec.]

hŏ'llow² (-ō) a., n., & *adv.* **1.** a. having a hole, not solid (*hollow* SQUARE¹); having a depression, sunken (*hollow cheeks*); empty, hungry; (of sound) echoing, as if made in or on a hollow container; (fig.) empty (*hollow triumph*), insincere, cynical (*hollow laugh*), false (*hollow promises*). **2.** n. hollow place, hole, valley, basin; **in the** ∼ **of** one's **hand**, entirely subservient to one. **3.** *adv.* completely (*beaten hollow*). **4.** ∼**-eyed**, with eyes deep sunk; ∼**-hearted**, insincere; ∼**-ware**, hollow articles of metal, china, etc., as pots, kettles, jugs, (opp. *flatware*). **5.** Hence ∼LY² *adv.*, ∼NESS n. [ME *holg*, *holu*, *hol(e)we* f. OE *holh* cave, cogn. w. HOLE¹]

hŏ'llow³ (-ō) *v.t.* ∼ (**out**), excavate; bend into hollow shape. [ME, f. prec.]

hŏ'llŷ *n.* evergreen shrub of genus *Ilex*, with prickly usu. dark-green leaves, small white flowers, and red berries, used to decorate houses and churches at Christmas; ~ **blue**, azure blue butterfly; ~ **fern** (with glossy fronds reminiscent of holly); ~ **oak**, holm-oak. [OE *hole(g)n*, cogn. w. OS, OHG *hulis*, OFrank. *huls]

hŏ'llŷhŏck *n.* tall plant (*Althaea rosa*) with large flowers of many varieties of colour. [ME, orig. = marsh mallow, f. HOLY + obs. *hock* mallow, OE *hoc*, of unkn. orig.]

Hŏ'llŷwŏŏd *n.* American cinema industry or its products. [~ in California, principal centre of the industry]

||**hŏlm**[1], **hŏlme**, (hōm) *n.* islet, esp. in river or near mainland; flat ground by river, submerged in time of flood. [f. ON *holmr*]

hŏlm[2] (hōm) *n.* ~(-**oak**), evergreen oak, *Quercus ilex*, with holly-like leaves. [ME alt. of obs. *holin* f. as HOLLY]

Hŏ'lmesïan (hō'mz-) *a.* reminiscent of the detective Sherlock Holmes. [f. *Holmes* (cf. SHERLOCK) + -IAN]

hŏ'lmïum *n.* (Chem.) metallic element of lanthanide series. [mod. L (*Holmia* Stockholm; see -IUM)]

hŏ'lo- *comb. form.* whole, as: **H~cene**, (Geol.) = RECENT; ~HE'DRAL, (Cryst.) having full number of planes given by complete symmetry; ~**meta'bolous**, (of insect) undergoing complete metamorphosis; ~**phote**, apparatus for making available nearly all the light of a lamp (in lighthouse etc.). [f. Gk *holos* whole, entire + -o-]

hŏ'locaust *n.* wholesale sacrifice (fig.) or destruction esp. by fire; (*H~*) mass murder of Jews by Nazis 1939–45. [ME, f. OF *holocauste* f. LL f. Gk HOLO- (*kauston* burnt f. *kaiō* burn)]

hŏ'lo|grăm *n.* (Phys.) pattern produced by interference between coherent light-beam and light diffracted etc. from same beam by an object; photograph of such pattern, which when suitably illuminated produces an image of the object in two or three dimensions; hence ~GRA'PHIC *a.*, ~GRAPHY (-ŏ'g-) *n.* [f. HOLO- + -GRAM]

hŏ'lograph[1] (-ahf) *v.t.* record as hologram. [back-form. f. prec., after *telegraph*]

hŏ'lograph[2] (-ahf) *a. & n.* (document) wholly written by person named as its author. [f. F *holographe* or f. LL f. Gk *holographos* (as HOLO-, -GRAPH)]

hŏlothūr'ïan *a. & n.* (animal) of the class Holothurioidea, sea cucumber. [f. mod. L *Holothuria* n. pl. f. Gk *holothourion*, a zoophyte + -AN]

hŏlp('en). See HELP[1].

||**hŏls** (-z) *n.* (colloq.) holidays. [abbr.]

***Hŏ'lstein** (-tīn) *a. & n.* = FRIESIAN. [~ in NW Germany]

hŏ'lster *n.* leather case for pistol, fixed to saddle or worn on belt or under arm. [17th c.; syn. w. Du. *holster*; orig. unkn.]

hŏlt[1] *n.* (arch. or dial.) wood, copse; wooded hill. [OE, = OS, ON *holt*, OHG *holz* f. Gmc *hultam f. IE *kldos]

hŏlt[2] *n.* animal's (esp. otter's) lair. [var. of HOLD[2]]

hŏlus-bō'lus *adv.* all in a lump, altogether. [app. sham L]

hō'lŷ *a. & n.* **1.** *a.* consecrated, sacred; morally and spiritually perfect; belonging to, empowered by, devoted to, God; of high moral excellence; (in trivial excl.: *holy cow! holy mackerel! holy smoke!*); **holier-than-thou**, (colloq.) having attitude of superior sanctity. **2.** *n.* ~ **of holies**, inner chamber of sanctuary in Jewish temple, separated by veil from outer chamber, (fig.) innermost shrine, thing regarded as most sacred. **3.** H~ **City**, (1) city held sacred by adherents of a religion, esp. Jerusalem, (2) Heaven; *Holy* COMMUNION; ~ **cross**, (of Christ); H~ **Cross Day**, festival of Exaltation of the Cross, 14 Sept.; ~ **day**, religious festival; H~ **Family**, the young Jesus with his mother and St. Joseph (often

with St. John Baptist, St. Anne, etc.) as grouped in pictures etc.; *Holy* FATHER[1]; H~ **Ghost**, = *Holy Spirit*; *Holy* GRAIL[2]; *Holy* INNOCENTS' *Day*; ~ **Joe**, (orig. Naut. sl.) clergyman, pious person; H~ **Land**, (1) W. Palestine, esp. Judaea, (2) region similarly revered in non-Christian religions; ~ **name**, (RC Ch.) name of Jesus as object of formal devotion; *Holy* OFFICE; *holy* ORDER[1]*s*; ~ **place**, outer chamber of sanctuary in Jewish temple, (in *pl.*) places to which religious pilgrimage is made; *Holy* ROMAN[2] *Empire*; H~ **Rood Day**, (1) festival of Invention of the Cross, (2) = *Holy Cross Day*; *Holy* SACRAMENT; H~ **Saturday**, Saturday in Holy Week; *Holy* SCRIPTURE, SEE[2]; H~ **Spirit**, Third Person of the Trinity, God as spiritually acting; *holy* TERROR; H~ **Thursday**, (Anglican Ch.) Ascension Day, (RC Ch. & pop.) Thursday in Holy Week; *Holy* TRINITY; *holy* WAR[1]; ~ **water**, water dedicated to holy uses, or blessed by a priest; H~ **Week** (before Easter Sunday); ~ **Willie**, hypocritically pious person; H~ **Writ**, holy writings collectively, esp. the Bible; H~ **Year**, (RC Ch.) = JUBILEE 1. [OE *hālig*, = OS *hēlag*, OHG *heilag*, ON *heilagr* f. Gmc *hailagaz (*hailaz WHOLE)]

hō'lŷstōne *n.*, & *v.t.* (scour with) soft sandstone used for scouring decks. [18th c., prob. f. prec. + STONE; the stones were called *bibles* etc., perh. because used while kneeling]

hōm, hō'ma, *n.* (sacred drink of Parsees, juice of) soma plant. [f. Pers. *hōm*, *hūm*, Avestan *haoma*]

hŏ'mage *n.* formal public acknowledgement of feudal allegiance; acknowledgement of superiority, dutiful reverence, (*pay* or *do homage to* person or his qualities). [ME f. OF (*h*)*omage* f. med. L *hominaticum* f. L *homo* -*minis* man; see -AGE]

***hombre** (ŏ'mbrā) *n.* man. [Sp.]

Hŏ'mbŭrg *n.* soft felt hat with narrow curled brim and lengthwise dent in crown. [~ in W. Germany, where first worn]

hōme[1] *n.*, *a.*, & *adv.* **1.** *n.* dwelling-place; fixed residence of family or household; (US, Can., Austral., NZ) dwelling-house; **long** or **last** ~, the grave; SECOND *home.* **2.** native land of oneself or one's ancestors, esp. Britain. **3.** place where thing is native or most common; ~ **of lost causes**, Oxford University. **4.** institution of refuge or rest for persons needing care (*children's*, CONVALESCENT, MENTAL[1], *home*; see NURSE[2]); (colloq.) mental home (*you ought to be in a home*). **5.** (In games) place to be reached by runner etc.; finishing-point in race; (Lacrosse) player in attacking position near opponents' goal. **6.** home match or win. **7. at** ~, in one's own house or native land, at ease as if in one's own home (*make yourself at home*), familiar or well informed (*in* or *on* or *with* subject etc.), available to callers; **at-ho'me** *n.*, reception of visitors within certain hours during which host or hostess or both have announced that they will be at home; FROM *home*; *a* ~ **from** ~, place other than one's home where one feels at home, place providing homelike amenities; **near** ~, (fig.) affecting one closely. **8.** *a.* of or connected with home; carried on or done at home; proceeding from home; in the neighbourhood of home (||H~ **Counties**, those nearest to London); played on one's own ground etc. (*home match, win*); carried on or produced in one's own country (*home industries, products*; *the home* TRADE or *market*, opp. *foreign*); treating of domestic affairs of person, country, etc., (||H~ **Office**, department of H~ **Secretary** or Secretary of State for the Home Department, dealing with law and order, immigration, etc., in England and Wales; building used for this); that comes home to one (*home question, truth, thrust*). **9.** *adv.* to one's home or country (*come* or *go home*); arrived at home (*he is home*); *at home (*stay home*); to the point aimed at (*the thrust went home*); as far as possible (*drive a nail home*; *press* one's *advantage home*); **come** ~ **to**, become fully realized by; *come home to* ROOST[1]; ~ **and dry**, having achieved one's purpose;

nothing to write ∼ about, (colloq.) unexciting, trivial. **10.** ∼**-bird,** ∼'**body,** person who likes to stay at home; ∼**-born,** native; ∼**-bred,** bred at home; ∼**-brewed,** (of beer) brewed at home; ∼**-coming,** arrival at home; ∼ **economics,** domestic science; ‖*home* FARM[1]; ∼**-felt,** felt intimately; ∼**-grown,** grown or produced at home; H∼ **Guard,** (member of) British citizen army organized 1940–57 to defend against possible invaders; ‖*home* HELP[2]; ∼'**land** (1) native land, esp. Britain, (2) Bantustan; ∼**-made,** made at home; ∼**-making,** creation of a (pleasant) home; ∼ **movie,** film made at home or of one's own activities; ∼ **perm,** permanent hair-wave made with equipment for home use; *home* PLATE[1] 12; ∼ **port** (from which ship originates); ∼ **rule,** government of a country by its own citizens; ∼ **run,** (Baseball) hit that allows batter to make complete circuit of bases; ∼'**sick,** depressed by longing for home during absence from it; so ∼'**sickness** *n.*; ∼ **signal** (indicating whether or not railway train may proceed into station or to next section of line); ∼ **straight** or *****stretch,** concluding stretch of racecourse; ∼ **town** (of one's birth or early life or present fixed residence); ∼'**work,** work (to be) done at home, esp. lessons to be done by a schoolchild at home, (fig.) necessary preparation for debate etc. (*do* one's *homework*). **11.** Hence ∼'LESS, ∼'LIKE, (-ml-) *adjs.* [OE *hām*, = OS *hēm*, OHG *heim,* ON *heimr,* Goth. *haims* f. Gmc *****haim-*]

home[2] *v.* 1. *v.i.* (Esp. of trained pigeon) go home; ∼ **(in),** (of vessel, missile, etc.) be guided to (or *on*) destination by landmark, radio beam, etc. **2.** *v.t.* send or guide homewards; furnish (person etc.) with a home. [f. prec.]

ho'mel|y (-mlĭ) *a.* simple, plain; primitive; unpretentious; *****(of person or features) not attractive in appearance, ugly; hence ∼ĭNESS *n.* [ME, f. HOME[1] + -LY[1]]
*****ho'meopath** etc. See HOMOEOPATH etc.

ho'mer *n.* homing pigeon; *****home run. [f. HOME[2] + -ER[1]]

Home'ric (ho-, hō-) *a.* **1.** of, or in the style of, Homer or the poems ascribed to him; ∼ **laughter** (like that of Homer's gods as they watched lame Hephaestus hobbling); ∼ **question** (of authorship of *Iliad* and *Odyssey*). **2.** large-scale, titanic, (*Homeric conflict*). [f. L f. Gk *Homērikos* (*Homēros* Homer, traditional author of *Iliad* and *Odyssey*; see -IC)]

ho'mespŭn (-ms-) *a.* & *n.* (cloth made of yarn) spun at home; (anything) plain, homely, unsophisticated, practical. [t. HOME[1] + SPUN]

ho'mestead (-mstĕd) *n.* house with outbuildings; farm; (Austral. & NZ) owner's residence on sheep or cattle station; *****area of land (usu. 160 acres) granted to settler as home. [OE *hāmstede* (as HOME[1], STEAD)]

ho'meward (-mw-) *adv.* & *a.,* **-wards** (-z) *adv.* (going, leading) towards home; ∼**-BOUND**[5], (esp. of ship) preparing to go, or on the way, home. [OE *hāmweard(es)* (as HOME[1], -WARD(s))]

ho'mey. Var. of HOMY.

ho'micīde *n.* **1.** one who kills a human being. **2.** killing of a human being esp. by another; justifiable ∼ (where no blame attaches to killer, e.g. in executing sentence of death). **3.** Hence **hŏmicī'dAL** *a.* [ME f. OF, f. L (1) *homicida,* (2) *homicidium* (HOMO[1] man; see -CIDE)]

hŏmilě'tic *a.* & *n.* **1.** *a.* of homilies. **2.** *n.* (usu. in *pl.*) art of preaching. [f. LL f. Gk *homilētikos* (*homileo* hold converse, consort, f. as foll.; see -ETIC)]

ho'milỹ *n.* sermon, esp. for spiritual edification of its hearer(s); tedious moralizing discourse; hence **homi'lIARY**[1] *n.,* book of homilies. [ME f. OF *omelie,* f. eccl. L f. Gk *homilia* (*homilos* crowd; see -Y[1])]

ho'ming *a.* that goes home (cf. HOME[2]); (of pigeon) trained to fly home, bred for long-distance racing. [f. HOME[2] + -ING[2]]

ho'minid *n.* & *a.* (member) of the zoological family Hominidae (incl. existing and fossil man). [f. mod. L Hominidae f. L HOMO[1] *hominis* man; see -ID[1]]

hŏ'minoid *n.* & *a.* manlike (animal); hominid or pongid. [f. as prec. + -OID]

hŏ'minỹ *n.* coarsely ground maize kernels esp. boiled with water or milk. [Algonquian]

Homo[1] (hŏ'mō) *n.* **1.** (Zool.) (name of genus including) man. **2.** the genus ∼, mankind; ∼ **sapiens** (*pr.* sā'piēnz; [L, = wise]), modern man regarded as a species. [L]

hŏ'mō[2] *n.* (*pl.* ∼s) & *a.* (colloq.) homosexual. [abbr.]

hŏ'mō- *comb. form.* same (freq. opp. to HETERO-), as: ∼**ce'ntric,** having same centre; ∼**-ero'tic,** homosexual; ∼**gamous** (-ŏ'g-), (Bot.) having all florets hermaphrodite or of same sex; ∼**gene'tic,** having common descent or origin; ∼**geny** (-ŏ'j-), similarity due to common descent; ∼**graft** (from another individual of same species); ∼**graph,** word spelt like another, but of different meaning or origin; ∼**mor'phic,** ∼**mor'phous,** of same or similar form; ∼**nomous** (-ŏ'n-), having same law of growth; ∼**phone,** (1) word having same sound as another, but of different meaning or origin (e.g. *pair, pear*), (2) symbol denoting same sound as another; ∼**pho'nic,** (Mus.) in unison, characterized by movement of all parts with same melody; ∼**phonous** (-ŏ'f-), (of music) homophonic, (of word or symbol) being homophone; ∼**phony** (-ŏ'f-), being homophone or homophonic, homophonic composition; ∼**pla'stic,** similar in structure but not in origin; ∼**tra'nsplant,** = *homograft*; ∼**zy'gote,** zygote of like gametes, Mendelian hybrid that is not a HETEROZYGOTE and so breeds true; so ∼**zy'gous** *a.* [f. Gk *homos* same + -o-]

hŏ'moeopath, ***-mèo-,** (-mī-) *n.* one who practises homoeopathy. [f. G *homöopath* (as foll.; see -PATH)]

homoe|o'pathy, ***-mē'o'-,** (-mī-) *n.* treatment of disease by drugs (usu. in minute doses) that in healthy person would produce symptoms like those of the disease; so ∼**opā'thıc** *a.* (often joc., = minute), ∼**o'pathıst** (3) *n.* [f. G *homöopathie* f. Gk *homoios* like; see -PATHY]

hŏmoeostā's|is, ***-mēo-,** (-mī-) *n.* (*pl.* ∼**es** *pr.* -ēz) tendency towards relatively stable equilibrium between interdependent elements, esp. as maintained by physiological processes. [mod. L, f. Gk *homoios* like + -STASIS]

hŏmogě'neous *a.* of the same kind; consisting of parts all of the same kind, uniform; (Math.) containing terms all of same dimension; hence or cogn. [f. med. L f. Gk *homogenes* f. HOMO- + *genos* kind) + -OUS]

hŏmogĕně'ITY, ∼NESS, *ns.,* ∼LY[2] *adv.* [f. med. L *homogeneus* f. Gk HOMO(*genēs* f. *genos* kind) + -OUS]

homo'gĕniz|e, -īs|e (-īz-), *v.t.* make homogeneous; treat (milk) so that fat droplets are emulsified and cream does not separate; hence ∼A'TION, ∼FR[1] (2), *ns.* [f. prec. + -IZE]

hŏmoiother'mic *a.* warm-blooded. [f. Gk *homoios* like + THERMIC]

hŏmoiou'sian *a.* & *n.* (one who held that Father and Son on the Godhead were) of like but not identical substance (cf. HOMOOUSIAN). [f. eccl. L f. Gk *homoiousios* (*homoios* like, *ousia* essence) + -AN]

homo'log|ate *v.t.* acknowledge, admit; confirm, accept; hence ∼A'TION *n.* [f. med. L *homologare* agree f. Gk HOMO(*logeō* f. *logos* word) + -ATE[3]]

homo'logize, -ise (-īz), *v.* **1.** *v.i.* be homologous, correspond. **2.** *v.t.* make homologous. [f. as foll. + -IZE]

homo'logous *a.* having the same relation, relative position, etc.; corresponding; (Biol.) similar in position and structure but not necessarily in function; (of chromosomes) pairing at meiosis, usu. containing same genes; (of chemical compounds) forming series with constant successive differences of composition. [f. med. L f. Gk HOMO(*logos* ratio, proportion)]

hŏ'mologue (-g), *****-lŏg,** *n.* homologous thing. [F, f. Gk *homologon* neut. a. (as prec.)]

homo'logỹ *n.* being homologous; correspondence, sameness of relation; hence **hŏmolŏ'gICAL** *a.* [f. HOMOLOGOUS + -Y[1]]

hŏ'mŏnўm *n.* word of same form as another but different sense (e.g. POLE[1], POLE[2]); homograph or homophone; namesake; so **hŏmonў'm**IC, **homŏ'-nўm**OUS, *adjs.* [f. L f. Gk *homōnumon*, neut. a. (as HOMO-, *onoma* name)]

hŏmŏou'sian, hŏmou's-, *a.* & *n.* (one who held the persons of the Trinity to be) of the same substance (cf. HOMOIOUSIAN). [f. eccl. L *homoousianus* f. LL f. Gk HOMO(*ousios* f. *ousia* essence) + -AN]

hŏmopŏ'lar *a.* having similar poles; (Electr.) generating direct current without use of commutators; (Chem.) covalent. [f. HOMO- + POLAR]

homŏ'pterous *a.* of the Homoptera, suborder of insects including aphids and cicadas, with wings of uniform texture. [f. HOMO- + *pteron* wing + -OUS]

hŏmosĕ'xŭal *a.* & *n.* (person) who is sexually attracted only by persons of his or her own sex; relating to same sex; hence ∼ITY (-ă'l-) *n.*, ∼LY[2] *adv.* [f. HOMO- + SEXUAL]

homŭ'ncŭl|e, homŭ'ncŭl|us (*pl.* ∼i *pr.* -ī), *n.* little man, manikin. [L *homunculus* (*homo -minis* man; see -CULE)]

hŏ'mў *a.* suggesting home, homelike. [f. HOME[1] + -Y[2]]

hon (hŭn) *n.* (colloq.) = HONEY 2. [abbr.]

Hon. *abbr.* Honorary; Hono(u)rable.

hōne *n.*, & *v.t.* **1.** *n.* whetstone, esp. for razors; one of various stones as material for this. **2.** *v.t.* sharpen (as) on hone. [OE *hān* stone, = ON *hein* f. Gmc **hainō*]

hŏ'nèst (ŏ'-) *a.* **1.** fair and righteous in speech and act, not lying, cheating, or stealing; sincere; (of act or feeling) showing righteousness; (with patronizing effect; cf. WORTHY) blameless but undistinguished; ∼ broker, mediator in international, industrial, etc., disputes [orig. of Bismarck]. **2.** (Of gain etc.) got by fair means (**turn** or **earn an** ∼ **penny,** earn money fairly); (of thing) unadulterated, unsophisticated. **3.** (arch., of woman). chaste, virtuous; **make an** ∼ **woman of,** marry (seduced woman). **4.** (colloq.). ∼(-to-God), ∼-to-goodness, ∼ Injun, genuine(ly), real(ly). **5.** Hence ∼LY[2] *adv.* [ME, f. OF (*h*)*oneste* f. L *honestus* (*honos* HONOUR[1])]

hŏ'nèstў (ŏ'-) *n.* being honest; truthfulness; plant of genus *Lunaria* with purple or white flowers, so called from its round translucent pods. [ME, f. OF (*h*)*onesté* f. L *honestas -tatis* (as prec.; see -TY[1])]

ho'ney (hŭ'-) *n.* **1.** sweet viscid yellow fluid, the nectar of flowers collected and treated by bees and other insects; colour of this; (fig.) sweetness, sweet thing; person or thing excellent of its kind. **2.** (usu. as *voc.*, esp. Ir. & US) sweetheart, darling. **3.** ∼-badger, ratel; ∼-bee, common hive-bee (*Apis mellifera*); ∼-buzzard, bird of prey of genus *Pernis* feeding on larvae of bees and wasps; ∼dew, (1) sweet sticky substance found on leaves and stems, excreted by aphides, (2) ideally sweet substance, (3) tobacco sweetened with molasses, (4) cultivar of musk-melon with smooth pale skin and sweet green flesh; ∼-eater, Australasian bird of family Meliphagidae with long tongue that can take nectar from flowers; ∼-fungus (with honey-coloured toadstools round trees whose roots it attacks); ∼-guide, (1) small bird of genus *Indicator* etc. showing way to bees' nests, (2) marking on corolla thought to guide bees to nectar; ∼-parrot, lorikeet; ∼-pot, (fig.) posture with hands clasped under hams, ant that can regurgitate food for others; ∼ sac, enlarged part of bee's gullet where honey is formed; ∼suckle, climbing shrub of genus *Lonicera* with fragrant yellow and pink flowers; ∼-sweet, sweet as honey; ∼-tube, tube on abdomen of aphis once thought to produce honeydew. **4.** Hence ∼ED[2] (-nĭd) (lit. or fig.). [OE *hunig*, = OS *honig*, OHG *hona*(*n*)*g*, ON *hunang* f. Gmc **huna*(*n*)*gam*]

ho'neycōmb (hŭ'nĭkōm) *n.*, & *v.t.* **1.** *n.* bees' wax structure of hexagonal cells for honey and eggs; second STOMACH of ruminant; cavernous flaw in metal, esp. guns; ornamental or other work hexagonally arranged; fabric made with pattern of raised hexagons etc. **2.** *v.t.* make full of cavities, undermine; mark with honeycomb pattern. [OE *hunigcamb* (as prec., COMB[1])]

ho'neymōōn (hŭ'nĭm-) *n.*, & *v.i.* **1.** *n.* holiday spent together by newly married couple; (fig.) initial period of ardour or enthusiasm; **second** ∼, honeymoon-like holiday by couple married for some years. **2.** *v.i.* spend honeymoon (*in* or *at* place). [f. HONEY + MOON[1], orig. w. ref. to waning affection, not to period of a month]

honied. Var. of HONEYed.

Ho'niton (hŏ'-, hŭ'-) *n.* ∼ lace (with floral sprigs sewn on net or joined by other lace). [∼ in Devon]

hŏnk *n.* & *v.* **1.** *n.* wild-goose's cry; harsh sound of (motor) horn. **2.** *v.i.* & *t.* (cause to) emit or give honk. [imit.]

*hŏ'nkў *n.* (Black sl., derog.) white man or men. [20th c.; orig. unkn.]

hŏ'nkў-tŏnk *n.* (colloq.) cheap night-club dance-hall, etc.; ragtime music as played in these. [20th c.; orig. unkn.]

honnête homme (ŏnāt ŏ'm) *n.* honest and decent man. [F]

*honor[1,2]. See HONOUR[1,2].

*honorable. See HONOURABLE.

hŏ'noránd (ŏ'-) *n.* person to be honoured, esp. with honorary degree. [f. L *honorandus* (as HONOUR[2]; see -ND[1])]

hŏnorār'ĭ|um (ŏ-) *n.* (*pl.* ∼ums *or* ∼a). (voluntary) fee esp. for professional services nominally rendered without payment. [L, neut. (as n.) of *honorarius* (see foll.)]

hŏ'norarў (ŏ'-) *a.* **1.** conferred as an honour (without the usual requirements, functions, etc.; *honorary* DEGREE). **2.** holding honorary title or position; ∼ secretary, treasurer, etc., (serving without pay). **3.** (Of obligation) depending on honour, not legally enforceable. [f. L *honorarius* (as HONOUR[1]; see -ARY[1])]

hŏnori'fĭc (ŏ-) *a.* & *n.* (form of words) implying respect (esp. of Oriental forms of address). [f. L *honorificus* (as HONOUR[1]; see -FIC)]

honoris causa (ŏnōris kow'za) *adv.* as a mark of esteem (esp. of degree awarded without examination). [L, = for the sake of honour]

||**hŏ'nour**[1], ***hŏ'nor**[1], (ŏ'ner) *n.* **1.** high respect; glory; credit, reputation, good name; nobleness of mind; special right (*have the honour to* do, *of* doing). **2.** allegiance to what is right or to conventional standard of conduct; (of woman) chastity, reputation for this; ∼ system (of examinations etc. without supervision, relying on persons' honour). **3.** exalted position (**your, his, H**∼, said to or of County-Court etc. judge, *mayor, and in rustic or Irish speech to or of any person of rank). **4.** thing conferred as distinction; (Golf) right of driving off first as having won last hole (*it is my honour*); (in *pl.*) civilities rendered to guests etc., esp. *do the honours of* (*the table, a house, the town,* etc.); (in *pl.*) special distinction for proficiency at examination, course of degree studies more specialized than for ordinary pass; ||BIRTHday *honours*; **last, funeral,** ∼**s,** observances of respect at funeral; **military** ∼**s,** marks of respect paid by troops at burial of soldier, to royalty, etc.; ∼**s of war,** privileges granted to capitulating force, as that of marching out with colours flying etc.; ∼**s list** (of persons awarded honours). **5.** person or thing that brings honour to another (*he is an honour to the school, to his profession*). **6.** (In Whist) ace, king, queen, and jack esp. of trumps (in Bridge the ten also, or the four aces at no trumps); ∼-**trick,** = QUICK trick; ∼**s are even,** there is equality in the contest (lit. or fig.). **7.** in ∼ (celebration) **of; in** ∼ **bound,** on one's ∼, under moral obligation (*to* do); (**up)on my** ∼, (colloq.) ∼ **bright,** (forms of asseveration); **code** or **law of** ∼, rules forming conventional standard of conduct; AFFAIR, ||COMPANION[1], DEBT, GUARD[1], LEGION, MAID, MATRON, POINT[1], WORD[1], *of honour;* ∼ **point** (Her.,

half-way between fesse point and top of shield). [ME, f. AF *an*(*o*)*ur*, OF (*h*)*onor* f. L *honor* -*oris* repute, office, beauty]

||**hŏ'nour²**, ***hŏ'nor²***, (ŏ'ner) *v.t.* respect highly; confer dignity upon; acknowledge; (Commerc.) accept or pay (bill, cheque) when due. [ME, f. OF *onorer* f. L *honorare* (as prec.)]

||**hŏ'nourable**, ***hŏ'norable***, (ŏ'ner-) *a*. **1.** worthy of honour; bringing honour to its possessor; consistent with honour; showing honour, not base; man's **intentions** (in courting woman) **are** ~, (colloq.) he has marriage in view; *honourable* MENTION¹. **2.** (As title indicating eminence or distinction, given to younger sons of Earls, children of Viscounts and Barons, Maids of Honour, Justices of High Court without higher title, Lords of Session, members of Government and judges in Dominions and Colonies, to Members of Parliament by one another; *to members of Congress, cabinet ministers, judges, etc.); ||**Most H**~ (title of Marquises, Privy Council, and Order of Bath); ||**Right H**~ (title of Earls, Viscounts, Barons, Privy Counsellors, Lords (Justices) of Appeal, Lord Mayor of London, York, or Belfast, Lord Provost of Edinburgh or Glasgow, etc.). **3.** Hence ~'ED¹·² *a*. (~ed crow, = HOODIE). [OE *hōd*, = OHG *huot* f. WG *hoda*, cogn. w. HAT]

hood² (hŏŏd, hōod) *n*. (sl.) gangster, gunman. [abbr. of HOODLUM]

-**hood** *suf.* forming *ns.* of condition or quality or grouping f. *ns.* & *adjs.* (*childhood, falsehood, sisterhood*). [OE -*hād*, = OS -*hēd*, OHG -*heit*; orig. an independent *n.*, OE *hād* person, condition, quality, OS *hēd*, OHG *heit*, ON *heithr* honour, Goth. *haidus* manner]

hŏŏ'die *n*. ~ (**crow**), piebald grey and black crow (*Corvus cornix*). [f. HOOD¹ + -IE]

hŏŏ'dlum *n*. street hooligan, young thug. [19th c.; orig. unkn.]

||**hŏŏ'dman-blind** *n*. (arch.) blind-man's-buff. [f. *hoodman* hooded man (HOOD¹, MAN¹) + BLIND¹]

hŏŏ'dōo *n*. & *v.t.* **1.** *n*. (thing or person that seems to cause) bad luck. **2.** *v.t.* make unlucky; bewitch. [alt. of VOODOO]

hŏŏ'dwink *v.t.* deceive, delude; (arch.) blindfold. [f. HOOD¹ n. + WINK v.]

hŏŏ'ey *n*. & *int*. (sl.) nonsense, humbug. [20th c.; orig. unkn.]

hŏŏf *n*. (*pl*. ~s, *or* hooves *pr*. -vz) & *v*. **1.** *n*. horny casing of foot of horse and other animals; *cloven hoof* (see CLEAVE¹); **on the** ~, (of cattle) not yet slaughtered; ||PAD² *the hoof*; ~-**pick** (for removing stones from hoof); hence (-)~ED² (-ft) *a*. **2.** *v.t.* strike with hoof; (sl., of person) kick (another) *out* etc. **3.** *v.i.* walk or dance; hence ~'ER¹ *n*., (sl.) professional dancer. [OE *hōf*, = OS *hōf*, OHG *huof*, ON *hófr* f. Gmc **hōfaz*]

hŏŏ'-ha (-ah) *n*. (colloq.) uproar, trouble. [20th c.; orig. unkn.]

hŏŏk¹ *n*. **1.** piece of metal or other material bent back at an angle with round bend, for catching hold of or for hanging things upon; (**fish**-)~, bent piece of wire, usu. barbed, for catching fish; ~ **and eye**, small metal hook and loop as dress-fastener; ~, **line, and**

sinker, (fig.) entire(ly). **2.** (fig.) trap, snare; (in *pl.*, sl.) fingers. **3.** stroke (see foll. 3) in cricket or golf; (Boxing) short swinging blow with elbow bent and rigid. **4.** curved cutting instrument, esp. *reaping-hook*. **5.** sharp bend, e.g. in river; sand-spit with curved end; projecting point of land, esp. *Hook of Holland* [cf. Du. *hoek* corner]; = POT¹-*hook*; (Mus.) added stroke transverse to stem in symbol for quaver etc. **6. by** ~ **or by crook,** by one device or another, by fair means or foul; **off the** ~, no longer in difficulty, (of telephone receiver) not on its rest, thus preventing incoming calls; **off the** ~**s**, (sl.) dead; **on** one's **own** ~, (sl.) on one's own account; **sling** or **take** one's ~, (sl.) = HOOK² *it*. **7.** ~-**nose(d)**, (having) aquiline nose; ~'**worm**, (disease caused by) kind of nematode worm infesting humans and animals, male of which has hooklike spines for attachment. **8.** Hence ~'**LESS** *a*., ~'**LET** *n*. [OE *hōc*, = MLG, MDu. *hōk* corner]

hŏŏk² *v*. **1.** *v.t.* grasp with hook; secure with hook(s); ~ **on, up,** etc., attach (as) with hook; **be** ~**ed** (**on**), (sl.) be addicted (to) or captivated (by). **2.** catch (fish or fig. husband etc.) with hook; (sl.) steal. **3.** (Golf) strike (ball, or abs.) so that it deviates towards the striker; (Cricket) play (ball) round from off to on side with upward stroke; (Rugby Footb.) secure and pass (ball) backward with foot in scrummage; (Boxing) strike (opponent) with elbow bent and rigid. **4.** *v.i.* be(come) attached (*on, up,* etc.) (as) by hook. **5.** ~ **it**, (sl.) make off, run away; ~-**up,** (colloq.) connection, esp. interconnection of broadcasting equipment for special transmissions. [ME, f. prec.]

hŏŏ'kah (-ka) *n*. oriental tobacco-pipe with long flexible or rigid tube, smoke being drawn through water in vase to which tube and bowl are attached. [Urdu, f. Arab. *ḥukkah* casket]

Hŏŏke *n*. ~ **coupling**, ~'**s joint**, (for transmitting rotary motion between shafts by universal joint); ~'**s law** (that strain in elastic body is proportional to applied stress). [f. R. ~, Engl. scientist d. 1703]

hŏŏked (-kt) *a*. **1.** hook-shaped (*hooked nose*); furnished with hook(s). **2.** In vbl senses; (of rug etc.) made by pulling woollen yarn through canvas with hook. [f. HOOK¹·² + -ED²·¹]

hŏŏ'ker¹ *n*. In vbl senses; (Rugby Footb.) player of each team in front row of scrummage who tries to get ball by hooking it; *(sl.) prostitute. [f. HOOK² + -ER¹]

hŏŏ'ker² *n*. small Dutch or Irish fishing-vessel (derog or fondly) any ship. [f. Du. *hoeker* (*hoek* HOOK¹; see -ER¹)]

hŏŏ'key, ***hŏŏ'ky***, *n*. **play** ~, (sl.) play truant; **blind** ~, gambling guessing-game at cards [19th c.; orig. unkn.]

hŏŏ'ligan *n*. young ruffian; one of gang of young roughs; hence ~ISM (3) *n*. [perh. orig. name of ruffianly Irish family in SE London]

hŏŏp¹ *n*. & *v.t.* **1.** *n*. circular band of metal, wood, etc., esp. for binding staves of casks etc.; wooden or iron ring trundled along by child; circle of flexible material for expanding a woman's petticoat or skirt; iron arch used in croquet; large ring usu. with paper stretched over it through which circus performer jumps (**go, be put, through the** ~(**s**), undergo an ordeal); ~-**iron** (in long thin strips for binding casks etc.); ~-**la**, game in which rings are thrown in attempt to encircle one of various prizes, (sl.) commotion, (sl.) pretentious nonsense; ~ (**petticoat**) (expanded by hoops). **2.** *v.t.* bind with hoop; surround (as) with hoop. [OE *hōp*, = MDu. *hoep* f. WG **hōpa*]

hŏŏp² *n*. Var. of WHOOP.

hŏŏ'poe (-ōō) *n*. S. Eur. etc. bird with variegated plumage and large erectile crest. [alt. of ME *hoop* f. OF *huppe* f. L *upupa*, imit. of its cry]

hŏŏray'. Var. of HURRAY.

hŏŏ'segow (-sg-) *n*. (sl.) prison. [f. Amer. Sp. *juzgao*, Sp. *juzgado* tribunal f. L *judicatum* neut. p.p. (as n.) of *judicare* JUDGE²]

*Hōō′sier (-zh*er*) *n.* (nickname for) native or in-habitant of Indiana. [19th c.; orig. unkn.]
hōot *v.* & *n.* **1.** *v.i.* make loud sounds, esp. of disapproval or derision or (colloq.) merriment (*at*, or abs.); (of owl) utter cry; (of steam whistle or motor horn) sound. **2.** *v.t.* assail (person etc.) with derisive shouts; drive (person) *out, away*, etc., by hooting; cause (motor horn etc.) to sound. **3.** *n.* inarticulate shout, esp. of derision or disapproval; owl's cry; sound of hooter; (colloq.) (cause of) laughter; *do not care, does not matter, is not worth*, **a** ∼ or **two** ∼**s**, (sl.) anything at all. [ME *hūten*, perh. imit.]
*hōō′tenănnÿ *n.* (colloq.) informal celebratory event esp. with folk-music. [orig. dial., = 'gadget' etc.]
hōō′ter *n.* In vbl senses; ‖siren, steam whistle, esp. as signal for work to begin or cease; ‖motor horn; (sl.) nose. [f. HOOT + -ER¹]
hōots *int.* (Sc. & N. Engl.) expr. dissatisfaction or impatience. [natural excl.; cf. Sw. *hut* begone, W *hwt* away, Ir. *ut* out, all in similar sense]
Hōō′ver *n.* & *v.t.* **1.** *n.* (P) vacuum cleaner (prop. one made by the Hoover company). **2.** *v.t.* (colloq.) clean (carpet etc.) with Hoover. [f. W. H. ∼, Amer. manufacturer d. 1932]
hooves. See HOOF.
hŏp¹ *n.* & *v.* (**-pp-**). **1.** *n.* climbing perennial plant (*Humulus lupulus*), cultivated for the cones borne by the female; (in *pl.*) ripe cones of this, used for giving bitter flavour to malt liquor etc., (Austral. & NZ sl.) beer; *(sl.) opium or other narcotic. **2.** ∼**-bind, -bine,** climbing stem of hop; ∼**-fly,** aphis destructive to hops; ‖∼**-garden, -yard,** field for cultivation of hops; *∼**′head,** (sl.) drug addict (Austral. & NZ sl.) drunkard; ∼**-picker,** labourer or machine employed to pick hops; ∼**-pillow** (stuffed with hops, to pro-duce sleep); ∼**-pole** (on which hop plant is trained); ∼**′sack(ing),** (1) (coarse material of hemp etc. for) sack(s) to contain hops, (2) coarse clothing fabric in loose plain weave. **3.** *v.t.* flavour with hops; *∼ **up,** (sl., esp. in *p.p.*) stimulate with drug. **4.** *v.i.* produce or pick hops. [ME *hoppe* f. MLG, MDu. *hoppe* = OS *-hoppo*, OHG *hopfo*]
hŏp² *v.* (**-pp-**). **1.** *v.i.* spring, (of person) on one foot, (of bird, frog, etc.) with all feet at once; (colloq.) make quick change of position or location; ∼ **in, out,** (colloq.) get into or out of motor car. **2.** *v.t.* hop over (ditch etc.); (colloq.) jump on to or into (vehicle), obtain (ride) thus; ∼ **the twig** or **stick,** (sl.) depart suddenly, die; ∼ **it,** (sl.) go away. **3.** pass quickly from one (place of specified type) to others, (esp. in *vbl n.* and of aircraft: CLOUD, HEDGE¹, *-hopping*). **4.** ∼**-o′-my-thumb,** dwarf, pygmy [*o′* = ON¹]; ∼**ping mad,** (colloq.) very angry; ∼**′scotch,** child's game of hopping on one foot and with it pushing (or other-wise moving) flat stone etc., over SCOTCH²es marked on ground; *∼**-toad,** toad. [OE *hoppian*, = MHG *hopfen*, ON *hoppa*]
hŏp³ *n.* **1.** (action of) hopping; **on the** ∼, (colloq.) (1) bustling about, (2) unprepared (*caught on the hop*). **2.** (colloq.) informal dance. **3.** distance travelled by air without landing; stage of a flight or journey. **4.** ∼, **skip** (or **step**), **and jump,** = TRIPLE *jump*; LONG¹ *hop.* [f. prec.]
hōpe¹ *n.* **1.** (in *sing.* or *pl.*) expectation and desire combined (*of thing, of doing, that*); (Bibl.) feeling of trust; SET¹ one's *hopes on.* **2.** ground of hope, promise, probability, (**hoping against** ∼, clinging to a mere possibility); person or thing that gives cause for hope; what is hoped for; FORLORN *hope*; **not a** ∼, (iron.) **some** ∼(s)!, (colloq.) no chance at all. **3.** *∼**chest,** = BOTTOM¹ *drawer* (fig.). [OE *hopa, tōhopa*, = OLG *tōhopa*, MLG, MDu. *hope*]
hōpe² *v.* **1.** (in *sing.* or *pl.*) expectation and desire (*for* thing, or abs.). **2.** *v.t.* expect and desire (*that, to* do); feel fairly confident *that.* [OE *hopian*, = MDu. *hopen*; cf. prec.]
hō′peful (-pf-) *a.* & *n.* **1.** *a.* feeling hope; inspiring

hope, promising; hence ∼NESS *n.* **2.** *n.* (**young**) ∼, young person likely to succeed or (iron.) be dis-appointed. [f. HOPE¹ + -FUL]
hō′pefullÿ (-pf-) *adv.* In adj. senses; (qualifying whole sentence; **D**) it is hoped that (*hopefully, the car will be ready by then*). [f. prec. + -LY²]
hō′peless (-pl-) *a.* feeling no hope; admitting no hope (*a hopeless* CASE¹); inadequate, incompetent (*am hopeless at tennis*); hence ∼LY² *adv.*, ∼NESS *n.* [f. HOPE¹ + -LESS]
hŏ′plīte *n.* heavy-armed foot-soldier of ancient Greece. [f. Gk *hoplitēs* (*hoplon* weapon; see -ITE¹)]
hŏ′pper¹ *n.* **1.** one who hops; hopping insect, esp. flea or cheese-maggot or young locust. **2.** inverted pyramid or cone (orig. with hopping motion) through which grain passes in mill; similar con-trivance in various machines. **3.** barge carrying away mud etc. from dredging-machine and discharging it; railway truck able to discharge coal etc. through floor. [ME, f. HOP² + -ER¹]
hŏ′pper² *n.* hop-picker. [f. HOP¹ + -ER¹]
hŏ′pple *v.t.*, & *n.* **1.** *v.t.* fasten together legs of (horse etc.). **2.** *n.* apparatus for this. [prob. f. LG; cf. early Flem. *hoppelen* = MDu. *hobelen* jump, dance]
‖Hŏ′ppus *n.* ∼ (**cubic**) **foot,** unit of timber volume measurement (1·27 cu. ft.) used when calculating from length and girth of tree etc. [f. E. ∼, 18th-c. Engl. surveyor]
hŏr′arÿ *a.* of the hours; occurring every hour. [f. med. L *horarius* f. L *hora* HOUR; see -ARY¹]
Horā′tian (-shan) *a.* of or like (the poems of) Horace. [f. L *Horatianus* (Q. *Horatius* Flaccus, Roman poet d. 8 BC; see -AN)]
hŏrde *n.* troop of Tartar or other nomads; (usu. derog.) numerous company, gang, troop. [f. Pol. *horda* f. Turki *ordī, ordū* camp; cf. URDU]
hŏr′ehound (hŏr′h-) *n.* herb (*Marrubium vulgare*) with white cottony covering on stem and leaves; its bitter aromatic juice used against coughs etc.; one of various herbs allied to this. [OE *hāre hūne* (*hār* HOAR, *hūne*, a plant)]
horī′zon *n.* **1.** line at which earth and sky appear to meet; **apparent, sensible, visible,** ∼, circle where earth's surface touches a cone whose vertex is at observer's eye; ARTIFICIAL *horizon*; **celestial, rational, true,** ∼, great circle of the celestial sphere, plane of which passes through centre of earth and is parallel to that of apparent horizon of a place. **2.** (fig.) limit of mental perception, experience, interest, etc.; **on the** ∼ (fig., of event) just imminent or becoming apparent. **3.** geological stratum or set of strata, or layer of soil, with particular characteristics; level at which particular group of archaeological remains is found. [ME f. OF *orizon(te)*, f. LL *horizon -ontis* f. Gk *horizōn* (*kuklos*) limiting (circle)]
hŏrīzŏn′tal *a.* & *n.* **1.** *a.* of or at the horizon; parallel to the plane of this, at right angles to the vertical (*horizontal plane*); (of machinery etc.) having its parts working in horizontal direction; combining firms engaged in same stage of production (*horizontal* INTEGRATION); involving social groups of equal status etc. **2.** Hence ∼ITY (-ă′l-) *n.*, ∼LY² *adv.* **3.** *n.* horizontal line, plane, etc. [F, or mod. L *horizontalis* (as prec.; see -AL)]
hŏr′mē *n.* (Psych.) vital or purposeful energy. [f. Gk *hormē* impulse]
hŏr′mōn|e *n.* (Biol.) substance, formed by internal secretion, that passes into the blood or sap and stimulates organs to action; synthetic substance with similar effect; hence ∼AL (hŏrmō′-, hŏr′mo-) *a.* [f. Gk *hormō-*, part of *hormaō* impel]
hŏrn¹ *n.* **1.** non-deciduous outgrowth, often curved and pointed, on head of cattle, sheep, goats, rhino-ceroses, giraffes, and other mammals, found in pairs, single, or one in front of another; *take the* BULL¹ *by the horns.* **2.** each of two deciduous branched appendages on head of (esp. male) deer. **3.** projection on head of other animals, as snail's tentacle, insect's antenna,

crest of horned owl; emblem of cuckold; **draw in** one's ∼**s**, restrain one's ambition or ardour, draw back. **4.** substance of which horns consist; GATE¹ *of horn*. **5.** thing made of horn; drinking-vessel, powder--flask, made of horn; SHOE¹*horn*; ∼ **of plenty**, cornucopia. **6.** wind instrument played by lip-vibration (now made not of horn but of brass; *hunting-horn*); **English** ∼, cor anglais; (**French**) ∼, orchestral instrument with coiled tube, valves, and wide bell; ∼('IST), its player. **7.** instrument for sounding warning signal (FOG²-*horn*, *motor horn*); cone-shaped part of gramophone etc. **8.** horn-shaped projection; extremity of moon or other crescent; arm or branch of bay, river, etc.; either alternative of a DILEMMA; (vulg.) erect penis; **the H**∼, Cape Horn; GOLDEN *Horn*. **9.** ∼'**beam**, tree of genus *Carpinus* with hard tough wood; ∼'**bill**, bird with hornlike excrescence on bill; ∼'**book**, (Hist.) paper containing alphabet, Lord's Prayer, etc., mounted on wooden tablet with handle, and protected by thin plate of horn; ∼**-mad**, (arch.) stark mad (orig. of horned beasts); ∼--**rimmed**, (esp. of spectacles) having rims made of horn or substance resembling it; ∼'**stone**, brittle siliceous rock; ∼'**wort**, aquatic plant with forked leaves. **10.** Hence ∼ED² (-nd), ∼'LESS, *adjs.*; ∼**ed owl** (with hornlike feathers on head); ∼**ed toad**, small Amer. spiny lizard [OE, = OS, OHG, ON *horn*, Goth. *haurn* f. Gmc **hornaz*, -*am*, cogn. w. L *cornu*]

horn² *v. 1. n.t* (esp. in *p.p.*) furnish with horns. **2.** gore with the horns; adjust (frame of ship) at right angles to line of keel. **3.** *v.i.* ∼ **in**, (sl.) intrude (*on*), interfere. [ME, f. prec.]

hŏr'nblĕnde *n.* dark-brown, black, or green mineral, a constituent of granite and many rocks, composed chiefly of silicates of calcium, magnesium, and iron. [G (as HORN¹, BLENDE)]

hŏr'ner *n.* maker of horn spoons, combs, etc.; one who blows a horn. [ME, f. HORN¹ + -ER¹]

hŏr'nėt *n.* large kind of wasp, inflicting serious sting; ∼**s' nest**, host of enemies or opponents (*bring a hornets' nest about one's ears*). [prob. f. MLG, MDu. *horn(e)te*; OE *hyrnet*, OS *hornut*, OHG *hornuz*, perh. rel. to HORN¹]

hŏr'npipe *n.* (music for) lively dance, usu. by one person (esp. associated with merry-making of sailors). [name of obs. wind instrument partly of horn, ME, f. HORN¹ + PIPE¹]

hŏr'nswŏggle *v.t.* (sl.) cheat, hoax. [19th c., of unkn. orig.]

hŏr'nȳ *a.* of or like horn; hard as horn, callous, (*horny--handed*); (sl.) *l*echerous; hence ∼iNESS *n.* [ME, f. HORN¹ + -Y²]

hŏ'rologe *n.* (arch.) timepiece, dial, clock. [ME f. OF *orloge*, f. L f. Gk *hōrologion* (*hōra* time, -*logos* -telling)]

horŏ'logȳ *n.* study of measuring time or making clocks, watches, etc.; so ∼ER¹ (3), ∼IST (3), *ns.*; **hŏrolŏ'gic**(AL) *adjs.* [f. Gk *hōra* time + -O- + -LOGY]

hŏ'roscōpe *n.* (Astrol.) observation of sky and planets at certain moment, esp. at person's birth; diagram showing configuration of planets etc. at particular moment (CAST¹ *a horoscope*); prediction of person's future based on this; hence **hŏroscŏ'pic**(AL) *adjs.*, **horŏ'scopy**¹ *n.* [F, f. L f. Gk *hōroskopos* (*hōra* time, *skopos* observer)]

horrĕ'ndous *a.* (colloq.) horrifying; hence ∼LY²*adv.* [f. L *horrendus* gerundive of *horrēre* (see HORRID), + -OUS]

hŏ'rrent *a.* (poet.) bristling; shuddering. [f. L *horrēre* (see prec., -ENT)]

hŏ'rrib|**le** *a.* exciting, or likely to excite, horror; hideous, shocking; (colloq.) excessive, unpleasant, (*horrible noise*, *weather*); hence ∼le**NESS** (-beln-) *n.*, ∼LY² *adv.* [ME, f. OF (*h*)*orrible* f. L *horribilis* (*horrēre*; see foll., -IBLE)]

hŏ'rrid *a.* terrible, frightful; (poet.) rough, bristling; (colloq.) disagreeable, objectionable, (*horrid weather*, *boys*); hence ∼LY² *adv.*, ∼NESS *n.* [f. L *horridus* (*horrēre* bristle, shudder; see -ID¹)]

horrī'f|**ic** *a.* horrifying; hence ∼iCALLY *adv.* [f. F *horrifique* or f. L *horrificus* (*horrēre*; see prec., -FIC)]

hŏ'rri|**fy** *v.t.* excite horror in; shock, scandalize; hence ∼FICA'TION *n.* [f. L *horrificare* (as prec.; see -FY)]

hŏrripilā'tion *n.* (literary). = GOOSE¹-*flesh*. [f. LL *horripilatio* f. L *horrēre* to bristle + *pilus* hair; see -ATION]

hŏ'rror *n.* & *a.* **1.** *n.* painful feeling of loathing and fear; terrified and revolted shuddering; intense dislike (*of*) or (colloq.) dismay (*at*). **2.** person or thing causing horror; **Chamber of H**∼**s**, place full of horrors (orig. room of criminals etc. in Tussaud's waxworks). **3.** (in *pl.*) ∼**s!** (excl. of dismay); **the** ∼**s**, fit of horror or depression, esp. as in delirium tremens. **4.** ∼--**struck** or -**stricken**, horrified, shocked. **5.** *a.* (Of literature, film, etc.) designed to attract by arousing pleasurable feelings of horror; ∼ **comic**, paper like comic but with much violence and sensationalism. [ME, f. OF (*h*)*orrour* f. L *horror-oris* (as prec.; see -OR)]

hors (ōr) *adv.* & *prep.* outside, as: ∼ **concours** (-kawṅkoor'), (of exhibit or exhibitor) not competing for prize, unrivalled; ∼ *de* **combat** (-dėkaw'ṅbah), out of the fight, disabled. [F]

hors-d'œuvre (ōrdĕr'vr, -v) *n.* extra dish served as appetizer before or (occas.) during meal. [F, – outside the work]

hŏrse¹ *n.* **1.** solid-hoofed herbivorous quadruped (*Equus caballus*) with flowing mane and tail, used as beast of burden and draught, and for riding on; (esp.) adult male horse, stallion or gelding; wooden etc. representation of horse; (collect. *sing.*) cavalry (LIGHT⁴ *horse*); SEA-*horse*. **2.** vaulting-block in gymnasium; frame (often with legs) on which something is supported, as CLOTHES-*horse*; (Naut.) rope or bar in various uses; (Mining) obstruction in vein; (colloq.) (unit of) horsepower; (sl.) heroin. **3.** *put the* CART *before the horse*; DARK¹ *horse*; FLOG *a dead horse*; look *a* GIFT--*horse in the mouth*; **on** one's **high** ∼, behaving with pretentiousness or arrogance; **hold your** ∼**s!**, (colloq.) pause for a moment; ∼ **of another colour**, thing significantly different; *eat*, *work*, **like a** ∼, with great vigour; (**straight**) **from the** ∼'**s mouth**, (of information) from person directly concerned or other authoritative source; SWAP *horses*; **to** ∼, (as command) mount your horses; WHITE¹ *horses*; WILD, WILLING², WOODEN, WRONG, *horse*. **4.** ***∼**-and-buggy**, (fig.) out of date; **on** ∼'**back**, mounted on a horse; ∼'**bean**, broad bean used as fodder; ∼**-block**, small platform of stone or wood for mounting a horse; ∼--**box**, closed vehicle for transporting horse(s); (joc.) large pew; *horse*-BRASS; ∼-**breaker**, one who breaks in horses; ∼-**che'stnut**, large ornamental tree with upright conical clusters of white or pink or red flowers, fruit of this (like edible chestnut, but with coarse bitter taste); ∼-**cloth** (used to cover horse, or as part of trappings); *horse*-COLLAR¹; *horse*-COPER; ∼-**doctor**, veterinary surgeon attending horses; ∼-**drawn**, (of vehicle) pulled by horse; ∼'**flesh**, (1) flesh of horse, esp. as food, (2) horses collectively; ∼-**fly**, dipterous insect (of various kinds) troublesome to horses; ||H∼ **Guards**, (1) cavalry brigade of household troops, esp. (*Royal Horse Guards*) second regiment of it, (2) headquarters of such cavalry, esp. a building in Whitehall; ∼'**hair**, hair from mane or tail of horse; ∼ **latitudes**, belt of calms at northern edge of NE trade winds; ∼-**laugh**, loud coarse laugh; ∼'**leech**, large kind of leech, insatiable person, (*daughters of the* ∼*leech*, Prov. 30:15); ∼-**mackerel**, large fish of the mackerel type, e.g. scad, tunny; ∼'**man**, (skilled) rider on horseback; ∼'**manship**, art of riding, skill in riding, on horseback; *horse* MARINE¹s; ∼-**mushroom** (coarse but edible variety with hollow stem); ***∼ **opera**, (sl.) western film; ∼-**pistol** (for use by horseman); ∼'**play**, boisterous play; ∼-**pond** (for watering and washing horses, prov. as ducking-place of obnoxious persons); ∼'**power**, (*pl.* same) (power measured in terms of) unit of rate of doing work, = 550 foot-

-pounds per second, about 750 watts; ∼-**race** (between horses with riders); ∼-**racing,** sport of conducting horse-races; ∼-**radish,** plant whose pungent root is scraped or grated as condiment, often made into sauce; ∼ **sense,** (colloq.) plain rough sagacity; ∼'**s neck,** (sl.) drink of flavoured ginger-ale usu. with spirits; ∼-**soldier** (mounted on horse); ∼-**tail,** (1) tail of horse (formerly used in Turkey as standard, or as ensign denoting rank of pasha), (2) cryptogamous plant of genus *Equisetum,* like horse's tail, with hollow jointed stem, (3) = PONY-*tail;* ∼-**trading,** *dealing in horses, (fig.) shrewd bargaining; ∼'**whip,** (n.) whip for horses, (*v.t.; -pp-*) chastise (person) with this; ∼'**woman,** woman who rides on horseback. **5.** Hence ∼'LESS (-sl-) *a.;* ∼**less carriage,** (arch.) motor car. [OE *hors,* = OS, OHG *hros,* ON *hross* f. Gmc **horsam, -az*]

hŏrse[2] *v.* **1.** *v.t.* provide (person, vehicle) with horse(s). **2.** *v.i.* mount or go on horseback; (colloq.) fool *around.* [f. prec.]

hŏr'seshoe (-s-shoō) *n.* iron shoe for horse shaped like outline of hard part of hoof; thing of this shape, C-shaped object, (e.g. magnet, table, arch in Spanish and Islamic Archit.); *∼ **crab,** king-crab. [ME, f. HORSE[1] + SHOE[1]]

hŏr'sey. Var. of HORSY.

hŏrst *n.* (Geol.) ridge of land with faults between it and lower regions on each side. [G, = heap]

hŏr's|y̆ *a.* resembling a horse; concerned with or devoted to horses or horse-racing; affectedly using dress and language of groom or jockey; hence ∼**iLY**[2] *adv.,* ∼**iNESS** *n.* [f. HORSE[1] + -Y[2]]

hŏr't|ative *a.* tending or serving to exhort; so ∼**A'TION** *n.,* ∼**atory** *a.* [f. L *hortativus* (*hortari* exhort; see -IVE)]

hŏrtĕ'nsia *n.* variety of hydrangea. [mod. L, f. *Hortense* Lepaute, 18th-c. Frenchwoman + -IA[1]]

hŏr'ticŭlture *n.* art of garden cultivation; hence **hŏrtĭcŭ'ltur**AL *a.,* **hŏrtĭcŭ'ltur**IST (3) *n.,* (-cher-). [f. L *hortus* garden, after *agriculture*]

hortus siccus (hŏr'tus sĭ'kus) *n.* arranged collection of dried plants; (fig.) collection of uninteresting facts etc. [L, = dry garden]

Hos. *abbr.* Hosea (OT).

hŏsā'nna (-z-) *n.* shout of adoration (Matt. 21: 9, 15, etc.). [ME, f. LL f. Gk *hōsanna* f. Heb. *hŏšá'nā* for *hŏšŭ'a-nnā* save now!]

hōse (-z) *n.,* & *v.t.* **1.** *n.* (collect. as *pl.,* or arch. *pl.* ho'sen; stockings; half-∼, socks. **2.** (Hist.) breeches (DOUBLET *and hose*). **3.** ∼(-**pipe**), flexible tube conveying water for watering plants etc., putting out fires, dispersing rioters, etc. **4.** *v.t.* provide with hose; drench or spray or water with hose. [OE = OS, OHG, ON *hosa* f. Gmc *husōn]

hŏ'si|er (-zher) *n.* dealer in hose (‖and knitted or woven underclothing); hence ∼ERY (1) *n.* [ME, f. HOSE + -IER]

hŏ'spice *n.* house of rest for travellers, esp. one kept by religious order; ‖home for destitute or (esp. terminally) ill. [F, f. L *hospitium* (as HOST[2])]

hŏspitab|le (hŏ'-; D-pĭ'-) *a.* giving, disposed to give, welcome and entertainment to strangers or guests; hence ∼LY[2] *adv.* [F (*hospiter* f. med. L *hospitare* entertain; as prec., -ABLE)]

hŏ'spital *n.* institution providing medical and surgical treatment for persons ill or injured (*go* ‖*to hospital,* *to the hospital; so *in* (*the*) *hospital*); charitable institution (in names, as *Christ's H*∼, public school formerly in London); (Hist.) hospice, establishment of Knights Hospitallers; ∼ **fever,** kind of typhus formerly prevalent in crowded hospitals; ∼ **ship** (to receive sick and wounded seamen, or to convey sick and wounded soldiers home); ∼ **train** (taking wounded soldiers from battlefield); hence ∼ISM *n.,* adverse effects of prolonged stay in hospital, ∼IZE *v.t.,* admit to or treat in hospital, ∼**ĪZA'TION** *n.* [ME f. OF, f. med. L *hospitale* neut. (as n.) of L *hospitalis* a. (as HOST[2]; see -AL)]

hŏspĭtă'lĭty *n.* friendly and generous reception of guests or strangers or (fig.) of new ideas etc. [ME, f. OF *hospitalité* f. L *hospitalitas -tatis* (as prec.; see -ITY)]

hŏ'spĭtaller, *-**aler,** *n.* member of charitable religious order; chaplain (in some London hospitals); **Knight H**∼, member of order of military monks founded at Jerusalem *c.* 1048. [ME, f. OF *hospitalier* f. med. L *hospitalarius* (as HOSPITAL; see -ARY[1], -ER[2] (2))]

hŏst[1] *n.* **1.** large number (*of*; person **is a** ∼ **in** himself, can do as much as a number of ordinary persons); (arch.) army. **2.** (Bibl.) **Lord** (**God**) **of** ∼**s** (earthly or heavenly armies); ∼(**s**) **of heaven, heavenly** ∼, (1) sun, moon, and stars, (2) the angels. [ME f. OF, f. L *hostis* stranger, enemy, in med. L 'army']

hŏst[2] *n.,* & *v.t.* **1.** *n.* one who receives or entertains another as guest; landlord of inn (*mine host*; **reckon without** one's ∼, neglect difficulty, opposition, etc.). **2.** (Biol.) animal or plant having parasite or commensal; animal that has received transplanted organ etc. **3.** *v.t.* act as host to (person) or at (event). [ME, f. OF *oste* f. L *hospes -pitis* host, guest]

hŏst[3] *n.* bread consecrated in the Eucharist. [ME, f. OF (*h*)*oiste* f. L *hostia* victim]

hŏ'sta *n.* ornamental perennial of genus *Hosta* (formerly *Funkia*), with clusters of drooping bell-shaped white, blue, or lilac flowers. [mod. L, f. N. T. *Host,* Austrian physician d. 1834 + -A]

hŏ'stage *n.* person given to or seized by another as pledge; pledge, security; ∼ **to fortune,** person or thing that one acquires and may then suffer by losing, esp. wife or child; hence ∼SHIP (-ĭjsh-) *n.* [ME, f. OF (*h*)*ostage* f. Rom. *obsidaticum f. LL *obsidatus* hostageship f. L *obses obsidis* hostage; see -AGE]

‖**hŏ'stel** *n.* house of residence for students or other special class (YOUTH *hostel*); (arch.) inn. [ME, f. OF (*h*)*ostel* f. med. L (as HOSPITAL)]

hŏ'stelry *n.* (arch. or literary) inn. [ME, f. OF (*h*)*ostelerie* f. (*h*)*ostelier* innkeeper (as prec.; see -ERY)]

hŏ'stĕss *n.* woman who acts as HOST[2]; woman employed to welcome and entertain customers at night-club etc.; woman employed as AIR[1] *hostess* or similarly in other role. [ME, f. OF (*h*)*ostesse* (as HOST[2], -ESS[1])]

hŏ'stĭle *a.* of an enemy; unfriendly, opposed, (*to*); witness (who gives evidence unfairly and appears hostile to party calling him); hence ∼LY[2] (-l-lĭ) *adv.* [F, or f. L *hostilis* (as HOST[2]; SEE -IL)]

hŏstĭ'lĭty *n.* enmity; state of warfare; (in *pl.*) acts of warfare; opposition (in thought etc.). [f. F *hostilité* or f. LL *hostilitas* (as prec.; see -ITY)]

hŏ'stler (ŏ'sler) *n.* **1.** = OSTLER. **2.** *person in charge of locomotives etc. when not in use. [ME, f. OF *hosteler* (as OSTLER)]

hŏt[1] *a.* & *adv.* **1.** *a.* of or at high temperature, very warm (RED, WHITE[1], -*hot*); (of food etc.) prepared by heating and served without cooling; communicating or feeling heat (∼ **under the collar,** angry, resentful, or embarrassed). **2.** producing the sensation of heat (*hot fever, blush*); (of pepper etc.) pungent, biting. **3.** ardent, passionate; eager (*for; in hot pursuit*), keen (*on*); lustful; angry; excited; exciting; **not so** ∼, (colloq.) only mediocre. **4.** (Of scent in hunting, etc.) = WARM[1] 8; (fig., of news etc.) fresh, recent; ‖(colloq., of Treasury bills) newly issued. **5.** (Of a hit, return, etc., in ball-games) difficult for opponent to deal with; (of competitor in race or other sporting event) strongly fancied to win (*a hot favourite*); (of player) very skilful. **6.** (Of jazz etc.) strongly rhythmical and emotional. **7.** (sl.) radioactive; (of goods) stolen, esp. easily identifiable and hence difficult to dispose of; (of person) wanted by police. **8.** BLOW[1] *hot and cold;* **give it him** ∼, (colloq.) chastise or reprimand him severely; ∼ **and bothered,** exasperated and agitated; ∼ **and cold** (of water-supply in hotel etc.); ∼ **and cold,** feel alternately hot and cold owing to fear etc.; ∼ **and** ∼, (arch., of food) served as soon as cooked; ∼ **and strong,** vehement(ly); **make it** or the place or things ∿ **for, too** ∿ (uncomfortable, by persecution) **for** or **to hold, him. 9.** *adv.* hotly, eagerly, angrily. **10.** ∿ **air,** (sl.) excited or boastful talk; ∿'**bed,** bed of earth heated by fermenting manure, (fig.) place favourable to growth *of* (vice etc.); ∿ **blast** (of heated air forced into furnace); ∿- **short,** ardent, passionate; *sell* etc. *like hot* CAKES; ∿ **cathode** (heated to emit electrons); ∿ **cockles,** (Hist.) rustic game in which blindfolded person guessed who struck him; *hot cross* BUN; ∿ **dog,** (colloq.) hot sausage sandwiched in roll of bread, *(as int.* of approval); *hot flash* or FLUSH³ 4; ∿'**foot** *adv., a.,* & *(colloq.) v.i.,* (go) in eager haste; *hot* GOSPELLER; ∿'**head,** impetuous person; ∿-**headed,** impetuous, excitable; ∿'**house,** heated building with glass roof and sides for growing plants out of season or in colder climate; ∿ **line,** direct channel of emergency communication, esp. between Washington and Moscow; ∿ **money,** capital transferred at frequent intervals; ∿'**plate,** heated metal plate etc. for cooking food or keeping it hot; ∿'**pot,** mutton, lamb, beef, with potatoes etc. cooked in oven in tight-lidded pot; *hot* POTATO; ∿-**press,** (*n.*) press of glazed boards and hot metal plates for smoothing paper or cloth, (*v.t.*) press (paper etc.) in this; ∿ **rod,** motor vehicle modified to have extra power and speed; ∿ **seat,** (sl.) (1) electric chair, (2) embarrassing or onerous situation; ∿- **short,** (of metal) brittle in its hot state [cf. COLD-SHORT]; ∿ **spot,** small region that is relatively hot (lit. or fig.), ∿ **spring,** = *hot well* (1); ∿'**spur,** rash person (sobriquet of Sir H. Percy, d. 1403); ∿ **stuff,** (sl.) person of high spirit, vigour, skill, or strong will or passions; ∿ **tip,** (colloq.) unusually reliable TIP² 8; ∿ **war** (with active hostilities); ∿ **water,** (colloq., fig.) trouble, disgrace, (*be in* or *get into hot water*); ∿- **wa'ter bottle** or *bag,* container of rubber, earthenware, etc., filled with hot water as source of warmth; ∿ **well,** (1) spring of naturally hot water, (2) reservoir in condensing steam-engine; ∿ **wire** *a.,* operated by expansion of heated wire. **11.** Hence ∿'**tish¹** 2 *a.,* ∿'**ly¹** *adv.,* ∿'**ness** *n.* [OE *hāt,* = OS *het,* OHG *heiz,* ON *heitr* f. Gmc *haitaz;* cf. HEAT¹]

‖**hŏt³** *v.* (-tt-). (colloq.) **1.** *v.t.* heat, warm *up,* make hot. **2.** *v.i.* become hot or (fig.) dangerous, lively, etc. [f. prec.]

hŏ'tchpŏtch, (esp. Law) **-pŏt,** *n.* **1.** dish of many mixed ingredients, esp. mutton broth or stew with vegetables. **2.** (Law). reunion and blending of properties for purpose of securing equal division (esp. of property of intestate parent). **3.** (confused) mixture, medley. [ME f. AF & OF *hochepot* f. OF (*hocher* shake, POT¹); -*potch* by assim.]

hotĕ'l (ho-, hō-, ō-, o-) *n.* house for accommodation of paying travellers etc., (usu. large) inn; (Austral. & NZ) public house. [f. F *hôtel,* later form of HOSTEL]

hotĕ'lier *n.* hotel-keeper. [f. F *hôtelier* f. OF *hostelier;* see HOSTELRY]

Hŏ'ttentŏt *n.* (member or language) of S. Afr. Negroid people formerly occupying region near the Cape. [Afrik., perh. = stammerer, w. ref. to their mode of pronunc.]

‖**hough** (hŏk) *n.,* & *v.t.* **1.** *n.* = HOCK¹; cut of beef etc. from this and leg above it. **2.** *v.t.* hamstring, whence ∿'**er¹** *n.* [ME *ho(u)gh* = OE *hōh* (heel) in *hōhsinu* hamstring]

hound¹ *n.* **1.** dog for hunting, esp. one tracking by scent; ‖**the** ∿**s,** pack of foxhounds; **ride to** ∿**s,** go fox-hunting on horseback. **2.** despicable man; runner who follows scent in HARE and hounds; person keen in pursuit of something (*news-hound*). **3.** dogfish (NURSE³- -*hound*). **4.** ∿'**s-tongue,** cynoglossum; ∿'**s-tooth,** check pattern with reversed diagonal threads giving notched effect. **5.** Hence ‖∿'**ish¹** *a.* [OE *hund,* = OS *hund,* OHG *hunt,* ON *hundr,* Goth. *hunds* f. Gmc *hundaz* f. IE *kwntós*]

hound² *v.t.* chase or pursue (as) with hound; set (hound, or fig. person) *at* (quarry etc.); urge (person) *on.* [f. prec.]

hour (owr) *n.* **1.** twenty-fourth part of day and night, 60 minutes, (*1700* etc.) ∿**s,** time of 17 etc. hours after zero on twenty-four-hour clock); **the** ∿, each time o'clock of whole number of hours (*bus leaves on the hour, on the half hour, at quarter past the hour*); *the* ELEVENTH *hour;* WATT-*hour.* **2.** short indefinite period of time; time for or of action etc. (*the hour has come*); the present time (*question of the hour*); EVIL *hour.* **3.** *the* time o'clock (*what is the hour?*); **a late** ∿, a time late at night. **4.** (in *pl.*) fixed time for daily work (*office hours are 9 to 5;* **after** ∿**s,** after closing-time); **till all** ∿**s,** till very late; **small** ∿**s,** 1, 2, etc., a.m.; **good** or **early, bad** or **late, regular,** ∿**s** (time for getting up or going to bed). **5.** (R C Ch.) (prayers to be said at) one of seven stated times of day appointed for prayer (*book of hours*). **6.** (Astron.) 15° of longitude or RA. **7.** distance traversed in one hour by (stated or implied) means of travel (*we are an hour from London*). **8.** ∿-**circle,** meridian (24 of which are usu. marked on globe); ∿'**glass,** sand-glass running for an hour; ∿-**hand** (showing hour on clock etc.); ∿-**long** *a.* & *adv.,* (lasting) for one hour. [ME *ure* etc. f. AF; OF *ore, eure* f. L f. Gk *hōra* season, hour]

hour'i (hoor'ī) *n.* nymph of Muslim Paradise; voluptuously beautiful woman. [F, f. Pers. *hūrī* f. Arab. *hūr* pl. of *hawrā‘* gazelle-like (in the eyes)]

hour'ly (owr'-) *a.* & *adv.* (occurring, done, reckoned) every hour; continual(ly), frequent(ly). [f. HOUR + -LY¹,²]

house¹ *n.* (*pl. pr.* -zĭz). **1.** building for human habitation or (usu. w. defining pref.) occupation etc. (ALMS*house,* BAKE*house,* LIGHT¹*house,* SUMMER¹-*house,* WORK¹*house;* ∿ **of God,** church, place of worship; *house of* REFUGE); inn (*a drink on the* ∿, at innkeeper's expense), place of public refreshment (ALE*house,* COFFEE-*house,* EATING-*house,* PUBLIC *house*); *brothel; (Sc.) dwelling that is one of several in a building. **2.** building for keeping animals or goods (*hen-house,* STORE*house,* WARE¹*house*); animal's den, shell, etc. **3.** (place of abode of) religious fraternity. **4.** (members of) university college, house. ‖**the H**∿, Christ Church, Oxford. **5.** = (boys or girls in) BOARDING-*house* of school; one of divisions of day-school for games etc. **6.** (building used by) legislative or deliberative assembly (LOWER³ *House,* UPPER *House; House of* COMMONS, LORDS, REPRESENTATIVES; *Houses of* PARLIAMENT; **keep** or **make a H**∿, secure presence of enough members for quorum or support in House of Commons); (place of business of) institution or mercantile firm (CLEARING-*house,* CUSTOM-*house;* also in name of building, as *Broadcasting House*); ‖**the H**∿, (colloq.) Stock Exchange, (Polit.) House of Commons or Lords (*a question was asked in the House*), (Hist., euphem.) the workhouse. **7.** (audience in) theatre (FULL¹ *house*); performance in theatre etc. (*second house starts at 9 o'clock*). **8.** household, family, dynasty (**the H**∿ **of Windsor,** British Royal Family). **9.** (Astrol.) twelfth part of heavens. **10.** ‖(Army sl.) gambling form of lotto. **11.** *attrib.* (Of animal) kept in, frequenting, infesting, houses (*house- -cat, -cricket, -fly, -sparrow*); living in hospital as member of staff (*house officer, physician, surgeon*). **12.** ∿ **of call** (where carriers call for commissions, where person may be heard of, etc.); ∿ **of cards** (built by child out of playing-cards; often fig. of insecure scheme etc.); ∿ **of ill fame,** (arch.) brothel; H∿ **of Keys,** elective branch of Manx legislature; ∿ **and home,** (emphat.) home; ∿-**to-**∿, carried to or performed at each house in turn; BRING *down the house;* **keep** ∿, maintain, provide for, a household; **keep open** ∿, provide general hospitality; **keep (to) the** ∿, not go outdoors; **like a** ∿ **on fire,** vigorously, fast, excellently; MAN¹ *of the house;* ‖MOVE² *house;* **play** ∿, play at being a family in its home; **put** or **set** one's ∿ **in order,** (fig.) introduce needed reforms; **as safe as** ∿**s,** perfectly safe; **set up** ∿, begin to live in a separate dwelling. **13.** ‖∿-**agent** (for sale and letting of houses); ∿ **arrest,** detention in one's own house etc., not in prison; ∼'**boat,** boat fitted up for living in; ∼'**bote,** (Law) tenant's right to timber for house--repairs [f. as BOOT²]; ∼-**bound,** unable to leave one's house through illness etc.; ∼'**boy,** boy or man as servant in house; ∼'**breaker,** (1) = burglar (formerly in daytime only), (2) ||man employed in demolishing old houses; so ∼'**breaking** *n.*; ∼--**broken,** = *house-trained*; ∼**carl**(**e**), (Hist.) member of bodyguard of Danish or English king or noble; ∼'**coat,** woman's usu. long-skirted garment for informal wear in house; ||∼'**craft,** skill in household management; ∼-**dog** (kept to guard house); ∼--**father,** ∼-**mother,** ∼-**parents,** (in charge of house, esp. of home for children); ∼-**flag** (flown by a firm's ship); ∼ **guest** (staying for some days in private house); ∼-**hunting,** seeking house to live in; ∼'**keep,** (colloq.) keep house; ∼'**keeper,** (1) woman managing affairs of household, (2) person in charge of house, office, etc.; ∼'**keeping,** management of household affairs, (colloq.) money allowed for this, (fig.) operations of maintenance, record-keeping, etc., in an organization; ∼'**leek,** plant (*Sempervivum tectorum*) with pink flowers growing on walls and roofs; ∼ **lights** (in theatre auditorium); ∼ **magazine** (published by firm and dealing mainly with the firm's activities); ∼'**maid,** female servant in house, esp. in charge of reception rooms and bed-rooms (∼*maid's knee*, inflammation of knee-cap due to kneeling); ∼'**man,** = *houseboy* or ||*house officer* (see sense 11); *house*-MARTIN; ∼'**master,** ∼'**mistress,** (of school boarding-house); ∼-**mother, -parents,** (see *house-father*); ∼ **party** (of guests staying at country house etc.); ∼-**plant** (grown indoors); ∼-**proud,** (unduly) preoccupied with the care and beautifica-tion of the home; ∼-**room,** accommodation in house (*would not give it* ∼-*room*, would not take it even as a gift); ∼ **style,** printer's particular choice between variant spellings etc.; ∼-**top,** roof of house (*proclaim from the* ∼-*tops,* publicly announce); ||∼-**trained,** (of domestic animals or infants) trained to be clean or behave well in the house; ∼-**warming,** celebration of occupation of new home; ∼'**work,** cleaning, cooking, etc. **14.** Hence ∼'FUL 2 (-sf-) *n.,* ∼'LESS (-sl-) *a.* [OE *hūs,* = OS, OHG *hūs,* ON *hús,* Goth. *-hūs* f. Gmc **hūsam*]

house² (-z) *v.t.* receive (person etc.), store (goods), in house or as house does; provide houses for (population); fix in socket, mortise, etc. [OE *hūsian* (as prec.)]

hou'sehōld (-s-h-) *n.* occupants of house; domestic establishment; ||*the* royal household; ∼ **gods,** (Rom. Ant.) lares and penates, (fig.) essentials of home life; ∼ **management,** art of managing domestic affairs; ∼ **stuff,** (arch.) furniture etc.; ||∼ **troops** (em-ployed nominally to guard sovereign's person); ∼ **word,** familiar saying or name. [ME, f. HOUSE¹ + HOLD²]

hou'sehōlder (-s-h-) *n.* one who occupies house as his own dwelling (esp. Hist. as entitled to franchise); head of household. [ME, f. HOUSE¹ + HOLDER]

housewife *n.* **1.** (how'swīf). (usu. married) woman directing household affairs (*good, bad*) domestic manager; hence **hou'sewife**LY¹ (-swīfli) *a.* **2.** (hŭ'zif). case for needles, thread, etc. [ME *hus*(*e*)*wif* f. HOUSE¹ + WIFE]

hou'sewiferȳ (-swīfri) *n.* housecraft; housekeeping. [ME, f. prec. + -RY]

||**hou'sey**(-**housey**), **-ie,** *n.* (Army sl.) = HOUSE¹ 10. [f. HOUSE¹ + -Y³, -IE]

hou'sing¹ (-z-) *n.* horse's cloth covering, for pro-tection or ornament. [ME, = covering, f. obs. *house* f. OF *houce* f. med. L *hultia* f. Gmc **hulftī*]

hou'sing² (-z-) *n.* In vbl senses; (provision of) dwelling-houses collectively; shelter, lodging; rigid casing for moving (or sensitive) mechanism etc.; ∼ **estate,** residential district planned as a unit. [f. HOUSE² + -ING¹]

hōve. See HEAVE¹.

hŏ'vel *n.* open shed, outhouse; miserable dwell-ing; conical building enclosing kiln. [ME, of unkn. orig.]

hŏ'ver *v.i.,* & *n.* **1.** *v.i.* (Of bird etc., esp. of hawk, or of helicopter etc.) hang in the air (*over* or *about* a spot); linger *about* or *round* (person, place); remain in undecided state *between.* **2.** *n.* hovering; state of suspense. **3.** ∼**craft,** vehicle or craft supported by air ejected downwards against surface (of land or sea) just beneath it; ∼**fly** (of family Syrphidae, hovering with rapidly beating wings); ||∼-**plane,** helicopter; ∼**port** (used by hovercraft); ∼**train** (progressing on air-cushion like hovercraft). [ME, f. obs. *hove* hover, linger + -ER⁵]

how *adv.* & *n.* **1.** *interrog. adv.* by what means? in what way? (*how does he do it?*; *ask him how he does it*; *but how to bridge the gap?*; *how could you do such a vile thing?*); in what condition?; ∼ **are you?,** ∼ **do you do?,** ∼ **do?,** what is your state of health? (or as merely formal greeting); ∼-**do-you-do,** ∼-**d'ye-do,** etc., embarrassing situa-tion; ∼ **is that for high, queer,** etc.? (colloq. invitation to wonder); ∼'**s that?,** what is your opinion or explanation of that?, (Cricket, to umpire) is batsman out or not?; ∼ **now?,** (arch.) what is the meaning of this?; ∼ (can you show that to be) **so?. 2.** (In indirect statement, rhet. or vulg. =) that (*told us how God was almighty*). **3.** (In question or exclamation) to what extent (*how far is it?*; *how far it is!*; *how many are there?*; *how many there are!*; *how would you like to take my place?*; *how he snores!*). **4.** *rel. adv.* in whatever way, as, (*do it how you can*). **5.** *n.* the way a thing is done (*the how of it*). **6. and** ∼!, (sl.) very much so (chiefly used ironically or intensively); **here's** ∼!, I drink to your good health; ∼ **about,** = WHAT *about; how* COME 7; ∼**e'ver,** in whatever way, to whatever extent, never-theless, (colloq.) = *how* EVER; ∼ **much?,** what price (*how much is it?*), what amount (*how much do I owe you?*), (joc.) what? (as request for repetition); ∼**soe'ver,** ∼**soe'er** (poet.), ∼ . . . **soever,** in whatsoever way, to whatsoever extent. [OE *hū,* = OS (*h*)*wō,* OHG *wuo,* f. WG **hwō* (**hwa-* WHO)]

howbē'it *adv.* (arch. or literary). nevertheless. [f. BOY + BE + IT³]

how'dah (-*a*) *n.* seat for two or more, usu. with canopy, on elephant's back. [f. Urdu *hawda* f. Arab. *hawdaj* litter]

*****how'dȳ** *int.* = HOW *do you do?* [corrupt.]

how'itzer (-ts-) *n.* short gun for high-angle firing of shells at low velocities. [f. Du. *houwitser* f. G *haubitze* f. Czech *houfnice* catapult]

howl¹ *v.* **1.** *v.i.* (Of animal) utter long loud doleful cry; (of person) utter long loud cry of pain, derision, merriment, etc., freq. of (esp. child's) loud weeping; (of wind etc.) make prolonged wailing noise. **2.** *v.t.* utter (words) with howling; ∼ **down,** reduce to silence by howls of derision. [ME *houle,* = MLG, MDu. *hūlen,* MHG *hiulen* (imit.); cf. OWL]

howl² *n.* long loud doleful cry of dog, wolf, etc.; loud cry of pain etc.; yell of derision or merriment; (Electr.) howling noise in loudspeaker due to buildup of sound at audio frequencies. [f. prec.]

how'ler *n.* In vbl senses; S. Amer. monkey of genus *Alouatta*; (colloq.) glaring blunder. [f. HOWL¹ + -ER¹]

how'ling *a.* that howls; *howling* DERVISH; (Bibl.) ∼ (dreary) **wilderness;** (sl.) extreme, glaring, (*a howl-ing shame*). [f. HOWL¹ + -ING²]

hoy¹ *n.* (Hist.) small vessel, usu. rigged as sloop, carrying passengers and goods esp. for short dis-tances. [f. MDu. *hoei, hoede,* of unkn. orig.]

hoy² *int.* used to call attention, drive animals, or (Naut.) hail or call aloft. [ME; natural cry]

hoy'a *n.* climbing shrub of genus *Hoya,* with pink, white, or yellow waxy flowers. [mod. L, f. T. *Hoy,* Engl. gardener d. 1821 + -A]

hoy'den *n.* boisterous girl; hence ∼ISH¹ *a.* [orig. = rude fellow, prob. f. MDu. *heiden* (= HEATHEN)]

Hoyle *n.* **according to** ∼, exact(ly), correct(ly). [f. E. ∼, Engl. writer on card-games d. 1769]

h.p. *abbr.* high pressure; hire-purchase; horsepower.

HQ *abbr.* headquarters.

*HR *abbr.* House of Representatives.

HRH *abbr.* Her or His Royal Highness.

hr(s). *abbr.* hour(s).

HSH *abbr.* Her or His Serene Highness.

HT *abbr.* high tension.

huanaco. Var. of GUANACO.

hub *n.* central part of wheel, rotating on or with axle, and from which spokes radiate; (fig.) central point of interest etc. (esp. *hub of the universe*); **~-cap,** cover for hub of vehicle's wheel. [16th c., perh. = HOB²]

hu'bble-bubble *n.* rudimentary form of hookah; bubbling sound; confused talk. [redupl. of BUBBLE¹; imit.]

hu'bbub *n.* confused din; disturbance, riot; confused yelling of war-cry. [perh. of Ir. orig.; cf. Gael. *ubub* int. of contempt, Ir. *abú,* a war-cry]

hu'bby *n.* (colloq.) husband. [abbr.; see -Y³]

hu'br|is *n.* insolent pride or presumption; (Gk Tragedy) overweening pride towards the gods, leading to nemesis; so **~i'stic** *a.* [Gk]

hu'ckaback *n.* stout linen or cotton fabric with rough surface, for towels etc. [17th c.; orig. unkn.]

hu'ckle *n.* hip; haunch; **~-back**(ed), humpback(ed); **~-bone,** hip-bone, knuckle-bone of quadruped. [f. obs. *huck* hip (perh. f. **huk-* be bent) +-LE 1]

hu'ckleberry (-kelb-) *n.* (blue or black fruit of) low berry-bearing shrub of genus *Gaylussacia* common in N. Amer. [prob. alt. of *hurtleberry,* WHORTLEBERRY]

hu'ckster|er¹ *n.* pedlar, hawker; mercenary person; *publicity agent esp. for broadcast material; hence **~ERY** (2) *n.* [ME, prob. f. LG; cf. dial. *huck* to bargain, HAWKER¹, -STER]

hu'ckster² *v.* **1.** *v.i.* bargain, haggle. **2.** *v.t.* carry on petty traffic in (lit. or fig.); adulterate; hence **~ER¹** *n.* [f. prec.]

hu'ddle *v. & n.* **1.** *v.t.* ‖heap together confusedly; crowd (things etc.) promiscuously *together, up, into,* etc.; coil one*self up;* put (clothes) *on* hurriedly; hurry *over* or *through,* botch *up,* (work etc.). **2.** *v.i.* nestle closely *together, against,* etc. **3.** *n.* confused mass; confusion, bustle; (colloq.) close or secret conference. [16th c., perh. f. LG and ult. rel. to **hūd-* HIDE²; see -LE 3]

Hudibra'stic *a.* in the metre or manner of S. Butler's *Hudibras,* mock-heroic poem 1663–78, esp. with comical compound rhymes. [after *fantastic* etc.]

hue¹ *n.* colour, tint; attribute by virtue of which a colour is red, green, etc.; variety of colour caused by admixture of another; hence **-hūED²** (hūd), **~'LESS** (hū'l-), *adjs.* [OE *hīew, hēw,* form etc., = Goth. *hiwi* f. Gmc **hiwam*; cf. ON *hȳ* down on plant]

hue² *n.* **~ and cry,** loud cry raised for pursuit of wrongdoer, outcry (*against*), clamour; (Hist.) proclamation for capture of criminal. [f. OF *hu* outcry (*huer,* imit.)]

huff¹ *v.* **1.** *v.t.* (arch.) bully, storm at; bully (person *into, out of,* doing or *do*ing). **2.** *v.t. & i.* (cause to) take offence. **3.** *v.t.* (Draughts) remove (opponent's man that could have made a capture) from board as forfeit (orig. after blowing on the piece). **4.** *v.i.* give out puffs of air etc., (fig.) bluster (*huffing and puffing*). [imit. of sound of blowing]

huff² *n.* fit of petulance (*in a huff*); (Draughts). act of huffing; hence **~'ISH¹, ~'Y²,** *adjs.* [f. prec.]

hug *v.t.* (-gg-), & *n.* **1.** *v.t.* squeeze tightly in one's arms, usu. with affection; (of bear) squeeze (man etc.) between its forelegs; delight in, cling to, (prejudices etc.); (arch.) exhibit fondness for (person); congratulate one*self* (*on* or *for*); keep close to (shore, kerb, etc.); **~-me-tight,** knitted close-fitting usu. sleeveless woollen wrap; hence **~'GABLE** *a.* **2.** *n.* strong clasp with arms; squeezing grip in wrestling. [16th c., prob. f. Scand.; cf. ON *hugga* console]

huge *a.* extremely large, enormous; (of immaterial things) very great; hence **~'NESS** (-jn-) *n.* [ME *huge,* *hoge* f. OF *ahuge, ahoge,* of unkn. orig.]

hu'gely (-jlĭ) *adv.* enormously; very much. [ME, f. prec. +-LY²]

hu'geous (-jus) *a.* (arch. or joc.) huge; hence **~LY²** *adv.,* **~NESS** *n.* [f. HUGE + -OUS]

hu'gger-mugger (-g-; -g-) *n., a., adv., & v.* **1.** *n.* secrecy; confusion. **2.** *a. & adv.* secret(ly); confused(ly). **3.** *v.t.* conceal, hush *up.* **4.** *v.i.* proceed in secret or muddled fashion. [prob. rel. to ME *hoder* huddle, *mokere* conceal; cf. syn. 15th-c. *hoder moder,* 16th-c. *hucker mucker*]

Hu'guenot (-genŏt, -nō) *n.* (Hist.) French Protestant. [F, assim. of *eiguenot* (f. Du. *eedgenot* f. Swiss G *eidgenoss* confederate) to name of Geneva burgomaster *Hugues*]

*huh (hŭ) *int.* expr. interrogation, contempt, etc. [imit.]

hu'la (hoo'-) *n., & v.i.* **~**(**-~**), (perform) orig. Hawaiian woman's dance; **~ hoop,** large hoop for spinning round body with hula-like movements; **~ skirt,** long grass skirt. [Hawaiian]

hulk *n.* body of dismantled ship, used as store vessel etc. or (in *pl.,* Hist.) as prison; unwieldy vessel; (fig.) big person or mass. [OE *hulc* (= OHG *holko*), & f. MLG, MDu. *hulk*(*e*); cf. Gk *holkas* cargo ship]

hu'lking *a.* (colloq.) bulky; clumsy. [f. prec. +-ING²]

hull¹ *n., & v.t.* **1.** *n.* outer covering of fruit, esp. pod of peas and beans, husk of grain, or green calyx of strawberry; (fig.) covering. **2.** *v.t.* remove hull(s) of. [OE *hulu* (hul-, weak grade of *helan* cover; cf. HELE)]

hull² *n., & v.t.* **1.** *n.* body or frame of ship, airship, flying boat, etc.; **~ down,** (of ship) so far away that hull is below horizon, (of tank) concealed apart from gun-turret. **2.** *v.t.* strike (ship) in hull with shot etc. [ME, perh. cogn. w. HOLD³, or spec. use of prec.]

hu'llaballoo' *n.* uproar, clamour. [18th c., redupl. of *hallo, hullo,* etc.]

hullo'. Var. of HALLO, HELLO.

hum¹ *v.* (-mm-). **1.** *v.i.* make continuous low-pitched sound, as of bee, spinning top, etc.; make slight inarticulate vocal sound, esp. (usu. **~ and haw** or **ha**) of hesitation; (colloq.) be in state of activity (*make things hum*); ‖(sl.) smell unpleasantly. **2.** *v.i. & t.* sing (tune etc.) with closed lips. [ME; imit.]

hum² *n.* humming sound esp. of hesitation (usu. **~s and haws** or **ha's**); applause, surprise, etc.; (humming sound caused by) unwanted low-frequency variation of electric current etc.; ‖(sl.) bad smell. [ME; imit.]

hum³ *int.* expr. hesitation, dissent, etc. [imit.]

hu'man *a. & n.* **1.** *a.* of or belonging to the genus *Homo,* distinguished from animals by superior mental development, power of articulate speech, and upright posture (*human* NATURE); that is human or consists of human beings (*human creature, race*). **2.** of humans as opp. to God (*to err is human, to forgive divine; after all, he is only human*). **3.** having or showing the (esp. better) qualities distinctive of humans (*a very human person*); of humans as opp. to animals, machines, mere objects, etc. **4.** *human* ENGINEER¹; **~ engineering,** (study of) management of industrial labour, esp. as regards man–machine relationships; **~ equation,** = *personal* EQUATION (fig.); **~ interest,** reference to personal emotions (in newspaper story etc.); **~ relations** (concerning people as individuals); **~ rights** (held to be justifiably claimed by any person). **5.** Hence **~NESS** (-n-n-) *n.* **6.** *n.* human being. [ME *humain*(*e*) f. OF, f. L *humanus* (*homo* human being; see -AN)]

huma'ne *a.* **1.** benevolent, compassionate; inflicting the minimum of pain (**~ killer,** instrument for painless slaughter of animals). **2.** (Of branch of study) tending to civilize or confer refinement, elegant. **3.** Hence **~LY²** (-nlĭ) *adv.,* **~NESS** (-n-n-) *n.* [different. f. prec. after 1700]

hu'manism *n.* devotion to human interests; system concerned with human (not divine or supernatural) matters, or with the human race (not the individual), or with man as a responsible and progressive intellectual being; literary culture, esp. that of the

Renaissance humanists; doctrine emphasizing importance of common human needs and abstention from profitless theorizing. [f. foll. + -ISM]

hū′manist *n.* adherent of humanism; humanitarian; student (esp. in 14th-16th c.) of Roman and Greek literature and antiquities, whence **hūmani′stɪc** *a.* [f. F *humaniste* f. It. *umanista* (as HUMAN; see -IST)]

hūmănĭtār′ian *n.* & *a.* **1.** *n.* one who advocates or practises humane action, philanthropist; one who seeks to promote human welfare. **2.** *a.* relating to or holding the views of humanitarians. **3.** Hence ∼ISM (3) *n.* [f. foll. + -ARIAN]

hūmă′nitȳ *n.* **1.** being human; (in *pl.*) human attributes. **2.** the human race; human beings collectively. **3.** humaneness, benevolence. **4.** (Sc. Univ.) study of Latin. **5.** (in *pl.*) learning or literature concerned with human culture, esp. study of Latin and Greek classics. [ME, f. OF *humanité* f. L *humanitas -tatis* (as HUMAN; see -ITY)]

hū′manīz|e, -īs|e (-īz), *v.t.* make human, give human character to (∼ed milk, cow's milk prepared to resemble human milk); make humane; hence ∼A′TION *n.* [f. F *humaniser* (as HUMAN; see -IZE)]

hū′mankind (-n-k-) *n.* mankind. [f. HUMAN + KIND[1]]

hū′manlȳ *adv.* in a human manner; by human means (*I will do it if it is humanly possible*); from a human point of view (*humanly speaking*); with human feelings. [f. HUMAN + -LY[2]]

hū′mble *a.*, & *v.t.* **1.** *a.* having or showing low estimate of one's own importance; offered with such estimate (*humble apologies, opinion*); *your humble* SERVANT. **2.** of lowly rank or condition; (of thing) of modest pretensions, dimensions, etc.; *eat* ∼ *pie*, make humble apology, submit to humiliation [f. UMBLES]. **3.** Hence ∼NESS (-beln-) *n.*, **hū′mbLY[2]** *adv.* **4.** *v.t.* make humble, bring low, abase (*oneself* etc.). [ME (*h*)*umble* f. OF, f. L *humilis* lowly (*humus* ground)]

hū′mble-bee *n.* bumble-bee. [ME, prob. f. MLG *hummelbē*, MDu. *hommel*, OHG *humbal*; see BEE]

hū′mbŭg *n.* & *v.* (-gg-). **1.** *n.* fraud, sham; deception; impostor. **2.** ‖kind of hard boiled sweetmeat usu. flavoured with peppermint. **3.** *v.t.* delude (person *into, out of*, thing or doing). **4.** *v.i.* be, behave like, impostor. **5.** Hence ∼GERY (4) (-g-) *n.* [18th c., of unkn. orig.]

hŭmdĭnger (hŭ′-, -ĭ′-) *n.* (sl.) excellent or remarkable person or thing. [20th c.; orig. unkn.]

hŭ′mdrŭm *a.* & *n.* commonplace(ness), dull(ness); monotonous (routine etc.). [16th c., prob. f. HUM[1] by redupl.]

hū′meral *a.* & *n.* **1.** *a.* of the humerus; of the shoulder. **2.** *a.* & *n.* ∼ (veil), oblong scarf worn on shoulders by officiants at Eucharist. [f. F *huméral* & f. LL *humeralis* (as foll.; see -AL)]

hū′mer|us *n.* (*pl.* ∼i *pr.* -ī). bone of the upper arm in man; corresponding bone in other vertebrates. [L, = shoulder]

hū′mic. See HUMUS.

hū′mid *a.* moist, damp; hence **hūmi′difIER[1]** *n.* (esp. device for keeping atmosphere moist), **hūmi′difY** *v.t.*, ∼LY[2] *adv.* [f. F *humide* or f. L *humidus* (*ume̅re* be moist; see -ID[1])]

hūmi′ditȳ *n.* humid state; moisture; degree of moisture esp. in atmosphere (relative ∼, proportion of this quantity to value for saturation at same temperature). [ME, f. OF *humidité* or f. L *humiditas* (as prec.; see -ITY)]

hū′midôr *n.* box, room, etc., for keeping cigars or tobacco moist. [f. HUMID after *cuspidor*]

hū′mifȳ. See HUMUS.

hūmi′li|āte *v.t.* make humble, injure the dignity or self-respect of; so ∼A′TION *n.* [f. LL *humiliare* (as HUMBLE) + -ATE[3]]

hūmi′litȳ *n.* humbleness, meekness; humble condition. [ME, f. OF *humilité* f. L *humilitas -tatis* (as HUMBLE; see -ITY)]

hŭ′mmel *a.* (Sc.), of cattle or stags) hornless. [ME; cf. LG *hummel* hornless animal]

hŭ′mming *a.* In vbl senses; ∼-bird (of family Trochilidae, making humming sound by vibration of wings); ∼-top (that hums when it spins). [f. HUM[1] + -ING[2]]

hŭ′mmock *n.* hillock, knoll; *rising ground, esp. in marsh; hump or ridge in ice-field; hence ∼Y[2] *a.* [16th c., of unkn. orig.]

hŭ′mmŭm. Var. of HAMMAM.

***hŭ′mor[1],[2].** See HUMOUR[1],[2].

hū′moral *a.* (Med.) of the bodily humours; relating to body fluids esp. as opp. cells. [F, or f. med. L *humoralis* (as HUMOUR[1]; see -AL)]

hŭmoreˇ′sque (-k) *n.* (Mus.) short light capricious composition. [f. G *humoreske* (*humor* f. HUMOUR[1], -*eske* -ESQUE)]

hū′morist *n.* facetious person; humorous talker, actor, or writer; hence **hūmori′stɪc** *a.* [f. HUMOUR[1] + -IST]

hū′morous *a.* showing (sense of) humour; facetious, comic; hence ∼LY[2] *adv.*, ∼NESS *n.* [f. foll. + -OUS]

‖hū′mour[1] (-mer), *hū′mor[1], *n.* **1.** state of mind, mood; inclination, whim, (*in the humour for fighting*). **2.** facetiousness, comicality (less intellectual and more sympathetic than wit; (sense of) ∼, faculty of perceiving this and enjoying what is ludicrous or amusing, whence ∼LESS *a.* **3.** out of ∼, displeased; bad, good, ill, ∼ (temper), whence -∼ED[2] (-erd) *a.* **4.** (cardinal) ∼, (Hist.) one of four chief fluids of the body (blood, phlegm, choler, melancholy), thought to determine person's physical and mental qualities; AQUEOUS, VITREOUS, humour. [ME, f. AF (*h*)*umour*, OF f. L (*h*)*umor* moisture (as HUMID; see -OR)]

‖hū′mour[2] (-mer), *hū′mor[2], *v.t.* gratify, indulge, (person, taste, temper, etc.); adapt oneself to, make concessions to. [f. prec.]

‖hū′moursome (-mer-), *-mor-, *a.* capricious; peevish; hence ∼NESS (-mn-) *n.* [f. HUMOUR[1] + -SOME[1]]

hū′mous. See HUMUS.

hŭmp *n.*, & *v.t.* **1.** *n.* protuberance, esp. on the back, as deformity or (in camel etc.) as normal feature; live on one's ∼, be self-sufficient [w. ref. to camel's hump as reserve of nourishment]. **2.** rounded raised mass of earth etc.; mound over which railway vehicles are pushed so as to run by gravity to desired place. **3.** (fig.) critical point (of undertaking, ordeal, etc.); over the ∼, over the worst, well begun. **4.** ‖(sl.) fit of depression or vexation (*it gives me the hump*). **5.** ∼′back, (1) (person having) back with a hump, (2) whale with dorsal fin forming hump; ∼′backed, having such a back; ∼(back) bridge (with steep approach to top). **6.** Hence ∼ED[2] (-pt), ∼′LESS, *adjs.* **7.** *v.t.* make hump-shaped; annoy, depress; (‖, esp. Austral.) hoist up, shoulder, (one's pack, etc.); (sl.) exert one*self*; (vulg.) copulate with. [17th c., *hump--backed* replacing *crump-backed*; perh. rel. to LG *humpe* hump, LG *humpe*, Du. *homp* lump, hunk (of bread)]

humph (hmf) *int.*, *n.*, & *v.i.* (utter) inarticulate sound expr. doubt or dissatisfaction. [imit.]

‖hū′mptȳ *n.* low padded cushion seat. [f. *humpty* a. humpbacked, perh. f. foll.]

Hŭmptȳ-Dŭ′mptȳ *n.* short dumpy person; [from nursery rhyme in which name is taken to mean an egg] person or thing that once overthrown cannot be restored; [from Lewis Carroll's *Through the Looking-Glass*] person who makes words mean what he chooses. [perh. f. foll. & DUMPY; -*ty* unexpl.]

hŭ′mpȳ[1] *a.* having hump(s); humplike. [f. HUMP + -Y[2]]

hŭ′mpȳ[2] *n.* (Australian Aboriginal) hut. [f. Aboriginal *oompi*, infl. by HUMP]

hū′m|us *n.* organic constituent of soil, formed by decomposition of plant materials; hence -IC, ∼OUS *adjs.*, ∼IFY *v.t.* & *i.* [L, = soil]

Hŭn *n.* one of an Asiatic warlike nomad race who invaded and ravaged Europe in 4th-5th c.; uncivilized devastator, vandal; (usu. derog.) German (esp. Prussian); hence ∼′nISH[1] *a.* [OE *Hūne* pl. f. LL *Hunni* f. Gk *Hounnoi* f. Turki *Hun-yü*]

hŭnch[1] *v.* **1.** *v.t.* bend or arch convexly; thrust out or up to form a hump. **2.** *v.i.* *sit thus. [16th c.; orig. unkn.]

hŭnch[2] *n.* **1.** hump; thick piece; ∿**back(ed)**, = *humpback(ed)*. **2.** hint; premonition, intuitive feeling. [f. *hunch-backed*, 16th c., of unkn. orig.]

hŭ'ndred *a.* & *n.* (*pl.* ∿ *or* ∿**s**). **1.** ten times ten (*a, one, six, several, hundred men*; *a, one, six hundred of them, of my friends*; *hundreds of men, of them*; *some, several, many*, (arch.) *six, hundreds of*); symbol for this (100, c, C); set of 100, £100, etc.; (**a**) ∿ (**and one**), large number of; *1700* etc. HOURS; *not a hundred* MILES *from*; **a** ∿ **to one**, a high probability; **a** *or* **one** ∿ **per cent**, entire(ly), complete(ly), (usu. *not*) fully recovered; (**a**) ∿ **and one** etc., one hundred plus one etc., w. corresp. ordinals ∿**-and-first** etc. **2.** ||(esp. Hist.; *pl.* ∿**s**). subdivision of county or shire, having its own court; ||CHILTERN HUNDREDS. **3.** = foll. **4.** great or long ∿, 120; ∿**s and thousands**, tiny coloured sweets used chiefly for decorating cakes etc.; H∿ **Years War** (between England and France, 1337–1453); **the seventeen-**∿**s**, years 1700–1799. **5.** Hence ∿FOLD *a.*, *adv.*, & *n.*, (-)∿TH[2] *a.* & *n.* (**Old H**∿**th**, hymn 'All people that . . .', metrical version of Ps. 100 or its tune). [OE, = OS *hunderod*, ON *hundrath* f. Gmc *hundam hundred + *rath number]

hŭ'ndredweight (-wat) *n.* (*pl.* ∿ *or* ∿**s**). (**long**) ∿, ||112 lb. avoirdupois; (**metric**) ∿, 50 kg.; (**short**) ∿, *100 lb. [f. prec. + WEIGHT[1]]

hŭng. See HANG[1].

Hŭngār'ian (-ngg-) *a.* & *n.* **1.** *a.* of Hungary or its inhabitants. **2.** *n.* native or inhabitant of Hungary; Magyar language. [f. med. L *Hungaria* f. (*H*)*ungari* Magyar nation; see -AN]

hŭ'nger[1] (-ngg-) *n.* uneasy or painful sensation, exhausted condition, caused by lack of food; (fig.) strong desire (*for, after*, etc.); ∿**-march** (undertaken by body of unemployed etc.) to call attention to their condition); ∿**-strike**, refusal of food in order to procure release from prison, improvement of conditions, etc. [OE *hungor*, – OS, OHG *hungar*, ON *hungr* f. Gmc *hungruz]

hŭ'nger[2] (-ngg-) *v.* **1.** *v.i.* feel hunger; have craving (*for, after*); (in *p.p.*, arch.) hungry. **2.** *v.t.* starve (*into* submission, *out of* place etc.). [OE *hyngran*, assim. to prec.]

hŭ'ngr'ÿ (-ngg-) *a.* **1.** feeling hunger; showing hunger (*a hungry look*); inducing hunger (*a hungry air*); ∿**y rĭce**, W. Afr. grain allied to millet. **2.** (fig.) eager, greedy; (of soil) poor, barren; ||H∿**y Forties**, (Hist.) decade 1840–9 in Britain, a period of great distress among the poor. **3.** Hence ∿ĬLY[2] *adv.*, ∿ĬNESS *n.* [OE *hungrig* (as HUNGER[1]; see -Y[2])]

hŭnk *n.* large piece cut off; thick or clumsy piece. [19th c., prob. f. LDu.]

hŭ'nker *v.i.* crouch, squat, (*down*). [orig. Sc.; cf. MLG *hūken*, ON *húka*]

hŭ'nkers (-z) *n.* *pl.* the hams (**on** one's ∿, in a squatting position). [orig. Sc., f. prec.]

hŭnks *n.* niggardly man, miser. [17th c.; orig. unkn.]

***hŭ'nkÿ** *n.* (sl., derog.) person from Central or E. Europe. [prob. f. HUNGARIAN + -Y[3]]

***hŭnkÿ-dōr'ÿ** *a.* (sl.) excellent. [19th c.; orig. unkn.]

hŭ'nnish. See HUN.

hŭnt[1] *v.* **1.** *v.i.* & *t.* pursue wild animals, esp. foxes; chase (these) for food or sport; (of animal) chase (its prey). **2.** *v.i.* seek after, *for*; oscillate; (of engine etc.) run alternately too fast and too slow. **3.** *v.t.* drive by pursuit (*away* etc.); scour (district) in pursuit of game; use (horse, hounds) in hunting; *shoot (game); (in *p.p.*, of look etc.) expressing terror as if one were being hunted. **4.** move place of (bell) in ringing changes (*up* to last place, *down* to first place). **5.** ∿ **down**, bring to bay; ∿ **out**, track out, find by search; ∿ **up**, search for and find; ∿ **the hare, slipper, squirrel, thimble**, games of pursuit or search. [OE *huntian*, weak grade of *hentan* seize]

hŭnt[2] *n.* hunting (lit. or fig.); association of persons hunting with a pack; hunting district; oscillatory motion; ∿ **ball** (given by members of hunt). [ME, f. prec.]

hŭ'nter *n.* one who hunts or (fig.) seeks something (FORTUNE[1]-*hunter*); horse for hunting; watch with hinged cover protecting glass or (**half-**∿) outer part of it; ∿**'s moon**, next full moon after harvest moon; hence **hŭ'ntrESS**[1] *n.* [ME, f. HUNT[2] + -ER[1]]

hŭ'nting. In vbl senses; ∿**-box**, small house for use during hunting-season; ∿**-cat**, cheetah; *hunting--CROP*[1]; ∿**-ground**, place where one hunts (lit. or fig.); *happy* ∿*-ground(s)*, life after death (esp. as expected by Amer. Indians), good place for hunting (fig.); ∿**-horn**, (1) horn used in hunting, (2) second pommel on near side of side-saddle; ∿ **leopard**, cheetah; ∿**-lodge**, accommodation for hunters; *hunting* PINK[1]. [OE *huntung* (as HUNT[1], -ING[1])]

Hunts. *abbr.* Huntingdonshire (former county in England).

hŭ'nts|man *n.* (*pl.* ∿**men**). hunter; man in charge of (esp. fox) hounds. [f. HUNT[2] + -'s 1 + MAN[1]]

hur'dle *n.*, & *v.t.* **1.** *n.* portable rectangular frame strengthened with withes or wooden bars, for temporary fence etc.; upright wooden frame to be jumped over in race; (in *pl.*) race over such frames; (fig.) obstacle, difficulty; (Hist.) frame on which traitors were dragged to execution. **2.** *v.t.* fence off etc. with hurdles; leap over (lit. or fig.). [OE *hyrdel* f. Gmc *hurdhilaz (*hurdhiz f. IE **krt-*; see -LE 1)]

hur'dler *n.* one who makes hurdles; one who races over hurdles. [f. prec. + -ER[1]]

hur'dÿ-gurdÿ *n.* musical instrument with droning sound, played by turning handle, esp. one with rosined wheel turned by right hand to sound drone--strings, and keys played by left hand; (colloq.) barrel-organ. [prob. imit.]

hurl *v.* & *n.* **1.** *v.t.* throw violently from some position (lit. or fig.); throw (missile etc., or fig.). **2.** *v.i.* play hurley; hence ∿'ING[1] *n.*, game of hurley. **3.** *n.* hurling; violent throw. [ME, prob. imit., but corresp. in form and partly sense w. LG *hurreln*]

hur'ley *n.* (stick used in) Irish form of hockey; broad sticks. [f. prec.]

hur'lÿ-burlÿ, (arch.) **hur'lÿ**, *ns.* commotion, tumult. [(redupl.) f. HURL V.]

hurrah', hurray' (hu-, hōō-) *int.*, *n.*, & *v.i.* **1.** *int.* expr. exultation or approbation. **2.** *n.*, & *v.i.* cry or shout 'hurrah', 'hurray'. [alt. of HUZZA]

hŭ'rricane (-an, -ān) *n.* storm with violent wind, esp. W. Ind. cyclone; (Meteorol.) wind with velocity of 73 m.p.h. or more; violent commotion; ∿**-bird**, frigate--bird; ∿**-deck**, light upper deck; ∿**-house**, shelter at mast-head or on deck; ∿**-lamp** (designed to resist high wind). [f. Sp. *huracan*, & Port. *furacão*, of Carib orig.]

hŭ'rrÿ[1] *n.* great haste; eagerness to get a thing done quickly; eagerness (*to do, for* thing); (w. neg. or interrog.) need for haste (*there is no hurry*); (colloq.) *you will not beat that* **in a** ∿ (easily), *shall not ask again* **in a** ∿ (willingly); ∿**-scurry**, (*adv., a.*, & *n.*) (in) disorderly haste, (*v.i.*) proceed thus. [16th c., imit.]

hŭ'rrÿ[2] *v.* **1.** *v.t.* carry, drive, (person etc. *away, along, into, into* doing, *on*, etc.) with undue haste; (in *p.p.*) hasty, done rapidly owing to lack of time. **2.** *v.i.* move or act with great or undue haste; ∿ **along, up**, (colloq.) make haste. [as prec.]

hŭrst *n.* hillock; sandbank in sea or river; wooded eminence; wood. [OE *hyrst*, rel. to OS, OHG *hurst, horst*]

hurt[1] *n.* bodily or material injury; harm, wrong; hence ∿'FUL, ∿'LESS, *adjs.* [ME, f. OF *hurt* (*hurter*; see foll.)]

hurt[2] *v.* (**hurt**). **1.** *v.t.* cause bodily injury or pain to; damage; inflict injury upon; wound, (person, his feelings, etc.). **2.** *v.i.* cause pain or harm; (colloq.) suffer pain (*does your hand hurt?*). [ME, f. OF *hurter* f. Gallo-Rom. *hurtare, perh. f. Gmc]

hŭr'tle v. **1.** v.i. strike *against*; move with clattering or rattling sound; come with a crash; move rapidly. **2.** v.t. hurl swiftly. [f. prec. in obs. sense 'strike forcibly' + -LE 3]

hŭ'sband[1] (-z-) n. married man esp. in relation to his wife (cf. WIFE 2); (arch.) **good, bad**, ~ (manager of his affairs); SHIP[1]'s *husband*; hence ~HOOD, ~SHIP, ns., ~LIKE a. [OE *hūsbonda* f. ON *húsbóndi* (as HOUSE[1], BOND[3])]

hŭ'sband[2] (-z-) v.t. manage thriftily, use economically; (arch.) till (ground), cultivate (plants); (arch.) provide with husband, marry, (woman). [ME, f. prec.]

hŭ'sband|man (-z-) n. (*pl.* ~men). (arch.) farmer. [ME, f. HUSBAND[1] + MAN[1]]

hŭ'sbandrў (-z-) n. farming; (*good, bad*) management of affairs; careful management. [ME, f. HUSBAND[1] + -RY]

hŭsh[1] n. stillness; silence; ~**-money** (paid to prevent disclosure). [f. foll.]

hŭsh[2] v. **1.** v.t. silence, quiet; ~ **up**, suppress public mention of (affair). **2.** v.i. be silent (esp. in *imper.* as *int.*). **3.** ~'**aby(e)** *int.* (used to lull child); ~-~, (colloq.) to be kept highly secret; ~ **puppy**, (1) *quickly fried maize bread, (2) (H- P-; **P**) light soft shoe. [back-form. f. obs. *husht* a. f. *hust*, WHIST[1], ints.]

hŭsk n., & v.t. **1.** n. dry outer covering of some fruits or seeds, esp. of nut or *maize; (fig.) worthless outside part of anything. **2.** v.t. remove husk(s) from. [ME, prob. f. LG *hūske* sheath, dim. of *hūs* HOUSE[1]]

hŭ'sk|ў[1] a. & n. **1.** a. of or full of husks; dry as a husk; (of voice or person) dry in the throat, hoarse, whence ~ĭLY[2] *adv.*, ~ĭNESS n. **2.** a. & *n.* (colloq.) tough, strong, hefty, (person). [f. prec. + -Y[2]]

hŭ'skў[2] n. = ESKIMO *dog.* [perh. contr. f. ESKIMO]

hŭss n. dogfish (esp. nurse-hound) as food. [ME *husk(e)*, of unkn. orig.]

hussăr' (hŏŏz-) n. soldier of light cavalry regiment; (orig.) Hungarian light horseman of 15th c. [f. Magyar *huszár* f. OSerb. *husar* f. It. *corsaro* CORSAIR]

Hŭ'ssīte n. (Hist.) follower of Huss. [f. John *Hus(s)*, Bohemian religious and nationalist reformer d. 1415 + -ITE[1]]

hŭ'ssў (-sĭ, -zĭ), **hŭ'zzў**, n. woman of light or worthless character; pert girl. [f. HOUSEWIFE]

hŭ'stings (-z) n. (Parliamentary) election proceedings; (Hist.) platform from which (before 1872) candidates for Parliament were nominated and addressed electors. [pl. of *husting*, OE, f. ON *hústhing* house of assembly (cf. HOUSE[1], THING)]

hŭ'stle (-sel) v. & n. **1.** v.t. push roughly, jostle; thrust (person etc. *into, out of*, etc.); impel unceremoniously (*into* thing or do*ing*); (sl.) obtain by forceful action; (sl.) swindle. **2.** v.i. push roughly *against*; push one's way; hurry, bustle. **3.** n. hustling. [f. MDu. *husselen* shake, toss, frequent. of *hutsen*, orig. imit.]

hŭ'stler (-sl-) n. In vbl senses; (sl.) prostitute. [f. prec. + -ER[1]]

hŭt n. & v. (-tt-). **1.** n. small simple or crude house or shelter; (Mil.) temporary wooden etc. house for troops; ~**-circle**, (Archaeol.) ring of stones or earth indicating site of prehistoric hut. **2.** v.t. place (troops etc.) in huts; furnish with huts. **3.** v.i. lodge in hut. **4.** Hence ~'MENT n., hutted encampment. [f. F *hutte* f. MHG *hütte*]

hŭtch n. boxlike pen for rabbits etc.; (derog.) hut, cabin, small house. [ME, = coffer, f. OF *huche* f. med. L *hutica*, of unkn. orig.]

Hŭ'tterīte n. member of (N. Amer. immigrant) sect of anabaptists. [f. J. *Hutter*, Moravian anabaptist d. 1536 + -ITE (1)]

Huzoor' n. (arch.) Title used by Indians in respectful address. [f. Arab. *ḥuḍūr* presence (*ḥaḍara* be present)]

huzza' (-ah) *int.*, *n.*, & v. (~**ed** or ~'**d**, *pr.* -ah'd). (arch.) **1.** *int.* expr. exultation, encouragement, or applause. **2.** *n.*, & v.i. & t. (make, greet with) the cry 'huzza'. [16th c., perh. orig. sailor's cry when hauling]

hŭ'zzў. See HUSSY.

h.w. *abbr.* hit wicket.

HWM *abbr.* high-water mark.

hw'ўl (hŏŏ'-) n. emotional quality inspiring impassioned eloquence. [W]

Hy. *abbr.* Henry.

hy'acĭnth n. **1.** bulbous plant of genus *Hyacinthus* with racemes of bell-shaped (esp. purplish-blue fragrant) flowers; GRAPE *hyacinth*; **wild** or **wood** ~, squill (*Scilla nonscripta*) with drooping bell-shaped flowers; so (esp. as Homeric epithet of doubtful sense for *locks, hair*) ~INE[2] (-sĭ'-) a. **2.** purplish-blue colour of hyacinth. **3.** precious stone, orange variety of zircon. [f. F *hyacinthe* f. L f. Gk *huakinthos*, flower and gem, also name of youth loved by Apollo]

Hy'adēs (-z) n. pl. group of stars in Taurus near Pleiades, whose heliacal rising was thought to foretell rain. [ME, f. Gk *Huades* (acc. to pop. etym., f. *huō* rain, but perh. f. *hus* pig)]

hyae'na. See HYENA.

hy'aline (-ĭn, -ēn) a. & n. **1.** a. glasslike, vitreous; ~ **degeneration** (in which body-tissues become translucent). **2.** n. (literary). smooth sea, clear sky, etc. [f. L f. Gk *hualinos* (*hualos* glass; see -INE[2])]

hy'alīte n. colourless variety of opal. [f. Gk *hualos* glass + -ITE[1]]

hy'aloid a. & n. (Anat.) glassy; ~ (**membrane**), transparent membrane enveloping vitreous humour of eye. [f. F *hyaloïde* f. LL f. Gk *hualoeidēs* (as prec.; see -OID)]

hy'brĭd n. & a. **1.** n. offspring of two animals or plants of different species or varieties; person of mixed origins; (fig.) thing composed of incongruous elements, esp. word with parts taken from different languages. **2.** a. bred as hybrid from different species or varieties; heterogeneous; ~ **vigour**, heterosis; hence ~ISM (1, 2), ~ITY (-ĭ'd-), ns. [f. L *hybrida*, (*h*)*ibrida* offspring of tame sow and wild boar, child of freeman and slave, etc.]

hy'brĭdīz|e, -īs|e (-īz), v. **1.** v.t. subject (species etc.) to cross-breeding. **2.** v.i. produce hybrids; (of animal or plant) interbreed. **3.** Hence ~ABLE a., ~A'TION n. [f. prec. + -IZE]

hy'datĭd n. (Path.) cyst containing watery fluid (esp. one formed by, and containing, a tapeworm larva); tapeworm larva; hence ~ĭFORM (-ĭ'd-) a. [f. mod. L f. Gk *hudatis -idos* watery vesicle (*hudōr hudatos* water; see -ID[2])]

hy'dra n. thing hard to extirpate; water-snake; freshwater polyp of genus *Hydra* etc., with tubular body and tentacles around mouth. [ME, f. L f. Gk *hudra* water-snake, in Gk Myth. one whose many heads grew again when cut off]

hydră'ngea (-nja) n. shrub of genus *Hydrangea* with globular clusters of white, blue, or pink flowers. [mod. L, f. Gk *hudōr* water + *aggos* vessel (from cup-shape of seed-capsule)]

hy'drant n. pipe (esp. in street) with nozzle to which hose can be attached, for drawing water from main. [irreg. f. HYDRO- + -ANT]

hy'drāte n. (Chem.) compound of water with another compound or an element. [F, f. Gk *hudōr* water; see -ATE[1]]

hy'dr|āte[2] v.t. combine chemically with water; cause to absorb water; hence ~A'TION n. [f. prec.]

hydrau'lic a. & n. **1.** a. of water or other liquid conveyed through pipes and channels; operated by movement of liquid (*hydraulic brakes, lift*); concerned with hydraulics (*hydraulic engineer*); ~ **press**, hydrostatic press; ~ **ram**, automatic pump in which kinetic energy of descending column of water raises some of the water above its original level. **2.** hardening under water (*hydraulic cement*). **3.** Hence **hydrau'lICALLY** *adv.* **4.** n. (in *pl.*, usu. treated as *sing.*) science of conveyance of liquids through pipes etc., esp. as motive power. [f. L f. Gk *hudraulikos* (*hudōr* water, *aulos* pipe; see -IC)]

hȳ′drazine (-ēn) *n.* (Chem.) colourless alkaline liquid, N_2H_4, used as reducing agent and rocket propellant. [f. HYDROGEN + AZO- + -INE⁵]

hȳ′dric *a.* (Chem.) of or containing hydrogen. [f. HYDROGEN + -IC]

hȳ′dride *n.* (Chem.) binary compound of hydrogen esp. with metal. [f. HYDROGEN + -IDE]

hȳdriŏ′dic *n.* (Chem.) containing hydrogen and iodine (∼ **acid,** HI). [f. HYDROGEN + IODINE + -IC]

hȳ′drō *n.* (*pl.* ∼s). (colloq.) hotel etc. providing hydropathic treatment; hydroelectric power plant. [abbr.]

hȳ′dro- *comb. form,* w. senses (1) having to do with water, (2, Path.) dropsical, affected with accumulation of serous fluid, (3, Chem.) combined with hydrogen, as: ∼**bro′mic,** containing hydrogen and bromine; ∼**car′bon,** compound of hydrogen and carbon; ∼**cele,** (Path.) accumulation of serous fluid; ∼**ce′phalus,** water on the brain, esp. in young children with resulting mental deficiency; ∼**chlor′ic,** containing hydrogen and chlorine (∼*chloric acid,* HCl); ∼**chlor′ide,** compound of organic base with hydrochloric acid; ∼**cya′nic,** containing hydrogen and cyanogen (∼*cyanic acid,* HCN, highly poisonous volatile liquid); ∼**cle′ctric,** developing electricity by utilization of water-power, (of electricity) produced thus; ∼**fluo′ric,** containing hydrogen and fluorine; ∼**grapher** (-ŏ′g-) person skilled in, ∼**gra′phic(al)** having to do with, ∼**graphy** (-ŏ′g-,), scientific study of seas, lakes, rivers, etc.; ∼**logy** (-ŏ′l-), science of the properties, laws, etc., of water, esp. of its movement on, under, and above land; ∼**magne′tic,** involving hydrodynamics and magnetism, magnetohydrodynamic; ∼**ma′nia,** craving for water; ∼**mecha′nics,** mechanics of liquids; ∼**phane,** opal that absorbs water and becomes transparent on immersion [f. Gk *phanēs* apparent]; ∼**phone,** instrument for detection of sound-waves in water; ∼**phyte,** aquatic plant (esp. alga), plant needing much moisture; ∼**plane,** finlike device enabling submarine to rise or fall, light fast motor boat designed to skim over surface, seaplane; ∼**pneuma′tic,** involving combined action of water and air; ∼**qui′none,** substance formed by reduction of quinone, used as photographic developer; ∼**sphere,** waters of the earth's surface; ∼**the′rapy,** hydropathy; ∼**ther′mal,** of the action of heated water on earth's crust; ∼**thor′ax,** dropsy of the chest; ∼**tropism** (-ŏ′t-), (of plant-roots etc.) tendency to turn to or from moisture. [f. Gk *hudro-* (*hudōr* water; see -o-)]

hȳdrodynȧ′m|ic(al) *adjs.* of forces acting on or exerted by liquids (esp. water); so ∼ics *n.* [f. mod. L *hydrodynamicus* (as HYDRO-, DYNAMIC)]

hȳ′drofoil *n.* (vessel fitted with) structure designed to generate (esp. lifting) force when moving through liquid, esp. under vessel's hull to lift it out of water at speed. [f. HYDRO-, after AEROfoil]

hȳ′drogen *n.* colourless tasteless odourless gaseous element, the lightest substance known, combining with oxygen to form water; ∼ **bomb,** immensely powerful bomb utilizing explosive fusion of hydrogen nuclei; *hydrogen* PEROXIDE; ∼ **sulphide,** colourless poisonous gas, H_2S, with disagreeable smell, formed by rotting animal matter; hence **hȳdrŏ′gĕn**OUS *a.* [f. F *hydrogène* (as HYDRO-, -GEN)]

hȳdrogen|āte (hī′droj-, -ŏ′j-) *v.t.* charge, cause (esp. unsaturated compound) to combine, with hydrogen; hence ∼A′TION *n.* [f. prec. + -ATE³]

hȳ′droid *a.* & *n.* (Zool.) (animal) like or allied to the hydra polyp. [f. HYDRA + -OID]

hȳdrŏ′lys|is *n.* (*pl.* ∼es *pr.* -ēz). decomposition by chemical reaction with water; so **hȳ′drolyse** (-z), *-**lyze,** *v.t.,* decompose thus; **hȳdrolȳ′t**IC *a.* [f. HYDRO- + -LYSIS]

hȳ′dromel *n.* mixture of honey and water. [ME, f. L f. Gk *hudromeli* (as HYDRO-, *meli* honey)]

hȳdrŏ′|mĕter *n.* instrument for determining density of liquids; so **hȳdromĕ′tr**IC *a.,* ∼METRY *n.* [f. HYDRO- + -METER]

hȳdrŏ′path|ȳ *n.* medical treatment by external and internal application of water; hence **hȳdropā′th**IC *a.,* ∼IST (3) *n.* [f. HYDRO-, after *homoeopathy* etc.]

hȳdrophi′lic *a.* having affinity for water; wettable by water. [f. HYDRO- + Gk *philos* loving + -IC]

hȳdrophō′bia *n.* aversion to water, esp. as symptom of rabies in man; rabies, esp. in man; morbid dread of water. [LL, f. Gk *hudrophobia* (as HYDRO-, -PHOBIA)]

hȳdrophō′bic *a.* 1. of or suffering from hydrophobia. 2. not readily wettable. [f. prec. + -IC]

hȳdrŏ′pic *a.* dropsical. [ME, f. OE *ydropique* f. L f. Gk *hudrōpikos* (as HYDROPSY; see -IC)]

hȳdropō′nics *n.* soilless culture, art of growing plants without soil, in (sand, etc. containing) water impregnated with nutrients. [f. HYDRO- + Gk *ponos* labour; see -ICS]

hȳ′drŏpsȳ *n.* (arch.) dropsy. [ME, f. OF *idropesie* f. med. L (*h*)*ydropisia* f. L *hydropisis* f. Gk *hudrōps* (*hudōr* water)]

hȳdrostȧ′tic *a.* & *n.* 1. *a.* of the equilibrium of liquids and the pressure exerted by liquids at rest; ∼ **paradox,** principle that any quantity of a perfect liquid, however small, may be made to balance any other quantity; ∼ **press,** machine in which pressure of a body of water gives increased force by transmission from small to larger cylinder; hence ∼AL *a.,* ∼ALLY *adv.* 2. *n.* (in *pl.,* usu. treated as *sing.*) branch of mechanics concerned with the pressure and equilibrium of liquids at rest. [prob. f. Gk *hudrostatēs* hydrostatic balance (as HYDRO-; see STATIC)]

hȳ′drous *a.* (Chem. & Min.) containing water. [f. Gk *hudōr hudro-* water + -OUS]

hȳdrŏ′xȳde *n.* (Chem.) compound of element or radical with hydroxyl. [f. HYDRO- + OXIDE]

hȳdrŏ′xȳl *n.* (Chem.) radical containing hydrogen and oxygen, OH; so **hȳdrŏ′xȳ-** *comb. form.* [f. HYDROGEN + OXYGEN + YL]

hȳdrozō′an *a.* & *n.* (animal) of class Hydrozoa of mainly marine coelenterates. [f. mod. L *Hydrozoa* (as HYDRA, Gk *zōion* animal); see -A) + -AN]

hȳē′na, hȳae′na, *n.* carnivorous strong-jawed quadruped of order Hyaenidae (**laughing** ∼, species whose howl is compared to fiendish laughter); cruel, treacherous, or rapacious person; Tasmanian wolf; ∼-**dog,** bright coloured hyena-like S. Afr. canine quadruped. [ME, f. OF *hyene* & f. L f. Gk *huaina* fem. of *hus* pig]

Hȳgei′|a (-jē′a) *n.* personification of health; hence **h**∼AN *a.* [f. Gk *Hugeia* goddess of health (*hugiēs* healthy)]

hȳ′gien|e (-jēn) *n.* principles of maintaining health; practice of these, e.g. by cleanliness; hence ∼IC *a.,* ∼ICALLY *adv.,* ∼ICS *n.,* (-jē′-), ∼IST (3) *n.* [f. F *hygiène* f. mod. L f. Gk *hugieinē* (*tekhnē* art) of health (*hugiēs* healthy)]

hȳ′gro- *comb. form.* moisture, as: ∼**logy** (-ŏ′l-), study of humidity of atmosphere etc.; ∼**meter** (-ŏ′m-), instrument for measuring humidity of air or gas; ∼**me′tric,** ∼**metry** (-ŏ′m-), concerned with, measurement of, humidity; ∼**philous** (-ŏ′f-), (of plant) growing in moist environment; ∼**phyte,** = HYDRO*phyte*; ∼**scope,** instrument indicating but not measuring humidity of air; ∼**sco′pic,** of the hygroscope, (of substance) tending to absorb moisture from the air. [f. Gk *hugro-* (*hugros* wet, moist; see -o-)]

hȳ′ing. See HIE.

Hȳ′ksŏs *n. pl.* Asiatic invaders who ruled Egypt approx. from 17th to 16th c. BC. [f. Gk *Huksōs* f. Egypt. *heqa khoswe* foreign rulers]

hȳ′lic *a.* of matter, material. [f. LL f. Gk *hulikos* (*hulē* matter; see -IC)]

hȳ′lo- *comb. form.* matter, as: ∼**mor′phism,** doctrine that primordial matter is first cause of the universe and combines with forms to produce bodies;

hȳ′pha n. (pl. ∼e). filament in mycelium of fungus. [mod. L, f. Gk huphē web]

hȳ′phen n., & v.t. **1.** n. sign (-) used to join two words together (rock-forming), to connect separated syllables of word broken at end of line, to divide word into parts, to begin or end an incomplete word (hyper-), to represent hesitant speech (b-b-but), etc. **2.** v.t. join (words) with hyphen; write (compound word) with hyphen. [LL, f. Gk huphen together (hupo under, hen one)]

hȳ′phen|āte v.t. = prec. 2 (∼ated Americans, of mixed nationality: Irish-Americans, etc.); hence ∼A′TION n. [f. prec. +-ATE³]

hȳ′pno- comb. form. sleep, hypnosis, as: ∼ge′nesis, induction of hypnotic state; ∼logy (-ŏ′l-), science of the phenomena of sleep; ∼pae′dia, learning by hearing while asleep; ∼the′rapy, treatment of disease by hypnosis. [f. Gk hupnos sleep+-o-]

hȳpnō′s|is n. (pl. ∼es pr. -ēz). sleep artificially produced; state produced by hypnotism. [mod. L, f. Gk hupnos sleep; see -OSIS]

hȳpnŏ′t|ic a. & n. **1.** a. of or producing hypnotism; (of drug) soporific; hence ∼ICALLY adv. **2.** n. thing that produces sleep; person under (or open to) influence of hypnotism. [f. F hypnotique f. LL f. Gk hupnōtikos (hupnoō put to sleep; see -OTIC)]

hȳ′pnot|ism n. (artificial production of) state resembling deep sleep, in which subject acts only on external suggestion; so ∼IST (1) n., ∼IZE (3) n.t. (lit. or fig.). [f. prec. +-ISM]

hȳ′pō¹ n. (Photog.) sodium thiosulphate (incorrectly called HYPOsulphite), used in fixing. [abbr.]

hȳ′pō² n. (pl. ∼s). = HYPODERMIC 3. [abbr.]

hȳpo- pref. (usu. hyp- bef. vowel or h) w. sense 'under' (hypodermic), 'below normal' (hypoxia; opp. HYPER-), 'slightly' (hypomania), (Chem.) containing element combined in low valence (hypochlorous, hypochlorite), (Mus., of mode) plagal, starting from dominant of, (hypo-Aeolian etc.). [Gk (hupo under)]

hȳ′poblast n. (Biol.) innermost layer of gastrula; endoderm. [f. mod. L hypoblastus (as HYPO-, -BLAST)]

hȳ′pocaust n. (Rom. Ant.) hollow space under floor in which heat from furnace was accumulated for heating house or bath. [f. L f. Gk hupokauston place heated from below (as HYPO-, kaiō, kau-, burn)]

hȳpochŏ′ndrĭa (-k-) n. morbid depression without real cause; (unnecessary) anxiety about one's health. [LL, f. Gk hupokhondria soft parts of the body below ribs (whence melancholy was thought to arise; as HYPO-, khondros sternal cartilage)]

hȳpochŏ′ndrĭăc (-k-) a. & n. **1.** a. of or affected by hypochondria. **2.** n. hypochondriac person. [f. F hypocondriaque f. Gk hupokhondriakos (as prec.; see -AC)]

hȳpocorī′stic a. (Gram.) of the nature of a pet name. [f. Gk hupokoristikos (hupokorizomai call by pet names)]

hȳpocŏ′tyl n. (Bot.) part of embryo or seedling below cotyledon(s). [f. HYPO-+COTYLEDON]

hȳpŏ′crisy n. simulation of virtue or goodness; dissimulation, pretence. [ME, f. OF ypocrisie f. eccl. L f. Gk hupokrisis acting of a part, pretence (hupokrinomai f. hupo- HYPO-+krinō decide, judge)]

hȳ′pocrit|e n. person guilty of hypocrisy; dissembler, pretender; so ∼ICAL (-ĭ′t-) a. [ME, f. OF ypocrite f. eccl. L f. Gk hupokritēs actor (as prec.)]

hȳpocȳ′cloid n. (Math.) curve traced by point on circumference of circle rolling on interior of another circle; hence ∼AL (-oi′d-) a. [f. HYPO-+CYCLOID]

hȳpodĕr′m|ic a. & n. **1.** a. (Med., of drug etc.) introduced beneath the skin (hypodermic injection); (of needle, needle-pointed syringe, etc.) used thus; hence ∼ICALLY adv. **2.** (Anat.) lying under the skin. **3.** n. hypodermic injection or syringe. [f. hypoderma subcutaneous tissue (mod. L f. as HYPO-+Gk derma skin) +-IC]

hȳpogā′str|ium n. (pl. ∼ia). lowest (esp. central) region of abdomen; so ∼IC a. [mod. L, f. Gk hupogastrion (as HYPO-, gastēr belly); see -IUM]

hȳpogē′al, hȳpogē′an, adjs. (existing or growing) underground. [f. LL hypogeus f. Gk hupogeios (as HYPO-, gē earth) +-AL, -AN]

hȳ′pogēne a. (Geol.) produced under surface of earth. [f. HYPO-+Gk gen- produce]

hȳpogē′|um n. (pl. ∼a). underground chamber. [L, f. Gk hupogeion neut. (as n.) of hupogeios (see HYPOGEAL)]

hȳ′poid n. gear with pinion off centre-line of wheel, to connect non-intersecting shafts. [perh. f. HYPER-BOLOID]

hȳpoli′mni|on n. (pl. ∼a). lower layer of water in stratified lakes. [f. HYPO-+Gk limnion dim. of limnē lake]

hȳpo|mā′nĭa n. minor form of mania; hence ∼mā′nIC a. [mod. L, f. G hypomanie (as HYPO-, MANIA)]

hȳ′ponăstȳ n. (Bot.) tendency in plant-organs to grow more rapidly on underside. [f. HYPO- + Gk nastos pressed +-y¹]

hȳpŏ′phȳs|is n. (pl. ∼es pr. -ēz). (Anat.) = PITUITARY gland; hence ∼èAL, ∼IAL, (-of ĭ′z-) adjs. [mod. L, f. Gk hupophusis offshoot (as HYPO-, phusis growth)]

hȳpŏ′stas|is n. (pl. ∼es pr. -ēz). **1.** (Med.) excess of blood in lower parts of organs. **2.** (Metaphys.) underlying substance, opp. to attributes or to what is unsubstantial; so ∼IZE (3), **hȳpŏ′stat**IZE (3), vbs. t. **3.** (Theol.) personality (of Christ), person (of the Godhead); so **hȳpostā′t**IC(AL) adjs. (hypostatic union, of divine and human natures in Christ). [eccl. L, f. Gk hupostasis (as HYPO-, STASIS standing, state)]

hȳ′postȳle a. (Archit.) having roof supported on pillars. [f. Gk hupostulos (as HYPO-, STYLE)]

hȳpotä′xis n. (Gram.) subordination of one clause to another; so **hȳpotä′ct**IC a. [f. Gk hupotaxis (as HYPO-, TAXIS arrangement)]

hȳpotĕ′ns|ion (-shŏn) n. abnormally low blood pressure; hence ∼IVE a. [f. HYPO-+TENSION]

hȳpŏ′tenūse (-z) n. side opposite right angle of right-angled triangle. [f. L f. Gk hupoteinousa (grammē) subtending (line) fem. part. of hupoteinō (as HYPO-, teinō stretch)]

hȳpothă′lamus n. (Anat.) organ below brain, controlling body-temperature etc. [mod. L, f. as HYPO-, THALAMUS]

hȳ′pothēc n. (Rom. & Sc. Law). right established by law over thing belonging to debtor; so **hȳpŏ′thēc**ARY¹ a. [f. F hypothèque f. LL f. Gk hupothēkē deposit (as HYPO-, tithēmi place)]

hȳpŏ′thēc|āte v.t. pledge, mortgage; hence ∼A′TION n. [f. med. L hypothecare (as prec.) +-ATE³]

hȳpothĕr′mĭa n. (Med.) condition of having body-temperature below normal. [f. HYPO- + Gk thermē heat +-IA¹]

hȳpŏ′thĕs|is n. (pl. ∼es pr. -ēz). proposition made as basis for reasoning, without assumption of its truth; supposition made as starting-point for further investigation from known facts (cf. THEORY); groundless assumption; so **hȳpothĕ′t**ICAL a. [LL, f. Gk hupothesis foundation (as HYPO-, THESIS)]

hȳpŏ′thĕsize, -īse (-īz), v. **1.** v.i. frame a hypothesis. **2.** v.t. assume as hypothesis. [f. prec. +-IZE]

hȳpŏ′x|ia n. (Med.) deficiency of oxygen; hence ∼IC a. [f. HYPO-+OX-+-IA¹]

hȳpsŏ′graphȳ n. description or mapping of contours of earth's surface; hence **hȳpsogră′ph**IC(AL) adjs. [f. Gk hupsos height; see -GRAPHY]

hȳpsŏ′mĕter n. instrument for estimating altitudes, esp. from boiling-point of water etc.; hence **hȳpsomĕ′tr**IC a. [f. as prec. +-METER]

hȳr′ăx n. small ungulate mammal of order Hyracoidea, e.g. Syrian rock-rabbit and Afr. rock-badger. [mod. L, f. Gk hurax shrew-mouse]

hȳ′son n. kind of green tea from China. [f. Chin. xichun, lit. bright spring]

hȳ′ssop n. small bushy aromatic herb of genus Hyssopus, esp. species used medicinally; (Bibl.) plant whose twigs were used for sprinkling in Jewish rites, bunch of this used in purification. [ME *ysope* f. OE & f. OF f. L f. Gk *hyssōpos*, of Semitic orig.]

hỹsterĕ'ctom|ỹ *n*. (Surg.) removal of womb; hence ⁓IZE (1) *v.t.* [f. Gk *hustera* womb + -ECTOMY]

hỹsterĕ's|is *n*. (*pl.* ⁓es *pr.* -ēz). (Phys.) lagging of effect when cause varies- in amount etc., esp. of magnetic induction behind magnetizing force. [f. Gk *husterēsis* (*hustereō* be behind f. *husteros* coming after)]

hỹstēr'ia *n*. psychoneurosis with anaesthesia, convulsions, etc., and usu. with disturbance of moral and intellectual faculties; uncontrolled or morbid excitement. [mod. L, f. as foll.; see -IA¹]

hỹstĕ'ric *a*. & *n*. **1**. *a*. = foll. **2**. *n*. hysterical person; (in *pl.*) hysterical fits or convulsions. [f. L f. Gk *husterikos* of the womb (*hustera*; see -IC), hysteria being thought to occur more frequently in women than in men]

hỹstĕ'rical *a*. of or affected with hysteria; morbidly or uncontrolledly emotional; hence ⁓LY² *adv.* [f. as prec. + -AL]

hỹsterŏn prŏ'terŏn *n*. (Rhet.) figure of speech in which what should come last is put first, inversion of natural order (*I die! I faint! I fail!*). [LL, f. Gk *husteron proteron* latter (put in place of) former]

Hz *abbr.* hertz.

I

I¹, i, (ī) *n.* (*pl.* **Is** *or* **I's**). ninth letter of alphabet; (as Roman numeral) = 1 (**ii** 2, **iii** 3, **iv** (rarely **iiii**) 4, **ix** 9); **I-beam,** girder of I-shaped section.

I² (ī) *pron.* (*obj.* **me** *pr.* mĭ *or, when stressed,* mē; *refl.* MYSELF, arch. **me;** *poss.* MY, MINE³; *pl.* WE etc.). **1.** Sing. *pron.* of 1st pers.; **me,** (colloq.) cf. HER¹ 2; (in excl.) *ah me!, dear me!, silly me!* **2.** *n.* **the I,** (Metaphys.) the ego, subject or object of self-consciousness. [OE *ic,* = OS *ik,* OHG *ih,* ON *ek,* Goth. *ik* f. Gmc *eka f. IE **egō; me* t. OE *me, mē* acc. & dat., = OS *mī,* OHG *mih, mir,* ON, Goth. *mik* f. IE *me]

I *abbr.* Island(s); Isle(s).

I *symb.* iodine.

-i *suf.* **1.** Forming *pl.* of *ns.* f. L in *-us* or It. in *-e* or *-o* (*foci, dilettanti, timpani*). **2.** Forming *adjs.* f. names of regions etc. in or near the Middle East (*Israeli, Pakistani*) [f. adj. suf. in Semitic & Indo-Iranian languages].

-i- connecting vowel esp. of wds in -ANA, -FEROUS, -FIC, -FORM, -FY, -GEROUS, -VOROUS; cf. -O-. [f. or after F f. L]

-ia¹ *suf.* forming *ns.* (1) abstract (*hydrophobia, mania, utopia*), esp. Path. (*anaemia, pneumonia*), (2) Bot. classes and genera (*dahlia, fuchsia*), (3) names of countries (*Australia, India*). [f. or after L & Gk; cf. -A 1]

-ia² *suf.* forming *pl.* of *ns.* (1) f. Gk in *-ion* or L in *-ium* or *-e* (*paraphernalia, atria, regalia*), (2) Zool. groups (*Mammalia*); cf. -A 2.

Ia. *abbr.* Iowa.

IA *abbr.* || Institute of Actuaries; Iowa.

IAEA *abbr.* International Atomic Energy Agency.

-ial *suf.* forming *adjs.* (*celestial, dictatorial, terrestrial, trivial, venial*). [f. or after F *-iel* or f. L. *-ialis;* cf. -AL]

I'ámb *n.* iambus. [Anglicized f. IAMBUS]

iă'mbĭc *a.* & *n.* (Pros.) **1.** *a.* of or using iambuses. **2.** *n.* (usu. in *pl.*) iambic verse. [f. F *iambique* f. LL f Gk *iambikos* (as foll.; see -IC)]

iă'mbǀus *n.* (*pl.* ∼**uses,** *or* ∼**i** *pr.* -ī). (Pros.) foot consisting of one short followed by one long syllable. [L, f. Gk *iambos* iambus, lampoon (*iaptō* assail in words, from use by Gk satirists)]

-ian *suf.* forming *adjs.* (often used as *ns.*) esp. f. names of persons and places (*Bostonian, Christian, Churchillian, Georgian, Oxonian, Virgilian; theologian*); cf. -AN. [f. or after F *-ien* or f. L. *-ianus*]

-ı'asis *suf.* See -ASIS.

IATA (īah'ta) *abbr.* International Air Transport Association.

iătrŏgě'nĭc *a.* (Of disease) caused by process of medical examination or treatment. [f. Gk *iatros* physician + -o- + -GENIC]

ib. *abbr. ibidem.*

IBA *abbr.* Independent Broadcasting Authority.

Ibē'riǀan (ī-) *a* & *n.* (inhabitant or language) of ancient Iberia, the peninsula now comprising Spain and Portugal; hence **Ibero-** (ī'berō, ībē'rŏ) *comb. form,* Iberian (and) (*Ibero-American*). [f. L *Iberia* f. Gk *Ibēres* Spaniards, + -IAN]

i'bĕx *n.* wild goat esp. of Alps and Apennines, with large ridged recurved horns. [L]

ibid. *abbr.* = foll.

ibidem (ĭ'bĭdĕm, ĭbī'dĕm) *adv.* in the same book, chapter, passage, etc. [L]

-ibi'lity *suf.* forming *ns.* f. *adjs.* in -IBLE (*possibility, credibility*). [f. F *-ibilité* or f. L *-ibilitas;* see -ITY]

i'bis *n.* wading bird of family Threskiornithidae with long curved bill, found in lakes and swamps of warm climates; **sacred** ∼, white species venerated by ancient Egyptians. [ME f. L f. Gk]

-ible *suf.* forming *adjs.* w. senses as -ABLE (*terrible, defensible, forcible, possible*). [F, or f. L *-ibilis* f. *-i-*

of second, third, and fourth conjugations + *-bilis* (see -BLE)]

-ibly *suf.* forming *advs.* corresp. to adjs. in *-ible.* [f. -IBLE + -LY²]

IBM *abbr.* International Business Machines.

I'bō (ē'-) *n.* (*pl.* same *or* ∼**s**). (member or language of) a Black people of SE Nigeria. [native name]

IBRD *abbr.* International Bank for Reconstruction and Development.

I'bsenism (ī'-) principles and aims of works examining and criticizing social conventions, written by Ibsen and his followers. [f. H. *Ibsen,* Norw. dramatist d. 1906 + -ISM]

-ic, (arch.) **-ick** *or* **-ique** (-k), *suf.* forming *adjs.* & *ns.* (*Arabic, civic, classic, poetic, public, romantic, scenic, tragic; critic, epic, mechanic, music*); (Chem.) in higher valence or degree of oxidation (*ferric, sulphuric;* cf. -OUS); see -ICS, -ITIC [f. or after F *-ique* or f. L *-icus* or Gk *-ikos;* cf. -ATIC, -ETIC, -FIC, -OTIC]

i/c *abbr.* in charge; in command; internal combustion.

-ical *suf.* forming *adjs.* corresp. to *ns.* or *adjs.* usu. in -IC (*classical, comical, farcical, economical, historical, musical*), or to *ns.* in -Y¹ (*pathological, theoretical*). [f. -IC + -AL]

-ically *suf.* forming *advs.* corresp. to *adjs.* in -IC or -ICAL (*comically, musically, phlegmatically, poetically, tragically*). [f. prec. + -LY²]

ICAO *abbr.* International Civil Aviation Organization.

ICBM *abbr.* intercontinental ballistic missile.

*ICC *abbr.* Indian Claims Commission; Interstate Commerce Commission.

ice¹ *n.* **1.** frozen water, a brittle transparent crystalline solid; sheet of this on surface of water; **break the** ∼, (fig.) make a beginning, break through reserve or stiffness; CUT² *no ice;* **dry** ∼, solid carbon dioxide; **on** ∼, (of entertainment etc.) performed by skaters, (colloq.) (1) in state of temporary suspension, held in reserve, (2) absolutely certain; **on thin** ∼, (fig.) in a risky situation. **2.** (portion of) frozen confection esp. ||ice-cream or water-ice; (sl.) diamonds. **3.** ∼-**age,** glacial period (esp. in Pleistocene); ∼-**axe** (used by mountain-climbers for cutting footholds); ∼-**bag,** ice-filled rubber bag for medical use; ∼'**blink,** luminous appearance on horizon, caused by reflection from ice; ∼-**blue,** very pale blue; ∼-**boat,** (1) boat mounted on runners for travelling on ice, (2) boat used for breaking ice on river etc.; ∼-**bound,** confined by ice; *∼'**box,** refrigerator, = ice-boat (2); ∼-**breaker,** = ice-boat (2); ∼-**cap,** permanent covering of ice in polar lands; ∼-**cold,** as cold as ice; ∼-**cream,** frozen flavoured cream or custard; ∼-**cube,** small block of ice made in refrigerator; ∼-**fall,** steep part of glacier like frozen waterfall; ∼-**field,** expanse of ice, esp. in polar regions; ∼-**fish,** capelin; *ice-*FLOE; ∼-**foot,** belt of ice along coast in Arctic regions; ∼' **hockey** (played on skates); ∼-**house,** building often partly or wholly underground for storing ice; ∼ **lolly,** water-ice on small stick; ∼-**machine** (for artificial production of ice); ∼'**man,** (1) man skilled in traversing ice, (2) maker of ices, (3) dealer in ice; ∼-**pack,** (1) = PACK¹ 7, (2) quantity of ice applied to body for medical etc. purposes; ∼-**pick,** needle-like implement with handle for splitting up table ice; ∼-**plant** (with leaves covered with watery vesicles looking like ice-specks); ∼-**show,** entertainment by skaters on ice; ∼-**water** (from or cooled by ice); ∼-**wool** (glossy kind used in knitting etc.); ∼-**yacht,** = *ice-boat* (1). [OE *īs,* = OS, OHG *īs,* ON *īss* f. Gmc *īsam]

ice² *v.* **1.** *v.t.* freeze; cover (as) with ice; mix with or cool in ice; cover (cake etc.) with icing; *iced* LOLLY. **2.** *v.i.* become covered (*over, up*) with ice, freeze *up*. [ME, f. prec.]

-ice *suf.* forming (esp. abstract) *ns.* (*avarice, cowardice, jaundice, justice, malice, notice, novice, precipice, service*); cf. -ISE². [f. or after OF, f. L -*itius, -itia, -itium*]

||**ICE** *abbr.* Institution of Civil Engineers; internal combustion engine.

i'ceberg (ī'sb-) *n.* huge floating mass of ice, detached portion of glacier carried out to sea; (fig.) unemotional or cold-blooded person; **tip of the** ∿, part of the iceberg (about one-ninth) that projects above surface of sea, (fig.) small evident part of something much larger. [prob. f. Du. *ijsberg* (*ijs* ice, *berg* hill)]

I'celand (ī'sl-) *n.* ∿ **lichen** or **moss**, edible species of lichen; ∿ **poppy**, yellow or red orig. Arctic poppy; ∿ **spar**, transparent variety of calcite with strong double refraction; hence ∿ER¹ (4) *n.* [∿, island in N. Atlantic]

Icelǎ'ndic (īsl-) *a.* & *n.* (language) of Iceland. [f. prec. + -IC]

I'chabǒd (ī'k-) *n.* (As excl. of regret =) the glory has departed. [Heb.; see 1 Sam. 4:21]

||**I.Chem.E.** *abbr.* Institution of Chemical Engineers.

i'ching (ē'ch-) *n.* ancient Chinese fortune-telling game based on 8 groups of three lines and 64 groups of six lines. [f. Chin. *yijing* book of changes]

ichneu'mon (īk-) *n.* **1.** mongoose of N. Africa etc., noted for destroying crocodiles' eggs. **2.** ∿(-**fly**), small hymenopterous insect depositing eggs in or on larva of another insect as food for its own larva. [L, f. Gk *ikhneumōn* spider-hunting wasp (*ikhneuō* trace f. *ikhnos* footstep)]

ichnǒ'graphy (īk-) *n.* (drawing of) ground-plan of building, map of region, etc. [f. F *ichnographie* or f. L f. Gk *ikhnographia* (*ikhnos* track; see -GRAPHY)]

i'chǒr (ī'k-) *n.* (Gk Myth.) fluid flowing like blood in veins of gods; (poet.) bloodlike fluid; (Path.) watery fetid discharge from wound etc.; hence ∿OUS (ī'ker-) *a.* [f. Gk *ikhōr*]

i'chthyǒ- (ī'k-) *comb. form.* fish, as: ∿**grapher**, ∿**graphy**, (-ŏ'g-), writer on, description of, fishes; ∿**latry** (-ŏ'l-), worship of a fish-god; ∿**lite**, fossil fish; ∿**logy** (-ŏ'l-), study of fishes, whence ∿**lo'gical**, ∿**logist** (-ŏ'l-); ∿**phagous** *a.*, ∿**phagy** *n.* (-ŏ'f-), fish-eating. [f. Gk *ikhthus* fish + -O-]

i'chthyoid (ī'k-) *a.* & *n.* **1.** *a.* fishlike. **2.** *n.* vertebrate of fish type. [f. as prec. + -OID]

ichthyosaur'us, i'chthyosaur, (īk-) *n.* extinct marine animal of order Ichthyosauria, with long head, tapering body, four paddles, and large tail. [f. ICHTHYO- + Gk *sauros* lizard]

ichthy'ǒ'sis (īk-) *n.* (pl. ∿**oses** pr. -ŏ'sēz). disease in which epidermis becomes dry and horny; hence ∿o'TIC *a.* [f. Gk *ikhthus* fish + -OSIS]

ICI *abbr.* Imperial Chemical Industries.

-i'cian (ī'shan) *suf.* forming *ns.* denoting persons skilled in or concerned with subjects having names (usu.) in -IC or -ICS (*logician, magician, physician* f. PHYSIC, *politician, statistician; mortician, academician*). [f. or after F -*icien* (as -IC, -IAN)]

i'cicle *n.* tapering hanging ice-formation, produced by freezing of successive ice-drops trickling from the point of attachment. [ME, f. ICE¹ + (now dial.) *ickle* icicle (= OE *gicel,* ON *jökull* f. Gmc *jakilaz*)]

i'cing *n.* In vbl senses; sugar etc. coating of cake etc.; formation of ice on aircraft; ||∿ **sugar** (finely powdered, for icing cakes etc.). [f. ICE² + -ING¹]

-icist *suf.* = -ICIAN (*classicist, physicist* f. PHYSICS, *publicist, romanticist*). [f. -IC + -IST]

-i'city *suf.* forming abstract *ns.* esp. f. *adjs.* in -IC (*authenticity, catholicity, electricity, publicity, toxicity*). [f. -IC + -ITY]

-ick. See -IC.

-icle. See -CULE.

i'con, i'kon, *n.* image, statue; (Orthodox Ch.) painting, mosaic, etc., of sacred personage, itself regarded as sacred. [L, f. Gk *eikōn* image]

icǒ'nic *a.* of (the nature of) an image or portrait; (of statue) following a conventional type. [f. L f. Gk *eikonikos* (as prec.; see -IC)]

icǒ'noclǎsm *n.* breaking of images (lit. or fig.; cf. foll.). [f. foll. after *enthusiasm* etc.]

icǒ'noclǎst *n.* breaker of images, esp. one who took part in movement in 8th–9th c. against use of images in religious worship in churches of the East, and Puritan of 16th–17th c.; (fig.) one who attacks cherished beliefs; hence ∿IC (-ǎ's-) *a.* [f. med. L f. eccl. Gk *eikonoklastēs* (*eikōn* image, *klaō* break)]

icǒnǒ'graph|ў *n.* illustration of subject by drawings or figures; book whose essence is pictures; treatise on pictures or statuary; study of portraits esp. of an individual; hence ∿ER¹ *n.*, **iconogrǎ'ph**ICAL *adj.* [f. Gk *eikonographia* sketch (*eikōn* image; see -GRAPHY)]

icǒnǒ'latrў *n.* worship of images; so **icǒnǒ'**LATER *n.* [f. eccl. Gk *eikonolatreia* (as ICON, -LATRY)]

icǒnǒ'logў *n.* study of icons; symbolism. [f. as ICON + -O- + -LOGY]

icǒnǒ'meter *n.* (Photog.) direct-vision view-finder (either fixed to camera, or detached and adjustable for various lenses and sizes of plate); (Surv.) optical instrument for ascertaining size or distance of an object; so **icǒnǒ'**METRY *n.* [f. as ICON + -O- + -METER]

icǒnǒ'stas|is *n.* (pl. ∿**es** pr. -ēz). (Orthodox Ch.) screen bearing icons and separating the sanctuary from the nave. [f. mod. Gk *eikonostasis* (as ICON, STASIS)]

icosahē'dr|on (-a-h-) *n.* solid figure with twenty faces; hence ∿AL *a.* [f. LL *icosahedrum* f. Gk *eikosaedron* (*eikosi* twenty; see -HEDRON)]

icǒsi-*pref.* twenty, as: ∿**dodecahe'dron,** solid figure with twenty triangular and twelve pentagonal faces. [f. Gk *eikosi* twenty]

-ics *suf.* forming *ns.* (treated variously as *pl.* or *sing.*) denoting arts or sciences or branches of study or action (*athletics, mathematics, politics, statics, tactics*), occas. w. corresp. form in -ic denoting a particular form or instance (*aesthetic, tactic*). [f. or after F pl. -*iques* or f. L pl. -*ica* or Gk pl. -*ika*]

ICS *abbr.* (Hist.) Indian Civil Service.

ICSU *abbr.* International Council of Scientific Unions

i'cterus *n.* (Path.) jaundice; so **ictē'**RIC *a.* [L, f. Gk *ikteros*]

i'ctus *n.* (Pros.) rhythmical or metrical stress. [L, = blow (*icere* strike)]

i'cў *a.* abounding in or covered with ice; very cold (lit., or fig.; *icy manners*); hence **i'ci**LY² *adv.*, **i'ci**NESS *n.* [f. ICE¹ + -Y²]

id *n.* (Psych.) inherited instinctive impulses of the individual as part of the unconscious. [L, = that, transl. G *es*]

-id¹ *suf.* forming *adjs.* (*arid, fluid, morbid, rapid, timid, vivid*). [f. F -*ide* f. L -*idus*]

-id² *suf.* forming *ns.* (*pyramid*), esp. (Biol.) of structural constituents (*plastid*), in Bot. of plant belonging to family with name in -aceae (*orchid*). [f. or after F -*ide* f. L -*is* -*idis* f. Gk -*is* -*ida* or -*idos*]

-id³ *suf.* forming *ns.* denoting: **1.** (Zool.) animal belonging to family with name in -ida or class with name in -ida (*canid, arachnid*). **2.** member of person's family (*Seleucid* f. Seleucus). **3.** (Astron.) meteor in group radiating from a specified constellation (*Leonid* f. Leo); star of class like one in a specified constellation (*cepheid*). [f. or after L -*ides*, pl. -*idae* or -*ida*]

-id⁴ *suf.* (US or arch.) = -IDE.

ID *abbr.* Idaho; *identification.

id. *abbr. idem.*

i.d. *abbr.* inner diameter.

IDA *abbr.* International Development Association.

IDB *abbr.* illicit diamond-buying.

ide *n.* freshwater fish allied to carp. [f. mod. L *idus* f. Sw. *id*]

-ide *suf.* (Chem.) forming *ns.* denoting (1) binary compounds of an element with another element or radical, the suf. -*ide* being added to the name (usu.

abbr.) of the more electronegative element etc. (*sodium chloride, potassium cyanide, calcium carbide*), or various other compounds (*amide, anhydride, peptide, saccharide*), (2) elements of a series (*actinide, lanthanide*). [orig. in OXIDE]

ĭdē′a *n.* **1.** conception, plan, of or *of* thing to be aimed at, created, discovered, etc., (**not my ∼ of,** (colloq.) something I regard as the opposite of *fun* etc.; **has no ∼,** (colloq.) is utterly ignorant or incompetent); plan of action; **the big ∼,** (usu. iron.) the important intention or scheme. **2.** thing conceived by the mind (**man of ∼s,** resourceful person; **get** or **have ∼s,** (colloq.) be ambitious, rebellious, etc.; **put ∼s into** person's **head,** suggest ambitions etc. he would not otherwise have imagined); way of thinking (**the young ∼,** the child's mind); vague belief, fancy, (*the idea of his doing such a thing; I had no, had an, idea (that) you were there, where you were*); **the very ∼!, what an ∼!,** etc., (colloq.) that is outrageous, quite impracticable, etc.; **that's an ∼,** (colloq.) that proposal etc. is worth considering. **3.** archetype, pattern, as distinguished from its realization in individuals; (Platonic Philos.) eternally existing pattern of which individual things in any class are imperfect copies. **4.** (Descartes, Locke) immediate object of thought or mental perception; (Kant) conception of reason transcending all experience; (Hegel) absolute truth of which all phenomenal existence is the expression. **5.** Hence **∼′n²,** **∼ED²,** (-ī′ad), **∼LESS,** *adjs.* [(in sense 3), f. Gk, = look, form, kind (*id-* 3cc)]

ĭdē′al *a.* & *n.* **1.** *a.* answering to one's highest conception, perfect or supremely excellent; embodying an idea; existing only in idea; visionary; relating to or consisting of (Platonic) ideas; **∼ gas** (without attraction between its molecules, and so obeying simple laws); hence **∼LY²** *adv.* **2.** *n.* perfect type; actual thing as standard for imitation [ME, f. F *idéal* f. LL *idealis* (as prec.; see -AL)]

idē′al|ism (-ī′-, -ē′-) *n.* **1.** representation of things in ideal or idealized form, imaginative treatment, practice of forming or following after ideals, (cf. REALISM). **2.** (Philos.) system of thought in which the object of external perception is held to consist of ideas (cf. REALISM). **3.** So **∼IST** (3) *n.,* **∼ī′stIC** *a.* [f. F *idéalisme* or G *idealismus* (as prec.; see -ISM)]

idē′a′lity *n.* quality of being ideal; ideal thing. [f. IDEAL + -ITY]

idē′alīz|e (-ī′-, -ē′-), **-īs|e** (-īz), *v.t.* represent (thing, person, or abs.) in ideal form or character; exalt to ideal perfection or excellence; hence **∼A′TION,** **∼ER¹,** *ns.* [f. IDEAL + -IZE]

ī′dē|āte *v.* **1.** *v.t.* imagine, conceive. **2.** *v.i.* form ideas. **3.** Hence **∼A′TION** *n.,* **∼ā′tionAL** *a.* [f. med. L *ideare* form idea (as IDEA) + -ATE³]

idée fixe (ēdā fē′ks) *n.* (*pl.* **idées fixes** *pr.* same). idea that dominates the mind, obsession. [F, lit. 'fixed idea']

idée reçue (ēdā resū′) *n.* (*pl.* **idées reçues** *pr.* same). generally accepted notion or opinion. [F]

ĭdem (ī′dĕm) *n.* & *adv.* (in) the same author; the same word. [ME f. L]

ĭdĕ′ntic *a.* **1.** (Diplom.) **∼ note,** simultaneous and uniformly worded expression of opinion from several powers to another. **2.** = foll. [f. med. L *identicus* (cf. IDENTITY)]

ĭdĕ′ntical *a.* (Of one thing viewed at different times) the very same; (of different things) agreeing in every detail (*with*); (of twins) developed from a single fertilized ovum, therefore of same sex and usu. very similar in appearance; (Logic & Math.) expressing an identity (**∼ proposition,** of the type *Man is man*); hence **∼LY²** *adv.,* **∼NESS** *n.* [f. as prec. + -AL]

ĭdĕ′nti|fỹ *v.* **1.** *v.t.* treat (thing) as identical (*with*); associate (person, one*self*) inseparably or very closely *with* (party, policy, etc.); establish identity of, recognize; select by consideration (*identify the best method of solution*). **2.** *v.i.* associate oneself *with*; regard oneself

as sharing characteristics *with* (another person). **3.** Hence **∼fīABLE** *a.,* **∼fīCA′TION** *n.* (**∼fication card,** disc, plate, etc., object worn or carried and bearing name or an assigned number etc.; **∼fication parade,** assembly of persons from whom suspect is to be identified). [f. med. L *identificare* (as IDENTITY; see -FY)]

Idĕ′ntikĭt *n.* (P) reconstructed picture of person (esp. sought by police) assembled from features described by witnesses. [f. IDENTITY + KIT¹]

idĕ′ntitỹ *n.* absolute sameness; individuality, personality; condition of being a specified person; (Alg.) equality of two expressions for all values of the literal quantities, expression of this, e.g. $(x+1)^2 = (or \equiv)x^2 + 2x + 1$; (Math.) transformation that leaves an object unchanged; **∼ card, parade,** etc. = *identification card* etc. (cf. IDENTIFY). [f. LL *identitas*, f. L *idem* same (see -ITY)]

ĭ′dēo|grăm, **ĭ′dēo|graph** (-ahf), *ns.* character symbolizing idea of a thing without expressing the sequence of sounds in its name (e.g. numeral, many Chinese characters); hence **∼GRA′PHIC(AL)** *adjs.,* **∼GRAPHY** (-ŏ′g-) *n.* [f. Gk IDEA + -O- + -GRAM, -GRAPH]

ĭ′dēŏlŏgue (-g) *n.* theorist, visionary; adherent of an ideology. [f. F *idéologue* f. Gk IDEA + -LOGUE]

ĭdēŏ′lŏg|ỹ *n.* **1.** (arch.) science of ideas; visionary speculation. **2.** manner of thinking characteristic of a class or individual, ideas at the basis of some economic or political theory or system, (*bourgeois, Marxist, ideology*). **3.** Hence **ĭdēŏlŏ′gICAL** *a.,* **∼IST** (1) *n.* [f. F *idéologie* (as prec.; see -LOGY)]

īdes (īdz) *n. pl.* eighth day after nones in ancient--Roman calendar (15th day of March, May, July, October, 13th of other months).[ME f. OF, f. L *idus* pl., perh. f. Etruscan]

id est (ĭd ĕ′st). that is to say. [L (*id* that, *est* is)]

ĭ′diŏcỹ *n.* extreme mental imbecility; utter foolishness, idiotic behaviour or action. [ME, f. IDIOT, prob. after *lunacy*]

ĭ′diŏlĕct *n.* language as used by an individual person. [f. Gk *idios* own + DIALECT]

ĭ′diŏm *n.* language of a people or country; specific character of this; form of expression peculiar to a language or person, peculiarity of phraseology approved by usage though having meaning not deducible from those of the separate words; characteristic mode of expression in music, art, etc. [f. F *idiome* or f. LL f. Gk *idiōma -matos* private property (*idioomai* make one's own f. *idios* own, private)]

ĭdiŏmă′t|ic *a.* characteristic of a particular language; relating to or conforming to idiom; hence **∼ICALLY** *adv.* [f. Gk *idiōmatikos* peculiar (as prec.; see -IC)]

ĭdiŏ′pathỹ *n.* (Path.) disease not preceded or occasioned by another, or by any known cause; hence **ĭdiopă′thIC** *a.* [f. mod. L f. Gk *idiopatheia* (*idios* own; see -PATHY)]

ĭdiosỹ′ncrasỹ *n.* mental constitution, view or feeling, mode of behaviour, peculiar to a person; mode of expression peculiar to an author; (Med.) physical constitution peculiar to a person; hence **idiosỹncra′tIC** *a.* [f. Gk *idiosugkrasia* (*idios* own, *sun* together, *krasis* mixture)]

ĭ′diŏt *n.* person so deficient in mind as to be permanently incapable of rational conduct; (colloq.) stupid person, utter fool, whence **idiŏ′tIC** *a.,* **idiŏ′tICALLY** *adv.* [ME f. OF, f. L *idiota* ignorant person f. Gk *idiōtēs* private person, layman, ignorant person (*idios* own, private)]

ī′dle *a.* & *v.* **1.** *a.* (Of action, thought, or word) ineffective, worthless, vain; groundless; having no special purpose (*idle talk, curiosity*); useless; not in use, not working, unemployed; (of time etc.) unoccupied; lazy, indolent; **∼ wheel,** intermediate wheel between two geared wheels, esp. to allow them to rotate in same direction; hence **∼NESS** (ī′dĕln-) *n.,* **ī′dLY²** *adv.* **2.** *v.i.* be idle; (of engine) run slowly without doing work. **3.** *v.t.* pass (time etc.) *away* in

idleness. [OE *īdel*, = OS *īdal*, OHG *ītal* empty, useless]

i′dler *n.* In vbl senses; = IDLE *wheel*. [f. prec. + -ER¹]

i′dlèsse *n.* idleness. [pseudo-arch. f. IDLE + -ESS²]

I′dō (ē′dō) *n.* artificial universal language based on Esperanto. [Ido, = offspring]

i′dol *n.* image of deity used as object of worship; false god; person or thing that is the object of excessive devotion; (arch.) phantom; (Logic) false mental conception (∼s **of the tribe, cave, market, theatre,** four classes of fallacies distinguished by Bacon (1620) referable respectively to limitations of human mind, prejudices of idiosyncrasy, influence of words, philosophical and logical prepossessions). [ME, f. OF *idole* f. L f. Gk *eidōlon* phantom (*eidos* form)]

idŏ′lat|er *n.* worshipper of idols; devoted admirer (*of*); hence or cogn. ∼rESS¹, ∼rY¹ (*honour* person **on this side of** ∼ry, short of making a god of him), *ns.*, ∼rOUS *a.* [ME *idolatrer* f. OF + -ER¹ or f. *idolatry* + -ER¹, or f. OF *idolâtre* f. Rom. *idolatra* f. LL f. Gk *eidōlolatrēs* (as IDOL; see -LATRY)]

i′dolīz|e, -īs|e (-īz), *v.* **1.** *v.t.* make an idol of; venerate or love to excess. **2.** *v.i.* practise idolatry. **3.** Hence ∼A′TION *n.* [f. IDOL + -IZE]

idŏ′l|um *n.* (*pl.* ∼a). mental image, idea; (Logic) fallacy (see IDOL). [L (as IDOL)]

i′dyll, i′dȳl, *n.* short description in verse or (**prose** ∼) in prose of picturesque scene or incident, esp. in rustic life; episode suitable for such treatment, freq. a love-story; hence **idȳ′llic** *a.*, ∼IST (1) *n.*, ∼IZE (1) *v.t.* [f. L f. Gk *eidullion* dim. of *eidos* form]

-ie *suf.* **1.** = -Y³ (*bookie, dearie, movie, nightie, oldie*), esp. Sc. & Austral. **2.** (arch.) = -Y¹,² (*litanie, prettie*). [earlier form of -Y]

i.e. *abbr.* that is to say. [f. L ID EST]

‖**IEE** *abbr.* Institution of Electrical Engineers.

-ier *suf.* forming personal *ns.* denoting occupation etc. (1) unstressed *pr.* -ĭer etc. (*collier, grazier, hosier*; cf. -YER), (2) stressed *pr.* ēr′ (*bombardier, cavalier*). [(1) ME of various orig.; (2) F, f. L -*arius*]

if *conj.* & *n.* **1.** *conj.* on the condition or supposition that, in the case or circumstances such that, (*if you are* (now) *tired we will sit down*; *if you* (hereafter) *see him give him the message*; *if he has found it he will send it*; *if he had fair warning he has nothing to complain of*); (w. past tense implying that condition is not fulfilled: *if I were you*; *if I knew what to do I should do it*; *if he had been warned he would have* (or *would have had*) *nothing to complain of*); **if and when,** at the future time (if any) that. **2.** whenever (*if I feel any doubt I inquire*; *if I felt any doubt I inquired*; *if I had been badly treated I complained*). **3.** whether (*ask, see, try, if you can turn the handle*). **4.** (In excl. of wish, surprise, etc., without apodosis: *if I only knew!*, *if only I knew!*, I wish I knew; *if I haven't lost my watch!*, I have, to my surprise or disgust; so in polite request: *if you wouldn't mind opening the door?*). **5. as if,** as the case would be if (*it seems as if he meant* (colloq. *means*) *business*; *he talks as* (he would) *if he were drunk*; *nodded, as if to say 'But of course'*; *as if you didn't know*, you know quite well). **6.** (With reduction of protasis to significant word: **if any, if anything, if not, if so,** = if there is or are any, if it is (not) so, etc.; **if at all, if then,** = and perhaps not at all, not even then; **if only because, if only to,** even if for no other reason than that, than to). **7.** = THOUGH 1, 2 (*I'll finish it if it kills me*); despite being (*a useful if cumbersome device*). **8.** *n.* condition, supposition, (*too many ifs about it*); hence **i′ffish**¹, **i′ffȳ**², *adjs.*, uncertain. [OE *gif*, = OS *ef* (*of*), OHG *ibu, oba,* ON *ef*, Goth. *ibai*]

IF *abbr.* intermediate frequency.

IFC *abbr.* International Finance Corporation.

‖**I. Gas E.** *abbr.* Institution of Gas Engineers.

Igbo. Var. of IBO.

i′gloo *n.* Eskimo dome-shaped hut, esp. one built of snow. [Eskimo, = house]

i′gnèous *a.* of fire, fiery; (Geol.) produced by volcanic or magmatic agency. [f. L *igneus* (*ignis* fire) + -OUS]

ignis fă′tuus *n.* (*pl.* **ignes fatui** *pr.* -ēz -ūī). will-o′-the-wisp. [mod. L, = foolish fire, f. its erratic movement]

ignī′t|e *v.* **1.** *v.t.* set fire to, cause to burn; (Chem.) heat to the point of combustion or chemical change; hence ∼ABLE *a.*, ∼ER¹ *n.* (esp. for causing electric arc, or combustion in engine cylinder). **2.** *v.i.* take fire. [f. L *ignire -it-* (*ignis* fire)]

ignī′tion *n.* igniting or being ignited; mechanism for, or act of, starting combustion of mixture in cylinder of internal combustion engine; ∼ **key** (to operate this mechanism, normally necessary to start engine). [F, or f. med. L *ignitio* (as prec.; see -ION)]

ignī′tron *n.* (Electr.) mercury-arc rectifier able to carry large currents. [f. IGNITE + -TRON]

ignō′b|le *a.* of low birth, position, or reputation; mean, base, dishonourable; hence ∼leNESS (-bln-) *n.*, ∼LY² *adv.* [F, or f. L *ignobilis* (as IN-², (*g*)*nobilis* noble)]

ignomi′nious *a.* causing or deserving ignominy; humiliating; hence ∼LY² *adv.* [ME, f. F *ignominieux* or f. L *ignominiosus* (as foll.; see -OUS)]

i′gnominȳ *n.* dishonour, infamy; (arch.) infamous conduct. [f. F *ignominie* or L *ignominia* (as IN-², (**g*)*nomen* name); see -Y¹]

ignorā′mus *n.* ignorant person. [L, = we do not know, (Law, of grand jury) we take no notice of (bill or indictment); mod. sense perh. f. character in Ruggle's 'Ignoramus' (1615) exposing lawyers' ignorance]

i′gnorance *n.* lack of knowledge (*of* thing, or in general). [ME f. OF, f. L *ignorantia* (as foll.; see -ANCE)]

i′gnorant *a.* lacking knowledge; behaving in uncouth manner through lack of knowledge; uninformed (*of* or *in* subject, *of* fact); hence ∼LY² *adv.* [ME f. OF, f. L (as IGNORE; see -ANT)]

ignoratio elenchi (īgnerāshiō ĭlĕ′ngkī) *n.* (Logic). argument that appears to refute opponent while actually disproving something not asserted by him. [med. L, transl. Gk *hē tou eleghkou agnoia*, = ignorance of conditions for valid proof]

ignō′r e *v.t.* refuse to take notice of or accept; intentionally disregard. [f. F *ignorer* or f. L *ignorare* not know, ignore (as IN-², *gno-* know)]

ignotum per ignotius (īgnōtum pēr īgnō′tĭus) *n.* explanation obscurer than the thing it is meant to explain. [L, = the unknown by the still less known]

igua′na (īgwah′-) *n.* large W. Ind. and S. Amer. arboreal lizard of family Iguanidae. [Sp., f. Carib *iwana*]

igua′nodŏn (īgwah′-) *n.* large extinct herbivorous dinosaur. [f. (resemblance to) prec., after *mastodon* etc.]

i.h.p. *abbr.* indicated horsepower.

IHS *abbr.* Jesus. [ME f. LL, repr. Gk *IHΣ* = *Iēs*(*ous*) Jesus; often taken as abbr. of various L wds]

ikêba′na (-ah′nah) *n.* art of Japanese flower arrangement, with formal display acc. to strict rules. [Jap., = living flowers]

i′kon. See ICON.

il-¹,² *prefs.*, assim. forms of IN-¹,² before *l.*

il, -īle, *suf.* forming adjs. or *ns.* denoting relation or capability (*civil, fossil, utensil*; *agile, erectile, fragile, quartile, sessile, versatile*). [OF, f. L -*ilis*]

IL *abbr.* Illinois; ‖Institute of Linguists.

ilang-ilang. Var. of YLANG-YLANG.

-ile. See -IL.

‖**ILEA** *abbr.* Inner London Education Authority.

i′le|um *n.* (*pl.* ∼a). (Anat.) third and last portion of small intestine; ∼AL *a.*, ∼I′TIS *n.* [var. of ILIUM, confused w. foll.]

i′leus *n.* (Path.) painful obstruction of intestine, esp. of ileum. [L, f. Gk (*e*)*ileos* colic]

i′lex *n.* holm-oak; tree or shrub of genus *Ilex*, including common holly. [ME f. L]

i′liăc *a.* of the flank or ilium (*iliac artery*); ∼ **passion,** (arch.) ileus. [f. LL *iliacus*, in form f. L *ilia* flanks (see -AC), in first sense f. L ILEUS]

I'liad (ĭ'-) *n.* long story esp. *of woes* etc.; story of martial feats. [title of epic poem attributed to Homer and describing climax of siege of Troy, f. L f. Gk *Ilias -ados* (*poiēsis*) (poem) of *Ilion* Ilium = Troy]

i'li|um *n.* (*pl.* ∼a). bone forming upper part of each half of human pelvis; corresponding bone in animals. [ME f. L]

ilk *a.* **1.** (Sc.) **of that** ∼, of the same (*Guthrie of that* ∼, Guthrie of Guthrie). **2.** (colloq.) (*that, his, the same,* etc.) ∼, family, class, or set. [OE *ilca* same (*i-* that, the same, **ilk-* (cf. LIKE[1], -LY[1])]

ill *a., n.,* & *adv.,* (WORSE, WORST). **1.** *a.* out of health, sick, (usu. *pred.*: *he is ill, was taken ill, fell ill, of* or *with* disease, *with anxiety* etc.; *mentally ill people*); (of health) unsound, disordered. **2.** morally bad (*ill* FAME[1]); hostile, unkind, (∼ **blood,** ∼ **feeling,** ∼ **will,** animosity, strife; ∼ **nature,** churlishness; ∼ **humour, temper,** moroseness, irritability). **3.** harmful (*ill effects*); **do an** ∼ **turn to** person, harm him or his interests. **4.** wretched, disastrous, (*ill fortune, ill luck*; **it's an** ∼ **wind that blows nobody good,** most happenings benefit someone). **5.** (arch.) difficult (*ill to please*). **6.** faulty, unskilful, (*ill taste, management*); (of manners or conduct) improper; **with an** ∼ **grace,** sullenly; ∼ **success,** partial or complete failure. **7.** *n.* evil, the opposite of good; harm, injury; **speak** ∼ (something unfavourable) **of;** (in *pl.*) misfortunes, causes of harm. **8.** *adv.* badly, wrongly, (*behaved ill*; TAKE[1] *thing ill*); unfavourably (*it would have gone ill with him*); imperfectly, scarcely, (*ill provided*; *it ill became him to speak; can ill afford to do this*); ∼ **at ease,** embarrassed, uneasy. **9.** ∼ **-advi'sed**(**ly** *pr.* -īdlĭ), imprudent(ly); ∼**-affected,** not well disposed *towards*; *ill*-ASSORTED; ∼**-behaved,** having bad manners or conduct; ∼**-bred,** badly brought up, rude; ∼ **breeding,** bad manners; ∼**-condi'tioned,** (1) of evil disposition, (2) in bad condition; ∼**-defined,** not clearly defined; ∼**-disposed,** (1) disposed to evil, malevolent, (2) unfavourably disposed (*towards*); ∼**-fa'ted,** destined to, or bringing, bad fortune; ∼**-favoured,** unattractive, displeasing, objectionable; *ill*-FOUND[1]*ed*; ∼**-gotten,** gained by evil or unlawful means; ∼**-hu'moured,** bad-tempered; ∼**-ju'dged,** unwise; ∼**-ma'nnered,** having bad manners, rude; ∼**-na'tured**(**ly**), churlish(ly); ∼**-o'mened,** attended by bad omens; ∼**-starred,** born under an evil star, unlucky; ∼**-te'mpered,** morose, peevish, irritable; ∼**-ti'med,** done or occurring at an inappropriate time; ∼**-trea't,-u'se,** treat badly: so ∼**-trea'tment,-u'se,** *ns.*; ∼**-wisher,** person who wishes evil to another. [ME, f. ON *illr,* of unkn. orig.]

Ill. *abbr.* Illinois.

illā'tion *n.* deduction, conclusion; thing deduced. [f. L *illatio* (*illatus* p.p. of *inferre* INFER; see -ATION)]

illa'tive (ĭlā'-, ĭ'la-) *a.* (Of word) stating or introducing an inference; inferential: (Gram., of case) denoting motion into; hence ∼LY[2] (-vlĭ) *adv.* [f. L *illativus* (as prec.; see -IVE)]

illē'gal *a.* not legal; contrary to law; hence or cogn. **illega'lity** *n.,* ∼LY[2] *adv.* [f. L *illēgal* or f. med. L IL[2](*legalis* LEGAL)]

illē'g|ible *a.* not legible; hence ∼IBI'LITY *n.,* ∼**ibLY**[2] *adv.* [f. IL-[2] + LEGIBLE]

illēgi'tim|ate[1] *a.* & *n.* **1.** *a.* not authorized by law; improper; not recognized as lawful offspring; bastard; wrongly inferred; naturally abnormal; hence ∼ACY *n.,* ∼**ate**LY[2] (-tlĭ) *adv.* **2.** *n.* one whose position is illegitimate, esp. bastard. [f. LL *illegitimus,* after LEGITIMATE[1]; used IL-[2]]

illēgi'tim|āte[2] *v.t.* declare illegitimate; hence or cogn. ∼A'TION *n.,* ∼**at**IZE, ∼IZE, *vbs.t.* [f. prec.]

illi'beral *a.* without liberal culture, unscholarly; vulgar, sordid; narrow-minded, bigoted; not generous, stingy: hence or cogn. ∼ITY (-ă'l-) *n.,* ∼LY[2] *adv.* [f. L *illiberal* f. IL[2](*liberalis* LIBERAL) mean, sordid]

illi'cit *a.* unlawful, forbidden, (*illicit dealings, inter-*

course, still); hence ∼LY[2] *adv.* [f. F *illicite* or f. L IL[2](*licitus* LICIT)]

illi'mit|able *a.* limitless; hence ∼ABI'LITY, ∼**able**NESS (-bəln-), *ns.,* ∼**ably** *adv.* [f. LL *illimitatus* f. as IL-[2] + L *limitatus* p.p. of *limitare* LIMIT[2]; see -ABLE]

illi'quid *a.* (Of assets) not easily converted into cash; hence ∼ITY (-ĭ'd-) *n.* [f. IL-[2] + LIQUID, or f. med. L **illiquidus*]

illi'ter|ate *a.* & *n.* **1.** *a.* uneducated, esp. unable to read; hence ∼ACY, ∼**ate**NESS (-tn-), *ns.,* ∼**ate**LY[2] (-tlĭ) *adv.* **2.** *n.* illiterate person. [f. L IL[2](*litteratus* LITERATE)]

i'llness *n.* unhealthy condition of body, state of being ill. [f. ILL + -NESS]

illo'gical *a.* devoid of or contrary to logic; hence ∼ITY (-ă'l-) *n.,* ∼LY[2] *adv.* [f. IL-[2] + LOGICAL]

illu'de (-ū'd, -ōō'd) *v.t.* (literary). trick, deceive. [ME, = mock, f. L (as ILLUSION)]

illu'me (-ū'm, -ōō'm) *v.t.* (poet.) light up, make bright, (lit. or fig.). [shortening of ILLUMINE]

illu'min|āte (-ū'-, -ōō'-) *v.t.* **1.** light up, make bright; hence ∼ANCE *n.,* amount of light reaching unit area of surface, ∼ANT *a.* & *n.* **2.** give spiritual or intellectual light to; help to explain (subject); shed lustre upon. **3.** decorate (buildings etc.) profusely with lights as sign of festivity; decorate (initial letter in manuscript etc.) with gold, silver, and brilliant colours. **4.** So ∼A'TION, ∼**ātor** *n.,* ∼**ative** *a.* [f. L IL[1](*luminare* f. *lumen luminis* light) + -ATE[3]]

illumin|a'ti (-ōōmĭnäh'-) *n.pl.* **1.** (*I*∼). secret society founded by Weishaupt in Bavaria in 1776, holding deistic and republican principles, and organized like Freemasons. **2.** persons claiming to possess special enlightenment. **3.** So ∼ISM (3), ∼IST (2), (-ōō'-) *ns.* [pl. of L *illuminatus* or It. *illuminato* p.p. (as prec.)]

illu'mine (-ū'-, -ōō'-) *v.t.* (literary). light up, make bright; enlighten spiritually. [ME, f. OF *illuminer* f. L (as ILLUMINATE)]

illu'sion (ĭlū'zhən, -lōō'-) *n.* deception, delusion; (instance of) sense-perception of an external object involving a false belief as to its nature; misapprehension of true state of affairs; transparent kind of tulle; hence ∼AL *a.* [ME, f. F f. L *illusio -onis* f. IL[1](*ludere lusplay*) mock; see -ION]

illu'sion|ist (ĭlū'zhən-, -lōō'-) *n.* **1.** one who disbelieves in objective existence; so ∼ISM (3) *n.* **2.** one who produces illusions, esp. conjurer. [f. prec. + -IST]

illu'sive (-ū'-, -ōō'-) *a.* = foll. [f. med. L *illusivus* (as ILLUSION; see -IVE)]

illu'sor|y (-ū'-, -ōō'-) *a.* deceptive (esp. as regards value or content); having the character of an illusion; hence ∼**i**LY[2] *adv.,* ∼**i**NESS *n.* [f. eccl. L *illusorius* (as ILLUSION; see -ORY)]

i'llustrāt|e *v.t.* make clear, explain; make clear by examples; serve as example of; elucidate (description etc.) by drawings or pictures; ornament (book, newspaper, etc.) thus; hence ∼OR *n.* [f. L IL[1](*lustrare* light up) + -ATE[3]]

illustrā'tion *n.* illustrating; example serving to elucidate; drawing or picture illustrating book, article in newspaper, etc. [ME f. OF, f. L *illustratio -onis* (as prec.; see -ATION)]

i'llustrative *a.* serving as explanation or example (*of*); hence ∼LY[2] (-vlĭ) *adv.* [f. ILLUSTRATE + -IVE]

illŭ'strious *a.* distinguished, renowned; hence ∼LY[2] *adv.,* ∼NESS *n.* [f. L IL[1](*lustris;* cf. ILLUSTRATE) + -OUS]

Illy'rian (ĭ-) *a.* & *n.* (native, inhabitant, or language) of Illyria; (*of*) language-group represented by modern Albanian. [f. L *Illyrius* (*Illyria* on Balkan coast of Adriatic) f. Gk *Illurios,* + -AN]

i'lmenīte *n.* black ore of titanium. [f. *Ilmen* mts. in Urals + -ITE[1] (2)]

ILO *abbr.* International Labour Organisation.

-ily *suf.* forming *advs.* corresp. to *adjs.* in -Y[2] etc. (*icily, stickily*); cf. -LY[2].

im-[1,2] *prefs.,* assim. forms of IN-[1,2] before *b, m, p.*

IM *abbr.* intramuscular.

i′mage[1] *n.* **1.** artificial imitation of the external form of an object, e.g. statue (esp. of saint etc. as object of veneration). **2.** optical appearance or counterpart produced by light or other radiation from object reflected in mirror, refracted through lens, etc.; (Math.) set formed by mapping. **3.** form, semblance; counterpart as regards appearance (*he is the image of his father*); typical example. **4.** simile, metaphor; mental representation; idea, conception; character of thing or person as perceived by the public. **5.** Hence ∿LESS (-ĭjl-) *a.* [ME f. OF, f. L *imago -ginis*, cogn w. IMITATE]

i′mage[2] *v.t.* make an image of, portray; reflect, mirror; picture (thing *to* one*self*); describe vividly; typify; hence ∿ABLE (-ja-) *a.* [ME, f. prec.]

i′magery (-ĭjerĭ, -jrĭ) *n.* images collectively; statuary, carving; mental images collectively; ornate figurative illustration, esp. as used by author for particular effect. [ME, f. OF *imagerie* (as IMAGE[1]; see -ERY)]

imă′ginab|le *a.* that can be imagined (*the greatest difficulty imaginable*; *took all the trouble imaginable*); hence ∿LY[2] *adv.* [ME, f. LL *imaginabilis* (as IMAGINE; see -ABLE)]

imă′ginal *a.* of image(s); (Entom.) of an imago. [f. L (as IMAGE[1]) + -AL]

imă′ginar|y *a.* existing only in imagination; (Math.) being the square root of a negative quantity, and plotted graphically in a direction usu. perpendicular to the axis of REAL[2] quantities; hence ∿ĭLY[2] *adv.* [ME, f. L *imaginarius* (as prec.; see -ARY[1])]

imăgină′tion *n.* imagining; mental faculty forming images or concepts of external objects not present to the senses; fancy; creative faculty of the mind. [ME f. OF, f. L *imaginatio -onis* (as IMAGINE; see -ATION)]

imă′ginative *a.* of, given to using, having or showing in a high degree, the faculty of imagination; hence ∿LY[2] (-vlĭ) *adv.*, ∿NESS (-vn-) *n.* [ME, f. OF *imaginatif -ive* f. med. L *imaginativus* (as foll.; see -ATIVE)]

imă′gine *v.t.* form mental image or concept of, picture to oneself (something non-existent or not present to the senses); think, conceive, (thing, thing or person *to* be or do, *that* it is, *how*, *what*, etc.); guess (*cannot imagine what he is doing all this time*);(colloq.) suppose, be of opinion, (*that*); take into one's head (idea, *that*); (in *imper.* as excl. of surprise) *imagine* (*that*)*!*. [ME, f. OF *imaginer* f. L *imaginari* (as IMAGE[1])]

i′mag|ist *n.* one of a group of early 20th-c. poets who, in revolt against romanticism, sought clarity of expression through the use of precise images; so ∿ISM (3) *n.* [f. IMAGE[1] + -IST]

imā′gō *n.* (*pl.* ima′gines *pr.* -jĭnēz, or ∿s). final and perfect stage of insect after all metamorphoses, e.g. butterfly; (Psych.) idealized mental picture of oneself or another person, esp. parent. [mod. L sense of *imago* IMAGE[1]]

ima′m (-ah′m) *n.* leader of prayers in mosque; title of various Muslim leaders, esp. of one succeeding Muhammad as leader of Islam; hence ∿ATE[1] *n.* [f. Arab. ′*imām* leader (′*amma* precede)]

‖**I.Mar.E.** *abbr.* Institute of Marine Engineers.

imbă′lance *n.* lack of balance; disproportion. [f. IM-[2] + BALANCE[1]]

i′mbécile (-ĕl, -ĭl) *a.* & *n.* **1.** *a.* mentally weak, stupid, idiotic; (arch.) physically weak; hence or cogn. ∿LY[2] (-l-lĭ) *adv.*, **imbéci′lic** *a.*, **imbĕci′l|ity** *n.* **2.** *n.* person of weak intellect, esp adult with intelligence equal to that of average child of about 5; stupid person. [f. F *imbécille* f. L *imbecillus* (as IM-[2], *becillum* f. *baculum* stick, orig. in sense 'without supporting staff')]

imbĕ′d. See EMBED.

imbī′be *v.t.* absorb, assimilate, (ideas etc.); drink (liquid, or abs. esp. of drinking alcoholic liquor); inhale (air etc.); absorb (moisture etc.); so **imbibi′-** TION *n.* [ME, f. L IM[1](*bibere* drink)]

i′mbric|āte[1] *v.t.* & *i.* arrange (leaves, scales of fish, etc.), be arranged, so as to overlap like tiles; hence

∿A′TION *n.* [f. L *imbricare* cover with rain-tiles (*imbrex -icis* rain-tile f. *imber* shower) + -ATE[3]]

i′mbrĭcate[2] *a.* having scales etc. arranged to overlap like tiles. [f. L *imbricatus* p.p. (as prec.; see -ATE[2])]

imbrō′gliō (-ō′lyō) *n.* (*pl.* ∿s). confused heap; confused or complicated (esp. political or dramatic) situation. [It. (*imbrogliare* confuse f. as EMBROIL)]

imbrue′ (-ōō′) *v.t.* stain (one's hand, sword, etc., *in* or *with* blood, slaughter, etc.). [f. OF *embr*(*o*)*uer* bedabble (em- IM-[1], *breu* f. Rom. **brodum* f. Gmc **brotham*; see BROTH)]

imbru′te (-ōō′t) *v.t.* brutalize. [f. IM-[1] + BRUTE]

imbūe′ *v.t.* saturate (*with*); dye (*with*); permeate, inspire, (*with* feelings etc.); = IMBRUE. [orig. as p.p., f. F *imbu* or f. L *imbutus* (*imbuere* moisten)]

IMCO *abbr.* Intergovernmental Maritime Consultative Organization.

‖**I.Mech.E.** *abbr.* Institution of Mechanical Engineers.

IMF *abbr.* International Monetary Fund.

i′mĭde *n.* (Chem.) compound formed from ammonia by replacing two hydrogen atoms by metal or acid radical. [orig. F; arbitr. alt. of AMIDE]

-i′mine (-ēn) (Chem.) compound formed from ammonia by replacing two hydrogen atoms by either one or two non-acidic radicals. [f. G *imin*, arbitr. alt. of *amin* AMINE]

‖**I.Min.E.** *abbr.* Institution of Mining Engineers.

i′mĭt|āte *v.t.* follow example of, copy action(s) of, mimic; make copy of, reproduce; be (consciously or not) like; so ∿ABLE *a.*, ∿ātOR *n.* [f. L *imitari* (cogn. w. *imago* IMAGE[1]) + -ATE[3]]

imĭtā′tion *n.* **1.** imitating (*imitation is the sincerest flattery*) or being imitated. **2.** copy; counterfeit (often *attrib.*: *imitation gold, leather*). **3.** (Mus.) repetition of melody etc., usu. at different pitch, in another part or voice. [F, or f. L *imitatio* (as prec.; see -ATION)]

i′mĭtative (-at-, -āt-) *a.* imitating, following model or example (*of*); counterfeit; ∿ **arts**, painting and sculpture; ∿ **word**, one that reproduces a natural sound (e.g. *fizz*) or whose sound is thought to correspond to appearances etc. of object or action described (e.g. BLOB, JAG[1,2], JAM[1], JERK[1,2]); hence ∿LY[2] (-vlĭ) *adv.*, ∿NESS (-vn-) *n.* [f. LL *imitativus* (as IMITATE; see -ATIVE)]

‖**IMM** *abbr.* Institution of Mining and Metallurgy.

immă′culate *a.* pure, spotless, perfectly clean; free from fault (usu. neg. or iron.); (Biol.) not spotted; I∿ **Conception** (of Virgin Mary, as conceived and remaining free from taint of original sin); hence **immă′cul|ACY**, ∿NESS (-tn-), *ns.*, ∿LY[2] (-tlĭ) *adv.* [ME, f. L IM[2](*maculatus* f. *macula* spot); see -ATE[2]]

i′mmanent *a.* indwelling, inherent, (*in*); (of God) permanently pervading the universe (opp. *transcendent*), whence ∿ISM (3), ∿IST (2) *ns.*; hence **i′mman**ENCE, **i′mman**ENCY, *ns.* [f. LL IM[1](*manēre* remain); see -ENT]

immatē′rial *a.* not material, incorporeal; of no essential consequence, unimportant; hence ∿ITY (-ă′l-) *n.*, ∿IZE (3) *v.t.* [ME, f. LL IM[2](*materialis* MATERIAL)]

immatē′rial|ism *n.* doctrine that matter does not exist in itself apart from perception; so ∿IST (2) *n.* [prec. + -ISM]

immatūr′|e *a.* not mature; unripe; so ∿ITY *n.* [f. L IM[2](*maturus* MATURE[1])]

immea′sur|able *a.* not measurable; immense; hence ∿ABI′LITY, ∿ableNESS (-beln-), *ns.*, ∿ABLY *adv.* [ME, f. IM-[2] + MEASURABLE]

immē′diate *a.* **1.** (Of person or thing in its relation to another) not separated by any intervening medium; (of relation or action) direct, without intervening medium; ∿ **inference** (drawn from single premiss, without intervention of middle term); ∿ **knowledge** (gained without reasoning). **2.** nearest, next, (*the immediate vicinity, future*; *my immediate family, neighbour, predecessor*; ∿ **constituent**, (Ling.) any of the main

For other words in *im-* **see** IM-[1] **or** (**esp.**) IM-[2].

grammatical or morphological subdivisions of a sentence, phrase, or word. **3.** occurring at once, without delay, (*an immediate reply*). **4.** Hence **immē'di**ACY, ∼NESS (-tn-) *ns.*, ∼LY² (-tlĭ) *adv.* & (colloq.) *conj.* (cf. DIRECTLY). [ME, f. F *immédiat* or f. LL IM²(*mediatus* MEDIATE¹)]

immě'dicab|le *a.* that cannot be healed or cured; hence ∼LY² *adv.* [f. L IM(*medicabilis* MEDICABLE)]

imměmōr'ial *a.* ancient beyond memory or record (*from* TIME¹ *immemorial*); very old; hence ∼LY² *adv.* [f. med. L IM²(*memorialis* MEMORIAL)]

immě'nse *a.* so great as to be unmeasured, huge; (colloq.) great (*made an immense difference*); (sl.) very good; hence or cogn. ∼NESS (-sn-), **imměʹns**ITY, *ns.* [ME f. F, f. L IM²(*mensus* p.p. of *metiri* measure) immeasurable]

immě'nsel̄y (-slĭ) *adv.* in an immense degree; (colloq.) very much (*enjoyed myself immensely*). [f. prec. + -LY²]

immêr'se *v.t.* dip, plunge, (*in* liquid); cause (person) to be entirely below surface of water, esp. baptize thus; bury, embed, (*in*); involve deeply, absorb, (*in* debt, difficulties, thought, etc.). [f. L IM¹(*mergere mersdip*)]

immêr'sion (-shon) *n.* immersing or being immersed; baptism by plunging whole person in water; (fig.) absorption (*in* thought etc.); (Astron.) disappearance of celestial body behind another or in its shadow; ∼ **heater**, electric heater designed for direct immersion in a liquid to be heated, esp. as fixture in hot-water tank. [ME, f. LL *immersio* (as prec.; see -ION)]

i'mmigr|āte *v.* **1.** *v.i.* come as permanent resident (*into* foreign country). **2.** *v.t.* bring in (person) thus. **3.** Hence or cogn. ∼ANT *a.* & *n.* (|| also loosely of descendants of (esp. coloured) immigrants), ∼A'TION *n.*, ∼ātORY *a.* [f. L IM¹(*migrare* MIGRATE) + -ATE³]

i'mmin|ent *a.* (Of event, esp. danger) impending, soon to happen; (arch.) overhanging; hence or cogn. ∼ENCE *n.*, ∼entLY² *adv.* [f. L IM¹(*minēre*; cf. EMINENT) overhang; see -ENT]

immi'sc|ible *a.* that cannot be mixed (*with*); hence ∼IBI'LITY *n.*, ∼IBLY² *adv.* [f. LL *immiscibilis* (as IM-², MISCIBLE)]

immi'tigab|le *a.* that cannot be mitigated; hence ∼LY² *adv.* [f. LL IM²(*mitigabilis*; see MITIGATE, -ABLE)]

immi'xture *n.* mixing up; being involved (*in*). [f. IM-¹ + MIXTURE]

immō'bile *a.* immovable; not mobile; motionless; so **immō'bil**ISM *n.*, policy of extreme conservatism, **immobi'l**ITY *n.* [ME f. OF, f. L IM²(*mobilis* MOBILE)]

immō'biliz|e, **-īs|e** (-īz), *v.t.* fix immovably; keep (limb, patient) restricted in movement for healing purposes; restrict free movement of; make (troops, vehicle) incapable of being shifted; withdraw (coins) from circulation to support banknotes; hence ∼A'TION *n.* [f. F *immobiliser* (as prec.; see -IZE)]

immō'derate *a.* excessive, lacking moderation; hence ∼LY² (-tlĭ) *adv.* [ME, f. L IM²(*moderatus* MODERATE¹)]

immō'dest *a.* having no modesty, forward, impudent; lacking due decency; hence or cogn. ∼LY² *adv.*, ∼Y¹ *n.* [f. F *immodeste* or f. L IM²(*modestus* MODEST)]

i'mmol|āte *v.t.* kill (victim) as sacrifice; (fig.) sacrifice (thing etc. *to* another); so ∼A'TION, ∼ātOR, *ns.* [f. L IM¹*molare* sprinkle with MEAL¹ (*mola*), sacrifice + -ATE³]

immō'ral *a.* not conforming to, or opposed to, morality; morally evil (esp. in sexual matters); depraved, dissolute; hence or cogn. **immorā'l**ITY *n.*, ∼LY² *adv.* [f. IM-² + MORAL]

immōr'tal *a.* & *n.* **1.** *a.* living for ever, not mortal; divine; unfading, incorruptible; that will be famous for all time; *the Immortal* MEMORY; so ∼ITY (-ă'l-) *n.*, ∼IZE (3) *v.t.*, ∼LY² *adv.* **2.** *n.* immortal being, esp. (in *pl.*) gods of antiquity; person esp. author of enduring fame, (*I*∼) member of French Academy; (in *pl.*) royal bodyguard of ancient Persia. [ME, f. L IM²(*mortalis* MORTAL)]

immōrtě'lle *n.* composite flower of papery texture

retaining shape and colour after being dried, esp. helichrysum. [F, fem. of *immortel* = prec.]

immo'v|able (īmoō'-) *a.* & *n.* **1.** *a.* that cannot be moved; motionless; not subject to change (*immovable* FEAST); steadfast, unyielding; emotionless; (Law, of property) consisting of land, houses, etc.; hence ∼ABI'LITY, ∼ableNESS (-bəln-), *ns.*, ∼ABLY *adv.* **2.** *n.* (in *pl.*) immovable property. [ME, f. IM-² + MOVABLE]

immū'ne *a.* having immunity (*from*, *against*, *to*, poison, infection, contagion, criticism, punishment, etc.); relating to immunity (*immune mechanism*; ∼ **body**, antibody). [ME, f. L IM²(*munis* ready for service) exempt from public service or charge; Med. use f. F *immun*]

immū'nit̄y *n.* **1.** (Law). exemption (*from* taxation, jurisdiction, etc.). **2.** freedom (*from*); condition of being proof against or exempt from or *from* infection etc.; property by which organisms resist and overcome infection. [ME, f. L *immunitas* (as prec.; see -ITY); Med. use f. F *immunité*]

i'mmūniz|e, **-īs|e** (-īz), *v.t.* render immune (*against* infection etc.); hence ∼A'TION *n.* [f. IMMUNE + -IZE]

immū'nō- *comb. form.* immunity to infection (*immunochemistry*). [f. IMMUNITY + -O-]

immūnō'log|y *n.* study of resistance to infection in man and animals; hence **immūnolō'g**IC(AL) *adjs.*, ∼IST (3) *n.* [f. as prec. + -LOGY]

immūr'e *v.t.* imprison; shut oneself up; hence ∼MENT (-ūr'm-) *n.* [f. F *emmurer* or f. med. L IM¹(*murare* f. *murus* wall)]

immū't|able *a.* unchangeable; not subject to variation in different cases; hence ∼ABI'LITY *n.*, ∼abLY² *adv.* [ME, f. L IM²(*mutabilis* MUTABLE)]

imp¹ *n.* child of the Devil; little devil; mischievous child; ||(arch.) child. [OE *impa*, *impe* young shoot, scion, conn. w. foll.]

imp² *v.t.* add feathers to (wing of falcon) so as to improve its flight; (arch.) enlarge, add by grafting [OE *impian* = OHG *impfōn*, *impitōn* f. Rom. *impotare f. med. L *impotus* graft f. Gk *emphutos* implanted, p.p. of *emphuō̌*]

i'mpáct¹ *n.* striking (*on*, *against*), collision (lit. or fig.); (strong) effect, influence; ∼ **strength**, ability of a material to resist breaking when struck. [f. L (as IMPINGE)]

impǎ'ct² *v.t.* press or fix firmly (*into*, *in*); (in *p.p.*, of tooth) wedged between another tooth and jaw, (of fractured bone) with parts pushed together; hence ∼ION *n.* [back-form. f. impacted f. L p.p. prec.) + -ED¹]

impair' *v.t.* damage; weaken; so ∼MENT *n.* [ME *empeire* f. OF *empeirier* f. Rom. *impejorare make worse f. as IM-¹ + LL *pejorare* (L *pejor* worse)]

impǎ'la (-ah'-, -ǎ'-) *n.* (*pl.* same) small S. Afr. antelope (*Aepyceros melampus*). [Zulu]

impā'le *v.t.* **1.** transfix (body etc. *upon* or *with* stake etc., esp. Hist. as form of torture or capital punishment). **2.** (Her.) combine (two coats of arms) by placing side by side one shield separated by vertical line down middle. **3.** So ∼MENT (-lm-) *n.* [f. F *empaler* or f. med. L IM¹(*palare* f. *palus* stake)]

impǎ'lp|able *a.* imperceptible to the touch; not easily grasped by the mind, intangible; (of powder) very fine, not containing grains that can be felt; hence ∼ABI'LITY *n.*, ∼abLY² *adv.* [F, or f. LL IM²(*palpabilis* PALPABLE)]

impǎ'nel. See EMPANEL.

impǎ'radīse *v.t.* bring into state of supreme happiness; enrapture; make a paradise of (place, state). [f. IM-¹ + PARADISE]

impärisy̆llǎ'bic *a.* & *n.* (Gram.) (noun) that has different numbers of syllables in different cases (e.g. L *lapis lapidis*). [f. L *impar* unequal + -I- + SYLLABIC]

impǎr'k *v.t.* enclose (animals) in park; enclose (land) for park. [ME, f. AF *enparker*, OF EM¹(*parquer* f. *parc* PARK)]

impăr't *v.t.* give share of (thing *to* person etc.); communicate (news etc. *to*); hence ∿A'TION, ∿MENT, *ns.* [ME, f. OF *impartir* f. L IM¹(*partire* f. *pars* PART¹)]

impăr'tial (-shǎl) *a.* not partial, unprejudiced, fair; hence ∿ITY (-shǐǎ'l-) *n.*, ∿LY² *adv.* [f. IM-² + PARTIAL]

impăr'tible *a.* (Law, esp. of estate) not divisible. [f. LL IM²(*partibilis* PARTIBLE)]

impa'ss|able (-pah'-) *a.* that cannot be traversed; hence ∿ABI'LITY, ∿ableNESS (-beln-), *ns.*, ∿ABLY *adv.* [f. IM-² + PASSABLE]

impa'sse (ămpah's) *n.* blind alley; position from which there is no escape; = DEAD*lock* (2). [F (as IM-², *passer* PASS¹)]

impă'ss|ible *a.* incapable of feeling or emotion; incapable of suffering injury; (Theol.) not subject to suffering; hence ∿IBI'LITY, ∿ibleNESS (-beln-), *ns.*, ∿IBLY *adv.* [ME f. OF, f. eccl. L IM²(*passibilis* PASSIBLE)]

impă'ssion (-shon) *v.t.* (esp. in *p.p.*) stir the passions of, excite strongly; fill with passion. [f. It. IM¹(*passionare* f. *passione* PASSION¹)]

impă'ssive *a.* **1.** deficient in or incapable of feeling emotion; undisturbed by passion, serene. **2.** without sensation; not subject to suffering. **3.** Hence ∿LY² (-vlǐ) *adv.*, ∿NESS (-vn-), **impăssi'vITY,** *ns.* [f. IM-² + PASSIVE]

impă'sto *n.* (*pl.* ∿s). laying on of paint thickly; this style of painting. [It. IM¹(*pastare* f. PASTA)]

impa'ti|ent (-shent) *a.* not enduring with composure (*at, with*); (of action) indicating such feeling; intolerant *of*; restlessly desirous (*for* thing, *to* do); hence or cogn. ∿ENCE (-shens) *n.*, ∿entLY² *adv.* [ME f. OF, f. L IM²(*patiens*; see PATIENT)]

impaw'n *v.t.* (arch.) put in pawn; (fig.) pledge, plight. [f. IM-¹ + PAWN²]

impea'ch *v.t.* call in question, disparage, (character etc.); accuse (person) *of*, charge (*with*); find fault with (thing); accuse of treason or other high crime before competent tribunal; hence or cogn. ∿ABLE *a.*, ∿MENT *n.* [ME, f. OF *empe(s)cher* impede f. LL IM¹(*pedicare* f. *pedica* fetter, f. *pes pedis* foot) entangle]

impe'cc|able *a.* not liable to sin; (of thing) faultless; hence or cogn. ∿ABI'LITY, ∿ABLY *adv.*, ∿ANCY *n.*, ∿ANT *a.* [f. L IM²(*peccabilis* f. *peccare* sin; see-ABLE)]

impecū'ni|ous *a.* having little or no money; hence ∿o'SITY *n.* [f. IM-² + obs. *pecunious* having money f. L *pecuniosus* (*pecunia* money f. *pecu* cattle; see -OUS)]

impe'dance *n.* total effective resistance of electric circuit etc. to alternating current, arising from ohmic resistance and reactance; analogous mechanical property. [f. foll. + -ANCE]

impe'de *v.t.* retard by obstructing, hinder. [f. L IM¹(*pedire* f. *pes* foot), lit. shackle the feet of]

impe'diment *n.* hindrance, obstruction; defect in one's speech, e.g. lisp or stammer; hence ∿AL (-ĕ'n-) *a.* [ME, f. L *impedimentum* (as prec.; see -MENT)]

impĕdimĕ'nta *n. pl.* encumbrances; travelling--equipment, esp. of army etc. [L, pl. of *impedimentum* (see prec.)]

impĕ'l *v.t.* (-ll-). drive, force, urge by moral action, (person etc. *to* action, *to* do); drive forward, propel; hence ∿lENT *a. & n.*, ∿lER¹ (2) *n.* [ME, f. L IM¹(*pellere puls-* drive)]

impĕ'nd *v.i.* hang, be suspended, (*over*); (fig., of danger) hang threateningly (*over*); be about to happen; so ∿ENCE, ∿ENCY, *ns.*, ∿ENT, ∿ING², *adjs.* [f. L IM¹(*pendēre* hang)]

impe'nĕtr|able *a.* that cannot be penetrated; inscrutable, unfathomable; impervious (*to, by* ideas etc.); having that property in virtue of which two bodies cannot occupy same place at same time; hence ∿ABI'LITY, **ableNESS** (-beln-), *ns.*, ∿ABLY *adv.* [ME, f. F *impénétrable* f. L IM²(*penetrabilis* PENETRABLE)]

impe'nĕtrāte *v.t.* penetrate deeply. [f. IM-¹ + PENETRATE]

impĕ'nĭt|ent *a.* not repentant or penitent; hence or cogn. ∿ENCE, ∿ENCY, *ns.*, ∿entLY² *adv.* [f. eccl. L IM²(*paenitens* PENITENT)]

impĕ'rative *a. & n.* **1.** *a.* (Gram., of mood) expressing command (*come here!*); commanding, peremptory; urgent; obligatory; hence ∿LY² (-vlǐ) *adv.*, ∿NESS (-vn-) *n.* **2.** *n.* (Gram.) imperative mood, whence **imperati'vAL** *a.*; command (CATEGORICAL *imperative*). [f. LL *imperativus* f. IM¹(*perare* = *parare* make ready) command; see -IVE; in Gram. transl. Gk *prostaktikē* (*egklisis* mood)]

impera'tŏr (-ah'-) *n.* (Rom. Hist.) commander (title conferred by salutation of soldiers on victorious general, under the Republic); emperor; so **impĕratŏr'IAL** *a.* [L (as prec.; see -OR)]

impercĕ'pt|ible *a.* that cannot be perceived; very slight, gradual, or subtle; hence ∿IBI'LITY *n.*, ∿IBLY *adv.* [F, or f. med. L IM²(*perceptibilis* PERCEPTIBLE)]

imperci'pi|ent *a.* lacking in perception; hence ∿ENCE *n.* [f. IM-² + PERCIPIENT]

imperfĕ'ct *a. & n.* **1.** *a.* not fully formed or done, incomplete; faulty; (Gram., of tense) denoting (usu. past) action going on but not completed (*he was singing*); imperfect RHYME¹; hence ∿LY² *adv.* **2.** *n.* imperfect tense. [ME *imparfit* etc., f. OF *imparfait* f. L *imperfectus* (as IM-², PERFECT¹)]

imperfĕ'ction *n.* incompleteness; faultiness; fault, blemish. [ME f. OF, or f. LL *imperfectio* as prec.; see -ION)]

imperfĕ'ctive *a. & n.* (Gram.) **1.** *a.* (Of verb aspect etc.) expressing action without reference to its completion (opp. *perfective*). **2.** *n.* imperfective aspect or form of verb. [f. IMPERFECT + -IVE]

impĕr'forate *a.* not perforated, esp. (Anat.) lacking the normal opening; (of sheet of postage stamps or single stamp) not provided with rows of perforations. [f. IM-² + PERFORATE²]

impēr'ial *a. & n.* **1.** *a.* of an empire or sovereign state ranking with an empire; (Hist.) of the British Empire (now COMMONWEALTH). **2.** of an emperor; supreme in authority; majestic, august; magnificent. **3.** (Of weights and measures) used (now or formerly) by statute in UK (*imperial* GALLON, *acre, etc.*). **4.** Hence ∿LY² *adv.* **5.** *n.* small part of beard left growing beneath lower lip [partly from Napoleon III of France, but founded in F 1829, E 1838]; (arch.) trunk for luggage, adapted for roof of coach; size of paper, 762 × 559 or *787 × 584 mm. [ME f. OF, f. L *imperialis* (IMPERIUM; see -AL)]

impēr'ial|ism *n.* rule of an emperor; (Hist.) extension of British Empire where trade required protection given by imperial rule; (Hist.) union of different parts of British Empire for purposes of warlike defence, internal commerce, etc.; (usu. derog.) (belief in desirability of) acquiring colonies and dependencies, or extending a country's influence through trade, diplomacy, etc.; hence ∿i'stIC *a.*, ∿IZE (3) *v.t.* [f. prec. + -ISM]

impēr'ialist *n.* adherent of an emperor, esp. (1600–1800) of Holy Roman Emperor; advocate of imperial rule; advocate or agent of (esp. British or American) imperialism. [f. IMPERIAL + -IST]

impĕ'ril *v.t.* (||-ll-). bring or put into danger. [f. IM-¹ + PERIL]

impĕr'ious *a.* overbearing, domineering; urgent; imperative; hence ∿LY² *adv.*, ∿NESS *n.* [f. L *imperiosus* (IMPERIUM; see -OUS)]

impĕr'ish|able *a.* that cannot perish; hence ∿ABI'LITY, ∿ableNESS (-beln-), *ns.*, ∿ABLY *adv.* [f. IM-² + PERISHABLE]

imperium (impēr'ĭum, -ĕ'r-) *n.* absolute power; empire; ∿ *in imperio,* supreme authority within jurisdiction of another authority. [L, = command, dominion]

impĕr'man|ent *a.* not permanent; hence ∿ENCE, ∿ENCY, *ns.* [f. IM-² + PERMANENT]

impĕr'me|able *a.* that cannot be penetrated through;

(Phys.) that does not permit passage of fluids; hence ~ABI'LITY *n.* [f. F *imperméable* or f. LL IM²(*permeabilis* PERMEABLE)]
impermi'ssible *a.* not allowable. [f. IM-² + PERMISSIBLE]
imperscri'ptible *a.* not backed by written authority. [f. IM-² + L PER(*scribere script-* write) register; see -IBLE]
imper'sonal *a.* **1.** (Gram.) ~ **verb** (used only in 3rd person singular without definite subject, e.g. *it snows, methinks*); *impersonal* PRONOUN. **2.** having no personality; having no personal feeling, reference, or tone. **3.** Hence ~ITY (-ă'l-) *n.*, ~LY² *adv.* [f. LL IM²(*personalis* PERSONAL)]
imper'son|āte *v.t.* represent in bodily form, personify; pretend to be (another person) for purpose of entertainment or fraud; act (character); hence ~A'TION, ~**ātor**, *ns.* [f. IM-¹ + L *persona* PERSON + -ATE³]
imperso'nify *v.* (arch.) personify. [f. IM-¹ + PERSONIFY, after prec.]
imper'tin|ent *a.* **1.** (esp. Law). irrelevant, intrusive. **2.** out of place, absurd. **3.** insolent, saucy, lacking proper respect. **4.** Hence or cogn. ~ENCE *n.*, ~**ent**LY² *adv.* [ME f. OF, or f. LL IM²(*pertinens* PERTINENT)]
impertur'b|able *a.* not excitable, calm; hence ~ABI'LITY, ~**able**NESS (-beln-), *ns.*, ~ABLY *adv.* [ME, f. LL IM²(*perturbabilis* f. as PERTURB + -ABLE)]
imper'vious *a.* not affording passage (*to* water etc.); (fig.) not responsive *to* (argument etc.); hence ~LY² *adv.*, ~NESS *n.* [f. L IM²(*pervius* PERVIOUS)]
impeti'gō *n.* (*pl.* ~s). contagious acute pustular disease of skin; so **impeti'gin**OUS *a.* [ME, f. L *impetigo -ginis* f. IM¹(*petere* seek) assail]
i'mpetr|āte *v.t.* (Theol.) obtain by request; so ~A'TION *n.*, ~**āt**ORY *a.* [f. L IM¹(*petrare* = *patrare* bring to pass) + -ATE³]
impe'tūous *a.* moving violently or rapidly; acting or done with rash or sudden energy; hence or cogn. **impetūo'**SITY, ~NESS, *ns.*, ~LY² *adv.* [ME, f. OF *impetueux* f. LL *impetuosus* (as foll.; see -OUS)]
i'mpetus *n.* force or energy with which a body moves; (fig.) moving force, impulse. [L, = assault, force, f. IM¹(*petere* seek) assail]
i'mpeyan (-pĭan) *a.* ~ **pheasant,** Indian pheasant of genus *Lophophorus*, with crested head and brilliant plumage. [f. Sir E. *Impey*, Engl. judge d. 1809 and his wife, who sought to naturalize it in England, + -AN]
i'mpi *n.* body of S. Afr. Bantu warriors. [Zulu]
impi'ety *n.* ungodliness; (act etc. showing) lack of dutifulness or reverence. [ME, f. OF *impieté* or f. L IM²(*pietas* f. *pius* PIOUS; see -TY¹)]
impi'gnorāte *v.t.* (Sc.) = PAWN³, mortgage. [f. L IM¹(*pignorare* f. *pignus* a pledge)]
impi'nge (-nj) *v.i.* & *t.* (cause to) make impact (*on, upon*); encroach (*on, upon*); hence ~MENT (-njm-) *n.* [f. L IM¹(*pingere pact-* = *pangere* fix, drive) drive (thing) at]
i'mpious *a.* not pious; wicked, profane; hence ~LY² *adv.* [f. L IM²(*pius* PIOUS)]
i'mpish *a.* of or like an imp, mischievous; hence ~LY² *adv.*, ~NESS *n.* [f. IMP¹ + -ISH¹]
implă'c|able *a.* that cannot be appeased, inexorable; hence or cogn. ~ABI'LITY *n.*, ~ABLY *adv.* [ME f. F, or f. L IM²(*placabilis* PLACABLE)]
impla'nt¹ (-ah'-) *v.t.* insert, fix, (*in*); instil (principle, idea, etc., *in* mind etc.); plant; (Med.) insert (tissue etc.) in a living body, (in *pass.*, of fertilized ovum) become attached to womb wall; hence ~A'TION *n.* [f. F *implanter* or f. LL IM¹(*plantare* PLANT²) engraft]
i'mplant² (-ah-) *n.* thing implanted, esp. in the body, e.g. piece of tissue or capsule containing radioactive material. [f. prec.]
implau's|ible (-z-) *a.* not plausible; hence or cogn. ~IBI'LITY *n.*, ~IBLY *adv.* [f. IM-² + PLAUSIBLE]
implea'd *v.t.* (Law). prosecute or take proceedings against (person); involve in suit. [ME, f. AF *empleder*, OF *empleidier* (as EM-¹, PLEAD)]
imple'dge *v.t.* (arch.) put in pledge, pawn. [f. IM-¹ + PLEDGE¹]
i'mplement¹ *n.* tool, instrument, utensil; (in *pl.*) equipment, articles of furniture, dress, etc.; (Sc. Law) full performance. [ME, f. med. L *implementa* pl. f. *implēre* employ f. L IM¹(*plēre plet-* fill); see -MENT]
i'mplement² *v.t.* complete (contract etc.); fulfil (undertaking); put (decision, plan, etc.) into effect; fill up, supplement; hence ~A'TION *n.* [f. prec.]
implē'tion *n.* (arch.) filling; fullness. [ME, f. LL *impletio* (as IMPLEMENT¹; see -ION)]
i'mplicate¹ *n.* thing implied. [f. L *implicatus* p.p. of IM¹(*plicare plicat-* or *plicit-* fold); see -ATE¹]
i'mplic|āte² *v.t.* lead to as consequence or inference, whence ~**āt**IVE *a.*; show (person) to be concerned (*in* charge, crime, etc.); (in *pass.*) be affected *in* (a thing's operation); (arch.) entwine, entangle. [ME, f. as prec. + -ATE³]
implicā'tion *n.* implicating or implying; what is involved or implied in something else; **by** ~, by what is implied, as a natural inference. [ME, f. L *implicatio* (as IMPLICATE¹; see -ATION)]
impli'cit *a.* implied though not plainly expressed; virtually contained (*in*); (Math., of function) not expressed directly in terms of independent variable(s); ~ **faith, obedience,** etc., (not independently reached by the individual, but resting on authority of Church etc., absolute, unquestioning; cf. EXPLICIT); hence ~LY² *adv.*, ~NESS *n.* [f. F *implicite* or f. L *implicitus* (as IMPLICATE¹)]
implō'de *v.i* & *t.* (cause to) burst inwards; so **implō'**SION (-zhon) *n.*, **implō'**SIVE (-s-, -z-) *a.* [f. IM-¹ + L *-plodere*, after EXPLODE]
implor'e *v.t.* beg earnestly for; entreat (person *to* do). [f. F *implorer* or f. L IM¹(*plorare* weep) invoke with tears]
imply' *v.t.* involve the truth or existence of (thing not expressly asserted; *that*); signify; insinuate, hint; hence **implied**LY² (-ī'īd-, -ī'd-) *adv.* [ME, f. OF *emplier* f. L *implicare* (see IMPLICATE¹)]
||**impō'lder** *v.t.* make a polder of; reclaim from the sea. [f. Du. *inpolderen* (as IN-¹, POLDER)]
impo'licy *n.* bad policy; inexpediency. [f. IM-² + POLICY¹, after *impolitic*]
impolī'te *a.* (-est). not courteous; ill-mannered, rude; hence ~LY² (-tlĭ) *adv.*, ~NESS (-tn-) *n.* [f. L IM²(*politus* POLITE)]
impo'litic *a.* not politic; inexpedient; hence ~LY² *adv.* [f. IM-² + POLITIC]
impŏnderabi'lia *n. pl.* imponderables. [mod. L, neut. pl. of *imponderabilis* — foll.]
impo'nderable *a.* & *n.* **1.** *a.* (Phys.) having no weight; very light; (fig.) that cannot be estimated. **2.** *n.* imponderable thing (esp. fig., in *pl.*, of qualities, emotions, etc.). [f. IM-² + PONDERABLE]
impō'nent *a.* & *n.* (person) that imposes a duty etc. [f. IMPOSE after *opponent* etc.]
impor't¹ *v.t.* **1.** bring, introduce, (thing, esp. goods from another country *into*); hence ~ABLE *a.*, ~A'TION, ~ER¹, *ns.* **2.** imply, indicate, signify, (thing, *that*); express, make known, (*that*). **3.** (arch.) be of consequence to (*it imports us to know*). [ME, f. L IM¹(*portare* carry) bring in, in med. L = imply, be of consequence]
i'mport² *n.* **1.** what is implied, meaning; importance. **2.** importation; (usu. in *pl.*) amount imported; imported article or commodity. [f. prec.]
impor'tance *n.* being important; weight, significance; personal consequence, dignity. [F, f. med. L *importantia* (as IMPORT¹; see -ANCE)]
impor'tant *a.* carrying with it great consequence (*to* person concerned or purpose etc.), weighty, momentous; (of person) having high rank; consequential, pompous; hence ~LY² *adv.* [F, f. med. L (as IMPORT¹; see -ANT)]

impŏr'tŭnate *a.* persistent, pressing, in solicitation; (of affairs) urgent; hence or cogn. ∿LY² (-tlĭ) *adv.*, **importū'nĭty** *n.* [f. L ɪᴍ²(*portunus* f. *portus* harbour) inconvenient + -ᴀᴛᴇ²]

importūne (-ōr'-, -ū'-) *v.t.* solicit pressingly (person, or abs.); solicit for immoral purpose. [f. F *importuner* or f. med. L *importunari* (as prec.)]

impŏ's|e (-z) *v.* **1.** *v.t.* lay (tax, duty, charge, obligation, on or upon); compel compliance with. **2.** palm off (thing *upon* person); force (one*self*) *on* attention etc. of (person). **3.** (Print.) lay (pages of type) in proper order and secure them in a ᴄʜᴀꜱᴇ⁵. **4.** (arch.) place (thing) *upon*. **5.** *v.i.* exert influence (*on* person) by impressive character or appearance; hence ∿ɪɴɢ² *a.* **6.** practise deception (*on* or *upon*); ∿e on or upon, take advantage of (person, esp. willing or good-natured or gullible one). [ME, f. F *imposer* f. L ɪᴍ¹- (*ponere posit-* put) inflict, deceive; see ᴘᴏꜱᴇ¹]

imposi'tion (-z-) *n.* imposing or being imposed; laying on *of hands* (in ordination etc.); impost, tax, duty; piece of deception or imposture or advantage-taking; ‖work set as punishment at school. [ME f. OF, or f. L *impositio* (*imponere*; see prec., -ɪᴛɪᴏɴ)]

impŏ'ss|ible *a.* not possible, that cannot be done or exist, (*such a thing is impossible*; *it is impossible to alter them*); (loosely) not easy, not convenient, not easily believable; (colloq.) outrageous, intolerable, (*an impossible hat, person*); hence or cogn. ∿ɪBɪ'ʟɪᴛʏ *n.*, ∿ɪBʟʏ *adv.* [ME f. OF, or f. L ɪᴍ²(*possibilis* ᴘᴏꜱꜱɪBʟᴇ)]

i'mpŏst¹ *n.* tax, duty, tribute; (sl.) weight carried by racehorse in handicap. [F, f. med. L *impostus, -um* masc. & neut. p.p. (as n.) of *imponere* (see ɪᴍᴘᴏꜱᴇ)]

i'mpŏst² *n.* upper course of pillar, carrying arch. [f. F *imposte* or f. It. *imposta* fem. p.p. (as n.) of *imporre* f. L *imponere* (see ɪᴍᴘᴏꜱᴇ)]

impŏ'st|or *n.* one who assumes a false character or passes himself off as someone else; swindler; hence ∿(o)ʀᴏᴜꜱ *a.* [f. F *imposteur* f. LL *impos*(*i*)*tor* (as ɪᴍᴘᴏꜱᴛ¹; see -ᴏʀ)]

impŏ'st(h)ūme (-tūm) *n.* (arch.) purulent swelling, abscess, (lit. or fig.). [ME, f. OF *empostume* f. L f. Gk ᴀᴘᴏ(*stēma* f. *sta-* stand) separation into abscess]

impŏ'sture *n.* fraudulent deception. [F, f. LL *impostura* (as ɪᴍᴘᴏꜱᴛ¹; see -ᴜʀᴇ)]

i'mpot|ent *a.* powerless; helpless, decrepit; (esp. of male) wholly lacking in sexual power, unable to copulate or reach orgasm or (pop.) to procreate; hence or cogn. ∿ᴇɴᴄᴇ, ∿ᴇɴᴄʏ, *ns.*, ∿ᴇɴᴛʟʏ² *adv.* [ME f. OF, f. L ɪᴍ²(*potens* ᴘᴏᴛᴇɴᴛ¹)]

impou'nd *v.t.* shut up (cattle) in pound; shut up (person, thing) as in pound; take legal possession of; confiscate; (of dam etc.) collect or confine (water). [f. ɪᴍ-¹ + ᴘᴏᴜɴᴅ²]

impŏ'verish *v.t.* make poor; exhaust strength or natural fertility of; hence ∿ᴍᴇɴᴛ *n.* [ME, f. OF ᴇᴍ¹- (*poverir* f. *povre* ᴘᴏᴏʀ); see -ɪꜱʜ²]

imprǎ'ctic|able *a.* impossible in practice; (of person or thing) unmanageable; (of road etc.) impassable; hence ∿ᴀBɪ'ʟɪᴛʏ, ∿ᴀBʟᴇɴᴇꜱꜱ (-beln-), *ns.*, ∿ᴀBʟʏ *adv.* [f. ɪᴍ-² + ᴘʀᴀᴄᴛɪᴄᴀBʟᴇ]

imprǎ'ctical *a.* not practical; not practicable; hence ∿ɪᴛʏ (-ǎ'l-) *n.* [f. ɪᴍ-² + ᴘʀᴀᴄᴛɪᴄᴀʟ]

i'mprecāte *v.t.* invoke, call down, (evil *upon* person etc.); so ∿ᴀ'ᴛɪᴏɴ *n.* (esp., spoken curse), ∿ᴀᴛᴏʀʏ *a.* [f. L ɪᴍ¹(*precari* pray) + -ᴀᴛᴇ³]

imprecī'se *a.* not precise; hence ∿ʟʏ² (-slĭ) *adv.*, **imprecī'sion** (-zhon) *n.* [f. ɪᴍ-² + ᴘʀᴇᴄɪꜱᴇ]

imprĕ'gn|able¹ *a.* (Of fortress etc.) that cannot be taken by force; (fig.) proof against attack; hence ∿ᴀBɪ'ʟɪᴛʏ *n.*, ∿ᴀBʟʏ *adv.* [ME f. OF *imprenable* (as ɪᴍ-², *prendre* take, -ᴀBʟᴇ)]

imprĕ'gnable² *a.* that can be impregnated. [f. ɪᴍ-ᴘʀᴇɢɴᴀᴛᴇ² + -ᴀBʟᴇ]

imprĕ'gnate¹ *a.* pregnant (lit. or fig.); permeated (*with*). [f. LL *impregnatus* p.p. of ɪᴍ¹(*pregnare* be ᴘʀᴇɢ-ɴᴀɴᴛ); see -ᴀᴛᴇ²]

imprĕgn|āte² (ĭ'-, -ĕ'-) *v.t.* **1.** make (female) pregnant; (Biol.) fertilize (female reproductive cell or ovum). **2.** fill, saturate, (*with*); imbue, fill, (*with* feelings, moral qualities, etc.). **3.** Hence or cogn. ∿ᴀᴛᴀBʟᴇ *a.*, ∿ᴀ'ᴛɪᴏɴ *n.* [f. as prec. + -ᴀᴛᴇ³]

imprĕsā'ri'ō *n.* (*pl.* ∿s). organizer of public entertainments, esp. manager of operatic or concert company. [It. (*impresa* undertaking, as ᴇᴍᴘʀɪꜱᴇ; see -ᴀʀʏ¹)]

imprĕscrī'ptible *a.* not subject to prescription, that cannot be legally taken away, (*imprescriptible right*). [f. med. L *imprescriptibilis* (as ɪᴍ-², ᴘʀᴇꜱᴄʀɪBᴇ, -ɪBʟᴇ)]

i'mprĕss¹ *n.* stamping; mark made by seal, stamp, etc.; (fig.) characteristic mark or quality; = ɪᴍᴘʀᴇꜱ-ꜱɪᴏɴ 3. [f. foll.]

imprĕ'ss² *v.t.* apply (mark etc.) with pressure, imprint, stamp, (*on*); imprint, enforce, (idea etc., *that*, *what*, etc., *on* person, his mind); mark (thing *with* stamp etc., lit. or fig.); affect or influence deeply, whence ∿ɪBʟᴇ *a.*; affect (person) favourably or strongly (*with* idea etc.); (Electr.) apply (voltage etc.) from outside. [ME, f. OF ᴇᴍ¹(*presser* ᴘʀᴇꜱꜱ²)]

imprĕ'ss³ *v.t.* (Hist.) force (men) to serve in army or navy, seize (goods etc.) for public service; (arch.) enlist, make use of, (thing) in argument etc.; hence ∿ᴍᴇɴᴛ *n.* [f. ɪᴍ-¹ + ᴘʀᴇꜱꜱ³]

imprĕ'ssion (-shon) *n.* **1.** impressing (of mark). **2.** mark impressed; print taken from type or engraving; (printing of) number of copies of book, newspaper, etc., issued at one time; unaltered reprint from standing type or plates (as opp. to *edition*). **3.** effect produced (esp. on mind or feelings); representation of this by artist, mimic, etc. **4.** notion, (vague or mistaken) belief, impressed on the mind, (*that is my impression*; *I was under the impression, had the impression, that*). [ME f. OF f. L *impressio -onis* f. ɪᴍ¹(*primere press- = premere* ᴘʀᴇꜱꜱ²)]

imprĕ'ssion|able *a.* susceptible of impressions, easily influenced; hence ∿ᴀBɪ'ʟɪᴛʏ *n.* [f. F *impressionnable* (*impressionner*, as prec.; see -ᴀBʟᴇ)]

imprĕ'ssion|ism (-shon-) *n.* style of painting, music, or writing, such as to give general tone and effect without elaborate finish or detail; so ∿ɪꜱᴛ (2) *n.*, ∿ɪ'ꜱᴛɪᴄ *a.* (also = subjective, unsystematic, after ɪᴍᴘʀᴇꜱꜱɪᴏɴ 4). [f. F *impressionnisme* (as ɪᴍᴘʀᴇꜱꜱɪᴏɴ; see -ɪꜱᴍ)]

imprĕ'ssive *a.* (Of language, scene, etc.) able to excite deep feeling; deeply impressing mind or senses, esp. so as to cause approval or admiration; hence ∿ʟʏ² (-vlĭ) *adv.*, ∿ɴᴇꜱꜱ (-vn-) *n.* [f. ɪᴍᴘʀᴇꜱꜱ² + -ɪᴠᴇ]

i'mprĕst *n.* money advanced to person for use in State business. [f. phr. *in prest* (OF *prest* loan, advance pay; see ᴘʀᴇꜱꜱ³)]

imprīma'tur (-ā'-, -ah'-) *n.* official licence to print (esp. works sanctioned by RC Ch.); (fig.) sanction. [L, = let it be printed]

imprimatura (ĭmprēmatoor'a) *n.* (Paint.) coloured transparent glaze as primer. [f. It. *imprimitura* (*imprimere* ɪᴍᴘʀᴇꜱꜱ²; see -ᴜʀᴇ)]

imprī'mis *adv.* (arch.) in the first place. [assim. f. L *in primis* among the first things]

i'mprint¹ *n.* impression, stamp, (lit. or fig.); **publisher's, printer's,** ∿ (name, place etc., on title-page or at end of book). [ME, f. F *empreinte* stamp, fem. p.p. (as n.) of *empreindre* (see foll.)]

imprī'nt² *v.t.* stamp (figure etc. *on*); impress (idea etc. *on* or *in* mind, memory, etc.); impress (quality etc. *on* or *in*); stamp (thing *with* figure); (Psych.) become recognized as object of attachment by (esp. young animal). [ME, f. OF *empreinter* f. *empreindre* f. L *imprimere* (see ɪᴍᴘʀᴇꜱꜱɪᴏɴ)]

impri'son (-z-) *v.t.* put into prison; (fig.) confine, shut up; so ∿ᴍᴇɴᴛ *n.* [ME, f. OF ᴇᴍ¹(*prisoner* f. ᴘʀɪꜱᴏɴ)]

improʹb|able *a.* not likely to be true or to happen; existing but not easy to believe true; hence ∿ᴀBɪ'ʟɪᴛʏ *n.*, ∿ᴀBʟʏ *adv.* [F, or f. L ɪᴍ²(*probabilis* ᴘʀᴏBᴀBʟᴇ)]

improʹbity *n.* wickedness, lack of moral integrity; dishonesty. [f. L *improbitas* (as ɪᴍ-², ᴘʀᴏBɪᴛʏ)]

For other words in *im-* see ɪᴍ-¹ or (esp.) ɪᴍ-².

imprŏ'mptū *adv.*, *n.*, & *a.* extempore (performance, composition, speech); musical composition having character of improvisation. [F, f. L *in promptu* in readiness (see PROMPT¹)]

imprŏ'per *a.* **1.** inaccurate, wrong; not properly so called; ∼ **fraction** (greater than unity, with numerator greater than denominator). **2.** unseemly, indecent; not in accordance with rules of conduct. **3.** Hence ∼LY² *adv.* [f. F *impropre* or f. L *improprius* (as IM-², PROPER)]

‖**imprŏ'pri|āte** *v.t.* annex (ecclesiastical benefice) to corporation or person as property; place (tithes, ecclesiastical property) in lay hands; so ∼A'TION *n.* [f. AL IM¹(*propriare* f. *proprius* own) + -ATE³]

‖**imprŏ'priātor** *n.* one to whom benefice is impropriated. [f. prec. | -OR]

impropri'ety *n.* incorrectness; unfitness; indecency; instance of improper conduct etc. [f. F *impropriété* or f. L IM²(*proprietas* f. *proprius* PROPER; see -TY¹)]

improv'v|able (-ōo'v-) *a.* that can be improved; suitable for cultivation; hence ∼ABI'LITY, ∼**ableNESS** (-beln-), *ns.* [f. foll. + -ABLE]

impro've (-ōo'v) *v.t.* & *i.* **1.** make or become better; (in *pres. part.*) giving moral benefit (*an improving book*). **2.** make good use of (*the occasion, the opportunity*); ∼ **on** or **upon**, produce something better than. [orig. *em* , *improv(e)* f. AF *emprower* f. OF EM-¹ + *prou* profit, infl. by PROVE]

impro'vement (-ōo'vm-) *n.* improving or being improved; addition or alteration that adds to value. [ME, f. AF *emprowement* (as prec.); see -MENT)]

impro'ver (-ōo'v-) *n.* In vbl senses; ‖one who works at trade for low wage or none to improve his skill. [f. IMPROVE + -ER¹]

impro-'vid|ent *a.* unforeseeing; heedless; thriftless; hence or cogn. ∼ENCE *n.*, ∼ent**LY²** *adv.* [F (as IM-², PROVIDENT)]

improvisātor (-z-), **improv(v)isatore** (ĭm-prŏvezȧtōo'ā) (*fem.* **-satrice** *pr.* -trē'chā; *pl.* **-satori** *pr.* -tōr'ē), *n.* one who improvises or composes extempore. [f. (foll. after) It. *improvvisatore* (*improvvisare*; see foll.; -OR)]

i'mproviš|e (-z) *v.t.* compose, utter, (verse, music, etc., or abs.) extempore; provide or construct (thing, or abs.) extempore; hence or cogn. ∼A'TION (-vǐ'z-) *n.*, **improvisător'IAL**, ‖**improvisatORY** (-vǐ'z-, -ā'-), (-z-) *adjs.*, ∼ER¹ *n.* [f. F *improviser* or f. It. *improvvisare* f. *improvviso* extempore, f. L IM²(*provisus* p.p. as PROVIDE)]

impru'd|ent *a.* rash, indiscreet; hence or cogn. ∼ENCE *n.*, ∼ent**LY²** *adv.* [ME, f. L IM²(*prudens* PRUDENT)]

i'mpud|ent *a.* shamelessly presumptuous; unblushing; insolently disrespectful; hence or cogn. ∼ENCE *n.*, ∼ent**LY²** *adv.* [ME, f. L IM²(*pudens* f. *pudēre* be ashamed; see -ENT)]

impudi'city *n.* shamelessness, immodesty. [f. F *impudicité* f. L IM²(*pudicus*, as prec.); see -ITY]

impū'gn (-ū'n) *v.t.* assail by words, call in question, (statement, action); hence ∼ABLE *a.*, ∼MENT *n.* [ME, f. L IM¹(*pugnare* fight) assail]

impū'iss|ant *a.* impotent, weak; so ∼ANCE *n.* [F (as IM-², PUISSANT)]

i'mpulse *n.* **1.** impelling, push; impetus; (Phys.) indefinitely large force acting for very short time but producing finite change of momentum (e.g. blow of hammer), change of momentum caused by such force or by any force; wave of excitation in nerve causing action or inaction of muscle. **2.** mental incitement; sudden tendency to act without reflection (*did it on* (*an*) *impulse*); ∼ **buying** of goods because of sudden temptation rather than previous intent). [f. L *impulsus* (as IMPEL)]

impŭ'lsion (-shon) *n.* impelling push; mental impulse; impetus. [ME f. OF, f. L *impulsio -onis* (as IMPEL; see -ION)]

impŭ'lsive *a.* tending to impel; (Phys.) acting as an impulse; (of person, conduct, etc.) apt to be moved,

prompted, by sudden impulse; hence ∼LY² (-vlĭ) *adv.*, ∼NESS (-vn-) *n.* [ME, f. F *impulsif -ive* or f. LL *impulsivus* (as prec.; see -IVE)]

impū'nitў *n.* being exempt(ed) from punishment, or from injury as consequence of act; **with** ∼, in such a way as to be thus exempt(ed). [f. L *impunitas* f. IM²(*punis* f. *poena* penalty); see -ITY]

impūr'e (*or* ĭ'-) *a.* dirty; unchaste; mixed with foreign matter, adulterated, (lit. or fig.); (of colour) mixed with another colour; hence or cogn. ∼LY² (-ūr'lĭ) *adv.*, **impūr'ITY** *n.* [ME, f. L IM²(*purus* pure)]

impū't|e *v.t.* ∼e **to**, regard (esp. something undesirable) as being done or caused or possessed by, (Theol.) ascribe (righteousness, guilt, etc.) to (person) by virtue of similar quality in another; so ∼A'TION *n.*, ∼ABLE, ∼ATIVE, *adjs.* [ME, f. OF *imputer* f. L IM²(*putare* reckon) enter in the account]

IMS *abbr.* Indian Medical Service.

‖**I.Mun.E.** *abbr.* Institution of Municipal Engineers.

in¹ *prep.* **1.** Expr. inclusion or position within limits of space, time, circumstance, etc., (*in Europe, England, London*), or any town, suburb, village, etc., of public or private importance, cf. AT; *in the house, the street, the car, the pond, a box, a crowd, the rain, school, PRISON, bed, exile, health, his sleep, sorrow, TEAR²s*); wearing as dress (*in flannels, SHIRT-sleeves, gumboots*); with respect to (*blind in one eye; good in parts; in ITSELF; weak in Latin; lacking in courage; dealer in furs; a change in the weather; seven in number; a mile in length*); as a proportionate part of (*one in three failed; gradient of one in six; she is one in a million, 40p in the pound*); as a member of (*serving in the army; has shares in the company*); as content of (*there is something in what you say*); (colloq.) as a kind of (*the latest thing in luxury*); that is etc. the person of (*found a friend in Mary*); concerned with or pertaining to (*in politics, fancy, my opinion*); (of animal) pregnant with (*in calf, pig*); under the influence of (*in liquor*); (Mus.) modulated according to (the key of) (*symphony in G*); (Gram.) having as beginning or ending (*words in 'pro-', in '-ation'*); occupied with, with the purpose of, (*in search of; in reply to; in honour of*); with the form or arrangement or language of (*falling in folds; in ORDER¹ 7; packed in tens; written in French*); with the instrument or material or means of (*drawn in pencil; modelled, worked, in bronze; coat in green velvet; in this way we succeeded*); during the time of (*in the night; in May; in summer; in 1976; in his fortie..; finished in in two days; drowned in crossing the river*); after the time of (*back in ten minutes*); within the ability of (*as far as in me lies*; **have it in one**, have the capacity to do). **2.** into (w. vbs. of motion or change: *put it in your pocket; cut it in two or half; throw it in the fire; slam the door in his face; sun was shining in my eyes*). **3.** (Introducing ind. obj.: *believe in, engage in, rejoice in, share in*). **4.** (Forming adv. phr.: *in any case, in common, in fact, in short, in truth, in vain*). **5. in it,** (usu. w. neg.) in the running, a serious competitor; **nothing, little, not much, in it,** no decided advantage to any competitor or race or difference between alternatives etc.; *in so* FAR *as*; **in that,** since, because, in so far as. [OE, = OS, OHG, Goth. *in*, ON f. IE *(*e*)*n*]

in² *adv.* **1.** Expr. position within certain limits or motion to point at such position (*come in, send him in, walk in*, = into room, house, enclosed ground, etc.); in the house, etc. at home (*will be in tomorrow*); in a publication (*looked for the word, but it was not in; is my article in?*); on or to the inward side (*coat with the woolly side in; rub, burn, it in*); so as to be enclosed (*hemmed, walled, locked, in*); in fashion, season, office, effective or favourable action, (*short skirts, oysters, the Tories, are in; get one's* EYE¹ *in; my luck was in;* TIDE¹ *is in; join in; functioning as batsman, elected candidate, etc.*); (of domestic fire) burning; (of train, boat, season, harvest, request, etc.) having arrived or been received. **2. in at,** present at (the finish etc.); **in between,** within the space(s) or interval(s) between; **in for,** (1) involved in, committed to, about to undergo, (usu. something unpleasant, esp. *it*), (2) engaged in competition for (race, prize, etc.); **have it in for,** seek revenge on (person); *in for a* PENNY; **in and in,** (of breeding) repeated(ly) within same stock; **in on,** (colloq.) sharing in, aware of (secret etc.); **in and out,** sometimes in and sometimes out;(**well**) **in with,** on friendly terms with. **3. day, week, year,** etc. **in, day** etc. **out,** throughout a long succession of days etc.; THROW[1] *in.* **4.** ‖~**-off,** (Bill.) losing HAZARD; ~**-swinger,** (Cricket) ball that swings towards batsman; ~**-tray** (for incoming documents etc.). **5.** (As *suf.* denoting persistent or prolonged action esp. by large numbers: SIT-*in,* TEACH-*in*). [(1) OE *in(n)* w. vbs. of motion, = OS, OHG *in,* ON, Goth. *inn,* (2) OE *inne* w. vbs. of position, = OS, OHG, Goth. *inna,* ON *inni*]

in[3] *a.* **1.** internal, living etc. inside; **in patient, in-patient,** one who remains as resident in hospital while under treatment. **2.** fashionable, sophisticated; esoteric; **in-group,** group of persons united by common interests. [f. prec. used attrib.]

in[4] *n.* **1.** (in *pl.*) political party in office. **2.** (colloq.) introduction to or influence with important person. **3. ins and outs,** turnings to and fro (usu. fig.), details (*of* procedure etc.). [f. IN[2]]

in-[1] *pref.* in, on, into, towards, within, (*incoming, induce, influx, ingredient, inlay, insight, intrude, inveterate*). [f. IN[1,2] or f. or after L (*in* IN[1])]

in-[2] *pref.,* = UN-[2] (*indirect(ly), indisposition, inedible, inobservance, insane, inseparable, insignificant, insoluble, invaluable, invisible*). [L]

-in *suf.* (Chem.) forming names of neutral substances (*casein, gelatin, papain, protein*) and of antibiotics (*penicillin*). [f. -INE[5]]

IN *abbr.* Indiana.

in. *abbr.* inch(es).

In *symb.* indium.

-ina (-ē′na) *suf.* (1) of fem. names and titles (*Georgina, tsarina*), (2) of names of musical instruments (*concertina*), (3) of Zool. groups (*globigerina*). [f. It. or Sp. or f. L]

inabi′lity *n.* being unable; lack of power or means. [ME, f. IN-[2] + ABILITY]

in absentia (ĭn ăbsĕ′ntĭa, -shĭa) *adv.* in (his or her or their) absence. [L]

inacce′ss|ible (-ks-) *a.* not accessible, that cannot be reached; (of person) not open to advances or influence, unapproachable; hence ~IBI′LITY *n.,* ~IBLY *adv.* [ME f. F, or f. LL IN[2]-(*accessibilis* ACCESSIBLE)]

ină′ccŭr|ate *a.* not accurate; hence ~ACY *n.,* ~ateLY[2] (-tlĭ) *adv.* [f. IN-[2] + ACCURATE]

ină′ct|ion *n.* absence of action; sluggishness, inertness. [f. IN-[2] + ACTION]

ină′ctiv|āte *v.t.* make inactive or inoperative; hence ~A′TION *n.* [f. IN-[2] + ACTIVATE]

ină′ctive *a.* not active or inclined to act; indolent; passive; hence or cogn. **inăcti′v**ITY *n.,* ~LY[2] (-vlĭ) *adv.* [f. IN-[2] + ACTIVE]

ină′dĕqu|ate *a.* not adequate (*to* purpose, *to* do); insufficient; incompetent; hence ~ACY *n.,* ~ateLY[2] (-tlĭ) *adv.* [f. IN-[2] + ADEQUATE]

inadmi′ss|ible *a.* that cannot be admitted or allowed; hence ~IBI′LITY *n.,* ~IBLY *adv.* [f. IN-[2] + ADMISSIBLE]

inadvĕ′rt|ent *a.* not properly attentive; negligent; (of action) unintentional; hence or cogn. ~ENCE, ~ENCY, *ns.,* ~ent LY[2] *adv.* [f. IN-[2] + obs. advertent attentive (as ADVERT[2]; see ~ENT)]

inadvī′sable (-z-) *a.* not advisable. [f. IN-[2] + ADVISABLE]

ină′lien|able *a.* not alienable; hence ~ABI′LITY *n.,* ~ABLY *adv.* [f. IN-[2] + ALIENABLE]

ină′lter|able (-aw′l-, -ŏ′l-) *a.* unalterable esp. hence ~ABI′LITY *n.,* ~ABLY *adv.* [f. med. L IN[2](*alterabilis* f. as ALTER; see -ABLE)]

inămora′t|ō (-rah′-) *n.* (*fem.* ~**a**). lover. [It., p.p. (as *n.*) of IN[1](*amorare* f. *amore* f. L *amor* love) enamour]

ină′ne *a.* & *n.* **1.** *a.* empty, void; silly, senseless; hence

or cogn. ~LY[2] (-nlĭ) *adv.,* **ină′n**ITY *n.* **2.** *n.* (arch.) empty space. [f. L *inanis* empty, vain]

i′nanga (ē′nah-) *n.* (NZ) freshwater fish of family Galaxiidae. [Maori]

ină′nimate *a.* destitute of life; not endowed with animal life (~ **nature,** everything other than the animal world); spiritless, dull; hence or cogn. ~LY[2] (-tlĭ) *adv.,* **inănim**A′TION *n.* [f. LL IN[2](*animatus* ANIMATE[1])]

inani′tion *n.* emptiness, esp. exhaustion from lack of nourishment. [ME, f. LL *inanitio* f. L *inanire* make empty (as INANE); see -TION]

inappe′llable *n.* that cannot be appealed against. [f. obs. F IN[2](*appelable* f. *appeler* APPEAL[1]; see -ABLE)]

ină′ppĕt|ent *a.* not appetent; so ~ENCE, ~ENCY, *ns.* [f. IN-[2] + APPETENT]

ină′pplic|able *a.* not applicable, unsuitable, (*to* case, purpose); hence ~ABI′LITY *n.,* ~ABLY *adv.* [f. IN-[2] + APPLICABLE]

ină′pposite (-z-) *a.* not apposite, out of place; hence ~LY[2] (-tlĭ) *adv.,* ~NESS (-tn-) *n.* [f. IN-[2] + APPOSITE]

inapprē′ciab|le (-sha-) *a.* imperceptible, not worth reckoning; that cannot be appreciated; hence ~LY[2] *adv.* [f. IN-[2] + APPRECIABLE]

inapprēciā′tion (-shī-) *n.* failure to appreciate; so **inapprē′ciat**IVE (-shī-) *a.* [f. IN-[2] + APPRECIATION]

inăpprĕhĕ′nsible *a.* that cannot be grasped (by senses or intellect). [f. IN-[2] + APPREHENSIBLE]

inapprō′priate *a.* not appropriate; hence ~LY[2] (-tlĭ) *adv.,* ~NESS (-tn-) *n.* [f. IN-[2] + APPROPRIATE[1]]

ină′pt *a.* not suitable; unskilful; hence or cogn. ~ITUDE, ~NESS, *ns.,* ~LY[2] *adv.* [f. IN-[2] + APT]

inăr′ch *v.t.* graft by connecting growing branch without separation from parent stock. [f. IN-[1] + ARCH[2]]

inăr′m *v.t.* (poet.) embrace. [f. IN-[1] + ARM[1]]

inărti′cŭlate *a.* not jointed; (of speech) not articulate, indistinctly pronounced; unable to speak distinctly or express oneself clearly; dumb; hence ~LY[2] (-tlĭ) *adv.,* ~NESS (-tn-) *n.* [f. LL IN[2](*articulatus* ARTICULATE[1])]

inărtifi′cial (-shăl) *a.* (arch.) lacking in art, inartistic; artless, natural; hence ~LY[2] *adv.* [f. IN-[2] + ARTIFICIAL]

inărti′st|ic *a.* not following the principles of art; unskilled in or not talented in or not appreciating art; hence ~ICALLY *adv.* [f. IN-[2] + ARTISTIC]

inasmŭ′ch (-az-) *adv.* **1.** ~ *as,* since, because. **2.** (arch.) in so FAR[1] *as.* [ME, orig. *in as much*]

inatte′nt|ive *n.* lacking in attention, heedless; neglecting to show courtesy; hence or cogn. ~ION, ~iveNESS (-vn-), *ns.,* ~iveLY[2] (-vlĭ) *adv.* [f. IN-[2] + ATTENTIVE]

inau′d|ible *a.* that cannot be heard; hence ~IBI′LITY *n.,* ~IBLY *adv.* [f. IN-[2] + AUDIBLE]

inau′gŭral *a.* & *n.* **1.** *a.* of inauguration; (of lecture etc.) given by person being inaugurated. **2.** *n.* inaugural speech etc. [F (*inaugurer,* f. as foll.)]

inau′gŭr|āte *v.t.* admit (person, *esp. President of US) to office etc. with ceremony; enter with ceremony upon (undertaking etc.); initiate public use of (building etc.); begin, introduce; hence or cogn. ~A′TION, ~ātor, *ns.,* ~atorY *a.* [f. L IN[1](*augurare* take omens, f. AUGUR[1]) + -ATE[3]]

inauspi′cious (-shus) *a.* not of good omen; unlucky; hence ~LY[2] *adv.,* ~NESS *n.* [f. IN-[2] + AUSPICIOUS]

i′nboard *adv.* & *a.* (situated) within sides of or towards centre of ship, aircraft, or vehicle. [f. IN[1] + BOARD[1]]

i′nbŏrn *a.* existing from birth, implanted by nature. [f. IN[2] + BORN]

inbrea′the (-dh) *v.t.* breathe (thing) in (lit. or fig.); inspire (person). [ME, f. IN-[1] + BREATHE]

inbree′d *v.t.* (inbre′d). breed within or in and in; (in *p.p.*) innate, naturally inherent. [f. IN-[1], IN[2] + BREED[1]]

i′n-built (-bĭ-) *a.* built-in. [f. IN[2] + BUILT]

*****Inc.** *abbr.* Incorporated.

I′nc|a (ĭ′-) *n.* emperor or king of Peru before Spanish conquest; one of royal race in Peru; member of Amer.

For other words in *in-* **see** IN-[1] **or** (esp.) IN-[2].

Ind. people in Peru etc. before Spanish conquest; hence ∿ā'ic, ∿an, *adjs.* [Quechua, = lord, royal person]

incă'lcŭl|able (ĭn-k-) *a.* too great for calculation; that cannot be reckoned beforehand; (of person, character, etc.) uncertain; hence ∿abi'lity *n.*, ∿ably *adv.* [f. in-² + calculable]

in camera. See camera.

incănde'sce (ĭn-k-) *v.i.* & *t.* (cause to) glow with heat. [back-form. f. foll.; cf. -esce]

incănde'sc|ent (ĭn-k-) *a.* glowing with heat; shining brightly; (of electric or other light) produced by glowing of white-hot filament etc.; hence ∿ence *n.* [F, f. L in¹(*candescere* incept. of *candēre* be white); see -ent]

incăntā'tion (ĭn-k-) *n.* (use of) magical formula; spell, charm. [ME f. OF, f. LL *incantatio -onis* f. in¹(*cantare* sing) chant, bewitch; see -ation]

incă'p|able (ĭn-k-) *a.* not capable (*of* conduct etc., *of* doing, esp. = too honest etc. to behave thus); not susceptible (*of* improvement etc.); lacking in ordinary powers (*drunk and incapable*); hence ∿abi'lity *n.*, ∿ably *adv.* [F, or f. LL in²*capabilis* capable)]

incapă'cĭt|āte (ĭn-k-) *v.t.* render incapable or unfit (*for* work etc.; *for, from,* doing); disqualify; hence ∿ant, ∿a'tion, *ns.* [f. foll. + -ate³]

incapă'cĭtÿ (ĭn-k-) *n.* inability (*for* doing, *for* work etc., *to* do, or abs.); legal disqualification. [f. F *incapacité* or f. LL in²(*capacitas* capacity)]

incăr'cer|āte (ĭn-k-) *v.t.* imprison (lit. or fig.); hence or cogn. ∿a'tion, ∿ātor, *ns.* [f. med. L in¹(*carcerare* f. L *carcer* prison) + -ate³]

incăr'nadine (ĭn-k-) *a.*, & *v.t.* (poet.) (dye) flesh--coloured or crimson. [f. F *incarnadin -ine* f. It. *incarnadino* (for *-tino*) f. *incarnato* incarnate¹]

incăr'nate¹ (ĭn-k-) *a.* (Of person, spirit, quality, etc.) embodied in flesh, in human form, (*he is an incarnate fiend, a devil incarnate*); embodied in recognizable or most perfect form. [ME, f. eccl. L *incarnatus* p.p. of in¹(*carnare* f. L *caro carnis* flesh); see -ate²]

incăr'nate⁰ (ĭ'-, -ā'-) *v.t.* embody in flesh, put (idea etc.) into concrete form, realize; (of person etc.) be living embodiment of (quality). [f. as prec. + -ate³]

incărnā'tion *n.* embodiment in (esp. human) flesh, esp. **the I∿** (of Christ); impersonation, living type, (*of* quality etc.); (Med.) process of forming new flesh. [ME f. OF, f. eccl. L *incarnatio -onis* (as prec.; see -ation)]

incase. Var. of encase.

incau'tious (ĭn-kaw'shŭs) *a.* heedless, rash; hence ∿ly² *adv.*, ∿ness *n.* [f. in-² + cautious]

incĕ'ndiar|ÿ *a.* & *n.* **1.** *a.* of, guilty of, the malicious setting on fire of property; ∿y **bomb** (filled with substance(s) for causing fire at point of impact). **2.** (fig.) tending to stir up strife, inflammatory. **3.** *n.* incendiary person (lit. or fig.); incendiary bomb. **4.** Hence ∿ism (2) *n.* [ME f. L *incendiarius* f. *incendium* conflagration f. in¹(*cendere cens-* = *candere* cause to glow) set fire to; see -ary¹]

i'ncĕnse¹ *n.* gum or spice producing sweet smell when burned; smoke of this, esp. in religious ceremonial; (fig.) praise, flattery. [ME, f. OF *encens* f. eccl. L *incensum* thing burnt, incense, neut. p.p. (as n.) of L *incendere*; see prec.]

i'ncĕns|e² *v.t.* fumigate (person, thing) with incense; burn incense to (deity etc.); suffuse with fragrance; hence ∿a'tion *n.* [ME, f. OF *encenser* (as prec.)]

incĕ'nse³ *v.t.* enrage, make angry, (*against, with, at*). [ME, f. OF *incenser* f. L *incendere* (see incendiary)]

i'ncĕnsorÿ *n.* censer. [f. med. L *incensorium* (as incense¹; see -ory)]

incĕ'ntive *a.* & *n.* **1.** *a.* tending to incite. & *n.* **2.** *n.* incitement (*to* action, *to* do, *to* doing), provocation, motive; payment or concession to stimulate greater output by workers. [ME, f. L *incentivus* setting the tune f. in¹(*cinere cent-* = *canere* sing) sing to; see -ive]

incĕ'pt *v.* **1.** *v.i.* (Hist.) take master's or doctor's degree at university; so ∿or *n.* **2.** *v.t.* (Biol.) take in (food etc.). [f. L in¹(*cipere cept-* = *capere* take) begin]

incĕ'ption *n.* beginning; (Hist.) incepting. [ME f. OF, or f. L *inceptio* (as prec.; see -ion)]

incĕ'ptive *a.* & *n.* **1.** *a.* beginning; initial; (Gram., of verb) that denotes the beginning of an action. **2.** *n.* inceptive verb. [f. LL *inceptivus* (as incept; see -ive)]

incĕr'titūde *n.* uncertainty, doubt. [F, or f. LL *incertitudo* (as in-², certitude)]

incĕ'ssant *a.* unceasing, continual, repeated; hence **incĕ'ss**ancy, ∿ness, *ns.*, ∿ly² *adv.* [F, or f. LL in²(*cessans* part. of L *cessare* cease¹; see -ant)]

i'ncĕst *n.* sexual intercourse between persons regarded as too closely related to marry each other. [ME, f. L *incestus* or in²(*cestum* neut. adj. = *castum* chaste)]

incĕ'stŭous *a.* involving, or guilty of, incest; hence ∿ly² *adv.* [f. LL *incestuosus* (as prec.; see -ous)]

inch¹ *n.* & *v.* **1.** *n.* twelfth part of foot¹ 6, 2.54 cm; (as unit of map-scale) 1 inch representing 1 mile on the ground (*a 2½-inch map*); (as unit of rainfall) quantity that would cover horizontal surface to depth of 1 inch; (of atmospheric or other pressure) amount that balances weight of column of mercury 1 inch high. **2.** small amount (*would not yield an inch*); ∿ **by** ∿, **by** ∿es, bit by bit, gradually; **every** ∿, entirely, the whole distance; *give him an inch and he'll take an* ELL; *flog person* **within an** ∿ **of his life,** almost to death. **3.** (in *pl.*) stature (*a man of your inches*). **4.** *v.t.* & *i.* move by inches, edge *in,* forward, etc. [OE *ynce* = OHG *unza,* Goth. *unkja* f. L *uncia* twelfth part; cf. ounce¹]

||inch² *n.* small (esp. Scottish) island (freq. in place--names). [ME f. Gael. *innis*]

i'nchōate¹ (ĭ'n-k-) *a.* just begun; undeveloped. [f. L *inchoatus* p.p. of in¹(*choare, cohare* begin); see -ate²]

i'nchō|āte² (ĭ'n-k-) *v.t.* begin; originate; so ∿a'tion *n.*, ∿ativE (-kōā-, -kō'a-) *a.*, (esp., Gram.) inceptive. [f. as prec. + -ate³]

i'ncidence *n.* falling on or contact with a thing; manner or range of occurrence or action (*of* disease, taxation, etc.); range, scope, or extent of influence; (Phys.) falling of line, or of thing moving in a line, upon a surface (**angle of** ∿, that which incident line, ray, etc., makes with perpendicular to surface at point of incidence). [ME f. OF, or f. med. L *incidentia* (as incident²; see -ence)]

i'ncident¹ *n.* subordinate or accessory event; event, occurrence; hostile clash of e.g. troops of countries at war (*frontier incident*); public event causing trouble etc.; detached event attracting general attention; distinct piece of action in play or poem; (Law) privilege, burden, etc., attaching to estate etc. [ME f. OF (as foll.)]

i'ncident² *a.* apt or liable to happen, naturally attaching, (*to*); (Law) attaching *to* (cf. prec.); (of light etc.) falling, striking, (*on, upon*). [ME f. F, or f. L in¹(*cidere = cadere* fall); see -ent]

incidĕ'ntal *a.* casual, not essential, (*to*); liable to happen *to*; ∿ (**up**)**on,** following as subordinate event; ∿ **music** (introduced during the action of a play, film, etc.) [f. prec. + -al]

incidĕ'ntallÿ *adv.* In adj. senses; by the way, parenthetically. [f. prec. + -ly²]

inci'ner|āte *v.t.* reduce to ashes; consume (body etc.) by fire; hence or cogn. ∿a'tion *n.*, ∿ātor *n.* (esp. apparatus for burning refuse etc. to ashes). [f. med. L in¹(*cinerare* f. *cinis -eris* ashes) + -ate³]

inci'pi|ent *a.* beginning; in an initial stage; hence ∿ence, ∿ency, *ns.*, ∿ently² *adv.* [f. L (as incept; see -ent)]

i'ncipit *n.* first words (of book etc., or fig.). [L = '(here) begins', formerly used by scribes to mark beginning of book or section]

inci'se (-z) *v.t.* make a cut in; engrave. [f. F *inciser* f. L in¹(*cidere cis- = caedere* cut)]

inci'sion (-zhon) *n.* cutting into a thing; cut, division produced by cutting, notch. [ME f. OF, or f. LL *incisio* as prec.; see -ion)]

inci'sive *a.* cutting, penetrating; (fig.) mentally sharp, acute; clear and effective; hence ∼LY² (-vlǐ) *adv.*, ∼NESS (-vn-) *n.* [f. med. L *incisivus* (as INCISE; see -IVE)]

inci′sor (-z-) *n.* cutting-tooth, any front tooth between the canine teeth in either jaw. [med. L, = cutter (as INCISE; see -OR)]

inci′te *v.t.* urge, stir up, (person etc. *to* action, *to* do); hence or cogn. **incita′TION, ∼MENT** (-tm-), *ns.* [ME, f. F *inciter* f. L IN¹(*citare* rouse; see CITE)]

incivi′litў *n.* (act of) rudeness or discourtesy. [f. F *incivilité* or f. LL IN²(*civilitas* CIVILITY)]

i′ncivism *n.* lack of loyalty to one's nation (esp. in French Revolution). [f. F IN²(*civisme* f. L *civis* citizen; see -ISM)]

inclě′m|ent (ĭn-k-) *a.* (Of weather or climate) severe, esp. cold or stormy; so ∼ENCY *n.* [f. F *inclément* or f. L IN²(*clemens* CLEMENT)]

incli′nable (ĭn-k-) *a.* inclined, disposed, (*to* thing, *to* do); favourable (*to*).[ME f. OF *enclinable* (as INCLINE¹; see -ABLE)]

inclina′tion (ĭn-k-) *n.* leaning, slope, slant; dip of magnetic needle; difference of direction of two lines or planes, esp. as measured by angle between them; disposition, propensity, (*to*, *for*, *towards*, thing; *to* do) liking, affection, (*for*). [ME f. OF, or f. L *inclinatio* (as foll.; see -ATION)]

incli′ne¹ (ĭn-k-) *v.* **1.** *v.t.* bend (head, body, one*self*) forward or downward; ∼ one's **ear,** listen favourably (*to* person, prayer, etc.). **2.** dispose (mind, heart, person, thing, *to* do, *to* or *for* thing; *incline our hearts to keep this law*; *I am inclined to think so*; *door is inclined to bang*). **3.** *v.i.* be disposed (*I incline to think so*); tend (*to* or *towards* fatness etc.). **4.** *v.t.* & *i.* (cause to) lean or turn away from the vertical etc. direction; ∼d **plane,** sloping plane (esp. as means of reducing force needed to raise load). [ME *encline* f. OF *encliner* f. L IN¹(*clinare* bend)]

incline² (ĭn-klī′n, ĭ′-) *n.* inclined plane; slope. [f. prec.]

inclinŏ′meter (ĭn-k-) *n.* instrument measuring vertical intensity of earth's magnetic field by dip of magnetic needle; instrument for measuring slope; instrument for measuring inclination of ship or aircraft to horizontal. [f. L *inclinare* INCLINE¹ + -O- + -METER]

inclose. See ENCLOSE.

inclosure. Var. of ENCLOSURE.

inclu′de (ĭn-klōō′d) *v.t.* comprise or embrace (thing etc.) as part of a whole; (in *pres. part.* in abs. constr.) if we include (*six members, including the chairman*); treat or regard as so comprised; (in *p.p.*) shut in, enclosed; ∼ **out,** (colloq. or joc.) (specifically) exclude; so **inclu′sION** (ĭn-klōō′zhŏn) *n.* [ME, f. L IN¹(*cludere clus- = claudere* shut)]

inclu′sive (ĭn-klōō′-) *a.* including, comprising, (*of*, or abs.); (as *adv.*) with inclusion of the extreme limits stated (*pages 7 to 26 inclusive*); including much or all (*inclusive terms* at hotel etc.); hence ∼LY² (-vlǐ) *adv.*, ∼NESS (-vn-) *n.* [f. med. L *inclusivus* (as prec.; see -IVE)]

incŏ′gnito (ĭn-kŏ′gnĭtō, -ē′tō) *a., adv.,* & *n.* (*pl.* ∼s). **1.** *a.* & *adv.* with one's name, character, etc., kept secret. **2.** *n.* (pretended identity, anonymous character, of) person who is incognito. [It., = unknown, f. L IN²(*cognitus* p.p. of *cognoscere* know)]

incŏ′gniz|ant (ĭn-kŏ′gn-, -kŏ′n-) *a.* unaware, unconscious *of*; so ∼ANCE *n.* [f. IN-² + COGNIZANT]

incohēr′|ent (ĭn-k-) *a.* not coherent (lit. or fig.); so ∼ENCE, ∼ENCY, *ns.*, ∼entLY² *adv.* [f. IN-² + COHERENT]

incombu′st|ible (ĭn-k-) *a.* that cannot be consumed by fire; hence ∼IBI′LITY *n.* [ME, f. med. L IN²(*combustibilis* COMBUSTIBLE)]

i′ncome (ĭ′n-k-) *n.* periodical (usu. total annual) receipts from one's business, lands, work, investments, etc.; ∼ **group,** section of population graded by income; ∼ **tax** (levied on this); **negative ∼ tax,** amount deducted from taxable income for certain

commitments and paid as supplementary income when exceeding taxable income; NATIONAL *income.* [f. IN² + COME]

i′ncomer (ĭ′n-kŭ-) *n.* one who comes in; immigrant; intruder; successor. [f. IN² + COMER]

i′ncoming¹ (ĭ′n-kŭ-) *n.* entrance, arrival; (usu. in *pl.*) revenue, income. [ME, f. IN² + *coming* (COME, -ING¹)]

i′ncoming² (ĭ′n-kŭ-) *a.* coming in (*incoming tide, telephone calls*); succeeding another person; immigrant; (of profit) accruing. [f. IN² + *coming* (COME, -ING²)]

incommě′nsur|able (ĭn-k-; -sher-, -syer-) *a.* (Of magnitude) having no common measure integral or fractional (*with* another); irrational, surd; not comparable in respect of magnitude; not worthy to be measured *with*; hence ∼ABI′LITY *n.*, ∼ABLY *adv.* [f. LL IN²(*commensurabilis* COMMENSURABLE)]

incommě′nsurate (ĭn-k-; -sher-, -syer-) *a.* out of proportion, inadequate, (*with, to*); = prec.; hence ∼LY² (-tlǐ) *adv.*, ∼NESS (-tn-) *n.* [f. IN-² + COMMENSURATE]

incommŏ′de (ĭn-k-) *v.t.* trouble, annoy; hinder, inconvenience. [f. F *incommoder* or f. L IN²(*commodare* f. *commodus* convenient; see COMMODE)]

incommŏ′dious (ĭn-k-) *a.* not affording good accommodation, uncomfortable; hence ∼NESS *n.* [f. IN-² + COMMODIOUS]

incommū′nic|able (ĭn-k-) *a.* that cannot be shared; that cannot be told; that does not communicate; hence ∼ABI′LITY *n.*, ∼ableNESS (-beln-), *ns.*, ∼ABLY *adv.* [f. LL IN²(*communicabilis* COMMUNICABLE)]

incommūnica′dō (ĭn-k-; -ah′-) *a.* without or deprived of means of communication with others; (of prisoner) in solitary confinement. [f. Sp. *incomunicado* p.p. of *incomunicar* deprive of communication]

incommū′nicative (ĭn-k-) *a.* not communicative, taciturn; hence ∼LY² (-vlǐ) *adv.*, ∼NESS (-vn-) *n.* [f. IN-² + COMMUNICATIVE]

incommū′tab|le (ĭn-k-) *a.* unchangeable; not commutable; hence ∼LY² *adv.* [ME, f. L IN²(*commutabilis* COMMUTABLE)]

incŏ′mparab|le (ĭn-k-) *a.* without an equal, matchless; not to be compared (*with, to*); hence ∼leNESS (-beln-) *n.*, ∼LY² *adv.* [ME f. OF, f. L IN²(*comparabilis* COMPARABLE)]

incompa′t|ible (ĭn-k-) *a.* opposed in character, discordant; (of persons) unable to live, work, etc., together in harmony; (of drugs) not suitable for taking at same time; inconsistent (*with*); hence ∼IBI′LITY *n.*, ∼IBLY *adv.* [f. med. L IN²(*compatibilis* COMPATIBLE)]

incŏ′mpět|ent (ĭn-k-) *a.* & *n.* **1.** *a.* not qualified or able (*to* do); lacking a desirable ability or qualification; not able to perform its function; not legally qualified; hence or cogn. ∼ENCE, ∼ENCY, *ns.*, ∼entLY² *adv.* **2.** *n.* incompetent person. [f. F *incompétent* or f. LL IN²(*competens* COMPETENT)]

incomplē′te (ĭn-k-) *a.* not complete; hence ∼LY² (-tlǐ) *adv.*, ∼NESS (-tn-) *n.* [ME, f. LL IN²(*completus* COMPLETE¹)]

incŏmprehě′ns|ible (ĭn-k-) *a.* ∼ (*to*), that cannot be understood (by); (arch.) that cannot be contained within limits; hence ∼IBI′LITY *n.*, ∼ibleNESS (-beln-), *ns.*, ∼IBLY *adv.* [ME, f. L IN²(*comprehensibilis* COMPREHENSIBLE)]

incŏmprehě′nsion (ĭn-k-, -shŏn) *n.* failure to understand. [f. IN-² + COMPREHENSION]

incompre′ss|ible (ĭn-k-) *a.* that cannot be compressed; hence ∼IBI′LITY *n.* [f. IN-² + COMPRESSIBLE]

incomunicado. Var. of INCOMMUNICADO.

inconcei′v|able (ĭn-kŏnsē′v-) *a.* that cannot be imagined; (colloq.) very remarkable; hence ∼ABI′LITY *n.*, ∼ABLY *adv.* [f. IN-² + CONCEIVABLE]

inconclu′sive (ĭn-kŏn-klōō′-) *a.* (Of argument, evidence, action) not decisive or convincing; hence ∼LY² (-vlǐ) *adv.*, ∼NESS (-vn-) *n.* [f. IN-² + CONCLUSIVE]

incondě′nsable (ĭn-k-) *a.* that cannot be condensed,

For other words in *in-* see IN-¹ or (esp.) IN-².

incondite   507   **inculcate**

esp. that cannot be reduced to liquid or solid condition. [f. IN-² + CONDENSABLE]

inco'ndite (ĭn-k-) *a.* (Of literary composition etc.) ill constructed; crude, unpolished. [f. L IN²(*conditus* p.p. of *condere* put together)]

inconfor'mity (ĭn-k-) *n.* (arch.) dissimilarity, lack of conformity, (*to, with*); nonconformity. [f. IN-² + CONFORMITY]

inco'ngruous (ĭn-kŏ'nggrōō-) *a.* disagreeing, out of keeping, (*with*); out of place, absurd; hence or cogn. **incongru'ity** (ĭn-konggrōō'-), ∼NESS, *ns.*, ∼LY² *adv.* [f. L IN²(*congruus* congruous)]

inconse'cutive (ĭn-k-) *a.* lacking sequence, inconsequent; hence ∼LY² (-vlĭ) *adv.*, ∼NESS (-vn-) *n.* [f. IN-² + CONSECUTIVE]

inco'nsequ|ent (ĭn-k-) *a.* not following naturally, irrelevant; lacking logical sequence; disconnected; hence or cogn. ∼ENCE *n.*, ∼ent LY² *adv.* [f. L IN²(*consequens* CONSEQUENT)]

inconse'que'ntial (ĭn-k-; -shal) *a.* unimportant; = prec.; hence ∼LY² *adv.* [f. IN-² + CONSEQUENTIAL]

inconsi'derab|le (ĭn-k-) *a.* not worth considering; of small size, value, etc.; hence ∼le NESS (-beln-) *n.*, ∼LY² *adv.* [f. obs. F *inconsidérable* or f. LL IN²(*considerabilis* CONSIDERABLE)]

inconsi'der|ate (ĭn-k-) *a.* (Of person or action) thoughtless, rash; lacking in regard for feelings etc. of others; hence or cogn. ∼ate LY² (-tlĭ) *adv.*, ∼ate NESS (-tn-), ∼A'TION, *ns.* [f. L IN²(*consideratus* CONSIDERATE)]

inconsi'st|ent (ĭn-k-) *a.* not in keeping, discordant, incompatible, (*with*); (of single thing) having inconsistent parts; acting at variance with one's own principles or former conduct; hence ∼ENCY *n.*, ∼ent LY² *adv.* [f. IN-² + CONSISTENT]

inconso'lab|le (ĭn-k-) *a.* (Of person, grief, etc.) that cannot be consoled; hence ∼LY² *adv.* [F, or f. L IN²(*consolabilis* f. *consolari* CONSOLE¹; see -ABLE)]

inco'nson|ant (ĭn-k-) *a.* not harmonious (*with, to*); hence ∼ANCE *n.* [f. IN-² + CONSONANT¹]

inconspi'cuous (ĭn-k-) *a.* not conspicuous; (Bot., of flowers) small, pale, or green; hence ∼LY² *adv.*, ∼NESS *n.* [f. L IN²(*conspicuus* CONSPICUOUS) + -OUS]

inco'nst|ant (ĭn-k-) *a.* (Of person) fickle, changeable; variable, irregular; hence or cogn. ∼ANCY *n.*, ∼ant LY² *adv.* [ME f. OF, f. L IN²(*constans* -*antis* CONSTANT)]

inconte'stab|le (ĭn-k-) *a.* that cannot be disputed; hence ∼LY² *adv.* [F, or f. med. L IN²(*contestabilis* f. L *contestari* CONTEST²; see -ABLE)]

inconti'n|ent (ĭn-k-) *a.* lacking self-restraint (esp. in regard to sexual desire); unable to control excretions voluntarily; ∼ of, unable to retain or control (secrets, tongue, excretions etc.); so ∼ENCE *n.* [ME f. OF, or f. L IN²(*continens* CONTINENT¹)]

inco'ntinently¹ (ĭn-k-) *adv.* In adj. senses. [f. prec. + -LY²]

inco'ntinently² (ĭn-k-) *adv.* (literary), at once, immediately. [f. arch. *incontinent* adv., ME, f. F *incontinent* f. LL *in continenti* (*tempore*) in continuous (time), + -LY²]

incontrover'tib|le (ĭn-kŏ'-, -êr'-) *a.* indisputable, indubitable; hence ∼LY² *adv.* [f. IN-² + CONTROVERTIBLE]

inconve'nience (ĭn-k-) *n.*, & *v.t.* **1.** *n.* lack of adaptation to personal requirement or ease; instance of this. **2.** *v.t.* put (person etc.) to inconvenience. [ME f. OF, f. LL *inconvenientia* (as foll.; see -ENCE)]

inconve'nient (ĭn-k-) *a.* unfavourable to ease or comfort; awkward, troublesome; hence ∼LY² *adv.* [ME f. OF f. L IN²(*conveniens* -*ntis* CONVENIENT)]

inconver't|ible (ĭn-k-) *a.* not convertible; (esp. of currency) not convertible into another form or demand; hence ∼IBI'LITY *n.*, ∼IBLY *adv.* [F, or f. LL IN²(*convertibilis* CONVERTIBLE)]

incoör'dina'tion (ĭn-k-) *n.* lack of co-ordination, esp. of muscular action. [f. IN-² + CO-ORDINATION]

incor'porate¹ (ĭn-k-) *a.* (Of company etc.) formed into a corporation; embodied. [ME, f. as foll.; see -ATE²]

incor'por|āte² (ĭn-k-) *v.* **1.** *v.t.* unite (*in* one body, *with* another thing); admit as member of company etc., esp. *ad eundem*; combine (ingredients) into one substance; constitute as a legal corporation; (in *p.p.*) forming a legal corporation. **2.** *v.i.* become incorporated (*with*). **3.** Hence or cogn. ∼A'TION, ∼ātOR, *ns.* [ME, f. LL IN¹(*corporare* f. L *corpus* -*oris* body) + -ATE³]

incorpor'eal (ĭn-k-) *a.* not composed of matter; of immaterial beings; (Law) having no material existence (*incorporeal hereditament*); hence or cogn. ∼ITY (-ǎ'l-), **incorpore'ity** (ĭn-k-), *ns.*, ∼LY² *adv.* [f. L IN²(*corporeus* f. *corpus* -*oris* body) + -AL]

incorre'ct (ĭn-k-) *a.* not in accordance with fact; (of style etc.) improper, faulty; hence ∼LY² *adv.*, ∼NESS *n.* [ME f. OF, or f. L IN²(*correctus* CORRECT²)]

inco'rrig|ible (ĭn-k-) *a.* (Of person or habit) incurably bad or depraved; not readily improved; hence ∼IBI'LITY *n.*, ∼IBLY *adv.* [ME f. OF, or f. L IN²(*corrigibilis* CORRIGIBLE)]

incorru'pt|ible (ĭn-k-) *a.* **1.** that cannot decay, everlasting; so (Bibl.) ∼ION *n.* **2.** that cannot be corrupted, esp. bribed. **3.** Hence ∼IBI'LITY *n.*, ∼IBLY *adv.* [ME f. OF, or f. eccl. L IN²(*corruptibilis* CORRUPTIBLE)]

incra'ssate (ĭn-k-) *a.* (Bot. & Zool.) of thick or swollen form. [f. LL *incrassatus* p.p. of IN¹(*crassare* f. L *crassus* thick); see -ATE²]

increa'se¹ (ĭn-k-) *v.* **1.** *v.i.* become greater in size, amount, etc.; grow in numbers, esp. by propagation; advance (*in* quality, attainment, etc.). **2.** *v.t.* make greater or more numerous; intensify (quality). [ME, f. OF *encreiss*- st. of *encreistre* f. L IN¹(*crescere* grow)]

i'ncrease² (ĭ'n-k-) *n.* growth, enlargement; profit, (arch.) crops; growth in numbers, multiplication (of people, animals, or plants); increased amount; **on the** ∼, increasing. [ME, f. prec.]

incre'd|ible (ĭn-k-) *a.* that cannot be believed; (colloq.) hard to believe, surprising; hence ∼IBI'LITY *n.*, ∼IBLY *adv.* [ME, f. L IN²(*credibilis* CREDIBLE)]

incre'dulous (ĭn-k-) *a.* ∼(of, *or* abs.), unwilling to believe, hence or cogn. **incredu'lity** (ĭn-k-) *n.*, ∼LY² *adv.* [f. L IN²(*credulus* CREDULOUS)]

i'ncrement (ĭ'n-k-) *n.* (amount of) increase; profit (UNEARNED *increment*); (Math.) small amount by which variable quantity increases. [ME, f. L *incrementum* (as INCREASE¹; see -MENT)]

incri'min|āte (ĭn-k-) *v.t.* charge with crime; involve in accusation; tend to prove guilt of (*incriminating evidence*); hence ∼A'TION *n.*, ∼atory *a.* [f. LL IN¹(*criminare* f. L *crimen*; see CRIME) + -ATE³]

incrust. See ENCRUST.

incrusta'tion (ĭn-k-) *n.* encrusting; crust, hard coating, esp. of fine material; facing of marble etc. on building; (undesired) concretion or deposit on a surface; (fig.) accretion of habit; scab. [F, or f. LL *incrustatio* (as ENCRUST; see -ATION)]

i'ncubāte (ĭ'n-k-) *v.* **1.** *v.t.* bring forth young birds etc. from (eggs) by sitting on them or by artificial heat; cause development of (bacteria etc.) by creating suitable conditions. **2.** *v.i.* sit on eggs, brood. [f. L IN¹(*cubare cubit*- *or cubat*- lie) + -ATE³]

incubā'tion (ĭn-k-) *n.* **1.** incubating; brooding. **2.** (Path.) phase through which germs of disease pass before development of first symptoms; period of this. **3.** So **i'ncubātive, i'ncubātory**, (ĭn-k-) *adjs.* [f. L *incubatio* (as prec.; see -ATION)]

i'ncubātor (ĭ'n-k-) *n.* apparatus for hatching eggs or for rearing children born prematurely or for developing micro-organisms. [f. INCUBATE + -OR]

i'ncub|us *n.* (*pl.* ∼uses, *or* ∼i *pr.* -ī). evil spirit supposed to descend on sleeping persons; nightmare; person or thing that oppresses like nightmare. [ME f. LL, = L *incubo* nightmare (as INCUBATE)]

i'nculc|āte (ĭ'n-k-) *v.t.* urge, impress, (fact, habit, idea) persistently (*upon* or *in* person or mind); hence ∼A'TION, ∼ãTOR, *ns.* [f. L IN¹(*culcare = calcare* tread f. *calx calcis* heel) +-ATE³]

i'nculp|ãte (ĭn-k-) *v.t.* accuse, blame; involve in charge; hence ∼A'TION *n.*, ∼atIVE, ∼atORY, (-ŭ'-) *adjs.* [f. LL IN¹(*culpare* blame f. *culpa* fault)+-ATE³]

incŭ'lt (ĭn-k-) *a.* unpolished, rude; (of person or manners) coarse. [f. L IN²(*cultus* p.p. of *colere* cultivate)]

incŭ'mbencў (ĭn-k-) *n.* office, tenure, sphere, of an incumbent. [f. as foll.; see -ENCY]

incŭ'mbent¹ (ĭn-k-) *n.* holder of ecclesiastical benefice; holder of any office or place. [ME, f. AL *incumbens* part. (as n.) of L *incumbere* (see foll.)]

incŭ'mbent² (ĭn-k-) *a.* lying, pressing, (*on*); resting (*up*)on (person) as duty (*it is incumbent on you to warn them*). [f. L IN¹(*cumbere = cubare* lie); see -ENT]

incŭ'nable (ĭn-k-) *n.* = foll. 2. [F, f. as foll.]

incūnā'būl|um (ĭn-k-) *n.* (*pl.* ∼a). 1. (in *pl.*) early stages of development of a thing. 2. book printed at early date, esp. before 1501. [f. L *incunabula* swaddling-clothes, cradle (as IN-¹, *cunae* cradle)]

incŭr' (ĭn-k-) *v.t.* (-rr-). fall into, bring on oneself, (danger, blame, punishment, displeasure, expense, etc.); hence ∼rABLE *a.* [ME, f. L IN¹(*currere curs-* run)]

incŭr'|able (ĭn-k-) *a.* & *n.* (person) that cannot be cured; hence ∼ABI'LITY, ∼ableNESS (-bĕln-), *ns.*, ∼ABLY *adv.* [ME f. OF, or f. LL IN²(*curabilis* CURABLE)]

incŭr'i|ous (ĭn-k-) *a.* devoid of curiosity; heedless, careless; hence ∼o'SITY *n.*, ∼ousLY² *adv.* [f. L IN²(*curiosus* careful; see CURIOUS)]

incŭr's|ion (ĭn-kêr'shon) *n.* hostile invasion; sudden attack; raid; so ∼IVE *a.* [ME, f. L *incursio* (as INCUR; see -ION)]

incŭr'v|e (ĭn-k-) *v.t.* bend into a curve; (esp. in *p.p.*) curve inwards; so ∼A'TION *n.* [f. L IN¹(*curvare* CURVE¹)]

i'ncu|s *n.* (*pl.* ∼des *pr.* -kū'dēz). anvil bone of ear, receiving vibrations from malleus. [L, = anvil]

incū'se¹ (-z) *a.* & *n.* (impression on coin etc.) hammered or stamped in. [f. L *incusus* p.p. of IN¹(*cudere* forge)]

incŭ'se² (-z) *v.t.* (esp. in *p.p.*) impress (figure etc.) by stamping; mark (coin etc.) with such figure. [f. as prec.]

Ind (ĭ-) *n.* (arch. or poet.) India. [ME, f. OF *Inde* f. L INDIA]

Ind. *abbr.* Independent; India(n); Indiana.

inda'ba (-ah'-) *n.* conference between or with members of S. Afr. native tribes. [Zulu, = business]

indě'bted (-dě't-) *a.* owing money (*to*); owing gratitude (*to* person, or fig. *to* thing, *for* benefit etc.); hence ∼NESS *n.* [ME, f. OF *endetté* p.p. of EN¹(*detter* f. *dette* DEBT) involve in debt+-ED¹]

indě'cent *a.* unbecoming, highly unsuitable, (*with indecent haste*); offending against recognized standards of decency (∼ *assault*, sexual attack not involving rape; *indecent* EXPOSURE); hence or cogn. **indě'cENCY** *n.*, ∼LY² *adv.* [f. F *indécent* or f. L IN²(*decens* DECENT)]

inděci'pherable *a.* that cannot be deciphered. [f. IN-² + DECIPHERABLE]

inděci'sion (-zhon) *n.* lack of decision, hesitation. [f. F IN²(*décision* DECISION)]

inděci'sive *a.* not decisive; undecided, hesitating; hence ∼LY² (-vlĭ) *adv.*, ∼NESS (-vn-) *n.* [f. IN-² + DECISIVE]

indě'clinable *a.* (Gram.) that cannot be declined; having no inflexions. [ME, f. F *indéclinable* f. L IN²(*declinabilis* DECLINABLE)]

indě'corous *a.* improper; in bad taste; hence ∼LY² *adv.*, ∼NESS *n.* [f. L IN²(*decorus* seemly); see -OUS]

inděcŏr'um *n.* lack of decorum; improper behaviour. [L, neut. a. (as n.); cf. prec.]

indee'd *adv.* 1. in truth, really, (*he was, indeed, a remarkable man*; (emphat.) *I shall be very glad indeed*; *this is quick work indeed*; *indeed it is*; *yes, indeed!*); in point of fact (*if indeed such a thing is possible*; *saw here recently, indeed*

yesterday). 2. (As approving or ironic echo: *Who is this Mr. Smith?—Who is he, indeed!* = you may well ask, or, do you really need to ask?). 3. admittedly (*there are indeed exceptions*). 4. (interrog.) really? is it so? 5. (As excl. expr. irony, contempt, incredulity, etc.: *He expects to win—Does he, indeed!*). [ME, f. IN¹+DEED]

indefã'tig|able *a.* (Of person, quality, etc.) that cannot be tired out, unwearying, unremitting; hence ∼ABI'LITY *n.*, ∼ABLY *adv.* [f. obs. F *indéfatigable* or f. L IN²(*defatigabilis* f. DEfatigare wear out; see FATIGUE, -ABLE)]

inděfea's|ible (-z-) *a.* (Esp. of claim, rights, etc.) that cannot be forfeited or annulled; hence ∼IBI'LITY *n.*, ∼IBLY *adv.* [f. IN-²+DEFEASIBLE]

inděfě'ctible *a.* unfailing, not liable to defect or decay; faultless. [f. IN-²+*defectible* f. LL *defectibilis* (as DEFECT; see -IBLE)]

inděfě'ns|ible *a.* that cannot be defended (by force of arms or by argument); hence ∼IBI'LITY *n.*, ∼IBLY *adv.*[f. IN-²+DEFENSIBLE]

inděfi'nab|le *a.* that cannot be defined or exactly described; hence ∼LY² *adv.* [f. IN-²+DEFINABLE]

indě'finite *a.* 1. vague, undefined; unlimited; *indefinite* INTEGRAL. 2. (Gram.) not determining the person, thing, time, etc., referred to (*indefinite* ARTICLE¹, PRONOUN); (of tense) denoting an action without specifying whether it is continuous or complete (e.g. Greek aorist, English past). 3. Hence ∼LY² (-tlĭ) *adv.*, (esp.) for unlimited time, ∼NESS (-tn-) *n.* [f. L IN²(*definitus* DEFINITE)]

inděhi'scent *a.* (Bot., of fruit) not splitting open when mature. [f. IN-²+DEHISCENT]

indě'l|ible *a.* (Of mark, stain, ink, etc., and fig. of disgrace, mental feeling, etc.) that cannot be blotted out or removed; (of pencil etc.) that makes such marks; hence ∼IBI'LITY *n.*, ∼IBLY *adv.* [f. F *indélébile* or f. L IN²(*delebilis* f. *delēre* efface; see -IBLE)]

indě'lic|ate *a.* coarse, unrefined; tending to indecency; tactless; hence ∼ACY *n.*, ∼ateLY² (-tlĭ) *adv.* [f. IN-²+DELICATE]

indě'mni|fy *v.t.* protect or secure (person *from* or *against* harm or loss); secure (person) against legal responsibility (*for* actions); compensate (person *for* loss, expenses incurred, etc.); hence ∼FICA'TION *n.* [f. L IN²(*demnis* f. *damnum* loss)+-FY]

indě'mnitў *n.* security against damage or loss; legal exemption from penalties etc. incurred; compensation for loss incurred; sum paid for this, esp. sum exacted by victorious belligerent as one condition of peace. [ME, f. F *indemnité* f. LL *indemnitas -tatis* (as prec.; see -ITY)]

indemonstrable (-dě'mon-, -dĭmŏ'n-) *a.* that cannot be proved (esp. of primary or axiomatic truths). [f. IN-²+DEMONSTRABLE]

indě'nt¹ *v.* 1. *v.t.* make toothlike notches in; form deep recesses in (coastline etc.). 2. divide (document drawn up in duplicate) into two halves with zigzag line; draw up (document) in exact duplicate. 3. (Print. etc.) set back (beginning of line) inwards from margin to mark new paragraph etc. 4. *v.i.* & *t.* ||make requisition (orig. written order with duplicate) (*on* or *upon* person *for* thing); order (goods) by an indent; hence ∼OR *n.* [ME, f. AF *endenter* f. AL IN¹(*dentare* f. *dens dentis* tooth)]

indě'nt² (ĭ'-, -ě'-) *n.* indentation; indenture; ||official requisition for stores; ||order (esp. from abroad) for goods. [f. prec.]

indě'nt³ *v.t.* make a dent in; impress (mark etc.). [ME, f. IN-¹+DENT²]

inděntã'tion *n.* indenting; cut, notch; zigzag; deep recess in coastline etc. [f. INDENT¹,³+-ATION]

indě'ntion *n.* indenting of line in printing etc.; = prec. [irreg. f. INDENT¹,³+-ION]

indě'nture *n.* & *v.t.* 1. *n.* indented document (see INDENT¹); any sealed agreement or contract, esp. (usu. in *pl.*) that which binds apprentice to master; formal list, certificate, etc.; indentation. 2. *v.t.* bind

For other words in *in-* see IN-¹ or (esp.) IN-².

(person) by indentures, esp. as apprentice. [ME (orig. Sc.), f. AF *endenture* (as INDENT[1]; see -URE)]
indépe′ndence *n.* **1.** being independent (*of, on, from,* or abs.); independent income. **2.** I~ **Day,** *4 July (date of declaration of independence of US in 1776), similar festival in other countries. [f. INDEPENDENT + -ENCE]
indépe′ndency *n.* **1.** (Hist.; *I*~). Congregationalism. **2.** (arch.) = prec. 1. **3.** independent State. [f. foll. +-ENCY]
indépe′ndent *a.* & *n.* **1.** *a.* not depending on authority or control (*of,* or abs.); self-governing; (Hist.; *I*~) Congregational. **2.** not depending on something else for its validity, efficiency, (Math.) value, etc., (in *dependent proof, research, observer, variable*); (of broadcasting) not financed by licence-fees or grant; not needing to earn one's livelihood; ~ **income, means,** etc., (making it unnecessary to earn one's livelihood; ||~ **school** (not receiving government grant and not controlled by a local authority). **3.** not depending on others for one's opinion or conduct; that is an independent in politics etc.; unwilling to be under obligation to others. **4.** Hence ~LY[2] *adv.* **5.** *n.* person who acts (in politics etc.) independently of any party, (Hist.; *I*~) Congregationalist. [f. IN-[2] + DEPENDENT]
indéscri′b|able *a.* vague, indefinite; too great, beautiful, bad, etc., to be described; hence ~ABI′LITY *n.,* ~ABLY *adv.* |†. IN-[2] + DESCRIBABLE]
indéstru′ct|ible *a.* that cannot be destroyed; hence, ~IBI′LITY *n.,* ~IBLY *adv.* [f. IN-[2] + DESTRUCTIBLE]
indéter′minable *a.* that cannot be ascertained; (of dispute etc.) that cannot be settled. [ME, f. LL IN[2]-(*determinabilis* f. L *determinare*; see DETERMINE, -ABLE)]
indéter′minate *a.* **1.** not fixed in extent, character, etc.; vague; left doubtful; ~ **sentence,** one that leaves prisoner's release dependent on his conduct etc.; *indeterminate* VOWEL. **2.** (Math., of quantity) not limited to fixed value(s) by the value(s) of another. **3.** Hence **indéter′min**ACY, ~NESS (-In-), *ns.,* ~LY[2] (-tlĭ) *adv.* [ME, f. LL IN[2](*determinatus* DETERMINATE)]
indétermina′tion *n.* lack of determination; being indeterminate. [f. prec. +-ATION]
indéter′min|ism *n.* doctrine that human action is not wholly determined by motives; so ~IST (2) *n.,* ~i′STIC *a.* [f. IN-[2] + DETERMINISM]
i′ndex *n.* (*pl.* ~es or, esp. tech., **i′ndices** *pr.* -ĭsēz), & *v.t.* **1.** *n.* ~ (**finger**), forefinger. **2.** (On instrument) pointer showing value of quantity or position on scale etc. **3.** ~ (**number**), quantity indicating relative level of prices or wages at a date taken as standard; ~**linked,** calculated in accordance with this. **4.** number expressing physical property etc. in terms of a standard (*refractive index*). **5.** guiding principle; thing pointing to a conclusion. **6.** alphabetical list, usu. at end of book, of names, subjects, etc., with references; CARD *index.* **7.** (Hist.; *I*~) list of books forbidden to Roman Catholics, or to be read by them only in expurgated editions [f. L *Index librorum prohibitorum*]. **8.** (Typ.) hand-shaped symbol used to draw attention to note etc. **9.** (Math.) exponent. **10.** Hence ~ICAL (-ĕ′-), ~LESS, *adjs.* **11.** *v.t.* furnish (book) with index; enter (word etc.) in index; relate (wages etc.) to value of price index, whence ~A′TION *n.;* (Engin.) move through aliquot part of complete turn or to some other predetermined position; hence ~ER[1] *n.* [ME f. L *index indicis* forefinger, informer, sign, (as IN-[1], *dicpoint out)]
I′ndia (ĭ′-) *n.* *~ **ink,** = INDIAN *ink*; ~**man,** (Hist.) ship engaged in trade with India or East Indies; ~ **paper,** (1) soft absorbent kind orig. imported from China, used for proofs of engravings, (2) thin tough opaque printing-paper; ~ **rubber,** i~**rubber,** = RUBBER[2]. [~ in Asia, OE f. L, f. Gk (*Indos* river Indus, f. Pers. *hind* = Skr. *sindhu* river; see -IA[1])]
I′ndian (ĭ′-) *a.* & *n.* **1.** (East) ~, (native or inhabitant)

of India or E. Indies. **2.** (**American**) ~, (one) of the aboriginal inhabitants of America or their descendants; ||RED *Indian*. **3.** West ~, (native or inhabitant) of W. Indies. **4.** (Hist.) European, esp. Englishman, formerly resident in India. **5.** ~ **clubs** (bottle-shaped, for use in gymnastics); ~ **cobra,** very venomous species of cobra (*Naja naja*); ~ **corn,** maize; ~ **cress,** tropaeolum; *Indian* FILE[3]; *Indian* HEMP; ||~ **ink,** black pigment made orig. in China and Japan, suspension of this in water etc.; ~ **meal** (made from Indian corn); ~ **millet,** durra; *~ **paintbrush,** plant of genus *Castilleja*; ~ **rope-trick,** supposed Indian feat of climbing unsupported rope; ~ **shot,** canna; ~ **summer,** period of calm dry hazy weather in late autumn in northern US and elsewhere, (fig.) tranquil late period of life etc.; ~ **tobacco,** a lobelia; ~ **weed,** tobacco. **6.** Hence ~IZE (3) *v.t.* [ME, f. prec. +-AN]
I′ndic (ĭ′-) *a.* Indian; of the group of Indo-European languages comprising Sanskrit and its modern descendants. [f. L f. Gk *Indikos* Indian (see INDIA, -IC)]
i′ndic|āte *v.t.* **1.** point out, make known, show; suggest, call for; (Med., in *pass.*) be desirable or necessary. **2.** state briefly; be a sign of, express presence of, (thing, *that,* etc.); (in *p.p.*) shown by indicator. **3.** So ~A′TION *n.* [f. L IN[1](*dicare* make known f. as INDEX) + -ATE[3]]
indi′cative *a.* & *n.* **1.** *a.* (Gram., of mood) stating a thing as a fact, not as conception, wish, command, etc., of speaker. **2.** (or i′ndĭkātĭv). suggestive, giving indications, *of.* **3.** Hence ~LY[2] (-vlĭ). **4.** *n.* indicative mood. [ME, f. F *indicatif -ive* f. LL *indicativus* transl. Gk *horistikē* (*egklisis* mood); see prec., -IVE]
i′ndicātor *n.* person or thing that points out; recording instrument attached to apparatus etc.; board giving information on current situation; (Chem.) substance changing colour at given stage in chemical reaction; radioactive tracer; device on vehicle to indicate intended change of direction of travel. [f. INDICATE +-OR]
i′ndicatory (-dĭ′-, ĭ′-) *a.* = INDICATIVE. 2. [f. INDICATE +-ORY]
i′ndices. *See* INDEX.
indi′ci|um (-shĭ-) *n.* (esp. in *pl.* ~a). indication, sign; identifying mark; *imprinted mark showing that postage has been paid. [L, f. as INDEX]
indi′ct (-ī′t) *v.t.* accuse (person *for* crime, *as* culprit, *on* charge), esp. by legal process. [ME, f. AF *enditer* indict f. OF *enditer* declare f. Rom. *IN[1](dictare*; see DICTATE[2])]
indi′ctable (-ī′t-) *a.* liable, (of action) rendering one liable, to be indicted. [f. prec. +-ABLE]
indi′ction *n.* **1.** cycle of 15 years instituted by Constantine as fiscal period in 313; assessment of property-tax by Roman emperors at beginning of each 15 years; this tax. **2.** (arch.) proclamation. [ME, f. L *indictio* f. IN[1](*dicere dict-* say) proclaim; see -ION]
indi′ctment (-ī′t-) *n.* formal accusation; legal process in which this is made; document containing charge; **bill of** ~, (Hist. & US) written accusation as presented to grand jury. [ME, f. AF *enditement* (as INDICT; see -MENT)]
I′ndies (ĭ′ndĭz) *n. pl.* **1. the** ~, (arch.) India and adjacent regions. **2. East** ~, islands etc. east of India. **3. West** ~, islands of Central America. [pl. of obs. *Indy* INDIA]
indi′fference *n.* absence of interest or attention (*to, towards,* or abs.); neutrality; unimportance (*a matter of indifference*). [f. L *indifferentia* (as foll.; see -ENCE)]
indi′fferent *a.* **1.** ~ **to,** having no partiality for or against, having no interest in or sympathy for. **2.** neither good nor bad; not especially good; fairly bad; **very** ~, definitely bad. **3.** chemically, magnetically, etc., neutral. **4.** Hence ~LY[2] *adv.* [ME f. OF, or f. L IN[2](*differens* DIFFERENT)]
indi′fferent|ism *n.* spirit of indifference, professed or practised, esp. in religious matters; so ~IST (2) *n.* [f. prec. +-ISM]

i'ndigēne *n.* (arch.) indigenous animal, plant, etc. [f. F *indigène* f. L *indigena* (*indi-* = IN-¹, *gen-* be born)]

indi'gĕnous *a.* born or (esp. of flora and fauna) produced naturally in a region; belonging naturally (*to* soil etc.; or fig.); hence ∿LY² *adv.* [f. L *indigena* (see prec.) + -OUS]

i'ndĭg|ent *a.* needy, poor; so ∿ENCE *n.* [ME f. OF, f. LL *indigēre* (*indi-* = IN-¹, *egēre* need); see -ENT]

indĭgĕ'stĕd *a.* shapeless; ill-considered; not digested. [f. IN-² + DIGEST² + -ED¹]

indĭgĕ'st|ĭble *a.* difficult or impossible to digest (lit. or fig.); hence ∿IBI'LITY *n.* [F, or f. LL IN²(*digestibilis* DIGESTIBLE)]

indĭgĕ'st|ion (-schon) *n.* (case of, pain from) difficulty in digesting food; mental state suggestive of this; undigested condition (lit. or fig.); so ∿IVE *a.* [ME f. OF, or f. LL IN²(*digestio* DIGESTION)]

indi'gn (-ī'n) *a.* (arch.) unworthy. [ME, f. OF *indigne* or f. L IN²(*dignus* worthy)]

indi'gnant *a.* moved by mingled anger and scorn or feeling of injured innocence (*at* thing, *with* person, *that, to find* etc., or abs.); hence ∿LY² *adv.* [f. L *indignari* regard as unworthy (as prec.); see -ANT]

indignā'tion *n.* anger excited by supposed meanness, injustice, wickedness, or misconduct, (*at* thing; *against, with* person); ∿-meeting (to express public indignation). [ME f. OF, or f. L *indignatio* (as prec.); see -ATION)]

indi'gnitÿ *n.* unworthy treatment; slight, insult; humiliating quality (*the indignity of my position*). [f. F *indignité* or f. L *indignitas* (as INDIGN; see -ITY)]

i'ndĭgō *n.* (*pl.* ∿s). (blue dye obtained from) plant of genus *Indigofera*; synthetic form of the dye; ∿ (blue), colour between blue and violet in spectrum; ∿-bird, ∿ bunting, N. Amer. species of finch with indigo head; ∿ snake, cribo; ∿ white, white crystalline powder formed by reduction of indigo; hence **indĭgŏ'tĭc** [-*t*- euphonic] *a.* [16th c. *indico* (f. Sp.), *indigo* (f. Port.), f. L f. Gk *indikon* INDIAN (dye)]

indĭrĕ'ct *a.* **1.** (Of road etc.) not straight; not going straight to the point. **2.** (Of lighting) from concealed source and diffusely reflected; (Econ., of tax) not direct, paid by consumer in form of increased price for taxed goods; ∿ aggression (by non-military means). **3.** (Gram.) ∿ object, person or thing affected by verbal action but not primarily acted on (e.g. *him* in *give him the book*); ∿ passive, passive having for subject the indirect or prepositional object of the active (e.g. *he* in *he was given the book, he was laughed at*); ∿ question, question in reported speech (*asked who I was*); ∿ speech, = REPORT²*ed speech.* **4.** not directly aimed at (*an indirect result*). **5.** Hence ∿LY² *adv.*, ∿NESS *n.* [ME f. OF, or f. med. L IN²(*directus* DIRECT²)]

indĭrĕ'ction *n.* roundabout means (esp. *by indirection*, after Shak. *Hamlet* II. i. 66); deceit, trickery. [f. prec. + -ION]

indĭscĕr'nĭb|le *a.* & *n.* (thing) that cannot be discerned or distinguished from another; hence ∿LY² *adv.* [f. IN-² + DISCERNIBLE]

indĭscĕr'pt|ĭble *a.* (literary). incapable of, not destructible by, separation of parts; hence ∿IBI'LITY *n.* [f. IN-² + DISCERPTIBLE]

indi'scĭpline *n.* lack of order or control by authority. [f. IN-² + DISCIPLINE¹, or thr. F]

indĭscree't *a.* injudicious, unwary; hence ∿LY² *adv.* [ME, f. LL IN²(*discretus*; see DISCREET)]

indĭscrē'te *a.* not divided into distinct parts. [f. L IN²(*discretus* separated; see DISCREET)]

indĭscrē'tion *n.* injudicious conduct; accidental or (calculated ∿) supposedly accidental revelation of official secret etc.; imprudence; imprudent immoral action. [ME f. OF, or f. LL IN²(*discretio* DISCRETION)]

indĭscrī'min|ate *a.* confused, promiscuous; making no distinctions; hence ∿ately² (-tlĭ) *adv.*, ∿ateNESS (-tn-), ∿A'TION, *ns.*, ∿ATIVE *a.* [f. IN-² + *discriminate* a. f. L *discriminatus* p.p. (as DISCRIMINATE; see -ATE²)]

indĭspĕ'ns|able *a.* that cannot be dispensed with, necessary (*to* or *for*); (of law, duty, etc.) that cannot be set aside; hence ∿ABI'LITY, ∿ableNESS (-bəln-), *ns.*, ∿ABLY *adv.* [f. med. L IN²(*dispensabilis* DISPENSABLE)]

indĭspō'se (-z) *v.t.* render unfit or unable (*for* thing; *to* do); make averse (*towards* or *from* thing; *to* do); (esp. in *p.p.*) make (slightly) unwell. [f. IN-² + DISPOSE]

indĭsposī'tion (-zī'-) *n.* ill health, ailment, (esp. slight or temporary); disinclination (*to* thing; *to* do); aversion (*to, towards*). [F, or f. IN-² + DISPOSITION]

indĭspūt'able (-ū'-, -dī'-) *a.* that cannot be disputed; unquestionable; hence ∿ABI'LITY, ∿ableNESS (-bəln-), *ns.*, ∿ABLY *adv.* [f. LL IN²(*disputabilis* DISPUTABLE)]

indĭssō'l'ūble *a.* lasting, stable, (*an indissoluble bond*); that cannot be dissolved or decomposed; hence ∿UBI'LITY *n.*, ∿UBLY *adv.* [f. L IN²(*dissolubilis* DISSOLUBLE)]

indĭsti'nct *a.* not distinct; confused, obscure; hence ∿LY² *adv.*, ∿NESS *n.* [ME, f. L IN²(*distinctus* DISTINCT)]

indĭsti'nctive *a.* not having distinctive features; hence ∿LY² (-vlĭ) *adv.* [f. IN-² + DISTINCTIVE]

indĭsti'nguishab|le (-nggw-) *a.* not distinguishable (*from*); hence ∿LY² *adv.* [f. IN-² + DISTINGUISHABLE]

indi'te *v.t.* put into words, compose, (poem, speech, etc.); (usu. *joc.*) write (letter etc.). [ME, f. OF *enditier*; see INDICT]

i'ndĭum *n.* (Chem.) rare silver-white soft metallic element occurring with zinc etc. [f. L *indicum* INDIGO w. ref. to its characteristic spectral lines, + -IUM]

indĭvĕr'tĭb|le *a.* that cannot be turned aside; hence ∿LY² *adv.* [f. IN-² + DIVERT + -IBLE]

indĭvi'dūal *a.* & *n.* **1.** *a.* single; particular, special, opp. to *general*; having distinct character; characteristic of particular person; designed for use by one person; (Psych.) of study of individuals, Adlerian. **2.** *n.* single member of class; single human being, opp. to *society, family*, etc.; (colloq.) person (*an exceedingly unpleasant individual*). [ME, = 'indivisible', f. med. L *individualis* f. L IN²(*dividuus* f. *dividere* DIVIDE¹)]

indĭvi'dūal|ism *n.* self-centred feeling or conduct, egoism; self-reliant individual action; social theory favouring free action of individuals; so ∿IST (2) *n.*, ∿i'stIC *a.* [f. prec. + -ISM]

individūā'lĭtÿ *n.* separate existence; individual character, esp. when strongly marked; (in *pl.*) individual tastes etc. [f. INDIVIDUAL + -ITY]

indĭvi'dūaliz|e, -īs|e (-īz), *v.t.* give individual character to; specify; hence ∿A'TION *n.* [f. INDIVIDUAL + -IZE]

indĭvi'dūallÿ *adv.* personally, in an individual capacity; in a distinctive manner; one by one, not collectively; ∿ different, different as individuals though perhaps identical in species. [f. INDIVIDUAL + -LY²]

indĭvi'dū|āte *v.t.* individualize, form into an individual; so ∿A'TION *n.* [f. med. L *individuare* (as INDIVIDUAL) + -ATE³]

indĭvi's|ĭble (-z-) *a.* not divisible; not distributable among a number; hence ∿IBI'LITY *n.*, ∿IBLY *adv.* [ME, f. LL IN²(*divisibilis* DIVISIBLE)]

i'ndō- (ĭ'-) *comb. form.* Indian (and); ∿-Ar'yan, (1) Indic (group), (2) Indic-speaking (person); ∿-Chine'se, (native or inhabitant) of Indo-China; ∿-Europe'an, ∿-Germa'nic, (speaker of one) of the family of languages spoken over greater part of Europe and Asia as far as N. India; ∿-Iranian, (of) the subfamily of Indo-European languages spoken chiefly in N. India and Iran; ∿-Portugue'se, modified Portuguese as used in India. [f. L f. Gk *Indos* + -O-]

indō'cīle *a.* not docile; hence **indocĭ'lITY** *n.* [F, or f. L IN²(*docilis* DOCILE)]

indŏ'ctrĭn|āte *v.t.* teach, instruct (*in* or *into* subject etc.); imbue with or with a doctrine, idea, or opinion; hence ∿A'TION *n.* [f. IN-¹ + DOCTRINE + -ATE³]

i'ndōle *n.* (Chem.) crystalline substance with unpleasant smell, found in faeces etc., and as product of reduction of indigo. [f. INDIGO + L *oleum* oil]

i′ndol|ent a. averse to exertion; (Med.) causing no pain (*indolent tumour*); hence or cogn. ∼ENCE *n.*, ∼entLY² *adv.* [f. LL IN²(*dolens* f. L *dolēre* suffer pain; see -ENT)]

Indŏ′log| y̆ (ĭ-) *n.* study of Indian history, literature, etc.; hence ∼IST (3) *n.* [f. INDO- + -LOGY]

indŏ′mitab|le a. that does not let oneself or itself be subdued, unyielding; stubbornly persistent; hence ∼LY² *adv.* [f. LL IN²(*domitabilis* f. L *domitare* tame; see DAUNT, -ABLE)]

Indonē′sian (ĭ′-; -shan) a. & *n.* (native or inhabitant) of Indonesia; (one) of chief pre-Malay population of E. Indies; (language) of language-group spoken in E. Indies, esp. official language of Indonesian Republic. [f. *Indonesia* (f. INDIES after *Polynesia*) + -AN]

i′ndoor (-dôr) a. situated, carried on, used, within a building or under cover (*indoor aerial, games*); (Hist.) within workhouse (*indoor relief*). [earlier *within-door*; cf. foll.]

indoor′s (-ôr′z) *adv.* within a building; under a roof. [earlier *within doors*]

indôr′se. See ENDORSE.

i′ndraught, *i′ndraft, (-ahft) *n.* drawing in; inward flow or current. [f. IN² + DRAUGHT¹]

i′ndrawn a. (Of breath etc.) drawn in; aloof. [f. IN² + DRAWN]

i′ndri *n.* babacoote. [f. Malagasy *indry* behold, mistaken for its name]

indŭ′bitab|le a. that cannot be doubted; hence ∼LY² *adv.* [f. F, or f. L IN²(*dubitabilis* f. *dubitare* to doubt; see -ABLE)]

indŭ′c|e v.t. prevail on, persuade, (*to* do; **nothing will** ∼e **me to,** I will never); bring about, give rise to; (Electr.) produce (current) by induction; (Phys.) cause (radioactivity) by bombardment; (esp. Med.) bring on by artificial means (*induce labour*); infer, derive as an induction; hence ∼IBLE a. [ME, f. L IN¹(*ducere duct-* lead)]

indŭ′cement (-sm-) *n.* what induces; attraction that leads one on (*to*). [f. prec. + -MENT]

indŭ′ct v.t. introduce formally into possession (*to* benefice); install (*into* seat, room, status, etc.); introduce, initiate, (*to, into*); *summon to military service, whence ∼EE′ *n.* [ME, as INDUCE]

indŭ′ctance *n.* (Electr.) amount of induction or self-induction of a circuit. [f. prec. + -ANCE]

indŭ′ction *n.* **1.** inducting or inducing; (arch.) preamble, prologue, introduction; (esp. Med.) bringing on by artificial means (*induction of labour*). **2.** production (*of* facts) to prove general statement; inferring of general law from particular instances (cf. *deduction*); **mathematical** ∼, proving truth of theorem by showing (1) that if true of any particular case it is true of the next case in a series, and (2) that it is true of one particular case. **3.** bringing about of electric or magnetic state in a body by proximity (without contact) of electrified or magnetized body; production of electric current in conductor by change of magnetic field; physical quantity measuring amount of such influence; ∼-**coil** (for generating intermittent high voltage from direct current); ∼ **heating** (by induced electric current). **4.** drawing of fuel mixture into cylinder(s) of internal combustion engine. [ME f. OF, or f. L *inductio* (as INDUCE; see -ION)]

indŭ′ctive a. (Of reasoning etc.) of, based on, induction; of electric or magnetic induction; hence ∼LY² (-vlĭ) *adv.*, ∼NESS (-vn-) *n.* [f. LL *inductivus* (as INDUCE; see -IVE)]

indŭ′ctor *n.* one who inducts clergyman; (Electr.) any part of induction apparatus, esp. reactor. [L (as INDUCE; see -OR)]

induē′. See ENDUE.

indŭ′lge v. **1.** v.t. please (person, one*self*) by compliance with wishes (*in* matter etc.); favour (person *with* thing given); yield freely to (desire etc.). **2.** v.i. take pleasure freely (*in* strong language, cycling, a cigar); (colloq.) partake (too) freely of intoxicants. [f. L *indulgēre indult-* give free rein to]

indŭ′lgence *n.* **1.** indulging (*in*); self-indulgence. **2.** privilege granted; **Declaration of I**∼, proclamation of religious liberties, esp. under Charles II in 1672 and James II in 1687. **3.** (RC Ch.) remission of temporal punishment still due for sins even after sacramental absolution. [ME f. OF, f. L *indulgentia* (as prec.; see -ENCE)]

indŭ′lgenced (-nst) a. (RC Ch.) (Of prayer, material object, etc.) procuring indulgence to the user. [f. prec. + -ED²]

indŭ′lgent a. indulging or tending to indulge; (too) ready to overlook faults etc.; hence ∼LY² *adv.* [F, or f. L (as INDULGE; see -ENT)]

indŭ′lt *n.* (RC Ch.) Pope's licence for thing not sanctioned by common law of Church. [F f. LL *indultum*, neut. p.p. (as n.) f. L (as INDULGE)]

indu′na (-ōō′-) *n.* (S.Afr.) Zulu headman; authoritative person. [Zulu]

i′ndūr|āte v.t. & i. make or become hard; make callous or unfeeling; become inveterate; hence or cogn. ∼A′TION *n.*, ∼ATIVE a. [f. L IN²(*durare* f. *durus* hard) + -ATE³]

indū′si|um (-z-) *n.* (*pl.* ∼a). membranous shield covering fruit-cluster of fern; collection of hairs enclosing stigma of some flowers; case of larva; hence ∼AL a. [L, = tunic, f. *induere* put on (garment)]

indŭ′strial a. & n. **1.** a. of industry or industries; ∼ **action,** strike, go-slow, or working to rule; *industrial* ARCHAEOLOGY, ESTATE 5; **the I**∼ **Revolution,** rapid development of British industry by use of machines in the late 18th and early 19th c.; **I**∼ **Workers of the World,** labour organization (1905-) advocating syndicalism and international socialism. **2.** designed, or fit only, for industrial use (*industrial alcohol*); characterized by highly developed industries (*the industrial nations*). **3.** *n.* (in *pl.*) shares in industrial companies. **4.** Hence ∼ISM (3), ∼IST (3) (esp., manufacturer), ∼IZA′TION, *ns.*, ∼IZE (3) *v.t.*, ∼LY² *adv.* [f. INDUSTRY + -AL; in 19th c. partly f. F *industriel*]

indŭ′strious a. diligent, hard-working; hence ∼LY² *adv.* [f. F *industrieux* or f. LL *industriosus* (as foll.; see -OUS)]

i′ndustry̆ *n.* diligence; habitual employment in useful work; branch of trade or manufacture, these as a whole (*incentives to industry*); (colloq.) the diligent study of a particular topic. [ME, = skill, f. F *industrie* or f. L *industria* diligence; see -Y¹]

indwe′ll v. (**indwe′lt**). **1.** v.t. (Usu. fig., of spirit, principle, etc.) inhabit, occupy. **2.** v.i. be permanently present *in*. **3.** Hence ∼ER¹ *n.* [ME, f. IN-¹ + DWELL]

-ine¹ (usu. ĭn) *suf.* forming *adjs.* w. sense 'pertaining to, of the nature of' (*Alpine, asinine, divine, equine, feminine, Florentine, marine, supine*). [f. or after F *-in -ine* or f. L *-inus*]

-ine² (usu. ĭn) *suf.* forming *adjs.* esp. f. names of minerals, plants, etc., (*crystalline, hyacinthine; pristine*). [f. L *-inus* f. or after Gk *-inos*]

-ine³ (ĭn, ēn) *suf.* forming *fem. ns.* (*heroine, margravine*). [F f. L *-ina* f. Gk *-inē*, f. G *-in*]

-ine⁴ *suf.* forming (esp. abstract) *ns.* (*discipline, medicine, rapine; concubine, nectarine*). [F, f. L *-ina* fem. = -INE¹]

-ine⁵ (ēn, ĭn) *suf.* (Chem.) forming *ns.* denoting derived substances, esp. alkaloids, halogens, amines, and amino-acids. [f. prec.]

inē′briate¹ a. & n. **1.** a. drunken. **2.** *n.* drunken person, esp. habitual drunkard. [ME, f. L *inebriatus* p.p. of IN¹(*ebriare* f. *ebrius* drunk); see -ATE²]

inē′bri|āte² v.t. make drunk, intoxicate (lit. or fig.); hence ∼A′TION *n.* [f. as prec. + -ATE³]

inēbri′ety̆ *n.* (habit of) drunkenness. [f. IN-¹ + *ebriety* drunkenness f. F *ébriété* or f. L *ebrietas* (*ebrius* drunk; see -TY¹)]

inĕ′d|ible a. not edible, esp. from its nature (cf. UNEATABLE); hence ∼IBI′LITY *n.* [f. IN-² + EDIBLE]

inē′dited a. not published; published without editorial alterations or additions. [f. IN-² + EDITed]

inĕ'dŭc|able *a.* incapable of being educated, esp. through mental retardation; hence ∼ABI'LITY *n.* [f. IN-² + EDUCABLE]

inĕ'ffab|le *a.* unutterable, too great for description in words; that must not be uttered; hence ∼LY² *adv.* [ME f. OF, or L IN²(*effabilis* f. EFfari speak out, utter; see -ABLE)]

inĕffā'ce|able (-sa-) *a.* that cannot be effaced; hence ∼ABI'LITY *n.*, ∼ABLY *adv.*, (-sa-). [f. IN-² + EFFACEABLE]

inĕffĕ'ctive *a.* not producing any effect or the desired effect; (of person) inefficient; lacking artistic effect; hence ∼LY² (-vlĭ) *adv.*, ∼NESS (-vn-) *n.* [f. IN-² + EFFECTIVE]

inĕffĕ'ctŭal *a.* without effect; not producing the desired or expected effect; hence ∼LY² *adv.*, ∼NESS *n.* [ME, f. med. L IN²(*effectualis* EFFECTUAL)]

inĕffĭcā'cious (-shus) *a.* (Of remedy etc.) not efficacious; hence or cogn. ∼LY² *adv.*, ∼NESS, **inĕ'ffĭc-ACY**, *ns.* [f. IN-² + EFFICACIOUS]

inĕffĭ'ci|ent (-shent) *a.* not efficient; (of person) not fully capable, not well qualified; hence or cogn. ∼ENCY *n.*, ∼entLY² *adv.* [f. IN-² + EFFICIENT]

inĕla'st|ic (-ă'-, -ah'-) *a.* not elastic; unadaptable, inflexible, unyielding; hence ∼ICALLY *adv.*, **in-ĕlasti'CITY** *n.* [f. IN-² + ELASTIC]

inĕ'lĕg|ant *a.* ungraceful; unrefined; (of style) unpolished; hence ∼ANCE *n.*, ∼antLY² *adv.* [f. F *inélégant* f. L IN²(*elegans* ELEGANT)]

inĕ'lig|ible *a.* not eligible; undesirable; hence ∼IBI'LITY *n.*, ∼IBLY *adv.* [f. IN-² + ELIGIBLE]

inĕlŭ'ctab|le *a.* that cannot be escaped from; against which it is useless to strive; hence ∼LY² *adv.* [f. L IN²(*eluctabilis* f. Eluctari struggle out; see -ABLE)]

inĕ'pt *a.* out of place; absurd, silly; unskilful; hence or cogn. ∼ĭTUDE, ∼NESS, *ns.*, ∼LY² *adv.* [f. L IN²(*eptus* = *aptus* APT)]

inĕ'quable *a.* not uniform; not fairly distributed. [f. L IN²(*aequabilis* EQUABLE) uneven]

inĕqua'lity (-ŏ'l-) *n.* lack of equality in magnitude, quality, rank, circumstances, etc.; variableness; (of surface) irregularity; (Astron.) deviation from uniformity in motion of heavenly body; (Math.) formula affirming that two expressions are not equal. [ME, f. OF *inequalité* or f. L IN²(*aequalitas* EQUALITY)]

inĕ'quitab|le *a.* unfair, unjust; hence ∼LY² *adv.* [f. IN-² + EQUITABLE]

inĕ'quity *n.* unfairness, bias. [f. IN-² + EQUITY]

inĕrā'dicab|le *a.* that cannot be rooted out; hence ∼LY² *adv.* [f. IN-² + ERADICABLE]

inĕ'rr|able, inĕ'rr|ant, *adjs.* not liable to err; hence or cogn. ∼ABI'LITY, ∼ANCY, *ns.*, ∼ABLY *adv.* [f. L IN²(*errabilis* & *errans* f. *errare* err; see -ABLE, -ANT)]

inĕr't *a.* without inherent power of action, motion, or resistance; without active chemical or other properties; sluggish, slow; ∼ **gas**, = NOBLE *gas*; hence ∼LY² *adv.*, ∼NESS *n.* [f. L IN²(*ers ertis* f. *ars* ART²)]

inĕr'tia (-sha, -shya) *n.* **1.** (Phys.) property of matter by which it continues in its existing state of rest or uniform motion in straight line, unless that state is changed by external force; MOMENT *of inertia*; ∼ **reel** (allowing automatic adjustment of safety-belt rolled round it). **2.** inertness, sloth; ∼ **selling**, sending of goods not ordered, in hope that recipients will not take action to refuse them and must later make payment. **3.** Hence ∼LESS *a.* [L (as prec.; see -IA¹)]

inĕr'tial (-shal) *a.* of inertia; (of navigation etc.) performed automatically in response to forces causing accelerations. [f. prec.+ -AL]

inĕscā'pable *a.* that cannot be escaped. [f. IN-² + ESCAPABLE]

inĕscŭ'tcheon (-chon) *n.* (Her.) small escutcheon placed on a larger one. [f. IN² + ESCUTCHEON]

-inĕss *suf.* forming *ns.* corresp. to *adjs.* in -Y² etc. (*iciness, stickiness*); cf. -NESS.

in esse (ĭn ĕ'sĭ) *a.* in actual existence (opp. IN POSSE). [L]

inĕssĕ'ntial (-shal) *a.* & *n.* **1.** *a.* not necessary; dispensable. **2.** *n.* inessential thing. [f. IN-² + ESSENTIAL]

inĕ'stĭmab|le *a.* too great, intense, precious, etc., to be estimated; hence ∼LY² *adv.* [ME f. OF, f. L IN²(*aestimabilis* ESTIMABLE)]

inĕ'vit|able *a.* unavoidable, sure to happen; that is bound to occur or appear; (colloq.) that is tiresomely familiar; (of character-drawing, development of plot, etc.) so true to nature etc. as to preclude alternative treatment or solution, convincing; hence ∼ABI'LITY, ∼ableNESS (-beln-), *ns.*, ∼ABLY *adv.* [f. L IN²(*evitabilis* f. Evitare avoid; see -ABLE)]

inĕxā'ct (-gz-) *a.* not exact; hence or cogn. ∼ĭTUDE, ∼NESS, *ns.*, ∼LY² *adv.* [f. IN-² + EXACT¹]

inĕxcū'sab|le (-z-) *a.* (Of person, action, etc.) that cannot be excused or justified; hence ∼LY² *adv.* [ME, f. L IN²(*excusabilis* EXCUSABLE)]

inĕxhau'st|ible (-ĭgzaw'-) *a.* that cannot be exhausted; hence ∼IBI'LITY *n.*, ∼IBLY *adv.* [f. IN-² + EXHAUSTIBLE]

inĕ'xor|able *a.* that cannot be persuaded by request or entreaty; relentless; hence ∼ABI'LITY *n.*, ∼ABLY *adv.* [F, or f. L IN²(*exorabilis* f. EX¹*orare* entreat; see -ABLE)]

inĕxpē'di|ent *a.* not expedient; hence ∼ENCY *n.* [f. IN-² + EXPEDIENT]

inĕxpē'nsive *a.* not expensive; offering good value for the price; hence ∼LY² (-vlĭ) *adv.*, ∼NESS (-vn-) *n.* [f. IN-² + EXPENSIVE]

inĕxpēr'ienc|e *n.* lack of (knowledge or skill gained from) experience; so ∼ED² (-st) *a.* [f. F *inexpérience* f. LL IN²(*experientia* EXPERIENCE)]

inĕ'xpêrt *a.* unskilled; hence ∼LY² *adv.*, ∼NESS *n.* [OF, f. L IN²(*expertus* EXPERT¹)]

inĕ'xpiab|le *a.* (Of offence) that cannot be expiated; (of resentment etc.) implacable; hence ∼LY² *adv.* [f. L IN²(*expiabilis* EXPIABLE)]

inĕxplic|able (-ĕ'-, -ĭ'k-) *a.* that cannot be explained or accounted for; hence ∼ABI'LITY *n.*, ∼ABLY *adv.* [F, or f. L IN²(*explicabilis* that cannot be unfolded; see EXPLICABLE)]

inĕxpli'cit *a.* not definitely or clearly expressed; hence ∼LY² *adv.*, ∼NESS *n.* [f. IN-² + EXPLICIT²]

inĕxprĕ'ssib|le *a.* & *n.* **1.** *a.* that cannot be expressed in words; hence ∼LY² *adv.* **2.** *n.* (in *pl.*, arch. colloq.) trousers. [f. IN-² + EXPRESSIBLE]

inĕxprĕ'ssive *a.* not expressive; (arch.) inexpressible; hence ∼LY² (-vlĭ) *adv.*, ∼NESS (-vn-) *n.* [f. IN-² + EXPRESSIVE]

inĕxpū'gnable *a.* impregnable, invincible, (lit. or fig.). [ME f. F, f. L IN²(*expugnabilis* f. EX¹*pugnare* take by storm; see -ABLE)]

inĕxpū'ngible (-nj-) *a.* that cannot be expunged or obliterated. [f. IN-² + EXPUNGE + -IBLE]

in extenso (ĭn ĕkstĕ'nsō) *adv.* in full, at full length. [L]

inĕxtī'nguishable (-nggw-) *a.* not quenchable, indestructible, (lit., or fig. of laughter etc.). [f. IN-² + EXTINGUISHABLE]

in extremis (ĭn ĕkstrē'mĭs) *a.* at the point of death; (fig.) in great difficulties. [L]

inĕ'xtricab|le *a.* (Of place, state, etc.) that cannot be escaped from; (of knot, problem, etc.) that cannot be unravelled or solved; intricately confused; hence ∼LY² *adv.* [ME, f. L IN²(*extricabilis* f. extricare EXTRICATE; see -ABLE)]

infa'llibil|ism *n.* principle of papal infallibility; so ∼IST (2) *n.* [f. LL *infallibilis* (see foll.) + -ISM]

infa'll|ible *a.* incapable of erring; (of method, test, proof, etc.) unfailing; hence ∼IBI'LITY *n.* (esp. as attribute of the Pope speaking *ex cathedra*, defined 1870 by the Vatican Council), ∼IBLY *adv.* [ME, f. F *infallibile* or f. LL *infallibilis* (see FALLIBLE)]

i'nfamīze, -īse (-īz) *v.t.* render infamous. [f. L *infamis* (see foll.) + -IZE]

i'nfamous *a.* of ill fame, notoriously vile or evil; abominable; (Law) deprived of all or some rights of citizen on account of serious crime; hence or cogn. ∼LY² adv., **i'nfam**Y¹ n. [ME, f. med. L *infamosus* f. L IN²(*famis* f. *fama* fame) + -OUS]

i'nfancy n. early childhood, babyhood; (Law) being a minor; early state of development. [f. L *infantia* (as foll.; see -ANCY)]

i'nfant n. child during earliest period of life; (Law) minor (under 18); (esp..*attrib.*) thing in early state of development; ∼ **mortality**, death before age 1; ∼ **prodigy**, very precocious child; ||∼ **school** (for young children, usu. under 7). [ME, f. OF *enfant* f. L IN²(*fans fantis* part. of *fari* speak) unable to speak]

infa'nta n. (Hist.) daughter of king and queen of Spain or Portugal (usu. eldest daughter who is not heir to throne); so **infa'nte** n. (second son). [Sp. & Port., -a fem., -e masc., f. L (as prec.)]

infa'nti|cide n. killing of infant soon after birth, esp. with mother's consent; custom of killing new-born infants; one who kills an infant; hence ∼**ci'd**AL a. [F f. LL *infanticidium*, -*cida* (as INFANT; see -CIDE)]

i'nfant|ile a. of or as of infants (∼**ile paralysis**, poliomyelitis) in its infancy; so ∼INE¹ a. [F, or f. L *infantilis* (as INFANT; see -IL)]

infa'ntilism n. infantile action etc.; (Path.) state of being mentally or physically undeveloped though of adult age. [f. prec. + -ISM]

i'nfantry n. soldiers marching and fighting on foot; ∼**man**, soldier of infantry regiment. [f. F *infanterie* f. It. *infanteria* (*infante* youth, infantryman, f. as INFANT; see -RY)]

i'nfarct n. (Path.) region of dead tissue caused by blocking of blood-circulation; so **infar'ction** n. [f. mod. L IN¹(*farctus* p.p. of L *farcire* stuff)]

infa'tu|ate v.t. affect (person) with extreme folly; inspire with extravagant (esp. amorous) passion; ∼**ated with**, having an unreasonably strong love for; hence ∼A'TION n. [f. L IN¹(*fatuare* f. *fatuus* foolish) + -ATE³]

i'nfauna n. animals living just below surface of sea-bed. [f. Da. *ifauna* (as IN-¹, FAUNA)]

infe'ct v.t. contaminate (air, water, etc.) with germs or other noxious matter; affect (person, body, mind, *with* disease etc. lit. or fig.); imbue (person *with* pernicious opinion etc.); so ∼IVE a. [ME, f. L IN¹(*ficere fect-* = *facere* make) taint]

infe'ction n. communication of disease, esp. by agency of air, water, etc.; moral contamination; diffusive influence of example, sympathy, etc. [ME f. OF, or f. LL *infectio* (as prec.; see -ION)]

infe'ctious (-shus) a. infecting with disease, pestilential; (of disease) liable to be transmitted by air, water, etc.; (of emotions etc.) apt to spread, quickly affecting others; hence ∼LY² adv., ∼NESS n. [f. prec. + -OUS]

infeli'citous a. not felicitous; hence ∼LY² adv. [f. IN-² + FELICITOUS]

infeli'city n. unhappiness; a misfortune; inaptness of expression etc. [ME, f. L IN²(*felicitas* FELICITY)]

infer' v.t. (-rr-). reach from or *from* facts and reasoning (opinion, *that, when*, etc.); hence ∼ABLE a. [f. L IN¹(*ferre* bring)]

i'nference n. inferring; (Logic) forming of conclusion from premisses; thing inferred; so **infere'nti**AL (-shal) a. [f. med. L *inferentia* (as prec.; see -ENCE)]

infer'ior a. & n. 1. a. lower, in lower position, of lower rank, quality, etc., (*to*, or abs.); of poor quality; (of planet) having orbit within the earth's; (Bot.) (of calyx) below ovary, (of ovary) below calyx; (of figures or letters) written or printed below the line; hence ∼LY² adv. 2. n. person inferior to another esp. in rank (*kind to his inferiors*); inferior letter or figure. [ME f. L, compar. of *inferus* that is below]

inferiò'rity n. state of being inferior; ∼ **complex**, unrealistic feeling of general inadequacy caused by actual or supposed inferiority in one sphere, sometimes with aggressive behaviour in compensation, (colloq.) exaggerated feeling of personal inadequacy. [f. prec. + -ITY]

infer'nal a. of hell; hellish, fiendish; (colloq.) detestable, tiresome; ∼ **machine**, (arch.) apparatus (usu. disguised) for producing explosion destructive of life or property; hence ∼LY² adv. [ME f. OF, f. LL *infernalis* f. L *infernus* situated below; see -AL]

infer'nò n. (*pl.* ∼s). hell (esp. w. ref. to Dante's *Divine Comedy*); scene of horror or distress, esp. conflagration. [It., f. LL *infernus* (see prec.)]

infer'rable. Var. of INFERABLE.

infer'tile a. not fertile; hence **inferti'l**ITY n. [F, or f. LL IN²(*fertilis* FERTILE)]

infe'st v.t. (Of vermin, pirates, disease, etc.) haunt, swarm in or about, (place) esp. with troublesome result or evil intent; so ∼A'TION n. [ME, f. F *infester* or f. L *infestare* assail (*infestus* hostile)]

||**infeuda'tion** n. (Hist.) enfeoffment; ∼ **of tithes**, granting of tithes to laymen. [ME, f. med. L *infeudatio* f. IN¹(*feudare* f. *feudum* FEE); see -ATION]

infibula'tion n. fastening with clasp, esp. of genitals to prevent sexual intercourse. [f. L IN¹(*fibulare* f. FIBULA) + -ATION]

i'nfidel n. & a. 1. n. one who does not believe in religion; (Hist.) adherent of religion opposed to Christianity, esp. Muslim; person not an adherent of one's own religion; unbeliever. 2. a. that is an infidel, of unbelievers. [ME, f. F *infidèle* or f. L IN²(*fidelis* faithful f. *fides* faith)]

infidè'lity n. disbelief in Christianity or other religion; disloyalty, unfaithfulness, esp. to husband or wife. [ME, f. F *infidélité* or f. L *infidelitas* (as prec.; see -ITY)]

i'nfield n. 1. farm land around or near homestead; arable land; land regularly manured and cropped. 2. (Cricket) part of the ground near the wicket, fieldsmen stationed there; (Baseball) area between the four bases, four fielders stationed on its boundaries; hence ∼ER¹, ∼**sman** (-z-), ns. [f. IN² + FIELD]

i'nfighting (-fīt-) n. boxing at closer quarters than arm's length; (fig.) hidden conflict within an organization. [f. IN² + FIGHTING]

i'nfill v.t. fill in (cavity etc.); hence ∼ING¹ n., (esp.) placing of buildings to occupy gaps between earlier ones. [f. IN² + FILL]

infiltr|ate (ĭ'n-, -fī'-) v. 1. v.t. introduce (fluid) by filtration (*into, through*). 2. v.t. & i. permeate by filtration; (cause to) enter gradually and imperceptibly (as settlers, occupying troops, spies, etc.). 3. Hence ∼A'TION, ∼**ator**, ns. [f. IN-¹ + FILTRATE²]

i'nfinite a. & n. 1. a. boundless, endless; very great; (w. *pl.* n.) innumerable, very many; (Math.) greater than any assignable quantity or countable number, (of series) that may be continued indefinitely; (Gram., of verb part) not limited by person or number, e.g. infinitive, gerund, participle; hence ∼LY² (-tlĭ) adv. 2. n. the I∼, God; the ∼, infinite space. [ME, f. L IN²(*finitus* FINITE)]

infini'tèsimal a. & n. infinitely or very small (amount); ∼ **calculus**, the differential and integral calculuses regarded as one subject; hence ∼LY² adv. [f. mod. L *infinitesimus* f. prec. (cf. CENTESIMAL)]

infi'nitive a. & n. (Gram.) (verb-form) that expresses verbal notion without predicating it of any subject (e.g. *ask, to ask*); so **infiniti'v**AL a. [f. L IN² (*finitivus* definite f. *finire* -*it*- define; see -IVE)]

infi'nitūde n. being infinite, boundlessness; boundless number or extent (*of*). [f. L *infinitus*; see INFINITE, -TUDE]

infi'nity n. = prec.; infinite distance; (Math.) infinite number or extent. [ME, f. OF *infinité* f. L *infinitas* (as INFINITE; see -ITY)]

infir'm a. physically weak, esp. through age; (of person, mind, judgement, etc.) weak; (infirm *of purpose*); hence or cogn. ∼ITY n., ∼LY² adv. [ME, f. L IN²(*firmus* FIRM²)]

infir'mary n. hospital; sick-quarters in monastery, school, etc.; hence **infirmā'r'**IAN n., person in charge of infirmary (esp. in monastery). [f. med. L *infirmaria* (as prec.; see -ARY¹)]

infix¹ v.t. fix (thing in another); impress (fact etc. in mind); (Gram.) insert (formative element) in body of word; hence ∼A'TION n. [f. IN-¹+FIX¹, or f. L IN¹(figere fix- fix)]

infix² n. (Gram.) formative element infixed in word. [f. IN-¹, after prefix, suffix]

in flagrante delicto (ĭn flǎgrǎntĭ dělǐ'ktō) a. in the very act of committing an offence. [L, = in blazing crime]

inflā'me v. 1. v.t. set ablaze; light up (as) with flame; excite passionately (inflamed with or by); make hot, esp. cause fever in (body etc.); cause inflammation in; aggravate. 2. v.i. catch fire; become excited; become morbidly inflamed. [ME, f. OF enflammer f. L IN¹-(flammare f. flamma flame)]

inflǎ'mm|able a. & n. 1. a. easily set on fire; easily excited; hence ∼ABI'LITY, ∼ableNESS (-beln-), ns. 2. n. (usu. in pl.) inflammable substance. [f. prec. + -ABLE, after F inflammable]

inflammā'tion n. inflaming (lit. or fig.); (Path.) condition of part of the body with heat, swelling, redness, and usu. pain, esp. as reaction to injury or infection. [f. L inflammatio (as INFLAME; see -ATION)]

inflǎ'mmatory a. tending to inflame with desire or passion (usu. in bad sense); of, tending to, inflammation of the body. [f. as prec. + -ORY]

inflā't|e v.t. distend with air or gas; puff up (person with pride etc.); (Econ.) bring about inflation of (the currency, or abs.), raise (prices) artificially; (in p.p., of language) bombastic; hence ∼ABLE a., ∼ER¹, ∼OR, ns. [f. L IN¹(flare blow)+-ATE³]

inflā'tion n. inflating or being inflated; (Econ.) general increase of prices and fall in purchasing value of money, increase in available currency resulting in this; hence ∼ARY¹ a. [ME, f. L inflatio (as prec.; see -ATION)]

inflě'ct v.t. bend inwards, curve; (Gram.) vary ending of (word) to express grammatical relation, whence ∼IVE a.; change pitch of (voice, musical note). [ME, f. L IN¹(flectere flex- bend)]

inflě'ction. See INFLEXION.

inflě'x|ible a. unbendable; (fig.) unbending, inexorable; hence ∼IBI'LITY n., ∼IBLY adv. [f. L IN²-(flexibilis FLEXIBLE)]

||inflě'xion (-kshon), **inflě'ction,** n. inflecting; inflected form of word; suffix etc. used to inflect; modulation of voice; (Geom.) change of curve from convex part to concave; hence ∼AL, ∼LESS, adjs. [F, or f. L inflexio (as INFLECT; see -ION)]

inflī'ct v.t. lay on (stroke, wound, defeat, on or upon); impose (suffering, penalty, oneself, one's company, etc., on or upon); hence or cogn. ∼ABLE a., ∼ION n. (esp., troublesome or boring experience), ∼OR n. [f. L IN¹(figere flict- strike)]

inflorě'scence n. (Bot.) arrangement of flowers of plant in relation to axis and to each other; collective flower of plant; flowering (lit. or fig.). [f. mod. L inflorescentia n. LL IN¹(florescere; see FLORESCENCE)]

i'nflow (-ō) n. flowing in; that which flows in; so ∼ING¹,² n. & a. [f. IN²+FLOW 3]

i'nfluence (-lōō-) n., & v.t. 1. n. action of person or thing on or upon another, perceptible only in its effects; ascendancy, moral power, (over, with, person etc.); thing or person exercising (usu. non-material) power; (colloq., ellipt.) under the ∼ (i.e. of alcohol); UNDUE influence. 2. (Astrol.) supposed flowing from stars of ethereal fluid affecting character and destiny of man. 3. (Electr., arch.) = INDUCTION. 4. v.t. exert influence upon, have effect upon. [ME f. OF, or f. med. L influentia inflow f. L IN¹(fluere flow); see -ENCE]

i'nfluent (-lōō-) a. & n. 1. a. flowing in (lit. or fig.). 2. n. tributary stream. [ME, f. L (as prec.; see -ENT)]

influě'ntial (-lōōě'nshal) a. having great influence; hence ∼LY² adv. [f. med. L influentia INFLUENCE + -AL]

influě'nza (-lōō-) n. acute contagious and infectious febrile disorder caused by virus. usu. with fever, rapid prostration, and severe aching and catarrh, often occurring in epidemics; **gastric** ∼, (pop.) intestinal disorder of unknown cause. [It., f. med. L influentia INFLUENCE]

i'nflux n. flowing in, esp. of stream etc. (into river etc.), or of persons or things (into place etc.). [f. F, or f. LL IN¹(fluxus FLUX)]

i'nfo n. (colloq.) information. [abbr.]

info'ld. Var. of ENFOLD.

infō'rm v. 1. v.t. inspire, imbue, (person, heart, thing, with feeling, principle, quality, etc.); impart its quality to, permeate. 2. tell (person of or about or on thing or subject, that, how, etc.); hence ∼ANT n. 3. v.i. bring charge or complaint (against or on person). [ME, f. OF enfo(u)rmer f. L IN¹(formare f. forma form) give shape to, fashion, describe]

infō'rmal a. not according to due form; without ceremony or formality; ∼ **vote,** (NZ & Austral.) invalid vote or voting-paper; hence ∼ITY (-ǎ'l-) n., ∼LY² adv. [f. IN-²+FORMAL]

in forma pauperis (in fōrma paw'perĭs) adv. (Law). as a poor person not liable for costs of action. [L]

informā'tion n. informing, telling; thing told, knowledge, (desired) items of knowledge, news, (on, about); (Law) charge or complaint lodged with court or magistrate (against); ∼ **retrieval,** tracing of information stored in books, computers, etc.; ∼ **science,** study of processes for storing and retrieving information; ∼ **theory,** quantitative study of transmission of information by signals etc.; hence ∼AL a. [ME f. OF, f. L informatio -onis (as INFORM; see -ATION)]

infō'mat|ive a. giving information, instructive; so ∼ORY a. [f. med. L informativus (as INFORM; see -ATIVE)]

infō'med (-md) a. instructed, knowing the facts, (WELL, ill, -informed); educated, intelligent. [p.p. of INFORM]

infō'mer n. In vbl senses; one who informs against another; (**common**) ∼, one who makes it his business to detect offenders and lay information against them. [ME, f. INFORM + -ER¹]

infra (ĭ'nfra) adv. below; lower down, further on, (in book or writing). [L, = below]

i'nfra- pref. below (opp. SUPRA-), esp. (Anat.) below or under a part (∼re'nal, beneath the kidneys). [f. or after L infra below, beneath]

infrǎ'ction n. violation, infringement. [f. L infractio (as INFRINGE; see -ION)]

infra dig. pred. a. (colloq.) beneath one's dignity, unbecoming. [abbr. L infra dignitatem]

infralǎpsā'rian n. & a. (Calvinist) holding doctrine that God's election of some to eternal life was consequent to his prescience of the Fall, or that it contemplated man as already fallen; hence ∼ISM (3) n. [f. L infra below + lapsus fall + -ARIAN]

infrǎ'ngible (-nj-) a. unbreakable; inviolable. [obs. F, or f. med. L IN²(frangibilis FRANGIBLE)]

infra-rě'd a. (Phys.) having wavelength (just) beyond red end of visible spectrum; of or using such radiation. [f. INFRA- + RED]

infrasō'n|ic a. of sound waves with pitch below lower limit of human audibility; hence ∼ICALLY adv. [f. INFRA- + SONIC]

i'nfrastructure n. subordinate parts of an undertaking, esp. permanent installations as basis for military etc. operations. [F (as INFRA-, STRUCTURE)]

infrě'qu|ent a. not frequent; hence or cogn. ∼ENCY n., ∼entLY² adv. [f. L IN²(frequens FREQUENT¹)]

infrǐ'nge (-nj) v. 1. v.t. act contrary to, violate, (law, oath, etc.); act in defiance of (another's rights etc.). 2. v.i. encroach, trespass, on or upon. 3. Hence ∼MENT (-jm-), n. [f. L IN¹(fringere fract- = frangere break)]

infrǔctě'scence n. (Bot.) fruit formed from an inflorescence. [F, f. L fructus FRUIT, after inflorescence]

i'nfula n. (pl. ∼e). (Eccl.) each of two ribbons of bishop's mitre. [L, = woollen fillet worn by priest etc.]

For other words in in- **see** IN-¹ **or** (esp.) IN-².

infŭndĭ'bŭlar *a.* funnel-shaped. [f. L *infundibulum* funnel f. IN¹(*fundere* pour)+-AR¹]

infŭr'iate¹ *a.* excited to fury, frantic. [f. med. L *infuriatus* p.p. (as foll.); see -ATE²]

infŭr'iāte² *v.t.* fill with fury, enrage. [f. med. L IN¹(*furiare* f. L *furia* FURY)+-ATE³]

infŭ's|e (-z) *v.* **1.** *v.t.* pour (thing *into*); (fig.) instil (grace, spirit, life, etc., *into*); imbue, pervade, (*with* quality etc.). **2.** steep (herb, tea, etc.) in liquid to extract its soluble constituents, whence ∼ER¹ (2) *n.* **3.** *v.i.* undergo infusion (*let it infuse for five minutes*). **4.** Hence ∼ABLE *a.* [ME, f. L IN¹(*fundere fus-* pour)]

infŭ's|ible (-z-) *a.* that cannot be fused or melted; hence ∼IBI'LITY *n.* [f. IN-²+FUSIBLE (see FUSE¹)]

infŭ'sion (-zhon) *n.* infusing (lit. or fig.); liquid extract thus obtained; infused element, admixture. [ME f. F, or f. L *infusio* (as INFUSE; see -ION)]

infŭsor'|ia (-z-, -s-) *n. pl.* (arch.) class of protozoa found in infusions of decaying animal or vegetable matter; hence ∼IAL *a.* (∼ial earth, kieselguhr), ∼IAN *a.* & *n.* [mod. L, neut. pl. (as *n.*) of *infusorius* (as INFUSE; see -ORY, -IA²)]

-ing¹ *suf.* forming *ns.* f. *vbs.* (occas. f. *ns.*) w. senses (1) vbl action (*asking, driving, fighting, foreboding*), sometimes as occupation (*banking, glass-blowing*) or event (*wedding*) or as inflicted or performed on (*thrashing, the wearing of the green*), (2) thing produced by vbl action (*building, carving, filings, learning*), (3) material for (*clothing, fencing, sacking, scaffolding*), (4) what is used for or affects vbl action (*binding, firm going*), (5) what is to undergo vbl action (*darning, washing*), (6) set or arrangement of (*colouring, feathering*). [OE *-ung, -ing* f. Gmc *-ungā*]

-ing² *suf.* forming *pres. part.* of *vbs.*, often used as *a.* (*appalling, charming, diverting, heart-breaking, strapping, well-meaning*), sometimes w. sense 'likely to' (*not a marrying man*) or 'suitable to undergo' (*cooking apple*); occas. as *prep.* etc. (*during, notwithstanding*); occas. f. *ns.* (*hulking*) & *adjs.* (*balding*) [f. OE *-ende* by confus. w. prec.]

-ing³ *suf.* forming *ns.* w. sense 'one belonging to', 'one having the quality of', or dim., (*farthing, gelding, herring,* RIDING²). [OE, f. Gmc *-inga*; cf. -LING¹]

inga'ther (in-gă'dh-) *v.t.* gather in, assemble; hence ∼ING¹ *n.*, (esp.) harvest. [f. IN²+GATHER]

ĭngĕ'mĭnāte (inj-) *v.t.* repeat, reiterate, (esp. ∼ **peace**, constantly urge it). [f. L IN¹(*geminare* GEMINATE²)]

ĭngĕ'nious (inj-) *a.* clever at inventing, constructing, organizing, etc.; cleverly contrived (*ingenious machine, explanation, theory*); hence ∼LY² *adv.* [ME, = 'talented', f. F *ingénieux* or f. L *ingeniosus* (*ingenium* cleverness; cf. ENGINE, -OUS)]

ĭngénue (ă'nzhānū) *n.* artless young woman, esp. as a stage role. [F, fem. of *ingénu* INGENUOUS]

ĭngĕnū'ĭty (inj-) *n.* being ingenious; skill in contriving. [f. L *ingenuitas* ingenuousness (as foll.; see -ITY); E meaning by confus. of INGENIOUS w. foll.]

ĭngĕ'nŭous (inj-) *a.* open, frank; innocent, artless; hence ∼LY² *adv.*, ∼NESS *n.* [f. L IN¹(*genuus* f. **gen-* beget) free-born, frank]

ĭngĕ'st (inj-) *v.t.* take in (food etc.) by swallowing or absorbing (lit. or fig.); hence or cogn. ∼ION (-schon) *n.*, ∼IVE *a.* [f. L IN¹(*gerere gest-* carry)]

i'ngle (i'nggel) *n.* fire burning on hearth; ∼-**nook**, chimney-corner. [orig. Sc., perh. f. Gael. *aingeal* fire, light]

ĭnglŏr'ious (in-g-) *a.* shameful, ignominious; not famous; hence ∼LY² *adv.* [f. L IN-²(*glorius* f. *gloria* glory)+-OUS, or f. IN-²+GLORIOUS]

-ingly *suf.* forming *advs.* esp. denoting manner of action or nature of condition (*charmingly, correspondingly, disgustingly, embarrassingly, heart-breakingly, increasingly, inquiringly, irritatingly, mockingly, slantingly, soothingly*). [f. -ING²+-LY²]

i'ngoing (in-g-) *a.* going in, entering; penetrating, thorough. [f. IN²+GOING²]

i'ngot (i'ngg-) *n.* mass (usu. oblong) of cast metal, esp. of gold, silver, or steel. [ME; perh. f. IN²+*goten* p.p. of OE *geotan* cast]

ingraft. See ENGRAFT.

i'ngrain (i'n-g-) *a.* dyed in GRAIN; inherent, inveterate, ingrained; ∼ **carpet** (reversible, with different colours interwoven). [f. *in* GRAIN]

i'ngrained (i'n-gránd before *n.*, -á'nd elsewhere) *a.* deeply rooted, inveterate; thorough; (of dirt etc.) deeply embedded; hence ∼LY² (-á'nĭd-) *adv.* [var. of ENGRAIN*ed*]

ingrāte (i'n-grāt, -á't) *a.* & *n.* (arch.) ungrateful (person). [ME, f. L IN²(*gratus* grateful)]

ingrā'tiāte (in-grā'shi-) *v.t.* bring one*self* into favour *with*. [f. L *in gratiam* into favour+-ATE³]

ingrā'titūde (in-g-) *n.* lack of due gratitude. [ME f. OF, or f. LL *ingratitudo* (as INGRATE; see -TUDE)]

ingravĕ'sc|ent (in-g-) *a.* (Med.) (Of disease etc.) growing worse; hence ∼ENCE *n.* [f. L IN¹(*gravescere* grow heavy f. *gravis* heavy); see -ENT]

ingrē'dient (in-g-) *n.* component part, element, in a mixture or combination. [ME, f. L IN¹(*gredi gress- = gradi* step) enter; see -ENT]

i'ngrĕss (i'n-g-) *n.* (right of) going in; (Astron.) start of eclipse or transit. [ME, f. L *ingressus* (as prec.)]

i'ngrowing (i'n-grōi-) *a.* growing inwards, esp. (of nail) growing into the flesh; so **i'ngrown** *a.*, **ingrowth** *n.*, (i'n-grō-). [f. IN²+GROW+-ING²]

i'nguinal (i'nggw-) *a.* of the groin. [f. L *inguinalis* (*inguen -inis* groin; see -AL)]

ingulf. Var. of ENGULF.

ingŭr'gĭt|āte (in-g-) *v.t.* swallow greedily; (fig.) engulf; so ∼A'TION *n.* [f. L IN¹(*gurgitare* f. *gurges gurgitis* whirlpool)+-ATE³]

inhā'bĭt *v.t.* (Of person or animal) dwell in, occupy, (region, town, house, or fig.); hence or cogn. ∼ABLE *a.*, ∼ANT, ∼A'TION, *ns.* [ME *inhabite, enhabite* f. OF *enhabiter* or f. L IN¹(*habitare* dwell; see HABIT²)]

inhă'bĭtancy *n.* residence as inhabitant, *n.* during specified period so as to acquire rights etc. [f. as prec.+-ANCY]

inhā'l|e *v.t.* breathe in (air, gas, etc., or abs.; lit. or fig.); take (esp. tobacco-smoke or abs. of this) into the lungs; hence or cogn. ∼ANT, ∼ER¹ (2), *ns.* (esp. Med. = agent, device, for inhaling), **inhal**A'TION *n.* [f. L IN¹(*halare* breathe)]

inhārmō'nic *a.* (esp. Mus.) not harmonic. [f. IN-²+ HARMONIC]

inhārmō'nious *a.* not harmonious; hence ∼LY² *adv.* [f. IN-²+HARMONIOUS]

inhēr'e *v.i.* (Of qualities etc.) exist, abide, essentially or permanently *in*; (of rights etc.) be vested *in* (person etc.). [f. L IN¹(*haerēre haes-* to stick)]

inhēr'|ent *a.* existing in or *in* something esp. as permanent or characteristic attribute; vested *in* (person etc.) as right or privilege; hence or cogn. ∼ENCE *n.*, ∼ent*LY²* *adv.* [f. L (as prec.; see -ENT)]

inhĕ'rĭt *v.t.* receive (property, rank, title) by legal descent or succession; derive (quality, character) from one's progenitors or predecessors; (abs.) succeed as heir; hence ∼OR, ∼FESS¹, **inhĕ'rĭ**TRIX, *ns.* [ME, f. OF *enheriter* f. LL IN¹(*hereditare* f. L *heres heredis* heir)]

inhĕ'rĭt|able *a.* capable of inheriting or of being inherited (lit. or fig.); hence ∼ABI'LITY *n.* [ME f. AF (as prec.; see -ABLE)]

inhĕ'rĭtance *n.* inheriting; what is inherited (lit. or fig.). [ME, f. AF *inheritaunce* (OF *enheriter*; see INHERIT, -ANCE)]

inhē'sion (-zhon) *n.* inhering. [f. LL *inhaesio* (as INHERE; see -ION)]

inhi'bĭt *v.t.* **1.** forbid, prohibit, (person etc. *from* doing; esp. in Eccl. Law); forbid (ecclesiastic) to exercise clerical functions. **2.** hinder, restrain, or prevent, (action, process); (in *p.p.*) subject to inhibition. **3.** Hence or cogn. ∼OR *n.*, ∼ORY *a.* [f. L IN¹(*hibēre hibit- = habēre* hold)]

inhĭbi'tion *n.* inhibiting or being inhibited; (Psych.) restraint of direct expression of an instinct; (colloq.) emotional resistance to thought or action. [ME f. OF, or f. L *inhibitio* (as prec.; see -TTION)]

inhŏmogē'nēous *a.* not homogeneous; hence **inhŏmogēnē'ITY** *n.* [f. IN-² + HOMOGENEOUS]

inhŏspĭtab|le (-ŏ'-, -pĭ'-) *a.* not hospitable; (of region, coast, etc.) not affording shelter etc.; hence ∼le**NESS** (-bǝln-) *n.*, ∼**LY²** *adv.* [obs. F (as IN-², HOSPITABLE)]

inhŏspĭtă'lĭty *n.* being inhospitable. [f. L *inhospitalitas* (as IN-², HOSPITALITY)]

i'n-house *a.* (done, existing) within an institution. [f. IN¹ + HOUSE¹]

inhŭ'man *a.* **1.** (Of person or conduct) brutal, unfeeling, barbarous; hence or cogn. ∼ITY (-ă'n-) *n.*, ∼**LY²** *adv.* **2.** not of the ordinary human type. [f. L IN²(*humanus* HUMAN)]

inhŭmā'ne *a.* not humane; hence ∼**LY²** (-nlĭ) *adv.* [f. L *inhumanus* (see prec.), & f. IN-² + HUMANE; orig. = prec.]

inhŭ'm|e *v.t.* (literary). bury; hence ∼A'TION *n.* [f. IN¹(*humare* f. *humus* ground)]

ini'mical *a.* hostile (*to*); harmful (*to*); hence ∼**LY²** *adv.* [f. L *inimicalis* f. L IN²(*imicus* = *amicus* friend); see -AL]

ini'mĭtab|le *a.* that defies imitation; hence ∼le**NESS** (-bǝln-) *n.*, ∼**LY²** *adv.* [F, or f. L IN²(*imitabilis* IMITABLE)]

ini'quĭt|ў *n.* unrighteousness, wickedness; gross injustice; hence ∼**OUS** *a.* [ME, f. OF *iniquité* f. L *iniquitas -tatis* f. IN²(*iquus* = *aequus* just); see -ITY]

ini'tial (-shǝl) *a., n.,* & *v.t.* (-ll- *or* -l-). **1.** *a.* of, existing or occurring at, the beginning, (*initial stage, expenses, difficulties*); ∼ **letter, consonant,** etc., (standing at beginning of word); ∼ **teaching alphabet,** 44-letter phonetic alphabet devised to help those learning to read and write English; hence ∼**LY²** *adv.* **2.** *n.* initial letter, esp. (in *pl.*) first letters of words of (esp. person's) name(s). 3. *v.t.* mark or sign with initials. [f. L *initialis* f. *initium* beginning f. IN¹(*ire it-* go); see -AL]

ini'ti|āte¹ (-shĭ-) *v.t.* begin, set going, originate; admit (person), esp. with introductory rites or forms, (*into* society, office, secret; *in* or *into* mysteries, science, etc.); hence or cogn. ∼A'TION, ∼**ātor, ns.,** ∼**atory** (-shya-, -sha-) *a.* [f. L *initiare* (*initium*; see prec.) f. -ATE³]

ini'ti|ate² (-shĭ-) *a.* & *n.* (person) who has been initiated. [f. as prec.; see -ATE²]

ini'tiative (-shya-, -sha-) *n.* & *a.* **1.** *n.* first step, origination; **take the** ∼, be the first to take action (*in* doing); **on** one's **own** ∼, without being prompted by others. **2.** power or right to begin something; **have the** ∼, (esp., Mil.) be able to make enemy conform to one's movements **3.** ability to initiate things, enterprise, (esp. w. neg., expressed or implied: *he lacks, has little,* or *no, initiative*). **4.** right of citizen(s) outside legislature to originate legislation (as in Switzerland). **5.** *a.* beginning, originating. [F (as INITIATE¹; see -IVE)]

inje'ct *v.t.* drive, force, (fluid, medicine, *into* cavity etc.) by or as by syringe; fill (cavity etc. *with*) by injecting; administer medicine etc. to (person) by injecting; place (object, quality, etc.) where needed in, or as part of, something; hence ∼**OR** *n.* [f. L IN¹(*jicere ject-* = *jecĕre* throw)]

inje'ction *n.* injecting; liquid or solution injected; FUEL *injection*; ∼ **moulding,** shaping of rubber or plastic articles by injecting heated material into mould. [F, or f. L *injectio* (as prec.; see -ION)]

injudi'cious (-jōōdĭ'shǝs) *a.* unwise, ill-judged; hence ∼**LY²** *adv.*, ∼**NESS** *n.* [f. IN-² + JUDICIOUS]

I'njun (ĭ'-) *n.* (colloq. or *dial.*) American Indian (HONEST *Injun*). [corrupt.]

inju'nction *n.* authoritative admonition or order; judicial process restraining person from wrongful act or compelling restitution etc. to injured party, whence **inju'nct** *v.t.* (colloq.). [f. LL *injunctio* f. L *injungere* ENJOIN; see -ION]

i'njure *v.t.* do wrong to; hurt (lit. or fig.), harm, impair. [back-form. f. INJURY]

i'njured (-jerd) *a.* In vbl senses; wronged; showing sense of wrong, offended, (*in an injured voice*). [p.p. of prec.]

injur'ia (-oor'-) *n.* (Law). infringement of another's rights. [L; see INJURY]

injur'ious (-oor'-) wrongful; (of language) insulting, calumnious; hurtful; hence ∼**LY²** *adv.*, ∼**NESS** *n.* [ME, f. F *injurieux* or f. L *injuriosus* (as foll.; see -OUS)]

i'njurў *n.* wrongful action or treatment; harm, damage; ||∼ **time,** (Footb.) extra playing-time allowed by referee to compensate for that lost when players have been hurt. [ME, f. AF *injurie* f. L IN²(*juria* f. *jus juris* right) wrong; see -Y¹]

injŭ'stice *n.* lack of equity, unfairness; unjust act; **do** person **an** ∼, judge him unfairly. [ME f. OF, f. L IN²(*justitia* JUSTICE)]

ink *n.* & *v.t.* **1.** *n.* fluid (black, red, etc.) for writing with pen or marking with rubber stamp etc.; MARKING--*ink*. **2.** viscous paste used to mark paper etc. in printing, duplicating, writing with ball-pen, etc. **3.** black liquid ejected by cuttlefish etc. to darken water and assist its escape. **4.** ∼**-blot test,** Rorschach test; ∼-**horn,** small vessel of horn formerly used for holding ink (∼*-horn term,* literary word); ∼**-pad,** ink-soaked block, usu. in box, for inking rubber stamp etc.; ∼-**slinger,** (derog.) professional writer; ∼**'stand,** stand for one or more bottles to hold ink, often with pen-tray etc.; ∼-**well** (pot fitted into hole in desk). **5.** Hence ∼**Y²** *a.,* of, black as, stained with, ink. **6.** *v.t.* mark (*in, over,* etc.) with ink; cover (printing types etc.) with ink so as to print from them; apply ink to; ∼ **out,** obliterate with ink; hence ∼'**ER¹** (1, 2) *n.* [ME *enke, inke* f. OF *enque* f. LL *encau(s)tum* f. Gk *egkauston* (as EN-², CAUSTIC) purple ink used by Roman emperors for signature]

i'nkling *n.* hint, slight knowledge or suspicion, (*of*). [f. ME *inkle* utter in an undertone + -ING¹; orig. unkn.]

inlai'd. See INLAY¹.

i'nland (-*a*-, -ă-) *n., a.,* & *adv.* **1.** *n.* interior of country, parts remote from sea or frontiers. **2.** *a.* placed in interior of country; carried on within limits of a country (*inland trade*); ∼ **duty** (on inland trade); *inland* NAVIGATION; ||∼ **revenue** (consisting of taxes and inland duties); ||**I**∼ **Revenue,** government department responsible for assessing and collecting these; *inland* SEA. **3.** *adv.* (-ă'-). in or towards interior of country. **4.** Hence ∼**ER¹** (4) *n.*, ∼**ISH¹** *a.* [f. IN² + LAND¹]

i'n-law *n.* (colloq., usu. in *pl.*) relative by marriage. [f. IN¹ + LAW¹]

inlay'¹ *v.t.* (**inlai'd**). embed (thing *in* another) so that their surfaces are even; ornament (thing *with* another inlaid); insert (page, illustration, etc.) in space cut in larger stouter page. [f. IN-¹ + LAY³]

i'nlay² *n.* inlaid work; material inlaid; filling shaped to fit tooth-cavity. [f. prec.]

i'nlet (-ĭt, -ĕt) *n.* small arm of sea, lake, or river; piece inserted; way of entry. [ME, f. IN² + LET² v.]

i'nlier *n.* (Geol.) space occupied by one formation and completely surrounded by later formation. [f. IN², after *outlier*]

in limine (ĭn lĭ'mĭnĭ) *adv.* at the outset. [L, = on the threshold]

in loco parentis (ĭn lŏkō perĕ'ntĭs) *adv.* in place of a parent. [L]

i'nlў *adv.* (poet.) inwardly, in the heart; intimately; thoroughly. [OE *innlīce* (as IN², -LY²)]

i'nlўing *a.* situated within, or near a centre. [IN² + LYING²]

i'nmāte *n.* occupant (*of* house etc.), esp. one of several; occupant of hospital, prison, or other institution. [prob. orig. f. INN + MATE², assoc. w. IN²]

in medias res (ĭn mēdĭahs rē'z) *adv.* into the midst of things; into the middle of a narrative, without preamble. [L]

in memoriam (ĭn mĭmōr'iăm) *prep.* & *n.* **1.** *prep.* in memory of. **2.** *n.* writing, notice, etc., in memory of a deceased person. [L]

i'nmost (-ō-, -o-) *a.* most inward; (fig.) deepest, most intimate. [f. OE *innemest* (as IN²; see -MOST)]

inn *n.* **1.** house providing lodging etc. for payment, esp. for travellers; house providing alcoholic liquor for consumption on the premises; ∿'**keeper**, one who keeps an inn. **2.** ‖**Inn of Court,** (building in London belonging to) one of four legal societies having exclusive right of admitting persons to practise at the English bar, similar society in Ireland; ‖**Inns of Chancery,** (Hist.) buildings in London formerly used as hostels for law students. [OE *inn* (as IN²)]

i'nnards (-z) *n. pl.* (colloq.) entrails. [f. dial. etc. pronunc. of *inwards* (see INWARD 2)]

innāte (-ā'-, ĭ'-) *a.* inborn, natural; (Philos.) originating in the mind; hence ∿LY² (-tlĭ) *adv.*, ∿NESS (-tn-) *n.* [ME, f. L IN¹(*natus* p.p. of *nasci* be born)]

i'nner *a.* & *n.* **1.** *a.* interior, internal, inward; ‖∿ **bar,** Queen's or ·King's·COUNSEL¹ collectively; ∿ **city,** central area of city, usu. with overcrowding and poverty; ∿-**directed,** governed by standards formed early in one's life; ∿ **man** or **woman,** soul or mind, (joc.) stomach; ∿ **space,** (1) region between earth and outer space, or below surface of sea, (2) part of mind not normally perceived consciously; *∿*∿-**spring,** − INTERIOR-*sprung*; *Inner* TEMPLE¹; ∿ tube, separate inflatable tube inside cover of pneumatic tyre; hence ∿MOST *a.* **2.** *n.* division of target next outside bull's-eye; shot that strikes this. [OE *innera* a., compar. of IN²]

innĕrv|āte (ĭ'-, -ēr'-) *v.t.* supply (organ etc.) with nerves; hence ∿A'TION *n.* [f. IN-¹+L *nervus* nerve+-ATE³]

***i'nning** *n.* innings at baseball etc. [f. *in* v. go in (f. IN²)+-ING¹]

i'nnings (z) *n.* (*pl.* same, or colloq. '∿es). **1.** (Cricket etc.) portion of game during which a side is in or batting; play of one batsman during his turn. **2.** (fig.) tenure of office, dominance, of political party, cause, etc.; period during which person has opportunity to achieve something. [pl. of prec.]

i'nnocent *a.* & *n.* **1.** *a.* free from moral wrong, sinless; unacquainted with evil. **2.** not guilty (*of* crime etc.); ∿ **of,** (colloq.) without. **3.** simple, guileless; harmless; naïve; pretending to be guileless. **4.** Hence or cogn. **i'nnoc**ENCE, **i'nnoc**ENCY, *ns.*, ∿LY² *adv.* **5.** *n.* innocent person, esp. young child; (in *pl.*) young children killed by Herod after birth of Jesus (Matt. 2: 16); (**Holy**) I∿s' **Day,** 28 Dec. [ME f. OF, or f. L IN²(*nocens* -ent- part. of *nocēre* hurt); see -ENT]

innŏ'cūous *a.* not injurious, harmless (esp. of snakes); inoffensive; hence or cogn. **innŏcū'**ITY, ∿NESS *ns.*, ∿LY² *adv.* [f. L IN²(*nocuus* f. as prec.)+-OUS]

innŏ'minate *a.* unnamed; ∿ **bone,** (Anat.) bone formed from three original bones: ilium, ischium, and pubis. [f. LL IN²(*nominatus* p.p. of *nominare*; see NOMINATE, -ATE²)]

i'nnov|āte *v.i.* bring in novelties; make changes *in*; hence or cogn. ∿A'TION, ∿ATOR, *ns.*, ∿**ā**tive, ∿**ā**tory, *adjs.* [f. L IN²(*novare* make new, alter, f. *novus* new)+-ATE³]

innŏ'xious (-kshus) *a.* harmless; hence ∿LY² *adv.*, ∿NESS *n.* [f. L IN²(*noxius* NOXIOUS)]

innuĕ'ndo *n.* (*pl.* ∿es or ∿s), & *v.i.* **1.** *n.* oblique hint, allusive remark (usu. depreciatory). **2.** *v.i.* make innuendoes. [L, abl. gerund of IN¹(*nuere* nod), = by nodding at, pointing to]

I'nnuit (ĭ'nōō-) *n.* (*pl.* ∿s or same). Canadian Eskimo. [f. Eskimo *inuit* people]

innŭ'merab|le *a.* too many to be counted; hence ∿LY² *adv.* [ME, f. L IN²(*numerabilis* NUMERABLE)]

innŭ'mer|ate *a.* not numerate; unacquainted with basic principles of mathematics and science; so ∿ACY *n.* [f. IN-²+NUMERATE]

innŭtr|ĭ'tion *n.* lack of nutrition; so ∿ĭ'TIOUS² *a.* [f. IN-²+NUTRITION]

inobsĕr'vance (-z-) *n.* inattention; non-observance (*of* law etc.). [F, or f. L IN²(*observantia* OBSERVANCE)]

inŏ'cūl|āte *v.t.* treat (person or animal) *with* agent of disease by injection etc. to induce milder form of it and so safeguard against its attacks; implant (disease etc.) thus (*on* or *into* person etc.); (fig.) imbue (person etc.) *with* opinions etc.; (arch.) insert (bud, scion) in plant, treat (plant) thus; hence or cogn. ∿ABLE, ∿ATIVE, *adjs.*, ∿A'TION, ∿**ā**TOR, *ns.* [ME in last sense, f. L IN¹(*oculare* f. *oculus* eye, bud) engraft+-ATE³]

inŏ'cūl|um *n.* (*pl.* ∿a). substance used for inoculation. [mod. L, f. as prec.]

inŏ'dorous *a.* having no odour. [f. L IN²(*odorus* ODOROUS), IN-²+ODOROUS]

inoffĕ'nsive *a.* unoffending; not objectionable; hence ∿LY² (-vlĭ) *adv.*, ∿NESS (-vn-) *n.* [f. IN-²+OFFENSIVE]

inoffĭ'cious *a.* (-shus) *a.* (Law). not in accordance with moral duty. [f. L IN²(*officiosus* dutiful; see OFFICIOUS), or f. IN-²+OFFICIOUS]

inŏ'perable *a.* (Surg.) that cannot suitably be operated on (*inoperable cancer*). [f. F *inopérable* (as IN-², OPERABLE)]

inŏ'perative *a.* not working or taking effect. [f. IN-² +OPERATIVE]

inŏ'pportūne *a.* not appropriate, esp. as regards time; unseasonable; hence ∿LY² (-nlĭ) *adv.*, ∿NESS (-n-n-) *n.* [f. L IN²(*opportunus* OPPORTUNE)]

inŏr'dinate *a.* immoderate, excessive; intemperate; disorderly; hence ∿LY² (-tlĭ) *adv.* [ME, f. L IN²-(*ordinatus* p.p. of *ordinare* ORDAIN)]

inŏrgā'nic *a.* **1.** having no organized physical structure. **2.** (Chem., of compound etc.) of mineral origin, not organic; ∿ **chemistry,** that of inorganic substances. **3.** not arising by natural growth, extraneous; (Philol.) not explainable by normal etymology. [f. IN-²+ORGANIC]

inŏ'scūl|āte *v.i.* & *t.* join by running together; join closely; hence ∿A'TION *n.* [f. IN-¹+L *osculare* furnish with mouth (*osculum* dim. of *os* mouth)+-ATE³]

in partibus (ĭn pär'tĭbus) *adv.* (Of RC titular bishop, or fig.) in heretical territory. [orig. *in partibus infidelium,* L — in the regions of the unbelievers]

in petto (ĭn pĕ'tō) *adv.* secretly (esp. of cardinals appointed but not named as such). [It., = in the breast]

in posse (ĭn pŏ'sĭ) *a.* in the condition of being possible (opp. IN ESSE). [L]

in propria persona (ĭn prōprĭa persō'na) *adv.* in his or her own person. [L]

in puris naturalibus (ĭn pūrĭs nātura'lĭbus) *a.* stark naked. [L]

i'nput (-ŏŏt) *n.*, & *v.t.* (-tt-; input or inputted). **1.** *n.* what is put in; place where energy, information, etc., enters a system. **2.** *v.t.* put in or into; supply (data, programs, etc., *to* computer). [f. IN²+PUT¹]

i'nquĕst (-nkw-, -ngkw-) *n.* **1.** legal or judicial inquiry to ascertain matter of fact; inquisition; inquiry by coroner's court into cause of death; (colloq.) discussion after conclusion (of game, election, etc.); **great** or **last** ∿, Last JUDGEMENT. **2.** coroner's jury; **grand** or **great** ∿, (Hist.) grand jury (‖*grand* ∿ *of the nation,* House of Commons). [ME f. OF *enqueste* f. Rom. *inquesta fem. p.p. (as n.) of *inquaerere (see INQUIRE)]

inqui'ĕtūde (-nkw-, -ngkw-) *n.* uneasiness of mind or body. [ME f. OF, or f. LL *inquietudo* f. L IN²(*quietus* QUIET²); see -TUDE]

i'nquilīne (-nkw-, -ngkw-) *n.* animal living in the home of another, commensal. [f. L *inquilinus* sojourner (IN-¹, *colere* dwell)]

inquīr'|e, ‖enquīr'|e, (-nkw-, -ngkw-) *v.* **1.** *v.i.* make search (*into* matter); seek information (*of* = from person; *about, after,* thing etc.); ∿**e after** or **for** person, ask how he is; ask *for* (goods in shop etc.). **2.** *v.t.* ask to be told (person's name, business, etc., *whether, how,* etc.). **3.** Hence ∿ER¹ *n.* [ME *enquere* f. OF *enquerre* f. Rom. **inquaerere* f. L IN¹(*quirere quisit-* ·= *quaerere* seek)]

inquir′y, ‖**enquir′ỹ,** (-nkw-, -ngkw-) *n.* asking; question; (official) investigation; **court of** ∼ (Mil., investigating circumstances of mishap etc.); ‖∼ **agent,** private detective; ∼ **office** (answering questions from callers etc.). [f. prec. +-Y¹]

inquisi′tion (-nkwĭz-, -ngkw-) *n.* search, investigation; judicial or official inquiry; **the I∼,** (Hist.) RC ecclesiastical tribunal for suppression of heresy, esp. very severe one in Spain; hence ∼AL *a.* [ME f. OF, f. L *inquisitio -onis* examination (as INQUIRE; see -ION)]

inqui′sitive (-nkwĭ′z-, -ngkw-) *a.* inquiring, seeking knowledge; unduly inquiring, prying; hence ∼LY² (-vlĭ) *adv.,* ∼NESS (-vn-) *n.* [ME, f. OF *inquisitif -ive* f. LL *inquisitivus* (as prec.; see -IVE)]

inqui′sitor (-nkwĭ′z-, -ngkw-) *n.* official investigator; (Hist.) officer of the Inquisition (**Grand I∼,** director of court of Inquisition in some countries; **I∼--General,** head of this in Spain). [f. F *inquisiteur* f. L *inquisitor -oris* (as INQUIRE; see -OR)]

inquisitor′ial (-nkwĭz-, -ngkw-) *a.* of or like an inquisitor; offensively prying; (Law, of criminal procedure) in which proceedings are secret or prosecutor is judge, opp. *accusatorial*; hence ∼LY² *adv.* [f. med. L *inquisitorius* (as prec.; see -ORY) +-AL]

inquor′āte (-nkw-, -ngkw-) *a.* not constituting a quorum. [f. IN-² + QUORATE]

in re (ĭn rē′) *prep.* = RE² 1. [L, = in the matter (of)]

INRI *abbr.* Jesus of Nazareth, King of the Jews. [f. L *Iesus Nazarenus Rex Iudaeorum*]

i′nroad *n.* hostile incursion, raid; (fig.) intrusion *on* or *into,* esp. so as to consume (*makes inroads on my time*). [f. IN² + ROAD¹ in sense 'riding']

i′nrush *n.* rushing in, influx. [f. IN² + RUSH²]

ins. *abbr.* inches; insurance.

insalu′br′ious (-lōō′-, -lŭ′-) *a.* (Of climate or place) unhealthy; so ∼ITY *n.* [f. L IN²(*salubris* SALUBRIOUS)]

insā′ne *a.* not of sound mind, mentally deranged; extremely foolish, irrational; (of asylum etc.) for insane persons; hence or cogn. ∼LY² (-nlĭ) *adv.,* **insā′nity** *n.* [f. L IN²(*sanus* healthy)]

insā′nitary *a.* not sanitary; harmful to health. [f. IN-² + SANITARY]

insā′ti|able (-sha-) *a.* that cannot be satisfied; inordinately greedy (*of*); hence ∼ABI′LITY *n.,* ∼ABLY *adv.* [ME f. OF *insaciable,* or f. L IN²(*satiabilis* SATIABLE)]

insā′tiate (-shyat) *a.* never satisfied. [f. L IN²(*satiatus*; see SATIATE¹)]

i′nscāpe *n.* inward essential unique quality of observed objects as embodied in literary, artistic, etc., expression. [perh. f. IN-¹ +-SCAPE]

inscrī′b|e *v.t.* write (words etc. *in* or *on* stone, metal, paper, book, etc.); enter name of (person) on list or in book; ‖(esp. in *p.p.*) issue (stock etc.) in form of shares with registered holders; mark (sheet, tablet, etc., *with* characters); place informal dedication (*to* person) in or on (book etc.); (Geom.) draw (figure) within another so that some particular points (or all angular points) of it lie on the boundary of that other (cf. CIRCUMSCRIBE), whence ∼ABLE *a.* [f. L IN¹(*scribere script-* write)]

inscri′ption *n.* 1. words inscribed, esp. on monument, coin, stone, etc.; informal dedication of book etc. (see prec.); hence or cogn. ∼AL, **inscri′p**tIVE, *adjs.* 2. ‖inscribing (*of* loan). [ME, f. L *inscriptio* (as prec.; see -ION)]

inscru′t|able (-rōō′-) *a.* that cannot be understood by investigation; wholly mysterious; hence ∼ABI′LITY, ∼ableNESS (-bǝln-), *ns.,* ∼ABLY *adv.* [ME, f. eccl. L IN²(*scrutabilis* f. *scrutari* search; see SCRUTINY, -ABLE)]

i′nsect *n.* small invertebrate segmented animal; arthropod of class Insecta, having head, thorax, abdomen, two antennae, three pairs of thoracic legs, and usu. one or two pairs of thoracic wings; (fig.) insignificant or contemptible person or creature;

∼**-powder** (for killing or driving away insects). [f. L *insectum* (*animal*) notched (animal) f. IN¹(*secare sect-* cut)]

insectār′ium, inse′ctary, *n.* place for keeping insects. [f. as prec. + -ARIUM, -ARY]

inse′cti|cīde *n.* insect-killer, esp. preparation used for killing insects; hence ∼cī′dAL *a.* [f. INSECT + -I- + -CIDE]

inse′cti|vŏre *n.* mammal of order Insectivora feeding on insects etc., e.g. hedgehog and mole; so ∼VOROUS (-ĭ′v-) *a.* (also of plants that capture and absorb insects). [F, f. mod. L *insectivorus* (as INSECT; see -VORE)]

insĕctŏ′logỹ *n.* science of insects, esp. in their economic relations to man. [f. F *insectologie* (as INSECT; see -LOGY)]

insĕcūr′|e *a.* unsafe; not firm; (of ice, ground, etc.) liable to give way; hence or cogn. ∼eLY² (-ūr′lĭ) *adv.,* ∼ITY *n.* [f. med. L IN²(*securus* SECURE), or f. IN-² + SECURE]

insĕ′min|āte *v.t.* sow (seed etc., lit. or fig., *in*); introduce semen into; hence ∼A′TION *n.* (ARTIFICIAL *insemination*). [f. L IN¹(*seminare* f. SEMEN) +-ATE³]

insĕ′nsāte *a.* without sensibility, unfeeling; stupid; without physical sensation; hence ∼LY² (-tlĭ) *adv.* [f. eccl. L IN²(*sensatus* f. *sensus* SENSE; see -ATE²)]

insĕnsĭbi′litỹ *n.* lack of mental feeling or emotion; indifference (*to*); unconsciousness. [f. F *insensibilité* or f. LL *insensibilitas* (as foll.; see -ITY)]

insĕ′nsĭb|le *a.* 1. too small or gradual to be perceived, inappreciable; hence ∼LY² *adv.* 2. without one's mental faculties, unconscious; deprived of sensation. 3. unaware (*of, to, how,* etc.); emotionless, callous. [ME f. OF, or f. L IN²(*sensibilis* SENSIBLE)]

insĕ′nsĭtive *a.* not sensitive (*to* touch, sight, light, mental or moral impressions); hence ∼LY² (-vlĭ) *adv.,* ∼NESS (-vn-), **insĕnsĭti′**VITY, *ns.* [f. IN-² + SENSITIVE]

insĕ′ntient (-shent) *a.* not sentient; inanimate. [f. IN-² + SENTIENT]

insĕ′par|able *a.* & *n.* 1. *a.* that cannot be separated; (Gram., of prefix, or verb in respect of it) that cannot be used as separate word (e.g. *dis-, mis-, un-*); hence ∼ABI′LITY *n.,* ∼ABLY *adv.* 2. *n.* (usu. in *pl.*) inseparable person or thing, esp. friend. [ME, f. L IN²(*separabilis* SEPARABLE)]

insĕr′t¹ *v.t.* place, fit, thrust, in (thing *in, into,* another, *between* edges etc.); introduce (letter, word, article, advertisement, *in* or *into* written matter, newspaper, etc.); (Anat. etc., in *p.p.*) attached (at specific point). [f. L IN¹(*serere sert-* join)]

i′nsĕr̄t² *n.* thing (to be) inserted. [f. prec. or foll.]

insĕr′tion *n.* inserting; thing inserted, esp. in writing or print; each appearance of an advertisement in newspaper etc.; ornamental needlework etc. inserted into plain material (*lace insertions*); (Anat. etc.) mode or place of attachment of muscle, organ, etc.; placing of spacecraft in desired orbit. [f. LL *insertio* (as INSERT; see -ION)]

i′nsĕt¹ *n.* extra page(s) inserted in folded sheet or in book; small map, photograph, etc., inserted within border of larger; piece let into dress. [f. IN² + SET²]

insĕ′t² *v.t.* (-tt-; ∼ or ∼ted) put in as an inset. [f. IN² + SET¹]

inshă′llah (-a-) *int.* if Allah wills it. [f. Arab. *inšā' Allah*]

inshŏr′e *adv.* & *a.* close to shore; ∼ **of,** nearer to shore than. [f. IN² + SHORE¹]

insīde *n., a., adv., & prep.* 1. *n.* (-ĭ′d). inner side or surface, (of path) side next to wall or away from road; inner part, interior; (colloq., in *sing.* or *pl.*) stomach and bowels; position affording inside information; (Hist.) passenger travelling inside coach etc.; ‖**the** ∼ (middle part) *of a week* etc.; *turned* **i′nside ou′t,** so that inner side becomes outer, (fig.) in utter confusion; *know* **i′nside ou′t** (thoroughly). 2. *a.* (ĭ′-). situated *on* or in, derived from, the inside; (Footb. & Hockey) nearer to centre of field (*inside forward*); ∼ **left, right,** inside forward on left, right, side); ∼ **information** (not accessible to outsiders); ∼ **job,** (colloq.)

For other words in *in-* see IN-¹ or (esp.) IN-².

burglary etc. of premises by person living or working there; ~ **track** (shorter because of curve). **3.** *adv.* (-ī′d). on or in or to the inside; (sl.) in prison; (colloq.) ~ **of** (in less than) *a week* etc. **4.** *prep.* (-ī′d). on the inner side of, within; in less than (*inside an hour*). [f. IN³ + SIDE¹]

insī′der *n.* one who is within some society, organization, etc. (cf. OUTSIDER); one who is in the secret, esp. so as to gain unfair advantage. [f. prec. + -ER¹]

insī′dious *a.* treacherous, crafty; proceeding or progressing secretly or subtly (*insidious disease*); hence ~LY² *adv.*, ~NESS *n.* [f. L *insidiosus* cunning f. IN¹(*sidiae* f. *sedēre* sit) ambush; see -OUS]

ī′nsīght (-īt) *n.* penetration (*into* character, circumstances, etc.) with the understanding; instance of this; hence ~FUL *a.* [ME, = 'discernment', prob. of Scand. & LG orig. (as IN-¹, SIGHT¹)]

insī′gn|e *n.* (*pl.* ~ia). badge. [L (see foll.)]

insī′gnia *n.* (as *sing.* or *pl.*) badges, distinguishing marks, (*of* office, honour, etc.). [L, pl. of *insigne* neut. (as n.) of IN¹(*signis* f. *signum* SIGN¹) distinguished; see -IA²]

insigni′fic|ant *a.* unimportant, trifling; contemptible; meaningless; hence ~ANCE, ~ANCY, *ns.*, ~antLY² *adv.* [f. IN-² + SIGNIFICANT]

insincēr′e *a.* not sincere; not candid; hence or cogn. ·~LY² (-cī′li) *adv.*, **insincē′rITY** *n.* [f. L IN²(*sincerus* SINCERE)]

insī′nu|āte *v.t.* introduce (thing, one*self*, *into* place; one*self*, person, *into* favour, office, etc.) gradually or subtly; convey indirectly, hint obliquely, (idea, *that*); hence or cogn. ~A′TION, ~ātOR, *ns.*, ~ATIVE *a.* [f. L IN¹(*sinuare* to curve) + -ATE³]

insī′pid *a.* tasteless; lacking flavour; lacking liveliness, dull, uninteresting; hence ~ITY (-ī′d-), ~NESS, *ns.*, ~LY² *adv.* [f. F *insipide* or f. LL IN²(*sipidus* = L *sapidus* SAPID)]

insī′st *v.* **1.** *v.i.* & *t.* ~ (**on**), maintain positively, (*insist on his innocence*; *insist* (*on it*) *that he is innocent*). **2.** *v.i.* make a stand *on* as essential (*I insist on being present, on your being present, on your presence, on it that you shall be present*). **3.** (arch.) write or speak long or emphatically (*on, upon*). [f. L IN¹(*sistere* stand) stand on, persist]

insī′st|ent *a.* insisting (*on*, or abs.); obtruding itself on one's attention; so ~ENCE, ~ENCY, *ns.*, ~entLY² *adv.* [f. prec. + -ENT]

in sī′tu (in sī′tū) *adv.* in its (original) place. [L]

insobrī′ety *n.* intemperance, esp. in drinking. [f. IN-² + SOBRIETY]

insofar′ *adv.* = *in so* FAR¹.

insolā′tion *n.* exposure to the sun's rays, esp. for purposes of bleaching etc., as medical treatment, or as cause of disease. [f. L *insolatio* f. IN¹(*solare* f. *sol* sun), see -ATION]

ī′nsōle *n.* = SOCK¹ 2; fixed inner sole of boot or shoe. [f. IN³ + SOLE¹]

ī′nsol|ent *a.* offensively contemptuous; insulting; hence or cogn. ~ENCE *n.*, ~entLY² *adv.* [ME, = 'arrogant', f. L IN²(*solens* pres. part. of *solēre* be accustomed); see -ENT]

insŏ′l|ūble *a.* that cannot be solved; that cannot be dissolved; hence ~UBI′LITY, ~ūbleNESS (-beln-), *ns.*, ~UBLY *adv.*, ~ūbīlIZE (3) *v.t.* [ME f. OF, or f. L IN²(*solubilis* SOLUBLE)]

insŏ′lv|ent *a.* & *n.* (debtor) unable to pay debts; relating to insolvency (*insolvent laws*); hence ~ENCY *n.* [f. IN-² + SOLVENT]

insŏ′mni|a *n.* habitual sleeplessness; hence ~AC *n.* & *a.* [L, f. IN²(*somnis* f. *somnus* sleep) sleepless; see -IA¹]

insomŭ′ch *adv.* to such an extent *that*; inasmuch *as*. [ME, orig. *in so much*]

insou′ci|ant (insōō′siant, ăŋsōō′syaṅ) *a.* carefree, unconcerned; so ~ANCE (-ns, -ṅs) *n.* [F (as IN-², *souciant* part. of *soucier* care)]

inspă′n *v.t.* & *i.* (-**nn**-). (S. Afr.) yoke (oxen etc.) in team to vehicle; harness animal(s) to (wagon). [f. Du. IN¹(*spannen* stretch f. as SPAN²)]

inspe′ct *v.t.* look closely into; examine officially

(*inspect passports*); so ~ION *n.* [f. L IN¹(*spicere spect-* = *specere* look at), or its frequent. *inspectare*]

inspe′ctor *n.* one who inspects; official employed to supervise a service and make reports; ||police officer below superintendent and above sergeant; ~ **general,** chief inspector; ||~ **of taxes,** official assessing income tax payable; hence ~ATE¹, ~SHIP, *ns.*, ~IAL (-ōī′-) *a.* [L (as prec.; see -OR)]

inspirā′tion *n.* **1.** drawing in of breath. **2.** inspiring; divine influence, esp. that which is thought to prompt poets etc. and that under which books of Scripture are held to have been written, whether **verbal** ~ (dictating every word), **plenary** ~ (covering all subjects treated), or **moral** ~ (confined to moral and religious teaching), whence ~ISM (3), ~IST (2), *ns.* **3.** thought etc. that is inspired, prompting; sudden brilliant or timely idea. **4.** inspiring principle. **5.** Hence ~AL *a.* [ME f. OF, f. LL *inspiratio -onis* (as INSPIRE; see -ATION)]

ī′nspirātor *n.* apparatus for drawing-in air or vapour. [LL (as foll.; see -OR)]

inspīr′e *v.t.* **1.** breathe in, inhale, (air etc., or abs.); hence **inspī′ratORY** *a.* **2.** instil thought or feeling into (person; esp. of divine or supernatural agency); animate (person etc. *with* feeling); instil (feeling *into* person etc.), create (feeling *in* person); (in *p.p.*) secretly suggested by or emanating from influential person etc., (of guess) intuitive but accurate. [ME, f. OF *inspirer* f. L IN¹(*spirare* breathe)]

inspī′rit *v.t.* put life into, animate; encourage (person *to* action, *to* do); hence ~ING² *a.* [f. IN-¹ | SPIRIT¹]

inspī′ss|āte *v.t.* (literary). thicken, condense; hence ~A′TION *n.* [f. LL IN¹(*spissare* f. L *spissus* thick) + -ATE³]

inst. *abbr.* instant (*the 6th inst.*); institute; institution.

instabī′lity *n.* lack of stability, being unstable. [ME, f. F *instabilité* f. L *instabilitas -tatis* f. IN²(*stabilis* STABLE¹); see -ITY]

instă′ll (-aw′l) *v.t.* **1.** place (person in office or rank) with ceremonies, whence ~ANT *a.* & *n.* **2.** establish (person, one*self*, in place, condition, etc.); place (heating or lighting apparatus etc.) in position for use. [f. med. L IN¹(*stallare* f. *stallum* STALL¹)]

installā′tion *n.* installing or being installed; apparatus etc. installed. [f. med. L *installatio* (as prec.; see -ATION)]

instă′lment, *instă′llment, (-aw′l-) *n.* each of several parts, successively falling due, of sum payable; each of several parts (esp. of serial story etc.) supplied, published, etc. at different times; *~ **plan,** payment by instalments, esp. hire-purchase. [alt. f. obs. *estallment* f. AF *estalement* (*estaler* fix; see -MENT), prob. assoc. w. prec.]

ī′nstance¹ *n.* **1.** fact illustrating a general truth, person or thing for which an assertion is valid, example; particular case (*in your, this, instance*); **for** ~, as an example. **2. at the** ~ (request, suggestion) **of**. **3.** (Law). process, suit; **court of first** ~ (primary jurisdiction). **4. in the first** ~, in the first place, at the first stage of a proceeding. [ME f. OF, f. L *instantia* (as INSTANT¹; see -ANCE)]

ī′nstance² *v.t.* cite (fact, case) as an instance; (usu. in *pass.*) exemplify. [f. prec.]

ī′nstancy *n.* urgency; pressing nature. [f. L *instantia* (see INSTANCE¹, -ANCY)]

ī′nstant¹ *a.* occurring immediately; (of food) that can be prepared easily for immediate use; (fig.) hurriedly produced; urgent, pressing, (Commerc.) of the current month (*the 6th instant*); (arch.) of the present moment. [ME f. F, f. L IN¹(*stare* stand) be present, press upon; see -ANT]

ī′nstant² *n.* **1.** precise (esp. the present) point of time, = MOMENT 1, (*come this instant*; *I went that instant* or *on the instant*; *I told you the* ~ (as soon as) *I knew*. **2.** short space of time, = MOMENT 1, (*in an instant*; *not an instant too soon*). [after med. L *instans* (*tempus*) present (time); see prec.]

instantā′neous *a.* occurring or done in an instant or instantly; (Phys.) existing at a particular instant;

hence ∼LY[2] adv., ∼NESS n. [f. med. L *instantaneus* f. L *instans* (see INSTANT[1]) after eccl. L *momentaneus*, + -OUS]

insta'nter adv. (arch. or joc.) immediately, at once. [L (*instans*; see INSTANT[1])]

insta'nti|āte (-shī-) v.t. represent by an instance; so ∼A'TION n. [f. L *instantia* (see INSTANCE[1]) + -ATE[3]]

i'nstantly adv. immediately, at once; (arch.) urgently, pressingly. [ME, f. INSTANT[1] + -LY[2]]

i'nstār n. stage in life of insect etc. between two ecdyses. [L, = form]

insta'te v.t. install, establish, *in* office etc. [f. IN-[1] + STATE[1]]

in statu pupillari (ĭn stătū pūpĭlār'ī) a. under guardianship; in junior status at university, not having master's degree. [L]

in statu quo (ĭn stătū kwō') a. in the same state as formerly. [L; cf. STATUS]

instaurā'tion n. (act of) restoration, renewal; so **i'nstaurātor** n. [f. L *instauratio* f. IN[1](*staurare*; cf. RESTORE, -ATION)]

instea'd (-ĕ'd) adv. as a substitute or alternative; in place of (*instead of this; instead of going*); cf. STEAD. [ME, f. IN[1] + STEAD]

i'nstěp n. upper surface of foot between toes and ankle; part of shoe etc. fitting over or under this; instep-shaped thing. [16th c., ult. f. as IN-[1] + STEP[1], but immed. orig. uncert.]

i'nstig|āte v.t. urge on, incite, (person *to* action, *to* do esp. something evil); bring about (revolt, murder, etc.) thus; hence or cogn. ∼A'TION, ∼ātor, ns. [f. L IN[1]*stigare*, + -ATE[3]]

insti'l, *insti'll, v.t. (-ll-). put in (liquid *into* thing) by drops; introduce (feeling, ideas, etc., *into* person, mind, etc.) gradually; hence or cogn. instilLA'TION, ∼MENT, ns. [f. L IN[1](*stillare* drop); cf. DISTIL]

i'nstinct[1] n. **1.** innate propensity to certain seemingly rational acts performed without conscious intention; innate usu. fixed pattern of behaviour esp. in response to certain simple stimuli; HERD[1] *instinct*. **2.** innate impulse; intuition, unconscious skill, (*for*). **3.** Hence **insti'nctive**, **insti'nctual**, adjs., **insti'nctively**[2] (-vlĭ) adv. [ME, = 'impulse', f. L *instinctus* f. IN[1]-(*stinguere stinct-* prick) incite]

insti'nct[2] pred. a. imbued, charged, (*with* life, beauty, force, etc.). [f. L p.p. (as prec.)]

i'nstitūte[1] n. **1.** society or organization for promotion of scientific, educational, or other public object; building used by this; *brief instruction-course for teachers etc. **2.** principle of instruction; (in *pl.*) digest of elements of a subject, esp. of jurisprudence, (*Institutes of Justinian*). [f. L *institutum* design, precept, neut. p.p. (as n.) of *instituere* (see foll.)]

i'nstitūte[2] v.t. establish, found; initiate (inquiry etc.); appoint (person *to* or *into* cure of souls). [ME, f. L IN[1](*stituere -tut-* = *statuere* set up) establish, arrange, teach]

institū'tion n. **1.** instituting; establishment (of person) in cure of souls. **2.** established law, custom, or practice; (colloq., of person etc.) familiar object. **3.** = INSTITUTE[1] 1, esp. for charitable or social purpose. [ME f. OF, f. L *institutio -onis* (as prec.; see -ION)]

institū'tional a. of or like institution(s); (of religion) expressed or organized through institutions (churches etc.); suggestive of typical charitable institutions; *(of advertising) intended to create prestige rather than immediate sales; hence ∼ISM (2) n. [f. prec. + -AL]

institū'tionalize, -ise (-īz), v.t. make institutional; place or keep (person needing care) in an institution; subject to institutional life. [f. prec. + -IZE]

||**Inst. P.** abbr. Institute of Physics.

instru'ct v.t. teach (person etc. *in* subject); inform (person *that, when*, etc.); (of client, solicitor) give information to (solicitor, counsel); direct, command, (person *to* do); so ∼OR (esp. *teacher ranking below professors), ∼FESS[1], ns. [ME, f. L IN[1](*struere struct-* pile up) build, teach]

instru'ction n. teaching; (esp. in *pl.*) making known to person what he is required to do, direction, order; (in *pl.*) directions to solicitor or counsel; expression in computer program defining and effecting an operation; hence ∼AL a. [ME f. OF, f. LL *instructio -onis* (as prec.; see -ION)]

instru'ctive a. tending to instruct, conveying a lesson; hence ∼LY[2] (-vlĭ) adv., ∼NESS (-vn-) n. [f. INSTRUCT + -IVE]

i'nstrument (-rōō-) n., & v.t. **1.** n. thing used in performing an action; person so made use of; tool, implement, esp. for delicate or scientific work; measuring-device, esp. in aeroplane and serving to determine position etc. when visibility is bad; (**musical**) ∼, contrivance for producing musical sounds by vibration of strings, membranes, etc., or of body of air in pipe etc.; formal, esp. legal, document; ∼ **board** or **panel**, surface containing dials etc. of measuring-instruments. **2.** v.t. arrange (music) for instruments; equip with (measuring-)instruments. [ME f. OF, or f. L *instrumentum* (as INSTRUCT; see -MENT)]

instrume'ntal (-rōō-) a. serving as instrument or means (*to* purpose, *in* work, *in* doing), whence ∼ITY (-ă'l-) n.; of, or arising from, an instrument (*instrumental error*); (of music) performed on instruments (opp. *vocal*), whence ∼IST (3) n.; (Gram., of case) denoting the means or instrument; hence ∼LY[2] adv. [ME f. F, f. med. L *instrumentalis* (as INSTRUMENT; see -AL)]

instrumentā'tion (-rōō-) n. arrangement or composition of music for instruments; provision or use of mechanical instruments in industry; operation with scientific, surgical, or other instrument; instrumentality. [F (*instrumenter* f. as INSTRUMENT; see -ATION)]

insubōr'din|ate a. disobedient, rebellious; so ∼A'TION n. [f. IN-[2] + SUBORDINATE[1]]

insubstā'ntial (-shal) a. not real; lacking solidity or substance; hence ∼ITY (-shĭă'l-) n. [f. LL IN[2](*substantialis* SUBSTANTIAL)]

insu'fferab|le a. intolerable; unbearably arrogant, conceited, etc.; hence ∼LY[2] adv. [f. IN-[2] + SUFFERABLE]

insuffi'ciency (-shen-) n. being insufficient; (Med.) inability of an organ to perform its normal function (*renal insufficiency*). [ME, f. LL *insufficientia* (as foll.; see -ENCY)]

insuffi'cient (-shent) a. not sufficient, inadequate; hence ∼LY[2] adv. [ME f. OF, f. LL IN[2](*sufficiens* SUFFICIENT)]

i'nsuffl|ate v.t. blow, breathe, (air, gas, powder, etc.) into cavity of the body etc.; treat (nose etc.) thus; (Eccl.) blow or breathe on (person) to symbolize spiritual influence; hence or cogn. ∼A'TION n., ∼ātor n.; (esp.) device for blowing powder on surface of object in order to make latent fingerprints visible. [f. LL IN[1](*sufflare* blow upon f. as SUB-+ L *flare* blow) + -ATE[3]]

i'nsular a. **1.** of (the nature of) an island or (Physiol.) islet (of Britain (esp. w. ref. to a development of Latin handwriting current in the British Isles in the early Middle Ages). **2.** of or like islanders; ignorant of or indifferent to other countries and their culture, narrow-minded; hence ∼ISM (2) n. **3.** Hence ∼ITY (-ă'r-) n., ∼LY[2] adv. [f. LL *insularis* (as foll.; see -AR[1])]

i'nsul|āte v.t. **1.** detach (person, thing) from surroundings, isolate. **2.** isolate (thing) by interposition of non-conductors, to prevent passage of electricity or heat or sound. **3.** (arch.) make (land) into an island. **4.** Hence ∼A'TION n. [f. L *insula* island + -ATE[3]]

i'nsulātor n. thing or substance used for insulation against electricity etc.; device to support telegraph-wires etc. or prevent contact between electrical conductors. [f. prec. + -OR]

i'nsulin n. hormone secreted by islets of Langerhans in vertebrates and controlling passage of sugar from blood to tissues. [f. L *insula* island + -IN]

i'nsult[1] n. insulting speech or action; (Med.) (agent causing) damage to the body. [f. F *insulte*, or f. eccl. L IN[1](*sultus* = *saltus* leap, as foll.)]

For other words in *in-* see IN-[1] or (esp.) IN-[2].

insŭ'lt² *v.t.* treat with scornful abuse, subject to indignity; (of person or thing) offend modesty or self--respect of. [f. L IN¹(*sultare = saltare*, frequent. of *salire* salt- leap)]

insu'per|able (-ŏŏ'-, -ū'-) *a.* (Of barrier etc. and fig. of difficulty etc.) that cannot be surmounted or overcome; hence ~ABI'LITY *n.*, ~ABLY *adv.* [ME f. OF, or f. L IN²(*superabilis* SUPERABLE)]

insuppŏr'tab|le *a.* that cannot be endured; unjustifiable; hence ~LY² *adv.* [F (as IN-², SUPPORT, -ABLE)]

insur'ance (-shoor'-) *n.* insuring; sum paid for this, premium; ||NATIONAL *Insurance*; ~ **agent, company,** etc., (undertaking insurance dealings for or as insurer); *insurance* POLICY²; ||~ **stamp** (certifying payment of regular amount for National Insurance). [earlier *ensurance* f. OF *enseürance* (as ENSURE; see -ANCE)]

insur'ant (-shoor'-) *n.* person to whom insurance policy is issued. [f. foll. + -ANT]

insur'|e (-shoor') *v.t.* **1.** secure payment of sum of money in event of or *against* loss of or damage or injury to (property, life, person, etc., or abs.; cf. ASSURANCE) on payment of premium; (of owner of property etc. or of insurance company etc.) secure payment of (sum of money) thus; **the ~ed,** the person in respect of whom such payment is secured. **2.** *ensure. **3.** Hence ~ABLE *a.* [ME, var. of ENSURE]

insur'er (-shoor'-) *n.* one who insures property in consideration of premium, underwriter. [f. prec. + -ER¹]

insur'g|ent *a.* & *n.* **1.** *a.* rising in active revolt; (of sea etc.) rushing in; hence ~ENCY *n.* **2.** *n.* rebel. [F, f. L IN¹(*surgere surrect*- rise); see -ENT]

insurmou'ntab|le *a.* that cannot be surmounted or overcome; hence ~LY² *adv.* [f. IN-² + SURMOUNTABLE]

insurre'ction *n.* rising in open resistance to established authority; incipient rebellion; hence ~AL, ~ARY¹, *adjs.*, ~IST (3) *n.* [ME f. OF, f. LL *insurrectio* -*onis* (as INSURGENT; see -ION)]

insusce'pt|ible *a.* not susceptible (*of* treatment, *to* agency, etc.); hence ~IBI'LITY *n.* [f. IN-² + SUSCEPT-IBLE]

int. *abbr.* interior; internal; international.

intă'ct *a.* untouched; entire; unimpaired. [ME, f. L IN²(*tactus* p.p. of *tangere* touch)]

intă'gliāted (-tä'l-) *a.* decorated with surface carving. [f. It. *intagliato* p.p. of IN¹(*tagliare* cut)]

intă'gliō (-tä'l-, -tah'l-) *n.* (*pl.* ~s), & *v.t.* **1.** *n.* engraved design; (esp. incised) carving in hard material; gem with incised design; process of printing from engraved design. **2.** *v.t.* engrave (material, design) in intaglio. [It. (as prec.)]

'ntăke *n.* action of taking in; place where water is taken into channel or pipe from river, where fuel or air enters engine, etc.; airway into mine; person(s) or thing(s) or quantity taken in or received; (N. Engl.) land reclaimed from moor etc. [f. IN² + TAKE¹]

intă'ngi|ble (-nj-) *a.* that cannot be touched; that cannot be grasped mentally; hence ~IBI'LITY *n.*, ~IBLY *adv.* [F, or f. med. L IN²(*tangibilis* TANGIBLE)]

intăr'sia *n.* mosaic woodwork made esp. in 15th-c. Italy. [f. It. *intarsio*]

'ntēger *n.* whole number; thing complete in itself. [L, adj. = untouched, whole (see ENTIRE)]

'ntēgral *a.* & *n.* **1.** *a.* of, or necessary to the completeness of, a whole; whole, complete; forming a whole (*integral design*). **2.** (Math.) of, or denoted by, an integer; involving only integers (e.g. as coefficients in a function); ~ **calculus** (dealing with finding and properties of integrals of functions; cf. DIFFERENTIAL). **3.** Hence or cogn. ~ITY (-ă'l-) *n.*, ~LY² *adv.* **4.** *n.* (Math.) quantity of which given function is the derivative, containing indeterminate additive constant (**indefinite** ~), or calculated as difference between its values at specified limits (**definite** ~); function satisfying given differential equation. [f. LL *integralis* (as prec.; see -AL)]

i'ntĕgrănd *n.* (Math.) function that is to be integrated. [f. L *integrandus* gerundive of *integrare*; see INTEGRATE², -ND¹]

i'ntĕgrant *a.* (Of parts) component, making up a whole. [f. F *intégrant* (*intégrer* f. as INTEGRATE²; see -ANT)]

i'ntĕgrate¹ *a.* made up of parts; whole, complete. [f. L *integratus* (as foll.; see -ATE²)]

i'ntĕgr|āte² *v.* **1.** *v.t.* complete (imperfect thing) by addition of parts; combine (parts) into a whole. **2.** (Math.) find the integral of; (esp. in *pres. part.*) indicate mean value or total sum of (temperature, area, etc.), whence ~ātor *n.* **3.** *v.t. & i.* bring or come into equal membership of society, esp. without regard to race or religion; end (racial) segregation (of or at). **4.** ~ated **circuit,** small chip etc. of material designed to replace conventional electrical circuit of many components. **5.** Hence ~ATIVE *a.* [f. L *integrare* make whole (as INTEGER) + -ATE³]

intĕgrā'tion *n.* integrating; ending of racial segregation, whence ~IST (2) *n.*; (Psych.) combination of diverse elements of perception etc.; **horizontal** ~ (of firms engaged in same stages or types of manufacture); **vertical** ~ (of firms engaged in successive stages in production of goods). [f. L *integratio* (as prec.; see -ATION)]

intĕ'grity *n.* wholeness; soundness; uprightness, honesty. [ME, f. F *intégrité* or f. L *integritas* (as INTEGER; see -ITY)]

intĕ'gŭment *n.* skin, husk, rind, or other (usu. natural) covering; hence ~AL, ~ARY¹, (-č'n-) *adjs.* [f. L *integumentum* f. IN¹(*tegere* cover); see -MENT]

i'ntĕllĕct *n.* faculty of knowing and reasoning; understanding; person, persons collectively, of good understanding. [ME f. OF, or f. L *intellectus* perception (as INTELLIGENT)]

intĕllĕ'ct|ion *n.* action or process of understanding, esp. as opp. to imagination; so ~IVE *a.* [ME, f. med. L *intellectio* (as INTELLIGENT; see -ION)]

intĕllĕ'ctŭal *a.* of, appealing to, requiring or given to the exercise of, intellect. **2.** *a.* & *n.* (person) possessing a good understanding and intelligence, enlightened (person). **3.** Hence or cogn. ~ITY (-ă'l-) *n.*, ~IZE (2, 3) *v.t. & i.*, ~LY² *adv.* [ME, f. L *intellectualis* (as INTELLECT; see -AL)]

intĕllĕ'ctŭal|ism *n.* doctrine that knowledge is wholly or mainly derived from pure reason; (excessive) exercise of intellect only; so ~IST (2) *n.* [f. prec. + -ISM]

intĕ'lligence *n.* **1.** intellect, understanding; hence **intĕlligĕ'ntIAL** (-shal) *a.* quickness of understanding, sagacity, (of person or animal), ~ **quotient,** number denoting ratio of given person's intelligence to the normal or average; ~ **test** (designed to measure intelligence rather than acquired knowledge). **3.** intelligent or rational being. **4.** information, news; (persons employed in) collecting information, esp. that of military value; hence **department** (engaged in collecting information esp. secretly). [ME f. OF, f. L *intelligentia* (as INTELLIGENT; see -ENCE)]

intĕ'lligencer *n.* bringer of news, informant; secret agent, spy. [f. prec. + -ER¹]

intĕ'lligent *a.* having or showing (usu. a high degree of) understanding; clever, quick of mind; hence ~LY² *adv.* [f. L *intelligere* -*lect*- understand (as INTER-, *legere* gather, pick out, read); see -ENT]

intĕlligĕ'ntsia *n.* class of intellectuals regarded as possessing culture and political initiative; class of persons doing intellectual work. [Russ., f. Pol. *inteligencja* f. L (as INTELLIGENCE)]

intĕ'llig|ible *a.* that can be understood, comprehensible *to*; (Philos.) that can be apprehended only by the intellect, not by the senses; hence ~IBI'LITY *n.*, ~IBLY *adv.* [f. L *intelligibilis* (as INTELLIGENT; see -IBLE)]

intĕ'mper|ate *a.* (Of person or conduct or speech) immoderate, unbridled, violent; excessive in the indulgence of an appetite; addicted to drinking; hence or cogn. ~ANCE *n.*, ~ate LY² (-tlĭ) *adv.* [ME, f. L IN²(*temperatus* TEMPERATE)]

intĕ'nd *v.t.* **1.** have as one's purpose (*we intend to go; we intend going; we intended no harm; we intend that it shall be done today*); (in *p.p.*) done on purpose; (in *pres. part.*) who intends to be (*intending visitor*). **2.** design, destine, (person, thing; *for* a purpose or *as* something: *we intend our son for the Bar; intend him to go; intend it as a stopgap*); *this bun is* ~ed *for you* (to eat), *this daub is* ~ed *for* (meant to represent) **me. 3.** mean (*what exactly do you intend by the word?*). [ME *entende, intende* f. OF *entendre, intendre* f. L IN¹(*tendere* tent- or tens- stretch, tend) strain, direct, purpose]

intĕ'nd|ant *n.* (Esp. as title of foreign officials) superintendent or manager of public business etc.; hence ~ANCY *n.* [F, f. L (as prec.; see -ANT)]

intĕ'ndĕd *n.* (colloq.) person one intends to marry, esp. fiancé(e) (*your, his, her, intended*). [f. p.p. of INTEND]

intĕ'ndment *n.* intention, meaning; true meaning as fixed by law. [ME, f. OF *entendement* meaning (as INTEND; see -MENT)]

intĕ'nse *a.* (~r, ~st). (Of quality etc.) existing in a high degree, violent, vehement; having some quality in high degree; (of feeling or action) eager, ardent; (of person) feeling, apt to feel, strong emotion; hence ~LY² (-slĭ) *adv.*, ~NESS (-sn-) *n.* [ME f. OF *intens*, or f. L *intensus* (as INTEND)]

intĕ'nsi|fy *v.t. & i.* make or become (more) intense; (Photog.) increase opacity of (negative); hence ~FICA'TION, ~fĪER¹, *ns.* [f. prec. +-I-+-FY]

intĕ'nsion (-shǒn) *n.* intensity, high degree, of a quality; strenuous exertion of mind or will; (Logic) internal content of a concept, whence ~AL *a.* [f. L *intensio* (as INTEND; see -ION)]

intĕ'nsity *n.* quality of being intense; (measurable) amount of some quality, e.g. force, brightness, magnetic field. [f. INTENSE +-ITY]

intĕ'nsive *a. & n.* **1.** *a.* of or relating to intensity as opp. to extent; producing intensity; (Gram.) expressing intensity, giving force; vigorous, thorough; concentrated, directed to a single point or area or subject, (*intensive bombardment, study*); (Econ.) serving to increase production from given area (*intensive methods, agriculture*); (as *suf.*) making much use of (*capital-intensive, labour-intensive*); ~ **care,** medical treatment with constant observation of patient; hence ~LY² (-vlĭ) *adv.* **2.** *n.* (Gram.) intensive word etc. [F *intensif -ive* or f. med. L *intensivus* (as INTEND; see -IVE)]

intĕ'nt¹ *n.* intention, purpose, (*with intent to defraud* etc.; *with malicious, good,* etc., *intent*); **to all** ~**s and purposes,** practically, virtually. [ME f. OF (1) *entent* f. L *intentus* n., (2) *entente* f. Rom. *intenta fem. p.p., both as INTEND]

intĕ'nt² *a.* resolved, bent, (*on* doing, *on* object); attentively occupied (*on*); (of faculties, looks, etc.) earnest, eager; hence ~LY² *adv.*, ~NESS *n.* [f. L *intentus* a. (as INTEND)]

intĕ'ntion *n.* **1.** intending, one's purpose *of* doing or *to* do; thing intended, object, purpose, whence (-)~ED² (-nd) *a.*; ultimate aim; (in *pl.*, colloq.) purposes in respect of proposal of marriage (cf. HONOURABLE). **2.** (Med.) **second** ~, healing of wound by granulation, **first** ~, healing without this by immediate reunion of parts; *intention* TREMOR. **3.** (Logic) conception, **first** ~s, primary conceptions of things (e.g. a tree, an oak), **second** ~s, secondary conceptions (e.g. difference, identity, species). **4.** (Theol.) special, particular, ~, special object for which mass is celebrated etc. [ME f. OF *entencion* f. L *intentio* stretching, purpose (as INTEND; see -ION)]

intĕ'ntional *a.* done on purpose; hence ~LY² *adv.* [f. F *intentionnel* or f. med. L *intentionalis* (as prec.; see -AL)]

intĕr' *v.t.* (-rr-). deposit (corpse etc.) in earth, tomb, etc.; bury. [ME, f. OF *enterrer* f. Rom. *IN¹(*terrare* f. terra earth)]

i'nter- *pref.* w. sense 'between', forming: **1.** *vbs., ns.,* & *adjs.,* expr. mutual or reciprocal action or relation, or with sense 'among', 'between', as: ~**a'llied,** pertaining to two or more allies (in war etc.); ~**be'd,** embed (thing) between others; ~**ce'nsal,** between two censuses; ~**city,** existing or travelling between cities; ~**colle'giate,** carried on etc. between colleges or *universities; ~**colo'nial,** carried on etc. between colonies; ~**colu'mnar,** placed or existing between two columns; ~**columna'tion,** placing of columns at intervals, such interval; ~**contine'ntal,** connecting, situated or travelling or existing between, different continents; ~**conver'tible,** interchangeable ~**cro'ss** *v.t. & i.,* lay or lie across each other, (cause to) breed with each other; ~**denomina'tional,** relating to more than one (religious) denomination ~**departme'ntal,** pertaining to more than one department; interlock like clasped fingers; ~**di'gitate** (-lĭ'-, -dĭ'-), of or between different branches of learning; ~**flow** *n., & v.i.,* flow into each other; ~**gala'ctic,** situated between galaxies; ~**governme'ntal,** pertaining to more than one government; ~**grada'tion,** gradual approximation; ~**grade,** (*v.i.*) pass into another form by intervening grades, (*n.*) such grade; ~**grow'th** growing of things into each other; ~**ja'cent,** lying between; ~**kni't,** intertwine; ~**la'p** *v.i.,* overlap ~**li'nk,** link together (things, one *with* another, or abs.); ~**me'sh,** = MESH² 2; ~**migra'tion,** reciprocal migration; ~**ocea'nic,** between or connecting two oceans; ~**per'sonal,** (of relations) between persons ~**plai't,** plait together; ~**pla'netary,** (pertaining to travel) between planets; ~**provi'ncial,** situated or carried on between provinces; ~**pu'nction,** (arch. punctuation; ~**ra'cial,** existing between different races; ~**ste'llar,** between stars; ~**ta'ngle,** tangle together; ~**te'xture,** interweaving; ~**tri'bal,** existing between different tribes; ~**twi'st,** twist together ~**vei'n,** intersect (as) with veins; ~**war,** existing in the period between two wars; ~**wor'k,** (*v.t.*) inter weave (lit. or fig.), (*v.i.*) work upon each other ~**wrea'the,** wreathe together. **2.** scientific terms esp. *adjs.,* w. sense 'between', as: ~**arti'cular** between contiguous surfaces of a joint; ~**ato'mic** between atoms; ~**co'stal,** between the ribs (of body or ship), between veins of leaf; ~**crur'al,** between the legs; ~**di'gital,** between fingers or toes; ~ **fa'cial,** included between two faces of crystal or other solid; ~**fe'moral,** between the thighs; ~ **fi'brillar,** between fibrils; ~**gla'cial,** between glacial periods; ~**lo'bular,** situated between lobes ~**mole'cular,** between molecules; ~**node,** (Bot. part of stem between two of the knots from which leaves arise, (Anat.) slender part between two joints esp. bone of finger or toe; ~**nu'clear,** between nuclei; ~**o'sculate,** inosculate; ~**o'sseous** between bones; ~**pari'etal,** between right and left parietal bones of skull; ~**se'ptal,** between septa o partitions; ~**speci'fic,** formed from different species ~**spi'nal,** ~**spi'nous,** between spines or spinous processes; ~**stratifica'tion,** ~**stra'tified,** inter spersion, interspersed, (*with* strata); ~**ver'tebra** between vertebrae. [f. OF *entre-* or f. L *inter* between among]

inter. *abbr.* intermediate.

i'nteräct¹ *n.* interval between two acts of play interlude. [f. INTER-+ACT¹, after F *entr'acte*]

interä'ct² *v.i.* act reciprocally, act on each other hence ~ANT *a. & n.,* ~ION *n.,* ~IVE *a.* [f. INTER +ACT²]

inter alia (ĭnter ā'lĭa) *adv.* amongst other things. [L]

interblĕ'nd *v.* **1.** *v.t.* mingle (things, one *with* another **2.** *v.i.* blend with each other. [f. INTER-+BLEND¹]

interbree'd *v.t. & i.* (-bre'd). (cause to) produce

hybrid person or animal or plant. [f. INTER-+ BREED¹]

intercalary (-ĕr´ka-, -erkă´-) a. (Of day or month) inserted in calendar to harmonize calendar with solar year, e.g. 29 Feb. in leap years; (of year) having such addition; interpolated, intervening. [f. L *intercalari(u)s* (as foll.; see -ARY¹)]

intēr´cal|āte v.t. insert (intercalary day etc., or abs.); interpose (anything out of ordinary course, esp. in *p.p.* of strata); so ∼A´TION n. [f. L INTER(*calare* proclaim) +-ATE³]

intercē´de v.i. interpose on behalf of another, plead (*with* one person *for* another). [f. F *intercéder* or f. L INTER(*cedere cess-* go) intervene]

intercē´pt¹ v.t. seize, catch, stop, (person, message, vehicle, etc.) on the way from place to place; cut off (light etc. *from*); check, stop, (motion etc.); (Math.) mark off (space) between two points etc.; hence ∼ION n., ∼IVE a., ∼OR n. (esp. aircraft seeking to intercept enemy raiders). [f. L INTER(*cipere cept-* = *capere* take)]

i´ntercĕpt² n. (Math.) part of line between two points of intersection with other lines. [f. prec.]

intercĕ´ssion (-shŏn) n. interceding, esp. by prayer; so ∼cĕ´ssor n., ∼cĕssōr´IAL, ∼cĕ´ssORY, adjs. [F, or f. L *intercessio* (as INTERCEDE; see ION)]

i´nterchānge¹ (-nj) n. reciprocal exchange (*of* things) between two persons etc.; alternation; road junction designed so that traffic streams do not intersect. [f. foll.]

intercha´nge² (-nj) v.t. (Of two persons) exchange (things) with each other; put each of (two things) in the other's place; alternate; hence or cogn. ∼**ableNESS** (-běln-), ns., ∼**ABLE** a., ∼**ABLY** adv., (-ja-). [ME, f. OF *entrechangier* (*entre-* INTER-, *changer* CHANGE²)]

i´ntercŏm n. (colloq.) system of intercommunication by radio or telephone, esp. in aircraft. [abbr.]

intercommū´nic|āte v.i. communicate mutually; (of rooms etc.) have free passage into each other; so ∼A´TION n. [f. AL INTER(*communicare;* see COMMUNICATE) +-ATE³]

intercommū´nion (-yŏn) n. mutual communion; mutual action or relation, esp. between religious bodies. [f. INTER-+COMMUNION]

intercommū´nity n. quality of being common to various groups etc.; having things in common. [f. INTER-+COMMUNITY]

interconnĕ´ct v.t. & i. connect with each other; so ∼ION n. [f. INTER-+CONNECT]

i´ntercourse (-ōrs) n. social communication, dealings, between individuals; communion between man and God; communication for trade purposes etc. between different countries etc.; − SEXUAL *intercourse.* [ME, f. OF *entrecours* exchange, commerce, f. L INTER(*cursus* f. *currere curs-* run)]

intercŭ´rr|ent a. (Of time or event) intervening; (of disease) (1) occurring during progress of another, (2) recurring at intervals; hence ∼ENCE n. [f. L (as prec.; see -ENT)]

i´ntercŭt v.t. (-tt-; -cut). (Cinemat.) alternate (shots) with contrast of distance etc. by cutting. [f. INTER-+ CUT²]

interdepē´nd v.i. depend on each other; so ∼ENCE, ∼ENCY, ns., ∼ENT a. [f. INTER-+DEPEND]

i´nterdict¹ n. authoritative prohibition; (Sc. Law) injunction; (RC Ch.) sentence debarring person or (esp.) place from ecclesiastical functions and privileges. [ME f. OF *entredit* f. L *interdictum* p.p. (as n.) of INTER(*dicere dict-* say) interpose, forbid by decree]

interdi´ct² v.t. prohibit (action); forbid use of; restrain (person *from doing*); forbid (thing *to* person); so ∼ION n., ∼ORY a. [ME, f. prec.]

i´nterĕst¹ (-tr-, -ter-) n. **1.** legal concern, title, right, (*in* property); pecuniary stake (*in* commercial undertaking etc.); **declare an** or one's ∼ (in an undertaking, before discussion of it); VEST²ed *interests.* **2.** advantage, profit, (*it is* (*in* or *to*) *your interest to go;* look

after one's *own interests*); **in the** ∼(**s**) **of,** as something that is advantageous to. **3.** thing in which one is concerned; principle in which a party is concerned; party having a common interest (*the brewing interest*). **4.** selfish pursuit of one's own welfare; self-interest. **5.** concern, curiosity, (*take an interest, no interest, in*); quality exciting these or holding one's attention (*this has no great interest for me, is of no interest to me*); LOSE *interest.* **6.** money paid for use of money lent or for not exacting repayment of debt; **at** ∼, on condition of such payment; **with** ∼, (fig.) with increased force etc., (*returned the blow, his kindness, with interest*); **simple** ∼ (reckoned on principal only, and paid at fixed intervals); **compound** ∼ (reckoned on principal and on accumulations of interest). [ME, earlier *interesse* f. AF f. med. L, alt. app. after OF *interest,* both f. L *interest,* 3rd sing. pres. of INTER(*esse* be) matter, make a difference]

i´nterĕst² (-tr-, -ter-) v.t. cause (person) to take personal interest or share (*in*); (in *p.p.*) having a private interest, not impartial or disinterested, (*interested parties, motives*); excite curiosity or attention of. [alt. (after prec.) f. earlier *interess,* f. F *intéresse* f. L *interesse* (see prec.)]

i´nterĕsting (-tr-, -ter-) a. causing curiosity, holding the attention, **in an** ∼ **condition,** (arch.) pregnant; hence ∼LY² adv. [f. prec. +-ING²]

i´nterfāce n. & v. **1.** n. surface forming common boundary between two regions. **2.** place, or piece of equipment, where interaction occurs between two systems, processes, etc. **3.** v.t. & i. connect *with* by interface. [f. INTER-+FACE¹]

i´nterfācing n. stiffish material between two layers of fabric in garment etc. [f. INTER-+FACING]

interfēr´|e v.i. (Of thing) come into collision or opposition or incompatibility (*with*); (of person) meddle (*with,* or abs.), whence ∼ING² a.; intervene, take part, (*in*); (Phys., of light-waves etc.) combine in different phases so as to cause partial or complete neutralization; (of horse) knock one leg against another; ∼**e with,** (euphem.) molest or assault sexually. [f. OF *s'entreferir* strike each other (*entre-* INTER-, *ferir* f. L *ferire* strike)]

interfēr´ence n. interfering (*with*); (Radio) fading of received signals by interference of waves from different sources or paths, or (esp.) by (intrusion of) atmospherics or unwanted signals; hence **interferē´ntIAL** (-shal) a. [irreg. f. prec. +-ENCE, after *difference* etc.]

interferŏ´meter n. instrument for measuring wavelengths etc. by means of interference phenomena; hence **interfērome´trIC** a., **interferŏ´METRY** n. [f. INTERFERE + -O- + -METER]

interfēr´on n. protein inhibiting development of virus in cell. [f. INTERFERE +-ON]

intēr´fluent (-ōō-) a. flowing into each other. [f. L INTER(*fluere* flow); see -ENT]

interfū´se (-z) v. **1.** v.t. intersperse, mix, (thing *with*); blend (things) together. **2.** v.i. (Of two things) blend with each other. **3.** So **interfū´sION** (-zhŏn) n. [f. L INTER(*fundere fus-* pour)]

i´nterim adv., n., & a. **1.** adv. (arch.) meanwhile. **2.** n. intervening time (*in the interim*); **the I**∼, (Eccl.) truce, pending a General Council, between German Protestants and the Papacy in 16th c. **3.** a. intervening; provisional, temporary; ∼ **dividend** (paid between two annual etc. balances and not in pursuance of a published balance-sheet). [L (INTER+adv. suf. *-im*)]

intēr´ior a. & n. **1.** a. inner (opp. *exterior*); situated within (relative *to*); remote from coast or frontier, inland; internal, domestic, (opp. *foreign*); existing in mind or soul, inward; coming from inside; drawn, photographed, etc., within a building; ∼ **angle** (between adjacent sides of rectilinear figure); ∼ **decoration, design,** (of interior of building or room); ∼ **monologue,** form of writing representing character's inner thoughts; ∼**-sprung,** (of mattress etc.) with springs inside; hence ∼IZE (3) v.t., ∼LY²

For other words in *in-* see IN-¹ or (esp.) IN-².

adv. **2.** *n.* interior part, inside; (picture of) inside of building or room; inner nature, soul; (department dealing with) home affairs of a country (*Minister of the Interior*). [L, compar. of *inter* among]

inter·je'ct *v.t.* throw in, interpose (remark etc.) abruptly; remark parenthetically. [f. L INTER (*jicere ject-* = *jacĕre* throw)]

interje'ction *n.* ejaculation, exclamation; natural ejaculation viewed as part of speech (e.g. *ah!*, *whew!*, *dear me!*); interposed remark; hence ∼AL, ∼ARY¹, **interje'ct**ORY, *adjs.* [ME f. OF, f. L *interjectio -onis* (as prec.; see -ION)]

interla'ce *v.* **1.** *v.t.* bind together intricately, entangle; interweave (often fig.); mingle (two things, one *with* another); present (lines forming television picture) in two sequences each containing alternate lines. **2.** *v.i.* cross each other intricately. **3.** Hence ∼MENT (-sm-) *n.* [ME, f. OF *entrelacier* (*entre-* INTER-, *lacier* LACE²)]

interlár'd *v.t.* mix (writing, speech, *with* foreign words etc.). [f. F *entrelarder* (*entre-* INTER-, *larder* LARD²)]

i'nterlea|f *n.* (*pl.* ∼ves). extra leaf (usu. blank) between leaves of book. [f. foll.]

interlea've *v.t.* insert (usu. blank) leaves between leaves of (book etc.; lit. or fig.). [f. INTER- + LEAF, *leaves*]

interli'ne¹ *v.t.* insert words between lines of (document etc.); insert (words) thus; so **interlinē**A'TION *n.* [ME, f. med. L INTER (*lineare* f. L *linea* LINE²)]

interli'n|e² *v.t.* put extra lining between ordinary lining and material of (garment); hence ∼ING¹ (2, 4) *n.* [f. INTER- + LINE⁴]

interli'near *a.* written or printed between the lines of a text. [ME, f. med. L INTER (*linearis* LINEAR)]

interlō'ck *v.*, *a.*, & *n.* **1.** *v.i.* engage with each other by overlapping etc. **2.** *v.t.* (usu. in *pass.*) lock or clasp within each other. **3.** connect (switches etc.) so that they cannot be operated independently or unsafely. **4.** *a.* (Of fabric) knitted with closely interlocking stitches. **5.** *n.* mechanism to interlock switches etc. [f. INTER- + LOCK³]

interlō'cū|tor *n.* one who takes part in dialogue or conversation (**my** ∼**tor**, the person in conversation with me); centre man of Negro minstrel troupe; hence or cogn. **interlocū'tion**, ∼**tr**ESS¹, ∼**trix**, *ns.* [mod. L, f. L INTER (*loqui locut-* speak); see -OR]

interlō'cūtory *a.* of dialogue or conversation; (of decree etc.) given in the course of a legal action. [f. med. L *interlocutorius* (as prec.; see -ORY)]

i'nterlōper *n.* intruder, one who (esp. for profit) thrusts himself into others' affairs; (Hist.) unauthorized trader; so **i'nterlōpe** *v.i.* [f. INTER- (as in *intermeddle*) + *loper* (as in *landloper*)]

i'nterlude (-ōōd, -ūd) *n.* **1.** pause between acts of play; what fills this up; (Mus.) instrumental piece played between verses of psalm or hymn etc. **2.** intervening time or space of different character. **3.** event, amusing incident, etc., interposed. **4.** (Hist.) dramatic or mimic representation between acts of miracle plays or moralities. [ME, = light dramatic item between acts of morality play, f. med. L INTER (*ludium* f. *ludus* play)]

intermä'rriage (-rĭj) *n.* marriage between members of different families, castes, tribes, etc., or (loosely) between near relations. [f. INTER- + MARRIAGE]

intermä'rry *v.i.* (Of tribes, nations, families, etc.) become connected by marriage (*with* other tribes etc.). [f. INTER- + MARRY¹]

interme'ddle *v.i.* concern oneself (*with*, *in*, esp. what is not one's business). [ME, f. AF *entremedler* (*entre-* INTER-; see MEDDLE)]

interme'diary *a.* & *n.* **1.** *a.* acting between parties, mediatory; intermediate. **2.** *n.* intermediary person or thing, esp. mediator. [f. F *intermédiaire* f. It. *intermediario* f. L *intermedius* (see foll., -ARY¹)]

interme'diate¹ *a.* & *n.* **1.** *a.* coming between two things in time, place, or order; (of missile's range) less than inter-continental; ∼ **frequency** (to which radio signal is converted during heterodyne reception); hence ∼LY² (-tlĭ) *adv.* **2.** *n.* intermediate thing;

(Chem.) compound formed by one reaction and then taking part in another, esp. during synthesis of commercial products. [f. med. L *intermediatus* (as INTERMEDIUM; see -ATE²)]

intermē'di|āte² *v.i.* act as intermediary, mediate, (*between*); hence ∼A'TION, ∼**āt**OR, *ns.* [f. INTER- + MEDIATE²]

intermē'di|um *n.* (*pl.* ∼**a** *or* ∼**ums**). intermediate thing, medium. [LL, neut. (as *n.*) of L INTER (*medius* middle)]

intĕr'ment *n.* burial. [ME, f. INTER² + -MENT]

intermĕ'zz|ō (-tsō) *n.* (*pl.* ∼**i** *pr.* -ē, *or* ∼**os**). short light dramatic or other performance between acts of drama or opera; short movement connecting main divisions of large musical work, or independent piece of this type. [It., f. L INTERMEDIUM]

intĕr'minab|le *a.* endless; tediously long; hence ∼**le**NESS (-bɪln-) *n.*, ∼**LY**² *adv.* [ME f. OF, or f. LL IN²(*terminabilis* f. L *terminare*; see TERMINATE, -ABLE)]

intermi'ngle (-nggel) *v.* **1.** *v.t.* mix together (two things, one *with* another). **2.** *v.i.* mingle (*with*). [f. INTER- + MINGLE]

intermi'ssion (-shon) *n.* pause, cessation; period of inactivity, *(musical selection during)* interval in theatre performance etc. [F, or f. L *intermissio* (as foll.; see -ION)]

intermi't *v.t.* & *i.* (-tt-). suspend, discontinue; stop for a time (esp. of fever, pain, etc., or of pulse). [f. L INTER (*mittere miss-* let go)]

intermi'tt|ent *a.* ceasing for a time; occurring at intervals, not continuous or steady; hence or cogn. ∼**ENCE** *n.*, ∼**ent**LY² *adv.* [f. L (as prec.; see -ENT)]

intermi'x *v.t.* & *i.* mix together, intermingle; so ∼**t**URE *n.* [back-form. f. *intermixed*, *intermixt* f. L *intermixtus* p.p. of INTER (*miscēre* mix)]

intĕr'n¹ *v.t.* oblige to reside within limits of country etc.; confine (esp. enemy alien or prisoner of war) within prescribed limits; hence ∼**EE**′, ∼**MENT**, *ns.* [f. F *interner* (*interne* f. L *internus* internal)]

***i'ntĕrn**² *n.*, & *v.i.* **1.** *n.* advanced student or recent graduate residing in hospital and acting as assistant physician or surgeon; teacher undergoing practical training; hence ∼**SHIP** *n.* **2.** *v.i.* serve as intern. [after F *interne* (see prec.)]

intĕr'nal *a.* & *n.* **1.** *a.* of, or situated in, the inside or invisible part (opp. *external*); (of the inner nature of a thing, intrinsic; (of remedy etc.) applied within the body; relating to the interior of the body (*internal injuries*, *organs*); of the domestic affairs of a State; pertaining to students attending a university as well as being examined there; of the mind or soul, inward, subjective; ∼ **clock**, biological clock; ∼**-combustion engine** (in which motive power is derived from explosion of mixture of gas, or vaporized oil or petrol, and air in the cylinder); ∼ **evidence** (derived from what is contained in thing discussed); *∼ (inland) revenue; internal* RHYME¹, WORK¹; hence ∼ITY (-ă'l-) *n.*, ∼IZE (3) *v.t.*, ∼LY² *adv.* **2.** *n.* (in *pl.*) intrinsic qualities. [f. mod. L *internalis* (as INTERN¹; see -AL)]

internat. *abbr.* = foll.

internä'tional *a.* & *n.* **1.** *a.* existing, or carried on, between different nations; agreed on by all or many nations (*international candle*, *date-line*, *driving licence*; ∼ **system of units**, system of physical units based on the metre, kilogram, second, ampere, kelvin, candela, and mole, with prefixes to indicate multiplication or division by a power of ten; ∼ **unit**, standard quantity of vitamin etc.); ∼ **law**, body of rules regarded by nations as governing their mutual behaviour in peace and war; hence ∼ITY (-ă'l-) *n.*, ∼LY² *adv.* **2.** *n.* contest (usu. in sports) between representatives of different nations; such representative. **3.** (*I*∼). one of four associations founded to promote socialist or communist action (1864–1876, 1889–, 1919–1943, 1938–). **4.** member of any of these associations. [f. INTER- + NATION + -AL]

Internätiona'le (ĭ-; -ah'l) *n.* **1.** the ∼, (orig. French)

For other words in *inter-* **see** INTER-.

revolutionary song adopted by socialists. **2.** = prec. **3.**
[F, fem. of *international* adj. f. prec.]

interna'tional∥ist *n.* **1.** one who advocates community of interests and friendly co-operation between nations; supporter of INTERNATIONAL 3; so ∼ISM (3) *n.* **2.** one versed in international law. [f. INTERNATIONAL + -IST]

interna'tionaliz∥e, -īs∥e (-īz), *v.t.* make international, esp. bring (territory etc.) under combined protection etc. of different nations; hence ∼A′TION *n.* [f. INTERNATIONAL + -IZE]

*****i'nterne.** Var. of INTERN².

interne'cine *a.* mutually destructive. [orig. = deadly, f. L *internecinus* f. *internecio* massacre f. INTER(*necare* kill) slaughter; see -INE¹]

internee'. See INTERN¹.

inte'r'nist *n.* specialist in internal diseases; *general practitioner. [f. INTERNAL + -IST]

inte'r'nment. See INTERN¹.

internu'ncial (-shǎl) *a.* of an internuncio; (of nerves) communicating between different parts of the system. [f. foll. + -AL]

internu'nciō (-shiō) *n.* (*pl.* ∼s). Pope's ambassador when or where no nuncio is employed; (Hist.) minister representing (esp. Austrian) government at Constantinople. [f. It. *internunzio* f. L INTER(*nuntius* messenger)]

interōcē'ptive *a.* (Biol.) relating to stimuli produced within an organism, esp. in the viscera [irreg. f. L *internus* interior + -o- + RECEPTIVE]

interpa'ge *v.t.* print or insert on intermediate pages. [f. INTER- + PAGE³]

inter'pĕll∥āte *v.t.* (In Continental etc. parliaments) interrupt order of the day by demanding explanation from (Minister concerned); so ∼A′TION, ∼ātor, *ns.* [f. L INTER(*pellare* thrust f. *pellere* drive) + -ATE³]

interpe'nĕtr∥āte *v.t.* & *i.* penetrate thoroughly, pervade; penetrate reciprocally; so ∼A′TION *n.*, ∼ATIVE *a.* [f. INTER- + PENETRATE]

i'nterplay *n.* reciprocal action; operation of two things on each other. [f. INTER- + PLAY³]

interplea'd *v.i.* & *t.* (cause to) litigate with each other in order to settle a point in which a third party is concerned. [ME, f. AF *enterpleder* (as INTER-, PLEAD)]

I'nterpŏl (I'-) *n.* International Criminal Police Commission. [abbr.]

inte'r'pol∥āte *v.t.* make insertions in (book etc.), esp. so as to give false impressions as to date etc.; introduce (words) thus; interpose orally; (Math. etc.) insert (intermediate terms) in series, estimate from known values etc. (others lying in the same range); so ∼A′TION, ∼ator, *ns.* [f. L INTER(*polare* cogn. w. *polire* POLISH¹) furbish up + -ATE³]

interpō's∥e (-z) *v.* **1.** *v.t.* insert, make intervene, (between); put forth, introduce, (veto, objection, authority, etc.) by way of interference; say (quoted words) as an interruption. **2.** *v.i.* intervene (between disputants etc.), make an interruption. **3.** Hence ∼AL *n.* [f. F *interposer* f. L INTER(*ponere* put; see POSE²]

interposi'tion (-z-) *n.* interposing; thing interposed; interference. [ME f. OF, or f. L *interpositio* f. INTER-(*ponere posit-* place); see -ITION]

inte'r'prĕt *v.* **1.** *v.t.* expound the meaning of (abstruse or foreign words, writings, dreams, etc.); make out the meaning of; bring out the meaning of; render, by artistic representation or performance; explain, understand, in specified manner (*we interpret this as a threat*). **2.** *v.i.* act as interpreter. **3.** Hence or cogn. ∼ABLE, ∼ATIVE, ∼IVE, *adjs.*, ∼A′TION *n.* [ME, f. OF *interpreter* or f. L *interpretari* explain, translate (INTERpres -pretis explainer)]

inte'r'prĕt∥er *n.* one who interprets; one whose office it is to translate the words of persons speaking different languages, esp. orally in their presence; hence ∼ership, ∼ress¹, *ns.* [ME f. AF *interpretour*, OF *interpreteur* f. LL *interpretator -oris* (as prec.; see -OR)]

interrĕ'gn∥um *n.* (*pl.* ∼ums or ∼a). period during

which State has no normal ruler, esp. between end of king's reign and accession of successor; interval, pause. [L INTER(*regnum* REIGN¹)]

interrĕlā't∥ĕd *a.* mutually related or connected; so ∼ION, ∼ionSHIP, *ns.* [f. INTER- + p.p. of RELATE]

intĕ'rrogāt∥e *v.t.* ask questions of (person etc.), esp. closely or formally; obtain information-signal from (automatic device); so ∼OR *n.* [ME, f. L INTER(*rogare* ask) + -ATE³]

interrogā'tion *n.* interrogating; question; ∼ point etc., QUESTION¹-mark. [ME f. F, or f. L *interrogatio* (as prec.; see -ATION)]

interro'gative *a.* & *n.* **1.** *a.* of, or having the form or force of, a question; of inquiry (*an interrogative tone*); (Gram.) used in questions (*interrogative* PRONOUN); hence ∼LY² (-vlĭ) *adv.* **2.** *n.* interrogative word, esp. pronoun. [f. LL *interrogativus* (as INTERROGATE; see -IVE)]

interro'gatory *a.* & *n.* **1.** *a.* of inquiry (*an interrogatory tone*). **2.** *n.* question, set of questions, esp. (Law) one formally put to accused person etc. [f. LL *interrogatorius* (as INTERROGATE; see -ORY)]

in terrōrem (ĭn tĕrōr'ĕm) *adv.* as a warning. [L]

interru'pt *v.t.* act so as to prevent from proceeding continuously (action, process, speech, person speaking, etc., or abs.); obstruct (view etc.); break the continuity of; hence or cogn. ∼ION *n.*, ∼IVE, ∼ORY, *adjs.* ∼ed screw (with part of thread cut away); hence or cogn. ∼ION *n.*, ∼IVE, ∼ORY, *adjs.* [ME, f. L INTER(*rumpere rupt-* break)]

interru'pt∥er, -or, *ns.* one who interrupts; device for interrupting esp. electric current. [f. prec. + -ER¹, -OR]

inter se (ĭnter sē') *adv.* between or among themselves. [L]

intersĕ'ct *v.* **1.** *v.t.* divide (thing) by passing or lying across it. **2.** *v.i.* (Of lines etc.) cross or cut each other. [f. L INTER(*secare sect-* cut)]

intersĕ'ction *n.* intersecting; point, line, elements, common to intersecting lines, surfaces, sets; place where two roads intersect; hence ∼AL *a.* [f. L *intersectio* (as prec.; see -ION)]

i'ntersĕx *n.* condition of being abnormally intermediate between male and female; individual in this condition. [f. INTER- + SEX]

intersĕ'xual (-ksŭ-, -kshŏŏ-) *a.* existing between the sexes; of intersex; so ∼ITY (-ă'l-) *n.*, ∼LY² *adv.* [f. INTER- + SEXUAL]

i'nterspāce *n.*, & *v.t.* **1.** *n.* interval of space or time. **2.** *v.t.* put interspace(s) between. [ME, f. INTER- + SPACE¹]

interspĕr's∥e *v.t.* scatter, place here and there (between, among); diversify (thing or things) *with* (others so scattered); hence ∼ION (-shon) *n.* [f. L INTER(*spergere spers-* = *spargere* scatter)]

*****i'nterstāte** *a.* existing, carried on, between States esp. of the US. [f. INTER- + STATE¹]

inte'r'stice *n.* intervening space; chink, crevice. [f. L *interstitium* f. INTER(*sistere stit-* stand)]

intersti'tial (-shǎl) *a.* of, forming, occupying, interstice(s). [f. as prec. + -AL]

intertrī'gō *n.* (*pl.* ∼s). (Path.) inflammation by rubbing of one area of skin on another. [L, f. INTER(*terere trit-* rub)]

intertwi'ne *v.* **1.** *v.t.* entwine (things, one *with* another). **2.** *v.i.* become entwined. **3.** Hence ∼MENT (-nm-) *n.* [f. INTER- + TWINE]

i'nterval *n.* **1.** intervening time or space; pause; break, gap, esp. in theatre etc. performance; ∼ signal (indicating continuity of radio transmission during short interval in broadcast programme); at ∼s, here and there and then and then. **2.** (Mus.) difference of pitch between two sounds, in melody or harmony. **3.** distance between persons or things in respect of qualities. **4.** Hence **interva'llic** *a.* [ME, ult. f. L INTER(*vallum* rampart) space between ramparts, interval]

intervē'n∥e *v.i.* come in as something extraneous;

occur in the mean time; (of person or thing) come between so as to prevent or modify result etc. (*between* persons, *in* affair); (Law) interpose in lawsuit to which one was not an original party (‖esp. of Queen's Proctor in divorce cases), whence ∼ER¹,⁴ *n*.; lie, be situated, *between*; so ∼ient *a.*, **interve'ntion** *n.*, **intervĕ'ntion**IST *n.*, one who favours intervention. [f. L INTER(*venire vent-* come)]

i'nterview (-vū) *n.*, & *v.t.* **1.** *n.* meeting of persons face to face, esp. for purpose of consultation; oral examination of candidate for employment etc.; meeting or conversation between journalist and person whose views are sought for publication; similar meeting as part of radio or television programme. **2.** *v.t.* have interview with (person); hence ∼EE', ∼ER¹, *ns.* [f. F *entrevue* f. *s'entrevoir* see each other (*entre-* INTER-, *voir* f. L *vidēre* see); cf. VIEW]

inter vivos (inter vī'vōs) *adv.* between living persons (esp. of gift as opp. legacy). [L]

intervŏ'lve *v.t.* (arch.) wind, roll up, (things) within each other. [f. INTER- + L *volvere* roll]

interwea've *v.t.* (-wo've; -wo'ven). weave together, interlace, (things, one *with* another); blend (things) intimately. [f. INTER- + WEAVE¹]

interwi'nd *v.t.* & *i.* (-wou'nd). wind together. [f. INTER- + WIND³]

intĕ'st|ate *a.* & *n.* **1.** *a.* (Of person) not having made a will (*he died intestate*); hence ∼ACY *n.* **2.** *n.* intestate person. [ME, f. L IN²(*testatus* p.p. of *testari* make will f. *testis* witness); see -ATE²]

intĕ'stin|e¹ *n.* (in sing. or *pl.*) lower part of alimentary canal from pyloric end of stomach to anus; **large** ∼e, caecum, colon, and rectum; **small** ∼e, duodenum, jejunum, and ileum; so ∼AL *a.* [f. L *intestinum* neut. adj. (as n.); see foll.]

intĕ'stine² *a.* (arch.) (Of war etc.) internal, domestic, civil. [f. L *intestinus* internal (*intus* within)]

*****inthrall.** Var. of ENTHRAL.

inthrŏnīzā'tion. See ENTHRONIZATION.

i'ntimacy *n.* state of being intimate; (euphem.) sexual intercourse. [f. foll. + -ACY]

i'ntimate¹ *a.* & *n.* **1.** *a.* close in acquaintance, familiar, (*intimate friend, friendship*); (euphem.) having sexual intercourse *with*; (of connection etc.) close; (of knowledge etc.) resulting from close familiarity; (of mixing etc.) thorough; essential, intrinsic; closely personal; (of diary) recording emotions etc. frankly; promoting close personal relationships; hence ∼LY² (-tlĭ) *adv.* **2.** *n.* intimate friend. [f. as foll.; see -ATE²]

i'ntim|āte² *v.t.* make known, state, announce, (fact, wish, *that*); imply, hint; so ∼A'TION *n.* [f. LL *intimare* announce f. L *intimus* inmost + -ATE³]

inti'mid|āte *v.t.* overawe with fear, esp. in order to influence conduct; hence ∼A'TION, ∼ĀTOR, *ns.* [f. med. L IN¹(*timidare* f. *timidus* TIMID) + -ATE³]

inti'nction *n.* dipping of the Eucharistic bread in the wine, to enable the communicant to receive both elements together. [f. LL *intinctio* f. L IN¹(*tingere tinct-* TINGE)]

‖**inti'tule** *v.t.* entitle (Act of Parliament etc.; usu. in *p.p.*). [f. OF *intituler* f. LL IN¹(*titulare* f. L *titulus* title)]

i'nto (bef. vowel -ŏŏ, bef. consonant -o) *prep.* **1.** Expr. motion or direction to a point within a thing, lit. or fig., (*come into the garden; throw it into the fire; look into the box, the matter, the future; inquire into it; get into trouble;* COME *into property; ran into a pillar; 4 (divided) into 20 = 5; watching far into the night*). **2.** Expr. change, condition, result, (*turn stones into gold; translate into English; grow into an adult; collect them into heaps; divide them into three classes; flogged into submission*). **3.** (colloq.) interested in; knowledgeable about. [OE *in(n)tō* (as IN², TO¹)]

intŏ'lerab|le *a.* that cannot be endured; hence ∼LENESS (-beln-), ∼LY² *adv.* [ME f. OF, or f. L IN²(*tolerabilis* TOLERABLE)]

intŏ'ler|ant *a.* not tolerant (*of*, esp. religious opinions differing from one's own); hence or cogn. ∼ANCE *n.*, ∼ANTLY² *adv.* [f. L IN²(*tolerans* TOLERANT)]

i'ntonāte *v.t.* intone. [f. med. L *intonare* (see INTONE) + -ATE³]

intonā'tion *n.* reciting in intoning voice; (Ch. Mus.) opening phrase of plainsong melody; utterance or production of musical tones; modulation of voice, accent. [f. med. L *intonatio* (as foll.; see -ATION)]

intō'ne *v.t.* recite (psalm, prayer, etc., or abs.) with prolonged sounds, esp. in monotone; utter with particular tone. [f. med. L IN¹(*tonare* f. L *tonus* TONE¹)]

in toto (in tō'tō) *adv.* completely. [L]

intŏ'xicant *a.* & *n.* intoxicating (liquor). [f. foll. + -ANT]

intŏ'xic|āte *v.t.* make drunk; excite, exhilarate, beyond self-control (*intoxicated with* or *by*); hence ∼ATING² *a.*, ∼A'TION *n.* [f. med. L IN¹(*toxicare* poison f. L *toxicum*; see TOXIC) + -ATE³]

intra- *pref.* forming *adjs.* usu. f. *adjs.*, w. senses 'on the inside, within' as: ∼cra'nial, within the skull; ∼mur'al, existing or done within walls, forming part of ordinary university teaching or studies; ∼mu'scular, in(to) muscle(s); ∼na'tional, (not inter)national; ∼-uterine, within the womb; ∼ve'nous, in(to) vein(s). [f. L *intra* inside]

inträ'ct|able *a.* not docile, refractory; (of thing) not easily dealt with; hence ∼ABI'LITY, ∼ABLENESS (-beln-), *ns.*, ∼ABLY *adv.* [f. L IN²(*tractabilis* TRACTABLE)]

intra'dŏs *n.* lower or inner curve of arch. [F INTRA(*dos* back f. L *dorsum*)]

inträ'nsig|ent (-s-, -z-) *a.* & *n.* **1.** *a.* uncompromising, esp. in politics; so ∼ENCE *n.* **2.** *n.* intransigent person. [f. F *intransigeant* f. Sp. *los intransigentes* extreme republicans in Cortes, ult. f. as IN-² + L TRANS(*igere* = *agere* act) come to an understanding; see -ENT]

intra'nsĭtive (-ă'-, -ah'-; -s-, -z-) *a.* (Gram.) that does not take a direct object (cf. TRANSITIVE); hence ∼LY² (-vlĭ) *adv.* [f. LL IN²(*transitivus* TRANSITIVE)]

i'ntrant *n.* (arch.) one who enters a college, association, religious order, etc. [L *intrare* enter; see -ANT]

intrĕ'pid *a.* fearless, brave; hence **intrepi'd**ITY *n.*, ∼LY² *adv.* [f. F *intrépide* or f. L IN²(*trepidus* alarmed)]

i'ntric|ate *a.* perplexingly entangled or complicated; involved; obscure; hence ∼ACY *n.*, ∼ately² (-tlĭ) *adv.* [ME, f. L IN¹(*tricare* f. *tricae* tricks); see -ATE²]

i'ntrigant *n.* (*fem.* ∼e). intriguer. [f. F *intriguant* (*intriguer*; see INTRIGUE¹, -ANT)]

intriguant(e). Var. of prec.

intri'gu|e¹ (-ē'g) *v.* **1.** *v.i.* carry on underhand plot; employ secret influence (*with*); (arch.) have secret amour (*with*); hence ∼ER¹ (-ē'ger) *n.* **2.** *v.t.* puzzle, rouse the interest or curiosity of. [f. F *intriguer* f. It. *intrigare* f. L (as INTRICATE)]

intri'gue² (-ē'g) *n.* underhand plotting or plot; (arch.) secret amour. [F, f. It. *intrigo* (*intrigare*; see prec.)]

intri'ns|ic *a.* belonging naturally, inherent, essential, (*intrinsic value*); hence ∼ICALLY *adv.* [ME, = interior, f. F *intrinsèque* f. LL *intrinsecus* f. L *intrinsecus* adv. inwardly]

i'ntrŏ *n.* (*pl.* ∼s). (colloq.) introduction. [abbr.]

intro- *pref.* w. sense 'into', as: ∼fle'xion, inward bending; ∼gre'ssion, going or coming in; ∼susce'ption, intussusception. [f. L *intro* to the inside]

introdū'ce *v.t.* **1.** bring in; place in, insert; bring into use (custom, idea, improvement, etc., into place, system, etc.). **2.** usher in, bring forward, (matter etc.); begin, come immediately before the start of. **3.** make known, esp. in formal manner (person, oneself, to another); present (broadcast programme etc.) to audience. **4.** draw attention or extend understanding of (person to subject etc.) for first time; bring (bill etc.) before Parliament etc. **5.** So **introdŭ'ct**ORY *a.* [ME, f. L INTRO(*ducere duct-* lead)]

introdū'ction *n.* introducing; thing introduced; preliminary explanatory matter prefixed to book, lecture, etc.; introductory treatise; formal presentation of one person to another; **letter of** ∼ (given by one person to another and introducing him to a third). [ME f. OF, or f. L *introductio* (as prec.; see -ION)]

introit (-oi't, ĭ'-) n. (Eccl.) psalm or antiphon sung or said while priest approaches altar to celebrate Eucharist. [ME f. OF, f. L *introitus* f. INTRO(*ire it-* go)]

introjĕ'ction n. (Psych.) unconscious incorporation of external ideas into one's own mind. [f. INTRO- after *projection*]

intromi't v.t. (-tt-). (arch.) let in, admit, (*into*); insert; so **intromi'ssion** (-shon) n., (esp. Sc. Law) intermeddling with the property of another, ~tENT a., (esp., Biol., of male organ) copulatory. [f. L INTRO(*mittere miss-* send) introduce]

introspĕ'ct v.i. examine one's own thoughts and feelings; hence ~ION n., examination or observation of one's own mental processes, ~IVE a. [f. L INTRO-(*spicere spect-* = *specere* look)]

introvĕr'sion n. introverting (esp. Psych., opp. EXTROVERSION; so **i'ntrovĕrt**[1] n. & a., **i'ntrovĕrtED**[1] a., (person) characterized by introversion, unsociable or reserved (person). [f. foll. after *eversion* etc.]

intro|vĕr't[2] v.t. turn (mind, thought) inwards upon itself; (esp. Zool.) withdraw (organ etc.) within its own tube or base, like finger of glove, so ~vĕr'sIBLE a.; hence ~vĕr'sIVE, ~vĕr'tIVE, adjs, [f. mod. L INTRO(*vertere* turn)]

intru'd|e (-rōō'd) v. 1. v.t. thrust, force, (thing *into*); force (thing, one*self*, *on* or *upon* person). 2. v.i. come uninvited, thrust oneself in, (*into* place, company, etc., *on* or *upon* person, his privacy, etc.). 3. impose ~ER[1] n. (e.g. burglar, raiding aircraft). [f. L IN[1]-(*trudere trus-* thrust)]

intru'sion (-rōō'zhon) n. intruding; forcing in; forcing oneself in (*into, on, upon*); (Geol.) body of rock forced between strata etc. while molten; (Law) occupation of vacant estate etc. to which one has no claim; (Hist.) settlement of minister of Church of Scotland without consent of congregation, whence ~IST (2) n.; so **intru'sIVE** (-rōō's-) a. [ME f. OF, or f. med. L *intrusio* (as prec.; see -ION)]

intrŭ'st. See ENTRUST.

i'ntŭb|āte v.t. (Med.) insert tube into (larynx etc.) to keep it open; hence ~A'TION n. [f. IN-[1] + L *tuba* tube + -ATE[3]]

intŭ'it v.t. & i. know by intuition; receive knowledge by direct perception. [f. L IN[1](*tuēri tuit-* look) consider]

intui'tion n. immediate apprehension by the mind without reasoning; immediate apprehension by a sense; immediate insight; hence ~AL a. [f. LL *intuitio* (as prec.; see -ION)]

intui'tion(al)|ism n. (Philos.) doctrine that the perception of truth is by intuition; doctrine that in perception external objects are known immediately by intuition; intuitivism; so ~IST (2) n. [f. INTUI-TION(AL) + -ISM]

intŭ'itive a. of, possessing, perceived by, intuition; hence ~LY[2] (-vlĭ) adv., ~NESS (-vn-) n. [f. med. L *intuitivus* (as INTUIT; see -IVE)]

intŭ'itiv|ism n. doctrine that ethical principles are matters of intuition; so ~IST (2) n. [f. prec. + -ISM]

intŭmĕ'sc|e v.i. swell up; so ~ENCE n., ~ENT a. [f. L IN[1](*tumescere* incept. of *tumēre* swell)]

intussuscĕ'ption n. 1. (Biol.) taking in of foreign matter by living organism, and its conversion into organic tissue. 2. (Path.) inversion of one portion of intestine within another. [F, or mod. L *intussusceptio*, f. L *intus* within + *susceptio* f. SUS(*cipere cept-* = *capere* take) take up; see -ION]

intwi'ne. Var. of ENTWINE.

Inuit. Var. of INNUIT.

inŭ'nction n. smearing or rubbing with oil. [ME, f. L IN[1](*unctio* UNCTION)]

i'nund|āte v.t. overflow, flood, (land etc. *with* water, or fig.: *inundated with inquiries*); so ~A'TION n. [f. IN[1](*undare* flow f. *unda* wave) + -ATE[3]]

inūr'e v. 1. v.t. accustom, habituate, (person etc. *to* esp. unpleasant thing, *to* do), whence ~MENT (-ūr'm-) n. 2. v.i. (esp. Law). come into operation, take effect. [ME, f. AF **eneurer* (**en eure* in use f. *en* in + **eure* f. OF *e(u)vre* work f. L OPERA[1])]

inūr'n v.t. (arch.) put (ashes of cremated body) in an urn. [f. IN-[1] + URN]

in utero (ĭn ū'terō) adv. in the womb, before birth. [L]

inŭ'tile a. (literary). useless; so **inūtĭ'lITY** n. [ME f. F, f. L IN[2](*utilis* useful f. *uti* use; see -IL)]

in vacuo (ĭn vă'kūō) adv. in a vacuum (lit. or fig.). [L]

invā'd|e v.t. make hostile inroad into (country etc.); swarm into; (fig., of sound, disease, feeling, etc.) assail; encroach upon (rights etc.); hence ~ER[1] n. [f. L IN[1](*vadere vas-* go)]

invă'gin|āte v.t. put in a sheath; turn (tube etc.) inside out; so ~A'TION n. [f. IN-[1] + L *vagina* sheath + -ATE[3]]

i'nvalid[1] (-ĭd, -ēd) a. & n. (person) enfeebled or disabled by illness or injury; ~ carriage, chair, diet, etc., (for use by invalids); hence ~ISM (2) n. [f. L IN[2](*validus*; see VALID); pronunc. (-ēd) after F *invalide*]

invalid[2] (ĭ'nvalĕd, -ē'd) v. 1. v.t. disable (person) by illness (usu. in *pass.*); treat as an invalid; remove from active service, send home etc., as an invalid. 2. v.i. become an invalid, go on the sick-list. [f. prec.]

invă'lid[3] a. not valid, esp. having no legal force; hence ~LY[2] adv. [f. as INVALID[1]]

invā'lid|āte v.t. make (esp. argument etc.) INVALID[3]; hence ~A'TION n. [f. med. L IN[2](*validare* f. *validus* VALID) + -ATE[3]]

invali'dĭtý n. lack of validity; bodily infirmity. [f. F *invalidité* or f. med. L *invaliditas* (as INVALID[1]; see -ITY)]

invă'lūab|le a. above valuation, inestimable; hence ~LY[2] adv. [f. IN-[2] + VALUABLE]

I'nvăr, ĭ'-, n. (P) iron-nickel alloy with negligible coefficient of expansion, used in manufacture of clocks and scientific instruments. [abbr. of foll.]

invăr'i|able a. unchangeable; always the same; (Math.) constant, fixed; hence ~ABI'LITY, ~ableNESS (-bln-), ns., ~ABLY adv. [f. F, or LL IN[2](*variabilis* VARIABLE)]

invăr'i|ant a. & n. 1. a. invariable; hence ~ANCE n. 2. n. (Math.) function remaining unchanged when specified transformation is applied. [f. IN-[2] + VARIANT]

invā'sion (-zhon) n. invading, encroachment; so **invā'sIVE** a. [F, or f. LL *invasio* (as INVADE; see -ION)]

invĕ'ctèd a. (Her.) bordered by or consisting of a series of small convex lobes. [f. as INVEIGH + -ED[1]]

invĕ'ctive n. violent attack in words; abusive oratory. [ME f. OF, f. LL *invectivus* a., *invectiva* (*oratio*) as n. (as foll.; see -IVE)]

invei'gh (-vā') v.i. speak violently, rail loudly, *against*. [f. L IN[1](*vehi* pass. of *vehere vect-* go into, assail]

invei'gle (-vē'-, -vā'-) v.t. entice, tempt, guilefully persuade, (*into* place, conduct, etc.; *into* doing); cajole; hence ~MENT (-gelm-) n. [earlier *enve(u)gle* f. AF *envegler*, OF *aveugler* to blind (*aveugle* blind prob. f. Rom. **ab oculis* without eyes)]

invĕ'nt v.t. create by thought, originate, (new method, instrument, etc.); concoct (false story etc.); so ~OR n. (esp. in Law, patentee of invention), ~RESS[1] n. [ME, = discover, f. L IN[1](*venire vent-* come) find, contrive]

invĕ'ntion n. inventing; thing invented, contrivance, esp. one for which patent is granted; fictitious story; (Mus.) short piece developing simple idea; inventiveness; **I~ of the Cross**, (festival on 3 May commemorating) reputed finding of the Cross by Helena mother of Constantine, AD 326. [ME, f. L *inventio* (as prec.; see -ION)]

invĕ'ntive a. able to invent, original in devising; showing originality in devising; hence ~LY[2] (-vlĭ) adv., ~NESS (-vn-) n. [ME f. F *inventif -ive* or f. med. L *inventivus* (as INVENT; see -IVE)]

i′nventory *n.*, & *v.t.* **1.** *n.* detailed list (of goods, furniture, etc.); stock of goods in this; *trader's stock. **2.** *v.t.* enter (goods etc.) in inventory; make inventory of. [ME, f. med. L *inventorium* f. LL *-arium* (as INVENT; see -ORY)]

Inverne′ss (ĭ-) *n.* ∼ **cloak** or **coat, i**∼, man's sleeveless cloak with removable cape. [∼ in Highland, Scotland]

inve′rse (-êr′-, ĭ′n-) *a.* & *n.* **1.** *a.* inverted in position, order, or relation; ∼ **ratio, proportion,** (between two quantities one of which increases in proportion as the other decreases); ∼ **square law** (by which intensity of gravitational force, illumination, etc., decreases in inverse proportion to square of distance); hence ∼LY² (-slĭ) *adv.* **2.** *n.* inverted state; thing that is the direct opposite (*of* another). [f. L *inversus* p.p. of *invertere* (see INVERT)]

inve′rsion (-shŏn) *n.* turning upside down; reversal of normal position, order, or relation, e.g. (Gram.) of order of words, (Meteorol.) of variation of air temperature with altitude; reversal of a ratio; (Mus.) process or result of inverting; (Chem.) reversal of direction of rotation of plane of polarized light; (**sexual**) ∼, homosexuality; so **inve′rsive** *a.* [f. L *inversio* (as foll.; see -ION)]

inve′rt¹ *v.t.* **1.** turn upside down; turn (foot) inwards; ∼**ed comma,** comma placed upside down (single or paired) above the line before quotation, ‖(in *pl.*) quotation-marks. **2.** reverse position, order, or relation, of; (Mus.) change relative position of notes of (chord, interval) by placing lowest note higher, usu. by an octave; subject to inversion; *inverted* PLEAT; ∼**ed snob,** one who admires what a snob dislikes and vice versa. [f. L IN¹(*vertere vers-* turn)]

i′nvert² *n.* inverted arch, as at bottom of sewer; homosexual; ∼ **sugar,** mixture of dextrose and laevulose. [f. prec.]

inve′rtebrate (-at, -āt) *a.* & *n.* **1.** *a.* not having backbone or spinal column or (usu.) notochord; (fig.) lacking firmness of character. **2.** *n.* invertebrate animal or (fig.) person. [f. mod. L IN²(*vertebrata* pl. f. as VERTEBRA; see -ATE²)]

inve′st *v.* **1.** *v.t.* clothe (person etc. *in* or *with*); cover as garment; clothe, endue, (person etc. *with* qualities, insignia of office, rank, etc.). **2.** lay siege to. **3.** employ (money *in* stocks etc.) esp. for profit. **4.** *v.i.* ∼ **in,** put money into (stocks), (colloq.) expend money on (*invest in a car*). **5.** Hence ∼OR *n.* [ME, f. F *investir* or f. L IN¹(*vestire vestit-* clothe f. *vestis* clothing); sense 3 f. It. *investire*]

inve′stig|ate *v.* **1.** *v.t.* examine, inquire into, study carefully; make official inquiry into. **2.** *v.i.* make search or systematic inquiry. **3.** Hence or cogn. ∼A′TION, ∼ātOR, *ns.*, ∼ātIVE, ∼ātORY, *adjs.* [f. L IN¹(*vestigare* track) + -ATE³]

inve′stiture *n.* formal investing of person (*with* office), esp. ceremony at which sovereign confers honours; enduing (*with* attributes). [ME, f. med. L *investitura* (as INVEST; see -URE)]

inve′stment *n.* investing of money; money invested; property in which money is invested; investiture; (arch.) clothing; (Mil.) act of besieging, blockade; ∼ **trust** (that buys and sells shares in selected companies to make profit for its members). [f. INVEST + -MENT]

inve′ter|ate *a.* long-established; (of disease, habit, prejudice, etc.) deep-rooted, obstinate; (of person) habitual (*an inveterate smoker*); hence ∼ACY *n.*, ∼ateLY² (-tlĭ) *adv.* [ME, f. L IN¹(*veterare* make old f. *vetus veteris* old); see -ATE²]

invi′dious *a.* (Of conduct etc.) giving or likely to give offence, esp. by real or seeming injustice etc.; (of thing) likely to excite ill feeling against the possessor; hence ∼LY² *adv.*, ∼NESS *n.* [f. L *invidiosus* (*invidia* ENVY¹; see -IOUS)]

invi′gil|ate *v.i.* keep watch; ‖supervise candidates at examination; hence ∼A′TION, ∼ātOR, *ns.* [f. L IN¹(*vigilare* watch f. *vigil* watchful) + -ATE³]

invi′gor|ate *v.t.* make vigorous; animate; hence ∼ATIVE *a.*, ∼A′TION, ∼ātOR, *ns.* [f. med. L *IN¹(vigorare* make strong) + -ATE³]

invi′nc|ible *a.* unconquerable (lit. or fig.); ∼ible **ignorance** (that cannot be overcome by the ignorant person himself); hence ∼IBI′LITY *n.*, ∼IBLY *adv.* [ME f. OF, f. L IN²(*vincibilis* VINCIBLE)]

invi′ol|able *a.* not to be violated; (of law, person, place, etc.) to be kept sacred from infraction, profanation, etc.; hence ∼ABI′LITY *n.*, ∼ABLY *adv.* [F, or f. L IN²(*violabilis* VIOLABLE)]

invi′olate *a.* (Of law, place, etc.) not violated; unbroken; unprofaned; hence **invi′ol**ACY, ∼NESS (-tn-), *ns.*, ∼LY² (-tlĭ) *adv.* [ME, f. L IN²(*violatus* p.p. of *violare* treat violently); see -ATE²]

invi′sib|le (-z-) *a.* that cannot be seen by the eye, either by nature or because hidden; too small to be seen; (arch.) not prepared to receive callers; ∼le **exports, imports,** items not appearing in lists of exported or imported goods but for which payment is made by or to another country, e.g. shipping and insurance services; ∼le **ink** (for writing words etc. that cannot be seen until the paper is heated or otherwise treated); ∼le **mending** (of clothing etc., so carefully done as to be undetectable); hence **invis**IBI′LITY (-z-), ∼le NESS (-bĕln-), *ns.*, ∼LY² *adv.* [ME f. OF, or f. L IN²(*visibilis* VISIBLE)]

invi′t|e *v.t.*, & *n.* **1.** *v.t.* request courteously to come (*to* dinner, *to* one's house, *in*, etc.); request courteously (*to* do what is presumably agreeable); solicit courteously (suggestions, opinions, confidences); bring on, tend to bring on, (thing) unintentionally; (of thing) present inducements, attract, whence ∼ING² *a.*; so **invit**A′TION, ∼EE′, *ns.*, ∼atORY *a.* **2.** *n.* (Ĭ′-, -ī′t). (colloq.) invitation. [f. F *inviter* f. L *invitare*]

in vitro (ĭn vĭ′trō, vē′-) *adv.* (Biol.) in a test-tube or other laboratory environment (opp. foll.). [L, = in glass]

in vivo (ĭn vē′vō) *adv.* (Biol.) in the living body. [L]

invocā′tion *n.* **1.** invoking, calling upon God etc. in prayer; **the** ∼, (esp. the words 'In the name of the Father' etc. as used by preacher before sermon. **2.** appeal to one's muse for inspiration or assistance in poem. **3.** Hence **invoca**TORY (ĭnvŏ′ka-, ĭ′nvokā-) *a.* [ME f. OF, f. L *invocatio -onis* (as INVOKE; see -ATION)]

i′nvoice *n.*, & *v.t.* **1.** *n.* list of goods shipped or sent, or services performed, with prices and charges. **2.** *v.t.* make invoice of (goods); send invoice to (person). [app. orig. *invoyes* pl. of *invoy* = ENVOY¹; *-ce* as in *dice, truce*]

invo′ke *v.t.* call on (deity etc.) in prayer as witness; appeal to (law, person's authority, etc.); summon (spirit) by charms; ask earnestly for (vengeance, help, etc.). [f. F *invoquer* f. L IN¹(*vocare* call)]

i′nvolucr|e (-lōō′ker, -lŭ′-) *n.* covering, envelope; (Anat.) membranous envelope; (Bot.) whorl of bracts surrounding inflorescence; hence ∼AL *a.* [F, or f. L *involucrum* (as INVOLVE)]

invo′luntar|y *a.* done without exercise of the will, unintentional; (of limb, muscle, movement) not controlled by the will; hence ∼iLY² *adv.*, ∼iNESS *n.* [f. LL IN²(*voluntarius* VOLUNTARY)]

i′nvolute (-ūt, -ōōt) *a.* & *n.* **1.** *a.* involved, intricate. **2.** curled spirally. (Bot.) rolled inwards at edges. **3.** *n.* (Geom.) locus of point fixed on straight line that rolls without sliding on a curve and is in the plane of that curve (cf. EVOLUTE). [f. L *involutus* p.p. of *involvere* (see INVOLVE)]

i′nvoluted (-ūt-, -ōōt-) *a.* complicated, abstruse; = prec. 2. [f. prec. + -ED¹]

involu′tion (-lōō′-) *n.* involving; entanglement; intricacy; curling inwards; part so curled; (Math.) raising of quantity to any power. [f. L *involutio* (as foll.; see -ION)]

invo′lve *v.t.* **1.** wrap (thing *in* another); wind spirally. **2.** entangle (person, thing, *in* difficulties, mystery, etc.); implicate (person *in* charge, crime, etc.);

For other words in *in-* see IN-¹ or (esp.) IN-².

include (*in*); imply, entail. **3.** (in *p.p.*) concerned (*in*), in question; complicated in thought or form (*an involved sentence*). [ME, f. L IN¹(*volvere volut-* roll)]

invŏ'lvement (-vm-) *n.* involving or being involved (*in*, *with*); financial embarrassment; complicated affair. [f. prec. + -MENT]

invŭ'lner|able *a.* that cannot be wounded or hurt (esp. fig.); hence ∼ABI'LITY *n.*, ∼ABLY *adv.* [f. L IN²(*vulnerabilis* VULNERABLE)]

i'nward *a.*, *n.*, & *adv.* **1.** *a.* situated within; mental, spiritual; directed towards the inside, coming in; fully acquainted *with*. **2.** *n.* (in *pl.*) entrails. **3.** *adv.* inwards. [OE *innanweard* (*innan* IN²; see -WARD)]

i'nwardly *adv.* on the inside; (of speaking) inaudibly, not aloud; in mind or spirit. [OE *inweardlīce* (as prec., -LY²)]

i'nwardness *n.* inner nature, essence; quality of being inward; spirituality; close familiarity. [f. INWARD + -NESS]

i'nwards (-z) *adv.* (Of motion or position) towards the inside; within the mind or soul. [ME, f. INWARD adv.; see -WARDS]

inwea've, enwea've, *v.t.* (-wo've; -wo'ven). weave in (thing *with* another, lit. or fig.). [f. IN-¹, EN-¹ + WEAVE¹]

inwrap. Var. of ENWRAP.

inwreathe. Var. of ENWREATHE.

inwrou'ght (ĭnraw't, before *n.* ĭ'n-) *a.* (Of fabric) decorated (*with* pattern); (of pattern) wrought (*in* or *on* fabric); (fig.) intimately blended (*with*). [f. IN² + WROUGHT]

inya'la (-ah'-) *n.* (*pl.* same.) large S. Afr. antelope (*Tragelaphus angasi*). [f. Zulu *inxala*]

iod-. See IODO-.

iŏ'dic *a.* containing iodine in chem. combination, esp. ∼ **acid** (HIO₃); hence **i'od**ATE¹ (3) *n.* [f. IODINE + -IC]

i'odide *n.* (Chem.) binary compound of iodine. [f. foll. + -IDE]

iodin|āte (ĭō'-, ī'o-) *v.t.* treat or impregnate with iodine; so ∼A'TION *n.* [f. foll. + -ATE²]

i'odin|e (-ēn, ĭn) *n.* non-metallic element forming black crystals and violet vapour, resembling chlorine and bromine in chemical properties, used in medicine and photography; alcoholic solution of this as antiseptic; hence ∼ISM (5) *n.*, ∼IZE (5) *v.t.* [f. F *iode* f. Gk *iōdēs* violet-like (*ion* violet; see -OID) + -INE⁵]

iodo-, (esp. bef. vowel) **iod-,** *comb. form.* (Chem.) iodine. [f. prec. + -O-]

iŏ'doform *n.* compound of iodine chemically analogous to chloroform, a pale yellow solid with antiseptic properties. [f. prec. after *chloroform*]

IOM *abbr.* Isle of Man.

i'on *n.* one of the electrically charged particles into which the atoms or molecules of certain substances (esp. salts, acids, and bases) are dissociated by solution in water, and which make such a solution a conductor of electricity; similar particle formed when neutral atom etc. loses or gains electron(s); charged molecule of gas occurring e.g. in air exposed to X-rays; ∼ **exchange**, reaction of interchange between ions of like charge, used in water-softening etc.; ∼ **exchanger**, substance or equipment for this process. [Gk, neut. pres. part. of *eimi* go]

-ion *suf.* forming *ns.* of action, condition, state, etc., usu. f. *vbs.* (*destruction*, *legion*, *objection*, a *suggestion*, *vexation*; cf. -SION, -TION, -XION), occas. corresp. to *adjs.* etc. (*communion*, *union*). [f. or after F, or f. L -*io* -*ionis*]

Iō'nian (ī-) *a.* & *n.* **1.** *a.* of Ionia. **2.** ∼ **mode**, (Mus.) (1) ancient Greek MODE, reputedly soft and effeminate in character, (2) eleventh of church modes (with C as final and G as dominant), corresp. to modern major key of C. **3.** *n.* native or inhabitant of Ionia, esp. member of part of the Hellenic people which occupied Attica, western Asia Minor, Ionian Isles etc. [f. L f. Gk *Iōnios* + -AN]

Iŏ'nic¹ (ī-) *a.* of Ionia; ∼ **dialect** (of Greek); ∼ **order**, (Archit.) Greek ORDER¹ characterized by two lateral volutes of the capital. [f. L f. Gk *Iōnikos*; see -IC]

iŏ'n|ic² *a.* of ions; using ions (*ionic propulsion*); hence ∼ICALLY *adv.* [f. ION + -IC]

iō'nium *n.* naturally occurring radioactive thorium isotope, of mass number 230. [f. ION + -IUM]

i'oniz|e -is|e (-īz), *v.t.* & *i.* convert or be converted into ion(s); ∼**ing radiation** (causing ionization when passing through matter); hence ∼ABLE *a.*, ∼A'TION *n.* [f. ION + -IZE]

iō'nosph|ēre *n.* ionized region of upper atmosphere, able to reflect radio waves for long-distance transmission round the earth; hence ∼ĕ'rIC *a.* [f. ION + -O- + SPHERE]

-ior¹ *suf.*, later or US spelling of -IOUR.

-ior² *suf.* forming *adjs.* of comparison (*senior*, *ulterior*). [L]

iō'ta *n.* ninth Greek letter (I, ι) = i (*iota* SUBSCRIPT); smallest amount, JOT¹. [Gk *iōta*]

IOU (īōū') *n.* signed document bearing these letters followed by specified sum, constituting formal acknowledgement of debt. [= *I owe you*]

-iour, *-ior, *suf.* forming *ns.*, = -I- representing some formative or stem element + -*our* -OR (*paviour*, *saviour*).

-ious *suf.* forming *adjs.* w. sense 'characterized by, full of', esp. corresp. to *ns.* in -*ion* (*cautious, contagious, curious, invidious, religious, spacious, specious, various*). [f. or after F -*ieux* f. L -*iosus* (as -I-, -OUS)]

IOW *abbr.* Isle of Wight.

IPA *abbr.* International Phonetic Alphabet (or Association).

i'pĕcăc *n.* (colloq.) = foll. [abbr.]

ipĕcăcuā'nha (-na) *n.* root of a S. Amer. shrub, used as emetic, diaphoretic, and purgative. [Port., f. Tupi-Guarani *ipekaaguéne* emetic creeper]

ipomoe'a (-ē'a) *n.* twining tropical plant of genus *Ipomoea*, with trumpet-shaped flower, esp. sweet potato. [mod. L, f. Gk *ips ipos* worm + *homoios* like; see -A]

i.p.s. *abbr.* inches per second.

ipse dixit (ĭpsī dĭ'ksĭt) *n.* dogmatic statement resting merely on speaker's authority. [L, = he himself (the master) said it, transl. Gk *autos epha* used of Pythagoras]

ipsilă'teral *a.* belonging to or occurring on same side of body. [irreg. f. L *ipse* self + -I- + LATERAL]

ipsissima verba (ĭpsĭsīma vĕr'ba) *n. pl.* the precise words. [L]

ipso facto (ĭpsō fă'ktō) *adv.* by that very fact or act; thereby. [L]

IQ *abbr.* intelligence quotient.

-ique. See -IC.

ir-¹,² *prefs.*, assim. forms of IN-¹,² before *r*.

IR *abbr.* infra-red.

Ir *symb.* iridium.

IRA *abbr.* Irish Republican Army.

ira'dĕ (-ah'dĭ) *n.* (Hist.) written decree of Sultan of Turkey. [Turk., f. Arab. '*irāda* will]

Irā'nian (ī-) *a.* & *n.* **1.** *a.* of Iran (Persia); (of languages) of the group of Indo-European languages including Persian, Pashto, Avestan, and Kurdish. **2.** *n.* Iranian person or language-group. [f. *īrān* native name of Persia + -IAN]

Ira'qi (Irah'kĭ) *a.* & *n.* (native, inhabitant, or modern Arabic dialect) of Iraq. [f. *Iraq* in SW Asia + -I]

irā'sc|ible (ĭr-, ĭr-) *a.* irritable, hot-tempered; hence ∼IBI'LITY *n.*, ∼IBLY *adv.* [ME f. F, f. LL *irascibilis* f. L *irasci* grow angry (*ira* anger; see -IBLE)]

irā'te (ĭr-, ĭr-) *a.* angry, enraged; hence ∼LY² (-tlĭ) *adv.* [f. L *iratus* (*ira* anger); see -ATE²]

IRBM *abbr.* intermediate-range ballistic missile.

īre *n.* (rhet. or poet.) anger; hence ∼'FUL (īr'f-) *a.* [ME f. OF, f. L *ira*]

irē'nic(al) (īr-, ĭr-) *adjs.* aiming or aimed at peace. [f. Gk *eirēnikos* (*eirēnē* peace, -IC, -ICAL)]

irē'nicŏn. Var of EIRENICON.

iridā'ceous (ĭr-, ĭr-; -shus) *a.* (Bot.) of the iris family (Iridaceae). [f. mod. L *iridaceus* (as IRIS; see -ACEOUS)]

iridĕ'sc|ent *a.* showing colours like those of rainbow;

changing colour with position; hence ∼ENCE *n*. [f. L
IRIS + -ESCENT]

iri′dium (ĭr-, īr-) *n*. white metallic element of the
platinum group used esp. in hard alloys. [mod. L, f. L
IRIS + -IUM]

īr′is *n*. **1.** flat circular coloured membrane behind
cornea of eye, with circular opening (PUPIL) in centre.
2. perennial herbaceous plant of genus *Iris* chiefly
with tuberous roots, sword-shaped leaves, and showy
flowers. **3.** ∼ (**diaphragm**), adjustable diaphragm
of thin overlapping plates for regulating size of
central hole, e.g. for admission of light to lens or lens
system. [ME f. L *iris iridis* f. Gk *iris iridos* (goddess of)
rainbow, iris]

Ir′ish (īr′-) *a*. & *n*. **1.** *a*. of or from Ireland or its
inhabitants; ||∼ **bridge**, open stone drain carrying
water across road; *Irish* BULL[4]; ∼ **coffee**, = GAELIC
coffee; ∼ **deer** or **elk**, large extinct deer of Ireland and
England; ∼ **Gaelic**, Irish (language); ∼**man**, (1)
man of Irish birth or descent, (2) prickly NZ shrub; ∼
moss, dried carrageen; ∼ **Sea** (between England
& Wales and Ireland); *Irish* STEW[2]; ∼ **terrier**
(rough-haired reddish-brown kind); ∼ **whisk(e)y**,
kind distilled in Ireland esp. from malted barley;
∼**woman**, woman of Irish birth or descent. **2.**
resembling the Irish, esp. w. ref. to their reputation
for illogicality (cf. BULL[4]). **3.** Hence ∼ER[1] *n*., (colloq.)
Irish person, ∼ISM (2, 4) *n*., ∼IZE (3) *v.t.*, ∼RY (5) *n*. **4.**
n. Celtic language of Ireland; (colloq.) bad temper;
the ∼, (pl.) persons of Irish birth or descent. [ME, f.
OE *Iras* the Irish + -ISH[1]]

īri′tis *n*. inflammation of the iris. [G, irreg. f. as
IRIS + -ITIS]

îrk *v.t.* disgust, tire, bore, esp. *it irks me, him*, etc. [ME,
of unkn. orig.]

îr′ksome *a*. tedious, tiresome; hence ∼LY[2] (-mlĭ) *adv.*,
∼NESS (-mn-) *n*. [ME, = tired etc., f. prec. + -SOME[1]]

||**IRO** *abbr.* Inland Revenue Office.

irŏ′kŏ *n*. (*pl.* ∼s). (wood of) Afr. tree of genus
Chlorophora. [Ibo]

iron[1] (ī′ern) *n*. & *a*. **1.** *n*. silver-white widely distributed
metal of great strength, much used for tools etc.; (fig.,
as type of unyieldingness: *a man of, a will of, iron*). **2.**
preparation of iron as tonic. **3.** tool or implement
made of iron (*branding, curling, grappling, -iron*); golf-
-club with iron or steel head and sloping face for
lofting ball; implement (orig. of iron) with smooth
flat base and means of heating used to smooth clothes
etc.; (usu. in *pl.*) fetter (esp. **in** ∼**s**, fettered at ankles
or handcuffed); (esp. in *pl.*) stirrup; (usu. in *pl.*) leg-
-support to rectify malformations etc. **4. the** ∼
entered into his soul [Ps. 105: 18, L mistranslation
of Heb. 'his person entered into the iron', i.e. fetters],
he became permanently affected by ill-treatment
etc.; **strike while the** ∼ **is hot**, act promptly at a
good opportunity; **have** (**too**) **many** ∼**s in the fire**
(undertakings or resources). **5.** *a*. of iron; very robust
(*iron constitution*); firm, unyielding, merciless, (*iron
will, rule*). **6. I**∼ **Age**, (esp. early part of) era of iron
implements and weapons; ∼**-bark**, species of
eucalyptus with thick solid bark and hard wood; ∼-
-bound, bound with iron, (of coast) rock-bound,
(fig.) rigorous, hard and fast; I∼ **Chancellor**,
Bismarck; ∼**clad**, (*a*.) clad in, protected with, iron,
(fig.) impregnable, rigorous, (*n*., Hist.) ship cased
with plates of iron; I∼ **Cross**, German military
decoration; I∼ **Curtain**, (fig.) barrier to passage of
persons and information at (esp. Western) limit of
Soviet sphere of influence; I∼ **Duke**, 1st Duke of
Wellington; ∼**-grey** *a*. & *n*., (of) the colour of freshly
broken iron; ∼ **horse**, (arch.) locomotive engine; ∼
lung, rigid case fitted over patient's body, used for
administering prolonged artificial respiration by
means of mechanical pumps; ∼**master**, manufacturer of iron; ∼**mould**, *∼**mold**, spot caused
by iron-rust or ink-stain; *iron* PYRITES; ∼ **ration**,
(soldier's) modicum of tinned etc. food to be used

only in emergency; I∼**sides**, man of great bravery,
esp. (as *pl*.) Cromwell's troopers in Civil War;
∼**stone**, (1) hard iron-ore, (2) kind of hard white
pottery; ∼**ware**, (esp. domestic) articles made of
iron; ∼**work**, work in iron, things made of iron;
∼**works** (as *sing.* or *pl*.), place where iron is smelted
or iron goods are made. [OE *īren, īsern*, = OS, OHG
īsarn, ON *īsarn*, Goth. *eisarn* f. Gmc **īsarnam*, prob.
f. Celt.]

iron[2] (ī′ern) *v.t.* furnish or cover with iron; shackle
with irons; smooth (clothes etc.) with flat-iron etc.
(see prec., sense 3), whence ∼ING[1] (1, 5) *n*. (∼**ing**-
-board, flat surface usu. on legs of adjustable height,
to support clothes etc. being ironed); ∼**on** *a*., that
can be attached to fabric by ironing; ∼ **out**, (fig.)
remove (difficulties etc.); hence ∼ER[1] (1, 2) *n*.
[ME, f. prec.]

irŏ′n‖ic(al) *adjs.* of (the nature of), using, said in,
addicted to, irony; hence ∼ICALLY *adv.* [f. F *ironique* or
f. LL f. Gk *eirōnikos* dissembling (as IRONY[1]; see -IC)]

ī′r‖on‖ist *n*. one who uses irony; so ∼IZE (2) *v.i.* [f. Gk
eirōn dissembler + -IST]

||**i′ronmong‖er** (ī′ernmŭngg-) *n*. dealer in hardware
etc.; hence ∼ERY (1, 2, 3) *n*., (also, sl., firearms). [f.
IRON[1] + MONGER]

ī′rony[1] *n*. expression of one's meaning by language of
opposite or different tendency, esp. simulated
adoption of another's point of view or laudatory
tone for purpose of ridicule; ill-timed or perverse
arrival of event or circumstance in itself desirable, as
if in mockery of the fitness of things; use of language
that has an inner meaning for a privileged audience
and an outer meaning for the persons addressed or
concerned (occas. including speaker; cf. TRAGIC
irony); SOCRATIC *irony*. [f. L f. Gk *eirōneia* simulated
ignorance (*eirōn* dissembler; see -Y[1])]

i′rony[2] (ī′ernĭ) *a*. of or like iron. [ME, f. IRON[1] + -Y[2]]

I′roquoi‖s (ĭ′rokwoi) *n*. (*pl*. same). Amer. Indian of
powerful confederacy of five tribes formerly
inhabiting New York State; hence ∼AN (-oi′an) *a*. &
n., (member or language-group) of Iroquois Indians.
[F, f. Algonquin]

irrā′di‖ant *a*. (rhet.) shining brightly; hence ∼ANCE *n*.
[f. as foll.; see -ANT]

irrā′diāt‖e *v.t.* shine upon; (fig.) throw light on
(subject); light up (face etc. *with* joy etc.); subject to
action of radiation (e.g. sunlight, ultraviolet rays, X-
-rays, or neutrons); hence ∼IVE *a*. [f. L IR[1](*radiare* f.
radius RAY[1] + -ATE[3]]

irrādiā′tion *n*. irradiating; shining, illumination, (lit.
or fig.); apparent extension of edges of illuminated
object seen against dark background. [F, or f. LL
irradiatio (as prec.; see -ATION)]

irrā′tional *a*. & *n*. **1.** *a*. unreasonable, illogical,
absurd; not endowed with reason; (Math., of root
etc.) not rational, not commensurable with the
natural numbers (e.g. non-terminating decimal);
hence ∼ITY (-ă′l-) *n*., ∼IZE (3) *v.t.*, ∼LY[2] *adv.* **2.** *n*.
irrational number, surd. [f. L IR[2](*rationalis* RATIONAL)]

irréclai′mab‖le *a*. that cannot be reclaimed or
reformed; hence ∼LY[2] *adv.* [f. IR-[2] + RECLAIMABLE]

irre′concil‖able *a*. & *n*. **1.** *a*. implacably hostile; (of
ideas etc.) incompatible; hence ∼ABI′LITY,
∼able NESS (-beln-) *ns*., ∼ABLY *adv.* **2.** *n*. uncompromising opponent of political measure etc. [f.
IR-[2] + RECONCILABLE]

irreco′verab‖le (-kŭ′-) *a*. that cannot be recovered or
remedied; hence ∼LY[2] *adv.* [f. IR-[2] + RECOVERABLE]

irrécū′sable (-z-) *a*. that must be accepted. [f. F
irrécusable or f. LL IR[2](*recusabilis* f. L *recusare* refuse; see
RECUSANT, -ABLE)]

irredee′mab‖le *a*. that cannot be redeemed; (of
government annuity) not terminable by repayment;
(of paper currency) for which issuing authority does
not undertake ever to pay coin; irreclaimable,
hopeless, absolute, whence ∼LY[2] *adv.* [f. IR-[2] +
REDEEMABLE]

irrĕdĕ'nt|ist *n.* **1.** (*I~*). advocate of return to Italy of all Italian-speaking districts. **2.** Greek, Pole, etc., of similar views. **3.** So *~*ISM (3) *n.* [f. It. *irredentista* f. (*Italia*) *irredenta* unredeemed (Italy)]

irrĕdū'c|ible *a.* that cannot be brought (*to* desired condition); that cannot be reduced (*irreducible minimum*); that cannot be simplified; hence *~*IBI'LITY *n.*, *~*IBLY *adv.* [f. IR-² + REDUCIBLE]

irrĕ'fragab|le *a.* (Of statement, argument, person) indisputable, unanswerable; (of rules etc.) inviolable; hence *~*LY² *adv.* [f. LL IR²(*refragabilis* f. REfragari oppose); see -ABLE]

irrĕfrǎ'ngĭble (-nj-) *a.* inviolable; (Opt.) incapable of being refracted. [f. IR-² + REFRANGIBLE]

irrĕfūt'able (-rĕ'fū-,-rĭfū'-) *a.* that cannot be refuted; hence *~*ABI'LITY *n.*, *~*ABLY *adv.* [f. LL IR²(*refutabilis* REFUTABLE)]

irrĕ'gūlar *a.* & *n.* **1.** *a.* not regular, contrary to rule or moral principle; abnormal; not of symmetrical form; (of surface) uneven; disorderly; uneven in duration, order, etc.; (of flower) having unequal petals etc.; (Gram., of verb, noun, etc.) not inflected normally; (of troops etc.) not pertaining to regular army; hence or cogn. *~*ITY (-ǎ'r-) *n.*, *~*LY² *adv.* **2.** *n.* (in *pl.*) irregular troops. [ME, f. OF *irreguler* f LL IR²(*regularis* REGULAR)]

irrĕ'lative *a.* unconnected, unrelated, (*to*); having no relations, absolute; irrelevant; hence *~*LY² (-vlĭ) *adv.* [f. IR-² + RELATIVE]

irrĕ'lĕv|ant *a.* not relevant, that does not apply (*to* matter in hand); hence *~*ANCE, *~*ANCY, *ns.*, *~*antLY² *adv.* [f. IR-² + RELEVANT]

irrĕli'g|ion (-jon) *n.* hostility to, or disregard of, religion; hence or cogn. *~*ionIST (2) *n.*, *~*IOUS (-jus) *a.* [f. F *irréligion* or f. L IR²(*religio* RELIGION)]

irrĕmĕ'diab|le *a.* that cannot be remedied; hence *~*LY² *adv.* [f. L IR²(*remediabilis* REMEDIABLE)]

irrĕmi'ssib|le *a.* unpardonable; unalterably obligatory; hence *~*LY² *adv.* [ME f. OF, or f. eccl. L IR²(*remissibilis* REMISSIBLE)]

irrĕmŏ'v|able (-mōō'-) *a.* that cannot be removed, esp. from office; hence *~*ABI'LITY *n.*, *~*ABLY *adv.* [f. IR-² + REMOVABLE)]

irrĕ'parab|le *a.* (Of injury, loss, etc.) that cannot be rectified or made good; hence *~*leNESS (-beln-) *n.*, *~*LY² *adv.* [ME f. OF, f. L IR²(*reparabilis* REPARABLE)]

irrĕplǎ'ceable (-sa-) *a.* not replaceable; of which the loss cannot be made good. [f IR-² + REPLACEABLE]

irrĕprĕ'ssib|le *a.* & *n.* **1.** *a.* that cannot be repressed or restrained; hence *~*LY² *adv.* **2.** *n.* (colloq.) irrepressible person. [f. IR-² + REPRESS +-IBLE]

irrĕproa'ch|able *a.* free from blame, faultless; hence *~*ABI'LITY *n.*, *~*ABLY *adv.* [f. F IR²(*réprochable*, as REPROACH; see -ABLE)]

irrĕsi'st|ible (-zĭ'-) *a.* too strong, convincing, delightful, etc., to be resisted; hence *~*IBI'LITY *n.*, *~*IBLY *adv.* [f. med. L IR²(*resistibilis*, as RESIST; see -IBLE), or f. IR-² + RESISTIBLE]

irrĕ'solute (-zolōōt, -ūt) *a.* undecided, hesitating; lacking in resoluteness; hence or cogn. *~*LY² (-tlĭ) *adv.*, *~*NESS (-tn-), irrĕsolU'TION (-zolōō'shon, -ū'-), *ns.* [f. IR-² + RESOLUTE]

irrĕsŏ'lvable (-z-) *a.* that cannot be resolved into parts; (of problem) that cannot be solved. [f. IR-² + RESOLVABLE]

irrĕspĕ'ctive *a.* *~* **of**, not taking into account, without reference to, (*the posts were filled irrespective of nationality*); hence *~*LY² (-vlĭ) *adv.* [f. IR-² + RESPECTIVE]

irrĕspŏ'ns|ible *a.* not responsible for (esp. one's own) conduct; acting or done without due sense of responsibility; hence *~*IBI'LITY *n.*, *~*IBLY *adv.* [f. IR-² + RESPONSIBLE]

irrĕspŏ'nsive *a.* not responsive (*to*); hence *~*NESS (-vn-) *n.* [f. IR-² + RESPONSIVE]

irrĕtĕ'ntive *a.* (Esp. of memory) not retentive; hence *~*NESS (-vn-) *n.* [f. IR-² + RETENTIVE]

irrĕtrie'v|able *a.* that cannot be retrieved; hence

*~*ABI'LITY *n.*, *~*ABLY *adv.* [f. IR-² + RETRIEVABLE]

irrĕ'ver|ent *a.* lacking reverence; hence or cogn. *~*ENCE *n.*, *~*ĕ'ntIAL (-shal) *a.*, *~*entLY² *adv.* [f. L IR²(*reverens* REVERENT)]

irrĕvĕr's|ible *a.* unalterable; not reversible; hence *~*IBI'LITY *n.*, *~*IBLY *adv.* [f. IR-² + REVERSIBLE]

irrĕ'voc|able *a.* unalterable; gone beyond recall; hence *~*ABI'LITY *n.*, *~*ABLY *adv.* [ME, f. L IR²(*revocabilis* REVOCABLE)]

i'rrig|āte *v.t.* (Of stream etc.) supply (land) with water; water (land) with channels etc.; (Med.) supply (wound etc.) with constant flow of liquid; (fig.) refresh as with moisture; hence or cogn. *~*ABLE, *~*ATIVE, *adjs.*, *~*A'TION, *~*ātOR, *ns.* [f. L IR²(*rigare* moisten) + -ATE³]

i'rrit|able *a.* **1.** quick to anger, touchy; hence *~*ABLY *adv.* **2.** (Of organ etc.) very sensitive to contact etc.; (Biol.) responding actively to physical stimulus. **3.** So *~*ABI'LITY *n.* [f. L *irritabilis* (as IRRITATE¹; see -ABLE)]

i'rrit|ant *a.* & *n.* **1.** *a.* irritating (esp. physically); hence *~*ANCY *n.* **2.** *n.* irritant substance or agent (lit. or fig.). [f. IRRITATE¹ or f. as IRRITATE², +-ANT]

i'rritāt|e¹ *v.t.* **1.** excite to anger, annoy, vex, (*irritated at, by, with, against, that, to find etc.*). **2.** excite, produce uneasy sensation in, (bodily organ etc.); (Biol.) stimulate (organ etc.) to action. **3.** Hence or cogn. irritA'TION *n.*, *~*IVE *a.* [f. L *irritare* i -ATE³]

i'rritāte² *v.t.* (Sc. etc. Law). make null and void, defeat. [f. LL *irritare* f. L IR²(*ritus = ratus* established) invalid + -ATE³]

irrŭ'pt *v.i.* enter forcibly or violently (*into*); so *~*ION *n.* [f. L IR¹(*rumpere rupt-* break)]

*IRS *abbr.* Internal Revenue Service.

Ir'vĭngīte (ẽr'v-) *n.* member of a religious body called by its members the Catholic (and) Apostolic Church. [f. E. *Irving*, minister of Ch. of Scotland d. 1834, on whose principles it was founded, + -ITE¹ (1)]

is. See BE.

Is. *abbr.* Island(s); Isle(s).

Is(a). *abbr.* Isaiah (OT).

Isabĕ'lla, i'sabĕl, (ĭz-) *a.* & *n.* greyish yellow; hence **isabĕ'llINE**¹ (ĭz-) *a.* [f. name *Isabella*, F *Isabelle*; immed. ref. unkn.]

isagŏ'g|ic *a.* introductory; hence *~*ICS *n. pl.*, study of literary and external history of Bible. [f. L f. Gk *eisagōgikos* f. *eisagōgē* introduction (*eis* into, *agōgē* leading f. *agō* to lead), see -IC]

i'satin *n.* (Chem.) crystalline reddish-yellow substance got from indigo by oxidation. [f. Gk *isatis* woad + -IN]

ISBN *abbr.* international standard book number.

ischae'm|ia, *ischē'm|ia, (-k-) *n.* (Med.) reduction of blood supply to part of body; hence *~*IC *a.* [mod. L, f. Gk *iskhaimos* (*iskhō* keep back); see -AEMIA]

i'schi|um (-k-) *n.* (*pl. ~*a). curved bone forming base of each half of pelvis; hence or cogn. *~*ǎ'dIC, *~*AL, *~*A'TIC, *adjs.* [L, f. Gk *iskhion* hip-joint; cf. SCIATIC]

-ise¹. See -IZE.

-ise². *suf.* forming *ns.* of quality, state, or function, (*exercise, expertise, franchise, merchandise*); cf. -ICE. [f. or after F or OF *-ise* f. L *-itia* etc.]

-ise³. See -ISH².

isentrŏ'pic *a.* having equal entropy. [f. ISO- + ENTROPY + -IC]

-ish¹ *suf.* forming *adjs.* (& *advs.*) f. *ns.* etc. **1.** Of nationality (*British, Danish*); w. sense 'belonging to, of the nature of' (*boyish, heathenish*), esp. derog. (*bookish, foppish, stand-offish, uppish*). **2.** With sense 'somewhat' (*reddish, roughish, soonish*). **3.** (colloq.) Denoting approximate time of day or age (*eightish, fortyish*). [OE *-isc, =* OS, OHG *-isc,* ON *-iskr*, Goth. *-isks*]

-ish², -ise³, *suf.* forming *vbs.* (*advertise, blemish, chastise, finish, perish, relish, vanish*). [f. or after F *-iss-* in extended stem of vbs. in *-ir*) f. L *-isc-* incept. suf.]

I'shmael (ĭ'-) *n.* outcast, one at war with society; hence *~*ITE¹ (1)) *n.* [name of son of Abraham and Hagar, Gen. 16: 12] ī′singlass (ī′zĭngglahs) n. 1. whitish semitransparent substance, a form of gelatin, got from viscera of some fish, esp. sturgeon, and used in making jellies, glue, etc. 2. mica. [corrupt. of obs. Du *huisenblas* sturgeon's bladder, assim. to GLASS¹]

Islam (ī′zlahm, -lăm, -lah′m) n. religion of the Muslims, revealed through Muhammad as Prophet of Allah; the Muslim world; hence ∾IC (-ă′m-), ∾ī′TIC, *adjs.*, ∾ISM (3), ∾IST (2, 3), ∾ITE¹ (1), *ns.* [f. Arab. *islām* submission (to God) (*aslama* resign oneself)]

ī′sland (ī′l-) n., & v.t. 1. n. piece of land surrounded by water; (fig.) anything detached or isolated, esp. woodland surrounded by prairie, TRAFFIC *island*; (Naut.) ship's superstructure, bridge, etc.; (Physiol.) detached portion of tissue or group of cells (cf. ISLET); hence ∾ER¹ (4) n. 2. v.t. make into an island, isolate; dot (as) with islands. [OE *īgland* (*ī(e)g* island, LAND¹); -s- by assoc. w. ISLE]

isle (īl) n., & v.t. 1. n. island (poet., or with proper name; *Isle of Wight, British Isles*; usu. of small islands, also of peninsulas, e.g. *Isle of Purbeck*). 2. v.t. (poet.) make into an isle; place (as) on isle. [ME f. OF *ile* f. L *insula*; later ME & OF *isle* after L]

ī′slĕt (ī′l-) n. little island; isolated tract or spot; detached portion of tissue (∾s of Langerhans, groups of pancreatic cells secreting insulin). [OF, dim. of *isle*; see prec., -ET¹]

ism n. (often derog.) any distinctive doctrine or practice (*isms and ologies*). [foll. used as n.]

-ism *suf.* forming abstract *ns.*: (1) of action or its result f. *vbs.* in -IZE (*baptism, organism*); (2) of typical conduct or condition f. *ns.* denoting classes or *adjs.* denoting qualities (*heroism, barbarism, diamagnetism*); (3) of system or principle f. name of subject or founder or connected catchword (*Conservatism, Arianism, jingoism*); (4) of peculiarity in language (*Americanism, Gallicism, archaism*); (5) of pathological condition, esp. induced by excessive use of drug etc. (*alcoholism, dwarfism, Parkinsonism*). [f. or after F -*isme* f. L f. Gk -*ismos* or -*isma* f. -*izō* -IZE]

Ismai′li (ĭzmī′-) n. member of Muslim sect that seceded from Shiah in 9th c., now regarding Aga Khan as their imam. [f. *Ismail* descendant of Muhammad's son-in-law d. 760 + -I]

isn't. See BE.

ī′so- *comb. form.* 1. equal, as: ∾cheim (-kīm), line on map connecting places with same average temperature in winter [f. Gk *kheima* winter weather]; ∾chroma′tic, of same colour; ∾chronous (-ŏ′k-), occupying equal time, occurring at same time; ∾cli′nal (-ī′-), ∾cli′nic (-ī′-), corresponding to equal values of magnetic dip; ∾dyna′mic, corresponding to equal values of (magnetic) force; ∾ge′o-therm, line or surface connecting points in interior of earth having same temperature; ∾gloss, line between areas that differ in one linguistic feature; ∾go′nic, corresponding to equal values of magnetic declination; ∾hel, line on map connecting places with same duration of sunshine [f. Gk *hēlios* sun]; ∾hy′et (-hī′et), line on map connecting places with same amount of rainfall [f. Gk *huetos* rain]; ∾nomy (-ŏ′n-), equality before the law; ∾phote, line of equal brightness or illumination; ∾pleth, line on map connecting places with equal incidence of a meteorological etc. feature [f. Gk *plēthos* fullness]; ∾sei′smal (-ī′z-) n. & a., (line on map) connecting places with equal strength of earthquake shock; ∾there (-ēr), line on map connecting places with same average temperature in summer [f. Gk *theros* summer]. 2. (Chem.) isomeric (esp. of hydrocarbon with branched chain of carbon atoms: *isobutane*). [f. Gk *isos* equal]

ISO *abbr.* ‖(Companion of the) Imperial Service Order; International Organization for Standardization.

ī′sob|ȧr n. line on map connecting places with same atmospheric pressure at a given time or on average

over a given period; curve or formula for physical system at constant pressure; one of two or more isotopes of different elements, with same atomic weight; hence ∾ȧ′rIC a. [f. Gk *isobarēs* of equal weight (as ISO-, *baros* weight)]

īsō′cracy̆ n. (system of government in which all have) equal political power; so ī**socrȧ′t**IC a. [f. Gk *isokratia* (as ISO-, -CRACY)]

īsocy̆′clic a. (Chem.) having molecular ring composed of atoms of one kind. [f. ISO- + CYCLIC]

ī′solāt|e v.t., & n. 1. v.t. place apart or alone; (Chem.) free (substance) from combination with all others; (Electr.) insulate; subject (person etc.) to quarantine; (in *p.p.*) untypical, unique; hence ∾ABLE, ī′solABLE, *adjs.*, ∾OR n. 2. n. isolated thing. [orig. in p.p., f. F *isolé* f. It. *isolato* f. LL *insulatus* f. L *insula* island; see -ATE³, -ED¹]

ī′solāting a. in vbl senses; (of language) having each element as an independent word without inflexions. [f. prec. + -ING²]

īsolā′tion n. isolating or being isolated; in ∾, considered without regard to relationships; ∾ hospital, ward, (for patients with contagious or infectious diseases); hence ∾ISM (3) n., policy of holding aloof from affairs of other countries or political groups, ∾IST (2) n., advocate of this policy. [f. ISOLATE + -ATION]

ī′solātive a. (Philol., of sound-change) occurring independently of neighbouring sounds. [f. ISOLATE + -IVE]

ī′som|ĕr n. (Chem.) one of two or more substances composed of molecules having the same atoms differently arranged and therefore different properties; (Phys.) nucleus in metastable excited state; hence or cogn. ∾ĕ′rIC a., īsō′merISM (2) n., īsō′-merIZE (3) v.t. [G, f. Gk *isomerēs* sharing equally (as ISO-, *meros* share)]

īsō′merous a. (Bot., of flower) having same number of petals in each whorl. [f. Gk *isomerēs* (see prec.) + -OUS]

īsome′tr|ic a. of equal measure; (Math., of transformation) without change of shape (so īsō′-mĕtry¹ n.); (of drawing etc.) with plane of projection at equal angles to three principal axes of object depicted; (Physiol., of muscle action) developing tension while muscle is prevented from contracting, whence ∾ICS n. *pl.*, system of physical exercises in which muscles are caused to act against each other or against a fixed object. [f. Gk *isometria* (as ISO-, -METRY) + -IC]

ī′somȯrph n. substance or organism isomorphic with another; hence or cogn. ∾IC, ∾OUS, (-ōr′-) *adjs.*, having same (esp. crystal) form, exactly corresponding in form and relations, ∾ISM (2) (-ōr′-) n. [f. ISO- + Gk *morphē* form]

-ison *suf.* forming *ns.*, w. senses of -ATION (*comparison, garrison, jettison, venison*). [f. OF -*aison* etc. f. L -*atio* etc. (see -ATION)]

ī′sopȯd n. crustacean of order Isopoda, incl. wood-lice and allied marine and freshwater species, often parasitic, with seven equal pairs of legs. [f. F *isopode* f. mod. L *Isopoda* (as ISO-, Gk *pous podos* foot)]

īsō′scelēs (-z) a. (Of triangle) having two sides equal. [LL, f. Gk ISO(*skelēs* f. *skelos* leg)]

īsō′stasy̆ n. (Geol.) general state of equilibrium of earth's crust, with rise and fall of land relative to sea; hence **īsos**TA′TIC a. [f. ISO- + Gk *stasis* station + -Y¹]

ī′sothĕrm n. line on map connecting places with same temperature at a given time or on average over a given period; curve or formula for changes in physical system at constant temperature; so ∾AL (-ēr′-) a. [f. F *isotherme* f. as ISO- + Gk *thermē* heat]

īsotȯ′nic a. having same osmotic pressure; (Physiol., of muscle action) taking place with normal contraction. [f. Gk *isotonos* (as ISO-, TONE¹) + -IC]

ī′sotōpe n. one of two or more forms of an element differing from each other in atomic weight, and in nuclear but not chemical properties; hence **īsotō′p**IC *a.*, **isŏ'topy¹** *n.* [f. ISO-+Gk *topos* place (i.e. in periodic table of elements)]

isotrŏ'p|ic *a.* having the same physical properties in all directions; hence ∼ICALLY *adv.*, **isŏ'tropy¹** *n.* [f. ISO-+Gk *tropos* turn+-IC]

I'srael (ĭ'zrāl, -rĭel) *n.* **1.** (**Children of**) ∼, Jewish or Hebrew nation or people; so ∼ITE¹ (1) *n.* **2.** (fig.) God's elect. [later name of Jacob, their traditional ancestor, eccl. L f. Gk *Israēl* f. Heb. *yisrā'ēl* he that strives with God (Gen. 32: 28)]

Israe'li (ĭzrā'-) *a.* & *n.* (inhabitant) of State of Israel in SW Asia. [f. as prec.+-I]

ISSN *abbr.* international standard serial number.

i'ssūant *a.* (Her., esp. of beast with only upper part shown) rising from bottom or top of a bearing. [f. ISSUE²+-ANT]

i'ssue¹ (ĭ'shōō, ĭ'sū) *n.* **1.** outgoing, outflow; termination (*of* action etc.); (arch.) discharge of blood etc., incision to procure this. **2.** way out, outlet; place of emergence of stream etc. **3.** (Law). progeny, children, (*without male issue*). **4.** result, outcome; **force the** ∼, compel decision; **in the** ∼, as things turn(ed) out. **5.** point in question, important topic for discussion (*make an issue of it; what are the real issues?*), esp. (Law) between contending parties in action, ∼ **of fact** (when fact is denied), ∼ **of law** (when application of the law is contested). **6. at** ∼, (of persons) at variance, (of things) in dispute; **join** or **take** ∼, proceed to argue (*with person on* point agreed upon as basis of dispute). **7.** giving out, issuing, (*of* bills of exchange, shares, notes, stamps, etc.), number or quantity of coins, notes, copies of newspaper, supplies, etc., issued at one time; whole number of copies of book etc. put on sale at one time; one of regular series of magazine etc. (*in the May issue*). **8.** Hence ∼LESS *a.* [ME f. OF, f. Rom. *exuta* fem. (as n.) of *exutus* for L *exitus* p.p. of *exire* (see EXIT²)]

i'ssu|e² (ĭ'shōō, ĭ'sū) *v.* **1.** *v.i.* go or come out (often *out, forth*); emerge from a condition; be derived, spring, (*from*); result (*from*); end, result, (*in*); come out, be published. **2.** *v.t.* send forth; publish, put into circulation, (notes, newspaper, etc.), whence ∼ABLE *a.*, ∼ANCE *n.*; give out (book *from* library, orders *to* subordinate, etc.); supply (thing *to* person, person *with* thing) esp. for official use. [ME, f. prec.]

-ist *suf.* forming personal *ns.*: (1) of agent, corresp. to Gk vbs. in *-izō* or (possible) E vbs. in *-IZE*, (*antagonist, circumlocutionist, plagiarist*); (2) of adherent of creed etc. in *-ISM* (*atheist, Darwinist, fatalist, nonconformist*); (3) of one concerned with any subject (*copyist, cyclist, dentist, parodist, pathologist, tobacconist*), e.g. as player of musical instrument (*violinist*). [= F *-iste*, L *-ista* f. Gk *-istēs* (*-izō* -IZE, *-tēs* agent-suf.)]

i'sthm|us (-sm-, -sthm-) *n.* narrow piece of land connecting two larger bodies of land; (Anat. & Bot.) narrow part connecting two larger bodies; so ∼IAN *a.* (esp. of Isthmus of Corinth; **I**∼**ian Games**, biennial national festival in ancient Greece). [L, f. Gk *isthmos*]

i'stle *n.* fibre used for cord, nets, etc., got from species of agave etc. [f. Mex. *ixtli*]

it¹ *pron.* (*obj.* **it**; *refl.* ITSELF or arch. **it**, *poss.* ITS, *pl.* THEY etc.). **1.** the thing previously mentioned or implied or easily identified; the person in question: **who is it** (that knocks etc.)?, **it** (the person that knocks etc.) **is I**; the animal or young child of unknown or immaterial sex. **2.** (As subj. of impers. v.) *it rains, it is cold; so it seems; it* (the season) *is winter; it* (the day) *is Ash Wednesday, it is Ash Wednesday today; it* (the time) *is 6 o'clock; it* (the distance) *is 6 miles to Oxford; it says in the Bible* (the Bible says) *that all men are liars; I would go if it were not* (would go but) *for the expense.* **3.** (As subj. anticipating deferred virtual subj. in more or less conscious apposition) *it is absurd talking* (or *to talk*) *like that; it is incredible that he should refuse; it is a dirty business, this meat-canning; is it difficult to learn Greek?.* **4.** (Anticipating deferred subj. introduced by THAT², separated from it by adv. predicate) *it is seldom*

that he fails; it is in vain that you quibble; it is to him that you must apply; (anticipating deferred obj. introduced by THAT²) *saw to it that they obeyed; I take it that you agree.* **5.** (As antecedent to relative of either number and any gender, separated by predicate) *it was a purse that he dropped; it was the Russians that began it.* **6.** (As indef. obj. w. *v.t.* or *i.*, or *prep.*) *face it out; carry it off successfully; confound it!; run for it; lord it over him; watch it!; give it him* (*hot*); AT *it*; *be* FOR *it*; WITH *it*; see DO¹ 2, HAVE¹ 12. **7.** exactly what is needed; the extreme limit of achievement etc.; (colloq.) sexual intercourse, sex appeal; **that's it**, (colloq.) that is (1) the problem, (2) what is wanted, (3) the end; **this is it**, (colloq.) the expected event is at hand. **8.** (In children's games) player who has to catch others. [OE *hit* neut. nom. & acc. of HE¹]

‖**it²** *n.* (colloq.) Italian vermouth (*gin and it*). [abbr.]

‖**ITA** *abbr.* Independent Television Authority.

i.t.a. *abbr.* initial teaching alphabet.

ital. *abbr.* italic (type).

Ita'lian (ĭtă'lyan) *a.* & *n.* **1.** *a.* of Italy; ∼ **handwriting** (developed in Italy and now current in almost all countries using Roman alphabet); ∼ **millet**, foxtail millet; ∼ **vermouth** (sweet); ‖∼ **warehouse(man)** (for supply of Italian groceries, fruits, olive oil, etc.). **2.** *n.* language or native or inhabitant of Italy. **3.** Hence or cogn. ∼ATE² *a.*, having Italian style or appearance, ∼ISM (2, 4) *n.*, ∼IZE (3) *v.t.* & *i.* [ME, f. It. *Italiano* (*Italia* Italy); see -AN]

itä'lic *a.* & *n.* **1.** *a.* (**I**∼). of ancient Italy (**I**∼ **languages**, Latin, Oscan and Umbrian). **2.** ∼ **hand-** (**writing**), (simulation of) original form of Italian handwriting; ∼ **type**, (Print.) sloping type introduced by Aldus Manutius of Venice (*c.* 1500), as *Italia* at end of this entry. **3.** *n.* italic type, letter in this (now used esp. for emphasis or distinction, e.g. to indicate foreign word). [f. L f. Gk *Italikos* (*Italia* Italy; see -IC)]

itä'licize, -ise (-īz), *v.t.* print (words) in italics, usu. for emphasis or distinction. [f. prec.+-IZE]

Itä'liot, -ōte, (ĭ-) *n.* & *a.* (inhabitant) of Greek colonies in ancient Italy. [f. Gk *Italiōtēs* (*Italia* Italy; see -OT²)]

Itä'lō- (ĭ-) *comb. form.* Italian (and), as *Italo-German*, ∼PHIL(E) *n.* & *a.* [f. ITALIAN+-O-]

itch¹ *n.* irritation in the skin; contagious disease accompanied by this and caused by the ∼**-mite**, which burrows in the skin; restless desire, hankering, (*for* thing, *to* do; SEVEN-year itch); hence ∼'Y² *a.* [OE *gycce* (as foll.)]

itch² *v.i.* **1.** feel irritation of skin, causing desire to scratch it, it ∼**es**, there is an itching. **2.** (Of person or his fingers) crave uneasily (*for* thing, *to* do); ∼**ing palm** etc., avariciousness. [OE *giccan, gyccan*, = OS *jukkian*, OHG *jucchen* f. WG **juk-*]

-ite¹ *suf.* forming *ns.* w. sense 'person or thing belonging to or connected with': (1) in names of persons (*Israelite, Stagirite, Luddite, Pre-Raphaelite*); (2) in names of fossil organisms (*ammonite, belemnite*), of minerals (*anthracite, calcite, graphite*), of constituent parts of body or organ (*somite*), of explosives (*cordite, dynamite*), of commercial products (*ebonite, vulcanite*), of salts of acids having names in *-ous* (*nitrite, sulphite*). [f. or after F *-ite* f. L f. Gk *-itēs*]

-ite² *suf.* forming *adjs.* (*erudite, favourite, composite*), *ns.* (*appetite*), & *vbs.* (*expedite, unite*). [f. or after L *-itus* p.p. of vbs. in *-ēre, -ere, -ire*]

i'tem *n.* & *adv.* **1.** *n.* article or unit included in enumeration (prop. not the first); entry of this in account etc.; short piece of news etc. in newspaper etc.; hence ∼IZE (3) *v.t.*, state by items. **2.** *adv.* likewise, also, (introducing mention of item). [n. f. adv., L, = in like manner, also]

i'ter|āte *v.t.* repeat (quoted words etc.); make (charge, assertion, objection, etc.) repeatedly; hence or cogn. ∼ANCE, ∼ANCY, ∼A'TION, *ns.*, ∼ATIVE *a.* (esp. Gram., = frequentative). [f. L *iterare* (*iterum* again)+-ATE³]

ithÿphä'llic *a.* & *n.* **1.** *a.* of the phallus carried in

Bacchic festivals; (of statue etc.) having erect penis; lewd; in the metre used for Bacchic hymns. **2.** *n.* poem in this metre; licentious poem. [f. LL f. Gk *ithuphallikos* (*ithus* straight, *phallos* PHALLUS; see -IC)]

-i′tic *suf.* forming *adjs.* & *ns.* corresp. to *ns.* in -ITE[1], -ITIS, etc., (*Semitic, arthritic, syphilitic*). [f. or after F -*itique* f. L f. Gk -*itikos*; see -IC]

ĭti′ner|ant *a.* & *n.* (person) travelling from place to place; (of justices) travelling on circuit; (of Methodist ministry) moving from circuit to circuit; hence ∼ACY, ∼ANCY, *ns.* [f. as ITINERATE; see -ANT]

ĭti′nerarў *n.* & *a.* **1.** *n.* route; record of travel; guidebook. **2.** *a.* of travelling; of roads. [f. LL *itinerarius* a., -*um* n. f. L *iter itineris* journey; see -ARY[1]]

ĭti′ner|āte *v.i.* travel from place to place; (of Methodist minister) move from circuit to circuit; hence ∼A′TION *n.* [f. LL *itinerari* (as prec.) +-ATE[3]]

-i′tion *suf.* forming *ns.* w. senses as -ATION (*admonition, perdition, position*). [f. or after F, or f. L -*itio -itionis* f. p.p. stems in -*it*- (cf. -ITE[2]); see -ION]

-i′tious[1] (-i′shŭs) *suf.* forming *adjs.* w. sense 'related to, having the nature of' (*excrementitious, supposititious*). [f. L -*icius*+-OUS, by confus. of *c* and *t* in LL and med. L MSS]

-i′tious[2] (-i′shŭs) *suf.* forming *adjs.* corresp. to *ns.* in -*ition* (*ambitious, nutritious, suppositious*). [f. L -*itio* etc. (cf. -ITION)+-OUS]

-i′tis *suf.* forming *ns.*, esp. names of inflammatory diseases (*appendicitis, bronchitis*) or (colloq.) of states of mind etc. fancifully regarded as diseases (*electionitis*). [Gk -*itis*, forming fem. of *adjs.* in -*itēs* (*nosos* disease)]

-itive *suf.* forming *adjs.* w. senses as -ATIVE (*positive, transitive*). [f. or after F -*itif* -*itive* or f. L -*itivus* f. p.p. stems in -*it*- (cf. -ITE[2]); see -IVE]

ITO *abbr.* International Trade Organization.

-itor *suf.* See -OR.

-itorў *suf.* See -ORY.

-itous *suf.* forming *adjs.* corresp. to *ns.* in -ITY (*calamitous, felicitous*). [f. or after F -*iteux* f. L -*itosus*]

its *poss. pron.* of it(self). [f. IT[1]+-S[3]]

it's = *it is.* [f. IT[1]+ 's[3]]

itsĕ′lf *pron.* Emphat. and refl. form corresp. to IT[1]; *a* LAW[1] *unto itself*; **by** ∼, automatically, apart from its surroundings; **in** ∼, apart from its surroundings, viewed in its essential qualities etc. (*not in itself a bad thing*). [OE, f. IT[1]+SELF, but often treated as ITS+SELF; cf. *its own self*]

itsў-bi′tsў, ittў-bi′ttў, *adjs.* (colloq., usu. derog.) tiny, insubstantial. [childish redupl. of LITTLE, infl. by BIT[2]]

ITU *abbr.* International Telecommunication Union.

||**ITV** *abbr.* independent television.

-itў *suf.* forming *ns.* denoting quality or condition (*authority, humility, purity, suavity*), or instance or degree of this (*a monstrosity, a profanity; humidity, porosity*). [f. or after F -*ité* f. L -*itas* -*itatis*; cf. -TY[1]]

IU *abbr.* international unit.

IU(C)D *abbr.* intra-uterine (contraceptive) device.

-ium *suf.* forming *ns.*: names of metallic elements (*sodium, uranium*; also **-um**, as *tantalum*), region of body (*pericardium, hypogastrium*), biological structure (*mycelium, prothallium*), and miscellaneous wds (*pandemonium, symposium*). [f. or after L -*ium* f. Gk -*ion*]

IV *abbr.* intravenous.

-ive *suf.* forming *adjs.* w. sense 'tending to, having the nature of' (*active, descriptive, evasive, reflexive*) & *ns.* (*adjective, captive*); see -ATIVE, -ITIVE; hence **-iveLY**[2] (-vlĭ) *adv. suf.*, **-iveNESS** (-vn-) *n. suf.* [f. or after F -*if* -*ive* f. L -*ivus*]

ī′vied (-ĭd) *a.* overgrown with ivy. [f. IVY+-ED[2]]

ī′vorў *n.* **1.** hard creamy-white substance composing main part of tusks of elephant, hippopotamus, walrus, narwhal, and (**fossil** ∼) mammoth; **vegetable** ∼, hard endosperm of seed of a COROZO palm (∼**-nut**), black ∼, (Hist.) African Negro slaves; GATE[1] *of ivory.* **2.** colour of ivory. **3.** (sl., in *pl.*) dice, billiard-balls, piano-keys, teeth. **4.** (in *pl.*) articles made of ivory. **5.** ∼ **black,** black pigment from calcined ivory; ∼ **gull** (*Pagophila eburnea*, flying very far north); ∼ **tower,** seclusion or withdrawal from (harsh realities of) the world. [ME, f. OF *yvoire* f. Rom. **eboreum* f. L *ebur -oris*]

ī′vў *n.* climbing evergreen shrub (*Hedera helix*) with usu. dark-green shining five-angled leaves; GROUND[1] *ivy*; ∼ **geranium,** pelargonium with leaves like ivy; **Ivy* **League,** group of famous colleges in eastern US; *ivy-leaved* TOADflax. [OE *ĭfig*, rel. to MLG *if(lōf)*, OHG *ebah*]

IWW *abbr.* Industrial Workers of the World.

ĭ′xia *n.* S. Afr. iridaceous plant of genus *Ixia*, with large showy flowers. [L f. Gk, a kind of thistle]

Ixiŏ′nian (ĭ-) *a.* of *Ixion*, king of Thessaly in Gk myth, punished by being bound to eternally revolving wheel in Hades. [f. Gk *Ixiōn*+-IAN]

ĭ′zard *n.* goatlike antelope of Pyrenees, allied to chamois. [f. F *isard*; orig. unkn.]

-ize, -ise[1] (-īz) *suf.* forming vbs. w. senses (1) *v.t.* treat in specified way (*catechize, monopolize*), (2) *v.i.* follow specified practice (*philosophize*), have specified feeling (*sympathize*), (3) *v.t.* & *i.* bring or come into specified state (*Anglicize, pulverize, volatilize*), (4) *v.t.* & *i.* treat or act according to method of (*bowdlerize, pasteurize*), (5) *v.t.* impregnate with or affect with or provide with (*oxidize, syphilize, accessorize*); so **-ĭZA′TION, -īZER**[1], *n. sufs.* [f. or after F -*iser* f. LL -*izare* f. Gk -*izō*]

ĭ′zzard *n.* (arch.) the letter Z (*from A to Izzard*). [var. of ZED]

ĭ′zzat *n.* (Ind. etc.) honour, reputation, self-respect. [Arab. '*izzah* glory]

J

J, j, (jā) *n.* (*pl.* **Js** *or* **J's**). tenth letter of alphabet; (as Roman numeral in prescriptions etc.) = *i* in final position (*ij*, *vj*).

J. *abbr.* jack; joule(s); Judge; Justice.

jăb *v.t.* (**-bb-**), & *n.* **1.** *v.t.* poke roughly; stab; thrust (thing) abruptly (*into*). **2.** *n.* abrupt blow with pointed thing or fist; (colloq.) hypodermic injection. [var. (orig. Sc.) of JOB³]

jă′bber *n.* & *n.* **1.** *v.i.* speak volubly and with little sense; chatter like monkeys etc. **2.** *v.t.* utter (words) rapidly and indistinctly. **3.** *n.* jabbering; gabble, gibberish. [imit.; see -ER⁵]

jă′bberwŏckў *n.* nonsensical writing or speech, esp. for comic effect. [f. title of poem in Lewis Carroll's *Through the Looking-Glass* (1871)]

jă′biru (-ōō) *n.* large tropical Amer. stork; similar bird of Old World. [f. Tupi-Guarani *jabirú*]

jăborā′ndi *n.* dried leaflets of S. Amer. shrub of genus *Pilocarpus*, with diuretic and sudorific properties [f Tupi-Guarani *jaburandi*]

jă′bŏt (zhă′bō) *n.* ornamental central frill of lace etc. on front of woman's bodice or in Highland dress; (Hist.) frill on man's shirt-front. [F, orig. = crop of bird, prob. f. *gab-* crop, maw]

jă′cana *n.* small tropical wading bird of family Jacanidae, with disproportionately large straight claws (enabling it to walk on floating leaves). [f. Port. *jaçanã* f. Tupi-Guarani *jasaná*]

jăcarä′nda *n.* **1.** tropical Amer. tree of genus *Dalbergia* etc. with hard scented wood. **2.** tropical Amer. etc. tree of genus *Jacaranda*, with trumpet-shaped blue flowers. [Tupi Guarani]

jă′cǐnth *n.* reddish-orange gem, variety of zircon. [ME *iacynt* etc. f. OF *iacinte* or f. med. L *jacint(h)us* f. L *hyacinthus* HYACINTH]

jăck¹ *n.* **1.** (J~) familiar form of man's Christian name *John*, esp. as type of common man; J~ **and Jill**, boy and girl, man and woman; **every man ~**, every individual man; **on one′s ~**, on one′s J~ **Jones**, (sl.) alone, on one's own [rhyming sl.]. **2.** = *Jack tar*; ||labourer, man who does odd jobs, etc.; CHEAP*jack*; LUMBER²*jack*; STEEPLE*jack*. **3.** court-card usu. ranking below king and queen. **4.** machine for turning spit in roasting meat; machine for lifting heavy weights; machine for lifting wheel of vehicle off ground while changing or cleaning it; figure of man striking bell on clock; device using quill to pluck string of harpsichord etc.; device using single plug to connect telephone circuits etc.; BOOT¹*jack*. **5.** (Bowls). small white ball for players to aim at. **6.** male of various animals; = PIKE³, esp. young or small one. **7.** (in *pl.*, treated as *sing.*) game played with jackstones. **8.** (sl.) detective, policeman; money. **9.** **~-a-dandy**, dandy; **~′ass**, male ass, stupid person (*~′assery*, stupid behaviour; *laughing ~ass*, giant kingfisher of Australia, with loud discordant cry); **~′boot**, large boot coming above knee, worn esp. by 17th–18th-c. cavalry and by Nazi soldiers, (fig.) oppressive behaviour; **~′daw**, thievish small bird of crow family haunting church towers [cf. DAW]; J~ **Frost**, frost personified; *~′hammer, pneumatic hammer; **~-in-office**, self-important official; **~-in-the-box**, toy figure that springs out of box when it is opened; J~**-in-the-green**, man or boy enclosed in framework covered with leaves in May-Day celebrations; ||J~ **Ketch**, common hangman [f. name of executioner 1663–86]; **~-knife**, large clasp-knife for the pocket, dive in which body is first doubled up and then straightened, accidental folding of articulated vehicle (also as *v.i.* & *t.*); **~ of all trades**, one who

can turn his hand to anything; **~-o′-lantern**, (1) will-o′-the-wisp (lit. or fig.), (2) lantern of pumpkin or turnip rind with holes cut to represent facial features; **~-plane** (medium-sized, for coarse joinery); **~-plug** (for use with jack; see sense 4); **~′pot**, (Poker) accumulating pool that can be opened only by player holding two jacks or better, large esp. accumulating prize in lottery etc. (*hit the ~pot*, be remarkably lucky); **~ pudding**, buffoon, clown; *~**-rabbit**, large prairie hare with very long ears and hind legs; **~-rafter**, short rafter in hip-roof; **before you can** or **could say** J~ **Robinson**, very quickly or suddenly; J~ **Russell**, type of terrier [named after *John Russell*, Engl. clergyman d. 1883]; **~-snipe**, small species of snipe; **~′stone**, small round pebble or metal object used with others in tossing-games; **~′straw**, spillikin; J~ **tar**, sailor, **~ towel**, roller towel. [ME *Iakke*, by-name for *John* (erron. assoc. w. F *Jacques* James)]

jăck² *v.t.* **~ (up)**, raise (as) with JACK¹ (sense 4); **~ in** or **~ up**, (sl.) abandon (attempt etc.). [f. prec.]

jăck³ *n.* ship's flag, smaller than ensign, esp. one flown at bow, indicating nationality; UNION *Jack*; **~-staff**, (1) staff at bow for jack, (2) staff carrying flag that is to show above mast-head. [prob. = JACK¹]

jăck⁴ *n.* (arch. or Hist.) foot-soldier's sleeveless padded tunic; = BLACK¹*jack* (1). [ME, f. OF *jaque*, of uncert. orig.]

jăck⁵ *n.* E. Ind. fruit, like bread-fruit but coarser. [f. Port. *jaca* f. Malayalam *chakka*]

jă′ckal (-awl) *n.* wild animal related to dog, esp. *Canis aureus*, of size of fox, formerly supposed to hunt up lion's prey for him; (fig.) person who does preparatory drudgery etc. or who assists another's immoral behaviour. [f. Turk. *çakal* f. Pers. *šagāl*]

jă′ckanāpes (-ps) *n.* pert fellow; coxcomb; pert child; (arch.) tame monkey [earliest form *Jack Napes* (1450), supposed to refer to Duke of Suffolk, whose badge was an ape's clog and chain]

jăckarōō′,jăckerōō′,*n.,* & *v.i.* (Austral. colloq.) (serve as) trainee on sheep-station etc. [f JACK¹ + KANGAROO]

jă′ckĕt *n.,* & *v.t.* **1.** *n.* sleeved short outer garment for man or woman (DUST² person's *jacket*); thing similarly worn (LIFE-*jacket*, STRAIT-*jacket*). **2.** outer covering round boiler etc. for protection, to maintain desired temperature, etc. **3.** paper wrapper, freq. coloured and artistically designed, in which bound book is issued. **4.** animal's coat; *potatoes cooked in their* **~s** (skins). **5.** *v.t.* cover with jacket. [ME, f. OF *ja(c)quet* dim. of *jaque* JACK⁴; see -ET¹]

Jā′cob *n.* **~′s ladder,** (1) plant with corymbs of blue or white flowers, and leaves suggesting ladder, (2, Naut.) rope ladder with wooden rungs, (3) endless chain of buckets; **~′s staff,** (1) surveyor's iron-shod rod used instead of tripod, (2) instrument for measuring distances and heights; **~ sheep** (ornamental piebald breed). [f. ~ in Genesis (w. ref. to 28:12, 30:40), f. Heb. *ya'ăķōḇ* supplanter]

Jăcobē′an *a.* & *n.* **1.** *a.* of the reign of James I (esp. Archit.); of St. James the Less or his Epistle; (of furniture) of the colour of dark oak. **2.** *n.* Jacobean person; = JACOBITE 2. [f. mod. L *Jacobaeus* f. eccl. L *Jacobus* James f. Gk *Iakōbos* = prec.; see -EAN]

Jă′cobin¹ *n.* **1.** Dominican friar [from convent near to church of S. Jacques in Paris]. **2.** member of extreme democratic club established in Paris in old Jacobin convent (1789); sympathizer with its principles; extreme radical; hence **~ic**(AL) (-ǐ′n-) *adjs.*, **~ism** (3) *n.,* **~ize** (3) *v.t.* [ME f. F, f. med. L *Jacobinus* f. eccl. L *Jacobus* (see prec., -INE¹)]

jă′cobin[2] *n.* pigeon with reversed feathers on back of neck, suggesting cowl. [f. F *jacobine*, fem. (as prec.)]

Jă′cob|īte *n.* **1.** adherent of James II after his abdication, or of his descendants or of the Stuarts; hence **i′t**ICAL *a.*, **∼īt**ISM (3) *n.* **2.** admirer of Henry James (Amer. novelist and critic d. 1916). **3.** follower of Jacobus Baradaeus (6th-c. Syrian Monophysite monk). [f. L *Jacobus* James (see JACOBEAN) + -ITE[1]]

jă′conĕt *n.* cotton cloth like cambric, esp. dyed waterproof kind for poulticing etc. [f. Urdu *jagannāthī* f. *Jagannath* (now Puri) in India, place of origin (see JUGGERNAUT)]

Jă′cquărd (-kärd) *n.* apparatus with perforated cards to facilitate weaving of figured fabrics; **∼** (**loom**), loom fitted with this; fabric thus made, with intricate variegated pattern. [f. J. M. **∼**, Fr. inventor d. 1834]

jacquerie (zhăkĕrē′) *n.* (revolt of) peasantry. [F, f. OF *jaquerie* (esp. of peasants' rising in N. France against nobles in 1357–8) f. *Jacques* James (see -ERY)]

jăctā′tion *n.* **1.** (literary). boasting. **2.** = foll. 2. [f. L *jactatio* (*jactare* frequent. of *jacĕre* throw; see -ATION)]

jăctitā′tion *n.* **1.** (Law). **∼ of marriage,** offence of falsely claiming to be a person's wife or husband. **2.** (Med.) restless tossing of body in illness; twitching of limb or muscle. [sense l f. med. L *jactitatio* false declaration f. L *jactitare* boast, frequent. of *jactare* (see prec., -ATION); sense 2 f. prec.]

jāde[1] *n.,* & *v.t.* **1.** *n.* inferior, wearied, or worn-out horse. **2.** (In reprobation, usu. playful) a woman. **3.** *v.t.* (esp. in *p.p.*) wear out with hard work or surfeit. [ME; orig. unkn.]

jāde[2] *n.* **1.** silicate of calcium and magnesium, a hard green, blue, or white stone, used as ornament or for implements. **2.** silicate of sodium and aluminium like this in appearance. **3.** green colour of jade. [F; *le jade* for *l′ejade* f. Sp. (*piedra de) ijada* (stone of) the colic, f. Rom. **iliata* f. L *ilia* flanks]

jă′deïte (-dīt) *n.* = prec. 2. [f. prec. + -ITE[1] (2)]

j′adoube (zhahdōō′b) *int.* (Chess) expr. intention not to move man that one is about to touch. [F, = I adjust]

jae′ger[1] (yā′ger) *n.* German or Austrian rifleman; skua. [f. G *jäger* hunter (*jagen* to hunt)]

Jae′ger[2] (yā′ger) *n.* (P for various textiles, esp.) kind of woollen clothing-material excluding all vegetable fibres as unwholesome; garment of this. [19th c.; f. G. **∼**, Ger. scientist d. 1917]

Jă′ffa *n.* **∼** (**orange**), large oval thick-skinned variety of orange. [**∼** in Israel, near where it was first grown]

jăg[1] *n.* sharp projection, e.g. point of rock; hence **∼′g**Y[2] (-gĭ) *a.* [f. foll.]

jăg[2] *v.t.* (-gg-). cut or tear in uneven manner; make indentations in; hence **∼′g**ER[1] (2) (-g-) *n.* [ME; prob. imit.]

jăg[3] *n.* (sl.) drinking-bout; spree; (colloq.) period of indulgence in activity, emotion, etc. [16th c., = load for one horse; orig. unkn.]

‖**jăg**[4] *n.* (colloq.) Jaguar (car). [abbr. of proprietary name]

jäger. Var. of JAEGER[1].

jă′ggèd[1] (-g-) *a.* with irregularly cut or torn edge; deeply indented; hence **∼**LY[2] *adv.,* **∼**NESS *n.* [ME, f. JAG[1],[2] + -ED[2],[1]]

*jăgged[2] (-gd) *a.* (sl.) drunk. [f. JAG[3] + -ED[2]]

jă′ggerỹ (-g-) *n.* coarse brown Indian sugar made from palm-sap; other crude sugar. [f. Indo-Port. *jag(a)ra* f. Kanarese *sharkare* f. Skr. *śarkarā* sugar]

jă′guar (-gūer, -gwer) *n.* large carnivorous spotted feline (*Panthera onca*) inhabiting some wooded parts of America. [Tupi-Guarani *yaguara*]

jăguarŭ′ndi (-gw-) *n.* grey long-tailed feline (*Felis jaguarondi*) of S. & Central America. [Tupi-Guarani]

Jah, **Jah′veh** (yah′vă), *n.* = JEHOVAH 1; hence **Jah′v**IST (2) *n.* = JEHOVIST. [Heb.]

jai alai (hī′alī) *n.* game like pelota played with large curved wicker baskets. [Sp. f. Basque]

jail etc. See GAOL etc.

Jain (jīn) *n.* & *a.* (member) of a non-Brahminical Indian religion, with doctrines like those of Buddhism; hence **∼′**ISM (3), **∼′**IST (2), *ns.* [Hindi, f. Skr. *jainas* of a Buddha or saint (*jinas* f. root *ji* conquer)]

jāke *a.* (sl.) all right, satisfactory. [20th c.; orig. uncert.]

jă′lap *n.* purgative drug got esp. from tuberous roots of a Mex. climbing plant (*Exogonium purga*). [F, f. Sp. *jalapa* f. *Jalapa, Xalapa,* Mex. city, f. Aztec *Xalapan* sand by the water (*xalli* sand, *atl* water, *pan* upon)]

jalŏ′pỹ *n.* dilapidated old motor vehicle or aircraft. [20th c.; orig. unkn.]

jă′lousie (zhă′lōōzē) *n.* slatted shutter or blind to admit air and light but not rain etc. [F (as JEALOUSY)]

jăm[1] *v.* (-mm-) & *n.* **1.** *v.t.* squeeze (thing) into space between two surfaces; cause (part of machine) to be no longer movable so that it cannot work, make (machine) unworkable in this way; squeeze (things) together in compact mass; thrust (thing) violently (*into* confined space); block, fill up, (passage etc.) by crowding into it; **∼ on,** apply (brakes) forcibly. **2.** *v.i.* become tightly wedged; (of machine) become unworkable by jamming of part; (Jazz colloq.) extemporize. **3.** *v.t.* (Radio). make (message, transmitter) unintelligible by causing interference. **4.** *n.* crush, squeeze, stoppage (of machine etc.) due to jamming; crowded mass (LOG[1]-*jam,* TRAFFIC *jam*); (colloq.) dilemma, awkward position. **5.** **∼-packed,** (colloq.) very full; **∼** (**session**), (Jazz colloq.) improvised playing by group. [imit.]

jăm[2] *n.,* & *v.t.* (-mm-). **1.** *n.* preparation of fruit, made by boiling it with sugar or other sweetener to a thick consistency (**∼ tomorrow,** pleasant thing continually promised but usu. never produced); ‖(colloq.) something easy or pleasant (MONEY *for jam*); hence **∼′my**[2] *a.* **2.** *v.t.* spread with jam; make into jam. [perh. = prec.]

Jam. *abbr.* Jamaica; James (NT).

Jamai′ca *n.* **∼ pepper,** allspice. [**∼** in W. Indies]

jămb (-m) *n.* side post of doorway, window, etc.; (in *pl.*) stone sides of fireplace. [ME, f. OF *jambe* f. Rom. **gamba* leg f. LL *gamba* hoof]

jămbalaya′a *n.* dish of rice with shrimps, chicken, etc. [Louisiana F, f. mod. Prov. *jambalaia*]

jămboree′ *n.* celebration, merry-making; large rally of Scouts. [19th c., of unkn. orig.]

jă′mmy. See JAM[2].

Jan. *abbr.* January.

jāne *n.* (sl.) woman. [f. Christian name *Jane*]

Jā′neïte (-nīt) *n.* admirer of Jane Austen's novels. [f. *Jane* Austen, Engl. novelist d. 1817 + -ITE[1] (1)]

jă′ngle (-nggel) *v.i.* & *t.,* & *n.* **1.** (make) harsh or discordant sound; cause (bell etc.) to do this; cause irritation to (nerves etc.) by discord; speak or utter in discordant or noisy way. **2.** (arch.) dispute, wrangle. [ME, f. OF *jangler,* of uncert. orig.]

jă′nitor *n.* door-keeper; caretaker of building; hence **∼**IAL (-ōr′-) *a.* [L (*janua* door; see -OR)]

jă′nizarỹ, jă′nissarỹ, *n.* (Hist.) member of body of Turkish infantry forming Sultan's guard and chief part of army (14th–19th c.); Turkish soldier; (fig.) devoted follower or supporter. [ult. f. Turk. *yeniçeri* (*yeni* new, *çeri* troops)]

jă′nkers (-z) *n.* (sl., esp. Mil.) punishment for defaulters. [20th c.; orig. unkn.]

‖**jă′nnock** *a.* (dial.) straightforward, honest, genuine. [19th c.; orig. unkn.]

Jă′nsen|ist *n.* (Hist.) member of party in RC Ch. esp. in France holding with Jansen the perverseness of the natural human will and its inability to do good; so **∼′**ISM (3) *n.,* **∼′i′st**IC *a.* [f. C. *Jansen,* Du. theologian d. 1638 + -IST]

Jă′nŭarỹ *n.* first month of year. [ME f. AF *Jenever,* f. L *Januarius* (*mensis* month) of Janus; see foll., -ARY[1]]

Jă′nus-fāced (-st) *a.* facing both ways at once; (fig.) hypocritical, insincere. [f. *Janus,* Rom. god of gates and beginnings, shown with faces on front and back of head, + FACE[1] + -ED[2]]

Jăp a. & n. (colloq., often derog.; **R**) Japanese. [abbr.]

japă'n[1] n. hard varnish, esp. kind brought orig. from Japan; work in Japanese style. [f. *Japan* in Asia, app. f. Malay *Japang*, *Japung* f. Chin. *Riben* (*ri* sun, *ben* origin)]

japă'n[2] v.t. (-nn-). varnish with japan; make black and glossy as with japan. [f. prec.]

Jăpanē'se (-z) a. & n. (*pl.* same). (native or inhabitant or language) of Japan; ∼ **cedar**, cryptomeria; ∼ **(flowering) cherry** (hybrid kind with pink or white usu. double flowers); ∼ **laurel**, species of laurel (*Aucuba japonica*) often with pale-blotched leaves; ∼ **maple**, ornamental purple-flowered maple (*Acer palmatus*); ∼ **medlar**, loquat; ∼ **print** (in water--colour from wood-blocks); ∼ **quince**, japonica; ∼ **silk**, habutai. [f. *Japan* (see JAPAN[1]) + -ESE]

jāpe v.i., & n. (practical) joke. [ME, of uncert. orig.]

Japhĕ'tic a. of, (supposedly) descended from, Japheth, third son of Noah (Gen. 10:2 ff.); (arch.) Indo-European. [f. mod. L *Japheti* descendants of *Japheth* + -IC]

Jă'plish n. language blending Japanese and English, used in Japan. [f. JAPANESE + ENGLISH[1]]

japŏ'nica n. ornamental usu. red-flowered variety of quince. [mod. L., fem. of *japonicus* Japanese]

jăr[1] n. harsh or grating sound; thrill of nerves or feelings, shock; lack of harmony, disagreement; quarrel. [as foll.]

jăr[2] v. (-rr-). **1.** v.i. sound discordantly; have discordant or painful effect (*on* or *upon* person, his ear, nerves, etc.); strike with grating sound (*on, upon, against,* object); (of body affected) vibrate or resound discordantly; (of opinion, statement, action) be out of harmony, disagree, (*with*); dispute, wrangle. **2.** v.t. cause (thing) to jar; send shock through (nerves). [16th c.; prob. imit.]

jăr[3] n. earthenware, stoneware, glass, or plastic vessel with or without handle(s), usu. cylindrical (LEYDEN *jar*); contents of this; ||(colloq.) glass of beer etc.; hence ∼'FUL 2 n. [f. F *jarre* f. Arab. *jarra*]

jăr[4] n. (arch. or colloq.) **on the** ∼, ajar. [late form of obs. *char*; see AJAR[1]]

jardinière (zhărdinyãr') n. ornamental pot or stand for display of growing flowers in room, on window--sill, etc.; dish of mixed vegetables. [F]

jă'rgon[1] n. unintelligible words, gibberish; barbarous or debased language; mode of speech familiar only to a group or profession (*critics' jargon*; *scientific, law, jargon*); (arch.) twittering of birds; hence ∼IC (-ŏ'n-), ∼i'stIC, *adjs.*, ∼IZE (2, 3) *v.t.* & i. [ME, f. OF, of unkn. orig.]

jă'rgon[2], **jărgōō'n**, n. translucent, colourless, or smoky variety of zircon. [F, f. It. *giargone*, prob. ult. as ZIRCON]

jărgonĕ'lle n. early-ripening variety of pear. [F, dim. of prec.]

jărl (y-) n. (Hist.) Norse or Danish chief. [ON, orig. man of noble birth; = EARL]

jă'rrah (-a) n. (durable timber of) Austral. mahogany gum-tree (*Eucalyptus marginata*). [f. Aboriginal *djarryl*]

Jas. abbr. James (also in NT).

jă'smĭn(e) (-s-, -z-), **jĕ'ssamĭn(e)**, n. shrub of genus *Jasminum* with white or yellow flowers, esp. **common** or **white** ∼, climbing shrub (*J. officinale*) with fragrant flowers; **red** ∼, a red-flowered frangipani (*Plumeria rubra*); **winter** ∼ (*J. nudiflorum*, with yellow flowers). [16th c., f. F *jasmin, jessemin* f. Arab. *yās(a)mīn* f. Pers. *yāsamīn*]

jă'spé (-ā) a. like jasper, randomly coloured (esp. of cotton fabric). [F, p.p. of *jasper* marble (*jaspe* JASPER)]

jă'sper n. opaque variety of quartz, usu. red, yellow, or brown. [ME, f. OF *jasp(r)e* f. L f. Gk *iaspis*, of oriental orig.]

Jat (jaht) n. member of Indo-Aryan people widely distributed in NW India. [f. Hindi *jāṭ*]

jā'tō n. (*pl.* ∼**s**). (Aeron.) jet-assisted take-off; auxiliary jet engine(s) to provide temporary extra thrust at take-off. [abbr.]

jau'ndice n., & v.t. **1.** n. (Path.) condition often caused by obstruction of bile and marked by yellowness of skin, fluids, and tissues, and occas. by disordered vision; (fig.) envy or jealousy. **2.** v.t. affect with jaundice; (fig., esp. in *p.p.*) affect (person, his judgement etc.) with envy or resentment or jealousy. [ME *iaunes* f. OF *jaunice* yellowness (*jaune* yellow; see -ICE)]

jaunt v.i., & n. (take) excursion or journey, esp. for pleasure; ∼'ing-car, light two-wheeled horse-drawn vehicle used in Ireland. [16th c.; orig. unkn.]

jau'nt|y a. & n. **1.** a. having or affecting easy sprightliness or airy self-satisfaction; hence ∼ILY[2] adv., ∼iNESS n. **2.** n. ||(colloq.) master-at-arms. [17th c. *jentee* repr. F *gentil* (see GENTLE); ASSIM. TO -Y[2]]

*ja'va[1] (jăh'-) n. (sl.) coffee. [f. *Java coffee* (as foll.)]

Ja'va[2] (jăh'-) n. *Java* MAN[3]; ∼ **sparrow**, a weaver--bird (*Padda oryzivora*). [name of island in Indonesia]

Ja'van (jăh'-). a. & n. (native) of Java. [f. prec. + -AN]

Javanē'se (jăh'-; -z) a. & n. (*pl.* same). = prec.; (of) the Malayan language of Java. [f. prec. + -ESE]

jă'velin (-vel-, -vl-) n. light spear thrown by hand as weapon or in athletic sport. [f. F *javeline, javelot,* f. Gallo-Rom. *gabalottus*]

Javĕ'lle (zh-) n. ∼ **water,** solution of sodium hypochlorite for bleaching, disinfecting, etc. [*Javel* in France]

jaw n. & v. **1.** n. upper or (usu.) lower jaw; **upper** ∼, **lower** ∼, one of the bones (or sets of bones) forming framework of mouth and biting and masticating apparatus in vertebrates; ∼-**bone,** (1) each of the two bones forming lower jaw in most mammals, (2) these two combined into one in others, (*3, sl.) = CREDIT[1] 3. **2.** (in *pl.*) bones of mouth including teeth, mouth; narrow mouth of valley, channel, etc.; gripping-members of machine, e.g. vice; (fig.) gripping--power (*of death* etc.). **3.** (colloq.) loquacity (**hold your** ∼, stop talking); sermonizing talk, lecture (esp. ||PI[2] *jaw*); ∼-**breaker,** word that is very long, or hard to pronounce. **4.** v.i. (sl.) speak esp. at tedious length. **5.** v.t. (sl.) persuade by talking; admonish, lecture, (person). [ME, f. OF *joe* cheek, jaw, of uncert. orig.]

jay n. noisy chattering arboreal European bird (*Garrulus glandarius*) with vivid blue, black, and white feathers; related bird of subfamily Garrulinae; (fig.) impertinent chatterer, simpleton; ∼-**walker,** pedestrian who crosses, or walks in, street or road without regard for traffic; ∼-**walk** v.i., behave thus. [ME f. OF, f. LL *gaius, gaia,* perh. f. L man's praenomen *Gaius* (cf. *jackdaw, robin*)]

jăz z n., a., & v. **1.** n. music and dance of US Negro origin with characteristic improvisation, syncopation, and strong rhythm; (sl.) deceptive talk, nonsense, matter (*all that jazz*); ∼ **band** (suitable for playing jazz, e.g. piano, trumpet, saxophone, banjo, bass, and drums); ∼'**man,** man who plays jazz; hence ∼'Y[2] a., of or like jazz, unrestrained, vivid. **2.** v.i. play, dance, indulge in, jazz. **3.** v.t. arrange (music) as jazz; make (pattern etc.) vivid or grotesque; brighten or liven *up.* [20th c.; perh. orig. = copulation]

||JCR abbr. Junior Combination Room; Junior Common Room.

jea'lous (jĕ'l-) a. solicitous *for* or for preservation *of* (rights etc.); feeling resentment or envy (*of* person, his advantages, etc.) on account of known or suspected rivalry esp. in sexual love; (Bibl., of God) intolerant of disloyalty; (of inquiry, supervision, etc.) vigilant; hence ∼LY[2] adv. [ME, f. OF *gelos* f. med. L *zelosus* (as ZEAL; see -OUS)]

jea'lousy (jĕ'lu-) n. quality or state of being jealous. [ME, f. OF *gelosie* (as prec.; see -Y[1])]

jean (jēn, jān) n. twilled cotton cloth; (in *pl.*) trousers of jean or denim, esp. tight-fitting informal trousers. [ME, attrib. use of *Jene* f. OF *Janne* f. med. L *Janua* Genoa]

Jeep n. (**P**) small and sturdy motor vehicle with four-wheel drive. [orig. US, f. *G.P.* = *general purposes*, infl. by 'Eugene the *Jeep*', animal in comic strip]

jeer[1] n. (Naut., usu. in *pl.*) tackle for hoisting and lowering yards. [ME; orig. unkn.]

jeer[2] *v. & n.* **1.** *v.i. & t.* scoff derisively (*at* or at); deride. **2.** *n.* gibe, taunt. [16th c.; orig. unkn.]

Jeez *int.* (sl.) = GEE[3]. [abbr. of JESUS]

jehad. See JIHAD.

Jĕhŏ′vah (-*a*), **Yah′veh** (-ā), **Yah′weh** (-ā), *ns.* **1.** Name of God in OT. **2.** **Jehovah's Witness**, member of fundamentalist millenary sect rejecting supremacy of State over religious principles. [repr. Heb. *YHVH* (given the vowels of *adonai* 'my lord' to indicate substitution of latter word in reading, hence erron. med. L *Iehoua(h)*), perh. = he that is]

Jĕhŏ′vĭst, Yah′vĭst, *ns.* author(s) of parts of Hexateuch where God is called 'Jehovah' (cf. ELOHIST); hence **Jĕhŏvĭ′stIC, Yahvĭ′stIC,** *adjs.* [f. prec. + -IST]

Jĕ′hū *n.* (joc.) driver, esp. reckless one. [2 Kgs. 9:20]

jĕju′ne (-ōō′n) *a.* meagre, scanty; (of land) barren; unsatisfying to the mind; puerile; hence ∿LY[2] (-nlĭ) *adv.,* ∿NESS (-n-n-) *n.* [orig. = fasting, f. L *jejunus*]

jĕju′num (-jōō′-) *n.* (Anat.) portion of small intestine between duodenum and ileum. [L, neut. of *jejunus* fasting]

Jĕkўll and Hў′de *n.* person in whom two personalities alternate. [f. R. L. Stevenson's story *The Strange Case of Dr. Jekyll and Mr. Hyde*]

jĕll *v.i.* (colloq.) set as jelly; (fig.) take definite form. [back-form. f. JELLY]

jĕ′llaba *n.* loose hooded cloak (as) worn by Arab men. [f. Arab. *jallaba, jallābīya*]

jĕ′llў *n. & v.* **1.** *n.* soft stiffish semitransparent food, consisting chiefly of gelatin, got from skin, bones, etc., by boiling and cooling; similar preparation of fruit--juice, sugar, etc.; substance of similar consistency; (sl.) gelignite [cf. GELLY ; ∿ **baby**, soft gelatinous sweetmeat moulded in shape of baby; ∿**bag** (for straining juice for jelly); ∿**fish**, usu. marine coelenterate with stinging tentacles and saucer-shaped gelatinous body, (fig.) spineless person; *∿ **roll**, Swiss roll made with jelly instead of jam. **2.** *v.t. & i.* (cause to) set as jelly, congeal; set (cooked eels etc.) in jelly. [ME, f. OF *gelee* frost, jelly, f. Rom. *gelata* (L *gelare* freeze f. *gelu* frost; see -Y[4])]

‖**jĕ′mmў** *n.* **1.** crowbar used by burglars, usu. made in sections. **2.** sheep's head as food. [pet-form of man's Christian name *James*; see -Y[3]]

je ne sais quoi (zhe ne sā kwah′) *n.* an indefinable something. [F, = I do not know what]

jĕ′nnĕt *n.* small Spanish horse. [f. F *genet* f. Sp. *jinete* light horseman f. Arab. *zenāta* Berber tribe famous as horsemen]

jĕ′nnў *n.* **1.** locomotive crane; = SPINNING-*jenny*; (Bill.) losing hazard down side of table into middle pocket (**short** ∿) or far corner pocket (**long** ∿); CREEPING *Jenny.* **2.** she-ass; ∿ **wren**, (esp. pop. and childish name for) wren. [pet-form of woman's Christian name *Janet*; see -Y[3]]

jeo′pardīze (jĕ′p-), **-īse** (-īz), *v.t.* put into jeopardy, endanger. [f. foll. + -IZE]

jeo′pardў (jĕ′p-) *n.* danger, esp. of severe loss or harm; danger resulting from being on trial for criminal offence. [ME *iuparti* f. OF *iu* (*ieu*) *parti* divided (i.e. even) game, f. L *jocus* game + *partitus* p.p. of *partiri* divide f. *pars partis* part]

jĕquï′rïtў *n.* twining shrub (*Abrus precatorius*) with particoloured red and black seeds used for ornament and in medicine. [f. F *jéquirity* f. Tupi-Guarani *jekiriti*]

Jer. *abbr.* Jeremiah (OT).

jĕr′bĭl. See GERBIL.

jĕrbŏ′a *n.* small Afr. desert rodent of family Dipodidae, with long hind legs and great jumping powers. [med. L, f. Arab. *yarbū′* flesh of loins, jerboa]

jĕrĕmī′ad *n.* lamentation, doleful complaint. [f. F *jérémiade* f. *Jérémie* Jeremiah f. eccl. L *Jeremias*, w. ref. to Lamentations of Jeremiah in OT; see -AD]

Jĕrĕmī′ah (-*a*) *n.* doleful prophet or denouncer of the present age. [w. ref. as prec.]

jerfalcon. Var. of GYRFALCON.

Jĕ′richŏ (-kō) *n.* **go to** ∿, (colloq., esp. in *imper.*) go to a distant place, go away. [∿ in ancient Palestine]

jĕrk[1] *n.* sharp sudden pull, twist, etc.; involuntary spasmodic contraction of muscle; (in *pl.*) spasmodic movements of limbs or face, esp. in religious excitement; PHYSICAL *jerks*; (sl.) stupid, foolish, or insignificant person. [16th c.; perh. imit.]

jĕrk[2] *v.* **1.** *v.t.* pull, thrust, twist, etc., with a jerk; throw with suddenly arrested motion; (of weight-lifter) raise (weight) from shoulder-level to above head; *∿***water** *n. & a.,* (colloq.) rustic (town), slow (train), unimportant (person etc.). **2.** *v.i.* move with a jerk; ∿ **off**, (sl.) masturbate. [as prec.]

jĕrk[2] *v.t.* cure (esp. beef) by cutting in long slices and drying in sun. [f. Amer. Sp. *charquear* (*charqui* f. Quechua *echarqui* dried flesh)]

jĕr′kin *n.* sleeveless jacket; (Hist.) man's close-fitting jacket, often of leather. [16th c.; of unkn. orig.]

jĕr′k|ў *a.* having sudden abrupt movements; spasmodic; hence ∿ĭLY[2] *adv.,* ∿ĭNESS *n.* [f. JERK[1] + -Y[2]]

jĕrobŏ′ăm *n.* winebottle of 6–12 times ordinary size. [f. name of 'a mighty man of valour' 'who made Israel to sin', 1 Kgs. 11:28, 14:16]

jĕ′rrў *n.* **1.** ‖(sl.) chamber-pot; (*J*∿) German (soldier), Germans collectively. **2.** ∿**-builder**, -**building**, builder, building, of unsubstantial houses with bad materials; ∿**-built**, so built; ∿**can, je′rri-can**, kind of (orig. German) 5-gallon can for petrol or water. [variously f. prec., *Jeremy, German*, etc.; see -Y[3]]

jĕrrўmă′nder. Var. of GERRYMANDER.

jĕr′sey (-zĭ) *n.* **1.** (*J*∿). (animal or) breed of dairy cattle from Jersey. **2.** plain knitted fabric. **3.** close--fitting woollen knitted pullover, esp. as worn by sailor etc.; similar garment worn as undervest. [f. *Jersey*, largest of Channel Islands]

Jeru′salem (-rōō′-) *n.* **the New** ∿, heavenly abode of the blessed; *Jerusalem* ARTICHOKE. [∿, holy city in Israel]

jĕss *n., & v.t.* **1.** *n.* short strap of leather, silk, etc., round leg of hawk used in falconry. **2.** *v.t.* put jesses on (hawk). [ME *ges* f. OF *ges* nom. sing. & acc. pl. of *get* f. Rom. **jectus* for L *jactus* throw (*jacēre jact-* to throw)]

jĕ′ssamin(e). See JASMINE.

Jĕ′ssĕ *n.* ∿ **window** (showing Christ's descent from Jesse, usu. in form of tree). [name of David's father (1 Sam. 16:12); see Is. 11:1, Matt. 1:6, 16]

jĕst[1] *n.* piece of raillery, taunt; joke (**break a** ∿, utter it); fun (**in** ∿, not seriously); object of derision (*a standing* jest); ∿**-book**, book of jests. [orig. = exploit, f. OF *geste* f. L *gesta*, neut. pl. p.p. of *gerere* do]

jĕst[2] *v.i.* joke; jeer; speak or act in trifling manner. [f. prec.]

jĕ′ster *n.* one who jests, esp. (Hist.) professional maker of amusement maintained in court or noble household. [f. prec. + -ER[1]]

Jĕ′sū (-zū) *n.* (arch.) (Voc. form of name of) JESUS. [ME, f. OF obl. case *Iesu*]

Jĕ′sūĭt (-z-) *n.* member of Society of Jesus, RC order initiated by Ignatius Loyola and others (1534); (derog., arch.) dissembling person, equivocator; ∿**s′** (cinchona) **bark**; hence **Jĕsūĭ′tICAL** (-z-) *a.* (lit. or derog.), ∿ISM (-z-), ∿RY (4), *ns.,* ∿IZE (3) *v.t. & i.* [f. F *jésuite* or f. mod. L *Jesuita* (*Jesus*; see foll., -ITE[1])]

Jĕ′sus (-z-) *n.* **Society of** ∿ (see prec.); ∿ (**Christ**)!, (vulg.) excl. expr. surprise, impatience, etc. [name of founder of Christian religion d. *c.* AD 30]

jĕt[1] *n. & a.* (made of) hard black lignite taking brilliant polish; ∿(**-black**), (of) colour of this, deep glossy black. [ME, f. AF *geet*, **jeet*, OF *jaiet* f. L f. Gk *gagatēs* (*Gagai* in Asia Minor)]

jĕt[2] *n.* **1.** stream of water, steam, gas, flame, etc., shot forward or upwards esp. from small opening; spout, nozzle, for emitting water etc. thus; (colloq.) jet engine or plane. **2.** ∿ **engine** (using jet propulsion for forward thrust, esp. of aircraft); ∿ **lag**, delayed bodily effects felt after long flight by jet aircraft (esp.

owing to difference of local time); ∼ **plane** (with jet engine); ∼**-propelled**, having jet propulsion, (fig.) very fast; ∼ **propulsion** (by backward ejection of high-speed jet of gas etc.); ∼ **set**, wealthy élite making frequent air journeys between social or business events; ∼ **stream**, jet from jet engine, (Meteorol.) strong wind blowing in narrow range of altitudes in the atmosphere. [f. foll. & F f. *jeter* (as foll.)]

jĕt³ *v.t.* & *i.* (-tt-). **1.** spurt out in jets; (cause to) project forward; ‖(in *p.p.*, of pocket) with edges of aperture bound, to prevent ravelling. **2.** (colloq.) send, travel, by jet plane. [f. F *jeter* throw f. Rom. **jectare* = L *jactare* frequent. of *jacĕre jact-* throw; sense 2 f. prec.]

jeté (zhĕtā´) *n.* (Ballet). hop accompanied by kick with other leg. [F, p.p. of *jeter* throw (see prec.)]

jĕ'tsam *n.* goods thrown overboard from ship to lighten it, esp. such as are washed ashore (cf. FLOTSAM). [contr. of foll.]

jĕ'ttison *n.*, & *v.t.* **1.** *n.* throwing of goods overboard, esp. to lighten ship in distress; dropping of objects to lighten aircraft in flight; (fig.) abandonment. **2.** *v.t.* throw (goods) overboard, drop (object), thus; (fig.) abandon. [ME, f. AF *getteson*, OF *getaison* f. L *jactatio -onis* (*jactare* throw; see JET³, -ISON)]

jĕ'tton *n.* counter with stamped or engraved device. [f. F *jeton* (*jeter* throw, add up accounts; see JET²)]

jĕ'ttў¹ *n.* pier or mole running out to protect harbour or coast; landing-pier. [ME, f. OF *jetee*, fem. p.p. (as n.) of *jeter*; see JET³, -Y¹]

jĕ'ttў² *a.* jet-black. [f. JET¹ + -Y²]

jeu (zhŏr) *n.* (*pl.* ∼*x pr.* same), ∼ **de mots** (de mō´), play on words, pun; ∼ **d'esprit** (dĕsprē´), witty or humorous (usu. literary) trifle. [F, = play, game, f. L *jocus* jest]

jeune premier (zhŏrn premyā´) *n.* (Theatr.) actor playing part of youthful hero. [F, lit. 'first young man']

jeunesse dorée (zhŏrnĕs dōr´ā) *n.* = GILD¹ed *youth*. [F]

Jew¹ (jōō) *n.* **1.** person of Hebrew descent; person whose religion is Judaism; WANDERing *Jew*. **2.** (derog., colloq.; R) person who drives hard bargains, usurer. **3.** ∼**-baiting**, systematic persecution of Jews; **jew- -fish**, large Austral. food-fish of various species, esp. mulloway; ∼**'s-ear**, edible cup-shaped fungus; ∼**'s harp**, small lyre-shaped musical instrument played by holding metal frame between teeth and striking metal tongue with finger. **4.** Hence ∼**'ESS¹** *n.*, ∼**'ISH¹** *a.* [ME, f. OF *giu* f. L *judaeus* f. Gk *ioudaios* f. Aram. *yᵉhûdai* = Heb. *yᵉhûdí* (*yᵉhûdâh* Judah)]

jew² (jōō) *v.t.* ∼ (**down**), (derog., colloq.; R) cheat, bargain with (person) to lower his price. [f. prec. 2]

jew'el (jōō´-) *n.*, & *v.t.* (‖-ll-). **1.** *n.* ornament containing precious stone(s), worn for personal adornment; precious stone (used also in watches because of hardness); highly prized person or thing; ∼**-fish**, scarlet and green tropical fish; hence ∼**lў²** *a.* **2.** *v.t.* (esp. in *p.p.*) adorn or furnish with jewels; bejewel; (watch) with jewels for the pivot-holes. [ME, f. AF *j(e)uel*, OF *joel*; orig. uncert.]

jew'eller, ***-eler**, (jōō´-) *n.* maker of or dealer in jewels or jewellery; ∼**'s rouge**, finely divided rouge for polishing. [ME, f. AF *jueler*, OF *juelier* (as prec.; see -ER²)]

jew'ellerў, **jew'elrў**, (jōō´elrĭ) *n.* jewels collectively or as adornment; gems or ornaments worn for personal adornment. [ME f. OF *juelerie* (as prec.; see -ERY), & f. JEWEL, JEWELLER + -ERY, -RY]

Jewrў (joor´ĭ) *n.* Jews collectively; (Hist.) Jews' quarter in town etc. [ME, f. AF *juerie*, OF *juierie* (as JEW¹; see -RY)]

jĕzai'l (-zī'l) *n.* long Afghan musket. [f. Urdu *jazā'īl*]

Jĕ'zĕbĕl (-bĕl, -bĕl) *n.* shameless or profligate woman; woman who puts garish colour on her face. [∼, wife of Ahab (1 Kgs. 16, 19, 21)]

*JG *abbr.* junior grade (esp. of rank in Navy).

jib¹ *n.* **1.** triangular staysail from outer end of jib-boom

to fore-topmast-head in large ships, from bowsprit to mast-head in smaller ones; **cut of his** ∼, his personal appearance; ∼**-boom**, spar run out from end of bowsprit. **2.** projecting arm of crane. [17th c., of unkn. orig.]

jib² *v.* (-bb-). **1.** *v.t.* pull (sail, yard) round from one side of ship to the other. **2.** *v.i.* (Of sail etc.) swing round thus. [17th c., of unkn. orig.]

jib³ *v.i.* (-bb-). **1.** (Of horse etc.) stop and refuse to go on, move backwards or sideways instead of going on; hence ∼**'bER¹** *n.* **2.** (fig.) refuse to proceed in some action; ∼ **at**, show repugnance to (course of action, person). [19th c., of unkn. orig.]

ji'bba(h) (-ba) *n.* long cloth coat (as) worn by Muslim men. [Egypt. var. of Arab. *jubba*]

ji'b-door (-ōr) *n.* door flush with wall, usu. painted etc. so as to be indistinguishable. [18th c.; orig. unkn.]

*jibe¹ *v.i.* (colloq.) fit or agree (*with*). [19th c., of unkn. orig.]

jibe². See GIBE, GYBE.

jiff('ў) *n.* (colloq.) very short time (*in a jiffy*; (*wait*) *half a jiff*). [18th c., of unkn. orig.]

jig¹ *n.* **1.** lively jumping dance; music for this, usu. in triple time. **2.** appliance that holds a piece of work and guides the tools operating upon it. **3.** (sl.) joke, trick; **the ∼ is up**, success is now impossible. [16th c., of unkn. orig.]

jig² *v.* (-gg-). **1.** *v.i.* dance a jig. **2.** *v.t.* & *i.* move up and down rapidly and jerkily. **3.** *v.t.* separate coarser and finer portions of (ore) by shaking it under water in box with perforated bottom. **4.** work upon with a jig; equip with jigs; ∼**'saw**, machine fretsaw; ∼**saw (puzzle)**, picture pasted on board and cut in irregular pieces with jigsaw to form puzzle of reassembling them. [prob. f. prec.]

ji'gger¹ (-g-) *n.* **1.** (Naut.) small tackle consisting of a double and single block with rope; small sail at stern; small smack having this. **2.** (Bill. sl.) device forming rest for cue; (Golf) iron club with narrow face. **3.** one who jigs ore. **4.** (sl.) contrivance, gadget. **5.** (small glass holding) measure of spirits etc. **6.** woman's short loose jacket. **7.** ∼**-mast**, (1) small mast at stern, (2) aftermost mast in four-master [partly f. prec. + -ER¹]

ji'gger² (-g-) *n.* = CHIGOE or *CHIGGER 2. [corrupt.]

ji'ggered (-gerd) *a.* (colloq.) (As mild oath) confounded (*I'll be jiggered*). [euphem.]

‖**ji'ggerў-pō'kerў** (-g-) *n.* (colloq.) underhand scheming; hocus-pocus, nonsense. [cf. Sc. *joukery- -pawkery* (*jouk* dodge, skulk)]

ji'ggle *v.t.* rock or jerk lightly. [f. JIG² + LE 3, or f. JOGGLE¹]

jiha'd, **jĕha'd**, (-ah'd) *n.* religious war of Muslims against unbelievers; (fig.) campaign for or against a doctrine etc. [f. Arab. *jihād*]

Jill. Var. of GILL⁴ (JACK¹ *and Jill*).

jillaroō', **jilleroō'**, *n.* (Austral. colloq.) girl jackaroo. [joc. f. prec. + JACKAROO]

jilt *n.*, & *v.t.* **1.** *n.* person (esp. woman) who capriciously casts off lover after encouraging him. **2.** *v.t.* act as jilt towards, be faithless to. [17th c., of unkn. orig.]

*Jim Crow¹ (-ō´) *n.* **1.** (derog.; R) a Black; racial segregation esp. of Blacks; hence ∼ISM (3) *n.* **2.** implement for straightening iron bars or rails by screw pressure. [nickname]

ji'm-jăms (-z) *n. pl.* (sl.) delirium tremens; fit of depression or nervousness. [fanciful redupl.]

*ji'mmў. Var. of JEMMY 1.

*ji'mson *n.* ∼ (**weed**), highly poisonous tall weed (*Datura stramonium*) with large trumpet-shaped flowers. [f. *Jamestown* in Virginia]

ji'ngle (-nggel) *n.* & *v.* **1.** *n.* mingled noise like that of small bells, links of chain, etc.; thing designed to make this; repetition of same or similar sounds in words, esp. if designed to catch the attention; short verse of this kind used in advertising etc.; words intended to attract by sound rather than sense; Irish and

Australian covered two-wheeled vehicle; ∼**-jangle,** continuous alternation of jingling sounds; hence **ji′ngl**y² *a.* **2.** *v.i.* & *t.* make, cause (keys etc.) to make, a jingle; (of writing) be full of alliterations, rhymes, etc. [ME; imit.]

ji′ngō (-nggō) *n.* (*pl.* ∼**es**). **1.** (In asseverations) **by (the living)** ∼**!. 2.** supporter of bellicose policy, blustering patriot (orig. supporter of Beaconsfield's policy in 1878, f. use of *by jingo* in popular song); hence ∼**ism** (2), ∼**ist** (2), *ns.,* ∼**i′stic** *a.* [17th c.; orig. conjurer's gibberish]

jink *v.* & *n.* **1.** *v.i.* move elusively, dodge; make tricky turn in Rugby football; (sl.) manœuvre aircraft, be manœuvred, jerkily to avoid anti-aircraft fire etc. **2.** *v.t.* elude by dodging. **3.** *n.* act of jinking; **high** ∼**s,** boisterous sport, merry-making. [orig. Sc.; prob. imit. of nimble motion]

jinnee′ (*pl.* **jinn**), **jinn,** *ns.* (Muslim Myth.) spirit lower than angels, able to appear in human and animal forms, and having supernatural power over men. [f. Arab. *jinnī*, pl. *jinn*; cf. GENIE]

jinri′cksha, jinri′kisha, *n.* (arch.) = RICKSHAW. [Jap. *jinrikisha* (see RICKSHAW)]

jinx *n.* (colloq.) person or thing that seems to cause bad luck. [perh. var. of *jynx* wryneck, charm]

jipija′pa (hĭpīhah′pa) *n.* = TOQUILLA. [Sp., f. *Jipijapa* in Ecuador]

*****ji′tney** *n.* (sl.) five cents; motor bus carrying passengers at low rates; thing of poor quality. [20th c., of unkn. orig.]

ji′tter *v.i.,* & *n.* (colloq.) **1.** *v.i.* be nervous, act nervously; ∼**bug,** (1) person addicted to dancing to hot music, (2) such dance, (3) nervous person. **2.** *n.* (in *pl.*) extreme nervousness; hence ∼**y²** *a.,* nervy, jumpy. [20th c., of unkn. orig.]

jiu-jitsu. Var. of JU-JITSU.

jive *n.,* & *v.i.* (sl.) **1.** *n.* fast, lively jazz music; lively dancing esp. to jazz. **2.** *v.i.* play jive; dance (to) jive. [20th c.; orig. uncert.]

Jno. *abbr.* John.

Jnr. *abbr.* Junior.

jō *n.* (*pl.* **joes**). (Sc.) sweetheart, beloved. [var. of JOY¹]

jŏb¹ *n.* **1.** piece of work, esp. one done for hire or profit; (sl.) a crime, esp. a robbery; product of work, esp. if well done. **2.** transaction in which private advantage prevails over duty or public interest. **3.** paid position of employment; (colloq.) anything one has to do; (colloq.) difficult task. **4. bad** ∼, unsatisfactory state of affairs (*make the best of a bad job*), thing on which labour or concern is wasted; **good** ∼, satisfactory or fortunate state of affairs; ∼**s for the boys,** (colloq.) profitable situations etc. to reward one's supporters; **just the** ∼, (sl.) precisely what is wanted; **make a (good)** ∼ **of,** do thoroughly or successfully; **on the** ∼, at work, in the course of doing a piece of work; **out of a** ∼, unemployed. **5.** ∥∼**′centre,** employment exchange displaying information about available jobs; ∼ **lot,** lot of goods bought as speculation, miscellaneous group of articles; ∥∼**′master,** one who lets out horses and carriages for limited periods; ∼**-sheet** (for recording details of jobs done); ∼**-work** (done and paid for by the job). **6.** Hence ∼LESS *a.,* unemployed. [16th c., of unkn. orig.]

jŏb² *v.* (**-bb-**). **1.** *v.i.* do jobs. **2.** *v.t.* ∥hire (horse, carriage) for definite time or job; let out on hire thus. **3.** *v.t.* & *i.* buy and sell (stock, goods) as middleman; deal in stocks; ∼ **backwards,** (fig.) use hindsight. **4.** turn position of trust to private advantage; deal corruptly with (matter), whence ∼**′bery** (4) *n.;* *(sl.) swindle. **5.** Hence ∼**′ber¹** *n.* (esp. = STOCKjobber or *wholesaler), ∼**′bing²** *a.* (esp. of carpenter, gardener, printer, etc.). [f. prec.]

jŏb³ *v.* (**-bb-**) & *n.* **1.** *v.t.* prod, stab slightly. **2.** *v.i.* thrust *at* (thing). **3.** *n.* prod, thrust, jerk at horse's bit. [ME, app. imit.; cf. JAB]

Jŏb⁴ *n.* patriarch, story of whose patience in adversity

forms Book of Job in OT (**would try the patience of** ∼, is vexatious); ∼**'s comforter,** one who under guise of comforting aggravates distress; ∼**'s tears,** seeds of a grass (*Coix lacryma-jobi*) used as beads.

∥**jōbā′tion** *n.* (colloq.) (Esp. lengthy) reprimand. [f. obs. *jobe* reprove (f. JOB⁴) + -ATION]

jŏ′bber. See JOB².

∥**jŏ′bbernowl** (-ōl) *n.* (colloq.) stupid head; stupid person. [f. obs. *jobard* (F, f. OF *jobe* silly) + (now dial.) *noll* head]

∥**Jŏck¹** *n.* (Army sl.) Scottish (esp. Highland) soldier. [Sc. form of JACK¹]

jŏck² *n.* (colloq.) jockey. [abbr.]

*****jŏck³** *n.* (sl.) = JOCK-STRAP. [abbr.]

jŏ′ckey¹ *n.* (esp. professional) rider in horse-races; ∼ **cap** (with long peak, as worn by jockeys); ∥**J**∼ **Club,** club established at Newmarket and controlling horse-racing; hence ∼DOM, ∼SHIP (3), *ns.* [dim. of JOCK¹; see -Y³]

jŏ′ckey² *v.* **1.** *v.t.* outwit, cheat; get (person etc.) *away, out, in,* etc., by trickery; manœuvre or cheat (person *into, out of, doing*). **2.** *v.i.* cheat; ∼ **for position,** try to gain an advantageous position esp. by skilful manœuvring or unfair action. [f. prec.]

jŏ′ck-străp *n.* support or protection for male genitals, worn esp. by sportsmen; *(sl.) athletic person. [f. vulg. *jock* genitals+STRAP]

jocō′se *a.* playful; fond of joking; waggish; hence ∼LY² (-slĭ) *adv.,* ∼NESS (-sn-), **jocō′sity,** *ns.* [f. L *jocosus* (*jocus* jest; see -OSE¹)]

jŏ′cūlar *a.* merry, fond of joking; of the nature of a joke, humorous; hence ∼ITY (-ă′r-) *n.,* ∼LY² *adv.* [f. L *jocularis* (*joculus* dim. of *jocus* jest; see -AR¹)]

jŏ′cund *a.* (literary). merry, cheerful, sprightly; pleasant; hence or cogn. **jocŭ′nd**ITY *n.,* ∼LY² *adv.* [ME f. OF, f. L *jocundus, jucundus* (*juvare* delight)]

jŏ′dhpurs (-dperz) *n. pl.* long breeches for riding etc., close-fitting from knee to ankle. [f. *Jodhpur* in India]

jŏ′ey *n.* (Austral.) young kangaroo; young animal. [f. Aboriginal *joè*]

jŏg *v.* (**-gg-**) & *n.* **1.** *v.t.* shake with push or jerk; nudge (person), esp. to arouse attention; stimulate (person's, or one's own, memory). **2.** *v.i.* move up and down with unsteady motion; (of horse) move at jogtrot; proceed laboriously, trudge, (*on, along*); go on one's way; proceed, get through the time, (*we must jog on somehow; matters jog along*); run at slow pace esp. as physical exercise, whence ∼**′ger¹** (-g-) *n.* **3.** ∼**′trot,** slow regular trot, (fig.) monotonous progression. **4.** *n.* shake, push, nudge; slow walk or trot. [ME; app. imit.]

jŏ′ggle¹ *v.* & *n.* **1.** *v.t.* & *i.* shake, move, (as) by repeated jerks. **2.** *n.* slight shake; act or action of joggling. [f. prec.+-LE 3]

jŏ′ggle² *n.,* & *v.t.* **1.** *n.* joint of two pieces of stone or timber, contrived to prevent their sliding on one another; notch in one of two pieces, projection in the other, or small piece let in between the two, for this purpose. **2.** *v.t.* join with joggle. [perh. f. *jog* = JAG¹]

Jŏhă′nnīne *a.* of the apostle John. [f. L (as JOHN; see -INE¹)]

Jŏhă′nnisbĕrger (-g-) *n.* fine white wine from *Johannisberg* in the Rheingau. [G]

John (jŏn) *n.* **1.** (J∼). (sl., derog.) policeman; *(sl.) lavatory; (sl.) prostitute's client. **2.** *John* BARLEYcorn; ∼ **Bull,** English nation, typical Englishman; ∼ **Chinaman,** (derog.) typical Chinese; ∼ **Citizen,** average man; ∼ **Collins,** Collins made with gin; ∼ **Doe,** fictitious character in law (cf. RICHARD *Roe*), *average man; *John* DORY¹; ∼-o′-*Groat's*(-House), extreme north of Scotland (*from* ∼-o′-*Groat's to* Land's *End*, through Great Britain); *∼ **Hancock, Henry,** person's signature. [man's Christian name; ME, f. L *Jo(h)annes* f. Gk *Iōannēs* f. Heb. *yôḥānān*]

jŏ′hnnȳ (jŏ′nĭ) *n.* ∥(colloq.) fellow, man; ∥**J**∼ **Armstrong,** (Naut. sl.) hand-power; **J**∼ **Raw,** novice; ∼**-cake,** cake of (US) maize-meal or (Austral.)

wheat-meal; ∼-come-lately, (colloq.) recently arrived person; *∼-jump-up, violet or pansy. [f. JOHN+-Y³]

John|sō′nian (jŏn-) *a.* of or like S. Johnson, esp. in using many long words of Latin derivation; so ∼sonE′SE *n.* [f. S. *Johnson*, Engl. man of letters and lexicographer d. 1784+-IAN]

joie de vivre (zhwah de vē′vr) *n.* feeling of healthy and exuberant enjoyment of life. [F, = joy of living]

join *v.* & *n.* **1.** *v.t.* put together, fasten, unite, (things, one *to* another, *together*); connect (two points) by (esp. straight) line; unite (persons, one *with* or *to* another) in marriage, friendship, alliance, etc. (*join* FORCE¹s). **2.** *v.i.* come together, be united, (*with, to,* or abs.); take part with others (*in* doing or action; ∼ **in**, take part); ∼ **up**, enlist in army etc. **3.** *v.t.* come into the company of (person); associate oneself with (person) *in* action, *for* meal, etc.; become member of (club, army, etc.); take or resume one's place in (regiment, ship, train, procession, company, etc.); be or become connected or continuous with (*the Cherwell joins the Thames at Oxford*). **4.** ∼ **battle**, begin fighting; ∼ **hands**, clasp one's hands together, clasp each other's hands, (fig.) combine in action or enterprise; *join* ISSUE¹. **5.** *n.* point, line, or surface of junction. [ME, f. OF *joindre* (st. *joign-*) f. L *jungere junct-* join f. IE *jug-; cf. YOKE]

joi′nder *n.* (law) joining, union. [AF, f. OF *joindre* to join; see prec., -ER¹]

joi′n|er *n.* In vbl senses; one who makes furniture, house fittings, and other woodwork that is lighter than carpenter's, whence ∼ERY (1, 2) *n.*; (colloq.) person who readily joins societies etc. [ME, f. AF *joignour*, OF *joigneor* (as JOIN; see -OR, -ER²)]

joint¹ *n.* **1.** place at which two things are joined together. **2.** structure in animal body by which two bones are fitted together; **out of** ∼, (of bone) dislocated, (fig.) out of order; *put* person's NOSE *out of joint*. **3.** part of stem from which leaf or branch grows. **4.** point at which, contrivance by which, two parts of artificial structure are joined, rigidly or so as to allow of movement; piece of flexible material as hinge of book-cover; (Geol.) fissure in mass of rock. **5.** one of the parts of which a body is made up; one of the parts into which butcher divides carcass, esp. as roasted and served at table. **6.** (sl.) place of meeting or resort; marijuana cigarette. **7.** ∼-**stool** [orig. *joined*-], (Hist.) one made of parts fitted by a joiner, night-stool, commode. **8.** Hence ∼′LESS *a.* [ME, f. OF, p.p. (as n.) of *joindre* JOIN]

joint² *a.* held or done by, belonging to, two or more persons etc. in conjunction (*joint* ACCOUNT², *action, opinion, estate*); (esp. of person) sharing (*with* others in possession, action, state, etc.; *joint author, favourite, heir, owner*); *joint and* SEVERAL; **during their** ∼ **lives**, while they are both or all alive; ∼ **stock**, capital held jointly, common fund, (*attrib.*) holding, formed on basis of a joint stock (*joint-stock bank, company*); hence ∼′LY⁰ *adv.* [ME f. OF p.p. (as prec.)]

joint³ *v.t.* connect by joints; fill up joints of (masonry etc.) with mortar etc., point; prepare (board etc.) for being joined to another by planing its edge; divide (body, member) at a joint or into joints. [f. JOINT¹]

joi′nter *n.* In vbl senses; plane for jointing; tool for jointing masonry; workman employed in jointing wires, pipes, etc. [f. prec.+-ER¹]

joi′ntress *n.* widow who holds a jointure. [f. obs. *jointer* joint possessor+-ESS¹]

joi′nture *n.*, & *v.t.* **1.** *n.* estate settled on wife for period during which she survives husband. **2.** *v.t.* provide (wife) with jointure. [ME f. OF, f. L *junctura* (as JOIN; see -URE)]

joist *n.* one of parallel timbers stretched on edge from wall to wall for ceiling laths or floor boards to be nailed to; hence ∼′ED² *a.* [ME f. OF *giste* f. Rom. *jacitum* neut. p.p. of L *jacēre* lie]

jōke¹ *n.* thing said or done to excite laughter; witticism, jest; ridiculous thing, person, or circumstance; **no** ∼,

a serious matter; **practical** ∼, trick played on person in order to have laugh at his expense; **standing** ∼, what is regarded as irremediably ridiculous; hence **jō′k(e)y²** *a.* [orig. sl., perh. f. L *jocus* jest]

jōk|e² *v.* **1.** *v.i.* make jokes; ∼ing **apart**, seriously (after there has been joking). **2.** *v.t.* poke fun at, banter. [f. prec. or f. L *jocari* to jest (as prec.)]

jō′ker *n.* one who jokes; (sl.) fellow, man; (Cards) odd (often blank) card in some games, counting as (highest) trump or as WILD card; *clause unobtrusively inserted in bill or document and affecting its operation in way not immediately apparent; unexpected factor or resource. [f. prec.+-ER¹]

jokul, jökull, (yŏ′kōōl, yēr′-) *n.* snow-mountain in Iceland. [Icel. *jökull* ICICLE]

jolie laide (zhŏlē lā′d) *n.* (*pl. jolies laides pr.* same). = BELLE LAIDE. [F (*jolie* pretty, *laide* ugly, fem. adjs.)]

jō′lli|fy *v.i.* make merry, esp. in drinking; hence ∼FICA′TION *n.* [f. JOLLY¹+-FY]

jō′llity *n.* merry-making, festivity. [ME, f. OF *joliveté* (as foll.; see -TY¹)]

jō′lly¹ *a., adv., n.,* & *v.t.* **1.** *a.* joyful; slightly drunk; festive, jovial, (**the** ∼ **god**, Bacchus; **J**∼ **Roger**, pirates' black flag usu. with skull and cross-bones). **2.** (colloq.) pleasant or thing) very pleasant, delightful, (often iron.: *he must be a jolly fool to do it*). **3.** *adv.* (colloq.) very (*he was jolly miserable, for he's a jolly good fellow; you will jolly well have to*). **4.** *n.* ||(sl.) Royal Marine. *v.t.* (colloq.) flatter, cajole, (usu. *jolly along*); chaff, banter. [ME f. OF *jolif* gay, pretty, perh. f. ON *jól* YULE]

jō′lly² *n.* ∼-(**-boat**), clinker-built ship's-boat, smaller than cutter. [18th c., of unkn. orig.; cf. 16th–17th c. *jolywat, gellywatte* and YAWL]

jōlt *v.* & *n.* **1.** *v.t.* shake (person etc.) with jerk from seat etc., esp. in locomotion; give mental shock to, perturb. **2.** *v.i.* (Of vehicle) move along with jerks, as on rough road. **3.** *n.* such jerk; surprise, shock; hence ∼′Y² *a.* [16th c., of unkn. orig.]

Jon. *abbr.* Jonah (OT); Jonathan.

Jō′nah (-a) *n.* person who seems to bring bad luck. [∼ in OT]

Jō′nathan *n.* **1.** ||(**Brother**) ∼, personified people of, typical citizen of, United States. **2.** kind of red-skinned Amer. dessert apple. [perh. f. ∼ Trumbull, 18th-c. governor of Connecticut]

Jōnes (-nz) *n.* KEEP¹ up with the *Joneses*. [common surname]

jongleur (zhaw′nglēr) *n.* (Hist.) itinerant minstrel. [F, var. of *jougleur* JUGGLER]

jō′nquil *n.* species of narcissus with rushlike leaves and clusters of fragrant white and yellow flowers. [f. mod. L *jonquilla* or F *jonquille* f. Sp. *junquillo* dim. of JUNCO]

Jōr′dan *n.* ∼ **almond**, fine almond esp. from Malaga. [ME, prob. f. OF or Sp. *jardin* GARDEN, assim. to name of river (see foll.)]

Jōrdā′nian *a.* & *n.* (native or inhabitant) of kingdom of the Jordan in SW Asia. [f. *Jordan*, river of Palestine flowing into Dead Sea,+-IAN]

jōr′um *n.* large drinking-bowl; its contents, esp. punch. [perh. f. *Joram* (2 Sam. 8:10)]

Jos. *abbr.* Joseph.

jōsh *n.* & *v.* (sl.) **1.** *n.* good-natured joke, leg-pull. **2.** *v.t.* hoax, banter. **3.** *v.i.* indulge in ridicule. **4.** Hence ∼′ER¹ *n.* [19th c.; orig. unkn.]

Josh. *abbr.* Joshua (OT).

Jō′shua (-shwa) *n.* ∼(-**tree**), many-branched yucca in western US. [prob. f. gestures of ∼ in OT (Josh. 8:18)]

jōss *n.* Chinese idol; ∼-**house**, Chinese temple; ∼-**stick**, (of fragrant tinder mixed with clay, as incense). [perh. ult. f. Port. *deos* f. L *deus* god]

||**jō′sser** *n.* (sl.) fool; fellow. [f. prec.+-ER¹; cf. Austral. sense 'clergyman']

jō′stle (-sel) *v.* & *n.* **1.** *v.i.* knock or push *against*; struggle *with* (person *for* thing). **2.** *v.t.* push against, elbow; push (person *away, from,* etc.). **3.** *n.* jostling; collision (lit. or fig.). [ME; earlier *justle,* f. JUST³, JOUST+-LE³]

jŏt¹ *n.* (Usu. w. neg. expressed or implied) small amount, whit (*not one jot or tittle*). [f. L f. Gk IOTA; cf. Matt. 5:18]

jŏt² *v.t.* (-tt-). write (usu. *down*) briefly or hastily; hence ∼'tER¹ *n.*, (esp.) small pad or notebook for memoranda etc., ∼'tING¹ (2) *n.* [f. prec.]

joule (jōōl) *n.* unit of work or energy, work done by force of one newton when its point of application moves one metre in the direction of action of the force, work done or heat generated by a current of one ampere flowing for one second against a resistance of one ohm. [f. J. P. *Joule*, Engl. physicist d. 1889]

jounce *v.t.* & *i.* bump, bounce, jolt. [ME, of unkn. orig.]

jour'nal (jer'-) *n.* **1.** (In bookkeeping by double entry) book in which each transaction is entered, with statement of accounts to which it is to be debited and credited. **2.** daily record of events; (Naut.) log-book; the J∼s, (Parl.) record of daily proceedings. **3.** daily or other newspaper; other periodical, esp. one dealing with current events or learned topics. **4.** part of shaft or axle that rests on bearings [hist. unexpl.]; ∼-bearing (supporting this); ∼-box (enclosing journal and bearings). [ME, f. OF *jurnal* f. LL *diurnalis* DIURNAL]

jour'nal|ist (jer'-) *n.* one whose business it is to edit, or write for, a journal (sense 3), esp. a newspaper; hence or cogn. ∼E'SE *n.*, style of language said to be characteristic of (hasty or inferior) newspaper writing, ∼ISM (2) *n.*, ∼ĭ'stIC *a.* [f. prec. + -IST]

jour'nalize (jer'-), **-ise** (-īz), *v.t.* & *i.* record in, or keep, private journal. [f. JOURNAL + -IZE]

jour'ney (jer'-) *n.*, & *v.i.* **1.** *n.* distance travelled in specified time (*a day's*, *4 days', journey*); act of going to some distance, round of travel (usu. by land; cf. VOYAGE; *take, undertake, perform, a journey*); travelling of vehicle along route at stated time; ∼man, qualified mechanic or artisan who works for another, reliable but not outstanding worker, (fig.) mere hireling; ∼*man clock*, secondary clock adjusted or controlled by another; ∼-work, work of a journeyman (esp. fig.). **2.** *v.i.* make a journey. [ME; (v. f. AF *journeyer*) f. OF *jornee* day, day's work or travel, f. Rom. **diurnata* day (LL *diurnum* day f. L *diurnus* daily); see -y⁴]

joust (jowst, jōōst), **jŭst³**, *v.i.*, & *n.* (engage in) combat between two knights etc. on horseback with lances. [ME, (n. f. OF *juste*) f. OF *juster* bring together f. Rom. **juxtare* approach f. L *juxta* near]

Jŏve *n.* Jupiter; **by ∼!** (excl. of surprise or approval). [ME, f. L *Jovis* gen. of OL *Jovis* used as gen. of JUPITER]

jŏ'vial *a.* merry; convivial; hearty and good-humoured; hence ∼ITY (-ă'l-) *n.*, ∼LY² *adv.* [F, f. LL *jovialis* of Jupiter (as prec.; see -AL), w. ref. to supposed influenced of planet Jupiter on those born under it]

Jŏ'vian *a.* of or like Jupiter; of the planet Jupiter. [f. as JOVE + -IAN]

jowar' *n.* durra. [f. Hindi *jawār*]

jowl *n.* **1.** jawbone; jaw; cheek, esp. CHEEK *by jowl*. **2.** external throat or neck when prominent, dewlap of cattle, crop of bird. **3.** head and shoulders of salmon and other fish. [(1) ME *chavel* jaw (f. OE *ceafl*); (2) ME *cholle* neck (f. OE *ceole*); (3) ME *cholle* head of man, beast, or fish]

joy¹ *n.* **1.** vivid emotion of pleasure, gladness, (*at, in, of*); **no ∼**, (colloq.) no satisfaction or success; WISH person *joy of it*. **2.** thing that causes delight. **3.** ∼-bells (rung on festive occasions); ∼-ride, (colloq.) pleasure-ride in motor car etc., usu. without its owner's permission; ∼'stick, (sl.) control-lever of aeroplane. **4.** Hence or cogn. ∼'LESS, ∼'OUS, *adjs.* [ME, f. OF *joie* f. Rom. **gaudia* fem. f. L *gaudia* pl. of *gaudium* (*gaudēre* rejoice)]

joy² *v.i.* & *t.* (chiefly poet.) rejoice; gladden. [ME, f. OF *joïr* rejoice f. Rom. **gaudire* for L *gaudēre* rejoice]

joy'ance *n.* (chiefly poet.) rejoicing; festivity; delight. [f. prec. + -ANCE]

Joy'cèan *a.* & *n.* **1.** *a.* of or characteristic of (the writings of) Joyce. **2.** *n.* specialist in or admirer of Joyce's works. [f. J. *Joyce*, Ir. poet and novelist d. 1941 + -EAN]

joy'ful *a.* full of, showing, or causing, joy; hence ∼LY² *adv.*, ∼NESS *n.* [ME, f. JOY¹ + -FUL]

JP *abbr.* Justice of the Peace.

Jr. *abbr.* Junior.

jt. *abbr.* joint.

ju'bil|āte (jōō'-) *v.i.* exult, make demonstrations of joy; hence or cogn. ∼ANCE, ∼A'TION, *ns.*, ∼ANT *a.* [f. L *jubilare* shout esp. for joy + -ATE³]

Jubilātè (De'ō) (jōōbĭlahtŭ dā'ō) *n.* canticle consisting of Ps. 100. [L, = shout ye to God, its first words]

ju'bĭlee (jōō'-) *n.* **1.** (Jewish Hist.) year of emancipation and restoration, kept every 50 years, (see Lev. 25). **2.** (RC Ch.) period of remission from penal consequences of sin, granted under certain conditions for a year usu. at intervals of 25 years. **3.** anniversary (esp. fiftieth, **golden** ∼); DIAMOND *jubilee*; SILVER¹ *jubilee*. **4.** season of rejoicing; exultant joy. [ME, f. OF *jubilé* f. LL *jubilaeus* (*annus year*) of jubilee f. Gk *iōbēlaios* (*iōbēlos* f. Heb. *yōbēl* ram, ram's-horn trumpet, jubilee) by assoc. w. L *jubilare* (see JUBILATE)]

Jud. *abbr.* Judith (Apocr.).

Judae'an, ***Judē'an***, (jōō-) *a.* & *n.* (inhabitant) of Judaea in Palestine. [f. *Judaea* + -AN]

Judae'o-, ***Judē'ō-***, (jōō-) *comb. form.* Jew(ish), as ∼-German, Yiddish; ∼PHOBE *n.* & *a.* [f. L *judaeus* Jew(ish) + -o-]

Judā'ic (jōō-) *a.* of or characteristic of Jews. [f. L f. Gk *Ioudaïkos* (*Ioudaios* JEW¹; see -IC)]

Ju'dā|ism (jōō'-) *n.* religion of the Jews, with belief in one God and based on Mosaic and rabbinical teachings; Jews collectively; hence ∼IST (2) *n.* [ME, f. LL *Judaismus* f. Gk *Ioudaïsmos* (as prec.; see -ISM)]

Ju'dāīze (jōō'-), **-īse** (-īz), *v.* **1.** *v.i.* follow Jewish customs or rites. **2.** *v.t.* make Jewish; convert to Judaism. [f. LL *judaizare* f. Gk *ioudaïzō* (as JUDAIC; see -IZE)]

Ju'das (jōō'-) *n.* infamous traitor; (*j*∼) peep-hole in door; ∼-colour(ed), (of beard etc.) red; ∼ kiss, act of betrayal (Matt. 26:48); ∼-tree (with purple flowers usu. appearing before the leaves). [name of apostle who betrayed Christ]

ju'dder *v.i.*, & *n.* **1.** *v.i.* (Esp. of mechanism) shake noisily or violently; (of singer's voice) oscillate in intensity. **2.** *n.* instance of juddering. [imit.; cf. SHUDDER]

Judg. *abbr.* Judges (OT).

judge¹ *n.* **1.** public officer appointed to hear and try causes in court of justice (SOBER *as a judge*); (of God) supreme arbiter (*as God is my judge*). **2.** (Jewish Hist.) officer having temporary authority in Israel in period between Joshua and the kings; (in *pl.*) seventh book of OT, containing history of this period. **3.** person appointed to decide dispute or contest; person who decides a question; person who is qualified to decide on merits of thing or question (*am no judge of that*; *good judge of claret*). **4.** J∼ **Advocate General**, civil officer in supreme control of courts martial in army or air force; ∼-made law, principles based on judges' decisions; ‖*judge's* MARSHAL¹; ‖J∼s' **Rules** (regarding admissibility of accused's statements in custody). **5.** Hence ∼'SHIP (1, 2) (-jsh-) *n.* [ME f. OF *juge* f. L *judex judicis* (*jus* law, *-dicus* speaking)]

judge² *v.* **1.** *v.t.* pronounce sentence on (person) in court of justice; try (cause); decide (question); have authority over as JUDGE¹ (esp. sense 2); act as JUDGE¹ (sense 3) of; form opinion about, estimate, appraise, (person etc. *by* his deeds etc.); (arch.) criticize, censure, (*judge not that ye be not judged*); conclude, consider, suppose, (thing *to be, that*, etc., *from* or *by* data). **2.** *v.i.* act as judge; form a judgement (*of* thing etc.). [ME, f. OF *jug(i)er* f. L *judicare* (*judex*; see prec.)]

jŭdgemă'tic(al) (-jm-) *adjs.* (colloq.) judicious, discerning; hence ∼ALLY *adv.* [f. JUDGE¹ after *dogmatic*]

ju'dgement, ju'dgment, (-jm-) *n.* **1.** sentence of court of justice, decision by judge; **J~ of Paris,** (Gk. Myth.) award of golden apple by Paris to Aphrodite, leading to abduction of Helen and to Trojan War; **the Last J~** (of mankind by God at end of world); sIT *in judgement.* **2.** misfortune viewed as sign of divine displeasure (often joc.: *it is a judgement on you for getting up late).* **3.** criticism; opinion, estimate, (*in my judgement*; **against** one's **better ~,** contrary to what one really feels to be advisable); critical faculty, discernment, (*error of judgement*); good sense; hence ~AL *a.* **4.** J~ **Day, day of ~,** (of God's final judgement); ~ **debt** (for whose payment a judgement has been given); ~ **creditor, debtor,** (for, against, whom judgement has been given); **~-seat,** judge's seat, tribunal; ||~ **summons** (for failure to pay judgement debt). [ME, f. OF *jugement* (as JUDGE²; see -MENT)]

ju'dicature (joō'-) *n.* **1.** administration of justice; **Supreme Court of J~** in England (consisting of Court of Appeal and High Court of Justice; the latter is composed of the Queen's Bench, the Chancery, and the Family divisions, and the Court of Appeal, Criminal division). **2.** judge's (term of) office; body of judges; court of justice. [f. med. L *judicatura* f. L *judicare*; see JUDGE², -URE]

judi'cial (joōdi'shal) *a.* **1.** of, done by, proper to, a court of law; ~ **factor,** (Sc.) official RECEIVER; ~ **murder,** legal but unjust death sentence; *judicial* SEPARATION. **2.** inflicted as a divine judgement. **3.** having the function of judgement (*a judicial assembly*). **4.** of, or proper to, a judge; expressing a judgement, critical; impartial. **5.** Hence ~LY² *adv.* [ME, f. L *judicialis* (as foll.; see -AL)]

judi'ciary (joōdi'sherī) *n.* the judges of a State collectively. [f. L *judiciarius* (*judicium* judgement f. *judex* JUDGE¹; see -ARY¹)]

judi'cious (joōdi'shus) *a.* sensible, prudent; sound in discernment and judgement; hence ~LY² *adv.,* ~NESS *n.* [f. F *judicieux* f. L *judicium* (as prec.); see -OUS]

ju'dō (joō'-) *n.* (*pl.* ~s). modern refined form of ju-jitsu; hence ~**ka** (*pl.* same), ~IST, student of or expert in judo. [Jap. (*jū* gentle, *dō* way)]

Ju'dy (joō'-) *n.* See PUNCH¹; (*or j~*; colloq.) woman. [pet-form of woman's Christian name *Judith*; see -Y³]

jug¹ *n.* **1.** deep vessel for holding liquids, with handle and often with spout or lip shaped for pouring; *large jar with narrow mouth; hence ~'FUL 2 *n.* **2.** (stone) ~, (sl.) prison [perh. f. *Jug,* pet-form of woman's Christian name *Joan* etc.]

jug² *v.t.* (-gg-). stew, boil, (hare, rabbit) in covered vessel; (usu. in *p.p.*); (sl.) imprison. [f. prec.]

jug³ *v.i.* (-gg-). (Of nightingale or other bird) utter sound *jug*; so **jug, jug-jug,** *ns.* [imit.]

Jugendstil (yoō'gentshtēl) *n.* German equivalent of ART² *nouveau.* [G (*jugend* youth, *stil* style)]

Ju'ggernaut (-g-) *n.* **1.** (Hind. Myth.) Krishna, eighth avatar of Vishnu; his idol at Puri in Orissa, annually dragged in procession on huge car, under wheels of which devotees are said to have formerly thrown themselves. **2.** (fig.) institution or notion to which persons blindly sacrifice themselves or others; (*j~*) large overpowering force or object, very large and heavy motor vehicle. [f. Hindi *Jagannath* f. Skr. *Jagannātha* (*jagat-* world, *nāthás* lord)]

ju'ggins (-gīnz) *n.* (sl.) simpleton. [perh. f. proper name *Juggins* (as JUG¹); cf. MUGGINS]

ju'ggle *v.* & *n.* **1.** *v.i.* perform conjuring tricks; perform feats of dexterity (*with* several objects tossed up and caught); ~ **with,** deceive (person), misrepresent (facts), rearrange adroitly. **2.** *v.t.* perform juggling feats with; cheat (person etc. *out of* thing); bring, get, change, (*away, into,* etc.) by trickery. **3.** *n.* piece of juggling, fraud. [ME, back-form. f. foll., or f. OF *jogler, jugler* f. L *joculari* jest (*joculus* dim. of *jocus* jest)]

ju'ggl|er *n.* one who juggles; conjuror; trickster, impostor; so ~ERY (2, 4) *n.* [ME, f. OF *jo(u)glere -eor* f. L *joculator -oris* (as prec.; see -ER²)]

Jugoslav. See YUGOSLAV.

ju'gular *a.* & *n.* **1.** *a.* of the neck or throat; ~ **veins,** great veins of neck, conveying blood from head. **2.** (Of fish) having ventral fins in front of pectoral. **3.** *n.* jugular vein. [f. LL *jugularis* f. L *jugulum* collar-bone, throat, dim. of *jugum* YOKE; see -AR¹]

ju'gulate *v.t.* kill by cutting throat; (fig.) arrest course of (disease etc.) by powerful remedy etc. [f. L *jugulare* (*jugulum*; see prec.) + -ATE³]

juice (joōs) *n.* liquid part of vegetables or fruits; fluid part of animal body or substance, esp. secretion (*gastric, pancreatic, juice*; STEW² *in* one's *own juice*); (fig.) essence or spirit of anything; (sl.) petrol or electricity used in engine etc.; hence ~'LESS (-sl-) *a.* [ME, f. OF *jus* f. L *jus* broth, juice]

jui'c|y (joō'-) *a.* full of juice, succulent; (colloq., of weather) wet; (colloq.) of rich intellectual quality, interesting, racy, scandalous; hence ~**iLY²** *adv.,* ~INESS *n.* [ME, f. prec. + -Y²]

ju-ji'tsu (joōji'tsoō) *n.* Japanese system of unarmed combat seeking to utilize opponent's strength and weight to his disadvantage. [f. Jap. *jūjutsu* (*jū* gentle, *jutsu* skill)]

ju-ju (joō'joō) *n.* (W. Afr.) charm or fetish; supernatural power attributed to this. [perh. f. F *joujou* toy]

ju'jube (joō'joōb) *n.* (edible acid berry-like drupe of) plant of genus *Zizyphus*; lozenge of gelatin etc. flavoured with or imitating this. [F, or f. med. L *jujuba* ult. f. Gk *zizyphon*]

ju-jutsu. Var. of JU-JITSU.

juke-box (joō'k-) *n.* machine that automatically plays selected gramophone record when coin is inserted. [f. Gullah *juke* disorderly + BOX²]

Jul. *abbr.* July.

ju'lep (joō'-) *n.* sweet drink, esp. as vehicle for medicine; medicated drink as mild stimulant etc.; *iced and flavoured spirit and water, esp. *mint julep.* [ME f. OF, f. Arab. *julāb* f. Pers. *gulāb* (*gul* rose, *āb* water)]

Ju'lian (joō'-) *a.* of Julius Caesar; ~ **calendar** (introduced by him, in which the year consisted of 365 days, every fourth year having 366; cf. GREGORIAN); ~ **day,** (Astron.) day as numbered in one sequence from 4713 BC (*Julian day 2444606 begins at noon on 1 Jan. 1981*); ~ **year,** (average length of) year of Julian calendar, (Astron.) year of Julian days. [f. L *Julianus* (*Julius*; see -AN)]

julie'nne (zhoō-, joō-) *a.* & *n.* (foodstuff, esp. vegetables) cut into thin strips; clear soup to which are added such vegetables already cooked. [F, f. name *Jules* or *Julien*]

Ju'liet (joō'-) *n.* ~ **cap,** small network ornamental cap worn by brides etc. [f. heroine of Shakespeare's *Romeo* & *Juliet*]

July' (joō-) *n.* (*pl.* ~s). seventh month of year. [ME, f. AF *julie* f. L *Julius* (*mensis* month), named after Julius Caesar]

*ju'mbal, *ju'mble¹, *n.* thin crisp sweet cake, usu. ring-shaped. [perh. var. of *gimmal* (see GIMBALS)]

ju'mble² *v.i.* & *t.* move about in disorder; mix *up,* confuse. [prob. imit.]

ju'mble³ *n.* confused assemblage; ||articles for jumble sale; muddle; jolting; ||~ **sale** (of miscellaneous cheap usu. second-hand articles at bazaar etc.); hence **ju'mbly²** *a.* [f. prec.]

ju'mbo *n.* (*pl.* ~s) & *a.* **1.** *n.* big clumsy person, animal, or thing; very large specimen; = *jumbo jet.* **2.** *a.* very large of its kind; ~ **jet,** large jet plane able to carry several hundred passengers. [prob. f. second element in MUMBO-JUMBO]

ju'mbuck *n.* (Austral.) sheep. [Aboriginal]

jump¹ *n.* **1.** act of jumping; *broad or ||LONG¹ *jump*; HIGH *jump*; **get the ~ on,** (sl.) get an advantage over by anticipation; **on the ~,** (colloq.) bustling about; **one ~ ahead,** having progressed one stage farther (than rival in plans etc.). **2.** sudden movement caused by shock or excitement; **the ~s,** (sl.) nervousness, the fidgets, delirium tremens. **3.** abrupt rise in amount, price, value, etc.; ∿ (**bid**), (Bridge) bid higher than is necessary to overcall in the relevant suit. **4.** sudden transition; gap in series, argument, etc. **5.** obstacle to be jumped by horse etc.; SKI-*jump*. **6.** ∿-**cut**, (Cinemat.) removal of middle part of shot to give discontinuity of action; ∿-**jet**, VTOL jet plane; ∿-**leads**, device for conveying current from one battery to recharge another; *∿-**rope**, skipping-rope; *∿ **seat**, folding seat in motor car; ∿ **suit**, one-piece garment for whole body, orig. worn by paratroops. [f. foll.] **jump**² *v.* **1.** *v.i.* move up off ground etc. by bending and sudden muscular extension of legs or (of fish) tail; move suddenly with jump or bound (*up* from seat etc., *from* high place, *out*, etc.; ∿ **in**, get quickly into vehicle etc.); give sudden movement from excitement, shock, etc., esp. *jump for joy.* **2.** rise suddenly in price etc. **3.** come *to*, arrive *at*, (conclusion) over-hastily; come suddenly *into* prominence etc. **4.** agree, coincide, (*together*, one *with* another). **5.** ∿ **at**, (fig.) (offer, bargain) eagerly; ∿ **down** person's **throat**, reprimand or contradict him fiercely; ∿ **in the lake**, (colloq., usu. in *imper.*) go away and cease being a nuisance; ∿-**off**, deciding round in horse-jumping contest; ∿**ing-o'ff** a., starting (*place, point*; lit. or fig.); ∿ **on**, attack crushingly (lit. or fig.); *jump out of* one's SKIN¹; *jump over* the BROOM*stick*; ∿ **to it**, make an energetic start; ∿-**ed-up** (-pt-) *a.*, upstart. **6.** *v.t.* pass over (gate etc.) by jumping; pass (red traffic-light etc.); (of train, tram, etc.) leave (the rails); move or pass over (intervening thing) to point beyond; *get on or off (train etc.) quickly, esp. in illegal manner; abandon contrary to one's undertaking (*jump* BAIL¹); ∿ **ship**, (of seaman) be deserter before end of his contract. **7.** help (child etc.) to jump *down* etc.; cause (thing) to jump; use (horse) for jumping. **8.** (esp. in *p.p.*) cook (potatoes etc.) in frying-pan, occasionally shaking them. **9.** pounce upon (person, thing); act before time prescribed by (*jump the* GUN; ‖∿ **the queue**, push forward out of one's turn, take precedence of others waiting). **10.** take summary possession of (claim allegedly abandoned or forfeited by former occupant). **11.** skip over (subject, part of book, etc.). **12.** drill (rock, hole in wall) with jumper. **13.** Hence ∿ᴬBLE *a.* [16th c.; prob. imit.]

ju'mper¹ *n.* In vbl senses; member of Welsh Methodist body (or later sects) who jump(ed) as part of worship; jumping insect, e.g. flea; (Electr.) short wire used to make or break circuit; rope made fast to keep yard, mast, etc., from jumping; heavy chisel-ended iron bar for drilling blasting-holes. [f. prec. + -ER¹]

ju'mper² *n.* loose outer jacket of canvas etc. worn by sailors etc.; ‖woman's knitted pullover; *pinafore dress. [prob. f. (17th c., now dial.) *jump* short coat perh. f. F *jupe* f. Arab. *jubba*; cf. JIBBAH]

ju'mping *a.* In vbl senses; ∿ **bean**, seed of Mexican plant that jumps owing to movement of enclosed larva; ∿ **deer**, N. Amer. black-tailed deer. [f. JUMP² + -ING²]

ju'mp‖y *a.* characterized by sudden movements esp. of nervous excitement; hence ∿ĭNESS *n.* [f. JUMP¹ + -Y²]

Jun. *abbr.* June; Junior.

ju'nco *n.* (*pl.* ∿s or ∿es). small Amer. finch of genus *Junco.* [Sp., f. L *juncus* rush plant]

ju'nction *n.* joining; joint, meeting-place; place where railway lines or roads meet and unite; (Electronics) region of transition in semiconductor between regions where conduction is mainly by electrons and mainly by holes; ∿ **box** (containing junction of electric cables etc.). [f. L *junctio* (as JOIN; see -ION)]

ju'ncture *n.* joining; place where things join; concurrence of events, state of affairs, (*at this juncture*). [ME, f. L *junctura* (as JOIN; see -URE)]

June (jōōn). *n.* sixth month of year; ∿'**berry** = SERVICE²-*berry* (2). [ME, f. OF *juin* & f. L *Junius* var. of *Junonius* sacred to JUNO]

Ju'ngian (yōō'-) *a.* & *n.* (disciple) of Jung or his system of analytical psychology with complex classification of personality types. [f. C. G. *Jung*, Swiss psychologist d. 1961 + -IAN]

ju'ngle (-nggel) *n.* (area of) land overgrown with underwood or tangled vegetation, esp. in tropics, (**law of the** ∿, state of ruthless competition); scene of ruthless struggle for survival (*blackboard jungle* in schools, *concrete jungle* in cities); wild tangled mass; ∿ **fever**, severe form of malaria; ∿ **gym**, structure of bars for children to climb on in playing; hence **ju'ngl**ED (-eld), **ju'ngl**Y², (-ngg-) *adjs.* [f. Hindi *jangal* f. Skr. *jangala* desert, forest]

ju'nior (jōō'-) *a.* & *n.* **1.** *a.* less advanced in age; inferior in age or standing to; of less or least standing, of lower or lowest position, (*junior partner*); (of school) having pupils in a younger age-range; *of year before final year at university, high school, etc.; *∿ **college** (offering two-year course esp. in preparation for completion at senior college); ‖∿ **combination** or **common room** (for use by junior members of college); hence ∿ITY (-ŏ'r-) *n.* **2.** (Appended to name for distinction, esp. of son from father) junior to another of same name. **3.** *n.* junior person; one's inferior in length of service etc. (*is my junior*); junior student; barrister who is not QC; *(colloq.) the son in a family. [L, compar. of *juvenis* young]

ju'niorate (jōō'-) *n.* (In Society of Jesus etc.) (place for) two-years' course attended by those intending to enter priesthood. [f. prec. + -ATE¹]

ju'niper (jōō'-) *n.* evergreen shrub or tree of genus *Juniperus,* esp. shrub with prickly leaves and dark purple berry-like cones yielding **oil of** ∿ (used in medicine and in flavouring gin etc.). [ME, f. L *juniperus*]

junk¹ *n.*, & *v.t.* **1.** *n.* old cables or ropes cut up for oakum etc.; discarded material, rubbish; ‖lump, chunk; (Naut.) hard salt meat; lump of tissue in sperm whale, containing spermaceti; (sl.) narcotic drug, esp. heroin, whence ∿'IE *n.*, drug addict; *∿ **mail**, unsolicited advertising matter sent by post; ∿-**shop** (selling cheap second-hand goods or (derog.) antiques). **2.** *v.t.* discard as junk. [ME, of unkn. orig.]

junk² *n.* flat-bottomed sailing vessel used in China seas, with prominent stem and lugsails. [f. obs. F *juncque,* Port. *junco,* or Du. *jonk,* f. Jav. *djong*]

junker (yōō'ngker) *n.* (Hist.) young German nobleman; member of exclusive (Prussian) aristocratic party. [G, earlier *junkher* (f. OHG as YOUNG, HERR); cf. YOUNKER]

ju'nket *n.*, & *v.i.* **1.** *n.* dish of sweetened and flavoured curds, often with fruit or cream; feast; *pleasure outing; *official's tour at public expense. **2.** *v.i.* feast, picnic; hence ∿ING¹ *n.* [ME *jonket,* f. OF *jonquette* rush-basket (used to carry junket; *jonc* rush f. L *juncus*)]

Ju'nō (jōō'-) *n.* (*pl.* ∿s). woman of stately beauty; hence ∿ᴇ'sQUE *a.*, (of woman) large and regal. [L, goddess of marriage, wife of Jupiter]

Junr. *abbr.* Junior.

ju'nta *n.* **1.** body of persons acting towards common aim, esp. political clique or faction after revolution or *coup d'état.* **2.** deliberative or administrative council in Spain or Italy. [Sp. & Port., f. L *juncta,* fem. p.p. (as JOIN)]

ju'ntō *n.* (*pl.* ∿s). = prec. 1. [erron. f. prec.]

Ju'piter (jōō'-) *n.* largest planet of solar system. [ME, f. L *Jup(p)iter* king of the gods (OL *Jovis pater,* cf. JOVE, PATER)]

jur'al (joor'-) *a.* of law, of (moral) rights and obligations. [f. L *jus juris* law, right + -AL]

Jura'ssic (joor-) *a.* & *n.* (Geol.) (of the) middle Mesozoic period or system, with prevalence of oolitic limestone as in Jura Mountains. [f. F *jurassique* (*Jura*); cf. *liassic, Triassic*]

‖**jur'at**¹ (joor'-) *n.* municipal officer (esp. of Cinque Ports) like alderman; honorary judge or magistrate in Channel Is. [ME, f. med. L *juratus* p.p. (as n.) of L *jurare* swear]

jur'at² (joor'-) *n.* statement of circumstances in which affidavit was made. [f. L *juratum* neut. p.p. (as n.); see prec.]

juri'dical (joor-) *n*. of judicial proceedings; relating to the law. [f. L *juridicus* (*jus juris* law, *-dicus* saying f. *dicere* say) +-AL]

jurisconsu'lt (joor-) *n*. one learned in law, jurist. [f. L *jurisconsultus* (*jus juris* law, *consultus* skilled; see CONSULT)]

jurisdi'ction (joor-) *n*. administration of justice (*over* or *of*); legal or other authority; extent of this, territory it extends over; hence ∼AL *a*. [ME *jure-*, *juri-*, *jurisdiccioun* f. OF *jure-*, *juridiction* & f. L *jurisdictio* (as prec.; see DICTION)]

jurispru'd|ence (joorĭsprōō'-) *n*. **1**. science or philosophy of human law; hence ∼ĕ'ntIAL (-ōōdĕ'nshal) *a*. **2**. skill in law; so ∼ENT *a*. & *n*. [f. L *jurisprudentia* (as prec., L *prudentia* knowledge; see PRUDENCE)]

jur'ist (joor'-) *n*. one versed in law; legal writer; student of or graduate in law; *lawyer; hence ∼IC(AL) (-ĭ's-) *adjs*. [f. F *juriste* or f. med. L *jurista* (*jus juris* law; see -IST)]

jur'or (joor-) *n*. member of jury; one who takes an oath (cf. NONjuror). [ME, f. AF *jurour*, OF *jureor* f. L *jurator -oris* (*jurare -at-* swear; see -OR)]

jur'ÿ (joor'ĭ) *n*. **1**. body of persons sworn to render verdict on question submitted to them in court of justice or coroner's court; GRAND *jury*; **petty** or **trial** ∼ (of 12 persons who try final issue of fact in civil or criminal cases and pronounce verdict); **special** ∼ (of persons of certain station in society, opp. **common** ∼); ∼ **of matrons** (Hist., in cases where pregnancy was pleaded to obtain stay of execution). **2**. body of persons selected to award prizes in competition. **3**. ∼-**box**, enclosure for jury in court; ∼**man**, ∼**woman**, member of jury. [ME, f. AF & OF *juree* oath, inquiry, f. *jurata* fem. p.p. (as n.) of L *jurare* swear; cf. -Y⁴]

jur'ÿ-|mast (joor'ĭmahst) *n*. (Naut.) temporary mast in place of broken or lost one; so ∼-**rigged** etc. of other makeshifts. [perh. f. *iuerie* f. OF *ajurie* aid]

ju'ssive *a*. (Gram.) expressing a command. [f. L *jubēre juss-* command +-IVE]

just¹ *a*. acting or done in accordance with what is morally right or proper (*to* person etc.; *the* SLEEP¹ *of the just*); (of treatment etc.) deserved (*a just reward*); (of feelings, opinions, etc.) well-grounded (*just resentment, fear*); right in amount etc., proper; hence ∼'LY² *adv.*, ∼'NESS *n*. [ME, f. OF *juste* f. L *justus* (*jus* right)]

just² *adv*. **1**. exactly (*just at that spot; just there; just three o'clock; just then; come just as you are; just as I opened the door; it is just as you say, just what I want*); (w. interrog. wds asking for precise information; *just how did you do it?*; *I wonder just how good he is*); ∼ **about**, (colloq.) almost (exactly), almost completely; **that is** ∼ **it** (precisely the point in question); ∼ **so**, (1) exactly arranged (*she likes everything just so*), (2) it is exactly as you say. **2**. barely, no more than, (*I just managed it*; ||*I just saw him*; (*wait*) *just a minute, please*). **3**. exactly or nearly at that or this moment (||*I have just seen him*; **I just saw him*); ∼ **now**, (1) at this moment, (2) a little time ago. **4**. (colloq.) simply, merely, (*it's just that I don't like him; just* (*you*) *wait till I catch you!*; *we are just good friends; it just doesn't make sense; just listen to that cheering!*); ∼ **in case**, as a precaution. **5**. (colloq.) positively (*it is just splendid*); quite (*not just yet*; *it is just as well that I checked*); (sl.) really, indeed, (*won't I just give him a pasting!*). [ME, f. prec.]

just³. See JOUST.

ju'stice *n*. **1**. just conduct; fairness; exercise of authority in maintenance of right; **poetic**(**al**) ∼, due allocation of reward of virtue and punishment of vice; ROUGH *justice*. **2**. judicial proceedings (*was duly brought to justice; Court of Justice*); **Department of J*∼ (headed by Attorney-General). **3**. magistrate; judge, esp. (in England) of Supreme Court of Judicature, whence ∼SHIP (-s-sh-) *n*.; LORD *Justice* (*of Appeal, Clerk, General*); ||Mr. or Mrs. J∼, form of address or reference to High Court judge; J∼ **of the Peace**, unpaid lay magistrate appointed to preserve peace in county, town, etc. **4**. **do** ∼ **to**, treat fairly, show due appreciation of; **do** oneself ∼, perform in manner worthy of one's abilities; **in** ∼ **to**, out of fairness to; **with** ∼, reasonably. [ME f. OF, f. L *justitia* (as JUST¹; see -ICE)]

justi'ciable (-shya-) *a*. subject to jurisdiction. [OF, f. *justicier* bring to trial f. med. L *justitiare* (as prec.); see -ABLE]

justi'ciar (-shyer) *n*. chief political and judicial officer under Norman and early Plantagenet kings. [as foll.; see -AR²]

justi'ciarÿ (-shyerĭ) *n*. & *a*. **1**. *n*. administrator of justice; ∼ prec.; **Court of J**∼, supreme criminal court in Scotland **2**. *a*. of the administration of justice. [f. med. L *justitiarius* f. L *justitia*; see JUSTICE, -ARY¹]

ju'stifi|able *a*. that can be legally or morally justified (*justifiable* HOMICIDE); hence ∼ABI'LITY *n*., ∼abLY⁰ *adv*. [F (*justifier*; see foll., -ABLE)]

ju'stifÿ *v.t*. show the justice or rightness of (person, act, etc.); demonstrate correctness of (assertion etc.); adduce adequate grounds for (conduct, claim, etc.); vindicate, (of circumstances, esp. in *pass*.) be such as to justify (*in p.p.*) just, right, (*am justified in assuming*); (Theol.) declare (person) free from penalty of sin on ground of Christ's righteousness or (RC) of the infusion of grace; (Print.) adjust (line of type) to fill a space neatly; ∼fÿ **bail**, show by oath of person furnishing bail that he has sufficient funds to do so; ∼FICA'TION *n*., ∼ficatORY *a*. [ME, f. F *justifier* f. LL *justificare* do justice to f. L *justus* JUST¹; see -FY]

jut¹ *n*., & *v.i.* (-**tt**-). **1**. *n*. projection, protruding point. **2**. *v.i*. protrude, project (often *out, forth*). [var. of JET²,³]

jute¹ (jōōt) *n*. fibre from bark of E. Ind. plants of genus *Corchorus*, used for sacking, mats, cords, etc. [f. Bengali *jhōto* f. Skr. *jūṭa = jaṭā* braid of hair]

Jute² (jōōt) *n*. member of Low German tribe that settled in Britain in 5th-6th c.; hence ∼'ISH¹ *a*. [repr. med. L *Jutae, Juti*, in OE *Eotas, Iotas* = Icel. *Iótar* people of Jutland (in Denmark)]

juvene'sc|ence (jōō-) *n*. (transition from infancy to) youth; so ∼ENT *a*. [f. L *juvenescere* reach age of youth (*juvenis* young); see -ENCE]

ju'venile (jōō'-) *a*. & *n*. **1**. *a*. young, youthful; suited to or characteristic of youth; ∼ **court** (for trial of persons below specified age); ∼**delinquent**, offender below age of legal responsibility; so ∼**delinquency**, offences by such; hence or cogn. ∼LY² (-l-lĭ) *adv.*, **juveni'l**ITY (jōō-) *n*. **2**. *n*. young person; (Commerc.) book intended for young people; actor playing part of youthful person. [f. L *juvenilis* (as prec.; see -IL)]

juveni'lia (jōō-) *n. pl*. works produced by author or artist in youth. [L, neut. pl. of *juvenilis* (see prec.)]

juxtapo'se (-z) *v.t*. place (things) side by side; place (thing) thus *to* or *with* another; so **juxta**POSI'TION (-z-) *n*. [f. F *juxtaposer* f. L *juxta* next; see POSE¹]

K

K, k, (kā) *n.* (*pl.* **Ks** *or* **K's**). eleventh letter of alphabet.

K. *abbr.* kelvin(s); King('s); Köchel.

k *abbr.* kilo-.

K *symb.* potassium. [f. mod. L *kalium* (as KALI; see -IUM)]

Ka'aba (kah'*aba*) *n.* sacred building at Mecca, Muslim Holy of Holies containing sacred black stone. [f. Arab. *ka'ba*]

kă'bbala. Var. of CABBALA.

kabŏ'b. Var. of KEBAB.

kabu'kĭ (-ōō'-) *n.* traditional popular Japanese drama with highly stylized song etc., acted by males only. [Jap. (*ka* song, *bu* dance, *ki* art)]

Kabŷ'le *n.* member or language of Berber tribe of Algeria, Morocco, and Tunis. [f. Arab. *ḳabā'īl* tribes]

kachi'na (-ē'-) *n.* Amer. Ind. ancestral spirit; ～ (**dancer**), one who represents kachina in ceremonial dances; ～ **doll,** wooden doll representing kachina. [Hopi, = supernatural]

Kă'ddĭsh *n.* Jewish mourner's prayer; doxology in the synagogue service. [f. Aram. *ḳaddīš* holy]

kadi. Var. of CADI.

*****kă'ffeeklätsch** (-fäkläch) *n.* meeting for informal conversation and drinking of coffee. [G (*kaffee* coffee, *klatsch* gossip)]

Kă'ffir, (arch.) **Că'ffre** (-fer), *n.* member or language of a S. Afr. people of Bantu family; (derog.; **R**) Bantu inhabitant of S. Africa; **k～** (**corn**), E. Afr. variety of sorghum, grown also in other dry regions; ～ **lily,** S. Afr. herbaceous plant (*Clivia miniata*) with showy flowers. [f. Arab. *kāfir* infidel (*kafara* not believe)]

kaffiyeh. Var. of KEFFIYEH.

Kă'fir *n.* native of Kafiristan in central Asia. [f. as KAFFIR]

Kă'fkaĕ'sque (-sk) *a.* resembling the writings of Kafka, esp. in nightmare quality. [f. F. *Kafka,* Austrian novelist d. 1924 + -ESQUE]

kă'ftan. See CAFTAN.

ka'gō (kah'-) *n.* (*pl.* ～s). Japanese basket-work palanquin slung on pole. [f. Jap. *kango*]

kail('yård). See KALE.

kai'nĭt(e) (kī'n-) *n.* hydrated magnesium and potassium chloride and sulphate, used as fertilizer. [G *kainit* f. Gk *kainos* new; see -ITE[1]]

kai'ser (kī'z-) *n.* (Hist.) emperor, esp. German Emperor, Emperor of Austria, or head of Holy Roman Empire; hence ～SHIP *n.* [in mod. E f. G *kaiser* and Du. *keizer*; in ME f. OE *cāsere* n. Gmc adoption (thr. Gk *kaisar*) of L CAESAR]

ka'ka (kah'-) *n.* large olive-brown New Zealand parrot; so ～**pō** *n.* (*pl.* ～s), New Zealand owl-like nocturnal parrot. [Maori (*po* = night)]

kăkĕmō'nō *n.* (*pl.* ～s). Japanese wall-picture (usu. painted or inscribed on paper or silk and mounted on rollers). [Jap. (*kake-* hang, *mono* thing)]

kala-azār' (kah-) *n.* infectious disease of oriental tropics, caused by protozoan parasite *Leishmania donovani* and transmitted by bite of fly. [Assamese (*kālā* black, *āzār* disease)]

kăle, kail, *n.* **1.** variety of cabbage, esp. one (**curly ～**) with wrinkled leaves and no compact head; **Scotch ～,** kind with purplish leaves; **sea-***kale.* **2.** broth made of this or other vegetables; ***** (sl.) money. **3.** ～'**yard,** (Sc.) kitchen-garden; ～**yard school,** writers of fiction describing, with much use of the vernacular, everyday life in Scotland. [ME; northern form of COLE]

kalei'do\|scōpe (-lī'd-) *n.* tube through which are seen symmetrical figures, produced by reflections of pieces of coloured glass etc., and varied by rotation of the tube; (fig.) constantly changing group of bright or interesting objects; hence ～**scŏ'pic**(AL) *adjs.* [f. Gk *kalos* beautiful + *eidos* form + -SCOPE]

kalends. Var. of CALENDS.

kă'lĭ *n.* glasswort (*Salsola kali*), from which potash was obtained. [f. Arab. *ḳalī* ALKALI]

kă'lmĭa *n.* evergreen showy-flowered N. Amer. shrub of genus *Kalmia.* [mod. L, f. P. *Kalm,* Sw. botanist d. 1779 + -IA[1]]

Kă'lmŭck *a.* & *n.* (member or language) of a Buddhist Mongol people living in western USSR. [f. Russ. *kalmyk*]

ka'lŏng (kah'-) *n.* Indonesian frugivorous fox-bat, largest known bat. [Malay]

kă'lpa *n.* (Hinduism). great age of the world; day of Brahma (4,320,000,000 years), after which world is destroyed. [Skr.]

Ka'ma (kah'-) *n.* Hindu god of love; ～ **Sutra,** ancient Sanskrit treatise on art of love. [Skr.]

kăme *n.* short ridge of sand and gravel deposited from water of melted glacier. [Sc. form of COMB[1]]

kămĭka'zĕ (-ah'-) *n.* (Hist.) Japanese aircraft laden with explosives and deliberately crashed by its pilot on its target; its pilot. [Jap. (*kami* divinity, *kaze* wind)]

kă'mpŏng *n.* Malayan enclosure or village. [Malay; cf. COMPOUND[3]]

Kan. *abbr.* Kansas.

ka'na (kah'-) *n.* one of various Japanese syllabaries. [Jap.]

kana'ka (-ă'-, -ah'-) *n.* South Sea Islander, esp. one formerly employed on forced labour in Australia. [Hawaiian, = man]

Kănarē'se (-z) *n.* (*pl.* same). (member of) Dravidian people living in western India; their language. [f. *Kanara* in India + -ESE]

kăngarōō' (-ngg-) *n.* **1.** herbivorous marsupial mammal of genus *Macropus* with strongly developed hindquarters and great leaping-power, found in Australia, Tasmania, etc.; ||Australian; ～ **dog** (for hunting kangaroos); ～ **hare,** ～ **mouse,** small marsupials like hare and mouse; ～ **paw,** Austral. herb with green and red woolly flowers; ～**rat,** (1) = RAT[1] *kangaroo,* (2) pouched nocturnal rodent of SW United States. **2.** ||～ **closure** (when chairman in committee selects some amendments for discussion and excludes others); ～ **court,** improperly constituted illegal court held by strikers etc. [f. Aboriginal name]

kă'nji *n.* Japanese writing using Chinese characters. [Jap. (*kan* Chinese, *ji* character)]

Kă'nnada *n.* Kanarese language. [f. Kanarese *kannaḍa*]

kanōō'n *n.* instrument like zither, with fifty to sixty strings. [f. Pers. or Arab. *ḳānūn*]

Kans. *abbr.* Kansas.

Kă'ntĭan *a.* of Kant or his philosophy esp. of a priori categories of thought whereby sense-impressions are co-ordinated; hence ～ISM (3) *n.* [f. I. *Kant,* Ger. philosopher d. 1804 + -IAN]

KANU (kah'nōō) *n.* Kenya African National Union. [abbr.]

kă'olĭn *n.* fine white clay produced by decomposition of felspar, used in making porcelain; hence ～IZE (3) *v.t.* [F, f. Chin. *gaoling* name of mountain (*gao* high, *ling* hill)]

kă'ŏn *n.* (Phys.) one of several mesons having mass several times that of electron. [f. K (letter used as symbol for the particle) + -ON]

kăpĕ'llmeister (-mī-) *n.* (*pl.* same). conductor of

orchestra, opera, choir, etc.; ~ **music,** uninspired music in routine style. [G (*kapelle* court orchestra f. It. *cappella* CHAPEL, *meister* master)]

ka′pŏk *n.* fine cotton-like material surrounding seeds of a tropical tree (*Ceiba pentandra*), used for stuffing cushions, soft toys, etc. [ult. f. Malay *kāpoq*]

kă′ppa *n.* tenth Greek letter (Κ, ϰ) = k. [Gk]

kăpu′t (-ŏŏ′t) *pred. a.* (sl.) done for, smashed, ruined, out of order. [f. G *kaputt*]

kărabi′ner (-ē′-) *n.* coupling link with safety closure, used by mountaineers. [G, lit. 'carbine']

Kăr′aïte *n.* member of Jewish sect in Crimea etc. that rejects rabbinical tradition and interprets scriptures literally. [f. Heb. ḳᵉrā'îm scripturalists (ḳārā read) + -ITE¹]

karakul. See CARACUL.

***kă′rat.** Var. of CARAT (esp. of gold quality).

kara′tè (-ah′-) *n.* Japanese system of unarmed combat using hands, feet, etc., as weapons. [Jap. (*kara* empty, *te* hand)]

kăr′m|a *n.* (Buddhism & Hinduism). sum of person's actions in one of his successive states of existence, viewed as deciding his fate for the next; destiny; hence ~IC *a.* [Skr., = action, fate]

karō′ss *n.* mantle of animals' skins with the hair on, used by S. Afr. tribesmen. [f. Afrik. *karos*, of uncert. orig.]

kă′rrï *n.* (hard dark-red timber) of tall W. Austral. tree (*Eucalyptus diversicolor*). [Aboriginal]

kar(r)ŏŏ′ *n.* elevated plateau of clayey soil in S. Africa, waterless in dry season. [Hottentot]

kărst *n.* region with underground drainage and many cavities etc. caused by dissolution of rock. [name of such region in Yugoslavia]

kărt *n.* = GO¹-*kart*. [abbr.]

kărtĕ′ll. Var. of CARTEL.

kă′ryo- *comb. form.* (Biol.) nucleus of cell, as: ~**plasm,** protoplasm of cell nucleus; ~**type,** character of cell nucleus as determined by nature of all chromosomes, systematized diagram of chromosomes. [f. Gk *karuon* kernel + -O-]

kasbah. See CASBAH.

kătabă′tic *a.* (Meteorol.) (Of wind) caused by air flowing downwards; cf. ANABATIC. [f. Gk *katabatikos* (*katabanō* go down; see -IC)]

kată′bolism, Var. of CATABOLISM.

kătaka′na (-ah′-) *n.* angular form of kana. [Jap., = side kana]

kăthermŏ′mèter *n.* instrument to determine cooling of air or rate of air-flow past evaporating liquid etc. [f. as CATA- + THERMOMETER]

kă′thŏde. Var. of CATHODE.

kă′tydid *n.* large green grasshopper common in US. [imit. of sound it makes]

kaur′ï (kowr′ï) *n.* coniferous tree (*Agathis australis*) of New Zealand, yielding valuable timber and a resin, ~-**gum.** [Maori]

ka′va (kah′-) *n.* (intoxicating beverage from crushed roots of) a Polynesian shrub, *Piper methysticum*. [Polynesian]

ka′wa-kawa (kah′wakah-) *n.* ornamental NZ shrub (*Piper excelsum*) with aromatic leaves. [Maori]

kay′ăk (kï′-) *n.* Eskimo one-man canoe of light wooden framework covered with sealskins; small covered canoe resembling this. [Eskimo]

kay′ŏ *v.t.,* & *n.* (*pl.* ~s). (colloq.) **1.** *v.t.* knock out, stun by blow. **2.** *n.* knock-out. [repr. pr. of *KO*]

kazŏŏ′ *n.* toy musical instrument into which player sings or hums. [19th c., app. w. ref. to sound produced]

KB *abbr.* King's Bench.

||**KBE** *abbr.* Knight Commander (of the Order) of the British Empire.

KC *abbr.* King's College; King's Counsel.

kc(/s) *abbr.* kilocycles (per second).

||**KCB** *abbr.* Knight Commander (of the Order) of the Bath.

||**KCIE** *abbr.* Knight Commander (of the Order) of the Indian Empire.

||**KCMG** *abbr.* Knight Commander (of the Order) of St. Michael & St. George.

||**KCSI** *abbr.* Knight Commander (of the Order) of the Star of India.

||**KCVO** *abbr.* Knight Commander of the Royal Victorian Order.

KD *abbr.* knocked down.

KE *abbr.* kinetic energy.

ke′a (kē′a, kā′a) *n.* green parrot (*Nestor notabilis*) of New Zealand. [Maori, imit.]

kĕba′b (-ă′b, -ah′b) *n.* (usu. in *pl.*) meat cooked in small pieces often with vegetables, ginger, garlic, etc., usu. on skewer. [f. Urdu f. Arab. *kabāb*]

kĕck *v.i.* make sound as if about to vomit; ~ **at,** reject (food etc.) with loathing. [imit.]

kĕdge *v.* & *n.* **1.** *v.i.* move ship by means of hawser attached to small anchor; (of ship) move thus. **2.** *v.t.* move (ship) thus. **3.** *n.* ~(-**anchor**), small anchor for this purpose. [perh. spec. use of obs. *cagge*, dial. *cadge* bind, tie]

kĕdgeree (kĕ′-, -ē′) *n.* Indian dish of rice, split pulse, onions, eggs, etc.; European dish of fish, rice, hard-boiled eggs, etc. [f. Hindi *khichrī*, Skr. *k'rsara* dish of rice and sesame]

keek *v.i.,* & *n.* (Sc.) peep. [ME *kike*; cf. MDu., MLG *kīken*]

keel¹ *n.* & *v.* **1.** *n.* lowest longitudinal timber of vessel, on which framework of the whole is built up; metal structure serving same purpose; (poet.) ship; EVEN² *keel*; **false** ~ (attached to bottom of true keel to protect it); ~-**blocks** (on which keel rests during building etc.); ~-**haul,** haul (person) under keel as punishment; (fig.) rebuke severely. **2.** ridge along breastbone of many birds; (Bot.) prow-shaped pair of petals in corolla, etc. **3.** Hence ~LESS (-l-l-) *a.* **4.** *v.t.* & *i.* ~ (**over**), (cause to) turn over or fall down. **5.** *v.t.* turn (ship) keel upwards. [ME *kele*, f. ON *kjolr* f. Gmc **keluz*]

||**keel²** *n.* flat-bottomed vessel, esp. of kind used on Tyne etc. for loading colliers; amount carried by this. [ME *kele* f. MDu. *kēl*, MDu. *kiel*, ship, boat, = OE *cēol* etc. f. Gmc **keulaz*]

kee′livïne *n.* (Sc.) lead pencil. [18th c., of unkn. orig.]

kee′lson. See KELSON.

keen¹ *n.* Irish funeral song accompanied with wailing. [f. Ir. *caoine* (as foll.)]

keen² *v.* **1.** *v.i.* utter the keen. **2.** *v.t.* bewail (person) thus; utter in wailing tone. **3.** Hence ~ER¹ *n.* (esp.) professional mourner at Irish funerals. [f. Ir. *caoinim* wail]

keen³ *a.* **1.** having sharp edge or point; (of edge etc.) sharp. **2.** (Of sound, light, etc.) penetrating, vivid, strong; (of wind, frost, etc.) piercingly cold; (of pain etc.) acute, bitter; ||(of price) exceptionally low because of competition; (colloq.) excellent. **3.** (Of person, desire, interest) eager, ardent, (*keen sportsman*; ~ **as mustard,** enthusiastic [w. later pun on *Keen's mustard*]; ~ **on,** (colloq.) much attracted by (person, thing, doing). **4.** (Of eyes, sight, smell) sharp, highly sensitive; intellectually acute. **5.** Hence ~LY² *adv.,* ~′NESS (-n-n-) *n.* [OE *cēne,* = OHG *kuoni* bold, ON *kœnn* skilful, f. Gmc **kōnjaz*]

keep¹ *v.* (**kept**). **1.** *v.t.* pay due regard to, observe, stand by, (law, promise, faith, treaty, appointment; *keep the* PEACE, one's WORD¹ 5). **2.** celebrate (feast, ceremony, etc.). **3.** guard, protect, (person, as *God keep you!*; fortress, town, etc., goal at football etc.); *keep* WICKET; (abs.) act as wicket-keeper. **4.** have charge of, retain possession of (*you may keep the change*), not lose or destroy; **you can** ~ **it,** (colloq.) I do not want what is being offered. **5.** maintain (place etc.) in proper order (*keep* HOUSE¹; *keep open* HOUSE¹); carry on, manage, (shop etc.); maintain (diary, accounts, books) by making requisite entries. **6.** provide for sustenance of (family, one*self*, etc.); own and manage (cows, bees, etc.); maintain in return for sexual favours; ～ person in, ensure his supply of. **7.** have (commodity) habitually on sale. **8.** preserve in being, continue to have or do, (keep COMPANY, PACE[1], STEP[2], TIME[1], GUARD[1], a LOOK-out, WATCH[1], ORDER[1] 12). **9.** maintain in proper or specified condition (often in spec. senses: keep the BALL[1] rolling, POT[1] boiling, one's COUNTENANCE[1], person's CONSCIENCE, one's HAIR on, one's HEAD[1]); ～ one's **balance**, not lose it (lit. or fig.); keep in MIND[1]. **10.** detain (person in prison, in custody, etc.; what kept you so long?); restrain (person, thing, oneself, from doing, from thing). **11.** reserve (thing for future time etc.). **12.** conceal (keep one's COUNSEL[1], a secret). **13.** continue to follow (way, course); ～ **track of**, follow the course or development of. **14.** remain in (one's bed or room, the HOUSE[1], one's seat); retain one's place in (the saddle, field, the stage, one's ground, etc.) against opposition; ～ one's **feet**, not fall. **15.** v.i. remain (indoors etc.); ||(colloq., esp. Camb. Univ.) reside (where do you keep?). **16.** remain in specified condition (keep fit, in good health, in TOUCH[2] with, cool, (colloq.) friends; I hope it keeps fine; **how are you** ～**ing?**, (colloq.) what is your state of health?); continue in specified direction, course, or action, (keep straight on for two miles; keep (to the) left; she keeps giggling). **17.** (Of food etc.) remain in good condition, not decay; (fig., of news etc.) admit of being reserved for later occasion. **18.** (w. preps.): ～ (work, cause to work, persistently) at; ～ (abstain or refrain) from; ～ off, avoid (subject etc.), not go on (the grass etc.), not (allow to) come close to or touch; ～ to, adhere to (course, promise), confine oneself to; ～ (thing etc.) to oneself, (1) refuse to share it with others, (2) not allow others to know of it; ～ oneself to oneself, avoid society. **19.** (w. advs.): ～ away, avoid coming, prevent from coming; ～ back, hold back, retard progress of, conceal, stay at a distance (from); ～ down, hold in subjection, keep low in amount, not vomit (food eaten), (Mil.) lie low in skirmishing; ～ in, confine, restrain, (feelings etc.), confine (child) in school after hours, keep (fire) burning, remain indoors, remain on good terms with; ～ one's HAND[1] in; ～ off, ward off, avert, not (allow to) come close or touch; ～ on, continue to hold, use, show, employ, etc., continue (doing), ||nag (at); ～ out, not let enter, stay outside; ～ together, remain, cause to remain, together; ～ under, hold in subjection; ～ up, prevent (one's spirits, prices, etc.) from sinking, maintain (keep one's END[1] up; ～ it up, not relax or slacken), keep in repair, in efficient or proper state, etc., (keep up appearances, your Greek), carry on (correspondence etc.), cause (person) to remain out of bed at night, not give way, proceed at equal pace with (～ up with the Joneses, strive to remain on terms of obvious social equality with one's neighbours). [OE cēpan, of unkn. orig.]

keep[2] n. **1.** (Hist.) tower, stronghold, donjon. **2.** maintenance, food required for this, (you don't earn your keep); pasture. **3. for** ～**s**, (colloq.) permanently. [f. prec.]

kee'per n. In vbl senses; = GAME[1]keeper, WICKET-keeper; custodian of museum, art gallery, forest, etc.; (arch.) lunatic's attendant; ring that keeps another, esp. wedding-ring, on the finger; plain ring to preserve hole in pierced ear-lobe; bar of soft iron across poles of horseshoe magnet to maintain its strength; fruit etc. that keeps (sense 17) well. [ME, f. KEEP[1]+-ER[1]]

kee'ping n. In vbl senses; custody, charge, (in safe keeping; in his keeping); agreement, harmony, (orig. esp. of painting; in, out of, ～ (with)). [ME, f. KEEP[1]+-ING[1]]

kee'psake n. thing kept for sake, or in remembrance, of giver. [f. KEEP[1]+SAKE[1]]

kee'shŏnd (kā's-h-) n. (breed of) Dutch dog with thick curly hair like large Pomeranian, once kept esp. on barges. [Du.]

kef n. drowsy state produced by bhang etc.; enjoyment of idleness; substance smoked to produce kef. [f. Arab. kayf enjoyment, well-being]

kĕffi'yeh (-fĕ'yā) n. bedouin Arab's kerchief worn as head-dress. [f. Arab. keffiya, kūfiyya, perh. f. LL cofea COIF]

kĕg n. small barrel, usu. of less than ||10 or *30 gal.; ～ beer (supplied from sealed metal container). [f. ME cag, f. ON kaggi, of unkn. orig.]

***kĕ'gler** n. player at skittles or similar game. [G (kegel skittle)]

kĕlp n. **1.** large brown seaweed burnt for ash. **2.** calcined ashes of seaweed used because of the sodium carbonate, iodine, etc., they contain, formerly in making soap and glass. [ME cülp(e), of unkn. orig.]

kĕ'lpĭe n. **1.** (Sc.) water-spirit, usu. in form of horse, reputed to delight in the drowning of travellers etc. **2.** Austral. sheep-dog orig. bred from Scottish collie. [18th c., of unkn. orig.]

kĕ'lson, kee'lson, n. line of timber fastening ship's floor-timbers to keel. [ME kelswayn, -sweyn, -syng, perh. f. LG kielswīn (kiel KEEL[1], prob. swīn SWINE used as name of a timber)]

Kĕlt[1]. Var. of CELT[1].

kĕlt[2] n. salmon or sea trout after spawning. [ME; orig. unkn.]

kĕ'lter. See KILTER.

kĕ'lvĭn n. degree (equal to Celsius degree) of K～ scale of temperature (with zero at absolute zero). [f. Lord Kelvin, Brit. physicist d. 1907]

kĕmp n. coarse hair in wool; hence ～'Y[2] a. [ME, f. ON kampr beard, whisker]

kĕmpt a. combed, neatly kept. [p.p. of (now dial.) kemb COMB[2], f. OE cemban f. Gmc *kambjan (as COMB[1])]

kĕn[1] n. range of sight or knowledge (in, out of, beyond, one's ken). [f. foll.]

kĕn[2] v.t. (-nn-; kent). (Sc. & N. Engl.) recognize at sight; know (person, thing, fact, that etc.). [OE cennan, = OS kennian, OHG kennen, ON kenna, Goth. kannjan f. Gmc *kann- know, CAN[2]]

kenā'f n. (fibre, used like jute, of) Asian plant (Hibiscus cannabinus). [Pers.]

kĕ'ndō n. Japanese sport of fencing with two-handed bamboo swords. [Jap., = sword-way]

kĕ'nnel[1] n. & v. (||-ll-). **1.** n. small structure for shelter of house-dog or hounds; (in pl.) breeding or boarding establishment for dogs; mean dwelling. **2.** v.i. live in, go to, kennel. **3.** v.t. put into, keep in, kennel. [ME, f. AF *kenil, OF chenil f. med. L *canile f. L canis dog]

kĕ'nnel[2] n. gutter in street etc. [earlier cannel f. ONF canel CHANNEL[1]]

kĕ'nning n. periphrastic expression in OE and ON poetry, e.g. 'oar-steed' = ship. [ME, = 'teaching' etc., f. KEN[2]+-ING[1]]

***kĕ'nō** n. (pl. ～s). game of chance resembling bingo. [19th c.; orig. unkn.]

kĕnō'sis n. (Theol.) renunciation of divine nature, at least in part, by Christ in the Incarnation; hence **kĕnō'tĭc** a. [Gk kenōsis (kenoō to empty f. kenos empty; see -OSIS]

kĕ'notrŏn n. (Electr.) type of high-vacuum diode rectifier. [f. Gk kenos empty+-o-+-TRON]

kĕ'nspĕckle a. (Sc.) conspicuous. [f. kenspeck, of Scand. orig. (cogn. w. KEN[2])+-LE 1]

kĕnt. See KEN[2].

Kĕ'ntish a. of Kent, England; ||～ **fire**, prolonged volley of rhythmic applause or demonstration of dissent; ～ **man** (esp. born W. of Medway, opp. man of Kent born E.); ～ **rag**, hard compact limestone found in Kent. [OE Centisc (Cent f. L Cantium; see -ISH[1])]

kĕ'ntlĕdge n. (Naut.) pig-iron etc. used as permanent ballast. [f. F quintelage ballast, assim. to kentle obs. var. of QUINTAL; see -AGE]

Kĕntŭ'ckў n. ～ **Derby**, annual race for 3-year-old horses at Louisville, Kentucky. [～ in US, prob. f. Iroquois]

Kĕ'nyan a. & n. (native or inhabitant) of Kenya. [f. Kenya in E. Africa+-AN]

ke'pi (kĕ'-, kā'-) n. French military cap with horizontal peak. [f. F képi f. Swiss G käppi dim. of kappe cap]

Kĕ'pler *n.* ~'s **laws,** three theorems about the nature of planetary motion; hence ~IAN (-ēr'-) *a.* [f. J. ~, Ger. astronomer d. 1630]

kĕpt. See KEEP[1].

kĕră'mĭc. Var. of CERAMIC.

kĕ'ratĭn *n.* protein forming the basis of horns, claws, nails, feathers, hair, etc. [f. Gk *keras keratos* horn + -IN]

kĕ'ratō-. See CERATO-.

kĕ'ratōse *a.* (Of sponge) composed of horny substance. [f. Gk *keras keratos* horn + -OSE[1]]

||**kĕrb** *n.* stone edging to pavement or raised path; ~**-crawling,** driving slowly along and seeking to persuade person on pavement to enter the vehicle; ~ **drill,** simple procedure to promote safety of pedestrian about to cross road; ~'**stone,** one of stones forming kerb; ~(*stone*) *market,* (place for) sale of securities after hours or of shares not dealt with on the Stock Exchange; ~ **weight** (of motor car without occupants or luggage). [var. of CURB]

kĕr'chief (-ĭf, -ēf) *n.* cloth used to cover head; (poet.) handkerchief; hence ~ED[2] (-ft) *a.* [ME *c(o)urchef* f. AF *courchef,* OF *couvrechief* (*couvrir* COVER[1], CHIEF[1] head)]

kĕrf *n.* slit made by cutting, esp. with saw; cut end of felled tree. [OE. *cyrf* f. Gmc **kurbhiz* (as CARVE)]

kerfu'ffle *n.* (colloq.) fuss, commotion. [Sc. *curfuffle* (*fuffle* to disorder); imit.]

kĕr'mĕs (-z) *n.* female of an insect, *Kermes ilicis,* formerly taken to be a berry, feeding on ~ (**oak**), an evergreen oak (*Quercus coccinea*) of S. Europe and N. Africa, red dyestuff consisting of dried bodies of these; ~ (**mineral**), bright red amorphous trisulphide of antimony. [f. F *kermès* f. Arab. & Pers. *ḳirmiz*; cogn. with CRIMSON]

kĕr'mis *n.* periodical fair in Holland etc., with much noisy merry-making; *charity bazaar. [Du. orig. = mass on anniversary of dedication of church, when yearly fair was held (*kerk* f. as CHURCH[1], *mis, misse* MASS[1])]

kĕrn[1] *n.* (Print.) part of metal type projecting beyond body or shank; hence ~ED[2] (-nd) *a.* [perh. f. F *carne* corner f. OF *charne* f. L *cardo cardinis* hinge]

kĕrn[2], kĕrne, *n.* (Hist.) light-armed Irish foot-soldier; peasant, boor. [ME, f. Ir. *ceithern*]

kĕr'nel *n.* softer (usu. edible) part within hard shell of nut or stone-fruit; body of seed within husk etc., e.g. grain of wheat; (esp. fig.) nucleus, centre of formation, essential part. [OE *cyrnel,* dim. of CORN[1]; see -LE 1]

kĕ'rosēne, -ine (-ēn) *n.* (US, Austral., NZ, or tech.) fuel-oil obtained by distillation of petroleum or from coal or bituminous shale, paraffin oil. [irreg. f. Gk *kēros* wax + -ENE]

Kĕ'rrў *n.* (one of) breed of very small black dairy cattle; ~ **blue,** (breed of) terrier with silky blue-grey coat. [~ in Ireland]

kĕr'sey (-zĭ) *n.* kind of coarse narrow cloth woven from long wool, usu. ribbed. [ME, prob. f. K~ in Suffolk]

kĕr'seymēre (-zĭ-) *n.* twilled fine woollen cloth. [alt. of *cassimere,* var. of CASHMERE, assim. to prec.]

kerý'gma *n.* (*pl.* ~**ta**). proclamation of religious truth, esp. of the Christian gospel, opp. *didache*; hence **kĕrygmă'tic** *a.* [Gk *kērugma -matos* proclamation (*kērussō* proclaim)]

kĕ'strel *n.* small falcon (esp. *Falco tinnunculus*) often hovering in the air with head to wind. [ME *castrell,* perh. f. F dial. *casserelle,* F *créc(er)elle,* perh. imit. of its cry]

kĕtch *n.* two-masted fore-and-aft rigged sailing-boat with mizen-mast stepped forward of rudder. [ME *catche,* prob. f. CATCH[1,2]]

kĕ'tchup *n.* sauce made from tomatoes, mushrooms, etc., with vinegar and other flavouring, used as condiment. [f. Chin. dial. *kōechiap* pickled-fish brine]

kĕ'tōne *n.* one of a class of organic compounds containing the group CO with double bond to carbon, of which acetone is the simplest. [f. G *keton* alt. of *aketon* ACETONE]

kĕ'ttle *n.* **1.** vessel, usu. of metal with spout and handle, for boiling water in; FISH[1]-*kettle*; **a** (**pretty** etc.) ~ **of fish,** (awkward) state of affairs. **2.** ~**drum**(mer), (player of) hollow brass or copper hemisphere, over edge of which parchment is stretched and tuned to definite note; ~-**holder,** piece of cloth etc. to protect hand from heat of kettle-handle. **3.** Hence ~FUL 2 (-tᵊlf-) *n.* [ME, f. ON *ketill* = OE *cetel, cietel,* OS *ketel,* OHG *kezzil,* Goth. *katils* f. Gmc **katilaz* f. L *catillus* dim. of *catinus* deep food-vessel]

keV *abbr.* kilo-electron-volt.

kew'pie *n.* small chubby doll with wings and curl or topknot. [*P, f. CUPID + -IE]

key[1] (kē) *n.* **1.** instrument, usu. of metal, for moving bolt of lock forwards or backwards to lock or unlock; GREEK, MASTER[1], SKELETON, *key.* **2.** HOUSE[1] *of Keys;* **St. Peter's** ~**s,** two keys crosswise as borne in papal coat of arms. **3.** what gives or precludes opportunity for or access to something; (*attrib.*) essential, of vital importance. **4.** (in *pl.*) ecclesiastical authority as transmitted to Pope as successor of St. Peter (cf. sense 2). **5.** place that by its position gives control of sea, territory, etc. **6.** solution, explanation; literal translation of foreign book; first move in chess-problem solution; book of solutions of mathematical problems etc.; word or system for solving cipher or code. **7.** (Mus.) system of notes definitely related to each other, based on particular note, and predominating in a piece of music (a *study in the key of C major*); (fig.) tone, style, of thought or expression (**high** ~, **low** ~, with mainly bright, dark, tones, lit. or fig.). **8.** piece of wood or metal inserted between others to secure them. **9.** part of first coat of wall plaster passing between laths and so securing the rest; roughness of surface helping adhesion of plaster etc. **10.** lever pressed by finger in playing organ, piano, flute, concertina, etc.; similar lever in typewriter, in punch for cards or tape, etc.; mechanical device for making or breaking electric circuit, e.g. in telegraphy or IGNITION. **11.** instrument for grasping screws, pegs, nuts, etc., esp. one for winding clock etc. **12.** samara of sycamore etc. **13.** ~'**bar,** rod carrying type in typewriter and moved by striking corresponding key; ~'**board,** set of keys on typewriter, piano, etc.; ~-**bugle** (Hist., fitted with keys to increase number of different sounds); ~'**hole** (by which key is put into lock); ~ **industry,** one essential to the carrying on of others, e.g. coal-mining, dyeing; ~ **man** (occupying vital position in an organization); ~ **map** (in bare outline, to simplify use of full map); ||~ **money,** payment demanded from incoming tenant for provision of key to premises; ~ **move,** (Chess) = sense 6; ~'**note,** (Mus.) note on which key is based, (fig.) prevailing tone or idea (~*note speech,* designed to set prevailing tone at conference, rally, etc.); ~-**pad,** set of numbered buttons used instead of telephone-dial; ~-**ring** (for keeping keys on); *key* SIGNATURE; ~'**stone,** voussoir at summit of arch locking the whole together, (fig.) central principle etc. on which all depends; *Keystone State,* Pennsylvania; ~'**way,** groove to receive key; ~'**word,** (1) key to cipher etc. (see sense 6), (2) significant word used in indexing (~*word in context,* listed with words next to it in source document). **14.** Hence ~'LESS *a.* [OE *cæg*(*e*), = OFris. *kei, kay,* of unkn. orig.]

key[2] (kē) *v.t.* fasten (in, on, etc.) with pin, wedge, bolt, etc.; regulate pitch of strings of (piano etc.); roughen (surface) to help adhesion of plaster etc.; identify by means of key; word (advertisement in particular periodical) so that answers to it can be identified (usu. by varying the form of address given); ~ **up,** (fig.) stimulate (person *to do,* to condition etc.), raise tone or standard of, brace up, raise (offer, demand, endeavour). [ME, f. prec.]

key[3] (kē) *n.* low island or reef, esp. in W. Indies. [f. Sp. *cayo* shoal, reef, infl. by QUAY]

Key'nesian (kā'nz-) *a.* & *n.* (adherent) of the economic theories of Keynes, esp. regarding State control of the economy through money and taxes; hence ∼-**ism** (3) *n*. [f. Lord *Keynes*, Brit. economist d. 1946 + -IAN]

‖**KG** *abbr.* Knight (of the Order) of the Garter.

kg. *abbr.* kilogram(s).

KGB (kājēbē′) *n*. USSR secret police since 1953. [Russ., abbr. of *Komitet Gosudarstvennoĭ Bezopasnosti* committee of State security]

Kgs. *abbr.* Kings (OT).

khă′ddar (kă′-) *n*. Indian homespun cloth. [Hindi]

kha′ki (kah′-) *a.* & *n*. **1.** *a.* dust-coloured, dull brownish-yellow. **2.** *n*. khaki fabric of twilled cotton or wool, used esp. in military dress. [f. Urdu *k̲h̲ākī* dust--coloured (*k̲ak̲* dust)]

khă′msĭn (kă′-) *n*. oppressive hot S. or SE wind in Egypt for about 50 days in March, April, and May. [Arab. *k̲amsīn* (*k̲amsūn* fifty)]

khan¹ (kăn, kahn) *n*. Title of rulers and officials in Central Asia, Afghanistan, etc.; (Hist.) supreme ruler of Turkish, Tartar, and Mongol tribes, and emperor of China, in Middle Ages; hence ∼′ATE¹ (1) *n*. [f. Turki *k̲ān* lord]

khan² (kăn, kahn) *n*. caravanserai. [f. Arab. *k̲ān* inn]

Khèdi′v|e (kĭdē′v) *n*. (Hist.) Title of viceroy of Egypt under Turkish Government 1867–1914; hence ∼(I)AL *adjs*. [f. F *khédive* ult. f. Pers. *k̲adīv* prince]

Khmer (kmār) *a.* & *n*. (native or language) of ancient Khmer kingdom in SE Asia or of modern Cambodia. [native name]

khuskhus. Var. of CUSCUS¹.

kHz *abbr.* kilohertz.

kiă′ng *n*. Tibetan ass with thick furry coat. [f. Tibetan *kyang*]

‖**ki′bble¹** *n*. iron hoisting-bucket used in mines. [f. G *kübel*, = OE *cyfel* f. med. L *cupellus* corn-measure, dim. of *cuppa* cup]

ki′bble² *v.t.* grind coarsely. [18th c.; orig. unkn.]

kibbu′tz (-ōō′ts) *n*. (*pl.* ∼im *pr.* -ē′m). communal esp. farming settlement in Israel; so ∼**nik** *n.*, member of kibbutz. [f. mod. Heb. *k̲ibbūṣ* gathering]

kībe *n*. ulcerated chilblain, esp. on heel. [ME, prob. f. W *cibi*]

ki′bitz (-ts) *v.i.* (colloq.) act as kibitzer. [Yiddish, f. G *kiebitzen* (as foll.)]

kibitzer (kĭ′bĭts-, -bĭ′-) *n*. (colloq.) meddlesome person, one who gives advice gratuitously; one who watches a game of cards from behind the players; meddlesome looker-on. [f. Yiddish *kibitser* f. G *kiebitz* lapwing, busybody]

ki′blah (-a) *n*. point to which Muslims turn at prayer, i.e. (direction of) the Kaaba; mihrab. [f. Arab. *k̲ibla* that which is opposite]

ki′bŏsh *n*. (sl.) nonsense; **put the** ∼ **on**, put an end to, finally dispose of. [19th c.; orig. unkn.]

kick¹ *n*. **1.** act of kicking; **more** ∼**s** (harshness) **than halfpence** (kindness); ∼ **in the pants** or **teeth**, (colloq.) humiliating set-back. **2.** (colloq.) resilience (*has no kick left*); sharp stimulant effect, pleasurable thrill, (*has some kick in it*; *get a kick out of this*; *did it for kicks*); specified temporary interest or enthusiasm (*on a health-food kick*). **3.** recoil of gun when discharged. **4.** (Footb.) ‖**good, bad,** etc., ∼ (kicker); ∼-**pleat** (in narrow skirt, to allow free movement); ∼′**sorter,** (colloq.) device for selecting and counting electrical pulses of specified amplitudes; ∼-**start(er)**, lever on motor cycle etc. for starting engine by downward push with foot; ∼-**turn**, form of standing turn in skiing. [f. foll.]

kick² *v.* **1.** *v.i.* strike out with the foot (esp. *at* object etc. to be moved); *kick against the* PRICK¹*s, over the* TRACE²*s*; ALIVE *and kicking*. **2.** show annoyance, dislike, etc., (*against, at,* proposal, treatment). **3.** *v.t.* strike with foot to propel or as sign of annoyance etc.; (sl.) abandon (habit); *kick the* BUCKET¹*s*, one's HEEL¹*s*. **4.** drive, move, (thing) by kicking. **5.** (Of cricket-ball) rise sharply from pitch; (Footb.) score (goal) by a kick. **6.** drive forcibly and contemptuously (*out,*

downstairs, etc.; ∼ person **upstairs**, fig., shelve him by giving him peerage or titular promotion). **7.** ∼ **about** or **around**, treat (person) roughly or scornfully, discuss (idea) unsystematically, move idly from place to place, be unused or unwanted; ∼′**back**, (1) recoil, (2) payment for help in making profit or for showing favour etc.; ∼-**down**, device for gear-changing in motor vehicle by full depression of accelerator; ∼ **in**, (sl.) contribute; ∼ **off**, remove (shoes) by kicking, (Footb.) begin game, (colloq.) start; ∼-*off* n., start of game by kicking ball; ∼ **up**, raise (dust), create (fuss, noise), ∼ *up its heels* (of playful horse). [ME *kike*, of unkn. orig.]

kick³ *n*. indentation in bottom of glass bottle. [19th c.; orig. unkn.]

ki′cker *n*. In vbl senses; horse given to kicking. [f. KICK² + -ER¹]

ki′ckshaw *n*. (arch.) fancy dish in cookery (usu. derog.); toy, trifle. [f. F *quelque chose* something]

kid¹ *n.*, & *v.i.* (-dd-). **1.** *n*. young goat; leather from skin of this, used for gloves, shoes, handbags, etc.; (sl.) child, **young person, whence ∼′dIE, ∼′do, ∼′dY³, ns.;* ∼ **brother, sister,** (sl.) younger brother, sister; ∼-**glove** *a.*, (1) over-dainty, avoiding everyday work etc., (2) using great tact, avoiding unnecessary violence; ∼(**s′**) **stuff,** (sl.) something very simple or easy. **2.** *v.i.* (Of goat) give birth to kid. [ME *kide* f. ON *kith* f. Gmc **kidhjam*]

kid² *v.t.* (-dd-), & *n.* (sl.) hoax, humbug, deceive (*don't kid yourself*), tease; **no** ∼**ding,** that is the truth. [perh. f. prec.]

kid³ *n*. small wooden tub esp. (formerly) sailor's mess--tub. [perh. var. of KIT¹]

Ki′dderminster *n*. ∼ **carpet** (ingrain, with pattern formed by intersection of two cloths of different colours). [∼ in Hereford & Worcester]

ki′ddie, ki′ddö, ki′ddӯ. See **kid¹.**

ki′ddle *n*. barrier in river with opening fitted with nets etc. to catch fish; arrangement of stake-nets on sea--beach. [ME, f. AF *kidel,* OF *quidel, guidel*]

ki′dnăp *v.t.* (-pp- *or* *-p-). steal (child); carry off (person etc.) by illegal force or fraud esp. to obtain ransom; so ∼**per¹,** *n*. [back-form. f. *kidnapper* (KID¹, *nap* = NAB, -ER¹)]

ki′dney *n*. **1.** either of the pair of glandular organs in abdominal cavity of mammals, birds, and reptiles, serving to excrete urine and so remove nitrogenous matter from blood; **artificial** ∼, apparatus performing functions of human kidneys in place of damaged organ. **2.** kidney of sheep, ox, or pig, as food. **3.** temperament, nature, kind, (*a man of that kidney, of the right kidney*). **4.** ∼ (**potato**), oval potato. **5.** ∼ **bean,** (1) dwarf French bean; (2) scarlet runner bean; ∼ **dish, table,** etc. (kidney-shaped); ∼ **machine,** = *artificial kidney* (see sense 1); ∼-**shaped,** oval but with one side concave and the other convex; *kidney*-VETCH. [ME *kidnei,* pl. *kidneiren,* app. partly f. *ei* EGG¹]

kie-kie (kē′kē) *n*. NZ climbing plant with edible bracts, and leaves used for baskets etc. [Maori]

kier *n*. vat in which cloth is boiled for bleaching etc. [f. ON *ker* tub, = OHG *kar,* Goth. *kas*]

kie′selguhr (-zēlgoor) *n*. diatomaceous earth used for polishing and as absorbent of nitro-glycerine in manufacture of dynamite. [G (*kiesel* gravel, dial. *guhr* earthy deposit)]

kif. Var. of KEF.

*kike *n*. (sl., derog.; **R**) Jew. [20th c.; orig. uncert.]

ki′lderkin *n*. cask for liquids etc., containing 16 or 18 gal.; this as measure. [ME, alt. of *kinderkin* f. MDu. *kinde(r)kin, kinneken,* dim. of *kintal* QUINTAL; see -KIN]

Kĭlkě′nnӯ *n*. ∼ **cats,** two cats said to have fought until only tails remained, (fig.) two combatants who annihilate each other. [∼ in Ireland)]

kill¹ *v.t.* **1.** deprive of life, put to death, slay (*kill two* BIRDS *with one stone*); (of disease, grief, shock, drink, poison, etc.) cause the death of; (colloq.) cause severe pain to (*my feet are killing me*); ∼ **off,** get rid of (number of persons etc.) by killing; ∼ one**self**, (colloq.) exert oneself unduly. **2.** (abs.) perform act of killing, do execution; **shoot to** ∼ (not only to warn or wound). **3.** obtain (meat) by killing animals. **4.** represent in fiction etc. as dead (*kill your villain in the last chapter*). **5.** destroy vitality of (plant, disease, etc.); destroy, put an end to, (feelings etc.); switch off (spotlight, engine, etc.); (colloq.) eat or drink, esp. consume whole contents of (bottle). **6.** neutralize (colour etc.) by contrast. **7.** spend (time) unprofitably while awaiting future event. **8.** overwhelm (person) with admiration, amusement, etc.; *dressed* etc. **to** ∼, showily or fascinatingly. **9.** (Lawn Tennis) strike (ball) so that it cannot be returned; (Footb.) stop (ball) dead. **10.** totally defeat (bill in Parliament). **11.** ∼ (fatally harm) **with kindness** (that is mistaken or excessive); ∼ or **cure** (of remedies that either cure completely or prove fatal; or fig.); ∼'**joy**, one who throws gloom over social enjoyment; ∼**time** *n.* & *a.* (occupation) intended to kill time. [ME *cülle*, *kille*, perh. ult. cogn. w. QUELL]

kill[2] *n.* act of killing; animal(s) killed, esp. by sportsman; destruction or disablement of submarine, aircraft, etc.; **in at the** ∼, (fig.) present at the time of victory. [f. prec.]

ki′lldeer *n.* large Amer. ring-plover (*Charadrius vociferus*) with plaintive note. [imit.]

ki′ller *n.* one who or that which kills; murderous ruffian; HUMANE *killer*; ∼ **whale**, voracious cetacean (esp. *Orcina orca*). [f. KILL[1] + -ER[1]]

ki′llick *n.* heavy stone used by small craft as anchor; small anchor; ǁ(Navy sl.) leading seaman. [17th c., of unkn. orig.]

ki′llifish *n.* small fish of family Cyprinodontidae used as bait; tropical fish of family Poeciliidae. [perh. f. *kill* stream (f. Du. *kil*) + FISH[1]]

ki′lling[1] *n.* In vbl senses; (fig.) great (esp. financial) success (*make a killing*); ∼**-bottle** (containing poisonous vapour to kill insects collected as specimens). [ME, f. KILL[1] + -ING[1]]

ki′lling[2] *a.* In vbl senses; (colloq.) overwhelmingly attractive, amusing, etc.; hence ∼LY[a] *adv.* [ME, f. KILL[1] + -ING[2]]

kiln *n.* furnace or oven for burning, baking, or drying, esp. (**lime-**∼) for calcining lime, or (**brick-**∼) for baking bricks; ∼**-dry** *v.t.*, dry in kiln. [OE *cylene* f. L *culina* kitchen]

ki′lo (kĭ′-, kē′-) *n.* (*pl.* ∼s). kilogram; kilometre. [F, abbr.]

ki′lo- *pref.* denoting factor of 1,000 as: ∼**cycle** (*per second*), ∼**hertz**, unit of frequency, = 1,000 cycles per second; ǁ∼**litre**, *∼**liter**, measure of 1,000 litres, approx. 35.31 cu. ft. or ǁ3.44 quarters; ∼**ton**(**ne**), (esp.) unit of explosive power equivalent to 1,000 tons of TNT; **kilovolt**; ∼**watt**, power of 1,000 watts, approx. 1.34 h.p.; ∼**watt-hour**, amount of energy equal to one kilowatt operating for one hour. [F, f. Gk *khilioi* thousand]

ki′logram, -gramme, *n.* unit of mass or weight in the metric system, equal to that of the international prototype kept at Sèvres near Paris, approx. 2.205 lb.; ∼**-metre**, quantity of energy that will raise one kilogram to height of one metre. [F *kilogramme* (as prec., GRAM[2])]

ǁ**kilometre**, *kilometer**, (kĭ′lomē-, D kēlŏ′mĭ-) *n.* distance of 1,000 metres, approx. 0.62 mile; hence **kilome′tr**IC *a.* [f. F *kilomètre* (as KILO-, METRE[2])]

kilt[1] *v.t.* tuck up (skirts) round body; (esp. in *p.p.*) gather in vertical pleats. [ME, of Scand. orig.; cf. Da. *kilte* (*op*) tuck (up), Sw. dial. *kilta* swathe, OIcel. *kilting*, *kjalta* skirt, lap]

kilt[2] *n.* skirtlike garment, usu. of tartan cloth, reaching from waist to knee, with many pleats at back and sides, part of Highland man's dress; similar garment worn by children and women; hence ∼**ED**[2] *a.*, ∼**IE** *n.*, wearer of a kilt, esp. kilted Highland soldier. [f. prec.]

*ki′lter, kě′lter**, *n.* good working order (**out of** ∼, not working properly). [17th c., of unkn. orig.]

ki′mberlite *n.* = BLUE[1] *ground*. [f. *Kimberley* in S. Afr. + -ITE[1] (2)]

kimō′nō *n.* (*pl.* ∼s). long loose Japanese robe with wide sleeves, held together by a sash; woman's dressing-gown or wrap modelled on this. [Jap.]

kin *n.* & *a.* **1.** *n.* ancestral stock, family, (*comes of good kin*); one's relative(s); KITH *and kin*. **2.** *pred. a.* related (*we are kin; he is kin to me*). **3. of** ∼, akin, related by blood ties or (fig.) in character; **near of** ∼, closely related; **NEXT** *of kin*. **4.** Hence ∼LESS *a.* [OE *cynn*, = OS, OHG *kunni*, ON *kyn*, Goth. *kuni* f. Gmc *kunjam* f. weak grade of *kin-*, *kan-*, *kun-* f. IE *gen- etc. produce]

-kin *suf.* forming dim. *ns.* (*catkin, lambkin, manikin, napkin*; also in names, as *Peterkin* or *Perkin*). [f. or after MDu. *-kijn*, *-ken*, OHG *-chin*]

kinaesthē′sia, *kinēsth‵ē′sia**, (‵isthē′z-) *n.* sense of muscular effort in voluntary movement of body; hence ∼**ē′t**IC *a.* [f. Gk *kineō* move + *aisthēsis* sensation + -IA[1]]

ki′ncob *n.* rich Indian fabric embroidered with gold or silver. [f. Urdu f. Pers. *kamkāb* (*kamkā* damask)]

kind[1] *n.* **1.** race, natural group, of animals, plants, etc., (*human kind; the rabbit kind*). **2.** class, SORT[1], variety, (*what kind, of what kind, is it?; of a different kind*); **something of the** ∼, something like the thing in question; **nothing of the** ∼, not at all like it; (of **a** ∼, (derog.) scarcely deserving the name (*we had coffee of a kind*); **two of a** ∼, two that are similar in some important respect. **3.** (Eccl.) each of the two elements in the Eucharist. **4.** (In transposed constr.) **what** ∼ **of** *tree is this?*, of what kind is this tree?, *this is* **the** ∼ **of** *thing I meant* (a thing of the kind I meant); **this** or (colloq.) **these** ∼ **of** *men* (men of this kind) *annoy me*. **5.** (Implying looseness, vagueness, exaggeration, etc., in the term used) *he is* **a** *kind of stockbroker, of millionaire; felt a kind of compunction*; (colloq.) *I* ∼ **of** (to some extent) *expected it, felt kind of sorry for him*. **6.** (arch.) nature in general (*the law of kind*); way, fashion, natural to person etc. (*they act after their kind*). **7.** character, quality; *they differ in* ∼ (not merely in degree). **8. in** ∼, (of payment) in goods or natural produce, not in money, (of repayment, esp. fig.) in the same form (*repay his insolence in kind* = with insolence). [OE *cynd*(*e*), *gecynd*(*e*) f. Gmc *gakundiz* (as Y-, KIN, *-diz* abstract suf.)]

kind[2] *a.* of gentle or benevolent nature; friendly in one's conduct *to* (person etc.); showing friendliness; affectionate; ∼**-hearted**, having a kind heart; hence ∼′NESS *n.* [OE *gecynde* (as prec.); orig. = 'natural', native']

ki′nda (colloq.) = *kind of*. [f. KIND[1] 5 + -A]

ki′ndergarten *n.* school for young children, esp. teaching by object-lessons, toys, games, etc. [G, = children's garden]

ki′ndle *v.* **1.** *v.t.* set on fire, light, (flame, fire, substance); (fig.) inflame, inspire, (passion etc.), stir up (person or emotion etc., to do). **2.** *v.i.* catch fire, burst into flame; (fig.) become animated, glow with passion etc. **3.** *v.t.* & *i.* make or become bright; ∼ (**up**), (cause to) glow. **4.** Hence **ki′ndl**ING[1] *n.*, (esp., in *sing.* or *pl.*) small wood for lighting fires. [ME, f. ON *kynda* kindle + -LE 3; cf. ON *kindill* candle, torch]

ki′ndly[1] *adv.* In adj. senses; (in polite request or iron. command: *kindly acknowledge this letter; will you kindly shut the door behind you*); **take** ∼, accept with pleasure; **take** ∼ **to**, be pleased by; **thank** ∼ (with hearty appreciation). [OE *gecyndelīce* (as KIND[1], -LY[2])]

ki′ndly[2] *a.* kind, kind-hearted; (of climate etc.) pleasant, genial, (arch.) native-born (*a kindly Scot*); hence ∼ILY[a] *adv.*, ∼iNESS *n.* [OE *gecyndelic* (as KIND[1], -LY[1])]

ki′ndred *n.* & *a.* **1.** *n.* blood relationship; (fig.) resemblance in character; one's relative(s). **2.** *a.* related by blood; (fig.) allied, connected, similar, (*frost and kindred phenomena*; ∼ **spirit**, person felt to be congenial). [ME, f. KIN + *-red* f. OE *rǣden* condition]

kine. See COW[1].

kinemǎ′tic *a.* of motion considered abstractly

without reference to force or mass; *kinematic* VISCOSITY; hence ～ICAL *a*., ～ICALLY *adv*., ～ICS *n*., science of pure motion. [f. Gk *kinēma -matos* motion (*kineō* move) + -IC]

kinematograph. Var. of CINEMATOGRAPH.

kinē′si|cs *n. pl.* (often treated as *sing.*) (study of) body movements etc. contributing to communication, e.g. shrug of shoulders; so ～ō′LOGY *n.*, study of mechanics of body movements. [f. Gk *kinēsis* motion (as foll.) + -ICS]

kinē′tic *a.* of or due to motion; ～ **art** (depending on movement for its effect); *kinetic* ENERGY; ～ **theory of heat, of gases,** (that heat, the gaseous state, is due to motion of particles); hence **kinē′t**ICS *n.*, science of the relations between the motions of bodies and the forces acting upon them. [f. Gk *kinētikos* (*kineō* move; see -ETIC)]

king[1] *n.* **1.** male sovereign (esp. hereditary) ruler of independent state; **Kings,** two books of OT dealing with history esp. of kingdom of Judah. **2. K～ Emperor** (Hist., of UK and India, or of Austria-Hungary); **K～ Log, K～ Stork,** rulers going to extremes of *laissez-faire*, active oppression, (w. ref. to fable of Jupiter and the frogs); **K～ of ～s,** (1) God, (2) title assumed by many Eastern kings; ～ **of terrors,** Death; **K～ Charles spaniel** (small black-and-tan kind); **K～ Charles's head,** *idée fixe* [f. Dickens's *David Copperfield*, ch. xiv]; ‖*King's* BENCH, BOUNTY, COLOUR[1], COUNSEL[1], ENGLISH[1], EVIDENCE, GUIDE[1], HIGHWAY, MESSENGER, PROCTOR, SCOUT[1], SHILLING, SPEECH; **K～ of the Castle,** children's game of seeking to displace rival from mound. **3.** great merchant, player, etc. (*fur, railway, tennis, king*; cf. LORD 1). **4.** ～ **of beasts,** lion; ～ **of birds,** eagle. **5.** best kind (*of* fruits, plants, etc.). **6.** piece in chess that has to be protected from checkmate (～'s **bishop, knight, pawn, rook,** those placed nearest king at start); piece in draughts made by crowning a man that has traversed the board and reached opponent's baseline; court-card bearing representation of king and usu. ranking next below ace. **7.** ～'**bird,** (1) kind of bird of paradise, (2) Amer. tyrant fly-catcher; ～'**bolt,** main or large bolt; ～ **cobra,** large very venomous hooded Indian snake (*Naja hannah*); ～-**crab,** (1) large marine arthropod esp. of genus *Limulus* having horseshoe-shaped carapace, (2) *large edible spider-crab; ～'**craft,** skilful exercise of kingship; ～'**cup,** (1) buttercup, (2) ‖marsh marigold; ～-**fish,** fish of remarkable size etc., esp. opah or mulloway; ～'**fisher,** small bird of family Alcedinidae with dagger-shaped bill and brilliant plumage, feeding on fish it captures by diving; *K～ **James**('s) **Bible** or **Version,** = AUTHORIZED *Version*; ～'**maker,** one who sets up kings by his power, esp. Earl of Warwick in reign of Henry VI; ‖K～ **of Arms,** chief herald (at College of Arms: Garter, Clarenceux, and Norroy & Ulster; in Scotland: Lyon); ～ **penguin** (large species *Aptenodytes patagonica*); ～'**pin,** = *kingbolt,* (fig.) essential or leading person or thing; ～-**post,** upright post from tie-beam to rafter-top; ～'s **evil,** scrofula, formerly held to be curable by royal touch; ～-**size(d)** *a.*, larger than normal, very large; ‖K～'s **Scholar** (holding scholarship on royal foundation). **8.** Hence ～'**hood** ～'LING[1], ～'SHIP (1), *ns.*, ～'LESS *a.*, ～'LET *n.*, (1) petty king, (2) small bird of family Regulidae, e.g. firecrest and goldcrest, ～'LIKE *a.* & *adv.*, ～'LY[1] *a.* [OE *cyning, cyng,* = OS, OHG *kuning* f. Gmc *kuningaz* (as KIN, -ING[3])]

king[2] *v.t.* make (person) king; ～ **it,** act the king, govern. [ME, f. prec.]

ki′ngdom *n.* **1.** organized community headed by king or queen; MIDDLE[1] *Kingdom*; UNITED *Kingdom.* **2.** territory subject to king; spiritual reign of God, sphere of this, (*the kingdom of heaven; thy kingdom come*); ～-**come,** (sl.) the next world; **till ～ come,** (sl.) for an indefinitely long time. **3.** domain; province of nature, esp. *animal, vegetable, mineral, kingdom.* **4.**

Hence ～ED[2] (-md) *a.* [OE *cyningdōm* (as KING[1], DOM)]

ki′nin *n.* peptide formed in blood after injury and causing sensation of pain; compound promoting cell division and inhibiting ageing in higher plants. [f. Gk *kineō* move + -IN]

kink *n.* & *v.* **1.** *n.* short backward twist in wire or chain or rope or tube or hair such as may cause obstruction or a break; (fig.) mental twist, crotchet. **2.** *v.i.* & *t.* (cause to) form kink. [f. MLG *kinke* f. **ki(n)k-* bend; vb. prob. f. Du. *kinken*]

ki′nkajou (-ōō) *n.* carnivorous nocturnal arboreal animal of central & S. America, with prehensile tail, allied to racoon. [f. F *quincajou* f. N. Amer. Ind.; cf. Algonquin *kwingwaage* wolverine]

ki′nk|ȳ *a.* having (many) kinks; (colloq.) bizarre, perverted (esp. sexually); hence ～iNESS *n.* [f. KINK + -Y[2]]

ki′nnikinic *n.* mixture of dried sumac-leaves, bark of willow, etc., as substitute for tobacco, or mixed with it; any plant used for this. [Algonquin, lit. 'mixture']

ki′nō (kē′-) *n.* (*pl.* ～s). gum of various trees, resembling catechu, and used in medicine and tanning as astringent. [W. Afr.]

-kins (-z) *suf.* = -KIN (w. suggestion of endearment, as *babykins*); cf. -s[4].

ki′ns|folk (-zfōk) *n. pl.* relations by blood; so ～'MAN (～'WOMAN, *ns.* [ME, f. KIN + 's l + FOLK]

ki′nship *n.* blood relationship; similarity or alliance in character. [f. KIN + -SHIP]

ki′osk (kē′-) *n.* light or open-fronted outdoor or ‖indoor structure for sale of newspapers, food, etc.; bandstand etc.; structure in street etc. for public telephone; light open pavilion in Turkey and Iran. [f. F *kiosque* f. Turk. *kiūshk* pavilion f. Pers. *gus̆*]

kip[1] *n.* hide of young or small animal as used for leather. [ME, of unkn. orig.]

kip[2] *n.*, & *v.i.* (-pp-). (sl.) **1.** *n.* common lodging-house; bed. **2.** *n.*, & *v.i.* sleep; (place to) lie down for sleep. [cf. Da. *kippe* mean hut]

ki′pper[1] *n.* **1.** male salmon in spawning season. **2.** kippered fish, esp. herring. [ME, of uncert. orig.]

ki′pper[2] *v.t.* cure (salmon, herring, etc.) by splitting open, cleaning, rubbing with salt, pepper, etc., and drying in open air or smoke. [f. prec.]

kir′by-grip *n.* type of hair-grip with spring. [f. *Kirbigrip* (P)]

Kirghi′z (kērgē′z) *a.* & *n.* (member or language) of a Mongol people living in central Asia between Volga and Irtysh rivers. [Kirghiz]

ki′ri *n.* Japanese paulownia(-wood). [Jap.]

‖**kirk** *n.* **1.** (Sc. & N. Engl.) church. **2. the K～ (of Scotland),** Church of Scotland as opp. to Church of England or to Episcopal Church in Scotland; ～'**man,** member of Church of Scotland; ～-**session,** lowest court in Church of Scotland and (Hist.) other Presbyterian Churches, composed of ministers and elders. [ME, f. ON *kirkja* f. OE *cir(i)ce* CHURCH[1]]

kir′sch(wasser) (kēr′shvahser) *n.* spirit distilled from fermented liquor of wild cherries. [G (*kirsche* cherry, *wasser* water)]

kir′tle *n.* (arch.) woman's gown or outer petticoat; man's tunic or coat. [OE *cyrtel,* = ON *kyrtill* tunic f. Gmc **kurtilaz,* ult. perh. f. L *curtus* short; see -LE 1]

ki′smět (-s-, -z-) *n.* destiny, fate. [Turk., f. Arab. *ḳisma(t)* (*ḳasama* divide)]

kiss[1] *n.* touch given with lips (as foll.; BLOW[1] *a kiss*); (Bill.) impact between moving balls; small sweetmeat or piece of confectionery; ～-**curl,** small curl of hair on forehead, in front of ear, or at nape; ～ **of death,** apparently friendly act causing ruin; ～ **of life,** mouth-to-mouth resuscitation; ～ **of peace,** ceremonial kiss in Eucharist as sign of unity. [ME, f. foll.]

kiss[2] *v.t.* **1.** touch with the lips, esp. as sign of love, affection, greeting, or reverence; express thus (*kiss me good night*); (abs., of two persons) touch each other's lips thus; (Bill., of ball) touch (ball) with KISS[1] (also abs. of two balls). **2.** ～ **away,** remove (tears etc.)

with kisses; ∼ **the book** (Bible, in taking oath); ∼ **the dust,** yield abject submission, be overthrown; ∼ **goodbye to,** (fig.) accept loss of; ∼ **the ground,** prostrate oneself in token of homage, (fig.) be brought low; ∼ one's **hand to,** BLOW¹ a kiss to; ∼ **hands** or **the hand** (of sovereign etc. as ceremonial salutation or on appointment to office); ∼ **the rod,** accept chastisement submissively; ∼**-in-the-ring,** game for young people in which one pursues and kisses another of opposite sex; ∼**-me-quick,** (1) small bonnet standing far back on head, (2) = KISS¹- -*curl.* **3.** Hence ∼´ABLE *a.* [OE *cyssan,* = OS *cussian,* OHG *kussen,* ON *kyssa* f. Gmc **kussjan* (**kussaz* a kiss)]

ki´sser *n.* In vbl senses; (sl.) face, mouth. [f. prec. + -ER¹]

ki´ssing¹ *a.* In vbl senses; ∼ **cousin,** ∼ **kin(d),** distant relative(s) given formal kiss at occasional meeting; ∼**-crust,** soft crust where loaf has touched another in baking. [ME, f. KISS² + -ING²]

ki´ssing² *n.* In vbl senses; ||∼**-gate** (hung in U- or V- -shaped enclosure). [f. KISS² + -ING¹]

kist. Var. of CIST¹.

Kiswahi´li (-swahhē´-) *n.* Swahili language. [Swahili (*ki-* pref. for abstract or inanimate object)]

kit¹ *n.* & *v.* (-tt-). **1.** *n.* ||wooden tub for various purposes, e.g. to hold fish. **2.** (articles carried in) soldier's etc. pack etc.; personal equipment, esp. as packed for travelling; workman's outfit of tools etc.; set of parts sold together from which thing may be made; clothing etc. for a particular activity or situation (*riding-kit; tropical kit*); ∼´**bag** for carrying soldier's or traveller's kit). **3.** *v.t.* & *i.* fit out, be fitted out, with kit (often *out* or *up*). [ME, f. MDu. *kitte* wooden vessel; orig. unkn.]

kit² *n.* kitten; young fox etc. [abbr.]

kit³ *n.* (Hist.) small fiddle used esp. by dancing- -master. [perh. f. L *cithara* (see CITHERN)]

ki´t-cǎt *n* ∼ **(portrait),** portrait of less than half- -length, but including hands. [*K*∼ *Club,* club of Whig politicians founded under James II, f. Christopher (or *Kit*) *Cat,* keeper of pie-house where club met]

ki´tchèn *n.* room or other place where food is prepared and cooked (SOUP-*kitchen*); (Mus. sl.) percussion department of orchestra; ∼ **cabinet,** (Polit.) group of unofficial advisers thought to be unduly influential; ∼ **garden** (for growing one's own fruit and vegetables); ∼**-maid,** maidservant employed in kitchen, usu. under cook; *kitchen* MIDDEN; *∼ **police,** (Mil.) enlisted men instructed to help cooks; ∼ **sink,** (fig.) extreme realism in painting, drama, etc., (*everything but the* ∼ *sink,* everything imaginable); ∼ **stuff,** kitchen requisites, esp. vegetables; ∼**-ware,** hard- ware used in kitchen. [OE *cycene,* = OS **kukina,* OHG *chuhhina* f. WG **kocina,* *cocina var. of LL *coquina* f. L *coquere* cook]

ki´tchener *n.* ||cooking-range; person in charge of monastery kitchen. [ME, f. prec. + -ER¹]

kitchěně´tte *n.* small room, alcove, etc., used as kitchen (and pantry). [f. KITCHEN + -ETTE]

kite *n.* & *v.* **1.** *n.* large bird of prey, of hawk family, with long wings, usu. forked tail, and no tooth in bill. **2.** rapacious person, sharper. **3.** toy consisting of light wooden etc. frame, usu. in form of symmetrical quadrilateral or of triangle with segment of circle on base, with paper, etc. stretched over it and usu. with long tail, flown in strong wind by string; BOX²-*kite;* FLY² *a kite.* **4.** (Commerc. sl.) accommodation bill (FLY² *a kite*); ||(sl.) aeroplane. **5.** (in *pl.*) highest sails of ship, set only in light wind. **6.** ∼ **balloon,** sausage- -shaped captive balloon for military observations; ||K∼´**mark,** official mark (representing a stylized kite) on goods approved by the British Standards Institution. **7.** *v.i.* soar or move like kite; *(colloq.) move quickly. **8.** *v.t.* cause to do this; (Commerc. sl.) convert into kite. [OE *cȳta,* of unkn. orig.]

kith *n.* ∼ **and kin,** friends and relations. [OE *cȳthth* f. Gmc **kunthithō* f. **kunth-* known; cf. UNCOUTH, -TH¹]

kitoo´l. See KITTUL.

kitsch (kĭch) *n.* worthless pretentiousness in art; art of this type; hence ∼´Y² *a.* [G]

ki´tten *n.* & *v.* **1.** *n.* young cat; young ferret etc.; skittish young girl; **have** ∼**s,** (colloq.) be very nervous or upset; hence ∼ISH¹ *a.* **2.** *v.t.* & *i.* give birth to (kittens). [ME *kito(u)n, ketoun* f. AF **kitoun, *ketoun,* OF *chitoun, chetoun* dim. of *chat* CAT¹, assim. to -EN²]

ki´ttiwāke *n.* small sea-gull of genus *Rissa.* [imit. of its cry]

ki´ttle *a.* ticklish, difficult to deal with, esp. ∼ **cattle** (usu. fig. of persons or things). [f. ME (now Sc. & dial.) *kittle* tickle, prob. f. ON *kitla* = OS *kitilon,* OHG *kizzilōn*]

kittu´l (-ōō´l), **kitoo´l,** *n.* E. Ind. palm-tree (*Caryota urens*); strong black fibre from leaf-stalks of this. [f. Sinh. *kitūl*]

ki´tty¹ *n.* (Pet-name for) kitten. [f. KIT² + -Y³]

ki´tty² *n.* pool in some card-games; joint fund (*how much is there left in the kitty?*); (Bowls) jack. [19th c.; orig. unkn.]

ki´wi (kē´wē) *n.* **1.** flightless NZ bird, = APTERYX; ∼ **berry, fruit,** Chinese gooseberry. **2.** (*K*∼; colloq.) New Zealander, esp. soldier or member of national sports team. [Maori]

*KKK *abbr.* Ku-Klux-Klan.

kl. *abbr.* kilolitre(s).

kla´xon *n.* powerful electric (motor-)horn. [P]

Klein (klīn) *n.* ∼ **bottle,** (Math.) closed surface with only one side, formed by passing neck of bottle through side of bottle to join hole in base. [f. F. ∼, Ger. mathematician d. 1925]

klěpht *n.* one of the Greeks who after Turkish conquest of Greece in 15th c. maintained independence in mountains; brigand. [f. mod. Gk *klephtēs* f. Gk *kleptēs* thief]

klěpto|mā´nia *n.* irresistible tendency to steal what one could afford to buy; hence ∼MA´NIAC *n.* & *a.* [f. Gk *kleptēs* thief + -O- + -MANIA]

klieg *n.* ∼ **(light),** powerful lamp in film studio etc. [f. A. T. & J. H. *Kliegl,* Amer. inventors d. 1927, 1959]

kli´pdas (-ahs) *n.* S. Afr. hyrax (*Procavia capensis*). [Afrik. (*klip* rock, *das* badger)]

kli´pspringer *n.* small S. Afr. antelope like chamois. [Afrik. (*klip* rock, *springer* jumper)]

Klō´ndīke *n.* source of valuable material. [f. ∼ in Yukon, Canada, where gold was found in 1896]

kloof *n.* ravine or valley in S. Africa. [Du., = cleft]

kly´strŏn *n.* (Electr.) device for amplifying or gen- erating microwaves by forming electrons into bunches as they cross a gap. [f. Gk *kluzō klus-* wash over + -TRON]

km. *abbr.* kilometre(s).

K-mě´sŏn (kǎmē´z-) *n.* = KAON. [f. K + MESON]

kn. *abbr.* knot(s) (see KNOT¹ 2).

knǎck *n.* acquired or intuitive faculty of doing a thing adroitly; trick or habit of action, speech, etc.; (arch.) ingenious device. [ME, prob. = ME *knack* sharp blow or sound, of LG orig., ult. imit.]

||**knǎ´ck|er** *n.,* & *v.t.* **1.** one who buys and slaughters useless horses, whence ∼ERY (3) *n.;* one who buys old houses, ships, etc., for the materials. **2.** *v.t.* (sl.) kill; (fig., esp. in *p.p.*) exhaust, wear out. [19th c.; orig. unkn.]

knǎg *n.* knot in wood, base of a branch; short dead branch, peg for hanging things on; hence ∼´**gy²** (-gĭ) *a.* [ME, perh. f. LG *knagge*]

knǎp¹ *n.* (chiefly dial.) crest of hill, rising ground. [OE *cnæp(p),* perh. cogn. w. ON *knappr* knob]

knǎp² *v.t.* (-pp-). break (flints for roads or building) with hammer, whence ∼´**per¹** (1, 2) *n.;* (arch.) knock, rap, snap asunder. [ME, imit.]

knǎ´psǎck *n.* soldier's or traveller's canvas or leather bag, strapped to back and used for carrying neces- saries. [MLG, prob. f. *knappen* bite + SACK¹]

knă'pweed *n.* common weed of genus *Centaurea*, esp. *C. nigra*, with hard stem and light purple flowers on dark globular head. [ME, orig. *knopweed* f. KNOP + WEED]

knȧr *n.* knot in wood, esp. protuberance covered with bark on trunk or at root of tree. [ME *knarre*, rel. to MLG, MDu., MHG *knorre* knobbed protuberance]

knȧv|e *n.* **1.** unprincipled or dishonest man, rogue; hence ∼'ERY (4) *n.*, ∼'ISH[1] *a.* **2.** (Cards) = JACK[1] 3. [OE *cnafa* boy, servant, = OHG *knabo* f. WG *knabho*]

knaw'el *n.* low-growing weed of genus *Scleranthus*. [f. G *knauel*]

knead *v.t.* work up (moist flour or clay) into dough or paste; make (bread, pottery) thus; (fig.) blend, weld together; operate on (muscles etc.) as if kneading, massage; hence ∼'ABLE *a.*, ∼'ER[1] (1, 2) *n.* [OE *cnedan*, = OS *knedan*, OHG *knetan*, ON *knotha* f. Gmc **kned-*, **knad-*]

knee[1] *n.* **1.** joint between thigh and lower leg in man; corresponding joint in animal; upper surface of thigh of sitting person (*hold child* etc. *on* one's *knee*); **bend** or **bow the** ∼, kneel esp. in submission; **on** one's ∼**s, on bended** ∼(**s**), kneeling esp. in worship, supplication, or submission; **give a** ∼ **to**, support (pugilist) on one's knee between rounds, act as second to; *on the knees of the* GODs; **bring** person **to his** ∼**s,** reduce him to submission. **2.** part of garment covering knee. **3.** thing like knee in shape or position, esp. piece of wood or iron with angular bend; sharp turn in graph. **4.** ∼**-breeches** (reaching down to or just below knee); ∼'**cap,** (1) convex bone in front of knee-joint, (2) protective covering for knee; ∼'**capping,** shooting in the legs as punishment; ∼**-deep,** immersed up to the knees, (fig.) deeply involved *in*; ∼**-deep,** ∼**-high,** so deep or high as to reach the knees; ∼**-hole,** space for knees, esp. between columns of drawers at each side of desk etc.; ∼ **holly,** butcher's-broom; ∼**-jerk,** sudden involuntary kick caused by motion on tendon below knee (also fig. of response regarded as predictable and unthinking); ∼**-joint,** (1) joint of knee, (2) joint of two pieces hinged together; ∼**-length,** so long as to reach the knees; ∼**-pan,** kneecap; ∼**s-up,** (colloq.) lively party with dancing. [OE *cnēo(w)*, = OS *knio*, OHG *kneo*, ON *kné*, Goth. *kniu* f. Gmc **knewam* f. IE **gneuom*]

knee[2] *v.t.* touch or strike with the knee; (colloq.) cause (trousers) to bulge at knees. [f. prec.]

kneel *v.i.* (**knelt** or ***∼**ed**). fall or rest on the knee(s) esp. in prayer or reverence (*to* person); hence ∼'ER[1] *n.*, (esp.) hassock etc. to kneel on. [OE *cnēowlian* (as KNEE[1])]

knĕll[1] *n.* sound of bell, esp. of one rung solemnly after a death or at funeral; (fig.) announcement, event, etc., regarded as an omen of death or extinction; **ring the** ∼, announce or herald abolition etc. *of.* [OE *cnyll* (as foll.)]

knĕll[2] *v.* (arch.) **1.** *v.i.* (Of bell) ring, esp. at death or funeral; give forth doleful sound; (fig.) sound ominously. **2.** *v.t.* proclaim as by a knell. [OE *cnyllan*; perh. infl. by *bell*]

knĕlt. See KNEEL.

knew. See KNOW[1].

kni'ckerböcker *n.* **1.** (*K*∼). New Yorker; descendant of original Dutch settlers in New York. **2.** (in *pl.*) loose-fitting breeches gathered in at knee. [f. Diedrich *K*∼, pretended author of W. Irving's *History of New York* (1809)]

kni'ckers (-z) *n.pl.* ‖woman's or girl's undergarment covering lower part of body and having separate legs or leg-holes; ***knickerbockers; ***boy's short trousers; ‖(as *int.*, vulg.) expr. contempt. [abbr. of prec.]

kni'ck-knăck (nĭ'knăk) *n.* light dainty article of furniture, dress, or food; trinket, toy, useless ornament; hence ∼ERY (2, 5) *n.*, ∼ISH[1] *a.* [redupl. of *knack* in obs. sense 'trinket']

knife *n.* (*pl.* **knives** *pr.* nīvz), & *v.t.* **1.** *n.* metal blade with sharpened longitudinal edge fixed in handle either rigidly or with hinge, used as cutting instrument or as weapon; **the** ∼, surgical operation(s); WAR[1] *to the knife*; **get** one's ∼ **into,** show malicious or vindictive spirit towards (person); **that one could cut with a** ∼, (colloq., of accent, atmosphere, etc.) very obvious or oppressive; **before you can say** ∼, (colloq.) very quickly or suddenly. **2.** cutting-blade forming part of machine. **3.** ∼**-board,** board on which knives are cleaned, ‖(Hist.) double bench placed lengthways on top of omnibus; ‖∼**-boy** (Hist., employed to clean table-knives); ∼**-edge** (1) edge of knife, (2) steel wedge on which pendulum etc. oscillates, (3) arête, (4) position of extreme uncertainty; ∼**-grinder,** (1) itinerant sharpener of knives etc., (2) one who grinds knives etc. in process of making; ∼**-machine** (for cleaning knives); ∼**-pleat** (narrow and flat, usu. overlapping another); **at** ∼**-point,** under threat of injury by knife; ∼**-rest,** metal or glass support for carving-knife or -fork at table; ∼**-throwing** (esp. with great accuracy, as entertainment). **4.** *v.t.* cut or stab with knife; ***(sl.) seek to defeat by underhand means. [OE *cnīf.* f. ON *knīfr*, = MLG *knīf*, MDu. *cnijf*, f. Gmc **knībhaz*]

knight (nīt) *n.*, & *v.t.* **1.** *n.* (Hist.) man, usu. one of noble birth who had served as page and squire, raised to honourable military rank by king or other qualified person. **2.** man on whom corresponding rank is conferred as reward for personal merit or services to Crown or country. **3.** (Hist. or fig.) military follower, esp. one devoted to service of lady as her attendant or champion in war or tournament; ∼**-service,** (Hist.) tenure of land by military service. **4.** (Hist.) ∼ (**of the shire**), gentleman representing shire or county in parliament. **5.** (Rom. Ant.) one of the class of *equites,* orig. cavalry of Roman army; (Gk Ant.) citizen of second class at Athens. **6.** chess piece, usu. with shape of horse's head. **7.** (w. following n. in apposition, etc.; *pl.* usu. ∼**s** —): *knight* BACHELOR, COMMANDER, HOSPITALLER, TEMPLAR; ∼ **errant,** medieval knight wandering in search of chivalrous adventures, (fig.) person of chivalrous or of quixotic spirit; ∼**-e'rrantry,** practice or conduct of a knight errant; *knight* MARSHAL[1]; ∼ **of the road,** (1) highwayman, (2) commercial traveller, (3) tramp. **8.** Hence ∼'HOOD (-t-h-) *n.*, ∼'LIKE, ∼'LY[1], *adjs.*, ∼'LY[2] *adv.* (poet.). **9.** *v.t.* confer knighthood on. [OE *cniht* boy, youth, hero, = OS, OHG *kneht* f. WG **knehta*]

kni'ghtage (nī't-) *n.* whole body of knights; list and account of knights. [f. prec. + -AGE]

knish (k-n-) *n.* dumpling of flaky dough filled with cheese etc. and baked or fried. [Yiddish f. Russ.]

knit *v.* (-tt-; ∼'ted *or*, esp. fig., **knit**) & *n.* **1.** *v.t.* form (close texture, garments etc. of this, or abs.) of interlocking loops of yarn or thread; make (a plain stitch) in knitting; contract (brow) in vertical wrinkles. **2.** *v.t.* & *i.* make or become close or compact (esp. WELL-knit); (fig.) unite (*together*) intimately by means of common interests, marriage, etc.; (of parts of broken bone) become joined (*together*) again as one. **3.** ∼ **up,** make or repair by knitting, (fig.) close up, conclude, (argument etc.); ∼'**wear,** knitted garments. **4.** *n.* knitted material or garment. [OE *cnyttan,* = MDu., MLG *knutten* f. WG **knuttjan* (**knutto* KNOT[1])]

kni'tting *n.* In vbl senses; work in process of being knitted; ∼**-machine** (for mechanical knitting of garments etc.); ∼**-needle,** slender pointed rod of steel, wood, plastic, etc., two or more of which are used together in knitting. [ME, f. prec. + -ING[1]]

knŏb & *v.* (-bb-). **1.** *n.* rounded protuberance, esp. at end on or surface of thing; such handle of door or drawer, attachment of this shape for pulling, turning, etc.; small lump (of butter, sugar, coal, etc.); ∼'**kerrie** [after Afrik. *knopkierie*], short stick with knobbed head as weapon of S. Afr. tribes; ∼'**stick,** knobbed stick used esp. as weapon, ‖(arch.) = SCAB 3; **with** ∼**s on,** (sl.) = that and more (phr. indicating ironic or emphatic agreement, or in retort to insult etc.); hence ∿'**by²** *a.* **2.** *v.t.* furnish with knob(s). **3.** *v.i.* bulge *out.* [ME f. MLG *knobbe* knot, knob, bud; cf. KNOP, NOB¹, NUB]

knŏ'bbl|e *n.* small knob; hence ∿**y²** *a.* [ME, dim. of prec.; cf. Du. & LG *knobbel*]

knŏck¹ *v.* **1.** *v.t.* & *i.* strike with audible sharp blow; strike door, strike *at the door* etc. to seek admittance; make by knocking (*knock a hole in*); **knock* (*on*) WOOD. **2.** *v.i.* (Of motor or other engine) make thumping or rattling noise as result of loose bearing or other mechanical defect; = PINK⁶. **3.** *v.t.* (sl.) criticize; ||make strong impression on, astonish; ||∿'**ing-shop,** (sl.) brothel. **4.** ∿ **on the head,** stun or kill (person etc.) by blow on head, (fig.) put an end to (scheme etc.); ∿ one's **head against,** (fig.) come into unpleasant collision with (unfavourable facts or conditions). **5.** drive (thing, person) *in, out, off,* etc., by striking (cf. sense 6); *knock into a* COCK²*ed hat;* ∿ person **into the middle of next week,** (colloq.) send him flying; *knock* SPOT¹*s off, the* BOTTOM¹ *out of.* **6.** ∿ **about,** strike repeatedly, treat roughly, be casually present, wander, lead irregular life; ∿'*about* a., boisterous (freq. of theatrical performance), wandering irregularly, (of clothes) suitable for rough use; ∿ **against,** collide with, come across casually; ||∿ **back,** (sl.) eat or drink esp. quickly, disconcert; ∿ **down,** strike (person etc.) to ground with blow, demolish, (fig.) cause to succumb, (at auction) dispose of (article *to* bidder) by knock with hammer, (colloq.) lower (prices), *(sl.) steal, (Commerc.) take (machinery, furniture, etc.) to pieces to save space in transport; ∿*-down* a., (of blow, lit. or fig.) overwhelming, (of price) very low, (of price at auction) reserve, (of furniture etc.) easily dismantled; ∿ **off,** (colloq.) strike off with blow, leave off work, leave off (work), (colloq.) dispatch (business) or rapidly compose (verses etc.), deduct (sum *from* price, bill, etc.), (sl.) steal, (sl.) copulate with (woman), (sl.) kill; ∿ **on,** (Rugby Footb.) propel (ball) with hand or arm towards opponents' goal-line, whence ∿*-on* n.; ∿ **out,** empty (one's tobacco-pipe) by tapping, make unconscious by hitting on head, disable (boxer) so that he cannot rise within usu. ten seconds, (fig.) defeat esp. in knock-out competition, make useless, (sl.) astonish, (sl.) exhaust one*self,* (colloq.) make (plan etc.) hastily; ∿*-out* n. & a., (blow) that knocks boxer etc. out, (competition) in which loser of each match is eliminated, (sl.) outstanding or irresistible person or thing; ∿*-out drops* (added to drink in order to make drinker unconscious); ∿ **sideways,** (colloq.) discomfit; ∿ **together,** put together hastily or roughly; ∿ **under,** submit, knuckle under; ∿ **up,** drive upwards with blow, make or arrange hastily, score (runs) rapidly at cricket, ||arouse (person) by knocking at door, exhaust, make ill, become exhausted or suffer breakdown, (sl.) make pregnant; ∿*-up* n., practice or casual game at tennis etc. **7.** ∿ **knees,** abnormal condition with leg(s) curved inward at the knee; so ∿**-knee**ED² *a.* [OE *cnocian,* = ON *knoka,* prob. imit.]

knŏck² *n.* act of knocking; sharp or audible blow; rap esp. at door; sound of knocking in motor etc. engine (see prec.); (colloq.) innings at cricket; ∿ **for** ∿ **agreement** (between insurers, whereby each pays his own policy-holders regardless of liability); **take a** or **the** ∿, be hard hit financially or emotionally. [ME, f. prec.]

knŏ'cker *n.* In vbl senses; appendage, usu. of iron or brass, so hinged to door that it may be struck against metal plate to call attention (||**up to the** ∿, sl., in good condition, to perfection); (in *pl.,* vulg.) woman's breasts; ||∿**-u'p,** person who goes from house to house awakening others at required time. [ME, f. KNOCK¹ + -ER¹]

knŏll¹ *n.* small hill, mound. [OE *cnoll* hilltop, rel. to MDu., MHG *knolle* clod, ON *knollr* hilltop]

knŏll² *v.t.* & *i.,* & *n.* (arch.) = KNELL¹·²; summon by sound of bell. [ME, var. of KNELL¹·², perh. imit.]

knŏp *n.* (ornamental) knob; ornamental loop or tuft in yarn; (arch.) flower-bud. [ME, f. MLG, MDu. *knoppe,* = OHG *knoph*]

knŏ'pkierie (k-n-) *n.* (S. Afr.) = KNOBKERRIE. [Afrik.]

knŏt¹ *n.* **1.** intertwining or tangling of parts of one or more ropes, strings, tresses, etc., to fasten them together; ribbon etc. so tied as ornament or adjunct to dress; **tie in** ∿**s,** (colloq.) render (person) completely baffled or confused. **2.** (Naut.) division marked by knots on log-line, as measure of speed; unit of ship's or aircraft's speed equivalent to one nautical MILE per hour; (pop.) one nautical mile; **at the rate of** ∿**s,** (colloq.) very fast. **3.** difficulty, problem, (GORDIAN *knot*); central point in problem or plot of story etc. **4.** that which forms or maintains a union (esp. of wedlock). **5.** hard lump in animal body; excrescence in stem, branch, or root, of plant; (hard mass formed in trunk at insertion of branch, causing) round cross-grained piece in board; node on stem of plant. **6.** group or cluster *of* persons or things. **7.** ||(**porter's**) ∿, double shoulder-pad and forehead-loop used for carrying loads. **8.** ∿**-garden,** intricately designed formal garden; ∿**-grass,** common weed (*Polygonium aviculare*) with intricate creeping stems and small pale pink flowers; ∿**-hole** (in board, where knot (sense 5) has fallen out); ∿'**work,** ornamental work representing or consisting of intertwined cords. **9.** Hence ∿'LESS *a.* [OE *cnotta,* = Du. *knot,* MHG *knotze* f. WG *knutto]

knŏt² *v.* (**-tt-**). **1.** *v.t.* tie (string etc.) in knot; knit (one's brows); unite closely or intricately; entangle; **get** ∿**ted!,** (sl.) stop annoying me. **2.** *v.i.* & *t.* make knots for fringes, make (fringe) thus; hence ∿'TING¹ *n.* [f. prec.]

knŏt³ *n.* small wading bird (esp. *Calidris canutus*) of sandpiper family. [ME; orig. unkn.]

knŏ'tt|y *a.* full of knots; (fig.) puzzling, hard to explain, (*knotty subject, question, point*); hence ∿ILY² *adv.,* ∿INESS *n.* [ME, f. KNOT¹ + -Y²]

knout (nowt, nōōt) *n.,* & *v.t.* (flog with) scourge formerly used in Russia, often fatal in its effects. [F, f. Russ. *knut* f. Icel. *knútr,* cogn. w. KNOT¹]

know¹ (nō) *v.* (**knew** *pr.* nū; ∿*n pr.* nōn). **1.** recognize, identify, (*I knew him at once; knew him for an American; would you know him again?*); be able to distinguish (one *from* another, a HAWK¹ *from a handsaw; not know* person *from* ADAM¹). **2.** be acquainted with (thing, place, person) *by* SIGHT¹, *to speak to,* etc. (∿ **by name,** (1) have heard the name of, (2) be able to give the name of); (Math., in *p.p.,* of quantity etc.) having value that can be stated; have personal experience of (fear etc.), be subject to (*her joy knew no bounds*); be on intimate terms with; (arch.) have sexual intercourse with. **3.** have in the mind, be able to recall, be aware of (fact), be aware, have learnt, (*that, how, what,* etc.); ∿ (person or thing) **to be** or **do** (that he etc. is or does; *let me know, let it be known,* (see LET² 5); (in *p.p.*) of which there is knowledge as a fact (*a known thief*). **4.** be able to use (a language etc.), have theoretical or practical understanding of (subject). **5.** all one ∿**s** (**how**), all one can, (*adv.*) to the utmost of one's power; **before** one ∿**s where** one **is,** with baffling rapidity; **don't I** ∿ **it,** (colloq., expr. rueful assent); **I don't** ∿ **that** *I like this,* (colloq.) I am fairly sure that . . . not; **don't you** ∿ (colloq. parenthetic expletive: *it's such a bore, don't you know*); **for all** or **aught I** ∿, so far as my knowledge is concerned; GOD or HEAVEN or *the* LORD (*only*) *knows;* **has been** ∿**n** to do, is known to have done; **I** ∿ **what,** I have a new idea or suggestion to propose; *I wouldn't know* (see WILL¹ 7); **I knew it,** I was sure that that would happen; **not if I** ∿ **it,** only against my will; **not what hit** one, be suddenly killed or utterly disconcerted; **not want to** ∿, refuse to take notice (of); **was not to** ∿, (1) was not to be told, (2) had no way of learning; **what do you** ∿ (**about that**)? (colloq. excl. of surprise); **you**

∼, (colloq., reminding hearer that he knows or should know a thing, or as mere gap-filler in conversation); **you ∼ something?** or **what?**, I am going to tell you something; **you ∼ what he** or **it is,** you are familiar with his or its characteristics, difficult nature, etc.; YOU-*know-what* or *-who*; **you never ∼,** nothing future is completely certain; **that's all you'** ∼ (about it), you are more ignorant than you think. **6.** ∼ **about,** have information about; ∼-**all,** (would--be) omniscient person; ∼ **better** (**than that, than to** do), be too wise or well-informed of the facts to believe that, too well-mannered to behave thus, etc.; ∼ **how,** know the way to do something; ∼-*how* n., faculty of knowing how, practical knowledge, technical expertness; ∼-**it-all,** (colloq.) = *know-all*; ∼-**nothing,** (1) ignorant person, (2) agnostic; ∼ **of,** be aware of, have heard of, (*not that I ∼ of*, not so far as I know); ∼ one's **own mind,** not vacillate; *know the* ROPES, one's STUFF; ∼ **a thing or two,** be experienced or shrewd; ∼ **what's what,** have proper knowledge of the world and of things in general; *know* WHO'*s who.* **7.** Hence ∼'ABLE *a.* [OE (*ge*)*cnāwan,* = OHG *-cnā*(*h*)*en,* ON *kná,* f. IE **gn-* etc., cogn. w. CAN², KEN²]

know² (nō) *n.* (colloq.) **in the ∼,** knowing (about) the thing in question or what is not generally known. [f. prec.]

knowe. Var. (Sc. & N. Engl.) of KNOLL¹.

know'ing¹ (nō'ĭ-) *n.* In vbl senses; **there is no ∼,** no one can tell. [ME, f. KNOW¹ + -ING¹]

know'ing² (nō'ĭ-) *a.* In vbl senses; showing knowledge, shrewd; (usu. derog.) cunning, wary; hence ∼NESS *n.* [ME, f. KNOW¹ + -ING²]

know'ingly (nō'ĭ-) *adv.* in a knowing manner; consciously, intentionally, (*I have never knowingly injured him*). [ME, f. prec. + -LY²]

know'ledge (nŏl'-) *n.* **1.** knowing, familiarity gained by experience, (*of* person, thing, fact); CARNAL *knowledge.* **2.** person's range of information; *it* **came to my ∼,** became known to me; **to my ∼,** (1) so far as I know, (2) as I know for certain. **3.** theoretical or practical understanding (*of* subject, language, etc.); the sum of what is known (*every branch of knowledge*); (Philos.) certain understanding, opp. to opinion. **4.** certain understanding, opp. to opinion. Hence ∼ABLE (nŏl'ĭja-) *a.,* (colloq.) well-informed, intelligent. [ME *knaulege,* w. earlier v. *knawlechen,* f. as KNOW¹ + OE *-lǣcan* (*lāc* as in WEDLOCK)]

known. See KNOW¹.

Knt. *abbr.* Knight.

knu'ckle *n.* & *v.* **1.** *n.* bone at finger-joint, esp. at root of finger; projection of carpal or tarsal joint of quadruped; joint of meat consisting of this with parts above and below it; RAP¹ *on* or *over the knuckles;* **near the ∼,** (colloq.) verging on the indecent; ∼-**bone,** bone forming knuckle, animal's limb-bone with ball--like end, knuckle of meat, sheep's metacarpal or metatarsal bone, (in *pl.*) these bones used in game of JACK¹s; ∼**duster,** metal instrument protecting knuckles from injury in striking, and increasing force of blow. **2.** *v.t.* strike, press, rub, with knuckles. **3.** *v.i.* ∼ (**down**), place knuckles on ground in playing at marbles; ∼ **down,** apply oneself earnestly (*to* work etc.); ∼ **down** or **under,** give in, submit (*to*). [ME *knokel* f. MLG, MDu. *knökel,* dim. of *knoke* bone]

knur, ‖**knurr,** *n.* hard excrescence on trunk of tree; hard concretion; hard ball used in game of *knur and* SPELL⁴. [ME *knorre,* var. of KNAR]

knurl *n.* small projecting knob, ridge, etc.; hence ∼ED² (-ld) *a.* [f. prec.]

KO *abbr.* kick-off; knock-out; ∼('d), knocked out.

kō'a *n.* (dark red wood of) Hawaiian tree (*Acacia koa*). [Hawaiian]

kōa'la (-ah'-) *n.* ∼ (**bear**), tailless arboreal Australian marsupial (*Phascolarctos cinereus*) with thick grey fur and large ears. [f. Aboriginal *kūl*(*l*)*a*]

kō'än *n.* riddle used in Zen to teach inadequacy of logical reasoning. [Jap., = public plan]

kŏ'bŏld *n.* (Gmc Myth.) familiar spirit, brownie; underground spirit in mines etc. [G]

Kö'chel (kēr'χel) *n.* ∼ **number** etc. (of a composition by Mozart as listed in Köchel's complete catalogue of his works). [f. L. von ∼, Austrian scientist d. 1877]

Kŏ'dăk *n.* (*P) (make of) small camera held in hand. [name of manufacturer]

Kŏ'dïăk *n.* ∼ (**bear**) (large brown Alaska species). [f. ∼ Island, Alaska]

koedoe. S. Afr. var. of KOODOO.

kŏ'el *n.* Indian or Australasian cuckoo of genus *Eudynamys.* [f. Hindi *kŏīl* f. Skr. *kokila*]

koh'-ï-noor (kō'ĭ-) *n.* large diamond; anything superb (*of* its class). [name of famous Indian diamond, property of British Crown since 1849, f. Pers. (*kūh* mountain, *i* of, *nūr* light)]

kohl (kōl) *n.* powder, usu. antimony sulphide or lead sulphide, used esp. in East to darken eyelids etc. [f. Arab. *kuḥl*]

kohlra'bi (kōlrah'-) *n.* cabbage with turnip-shaped edible stem. [G, f. It. *cavoli rape* pl. f. med. L *caulorapa* (see COLE, RAPE³)]

koi'nē *n.* common language of Greeks from close of classical period to Byzantine era; common language shared by various peoples, lingua franca. [f. Gk *koinē* (*dialektos*) common (language)]

kōla. See COLA.

koli'nský *n.* (fur of) Siberian mink. [f. Russ. *kolinskii* (*Kola* in NW Russia)]

kŏ'lkhŏz (-kŏz) *n.* collective farm in USSR. [Russ., f. *kollektivnoe khozyaĭstvo* collective farm]

kŏ'llergäng *n.* mill with vertical rollers for crushing paper-pulp. [G]

kŏmĭtä'(d)jï. Var. of COMITADJI.

komŏ'dō *n.* ∼ **dragon** or **lizard,** very large monitor lizard (*Varanus komodoensis*). [f. K∼ Island in Indonesia]

Kŏ'msomŏl *n.* (member of) USSR organization for young people. [Russ., f. *Kommunisticheskiĭ Soyuz Molodezhi* Communist League of Youth]

kōo'dōo, kudu (kōō'dōō), *n.* large white-striped spiral-horned Afr. antelope of genus *Strepsiceros.* [Xhosa-Kaffir *iqudu*]

*kŏŏk *n.* & *a.* (sl.) crazy or eccentric (person); hence ∼'Y² *a.* [20th c.; prob. f. CUCKOO]

kōo'kaburra *n.* (Austral.) laughing JACK¹ass. [Aboriginal]

kŏ'pĕ(c)k. Var. of COPECK.

kŏ'pje (-pĭ), **kŏ'ppïe,** *n.* (S. Afr.) small hill. [Du. *kopje,* Afrik. *koppie,* dim. of *kop* head]

Kora'n (kōrah'n, kor-) *n.* sacred book of the Muslims, collection of Muhammad's oral revelations, written in Arabic; hence ∼IC (-ah'-, -ä'-) *a.* [f. Arab. *ḳur'an* recitation (*ḳara'a* read)]

Korē'an *a.* & *n.* (native or language) of Korea. [f. *Korea* in E. Asia + -AN]

kŏr'fball (-awl) *n.* game like basketball played by teams of 6 men and 6 women. [f. Du. *korfbal* (*korf* basket, *bal* ball)]

kŏ'sher *a.* & *n.* **1.** *a.* (Of food or shop where food is sold or used) fulfilling requirements of Jewish law; (colloq.) correct, genuine, legitimate. **2.** *n.* kosher food or shop. [f. Heb. *kāšēr* proper]

kŏ'tō *n.* (*pl.* ∼s). Japanese musical instrument with 13 long silk etc. strings. [Jap.]

kōtow'. See KOWTOW.

kou'miss (kōō'-) *n.* fermented liquor prepared from mare's or other milk, used by Asian nomads or medicinally. [f. Tartar *kumiz*]

kour'bäsh (koor'-) *n.* whip of (esp. hippopotamus) hide as instrument of punishment in Turkey and Egypt. [f. Arab. *ḳurbāj* f. Turk. *ḳɪrbāç* whip]

kowhai (kō'ī, kŏ'wī) *n.* golden-flowered NZ tree or shrub of genus *Sophora.* [Maori]

kowtow', kōtow', *n.,* & *v.i.* **1.** *n.* Chinese custom of touching ground with forehead as sign of worship or absolute submission. **2.** *v.i.* perform the kowtow; act obsequiously (*to* person etc.). [f. Chin. *ketou* (*ke* knock, *tou* head)]

||**KP** *abbr.* Knight (of the Order) of St. Patrick.

k.p.h. *abbr.* kilometres per hour.

Kr *symb.* krypton.

kraal (-ahl) *n.* S. Afr. village of huts enclosed by fence; enclosure for cattle or sheep. [Afrik., f. Port. *curral*, of Hottentot orig.]

kraft (-ahft) *n.* ~ (**paper**), strong smooth brown (wrapping-)paper [G f. Sw., = strength]

krait (-īt) *n.* highly venomous E. Asian snake of genus *Bungarus.* [f. Hindi *karait*]

kra'ken (-ah'-) *n.* mythical sea-monster said to appear off coast of Norway. [Norw.]

krans (-ah-) *n.* (S. Afr.) precipitous or overhanging wall of rocks. [Afrik., f. Du. *krans* coronet]

Kraut (-owt) *n.* (sl., derog.) German. [f. SAUERKRAUT]

krĕ'mlin *n.* citadel within Russian town, esp. that of Moscow; **the K**~, the USSR Government; hence **K**~**ŏ'**LOGY *n.*, study and analysis of Soviet policies. [F, f. Russ. *kreml'*, of Tartar origin]

krie'gspiel *n.* war-game in which blocks representing troops etc. are moved about on maps; form of chess with umpire, in which each player has only limited information about opponent's moves. [G (*krieg* war, *spiel* game)]

krill *n.* tiny planktonic crustaceans eaten by whales etc. [f. Norw. *kril* tiny fish]

krī'mmer *n.* grey or black fur from wool of young Crimean lambs. [G (*Krim* Crimea)]

kris, crease², creese, (krēs) *n.* Malay or Indonesian dagger with wavy blade. [ult. f. Malay *k(i)rīs*]

Krī'shnaïsm *n.* worship of Krishna, great deity of later Hinduism, worshipped as incarnation of Vishnu. [f. *Krishna* + -ISM]

kromĕ'skÿ *n.* minced meat or fish rolled in bacon and fried. [app. f. Pol. *kromeczka* small slice]

krō'n|a *n.* monetary unit of Sweden (*pl.* ~**or**) and of Iceland (*pl.* ~**ur**). [Sw. & Icel., = CROWN¹]

krō'ne (-*e*) *n.* (*pl.* ~**r**). monetary unit of Denmark and of Norway. [Da. & Norw., = CROWN¹]

Kru, Krōō, (-ōō), *n.* & *a.* (member) of a Black people on coast of Liberia, skilful as seamen. [W. Afr.]

kru'gerrand (-ōō'gerahnt) *n.* S. Afr. gold coin depicting President Kruger. [f. S. J. P. *Kruger*, S. Afr. statesman d. 1904, + RAND²]

kru'mmhŏrn *n.* medieval wind instrument with double reed and curved end. [G (*krumm* crooked, *horn* HORN¹)]

krÿ'ptŏn *n.* (Chem.) rare inert gaseous element. [f. Gk *krupton* hidden, neut. adj. f. *kruptō* hide]

KS *abbr.* Kansas; ||King's Scholar.

Ksha'trïya (-ah'-) *n.* member of second of four great Hindu castes, the military caste. [Skr. (*kshatra* rule)]

K.St.J. *abbr.* Knight (of the Order) of St. John.

KT *abbr.* Knight Templar; ||Knight (of the Order) of the Thistle.

Kt. *abbr.* Knight.

Ku *symb.* kurchatovium.

kŭ'dŏs *n.* (colloq.) glory, renown. [Gk]

kudu. See KOODOO.

Kŭ'fic. See CUFIC.

***Kū'-Klŭx(-Klā'n)** n.* secret society hostile to Negroes, orig. formed in southern States after Civil War. [perh. f. Gk *kuklos* circle, + CLAN]

ku'krī (kōō'-) *n.* curved knife broadening towards point, used by Gurkhas. [f. Hindi *kukrī*]

ku'lăk (kōō'-) *n.* peasant working for his own profit in Soviet Russia. [Russ., = fist, tight-fisted person]

ku'lan (kōō'-) *n.* wild ass of SW Asia, closely related to kiang. [Tartar]

kultur (kooltoor') *n.* (esp. derog.) civilization as conceived by the Germans (with implication of racial arrogance and militarism); ~**kampf,** conflict between civil and ecclesiastical authorities esp. as regards control of schools. [G, f. L *cultura* CULTURE]

ku'mara (kōō'-) *n.* (NZ) sweet POTATO. [Maori]

kumis(s). Var. of KOUMISS.

kŭmmel (kōō'mel) *n.* sweet liqueur flavoured with caraway and cumin seeds. [G, f. as CUMIN]

kumquat. See CUMQUAT.

kung fu (kōōngfōō', kŭ-) *n.* Chinese form of karate. [f. Chin. *gongfu* (*gong* merit, *fu* master)]

kurbash. Var. of KOURBASH.

kŭrchatŏ'vium *n.* (Chem.) artificially produced transuranic metallic element. [f. I. V. *Kurchatov,* Russ. physicist d. 1960 + -IUM]

Kurd (kērd, koord) *n.* one of a tall pastoral people in Kurdistan etc.; hence ~'ISH¹ *a.* & *n.*, (Iranian language) of the Kurds. [Kurdish]

kŭ'rrajŏng *n.* Austral. tree yielding tough bast fibre. [Aboriginal]

kursaal (koor'zahl) *n.* building for use of visitors at (esp. German) health resort; casino. [G (*kur* CURE¹, *saal* room)]

kŭrtō'sis *n.* (Statistics). sharpness of peak of frequency-distribution curve. [mod. L, f. Gk *kurtōsis* bulging (*kurtos* convex f. *kurtos, kurtē* lobster-pot)]

kV *abbr.* kilovolt(s).

kvàss *n.* Russian rye-beer. [f. Russ. *kvas*]

kW *abbr.* kilowatt(s).

kwashiŏr'kŏr (kwŏ-) *n.* (Path.) tropical disease of children, caused by insufficiency of protein in diet. [native name in Ghana]

kWh *abbr.* kilowatt-hour(s).

KWIC *abbr.* keyword in context.

KWOC *abbr.* keyword out of context.

KY, Ky., *abbr.* Kentucky.

kÿ'anīte *n.* aluminium silicate as blue crystalline mineral. [f. Gk *kuanos* dark blue + -ITE¹]

kÿ'anīze, -īse (-īz), *v.t.* treat (wood) with solution of corrosive sublimate to prevent decay. [f. J. H. *Kyan,* Engl. inventor d. 1850 + -IZE]

kÿ'bŏsh. Var. of KIBOSH.

kÿle *n.* narrow channel between island and island or mainland in W. Scotland. [f. Gael. *caol* strait]

ky'lin (kē'-) *n.* fabulous composite animal figured on Chinese and Japanese pottery. [f. Chin. *qilin* (*qi* male, *lin* female)]

||**kÿ'löe** *n.* one of breed of small long-horned Highland cattle. [K~ in Northumberland]

kÿ'mograph (-ahf) *n.* instrument recording variations in pressure, e.g. in sound-waves, or successive positions of moving object, e.g. heart. [f. Gk *kuma* wave + -o- + -GRAPH]

kÿph|ō'sis *n.* (*pl.* ~**oses** -ō'sēz). (Med.) curvature of spine, convex backwards (opp. *lordosis*); hence ~**o'**TIC *a.* [mod. L, f. Gk *kuphōsis* (*kuphos* bent; see -OSIS)]

***Kyrie** (**eleison**)* (kēr'ĭ ĭlā'īson, -ĭā -ŏn, kī'rĭē) *n.* **1.** (First word(s) of) short petition used in Roman and Orthodox Churches, esp. at beginning of Mass; musical setting of these. **2.** response to commandments, sometimes used in Anglican Communion Service. [ME f. med. L, f. Gk *Kurie eleēson* Lord, have mercy]

L

L, l, (ĕl) *n.* (*pl.* **Ls** *or* **L's**). twelfth letter of alphabet; right-angled joint of pipes etc.; (as Roman numeral) 50 (**li** 51, **lv** 55, **lx** 60); (*colloq.) elevated railway (cf. EL).

L. *abbr.* Lake; |||learner-driver; Liberal; Licentiate; (Biol.) Linnaeus; lire.

£ *abbr.* = POUND¹ 2, POUNDS (£5; £*E* = Egyptian pound(s), etc.). [f. L *libra*]

l. *abbr.* left; line; litre(s); (arch.) POUND¹ 2.

la. See LAH.

LA *abbr.* Library Association; Los Angeles.

La., LA, *abbrs.* Louisiana.

La *symb.* lanthanum.

laa'ger (lah'g-) *n.* & *v.* **1.** *n.* camp, encampment, esp. in circle of wagons; (Mil.) park for armoured vehicles. **2.** *v.t.* form (vehicles) into laager; encamp (persons) in laager. **3.** *v.i.* encamp. [Afrik., f. Du. *leger*; see LEAGUER¹]

lăb *n.* (colloq.) laboratory. [abbr.]

Lab. *abbr.* Labour; Labrador.

lă'barum *n.* Constantine the Great's imperial standard, with Christian symbols added to Roman military symbols; symbolic banner. [LL, of unkn. orig.]

lă'bdanum. Var. of LADANUM.

lăbėfă'ction *n.* (literary). shaking, weakening, downfall. [f. L *labefacere* weaken (*labi* fall, *facere* make); see -FACTION]

lā'bel *n.*, & *v.t.* (||-ll-). **1.** *n.* slip of paper, card, linen, metal, etc., for attaching to object and indicating its nature, owner, name, destination, etc.; piece of paper on centre of gramophone record describing its contents, company manufacturing gramophone records with distinctive label; (fig.) short classifying phrase or name applied to persons etc. (freq. derog. in literary or artistic criticism); adhesive stamp; (Archit.) dripstone; (Her.) mark of eldest son, consisting of superimposed horizontal bar with (usu. 3) downward projections. **2.** *v.t.* attach label to; assign to a category *as,* or abs.); replace (atom) by atom of a (usu. radioactive) isotope as means of identification; replace atom in (molecule) or atoms in molecules of (substance) thus; (in *p.p.*) made identifiable thus. [ME f. OF, = ribbon, prob. f. Gmc (as LAP¹) + dim. -EL]

lā'bia. See LABIUM.

lā'bial *a.* & *n.* **1.** *a.* of the lips; (Anat. & Zool.) of like, serving as, a lip, liplike part, or labium. **2.** (Mus.) ~ **pipe** in organ, one furnished with lips, flue-pipe. **3.** *a.* & *n.* (Phonet.) (sound) requiring partial or complete closure of lips (*p, b, f, v, m, w,* and vowels in which lips are rounded, as ōō); hence ~ISM (1) *n.*, ~IZE (3) *v.t.* [f. med. L *labialis* f. L *labia* lips; see -AL]

lā'biate *a.* & *n.* **1.** (Bot.) (plant) with corolla or calyx divided into two parts suggesting lips. **2.** *a.* (Bot. & Zool.) like lip or labium. [f. mod. L *labiatus* (as LABIUM; see -ATE²)]

lā'bile *a.* (Phys. & Chem.) unstable, liable to displacement or change; hence **labi'lITY** *n.* [ME, f. LL *labilis* (*labi* to fall; see -IL)]

lā'biŏ- *comb. form.* of the lip(s) (and), as: ~**de'ntal**, (sound) made with lip and teeth, e.g. *f, v;* ~**ve'lar,** (sound) made with lips and soft palate, e.g. *w.* [f. as foll. + -o-]

lā'bi|um *n.* (*pl.* ~**a**). **1.** (Anat., usu. in *pl.*) lip of female pudendum; ~**a major'a, minor'a,** outer, inner, folds of labia. **2.** lower part of mouth of insect, crustacean, etc.; inner lip of univalve shell. **3.** lip, esp. the lower one, of labiate plant's corolla. [L, = lip]

***lā'bor** etc. See LABOUR¹,² etc.

laboratorў (labŏ'r-, lă'ber-) *n.* room or building used for experiments in natural science, esp. chemistry, or for research (lit., or fig.: *laboratory of the mind* etc.); LANGUAGE *laboratory;* ~ **animal** (of species commonly used for laboratory experiments). [f. med. L *laboratorium* (L *laborare* LABOUR²; see -ORY)]

labŏr'ious *a.* hard-working; toilsome; (of style etc.) showing signs of toil, not facile or fluent; hence ~LY² *adv.,* ~NESS *n.* [ME, f. OF *laborieus* f. L *laboriosus* (as foll.; see -IOUS)]

||**lā'bour¹** (-ber), ***lā'bor¹,** *n.* **1.** bodily or mental work, exertion, (HARD *labour;* ~ **in vain, lost** ~, fruitless efforts; ~ **of love,** task one delights in or does for love of someone). **2.** toil tending to supply wants of the community; body of those who contribute by toil to production, labourers; the labouring classes as a political force; (*L*~) the Labour Party. **3.** task (~ **of Hercules,** one needing enormous strength etc.). **4.** pains of childbirth, (uterine contractions in) process of giving birth, (*in labour*). **5.** ~ **camp,** penal settlement with forced labour by prisoners; L~ **Day** (celebrated in honour of workers, esp. 1 May or *first Monday in Sept.); L~ **Exchange,** (colloq. or Hist.) employment exchange; ~ **force,** body of workers employed; *labour-*INTENSIVE; ~**market,** supply of labour with reference to demand on it; L~ **Party,** (Polit.) party representing interests esp. of workers; ~**-saving,** designed to reduce or eliminate work; *~ **union,** trade union. [ME, f. OF *labo(u)r* f. L *labor -oris*]

||**lā'bour²** (-ber), ***lā'bor²,** *v.* **1.** *v.i.* use labour, exert oneself, work hard (~**ing man,** labourer); strive *for* purpose, *to* do; advance with difficulty (*wheels labour in the sand*); be troubled (*her labouring heart*) or impeded; suffer *under* (delusion etc.); (of ship) roll or pitch heavily. **2.** *v.t.* (arch. or poet.) till (ground). **3.** elaborate, work out in (excessive) detail, treat at (great) length, (*I will not labour the point*); (in *p.p.*) much elaborated, showing signs of labour, done with great effort, not spontaneous. [ME, f. OF *labourer* f. L *laborare* (*labor* LABOUR¹)]

||**lā'bourer** (-ber-), ***lā'borer,** *n.* one who labours, (esp.) person doing for wages work that requires strength or patience rather than skill or training, or assisting skilled worker. [ME, f. OF *laboureur* (as prec.; see -ER²)]

||**lā'bourite** (-ber-), ***lā'borite,** *n.* member or adherent of Labour Party. [f. LABOUR¹ + -ITE¹ (1)]

Lă'bradŏr *n.* ~ (**dog, retriever**), (animal of) breed of retriever with black or golden coat. [~ in Canada]

lā'brėt *n.* piece of shell, bone, etc., inserted in lip as ornament. [f. foll. + -ET¹]

lā'br|um *n.* (*pl.* ~**a**). upper lip of insect. [L, = lip, cogn. W. LABIUM]

labŭr'num *n.* small leguminous tree of genus *Laburnum,* with poisonous seeds, esp. an ornamental species (*L. anagyroides*) with pendulous racemes of bright yellow flowers. [L]

lă'byrinth *n.* complicated irregular structure with many passages hard to find way through or about without guidance, maze; intricate or tortuous arrangement; (Anat.) complex cavity of internal ear, with membranous structure within bony case; entangled state of affairs; hence ~INE² (-ĭ'nthīn) *a.* [f. F *labyrinthe* or f. L f. Gk *laburinthos*]

lăc¹ *n.* resinous substance secreted on trees by ~ **insect** of SE Asia as protective covering, used as varnish etc. [ult. f. Hind. *lākh* f. Prakrit *lakkha* f. Skr. *lākṣā*]

lăc². See LAKH.

‖**LAC** *abbr.* Leading Aircraftman.

lă′ccolĭth *n.* (Geol.) dome-shaped intrusion of igneous rock from beneath sedimentary rocks. [f. Gk *lakkos* reservoir + -LITH]

lăce¹ *n.* **1.** cord or leather strip for fastening or tightening opposite edges of shoes, corsets, etc., by help of eyelets or hooks; braid for trimming men's coats etc. (usu. *gold* or *silver lace*). **2.** fine open fabric of linen, cotton, silk, woollen, or metal threads usu. with inwrought or applied patterns; hence **lă′cy**² *a.* **3.** ∼-**glass** (Venetian, with lacelike designs); ∼-**pillow**, pad laid on lap of person making lace; ∼′**wing**, neuropterous fly; ∼′**wood**, timber of plane tree. [ME, f. OF *laz*, *las*, f. Rom. **lacium* f. L *laqueus* noose]

lăce² *v.* **1.** *v.t.* ∼ (**up**), fasten or tighten (shoe, corsets, etc.) with lace(s); compress waist of (person) thus with corset-laces; ∼-**up** *a.* & *n.*, (shoe) provided with lace. **2.** interlace or embroider (fabric) *with* thread etc.; pass (cord etc.) *through*. **3.** trim with lace; diversify *with* streaks of colour. **4.** lash, beat, defeat. **5.** flavour, fortify, (coffee, beer, etc.) with dash of spirits. **6.** *v.i.* ∼ **into**, = sense 4. **7.** Hence **lă′cɪng**¹ (1, 3, 6) *n.* [ME, f. OF *lacier* f. Rom. **laciare* (as prec.)]

lă′cer|āte *v.t.* mangle, tear, (esp. flesh or tissues); (fig.) afflict, distress, (heart, feelings); hence or cogn. ∼**ABLE** *a.*, ∼**A′TION** *n.* [f. L *lacerare* (*lacer* torn) + -ATE²]

lacĕr′tian, -tĭ′lian, -tīne, *adjs.* of lizards; lizard-like. [f. L *lacerta* lizard + -IAN, -IL, -INE¹]

lă′chĕs (-z) *n.* (Law) negligence in performing a legal duty, delay in asserting right, claiming privilege, etc.; culpable negligence. [ME, f. AF *laches(se)*, OF *laschesse* (*lasche* f. Rom. **lascus* for L *laxus* loose)]

lăchrȳma Chrī′stī (lăk-; krī′-) *n.* strong sweet red wine of S. Italy. [L, = Christ's tear]

lă′chrȳmal (-k-) *a.* & *n.* **1.** *a.* of or for tears; ∼ *vase* (to hold tears of mourners etc.). **2.** (Anat.) concerned in secretion of tears (*lachrymal canal*, *duct*, *gland*, *sac*). **3.** *n.* lachrymal vase; (in *pl.*) lachrymal organs. [ME, f. med. L *lachrymalis* f. L *lacrima* tear]

lăchrȳmā′tion (-k-) *n.* flow of tears. [f. L *lacrimatio* (*lacrimare* weep, as prec.; see -ATION)]

lă′chrȳmātor (-k-) *n.* tear-gas. [f. as foll. + -OR]

lă′chrȳmātory (-k-) *a.* & *n.* **1.** *a.* of or causing tears. **2.** *n.* phial of kind found in ancient Roman tombs and conjectured to be lachrymal vases. [f. L *lacrima* tear + -ORY]

lă′chrȳmōse (-k-) *a.* tearful, given to weeping; hence ∼LY² (-slī) *adv.* [f. L *lacrimosus* (*lacrima* tear; see -OSE¹)]

lacĭ′niate, lacĭ′niāted, *adjs.* (Bot. & Zool.) divided into deep narrow irregular segments. [f. L *lacinia* flap of garment; see -ATE², -ED¹]

lăck *n.* & *v.* **1.** *n.* not having; want, need, *of* (**no** ∼', plenty *of*; **for** ∼, owing to want or absence *of*). **2.** *v.t.* be without, not have when needed, be deficient in, (*lacks money, courage*). **3.** *v.i.* ∼ **for**, have none or insufficient of; ∼′ɪNG² *a.*, undesirably absent or deficient (*money was lacking; is lacking in courage*), (colloq.) deficient in intellect. **4.** ∼**land**, (person) having no land, (L-) nickname of King John; ∼-**lustre**, (of eye etc.) dull. [ME *lac*, *lacen*, corresp. to MDu., MLG *lak* deficiency, MDu. *laken* to lack]

lăckadai′sical (-z-) *a.* languishing, affected, given to airs and graces, feebly sentimental; unenthusiastic, listless; hence ∼LY² *adv.*, ∼NESS *n.* [f. arch. *lackaday*, *-daisy*, int. (ALACK) + -ICAL]

lă′cker. Var. of LACQUER.

lă′ckey *n.*, & *v.t.* **1.** *n.* footman, manservant (usu. liveried); servant; obsequious person, parasite; servile political follower; ∼ **moth** (whose striped caterpillars resemble footman's livery). **2.** *v.t.* dance attendance on, behave servilely to. [f. F *laquais*, obs. *alaquais* f. Cat. *alacay* = Sp. ALCALDE]

Lacō′nian *a.* & *n.* (inhabitant or dialect) of Laconia, Spartan. [f. L *Laconia* Sparta f. Gk *Lakōn* Spartan, + -AN]

lacō′n|ic *a.* brief, concise, sententious; given to such speech or style; hence ∼ICALLY *adv.*, ∼ICISM (2) *n.*

[f. L f. Gk *Lakōnikos* (*Lakōn* Spartan; see -IC), the Spartans being known for their terse speech]

lă′conĭsm *n.* brevity of speech; short pithy saying. [f. Gk *lakōnismos* (*lakōnizō* behave like Spartan; see prec., -ISM)]

lă′cquer (-ker) *n.*, & *v.t.* **1.** *n.* coloured varnish of shellac dissolved in alcohol used esp. as coating for brass; sap of ∼-**tree** (*Rhus vernicifera*) taking hard polish and used to varnish wood etc.; synthetic liquid that dries to form protective film; substance sprayed on hair to keep it in place. **2.** *v.t.* coat with lacquer. [f. obs. F *lacre* sealing-wax, f. unexpl. var. of Port. *laca* LAC¹]

lacquey. Var. of LACKEY.

lacrim-, lacrym-. Vars. of LACHRYM-.

lacro′sse (-ŏ′s, -aw′s) *n.* game like hockey, but with ball driven by and caught and carried in crosse. [F (*la* the, CROSSE)]

lă′ctāte¹ *n.* (Chem.) salt or ester of lactic acid. [f. LACTIC + -ATE¹ (3)]

lăctā′te² *v.i.* secrete milk. [f. as foll. + -ATE³]

lăctā′tion *n.* suckling; secreting of milk. [f. L *lactare* suckle (*lac lactis* milk) + -ATION]

lă′cteal *a.* & *n.* **1.** *a.* of milk; conveying chyle or other milky fluid. **2.** *n.* (in *pl.*) lymphatic vessels of mesentery conveying chyle. [f. L *lacteus* (*lac*; see prec.) + -AL]

lăctĕ′scence *n.*, **lăctĕ′scent** *a.* milky (appearance); (yielding) milky juice. [f. L *lactescere* (*lactēre* be milky f. as foll.); see -ESCENCE, -ESCENT]

lă′ctic *a.* (Chem.) of milk; ∼ **acid** (formed in sour milk). [f. L *lac lactis* milk + -IC]

lăctĭ′ferous *a.* yielding milk or milky fluid. [f. LL *lactifer* (as prec.; see -FEROUS)]

lă′ctō- *comb. form.* milk, as: ∼METER (-ŏ′m-), instrument for testing density of milk; ∼**pro′tein**, albuminous constituent of milk. [f. L *lac lactis* milk + -O-]

lă′ctōse *n.* sugar present in milk, less sweet than sucrose. [f. as prec. + -OSE²]

lacŭ′n|a *n.* (*pl.* ∼**ae** or ∼**as**). hiatus, blank, missing portion (esp. in ancient MS, book, etc.), empty part; cavity in bone, tissue, etc.; hence ∼AL, ∼AR¹, ∼ARY¹, ∼OSE¹, *adjs.* [L, = pool (*lacus* LAKE¹)]

lacŭ′strine *a.* of, dwelling or growing in, lake(s); ∼ **age** (of LAKE¹-dwellings). [f. L *lacus* LAKE¹ (after *palustris* marshy) + -INE¹]

‖**LACW** *abbr.* Leading Aircraftwoman.

lă′cȳ. See LACE¹.

lăd *n.* boy, youth, young fellow, young son; man, fellow; spirited person (*quite a lad*); ‖stable man or woman (of any age); **my**∼, **the**∼**s**, (cf. BOY); ∼**′s love**, southernwood; hence ∼**′dɪE** *n.* [ME *ladde*, of unkn. orig.]

lă′danum *n.* gum resin from plants of genus *Cistus*, used in perfumery etc. [L, f. Gk *ladanon* (*lēdon* mastic)]

lă′dder *n.* & *v.* **1.** *n.* set of steps (called *rungs*) inserted usu. in two long supports of wood or metal or in two cords to serve as (usu. portable) means of ascending building etc.; SALMON-*ladder*; SNAKES *and* ladders; STEP²-*ladder*. **2.** ‖vertical flaw in stocking etc. caused by stitch(es) becoming undone through several rows; hence ∼PROOF² *a.* **3.** (fig.) means of rising in the world or attaining object (**kick down the** ∼, abandon friends or occupation that have helped one to rise); see RUNG¹. **4.** ∼**back**, (chair) with back made of horizontal bars between uprights; ∼-**dredge** (with buckets carried round on ladder-like chain); ∼-**stitch**, transverse bars in embroidery; ∼ **tournament** (with contestants listed and each entitled to gain higher place if he can defeat one just above him). **5.** *v.i.* ‖develop ladder (sense 2). **6.** *v.t.* ‖cause ladder (sense 2) in. [OE *hlǣd(d)er*, = MDu. *lēdere*, OHG *leitara* f. WG **hlaidr-* f. Gmc **hli-*, **hlai-* (LEAN²)]

lāde *v.t.* (*p.p.* **la′den**). **1.** put cargo on board (ship); ship (goods) as cargo (BILL⁴ *of lading*), whence **lā′dɪNG**¹ (3) *n.* **2.** (in *p.p.*) (Of vehicle, beast of burden, person, tree, branch, table, etc.) loaded (*with*); (painfully burdened *with* sin, sorrow, etc. [OE *hladan*, = OS, OHG *hladan*, ON *hlatha*, Goth. *-hlathan*; cf. LAST²]

la-di-da′ (lahdĭdah′) *n.* & *a.* **1.** *n.* (person given to) swagger or pretension in manners and pronunciation. **2.** *a.* pretentious in this way. [imit. of pronunc. used]

ladies. See LADY.

lā′dĭfy. See LADYFY.

Ladi′n (-ē′n) *n.* Rhaeto-Romanic of the Engadine. [Romansh, f. L *latinus* LATIN]

Ladi′nō (-ē′-) *n.* (*pl.* ∼s). **1.** Spanish dialect of Sephardic Jews. **2.** mestizo or white person in Central America. [Sp., orig. = Latin, f. L (as prec.)]

lā′dle *n.*, & *v.t.* **1.** *n.* utensil with large cup-shaped bowl and long handle, for transferring liquids; vessel for transporting molten metal in foundry; hence ∼FUL 2 (-del-f-) *n.* **2.** *v.t.* transfer (liquid) with ladle from one receptacle to another; ∼ **out**, (fig.) distribute, esp. lavishly. [OE *hlædel* (*hladan* LADE, -LE 1)]

lā′dy̆ *n.* **1.** ruling woman (*lady of the house* or *manor*; *Lady* SUPERIOR; *our sovereign lady*); **find the** ∼, = THREE-*card trick*. **2.** woman to whom man is chivalrously devoted; mistress. **3. Our L**∼, Virgin Mary; hence *Lady's bed-straw, finger,* etc. (see sense 13). **4.** woman belonging to the upper class or fitted for it by manners, habits, and sentiments, (corresp. to *gentleman*; ‖∼ **of the bedchamber,** ∼**-in-waiting,** lady attending queen or princess). **5.** (courteous or formal synonym for) woman (when used as *voc.*, only poet. or vulg. in *sing.*, but usu. form of address in *pl.*); **ladies and gentlemen** (in addressing company of both sexes); TEA-*lady*; YOUNG *lady*. **6.** ‖(*L*∼, title used as less formal prefix for) Marchioness (of), Countess (of), Viscountess, Baroness, (also prefixed to Christian name of) daughter of duke, marquis, or earl, (or to husband's Christian name of) wife or widow of holder of courtesy title *Lord* William etc., (or to surname of) wife or widow of baronet or knight; **L**∼ **Mayoress,** wife of Lord Mayor. **7. my** ∼, form of address used chiefly by servants etc. to holders of the title *Lady*; **my dear** or **good** ∼ (as *voc.* in gen. use); OLD *lady*. **8.** wife (arch. or vulg., exc. of those who hold title *Lady* or in respectful ref.; *my* or *your lady wife*); **your good** ∼, your wife. **9.** (*attrib.*, usu. courteous or formal) female (*lady clerk, doctor, friend, president, dog,* etc.). **10. ladies' room,** ‖**the Ladies(**′**)** (as *sing. n.*), women's public lavatory. **11. ladies' chain,** figure in quadrille etc.; **Ladies' Gallery** (in House of Commons, reserved for ladies). **12.** *lady of* EASY *virtue*; PAINT²*ed lady.* **13. L**∼**-altar** (in Lady chapel); ∼**bird,** *****∼**bug,** coleopterous insect of family Coccinellidae, usu. reddish--brown with black spots; **L**∼ **Bountiful,** beneficent lady in village etc. [character in Farquhar's *Beaux' Stratagem*]; ∼**-chair,** seat made by two persons' interlaced hands to carry wounded man etc.; **L**∼ **chapel** (in large church, often E. of high altar, dedicated to Virgin Mary); ∼**-clock, -cow,** ladybird; **L**∼ **Day,** Feast of the Annunciation, 25 Mar.; ∼**-fern** (slender kind); *****∼**finger,** finger-shaped sponge--cake; ‖*lady* HELP²; ∼**-killer,** man devoting himself to making conquests of women; ∼**-love,** man's sweetheart; *Lady's* BED¹*straw*; ∼**'s companion,** roll containing cottons etc.; **L**∼**'s finger,** kidney-VETCH; **L**∼**'s laces,** kind of striped grass; ∼**'s-maid,** personal maidservant of lady; **ladies' man,** ∼**'s man,** (fond of female society); **L**∼**'s mantle,** rosaceous plant of genus *Alchemilla* with yellowish--green clustered flowers; ∼**-smock,** = cuckoo flower (1); ∼**'s slipper,** orchidaceous wild and garden plant with usu. yellow bag- or slipper-shaped flowers; **L**∼**'s tresses,** white-flowered orchis of genus *Spiranthes*. **14.** Hence ∼HOOD *n.* [OE *hlæfdige* (*hlāf* LOAF¹, *****dig-* knead; cf. DOUGH); in *Lady Day* etc. f. OE gen. *hlæfdigan* (Our) Lady's]

lā′dyfy, lā′dĭfy, *v.t.* make lady of; call 'lady'; (in *p.p.*) having the airs of a FINE² lady. [f. prec.+-FY]

lā′dy̆like *a.* with manners etc. of a lady; (of man) effeminate; befitting a lady. [f. LADY+-LIKE]

lā′dy̆ship *n.* being a lady; **her, your,** ∼, **their** ∼**s,** she, you, they, (in respectful mention of or address to

holder(s) of title *Lady*; also iron.). [ME, f. LADY + -SHIP]

l(a)e′vō- (lē′-) *comb. form.* left, esp. (Chem.) w. ref. to property of causing plane of polarized light ray to rotate to left (opp. DEXTRO-); **levodo′pa,** this form of DOPA; ∼**ro′tatory,** (of substance) having this property; ∼**tartaric acid** etc. (form having this property). [f. L *laevus* left+-o-]

l(a)e′vŭlōse (lē′v-) *n.* (Chem.) laevorotatory fructose in fruit and honey. [f. as prec.+-ULE+-OSE²]

LAFTA *abbr.* Latin-American Free Trade Association.

lăg¹ *v.i.* (-**gg**-), & *n.* **1.** *v.i.* go too slow, not keep pace, fall behind or *behind* (adv. or prep.); * = STRING 15. **2.** *n.* lagging, delay; (Phys.) (amount of) retardation in current or movement (∼ **of tide,** interval by which it falls behind mean time at 1st and 3rd quarters of moon; cf. PRIMING²); TIME¹-*lag.* **3.** Hence ∼′GARD *n.* & *a.*, ∼′GER¹ *n.*, ∼′GING² *a.*, (-g-). [orig. 'hindmost person', 'hang back'; perh. f. a fanciful distortion of LAST³ in children's game (*fog, seg, lag,* = 1st, 2nd, last, in dial.)]

lăg² *v.t.* (-**gg**-), & *n.* (sl.) **1.** *v.t.* send to prison; ‖apprehend, arrest; hence ∼′GING¹ (-g-) *n.*, term of imprisonment. **2.** *n.* convict, esp. *old lag.* [19th c.; orig. unkn.]

lăg³ *n.*, & *v.t.* (-**gg**-). **1.** *n.* (piece of) non-heat--conducting cover of boiler etc. **2.** *v.t.* enclose in lags; hence ∼′GING¹ (1, 3) (-g-) *n.* [prob. f. Scand.; cf. ON *lögg* barrel-rim, cogn. w. LAY³]

lä′gan *n.* (Law). goods or wreckage lying on bed of sea, sometimes with buoy etc. for later retrieval of them. [OF, perh. of Scand. orig., f. root of LIE³, LAY³]

la′ger (lah′g-) *n.* light kind of (orig. German or Bohemian) beer. [f. G *lager-bier* beer brewed for keeping (*lager* store)]

lä′ggard etc. See LAG¹,²,³.

*****lagnĭăppe** (lă′nyăp, lahnyă′p) *n.* thing given as bonus or gratuity. [Louisiana F, f. Sp. *la ñapa*]

lä′gomŏrph *n.* (Zool.) mammal of order Lagomorpha, e.g. hare or rabbit. [f. Gk *lagōs* hare+*morphē* form]

lagoō′n *n.* stretch of salt water separated from sea by low sandbank; enclosed water of atoll; (US, Austral., & NZ) small freshwater lake near larger lake or river; artificial shallow pool for treatment of effluent. [f. F *lagune* or f. It. & Sp. *laguna* f. L LACUNA]

lah, la, (lah) *n.* (Mus.) sixth note of scale in movable--doh system; the note A in fixed-doh system. [ME, f. L *labii*; see GAMUT]

la′har (lah′-h-) *n.* flow of volcanic mud. [Jav.]

lā′ic *a.* & *n.* non-cleric(al), lay(man), secular, temporal; so ∼AL *a.*, ∼ALLY *adv.* [f. LL f. Gk *laikos* (*laos* people; see -IC)]

laī′city *n.* principles or influence of laity. [f. prec.+ -ITY]

lā′iciz|e, -īs|e (-īz), *v.t.* make LAY²; subject (school etc.) to control, make (office) tenable, by laymen; hence ∼A′TION *n.* [f. LAIC+-IZE]

laid. See LAY³.

lain. See LIE³.

lair *n.* & *v.* **1.** *n.* place where domestic animals lie down; ‖shed or enclosure for cattle on way to market, whence ∼′AGE (1, 3) *n.*; wild animal's lying-place, (fig.) person's hiding-place. **2.** *v.i.* & *t.* go to, rest or place in, lair. [OE *leger,* = OS *legar,* OHG *leger* bed, camp, Goth. *ligrs* bed f. Gmc *****leg-* LIE³]

laird *n.* (Sc.) landed proprietor; hence ∼′SHIP *n.* [Sc. form of LORD]

laissez-aller, laisser-, (lāsā ä′lā) *n.* unconstrained freedom, absence of constraint. [F, = let go]

laissez-faire, laisser-, (lāsāfār′) *n.* government abstention from interference with individual action esp. in commerce. [F, = let act]

laissez-passer, laisser-, (lāsăpä′sā) *n.* permit, document allowing holder to pass. [F, = let pass]

lā′ĭty *n.* body of those who are laymen in respect of religion or a profession. [ME, f. LAY²+-ITY]

lāke¹ *n.* large body of water entirely surrounded by land; **the Great L∼s**, Superior, Huron, Michigan, Erie, and Ontario, along boundary of US and Canada; ∼-**country**, L∼ **District**, L∼'**land, the** L∼s, region of English lakes in Cumbria; ∼-**dweller**, prehistoric inhabitant of ∼-**dwellings**, built on piles driven into bed or shore of lake; L∼ **Poets**, Coleridge, Southey, and Wordsworth, who lived in Lake District; L∼**land terrier**, (breed of) small stocky terrier originating in Lakeland; hence ∼'**LESS** *a.*, ∼'**LET** *n.*, (-kl-). [ME f. OF *lac* f. L *lacus* basin, pool, lake]

lāke² *n.* reddish pigment, orig. made from lac; pigment made from dye on inert base of metal oxide; any insoluble product of soluble dye and mordant. [var. of LAC¹]

läkh (-k), **läc²**, *n.* (Ind.) a hundred thousand (*of* rupees etc.). [f. Hind. *lākh* f. Skr. *lakṣa*]

Lä'llan *a.* & *n.* (Sc.) **1.** *a.* of the Lowlands of Scotland. **2.** *n.* ∼(s), Lowland Scots dialect, esp. as literary language. [var. of LOWLAND]

lällā'tion *n.* pronunciation of *r* as *l*; imperfect speech (as) of young children. [f. L *lallare* sing lullaby + -ATION]

***lä'llygäg** *v.i.* (-gg-). (sl.) loiter; cuddle amorously. [20th c.; orig. unkn.]

läm¹ *v.* (-mm-). (sl.) thrash, hit (*into*) hard with stick etc. [perh. f. Scand.; cf. ON *lemja* beat so as to LAME]

***läm²** *n.* (sl.) **on the** ∼, fleeing. [20th c., orig. unkn.]

Lam. *abbr.* Lamentations (OT).

la'ma (lah'-) *n.* Tibetan or Mongolian Buddhist priest; **Dalai L**∼ (dä'lī), chief lama of Tibet; **Pa'nchen** or **Ta'shi L**∼, lama ranking next after Dalai Lama; hence ∼ISM (3) *n.*, ∼IST (2) *n.* & *a.*, (-a-ĭ-). [f. Tibetan *blama* w. silent *b*)]

Lamär'ck|ian *a.* & *n.* (follower) of Lamarck or his theory of organic evolution by the inheritance of acquired characters; so ∼ISM (3) *n.* [f. J.-B. *Lamarck*, Fr. botanist and zoologist d. 1829 + -IAN]

lama'serý (-mah'-) *n.* monastery of lamas. [f. F *lamaserie* irreg. f. *lama* LAMA]

lämb (-m) *n.* & *v.* **1.** *n.* young sheep; **as well be hanged or hung for a sheep as** (for) **a** ∼, sin boldly, go the whole hog; **like a** ∼ (**to the slaughter**), unresistingly. **2.** flesh of lamb as food. **3.** young member of church flock; meek, gentle, innocent, weak, or dear person; **The L**∼ (**of God**), Christ. **4.** ∼'**s fry**, lamb's testicles or other offal as food; ∼'**skin** (with wool on, or as leather); ∼'**s lettuce**, salad-plant of genus *Valerianella*; ||∼'**s-tails**, hazel catkins; ∼'**s-wool**, soft fine wool used in knitted garments. **5.** Hence ∼'HOOD (-mh-), ∼'KIN (-mk-), *ns.*, ∼'LIKE (-ml-) *a.* **6.** *v.t.* (In pass., of lamb) be brought forth; tend (lambing ewes), whence ∼'ER¹ (-mer) *n.* **7.** *v.i.* give birth to lamb. [OE, = OS, OHG, ON, Goth. *lamb* f. Gmc **lambaz*]

lämbä'ste, -bä'st, *v.t.* (colloq.) thrash, beat; criticize severely. [|. LAM¹ + BASTE³]

lä'mbda (-mda) *n.* eleventh Greek letter (Λ, λ) = 1; ∼ **moth** (with Λ-shaped mark on wings). [ME, f. Gk *la(m)bda*]

lä'mb|ent *a.* (Of flame or light) playing on surface without burning it, with soft radiance; (of eyes, sky, etc.) softly radiant; (of wit etc.) lightly brilliant; hence ∼ENCY *n.*, ∼ently² *adv.* [f. L *lambere* lick; see -ENT]

lä'mbert *n.* unit of surface brightness, corresponding to emission of one lumen per square centimetre. [f. J. H. *Lambert*, Ger. physicist d. 1777]

Lä'mbeth *n.* ∼ **Conference**, regular assembly of all bishops of Anglican Communion; ∼ **degree**, honorary degree conferred by Archbishop of Canterbury. [f. Archbishop of Canterbury's palace at ∼ in London]

lä'mbrèquin (-kǐn) *n.* *short piece of drapery over top of door or window, or hung from mantelpiece; (Her.) mantling. [F, f. Du. **lamperkin*, dim. of *lamper* veil; see -KIN]

lāme *a.*, & *v.t.* **1.** *a.* disabled by injury or defect in a limb, esp. foot or leg, limping or unable to walk normally, (of person, animal, limb, one's steps, etc.; *lame of*, or *in, a leg* etc.). **2.** (Of argument, story, excuse) imperfect, unsatisfactory, unconvincing; (of verse) halting; *∼-brain, stupid person; ∼ duck, disabled person, defaulter on Stock Exchange, firm etc. unable to meet its financial obligations, *official about to retire after not being re-elected. **3.** Hence lä'mish¹ 2 *a.*, ∼LY² (-mlĭ) *adv.*, ∼'NESS (-mn-) *n.* **4.** *v.t.* make lame, disable, (lit. or fig.). [OE *lama*, = OS *lamo*, OHG *lam*, ON *lami* f. Gmc **lamaz*]

lamé (lah'mā) *n.* (material) with gold or silver thread inwoven. [F]

lamě'll|a *n.* (*pl.* ∼ae). thin plate, scale, layer, or film, esp. of bone or tissue; hence ∼AR¹, lä'mellATE², ∼ĬFORM, ∼OSE¹, *adjs.* [L, dim. of LAMINA]

lamě'llibränch (-ngk) *n.* bivalve mollusc of class Lamellibranchia, e.g. oyster. [f. as prec. + -I- + Gk *bragkhia* gills]

lamě'llicŏrn *n.* & *a.* (beetle) having lamelliform antennae, e.g. stag-beetle. [f. mod. L *lamellicornis* f. L LAMELLA + *cornu* horn]

lamě'nt *n.* & *v.* **1.** *n.* passionate expression of grief; elegy, dirge. **2.** *v.t.* express or feel grief for or about, (in *p.p.*) mourned for (esp. conventionally of the dead: *your late lamented father*). **3.** *v.i.* ∼ **for** or **over**, or abs., = sense 2. [n. f. L *lamentum*, or f. v. f. F *lamenter* or f. L *lamentari*]

lä'mentab|le *a.* (Of event, fate, condition, character, etc.) deplorable, regrettable; (arch.) mournful; hence ∼LY² *adv.* [ME f. OF, or f. L *lamentabilis* (as prec.; see -ABLE)]

lämentā'tion *n.* lamenting, lament; L∼s (of Jeremiah), OT book on destruction of Jerusalem in 6th c. BC. [ME f. OF, or f. L *lamentatio* (as LAMENT; see -ATION)]

lä'min|a *n.* (*pl.* ∼ae). thin plate, scale, layer, or flake, of metal, bone, membrane, stratified rock, vegetable tissue, etc.; hence ∼OSE¹ *a.* [L]

lä'minar *a.* consisting of laminae; (Phys., of flow) taking place along fixed streamlines, not turbulent. [f. prec. + -AR¹]

lä'min|āte¹ *v.* **1.** *v.t.* beat or roll (metal) into thin plates; overlay with metal plates; manufacture by placing layer on layer. **2.** *v.t.* & *i.* split into layers or leaves. **3.** Hence ∼A'TION *n.* [f. LAMINA + -ATE³]

lä'minate² *n.* in form of lamina(e). **2.** *n.* laminated structure or material, esp. of layers fixed together to form rigid or flexible material. [f. LAMINA + -ATE²]

Lä'mmas *n.* first day of August, formerly observed as harvest festival (latter ∼, non-existent date, day that will never come). [OE *hlāfmæsse* (as LOAF¹, MASS¹)]

lä'mmergeyer (-gīer) *n.* bearded vulture, largest European bird of prey. [f. G *lämmergeier* (*lämmer* lambs, *geier* vulture)]

lämp *n.* & *v.* **1.** *n.* vessel with oil and wick for giving light; transparent vessel enclosing candle, gas-jet, wire made incandescent by electricity when required, or other illuminant; this with support and shade; **smell of the** ∼, betray nocturnal study, be laborious in style etc.; FLUORESCENT, NEON, SAFETY, SPIRIT¹-, SUN-, *lamp*. **2.** (fig.) sun, moon, star; source of spiritual or intellectual light, hope, etc. **3.** ∼'**black**, pigment made from soot; ∼'**chimney**, glass cylinder making draught for lamp-flame; ∼'**holder**, device for supporting (esp. electric) lamp; ∼'**light** (given by lamp(s)); ∼'**lighter**, man who lights street lamps (usu. Hist.; *like a* ∼*lighter*, with great speed), *spill for lighting lamps; ∼'**post**, ∼-**standard**, (supporting street lamp); ∼'**shade** (placed over lamp to soften or intercept its light). **4.** Hence ∼'LESS *a.* **5.** *v.i.* shine. **6.** *v.t.* supply with lamps; illuminate; *(sl.) look at. [ME, f. OF *lampe* f. LL *lampada* f. acc. of L f. Gk *lampas* torch]

lämpōō'n *n.*, & *v.t.* **1.** *n.* virulent or scurrilous piece of satire against a person; hence ∼IST (1) *n.* **2.** *v.t.* write lampoon(s) against; hence ∼ER¹ *n.* [f. F *lampon*, conjectured to be f. *lampons* let us drink (*lamper* gulp down f. *laper* LAP⁵)]

lă′mprey *n.* eel-like aquatic vertebrate with sucker mouth, gill-pouches, and opening on top of head. [ME, f. OF *lampreie* f. med. L *lampreda*; cf. LL *lampetra*, perh. f. L *lambere* lick + *petra* stone]

Lăncă′strian *a.* & *n.* **1.** (inhabitant or native) of Lancashire or Lancaster. **2.** (adherent) of family descended from John of Gaunt Duke of Lancaster (4th son of Edward III), or of the Red Rose party supporting it in the Wars of the Roses; cf. YORK¹. [f. *Lancaster* + -IAN]

lance¹ (lah-) *n.* **1.** weapon with long wooden shaft and pointed steel head used by horseman in charging; similar implement for spearing fish or killing harpooned whale; metal pipe supplying oxygen to burn metal; FREE¹ *lance*; **break a** ∼, argue *for* or *with*. **2.** lancer. **3.** ∼**-corporal**, (in RA) ∼**-bombardier**, ||(sl.) ∼**-jack**, NCO below corporal or bombardier; ∼**-sergeant**, corporal acting as sergeant. **4.** ∼**-fish**, sand-eel; ∼**-snake**, venomous Amer. snake of genus *Bothrops*, fer de lance; ∼**′wood**, tough elastic W. Ind. wood used for carriage-shafts, fishing-rods, etc. [ME f. OF, f. L *lancea*; *lance-corporal* on anal. of obs. *lancepesade* lowest grade of NCO ult. f. It. *lancia spezzata* broken lance]

lance² (lah-) *v.t.* **1.** (poet.) fling, launch. **2.** (Surg.) prick or cut open with lancet. **3.** pierce with lance. [ME, f. OF *lancier* (*lance*; see prec.)]

la′ncelet (lah′nsl-) *n.* small marine animal of genus *Branchiostoma* etc. burrowing in sand. [f. LANCE¹ + -LET]

lă′ncĕolate *a.* shaped like lance-head, tapering to each end. [f. LL *lanceolatus* (*lanceola* dim. of *lancea* lance; see -ATE²)]

la′ncer (lah′-) *n.* soldier of cavalry regiment orig. armed with lances; (in *pl.*) quadrille for 8 or 16 pairs, music for it. [f. F *lancier* (as LANCE¹; see -ER²)]

la′ncet (lah′-) *n.* **1.** surgical instrument usu. with two edges and point for small incisions. **2.** ∼ (**arch, light, window,** etc.), narrow arch or window with pointed head; hence ∼ED² *a.* [ME, f. OF *lancette* (as LANCE¹; see -ET¹)]

la′ncĭnāting (lah′-) *a.* (Of pain) acute, shooting. [f. *lancinate* pierce f. L *lancinare* to tear; see -ATE³, -ING²]

Lancs. *abbr.* Lancashire.

lănd¹ *n.* **1.** solid part of earth's surface (opp. *sea, water, air; travel by land*); **how the** ∼ **lies,** (fig.) what is the state of affairs. **2.** ground, soil, expanse of country (||LIE⁴, *LAY³, *of the land*); this as basis for agriculture, building, etc. **3.** country, nation, State, (*land of hope and glory*); *land of* CAKEs; ∼ **of the leal,** heaven; *in the land of the* LIVING²; *land of* PROMISE¹. **4.** landed property, (in *pl.*) estates; (Sc.) building containing several dwellings. **5.** (S. Afr.) ground fenced off for tillage. **6.** strip of plough or pasture land parted from others by drain-furrows. **7.** space between rifling-grooves in gun. **8.** ∼**-agent, -agency,** (1) ||steward-(ship) of estate, (2) agent, agency, for sale etc. of estates; ∼**-bank** (issuing banknotes on securities of landed property); ∼**-breeze** (blowing seaward from land); ∼**-bridge**, neck of land between two land masses; ∼**′fall,** approach to land esp. for first time on sea or air voyage; ∼**′force(s)** (military, not naval or air); ∼**-form,** natural feature of earth's surface; ||∼**-girl,** woman doing farm work, esp. in wartime; ∼**-grabber,** illegal seizer of land; (esp.) man who took Irish farm after eviction of tenant; *∼ **grant,** grant of public land (*∼**-grant college,** state college granted such land under acts of 1862 and 1890); ∼**-holder,** proprietor or (usu.) tenant of land; ∼**-hunger, -hungry,** eager(ness) to acquire land; ∼**′lady,** (1) woman keeping inn, boarding-house, or lodgings, (2) woman having tenants; ∼**-law,** (usu. in *pl.*) law of

landed property; ∼**-line,** means of telecommunication over land; ∼**-locked,** almost or quite enclosed by land; ∼**′lubber,** (Naut.) person unfamiliar with the sea and ships; ∼**′mark,** (1) object marking boundary of country, estate, etc., (2) conspicuous object in district etc., (3) object or event or change marking stage in process or turning-point in history; ∼ **mass,** large area of land; ∼**-mine,** (1) explosive mine laid in or on ground, (2) parachute mine; *∼ **office** (recording dealings in public land); *∼**-office business,** enormous trade; ∼**′owner,** owner of land; ∼**′rail,** corncrake; L∼**′s End,** western point of Cornwall; ∼**-shark,** (1) one who lives by swindling seamen ashore, (2) = *land-grabber*; ∼**-slater,** wood-louse; ∼**′slide,** = *landslip*, (fig.) overwhelming majority of votes for one side, esp. in an election; ∼**′slip,** sliding down of mass of land on cliff or mountain; ∼**′sman** (-z-), non-sailor; ∼**-tax** (assessed on landed property); ∼**-tie,** rod, beam, or piece of masonry, securing or supporting wall etc. by connecting some part of it with the ground; ∼**-wind** (blowing seaward from land). **9.** Hence ∼**LESS** *a.,* ∼**′WARD** *a., adv.,* & *n.,* ∼**′WARDS** *adv.* [OE, = OS *land*, OHG *lant*, ON, Goth. *land* f. Gmc *landam*]

lănd² *v.* **1.** *v.t.* & *i.* set or go ashore (in *p.p.* = having come ashore; see -ED¹ (2)), disembark (*at*). **2.** bring (aircraft, its passengers etc.), (of aircraft etc.) come down, to ground or surface of water; hence ∼′ER¹ *n.,* spacecraft (planned to be) landed on planet. **3.** bring to, (also ∼ **up**) reach or find oneself in, a certain place, stage, or position. **4.** *v.t.* deal (person blow etc.; *landed him one in the eye*); present (*with* problem etc.). **5.** set down from vehicle; bring (fish) to land, (fig.) win (prize etc.), obtain (appointment etc.), esp. against strong competition. **6.** *v.i.* alight after jump etc. (lit. or fig.); ∼ **on** one's **feet,** get well out of difficulty by luck. [ME, f. prec.]

Land³ (lahnt) *n.* (*pl.* **Länder** *pr.* lĕ′n-). province of (Federal Republic of) Germany; province of Austria. [G (as LAND¹)]

lă′ndau *n.* four-wheeled carriage with top, such that the back half of the top can be raised and lowered and the front half removed. [L∼ near Karlsruhe, where first made]

lăndaulĕ′t *n.* small landau; motor car with folding hood over rear seats. [f. prec. + -LET]

lă′nddrŏst (-d-d-) *n.* (Hist.) rural magistrate in S. Africa. [Afrik. (*land* LAND¹, *drost* bailiff)]

lă′ndĕd *a.* possessed of land (**the** ∼ **interest,** owners and holders of land); consisting of land (*landed estate, property*). [ME, f. LAND¹ + -ED²]

lă′ndgrāve *n.* (*fem.* ∼avine *pr.* -avēn). (Hist.) German title of nobility; hence ∼**ā′vĬATE¹** (1) *n.* [MLG; MHG *lantgrāve* (as LAND¹, G *graf* COUNT²)]

lă′nding *n.* In vbl senses; ∼(**-place**), place for disembarking; platform between two flights of stairs or at top of flight, passage leading to upstairs rooms; HARD, SOFT, LANDING; ∼**-craft,** any of numerous types of naval craft esp. designed for putting ashore troops and equipment; ∼**-gear,** undercarriage; ∼**-net** (for landing large fish that has been hooked); ∼**-stage,** platform, often floating, on which passengers and goods are disembarked; ∼**-strip,** airstrip. [ME, f. LAND² + -ING¹]

lă′ndler (lĕ′ndler) *n.* (music for) Austrian dance in triple time, precursor of waltz. [G (*Landl* Upper Austria; see -ER¹)]

lă′ndlöper *n.* (esp. Sc.) vagabond. [f. MDu. *landlooper* (as LAND¹, *loopen* run f. as LEAP¹, -ER¹)]

lă′ndlŏrd *n.* person who lets land or (part of) building to tenant; keeper of inn, boarding-house, or lodgings; hence ∼ISM *n.,* system by which land is owned by landlords receiving fixed rents from tenants (usu. derog. of former Irish system), advocacy of this. [ME, f. LAND¹ + LORD]

lăndŏ′cracy *n.* (joc.) the landed class; so **lă′ndo**CRAT *n.* [f. LAND¹ + -O- + -CRACY]

lǎ′ndscāpe (-ns-, -nds-) *n.* & *v.* **1.** *n.* (picture representing, art reproducing, or actual piece of) inland scenery; ∼ **architecture** or ∼ **gardening**, architect or gardener, laying-out of, one who lays out, grounds attractively or in imitation of natural scenery; ∼**-marble** (with treelike markings); ∼**-painter** (who paints landscapes), so **lǎ′ndscāpɪsт** (1) *n.* **2.** *v.t.* & *i.* improve by, engage in, landscape gardening or architecture. [f. MDu. *landscap* (as LAND[1], -SHIP)]

lāne *n.* **1.** narrow road usu. between hedges (**it is a long ∼ that has no turning**, change is sure to come); narrow street. **2.** passage made or left between rows of persons. **3.** strip of road for single line of traffic; strip of track or water for runner, rower, or swimmer in race. **4.** course prescribed for or regularly followed by ships (**ocean ∼**) or aircraft. [OE, = OFris. *lana, laen*, MDu. *lāne*, of unkn. orig.]

lǎng sýne (lahñ *se.*) *adv.* & *n.* (Sc.) (in) the old days; cf. AULD. [= *long since*]

lǎ′nguage (-nggwǐj) *n.* **1.** a vocabulary and way of using it prevalent in one or more countries; ARTIFICIAL, DEAD, *language*. **2.** method of expression (**finger** or DEAF-*and-dumb* ∼; ∼ **of flowers**, symbolic meanings attached to various kinds); system of symbols and rules for writing computer programs. **3.** words and their use; faculty of speech; person's style of expressing himself; (**bad**) ∼, oaths and abusive talk; STRONG *language*; **speak the same** ∼, have similar outlook and way of expressing oneself. **4.** professional or sectional vocabulary. **5.** literary style, wording. **6.** ∼ **laboratory**, room equipped with tape-recorders etc. for learning foreign languages by repeated practice; ∼**-master**, teacher of (usu. mod. foreign) language(s). [ME f. OF *langage* f. Gallo-Rom. **linguaticum* f. L *lingua* tongue; see -AGE]

langue de chat (lahñ de shah′) *n.* very thin finger--shaped piece of chocolate or crisp biscuit. [F, = cat's tongue]

langue d'oc (lahñgedŏ′k), **langue d'oïl** (lahñgedoi′l), *ns.* medieval French as spoken south, north, of the Loire, the basis of modern Provençal and modern French respectively. [f. OF *langue* language f. L *lingua* tongue, *de* of, *oc* (f. L *hoc*), *oïl* (f. L *hoc ille*), these being the respective forms for *yes*]

lǎ′nguid (-nggwǐd) *a.* inert, lacking vigour; indisposed to exertion; spiritless, apathetic; (of ideas etc.) not vivid, uninteresting; (of trade etc.) sluggish, slow--moving; faint, weak; hence ∼LY[2] *adv.*, ∼NESS *n.* [f. F *languide* or f. L *languidus* (as foll.; see -ID[1])]

lǎ′nguish (-nggw-) *v.i.* grow or be feeble, lose or lack vitality; live *under* enfeebling or depressing conditions; grow slack, lose intensity; droop, pine (*for*); put on languid look, affect sentimental tenderness, whence ∼INGLY *adv.*; hence ∼MENT *n.* [ME, f. OF *languir* (-ISH[2]) f. Rom. **languire* for L *languēre*, rel. to LAX[1]]

lǎ′nguor (-ngger) *n.* faintness, fatigue; inertia, lack of alertness; soft or tender mood or effect; slackness, dullness, drooping state; (of air etc.) oppressive stillness; so ∼OUS *a.* [ME f. OF, f. L *languor* -*oris* (as prec.; see -OR)]

langur′ (langgoor′) *n.* Asian long-tailed monkey esp. of genus *Presbytis*. [Hindi]

lǎ′niary *a.* & *n.* (tooth) adapted for tearing, canine. [f. L *laniarius* (*lanius* butcher f. *laniare* to tear; see -ARY[1])]

lani′ferous, lani′gerous, *adjs.* wool-bearing. [f. L *lanifer, -ger* (*lana* wool; see -FEROUS, -GEROUS)]

lǎnk *a.* shrunken, spare; tall and lean; (of grass etc.) long and flaccid; (of hair) straight and limp, not wavy or curly. [OE *hlanc* f. Gmc **hlank-*; cf. FLANK, LINK[1]]

lǎ′nk|ȳ *a.* (Of person or limbs) ungracefully lean and long or tall; hence ∼ɪLY[2] *adv.*, ∼ɪNESS *n.* [f. prec.+-Y[2]]

lǎ′nner *n.* (female) S. Eur. falcon of species *Falco biarmicus*. [ME, f. OF *lanier* perh. f. OF *lanier* cowardly, orig. = weaver f. L *lanarius* wool-merchant (*lana* wool; see -ER[2])]

lǎ′nnerèt *n.* male lanner (smaller than female). [ME, f. OF *laneret* (as prec.; see -ET[1])]

lǎ′nolin *n.* fat which permeates sheep's wool, extracted as basis for ointments etc. [G, f. L *lana* wool + *oleum* oil + -IN]

lǎ′nsquěnět (-kǐ-) *n.* card-game of German origin; German mercenary soldier in 16th–17th c. [F, f. G *landsknecht* (as LAND[1], *knecht* soldier f. OHG *kneht*; see KNIGHT)]

lǎ′ntern *n.* **1.** (lamp with) transparent case protecting flame of candle etc.; = MAGIC *lantern*, whence ∼IST (3) *n.*; ‖**parish** ∼, the moon. **2.** light-chamber of lighthouse; structure on top of dome or room with glazed sides to admit light, similar structure for ventilation etc.; proboscis of lantern-fly. **3.** ∼**-fly**, insect of family Fulgoridae, formerly thought to be luminous; ∼ **jaws** (long and thin, giving hollow look to face); ∼**-slide**, SLIDE[2] 6 for projection by magic lantern etc.; ∼**-wheel**, lantern-shaped gear-wheel, trundle. [ME, f. OF *lanterne* f. L *lanterna* f. Gk *lamptēr* torch, lamp]

lǎ′nthanīde *n.* (Chem.) element of the ∼ **series** from lanthanum or cerium to lutetium (atomic numbers 57–71), all being metals with similar chemical properties. [f. G *lanthanid* (as foll., see -IDE)]

lǎ′nthanum *n.* (Chem.) metallic element, first of lanthanide series. [f. Gk *lanthanō* escape notice + -UM, from having remained undetected in cerium oxide]

‖**lǎ′nthorn** (-tern) *n.* lantern. ‖pop. assim. of *lantern* to *horn*, common former material]

lanū′gō *n.* (*pl.* ∼s). fine soft hair esp. on human foetus. [L, = down (*lana* wool)]

lǎ′nyard *n.* **1.** (Naut.) short rope or line attached to something to secure it. **2.** cord attached to breech mechanism for firing gun. **3.** cord hanging round neck or looped round shoulder, to which knife, whistle, etc., may be attached. [ME, f. OF *laniere*, *lasniere*; assim. to YARD[1]]

Lāodicē′an *a.* & *n.* (person who is) lukewarm, esp. in religion or politics. [f. L *Laodicea* in Asia Minor + -AN; see Rev. 3:16]

Lao′tian (low′shan, lahō′shan) *a.* & *n.* (native, inhabitant, or language) of Laos. [f. *Laos* in SE Asia + -IAN]

lǎp[1] *n.* **1.** hanging part or flap of garment, saddle, etc.; lobe of ear. **2.** front part of skirt held up to contain something; front of body from waist to knees of sitting person, with dress, as place on which child is nursed or object held (lit., or fig. *in the lap of luxury* etc.); **in** or **on** person's ∼, (fig.) as his responsibility (*in the lap of the* GODS); hence ∼′FUL 2 *n.* **3.** hollow among hills. **4.** ∼**-dog**, small pet dog; ***∼′**robe**, travelling-rug; ∼′**stone**, shoemaker's stone held in lap to beat leather on. [OE *læppa*, = OS *lappo*, OHG *lappa*; cf. ON *leppr* rag]

lǎp[2] *v.* (**-pp-**). **1.** *v.t.* coil, fold, wrap, (garment etc. *about, round*, as advs. or preps.); enfold, swathe, *in* wraps etc.; (of influence etc.) surround, encircle; (esp. in *pass.*) enfold caressingly. **2.** cause to overlap; lead (competitor in race) by one or more laps. **3.** *v.i.* project *over* (thing, or abs.). [ME, prob. f. prec.]

lǎp[3] *n.* **1.** amount of overlapping, overlapping part, (**half-**∼, joining of rails, shafts, etc., by halving thickness of each at end and fitting together). **2.** layer or sheet (of cotton etc. being made) wound on roller; single turn of rope, silk, thread, etc., round drum or reel; one circuit of race-track etc. (∼ **of honour**, ceremonial circuit of football pitch etc. by winners), (fig.) section of journey etc., esp. *last lap*. **3.** ∼**-joint**, = *half-lap* (see above); ∼**-strake**, clinker--built (boat); ∼**-weld** *n.*, & *v.t.*, (with overlapping edges). [ME, f. prec.]

lǎp[4] *n.*, & *v.t.* (**-pp-**). **1.** *n.* rotating disc for polishing gem or metal. **2.** *v.t.* polish with lap. [perh. f. prec.]

lǎp[5] *v.* (**-pp-**) & *n.* **1.** *v.i.* & *t.* take up liquid, drink (*up* liquid), with tongue as cat does; consume (liquid, or fig.) greedily (usu. *up* or *down*); (of water) move, beat upon (shore), with rippling sound of lapping. **2.** *n.*

liquid food for dogs, (sl.) weak beverage, any liquor; single act of lapping, amount taken up by it; sound of wavelets on beach etc. [OE *lapian*, = MLG, MDu. *lapen*, OHG *laffan* f. Gmc *lap-]

lă′paro- *comb. form.* (Anat. & Surg.) flank, as ∼TOMY (-ŏ′t-) *n.*, cutting of abdominal walls for access to cavity of abdomen. [f. Gk *lapara* flank (*laparos* soft)]

lapĕ′l *n.* part of front of coat etc. folded back; hence ∼lED² (-ld) *a.* [f. LAP¹ + -EL]

lă′picīde *n.* cutter of stones or inscriptions on stone. [f. L *lapicida* irreg. f. *lapis -idis* stone; see -CIDE]

lă′pidarȳ *a.* & *n.* **1.** *a.* concerned with stones; engraved on stone, (of style) suitable for inscriptions, dignified and concise. **2.** *n.* cutter, polisher, or engraver, of gems. [ME, f. L *lapidarius* (*lapis -idis* stone; see -ARY¹)]

lă′pid|āte *v.t.* (literary). throw stones at; stone to death; so ∼A′TION *n.* [f. L *lapidare* (as prec.) + -ATE³]

lapi′llī *n. pl.* stone fragments ejected from volcanoes. [It. f. L, pl. dim. of *lapis* stone]

lăpĭs (**lă′zūlī**) *n.* sodium aluminium silicate-sulphate used as gem; bright blue pigment from it; its colour. [ME, f. L *lapis* stone + med. L *lazuli* gen. of *lazulum* f. Pers. (as AZURE)]

Lă′plănder *n.* inhabitant of Lapland. [f. *Lapland* f. Sw. *Lappland* (as LAPP, LAND¹), + -ER¹]

Lăpp *n.* & *a.* **1.** *n.* one of nomadic race of northern Scandinavia; their language. **2.** *a.* of the Lapps or their language. [f. Sw. *Lapp*, perh. orig. term of contempt; cf. MHG *lappe* simpleton]

lă′ppĕt *n.* flap, fold; loose or overlapping piece of garment, flesh, membrane, etc.; lobe of ear etc; streamer of woman's head-dress; ∼-(-moth), kind of large moth, whose caterpillars have side-lobes; hence ∼ED² *a.* [f. LAP¹ + -ET¹]

Lă′ppĭsh *a.* & *n.* **1.** *a.* Lapp. **2.** *n.* Lapp language. [f. LAPP + -ISH¹]

lăpse¹ *n.* slip of memory, tongue, or pen, slight mistake; weak or careless deviation from what is right, moral slip; falling away *from* faith or *into* heresy; decline to lower state; passage or interval *of* time; (Law) termination of right or privilege through disuse; (arch., of water) gentle flow; ∼ **rate,** (Meteorol.) rate of fall of temperature with increasing height. [f. L *lapsus* (*labi laps-* glide, slip, fall)]

lăpse² *v.i.* fail to maintain position or state for want of effort or vigour; fall *back* or *away* (*into* inferior or previous or ordinary state); (of benefice, estate, right, etc.) become void, revert *to* someone, by non-fulfilment of conditions, absence of heirs, etc.; glide, flow, subside, pass *away*; (in *p.p.*) that has lapsed (see -ED¹ (2)). [partly f. L *lapsare* (as prec.), partly f. prec.]

lapsus (**lă′psus**) *n.* (*pl.* same). slip (usu. in ∼ **linguae** *pr.* lĭ′nggwē, slip of the tongue, ∼ **calami** *pr.* kă′lamī, slip of the pen). [L; see LAPSE¹]

Lapū′tan *a.* chimerical, visionary, absurd. [f. *Laputa* in Swift's 'Gulliver's Travels', whose inhabitants engaged in visionary projects, + -AN]

lă′pwing *n.* bird of plover family (*Vanellus vanellus*), with crested head and shrill cry, pewit. [OE *hlēapewince* (*hlēapan* LEAP¹, as WINK, w. ref. to manner of flight), assim. to LAP², WING]

lār *n.* **1.** (*pl.* **lar′es** *pr.* lār′ēz, lār′āz). ancient-Roman household deity; **lares** (**and penates**), the home. **2.** (*pl.* ∼**s** *pr.* -z). white-handed gibbon (*Hylobates lar*) of SE Asia. [L]

lăr′board (-berd) *n.* & *a.* (Naut.; arch. or US) = PORT⁵. [ME *lad*(*d*)*e*-, *lathe*- (perh. = LADE + BOARD¹), later assim. to *starboard*]

lăr′cen|ȳ *n.* theft; (Law) felonious taking away of another's personal goods with intent to convert them to one's own use (**grand, petty,** ∼**y,** of property above, below, value of 12d. (5p), or of $200); hence ∼ER¹, ∼IST (1) *ns.*, ∼OUS *a.* [f. AF *larcenie*, f. OF *larcin* f. L *latrocinium* (*latro* robber, mercenary f. Gk *latreus*); see -Y¹]

lărch *n.* bright-foliaged deciduous coniferous tree of genus *Larix*, yielding turpentine, tough timber, and

bark used in tanning; ∼(′wood), its wood. [f. MHG *larche*, f. OHG *larihha* f. L *larix -icis*]

lărd¹ *n.* internal fat of abdomen of pigs esp. when rendered and clarified for use in cooking and pharmacy; hence ∼′Y² *a.* (∼**y-cake,** cake made with lard, currants, etc.). [ME, f. OF *lard* bacon, f. L *lar*(*i*)*dum* cogn. w. Gk *larinos* fat]

lărd² *v.t.* **1.** insert strips of bacon in (meat etc.) before cooking (∼′**ing-needle, -pin,** instrument for doing this). **2.** garnish (talk, writing) *with* metaphors, technical terms, foreign words, etc. [ME, f. OF *larder* (as prec.)]

lăr′der *n.* room or cupboard for storing meat and other provisions. [ME f. AF; OF *lardier* f. med. L *lardarium* (as LARD¹, -ER² (2))]

lăr′don, lărdŏŏ′n, *n.* strip of bacon or pork used to lard meat. [ME f. F *lardon* (as LARD¹; see -OON)]

lărdȳ-dăr′dȳ *a.* (sl.) affected and languidly dandified. [cf. LA-DI-DA]

lares. See LAR.

lărge *a.*, *n.*, & *adv.* **1.** *a.* of considerable or relatively great magnitude (more formal than *big*, and without emotional implications of *great*); *as large as, larger than,* LIFE; ∼ **of limb,** with large limbs. **2.** (Of agent) doing thing on a large scale (*large and small farmers*); (as distinctive epithet) of the larger kind (*large* INTESTINE¹). **3.** of wide range, comprehensive, (*large powers, discretion*); (of artistic treatment) free, sweeping, broad. **4.** ∼**-handed,** generous; ∼**-hearted,** ∼**-souled,** kindly; ∼**-minded,** liberal, not narrow-minded; ∼**-scale,** made or occurring on a large SCALE³ or in large amounts. **5.** Hence lăr′gĬsh¹ 2 *a.*, ∼′NESS (-jn-) *n.*, lăr′gEN⁶ *v.i.* & *t.* (poet.). **6.** *n.* at ∼, at liberty, free, (of narration etc.) at full length with details, as a body or whole (*popular with the people at large*), *representing a whole State etc. and not merely a part of it, without particularizing, without specific aim (*scatters imputations at large*); *ambassador at ∼ (appointed for special duties, not to any one country); gentleman at ∼, gentleman attached to the court without special duties, person who has no occupation; STATUTES *at large;* **in** ∼, on a large scale (opp. *in little*). [ME. BY¹ and *large;* BULK², LOOM², *large;* WRIT² *large*. [ME f. OF, f. fem. of L *largus* copious]

lăr′gelȳ (-jlĭ) *adv.* In adj. senses; to a great or preponderating extent (*is largely due to*). [f. prec. + -LY²]

lărgess, -esse (lärjĕ′s, lär′jĭs, -zh-) *n.* money or gifts freely bestowed esp. by great person on occasion of rejoicing; generous or plentiful bestowal. [ME, f. OF *largesse* f. Rom. *largitia* f. L *largus* copious; see -ESS²]

lărghĕ′tto (-gĕ′-) *adv.*, *a.*, & *n.* (*pl.* ∼**s**). (Mus.) (movement) in fairly slow time. [It., dim. of foll.]

lăr′gŏ *adv.,a.,*& *n.* (*pl.* ∼**s**). (Mus.) (movement) in slow time with broad dignified treatment. [It., = broad]

lă′riat *n.* rope for tethering horse etc.; lasso. [f. Sp. *la reata* (*reatar* tie again f. as RE- + L *aptare* adjust f. *aptus* APT, fit)]

lărk¹ *n.* **1.** small bird of family Alaudidae, with sandy-brown plumage and long hind-claws, esp. the sky-lark; **rise with the** ∼, get up early; ∼**-heel,** ∼′**spur,** plant of genus *Delphinium* with spur-shaped calyx. **2.** bird of some other families (*meadow-lark, titlark*). [OE *lāferce, læwerce* = MLG, MDu. *lēwer*(*i*)*ke*, OHG *lērihha*, ON *lævirki*, of unkn. orig.]

lărk² *n.*, & *v.i.* (colloq.) **1.** *n.* frolic, spree, amusing incident (**what a** ∼!, how amusing!), whence ∼′Y² *a.* ‖type of activity etc. **2.** *v.i.* play tricks, frolic (*about*). [19th c.; orig. uncert.]

lărn *v.t.* & *i.* **1.** (joc. or vulg.) = LEARN. **2.** *v.t.* (colloq.) teach, instruct, (*that'll larn you*). [dial. form of LEARN]

lă′rrikin *n.* (Austral.) young street rowdy, hooligan. [perh. f. man's Christian name *Larry* (pet-form of *Lawrence*) + -KIN]

lă′rrup *v.t.* (colloq.) thrash. [dial., perh. f. LATHER]

Lă′rrȳ *n.* (as) **happy as** ∼, extremely happy. [20th c., of uncert. orig.; cf. LARRIKIN]

lă′rum Var. (arch.) of ALARM¹; cf. ALARUM.

lär'v|a *n.* (*pl.* ∼**ae**). insect from time of leaving egg till transformation into pupa, grub; immature form of other animals that undergo some metamorphosis; hence ∼AL *a.*, ∼ĬCIDE (1) *n.* [L, = ghost, mask]

laryng-. See LARYNX.

lary'ngoscöpe (-ngg-) *n.* mirror apparatus for examining larynx. [f. LARYNX + -O- + SCOPE]

lăryngö'tomy̆ (-ngg-) *n.* cutting into larynx from without, esp. to provide breathing-channel. [f. as prec. + -TOMY]

lă'rȳn|x *n.* (*pl.* ∼**ges** *pr.* -ĭ'njēz). cavity in throat containing vocal cords; hence ∼gèAL (-ĭ'nj-) *a.*, & *n.*, hypothetical phonetic element of laryngeal quality supposed to have existed in Proto-Indo-European, ∼gIC (-ĭ'nj-) *a.*, ∼gI'TIS (-nj-), ∼gö'LOGY (-ngg-), *ns.* [mod. L, f. Gk *larugx -ggos*]

lasă'gnĕ (-ă'nyĕ, -ah'-) *n. pl.* pasta in wide ribbon form, esp. as served with minced meat and sauce. [It., pl. of *lasagna* f. L *lasanum* cooking-pot]

Lä'scar *n.* E. Indian sailor. [ult. f. Urdu & Pers. *laškar* = 'army', misapplied; cf. LASHKAR]

lascï'vious *a.* lustful, wanton; inciting to lust; hence ∼LY² *adv.*, ∼NESS *n.* [ME, f. LL *lasciviosus* f. L *lascivia* lustfulness (*lascivus* sportive, wanton; see -OUS)]

läse (-z) *v.i.* function as or in laser; (of substance etc.) undergo physical processes employed in laser. [back-form. f. foll.]

lä'ser (-z-) *n.* device generating intense beam of highly coherent monochromatic radiation in one direction, by stimulation of emission from excited atoms etc., optical MASER. [f. *light amplification by stimulated emission of radiation*; cf. MASER]

läsh¹ *v.* **1.** *v.i.* make sudden violent movement of limb, tail, whip, etc.; pour or rush vehemently; strike violently *at* or *against*; hit or (of horse) kick *out*; break *out* into excess, strong language, etc. **2.** *v.t.* beat with thong, flog; move suddenly and forcefully (*lashed its tail*); (of waves or rain) beat upon; castigate in words, rebuke, satirize; urge as with lashes (∼ *oneself into a fury*, work up a rage). **3.** fasten (*down, on, together, to something*) with cord, twine, etc.; ∼**-up** *a.* & *n.*, makeshift, improvised (structure), (sl.) muddle(d), failure. [sense 1 ME, prob. imit.; sense 2 f. foll.; sense 3 ME, perh. of LG orig.]

läsh² *n.* stroke with thong, whip, etc.; flexible part of whip (**the** ∼, punishment of flogging); (csp. in *pl.*) eyelash, whence ∼'LESS *a.*; goading influence. [f. prec. 1]

lä'sher *n.* In vbl senses; ||esp. (water rushing over) weir, pool below weir. [f. LASH¹ + -ER¹]

lä'shing *n.* In vbl senses; cord used for lashing; (in *pl.*, sl.) plenty, abundance, (*of*). [f. LASH¹ + -ING¹]

lä'shkar *n.* body of armed Indian tribesmen. [f. Urdu (as LASCAR)]

lasque (lahsk) *n.* flat, ill-formed, or veiny diamond. [perh. f. Pers. *lašk* piece]

läss *n.* girl (esp. Sc., N. Engl., or poet.); man's sweetheart; hence ∼'IE *n.* [ME *lasce* f. **lask* f. ON *laskwa* unmarried (fem.)]

Lä'ssa *n.* ∼ **fever,** acute febrile virus disease of tropical Africa. [∼ in Nigeria]

lä'ssitüde *n.* weariness, languor, disinclination to exert or interest oneself. [F, or f. L *lassitudo* (*lassus* tired; see -TUDE)]

lasso (lasö̆', lă'sö̆) *n.* (*pl.* ∼**s** or ∼**es**), & *v.t.* **1.** *n.* Sp. Amer. noosed rope of untanned hide etc. for catching cattle etc. **2.** *v.t.* catch with lasso. [f. Sp. *lazo* LACE¹]

läst¹ (lah-) *n.* shoemaker's wooden or metal model for shaping shoe etc. on; **stick to** one's ∼, not meddle with things one does not understand (w. ref. to L *ne sutor ultra crepidam*). [OE *lǣste* last, *lǣst* boot, *läst* footprint; cf. OHG *leist* last, Goth. *laists*- track, ON *leistr* foot f. Gmc **laist*-; cf. LAST⁴]

ast² (lah-) *n.* commercial measure of weight, capacity, or quantity, varying with place and goods (∼ **of wool,** 12 sacks or 4,368 lb.; ∼ **of herrings,** 12 barrels; ∼ **of malt,** 10 qr. or 80 bushels). [OE *hlǣst*

load, = MLG, MDu. *last*, OHG *hlast* f. WG **hlatsta* f. Gmc **hlath-* LADE]

last³ (lah-) *a.*, *n.*, & *adv.* **1.** *a.* after all others, coming at the end, (**the** ∼ **two** etc., the last and the last but one etc.; **second** ∼, ∼ **but one,** next to the last; ∼ **but not least,** last in order of mention or occurrence but not of importance); ∼**-across,** children's game of being last to cross road in front of approaching vehicle; *last* DITCH; ∼ **minute** or **moment,** time immediately before a decisive event; ∼ **name,** surname; *last* ||POST⁴, QUARTER¹ 9, STRAW¹; ∼ **thing** (*adv.*, colloq.), as final act (esp. before going to bed); ∼ **word,** conclusive or definitive statement, final contribution to dispute, latest fashion. **2.** belonging to the end, esp. of life or the world; L∼ **Day,** Judgement Day; *last* HOME¹, HONOUR¹*s*, INQUEST; *Last* JUDGEMENT; *on* one's *last* LEGS; *last* RESPECT¹*s*; ∼ **rites,** religious ceremony for person near death; ∼ **sleep,** death; L∼ **Supper** (of Christ and his disciples on eve of Crucifixion); **the four** ∼ **things,** death, judgement, heaven, and hell; ∼ **trump,** trumpet to wake the dead on Judgement Day; ∼ **words,** person's dying words. **3.** next before expressed or implied point of time, latest up to now or then, most recent, (*in the last fortnight*; *last Christmas*; *last Tuesday* or *Tuesday last*); ∼ **evening, night, week, month, year,** *ns.* & *advs.*, (during) the evening etc. most recently past. **4.** lowest, of least rank or estimation. **5.** only remaining (*last chance, crust, resource*). **6.** least likely, willing, suitable, etc., to (*should be the last to do it*; *is the last thing to try*). **7.** utmost, extreme, (*is of the last importance*). **8.** *n.* last-mentioned person or thing (*the, this, these, which, last*); most recent letter etc.; last day or moments, death, (*the or his* etc. *last*); last day of month; last performance of certain acts (*breathe, look,* one's *last*); last mention or sight (*shall never hear the last of it, see the last of him*); **at** (**long**) ∼, in the end, after much delay; **to** or **till the** ∼, to the end, esp. till death. **9.** *adv.* after all others (esp. in comb., as *last-mentioned*); on the last occasion before the present (*when did you see him last?* or *last see him?*); (in enumerations) in the last place, finally. [OE *latost* superl. of *lǣt* a., *late* adv.; see LATE¹, -EST¹; loss of *-t-* as in BEST¹]

last⁴ (lah-) *v.* **1.** *v.i.* continue, remain unexhausted or adequate or alive for specified or long time; suffice (*will last me eight months*; *will last my time*). **2.** *v.t.* ∼ **out,** continue esp. in vigour or use at least as long as. [OE *lǣstan*, = OS *lēstian* execute, OHG *leisten* afford, Goth. *laistjan* follow f. Gmc **laist-* LAST¹]

la'sting (lah'-) *a.* & *n.* **1.** *a.* enduring, permanent, (*no lasting benefit*); durable; hence ∼LY² *adv.*, ∼NESS *n.* **2.** *n.* kind of durable cloth. [ME, f. prec. + -ING²]

la'stly̆ (lah'-) *adv.* in the last place, finally. [ME, f. LAST³ + -LY²]

lat. *abbr.* latitude.

Lătaki'a (-ē'a) *n.* kind of Turkish tobacco chiefly used in mixtures. [∼ (ancient *Laodicea*) in Syria]

lätch *n.* & *v.* **1.** *n.* small bar falling into catch and lifted by lever etc. from outside, as fastening for door or gate; small spring-lock of outer door catching when door is closed and worked from outside by key; ∼'**key,** any outer-door key, (fig.) symbol of emancipation, (∼*key child*, child given key to enter home on return from school etc., when mother is absent); **on the** ∼, fastened by latch only, not locked. **2.** *v.t.* & *i.* fasten (itself) with latch. **3.** *v.i.* (colloq.) ∼ *on* to, (1) attach oneself to, (2) understand. [prob. f. (now dial.) *latch* v. seize f. OE *lǣccan* f. Gmc **lakk-*]

lä'tchet *n.* (arch.) thong for fastening shoe. [ME, f. OF *lachet*, var. of *lacet* dim. of *laz* LACE¹]

läte¹ *a.* (*compar.* **la'ter** or LATTER; *superl.* **la'test** or LAST³) *a.* & *n.* **1.** *a.* after the due or usual time (*was late for dinner*; *it is too late to go*); (of agent or action) doing or done after proper time (*late comer*; *late rising*). **2.** backward in flowering, ripening, etc. **3.** far on in day or night (∼**dinner,** in evening; ∼**hours,** after usual time for rising or going to bed); far on in time (*on*

Wednesday **at** ∼**st,** then if not before); far on in a period, development, etc., *(late stained glass; in the late 19th century; late* LATIN). **4.** no longer alive, no longer having specified status etc., that was recently so-and--so, **(the** ∼ *prime minister,* dead or resigned; *my late husband, residence).* **5.** of recent date *(the late floods, war;* **of** ∼ **years,** in the last few years); ∼**st,** most recent (news etc., or abs.). **6.** ‖∼ **fee** (on letter posted after ordinary collection time). **7.** Hence **lā′**TEN⁶ *v.t.* & *i.,* ∼′NESS (-tn-) *n.*, **lā′**TISH¹ 2 *a.* & *adv.* **8.** *n.* **of** ∼, recently. [OE *lǣt,* = OS *lat,* OHG *laz,* ON *latr,* Goth. *lats* f. Gmc **lataz* slow (**lat-* f. IE **lad-,* cogn. w. LET¹)]

lāte² *adv.* (**la′ter; la′test,** LAST³). after proper time *(better late than never);* far on in time *(this happened later on;* **sooner or** ∼**r, early or** ∼**, soon or** ∼, at some future time, eventually); at or till late hour *(we sat late);* (poet.) recently, lately, *(I sent thee late a rosy wreath);* formerly but not now *(late of Oxford);* at late stage of development etc. *(traces remained as late as Stuart times);* ∼ **in the day,** (colloq.) at a late stage, esp. unreasonably late in the proceedings etc. [OE *late,* adv. form of prec.]

lateen′n *a.* ∼ **sail** (triangular on long yard at angle of 45° to mast); (of ship etc.) so rigged. [f. F *(voile) latine* Latin (sail), named as common in Mediterranean]

lā′telȳ (-tlĭ) *adv.* not long ago, recently, in recent times. [OE *lǣtlīce* (as LATE¹, -LY²)]

La Tène (lah tĕn) *a.* relating to the second Iron-Age culture of central & W. Europe. (∼ in Switzerland, where remains of it were first identified]

lā′tent *a.* hidden, concealed; existing but not developed or manifest; dormant; *latent* HEAT¹; ∼ **image,** (Photog.) invisible image that may be developed; hence **lā′t**ENCY *n.,* ∼LY² *adv.* [f. L *latēre* be hidden; see -ENT]

-later *suf.* See -LATRY.

lā′teral *a.* & *n.* **1.** *a.* of, at, towards, from, the side, side-; ∼ **branch** of family (descended from brother or sister of person in direct line); ∼ **thinking,** seeking to solve problems by unorthodox or apparently illogical methods; hence ∼LY² *adv.* **2.** *n.* side part, member, or object, esp. lateral shoot or branch. [f. L *lateralis (latus lateris* side; see -AL)]

Lā′teran *a.* ∼ **Council,** one of five general councils of Western Church held in cathedral of St. John Lateran, Rome. [f. L *Laterana, -num,* district of Rome where family of Plautii *Laterani* resided]

lā′ter‖īte *n.* red or yellow friable ferruginous surface clay hardening in air, much used for road-making in tropics; hence ∼ī′TIC *a.* [f. L *later* brick + -ITE¹ (2)]

lā′tĕx *n.* (*pl.* ∼**es,** or **la′tices** *pr.* -ĭsēz). milky fluid of (esp. rubber) plant; synthetic product resembling this. [L, = liquid]

lath (lah-) *n.* (*pl. pr.* -ths, -dhz), & *v.t.* **1.** *n.* piece of sawn or split timber in form of thin strip about an inch wide esp. for use as support for slates or plaster or as material for trellis or Venetian blind (**as thin as a** ∼, of persons, whence ∼′Y² *a.*); ∼ **and plaster,** material for interior wall-facings, ceilings, partitions, etc. **2.** *v.t.* provide (wall, ceiling) with laths; hence ∼′ING¹ (3) *n.* [OE *lætt,* **læthth-,* = OS, OHG *latta*]

‖**lāthe¹** (-dh) *n.* (Hist.) administrative district of Kent. [OE *lǣth* estate, = ON *láth*]

lāthe² (-dh) *n.* machine for shaping wood, metal, ivory, etc., by rotating article against tools used; ∼-**bed,** lower framework of lathe with slot from end to end for adjustment; ∼-**head,** headstock of lathe. [prob. rel. to ODa. *lad* structure, frame, f. ON *hlath,* rel. to *hlatha* LADE]

la′ther (lah′dh-, lā′-) *n.* & *v.* **1.** *n.* froth of soap etc. and water; frothy sweat esp. of horse; (fig.) state of agitation; hence ∼Y² *a.* **2.** *v.t.* cover (esp. chin etc. for shaving) with lather; beat, thrash, whence ∼ING¹ (1) *n.* **3.** *v.i.* (Of horse) become covered with lather; (of soap etc.) form lather. [OE *lēathor* n., *lēthran* v., = ON *lauthr* washing-soda, *leythra* to lather f. Gmc (**lauthrian* v. f.) **lauthram* f. IE **loutrom*]

la′thĭ (lah′tĭ) *n.* (Ind.) long heavy iron-bound bamboo stick used as weapon esp. by police. [f. Hindi *lāthī*]

lătĭfŭ′ndia *n. pl.* large estates, esp. as characterizing a country's social system. [L *(latus* broad, *fundus* estate)]

Lă′tĭn *a.* & *n.* **1.** *a.* of Latium or its ancient inhabitants; of ancient Romans; of, like, in, the Indo-European language of the ancient Romans. **2.** of the Roman Catholic Church; ∼ (= WESTERN) **Church;** ∼ **rite,** religious ceremonial using Latin, esp. in Western Church. **3.** (Of peoples) inheriting Roman customs etc., speaking one of the languages descended from Latin; ∼ **America,** parts of Central & S. America where Spanish or Portuguese is main language, whence *L*∼*-Amé′rican a.* & *n.;* ∼ **cross,** plain cross with lowest arm longer than the other three; **the** ∼ **peoples,** inhabitants of France, Spain, Portugal, Italy, etc.; ∼ **Quarter** [F *Quartier Latin*], educational centre of Paris, where Latin was spoken in the Middle Ages, noted for its unconventional mode of life; ∼ **square,** arrangement of *n* letters etc. each occurring *n* times, in a square array of *n²* compartments so that no letter appears twice in same row or column. **4.** *n.* the Latin language; **old** ∼ (before about 75 BC, pre--classical); **classical** ∼, that of leading writers of late republican and early imperial Rome, about 75 BC to AD 200; **late** ∼ (about AD 200 to 600); **medieval** ∼ (about AD 600 to 1500); **modern** ∼ (since AD 1500, used esp. in scientific classifications); DOG¹ *Latin;* LAW¹ *Latin;* **low** ∼, medieval, or late and medieval, Latin; PIG *Latin;* **popular** ∼ (informal, of classical times); **silver** ∼ (literary language of 1st c. AD); **thieves'** ∼, secret cant of thieves etc.; **vulgar** ∼ (informal, of classical times); hence or cogn. ∼ISM (4), ∼IST (3), *ns.,* ∼LESS *a.* **5.** inhabitant of Latium; (Rom. Ant.) Italian with rights of citizenship. [ME f. OF and f. L *Latinus (Latium* district of Italy including Rome)]

Lă′tināte *a.* having the character of Latin. [f. prec. + -ATE²]

lă′tinē *adv.* in Latin (giving Latin equivalent of word etc.). [L]

Latĭ′nĭtȳ *n.* way a person speaks or writes Latin; quality of Latin style or grammar. [f. L *latinitas* (as LATIN; see -ITY)]

Lă′tĭnīz‖e, -īs‖e (-ĭz), *v.* **1.** *v.t.* give Latin form to (word), put into Latin; make conformable to ideas, customs, etc., of the ancient Romans, Latin peoples, or Latin Church. **2.** *v.i.* use Latin forms, idioms, etc. **3.** Hence ∼A′TION, ∼ER¹, *ns.* [f. LL *latinizare* (as LATIN; see -IZE)]

*Latī′nō (-ē′-) *n.* (*pl.* ∼**s**). Latin-American inhabitant of US. [Amer. Sp.]

lă′tĭsh. See LATE¹.

lă′tĭtūde *n.* **1.** freedom from narrowness, liberality of interpretation, tolerated variety of action or opinion. **2.** (Geog.) angular distance on a meridian *(degree, minute,* etc., *of latitude);* place's angular distance on its meridian N. or S. of equator *(latitude* 40° *N.* etc.); (usu. in *pl.*) regions, climes, esp. w. ref. to temperature, **(high** ∼**s,** near N. or S. pole; **low** ∼**s,** near equator); hence **lătĭtū′din**AL *a.* **3.** (Astron.) angular distance of heavenly body or point esp. from ecliptic. **4.** (arch.) breadth, scope. [ME, = breadth, f. L *latitudo -dinis (latus* broad; see -TUDE)]

lătĭtūdĭnār′ian *a.* & *n.* (person) allowing latitude esp. in religion, (one who is) indifferent as to particular creeds and forms of worship; hence ∼ISM (3) *n.* [f. L (as prec.) + -ARIAN]

lā′tria *n.* (RC Ch.) supreme worship due to God alone. [L, f. Gk *latreia* worship *(latreuō* serve)]

latri′ne (-ē′n) *n.* place for urination and defecation, esp. in camp, barracks, hospital, etc.; ∼ **rumour,** (sl.) wild rumour arising from gossip in latrines. [F, f. L *latrina* for *lavatrina (lavare* wash)]

-latrȳ *suf.* forming *ns.* denoting worship *(idolatry, Mariolatry,* & joc. *Bardolatry* etc.), w. corresp. *ns.* in

-*later* denoting worshipper. [f. Gk (as LATRIA, and -*latrēs* -worshipper)]

lă′tten *n.* alloy of copper, zinc, lead, and tin, formerly used for monumental brasses and church articles. [ME *latoun*, f. OF *laton, leiton*]

lă′tter *attrib. a.* **1.** following another (*the latter part of the year*); second-mentioned of two (opp. FORMER[1]); last--mentioned of three or more; **the** ∼, second- or last-mentioned thing or person. **2.** belonging to end of period, world, etc., (**in these** ∼ **days**, at this late period of the world's history; ∼ **end**, conclusion of a period, esp. death). **3.** (arch.) later, second, (∼ **grass,** ∼**math**, aftermath). **4.** ∼ **day,** Judgement Day; ∼**-day,** modern (*L*∼*-day Saints*, Mormons' name for themselves); *∼-wit, thinking of rejoinder etc. after opportunity of making it is lost. [OE *lætra*, compar. of *læt* LATE[1]]

lă′tterlỹ *adv.* towards the end of life or some period; nowadays, of late. [f. prec. + -LY[2]]

lă′ttice *n.* **1.** structure of cross laths with interstices, serving as screen, door, etc.; ∼(-**work**), laths so arranged. **2.** regular arrangement of atoms or molecules in a crystal. **3.** ∼ **frame** or **girder**, girder made of two flanges connected by iron lattice-work; ∼ **window,** one having lattice, or small panes set in diagonally crossing strips of lead. **4.** Hence **lă′tticeᴰ** (-st) *a.*, **lă′tticing**[1] (6) *n.* [ME, f. OF *lattis* (*latte* lath f. WG *latta, -is* ICE)]

Lă′tvian *a.* & *n.* (native or inhabitant) of Latvia; Lettish. [f. *Latvia*, republic of USSR + -AN]

laud *n.*, & *v.t.* **1.** *n.* (Esp. in hymns) praise; hymn of praise. **2.** (Eccl., in *pl.*) (office of) first of the canonical hours of prayer, often said together with matins. **3.** *v.t.* (literary). praise, celebrate. **4.** So ∼A′TION, ∼ā′TOR, *ns.*, ∼ATIVE, ∼ATORY, *adjs.* [ME, n. f. OF *laude*, v. f. L *laudare*, f. L *laus laudis* praise]

laud′d|able *a.* commendable, praiseworthy; (Med., of secretion) healthy, sound; hence ∼ABI′LITY *n.*, ∼ABLY *adv.* [ME, f. L *laudabilis* (as prec.; see -ABLE)]

lau′danum (law′dn-, lŏ′-)' *n.* tincture of opium. [mod. L, name given by Paracelsus to a costly medicament, later applied to preparations containing opium; perh. var. of LADANUM]

laugh (lahf) *v.* & *n.* **1.** *v.i.* make the sounds and movements of face and body by which lively amusement, sense of the ludicrous, exultation, and scorn, are instinctively expressed; have these emotions; (in person's face, show upon contempt for him; ∼ in or up one's sleeve, be secretly amused; **don't make me** ∼, (colloq., iron.) that is ridiculous; ∼ **on the other** or **wrong side of** one's **face** or **mouth,** change from joy or amusement to sorrow or vexation; **he** ∼**s best who** ∼**s last** (warning against premature exultation). **2.** (poet. or rhet.) (Of water, landscape, corn, etc.) be lively with play of movement or light. **3.** *v.t.* utter laughingly; hold up *to scorn*; get (person) *out of* habit, belief, etc., by ridicule (∼ *person*, *opinion*, etc., **out of court,** deprive of a hearing by ridicule). **4.** ∼ **at,** (1) make fun of, ridicule, (2) look pleasantly or smile at; ∼ **away,** dismiss (subject) with a laugh; ∼ **down,** silence with laughter; ∼ **off,** get rid of (embarrassment etc.) with a jest; ∼ **over,** discuss with laughter. **5.** Hence ∼′ER[1] *n.* **6.** *n.* act of laughing (**join in the** ∼, esp. of person taking banter good-humouredly; **have** or **get the** ∼ **of** or **on** person, **have the** ∼ **on** one's **side,** turn the tables on opponent; **have the last** ∼, be ultimately the victor); (colloq.) comical thing (*that's a laugh*); person's manner of laughing. [OE *hlæhhan, hliehhan*, = OS *hlahhian*, OHG *hlahhan*, ON *hlæja*, Goth. *hlahjan* f. Gmc *hlah-* f. IE *klak-*, imit.]

lau′ghab|le (lah′f-) *a.* exciting laughter, amusing; hence ∼LY[2] *adv.* [f. prec. (n. or v.) + -ABLE]

lau′ghing[1] (lah′f-) *n.* **1.** In vbl senses; **no** ∼ **matter,** serious thing, not a fit subject for laughter. **2.** ∼**-gas,** nitrous oxide (with exhilarating effect when inhaled) used as anaesthetic; ∼**-stock,** person or thing generally ridiculed. [ME, f. LAUGH + -ING[1]]

lau′ghing[2] (lah′f-) *a.* In vbl senses; *laughing* HYENA; *laughing* JACK[1]*ass*; (sl.) satisfactorily placed; hence ∼LY[2] *adv.* [ME, f. LAUGH + -ING[2]]

lau′ghter (lah′f-) *n.* action of laughing; Homeric *laughter*. [OE *hleahtor*, = OHG *hlahtar*, ON *hlátr* f. Gmc *hlahtraz* (as LAUGH)]

launce (lahns, lăns) *n.* sand-eel. [perh. f. LANCE[1]; cf. *garfish*]

launch[1] (law-, lah-) *v.* & *n.* **1.** *v.t.* hurl, discharge, send forth, (missile, blow, censure, threat, decree). **2.** set (vessel) afloat; send off, start, (person, enterprise, rocket, etc.) on a course. **3.** *v.i.* burst (usu. **out**) *into* expense, strong language, etc.; ∼ **out,** spend money freely, expatiate in words. **4.** go *forth*, *out*, on an enterprise. **5.** Hence ∼′ER[1] *n.*, (esp.) structure to hold rocket etc. during launching, rocket releasing satellite into orbit; ∼**′ing pad, site,** etc., (from which rockets are launched). **6.** *n.* process of launching ship, rocket, etc.; ∼ **pad** etc. = *launching pad* etc. [ME, f. AF *launcher*, ONF *lancher*, OF *lancier* LANCE[2]]

launch[2] (law-, lah-) *n.* man-of-war's largest boat, used for shore-going, visiting other ships, etc.; motor--driven pleasure-boat on rivers etc. [f. Sp. *lancha* pinnace perh. f. Malay *lancharan* (*lanchār* swift)]

lau′nder *v.t.* wash, starch, iron, etc., (linen etc.); wash (clothes etc.); transfer (funds) to make their source seem legitimate; hence ∼E′TTE, **laundre′tte,** *laun′dromat,* establishment with automatic washing-machines available for public use. [f. ME *launder* n., washer of linen, contr. of *lavander* f. OF *lavandier* f. Rom. *lavandārius* f. L *lavanda* things to be washed, neut. pl. gerundive of *lavare* wash]

lau′ndress *n.* woman who launders linen etc. as occupation. [f. *launder* n. (see prec.) + -ESS[1]]

lau′ndry *n.* establishment for laundering linen etc.; batch of clothes sent to or from laundry. [contr. f. *lavendry* (f. OF *lavanderie*) after LAUNDER; see -RY]

laur′a *n.* (Hist.) group of hermits' cells in Egypt etc. [Gk, = alley]

laur′eate (lŏr′-, lŏ′r-) *a.* & *n.* **1.** *a.* wreathed with, (of wreath) consisting of, laurel; worthy of laurels as poet. **2.** *a.* & *n.* one who wins laurels (fig.; *Nobel laureate*); (**Poet**) L∼, poet receiving stipend as member of British Royal Household writing poems for State occasions; hence ∼SHIP (-tsh-) *n.* [f. L *laureatus* (*laurea* laurel-wreath f. *laurus* laurel; see -ATE[2])]

laur′el (lŏ′-) *n.*, & *v.t.* (||-ll-), **1.** *n.* (arch.) bay-tree. **2.** foliage of bay-tree as emblem of victory or distinction in poetry (collect. *sing.*, or *pl.*; usu. fig.; *reap, win, laurels*; **look to** one's ∼**s,** beware of losing pre-eminence; **rest on** one's ∼**s,** cease to strive for further glory). **3.** plant with dark-green glossy leaves like bay-tree, e.g. (CHERRY-)*laurel*, (JAPANESE) *laurel*, MOUNTAIN *laurel*, SPURGE *laurel*. **4.** *v.t.* wreathe with laurel. [ME *lorer* f. OF *lorier* f. Prov. *laurier* (*laur* f. L *laurus*); -*l* by dissim.]

laurusti′nus (lŏ-) *n.* evergreen winter-flowering shrub (*Viburnum tinus*). [mod. L f. L *laurus* laurel + *tinus* wild laurel]

lăv *n.* (colloq.) lavatory. [abbr.]

la′va (lah′-) *n.* matter flowing from volcano; solid substance it cools into; kind or bed of lava. [It. (*lavare* wash f. L]

lava′bo (-ā′-, -vah′-) *n.* (*pl.* ∼**s**). ritual washing of celebrant's hands at offertory; towel or basin used for this; monastery washing-trough; wash-basin. [L, = I will wash, first wd of Ps. 26:6]

lă′vage *n.* (Med.) washing-out of an organ. [F (*laver* wash, f. as LAVE; see -AGE)]

lavā′tion *n.* washing. [f. L *lavatio* (*lavare* wash; see -ATION)]

lă′vatorỹ *n.* **1.** (room or building or compartment with) receptacle for urine and (usu.) faeces, usu. with means of disposing of them; ∼ **paper,** = TOILET--*paper*. **2.** *(room or compartment with) equipment for washing face and hands. **3.** (arch.) vessel for washing hands etc. [ME, in sense 3, f. LL *lavatorium* f. L *lavare -at-* wash; see -ORY]

lāve[1] *v.t.* (poet. or literary). wash, bathe; (of stream etc.) wash against, flow along. [ME, f. OF *laver* f. L *lavare* wash, perh. coalescing w. OE *lafian* wash by pouring water on, rel. to MDu. *laven*, OHG *labōn* refresh f. L *lavare*]

lāve[2] *n.* (Sc.) remainder. [OE *lāf*, = OHG *leiba*, ON *leif*, Goth. *laibo* f. Gmc *laibhō* (as LEAVE[2])]

lă'vénder *n.*, & *v.t.* **1.** *n.* small shrub of genus *Lavandula*, with narrow leaves and lilac or purple flowers, cultivated for perfume; its flowers and stalks laid among linen etc.; **lay up in** ∼, (fig.) preserve piously for future use. **2.** pale blue colour with trace of red. **3.** ∼ **cotton**, shrub with strongly scented leaves; ∼-**water**, perfume of distilled lavender, alcohol, and ambergris. **4.** *v.t.* put lavender among (linen). [ME, f. AF *lavendre*, ult. dissim. f. med. L *lavandula* etc.]

lă'ver[1] *n.* edible seaweed of various species. [L]

lā'ver[2] *n.* **1.** (Bibl.) large brazen vessel for Jewish priests' ablutions. **2.** (arch.) washing or fountain basin; font. [ME *lavo(u)r* f. OF *laveo(i)r* f. LL (as LAVATORY)]

lă'verock. Sc. var. of LARK[1].

lă'vish *a.*, & *v.t.* **1.** *a.* giving or producing without stint, profuse, prodigal, (*of* money etc., *in* giving); very or over abundant; hence ∼LY[2] *adv.*, ∼NESS *n.* **2.** *v.t.* bestow or spend (money, effort, blood, admiration, etc.) profusely. [ME, f. obs. *lavish*, *lavas* n. profusion, f. OF *lavasse* deluge of rain (*laver* wash; see -ISH[2])]

law[1] *n.* **1.** body of enacted or customary rules recognized by a community as binding, this personified, (*forbidden by* or *under British law*; *the law forbids, allows*; *the law of the land*); **the** ∼ **of the Medes and Persians**, unalterable law [Dan. 6:12]; **lay down the** ∼, talk authoritatively, hector. **2.** one of these rules. **3.** their controlling influence, law-abiding state of society, (*law and order*); **necessity knows no** ∼ (takes precedence over the laws); **be a** ∼ **unto** one**self**, do what one feels is right, take one's own line, disregard convention; **a** ∼ **unto itself**, thing that does not behave in customary manner. **4.** the laws as a social system (‖BARRISTER-*at-law*; COURT[1] *of law*) as subject of study (*read law*, ‖*study the law*, *study law*); **at** or **in** ∼, according to the laws, whence SON-*in-law* etc. (orig. w. ref. to lawful wedlock); MATTER[1] *of law*. **5.** binding injunctions (**give the** ∼ **to**, impose one's will upon; *his word is law*). **6.** (With defining word) one of the branches of the study of law, the laws concerning specified subject (*commercial law*; *the law of contract, of evidence*; CANON, CIVIL, COMMON[1], MARTIAL, STATUTE, *law*); INTERNATIONAL *law* or ∼ **of nations; bachelor, doctor,** etc., **of** ∼s (= in jurisprudence, orig. w. ref. to canon and civil law). **7.** the statute and common law (opp. *equity*). **8.** (In pred. use, of decisions, opinions, etc.; also **good, bad,** etc., ∼) borne out, or not, by the relevant laws (*it may be common sense, but it is not law*). **9.** *the* legal profession; legal knowledge. **10.** judicial remedy, lawcourts as providing it, litigation, (*go to law*; **have** or **take the** ∼ **of** or on person, sue him; **take the** ∼ **into one's own hands**, redress one's grievance by force); **the Law Courts**, ‖(esp.) London building where the higher courts are held. **11.** God's commandments as expressed in the Bible or implanted by nature in the human mind; ∼ (**of Moses**), (precepts of) Pentateuch, Mosaic dispensation. **12.** rule of action or procedure, esp. in an art, department of life, or game; *law of* HONOUR[1]; *laws of* WAR[1]. **13.** ∼ (**of nature**), **natural** ∼, correct statement of invariable sequence observed under specified conditions and specified phenomenon (cf. GRESHAM, GRIMM, KEPLER, NEWTON, PARKINSON[2], etc.); laws of nature, regularity in nature (*where they saw chance, we see law*). **14.** allowance or start given to hunted animal or competitor in race; time of grace, respite. **15.** ∼-**abiding** (**ness**), obedient, obedience, to law; *law* AGENT; ∼-**breaker**, one who violates the law; ∼ **calf**, unstained calf-leather used for binding law-books;

*law*COURT[1]; ∼ **French**, the Anglo-Norman terms used in English law(-books); ∼'**giver**, one who makes (esp. code of) laws; ‖∼-**hand**, handwriting used in legal documents; ∼ **Latin**, barbarous Latin of early English statutes; ‖**Law Lord**, Lord of Appeal in Ordinary or other member of House of Lords qualified to perform its legal work; ∼'**maker**, legislator; *∼'**man**, police officer, sheriff, etc.; ∼ **merchant**, mercantile law; ∼ **officer**, legal functionary, ‖esp. Attorney-General or Solicitor-General or Lord Advocate; ∼-**stationer** (selling stationery needed by lawyers ‖and undertaking engrossing of documents); ∼'**suit**, prosecution of claim in lawcourt; ∼-**term**, (1) word or expression used in law, (2) period appointed for sitting of lawcourts. [OE *lagu* f. ON *lagu* pl. of *lag* something 'laid down' or fixed, cogn. w. LAY[3]]

law[2]. Var. of LAWK.

law'ful *a.* permitted, appointed, qualified, or recognized, by law, not illegal or (of child) illegitimate; *lawful* WIFE; hence ∼LY[2] *adv.*, ∼NESS *n.* [ME, f. LAW[1] + -FUL]

lawk(s) *int.* (vulg.) expr. astonishment; **lawk-a-mussy**, (vulg.) = Lord have mercy. [corrupt. of LORD, perh. after ALACK]

law'less *a.* (Of country etc.) where law is non-existent or inoperative; regardless of, disobedient to, uncontrolled by, law; unbridled, licentious; hence ∼LY[2] *adv.*, ∼NESS *n.* [ME, f. LAW[1] + -LESS]

lawn[1] *n.* fine woven linen or cotton, used e.g. for bishop's sleeves; hence ∼'Y[2] *a.* [ME, prob. f. *Laon* in France]

lawn[2] *n.* **1.** (expanse of) grass-covered land; close-mown turf-covered piece of pleasure-ground or garden; (arch.) glade. **2.** *∼ **bowling**, the game of BOWL[2]s; ∼-**mower**, machine with revolving cutters for mowing lawns; ‖∼ **sand**, mixture of sand with weed-killers and fertilizers for use on lawns; ∼-**sprinkler**, machine for watering lawns etc.; ∼ **tennis**, modification of tennis played by two persons (*singles*) or four (*doubles*) on usu. outdoor court ('grass' or 'hard') without walls. [f. ME *laund(e)* = glade, f. OF *launde* f. OCelt. *landā* LAND[1]]

lawrĕ'ncium (*ler-*) *n.* (Chem.) artificially produced transuranic metallic element. [f. E. O. *Lawrence*, Amer. physicist d. 1958 + -IUM]

Lawrĕ'ntian (*lerĕ'nshan*) *a.* of or pertaining to (the work of) T. E. or D. H. *Lawrence*. [f. T. E. *Lawrence*, Engl. military leader and author d. 1935, or D. H. *Lawrence*, Engl. author d. 1930, + -IAN, after L *Laurentius* Laurence]

lawyer (law'yer, loi'er) *n.* member of legal profession, esp. solicitor or ‖solicitor; person versed in law (*good, no,* etc., *lawyer*); **Penang** ∼, walking-stick of Penang palm [perh. f. native tree-name]; SEA *lawyer*. [ME *law(i)er* f. LAW[1]; see -ER[1], -YER]

lăx[1] *a.* loose, relaxed, not compact; negligent, careless, not strict, vague; (Phonet.) pronounced with vocal muscles relaxed; hence or cogn. ∼'ITY *n.*, ∼'LY[2] *adv.* [ME, f. L *laxus*, cogn. w. SLACK]

lăx[2] *n.* (Swedish or Norwegian) salmon. [OE *leax*, *læx*, = OHG *lahs*, ON *lax* f. Gmc *lahs-*]

lă'xative *a.* & *n.* (medicine) tending to cause evacuation of the bowels. [ME, f. OF *laxatif -ive* or f. LL *laxativus* f. L *laxare* loosen (as LAX[1]; see -ATIVE)]

lay[1] *n.* short lyric or narrative poem meant to be sung; narrative poem; song; (poet.) song of birds. [ME, f. OF *lai*, Prov. *lais*, of unkn. orig.]

lay[2] *a.* **1.** non-clerical, not in orders; of or done by layman or laity; non-professional, not expert, (esp. w. ref. to law or medicine). **2.** ∼ **brother,** ∼ **sister,** person who has taken habit and vows of religious order but is employed in manual labour and excused other duties; ∼ **clerk,** singing man in cathedral or collegiate church, parish clerk; ∼ **communion,** (1) membership of church as layman, (2) communicating of laity in Eucharist; ∼ **deacon,** man in deacon's order but also following secular employment; ∥∼ **lord,** peer who is not a LAW¹ Lord; ∼'**man,** one of the laity, non-expert in regard to some profession, art, or science, (esp. law or medicine); ∼ **reader,** layman licensed to conduct parts of Protestant religious services, non-professional reader (of book etc.); ∼ **rector,** layman receiving rectorial tithes; ∼ **sister** (see *lay brother*); *lay* VICAR. [ME, f. F *lai* f. eccl. L f. Gk *laïkos* LAIC]

lay³ *v.* (**laid**) & *n.* **1.** *v.t.* make prostrate (*lay* LOW¹); (of wind or rain) beat down (crops); cause (sea, wind, dust, misgivings, ghost) to subside, (Naut.) sail so far as to bring (land etc.) below horizon, (opp. RAISE). **2.** deposit; place in recumbent posture (∼ **to sleep** or **rest,** lit., or fig. = bury; ∼ one's **bones,** be buried *in* specified place); (of hen bird) produce (egg, or abs.); put down (amount, one's head or life, etc.) as wager, stake, (abs.) announce readiness to bet (*that*); (sl.) copulate with (usu. woman). **3.** place, set, apply, put, (∼ **heads together,** consult one another; *lay to* HEART; *lay hounds on scent*; ∼ **hold on** or **of,** seize, grasp, (fig.) benefit from (opponent's weak point etc.); *lay* one's *hopes on*; *lay* SIEGE *to*; *lay snare, trap, ambush*; *lay great* STORE *by* or *on*; *lay* WAIT²); locate (*scene*; *scene of tale is laid in London*); put (limb etc.) in specified position (*horse laid his ears back*; *lay* one's HAND¹ *on*; ∼ **hands on,** (1) seize, appropriate, (2) do violence to, esp. one*self* = commit suicide, (3) find: *cannot lay my hands on it*, (4) confirm or ordain by imposition of hands; aim (large gun); (w. compl.) bring into specified state (*lay land fallow*, *under water*); ∼ **person under obligation,** oblige him, **under necessity,** compel him, **under contribution,** make him contribute; *lay by the* HEEL¹*s*; ∼ **bare,** denude, reveal; ∼ **open,** (1) reveal, explain, (2) break skin of (part of body); ∼ **waste,** ravage. **4.** present, put forward, (*lay claim to*; ∼ **a charge,** make accusation; ∼ **an information,** bring indictment in legal form); place (facts, question) for consideration *before* person; ∥(Parl.) = *lay on* the TABLE 10 (to give information to the House of Commons); (of plaintiff) fix claim for (damages) *at* certain sum; impute (fault) *to* person's *charge, at* or *to* his *door*, (arch.) *to* him; represent (evil) as consequent *on* some cause. **5.** impose (penalty, command, obligation, burden, tax), cast (blame), (*up*)*on* (∼ **emphasis,** STRESS, **weight, on,** emphasize, treat as important); bring (stick etc.) down *on*; (abs.) ∼ **about** (colloq.) or **into** (sl.), belabour, ∼ **about** one, hit out on all sides, lit. or fig. **6.** dispose, arrange, esp. horizontally (foundation, floor, bricks, submarine cable; ∼ **table, cloth,** or **breakfast** etc., prepare table for meal; ∼ **the fire,** put fuel ready for lighting); make (strand, rope) by twisting yarn or strands; fix outlines of, devise (plan, plot); put (colour etc.) on a surface in layers; cover, coat, strew, (surface) *with* carpet, metal, straw, etc.; **laid paper** (with ribbed surface owing to wires used in making); **laid work,** embroidery with sewed-down thread along lines. **7.** *v.i.* (Naut. or vulg.) = LIE³; ∼ **on your oars,** stop rowing but keep oars out; ∥∼'**about,** habitual loafer or tramp. **8.** ∼ **aside,** put away, cease to use or practise or think of, abandon, save (money etc.) for future needs; ∼ **back,** cause to slope back from vertical (*laid-back* (sl.), relaxed); ∼ **by,** = *lay aside*; ∼-*by n.* (pl. ∼-*bys*), ∥extra strip alongside road to provide place for vehicles to stop without obstructing other traffic, similar arrangement on canal or railway, (Austral. & NZ) system of reserving article by deposit for later purchase; ∼ **down,** put on the ground etc. (∼ *down* one's *arms*, surrender), relinquish (office, hopes), pay or wager (money), sacrifice (one's life), (begin to) construct (ship, railway), formulate (rule, principle, course; *lay down the* LAW¹), set down (chart etc.) on paper, convert (land) into pasture (*in, to, under, with,* grass, clover, etc.), store (wine) in cellar; ∼ **in,** provide oneself with stock of; ∼ **off,** discharge (temporarily) owing to shortage of

work, (colloq.) desist; ∼-*off n.*, (period of) such temporary discharge, time of reduced activity; ∼ **on,** impose (tax, command, penalty), deal blows, inflict (blows, or *it*), ply (lash etc.), apply coat of (paint etc.; *lay it on* THICK or *with a* TROWEL), provide pipes etc. supplying (gas, water, electricity), provide (refreshments, entertainment, means of transport, etc.); ∼ **out,** spread, expose to view etc., prepare (body) for burial, (sl.) kill, (colloq.) put (person) out of action temporarily at football etc., expend (money), dispose (grounds, garden) according to a plan, (*refl.*) take pains *to* do; ∼'*out n.*, disposing or arrangement of ground etc., (in plans etc.) drawing showing arrangement, make-up of book, newspaper, advertisement, etc.; ∼ **up,** store, put by, save (money, or abs.), take (vehicle, ship) out of service, lay (rope; see sense 6), confine to bed or house. **9.** *n.* direction or amount of twist in rope-strands; way, position, or direction, in which something (esp. country) lies, lie (*∗lay of the land*); (sl.) line of business, job; (sl.) (partner, usu. woman, in) copulation; **in ∼,** (of hen) in condition to lay eggs; ∼-**day** (allowed for loading or unloading cargo); ∼'**shaft,** secondary or intermediate shaft for transmission of power in machine. [OE *lecgan*, = OS *leggian*, OHG *legen, lecken*, ON *leggja*, Goth. *lagjan* f. Gmc *∗leg-, ∗lag-* LIE³]

lay⁴. See LIE³.

lay'er *n.* & *v.* **1,** *n.* In vbl senses. **2.** thickness of matter (esp. one of several) spread over surface; ∼ **cake** (made in layers with filling between). **3.** (Hort.) shoot fastened into earth to strike root while attached to parent plant; ∼**stool,** root from which layers are produced. **4.** Hence ∼ED² (-erd) *a.* **5.** *v.t.* (Hort.) propagate as layer. **6.** *v.i.* (Of crops) be laid by wind or rain. [ME, f. LAY³+-ER¹]

layë'tte *n.* clothes, toilet articles, and bedding, needed for new-born child. [F, dim. of OF *laie* drawer f. MDu. *laege*; see -ETTE]

lay' figure (-ger) *n.* jointed wooden figure of human body used by artists for arranging drapery on etc.; unimportant person, nonentity, unreal character in novel etc. [*lay* f. obs. *layman* lay figure f. Du. *leeman* (obs. *led* joint)]

∥**lay'stall** (-awl) *n.* refuse heap. [f. LAY³+STALL¹]

lā'zar *n.* (arch.) poor and diseased person, esp. leper; ∼-**house,** = foll. [ME, f. med. L *lazarus* f. proper name (Luke 16:20)]

lazare't, -e'tto (*pl.* -os), *n.* hospital for diseased poor, esp. lepers; building or ship for quarantine; after part of ship's hold, used for stores. [(F *lazaret*) f. It. *lazzaretto* (*lazzaro* LAZAR)]

laze *v.* & *n.* (colloq.) **1.** *v.i.* be lazy **2.** *v.t.* pass (time) *away* in laziness. **3.** *n.* time spent in lazing. [back form. f. LAZY]

lä'zŭlī *n.* = LAPIS LAZULI. [abbr.]

lā'zÿ *a.* & *v.* **1.** *a.* unwilling to work; appropriate to or inducing indolence; (of river etc.) slow-moving. **2.** ∼-**bones,** lazy person; ∼ **Susan,** revolving food-stand for table; ∼-**tongs,** arrangement of zigzag levers for picking up distant objects. **3.** Hence **lā'zILÿ²** *adv.*, **lā'zINESS** *n.* **4.** *v.i.* & *t.* laze. [earlier *laysie, lasie, laesy,* perh. of LG orig.; cf. LG *lasich* idle]

lb. *abbr.* POUND¹ 1, pounds. [f. L *libra*]

l.b. *abbr.* leg-bye(s).

L/Bdr. *abbr.* Lance-Bombardier.

l.b.w. *abbr.* leg before wicket.

l.c. *abbr.* letter of credit; *loco citato*; lower case.

∥**LCC** *abbr.* (Hist.) London County Council.

∥**LCJ** *abbr.* Lord Chief Justice.

LCM *abbr.* least (or lowest) common MULTIPLE.

L/Cpl. *abbr.* Lance-Corporal.

Ld. *abbr.* Lord.

Ldg. *abbr.* Leading (Seaman etc.).

LDS *abbr.* Licentiate in Dental Surgery.

-le, -el, *suf.* **1.** Forming *ns.* w. dim. sense (*bramble*) or denoting appliance (*thimble, handle, bridle, girdle*), agent (*beadle*), etc., and *adjs.* f. *vbs.*, w. sense 'apt or liable to' (*brittle, fickle, nimble*) [ME f. OE -*el*(*a*), -(*e*)*le* n., -*ol*, -*ul*, -*el* a.]. **2.** Forming *ns.* mainly w. (orig.) dim. sense (*angle, castle, mantle, novel, tunnel*) or sense as -AL (*battle, cattle*) [ME -*el*(*le*) f. OF -*el* f. L -*ellus*,-*ellum* or OF -*ele* f. L -*ale*, or f. L -*aille* f. L -*alia* (as -AL), or f. F -*eille* f. L -*icula*, or f. L -*ulus* etc.]. **3.** Forming *vbs.* w. frequent. or dim. sense (*crumple, dazzle, nestle, snarl, twinkle, wriggle*) [ME -(*e*)*len* f. OE -*lian* f. Gmc *-*ilōjan*].

lea[1] *n.* (poet.) tract of open ground, esp. grassland. [OE *lēa*(*h*), cogn. w. OHG *lōh* grove, f. Gmc *-*lauh*- f. IE *-*louq*-]

lea[2] *n.* measure of yarn (300, 200, 120, or 80 yards, according to type and place). [ME *lee*, perh. f. F *lier* f. L *ligare* to bind]

LEA *abbr.* Local Education Authority.

leach *v.t. & i.* make (liquid) percolate through some material; subject (bark, ore, ash, soil) to action of percolating fluid; remove (soluble matter *away* or *out*) by such means, be removed thus. [prob. repr. OE *leccan* to water, f. WG *-*lakkjan*]

lead[1] (lĕd) *n., & v.t.* **1.** *n.* heavy easily fusible soft malleable base metal of dull pale bluish-grey colour (RED *lead*; **white** ~, mixture of lead carbonate and hydrated lead oxide used as pigment); = BLACK[1]*lead*, (hence) thin stick of graphite in or for pencil; bullet(s). **2.** lump of lead used in SOUND[2]ing water (**cast** or **heave the** ~, lower it from ship; ||SWING *the lead*). **3.** ||(in *pl.*) strips of lead used to cover roof, piece of (esp. horizontal) lead-covered roof; lead frames or cames holding glass of lattice or stained-glass window. **4.** (Print.) metal strip to give space between lines. **5.** ~ **pencil** (of graphite usu. enclosed in wood or in metal case); ~-**poisoning**, acute or chronic poisoning by taking of lead into the body; ~ **shot**, = SHOT[1] 2; ~'**sman** (-z-), sailor who heaves the lead; ~ **tetraethyl**, = TETRA*ethyl lead*; ~ **wool**, lead in a fibrous state, used for jointing water-pipes; ~-**work**, plumber's or glazier's work; ~-**works**, place where lead ore is smelted; ~'**wort**, = PLUMBAGO 2. **6.** Hence ~'LESS *a.* **7.** *v.t.* (esp. in *p.p.*) cover, weight, frame (panes), with lead; (Print.) separate lines of (printed matter) with leads; add lead (compound) to (petrol etc.). [OE *lēad*, = MLG *lōd*, MHG *lōt* plummet f. WG *-*lauda*]

lead[2] *v.* (**led**). **1.** *v.t.* cause to go with one (~ **captive**, take away as prisoner). **2.** (Of person, or fig. of motive, circumstance, etc.) conduct, guide, esp. by going in front (*led me to the house I was looking for; curiosity, chance, led him to Rome*); *lead* person a DANCE[2]; ~ person a (**dog's**) **life**, harass him constantly; *lead the* WAY 2. **3.** (Of commander) direct movements of. **4.** guide (person) by the hand or by contact, (animal) by halter etc., (**led horse**, spare horse led by groom etc.; **led captain**, hanger-on, toady, parasite); guide by persuasion (*is easier led than driven*; ~ **astray**, tempt to sin etc.; ~ **by the hand**, guide like a child; ~ **by the nose**, induce to do submissively all one wishes). **5.** guide actions or opinions of, bring by argument etc. *to* conclusions, induce *to do* (~ person **to suppose** etc., deceive him into thinking *that*); ply (witness) with leading questions. **6.** (Of road etc.) be route for (person, or usu. abs.) *to* or *into* place (*all roads lead to Rome*); ~ **to**, (fig.) have as result (*this led to confusion*). **7.** make (rope, water, etc.) go *through* pulley, channel, etc. **8.** pass, go through, spend, (life etc., esp. w. epithet: *lead a miserable existence, a double life*). **9.** have first place in (*lead the dance, the van, the world in sugar production*); (abs.) go first, be first at some point in race, be ahead in game (*Kent led on the first innings*), make one's start *with*. **10.** direct by example (*lead orchestra, band, chorus,* etc.), set (fashion); be official director or spokesman of (party), ||act as leading counsel in (case, or usu. abs.). **11.** *v.t. & i.* (Cards). play as first card, be first player, in trick; play one of (suit) when leading; ~ **away from**, lead card of suit-holding including (ace etc., usu. to one's

disadvantage); ~ **through,** cause holder of (ace etc.) to play to trick before another player (usu. to one's advantage); ~ **up to,** allow holder of (ace etc.) to play to trick after another player (usu. to one's disadvantage). **12.** ~ **away,** (usu. in *pass.*) induce to follow unthinkingly; ~-**in** *n.*, introductory matter, (Electr.) wire connecting radio receiver to external aerial; ~ **off,** begin (dance, conversation, or abs.); ~-**off** *n.*, commencement; ~ **on,** entice into going farther than was intended; *lead up the* GARDEN (*path*); ~ **up to,** form preparation for, serve to introduce, direct conversation towards, (subject). **13.** Hence ~'ABLE *a.* [OE *lǣdan*, = OHG *leiten*, OS *lēdjan*, ON *leitha* f. Gmc *-*laidhjan* (*-*laidhō* LOAD[1])]

lead[3] *n.* **1.** guidance given by going in front, example, (*follow the lead of*; **give** person **a** ~, encourage him by doing thing, e.g. leaping fence in hunting, first, (fig.) provide with clue). **2.** leading place, leadership, (*is in the lead; take the lead*; amount by which competitor is ahead of others (*a lead of five minutes, five miles*). **3.** artificial watercourse, esp. one leading to mill; (Electr.) conductor conveying current from source to place of use; distance advanced by screw in one turn; channel in ice-field; thong, string, strap, etc., for leading or controlling a dog; (Cards) act or right of playing first in game or to trick (**return** ~, lead suit already led by partner), card led; (Theatr.) (player of) chief part. **4.** ~ **screw** (moving the carriage of a lathe); ~ **story,** item of news given greatest prominence in newspaper etc.; ~ **time** (between initiation and completion of production process). [ME, f. prec.]

lea'den (lĕ'd-) *a.* (as) of lead; heavy, slow, burdensome, (*leaden limbs*); inert, depressing, (*leaden rule*); lead-coloured (*leaden skies*); *leaden* SEAL[2]. [OE *lēaden* (as LEAD[1], -EN[5])]

lea'der *n.* In vbl senses (FOLLOW-*my-leader*); **L~ of House** (**of Commons** or **of Lords**), member of Government with official initiative in business; || = LEADING[2] *counsel*; front horse in team or tandem (cf. WHEELER); *-conductor of orchestra; leading performer in orchestra, quartet, choir, etc., ||esp. leading first-violin player; shoot growing at apex of stem or principal branch; || = LEADING[2] *article*; tab to assist threading of film, tape, etc., on reel; (Print., in *pl.*) line of dots or dashes to guide eye; hence ~LESS *a.*, ~SHIP (1, 3, 4) *n.* [OE *lǣdere* (as LEAD[2], -ER[1])]

lea'ding[1] *n.* In vbl senses; *men* **of light and** ~, deservedly influential; ~-**rein** (to lead horse with); ~-**staff** (attached to ring in bull's nose); ~-**strings,** strings with which children were taught formerly to walk (*in* ~-*strings*, in state of pupillage). [ME, f. LEAD[2]+-ING[1]]

lea'ding[2] *a.* In vbl senses; ||ranking just below NCO (*leading aircraftman, seaman*); ||~ **article,** editorial expression of opinion at full length in newspaper; ~ **case,** (Law) case serving as precedent for deciding others; ||~ **counsel,** (1) senior barrister of two or more for one party on a case, (2) QC or senior counsel of circuit; ~ **edge,** foremost edge of aircraft's wing, etc., forward edge of propeller-blade, (Electr.) part of pulse in which amplitude increases, (opp. *trailing edge*); ~ **lady, man,** (taking chief part in play); ~ **light,** prominent influential person; ~ **motive,** leitmotiv; ~ **note** or *-tone,** seventh note of diatonic scale of any key, semitone below keynote; ~ **question** (prompting desired answer). [f. LEAD[2]+-ING[2]]

lea'ding[3] (lĕ'-) *n.* In vbl senses (esp. Print.). [f. LEAD[1]+-ING[1]]

leaf *n.* (*pl.* **leaves** *pr.* -vz) & *v.* **1.** *n.* relatively broad flat organ (usu. green) of plant springing from side of stem or branch or direct from root; (pop.) petal (cf. *rose-leaf*); (collect.) foliage (**fall of the** ~, autumn); state of having leaves out (*is in, comes into, leaf*); (collect.) leaves of tobacco or tea. **2.** single thickness of folded paper, esp. (= 2 pages) in book (*take a leaf out of* person's BOOK[1]; **turn over a new** ~, improve one's conduct). **3.** very thin sheet of metal, esp. gold or silver, or of horn, marble, talc, etc. **4.** hinged part or flap of door, shutter, table (also used of extra section inserted in expansible table), bridge (= bascule), or rifle-sight. **5.** *layer of fat around pig's kidneys. **6.** ∼-**green**, (of) the colour of green leaves; ∼-**insect** (having wings resembling leaf of plant); *∼-**lard** (made from leaf, sense 5); ∼-**miner**, caterpillar eating through leaves; ∼-**monkey**, langur; ∼-**mould**, soil composed chiefly of decaying leaves; ∼-**nosed bat** (with leaflike appendage to snout); ∼ **spring** (made of strips of metal); ∼-**stalk**, petiole. **7.** Hence ∼'AGE (1) *n.*, (-)∼ED² (-ft), ∼'LESS, ∼'Y², *adjs.* **8.** *v.i.* put forth leaves; ∼ **through**, = sense 9. **9.** *v.t.* *turn over leaves or pages of (book etc.). [OE *lēaf*, = OS *lōf*, OHG *loup*, ON *lauf*, Goth. *laufs* f. Gmc *laubhaʒ-, -am*]

lea′flèt *n.* **1.** young leaf; (Bot.) one division of compound leaf. **2.** small leaf of paper, or sheet or leaves folded but not stitched, with printed matter, esp. for distribution free of charge. [f. prec. + -LET]

league¹ (-g) *n.* (arch.) varying measure of travelling-distance, usu. about three miles. [ME, ult. f. LL *leuga, leuca*, of Gaulish orig.]

league² (-g) *n.* & *v.* **1.** *n.* agreement made for mutual protection and assistance or prosecution of common interests, parties (whether States or individuals) to such compact, (Solemn League and Covenant; ||Primrose League; **in** ∼ **with**, allied with). **2.** group of sports clubs who compete with each other for championship; class of contestants (in sports, or fig.: *in the big league*); ∼ **table**, list of these in order of rank; ||Rugby League. **3.** L∼ **of Nations** (established by the treaty of peace 1919 to try to prevent war, now replaced by United Nations). **4.** *v.t.* & *i.* join in league (*with*). [f. F *ligue* or f. It. *liga*, var. of *lega* f. *legare* bind f. L *ligare*]

lea′guer¹ (-ger) *n.* & *v.* = LAAGER. [f. Du. *leger* camp, cogn. w. LAIR]

lea′guer² (-ger) *n.* member of league. [f. LEAGUE² + -ER¹]

leak *n.*, & *v.* **1.** *n.* hole caused by injury, wear, etc., through which fluid makes way into or out of vessel that is immersed in or contains it or through a dike (SPRING¹ *a leak*); fluid thus passing through; such passage (**take a** ∼, (sl.) urinate); (escape of) electric charge from imperfectly insulated conductor, device controlling this; improper disclosure of secret information. **2.** *v.i.* & *i.* let fluid, (of fluid) pass, out or in through leak; improperly disclose (secret etc.); ∼ (**out**), (of secret etc.) be thus disclosed. **3.** Hence ∼'AGE *n.*, action of leaking, what leaks out or in, improper disclosure of secrets. [ME, prob. of LG orig.; cf. MDu. *lek* n. (cogn. w. ON *leki*), *lēken* v. (ON *leka*), f. Gmc *lek-*, *lak-* LACK]

lea′kŷ *a.* having leak(s); given to letting out secrets; hence ∼iNESS n. [f. prec. + -Y²]

leal *a.* (Sc.) loyal, honest, (LAND¹ *of the leal*). [ME f. AF; OF *leel, loial*, as LOYAL]

lean¹ *a.* & *n.* **1.** *a.* (Of person) thin, not plump; meagre, of poor quality, not nourishing, (*lean crops, diet*; ∼ **years**, years of scarcity); unremunerative; (of meat) consisting chiefly of muscular tissue, not of fat; hence ∼'NESS (-n-n-) *n.* **2.** *n.* lean part of meat. [OE *hlæne* f. Gmc *hlainjaʒ*]

lean² *v.* (∼ed *pr.* lēnd or lĕnt, *or* ||∼t *pr.* lĕnt) & *n.* **1.** *v.i.* incline one's body against something for support, support oneself, (of thing) be supported in sloping position, *against* or *on*; ∼ **on**, (sl.) try to coerce; ∼ **upon**, (Mil.) have as protection on flank. **2.** rely or depend (*up*)*on* (*lean on a* REED¹). **3.** incline body *back, forward, over, towards*, etc., (*lean over* BACKWARDS). **4.** stand obliquely, out of the perpendicular, (*leaning tower*). **5.** have tendency (*to* mercy etc.), be partial *to* or *towards* cause, opinion, or person, whence ∼'ING¹ (1) *n.* **6.** *v.t.* place (thing) in leaning position. **7.** ∼-**to**, (pl. ∼-*tos*) building with roof resting against side of larger building or wall. **8.** *n.* inclination, slope, (*has a decided*

lean to the right). [OE *hleonian, hlinian*, = OS *hlinon*, OHG (*h*)*linēn* f. Gmc *hli-*]

leap¹ *v.* (∼ed *pr.* lēpt *or* lĕpt, *or* ∼t *pr.* lĕpt). **1.** *v.i.* & *t.* jump (*leapt at the offer, into prominence; heart leaps up*; ∼ **to the eye**, be very obvious; LOOK¹ *before you leap*). **2.** ∼-**frog**, (*n.*) game in which player vaults with parted legs over another bending down, (*v.t.* & *i.*; -gg-) perform such vault (over), (fig.) overtake alternately. **3.** Hence ∼'ER¹ *n.* [OE *hlēapan* = OS -*hlōpan*, OHG *loufan*, ON *hlaupa*, Goth. -*hlaupan* f. Gmc *hlaupan*]

leap² *n.* jump (*leap in the* DARK²; **by** ∼**s and bounds**, with startlingly rapid progress); thing to be jumped; (Geol.) fault; ∼-**day**, 29 Feb.; ∼ **year**, (1) year with extra day, now 29 Feb. [perh. because fixed festivals after February in leap year fall two days of the week, instead of as usual one, later than in the preceding year], (2) intercalary year; ∼-*year proposal*, (joc.) proposal of marriage by woman to man, traditionally allowable only in leap year. [OE *hlȳp*, *hliep*, = OHG *hlouf*, ON *hlaup* f. Gmc *hlaupiʒ* (as prec.)]

learn (lĕrn) *v.* (∼ed *pr.* -nd *or* -nt, *or* ∼t). **1.** *v.t.* get knowledge of (subject) or skill in (art etc.) or ability *to* do, by study, experience, or being taught, (*from* study etc., *from* or *of* teacher). **2.** commit to memory (esp. ∼ **by heart** or rote). **3.** become aware by information or from observation *that, how*, etc. (**I am** or **have yet to** ∼, I do not know, usu. w. implication of disbelief); be informed of, ascertain. **4.** (arch., joc., or vulg.) teach. **5.** *v.i.* receive instruction, get knowledge or skill; become informed *of*. **6.** Hence ∼'ABLE *a.*, ∼'ER¹ *n.*; ∼er(-**driver**), one who has begun to drive a motor vehicle but has not yet passed the driving test. [OE *leornian* = OS *līnōn*, OHG *lirnēn, lernēn* f. Gmc *lis-*, *lais-*; cf. LORE¹]

lear′nèd (lĕr′-) *a.* having learned much by study; showing profound knowledge; ||(in conventionally courteous mention of lawyer in House of Commons, lawcourts, etc.) learned in the law (esp. *my learned* FRIEND *or brother*); (of language, PROFESSION, etc.) pursued or studied by, (of words in a language) introduced by, (of publication or society) concerned with interests of, learned persons; hence ∼LY² *adv.* [ME, f. prec. in sense 'teach' + -ED¹]

lear′ning (lĕr′-) *n.* In vbl senses; (possession of) knowledge got by study, esp. of language or literature or history as subjects of systematic investigation (**the new** ∼, studies, esp. of Greek, introduced into England in 16th c., the Renaissance. [OE *leornung* (as LEARN, -ING¹)]

lease *n.*, & *v.t.* **1.** *n.* contract by which one party (*lessor*), usu. in consideration of rent, conveys land or tenement to another (*lessee*) for specified time (*put out to, take a, lease; by* or *on lease*); **a new** ∼ **of** or ***on life**, prospect of continued (vigorous) living due to recovered health or removal of anxiety etc., or of further use of (thing) after repair etc.; ∼'hold(er), (person having) tenure, property held, by lease; L∼-**Lend**, = LEND-*Lease*. **2.** *v.t.* grant or take lease of; ∼'back, sale of property followed by lease of it back to vendor so that rent to buyer compensates cost of purchase. [ME, f. AF *les*, OF *lais, leis*, (*lesser, laissier* leave, f. L *laxare* make loose (*laxus*))]

leash *n.*, & *v.t.* **1.** *n.* thong by which hounds or coursing-dogs are held (**hold in** ∼, control; **straining at the** ∼, eager to begin); group of three hounds, hares, etc.; *dog*-LEAD³ 3; (Weaving) cord with eye to receive warp-thread extending between parallel laths of loom-heddle. **2.** *v.t.* connect, hold in, with leash. [ME, f. OF *lesse, laisse* f. spec. use of *laisser* let run on slack lead; see LEASE]

least, *a.*, *n.*, & *adv.* **1.** *a.* smallest, slightest, (**the** ∼, esp. after neg., any however small; least common MULTIPLE; *line of least* RESISTANCE); very small (species or variety, e.g. *least tern*). **2.** *n.* least amount (**to say the** ∼ (**of it**), to put the case moderately; ∼ **said soonest mended**, discussion will only make things worse); **at** ∼, at all events, even if a wider statement is disputable; **at (the)** ~, at the lowest computation; **(in) the** ~, in the smallest degree, at all. **3.** *adv.* in the least degree. [OE *lǣst, lǣsest* f. Gmc *laisistaz*, superl. of *laisiz* (LESS; see -EST¹)]

lea'stways (-z), **lea'stwīse** (-z), *advs.* (dial. or vulg.) or at least, or rather. [f. prec. + -WAYS, -WISE]

||**leat** *n.* open watercourse conducting water to mill etc. [OE *-gelǣt* (as Y- + root of LET²)]

lea'ther (lĕ'dh-) *n.*, & *v.t.* **1.** *n.* skin of animal prepared for use by tanning or similar process; **patent** ~ (with fine varnished surface); ~ **and** (prop. **or**) *prunella*, a matter of indifference, a difference in clothes only [see Pope *Essay on Man* iv. 204]; **nothing like** ~, one's own goods will serve all purposes. **2.** article, or part of one, made of leather; piece of leather for polishing with; thong (esp. *stirrup-leather*); (sl.) cricket-ball or football; (in *pl.*) leggings or breeches. **3.** ~-**back,** largest existing turtle, with flexible shell; ~ **carp** (scaleless variety); ~**cloth,** strong fabric coated to resemble leather; ~-**head,** (sl.) stupid person; ~-**jacket,** ||crane-fly grub with tough skin; ~-**neck,** (Naut. sl.) soldier or (esp. US) marine [w. ref. to leather stock formerly worn]. **4.** Hence ~E'TTE (2) *n.,* ~**n** (arch.) [-EN⁵], ~Y² (esp. of meat etc., tough), *adjs.* **5.** *v.t.* cover with leather; wipe or polish with leather; beat, thrash, (orig. w. leather thong). [OE *lether,* = OS *lethar,* OHG *ledar,* ON *lethr* f. Gmc *lethram* f. IE *letrom*]

lea'theroid (lĕ'dh-) *n.* cotton paper chemically treated and resembling rawhide. [f. prec. + -OID]

leave¹ *n.* **1.** permission (*to* do); **by your** ~ (apology, often iron., for taking liberty, making unwelcome statement, etc.; *without a 'with your* ~' *or a 'by your* ~', (colloq.) without even asking permission); **take** ~ **to,** venture or presume to. **2.** (In Services, offices, schools) ~ (**of absence**), permission to be absent from duty, period for which this lasts (**on** ~, absent thus; SICK¹- -*leave;* ||TICKET *of leave*). **3. take** (one's) ~ (**of**), bid farewell (to); **take** ~ **of** one's **senses,** go mad; hence ~-**tāk**ING¹ (1) *n.* **4.** FRENCH *leave;* WAY-*leave.* [OE *lēaf,* = OHG *louba* f. WG *laubha;* cf. LIEF, LOVE¹]

leave² *v.t.* (**left**), & *n.* **1.** *v.t.* cause to or let remain, depart without taking, have at time of one's death, (*leaves a wife and three sons; has left his gloves, a slimy trail, a permanent scar, a bad impression on us; six from seven leaves one;* ~ **much** etc. **to be desired,** be unsatisfactory); bequeath; **be left with,** retain (feeling etc.), be burdened with (responsibility etc.). **2.** abstain from consuming or dealing with; (in *pass.*) remain over or *over;* **left-overs,** (esp.) food not consumed at earlier meal. **3.** let remain in specified state; *this* ~**s me cool** or **cold,** does not impress or excite me; ~ **it at that,** (colloq.) abstain from comment or further action; **be well** etc. **left** (provided for by legacy etc.); ~ **undone, unsaid,** etc., not do (up), refrain from saying, etc. **4.** commit or refer *to* another agent etc. than oneself (*nothing was left to chance*); ~ **him to himself,** do not try to control him; ~ **it to me,** let me deal with it. **5.** allow (person or thing) *to* do something without interference or assistance (*leave the future to take care of itself*); ~ **be,** (colloq.) not interfere with. **6.** deposit, entrust, (thing, instructions, message), station (person), to be seen to, delivered, etc., or to discharge function, in one's absence; ||**left luggage** (deposited at railway office etc. for later retrieval); ~ **card on** person (arch., as equivalent of formal call). **7.** go away from, cease to remain in or on, (*left him quite well an hour ago; leave this* or *here; leave the track, the* ROOM); (abs.) depart (*we leave tomorrow; often for* destination). **8.** pass (object) so that it is in specified relative direction (*leave the church on the left*). **9.** cease to reside at (place), attend (school), belong to (society), or serve (employer); also abs. (*I am leaving at Christmas*). **10.** abandon, forsake, desert, (esp. *leave in the* LURCH¹); **get left,** (colloq.) be deserted or worsted; **left at the post,** beaten from start of race; **left for dead** etc., abandoned as being beyond rescue. **11.** ~

alone, not have dealings with, not interfere with (*leave* WELL³ *alone*); ~ **behind,** go away without, leave as consequence or visible sign of passage, pass; ~ **go,** (vulg.) relax one's hold; ~ **hold of,** cease holding; ~ **off,** cease to wear, discontinue (habit, do*ing, work*), (abs.) come to or make an end; ~ **out,** omit, not include; ||~ **over,** let stand over for the time being. **12.** Hence **lea'ver¹** *n.,* **lea'ving¹** (2) *n.* (usu. in *pl.*). **13.** *n.* position in which player leaves the balls in billiards, croquet, etc. [OE *lǣfan,* = OS *-lēbian,* OHG *leiban,* ON *leifa,* Goth. *-laibjan* f. Gmc *laibhjan* remain (*laibhō* remainder)]

leaved (-vd) *a.* having leaves; (in *comb.*) having leaf or leaves of specified kind or number (*four-leaved clover*). [ME, f. LEAF + -ED²]

lea'ven (lĕ'-) *n.,* & *v.t.* **1.** *n.* substance added to dough to produce fermentation, esp. yeast, or fermenting dough reserved for purpose; (fig.) spreading and transforming influence (Matt. 13:33), tinge or admixture *of* some quality; **the old** ~, traces of unregenerate state (1 Cor. 5:6, 7). **2.** *v.t.* ferment (dough) with leaven; permeate and transform, modify *with* tempering element. [ME f. OF *levain* f. Gallo- -Rom. spec. use of L *levamen* relief (*levare* lift)]

leaves. See LEAF.

Lëbane'se (-z) *a.* & *n.* (*pl.* same). (native or inhabitant) of Lebanon. [f. *Lebanon* in SW Asia + -ESE]

lebensraum (lā'benzrowm) *n.* (Hist. or fig.) territory which the Germans believed was needed for their natural development as a nation. [G, = living-space]

lĕ'cher *n.* lewd or unchaste man, fornicator, debauchee; so ~OUS *a.,* **lĕ'chERY** (4) *n.* [ME, f. OF *lecheor* etc. (*lechier* live in debauchery or gluttony, f. Frank. *likkōn* f. Gmc *likkōjan* lick)]

lĕ'cithin *n.* complex fatty substance containing phosphorus and found in egg-yolk etc.; preparation of this, used to emulsify foods etc. [f. Gk *lekithos* egg-yolk + -IN]

lĕ'ctern *n.* reading-desk or singing-desk in church, esp. that for the lessons; *similar desk for lecturer etc. [ME *lettorne* f. OF *let(t)run,* med. L *lectrum* (*legere lect-* read)]

lĕ'ction *n.* text-reading found in particular copy or edition. [f. L *lectio* reading (as prec.; see -ION)]

lĕ'ctionarў *n.* book containing, list of, portions of Scripture appointed to be read at divine service. [ME, f. med. L *lectionarium* (as prec.; see -ARY¹)]

lĕ'ctor *n.* reader (esp. of lessons in church service, or in university). [L (*legere lect-* read; see -OR)]

lĕ'cture *n.* & *v.* **1.** *n.* discourse before audience or class on given subject, usu. by way of instruction; admonition, reproof, (**read** person **a** ~, reprove him). **2.** *v.i.* deliver lecture(s) (*on* subject). **3.** *v.t.* instruct or entertain (class, audience, etc.) by lecture; admonish, reprimand. **4.** Hence **lĕ'ctur**ER¹ (-kcher-) *n.* [ME f. OF, or f. med. L *lectura* f. L (as prec.; see -URE)]

lĕ'ctureship (-kchersh-) *n.* office of lecturer. [f. prec. + -SHIP (irreg. formation)]

lĕ'cўth|**us** *n.* (*pl.* ~**i** *pr.* -ī). (Gk Ant.) narrow-necked vase or flask. [f. Gk *lēkuthos*]

lĕd. See LEAD².

LED *abbr.* light-emitting diode.

le'derhōsen (lā-; -z-) *n.* leather shorts as worn by men in Bavaria etc. [G, = leather trousers]

lĕdge *n.* narrow horizontal surface projecting from wall etc.; shelflike projection on side of rock or mountain; ridge of rocks, esp. below water; (Mining) stratum of metal-bearing rock; hence **lĕ'dg**Y², **lĕdg**ED² (-jd), *adjs.* [perh. f. ME *legge* LAY³]

lĕ'dger *n.* & *a.* **1.** *n.* principal book of the set used for recording trade transactions, containing debtor-and- -creditor accounts; horizontal timber in scaffolding, parallel to face of building; flat gravestone; ~-**tackle,** kind of fishing-tackle in which lead weight keeps bait on bottom. **2.** *a.* (Mus.) = LEGER. [ME, f. senses of Du. *ligger* and *legger* (*liggen* LIE³, *leggen* LAY³; see -ER¹), & pronunc. of ME *ligge, legge,* (-je)]

lee *n.* shelter given by neighbouring object (*under the* *lee of*); ∼ **(side)**, sheltered side, side away from wind, (opp. *windward, weather side*); ∼**-board,** plank frame fixed to side of flat-bottomed vessel and let down into water to diminish leeway; *lee gage* or GAUGE¹ 2; *lee* HELM²; ∼ **shore,** shore to leeward of ship; ∼'**way,** lateral drift of ship to leeward of desired course, (fig.) allowable deviation, *margin of safety; make up* ∼*way,* (fig.) struggle out of bad position, recover lost time etc. [OE *hlēo,* = OS *hleo, hlea,* ON *hlé* f. Gmc *hlēw-]

leech¹ *n.* (arch., poet., or joc.) physician, healer; ∼'**craft,** art of healing. [OE *lǣce,* = OS *lāki,* OHG *lāhhi,* Goth. *lēkeis* f. Gmc *lǣkjaz* f. IE *lēgios*]

leech² *n.* **1.** aquatic blood-sucking worm of class Hirudinea, esp. *Hirudo medicinalis* formerly much used medicinally for bleeding; **stick like a** ∼ (persistently). **2.** person who extorts profit from others. [OE *lǣce,* = MDu. *lake,* assim. to prec.]

leech³ *n.* perpendicular or sloping side of square sail; side of fore-and-aft sail away from mast or stay. [ME, perh. rel. to ON *lik,* a nautical term of uncert. meaning]

Lee-E'nfield (-ě'-) *n.* type of rifle in use by British and other armies since 1900. [f. J. P. *Lee,* Amer. designer of bolt action d. 1904, + *Enfield* near London, where form of rifling was designed]

leek *n.* vegetable *(Allium porrum)* related to onion, but with lower leaves and bulb in cylindrical white form; this as Welsh national emblem; **eat the** ∼, pocket affront (see Shak. *Henry V* v. 1. 10). [OE *lēac,* = OHG *louh,* ON *laukr* f. Gmc *laukaz, -am*]

leer¹ *v.i.,* & *n.* glance (esp. sideways) with sly, lascivious, or malign expression. [perh. f. obs. *leer* cheek f. OE *hlēor,* as though 'to glance over one's cheek']

leer². Var. of LEHR.

leer'y *a.* (sl.) knowing, sly; wary *of.* [perh. f. obs. *leer* looking askance f. LEER¹, + -Y²]

lees (-z) *n. pl.* sediment of wine etc. (**drink, drain, to the** ∼, lit. or fig.); dregs, refuse. [pl. of MF f. OF *lie,* f. med. L *lia* f. Gaulish *lig(j)a*]

leet¹ *n.* (esp. Hist.) (**Court**) ∼, yearly or half-yearly court of record that lords of certain manors might hold; its jurisdiction or district. [ME, f. AF *lete* (= AL *leta*), of unkn. orig.]

leet² *n.* (Sc.) selected list of candidates for some office; **short** ∼, = SHORT list. [ME *lite* etc., prob. f. AF & OF *lit(t)e,* var. of *liste* LIST¹]

lee'ward (or, esp. Naut., loo'erd) *a., adv.,* & *n.* **1.** *a.* & *adv.* on or towards the sheltered side (opp. *windward*). **2.** *n.* this direction *(to leeward; on the leeward of*); hence ∼LY¹ *a.,* (of ship) apt to fall to leeward. [f. LEE + -WARD]

left¹ *a., adv.,* & *n.* **1.** *a.* (opp. RIGHT¹). on or towards that side of human body which in the majority of persons has the less-used hand, on or towards that part of an object which is analogous to person's left side or (with opposite sense) which is nearer to spectator's left hand *(left side, eye,* etc.; *left flank* of army etc.); *left* BANK¹, BOWER³; (Polit., often L∼) of the left (see sense 4); **have two** ∼ **feet,** be clumsy; ∼ **field,** (Baseball) part of field on third-base side, to catcher's left; ∼ **hand,** hand of left side, region or direction on left side of person *(at, on, to,* one's *left hand*); *marry* **with the** ∼ **hand,** morganatically (see LEFT-HANDED); ∼**-hand,** placed on the left hand *(left-hand* DRIVE²), done with the left hand *(left-hand blow),* (of rope) twisted counter-clockwise; ∼**-hand screw,** LEFT-HANDED screw; **over the** ∼ **(shoulder,** now rare), sl. phr. denoting that what is said is to be taken with a negative; ∼ **turn** (that brings one's front to face as one's left side did before); ∼ **wing** (of army, football etc. team, or political party, cf. sense 4), whence ∼**-wi'nger,** member of this; hence ∼'MOST *a.,* ∼'WARD *a.* & *adv.,* ∼'WARDS *adv.* **2.** *adv.* on or to the left side; ∼ **and right,** = RIGHT⁴ *and left.* **3.** *n.* left--hand part or region or direction; left-hand side of stage when facing audience; (Boxing) (blow with) left

hand; (in marching etc.) left foot; left wing of army. **4.** (Polit., often L∼). (In continental legislatures) more radical section of legislative chamber seated on president's left; radicals collectively; more advanced or innovative section of any group; hence ∼'ISH¹ *a.,* ∼'ISM (3) *n.,* principles or policy of the political left, ∼'IST (2) *n.* [ME *lüft, lift, left,* f. OE *lyft,* orig. sense 'weak, worthless' in OE *lyft-ādl* paralysis]

left². See LEAVE².

left-hä'ndèd *a.* **1.** having left hand more serviceable than right, using it by preference; awkward, clumsy; ambiguous, double-edged, of doubtful sincerity or validity, (esp. of compliment, also occas. of marriage); (of marriage) morganatic [from German custom by which bridegroom gave bride his left hand in such marriages]. **2.** (Of tool etc.) made to suit use of, (of blow) struck with, left hand; towards the left, turning to left; (of screw) advanced by turning to left. **3.** Hence ∼LY² *adv.,* ∼NESS *n.* [f. LEFT¹ *hand* + -ED²]

left-hä'nder *n.* left-handed person (esp. in games) or blow. [f. LEFT¹ *hand* + -ER¹]

le'fty, le'ftie, *n.* (colloq.) left-handed person; left--winger in politics. [f. LEFT¹ + -Y³]

leg *n.,* & *v.t.* (**-gg-**). **1.** *n.* organ of support and locomotion in animal, esp. lower limb of human, body, part of this from hip to ankle; SEA-*legs.* **2.** the BOOT¹ *is on the other leg; feel* or **find** one's ∼s, become able to stand or walk; **give** person **a** ∼ **up,** help him to mount or to get over obstacle (lit. or fig.); **have no** ∼**s,** (of golf-ball etc., colloq.) have not enough momentum to reach desired point; **have the** ∼**s of,** be able to go faster than; **keep** one's ∼**s,** not fall; **on** one's or **its last** ∼**s,** near death or end of usefulness etc.; **on** one's ∼**s,** (1) standing esp. to make speech, (2) well enough to walk about; **pull** person's ∼, deceive him jokingly; **shake a** ∼, (sl.) (1) dance, (2) make a start; **show a** ∼, (sl.) get out of bed; **stand on** one's **own** ∼**s,** be self-reliant or independent; **has not a** ∼ **to stand on,** cannot support argument by facts or sound reasons; **stretch** one's ∼**s,** take walking exercise; **take** to one's ∼**s,** run away. **3.** (esp. hind) leg of animal as food; leg of bird as food; ∼**-of-mutton sail,** sleeve, (so shaped). **4.** (arch.) obeisance made by drawing back one leg and bending other. **5.** (Cricket). part of field on playing batsman's side and behind or just in front of his wicket (opp. OFF; *hit to leg;* ∼ **stump,** stump nearest this; ∼ **break** etc., deviation of ball from leg side; *leg* SLIP², LONG¹, SHORT, SQUARE², *leg,* fieldsmen at various positions there). **6.** artificial leg *(cork, wooden,* etc., *leg).* **7.** part of garment covering (part of) leg. **8.** more or less leg-shaped support, pole, prop, of machine etc., or support of chair, table, bed, etc.; one branch of forked object; side of triangle other than base or hypotenuse. **9.** (Naut.) run made on single tack (usu. *long, short, leg).* **10.** (colloq.) one of two or three games constituting a round; section of relay race; hop or stage of long-distance flight or journey. **11.** *leg* BAIL¹; ∼ **before wicket,** (of batsman) out because of illegally obstructing ball with part of body other than hand; *leg-*BYE¹; ∼**-guard,** pad in cricket; *leg-*IRON¹; ∼'**man,** person employed to go about gathering news etc.; ∼**-pull,** (colloq.) joking attempt to deceive person; ∼**-rest,** support for seated invalid's leg; ∼**-room,** space to extend legs of seated person; ∼**--show,** theatrical performance by scantily dressed women; ∼ **theory,** (Cricket) bowling to leg with fieldsmen massed on that side; ∼ **trap,** (Cricket) group of fieldsmen near wicket on leg side. **12.** Hence (-)∼GED² (-gd), ∼'LESS, *adjs.* **13.** *v.t.* ∼ **it,** walk or run hard. **14.** propel (boat) through canal--tunnel by pushing with legs against tunnel-sides, whence ∼'GER¹ (-g-) *n.* [ME, f. ON *leggr* f. Gmc *lagjaz*]

le'gacy *n.* sum of money or article bequeathed; material or immaterial thing handed down by predecessor; ∼**-hunter,** person who pays court to another to secure legacy. [ME, f. OF *legacie* legateship, f. med. L *legatia* (as LEGATE[2]; see -ACY)]

le′gal *a.* **1.** of, based on, falling within province of, occupied with, law; ∼ **aid,** payment from public funds allowed, in cases of need, to help pay for legal advice or proceedings; ∼ **fiction,** assertion accepted as true (though probably fictitious) to achieve useful purpose esp. in legal matters; *legal* PROCEEDINGS, SEPARATION. **2.** required or appointed by law; *∼ **holiday,** = ||BANK[3] *holiday*; *legal* TENDER[2]. **3.** recognized by law, as distinguished from equity. **4.** lawful; hence ∼IZE (3) *v.t.* **5.** (Theol.) of the Mosaic law; of salvation by works not faith. **6.** Hence ∼LY[2] *adv.* [f. F *légal* or f. L *legalis* (*lex legis* law; see -AL), cf. LEAL, LOYAL]

le′gal|ism *n.* exaltation of law or formula, red tape; (Theol.) preference of the Law to the Gospel, doctrine of justification by works; so ∼IST (2) *n.*, ∼i′stIC *a.* [f. prec. + -ISM]

lega′lity *n.* lawfulness; = prec. [f. F *légalité* or f. med. L *legalitas* (as LEGAL; see -ITY)]

le′gate[1] *n.* **1.** ecclesiastic deputed to represent pope; ∼ **a latere** (ah lă′terā), one of highest class and full powers; hence **le′gat**INE[1] (-īn) *a.* **2.** (Rom. Hist.) deputy of general, (deputy of) governor of province. **3.** (arch.) ambassador, delegate. **4.** Hence ∼SHIP (-tsh-) *n.* [OE, f. OF *legat* f. L *legatus* p.p. (as n.) of *legare* commission]

lega′t|e[2] *v.t.* bequeath (often *give and legate*); so ∼OR *n.* [f. L *legare* bequeath + -ATE[3]]

legatee′ *n.* recipient of legacy. [f. prec. + -EE]

lega′tion *n.* sending of legate or deputy; body of deputies; diplomatic minister and his suite (esp. when he does not rank as ambassador), his official residence; legateship. [ME f. OF, or f. L *legatio* (as LEGATE[1]; see -ION)]

lega′tō (-ah′-) *a., adv.,* & *n.* (*pl.* ∼s). (Mus.) (passage to be performed) in smooth connected manner, without breaks. [It., = bound, p.p. of *legare* f. L *ligare* bind]

le′gend *n.* **1.** traditional story popularly regarded as historical, myth, such literature or tradition; (colloq.) (subject of) popular but unfounded belief(s) (*became a legend in his own lifetime*); hence ∼RY (5) *n.* **2.** inscription or motto, esp. on coin or medal; (Print.) caption; wording on map etc. explaining symbols used. **3.** (Hist.) story of a saint's life, collection of lives of saints or similar stories, esp. **the (Golden) L**∼, a particular 13th-c. collection. [ME in sense 3, f. OF *legende* f. med. L *legenda* what is to be read, neut. pl. gerundive of L *legere* read]

le′gendary *a.* of or connected with legends; described in legend; (colloq.) remarkable enough to be a subject of legend. [f. med. L *legendarius* (as prec.; see -ARY[1])]

le′ger *a.* (Mus.) ∼ **line,** short line added for notes above or below range of staff. [var. of LEDGER]

le′gerdemain *n.* sleight of hand, conjuring tricks, juggling; trickery, sophistry. [ME, f. F *léger de main* light of hand, dextrous]

le′gging (-g-) *n.* (usu. in *pl.*). outer covering of leather etc. for leg from knee to ankle. [f. LEG + -ING[1]]

le′gg|y (-gī) *a.* lanky-legged (esp. of boy, colt, puppy); (of woman) having attractively long legs; hence ∼INESS *n.* [f. LEG + -Y[2]]

leghŏrn (-gŏ′rn) *n.* (hat of) fine plaited straw; (*L*∼) (bird of) small hardy breed of domestic fowl. [imported f. *L*∼ (*Livorno*) in Italy]

le′g|ible *a.* (Of handwriting or print) clear, capable of being read; hence ∼IBI′LITY *n.*, ∼IBLY *adv.* [ME, f. LL *legibilis* (*legere* read; see -IBLE)]

le′gion (-jŏn) *n.* **1.** division of 3,000–6,000 men, including complement of cavalry, in ancient Roman army; ||**Royal British L**∼, national association of ex-service men (and now women) formed 1921; ***American L**∼, similar association formed 1919; **foreign** ∼, body of foreign volunteers in modern, esp. French, army. **2.** vast host, multitude, or number (**their name is L**∼, **they are** ∼, they are number-

less; cf. Mark 5:9). **3. L**∼ **of Honour,** French order of distinction founded 1802. **4.** Hence ∼ED[2] (-nd) *a.*, (poet.) arrayed in legions. [ME f. OF, f. L *legio -onis* (*legere* choose; see -ION)]

le′gionary (-jŏ-) *a.* & *n.* **1.** *a.* of legion(s). **2.** *n.* member of a legion. [f. L *legionarius* (as prec.; see -ARY[1])]

lēgionnair′e (-jŏ-) *n.* member of foreign legion; member of American or Royal British Legion; ∼**s′ disease,** form of bacterial pneumonia first identified after outbreak at American Legion meeting 1976. [f. F *légionnaire* (as LEGION)]

le′gislāte *v.i.* enact laws; make provision by laws *for*. [back-form. f. foll.]

lēgislā′tion *n.* (enacting of) laws; hence **le′gisl**ATIVE *a.* [f. LL *legis latio* (*lex legis* law, *latio* proposing f. *lat-* p.p. st. of *ferre* bring; see -ION)]

le′gislātor *n.* lawgiver; member of legislative body. [as LEGISLATION; see -OR)]

le′gislāture *n.* legislative body of a State. [f. prec. + -URE]

le′gist *n.* person versed in law. [ME, f. F *légiste* or f. med. L *legista* f. L *lex legis* law; see -IST]

legit′ *a.* & *n.* (colloq.) legitimate (drama or theatre). [abbr.]

legi′tim|ate[1] *a.* **1.** (Of child) lawfully begotten and born, esp. by persons lawfully married to each other; (of parent, birth, descent, etc.) with, of, through, etc., legitimate children. **2.** lawful, proper, regular, conforming to standard type; the ∼**ate drama** or **theatre,** body of plays of recognized merit, normal comedy and tragedy as dist. from musical comedy, farce, revue, etc. **3.** (Of sovereign's title) based on strict hereditary right; (of sovereign etc.) having legitimate title. **4.** logically admissible. **5.** Hence ∼ACY *n.*, ∼**ate**LY[2] (-tlī) *adv.*, ∼**at**IZE (3) *v.t.* [f. med. L *legitimatus*, p.p. of *legitimare* (see foll., -ATE[2])]

legi′tim|āte[2] *v.t.* make legitimate by decree, enactment, or proof; justify, serve as justification for; hence ∼A′TION *n.* [f. med. L *legitimare* f. L *legitimus* lawful (*lex legis* law) + -ATE[3]]

legi′tim|ism *n.* adherence to sovereign or pretender whose claim is based on direct descent (esp. in Spanish and French politics); so ∼IST (2) *n.* & *a.* [f. F *légitimisme* (*légitime* legitimate f. L; see prec., -ISM)]

legi′tim|īz|e, -īs|e (-īz), *v.t.* make legitimate; hence ∼A′TION *n.* [f. as LEGITIMATE[2], + -IZE]

le′gūme *n.* edible pod of leguminous plant; vegetable used for food. [f. F *légume* f. L *legumen -minis* (*legere* pick), because pickable by hand]

legū′minous *a.* of or like the botanical family Leguminosae (e.g. pea and bean), having seeds in pods and usu. root-nodules able to fix nitrogen. [f. mod. L *leguminosus* (as prec.; see -OUS)]

lehr (lēr) *n.* annealing-furnace for glass. [17th c.; orig. unkn.]

lei (lā, lā′ē) *n.* Polynesian garland of flowers. [Hawaiian]

Leibni′zian (lībnī′ts-) *a.* & *n.* (follower) of the philosophy of Leibniz (regarding matter as a multitude of monads and assuming pre-established harmony between spirit and matter). [f. G. W. *Leibniz*, Ger. philosopher d. 1716 + -IAN]

Lei′cester (le′ster) *n.* kind of firm usu. orange-coloured cheese orig. made in Leicestershire. [∼ in England]

Leics. *abbr.* Leicestershire.

leishmani′as|is (lē-) (*pl.* ∼es *pr.* -ēz). disease due to parasitic protozoan of genus *Leishmania*. [f. W. B. *Leishman*, Brit. physician d. 1926 + -I- + -ASIS]

lei′ster (lē′-) *n.*, & *v.t.* (pierce with) pronged salmon-spear. [f. ON *ljóstr* (*ljósta* to strike)]

lei′sure (le′zher) *n.* (opportunity to do, for, afforded by) free time, time at one's own disposal; **wait** etc. person's ∼, wait till he has leisure; **at** ∼, (1) not occupied, (2) deliberately, without hurry; **at** one's ∼, when one has time; hence ∼LESS (-erl-) *a.* [ME f. AF *leisour*, OF *leisir* f. n. use of L *licēre* be allowed; see -URE]

lei′sured (lĕ′zherd) *a.* having (ample) leisure. [f. prec. + -ED²]

lei′surel|y (lĕ′zher-) *a.* & *adv.* **1.** *a.* having, acting or done at, leisure, deliberate; hence ~iNESS *n.* **2.** *adv.* deliberately, without haste. [f. LEISURE + -LY¹,²]

lei′tmōtiv, -if, (lī′tmōtēf) *n.* (Mus. etc.) theme associated throughout piece or work with some person, situation, or sentiment. [G (as LEAD², MOTIVE¹)]

LEM *abbr.* lunar excursion module.

lĕ′man *n.* (arch.) lover, sweetheart; unlawful lover or (now usu.) mistress. [ME *leofman* (as LIEF, MAN¹)]

lĕ′mma *n.* (*pl.* ~**ta** *or* ~**s**). assumed or demonstrated proposition used in argument or proof; argument or subject of literary composition, dictionary entry, annotation, etc., prefixed as heading; motto appended to picture etc. [L, f. Gk *lēmma -matos* thing assumed, f. root of *lambanō* take]

lĕ′mmė *v.* (colloq.) = *let me*. [contr.]

lĕ′mming *n.* small arctic rodent of genus *Lemmus* etc., of which one species migrates in large numbers and has been reputed to continue headlong into the sea and drown. [Norw.]

lĕ′mon¹ *n.* **1.** pale-yellow oval acid-juiced fruit; **salt(s) of** ~, potassium oxalate used in removing ink-stains or rust. **2.** tree (*Citrus limon*) bearing lemons **3.** pale-yellow colour. **4.** (sl.) unattractive girl, unsatisfactory person or thing, simpleton, failure. **5.** ~ **balm,** mint plant (*Melissa officinalis*) with leaves smelling and tasting of lemon; *lemon* CHEESE¹ or *curd*; ~**-drop,** boiled sweet flavoured with lemon; ~ **grass,** fragrant tropical grass of genus *Cymbopogon* yielding oil smelling of lemon; ~**-plant,** lemon VERBENA; ~ **pudding** (flavoured with lemon); ||~ **squash,** drink of lemon-juice, crushed lemons, and other ingredients, often sold in concentrated form; ~**-squeezer,** instrument for pressing juice out of lemon; *lemon* THYME, VERBENA. **6.** Hence ~Y² *a.* [ME, f. OF *limon* f. Arab. *līma*; cf. LIME²]

lĕ′mon² *n.* ~ (**sole**), kind of plaice resembling sole. [f. F *limande*]

lĕmonȧ′de *n.* effervescent or still drink of lemon juice etc.; synthetic substitute for this. [f. LEMON¹ + -ADE 1]

lĕ′mur *n.* nocturnal mammal of Madagascar, of genus *Lemur*, allied to monkeys but with pointed muzzle; hence **lĕ′mur**INE¹, **lĕ′mur**OID, *adjs.* & *ns.* [mod. L, f. L *lemures* pl. spirits of the dead, from its spectre-like face]

lĕnd *v.t.* (lent). **1.** grant (*to* person) use of (thing) on understanding that it or its equivalent shall be returned; allow use of (money) at interest; *lending* LIBRARY. **2.** bestow, contribute, (something of temporary service or effect, as enchantment, aid, dignity); ~ **an ear** or one's **ears,** listen, ~ **a** (helping) **hand,** help. **3.** accommodate one*self* to some policy or purpose; (of thing) ~ *itself* to, be serviceable for. **4.** L~-Lease, arrangement (1941) whereby US supplied equipment etc. to UK and allies, orig. as loan in return for use of British-owned military bases. **5.** Hence ~′ABLE *a.,* ~′ER¹, ~′ING¹ (1, 4), *ns.* [ME, earlier *lĕne*(*n*) f. OE *lǣnan* (*lǣn* LOAN¹)]

lĕngth (-ngth, -ngkth) *n.* **1.** measurement from end to end; greater of two or greatest of three dimensions of a body; extent of a garment in vertical direction when worn; MEASURE² one's *length*. **2.** extent in, of, or with regard to, time (*a stay of some length; the length of a speech*). **3.** distance thing extends (*at* ARM¹'*s length; ships a cable's length apart*); length of horse, boat, etc., as measure of lead in race. **4.** degree of thoroughness in action (usu. w. *go; prepared to go* (to) *all lengths* or *any length*; *went to great lengths; will not go the length of asserting*). **5.** (Pros.) vowel's or syllable's quantity. **6.** (Cricket). distance from batsman at which ball pitches (*bowler keeps a good length*); proper amount of this (~ or **good-**~ **ball,** that pitches at right length). **7.** long stretch or extent; piece of material of certain length; full extent of one's body. **8.** **at** ~, at last or after a long time; **at** (FULL¹, great, some) ~, in detail, without curtailment. **9.** ||~′**man,** employee

with duty of maintaining section of railway or road. **10.** Hence ~′WAYS *adv.,* ~′WISE *adv.* & *a.* [OE *lengthu,* = Du. *lengte,* ON *lengd* f. Gmc **langithō* (as LONG¹, -TH¹)]

lĕ′ngthen (-ngth-, -ngkth-) *v.t.* & *i.* make or become longer; (Pros.) make (vowel) long. [ME, f. prec. + -EN⁶]

lĕ′ngth|y (-ngthĭ, -ngkthĭ) *a.* (Of speech, writing, style, speaker, etc.) of unusual length, prolix, tedious; hence ~iLY² *adv.,* ~iNESS *n.* [f. LENGTH + -Y²; 18th c., orig. US]

lē′ni|ent *a.* tolerant, gentle, not disposed to severity; (of punishment etc.) mild; (arch.) emollient; hence ~ENCE, ~ENCY, *ns.,* ~entLY² *adv.* [f. L *lenire lenit-* soothe (*lenis* gentle); see -ENT]

Lĕ′nin|ism *n.* policy and (esp. communistic) economic principles of Lenin; so ~IST (2), ~ITE¹ (1), *ns.* [f. V. I. *Lenin* (name assumed by V. I. Ulyanov), Russ. statesman d. 1924 + -ISM]

lē′nitive *a.* & *n.* L soothing (drug, appliance), palliative. [ME, f. med. L *lenitivus* (as LENIENT; see -IVE)]

lē′nitỹ *n.* mercifulness; act of mercy. [f. F *lénité* or f. L *lenitas* (*lenis* gentle; see -ITY)]

lē′nō *n.* (*pl.* ~**s**). open-work fabric with warp threads twisted in pairs before weaving. [f. F *linon* (*lin* flax f. L *linum*)]

lĕns (-z) *n.* piece of glass or other transparent substance with both sides (or one only) curved for concentrating or dispersing light-rays in telescope, spectacles, etc.; combination of lenses in photography; (Anat.) = CRYSTALLINE *lens*; (Zool.) one facet of compound eye; (Phys.) device for focusing or otherwise modifying direction of movement of sound, electrons, etc.; hence ~ED² (-zd), ~′LESS, *adjs.* [L *lens lentis* lentil (from similarity of shape)]

Lĕnt¹ *n.* period from Ash Wednesday to Easter Eve of which the 40 weekdays are devoted to fasting and penitence in commemoration of Christ's fasting in the wilderness; ||(in *pl.*) Lent-term boat-races at Cambridge; ||~ **lily,** (esp. wild) daffodil; ||~ **term,** university etc. term in which Lent falls. [ME, f. LENTEN]

lĕnt². See LEND.

-lent *suf.* forming *adjs.* (*pestilent, violent*; cf. -ULENT). [f. L *-lentus -ful*]

Lĕ′nten *a.* of, in, or appropriate to, Lent; ~ **face,** dismal look; ~ **fare** (without meat). [orig. *n.* = 'spring', f. OE *lencten,* prob. f. WG **lang-* LONG¹, perh. w. ref. to lengthening of day in spring; now regarded as a. f. LENT¹ + -EN⁵]

lĕ′ntic̑el *n.* (Bot.) aeration-pore in stems and some roots. [f. mod. L *lenticella* dim. of L LENS]

lĕntı̆′cŭlar *a.* **1.** shaped like lentil or lens, biconvex. **2.** of the lens of the eye. [f. L *lenticularis* (as foll.; see -AR¹)]

lĕ′ntil *n.* (biconvex seed of) leguminous plant (*Lens esculenta*) grown for food. [ME f. OF *lentille* f. L *lenticula* (as LENS; see -CULE)]

lĕ′ntisk *n.* mastic tree. [ME, f. L *lentiscus*]

lĕ′ntō *a.* & *adv.* (Mus.) slow(ly). [It.]

lĕ′ntoid *a.* = LENTICULAR 1. [f. L LENS + -OID]

Lē′ō *n.* (*pl.* ~**s**). (person born under) sign of the ZODIAC, the Lion. [OE f. L, = LION]

Lē′onid *n.* one of the meteors that seem to radiate from the constellation Leo. [f. L *Leo leonis* + -ID³]

lē′onīne¹ *a.* lion-like; of lions. [ME, f. OF *leonin -ine* or f. L *leoninus* (as prec.; see -INE¹)]

Lē′onīne² *a.* & *n.* **1.** *a.* of, made or invented by, Leo; ~ **City,** part of Rome round Vatican fortified by Leo IV; l~ **verse,** (1) medieval Latin verse in hexameter or elegiac metre with internal rhyme (e.g. *Daemon languebat, monachus tunc esse volebat*), (2) English verse with internal rhymes (e.g. *The fair breeze blew, the white foam flew*). **2.** *n.* (in *pl.*) leonine verse. [f. *Leo,* man's Christian name, as prec.]

leo′pard (lĕ′p-) *n.* **1.** large African and S. Asian carnivorous quadruped (*Panthera pardus*) with dark-spotted yellowish-fawn or (**black** ~) black coat, panther; **hunting** ~, cheetah; **snow-**~, OUNCE²; **can the** ~ **change his spots?,** innate character persists [Jer. 13:23]. **2.** (Her.) lion passant guardant as in arms of England. **3.** (*attrib.*, in names of animals etc.) spotted like leopard. **4.** ~'s **bane,** (1) yellow-flowered plant of genus *Doronicum*, (2) herb Paris. **5.** Hence ~ESS¹ *n*. [ME f. OF, f. LL f. late Gk *leopardos* (as LION, PARD¹)]

le'otard *n*. close-fitting one-piece garment worn by ballet-dancers, acrobats, etc. [f. J. *Léotard*, Fr. trapeze performer d. 1870]

le'per *n*. person suffering from leprosy; (fig.) person shunned on moral grounds. [ME, prob. attrib. use of *leper* leprosy f. OF *lepre* f. L f. Gk *lepra* fem. (as n.) of *lepros* scaly (*lepos* scale)]

lepido'pter|ous *a*. of the Lepidoptera, order of insects with four membranous scale-covered wings, including butterflies and moths; hence ~AN *a*. & *n*., ~IST (3) *n*. [f. Gk *lepis -idos* scale + *pteron* wing + -OUS]

le'porine *a*. of or like hares. [f. L *leporinus* (*lepus -oris* hare; see -INE¹)]

le'prechaun (-k-) *n*. (Ir.) small mischievous sprite. [f. OIr. *luchorpán* (*lu* small, *corp* body)]

le'prosy *n*. chronic infectious bacterial disease affecting skin and nerves, resulting in mutilations and deformities; (fig.) moral corruption or contagion. [f. foll. + -Y¹]

le'prous *a*. having, like, (as) of, leprosy. [ME f. OF, f. LL *leprosus* (*lepra*; see LEPER, -OSE¹)]

le'pto- comb. form. small, narrow, as: ~**cepha'lic,** ~**ce'phalous,** narrow-skulled; ~**da'ctyl** *n*. & *a*., (bird) with long slender toes; ~**spiro'sis,** infectious disease caused by spirochaete of genus *Leptospira*. [f. Gk *leptos* fine, small, thin, delicate + -o-]

le'pt|on¹ *n*. (*pl.* ~**a**). Greek coin worth $\frac{1}{100}$ of a drachma. [f. Gk *lepton* (*nomisma* coin) neut. of *leptos* small]

le'ptŏn² *n*. (Phys.) elementary particle without strong interaction. [f. as LEPTO- + -ON]

Le'sbian (-z-) *a*. & *n*. **1.** *a*. of Lesbos. **2.** of homosexuality in women. **3.** *n*. (or *l*~). homosexual woman; hence ~ISM (2) *n*. [f. L f. Gk *Lesbios* f. *Lesbos*, island in Aegean Sea, home of Sappho (see SAPPHISM), + -IAN]

lèse-majesté (lāzmă'zhĕstā), **lèse-mǎ'jĕstў** (-zm-), *n*. treason; affront to sovereign or ruler; (joc.) presumptuous conduct. [(f.) F *lèse-majesté* f. L *laesa majestas* injured sovereignty (*laedere laes-* injure, *majestas* MAJESTY)]

le'sion (-zhon) *n*. damage, injury; (Path.) morbid change in functioning or texture of organ etc. [ME f. OF, f. L *laesio -onis* (*laedere laes-* injure; see -ION)]

less *a., prep., n.,* & *adv*. **1.** *a*. (Of size, degree, duration, number, etc.) smaller (opp. *greater; in a less degree, of less magnitude* or *importance; of two evils choose the less; may your* SHADOW¹ *never grow less*). **2.** of smaller quantity, not so much, not so much of, (opp. *more; find less difficulty; eat less meat*); (**D**) fewer. **3.** of lower rank etc. (*no less a person than; James, Ajax, the Less*). **4.** *prep*. minus, deducting, (*a year less three days; dividend paid less tax*). **5.** *n*. smaller amount, quantity, or number (*cannot take (much) less; for (far or much) less than £100; is little less than disgraceful*); NOTHING *less than*; **in** ~ **than no time,** (joc.) very quickly or soon; ~ **of,** (colloq.) reduce or eliminate (imper.; *less of your impudence!* etc.). **6.** *adv*. to smaller extent, in lower degree, (NO³ *less*; NONE *the less*); **much** or **still** ~, with even greater force of denial (*do not suspect him of negligence, still* or *much less of dishonesty*). [OE *lǣssa* a., *lǣs* adv., f. Gmc *laisizō, *laisiz* compar. f. *laisa-* f. IE *loiso-]

-less *suf*. forming *adjs*. & *advs*. f. *ns.*, w. sense 'not having, without, free from', and f. *vbs.*, w. sense 'unable to be —ed', (*doubtless, guileless, homeless, numberless, powerless, shell-less; fathomless, relentless, tireless*); hence **-less**LY² *adv. suf.*, **-less**NESS *n. suf*. [OE *-lēas* (*lēas* devoid of)]

lessee' *n*. holder of, tenant (of house, theatre, etc.) under, lease; hence ~SHIP *n*. [ME f. AF p.p., OF *lessé* (as LEASE; see -EE)]

le'ssen *v.i.* & *t*. decrease, diminish. [ME, f. LESS + -EN⁶]

le'sser *attrib. a*. not so great as the other or the rest, minor, (*the lesser evils of life*). [double compar., f. LESS + -ER³]

le'sson *n.*, & *v.t*. **1.** *n*. thing to be learnt by pupil; amount of teaching given at one time, time assigned to it, (in *pl.*) systematic instruction in subject (*give* or *take lessons in*). **2.** occurrence, example, rebuke, or punishment, that serves or should serve as encouragement or warning; thing inculcated by experience or study. **3.** portion of Scripture etc. read aloud at divine service, esp. one of two readings from OT (**first** ~) and NT (**second** ~) at morning and evening prayer in Church of England. **4.** *v.t.* (arch.) instruct; admonish, rebuke. [ME, f. OF *leçon* f. L *lectio -onis* (see LECTION)]

le'ssōr *n*. person who lets on lease. [AF (*lesser*; see LEASE, -OR)]

lest *conj*. in order that not, for fear that, (*lest we forget*); (*fear* etc.) ~, that. [OE *thy̆ lǣs the* whereby less that, later *the lǣste*, ME *lest(e)*]

let¹ *v.t.* (-tt-; ~'**ted** or ~), & *n*. **1.** *v.t.* (arch.) hinder, obstruct. **2.** *n*. stoppage, hindrance, (arch. exc. in *without let or hindrance*). **3.** (Rackets, Lawn Tennis, etc.) obstruction of ball or player in certain ways, requiring ball to be served again. [OE *lettan*, = OS *lettian*, OHG *lezzen*, ON *letja*, Goth. *latjan* hinder, f. Gmc *lata-* LATE¹]

let² *v*. (-tt-; **let**) & *n*. **1.** *v.t.* allow or cause (liquid, air) to escape (*let blood*). **2.** ||grant use of (rooms, land, etc.) for rent or hire (*to pay for* period; **to** ~, offered for rent). **3.** award (contract for work). **4.** allow to, not prevent or forbid, (*we let them go; will go if you will let me;* LIVE² *and let live*). **5.** cause to know or be known. **6.** *v.t.* & *i*. ~ **alone,** not interfere with, attend to, or do (*let* WELL³ *alone*), in (*imper.*) not to mention, far less or more (*hasn't got a radio, let alone television*); ~ **be,** not interfere with, attend to, or do; ~ **down,** lower, fail to support (another, or user) at need, disappoint (~ *him down gently*, avoid humiliating him abruptly), deflate (tyre), lengthen (garment); ~**down** *n.*, disappointment; ~ **drop** or **fall,** drop (lit., or fig. hint, significant word) intentionally or by accident, (Geom.) draw (perpendicular) from outside point (*up*)on or to line; *let* FLY²; ~ **go,** release, set at liberty, lose hold of, lose or relinquish hold (*of*), dismiss from thought, cease discussion of, cease to restrain (~ *oneself go*, (1) relax, cease to take trouble, (2) give way to enthusiasm, impulse, etc.); ~ **in,** admit or open door to (lit., or fig.: *let in a flood of light; this would let in all sorts of evils;* ~ *oneself in*, with latchkey) etc., involve in loss etc., inlay in something; ~ **in for,** involve in (loss or difficulty); ~ **in on,** allow to share; ~ **into,** allow to enter, inlay in, make acquainted with (secret etc.); ~ **loose,** release or unchain (dog, fury, maniac, etc.); ~ **off** (*adv.*), discharge (gun, firework, or fig. joke etc.), not punish or compel, punish *with* light penalty, allow or cause (liquid, steam, etc.) to escape, ||let (part of house etc.); ~**off** *n.*, being allowed to escape something (esp. in cricket, not being caught etc. when there is a chance); ~ **off** (*prep.*), excuse (person penalty); ~ **on,** (sl.) reveal secret, pretend (*let on that he had succeeded*); ~ **out,** open door for exit of, exculpate, allow (person etc., secret or *that*) to depart or escape (*let the* CAT¹ *out of the bag*), release from restraint, make (garment) looser esp. by adjustment at seams, put out to rent esp. to several tenants, or to contract; ~-**out** *n.*, opportunity to escape; *let* RIP²; *let me* SEE¹ 13; *let* SLIP¹ 3; ~ **through,** allow to pass; ~ **up,** (colloq.) become less severe, diminish, relax one's efforts; ~-**up** *n.*, cessation, diminution. **7.** *v. aux*. supplying 1st and 3rd persons of imper. in exhortations (*let us pray; let you and me, let us*, colloq. *let's, try now; let us not*, colloq. *let's not* or *don't let's, be greedy*), commands (*let it be done, let him do it, at once; let there be light*); assumptions (*let AB be equal to CD*), and permission or challenge (*let him do his worst*). **8.** *n*. ||act of letting (sense 2). [OE *lǣtan*, = OS *lātan*, OHG *lāzan*, ON *láta*, Goth. *lētan* f. Gmc **lǣt-* rel. to **lat-* LATE¹]

-let (-lĭt, -lĕt) *suf.* forming *ns.* usu. dim. (*leaflet, ringlet, tartlet*) or denoting articles of attire etc. (*armlet*). [orig. f. OF *-elet* (as -LE 2, -ET¹) wrongly understood in wds such as *crosslet, hamlet*]

lē'thal *a.* causing, sufficient or designed to cause, death; ∼ **chamber** (for killing animals painlessly); hence **lĕthă'lıTY** *n.*, ∼LY² *adv.* [f. L *let(h)alis* (*letum* death; see -AL)]

lē'thargy *n.* morbid drowsiness, prolonged and unnatural sleep; torpid, inert, or apathetic state, lack of interest and energy; so **lĕthâr'gıC** *a.* [ME f. OF *litargie*, f. LL f. Gk *lēthargia* (*lēthargos* forgetful f. *lēth-, lanthanomai* forget); see -Y¹]

Lē'thē *n.* (river in Hades in Gk Myth. producing) forgetfulness of the past; hence **Lēthē'AN** *a.* [L, use of Gk *lēthē* forgetfulness (as prec.)]

Lĕtt *n.* member of a people living near the Baltic, mainly in Latvia; Lettish language. [f. G *Lette* f. Lettish *Latvi*]

lē'tter *n.*, & *v.t.* **1.** *n.* character representing one or more of the simple or compound sounds used in speech, one of the alphabetic symbols; (in *pl.*, colloq.) initials of degree etc. after holder's name, *school or college initial as mark of proficiency in games etc.; (Print.) type(s), fount of type, (BLACK¹ *letter*); PROOF¹ *before letters*. **2.** written or printed message addressed to person(s), usu. sent by post or messenger and fairly long; *letter of* CREDIT¹, *of* INTRODUCTION or CREDENCE; (in *pl.*) addressed document of legal or formal kind for various purposes (*letters* MISSIVE, ||PATENT¹, *of* ADMINISTRATION, *of* MARQUE¹, etc.). **3.** precise terms of statement (**to the** ∼, with adherence to every detail), strict verbal interpretation (opp. *spirit*; esp. **in** ∼ **and in spirit**, in form and substance; *according to the letter of the law*). **4.** (in *pl.*) literature, acquaintance with books, erudition, (*Bachelor etc. of Letters*; **man of** ∼**s**, scholar, author; **the commonwealth** or **republic of** ∼**s**, authors as a body, literature; **the profession of** ∼**s**, authorship); hence ∼ED² (-erd) *a.* **5.** ∼-**balance** (for ascertaining postage from weight of letters); ∼-**bomb**, terrorist explosive device sent by post; ∼-**book** (in which copies of correspondence are kept); ∼-**box**, box or slot into which letters are delivered or posted; ∼-**card**, folded card with gummed edge for posting as letter; ∼-**case**, pocket-book for holding letters; ∼ **head(ing)**, printed (heading on) stationery; ∼-**lock**, kind of lock opened by choosing out of certain letters on it a word or other combination that has been previously made when closing it; ∼-**paper**, paper for letters, ∼-**perfect**, (Theatr.) knowing one's part perfectly; ∼-**press**, (1) contents of illustrated book other than the illustrations, (2) printed matter relating to illustrations, (3) printing from raised type, not from plates, blocks, etc.; ∼-**scale(s)**, = *letter-balance*; ∼-**writer**, (1) person who writes letters, (2) book giving guidance on writing letters. **6.** Hence ∼LESS *a.* **7.** *v.t.* impress title etc. on (book-cover); inscribe letters on; classify with letters of the alphabet; hence ∼ING¹ (1, 6) *n.* [ME, f. OF *lettre* f. L *litera, littera* letter of alphabet, (in pl.) epistle, literature]

Lĕ'ttic *a.* & *n.* = foll.; = BALTIC 2. [f. LETT + -IC]

Lĕ'ttish *a.* & *n.* (language) of the Letts. [f. LETT + -ISH¹]

lettre de cachet (lĕtr de kă'shā) *n.* official order (orig. from French king) for imprisonment, exile, etc. [F, = sealed letter]

lĕ'ttuce (-tĭs) *n.* garden herb of genus *Lactuca* with crisp leaves much used in salad; plant of similar type eaten by animals (LAMB'*s lettuce*); (sl.) money. [ME *letus(e)*, rel. to OF *laitue* f. L *lactuca* (*lac lactis* milk, w. ref. to its milky juice)]

leu'co- *comb. form.* white, as: ∼**blast**, immature leucocyte; ∼**cyte**, white or colourless corpuscle of blood or found in lymph etc.; ∼**rrhoe'a** (-rē'a),

mucous discharge from female genitals; ∼**tome**, instrument for ∼**tomy** (-ŏ't-), incision into white tissue of frontal lobe of brain to relieve some cases of mental disorder. [f. Gk *leukos* white + -O-]

leuco'ma *n.* (Path.) white opacity of cornea. [f. as prec. + -OMA]

leukae'm|ĭa, *leukē'm|ĭa, *n.* (Med.) disease in which there is an excess of white corpuscles in tissues and usu. in the blood; hence ∼IC *a.* [mod. L, f. G *leukämie* f. Gk *leukos* white + *haima* blood; see -IA¹]

Lev. *abbr.* Leviticus (OT).

Lĕvă'nt¹ *n.* eastern part of Mediterranean with its islands and neighbouring countries; *Levant* MOROCCO. [F, part. of *lever* rise, used as n. = point of sunrise, east]

||**lĕvă'nt²** *v.i.* abscond, bolt, esp. with betting or gaming losses unpaid; hence **lĕvă'nter¹** [-ER¹] *n.* [perh. f. prec.]

lĕvă'nter² *n.* (L∼) inhabitant of Levant; strong easterly Mediterranean wind. [f. LEVANT¹ + -ER¹]

Levantīne (lĭvă'n-, lĕ'van-) *a.* & *n.* of, trading to, inhabitant of, the Levant. [f. LEVANT¹ + -INE¹]

lĕvă'tor *n.* (Anat.) muscle that raises structure or organ. [mod. L, f. L = one who lifts (*levare* raise)]

lĕ'vee¹ (-vĭ) *n.* **1.** (Hist.) reception of visitors on rising from bed. **2.** ||assembly held by sovereign or his representative at which men only are received; assembly of visitors or guests esp. at formal reception. [f. F *levé* var. of *lever* rising (*lever* to rise; see LEVY, -EE)]

*levee² (lĭvē', lĕ'vĭ) *n.* embankment against river floods; natural embankment built up by river; landing-place. [f. F *levée* fem. p.p. of *lever* raise (see LEVY, -EE)]

lĕ'vel *n.*, *a.*, & *v.* (||-ll-). **1.** *n.* instrument giving line parallel to plane of horizon for testing whether things are horizontal; surveyor's instrument for giving horizontal line or plane (**on a** ∼ **with**, in same horizontal plane as, (fig.) equal with; **on the** ∼, (colloq.) truthful(ly), honest(ly); **find** one's ∼, reach right social, intellectual, etc. place with regard to others; **water finds its** ∼, its surface in communicating receptacles or regions will be at same height unless they have no common level). **3.** plane or standard in social, moral, or intellectual matters; plane of rank or authority (*consultations at Cabinet level*); height or value reached (*eye level*, SEA-*level*; *sugar level in blood*). **4.** more or less level surface; flat country. **5.** *a.* horizontal, perpendicular to the plumb-line, on a level or equality (*with*, or abs.); ||∼ **crossing** of railway and road, or two railways, at same level; *level* PEG²*ging*; ∼ **race** (in which leading competitors are close together). **6.** even, equable, uniform, well-balanced, in quality, style, temper, judgement, etc.; ∼-**headed**, mentally well-balanced, cool; **do** one's ∼ **best**, (colloq.) not be remiss, make all possible efforts. **7.** Hence ∼LY² *adv.*, ∼NESS *n.* **8.** *v.t.* make level, even, or uniform; place on same level, bring *up* or *down* to a standard; raze, lay low, (*to* or *with the ground*, *in the dust*, or abs.); knock (person) down; abolish (distinctions); aim (missile, gun, or abs.), lay (gun), direct (satire, criticism, accusation, or abs.), (*at* or *against*); (Surv.) ascertain differences of height of (land, or abs.). **9.** *v.t.* & *v.* ∼ **off**, make or become level or smooth; ∼ **out**, make or become level, remove differences from. **10.** *v.i.* (sl.) be frank or honest (*with* person). **11.** ∼**ling-screw** *n.* for adjusting parts of machine etc. to exact level). [ME, f. OF *livel* f. Rom. **libellum* for L *libella* dim. of *libra* scales, balance]

lĕ'veller, *lĕ'veler, *n.* In vbl senses: person who would abolish social distinctions, advocate of equality; (*L*∼) extreme radical dissenter in 17th-c. England. [f. prec. + -ER¹]

lĕ'ver *n.* & *v.* **1.** *n.* bar resting on pivot and used to raise heavy or firmly fixed object; (Mech.) device consisting of straight bar or other rigid structure of which one point (*fulcrum*) is fixed, another is connected with the force (*weight*) to be resisted or acted upon, and a third is connected with the force (*power*) applied (∾ **of first order** with fulcrum, **of second order** with weight, **of third order** with power, between the other two); projecting handle moved to operate mechanism; (fig.) means of exerting moral force; ∾ **escapement** (with connection between escape wheel and balance made by two levers); ∾ **watch** (with lever escapement). **2.** *v.i.* use lever. **3.** *v.t.* lift, move, act on, with lever (*along, away, out, over, up*, etc.). [ME f. AF; OF *levier, leveor* (*lever* raise; see LEVY)]

lē′verage *n.* action of, way of applying, lever; set or system of levers; power, mechanical advantage gained by use, of lever; means of accomplishing a purpose, power, influence; *(Finance) gearing. [f. prec. + -AGE]

lĕ′verét *n.* young (esp. first-year) hare. [ME f. AF, dim. of *levre*, OF *lievre* f. L *lepus leporis* hare; see -ET¹]

lē′viable. See LEVY.

lèvī′athan *n.* **1.** (Bibl.) sea-monster. **2.** huge ship; anything very large of its kind; (in allusion to book by Hobbes, 1651) autocratic monarch or State. [ME f. LL, f. Heb. *liwyāṯān*]

lĕ′vigǀāte *v.t.* reduce to fine smooth powder; make smooth paste of; hence ∾A′TION *n.* [f. L *levigare* (*levis* smooth) + -ATE³]

lĕ′vin *n.* (arch. or poet.) (flash of) lightning. [ME *leven*(*e*), prob. f. ON]

lĕ′virǀate *n.* ancient-Jewish etc. custom by which dead man's brother or next of kin had to marry the widow; hence ∾ā′tIC(AL) *adjs.* [f. L *levir* brother-in-law + -ATE¹]

Lē′vis (-z) *n. pl.* (**P**) type of (orig. blue) denim jeans or overalls reinforced with rivets. [f. *Levi* Strauss, orig. US manufacturer in 1860s]

lĕ′vitǀāte *v.i.* & *t.* (cause to) rise and float in air (esp. w. ref. to spiritualism); hence ∾A′TION *n.* [f. L *levis* light, after *gravitate*]

Lē′vīte *n.* one of tribe of Levi, esp. of that part of it which provided assistants to priests in worship in Jewish temple. [ME, f. LL *levita* f. Gk *leuitēs* (*Leui* f. Heb. *lēwī* Levi)]

Lèvi′tǀicǀal *a.* of Levites or the tribe of Levi; of Levites' ritual; of Leviticus. [f. LL *leviticus* f. Gk *leuitikos* (as prec.; see -IC) + -AL]

Lèvī′ticus *n.* third book of Pentateuch, with Levitical law and ritual. [ME f. LL *Leviticus* (sc. *liber* book); see prec.]

lĕ′vitУ *n.* lack of serious thought, frivolity, unbecoming jocularity; inconstancy; undignified behaviour; (arch.) lightness of weight. [f. L *levitas* (*levis* light; see -ITY)]

lē′vo-, lē′vulōse. See LAEVO-, LAEVULOSE.

lĕ′vУ *n.*, & *v.t.* **1.** *n.* collecting of contribution, tax, etc., (**capital** ∾, appropriation by the State of a fixed proportion of all or some of the wealth in the country), or of property to satisfy legal judgement. **2.** enrolling of men for war etc.; amount or number thus enrolled, body of men enrolled, (in *pl.*) men enrolled. **3.** *v.t.* raise (contribution, taxes), impose (rate, toll), whence **lĕ′vÍABLE** *a.*; raise (sum, or abs.) by legal execution or process *on* person's goods; seize (goods) thus; extort (*levy blackmail*). **4.** enlist, enrol, (soldiers, army); collect men and munitions for, proceed to make, (war; usu. *upon* or *against*). [ME, f. OF *levee* fem. p.p. (as n.) of *lever* f. L *levare* raise (*levis* light); see -Y⁴]

lewd *a.* lascivious, unchaste, indecent, obscene; hence ∾′LY² *adv.*, ∾′NESS *n.* [OE *lǣwede* LAY²; orig. unkn.]

lew′is¹ (lōo′-) *n.* iron contrivance for gripping heavy blocks of stone for lifting. [18th c.; orig. unkn.]

Lew′is² (lōo′-) *n.* ∾ **gun**, light machine-gun with magazine, air cooling, and operation by gas from its own firing. [f. I. N. ∾, Amer. soldier d. 1931, its inventor]

lew′isīte (lōo′-) *n.* irritant and vesicant poison gas developed for use in chemical warfare. [f. W. L. *Lewis*, Amer. chemist d. 1943 + -ITE¹ (2)]

lĕ′xical *a.* of the words of a language (opp. *grammatical*); (as) of a lexicon; hence ∾LY² *adv.* [f. Gk *lexikos* & as LEXICON + -AL]

lĕxicŏ′ǀgraphУ *n.* dictionary-making; so ∾GRAPHER *n.*, **lĕxicoGRA′PHICAL** *a.* [f. foll. + -GRAPHY]

lĕ′xicon *n.* dictionary, esp. of Greek, Hebrew, Syriac, or Arabic; (fig.) vocabulary of a person, of a language, of a branch of knowledge, etc. [mod. L, f. Gk *lexikon* (*biblion* book), neut. of *lexikos* (*lexis* word f. *legō* speak; see -IC)]

lĕxi′graphУ *n.* system of writing in which each character represents a word. [f. Gk *lexis* (see prec.) + -GRAPHY]

lĕ′xis *n.* words, vocabulary; total stock of words in a language. [Gk; see LEXICON]

lex talionis (lĕks tălĭŏ′nĭs) *n.* law of retaliation (whereby punishment resembles offence committed, in kind and degree). [L]

ley¹ (lā) *n.* land temporarily under grass; ∾ **farming**, alternate growing of crops and grass. [ME, orig. adj., perh. f. OE *lǣge, cogn. w. LAY³, LIE³]

ley² (lē, lā) *n.* supposed straight line of prehistoric track usu. between hilltops. [var. of LEA¹]

Ley′den (lī′-) *n.* ∾ **jar**, kind of capacitor with glass jar as dielectric between sheets of tin foil. [f. ∾ (now *Leiden*) in Holland, where it was invented (1745)]

LF *abbr.* low frequency.

l.h. *abbr.* left hand.

li (lē) *n.* Chinese unit of distance, about ⅓ mile. [Chin.]

LI *abbr.* Light Infantry; *Long Island.

Li *symb.* lithium.

liabi′litУ *n.* being liable (‖**limited** ∾, being legally responsible only to limited amount for debts of trading company to which one belongs); what one is liable for, (in *pl.*) debts or pecuniary obligations; person or thing that causes disadvantage through one's responsibility therefor. [f. foll. + -ITY]

lī′able *pred. a.* legally bound, answerable *for*, subject or amenable *to* tax or penalty, under obligation *to* do; exposed or open *to*, apt *to* do or suffer, something undesirable (*difficulties are liable to occur*). [ME, perh. f. AF *liable that may be bound, f. OF *lier* f. L *ligare* bind; see -ABLE]

liai′se (-z) *v.i.* (colloq.) make liaison (sense 3) *with* or *between*. [back-form. f. foll.]

liai′son (-z-) *n.* **1.** illicit sexual association between a man and a woman. **2.** sounding of ordinarily silent final consonant before vowel beginning following word (or mute *h* in French). **3.** (Mil. etc.) connection, co-operation; ∾ **officer** (acting as go-between for allied forces or units of the same force). **4.** egg-yolk thickening for sauces. [F (*lier* bind f. L *ligare*; see -ISON)]

lia′na (-ah′-), **lia′ne** (-ah′n), *n.* climbing and twining plant of tropical forest etc. [F *liane, lierne* clematis, of uncert. orig.]

lī′ar *n.* teller (esp. habitual) of lie(s); ∾ **dice**, game with poker dice in which false result of throw may be announced. [OE *lēogere* (as LIE², -AR³)]

lī′as *n.* blue limestone rock in SW England; (Geol., *L*∾) lower strata of Jurassic series, blue argillaceous limestone rich in fossils; hence **liā′ssIC** *a.* [ME, f. OF *liois* hard limestone, prob. of Gmc orig.]

Lib. *abbr.* Liberal; (*Lib*) (colloq.) liberation (cf. WOMAN); **Lib-Lab**, Liberal and Labour (Parties).

libā′tion *n.* (pouring of) drink-offering to god; (joc.) potation. [ME, f. L *libatio* (*libare* pour as offering; see -ATION)]

lī′bel *n.*, & *v.t.* (‖-ll-). **1.** (Law). published false statement damaging to person's reputation; act of publishing it; **criminal** ∾, deliberate defamatory statement in permanent form; (**public**) ∾, publication of what is blasphemous, obscene, seditious, or treasonable; cf. SLANDER. **2.** (pop.) false and defamatory oral or written statement; thing that brings discredit *on* by misrepresentation etc. (*the portrait is a libel on him; the book, play, is a libel on human nature*).

3. (Civil & Eccl. Law) plaintiff's written declaration; (Sc. Law) statement of grounds of charge. **4.** Hence ∼1IST (1) *n.*, ∼1OUS *a.* **5.** *v.t.* defame by libellous statements; accuse falsely and maliciously; (Law) publish libel against, whence ∼1ER¹ *n.*; (Eccl. etc. Law) bring suit against, whence ∼1ANT (1), ∼1EE′, *ns.* [ME f. OF, f. L *libellus* dim. of *liber* book; see -EL, -LE 2]

li′ber *n.* bast. [L, = bark]

li′beral *a.* & *n.* **1.** *a.* directed to general broadening of mind, not professional or technical (*liberal culture, education, studies*); ∼ **arts,** medieval trivium and quadrivium, *arts as dist. from science and technology. **2.** giving freely, generous, not sparing *of*; given freely, ample, abundant; not rigorous or literal; open-minded, candid, unprejudiced. **3.** (Polit.) favourable to democratic reform and individual liberty, (moderately) progressive (*the Liberal Party*); hence ∼ISM (3), ∼IST (2), *ns.*, ∼i′STIC *a.*, ∼IZE (3) *v.t.* & *i.* **4.** Hence ∼LY² *adv.* **5.** *n.* (*L*∼). member of (esp. the British) Liberal Party. [ME, orig. 'befitting a free man', f. OF f. L *liberalis* (*liber* free (man); see -AL)]

libera′lity *n.* free giving, munificence; freedom from prejudice, breadth of mind. [ME, f. OF *liberalité* or f. L *liberalitas* (as prec.; see -ITY)]

li′ber|āte *v.t.* set at liberty, set free *from*; (Chem.) release from state of combination; free (country) from enemy occupation, (sl.) steal; so ∼A′TION, ∼ator, *ns.* [f. L *liberare* (*liber* free) + -ATE³]

libertā′rian *n.* & *a.* believer, believing, in free will (opp. *necessitarian*); advocate of liberty; hence ∼ISM (3) *n.* [f. LIBERTY + -ARIAN]

liber′ticide *n.* & *a.* (literary) destroyer, destructive, of liberty. [F (as LIBERTY; see -CIDE)]

li′bertin|e (-ēn, -īn) *n.* & *a.* free thinker, free-thinking, on religion; (one) who follows his own inclinations; dissolute, licentious, (man); CHARTER²ed *libertine*; hence ∼AGE (2), ∼ISM (2), *ns.* [f. L *libertinus* freedman (*libertus* made free, f. *liber* free; see -INE¹)]

li′berty *n.* **1.** being free from captivity, imprisonment, slavery, or despotic control; personification of this; CAP¹ *of liberty*; civil ∼, being subject only to laws established on behalf of community; *liberty of* CON-SCIENCE, *of the* PRESS¹ 5; ∼ **of the subject,** rights of subject under constitutional rule. **2.** right or power to do as one pleases or *to* do something; (Philos.) freedom from control of fate or necessity. **3.** setting aside of rules, licence; **take the** ∼ **to** do, **of** doing, presume or venture to do; **take liberties,** behave in improperly familiar manner (*with* person, or abs.), deal (unduly) freely *with* rules or facts. **4.** (in *pl.*) privileges, immunities, or rights, enjoyed by prescription or grant; (Hist., in *sing.*, or *pl.*) area having such privileges etc., district controlled by city though outside its boundary, area outside prison where some prisoners might reside. **5. at** ∼, free (*set at liberty*), having the right to do, disengaged. **6.** *L∼ **Bell** (in Philadelphia, rung at adoption of Declaration of Independence); ‖∼ **boat** (Naut., carrying liberty men); ∼ **bodice,** close-fitting under-bodice; L∼ **Hall,** place where one may do as one likes; ∼ **horse** (performing in circus without rider); ‖∼ **man,** sailor with leave to go ashore; L∼ **ship,** prefabricated US-built freighter of 1939-45 war. [ME, f. OF *liberté* f. L *libertas* -tatis (*liber* free; see -TY¹)]

libi′dinous *a.* lustful; hence ∼LY² *adv.* [ME, f. L *libidinosus* (*libido* -dinis lust; see -OUS)]

libi′dō (-ē′-, -ī′-) *n.* (*pl.* ∼s). psychic drive or energy, esp. that associated with sex instinct; hence **libi′din**AL *a.* [L; see prec.]

Li′br|a (lī′-, lē′-) *n.* (person born under) sign of the ZODIAC, the Balance or Scales; hence ∼AN *a.* & *n.*, (person) born under Libra. [ME, f. L, orig. = pound weight]

librā′rian *n.* custodian of or assistant in library; hence ∼SHIP (1, 3) *n.* [f. L *librarius* (see foll.) + -AN]

li′brary *n.* **1.** room or building containing books for reading or reference; room in large house devoted to

books. **2.** a collection of books for use by the public or by some class of persons; similar collection of films, records, computer routines, etc.; public institution charged with care of such collection; **lending** ∼ (from which books may be temporarily taken away with or ‖without payment); **reference** ∼ (in which books may be consulted but not taken away); ‖**free** ∼, **public** ∼, (used by public without payment and usu. supported by local rates); *circulating library* (see CIRCULATE); *RENTAL *library*. **3.** person's book-collection; series of books issued by publisher in similar bindings etc. as being connected in some way. **4.** ∼ **edition** (of good size and print and strongly bound); ∼ **science,** study of librarianship; ∼ **school** (teaching librarianship). [ME, f. OF *librairie* f. L *libraria* (*taberna* shop), fem. of *librarius* bookseller's, of books (*liber libri* book; see -ARY¹, -Y¹)]

librā′te *v.i.* oscillate like balance-beam; be poised, balance; sway, quiver; hence **li′brat**ORY *a.* [f. L *librare* (*libra* balance) + -ATE³]

librā′tion *n.* librating; ∼ **of moon,** apparent oscillation by which parts near edge of disc are alternately visible and invisible. [f. L *libratio* (as prec.; see -ATION)]

libre′tt|ō *n.* (*pl.* ∼i *pr.* -ē, or ∼os). text of opera or other long musical vocal work; hence ∼IST (1) *n.* [It., dim. of *libro* book f. L *liber* book]

Li′byan (-ian, -yan) *a.* & *n.* (inhabitant or native) of ancient N. Africa W. of Egypt, or of modern Libya; (poet.) N. African; (of) the Berber language or the group of Hamitic languages to which it belongs. [f. L *Libya* f. Gk *Libue* + -AN]

lice. See LOUSE.

li′cence¹, ***li′cense¹,** *n.* **1.** permit from authority to marry, print something, preach, be driver or owner of vehicle on public road, own a dog, gun, or television set, carry on some trade (esp. that in alcoholic liquor), etc.; university certificate of competence in some faculty; *∼ **plate,** number plate of licensed vehicle. **2.** leave, permission, (*have I your licence to remove the fence?*). **3.** liberty of action esp. when excessive, abuse of freedom, disregard of law or propriety; licentiousness. **4.** writer's or artist's irregularity in grammar, metre, perspective, etc., esp. for sake of effect (*poetic licence*). [ME f. OF, f. L *licentia* (*licēre* be lawful; see -ENCE); *-se* by confus. w. foll.]

li′cense², -**ce²,** *v.t.* **1.** grant permit (see prec. 1) to (person; ‖*licensed* VICTUALLER); authorize use of (premises) for certain purpose, esp. sale and consumption of alcoholic liquor; authorize publication of (book etc.) or performance of (play). **2.** (arch.) allow (person *to* do, thing to be done); (in *p.p.*) allow complete freedom to (*a licensed libertine*). **3.** Hence **licens**EE′ *n.* (esp.) one who holds a licence to sell alcoholic liquor, **li′cens**ER¹ *n.*, (esp.) official licensing publication of books or performance of plays. [ME, f. prec.; -*se* on anal. of *practise, prophesy,* vbs., cf. *practice, prophecy,* ns.; perh. after *advise, advice,* where the sound differs]

lice′ntiate (-shiat) *n.* holder of university licence or attestation of competence from collegiate or examining body; licensed preacher not yet having appointment, esp. in Presbyterian Church. [ME, f. med. L *licentiatus* p.p. (as n.) of *licentiare* f. L *licentia* (see LICENCE¹) + -ATE¹]

lice′ntious (-shus) *a.* immoral in sexual relations; (arch.) disregarding accepted rules or conventions; hence ∼LY² *adv.*, ∼NESS *n.* [f. L *licentiosus* (*licentia*; see LICENCE¹, -OUS)]

lich, lych, *n.* ∼**gate,** roofed gateway of churchyard where coffin awaits clergyman's arrival; ∼**house,** mortuary; ‖∼**owl,** screech-owl (boding death); ∼**stone** (to place coffin on at lich-gate). [OE *līc* corpse, = OS *līk*, OHG *lih*, ON *līk*, Goth. *leik* f. Gmc *līkam body, form, appearance]

lichee, lichi. Vars. of LITCHI.

li′chen (lī′k-, li′ch-) *n.* **1.** plant organism of group Lichenes, composed of fungus and alga in association, usu. of green, grey, or yellow tint growing on and

colouring rocks, tree-trunks, roofs, wall, etc.; hence
∿ED² (-nd) *a*., ∿ó'LOGY *n*. **2.** skin-disease with
reddish eruption. **3.** Hence ∿OUS *a*. [L, f. Gk *leikhēn*]
li'cit *a*. lawful, not forbidden; hence ∿LY² *adv*. [f. L
licitus p.p. of *licēre* be lawful]
lick *v.t*., & *n*. **1.** *v.t*. pass tongue over to taste, moisten,
clean, etc.; ∿ one's **chops** or **lips** (in relish or
anticipation of food); ∿ **into shape**, give proper
form to, make presentable or efficient [f. bears'
supposed treatment of their cubs]; ∿ person's **boots**
or **shoes**, show servility to him; ∿ one's **wounds**,
(fig.) remain in retirement after defeat. **2.** take *up* or
off, make *clean*, by licking; (of waves, flame, etc.) play
lightly over, (of flame) swallow *up* in passing. **3.** (sl.)
thrash (person, fault *out of* person), beat in fight or
competition, excel, whence ∿ING¹ (1) *n*.; surpass
comprehension of (*this licks me, has got me licked*). **4.**
∿'**spittle**, toady. **5.** *n*. act of licking with tongue (**a** ∿
and a promise, (colloq.) hasty performance of task,
esp. of washing oneself); = SALT-*lick*; smart blow with
stick etc.; (sl.) pace (*at a great lick; full* or *at full lick*).
[OE *liccian*, = OS *liccon, leccon*, OHG *leckōn* f. WG
likkōjan ult. f. IE *ligh-*]
li'ckerish, li'quorish, (-*ker*-) *a*. fond of fine food;
greedy, longing; lecherous. [alt. f. ME *lickerous* f. AF
likerous, OF *lecheros*; see LECHER, -OUS]
lickety-spli't *adv*. (colloq.) at full speed, headlong.
[prob. f. LICK (cf. *at full lick*) + SPLIT¹]
li'corice. See LIQUORICE.
li'ctor *n*. (Rom. Hist.; usu. in pl.) officer attending
consul or other magistrate, bearing fasces, and
executing sentence on offenders. [ME f. L, perh. rel.
to *ligare* bind]
lid *n*. **1.** hinged or detached part to cover opening or
close aperture, esp. for opening at top of vessel; with
the ∿ **off**, (fig.) with all horrors etc. exposed to view;
||**put the** (**tin**) ∿ **on**, (sl.) (1) be the culmination (of),
surpass all, (2) put a stop to. **2.** operculum of shell or
plant; = EYE¹*lid*; (sl.) hat. **3.** Hence (-)∿'dED²,
∿'LESS, *adjs*. [OE *hlid*, = OHG (*h*)*lit*, ON *hlith* f. Gmc
hlidham (*hlidh-* cover)]
li'dō (lē'-) *n*. (*pl*. ∿s). public open-air swimming-pool
or pleasure-beach. [It., name of bathing-beach near
Venice, f. L *litus* shore]
lie¹ *n*. **1.** intentional false statement; **tell a** ∿, utter
this; **act a** ∿, deceive without verbal lying; **white** ∿
(excused or justified by its motive); **give** person **the**
∿ (**in his throat**), accuse him of lying (grossly); **give
the** ∿ **to** supposition etc., serve to show its falsity. **2.**
imposture, thing that deceives. **3.** ∿-**detector**,
instrument for measuring pulse-rate, respiration,
etc., so as to detect physiological changes accompanying tension due to telling of lies. [OE *lyge* f. Gmc
leug- etc., assim. to foll.]
lie² *v*. (*part*. LYING²). **1.** *v.i*. speak falsely, tell lie(s) (*to*
person); ∿ **in** one's **teeth** or **throat**, (arch. or joc.) lie
outrageously or infamously. **2.** (of thing) be deceptive
(*the camera cannot lie*). **3.** *v.t*. get (one*self*, person) *into* or
out of by lying. [OE *lēogan*, = OS, OHG *liogan*, ON
ljúga, Goth. *liugan* f. Gmc *l(e)ug-*]
lie³ *v.i*. (*part*. LYING²; *past* **lay**; *p.p*. **lain**, Bibl. **li'en**). **1.**
(Of person or animal) have one's body in more or less
horizontal position along ground or surface (*lie asleep,
sick, dying, dead*, etc.; *lie* DOGGO; *let* SLEEP²*ing dogs lie; lie
in the* BED¹ *one has made*). **2.** (arch.) have sexual
intercourse *with*. **3.** (Of the dead) be buried *at* or *in*; *lie
in* STATE¹. **4.** take lying position (*down* etc.); be kept or
remain in specified state (*lie in prison, at the mercy of,
helpless, fallow*, WASTE¹, *idle*, CLOSE¹, LOW¹, PERDU, *in
ambush, in* WAIT²); (of game-bird) not rise; (of troops)
be encamped *at, in, near*, a place. **5.** (Of thing) be at
rest, usu. more or less horizontally, on surface (*lie at
the* DOOR *of*; ∿ **in ruins** or **in the dust**, be
overthrown or fallen; ∿ **on the table**, be laid on the
TABLE 10; ∿ **heavy**, be a weight on one's stomach or
conscience); be stored up in specified place (*money
lying at the bank*); be situated (*land lying high, to the east*,

round; how the LAND¹ *lies*); be spread out to view (*lie on
the surface, before us, open*); (of road, course of travel,
etc.) lead *through, by, along, among*, etc.; (of ship) float
in berth or at anchor; (of abstract thing) exist, be
found, reside, be arranged or related, in some
position or manner (*the choice lies between these three; my
sympathy lies with Mary; knows where his interest lies; how
do these facts lie to each other?; the remedy lies in education;
her strength lay in her weakness*; **as far as in me** ∿**s**, to
the best of my power; ∿**s with you**, is your business
or right *to do*); (Law) be admissible or sustainable
(*action, appeal, objection, will not lie*). **6.** ∿ **about**, be left
carelessly out of place; ∿ **back**, recline so as to rest; ∿
by, be unused, keep quiet or retired; ∿ **down**, have
brief rest in or on bed etc., whence ∿-*down n.*; ∿
down under, accept without protest; **lying down**,
in abject manner, not standing up to opponent etc.,
(*take defeat* etc., esp. *it, lying down*); ∿ **in**, (1) be
brought to bed in childbirth (*lying-in hospital*), (2)
||(colloq.) lie idly in bed late in the morning, whence
∿-*in n.*; ∿ **off**, (Naut.) stand some distance from
shore or other ship; ∿ **over**, be deferred; ∿ **to**,
(Naut.) come almost to a stop with head near wind
by backing or shortening sail; ∿ **up**, go into or be in
hiding, take to one's bed or room, (of ship) go into
dock or be out of commission. **7.** ∿-**abed**, late riser.
[OE *licgan*, = OS *liggian*, OHG *liggen*, ON *liggja* f.
Gmc *ligjan* (*leg-*, *lag-*, *lǣg-*, f. IE *legh-*, *logh-*)]
lie⁴ *n*. way, direction, or position, in which thing lies
(||∿ **of the land**, (fig.) state of affairs); position of
golf-ball to be struck (*recovered well from a bad lie*); place
where animal or bird is accustomed to lie. [f. prec.]
Liebfraumilch (lē'pfrowmilχ) *n*. mild white Rhine
wine. [G (*Liebfrau* Virgin Mary, patroness of convent
where it was first made, *milch* milk)]
lied (lēt) *n*. (*pl*. ∿'*er pr*. lē'der). German song esp. of
Romantic period. [G]
lief *adv*. (arch.) gladly, willingly, (usu. I *had* or *would as
lief* do one thing *as* another). [orig. adj., f. OE *lēof*
dear, pleasant, = OS *liof*, OHG *liub*, ON *ljúfr*, Goth.
liufs f. Gmc *leubhaz*; cf. LEAVE¹, LOVE¹]
liege *a*. & *n*. (usu. Hist.) **1.** *a*. (Of superior) entitled to
receive, (of vassal) bound to give, feudal service or
allegiance; ∿ **lord**, feudal superior, sovereign;
∿'**man**, sworn vassal, faithful follower. **2.** *n*. liege lord
(esp. *my liege* in voc.); (usu. in *pl*.) vassal, subject. [ME,
f. OF *li*(*e*)*ge* f. med. L *laeticus* (*letus, litus*, prob. f. Gmc)]
li'en¹ (lē'en) *n*. right or property to keep possession
of it till debt due in respect of it is discharged. [F,
f. OF *loien* f. L *ligamen* bond (*ligare* bind)]
li'en². See LIE³.
liĕr'ne *n*. short rib connecting bosses and intersections
of vaulting-ribs. [ME f. F; cf. LIANA]
lieu (lū) *n*. **in** ∿, in the place, instead, (*of*). [ME f. F,
L *locus* place]
Lieut. *abbr*. Lieutenant.
lieutĕ'n|ant (lĕft-, lĕft-) *n*. **1.** deputy, substitute, acting
for a superior (L∿ant of the Tower, acting commandant of Tower of London; ||LORD *Lieutenant*,
||DEPUTY *lieutenant*); (*first*) ∿ant, army (*or air
force) officer next below captain; navy officer next
below lieutenant-commander; *policeman next
below captain; ||FLIGHT¹ *lieutenant*; SECOND *lieutenant*;
∿ant-colonel, -commander, -general, officers
ranking just below colonel etc.; ∿ant-governor,
acting or deputy governor of state, province, etc.,
under governor(-general). **2.** Hence ∿ANCY *n*. [ME f.
OF (*lieu* place, TENANT hold)]
life *n*. (*pl*. lives *pr*. -vz). **1.** state of functional activity
and continual change peculiar to organized matter,
and esp. to the portion of it constituting an animal or
plant before death, animate existence, being alive; **a
matter of** ∿ **and death**, something on which it
depends whether one shall live or die, (fig.) something of vital importance; *life and* LIMB¹; **come to** ∿,
emerge from unconsciousness or inactivity; **for** one's
∿, **for dear** ∿, (as if) to escape death; **cannot for**

the ∿ of me, could not even if my life depended on it; lay down one's ∿, accept being killed; lose one's ∿, be killed (*many lives were lost*, many were killed); *a new* LEASE *of life*; not on your ∿, (colloq.) most certainly not; *a* PRICE *on his life*; save one's ∿, avoid death; save person's ∿, prevent his dying; SELL one's *life dear*(*ly*); STAFF[1] *of life*; take ∿, kill person(s) or animal(s); take one's (own) ∿, kill oneself; take one's ∿ in one's hands, risk it; upon my ∿ (form of asseveration). **2.** energy, liveliness, vivacity, animation; vivifying influence (*was the life*, or, *life and soul, of the party*); put some ∿ into it, (colloq.) act more energetically. **3.** living things and their activity (*very little life to be seen*); the living form or (esp. nude) model, life-size figure etc., (*taken from the life*); as large as ∿, (1) life-size, (2) in person (*here he is, as large as life*); larger than ∿, exaggerated; *portray* etc. to the ∿, with fidelity to the original; true to ∿, with accurate representation of persons' behaviour etc.; hence ∿'LIKE (-fl-) *a.* **4.** period from birth to death, birth to present time (*have done it all my life*), or present time to death; get the fright, have the TIME[1], etc., of one's ∿, (colloq.) be frightened, enjoy oneself, etc., as never before; ∿ (sentence), annuity, ∿ membership, etc., (to continue for rest of person's life); for ∿, for the rest of one's life. **5.** INSURE one's *life*; expectation of ∿, average period that person at specified age may expect to live; a good, bad, ∿, person likely to pass, fall short of, this average. **6.** fresh start after narrowly escaped death (usu. fig.); cat has nine lives (is hard to kill); *batsman* etc. is given a ∿, not put out when he gives a chance; *player in game has three* lives, successive chances before being put out. **7.** individual's actions and fortunes, manner of existence; particular aspect or type of this (*his* SEX *life, private life; village life*); make ∿ easy, not create problems; in ∿, to be experienced anywhere (*nothing in life surpasses that*); this ∿ (on earth); the other, the future, ∿, state of existence after death; eternal, everlasting, ∿ (in heaven); *the* SIMPLE *life*; this is the ∿ (expr. contentment); what a ∿! (expr. discontent). **8.** written story of person's life, biography. **9.** active part of existence, business and pleasures of the world; HIGH, LOW[1], *life*; SEE[1] *life.* **10.** (Theol.) salvation, regenerate condition; WATER[1] *of life.* **11.** time for which an inanimate thing exists or continues to function (*battery has a life of two years*) or be saleable or valid. **12.** ∿-and-death, vitally important; ∿'belt (of buoyant material to support body in water); ∿-blood, blood necessary to life, vitalizing influence; ∿'boat (of special construction for saving life at sea); ∿-breath, inspiring influence, sustaining principle; *life*BUOY[1]; ∿ cycle, series of forms of an organism between successive occurrences of a given form, or between coming into existence and death; ∿ estate, property that one holds for life but cannot dispose of further; ∿ expectancy, expectation of life (see sense 5); ∿-giving, that gives, sustains, or restores, physical or spiritual life; ∿-guard, (1) bodyguard of soldiers, (2) expert swimmer to rescue bathers from drowning; ||L∿ Guards, regiment of household cavalry (now armoured corps); ∿ history, (1) history of person's life, (2) series of developments of organism from egg etc. to death; ∿ insurance (for payment on death of insured person); ∿ interest, right to life estate; ∿-jacket (as *life*belt); ∿'line, (1) rope used for life-saving, e.g. that attached to lifebuoy, diver's signalling line, (fig.) sole means of communication, (2) (Palmistry) = LINE[2] *of life*; ∿'long, continued throughout a life; ∿-office (dealing in life insurance); ∿ peer(age) (with title lapsing at death); ∿-preserver, (1) short stick with heavily loaded end, (2) life-jacket etc.; ∿-raft, = RAFT[2] (often inflatable); ∿-saver, person or thing that saves from death or from serious difficulty, esp. (Austral. & NZ) = *life*-guard (2); ∿ sciences, biology and kindred

subjects; ∿-size(d), of the same size as the living person etc.; ∿-style, individual's way of life; ∿-support *a.*, (of equipment) allowing vital functions to continue in adverse environment or during severe disablement; ∿-table, statistics of expectation of life; ∿'time, duration of person's life (*chance* etc. *of a ∿time*, such as occurs only once in a person's life), duration of existence (= sense 11); ∿-work, task pursued throughout life. [OE *līf*, = OS *līf*, ON *līf*, OHG *līb* life, body, f. Gmc **lībham* (**lībh-*; cf. LIVE[2])]

li'feless (-fl-) *a.* no longer living; unconscious; not having life, inanimate; lacking animation or vigour; hence ∿LY[2] *adv.*, ∿NESS *n.* [OE *līfleas* (as LIFE, -LESS)]

li'fer *n.* (sl.) person sentenced to, sentence of, imprisonment for life. [f. LIFE + -ER[1]]

lift *v. & n.* **1.** *v.t.* raise to higher position, take up, hoist, (*up, off, out*); elevate to higher plane of thought or feeling; give upward direction to (eyes, face); dig up (potatoes etc. at harvest); hit (cricket-ball) into air; ∿ (up) one's hands or heart (in prayer etc.); ∿ one's hand (to take oath); ∿ a hand, make the slightest effort, usu. *to do*; ∿ a hand against, strike (person); ∿ up one's head, recover vigour after prostration; ∿ down, pick up and bring to lower position; ∿-off, (*a.*) removable simply by lifting, (*n.*) vertical take-off of spacecraft or rocket; ∿ up one's voice, (1) sing or speak, (2) cry out. **2.** hold or have on high (*church lifts its spire*); steal (esp. cattle), take (passage, information) as plagiarist; strike (tent etc.); remove (barrier, restriction); carry without charge as passenger in vehicle; have one's face ∿ed, undergo face-lifting. **3.** *v.i.* yield to upward force (*window will not lift*); (of cloud, fog, darkness) rise, disperse; (of floor) swell upwards, bulge. **4.** *n.* lifting; carrying of person without charge as passenger in vehicle; transport by air, quantity thus transported; one layer of leather in heel of boot or shoe; ||apparatus for raising and lowering persons or things to other floor of building; apparatus for carrying persons up or down mountain etc.; supporting or elevating influence; amount of rise of water in canal lock; rise in level of ground; upward pressure which the air exerts on an aircraft, counteracting the force of gravity. [ME, f. ON *lypta* f. Gmc **luftjan* (**luftuz* air)]

li'gament *n.* **1.** (Anat.) short band of tough flexible fibrous tissue binding bones together; any membranous fold keeping organ in position. **2.** similar structure in oyster etc. **3.** (arch.) bond of union. **4.** Hence ∿AL, ∿ARY[1], ∿OUS, (-mĕ'n-) *adjs.* [ME, f. L *ligamentum* (*ligare* bind; see -MENT)]

li'ga'te *v.t.* (Surg.) tie up (bleeding artery etc.); hence ∿A'TION *n.* [f. L *ligare* + -ATE[3]]

li'gature *n., & v.t.* **1.** *n.* thing used in tying, esp. band or cord used to tie up bleeding artery, strangulate tumour, etc.; thing that unites, bond; tying, ligation; (Mus.) slur, tie; (Print.) two or more letters joined (*fi* etc.). **2.** *v.t.* bind with ligature. [ME, f. LL *ligatura* (as prec.; see -URE)]

li'ger (-g-) *n.* offspring of lion and tigress. [portmanteau wd f. LION + TIGER]

light[1] *n.* **1.** the natural agent that stimulates the sense of sight; visible or other electromagnetic radiation from sun, fire, lamp, etc. **2.** medium or condition of space in which this is present and therefore sight is possible (opp. *darkness*). **3.** appearance of brightness (*saw a distant light*; NORTHERN, SOUTHERN, *lights*; ZODIACAL *light*). **4.** amount of illumination in place (in a good ∿, easily visible; *bad light stopped play*); one's fair or ordinary share of this (stand in person's ∿, deprive him of this, (fig.) prejudice his chances). **5.** vivacity, enthusiasm, or inspiration in person's eyes; ∿ of person's countenance, his favour, approving presence, or sanction (often iron.). **6.** sun's direct or diffused or reflected rays, daylight; SEE[1] the light (of day). **7.** being visible or exposed; come, bring, to ∿, be revealed, reveal; come to ∿ with, (Austral. & NZ colloq.) produce (money etc.). **8.** object from which brightness emanates (∼ of one's **eyes** or **life**, beloved person), sun or other heavenly body, ignited candle or lamp or the like (GREEN¹, RED, *light*); (collect.) lamps etc. illuminating place; beacon lamp esp. of ship or lighthouse; lighthouse; traffic-light; (fig.) eminent person, luminary; *light under* BUSHEL¹; **festival of** ∼**s**, Hanukkah; **out like a** ∼, deeply asleep (or otherwise unconscious); ∼**s out**, bedtime in school etc., (Mil.) last bugle-call of day. **9.** mental illumination, elucidation (**throw** or **shed** ∼ **upon** or **on**, help to explain), enlightenment (**by the** ∼ **of nature**, without aid of revelation or teaching; *light and* LEADING¹; SEE¹ *the light*); (in *pl.*) facts or discoveries serving to explain subject (*we have many new lights upon it since then*); (in *pl.*) one's natural or acquired mental attitude and ability (usu. *do one's best* etc. *according to* one's *lights*). **10.** aspect in which thing is viewed (**in the** ∼ **of** *these facts*, with the help given by; **appeared in the** ∼ **of** *a scoundrel*, seemed to be; **place in a good** ∼, represent favourably). **11.** (In crossword etc.) one of the words to be deduced from clues. **12.** (Theol.) brightness of heaven, illumination of soul by divine truth. **13.** window or opening in wall for admission of light; perpendicular division of mullioned window; window of vehicle (∥QUARTER¹- -*light*); glazed compartment of side or roof in greenhouse. **14.** (Paint.) illuminated surface; part of picture represented as lighted up. **15.** (Law). light falling on windows, the obstruction of which by neighbour is illegal (ANCIENT¹ *lights*). **16.** flame or spark serving to ignite (**strike a** ∼, produce this with match etc., also ∥as sl. *int.* of surprise etc.); thing used for igniting, spill, taper, match. **17.** ∼ **due, duty**, toll on ships for maintenance of lighthouses and lightships; ∼'**house**, tower or other structure containing beacon light to warn or guide ships at sea; ∼ **meter**, instrument for measuring intensity of light, esp. exposure meter; ∼ **pen**, photoelectric device for communicating with computer by movement esp. over screen of cathode-ray tube; *light*- -PROOF²; ∼'**ship**, moored or anchored ship with beacon light; ∼ **show**, display of changing coloured lights for entertainment; *light*-TIGHT; ∼-**year**, (Astron.) distance light travels in one year, about 6 million million miles. **18.** Hence ∼'LESS *a*. [OE *lēoht*, *līht*, = OS, OHG *lioht* f. WG **leuhta* f. IE **leuktom* (**leuk-* white)]

light² (līt) *a*. well provided with light, not dark; pale (often prefixed to *adjs*. & *ns*. of colour: *light-blue ribbon*; *I prefer light blue*; *light* BLUE²). [f. as prec.]

light³ (līt) *v*. (**lit** or ∼'**ed**; as attrib. *a*. usu. ∼*ed*). **1.** *v.t.* set (lamp etc., fire, fuel, tobacco, etc.) burning. **2.** give light to (room, street, etc.); cause (eyes, face, etc.) to light (sense 5). **3.** show (person his) way or surroundings with a light. **4.** *v.i.* (Of fuel, lamp, etc.) take fire, begin to burn or be bright. **5.** (Of eyes, face, etc.) brighten with animation. **6.** ∼ **up**, (1) = sense 1, (abs.) begin to smoke cigarette, pipe, etc., kindle lights in street or room at dusk, (2) light (room etc.) brightly, make conspicuous by light, (3) = sense 5; ∼**ing-u'p time** (after which vehicles on road must show prescribed lights); **lit up**, (sl.) drunk. **7.** Hence ∼'ING (1, 2, 6) *n*. [OE *līhtan* = OS *liuhtian*, Goth. *liuhtjan* f. Gmc (**leuht-* LIGHT¹)]

light⁴ (līt) *a*. & *adv*. **1.** *a*. of little weight, not heavy; (Phys., of isotope etc.) having not more than the usual mass; deficient in weight (*light coin* etc.); not abundant (*light traffic*). **2.** of low density (*light metal*). **3.** having, or intended for, a small load; (of ship) unladen; (of guns, battleship, etc.) of the smaller or light-armed kind; (of locomotive) with no train attached; (of railway) for transport of light loads only; (Mil.) carrying only light arms (*light brigade*); (of ship, cart, etc.) made lightly for small loads and quick movement. **4.** (Of building) not looking heavy, graceful, elegant; (Print., of type) not heavy or bold. **5.** acting gently, applied delicately, not violent, (*light*

touch, blow, rain, wind, step, etc.); ∼ **hand**, lit., or fig. = tactful management. **6.** not dense or tenacious; porous, friable, (*light soil, pastry*). **7.** easy to digest (*light meal*); (of wine or beer) not strong. **8.** not important (**make** ∼ **of**, treat as of no consequence); slight, not severe. **9.** trivial, venial, not grave; jesting, thoughtless, frivolous. **10.** wanton, unchaste, (esp. of woman or her conduct). **11.** nimble, quick-moving, (*light of foot*; *light heels, movements, rhythm*); ∼ **fingers** (good at stealing). **12.** easily borne (*light punishment, taxation, rule, expense*) or done (*light work, task*). **13.** aimed or aiming merely at entertainment (*light literature, writer, comedy, comedian, programme, relief*). **14.** (Of sleep) easily disturbed, not profound, (so *light sleeper*). **15.** free from sorrow, cheerful, hopeful, (*light heart*). **16.** giddy (*light in the head*). **17.** ∼-**armed**, with light weapons or armour; ∼**er-than-air'**, (of aircraft) weighing less than the air it displaces; ∼-**fingered**, apt to steal; ∼'**foot(ed)**, nimble; ∼-**hea'ded**, giddy, delirious, frivolous; ∼-**hea'rted**, (1) cheerful, gay, (2) (unduly) optimistic or casual; ∼ **horse(man)**, (member of) light-armed cavalry; ∼ **industry** (producing small or light articles); ∼ **infantry** (with light weapons); ∼-**mi'nded**, frivolous; ∼ **oil**, a lighter-than-water oil obtained from coal tar by distillation at low temperature; ∼-**o'-love**, fickle woman, prostitute; *light* OPERA¹; ∼'**weight** *a*. & *n*., (person or animal or garment) below average weight (see BOX⁵), (fig.) (person) of little ability or importance. **18.** Hence ∼'LY² *adv*. **19.** *adv*. in light manner (*tread, sleep, light*); with minimum load (*travel light*); ∼ **come** ∼ **go**, = EASY *come easy go*. [OE *lēoht*, *līht*, = OS *-līht*, OHG *līht(i)*, ON *léttr*, Goth. *leihts* f. Gmc **linhtaz* (**lingw-* f. IE **leñgh* ʷ.)]

light⁵ (līt) *v.i.* (**lit** or ∼'**ed**). **1.** (arch.) alight, descend, come down. **2.** chance, come by chance, (*up*)*on*. **3.** (sl.) ∼ **into**, attack; ∼ **out**, depart. [OE *līhtan*, = OHG *līhten*, ON *létta* f. Gmc **līhtjan* (**linht-* LIGHT⁴); sense f. idea of relieving horse etc. of weight)]

li'ghten¹ (lī't-) *v*. **1.** *v.t.* reduce load of (ship etc.); bring relief to (mind, heart, etc.); reduce weight of, (fig.) mitigate. **2.** *v.i.* grow lighter in weight etc. [ME, f. LIGHT⁴ + -EN⁶]

li'ghten² (lī't-) *v*. **1.** *v.t.* shed light upon, make bright (lit., or fig., *lighten our darkness*). **2.** *v.i.* (Of face, eyes, sky, etc.) grow bright, shine, flash; (of sky, clouds, or *it*) emit lightning. [ME, f. LIGHT² + -EN⁶]

li'ghter¹ (lī't-) *n*. In vbl senses; device for lighting cigarettes etc. e.g. with flint, steel, and fuel, or electrically. [f. LIGHT³ + -ER¹]

li'ghter² (lī't-) *n*. & *v.t.* **1.** *n*. boat, usu. flat-bottomed, for unloading and loading ships not brought to wharf and for transporting goods in harbour; ∼'**man**, worker in lighter; hence ∼AGE (4) *n*. **2.** *v.t.* remove (goods) in lighter. [ME, f. MDu. *lichter* (as LIGHT⁵ in sense 'unload': see -ER¹)]

li'ghtish¹·² *adjs*., **li'ghtnèss¹·²** *ns*., (lī't-). In adj. senses. [f. LIGHT²·⁴ + -ISH¹ 2, -NESS]

li'ghtning (līt'-) *n*. & *a*. **1.** *n*. visible electric discharge between clouds or cloud and ground (BALL¹ *lightning*; **forked** ∼, lightning-flash in form of zigzag or branching line; **sheet** ∼, lightning-flash of diffused brightness; **summer** ∼, sheet lightning without audible thunder, result of distant storm); **like** (**greased**) colloq.) ∼, with greatest conceivable speed; ***∼**-bug**, firefly; ∼**-conductor**, ***∼**-rod**, metal rod or wire fixed to exposed part of building or to mast to divert lightning into earth or sea. **2.** *a*. very quick (*with lightning speed*); ∼ **chess** (in which moves must be made at very short intervals); ∼ **strike**, (1) being struck by lightning, (2) labour strike at short notice by way of surprise. [ME, different. f. *lightening* vbl n. of LIGHTEN²]

lights (līts) *n. pl.* lungs of sheep, pigs, bullocks, etc., used as a food esp. for cats and dogs. [ME, n. use of LIGHT⁴; cf. LUNG]

li'ghtsome¹ (lī't-) *a*. light, graceful, elegant, in

appearance; light-hearted, merry; nimble; hence ~LY² (-mlĭ) adv., ~NESS (-mn-) n. [ME, f. LIGHT⁴ + -SOME¹]

li′ghtsome² (lī′t-) a. light-giving, luminous; well lighted, bright. [ME, f. LIGHT¹ + -SOME¹]

li′ghtwŏŏd (lī′t-) n. tree with light wood; *(tree with) wood that burns with bright flame. [f. LIGHT⁴·¹ + WOOD]

līgn-ä′lŏes (līnă′lōz) n. the drug aloes; aromatic E. Ind. wood from tree of genus *Aquilaria*; aromatic Mexican wood from tree of genus *Bursera*. [ME, f. LL *lignum aloes* wood of the ALOE]

li′gnĕous a. (Of plant) woody (opp. *herbaceous*). [f. L *ligneus* (as foll.) + -OUS]

li′gni- comb. form. wood, as: ~FEROUS (-ĭ′f-), ~FORM, adjs., ~FY v.t. & i. [f. L *lignum* wood + -I-]

li′gnin n. (Bot.) stiffening material in cell-walls of woody tissue. [f. as prec. + -IN]

li′gnīte n. brown coal showing traces of plant structure, intermediate between bituminous coal and peat. [F, f. as LIGNI- + -ITE¹ (2)]

lignum vi′tae (-vī′tē, -vē′tī) n. = GUAIACUM 2. [L, = wood of life]

li′grŏin n. solvent derived from petroleum. [20th c., of unkn. orig.]

li′gūlate a. (Bot.) with strap-shaped florets. [f. as foll. ¦ -ATE²]

li′gūle n. (Bot.) narrow projection from top of leaf--sheath of grass. [f. L *ligula* strap, spoon (*lingere* lick; see -ULE)]

li′kable. Var. of LIKE²*able*.

līke¹ a., prep., adv., conj., & n. **1.** a. (often governing n. as if trans. part.; **more**, **most**, ~, occas., esp. poet., **li′ker, li′kest**). having feature(s) in common with something or each other or the original, (*in like manner; on this and the like subjects; the two letters are very like; as like as two peas; the picture is not like*); ~ **father** ~ **son**, ~ **master** ~ **man**, etc., as the one is so will the other be. **2.** (Alg. etc.) ~ **charges, signs** (both positive or both negative); ~ **quantities** (expressed by same letters). **3.** (arch.) ~ **with** or **to**, similar to (*beings of like passions with us; like to the lark at break of day arising*). **4.** resembling, such as, as good as; **what is he, it,** ~?, what sort of person is he, thing is it?; LOOK *like*; *like* THAT¹; **more** ~ **it**, nearer what is required; *a critic* ~ **you**, of the class that you exemplify; **nothing** ~′ (*as or so good, as or so many*, etc., or abs.) not nearly; SOMETHING *like*. **5.** characteristic of (*that is like your impudence; it was like him to think of himself last*). **6.** in suitable state or right mood for doing (LOOK *like*; *feel like working* or *stopping work*), or for having (*feel like a rest, a cup of tea*). **7.** (arch. or colloq.) likely (*as like as not; like enough*; *be* or **have** ~ *to* do, be on the point of doing; **had** ~ **to have done**, narrowly escaped doing). **8.** ~**-minded**, having same tastes, views, etc. **9.** prep. in the manner of, to the same degree as, (*cannot do it like you; do not talk like* THAT¹; *like a* SHOT¹; *like* MAD¹; *like* HELL; ~ **so**, (colloq.) in this manner; ~ **fun, anything**, etc., vigorously, intensely). **10.** (In proverbial or joc. pseudo-proverbial phrs., emphasizing vbs.) *blush like a peony, drink like a fish, fit like a glove, get on like a house on fire, smoke* (i.e. tobacco) *like a chimney, spread like wildfire, swear like a trooper, swim like a duck; hate person etc. like poison, scatter them like chaff*. **11.** adv. (arch. or colloq.) likely (*he will come, like enough*; cf. sense 7). **12.** (arch.) ~ **as**, in the same manner as. **13.** (vulg.) so to speak (*by way of argument, like*). **14.** conj. (colloq.; **D**) as (*cannot do it like you do; the snow is falling like in January*); *as if (ate like he had starved for days*); **tell it** ~ **it is**, give the facts. **15.** n. counterpart, equal, like thing or person, (*mix with your likes; shall not see his like again; did you ever see the like of it?; compare like with like*); **the** ~**s of me,** (colloq.) persons so humble as I; **the** ~**s of you**, (colloq.) persons so distinguished as you. **16.** (Golf). *the* stroke that equalizes number of strokes played by each side. **17.** (ellipt. use of a.; pl. same). thing(s) of the same kind (*will never do the like*

again); **and the** ~, and similar things, et cetera, (*music, painting, and the like*); **or the** ~, or other thing(s) of the same kind. [ME *līc, līk*, shortened form (= ON *līkr*) of OE *gelīc* = OS *gelīc*, OHG *gilīh*, ON *glīkr*, Goth. *galeiks* f. Gmc *galīkaz*; see Y-, LICH]

līke² v.t., & n. **1.** v.t. (arch. or joc.) be pleasing to (usu. impers.: *it likes me not, well*, etc.). **2.** find agreeable, congenial, or satisfactory, feel attracted by, wish for, prefer, (*I like you, the offer, his visits*, (iron.) *his impudence* or *that, her to be within reach, to see* or *seeing them now and then; do not like such subjects discussed; should* (*very*) *much like to come, like you to come; should like time to consider it; like my coffee black*); **should** ~ **to know** or **see**, (iron.) think you will find it hard to tell me, am not likely to see; **how do you** ~ **it?**, do you like it much or little or dislike it?; hence ~′ABLE (-ka-) a. **3. if you** ~ (expr. consent to request: *I will come if you like, you may come if you like*, or limited assent: *I am* shy *if you like*, i.e. but not misanthropic, or emphatic selection: I am *shy if you like*, i.e. but someone else is not). **4.** n. (usu. in *pl.*) liking's, predilection's (esp. *likes and dislikes*). [OE *līcian*, = OS *līkon*, OHG *līhhēn*, ON *līka*, Goth. *leikan* f. Gmc *līkōjan* *līkam*; see LICH]

-līke suf. forming adjs. f. *ns.*, w. sense 'similar to', 'characteristic of' (*godlike, ladylike, plumbago-like, shell--like*). [f. LIKE¹]

li′kelihŏŏd (-kl-) n. being likely (**in all** ~, very probably). [ME, f. foll. + -HOOD]

li′kely (-klĭ) a. & adv. **1.** a. such as might well happen, or be or prove true, or turn out to be the thing specified, probable, (*a likely story*, often iron.; *it is not likely* (*that*) *he will come; his most likely destination is London*). **2.** to be reasonably expected *to* (*he or this is or was not likely to come* or *happen*); promising, apparently suitable for purpose or *to* do or be, capable-looking, (*called at every likely house; six likely young fellows; the likeliest place for smugglers* or *to find him*). **3.** adv. probably (*it is more* or *most* or *quite* or *very likely right;* *it is likely right*). **4. as** ~ **as not**, with equal chances of happening etc. or not; **not** ~!, (colloq.) that is quite impossible. **5.** Hence **li′keliness** (-kl-) n. [ME, f. ON *līkligr* (as LIKE¹, -LY¹)]

li′ken v.t. find or point out resemblance in (thing or person) *to*. [ME, f. LIKE¹ + -EN⁶]

li′keness (-kn-) n. being like, resemblance (*between, to*); semblance, guise, form (*in the likeness of*); representation, copy, portrait (*take person's* ~, portray him). [OE *gelīknes* (as LIKE¹, -NESS)]

li′kewīse (-kwīz) adv. also, moreover, too; **do** ~, act similarly. [for *in like wise*]

li′king n. what one likes, one's taste (*is it to your liking?*); regard, fondness, taste, fancy, *for* (*have a liking for him, for precise statements; no liking for flattery*). [OE *līcung* (as LIKE², -ING¹)]

li′lac n. & a. **1.** n. shrub of genus *Syringa*, esp. *S. vulgaris* with fragrant pale pinkish-violet or white, blossoms. **2.** a. & n. (of) pale pinkish-violet colour. [obs. F f. Sp., f. Arab. *līlāk* f. Pers. *līlak* var. of *nīlak* bluish (*nīl* blue)]

liliä′ceous (-shŭs) a. of the lily family Liliaceae; lily--like. [f. LL *liliaceus* f. L *lilium* lily; see -ACEOUS]

lillipū′tian (-shan) a. & n. diminutive (person or thing). [f. *Lilliput* in Swift's *Gulliver's Travels* + -IAN]

lilt v. & n. (Sc. or literary). **1.** v.t. & i. sing or speak merrily or very rhythmically. **2.** n. (song with) marked rhythmical cadence or swing; light springing gait. [ME *lilte, lülte*, of unkn. orig.]

li′lỹ n. **1.** (flower of) bulbous herb of genus *Lilium* bearing large showy white or reddish or purplish often spotted flowers on tall slender stem, esp. *L. candidum*, the white or madonna lily; plant of family Liliaceae with similar flowers; **gild** or **paint the** ~, try to improve what is already quite satisfactory; ~ **of the valley**, spring herb with two large leaves and racemes of white bell-shaped fragrant flowers; WATER¹-*lily*. **2.** person or thing of special whiteness or purity (**lilies and roses**, fair complexion); heraldic fleur-de-lis (**the lilies**, arms of old French monarchy,

Bourbon dynasty). **3.** (*attrib.*) delicately white (*lily maid, hand*, etc.); pallid. **4.** ∼**-iron,** harpoon with detachable head for killing swordfish; ∼**-livered,** cowardly; ∼**-pad,** floating leaf of water-lily; ∼**-white,** white as a lily, (fig.) faultless, *excluding Blacks. **5.** Hence **li′li**ED² (-lid) *a.* [OE *lilie* f. L *lilium* prob. f. Gk *leirion*]

li′ma (lē′-) *n.* ∼ (**bean**), (flat white seed of) *Phaseolus limensis* of tropical America. [f. *L*∼ in Peru]

limb¹ (-m) *n.*, & *v.t.* **1.** *n.* projecting part of animal body used in movement or grasping; *escape* **with life and** ∼, without grave injury; *tear* ∼ *from* ∼, completely dismember with violence. **2.** (orig. ∼ **of the devil** or **Satan**) mischievous child; ∼ **of the law,** lawyer, policeman, etc. **3.** large branch of tree (**out on a** ∼, (fig.) isolated, stranded, at a disadvantage); one of four branches of cross; clause of sentence; spur of mountain. **4.** Hence (-)∼ED² (-md), ∼′LESS, *adjs.* **5.** *v.t.* dismember (body). [OE *lim*, = ON *limr*, prob. f. Gmc *li-* as in dial. *lith*]

limb² (-m) *n.* graduated edge of quadrant etc.; edge (*eastern, lower*, etc., *limb*) of sun, moon, etc.; broad part of petal, sepal, or leaf. [f. F *limbe* or f. L *limbus* hem, border]

li′mbĕck. Var. (arch.) of ALEMBIC.

li′mber¹ *n.*, & *v.t.* **1.** *n.* detachable front of gun-carriage (two wheels, axle, pole, and ammunition-box as seat). **2.** *v.t.* ∼ (**up**), attach limber to (gun), fasten together two parts of (gun-carriage, or abs.). [ME *limo(u)r*, app. rel. to med. L *limonarius* (*limo -onis* shaft); for *-b-* cf. *slumber*]

li′mber² *n.* (Naut.) gutter on either side of keelson for drainage to pump-well. [f. F *lumière* light, hole, limber, f. Rom. *luminaria* f. pl. of L *luminare* lamp (LUMEN)]

li′mber³ *a.* & *v.* **1.** *a.* flexible; lithe, nimble. **2.** *v.t.* ∼ (**up**), make limber (person, body). **3.** *v.i.* ∼ (**up**), make oneself limber. [perh. f. LIMBER¹, w. ref. to movement of shafts]

li′mbo¹ *n.* (*pl.* ∼s). region on border of hell, supposed abode of souls of pre-Christian righteous persons and unbaptized infants; prison, confinement; condition of neglect or oblivion. [ME, f. med. L phr. *in limbo*, f. *limbus* (see LIMB²)]

li′mbo² *n.* (*pl.* ∼s). W. Ind. dance in which dancer bends backwards and passes repeatedly under horizontal bar gradually lowered to just above ground. [Caribbean name]

Li′mbŭrger (-g-) *n.* soft white cheese with characteristic strong smell, orig. made in Limburg. [Du., f. *Limburg* in Belgium; see -ER¹]

lime¹ *n.*, & *v.t.* **1.** *n.* bir′d∼, (arch.) ∼, sticky substance made from holly bark and spread on twigs to catch small birds. **2.** (qui′ck)∼, white caustic alkaline earth (calcium oxide) got by heating limestone etc. and used for making mortar, as fertilizer, etc.; **slaked** ∼, this after combination with water, calcium hydroxide; hence ∼′LESS (-ml-), **li′m**Y², *adjs.* **3.** ∼**-burner,** maker of lime; ∼**-kiln** (for heating limestone); ∼′**light,** intense white light got by heating cylinder of lime in oxyhydrogen flame; *the* ∼*light*, (fig., w. ref. to former use in theatre) full glare of publicity; ∼**-pit** (for steeping hides to remove hair); ∼′**stone,** rock composed mainly of calcium carbonate; ∼**-twig** (smeared with birdlime); ∼**-wash,** mixture of lime and water for coating walls; ∼ **water,** solution of calcium hydroxide as antacid or to detect carbon dioxide by white precipitate of calcium carbonate. **4.** *v.t.* smear (twigs), catch (bird), with birdlime; trap as if with birdlime; treat, dress (land), with lime; steep (skins) in lime and water; bleach (wood) by treating with lime. [OE *līm*, = MDu., OHG *līm*, ON *līm* f. Gmc *līm* cogn. w. *laim-* LOAM]

lime² *n.* round fruit of tree *Citrus medica*, like lemon but smaller and more acid; ∼(**-green**), its yellowish-green colour; ∼(**-juice**), its juice (used as drink and esp. as antiscorbutic). [F, f. mod. Prov. *limo*, Sp. *lima* f. Arab. *līma*; cf. LEMON¹]

lime³ *n.* (-tree), ornamental tree of genus *Tilia* esp. *T. europaea* with heart-shaped leaves and small fragrant yellowish blossom. [alt. of *line* = *lind*; see LINDEN]

li′mĕn *n.* (Psych.) = THRESHOLD; hence **li′min**AL *a.* [L *limen liminis* = threshold, representing G *schwelle*]

li′merick *n.* kind of humorous verse, esp. five-line form often epigrammatic or indecent, with rhymes *aabba* (popularized by Edward Lear's nursery rhymes). [said to be f. chorus 'Will you come up to Limerick?' sung after extempore verses contributed by each member of party, f. *L*∼ in Ireland]

‖**li′me-wort,** ‖**li′mpwort,** (-ẽrt) *n.* = BROOK¹*lime*. [f. *lime*, *lempe*, OE *hleomoce*, + WORT]

*****Li′mey** *n.* (sl. derog.) British person esp. sailor; British ship. [f. *lime-juicer* in same senses (because use of *lime*²-juice was enforced in British Navy) + -Y³]

li′mit *n.* bounding line, terminal point (**upper, lower,** ∼, largest and smallest possible or permissible amount); line or point that may not or cannot be passed (**within** ∼**s,** to some extent but not unrestrictedly; **without** ∼, unlimited(ly); **is the** ∼, (sl.) is the last straw, intolerable, etc.; *****off** ∼**s,** out of bounds); (Math.) quantity which function or sum of series can be made to approach as closely as desired; ∼ **man** (receiving longest start allowed in handicap, opp. *scratch*); hence ∼LESS *a.* [ME, f. L *limes limitis* boundary, frontier]

li′mit *v.t.* confine within limits, set (usu. non-material) bounds to, restrict *to*; serve as limit to; (in *p.p.*) few or scanty; ‖*limited* (LIABILITY) *company*; ∼ed **edition** (with limited number of copies); ∼ed **monarchy** etc. (subject to constitutional restrictions, opp. *absolute*); *****∼ed** (**train**), fast train with limited accommodation and stops; so ∼ATIVE *a.* [ME, f. OF *limiter*, or f. L *limitare* (as prec.)]

li′mitary *a.* subject to restriction; of, on, serving as limit. [f., or f. L *limitaris* as, LIMIT¹ + -ARY²]

li′mita′tion *n.* limiting; limited condition, disability or inability, (**has his** ∼**s,** is untalented in some directions); limiting rule or circumstance; legally specified period beyond which action cannot be brought, estate or law is not to continue, etc., (**statute of** ∼**s,** any statute that fixes such period). [ME, f. L *limitatio* (as LIMIT²; see -ATION)]

li′mitrophe *a.* (Of district etc.) on frontier, adjacent *to*. [F, f. LL *limitrophus* f. L *limes* limit + Gk *-trophos* -feeding, orig. of lands set apart for support of frontier troops]

limn (-m) *v.t.* (arch. or literary). paint (picture); depict, portray; hence **li′mn**ER¹ *n.* [f. obs. *lumine* illuminate (MSS.), f. OF *luminer* f. L *luminare* (LUMEN)]

limnŏ′log‖**ў** *n.* study of physical phenomena of lakes and other fresh waters; hence **limnolŏ′g**ICAL *a.*, ∼IST (3) *n.* [f. Gk *limnē* lake + -o- + -LOGY]

li′mousine (-ōozēn) *n.* motor car with enclosed body and partition behind driver; luxurious motor car. [F, orig. caped cloak worn in former French province of *Limousin*]

limp¹ *v.i.*, & *n.* **1.** *v.i.* walk lamely, (of verse) halt; (of damaged ship, aircraft, etc.) proceed slowly or with difficulty. **2.** *n.* lame walk. [cogn. w. OE *lemp-healt* lame, MHG *limpfen* limp, f. WG *lamp-* f. IE *lomb-*]

limp² *a.* not stiff, flexible, (of bookbinding) not stiffened with millboard; (fig.) lacking energy; hence ∼′LY² *adv.*, ∼′NESS *n.* [18th c., of unkn. orig., perh. rel. to prec., w. sense 'hanging loose']

li′mpĕt *n.* marine gastropod mollusc with shallow conical shell sticking tightly to rocks; (fig.) person, esp. State employee, who clings to office; ∼ **mine** (attached to ship's hull and exploding after set time). [OE *lempedu* f. med. L *lampreda* limpet, LAMPREY]

li′mpid *a.* (Of liquid, atmosphere, eyes, literary style) pellucid, clear, not turbid; hence or cogn. ∼LY² *adv.*, ∼ITY (-ĭ′d-), ∼NESS, *ns.* [f. F *limpide* or f. L *limpidus*, perh. cogn. w. LYMPH]

li'mpkin *n.* wading-bird of genus *Aramus*, intermediate between crane and rail. [f. LIMP¹ + -KIN, from its movements]

limpwort. See LIME-WORT.

li'mūl|us *n.* (*pl.* ∼i *pr.* -ī). = KING¹-*crab* (1). [mod. L, f. L *limulus* dim. of *limus* askew]

li'mÿ. See LIME¹.

li'nage *n.* number of lines in printed matter; payment according to this. [f. LINE² + -AGE]

li'nchpin *n.* pin passed through axle-end to keep wheel in place; (fig.) element or person vital to an organization etc. [f. ME *linch* f. OE *lynis*, = OS *lunisa*, + PIN¹]

Li'ncoln (-ngkon) *n.* ∼ **green**, bright green cloth made at Lincoln, formerly worn by outlaws etc. in Sherwood Forest. [∼ in England]

Lincru'sta (-n-k-) *n.* (**P**) wallpaper covered with embossed linoleum. [f. L *linum* flax + *crusta* rind]

Lincs. *abbr.* Lincolnshire.

li'nctus *n.* medicine to be licked up; soothing syrupy cough-mixture. [L (*lingere* lick)]

li'ndāne *n.* colourless crystalline isomer of benzene hexachloride used as insecticide. [f. T. van der *Linden*, Du. chemist b. 1884 + -ANE]

li'nden *n.* lime-tree [orig a , f. OE *lind* lime-tree (= OHG *linta*, ON *lind*), + -EN⁵; cf. LIME³]

line¹ *n.* fine long flax separated from the tow by hackling. [OE *līn*, = OS, OHG, ON *līn*, Goth. *lein* f. Gmc *līnam*, cogn. w. or f. L *linum* flax]

line² *n.* **1.** piece of rope (esp. Naut., e.g. for sounding; so prob. **hard** ∼**s**, bad luck, hardship); = CLOTHES-*line.* **2.** wire or cable for telegraph or telephone, connection by this (HOLD¹ *the line; the line is bad*; PARTY¹ *line*); ∼**man** (employed to keep such wire etc. in repair); **get** one's or **the** ∼**s** (= WIRES) **crossed. 3.** cord bearing fish-hook(s); ∼**fishing** (opp. *net-fishing*); HOOK¹, *line, and sinker*; **give** person ∼ **enough**, let him go his own way for a time in order to secure or detect him later. **4.** cord for measuring, levelling, etc. (PLUMB¹ *line*); **by rule and** ∼, with precision. **5.** (in *pl.*) one's lot in life [Ps. 16:6, w. ref. to marking out land]; *reins for horse etc. **6.** long narrow mark traced on surface; use of these in draughtsmanship (*boldness, purity, of line; translate life* etc. *into line and colour*); ∼**-drawing** (done with pen or pencil); ∼**-engraving** (done with incised lines, opp. *etching* and *mezzotint*); ∼**-work** (with pen or pencil, not wash etc.); ∼ **of beauty**, line with two opposite curves like elongated S. **7.** one of the very narrow horizontal sections in which televised scenes are photographed and reproduced. **8.** narrow range of spectrum that is noticeably brighter or darker than adjacent parts. **9.** (Games). mark limiting court or ground or special parts of them. **10.** thing resembling traced mark, band of colour, seam, furrow, wrinkle (∼ *of life, fortune*, etc., folds in palm of hand regarded as significant in palmistry). **11.** (Math.) straight or curved continuous extent of length without breadth; track of moving point. **12.** curve connecting all points having specified common property; **the L**∼, the equator; *line* SQUALL; ∼ **of force**, (Phys.) curve whose direction at each point is that of electric etc. force there. **13.** straight line; *the* (usu. imaginary) horizontal straight line through feet of most letters (*on the line*; g *and* y *extend below the line*); ∼ **drive**, low straight hit at baseball; *line of* FIRE¹; **in** ∼, so as to form a straight line (*with*); *picture* **hung on the** ∼, exhibited with its centre about level with spectator's eye; ∼ **of sight** or **vision** (along which observer looks). **14.** contour, outline, lineament (*the savage lines of his mouth*); shape to which garment is designed; (in *pl.*) plan or draft (esp. of ship in horizontal, vertical, and oblique sections) or manner of procedure (*on conservative, political, the same*, etc., *lines; on or along the lines laid down by* person). **15.** (As measure) ¹⁄₁₂ inch. **16.** limit, boundary, (*dividing line*); **above the** ∼, (Bridge) not scoring towards game, (Econ.) relating

to current expenditure; DRAW¹ *the line*; **on the** ∼, (1) not clearly one thing or the other, (2) offered without reserve (*put* or *lay on the line*). **17.** row of persons or things; **come, bring, into** ∼, agree or conform or co-operate, induce to do so; **in** ∼ **for**, likely to get; **in** ∼ **with**, in accordance with; **out of** ∼, discordant; *stand in* ∼, form queue; TOE *the line*. **18.** (Mil.) connected series of field-works (esp. in *pl.*, of defences facing enemy); row of tents or huts in camp; **up the** ∼, to the battle-front; HOLD¹ *the line*. **19.** (Naut.) ∼ **abreast**, number of parallel ships ranged on line crossing keels at right angles; ∼ **ahead**, ships following in a string; ∼ (**of battle**), ships drawn up in battle array. **20.** (Mil.) double row (front and rear ranks) of men ranged side by side, arrangement of companies side by side (opp. *column; drawn up in, form, wheel into, line*); **all along the** ∼, at every point, (lit., or fig. of success etc.). **21. the** ∼, regular and numbered army regiments (not auxiliary forces or Guards). **22.** *group of football players forming line before scrimmage (∼'man, member of this); ∼'backer, player just behind defensive line. **23.** row of words in page or newspaper column (READ *between the lines*); (in *pl.*) = MARRIAGE *lines*; ∼**-filling**, flourish or ornament in blank space at end of line in MS; ∼**-printer**, machine for printing results from computer etc. a line at a time. **24.** short letter (*just a line to tell you the news*). **25.** single verse of poetry; (in *pl.*) piece of poetry (often *upon* subject or *to* person); (in *pl.*) specified amount (*100* etc. *lines*) of verse, repeated admonition, etc., to be written out as school punishment; (in *pl.*) words of actor's part. **26.** series or regular succession of steamers, buses, aircraft, etc., plying between certain places; company conducting this (*shipping line; airline*). **27.** connected series of persons or things following one another in time (*can show a long line of heroes*), esp. several generations of family (*male, female, direct*, etc., *line*); family, lineage, stock (*comes of a good line*). **28.** direction, course, track, (*line of* MARCH⁴, *communication*, etc.; ASSEMBLY *line*) **29.** (Railways). single track of rails (**up, down,** ∼, for UP, DOWN⁵, trains); one branch of system (*main, branch, loop, line*) or whole system under one management; **the end of the** ∼, (fig.) point at which further effort becomes fruitless. **30.** course followed esp. in riding to hounds (*take, keep to*, one's *own line*; often also fig.; **get a** ∼ **on**, (colloq.) learn something about; *line of least* RESISTANCE). **31.** course of procedure, conduct, thought, etc., (HARD *line*; PARTY¹ *line*). **32.** department of activity, province, branch of business, (*line of* COUNTRY; **in the** ∼ **of** *duty* etc., a proper part of; *something* **in, out of,** one's ∼, that interests or concerns one, or not; SHOOT¹ *a line*). **33.** (Commerc.) class of goods; order for or stock of this. [ME *li(g)ne* f. OF *ligne* f. Rom. *linja* f. L *linea* (*linum* flax), & f. OE *līne* rope, series, = OHG *līna*, f. Gmc f. L *linea*]

line³ *n.* **1.** *v.t.* mark in, off, out, with lines on paper etc.; cover with lines (*a face lined with pain*). **2.** draw (persons or things) *up* in line (*with*). **3.** *v.t.* & *i.* spread *out* in line, come *up* to line. **4.** *v.t.* post troops etc. along (road, hedge, etc.), (of troops) form open or close line along (pass etc.), (of persons or things) stand at fairly short intervals along (street, wall, etc.). **5.** ∼**-out**, (Rugby Union) parallel lines of opposing forwards at right angles to touch-line when ball is thrown in; ∼**-up**, line of persons for inspection, arrangement of persons in team etc. [ME, f. prec.]

line⁴ *v.t.* attach layer of (usu. different) material to inside of (garment, box, vessel, bag, etc.); fill (purse, pocket, stomach, etc.); serve as lining for; hence **li'ning** (2, 4) *n.* (*every cloud has a* SILVER¹ *lining*). [ME, f. LINE², w. ref. to use of linen for linings]

line⁵ *v.t.* (Of dog, wolf, etc.) copulate with (bitch). [ME, f. OF *ligner*]

li'neage *n.* lineal descent, ancestry, pedigree. [ME f. OF *li(g)nage* f. Rom. *lineaticum* f. L *linea* LINE²; see -AGE]

li'nëal *a.* in the direct line of descent or ancestry (opp. *collateral*); of or in line(s), linear; hence ∿LY² *adv.* [ME f. OF, f. LL *linealis* (as LINE²; see -AL)]

li'nèament *n.* (usu. in *pl.*) distinctive feature or characteristic, esp. feature of face. [ME, f. L *lineamentum* (*lineare* make straight f. *linea* LINE²); see -MENT]

li'near *a.* **1.** of or in line(s) (*linear perspective*); of length (*linear extent*). **2.** (Math. & Phys.) involving one dimension only; ∿ **accelerator** (in which particles travel in straight lines, not in closed orbits); ∿ **equation** (of first degree); hence ∿IZE (3) *v.t.* **3.** long, narrow, and of uniform breadth. **4.** (Paint.) using clear outlines, expressed in lines rather than masses. **5.** L∿ **A, B,** two related forms of ancient writing discovered in Crete and Greece. **6.** Hence ∿ITY (-ă'r-) *n.*, ∿LY² *adv.* [f. L *linearis* (*linea* LINE²; see -AR²)]

lineā'tion *n.* drawing of, marking with, arrangement of, lines. [ME, f. L *lineatio* (*lineare*; see LINEAMENT, -ATION)]

li'nèn *a.* & *n.* **1.** *a.* made of flax (*linen cloth*). **2.** *n.* cloth woven from flax; particular kind of this; (collect.) shirts, sheets, cloths, etc., of linen, calico, etc., (**wash** one's **dirty** ∿ **at home, in public,** keep, not keep, quiet about domestic quarrels etc.); undergarments; sheets and pillowcases; table-linen. **3.** ‖∿**-basket** (for soiled clothes); ‖∿**-draper,** dealer in linen, calico, etc.; ∿**fold,** carved or moulded ornament representing a fold or scroll of linen. [OE *linen,* = OS, OHG *linin* f. WG (as LINE¹; see -EN⁵)]

li'ner¹ *n.* In vbl senses; removable metal lining to avoid wear and tear in machinery etc. [f. LINE⁴ + -ER¹]

li'ner² *n.* ship, usu. steamer, belonging to line of passenger ships; aircraft belonging to a regular line, used esp. for passenger transport, air liner; train belonging to regular line; ∿ **train** (transporting containers on permanently coupled wagons). [f. LINE² 26 + -ER¹]

li'nes|man (-nz-) *n.* (*pl.* ∿**men**). ‖soldier of line regiment; (Lawn Tennis, Footb., etc.) official assisting umpire or referee esp. by deciding whether or where ball touches or crosses line; ‖man employed to test safety of railway lines; = *lineman* (LINE² 2). [f. LINE² + 's 1 + MAN¹]

ling¹ *n.* long slender N. Eur. sea-fish (*Molva molva*) used (usu. cured) for food. [ME *leng(e),* prob. f. MDu.; cogn. w. LONG¹]

ling² *n.* heather of various species, esp. *Calluna vulgaris;* hence ∿'Y² *a.* [ME f. ON *lyng*]

-ling¹ *suf.* forming *ns.* **1.** Denoting person or thing connected with (*hireling, nursling, sapling*) or having the property of being (*grayling, underling*) or undergoing (*starveling*). **2.** Denoting diminutive (*codling, duckling*), often derog. (*lordling*). [OE, f. as -LE 1 + -ING³; sense 2 f. ON]

-ling² *suf.* forming *advs.* & *adjs.* (*darkling, grovelling*); cf. -LONG. [OE, f. Gmc **ling-* extend]

li'nga(m) (-ngg-) *n.* phallus (esp. as symbol of Siva). [Skr. *lingam,* lit. 'mark']

li'nger (-ngg-) *v.* **1.** *v.i.* put off departure esp. because of reluctance to go; stay about, not depart or arrive at expected or right time; dally *round* place or *over* or (*up*)*on* subject; (of invalid or moribund custom) drag *on* a feeble existence; be protracted (*lingering disease, agonies*); be tardy, delay. **2.** *v.t.* ∿ (**out**), pass (time) slowly; throw (time) *away* in delays. **3.** Hence ∿ER¹ *n.* [ME *lenger,* frequent. of *leng* f. OE *lengan,* = OHG *lengen* f. Gmc **langjan* lengthen (**lang-* LONG¹); see -ER⁵]

li'ngerie (lǎ'nzherē) *n.* women's underwear and night-clothes. [F (*linge* linen; see -ERY)]

li'ngo (-nggō) *n.* (*pl.* ∿**es**). (derog. or joc.) foreign language; vocabulary of special subject or class of people. [prob. f. Port. *lingoa* f. L *lingua* tongue]

lingua frä'nca (-nggwa) *n.* mixture of Italian with French, Greek, Arabic, and Spanish, used in the Levant; any language serving as medium between

different nations whose own languages are not the same; system providing mutual understanding. [It. = Frankish tongue]

li'ngual (-nggwal) *a.* **1.** (Anat.) of the tongue. **2.** (Phonet.) formed by the tongue; hence ∿IZE (3) *v.t.* **3.** of speech or languages. [f. med. L *lingualis* f. L *lingua* tongue; see -AL]

li'nguifórm (-nggw-) *a.* (Bot., Anat., & Zool. tongue-shaped. [f. L *lingua* tongue + -I- + -FORM]

li'nguist (-nggwist) *n.* person skilled in foreign languages (*good, bad, no, linguist*) or in linguistics. [f. L *lingua* language + -IST]

lingui'st|ic (-nggwĭ'-) *a.* of the study of languages; of language; hence ∿ICALLY *adv.* [f. prec. + -IG]

lingui'st|ics (-nggwĭ'-) *n.* science of language(s) as regards nature and structure; hence ∿I'CIAN *n.* [f. linguistique or G linguistik (as prec.; see -ICS)]

li'nguo- (-nggwo) *comb. form.* tongue, as: ∿**de'ntal** (of sound) made with tongue and teeth. [f. L *lingua* tongue + -o-]

‖**li'nhay** (lĭ'nĭ) *n.* (dial.) farm-shed or outbuilding open along front. [17th c., orig. unkn.; first element perh. f. LEAN²]

li'niment *n.* embrocation, usu. made with oil. [f. LL *linimentum* f. L *linire* smear; see -MENT]

li'ning. See LINE⁴.

link¹ *n.* & *v.* **1.** *n.* one ring or loop of chain; measure equal to 1/100 of surveying chain or 7.92 in. = CUFF¹-*link;* loop in knitting etc.; connecting part thing or person that unites others, filler of gap member of series (MISSING *link*); ∿('**man**), playe between forwards and half-backs or strikers and backs in football etc., person providing continuity i broadcast programme. **2.** *v.t.* connect, join, (things persons) *together* or (thing, person) *to;* clasp (hands) hook (arm *in* or *through* another's, or arms). **3.** *v.i* attach oneself *on* or *in* to system, company, etc. **4.** ∿ **up,** connect, combine; ∿-*up* n., act or result of linking up. **5.** Hence ∿'AGE (1, 3) *n.* [ME, f. ON **hlenkr* Gmc **hlankjaz,* cogn. w. LANK]

link² *n.* torch of pitch and tow formerly used for lighting people along streets; ∿'**boy,** ∿'**man** (employed to carry links). [16th c., perh. f. med. *li(n)chinus* wick f. Gk *lukhnos* light]

links *n. pl.* **1.** (Sc.) level or undulating sandy groun near sea-shore, with turf and coarse grass. **2.** (as *sing* or *pl.*) golf-course, esp. one resembling sense 1. [pl. c *link* 'rising ground' f. OE *hlinc* perh. cogn. w. LEAN²]

linn *n.* (Sc.) waterfall; pool below this; precipice ravine. [f. Gael. *linne*]

Linn. *abbr.* (Biol.) Linnaeus.

Linnae'an *a.* & *n.* (follower) of Linnaeus or his syster of classifying plants; **Linne'an Society,** Englis society publishing journals etc. on natural history. [*Linnaeus,* Sw. naturalist, ennobled von *Linné,* 1778 + -AN]

li'nnèt *n.* common brown or grey songbird (a finch *Carduelis cannabina*); **green** ∿, greenfinch. [f. O *linette* (*lin* flax, f. its food)]

linn(e)y. Var. of LINHAY.

li'nō *n.* (*pl.* ∿s). linoleum; ∿**cut,** (print made from design cut in relief on piece of linoleum. [abbr.]

linō'lèum *n.* floor-covering of canvas with thick coa of solidified linseed oil etc.; hence ∿ED² (-md) *a.* [f. l *linum* flax + *oleum* oil]

Li'notype *n.* (P) machine for producing lines of word at one casting as substitute for type-setting with singl types, used in printing newspapers. [= *line o' type*]

li'nsäng *n.* civet-cat of genus *Linsang* in E. Indies o *Poiana* in Africa. [Jav.]

li'nseed *n.* seed of flax; ∿ **cake,** linseed (with th ∿ **oil** pressed out for use in paint etc.) as cattle-foo ∿ **meal,** ground linseed. [OE *lïnsæd* (as LINE SEED)]

linsey-wōo'lsey (-z-; -zĭ) *n.* dress material of coars inferior wool woven on cotton warp (orig. of wo and flax); (fig.) strange medley, nonsense. [ME, *linsey* coarse linen, prob. f. *Lindsey* in Suffolk, + WOOL, w. jingling termination]

li′nstŏck *n.* (Hist.) match-holder used to fire cannon. [earlier *lintstock* f. Du. *lontstok* (*lont* match, *stok* stick), w. assim. to LINT]

lint *n.* soft material for dressing wounds, made by ravelling or scraping linen cloth; fluff; (Sc.) flax; ∼-**white**, flaxen in colour. [ME *lyn(n)et*, perh. f. OF *linette* linseed (*lin* flax; see LINE¹, -ET¹)]

li′ntel *n.* horizontal timber or stone over door or other aperture; hence ∼lED², *∼ED², (-ld) *a.* [ME f. OF *lintel* threshold, f. Rom. *limitale* (cf. var. OF *lintier* f. *limitare*) by confus. w. LL *liminare* f. L *limen* threshold; see LIMIT¹, -LE 2]

*****li′nter** *n.* machine for removing short fibres from cotton seeds after ginning; (in *pl.*) these fibres. [f. LINT + -ER¹]

li′nÿ *a.* marked with lines; wrinkled; (Art) using line too much. [f. LINE² + -Y²]

li′on *n.* **1.** large powerful tawny African and S. Asian (formerly also European) carnivorous mammal (*Panthera leo*) with tufted tail and (in the male) flowing shaggy mane; ∼ **in the way or path**, obstacle, esp. imaginary [Prov. 26:13]; ∼**'s mouth**, perilous position; ∼**'s provider**, (arch.) jackal (lit. or fig.); ∼**'s share**, largest or best part. **2.** ∼ (-heart), courageous person (esp. as sobriquet of Richard I); ∼**-hearted**, brave (and generous). **3.** (in *pl.*) sights worth seeing in town etc. [from custom of showing country visitors the lions formerly kept in Tower of London]. **4.** person of literary or other celebrity sought after to be shown off at social gatherings; ∼**-hunter**, host or hostess depending much on such persons; hence ∼'HOOD, ∼'SHIP, *ns.* **5.** national emblem of Great Britain (**the British L**∼, the nation personified; ∼ **and unicorn**, supporters of British royal coat of arms; **twist the** ∼**'s tail**, defy or insult Britain; **L**∼**s**, British international Rugby Union team); representation of lion (esp. Her.). **6.** (*L*∼) member of an international organization for service to community; *the* zodiacal sign Leo. **7.** Hence ∼ESS¹, ∼ET¹, *ns.*, ∼-LIKE *a.* [ME, f. AF *liun* f. L *leo -onis* f. Gk *leōn leontos*]

li′onīze, -īse (-īz), *v.t.* treat (person) as celebrity, make a lion (see prec. 4) of. [f. LION + -IZE]

lip *n.*, & *v.t.* (-pp-). **1.** *n.* one of the fleshy parts forming edges of opening of mouth (*upper, lower or under, lip*); pink portion of this (*redden one's lips*), bite one's ∼ (in vexation or to repress emotion or retort, stifle laugh, etc.); curl one's ∼ (in scorn); escape one's ∼s, be uttered thoughtlessly; hang one's ∼ (in humiliation); hang on person's ∼s, listen with rapt attention to all he says; lick or smack one's ∼s (in enjoyment or anticipation of food, or fig.); pass person's ∼s, be eaten, spoken, etc.; stiff upper ∼, firmness or fortitude. **2.** (sl.) saucy talk, impudence; (*none of your lip!*). **3.** edge of cup, vessel, cavity, wound, etc., esp. part that is shaped for pouring from. **4.** (In *comb.*) from the lips only, professed, not heartfelt or sincere, (*lip-Christian, -worship*). **5.** ∼-**deep**, superficial, insincere; ∼-**language, -reading, -speaking**, use and interpretation of motions of lips to and by the deaf or when hearing is prevented by noise etc.; ∼-**read** *v.t.* & *i.*, understand by, use, lip-reading; ∼'**salve**, ointment to cure or prevent sore lips, (fig.) flattery; ∼-**service** (proffered but not performed); ∼'**stick**, (*n.*) (stick of) cosmetic for colouring lips, (*v.t.*) apply lipstick to. **6.** Hence (-)∼pED² (-pt), ∼'LESS, *adjs.* **7.** *v.t.* touch with lips, apply lips to; (of water) just touch, lap; (Golf) hit ball just to edge of (hole), (of ball) reach edge of (hole) but fail to drop in. [OE *lippa*, = MLG, MDu. *lippe* f. Gmc *lipjon*, rel. to *lep-* f. IE *leb-*]

li′pāse *n.* (Chem.) enzyme able to decompose fats. [f. Gk *lipos* fat + -ASE]

li′pĭd, li′pīde, *n.* (Chem.) fat or fatlike substance, e.g. ester of a higher aliphatic acid. [F *lipide* (as prec.; see -IDE)]

lipŏ′graphÿ *n.* omission of letter(s) or word(s) in writing. [f. Gk *lip-* st. of *leipō* omit + -O- + -GRAPHY]

Lippiza′ner (-tsah′-) *n.* horse of fine white breed used esp. in displays of dressage. [G (*Lippiza* in Yugoslavia)]

liqu|ā′te *v.t.* separate or purify (metals) by liquefying; hence ∼A′TION *n.* [f. L *liquare* melt (cogn. w. LIQUOR) + -ATE³]

li′que|fÿ *v.t.* & *i.* bring (solid or gas) or come into liquid condition; hence or cogn. ∼FA′CIENT *a.* & *n.*, ∼FA′CTION *n.*, ∼fā′ctIVE, ∼fīABLE, *adjs.*, ∼fīER¹ (1, 2) *n.* [f. F *liquéfier* f. L *liquefacere* (*liquēre* be liquid; see -FY)]

liquĕ′scent *a.* becoming, or apt to become, liquid. [f. L *liquescere* (as prec.; see -ESCENT)]

liqueur′ (-kūr′) *n.* strong spirituous liquor sweetened and flavoured with aromatic substances and usu. drunk in small quantities after meals; mixture of sugar and alcohol or wines used to flavour champagne; ∼ **brandy** (of special quality for drinking as liqueur); ∼-**glass**, very small glass for liqueurs. [F, = LIQUOR]

li′quĭd *a.* & *n.* **1.** (substance that is) incompressible but offering no resistance to change of shape, neither solid nor gaseous, resembling water or oil in normal state; ∼ **air, oxygen**, etc., (reduced to liquid state by intense cold); ∼ **crystal**, turbid liquid in intermediate state between crystalline solid and ordinary liquid; ∼ **fire**, burning oil etc. projected from flame-thrower; ∼ **measure**, (unit for) measurement of volume of liquids. **2.** *a.* watery; having the transparency, translucence, or brightness, of pure water (*liquid lustre, eyes, sky, air, blue*). **3.** (Of sounds) flowing clear, fluent, pure, not grating or discordant, not guttural, vowel-like, (*blackbird's liquid notes; in his liquid Italian*). **4.** not fixed, unstable, (*has very liquid convictions or principles*). **5.** (Of assets) easily converted into cash. **6.** Hence ∼IZE (3) *v.t.*, ∼LY² *adv.*, ∼NESS *n.*; ∼īzER¹ *n.* machine used to make food into purée etc. **7.** *n.* (Phonet.) sound denoted by one of the letters *l, r*, and occas. *m, n.* [ME, f. L *liquidus* (*liquēre* be liquid; see -ID¹)]

liquĭdā′mbar *n.* (tree of genus *Liquidambar* yielding) resinous gum. [mod. L, app. f. L *liquidus* (see prec.) + med. L *ambar* amber]

li′quĭd|āte *v.t.* **1.** *v.t.* pay, clear off, (debt). **2.** put an end to, suppress, get rid of (often by violent means). **3.** wind up, ascertain liabilities and apportion assets of, (company, firm); hence ∼ātor *n.* **4.** *v.i.* (Of company) be liquidated. **5.** Hence ∼A′TION *n.*; **go into** ∼**ation**, (of company) have its affairs wound up, become bankrupt. [f. med. L *liquidare* make clear (as LIQUID) + -ATE³]

liqui′dity *n.* state of being liquid; state of having liquid assets. [f. F *liquidité* or f. med. L *liquiditas* (as LIQUID, -ITY)]

li′quidus *n.* ∼ (**curve**), curve in graph of temperature and composition of a mixture, above which the substance is entirely liquid. [L (see LIQUID)]

li′quor (-ker) *n.* & *v.* **1.** *n.* liquid part of secretion or product of operation; liquid used as wash etc. **2.** water used in brewing; liquid (usu. fermented or distilled) for drinking (MALT¹, SPIRITUOUS, *liquor*; **in** ∼, **the worse for** ∼, more or less drunk). **3.** water in which food has been boiled; (Pharm., *pr.* lī′kwor) solution of specified drug in water (*liquor ammoniae* etc.). **4.** *v.t.* dress (leather, shoes) with grease or oil; steep (malt etc.) in water. **5.** *v.t.* & *i.* (sl.) ∼ (**up**), (cause to) drink large amount of alcoholic liquor. [ME f. OF *lic(o)ur*, f. L *liquor -oris* (*liquēre* see LIQUID, -OR)]

li′quorice (-ker-), **li′corice**, *n.* (black substance used in medicine and as sweetmeat made from) root of leguminous plant *Glycyrrhiza glabra*; the plant. [ME, f. AF *lycorys*, OF *licoresse* f. LL *liquiritia* f. Gk *glukurrhiza* (*glukus* sweet, *rhiza* root)]

li′quorish (-ker-) *a.* = LICKERISH; fond of, indicating fondness for, liquor; hence ∼LY² *adv.*, ∼NESS *n.* [var. of LICKERISH, misapplied]

lir′a (lēr′a) *n.* Italian monetary unit (*pl.* usu. **lire** *pr.*

-ā); Turkish monetary unit. [It., f. Prov. *liura* f. L *libra* POUND¹ 2]

lisle (līl) *n*. ~ (**thread**), fine smooth cotton thread for stockings etc. [f. L~, former sp. of *Lille* in NE France, where orig. made]

lisp *v*. & *n*. **1.** *v.i.* substitute sound like (th) or (dh) for sibilants in speaking; (of child) speak with imperfect pronunciation. **2.** *v.t.* ~ (**out**), say with a lisp. **3.** *n*. lisping pronunciation; rippling of waters, rustling of leaves. [OE *wlispian (*wlisp* a. lisping, = OHG *lisp* stammering, *lispen* to lisp; imit.)]

li′ssom, li′ssome, *a*. lithe, supple, agile; hence ~NESS (-mn-) *n*. [contr. of *lithsom (as LITHE, -SOME¹)]

list¹ *n*., & *v.t.* **1.** *n*. roll or catalogue of names, of persons or things belonging to a class, of articles with prices, of things to be done, etc.; **active** ~ (of officers in army or navy or air force liable to be called on for service); ||CIVIL, FREE¹, SICK¹-, *list*; ~ **price** (as shown in published list). **2.** (in *pl*.) palisades enclosing tilt-yard; (fig.) scene of contest (**enter the ~s against,** challenge or accept challenge of, usu. to controversy). **3.** ||selvage or edge of cloth, usu. of different material; such edges used as a material (*list slippers*). **4.** *v.t.* enter in list; (in *p.p.*, of securities) approved for dealings on stock exchange; ||~**ed building** (included in official list of buildings with architectural or historical importance, and thus protected from demolition etc.). **5.** *v.t.* & *i.* (arch.) enlist. [OE *līste* border, = OHG *līsta* f. Gmc *līstōn; in sense 2 thr. OF *lisse*, in sense 1 thr. F *lisse* w. sense 'strip of paper']

list² *v.t.* (3 *sing. pres.* ~ or ~′eth; *past* ~ or ~′ed). (arch.) **1.** (*impers.*) be pleasing to (*shall do what him listeth; did as him list*). **2.** desire, choose, (*to do, or abs.; ye who list to hear; wind bloweth where it listeth*). [OE *lystan,* = OS *lustian,* OHG *lusten,* ON *lysta* f. Gmc *lustjan (*lust-; cf. LUST)]

list³ *n*., & *v.i.* lean(ing) over to one side (of ship, owing to leak, shifting cargo, subsidence, etc.; cf. HEEL³; also of building, fence, etc.). [17th c., of unkn. orig.]

list⁴ *v.i.* & *t.* (arch.) listen (to), hear. [OE *hlystan (hlyst* sense of hearing, = OS, ON *hlust* f. Gmc *hlustiz* f. IE *klustis* f. *klu-* hear)]

li′sten (-sen) *v.i.* make effort to hear something, hear with attention person speaking; give attention with ear *to* (person or sound or story); yield *to* (person furnishing) temptation or request; ~ (**out**) **for,** seek to hear (sound etc.) by waiting alertly for it; ~ **in,** tap telephonic communication, use radio receiving set (*to* transmitter); ~**ing-post,** point near enemy's lines for detecting his movements by sound, (fig.) place for gathering of information from reports etc.; hence ~ER¹ (-sn-) *n*., (1) one who listens (**good ~er,** one who habitually listens with interest or sympathy), (2) person receiving broadcast radio programmes. [OE *hlysnan,* = MHG *lüsenen* f. WG *hlusinōjan (*hlus-; see prec.)]

*****li′ster** *n*. plough with double mould-board. [f. *list* prepare land for crop + -ER¹]

li′sting *n*. (drawing up of) LIST¹ 1; ||selvage (see LIST¹ 3). [f. LIST¹ + -ING¹]

li′stless *a*. languid, indifferent, uninterested, (such that one is) disinclined for exertion; hence ~LY² *adv*., ~NESS *n*. [ME, f. obs. *list* inclination f. LIST², + -LESS]

lit. See LIGHT³,⁵.

li′tany *n*. series of petitions for use in church services or processions recited by clergy and responded to usu. in recurring formula(s) by people; **the L~,** that contained in the Book of Common Prayer; ~**-desk, -stool,** (at which reciter of litany kneels). [ME f. OF *letanie,* f. eccl. L f. Gk *litaneia* prayer (*litē* supplication)]

litchi′, lychee′, (lēchē′) *n*. (sweetish pulpy shelled fruit of) tree *Litchi chinensis,* orig. from China. [f. Chin. *lizhi*]

-lite *suf*. forming names of minerals (*rhyolite, zeolite*). [F, f. Gk *lithos* stone]

*****liter.** See LITRE.

li′teracy *n*. ability to read and write. [f. LITERATE + -CY, after *illiteracy*]

||**literae hūmāniōr′ēs** (-z) *n*. = POLITE letters (esp. as name of school of classics and philosophy at Oxford). [L, = the more humane studies]

li′teral *a*. & *n*. **1.** *a*. of, in, expressed by, letter(s) of alphabet; (Alg.) not numerical; ~ **error,** misprint of a letter. **2.** following the letter, text, or exact or original words (*literal translation, transcript,* etc.); hence ~ISM (4) *n*. **3.** taking words in their usual or primary sense and applying the ordinary rules of grammar, without mysticism or allegory or metaphor, (*literal interpretation;* **I hear nothing in the ~ sense of the word,** with the ears as opp. other means of getting news); hence ~ISM (3), ~IST (2), *ns.,* ~IZE (3) *v.t.* **4.** ~(-**minded**), (of person) prosaic, matter-of-fact. **5.** not exaggerated (*the literal truth*); so called without exaggeration (*literal extermination*); (colloq.; **D**) so called with some exaggeration (*a literal flood of pamphlets*). **6.** Hence ~ITY (-ă′l-), ~NESS, *ns.,* ~LY² *adv*. **7.** *n*. literal error. [ME f. OF, or f. LL *litteralis* f. L (as LETTER; see -AL)]

li′terar∥y *a*. **1.** of, constituting, occupied with, literature or books and written composition esp. of the kind valued for quality of form; *literary* EXECUTOR; ~**y history** of a thing, history of its treatment in literature; ~**y man,** author, scholar; ~**y property,** exclusive right of publication, books etc. subject to this. **2.** (Of word or idiom) non-colloquial, used chiefly by writers. **3.** Hence ~iLY² *adv.,* ~iNESS *n*. [f. L *litterarius* (as LETTER; see -ARY¹)]

li′terate *a*. & *n*. **1.** (person) able to read and write. **2.** *n*. ||man admitted to Anglican orders without university degree. [ME, f. L *litteratus* (as LETTER; see -ATE²)]

litera′ti (-ah′ tē) *n. pl.* men of letters, the learned class. [L, pl. of *lit(t)eratus* (see prec.)]

literatim (līterā′tim, -ah′-) *adv*. letter for letter, textually, literally. [med. L]

litera′tion *n*. representation of sounds etc. by letter(s) of alphabet. [f. L (as LETTER) + -ATION]

li′terator *n*. = LITTÉRATEUR. [L, = teacher of ABC, grammarian (as LITERATE; see -OR)]

li′terature (-ter-, -tr-) *n*. literary production (*engaged in literature*); realm of letters, writings of country or period; writings whose value lies in beauty of form or emotional effect; *the* books etc. treating *of* a subject; (colloq.) printed matter; (arch.) acquaintance with books. [ME, = literary culture, f. L *litteratura* (as LITERATE; see -URE)]

-lith *suf*. denoting types of stone (*laccolith, monolith*). [f. Gk *lithos* stone]

li′tharge *n*. lead monoxide esp. in red form. [ME f. OF *litarge,* f. L f. Gk *litharguros (lithos* stone, *arguros* silver)]

lithe (-dh) *a*. flexible, supple; hence ~ NESS (-dhn-) *n.,* ~′SOME (-dhs-) *a*. [OE *līthe,* = OS *līthi,* OHG *lindi* soft, f. WG *linthja-* f. Gmc & IE *len-*]

li′thia *n*. lithium oxide; ~ **water** (containing lithium salts and used against gout). [mod. L, alt. of earlier *lithion* f. Gk neut. of *litheios (lithos* stone), after *soda* etc.]

li′thic¹ *a*. of stone; (Path.) of the STONE (sense 5). [f. Gk *lithikos* as prec.; see -IC]

li′thic² *a*. (Chem.) of lithium. [f. foll. + -IC]

li′thium *n*. (Chem.) soft silver-white metallic element, the lightest alkali metal. [f. LITHIA + -IUM]

li′thō *n*. (*pl*. ~s), *a*., & *v.t.* (colloq.) (produce by) lithographic (process). [abbr.]

li′tho- *comb. form.* stone, esp. (1) Path. w. ref. to the STONE (sense 5), (2) Path. w. ref. to use of STONE (sense 4). [f. Gk *lithos* stone + -O-]

li′thograph (-ahf) *n*., & *v.t.* **1.** *n*. lithographic print. **2.** *v.t.* print by lithography; write or engrave on stone. [back-form. f. foll.; see -GRAPH]

lithō′graphy *n*. process of obtaining prints from stone or metal surface so treated that what is to be printed can be inked but the remaining area rejects ink; hence **lithō′**GRAPHER *n.,* **litho**GRA′PHIC *a*. [f. Gk *lithographie* (as LITHO-, -GRAPHY)]

lithŏ′logȳ *n.* science of the nature and composition of stones and rocks; hence **litholŏ′gical** *a.* [f. LITHO- + -LOGY]

li′thophȳte *n.* (Bot.) plant that grows on stone. [f. LITHO- + -PHYTE]

li′thopōne *n.* white pigment of zinc sulphide and barium sulphate. [f. LITHO- + Gk *ponos* work]

li′tho|sphēre *n.* Earth's crust; solid earth (opp. hydrosphere and atmosphere); hence ∼**sphĕ′ric** *a.* [f. LITHO- + SPHERE]

lithŏ′tom|ȳ *n.* operation of cutting into bladder to remove stone; hence ∼IST (1) *n.*, ∼IZE (1) *v.t.* [f. LL f. Gk *lithotomia* (as LITHO-, -TOMY)]

lithŏ′trit|ȳ *n.* operation of crushing stone in bladder into small particles that can be passed through urethra; hence ∼IST (1) *n.*, ∼IZE (1) *v.t.* [f. LITHO- + L *terere* trit- rub + -Y¹]

Lithūā′nian *a.* & *n.* (native, inhabitant, or language) of Lithuania. [f. *Lithuania*, republic of USSR + -AN]

li′tig|āte *v.* 1. *v.i.* go to law, be party to lawsuit. 2. *v.t.* contest (point) in lawcourt; hence ∼ABLE *a.* 3. Hence ∼ANT (1) *n.* & *a.*, ∼A′TION *n.* [f. L *litigare* (*lis litis* lawsuit) + -ATE³]

liti′gious (-jus) *a.* given to litigation, fond of going to law; disputable in lawcourt, offering matter for lawsuit; of lawsuits; hence ∼LY² *adv.*, ∼NESS *n.* [ME, f. OF *litigieux* or f. L *litigiosus* (*litigium* litigation); cf. prec., -OUS)]

li′tmus *n.* blue colouring-matter got from lichens that is turned red by acid and restored to blue by alkali; ∼**-paper** (unsized and stained with litmus as test for acids or alkalis). [ME, f. ONorw. *litmosi* f. ON *litr* dye + *mosi* moss]

li′totēs (-z) *n.* ironical understatement, esp. expressing of an affirmative by the negative of its contrary (*I shan't be sorry* for *I shall be glad*; *not a* LITTLE 10). [LL, f. Gk *litotēs* (*litos* plain, meagre)]

||li′tre, *li′ter, (lē′ter) *n.* unit of capacity in metric system, volume of one kilogram of water under standard conditions, 1 cubic decimetre or about 1¾ pints; hence ∼AGE (1) (lē′terĭj) *n.* [F (*litron*, an obs. measure of capacity, f. med. L f. Gk *litra* Sicilian monetary unit)]

Litt. D. *abbr.* Doctor of Letters. [f. L *Litterarum Doctor*]

li′tter *n.,* & *v.t.* 1. *n.* vehicle containing couch shut in by curtains and carried on men's shoulders or by beasts of burden; framework with couch for transporting sick and wounded. 2. straw, rushes, etc., as bedding esp. for animals; straw and dung of farmyard. 3. odds and ends, leavings, state of untidiness, disorderly accumulation of papers etc.; hence ∼Y² *a.* 4. the young animals brought forth at a birth. 5. ∼**-basket, -bin,** (for deposit of waste paper, etc.); *∼**-bug,** ∼**-lout,** person who carelessly leaves refuse in street etc. 6. *v.t.* ∼ (**down**), provide (horse etc.) with litter as bed, spread litter or straw on (floor) or in (stable). 7. (Of objects lying about, or of person *with* these) make (place) untidy; scatter and leave lying. 8. give birth to (whelps etc., or abs.). [ME, f. AF *litere*, OF *litiere* f. med. L *lectaria* f. L *lectus* bed; see -ER² (2)]

littérateur (lĕtĕrahtĕr′) *n.* literary man. [F]

li′ttle *a.* (LESS, LESSER, **li′ttler;** LEAST, **li′ttlest;** *also* **smaller, smallest),** *n.,* & *adv.* (LESS, LEAST). 1. *a.* small (often with emotional implications not given by *small*; cf. GREAT), not great or big; working etc. on only a small scale (*the little shopkeeper is being put out of business by the supermarkets*); (as distinctive epithet) of smaller or smallest size etc. (*little* AUK, BEAR¹, FINGER, SLAM², *toe*); ∼ **Switzerland** etc. (small area reminiscent of). 2. young (*a little boy, girl, child*; **the** ∼ **Joneses,** the Jones children; ∼ **man** or **woman,** boy or girl (esp. as joc. or affectionate *voc.*); ∼ **ones,** children, cubs, etc.); younger (*little brother, sister*). 3. as of a child, evoking tenderness, condescension, amusement, etc., (*her poor little efforts to please; we know his little ways*); so *that's* **your** ∼ **game,** what you are hoping to do unbeknown; **the** ∼ **woman,** (colloq.) one's wife.

4. short in stature, distance, or time, (*a little man; will go a little way with you; wait a little while*). 5. trivial, unimportant, (*exaggerates every little difficulty*); mean, paltry, contemptible, (*with the little cunning of little minds; you little sneak*). 6. not much (*gained little advantage from it*; *very little butter left; did little or no damage; has but little faith in it*). 7. **a** ∼, some though not much, even a small amount of, [prob. f. sense 10 w. ellipsis of *of*] (*give me a little butter; a little care would have prevented it*); **in** ∼, on a small scale; **no** ∼, considerable, a good deal of, (*took no little trouble over it*). 8. *∼ **dipper,** = Little BEAR¹; ∼**-ease,** (Hist.) prison-cell too small to stand or lie full-length in; ∼ **end,** smaller end of connecting-rod, attached to piston; *Little* ENGLANDER; ||∼**-go,** (Hist. colloq.) first examination for BA degree at Cambridge or Oxford; *L*∼ **League,** baseball league for boys of 8–12; ∼ **magazine** (literary, usu. with experimental writing and in small format); ∼ **Mary,** (colloq.) the stomach; L∼ **Masters,** group of 16th-c. German engravers, followers of Dürer, named from size of their prints; *∼little* OLD 5; **the** ∼ **people,** fairies; *Little* RUSSIAN; ∼ **theatre** (esp. for experimental productions). 9. Hence ∼NESS (-teln-) *n.* 10. *n.* not much, only a small amount, a mere trifle, (*got but, nay, rather, little out of it; the little of his work that remains; did what little I could;* ∼ **or nothing,** hardly anything; *did* **not a** ∼ *for the cause,* much; THINK *little of*); *a* certain but no great amount (*knows a little of everything;* **a** ∼, rather, somewhat; **not a** ∼, extremely); short time or distance (*after, for, a little;* ∼ **by,** ∼ **by** ∼ **and** ∼, by degrees). 11. *adv.* to a small extent only (*little-known authors; is little more than speculation*); not at all (*he little knows, thought,* etc.). [OE *lȳtel*, = OS *luttil*, OHG *luzzil* f. WG *∗luttila* f. Gmc *∗lut-*]

li′ttoral *a.* & *n.* 1. *a.* of or on the shore. 2. *n.* region lying along the shore. [a. f. L *lit*(*t*)*oralis* (*litus* -*oris* shore; see -AL); n. thr. F, or It. *littorale*]

litŭr′g|ical *a.* of or related to liturgies or public worship; hence or cogn. ∼ICALLY *adv.,* ∼ICS, ∼iö′turgy, **li′turgIST** (3), *ns.* [f. med. L f. Gk *leitourgikos* (as foll.; see -ICAL)]

li′turgȳ *n.* 1. Communion office of Orthodox Church. 2. form of public worship; set of formularies for this; *the* Book of Common Prayer. 3. (Gk Ant.) public office or duty performed gratuitously by rich Athenian. [f. F *liturgie* or f. LL f. Gk *leitourgia* public worship (*leitourgos* minister f. *∗leitos* public + *-ergos* performing)]

li′vable. Var. of LIVEABLE.

live¹ *a.* 1. *attrib.* that is alive, living, (joc.) actual, not pretended or pictured or toy (*a real live burglar, steam -engine, mountain*); (of broadcast; also *pred.*) heard or seen during the occurrence of an event, not recorded or edited. 2. full of power, energy, or importance, not obsolete or exhausted, (*make the question a live issue*); glowing (*live coals*); (of shell, match, wire, etc.) unexploded, unkindled, charged with or carrying electricity; (of rock) not detached, seeming to form part of the earth's frame; (of wheel, axle, etc. in machinery) moving or imparting motion. 3. *live* BAIT²; ∼ **birth** (of living child, opp. *still birth*); ∼**load,** weight of persons or goods in building or vehicle; ∼**-oak,** Amer. evergreen tree (*Quercus virginiana*); ∼ **steam** (direct from boiler); ∼**stock,** animals kept or dealt in for use or profit; ∼ **weight** (of animal before being killed); ∼ **wire,** (fig.) highly energetic forceful person. [f. ALIVE]

live² *v.* 1. *v.i.* be alive, have animal or vegetable life. 2. subsist (*up*)*on* (*lives on fruit*); depend for subsistence (*lives on his wife, on* or *off his wife's earnings, the* FAT *of the land,* etc.); (fig.) sustain one's position or repute (*up*)*on* (*lives on his reputation*), get livelihood *by* or on one's wits etc. or *by doing;* ∼ **on air,** (appear to) take no food; ∼ **and let** ∼, condone others' failings so as to secure same treatment for oneself; *live from* HAND¹ *to mouth.* 3. conduct oneself (honestly, viciously, like a saint, etc.; ∼ **up to** one's **principles, faith,** etc., put them into practice; ~ **up** to one's **promise, reputation,** etc., not fall short of it; ~ **up** to one's **income** etc., spend it all). **4.** arrange one's habits, expenditure, feeding, etc.; ~ **in a small way** (cheaply and quietly); ~ **out of a suitcase** etc. (keeping all one's belongings in it during temporary residence); ~ **to** one**self** (in isolation); ~ **well** (on luxurious food, or virtuously). **5.** *v.t.* (w. cogn. obj.) spend, pass, experience, (*live a virtuous,* DOUBLE[1], *life*; *he lived what he narrated*); ~ **it up,** live gaily and extravagantly; ~ **out,** survive. **6.** wear *down* (scandal, prejudice, effect of past guilt) by blameless course of life. **7.** express in one's life (*live a lie*). **8.** *v.i.* enjoy life intensely or to the full (*you haven't lived till you've drunk champagne*). **9.** continue alive, have one's life prolonged, (*patient cannot live; lived to regret his decision, to see his children's children*); ~ **and learn,** continually discover new facts as one lives; ~ **through,** survive, remain alive at the end of; ~ **to,** survive and reach (*lived to a great age*); **long** ~ **the Queen!** (excl. of loyalty). **10.** (Of thing) survive (*his memory lives*); (of ship) escape destruction. **11.** make one's permanent abode (||~ **in, out,** of shop-assistant or domestic servant residing on premises or not); spend daytime *in* room (*room does not seem to be lived in*); ~ **together,** (esp. of man and woman not his wife) share dwelling-place; ~ **with,** (1) share dwelling-place with (esp. as *live together*), (2) tolerate, find congenial. [OE *libban, lifian,* = OS *libbian,* OHG *leben,* ON *lifa,* Goth. *liban* f. Gmc *libh-* remain]

li'veable (-va-) *a.* (Of house, room, climate, etc.) fit to live in; (of life) worth living; ~ (**with**), companion- able, easy to live with. [f. prec. + -ABLE]

li'velihŏŏd (-vl-) *n.* means of living, sustenance. [OE *līflād* (*līf* LIFE, *lād* course; see LOAD[1]), assim. to obs. *livelihood* liveliness]

li'velŏng[1] (-vl-) *a.* (poet. or rhet.) whole length of (**the** ~ **day, night, summer,** with implication of weari- ness or delight). [ME *lefe longe* (as LIEF, LONG[1]), assim. to LIVE[2]]

li'velŏng[2] (-vl-) *n.* orpine. [f. LIVE[2] + LONG[2]]

li'vel|y̆ (-vlĭ) *a.* lifelike, realistic, (*a lively description*); full of life, vigorous, energetic, brisk, vivid, interest- ing, (*lively horse, dance, recollection, discussion*; **look** ~, move more quickly or energetically); (joc.) exciting, dangerous, difficult, (*police had a lively time*; *press is making it* or *things lively for them*); (of colour) bright; gay, vivacious; (of boat etc.) rising lightly to waves; hence ~ILY[2] *adv.,* ~iNESS *n.* [OE *līflic* (as LIFE, -LY[1])]

li'ven *v.t.* & *i.* (colloq.) ~ (**up**), brighten, cheer. [f. LIFE + -EN[6]]

li'ver[1] *n.* **1.** large glandular organ in abdomen of vertebrates, secreting bile. **2.** disordered state of liver; biliousness. **3.** ~(-**colour**), dark reddish brown. **4.** flesh of some animals' liver used as food. **5.** (arch.) liver as seat of emotion (**white** or **lily** ~, cowardice). **6.** *liver* CHESTNUT; ||~ **salts** (to cure dyspepsia or biliousness); ~ **sausage** (filled with cooked liver etc.); ~ **of sulphur,** liver-coloured mixture of potassium sulphides etc., used as lotion in skin disease; ~**wort,** lichen-like plant with liver-shaped leaves. **7.** Hence ~LESS *a.* [OE *lifer,* = MDu. *lever,* OHG *libara,* ON *lifr* f. Gmc *librō*]

li'ver[2] *n.* one who lives in specified way (*clean, loose, liver*); **good** ~, (1) virtuous person, (2) person given to good LIVING[1]. [ME, f. LIVE[2] + -ER[1]]

li'verish *a.* suffering from disorder of liver; peevish, glum; hence ~NESS *n.* [f. LIVER[1] + -ISH]

Liverpŭ'dlian *a.* & *n.* (native or inhabitant) of Liverpool. [joc. f. *Liverpool* in Merseyside + PUDDLE[1] + -IAN]

li'very[1] *n.* **1.** allowance of provender for horses; *place where horses can be hired; (Hist.) provision of food or clothing for retainers etc.; **at** ~, (of horse) kept for owner and fed and groomed for fixed charge. **2.** distinctive clothes worn by member of City Company or person's manservant (**in, out of,** ~, of servant, so

attired or in plain clothes), (fig.) distinctive guise or marking (*birds in their winter livery; the livery of grief*); hence **li'veri**ED[2] (-ĭd) *a.* **3.** membership of City livery company (**take up** one's ~, become liveryman). **4.** (Law). legal delivery of property; writ allowing this. **5.** ||~ **company,** one of London City Companies that formerly had distinctive costume; ~ **cupboard,** small cupboard for keeping food etc. overnight; ||~ **fine,** payment for becoming member of livery company; ~**man,** (1) ||member of livery company, (2) keeper of or attendant in livery stable; ~ **servant** (wearing livery); ~ **stable** (where horses are kept at livery or let out for hire). [ME, f. AF *liveré,* OF *livrée,* fem. p.p. (as n.) of *livrer* DELIVER; see -Y[4]]

li'very[2] *a.* of the consistency or colour of liver; ||(of soil) tenacious; (colloq.) liverish. [f. LIVER[1] + -Y[2]]

li'vid *a.* of bluish leaden colour; discoloured as by bruise; ||(colloq.) furiously angry; hence or cogn. ~ITY (-ĭ'd-), ~NESS, *ns.,* ~LY[2] *adv.* [f. F *livide* or f. L *lividus* (*livēre* be bluish; see -ID[1])]

li'ving *n.* **1.** In vbl senses; **cost of** ~ (of basic necessities of life); STANDARD *of living.* **2.** livelihood, maintenance, (*make one's living as* teacher etc., *out of* or *by* begging etc.); **it's a** ~, (joc.) the work provides subsistence though not inspiration. **3.** ||(Eccl.) posi- tion as vicar or rector with income and/or property. **4. good** ~, luxurious feeding; **plain** ~ **and high thinking,** frugal and philosophic life. **5.** ~-**room** (for general day use); ~-**space,** = LEBENSRAUM; *living* WAGE[1]. [ME, f. LIVE[2] + -ING[1]]

li'ving[2] *a.* In vbl senses; contemporary, now existent, (*no man living could do better; the greatest living master of irony;* **the** ~, those now alive; **in the land of the** ~, alive); (of likeness or image of person) exact; (of water) perennially flowing; (of rock etc.) = LIVE[1] 2; (of language) still in vernacular use; ~ **death,** state of hopeless misery; **within** ~ **memory** (that of some persons still living); ~ **theatre** (opp. cinema). [OE *lifende* (as LIVE[2], -ING[2])]

lixi'vi|āte *v.t.* separate (substance) into soluble and insoluble constituents by percolation of liquid; hence ~A'TION *n.* [f. L *lixivius* made into lye (*lix*) + -ATE[3]]

li'zard *n.* reptile of suborder Lacertilia having usu. long body and tail, four legs, movable eyelids, and scaly or granulated hide. [ME f. OF *lesard(e)* f. L *lacertus;* assim. to -ARD]

||**LJ** *abbr.* (*pl.* **L JJ**) Lord Justice.

'll *v.* (chiefly after pronouns) = SHALL or WILL[1] (*I'll, he'll, that'll*). [abbr.]

LL *abbr.* Lord Lieutenant.

ll. *abbr.* lines.

lla'ma (lah'-) *n.* S. Amer. ruminant allied to camel but smaller, humpless, and woolly-haired, used as beast of burden, esp. variety of guanaco; (material made of) its wool. [Sp., prob. f. Quechua]

lla'nŏ (lah'-, lyah'-) *n.* (*pl.* ~s). S. Amer. treeless grassy plain or steppe; hence **llaner'ŏ** (lyahnār'ō) *n.* (*pl.* ~s), inhabitant of the llanos. [Sp., f. L *planum* PLAIN[1] 7]

LL B, LL D, LL M, *abbrs.* Bachelor, Doctor, Master, of Laws. [f. L *legum baccalaureus, doctor, magister;* cf. LAW[1] 6]

Lloyd's (loidz) *n.* incorporated society of underwriters in London; ~ **List,** daily publication devoted to shipping news; ~ **Register,** (society producing) annual alphabetical list of ships assigned to various classes. [orig. meeting in coffee-house established (1688) by Edward *Lloyd*]

LM *abbr.* long metre; lunar module.

lm *abbr.* lumen(s).

||**LMBC** *abbr.* Lady Margaret Boat Club (St. John's College, Cambridge).

LMH *abbr.* Lady Margaret Hall.

||**LMS** *abbr.* London Mathematical Society; (Hist.) London, Midland, & Scottish, London Missionary Society.

ln *abbr.* natural logarithm. [f. mod. L *logarithmus naturalis*]

lō *int.* **1.** (arch.) look!, see!, behold!. **2. lo and behold!**, (joc.) here is a surprising fact. [OE *lā* int. of surprise etc., & ME *lō* = *lōke* LOOK]

loach *n.* small edible freshwater fish of family Cobitidae. [ME, f. OF *loche*, of unkn. orig.]

load¹ *n.* **1.** what is (to be) carried, burden; amount usu. or actually carried (*cart-load of bricks*; *plane-load of people were killed*); unit of measure or weight of certain substances; **get a ～ of**, (sl.) notice, listen attentively to. **2.** material object or force acting as weight or clog; resistance of machinery to motive power; pressure of superstructure on arch etc.; (Electr.) amount of power supplied by dynamo or generating station at any given time. **3.** burden of responsibility, care, grief, etc., (**take a ～ off** person's **mind**, relieve him of anxiety). **4.** (in *pl.*, colloq.) plenty, superabundance, heaps, a lot, *of.* **5. ～-displacement, -draught,** (of ship when laden); **～ line,** Plimsoll line; **～-shedding,** temporary curtailment of supply of electricity to a specific area to prevent excessive load on generating plant; **～'star,** = LODEstar; **～'stone, lo'destone,** magnetic oxide of iron, piece of it used as magnet, thing that attracts, [= *way stone*; see etym.]. [OE *lād* way, journey, conveyance, = OHG *leita*, ON *leith* way, course, f. Gmc *laidhō* (cf. LEAD², LODE)]

load² *v.* **1.** *v.t.* put load on or aboard (person, vehicle, ship, etc.); place (load, cargo) aboard ship, on vehicle, etc. **2.** add weight to, be burden upon, oppress *with* (*stomach loaded with food*); weight with lead (*a loaded cane*); (in *p.p.*, of dice etc.) so weighted as to fall more often than usual with a certain face up, (fig.) not giving one a fair chance. **3.** strain bearing--capacity of (*table loaded with food*). **4.** supply or assail overwhelmingly *with* (*loaded her with gifts, praise, work, abuse*; *air loaded with soot*); (in *p.p.*, sl.) rich or drunk or *drugged. **5.** charge (firearm; **am ～ed,** have my gun etc. charged; *loaded for* BEAR¹]; insert film in (camera). **6.** charge with some hidden implication (esp. in *p.p.*; *a loaded question*). **7.** add extra charge to (insurance premium) for special reason(s). **8.** *v.i.* ～ (**up,** (of ship, vehicle, or person) take load aboard. [ME, f. prec.]

loa'der *n.* In vbl senses; attendant loading sportsman's guns; loading-machine; (in comb.) gun, machine, etc., loaded in specified way (*breech, muzzle, front, top, -loader*), so **-loa'dING²** *a.* [f. prec. + -ER¹]

loa'ding *n.* In vbl senses; (Electr.) maximum current or power taken by an appliance. [ME, f. LOAD² + -ING¹]

loaf¹ *n.* (*pl.* loaves *pr.* -vz). **1.** quantity of bread baked alone or as separate or separable part of batch, usu. of some standard weight; **brown, white, ～** (of brown, white, bread); **loaves and fishes,** personal profit as inducement to religious profession or public service [see John 6:26]; **half a ～ is better than no bread** (motto of compromise, opp. *all or nothing*). **2.** (sl.) head (**use** one's **～,** use one's common sense). **3.** (**sugar-)～,** conical moulded mass of sugar (**～ sugar,** this as whole or cut into lumps). **4.** (**meat** etc.) **～,** minced or chopped meat moulded into loaflike shape and cooked, usu. to be eaten cold. [OE *hlāf*, = OHG *leip*, ON *hleifr*, Goth. *hlaifs* f. Gmc *hlaibhaz*]

loaf² *v.* & *n.* **1.** *v.i.* spend time idly; saunter. **2.** *v.t.* ～ away, spend (time) in loafing. **3.** *n.* act or spell of loafing. [prob. back-form. f. foll.]

loa'fer *n.* person who loafs; (*L～*; *P*) leather shoe shaped like moccasin with flat heel. [perh. f. G *landläufer* vagabond]

loam *n.* paste of clay and water, composition of moistened clay and sand with chopped straw etc. used in making bricks, plastering, etc.; fertile soil of clay and sand with admixture of decayed vegetable matter, whence ～'Y² *a.* [OE *lām*, = MDu. *leem*, OHG *leimo* f. WG *laima* (*lai-* be sticky; cf. LIME¹)]

loan¹ *n.*, & *v.t.* **1.** *n.* thing, esp. sum of money, lent to be returned with or without interest; word, custom, etc., adopted by one people from another. **2.** lending or

being lent (*on loan*; **may I have the ～ of,** may I borrow). **3.** money contribution from individuals or public bodies to State expenses that is acknowledged as debt; arrangement or contract by which a government receives advances of money usu. for stipulated interest. **4.** ～ **collection** (of pictures etc. lent by owners for exhibition); **～-holder,** person holding debentures or other acknowledgements of loan, mortgagee; *～ **shark,** (colloq.) one who lends money at usurious interest; **～-translation,** expression adopted by one language from another in more or less literally translated form (e.g. *reason of State* f. F *raison d'état*, F *gratte-ciel* f. *skyscraper*); **～-word,** word adopted by one language from another in more or less modified form (e.g. *morale, naïve*). **5.** *v.t.* grant loan of; hence ～'ABLE *a.*, ～EE', ～'ER¹, *ns.* [ON *lán*, = OE *læn* (cf. LEND). MDu. *lēne*, OHG *lēhan* f. Gmc *laihwn-*]

loan², loa'ning, *ns.* (Sc.) lane; open place where cows are milked. [ME var. of LANE, + -ING¹]

loath, lōth, *pred. a.* disinclined, reluctant, unwilling, (usu. *to do*, or abs.; *for* person *to do*, or *that*); **nothing ～,** quite willing(ly); **～-to-depart,** (arch.) tune played as farewell. [OE *lāth*, = OS *lēth*, OHG *leid*, ON *leithr* f. Gmc *laithaz*]

loath|e (-dh) *v.t.* regard with disgust, abominate, detest; hence ～'ING¹ (1) *n.* [OE *lāthian* f. Gmc *laithōjan* (as prec.)]

loa'thl|y (-dh-) (arch. or literary) = foll.; hence ～iNESS *n.* [OE *lāthlic* (as LOATH, -LY¹)]

loa'thsome (-dh-) *a.* causing nausea or disgust, offensive to the senses, sickening, repulsive, odious; hence ～LY² (-mlĭ) *adv.*, ～NESS (-mn-) *n.* [ME, f. *loath* n. disgust (f. LOATHE) + -SOME¹]

loaves. See LOAF¹.

lōb *v.* (-bb-) & *n.* **1.** *v.i.* (arch.) walk, run, or move, heavily or clumsily or slowly. **2.** *v.t.* toss, bowl, or send, (ball) with slow or high-pitched motion. **3.** *n.* ball high in air at lawn tennis, table-tennis, etc.; (Cricket) slow underhand ball. [v. f. n., prob. f. LDu.]

lō'b|āte *a.* (Biol.) having lobe(s); hence ～A'TION *n.* [f. LOBE + -ATE²]

lō'bby *n.* & *v.* **1.** *n.* porch, ante-room, entrance-hall, corridor; (in House of Commons etc.) large hall open to public used esp. for interviews between MPs and others, (also **division ～**) one of two corridors to which members retire to vote; body of those who lobby. **2.** *v.t.* seek to influence (members of legislature), get (bill etc.) *through,* by interviews etc. in lobby; solicit support of (influential person). **3.** *v.i.* frequent lobby of legislature, solicit members' votes; hence ～IST (1) *n.* [f. med. L *lobia, lobium* LODGE¹]

lōbe *n.* roundish and flattish projecting or pendulous part, often one of two or more such parts divided by fissure (*lobe of liver* or *lungs*; *lobes of brain*); lower soft pendulous external part of ear; hence **lō'bAR¹** *a.* (esp. of the lungs, as *lobar pneumonia*), **lōbED²** (-bd), ～'LESS (-bl-), *adjs.* [f. LL f. Gk *lobos* lobe, pod]

lobe'ctomy *n.* (Med.) excision of lobe of an organ, as of a lung, thyroid gland, etc. [f. prec. + -ECTOMY]

lobē'lia *n.* herbaceous plant of genus Lobelia with blue, scarlet, white, or purple flowers having deeply cleft corolla. [f. M. de *Lobel*, Flemish botanist in England d. 1616 + -IA¹]

lō'blŏlly *n.* **1.** ～ **boy, man,** (Naut.) surgeon's attendant, surgeon's mate. **2.** ～ **pine,** *Pinus taeda,* growing in swamps of southern US. [perh. f. dial. *lob* eat up noisily + dial. *lolly* soup]

lōbŏ'tom|y *n.* (Med.) = LEUCOtomy. [f. LOBE + -O- + -TOMY]

lō'bscouse *n.* sailor's dish of meat stewed with vegetables and ship's biscuit. [18th c., of unkn. orig.; cf. Du. *lapskous*, Da., Norw., G *lapskaus*]

lō'bster *n.,* & *v.i.* **1.** *n.* large marine stalk-eyed ten-footed long-tailed edible crustacean of family Homaridae, with large claws formed by first pair of feet, bluish black before and scarlet after boiling; its flesh as food (*lobster* NEWBURG, THERMIDOR); ∼-**pot,** basket in which lobsters are trapped. **2.** *v.i.* catch lobsters. [OE *lopustre*, corrupt. of L *locusta* crustacean, LOCUST, assim. to -STER]

lo′bŭl∥e *n.* small lobe; hence ∼AR¹ *a.* [f. LOBE + -ULE]

lŏ′bworm (-wẽrm) *n.* large earthworm used as fishing-bait; LUG¹worm. [f. LOB in obs. sense 'pendulous object']

local¹. Var. of LOCALE.

lō′cal² *a.* & *n.* **1.** *a.* in regard to place; ∼ **habitation,** position in space as test of thing's material existence; ∼ **surname** (derived from name of place). **2.** belonging to, existing in, or peculiar to certain place(s); of the neighbourhood (*the local lawyer*); of affecting a part and not the whole (*local pain*); ‖(on envelope) for delivery in this town or district; not widely distributed (*the globe-flower is very local*); ∼ **action,** (Law) one that must relate to a specific place, e.g. trespass; ∼ **anaesthetic** (acting on only a small area of the body); ‖∼ **authority,** body charged with administration of local government; ∼ **call,** telephone call to nearby place, charged at low rate; ∼ **colour,** details characteristic of scene or time of novel etc. and added to give realism, (Paint.) colouring of separate objects in picture; *local* DERBY; ‖L∼ **Examinations** (set by university board and held in various places); ‖∼ **government,** system of administration of county, district, parish, etc., by elected representatives of those who live there; ∼ **option** or **veto,** system whereby inhabitants of a district may prohibit sale of alcoholic liquor there; ∼ **preacher,** Methodist layman authorized to preach in his own circuit; ∼ **time** (measured from sun's transit over meridian of place); ∼ **train** (stopping at all stations). **3.** Hence ∼LY² *adv.* **4.** *n.* inhabitant of, professional person practising in, particular district; local preacher; (item of) local news in newspaper; postage stamp current only in limited district; local train; ‖(colloq.) the local public house; ‖(in *pl.*) Local Examination(s); *local branch of trade union. [ME f. OF, f. LL *localis* f. L *locus* place; see -AL]

loca′le (-ah′l) *n.* scene or locality of operations or events. [f. F *local* n. f. as foll., respelt to indicate stress; cf. MORALE]

lō′calism *n.* attachment to a place; limitation of ideas etc. resulting from this; favouring of what is local; a local idiom, custom, etc. [f. LOCAL² + -ISM]

locā′lĭtў *n.* position of a thing, place where it is; (district near) site or scene of something; faculty of remembering and recognizing district or places, finding one's way, etc., (BUMP² *of locality*). [f. F *localité* or f. LL *localitas* (as LOCAL²; see -ITY)]

lō′calīz∥e, -īs∥e (-īz), *v.t.* invest with the characteristics of a particular place; restrict or assign to particular place; attach to districts, decentralize; hence ∼ABLE *a.,* ∼A′TION *n.* [f. LOCAL² + -IZE]

locā′t∥e *v.* **1.** *v.t.* establish in (proper) place, (in *pass.*) be situated. **2.** state locality of; discover exact place of (*locate the enemy's camp*). **3.** *v.i.* *take up residence or business (*in* place). **4.** Hence ∼OR *n.* [f. L *locare* (*locus* place) + -ATE³]

locā′tion *n.* locating or being located; (position in) a particular place; (S. Afr.) area where African natives are obliged to live; (Cinemat.) place, other than studio, where (part of) film is made (*on location*). [f. L *locatio* (as prec.; see -ATION)]

lō′cative *a.* & *n.* (Gram.) (case of nouns etc.) denoting place where. [f. as LOCATE + -IVE, after *vocative*]

loc. cit. *abbr.* in the passage already quoted. [f. LOCO CITATO]

lŏch (lŏχ, lŏk) *n.* (Sc.) **1.** lake. **2.** arm of the sea, esp. when narrow or partially land-locked. **3.** So ∼′an *n.,* small loch. [ME f. Gael.]

lŏ′chĭ∥a (-k-) *n.* discharge from uterus after childbirth; hence ∼AL *a.* [mod. L, f. Gk *lokhia* neut. pl. (as n.) of *lokhios* of childbirth]

lō′cī. See LOCUS.

lŏck¹ *n.* portion of fairly long hair that hangs together; (in *pl.*) hair of head; tuft of wool or cotton; hence ∼ED² (-kt) *a.* [OE *locc,* = OS *lok,* OHG *loc,* ON *lokkr* f. Gmc *lokkaz*]

lŏck² *n.* **1.** mechanism for fastening door, lid, etc., with bolt that requires key of particular shape to work it (**under** ∼ **and key,** locked up); appliance to keep wheel from revolving or slewing; wrestling-hold that keeps opponent's arm etc. fixed; ∼ (**forward**), (Rugby Footb.) player in second row of scrum. **2.** mechanism for exploding charge of gun (∼, **stock, and barrel,** whole of thing, completely). **3.** confined section of canal or river where level can be changed for raising and lowering boats between adjacent sections by use of gates and sluices. **4.** = AIR¹*lock* (2). **5.** interlocking, e.g. block or jam of vehicles in street. **6.** turning of front wheels of vehicle to change its direction of motion (**full** ∼, maximum extent of this). **7.** ‖∼ (**hospital**), hospital for venereal disease. **8.** ∼′**fast,** (Sc.) secured with lock; ∼-**keeper,** ∼′**sman,** keeper of canal etc. lock; ∼-**knit,** (fabric) knitted with interlocking stitch; ∼-**nut,** (Mech.) nut screwed down on another to keep it tight; ∼′**smith,** maker and mender of locks; ∼-**step,** marching with each man as close as possible to the one in front; ∼-**stitch** (made by sewing--machine by firmly locking together two threads or stitches). **9.** Hence ∼′LESS *a.* [OE *loc,* = OS *lok,* OHG *loh* hole, ON *lok* lid, end, f. Gmc *lokam*]

lŏck³ *v.* **1.** *v.t.* fasten (door, box, etc.) with lock, shut *up* (house etc.) by fastening doors thus; ∼ (or **shut**) **the stable door after** (or **when**) **the horse has bolted** or **been stolen,** take precautions too late. **2.** shut (person, thing) *up, in,* or *into,* (as if) with lock; (of land, hills, etc., usu. in *pass.*) enclose; (fig.) store (*up or away*) inaccessibly (*facts locked up in hieroglyphics*; *capital locked up in land*); hold fast in sleep, enchantment, etc.; keep (person) *out* by locking door (esp. of employer coercing workmen by refusing them work until they accept his conditions; ∼-**out** *n.,* this procedure, cf. STRIKE 12). **3.** *v.t.* & *i.* bring or come into rigidly fixed position, stop moving or revolving, engage, (cause to) catch, fasten by interlacing or fitting of corresponding parts, entangle; (in *p.p.*) joined *in* hostile or other embrace; ∼ **on to,** (cause to) locate by radar etc. and then track. **4.** *v.t.* provide (canal etc.) with locks; convey (boat) *up* or *down* through lock. **5.** *v.i.* (Of door, box, etc.) have means of being fastened with lock; go through canal etc. lock. **6.** ∼′**jaw,** (pop. name for) trismus, variety of tetanus, tonic spasm of muscles of mastication causing jaws to remain rigidly closed; ∼-**up,** (time of) locking up school etc. for night, unrealizable state of invested capital or amount of capital locked up, house or room for temporary detention of prisoners, ‖(premises etc.) that can be locked up. [ME, f. prec.]

lŏ′ckage *n.* amount of rise or fall effected by canal locks; toll for use of lock; use or number of locks. [f. LOCK² + -AGE]

lŏ′cker *n.* In vbl senses; small cupboard, esp. one of many reserved or reservable each for individual's use in public place, e.g. in ∼-**room** of cricket pavilion or in schoolroom; (Naut.) chest or compartment for clothes, stores, ammunition, etc., (**not a shot in** one's or **the** ∼, no money in one's pocket, no chance left; DAVY JONES'*s locker*). [ME, f. LOCK³ + -ER¹]

lŏ′ckĕt *n.* metal plate or band on scabbard; small ornamental case holding portrait, lock of hair, etc., and usu. hung from neck. [f. OF *locquet* dim. of *loc*]

lŏck′up. See LOCK³.

lō′cō¹ *n.* (*pl.* ∼s). (colloq.) locomotive engine. [abbr.]

lō′cō² *n.* (*pl.* ∼es or ∼s) & *a.* **1.** *n.* ∼ (-weed), poisonous leguminous plant of US causing brain disease in cattle eating it. **2.** *a.* (sl.) crazy. [Sp., = insane]

loco citato (lŏkō sĭtä′tō, -ah′-) *adv.* in the passage already quoted. [L, = in the place cited]

lōcomō′t|ion *n.* (power of) motion from place to place; travel, way (esp. artificial) of travelling; so ∼**ORY** *a.* [f. L *loco* abl. of *locus* place + *motio* MOTION[1]; suggested by the scholastic phr. *in loco movēri* move in space]

lōcomōtive (lō′-, -mō′-) *a.* & *n.* **1.** *a.* of locomotion (*locomotive power*), (joc.) of travel (*in these locomotive days*). **2.** having power of or given to locomotion, not stationary, (*locomotive bivalves, crane*); ∼ **engine** (that goes from place to place by its own power, esp. for drawing train along rails). **3.** *n.* locomotive engine. [f. as prec.; see -IVE]

lō′comōtor *a.* of locomotion (*locomotor* ATAXY). [f. as prec. + MOTOR]

lō′cŭl|us *n.* (*pl.* ∼**i** *pr.* -ī). (Zool., Anat., & Bot.) one of a number of small separate cavities; hence ∼**AR**[1] *a.* [L, dim. of LOCUS]

lo′cum *n.* (colloq.) = foll. [abbr.]

lōcum tĕ′nĕn|s (-z) *n.* (*pl.* ∼**tes** *pr.* -ĕ′ntēz). deputy acting esp. for clergyman or doctor; hence **lōcum--tĕ′nen**CY *n.* [med. L, (one) holding place; cf. foll. & TENANT]

lō′cus *n.* (*pl.* **lo′ci** *pr.* -sī). **1.** (Math.) curve etc. formed by all points satisfying particular equation of relation between coordinates, or by point, line, or surface, moving according to mathematically defined conditions. **2.** (Biol.) normal position of gene on chromosome. **3.** ∼ *classicus,* best-known or most authoritative passage on a subject; ∼ *in quo,* scene of event; ∼ *standi,* recognized position, right to intervene, appear in court, etc. [L, = place]

lō′cust *n.* **1.** any of various African and Asian short--horned edible grasshoppers of family Acrididae, migrating in swarms and consuming all vegetation of districts; (fig.) person of devouring or destructive propensities; *cicada. **2.** ∼ (**bean**), carob; ∼ (**tree**), (1) carob tree, (2) false acacia, (3) kowhai. **3.** ∼--**bird, -eater,** any of various birds feeding on locusts. [ME, f. OF *locuste* f. L *locusta* lobster, locust]

locū′tion *n.* style of speech; word or phrase considered in regard to style, idiom. [ME f. OF, or f. L *locutio* (*loqui locut-* speak, see -ION)]

lo′cŭtorў *n.* parlour or conversation-room in monastery; grille for interviews between inmates of monastery and outsiders. [f. med. L *locutorium* (as prec.; see -ORY)]

lōde *n.* vein of metal ore; ∼′**star, loa′dstar,** star that is steered by, esp. the pole-star, (fig.) guiding principle, object of pursuit; ∼′**stone,** = LOAD[1]*stone* [var. of LOAD[1]]

lō′den *n.* thick waterproof woollen cloth; dark green colour in which this is often made. [G]

lōdge[1] *n.* **1.** (arch.) small esp. temporary dwelling, **2.** cottage at gates of park or in grounds of large house, occupied by gardener or other servant; house (e.g. in Scottish Highlands) occupied in the hunting or shooting season; large house; hotel esp. at resort. **3.** porter's room(s) at gate of college, factory, or house of chambers or flats. **4.** (Freemasonry, Friendly Societies, etc.) (place of meeting for) members of branch; **grand** ∼, governing body of Freemasons or similar society. **5.** residence of head of college at Cambridge (cf. LODGINGS). **6.** beaver's or otter's lair. **7.** N. Amer. Indian's tent or wigwam (∼-**pole pine,** with trunk used to support this). **8.** local branch of trade union. [ME *log*(*g*)*e* f. OF *loge* arbour, hut, f. med. L *laubia, lobia* (cf. LOBBY), f. Gmc *laubja (*laubham* LEAF)]

lōdg|e *v.* **1.** *v.t.* provide with sleeping-quarters; receive as guest or inmate; establish as resident in house or room(s). **2.** serve as habitation for, contain; (in *pass.*) be contained *in.* **3.** leave *in* place or *with* person for safety. **4.** deposit in court or with official a formal statement of (complaint, information); bring forward (objection etc.). **5.** place (power etc.) *in, with, in the hands of,* (person). **6.** (Of wind or rain) lay (crops) flat. **7.** *v.t.* & *i.* (make, let) stick or remain in place without falling or going further (*lodged a bullet,*

bullet lodged, in his brain; tide lodges mud in the cavities). **8.** *v.i.* reside, be situated; be inmate paying for accommodation in another's house, whence ∼′**ER**[1] *n.* **9.** (Of crops) be laid flat by wind or rain. [ME, f. OF *logier* (as prec.)]

lō′dgement, lō′dgment, (-jm-) *n.* **1.** (Mil.) temporary defensive work on captured part of enemy's works; establishing oneself on enemy's ground. **2.** stable position gained, foothold, (*make, effect, a lodgement*). **3.** (Law) deposit(ing) of money. **4.** accumulation of matter intercepted in fall or transit. [f. F *logement* (as prec.; see -MENT)]

lō′dging *n.* In vbl senses; accommodation in hired rooms; dwelling-place, abode, (in *pl.*) room(s) hired elsewhere than in hotel for residing in, (in *pl.*) residence of head of college at Oxford (cf. LODGE[1]); ∼-**house** (in which lodgings are let); ||*common* ∼-*house* (usu. one with dormitory in which bed can be had for the night); ∼ **turn,** spell of duty in railway service or vehicle-driving during which employee sleeps away from home for a night. [ME, f. LODGE[2] + -ING]

lō′ĕss, löss (lērs), *n.* deposit of fine light-coloured wind-blown dust in Rhine, Mississippi, and other river valleys, very fertile when irrigated. [f. G *löss* f. Swiss G. *lösch* loose (*lösen* loosen)]

loft (lŏft, lawft) *n.,* & *v.t,* **1,** *n,* attic, esp. for storage etc.; *upstairs room; room over stable esp. for hay and straw; pigeon-house; gallery in church or hall (*organ loft, rood-loft*). **2.** (Golf.) backward slope in club-head, lofting stroke. **3.** *v.t.* hit, throw, kick, etc., (ball) high up, clear (obstacle) thus; (esp. in *p.p.*) give loft to (golf-club). [OE f. ON *lopt* (pr. lawft) air, sky, upper room, f. Gmc (as LIFT)]

lō′fter (lŏ′-, law′-) *n.* golf-club for lofting the ball. [f. prec. + -ER[1]]

lō′ft|ў (lŏ′-, law′-) *a.* of imposing height, towering, soaring, (*lofty mountain, flight, stature*; not used of persons); consciously superior or dignified (*lofty contempt, good humour*); exalted, distinguished, high--flying, high-flown; elevated, sublime, grandiose; hence ∼**i**LY[2] *adv.,* ∼**i**NESS *n.* [ME, f. LOFT (as in *aloft*) + -Y[2]]

lŏg[1] *n.,* & *v.t.* (-gg-). **1.** *n.* unhewn piece of felled tree, or similar rough mass of wood esp. cut for firewood; **in the** ∼, unhewn; KING[1] *Log; float, lie, fall,* **like a** ∼, in helpless or stunned state; **sleep like a** ∼ (soundly). **2.** float attached to line wound on reel for gauging speed of ship, other apparatus for same purpose, (**heave, throw, the** ∼, use this; **sail by the** ∼, calculate ship's position by it); PATENT[1] *log*. **3.** ∼ (-**book**), (1) book with permanent record made of all events occurring during ship's or aircraft's voyage(s) (including rate of ship's progress shown by log), (2) traveller's diary etc., (3) regularly maintained record of progress or performance; ∼-**book,** ||book showing registration details of motor vehicle; ∼ **cabin,** hut built of logs; ∼-**jam,** crowded mass of logs in river, (fig.) deadlock; ∼-**line** (to which float of ship's log is attached); ∼-**rolling,** (1) mutual help, esp. to assist each other's political projects [f. phr. *you roll my log and I'll roll yours*], (2) sport of trying to knock opponent off floating log on which both stand; ∼′**wood,** (wood, used in dyeing, of) W. Ind. tree (*Haematoxylon campechianum*). **4.** *v.t.* cut into logs; enter (distance made etc.) in ship's log-book, (of ship) make (distance); enter (seaman's name with offence committed) in log-book, fine (offender); enter (data etc.) in regular record; attain (cumulative total of time etc. thus recorded). [ME, of unkn. orig.]

lŏg[2] *n.* logarithm (esp. prefixed to number or algebraic symbol whose logarithm is to be indicated). [abbr.]

***-lŏg.** See -LOGUE.

lō′ganbĕrrў *n.* fruit got by cross between raspberry and dewberry. [f. J. H. *Logan,* Amer. horticulturist d. 1928 + BERRY[1]]

lō′gan(-stōne) *n.* poised heavy stone rocking at a touch. [= *logging* (dial. *log* to rock) + STONE]

lŏgaoe′dĭc (-aē′-) *a.* & *n.* (line of verse) composed of mixed dactyls and trochees, or anapaests and iambuses. [f. LL f. Gk *logaoidikos* (*logos* speech, *aoidē* song; see -IC)]

lŏ′garĭthm (-dhĕm, -thĕm) *n.* one of a class of arithmetical functions tabulated to assist calculation by substituting addition and subtraction for multiplication and division, and the latter two for involution and evolution; power to which fixed number (the *base*) must be raised to produce given number (*the logarithm of 1000 to base 10 is 3*); **common** ∼ (to base 10); **Napierian** or **natural** ∼ (to base denoted by *e*, about 2.72); hence **lŏgari′thmIC** (-dh-, -th-) *a.* [f. mod. L *logarithmus* f. Gk *logos* reckoning, ratio + *arithmos* number]

loge (lōzh, lōj) *n.* box in theatre etc. [F]

-loger *suf.* forming *ns.* = -LOGIST (*astrologer, campanologer*). [after ASTROLOGER]

*lŏ′gger (-g-) *n.* lumberjack. [f. LOG¹ + -ER¹]

lŏ′ggerhead (-gerhĕd) *n.* **1.** (arch.) blockhead, fool. **2.** iron instrument with ball at end heated for melting pitch etc. **3.** large-headed turtle (esp. *Caretta caretta*). **4. at** ∼**s,** disagreeing or disputing (*with*). [prob. f. dial. *logger* block of wood for hobbling a horse, + HEAD¹]

lŏ′ggia (-jya) *n.* open-sided gallery or arcade; open-sided extension of house. [It., = LODGE¹]

lŏ′ggĭng (-g-) *n.* lumbering (see LUMBER² 5). [f. LOG¹ + -ING¹]

lŏ′gĭc *n.* science of reasoning, proof, thinking, or inference; particular scheme of or treatise on this; chain of reasoning, correct or incorrect use of reasoning, ability in reasoning, arguments (CHOP⁴ *logic*; *argues with great learning and logic*; *is not governed by logic*); inexorable force, converting-power, compulsion, (*the logic of events, facts, necessity, war*, etc.); arrangement of elements in computer to perform specified task; so **logi′CIAN** *n.* [ME, f. OF *logique* f. LL *logica* f. Gk *logikē* (*tekhnē* art) of reason (LOGOS; see -IC)]

-lŏ′gĭc, -lŏ′gĭcal, *sufs.* forming *adjs.* corresp. esp. to *ns.* in -LOGY: *pathological, physiologic(al), theological, zoological.* [f. or after Gk -*logikos* f. adjs. & ns. in -*logos,* -*logia* -LOGY; see -IC, -ICAL]

lŏ′gĭcal *a.* of logic or formal argument; not contravening the laws of thought, correctly reasoned; deducible, defensible on ground of consistency, reasonably to be believed or done; capable of correct reasoning; ∼ **atomism,** (Philos.) theory that all propositions can be analysed into simple independent elements; ∼ **empiricism** or **positivism,** form of positivism in which symbolic logic is used and linguistic problems of meaning are emphasized; *logical* NECESSITY; hence ∼ITY (-ă′l-) *n.*, ∼LY² *adv.* [f. med. L *logicalis* f. LL *logica* (see LOGIC, -AL)]

lo′gi|on (lō′j-, lŏ′g-) *n.* (*pl.* ∼**a**). saying of Christ not recorded in canonical Gospels but preserved elsewhere. [Gk, = oracle (LOGOS)]

-logist *suf.* forming *ns.* meaning 'person skilled in -*logy*' (*etymologist, geologist, zoologist*). [f. (or f. as) -LOGY + -IST]

logi′stics *n. pl.* art of moving, lodging, and supplying troops and equipment; so **logi′stIC** *a.* [f. F *logistique* (*loger* LODGE²; see -ICS)]

lŏ′gŏ *n.* (*pl.* ∼**s**), (colloq.) = LOGOTYPE 2. [abbr.]

lŏ′gogram *n.* sign or character representing a word, esp. in shorthand. [f. Gk *logos* word + -GRAM]

logo′grapher *n.* (Gk Ant.) one of the Greek prose historians before Herodotus; ancient-Greek professional speech-writer for lawcourts. [f. LL *logographus* accountant or f. Gk *logographos* prose-writer (see LOGOS, -GRAPHER)]

logŏ′machy (-kĭ) *n.* (literary). dispute about words, controversy turning on merely verbal points. [f. Gk *logomakhia* (LOGOS, -*makhia* -fighting)]

lŏgorrhoe′a, *-rhē′a, (-rē′a) *n.* excessive flow of words esp. in mental illness. [f. as foll. + Gk *rhoia* flow]

Lŏ′gŏs *n.* the Word of God, or Second Person of the Trinity. [Gk, = word, reason, account, cogn. w. *legō* speak, choose, used in mystic sense by Hellenistic and Neoplatonist philosophers and by St. John]

lŏ′gotȳpe *n.* **1.** word, or more letters than one, cast in one piece but not as ligature, for use in printing. **2.** (single piece of type bearing) non-heraldic device chosen as badge of organization and used in advertisements, on notepaper, etc. [f. Gk *logos* word + TYPE¹]

-lŏgue (-g), ***-lŏg,** *suf.* forming *ns.* denoting talk (*dialogue, monologue*), compilation (*catalogue*), or occas. = -LOGIST (*ideologue, sinologue*). [f. or after F -*logue* f. Gk -*logos,* -*logon*]

*lŏ′g|ў (-gĭ) *a.* lethargic, sluggish; dull, inert; hence ∼ILY² *adv.*, ∼INESS *n.* [19th c., of unkn. orig.]

-logŷ *suf.* forming *ns.* denoting (1) character of speech or language (*tautology*), (2) subject of study (*mineralogy, sociology, theology, geology*), (3) discourse (*trilogy*). [f. F -*logie* or med. L or f. Gk -*logia* (as LOGOS; see -Y¹)]

loin *n.* **1.** (in *pl.*) part of body on both sides of spine between false ribs and hip-bones (**gird up** one's ∼**s,** prepare for journey or effort; **fruit, child,** etc., **of, sprung from,** etc., one's ∼**s,** one's begotten offspring). **2.** joint of meat that includes the loin vertebrae. **3.** ∼**′cloth,** cloth worn round loins esp. as sole garment. [ME, f. OF *loigne* f. Rom. **lumbea* fem. of **lumbeus* a. f. L *lumbus*]

loir (loi′er) *n.* large species of dormouse. [F, f. pop. L **lēre,* f. L *glis gliris*]

loi′ter *v.* **1.** *v.i.* linger on the way, hang about; travel indolently and with frequent pauses. **2.** *v.t.* pass (time etc.) *away* in loitering. **3.** Hence ∼ER¹ *n.* [ME, f. MDu. *loteren* wag about]

lŏll *v.* **1.** *v.t.* hang (one's tongue) out; let (one's head or limbs) rest lazily on something. **2.** *v.i.* (Of tongue) hang (*out*); stand, sit, or recline, in lazy attitude. [ME; prob. imit.]

Lŏ′llard *n.* one of the 14th-c. heretics who followed Wyclif or held opinions like his; hence ∼ISM (3) *n.* [f. MDu. *lollaerd* (*lollen* mumble; see -ARD)]

lŏ′llipŏp *n.* large usu. flat rounded boiled sweet on small stick; ||∼ **man** etc., (colloq.) official using circular sign on stick to stop traffic so that children may cross road. [perh. f. dial. *lolly* tongue + POP²]

lŏ′llop *v.i.* (colloq.) flop about; move or proceed in a lounging or ungainly way. [prob. f. LOLL, assoc. w. TROLLOP]

lŏ′llў *n.* **1.** (colloq.) lollipop; (Austral.) a sweet; **ice(d)** ∼, water-ice or ice-cream on small stick. **2.** (sl.) money. [abbr. of LOLLIPOP]

Lŏ′mbard *n.* & *a.* **1.** *n.* one of the Germanic 6th-c. conquerors of Italy; native or dialect of Lombardy. **2.** *a.* of the Lombards or Lombardy, Lombardic; ∼ **Street,** a London street formerly occupied by Lombard bankers, and still containing many of chief London banks, (transf.) the money market, financiers as a body, (∼ **Street to a China orange,** great wealth against one ordinary object, virtual certainty). [ME, f. OF *lombard* or MDu. *lombaerd,* f. It. *lombardo* f. med. L *Longobardus,* L *Lango-,* f. Gmc **Langbardhaz* (LONG¹, L *Bardi* name of the people)]

Lŏmbâ′rdĭc *a.* of the Lombards or Lombardy (esp. of N. Ital. 7th–13th-c. architecture and 15th–16th-c. painting). [f. prec. + -IC]

Lŏ′mbardў ∼ **poplar** (variety with especially tall slender form). [∼ in N. Italy]

lŏ′mĕnt *n.* (Bot.) kind of pod that breaks up when mature into one-seeded joints; hence ∼A′CEOUS *a.* [f. L *lomentum* bean-meal (orig. cosmetic) f. *lavare* wash]

Lo′ndon (lŭ′-) *n.* ∼ **clay,** geological formation in lower division of Eocene in SE England; ∼ **particular,** (arch.) kind of thick fog peculiar to London; ∼ **plane,** hybrid plane-tree resistant to smoke and often planted in streets; ∼ **pride,** a pink-flowered saxifrage; ∼ **smoke,** dull grey colour; hence ∼ER¹ (4), ∼ISM (4), *ns.,* ∼IZE (3) *v.t.* [∼, capital of UK]

lōne *attrib. a.* **1.** (poet. or rhet.) solitary, companionless, unfrequented, uninhabited, lonely. **2.** ~ **hand,** hand played or player playing against the rest at quadrille and euchre, (fig.) person or action without allies; ~ **scout,** Scout who does not have regular access to a Scout troop; *L~ **Star** (**State**), Texas; *lone* WOLF. **3.** feeling or making feel lonely. **4.** (Of woman) single or widowed. [ME, f. ALONE]

lō′nel‖y̆ (-nlĭ) *a.* solitary, companionless, isolated; unfrequented; sad because without friends or company (~y **heart,** such person); hence ~iNESS *n.* [f. prec.+-LY¹]

lō′ner *n.* person or animal that prefers not to associate with others. [f. LONE+-ER¹]

lō′nesome (-ns-) *a.* solitary, lonely; feeling lonely or forlorn; causing such feeling; **by** or **on** one's ~, all alone; hence ~LY² (-mlĭ) *adv.,* ~NESS (-mn-) *n.* [f. LONE+-SOME¹]

lŏng¹ (~′er, ~′est, *pr.* -ngg-) & *n.* **1.** *a.* measuring much from end to end in space or time, not soon traversed or finished, (*a long line, journey, way off; a long life, time ago*); (seemingly) more than the stated amount (*ten long miles*); (colloq., of person) tall; *as long as my* ARM¹; *long in the* TOOTH. **2.** far-reaching, acting at a distance, involving great interval or difference, (*little* PITCHER¹*s have long ears*); (of a chance) involving much risk; (of bill of exchange) maturing at distant date; (of person's memory) retaining things for a long time. **3.** (Usu. appended to measurement) having specified length or duration (*tail 6 in. long; vacation is two months long; as* BROAD *as it is long*) **4.** of elongated shape; remarkable for or distinguished by or concerned with length or duration. **5.** expressed by many digits or consisting of many individuals (~ **figure** or **price,** heavy cost); (of family) having many children; (of bill) containing many or exorbitant items. **6.** lengthy, prolix, tedious. **7.** of more than the usual numerical amount (*long* DOZEN, HUNDRED(WEIGHT), TON¹). **8.** lasting, going far back or forward in time, (*a long friendship, farewell*). **9.** (Phonet. & Pros.) (Of vowel or syllable) (1) having the greater of the two recognized durations, (2) stressed; (of Engl. vowel) having the pronunciation shown in its name (e.g. *pile* and *cute* have long, *pill,* and *cut* short, *i* and *u*). **10.** (St. Exch. etc.; of stocks, stockbroker, etc.) bought, buying, etc., in large quantities in advance, with expectation of rise in price. **11.** ~**-and-short work,** (Archit.) alternation of tall quoins with flat slabs; ~ **arm,** (1) far-reaching power, (2) pole with hook etc. for use at height beyond ordinary reach; *make a* ~ *arm,* reach out for something; ~**-bill,** bird with long bill, esp. snipe; ~′**boat,** sailing-ship's largest boat; ~′**bow** (drawn by hand and shooting long feathered arrow; *draw the* ~*bow,* tell exaggerated or invented stories; ~**-case** (grandfather) **clock;** ~**-chain,** (of molecule) containing chain of many carbon atoms; ‖*by a long* CHALK¹; ~ **clay,** churchwarden pipe; ~**-clothes,** (arch.) ~**-coats,** clothes of baby in arms; ~**-dated,** not due for early payment or redemption; ~**-day,** (of plant) needing long daily period of light to cause flowering; ~**-distance,** (of weather forecast) long--range, (of telephone call, public transport, etc.) between distant places; *long* DIVISION; ~ **drink** (served in tall glass); ~**-eared,** stupid (like an ass), (of owl) having long ear-tufts; ~ **face,** dismal expression; ~ **field,** (1) = *long off* or *long on,* (2) part of field behind bowler; ~ **finger,** middle finger; ‖~ **firm,** swindlers who obtain goods but do not pay; ~ **game,** (Golf) driving and play before approaching the green; *the ~ green,* (sl.) money; ~**-hair(ed),** (person) with hair longer than usual, esp. intellectual or hippie; ~′**hand,** ordinary writing (opp. shorthand or typing or printing); **the ~ handle,** (Cricket) hitting freely; ~ **haul,** transport of goods, or other effort made, over a long distance; ~**-hea′ded,** shrewd, far-seeing, sagacious; *long* HOME¹; ~ **hop,** short-pitched ball in cricket, easily hit; ~′**horn,** one

of a breed of cattle with long horns, beetle of family Cerambycidae with very long antennae; ~ **johns,** (colloq.) underpants with full-length legs; ‖~ **jump,** athletic contest of jumping as far as possible along the ground in one leap; *at long* LAST³ 8; ~ **leg,** (position of) cricket fieldsman far behind batsman on leg side; ~**-legged,** (fig.) speedy; ~ **lens** (with great focal length); ~**-lived** (-ĭvd), having a long life, durable; ~ **mark,** macron; ~ **measure,** measure of length (metres, miles, etc.); ~ **metre,** (1) hymn stanza of four lines with 8 syllables each, (2) quatrain of iambic tetrameters with alternate lines rhyming; **make a** ~ **nose,** cock a SNOOK²; ~ **odds,** very unequal stakes or chances in betting; ~ **off,** ~ **on,** (position of) cricket fieldsman far behind bowler and towards off, on, side; ~ **on,** (colloq.) well supplied with; L~ **Parliament,** English parliament elected 1640 and dissolved 1660; ~ **pig,** (transl. of cannibals' name for) human flesh as food; ~**-player,** = LONG²-playing record; ~ **purse,** plenty of money; ~**-range,** having a long range, relating to a long period of future time; ~ **robe,** legal profession; **in the ~ run,** in the end, as the ultimate outcome (after all vicissitudes); *long* SEA; ~ **service,** prolonged service in one post, esp. (Mil.) enlistment for many years; ~′**shanks,** (1) = STILT 3, (2, *L.-*) nickname of Edward I; ~ **ship,** (Hist.) warship with many rowers; ~**-short story,** short story longer than the average; ~ **shot,** wild guess or venture, bet at long odds, (Cinemat.) shot including objects at a distance; *not by a* ~ *shot,* far from, by no means; ~ **sight,** ability to see clearly only what is comparatively distant; ~**-sighted,** having long sight, (fig.) having imagination or foresight; ~**-sleeved,** with sleeves reaching below elbow; *of long* STANDING¹; ~′**stop,** (position of) cricket fieldsman directly behind wicket-keeper, (fig.) last resort; ~ **suit,** many cards of one suit in a hand (esp. more than 3 or 4 in hand of 13), (fig.) thing at which one excels; *long* TERM; ~**-term,** occurring in or relating to a long period of time; ~ **time** *adv.,* (arch.) for a long time; ~**-time,** that has been such for a long time; ~ **tongue,** loquacity; ~ **trousers** (opp. *shorts*); ‖~ **vacation,** summer vacation of lawcourts and universities; ~ **view(s),** consideration of remote effects; ~ **waist,** low or deep waist of dress or body; ~ **wave,** radio wave of more than 1,000 metres wavelength; *long* WHIST³; ~ **wind,** ability to run a long distance without rest or (fig.) to talk or write at tedious length; ~**-winded,** having such ability. **12.** Hence ~′ISH¹ 2 *a.,* ~′WAYS, ~′WISE, *advs.* **13.** *n.* a long interval or period (*shall see you before long; shall not be away for long; will not take long; it is long since I saw him*); **at (the)** ~**est,** to mention the most distant date possible. **14.** recital at length (**the ~ and the short of it,** all that can or need be said, the total upshot). **15.** long syllable or vowel; mark indicating that vowel is long; (St. Exch.) long-dated stock, person who buys long; ‖ = *long vacation;* ~**s and shorts,** quantitative verse, (Archit.) = *long-and-shortwork.* [OE *long, lang,* = OS, OHG *lang,* ON *langr,* Goth. *laggs* f. Gmc *langaz*]

lŏng² *adv.* (~′er, ~′est, *pr.* -ngg-). **1.** for a long time (*have long thought so*); *long* LIVE² . . . .!; **so** or **as ~ as,** during the whole time that, provided that, if only; **so¹** *long!,* goodbye. **2. be ~ doing,** (prob. by confus. of *adv.* & *a.*) **be ~ in doing,** (ellipt.) **be ~,** take a long time, be slow, to do, (*he was long finding it out; the chance was long in coming; wait here, for I shall not be long*); **not be ~ for this world,** have only short time to live. **3.** by a long time (*long before, after, since* or *ago*); (appended to *ns.* of duration) throughout specified time (*all day long, his life long*). **4.** In *compar.,* with *no, any, much,* etc.) after implied point of time (*shall not wait any longer*); **no ~er,** not now or henceforth as formerly. **5.** ~**-ago** *a.* & *n.,* (belonging to) the distant past; ~**-drawn-(-out),** (unduly) prolonged; ~**-playing,** (of gramophone record) playing for about 10 to 30 minutes on each side; ~**-running,** continuing for a long time;

long-STANDING²; ∿-**suffering** *n.* & *a.*, bearing provocation patiently. [OE *lange* (as prec.)]

lŏng² *v.i.* wish earnestly or vehemently *for* thing or *to* do; hence ∿'ING¹ (1) *n.*, ∿'ING² *a.*, ∿'INGLY *adv.* [OE *langian* seem LONG¹ to]

-**lŏng** *suf.* forming *adjs.* & *advs.* (1) w. sense as LONG² 3 (*day-long, lifelong*), (2) = -LING² (*headlong, sidelong*). [f. LONG¹]

long. *abbr.* longitude.

longaeval. Var. of LONGEVAL.

lŏngani'mitў (-ngg-) *n.* (arch.) long-suffering, forbearance. [ME, f. LL *longanimitas* (LL (*longanimis* f. L *longus* long + *animus* spirit, after Gk *makrothumia*; see -ITY)]

longe. See LUNGE¹.

lŏ'ngeron (-nj-) *n.* (usu. in *pl.*) longitudinal member of aeroplane's fuselage. [F, = girder]

lŏngē'val (-nj-) *a.* (arch.) long-lived, long-lasting. [f. L *longaevus* (*longus* long, *aevum* age) + -AL]

lŏngē'vitў (-nj-) *n.* long life. [f. LL *longaevitas* (as prec.; see -ITY)]

lŏ'ngicŏrn (-nj-) *n.* longhorn beetle. [f. mod. L *longicornis* f. L *longus* long + -I- + *cornu* horn]

lŏ'ngitŭde (-nj-, -ngg-) *n.* **1.** (Geog.) angular distance east or west from a standard meridian, e.g. that of Greenwich, to the meridian of any place, reckoned up to 180° E. or W. **2.** (Astron.) angular distance eastward on ecliptic from vernal equinoctial point to point within 90° of any body or point and on great circle through it perpendicular to ecliptic; similar distance in other reference systems. **3.** (arch. or joc.) length. [ME, f. L *longitudo -dinis* (*longus* long; see -TUDE)]

lŏngĭtŭ'dĭnal (-nj-, -ngg-) *a.* of or in length; running lengthwise; of longitude; ∿ **wave** (vibrating in direction of propagation); hence ∿LY² *adv.* [f. as prec. + -AL]

Lŏ'ngobărd *n.* = LOMBARD 1. [f. med. L *Longobardi* (see LOMBARD)]

lŏ'ng-shŏre *a.* existing or found or employed on, frequenting, directed along, the shore; ∿**man,** landsman employed in loading and unloading ships, shore-fishing, etc. [f. *along shore*]

longueur (lawṅgēr') *n.* tedious passage in book etc.; tedious stretch of time. [F, = length]

loni'cera *n.* shrub of genus *Lonicera*, honeysuckle. [f. A. *Lonicerus*, Ger. botanist d. 1586 + -A]

loō¹ *n.* round card-game with penalties paid to the pool; (having to pay) this penalty; ∿ **table** (circular kind). [abbr. of obs. *lanterloo* f. F *lantur(e)lu*, refrain of a song]

||**loō²** *n.* (colloq.) lavatory. [20th c.; orig. uncert.]

loō'bў *n.* lazy or stupid person. [ME, of unkn. orig.]

loōf. Var. of LUFF.

loō'fah (-a) *n.* pod of the plant *Luffa aegyptiaca* used as flesh-brush or sponge. [f. Egypt. Arab. *lūfa*, the plant]

loōk *v.* & *n.* **1.** *v.i.* use one's sight, turn eyes in some direction; ∿ **before you leap,** avoid precipitate action. **2.** *v.t.* contemplate, examine; ∿ person **through and through,** observe him searchingly; look (person, *death*, etc.) *in the* EYE¹(*s*) or *in the* FACE¹; look *a* GIFT-*horse in the mouth*; ∿'**ing-glass,** glass mirror. **3.** express, threaten, show, by one's looks (*look compassion, death,* DAGGERS, etc.). **4.** ascertain or observe by sight *what, who, how, whether,* etc.; ∿ **what you've done!, who's here!,** etc., (excl. of rebuke or surprise). **5.** *v.i.* make visual or (fig.) mental search (*I'll look in the morning; instead of reforming others let him look at home*); inquire (*when one looks deeper*); take care or make sure *that*, expect *to* do; ∿ (**here**)! (demanding attention or expostulating); ∿-**see,** (sl.) survey, inspection; ∿ **sharp,** [orig. = keep strict watch] lose no time, bestir oneself; ∿ **you!,** observe this fact. **6.** (Of thing) face, be turned, have or afford outlook, in some direction (*towards, on to, into, over, down*, etc.). **7.** have specified appearance, seem, (*look a*

fool, foolish, to be real, every inch a king, one's BEST¹); *∿-**alike,** person or thing closely resembling another; *look* ALIVE; ∿**small,** be exposed as mean etc.; ∿ **well** or **ill,** (1) seem in good or bad health, (2) of thing; also ∿ **good** or **bad**) seem to be progressing well or badly; ∿ **as if,** suggest by appearance the belief that; ∿ **like,** have appearance of, ||seem to be, threaten or promise, indicate presence of, (*it looks like this, like rain, like rats*; *he looks like an angel, a policeman, biting, winning*); hence -∿'ING² *a.* (*good-looking, grave--looking*, etc.). **8.** seem to be (∿ one's **age,** seem as old as one really is; ∿ one**self again,** seem recovered). **9.** (w. *preps.*): ∿ **about** one, examine one's surroundings, take time to form plans; ∿ **after,** follow with the eye, seek for, attend to, take care of; ∿ **at,** direct one's eyes or attention at, examine or consider thus; *to* ∿ *at*, in outward appearance; *to* ∿ *at him* etc., judging by his etc. appearance; *will not* ∿ *at*, refuses to take, rejects, scorns; ∿ *down* one's *nose at*, (colloq.) regard with contempt or with covert displeasure; ∿ **for,** expect, hope or be on the watch for, search for (*look for* TROUBLE); ∿ **into,** examine the inside of (box etc.), dip into (book), investigate; ∿ **on,** regard *as*, regard (coldly, *with* distrust etc.); ∿ **over,** inspect, (arch.) overlook or pardon; ∿ **through,** direct one's sight through (window etc.), penetrate (veil etc.) with sight or (pretence or pretender) with insight, inspect exhaustively or successively, ignore by pretending not to see, glance through (book etc.); ∿ **to,** consider, take care of, be careful about (*look to your manners*; *look to it that*), keep watch over, rely on (person or thing) *for*, expect, count upon, aim at; ∿ **upon,** = *look on* (see above). **10.** (w. *advs.*): ∿ **about** or **around,** be on the watch, make search *for*, let one's eyes rove; ∿ **back,** be half-hearted about enterprise one has begun (usu. w. neg.), turn one's thoughts (*up*)*on* or *to* something past, cease to progress (usu. w. neg.); ||make a second call later; ∿ **down** (**up**)**on,** consider oneself superior to; ∿ **forward to,** anticipate (usu. with pleasure, also *with apprehension* etc.); ∿ **in,** make short visit or call, (colloq.) watch television; ∿-*in n.,* informal call or visit, chance of participation or success; ∿ **on,** be (mere) spectator; ∿ **out,** direct one's sight or put one's head out of window etc., be vigilant, keep one's eyes open *for* expected person, be prepared *for* squalls etc., have or afford outlook *on, over,* etc., ||select or find by inspection; ∿-*out n.,* watch, looking out, (*keep a good look-out; on the look-out for* or *to* do), post of observation, man or party or boat stationed to look out, view over landscape, prospect of luck (*it's a bad* or *poor look-out for him*), person's own concern (*that is his* ∿*-out,* he must deal with that himself); ∿ **over,** inspect one by one or part by part (*must look them over soon*); ∿ **round,** look in every or another direction, examine objects of interest in a place, or possibilities etc. with a view to deciding on a course of action; ∿ **through,** survey with searching glance (*looked him through*), inspect exhaustively or successively; ∿ **up,** improve in price or prosperity, search for (esp. word in dictionary or facts in book of reference), (colloq.) go to visit (person), raise eyes; ∿ *up to,* respect, venerate; ∿ person *up and down,* scrutinize him keenly or contemptuously. **11.** *n.* act of looking, directing of eyes to look at thing or person, glance, (*a kind, scornful, look*); (in *sing.* or *pl.*) appearance of face, expression, personal aspect, (**good** ∿**s,** beauty); (of thing) appearance (*the place has a European look; the peasant look in knitwear*; **for the** ∿ **of the thing,** (colloq.) to keep up appearances; **don't like the** ∿ **of this,** find it alarming). [OE *lōcian,* = OS *lōkon* f. WG **lōk-, *lōg-*]

loō'ker *n.* In vbl senses; person having specified appearance (*good-looker*); (colloq.) attractive woman; ∿-**o'n,** one who is a mere spectator. [ME, f. prec. + -ER¹]

loōm¹ *n.* apparatus for weaving yarn or thread

crosswise into fabric. [ME *lōme* f. OE *gelōma* tool (as Y-, *lōma* apparatus)]

lōom² *v.i.*, & *n.* **1.** *v.i.* ~ (**up**), appear indistinctly, be seen in vague and often magnified or threatening shape, (lit. or fig.; often *loom large* etc.). **2.** *n.* vague often exaggerated first appearance of land at sea etc. [prob. f. LDu.; cf. EFris. *lōmen* move slowly, MHG *lüemen* be weary]

lōom³. Var. of LOON².

lōom⁴ *n.* (inboard part of) shaft of oar. [f. Scand.; cf. Norw. *lumm*]

lōon¹ *n.* (Sc. or arch.) scamp, idler; lad. [ME, of unkn. orig.]

lōon² *n.* diving bird, esp. grebe or large diver; crazy person (cf. foll.). [alt. f. *loom* f. ON *lómr*]

lōo'ný *n.* & *a.* lunatic; ~-**bin**, mental home or hospital. [abbr.; see -Y²]

lōop¹ *n.* & *v.* **1.** *n.* figure produced by a curve, or doubled string etc., that crosses itself; attachment or ornament formed of cord, thread, etc., so crossed and fastened at crossing; ring or curved piece of material as handle etc.; contraceptive coil; ~(-**line**), railway or telegraph line that diverges from main line and joins it again; manœuvre in which aeroplane is flown upside down between climb and dive; (Skating) curve crossing itself made on single edge; (Electr.) complete circuit for current; endless strip of tape or film allowing continuous repetition; (Computers) sequence of operations repeated till some condition is satisfied; hence ~'Y² *a.*, (sl.) crazy. **2.** *v.t.* form (string etc.) into loop(s); enclose (as) with loop; fasten (*up, back*) or join (*together*) with loop(s); ~ **the** ~, (Aeron.) perform loop. **3.** *v.i.* (Esp. of looper larvae) form loop. [ME, of unkn. orig.]

lōop² *n.* = LOOPHOLE. [ME, of unkn. orig.]

lōo'per *n.* caterpillar of geometer moth, progressing by arching itself into loops; contrivance in sewing--machine etc. for making loops. [f. LOOP¹ + -ER¹]

lōo'phŏle (-p-h-) *n.*, & *v.t.* **1.** *n.* narrow vertical slit in wall for shooting or looking through or to admit light or air; outlet, means of evading rule etc. **2.** *v.t.* make loopholes in (wall etc.). [f. LOOP² + HOLE¹]

lōose¹ *a.* **1.** released from bonds or restraint; (of animal) not confined or tethered etc.; LET² *loose*. **2.** detached or detachable from its place (*come, get, work, loose*); **cut** ~, begin to act freely; *play* FAST⁴ *and loose*. **3.** hanging partly free (esp. *loose end*; **at a** ~ **end**, ***at** ~ **ends**, without definite occupation); not rigidly fixed, apt to shift, (*have a* SCREW *loose*); not fastened together or held in container etc. (*loose papers, hair, tea*). **4.** slack, relaxed, not tense or tight, (**with a** ~ **rein**, lit. of riding, fig. indulgently); (of tongue) likely to speak indiscreetly; (of bowels) tending to diarrhoea; ~ **build** or **make**, ungainly figure; ~-**limbed**, having supple limbs. **5.** not compact, dense, or serried (*loose soil, fabric*; ~ **order**, arrangement of soldiers etc. with wide intervals); (Footb., of ball) not in any player's possession, (of play etc.) with players not close together. **6.** (Of statement, idea, etc.) inexact, indefinite, vague, incorrect; (of translation) not close or faithful; (of style) ungrammatical; (of agent) doing the act loosely (*loose thinker*); (Cricket, of bowling) inaccurately pitched, (of fielding) careless or bungling. **7.** morally lax, dissolute, promiscuous, wanton in speech or act. **8.** *loose* BOX²; ~ **change**, money as coins in pocket etc. for casual use; ||~ **cover**, removable cover for chair etc.; ~-**leaf** *a.*, (of ledger, notebook, etc.) with each leaf separate and removable; (in comb.) loosely (*loose-flowing, -fitting*). **9.** Hence ~'LY² (-slī) *adv.*, ~'NESS (-sn-) *n.*, **lōo'sISH**¹ 2 *a.* [ME *lōs* f. ON *lauss* (= OE *lēas* untrue, OS, OHG *lōs*, Goth. *laus*), f. Gmc *lausaz*]

lōose² *v.t.* release, set free, free from constraint; untie, undo, (knot, fetters, seal, hair of head); detach from moorings; ~ (**off**), discharge (arrow), (abs.) discharge gun (*at*); relax (*loose hold*). [ME, f. prec.]

lōose³ *n.* **1.** loose play in football (*in the loose*); state of

freedom or unrestrainedness (**on the** ~, having a spree). **2.** free expression (*give a loose to* one's *feelings*). [f. LOOSE¹,²]

lōo'sen *v.t.* & *i.* make or become less tight or compact or firm; relieve (bowels) from constipation or (cough) from dryness; relax (discipline etc.); ~ person's **tongue**, make him speak freely; ~ **up**, = LIMBER³ *up*. [ME, f. LOOSE¹ + -EN⁶]

lōo'sestrife (-s-s-) *n.* marsh plant of genus *Lysimachia*, esp. *L. vulgaris* (**golden** or **yellow** ~); marsh plant of genus *Lythrum*, esp. *L. salicaria* (**purple** or **red** or **spiked** ~). [f. LOOSE² + STRIFE, mistransl. of L f. Gk *lusimakhion* (Gk pers. name of discoverer *Lusimakhos*), as if directly f. *luō* undo, *makhē* battle]

lōot *n.*, & *v.t.* **1.** *n.* goods taken from enemy, spoil; booty, illicit gains made by official; (sl.) money. **2.** *v.t.* plunder, sack, (city, building, etc., or abs.); carry off as booty; steal (goods), rob (house), left unprotected after violent events; hence ~'ER¹ *n.* [f. Hindi *lūt*]

lŏp¹ *v.* (**-pp-**) & *n.* **1.** *v.t.* cut off branches and twigs and rarely top of (tree); strip tree of (branches etc. *off, away*); cut *off* or off (person's limb or head), (fig.) remove (items) as superfluous. **2.** *v.i.* make lopping strokes *at.* **3.** *n.* smaller branches and twigs of trees (~ **and top**, ~ **and crop**, trimmings of tree). [ME, f. OE *loppian*; cf. obs. *lip* to prune]

lŏp² *v.* (**-pp-**) & *n.* **1.** *v.i.* & *t.* hang limply; (of animal) let (ears) hang. **2.** *n.i* slouch, dawdle, hang *about*; move with short bounds. **3.** ~-**ears**, drooping ears; so ~-**eared** *a.*; ~-**ear**, = sense 5. **4.** Hence ~'PY² *a.* **5.** *n.* lop-eared rabbit. [cogn. w. LOB]

lōpe *v.i.*, & *n.* (run with) long bounding stride (esp. of animals). [ME, var. of Sc. *loup* f. ON *hlaupa* LEAP¹]

lō'pho- comb. form. crested, as: ~**branch** (-ăngk), (fish) with gills arranged in tufts; ~**dont**, (animal) with transverse ridges on crowns of molars; ~**phore**, tentacled disc at mouth of bryozoan. [f. Gk *lophos* crest + -o-]

lŏpsī'dĕd *a.* with one side lower or smaller than the other, unevenly balanced; hence ~'LY² *adv.*, ~'NESS *n.* [f. LOP² + SIDE¹ + -ED²]

loq. *abbr. loquitur.*

loquā'cious (-shus) *a.* talkative; (of birds, water) chattering, babbling; hence or cogn. ~'LY² *adv.*, ~'NESS, **loquā'city**, *ns.* [L *loquax -acis* (*loqui* talk); see -ACIOUS]

lō'quat (-ŏt) *n.* (small reddish fruit of) orig. Chinese and Japanese tree, *Eriobotrya japonica*. [f. Chin. dial. *luh kwat* rush orange]

lo'quitur (lŏ'kwĭtẽr) *v.i.* 3 *sing. pres.* speaks (with speaker's name added, as stage-direction or to inform reader). [L]

||**lŏr** *int.* (vulg.) = LORD 6. [abbr.]

lōr'al *a.* of the LORE². [f. LORE² + -AL]

lōr'an *n.* system of navigation using signal pulses from four radio transmitters. [f. *long-range navigation*]

lōr'cha *n.* ship with hull of European shape but Chinese rig. [Port.]

lōrd *n.*, *int.*, & *v.t.* **1.** *n.* master, ruler, chief, prince, sovereign, (*our sovereign lord the King*; *Lord of* MISRULE; ~**s of creation**, (1) mankind, (2, joc.) men as opp. women); (poet. or rhet.) owner (*lord of a few acres*; cf. LANDLORD; magnate in some trade (*the cotton lords*; cf. KING¹ 3). **2.** feudal superior (MESNE *lord*; *lord of the* MANOR). **3.** ~ (**and master**), (poet. or joc.) husband. **4.** (Astrol.) dominant planet. **5.** L~ (**God**), (usu. with the, exc. in *voc.*) God (*the Lord gave, and the Lord hath taken away*; *blessed be the name of the Lord*); **L**~ (**only**) **knows**, (colloq.) = GOD *knows* (1). **6.** *int.* (colloq.) (**oh**) L~(**y**)!, **good L~**!, (expr. surprise or consternation); L~ **have mercy**, L~ **bless me** or **my soul** or **you** or **us**, *Lord* LOVE² *you*, (expr. surprise). **7.** *n.* **Our L**~, the L~, Christ; **in the year of our L**~ (of the Christian era); L~'**s day**, Sunday; **the L**~'**s Prayer**, the Our Father, prayer taught by Christ to his disciples (Matt. 6:9-13); **the L**~'**s Supper**, the Eucharist; **the L**~'**s table**, (1) Christian altar, (2) Eucharist. **8.** nobleman, peer of the realm or person entitled by courtesy to the title *Lord* (see below) as part of his ordinary style (**live, treat, like a ~,** fare, entertain, sumptuously; *drunk* **as,** *swear* **like, a ~,** excessively; ||**~-in-waiting, ~ of the bedchamber,** nobleman attending queen, king); **the L~s,** the TEMPORAL and SPIRITUAL peers of Parliament; **House of L~s,** (1) upper legislative chamber of United Kingdom, (2) committee of specially qualified members of this appointed as ultimate judicial appeal court, (3) building where these bodies meet. **9.** ||**L~s** (**Commissioners**), members of board performing duties of high State office put in commission; **First L~,** president of such board; **Sea L~,** naval member of Admiralty Board; **L~s of Session,** judges of Scottish Court of Session. **10.** *Lord* ADVOCATE[1]; **L~ of Appeal** (**in Ordinary**), member of House of Lords (2) (see sense 8); **L~ Bishop** (ceremonious title of any bishop); ||*Lord* CHAMBERLAIN, (*High*) CHANCELLOR; ||**L~ Chief Justice,** president of Queen's Bench Division; *Lord* (*High*) COMMISSIONER; ||**L~ Justice** (**of Appeal**), judge in Court of Appeal; **L~ Justice Clerk,** vice--president of Scottish Court of Session; **L~ Justice General,** Lord President as head of Scottish Court of Justiciary; ||**L~ Lieutenant,** (1) viceroy of Ireland till 1922, (2) chief executive authority and head of magistrates in each county; *Lord* ||LYON, MAYOR, ||PRESIDENT, ||PRIVY Seal, ||PROVOST, ||RECTOR, ||(*High*) STEWARD. **11.** ||(Prefixed as part of less formal personal designation of) marquis, earl, viscount, or baron, (whether peer, or peer's eldest son holding his father's second title by courtesy; never with *of*: the Earl of Derby or (*the*) *Lord Derby*; always used in place of *Baron* except very formally). **12.** (Prefixed to Christian name, with or without sur-name, of) younger son of duke or marquis. **13. My ~,** respectful or polite form of address or (arch.) reference to nobleman (below duke), bishop, lord mayor, lord provost, or judge of supreme court. **14. ~s and ladies,** wild arum. **15.** Hence **~'**LESS *a.,* **~'**LING'[2] *n.* **16.** *v.t.* rule *over* like a lord (usu. in *pass.: will not be lorded over,* or with *it*: *lording it over his household*); ennoble, confer title of *Lord* upon. [OE *hláford* f. *hláfweard* = bread-keeper (as LOAF[1], WARD[1])]

lōr'dl|y *a.* haughty, imperious, lofty, disdainful; grand, magnificent, fit for or belonging to a lord; hence **~**ÍNESS *n.* [OE *hláfordlíc* (as prec., -LY[1])]

lōrd|ō'sis *n.* (*pl.* **~oses** *pr.* -ō'sēz). (Med.) curvature of spine, convex forwards (opp. *kyphosis*); hence **~**o'TIC *a.* [mod. L, f. Gk *lordōsis* (*lordos* bent back-wards; see -OSIS)]

lōr'dshĭp *n.* dominion, rule, ownership *of* or *over*; domain, estate, manor; being a lord; **his, your, ~, their ~s,** he, you, they, (in respectful mention of or address to holder(s) of title *Lord*; also iron.). [OE *hláfordscipe* (as LORD, -SHIP)]

Lōr'dÿ *int.* See LORD 6. [f. LORD + -Y[3]]

lōre[1] *n.* **1.** body of traditions and knowledge on a subject (*ghost, bird, sacred, lore*) or held by a group (*gypsy lore*). **2.** (arch.) doctrine; erudition, scholar-ship. [OE *lár,* = OS, OHG *léra* f. WG **laiza* f. Gmc **laizō* (**lais-* LEARN)]

lōre[2] *n.* (Zool.) straplike surface, in birds between eye and upper mandible, in snakes between eye and nostril. [f. L *lorum* strap]

lōrgnĕ'tte (-nyě't), **lōr'gnon** (-nyawn), *ns.* (in *sing.* or *pl.*) pair of eyeglasses or opera-glasses held by long handle. [F (*lorgner* to squint; see -ETTE)]

lŏ'ricate *a.* & *n.* (Zool.) (animal) having defensive armour of bone, plates, scales, etc. [f. L *loricatus* (*lorica* breastplate f. *lorum* strap; see -ATE[2])]

lŏrikeet (lŏ'-, -ē't) *n.* small brightly-coloured Poly-nesian parrot allied to the lory. [dim. of LORY, after *parakeet*]

lŏ'rimer, lŏ'riner, *n.* (Hist.) bit-maker, spurrier, (now only in title of a livery company). [ME, f. OF

loremier, -nier (*lorain* harness-strap f. Rom. **loranum* f. L *lorum* thong); see -ER[2] (2)]

lōr'ĭs *n.* small slender tailless nocturnal arboreal lemur (**slender ~,** *Loris gracilis* of S. India etc.; **slow ~,** *Bradicebus tardigradus* of E. Indies etc.). [F, perh. f. obs. Du. *loeris* clown]

lōrn *a.* (arch. or joc.) desolate, forlorn. [p.p. of obs. *leese* f. OE -*léosan* lose]

||**lŏ'rrÿ** *n.* motor truck for transporting goods, troops, etc.; long flat low wagon; truck used on railways and tramways. [19th c., orig. N. Engl., perh. f. name *Laurie*]

lōr'ÿ *n.* bright-plumaged parrot-like Asian bird. [f. Malay *lūrī*]

lose (lōōz) *v.* (**lost** *pr.* lŏst *or* lawst). **1.** *v.t.* be deprived of, cease by negligence, misadventure, separation, death, etc., to possess or have, (*property, honour,* person's *confidence, limb, father, friend,* etc.); get rid of (a cold etc.); vomit (recently eaten meal); *lose* FACE[1], GROUND[1] 7, one's HEAD[1] 22, (one's) HEART; **~ interest,** (of person) cease to be interested, (of thing) cease to interest; *lost* LABOUR[1]; *lose* one's LIFE, one's MIND[1]; **lost motion,** imperfect transmission of mechanical motion owing to looseness etc.; *lose* one's PATIENCE, one's TEMPER[2]; **lost wax,** *cire perdue*; **~ way,** (of ship or boat) begin to move less quickly. **2.** (in *pass.*) disappear, perish, die or be dead, (*letter--writing is a lost art*; *the ship and all hands were lost*); **lost** to person, taken from his possession; **lost** to *sense of duty, shame,* etc., no longer affected by them; **lost soul** (damned). **3.** *v.i.* suffer loss or detriment, incur disadvantage, be the worse off in money or otherwise *by* transaction etc., (*the publisher lost by it*; *I lost on the deal*); (of clock etc.) become slow, indicate time earlier than correct time; *story* **does not ~ in the telling,** is, if anything, exaggerated; **~ in,** suffer loss as regards (*the work loses in freshness*); **~ out,** (colloq.) be unsuccessful, suffer loss; **you can't ~,** (colloq.) you must inevitably profit. **4.** *v.t.* become unable to find, fail to keep in sight or follow or mentally grasp, (*lose a document,* one's *way,* the *thread of a discourse,* a *person* etc. under observation); (in *p.p.*) having strayed or become separated from owner etc. (*lost dog*); **get lost,** (sl., usu. in *imper.*) cease to be annoying; **lost generation,** culturally and emotion-ally unstable generation reaching maturity *c.* 1915-25; **~** one**self in, be lost in,** be engrossed in (book etc.); **~ itself in, be lost in,** be obscured or merged in; *lose* SIGHT[1] *of; Lost* TRIBES. **5.** spend (time, opportunities, efforts) to no purpose, waste; **be lost** (**up**)**on,** fail to influence or draw the attention of. **6.** fail to obtain, catch, see, or hear, (*lose* one's *train,* a *legacy,* a *word* or *remark,* a *fox*); fail to carry (motion); forfeit (stake, right to thing); be defeated in (game, race, battle, bet, lawsuit, or abs.); *lost* CAUSE[1]; **losing battle, game,** (in which defeat seems inevitable); **losing game,** test of skill in forcing opponent to win; *losing* HAZARD; *lose* the TOSS. **7.** cause (person) the loss of, cost, (*will lose you your place*); (colloq., esp. in *p.p.*) cause (person) to fail to follow one's train of thought (*wait a moment, you've lost me there* or *I'm lost*). **8.** Hence **lo'**SABLE (lōō'z-) *a.* [OE *losian* perish, destroy (*los* loss); later sense-development infl. by obs. (cogn.) *leese,* and pronunc. prob. by LOOSE[1]]

lŏ'sel (-z-) *n.* (arch.) profligate, rake; ne'er-do-well. [ME, app. f. *los-,* stem of *leese*; see LORN]

lo'ser (lōō'z-) *n.* In vbl senses (**be a ~ by,** suffer loss by; **good ~,** person not dejected or angered by losing game etc.); person, horse, etc., that loses race etc.; consistently unsuccessful person; ||(Bill.) losing HAZARD; (Bridge) card that will not take a trick. [ME, f. LOSE + -ER[1]]

loss (lŏs, laws) *n.* **1.** losing or being lost (see LOSE). **2.** person, thing, or amount lost (CUT[2] one's *losses*; *loss in weight on heating*; *suffered heavy losses*). **3.** detriment, disadvantage, resulting from loss (person etc. **is a great, no,** etc., **~,** the loss of him is a serious blow, a matter of indifference, etc.). **4. at a** ~ (*for, to discover*, etc.), puzzled, not knowing what to do; **at a** ~, (*sold* etc.) for less than was paid for it; DEAD *loss*; PROFIT¹ *and loss*; ~**-leader**, article sold at a loss to attract customers for other articles. [ME *los*, *loss(e)*, prob. back-form. f. *lost*, p.p. of LOSE]

löss. See LOESS.

lost. See LOSE.

löt *n*., & *v.t.* (**-tt-**). **1.** *n*. one of a set of objects used to secure a chance decision in dividing goods, selecting officials, etc., (*draw* or *cast* or *throw lots* usu. *between, for, who*, etc.; **cast** or **throw in** one's ~ **with**, decide to share fortunes of). **2.** this method of deciding (*chosen by lot*); choice resulting from it (*the lot fell upon me*). **3.** what falls to person by lot, share (*have neither* PART¹ *nor lot in*); person's destiny, fortune, condition, (*the lot falls to me, it falls to* or *is my lot, it falls to me as my lot*, to do). **4.** ||tax, due, (SCOT¹ *and lot*). **5.** plot or allotment of land, *across* ~s, over fields etc. as short cut. **6.** article or set of articles offered separately at sale, item at auction; **bad** ~, disreputable or vicious person. **7.** number or quantity of persons or things of same kind or associated in some way; **the** (**whole**) ~, the total number or quantity; **that's the** ~, (colloq.) there is no more to come. **8.** (colloq.) considerable number or amount, *a good or great deal* (*saw a lot of accidents*; *goes to the theatre a lot*); (in *pl*.) a great quantity or number (*there is lots of soup left*; *has lots of friends*). **9.** *v.t.* divide (land, usu. *out*, or goods for sale) into lots. [OE *hlot* portion, choice, f. Gmc **hleut-*, **hlaut-*, **hlut-*]

löth. See LOATH.

Lothar'ı̈ö (-ār'-, -ār'-) *n*. (*pl*. ~**s**). libertine, rake. [character in Rowe's *Fair Penitent* (1703)]

lö'tion *n*. liquid preparation used externally to heal wound, beautify skin, etc. [ME f. OF, or f. L *lotio* (*lavare lot-* wash; see -ION)]

lö'ttery *n*. arrangement for distributing prizes by chance among purchasers of numbered tickets (~**-wheel**, wheel with box used for shuffling numbers corresponding to those on tickets); (fig.) thing that defies calculation (*life, marriage, is a lottery*). [prob. f. Du. *loterij* (as LOT, -ERY)]

lö'ttö *n*. game of chance with drawing of numbers, as in lottery, and cards bearing various rows of numbers, winner being first to have card with a row of numbers all of which have been drawn. [It.]

lö'tus *n*. **1.** (plant bearing) fruit represented in ancient Greek legend as inducing luxurious dreaminess and distaste for active life; ~**-eater**, ~**-land**, person given to, place of, indolent enjoyment. **2.** Egyptian water-lily of genus *Nymphaea*; Indian water-lily with large pink flowers, of genus *Nelumbo*; this as used symbolically in Hinduism and Buddhism (~ **position**, cross-legged position of meditation); bird's-foot trefoil or other plant of genus *Lotus*. [L, f. Gk *lōtos*, of Semitic origin]

louche (lōōsh) *a*. oblique; disreputable, shifty. [F, = squinting]

loud *a*. & *adv*. **1.** *a*. strongly audible; *loud* PEDAL¹; ~**spea'ker**, (esp. Naut.) ~ **hailer**, apparatus that converts (sound through) electrical impulses into sound loud enough to be heard at some distance. **2.** clamorous, noisy; (of colour, dress, pattern, manners) obtrusive, conspicuous, flashy; ~**-mouthed**, noisily self-assertive. **3.** Hence ~'EN⁶ *v.i.*, ~'ISH 2 *a*., ~'LY² *adv*., ~'NESS *n*. **4.** *adv*. loudly (*don't talk so loud*; *laughed loud and long*); **out** ~, aloud (*laughed out loud when I read it*); *loud-spoken* (see SPEAK 10). [OE *hlūd*, = OS *hlūd*, OHG *hlūt* f. WG *hludha f. IE *klutos (**klu-* hear)]

lough (lŏx, lŏk) *n*. (Ir.) lake, arm of sea. [f. Ir. *loch* LOCH, W. spelling of obs. *lough* lake, ME f. same source]

louis (lōō'ĭ) *n*. (*pl*. same *pr*. -z). **1.** ~**(-d'or)** (-dōr), (Hist.) French gold coin of (about) 20 francs. **2.** L~ **Treize** (trāz), **Quatorze** (kătōr'z), **Quinze** (kănz), **Seize** (sāz), styles of furniture etc. prevalent in reigns

of kings Louis XIII, XIV, XV, XVI, of France. [f. *Louis*, Christian name of many kings of France]

loung|e (-nj) *v.i.*, & *n*. **1.** *v.i.* go lazily, saunter; loll, recline; idle; hence ~'ER¹ *n*. **2.** *n*. spell of lounging, saunter, stroll. **3.** place where one can lounge, esp. entrance-hall or gallery furnished for the purpose; place at airport etc. with seats for waiting passengers; sitting-room in house. **4.** sofa or deep chair. **5.** ~**e chair**, comfortable easy chair; ~**e lizard**, (sl.) idler in fashionable society; ||~**e suit**, man's ordinary suit for day wear in offices etc., with tailless jacket. [perh. f. obs. *lungis* lout]

loupe (lōōp) *n*. watchmaker's or jeweller's small magnifying glass. [F]

lour, lower², (lowr) *v.i.*, & *n*. **1.** *v.i.* frown, scowl, look sullen, (*on, upon, at*); (of clouds, sky, storm) look dark and threatening. **2.** *n*. scowl; gloominess of sky etc., whence ~'Y² *a*. [ME *loure*, of unkn. orig.]

louse *n*., & *v.t.* **1.** *n*. (*pl*. **lice**). parasitic insect (*Pediculus humanus*) infesting human hair and skin and transmitting many diseases; other insect of order Anoplura or Mallophaga parasitic on mammals, birds, fish, or plants; ~**'wort**, plant of genus *Pedicularis* with purple-pink flowers found in marshes and wet fields. **2.** (sl., *pl*.) contemptible person. **3.** *v.t.* remove lice from; ~ **up**, (sl.) make a mess of. [OE *lūs*, pl. *lýs*, = OHG *lūs*, ON *lús*]

lou's|ý (-zĭ) *a*. **1.** infested with lice. **2.** (sl.) disgusting; disgustingly bad or ill (*I feel lousy today*); abundantly supplied *with* (money etc.), swarming *with*. **3.** Hence ~'ı̈.Y² *adv*., ~'ıNESS *n*. [ME, f. prec. + -Y²]

lout¹ *n*. awkward fellow, bumpkin; rough-mannered or unpleasantly aggressive man; hence ~'ISH¹ *a*. [perh. f. foll.]

lout² *v.i.* (arch.) bow, make obeisance. [OE *lūtan*, = ON *lúta* f. Gmc **leut-*]

lou'ver, lou'vre, (lōō'ver) *n*. domed turret-like erection on hall-roof etc. with side openings to let smoke out or air in; ~**s**, ~**-boards**, arrangement of overlapping boards (or strips of glass etc.) to admit air but exclude light or rain; arrangement of overlapping strips of metal to admit cooling air to engine; hence **lou'v(e)red²** (lōō'verd) *a*. [ME, f. OF *lov(i)er* skylight, prob. f. Gmc & cogn. w. LODGE¹]

lo'vab|le (lŭ'-) *a*. deserving love, amiable; hence ~**leNESS** (-bəln-) *n*., ~**LY²** *adv*. [f. LOVE² + -ABLE]

lo'vage (lŭ'-) *n*. S. European herb (*Levisticum officinale*) grown for use in flavouring etc; white-flowered herb of genus *Ligustrum*. [ME *loveache* alt. f. OF *levesche* f. LL *levisticum* f. L *ligusticum* neut. of *ligusticus* Ligurian]

love¹ (lŭv) *n*. **1.** warm affection, attachment, liking, or fondness, paternal benevolence (esp. of God), affectionate devotion, (*of, for, to*, or *towards* person; *of, for*, or *to* thing); **give** person's ~ **to**, convey affectionate message from him to (another); **send** one's ~, send such message (*to*); **for the** ~ **of**, for the sake or in the name of (*God, Heaven*, (sl.) MIKE³, etc.), esp. in adjurations; *play for* ~, for the pleasure of it, not for stakes; **for** ~ **or money**, by any means, esp. *cannot get it* etc. *for love or money*; LABOUR¹ *of love*; **there's no** ~ lost between them, they dislike each other. **2.** sexual affection or passion or desire, relation between sweethearts; this feeling as a literary subject, a personified influence, or a god; representation of Cupid, or of naked winged child, symbolizing love; **in** ~, inspired by sexual love; **in** ~ **with**, feeling such love for, (fig.) fond of (a pursuit, thing, etc.); **fall in** ~, enter state of being in love; **out of** ~, no longer in love (*with*); *all's* FAIR² *in love and war*; ~ **in a cottage**, marriage on insufficient means; **make** ~ (**to**), (1) pay amorous attentions (to), (2) have or seek sexual intercourse (with). **3.** beloved one, sweetheart, (esp. of woman); (as colloq. form of address by or to woman or to child); **my** ~, (as form of address between husband and wife, sweethearts, etc.). **4.** (colloq.) delightful person or pretty thing (*he is an old love*; *what loves of teacups!*). **5.** (In games) no score, nothing, nil;

∼ **all,** neither side has yet scored; ∼ **game, set,** (in which loser has not scored). **6.** ∼ **affair,** (usu. temporary) relationship between two people in love; ∼**-apple,** (arch.) tomato; ∼**-begotten,** illegitimate; ∼**-bird,** parakeet esp. of genus *Agapornis* said to pine away at death of its mate, (fig.) = LOVER[1]; ∼**-child** (illegitimate); ∼**-feast,** (1) meal in token of brotherly love among early Christians, (2) religious service among Methodists etc. imitating this; ∼**-hate (relationship),** intense emotional response involving both love and hate; ∼**-in-a-mist,** garden plant (*Nigella damascena*) with blue flowers and green bracts; ∼**-in-idleness,** wild pansy; ∼**-knot,** = TRUE-*love knot*; ∼**-letter** (between sweethearts and concerned with love); ∼**-lies-bleeding,** garden plant of genus *Amaranthus* with long drooping spike of purple-red bloom; ∼'**lock,** trees or curl worn on temple or forehead; ∼'**lorn,** pining with love, deserted by one's lover; ∼**-making,** (1) courtship, (2) sexual intercourse; ∼**-match,** marriage made for love's sake; ∼**-nest,** place of intimate love-making; ∼**-philtre,** philtre; ∼**-seat,** armchair or sofa for two persons; ∼'**sick,** languishing with love; ∼**-song** (about or expressing love); ∼**-story,** novel etc. of which main theme is love, facts of a wooing etc.; ∼**-token,** thing given as sign of love. **7.** Hence ∼'SOME[1] (-vs-) *a.* (literary), lovable, lovely, loving, ∼'WORTHY (-vw-) *a.* [OE *lufu,* = OHG *luba,* Goth. *-lubō* f. Gmc **leubh-, *laubh-, *lubh-;* cf. LIEF, LEAVE[1], BELIEVE]

love[2] (lŭv) *v.* **1.** *v.t.* hold dear, bear or make love to, be in love with, be fond of; *love me, love my* DOG[1]; *Lord* ∼ *you!* (excl. of surprise at person's mistake etc.). **2.** *v.i.* be in love. **3.** *v.t.* cling to, delight in, enjoy having, be addicted to, admire or be glad of the existence of, (life, honour, comfort, golf, do*ing,* virtue, man who knows his own mind, etc.). **4.** (w. inf. or gerund) be (habitually) inclined (*children love to ape their elders*); (colloq.) like, be delighted, (*he simply loves to find* or *finding mistakes*; *Will you come?—I should love to*). [OE *lufian* (as prec.)]

lo've̍lèss (lŭ'vl-) *a.* unloving; unloved; hence ∼LY[2] *adv.,* ∼NESS *n.* [ME, f. LOVE[1] +-LESS]

lo'vel|y̆ (lŭ'vlĭ) *a.* & *n.* **1.** *a.* attractively or admirably beautiful, *beautiful in moral quality; (colloq.) delightful, very pleasing to any of the senses, intensely amusing; ∼**y and,** (colloq.) delightfully (*lovely and warm*); hence ∼iLY[2] *adv.,* ∼iNESS *n.* **2.** *n.* glamorously beautiful woman or girl, esp. showgirl. [OE *luflic* (as LOVE[1], -LY[1])]

lo'ver (lŭ'-) *n.* **1.** person (esp. man) in love with another (*it was a lover and his lass*), (in *pl.*) pair in love; ∼'**s knot,** = LOVE[1]-*knot.* **2.** person (esp. man) having illicit love affair. **3.** admirer, devotee, *of* thing, action, or idea, (*lover of music, cleanliness*; *music-lover*). **4.** Hence ∼LESS *a.,* ∼LIKE, ∼LY[1,2], *adjs.* & *advs.* [ME, f. LOVE[2] +-ER[1]]

lo'vey (lŭ'-) *n.* (colloq.) = LOVE[1] 3; ∼**-dovey,** (*n.*) = *lovey,* (*a.*) fondly affectionate, esp. unduly sentimental. [f. LOVE[1] +-Y[3]]

lo'ving (lŭ'-) *a.* that loves, affectionate; manifesting or proceeding from love; ∼**-cup,** large drinking-vessel with two or more handles, passed round at banquet; ∼**-kindness,** tenderness and consideration; hence ∼LY[2] *adv.,* ∼NESS *n.* [OE *lufiende;* see LOVE[2], -ING[2]]

low[1] (lō) *a., n.,* & *adv.* **1.** *a.* (Of thing) not reaching far up, not reaching the normal or average level, not high or tall, (*low hills, house, shoe, forehead, flying, stature*); (of dress, neckline, etc.) leaving wearer's neck and part of shoulders and breast exposed. **2.** not elevated in geographical etc. position; (of sun, moon, etc.) near horizon; (of person's BOW[4]) with head close to ground. **3.** of or in humble rank or position (*of low birth*; HIGH *and* low). **4.** not exalted or sublime, commonplace, undignified, uncivilized, not highly organized; abject, mean, degraded, coarse, vulgar, (*low cunning*; *low slang*); (of playing-card) that

outranks few or no others. **5.** poorly nourished, not nourishing, indicative of poor nutrition, lacking vigour, dejected, (*low condition, diet*; *low* SPIRIT[1]*s*; *low-* -SPIRITED). **6.** not intense (*low fever*); of small or less than normal amount as measured by a scale or degrees (*low attendances, prices, wages, rates, temperature*); (of latitude) near equator; ∼ *opinion of* (very unfavourable); **at** ∼**est,** to mention the least possible amount etc.; *lowest common* DENOMINATOR, MULTIPLE. **7.** (Of sound) not shrill or high up, having slow vibrations; not loud (*a low whisper*); (of vowel) = OPEN[1]. **8.** (Of liquid, receptacle, supply of anything, esp. fig. of purse or money) nearly exhausted or empty. **9.** ∼**-born,** of humble birth; *∼'**boy,** table with drawers and fairly short legs; ∼**-bred,** having vulgar manners; ∼'**brow** *a.* & *n.,* (colloq.) (one who is) not highly intellectual or cultured (opp. *highbrow*); ∼**-browed,** lit., also (of rocks) beetling, (of building etc.) with low entrance, gloomy; **Low Church,** party or principles giving only low place to ritual, authority of bishops and priests, saving grace of sacraments, etc., approximating to Protestant nonconformity; **Low-Chur'chman,** holder of such principles; ∼**-class,** of low quality or social class; ∼ **comedian,** actor in ∼ **comedy** (in which subject and treatment border on farce); **Low Countries,** Netherlands (Holland), Belgium, and Luxembourg; ∼**-cut,** (of neckline etc.) = sense 1; ∼**-down,** (*a.*) abject, mean, dishonourable, (*n.,* sl.) true facts, inside information (*on*); *Low* DUTCH[1]; ∼ **frequency** (esp. in Radio, 30 to 300 kilohertz); *low* GEAR; *Low* GERMAN[2]; ∼**-grade,** of low quality; ∼**-key,** restrained, (Photog.) consisting of dark tones; *low* LATIN; ∼ **life,** that of the lower classes; ||∼**-loader,** lorry with low floor and no sides, for heavy loads; ∼**-lying,** at low altitude (above sea-level etc.); *low* MASS[1]; ∼**-pitched,** (of sound) low, (of roof) not very steep; ∼ **point,** minimum or worst state reached; ∼**-powered,** having little power or energy; *low* PRESSURE, PROFILE, RELIEF[2]; *∼**-rise,** (of building) having few storeys; ∼ **season,** period of relatively few visitors at resort etc.; **Low Sunday** (next after Easter); ∼ **tension,** = *low voltage*; *low* TIDE[1]; ∼ **voltage,** electric potential that is safe for general use; ∼ **water,** state of tide when water is lowest, time of extreme ebb (*in* ∼ *water,* short of money or other assets); ∼**-wa'ter mark,** level reached at low water, (fig.) minimum recorded value, point of least excellence, etc.; **Low Week** (beginning with Low Sunday). **10.** Hence ∼'ISH[1] 2 *a.,* ∼'NESS *n.* **11.** *n.* a low or the lowest level or figure; area of low barometric pressure. **12.** *adv.* in or to a low position (lit. or fig.; *hangs low; aim low; bowed low; never fell so low as that*); in low tone (*talk low*); (of sound) at or to a low pitch. **13. bring** ∼, depress or reduce, in health, wealth, or position; BURN[2] *low;* **lay** ∼, overthrow, bring down, humble; **lie** ∼, crouch, be prostrate or dead or abased, keep quiet or out of the way, say nothing, bide one's time; **play** ∼, (1) gamble for small stakes, (2) play low-ranking card; RUN[1] *low;* **tackle** ∼ (Rugby Footb., at or below waist). [ME *lāh,* f. ON *lágr,* = MDu. *lage,* MHG *læge* f. Gmc **læg-* (LIE[3])]

low[2] (lō) *v.* & *n.* **1.** *v.i.* utter cry (as) of cattle, moo. **2.** *v.t.* say with lowing sound. **3.** *n.* cry of cattle. [OE *hlōwan,* = OS *hlōian,* OHG *hluoen,* f. Gmc **hlō-* f. IE **klā-*]

low'er[1] (lō'er) *v.* **1.** *v.t.* let or haul down; cause to descend; (colloq.) drink; ∼ (**away**), (Naut. abs.) let down boat, haul down sail, etc. **2.** diminish height or elevation of (*lower* one's *eyes,* one's SIGHT[1]*s,* one's *gun*); reduce strength of; diminish (price etc.); degrade, disgrace. **3.** *v.t.* & *i.* diminish in intensity or pitch (*lower your voice*). **4.** *v.i.* sink, descend, slope downwards; (of price etc.) come down. [ME, f. LOWER[3]]

lower[2]. See LOUR.

low'er[3] (lō'er) *a.* & *adv.* **1.** *a.* less high in place, situated below another part, (*lower lip, atmosphere, Jurassic,* etc.), situated on less high land (*Lower Egypt*) or to the south (*Lower California*); *lower* CASE[2]; ~ **deck**, deck immediately over hold, ||petty officers and men of Navy or of ship; *lower* JAW; ~ **regions**, hell, realm of the dead; ~ **world**, (1) the earth, (2) hell. **2.** less high in rank, dignity, etc., (*the lower classes*, *servants*); L~ **Chamber**, = *Lower House*; ~ **court** (subject to overruling by another on appeal etc.); *lower* CRITICISM; L~ **Empire**, Roman Empire from reign of Constantine onwards; **the L~ House** (in legislature, esp.) House of Commons, clergy in Convocation; ~ **mammal, plant**, etc., (evolved to only slight degree, e.g. platypus, fungus). **3.** Hence ~MOST *a*. **4.** *adv*. in or to lower position etc. (cf. LOW[1] 12). [ME, compar. of LOW[1]]

low'land (lō'l-) *n*. & *a*. **1.** *n*. low land (usu. in *pl*., esp. of part of Scotland lying S. and E. of Highlands). **2.** *a*. of or in lowland or the Scottish Lowlands. **3.** Hence ~ER[1] (4) *n*. [f. LOW[1] + LAND[1]]

low'li|y (lō'-) *a*. & *adv*. **1.** *a*. humble in feeling, behaviour, rank, or condition, modest, unpretending; (of organism etc.) evolved to only slight degree; hence ~iLY[2] *adv*., ~iNESS *n*. **2.** *adv*. in lowly manner. [ME, f. LOW[1] + -LY[1,2]]

lŏx[1] *n*. liquid oxygen. [abbr.]

*lŏx[2] *n*. smoked salmon. [f. Yiddish *laks*, cogn. w. LAX[2]]

lŏ'xodr|ōme *n*. rhumb-line; so ~o'mIC *a*., of (sailing by) rhumb-lines. [f. Gk *loxos* oblique + *dromos* course]

loy'al *a*. true, faithful, to duty, love, or obligation (*to* person etc.); faithful in allegiance to sovereign, government, or mother country, (~ **toast**, toast drunk as evidence of allegiance to sovereign etc.); exhibiting loyalty; hence or cogn. ~ISM (3), ~IST (2), ~TY[1], *ns*., ~IZE (3) *v.t*., ~LY[2] *adv*. [F, f. OF *loial* etc. f. L *legalis* LEGAL]

lŏ'zènge (-nj) *n*. **1.** rhombus, diamond figure, esp. as bearing in heraldry; lozenge-shaped shield for spinster's or widow's coat of arms; lozenge-shaped facet of cut gem; lozenge-shaped pane in casement. **2.** small tablet (orig. lozenge-shaped) of flavoured sugar, medicine, meat essence, etc., to be dissolved in mouth. [ME, f. OF *losenge*, perh. deriv. of Rom. *lausa (cf. Prov. *lausa* tombstone), of Gaulish or Iberian origin]

lŏ'zènged (-njd) *a*. with lozenges of alternate colours; with lozenge panes. [f. prec. + -ED[2]]

lŏ'zèngy (-nji) *a*. (Her.) divided into lozenges. [f. OF *losengie* (as LOZENGE; see -Y[4])]

LP *abbr*. long-playing (record); low pressure.

LPG *abbr*. liquefied petroleum gas.

||L-plāte (ĕ'lp-) *n*. sign bearing letter L, affixed to front or rear of motor vehicle to indicate that it is being driven by learner. [f. L + PLATE[1]]

||L'pool *abbr*. Liverpool.

Lr *symb*. lawrencium.

LS *abbr*. Linnean Society.

l.s. *abbr*. place of the seal (on document). [f. L *locus sigilli*]

LSD *abbr*. lysergic acid diethylamide.

£.s.d. (ĕlĕsdē') *n*. pounds, shillings, and pence (in former British currency); money, riches. [f. L *librae, solidi, denarii* pounds, shillings, pence]

LSE *abbr*. London School of Economics.

'lt *v*. (arch.) = *wilt* (*thou'lt*). [abbr.]

LT *abbr*. low tension.

Lt. *abbr*. Lieutenant(-); light.

LTA *abbr*. Lawn Tennis Association.

Ltd. *abbr*. Limited.

Lu *symb*. lutetium.

*luau (lōō-ow') *n*. Hawaiian-style party or feast. [f. Hawaiian *lu'au*]

lŭ'bber *n*. big clumsy fellow, lout; clumsy seaman; ~'s **hole**, (Naut.) hole in platform of ship's TOP[1] (sense 7), used to avoid climbing by futtock shrouds; ~('s) **line**, (Naut.) line marked on compass showing direction of ship's head; hence ~LIKE *a*., ~LY[1,2] *a*. &

adv. [ME, perh. f. OF *lobeor* swindler, parasite (*lober* deceive)]

lu'bric|āte (lōō'-, lū'-) *v.t*. make slippery or smooth by applying fluid or unguent; minimize friction of (machinery) with grease etc. (lit. or fig.); hence ~ANT *a*. & *n*., ~ātor, ~a'tion, *ns*. [f. L *lubricare* (*lubricus* slippery) + -ATE[3]]

lūbri'cious (-shus), **lū'bricous**, (lōō-, lū-), *adjs*. slippery, smooth, oily, (lit. or fig.); lewd, wanton. [f. L *lubricus* slippery + -IOUS, -OUS]

lubri'cit|y (lōō'-, lū'-) *n*. slipperiness, smoothness, oiliness, (lit. or fig.); lewdness, wantonness. [ME, f. F *lubricité* or f. LL *lubricitas* (as prec.; see -ITY)]

*lubrĭtōr'ium (lōō-) *n*. place where motor vehicles are lubricated. [f. LUBRICATE after *sanatorium*]

Lu'can (lōō'-, lū'-) *a*. of St. Luke. [f. eccl. L *Lucas* f. Gk *Loukas* Luke, + -AN]

lucār'ne (lōō-, lū-) *n*. dormer window. [F, f. Prov. *lucana*]

luce (lōōs, lūs) *n*. = PIKE[3] (esp. when full-grown). [ME, f. OF *lu(i)s* f. LL *lucius*]

lu'c|ent (lōō'-, lū'-) *a*. shining, luminous; translucent; hence ~ENCY *n*. [f. L *lucēre* shine (as LUX); see -ENT]

||lucěr'ne, **||lucěr'n**, (lōō-, lū-) *n*. leguminous European plant (*Medicago sativa*) with clover-like leaves and flowers, used for fodder, alfalfa. [f. F *luzerne*, f. mod. Prov. *luzerno* glow-worm, w. ref. to the shiny seeds]

Lucia'nic (lōō'-) *a*. after the manner of Lucian, witty and scoffing. [f. Gk *Loukianos* Lucian, Gk writer d. *c*. AD 190, + -IC]

lu'cid (lōō'-, lū'-) *a*. **1.** clear, pellucid, (usu. fig. of reasoning, literary style, etc.); ~ **interval**, period of sanity between attacks of madness, or of quiet between disturbances. **2.** (poet.) bright. **3.** (Entom. & Bot.) with smooth shining surface. **4.** Hence or cogn. ~ITY (-i'd-） *n*., ~LY[2] *adv*. [f. L *lucide* or f. L *lucidus* bright (*lucēre* shine f. as LUX; see -ID[1])]

Lu'cifer (lōō'-, lū'-) *n*. **1.** (planet Venus) morning star. **2.** the chief rebel angel, Satan, before his fall (*as proud as Lucifer*) [f. misunderstanding of Is. 14:12]. **3.** (arch.) l~ (**match**), friction MATCH[2]. [OE f. L, = light-bringing, morning-star, (as LUX, -fer f. *ferre* bring)]

luci'fugous (lōō-) *a*. (literary or tech.) avoiding the light. [f. L *lucifugus* (as LUX, *fugere* flee) + -OUS]

Lu'cīte (lōō'-) *n*. (P) = PERSPEX. [f. as prec. + -ITE[1] (2)]

lŭck *n*. **1.** (chance as bestower of) good or ill fortune, fortuitous events affecting one's interests, person's apparent tendency to be (un)fortunate, supposed tendency of chance to bring a succession of (un)-favourable events; **as ~ would have it**, (un)fortunately; **bad ~**, (omen of) ill fortune (*bad ~ to him!*, as imprecation); **down on one's ~**, dispirited by misfortune, temporarily unfortunate; **good ~**, (omen of) good fortune; *good ~ to you*, (1) I wish you well, (2) you are being rash; HARD *luck*; **just my ~**, I am unlucky as usual; PUSH[1] one's *luck*; **try one's ~**, make a venture; WORSE *luck!*; **you never know your ~**, you may be lucky. **2.** good fortune, success due to chance: **for ~**, to bring good fortune; **have the ~**, be fortunate enough *to*; **in ~('s way)**, having good fortune; **no ~**, lack of success; **no such ~**, unfortunately not; **out of ~**, unsuccessful; STROKE[1] of *luck*; **with ~**, if all goes well; hence ~LESS *a*. **3.** ||~--**penny**, ||-**penny**, (1) piece of money kept for luck, (2) sum returned by seller to buyer. [ME, f. LG *luk*, f. MLG *geluke*, = MDu. *ghelucke*, MHG *gelücke*]

lŭ'ckĭly *adv*. **1.** by luck; in a fortunate manner. **2.** (Qualifying whole sentence or clause) which is etc. a fortunate thing, thank goodness, (*luckily for me I was wrong*; *needed a book which was luckily still available*). [ME, f. foll. + -LY[2]]

lŭ'cky[1] *a*. constantly attended by good luck, enjoying it on a particular occasion, having as much success or happiness as one deserves and more; right by luck, of the nature of a fluke, (*lucky guess, hit, shot*); coming in the nick of time; presaging, bringing, worn etc. for, good luck, well-omened, (*lucky charm, penny, stone, day*); ∿**-bag**, (1) of sweets etc. bought without full knowledge of its contents, (2) = ‖∿ **dip, -tub,** (at bazaars etc., containing articles of more or less value for one of which payer of small sum may dip; fig. of miscellany or medley from which one obtains something by chance); *lucky* STAR[1] 4; hence **lŭ′cki**NESS *n.* [f. LUCK + -Y²]

‖**lŭ′ckȳ²** *n.* (sl.) cut one's ∿, escape, make off. [19th c.; orig. unkn.]

lŭ′ckȳ³ *n.* (Sc.) elderly woman. [f. LUCKY¹ as term of endearment]

lu′crative (loo′-) *a.* yielding gain, profitable; hence ∿LY² (-vli) *adv.*, ∿NESS (-vn-) *n.* [ME, f. L *lucrativus* (*lucrari* to gain; see foll., -ATIVE)]

lu′cre (loo′ker) *n.* (derog.) pecuniary profit or gain (FILTHY *lucre*). [ME f. F, or f. L *lucrum*]

lu′cŭbrāt|e (loo′-) *v.i.* express one's meditations in writing; produce lucubrations; hence ∿OR *n.* [f. L *lucubrare* work by lamplight (as LUX) + -ATE³]

lucŭbrā′tion (loo-) *n.* nocturnal study or meditation; literary work esp. of pedantic or elaborate character. [f. L *lucubratio* (as prec.; see -ATION)]

lu′cŭlent (loo′-) *a.* (arch.) clear, convincing, lucid, (*luculent proof, instance, explanation*); hence ∿LY² *adv.* [ME, = 'shining', f. L *luculentus* (as LUX; cf. -ULENT)]

Lucŭ′llan (loo-, lū-) *a.* profusely luxurious. [f. L. L. *Lucullus*, Roman general of 1st c. BC famous for his lavish banquets, + -AN]

lucus a non lucendo (lookus ah nŏn lookĕ′ndō, lū-, ā, -sĕ′-) *n.* paradoxical derivation; reference of effect to paradoxical cause, explanation by contraries. [L, = *lucus* (grove) is derived from *lucĕre* (shine) because there is no light there]

‖**lŭd** *n.* = LORD (in **my** ∿, **m′**∿, repr. counsel's pronunc. in addressing judge).

Lŭ′ddīte *n.* & *a.* (member) of bands of English artisans (1811–16) who raised riots for destruction of machinery; (person) similarly engaged in seeking to obstruct progress. [perh. f. Ned *Lud*, insane person who destroyed two stocking-frames about 1779; see -ITE¹]

lu′dicrous (loo′-, lŭ′-) *a.* absurd, ridiculous; exciting or deserving derision; hence ∿LY² *adv.*, ∿NESS *n.* [f. L *ludicrus* prob. f. *ludicrum* stage-play (*ludere* play; see -OUS)]

lues (loo′ēz) *n.* plague; ∿ (**venerea** *pr.* vĭnēr′ia), syphilis; hence (irreg.) **lue**′TIC (looĕ′t-) *a.* [L]

lŭff *n.* & *v.* (Naut.) **1.** *n.* side of fore-and-aft sail next to mast or stay; ‖broadest part of ship's bow where sides begin to curve in. **2.** *v.t.* & *i.* bring ship's head, bring head of (ship), nearer wind; turn (helm) so as to secure this; (yacht-racing) get windward side of (opponent); raise or lower (jib of crane). [ME *lo(o)f* f. OF *lof*, prob. f. LG]

lŭ′ffa. Var. of LOOFAH.

Luftwaffe (loo′ftvahfe) *n.* (Hist.) German Air Force. [G]

lŭg¹ *n.* ∿(**′worm**), large marine worm used as bait. [17th c.; orig. unkn.]

lŭg² *n.* = LUGSAIL. [abbr.]

lŭg³ *v.* (-**gg**-) & *n.* **1.** *v.t.* drag or tug (heavy object) with effort or violence; bring (subject etc.) irrelevantly *in* or *into*; force (person) *along, to* place, etc. **2.** *v.i.* pull hard at. **3.** *n.* hard or rough pull; (**in pl.*) affectation. [ME, prob. f. Scand.; cf. Sw. *lugga* pull person's hair (*lugg* forelock)]

lŭg⁴ *n.* **1.** (colloq. or joc., esp. Sc. & N. Engl.) ear; ∿**′hole,** ear orifice. **2.** projection on an object by which it may be carried, fixed in place, etc. **3.** * (sl.) stupid or commonplace person. [prob. of Scand. orig.; cf. prec.]

luge (loozh) *n.,* & *v.i.* **1.** *n.* short raised toboggan for one person seated. **2.** *v.i.* ride on luge. [Swiss F]

Lu′ger (loo′g-) *n.* German type of automatic pistol. [f. G. ∿, Ger. firearms expert d. 1922]

lŭ′ggage *n.* suitcases, bags, etc., (for) containing traveller's belongings; ∿**-van,** railway carriage for passengers' luggage. [f. LUG³ + -AGE]

lŭ′gger (-g-) *n.* small ship with four-cornered sails set fore and aft. [f. foll. + -ER¹]

lŭ′gsail (-sāl, -sal) *n.* four-cornered sail bent on yard slung at a third or quarter of its length from one end. [prob. f. LUG⁴ + SAIL¹]

lugu′brious (loogoo′-, loo-, -gū′-) *a.* doleful, dismal, mournful; hence ∿LY² *adv.*, ∿NESS *n.* [f. L *lugubris* (*lugēre* mourn) + -OUS]

lu′kewarm (loo′kwŏrm, -ōr′m) *a.* moderately warm, tepid; not zealous, indifferent; hence ∿LY² ∿NESS *n.* [ME, f. (now dial.) *luke, lew,* f. OE **hlēow,* = ON *hlȳr* warm, + WARM¹]

lŭll *v.* & *n.* **1.** *v.t.* soothe or send to sleep by sounds or caresses, quiet (suspicion etc.) usu. by deception; (in *pass.*) be deluded *into* (undue confidence), (of sea, storm) be made quiescent. **2.** *v.i.* (Of storm or noise) lessen, fall quiet. **3.** *n.* intermission in storm (lit. or fig.) or in any activity. [ME, imit. of sounds used in lulling child]

lŭ′llabȳ *n.,* & *v.t.* **1.** *n.* soothing refrain or song to put child to sleep. **2.** *v.t.* sing to sleep. [f. as prec. + -*by* as in BYE-BYE¹]

lu′lu (loo′loo) *n.* (sl.) remarkable or excellent person or thing. [19th c., perh. f. *Lulu*, pet-form of *Louise*]

lŭmbā′gō *n.* (*pl.* ∿s). rheumatic affection in muscles of loins. [L (*lumbus* loin)]

lŭ′mbar *a.* (Of artery, vein, nerve, vertebra, etc.) of or in loin(s); ∿ **puncture,** spinal puncture in this area. [f. med. L *lumbaris* f. L *lumbus* loin; see -AR¹]

lŭ′mber¹ *v.i.* move in clumsy blundering noisy way (*along, past, by,* etc.); hence ∿ING² *a.* (esp., ponderous), ∿SOME¹ *a.* [ME *lomere,* perh. imit.]

lŭ′mber² *n.* & *v.* **1.** *n.* disused articles of furniture etc. inconveniently taking up space (∿**-room,** in which such things are kept); useless or cumbrous material. **2.** *partly prepared timber; ∿**jack,** ∿**man,** feller, dresser, or conveyer of lumber. **3.** ∿**-jacket,** hip-length stout jacket fastening up to neck. **4.** *v.t.* fill *up* inconveniently, obstruct, (room, place); encumber *with*; heap together, treat, as lumber. **5.** *v.i.* cut and prepare forest timber; hence ∿ER¹, ∿ING¹, *ns.* [perh. f. prec.; later assoc. w. obs. *lumber* pawnbroker's shop]

lŭ′mbrical *a.* & *n.* ∿ (**muscle**), one of the muscles flexing fingers or toes. [f. mod. L *lumbricalis* f. L *lumbricus* earthworm, w. ref. to the shape]

lu′měn (loo′-, lū′-) *n.* **1.** (Phys.) unit of light flux, flux per unit solid angle from uniform source of one candela. **2.** (*pl.* **lu′mina**). (Anat., Bot., etc.) cavity within tube, cell, etc. [L *lumen luminis* a light, an opening]

Lu′minal (loo′-, lū′-) *n.* (P) phenobarbitone. [f. as prec. + -*al* as in *veronal*]

lu′minance (loo′-, lū′-) *n.* amount of light emitted from surface per unit area in given direction. [f. L *luminare* illuminate (as LUMEN) + -ANCE]

lu′minarȳ (loo′-, lū′-) *n.* natural light-giving body, esp. sun or moon; person having much intellectual, moral, or spiritual influence. [ME, f. OF *luminarie* or f. LL *luminarium* f. L LUMEN; see -ARY¹]

lumině′sc|ent (loo′-, lū-) *a.* emitting light without being hot; hence ∿ENCE *n.* [f. as LUMEN + -ESCENT]

lumini′ferous (loo′-, lū-) *a.* producing or transmitting light. [f. as LUMEN + -I- + -FEROUS]

lu′minous (loo′-, lū′-) *a.* **1.** emitting or full of light, bright, shining, (∿ **paint,** phosphorescent kind making thing visible in darkness); hence **lumino′sity** *n.* (loo′-, lū′-). **2.** of light (*luminous intensity*). **3.** (Of lectures etc.) throwing light upon subject. **4.** Hence ∿LY² *adv.*, ∿NESS *n.* [ME f. OF *lumineux* or f. L *luminosus* (as LUMEN; see -OUS)]

‖**lŭ′mmĕ** *int.* (vulg.) of surprise or emphasis. [= (*Lord*) *love me*]

*lŭ′mmox n. (colloq.) clumsy or stupid person. [19th c. in US & dial.; orig. unkn.]

lŭmp¹ n. & v. **1.** n. compact shapeless or unshapely mass (∼ **in throat,** feeling of pressure there caused by emotion); (sl.) great quantity, lot, heap; mass of clay or dough ready for moulding or baking; protuberance, excrescence, swelling, bruise; heavy dull or ungainly person; ‖**the** ∼, casual workers in building and other trades; **in the** ∼, taking things as a whole, in a general manner; ∼ **sugar** (broken or cut or shaped into lumps or cubes); ∼ **sum,** (1) sum covering number of items, (2) money paid down at once (opp. instalments). **2.** v.t. put together in one lump, mass together, treat as all alike, disregard differences between or among, (together, with, in with, under title etc.). **3.** v.i. rise or collect into lumps; go heavily along, sit heavily down. [ME, perh. of Scand. orig.]

lŭmp² n. ∼('**fish**), ugly spiny-finned leaden-blue fish (Cyclopterus lumpus) clinging tightly to objects by sucking-disc on belly; ∼-**sucker,** this or a related fish. [f. MLG lumpen, MDu. lumpe, perh. = prec.]

lŭmp³ v.t. (colloq.) be displeased at, put up with ungraciously, (used in antithesis with like: if you don't like it you can lump it, I don't care whether you like it or not). [imit.; cf. dump, grump, etc.]

lŭ′mpenprŏlĕtā′riat n. (derog.) ignorantly contented lower orders of society uninterested in revolutionary advancement; so **lŭ′mpen** a., characteristic of these. [G (lumpen rag, rogue; see PROLETARIAT)]

lŭ′mpish a. heavy and clumsy; stupid, lethargic; hence ∼LY² adv., ∼NESS n. [f. LUMP¹+-ISH¹]

lŭ′mpý a. full of or covered with lumps; (of water) cut up by wind into small waves; hence ∼ĬLY² adv., ∼ĬNESS n. [f. LUMP¹+-Y²]

lu′na (lōō′-) n. ∼ (**moth**), N. Amer. moth (Actias luna) with crescent-shaped spots on wings. [L, = moon]

lu′nacÿ (lōō′-) n. being a lunatic, insanity [orig. of the intermittent kind attributed to changes of moon], (Law) such mental unsoundness as interferes with civil rights or transactions (‖**Master in L**∼, (Hist.) officer investigating cases of alleged lunacy); great folly. [f. LUNATIC+-ACY]

lu′nar (lōō′-, lū′-) a. **1.** of, in, as of, concerned with, determined by, the moon; ∼ **cycle,** Metonic cycle; ∼ **distance,** angular distance of moon from sun, planet, or star, used in finding longitude at sea; ∼ (**excursion**) **module,** module for journey from spacecraft in orbit round moon to moon's surface and back; ∼ **month,** period of moon's revolution, esp. interval between new moons of about 29¼ days, (pop.) period of four weeks; ∼ **nodes,** points at which moon's orbit cuts ecliptic; ∼ **observation,** finding of longitude by lunar distance; ∼ **rainbow** (made by moon's rays); lunar YEAR. **2.** (Of light, glory, etc.) pale, feeble; crescent-shaped, lunate, (esp. ∼ **bone** in wrist); of or containing silver (from alchemists' use of luna 'moon' for silver; ∼ **caustic,** silver nitrate esp. in stick form). [f. L lunaris (as LUNA; see -AR¹)]

lu′nāte (lōō′-, lū′-) a. & n. **1.** a. crescent-shaped (∼ **bone** in wrist). **2.** n. crescent-shaped prehistoric implement etc. [f. L lunatus (as LUNA; see -ATE²)]

lu′natic (lōō′-) a. & n. insane (person; see LUNACY), mad(man); (of action etc.) outrageously foolish; eccentric, foolish, (person); ∼ **asylum,** (Hist.) mental home or hospital; lunatic FRINGE. [ME, f. OF lunatique f. LL lunaticus f. L LUNA; see -ATIC]

lunā′tion (lōō-, lū-) n. interval between new moons, about 29½ days. [ME, f. med. L lunatio (as prec.; see -ATION)]

lŭnch n. & v. **1.** n. midday meal; light refreshment taken between breakfast and dinner (where latter is taken at midday); ∼-**hour,** ∼-**time,** (when lunch is taken); ∼-**room,** restaurant with quick service of lunches. **2.** v.t. provide lunch for. **3.** v.i. take lunch. [f. foll.]

lŭ′ncheon (-nchŏn) n. **1.** (formal). = prec. 1, *light meal taken at any time of day. **2.** ∼ **meat,** meat in loaf form ready to cut and eat; ‖∼ **voucher** (given to employee as part of pay and exchangeable for food at many restaurants). **3.** Hence *∼E′TTE n., establishment serving light lunches. [17th c., of uncert. orig.]

lune (lōōn, lūn) n. (Geom.) crescent-shaped figure formed on sphere or plane by two arcs intersecting at two points. [F, f. L LUNA]

lunĕ′tte (lōō-, lū-) n. arched aperture in concave ceiling to admit light; crescent-shaped or semicircular space in dome or ceiling decorated with painting etc.; (Fortif.) work larger than redan, with two faces and two flanks; watch-glass of flattened shape. [F, dim. of lune (see prec., -ETTE)]

lŭng n. either of the pair of organs used to draw in air and bring it into contact with the blood in man and most vertebrates (**good** ∼**s,** ability to use exhaled air to produce strong voice); IRON¹ lung; ∼**s of London** etc., parks and open spaces in or close to great city; ∼-**fish** (having lungs as well as gills); ∼-**power,** power of voice; ∼′**wort,** (1) herb Pulmonaria officinalis, with white-spotted leaves likened to diseased lung, (2) lichen (Lobaria pulmonaria) once supposed to be good for lung-disease; hence ∼ED⁹ (-ngd), ∼′LESS, adjs., ∼′FUL 2 n. [OE lungen, ∼s MLG lunge, OHG lungun, ON lunga f. Gmc *lung- f. IE *lngh-, cogn. w. LIGHT¹]

lŭnge¹, longe, (lunj) n., & v.t. **1.** n. long rope with which horse-breaker holds horse while he makes it canter in circle; circular exercise-ground for training horses. **2.** v.t. exercise (horse) with or in lunge. [F longe, allonge (as foll.)]

lŭnge² (-nj) n. & v. **1.** n. thrust with sword etc. esp. in fencing; sudden forward movement, plunge, rush; gymnastic movement of foot with knee bent while other foot remains fixed. **2.** v.i. make lunge in fencing etc., deliver blow from shoulder in boxing, (at, out). **3.** v.t. drive (weapon, sting, etc.) violently in some direction. [f. earlier allonge, F, f. allonger lengthen (à to, long LONG¹)]

lu′ngi (lōō′nggē) n. (Ind.) (cotton material for) man's loincloth. [Urdu]

lunisŏ′lar (lōō-, lū-) a. of sun and moon; ∼ **period** (of 532 years between repetitions of both solar and lunar cycles); ∼ **precession** (due to joint action of sun and moon); ∼ **year** (with divisions regulated by changes of moon, and average length made to agree with solar year). [f. L luna moon+-I-+L sol sun +-AR¹]

lu′nūla (lōō′-, lū′-) n. (pl. ∼e). crescent-shaped mark, esp. white mark at base of finger-nail; crescent-shaped Bronze Age ornament. [L, dim. of LUNA]

lu′pin, lu′pine¹, (lōō′-) n. garden or fodder plant of genus Lupinus, with long tapering spikes of blue, purple, pink, white, or yellow flowers; (in pl.) seeds of lupin. [ME, f. L lupinus]

lu′pine² (lōō′-, lū′-) a. of wolf or wolves; wolflike. [f. L lupinus (lupus wolf; see -INE¹)]

lu′p|us (lōō′-) n. ulcerous disease of skin, esp. tuberculosis of skin; hence ∼ĬFORM, ∼OID, ∼OUS, adjs. [L, = wolf]

lur (loor) n. bronze S-shaped trumpet of prehistoric times, still used in Scandinavia to call cattle. [Da. & Norw.]

lŭrch¹ n. **leave in the** ∼, desert (friend, ally) in difficulties. [orig. = state of score in some games in which winner was far ahead of loser, f. F lourche game like backgammon, also bad defeat in this]

lŭrch² n., & v.i. **1.** n. sudden lean or deviation to one side, stagger. **2.** v.i. make lurch(es), stagger. [orig. Naut., lee-lurch alt. of lee-latch drifting to leeward]

lŭr′cher n. **1.** ‖cross-bred dog between collie or sheep-dog and greyhound, used esp. by poachers. **2.** (arch.) petty thief, swindler; spy. [f. obs. lurch v. var. of LURK, +-ER¹]

lure (lūr, loor) n., & v.t. **1.** n. falconer's apparatus for recalling hawk (bunch of feathers, within which it finds its food while being trained, attached to thong); thing used to entice, decoy; enticing quality *of* a pursuit etc. **2.** *v.t.* recall (hawk) with lure; entice (person, animal; usu. *away* or *into*). [ME, f. OF *luere* f. Gmc *lōthr- (cf. *lathōn invite)]

lure². Var. of LUR.

lur′id (lūr′-, loor′-) *a.* **1.** ghastly, wan, glaring, unnatural, stormy, terrible, in colour or combination of colours or lights (of complexion, landscape, sky, lightning, thunder-clouds, smoky flame, glance, etc.); **cast a ~ light on,** explain or reveal (facts or character) in tragic or terrible way. **2.** sensational, horrifying, (*lurid details*); showy, gaudy, (*paperbacks with lurid covers*). **3.** (Bot. etc.) of dingy yellowish brown. **4.** Hence ~LY² *adv.*, ~NESS *n.* [f. L *luridus* (*luror* wan or yellow colour; see -ID¹)]

lurk *v.i.* be hidden *in, under, about,* etc.; escape notice, exist unobserved, be latent, (*have a lurking sympathy for*); ~**′ing-place,** hiding-place. [ME, perh. f. LOUR w. frequent. *-k* as in *talk*]

lŭ′scious (-shŭs) *a.* richly sweet in taste or smell; excessively sweet, cloying; (of language or literary style) over-rich in sound, imagery, or voluptuous suggestion; appealing to the senses, voluptuously attractive; hence ~LY² *adv.*, ~NESS *n.* [ME, perh. alt. of obs. *licious* f. DELICIOUS]

lŭsh¹ *a.* (Of vegetation, esp. grass) luxuriant and succulent; (fig.) luxurious. [ME, perh. var. of obs. *lash* soft, f. OF *lasche* lax (see LACHES); assoc. w. prec.]

lŭsh² *n.* & *v.* (sl.) **1.** *n.* liquor, drink; *alcoholic drunkard. **2.** *v.* & *i.* ply with, or drink, alcoholic liquor. [18th c., perh. joc. use of prec.]

Lus‖itā′nian (lōō-) *a.* & *n.* (inhabitant) of ancient Lusitania or modern Portugal; so ~o- *comb. form.* [f. *Lusitania*, ancient province mainly corresponding to Portugal]

lŭst *n.*, & *v.i.* **1.** *n.* animal desire for sexual indulgence, lascivious passion, whence ~′FUL *a.*; passionate enjoyment *of* or desire *of* or *for* (*lust of battle, for power*); (Bibl. & Theol.) sensuous appetite regarded as sinful (*lusts of the flesh*). **2.** *v.i.* have strong or excessive (esp. sexual) desire (usu. *after* or *for*). [OE, = OHG *lust*, ON *losti*, Goth. *lustus* f. Gmc *lust-; cf. LIST²]

*lŭ′ster¹,². See LUSTRE¹,².

lŭ′stral *a.* of, or used in, ceremonial purification. [f. L *lustralis* (as LUSTRUM; see -AL)]

lŭ′str‖āte *v.t.* purify by expiatory sacrifice, ceremonial washing, or other such rite; so ~A′TION *n.* [f. L *lustrare* (as LUSTRUM) + -ATE³]

‖lŭ′stre¹ (-ter), ***lŭ′ster¹,** *n.,* & *v.t.* **1.** *n.* gloss, refulgence; shining surface, brilliance, bright light, radiant beauty; hence ~LESS, **lŭ′strous,** *adjs.* **2.** splendour, glory, distinction, (*add lustre to; throw* or *shed lustre on*). **3.** (prismatic glass pendant of) chandelier. **4.** ‖thin dress-material with cotton warp, woollen weft, and lustrous surface. **5.** iridescent glaze on pottery and porcelain; ~(**ware**) (provided with this). **6.** *v.t.* put lustre on (cloth, pottery, etc.). [F, f. It. *lustro* (*lustrare* f. L *lustrare* illuminate)]

‖lŭ′stre² (-ter), ***lŭ′ster²,** *n.* = LUSTRUM. [ME, Anglicized f. foll.]

lŭ′str‖um *n.* (*pl.* ~**a** *or* ~**ums**). period of five years. [L, orig. purificatory sacrifice after quinquennial census]

lŭ′st‖ȳ *a.* healthy and strong; vigorous, lively; hence ~**ĬHOOD** (arch.), ~**ĬNESS,** *ns.,* ~**ĬLY²** *adv.* [ME, f. LUST + -Y²]

lusus (naturae) (lū′sŭs natūr′ē, lōō′-, -toor′ī) *n.* sport or freak of nature, strikingly abnormal natural production. [L]

lu′tanist, lu′tenist, (lōō-, lū′-) *n.* lute-player. [f. med. L *lutanista* (*lutana* LUTE¹; see -IST)]

lute¹ (lōōt, lūt) *n.* guitar-like instrument much used in 14th–17th c., with pear-shaped body. [ME, f. F *lut, leüt,* prob. f. Prov. *laüt* f. Arab. *al-'ūd*]

lut‖e² (lōōt, lūt) *n.,* & *v.t.* **1.** *n.* clay or cement used to

stop hole, make joint airtight, coat crucible, protect graft, etc.; rubber seal for jar etc. **2.** *v.t.* apply lute to. **3.** Hence ~′ING¹ (3) *n.* [ME; n. f. OF *lut* f. L *lutum* mud, clay; v. f. L *lutare*]

lutecium. Var. of LUTETIUM.

lu′tèo- (lōō′-, lū′-) *comb. form.* orange-coloured, as: ~**fu′lvous,** orange-tawny. [f. as foll. + -O-]

lu′tèous (lōō′-, lū′-) *a.* of deep orange yellow or greenish yellow. [f. L *luteus* (*lutum* WELD¹) + -OUS]

lu′testring (lōō′ts-, lū′-) *n.* (arch.) glossy silk fabric. [app. f. *lustring* f. F *lustrine* or f. It. *lustrino* (*lustro* LUSTRE¹), assim. to LUTE¹, STRING]

Lutè′tian (lōō-, lū-; -shan) *a.* (arch.) Parisian. [f. L *Lutetia* ancient name of Paris + -AN]

lutè′tium (lōō-, lū-; -shŭm) *n.* (Chem.) heaviest element of lanthanide series. [f. F *lutécium* f. as prec. + -IUM]

Lu′theran (lōō′-, lū′-) *a.* & *n.* (follower) of Martin Luther; (member) of Church accepting the Augsburg confession of 1530, with justification by faith alone as cardinal doctrine; hence ~ISM (3) *n.*, ~IZE (2, 3) *v.i.* & *t.* [f. M. *Luther,* Ger. religious leader d. 1546 + -AN]

Lu′tine (lōō′tēn) *a.* ~ **bell** (at Lloyd's, rung to announce loss of a ship or arrival of overdue ship). [name of ship wrecked 1799]

lŭx *n.* (*pl.* same). (Phys.) unit of illumination, one lumen per square metre. [L *lux lucis* light]

lŭx′‖āte *v.t.* dislocate (joint etc.); so ~A′TION *n.* [f. L *luxare* + -ATE³]

luxe (lōōks, lŭks) *n.* luxury; see DE LUXE. [F, f. L *luxus*]

lŭxur′i‖ant (-gzūr′-, -ks-, -gzhoor′-) *a.* prolific (lit., or fig.) of imagination etc.); profuse in growth, exuberant, rank; (of literary or artistic style) florid, richly ornamented; hence ~ANCE *n.*, ~**ant**LY² *adv.* [f. L *luxuriare* grow rank (*luxuria* LUXURY); see -ANT]

lŭxur′iāte (-gzūr′-, -ks-, -gzhoor′-) *v.i.* revel, feel keen delight, *in* or *on*; take one's ease, be luxurious. [f. as prec. + -ATE³]

lŭxur′ious (-gzūr′-, -ks-, -gzhoor′-) *a.* fond of or contributing to luxury; self-indulgent, voluptuous; very comfortable; hence ~LY² *adv.*, ~NESS *n.* [ME, f. OF *luxurios* f. L *luxuriosus* (as foll.; see -OUS)]

lŭ′xurȳ (-ksherĭ) *n.* (habitual use of) choice or costly food, dress, furniture, etc.; thing that one enjoys; thing desirable for comfort or enjoyment but not indispensable; luxuriousness; (*attrib.*) relating to luxuries, comfortable and expensive (*a luxury flat*). [ME, f. OF *luxurie, luxure* f. L *luxuria* (*luxus* abundance); see -Y¹]

‖LV *abbr.* luncheon voucher.

Lw *symb.* lawrencium.

LWM *abbr.* low-water mark.

lx *abbr.* lux(es).

LXX *abbr.* & *symb.* Septuagint; seventy.

-lȳ¹ *suf.* forming *adjs.* esp. f. *ns.*, w. sense 'having the qualities of' (*kingly, lovely, motherly, rascally*), or 'recurring at intervals of' (*daily, hourly*). [f. or after OE *-lic,* = OS *-līk,* OHG *-līh,* ON *-ligr, -legr,* Goth. *-leiks* f. Gmc *likam form]

-lȳ² *suf.* forming *advs.* f. *adjs.* (orig. corresp. to those in -LY¹, now f. those of almost any kind; *beastly cold, ghastly pale, hourly, purposely; boldly, feebly, nastily, pathetically, volubly*); often as part of compd. suf., e.g. *-ably, -edly, -fully, -ically, -ily, -ingly, -ously.* [f. or after OE *-līce,* = OS *-līko,* OHG *-līhho,* ON *-liga,* Goth. *-leikō* f. as prec.]

lȳcā′nthropy *n.* mythical transformation of person into wolf (cf. WEREWOLF); form of madness in which patient imagines himself an animal and exhibits depraved appetites, change of voice, etc.; hence **lȳ′canthrōpe** *n.*, person exhibiting lycanthropy. [f. mod. L f. Gk *lukanthrōpia* (*lukos* wolf, *anthrōpos* man; see -Y¹)]

lycée (lē′sā) *n.* State secondary school in France. [F, f. L (as foll.)]

Lȳcē′um *n.* garden at Athens in which Aristotle

taught, his philosophy and followers (cf. ACADEMY, GARDEN, PORCH); (*l*-; US or Hist.) literary institution, lecture-hall, teaching-place. [L, f. Gk *Lukeion* neut. of *Lukeios* epithet of Apollo (from whose neighbouring temple the Lyceum was named)]

lȳch. See LICH.

lychee. See LITCHI.

lȳ'chnis (-k-) *n*. perennial herb of genus *Lychnis*, e.g. ragged robin. [L, f. Gk *lukhnis* a red flower (*lukhnos* lamp)]

lȳ'copŏd *n*. club-moss, esp. of genus *Lycopodium*. [Anglicized f. foll.]

lȳcopŏ'dium *n*. = prec.; fine powder from spores of this, used as absorbent in surgery, and in making fireworks etc. [mod. L f. Gk *lukos* wolf + *pous podos* foot; see -IUM]

Lȳ'dian *a*. & *n*. (language or inhabitant) of ancient Lydia; ~ **mode**, (1) ancient Greek MODE, reputedly effeminate in character, (2) fifth of church modes (with F as final and C as dominant). [f. L f. Gk *Ludios* of Lydia in Asia Minor + -AN]

lye *n*. water made alkaline by lixiviation of vegetable ashes; any strong alkaline solution esp. for washing; any cleansing substance. [OE *lēag*, = MDu. *lōghe*, OHG *louga*, ON *laug* hot bath f. Gmc *laugō* (*lau*- f IE *lou*- wash; cf. LATHER)]

lȳ'ing[1] *n*. In vbl senses; place to lie (*dry lying*); *lying in* (see LIE[3] 6); *lying in* STATE[1]. [ME, f. LIE[2,3] + -ING[1]]

lȳ'ing[2] *a*. In vbl senses; deceitful, false; whence ~LY[9] *adv*.; *lying down* (see LIE[3] 6); LOW[1]-*lying*. [f. LIE[2,3] + -ING[2]]

||lȳ'ke-wāke *n*. watch kept at night over dead body. [perh. f. ON *līkavaka*; cf. LICH, WAKE[2]]

lȳ'me-grass (-ahs) *n*. blue-green grass of genus *Elymus*, planted on sand to keep it from shifting. [perh. f. LIME[1], w. ref. to its binding effect, + GRASS]

lymph *n*. **1**. (Physiol.) colourless alkaline fluid from tissues or organs of body, like blood but without red corpuscles; ~ **gland** or **node**, small mass of tissue where lymph is purified and lymphocytes are formed. **2**. exudation from sore etc.; (*calf* or *vaccine*) ~, = vaccine 2. **3**. (poet.) pure water. **4**. Hence ~'OID, ~'OUS, *adjs*. [f. F *lymphe* or f. L *lympha*, *limpa* water]

lymphǎ'tic *a*. & *n*. **1**. *a*. of, secreting, conveying, lymph (*lymphatic gland*, *system*). **2**. (Of person or TEMPERAMENT) flabby, pale, sluggish, (qualities formerly attributed to excess of lymph). **3**. *n*. veinlike vessel conveying lymph. [orig. = 'frenzied', f. L *lymphaticus* mad f. Gk *numpholēptos* seized by nymphs, now assoc. w. LYMPH (on anal. of *spermatic* etc.)]

lȳ'mphocȳte *n*. form of leucocyte occurring in lymph. [f. LYMPH + -O- + -CYTE]

lynce'an *a*. lynx-eyed, keen-sighted. [f. L f. Gk *lugkeios* (*lugx* lynx) + -AN]

lynch *n*., & *v.t*. **1**. ~ **law**, procedure of self-constituted illegal court that summarily executes or otherwise punishes person charged with offence. **2**. *v.t*. execute (person) thus. [orig. US, earlier *Lynch's law*, named after Capt. W. Lynch of Virginia *c*. 1780]

||lȳ'nchet *n*. ridge or ledge formed by prehistoric ploughing on slope. [f. *linch* f. OE *hlinc*; cf. LINKS]

lȳ'nchpin. Var. of LINCHPIN.

lynx *n*. animal of subgenus *Lynx* of cat genus, with tufted ear-tips, short tail, spotted fur, and proverbially keen sight; its fur; ~-**eyed**, keen-sighted. [ME f. L, f. Gk *lugx*]

Lȳ'on *n*. (Lord) ~, ~ **King of Arms**, chief herald of Scotland, presiding over ~ **Court** (cf. KING[1] 7). [arch. form of LION; named f. lion on royal shield]

lȳophi'lic *a*. (Of colloid) readily dispersed by solvent; hence **lȳŏ'philIZE** *v.t*., freeze-dry. [f. Gk *luō* loosen, dissolve + Gk *philos* loving + -IC]

lȳophŏ'bic *a*. (Of colloid) not lyophilic. [f. as prec. + -PHOBE + -IC]

lȳr'ate *a*. (Biol.) lyre-shaped. [f. as foll. + -ATE[2]]

lȳre *n*. (Gk Ant.) instrument like harp but of size to be held up in left hand and played with plectrum, and with strings supported by two symmetrically curved and yoked horns, chiefly used for accompanying voice; ~-**bird**, Australian bird of genus *Menura*, the male with lyre-shaped tail display; ~ **flower**, bleeding heart. [ME, f. OF *lire* f. L f. Gk *lura*]

lȳ'ric *a*. & *n*. **1**. *a*. of or for the lyre, meant to be sung, of the nature of, expressed or fit to be expressed in, song (*lyric drama*, *opera*); (of poem) expressing writer's own thoughts and sentiments usu. briefly and in stanzas or strophes; (of poet) writing in this manner. **2**. *n*. lyric poem; (in *pl*.) lyric verses; (Theatr.) words of song. [f. F *lyrique* or f. L f. Gk *lurikos* (as prec.; see -IC)]

lȳ'rical *a*. = prec.; resembling, couched in or using language appropriate to, lyric poetry; (colloq.) highly enthusiastic; hence ~LY[2] *adv*. [f. as prec. + -AL]

lȳ'ricism *n*. lyric character; a lyrical expression; high-flown sentiments. [f. LYRIC + -ISM]

lyr'ist *n*. **1**. (līr'-). player on lyre. **2**. (lĭr'-). lyric poet. [f. L f. Gk *luristēs* (*lura* lyre)]

lȳsėr'gic *a*. ~ **acid**, crystalline acid got from ergot or synthetically; ~ **acid diethylamide**, a powerful hallucinogenic drug. [f. hydro*lysis* + *ergot* + -IC]

lȳ'sis *n*. (*pl*. ~es *pr*. -ēz). (Physiol.) disintegration of bacterial or other cells; so ~IN *n*., substance able to cause lysis. [L, f. Gk *lusis* loosening (*luō* loosen)]

-lȳsis *suf*. (*pl*. ~es *pr*. -ēz) forming *ns*. denoting disintegration or decomposition (*electrolysis*, *haemolysis*). [f. as prec.]

Lȳ'sŏl *n*. (*P) mixture of cresols and soft soap, used as disinfectant. [f. Gk *lusis* (see LYSIS) + -OL]

lythe (-dh) *n*. (Sc.) pollack. [18th c., of unkn. orig.]

-lȳ'tic *suf*. forming *adjs*. corresp. to *ns*. in -LYSIS. [f. Gk *lutikos* (as LYSIS; see -IC)]

lȳ'tta *n*. (*pl*. ~e). = WORM[1] 4. [L, f. Gk, orig. = rabies]

M

M, m, (ĕm) *n.* (*pl.* **Ms** *or* **M's**). thirteenth letter of alphabet; (as Roman numeral) 1,000 (**mi** 1,001; **mm** 2,000; **mcmlxxxi** 1,981); (Print.) em.
M. *abbr.* Master; mega-; Member of; *Monsieur*; ||motorway.
m. maiden (over); male; mare; mark(s) (as monetary unit); married; masculine; metre(s); mile(s); milli-; million(s); minute(s).
m' *a.* = *my* in *m'lud*, *m'tutor*, etc.
'm *v.* & *n.* (colloq.) = *am* in *I'm*; = *madam* in *yes'm* etc. [abbr.]
ma (mah) *n.* (vulg.) mother. [abbr. of MAMMA¹]
MA *abbr.*, Master of Arts; Massachusetts.
ma'am (mahm, măm, mum) *n.* madam (esp. used by servants or in addressing Queen or royal princess or officer in WRAC etc. [abbr.]
maar (mār) *n.* volcanic crater formed by explosion. [G]
măc¹. See MACK¹.
Măc² *n.* (colloq.) Scotsman; *man (esp. as *voc.*). [f. *Mac-* as patronymic prefix in many Scottish & Irish surnames]
maca'bre (-ah'br) *a.* grim, gruesome. [ME, f. OF *macabré*, perh. f. *Macabé* Maccabee, w. ref. to miracle play containing slaughter of the Maccabees]
macă'cō¹ *n.* (*pl* ~s). macaque or similar monkey. [Port., = monkey, f. Fiot *makaku* some monkeys (*kaku* monkey)]
macă'cō² *n.* (*pl.* ~s). lemur, esp. of genus *Lemur*. [f. F *mococo*, of unkn. orig.; cf. F *maki* lemur f. Malagasy *maka*]
macă'dam *n.* material for road-making with successive layers of broken stone of nearly uniform size, each subjected to pressure before next is laid; TAR¹ *macadam*; hence ~IZE (1) *v.t.* [f. J. L. *McAdam*, Brit. surveyor d. 1836, who advocated this method]
măcadā'mia *n.* Austral. evergreen nut-tree of genus *Macadamia*. [f. J. *Macadam*, Austral. chemist d. 1865 + -IA¹]
maca'que (-ah'k) *n.* monkey of genus *Macaca*, e.g. rhesus. [F, f. as MACACO¹]
măcarō'ni *n.* **1.** pasta formed into long tubes, used as food; ~ (*and) cheese, savoury dish containing mainly macaroni and cheese. **2.** (*pl.* ~es). (Hist.) 18th-c. dandy imitating continental fashions. [f. It. *maccaroni*, f. late Gk *makaria* barley food]
măcarō'nic *a.,* & *n.* in *pl.* (verses) of burlesque form containing Latin (or other foreign) words and vernacular words with Latin etc. terminations. [f. mod. L *macaronicus* f. obs. It. *macaronico*, joc. f. as prec.; cf. -IC]
măcarōo'n *n.* small cake or biscuit of ground almonds, white of egg, sugar, etc. [f. F *macaron* f. It. (as MACARONI)]
Macă'ssar *a.* & *n.* ~ (oil), (Hist.) kind of oil for the hair. [f. *Macassar*, district in Sulawesi, whence its ingredients were said to come]
macaw'¹ *n.* long-tailed brightly coloured Amer. parrot of genus *Ara* etc. [f. Port. *macao*, of unkn. orig.]
macaw'² *n.* palm-tree of genus *Acrocomia*, with nuts yielding fragrant oil. [Carib]
Macc. *abbr.* Maccabees (Apocrypha).
Mă'ccabees (-z) *n. pl.* (**Books of the**) ~, four books of Jewish history and theology, of which first and second are in Apocrypha; so **Măccabē'AN** *a.* [name of Jewish family that led revolt *c.* 170 BC under Judas *Maccabaeus*]
McCăr'thyism (makăr'-) *n.* policy of hunting out (suspected) Communists and removing them esp. from Government departments. [f. J. R. *McCarthy*, US senator d. 1957 + -ISM]

McCoy' (makoi') *n.* (colloq.) **the real** ~, the real thing, the genuine article. [19th c., of uncert. orig.]
măce¹ *n.* **1.** (Hist.) heavy usu. metal-headed and spiked club. **2.** heavy club used by policeman etc. **3.** staff of office resembling this; ||symbol of Speaker's authority in House of Commons; ~(-**bearer**), official carrying mace. **4.** stick used in game of bagatelle. [ME, f. OF *mace, masse* f. Rom. **mattea* club]
măce² *n.* dried outer covering of nutmeg, used as spice. [ME *macis* (taken as pl.) f. OF *macis*, f. L *macir* a red spicy bark]
măcédoine (mă'sĭdwahn) *n.* mixed fruit or vegetables esp. cut up small or in jelly. [F, = Macedonia, w. ref. to mixture of peoples there]
mā'cer *n.* mace-bearer, esp. (Sc.) lawcourt official keeping order. [ME, f. OF *massier* (*masse*; see MACE¹, -ER²)]
mā'cer|āte *v.t.* & *i.* soften by soaking; waste away by fasting; hence ~A'TION, ~ātor, *ns.* [f. L *macerare* + -ATE³]
Mach (mahχ, măk, mahk) *n.* ~ (**number**), ratio of the speed of a body to the speed of sound in the surrounding medium; ~'**meter,** indicator of air speed as Mach number; ~ **one, two,** etc., speed corresponding to Mach number of one, two, etc. [f. E. ~, Austrian physicist d. 1916]
macha'n (-ah'n) *n.* (Anglo-Ind.) elevated platform used in tiger-shooting etc. [Hindi]
mache'tè (-ĕ'-, -ā'-), **mă'tchĕt,** *n.* broad heavy knife used in Central America and W. Indies as implement and weapon. [Sp. (*macho* hammer f. LL *marcus*)]
măchiavĕ'llian (-k-) *a.* deceitful, perfidious, cunning; hence ~ISM (1) *n.* [f. N. dei *Machiavelli*, Florentine philosopher d. 1527, author of *Il Principe*, treatise on statecraft advocating use of sometimes unscrupulous means to strengthen the State]
machi'col|āte *v.t.* (usu. in *p.p.*) furnish (parapet etc.) with openings between supporting corbels for dropping stones etc. on assailants; hence ~A'TION *n.* [f. OF *machicoler*, ult. f. Prov. *machacol* (*macar* crush, *col* neck)]
machicoulis (mahshĭkōō'lĭ) *n.* machicolation. [f. F *machicoulis* (as prec.)]
mă'chĭn|āte (-k-) *v.i.* lay plots, intrigue; so ~A'TION, ~ātor, *ns.* [f. L *machinari* contrive (as foll.) + -ATE³]
machi'ne (-shē'n) *n.,* & *v.t.* **1.** *n.* apparatus for applying mechanical power, having several parts each with definite function; bicycle, motor cycle, etc.; aircraft; computer; *bathing-machine* (see BATHE¹). **2.** person who acts mechanically and without intelligence, or with unfailing regularity. **3.** (Mech.) instrument that transmits force or directs its application; **simple** ~, one without combination of parts, e.g. lever. **4.** controlling system of an organization (*party, political, propaganda, war, machine*). **5.** ~ **age,** era of many mechanical devices; ~-**gun,** (*n.*) mounted automatic gun delivering continuous fire, (*v.t.*; *-nn-*) shoot at with machine-gun; ~-**made,** (1) made by machine; ~-**pistol,** sub-machine-gun; ~-**readable,** in form that computer can respond to; ~ **tool,** mechanically operated tool for working on metal, wood, or plastics. **6.** *v.t.* make or operate on with machine (esp. of sewing and printing). [F, f. L *machina* f. Gk *makhana* (Doric), *mēkhanē* (*mēkhos* contrivance, cogn. w. MAY¹)]
machi'nery (-shē'-) *n.* machines; works of a machine, mechanism; organized system, means arranged *for* doing; group of contrivances, esp. supernatural persons and incidents, used in literary work. [f. prec. + -ERY]
machi'nist (-shē'-) *n.* one who makes or controls

machinery or machine tools; one who works (esp. sewing-)machine. [f. F *machiniste* & f. MACHINE + -IST]
mach|i′smō (-ĕ′z-) *n*. (show of) virility or courage; so **ma′chō** (mah′-, mă′-) *n*. (*pl.* ∼os) & *a.*, (man) exhibiting this. [Sp. (*macho* MALE f. L *masculus*; see -ISM)]
machtpolitik (mahχtpŏlītĕ′k) *n*. = POWER *politics*. [G]
macintosh. Var. of MACKINTOSH.
măck¹, **măc¹**, *n*. (colloq.) ||mackintosh (coat); *mackinaw. [abbr.]
măck² *n*. (sl.) pimp, procurer. [abbr. of obs. *mackerel* f. OF *maquerel*, *makeler* f. MDu. *makelaer* broker]
mă′ckerel *n*. (*pl.* ∼ or ∼s). N. Atlantic sea-fish (*Scomber scombrus*) used as food and approaching shore in shoals in summer to spawn; ∼ **breeze** or **gale** (strong, and thus favourable to mackerel-catching); ∼ **shark**, porbeagle; ∼ **sky** (dappled with rows of small white fleecy clouds, like pattern on mackerel′s back). [ME, f. AF *makerel*, OF *maquerel*]
***mă′ckinaw** *n*. heavy woollen cloth; warm belted coat of this. [f. M∼ City, Michigan]
mă′ckintŏsh *n*. waterproof material of rubber and cloth for garments, esp. that patented by C. *Macintosh*, Sc. inventor d. 1843; ||cloak or coat of this, or of any waterproof material.
mă′ckle *n*. blurred impression in printing. [f. F *macule* f. L MACULA]
mă′cle *n*. twin crystal; dark spot in mineral. [F, f. L MACULA]
||**M′Naghten** (maknaw′ten) ∼ **rules** (governing decision as to criminal responsibility of insane person). [f. name of 19th-c. accused]
Mâcon (mahkaw′ń) *n*. white or red burgundy produced in the neighbourhood of *Mâcon* in France.
macramé (-rah′mī) *n*. fringe or trimming or lace of knotted thread or cord; art of making this. [f. Turk. *makrama* bedspread f. Arab. *miḳrama*]
mă′crō- *comb. form*. long, large, large-scale, as: ∼**bio′tic**, relating to a diet of pure vegetable foods etc. intended to prolong life, ∼**cepha′lic**, ∼**ce′phalous**, having a long or large head, ∼**cosm**, the great world, the universe, any great whole; ∼**-economics**, study of general economics of large units; ∼**molecule**, (Chem.) molecule containing very large number of atoms; ∼**photography** (at fairly low magnification); ∼**sco′pic**, (1) visible to the naked eye, (2) regarded in terms of large units. [f. Gk *makro-* (*makros* long, large; see -o-)]
mă′crŏn *n*. written or printed mark (⁻) of long or stressed vowel. [f. Gk *makron* neut. a. (as prec.)]
mă′cul|a *n*. (*pl.* ∼ae). dark spot; spot. permanent one, in skin, whence ∼AR¹ *a.*, ∼A′TION *n.*; ∼a (**lutea** *pr.* lōō′tĭa), region of greatest visual acuity in retina. [ME f. L, = spot, mesh]
măd¹ *a*. **1.** with disordered mind, insane; frenzied; extravagantly gay; (of person or conduct or idea) wildly foolish, **like** ∼, furiously, violently, (*I ran like mad*). **2.** wildly excited, infatuated, (*after, about, for, on*, thing, subject, etc.; *cricket-mad*); (colloq.) annoyed (*I was mad at missing my train*). **3.** (Of animal) rabid (*mad bull, dog*). **4.** ∼′**cap** *n*. & *a.*, wildly impulsive (person); ∼**-doctor**, (arch.) physician treating the insane; ∼′**house**, mental home or hospital, (fig.) confused uproar; ∼ **keen**, (sl.) extremely eager; ∼′**man**, ∼′**woman**, mad person. **5.** Hence ∼′LY² *adv.* (also, colloq., passionately or extremely), ∼′NESS *n*. [OE *gemǣd(e)d*, p.p. of *gemǣden* f. *gemǣd* mad, = OS *gimēd*, OHG *gameit* foolish, boastful, Goth. *gamaiths* crippled, f. Gmc *gamaidhaz*]
măd² *v*. (-dd-) **1.** *v.t.* *make angry. **2.** *v.i.* (arch.) be mad, act madly; **the** ∼**ding crowd** (frenzied, in Gray′s *Elegy*; now often taken as = maddening). [ME, f. prec.]
mă′dam *n*. **1.** polite or respectful formal address or mode of reference to woman (also prefixed to designation of office etc., *Madam Chairman*; cf. MR). **2.**

(euphem.) woman brothel-keeper. **3.** (derog.) conceited, pert, etc., young woman. [ME, f. OF *ma dame* my lady]
Madame (madah′m, mă′dam) *n*. (*pl.* **Mesdames** *pr.* mādā′m, mādah′m). Title used of or to French-speaking woman, corresponding to Mrs or madam; (*m*∼) = prec. 1. [F, as prec.]
mă′dden *v.t.* & *i*. make or become mad; irritate. [ME, f. MAD¹ + -EN⁶]
mă′dder *n*. herbaceous plant (*Rubia tinctorum*) with yellowish flowers; red dye got from its root; synthetic substitute for this dye. [OE *mædere*, = ON *mathra*, OHG *matara*]
māde. See MAKE¹.
Madeir′a (-ēr′a) *n*. fortified white wine produced in Madeira; ∼ **cake**, kind of rich sweet sponge-cake. [∼, island in Atlantic; Port., = timber, f. L *materia* MATTER¹, from its thick woods]
mă′deleine (-dlān) *n*. small rich cake. [F]
Mademoiselle (mădam(w)azĕ′l) *n*. (*pl.* **Mesdemoiselles** *pr.* mādmwazĕ′l). Title used of or to unmarried French-speaking woman, corresponding to Miss or madam; (*m*∼) young Frenchwoman, French governess. [F (*ma my*, *demoiselle* DAMSEL)]
Mădison A′vĕnūe (-ă′-) *n*. American publicity and advertising industry. [street in New York]
madŏ′nna *n*. (picture or statue of) Virgin Mary; ∼ **lily** (white *Lilium candidum*, as in pictures of the Virgin Mary). [It. (*ma* − *mia* my, *donna* lady f. L *domina*)]
mă′dre′s *n*. cotton fabric with coloured or white stripes etc. [f. M∼ in India]
mă′drĕ|pŏre *n*. perforated coral of genus *Madrepora*; animal producing this; hence ∼**pŏ′ric** *a*. [f. F *madrépore* or mod. L *madrepora* f. It. *madrepora* (*madre* mother, *poro* PORE¹)]
mă′drĭg|al *n*. short amatory poem; part-song for several voices, prop. with elaborate contrapuntal imitation and without instrumental accompaniment; hence ∼**ā′lIAN**, ∼**alE′sQUE**, *adjs.* [f. It. *madrigale* f. med. L *matricalis* mother- f. as MATRIX, -AL (cf. *mother church*)]
Mădurĕ′se (-z) *a*. & *n*. (*pl.* same). (language or member) of an Indonesian people in Java etc. [f. *Madura* province + -ESE]
maduro (mahdoor′ō) *a*. & *n*. (*pl.* ∼**s**). full-flavoured (cigar) [Sp., = matured f. L (as MATURE¹)]
Maecē′nas *n*. generous patron of literature or art. [f. *Gaius* ∼, Roman statesman d. 8 BC, patron of Horace and Virgil]
mae′lstrom (mā′l-) *n*. whirlpool on W. coast of Norway; great whirlpool (lit. or fig.). [early mod Du., f. *malen* grind, whirl + *stroom* STREAM]
mae′năd *n*. bacchante (lit. or fig.). [f. L f. Gk *Mainas* -ados (*mainomai* rave)]
maestoso (mīstō′sō, mahĕs-) *adv*. (Mus.) majestically. [It.]
maestr|ō (mahĕ′s-, mī′s-) *n*. (*pl.* ∼**os**, or ∼**i** *pr.* -ē). great musical composer, teacher, or conductor; masterly performer in any sphere. [It., = master]
Mae Wĕ′st (mā-) *n*. (sl.) inflatable life-jacket. [professional name of Amer. film actress d. 1980, noted for her large bust]
mă′ffĭck *v.i.* exult riotously. [back-form. f. *Mafeking* (pr. mă′fĭkĭng) in S. Africa (relief of which in 1900 was celebrated extravagantly in London etc.), treated as gerund]
ma′fia (mă′-, mah′-) *n*. **1.** hostility to law and its ministers among Sicilian population, often shown in crimes; those who share in this. **2.** (*M*∼). organized international body of criminals esp. in US and orig. among Italian immigrants. **3.** organization regarded as exerting hidden influence. [It. dial. (Sicilian), = bragging]
mafĭō′s|ō (mah-) *n*. (*pl.* ∼**i** *pr.* -ē). member of mafia. [It. (as prec.)]
măg *n*. (colloq.) magazine (sense 2); magnesium; magnetic; magneto. [abbr.]

măgazi'ne (-zē'n) *n.* **1.** store for arms, ammunition, and provisions, for use in war; store for gunpowder or other explosives; chamber containing supply of cartridges fed automatically to breech of gun; similar device in camera, slide-projector, etc. **2.** periodical publication (now usu. illustrated) containing contributions by various writers. [f. F *magasin* f. It. *magazzino* f. Arab. *maḵāzin* pl. of *maḵzan* storehouse (*ḵazana* store up)]

mă'gdalèn *n.* reformed prostitute; home for magdalens. [f. Mary *Magdalen*(*e*) of Magdala in Galilee (Luke 8: 2), identified with the sinner of Luke 7: 37; f. eccl. L *Magdalena* f. Gk *Magdalēnē*]

Măgdalē'nian *a.* & *n.* (Archaeol.) (culture) of the (latest) palaeolithic period in Europe, with horn and bone tools. [f. F *Magdalénien* of La *Madeleine*, Dordogne, France, where remains were found, + -IAN]

Mă'gdebûrg. See HEMISPHERE. [~ in E. Germany]

măge *n.* (arch.) magician; learned person. [ME, Anglicized f. MAGUS]

Măgĕllă'nic *a.* of Magellan, ~ **clouds,** two galaxies visible in the southern sky that are the nearest to the Galaxy. [f. F. *Magellan,* Port. explorer d. 1521, + -IC]

magĕ'nta *n.* & *a.* **1.** *n.* brilliant crimson aniline dye, fuchsine; colour of this. **2.** *a.* coloured with or like magenta. [f. *M*~ in N. Italy, site of battle (1859) shortly before the dye was discovered]

mă'ggot *n.* **1.** larva, esp. of cheese-fly or bluebottle; **red** ~, larva of wheat-midge. **2.** whimsical fancy. **3.** Hence ~Y² *a.* [ME, perh. alt. f. *maddock,* earlier *mathek* f. ON *mathkr*; cf. MAWKISH]

Magi. See MAGUS.

Mā'gian *a.* & *n.* (one) of the Magi or magi; magician; hence ~ISM (3) *n.* [f. L MAGUS + -IAN]

mă'gĭc *n.,* *a.,* & *v.t.* (-ck-). **1.** *n.* supposed art of influencing course of events by occult control of nature or of spirits, witchcraft, (**black, white, natural,** ~, involving invocation of devils, angels, no personal spirit; SYMPATHETIC *magic*); conjuring tricks; inexplicable or remarkable influence producing surprising results (**like** ~, very rapidly). **2.** *a.* of magic; used or usable in magic; producing surprising results; ~ **carpet,** mythical carpet able to transport person on it to any place; ~ **eye,** (1) small cathode-ray tube used to indicate correct tuning of radio receiver, (2) photoelectric device used for automatic control; ~ **lantern,** simple form of image--projector using slides; ~ **square,** one divided into smaller squares each containing a (usu. different) number, so arranged that sum of vertical, horizontal, or diagonal row is always same. **3.** *v.t.* change or make (as if) by magic; ~ **away,** cause to disappear thus. [ME, f. OF *magique* a. & n. f. L *magicus* a., LL *magica* n., f. Gk *magikos* (as MAGUS; see -IC)]

mă'gĭcal *a.* of magic; resembling, or produced as if by, magic; hence ~LY² *adv.* [f. prec. + -AL]

magĭ'cian (-shan) *n.* one skilled in magic, wizard, conjurer. [ME, f. OF *magicien* f. LL *magica* as prec.; see -ICIAN]

magilp. Var. of MEGILP.

Mă'gĭnŏt (-nō) *n.* ~ **Line,** line of fortifications on NE border of France before 1940, (fig.) line of defence on which one blindly relies; ~**-minded,** obsessed with defence of *status quo.* [f. A. ~, Fr. minister of war d. 1932]

măgistēr'ĭal *a.* of, or conducted by, a magistrate; invested with authority; dictatorial; (of opinion, writings, etc.) authoritative; hence ~LY² *adv.* [f. med. L *magisterialis* f. LL *magisterius* f. L *magister* MASTER¹]

magĭ'stral *a.* of a master or masters; (Pharm., of remedy etc.) devised by physician for particular case, not included in the pharmacopoeia (cf. OFFICINAL). [F, or f. L *magistralis* (*magister* MASTER¹; see -AL)]

mă'gĭstr|āte *n.* civil officer administering law; person conducting court of summary jurisdiction (||STIP-ENDIARY or JUSTICE of the Peace); ~**ates' court** (for minor cases and preliminary hearings); hence or cogn. ~ACY, ~āteSHIP (-tsh-), ~atURE, *ns.* [ME, f. L *magistratus* (orig. office of) magistrate (as prec.; see -ATE¹)]

Măglemō'sian (-z-) *a.* & *n.* (of) a N. European mesolithic culture, with bone and stone implements. [f. *Maglemose* in Denmark, where articles from it were found, + -IAN]

mă'gma *n.* (*pl.* ~**ta** *or* ~**s**). crude pasty mixture of mineral or organic matter; (semi-)molten stratum under solid crust of earth, from which igneous rock is formed by cooling; hence **măgmă'tic** *a.* [ME, = solid residue; L f. Gk *magma -atos* f. root of *massō* knead]

Măgna Chār'ta (k-) *or* **Cär'ta** *n.* great charter of English personal and political liberty obtained from King John in 1215; any similar document establishing rights. [med. L, = great charter]

măgnă'nimous *a.* noble, generous, not petty, in feelings or conduct; showing magnanimity; hence or cogn. **măgnani'mITY** *n.,* ~LY² *adv.* [f. L *magnanimus* (*magnus* great, *animus* mind) + -OUS]

mă'gnāte *n.* wealthy or eminent man (*cotton, financial, magnate*). [ME, f. LL *magnas -atis* f. L *magnus* great]

măgnē'si|a (-sha) *n.* **1.** magnesium oxide. **2.** (pop.) hydrated magnesium carbonate, white powder used as antacid and laxative; MILK¹ *of magnesia.* **3.** Hence ~AN (-shan) *a.* [ME f. med. L, f. Gk *Magnēsia* (*lithos* stone) of Magnesia in Asia Minor, orig. ref. to load-stone]

măgnē'sĭum (-z-, -s-) *n.* silver-white metallic element present in magnesia; ~ **flare, light,** blinding light got by burning magnesium wire. [f. prec.; see -IUM]

mă'gnĕt *n.* **1.** piece of iron, steel, alloy, ore, etc., having the properties of attracting iron and of pointing approximately north and south when suspended, natural (as in loadstone) or induced by contact with a magnet, by magnetic induction, or by electric current; **bar** ~ (in form of straight bar); **horseshoe** ~ (in shape of bar bent till ends nearly meet); PERMANENT *magnet.* **2.** = LOAD¹*stone.* **3.** (fig.) person or thing that attracts. [ME, f. L *magnes magnetis* f. Gk *magnēs* = *Magnēs -ētos* (*lithos* stone) of Magnesia (cf. MAGNESIA)]

măgnĕ'tic *a.* **1.** having properties of magnet; producing, produced by, acting by, magnetism; ~ **compass,** = COMPASS¹ 3; ~ **equator,** aclinic line; *magnetic* FIELD 6; ~ **inclination,** = *magnetic* DIP²; ~ **mine,** submarine mine detonated by approach of large mass of metal, e.g. ship; *magnetic* MOMENT, NEEDLE, NORTH, POLE²; ~ **storm,** disturbance of earth's magnetic field by charged particles from sun etc.; *magnetic* TAPE. **2.** capable of acquiring properties of, or being attracted by, a magnet. **3.** (fig.) very attractive; (arch.) mesmeric. **4.** Hence **măgnĕ'tICALLY** *adv.* [f. LL *magneticus* (as prec.; see -IC)]

mă'gnĕtĭsm *n.* **1.** (science of) magnetic phenomena; natural agency producing these; ANIMAL *magnetism*; **terrestrial** ~, magnetic properties of the earth as a whole. **2.** (fig.) attraction, personal charm. **3.** So **mă'gnĕtIST** (3) *n.* [f. mod. L *magnetismus* (as MAGNET); see -ISM)]

mă'gnĕtīte *n.* magnetic iron oxide. [f. G *magnetit* (as MAGNET, -ITE¹ (2))]

mă'gnĕtīz|e, -īs|e (-īz), *v.t.* give magnetic properties to; make into a magnet; attract (lit. or fig.) as magnet does; hence ~ABLE *a.,* ~A'TION *n.* [f. MAGNET + -IZE]

măgnē'tō *n.* (*pl.* ~**s**). electric generator using permanent magnets (esp. for ignition in internal combustion engines, producing the required intermittent high-tension current independently of a battery). [abbr. of MAGNETO-*electric*]

măgnĕ'tō- comb. form: magneto, magnetism, as: ~**-ele'ctric,** (of electric generator) using permanent magnets, so ~**-electri'city;** ~**graph,** instrument recording variation of magnetic quantities; ~**hydrodyna'mic,** relating to movement of electrically conducting fluid in magnetic field; ∼**meter** (-ŏ'm-), instrument measuring magnetic forces, esp. terrestrial magnetism; ∼**-mo'tive force,** sum of magnetizing forces along circuit; ∼**sphere,** region in which earth's magnetic field is effective; ∼**stri'ction,** change in size caused by magnetization. [f. Gk *magnēs* (see MAGNET) + -o-]

mă'gnětŏn *n.* (Phys.) unit of magnetic MOMENT of atom etc. [f. F *magnéton* (as MAGNETIC; see -ON)]

mă'gnětrŏn *n.* electron tube for amplifying or generating microwaves, with flow of electrons controlled by external magnetic field. [f. MAGNET + -TRON]

măgni'fic(al) *adjs.* (arch.) magnificent, sublime. [ME, f. F *magnifique* or f. L *magnificus* (*magnus* great; see -FIC), + -AL]

măgni'ficăt *n.* song of praise; (*M*∼) a canticle (see etym.). [f. hymn of Virgin Mary in Luke 1: 46–55, used as canticle, and beginning thus in Vulgate; L, 3rd sing. of *magnificare* MAGNIFY]

măgnificā'tion *n.* magnifying or being magnified; amount of this, apparent enlargement of object by lens. [f. MAGNIFY + -FICATION]

măgni'fic|ent *a.* splendid, stately; sumptuously constructed or adorned; splendidly lavish; (colloq.) fine, excellent; hence or cogn. ∼ENCE *n.,* ∼**entLY²** *adv.* [F, or f. L *magnificent-* stem seen in compar. and superl. of *magnificus* MAGNIFIC]

măgni'ficō *n.* (*pl.* ∼**es**). Venetian magnate; grandee. [It., = MAGNIFIC]

mă'gni|fý *v.t.* increase apparent size of (thing), as with lens (∼**fying glass**) or microscope; exaggerate; intensify; (arch.) extol; hence ∼**fīER¹** (2) *n.* [ME, f. OF *magnifier* or f. L *magnificare* (*magnificus*; see MAGNIFIC, -FY)]

măgni'loqu|ent *a.* lofty in expression; boastful; hence ∼ENCE *n.,* ∼**entLY²** *adv.* [f. L *magniloquus* (*magnus* great, *-loquus* -speaking) + -ENT]

mă'gnitūde *n.* largeness; size; importance; (Astron.) (class of fixed stars arranged according to) degree of brightness (*first, seventh,* etc., *magnitude*); **apparent** ∼, as seen from the earth; **absolute** ∼, as seen at standard distance of ten parsecs, giving a measure of intrinsic luminosity); (fig.) **of the first** ∼ (importance). [ME, f. L *magnitudo* (*magnus* great; see -TUDE)]

măgnō'lĭa *n.* tree of genus *Magnolia,* cultivated for its dark-green foliage and waxlike flowers; *M∼ **State,** Mississippi. [mod. L, f. P. *Magnol,* Fr. botanist d. 1715 + -IA¹]

mă'gnum *n.* (bottle containing) two reputed quarts (⅔ imperial gal. or *⅖ US gal.) of wine or spirits. [L, neut. (as n.) of *magnus* great]

magnum opus. See OPUS.

mă'gpīe *n.* **1.** Eur. & Amer. crow (*Pica pica*) with long pointed tail and black-and-white plumage; idle chatterer; random collector. **2.** bird with plumage like magpie (e.g. Austral. bird of genus *Gymnorhina*); (rifle shot that strikes) next-to-outermost division of target. [f. *Mag* abbr. of woman's Christian name *Margaret* + PIE¹]

mă'guey (-gwā) *n.* agave plant, esp. that which yields pulque. [Sp., f. Haitian]

mă'g|us *n.* (*pl.* ∼i *pr.* -ī). member of ancient Persian priestly caste; sorcerer; **the (three) Magi,** the 'wise men' from the East who brought offerings to the infant Christ (Matt. 2:1). [ME f. L, f. Gk *magos* f. OPers. *magus*]

Mă'gyăr *n.* & *a.* **1.** (or mŏ'dyer). (member or language) of the people now predominant in Hungary; Hungarian. **2.** ∼ (**blouse**), blouse with ∼ **sleeves** (cut in one piece with main part of garment). [native name]

ma'halěb (mah'-h-) *n.* small cherry (*Prunus mahaleb*) with kernels yielding oil for perfume. [earlier *macaleb* f. F, f. Arab. *mahlab*]

mahara'ja, -jah, (mah-harah'ja) *n.* (Hist.) title of some Indian princes. [f. Hindi *mahārājā* (*mahā* great; see RAJA)]

mahara'nee, -ra'nī, (mah-harah'nī) *n.* (Hist.) maharaja's wife or widow. [f. Hindi *mahārānī* (*mahā* great; see RANEE)]

mahari'shi (mah-ha-) *n.* great Hindu sage. [f. Hindi (as prec., RISHI)]

mahā'tma (ma-h-) *n.* (Buddhism) one of a class of persons with preternatural powers, supposed to exist in India and Tibet; (Theosophy) sage or adept; person regarded with reverence. [f. Skr. *mahātman* (*mahā* great, *ātmán* soul)]

Mahaya'na (mah-hayah'na) *n.* school of Buddhism with syncretistic features and worship of gods, practised in China, Japan, and Tibet. [Skr. (*mahā* great, *yāna* vehicle)]

Mah'd|ī *n.* spiritual and temporal leader expected by Muslims; claimant of this title, esp. one of several leaders of insurrection in Sudan; hence ∼ISM (3), ∼IST (2), *ns.* [f. Arab. *mahdīy* he who is guided right, p.p. of *hadā* guide]

mah-jŏ'ng, -ngg (-ng), *n.* game (orig. Chinese) for four played with 136 or 144 pieces called tiles. [f. Chin. dial. *ma-tsiang* sparrows]

mah'lstick. See MAULSTICK.

mahŏ'ganў (ma-h-) *n.* reddish-brown wood from tropical tree (esp. W. Ind. tree of genus *Swietenia*), much used for furniture, and taking high polish; tree yielding mahogany; (arch.) dining-table (**have one's knees under** person's ∼, be dining with him); colour of mahogany, reddish-brown. [17th c.; orig. unkn.]

Mahometan (ma-hŏ'mĭtan). Var. of MUHAMMADAN.

Mahou'nd (ma-hōō'nd) *n.* (arch.) Muhammad (regarded mistakenly as a god). [ME f. OF *Mahun* (*Mahomet* Muhammad)]

mahou't (ma-how't) *n.* elephant-driver. [f. Hindi *mahāut* f. Skr. *mahāmātra* high official, lit. 'great in measure']

Mahratta. See MARATHA.

mah'seer *n.* large Indian freshwater game-fish (*Barbus mosal*). [f. Hindi *mahāsīr*]

maid *n.* **1.** (arch. or poet.) girl; young (unmarried) woman, virgin; spinster. **2.** (rhet.) young woman; **the M∼ (of Orleans),** Joan of Arc. **3.** ∼('**servant,** female servant esp. for indoor work (HOUSE¹maid, NURSE¹maid). **4.** ∼ **of all work,** female servant doing general housework, (fig.) person doing many jobs; ∼ **of honour,** (1) unmarried lady attending queen or princess, (2) kind of custard tartlet, (3) *principal bridesmaid; OLD *maid.* **5.** Hence ∼'ISH¹ *a.,* ∼'Y³ *n.* [ME, abbr. of MAIDEN]

maidan (mīdah'n) *n.* (Anglo-Ind.) open space in or near town; parade-ground. [f. Urdu f. Arab. *maydān*]

mai'den *n.* & *a.* **1.** *n.* (arch. or poet.) = MAID **1.2.** (Hist.) kind of guillotine used at Edinburgh. **3.** = *maiden over*; maiden horse. **4.** *a.* unmarried (*maiden aunt, lady*); ∼ **name** (before marriage). **5.** (Of female animal) unmated; (of horse) that has never won prize, (of race) open only to such horses; (of plant) grown from seed; (of speech by MP, voyage, etc.) first; (of fortress etc.) never captured; (of soldier, sword, etc.) untried. **6.** ‖∼ **assize,** one with no cases for trial; ∼ **over,** (Cricket) over in which no runs are scored. **7.** ∼**hair,** fern of genus *Adiantum* with fine hairlike stalks and delicate fronds; ∼**hair tree,** ginkgo; ∼**head** [see -HEAD], (1) virginity, (2) = HYMEN². **8.** Hence ∼HOOD *n.,* ∼ISH¹, ∼LIKE, ∼LY¹, *adjs.* [OE *mægden,* dim. (-EN²) f. *mægeth* = OS *magath,* OHG *magad,* Goth. *magaths* f. Gmc *magadiz maid]

maieu'tic (māū'-) *a.* (Of Socratic mode of inquiry) serving to bring out a person's latent ideas into clear consciousness. [f. Gk *maieutikos* (*maieuomai* act as midwife (*maia*); see -IC)]

mai'gre¹ (-ger) *a.* (RC Ch.) (Of day) on which abstinence from meat is ordered; (of food) suitable for eating on maigre days. [F, lit. lean; cf. MEAGRE]

mai'gre², *mai'ger, (-ger) *n.* fish of family Sciaenidae, esp. BAR³. [F]

mail[1] *n.* **1.** armour composed of rings or chains or plates, defensive armour for the body; **coat of** ~, jacket covered with this. **2.** protective shell or scales of animals. **3.** Hence ~ED[2] (-ld) *a.* (~**ed fist,** physical force). [ME, f. OF *maille* f. L *macula* spot, mesh]

mail[2] *v.t.* clothe (as) with mail. [f. prec.]

mail[3] *n.,* & *v.t.* **1.** *n.* bag of letters for conveyance by post; this system of conveyance, the POST[2]; matter so conveyed; all that is so conveyed on one occasion; ~ (**coach, train,** etc.), vehicle carrying this; letters etc. delivered at one place on one occasion; (as newspaper name: *Daily Mail, Oxford Mail*). **2.** ~**-bag,** large bag for carrying mail; ~**-boat** (carrying mail); *~'**box,** letter-box; *~ **carrier,** postman; ||~**-cart,** (1) cart for carrying mail by road, (2) light vehicle for carrying children; *~ **drop,** receptacle for mail; *~'**man,** postman; ~ **order,** order for goods to be sent by post (~*-order firm,* firm doing business mainly on this system). **3.** *v.t.* send (letters etc.) by post; hence *~'**ABLE** a.,* acceptable for conveyance by post. **4.** ~'**ing list** (of persons to whom advertising matter etc. is to be posted). [ME f. OF *male* wallet f. WG (= OHG) **malha*]

maillot (măyō') *n.* dancer's or gymnast's tights; woman's one-piece bathing-suit; = JERSEY 3. [F]

maim *v.t.* mutilate, cripple, (lit. or fig.). [ME *maynhe* etc. f. OF *mahaignier* etc., of unkn. orig.]

main[1] *n.* (In game of hazard) number (5, 6, 7, 8, or 9) called by player before dice are thrown; match between fighting-cocks. [16th c.; prob. orig. MAIN[3] *chance*]

main[2] *n.* **1.** principal channel, duct, etc., for water, sewage, etc., or (usu. in *pl.*) for supply of electricity. **2.** (arch. or poet.) mainland; high seas; SPANISH *Main.* **3.** **in the** ~, for the most part. **4.** **with might and** ~, with all one's force. [f. foll.; orig. = physical force (as in sense 4); OE *magen*, OHG *magan*, ON *magn* f. Gmc **mag-*; cf. MAY[1]]

main[3] *attrib. a.* **1.** exerted to the full (*by main force*); chief in size or extent (*the main body of an army* etc.); principal, most important, as *the main point* (in argument). *the main road* (in district), *the main clause* (in sentence), whence ~'LY[2] *adv.* **2.** have *an eye to the* ~ **chance,** one's own interests; ~'**land,** large continuous extent of land, excluding neighbouring islands etc., (*M*-) largest island in Orkney and in Shetland; ~ **line,** (1) chief railway line, (2) *chief road or street, (3, sl.) principal vein esp. as site of drug injection; ~'**line** *v.i.*, (sl.) take drugs thus; ~'**spring,** principal spring of watch, clock, etc., (fig.) chief motive power or incentive; *~ **stem,** (colloq.) main street; ~'**stream,** principal current of river etc., (fig.) prevailing trend of opinion, fashion, etc., (of jazz) neither traditional nor modern; ~ **street,** principal street of town, (fig., after S. Lewis's novel *Main Street*, 1920) materialistic ideals. **3.** (Naut.) ~ **brace** (attached to main yard; *splice the* ~ *brace,* (Hist.) serve extra rum ration); *main* COURSE[1]; ~ **deck,** (in man-of-war) deck next below spar-deck, (in merchantman) upper deck between poop and forecastle; ~'**mast,** principal mast; ~'**sail** (-săl, -sal), (in square-rigged vessel) lowest sail on main-mast, (in fore-and-aft rigged vessel) sail set on after part of mainmast; (fig.) chief support; ~'**stay,** stay from maintop to foot of foremast, (fig.) chief support; ~'**top,** platform above, ~-**to'pmast,** mast above, head of lower mainmast; ~ **yard,** yard on which mainsail is extended. [ME, partly f. ON *megenn, megn* a., partly f. OE *magen-* (as prec.)]

maintai'n *v.t.* cause to continue, continue one's action in, retain in being, (war, contest, lawsuit, condition, position, attitude, relations, correspondence, etc.); cause (person etc.) to continue in (condition, possession of thing, etc.); support (life, one's state in life) by nourishment, expenditure, etc.; furnish (one*self*, one's family, etc.) with means of subsistence; provide means for (garrison etc. to be equipped, building or

road to be repaired, etc.; ||~**ed school,** one supported from public funds); take action to preserve (machine etc.) in good order; give aid to (cause, party); assert as true (opinion, statement, *that*); hence ~ABLE *a.,* ~ER[1], ~OR, *ns.,* (esp. Law, one guilty of MAINTENANCE). [ME, f. OF *maintenir* f. Rom. **manu-tenēre* f. L *manu tenēre* hold in the hand]

mai'ntènance *n.* maintaining or being maintained; (provision of) enough to support life (SEPARATE[1] *maintenance*); = ALIMONY 2; (Law) former offence of aiding a party in litigation without lawful cause; **cap of** ~, cap or hat worn as symbol of official dignity or carried before a sovereign etc.; ~ **worker** (employed to keep equipment etc. in repair). [ME f. OF *maintenir*; see prec., -ANCE)]

maiolica. See MAJOLICA.

maisonè'tte, -nn-, (-z-) *n.* small house; part of house used separately (usu. not all on one floor). [F *maisonnette*, dim. of *maison* house; see -ETTE]

maître d'hôtel (mātr dōtĕ'l) *n.* major-domo; head waiter; ~ **butter, sauce,** (containing lemon-juice and chopped parsley). [F, = master of house]

maize *n.* (orig. N. Amer.) cereal *Zea mays*; its cobs or grains; yellow colour of maize cobs. [f. F *maïs* or f. Sp. *maiz*, of Carib orig.]

Maj. *abbr.* Major(-).

maje'st|ic *a.* possessing stateliness or grandeur, imposing; hence ~ICALLY *adv.* [f. foll. + -IC]

mā'jèstý *n.* **1.** impressive stateliness of aspect, bearing, language, etc. **2.** sovereign power; **Your, His, Her, M**~ (forms used in speaking to or of sovereign or sovereign's wife or widow: *Her Majesty the Queen*; *Her Majesty the Queen Mother*; *Her Majesty's Stationery Office*; *Her Britannic Majesty*). **3.** representation of God or Christ enthroned within aureole. [ME, f. OF *majesté* f. L *majestas -tatis* (as MAJOR[2]; see -TY[1])]

Mäjli's *n.* parliament of various N. Afr. or Middle Eastern countries, esp. Iran. [Pers., = assembly]

majō'lica, maiŏ'- (mayŏ'-) *n.* Renaissance Italian earthenware with coloured ornamentation on opaque white glaze; modern imitation of this. [f. It. *majolica,* f. former name of island of Majorca]

mā'jor[1] *n.* officer next below lieutenant-colonel and above captain; ~**-general,** officer next below lieutenant-general; hence ~SHIP *n.* [F, short for *sergent-major* SERGEANT-major, orig. a high rank (f. as foll.)]

mā'jor[2] *a., n.,* & *v.i.* **1.** *a.* greater (not followed by *than*) of two things, classes, etc.; of full age; ||(in schools) *Smith* etc. ~, the elder of the two Smiths or the first to enter the school; ~ **axis** (of conic, passing through its foci); *~ **league,** highest-ranking baseball etc. league (or fig.); ~ **part,** majority (*of*); *major* PLANET[1], PROPHET; ~ **suit,** (Bridge) spades or hearts; FRIARS *Major.* **2.** unusually important or serious or significant (*major road, war*); (of operation) presenting possible danger to patient's life. **3.** (Logic). (Of term) occurring in predicate of conclusion of syllogism; (of premiss) containing major term. **4.** (Mus.) (Of interval) normal or perfect (cf. MINOR), as in major scale, (*major third*); (of key) in which scale has major third; (of scale) with semitones above third and seventh notes. **5.** *n.* (Mil.) officer in charge of section of band instruments (DRUM[1] *major*, PIPE[1] *major*, TRUMPET-*major*); SERGEANT-*major.* **6.** person of full age; (Logic) major term or premiss; *student's special subject or course; *student specializing in a subject (*is a philosophy major*). **7.** *v.i.* ~ (Of student) undertake study or qualify *in* as special subject. [ME f. L, compar. of *magnus* great]

mājor-dō'mō *n.* (*pl.* ~s). chief official of Italian or Spanish princely household; house-steward, butler. [orig. *mayordome* f. Sp. *mayordomo*, It. *maggiordomo* f. med. L *major domus* highest official of the household (as prec., DOME)]

mājorĕ'tte *n.* = DRUM[1] *majorette.* [abbr.]

majŏ'rity *n.* **1.** greater number or part (*of*); **the great**

∼, much the greater number; **the (great)** ∼, the dead (esp. *join the (great)* ∼, *die*); ABSOLUTE or *overall majority*; ∼ **rule**, principle that greater number should exercise greater power; ∼ **verdict** (given by more than half of jury, but not unanimous). **2.** number by which votes cast for one party etc. exceed those for the next in rank; party etc. receiving greater number of votes (**in the** ∼, belonging to or constituting this). **3.** full age (*attained his majority*). **4.** rank of MAJOR[1]. [f. F *majorité* f. med. L *majoritas -tatis* (as MAJOR[2]; see -ITY)]

ma'juscul‖e *a. & n.* (Palaeog.) large (letter), whether capital or uncial; (written in) large lettering; hence ∼AR[1] (-ŭ's-) *a.* [F, f. L *majuscula* (*littera* letter), dim. of MAJOR[2]; see -CULE]

ma'kable. See MAKE[1] 29.

make[1] *v.* (**made**). **1.** *v.t.* construct, frame, create, from parts or other substances, (*God made man* (*a rational creature*); *bees make cells of wax*; *made in England*; *can make almost anything out of bamboo*; *hydrogen and nitrogen make ammonia*); **made,** (of person) built, formed, (WELL--made, *loosely-made*); **made dish,** food prepared from several separate foods; **made road** (artificially prepared, with surfacing-materials added); **be made for,** be ideally suited to; **be made of,** consist of (*pipes are made of clay*), **have it made,** (sl.) be sure of success; ‖*made to* MEASURE[1]; *made to* ORDER[1] 17. **2.** compose, write, (book etc.); prepare (will etc.). **3.** prepare (tea, coffee, etc.) for use; shuffle (pack of cards) for dealing; arrange and light materials for (a fire); arrange bedclothes on (bed) for further use; *make* HAY[1]. **4.** cause to exist, bring about, (disturbance, difficulties, trouble, an enemy, sport, noise, one's mark in the world, a corner in wheat, etc.); *make no* BONE[1]*s*; *make* CONVERSATION, FRIENDS, FUN or GAME[1] *of*, a NAME[1] *for* one*self*, PEACE, *place* or ROOM (*for*), a *point of* (see POINT[1] 11); ∼ **time,** find an occasion when time is available (*for doing* or *to do*), *(sl.)* make sexual advances; *make* (*one's* or *its*) WAY. **5.** (Electr.) complete, close, (circuit; opp. *break*). **6.** result in (*it makes a difference*; '*find*' *makes in the past tense* '*found*'); amount to (*2 and 2 make 4*); constitute (*one* SWALLOW[2] *does not make a summer*). **7.** establish, enact, (distinctions, rules, laws). **8.** collect, get together, (a HOUSE[1], a quorum); ∼ **a bag,** kill number of game; ∼ **a book,** arrange series of bets on an event; ∼ **sail,** spread (additional) sail(s), start on voyage; *make* WATER[1]. **9.** cause (obj. of prep. *of*) to become (*make an* EXAMPLE[1], *an* EXHIBITION, *a* FOOL[1], *of* person or one*self*); *make a* HABIT[1], *a* PRACTICE[1], *of*; ∼ **a day,** NIGHT, **week,** etc., **of it,** carry activity etc. on through the day etc. **10.** frame in the mind (*make a judgement of*); feel (doubt, scruples, *of* or *about*). **11.** (Naut.) discern, come in sight of. **12.** arrive at; achieve place in (team, prize-list, etc.); (sl.) catch (a train etc.), win affections of, esp. seduce (person); ∼ **it,** succeed in traversing a certain distance, (fig.) be successful, (sl.) achieve copulation (*with*). **13.** form, be counted as, (*this makes the tenth time*; *will you make one of the party?*); serve for (*this makes pleasant reading*); become by development or training (*she will make a good wife*; *he would make a good preacher*). **14.** gain, acquire, procure, (*money, a living, a profit,* one's *fortune*); (Cards) win (trick), play (card) to advantage, win number of tricks that fulfils (contract); obtain as result (*made a loss on the transaction*); (Cricket) score (runs). **15.** secure the advancement of; **made man,** one who has attained success in life; SELF-*made*; ∼ **or break,** ∼ **or mar,** cause success or ruin of; ∼ one's **day** etc., be essential factor in success of it. **16.** cause to be (*make it hot, known, plain*; *make* one*self a martyr*; *make* one*self* SCARCE; *make him a duke*); convert *into*; choose as (*shall we make it Tuesday then?*); bring to (chosen value etc.; *add one and make it a round dozen*). **17.** consider to be (*what do you make the time?*; *I make it 5 miles*); consider (*what bird do you make that to be?*). **18.** cause, compel, (to) (*make him repeat it*; *he was made to repeat it*); *make* BELIEVE (and see 28); ∼ **do,** use

(with) temporary expedients, manage *with* (something) as an inferior or temporary substitute. **19.** represent as, cause to appear to do or be, (*he makes Richard the king's son*). **20.** execute (bodily movement, *a* BACK[1], BOW[4], FACE[1], LEG); perform (journey etc., and with many ns. expr. vbl action, as *an acquisition, attempt, blunder, demand, effort, mistake, offer, promise, purchase, speech, start*); wage (war *on, against, with*); travel along (*make a bee-line for*); accomplish (distance, speed, etc.); ∼ (eat) **a good breakfast** etc.; *make* HEAD[1] 22, LOVE[1], SHIFT[2]. **21.** ∼ **of,** construct from, (fig.) conclude to be the meaning or character of (*can you make anything of it?*; *what am I to make of your behaviour?*); **made of money,** (colloq.) very rich; ∼ **much, little, the best,** etc., **of,** (1) derive much etc. advantage from, (2) give much etc. attention to, attach much etc. importance to; *make* LIGHT[4] *of, a* HASH[2] *of*, HEAD[1] *or tail of*, *a* MEAL[2] *of*, THE MOST *of*, NOTHING *of*. **22.** *v.i.* proceed (*towards* etc.); ∼ **after,** (arch.) pursue; ∼ **away** or **off,** depart hastily; ∼ **off with,** carry away, steal. **23.** act as if with intention *to* do (*he made to go*); ∼ **as if** or **though,** act as if one were about *to* do or as one would if one *had* etc.; *make* BOLD, CERTAIN, FREE[1], GOOD, MERRY[2], SURE. **24.** (Of tide) begin to flow or ebb. **25.** ∼ **against,** be unfavourable to; ∼ **away with,** get rid of, kill, squander; ∼ **for,** conduce to (happiness etc.), confirm (view), proceed towards (place), assail; ∼ **over,** transfer possession of (thing *to* person), refashion (garment etc.); *∗*∼ **with,** (sl.) (exert oneself *to*) supply. **26.** ∼ **out,** draw up, write out, (list, document, cheque *to*, or *in favour of*, person), get together with difficulty (*articles put in to make out a volume*), (try to) prove (*how do you make that out?*, *you make me out* (*to be*) *a hypocrite*), understand (*I can't make him out, can't make out what he wants*), decipher (handwriting etc.), distinguish by sight or hearing (*I made out a figure in the distance*); (colloq.) make progress, fare, (*how did you make out?*), assert or pretend (*he made out that he liked it*). **27.** ∼ **up,** serve or act to overcome (deficiency), complete (amount, party), compensate (*make up lost ground*; *make up for lost time*; *we must* ∼ **it up to** (compensate) *him somehow*), compound, put together, prepare, (medicine, hay *into* bundles, butter, beds for use, etc.), sew together (parts of garment etc.), get together (company, sum of money), arrange (type) in pages, compile (list, account, document), concoct (story), (of parts) compose (whole), prepare (actor) for his part by dressing, false hair, etc., apply cosmetics (to), arrange (marriage etc.), settle (dispute); ∼ (**it**) **up,** be reconciled; *make up* one's MIND[1]; ∼ **up to,** court, curry favour with; ∼**-up** *n.*, disguise of actor, cosmetics etc. used for this, making up of type, type made up, (cosmetics for) woman's facial adornment, composition or constitution, person's character and temperament. **28.** ∼'**bate,** (arch.) one who foments strife; ∼-belief *n.*, ∼-**believe** *n. & a.*, pretence, pretended; ∼'**ready,** (Print.) final preparation for printing; ∼'**shift** *a. & n.*, (serving as) temporary substitute or device; ∼'**weight,** small quantity added to make full weight (lit., or fig. of extra person), (fig.) unimportant point added to make argument seem stronger. **29.** Hence **ma'kable** *a.* [OE *macian*, = OS *makon*, OHG *mahhōn* f. WG *∗makōjan* (*∗mak-* fit, suitable, cogn. w. MATCH[1])]

make[2] *n.* **1.** (Of natural or manufactured thing) kind of structure or composition; build of body; mental or moral disposition; (particular) origin or type of manufacture (*British make*; *our own make of shoes*; *different makes of car*); shuffling of cards; **on the** ∼, (sl.) intent on gain, *∗*(sl.) looking for sexual partners. **2.** (Electr.) making of contact, position in which this is made. [ME, f. prec.]

ma'ker *n.* In vbl senses; **the, our,** etc., M∼, God; (arch.) poet. [ME, f. MAKE[1] + -ER[1]]

ma'king *n.* **1.** In vbl senses; **be the** ∼ **of,** ensure success or favourable development of; **in the** ∼, in course of being made or formed. **2.** (in *pl.*) earnings, profits; essential qualities for becoming (*he has the makings of a general*); (US & Austral.) paper and tobacco for rolling a cigarette. [OE *macung* (as MAKE[1], -ING[1])]

ma′kō[1] (mah′-) *n.* (*pl.* ∼s). blue Pacific shark (*Isurus glaucus*). [Maori]

ma′kō[2] (mah′-) *n.* (*pl.* ∼s). small NZ tree with clusters of dark-red berries and large racemes of pink flowers. [Maori]

măl- *pref.* **1.** bad(ly) (*malpractice, maltreat*), faulty (*malfunction*). **2.** not (*maladroit, malcontent*). [f. F *mal* badly f. L *male*]

Mal. *abbr.* Malachi (OT).

Mală′cca *n.* ∼ **cane,** rich-brown cane from stem of palm-tree *Calamus rotang*, used for walking-sticks etc. [∼ in Malaysia]

mä′lachīte (-kīt) *n.* hydrated copper carbonate as bright-green mineral taking high polish and used for ornament. [f. OF *melochite* f. L *molochites* f. Gk *molokhitis* (*molokhē* = *malakhē* mallow; see -ITE[1])]

mä′laco- *comb. form.* soft, as: ∼**derm,** soft-skinned reptile etc.; ∼**logy** (-ŏ′l-), science of molluscs; ∼**ptery′gian** *a.* & *n.,* soft-finned (fish). [f. Gk *malakos* soft + -o-]

mălacŏ′stracan *a.* & *n.* (member) of the crustacean order Malacostraca, e.g. crab, lobster, shrimp. [f. as prec. + Gk *ostrakon* shell + -AN]

măladjŭ′st|ĕd *a.* not correctly adjusted; (of person) not satisfactorily adjusted to one's environment and conditions of life; so ∼MENT *n.* [f. MAL- + p.p. of ADJUST]

măladmi′nĭst|er *v.t.* administer or manage inefficiently or badly or improperly; so ∼RA′TION *n.* [f. MAL- + ADMINISTER]

măladroit (-oi′t, mă′-) *a.* clumsy, bungling; hence ∼LY[2] *adv.,* ∼NESS *n.* [F (as MAL-, ADROIT)]

mä′lady *n.* ailment, disease, (lit. or fig.). [ME, f. OF *maladie* (*malade* sick f. Rom. *male habitus f. L *male* ill, *habitus* p.p. of *habēre* have)]

māla fī′dē *adv.* & *a.* (acting, done) in bad faith. [L]

Mă′laga *n.* white or red fortified wine from Málaga. [*Málaga* in S. Spain]

Mălagă′sў *a.* & *n.* (language or native or inhabitant) of Madagascar. [orig. *Malegass, Madegass* f. *Madagascar*]

malai′se (-z) *n.* bodily discomfort, esp. without development of specific disease; feeling of uneasiness. [F, f. OF *mal* bad + *aise* EASE[1]]

mă′lamūte, mă′lemūte, *n.* Eskimo dog. [name of Alaskan Eskimo tribe]

malanders. Var. of MALLENDERS.

mă′lapêrt *a.* & *n.* (arch.) impudent, saucy, (person). [ME f. OF (as MAL-, *apert* = *espert* EXPERT[1])]

mă′laprŏp(ism) *ns.* ludicrous misuse of word, esp. in mistake for one resembling it (e.g. *derangement of epitaphs* for *arrangement of epithets*). [f. Mrs. *Malaprop* (f. foll.) in Sheridan's 'The Rivals']

mălăpropō′s (-pō′) *adv., a.,* & *n.* (thing) inopportunely (said, done, or happening). [f. F *mal à propos* (mal ill; see APROPOS)]

mă′lar *a.* & *n.* (bone) of the cheek. [f. mod. L *malaris* f. L *mala* jaw; see -AR[1]]

malăr′|ia *n.* intermittent and remittent fever caused by bite of mosquito, which conveys protozoan parasite of genus *Plasmodium*; unwholesome atmosphere caused by exhalations of marshes, to which these fevers were formerly attributed; hence ∼IAL, ∼IAN, ∼IOUS, *adjs.* [f. It. *mal′aria* bad air]

malăr′key *n.* (sl.) humbug, nonsense. [20th c.; orig. unkn.]

mălathi′on *n.* insecticide containing phosphorus, with low toxicity to plants and mammals. [f. diethyl *maleate* + *thio*-acid + -ON]

Malay′ *a.* & *n.* (language or member) of a people predominating in Malaysia and Indonesia; hence ∼AN *a.* & *n.,* ∼O- *comb. form.* [f. Malay *malāyu*]

Mălaya′lam (-yah′-) *n.* Dravidian language of Malabar district of S. India. [native]

mă′lcontĕnt *a.* & *n.* discontented (person), (one) inclined to rebellion. [F (as MAL-, CONTENT[3])]

mal de mer (măl de mār′) *n.* seasickness. [F, = sickness of sea]

māle *a.* & *n.* **1.** *a.* of the sex that can beget offspring by performing the fertilizing function (*male child, slave, dog*; *male* CHAUVINIST, MENOPAUSE, *nurse*); (of plants or their parts) containing only fecundating organs, or thought of as male because of colour etc. (∼ **fern,** *Dryopteris filixmas*, commonest lowland fern in UK); of men or male animals or plants (*the male sex*; *male* (*voice*) *choir*); (of parts of machinery etc.) designed to enter or fill the corresponding female part (*male screw*); *male* RHYME[1]; hence ∼′NESS (-ln-) *n.* **2.** *n.* male person or animal. [ME f. OF *ma(s)le,* f. L *masculus* (*mas* a male; see -CULE)]

mălĕdi′ct|ion *n.* (utterance of) curse; so ∼IVE, ∼ORY, *adjs.* [ME, f. L *maledictio* f. *maledicere* speak evil of (*male* ill, *dicere dict-* speak); see -ION]

mă′lefăctor *n.* criminal; evil-doer; so **mălĕfă′ctION** *n.* [ME f. L, f. *malefacere* (*male* ill, *facere fact-* do); see -OR]

malĕ′fic *a.* (Of magical arts etc.) harmful, baleful. [L *maleficus* (*male* ill; see -FIC)]

malĕ′fic|ent *a.* hurtful (*to*); criminal; so ∼ENCE *n.* *maleficence* f. as prec. after *malevolence*]

mä′lemūte. See MALAMUTE.

malĕ′vol|ent *a.* desirous of evil to others; hence or cogn. ∼ENCE *n.,* ∼ent LY[2] *adv.* [f. OF *malivolent* or f. L *malevolens* (*male* ill, *volens* willing, part. of *velle*)]

mălfea′s|ance (-ē′z-) *n.* (Law). evil-doing, esp. official misconduct; so ∼ANT *a.* & *n.* [f. AF *malfaisance* f. OF MAL(*faisant* part. of *faire* do f. L *facere*); see -ANCE; cf. MISFEASANCE]

mălfŏrmā′tion *n.* faulty formation; so **mălfŏr′mED**[1] (-md) *a.* [f. MAL- + FORMATION]

mălfŭ′nction *n.,* & *v.i.* fail(ure) to function in normal or satisfactory manner. [f. MAL- + FUNCTION]

ma′li (mah′lē) *n.* (Ind.) member of gardener caste. [Hindi]

mā′lic *a.* (Chem.) ∼ **acid** (derived from unripe apples and other fruits). [f. F *malique* f. L *malum* apple; see -IC]

mā′lice *n.* **1.** active ill will; desire to tease; **bear** ∼ (**to** or **towards** or **against**), cherish vindictive feelings (*against*). **2.** (Law). wrongful intention, esp. as increasing guilt of certain offences, esp. murder; *malice* AFORE*thought* or PREPENSE. **3.** So **mali′c**IOUS (-shus) *a.,* given to or arising from malice. [ME f. OF, f. L *malitia* (*malus* bad; see -ICE)]

mali′gn[1] (-ī′n) *a.* (Of thing) injurious; (of disease) malignant; malevolent; hence or cogn. **mali′gn**ITY *n.,* ∼LY[2] *adv.* [ME, f. OF *malin maligne* or f. L *malignus* (*malus* bad; cf. BENIGN)]

mali′gn[2] (-ī′n) *v.t.* speak ill of, slander. [ME, f. OF *malignier* f. LL *malignare* contrive maliciously f. L *malignus* (see prec.)]

mali′gn|ant *a.* & *n.* **1.** *a.* (Of disease) very virulent or infectious (*malignant cholera*); (of tumour) tending to spread and to recur after removal, cancerous; *malignant* PUSTULE. **2.** harmful; feeling or showing intense ill will. **3.** *n.* & *a.* (Hist.) supporter of, supporting, Charles I against Parliament. **4.** Hence ∼ANCY *n.,* ∼ant LY[2] *adv.* [f. LL *malignare* (as prec.; see -ANT)]

mali′nger (-ngg-) *v.i.* pretend, produce, or protract, illness in order to escape duty (esp. of soldiers, sailors, etc.); so ∼ER[1] *n.* [back-form. f. *malingerer* app. f. F *malingre,* perh. f. as MAL- + *haingre* weak]

mā′lism *n.* doctrine that the world is a bad one. [f. L *malus* bad + -ISM]

mā′lison (-z-) *n.* (arch.) curse. [ME, f. OF *mal*(*e*)*isonf.* L (as MALEDICTION)]

mall (mŏl, mawl) *n.* **1.** sheltered walk as promenade; *shopping precinct. **2.** (Hist.) game of pall-mall; alley for it; mallet for it. [var. of MAUL[1]; applied to *The*

Mall in London (orig. a pall-mall alley), whence sense 1]

ma'llard n. (*pl.* same). wild drake or duck (*Anas platyrhynchos*); its flesh. [ME f. OF, prob. f. **maslart* (as MALE; see -ARD)]

ma'lleable a. (Of metal etc.) that can be hammered or pressed out of shape without tendency to return to it or to fracture; (fig.) adaptable, pliable; hence **mälleABI'LITY** n. [ME f. OF, f. med. L *malleabilis* f. L *malleare* to hammer (MALLEUS); see -ABLE]

ma'llee n. (Austral.) (scrub formed by) one of various eucalyptuses flourishing in arid areas; **∼-bird**, **-fowl**, **-hen**, megapode (*Leipoa ocellata*) like small turkey. [Aboriginal]

mä'llěmŭck, mö'llỹmawk, n. fulmar, petrel, or similar bird. [f. Du. *mallemok* (*mal* foolish, *mok* gull)]

mä'llenders (-z) n. *pl.* dry scabby eruption behind horse's knee. [ME, f. OF *malandre* sing. f. L *malandria* pl. neck-pustules]

mallě'ol|us n. (*pl.* ∼i *pr.* -ī). (Anat.) bone of hammer--head shape, esp. one forming projection on either side of ankle. [L, dim. of MALLEUS]

mä'llět n. hammer, usu. of wood; implement for striking croquet or polo ball. [ME, f. OF *maillet* (*mailler* to hammer f. *mail* hammer f. L *malleus*)]

mä'llě|us n. (*pl* ∼i *pr.* -ī). bone of middle ear transmitting vibrations of tympanum to incus. [L, = hammer]

mä'llow (-ō) n. plant of genus *Malva*, esp. species with hairy stems and leaves and purple flowers. [OE *meal(u)we* f. L *malva*]

malm (mahm) n. soft chalky rock; loamy soil from disintegration of this; fine-quality brick made originally from malm, marl, or similar chalky clay. [OE **mealm*, = ON *malmr* ore, Goth. *malma* sand f. Gmc **mel-* grind (cf. MEAL[1])]

mälmai'son (-z-) n. large usu. pink variety of car-nation. [f. F *Souvenirs de Malmaison* memories of Mal-maison (château of Empress Josephine near Paris)]

ma'lmsey (mah'mzĭ) n. strong sweet wine from Greece, Spain, Madeira, etc. [ME, f. MDu., MLG *malmesie, -eye*, f. Monemvasia in the Morea, Greece; cf. MALVOISIE]

mälnūtri'tion n. insufficient nutrition; condition where diet omits some foods necessary for health; so **mälNOU'RISHMENT** n. [f. MAL- + NUTRITION]

mälō'dorous a. evil-smelling. [f. MAL- + ODOROUS]

Mälpi'ghian (-gī-) a. ∼ **layer** (of developing cells in epidermis). [f. M. *Malpighi*, It. physician d. 1694 + -AN]

mälprä'ctice n. wrongdoing; (Law) physician's im-proper or negligent treatment of patient; (Law) illegal action for one's own benefit while in (esp. official) position of trust. [f. MAL- + PRACTICE[1]]

malt[1] (mawlt, mŏlt) n. barley or other grain prepared by steeping, germination, and drying for brewing or distilling or vinegar-making; (colloq.) malt liquor, malt whisky; ∼ **house** (for preparing and storing malt); ∼ **liquor** (made from malt by fermentation, not distillation, e.g. beer, stout); ∼ **whisky** (made from malted barley). [OE *m(e)alt*, = OS *malt*, OHG *malz*, ON *malt* f. Gmc **maltaz*, cogn. w. MELT[2]]

malt[2] (mawlt, mŏlt) v. 1. v.t. convert (grain) into malt; ∼**ed milk** (made from dried milk and prepara-tion of malt). 2. v.i. (Of seeds) become malt when germination is checked by drought. [ME, f. prec.]

Ma'lta (maw'-, mŏ'-) n. ∼ **fever**, brucellosis in humans or goats. [∼, island in Mediterranean, where it was common]

Maltě'se (mawltē'z, mŏ-) a. & n. (*pl.* same). (lan-guage, native, or inhabitant) of Malta; ∼ **cat** (bluish-grey short-haired breed); ∼ **cross** (with arms broadened outwards, often indented at ends); ∼ **dog, terrier**, small breed of spaniel, or terrier. [f. prec. + -ESE]

mä'ltha n. cement of pitch and wax or other in-gredients. [L f. Gk]

Mälthū'sian (-z-) a. & n. (follower) of Malthus; hence **∼ISM** (3) n. [f. T. R. *Malthus*, Engl. clergyman d. 1834, who advocated moral restraint as means of preventing increase of population beyond means of subsistence, + -IAN]

ma'lting (maw'-, mŏ'-) n. In vbl senses; malt-house. [ME, f. MALT[2] + -ING[1]]

ma'ltōse (maw'-, mŏ'-) n. (Chem.) sugar produced by hydrolysis of starch under action of malt, saliva, etc. [F (as MALT[1], -OSE[2])]

mältrea't v.t. ill-treat; hence ∼MENT n. [f. F MAL (*traiter* TREAT)]

ma'ltster (maw'l(t)ster, mŏ'-) n. one who makes malt. [ME, f. MALT[1] + -STER]

mälvä'ceous (-shus) a. (Bot.) of the genus *Malva*; of the family Malvaceae. [f. L *malvaceus* (as MALLOW; see -ACEOUS)]

mälversä'tion n. corrupt behaviour in position of trust; corrupt administration (of public money etc.). [F (*malverser* f. L *male* badly + *versari* behave; see -ATION)]

mälvoisie' (-vwazē') n. malmsey. [ME f. OF *malvesie* f. F form of *Monemvasia*; see MALMSEY]

mäm n. (colloq. or childish). mother. [f. as MAMMA[1]]

mama. See MAMMA[1].

mä'mba n. venomous S. African snake of genus *Dendroaspis*. [f. Zulu *imamba*]

mä'mbō n. (*pl.* ∼s). Latin-Amer. dance like rumba; music for it. [Amer. Sp., prob. f. Haitian]

mä'melon n. small rounded hillock. [F, = nipple (*mamelle* breast f. L MAMILLA)]

Mä'měluke (-ōōk) n. (Hist.) member of military body (orig. Circassian slaves) that ruled Egypt 1254–1811. [f. F *mameluk*, ult. f. Arab. *mamlūk* slave (*malaka* possess)]

mami'll|a, *mamm-, n. (*pl.* ∼ae). nipple of woman's breast; nipple-shaped organ etc.; hence ∼ARY[1], ∼ATE[2], *adjs.* [L, dim. of MAMMA[2]]

mamma'[1], mama', (-ah') n. (Child's name for) mother; ∼'s **boy**, boy or man who has been unduly cosseted by his mother. [imit. of child's *ma, ma*]

mä'mm|a[2] n. (*pl.* ∼ae). milk-secreting organ of female in mammals; corresponding non-secreting structure in males; hence ∼ARY[1], ∼iFORM, *adjs.* [OF. f. L]

mä'mmal n. animal of class Mammalia, having mammae for nourishment of young, and usu. quad-ruped with hair or fur, e.g. man, dog, rabbit, whale; hence **mammä'lIAN** a. & n., **mammä'LOGY** n. [Anglicized f. mod. L *mammalia* neut. pl. of L *mammalis* (as MAMMA[2]; see -AL)]

mä'mmaliferous a. (Geol.) containing mammalian remains. [f. prec. + -I- + -FEROUS]

mä'mmarȳ. See MAMMA[2].

mä'mmee' n. tropical American tree with large red--rinded yellow-pulped fruit. [f. Sp. *mamei* f. Haitian]

*mammi'lla. See MAMILLA.

Ma'mmon n. wealth regarded as idol or evil in-fluence; the worldly rich; **the ∼ of unrighteous-ness**, wealth ill used or ill gotten; hence ∼ISH[1] a., ∼ISM (3), ∼IST (2), ∼ITE[1], *ns.* [ME, f. LL *Mam(m)ona* f. Gk *mamōnas* f. Aram. *māmōn* riches; see Matt. 6: 24, Luke 16: 9–13]

mä'mmoth n. & a. 1. n. large extinct elephant, with hairy coat and curved tusks. 2. a. huge. [f. Russ. *mamo(n)t*, prob. f. Siberian orig.]

mä'mmȳ n. (Child's word for) mother; *Black woman in charge of white children. [f. as MAMMA[1] + -Y[3]]

män[1] n. (*pl.* **men**). 1. human being (**a ∼ and a brother**, a fellow human being); (in indefinite or general application) person (*any, no, man; some, few, men*); (**all**) **to a ∼**, all without exception. 2. the human race (*man is born with trouble; man is a political animal*); **rights of ∼**, = HUMAN rights. 3. human being of specified historical period (*Renaissance man*), esp. prehistoric type named from place where re-mains were found (*Heidelberg, Java, Peking, Piltdown,*

Man); INNER, NEW[1], OLD, OUTER, *man*. **4.** adult human male, opp. to woman, boy, or both; ∼ **and boy**, (*adv.*) from boyhood upwards; **be a** ∼, **play the** ∼, be manly, not show fear; ∼ **to** ∼, (*adv.*) with candour; **separate** or **sort out the men from the boys**, (colloq.) find those who are truly virile or competent; LITTLE *man*. **5.** (As *voc.*, expr. impatience) *nonsense, man!*; (as general mode of address among hippies etc.) *dig that, man*; **my (good)** ∼ (patronizing); *man* ALIVE!. **6. a** ∼, one (*what can a man do in such a case?*). **7.** individual (male) person; one's opponent, allocated assistant, etc.; **as one** ∼, in unison; **as a** ∼, viewed simply in regard to his personal character; **the (very)** ∼, the most suitable man *for*; *if you want noise*, **he is your** ∼ (can supply you); **I'm your** ∼ (accept your offer etc.); **be one's own** ∼, (1) be free to act, be independent, (2) be in full possession of one's faculties, senses, etc.; *man* FRIDAY; *every man* JACK[1]; ∼ **of God**, saint or clergyman; *man of* HONOUR[1] 1; ∼ **of the house**, householder; ∼ **of Kent** (see KENTISH); *man of* LETTERS, *of the* MOMENT; ∼ **in the moon**, semblance of man seen in full moon; *man of* PLEASURE, SIN[1]; ∼ **in** or ***on the street**, ordinary average man (esp. as opp. expert); *man of* STRAW[1], *about* TOWN; ∼-**of-war**, armed ship of country's navy (PORTUGUESE *man-of-war*); *man of the* WORLD; BEST[1] *man*; HANDY*man*. **8.** *suf.* man concerned or dealing or skilful with or describable as (*clergyman, countryman, Dutchman*, GENTLEMAN, HORSE[1]*man, oarsman*, POST[2]-*man*); ship of specified type (INDIA*man*, MERCHANT-*man*). **9. *the Man,** (sl.) the police, (Black sl.) white men. **10.** husband (*man and wife*). **11.** manservant, valet; workman (*the employers held a meeting with the men*); (Hist.) vassal. **12.** (usu. in *pl.*) soldiers, sailors, etc., esp. those not officers. **13.** one of a set of objects of same or different forms used in playing chess, draughts, etc. **14.** ∼-**at-arms**, (arch.) soldier, esp. heavy-armed and mounted; ∼-**child**, (arch.) male child; ∼-**day** (as *man-hour*); ∼-**eater**, ∼-**eating** *a.*, (cannibal, shark or tiger) eating human flesh; **me′n-folk**, men in general, the men of one's family; ∼′**handle**, move by human effort alone, (sl.) handle roughly; ∼-**hater**, one who hates mankind or the male sex; ∼′**hole**, opening in floor, sewer, etc., for man to pass through; ∼-**hour**, work done by one man in one hour; ∼-**hunt**, organized search for person (esp. criminal); ∼-**made**, (of textile etc.) artificially made, synthetic; *man*-MILLINER; ∼′**power**, (1) power of man in work, (2) number of persons available for military or other service; **men's (room)**, lavatory for men; ∼′**servant** (pl. *me′n-servants*), male servant; ∼-**size(d)**, of size of or adequate to a man; ∼′**slaughter**, killing of human being, (Law) unlawful killing of human being without malice aforethought; ∼-**tailored**, (of women's clothes) tailored in style of men's clothes; ∼′**trap** (for catching men, esp. trespassers); **me′nswear** (-z-), clothes for men; ∼-**week**, -**year**, (as *man-hour*). **15.** Hence ∼′LESS *a.* [OE *man*(*n*), pl. *menn*, = OS, OHG *man*, ON *mathr*, Goth. *manna* f. Gmc **man*-, **mannon*-]

măn[2] *v.t.* (**-nn-**). furnish (fort, ship, industrial undertaking, etc.) with man or men for service or defence; act thus in respect of (*man the pumps*); (Naut.) place men at (part of ship); fill (post); fortify spirits or courage of (esp. one*self*). [OE *mannian* (as prec.)]

Man. *abbr.* Manitoba.

ma′na (mah′-) *n.* power, authority, prestige; supernatural or magical power. [Maori]

mă′nacle *n.*, & *v.t.* **1.** *n.* (usu. in *pl.*) fetter for the hand, handcuff, (fig.) restraint. **2.** *v.t.* fetter with manacles. [ME f. OF *manicle* handcuff f. L *manicula* dim. of *manus* hand]

mă′nage[1] *n.* (arch.) training of horse; trained movements of horse; riding-school. [f. It. *maneggio* (as foll.); cf. MANÈGE]

mă′nage[2] *v.* **1.** *v.t.* handle, wield, (tool etc.); conduct (undertaking etc.); organize, regulate, be manager of,

(household, institution, State); be manager of (team etc.); take charge of (cattle etc.); take control of (person, animal); gain one's ends with (person etc.) by tact, flattery, dictation, etc.; succeed in achieving (*she managed a smile*); contrive (*to* do; often iron.: *he managed to muddle it*). **2.** *v.i.* succeed in one's aim (often *with* inadequate material etc.). **3.** *v.t.* (With *can* or *be able to*) cope with, make proper use of, do what is suggested or appropriate regarding, (*can you manage this matter, another slice, lunch next Saturday?*, or abs., *you manage by yourself?*). [f. It. *maneggiare* f. Rom. **manidiare* f. L *manus* hand]

mă′nage|able (-nĭja-) *a.* that can be managed; easily controlled, wielded, accomplished, etc.; hence ∼ABI′LITY, ∼**able**NESS (-bĕln-), *ns.*, ∼**ably** *adv.* [f. prec. + -ABLE]

mă′nagement (-nĭjm-) *n.* In vbl senses; trickery, deceit; administration of business concerns or public undertakings; persons engaged in this (**the** ∼, governing body, board of directors, etc.); (Med.) technique of treatment *of* disease etc. [f. MANAGE[2] + -MENT]

mă′nager (-nĭj-) *n.* **1.** person conducting a business, institution, etc.; person controlling activities of person or team in sports, entertainment, etc. **2.** ∥member of either House of Parliament appointed with others for some duty in which both Houses are concerned. **3.** good, bad, etc., ∼ (of money, household affairs, etc.). **4.** ∥(Law). person appointed, usu. by Court of Chancery, to manage a business for benefit of creditors etc. **5.** Hence ∼ESS[1] (*or* -ĕ′s), ∼SHIP, *ns.*, **mănagē′r**IAL *a.* [f. MANAGE[2] + -ER[1]]

mă′naging (-nĭj-) *a.* In vbl senses; having executive control or authority (*managing director*); fond of being in control of affairs; (arch.) economical. [f. MANAGE[2] + -ING[2]]

mă′nakin *n.* brightly-coloured small tropical Amer. bird of family Pipridae. [var. of MANIKIN]

mañana (manyah′na) *adv.* & *n.* tomorrow (as symbol of easy-going procrastination in Spanish-speaking countries); the indefinite future. [Sp.]

mănatee′ *n.* sirenian of genus *Trichechus*. [f. Sp. *manati* f. Carib *manattouí*]

Mă′nchèster *n.* ∥∼ **goods**, cotton textiles; ∼ **School**, (Hist.) adherents of doctrines of free trade and *laissez-faire*. [∼ in NW England]

mănchinee′l *n.* W. Ind. tree (*Hippomane mancinella*) with poisonous and caustic milky sap and acrid apple-like fruit. [f. F *mancenille* f. Sp. *manzanilla* dim. of *manzana* apple]

Mănchu′ (-ōō′) *a.* & *n.* (member) of Tartar people forming last Chinese imperial dynasty (1644–1912); (of) their language, now spoken in part of NE China. [Manchu, = pure]

mă′nciple *n.* officer who buys provisions for college, one of the Inns of Court, etc. [ME f. AF & OF, f. L *mancipium* purchase (*manceps* buyer f. *manus* hand + *capere* take)]

Măncū′nian *a.* & *n.* (inhabitant) of Manchester; (past or present member) of Manchester Grammar School. [f. L *Mancunium* name of settlement on site of MANCHESTER + -AN]

-măncў *suf.* forming *ns.* w. sense 'divination by' (GEOmancy, NECROMANCY). [f. OF *-mancie* f. LL *-mantia* f. Gk *manteia* divination; see -CY]

Măndae′an *a.* & *n.* (member or language) of a Gnostic sect hostile to Christianity, surviving in Iraq. [f. Aram. *mandaiia* Gnostics (*manda* knowledge) + -AN]

mă′ndala *n.* symbolic circular figure as religious symbol of universe; (Psych.) such symbol in dream, representing dreamer's search for completeness and self-unity. [f. Skr. *máṇḍala* disc]

măndā′mus *n.* judicial writ issued as command to inferior court, or ordering person to perform public or statutory duty. [L, = we command]

mă′ndarin[1] *n.* **1.** (Hist.) Chinese official in any of 9 grades. **2.** (*M*~). standard spoken Chinese language. **3.** party leader; bureaucrat; respected (esp. reactionary) person. **4.** nodding toy figure in Chinese costume. **5.** ~ **collar**, high upright collar not quite meeting in front; ~ **duck**, small Chinese duck (*Aix galericulata*) noted for its bright plumage; ~ **sleeve** (loose and open below elbow). **6.** Hence ~ATE¹ (1, 4) *n*. [f. Port. *mandarim* f. Malay f. Hindi *mantrī* f. Skr. *mantrin* counsellor]

mă'ndarin², -ine (-ēn), *n*. ~ (**orange**), small flat loose-skinned deep-coloured orange. [F *mandarine* perh. f. as prec. 1, w. ref. to yellow robes]

mă'ndatarў *n*. **1.** (Law). one to whom a MANDATE¹ is given. **2.** (Hist.) State receiving mandate. [f. LL *mandatarius* (as foll.; see -ARY¹)]

mă'ndāte¹ *n*. judicial or legal command from superior; commission to act for another, esp. (Hist.) one from League of Nations to a State (the mandatory) to govern former German etc. colony; papal rescript; (poet.) command; (Law) commission by which mandatary undertakes to perform gratuitously some service, with indemnity against loss by him; [after F *mandat*] political authority supposed to be given by electors to (party in) parliament. [f. L *mandatum*, neut. p.p. (as n.) of *mandare* command (*manus* hand, *dare* give); see -ATE¹]

mă'ndā'te² *v.t.* commit (territory etc. *to* mandatary). [f. as prec. + -ATE³]

mă'ndatorў *a.* & *n.* **1.** *a.* of or conveying a command; compulsory. **2.** *n.* = MANDATARY. [f. LL *mandatorius* f. L (as MANDATE¹; see -ORY)]

mă'ndible *n.* jaw, esp. lower jaw in mammals and fishes; upper or lower part of bird's beak; either half of crushing organ in arthropod's mouth-parts; so **mă'ndi'bulAR¹, mă'ndi'bulATE²**, *adjs.* [ME f. OF, or f. LL *mandibula* (*mandere* chew)]

mă'ndō'la *n.* large early form of mandolin. [It.]

mă'ndolin, -ine, *n.* musical instrument of lute kind with paired metal strings, played with plectrum. [F *mandoline* f. It. *mandolino* dim. (as prec.)]

mă'ndō'ra. Var. of MANDOLA.

mă'ndō'rla *n.* = VESICA 2. [It., = almond]

mandrā'gora *n.* = foll., esp. as type of narcotic (Shak. *Othello* III. iii. 330). [OE f. med. L, f. L f. Gk *mandragoras*]

mă'ndrāke *n.* poisonous plant with white or purple flowers and large yellow fruit, and having emetic and narcotic properties, with root once thought to resemble human form and to shriek when plucked. [ME *mandrag(g)e*, prob. f. MDu. *mandrag(r)e* f. med. L as prec., assoc. w. MAN¹, *drake* dragon; cf. DRAKE¹]

mă'ndrel *n.* (In lathe) shaft to which work is fixed while being turned; cylindrical rod round which metal or other material is forged or shaped; ‖miner's pick. [16th c.; orig. unkn.]

mă'ndrill *n.* large fierce W. Afr. baboon (*Mandrillus sphinx*). [prob. f. MAN¹ + DRILL³]

mă'ndūc|āte *v.t.* (literary). chew, eat; so ~A'TION *n.*, ~ātorў *a.* [f. L *manducare* chew (*manduco* guzzler f. *mandere* chew) + -ATE³]

māne *n.* long hair on neck of horse, lion, etc., (fig.) long hair of person; hence **(-)mānED²** (-nd), ~'LESS (-nl-), *adjs.* [OE *manu*, = OHG *mana*, ON *mén* f. Gmc **manō*]

manège, manege, (manā'zh) *n.* riding-school; movements of trained horse; horsemanship. [F *manège* f. It. (as MANAGE¹)]

ma'nes (mah'nāz, mā'nēz) *n. pl.* deified souls of departed ancestors; (as *sing.*) shade of departed person, as object of reverence. [ME f. L]

*maneuver¹·². See MANŒUVRE¹·².

mă'nful *a.* brave, resolute; hence ~LY² *adv.*, ~NESS *n.* [ME, f. MAN¹ + -FUL]

mă'ngabey (-nggabā) *n.* small long-tailed W. Afr. monkey of genus *Cercocebus*. [f. *M*~, region of Madagascar]

mănganēse (mă'nggganēz, -ē'z) *n.* **1.** black mineral used in glass-making etc. **2.** (Chem.) metallic element of which this is the oxide. **3.** Hence **măngă'nIC, mă'nganous**, (-ngg-) *adjs.* [f. F *manganèse*, f. It. *manganese*, alt. f. MAGNESIA]

mānge (-nj) *n.* skin disease in hairy and woolly animals, caused by an arachnid parasite and occas. communicated to man. [ME *mangie, maniewe* f. OF *manjue, mangeue* itch f. *mangier manju-* eat f. L (as MANDUCATE)]

mă'ngel(-wŭrzel), mă'ngold(-wŭrzel), (-ngg-) *n.* large kind of beet, used as cattle food. [G *mangold-wurzel* (*mangold* beet, *wurzel* root)]

mā'nger (-nj-) *n.* long open box or trough in stable etc. for horses or cattle to eat from; DOG¹ *in the manger.* [ME, f. OF *mangeoire, mangeure* f. Rom. *manducatoria f. L (as MANDUCATE; see -ORY)]

ma'nge-tout (mah'nzhtoo) *n.* sugar-pea. [F, = eat-all]

mă'ngle¹ (-nggel) *n.*, & *v.t.* **1.** *n.* machine of two or more cylinders for squeezing water from and pressing washed clothes. **2.** *v.t.* press (clothes) in mangle. [f. Du. *mangel(stok)* (*mangelen* to mangle ult. f. Gk *magganon*; *stok* staff, STOCK)]

mă'ngle² (-nggel) *v.t.* hack, cut about, mutilate, by blows; cut roughly so as to disfigure; spoil (quotation, text, etc.) by gross blunders, make (words) unrecognizable by mispronouncing. [f. AF *ma(ha)ngler*, app. frequent. of *mahaignier* MAIM]

mă'ngō (nggō) *n.* (*pl.* ~es *or* ~s). (Indian tree *Mangifera indica*, bearing) fleshy fruit yellowish-red in colour, eaten ripe or used green for pickles etc. [f. Port. *manga* f. Malay *mangā* f. Tamil *mānkāy* (*mān* mango-tree, *kāy* fruit)]

mangold(-wurzel). See MANGEL.

mă'ngonel (-ngg-) *n.* (Hist.) military engine for throwing stones etc. [ME, f. OF *mangonel(le)*, f. med. L *manganellus* dim. of LL *manganum* f. Gk *magganon*]

mă'ngosteen (-ngg-) *n.* (E. Ind. tree *Garcinia mangostana*, bearing) fruit with thick reddish-brown rind and white juicy pulp. [f. Malay *manggustan*]

mă'ngrove (-ngg-) *n.* tropical tree or shrub of genus *Rhizophora* growing in shore-mud with many tangled roots above ground. [17th c., of uncert. orig.; assim. to GROVE]

mā'ng|ў (-njī) *a.* having the mange; squalid, shabby; hence ~iLY² *adv.*, ~iNESS *n.* [f. MANGE + -Y²]

mănhă'ttan *n.* cocktail made of vermouth, whisky, etc. [f. *M*~, borough of New York]

mă'nhōōd *n.* state of being a man (in any sense; *manhood* SUFFRAGE); manliness, courage; the men of a country. [ME, f. MAN¹ + -HOOD]

mā'nia *n.* mental derangement marked by excitement and violence; excessive enthusiasm (*for* thing, *for* doing). [ME f. LL f. Gk, = madness (*mainomai* be mad, cogn. w. MIND¹; see -IA¹)]

-mā'nia *suf.* denoting (scientifically) a special type of madness (*kleptomania, megalomania, nymphomania*), (pop.) eager pursuit (*bibliomania*) or admiration (*Anglomania*). [f. as prec.]

mā'niăc *a.* & *n.* (person) affected with mania; raving mad(man); hence **mani'acAL** *a.*, **mani'acAL**LY² *adv.* [f. LL f. late Gk *maniakos* (as MANIA; see -AC)]

-mā'niăc *suf.* forming *adjs.* & *ns.* w. sense '(person) affected with -MANIA' (*nymphomaniac*). [f. as prec.]

mā'nic *a.* of or affected by mania; ~**-depressive**, (*a.*) relating to mental disorder with alternating periods of elation and depression, (*n.*) person having such disorder. [f. MANIA + -IC]

Mănichee' (-kē') *n.* adherent of religious system (3rd–5th c.) that represented Satan as coeternal with God; (Philos.) dualist; hence **Mănich(a)e'AN** *a.* & *n.*, **Mănich(a)e'ISM** (3) *n.*, (-kē'-). [f. LL f. late Gk *Manikhaios*, f. *Manes* or *Manichaeus* Persian founder of sect]

mă'nicūr|e *n.*, & *v.t.* **1.** *n.* (one who undertakes professional) cosmetic treatment of hands and finger-nails. **2.** *v.t.* apply manicure treatment to (hands, person). **3.** Hence ∿ist (3) *n.* [F, f. L *manus* hand + *cura* care]

mă'nĭfĕst[1] *n.* cargo-list for use of Customs officers; list of passengers in aircraft or of trucks etc. in goods train. [f. It. MANIFESTO]

mă'nĭfĕst[2] *a.* clear, obvious, to eye or mind; hence ∿LY[2] *adv.* [ME, f. OF *manifeste* or f. L *manifestus* (*manus* hand, *festus* struck)]

mă'nĭfĕst[3] *v.* **1.** *v.t.* show plainly to eye or mind; be evidence of, prove; display, evince, (quality, feeling) by one's acts etc.; (of thing) reveal *itself*; record in a manifest. **2.** *v.i.* (Of ghost) appear. **3.** So ∿ᴀ'ᴛɪᴏɴ *n.*, ∿ᴀᴛɪᴠᴇ (-ĕ's-) *a.* [ME, f. OF *manifester* or f. L *manifestare* (as prec.)]

mănĭfĕ'stō *n.* (*pl.* ∿s). public declaration of policy by sovereign, State, political party, candidate, etc. [It. (*manifestare* f. L, as MANIFEST[2])]

mă'nĭfōld *a.* & *n.* **1.** *a.* (Literary). having various forms, applications, component parts, etc.; performing several functions at once; many and various (*manifold vexations*); hence ∿LY[2] *adv.*, ∿ɴᴇss *n.* **2.** *n.* manifold thing; (Mech.) pipe or chamber with several openings. [OE *manigfeald*, = OHG *managfalt*, Goth. *managfalths* (as MANY, -FOLD)]

mă'nĭkĭn *n.* little man, dwarf; artist's lay figure; anatomical model of the body; = MANAKIN. [f. Du. *manneken*, dim. of *man* MAN[1]; see -KIN]

Manĭ'la *n.* cigar or cheroot as made in Manila; ∿ (**hemp**), strong fibre of a Philippine tree (*Musa textilis*); **m**∿ (**paper**), brown wrapping-paper made from Manila hemp or other material. [∿ in Philippines]

manĭ'lla[1] *n.* metal bracelet used by Afr. tribes as medium of exchange. [Sp., prob. dim. of *mano* hand f. L *manus*]

Manĭ'lla[2]. Var. of MANILA.

manĭ'lle *n.* second best trump or honour in ombre and quadrille. [F, f. Sp. *malilla* dim. of *mala* bad f. L *malus*]

mă'nĭŏc *n.* cassava; flour made from it. [f. Tupi *mandioca*]

mă'nĭple *n.* **1.** (Rom. Ant.) subdivision of legion, containing 120 or 60 men. **2.** Eucharistic vestment, strip hanging from left arm. [OF, or f. L *manipulus* handful, troop, (*manus* hand)]

manĭ'pūl|āte *v.t.* handle, treat, esp. with skill (material, thing, question); manage (person, property, etc.) by dextrous (esp. unfair) use of influence etc.; (Surg.) manually examine and treat part of body for fracture etc.; hence or cogn. ∿ABLE *a.*, ∿ᴀ'ᴛɪᴏɴ, ∿ᴀᴛᴏʀ, *ns.*, ∿ᴀᴛɪᴠᴇ, ∿ᴀᴛᴏʀʏ, *adjs.* [back-form. f. *manipulation* f. F f. mod. L *manipulatio* (*manipulare* f. as prec.), after F *manipuler*; see -ATE[3]]

Manit. *abbr.* Manitoba.

mă'nĭtou (-ōō) *n.* (Amer. Ind.) good or evil spirit as object of reverence; thing having supernatural power. [f. Algonquin *manito, -tu* he has surpassed]

mănkĭnd (-n-k-) *n.* **1.** (-ī'-). human species. **2.** (mă'-). men in general. [ME, f. MAN[1]+KIND[1]]

mă'nlīke *a.* having (good or bad) qualities of a man; (of woman) mannish; (of animal) resembling a human being. [ME, f. MAN[1]+-LIKE]

mă'nl|ȳ *a.* having a man's virtues, courage, frankness, etc.; (of woman) having a man's qualities; (of things, quality, etc.) befitting a man; hence ∿ɪɴᴇss *n.* [ME, f. MAN[1]+-LY[1]]

mă'nna *n.* substance miraculously supplied as food to Israelites in the wilderness (Exod. 16); spiritual nourishment, esp. the Eucharist; sweet dried juice from ∿-ash (*Fraxinus ornus*) and other plants, used as mild laxative; unexpected benefit. [OE f. LL f. Gk, f. Aram. *mannā* f. Heb. *mān*, explained as = *mān hū?* what is it?, but prob. = Arab. *mann* exudation of common tamarisk (*Tamarix gallica*)]

mănned (-nd) *a.* (Of aircraft, spacecraft, etc.) containing human crew. [p.p. of MAN[2]]

mă'nnĕquin (-kĭn) *n.* person, usu. woman, employed by dressmaker etc. to display clothes by wearing them; dummy for display of clothes in shop. [F, = MANIKIN]

mă'nner *n.* **1.** way a thing is done or happens (*in* or *after this manner*); **adverb of** ∿, one that asks or tells how; **to the** ∿ **born**, (Shak. *Hamlet* ɪ. iv. 15) destined by birth to be subject to the custom, (colloq.) naturally fitted for the position etc. **2.** (in *pl.*) modes of life, conditions of society; **comedy of** ∿s (with satirical portrayal of these in a society). **3.** outward bearing, style of utterance etc. **4.** (in *pl.*) behaviour in social intercourse (*good, bad*, etc., *manners*); polite social behaviour, habits indicating good breeding (*he has no manners*); hence ∿ʟᴇss *a.* **5.** style in literature or art (*sketch in the manner of Rembrandt*); mannerism. **6.** (arch.) kind, sort, (*what manner of man is he?*). **7. all** ∿ **of**, (see ALL 1); **no** ∿ **of**, no . . . at all; **in a** ∿ (of speaking), in some sense, to some extent, so[1] to speak; *manner of means* (see MEAN[1] 5). [ME f. AF *manere*, OF *maniere* f. Rom. *manuaria mode of handling, fem. (as n.) of L *manuarius* of the hand (*manus*); see -ARY[1]]

mă'nnered (-erd) *a.* behaving (in specified way: *ill*, WELL-, *rough*, *-mannered*); (of style, artist, writer) showing mannerism. [ME, f. prec.+-ED[2]]

mă'nner|ism *n.* excessive addiction to a distinctive manner in art or literature; trick of style; trick or gesture of speech (esp. of an actor); style of Italian art preceding Baroque, with contorted figures; hence ∿ist (2) *n.*, ∿i'stic(AL) *adjs.* [f. MANNER+-ISM]

mă'nnerl|ȳ *a.* & *adv.* **1.** *a.* well-mannered, polite; hence ∿ɪɴᴇss *n.* **2.** *adv.* politely. [f. MANNER+-LY[1,2]]

mă'nnĭkĭn. Var. of MANIKIN.

mă'nnĭsh *a.* (Of woman, usu. derog.) masculine; characteristic of man as opp. to woman (*his mannish air of superiority*); hence ∿ɴᴇss *n.* [OE *mennisc* f. (& assim. to) MAN[1]+-ISH[1]]

‖**manœu'vre**[1], ***maneu'ver**[1], (-nōō'ver) *n.* planned and controlled movement, (in *pl.*) large-scale exercise, of troops, warships, etc.; deceptive or elusive movement; skilful plan; MASS[2] *of manœuvre*. [F *manœuvre* (as foll.)]

‖**manœu'vr|e**[2], ***maneu'ver**[2], (-nōō'ver) *v.i.* & *t.* perform, cause (troops etc.) to perform, manœuvres; employ artifice; force, drive, manipulate, (person, thing, *into, out, away*, etc.) by scheming or adroitness; hence ∿ABLE *a.*, ∿ER[1] *n.* [f. F *manœuvrer* f. med. L *man(u)operare* f. L *manus* hand + *operari* to work]

manŏ'mĕter *n.* pressure-gauge for gases and liquids; hence **mănomĕ'tr**ɪc *a.* [f. F *manomètre* f. Gk *manos* thin; see -METER]

ma non troppo. See TROPPO.

mă'nor *n.* **1.** English territorial unit, orig. of nature of feudal lordship, now consisting of lord's demesne and of lands from whose holders he may exact certain fees etc.; **lord of the** ∿, person or corporation having rights of this; ∿(-house), his mansion; hence **manor'**IAL *a.* **2.** (sl.) unit area of police administration. [ME, f. AF *maner*, OF *maneir*, f. L *manēre* remain]

manqué (mah'nkā) *a.* (placed after *n.*) that might have been but is not, that has missed being, (*a Napoleon, comic actor, manqué*). [F, p.p. of *manquer* lack]

mă'nsard *n.* ∿ (**roof**), roof of which each face has two slopes, the lower one steeper. [f. F *mansarde* f. Mansard, Fr. architect d. 1666]

mănse *n.* ecclesiastical residence, esp. Scottish Presbyterian minister's house; **son** or **daughter of the** ∿, child of Presbyterian etc. minister. [ME, f. med. L *mansus, -sa, -sum*, house (*manēre* mans- remain)]

-manship *suf.* forming *ns.* denoting skill in subject or activity, esp. when used to disconcert another person. [orig. in GAMESMANSHIP after *craftsmanship*, *sportsmanship*, etc.]

mă'nsion (-shon) *n.* large residence (‖in *pl.* often of large buildings divided into flats); ‖∿-house, house of lord of manor or landed proprietor, official residence, esp. (**the M**∿ **House**) of Lord Mayor of London. [ME f. OF f. L *mansio -onis* a staying (as MANSE; see -ION)]

mä'nsuetüde (-swĭ-) *n.* (arch.) meekness, docility, gentleness. [ME f. OF, or f. L *mansuetudo* (*mansuetus* gentle, tame f. *manus* hand + *suetus* accustomed; see -TUDE)]

mä'nta *n.* large RAY[3] of genus *Manta*. [Amer. Sp., = blanket]

mä'ntel *n.* ～(**piece**), (1) structure of wood, marble, etc., above and around fireplace, (2) = *mantelshelf*; ～(**shelf**), shelf projecting from wall above fireplace. [var. of MANTLE[1]]

mä'ntelet *n.* (Hist.) short loose sleeveless mantle etc.; bullet-proof screen for gunners. [ME f. OF, dim. of *mantel* MANTLE[1]; see -ET[1]]

mä'ntic *a.* of divination. [f. Gk *mantikos* (*mantis* prophet; see -IC)]

-mä'ntic *suf.* forming *adjs.* corresp. to *ns.* in -MANCY (*necromantic*). [f. as prec.]

mäntï'lla *n.* lace scarf worn by Spanish woman over hair and shoulders. [Sp., dim. of *manta* MANTLE[1]]

mä'ntis *n.* (*pl.* same). orthopterous insect of genus *Mantis*; **praying** ～, species that holds forelegs in position suggesting hands folded in prayer. [Gk, = prophet]

mäntï'ssa *n.* fractional part of logarithm. [L, = makeweight]

mä'ntle[1] *n.* **1.** loose sleeveless cloak esp. of woman; (fig.) covering. **2.** fragile lacelike tube fixed round gas-jet to give incandescent light. **3.** outer fold of skin enclosing mollusc's viscera. **4.** bird's back, scapulars, and wing-coverts esp. if of distinctive colour. **5.** (Geol.) region between crust and core of earth. [ME f. OF, f. L *mantellum* cloak]

mä'ntle[2] *v.* **1.** *v.t.* clothe (as) in mantle; cover, conceal, envelop. **2.** *v.i.* (Of liquid) become covered with coating or scum; (of blood) suffuse cheeks, (of face) glow, with blush. [ME, f. prec.]

mä'ntlet. Var. of MANTELET.

mä'ntling *n.* (Her.) ornamental (representation of) drapery etc. behind and around shield. [f. MANTLE[1],[2] + -ING[1]]

mä'ntra *n.* Vedic hymn; Hindu or Buddhist devotional incantation. [Skr., = instrument of thought (*man* think)]

mä'ntua *n.* (Hist.) woman's loose gown in 17th–18th c.; ～**-maker**, dressmaker. [corrupt. of *manteau* (F, as MANTLE[1]), after *M*～ in Italy]

mä'nual *a.* & *n.* **1.** *a.* of, done with, the hands (*manual labour*); worked by hand, not by automatic equipment, (*manual fire-engine, gear-change, telephone exchange*); ～ **alphabet,** deaf-and-dumb alphabet; SIGN[1] *manual*; hence ～LY[2] *adv.* **2.** *n.* small book for handy use; reference book, textbook, handbook; organ keyboard played with hands not feet; (Mil.) exercise in handling rifle etc.; (Hist.) book of the forms to be used by priests in the administration of the Sacraments. [ME f. OF *manuel*, f. (& later assim. to) L *manualis* (*manus* hand; see -AL)]

mänüfa'ctory *n.* place where product is manufactured; factory, workshop. [f. foll., after *factory*]

mänüfa'cture[1] *n.* making of articles by physical labour or machinery, esp. on large scale; branch of such industry (*woollen manufacture*; **of home, English,** etc., ～, made at home etc.); (derog.) merely mechanical production (*of* literature etc.). [F, f. It. *manifattura*, & L *manufactum* made by hand; see -URE]

mänüfa'cture|e[2] *v.t.* bring (material) into form fit for use; produce (articles) by labour, esp. by machinery on large scale, (derog.) of literary work etc.; invent, fabricate, (evidence, story); hence ～ER[1] *n.* [f. prec.]

manu'ka (manoō'-, mah'nu-) *n.* (Austral. & NZ) tree or shrub of genus *Leptospermum*, with aromatic leaves and hard timber. [Maori]

mänümï't *v.t.* (-tt-). (Hist.) set (slave) free; so **mänümï'ssion** *n.* [ME, f. L *manumittere* (*manus* hand, *emittere* emiss- send forth)]

manür'e[1] *n.* any substance, e.g. dung or compost or

artificial material, (to be) spread over or mixed with soil to fertilize it; hence **manür'ial** *a.* [f. foll.]

manür'e[2] *v.t.* apply manure to (land etc., or abs.; lit. or fig.). [ME, f. AF *mainoverer* = OF *manouvrer* MANŒUVRE[2]]

mä'nüscript *a.* & *n.* (book, document, state of being) written by hand or typed, not printed; author's copy in this form, submitted for publication. [f. med. L *manuscriptus* (*manu* by hand, *scriptus* p.p. of *scribere* write)]

mä'nward *a.* (arch.) tending or directed towards man. [ME, f. MAN[1] + -WARD]

Mänx *a.* & *n.* **1.** *a.* of the Isle of Man; ～ **cat,** tailless variety; ～'**man,** native or inhabitant of Isle of Man. **2.** *n.* Celtic language of Isle of Man; (as *pl.*) the Manx people. [f. ON *Mänskr (*Mön Man-* f. OIr. *Manu* Isle of Man, -*skr* -ISH[1])]

ma'nÿ (mĕ'-) *a.* (MORE, MOST) & *n.* great in number, numerous, (*many times*; (poet. or rhet.) *many a time* (*and oft*), *many and many a time*; *many people wish, many wish, many of us wish, a man wishes*; *how many* (*of them*) *can I have?*; *as many* (*of them*) *as you like*; *his reasons were many and good*); **as** ～, that number of (*six mistakes in as many lines*); **as** ～ **again,** the same number additionally (*sixty here and as many again in London*); ～'**s the,** there are many — s that (*many's the tale he has told us*); ～'**s the time,** often (*many's the time I have seen you do it*); **the** ～, the multitude of people; **the one and the** ～, (Philos.) unity and plurality; **one too** ～, not wanted, in the way; **be (one) too** ～ **for,** outwit, baffle; **a good, a great,** ～, a fair, a large, number; ～**-headed beast, monster,** the populace; ～**plies,** third STOMACH of ruminant; ～**-sided,** having many sides, aspects, capabilities, interests, etc. [OE *manig*, = OS, OHG *manag*, Goth. *manags* f. Gmc *managaz]

mänzanï'lla *n.* pale very dry Spanish sherry. [Sp., lit. 'camomile']

mänzanï'ta (-ē'-) *n.* Californian shrub of genus *Arctostaphylos*. [Sp., dim. of *manzana* apple]

Mao (mow) *a.* of style worn in Communist China (*Mao cap, jacket,* etc.). [f. Mao Zedong, Chinese Communist statesman d. 1976]

Mao'|ism (mow'-) *n.* Communist doctrines of Mao Zedong; hence ～IST (2) *n.* [f. as prec. + -ISM]

Maor'i (mowr'ĭ) *n.* & *a.* (member or language) of brown Polynesian aboriginal race in New Zealand; ～**land,** New Zealand. [native name]

mäp[1] *n.* representation (usu. on plane surface, cf *globe*) of (part of) earth's surface, showing physical and political features etc., or of the heavens, showing positions of stars etc.; (sl.) face; (**wipe**) **off the** ～, (colloq.) (render) of no account, obsolete, in(to) oblivion, very distant; **on the** ～, (colloq.) to be reckoned with, prominent, important (*put on the* ～, make prominent etc.); hence ～'LESS *a.* [f. L *mappa* napkin; in med. L *mappa* (*mundi*) map of world]

mäp[2] *v.t.* (-pp-). represent on map; (Math.) associate each element of (set) with one element of another set; ～ **out,** plan, arrange in detail (course of conduct, one's time, etc.). [f. prec.]

mä'ple *n.* tree or shrub of genus *Acer* grown for shade, ornament, wood, or sugar; its wood; ～**-leaf,** emblem of Canada; ～ **sugar** (got by evaporating sap of sugar maple etc.); *maple* SYRUP. [ME *mapul* etc., f. OE *mapeltrēow, mapulder*]

maquë'tte (-k-) *n.* sculptor's small preliminary model in wax, clay, etc.; preliminary sketch. [F, f. It. *machietta* dim. of *macchia* spot]

maquïllage (mahkĭyah'zh) *n.* (applying of) make-up or cosmetics. [F (*maquiller* make up f. OF *masquiller* stain; see -AGE)]

Ma'quis (mah'kē) *n.* secret army of patriots in France during German occupation (1940–45); member of this. [F, = brushwood, f. Corsican It. *macchia* thicket]

mär *v.t.* (-rr-). impair fatally, ruin, esp. *make* (or *mend*) *or mar*; spoil, disfigure, impair perfection of; ～'**plot,**

one who hinders undertaking by officiousness. [OE *merran*, = OS *merrian* hinder, OHG *merren*, ON *merja* bruise, Goth. *marzjan* cause to stumble]

Mar. *abbr.* March.

ma᷅'rabou (-boo) *n.* large W. Afr. stork; = ADJUTANT 2; tuft of down from wing or tail of marabou as trimming for hat etc. [F, f. Arab. (as foll.), the stork being regarded as holy]

ma᷅'rabout[1] (-boot) *n.* Muslim hermit or monk, esp. in N. Africa; shrine marking marabout's burial--place. [F, f. Port. *marabuto* f. Arab. *murābiṭ* holy man (*ribāṭ* frontier station, where he acquired merit by combat against the infidel)]

marabout[2]. Var. of MARABOU.

mara᷅'ca *n.* hand-held clublike gourd containing beans, beads, etc., shaken (usu. in pairs) as percussion instrument. [f. Port. *maracá*, prob. f. Tupi]

maraschi'no (-kē'-) *n.* (*pl.* ~s). strong sweet liqueur from a small black Dalmatian cherry; ~ **cherry** (preserved in this). [It. (*marasca* small black cherry, for *amarasca* f. *amaro* bitter f. L *amarus*)]

mara᷅'sm|us (-z-) *n.* wasting away of body; hence ~IC *a.* [mod. L, f. Gk *marasmos* (*maraino* wither)]

Mara᷅'tha, Mahra'tta, (mara᷅'-, -rah'-) *n.* member of a warlike Indian race; so **Mara'thi, Mahra'tti,** (mara᷅'tī, -rah'-) *n.*, their language. [f. Hindi *Marhaṭṭa* f. Skr. *Māhārāshṭra* great kingdom]

ma᷅'rathon *n.* long-distance road race, esp. of 26 miles 385 yards (42.195 km.) as a principal event of modern Olympic Games; feat of endurance, undertaking of long duration (often *attrib.*). [f. *M*~ in Greece, scene of decisive battle in 490 BC, whence messenger ran with news to Athens]

marau'd *v.i.* & *t.* make plundering raid (on); go about pilfering; plunder; hence ~ER[1] *n.* [f. F *marauder* (*maraud* rogue)]

ma᷅rave'di (-va᷅'-) *n.* (Hist.) gold or copper Spanish coin. [ME f. Sp., f. Arab. *Murābiṭīn* MARABOUT[1]'s, Moorish dynasty at Cordova 1087–1147]

ma᷅r'ble *n.*, & *v.t.* **1.** *n.* limestone in metamorphic crystalline (or granular) state and capable of taking polish, used in sculpture and architecture; this as type of hardness or durability or smoothness (often *attrib.*); (in *pl.*) collection of sculptures (*Elgin Marbles*); ~ **cake** (with mottled appearance, made of light and dark sponge). **2.** small ball of marble, clay, glass, etc., as toy; (in *pl.*) game using these, *(sl.)* one's mental faculties. **3.** Hence **ma᷅r'bly**[2] *a.* **4.** *v.t.* (esp. in *p.p.*) stain, colour, (paper, edges of book, soap) to look like variegated marble; (in *p.p.*, of meat) streaked with alternating layers of lean and fat. [ME, f. OF *marbre*, *marble*, f. L *marmor* f. Gk *marmaros* shining stone]

ma᷅rc *n.* refuse of pressed grapes etc.; brandy made from this. [F (*marcher* tread, MARCH[5])]

Ma᷅r'can *a.* of St. Mark. [f. L *Marcus* Mark + -AN]

ma᷅r'casīte *n.* crystallized iron pyrites; piece of this as adornment. [ME, f. med. L *marcasita*, f. Arab. *markaṣīṭā* f. Pers.; assoc. w. -ITE[1] (2)]

marca'tō (-ah'-) *adv.* & *a.* (Mus.) (with each note) played with emphasis. [It., = marked]

ma᷅rce'l *n.*, & *v.t.* (-ll-). **1.** *n.* ~ (**wave**), kind of deep wave in hair. **2.** *v.t.* wave (hair) thus. [f. *Marcel* Grateau, Paris hairdresser d. 1936, who invented the method]

marce'sc|ent *a.* (Of part of plant) withering but not falling; hence ~ENCE *n.* [f. L *marcescere* incept. of *marcēre* wither; see -ESCENT]

Ma᷅rch[1] *n.* third month of year; March HARE. [ME, f. OF *march*(*e*), dial. var. of *marz*, *mars*, f. L *Martius* (*mensis* month) of Mars]

ma᷅rch[2] *n.* (Hist.) boundary, frontiers, (often in *pl.*, esp. of borderland between England and Scotland or Wales); tract of (often disputed) land between two countries; hence **ma᷅r'cher**[1] [-ER[1] (4)] *n.* [ME, f. OF *marche* f. Rom. *marca* f. OFrank. *marka f. Gmc *markō MARK[1]]

ma᷅rch[3] *v.i.* (Of country, estate, etc.) border *upon*, have

common frontier *with*. [ME, f. OF *marchir* (*marche*; see prec.)]

ma᷅rch[4] *n.* **1.** (Mil.) marching of troops; **line** (route) **of** ~; ~ **past**, marching of troops in line past saluting-point at review; **on the** ~, marching, (fig.) in steady progress. **2.** long toilsome walk; procession as protest or demonstration; progress (*of* events, time, intellect, mind). **3.** distance covered by troops in a day; FORCE[2]*d march*; STEAL *a march on*. **4.** uniform step of troops etc. (*quick*, *slow*, *march*). **5.** (Mus.) composition meant to accompany march (DEAD *march*). [f. foll. or F *marche* (*marcher*; see foll.)]

ma᷅rch[5] *v.* **1.** *v.i.* walk *away*, *forth*, *past* (reviewing officer or sovereign), *out*, etc., in military manner with regular and measured tread; advance thus *on* (place to be attacked). **2.** walk or proceed steadily (also fig. of events). **3.** ||~**ing order,** equipment or formation for marching; ~**ing orders,** direction for troops to depart for war etc., (fig.) dismissal. **4.** *v.t.* cause to march or go *away*, *on*, *off*, etc. **5.** Hence **ma᷅r'cher**[2] [-ER[1]] *n.* [f. F *marcher*, f. Gallo-Rom. *marcare f. LL *marcus* hammer]

ma᷅r'cher[1,2]. See MARCH[2,5].

ma᷅r'chioness (-sho-) *n.* marquis's wife or widow; woman holding rank of marquis in her own right. [f. med. L *marchionissa* (*marchio -onis* captain of the marches f. as MARCH[2]; see -ESS[1])]

ma᷅r'chpāne. Var. (arch.) of MARZIPAN.

ma᷅rcō'ni *n.* & *v.* (arch.). **1.** *n.* = foll. **2.** *v.t.* & *i.* send (message) thus. [f. G. *Marconi*, It. inventor of system of wireless telegraphy d. 1937]

ma᷅rcō'nigram *n.* (arch.) message sent by Marconi's system of wireless telegraphy. [f. as prec. + -GRAM]

Ma᷅rdi Gra's (ma᷅rdē grah') *n.* (merry-making on) Shrove Tuesday; last day of carnival. [F, = fat Tuesday]

ma᷅r'e[1] *n.* (*pl.* maria *pr.* ma᷅r'īa). **1.** ~ **clau'sum,** sea under jurisdiction of particular country; ~ **li'berum,** sea open to all nations. **2.** (Astron.) large dark flat area on moon, once thought to be sea; similar area on Mars. [L, = sea]

ma᷅re[2] *n.* female of equine animal, esp. horse; GREY[1] *mare*; SHANKS's *mare*; ~'s **nest,** illusory discovery; ~'s-**tail,** (1) tall slender marsh plant (*Hippuris vulgaris*), (2, in *pl.*) long straight streaks of cirrus cloud. [OE *mēre etc., = MDu., MLG *mer(r)ie*, OHG *mar(i)ha*, ON *merr* f. Gmc *marhjōn (*marhaz horse f. IE *markos; cf. MARSHAL[1])]

ma᷅re'mma *n.* low marshy unhealthy country by seashore. [It., f. L *maritima* (as MARITIME)]

ma᷅rgarine (ma᷅rjerē'n, -g-, ma᷅r'-) *n.* butter--substitute made from edible oils and animal fats with milk etc. [F, misapplication of a chem. term, f. *margarique* f. Gk *margaron* pearl; see -IC, -IN[1], -INE[5]]

ma᷅r'gay *n.* small S. Amer. tiger-cat (*Felis tigrina*). [f. Tupi *mbaracaïa*]

ma᷅rge[1] *n.* (poet.) margin. [F, f. L (as MARGIN)]

ma᷅rge[2] *n.* (colloq.) margarine. [abbr.]

ma᷅r'gent *n.* (arch. or poet.) = foll. [alt. as in *ancient*, *pageant*, etc.]

ma᷅r'gin *n.*, & *v.t.* **1.** edge or border of surface; hence ~ATE[2], ~āt ED[1], *adjs.* **2.** condition near the limit below or beyond which a thing ceases to be possible etc.; extra amount (of time, money, etc.) over and above the necessary or minimum (*by a narrow margin*; *margin of profit*, *of safety*); sum deposited with stock-broker to cover risk of loss on transaction on account; ~ **of error,** (slight) difference allowed for miscalculation or mischance. **3.** plain space beside main body of print etc. on page; ~ **release,** device on typewriter to continue word etc. into margin normally imposed by adjustable stop. **4.** *v.t.* furnish with margin or marginal notes. [ME, f. L *margo -ginis*]

ma᷅r'ginal *a.* of, written in, the margin; having marginal notes; of, at, the edge; (of sea) adjacent to shore of a State; (of land) difficult to cultivate and yielding little profit; close to the limit (esp. of no further profit etc.); barely adequate or provided for (‖∼ **seat**, one where MP has only small majority and is likely to be unseated at next election); ∼ **cost** (added by making one extra copy, etc.). [f. med. L *marginalis* (as prec.; see -AL)]

margina′lia *n. pl.* marginal notes. [med. L, neut. pl. of *marginalis*; see prec., -IA²]

mar′grave *n.* (Hist.) hereditary title of some princes of Holy Roman Empire (orig. military governor of border province). [f. MDu. *markgrave* border count (as MARK¹, *grave* COUNT³ f. OLG *grēve*)]

mar′gravine (-ēn) *n.* margrave's wife. [f. Du. *markgravin* (as prec.; see -INE³)]

mar′gueri′te (-gerē′t) *n.* ox-eye daisy. [F, f. L *margarita* f. Gk *margaritēs* (*margaron* pearl; see -ITE¹)]

mar′ia. See MARE¹.

mariage de convenance (mǎrīahzh de kaw′n-venahns) *n.* = *marriage of* CONVENIENCE. [F]

Mar′ian *a.* & *n.* (devotee) of the Virgin Mary, Mary I Queen of England, or Mary Queen of Scots; English Catholic of 1553–58. [f. L *Maria* Mary + -AN]

ma′rigold *n.* plant of genus *Calendula* or *Tagetes*, with golden or bright yellow flowers; CORN¹ *marigold*; MARSH *marigold*. [ME, f. *Mary* (prob. the Virgin) + dial. *gold* marigold]

marijua′na, -hua′na, (mǎrīhwah′na) *n.* dried leaves, flowering tops, and stems of HEMP (sense 1), used to make a hallucinogenic drug esp. for cigarettes (*reefers*). [Amer. Sp.]

mari′mba *n.* xylophone of Afr. & Central-Amer. natives; modern orchestral instrument evolved from this. [Congo]

mari′na (-ē′-) *n.* place with moorings for pleasure-yachts etc. [It. & Sp. fem. a., f. *marino* f. L (as MARINE)]

marina′de *n.*, & *v.t.* **1.** *n.* mixture of wine, vinegar, oil, herbs, spices, etc. used to enhance flavour; fish or meat treated with this **2.** *v.t.* steep in marinade. [F, f. Sp. *marinada* (*marinar* pickle in brine, f *marino*, as MARINE, see -ADE)]

ma′rinate *v.t.* = prec. 2. [f. It. *marinare* or F *mariner* (as foll.) + -ATE³]

mari′ne (-ē′n) *a.* & *n.* **1.** *a.* of, found in, produced by, the sea; of shipping or naval matters (*marine insurance*; ∼ **stores**, new or old ships' material and similar odds and ends as merchandise); for use at sea; *marine* TRUMPET, **2.** *n.* country's shipping, fleet, or navy, (*esp. mercantile* or *merchant marine*). **3.** sea picture. **4.** member of body of troops trained to serve on land or sea (‖ROYAL *Marines*); **tell that to the (horse)** ∼**s**, (colloq.) you will not deceive me with that. [MF, f OF *marin* marine f. L *marinus* (*mare* sea; see -INE¹)]

ma′riner *n.* seaman; **master** ∼, (seaman certified competent to be) captain of merchant ship; ∼**'s compass**, = COMPASS 3. [ME f. AF; OF *marinier* f. med. L *marinarius* f. L (as prec.; see -ER²)]

Mă′riŏ′latrў *n.* (derog.) worship of the Virgin Mary. [f. L *Maria* Mary + -LATRY, after *idolatry*]

mǎrionĕ′tte *n.* puppet worked by strings. [f. F *marionnette* (*Marion* dim. of *Marie* Mary; see -ETTE)]

ma′rish *n.* & *a.* (arch.) marsh(y). [ME & OF *mareis* f. med. L *mariscus* f. WG (as MARSH)]

Mar′ist *n.* member of RC Society of Mary. [f. F *Mariste* (*Marie* Mary; see -IST)]

marital (mǎ′rĭt-, merī′t-) *a.* of a husband; of or between husband and wife; of marriage; hence ∼**LY²** *adv.* [f. L *maritalis* (*maritus* husband; see -AL)]

ma′ritime *a.* living or found near the sea; connected with the sea or seafaring (*maritime insurance*). [f. L *maritimus* (*mare* sea)]

mar′joram *n.* aromatic herb of genus *Origanum* or *Majorana*, used in cookery. [ME & OF *majorane*, f. med. L *majorana*, of unkn. orig.]

mark¹ *n.* **1.** target or other object to be aimed at; (sl.) intended victim of swindler etc.; (Boxing) pit of stomach; **beside, off, wide of, the** ∼, not hitting it,

(fig.) not to the point, irrelevant; EASY *mark*. **2.** desired object (*hit, miss,* OVERSHOOT¹, *the mark*); one's ∼, (sl.) what one prefers. **3.** sign, indication, (*of* quality, character, feeling, etc.); ∼ **of mouth**, depression in horse's incisor tooth indicating age; *mark of the* BEAST. **4.** affixed or impressed sign, seal, etc. for distinction or identification; (followed by numeral) particular design of piece of equipment etc. **5.** cross etc. made in place of signature by illiterate person. **6.** written or printed symbol; this as sign of good or bad conduct, or as characterizing quality of work; EXCLAMATION, PUNCTUATION, QUESTION¹, *mark*; BLACK¹ *mark*. **7.** unit of numerical award of merit in examination (*he gained 46 marks,* FULL¹ *marks*). **8.** line etc. serving to indicate position; piece of material used to indicate position on SOUND³ing-line; runner's starting-point in race (*get on your marks*); **off the** ∼, having made a start; **on the** ∼, (smartly) ready to start; **below, up to,** etc., **the** ∼ (the usual standard, esp. of person's health). **9.** (Rugby & Austral. Footb.) heel-mark on ground made by player who has caught the ball direct from kick or knock-on or throw-forward by opponent. **10.** trace, visible sign, left by person or thing; stain, scar, etc.; BIRTHmark; **make** one's ∼, attain distinction; **of** ∼, noteworthy; (as apology for mentioning anything horrible etc.) **(God) save the** ∼ (freq. sarcastic or impatiently scornful). **11.** (Hist.) tract of land held in common by Teutonic or medieval German village community. [OE *me(a)rc,* = OS *marka,* OHG *marcha,* ON *mörk,* Goth. *marka* f. Gmc **markō* boundary]

mark² *v.t.* **1.** make a mark on (thing or person) by stamping, cutting, writing, hitting, etc.; put distinguishing or identifying mark or name to or on (clothes etc.); give distinctive character to (*to mark the occasion*); attach figures indicating prices to (goods); (in *pass.*) have natural marks (*is marked with silver spots*). **2.** ∼ **out**, trace out boundaries for (ground), plan (course), destine (*marked out for slaughter*). **3.** ∼ **off**, separate (thing *from* another, lit. or fig.) by boundary. **4.** name or indicate (place on map, length of syllable) by signs or marks. **5.** record (points gained in games); allot marks to (student's work etc.); = READ 10. **6.** manifest (one's displeasure etc. *by*). **7.** accompany, be a feature of, (*no triumph marks her manner; day was marked by severe storms*). **8.** ∼ **time**, move feet as in marching, but without advancing, (fig.) act routinely or unprogressively, await opportunity to advance. **9.** see, notice; observe mentally (*mark my words; without any obligation, mark you*); ∼ **(down),** note and remember spot where (grouse etc.) has settled, choose as one's victim etc. **10.** ‖(Footb. etc.) keep close to (opponent) so as to hamper him if he receives ball. **11.** ∼ **down,** mark at a lower price; ∼ **up,** mark at a higher price; ∼-*up n.,* amount added by shopkeeper to cost-price of goods to cover overhead charges and profit. [OE *mearcian* = OS *markon,* OHG *marchōn,* ON *marka* observe, f. WG **markōjan* (as prec.)]

mark³ *n.* **1.** (Hist.) denomination of weight for gold and silver; English money of account. **2.** monetary unit in Germany and Finland. [OE *marc,* = MDu. *marc,* MHG *marke,* ON *mörk,* prob. rel. to med. L *marca, marcus*]

mark|ed (-kt) *a.* In vbl senses; (clearly) noticeable or evident (*a marked difference*), whence ∼'**edLY²** *adv.,* ∼'**edNESS** *n.;* (of playing-cards) given distinctive marks on their backs to assist cheating; **∼ed man,** (1) one whose conduct is watched with suspicion or hostility, (2) one expected to reach eminence. [OE (p.p. of MARK²)]

mar′ker *n.* In vbl senses; one who marks down game; one who records score, esp. in billiards; flare etc. to direct aircraft pilot to target; bookmark; memorial stone etc.; thing to mark place reached. [ME, f. MARK² + -ER¹]

mar′ket¹ *n.* **1.** gathering of people for purchase and sale of provisions, livestock, etc.; time of this; **bring**

one's **eggs** or **hogs to a bad** ∼, fail in one's schemes. **2.** open space or covered building in which provisions, cattle, etc., are exposed for sale. **3. make a** ∼ **of,** (fig.) barter away. **4.** demand (*for* commodity or service; *goods find a ready market*); place or class where there is such demand; conditions as regards, opportunity for, buying or selling; *the* (corn etc.) trade; **be in the** ∼ **for,** wish to buy; **be on the** ∼, **come into the** ∼, be offered for sale; **put on the** ∼, offer for sale; BUYer's, SELLer's, market. **5.** BLACK[1] market; (European) **Common M**∼, ‖**the M**∼, the European Economic Community, an economic and political association of certain European countries as a unit with internal free trade and common external tariffs; MONEY-market; STOCK-market. **6.** rate of purchase and sale, market value, (*the market fell*); PLAY[1] *the market*; **down-**∼, **up-**∼, in the direction of lower-priced, higher-priced, goods. **7.** ∼ **cross** (erected in market-place); ∼**-day** (on which market is held, usu. weekly); ‖∼ **garden** (in which vegetables are grown for market); ∼ **overt,** open market; ∼**-place,** open space in town, where market is held, (fig.) scene of actual dealings; ∼ **price** (in current dealings); ∼ **research,** study of possible buyers for one's goods; ∼ **town** (where market is held); ∼ **value,** value as saleable thing (dist. from cost and from BOOK[1] value). [ME f. OS -*market*, OHG -*marchāt* f. L *mercatus* (*mercari* buy; see MERCHANT)]

mar'ket[2] v. **1.** v.i. buy or sell in market. **2.** v.t. sell (goods) in market or elsewhere; hence ∼ABLE a., ∼ING[1] (1) n. [ME, f. prec.]

mar'khor (-kōr) n. large spiral-horned wild goat of N. India. [f. Pers. *mār-ḳwār* (*mār* serpent, *ḳwār* -eating)]

mar'king n. In vbl senses; colouring of feathers, skin, etc.; identification symbol on aircraft etc.; ∼**-ink** (indelible, for marking linen etc.). [ME, f. MARK[2] + -ING[1]]

mar'ksman n. (*pl.* -men). one skilled or practised in aiming at mark, esp. one who attains certain standard of proficiency in rifle practice; hence ∼SHIP (1, 3) n. [f. MARK[1] + 's l + MAN[1]]

marl[1] n., & v.t. **1.** n. soil consisting of clay and lime, a valuable fertilizer; hence ∼'Y[2] a. **2.** v.t. apply marl to (ground). [ME, f. OF *marle* f. med. L *margila* f. L *marga*]

marl[2] n. mottled yarn of differently coloured threads; fabric made from it. [f. MARBLEd]

Marlbur'ian (mär-, môr-) a. & n. (past or present member) of Marlborough College. [f. *Marlborough* (as if *Marlbury*) + -IAN]

*****mar'lin** n. large sea-fish of genus *Makaira*. [f. MARLINSPIKE, w. ref. to its pointed snout]

mar'line n. (Naut.) thin line of two strands; ∼**-spike,** = foll. [ME, f. Du. *marlijn* (*marren* bind, *lijn* LINE[2])]

mar'linspike n. (Naut.) pointed iron tool used to separate strands of rope or wire. [orig. app. *marling-spike* f. *marl* fasten with marline (f. Du. *marlen* frequent. of MDu. *marren* bind) + -ING[1] + SPIKE[1]]

mar'lite n. kind of marl that is not reduced to powder by action of air. [f. MARL[1] + -ITE[1]]

mar'malade n. preserve of oranges or other citrus fruit, made like jam; ∼ **cat** (with orange fur). [f. F *marmelade* f. Port. *marmelada* quince jam (*marmelo* quince f. L f. Gk *melimēlon* f. *meli* honey + *mēlon* apple; see -ADE)]

mar'mite n. **1.** (*M*∼; P). flavouring extract made from fresh brewer's yeast. **2.** (or *mârmē't*). earthenware cooking-vessel. [F, = cooking-pot]

mar'molite n. laminated pale-green serpentine. [irreg. f. Gk *marmairō* shine; see -LITE]

marmor'eal a. (poet.) of or like marble. [f. L *marmoreus* (as MARBLE) + -AL]

mar'moset (-z-) n. small tropical Amer. monkey of family Callithricidae, with bushy tail. [f. OF *marmouset* grotesque image, of unkn. orig.]

mar'mot n. burrowing rodent of genus *Marmota*. [f. F

marmotte prob. f. Romansh *murmont* f. L *murem* (nom. *mus*) *montis* mountain mouse]

ma'rocain n. dress-fabric of crêpe type made in silk (or other materials). [F, = Moroccan (*Maroc* Morocco)]

Ma'ronite n. one of a sect of Syrian Christians dwelling chiefly in Lebanon. [f. med. L *Maronita* (*Maro* 5th-c. Syrian founder; see -ITE[1])]

maroo'n[1] a. & n. **1.** (of) brownish-crimson colour. **2.** n. explosive device giving loud report. [f. F *marron* chestnut f. It. *marrone* f. med. Gk *maraon*]

maroo'n[2] n. one of class of Blacks, orig. fugitive slaves, in mountains and forests of Surinam and W. Indies; marooned person. [f. F *marron*, f. Sp. *cimarrón* wild (*cima* peak; see -OON)]

maroo'n[3] v. **1.** v.t. put (person) ashore and leave him on desolate island or coast as punishment; (of floods etc.) make (person) unable to leave place safely. **2.** v.i. idle, hang about. [f. prec.]

marque[1] (-k) n. (Hist.) **letter(s) of** ∼ (**and reprisal**), licence to fit out armed vessel and employ it in capture of enemy's merchant shipping, (in *sing.*) ship carrying such licence. [ME f. F, f. Prov. *marca* (*marcar* seize as a pledge)]

marque[2] (-k) n. make of motor car, as opp. to specific type (*the Jaguar marque*). [F, = MARK[1]]

marquee' (-kē') n. large tent; *canopy over entrance to large building. [f. MARQUISE 3, taken as pl. & assim. to -EE]

mar'quetry, -terie, (-kītrī) n. inlaid work in wood, ivory, etc. [F *marqueterie* (*marqueter* variegate f. MARQUE[2]; see -RY)]

mar'quis, mar'quess, n. nobleman ranking between duke and (in UK) earl or (elsewhere) count; hence ∼ATE[1] (1) n. [ME, f. OF *marchis* f. Rom. **marchensis* (as MARCH[2], -ESE)]

marqui'se (-kē'z) n. **1.** (In foreign nobility) marchioness. **2.** finger-ring set with oval pointed cluster of gems. **3.** (arch.) tent, marquee. [F, fem. of *marquis* (as prec.)]

marquise'tte (-kīz-) n. fine light cotton, rayon, or silk fabric for net curtains etc. [F, dim. of *marquise*; see prec., -ETTE]

ma'rram n. shore grass (*Ammophila arenaria*) that binds sand with its tough rhizome. [f. ON *marálmr* (*marr* sea, *hálmr* HAULM)]

Marra'no (-ah-') n. (*pl.* ∼s). (Hist.) Jew or Moor in medieval Spain accepting, or simulating acceptance of, Christianity, esp. to avoid persecution. [Sp.]

ma'rriage (-rij) n. **1.** condition of man and woman legally united for purpose of living together and usu. procreating lawful offspring; act or ceremony or procedure establishing this condition; one particular such union (*by a previous marriage*); **by** ∼, as result of this (*related by marriage*); **give** or **take in** ∼, as husband or wife; *marriage of* CONVENIENCE; CIVIL *marriage*. **2.** (fig.) intimate union (*the marriage of true minds*); (Cards) union of king and queen of same suit. **3.** ∼ **articles,** antenuptial agreement respecting rights of property and succession; ∼**-bed,** (fig.) marital intercourse; ∼**-broker,** one who arranges marriages for payment; ∼ **bureau,** establishment arranging introductions between persons wishing to marry; ∼ **certificate** (stating that marriage ceremony has taken place, with names, date, etc.); ∼ **guidance,** assistance to married couples who have problems in living together harmoniously; ∼ **licence,** LICENCE[1] to marry; ‖∼ **lines,** marriage certificate; ∼ **market,** supply and demand of eligible partners for marriage; ∼ **portion,** dowry; *marriage* SETTLEMENT. [ME f. OF *mariage* (*marier* MARRY[1]; see -AGE)]

ma'rriageable (-rija-) a. old enough to marry; (of age) fit for marriage. [f. prec. + -ABLE]

ma'rried (-īd) a. & n. **1.** a. united in marriage; of person(s) so united (*married life, love, name*). **2.** n. married person (*young marrieds*). [ME, p.p. of MARRY[1]]

mărrŏn glacé (glah´sā) *n.* chestnut preserved in and coated with sugar as sweetmeat. [F, = iced chestnut; cf. GLACÉ]

mă´rrow (-ō) *n.* **1.** soft fatty substance in cavities of bones, often taken as typifying rich food or vitality, (*chilled* **to the** ∼, right through); **spinal** ∼, substance forming spinal cord. **2.** essential part (*pith and marrow*). **3.** (**vegetable**) ∼, white-fleshed edible gourd, the fruit of *Cucurbita pepo*. **4.** ∼**bone,** bone containing edible marrow; *on* one's ∼*bones,* (joc.) on one's knees; ∼(**fat**), kind of large pea; *∼* **squash,** vegetable marrow. **5.** Hence ∼LESS, ∼Y², *adjs.* [OE *mearg,mærg,* = OS,OHG *marg,*ON *mergr* f. Gmc *mazg-*]

mă´rry¹ *v.* **1.** *v.t.* (Of priest etc. or in *p.p.*) join (persons, one *to* another) in marriage; (of parent or guardian) give (son, daughter, etc.) in marriage; (of person) take as wife or husband in marriage; ∼ **off,** find wife or husband for (one's son or daughter). **2.** (fig.) unite intimately; correlate (things) as pair; (Naut.) splice (rope-ends) together without increasing girth. **3.** *v.i.* take husband or wife; ∼ **into,** become member of (family) by marriage; hence ∼ING² *a.,* (esp.) likely to marry (*not a marrying man*). [ME, f. OF *marier* f. L *maritare* (*maritus* husband)]

mă´rry² *int.* (arch.) expr. surprise, asseveration, indignation, etc.; ∼ **come up** (expr. indignant or contemptuous surprise). [ME, = (the Virgin) *Mary*]

Mărs (-z) *n.* planet fourth in order of distance from sun, next beyond earth. [L *Mars Martis,* name of Roman god of war]

Mărsa´la (-sah´-) *n.* dark sweet fortified wine like light sherry. [∼ in Sicily, where orig. made]

Mărseillai´se (-selā´z, -sāyā´z) *n.* national anthem of France, first sung in Paris by Marseilles patriots. [F, fem. adj. f. *Marseille* Marseilles; cf. -ESE]

mărsh *n.* **1.** low land flooded in wet weather and usu. watery at all times; (*attrib.,* in many names of plants and animals found in marshes). **2.** ∼ **fever,** malaria; ∼ **gas,** methane; ∼**-harrier,** species of HARRIER³; ∼**'land,** land consisting of marshes; ∼ **mallow,** (confection made from root of) shrubby herb (*Althaea officinalis*) growing near salt marshes, ∼´*mallow,* soft sweet made from sugar, albumen, gelatin, etc.; ∼ **marigold,** golden-flowered ranunculaceous plant (*Caltha palustris*) growing in moist meadows etc.; ∼ **tit,** grey tit (*Parus palustris*) inhabiting marshland; ∼ **trefoil,** buckbean. **3.** Hence ∼´Y² *a.* [OE *mer(i)sc,* = MLG, MDu. *mersch* f. WG **marisk-*]

măr´shal¹ *n.* **1.** high officer of state (∥EARL *Marshal*); officer of highest rank in some armies; ∥AIR¹ *Marshal;* ∥FIELD *Marshal;* ∥M∼ **of the Royal Air Force** (officer of highest rank); **knight** ∼, (Hist.) officer of royal household with judicial functions; ∥(**judge's**) ∼, official accompanying judge on circuit, with secretarial duties. **2.** officer arranging ceremonies, controlling procedure at races, etc.; *head of police or fire department; PROVOST *marshal;* hence ∼SHIP *n.* [ME f. OF *mareschal,* f. LL *mariscalcus* f. Gmc **marhaskalkaz* (**marhaz* horse; see MARE²; **skalkaz* servant)]

măr´shal² *v.* (∥-ll-). **1.** *v.t.* arrange in due order (persons at table etc., soldiers, facts, one's thoughts, etc.); (Her.) combine (coats of arms); conduct (person) ceremoniously (*into* etc.). **2.** *v.i.* take up positions in due arrangement; ∼**ling yard,** = RAILWAY-yard (in which goods trains etc. are assembled). [ME. f. prec.]

măr´shalsea *n.* (Hist.) court held, prison in Southwark (London) controlled, by knight marshal. [alt. f. *marshalcy* f. MARSHAL¹ + -CY]

mărsu´pial (-ū´-, -ōō´-) *a.* & *n.* **1.** *a.* (Anat.) of or like a pouch (*marsupial muscle*). **2.** *a.* & *n.* (animal) of the class of mammals characterized by the females' having a pouch in which to carry their young, which are born incompletely developed. [f. mod. L *marsupialis* f. L f. Gk *marsupion* pouch dim. of *marsipos* purse; see -AL]

mărt *n.* market-place; auction room; trade centre. [ME, f. obs. Du. *mart,* var. of *markt* MARKET]

măr´tagon *n.* lily (*Lilium martagon*) with small purple turban-like flowers. [F, f. Turk. *martagān* a form of turban]

Mărtě´llō *n.* (*pl.* ∼s). ∼ (**tower**), small circular fort, usu. on coast to prevent hostile landing. [alt. f. Cape *Mortella* in Corsica, where such a tower proved difficult to capture in 1794]

măr´těn *n.* animal of genus *Martes,* like weasel, with valuable fur. [ME, f. MDu. *martren* f. OF (*peau* skin) *martrine,* fem. adj. f. *martre* f. WG **marthr-* f. Gmc **marthuz*]

măr´těnsīte (-z-) *n.* chief constituent of hardened steel. [f. A. *Martens,* Ger. metallurgist d. 1914 + -ITE¹]

măr´tial (-shal) *a.* **1.** of, suitable for, appropriate to, warfare; hence ∼IZE (3) *v.t.* **2.** ∼ **arts,** fighting sports such as judo and karate; ∼ **law,** military government, by which ordinary law is suspended. **3.** warlike, brave; fond of fighting. **4.** (*M*∼). Martian. **5.** Hence ∼LY² *adv.* [ME f. OF, or f. L *martialis* of MARS; see -IAL]

Măr´tian (-shan) *a.* & *n.* (hypothetical inhabitant) of Mars. [ME, f. OF *martien* or f. L *Martianus* (MARS; see -IAN)]

măr´tin *n.* bird of swallow family, esp. **house-**∼ (*Delichon urbica*), which builds mud nest on house walls etc., and ∥SAND-*martin.* [prob. f. St. *Martin* (see MARTINMAS)]

martině´t *n.* strict (esp. military or naval) disciplinarian; hence ∼(**t**)ISH¹ *a.* [f. J. *Martinet,* 17th-c. French drill-master]

măr´tingāle (-ngg-) *n.* **1.** strap, or set of straps, fastened at one end to nose-band, at other end to girth, of horse to prevent rearing etc.; (Naut.) rope for holding down jib-boom. **2.** gambling system of continually doubling stakes in hope of eventual win that must yield net profit. [F, of uncert. orig.]

Mărti´ni (-ē´nĭ) *n.* (**P**) cocktail of gin, French vermouth, orange bitters, etc.; **dry** ∼ (containing much gin). [f. *Martini* & Rossi, It. firm selling vermouth]

Măr´tinmas *n.* St. Martin's day, 11 Nov.; ∼ **summer,** St. Martin's summer¹. [ME, f. St. *Martin,* bishop of Tours in 4th c., + MASS¹]

măr´tlět *n.* **1.** (arch.) swift or house-MARTIN. **2.** (Her.) imaginary footless bird as charge. [f. F *martelet* alt. f. *martinet* dim. f. MARTIN]

măr´tyr *n.,* & *v.t.* **1.** *n.* one who undergoes penalty of death for persistence in Christian faith or obedience to law of Church, or undergoes death or suffering for any great cause; ∼ **to,** constant sufferer from (ailment); **make a** ∼ **of** oneself, (pretend to) accept discomfort etc., in order to be more highly thought of. **2.** *v.t.* put to death as martyr; torment. [OE *martir* f. eccl. L f. Gk *martur, martus -uros* witness]

măr´tyrdom *n.* sufferings and death of martyr; torment. [OE *martyrdōm* (as prec., -DOM)]

măr´tyrīze, -**is**∣**e** (-īz), *v.t.* make a martyr of (oneself, person); hence ∼A´TION *n.* [ME, f. LL *martyrizare* (as MARTYR; see -IZE)]

mărtyr∣ŏ´logy *n.* list or register, history, of martyrs; hence ∼OLO´GICAL *a.,* ∼Ŏ´LOGIST *n.* [f. med. L f. eccl. Gk *marturologion* (as MARTYR, *logos* account; see -LOGY)]

măr´tyry *n.* shrine or church erected in honour of martyr. [ME, f. med. L f. Gk *marturion* martyrdom (as MARTYR)]

măr´vel¹ *n.* wonderful thing; wonderful example *of* (quality); (arch.) astonishment; ∼ **of Peru,** showy garden plant (*Mirabilis jalapa*) with flowers opening in afternoon. [ME, f. OF *merveille* f. LL *mirabilia* neut. pl. of L *mirabilis* (*mirari* wonder; see MIRACLE, -ABLE)]

măr´vel² *v.i.* (∥-ll-). (literary). be surprised (*at, that*); wonder (*how, why,* etc.). [ME, f. OF *merveiller* (*merveille* as prec.)]

măr´vellous, *măr´velous, *a.* astonishing; extremely improbable; excellent; hence ~LY² *adv.*, ~NESS *n.* [ME, f. OF *merveillos* (*merveille*; see MARVEL¹, -OUS)]

Mār'xian *a.* & *n.* (adherent) of the doctrines of Marx. [f. K. *Marx*, Ger. socialist d. 1883 + -IAN]

Mār'x|ism *n.* political and economic theory of Marx, predicting abolition of private ownership of means of production, with provision of work and subsistence for all; ~ism-Le'ninism, this as developed by Lenin (cf. LENINISM); so ~IST (2) *n.* (often *attrib.*). [f. as prec. + -ISM]

mār'zipǎn *n.* paste of ground almonds, sugar, etc., made up into small cakes, etc. or used on top of large cakes; piece of marzipan. [G, f. It. *marzapane*]

mǎscâr'a *n.* cosmetic for darkening the eyelashes, eyebrows, etc. [It. *mascara, maschera* MASK¹]

mǎ'scle (-skel) *n.* (Her.) lozenge voided, with central lozenge-shaped aperture. [ME f. AF, f. AL *ma(s)cula* f. L MACULA]

mǎ'scŏn *n.* (Astron.) concentration of dense matter with strong gravitational pull below moon's surface. [f. *mass* concentration]

mǎ'scŏt *n.* person or animal or thing that is supposed to bring luck. [f. F *mascotte* f. mod. Prov. *mascotto* fem. dim. of *masco* witch]

ma'sculine (mǎ'-, mah'-) *a.* & *n.* 1. *a.* of men; manly, vigorous; (of woman) having qualities appropriate to a man. 2. (Gram.) having gender proper to men's names. 3. (Pros.) ~ **rhyme** (between words ending in stressed syllables); ~ **ending**, ending of line with stressed syllable. 4. Hence ~LY² (-nlī) *adv.*, ~NESS (-n-n-), **mascūli'nITY** (mǎ-, mah-), *ns.* 5. *n.* masculine gender or word. [ME, f. OF *masculin -ine* f. L *masculinus* (as MALE; see -INE¹)]

mǎ'ser (-z-) *n.* device using stimulated emission of radiation by excited atoms etc. to amplify or generate highly monochromatic electromagnetic radiation, esp. microwaves; cf. LASER. [f. microwave amplification by stimulated emission of radiation]

mǎsh¹ *n.* malt mixed with hot water to form wort for brewing; mixture of boiled grain, bran, etc., given warm to horses etc.; soft pulp made by crushing, mixing with water, etc.; ||(colloq.) mashed potatoes (*sausage and mash*); confused mixture; ~-**tub** (in which malt is mashed). [OE *māsc* = MLG *mēsch*, MHG *meisch* crushed grapes, f. WG **maisk-*, perh. cogn. w. MIX]

mǎsh² *v.t.* mix (malt) with hot water to form wort; crush or pound to a pulp; reduce (potatoes etc.) to uniform mass by crushing. [ME, f. prec.]

mǎsh³ *v.t.*, & *n.* (arch. sl.) 1. *v.t.* excite sentimental admiration in (person of opposite sex); be ~ed **on**, have such admiration for; so ~'ER¹ *n.*, man who poses as dashing beau. 2. *n.* person thus admired; such admiration. [back-form. f. *masher*, prob. f. prec.]

mǎ'shie *n.* (Golf). iron used for lofting or for medium distances; ~ **niblick**, club intermediate between mashie and niblick. [perh. f. F *massue* club]

mask¹ (mah-) *n.* covering, usu. of velvet or silk, for concealing face at balls etc., or of wire, gauze, etc., for protection e.g. of fencer, or worn by surgeon to prevent infection of patient, etc., or of any material to disguise or for grotesque appearance to amuse or terrify; respirator used to filter inhaled air or to supply gas for inhalation; hollow figure of human head worn by ancient Greek and Roman actors; likeness of person's face, esp. one made by taking mould from face (DEATH-*mask*); (fig.) disguise (*throw off the mask*); (arch.) masked person; (Photog.) screen used to exclude part of image; face or head of fox; = PACK¹ 10 for face. [f. F *masque* f. It. *maschera* f. Arab. *maskara* buffoon (*sakira* to ridicule)]

mask² (mah-) *v.t.* 1. cover (face etc.) with mask; (in *pass.*) be disguised with mask. 2. (Mil.) conceal (battery etc.) from enemy's view, hinder (army etc.) from action by observing with adequate force, hinder (friendly force) by standing in its line of fire. 3.

disguise, conceal, (taste, one's feelings, etc.); protect from some process. 4. ~ed **ball** (at which masks are worn). [f. prec.]

ma'sker, ma'squer, (mah'sk-) *n.* one who takes part in masquerade or masque. [f. prec. + -ER¹]

mǎskinö'nge (-nj, -njī) *n.* large N. Amer. pike esp. in Great Lakes. [ult. f. Ojibwa, = great fish]

mǎ'soch|ism (-k-) *n.* form of (esp. sexual) perversion in which person derives pleasure from his own pain or humiliation (opp. SADISM); (colloq.) enjoyment of what appears to be painful or tiresome; so ~IST (2) *n.*, ~i'stIC *a.* [f. L. von Sacher-*Masoch*, Austrian novelist d. 1895, who described cases of it, + -ISM]

mā'son *n.*, & *v.t.* 1. *n.* one who builds with stone; ~'s **mark**, device carved on stone by mason who dressed it. 2. (*M~*). Freemason; hence **Masö'nIC** *a.* 3. *v.t.* build or strengthen with masonry. [ME, f. OF (*maçon-ner* v. f.) *maçon, ONF machun,* f. Rom. **matio, *macio, -onis,* prob. f. Gmc **mattjon*]

Māson-Dī'xon *a.* ~ **line**, boundary between Maryland and Pennsylvania, taken as northern limit of slave-owning states before abolition of slavery in US. [f. C. *Mason* & J. *Dixon,* 18th-c. Engl. astronomers who partly surveyed it]

mā'sonrÿ *n.* 1. mason's work. 2. (*M~*). Freemasonry. [ME, f. OF *maçonerie* (as MASON; see -ERY)]

Mā'sorah (-*a*) *n.* body of traditional information and comment on text of Hebrew Bible. [f. Heb. *māsōret,* perh. = bond]

Mā'sor|ēte *n.* Jewish scholar contributing to the Masorah; hence ~e'TIC *a.* [f. F *Massoret* & mod. L *Massoreta,* orig. misuse of Heb. (see prec.), assim. to -ETE]

masque (mahsk) *n.* amateur dramatic and musical entertainment esp. in 16th–17th c., orig. in dumb show, later with metrical dialogue; dramatic composition for this. [var. of MASK¹]

masquer. See MASKER.

masquerā'de¹ (mǎsk-, mah-) *n.* masked ball; false show, pretence. [f. F *mascarade* f. Sp. *mascarada* (*máscara* mask; see -ADE)]

masquerā'de² (mǎsk-, mah-) *v.i.* appear in disguise, assume false appearance, (*as*). [f. prec.]

mass¹ (mǎs, mahs) *n.* (a) celebration (usu. RC) of the Eucharist (*mass was said; we attend, go to, hear, mass; masses were said for his soul*); liturgy used in this; musical setting of parts of this; **high** ~ (with incense, music, and assistance of deacon and subdeacon); **low** ~ (with no music and minimum of ceremony). [OE *mæsse* f. eccl. L *missa,* f. L *mittere miss-* dismiss, perh. f. concluding dismissory words *Ite, missa est*]

mǎss² *n.* & *v.* 1. *n.* coherent body of matter of indefinite shape; dense aggregation of objects (*a mass of fibres*); (in *sing.* or *pl.*) large number or amount (*of*); a main portion (of a painting etc.) as perceived by the eye; unbroken expanse (*of* colour etc.); **a** ~ **of,** full of or covered with (mistakes, bruises, etc.); **the** (**great**) ~, the majority (*of*); **the** ~**es,** the ordinary people; **in the** ~, in the aggregate. 2. (Phys.) quantity of matter a body contains, as measured by its acceleration under a given force, or by the changes in velocity when it strikes a given body; **centre of** ~, point representing mean position of matter in a body or system. 3. (*attrib.*) relating to large numbers of persons or things, large-scale, (*mass audience, murder*); ~ **action,** action by large numbers (*law of* ~ *action,* Chem. law that reaction rate is proportional to concentration of reacting substances); ~ **defect,** (Phys.) difference between mass and mass number of isotope; *mass* ENERGY; ~ **grave** (in which many persons are buried at same time); ~ **hysteria** (affecting many persons at same time); ~ **of manœuvre,** body of troops kept free to meet strategic needs; ~ **media,** means of communication (e.g. newspapers or broadcasting) to large numbers of people; ~ **medication,** administration of medicinal substance to many persons at once, e.g.

through water supply; ~ **meeting,** large assembly of people to express political etc. views; ~ **number,** (Phys.) total number of protons and neutrons in atomic nucleus; ||~ **observation,** study and recording of social habits and opinions of ordinary people; ~-**produ′ced,** ~ **production** (of large quantities of a standardized article by standardized mechanical processes); ~ **radiography,** quick routine radiographic examination of the chests of large numbers of people; ~ **spectrograph,** apparatus separating isotopes according to mass by passage in ionic form through electric and magnetic fields, and detecting them photographically; ~ **spectrometer,** similar device with electrical detection; ~ **spectrum,** distribution of isotopes shown by these instruments; ~ **transport,** public transport as opp. private cars etc. **4.** Hence ~′LESS *a.* **5.** *v.t.* & *i.* gather into mass; assemble as one body (*massed bands*); (Mil.) concentrate (troops). [ME; (v. f. OF *masser*) f. OF *masse* f. L *massa* f. Gk *maza* barley-cake (perh. rel. to *massō* knead)]

Mass. *abbr.* Massachusetts.

mä′ssacre (-ker) *n.,* & *v.t.* **1.** *n.* general slaughter, carnage, (of persons, occas. of animals); utter defeat or destruction. **2.** *v.t.* make a massacre of; murder cruelly or violently (a number of persons). [(v. f. F *massacrer* †.) F *massacre*; in OF *maçacre*, shambles, butchery; orig. unkn.]

mä′ssage (-ahzh) *n.,* & *v.t.* **1.** *n.* rubbing, kneading, etc., of muscles and joints of the body with the hands, to stimulate their action, cure strains, etc. **2.** *v.t.* treat (part, person) thus. [F (*masser* treat with massage, perh. f. Port. *amassar* knead, f. *massa* dough; see MASS², -AGE)]

mässasau′ga *n.* small N. Amer. rattlesnake of genus *Sistrurus.* [irreg. f. *Missisauga* River, Ontario]

mässé (mä′sā) *n.* (Bill.) stroke made with cue held vertical. [F, p.p. of *masser* make such stroke (as MACE¹)]

mässe′ter *n.* one of two chewing-muscles from temporal bone to lower jaw. [f. Gk *masētēr* (*masaomai* chew)]

mässeu|r′ (-êr′) *n.* (*fem.* ~**se** *pr.* -êr′z). one who provides massage professionally. [F (*masser*; see MASSAGE)]

mä′ssicot *n.* yellow lead monoxide, used as pigment. [F, perh. rel. to It. *marzacotto* unguent prob. f. Arab. *mashakūnyā*]

mässif (mä′sēf, -ē′f) *n.* mountain heights forming a compact group. [F adj. (see foll.) as n.]

mä′ssive *a.* **1.** large and heavy or solid; (of features, head, etc.) relatively large, of solid build; (Min.) not definitely crystalline; (Geol.) without structural divisions. **2.** (fig.) solid, substantial; impressive, imposing; unusually large. **3.** Hence ~LY² (-vlī) *adv.,* ~NESS (-vn-) *n.* [ME f. F *massif -ive* f. OF *massiz* (see MASSY, -IVE)]

Massorah, Massorete, etc. Vars. of MASORAH etc.

mä′ss|y̆ *a.* (arch. or rhet.) solid; weighty; hence ~ĬNESS *n.* [ME, perh. f. OF *massiz* f. pop. L **massiceus* f. L *massa* MASS²; see -Y²]

mast¹ (mah-) *n.,* & *v.t.* **1.** *n.* long pole of timber, iron, etc., set up on ship's keel to support sails; flag-pole; **before the ~,** serving as ordinary seaman (quartered in forecastle); HALF-mast (*high*); hence (of ship) -~′ED a., -~′ER¹ *n.* **2.** ~-**head,** (1) highest part of mast, esp. of lower mast as place of observation or punishment, (2) title etc. of newspaper etc. at head of front or editorial page, (3, *v.t.*) send (sailor) to mast-head, raise (sail) to position on mast. **3.** post, or lattice-work upright, for supporting a radio or television aerial; (**mooring-**)~, strong steel tower to top of which an airship can be moored. **4.** *v.t.* furnish with masts. [OE *mæst*, = OHG *mast* f. WG **masta* f. IE **mazdos*]

mast² (mah-) *n.* fruit of beech, oak, chestnut, and other forest-trees, esp. as food for pigs. [OE *mæst*, =

MDu., OHG *mast*, WG **masta* f. IE **mazdos*, prob. cogn. w. MEAT]

mä′staba *n.* **1.** (Archaeol.) ancient Egyptian tomb with sloping sides and flat roof. **2.** stone etc. bench attached to house in Islamic countries. [f. Arab. *maṣṭabah*]

mästě′ctomy̆ *n.* (Surg.) excision or amputation of a breast. [f. Gk *mastos* breast + -ECTOMY]

ma′ster¹ (mah′-) *n.* & *a.* **1.** *n.* person having control; (Naut.) captain of merchant ship (*master* MARINER); employer; owner of dog, horse, etc.; owner of slave; person in control of pack (*of foxhounds* etc.); male head of household (*master of the house*); ||official of Supreme Court; (*M*~) courtesy title of eldest son of Sc. viscount or baron (*the Master of Falkland*); **be ~ of,** have at one's disposal, know how to control; **be** one's **own ~,** be independent or free to do as one wishes; **make** oneself ~ **of,** acquire thorough knowledge of or facility in using. **2.** one who has or gets the upper hand (*we will see which of us is master*). **3.** male teacher or tutor, esp. SCHOOL¹master; revered teacher in philosophy etc.; holder of university degree orig. giving him authority to teach in university (*Master of Arts* etc.); **the M**~, Christ. **4.** skilled workman, or one in business on his own account, (*master carpentor, mason*). **5.** great artist (LITTLE *Masters*; OLD *master*); picture etc. by a master; (Chess etc.) player of proved ability at international level. **6.** head of college, school, etc.; presiding officer of livery company, Masonic lodge, etc. **7.** thing from which series of copies (of film, gramophone record, etc.) is made. **8.** part of machine directly controlling another (cf. SLAVE). **9.** (As title of functionaries) *Master of Ceremonies* (see CEREMONY); **M**~ **in Chancery,** chief clerk of Chancery Division; **M**~ **of the Horse,** third official in Royal Household, attending sovereign on State occasions; ||*Master in* LUNACY; *Master of* MISRULE; **M**~ (organizer, leader, esp. in Royal Household and Inns of Court) **of the Revels;** ||*Master of the* ROLL¹s. **10.** (Prefixed, esp. by servants and in address of letter, to name of boy or young man not old enough for *Mr*) *Master Tom, Master* (*Tom or T.*) *Jones*; (arch. as title of man of high rank, learning, etc.). **11.** ~ **aircrew,** RAF rank equivalent to warrant-officer; ~-**at-arms,** chief police officer on man-of-war or merchant ship; *Master* GUNNER; ~-**hand,** (action of) person having commanding power or great skill; ~-**key** (opening many locks, each also opened by separate key); ~ **mason,** (1) (see sense 4), (2) fully qualified Freemason, who has passed third degree; ~-**mind,** (*n.*) (possessor of) outstanding intellect, person directing an enterprise, (*v.t.*) plan and direct (an enterprise); ~-**piece,** consummate piece of workmanship, one's best work; ~-**singer,** = MEISTERSINGER; ~-**stroke,** surpassingly skilful act (of policy etc.); ~-**switch,** switch controlling electricity etc. supply to an entire system; ~ **touch,** masterly manner of dealing with something; ~-**work,** masterpiece. **12.** Hence ~DOM, ~HOOD, *ns.,* ~LESS *a.* **13.** *a.* commanding, superior, (*a master spirit*); main, principal, (*master bedroom*); controlling others (*master plan*). [OE *mægester* (later also f. OF *maistre*) f. L *magister,* prob. cogn. w. *magis* more]

ma′ster² (mah′-) *v.t.* overcome, defeat; reduce to subjection; acquire complete knowledge of (subject) or facility in using (instrument etc.); rule as a master. [ME, f. prec.]

ma′sterful (mah′-) *a.* self-willed, imperious; masterly; hence ~LY² *adv.,* ~NESS *n.* [ME, f. MASTER¹ + -FUL]

ma′sterl|y̆ (mah′-) *a.* worthy of a master, very skilful; hence ~ĬNESS *n.* [f. MASTER¹ + -LY¹]

ma′stership (mah′-) *n.* dominion, control; office or function of (esp. school)master. [ME, f. MASTER¹ + -SHIP]

ma′stery̆ (mah′-) *n.* sway, dominion; *the* upper hand; masterly skill; masterly use or knowledge (*of* instrument, subject). [ME, f. OF *maistrie* (as MASTER[1]; see -Y[1])]

mă′stic *n.* gum or resin exuding from bark of certain trees (esp. *Pistacia lentiscus*), used in making varnish; ∼ (**tree**), tree yielding this; type of cement esp. made with asphalt; liquor flavoured with mastic gum, made in Turkey and Greece. [ME f. OF, f. LL *mastichum* f. L f. Gk *mastikhē*, perh. f. *mastikhaō* (w. ref. to its use as chewing-gum; see foll.)]

mă′stic|āte *v.t.* grind (food) with teeth, chew; hence or cogn. ∼A′TION, ∼ātOR, *ns.*, ∼ātORY *a.* [f. LL *masticare* f. Gk *mastikhaō* gnash the teeth + -ATE[3]]

ma′stiff (mah′-) *n.* large strong dog with drooping ears and pendulous lips. [ME, ult. f. OF *mastin* f. Rom. **mansuetinus* f. L *mansuetus* tame; see MANSUETUDE]

măstī′tis *n.* inflammation of mammary gland (breast or udder). [f. Gk *mastos* breast + -ITIS]

mă′stodŏn *n.* large extinct mammal of genus *Mammut*, like elephant, with nipple-shaped tubercles on crowns of molar teeth; hence **măstodŏ′ntIC** *a.* [mod. L, f. Gk *mastos* breast + *odous odontos* tooth]

mă′stoid *a.* & *n.* (Anat.) **1.** *a.* shaped like woman's breast; ∼ **process,** conical prominence on temporal bone behind ear, to which muscles are attached. **2.** *n.* mastoid process; (colloq.) mastoiditis; hence ∼I′TIS *n.*, inflammation of mastoid process. [f. F *mastoïde* or mod. L *mastoides* f. Gk *mastoeidēs* (*mastos* breast; see -OID)]

mă′sturb|āte *v.i.* & *t.* produce sexual orgasm or arousal (of) by manual stimulation of genitals etc., not by sexual intercourse; so ∼A′TION *n.*, ∼ātORY *a.* [f. L *masturbari* + -ATE[3]]

măt[1] *n.* piece of coarse fabric of plaited rushes, straw, etc., for lying upon, packing furniture, etc.; piece of this or other material for wiping shoes upon, esp. door-mat; piece of cork, rubber, plastic, etc., to protect surface from heat or moisture of object placed on it; small rug; piece of resilient material to protect falling jumper, wrestler, etc.; **on the** ∼, (sl.) in trouble (orig. in army, on the orderly-room mat before the CO). [OE *m(e)att(e)*, = OHG *matta* f. WG f. LL *matta*]

măt[2] *v.* (-tt-). **1.** *v.t.* cover or furnish with mats; entangle (*together*) in thick mass (esp. in *p.p.*; *matted hair*). **2.** *v.i.* become matted. [f. prec.]

măt[3]. See MATT.

mă′tadŏr *n.* man appointed to kill bull in bullfight; a principal card in ombre, quadrille, etc.; domino game in which piece played must make total of seven. [Sp. (*matar* kill f. Pers. *māt* dead)]

mătch[1] *n.* **1.** person able to contend with another as an equal (*find, meet*, one's *match*; *be* (*more than*) *a match for*); person equal to another in some quality (*we shall never see his match*); person or thing exactly like or corresponding to another. **2.** contest of skill etc. in which persons or teams strive against each other. **3.** matrimonial alliance; **make a** ∼, bring this about. **4.** person viewed in regard to his or her eligibility for marriage, esp. as to rank or fortune, (*he is an excellent match*). **5.** ∼′**board,** one with tongue cut along one edge and groove along another, so as to fit with similar boards; ∼′**maker,** person fond of scheming to bring about marriages; ∼ **play,** (Golf) play in which the score is reckoned by counting the holes won by each side, opp. *medal play*; ∼ **point,** state of a game when one side needs only one more point to win the match, this point, (Bridge) unit of scoring in matches and tournaments. [OE *gemæcca* mate, companion, f. Gmc **gamakjon* fit, suitable; cf. MAKE[1]]

mătch[2] *v.* **1.** *v.t.* (arch.) join (person *with* another) in marriage. **2.** prove to be a match for; place (person etc.) in conflict or contest *against* another (**well** ∼**ed,** fit to contend with each other, live together, etc., on equal terms); place (person, thing) in competition *with.* **3.** *v.t.* & *i.* be equal, correspond in quantity, quality, colour, etc., to or *with* (thing etc., or abs.; *the*

carpets match the wallpaper*; these ribbons do not match, do not match (with) your hat*; *trimmed with velvet to match*); find material etc. that matches with (another; *can you match this silk?*); find person or thing suitable for another (*matching unemployed workers with vacant posts*); **to** ∼, (fig.) corresponding in quality, number, etc., with what has been mentioned. **4.** (Electr.) produce or have adjustment of (circuits) such that maximum power is transmitted between them. **5.** Hence ∼′ABLE *a.* [ME, f. prec.]

mă′tch[3] *n.* short thin piece of wood (∼′**stick**), wax, etc., tipped with composition that bursts into flame when rubbed on rough or (**safety** ∼) specially prepared surface; piece of wick, cord, etc., designed to burn at uniform rate, for firing cannon etc.; ∼′**box** (for holding matches); ∼′**lock,** (gun with) lock in which match is placed for igniting powder; ∼′**wood,** wood suitable for matches, minute splinters, (*make* ∼*wood of*, utterly smash). [ME, f. OF *mesche, meiche,* perh. f. L *myxa* lamp-nozzle]

mă′tchĕt. See MACHETE.

mă′tchlèss *a.* without an equal, peerless; hence ∼LY[2] *adv.* [f. MATCH[1] + -LESS]

māte[1] *n.*, & *v.t.* (Chess). = CHECKMATE; **fool's** ∼ (in which first player is mated at opponent's second move); **scholar's** ∼ (in which second player is mated at opponent's fourth move); **self-**∼, **sui-**∼, (in which player forces opponent to mate him); SMOTHER*ed mate*; STALEMATE. [ME, f. F *mat*(*er*); see CHECKMATE]

māte[2] *n.* **1.** companion, fellow worker; (as general colloq. form of address among equals, esp. sailors or labourers). **2.** one of a pair, esp. of birds; fitting partner in marriage; (in *comb.*) fellow member or joint occupant of (*team-mate, room-mate*). **3.** (Naut.) officer on merchant ship subordinate to master. **4.** assistant to a worker (*cook's, plumber's, surgeon's, mate*). **5.** Hence ∼′LESS (-tl-) *a.* [ME, f. MLG *mate* (*gemate* f.) WG **gamato* messmate f. **ga-* Y-, **mat* MEAT]

māte[3] *v.t.* & *i.* join (two persons, one *with* another) in marriage; marry (*with*, or abs.); come or bring together for breeding (of animals); pair (birds), (of birds) pair; keep company, (Mech.) fit well, (*with*). [f. prec.]

mă′té (-ā) *n.* (vessel for) infusion of leaves of a S. Amer. shrub (*Ilex paraguayensis*); the shrub, or its leaves. [f. Sp. *mate* f. Quechua *mati*]

∥**mă′telŏt,** ∥**mă′tlo(w),** (mă′tlō) *n.* (sl.) sailor. [F *matelot*]

matelote (mă′telŏt) *n.* dish of fish etc. with sauce of wine, onions, etc. [F, f. as prec.]

mā′ter *n.* ∥(sl.) mother; DURA MATER, PIA MATER; ∼**fami′lias,** woman head of family or household (cf. PATERFAMILIAS). [L]

matēr′ial *a.* & *n.* **1.** *a.* concerned with the matter, not the form, of reasoning; of matter, corporeal; ∼ **theory of heat** (that it is a material substance). **2.** (Of conduct, point of view, etc.) not spiritual; concerned with bodily comfort etc. (*material well-being*). **3.** important, essential, (*to*, or abs.; *at the material time*). **4.** Hence ∼ITY (-ă′l-) *n.*, ∼LY[2] *adv.* **5.** *n.* matter from which thing is made (RAW *material*); (in *sing.* or *pl.*) elements, constituent parts, (*of* substance, *for* historical composition etc.; cloth, fabric; (in *pl.*) things needed for an activity (*building, cleaning, writing, materials*); person(s) or thing(s) suitable to receive a given training, got from a specified source, etc. (*academic, experimental, material*). [ME, f. OF *materiel, -al,* f. LL *materialis* f. L (as MATTER[1]; see -AL)]

matēr′ial|ism *n.* opinion that nothing exists but matter and its movements and modifications; doctrine that consciousness and will are wholly due to material agency; (Art) tendency to lay stress on material aspect of objects; tendency to prefer material possessions and physical comfort to spiritual values; so ∼IST (2) *n.*, ∼ī′stIC *a.* [f. prec. + -ISM]

matēr′ializ|e, -īs|e (-īz) *v.* **1.** *v.t.* make, or represent as, material; make materialistic. **2.** *v.t.* & *i.* cause (spirit) to appear, (of spirit) appear, in bodily form; make or become actual fact; (colloq.) be present when expected. **3.** Hence ∼A′TION *n.* [f. MATERIAL + -IZE]

matēria mĕ′dica *n.* (science of origin and properties of) remedial substances used in practice of medicine. [mod. L, transl. Gk *hulē iatrikē* healing material]

matériel (matēriě′l) *n.* stock-in-trade, available means, esp. materials and equipment in warfare (opp. *personnel*). [F, adj. as n. (as MATERIAL)]

matĕr′nal *a.* of or like a mother; motherly; related through the mother (∼ **uncle,** mother's brother); of the mother in pregnancy and childbirth; hence ∼LY² *adv.* [ME, f. OF *maternel* or f. L *maternus* (*mater* mother); see -AL]

matĕr′nitў *n.* motherhood; motherliness; ∼ **home, hospital, nurse, ward,** (for women during and just after childbirth); ∼ **dress, wear,** (suitable for pregnant woman). [f. F *maternité* f. med. L *maternitas -tatis* f. L *maternus* (see prec., -ITY)]

mā′t|ey, mā′t|ў, *a.* (∼ier, ∼iest) & *n.* **1.** *a.* sociable, familiar and friendly (*with*); hence ∼eyNESS, ∼īNESS, (-ĭn-) *n.* **2.** *n.* (esp. as colloq. *voc.*) ||mate, companion. [f. MATE² + -Y²,³]

*māth *n.* (colloq.) mathematics. [abbr.]

māthema′tical *a.* of mathematics; (of proof etc.) rigorously precise; *mathematical* INDUCTION, TABLES; hence ∼LY² *adv.* [f. F *mathématique* or f. L f. Gk *mathēmatikos* (*mathēma -matos* science f. *manthanō*, root **math-*, learn; see -ICAL)]

māthĕmă′tics *n. pl.* (also treated as *sing.*) (**pure**) ∼, abstract science of space, number, and quantity; (**applied**) ∼, this applied to branches of physics, astronomy, etc.; (as *pl.*) use of mathematics in calculation etc.; so **māthĕmati′cian** *n.* [prob. f. F *mathématiques* pl. f. L f. Gk *mathēmatika* (as prec.; see -ICS)]

||**māths** *n.* (colloq.) mathematics. [abbr.]

mati′cō (-tē′-) *n.* (*pl.* ∼s). tropical Amer. wild pepper; its leaves used as styptic. [Sp., dim. of *Mateo* Matthew, said to be f. name of a soldier who discovered its properties]

Mati′lda *n.* (Austral.) bushman's bundle, swag; **walk** or **waltz** ∼, carry this. [f. woman's Christian name]

mā′tin *n.* **1.** (in *pl.*) office of one of the canonical hours of prayer, prop. a night office, but also recited with lauds at daybreak or on previous evening. **2.** (in *pl.*) morning prayer in Church of England. **3.** (poet.; in *sing.* or *pl.*) morning song of birds. [ME f. OF *matines* f. eccl. L *matutinas*, acc. fem. pl. a. (as n.) f. L *matutinus* of the morning (*Matuta* dawn-goddess; see -INE¹)]

mā′tinée, *-nee, (-nā) *n.* afternoon theatrical or cinema or musical performance; ∼ **coat,** baby's short coat; ∼ **idol,** handsome actor appealing to feminine playgoers etc. [F, = what occupies a morning (MATIN morning)]

||**matlo(w).** See MATELOT.

mā′trass *n.* long-necked glass vessel with round or oval body, used for distilling etc. [f. F *matras*, of uncert. orig.]

mā′triǎrch (-k) *n.* woman corresponding in status to patriarch (usu. joc.); hence **mātriǎr′chal** (-k-) *a.* [f. L *mater* mother on false anal. of PATRIARCH]

mā′triǎrchў (-kĭ) *n.* social organization in which mother is head of family and descent is reckoned through female line. [f. prec. after PATRIARCHY]

||**matrī′c n.** (colloq.) matriculation. [abbr.]

mā′tricīd|e *n.* one who kills his, killing of one's, mother; hence ∼AL *a.* [f. L *matricida, matricidium* (*mater* mother; see -CIDE)]

matri′cŭl|āte *v.t.* & *i.* admit (student) to membership of university; be thus admitted; hence ∼A′TION *n.* (also as name of examination to qualify for this), ∼ātORY *a.* [f. med. L *matriculare* enrol f. LL *matricula* register, dim. of L MATRIX, + -ATE³]

mātrĭli′néal *a.* of or based on (kinship with) the

mother or the female line. [f. L *mater matris* mother + LINEAL]

mātrĭlō′cal *a.* of system of marriage where husband goes to live with wife's group. [f. as prec. + LOCAL²]

mă′trimonў *n.* **1.** rite of marriage; state of being married. **2.** a card-game; combination of king and queen of trumps in some card-games. **3.** So **mātrĭmō′nĭAL** *a.* [ME, f. AF *matrimonie*, OF *matremoi(g)ne* f. L *matrimonium* (*mater matris* mother; see -MONY)]

mā′tr|ix *n.* (*pl.* ∼ices *pr.* -īsēz, *or* ∼ixes). **1.** womb; place in which thing is developed; formative part of animal organ. **2.** mass of rock etc. enclosing gems etc. **3.** (Biol.) substance between cells. **4.** mould in which printer's types, gramophone records, etc., are cast or shaped. **5.** (Math.) rectangular array of quantities in rows and columns that is treated as a single quantity. [L, = breeding-female, womb, register (*mater matris* mother; cf. -TRIX)]

mā′tron *n.* **1.** married woman, esp. one of dignity and sobriety; ∼ **of honour,** married woman attending bride at wedding; JURY *of matrons.* **2.** woman managing domestic arrangements of school etc.; woman in charge of nurses in hospital. **3.** Hence ∼AGE (1, 2), ∼HOOD, ∼SHIP, *ns.,* ∼AL, ∼LY¹ (esp. w. ref. to staidness or portliness), *adjs.* [ME, f. OF *matrone* f. L *matrona* (*mater matris* mother)]

mătt, mǎtt³, *a., n.,* & *v.t.* (-tt-). **1.** *a.* (Of colour, surface, etc.) dull, without lustre. **2.** *n.* border of dull gold round framed picture; appearance of unburnished gold. **3.** *v.t.* make (gilding etc.) dull; frost (glass). [(v. f. F *matir*) f. F *mat* n. & a., identical w. *mat* MATE¹; see CHECKMATE]

Matt. *abbr.* Matthew (also in NT).

mă′ttamôre *n.* subterranean dwelling or storehouse. [f. F *matamore* f. Arab. *matmūra* (*tamara* bury)]

mătte *n.* impure product of smelting of sulphide ores, esp. those of copper or nickel. [F]

mă′tter¹ *n.* **1.** that which has mass and occupies space; physical substance in general, as opp. to *spirit, mind,* etc. **2.** (Physiol.) substance in or from the body (*faecal matter*; GREY, WHITE¹, *matter*); purulent discharge. **3.** (Logic.) particular content of proposition, distinguished from its form. **4.** material for thought or expression; substance of book, speech, etc., (often opp. to *manner* or *form*). **5.** what is or may be a good reason (*of or for* complaint, regret, etc.). **6.** thing(s) esp. of specified kind (*postal, printed, reading, matter*); (Print.) body of a printed work, as type or as printed sheets; **no** ∼, it is of no importance (*when, how,* etc., or abs.; *will do it no matter what the consequences*); **what** ∼?, that need not disquiet us. **7.** affair, thing to be done or considered, esp. of specified kind (*a* HANGING¹ *matter; no* LAUGHING¹ *matter; money matters*); **a** ∼ **of,** thing that pertains to or depends (solely) on (*a matter of common knowledge; it is only a matter of time before he gives in; that is a matter of habit*), approximately (*for a matter of 40 years; a matter of* COURSE¹; **a** ∼ **of fact,** what pertains to the sphere of fact (opp. to *opinion* etc.), esp. *as a matter of fact* (often in correcting another's misunderstanding), (Law) part of judicial inquiry concerned with truth of alleged facts (opp. to ∼ *of law*); ∼-*of--fact a.*, unimaginative, prosaic; *a matter of* FORM¹, of RECORD²; **the** ∼, thing that is amiss (*with; something is the matter; there is something the matter with him*); **what is the** ∼ **with,** surely there is no objection to; **for that** ∼, **for the** ∼ **of that,** (1) so far as that is concerned, (2) and indeed also (something further); **in the** ∼ **of,** as regards. [ME f. AF *mater(i)e*, OF *matiere* f. L *materia* timber, substance, subject of discourse]

mă′tter² *v.i.* **1.** be of importance, signify, (*to* person etc.; *it matters how, when,* etc.; esp. w. neg.). **2.** secrete or discharge pus. [f. prec.]

mă′tterў *a.* purulent, festering. [ME, f. MATTER¹ + -Y²]

Mă′tthew (-thū) *n.* ∼ **principle,** 'unto every one that hath shall be given' (Matt. 25:29). [f. St. ∼, traditional author of 1st Gospel]

mǎ'ttǐng *n.* In vbl senses; fabric of hemp, bast, grass, etc., for mats (*coconut matting*). [f. MAT[1,2] + -ING[1]]
||**mattins.** Var. of MATIN (sense 2).

mǎ'ttock *n.* agricultural tool of PICK[1] shape, with an adze and a chisel edge as ends of head. [OE *mattuc*, of unkn. orig.]

mǎ'ttoid *n.* person of erratic mind, mixture of genius and fool. [f. It. *mattoide* (*matto* insane; see -OID)]

mǎ'ttréss *n.* fabric case stuffed with hair, straw, feathers, foam rubber, etc., or filled with air or water, as bed or support for bed; SPRING[2], WIRE, *mattress*. [ME f. OF *materas* f. It. *materasso* f. Arab. *almaṭraḥ* the place, the cushion (*ṭaraḥa* throw)]

mǎ'tūrāte *v.i.* (Med.) (Of boil etc.) come to maturation. [f. L (as MATURE[2]) + -ATE[3]]

mǎtūrā'tion *n.* **1.** (Med.) formation of purulent matter; causing of this, whence **matūr'ative** *a.* **2.** ripening of fruit; maturing, development. [ME f. F, or f. med. L *maturatio* f. L (as MATURE[2]; see -ATION)]

matūr'e¹ *a.* (~r, ~st). complete in natural development, ripe; with fully developed powers of body and mind, adult; (of thought, intentions, etc.) duly careful and adequate; (of bill etc.) due for payment; hence or cogn. ~LY[2] (-ūr'lĭ) *adv.*, ~NESS (-ūr'n-), **matūr'ITY**, *ns.* [ME, f. L *maturus* timely, early]

matūr'e² *v.t.* & *i.* develop fully; ripen; perfect (plan etc.); come to maturity; (of bill etc.) become due for payment. [ME, f. L *maturare* (as prec.)]

matutinal (mǎtūtī'-, matū'tǐ-) *a.* of, or occurring in, the morning; early. [f. LL *matutinalis* f. L *matutinus* (see MATIN)]

mǎ'tỹ. See MATEY.

ma'tzō (mah'tsō) *n.* (*pl.* ~s, *or* ~th *pr.* -t). (wafer of) unleavened bread for Passover. [Yiddish, f. Heb. *maṣṣāh*]

maud *n.* Scots shepherd's grey striped plaid; travelling-rug like this. [18th c.; orig. unkn.]

mau'dlin *a.* & *n.* **1.** *a.* weakly or tearfully sentimental, esp. of tearful and effusive stage of drunkenness. **2.** *n.* weak or mawkish sentiment. [a. f. n. (w. ref. to pictures of weeping Mary Magdalen), ME f. OF *Madeleine* f. eccl. L *Magdalena* MAGDALEN]

mau'gre (-ger) *prep.* (arch.) in spite of. [ME, = ill will, f. OF *maugré* (*mal* bad f. L *malus*, *gré* pleasure f. L *gratus* pleasing)]

maul¹ *n.* special heavy hammer, commonly of wood, esp. for driving piles. [ME, f. OF *mail* f. L *malleus* hammer]

maul² *v.t.*, & *n.* **1.** *v.t.* beat and bruise; handle (thing, subject, quotation) roughly or carelessly; damage by criticism. **2.** *n.* brawl; (Rugby Footb.) loose scrum with ball off ground. [ME, f. prec.]

mau'lstick, mah'lstick, *n.* light stick held by (right-handed) painter in left hand as support for right, with padded leather ball at one end. [f. Du. *maalstok* (*malen* to paint, *stok* stick)]

mau'nder *v.i.* move or act listlessly or idly; talk in dreamy or rambling manner. [perh. f. obs. *maunder* beggar, to beg]

Mau'ndỹ *n.* **1.** ||distribution of ~ **money** (specially minted silver coins) by the Queen to the poor on ~ **Thursday** (next before Easter). **2.** (RC Ch.) ceremony of washing the feet of poor people (John 13:14). [ME, f. OF *mandé* f. L *mandatum* MANDATE[1], commandment (John 13:34)]

Mau'rist (mō'-) *n.* member of congregation of French Benedictine monks founded 1618, famous for scholarship and literary industry. [f. St. *Maur*, disciple of St. Benedict d. 584 + -IST]

Mauri'tian (merǐ'shan) *a.* & *n.* (native or inhabitant) of Mauritius. [f. *Mauritius*, island in Ind. Ocean + -AN]

mausolē'um *n.* magnificent tomb, orig. that of *Mausolus* king of Caria erected at his order by his queen Artemisia in 4th c. BC. [L, f. Gk *Mausōleion* (*Mausōlos* Mausolus)]

mauvaise honte (mōvāz awʹṅt) *n.* unjustified shame; painful diffidence. [F, = ill shame]

mauvais quart d'heure (mōvā kārdēr') *n.* short but unpleasant experience, interview, etc. [F, = bad quarter of an hour]

mauve (mōv) *n.* & *a.* **1.** *n.* bright but delicate pale purple dye from coal-tar aniline. **2.** *a.* of the colour of this. [F, lit. = mallow, f. L *malva*]

*****mā'ven** *n.* (colloq.) expert, connoisseur. [f. Heb. *mēḇĭn*]

mǎ'verick *n.* unbranded calf or yearling; unorthodox or independent-minded person. [f. S. A. *Maverick*, Texas engineer who owned but did not brand cattle *c.* 1850]

mā'vis *n.* (poet. or dial.) song-THRUSH[1]. [ME, f. OF *mauvis*, of uncert. orig.]

mavour'neen (-oor'-) *n.* & *int.* (Ir.) my darling. [f. Ir. *mo mhuirnín* (*mo* my, *muirnín* dim. of *muirn* love; see -EEN)]

maw *n.* stomach of animal or (joc.) person, esp. last of ruminant's four stomachs; jaws or throat of voracious animal; ~'worm, intestinal worm. [OE *maga*, = MDu. *maghe*, OHG *mago*, ON *magi* f. Gmc *magon*]

maw'kish *a.* of faint sickly flavour; feebly or falsely sentimental; hence ~LY[2] *adv.*, ~NESS *n.* [f. obs. *mawk* maggot f. ON *mathkr* f. Gmc *mathon*, + -ISH[1]]

mawl. Var. of MAUL[1].

max. *abbr.* maximum.

mǎ'xi *n.* (colloq.) maxi-coat, -skirt, etc. [abbr.]

mǎ'xi- *comb. form.* very large or long (*maxi-coat*). [abbr. of MAXIMUM; cf. MINI-]

mǎxi'll|a *n.* (*pl.* ~ae). jaw(bone), esp. upper jaw in most vertebrates; masticatory mouth-part of many arthropods; hence ~ARY[1] *a.* [L, = jaw]

mǎ'xim¹ *n.* a general truth drawn from science or experience; principle, rule of conduct. [ME, f. F. *maxime* or f. med. L *maxima* (*propositio*), fem. a. (as MAXIMUM)]

Mǎ'xim² *n.* single-barrelled quick-firing machine-gun, with water round barrel to keep parts cool. [f. Sir H. S. ~, its Amer.-born inventor d. 1916]

mǎ'ximal *a.* being or relating to a maximum; greatest possible in size, duration, etc.; hence ~LY[2] *adv.* [f. MAXIMUM + -AL]

mǎ'ximalist *n.* person who holds out for the maximum of his demands and rejects compromises. [f. as prec. + -IST, orig. as transl. of Russ. (see BOLSHEVIK)]

mǎ'ximiz|e, -īs|e (-īz), *v.t.* increase or enhance to the utmost; hence ~A'TION *n.* [f. L *maximus* (see foll.) + -IZE]

mǎ'ximum *n.* (*pl.* ma'xima) & *a.* highest (amount) possible, attained or attainable, usual, etc., (*reaches a, its, the maximum at noon*); ~ **price** (that may not by law etc. be exceeded); ~ **thermometer** (automatically recording highest temperature within given period); ~ **and minimum thermometer** (combining this and MINIMUM thermometer). [mod. L, neut. (as n.) of L *maximus* superl. of *magnus* great]

mǎ'xwěll *n.* unit of magnetic flux, corresponding to induction of one gauss. [f. J. C. *Maxwell*, Brit. physicist d. 1879]

may¹ *v. aux.* (*pres.* may exc. 2 *sing.* (arch.) **mayst** or **may'est**, *neg.* **mayn't**, (colloq.) **mayn't**; *past* **might** *pr.* mīt exc. 2 *sing.* (arch.) **mi'ghtest**, *neg.* **might not**, (colloq.) **mightn't** *pr.* mī'tent; no other parts used). **1.** Expr. possibility (*it may be true*, opp. *it cannot be true*; *it may not be true*, opp. *it must be true*; *it may or may not be true*; *you may* (WELL[3]) *walk ten miles without seeing one*); he ~ or **might** (= will perhaps) *lose his way*; *I* ~ **have been** (= was perhaps) *wrong*; *I was afraid he might* (= would perhaps) *lose his way*; *afraid he might* **have** (= had perhaps) *lost it*; *we* ~ or **might as well** *go* (as not); **that is as** ~ **be**, the truth of that is not yet determined; **be that as it** ~, irrespective of the situation regarding that. **2.** Expr. permission (*you may go*, opp. *you may not* or *must not or cannot go*; *I wish I might*); **you might** (= I request you to) *call at the baker's*; **you** etc. **might** (= you etc. ought to, yet do not) *offer to help*; **you** etc. **might**

(= you etc. ought to) *have offered*; (iron.) *who are you, may* or *might I ask?* **3.** (In purpose-clauses, and after *wish, fear,* etc.) *take, took, such a course as may, might, avert the danger*; *I hope he may, hoped he might, succeed.* **4.** (Expr. wish) *may you live to repent it!*; *may the best man win!*; *may it please your ladyship.* **5.** (In questions, emphasizing uncertainty) *who may* or *might you be?.* **6. might-have-been,** a past possibility, a person who might have been more eminent. [OE (1 sing.) *mæg,* of preterite-present form; OS, OHG, Goth. *mag,* ON *má,* f. Gmc **mag-* be strong f. IE **mogh-, *megh-*; cf. MAIN², MIGHT¹]

may² *n.* (poet.) maiden. [ME, perh. f. ON *mær,* Goth. *mawi* f. Gmc **maujō*]

May³ *n.* **1.** fifth month of year; (poet.) bloom, prime; **Queen of the ~,** girl chosen to be queen of games on May Day. **2.** (*may*). hawthorn (blossom). **3.** ||(Camb. Univ.; in *pl.*) examinations held in May; boat-races held during **~ Week** (late in May or early in June). **4. ~-apple,** Amer. herb bearing yellow egg-shaped fruit in May; **~-bug,** cockchafer; **~ Day,** 1 May esp. as festival with dancing, or as international holiday in honour of workers; **~'day,** international radio distress-signal [repr. pr. of F *m'aider* help me]; ||**~'fair,** opulent district in West End of London [named from fair formerly held there in May]; **~'flower,** any flower that blooms in May; **may'fly,** insect of order Ephemeroptera, living briefly in spring; **may'pole,** pole painted and decked with flowers and ribbons, for dancing round on May Day; **~ queen,** Queen of the May. [ME, f. OF *mai* f. L *Maius (mensis* month) of the goddess *Maia*]

ma'ya¹ (mah'-) *n.* (Hindu Philos.) illusion, esp. the material world regarded as unreal. [f. Skr. *māyā*]

Ma'y|a² (mah'-) *n.* member or language of an Amer. Ind. people of Guatemala and Mexico until 15th c.; hence **~an** *a.* [native name]

may'be (-bē, -bi), (arch.) **mayhă'p,** *advs.* perhaps, possibly. [ME, f. *it may be, it may hap*]

may'hem *n.* **1.** (Hist.) crime of maiming person so as to render him partly or wholly defenceless. **2.** (fig.) violent and damaging action. [f. AF *mahem,* OF *mayhem* (as MAIM)]

may'ing *n.* & *a.* participating in May Day festivities. [ME, f. MAY³ + -ING¹]

mayonnai'se (-ā'z) *n.* (dish of salmon, chicken, etc., with) dressing of egg-yolks, oil, vinegar, etc. [F, perh. f. *mahonnais -aise* of Port Mahon in Minorca]

mayor (mār) *n.* head of municipal corporation of city or borough (||in some large cities **Lord M~**; *Lord Mayor's* SHOW²); ||head of district council with status of borough; **~ of the palace,** (orig. under Merovingian kings) nominal subordinate to whom the power of his titular superior has passed; hence **may'oral** *a.* [ME, f. OF *maire* f. L (as MAJOR²)]

mayor'alty (mār'-) *n.* mayor's (period of) office. [ME, f. OF *mairalté* (as prec.; see -AL, -TY¹)]

mayor'ess (mar'-) *n.* mayor's wife (LADY *Mayoress*); female mayor; lady fulfilling ceremonial duties of mayor's wife. [f. MAYOR + -ESS¹]

may'weed *n.* stinking camomile, *Anthemis cotula.* [earlier *maidwede* f. obs. *maithe(n)* f. OE *magothe, mægtha* + WEED]

mă'zard, mă'zzard, *n.* **1.** (arch.) head, face. **2.** wild sweet cherry (*Prunus avium*) of Europe. [alt. of MAZER; cf. -ARD]

măzari'ne (-ē'n) *n.* & *a.* deep rich blue. [17th c., perh. f. name of Cardinal *Mazarin,* Fr. statesman d. 1661, or Duchesse de *Mazarin,* Fr. noblewoman d. 1699]

Mă'zdaism *n.* Zoroastrianism. [f. Avestan *mazda,* the good principle in ancient-Persian theology]

māze *n.,* & *v.t.* **1.** *n.* complex network of paths, labyrinth; network of paths and hedges designed as puzzle for those who try to penetrate it; (fig.) confusion, confused mass, etc. **2.** *v.t.* (esp. in *p.p.*) bewilder, confuse. [ME, n. f. v., orig. in p.p.; cogn. w. AMAZE]

mă'zer *n.* (Hist.) hardwood drinking-bowl, usu.

silver-mounted. [ME, f. OF *masere,* of Gmc orig.; cf. OHG *masar* maple, excrescence on tree f. **mas-* spot (cf. MEASLES)]

*mazu'ma (-ōō'-) *n.* (sl.) money. [Yiddish]

mazŭr'ka *n.* lively Polish dance in triple time; music for this. [F, or f. G *masurka,* f. Pol. *mazurka* woman of province *Mazovia*]

mā'z|y *a.* resembling a maze; full of turnings; hence **~ĭLY²** *adv.,* **~ĭNESS** *n.* [f. MAZE + -Y²]

mă'zzard. See MAZARD.

MB *abbr.* Bachelor of Medicine. [f. L *Medicinae Baccalaureus*]

MBA *abbr.* Master of Business Administration.

||**MBE** *abbr.* Member (of the Order) of the British Empire.

MC *abbr.* master of ceremonies; *Member of Congress; ||Military Cross.

Mc(/s) *abbr.* megacycles (per second).

MCC *abbr.* Marylebone Cricket Club.

McCarthyism, McCoy. See MacC-.

M.Ch(ir). *abbr.* Master of Surgery. [f. L *Magister Chirurgiae*]

M.Com. *abbr.* Master of Commerce.

MCP *abbr.* male chauvinist pig.

||**MCR** *abbr.* Middle Common Room.

MD *abbr.* Doctor of Medicine. [f. L *Medicinae Doctor*]; Managing Director; mentally deficient.

MD, Md., *abbrs.* Maryland.

Md *symb.* mendelevium.

*MDT *abbr.* Mountain Daylight Time.

me¹. See I².

mē², mi (mē), *n.* (Mus.) third note of scale in movable-doh system; the note E in fixed-doh system. [ME, f. L *mira*; see GAMUT]

ME *abbr.* Maine.

Me. *abbr.* Maine; *Maître* (title of Fr. advocate).

mea culpa (mēa kŭ'lpa, māa kŏŏ'lpa) *n.* & *int.* (expr.) acknowledgement of one's fault or error. [L, = by my fault]

mead¹ *n.* alcoholic liquor of fermented honey and water. [OE *me(o)du* = MLG *mede,* OHG *metu, mitu,* ON *mjöthr* f. Gmc **meduz* f. IE **medhu-*]

mead² *n.* (poet. or arch.) = foll. [OE *mæd* f. Gmc **mædwō* (**mētwā* mowed land, cogn. w MOW³)]

mea'dow (mě'dō) *n.* piece of grassland, esp. one used for hay; low well-watered ground, esp. near river; **~ brown,** common brown butterfly; **~-grass** (of genus *Poa*); *~ **lark,** bird of genus *Sturnella,* akin to bobolink; **~ pipit,** brown and white Old World pipit (*Anthus pratensis*); **~ rue,** ranunculaceous plant of genus *Thalictrum*; **~ saffron,** perennial plant (*Colchicum autumnale*) abundant in meadows, with lilac flowers; **~sweet,** rosaceous plant of genus *Filipendula* or *Spiraea,* common in meadows, with creamy-white fragrant flowers; hence **~y²** *a.* [OE *mædwe,* obl. case of *mæd* (see prec.)]

||**mea'gre, *mea'ger,** (-ger) *a.* (Of person etc.) lean, thin; (esp. of meals) poor, scanty; (of literary composition, ideas, etc.) lacking fullness, unsatisfying; hence **~LY²** *adv.,* **~NESS** *n.* [ME f. AF *megre,* OF *maigre* f. L *macer*]

meal¹ *n.* edible part of any grain or pulse (usu. exc. wheat) ground to powder; (Sc.) oatmeal; *maize flour; powdery substance made by grinding; **~-beetle,** insect (*Tenebrio molitor*) infesting granaries etc.; **~-worm,** its larva. [OE *melu,* = OS, OHG *melo,* ON *mjöl* f. Gmc **melwam* (**mel-* etc. f. IE)]

meal² *n.* customary (or any) occasion of taking food; food so taken; **make a ~ of,** (1) consume as meal, (2) make (task etc.) seem unduly laborious; **~-ticket,** ticket entitling one to meal, esp. at specified place with reduced cost, (fig.) thing or person that provides for one; **~'time,** usual time of eating. [OE *mæl* mark, fixed time, meal, = OS, OHG, ON *māl,* Goth. *mēl* f. Gmc **mælam* f. IE **mē-* to measure]

mea'lie *n.* (usu. in *pl.*) (S. Afr.) maize; corn-cob. [f. Afrik. *milie* f. Port. *milho* maize, millet f. L *milium*]

mea′ly *a.* **1.** of, like, containing, meal; (of boiled potatoes) dry and powdery; ∼-**bug,** insect infesting vines etc., whose body is covered with white powder. **2.** (Of horse) spotty; (of complexion) pale; ∼(-**mouthed**), not outspoken, afraid to use plain expressions. **3.** Hence **mea′li**NESS *n.* [f. MEAL[1] + -Y[2]]

mean[1] *n.* **1.** condition, quality, virtue, course of action, equally removed from two opposite (usu. blameworthy) extremes; GOLDEN *mean.* **2.** (Math.) term, or one of terms, between first and last terms of arithmetical, geometrical, etc., progression (*2 and 8 have arithmetic mean 5, geometric mean 4*); quotient of the sum of several quantities and their number. **3.** (in *pl.,* often treated as *sing.*) that by which a result is brought about (*it has been a means of extending our trade*; *by fair means or foul*); WAYS *and means*; ∼**s of grace,** sacraments etc. **4.** (in *pl.*) money resources (*he lives beyond his, on his own, means*; ∼**s test,** official inquiry as to proof of need before financial assistance is given); wealth (*a man of means*). **5. by all** (**manner of**) ∼**s,** in every possible way, at any cost, certainly; **by no** (**manner of**) ∼**s, not by any** (**manner of**) ∼**s,** not at all, certainly not; **by** ∼**s** (the agency, instrumentality) **of** (person, thing, do*ing*). [ME, f. foll., partly thr. F]

mean[2] *a.* (Of quantity) equally far from two extremes; calculated as MEAN[1] 2; ∼ **free path,** average distance travelled by gas molecule etc. between collisions; ∼ **proportional,** geometric MEAN[1] of two quantities; ∼ **sea level** (half-way between mean levels of high and low water); ∼ **sun,** fictitious sun moving in celestial equator at mean rate of real sun; ∼ **time** (based on mean sun); **in the** ∼ (intervening) **time** or **while;** ∼**′time,** ∼**′while,** *advs.,* in the mean time. [ME, f. AF *me(e)n,* f. OF *meien, moien* f. L *medianus* MEDIAN]

mean[3] *a.* **1.** (Of capacity, understanding, etc.) inferior, poor; ∼ **white,** = POOR *white.* **2.** not imposing in appearance, shabby; **no** ∼, a very good (*he is no mean scholar*). **3.** ignoble, small-minded, (*a mean trick*): malicious, ill-tempered; *vicious, nastily behaved; *(colloq.) (1) unwell, (2) secretly ashamed, (*feel mean*); *(sl.) skilful. **4.** niggardly, not generous or liberal. **5.** Hence ∼′LY[2] *adv.,* ∼′NESS -n-n-) *n.* [OE *(ge)mǣne,* = OS *gimēni,* OHG *gimeini,* Goth. *gamains* f. Gmc *gamainiz* (*ga-* Y-, *mainiz* f. *moinis* f. *moi-, *mei-* exchange)]

mean[4] *v.t.* (∼t *pr.* mĕnt). **1.** have as one's purpose, have in mind, (*mischief,* BUSINESS, *to* do). **2.** design, destine, for a purpose etc. (*mean it to be used*; *mean it for a stopgap*); *he* **was** ∼t (by parents etc., or by Providence) *for a soldier*; *it is* ∼t **for** *you,* you are to receive it or take note of it; *I* ∼ *you* to (am determined that you shall) *go*; *am I* ∼t (intended, expected) to *go?*; ∼ **well** (**to, towards, by**), be kindly disposed (towards). **3.** intend to convey (specified sense) or indicate (object) or refer to (thing) (*I mean that it is impossible*; *I mean his father, his own hat, Richmond in Surrey*); ∼ **it,** not be joking or exaggerating. **4.** be of some (specified) importance *to* (person), esp. as source of benefit or object of affection etc. **5.** (Of words or event or person) signify, import, (thing, *that*); have as equivalent in another language ('*mensa*' *means* '*table*'); entail, involve, (*it means catching the early train*); portend (*this means war*); **what do you** ∼ **by** it?, can you justify such behaviour etc.?. [OE *mǣnan,* = OS *mēnian,* OHG *meinen* f. WG *mainjan* f. IE **mēn-*; cf. MIND[1]]

meä′nder *n.,* & *v.i.* **1.** *n.* (in *pl.*) sinuous windings of river; winding paths. **2.** circuitous journey; ornamental pattern of lines winding in and out, fret. **3.** *v.i.* wander at random; (of stream) wind about. [f. L *maeander* f. Gk *Maiandros,* winding river in Phrygia]

meä′ndrine *a.* full of windings (esp. of corals of genus *Maeandra,* with surface like human brain). [f. prec. + -INE[1]]

mea′nie, mea′nỹ, *n.* (colloq.) niggardly or small-minded person. [f. MEAN[3] + -IE, -Y[3]]

mea′ning *n.* what is meant; significance; importance; **with** ∼, significantly; hence ∼FUL, ∼LESS, *adjs.* [ME, f. MEAN[4] + -ING[1]]

mea′ning[2] *a.* expressive, significant, whence ∼LY[2] *adv.*; WELL-*meaning.* [f. MEAN[4] + -ING[2]]

means. See MEAN[1].

meant. See MEAN[4].

mea′nỹ. See MEANIE.

mea′sles (-ze*l*z) *n.* (as *pl.* or *sing.*) acute infectious virus disease marked by red spots on skin; such spots; tapeworm disease of pigs; GERMAN[2] *measles.* [ME *masele(s)* f. MLG *masele,* MDu. *masel* pustule, OHG *masala,* cogn. w. MAZER]

mea′slỹ (-z-) *a.* of or affected with measles; (of pork) infested with tapeworms; (sl.) inferior, contemptible, worthless. [f. prec. + -Y[2]]

mea′surab|**le** (mĕ′zher-) *a.* that can be measured; **within a** ∼**le distance of,** getting near (something undesirable); hence ∼LY[2] *adv.*; [ME, f. OF *mesurable* f. LL *mensurabilis* f. L *mensurare* (as foll.; see -ABLE)]

mea′sure[1] (mĕ′zher) *n.* **1.** size or quantity found by measuring; **for good** ∼, as something beyond the minimum, as a finishing touch; **short, full,** ∼, less, not less, than professed amount; ‖*clothes* **made to** ∼ (in accordance with measurements taken); **take** person's ∼, measure him for clothes etc., (fig.) gauge his character, abilities, etc. **2.** degree, extent, amount, (esp. **in a** or **in some** ∼, partly); **a** ∼ **of,** some degree of. **3.** vessel of standard capacity for transferring fixed quantities of liquids etc. (*pint measure*). **4.** rod, tape, etc., for measuring (TAPE-*measure*; *yard-measure*). **5.** unit of capacity, e.g. bushel (*20 measures of wheat*). **6.** system of measuring (*liquid, linear,* LONG[1], *measure*). **7.** that by which a thing is computed (*a chain's weakest link is the measure of its strength*). **8.** quantity contained in another an exact number of times; **greatest common** ∼, greatest number that is a factor of each of given numbers. **9.** prescribed extent or quantity (**set** ∼**s to,** limit; **beyond** ∼, excessively); (Print.) width of page or column of type. **10.** poetical rhythm, metre; metrical group of dactyl or two iambuses, trochees, spondees, etc.; time of piece of music; (Mus.) bar; (arch.) dance (*tread a measure*). **11.** suitable action (*take measures to ensure that*). **12.** legislative enactment. **13.** mineral stratum (COAL *measures*). [ME f. OF *mesure* f. L *mensura* (metiri mens- measure; see -URE)]

mea′sure[2] (mĕ′zher) *v.* **1.** *v.t.* ascertain extent or quantity of (thing) by comparison with fixed unit or with object of known size; ascertain size and proportions of (person) for clothes. **2.** look (person) up and down (*with one's eye*). **3.** mark off or *off* (line etc. of given length). **4.** ∼ one's **length,** accidentally fall flat on the ground; ∼ **swords,** (of duellists) see that swords are of equal length, (fig.) try one's strength *with* (person). **5.** estimate (quality, person's character, etc.) by some standard or rule. **6.** deal *out* (thing *to* person). **7.** bring (one*self,* one's strength etc.) into competition *with.* **8.** (poet.) traverse (distance). **9.** *v.i.* take measurements; be of specified size (*it measures six inches*); ∼ **up** (**to**), have necessary qualifications (for); **mea′suring-jug, -tape,** etc., (marked at various points to assist measurement); **mea′suring-worm,** caterpillar of geometer moth. [ME, f. OF *mesurer* f. L *mensurare* (as prec.)]

mea′sured (mĕ′zherd) *a.* In vbl senses: rhythmical, regular in movement, (*measured tread*); (of language) carefully weighed; hence ∼LY[2] *adv.* [p.p. of prec.]

mea′sureless (mĕ′zher*l*-) *a.* not measurable, infinite. [ME, f. MEASURE[1] + -LESS]

mea′surement (mĕ′zherm-) *n.* act or result of measuring; (in *pl.*) detailed dimensions. [f. MEASURE[2] + -MENT]

meat *n.* **1.** animal flesh as food, usu. (cf. BUTCHER[1]*'s meat*) excluding fish and poultry; *edible part of fruits, nuts, eggs, shellfish, etc.; **green** ∼, grass, green vegetables, as food; WHITE[1] *meat.* **2.** (arch.) food of any kind. **3. one man's** ∼ **is another man's poison,**

not everybody likes the same things; *this was* ∿ **and drink** (a source of great pleasure) *to him.* **4.** (arch.) a meal (*before, at, after, meat*). **5.** (fig.) principal or interesting or most useful part *of.* **6.** ∿**-axe,** butcher's cleaver; *meat* BALL¹ 5; ∿**-fly** (breeding in meat); *meat* LOAF¹; ∿**-man,** butcher; ∿**-safe,** cupboard for storing meat, usu. of wire gauze etc.; ||∿ **tea,** tea at which meat is served, high TEA. **7.** Hence ∿'LESS *a.* [OE *mete* food, = OS *meti, mat,* OHG *maz,* ON *matr,* Goth. *mats* f. Gmc **matiz, *matam,* (**mat-* measure; cf. METE²)]

mēā′tus *n.* (*pl.* ∿ *or* ∿**es**). (Anat.) (orifice of) channel or passage in the body; **auditory** ∿, channel of the ear. [L, = passage (*meare* flow, run)]

mea′t|y *a.* full of meat, fleshy; (fig.) full of substance; of or like meat; hence ∿ĬLY² *adv.,* ∿ĬNESS *n.* [f. MEAT + -Y²]

Mĕ′cca *n.* place one aspires to visit; birthplace of a faith, policy, pursuit, etc. [∿ in Arabia, birthplace of Muhammad and chief place of Muslim pilgrimage]

Mĕcca′nō (-ah′-) *n.* (P) set of miniature usu. metal parts from which engineering models can be constructed. [cf. foll.]

mĕchă′nĭc (-k-) *n.* **1.** skilled worker, esp. one who makes or uses or repairs machinery. **2.** (in *pl.,* usu. treated as *sing.*) branch of applied mathematics dealing with motion and tendencies to motion; science of machinery; method of construction or routine operation. [orig. a., ME, f. OF *mecanique* or f. L f. Gk *mēkhanikos* (as MACHINE; see -IC)]

mĕchă′nĭcal (-kă′-) *a.* **1.** of machines or mechanism. **2.** (arch.) of the nature of handicraft. **3.** working or produced by machinery. **4.** ∿ **advantage,** ratio of exerted to applied force in machine; ∿ **drawing** (done with compasses etc.); *mechanical* ENGINEER¹ 4; ∿ **equivalent,** value of unit (*of heat*) in terms of mechanical work; *mechanical* MIXTURE, POWERS; ∿ **transport,** motor branch of RCT. **5.** (Of person or action) like a machine, automatic, lacking originality **6.** (Of agency, principle, etc.) belonging to mechanics; (of theory etc.) explaining phenomena by assumption of mechanical action, whence ∿ISM (3) *n.* **7.** of mechanics as a science. **8.** Hence ∿LY² *adv.,* ∿NESS *n.,* **mĕchă′nĭco-** (-kă′-) *comb. form.* [ME, f. L (as prec.; see -AL)]

mĕchani′cian (-kanĭ′shan) *n.* one skilled in constructing machinery. [f. MECHANIC + -IAN]

mĕ′chanĭsm (-k-) *n.* structure, adaptation of parts, of machine (lit. or fig.); system of mutually adapted parts working together (as) in machine; mode of operation of a process; (Art) mechanical execution, technique; (Philos.) doctrine that all natural phenomena, including life, allow mechanical explanation by physics and chemistry. [f. mod. L *mechanismus* f. Gk (as MACHINE; see -ISM)]

mĕ′chan|ist (-k-) *n.* mechanician; expert in mechanics; (Philos.) one who holds the doctrine of mechanism, whence ∿ĭ′stĭc *a.* [f. MECHANIC + -IST]

mĕ′chanĭz|e (-k-), **-ĭs|e** (-īz), *v.t.* give mechanical character to; introduce machines in; (Mil.) re-equip by substituting motor transport for horse-drawn vehicles, replacing cavalry by tanks and armoured cars, etc. [f. MECHANIC + -IZE]

Mĕ′chlĭn (-k-) *n.* ∿ (*lace*), lace made at *Mechlin* (now *Mechelen* or *Malines*) in Belgium.

M.Econ. *abbr.* Master of Economics.

mĕcō′nĭum *n.* (Med.) dark substance forming first faeces of new-born infant. [L, lit. poppy-juice, f. Gk *mēkōnion* (*mēkōn* poppy)]

Mĕd *n.* (colloq.) Mediterranean Sea. [abbr.]

M.Ed. *abbr.* Master of Education.

med. *abbr.* medium.

mĕ′dal *n.* piece of metal, usu. in form of coin, struck or cast with inscription and device to commemorate event etc., or awarded as distinction to soldier, scholar, athlete, etc., for services rendered, proficiency, etc.; **the reverse of the** ∿, the other side of a question; ∿ **play,** (Golf) play in which the score is

reckoned by counting the number of strokes taken for the round, opp. *match play*; hence ∿IED² (-ld), **mĕdă′llĭc,** *adjs.* [f. F *médaille* f. It. *medaglia* f. Rom. **medallia* f. pop. L **metallea* n. pl. f. L *metallum* METAL]

mĕdă′llion (-yon) *n.* large medal; thing so shaped, e.g. decorative panel or tablet, portrait, etc. [f. F *médaillon* f. It. *medaglione* augment. of *medaglia* (see prec., -OON)]

mĕ′dallist, *mĕ′dalist, *n.* engraver or designer of medals; recipient of (specified) medal (*gold medallist*). [f. MEDAL + -IST]

mĕ′ddl|e *v.i.* busy oneself unduly *with,* interfere *in*; hence ∿ER¹ *n.,* ∿ESOME¹ (-dels-) *a.* [ME, f. OF *medler,* var. of *mesler* f. Rom. **misculare* f. L *miscēre* mix]

Mēde *n.* one of the earliest Iranian inhabitants of Media in Persia; **law of the** ∿**s and Persians,** immutable law (Dan. 6: 8). [ME, f. L *Medi* pl. f. Gk *Mēdoi*]

mē′dia¹ *n.* (*pl.* ∿**e**). **1.** (Phonet.) voiced stop, e.g. *g, b, d.* **2.** (Biol.) middle membrane enclosing artery or other vessel. [L, fem. of *medius* middle]

mē′dia² *n. pl.* of MEDIUM (esp. sense 6).

mediae′val. See MEDIEVAL.

mē′dial *a.* situated in the middle; of average size; hence ∿LY² *adv.* [f. LL *medialis* f. L *medius* middle; see -AL]

mē′dian¹ *a. & n.* **1.** *a.* situated in the middle. **2.** *n.* (Anat.) median artery, vein, nerve, etc.; (Geom.) straight line drawn from any vertex of triangle to middle of opposite side; (Statistics) value of a quantity such that exactly half of a given population have greater values of that quantity. [f. F *médiane* or f. L *medianus* (as prec.; see -AN)]

Mē′dian² *a. & n.* (one) of the Medes; (inhabitant) of ancient Media. [f. MEDE + -IAN]

mē′diant *n.* (Mus.) third note of diatonic scale of any key. [f. F *médiante* f. It. *mediante* part. (as n.) of obs. *mediare* come between, f. L (as MEDIATE²; see -ANT)]

mēdiăstī′u|um *n.* (*pl.* ∿**a**). (Anat.) membranous middle septum, esp. between lungs; hence ∿AL *a.* [mod. L, f. med. L *mediastinus* medial, after L *mediastinus* drudge (*medius* middle)]

mē′diate¹ *a.* connected not directly but through some other person or thing; involving intermediate agency; hence ∿LY² (-tlĭ) *adv.* [ME, f. L *mediatus* p.p. of *mediare* (see foll., -ATE³)]

mē′di|āte² *v.* **1.** *v.t.* form connecting link between; be the medium for bringing about (result) or conveying (gift etc.). **2.** *v.t.* intervene (*between* two persons) for purpose of reconciling them. **3.** So ∿A′TION *n.* [f. LL *mediare* f. L *medius* middle, + -ATE³]

mē′diatĭz|e, -īs|e (-īz), *v.t.* annex (State) to another State, leaving former sovereign his title and some rights of government; hence ∿A′TION *n.* [f. F *médiatiser* (*médiat* f. as MEDIATE¹; see -IZE)]

mē′diātor *n.* one who mediates, esp. Christ as mediating between God and man; hence *or cogn.* **mediatō′rIAL,** **mē′diatory,** *adjs.,* **mē′diātrix** *n.* (esp. Virgin Mary). [ME, f. OF *mediatour* f. LL *mediator -oris* (as MEDIATE²; see -OR)]

mē′dĭc¹ *n.* (sl.) medical practitioner or student. [f. L *medicus* physician (*medēri* heal)]

mē′dĭc². Var. of MEDICK.

mē′dicable *a.* admitting of remedial treatment. [f. L *medicabilis* (as MEDICATE; see -ABLE)]

*Mĕ′dicaid *n.* Federal system of health insurance for the poor. [f. foll. + AID²]

mĕ′dical *a. & n.* **1.** *a.* of the art of medicine in general or as opp. to surgery, obstetrics, etc.; ∿ **attendant,** one's physician; ∿ **certificate** (of fitness or unfitness to work etc.); ∿ **examination** (to determine person's physical fitness); ∿ **examiner,** physician making medical examinations of eg *acting like* coroner; ∿ **jurisprudence,** forensic medicine; ∿ **man,** ∿ **practitioner,** physician or surgeon; ||∿ **officer,** person in charge of health services of local authority or other organization; ∿ **school** (in which physicians etc. are trained); ∼ **student,** person studying for qualification in medicine. **2.** (Of disease) requiring medical, not surgical, treatment; (of hospital ward etc.) used for patients receiving such treatment. **3.** Hence ∼LY² *adv.* **4.** *n.* (colloq.) medical examination; medical student. [f. F *médical* or f. med. L *medicalis* f. L *medicus*; see MEDIC¹, -AL]

medicament (mĭdĭ'-, mĕ'dĭ-) *n.* substance used in curative treatment. [f. F *médicament* or f. L *medicamentum* (as MEDICATE; see -MENT)]

*Mĕ'dĭcāre *n.* Federal system of health insurance for those over 65. [f. MEDICAL + CARE¹]

mĕ'dĭc|āte *v.t.* treat medically; impregnate with medicinal substance; hence or cogn. ∼A'TION *n.,* ∼ATIVE *a.* [f. L *medicari* administer remedies to (*medicus*; see MEDIC¹, -ATE³)]

Mĕdĭcē'an *a.* of the Medici family, rulers of Florence in 15th c. [f. mod. L *Medicei* f. It. *Medici,* + -AN]

mĕdĭ'cĭnal *a.* & *n.* of medicine; (substance) having healing properties; hence ∼LY² *adv.* [ME f. OF, f. L *medicinalis* (as foll.; see -AL)]

mĕ'dĭcine (mĕ'dsĭn, mĕ'dĭsĭn) *n.,* & *v.t.* **1.** *n.* art of restoring and preserving health, esp. by means of remedial substances and regulation of diet etc., as opp. to surgery and obstetrics. **2.** substance, esp. one taken internally, used in this; (among primitive peoples) spell, charm, fetish, (∼-man, magician). **3. a dose** etc. **of** one's **own** ∼, treatment such as one is accustomed to giving others; **take** one's ∼, submit to disagreeable thing; ∼ **ball,** stuffed leather ball thrown and caught as means of exercise; ∼ **chest,** box containing remedies. **4.** *v.t.* (arch.) give medicine to; cure with medicine. [ME, (v. f. OF *medeciner*) f. OF *medecine* f. L *medicina* (*medicus*; see MEDIC¹, -INE⁴)]

mĕ'dick *n.* leguminous plant of genus *Medicago,* esp. lucerne. [ME, f. L *medica* f. Gk *Mēdĭkē poa* Median grass]

mĕ'dĭcō *n.* (*pl.* ∼s). (colloq.) medical practitioner or student. [It., f. L (as MEDIC¹)]

mĕ'dĭcō- *comb. form.* medical (and) (*medico-legal*). [f. L *medicus* (see MEDIC¹) + -O-]

mĕdĭē'val, mĕdĭae'val, *a.* of or imitating the Middle Ages; (fig.) old-fashioned; ∼ **history** (of 5th–15th c.); *medieval* LATIN; hence ∼ISM (2), ∼IST (3), *ns.,* ∼IZE (2, 3) *v.t.* & *i.,* ∼LY² *adv.* [f. mod. L *medium aevum* f. L *medius* middle + *aevum* age, + -AL]

mĕdĭŏ'cre (-ker) *a.* of middling quality, neither good nor bad; fairly bad. [f. F *médiocre* or f. L *mediocris* of middle height or degree (*medius* middle, *ocris* rugged mountain)]

mĕdĭŏ'crĭtў *n.* In adj. senses; mediocre person. [ME, f. F *médiocrité* f. L *mediocritas* (as prec.; see -ITY)]

mĕ'dĭtāt|e *v.* **1.** *v.t.* plan mentally; design. **2.** *v.i.* exercise the mind in (esp. religious) contemplation (*on* or *upon* subject). **3.** Hence or cogn. **mĕdĭtā'TION,** ∼OR, *ns.* [f. L *meditari,* frequent. f. IE **med-* measure, + -ATE³]

mĕ'dĭtative *a.* inclined to meditate; indicative of meditation; hence ∼LY² (-vlĭ) *adv.,* ∼NESS (-vn-) *n.* [f. prec. + -IVE]

mĕdĭterrā'nèan *a.* & *n.* **1.** *a.* & *n.* (Of water area) land-locked; M∼ (**Sea**), that which separates Europe from Africa. **2.** *a.* of the region of the Mediterranean Sea; (of person) dark-complexioned and not tall. **3.** (arch.) (Of land) remote from coast. [f. L *mediterraneus* inland (*medius* middle, *terra* land) + -AN]

mĕ'dĭum *n.* (*pl.* me'dia *or* ∼s) & *a.* **1.** *n.* middle quality, degree, etc., (*between* extremes, or abs.); HAPPY *medium.* **2.** intervening substance through which impressions are conveyed to senses etc., e.g. air; (fig.) environment, conditions of life. **3.** agency, means, (*by* or *through the medium of*); ∼ **of circulation,** what serves as instrument of commercial transactions, e.g. coin. **4.** liquid, e.g. oil, water, with which pigments are mixed for use in painting. **5.** (*pl.* ∼s). person claiming to have communication with the spirits of the dead etc. and reveal its results to others;

hence ∼ISM (3) *n.,* ∼ï'stIC *a.* **6.** means by which something is communicated; material or form used by artist, musical composer, etc.; (in *pl.,* or erron. as *sing.*) = MASS² *media.* **7.** *a.* intermediate between two degrees or amounts, average, moderate; ∼ **bowler,** ∼ **pace,** (Cricket, neither fast nor slow); *medium* TERM¹; ∼ **wave,** radio wave having wavelength between 100 and 1,000 metres. [L, = middle, neut. (as n.) of *medius* middle]

mĕ'dlar *n.* (tree, *Mespilus germanica,* with) fruit like small brown apple, eaten when decayed; **Japan(ese)** ∼, loquat. [ME, f. OF *medler* (**medle,* *mesdle f. *mesle* f. L f. Gk *mespilē, -on*)]

mĕ'dley *n., a.,* & *v.t.* **1.** *n.* heterogeneous mixture; mixed company; literary miscellany; musical composition made from various previous ones; ∼ **relay,** relay race between teams in which each member runs a different distance or uses a different swimming-stroke. **2.** *a.* (arch.) mixed, motley. **3.** *v.t.* (arch.) make a medley of, intermix. [ME, f. OF *medlee* var. of *meslee* f. Rom. *misculata (as MEDDLE)]

Mĕdŏ'c (mā-) *n.* red Bordeaux wine from *Médoc* district in SW France.

mĕdŭ'lla *n.* marrow of bone; spinal marrow; ∼ (**oblongata** *pr.* ŏblŏnggah'ta; L, = prolonged), hindmost segment of brain; central part of some organs, esp. hair or kidney; soft internal tissue of plants; hence **mĕdŭ'llARY²** *a.* [L, = pith, marrow, prob. cogn. w. *medius* middle]

mĕdŭ'sa *n.* (*pl.* ∼e *or* ∼s). (Zool.) jellyfish; sexually reproductive form of hydrozoan or scyphozoan, with jelly-like body and stinging tentacles; hence **mĕdŭ'sAN** *a.* [L, f. Gk *Medousa,* name of a Gorgon with snakes for hair]

meed *n.* (literary or arch.) reward; merited portion (*of* praise etc.). [OE *mēd,* = OS *mēda,* OHG *mēta* f. WG *mēda cogn. w. Goth. *mizdō,* Gk *misthos* reward]

meek *a.* piously humble and submissive; submitting tamely to injury etc.; hence ∼LY² *adv.,* ∼NESS *n.* [ME *me(o)c* f. ON **miúkr, mjúkr* soft, gentle]

meer'kăt *n.* suricate. [Du., = sea-cat]

meer'schaum (-shəm) *n.* hydrated magnesium silicate, found in soft white masses chiefly in Turkey; tobacco-pipe with bowl made from this. [G, = sea-foam (*meer* sea, *schaum* foam), transl. Pers. *kef-i-daryā,* w. ref. to its frothiness]

meet¹ *n.* meeting of hounds and persons for hunt, or of cyclists, athletes, etc., for competition; *meeting-place of railway trains. [f. foll.]

meet² *v.* (**met**). **1.** *v.t.* come face to face with (person coming from opposite direction); go to place to be present at arrival of (person, train, etc.); make the acquaintance of (*pleased to meet you;* **John, meet Mary*); ∼ (person) **half-way,** (fig.) respond to friendly advances of, make a compromise with; WELL³ *met!.* **2.** (Of line, road, river, moving object, etc.) reach point of contact with (another line etc.); ∼ **the eye, ear,** be visible, audible; ∼ person's **eye,** see he is looking at one, look at him in one's turn; **more in it than** ∼s **the eye,** hidden qualities or complications. **3.** oppose in battle or duel or contest; grapple with (evils etc.). **4.** come by accident or design into the company of. **5.** experience, receive, suffer, (one's death, fate, etc.). **6.** come into conformity with (person, his wishes). **7.** satisfy (demand; ∼ **the case,** be adequate); give valid answer to (objection etc.); pay (cost); provide funds required by (cheque, bill at maturity). **8.** *v.i.* (Of two or more persons) come face to face; be in opposition in contest etc.; come *together* (*they had* or *were met together*); assemble for purpose of conference, business, etc. **9.** come into contact (*waistcoat* **won't** ∼, is too small in girth to be fastened); (of qualities) unite in same person; *make* END³ *s meet.* **10.** ∼ **with,** happen to meet (person, obstacle, etc.). = sense 5, * = sense 4; ∼ **up** (colloq.) happen to meet (*with* person). [OE *mētan,* = OS *mōtian,* ON *mœta,* Goth. *gamotjan* f. Gmc *gamōtjan (*mōtam meeting; cf. MOOT)]

meet³ *a.* (arch.) suitable, fit, proper, (*for* thing, *to* do, *to* be done); *it is* ∼ (proper) *that*; hence ∼'LY² *adv.*, ∼'NESS *n.* [ME (*i*)*mete* repr. OE *gemǣte* f. Gmc **gamǣtja-* (**ga-* Y-, **mæt-* METE²)]

mee'ting *n.* In vbl senses; race-meeting; assembly of people for entertainment, discussion, etc.; assembly (esp. of Quakers) for worship; persons assembled (*address the meeting*); (arch.) duel; ∼**-house**, place of worship (US, or derog. exc. of Quakers); ∼**-place** (appointed for meeting). [ME, f. MEET² + -ING¹]

mě'ga- *comb. form.* **1.** large, as: ∼**cepha'lic**, large--headed; ∼**lith**, (Archaeol.) large stone, esp. as monument; ∼**li'thic**, made of, marked by use of, large stones; ∼**sco'pic**, visible to naked eye; ∼**ther'ium**, huge extinct herbivorous slothlike animal. **2.** Denoting factor of one million (10^6), as: ∼**death**, death of one million persons (esp. as unit of results of war); *megahertz*; ∼**ton(ne)**, one million tons, esp. = this quantity of TNT as unit of equivalent explosive power; *megavolt*; *megawatt*. [Gk (*megas* great)]

mě'galo- *comb. form.* great, as ∼**ma'nia**, insanity of self-exaltation, passion for grandiose things; ∼**saur'us**, huge extinct carnivorous lizard. [Gk (*megas megal-* great; see -O-)]

mĕgalŏ'polis *n.* a great city or its way of life; populous area surrounding one or more cities. [f. prec. + Gk *polis* city]

mě'gaphōne *n.* large speaking-trumpet for sending sound of voice to a distance. [f. MEGA- + -PHONE]

mě'gapŏde, mě'gapŏd, *n.* bird of mainly Australasian family Megapodidae, building mound of debris in which eggs are laid and hatched. [f. mod. L *Megapodius* (genus-name) f. as MEGA- + Gk *pous podos* foot]

||**Mě'gger** (-g-) *n.* (Electr.; **P**) apparatus for measuring insulation resistance. [cf. MEGOHM]

mĕgi'lp (-g-) *n.* vehicle (usu. linseed oil and varnish) for oil colours. [18th c.; orig. unkn.]

mě'gohm (-ōm) *n.* (Electr.) unit of resistance, one million ohms. [f. MEGA- 2 + OHM]

mě'grim¹ *n.* (arch.) migraine; whim, fancy; (in *pl.*) depression, low spirits; (in *pl.*) staggers, vertigo, in horses etc. [ME *mygrane* (f. MIGRAINE]

mě'grim² *n.* small flounder or similar flat-fish. [19th c.; orig. unkn.]

mei'nie (mā'-) *n.* (arch.) family; retinue; multitude of persons. [ME, f. OF *meinee, mesnee* f. Rom. *mansionata f. L (as MANSION)]

mei|o'sis (mī-) *n.* (*pl.* ∼**o'ses** *pr.* -ō'sēz). **1.** = LITOTES. **2.** (Biol.) process of division of cell nuclei whereby diploid number of chromosomes is halved, to be combined with another half-set at fertilization; cf. MITOSIS. **3.** Hence ∼**o'tic** *a.* [mod. L, f. Gk *meiōsis* (*meioō* lessen, f. *meiōn* less; see -OSIS)]

Mei'stersinger (mī's-) *n.* (*pl.* same). one of the German lyric poets and musicians of 14th-16th c. organized in guilds and having elaborate technique. [G (*meister* MASTER¹, *singer* SINGER)]

mě'lamine (-ēn) *n.* white crystalline organic base, a polymer of cyanamide; ∼ (**resin**), plastic made from melamine and an aldehyde. [f. *melam* (arbitrary) + AMINE]

mělanchō'lia (-n-k-) *n.* mental illness marked by depression and ill-founded fears. [LL; see MELANCHOLY]

mělanchō'lic (-n-k-) *a.* melancholy; liable to melancholy; *melancholic* TEMPERAMENT. [ME, f. OF *melancolique* f. L f. Gk *melagkholikos* (as foll.; see -IC)]

mě'lancholy (-n-k-) *n. & a.* **1.** *n.* (habitual or constitutional tendency to) sadness and depression; pensive sadness; (Hist.) one of the four HUMOUR¹s, black bile. **2.** *a.* (Of person) sad, gloomy; (of thing) saddening, depressing; (of words etc.) expressing sadness. [ME, f. OF *melancolie* f. LL f. Gk *melagkholia* (*melas melanos* black, *kholē* bile); see -Y¹]

Mělanē'sian (-shən) *a. & n.* (member or language) of dark-skinned and frizzy-haired dominant race in

Melanesia. [f. *Melanesia*, island-group in W. Pacific (f. Gk *melas* black + *nēsos* island + -IA¹) + -AN]

mélange (mālah'nzh) *n.* mixture, medley. [F (*mêler* mix, as MEDDLE)]

mě'lanin *n.* dark-brown or black pigment in hair, skin, etc., of coloured races or melanotic patient or in melanism. [f. Gk *melas melanos* black + -in]

mě'lanism *n.* darkness of colour (esp. of animals) resulting from abnormal development of black pigment in skin, hair, etc. [f. as prec. + -ISM]

mělan|ō'sis *n.* (*pl.* ∼**oses** *pr.* -ō'sēz). morbid deposit, abnormal development, of black pigment in tissue; hence ∼**o'tic** *a.* [mod. L, f. Gk (as MELANIN) + -OSIS]

Mě'lba *n.* ∼ **toast**, thin crisp toast; PEACH¹ *Melba*. [f. Dame N. ∼, Austral. soprano d. 1931]

***měld**¹ *v.t. & i.* merge, blend, combine. [perh. f. MELT² + WELD²]

měld² *v. & n.* **1.** *v.t. & i.* (In some card-games) declare for a score. **2.** *n.* act of melding; group of cards (to be) melded. [f. G *melden* announce]

mêlée, *mê'lee, (mě'lā) *n.* confused fight, skirmish, scuffle; muddle. [F (as MEDLEY)]

mě'lic¹ *a.* (Of poem, esp. Gk lyric) meant to be sung. [f. L f. Gk *melikos* (*melos* song; see -IC)]

mě'lic² *n.* grass of genus *Melica*. [f. mod. L *melica* f. It., = sorghum]

mē'lior|āte *v.t. & i.* improve; hence ∼**A'TION** *n.*, ∼**ātive** *a.* [f. LL *meliorare* (as foll.) + -ATE³]

mē'lior|ism *n.* doctrine that the world may be made better by human effort, so ∼**IST** (2) *n.* [f. L *melior* better + -ISM]

měli'sma (-z-) *n.* (*pl.* ∼**ta**). (Mus.) melodic music or tune; hence **mělismă'tic** (-z-) *a.* [Gk]

mělli'ferous *a.* yielding or producing honey. [f. L *mellifer* (*mel* honey; see -FEROUS)]

mělli'flu|ous (-lōō-) *a.* (Of voice, words) sweet as honey; so ∼**ENCE** *n.*, ∼**ENT** *a.*, ∼**ous**LY² *adv.*, ∼**ous**-NESS *n.* [ME, f. OF *melliflue* or f. LL *mellifluus* (*mel* honey, *fluere* flow) + -OUS]

mě'llow (-ō) *a. & v.* **1.** *a.* (Of fruit) soft, sweet, and juicy; (of wine) well-matured; (of earth) rich, loamy; (of character) softened by age or experience; (of sound, colour, light) full and pure without harshness; genial, jovial; partly intoxicated; hence ∼**LY²** *adv.*, ∼**NESS** *n.* **2.** *v.t. & i.* Make or become mellow. [ME, perh. f. attrib. use of OE *melu* memu MEAL¹]

mělŏ'dēon, -dion, *n.* American organ. [f. MELODY + HARMONIUM, w Graecized ending]

mělŏ'dic *a.* of or relating to melody; ∼ **minor**, (Mus.) scale with major 6th and 7th ascending, minor 6th and 7th descending. [f. F *mélodique* f. LL *melodicus* f. Gk *melōidikos* (as MELODY; see -IC)]

mělŏ'dious *a.* of or producing melody; sweet--sounding; hence ∼**LY²** *adv.*, ∼**NESS** *n.* [ME, f. OF *melodieus* (as MELODY; see -OUS)]

mě'lodist *n.* singer; composer of melodies. [f. MELODY + -IST]

me'lodize, -ise (-īz), *v.* **1.** *v.i.* make melody. **2.** *v.t.* make melodious. [f. MELODY + -IZE]

mě'lodrama (-rah-) *n.* sensational dramatic piece with crude appeals to emotions and usu. happy ending; genre of drama of this type; language or behaviour or occurrence suggestive of this; (Hist.) play with songs interspersed and with orchestral music accompanying the action; hence **mělodramă'tic** *a.*, **mělodramă'tically** *adv.*, **mělŏdră'matist** (1) *n.*, **mělŏdră'matize** (1, 3) *v.t.* [earlier *-drame* f. F *mélodrame* f. *melos* music + F *drame* DRAMA]

mě'lody *n.* sweet music; musical arrangement of words; arrangement of single notes in musically expressive succession; principal part in harmonized music. [ME, f. OF *melodie* f. LL *melodia* f. Gk *melōidia* (*melos* song; see ODE, -Y¹)]

mě'lon *n.* (sweet fruit of) gourd, esp. MUSK-*melon* or WATER¹-*melon*; (sl.) spoils or profits to be shared. [ME f. OF, f. LL *melo -onis*, abbr. of L *melopepo* f. Gk *mēlopepōn* (*mēlon* apple, *pepōn* gourd f. *pepōn* ripe)]

melt[1] *n.* melted metal etc.; amount melted at a time; process of melting; ~-**water** (formed by melting of snow and ice, esp. from glacier). [f. foll.]

melt[2] *v.* (*p.p.* ~'**ed** or, as *a.* of substances not easily melted, **mo'lten** *pr.* mō'-). **1.** *v.i.* become liquefied by heat; (colloq., of person) suffer extreme heat; (of food) be easily dissolved *in the mouth*; (of clouds) break *into rain*; (of person, heart, feelings) be softened by or *with* pity or love, dissolve *into tears*, (*the melting mood*); (of sound) be soft and liquid; pass by imperceptible degrees *into* (another form); ~ **away**, disappear by liquefaction, dwindle away, (colloq., of person) depart unobtrusively; ~ **down**, become liquid and lose structure, whence ~-*down* n. **2.** *v.t.* change to liquid condition by heat; soften (person, feelings); ~ **down** (coin, plate, etc., to use the metal as raw material). **3.** ~'**ing-point,** temperature at which solid melts; ~'**ing-pot,** (fig.) place of reconstruction or vigorous mixing. [OE *meltan, mieltan,* = ON *melta* digest f. Gmc **maltjan* dissolve (**melt-* f. IE **meld-*; cogn. w. MALT[1])]

me'lton *n.* cloth with close-cut nap, for overcoats etc.; ‖M~ **Mow'bray** (mō'b-) **pie,** kind of raised meat pie. [f. *M~ Mowbray* in Leics.]

me'mber *n.* **1.** part or organ of body, esp. limb; **unruly** ~, (arch.) the tongue [Jas. 3: 5–8]; ~ **of Christ,** (fig.) Christian. **2.** constituent portion of complex structure; person belonging to a society etc.; M~ (one formally elected to take part in proceedings) **of Parliament, *of Congress;** person admitted to lowest grade of order, e.g. to Order of the British Empire, 5th class (MBE), or to Royal Victorian Order, 4th or 5th class (MVO). **3.** part or branch of political body. **4.** division or clause of sentence; group of figures, part of numerical expression; one side of equation. **5.** Hence (-)~ED[2] (-erd), ~LESS, *adjs.* [ME f. OF *membre* f. L *membrum* limb]

me'mbership *n.* being a member; number of members; body of members. [f. prec. + -SHIP]

me'mbrāne *n.* pliable sheetlike connective tissue or lining in animal or vegetable body; similar structure formed in some diseases; skin of parchment, forming part of a roll; so **membranᴀ'ceous, membrā'neous, me'mbranous,** *adjs.* [f. L *membrana* skin of body, parchment, (as MEMBER)]

membrum virile (mĕmbrŭm vīrī'lī) *n.* (arch.) penis. [L, = male member]

mĕme'ntō *n.* (*pl.* ~ **es** *or* ~**s**). object serving as reminder or warning, or kept as memorial of person or event; ~ *mori* (mōr'ī; L, = remember you must die), warning or reminder of death (e.g. skull). [L, imper. of *meminisse* remember]

mĕ'mō *n.* (*pl.* ~**s**). (colloq.) memorandum. [abbr.]

mĕ'moir (-wār) *n.* record of events; history written from personal knowledge or special sources of information; (esp. in *pl.*) (auto)biography; essay on learned subject specially studied by the writer; hence ~IST (1) *n.* [f. F *mémoire* masc., spec. use of *mémoire* fem. MEMORY]

memorabī'lia *n. pl.* memorable things. [L, neut. pl. (as foll.)]

mĕ'mor|able *a.* worth remembering, not to be forgotten, easily remembered; hence ~ABI'LITY *n.,* ~ABLY *adv.* [ME, f. F *mémorable* or f. L *memorabilis* (*memorare* bring to mind f. *memor* mindful; see -ABLE)]

memorā'nd|um *n.* (*pl.* ~**a** *or* ~**ums**). note to help the memory; record of events etc. for future use; (Law) document recording terms of contract, agreement, establishment of company, etc.; informal letter without signature; informal diplomatic message. [ME, f. L, neut. sing. gerundive of *memorare* (see prec.)]

memŏr'ial *a.* & *n.* **1.** *a.* (Of statue, festival, building, religious service, etc.) serving to commemorate; of memory; *M~ **Day,** day (usu. last Mon. in May) commemorating those who died on active service. **2.**

n. memorial object, custom, etc.; (usu. in *pl.*) record, chronicle; informal diplomatic paper; statement of facts as basis of petition etc. **3.** Hence ~IST (1) *n.* [ME f. OF, or f. L *memorialis* (as MEMORY; see -AL)]

memŏr'ialīze, -ise (-īz), *v.t.* commemorate; address memorial to (person or body). [f. prec. + -IZE]

memŏ'ria te'chnica (tĕ'k-) *n.* system or contrivance used to assist memory. [mod. L, = artificial memory]

me'morīze, -ise (-īz), *v.t.* commit to memory. [f. foll. + -IZE]

me'mory *n.* **1.** faculty by which things are recalled to or kept in the mind; this in an individual (**a good** ~, ability to retain and recall much); **commit to** ~, learn so as to be able to recall. **2.** recovery of one's knowledge by mental effort; recollection, remembrance; **from** ~, without verification in books etc.; **in** ~ **of,** as a record of, to keep alive the remembrance of. **3.** (In computer) = STORE 3. **4.** act of remembering; person or thing remembered. **5.** posthumous repute (*his memory has been censured*; *of happy memory*); **the Immortal M**~ (toast to Sc. poet Robert Burns d. 1796). **6.** length of time over which memory extends (*beyond, within, the memory of men; within* LIVING[2] *memory*). [ME, f. OF *memorie, memoire* f. L *memoria* (*memor* mindful, remembering, cogn. w. MOURN; see -Y[1])]

me'msahib *n.* (Anglo-Ind., Hist.) European married lady as spoken of or to by Indians. [f. MA'AM + SAHIB]

mĕn. See MAN[1].

me'nace *n.* **1.** (literary) threat. **2.** dangerous or obnoxious thing or person. [ME, f. Rom. **minacia* = L *minaciae* pl. (*minax* threatening f. *minari* threaten)]

me'nace[2] *v.t.* & *i.* threaten, esp. in malignant or hostile manner. [ME, f. AF *manasser,* OF *menacier* f. Rom. **minaciare* (as prec.)]

mé'nage (mānah'zh) *n.* domestic establishment; ~ *à trois* (ah trwah), household consisting of husband, wife, and lover of one of these. [f. OF *manaige* f. Rom. **mansionaticum* f. L (as MANSION; see -AGE)]

mĕnà'gerie *n.* collection of wild animals in captivity for exhibition etc. [f. F *ménagerie* (as prec.; see -ERY)]

menār'che (-kī) *n.* onset of first menstruation. [mod. L, f. as MENO- + Gk *arkhē* beginning]

mĕnd[1] *n.* repaired hole in material etc.; **on the** ~, improving in health or (of affairs etc.) condition. [f. foll.]

mĕnd[2] *v.* **1.** *v.t.* restore to sound condition, repair, (broken article; torn clothes, whence ~'ING[1] (5) *n.*; damaged road, etc.); add fuel to (fire); cut (worn quill pen) to required shape; (*least said soonest mended*; *mend* one's FENCE[1]*s*; ~ **or end,** improve or abolish; LEAST *said soonest mended*; *mend* one's FENCE[1]*s*; ~ **one's manners** *or* **ways,** improve them; ~ **matters,** rectify or improve state of affairs; ~ **one's pace,** walk more quickly; hence ~'ABLE *a.,* ~'ER[1] *n.* **2.** *v.i.* regain health. [ME, f. AF *mender* (*amender* AMEND)]

mĕndā'cious (-shŭs) *a.* lying, untruthful; hence or cogn. ~LY[2] *adv.,* **mĕndā'city** *n.* [f. L *mendax -dacis* perh. f. *mendum* fault; see -ACIOUS]

mĕndelē'vium *n.* (Chem.) artificially produced transuranic element. [f. D. I. *Mendeleev,* Russ. chemist d. 1907 + -IUM]

Mĕ'ndelism *n.* theory of heredity showing that recurrence of certain inherited characters depends on presence of genes; so **Mĕnde'lian** *a.* & *n.,* **Mĕnde'lianism** (3) *n.* [f. G. J. *Mendel,* Austrian botanist d. 1884 + -ISM]

mĕ'ndic|ant *a.* & *n.* **1.** *a.* begging (living solely on alms); hence or cogn. ~ANCY, **mĕndi'city,** *ns.* **2.** *n.* beggar; mendicant friar. [f. L *mendicare* beg (*mendicus* beggar f. *mendum* fault); see -ANT]

menfolk. See MAN[1].

mĕnhā'den *n.* large herring of genus *Brevoortia* on E. coast of N. America, used for manure, and yielding valuable oil. [Algonquian; cf. Narragansett *munnawhatteaúg*]

me'nhir (-ēr) *n.* (Archaeol.) tall upright usu.

prehistoric monumental stone. [f. Breton *men hir* (*men* stone, *hir* long)]

mē′nial *a.* & *n.* **1.** *a.* (Of service) degrading, servile; (of servant, usu. derog.) domestic; hence ∿LY² *adv.* **2.** *n.* menial servant. [ME f. AF (MEINIE; see -AL)]

mē′ninx *n.* (usu. in *pl.* **meni′nges** *pr.* mĭnĭ′njĕz). any of three membranes enveloping brain and spinal cord (dura mater, arachnoid, pia mater); hence **mēni′nge**AL *a.*, **mēningi′**TIS *n.*, (-nj-), **mēni′ngo**-CELE (-ngg-) *n.*, hernia of meninges. [mod. L, f. Gk *mēnigx -iggos* membrane]

mēni′sc|us *n.* (*pl.* ∿i *pr.* -sī). lens convex on one side, concave on the other; (Math.) figure of crescent form; (Phys.) curved upper surface of liquid in tube. [mod. L, f. Gk *mēniskos* crescent dim. of *mēnē* moon]

Mē′nnonīte *n.* member of a Protestant sect that arose in Friesland in 16th c. with tenets resembling those of Quakers and Baptists. [f. *Menno* Simons, founder d. 1559]

mē′no- *comb. form.* menstruation, as: ∿rrha′gia (-rā′-) excessive flow, ∿rrhoe′a (-rē′a) ordinary flow, of the menses. [f. Gk *mēn mēnos* month]

mēnŏ′logў *n.* calendar, esp. that of Greek Church, with biographies of saints. [f. mod. L *menologium* f. eccl. Gk *mēnologion* (*mēn* month, *logos* account); see -Y¹]

mē′nopaus|e (-z) *n.* final cessation of menses; period of woman's life (usu. between 40 and 50) when this occurs; **male** ∿e, climacteric period of man's life; hence ∿AL *a.* [f. mod. L *menopausis* (as MENO-, PAUSE)]

mēnŏr′ah (-a) *n.* seven-branched candelabrum used in Jewish worship. [Heb., = candlestick]

mē′nsēs (-z) *n. pl.* flow of blood etc. from mucous lining of human or primate womb, occurring in women at intervals of about one lunar month. [L, *pl.* of *mensis* month]

Mē′nshĕvīk *n.* (Hist.) Russian socialist of the more moderate party (cf. BOLSHEVIK). [f. Russ. *Men'shevik* member of minority (*men'she* less)]

mens rea (mĕnz rē′a) *n.* criminal intent of an action. [L, = guilty mind]

mē′nstrual (-ŏŏ-) *a.* of the menses. [ME, f. L *menstrualis* (as MENSTRUUM; see -AL)]

mē′nstru|āte (-ŏŏ-) *v.i.* discharge the menses; hence ∿A′TION *n.* [f. LL *menstruare* (as foll.) + -ATE³]

mē′nstruous (-ŏŏ-) *a.* of the menses; menstruating. [ME, f. OF *menstrueus* or f. LL *menstruosus* (as foll.; see -OUS)]

mē′nstru|um (-ŏŏ-) *n.* (*pl.* ∿a). solvent (lit. or fig.). [ME f. L, neut. (as n.) of *menstruus* monthly (*mensis* month) f. alchemical parallel between transmutation into gold and supposed action of menses on ovum]

mē′nsūrable *a.* measurable, having fixed limits; (Mus.) having fixed rhythm and notes of definite duration. [F, or f. LL *mensurabilis* (*mensurare* to measure f. L *mensura* MEASURE¹; see -ABLE)]

mē′nsūral *a.* of measure; (Mus.) = prec. [f. L *mensuralis* (*mensura* MEASURE¹; see -AL)]

mēnsūrā′tion *n.* measuring; (Math.) rules for finding lengths, areas, and volumes. [f. LL *mensuratio* (as MENSURABLE; see -ATION)]

-ment *suf.* forming ns. expr. result or means of vbl action (*fragment, implement, ligament, ornament*; *abridgement, amazement, embankment, treatment*); also f. adjs. (*merriment, oddment*). [f. or after F f. L *-mentum*]

mē′ntal¹ *a.* & *n.* **1.** *a.* of the mind; done by the mind; ||(colloq.) affected with mental disorder. **2.** ∿ **age**, degree of person's mental development expressed as age at which same degree is attained by average child; ∿ **arithmetic** (performed without use of written figures); ∿ **asylum, home, hospital**, establishment for care of mental patients; *mental* BLOCK¹; ∿ **cruelty**, infliction of suffering on another's mind, esp. as grounds for divorce; ∿ **defective, deficiency**, (condition of) person mentally unable to deal with his ordinary affairs; ∿ **illness**, disorder of the mind; ∿ **patient**, sufferer

from mental illness; *mental* RESERVATION. **3.** Hence ∿LY² *adv.* **4.** *n.* (colloq.) mental patient. [ME f. OF, or f. LL *mentalis* f. L *mens -ntis* mind; see -AL]

mē′ntal² *a.* of the chin. [F, f. L *mentum* chin; see -AL]

mē′ntal|ism *n.* (Philos.) doctrine that mind, and not the material world, is real; (Psych.) doctrine that the mind may be studied by introspection; so ∿IST (2) *n.* [f. MENTAL¹ + -ISM]

mēntă′litў *n.* what is mental or in or of the mind; (degree of) intellectual power; mental character or outlook. [f. MENTAL¹ + -ITY]

mēntā′tion *n.* mental action; state of mind. [f. L *mens -ntis* mind + -ATION]

mē′nthŏl *n.* camphor-like substance got from oil of peppermint etc., used as flavouring and to relieve local pain etc.; hence ∿ātED¹ *a.*, treated with or containing menthol. [G, f. L *mentha* MINT³; see -OL 2]

mē′ntion¹ *n.* mentioning, naming, (*of* thing); formal reference to meritorious person (in mil. dispatches etc.; **honourable** ∿, award of merit to candidate in examination, work of art, etc., not entitled to prize); **make (no)** ∿ **of**, (not) refer to. [ME f. OF, f. L *mentio -onis* (*men-* root of *mens* mind; see -ION)]

mē′ntion² *v.t.* refer to, remark upon, specify by name (esp. thing not obviously essential to context; *this was expressly mentioned*); (in deprecation of apology or thanks) **don't** ∿ **it**; (introducing fact or thing of secondary or, as rhet. artifice, of primary importance) **not to** ∿; hence ∿ABLE *a.* [F *mentionner* (*mention*; see prec.)]

mē′ntŏr *n.* experienced and trusted adviser. [F, f. L f. Gk *Mentōr* adviser of the young Telemachus in Homer's 'Odyssey' and Fénelon's 'Télémaque' (root *men-* think)]

mē′nū *n.* list of dishes to be served or available in restaurant etc. [F adj. (as n., = detailed list) f. L *minutus* MINUTE³]

MEP *abbr.* Member of the European Parliament.

||**mē′pacrine** (-ēn) *n.* quinacrine. [f. methyl + *paludism* (= malaria) + *acridine*]

Mēphist|o′phĕlēs (-z) *n.* evil spirit to whom Faust, in German legend, sold his soul; fiendish person; hence ∿ŏphĕlE′AN, ∿ophĕ′lIAN, *adjs.* [G, 16th c., of unkn. orig.]

mēphī′tis *n.* noxious emanation, esp. from the earth; noisome or poisonous stench; so **mēphī′t**IC *a.* [L]

-mer *suf.* (Chem.) forming ns. denoting substance of a specified class, esp. polymer, (*dimer, isomer, tautomer*). [f. Gk *meros* part, share]

mē̌r′cantīle *a.* of trade, commercial; trading; mercenary, fond of bargaining; ∿ **marine**, shipping employed in commerce not war. [F, f. It. (*mercante* MERCHANT; see -IL)]

mē̌r′cantil|ism *n.* old economical theory that money is the only form of wealth; so ∿IST (2) *n.* [f. prec. + -ISM]

mē̌rcă′ptan *n.* (Chem.) substance like an alcohol but with sulphur in place of oxygen. [f. mod. L *mercurium captans* capturing mercury]

Mē̌rcā′tor *n.* ∿'s **projection**, map projection of globe on cylinder, with straight lines of latitude and longitude at right angles. [f. G. ∿ (Latinized f. Kremer), Flemish-born geographer d. 1594]

mē̌r′cenar|ў *a.* & *n.* **1.** *a.* working merely for money or other reward; hired; hence ∿INESS *n.* **2.** *n.* hired soldier in foreign service. [ME, f. L *mercenarius* (*merces -edis* reward); see -ARY¹)]

||**mē̌r′c|er** *n.* dealer in textile fabrics, esp. silks and other costly materials; hence ∿ERY (1) *n.* [ME f. AF; OF *mercier* f. Rom. *merciarius f. L *merx mercis* goods; see -ER² (2)]

mē̌r′cerīze, -īse (-īz), *v.t.* treat (cotton fabric or thread) under tension with caustic alkali to give greater strength and impart lustre. [f. J. *Mercer*, alleged inventor of the process d. 1866 + -IZE]

mē̌r′chandīse (-z) *n.* & *v.* **1.** *n.* commodities of commerce, goods for sale. **2.** *v.i.* & *t.* trade (in);

promote sales (of). [ME, f. OF *marchandise* (*marchand*; see foll., -ISE²)]

mer′chant *n.* **1.** wholesale trader, esp. with foreign countries; (esp. US & Sc.) retail trader. **2.** ~ **bank** (dealing in commercial loans and financing); ~ **fleet,** *marine,* ∥**navy, service,** mercantile marine; ~**man,** ~ **ship,** ship conveying merchandise; ~ **prince,** wealthy merchant; LAW¹ *merchant.* **3.** (sl.) person fond of an activity etc. (SPEED-*merchant*). [ME, f. OF *marchand, marchant* f. Rom. *mercatare* frequent. of L *mercari* trade (*merx mercis* merchandise); see -ANT]

mer′chantable *a.* saleable, marketable. [ME, f. *merchant* v. f. OF *march*(*ĕ*)*ander* (*marchand*; see prec.) + -ABLE]

mer′ciful *a.* having, showing, or feeling mercy; hence ~LY² *adv.,* ~NESS *n.* [ME, f. MERCY + -FUL]

mer′ciless *a.* pitiless; showing no mercy; hence ~LY² *adv.,* ~NESS *n.* [ME, f. MERCY + -LESS]

mercur′ial *a.* & *n.* **1.** *a.* (Of person) sprightly, ready-witted, volatile; hence ~ITY (-ă′l-) *n.* **2.** of or containing mercury; (*M*~) of the planet Mercury; hence ~LY² *adv.* **3.** *n.* mercurial drug; hence ~ISM (5) *n.,* ~IZE (5) *v.t.* [ME, f. OF *mercuriel* or f. L *mercurialis* (as foll.; see -AL)]

mer′cury *n.* **1.** (*M*~). Roman god of eloquence, skill, thieving, etc., and messenger of gods; guide, messenger, (arch., exc. in newspaper titles). **2.** (*M*~). planet nearest to sun. **3.** silvery-white heavy normally liquid metal usu. got from cinnabar and used in barometers, thermometers, amalgams, and mirrors, (**the** ~ **is rising,** weather is improving), quicksilver; hence **mercur′ic, mercur′ous** (*or* mer′-), *adjs.* (Chem.). **4.** herb of genus *Mercurialis.* [ME, f. L *Mercurius* (*merx mercis* merchandise)]

mer′cy *n.* & *a.* **1.** *n.* compassion, forbearance, shown by one to another (esp. offender) who is in his power and has no claim to kindness; God's forbearance and forgiveness of sins; **have** ~ **on** or **upon,** show mercy to; ~ (**me**)!, ~ **on** or **upon us,** (excl. of terror or surprise). **2.** compassionateness; ERRAND *of mercy;* **at the** ~ **of,** wholly in the power of, liable to danger or harm from. **3.** act of mercy; **small** ~, minor piece of good fortune; **that is a** ~ (blessing, thing to be thankful for); **left to the tender mercies of,** at the mercy of, (usu., iron.) exposed to probable rough handling by. **4.** ~-**seat,** golden covering of Ark of Covenant, throne of God, Christ as propitiation. **5.** *a.* administered or performed out of mercy or pity for suffering person (*mercy killing*). [ME f. OF *merci* f. L *merces -edis* reward, in LL pity, thanks]

mere¹ *n.* lake, pond, (arch. or poet., exc. in place names). [OE, = OS, OHG *meri,* ON *marr* sea, Goth. *mari-* f. Gmc *mari* f. IE *mori-*]

mere² *attrib. a.* that is solely or no more or better than (what the noun implies) (*a mere swindler; the merest trace* or *buffoonery*); **no** ~, by no means only a; (Law) ~ **right** (without possession); hence ~LY² (mēr′li) *adv.* [ME, f. AF *meer,* OF *mier* f. L *merus* unmixed]

me′rĕ³ *n.* Maori war-club, esp. one made of greenstone. [Maori]

meretri′cious (-shŭs) *a.* of or befitting a prostitute; (of ornament, literary style, etc.) showily but falsely attractive; hence ~LY² *adv.,* ~NESS *n.* [f. L *meretricius* f. *meretrix -tricis* harlot (*merēri* hire; see -TRIX) + -OUS]

mergăn′ser *n.* diving fish-eating northern duck of genus *Mergus* etc., with long narrow serrated hooked bill. [mod. L, f. L *mergus* diver (*mergere* dive) + *anser* goose]

merg|e *v.i.* & *t.* lose, cause (thing) to lose, character or identity *in* (another); embody (title, estate, *in* greater one); join or blend gradually; combine (*with*); hence ~′ENCE *n.* [f. L *mergere mers-* dip, plunge, partly thr. legal AF *merger*]

mer′ger *n.* merging, esp. of estate in another; combining of two commercial companies etc. into one;

absorbing of minor offence in a greater one. [f. AF (as prec.; see -ER⁴)]

meri′dian *n.* & *a.* **1.** *n.* circle passing through celestial poles and zenith of any place on earth's surface; circle of constant longitude, passing through given place and the terrestrial poles (**prime** ~, that from which longitude is reckoned, esp. Greenwich meridian); corresponding line on map; (arch.) point at which sun or star attains highest altitude; (fig.) prime, full splendour. **2.** *a.* of noon; (fig.) of the period of greatest splendour, vigour, etc. [ME, f. OF *meridien* or f. L *meridianus* a. (*meridies* midday f. *medius* middle + *dies* day; see -AN)]

meri′dional *a.* & *n.* **1.** *a.* of (the inhabitants of) the south (esp. of Europe); of a meridian. **2.** *n.* inhabitant of the south (esp. of France). [ME f. OF, f. LL *meridionalis* (irreg. f. L *meridies*; see prec., -AL)]

meri′ngue (-ă′ng) *n.* confection of sugar, white of eggs, etc., baked crisp; small cake or shell of this, usu. decorated or filled with whipped cream etc. [F, of unkn. orig.]

meri′nō (-rē′-) *n.* (*pl.* ~**s**). ~ (**sheep**), variety of sheep with fine wool; soft woollen or wool-and-cotton material like cashmere, orig. of merino wool; fine woollen yarn. [Sp., of uncert. orig.]

mĕ′ristĕm *n.* (Bot.) growing tissue of small cells in plants; hence ~A′TIC *a.* [f. Gk *meristos* divisible (*merizō* divide f. *meros* part), after *xylem*]

mĕ′rit *n.,* & *v.t.* **1.** *n.* quality of deserving well; excellence, worth; (Theol.) good deeds as entitling to future reward; (usu. in *pl.*). thing that entitles to reward or gratitude; **make a** ~ **of,** view, represent, (one's own conduct) as meritorious; **the** ~**s,** the intrinsic rights and wrongs (*of* case etc., esp. Law); *judge* (proposal etc.) **on its** ~**s,** with regard only to its intrinsic excellences etc.; ∥**Order of M**~ (founded 1902, for distinguished achievement; *~ **system,** practice of giving public office to those most competent for it. **2.** *v.t.* deserve, be worthy of, (reward, punishment, consideration, etc.). [ME; (v. f. F *mériter*) f. OF *merite* f. L *meritum* price, value, neut. p.p. (as n.) of *merēri* earn, deserve]

mĕritŏ′cracy *n.* government by persons selected according to merit in competition; group of persons thus selected; society thus governed. [f. prec. + -o- + -CRACY]

mĕritŏr′ious *a.* (Of person or act) having merit, deserving reward, praise, or gratitude; deserving commendation for thoroughness etc.; hence ~LY² *adv.,* ~NESS *n.* [ME, f. L *meritorius* (*merēri* merit-earn; see -ORY) + -OUS]

merle *n.* (arch. or Sc.) blackbird. [ME f. F, f. L *merulus, -la*]

mer′lin *n.* small Eur. or N. Amer. falcon (*Falco columbarius*). [ME, f. AF *merilun* f. OF *esmerilon* augment. f. *esmeril* f. Frank. *smeril*]

mer′lon *n.* solid part of embattled parapet, between two embrasures. [F, f. It. *merlone* (*merlo* battlement)]

mer′maid *n.* imaginary half-human sea creature, with head and trunk of woman and tail of fish; ~**′s purse,** = SEA-*purse*; so **mer′MAN¹** *n.* [ME, f. MERE¹ in obs. sense 'sea' + MAID]

mĕ′ro- *comb. form.* partly, partial, as: ~**blast,** ovum that is partly germinal, partly nutritive; ~**HE′DRAL,** (of crystal) having less than full number of faces corresponding to its symmetry. [f. Gk *meros* part + -o-]

-merous *suf.* (esp. Bot. & Entom.) having so many parts (*dimerous, 5-merous*). [f. Gk (as prec.) + -OUS]

Mĕrovi′ngian (-nj-) *a.* & *n.* (member) of the Frankish dynasty founded by Clovis and reigning in Gaul and Germany *c.* 500–750. [f. F *mérovingien* f. med. L *Merovingi* f. L *Meroveus* name of reputed founder; see -ING³, -IAN]

mĕ′rriment *n.* hilarious enjoyment; mirth, fun. [f. MERRY² + -MENT]

mĕ′rry¹ *n.* gean. [f. F *merise,* taken as pl. (cf. CHERRY)]

mĕ'rrў² *a.* joyous; full of laughter or gaiety; (colloq.) slightly tipsy; **make ∼**, be festive; **make ∼ over**, make fun of; **∼ andrew**, mountebank's assistant, clown, buffoon, (lit. or fig.); **∼ Christmas!** (as salutation); ||*merry* DANCER*s*; **∼** or **merrie** (pleasant) **England; ∼-go-round**, revolving machine with wooden horses or cars for riding on at fair etc., revolving device in playground, (fig.) cycle of bustling activities; **∼ hell**, (sl.) great disturbance (*play merry hell with*); **∼-making**, festivity; **∼ men**, companions of outlaw etc., (joc.) person's assistants; **the M∼** Monarch, Charles II; **∼thought**, wishbone of bird; hence **mě'rrі**LY² *adv.* [OE *myr(i)ge* f. Gmc **murgjaz* (cf. MIRTH); perh. = Gmc **murgjaz* short]

*me'sa (mā'-) *n.* high rocky tableland with precipitous sides. [Sp., lit. 'table', f. L *mensa*]

mésalliance (māzǎ'lïahn̄s) *n.* marriage with person of inferior social position. [F (*més-* MIS-; see ALLIANCE)]

mě'scăl *n.* **1.** (liquor got from) maguey plant. **2.** peyote cactus; **∼ buttons**, its disc-shaped dried tops. [f. Sp. *mezcal* f. Nahuatl *mexcalli*]

mě'scaline (-ēn), **-in**, *n.* hallucinogenic alkaloid present in mescal buttons. [f. prec.+-INE⁵]

Mesdames, Mesdemoiselles. See MADAME, MRS; MADEMOISELLE.

mėsee'ms (-z) *v.i.* impers. (arch.) it seems to me. [ME, f. *me* dat.+SEEMS]

mĕsĕmbrŷä'nthĕmum (-z-) *n.* S. Afr. plant of genus *Mesembryanthemum*, with bright pink or white flowers opening at about noon. [mod. L, f. Gk *mesēmbria* noon+*anthemon* flower]

mĕsĕncĕ'phalŏn *n.* midbrain. [f. Gk *mesos* middle+ *encephalon* (see ENCEPHALIC)]

mě'senterў *n.* fold of peritoneum attaching some part of intestinal canal to posterior wall of abdomen; hence **mĕsĕntĕ'rIC** *a.*, **mĕsĕnteri'TIS** *n.* [f. med. L f. Gk *mesenterion* (as MESO-, *enteron* intestine)]

mĕsh¹ *n.* open space, interstice, of net, sieve, etc.; (in *pl.*) network, (fig.) snare; network fabric; (Physiol., in *pl.*) interlaced structure; **in ∼**, (of teeth of wheels) engaged. [earlier *meish*, *meash*, *mash* f. MDu. *maesche*, *masche* f. Gmc **mǣsk-*, **mask-*]

mĕsh² *v.* **1.** *v.t.* catch in net (lit. or fig.). **2.** *v.i.* (of teeth of wheel) be engaged (*with* others), (fig.) be harmonious. [f. prec.]

mě'sial (-z-) *a.* of, in, directed towards, middle line of a body; hence **∼**LY² *adv.* [irreg. f. Gk *mesos* middle+ -IAL]

mesic. See MESON.

mě'smer|ism (mĕ'z-) *n.* (arch. or fig.) hypnotic state produced in patient by operator's influence over will and nervous system; doctrine concerning, influence producing, this; hence **mĕsmĕ'rIC** *a.*, **∼IST** (1) *n.*, **∼IZE** (4) *v.t.*, (mĕz-). [f. F. A. *Mesmer*, Austrian physician d. 1815+-ISM]

mĕsne (mēn) *a.* Intermediate; **∼ lord** (holding estate from superior feudal lord); **∼ process**, proceedings in suit intervening between primary and final process; **∼ profits** (received from estate by tenant between two dates). [ME f. law F, var. of AF *meen*, MEAN²; cf. DEMESNE]

mě'so- (-s-, -z-) *comb. form.* middle, intermediate, as: **∼-American**, of region from Mexico to Nicaragua; **∼blast**, middle germ-layer of embryo; **∼carp**, middle layer of pericarp; **∼cepha'lic**, (of skull) intermediate between brachycephalic and dolichocephalic; **∼derm**, = mesoblast; **∼ga'ster**, membrane attaching stomach to dorsal wall of abdomen; **∼li'thic**, of Stone Age between palaeolithic and neolithic; **∼morph**, person with compact muscular body-build; **∼phyll**, inner tissue of leaf; **∼phyte**, plant needing moderate amount of moisture; **∼sphere**, region of atmosphere from top of stratosphere to altitude about 50 miles; **∼tron**, orig. name of MESON; **M∼zo'ic**, of second geological

era (cf. CAINOZOIC, PALAEOZOIC). [f. Gk *mesos* middle +-o-]

mě'sŏn (-z-) *n.* (Phys.) elementary unstable particle intermediate in mass between proton and electron, found in cosmic rays and atomic nuclei; hence **mě'sIC**, **mĕsŏ'nIC**, (-z-) *adjs.* [f. MESOTRON; see -ON]

mě'squite, -quit, (-kēt) *n.* N. Amer. leguminous tree of genus *Prosopis*, with pods (**∼ beans**) used as fodder; **∼ grass**, (of genus *Bouteloua*, found near mesquite tree). [f. Mex. Sp. *mezquite*]

mĕss¹ *n.* **1.** portion of liquid or pulpy food (freq. *savoury mess*); **∼ of pottage**, material comfort etc. for which something higher is sacrificed (Gen. 25: 29–34). **2.** liquid or mixed food for hounds etc.; (derog.) disagreeable concoction or medley. **3.** dirty or untidy state of things; spilt liquid etc.; domestic animal's excreta; state of confusion, embarrassment, or trouble; **make a ∼ of**, bungle (undertaking). **4.** company of persons who take meals together, esp. in the fighting services; meal so taken; place where such meals are taken; **∼-jacket**, short close-fitting coat worn at mess; **∼-kit**, soldier's cooking and eating utensils; **∼'mate**, one of the same (usu. ship's) mess; **∼ tin**, small oval bucket as part of mess-kit. [ME, f. OF *mes* portion of food f. LL *missus* course at dinner, p.p. of *mittere* send]

mĕss² *v.* **1.** *v.t.* **∼** (**up**), make a mess of, dirty, interfere with, muddle (business). **2.** *v.i.* potter *about* or *around*; take one's meals (*with*, or abs.). [f. prec.]

mě'ssage¹ *n.* oral or written communication sent or transmitted by one person to another; mission, errand; prophet's, writer's, or preacher's, inspired or significant communication; **get the ∼**, (colloq.) understand what is meant. [ME f. OF, f. Rom. **missaticum* f. L *mittere* miss- send; see -AGE]

mě'ssage² *v.t.* send as a message; transmit (plan etc.) by signalling etc. [f. prec.]

Messeigneurs. See MONSEIGNEUR.

mě'ssėnger (-nj-) *n.* one who carries a message; person employed to carry messages; **King's** or **Queen's M∼**, courier in diplomatic service; **∼ RNA** (carrying genetic information from gene to ribosome). [ME & OF *messager* (as MESSAGE¹; see -ER²); -n- as in harbinger, passenger, porringer, scavenger, wharfinger]

Mėssī'ah (-a) *n.* promised deliverer of Jews; Christ regarded as this; (would-be) liberator of oppressed people or country; hence **∼**SHIP *n.* [ME f. OF *Messie* f. LL f. Gk *Messias* f. Aram. *m'shīḥā*, Heb. *māšīaḥ* anointed (*māšaḥ* anoint); *Messiah* alt. sp. to give the wd a more Hebraic appearance]

Mĕssiä'nIC *a.* of the, inspired by hope or belief in a, Messiah; so **Mĕssī'ANISM** (3) *n.* [f. F *messianique* (as prec., after *rabbinique* rabbinical)]

Messieurs. See MONSIEUR.

Mĕ'ssrs (-serz) *n.* (used as *pl.* of MR, esp. as prefix to name of firm or to list of men's names). [abbr. of prec.]

mě'ssuage (-swïj) *n.* (Law). dwelling-house with outbuildings and land assigned to its use. [ME, f. AF *mes(s)uage*, perh. alt. sp. f. *mesnage* dwelling f. OF *manaige*; see MÉNAGE]

mě'ss|ў *a.* that is, or is accompanied by, a mess (sense 3); untidy, slovenly, difficult to deal with; hence **∼**ILY² *adv.*, **∼**INESS *n.* [f. MESS¹+-Y²]

mĕsti'zō (-tē'-) *n.* (*pl.* **∼s**). Spanish or Portuguese half-caste, esp. offspring of Spaniard and Amer. Indian. [Sp., f. Rom. **mixticius* f. L *mixtus* p.p. of *miscēre* mix]

mĕt¹. See MEET².

mĕt². *a.* (colloq.) meteorological, metropolitan, etc.; **the Met**, ||the Meteorological Office, **the Metropolitan Opera House (New York). [abbr.]

mě'ta- *pref.* (usu. **met-** bef. vowel or *h*), w. sense of change of position or condition (*metabolism*), behind, after (*metaphysics*), beyond (*metacarpus*) of a higher or second-order kind (*metalanguage*). (Chem.) (1) relating to two carbon atoms separated by one other in a benzene ring, (2) relating to a compound formed by dehydration (*metaphosphate*). [Gk *meta-, met-, meth-* (*meta* with, after)]

mĕtă′bolism *n.* process, in organism or single cell, by which nutritive material is built up into living matter (**constructive** ∼) or protoplasm is broken down into simpler substances for special functions (**destructive** ∼); **basal** ∼, this process as occurring in organism completely at rest; so **mĕtabŏ′lic** *a.*, **mĕtă′bolize** (3) *v.t.* [f. Gk *metabolē* change f. META- (*ballō* throw) change + -ISM]

mĕtacăr′p|us *n.* (*pl.* ∼i *pr.* -ī). part of hand between wrist and fingers; set of bones in this; hence ∼AL *a.* [mod. L, f. Gk *metakarpon* (as META-, CARPUS)]

||mĕ′tacĕntre, *-ter, *n.* point of intersection between line (vertical in equilibrium) through centre of gravity of floating body and vertical line through centre of pressure after slight angular displacement, which must be above the centre of gravity to ensure stability; hence **mĕtacĕ′ntr**IC *a.* [f. F *métacentre* (as META-, CENTRE[1])]

mĕ′tage *n.* official measuring of load of coal etc.; duty paid for this. [f. METE[2] + -AGE]

mĕtagĕ′nĕsis *n.* alternation of generations between sexual and asexual reproduction; so **mĕtagĕnE′TIC** *a.* [mod. L (as META-, GENESIS)]

mĕ′tal *n., a.,* & *v.t.* (||-ll-). **1.** *n.* any of a class of elements such as gold, silver, copper, iron, lead, tin, aluminium, uranium, etc., all of which are crystalline when solid and many of which are opaque, ductile, malleable, dense, good conductors of heat and electricity, and characterized by a peculiar lustre; alloy of these; BELL[1]-, BRITANNIA, GUN-, TYPE[1]-, WHITE[1], YELLOW, *metal*; HEAVY *metal*. **2.** (Mil.) tanks, armoured vehicles, etc. **3.** material used for making glass, in molten state; ROAD[1]-*metal*; ||(in *pl.*) rails of a railway line (*train* **leaves the** ∼**s**, is derailed). **4.** (Her.) gold or silver as tincture. **5.** ∼**work**, (product of) shaping objects from metal. **6.** *a.* made of metal. **7.** *v.t.* furnish or fit with metal; ||make or mend (road) with road-metal. [ME f. OF, or L f. Gk *metallon* mine]

mĕ′talănguage (-nggwĭj) *n.* language used to discuss a language; system of propositions about propositions. [f. META- + LANGUAGE]

mĕtă′llic *a.* **1.** of metal(s); ∼ **currency**, gold, silver, copper, etc., cf. PAPER[1]. **2.** characteristic of metals; ∼ **lustre**, peculiar sheen of metals; ∼ **sound** (like struck metal, sharp and ringing); ∼ **voice** (harsh and unmusical). **3.** Hence or cogn. **mĕtă′llic**ALLY *adv.*, **mĕtăllĭ′FEROUS, mĕ′tall**INE[1], *adjs.* [f. F *métallique* f. L f. Gk *metallikos* (as METAL; see -IC)]

mĕ′talliz|e, *-ise (-īz), ***-alize,** *v.t.* render metallic; coat with thin layer of metal; hence ∼A′TION *n.* [f. METAL + -IZE]

mĕtallŏ′graphy *n.* descriptive science of structure and properties of metals. [f. as METAL + -O- + -GRAPHY]

mĕ′talloid *a.* & *n.* **1.** *a.* having form or appearance of metal. **2.** *n.* element with characteristics both of metals and non-metals. [f. METAL + -OID]

mĕtă′llophŏne *n.* (Mus.) instrument like xylophone but with metal bars. [f. METAL + -O- + -PHONE]

metallurg|y (mĭtă′ler-, mĕ′taler-) *n.* art of working metals, esp. of extracting metals from their ores; science of the properties of metals; hence **mĕtallŭr′g**IC(AL) *adjs.*, ∼IST (3) *n.* [f. Gk *metallon* metal + *-ourgia* working; see -Y[1]]

mĕ′tamēre *n.* (Zool.) one of several similar segments of animal body. [f. META- + Gk *meros* part]

mĕtamĕ′ric *a.* (Chem.) having same proportional composition and molecular weight, but different chemical properties; (Zool.) of metameres; so **mĕ′tamER, mĕtă′mer**ISM (2), *ns.* [f. as prec. + -IC]

mĕtamŏr′ph|ic *a.* of, or marked by, metamorphosis; (Geol., of rock) that has undergone transformation by natural agencies, whence ∼ISM (1) *n.* [f. META- + Gk *morphē* form + -IC]

mĕtamŏr′phŏse (-z) *v.t.* change in form, turn (*to* or *into* new form); change nature of. [f. F *métamorphoser* (*métamorphose* = foll.)]

mĕtamŏr′phos|is (-ŏr′fo-, -ŏrfŏ′-) *n.* (*pl.* ∼es *pr.* ∼ēz). change of form (by magic or by matural development etc.); changed form; change of character, conditions, etc.; (Zool.) change (usu. rapid) between immature form and adult, e.g. of insect. [L, f. Gk *metamorphōsis* f. META-(*morphoō* f. *morphē* form) transform; see -OSIS]

mĕ′taph|or *n.* application of name or descriptive term or phrase to an object or action to which it is imaginatively but not literally applicable (e.g. *a glaring error, food for thought, leave no stone unturned*); instance of this; **mixed** ∼**or**, combination of inconsistent metaphors (*this tower of strength will forge ahead*); hence ∼ŏ′ric(AL) *adjs.*, ∼ŏ′rical*LY*[2] *adv.* [f. F *métaphore* or f. L f. Gk *metaphora* f. META(*pherō* carry) transfer]

mĕ′taphr|āse (-z) *n.,* & *v.t.* **1.** *n.* translation, esp. word-for-word, opp. *paraphrase*. **2.** *v.t.* put into other words. **3.** So ∼**a′st**IC *a.* [f. mod. L f. Gk *metaphrasis* (*metaphrazō* translate; see META-, PHRASE)]

mĕtaphy′sic (-z-) *n.* (system of) metaphysics. [ME; see METAPHYSICS]

mĕtaphy′sical (-z-) *a.* & *n.* **1.** *a.* of metaphysics; based on abstract general reasoning; over-subtle; incorporeal; supernatural; visionary; (of some 17th-c. poets, esp. Cowley and Donne) addicted to fanciful conceits and far-fetched imagery; hence ∼LY[2] *adv.* **2.** *n.* (esp. in *pl.*) **the M**∼**s**, the metaphysical poets. [f. as foll. + -AL]

mĕtaphy′s|ics (-z-) *n. pl.* (often treated as *sing.*) theoretical philosophy of being and knowing; philosophy of mind; (pop.) abstract or subtle talk, mere theory; so ∼I′CIAN *n.*, ∼icIZE (2) *v.i.* [ME *metaphysic*, later -ics, f. OF *métaphysique* f. med. L *metaphysica* fem. sing. & neut. pl., f. med. Gk *metaphusika* f. Gk *ta meta ta phusika* the works (of Aristotle) placed after (META-) the *Physics*]

mĕtapl|ā′sia (-z-) *n.* (Physiol.) transformation of one form of tissue into another; so ∼**a′st**IC *a.* [mod. L, f. Gk *metaplase* f. Gk META (*plasis* f. *plassō* to mould); see -IA[1]]

mĕ′taplăsm *n.* (Biol.) non-living part of protoplasm. [f. META- after PROTOPLASM]

mĕtapŏ′litics *n. pl.* (often derog.) abstract political science. [f. META- after METAPHYSICS]

mĕta|stă′ble *a.* (Of state of equilibrium) stable only under small disturbances; passing to another state so slowly as to seem stable; hence ∼STABI′LITY *n.* [f. META- + STABLE[1]]

mĕtă′stas|is *n.* (*pl.* -es *pr.* -ēz). (Physiol.) transference of bodily function, disease, etc., from one part or organ to another; transformation of chemical compounds into others in process of assimilation by an organism; hence ∼IZE (3) *v.i.*, **mĕtastă′t**IC *a.* [f. Gk (*methistēmi* change; see META-, STASIS)]

mĕtatăr′s|us *n.* (*pl.* ∼i *pr.* -ī). part of foot between ankle and toes; set of bones in this; hence ∼AL *a.* [mod. L (as META-, TARSUS)]

mĕtă′thĕs|is *n.* (*pl.* ∼es *pr.* -ēz). (Gram.) transposition of sounds or letters in word; (Chem.) interchange of (groups of) atoms between two molecules; so **mĕtathĕ′t**IC(AL) *adjs.* [LL, f. Gk, f. META(*tithēmi* place) transpose; see THESIS]

métayage (mĕ′tāyahzh) *n.* land tenure in which farmer pays part (usu. half) of produce as rent to owner, who furnishes stock and seed. [F (as foll.; see -AGE)]

métayer (mĕ′tāyā) *n.* tenant of land on *métayage* system. [F, f. med. L *medietarius* f. L *medietas* half; see MOIETY, -ARY[1]]

mĕtazō′an *a.* & *n.* (Zool.) (member) of the sub-kingdom Metazoa, comprising multicellular animals with differentiated tissues. [f. *Metazoa* f. Gk META- + *zōia* pl. of *zōion* animal, + -AN]

mēte[1] *n.* boundary, boundary stone, esp. (Law) *metes and bounds*. [ME f. OF, f. L *meta* boundary, goal]

mēte[2] *v.t.* (literary) apportion, allot, (punishment, reward, usu. *out*); (poet. or Bibl.) measure; ∼-**wand**, **-yard**, (fig.) standard of estimation. [OE *metan,* = OS *metan,* OHG *mezzan,* ON *meta,* Goth. *mitan* f. Gmc **met-, *mæt-* MEET[3] f. IE **med-, *mod-*]

mĕtĕmpsȳchŏ'sĭis (-k-) *n.* (*pl.* ∼es *pr.* -ēz). supposed transmigration of soul of human being or animal at death into new body of same or different species; hence ∼IST (2) *n.* [LL, f. Gk *metempsukhōsis* (as META-, EN-[2], *psukhē* soul, -OSIS)]

mē'tĕor *n.* (any atmospheric phenomenon, esp.) bright moving body formed by small mass of matter from outer space rendered luminous by compression of air on entering earth's atmosphere; (*attrib.*) = foll. 2; ∼ **shower**, group of meteors appearing to come from one point in sky. [ME, f. mod. L *meteōrum* f. Gk *meteōron* neut. (as n.) of *meteōros* lofty (as META-, *aeirō* raise)]

mĕtĕŏ'ric *a.* **1.** of the atmosphere; dependent on atmospheric conditions. **2.** of meteors; (fig.) like a meteor, dazzling, rapid, transient. **3.** ∼ **stone**, meteorite. [partly f. prec. + -IC; partly f. med. L *meteoricus* f. as prec.]

mē'tĕorīte *n.* fallen meteor, fragment of rock or metal reaching earth's surface from outer space. [f. METEOR + -ITE[1]]

mē'tĕorograph (-aht) *n.* apparatus recording several meteorological phenomena at same time. [f. F *météorographe* (as METEOR, -GRAPH)]

mē'tĕor|oid *n.* body moving through space, of same nature as those which by passing through earth's atmosphere become visible as meteors; hence ∼**oi'dAL** *a.* [f. METEOR + -OID]

mĕtĕorolo'gical *a.* of meteorology; ‖**M**∼ **Office**, government department providing weather forecasts etc.; *meteorological* TIDE[1]; hence ∼**LY**[2] *adv.* [f. foll. + -ICAL]

mĕtĕorŏ'log|ȳ *n.* study of motions and phenomena of atmosphere, esp. for weather forecasting; atmospheric character (*of region*); so ∼IST (3) *n.* [f. Gk *meteōrologia* (as METEOR, see -LOGY)]

mē'ter[1] *n.,* & *v.t.* **1.** *n.* person or thing that measures esp. instrument for recording quantity supplied (GAS[1], WATER[1], *meter*) or present (*humidity meter*) or needed (*exposure meter*); = PARK[2]*ing-meter,* TAXI-METER; ∼ **maid**, woman employed to report offences against parking-meter regulations. **2.** *v.t.* measure by meter. [ME, f. METE[2] + -ER[1]]

*mē'ter[2,3]. See METRE[1,2].

-meter (-mĭ-, -mē-) *suf.* **1.** Forming names of automatic measuring instruments (*barometer, calorimeter, galvanometer, thermometer, voltmeter*). **2.** (Pros.) Forming names of lines with specified number of measures (*dimeter, pentameter*). [f. Gk *metron* measure]

mē'thadōne *n.* powerful synthetic analgesic drug used as substitute for morphine or heroin. [f. 6-dimethylamino-4, 4-diphenyl-3-heptan*one*]

mĕthămphĕ'tamine (-in, -en) *n.* amphetamine derivative with quicker and longer action, used as stimulant. [f. METHYL + AMPHETAMINE]

mē'thāne *n.* (Chem.) odourless colourless inflammable gaseous hydrocarbon, CH_4, simplest member of paraffin series. [f. METHYL + -ANE]

mē'thanŏl *n.* (Chem.) methyl alcohol. [f. prec. + ALCOHOL]

Mĕ'thedrine (-ēn, -ĭn) *n.* (P) methamphetamine in hydrochloride form. [f. METHYL + BENZEDRINE]

mĕthĕ'glin *n.* (Hist. or dial.) spiced or medicated kind of mead. [f. W *meddyglyn* (*meddyg* healing f. L *medicus, llyn* liquor)]

mĕthi'nks *v.i.* impers. (*past* **methou'ght** *pr.* -aw't). (arch.) it seems to me. [OE *mē thyncth* (*mē* dat. ME[1], *thyncth* 3rd sing. of *thyncan* seem, THINK)]

mĕ'thod *n.* special form of procedure esp. in any branch of mental activity; (Theatr.) technique of acting based on actor's thorough emotional identification with character; (∼ *in* MADNESS) orderly arrangement of ideas; scheme of classification; orderliness, regular habits; **there's** ∼ **in his** etc. **madness,** (joc.) his etc. conduct or proposal is not so mad as it seems. [f. F *méthode* or f. L f. Gk *methodos* pursuit of knowledge (as META-, *hodos* way)]

*mĕthŏ'dic *a.* methodical; methodological. [f. LL f. Gk *methodikos* (*methodos* METHOD; see -IC)]

mĕthŏ'dical *a.* characterized by method or order; hence ∼LY[2] *adv.* [f. as prec.; see -ICAL]

Mĕ'thodist *n.* **1.** member of any of several Protestant religious bodies (now united) originating in the 18th-c. evangelistic movement of Charles and John Wesley and George Whitefield; hence **Mĕ'thod**ISM (3) *n.,* **Mĕthodi'st**IC(AL) *adjs.* **2.** (*m*∼). one who follows or advocates a method or system of procedure. [f. mod. L *methodista* (as METHOD; see -IST); sense 1 prob. f. following a specified 'method' of devotional study]

mĕ'thodīze, -īse (-īz), *v.t.* reduce to order; arrange in orderly manner. [f. METHOD + -IZE]

mĕthodŏ'logȳ *n.* science of method; body of methods used in a particular branch of activity; so **mĕthodo-LO'GICAL** *a.* [f. mod. L *methodologia* or F *méthodologie* (as METHOD, -O-, -LOGY)]

methought. See METHINKS.

‖mĕths *n.* (colloq.) methylated spirit; ∼-**drinker** (addicted to drinking this). [abbr.]

Mĕthu'selah (-ū'zela, -ōō'-) *n.* pre-Noachian patriarch stated (Gen. 5: 27) to have lived 969 years (hence as type of longevity); very large winebottle. [ME, f. Bibl. Heb. *m*[e]*tūšelah*]

mē'thyl (mĕ'thĭl, mē'thĭl) *n.* (Chem.) hydrocarbon radical CH_3, present in methane and many organic compounds; ∼ **alcohol,** colourless volatile inflammable liquid CH_3OH, the simplest alcohol; hence **mĕthȳ'l**IC *a.* [G, or F *méthyle,* back-form. f. G *methylen,* F *méthylène* (see METHYLENE)]

mĕ'thylāte *v.t.* mix, impregnate, (esp. alcohol to make it unfit for drinking and so exempt it from duty) with methyl alcohol (*methylated spirit(s)*). [f. prec. + -ATE[3]]

mĕ'thylēne *n.* (Chem.) hydrocarbon radical CH_2, present in many polymers. [f. F *méthylène* f. Gk *methu* wine + *hulē* wood; see -ENE]

mĕ'tic *n.* (Gk Ant.) alien living in Greek city with some privileges of citizenship. [irreg. f. Gk *metoikos* (as META-, *-oikos* dwelling)]

mĕti'cŭlous *a.* (over-)scrupulous about minute details; (colloq.) very careful, accurate; hence ∼LY[2] *adv.,* ∼NESS *n.* [f. L *meticulosus* (*metus* fear); see -OUS]

métier *n.* one's trade, profession, or department of activity; one's forte. [F, f. Rom. **misterium* for L *ministerium* service (MINISTER[1])]

mē'tif (mā'-) *n.* offspring of white person and quadroon; = foll. [F *métif,* alt. of *métis* (see foll.)]

mē'tis (mā'-) *n.* offspring of white person and Amer. Indian, esp. in Canada. [f. F *métis,* OF *mestis* f. Rom. **mixticius* (see MESTIZO)]

mĕ'töl *n.* white soluble powder used as photographic developer. [G, an arbitr. name]

Mĕtŏ'nic *a.* ∼ **cycle**, period of 19 years (235 lunar months) covering all the changes of the moon's position relative to the sun and the earth. [f. Gk *Metōn,* Athenian astronomer of 5th *c.* BC + -IC]

mĕ'tonȳm *n.* word used by metonymy. [back-form. f. foll., after *synonym*]

mĕtŏ'nȳmȳ *n.* substitution of the name of an attribute or adjunct for that of the thing meant (e.g. *crown* for *king,* the *turf* for *horse-racing*); hence **mĕtonȳ'm**ICAL *a.* [f. LL f. Gk *metōnumia* (as META-, *onoma, onuma* name)]

mĕ'tōpe *n.* (Archit.) square space between triglyphs in Doric frieze. [f. L f. Gk *metopē* (as META-, *opē* hole for beam-end)]

‖mĕ'tre[1] (-ter), ***mĕ'ter**[2], *n.* any form of poetic rhythm, determined by character and number of feet; metrical group, measure; hence **mĕtri'c**IAN,

mĕ′trɪcs, mĕ′trɪst (3), *ns.* [OE f. OF, & f. L f. Gk *metron* measure f. IE *me-]

||**mĕ′tre²** (-*ter*), ***mĕ′ter³,** *n.* unit of length in metric system (about 39.4 in.); CUBIC *metre,* SQUARE² *metre*; ∼-**candle,** unit of illumination equal to that at one metre from a source of one candela; hence ∼AGE (1) (-*terĭj*) *n.* [f. F *mètre* (as prec.)]

mĕ′trĭc *a.* of the METRE²; ∼ **system,** decimal measuring-system with the metre, and the litre and (kilo)gram determined by it, as units of length, capacity, and weight or mass; **go** ∼, (colloq.) adopt the metric system; *metric* HUNDREDWEIGHT, TON¹. [f. F *métrique* (as prec.; see -IC)] **-mĕ′tric(al)** *sufs.* forming *adjs.* corresp. to *ns.* in -METER, -METRY, (*geometric, geometrical, thermometric*); hence **-mĕ′trical**LY² *adv. suf.* [f. or after F *-métrique* f. L (as foll.)]

mĕ′trical *a.* of, or composed in, metre (*metrical psalms*); of, or involving, measurement (*metrical geometry*); hence ∼LY² *adv.* [ME, f. L f. Gk *metrikos* (as METRE¹; SEE -ICAL)]

mĕ′tric|**āte** *v.i.* & *t.* change or adapt to metric system of measurement; so ∼A′TION *n.,* ∼IZE (3) *v.t.* [f. METRIC+-ATE³]

metrician, metrics, metrist. See METRE¹.

mĕtrī′tĭs *n.* inflammation of womb. [f. Gk *mētra* womb+-ITIS]

Mĕ′trō, Métro, *n.* (*pl.* ∼*s*). (colloq.) underground railway (esp. in Paris). [abbr. of F *métropolitain* METROPOLITAN]

mĕtrŏ′logў *n.* science or system of weights and measures; hence **mĕtrolŏ′gɪc(al)** *adjs.* [f. Gk (as METRE¹)+-LOGY]

mĕ′tronōme *n.* (Mus.) instrument marking time at selected rate by means of pendulum etc.; hence **mĕtronŏ′mɪc** *a.* [f. Gk *metron* measure+*nomos* law]

mĕtronў′mic *a.* & *n.* (name) derived from name of a mother or female ancestor. [f. Gk *mētēr mētros* mother, after *patronymic*]

mĕtrŏ′polis *n.* chief city of a country, capital, (|||the ∼, London); metropolitan bishop's see; centre of activity. [LL, f. Gk *mētropolis* parent State (*mētēr mētros* mother, *polis* city)]

mĕtropŏ′lītan *a.* & *n.* **1.** *a.* of or the metropolis; belonging to, forming (part of), mother country as dist. from its colonies etc.; of an ecclesiastical metropolis. **2.** *a.* & *n.* ∼ (**bishop**), bishop having authority over bishops of a province, in the Western Church equivalent to archbishop, in the Orthodox Church ranking above archbishop and below patriarch, whence ∼ATE¹ *n.*; ||∼ **magistrate,** paid professional magistrate in London (cf. STIPENDIARY). **3.** *n.* inhabitant of a metropolis. [ME, f. LL *metropolitanus* f. Gk *mētropolitēs* (as prec.; see -ITE¹, -AN)]

mĕtrŏrrha′gia (-ōrā′-) *n.* bleeding from womb. [mod. L, f. Gk *mētra* womb+as HAEMORRHAGE]

-mĕtrў *suf.* forming names of procedures and systems corresp. to instruments in -METER (*calorimetry, thermometry*). [after *geometry* etc. f. Gk *-metria* (-*metrēs* measurer, as METRE¹); see -Y¹]

mĕ′ttl|**e** *n.* quality of person's disposition or temperament; natural ardour; spirit, courage; **on** one's ∼**e,** incited to do one's best; hence (-)∼ED² (-*teld*), ∼**eSOME**¹ (-*tels*-), *adjs.* [var. of METAL *n.*]

meu *n.* baldmoney. [irreg. f. L *meum* f. Gk *mēon*]

meum (mē′um) *n.* ∼ **and tuum** (tū′um), mine and thine (used to express rights of property). [L, neut. of *meus* mine]

MeV *abbr.* mega-electron-volt(s).

mew¹ *n.* gull, esp. common gull (*Larus canus*). [OE *mæw,* = OS *mēu,* MDu., MLG *mēwe* f. Gmc **mai(g)wiz*]

mew² *n.,* & *v.t.* **1.** *n.* cage for hawks, esp. while moulting. **2.** *v.t.* put (hawk) in mew; (fig.) shut *up,* confine. [ME, f. OF *mue* (*muer;* see foll.)]

mew³ *v.t.* (arch.) (Of hawk) moult, shed, (feathers). ME, f. OF *muer* f. L *mutare* change]

mew⁴ *v.i.,* & *n.* **1.** *v.i.* (Of cat or sea-bird) utter sound *mew.* **2.** *n.* this sound, esp. of cat. [ME; imit.]

mew⁵. Var. of MEU.

mewl *v.i.* cry feebly, whimper; mew like cat. [imit.; cf. MIAUL]

||**mews** (-z) *n.* set of stabling round open yard or along lane, now often converted into dwellings. [pl. (now used as sing.) of MEW², orig. of royal stables on site of hawks' mews at Charing Cross]

Mĕ′xĭcan *a.* & *n.* (native or inhabitant) of Mexico; (person) of Mexican descent; (language) spoken in Mexico, esp. Nahuatl. [f. Sp. *mexicano* (*Mexico* f. *Mexitli* Aztec war-god; see -AN)]

mĕzēr′éon *n.* small Eur. & Asian shrub (*Daphne mezereum*) with fragrant purple or pink flowers and red berries. [med. L, f. Arab. *māzaryūn*]

mĕzu′z|**ah** (-ōō′za) *n.* (*pl.* ∼**oth** *pr.* -ōth). parchment inscribed with religious texts and attached in case to doorpost of Jewish house. [f. Heb. *mᵉzûzāh* doorpost]

mĕ′zzanine (mĕ′tsanēn, mĕ′za-) *n.* low storey between two others (usu. between ground and first floors); (Theatr.) floor beneath stage, *dress circle. [F, f. It. *mezzanino* dim. of *mezzano* middle f. L *medianus* MEDIAN¹]

mezza voce (mĕdza vō′chā, -tsa) *adv.* (Mus.) with less than full strength of voice or sound. [It., = half voice]

mezzo (mĕ′dzō, -tsō) *adv.* (esp. Mus.) half, moderately; ∼ **forte,** fairly loud; ∼ **piano,** fairly soft; ∼-**rilievo** (-rīlyä′vō), half-relief, in which figures project half their true proportions; ∼(-**soprano**), (person with, part for) voice between soprano and contralto. [It., f. L *medius* middle]

mĕ′zzŏtĭnt (-dzō-, -tsō-) *n.,* & *v.t.* **1.** *n.* method of engraving in which plate is roughened uniformly, lights and half-lights being given by scraping away the roughness thus produced, deep shadows by leaving it; print produced by this. **2.** *v.t.* engrave in mezzotint; hence ∼ER¹ *n.* [f. It. *mezzotinto* f. *mezzo* half (see prec.) + *tinto* TINT]

MF *abbr.* medium frequency.

mf *abbr.* mezzo forte.

||**MFH** *abbr.* Master of Foxhounds.

MG *abbr.* machine-gun; Morris Garages.

mg. *abbr.* milligram(s).

Mg *symb.* magnesium.

MGB *abbr.* motor gun-boat.

Mgr. *abbr.* Manager; *Monseigneur; Monsignor.*

***MH** *abbr.* Medal of Honor.

MHD *abbr.* magnetohydrodynamics.

mhŏ (mō) *n.* (*pl.* ∼s). (Electr.) unit of conductance, reciprocal of ohm. [OHM reversed]

MHR *abbr.* Member of the House of Representatives.

MHz *abbr.* megahertz.

mi. See ME².

MI *abbr.* Michigan; ||(Hist. or colloq.) Military Intelligence (**M.I.5,** security service; **M.I.6,** espionage department); Mounted Infantry.

***mi.** *abbr.* mile(s).

miaow (mǐow′) *n.,* & *v.i.* (make) cry of cat, mew. [imit.]

miä′sm|**a** (-z-) *n.* (*pl.* ∼**ata** *or* ∼**as**). infectious or noxious emanation; hence ∼AL, ∼A′TIC, *adjs.* [Gk, = defilement (*miainō* pollute)]

miau′l *v.i.* cry like cat, mew. [f. F *miauler;* imit.]

Mic. *abbr.* Micah (OT).

mi′ca *n.* one of several minerals composed of aluminium silicate with other silicates, found as small glittering scales in granite etc., or in crystals that can be separated into thin transparent plates; ∼-**schist,** -**slate,** slaty rock of quartz and mica; hence MĬCA′CEOUS *a.* [L, = crumb]

Micaw′ber *n.* person perpetually idling and trusting that something good will turn up; hence ∼ISH¹ *a.,* ∼ISM (3) *n.* [character in Dickens's *David Copperfield*]

mice. See MOUSE¹.

MICE *abbr.* Member of the Institution of Civil Engineers.

micě'lle n. (Chem.) minute aggregation of molecules in some colloidal solutions. [f. mod. L *micella* dim. of L *mica* crumb]

Mich. *abbr.* Michaelmas; Michigan.

Mi'chaelmas (-kel-) n. feast of St. Michael, 29 Sept.; ~ **daisy,** aster flowering at Michaelmas; ||~ **term** (in university etc., beginning at or near Michaelmas). [f. St. *Michael* (OE, f. Heb. *mīḵā'ēl* who is like God?) + MASS[1]]

M.I.Chem.E. *abbr.* Member of the Institution of Chemical Engineers.

*Mi'chigan (-shĭ-) n. = NEWMARKET 2. [~ in US]

mick n. (sl., derog.; **R**) Irishman; Roman Catholic. [f. man's Christian name *Michael*]

mi'ckey[1], mi'ckȳ, n. (sl.) **take the** ~ (**out of**), act disrespectfully or teasingly (towards). [20th c.; orig. uncert.]

Mi'ckey[2] (Fĭ'nn) n. (sl.) strong alcoholic drink, esp. containing narcotic or laxative. [20th c.; orig. uncert.]

mi'ckle, mŭ'ckle, a. & n. (arch. or Sc.) **1.** a. much, great. **2.** n. large amount (in prov. *many a little,* or *pickle, makes a mickle,* or orig. erron. *many a mickle makes a muckle*). [ME, f. ON *mikell,* = OE *micel,* OS *mikil,* OHG *michil,* Goth. *mikils* f. Gmc *mikilaz f. IE **meg-*]

mi'crō- *comb. form.* **1.** small, as: ~**bio'logy,** study of micro-organisms; (**M**)~**card,** (**P**) opaque card bearing microphotograph of document etc.; ~**cepha'lic** *a.* & *n.,* ~**ce'phalous** *a.,* (person) with abnormally small head; ~**chip,** tiny piece of semiconductor carrying many electrical circuits; ~**circuit,** integrated circuit or other very small circuit; ~**climate,** climate of small area; ~**cline,** green and blue felspar [from its cleavage planes' being at not quite 90°]; ~**cry'stalline,** having crystalline structure visible only under the microscope; ~**dot,** photograph of document etc. reduced to size of dot; ~**-electro'nics,** design, manufacture, and use of microcircuits; ~**fiche** (*pl* same), piece of film bearing microphotograph of document etc.; ~**film,** (*n.,* & *v.t.*) (photograph on) length of film bearing microphotograph of document etc.; ~**graph,** photograph taken with microscope; ~**groove,** (gramophone record having) very narrow groove; ~**lith,** (Archaeol.) minute worked flint usu. as part of composite tool; ~**meter** (-ŏ'm-), instrument for measuring small objects or angular distances; ~**miniaturiza'tion,** making of electronic devices with greatly reduced size; ~**organism,** organism not visible to naked eye, e.g. bacterium or virus; ~**pho'tograph,** photograph reduced to very small size; ~**phyte,** microscopic plant; ~**processor,** data processor contained on one chip or a few chips; ~**pyle,** (Bot.) hole in ovule for pollen to enter [Gk *pulē* gate]; ~**seism,** very slight earthquake tremor; ~**some,** minute granule in protoplasm; ~**spore,** (parasitic fungus with) small spore; ~**structure,** arrangement of metal etc. crystals visible under microscope; ~**technique,** skill in use of microscope; ~**tome,** instrument for cutting thin sections for microscope; ~**tone,** (Mus.) interval smaller than semitone; ~**wave,** electromagnetic wave of length between about 50 cm. and 1 mm. (~*wave oven,* using such waves to heat food quickly). **2.** denoting factor of one millionth (10^{-6}: *microgram, microsecond, microwatt*). [f. Gk *mikro-* (*mikros* small)]

mi'crōbe n. minute living being, micro-organism (esp. of bacteria causing diseases and fermentation); hence **micrō'bIAL, microbIC,** adjs. [F, f. Gk *mikros* small + *bios* life]

mi'crocŏsm n. man viewed as epitome of the universe; any community or complex unity so viewed; miniature representation (*of*); hence **microcŏ'smIC** (-z-) a. [ME, f. F *microcosme* or f. med. L *micro(s)cosmus* f. Gk *mikros kosmos* little world]

mi'crŏn n. one millionth of a metre. [f. Gk *mikron* neut. of *mikros* small; cf. MICRO- 2]

Micrōnē'sian (-shan) a. & n. (inhabitant or language) of Micronesia. [f. *Micronesia,* island-group in W. Pacific (f. as MICRO- + Gk *nēsos* island + -IA[1]) + -AN]

mi'crophōne n. instrument for intensifying small sounds or converting sound waves into electrical energy variations which may be reconverted into sound after transmission by wire or radio or after recording. [f. MICRO- + -PHONE]

mi'croscōpe n. instrument magnifying small objects by means of lens(es) so as to reveal details invisible to naked eye. [f. mod. L *microscopium* (as MICRO-, -SCOPE)]

microscŏ'p|ic a. **1.** of the microscope; so ~ICAL a. **2.** too small to be visible (in detail) without microscope; (fig.) extremely small; regarded in terms of small units. **3.** Hence ~ICALLY adv. [f. prec. + -IC]

micrŏ'scop|ȳ n. use of the microscope; so ~IST (3) n. [f. MICROSCOPE + -Y[1]]

mi'crūrgȳ n. manipulation of individual cells etc. under microscope. [f. MICRO- + Gk *-ourgia* work]

mictūri'tion n. urination; (arch.) unduly frequent desire to urinate. [f. L *micturire -it-,* desiderative f. *mingere mict-* urinate; see -ION]

mid[1] a. (superl. ~'most). **1.** that is the middle of (usu. as comb. after in: *in mid-air, career, Channel, course, ocean, stream, week: from mid-June to mid-August; the mid--term examinations*). **2.** that is in the middle, medium, half; (Phonet., of vowel) pronounced with tongue neither high nor low. **3.** ~'brain, part of brain developing from middle of primitive or embryonic brain; ***Mideast,** Middle East; ~'field, (Footb.) part of field away from goals; ~'iron, (Golf) iron with medium loft; ~'line, median line; ~'o'ff, -o'n, (Cricket) (position of) fieldsman near bowler on off, on, side; ~'rib, central rib of leaf; *~'town, region between downtown and uptown; ~'way (*or -ā'*) *adv.,* in middle of distance between places; ***Midwest,** Middle West; ~wi'cket, (Cricket) (position of) fieldsman on leg side opposite middle of pitch [OE, **midd,* = OS *middi,* OHG *mitti,* ON *mithr,* Goth. *midjis* f. Gmc **midhja-,* **medhja-* f. IE **medhjo-*]

mid[2]. Var. (poet.) of AMID.

Mi'das n. ~ touch, ability to make money in all one's activities. [f. ~, fabled king of Phrygia, whose touch turned all things to gold]

mi'dday (-d-d-) n. noon; time near noon. [OE *middæg* (as MID[1], DAY)]

mi'dden n. dunghill; refuse heap near dwelling; **kitchen** ~, prehistoric refuse-heap, chiefly of shells and bones. [ME *myddyng,* of Scand. orig.; cf. Da. *mødding* (*møg* MUCK[1], *dynge* heap)]

mi'ddle attrib. a., & n. **1.** a. (Of member of group) so placed as to have same number of members on each side; equidistant from extremities; intermediate in rank, quality, etc.; average (*a man of middle height*); (of language) pertaining to period between old and modern forms (*Middle* ENGLISH[1]). **2.** ~ **age,** (between youth and old age); ~**-aged**(*d*) SPREAD[2]; **the M~ Ages** (about 1000–1400, or in a wider sense 600–1500); **M~ America,** (1) Mexico and Central America, (2) the American middle class; ||~ **article,** brief essay of literary kind in weekly or other journal, often placed between leading articles and book-reviews; ~**-brow** a. & n., (colloq.) (person) claiming to be or regarded as only moderately intellectual; ~ **C,** (Mus.) C near middle of piano keyboard, note between treble and bass staves, at about 260 hertz frequency; ~ **class,** class of society between upper and lower, incl. professional and business workers and their families; ||~ **common room** (for use by graduate members of college who are not fellows); ~ **course,** a compromise between two extremes; *middle* DISTANCE; ~ **ear,** cavity of central part of ear behind drum; ~ **earth,** world as between heaven and hell; *Middle* EAST(ERN); *middle* FINGER; ~ **game,** central phase of chess game;

M∿ Kingdom, China (orig. of Honan as central and sovereign State), or Egypt *c.* 2000–1800 BC; ∿ life, the middle part of life, middle age; ∿man, any of the traders who handle a commodity between its producer and consumer; ∿ name, name between first name and surname, (fig.) person's most characteristic quality (*sobriety is his middle name*); ∿-of-the--road, (of person or course of action) moderate, avoiding extremes; ∿ passage, sea journey between W. Africa and W. Indies (w. ref. to the slave trade); ∿ school, (1) middle forms of independent or grammar school, (2) school for children from about 9 to 13 years old; ∿-sized, of medium size; *Middle* TEMPLE¹; ∿ term, (Logic) term common to both premisses; ∿ voice, (Gram.) voice of (esp. Gk) verbs expr. reciprocal or reflexive action; ∿ watch (from midnight to 4 a.m.); ∿ way, (1) = *middle course,* (2) eightfold path of Buddhism between indulgence and asceticism; ∿weight (see BOX⁵*ing weights*); *Middle* WEST(ERN). 3. *n.* middle point or position or part (of); waist; middle voice; middle term; ||middle article; EXCLUDEd *middle*; KNOCK¹ *into the middle of next week*; in the ∿ of, while (do*ing*), during (process). [OE *middel,* = OS *middil,* OHG *mittil* f. WG **middila* f. Gmc **midjha-* MID¹; see -LE 1]

mi′ddle² *v.t.* place in the middle; (Footb.) return (ball, or abs.) from wing to midfield in front of goal; (Cricket) strike (ball) with middle of bat; (Naut.) fold in the middle. [f. prec.]

mi′ddling *a., n.,* & *adv.* **1.** *a.* (Commerc., of goods) of the second of three grades; (fair to) ∿, moderately good; second-rate; (colloq.) fairly well (in health); hence ∿LY² *adv.* **2.** *n.* (in *pl.*) middling goods, esp. flour of medium fineness. **3.** *adv.* fairly or moderately (*middling good, fast*). [ME, of Sc. orig., prob. f. MID¹ + -LING²]

Middx. *abbr.* Middlesex.

mi′ddy¹ *n.* (colloq.) midshipman; ∿ (blouse), woman's or child's loose blouse with collar as worn by sailors. [abbr.; cf. -Y³]

mi′ddy² *n.* (Austral.) measure of beer. [20th c.; orig. unkn.]

midge *n.* gnatlike insect; small person; (Zool.) dipterous insect of family Chironomidae. [OE *mycg(e),* = OS *muggia,* OHG *mucca,* ON *mý* f. Gmc **mugjaz, *mugjōn*]

mi′dget *n.* & *a.* extremely small person, esp. when exhibited as curiosity; very small (thing). [f. prec. + -ET¹]

mi′di *n.* garment of medium length, between maxi and mini. [f. MID¹ after MINI]

midine′tte *n.* Parisian shop-girl (esp. milliner's assistant. [F (*midi* midday, *dînette* light dinner)]

mi′dland *n.* & *a.* **1.** *n.* middle part of country; the M∿s, the inland counties of central England. **2.** *a.* of or in the midland or Midlands; Mediterranean. **3.** Hence ∿ER¹ (4) *n.* [f. MID¹ + LAND¹]

mi′dmōst. See MID¹.

mi′dnīght (-nīt) *n.* the middle of the night, (time near) 12 o'clock at night; intense darkness; ∿ blue, very dark blue; *midnight* OIL¹; ∿ sun, sun visible at midnight during summer in polar regions. [OE *midniht* (as MID¹, NIGHT)]

Mi′drāsh *n.* (*pl.* ∿im *pr.* -ā′shēm). ancient Jewish commentary on part of Hebrew scriptures. [f. Bibl. Heb. *miḏrāš* commentary (*dāraš* study)]

mi′driff *n.* diaphragm between thorax and abdomen; region of front of body over this; (part of) garment fitted to this region. [OE *midhrif* (as MID¹, *hrif* belly)]

mi′dship *n.* middle part of ship or boat; ∿man, ||rank between naval cadet and sub-lieutenant, *naval cadet; ∿s, = AMIDSHIPS. [f. MID¹ + SHIP¹]

midst *n., adv.,* & *prep.* **1.** *n.* in the ∿ of, among, in the MIDDLE¹ of; in our, their, your, ∿, among us, them, you. **2.** *adv.* (arch.) first, ∿, and last, throughout. **3.** *prep.* (poet.) amidst. [ME *middest, middes* f. *in middes, in middan* (IN¹, MID¹ as n.)]

midsŭmmer (mĭ′-, -ŭ′-) *n.* period of or near summer solstice, about 21 June; M∿(′s) Day, 24 June; ∿ madness, extreme folly. [OE *midsumor* (as MID¹, SUMMER¹)]

mi′dwī|fe *n.* (*pl.* ∿ves *pr.* -vz). person (usu. woman) trained to assist others in giving birth; hence **mi′d-wif**ERY (2) (-frĭ) *n.* [ME, prob. f. obs. prep. *mid* with (OE; cf. G *mit*) + WIFE woman, in sense 'one who is with the mother']

midwi′nter *n.* period of or near winter solstice, about 22 Dec. [OE (as MID¹, WINTER)]

MIEE *abbr.* Member of the Institution of Electrical Engineers.

mie′lie. Var. of MEALIE.

mien *n.* (literary). look or bearing of person, as showing character or mood. [prob. f. obs. *demean* n. f. DEMEAN¹, assim. to F *mine* expression]

miff *n.,* & *v.t.* (colloq.) **1.** *n.* petty quarrel; huff. **2.** *v.t.* put out of humour, offend. [perh. imit.; cf. G *muff,* excl. of disgust]

might¹ (mīt) *n.* great (bodily or mental) strength; power to enforce one's will (usu. in contrast with *right*); with all one's ∿, to the utmost of one's power; *with might and* MAIN². [OE *miht, mieht,* = OS, OHG *maht,* Goth. *mahts* f. Gmc **mahtiz* (**mag-* MAY¹, be able)]

might². See MAY¹.

mi′ght|ў (mī′tĭ) *a.* & *adv.* **1.** *a.* powerful, strong, in body or mind; ∿y works, (Bibl.) miracles. **2.** massive, bulky; (colloq.) great, considerable; HIGH *and mighty.* **3.** Hence ∿ILY² *adv.,* ∿iNESS *n.* **4.** *adv.* (colloq.) very (*that is mighty easy*). [OE *mihtig* (as MIGHT¹, -Y²)]

mignonne′tte (mĭnyo-) *n.* **1.** annual plant of genus *Reseda.* esp. a species (*R. odorata*) with fragrant grey--green flowers; colour of these. **2.** light fine narrow pillow-lace. [f. F *mignonnette* dim. of *mignon* small; see -ETTE]

mi′grain|e (mē′-, mĭ-) *n.* recurrent paroxysmal headache often with nausea and disturbance of vision; hence ∿OUS *a.* [F, f. LL f. Gk *hēmicrania* (as HEMI-, CRANIUM, -IA¹); orig. of headache confined to one side of head]

mi′grāte (-ā′t, mī′-) *v.i.* move from one place (country, town, college, house) to another; (of bird or fish) come and go with the seasons; move under natural forces; hence or cogn. **mi′gr**ANT *a.* & *n.,* **migr**A′TION, **migrā′t**OR, *ns.,* **mi′grat**ORY *a.* [f. L *migrare* + -ATE²]

mih′rab (mē′rahb) *n.* niche or slab in mosque, used to show direction of Mecca. [f. Arab. *miḥrāb* praying--place]

mika′dō (-kah′-) *n.* (*pl.* ∿s). emperor of Japan. [Jap. (*mi* august, *kado* door)]

||mike¹ *v.t.,* & *n.* (sl.) **1.** *v.t.* shirk work, idle. **2.** *n.* idling (*on the mike*). [19th c.; orig. unkn.]

mike² *n.* (colloq.) microphone. [abbr.]

mike³ *n.* (sl.) = MICK; for the love of Mike, for Heaven's SAKE¹. [abbr. of man's Christian name *Michael*]

mil *n.* one-thousandth of an inch, as unit measure for diameter of wire etc. [f. L *millesimum* thousandth (*mille* thousand)]

mila′dў *n.* (Form used in speaking of or to) English noblewoman or great lady. [F, f. E *my lady*; cf. MILORD]

mi′lage. Var. of MILEAGE.

Milanē′se (-z) *a.* & *n.* (*pl.* same). (native or inhabitant) of Milan; ∿ silk, finely woven silk or rayon. [It. (*Milano* Milan in Lombardy; see -ESE]

milch *a.* (Of domestic mammal) giving, or kept for, milk; ∿ cow, (fig.) source of regular (and easy) profit, esp. person from whom money is easily obtained. [ME *m(i)elche,* OE **mielce* f. Gmc **melukjað* (as MILK¹)]

mīld *a.* **1.** gentle and conciliatory; (of rule, punishment, illness, feeling, etc.) moderate, not severe. **2.** (Of weather, esp. in winter) moderately warm; (of medicine) operating gently; (of food, tobacco, etc.) not sharp or strong in taste etc.; (of beer) not strongly flavoured with hops, opp. to *bitter* (||∼ **and bitter,** mixture of mild and bitter beer; DRAW[1] *it mild*). **3.** tame, feeble, lacking energy or vivacity. **4.** ∼ **steel** (containing small percentage of carbon, strong and tough, but not readily tempered). **5.** Hence ∼'EN[6] *v.t.* & *i.*, ∼'LY[2] *adv.* **(to put it** ∼**ly,** without any exaggeration), ∼'NESS *n.* [OE *milde*, = OS *mildi*, OHG *milti*, ON *mildr*, Goth. *-milds* f. Gmc **mildh-* f. IE **meldh-*, **moldh-*]

mi'ldew *n.* & *v.* **1.** *n.* destructive growth of minute fungi on plants; similar growth on paper, leather, etc., exposed to damp; hence ∼Y[2] *a.* **2.** *v.t.* & *i.* taint, be tainted, with mildew. [OE *mildēaw, meledēaw*, = OHG *militou* f. Gmc **melith* honey + **dawwaz* DEW[1]]

mile *n.* **1.** unit of linear measure, now (**statute** ∼) 1,760 yards, about 1.609 kilometre, (orig.) Roman measure of 1,000 paces, about 1,620 yards; ||**Admiralty, air, geographical, nautical, sea,** ∼, unit of approx. 2,025 yards (= 1,852 metres) or one minute of great circle of earth; SQUARE[2] *mile*; **not a hundred** or **a million** ∼**s from,** (joc.) in or at or close to. **2.** (colloq.) great distance or amount (STICK[1] *out a mile*; *miles apart, away, better, too big*; *beat him by miles*). **3.** race extending over a mile. **4.** ∼**-post** (placed at distance of one mile from finishing-point of race etc.); ∼'**stone,** stone set up on road to mark distance in miles, (fig.) stage or event in life, progress, etc. [OE *mīl*, = OHG *mīl(l)a*, ON *míla* f. WG **mīlja* f. L *mil(l)ia* pl. of *mille* thousand]

mi'leage (mī'lij) *n.* number of miles travelled, used, etc.; number of miles travelled by vehicle per gallon etc. of fuel; travelling expenses (per mile); (fig.) benefit, profit. [f. prec. + -AGE]

mi'ler *n.* (colloq.) man or horse qualified or trained specially to run a mile; HALF-*miler*, QUARTER[1]-*miler*. [f. MILE + -ER[1]]

Mile'sian[1] (-zyan) *a.* & *n.* (inhabitant or native) of Miletus; ∼ **tale,** one of a set of short erotic stories in ancient times. [f. L f. Gk *Milēsios* (*Milētos* Miletus, city of Asia Minor) + -AN]

Mile'sian[2] (-zyan) *a.* & *n.* (joc.) Irish(man). [f. *Milesius*, fabulous Sp. king whose sons are said to have conquered Ireland *c.* 1300 BC, + -AN]

mi'lfoil *n.* common yarrow, *Achillea millefolium*, with small white flowers and finely divided leaves. [ME f. OF, f. L *millefolium* (*mille* thousand, *folium* leaf), after Gk *muriophullon*]

mi'liary *a.* (Path.) like millet-seed in size or form; ∼ **fever** (marked by rash like measles, with vesicles of form of millet-seed); ∼ **tuberculosis** (with small tubercular nodules throughout body). [f. L *miliarius* (*milium* millet; see -ARY[1])]

milieu (mē'lyèr) *n.* (*pl.* ∼**x** or ∼**s**, *pr.* -z). environment, state of life, social surroundings. [F (*mi* MID[1], LIEU place)]

mi'litant *a.* & *n.* **1.** *a.* engaged in warfare (CHURCH *militant*); combative, aggressively active; hence **mi'litANCY** *n.*, ∼LY[2] *adv.* **2.** *n.* militant person. [ME f. OF, f. L (as MILITATE; see -ANT)]

mi'litar|ism *n.* spirit or tendencies of the professional soldier; undue prevalence of military spirit or ideals; hence ∼i'stIC *a.* [f. F *militarisme* (as MILITARY; see -ISM)]

mi'litarist *n.* student of military science; one dominated by military ideas. [f. MILITARY + -IST]

mi'litariz|e, -is|e (-īz), *v.t.* make military or warlike; equip with military resources; imbue with militarism; hence ∼A'TION *n.* [f. foll. + -IZE]

mi'litary *a.* & *n.* **1.** *a.* of, done by, befitting, soldiers, the army, or all armed forces (*military service*); ∼ **academy** (for training army officers); ∼ **band,** wood-wind, brass, and percussion combination; ∼ **chest,** treasury of army; ∼ **fever,** enteric; *military* HONOUR[1]*s*; ∼ **orchis** (having fancied resemblance to soldier); ∼ **police** (fulfilling functions of police

among soldiers); ∼ **tenure,** feudal holding of land in return for service as soldier; ∼ **testament,** soldier's will made orally; hence **mi'litariLY**[2] *adv.* **2.** *n.* (as *sing.* or *pl.*) soldiers, *the army* or *the armed forces* (opp. police or civilians). [f. F *militaire* or f. L *militaris* (*miles militis* soldier; see -ARY[2])]

mi'litāte *v.i.* (Of facts, evidence) have force, tell, (*against*, rarely *in favour of*, conclusion etc.). [f. L *militare* (*miles militis* soldier) + -ATE[3]]

mili'tia (-sha) *n.* military force, esp. one raised from among civil population and supplementing regular army in emergency; ∼**man,** member of the militia. [L, = military service (*miles*; see prec., -IA[1])]

milk[1] *n.* **1.** opaque white fluid secreted by female mammals for nourishment of their young; milk of cow etc. as food; ∼ **for babes,** simple forms of literature, doctrine, etc., opp. to *strong meat*; CONDENSEd *milk*; *dried* or *powdered milk* (cf. DRY[2]); ∼ **and honey,** abundant means of prosperity; **in** ∼, secreting it; ∼ **of human kindness,** kindness natural to humanity; **no use crying over spilt** ∼ (irremediable loss or error); ∼ **and water,** feeble or insipid or mawkish discourse or sentiment. **2.** milklike juice of plants, e.g. in coconut; milklike preparation of herbs, drugs, etc.; **M**∼ **of Magnesia,** (||P) white suspension of magnesium hydroxide in water as antacid or laxative; ∼ **of sulphur,** amorphous powder of sulphur formed by precipitation. **3.** ∼ **bar** (for sale of beverages made from milk, other non-alcoholic drinks, ice-cream, etc.); ∼ **chocolate** (for eating, made with milk); ∼ **fever,** mild fever shortly after parturition; ||∼**-float,** light low vehicle used in delivering milk; ∼**-leg,** painful swelling, esp. of legs, after childbirth; ∼**-loaf** (made with milk); ∼'**maid,** woman who milks or works in dairy; ∼'**man,** man who sells or delivers milk; ∼**-powder,** milk dehydrated by evaporation; ∼ **pudding** (of rice, sago, tapioca, etc., baked with milk in dish); ∼ **punch,** drink made of spirits and milk; ∼ **run,** (fig.) routine expedition or service journey; ∼ **shake,** drink of milk, flavouring, etc., mixed by shaking or whisking; ∼'**sop,** spiritless man or youth; ∼ **sugar,** lactose; ∼ **thistle,** sow[2]*thistle*; ∼**-tooth,** temporary tooth in young mammals; ∼**-vetch,** leguminous yellow-flowered plant of genus *Astragalus*; ∼**-walk,** milkman's round; ∼**-weed,** one of various wild plants with milky juice; ∼**-white,** white like milk; ∼'**wort,** plant of genus *Polygala* formerly supposed to increase women's milk. [OE *milc, meol(o)c*, = OS *miluk*, OHG *miluh*, ON *mjolk*, Goth. *miluks* f. Gmc **meluks* (**melk-* to milk f. IE **melg-*)]

milk[2] *v.t.* draw milk from (cow, ewe, goat, etc.); get money out of, exploit, (person); (sl.) tap (telegraph or telephone wires etc.); extract juice, venom, etc., from (tree, snake, etc.); ∼'**ing-machine,** device for milking cows mechanically. [OE *milcian* (as prec.)]

mi'lk|y *a.* of, like, mixed with, milk; (of gem or liquid) cloudy, not clear; effeminate, weakly amiable; **M**∼**y Way,** faintly luminous band of countless stars encircling the heavens, the Galaxy; hence ∼iNESS *n.* [ME, f. MILK[1] + -Y[2]]

mill[1] *n.* **1.** building fitted with machinery for grinding corn (WATER[1]-*mill*; WINDMILL); **put, go, through the** ∼, subject to, undergo, training or experience or suffering; **the** ∼**s of God grind slowly,** retribution is often delayed. **2.** any mechanical apparatus for grinding corn; apparatus for grinding any solid substance to powder or pulp (COFFEE, PEPPER[1], *powder, -mill*). **3.** any machine or building fitted with machinery for manufacturing-processes etc., (*cotton,* PAPER[1], *silk, -mill*; ROLL[2]*ing, saw, -mill*). **4.** boxing--match; fist fight. **5.** ∼'**board,** stout pasteboard for bookbinding etc.; ∼**-dam,** dam put across stream to make it usable by mill; ∼**-hand,** worker in mill or factory; ∼**-pond,** water retained by mill-dam (*like a* ∼*-pond*, said of calm sea); ∼**-race,** current of water that drives mill-wheel; ∼**-rind,** iron support of upper millstone; ~'**stone**, one of pair of circular stones for grinding corn, (fig.) heavy burden (cf. Matt. 18: 6); *see far into a* ~*stone*, (usu. iron.) be extraordinarily acute; *nether* ~*stone*, (fig.) hard heart etc.; *between upper and nether* ~*stone*, subject to irresistible pressure; ~*stone grit*, a hard siliceous Carboniferous rock just below coal strata; ~**-wheel**, wheel used to drive water-mill; ~'**wright**, one who designs or erects mills. [OE *mylen* f. Gmc **mulino, -na* f. LL *molinum, -na* f. L *mola* grindstone, mill (*molere* grind)]

mill² *v.* **1.** *v.t.* thicken (cloth etc.) by fulling; grind (corn), produce (flour), hull (seeds), in mill; (esp. in *p.p.*) produce regular markings on edge of (coin); cut or shape (metal) with rotating tool; beat (chocolate etc.) to froth; (sl.) beat, strike, fight, (person). **2.** *v.i.* (Of cattle or persons) move round and round in a confused mass. [f. prec.]

*mill³ *n.* one-thousandth of a dollar as money of account. [f. L *millesimum* thousandth (see MIL), on anal. of CENT]

mille-feuille (mēlfü'ĭ) *n.* rich confection of puff pastry split and filled with jam, cream, etc. [F, = thousand-leaf]

millénār'ian *a. & n.* of the millennium; (person) believing in this; hence ~ISM (3) *n.* [f. as foll. + -AN]

millenary (mĭlĕ'-, mĭ'lĭ-) *a. & n.* (period) of 1,000 years; (festival) of the thousandth anniversary; of, (person) believing in the, the millennium. [f. LL *millenarius* consisting of a thousand (*milleni* distrib. of *mille* thousand; see -ARY¹)]

mille'nni|um *n.* (*pl.* ~**ums** *or* ~**a**). period of a thousand years, esp. that of Christ's prophesied reign in person on earth (Rev. 20: 1–5); (fig.) period of good government, great happiness, and prosperity; hence ~AL *a.* [mod. L, f. L *mille* thousand after BIENNIUM]

mi'llepēde, mi'llipēde, *n.* myriapod of class Diplopoda with legs usu. placed on each segment in double pairs; terrestrial isopod crustacean, esp. common wood-louse. [f. L *millepeda* wood-louse (*mille* thousand, *pes pedis* foot)]

mi'llepore *n.* reef-building coral of genus *Millepora*. [f. F *millépore* or mod. L *millepora* (L *mille* thousand, *porus* PORE¹)]

mi'ller *n.* proprietor or tenant of corn-mill; one who works or owns any mill; ~'**s thumb**, small freshwater fish of genus *Cottus*, a bullhead. [ME *mylnere*, prob. f. MLG, MDu. *molner, mulner*, OS *mulineri* f. LL *molinarius* (*molina* MILL¹); assim. to MILL¹]

mille'simal *a. & n.* thousandth (part); consisting of thousandths; hence ~LY² *adv.* [f. L *millesimus* (*mille* thousand) + -AL]

mi'llet *n.* cereal plant, esp. *Panicum miliaceum*, bearing large crop of small nutritious seeds; its seed; ~**-grass**, tall woodland grass, *Milium effusum*. [ME f. F, dim. of *mil* f. L *milium*]

mi'lli- *comb. form.* thousand, esp. denoting factor of one thousandth, as: ~**a'mmeter** (for measuring current in **milliamperes**); *milli*BAR¹; ~**gram** (about .015 of English grain); ~**litre** (about .061 cu. in.); ~**metre** (about .039 in.); *milli*second; *milli*volt; *milli*watt. [f. L *mille* thousand + -I-]

‖**mi'lliard** (-yerd) *n.* one thousand millions. [F (*mille* thousand)]

mi'llin|er *n.* person (usu. woman) who makes or sells women's hats; **man-**~**er**, (fig.) man busied in trifling occupations; hence ~ERY (1) *n.* [f. *Milan* + -ER¹; orig. = vendor of goods from Milan]

mi'llion (-yon) *a. & n.* (for *pl.* usage see HUNDRED). one thousand thousand (things, *of* things, or abs.); a million ‖pounds or *dollars; enormous number (*not a million* MILES *from*; cf. HUNDRED, THOUSAND); **the** ~, the bulk of the population; hence ~FOLD *a. & adv.*, (-)~TH² *a. & n.* [ME f. OF, prob. f. It. *millione* (*mille* thousand, *-one* augment. suf.; see -OON)]

millionair'e (-yon-) *n.* person possessing a million

pounds, dollars, francs, etc.; person of great wealth. [f. F *millionnaire* (as prec.; see -ARY¹)]

mi'llipēde. See MILLEPEDE.

Mills (-z) *n.* ~ **bomb**, oval hand-grenade. [f. Sir W. ~, its inventor (d. 1932)]

milo'meter *n.* instrument for measuring number of miles travelled by a vehicle. [f. MILE + -O- + -METER]

milōr'd *n.* (Esp. French word for) English lord or wealthy Englishman. [F, f. E *my lord*; cf. MILADY]

milt *n.* spleen in mammals; analogous organ in other vertebrates; seed-filled reproductive gland of male fish. [OE *milt(e)* = MDu. *milte*, OHG *milzi*, ON *milti* f. Gmc **miltjaz, *miltjōn*, perh. cogn. w. MELT²]

mi'lter *n.* male fish in spawning-time. [f. prec. + -ER¹]

Miltō'nian, Miltō'nic, *adjs.* of, or in the manner of, Milton. [f. J. *Milton*, Engl. poet. d. 1674 + -IAN, -IC]

mi'mbar *n.* pulpit in mosque. [f. Arab. *minbar*]

mime *n. & v.* **1.** *n.* (Gk & Rom. Ant.) simple farcical drama marked by mimicry; similar modern performance with gestures and usu. without words. **2.** performer in this; pantomimist, buffoon. **3.** *v.i. & t.* act with mimic gestures, usu. without words. [f. L f. Gk *mimos*]

M.I.Mech.E. *abbr.* Member of the Institution of Mechanical Engineers.

mi'méograph (-ahf) *n., & v.t.* (reproduce by) apparatus for holding stencils of written pages, from which many copies may be taken. [irreg. f. Gk *mimeomai* imitate; see -GRAPH]

mimē'sis *n.* (Biol.) close external resemblance of an animal to another that is distasteful or harmful to predators of the first. [f. Gk *mimēsis* imitation (as prec.)]

mimē't|ic *a.* of, or addicted to, imitation, mimicry, or mimesis; hence ~ICALLY *adv.* [f. Gk *mimētikos* (as prec.; see -ETIC]

mi'mic¹ *a. & v. n.* **1.** *a.* having aptitude for mimicry; imitating; imitative, esp. for amusement, **2.** *n.* person skilled in ludicrous imitation. [f. L f. Gk *mimikos* (as MIME; see -IC)]

mi'mic² *v.t.* (-ck-). ridicule by imitating (person, manner, etc.); copy minutely or servilely; (of. thing) resemble closely. [f. prec.]

mi'micry *n.* mimicking; thing that mimics another; (Zool.) mimesis. [f. MIMIC¹ + -RY]

M.I.Min.E. *abbr.* Member of the Institution of Mining Engineers.

miminy-pi'miny *a.* over-refined, finical. [imit.]

mimō'sa (-za) *n.* leguminous shrub of genus *Mimosa* with globular flower-heads, incl. common sensitive plant (*M. pudica*); acacia. [mod. L, app. f. L (as MIME, from being as sensitive as animals) + -*osa* fem. suf.; see -OSE¹]

mi'mulus *n.* any of the flowering plants of genus *Mimulus*, incl. musk and monkey-flower. [mod. L, app. dim. of L (as MIME, perh. w. ref. to masklike flowers)]

M.I.Mun.E. *abbr.* Member of the Institution of Municipal Engineers.

Min *n.* Chinese dialect of Fukien province in SE China. [Chin.]

Min. *abbr.* Minister; Ministry.

min. *abbr.* minim; minimum; minute(s).

mi'na¹ *n.* (*pl.* ~**e**). ancient monetary unit in Greek--speaking countries; ancient unit of weight in Greece, Egypt, etc., about 1 lb. [L, f. Gk *mna*]

mi'na², my'na, my'nah (-a), *n.* bird of starling family in SE Asia, esp. talking species *Gracula religiosa*. [f. Hindi *mainā*]

minā'cious (-shus) *a.* threatening, menacing; hence ~LY² *adv.*, **mina'city** *n.* [f. L *minax minacis* (*minari* threaten); see -ACIOUS]

minarĕt (mĭ'-, -ĕ't) *n.* slender turret connected with mosque and having balcony from which muezzin calls at hours of prayer. [F, or Sp. *minarete* f. Turk. *minare* f. Arab. *manār(a)* lighthouse, minaret (*nār* fire, light)]

mǐ'natorў *a.* threatening, menacing; expressing threat. [f. LL *minatorius* (*minari* -*at*- threaten; see -ORY)]

mǐ'nbăr. Var. of MIMBAR.

mince[1] *n.* minced meat; ∼'**meat,** mixture of currants, raisins, sugar, apples, candied peel, spices, etc., for ∼ **pie** (usu. small round pie, containing this); *make* ∼-*meat of*, utterly defeat (person, argument, etc.). [f. foll.]

mince[2] *v.* **1.** *v.t.* cut (meat etc.) very small; (usu. w. neg.) ∼ **matters,** use polite expressions in condemnation. **2.** restrain (one's words) within bounds of politeness. **3.** *v.t.* & *i.* utter (words), walk, with affected delicacy; hence **mǐ'ncing**LY[2] *adv.* **4.** Hence **mǐ'ncER**[1] (1, 2) *n.* [ME, f. OF *mincier* f. Rom. **minutiare* f. L (as MINUTIA)]

mind[1] *n.* **1.** remembrance (*bear, have, in mind*); **bring or call to** ∼, remember, cause to be remembered; **come to** ∼, **come into person's** ∼, be remembered; **go out of** person's ∼, be forgotten by him; **keep in** ∼, remember; MONTH'*s* ∼; **put** person **in** ∼ **of,** make him remember; **put out of** one's ∼, deliberately forget about; *out of* SIGHT[1] *out of mind*; TIME[1] *out of mind*. **2.** candid opinion; SPEAK one's *mind*; **give** person **a piece of** one's ∼, scold or reproach him. **3.** opinion (*in or to my mind he is a genius*); **be in** (or **of**) **a** or **one** or **the same** ∼, agree in opinion; **be in two** ∼**s,** be undecided (*about*); **change** one's ∼, adopt new plan or opinion; **have a** ∼ **of** one's **own,** be capable of forming opinions independently of others; **have a good** or **great,** (**half**) **a,** ∼ **to,** feel much, somewhat, tempted or inclined to; **know** one's **own** ∼, not vacillate; **make up** one's ∼, decide, resolve, (*to do, to course of action* etc., or abs.), reconcile oneself *to* inevitable fact; **read** person's ∼, know what he is thinking, without being told. **4.** direction of thoughts or desires; ABSENCE *of mind*; **cast** one's ∼ **back,** recall an earlier time; **give** or **put** or **set** or **turn** one's ∼ **to,** direct one's attention to; **have it in** ∼, intend; **have on** one's ∼, be troubled by thought of; **keep** one's ∼ **on,** continue to think about; **open** or **close** one's ∼ **to,** be willing, unwilling, to consider; PRESENCE *of mind*; **set** one's ∼ **on,** desire to attain; **to** one's ∼, as one would like it. **5.** way of thinking and feeling (*frame, state, of mind; the Victorian mind*). **6.** seat of consciousness, thought, volition and feeling. **7.** soul, opp. to body or material things (*mind may triumph over matter*); ∼'**s eye,** mental view. **8.** person, as embodying mental qualities. **9.** intellectual powers, opp. to will and emotions; hence ∼'LESS *a.,* (esp.) stupidly ill-behaved. **10.** normal condition of mental faculties; **lose** one's ∼, become insane; **out of** one's ∼, insane; **in** one's **right** ∼, sane. **11.** ∼-**boggling,** (colloq.) causing the mind to boggle; ∼-**reader,** = THOUGHT[1]-*reader*; ∼-**set,** (fixed) direction of thought; ∼-**stuff,** (Philos.) supposed rudimentary form of psychical existence regarded as the reality of which matter is an aspect. [ME *mynd* f. OE *gemynd*, = OHG *gimunt*, Goth. *gamunds* f. Gmc **gamundhiz* (as Y-, **mun*- weak grade of **men*- etc. f. IE **men*-, **mon*-, **mn*- think)]

mind[2] *v.t.* & *i.* **1.** bear in mind (chiefly in *imper.*); ∼ (**you**), (parenth.) please take note; give heed to (*never mind the expense*); **be obedient to. **2.** concern oneself about; **never** (**you**) ∼, (*imper.*), (1) do not be troubled, take comfort, (2) I refuse to answer your question; ∼ one's **P's and Q's,** be careful as to speech or behaviour; *mind* (= WATCH[2]) one's *step*. **3.** apply oneself to (business etc.; *mind your own BUSINESS*). **4.** (usu. w. neg. or interrog.) object to (thing, person, *that*, do*ing*; *would you mind ringing?*); **I should not** ∼, **don't** ∼ **if I have,** (should like) *a cup of tea*; **if you don't** ∼ (have no objection); **do you** ∼?, (iron.) please stop that. **5.** remember and take care (*mind* (*that*) thing is done). **6.** ∼, ∼ **out for** (or abs.), be on one's guard against or about, remember existence of (*mind the step*); ∼ **away** or **out,** ∼ **your back,** (colloq.) let me pass. **7.** have charge of; ∼ **the shop** or **store,* (fig.) have charge of affairs. **8.** Hence

∼'ER[1] *n.,* one whose business it is to attend to something, esp. child or machinery. [ME, f. prec.]

mǐ'ndĕd *a.* disposed (*to* do); inclined to think (in specified way: *mechanically, politically, minded*); (in *comb.*) having (specified kind of) mind (*high-minded; small-minded*), inclined to concern oneself with (*car-minded*). [f. MIND[1] + -ED[2]]

mǐ'ndful *a.* taking thought or care (*of,* or abs.); hence ∼LY[2] *adv.,* ∼NESS *n.* [ME, f. MIND[1] + -FUL]

mǐne[1] *n.* **1.** excavation in earth for extracting metal, coal, salt, etc., (∼'**worker,** one who works in this); (fig.) abundant source (*of* information etc.); ‖iron ore. **2.** (Mil. etc.) subterranean gallery in which explosive is placed to blow up fortifications, (formerly) subterranean passage under wall of besieged fortress. **3.** receptacle filled with explosive placed in or on ground for destroying enemy personnel or material, or moored beneath or floating on or near surface of water for destroying or impeding enemy ships; ∼-**detector,** instrument indicating presence of mines; ∼'**field,** area of land or sea in which mines have been laid, (fig.) area presenting many unseen hazards; ∼-**layer,** ship or aircraft for laying mines; ∼'**sweeper,** ship for clearing away floating or submarine mines. [ME, f. OF *mine,* (perh. f. *miner*; see foll.), or f. foll.]

mǐne[2] *v.t.* & *i.* **1.** burrow in (earth); make (hole) underground; make subterranean passages under; (fig.) undermine. **2.** (Mil. etc.) lay mines under or in. **3.** obtain (metal, coal, etc.) from mine; dig in (earth etc., or abs.) for or *for* ore etc. **4.** Hence **mǐ'nING**[1] (1) *n.* [ME, f. OF *miner,* perh. f. Celt.]

mǐne[3] *poss. pron.* see MY. [OE *mīn,* = OS *mīn,* OHG *mīn,* ON *mínn,* Goth. *meins* f. Gmc **mīnaz* f. IE **mei* locative of **me* ME[1] (cf. I[2]) + adj. suf. **-no*-]

mǐ'ner *n.* one who works in a mine; soldier whose duty it is to lay mines; burrowing insect or grub. [ME, f. OF *minĕor, minour* (as MINE[2]; see -OR)]

mǐ'neral *a.* & *n.* **1.** *a.* obtained by mining; belonging to any of the species into which inorganic substances are classified; *mineral* KINGDOM; ∼ **oil,** petroleum or one of its distillation products; ∼ **water,** (1) water found in nature impregnated with mineral substance, (2) artificial imitation of this, esp. soda-water, (3) other effervescent drink, e.g. ginger-beer; *mineral* WAX[1], WOOL. **2.** *n.* mineral substance or object; ‖(esp. in *pl.*) = *mineral water* (2, 3). **3.** Hence ∼IZE (3) *v.t.* & *i.*, change (partly) into mineral. [ME f. OF, or f. med. L *mineralis* (*minera* ore f. OF *miniere* mine f. Rom. **minaria* f. **mina*(*re*) MINE[1,2])]

miner|ă'logў *n.* Science of minerals; hence ∼alŏ'gI- CAL *a.,* ∼a'logIST (3) *n.* [irreg. f. prec. + -LOGY]

minĕstrŏ'nĕ *n.* thick soup containing vegetables and pasta or rice. [It.]

mǐ'nĕver. Var. of MINIVER.

Mǐng *n.* (Chinese porcelain contemporary with) Chinese ruling dynasty 1368–1644. [Chin.]

mǐ'ngle (-nggel) *v.t.* & *i.* mix, blend; ∼ **their** etc. **tears,** weep together; ∼ **with,** go about among. [ME *mengel* f. obs. *meng* f. OE *mengan,* cogn. w. AMONG, + -LE[3]]

‖**mǐ'ngў** (-njĭ) *a.* (colloq.) mean, stingy. [perh. f. MEAN[3] and STINGY]

mǐ'ni *n.* (colloq.) minicar, miniskirt, etc.; (M∼; P) make of small car. [abbr.]

mǐ'ni- *comb. form.* miniature, very small of its kind, (*minibus, minicar*); ∼**cab,** car like taxi but available only if ordered in advance; ∼**skirt** (ending well above the knees). [abbr.]

mǐ'niăte *v.t.* paint with vermilion; illuminate (manuscript). [f. L *miniare* (MINIUM) + -ATE[3]]

mǐ'niatur|e (-nĭcher) *n., a.,* & *v.t.* **1.** *n.* picture in illuminated manuscript; small-scale minutely finished portrait, usu. on ivory or vellum; this branch of painting (*portrait in miniature*), whence ∼IST (3) *n.*; reduced image; **in** ∼**e,** on a small scale. **2.** *a.* represented on small scale; small-scale; much smaller than normal; ∼e **camera** (producing small negatives). **3.** *v.t.* represent in miniature. [f. It. f. med. L *miniatura* f. L *miniare* (as prec.; see -URE)]

mi'niatūrīz|e (-nĭcher-), **-īs|e** (-īz), *v.t.* make miniature; produce in smaller version. [f. prec. + -IZE]

mi'nifȳ *v.t.* represent as smaller or less important than it is; lessen in size or importance. [irreg. f. L *minor* less, *minimus* least, after MAGNIFY]

mi'nikin *n.* & *a.* diminutive (creature); affected, mincing. [f. obs. Du. *minneken* (*minne* love, -*ken*, -*kijn* -KIN)]

mi'nim *n.* ∥(Mus.) note half as long as semibreve; single down-stroke of pen; object or portion of the smallest size or importance; sixtieth part of fluid drachm, about a drop. [ME, f. L *minimus* smallest]

mi'nimal *a.* very minute or slight; being or relating to a minimum; least possible in size, duration, etc.; hence ∼LY² *adv.* [f. as prec. + -AL]

mi'nimalist *n.* person ready to accept a minimum provisionally (opp. MAXIMALIST). [f. prec. + -IST, orig. as transl. of Russ. (see MENSHEVIK)]

mi'nimīz|e (-īs|e (-īz), *v.t.* reduce to, or estimate at, smallest possible amount or degree; estimate or represent at less than the true value or importance; hence ∼A'TION *n.* [f. as MINIM + -IZE]

mi'nim|um *n.* (*pl.* ∼a) & *a.* least (amount) possible, attained or attainable, usual, etc., (*reaches a, its, the* minimum at midnight*); ∼um **lending rate,** announced minimum percentage at which central bank will discount bills; ∼um **thermometer** (automatically recording lowest temperature within given period); ∼um **wage** (than which, by law or agreement, less is not to be offered). [L, neut. (as n.) of *minimus* least]

mi'ning. See MINE².

mi'nion (-yon) *n.* (derog.) favourite child, servant, animal, etc.; favourite of king etc.; servile agent, slave; ∼s **of the law,** gaolers, police, etc. [f. F *mignon,* OF *mignot,* of Gaulish orig.]

mi'niscūle *a.* (erron.) = MINUSCULE.

mi'nish *v.t.* & *i.* (arch.) diminish; reduce in power etc. [ME, f. OF *menu(i)sier* f. Rom. *minutiare* (see MINCE²); assim. to -ISH²]

mi'nister¹ *n.* **1.** person employed in execution *of* (purpose, will, etc.). **2.** person at head of (main branch of) government department. **3.** diplomatic agent accredited by one State to another, usu. ranking below ambassador. **4.** ∼ (**of religion**), clergyman ∥esp. in Presbyterian and Nonconformist Churches; ∼ (**general**), superior of some religious orders. **5.** PRIME² *minister*; ∥M∼ **of the Crown,** member of Cabinet; ∥M∼ **of State,** departmental senior minister intermediate between head of department and junior minister. [ME, f. OF *ministre* f. L *minister* servant (*minus* less); cf. MASTER¹]

mi'nister² *v.* **1.** *v.i.* render aid or service (*to* person, cause, etc.; ∼ing **angel,** w. ref. to Mark 1: 13, esp. of sick-nurse etc.); (arch.) be helpful, contribute, (*to* result). **2.** *v.t.* (arch.) furnish, supply, (help etc.). [ME, f. OF *ministrer* f. L *ministrare* (as prec.)]

ministēr'ial *a.* **1.** of a minister of religion or his office. **2.** of a governmental minister; siding with the Ministry against the Opposition, whence ∼IST (2) *n.* **3.** (arch.) concerned with the execution of orders or law; subsidiary, instrumental. **4.** Hence ∼LY² *adv.* [f. F *ministériel* or f. LL *ministerialis* f. L (as MINISTRY; see -AL)]

ministrā'tion *n.* giving aid or service; ministering, esp. in religious matters; supplying (*of*); so **mi'ni-stranT** *a.* & *n.,* **mi'nistrative** *a.* [ME f. OF, or f. L *ministratio* (as MINISTER²; see -ATION)]

mi'nistrȳ *n.* **1.** ministering, ministration. **2.** *the* body of ministers of the government or of religion; *the* profession of clergyman. **3.** Government department headed by minister (*Ministry of Defence*); building occupied by it. **4.** office as religious minister, priest, etc.; period of tenure of this. [ME, f. L *ministerium* (MINISTER¹)]

mi'nium *n.* (Hist.) red lead; vermilion. [ME f. L]

mi'niver *n.* plain white fur used in ceremonial costume. [ME, f. AF *menuver,* OF *menu vair* (as MENU, VAIR)]

mink *n.* small semi-aquatic stoatlike animal of family Mustelidae, esp. *Mustela vison*; its thick brown fur; coat made of this. [cf. Sw. *mänk, menk*]

mi'nke (-n-ke) *n.* small rorqual with pointed snout. [f. *Meincke,* Norw. whaler]

Minn. *abbr.* Minnesota.

mi'nnesinger *n.* German lyric poet and singer in 12th–14th c. [G *(minne* love, obs. *singer* singer), f. love's being their chief theme]

mi'nnow (-ō) *n.* small freshwater fish (esp. ∥*Phoxinus phoxinus*); **Triton among the** ∼**s,** one who seems great from insignificance of others. [late ME *menow,* perh. repr. OE **mynwe, myne,* OHG *muniwa*; infl. by ME *menuse* f. OF *menuise* f. Rom. **minutia* pl. small objects (as MINUTIA)]

Mino'an *a.* & *n.* (Archaeol.) (person) of the Cretan Bronze-Age civilization (*c.* 3000–1100 BC) named from excavations at palace of (legendary king) Minos at Knossos. [f. Gk *Minōs* + -AN]

mi'nor *a., n.,* & *v.i.* **1.** *a.* lesser (not followed by *than*) of two things, classes, etc.; not yet of full age; ∥(in schools) *Smith* etc. ∼, the younger of the two Smiths or the second to enter the school; FRIARS *Minor*; ∼ **axis** (of conic, perpendicular to major axis); ∼ **canon,** clergyman not member of chapter, assisting in daily cathedral service; ***∼ **league** (in baseball, or fig.; opp. MAJOR² *league*); *minor* ORDER¹*s*; ∼ **piece,** (Chess) bishop or knight; ∼ **planet,** asteroid; *minor* PROPHET; ∼ **suit,** (Bridge) diamonds or clubs. **2.** comparatively unimportant (*minor poet*); (of operation) presenting no danger to patient's life. **3.** (Logic). (Of term) occurring as subject of conclusion of syllogism; (-ō) (of premiss) containing minor term. **4.** (Mus.) (of interval) less by a semitone than major interval; (of key) in which scale has minor third (**in a** ∼ **key,** (fig.) doleful(ly)); HARMONIC, MELODIC, *minor scale.* **5.** *n.* = MINORITE; (Logic) minor term or premiss; minor key etc.; person under full age; ***student's subsidiary subject or course. **6.** *v.i.* ***(Of student) undertake study *in* as minor subject etc. [L, = less, cogn. w. *minuere* lessen]

Minor'ca *n.* ∼ (**fowl**), black variety of domestic fowl brought from Spain. [f. Sp. *Menorca* Minorca, second largest of the Balearic Islands]

Mi'norėss *n.* (Hist.) nun of order founded by St. Clare and St. Francis. [f. OF *menouresse* (*menour* f. L MINOR; see -ESS¹)]

Mi'norite *n.* Franciscan friar. [f. MINOR (because regarding themselves as a humble order) + -ITE¹]

mino'ritȳ *n.* **1.** state of being under full age, period of this. **2.** smaller number or part (*of*), esp. smaller party voting together against majority; number of votes cast for this; state of having less than half the votes. **3.** small group of persons differing from others in race, religion, language, opinion on a topic, etc. & (attrib.) relating to or done by a minority. [f. F *minorité* or f. med. L *minoritas* f. L MINOR; see -ITY]

Mi'notaur *n.* (Gk Myth.) bull-headed man kept in Cretan labyrinth and fed with human flesh. [ME f. OF, f. L f. Gk *Minōtauros* (*Minōs,* legendary king of Crete, husband of Minotaur's mother, + *tauros* bull)]

mi'nster *n.* church of a monastery; name given to some large or important churches. [OE *mynster* = OHG *munstari,* ON *mustari* f. pop. L **monisterium* f. eccl. L f. Gk *monastērion* MONASTERY]

mi'nstrel *n.* **1.** medieval singer or musician, who sang or recited (often his own) poetry; (Hist.) person who entertained his patrons with singing, buffoonery, etc. **2.** (usu. in *pl.*) one of a band of public entertainers, with blackened faces etc., performing songs and music ostensibly of Negro origin. [ME, f. OF *menestral* entertainer, servant, f. Prov. *menest(ai)ral* officer, employee, musician, f. LL *ministerialis* official, officer (see MINISTERIAL)]

mǐ′nstrelsў *n.* minstrel's art; body of minstrels; minstrel poetry. [ME, f. OF *menestralsie* (as prec.)]

mint[1] *n.* place where money is coined, usu. under State authority; vast sum *of money*; (fig.) source of invention etc.; **in ~ condition, state,** (as if) fresh from the mint, (of book, print, postage stamp, etc.) fresh, unsoiled, perfect; **~-mark,** mark placed on coin to show at what mint it was struck (also fig.); **~-master,** superintendent of coinage at mint. [OE *mynet,* = OS *munita,* OHG *muniz*(*za*) f. WG **munita* f. L *moneta* MONEY]

mint[2] *v.t.* make (coin) by stamping metal; invent, coin, (word, phrase, etc.); hence ~′AGE (3, 4) *n.* [ME, f. prec.]

mint[3] *n.* aromatic plant of genus *Mentha,* esp. spearmint; peppermint (lozenge or sweetmeat); *mint* JULEP; ~ **sauce** (of finely chopped spearmint leaves with vinegar and sugar, eaten esp. with roast lamb); hence ~′Y[2] *a.* [OE *minte,* = OHG *minza* f. WG **minta* f. L *ment*(*h*)*a* f. Gk *minthē*]

Mǐ′nton *n.* type of fine pottery or porcelain. [f. T. ~, Engl. maker of china d. 1836]

mǐ′nŭĕnd *n.* (Math.) quantity or number from which another is to be subtracted. [f. L *minuendus* gerundive of *minuere* diminish]

minŭĕ′t *n.* slow stately dance for two in triple measure; music for this, or in same rhythm and style (often as movement in suite, sonata, or symphony). [f. F *menuet* (*menuet* a. = fine, delicate, dim. of MENU; see -ET[1])]

mǐ′nus *prep.,* *a.,* & *n.* **1.** *prep.* with the subtraction of (symbol −); below zero (*temperature of minus ten degrees*); (colloq.) lacking, deprived of, (*returned minus shoes and stockings*). **2.** *a.* (Math.) negative; (Electr.) having negative charge; *minus* SIGN[1]. **3.** *n.* the symbol (−); negative quantity; disadvantage. [L, neut. of MINOR]

mǐ′nuscūl|e *a.* & *n.* **1.** (Palaeog., of kind of cursive script developed in 7th c.) small (letter). **2.** lower-case (letter); extremely small. **3.** Hence ~AR[1] (-ŭ′s-) *a.* [F, f. L *minuscula* (*littera* letter), dim. of MINOR; see -CULE]

mǐ′nute[1] (-ĭt) *n.* **1.** sixtieth part of an hour; distance traversed in one minute (cf. HOUR; *twenty minutes from the station*); = MOMENT; short time, instant; exact point of time; **the ~,** (colloq.) the present time (cf. MOMENT); **up to the ~,** having latest information, in the latest fashion; **the ~ (that),** as soon as; **just a ~, wait a ~,** (colloq.) (1) I shall not keep you waiting for long, (2) I wish to comment or object; LAST[3] *minuto.* **2.** sixtieth part of angular degree. **3.** rough draft, memorandum; (in *pl.*) brief summary of proceedings of assembly, committee, etc.; official memorandum authorizing or recommending a course of action. **4.** ~-**book** (for writing minutes in); ~-**gun** (fired at intervals of a minute at funeral etc.); ~-**hand** (indicating minutes on watch or clock); ***~-**man,** (Hist.) American militiaman of revolutionary period (because ready to march at a minute's notice); ~-**mark** (′, also denoting linear feet; cf. SECOND-*mark*); ~ **steak** (thin slice, that can be cooked quickly). [ME f. OF, f. LL *minuta* n., f. fem. of *minutus* MINUTE[3]; senses 1 & 2 f. med. L *pars minuta prima* first minute part, cf. SECOND; sense 3 perh. f. med. L *minuta scriptura* draft in small writing]

mǐ′nute[2] (-ĭt) *v.t.* **1.** (arch.) find the exact time of. **2.** record in minutes; send minute to (person); ~ (**down**), make a note of. [f. prec.]

mǐnū′te[3] *a.* (~r, ~st). very small; trifling, petty; (of inquiry, inquirer, etc.) accurate, detailed, precise; hence ~LY[2] (-tlĭ) *adv.,* ~NESS (-tn-) *n.* [ME, f. L *minutus,* p.p. of *minuere* lessen]

mǐnū′tia (-shĭa) *n.* (usu. in *pl.* ~e). precise or trivial or minor detail. [L, = smallness, in pl. trifles (*minutus*; see prec.)]

minx *n.* pert or sly girl. [16th c., of unkn. orig.]

Mǐ′ocēne *a.* & *n.* (Geol.) (of the) division of the

Tertiary below the Pliocene. [irreg. f. Gk *meiōn* less + *kainos* new]

mǐ|ō′sĭs, mў|ō′sĭs, *n.* (*pl.* ~oses *pr.* -ō′sēz). excessive contraction of eye-pupil; hence ~o′TIC *a.* [f. Gk *muō* shut the eyes + -OSIS]

M.I.Prod.E. *abbr.* Member of the Institution of Production Engineers.

mir (mēr) *n.* Russian pre-Communist village community. [Russ.]

mirabě′lle *n.* (small round yellow fruit of) a Eur. species of plum-tree similar to bullace and damson; liqueur distilled from it. [F]

mirabile dictu (mĭrahbĭlā dĭ′ktōō) *adv.* wonderful to relate. [L]

mǐ′racle *n.* **1.** marvellous event due to some supposed supernatural agency; remarkable occurrence; remarkable specimen (of ingenuity, impudence, etc.); **to a ~,** (arch.) surprisingly well. **2.** ~ (**play**), dramatic representation in Middle Ages, based on Bible or lives of saints. [ME f. OF, f. L *miraculum* object of wonder (*mirari* wonder f. *mirus* wonderful)]

mǐrǎ′cūlous *a.* of the nature of a miracle; supernatural; surprising; hence ~LY[2] *adv.,* ~NESS *n.* [f. F *miraculeux* or f. med. L *miraculosus* f. L (as prec.; see -OUS)]

mǐradôr′ *n.* belvedere on Spanish house. [Sp. (*mirar* to look)]

mǐrage (mĭrahzh, -ah′-) *n.* optical illusion caused by atmospheric conditions, esp. appearance of sheet of water in desert or on hot road; illusory thing. [F (*se mirer* be reflected, f. L *mirare* look at; see -AGE)]

mīre[1] *n.* **1.** swampy ground, bog; *stick, find one self,* **in the ~,** (fig.) in difficulties. **2.** mud, dirt. [ME, f. ON *mýrr* f. Gmc **meus-, *mus-,* cogn. w. MOSS]

mīre[2] *v.t.* **1.** plunge in mire; (fig.) involve in difficulties. **2.** defile, bespatter, (lit. or fig.). [ME, f. prec.]

mirepoix (mēr′pwah) *n.* sauté chopped vegetables used in sauces etc. [F, f. Duc de *Mirepoix,* Fr. general d. 1757]

mǐrk. Var. of MURK.

mǐ′rror *n.,* & *v.t.* **1.** *n.* polished surface (usu. of amalgam-coated glass, or metal) reflecting image, looking-glass; (fig.) what gives faithful reflection or true description of thing (*hold the mirror up to*); newspaper (used in titles; *Daily Mirror*); ~ **carp** (with large shiny scales); ~ **image** (with structure reversed, or occas. identical); ~ **symmetry** (as of object and its image in mirror); ~ **writing** (backwards, with result like mirror reflection of ordinary writing). **2.** *v.t.* reflect as in mirror (lit. or fig.). [ME f. OF *mirour,* f. Rom. **miratorium* f. L *mirare* look at]

mǐrth *n.* merriment, laughter, hence ~′FUL, ~′LESS, *adjs.* [OE *myrgth* (as MERRY[2], -TH[1])]

MIRV *abbr.* multiple independently targeted re-entry vehicle (type of missile).

mīr′ў *a.* muddy; vile. [ME, f. MIRE[1] + -Y[2]]

mis-[1] *pref.* to *vbs.* and vbl derivs., w. sense 'amiss', 'badly', 'wrongly', 'unfavourably', (*mislead, misshapen, mistrust*), or intensifying unfavourable meaning contained in *v.* (*misdoubt*). [OE, = OS, ON *mis-,* OHG, Goth. *missa-* f. Gmc **missa-* (1) divergent (2) mutual]

mis-[2] *pref.* to *vbs., adjs.,* & *ns.,* w. sense 'amiss', 'badly', 'wrongly', or negative, (*misadventure, mischief*). [f. OF *mes-* f. Rom. **minus-* f. L MINUS]

misadvě′nture *n.* (piece of) bad luck; (Law) death due to accident without crime or negligence. [ME, f. OF *mesaventure* (*mesavenir* turn out badly f. as MIS-[2] + ADVENT; cf. ADVENTURE)]

misalī′gn (-ī′n) *v.t.* give wrong alignment to; so ~MENT *n.* [f. MIS-[1] + ALIGN]

misallī′ance *n.* unsuitable alliance, esp. unsuitable marriage. [f. MIS-[1] + ALLIANCE, after MÉSALLIANCE]

mǐ′santhrōpe (-z-, -s-) *n.* hater of mankind; one who avoids human society; hence or *anal.* **misǎnthrŏ′p**ic(AL), *adjs.,* **misǎ′nthrop**IST (1), **misǎ′nthrop**Y[1], *ns.,* **misǎ′nthrop**IZE (2) *v.i.,* (-z-, -s-). [F, f. Gk *misanthrōpos* (*misos* hatred, *anthrōpos* man)]

misapplỹ' v.t. apply (esp. funds) wrongly; so **mis-APPLICA'TION** n. [f. MIS-¹+APPLY]

misâpprêhě'n|d v.t. misunderstand (words, person); so ∼SION (-shon) n., ∼SIVE a. [f. MIS-¹+APPRE-HEND]

misapprŏ'pri|āte v.t. apply (usu. another's money) to wrong (esp. one's own) use; so ∼A'TION n. [f. MIS-¹ +APPROPRIATE²]

misbĕc|o'me (-ŭ'm) v.t. (∼a'me; ∼o'me). be unsuitable or unbecoming to. [f. MIS-¹+BECOME]

misbĕgŏ'tten a. illegitimate, bastard; contemptible, disreputable. [f. MIS-¹+begotten p.p. of BEGET]

misbĕhă've v.t. behave (oneself, or abs.) improperly; so **misBEHA'VIOUR** n. [ME, f. MIS-¹+BEHAVE]

misbĕlie'f n. wrong religious belief; false opinion. [ME, f. MIS-¹+BELIEF]

misbĕsee'm v.t. (arch.) misbecome. [f. MIS-¹+BESEEM]

misc. abbr. miscellaneous.

miscă'lcūl|āte v.t. calculate (amount, results, etc., or abs.) wrongly; so ∼A'TION n. [f. MIS-¹+CALCULATE]

miscă'll (-aw'l) v.t. call by wrong or inappropriate name; (arch. or dial.) call (person) names. [ME, f. MIS-¹+CALL¹]

miscă'rriage (-rĭj) n. **1.** miscarrying (of letter, scheme, etc.); ∼ (failure of court to attain the ends) **of justice. 2.** untimely delivery (of pregnant woman), abortion (esp. if spontaneous); (Med.) delivery of (prob. non-viable) foetus in 12th–28th week of pregnancy. [f. foll., after CARRIAGE]

miscă'rrỹ v.i. (Of person or business or scheme) fail, be unsuccessful; (of woman) have miscarriage, be delivered prematurely (of child); (of letter) fail to reach destination. [ME, f. MIS-¹+CARRY¹]

miscă'st (-kah'-) v.t. (miscă'st) add (accounts etc.) wrongly; allot unsuitable part to (actor). [f. MIS¹-+CAST¹]

miscĕgĕnă'tion n. interbreeding of races, esp. of Whites with non-Whites. [irreg. f. L miscēre mix+genus race+-ATION]

miscellā'nĕa n. pl. literary miscellany; collection of miscellaneous items. [L, neut. pl. (as foll.)]

miscellā'nĕous a. of mixed composition or character; (w. pl. n.) of various kinds; (of persons) many-sided; hence ∼LY² adv., ∼NESS n. [f. L miscellaneus (miscellus mixed f. miscēre mix) see -ANEOUS)]

miscellanỹ (mĭsĕ'l-, mĭ'sel-) n. mixture, medley; book containing collection of studies etc. or various literary compositions; hence **miscĕ'llan**IST (3) n. [f. F miscellanées fem. pl., or f. L MISCELLANEA, assim. to -Y¹]

mischa'nce (-ah'ns) n. (piece of) bad luck. [ME, f. OF mesch(e)ance (mescheoir; see MIS-², CHANCE¹)]

mi'schief (-chǐf) n. **1.** harm or injury caused by person or other agent (do person a ∼, wound or kill him); **make** ∼, create discord; **the** ∼ (annoying part) of it is that etc. **2.** causer or cause of harm or annoyance. **3.** vexatious but not malicious conduct, esp. of children; pranks, scrapes, (get into, keep out of, mischief). **4.** playful malice, archless, satire, (eyes full of mischief). **5. the** ∼, (colloq.) the Devil (where the mischief have you been?). [ME, f. OF meschief (meschever f. as MIS-², chever come to end f. chef head; see CHIEF¹)]

mi'schievous (-chǐv-) a. (of thing) having harmful effects; (of person, conduct, etc.) disposed to acts of playful malice or mild vexatiousness; hence ∼LY² adv., ∼NESS n. [ME, f. AF meschevous f. OF meschever (see prec., -OUS)]

mi'schmĕtall (-shm-) n. alloy of lanthanide metals that ignites on exposure to air. [G mischen mix, metall metal)]

mi'scI|ble a. that can be mixed (with); hence ∼IBI'LITY n. [f. med. L miscibilis f. L miscēre mix; see -IBLE]

misconcei've (-sē'v) v. **1.** v.i. have a wrong idea or conception (of, or abs.). **2.** v.t. misunderstand (word,

person). **3.** So **misCONCE'PTION** n. [ME, f. MIS-¹+CONCEIVE]

miscŏ'nduct n. improper conduct, esp. adultery; bad management; so **misCONDU'CT²** v.t. & refl. [f. MIS-¹+CONDUCT¹]

misconstrue' (-ōō') v.t. put wrong construction on (word, action); mistake meaning of (person); so **misCONSTRU'CTION** n. [ME, f. MIS-¹+CONSTRUE]

miscŏ'pỹ v.t. copy incorrectly. [f. MIS-¹+COPY²]

miscou'nt n., & v.t. & i. (make) wrong count, esp. of votes; count (things) wrongly. [ME, f. MIS-¹+COUNT¹,²]

mi'scrĕant a. & n. **1.** a. depraved; (arch.) heretical. **2.** n. vile wretch, villain; (arch.) heretic. [ME, f. OF mescreant (as MIS-², creant part. of croire f. L credere believe; see -ANT)]

miscūe' n., & v.i. (Bill. etc.) **1.** n. failure to strike ball properly with cue. **2.** v.i. make a miscue. [f. MIS-¹ or MISS²+CUE²]

misdā'te v.t. date (event, letter, etc.) wrongly. [f. MIS-¹+DATE³]

misdea'l v. (misdea'lt pr. -dĕ'-) & n. **1.** v.i. & t. make mistake in dealing (cards). **2.** n. mistake in dealing cards; misdealt hand. [f. MIS-¹+DEAL²]

misdee'd n. evil deed; crime. [OE misdǣd (as MIS-¹, DEED)]

misdee'm v. (arch. or poet.) **1.** v.t. have wrong opinion of; mistake (person, thing for another). **2.** v.i. form wrong judgement (of). [ME; cf. ON misdœma (see MIS-¹, DEEM)]

misdĕmea'nant n. person convicted of misdemeanour or guilty of misconduct. [f. arch. misdemean misbehave (MIS-¹, DEMEAN¹)+-ANT]

misdĕmea'nour (-ner), *-or, n. **1.** (Law) indictable offence, (in UK formerly) less heinous than felony. **2.** offence, misdeed. [ME, f. MIS-¹+DEMEANOUR]

misdĭrĕ'ct v.t. direct (person, letter, blow, etc.) wrongly; (of judge) instruct (jury) wrongly; so **misDIRE'CTION** n. [f. MIS-¹+DIRECT¹]

misdo'ing (-dōō'-) n. misdeed. [ME, f. MIS-¹+DOING]

misdou'bt (-ow't) v.t. have doubts as to the truth or existence of; have misgivings, be suspicious, about; suspect (that). [f. MIS-¹+DOUBT²]

mise (mēz, mīz) n. **1.** (Hist.) settlement by agreement, as **M**∼ **of Lewes** (between Henry III and barons, 1264). **2.** ∼ **en scène** (mēz ahñ sā'n), scenery and properties of acted play, (fig.) surroundings of an event. [ME f. OF, fem. p.p. (as n.) of mettre put f. L mittere miss- send, put]

mi'ser (-z-) n. one who hoards wealth and lives miserably; avaricious person. [L, = wretched]

mi'serab|le (-z-) a. wretchedly unhappy or uncomfortable; (of event etc.) causing wretchedness; contemptible, mean, (a miserable hovel); hence ∼LY² adv. [ME, f. F misérable f. L miserabilis pitiable (miserari to pity f. miser wretched; see -ABLE)]

misère (mĭzār') n. (Cards) declaration undertaking to win no tricks. [F, = poverty, MISERY]

miserer'è (-zerēr'ĭ, -ār'ĭ) n. cry for mercy; = foll. 3. [ME, f. L, imper. of miserēri have mercy (as MISER); first word of Ps. 51 in L]

mise'ricŏrd (-z-) n. **1.** apartment in monastery in which some relaxations of rule were permitted. **2.** dagger for giving the coup de grâce. **3.** shelving projection on under side of hinged seat in choir stall, serving (when seat was turned up) to help support person standing. [ME, f. OF misericorde f. L misericordia (misericors compassionate f. stem of miserēri pity+cor cordis heart)]

mi'serlỹ (-z-) a. like a miser, niggardly; hence ∼iNESS a. [f. MISER+-LY¹]

mi'serỹ (-z-) n. wretched state of mind or of outward circumstances; thing causing this; misère; wretched or (colloq.) discontented or grumpy person; **out of its**

∼, (of animal) released from suffering, esp. by being killed. [ME, f. AF *miserie*, OF *misere*, or f. L *miseria* (as MISER; see -Y¹)]

misfea'sance (-za-) *n.* (Law). transgression, esp. wrongful exercise of lawful authority. [ME, f. OF *mesfaisance* (*mesfaire* misdo f. as MIS-²+*faire* do f. L *facere*); see -ANCE; cf. MALFEASANCE]

misf īr'e *v.i.*, & *n.* (Of gun, motor engine, etc.) fail(ing) to go off or start action or function regularly; fail(ing) to have intended effect. [f. MIS-¹+FIRE²,¹; cf. MISS² *fire*]

mi'sfit *n.* garment etc. that does not fit the person it is meant for; person unsuited to his environment, his work, etc.; ∼ (**stream**), (Geog.) stream whose size is not as expected from that of its valley. [f. MIS-¹+FIT²]

misfôr'tune (-chun, -chōon) *n.* bad luck (*more his misfortune than his fault*); instance of this. [f. MIS-¹+FORTUNE¹]

misgi've (-g-) *v.t.* (**misga've**; **misgi'ven**). (Of person's mind, heart, etc.) fill (him) with suspicion or foreboding (*about* thing, *that*). [f. MIS-¹+GIVE¹]

misgi'ving (-g-) *n.* feeling of mistrust or apprehension. [f. prec.+-ING¹]

misgo'vern (-gŭ'-) *v.t.* govern (State etc.) badly; so ∼MENT *n.* [ME, f. MIS-¹+GOVERN]

misgui'd|**e** (-gī'd) *v.t.* (chiefly in *p.p.*) mislead, cause to err in thought or action; hence ∼**ĕdLY²** *adv.* [ME, f. MIS-¹+GUIDE²]

mishā'ndle (-s-h-) *v.t.* handle (person, thing) roughly or rudely, ill-treat; deal with incorrectly or ineffectively. [f. MIS-¹+HANDLE²]

mishăp (mĭs-h-, -ă'p) *n.* unlucky accident. [ME, f. MIS-¹+HAP¹]

mishear' (-s-h-) *v.t.* (**mishear'd** *pr.* -hēr'd). hear incorrectly or imperfectly. [ME, f. MIS-¹+HEAR]

mishit (-s-h-) *n.*, & *v.t.* (-tt-; **mishit**). **1.** *n.* (mĭ'-). faulty or bad hit. **2.** *v.t.* (-ī't). hit (a ball) faultily. [f. MIS-¹+HIT²,¹]

mi'shmăsh *n.* confused mixture. [ME; redupl. of MASH¹]

Mi'shnah (-a) *n.* collection of precepts forming basis of Talmud, and embodying Jewish oral law; hence **Mishnā'IC** *a.* [f. Heb. *mišnāh* (teaching by) repetition]

misinfôr'm *v.t.* give wrong information to, mislead; so **misINFORMA'TION** *n.* [ME, f. MIS-¹+INFORM]

misintĕr'prĕt *v.t.* give wrong interpretation to; make wrong inference from; so ∼A'TION *n.* [f. MIS-¹+INTERPRET]

misjŭ'dge *v.t.* & *i.* judge wrongly; have wrong opinion of or *of*; so **misJU'DG(E)MENT** *n.* [f. MIS¹+JUDGE²]

mislay' *v.t.* (**mislai'd**). put (thing) by accident where it cannot readily be found; (euphem.) lose. [ME, f. MIS-¹+LAY³]

mislea'd *v.t.* (**misle'd**). lead astray, cause to go wrong, in conduct or belief. [OE *mislǣdan* (as MIS-¹, LEAD²)]

misli'ke *v.t.* (arch.) dislike. [OE *mislīcian* (as MIS-¹, LIKE²)]

mismă'nage *v.t.* manage badly or wrongly; so ∼MENT (-ĭjm-) *n.* [f. MIS-¹+MANAGE²]

mismătch *v.t.*, & *n.* **1.** *v.t.* (-ă'ch). match unsuitably or incorrectly. **2.** *n.* (mĭ'-). bad match. [f. MIS-¹+MATCH²,¹]

misnā'me *v.t.* = MISCALL. [f. MIS-¹+NAME²]

misno'mer *n.* use of wrong name; wrong (use of) name or term. [ME f. AF, f. OF *mesnom(m)er* (as MIS-², *nommer* name f. as NOMINATE; see -ER⁴)]

misŏ'gam|**ў** *n.* hatred of marriage; hence ∼IST (2) *n.* [f. Gk *misos* hatred+*gamos* marriage+-Y¹]

misŏ'gyn|**ist** (-j-, -g-) *n.* one who hates all women; so ∼Y¹ *n.* [f. as prec.+Gk *gunē* woman+-IST]

misŏ'log|**ў** *n.* hatred of reason, discussion, or knowledge; hence ∼IST (2) *n.* [f. Gk *misos* hatred+-LOGY]

misonē'|**ism** *n.* hatred of what is new; hence ∼IST (2) *n.* [f. as prec.+Gk *neos* new+-ISM]

mi'spickel *n.* (Min.) arsenical pyrites. [G]

misplā'ce *v.t.* put in wrong place or hands; bestow (affections) on wrong object; place (confidence) amiss; time (words, action) badly; so ∼MENT (-sm-) *n.* [f. MIS-¹+PLACE²]

misplay' *n.*, & *v.t.* play(ing) in wrong or ineffective manner. [f. MIS-¹+PLAY²,¹]

misprint *n.*, & *v.t.* **1.** *n.* (mĭ'-). mistake in printing. **2.** *v.t.* (-ī'nt). print wrongly. [n. f. v., f. MIS-¹+PRINT²]

mispri'sion¹ (-zhon) *n.* (Law). wrong action or omission, esp. ∼ **of treason** or **felony**, (orig.) minor form of these, (now) concealment of one's knowledge of treasonable intent etc. [ME, f. AF *mesprisioun* f. OF *mesprison* error (*mesprendre* to mistake f. as MIS-², *prendre* take)]

mispri'sion² (-zhon) *n.* (arch.) contempt; failure to appreciate the value (*of*). [f. foll., after prec.]

mispri'ze *v.t.* despise; fail to appreciate. [ME, f. OF *mesprisier* (as MIS-², PRIZE¹)]

mispronou'nce *v.t.* pronounce (word etc.) wrongly; so **misPRONUNCIA'TION** *n.* [f. MIS-¹+PRONOUNCE]

misquō'te *v.t.* quote wrongly; so **misQUOTA'TION** *n.* [f. MIS ¹+QUOTE]

misrea'd *v.t.* (**misrea'd** *pr.* -rĕ'd). read or interpret wrongly. [f. MIS-¹+READ]

misrĕmĕ'mber *v.t.* remember imperfectly or incorrectly. [f. MIS-¹+REMEMBER]

misrĕpôr't *n.*, & *v.t.* (give) false or incorrect report (of). [ME, f. MIS-¹+REPORT²,¹]

misrĕprĕsĕ'nt (-zĕ'-) *v.t.* represent wrongly, give false account of; so ∼A'TION *n.* [f. MIS-¹+REPRESENT]

misru'le (-ōō'l) *n.*, & *v.t.* **1.** *n.* bad government; disorder; **Lord, Master, of M**∼, (Hist.) person presiding over Christmas revels in nobleman's house, Inn of Court, etc. **2.** *v.t.* govern badly. [ME, f. MIS-¹+RULE]

miss¹ *n.* **1.** failure to hit or attain; **a** ∼ **is as good as a mile**, failure or escape is about alike, is however narrow the margin; NEAR² *miss*. **2.** (Bill.) failure to hit object-ball (**give a** ∼, avoid hitting object-ball so as to leave one's own in safe position); **give** (thing) **a** ∼, avoid, leave alone, (*shall give the party, the prunes, a miss*). **3.** (colloq.) = MISCARRIAGE 2. [OE, = loss, cogn. w. foll.]

miss² *v.* **1.** *v.t.* (Of person or missile) fail to hit (mark etc., or abs.), fail to reach, find, get, or meet; let slip (opportunity); fail to catch (train etc.; ∼ **the boat** or **the bus**, lose an opportunity). **2.** fail to see (event) or hear or understand (remark, joke, etc.); **not** ∼ **much**, be alert. **3.** ∼ (**out**), leave out (words etc. in reading, writing, etc.); fail to keep (appointment) or perform. **4.** notice esp. with regret the absence of, feel the want of; **be** ∼'**ing**, not be there. **5.** *v.i.* (Of internal combustion engine) misfire. **6.** ∼ **fire**, (of gun) fail to go off, (fig.) fail in one's object, fail to have intended effect; ∼ **out** (on), (colloq.) fail to get (something), be unsuccessful; miss STAY²5. **7.** Hence ∼'ABLE *a.* [OE *missan*, = OHG *missen*, ON *missa* f. Gmc **missjan* (**missa-* MIS-¹)]

miss³ *n.* (M∼). (As title of unmarried woman or girl without higher title, or retained by married woman for professional etc. reasons) *Miss Smith* (pl. *the Miss Smiths*, *the Misses Smith*; (as title of beauty queen from specified region) *Miss France*, *Miss World*; as *voc.* without name, to teacher or shop assistant, or from servant etc.) young woman. **2.** (usu. derog. or playful). girl, esp. schoolgirl, often w. implication of silliness or sentimentality; whence ∼'ISH¹ *a.* **3.** (Commerc.) garment (of) size suitable for young women. [abbr. of MISTRESS]

Miss. *abbr.* Mississippi.

mi'ssal *n.* (RC Ch.) book containing service of Mass for whole year; book of prayers, esp. illuminated one. [ME, f. med. L *missale* neut. (as n.) of eccl. L *missalis* of the mass (*missa* MASS¹; see -AL)]

mi′ssel *n.* (-thrush), large thrush (*Turdus viscivorus*) that feeds on mistletoe etc. berries. [OE *mistel* basil, mistletoe, = OHG, ON *mistil*; orig. unkn.]

misshāpe (-s-sh-) *v.t.* give bad shape or form to (lit. or fig.). [ME, f. MIS-¹+SHAPE¹]

misshā′pen (-s-sh-) *a.* ill-shaped, deformed, distorted. [ME, f. MIS-¹+*shapen* arch. p.p. of SHAPE¹]

mi′ssīle *a.* & *n.* (object or weapon) suitable for throwing at a target or for discharge from machine; self-propelled weapon directed by remote control (GUIDE²*d missile*) or automatically; hence ∿RY (1, 5) (-lrĭ) *n.* [f. L *missilis* (*mittere miss-* send; see -IL)]

mi′ssing *a.* In vbl senses; not found, not in its place, (*there is a page missing*; *a page is missing*; *here is the missing page*; cf. MISS² 4); (of soldier etc.) neither present after battle etc. nor known to have been killed or wounded or captured; ∿ link, thing lacking to complete a series, hypothetical intermediate type, esp. between man and anthropoid apes. [f. MISS²+-ING²]

mi′ssion (-shon) *n.* 1. body of persons sent to foreign country to conduct negotiations etc. 2. body sent by religious community to propagate its faith; field of missionary activity; missionary post; organization in a district for conversion of the people; course of religious services etc. for this purpose. 3. task to be performed; journey for such purpose; military operation, esp. dispatch of aircraft or spacecraft. 4. person's vocation or divinely appointed work in life. [F, or f. L *missio* (*mittere miss-* send; see -ION)]

mi′ssionary (-sho-) *a.* & *n.* 1. *a.* of, concerned with, characteristic of, religious or similar missions. 2. *n.* person who goes on missionary work. [f. mod. L *missionarius* f. L (as prec.; see -ARY¹)]

mi′ssioner (-sho-) *n.* missionary; person in charge of parochial mission. [f. MISSION+-ER¹]

mi′ssis, mi′ssus (-sĭz) *n.* 1. (vulg. or joc.) wife; **the** ∿, my or your wife. 2. (vulg., as *voc.*) Form of address to woman. [corrupt. of MISTRESS; cf. MRS]

mi′ssive *a.* & *n.* 1. *a.* letter(s) ∿, letter from sovereign to dean and chapter nominating person to be elected bishop. 2. *n.* = LETTER 2, esp. official one or (joc.) long or serious one. [ME, f. med. L *missivus* f. L (as MISSION; see -IVE)]

misspě′ll (-s-s-) *v.t.* (for forms see SPELL²). spell wrongly; hence ∿ING¹ *n.* [f. MIS-¹+SPELL²]

misspě′nd (-s-s-) *v.t.* (**misspe′nt**). spend amiss or wastefully (esp. in *p.p.*). [ME, f. MIS-¹+SPEND]

misstā′te (-s-s-) *v.t.* state wrongly; so ∿MENT (-tm-) *n.* [f. MIS-¹+STATE²]

misstě′p (-s-s-) *n.* wrong step or action; *faux pas.* [f. MIS-+STEP²]

missus. See MISSIS.

mi′ssy *n.* affectionate, playful, or derog., form of address to young girl. [f. MISS³+-Y³]

mist *n.* & *v.* 1. *n.* water vapour near ground in droplets smaller than raindrops and causing obscuration of the atmosphere; Scotch ∿, thick mist and drizzle (frequent on Scottish hills). 2. dimness or blurring of sight caused by bodily disorder or by tears; condensed vapour obscuring windscreen etc.; cloud of particles resembling mist. 3. Hence ∿FUL *a.*, ∿LIKE *a.* & *adv.* 4. *v.t.* & *i.* cover, be covered, (as) with mist. [OE *mist*, = MLG, MDu. *mist*, Icel. *mistur* f. Gmc **mihstaz*]

mistā′ke¹ *n.* misunderstanding of a thing's meaning; thing incorrectly done or thought through ignorance or inadvertence; **and,** or **make, no** ∿, undoubtedly (emphasizing statement). [f. foll.]

mistā′ke² *v.* (**mistoo′k**; ∿n). 1. *v.t.* misunderstand meaning or intention of (person, statement, purpose); choose wrongly (*mistake* one's *vocation*); wrongly take (one *for* another); **there is no mista′king,** one is sure to recognize (person or thing). 2. *v.i.* err in opinion. 3. (in *p.p.*) wrong in opinion, (of action etc.) ill-judged, (*you are mistaken*; *mistaken kind-*

ness); hence ∿nLY² *adv.*, ∿nNESS (-n-n-) *n.* 4. Hence **mistā′kable** *a.* [ME, f. ON *mistaka* (as MIS-¹, *taka* TAKE¹)]

mi′ster *n.*, & *v.t.* 1. *n.* (vulg., as *voc.*) Form of address to man. 2. person without title of nobility etc. (*a mere mister*). 3. *v.t.* address or speak of as *Mr.* [weakened form of MASTER¹ in unstressed use before name; cf. MR]

mi′stigris *n.* (Cards). (blank card in) a variety of poker. [f. F *mistigri* jack of clubs]

misti′me *v.t.* say, do, (thing) at wrong time. [OE *mistīmian* (as MIS-¹, TIME²)]

mistle. Var. of MISSEL.

mi′stletōe (-seltō) *n.* parasitic plant (*Viscum album*) growing on apple and other trees, and bearing white glutinous berries used in making birdlime; **kiss under the** ∿ (w. ref. to custom permitting kissing of girl standing below mistletoe hung as Christmas decoration). [OE *misteltān* (= ON *mistilteinn*; see MISSEL, *tān* twig)]

mistŏŏ′k. See MISTAKE².

mistral (mĭ′-, -trah′l) *n.* cold N. or NW wind in Mediterranean provinces of France etc. [F & Prov., f. L (as MAGISTRAL)]

mistrans|lā′te (-rā-, -rah-; -s-, -z-) *v.t.* translate incorrectly; so ∿lā′TION *n.* [f. MIS-¹+TRANSLATE]

mistrea′t *v.t.* treat badly; hence ∿MENT *n.* [ME, MIS-¹+TREAT]

mi′stress *n.* 1. woman in authority over servants; female head of household. 2. woman who has power to control or dispose *of* (*you are mistress of the situation, of yourself*; *you are your own, the dog's, mistress*; cf. MASTER¹); woman head of college, school, etc.; (fig.) ∿ **of the seas,** chief naval power. 3. woman who has thorough knowledge (*of* subject). 4. woman loved and courted by a man; woman illicitly occupying place of wife or having permanent illicit sexual relationship with man. 5. ||female teacher in school or of special subject (*music mistress*). 6. ||M∿ **of the Robes,** lady charged with care of Queen's wardrobe; WARDROBE *mistress*. 7. (arch. or dial., as title) = MRS. 8. Hence ∿-SHIP *n.* [ME f. OF *maistresse* (*maistre* MASTER¹; see -ESS¹)]

mistri′al *n.* trial vitiated by error; **inconclusive trial. [f. MIS-¹+TRIAL]

mistrů′st *v.t.*, & *n.* 1. *v.t.* feel no confidence in (person, one*self*, one's powers, etc.); be suspicious of. 2. *n.* lack of confidence; suspicion. [ME, f. MIS-¹+TRUST]

mistrů′stful *a.* lacking confidence or trust; suspicious *of*; hence ∿LY² *adv.*, ∿NESS *n.* [f. prec. 2+-FUL]

mi′st|y *a.* of, or covered with, mist; indistinct in form; (fig.) obscure, vague, (*a misty idea*); hence ∿iLY² *adv.*, ∿iNESS *n.* [OE *mistig* (as MIST, -Y²)]

misůnderstā′nd *v.t.* (-stoo′d). take (words etc., or abs.) in wrong sense; (esp. in *p.p.*). misinterpret words or actions of (person); so ∿ING¹ *n.* [ME, f. MIS-¹+UNDERSTAND]

misū′sage (-ū′z-, -ū′s-) *n.* wrong or improper usage; ill-treatment. [f. MIS-¹+USAGE]

misū′s|e¹ (-z) *v.t.* use wrongly, apply to wrong purpose; ill-treat; hence ∿ER¹ *n.* [ME, f. MIS-¹+USE²]

misū′se² *n.* wrong or improper use or application. [ME, f. MIS-¹+USE¹]

MIT *abbr.* Massachusetts Institute of Technology.

mīte *n.* 1. small arachnid of order Acari, esp. **cheese-** ∿ (found in cheese), ITCH¹-*mite*; hence **mī′t**Y² *a.* 2. (Hist.) Flemish copper coin of small value; (pop.) half a farthing (as in Mark 12: 42); modest contribution, the best one can do, (*let me offer my mite of comfort*); **a** ∿, (*adv.*, colloq.) somewhat (**not a** ∿, not at all). 3. small object, esp. child; **a** ∿ **of a** (a tiny) *child* etc. [sense 1 f. OE *mīte*, = MLG, MDu. *mīte*, OHG *mīza* gnat f. Gmc **mītōn*; sense 2 ME, f. MLG, MDu. *mīte*, prob. of same orig.]

**mī′ter¹,². See MITRE¹,².

Mi′th|ras *n.* Persian god identified with sun, worshipped in Europe during first three centuries AD;

For other words in *mis-* see MIS-¹,².

hence ~rā′ıc a., ~rāısm (3), ~rāıst (2), ns. [L f. Gk, f. OPers. *Mithra* f. Skr. *Mitra* a Vedic god]

mithri′dat|ize, -i̇|se (-īz), *v.t.* render proof against poison by gradually increasing doses of it; so **mithri′dă′tıc** *a.*, ~ısм (1) *n.* [f. *mithridate* supposed universal antidote (*Mithridates* VI, king of Pontus d. 63 BC, supposed to have used this method) + -ize]

mi′tig|āte *v.t.* appease (anger etc.); alleviate (pain, grief); reduce severity of (punishment); moderate (heat, cold, severity, guilt, etc.); so ~ABLE *a.*, ~A′TION *n.*, ~ātory *a.* [ME, f. L *mitigare* (*mitis* mild) + -ATE³]

mitŏchŏ′ndri̇|on (-k-) *n.* (*pl.* ~a). (Biol.) organelle in most cells, containing enzymes needed for metabolic processes. [mod. L, f. Gk *mitos* thread + *khondrion* dim. of *khondros* granule]

mit|ō′si̇s *n.* (*pl.* ~oses *pr.* -ō′sēz). (Biol.) division of a cell or nucleus with longitudinal splitting of all chromosomes into pairs distributed equally between resulting two cells or nuclei; hence ~o′tıc *a.* [mod. L, f. Gk *mitos* thread; see -OSIS]

mitrailleu′se (-trahyêr′z) *n.* many-barrelled breech-loading machine-gun discharging small missiles simultaneously or in rapid succession. [F, fem. agent-n. f. *mitrailler* (*mitraille* small missiles f. OF *mi*(*s*)*traille* small money, f. *mite* MITE)]

mi′tral *a.* of or like a mitre; ~ **valve,** two-cusped valve between left atrium and left ventricle of heart. [f. mod. L *mitralis* f. L (as foll.; see -AL)]

||**mi′tre¹** (-ter), *mi′ter¹, n.* **1.** bishop's and abbot's tall cap, deeply cleft at top, esp. as symbol of episcopal office; hence **mi′t(e)rED²** (-terd) *a.* **2.** [perh. diff. wd]. joint of two pieces of wood etc. at angle of 90°, such that line of junction bisects this angle (~-block, -board, -box, guide for saw in cutting mitre-joints; ~-wheels, pair of bevelled cog-wheels with teeth set at 45° and axes at right angles); similar joint of pieces of cloth etc. [ME f. OF, f. L f. Gk *mitra* girdle, turban]

||**mi′tre²** (-ter), *mi′ter², v.* **1.** *v.t.* bestow mitre on. **2.** *v.t. & i.* join with mitre. [ME, f. prec.]

mitt *n.* lace or knitted glove not covering fingers; mitten; baseball glove for catching ball; *** (sl.) hand (**frozen ~,** chilly reception) [abbr. of foll.]

mi′tten *n.* kind of glove with thumb but no (or no separate) fingers, for warmth or protection in hedgers' work etc.; (in *pl.*, *sl.*) boxing-gloves; **give, get, the (frozen) mitten,** (sl.) dismiss (person), be dismissed; hence ~ED² (-nd) *a.* [ME, f. OF *mitaine*, f. Rom. *medietana (sc. *muffula* MUFFLE²) f. L *medietas* half (see MOIETY)]

mi′ttimus *n.* warrant committing person to prison or (Hist.) ordering documents to be sent to another court; (arch. colloq.) dismissal from office. [ME f. L, = we send]

Mi′ttȳ *n.* (*pl.* ~s). (Walter) ~, person given to extravagant day-dreams of his own triumphs. [hero of story by J. Thurber]

mix *v. & n.* **1.** *v.t.* put together, combine (two or more substances or groups or qualities etc., one *with* another) so that the particles or members or constituent parts of each are diffused among those of the others; prepare (compound, cocktail, etc.) by mixing ingredients; ~ one's **drinks,** drink different alcoholic liquors in succession. **2.** *v.i.* join, be mixed (*oil will not mix with water*); (of persons) be harmonious or sociable (*with*), have dealings *with*, participate *in*; (of things) be compatible. **3.** ~ **in,** ~ **it,** (colloq.) start fighting; ~ **up,** (1) mix thoroughly, (2) confuse esp. in thought, so ~-*up* n.; **be ~ed up,** be involved (*in* or *with* shady dealings etc.). **4.** *n.* (colloq.) mixture; proportion of materials in a mixture; merging of film pictures or sounds; ingredients prepared commercially for making cake etc. or for a process such as concrete-making. [back-form. f. foll. taken as p.p.]

mixed (-kst) *a.* In vbl senses (see prec.); of diverse qualities or elements; (of group of persons) contain-

ing persons from various classes, esp. of doubtful status; tangled; ~(up), (colloq.) mentally confused, muddled, ill-adjusted; for persons of both sexes (*mixed school, bathing*); ~ **bag,** assortment of diverse things or persons; ~ **blessing,** thing having advantages but also disadvantages; ~ **chalice,** sacramental wine with ceremonial addition of water; ~ **crystal** (formed from more than one substance); ~ **doubles,** (Tennis etc.) doubles game with man and woman as partners on each side; ~ **farming** (with both crops and livestock); ~ **feelings** (e.g. some pleasure and some dismay at same event); ~ **grill,** dish of various grilled meats and vegetables; ~ **marriage** (between persons of different race or religion); *mixed* META-PHOR; ~ **number** (containing integer and fraction); ||~ **tithe** (from animals fed on the land); hence **mi′xedNESS** *n.* [ME *mixt* f. OF *mixte* f. L *mixtus* p.p. of *miscēre* mix]

||**mi′xen** *n.* (arch. or dial.) dunghill. [OE, f. Gmc *mihsa; see -EN³]

mi′xer *n.* In vbl senses; apparatus for mixing foods etc.; apparatus for merging pictures in television or cinematography; apparatus controlling combination of various sounds in preparation of sound films or in broadcasting; drink to be mixed with another; **good, bad,** ~, (colloq.) one who gets on well, badly, with other people (esp. those of a different social class). [f. MIX + -ER¹]

Mixoly′dian *a.* ~ **mode,** (1) ancient Greek MODE, (2) seventh of church modes (with G as final and D as dominant). [f. Gk *mixoludios* half-Lydian (*mixos* mixed; see LYDIAN)]

mi′xture *n.* **1.** mixing or being mixed. **2.** thing or (fig.) person that is the result of mixing; medicinal preparation of this kind (*cough mixture*; **the ~ as before,** (fig.) the same treatment repeated); (**mechanical**) ~, (product of) mechanical mixing of two substances, involving no change in their character, opp. to chemical compound or combination; gas or vaporized petrol or oil mixed with air, forming explosive charge in internal-combustion engine; HEATHER *mixture*. [ME f. F, or f. L *mixtura* (as MIXED); see -URE]

mi′zen, mi′zzen, *n.* (Naut.) ~ (-sail), lowest fore-and-aft sail of full-rigged ship's ~-mast (next aft of main-mast); ~ **yard** (on which mizen is extended). [ME, f. F *misaine* f. It. *mezzana* mizen-sail, fem. of *mezzano* middle; see MEZZANINE]

mi′zzle¹ *v.i. impers.*, & *n.* drizzle; hence **mi′zzlY²** *a.* [ME, prob. f. LG *miseln*; cf. MDu. *miezelen*]

||**mi′zzle²** *v.i.* (sl.) run away, decamp. [18th c.; orig. unkn.]

MJI *abbr.* Member of the Institute of Journalists.

Mk. *abbr.* mark.

MKS(A) *abbrs.* metre-kilogram-second(-ampere) system of measurement.

Mkt. *abbr.* Market.

ml. *abbr.* mile(s); millilitre(s).

MLA *abbr.* Member of Legislative Assembly; Modern Language Association (of America).

MLC *abbr.* Member of Legislative Council.

MLF *abbr.* multilateral (nuclear) force.

M.Litt. *abbr.* Master of Letters. [f. L *Magister Litterarum*]

Mlle *abbr.* Mademoiselle.

Mlles *abbr.* Mesdemoiselles.

MLR *abbr.* minimum lending rate.

MM *abbr.* Maelzel's metronome; *Messieurs*; ||Military Medal.

mm. *abbr.* millimetre(s).

Mme *abbr.* Madame.

Mmes *abbr.* Mesdames.

m.m.f. *abbr.* magnetomotive force.

M.Mus. *abbr.* Master of Music.

MN *abbr.* ||Merchant Navy; Minnesota.

Mn *symb.* manganese.

||**M'Naghten.** See MacN-.

mnĕmŏ'nic (n-) *a.* & *n.* **1.** *a.* of, or designed to aid, the memory. **2.** *n.* mnemonic device; (in *pl.*, usu. treated as *sing.*) art of, system for, improving memory. **3.** Hence **mnē'monIST** (3) (n-) *n.* [f. med. L f. Gk *mnēmonikos* (*mnēmōn* mindful f. *mna-* remember; see -IC)]

mō *n.* (*pl.* **mos**). (sl.) moment (*wait a mo*). [abbr.]

MO *abbr.* Medical Officer; money order.

MO, Mo., *abbrs.* Missouri.

*mo. *abbr.* month.

Mo *symb.* molybdenum.

mō'a *n.* extinct flightless NZ bird of family Dinornithidae, more or less resembling ostrich; cf. DINORNIS. [Maori]

moan¹ *n.* **1.** long murmur expr. physical or mental suffering; low plaintive sound of wind etc. **2.** complaint, grievance; suffering; **make** (one's) ∼, (arch.) complain. **3.** Hence ∼'FUL *a.* [ME, f. OE *mān f. Gmc **main-*]

moan² *v.* **1.** *v.i.* make moan(s). **2.** *v.t.* utter (words) with moans; lament (misfortune etc.); lament for (dead person etc.). [f. prec.]

moat *n.*, & *v.t.* **1.** *n.* deep wide ditch surrounding house, castle, etc., usu. filled with water. **2.** *v.t.* surround (as) with moat. [ME *mot(e)* f. OF *mot(t)e* mound]

mŏb¹ *n.* **1.** *the* populace; rabble, tumultuous crowd; promiscuous assemblage of persons; (Austral.) flock or herd; (sl.) associated group of persons. **2.** ∼ **law,** ∼ **rule,** (imposed and enforced by mob); ||∼'**sman** (-z-), (arch.) well-dressed pickpocket; ∼'**ster,** (sl.) gangster; ||SWELL *mob.* **3.** Hence ∼'**bISH¹** *a.,* ∼-ŏ'CRACY *n.* [abbr. of *mobile* n. (17th c.) short for *mobile vulgus,* L, = excitable crowd (MOBILE)]

mŏb² *v.* (-bb-). **1.** *v.t.* (Of mob) attack; crowd round and molest or acclaim. **2.** *v.i.* assemble in a mob. [f. prec.]

mŏ'b-cǎp *n.* woman's large indoor cap covering whole of hair, worn in 18th and early 19th c. [f. obs. (18th c.) *mob,* orig. = slut, +CAP¹]

mō'bīle *a.* & *n.* **1.** *a.* movable, not fixed, free to move, able to move or flow easily; (of face etc.) readily changing its expression; (of person or mind) changing (too) easily; (of troops) that my be easily moved from place to place; (of shop etc.) accommodated in vehicle so as to serve various places; (of person) able to change one's social status; so **mobi'lITY** *n.* **2.** light structure of metal, plastic, cardboard, etc., that may be hung so as to turn freely. [ME f. F, f. L *mobilis* (*movēre* move; see -IL)]

mobi'liary *a.* (Law). relating to movable property. [f. F *mobiliaire* f. L (as prec.; see -ARY¹)]

mō'bīliz|e, -īs|e (-īz), *v.t.* render movable, bring into circulation; prepare (forces, or abs.) for active service; hence or cogn. ∼ABLE *a.,* ∼A'TION *n.* [f. F *mobiliser* (as MOBILE; see -IZE)]

Mö'bius (mēr'-) *n.* ∼ **strip** etc., (Math.) surface with only one side and edge formed by joining ends of rectangle after twisting one end through 180°. [f. A. F. ∼, Ger. mathematician d. 1868]

mobsman, mobster. See MOB¹.

mŏ'ccasin *n.* footwear of soft deerskin etc. worn by N. Amer. Indians, trappers, etc., with sole joined to U--shaped flat vamp and no heel; similar shoe in ordinary wear; Amer. viper of genus *Agkistrodon.* [f. Powhatan *mockasin,* Ojibwa *makisin*]

Mō'cha¹ (-kä) *n.* moss agate. [prob. f. as foll.]

mō'cha² (-ka) *n.* fine quality of coffee; coffee (and chocolate) flavouring; soft kind of sheepskin. [f. *M*∼, Arabian port at entrance of Red Sea, whence the coffee orig. came]

mŏck¹ *n.* (arch.) derision; thing deserving scorn (**make** (a) ∼ **of,** ridicule); imitation, counterfeit. [ME, f. MOCK³]

mŏck² *attrib. a.* sham, imitation (esp. without intent to deceive), pretended; ∼ **duck** or **goose,** pork with sage-and-onion stuffing; ∼-**heroic** *a.* & *n.,*

burlesquing (of) heroic style; ∼ **moon,** paraselene; *mock* ORANGE¹; ∼ **sun,** parhelion; ∼ **turtle soup** (made from calf's head etc.). [f. prec. & foll.]

mŏck³ *v.* **1.** *v.t.* subject to ridicule; defy contemptuously; delude; ridicule by imitation; mimic, counterfeit. **2.** *v.i.* scoff *at.* **3.** ∼'**ing-bird,** bird that mimics notes of other birds, esp. Amer. songbird (*Mimus polyglottos*); ∼-**up,** experimental model showing appearance of (part of) proposed book, ship, etc. **4.** Hence ∼'ER¹ *n.*; **put the** ∼**ers on,** (sl.) bring bad luck to. [ME *mokke, mocque,* f. OF *mo(c)quer* deride f. Rom. *moccare]

mŏ'ckerÿ *n.* derision; subject or occasion of this; counterfeit or absurdly inadequate representation (*of*); ludicrously or insultingly futile action etc. [ME, f. OF *moquerie* (as prec.; see -ERY)]

mŏd¹ *n.* Gaelic congress for music and poetry. [f. Gael. *mōd*]

mŏd² *n.* & *a.* (colloq.) & *prep.* **1.** *n.* modification; ||(*Mod*) teenager of group notable for sophistication and tidiness [f. MODERN]. **2.** *a.* modern; ∼ **cons,** modern conveniences. **3.** *prep.* modulo. [abbr.]

mō'dal *a.* of mode or form as opp. to substance; (of legacy etc.) having directions as to mode in which it is to be applied; (Gram.) of the mood of a verb, (of verb, e.g. *would,* called ∼ **auxiliary**) used to express mood of another verb, (of particle) denoting manner; (Logic, of proposition) in which predicate is affirmed of subject with some qualification, or which involves affirmation of possibility, impossibility, necessity, or contingency; (Statistics & Mus.) of mode(s); hence ∼LY² *adv.* [f. med. L *modalis* f. L (as MODE; see -AL)]

modă'lity *n.* being modal; (in *sing.* or *pl.*) (prescribed) method of procedure. [f. med. L *modalitas* (as prec.; see -ITY)]

mōde *n.* **1.** way, manner, in which thing is done; method of procedure; prevailing fashion or custom; **the** ∼, (arch.) the fashion in dress etc. **2.** (Mus.) ancient Greek scale system used in diatonic composition (DORIAN, LYDIAN, etc., *mode*); medieval scale for composition of church plainsong; each of the two chief scale systems in more modern music (MAJOR², MINOR, *mode*). **3.** (Logic). character of modal proposition; = MOOD². **4.** *(Gram.) = MOOD². **5.** (Statistics). value of variable corresponding to its greatest frequency of occurrence. [F, & f. L *modus* measure f. IE **mod-,* **med-*]

mŏ'del¹ *n.* & *a.* **1.** *n.* representation in three dimensions of existing or proposed structure etc. esp. on smaller scale (WORKING² *model*); simplified description of system etc. to assist calculations and predictions. **2.** figure in clay, wax, etc., to be reproduced in other material; (copy of) garment etc. by well-known designer. **3.** design, style of structure, esp. of motor vehicle. **4.** person or thing proposed for imitation; person employed to pose for artist; mannequin, person employed to display clothes etc. by wearing them. **5. the New M**∼, plan for reorganization of Parliamentary army in England 1644-5. **6.** *a.* exemplary, ideally perfect. [f. F *modelle* f. It. *modello* f. Rom. *modellus f. L MODULUS]

mŏ'del² *v.* (||-ll-). **1.** *v.t.* fashion, shape, (figure) in clay, wax, etc.; give shape to, frame, (document, argument, etc.); (Art) cause to appear three-dimensional; form (thing) *after, on, upon,* a model; (of person acting as model) display (garment) by wearing it. **2.** *v.i.* act or pose as model (see prec. 4). [f. prec.]

mō'dem *n.* combined device for modulation and demodulation, e.g. between computer and telephone line. [portmanteau wd]

mŏ'derat|e *a.* & *n.* **1.** *a.* avoiding extremes, temperate in conduct or expression; (of wind) of medium strength; fairly or tolerably large or good; (of prices) low; hence ∼eLY² (-tlī) *adv.,* ∼eNESS (-tn-) *n.* **2.** *n.* one who holds moderate opinion in politics etc.; hence

~ISM (3) *n*. [ME, f. L *moderatus* p.p. of *moderare* reduce, control, cogn. w. MODEST; see -ATE²]

mŏ′derāte² *v*. 1. *v.t.* render less violent, intense, rigorous, etc. 2. *v.i.* (Of fury, scorn, storm, etc.) become less vehement. 3. *v.t.* & *i.* act as moderator (of or to). [f. as prec. +-ATE³]

mŏderā′tion *n*. 1. moderating; moderateness; in ~, in a moderate manner or degree. 2. (M~; in *pl*.) first public examination in some faculties for Oxford BA degree. 3. retardation of neutrons by MODERATOR 2. [ME f. OF, f. L *moderatio -onis* (as MODERATE¹; see -ATION)]

mŏderā′tō (-ah′-) *adv*. (Mus.) at moderate pace. [It. (as MODERATE¹)]

mŏ′derātor *n*. 1. arbitrator; mediator; presiding officer; examiner for Moderations; Presbyterian minister presiding over any ecclesiastical body; Dublin graduate with first or second class honours; hence ~SHIP *n*. 2. substance used in nuclear reactor to retard neutrons. [ME f. L (as MODERATE¹; see -OR)]

mŏ′dern *a*. & *n*. 1. *a*. of the present and recent times; ~ English (from 1500 onwards); ~ history (subsequent to Middle Ages); ~ languages (as subject of study, those spoken at present time, esp. in Europe); modern LATIN; ||~ school (in which modern arts, not classical or technical, subjects are chiefly or exclusively taught). 2. in current fashion, not antiquated. 3. Hence or cogn. modḗr′nĭty, ~ĭzā′tion, ~NESS (-n-n-), *ns*., ~IZE (3) *n.t.* & *i.*, ~LY² *adv*. 4. *n*. (usu. in *pl*.) person living in modern times. [f. F *moderne* or f. LL *modernus* f. L *modo* just now]

mŏ′dern|ism *n*. 1. modern view(s) or method(s), esp. tendency in matters of religious belief to subordinate tradition to harmony with modern thought; so ~IST (2) *n*., ~i′stIC *a*. 2. modern term or expression. [f. prec. +-ISM]

mŏ′dĕst *a*. having a humble or moderate estimate of one's own merits; diffident, retiring, bashful; (esp. of woman) decorous in manner and conduct, scrupulously chaste; (of demand, statement, etc.) not excessive or exaggerated (freq. iron.); (of thing) unpretentious in appearance, amount, etc.; hence or cogn. ~LY² *adv*., ~Y¹ *n*.; ~y (vest), garment or piece of lace etc. to show at woman's neck and conceal bosom. [f. F *modeste* f. L *modestus* keeping due measure]

mŏ′dicum *n*. small quantity (*of* food, truth, etc.). [L, = short distance or time, neut. (as n.) of *modicus* moderate (*modus* measure)]

mŏdĭfĭcā′tion *n*. modifying or being modified; change made. [F, or f. L *modificatio* (as foll.; see -FICATION)]

mŏ′dĭ|fy *v.t.* make less severe or decided, tone down; make partial changes in; (Gram.) qualify sense of (word etc.); change (vowel) by umlaut; hence or cogn. ~fIABLE, ~fiātorY, *adjs*., ~fIER¹ *n*. [ME, f. OF *modifier* f. L *modificare* (as MODE; see -FY)]

modī′llion (-yon) *n*. (Archit.) projecting bracket under corona of cornice in Corinthian and other orders. [f. F *modillon* f. It. *modiglione* f. Rom. *mutellio -onis (*mutellus for L *mutulus* mutule)]

mŏ′dish *a*. (Usu. derog. of person) fashionable; hence ~LY² *adv*., ~NESS *n*. [f. MODE +-ISH¹]

mŏdi′ste (-ē′st) *n*. milliner, dressmaker. [F (as MODE; see -IST)]

Mŏds (-z) *n*. (colloq.) = MODERATIONs. [abbr.]

mŏ′dŭlar *a*. of, or consisting of, modules or moduli. [f. mod. L *modularis* f. L MODULUS; see -AR¹]

mŏ′dŭl|āte *v*. 1. *v.t.* regulate, adjust; moderate. 2. adjust or vary tone or pitch of (speaking voice); alter amplitude or frequency or phase of (wave) by wave of a lower frequency to convey a signal. 3. *v.i.* (Mus.) pass (*from* one key *to* another). 4. Hence or cogn. ~A′TION, ~ātOR, *ns*. [f. L *modulari* measure, adjust to rhythm (MODULUS) +-ATE³]

mŏ′dŭle *n*. standard or unit for measuring; (Archit.) unit of length for expressing proportions, e.g. semidiameter of column at base; standardized part or

independent unit in construction esp. of furniture, building, spacecraft, or electronic system. [F, or f. L (as MODULUS); see -ULE]

mŏ′dŭlō *prep*. & *a*. (Math.) 1. *prep*. with respect to MODULUS 2 of. 2. *a*. using moduli (see foll. 2). [L, abl. of foll.]

mŏ′dŭl|us *n*. (*pl*. ~i *pr*. -ī). (Math. & Phys.) 1. constant multiplier or coefficient; constant that gives ratio between amount of physical effect and that of force producing it. 2. number used as divisor for considering numbers in sets giving same remainder when divided by it. 3. magnitude of vector or of complex number treated as such. [L, = measure, dim. of foll.]

modus (mō′dus) *n*. ~ operandi (ŏperă′ndī), way a person goes about a task, way a thing operates; ~ vivendi (vīvĕ′ndī), arrangement between disputants pending settlement of debate, arrangement between people(s) who agree to differ. [L (see MODE; *operandi* of operating, *vivendi* of living)]

Moebius. Var. of MÖBIUS.

mofĕ′tte *n*. (fissure in earth from which issues) exhalation of mephitic or volcanic gas. [F, or f. It. (Naples) *mofetta*]

mŏg, mŏ′ggĭe (-gī), *ns*. (sl.) cat. [20th c., of dial. orig.]

Mŏgŭl (mō′-, -ŭ′l) *n*. & *a*. 1. Mongolian; ~ empire, empire established in India by Mongolians under the (Great or Grand) ~, emperor of Delhi in 16th–19th c. 2. *n*. (colloq.; m~) important or influential person. [f. Pers. & Arab. *muğul* f. as MONGOL]

MOH *abbr*. ||Master of Otter-hounds; Medical Officer of Health.

mō′hair *n*. (yarn or fabric from) hair of angora goat; mixture of this with wool or cotton. [ult. f. Arab. *muḳayyar*, lit. choice, select (*ḳayyara* choose)]

Mohă′mmĕdan. See MUHAMMADAN.

Mŏ′hawk *n*. member or language of a tribe of N. Amer. Indians; (Skating) step from either edge of skate to same edge on other foot in opposite direction (cf. CHOCTAW). [native name]

mo′ho *n*. (*pl*. ~s). discontinuity between earth's crust and mantle. [f. A. *Mohorovičić*, Yugoslav seismologist d. 1936]

Mŏ′hŏck *n*. (Hist.) one of a class of aristocratic ruffians infesting London streets at night in 18th c. [f. MOHAWK]

mŏ′hŏle *n*. proposed hole to be drilled through sea-bed to earth's mantle. [f. MOHO +HOLE¹]

||moi′der, ||moi′ther (-dh-), *v.t.* (dial.) perplex, confuse, worry, (esp. in *p.p.*). [17th c.; orig. unkn.]

moi′dore *n*. former Portuguese gold coin, current in England in 18th c. [f. Port. *moeda d'ouro* (*moeda* money, *de* of, *ouro* gold)]

moi′etȳ *n*. (Law or literary) half; (loosely) one of two parts into which thing is divided. [ME, f. OF *moit(i)é* f. L *medietas -tatis* middle (*medius* a. middle; see -TY¹)]

moil *v.i.*, & *n*. drudge(ry), esp. *toil and moil*. [ME, f. OF *moillier* moisten, paddle in mud, f. Rom. *molliare f. L *mollis* soft]

moire (mwär) *n*. ~ (antique), watered fabric, usu. silk, orig. mohair. [f. earlier *mouaire*, f. MOHAIR]

moiré (mwär′ā) *a*. & *n*. 1. *a*. (Of silk) watered; (of metal) having clouded appearance like watered silk. 2. *n*. this appearance; = prec. [F, p.p. of *moirer*, f. as prec.]

moist *a*. slightly wet, damp; (of season etc.) rainy; (of disease) marked by discharge of matter etc.; hence ~LY² *adv*., ~NESS *n*. [ME, f. OF *moiste*, perh. f. Rom. *muscidus mouldy, wet, f. L *mucidus* (cf. MUCUS) and *musteus* fresh (as MUST¹)]

moi′sten (-sen) *v.t.* & *i.* make or become moist. [f. prec. +-EN⁶]

moi′sture *n*. water or other liquid diffused in small quantity as vapour, within solid, condensed on surface, etc.; hence ~LESS (-cherl-) *a*. [ME, f. OF *moistour* (as MOIST; see -URE)]

moi′sturīz|e, -īs|e (-īz), (-stūr-, -scher-) *v.t.* make less dry (esp. skin by use of cosmetic); hence ∿ER¹ (2) *n*. [f. prec. + -IZE]

moither. See MOIDER.

mōke *n*. (sl.) ‖donkey; (Austral.) very poor horse; *(derog.) Black. [19th c., perh. f. a proper name]

mō′kō *n*. (*pl.* ∿s). Maori system of tattooing. [Maori]

mō′ksa *n*. (Hinduism etc.) release from cycle of existences. [f. Skr. *mokṣa*]

mōl *abbr.* MOLE⁴(s).

mō′lal *a.* (Chem., of solution) containing one mole of solute per kilogram of solvent. [f. MOLE⁴ + -AL]

mō′lar¹ *a.* & *n.* **1.** *a.* (Usu. of mammal's back teeth) serving to grind. **2.** *n.* molar tooth. [f. L *molaris* (*mola* millstone; see -AR¹)]

mō′lar² *a.* of mass; acting on or by means of large masses or units. [f. L *moles* mass + -AR¹]

mō′lar³ *a.* (Chem.) of MOLE⁴(s); (of solution) containing one mole of solute per litre; hence **molǎ′rity** *n*. [f. MOLE⁴ + -AR¹]

molǎ′ssès (-z) *n*. uncrystallized syrup drained from raw sugar; *syrup got from sugar in process of refining, treacle. [f. Port. *melaço* f. LL *mellaceum* MUST¹ (*mel* honey; see -ACEOUS)]

***mōld¹⁻⁴, *mō′lder**¹,², etc. See MOULD¹⁻⁴, MOULDER¹,², etc.

mōle¹ *n*. abnormal pigmented prominence on human skin. [OE *māl*, = OHG *meil*(*a*), Goth. *mail* f. Gmc *mail-*]

mōle² *n*. small burrowing insectivore of genus *Talpa* with (usu. blackish) velvety fur and very small eyes, formerly thought to be blind; any mammal of family Talpidae; ∿-**cricket,** nocturnal burrowing insect; ∿ **drain,** hollow drainage channel like mole's burrow; ∿′**hill,** small mound thrown up by mole in burrowing (*make a mountain out of a* ∿*hill,* exaggerate obstacle etc.); ∿′**skin,** (1) skin of mole as fur, (2) kind of cotton fustian with surface shaved before dyeing, (3, in *pl.*) clothes, esp. trousers, of this. [ME *molle,* prob. f. MDu. *moll*(*e*), *mol,* MLG *mol, mul*]

mōle³ *n.* massive structure, usu. of stone, as pier, breakwater, or junction between places separated by water; artificial harbour. [f. F *môle* f. L *moles* mass]

mōle⁴ *n.* (Chem.) = GRAM²-*molecule,* quantity containing as many molecules as there are atoms in 0.012 kg of the isotope carbon-12. [f. G *mol* (*molekül* MOLECULE)]

mōle⁵ *n.* (Med.) abnormal mass of tissue in uterus. [f. F *môle* f. L *mola* millstone]

• **molé′cūlar** *a.* of, relating to, consisting of, molecules; ∿ **weight,** ratio between mass of one molecule of a substance and one-twelfth of mass of an atom of the isotope carbon-12; hence ∿ITY (-ă′r-) *n.*, ∿LY² *adv.* [f. foll. + -AR¹]

mō′lecūle *n.* (Phys. & Chem.) one of the minute groups of atoms (in some elements, esp. the noble gases, one of the single atoms) of which material substances consist, the smallest portion to which a substance can be reduced by subdivision without losing its chemical identity; (loosely) small particle. [f. F *molécule* f. mod. L *molecula* dim. of L *moles* mass; see -CULE]

molé′st *v.t.* meddle hostilely or injuriously with (person); so **molèsta′tion** *n.* [f. OF *molester* or f. L *molestare* annoy (*molestus* troublesome)]

molī′ne *a.* (Her., of cross) having each extremity broadened and curved back like ends of mill-rind. [prob. f. AF *moliné* (*molin* MILL¹)]

Mō′lin‖ism *n.* **1.** doctrine of Luis *Molina,* Sp. Jesuit d. 1600, that efficacy of grace depends on the will that freely accepts it. **2.** doctrine of Miguel de *Molinos,* Sp. priest d. 1696; quietism. **3.** Hence ∿IST (2) *n.* [f. *Molina, Molinos,* + -ISM]

mōll *n.* (colloq.) prostitute; gangster's female companion. [pet-form of woman's Christian name *Mary*]

mŏ′lli‖fy̆ *v.t.* appease, soften; so ∿FICA′TION *n.* [ME, f. F *mollifier* or f. L *mollificare* (*mollis* soft; see -FY)]

mŏ′llusc, *-sk, *n.* animal belonging to the phylum Mollusca of soft-bodied and usu. hard-shelled animals, including limpets, snails, cuttlefish, oysters, mussels, etc.; hence **mollŭ′scAN, mollŭ′scOUS,** *adjs.,* **mollŭ′scOID** *a.* & *n.* [f. mod. L *mollusca,* neut. pl. (as n.) of L *molluscus* (*mollis* soft)]

mŏ′lly̆ *n.* effeminate man or boy, milksop; ∿**coddle,** (*n.*) milksop, (*v.t.*) coddle, pamper. [f. as MOLL + -Y³]

mŏ′lly̆mawk. See MALLEMUCK.

Mō′lŏch (-k) *n.* Canaanite idol to whom children were sacrificed; (fig.) tyrannical object of sacrifices; (*m*∿) spiny slow-moving grotesque-looking Austral. reptile of genus *Moloch.* [LL, f. Gk *Molokh* f. Heb. *mōlek*]

molŏ′ss‖us *n.* (*pl.* ∿**i** *pr.* -ī). (Pros.) foot consisting of three long syllables. [L, f. Gk *Molossos* of Molossia in Epirus]

Mŏ′lotŏv (-f) *n.* ∿ **bread-basket,** explosive container scattering incendiary bombs; ∿ **cocktail,** anti-tank incendiary hand-grenade. [f. V. M. ∿, Russ. statesman b. 1890]

***mŏlt.** See MOULT.

mŏ′lten. See MELT².

mŏ′ltō *adv.* (Mus.) very (preceding or following direction: *molto sostenuto; allegro molto*). [It., f. L *multus* much]

mŏ′ly̆ *n.* fabulous herb with white flower and black root, endowed with magic properties; a yellow-flowered wild garlic (*Allium moly*). [L, f. Gk *mōlu*]

molў′bdenīte *n.* molybdenum disulphide as ore. [f. as foll. + -ITE¹]

molў′bdènum *n.* silver-white brittle metallic element used in steel for making high-speed tools etc. [mod. L, earlier -*dena,* orig. molybdenite, lead ore, L f. Gk *molubdaina* plummet (*molubdos* lead); see -UM]

***mŏm** *n.* (colloq.) = MUMMY²; hence ∿′ISM *n.,* excessive reverence for one's mother. [abbr. of MOMMA]

mŏ′ment *n.* **1.** very brief portion of time, instant; short period of time (*wait a moment*); exact point of time; **one** ∿, **half a** ∿, **just a** ∿, (ellipt.) wait a MINUTE¹; **in a** ∿, (1) instantly, (2) very soon; **not for a** ∿, never; *came the* (**very**) ∿ (as soon as) *I heard of it; timed* **to the** ∿ (with absolute accuracy); **the** ∿ (time that affords an opportunity); *am, was, busy* **at the** ∿ (just now, then); *man* **of the** ∿ (important at the time in question); LAST³ *moment;* PSYCHOLOGICAL *moment;* **this** ∿, immediately (*come here this moment*); ∿ **of truth,** time of final sword-thrust in bullfight, (fig.) time of crisis or test. **2.** (Phys.) product of force and distance from its line of action to a point, expressing its power of causing rotation about that point; product of charge etc. and length of dipole; property of magnet that interacts with applied field to give mechanical moment; ∿ **of inertia,** quantity by which angular acceleration of a body must be multiplied to give corresponding torque; ∿ **of momentum,** ANGULAR momentum. **3.** importance (*of great, little, moment*). [ME f. OF, f. L MOMENTUM]

mŏ′mentar‖y̆ *a.* lasting only a moment; short-lived, transitory; hence ∿ILY² *adv.* (* = foll.), ∿INESS *n.* [f. L *momentarius* (as prec.; see -ARY¹)]

mŏ′mently̆ *adv.* (literary) from moment to moment; every moment; for a moment. [f. MOMENT + -LY²]

momĕ′ntous *a.* having great importance; hence ∿LY² *adv.,* ∿NESS *n.* [f. MOMENT + -OUS]

momĕ′nt‖um *n.* (*pl.* ∿**a**). **1.** (Mech.) quantity of motion of moving body, product of its mass and its velocity; ANGULAR *momentum;* CONSERVATION of *momentum.* **2.** impetus gained by movement (lit. or fig.). **3.** (*momentum* f. movēre move; see -MENT)]

mŏ′mma, *mŏ′mmy̆, *ns.* = MAMMA¹. [var. of MAMMA¹, MUMMY²]

Mō′mus *n.* fault-finder, captious critic. [f. Gk *Mōmos* god of ridicule]

Mon. *abbr.* Monday; Monmouthshire (former county in England).

mŏ′nachal (-k-), **mŏ′nacal,** *a.* monastic; monkish; so

mŏ'nachISM (3) (-k-) *n.* [f. F *monacal* or eccl. L *monachalis* f. LL (as MONK; see -AL)]

mō'nad (-ăd, -ad) *n.* the number one, unit; ultimate unit of being (e.g. a soul, an atom, a person, God), esp. in philosophy of Leibniz, whence ∼ISM (3) *n.*; (Biol.) simple organism, e.g. one assumed as first term in genealogy of living beings; so **monǎ'd**IC *a.* [f. F *monade* or f. LL f. Gk *monas -ados* unit (*monos* alone; see -AD)]

mŏnadĕ'lphous *a.* (Bot.) (Of stamens) having filaments united into one bundle; (of plant) with such stamens. [f. Gk *monos* one + *adelphos* brother + -OUS]

monǎ'ndrous *a.* (Bot.) having (flowers with) a single stamen. [f. Gk *monandros* (*monos* one, *anēr andros* male) + -OUS]

monǎ'ndrў *n.* custom of having only one husband at a time. [f. MONO- after *polyandry*]

mŏ'narch (-k) *n.* **1.** sovereign with title of king, queen, emperor, empress, or equivalent; supreme ruler (lit. or fig.). **2.** large orange and black butterfly (*Danaus plexippus*). **3.** Hence **monǎr'ch**AL, **monǎr'ch**IC(AL), (-k-) *adjs.* [ME, f. F *monarque* or f. LL *monarcha* f. Gk *monarkhēs, -os,* (*monos* alone, *arkhō* to rule)]

mŏ'narch|ism (-k-) *n.* principles of, attachment to, monarchy; so ∼IST (2) *n.* [f. F *monarchisme* (as foll.; see -ISM)]

mŏ'narchў (-kĭ) *n.* (State under) monarchical government; *constitutional* or LIMIT[2]*ed monarchy.* [ME, f. OF *monarchie* f. LL f. Gk *monarkhia* rule of one (as MONARCH; see -Y[1])]

mŏ'nasterў *n.* residence of community (usu. of monks) living secluded under religious vows. [ME, f. eccl. L f. eccl. Gk *monastērion* (*monazō* live alone f. *monos* alone)]

monǎ'st|ic *a.* of or like monks, nuns, friars, etc.; of monasteries; *monastic* vow; hence ∼ICALLY *adv.*, ∼icISM (3) *n.*, ∼icIZE (3) *v.t.* [f. F *monastique* or f. LL f. Gk *monastikos* (*monazō*; see prec., -IC)]

mŏnatŏ'mic *a.* (Chem.) consisting of (molecules each containing) one atom; having one replaceable atom or radical. [f. MONO- + ATOM + -IC]

monaur'al *a.* = MONOphonic. [f. MONO- + AURAL[2]]

mŏ'nazite *n.* phosphate mineral from India, Brazil, etc., containing rare-earth elements and thorium. [f. G *monazit* f. Gk *monazō* (see MONASTERY), f. its rarity; see -ITE[1]]

mondaine (mawndă'n) *n.* & *a.* (woman) of the fashionable world; worldly (woman). [F, fem. of *mondain* (see MUNDANE)]

Mo'nday (mŭ'ndā, -dĭ) *n.* & *adv.* **1.** *n.* day of week, following Sunday; **St.** ∼, Monday on which little work is done, as if regarded as saint's day. **2.** *adv.* (cf. FRIDAY?) [OE *mōnandæg* day of the moon, transl. LL *lunae dies* after Gk *hēmera Selēnēs*]

Mo'ndayish (mŭ'ndĭish) *a.* (Of clergy) indisposed as result of Sunday work; (of others) slack as result of Sunday holiday. [f. prec. + -ISH[1]]

monde (mawnd) *n.* the fashionable world; society; the set in which one moves. [F, = world, f. L (as foll.)]

mŏ'ndial *a.* world-wide. [F, f. eccl. L *mundialis* f. L *mundus* world; see -IAL]

Mŏ'nel *n.* ∼ (metal), nickel-copper alloy with high tensile strength. [f. A. *Monell*, US business man d. 1921]

mo'nĕtar|ў (mŭ'-) *a.* of the currency in use; (consisting) of money; hence ∼ISM *n.*, belief in control of money as chief method of stabilizing the economy, ∼IST *n.*, advocate of this. [f. F *monétaire* or f. LL *monetarius* f. L (as MONEY; see -ARY[1])]

mo'nĕtiz|e (mŭ'-), **-is|e** (-īz), *v.t.* put (a metal) into circulation as money; give fixed value as currency; hence ∼A'TION *n.* [f. F *monétiser* f. L (as foll.; see -IZE)]

mo'ney (mŭ'-) *n.* **1.** current medium of exchange in form of portable pieces of stamped metal; this and promissory documents representing it (**paper** ∼), esp. government and bank notes; particular form of money; (in *pl.*; also **monies**) sums of money;

property viewed as convertible into money; rich person(s) (*marry money*); purchasing power of money. **2.** *money of* ACCOUNT[2]; BIG *money*; COIN[2] *money*; CONSCIENCE *money*; **in the** ∼, (colloq.) (1) winning money prizes, (2) having plenty of money; **there is** ∼ **in,** profit can be had from; ||∼ **for jam** or **old rope,** (sl.) profit for little or no trouble; *for* LOVE[1] *or money*; **make** ∼, acquire wealth; ∼ **makes the mare go** (provides a motive for action); **the one for my** ∼ (that I prefer); **put** ∼ **into,** make investment in; *a* RUN[2] *for* one's *money*; **time is** ∼, waste of time means loss of profit. **3.** ∼**-back,** (of guarantee) offering return of money paid, if buyer is not satisfied; ∼**-bag,** bag for money, (in *pl.*) wealth; ∼**-bags,** (as *sing.*) wealthy or avaricious person; ∼**-bill,** proposed legislation for grant of funds; ∼**-box,** closed box into which savings or contributions are dropped through slit; ∼**-changer,** one whose business it is to change money at stated rate; ∼**-grubber,** person sordidly intent on amassing money; ∼**-grubbing** *a.* & *n.*, (given to) this practice; ∼**-lender,** one whose business it is to lend money at interest; ∼**-making** *a.* & *n.*, (allowing) acquisition of wealth; ∼**-market,** sphere of operation of dealers in short-dated loans, stocks, etc.; *money* ORDER[1] 16 ||∼**-spinner,** small red spider thought to bring good luck, (fig.) something that brings in much money, e.g. successful book, film, play, etc.; ∼'**s-worth,** anything recognized as equivalent to money, good value for one's money; ∼**wort,** plant with round glossy leaves. **4.** Hence ∼LESS (mŭ'nĭl-) *a.* [ME, f. OF *moneie* f. L *moneta* mint, money, orig. title of Juno, in whose temple at Rome money was minted]

mo'neyed (mŭ'nĭd) *a.* rich; consisting of money, (*moneyed resources, assistance*); ∼ **interest,** the class concerned with money as a possession. [ME, f. prec. + -ED[2]]

mo'neyer (mŭ'nĭer) *n.* (Hist.) one who makes metal into coins. [ME, f. OF *mon(n)ier* f. LL *monetarius* f. L (as MONEY; see -ER[2])]

'mong. Var. (poet.) of AMONG.

mo'nger (mŭ'ngg-) *n.* dealer, trader, (chiefly in *comb.*; lit., as *fishmonger, ironmonger,* or fig., usu. derog., as *scandalmonger, verse-monger*). [OE *mangere* (*mangian* to traffic f. Gmc *mangōjan f. L *mango* dealer; see -ER[1])]

Mŏ'ngol (-ngg-) *n.* & *a.* **1.** (member) of Asian people now inhabiting Mongolia, formerly extending to E. Europe. **2.** (person) with Mongoloid characteristics. **3.** (*m*∼). (person) suffering from mongolism. [native name, perh. f. *mong* brave]

Mŏngō'lian (-ngg-) *a.* & *n.* (native or language) of Mongolia, Mongol; Mongoloid. [f. prec. + -IAN]

mŏ'ngolism *n.* congenital mental deficiency with Mongoloid appearance. [f. MONGOL + -ISM]

Mŏ'ngoloid (-ngg-) *a.* & *n.* (person) resembling Mongolians in racial origin or in having broad flat (yellowish) face; = MONGOL 3. [f. MONGOL + -OID]

mŏ'ngoose (-ngg-) *n.* (*pl.* ∼s). small carnivorous tropical mammal of genus *Herpestes,* esp. a species common in India, able to kill venomous snakes unharmed; species of lemur (*Lemur mongoz*). [f. Marathi *mangūs*]

mo'ngrel (mŭ'ngg-) *n.* & *a.* **1.** *n.* dog of no definable type or breed, other animal or plant resulting from crossing of different breeds or types; (derog.) person not of pure race. **2.** *a.* of mixed origin, nature, or character. **3.** Hence ∼ISM (2) *n.*, ∼IZE (3) *v.t.*, ∼LY[1] *a.* [app. f. root **mang-,* **meng-,* **mong-,* mix; cf. MINGLE, -REL]

'mongst. Var. (poet.) of AMONGST.

mŏ'nial *n.* mullion. [ME, f. OF *moinel* middle (*moien* MEAN[2]; see -AL)]

mŏ'ni(c)ker *n.* (sl.) name. [19th c.; orig. unkn.]

monies. See MONEY 1.

moni'lifōrm *a.* with form suggesting necklace or

string of beads. [f. F *moniliforme* or mod. L *moniliformis* f. L *monile* necklace; see -FORM]

mŏ′n∣ism *n.* doctrine that only one ultimate principle or being exists; any of the theories that deny the duality of matter and mind; hence ∼IST (2) *n.*, **moni′stic** *a.* [f. mod. L *monismus* f. Gk *monos* single; see -ISM]

moni′tion *n.* warning (*of* danger); formal notice from bishop or ecclesiastical court admonishing person to refrain from some offence. [ME f. OF, f. L *monitio -onis* (*monēre monit-* warn; see -ITION)]

mŏ′nitor *n.* & *v.* **1.** *n.* (arch.) one who admonishes. **2.** senior pupil in school with duties of keeping order etc., = PREFECT 3; pupil given specified duties in class etc.; hence **mŏnitŏr′IAL** *a.*, ∼SHIP *n.* **3.** tropical lizard of genus *Varanus*, supposed to give warning of approach of crocodiles. **4.** shallow-draught warship of heavy gunpower. **5.** one who listens to and reports on foreign broadcasts, misuse of official telephones, etc. **6.** detector of radioactive contamination, esp. in workers in an atomic plant. **7.** television receiver used in selecting or verifying the broadcast picture. **8.** Hence **mŏ′nitr**ESS¹ *n.* **9.** *v.t.* & *i.* act as monitor (of); regulate strength of (recorded or transmitted signal); maintain regular surveillance (over). [L (as prec.; see -OR)]

mŏ′nitorȳ *a.* & *n.* **1.** *a.* warning, admonitory. **2.** *n.* bishop's or pope's letter of admonition. [f. L *monitorius* (as MONITION; see -ORY)]

monk (mŭ-) *n.* member of community of men living apart from the world under vows of poverty, chastity, and obedience; ∼′**fish**, angler-fish; ∼′**s cloth**, rough cotton cloth in basket weave; ∼ **shoe** (with strap over instep); ∼′**shood** (-s-h-), poisonous plant (*Aconitum napellus*) with hood-shaped flowers; hence ∼′HOOD, ∼′SHIP, *ns.* [OE *munuc*, = OS *munik*, OHG *munih*, ON *múnkr* f. pop. L **monicus* var. of LL f. Gk *monakhos* solitary (*monos* alone)]

mo′nkerȳ (mŭ′-) *n.* (derog.) monastic life; monastery; monks; monkish practices. [f. prec. + -ERY]

mo′nkey (mŭ′-) *n.* & *v.* **1.** *n.* mammal of a group closely allied to and resembling man, ranging from anthropoid apes to marmosets; (esp.) small long--tailed member of order Primates; (as term of playful contempt, to or of person) *young monkey* etc.; POWDER--*monkey.* **2.** ∼ (**engine**), machine hammer for pile--driving etc.; globular earthenware water-vessel with straight upright neck. **3.** (sl.) **have a** ∼ **on** one's **back**, be a drug addict; **make a** ∼ **of**, humiliate by making appear ridiculous; ‖**get** one's ∼ **up**, become angry. **4.** (sl.) ‖£500; **$500. **5.** ∼**-bread**, (fruit of) baobab tree; ∼ **business**, (sl.) mischief; ∼**-cup**, pitcher-plant; ∼**-flower**, kind of mimulus with bright yellow flowers; ∼**-jacket**, short close-fitting one worn by sailors etc. or at mess; ∼**-nut**, peanut; ∼**-puzzle**, prickly tree of genus *Araucaria* with inter-laced branches; **∼**shines**, ‖∼**-tricks**, (sl.) mischief; ∼**-wrench**, one with adjustable jaw. **6.** Hence ∼ISH¹ (-kǐ-) *a.* **7.** *v.t.* mimic, mock. **8.** *v.i.* play mischievous tricks (*with*), fool *about* or *around* (*with*). [16th c., of unkn. (perh. LG) orig.]

mo′nkish (mŭ′-) *a.* of monks, monastic; (usu. derog.) characteristic of monks. [f. MONK + -ISH¹]

mŏ′nniker. Var. of MONICKER.

mŏ′nō *a.* & *n.* (*pl.* ∼s). (colloq.) monophonic (reproduction, record, etc.); mononucleosis. [abbr.]

mŏ′no- *comb. form.* (bef. vowel usu. **mon-**). one, alone, single, (Chem., forming names of compounds) containing one atom or group of a specified kind, as: ∼ba′sic, (Chem.) having one replaceable hydrogen atom; ∼car′pic, ∼car′pous, bearing fruit only once; ∼ce′phalous, (Bot.) having only one head; ∼cli′nal (-ī′-), (of strata) dipping in one and the same direction; ∼cli′nic (-ĭ′-), (of crystal) having one axial intersection oblique; ∼cot, ∼cotyle′don(ous), (flowering plant) with single cotyledon; ∼cracy (-ŏ′k-), government by one

person only; ∼cro′tic, (of pulse) with single beat; **mono′cular** (-ŏ′k-) *a.* & *n.*, with, (device) adapted to, one eye; ∼culture, cultivation of only one crop; ∼cycle, unicycle; ∼cyte, large type of leucocyte; ∼da′ctylous, having one finger, toe, or claw; ∼drama, dramatic piece for one performer; ∼ge′nesis, development of all beings from single cell; so ∼gene′tic *a.*; ∼geny (-ŏ′j-), theoretical descent of mankind from one pair of ancestors; ∼glot *a.* & *n.*, (person) using only one language; ∼gynous (-ŏ′j-), having only one pistil; ∼gyny (-ŏ′j-), custom of having only one wife at a time; ∼hull, boat with single hull, opp. *catamaran* etc.; ∼hy′brid (with respect to only one allele); ∼hy′dric, (Chem.) containing one hydroxyl group; ∼latry (-ŏ′l-), worship of one god without denying that others may exist; ∼layer, monomolecular layer; ∼li′ngual, = *monoglot* a.; ∼me′tallism, standard of currency based on one metal; ∼mole′cular, (of layer) only one molecule in thickness; ∼mor′phic, ∼mor′phous, not changing form during development; ∼nucleo′sis, glandular fever; ∼pe′talous, having corolla in one piece, or petals united into tube; ∼pho′nic, (of sound-reproduction) using only one channel of transmission (cf. STEREOPHONIC), (Mus.) homophonic; ∼phthong, single vowel sound (cf. DIPHTHONG), whence ∼phtho′ngal (-ngg-) *a.*; ∼-plane, aeroplane with one set of wings (cf. BIPLANE); **mono′psony**, exclusive possession of the buying of some commodity or service [f. Gk *opsōneō* buy provisions]; ∼psy′chism (-osī′k-), theory that all souls are one; ∼rhyme, poem in which all lines have same rhyme; ∼sa′ccharide, (Chem.) sugar with one carbonyl group in each molecule; ∼sper′mous, (Bot.) having one seed; ∼stichous (-ŏ′stĭk-), (Bot. & Zool.) arranged in, or consisting of, one layer or row; ∼stro′phic, consisting of repetitions of one strophic arrangement; ∼tint, monochrome; ∼ty′pic, having only one type or representative; ∼va′lent, (Chem.) univalent. [Gk (*monos* alone; see -o-)]

mŏ′nochŏrd (-k-) *n.* (Mus.) instrument with single string, esp. for determination of musical intervals. [ME, f. OF *monocorde* f. LL f. Gk MONO(*khordon* f. *chordē* CHORD¹)]

mŏnochromă′tic (-k-) *a.* (Of light or other radiation) containing only one colour or wavelength or energy; executed in monochrome. [f. MONO-+ CHROMATIC]

mŏ′nochrōme (-k-) *n.* & *a.* **1.** *n.* picture done in (different tints of) one colour, or in black and white only; representation in one colour. **2.** *a.* having or using only one colour, (esp.) in black and white only. [ult. f. Gk MONO(*khrōmatos* f. *khrōma* colour)]

mŏ′nocle *n.* single eyeglass. [F, orig. a. f. LL *monoculus* one-eyed (as MONO-, *oculus* eye)]

mŏ′nocŏque (-k) *n.* aircraft or vehicle structure with chassis not separate from body. [F (as MONO-, *coque* shell)]

mŏ′nod∣ȳ *n.* ode sung by single actor in Greek tragedy; poem in which mourner bewails someone's death; (Mus.) composition with only one melodic line; hence or cogn. **monŏ′dic** *a.*, ∼IST (1) *n.* [f. LL *monodia* f. Gk *monōidia* f. *monōidos* singing alone (as MONO-, ODE); see -Y¹]

monoe′cious (-nē′shus) *a.* **1.** (Bot.) with unisexual male and female organs on same plant. **2.** (Zool.) hermaphrodite. [f. mod. L *Monoecia* class of such plants (Linnaeus) f. Gk *monos* single + *oikos* house; see -IA²]

monŏ′gam∣ȳ *n.* practice or state of being married to one person at a time; (Zool.) habit of having only one mate at a time; hence or cogn. ∼IST (2) *n.*, ∼OUS *a.* [f. F *monogamie* f. eccl. L f. Gk MONO(*gamia* f. *gamos* marriage); see -Y¹]

mŏ′nogrăm *n.* two or more letters, esp. person's initials, interwoven as device; hence **mŏnogram-**

mä′tic, ∼med² (-md), *adjs.* [f. F *monogramme* f. LL *monogramma* f. Gk **monogrammos* (as MONO-, -GRAM)]

mŏ′nograph (-ahf) *n.*, & *v.t.* **1.** *n.* separate treatise on single object or class of objects. **2.** *v.t.* write monograph on. **3.** Hence **monŏ′graph**ER¹, **monŏ′graph**IST (1), *ns.*, **mŏnogră′ph**IC *a.* [earlier *monography* f. mod. L *monographia* (*monographus* writer on single genus or species); see MONO-, -GRAPH, -GRAPHY]

mŏ′nolith *n.* single block of stone, esp. shaped into pillar or monument; large block of concrete; person or thing like monolith in being massive, immovable, or solidly uniform; hence **mŏnoli′th**IC *a.* [f. F *monolithe* f. Gk MONO(*lithos* stone)]

mŏ′nologu|e (-ŏg) *n.* scene in drama in which a person speaks alone; dramatic composition for one performer; long speech by one person in a company; hence **mŏnolŏ′g**IC(AL) *adjs.*, **monŏ′log**IST (1), ∼IST (1) (-gĭ-), *ns.*, **monŏ′log**IZE (2) *v.i.* [F, = one who likes to hear himself talk, f. Gk MONO*logos* speaking alone; see -LOGUE]

mŏnomā′ni|a *n.* obsession of mind by one idea or interest; hence ∼AC *n.*, ∼ACAL (-manī′-) *a.* [f. F *monomanie* (as MONO-, -MANIA)]

‖**mŏ′nomārk** *n.* combination of letters and/or figures registered as identification mark for goods, articles, addresses, etc. [f. MONO-+MARK¹]

mŏ′nomer *n.* (Chem.) unit in polymer molecule; compound that can be polymerized; hence **mŏnome′r**IC *a.* [f. MONO-+-MER]

monŏ′mial *n.* & *a.* (Alg.) (expression) consisting of one term. [f. MONO- after *binomial*]

Monŏ′physite *n.* one who holds there is only one nature (partly divine, partly and subordinately human) in the person of Christ. [f. eccl. L f. eccl. Gk MONO(*phusitēs* f. *phusis* nature; see -ITE¹)]

monŏ′pol|ist *n.* one who favours monopoly; one who has monopoly (*of*); so ∼i′st**IC** *a.* [f. MONOPOLY+-IST]

monŏ′poliz|e, -is|e (-īz), *v.t.* obtain exclusive possession or control of (trade, commodity, the conversation, person's attention, etc.); hence ∼A′TION *n.* [f. foll. +-IZE]

monŏ′poly *n.* exclusive possession of the selling of some commodity or service; this conferred as privilege by State; exclusive possession, control, or exercise (*of* or **on*); thing that is monopolized; (*M*∼; **P**) board-game of simulated property-dealings with imitation money. [f. L f. Gk MONO(*pōlion* f. *pōleō* sell)]

mo′norail *n.* railway in which track consists of a single rail. [f. MONO-+RAIL¹]

mŏ′nosyll|able *n.* word of one syllable; **speak in** ∼ables, answer little but *Yes* or *No*; so ∼ă′bIC *a.* [f. MONO-+SYLLABLE]

mŏ′nothē|ism *n.* doctrine that there is only one God; hence ∼IST (2) *n.*, ∼i′st**IC** *a.* [f. MONO-+Gk *theos* god +-ISM]

Monŏ′thēlite *n.* one who holds that Christ had only one will but two natures (cf. MONOPHYSITE). [ME, f. med. L *monothelita* f. late Gk MONO(*thelētēs* f. Gk *thelō* to will)]

mŏ′notōne *a.* & *n.*, & *v.t.* **1.** *a.* & *n.* (utterance of) successive syllables) without change of pitch. **2.** *a.* (Math.) = foll. **3.** *n.* sameness of style in writing. **4.** *v.t.* recite, speak, sing, in unvaried tone. [f. mod. L f. late Gk MONO(*tonos* TONE¹)]

mŏnotŏ′n|ic *a.* uttered in monotone; (Math.) either never decreasing or never increasing; hence ∼ICALLY *adv.* [f. prec. +-IC]

monŏ′ton|ous *a.* (Of sound or utterance) without variation in tone or cadence; lacking in variety, wearisome through sameness; hence or cogn. ∼IZE (3) *v.t.*, ∼ousLY² *adv.*, ∼ousNESS, ∼Y¹, *ns.* [f. prec. +-OUS]

mŏ′notrēme *n.* (Zool.) mammal of subclass Monotremata of primitive egg-laying Australasian animals with single vent. [f. MONO-+Gk *trēma -matos* hole]

mŏ′notype *n.* impression on paper from inked design on glass etc.; (*M*∼; **P**) composing-machine that casts and sets up single types. [f. MONO-+TYPE¹]

monŏ′xīde *n.* (Chem.) oxide containing one oxygen atom (*carbon monoxide*). [f. MONO-+OXIDE]

Monrōe′ *n.* ∼ **doctrine**, ∼ism (-ō′ĭ-), US policy of objecting to interference by European powers in the Americas and to further colonization there, similar policy elsewhere; hence ∼IST (2) (-ō′ĭ-) *n.* [f. J. ∼, US President d. 1831, who formulated the policy (1823)]

Monseigneur (mawn̄sēnyēr′) *n.* (*pl. Messeigneurs* pr. mēsēnyēr′). Title given to eminent French person, esp. prince, cardinal, archbishop, or bishop. [F (*mon* my, *seigneur* lord)]

Monsieur (mosyēr′) *n.* (*pl. Messieurs* pr. mēsyēr′). Title used of or to French-speaking man, corresponding to Mr. or sir; Frenchman; (Hist.) title of second son or next younger brother of French king. [F (*mon* my, *sieur* lord)]

Monsignor (mŏnsēnyōr′) *n.* (*pl.* ∼*i*). Title of some RC prelates, officers of papal court, and others. [It., after MONSEIGNEUR; see SIGNOR]

mŏnsōō′n *n.* wind in S. Asia, esp. in Indian Ocean, blowing from SW in summer (**wet** ∼) and NE in winter (**dry** ∼); rainy season accompanying wet monsoon; other wind with periodic alternations; hence ∼AL *a.* [f. obs. Du. *monssoen* f. Port. *monção* f. Arab. *mawsim* fixed season (*wasama* to mark)]

mŏ′nster *n.* & *a.* **1.** *n.* misshapen animal or plant; grossly malformed foetus etc. **2.** imaginary animal compounded of incongruous elements, e.g. centaur, sphinx, griffin. **3.** inhumanly cruel or wicked person, inhuman example *of* (cruelty etc.). **4.** animal or thing of huge size. **5.** *a.* huge. [ME, f. OF *monstre* f. L *monstrum* portent, monster (*monēre* warn)]

mŏ′nstrance *n.* (RC Ch.) open or transparent vessel with gold or silver frame, in which the Host is exposed for veneration. [ME, = demonstration, f. med. L *monstrantia* L *monstrare* show; see -ANCE]

mŏnstrŏ′sity *n.* monstrousness; = MONSTER 1, 2; outrageous thing. [f. LL *monstrositas* (as foll.; see -ITY)]

mŏ′nstrous *a.* & *adv.* **1.** *a.* abnormally formed, of the nature of a monster; huge; outrageously wrong or absurd; atrocious; hence ∼LY² *adv.*, ∼NESS *n.* **2.** *adv.* (arch.) extremely. [ME, f. OF *monstreux* or f. L *monstrosus* (as MONSTER; see -OUS)]

mōns Vě′neris (-nz-) *n.* rounded mass of fat on woman's abdomen above vulva. [L, = mount of Venus]

Mont. *abbr.* Montana.

mŏ′ntage (-ahzh) *n.* selection, cutting, and piecing together as a consecutive whole of separate sections of cinema or television film; (production of) composite picture made from various elements; (production of) composite whole from juxtaposed pieces of music, painting, photographs, etc. [F (*monter* MOUNT²; see -AGE)]

mŏ′ntāne *a.* of or inhabiting mountainous country. [f. L *montanus* (as MOUNT¹; see -ANE)]

mŏntbrē′tia (-nbrē′sha) *n.* iridaceous hybrid plant of genus *Crocosmia*, with bright orange-coloured flowers. [mod. L, f. A. F. E. Coquebert de *Montbret*, Fr. botanist d. 1801 +-IA¹]

mŏ′nte *n.* Spanish game of chance, played with 45 cards; **three-card** ∼, game of Mexican origin played with 3 cards, similar to THREE-card trick. [Sp., = mountain, heap of cards]

Mŏntěně′grin *n.* & *a.* (inhabitant) of Montenegro in SW Yugoslavia. [f. *Montenegro* (Venetian It., = black mountain); cf. -INE¹]

Mŏntěssō′ri *n.* ∼ **system** (of educating very young children by direction of their natural activities rather than strict control). [f. M. ∼, It. educationalist d. 1952, who initiated it *c.* 1900]

month (mŭ-) *n.* (calendar) ∼, any of usu. twelve portions into which year is divided or any period between same dates in successive such portions; period of 28 days; LUNAR *month*; *month of* SUNDAYS;

THIS *day month*; ∼'s **mind,** mass etc. in commemoration of deceased person a month after death, ‖(arch.) strong inclination, liking. [OE *mōnath,* = OS *mānoth,* OHG *mānōd,* ON *mánuthr,* Goth. *mēnōths* f. Gmc *mēnōth-,* cogn. w. MOON[1]]

mo'nthly (mŭ'n-) *a., adv.,* & *n.* **1.** *a.* & *adv.* (occurring, published, done, etc.) once a month; ∼ **nurse** (attending woman during first month after childbirth); ∼ **rose,** China rose supposed to flower monthly. **2.** *n.* monthly periodical; (in *pl.,* arch.) menses. [f. prec. + -LY[1,2]]

mŏ'ntĭcūle *n.* small hill; small mound caused by volcanic eruption; slight protuberance on surface of animal etc. [F, f. LL *monticulus* dim. of *mons* MOUNT[1]; see -CULE]

mŏ'nŭment *n.* written record; anything enduring that serves to commemorate or make celebrated, esp. structure or building (‖**the M**∼, column in London commemorating fire of 1666); stone or other structure placed over grave or in church etc. in memory of the dead; ‖ANCIENT[1] *monument.* [ME f. F f. L, *monu-, monimentum* (*monēre* remind; see -MENT)]

mŏnūmĕ'ntal *a.* **1.** of, or serving as, a monument; ∼ **mason,** maker of tombstones etc. **2.** (Of literary work) massive and permanent; extremely great, stupendous, (*monumental achievement, blunder, ignorance*). **3.** Hence ∼LY[2] *adv.* [f. prec. + -AL]

mŏnūmĕ'ntalīze, -īse (-īz) *v.t.* record or commemorate (as) by monument. [f. prec. + -IZE]

-mony *suf.* forming *ns.* esp. denoting abstract state or quality (*acrimony, matrimony, testimony*). [f. L *-monia, -monium,* cogn. w. -MENT]

moo *v.i.,* & *n.* (make) characteristic vocal sound of cattle, = LOW[2]; ∼**cow,** (childish name for) cow. [imit.]

mooch *v.* (sl.) **1.** *v.i.* loiter *about,* walk slowly *along.* **2.** *v.t.* steal; *beg. [ME, prob. f. OF *muchier* hide, skulk]

mood[1] *n.* state of mind or feeling; (in *pl.*) fits of melancholy or bad temper; (*attrib.*) inducing a particular mood (*mood music*); **in the** ∼, **in no** ∼, inclined, disinclined, (*for* thing, *to* do). [OE *mōd* mind, thought, = OS *mōd,* OHG *muot,* ON *móthr* anger, grief, Goth. *mōths* f. Gmc *mōdhaz, -am*]

mood[2] *n.* **1.** (Gram.) form(s) of verb serving to indicate whether it is to express fact, command, wish, etc., (*indicative, imperative, subjunctive, mood*); (distinction of meaning expressed by) group of such forms. **2.** (Logic) any of the classes into which each of the figures of valid categorical syllogism is subdivided. [var. of MODE, assoc. w. prec.]

moo'd/y *a.* gloomy, sullen; hence ∼ĭLY[2] *adv.,* ∼ĭNESS *n.* [OE *mōdig* brave (as MOOD[1], -Y[2])]

moo'lah (-*a*) *n.* (sl.) money. [20th c.; orig. unkn.]

moo'lvi(e) *n.* Muslim doctor of the law; learned person, teacher, (esp. as term of respect among Muslims in India). [f. Urdu *mulvī* f. Arab. *mawlawīy* judicial; cf. MULLAH]

moon[1] *n.* **1.** satellite of the earth, revolving round it monthly, illuminated by sun and reflecting some light to earth; this in particular month, regarded as a distinct object from that visible in other months (*age of the moon*; FULL[1], NEW[1], HARVEST, HUNTER'*s, moon*), or when visible (*there is no moon tonight*); (poet.) month (*in the moon when nights are brightest*); satellite of any planet; **the** ∼, thing unlikely to be attained (*cry for the moon*), anything no matter how unattainable (*promised her the moon*); *once in a* BLUE[1] *moon*; MAN[1] *in the moon*; **old** ∼ **in new** ∼'s **arms** (during first quarter, when dark part is faintly seen by earth--light); **over the** ∼, (colloq.) in raptures, highly excited; ‖SHOOT[1] *the moon.* **2.** ∼**beam,** ray of moon-light; ∼**calf,** born fool; ‖∼-**daisy** (ox-eye); ∼**-face** (round like full moon); ∼**-fish,** opah; ‖∼'-**flower,** ox-eye daisy; ∼'**light,** (*n.*) light of moon, (*a.*) lighted by the moon (∼*light flit(ting),* removal of household goods by night to avoid paying rent), (*v.i.,* colloq.) have two paid occupations, esp. one by day and one by night; ∼'**lit,** lighted by the moon;

∼'**quake,** tremor of moon's surface; ∼'**rise,** ∼'**set,** (moment of) moon's rising, setting; ∼'**shine,** (1) visionary talk or ideas, (2) illicitly distilled or smuggled alcoholic liquor; *∼'**shiner,** (sl.) illicit distiller, liquor-smuggler; ∼-**shot,** (launching of) spacecraft travelling to moon; ∼'**stone,** feldspar of pearly appearance; ∼'**struck,** deranged in mind. **3.** Hence ∼LESS *a.* [OE *mōna,* = OS, OHG *māno,* ON *máni,* Goth. *mēna* f. Gmc *∼mēnon,* cogn. w. MONTH]

moon[2] *v.* **1.** *v.i.* move or look listlessly (*about, around,* etc.); ∼ **over,** be inactive or inattentive because infatuated by. **2.** *v.t.* pass *away* (time) in listless manner. [f. prec.]

Moon[3] *n.* ∼ **type,** system of writing and printing for the blind, in which the characters are represented by large raised lines. [f. W. ∼, Engl. inventor d. 1894]

moo'nshee *n.* secretary or language-teacher in India. [f. Urdu *munshī* f. Arab. *munśi'* writer]

moo'ny *a.* of or like the moon; listless, stupidly dreamy. [f. MOON[1,2] + -Y[2]]

moor[1] (moor, mŏr) *n.* tract of open waste ground, esp. if covered with heather; tract of ground preserved for shooting; *fen; ∼'**fowl,** ∼ **game,** red grouse; ∼'-**cock,** male of this; ∼'**hen,** (1) female of this, (2) water-hen; ∼'**land,** country abounding in heather; hence ∼ISH[1], ∼'Y[2], *adjs.* [OE *mōr* waste land, marsh, mountain, = OS *mōr* marsh, OHG *muor* f. Gmc *mōraz, *mōram*]

Moor[2] (moor, mŏr) *n.* one of a Muslim people of mixed Berber and Arab descent, inhabiting NW Africa; ∼'('man,** Indian or Sri Lankan Muslim; hence ∼ISH[1] *a.* (∼**ish idol,** brightly-coloured Pacific fish of genus *Zanclus*). [ME f. OF *More* f. L f. Gk *Mauros* inhabitant of Mauretania, region of N. Africa]

moor[3] (moor, mŏr) *v.t.* attach (boat or other floating thing) to fixed object; hence ∼'AGE (3, 4) *n.* [ME *more,* prob. f. (M)LG *mōren*]

moor'ing (moor'-, mŏr'-) *n.* **1.** In vbl senses; *mooring--MAST[1].* **2.** (usu. in *pl.*) permanent anchors and chains laid down for ships to be moored to; what a floating object is moored to. **3.** (in *pl.*) place where vessel is moored. [ME, f. prec. + -ING[1]]

moo'se *n.* (*pl.* same). N. Amer. animal closely allied to or same as European elk. [f. Narragansett *moos*]

moot *n., a.,* & *v.t.* **1.** *n.* (Hist.) assembly; (law) students' discussion of hypothetical case for practice. **2.** *a.* debatable, undecided, (*that is a moot point*); *(Law) having no practical significance. **3.** *v.t.* raise (question) for discussion. [(v. f. OE *mōtian* converse) f. OE (*ge*)*mōt* f. Gmc *(ga)mōtam,* cogn. w. MEET[1]]

mŏp[1] *n.* bundle of coarse yarn or cloth fastened at end of stick, for cleaning floors etc.; similarly-shaped large or small instrument for various purposes; thick mass of hair like mop; ∼'('head,** (person with) this; ‖**Mrs Mop(p),** (joc.) charwoman; hence ∼'**py[2]** *a.* [ME *mappe,* perh. ult. conn. w. L *mappa* napkin]

mŏp[2] *v.t.* (-**pp-**). wipe or clean (as) with mop; wipe tears, sweat, etc., from (face, brow, etc.); wipe (tears etc.) thus; ∼ **the floor with,** (sl.) = WIPE *the floor with;* ∼ **up,** wipe up (as) with mop, (sl.) absorb (profits etc.), dispatch, make an end of, (Mil.) complete the occupation of (district etc.) by capturing or killing troops left there, capture or kill (stragglers). [f. prec.]

mŏp[3] *v.i.* (-**pp-**), & *n.* (arch. or literary) ∼ **and mow,** make grimaces; ∼ **and mows,** grimaces. [perh. imit. of pout; see MOW[2]]

‖**mŏp[4]** *n.* (Hist.) a fair or gathering in the autumn at which farm-hands and servants were hired. [perh. = *mop-fair* (at which MOP[1] was carried by maidservant seeking employment)]

mōpe *v.* & *n.* **1.** *v.i.* abandon oneself to listless condition; (arch., *refl.* or *pass.*) make one*self,* be, the victim of ennui. **2.** *n.* one who mopes; **the** ∼**s,** depression of spirits. **3.** Hence **mō'pish[1]** *a.* [16th c.; orig. unkn.]

mō′pĕd n. motorized bicycle, esp. with engine capacity below 50 c.c. [Sw. (*motor*, *pedaler* pedals)]

mō′pōke, mōr′epŏrk (mōr′p-) n. **1.** (NZ) spotted brown owl. **2.** (Austral.) small brown owl of genus *Ninox*; Tasmanian nightjar. [imit. of bird's note] ||**Mŏpp.** See MOP[1].

mŏ′ppĕt n. (Endearing term for) baby, little girl, etc.; (colloq.) child. [f. obs. *moppe* baby, doll, + -ET[1]]

moquĕ′tte (-kĕ′t) n. material of wool on cotton, with pile or loops, used for carpets and upholstery. [F, perh. f. obs. It. *mocaiardo* mohair]

mōr n. humus formed under acid conditions. [Da.]

mōr′a, mōr′ra, n. Italian game in which player guesses number of fingers held up at that moment by another. [It. *mora*]

morai′n|e n. area of debris carried down and deposited by glacier; hence ∼AL, ∼IC, adjs. [F, f. It. dial. *morena* f. F dial. *mor(re)* snout f. Rom. **murrum* round object]

mō′ral a. & n. **1.** a. concerned with goodness or badness of character or disposition, or with the distinction between right and wrong; (of literary work etc.) dealing with regulation of conduct; concerned with rules of morality; virtuous in general conduct; (of rights etc.) founded on moral law; capable of moral action (*man is a moral agent*). **2.** ∼ **certainty,** probability so great as to allow no reasonable doubt; ∼ **courage** (to meet contempt etc. rather than abandon right course of action); ∼ **cowardice,** fear of others' disapproval; *moral* IN-SPIRATION; ∼ **law,** conditions to be satisfied by any right course of action; *moral* PHILOSOPHY; ∼ **pressure,** persuasion through moral sense; **M**∼ Re--Armament, (beliefs of) Oxford Group, esp. as applied to international relations; *moral* SCIENCE; ∼ **sense,** ability to distinguish right and wrong; ∼ **support** (giving psychological rather than physical help); ∼ **theology,** ethics as branch of theology; ∼ **victory,** defeat that has some of the satisfactory elements of victory. **3.** Hence ∼LY[2] adv. **4.** n. moral lesson (esp. at end) of fable, story, event, etc. (**draw the** ∼, show what it is); moral maxim or principle (**point a** ∼, illustrate or apply it); (in pl.) moral habits, e.g. sexual conduct. [ME, f. L *moralis* (*mos moris* custom, pl. *mores* morals; see -AL)]

mora′le (-ah′l) n. moral condition, esp. (of troops or workers) as regards discipline and confidence. [f. F *moral* respelt to preserve pronunc.; cf. LOCALE]

mo′ralism n. natural system of morality, religion reduced to moral practice. [f. MORAL + -ISM]

mō′ral|ist n. one who practises or teaches morality; one who follows a natural system of ethics; hence ∼ĭ′stic a. [f. MORAL + -IST]

morā′lity n. moral science; (in pl.) moral principles, points of ethics; particular system of morals (*commercial morality*); degree of conformity to moral principles; (esp. good) moral conduct; moralizing; ∼ (**play**), (Hist.) kind of drama with abstract qualities as main characters and inculcating moral lesson, popular in 16th c. [ME, f. OF *moralité* or f. LL *moralitas* f. L (as MORAL; see -ITY)]

mō′raliz|e, -is|e (-īz), v. **1.** v.i. indulge in moral reflection or talk (*on* subject). **2.** v.t. interpret morally, point the moral of; make (more) moral. **3.** Hence ∼A′TION n. [f. F *moraliser* or f. med. L *moralizare* f. L (as MORAL; see -IZE)]

morǎ′ss n. (literary.) bog, marsh; (fig.) entanglement (*morass of vice*). [f. Du. *moeras* (assim. to *moer* MOOR[1]) f. MDu. *marasch* f. OF (as MARISH)]

mŏratōr′i|um n. (pl. ∼ums or ∼a). (period of) legal authorization to debtors to postpone payment; temporary prohibition or suspension (*on* activity). [mod. L, neut. (as n.) of LL *moratorius* delaying f. L *morari -at-* to delay (*mora* delay; see -ORY)]

Morā′vian a. & n. (native or inhabitant) of Moravia; (one) of Protestant sect holding Hussite doctrines and accepting Bible as only source of faith, founded in Saxony by emigrants from Moravia. [f. *Moravia*, now part of Czechoslovakia + -AN]

moray′ n. tropical eel of family Muraenidae. [f. Port. *moreia* f. L f. Gk *muraina*]

mōr′bid a. (Of mind, ideas, etc.) unwholesome, sickly; given to morbid feelings; (colloq.) melancholy; (Med.) of the nature, or indicative, of disease; ∼ **anatomy** (of diseased organs etc.); hence ∼LY[2] adv., ∼ITY (-ĭ′d-), ∼NESS, ns. [f. L *morbidus* (*morbus* disease; see -ID[1])]

morbidezza (mōrbĭdĕ′tsa) n. extreme delicacy in art; (Paint.) lifelike delicacy in flesh-tints. [It. (*morbido* tender, f. as prec.)]

mōrbi′fic a. causing disease. [f. F *morbifique* or mod. L *morbificus* f. L *morbus* disease; see -FIC]

mōrbi′lli n. pl. (spots characteristic of) measles. [L, pl. of *morbillus* pustule (*morbus* disease)]

morceau (mōrsō′) n. (pl. ∼x pr. -z). short literary or musical composition. [F (as MORSEL)]

mōrd|ā′cious (-shus) a. = foll.; so ∼A′CITY n. [f. L *mordax -acis* (*mordēre* bite; see -ACIOUS)]

mōr′d|ant a. & n. **1.** a. (Of sarcasm etc.) caustic, biting; hence ∼ANCY n. **2.** pungent, smarting. **3.** a. & n. corrosive or cleansing (acid). **4.** (substance) serving to fix colouring-matter or gold-leaf on another substance. [ME f. F, part. of *mordre* bite f. L *mordēre*; see -ANT]

mōr′dent n (Mus.) grace consisting of one rapid alternation of written note with note immediately below it; pralltriller. [G, f. It. *mordente* part. of *mordere* bite (as prec.; see -ENT)]

mōre a., n., & adv. **1.** a. existing in greater or additional quantity, amount, or degree, (*there is more truth in it than you think*; *10 is 2 more than 8*; *added one more line*; *bring some more water*); greater in degree (*more's the pity*; *the more fool you*). **2.** n. greater quantity or number (*more in it than* MEET[2]*s the eye*; *hope to see more of you* (see you more often); *more than one person has found it so*). **3.** adv. in greater degree (*you must attend more to details*; *more in sorrow than in anger*; *more frightened than hurt*); moreover; again (*once, twice, etc., never, more*). **4.** (Forming compar. of adjs. & advs., esp. those of more than one syllable) *more absurd(ly)*, *more curious, more easily, more truly* **5.** ∼ **and** ∼, in an increasing degree; *more* LIKE[1] *it*; ∼ **of,** to a greater extent (*more of a poet than a musician*); ∼ **or less,** (1) in greater or less degree, (2) or thereabouts; ∼ **so,** (the same) to a greater degree; ∼ **than,** (colloq.) (1) exceedingly (*happy* etc.), (2) thing that . . . not (*you remembered to thank her, which is more than I did*); **any** ∼, (to) any greater or further quantity or extent; **neither** ∼ **nor less than,** simply, literally, (*absurd, cheating*, etc.); NO[3] *more; or* ∼, at least (*six or more; moved a foot or more*); THE *more*; WHAT *is more*. [OE *māra*, = OS, OHG *mēro*, ON *meiri*, Goth. *maiza* f. Gmc **maizon* (**maiz* adv. f. IE **meis*)]

moree′n n. strong ribbed woollen or (woollen and) cotton material for curtains etc. [perh. fanciful f. MOIRE]

mōr′eish (mōr′ī-) a. (colloq.) pleasant to eat, causing desire for more. [f. MORE + -ISH[1]]

morĕ′l[1] n. (esp. black) nightshade. [ME, f. OF *morele*, fem. (as n.) of *morel* dark brown f. Rom. **maurellus* f. L *Maurus* MOOR[2]]

morĕ′l[2] n. edible fungus of genus *Morchella*. [f. F *morille* f. Du. *morilje*]

morĕ′llō n. (pl. ∼s). bitter kind of dark cherry. [f. It. *morello* blackish f. med. L *morellus* f. L (as MOREL[1])]

mōreō′ver (mōrō′v-) adv. (literary). further, besides, (introducing or accompanying new statement). [ME, f. MORE + OVER]

morepork. See MOPOKE.

mōr′ēs (-ēz, -āz) n. pl. customs or conventions regarded as essential to or characteristic of a community. [L, pl. of *mos* custom]

Morĕ′scō. Var. of MORISCO.

Morĕ'sque (-k) *a*. Moorish in style or design. [F, f. It. *moresco* (*Moro* MOOR²; see -ESQUE)]

mŏrgană't|ic *a*. (Of marriage) between man of high rank and woman of lower rank, who remains in her former station, their issue having no claim to succeed to possessions or title of father; (of wife) so married; hence ∼ICALLY *adv*. [f. F *morganatique* or G *morganatisch* f. med. L *morganaticus* (*matrimonium ad morganaticam*, prob. f. Gmc *morgangeba* morning gift from husband to wife on morning after consummation of marriage, this being such wife's only claim on husband's possessions)]

mŏr'gen (-g-) *n*. (S. Afr.) area of land, about two acres. [Du., = morning, app. as being area ploughed in a morning]

mŏrgue¹ (-g) *n*. mortuary; (Journ.) repository where miscellaneous material for reference (esp. drafted obituaries) is kept. [F, orig. name of Paris building in which bodies of persons found dead were exposed for identification, perh. = foll.]

morgue² (môrg) *n*. haughty demeanour, esp. as English characteristic. [F, of unkn. orig.]

mŏ'ribŭnd *a*. at the point of death (lit. or fig.). [f. L *moribundus* (*mori* die)]

mŏ'rion *n*. (Hist.) helmet without beaver or visor. [F, f. Sp. *morrion* (*morro* f. Rom. *murrum* round object)]

Mori'scō *a*. & *n*. (*pl.* ∼s or ∼es). **1.** *a*. Moorish. **2.** *n*. Moor², esp. in Spain; morris dance. [Sp. (*Moro* MOOR²)]

mŏr'ish. Var. of MOREISH.

Mŏr'mon *n*. (Nickname for) member of millenary religious body (Church of Jesus Christ of Latter-day Saints) founded 1830 by Joseph Smith on basis of revelations in **Book of** ∼ (named from its supposed author); hence ∼ISM (3) *n*.

mŏrn *n*. **1.** (poet.) morning; dawn. **2.** (Sc.) morrow (**the** ∼, tomorrow; **the** ∼**'s** ∼, tomorrow morning). [OE *morgen* = OS, OHG *morgan* f. Gmc *murganaz*]

mŏr'nay *n*. cheese-flavoured white sauce. [20th c.; orig. uncert.]

mŏr'ning *n*. early part of day, ending at noon, or at hour of midday meal (*in* or *during the morning*; **in the** ∼, (also, colloq.) tomorrow; *on Monday morning*); this time spent in a particular way; (colloq.) = GOOD *morning*; (fig.) early part (*of life* etc.); (poet.) dawn; (*attrib.*) occurring or done in the morning, (of clothes) conventionally worn in the morning; ∼ **after**, (colloq.) hangover; ∼**-after pill**, contraceptive pill effective when taken some hours after intercourse; ∼ **coat** (with front cut away to form tails); ∼ **dress**, (1) daytime wear, (2) man's morning coat and striped trousers; ∼ **gift** (see MORGANATIC, etym.); ∼ **glory**, twining plant of genus *Ipomoea*, with trumpet-shaped flowers; ∼ **paper**, newspaper published in the morning; *morning* PRAYER¹; ∼**-room**, sitting-room for the morning; ∼ **sickness**, nausea in morning in early pregnancy; ∼ **star**, Venus (or other planet or bright star) seen in east before sunrise; ∼ **watch**, (Naut.) 4–8 a.m. watch. [ME *mor(we)ning* f. *morwen* MORN + -ING¹, after *evening*]

Mŏr'o *n*. (*pl.* ∼s). Muslim of the Philippines. [Sp., = MOOR²]

Morŏ'ccan *a*. & *n*. (native or inhabitant) of Morocco. [f. as foll. + -AN]

morŏ'ccō *n*. (*pl.* ∼s). fine flexible leather made (orig. in Morocco) from goatskins tanned with sumac (**French** ∼, inferior small-grained kind; **Levant** ∼, high-grade large-grained kind); imitation of this in grained calf etc. [∼ in NW Africa, f. It. *Marocco* f. name of chief city *Marrakesh*]

mŏr'ŏn *n*. adult with intelligence equal to that of average child of 8–12; (colloq.) very stupid or degenerate person; hence **morŏ'nıc** *a*. [f. Gk *mōron*, neut. of *mōros* foolish]

morŏ'se *a*. sullen, gloomy, and unsocial; hence ∼LY² (-slī) *adv.*, ∼NESS (-sn-) *n*. [f. L *morosus* peevish etc. (*mos moris* manner; see -OSE¹)]

mŏrph *n*. allomorph. [back-form.]

mŏr'phème *n*. (Ling.) morphological element considered in respect of its functional relations in a linguistic system; smallest meaningful morphological unit of a language (e.g. *in*, *come*, *-ing*, opp. *income*, *incoming*, etc.); hence **mŏrphē'mıc** *a.*, **mŏrphē'mıcs** *n*., study of word-structure. [f. F *morphème* (as PHONEME, f. Gk *morphē* form)]

Mŏr'pheus *n*. god of dreams or sleep; **in the arms of** ∼, asleep. [ME f. L]

mŏr'phine (-ēn), (pop.) **mŏr'phia**, *ns*. alkaloid narcotic principle of opium, used to alleviate pain; hence **mŏr'phinısm** (5) *n*. [f. G *morphin* & mod. L *morphia*, f. prec.; see -INE⁵, -IA¹]

mŏrphogĕ'nĕsis *n*. (Biol.) development of form in organisms. [mod. L, f. as foll. + GENESIS]

mŏrphŏ'log|ў *n*. study of the forms of things, esp. (Biol.) study of the form of animals and plants, (Philol.) study of the form of words, system of forms in a language; hence **mŏrpholŏ'gıcal** *a.*, ∼IST (3) *n*. [f. Gk *morphē* form + -O- + -LOGY]

mŏr'ra. See MORA.

mŏ'rris¹ *a*. & *n*. ||∼ (**dance**), traditional dance by persons in fancy costume, usu. as characters in legend, with ribbons and bells; ∼ **dancer**, ∼ **man**, performer in this; ∼**-pike**, (Hist.) form of pike supposed to be of Moorish origin. [f. *morys*, var. of MOORISH]

Mŏ'rris² *n*. ∼ **chair**, type of plain easy chair with adjustable back. [f. William ∼, Engl. poet and craftsman d. 1896]

mŏ'rrow (-ō) *n*. (literary). **the** ∼, the following day; ||GOOD *morrow*; **on the** ∼ **of**, (fig.) in the time just following. [ME *morwe*, *moru*, f. as MORN; cf. SORROW]

mŏrse¹ *n*. walrus. [ult. f. Lappish *morssa*]

Mŏrse² *n.*, *a.*, & *v.* **1.** *n*. & *a*. (of) the alphabet or code invented by S. F. B. *Morse*, Amer. electrician d. 1872, in which letters are represented by various combinations of two signs, e.g. dot and dash, long and short flash. **2.** *v.t.* & *i.* signal by Morse code.

mŏrse³ *n*. clasp, often jewelled etc., of cope. [ME, f. OF *mors* f. L *morsus* bite, catch (*mordēre mors-* to bite)]

mŏr'sel *n*. mouthful, small piece (*of* food etc.); fragment. [ME f. OF, dim. of *mors* a bite (as prec.; see -LE 2)]

mŏrt¹ *n*. note sounded on hunting-horn at death of deer etc. [ME f. OF, f. L *mors mortis* death]

mŏrt² *n*. salmon in third year. [16th c.; orig. unkn.]

mŏrt³ *n*. (dial.) a great amount or number *of*. [perh. f. N. Engl. *murth* f. ON *mergth* multitude, assoc. w. foll.]

mŏr'tal *a*. & *n*. **1.** *a*. subject to death; causing death, fatal, (*to*, lit. or fig.; *mortal* SIN¹); (of battle) fought to the death; (of enemy) implacable; (of pain, fear, affront, etc.) intense, very serious; accompanying death (*mortal agony*); (sl.) very great (*in a mortal hurry*); (sl.) long and tedious (*for two mortal hours*); (sl.) whatsoever (*every mortal thing*; **no** ∼ *use* etc., no use etc. at all). **2.** Hence ∼LY² *adv.* **3.** *n*. mortal (esp. human) being; (joc.) person (*a thirsty mortal*). [ME, f. OF *mortal*, *mortel* or f. L *mortalis* (*mors mortis* death; see -AL)]

mŏrtă'lity *n*. mortal nature; loss of life on large scale; number of deaths in given period etc.; ∼ (**rate**), death rate; ∼ **tables** (showing expectation of life at various ages etc.). [ME, f. OF *mortalité* f. L *mortalitas -tatis* (as prec.; see -ITY)]

mŏr'tar *n.*, & *v.t.* **1.** *n*. vessel of hard material, e.g. marble, in which ingredients are pounded with pestle. **2.** short large-bore cannon for throwing shells at high angles; contrivance for firing lifeline or firework. **3.** mixture of lime or cement, sand, and water, (orig. made in a mortar) for joining stones or bricks; **bricks and** ∼, buildings; hence ∼LESS, ∼Y², *adjs.* **4.** ∼**-board**, board for holding mortar, academic cap with stiff flat square top. **5.** *v.t.* plaster or join with mortar; attack or bombard with mortars. [ME, f. AF *morter*, OF *mortier* f. L *mortarium*; partly f. LG]

mŏr′tgage[1] (mŏr′gĭj) *n.* conveyance of property by debtor to creditor as security for debt (esp. incurred by purchase of the property), with proviso that it shall be returned on payment of debt within certain period; deed effecting this; (loan resulting in) such debt. [ME f. OF, = dead pledge (*mort* f. L *mortuus* dead, *gage* GAGE[1])]

mŏr′tgag|e[2] (mŏr′gĭj) *v.t.* convey (property) by mortgage; pledge (oneself, one's powers etc., *to* object etc.); hence ∼EE′ (-jē′) *n.*, creditor in mortgage, ∼ER[1] (-jer), ∼OR′ (-jōr′), *ns.*, debtor in mortgage. [f. prec.]

mŏr′tice. See MORTISE.

*mŏrti′cian (-shan) *n.* undertaker, manager of funerals. [f. L *mors mortis* death + -ICIAN]

mŏr′ti|fy̌ *v.* **1.** *v.t.* bring (body, the flesh, passions, etc.) into subjection by self-denial or discipline; cause (person) to feel humiliated, wound (feelings). **2.** *v.i.* (Of flesh) be affected by gangrene or necrosis. **3.** So ∼FICA′TION *n.* [ME, f. OF *mortifier* f. eccl. L *mortificare* kill, subdue (*mors mortis* death; see -FY)]

mŏr′tise, -ice, *n.*, & *v.t.* **1.** *n.* hole in a framework designed to receive the end of some other part, esp. a TENON; ∼ **chisel** (with stout blade, for cutting mortises); ∼ **lock** (recessed in frame of door etc.). **2.** *v.t.* join (things *together*, one *to* or *into* another) securely, esp. by mortise and tenon; cut mortise in. [ME, f. OF *mortoise* f. Arab. *murtazz* fixed in]

mŏr′tmain *n.* (Law). (condition of) lands or tenements held inalienably by ecclesiastical or other corporation; **in** ∼, (fig.) as if under posthumous control. [ME, f. AF, OF *mortemain* f. med. L *mortua manus* dead hand, prob. in allusion to impersonal ownership]

mŏr′tūary̌ *a.* & *n.* **1.** *a.* of death or burial. **2.** *n.* building in which dead bodies may be kept for a time. [ME; (n. f. AF *mortuarie* f. med. L *mortuarium*) f. L *mortuarius* (*mortuus* dead; see -ARY[1])]

mŏr′ula *n.* (*pl.* ∼e). (Zool.) fully segmented ovum from which blastula is formed. [mod. L, dim. of L *morum* mulberry]

mor′wŏng *n.* Australasian food-fish of genus *Cheilodactylus.* [Aboriginal]

mosā′ic[1] (-z-) *a.*, *n.*, & *v.t.* (-ck-). **1.** *a.* & *n.* (form or work of art) in which pictures or patterns are produced by joining together small pieces of stone, glass, etc., of different colours; arrangement of photosensitive elements in television camera; (Biol.) chimera; (fig.) diversified (thing). **2.** ∼ (**disease**), virus disease causing leaf-mottling in plants, esp. tobacco, maize, and sugar-cane; ∼ **gold**, (1) tin disulphide, (2) alloy of copper and zinc used in cheap jewellery etc. **3.** Hence ∼IST (3) *n.* **4.** *v.t.* adorn with mosaics; combine (as) into mosaic. [ME, f. F *mosaïque* f. It. *mosaico* f. med. L *mosaicus, musaicus* f. Gk *mousa*(*e*)*ion* mosaic work (*mousa* MUSE[1])]

Mosā′ic[2] (-z-) *a.* of Moses, the ∼ **Law** (in Pentateuch). [f. F *mosaïque* or mod. L *Mosaicus* (*Moses, Moyses* f. Hcb. *Mōšeh*)]

mŏsasaur′us *n.* large extinct marine reptile. [mod. L, f. *Mosa* river Meuse (near which it was first discovered) + Gk *sauros* lizard]

mŏschatĕ′l (-k-) *n.* small plant (*Adoxa moschatellina*) with pale-green flowers and musky smell. [f. F *moscatelle* f. It. *moscatella* (*moscato* musk)]

mŏsĕ′lle (-z-) *n.* dry white wine produced near the river *Moselle* in Germany.

mō′sey (-zĭ) *v.i.* walk (*along*) in leisurely or aimless manner. [19th c.; orig. unkn.]

mŏsha′v (-ah′v) *n.* (*pl.* ∼im). co-operative association of Israeli smallholders. [f. Heb. *mošāb*, lit. 'dwelling']

Moslem. See MUSLIM.

mŏsque (-k) *n.* Muslim place of worship. [f. F *mosquée* f. It. *moschea* f. Arab. *masjid*]

mŏsqui′tō (-kē′-) *n.* (*pl.* ∼es). **1.** gnat esp. of genus *Culex* or *Anopheles*, female of which punctures skins of man and animals with long proboscis and sucks their blood; ∼**-net** (to keep off mosquitoes). **2.** *∼ **boat**, motor torpedo-boat; ∼ **craft**, small light nimble naval vessels. [Sp. & Port., dim. of *mosca* f. L *musca* fly]

mŏss *n.*, & *v.t.* **1.** *n.* small herbaceous cryptogam of class Musci, some growing in bogs, others on surface of ground, trees, stones, etc., in crowded masses; **rolling stone gathers no** ∼, one who constantly changes his place or employment will not grow rich; hence ∼′y̌[2] *a.* **2.** (Sc. & N. Engl.) (peat-)bog. **3.** ∼ **agate**, agate with mosslike dendritic markings; ∼**-grown**, overgrown with moss; ∼**-hag**, (Sc.) broken ground from which peat has been taken; ∼**-rose**, garden variety of cabbage rose, with mosslike growth on calyx and stalk; ∼**-stitch**, alternate plain and purl in knitting; ∼**trooper**, freebooter of Scottish Border in 17th c. **4.** *v.t.* cover with moss. [OE *mos* bog, moss, = OHG *mos* f. Gmc *musam]

*mŏ′ssbŭnker *n.* menhaden. [f. Du. *marsbanker*, of unkn. orig.]

mŏ′ssō *adv.* (Mus.) with animation or speed. [It., p.p. of *muovere* move]

mōst *a.*, *n.*, & *adv.* **1.** *a.* existing in greatest quantity or degree (*you have made most mistakes; see who can make the most noise*). **2.** *n.* greatest quantity or number (*this is the most I can do*); (sl.) *the* best of all; **make the** ∼ **of**, (1) employ to the best advantage, (2) represent at its best or worst. **3.** *a.* & *n.* the majority (of) (*most people think so; most of it is, of them are, missing; his singing is better than most*); **for the** ∼ **part**, as regards the greater part, usually; hence ∼′LY[2] *adv.* **4.** *adv.* in the highest degree (*this is most interesting; what most annoys me*). **5.** (Forming superl. of *adjs.* & *advs.*, esp. those of more than one syllable) *most ludicrous*(*ly*), *most certain*(*ly*); *most favoured* NATION; ||*Most* HONOURABLE; *Most* REVEREND. **6.** **at** (**the**) ∼, as the greatest amount; **ten at** (**the**) ∼, not more than ten; *this is at* ∼ (no better than) *a makeshift.* **7.** *(colloq.) almost. [OE *māst*, = OS *mēst*, OHG *meist*, ON *mestr*, Goth. *maists* f. Gmc *maistaz (*mais more; see -EST[1])]

-most (*most, mōst*) *suf* forming *adjs.* w. superl. sense f. *preps.* & other *wds* indicating relative position (*foremost, inmost, topmost, uttermost*). [OE *-mest* f. Gmc **-mo- + *-isto* -EST[1]]

mot (mō) *n.* (*pl. pr.* mōz). witty saying; BON MOT; ∼ **juste** (zhōō′st), the expression that conveys a desired shade of meaning with more precision than any other. [F, = word, f. Gallo-Rom. *mottum for L *muttum* uttered sound (*muttire* murmur)]

||MOT *abbr.* Ministry of Transport; ∼ **test**, (colloq.) compulsory annual test of motor vehicles of more than a specified age.

mōte *n.* particle of dust; ∼ **in** person's **eye**, fault that is trifling compared to one's own (see Matt. 7: 3). [OE *mot*, corresp. to Du. *mot* dust, sawdust, of unkn. orig.]

mōtĕ′l *n.* hotel or group of furnished cabins by the roadside, where motorists and their vehicles may be accommodated. [portmanteau wd f. MOTOR + HOTEL]

mōtĕ′t *n.* (Mus.) anthem (usu. unaccompanied) in RC or Lutheran Church. [ME f. OF, dim. of MOT; see -ET[1]]

mŏth *n.* **1.** small nocturnal lepidopterous insect of family Tineidae breeding in cloth etc., on which its larva feeds; (**the**) ∼, (ravages of) such insects; hence ∼′y̌[2] *a.* **2.** insect of order Lepidoptera excluding butterflies, without clubbed antennae and mainly nocturnal, apt to scorch itself by fluttering about light; (fig.) person hovering around temptation. **3.** ∼**-ball**, (n.) ball of naphthalene etc. for keeping moths away from clothes (*in* ∼-*balls*, (fig.) stored out of use for considerable time), (*v.t.*) place in moth-balls; ∼**-eaten**, destroyed by moths, (fig.) antiquated, time-worn; *moth-*PROOF[2] *a.*, & *v.t.* [OE *moththe*; cf. MDu., MLG, MHG *motte*, ON *motti*]

mo′ther[1] (mŭ′dh-) *n.* **1.** female parent; (**adoptive**) ∼, woman who has adopted a child; EXPECTANT or *pregnant mother.* **2.** quality, condition, etc., that gives rise to another (*necessity is the mother of invention*).

3. head of female religious community (often *Mother* Superior). **4.** (Title used of or to) elderly woman of lower class. **5.** (**artificial**) ∼, apparatus for rearing chickens without hen. **6.** M∼ Carey's chicken, stormy petrel; M∼ Carey's goose, largest species of petrel; M∼ Church (as of maternal authority); M∼-Church (whence others have sprung); ∼ country, country in relation to its colonies; ∼craft, skill in looking after one's children as a mother; ∼ earth, earth as mother of its inhabitants etc., (joc.) the ground; ∼(-fucker), (vulg.) despicable or unpleasant person; *M∼ Goose rhyme, nursery rhyme; M∼ Hubbard, loose cloak or overall [f. nursery-rhyme character]; ∼-in-law, mother of one's wife or husband; ∼-in-law's tongue, plant of genus *Sansevieria* with long pointed leaves; ∼land, native country; ∼-naked, stark naked; M∼ of God, Virgin Mary; ∼-of-pearl, smooth shining iridescent substance forming inner layer of oyster etc. shell; ∼- -of-thousands or -millions, ivy-leaved toadflax; M∼'s Day, || = Mother²*ing Sunday*, *similar festival on second Sunday in May; ||*mother's* help²; ||∼ ship (in charge of torpedo-boats, submarines, etc.); ||∼s' meeting (in parish etc. for pastoral instruction, or fig. for agitated discussion); ∼'s ruin, (sl.) gin; ∼'s son, man, esp. *every mother's son of* (*you* etc.); ∼ tongue, (1) one's native language, (2) language from which others spring; ∼ wit, native wit, common sense. **7.** Hence ∼hood n., ∼less a., with dead or unknown mother, ∼like a. & adv. [OE mōdor, = OS mōdar, OHG muotar, ON mōthir f. Gmc *mōthar- f. IE *māter-]

mo'ther² (mŭ'dh-) v.t. give birth to (usu. fig.); protect as a mother; acknowledge or profess oneself the mother of (child, lit. or fig.); ||M∼ing Sunday, 4th Sunday in Lent, with old custom of visiting parents with gifts. [f. prec.]

mo'ther³ (mŭ'dh-) n. ∼ (**of vinegar**), mucilaginous substance produced in vinegar during fermentation by mould-fungus; hence ∼y² a. [prob. = mother¹; cf. MDu. *moeder*, G *mutter* in same sense]

mo'therl|y (mŭ'dh-) a. having or showing the good (esp. tender or kind) qualities of a mother; hence ∼iness n. [OE mōdorlic (as mother¹, -ly¹)]

mōti'f (-ē'f) n. distinctive feature, dominant idea, in artistic or literary composition; (Mus.) = figure¹ 8; ornament of lace etc. sewn separately on garment; ornament on vehicle identifying maker etc. [F (as motive)]

mō'tile a. (Zool. & Bot.) capable of motion; hence **moti'l|ity** n. [f. L motus motion (as move²); see -il]

mō'tion¹ n. **1.** moving, change of place; manner of moving the body in walking etc.; change of posture; gesture; **go through the** ∼s, simulate an action by gestures, (fig.) make pretence, do something only superficially; **in** ∼, moving, not at rest; **put or set in** ∼, set going or working; ∼ **picture,** = film 3; time¹-*and-motion.* **2.** formal proposal in deliberative assembly; (Law) application by party etc. for rule or order of court. **3.** evacuation of bowels; (in *sing.* or *pl.*) faeces. **4.** piece of moving mechanism; ∼-**work,** mechanism of hands of clock or watch. **5.** Hence ∼al, ∼less, adjs. [ME f. OF, f. L motio -onis (as move²; see -ion)]

mō'tion² v. **1.** v.t. direct (person *to*, *towards, away,* etc.; *to* do) by sign or gesture. **2.** v.i. make gesture (*to* person) directing him (*to* do). [f. prec.]

mō'tiv|āte v.t. supply a motive to, be the motive of; cause (person) to act in a particular way; stimulate interest of (person in studying etc.); hence ∼a'tion n. [f. foll. 3 + -ate³]

mō'tive¹ a. & n. **1.** a. tending to initiate movement, whence **mōti'vity** n.; ∼ **power,** moving or impelling power, esp. agent whose energy is used to drive machinery, e.g. steam, electricity. **2.** concerned with movement. **3.** n. what induces a person to act, e.g. desire, fear, circumstance; hence ∼less (-vl-) a.

4. = motif. [ME, f. OF *motif* a. & n. f. LL *motivus* a. (as move²; see -ive)]

mō'tive² v.t. = motivate. [f. prec. 3]

mō'tley a. & n. **1.** a. diversified in colour; of varied character (*a motley crew*). **2.** n. incongruous mixture; (Hist.) jester's particoloured dress; **wear** ∼, play the fool. [ME *mottelay*, perh. f. AF *motelé*, f. mote]

mō'tō-cròss n. cross-country racing on motor cycles. [f. foll. + cross- (4)]

mō'tor n., a., & v. **1.** n. what imparts motion; machine supplying motive power for carriage or vessel, esp. internal combustion engine, or for other device with moving parts; || = *motor car*; ∼'man, driver of tram, underground train, etc. **2.** a. giving, imparting, or producing motion; ∼ area, part of frontal lobe of brain associated with initiation of muscular action; ∼ nerve (carrying impulses from brain or spinal cord to muscle); hence motōr'ial, mō'tory, adjs. **3.** driven by motor (*motor boat*, *mower*, *ship*); ∼ bicycle, motor cycle or moped; ∼ bike, (colloq.) = *motor cycle*; ∼ bus, bus with motor engine; ||∼ car, car with motor engine for use on ordinary roads; ∼ coach, long- -distance motor bus; ∼ cycle, two-wheeled motor- -driven road vehicle without pedal propulsion; hence ∼-cyclist; motor scooter; ∼ vehicle, vehicle with motor engine for use on ordinary roads. **4.** of or for motor vehicles; ||∼ spirit, petrol or other fuel for internal combustion engines. **5.** v.i. & t. ||go or convey in motor car; hence ∼able a., (of road) that can be traversed by motor vehicles. [L, = mover (as move²; see -or)]

mō'torcāde n. procession or parade of motor cars. [f. prec., after *cavalcade*]

mō'torist n. driver of motor car. [f. motor + -ist]

mō'toriz|e, -īs|e (-īz), v.t. equip (troops etc.) with motor transport; furnish with motor for propulsion etc.; hence ∼a'tion n. [f. motor + -ize]

||**mō'torway** n. road specially constructed and controlled for fast motor traffic. [f. motor + way]

mōtte n. mound forming site of castle, camp, etc. [ME f. OF *mote* (as moat)]

mō'ttle n., a., & v.t. **1.** n. irregular arrangement of spots or confluent blotches of colour; such spot. **2.** v.t. (usu. in *p.p.*) mark (soap etc.) with mottle. [prob. back- -form. f. motley]

mō'ttō n. (*pl.* ∼es). sentence inscribed on some object and expressing appropriate sentiment; word or sentence accompanying coat of arms or crest; maxim adopted as rule of conduct; verses etc. in paper cracker; quotation prefixed to book or chapter; (Mus.) recurrent phrase having some symbolical significance. [It., as mot]

motu proprio (mōtū prō'prīō) n. (*pl.* ∼s). administrative papal bull without seal. [L, = of our own accord]

||**mouch.** Var. of mooch.

mouchoir (mōō'shwär) n. handkerchief. [F]

moue (mōō) n. = pout². [F; see mow²]

mou'fflon (mōō'-) n. wild mountain sheep (*Ovis musimon*) of S. Europe. [F *mouflon* f. It. *muflone* f. Rom. *mufro -onis*]

mouillé (mōō'yā) a. (Phonet., of consonant) palatalized. [F, = wetted]

mou'jik, mu'zhïk, (mōō'zhĭk) n. (Hist.) Russian peasant. [Russ. *muzhik*]

mould¹ (mōld), *mōld¹, n. loose earth; upper soil of cultivated land, esp. if rich in organic matter; **man of** ∼, mere mortal; ∼-**board,** board in plough that turns over the furrow-slice. [OE *molde*, = MDu. *moude*, OHG *molta*, ON *mold*, Goth. *mulda* f. Gmc *moldō* (*mul-*, *mel-* grind; cf. meal¹)]

mould² (mōld), *mōld², n. **1.** pattern or template used by mason, bricklayer, etc., as guide in shaping mouldings; hollow form into which molten metal etc. is poured or soft material is pressed to harden in required shape; metal or earthenware vessel used to give shape to puddings etc., pudding etc. so shaped;

(fig.) **cast in** *heroic* etc. ∼, of such character. **2.** form, shape, esp. of animal body; (Archit.) moulding, group of mouldings. [ME *mold(e)*, app. f. OF *modle* f. L MODULUS]

mould³ (mōld), ***mōld³***, *v.t.* produce (object) in certain shape, *out of* (elements), *on* or *upon* (pattern), lit. or fig.; bring into certain shape; shape (bread) into loaves. [ME, f. prec.]

mould⁴ (mōld), ***mōld⁴***, *n.* woolly or furry growth of minute fungi on things of animal or vegetable origin that lie for some time esp. in moist warm air. [ME prob. f. obs. *mould* a., p.p. of *moul* grow mouldy f. ON *mugla, mygla*]

mou'lder¹ (mō'l-), ***mō'lder¹***, *n.* one who moulds, esp. workman making moulds for casting. [ME, f. MOULD³+-ER¹]

mou'lder² (mō'l-), ***mō'lder²***, *v.t.* decay to dust, rot *away*, (lit. or fig.). [perh. f. MOULD¹+-ER⁵, but cf. Norw. dial. *muldra* crumble]

mou'lding (mō'l-), ***mō'lding***, *n.* In vbl senses; moulded object, esp. ornamental variety of outline in cornices etc. of building, or similar shape of woodwork etc.; strip of wood thus shaped for attachment; ∼-**board** (on which dough is kneaded); ∼-**plane** (for shaping mouldings); **picture-**∼ (for framing pictures, or along wall for hanging framed pictures from). [ME, f. MOULD³+-ING¹]

mou'ld|ў (mō'l-), ***mō'ld|ў***, *a.* overgrown with mould; (fig.) stale, out-of-date; (sl.) dull, miserable, boring; hence ∼**ĭNESS** *n.* [ME, f. MOULD⁴+-Y²]

moulin (mōōlǎ'n) *n.* nearly vertical shaft in glacier, formed by surface water falling through crack in ice. [F, lit. = mill]

moult (mōlt), ***mōlt***, *v.* & *n.* **1.** *v.t.* & *i.* (of bird) shed (feathers), shed feathers, in changing plumage (lit. or fig.); (of animal) shed hair, shell, etc. **2.** *n.* moulting. [ME *moute* f. OE *mutian*, = OHG *mūzzōn*, WG f. L *mutare* change; *-l-* after *fault* etc.]

mound¹ *n.* ball of gold etc. representing earth, surmounting crown etc., and used in heraldry. [ME, f. OF *monde* f. L *mundus* world]

mound² *n.*, & *v.t.* **1.** *n.* elevation of earth or stones, esp. of earth heaped on grave; hillock; heap, pile; (Baseball) slight elevation on which pitcher stands; ∼-**builder**, (1) one of prehistoric N. Amer. Indian race who erected mounds, (2) megapode bird. **2.** *v.t.* enclose with, heap up in, mounds. [orig. = hedge or fence; 16th c., of unkn. orig.]

mount¹ *n.* **1.** mountain, hill, (arch. exc. before name, as *Mount Everest, Mount of Olives*); SERMON *on the Mount*. **2.** (Palmistry): fleshy prominence on palm of hand. [ME, f. OE *munt* & OF *mont* f. L *mons montis* mountain]

mount² *v.* **1.** *v.t.* ascend (hill, stairs, etc., or abs.). **2.** get on (horse etc., or abs.) for purpose of riding; put (person) on horse etc.; furnish (person) with horse; (in *p.p.*) serving on horseback or bicycle (*mounted police, infantry*). **3.** (Esp. of animal) get upon for copulation. **4.** raise (guns) into position on a fixed mounting; place (object) *on* elevated support; bring into readiness for operation; put (picture etc.) in a MOUNT³; fit (gem etc.) in gold etc.; fix (object) on microscope slide. **5.** put (play) on stage; display (article of costume); prepare (specimens etc.) for display or preservation. **6.** take action to effect (effort, programme, etc.; orig. Mil. of offensive); ∼ **guard**, perform duty of guarding (*over* thing etc.). **7.** *v.i.* move upwards; (of blood) rise into cheeks; ∼ (**up**), (fig.) increase in amount or intensity. **8.** rise to higher level of rank, power, etc. **9.** Hence ∼ING¹ (1, 4) *n.* (∼**ing-block**, block of stone provided to help in mounting one's horse). [ME, f. OF *munter, monter* f. Rom. *montare* f. L (as prec.)]

mount³ *n.* margin surrounding picture or photograph; card on which drawing is mounted; setting for gem etc.; ornamental metal parts of thing; stamp-HINGE; horse for person's riding; chance of riding, esp. as jockey. [f. prec.]

mou'ntain (-tĭn) *n.* **1.** large natural elevation of earth's surface, large or high and steep hill, esp. one over 1,000 ft. high; *waves ran* ∼**s** (very) **high,** ∼-**high. 2.** large heap or pile, huge quantity *of*; large surplus stock esp. of a commodity. **3. the M∼**, extreme party in French Revolution (1792) occupying elevated position in chamber of assembly. **4.** *make a mountain out of a* MOLE²*hill*; (**re**)**move** ∼**s**, do miracles, make every possible effort. **5.** ∼ **ash,** (1) tree of genus *Sorbus* with delicate pinnate leaves and scarlet berries, rowan, (2) eucalyptus like old ash-tree; ∼ **chain,** connected series of mountains; ∼ **cock**, capercaillie; ∼ **devil**, moloch; ∼ **dew**, (colloq.) Scotch whisky esp. illicitly distilled; ∼ **goat**, white goatlike animal (*Oreamnos montanus*) of Rocky Mountains etc.; ∼ **laurel**, N. Amer. shrub *Kalmia latifolia*; ∼ **linnet**, twite; ∼ **lion**, puma; ∼ **panther**, ounce; ∼ **range**, line of mountains connected by high ground; ∼ **sickness**, malady caused by rarefied air at great heights; ∼**side**, slope of mountain below summit; *M∼ **Time**, standard time of parts of Canada and US in or near Rocky Mountains; ∼ **tobacco**, a species of arnica; ∼ **trout**, (Austral.) small minnow popular in aquariums. [ME, f. OF *montaigne* f. Rom. *montania* fem. (or neut. pl.) of *montanius* a. f. L (as MOUNT¹)]

mountaineer' (-tĭn-) *n.* dweller amongst mountains; one skilled in mountain climbing, whence ∼ING¹ *n.* [f. prec.+-EER.]

mou'ntainous (-tĭn-) *a.* abounding in mountains; huge. [f. MOUNTAIN+-OUS]

mou'ntebank *n.* itinerant quack appealing to audience from platform; clown; charlatan; hence ∼ERY (4) *n.* [f. It. *montambanco* = *monta in banco* MOUNT² on bench]

Mou'ntie *n.* (colloq.) member of Royal Canadian Mounted Police. [f. MOUNT²*ed*+-IE]

mourn (môrn) *v.* **1.** *v.i.* feel sorrow or regret (*for* or *over* dead person, lost thing, loss, misfortune, etc.); show conventional signs of grief for period after person's death. **2.** *v.t.* sorrow for (dead person, regretted or past thing). [OE *murnan*, = OS *mornon*, OHG *mornēn* be anxious, ON *morna*, Goth. *maurnan*]

mour'ner (môr'-) *n.* one who mourns, esp. who attends funeral of friend or relation; person hired to attend funeral. [ME, f. prec.+-ER¹]

mour'nful (môr'-) *a.* expressing mourning; doleful, sad, sorrowful; hence ∼LY² *adv.*, ∼NESS *n.* [f. MOURN+-FUL]

mour'ning (môr'-) *n.* In vbl senses; (wearing of) black clothes as sign of mourning; DEEP¹, HALF, *mourning*; **in** ∼, wearing such garments, (sl.) (of eye) blacked in fighting, (sl., of finger-nails) dirty; ∼-**band** (of black crape etc. round sleeve or hat as token of mourning); ∼-**coach** (attending funeral); ∼ **dove**, Amer. dove with plaintive note; ∼-**paper**, notepaper with black edge; ∼-**ring** (worn as memorial of deceased person). [ME, f. MOURN+-ING¹]

mousaka. Var. of MOUSSAKA.

mouse¹ (mows) *n.* (*pl.* **mice**). small rodent esp. of genus *Mus*, or small shrew or vole; timid, shy, or retiring person; (sl.) black eye; ∼-**colour(ed)**, dark grey with yellow tinge; ∼ **deer**, chevrotain; ∼-**ear**, (1) a hawkweed, (2) forget-me-not; ∼ **hare**, pika; ∼'**trap** (for catching mice; ∼*trap cheese*, of poor quality); hence **mou'sy²** *a.* [OE *mūs*, pl. *mȳs*, = OS, OHG *mūs*, ON *mús* f. Gmc f. IE **mūs-*]

mous|e² (-z, -s) *v.i.* (Of cat or owl) hunt for or catch mice, whence ∼ER¹ *n.*; search industriously, prowl *about* (as if) in search of something. [ME, f. prec.]

moussa'ka (mōōsah'-) *n.* Greek dish of minced meat, aubergine, eggs, etc. [Gk or Turk.]

mousse (mōōs) *n.* dish of cold whipped cream or eggs or creamlike substance flavoured with fruit, chocolate, etc.; meat or fish purée with whipped cream etc. incorporated. [F, = moss, froth]

mousseli´ne (mōōslē´n) n. muslin-like fabric of silk etc.; sauce of seasoned or sweetened eggs and cream; ∼-de-laine, dress material of wool and cotton; ∼--de-soie (-swah), thin silk fabric of muslin-like texture. [F; see MUSLIN, DELAINE]

mousta´ch|e, *mus-, (mustah´sh) n. hair on either half (usu. in pl.) or whole of (usu. man's) upper lip; similar hair round mouths of some animals; ∼e-cup (with partial cover to protect moustache when drinking); hence ∼ED² (-sht) a. [F, f. It. mostaccio f. Gk mustax -akos]

Mousté´rian (mōō-) a. (Archaeol.) of a middle palaeolithic epoch with flints worked on one side only. [f. F moustérien (Le Moustier in SW France, where remains of it were found) + -IAN]

mou´sў. See MOUSE¹.

mouth¹ n. (pl. pr. -dhz). **1.** external orifice in head, with cavity behind it containing apparatus of biting and mastication and vocal organs; this cavity. **2.** (sl.) talkativeness; impudent talk, cheek. **3.** (Of horse, with reference to his readiness to feel and obey pressure of bit) good, bad, hard, mouth. **4.** ∼ to feed, person who consumes food but does no useful work in return; mouth WATER²s; DOWN³ in the mouth; give ∼, (of dog) bark, bay; in person's ∼, when said by him (that sounds strange in your mouth); keep one's ∼ shut, (sl.) not reveal secret; LAUGH on the other or wrong side of one's mouth; make a wry ∼, grimace in disgust; put one's money where one's ∼ is, (sl.) be ready to support one's opinions by action; not OPEN² one's mouth; out of person's own ∼, using his actual words; put words into person's ∼, (1) tell him what to say, (2) represent him as having said them; shut person's ∼, (sl.) prevent him from revealing something; take words out of person's ∼, say what he was about to say; WORD¹ of mouth. **5.** opening of bag, sack, cave, furnace, cannon, trumpet, volcano, etc.; place where river enters sea. **6.** ∼-breeder, fish carrying eggs and young in mouth; ∼-filling, bombastic; ∼-organ, thin rectangular box containing metal reeds, each tuned to a note, moved along lips while air is blown or sucked through it to play tunes; ∼'piece, (1) part attached as outlet, (2) part of pipe, musical instrument, telephone, etc., placed between or near lips, (3) one who speaks for another or others (sl., lawyer); ∼-to-∼, (of resuscitation) in which person breathes into patient's lungs through mouth; ∼'wash, liquid antiseptic etc. for use in mouth. **7.** Hence (-)∼ED² (-dhd), ∼'LESS, adjs. [OE mūth, = OS mūth, OS, OHG mund, ON munnr, muthr, Goth. munths f. Gmc *munthaz f. IE *mntos]

mouth² (-dh) v. **1.** v.t. utter (words or abs.) esp. pompously or very distinctly, rant, declaim; take (food) in, touch with, the mouth; train mouth of (horse). **2.** v.i. grimace; move lips silently. [ME, f. prec.]

mou´thful (-ōōl) n. quantity that fills the mouth; small quantity (of food etc.); something difficult to say; *(sl.) something important said. [f. MOUTH¹ + -FUL]

mou´thў (-dhī) a. railing, ranting; bombastic. [f. MOUTH¹ + -Y²]

mo´v|able (mōō´-) a. & n. **1.** a. that can be moved; (Law, of property) that can be removed, personal as opp. to REAL²; movable DOH, FEAST; hence ∼ABI´LITY, ∼ableNESS (-beln-), ns. **2.** n. article of furniture that may be removed from the house, opp. to fixture; (in pl.) personal property. [ME, f. OF (as MOVE²; see -ABLE)]

move¹ (mōōv) n. moving of a man in chess or other game; player's turn to do this; change of residence, business premises, etc.; device, step taken to secure object; on the ∼, (1) progressing, (2) moving about; make a ∼, initiate action, e.g. rise and go from dinner-table etc.; get a ∼ on, (colloq.) hurry up, bestir oneself. [ME, f. foll.]

move² (mōōv) v. **1.** v.t. change position of; change

position of (man) in chess etc.; put or keep in motion, shake, stir; move HEAVEN and earth, MOUNTAINs; ||∼ house, change one's place of residence. **2.** change posture of (one's body, limbs, etc.); cause (bowels) to be evacuated. **3.** provoke (laughter, anger, etc., in person, person to these); affect (person) with (usu. tender or sympathetic) emotion. **4.** prompt, incline, (person to action, to do); the spirit (orig. in Quaker use, = Holy Spirit) ∼s person, he feels inclined (to do). **5.** make formal application to (court etc. for); propose (question, resolution, that thing be done) in deliberative assembly. **6.** v.i. go or pass (about, away, etc.) from place to place; make progress (the work moves slowly); (of merchandise) be sold; make a move at chess etc.; (fig.) initiate action (moved to halt inflation); live, be socially active, in specified group etc. (moves in the best circles). **7.** change one's place of residence; ∼ about, do this often; ∼ in, take possession of new abode, begin new job, etc.; so ∼ out. **8.** ∼ along or on, go to new place (e.g. as policeman's order to person who stands too long in one place); ∼ over or up, adjust one's position to make room for another. **9.** (Of person or part of body) change posture; (of inanimate thing) undergo change of position. **10.** (Of bowels) be moved. **11.** make request or application (for). **12.** Hence ∼'LESS (-vl-) a., (literary) motionless. [ME, f. AF mover, OF moveir f. L movēre mot-]

moveable. Var. (esp. Law) of MOVABLE.

mo´vement (mōō´vm-) n. moving; military evolution; moving parts of mechanism (esp. of clock or watch), particular group of these; mental impulse; progressive development of poem, story, etc.; (Mus.) principal division of a musical work (e.g. suite, sonata, symphony), having a distinctive structure of its own; (series of combined actions and endeavours of) body of persons for special object (the OXFORD Movement; the Labour movement); activity in market for some commodity, rise or fall in price; = MOTION¹ 3. [ME f. OF, f. med. L movimentum (as MOVE²; see -MENT)]

mo´ver (mōō´-) n. In vbl senses; one who moves proposition; *remover of furniture; prime ∼, initial source (natural or mechanical) of motive power, (fig.) author of fruitful idea. [ME, f. MOVE² + -ER¹]

***mo´vie** (mōō´-) n. (colloq.) = FILM 3; (∼-house), cinema. [f. MOVING picture + -IE]

mo´ving (mōō´-) n. In vbl senses; affecting with emotion (cf. MOVE² 3), whence ∼LY² adv.; ∼ ||pavement or *sidewalk, structure like conveyor belt for pedestrians; ∼ picture, continuous picture of events (e.g. FILM 3) obtained by projecting on screen etc. a sequence of photographs taken at very short intervals; ∼ staircase, escalator. [ME, f. MOVE² + -ING²]

mow¹ (mō) n. (US or dial.) stack of hay, corn, etc.; place in barn where hay etc. is heaped; ∼'burnt, spoilt by becoming overheated in the mow. [OE mūga, = ON múgi swath, crowd]

mow² (mow, mō) n., & v.i. See MOP³. [ME, prob. f. OF mo(u)e mouth, lip, pout, or f. MDu. mouwe, in same senses]

mow³ (mō) v.t. (p.p. ∼ed pr. mōd, or ∼n). cut down (grass etc. or abs.) with scythe or machine; cut down produce of (field) or grass etc. of (lawn) thus; destroy sweepingly; ∼ down, kill or destroy randomly or in great numbers; hence ∼'ER¹ (1, 2) (mō´er) n. [OE māwan, = OHG māen f. Gmc *mǣ-; cf. MEAD²]

mö´xa n. down from dried leaves of Artemisia moxa, etc., burnt on skin as counter-irritant. [f. Jap. mogusa (moe kusa burning herb)]

***mö´xie** n. (sl.) energy, courage, daring. [f. trade name of a drink]

moy´a n. volcanic mud. [former name of mountain in Ecuador]

Mözǎ´rab n. (Hist.) Christian owning allegiance to Moorish king but allowed his own religion; hence ∼IC a. [f. Sp. Mozarabe f. Arab. musta'rib would-be Arab]

MP *abbr.* Member of Parliament; military police-(man).

mp *abbr.* mezzo piano.

m.p. *abbr.* melting-point.

m.p.g. *abbr.* miles per gallon.

m.p.h. *abbr.* miles per hour.

M.Phil. *abbr.* Master of Philosophy.

MPS *abbr.* Member of the Pharmaceutical Society.

Mr (mǐ'ster) *n.* (*pl.* MESSRS) Title of man without higher title, or prefixed to designation of office etc., (*Mr Jones, Mr Secretary, Mr Speaker*); **Mr Right,** (joc.) destined husband. [abbr. of MISTER]

MR *abbr.* Master of the Rolls.

MRA *abbr.* Moral Re-Armament.

MRBM *abbr.* medium-range ballistic missile.

‖**MRC** *abbr.* Medical Research Council.

MRCA *abbr.* multi-role combat aircraft.

Mrs (mǐ'sǐz) *n.* (*pl.* same or MESDAMES). Title of married woman without higher title; *Mrs* GRUNDY; ‖*Mrs* MOP¹(P). [abbr. of MISTRESS; cf. MISSIS]

Ms (mǐz) *n.* Title of woman without higher title, used like MR without distinction between married and unmarried (cf. MRS, MISS³). [by comb. of these earlier forms]

MS *abbr.* manuscript; Master of Science or Surgery; Mississippi; *motor ship; multiple sclerosis.

M.Sc. *abbr.* Master of Science.

*Msgr. *abbr.* *Monseigneur; Monsignor*

MSS (ĕmĕ'sǐz) *abbr.* manuscripts.

*MST *abbr.* Mountain Standard Time.

MT *abbr.* mechanical transport; Montana.

Mt. *abbr.* Mount.

MTB *abbr.* motor torpedo-boat.

M.Tech. *abbr.* Master of Technology.

mū *n.* twelfth Greek letter (M, μ) = m; μ (as symbol) = MICRO- 2; **mu-meson,** = MUON. [Gk]

much *a., n., & adv.,* (MORE, MOST). **1.** *a.* existing in great quantity (*much trouble; too much noise; not much rain*); **a bit ~,** (colloq.) somewhat excessive or immoderate; HOW much; so much; THIS much, THAT¹ much; too ~ for, (1) more than a match for, (2) beyond what is endurable by; hence ~'LY² *adv.* (joc.). **2.** *n.* great quantity (*I have put up with much; much of what you say is true*), MAKE¹, THINK, *much of; not much* IN¹ *it*; not ~ of a, (colloq.) not a great, a somewhat poor, (*am not much of a scholar; it was not much of a party*); not ~ to look at, insignificant or unpleasing in appearance; not come to ~, have little success. **3.** *adv.* in a great degree (*much to my surprise;* qualifying *v.* or *p.p.,* cf. VERY¹; *I much regret the mistake; was much annoyed;* qualifying compar. or superl. adj.: *much better; much the most likely*); approximately (*much the* SAME; ~ of a size, about the same size); for a large part of one's time (*is much in society*); ~ as, though . . . much (*cannot come, much as I should like to*); *much* LESS; *much* OBLIGED; as ~, that (quantity etc.; *I thought as ~,* I thought so; *as ~ again,* such as will double the amount); not ~, (sl.) certainly not, (iron.) very much. [ME, f. *muchel* MICKLE; for shortening cf. BAD, WENCH]

mu'chness *n.* greatness in quantity or degree; **much of a ~,** very nearly the same or alike. [ME, f. prec. + -NESS]

mu'cilage *n.* viscous substance obtained from plant seeds etc. by maceration; *solution of gum; so **mucila'gin**ous *a.* [ME f. F, f. LL *mucilago -ginis* musty juice (MUCUS)]

muck¹ *n.* farmyard manure; (colloq.) dirt, filth, anything disgusting; (colloq.) untidy state, mess, (**make a ~ of,** bungle); **~-rake** (for collecting muck, usu. fig. of predilection for worthless or unsavoury matters, whence **~-raking** *a.* & *n.*); ‖**~ sweat** (profuse); ~'**worm,** worm that lives in muck, (fig.) miser; hence ~'Y² *a.* [ME *muk,* prob. f. Scand.; cf. ON *myki* dung, cogn. w. MEEK]

muck² *v.* **1.** *v.t.* make dirty; remove muck (*out*) from; manure with muck; ‖**~ (up),** (sl.) bungle (job). **2.** *v.i.*

(sl.) ‖go aimlessly *about*; ‖fool *about with*; ~ **in,** share tasks etc. equally (*with* another). [ME, f. prec.]

mu'cker *n.* (sl.) ‖heavy fall (lit. or fig.; **come a ~,** experience this); *rough or coarse person; friend, companion. [f. MUCK¹ + -ER¹]

mu'ckle. See MICKLE.

mūcō'sa *n.* mucous membrane. [mod. L, fem. of *mucosus* (see foll.)]

mū'cous *a.* of or covered with mucus; ~ **membrane,** internal prolongation of the skin so covered; so **mūco'sITY** *n.* [f. L *mucosus* (as MUCUS; see -OUS)]

mū'crō *n.* (*pl.* ~**nes** *pr.* ō'nēz). (Bot. & Zool.) sharp-pointed part or organ; so **mū'cron**ATE² *a.* [L *mucro -onis* sharp point]

mū'cus *n.* slimy substance secreted by mucous membrane; gummy substance found in all plants; slimy substance exuded by some animals, esp. fishes. [L]

mŭd *n.* **1.** wet soft earthy matter; hard ground from drying of area of this; (fig.) what is worthless or polluting (one's *name is* ~, one is disgraced or discredited); **as clear as ~,** (joc.) not at all clear; **fling, sling, throw, ~,** make disgraceful imputations; **here's ~ in your eye!** (sl. drinking toast); STICK¹ *in the mud.* **2.** ~ **bath** (in mud of mineral springs, for rheumatism etc., or gen. of game etc. taking place amid much mud); ~'**fish** (burrowing in mud, esp. NZ *Neochanna apoda*); ~**-flap** (behind wheel of vehicle, to catch mud etc. thrown up); ~**-flat,** stretch of muddy land left uncovered at low tide; ~'**guard,** (metal) hood covering wheel of cycle, car, etc., to protect rider, pedestrians, etc., from mud; ~'**lark,** one who dabbles, works, or (of bird) lives, in mud, esp. street urchin; ~ **pack,** cosmetic paste applied thickly to face; ~ **pie,** mud made into pie shape by child; *~ **puppy,** large salamander; ~ **skipper,** fish able to leave water and leap on mud; ~ **volcano** (discharging mud). [ME *mode, mudde,* prob. f. MLG *mudde,* MHG *mot* bog]

mu'ddle¹ *n.* disorder; muddled condition, **make a ~ of,** bungle; ~**-headed(ness),** stupid(ity), confused (state). [f. foll.]

mu'ddle¹ (2) *v.t.* **1.** *v.t.* bewilder, esp. with drink; mix (*things up, together*) blunderingly; mismanage (affair); *crush and mix (ingredients for drink), whence **mu'ddl**ER¹ (2) *n.* **2.** *v.i.* busy oneself (*with*) in confused and ineffective way; ~ **along** or **on,** progress in haphazard way; ~ **through,** attain one's end by tenacity not skill or efficiency. [perh. f. MDu. *moddelen,* frequent. of *modden* dabble in mud (as MUD; see -LE 3)]

mu'ddly *adj.,* & *v.t.* **1.** *a.* like, abounding in, covered with, mud; (of liquid) turbid; (of light) dull; (of colour) impure; mentally confused; obscure; hence ~iLY² *adv.,* ~iNESS *n.* **2.** *v.t.* make muddy. [ME, f. MUD + -Y²]

Mudéjar (mōōdhā'här) *n. & a.* **1.** *n.* Christianized Moor in medieval Spain. **2.** *a.* of style of architecture originated by these. [Sp., f. Arab. *mudajjan* allowed to remain]

mue'sli (mōō'zlǐ) *n.* food of crushed cereals, dried fruit, nuts, honey, etc. [Swiss G]

mue'zzin (mōō-) *n.* Muslim crier who proclaims hours of prayer usu. from minaret. [f. Arab. *mu'addin* part. of '*addana* proclaim (*'udn* ear)]

muff¹ *n.* woman's fur or other covering (usu. cylindrical) into which both hands are thrust from opposite ends to keep them warm; EAR¹-*muff,* FOOT¹-*muff.* [f. Du. *mof,* MDu. *moffel, muffel* f. med. L *muff(u)la,* of unkn. orig.]

muff² *n., & v.t.* **1.** *n.* person who is awkward or stupid, orig. in some athletic sport; failure, esp. to catch ball at cricket etc.; hence ~'ISH¹ *a.* **2.** *v.t.* bungle, miss (catch, ball, etc.); blunder in (theatrical part etc.). [19th c., of unkn. orig.]

‖**mu'ffetee'** *n.* worsted cuff worn on wrist. [app. irreg. f. MUFF¹]

mŭ'ffin n. (*English) ~, light flat round spongy cake, eaten toasted and buttered; *similar round cake made from batter or dough; ||~-**bell** (Hist., rung by ~-**man,** seller of muffins in street). [18th c.; orig. unkn.]

mŭff'ineer' n. small castor for sprinkling salt or sugar on muffins. [f. prec. + -EER]

mŭ'ffle[1] n. thick part of upper lip and nose of ruminants and rodents. [f. F mufle, of unkn. orig.]

mŭ'ffle[2] n. receptacle in furnace where substances may be heated without contact with combustion products; similar chamber in kiln for baking painted pottery. [f. F moufle mitten; cf. MUFF[1]]

mŭ'ffle[3] v.t. wrap, cover up, (oneself, one's throat etc., or abs.) for warmth; prevent from speaking; wrap up (oars at rowlocks, bell, drum, horse's hoofs) to deaden sound for secrecy or solemnity; (usu. in p.p.) repress, deaden, sound of (curse etc.). [ME, perh. f. OF enmoufler (moufle thick glove, as MUFF[1])]

mŭ'ffler n. wrap or scarf worn for warmth; thing used to deaden sound, esp. felt pad between hammer and string of piano; *silencer of motor vehicle. [f. prec. + -ER[1]]

mŭ'ftï n. **1.** Muslim priest or expounder of law. **2.** plain clothes worn by one who has right to wear uniform (esp. in mufti). [f. Arab. muftī, part. of 'aftā decide point of law]

mŭg[1] n. **1.** drinking-vessel, usu. cylindrical and with handle; its contents; hence ~'FUL 2 n. **2.** (sl.) face, mouth; *hoodlum; ~ **shot,** photograph of face. [prob. f. Scand.; sense 2 prob. f. grotesque faces on mugs]

||**mŭg**[2] n. (sl.) simpleton; gullible person; **a** ~'s **game,** senseless or unprofitable activity. [perh. f. prec. w. ref. to look of stupidity]

||**mŭg**[3] v. (-gg-) & n. (sl.) **1.** v.i. study hard (at subject, or abs.). **2.** v.t. ~ (**up**), learn (subject) by hard study. **3.** n. one who studies hard. [19th c.; orig. unkn.]

mŭg[4] v.t. (-gg-). thrash; strangle; rob with violence esp. in public place; hence ~'gING[1] (-g-) n. [prob. f. MUG[1] 2]

mŭg[5] v.i. (-gg-). (sl.) make faces, esp. before audience, camera, etc. [f. MUG[1] 2]

mŭ'gger[1] (-g-) n. In vbl senses. [f. MUG[3-5] + -ER[1]]

mŭ'gger[2] (-g-) n. broad-nosed Indian crocodile (Crocodylus palustris) venerated by many Hindus. [f. Hindi magar]

mŭ'ggins (-gĭnz) n. (pl. ~es or same). (colloq.) simpleton; person who allows himself to be outwitted; card-game like snap. [perh. the surname M~, w. allus. to MUG[2]]

Mŭggletō'nian (-gelt-) a. & n. (member) of sect founded by, and believing in personal inspiration of, L. Muggleton and John Reeve, c. 1650. [f. Lodowick Muggleton, Engl. preacher d. 1698 + -IAN]

mŭ'gg|ў (-gĭ) a. (Of weather, day, etc.) oppressively damp and warm; hence ~ĭNESS n. [f. dial. mug mist, drizzle f. ON mugga, + -Y[2]]

Mughal. Var. of MOGUL 1.

mŭ'gwort (-ĕrt) n. wormwood plant, esp. Artemisia vulgaris. [OE mucgwyrt (as MIDGE, WORT)]

***mŭ'gwŭmp** n. great man, boss; one who holds aloof from party politics; one who sits on the fence. [f. Algonquin mugquomp great chief]

Muhă'mmadan, Mohă'mmĕdan, n. & a. Muslim; hence ~ISM (3) n., ~IZE (3) v.t. [f. Muhammad, Arabian prophet d. 632 + -AN]

mŭlä'ttō n. (pl. ~s or *~es) & a. **1.** n. offspring or descendant of White and Black persons. **2.** a. of colour of mulattos, tawny. [f. Sp. mulato young mule, mulatto, irreg. f. mulo MULE[1]]

mŭ'lberrў n. tree of genus Morus, leaves of which are much used for feeding silkworms; its purple or white fruit; **paper** ~, small Asiatic tree (Broussonetia papyrifera) of same family, whose bark is used for paper-making. [ME mol-, mool-, mulberry, dissim. f. murberie f. OE *murberie, mōrberie, = OHG mōrberi, murberi f. L morum; see BERRY[1]]

mŭ'lch (-lch, -lsh) n., & v.t. **1.** n. mixture of wet straw, leaves, etc., spread to protect roots of newly planted trees etc. **2.** v.t. treat with mulch. [prob. use as n. of mulsh soft; cf. dial. melsh mild f. OE melsc]

mŭlct n., & v.t. (literary). **1.** n. fine imposed for offence. **2.** v.t. punish (person) by fine (in amount), fine (person amount); deprive (person etc. of); swindle (person), obtain by swindling. [earlier mult(e) f. L mul(c)ta; v. thr. F mul(c)ter & L mulctare]

mūle[1] n. **1.** offspring (usu. sterile) of he-ass and mare, or (pop.) of she-ass and stallion (prop. hinny), used as beast of draught and burden and undeservedly noted for obstinacy; stupid or obstinate person; hybrid plant or animal; ~ **canary,** cross between canary and other finch. **2.** kind of spinning-machine invented by Crompton, intermediate between earlier types. [ME f. OF mul(e) f. L mulus mula]

mūle[2]. Var. of MEWL.

mūle[3] n. backless slipper. [F]

mülêteer' n. mule-driver. [f. F muletier (mulet dim. of OF mul MULE[1]; see -ET[1], -EER)]

mū'lga n. (Austral.) widely distributed shrubby acacia (Acacia aneura); its wood; scrub, bush; (colloq.) outback. [Aboriginal]

muliē'britý n. womanhood; normal characteristics of a woman (opp. virility); softness, effeminacy. [f. LL muliebritas f. L mulier woman; see -ITY]

mū'lish a. like a mule; stubborn; hence ~LY[2] adv., ~NESS n. [f. MULE[1] + -ISH[1]]

mŭll[1] n. thin soft plain muslin. [abbr. of mulmull f. Hindi malmal]

mŭll[2] n. & v. (colloq.). **1.** n. ||muddle, mess, (make a mull of). **2.** v.t. ||make a mull of (catch at cricket etc.). **3.** v.t. & i. ponder (over). [perh. f. mull grind to powder, ME mul dust f. MDu.]

mŭll[3] v.t. make (wine, beer) into hot drink with sugar, spices, egg-yolk, etc. [17th c.; orig. unkn.]

mŭll[4] n. (Sc.) promontory (Mull of Kintyre). [ME; cf. Gael. maol, Icel. múli]

mŭll[5] n. (Sc.) snuff-box. [var. of MILL[1], box orig. having a grinder]

mŭll[6] n. humus formed under non-acid conditions. [G, f. Da. muld]

mŭ'llah (-a) n. Muslim learned in Islamic theology and sacred law. [f. Pers., Turk., Urdu mullā f. Arab. mawlā]

mŭ'llein (-lĭn) n. herbaceous plant of genus Verbascum, with woolly leaves and yellow flowers. [ME, f. OF moleine f. Gaulish *melena]

mŭ'ller n. stone etc. used for grinding powders etc. on slab. [ME, perh. f. AF *moloir (moldre grind; see -ER[2])]

mŭ'llet n. fish of family Mullidae (**red** ~) or Mugilidae (**grey** ~), valued for food. [ME, f. OF mulet dim. f. L mullus red mullet f. Gk mollos]

***mŭ'lligan** n. (colloq.) stew of odds and ends of food. [perh. f. name Mulligan]

mŭlligataw'nў n. highly seasoned soup orig. from India; ~ **paste,** curry paste used for this. [f. Tamil milagutannir pepper-water]

mŭ'lligrŭbs (-z) n. pl. depression of spirits; stomach-ache. [16th c.; mulliegrums, of unkn. orig.]

mŭ'llion (-yon) n. vertical bar dividing lights in window (cf. TRANSOM); hence ~ED[2] (-yond) a. [prob. metathetic f. MONIAL]

mŭ'llock n. **1.** (Austral. & dial.) refuse, rubbish. **2.** (Austral.) rock containing no gold; refuse from which gold has been extracted; ridicule. [ME dim. of mul dust, rubbish, f. MDu.; see -OCK]

mŭ'lloway (-owā) n. (Austral.) large marine food-fish (Sciaena antarctica). [19th c.; orig. unkn.]

mŭltă'ngūlar (-ngg-) a. many-angled. [f. med. L multangularis (as MULTI-, ANGULAR)]

mŭltē'itў n. (arch.) manifoldness. [f. L multus many; cf HAECCEITY]

mŭ'lti- pref. many; as: ~**colour(ed),** of many colours; ~**fid,** (Bot. & Zool.) cleft into many parts; ~**foil,** (Archit.) ornament consisting of more than 5 foils;

~form, having many forms, of many kinds; so **~for′mity** *n.*; **~la′teral,** having many sides, (of agreement, treaty, etc.) in which three or more parties participate; **~li′ngual,** in or using many languages; **~millionair′e,** person with fortune of several millions; **~na′tional,** operating in several countries; **~no′mial** *a.* & *n.*, = POLYNOMIAL [after *binomial*]; **~parous** (-ĭ′p-), (1) bringing forth many young at a birth, (2) having borne more than one child; **~par′tite,** divided into many parts; **~phase,** (Electr.) = POLYPHASE; **~po′lar,** having many POLE²s; **~-purpose,** serving more than one purpose; **~ra′cial,** (composed) of many human races; **~-role,** having more than one role or function; **~-stage,** (of rocket etc.) having several stages of operation; **~-storey,** having several (esp. similarly designed) storeys; **~va′lent,** (Chem.) having a valence of more than two, or a variable valence; **~valve,** (of shell etc.) having several valves; **~vocal** (-ĭ′v-), having many meanings; **~-way,** having several paths of communication etc. [L (*multus* much, many; see -I-)]

multifār′ious *a.* having great variety; (w. *pl. n.*) many and various; hence **~LY²** *adv.*, **~NESS** *n.* [f. L *multifarius* + -OUS]

mŭ′ltiple *a.* & *n.* **1.** *a.* having several or many parts, elements, or individual components; (Bot., of fruit) collective; (w. *pl. n.*) many and various. **2.** **~-choice,** (of question in examination) accompanied by several possible answers from which what is incorrect is to be deleted; *multiple* PERSONALITY; **~poi′nding,** (Sc. Law) action by holder of goods etc. claimed by more than one other person, causing them to interplead; *multiple* SCLEROSIS; ||**~ shop** or **store** (with branches in various places); *multiple* STANDARD; **~ star,** several stars so close as to seem one, esp. when forming a connected system. **3.** *n.* quantity that contains another some number of times without remainder (*56 is a multiple of 7*; **least** or **lowest common ~,** least quantity that is a multiple of two or more given quantities); *multiple shop or store.* [F, f. LL *multiplus* f. L (as foll.)]

mŭ′ltiplĕx *a.*, & *v.t.* **1.** *a.* manifold, of many elements; involving simultaneous transmission of several messages along a channel of communication. **2.** *v.t.* transmit thus. [L (as MULTI-, *-plex -plicis* -fold)]

mŭ′ltipliable. See MULTIPLY¹.

mŭ′ltiplicable *a.* multipliable. [OF, or f. med. L *multiplicabilis* l. L (as MULTIPLY¹; see -ABLE)]

mŭltiplică′nd *n.* quantity to be multiplied by MULTI-PLIER. [f. med. L *multiplicandus* gerundive of L *multiplicare* (as MULTIPLY¹; see -ND¹)]

mŭltiplicā′tion *n.* multiplying, esp. the arithmetical process; **~ sign,** ×, as in 2 × 3; **~ table,** table of products of factors (esp. from 1 to 12) taken in pairs; so **mŭltipli′cative** *a.* [ME f. OF, or f. L *multiplicatio* (as MULTIPLY¹; see -ATION)]

mŭltipli′cĭty *n.* manifold variety, **a, the, ~** (great number) **of.** [f. LL *multiplicitas* (as MULTIPLEX; see -ITY)]

mŭ′ltipliēr *n.* In vbl senses; quantity by which MULTIPLICAND is multiplied; (Econ.) factor by which an increment of income exceeds the resulting increment of saving or investment; (Electr.) instrument for increasing a small current etc. so as to make it more easily used or measured. [ME, f. foll. + -ER¹]

mŭ′ltipl|ȳ¹ *v.* **1.** *v.t.* produce large number of (instances etc.); breed (animals), propagate (plants). **2.** *v.i.* increase in number esp. by procreation. **3.** *v.t.* obtain from (number, or abs.) another that is a specified number of times its value (*multiply 6 by 4 or 4 by 6* or arch. *6 into 4 and get 24*; *multiplying by ⅓ is the same as dividing by 3*). **4.** Hence **~ĪABLE** *a.* [ME, f. OF *multiplier* f. L *multiplicare* (as MULTIPLEX)]

mŭ′ltiplȳ² *adv.* In adj. senses. [f. MULTIPLE + -LY²]

mŭ′ltitūde *n.* numerousness; great number (*of*); large gathering of people, crowd; **the ~,** the common

---

people; **noun of ~,** collective noun. [ME f. OF, f. L *multitudo -dinis* (*multus* many; see -TUDE)]

mŭltitū′dinous *a.* very numerous; consisting of many individuals or elements; (of ocean etc.) vast; hence **~LY²** *adv.*, **~NESS** *n.* [f. L (as prec.) + -OUS]

mŭltivēr′sĭtȳ *n.* large university with many different departments. [f. MULTI- + UNIVERSITY]

multum in parvo (mŏoltum ĭn pār′vŏ, mŭ-) *n.* much in small compass. [L = much in little]

||**mŭ′lture** *n.* toll of grain or flour paid to miller. [ME, f. OF *mo(u)lture* f. med. L *molitura* (*molere molit-* grind; see -URE)]

mŭm¹ *int.* & *a.* (colloq.) **1.** *int.* silence! (esp. *mum′s the word*). **2.** *a.* silent (*keep mum*). [ME, imit. of closed lips]

mŭm² *v.i.* (-mm-). act in dumb show. [cf. prec., and MLG *mummen*]

mŭm³ *n.* (Hist.) kind of beer orig. brewed in Brunswick. [f. G *mumme*]

||**mŭm⁴** *n.* (colloq.) = MUMMY². [abbr.]

mŭ′mble *v.* & *n.* **1.** *v.i.* speak indistinctly. **2.** *v.t.* utter indistinctly; bite, chew, (as) with toothless gums. **3.** *n.* indistinct utterance. [ME *momele*, as MUM¹, -LE 3; cf. LG *mummelen*]

mŭmbō-jŭ′mbō *n.* (*pl.* **~s**). meaningless ritual; language or action intended to mystify or confuse; object of senseless veneration. [f. *Mumbo Jumbo,* grotesque idol said to have been worshipped by some Negro tribes]

mŭ′mchance (-ahns) *a.* & *adv.* (arch., literary, or dial.) silent(ly), saying nothing. [orig. *n.*, = dumb show, f. MLG *mummenschanze* masked serenade (*mummen* f. OF as foll.; *schanz* f. OF CHANCE¹)]

mŭ′mmer *n.* actor in traditional dumb show or (arch. sl.) in theatre. [ME, f. OF *momeur* (*momer* MUM²; see -ER²)]

mŭ′mmerȳ *n.* performance by mummers; ridiculous (esp. religious) ceremonial. [f. OF *momerie* (as prec.; see -ERY)]

mŭ′mmi|fȳ *v.t.* preserve (body) as mummy; shrivel, dry up, (tissues etc., esp. in *p.p.*); hence **~FICA′TION** *n.* [f. foll. + -FY]

mŭ′mmȳ¹ *n.* **1.** body of human being or animal embalmed for burial esp. in ancient Egypt; dried-up body. **2.** pulpy substance or mass, esp. *beat* (thing) *to a mummy.* **3.** rich brown pigment. [f. F *momie* f. med. L *mumia* f. Arab. *mūmiyā* f. Pers. *mūm* wax]

||**mŭ′mmȳ²** *n.* (colloq.) mother. [imit. of child's *pronunc*; cf MAMMA¹, -Y³]

mŭmp¹ *v.i.* (arch. or dial.) be silent and sullen; assume demure expression, whence **~′ING²** *a.* [imit. of mouth-shape]

||**mŭmp²** *v.i.* (arch. or dial.) beg, go about begging. [prob. f. obs. Du. *mompen* cheat]

mŭmps *n. pl.* (treated as *sing.*) contagious and infectious virus disease with swelling of parotid glands; sulks, whence **mŭ′mpISH¹** *a.* [16th c., f. MUMP¹]

mŭnch *v.t.* eat (food, or abs.) with much action of jaws, as cattle chew fodder, and usu. with evident enjoyment. [ME, imit.; cf. CRUNCH]

Münchau′sen (-z-) *n.* extravagantly mendacious story(-teller). [f. Baron **~,** hero of book of fantastic adventures written in English by R. E. Raspe, a German (1785), perh. based on life of Baron K. F. von *Münchhausen,* Ger. soldier d. 1797]

mŭ′ndāne *a.* of this world, worldly; of the universe, cosmic; dull, routine; hence **~LY²** (-nlĭ) *adv.*, **~NESS** (-n-n-) *n.* [ME, f. OF *mondain* f. LL *mundanus* f. L *mundus* world; see -ANE]

mŭ′ngo (-nggō) *n.* (*pl.* **~s**). wool from heavily felted substance, used in making cloth of poorer quality than shoddy. [poss. f. dial. *mong* mixture & Sc. man's Christian name *Mungo* applied to Yorks. dogs]

Mŭ′nich (-k) *n.* act of appeasement between nations or other groups. [f. the agreement to dismember Czechoslovakia made in 1938 at **~** in S. Germany]

mŭni′cipal *a.* **1.** of or under local self-government or corporate government of city or town; hence ∼ISM (2), ∼IST (2, 3), *ns.*, ∼IZE (3) *v.t.* **2.** carried on etc. by a municipality (*municipal debt, restaurant, trading, undertaking*); *municipal* CORPORATION. **3.** of particular State, opp. to international. **4.** Hence ∼LY² *adv.* [f. L *municipalis* (*municipium* f. *municeps -cipis* citizen who had privileges of Roman citizens f. *munia* civic offices + root of *capere* take); see -AL]

munici̇pa'li̇ty̆ *n.* town or district, having local self--government; governing body of this. [f. F *municipalité* (*municipal*, as prec.; see -ITY)]

muni'fic|ent *a.* splendidly generous, bountiful; hence or cogn. ∼ENCE *n.*, ∼entLY² *adv.* [f. L *munificent-*, var. stem of *munificus* (*munus* gift; see -FIC, -ENT)]

mu'niment *n.* (usu. in *pl.*) document kept as evidence of rights or privileges; archives. [ME f. OF, f. L *munimentum* defence, in med. L title-deed (*munire -it-* fortify; see -MENT)]

muni'tion *n.*, & *v.t.* **1.** *n.* (in *pl.*) military weapons, ammunition, equipment, and stores; hence ∼ER¹ *n.*, person who makes or supplies munitions. **2.** *v.t.* supply with munitions. [F, f. L *munitio -onis* fortification (as prec.; see -ITION)]

munnion. Var. of MULLION.

munshi. Var. of MOONSHEE.

munt (moŏ-) *n.* (S. Afr. sl., derog.; **R**). Black African. [f. Bantu *umuntu* person]

mu'ntjăk, -ăc, *n.* small deer orig. of SE Asia, of genus *Muntiacus*, the male with tusks and small antlers. [f. Sundanese *minchek*]

Muntz (-ts) *n.* ∼ (**metal**), alloy (60% copper, 40% zinc) used for sheathing ships etc. [f. G. F. ∼, Engl. manufacturer d. 1857]

mu'ŏn *n.* (Phys.) unstable elementary particle like electron but with mass about 200 times greater. [f. μ (MU) as symbol for it +-ON]

mur'age *n.* (Hist.) tax levied for building or repairing walls of town. [ME f. OF, in med. L *muragium* f. OF *mur* f. L *murus* wall; see -AGE]

mur'al *a.* & *n.* **1.** *a.* of or like a wall; on a wall (*mural paintings*); ∼ **crown,** (Rom. Ant.) crown or garland given to soldier who first scaled wall of besieged town. **2.** *n.* mural painting etc. [F, f. L *muralis* (*murus* wall; see -AL)]

mur'der¹ *n.* unlawful killing of human being with malice aforethought; (fig.) highly dangerous or troublesome state of affairs; (as *int.*, expr. alarm; **cry blue** ∼, (sl.) make extravagant outcry); **get away with** ∼, (colloq.) do whatever one wishes; JUDICIAL *murder*; (prov.) ∼ **will out** (cannot be hidden). [OE *morthor,* = Goth. *maurthr* f. Gmc *murthram* f. IE *mrt–*, & OF *murdre* f. Gmc]

mur'der² *v.t.* kill (human being) unlawfully with malice aforethought; kill wickedly or inhumanly; (colloq.) utterly defeat, spoil by bad performance, mispronunciation, etc.; hence ∼ER¹, ∼ESS¹, *ns.* [ME, f. prec.]

mur'derous *a.* (Of person, weapon, action, etc.) capable of, bent on, involving, murder or great harm; hence ∼LY² *adv.* [f. MURDER¹ + -OUS]

mure *v.t.* immure; wall or shut *up.* [ME, f. OF *murer* (*mur*; SEE MURAGE)]

mur'|ex *n.* (*pl.* ∼**ices** *pr.* -īsēz, *or* ∼**exes**). mollusc of genus *Murex*, yielding purple dye. [L]

muri̇ä'ti̇c *a.* (arch.) hydrochloric *acid*; so **mur'i̇ATE¹** (3) *n.*, chloride. [f. L *muriaticus* pickled in brine (*muria*; see -ATIC)]

mur'ine *a.* of or like mice. [f. L *murinus* (*mus muris* mouse; see -INE¹)]

murk *n.* & *a.* **1.** *n.* darkness; air obscured by fog etc. **2.** *a.* (arch.) (Of night, day, place, etc.) dark; misty, dense. [prob. f. Scand.; cf. ON *myrkr*]

mur'k|y̆ *a.* dark, gloomy; (of darkness) thick; dirty; suspiciously obscure (*murky past*); hence ∼i̇LY² *adv.*, ∼i̇NESS *n.* [ME, f. prec. + -Y²]

mur'mur¹ *n.* subdued continuous sound, as of waves, brook, etc.; (Med.) such sound heard in auscultation

of heart and indicating abnormality; subdued expression of discontent; softly spoken or nearly inarticulate word or speech; hence ∼ous *a.* [ME, f. OF *murmure* or f. L *murmur*; cf. foll.]

mur'mur² *v.* **1.** *v.i.* make subdued continuous sound; complain in low tones, grumble, (*at, against*). **2.** *v.t.* utter (words) in low voice. [ME, f. OF *murmurer* f. L *murmurare*; cf. Gk *mormurō* (of water) roar, Skr. *marmaras* noisy]

mur'phy̆ *n.* (sl.) potato. [Ir. surname]

mu'rra. See MURRHINE.

mur'rain (-rĭn) *n.* infectious disease in cattle; (arch.) **a** ∼ (plague) **on** you! [ME, f. AF *moryn*, OF *morine* (*morir* f. Rom. **morire* for L *mori* die)]

mur'rey *a.* & *n.* (arch.) (of) the colour of a mulberry, purple-red. [ME, f. OF *moré* f. med. L *moratus* (*morum* mulberry; see -Y⁴)]

mur'rhine (-rĭn) *a.* of a precious substance called **murra,** used in ancient Rome; ∼ **glass,** modern delicate glassware from the East, with coloured metal particles embedded in it. [f. L *murr(h)inus* (*murra* f. late Gk *morria*; see -INE¹)]

murther. Var. (arch.) of MURDER¹,².

Mus. B(ac). *abbrs.* Bachelor of Music. [f. L *Musicae Baccalaureus*]

mu'scadine *n.* musk-flavoured kind of grape. [perh. Engl. form. f. Prov. MUSCAT; see -INE⁴]

mu'scarine *n.* poisonous alkaloid from fungus *Amanita muscaria.* [f. L *muscarius* (*musca* fly; see -ARY¹, -INE⁵)]

mu'scat *n.* muscadine; strong sweet white wine from muscadines. [F, f. Prov. *muscat muscade* a. (*musc* MUSK; see -ATE¹)]

muscatě'l, -dě'l, *ns.* = prec.; raisin from muscadine. [ME f. OF, f. Prov. **muscadel* dim. of *muscat* (see prec.)]

mu'scle (-sel) *n.*, & *v.i.* **1.** *n.* any of the contractile fibrous bands or bundles that produce movement in animal body; **not move a** ∼, be perfectly motionless. **2.** that part of the animal body which is composed of muscles, chief constituent of flesh; (muscular) power. **3.** ∼**-bound,** with muscles stiff and inelastic through excessive exercise or training; ∼**man** (with highly developed muscles, esp. as intimidator). **4.** Hence ∼LESS (-l-l-) *a.* **5.** *v.i.* (sl.) ∼ **in,** intrude by violent means. [F, f. L *musculus* dim. of *mus* mouse, f. fancied mouselike form of some muscles]

mu̇sco'log|y̆ *n.* bryology; so ∼IST (3) *n.* [f. mod. L *muscologia* f. L *muscus* moss; see -LOGY]

mu̇scova'do (-vah'-) *n.* (*pl.* ∼s). unrefined sugar got from juice of sugar-cane by evaporation and draining off molasses. [f. Sp. *mascabado* (sugar) of lowest quality]

mu̇'scovite¹ *n.* common mica. [f. obs. syn. MUSCOVY *glass* + -ITE¹]

Mu̇'scovite² *n.* & *a.* (arch.) Russian; (citizen) of Moscow. [f. mod. L *Muscovita* (*Muscovia* = foll.; see -ITE¹)]

Mu̇'scovy̆ *n.* **1.** (arch.) Russia. **2.** ∼ **duck,** tropical Amer. duck (*Cairina moschata*) with slight smell of musk. [f. obs. F *Muscovie* f. med. L *Moscovia* f. Russ. *Moskva* Moscow]

mu̇'scular *a.* of or affecting the muscles; having well--developed muscles; ∼ **Christianity,** Christian life of cheerful physical activity as described in writings of C. Kingsley; *muscular* DYSTROPHY, STOMACH; hence **mu̇scula'rity** *n.* [f. earlier *musculous* (as MUSCLE; see -AR¹)]

mu̇'sculature *n.* muscular system of body or organ. [F, f. L (as MUSCLE; see -URE)]

Mus.D(oc). *abbrs.* Doctor of Music. [f. L *Musicae Doctor*]

muse¹ (-z) *n.* **1.** the Muses, (Gk & Rom. Myth.) nine goddesses, daughters of Zeus and Mnemosyne, inspirers of poetry, music, drama, etc. **2.** (**the**) ∼, poet's inspiring goddess, poet's genius. [ME f. OF, of f. L f. Gk *mousa*]

mūse[2] (-z) *v. & n.* (literary). **1.** *v.i.* ponder, reflect, (*on, upon*); gaze meditatively (*on* scene etc.). **2.** *v.t.* say meditatively. **3.** *n.* (arch.) fit of abstraction. [ME, f. OF *muser* to waste time f. Rom. *musare, perh. f. med. L *musum* muzzle]

mūse'tte (-z-) *n.* kind of small bagpipe with bellows; soft pastoral tune imitating bagpipe's sound; dance for which this served; reed stop on organ; *small knapsack. [ME f. OF, dim. of *muse* bagpipe; see -ETTE]

mūse'um (-z-) *n.* building used for storing and exhibition of objects illustrating antiquities, natural history, arts, etc.; ~ **piece,** specimen of art, manufacture, etc., fit for a museum, (derog.) old-fashioned or quaint person, machine, etc.; hence **mūsĕŏ'LOGY** (-z-) *n.* [L, f. Gk *mouseion* seat of the Muses (*mousa*)]

mŭsh[1] *n.* soft pulp; *maize porridge; feeble sentimentality; hence ~'Y[2] *a.* [app. var. of MASH[1]]

mŭsh[2] *v.i.*, & *n.* (N. Amer.) (go on) journey across snow with dog-sledge; (in *imper.*, as command to dogs pulling sledge) get moving. [prob. corrupt. f. F *marchons* imper. of *marcher* advance]

mŭ'shroom (-ŏŏm, -ŏŏm) *n.*, & *v.i.* **1.** *n.* edible fungus, esp. *Agaricus campestris*, with stem and domed cap, proverbial for rapid growth (~ **growth** etc., sudden development or thing suddenly developed); (fig.) upstart; ~ (**cloud**), cloud of mushroom shape esp. from nuclear explosion; ~-**colour**(**ed**), pale yellowish-brown. **2.** *v.i.* gather mushrooms; spring up rapidly; expand and flatten like mushroom cap. [ME, f. OF *mousseron* f. LL *mussirio -onis*]

mŭ'sic (-z-) *n.* **1.** art of combining sounds of voice(s) or instrument(s) to achieve beauty of form and expression of emotion; sounds so produced; pleasant sound, e.g. song of bird, murmur of brook, cry of hounds; SET[1] 9 *to music*; ~ **to** one's **ears,** something very pleasant to hear; *music of the* SPHERES. **2.** musical compositions; written or printed score of musical composition. **3.** FACE[2] *the music*; **rough** ~, noisy uproar, esp. with vexatious intention. **4.** *~ **box,** = MUSICAL *box*; ~ **centre,** equipment combining radio, record-player, and tape-recorder; ~ **drama,** opera without formal arias etc. and governed by dramatic considerations; ||~-**hall,** (place for) singing, dancing, variety, and other entertainments; ~-**paper** (with printed staves etc. for writing music score). [ME, f. OF *musique* f. L f. Gk *mousikē* (*tekhnē* art) of the Muses (*mousa* MUSE[1]; see -IC)]

mŭ'sical (-z-) *a. & n.* **1.** *a.* of music; (of sounds, voice, etc.) melodious, harmonious; fond of or skilled in music; set to or accompanied by music. **2.** ||~ **box,** mechanical musical instrument played by causing toothed cylinder to strike comblike metal plate within box; ~ **chairs,** parlour game in which players circulate round chairs one fewer than they till music ceases, when the one who finds no seat is eliminated, and a chair is removed before the next round; ~ **comedy,** light dramatic entertainment of songs, dialogue, and dancing connected by a slender plot; ~ **film** (in which music is an important feature); ~ **glasses,** instrument in which notes are produced by rubbing graduated glass bowls or tubes; *musical* INSTRUMENT; ~ **saw,** bent saw played with violin-bow; *musical* SOUND[2]. **3.** Hence ~ITY (-ă'l-), ~NESS *ns.*, ~LY[2] *adv.* **4.** *n.* musical film or comedy. [ME f. OF, f. med. L *musicalis* f. L *musica*; see prec., -AL]

***mūsica'le** (-zīkah'l) *n.* musical party. [F, fem. a. (as prec.)]

mŭsi'cian (-zī'shan) *n.* person skilled in science or practice of music. [ME, f. OF *musicien* (*musique*; see MUSIC, -ICIAN)]

mŭsicŏ'log|y̆ (-z-) *n.* study of music other than that directed to proficiency in performance or composition; hence ~IST (3) *n.*, **mŭsicŏlŏ'gICAL** (-z-) *a.* [f. F *musicologie* or MUSIC + -o- + -LOGY]

musique concrète (mūzēk kawṅkrĕ't) *n.* = CONCRETE[1] *music*. [F]

mŭsk *n.* **1.** odoriferous reddish-brown substance secreted in gland by male musk-deer, used as basis of perfumes and as stimulant etc.; plant with musky smell, or *Mimulus moschatus* (which formerly smelt of musk). **2.** ~-**deer,** small hornless ruminant of Central Asia, of genus *Moschus*; ~-**duck,** (1) = MUSCOVY *duck*, (2) Australian duck (*Biziura lobata*) with musky smell; ~-**melon,** common yellow melon (*Cucumis melo*); ~-**ox,** shaggy ruminant with curved horns (*Ovibos moschatus*) found in Arctic America; ~-**rat,** (fur of) large N. Amer. aquatic rodent (*Ondatra zibethica*) with musky smell; ~-**rose,** rambling rose (*Rosa moschata* etc.) with large white flowers having musky fragrance; ~-**thistle,** nodding thistle (*Carduus nutans*), whose flowers have musky fragrance; ~-**tree, -wood,** Australian tree. esp. of genus *Olearia*, with musky smell. **3.** Hence ~'Y[2] *a.* [ME, f. LL *muscus* f. Pers. *mušk*, perh. f. Skr. *muṣka* scrotum (from shape of musk-deer's gland)]

mŭ'skĕg *n.* level swamp or bog in Canada. [Cree]

***mŭ'skellŭnge** (-nj) *n.* = MASKINONGE. [Algonquian]

mŭ'skĕt *n.* (Hist.) infantry soldier's (esp. smooth-bored) light gun; ~-**shot,** (range of) shot fired from musket; hence or cogn. ~EER' *n.*, soldier armed with musket, ~OO'N *n.*, short musket with wide bore, ~RY (1, 5) *n.* [f. F *mousquet* f. It. *moschetto* crossbow bolt (*mosca* fly)]

Mu'slim (mŏŏ'-, mŭ'-), **Mŏ'slem,** (-s-, -z-) *a. & n.* believer in Islam. [f. Arab. *muslim*, part. of *aslama*; see ISLAM]

mŭ'slin (-z-) *n.* fine delicately woven cotton fabric; *cotton cloth in plain weave; hence ~ED[2] (-nd) *a.* [f. F *mousseline* f. It. *mussolina* (*Mussolo* Mosul in Iraq, where it was made; see -INE[1])]

mŭ'smon *n.* moufflon. [f. L *musimo* f. Gk *mousmōn*]

mŭ'squash (-ŏsh) *n.* (fur of) MUSK-rat. [Algonquian]

***mŭss** *v.t.*, & *n.* (colloq.) **1.** *v.t.* ~ (**up**), disarrange, throw into disorder. **2.** *n.* state of confusion, untidiness, mess; hence ~'Y[2] *a.* [app. var. of MESS[1]]

mŭ'ssel *n.* bivalve mollusc of genus *Mytilus* (marine, edible), *Unio* (freshwater, pearl-forming), etc.; ~ **plum,** (arch.) dark purple plum. [ME, f. OE *mus*(*c*)*le*, = OS, OHG *muscula*, & f. MLG *mussel*, f. Rom. *muscula bivalve, fem corresp. to L *musculus* (as MUSCLE)]

Mŭ'ssulman *n.* (*pl.* ~**mans** or ~**men**) & *a.* (arch.) Muslim. [f. Pers. *musulmān*, orig. a. f. *muslim* (as MUSLIM)]

mŭst[1] *n.* new wine; grape-juice before fermentation is complete. [OE, f. L *mustum* neut. (as n.) of *mustus* new]

mŭst[2] *n.* mustiness, mould. [back-form. f. MUSTY]

mŭst[3], **mŭsth** (-t), *a. & n.* **1.** *a.* (Of male elephant or camel) in state of frenzy. **2.** *n.* this state. [f. Urdu f. Pers. *mast* intoxicated]

mŭst[4] (or, *when unstressed*, must) *v. aux.* (*pres.* and *past* **must,** *neg.* **must not,** (colloq.) **mustn't** *pr.* mŭ'sent; no other parts used) & *n.* **1.** *v.* be obliged to (do) (*you must find it,* opp. *you do not have to or need not find it, past you had to find it; you knew you must find it; it must be found*); (interrog., iron.) *must you slam the door?*; (ellipt.) *I must* (go) *away; if I must, I will; I must down to the seas again.* **2.** ought to (do) (w. necessity less emphasized: *we must see what can be done; I must ask you to retract that*); **you** ~ **know,** I now tell you; I ~ **say** (cannot refrain from saying). **3.** be certain to (do) (*you must lose whichever happens,* opp. *you cannot lose*); *you* ~ **be** (surely are) *aware of this, joking, the secretary; he* ~ **be** (clearly is) *mad*; past tense, reporting reflection made at the time) *it was too late now to retreat, he must make good his word or incur lasting disgrace*; (as past or historic present, w. reference to perverse destiny) *just as I was getting better, what must I do but break my leg?, just as I was busiest, he must come worrying.* **4.** ~ **have** done (1) surely did or has done (*you must have known quite well what I meant; it must have stopped raining by now*), (2) necessarily would have done (*you must have caught it if you had run*); must NEEDS

5. (w. neg. belonging in sense to dependent vb.; cf. MAY¹) *you must not do it*, opp. *you may do it*; *it must not be done*; *you must not infer* (must avoid the inference); *you must never contradict*. **6.** *n.* (colloq.) *a* thing that cannot or should not be overlooked or missed. [OE *mōste* past of *mōt* may, pret.-pres. = OS *mōt, muot*, OHG *muoz*, Goth. *gamōtan* find room]

*mustache. See MOUSTACHE.

musta′chio (-ah′shō) *n.* (*pl.* ∿s). (arch.) moustache; hence ∿ED² (-ōd) *a.* [f. Sp. *mostacho* & f. It. (as MOUSTACHE)]

mŭ′stăng *n.* wild horse of Mexico and California; ∿ (small red Texas) **grape.** [f. Sp. *mestengo* f. *mesta* company of graziers, & Sp. *mostrenco*]

mŭ′stard *n.* plant of genus *Brassica* with pods and yellow flowers, esp. **black and white** ∿, seeds of which are ground, made into paste, and used as condiment (‖**English** ∿) or for poultice or ∿ **plaster;** brownish-yellow colour; *(sl.) thing that provides zest; ***cut the** ∿, (sl.) reach requisite standard; **grain of** ∿ **seed,** small thing capable of vast development (Matt. 13:31); KEEN³ *as mustard*; ‖∿ **and cress,** white mustard with cress used in seed-leaf for salad; **field** ∿, charlock; ‖**French** ∿ (mixed with vinegar); ∿ **gas,** colourless oily liquid, whose vapour is a powerful irritant and vesicant; ∿-**pot** (for table mustard). [ME, f. OF *mo(u)starde,* f. Rom. *mosto MUST¹; orig. the condiment as prepared w. must]

mŭ′ster¹ *n.* assembling of persons for inspection etc. (**pass** ∿, be accepted as adequate); assembly, collection; ∿-**book** (for registering military forces); ∿-**roll,** official list of officers and men in army or ship's company (lit. or fig.). [ME f. OF *mo(u)stre* f. Rom. n. (*mostrare v. f. L *monstrare* show)]

mŭ′ster² *v.* **1.** *v.t.* collect (orig. soldiers) for inspection, to check numbers, etc.; *∿ **in,** enrol (recruits); *∿ **out,** discharge (soldiers). **2.** *v.t.* & *i.* collect, get together. **3.** *v.t.* ∿ (**up**), summon (courage, strength, etc.). [ME, f. OF *mo(u)strer* f. L (as prec.)]

musth. See MUST³.

mŭ′st|ў *a.* mouldy; of mouldy or stale smell or taste; (fig.) stale, antiquated; hence ∿iNESS *n.* [perh. alt. f. *moisty* (MOIST) by assoc. w. MUST¹]

mū′table *a.* liable to change; fickle; hence **mūt-** ABI′LITY *n.* [f. L *mutabilis* (*mutare* change; see -ABLE)]

mū′tagen *n.* (Biol.) agent causing mutation; hence ∿IC (-ĕ′n-) *a.* [f. MUTATION + -GEN]

mū′tant *a.* & *n.* (Biol.) (form) resulting from mutation. [f. L *mutare* change; see -ANT]

mūtā′te *v.t.* & *i.* (cause to) undergo mutation. [back-form. f. foll.]

mūtā′tion *n.* **1.** change, alteration; (Biol.) genetic change which when transmitted to offspring gives rise to heritable variation; mutant; ∿ **stop,** (Mus.) organ stop in which notes produced are not at normal pitch but at that of some harmonic (other than mere octaves). **2.** (Gram., of vowel) = UMLAUT, (of consonant in Celtic language) change determined by preceding word. [ME, f. L *mutatio* (*mutare* change; see -ATION)]

mutatis mutandis (mootahtĭs mootă′ndĭs) *adv.* with due alteration of details (in comparing cases). [L]

mŭtch *n.* (dial.) woman's or child's linen cap. [ME, f. MDu. *mutse,* MHG *mütze* f. med. L *almucia* AMICE²]

mūte¹ *a.* & *n.* **1.** *a.* silent; not emitting articulate sound; (of hounds) not giving tongue; (Law) **stand** ∿ **of malice,** deliberately refuse to plead. **2.** (Of person or animal) dumb; not expressed in speech (*mute appeal, adoration*); temporarily bereft of speech; ∿ **swan,** common white swan. **3.** (Of consonant) plosive; (of letter) silent. **4.** Hence ∿LY² (-tlī) *adv.,* ∿′NESS (-tn-) *n.* **5.** *n.* mute consonant; dumb person (DEAF *mute*); actor whose part is in dumb show; dumb servant in oriental countries; hired mourner; clamp on bridge for deadening resonance of strings of violin

etc., pad or cone for deadening sound of wind instrument. [ME f. OF *muet,* dim. of *mu* f. L *mutus;* assim. to L]

mūte² *v.t.* deaden, muffle, the sound of (esp. musical instrument); tone down, (in *p.p.,* of colour etc.) subdued. [f. prec.]

mūte³ *v.i.* & *t.* (arch.) (Of bird) void faeces, discharge thus. [ME, f. OF *meutir, esmeutir, esmeltir* f. Frank. *smeltjan SMELT¹]

mū′til|āte *v.t.* deprive (person etc.) of limb or organ; cut off, destroy the use of, (limb etc.); render (book etc.) imperfect by excision etc.; hence or cogn. ∿A′TION, ∿āTOR, *ns.* [f. L *mutilare* (*mutilus* maimed) + -ATE³]

mūtineer′ *n.* one who mutinies. [f. F *mutinier* (*mutin* rebellious f. *muete* movement f. Rom. *movita f. L *movēre* move)]

mū′tinous *a.* rebellious; tending to mutiny; hence ∿LY² *adv.* [f. obs. *mutine* rebellion f. F *mutin* (see prec.) + -OUS]

mū′tinȳ *n.,* & *v.i.* **1.** *n.* open revolt against constituted authority, esp. by soldiers etc. against officers; **the** (**Indian** or **Sepoy**) **M**∿, revolt of Bengal native troops, 1857–8; ‖**M**∿ **Act,** (Hist.) annual ordinance dealing with offences against military and naval discipline. **2.** *v.i.* revolt, engage in mutiny, (*against,* or abs.). [f. obs. *mutine* v. or n. f. as prec., + -Y¹]

mū′tism *n.* muteness; silence; dumbness. [f. F *mutisme* f. L (as MUTE¹); see -ISM]

mŭtt *n.* (sl.) ignorant, stupid, or blundering person; (derog.) dog. [abbr. of *mutton-head*]

mū′tter *v.* & *n.* **1.** *v.i.* speak low in barely audible manner; murmur, grumble, (*against, at*). **2.** *v.t.* utter (words etc.) in low tone; (fig.) say in secret. **3.** *n.* muttering; muttered words. [ME, rel. to MUTE¹; see -ER⁵]

mŭ′tton *n.* flesh of sheep as food; (joc.) sheep (**return to** one's ∿**s,** [after F phr.] come back to one's main topic; DEAD *as mutton;* **eat** person's ∿, (arch.) dine with him; LEG *of mutton;* ∿-**bird,** (Austral.) sooty shearwater; ∿ **chop,** (1) piece of mutton (usu. rib and half vertebra to which it is attached) for frying etc., (2) side-whiskers shaped like this; ∿ **dressed as lamb,** (colloq.) elderly woman got up to look young; ∿-**head,** (colloq.) dull, stupid person; hence ∿Y² *a.* [ME f. OF *moton,* f. med. L *multo-onis* prob. f. Gaulish]

mū′tūal *a.* **1.** (Of feeling, action, etc.) felt, done, by each to(wards) the other (*mutual affection, benefit, suspicion*); standing in (specified) relation to each other (*mutual well-wishers*); ∿ **admiration society,** set of persons who overestimate each other's merits; *∿ **fund,** unit trust; ∿ **induction** (Electr., between adjacent circuits); ∿ **insurance company** (in which some or all of the profits are divided among the policy-holders). **2.** (colloq.) common to two or more persons (*our mutual friend, interest*). **3.** Hence ∿ITY (-ă′l-) *n.,* ∿LY² *adv.* [ME, f. OF *mutuel* f. L *mutuus* mutual, borrowed, cogn. w. *mutare* change; see -AL]

mū′tūal‖ism *n.* doctrine that mutual dependence is necessary for social well-being; mutually beneficial symbiosis; so ∿IST (2) *n.* [f. prec. + -ISM]

*mū′tūel *n.* totalizator. [abbr. of PARI-MUTUEL]

mū′tūle *n.* (Archit.) block projecting under cornice in Doric order. [f. L *mutulus*]

muu-muu (mōō′mōō) *n.* woman's loose brightly-coloured dress. [Hawaiian]

Mū′zak *n.* (P) system of music transmission by wire or cable for playing in public place; recorded light music as background. [cf. MUSIC]

muzhik. See MOUJIK.

‖mŭzz *v.t.* (sl.) make muzzy. [18th c., of unkn. orig.]

mŭ′zzle¹ *n.* projecting part of animal's head including nose and mouth; open end of firearm; contrivance of strap or wire put over animal's head to prevent its biting, eating, etc.; ∿-**loader,** gun that is loaded through the muzzle; ∿ **velocity** (with which projectile leaves muzzle of gun). [ME, f. OF *musel* f.

Gallo-Rom. *musellum dim. of med. L musum; cf. MUSE²]

mŭ′zzle² v.t. put muzzle on (animal, its mouth, or fig. a person); impose silence upon; (Naut.) take in (sail). [ME, f. prec.]

mŭ′zz|y̆ a. dull, spiritless; mentally hazy; stupid from liquor-drinking; hence ∼ĭLY² adv., ∼ĭNESS n. [18th c., of unkn. orig.; cf. MUZZ]

MV abbr. motor vessel; muzzle velocity.

Mv symb. (arch.) mendelevium.

||MVO abbr. Member of the Royal Victorian Order.

MW abbr. megawatt(s).

mW abbr. milliwatt(s).

Mx. abbr. maxwell(s); Middlesex (former county in England).

my̆ (when unstressed mī or mĭ) poss. pron. attrib. of me (in pred. & abs. use, & arch. before vowel, **mine**: my house; mine eyes have seen; this one is mine; for phrs. see HER², HERS); my LADY, LORD; **me and mine** (my relatives); (in affectionate, sympathetic, jocular, or patronizing use, prefixed to some wds in voc.) my boy, child, dear (fellow), friend, man; (in excl. of surprise) my!, oh my!, my GOD!, my WORD¹!, etc. [ME mī, reduced f. mīn MINE³]

MY abbr. motor yacht.

my̆ă′lgia (-ja) n. (Path.) pain in muscle(s). [mod. L, f. Gk mus muscle; see -ALGIA]

my̆′alism n. sorcery akin to obeah, practised esp. in W. Indies [f. myal, prob. of W. Afr. orig., | -ISM]

my̆′all n. Austral. acacia, with hard scented wood used for fences and tobacco-pipes. [f. Aboriginal maiāl]

my̆asthē′nia n. weakness of muscles. [mod. L, f. Gk mus muscle; cf. ASTHENIA]

my̆cē′li|um n. (pl. ∼a). (Bot.) vegetative part of fungus, consisting of microscopic threadlike hyphae; hence ∼AL a. [mod. L, f. Gk mukēs mushroom, after EPITHELIUM]

My̆cēnae′an a. (Archaeol.) of the late Helladic culture (c. 1500–1100 BC) illustrated by remains at Mycenae in Greece, and by Homer. [f. L Mycenaeus + -AN]

my̆cŏ′log|y̆ n. study of fungi; hence ∼IST (3) n. [f. Gk mukēs mushroom + -o- + -LOGY]

my̆corrhī′z|a (-orī′-) n. (pl. ∼ae). symbiotic fungus in plant roots; hence ∼AL a. [mod. L, f. as prec. + Gk rhiza root]

my̆cō′s|is n. (pl. ∼es pr. -ēz). presence of, disease caused by, parasitic fungi. [f. as MYCOLOGY + -OSIS]

my̆cŏ′trophy̆ n. condition of plant having mycorrhizae in its roots and perhaps thus being helped to assimilate nutrients. [f. G mykotrophie f. as MYCO-LOGY + Gk trophē nourishment]

my̆drī′asis n. excessive dilatation of eye-pupil. [L, f. Gk mudriasis]

my̆′ĕlin n. white substance forming sheath of nerve--fibres. [f. as foll. + -IN]

my̆ĕlī′tis n. inflammation of spinal cord. [mod. L, f. Gk muelos marrow; see -ITIS]

my̆ĕlō′ma n. (pl. ∼s or ∼ta). tumour of bone--marrow. [f. as prec. + -OMA]

my̆′lodŏn n. extinct gigantic sloth of genus Mylodon, with cylindrical teeth. [mod. L, f. Gk mule mill, molar, + odous odontos tooth]

myna(h). See MINA².

my̆nheer′ n. Title used of or to Dutch-speaking man, corresponding to Mr or Sir; Dutchman. [f. Du. mijnheer (mijn my, heer master)]

my̆o- comb. form. muscle, as: ∼**car′dium**, muscular substance of heart; ∼**logy** (-ŏ′l-), science of muscles. [f. Gk mus muos muscle + -o-]

my̆′ōpe n. short-sighted person. [F, f. LL f. Gk muōps (muŏ shut, ōps eye)]

my̆ō′pia n. short-sightedness (lit. or fig.); hence **my̆ŏ′p**IC a. [mod. L, f. as prec.; see -IA¹]

my̆ō′sis. See MIOSIS.

my̆osō′tis, my̆′osōte, n. small plant of genus Myosotis

with blue, pink, or white flowers, esp. forget-me-not. [f. L f. Gk muosōtis (mus muos mouse, ous ōtos ear)]

my̆′riad a. & n. (poet. or rhet.) ten thousand; (of) indefinitely great number. [f. LL f. Gk murias -ados (murioi 10,000)]

my̆′riapŏd, my̆′riopŏd, a. & n. (small crawling arthropod) with many legs, of the group Myriapoda comprising centipedes and millepedes. [f. mod. L Myriapoda f. as prec. + Gk pous podos foot]

my̆r′midon n. hired ruffian; base servant (∼ **of the law**, policeman, bailiff, etc.). [f. L f. Gk Murmidones pl., warlike Thessalian people who followed Achilles to Troy]

my̆rŏ′balan n. astringent plumlike fruit of E. Ind. tree of genus Terminalia, used in ink and in dyeing, tanning, etc. [F, or f. L myrobalanum f. Gk murobalanos (muron unguent, balanos acorn)]

myrrh¹ (mêr) n. gum resin from trees of genus Commiphora, used in perfumery and medicine, and in incense; hence ∼IC, ∼′Y², adjs. [OE myrra, myrre, = OS, OHG myrra f. L myrr(h)a f. Gk murra, of Semitic orig.]

myrrh² (mêr) n. SWEET cicely. [f. L f. Gk murris]

myr′tle n. plant of genus Myrtus, esp. **common** ∼, shrub with dark shiny evergreen leaves, white scented flowers, and black berries, sacred to Venus; *peri-winkle plant; BOG¹ myrtle; so **myrta′ceous** (mêrtā′shus) a., of family Myrtaceae including myrtles. [ME, f. med. L myrtilla, -us, dim. of L f. Gk murtos]

my̆sĕ′lf pron. **1.** Emphat. form corresp. to I² or ME¹ (I saw it myself); I ∼ (for my part) am doubtful; for phrs. see HERSELF 1. **2.** Refl. form corresp. to ME¹ (cf. HER-SELF 2). **3.** (poet.) = I² (myself am blind). [f. ME¹ + SELF; my- partly after herself regarded as f. HER²]

my̆′stagŏgue (-ŏg) n. teacher of mystical doctrines, esp. (Gk Ant.) to candidates for initiation in Eleusinian and other mysteries; hence **my̆stagŏ′g-**IC(AL) adjs. [F, or f. L f. Gk mustagōgos (mustēs, see MYSTIC; agōgos -leading)]

my̆stēr′ious a. full of, or wrapped in, mystery; (of person) delighting in mystery; hence ∼LY² adv., ∼NESS n. [f. F mystérieux (mystère f. OF as foll.; see -OUS)]

my̆′stery̆¹ n. **1.** hidden or inexplicable matter; **make a** ∼ **of**, treat as impressive secret. **2.** secrecy, obscurity, (is wrapped in mystery); (practice of) making a secret of (unimportant) things. **3.** religious truth divinely revealed, esp. one beyond human reason; religious rite, esp. (in pl.) Eucharist. **4.** (in pl.) secret religious rites of Greeks, Romans, etc. **5.** miracle play. **6.** ∼ (**novel, play,** etc.), fictional work in which reader etc. is invited to try to identify murderer etc.; ∼ **ship,** warship disguised as tramp steamer etc. to decoy submarines in 1914–18 war; ∼ **tour** or **trip,** pleasure excursion to unspecified destination. [ME, f. AF *misterie, OF mistere or f. L f. Gk mustērion, cogn. w. MYSTIC]

my̆′stery̆² n. (arch.) handicraft, trade, esp. (in in-dentures) art and mystery. [ME, f. med. L mi(ni)sterium (MINISTRY), assoc. w. prec.]

my̆′stic a. & n. **1.** a. spiritually allegorical or symbolic; occult, esoteric; of hidden meaning, mysterious; mysterious and awe-inspiring. **2.** n. one who seeks by contemplation and self-surrender to obtain union with or absorption into the Deity, or who believes in spiritual apprehension of truths beyond the under-standing. **3.** Hence ∼ISM (3) n. (often derog.). [ME, f. OF mystique or f. L f. Gk mustikos (mustēs initiated person f. muō close eyes or lips, initiate; see -IC)]

my̆′stical a. of mystics or mysticism; having direct spiritual significance; hence ∼LY² adv. [ME, f. as prec. + -ICAL]

my̆′sti|fy̆ v.t. hoax, make use of credulity of; bewilder; wrap up in mystery; so ∼FICA′TION n. [f. F mystifier (irreg. f. as MYSTIC or MYSTERY¹; see -FY)]

my̆sti′que (-tē′k) n. atmosphere of mystery and

veneration investing some creeds, doctrines, arts, professions, etc., or personages; any professional skill or technique which mystifies and impresses the layman. [F, f. OF as MYSTIC]

mȳth n. traditional narrative usu. involving supernatural or fancied persons etc. and embodying popular ideas on natural or social phenomena etc.; such narratives collectively; allegory (*Platonic myth*); fictitious person or thing or idea; so ∼IC(AL) *adjs.*, ∼'ICALLY *adv.* [f. mod. L *mythus* f. LL *mythos* f. Gk *muthos*]

mȳ'thic|ize, -|īse (-īz), *v.t.* treat (story etc.) as a myth, interpret mythically; so ∼ISM (1), ∼IST (1), *ns.* [f. MYTHIC + -IZE]

mȳtho- *comb. form.* myth, as: ∼**ge'nesis,** production of myths; ∼**grapher** (-ŏ'g-), compiler of myths; ∼**graphy** (-ŏ'g-), representation of myths in plastic art; ∼**ma'nia,** excessive tendency to tell lies;

∼**poe'ia** (-pē'a), construction of myths; ∼**poe'ic** (-pē'ĭk), making, or productive of, myths. [f. Gk *muthos* myth + -o-]

mȳthŏ'log|ȳ n. body of myths, esp. relating to particular person or subject; study of myths; hence or cogn. ∼ER[1], ∼IST (3), *ns.*, **mȳtholŏ'gic(AL)** *adjs.*, ∼IZE (2, 3) *v.t. & i.* [ME, f. F *mythologie* or f. LL f. Gk *muthologia* (as prec.; see -LOGY)]

mȳ'th|us n. (*pl.* ∼**i** *pr.* -ī). (arch.) myth. [mod. L (see MYTH)]

mȳxoedē'ma, *mȳxed-, (-ed-) *n.* metabolic disease caused by deficient action of thyroid gland, with thickening of subcutaneous tissues and loss of physical and mental energy. [f. Gk *muxa* mucus + OEDEMA]

mȳxō'ma n. (*pl.* ∼**s** or ∼**ta**). tumour of mucous or gelatinous tissue; hence ∼**to'sis** (-ōm-, -om-) *n.*, virus disease causing myxomas in rabbits. [mod. L, f. Gk *muxa* mucus; see -OMA]

N

N, n, (ĕn) *n.* (*pl.* **Ns** *or* **N's**). fourteenth letter of alphabet; (Print.) en; (Math.) indefinite number; **to the nth (degree),** to any required power, (fig.) to any extent, to the utmost.

'n, 'n', *conj.* (colloq.) and.

-n^{1,2}. See **-EN**^{1,5}.

N. *abbr.* (Chess) knight; New; newton(s); North(ern); nuclear.

n. *abbr.* name; nano-; neuter; noon; note.

N *symb.* nitrogen.

na *adv.* (Sc.) **1.** (nah). = **NO**^{4}. **2.** (na, after *v. aux.*). = **NOT** (*canna, didna*).

n/a *abbr.* not applicable; not available.

Na *symb.* sodium. [f. mod. L *natrium* (as **NATRON**; see **-IUM**)]

***NAACP** *abbr.* National Association for the Advancement of Colored People.

‖NAAFI (nă'fĭ) *abbr.* Navy, Army, and Air Force Institutes (canteen for servicemen).

nab *v.t.* (**-bb-**).(sl.) apprehend, arrest; catch in wrongdoing. [17th c., also *napp*, as in **KIDNAP**; orig. unkn.]

nā'bŏb *n.* **1.** (Hist.) Muslim official or governor under Mogul empire. **2.** (arch.) wealthy luxury-loving person, esp. one who has returned from India with fortune. [f. Port. *nababo* or Sp. *nabab*, f. Urdu (as **NAWAB**)]

nă'carăt *n.* bright orange-red colour. [F, perh. f. Sp. & Port. *nacardo* (*nacar* **NACRE**)]

nacĕ'lle *n.* outer casing of aeroplane's engine; car of airship. [F, f. LL *navicella* dim. of L *navis* ship]

nā'cre (-ker) *n.* (shellfish yielding) mother-of-pearl; hence **nā'créous, nā'crous,** *adjs.* [F]

nā'dir (-ēr, -er) *n.* point of heavens directly under observer (opp. **ZENITH**); (transf.) lowest point, place or time of greatest depression etc. [ME f. OF, f. Arab. *nazīr* (*as-samt*) opposite (to zenith)]

nae'v|us, *n.* *pl.* ~i *pr.* -ī). birthmark in form of sharply defined red patch in skin; = **MOLE**^{1}. [L]

Nā'ffy *n.* (sl.) = **NAAFI**. [phonet. sp.]

năg^1 *n.* small riding-horse or pony; (colloq.) horse. [ME, of unkn. orig.]

năg^2 *v.* (**-gg-**). **1.** *v.i.* find fault or scold persistently (*at* person); (of pain etc.) be persistently felt. **2.** *v.t.* annoy by nagging. [of dial., orig. perh. Scand. or LG, orig.; cf. Norw. & Sw. *nagga* gnaw, irritate, LG (*g*)*naggen* provoke]

Na'ga (nah'-) *n.* **1.** (Hindu Myth.) one of a race of semi-human serpents, genii of rain, rivers, etc. **2.** member of group of tribes in or near Naga Hills of Burma. [f. Skr. *naga* serpent]

naga'na (-ah'na) *n.* disease of livestock in Africa, caused by a trypanosome and transmitted by tsetse fly. [f. Zulu *nakane*]

nā'gŏr *n.* Senegal antelope (*Redunca redunca*). [F, arbitr. form. by Buffon f. earlier *nanguer*]

Nah. *abbr.* Nahum (OT).

Nahua'tl (nahwah'-) *a.* & *n.* (member or language) of group of peoples in S. Mexico and Central America, incl. Aztecs; hence ~**AN** *a.* [Sp. f. Nahuatl]

nai'ad (nī'-) *n.* (*pl.* ~**s**, *or* ~**es** *pr.* -ēz). water-nymph; nymph of dragonfly etc. [f. L f. Gk *Naias -ados* (*naō* flow; see **-AD** 1)]

naif (nahē'f) *a.* & *n.* = **NAÏVE** (person). [F masc. *a.*]

nail^1 *n.* **1.** horny covering of upper surface of tip of finger or toe; **bite** one's ~**s** (as habit, or in impatience or frustration); **TOOTH** *and* **nail;** ~**-biting,** (fig.) that causes helpless anxiety; ~**brush** (for cleaning nails); *~* **enamel,** ~ **polish,** ‖~ **varnish,** (for making nails lustrous); ~**-file,** ~**-scissors,** (for

trimming nails); hence ~**ED**^{2} (-ld) *a.* **2.** claw, talon; hard excrescence on upper mandible of some soft-billed birds. **3.** small metal spike usu. with point and broadened head driven in with hammer to hold things together or as peg or protection (cf. **HOBNAIL**) or ornament; **hard as** ~**s,** (1) in good physical condition, (2) callous; **hit the (right)** ~ **on the head,** give true explanation, propose or do right thing; hit the mark; *nail in* person's **COFFIN; on the** ~, without delay, esp. of payment; ~**-head,** architectural ornament like head of nail; ~**-punch, -set,** tool for sinking head of nail below surface. **4.** old measure of cloth length (2¼ in.). **5.** Hence ~**LESS** (-l-l-) *a.* [OE *nægel*, = OS, OHG *nagal*, ON *nagl* f. Gmc **naglaz* f. IE **nogh-*]

nail^2 *v.t.* **1.** fasten with nail(s) (*on, to, together, down, in,* etc.); *nail* **COLOUR**^{1}*s to mast;* ~ (**to counter** or **to barn door**), expose as spurious or vile; ~ **up,** close, or affix at height, with nail(s). **2.** fix or keep fixed (person, attention, etc.); secure, catch, engage, succeed in getting hold of, (person or thing); ~ **down,** define precisely, b'nd (person *to* promise etc.). [OE *næglan* (as prec.)]

nai'ler *n.* nail-maker; hence **nai'lERY** (3) *n.* [f. **NAIL**^{2} + -**ER**^{1}]

nai'nsŏŏk *n.* fine soft cotton fabric, orig. Indian. [f. Hindi *nainsukh* (*nain* eye, *sukh* pleasure)]

naï've (nahē'v, nīē'v), **naive** (nāv), *a.* artless, innocent, unaffected; unconsciously and amusingly simple; hence ~**LY**^{2} (-vlĭ) *adv.* [F, fem. of *naïf* f. L *nativus* **NATIVE**^{2}]

naï'vetý (nahē'vtĭ), **nai'vetý** (nā'vetĭ), **naïveté** (nahē'vtà), *n.* state or quality of being naïve; naïve action. [F *naïveté* (as prec.; see -**TY**^{1})]

nā'kéd *a.* **1.** without clothes, nude, (*as naked as my mother bore me*). **2.** defenceless; (of sword etc.) unsheathed; plain, undisguised, (*the naked truth; naked facts; in its naked absurdity*); exposed for examination (*his naked soul*). **3.** devoid of; treeless, leafless, barren; (of rock) exposed, without soil or vegetation; (of room) without furnishings; without ornament. **4.** (of light, flame, etc.) exposed to air, not protected from wind etc. or from contact with inflammable vapour etc., unshaded. **5.** without leaves, hairs, scales, shell, etc.; without addition, comment, support, evidence, etc., (*naked faith, quotations, word, assertion*); unassisted; ~ **eye** (without telescope, microscope, etc.). **6.** ~ **boys,** ~ **lady,** ~ **ladies,** meadow saffron, flowering while leafless. **7.** Hence ~**LY**^{2} *adv.,* ~**NESS** *n.* [OE *nacod,* = OHG *nackut,* ON *nökkvithr,* Goth. *naqad-* f. Gmc **naquadhaz*]

nā'ker *n.* (Hist.) kettledrum. [ME, f. OF *nacre, nacaire* f. Arab. *nakkāra* drum]

‖NALGO (nā'lgō) *abbr.* National and Local Government Officers' Association.

***NAM** *abbr.* National Association of Manufacturers.

nămbý-pă'mbý *a.* & *n.* **1.** insipidly pretty, weakly sentimental, lacking vigour. **2.** *n.* talk or person of this kind. [fanciful form. on name of Ambrose Philips, Engl. pastoral writer d. 1749]

nāme^1 *n.* **1.** word by which individual person, animal, place, or thing, is spoken of or to (*mention person by name*); **by** ~, called (*Tom by name*); **in all but** ~, virtually; **KNOW**^{1} *by name;* **of** (or **by**) **the** ~ **of,** called; **the** ~ **of the game,** (colloq.) purpose or essence of action etc.; **put** one's ~ **down for,** apply as candidate etc., promise to subscribe; **keep** one's ~ **on,** take one's ~ **off, the books,** remain, cease to be, member of college, club, etc.; **have to** one's ~, possess; **TAKE**^{1} person's *name in vain;* **USE**^{2} person's *name*; **what's in a** ∼?, names are arbitrary labels; WHAT*'s-its*(or *his*)*-name*. **2.** word denoting any object of thought, esp. one applicable to many individuals; CALL¹ person *names*; PROPER *name*. **3.** person as known, famed, or spoken of, (*adore the name of God*; *Nelson himself and many great names were there*). **4.** all who go under one name; family, clan, people. **5.** reputation (*has an ill, a good, name*; *give a* DOG¹ *a bad name*; *has a name for honesty, the name of being honest*; one's *good name*); (*attrib.*) widely known and esteemed (*a name brand*); **make a** ∼ **for** oneself, **win** oneself **a** ∼, become famous. **6.** merely nominal existence, practically non- -existent thing, (opp. *fact, reality, deed*; *virtuous in name* (*only*); *honour had become a name*). **7. in** person's ∼, **in the** ∼ **of,** invoking, relying upon, calling to witness, (*in God's* or *Heaven's name*; *in the name of goodness, common sense*), acting as deputy for or in the interest of (*open, in the name of the law!*; *did it in the name of friendship*); **in** one's **own** ∼, independently, without authority. **8.** ∼- -**calling,** (merely) abusive language; ∼-**child,** one named after (*of*) another person; ∼-**day,** (1) day of saint after whom person is named, (2)∥ = TICKET-*day*; ∼-**dropping,** familiar mention of names of the famous as form of boasting; ∼-**part,** title-role; ∼- -**plate** (affixed with name of occupant etc.); ∼'*sake* (-ms-), person or thing with same name as another (*his namesake*) [prob. f. phr. *for the name's sake*]; ∼-**tape** (for garment etc., with name of owner). [OE *nama*, *noma*, = OS, OHG *namo*, ON *nafn*, *namn*, Goth. *namo* f. Gmc *namon f. IE; cogn. w. L *nomen*, Gk *onoma*]

nāme² *v.t.* **1.** give name to (*after*, *for, *from*), call by (specified name); call (person or thing) by right name. **2.** nominate, appoint (*to* office etc.). **3.** mention, specify; cite as instance; **you** ∼ **it,** (colloq.) no matter what; ∼ **names,** mention specific persons' names (esp. in accusation). **4.** ∥(Of Speaker) mention (MP) as disobedient to the chair. **5.** specify as something desired; ∼ **the day,** arrange date (esp. of woman fixing date for her wedding). **6.** Hence **nā'me**ABLE (-ma-) *a.* [OE (*ge*)*namian* as prec.)]

nā'mel̇ėss (-ml-) *a.* having no name, bearing no name-inscription; obscure, inglorious; not mentioned by name, left unnamed on purpose (esp. *who shall be nameless*); anonymous, unknown; inexpressible, indefinable; too bad to be named, abominable, loathsome, (esp. *nameless vices*); hence ∼LY² *adv.*, ∼NESS *n.* [ME, = undistinguished, f. NAME¹ +-LESS]

nā'melẏ (-mlī) *adv.* that is to say, in other words. [ME, f. NAME¹ +-LY²]

năn *n.* (colloq.) grandmother. [childish pronunc.]

nănce, nă'ncẏ, *n.* & *a.* (sl.) effeminate (man or boy); male homosexual. [woman's Christian name, pet- -form of *Ann*]

nănkee'n (-ngk-, -n-k-) *n.* yellow cotton cloth; colour or (in *pl.*) trousers of this. [f. *Nankin*(g) in China, where orig. made]

nă'nnẏ *n.* **1.** ∼ (-goat), female goat. **2.** ∥child's nurse; (fig.) unduly protective person. [f. as NANCY]

nā'nō- *pref.* denoting factor of 10^{-9} (*nanosecond*). [f. L f. Gk *nanos* dwarf+-o-]

nā'ŏs *n.* (*pl.* **na'oi**). (Gk Ant. etc.) inner part of temple. [Gk, = temple]

năp¹ *v.i.* (-pp-), & *n.* **1.** *v.i.* sleep lightly or briefly; **catch** ∼'**ping,** find asleep, take unawares or off guard, detect in negligence or error. **2.** *n.* short sleep, doze, esp. by day (often *take a nap*). [OE *hnappian*, rel. to OHG (*h*)*naffezan* to slumber]

năp² *n.*, & *v.t.* (-pp-). **1.** *n.* surface given to cloth by raising and then cutting and smoothing the short fibres, pile, whence ∼'*LESS a.*; soft or downy surface. **2.** *v.t.* raise nap on (cloth). [ME *noppe* f. MDu., MLG *noppe* nap, *noppen* trim nap from]

năp³ *n.*, & *v.t.* (-pp-). **1.** *n.* card-game in which players declare numbers of tricks they expect to take, up to maximum of five; call of five in this game; ∼ **hand,** (fig.) position that justifies confident expectation of winning if one takes a risk; **go** ∼, risk attempting to

take all five tricks in nap, (fig.) risk everything, win all matches etc. in a series. **2.** betting of all one's money on one chance; tipster's choice for this. **3.** *v.t.* name (horse) as probable winner. [abbr. of orig. name of game NAPOLEON]

nā'pa. See NAPPA.

nā'palm (-ahm) *n.*, & *v.t.* **1.** *n.* thickening agent made from naphthalene and coconut oil; jellied petrol made from this, used in bombs. **2.** *v.t.* attack with napalm bombs. [f. NAPHTHENIC +*palmitic acid* in coconut oil]

nāpe *n.* back of or usu. *of* neck. [ME, of unkn. orig.]

nā'perẏ *n.* (Sc. or arch.) household, esp. table, linen. [ME, f. OF *naperie* (*nape* as NAPKIN; see -ERY)]

nă'phtha *n.* inflammable oil got by dry distillation of organic substances, such as coal, shale, or petroleum. [L, f. Gk, = inflammable volatile liquid issuing from earth, of Oriental orig.]

nă'phthalēne *n.* white crystalline substance got in distilling coal-tar and used in manufacture of dyes etc. and in moth-balls; hence **năphthă'**lIC *a.* [f. prec. +-*l-*+-ENE]

nă'phthēn|e *n.* (Chem.) saturated cyclic hydro- carbon; hence ∼IC (-ē'n-) *a.* (∼**ic acid,** any carboxylic acid from refining of petroleum). [f. NAPHTHA +-ENE]

Nā'pier *n.* ∼'**s bones,** slips of bone etc. marked for use in arithmetical calculations; hence ∼IAN (-pēr'ian) *a.* (see LOGARITHM). [f. J. ∼, Sc. mathe- matician d. 1617]

nă'pkin *n.* (**table-**)∼, square piece of linen, paper, etc., for wiping lips or fingers at meals, or serving fish etc. on; small towel; ∥baby's nappy; *SANITARY *napkin*; **lay up** etc. **in a** ∼, make no use of (Luke 19:20); ∼-**ring,** ring to hold (and distinguish) person's table-napkin when not in use. [ME, f. OF *nappe* f. L *mappa* (MAP¹), +-KIN]

napŏ'léon *n.* French gold twenty-franc piece of Napoleon I (**double** ∼, forty-franc piece); 19th-c. form of high boot; for the game NAP³; *mille-feuille. [f. F *napoléon* (*Napoléon*, name of 19th-c. French emperors]

Napŏlèŏ'n|ic *a.* of, like, etc., Napoleon I or the Napoleon family; hence or cogn. ∼ICALLY² *adv.*, **Napŏ'léon**ISM (3), **Napŏ'léon**IST (2), *ns.* [f. as prec. +-IC]

nă'p(p)a *n.* leather made by special process from skin of sheep or goat. [f. *Napa* in California]

∥**nă'pper** *n.* (sl.) head. [18th c.; orig. uncert.]

∥**nă'ppẏ¹** *a.* & *n.* (arch.) foaming (ale etc.); heady, strong. [app. f. NAP² +-Y²]

∥**nă'ppẏ²** *n.* piece of towelling etc. worn by baby to absorb or retain excreta. [abbr. of NAPKIN; see -Y³]

na'pu (nah'pōō) *n.* chevrotain of Malaya. [f. Malay *nāpu*]

nār'cèine *n.* narcotic alkaloid got from opium. [f. F *narcéine* f. Gk *narkē* numbness +-INE⁵]

nārcǐ'ss|ism *n.* (Psych.) tendency to self-worship, excessive or erotic interest in one's own personal features; hence ∼ǐ'stIC *a.* [f. *Narcissus* (Gk *Narkissos*), youth who fell in love with his reflection in water, +-ISM]

nārcǐ'ss|us *n.* (*pl.* ∼i *pr.* -ī, or ∼uses). bulbous plant of genus *Narcissus*, esp. *N. poeticus* bearing heavily scented single white spring flower with undivided corona edged with crimson and yellow. [L, f. Gk *narkissos*, perh. f. *narkē* numbness, w. ref. to its narcotic effects]

nār'colĕpsẏ *n.* disease with fits of somnolence; hence **nārcolĕ'pt**ıc *a. & n.*, (patient) having this disease. [f. as foll., after EPILEPSY]

nārcō's|is *n.* (*pl.* ∼es *pr.* -ēz). operation or effects of soporific narcotics; state of insensibility. [f. Gk *narkōsis* (*narkoō* benumb); see -OSIS]

nārcŏ't|ic *a.* & *n.* (substance) inducing drowsiness, sleep, stupor, or insensibility; (fig.) soporific; (of narcosis; (drug, e.g. stimulant or hallucinogen) affecting the mind; hence ∼ICALLY *adv.*, **nār'cot**ISM

(5) *n.*, **nār′cot**ize (3, 5) *v.t.* [ME, f. OF *narcotique* or f. med. L f. Gk *narkōtikos* (as prec.; see -OTIC)]

nārd *n.* (plant yielding) aromatic balsam of ancients; spikenard. [ME, f. L f. Gk *nardos* f. Semitic wd]

nārdōō′ *n.* (Aboriginal food of spores of) Austral. clover-like plant (*Marsilea drummondii*). [Aboriginal]

nār′|ēs (-z) *n. pl.* (Anat.) nostrils; hence ∼IAL *a.* [pl. of L *naris*]

nār′ghilė (-gĭ-) *n.* oriental tobacco-pipe with smoke drawn through water, HOOKAH. [f. Pers. *nārgīleh* (*nārgīl* coconut)]

||**nārk** *n.*, & *v.t.* (sl.) **1.** *n.* police decoy or spy; (Austral.) annoying person or thing; hence ∼′Y² *a.*, bad-tempered, irritable. **2.** *v.t.* annoy, infuriate; ∼ **it**, (*imper.*) stop that. [f. Romany *nāk* nose]

narr|ā′te *v.t.* give continuous story or account of; (abs.) utter or write narrative; so ∼A′TION *n.* [f. L *narrare* + -ATE³]

nā′rrative *n.* & *a.* **1.** *n.* tale, story, recital of facts, esp. story told in first person; kind of composition or talk that confines itself to these. **2.** *a.* in the form of, or concerned with, narration; hence ∼LY² (-vlĭ) *adv.* [f. F *narratif* -*ive* f. LL *narrativus* (as prec.; see -IVE)]

narrā′tor *n.* person who narrates, e.g. by describing events between speeches in broadcast play or by commentary during film. [L (as NARRATE; see -OR)]

nā′rrow (-ō) *a.*, *n.*, & *v.* **1.** *a.* of small width in proportion to length, lacking breadth, constricted; (of vowel) tense; of small size, confined or confining, (*within narrow bounds* etc.). **2.** of limited scope, restricted, (*in the narrowest sense*); with little margin (*a narrow majority*, *escape*). **3.** lacking in breadth of view or sympathy, illiberal, prejudiced, exclusive, self-centred. **4.** searching, precise, exact, (*after a narrow examination*). **5.** ∼ **bed, cell, house,** the grave; ||∼ **boat,** canal boat (esp. less than 7 ft. wide); ∼ **circumstances,** poverty; ∼ **cloth** (less than 52 in. wide); ∼-**mi′nded,** = sense 3; ||∼ **seas,** English Channel and Irish Sea; *narrow* SQUEAK; ∼ **way,** righteousness (Matt 7·14). **6.** Hence ∼·ISH¹ ² *a.*, ∼LY² *adv.*, ∼NESS *n.* **7.** *n.* (usu. in *pl.*) narrow part of a sound, strait, river, pass, or street. **8.** *v.t.* & *i.* make or become narrower, diminish, lessen, contract, restrict. [OE *nearu nearw-,* = OS *naru* f. Gmc **narwaz*]

nār′thĕx *n.* railed-off western porch etc. in early Christian church, used by women, penitents, catechumens, etc. [L, f. Gk *narthēx* giant fennel, stick, casket, narthex]

nār′whal (-wal) *n.* Arctic delphinoid cetacean (*Monodon monoceros*), the male with long straight horn(s) developed from one or both of its two teeth. [f. Du. *narwal* f. Da. *narhval* (*hval* whale); cf. ON *náhvalr* (perh. f. *nár* corpse, w. ref. to skin-colour)]

nār′ȳ *a.* (colloq.) not a, no; ∼ **a,** not one. [f. *ne'er a*]

||**NAS** *abbr.* National Association of Schoolmasters; Noise Abatement Society.

*****NASA** (nă′sa) *abbr.* National Aeronautics and Space Administration.

nā′sal (-z-) *a.* & *n.* **1.** *a.* of the nose; ∼ **organ,** (joc.) nose. **2.** (Of letter or sound) pronounced with nose passage open, e.g. *m, n, ng,* or Fr. *en, un,* etc.; (of voice or speech) having the intonation due to passage of breath through the nose; hence ∼IZE (2, 3) *v.i.* & *t.* **3.** Hence **nāsā′l**ITY (-z-) *n.*, ∼LY² *adv.* **4.** *n.* nasal letter or sound; nose-piece on helmet. [F, or f. med. L *nasalis* f. L *nasus* nose; see -AL]

nā′sc|ent *a.* in the act of being born, just beginning to be, not yet mature; (Chem.) just being formed and therefore unusually reactive (*nascent hydrogen*); so ∼ENCY *n.* [f. L *nasci* be born; see -ENT]

nā′seberrȳ (-zb-) *n.* sapodilla. [f. Sp. & Port. *néspera* medlar f. L (see MEDLAR); assim. to BERRY¹]

nā′sō- (-z-) *comb. form.* nose, as: ∼-**frontal,** of nose and forehead. [f. L *nasus* nose + -O-]

nā′stic *a.* (Bot.) of movement not determined by external stimulus. [f. Gk *nastos* squeezed together (*nassō* to press); see -IC]

nastū′rtium (-shum) *n.* **1.** (Bot.) pungent-tasting cruciferous plant of genus *Nasturtium,* e.g. watercress. **2.** (pop.) trailing garden plant of genus *Tropaeolum,* with bright orange, yellow, or red flowers and pungent-tasting leaves. [L]

na′st|ȳ (nah′-) *a.* disgustingly dirty, filthy; obscene, delighting in obscenity; disagreeable to smell or taste, unpalatable (lit. or fig.); annoying, objectionable (∼**y bit** or **piece of work,** (colloq.) unpleasant or contemptible person); (of weather etc.) foul, wet, stormy; hard to deal with or get rid of, serious (*a nasty sea, fence, blow, illness;* **a** ∼**y one,** rebuff, snub, awkward question, disabling blow, etc.); ill-natured, ill-tempered, spiteful *to;* hence ∼iLY² *adv.*, ∼iNESS *n.* [ME, of unkn. orig.]

Nat. *abbr.* National; Nationalist; Natural.

nā′tal *a.* of or from one's birth. [ME, f. L *natalis* (as NATION; see -AL)]

natā′lity *n.* birth rate. [f. F *natalité* (as prec.; see -ITY)]

natā′tion *n.* (literary). act or art of swimming. [f. L *natatio* (*natare* swim; see -ATION)]

nātatōr′ial, nā′tatorȳ, *adjs.* swimming; of swimming. [f. LL *natatorius* f. L *natator* swimmer (as prec.; see -ORY, -AL)]

*****nātatōr′ium** *n.* (esp. indoor) swimming-pool. [LL, neut. (as *n.*) of *natatorius* (see prec.)]

nātch *adv.* (colloq.) = NATURALLY 2. [abbr.]

nā′tēs (-z) *n. pl.* (Anat.) buttocks; anterior pair of optic lobes in brain. [L]

na′th(e)lèss (-thl-) *adv.* (arch.) nevertheless. [ME, f. OE *ná* not (*ne* not, *á* ever) + THE 2 + *lǣs* LESS 6]

nā′tion *n.* **1.** large number of people of mainly common descent, language, history, etc., usu. inhabiting a territory bounded by defined limits and forming a society under one government; **most favoured** ∼ (to which State accords lowest scale of import duties); ∼-**wide** *a.*, extending over whole nation. **2.** tribe of N. Amer. Indians; ||(in medieval and some St. universities) body of students from particular country or district. **3. law of** ∼**s,** international law; LEAGUE² *of Nations;* UNITED *Nations.* **4.** Hence ∼HOOD *n.* [ME f. OF, f. L *natio -onis* (*nasci* nat- be born; see -ION)]

nā′tional *a.* & *n.* **1.** *a.* of a or the nation, common to the whole nation; peculiar to or characteristic of a particular nation. **2.** ∼ **anthem,** song adopted by nation to express patriotism or loyalty, e.g. 'God save the Queen'; N∼ **Assembly,** elected house of legislature in various countries, esp. (Hist.) in France 1789–91; ||N∼ **Assistance,** (former official name for) supplementary benefits under National Insurance; *****∼ **bank** (chartered under federal government); *****∼ **convention** (of major political party, nominating candidates for presidency etc.); *National* DEBT; ∼ **football,** (Austral.) Australian Rules; N∼ **Front,** UK organization with extreme reactionary views on immigration etc.; ||N∼ **Government,** coalition government under MacDonald 1931–5; ||∼ **grid,** (1) network of high-voltage electric power lines between major power-stations, (2) metric system of geographical co-ordinates used in maps of British Isles; *****N∼ **Guard,** primary reserve force partly maintained by the states but available for federal use; ||N∼ **Health (Service),** system of national medical service paid for mainly by taxation (1948–); ∼ **holiday** (observed throughout a country); ∼ **income,** total money earned within a nation; ||N∼ **Insurance,** system of compulsory contribution from all adults below pension age and from employers to provide State assistance in sickness, unemployment, retirement, etc.; ∼ **newspaper** (circulating throughout the country); ∼ **park,** area of countryside subject to strict control of building etc. and under State supervision to maintain its value to the public; ||∼ **service,** service in armed forces under conscription; N∼ **Socialist,** member of highly nationalistic totalitarian party in power in Germany 1933–45;

||N~ **Trust**, private body for preserving historic or beautiful places. **3.** Hence ~LY² *adv.* **4.** *n.* ||(*N*~) = GRAND *National*. **5.** one's fellow countryman (*consul's powers over his own nationals*); citizen of a specified country. [F (as prec.; see -AL)]

nä′tional|ism *n.* patriotic feeling, principles, or efforts; policy of national independence; so ~IST (2) *n.*, ~ĭ′stIC *a.* [f. prec. +-ISM]

nätionă′litў *n.* being national, national quality; patriotic sentiment; one's nation of origin (*what is his nationality?*); a nation (*men of all nationalities*); existence as a nation; ethnic group forming part of one or more political nations. [f. NATIONAL +-ITY]

nä′tionalīz|e, **-is|e** (-īz), *v.t.* make national; make into a nation; naturalize (foreigner); convert (land, railways, coal-mines, steel industry, firm etc.) into national property or undertakings; hence ~A′TION *n.* [f. F *nationaliser* (as NATIONAL; see -IZE)]

nä′tive¹ *n.* **1.** ~ **of**, person born, or whose parents are domiciled at his birth, in (place). **2.** local inhabitant; (Austral.) white person born in Australia. **3.** member of non-European or less civilized indigenous people; (S. Afr.) Black. **4.** indigenous animal or plant; oyster reared wholly or partly in British waters, esp. in artificial beds. [ME, orig. = person born as slave, f. AL *nativus* n. f. L *nativus* a. (see foll.)]

nä′tive² *a.* **1.** belonging to a person or thing by nature, innate, inherent, natural *to*; hence ~LY² (-vlĭ) *adv.* **2.** unadorned, simple, artless. **3.** of one's birth, where one was born; belonging to one by right of birth. **4.** (Of metal etc.) found in pure or uncombined state; ~ **rock** (in its original place). **5.** born in a place (esp. of non-Europeans), indigenous, not exotic; of the natives of a place; (Austral. & NZ) resembling an animal or plant familiar elsewhere (~ **bear**, = KOALA); **go** ~, (of white person) adopt (less civilized) mode of life of natives where one lives. [ME, f. OF *natif -ive* or f. L *nativus* (as NATION; see -IVE)]

nä′tiv|ism *n.* (Philos.) doctrine of innate ideas; so ~IST (2) *n.* [f. prec. +-ISM]

nati′vitў *n.* birth of Christ, the Virgin Mary, or St. John the Baptist; picture of the Nativity of Christ; festival of Christ's Nativity, Christmas, or of birth of Virgin (8 Sept.) or St. John (24 June); birth; (Astrol.) horoscope at birth; ~ **play** (dealing with birth of Christ). [ME, f. OF *nativité* f. LL *nativitas -tatis* f. L (as NATIVE²; see -ITY)]

NATO, Nato, (nā′tō) *abbr.* North Atlantic Treaty Organization.

nä′tron *n.* native hydrated sodium carbonate. [F, f. Sp. *natrón* f. Arab. *naṭrūn* f. Gk *nitron* NITRE]

||**NATSOPA** (nătsō′pa) *abbr.* National Society of Operative Printers, Graphical & Media Personnel (orig. Printers and Assistants).

nä′tter *v.i.*, & *n.* (colloq.) **1.** *v.i.* chatter idly; grumble, talk fretfully. **2.** *n.* aimless chatter; grumbling talk. [orig. Sc., imit.]

nä′tterjăck *n.* species of small toad (*Bufo calamita*) with yellow stripe down back and running instead of hopping. [perh. f. prec., from its loud croak, +JACK¹]

nä′ttier blue (-ōō) *n.* soft shade of blue. [much used by J. M. *Nattier*, Fr. painter d. 1766]

nä′tt|ў *a.* spruce, trim, daintily tidy; deft-handed; showing deftness; hence ~ILY² *adv.*, ~iNESS *n.* [orig. sl., perh. rel. to NEAT²; see -Y²]

nä′tural (-cher-) *a.* & *n.* **1.** *a.* based on the innate moral sense, instinctive, (*natural law, justice*, VIRTUES). **2.** established by nature (*natural resources; natural* YEAR); ~ **numbers**, 1, 2, 3, etc.; *natural* LOGARITHM; ~ **selection**, process favouring survival of organisms best adapted to their environment. **3.** (Mus.) ~ **note**, not sharp or flat, so *B natural, F natural*, etc.; ~ **key** or **scale** (having no sharps or flats, i.e. C major or A minor). **4.** ~ **classification**, scientific arrangement according to natural features, esp. (Bot.) Jussieu's arrangement of species in ~ **orders** according to likeness as opp. Linnaeus's sexual system. **5.** normal,

conformable to the ordinary course of nature, not exceptional or miraculous or irregular; ~ **death** (by age or disease, not accident, poison, or violence); *natural* MAGIC. **6.** not enlightened or communicated by revelation (*the natural man*); ~ **religion**, deism (opp. *revealed religion*); ~ **theology**, knowledge of God as gained by reason and light of nature. **7.** physically existing, not spiritual or intellectual or fictitious, concerned with physical things, (*the natural world*); one's ~ **life**, duration of one's life on earth; *natural* LAW¹. **8.** existing in or by nature, not artificial, innate, inherent, self-sown, uncultivated, (*in its natural state*); ~ **childbirth** (with mother taught to relax and so not needing anaesthesia etc.); ~ **food** (without preservatives etc.); *natural* GAS¹; ~ **language** (opp. artificial language or code); ~ **uranium** (not enriched). **9.** lifelike; unaffected, easy-mannered, not disfigured or disguised. **10.** not surprising, to be expected. **11.** spontaneous or easy to (*comes natural to him*). **12.** destined to be such by nature (*natural enemies, antithesis; is a natural linguist*). **13.** so related by nature only, illegitimate, (*natural son, child, brother*, etc.). **14.** dealing with nature as a study; ~ **history,** (1) study of natural objects, esp. of animal or vegetable life, and esp. as set forth for popular use, (2) aggregate of facts about the natural objects or the characteristics of a place or class; ~ **historian**, writer on natural history; ~ **philosopher**, physicist; ~ **philosophy**, physics; *natural* SCIENCE. **15.** ~**-born**, having the character or position by birth; ~**-coloured**, not given any artificial colouring. **16.** Hence ~NESS *n.* **17.** *n.* person mentally deficient from birth; person who is naturally expert in some respect or endowed (*for a* role or activity); thing that is by nature suitable (*for*) or successful, a certainty. **18.** (Mus.) sign denoting return to natural pitch after sharp or flat; natural note, white key on piano. **19.** hand making 21 as first dealt in *vingt-et-un*; throw of 7 or 11 at craps. **20.** pale fawn colour. [ME f. OF *naturel* f. L *naturalis* (as NATURE; see -AL)]

nä′turalism *n.* (-cher-) *n.* action based on natural instincts; moral or religious system on purely natural basis; (Philos.) view of the world that excludes the supernatural or spiritual; realistic method, adherence to nature, in literature and art; indifference to conventions. [f. prec. +-ISM, in Philos. after F *naturalisme*]

nä′turalist (-cher-)*n.* & *a.* **1.** *n.* one who believes in or practises naturalism; student of animals or plants. **2.** *a.* = foll. [f. F *naturaliste*, & NATURAL +-IST]

näturali′st|ic (-cher-) *a.* of, or according to, naturalism; of natural history; hence ~ICALLY *adv.* [f. prec. +-IC]

nä′turalīz|e (-cher-), **-ĭs|e** (-īz), *v.* **1.** *v.t.* admit (alien) to citizenship; adopt (foreign word, custom, etc.); introduce (animal, plant) into another region so as to appear native or wild. **2.** *v.i.* become naturalized. **3.** *v.t.* free from conventions, make natural; exclude from the miraculous, place on naturalistic basis; cause to appear natural. **4.** *v.i.* study natural history. **5.** Hence ~A′TION *n.* [f. F *naturaliser* (as NATURAL; see -IZE)]

nä′turallў (-cher-) *adv.* **1.** In adj. senses. **2.** as a natural result; as might be expected, of course. [f. NATURAL +-LY²]

nä′ture *n.* **1.** thing's essential qualities (**in** or **by** or **from the** (**very**) ~ **of the case** or **of things,** inevitably if one considers these qualities); person's or animal's innate qualities or character (*it is not (in) her nature to act like that*; **by** ~, innately, GOOD, ILL, SECOND, *nature*; hence **-nä′tur**ED² (-cherd) *a.*); (**human**) ~, general characteristics and feelings of mankind (TOUCH² *of nature*); specified element of human character (*the rational, animal, moral, nature*); person of specified character (*sanguine natures do not feel this*). **2.** kind, sort, class, (*things of this nature; is in* or *of the nature of a command*). **3.** inherent impulses determining character or action (**against** ~, unnatural, immoral;

see also sense 5). **4.** vital force or functions or needs (*nature is exhausted; such a diet will not support nature;* CALL² *of nature,* EASE² or RELIEVE *nature*). **5.** physical power causing phenomena of material world, these phenomena as a whole, (**N~**, these personified; *all nature looks gay*; *Nature is the best physician*); **against** or **contrary to ~**, miraculous(ly); **back to ~**, returning to what are regarded as natural conditions of living; *in the* COURSE¹ *of nature*; DEBT *of nature*; **from ~**, using natural objects as models (*paint from nature*); **in ~**, (1) actually existing, (2) anywhere, at all; LAW¹ *of nature*; **one of N~'s**, a natural member of the class of (*gentlemen* etc.); **state of ~**, (1) unregenerate condition (opp. *state of* GRACE), (2) condition of man before society is organized, (3) uncultivated or undomesticated state of plants or animals, natural occurrence of minerals, (3) bodily nakedness. **6. ~ cure**, naturopathy; **~-printing**, method of producing print of leaves etc. by pressing them on prepared plate; **~ study** (as school subject), practical study of plant and animal life, physical phenomena, etc.; **~ trail**, path through woods etc. designed to draw attention to interesting natural objects. [ME f. OF, f. L *natura* (*nasci nat-* be born; see -URE)]

nā′tur|ism (-cher-) *n.* naturalism; worship of natural objects; nudism; so **~IST** (2) *n.* [f. prec. + -ISM]

nātur̆ō′pathy̆ (-cher-) *n.* treatment of disease by seeking to assist natural recovery; so **nā′turo**PATH 1 *n.*, **nāturopā′th**IC *a.*, (-cher-). [f. NATURE + -o- + -PATHY]

naught (nawt) *n. & pred. a.* (arch.) **1.** *n.* nothing, NOUGHT; **bring to ~**, ruin, baffle; **come to ~**, be ruined or baffled; **set at ~**, disregard, despise. **2.** *a.* worthless, useless. [OE *nāwiht, -wuht* (*nā*, see NO²; *wiht* WIGHT)]

nau′ght|y̆ (naw′tĭ) *a.* (Used of, to, or by children, or in imit. of childish speech). wayward, disobedient, badly behaved; wicked, blameworthy, unbecoming, indecent; hence **~ILY²** *adv.*, **~iNESS** *n.* [ME, f. prec. + -Y²]

nau′pli|us *n.* (*pl.* **~i** *pr. -ī*). larva of some crustaceans. [L, a kind of shellfish, or (*N~*) f. Gk *Nauplios* son of Poseidon]

nau′sèa (-s-, -z-) *n.* feeling of sickness with inclination to vomit; sea-sickness; loathing. [L, f. Gk *nausia* (*naus* ship)]

nau′sèat|e (-s-, -z-) *v.* **1.** *v.t.* reject (food; usu. fig.) with loathing; affect with nausea, whence **~ING²** *a.* **2.** *v.i.* feel sick (*at*), loathe food, occupation, etc. [f. L *nauseare* (as prec.) + -ATE³]

nau′sèous (-s-, -z-) *a.* causing nausea; offensive to taste or smell, nasty; disgusting, loathsome; hence **~LY²** *adv.*, **~NESS** *n.* [f. L *nauseosus* (as NAUSEA; see -OUS)]

nautch *n.* Indian exhibition of professional dancing--girls (**~-girl**, one of these). [f. Urdu (Hindi) *nāch* f. Prakrit *nachcha* f. Skr. *nṛitja* dancing]

nau′tical *a.* of sailors or navigation, naval, maritime; **~ almanac**, year-book containing astronomical and tidal information for navigators etc.; *nautical* MILE; hence **~LY²** *adv.* [f. F *nautique* or f. L f. Gk *nautikos* (*nautēs* sailor f. *naus* ship); see -ICAL]

nau′tilus *n.* (*pl.* **~es**, *or* **nau′tili** *pr. -ī*). **paper ~**, small cephalopod of genus *Argonauta*, of which the female has very thin shell and webbed sail-like arms; **pearly ~**, cephalopod of genus *Nautilus*, with chambered shell having nacreous septa. [L, f. Gk *nautilos*, lit. sailor (as prec.)]

Nă′vajŏ, Nă′vahŏ, (-ahō) *n.* (*pl.* **~s**). (member or language of) Amer. Ind. people in New Mexico and Arizona. [Sp., = pueblo]

nā′val *a.* of, in, for, etc., ships or (usu.) the or a navy (**~ academy** (for training naval officers); **~ architect**, designer of ships; **~ officer**, officer in navy; **~ stores**, all materials used in shipping); fought, won, etc., by or consisting of or based on ships of war; hence **~LY²** *adv.* [f. L *navalis* (*navis* ship; see -AL)]

nă′varin (-ăṅ) *n.* casserole of lamb or mutton with vegetables. [F]

nāve¹ *n.* hub of wheel. [OE *nafu, nafa,* = OHG *naba,* ON *nöf* f. Gmc **nabō* f. IE **nobhā;* cf. NAVEL]

nāve² *n.* body of church esp. from west door to chancel, usu. separated by pillars from aisles. [f. med. L *navis* f. L *navis* ship]

nā′vel *n.* depression in front of belly left by detachment of umbilical cord (**contemplate** one's **~**, indulge in complacent philosophical quietism); central point of anything; **~ orange**, large orange with navel-like formation at top; **~-string**, umbilical cord; **~wort**, pennywort or other plant with round centrally-depressed leaves. [OE *nafela,* = OHG *nabalo,* ON *nafli* f. Gmc **nabhalon* f. IE **(o)nobh-;* cf. NAVE¹]

navi′cŭlar *a. & n.* **1.** *a.* boat-shaped (of shrines, and of parts of plants or body); **~ bone** in hand or usu. foot; **~ disease** (in horse's navicular bone). **2.** *n.* navicular bone or disease. [f. F *naviculaire* or f. LL *navicularis* f. L *navicula* dim. of *navis* ship; see -AR¹]

nă′vig|able *a.* (Of river, sea, etc.) affording passage for ships; seaworthy (*in navigable condition*); (of balloon) steerable, dirigible; hence **~ABI′LITY** *n.* [F, or f. L *navigabilis* (as foll.; see -ABLE)]

nă′vigāte *v.* **1.** *v.i.* sail (in) ship; (of passenger in vehicle) assist driver by indicating correct route. **2.** *v.t.* sail over or up or down (sea, river); manage, direct course of, (ship or aircraft). [f. L *navigare* (*navis* ship, *agere* drive) + -ATE³]

năvigā′tion *n.* navigating (**inland ~**, communication by canals and rivers, methods of determining ship's or aircraft's position and course by geometry and astronomy; voyage; **~-coal**, steam-coal; **~ lights** (on ship or aircraft at night, indicating its position and direction of movement). [F, or f. L *navigatio* (as prec.; see -ATION)]

nă′vigātor *n.* one charged with or skilled in navigation; sea explorer; ||(arch.) navvy. [L (as NAVIGATE; see -OR)]

||**nă′vvy̆** *n.,* & *v.i.* **1.** *n.* labourer employed in excavating etc, for canals, railways, roads, etc.; = STEAM *navvy*. **2.** *v.i.* work as navvy. [abbr. of prec.]

nā′vy̆ *n.* **1.** whole body of State's ships of war with their crews and all the organization for their maintenance; officers and men of this; (poet.) fleet; ||MERCHANT *navy.* **2. ~** (**blue**), dark blue used in naval uniform; ||**N~ Cut, (P)** cake tobacco finely sliced; ***N~ Department,** government department in charge of navy; ||**N~ List,** official book with all naval officers' names and other information; ***~ yard,** government shipyard with civilian labour. [ME, = fleet, f. OF *navie* ship, fleet f. Rom. & pop. L *navia* ship, f. L *navis*]

nawa′b (nawah′b, -aw′b) *n.* **1.** (Hist.) Title of governor or nobleman in India. **2.** Title of distinguished Muslim in Pakistan. [f. Urdu *nawwāb* pl. f. Arab. *nā′ib* deputy; cf. NABOB]

nay *adv. & n.* **1.** *adv.* (arch.) = NO⁴; why, well, (vaguely introducing comment on another's statement etc.). **2.** or rather, and even, and more than that, (*weighty, nay, unanswerable*). **3.** *n.* the word 'nay'; negative vote; **will not take ~**, disregards refusals; **say ~, ~'say,** utter denial or usu. refusal, refuse or contradict (*cannot say him nay*); cf. YEA. [ME, f. ON *nei* (*ne* not, *ei* AYE²)]

Năzarēne (nă′-, -ē′n) *n. & a.* (native or inhabitant) of Nazareth, esp. Christ; (in Jewish or Muslim use) Christian; (member) of an early Jewish-Christian sect or a 20th-c. Protestant sect. [ME, f. LL f. Gk *Nazarēnos* (*Nazaret* Nazareth; see -ENE 2)]

Nă′zarīte¹ *n.* native or inhabitant of Nazareth. [f. LL *Nazaraeus* f. Gk *Nazaraios* + -ITE¹ (1)]

Nă′zarīte², Nă′zirīte, *n.* Hebrew who had taken certain vows of abstinence (Num. 6). [f. LL *Nazaraeus* f. Heb. *nāzīr* (*nāzar* to separate or consecrate oneself) + -ITE¹ (1)]

nāze *n.* promontory, headland. [f. place-names; cf. NESS]

Na′z|i (nah′tsĭ, nah′zĭ) *n. & a.* (member) of the German National Socialist party; (person) belonging to similar organization or holding similar views on racial superiority etc.; hence ∿IDOM, ∿(I)ISM (3), *ns.*, ∿IFY *v.t.* [repr. pronunc. of *Nati-* in G *Nationalsozialist*]

NB *abbr.* Nebraska; New Brunswick; no ball; Scotland (North Britain); *nota bene.*

Nb *symb.* niobium.

*NBC *abbr.* National Broadcasting Company.

||NBG *abbr.* (colloq.) no bloody good.

N. by E., N. by W., *abbrs.* North by East, West.

NC *abbr.* North Carolina.

||NCB *abbr.* National Coal Board.

NCO *abbr.* non-commissioned officer.

NCR *abbr.* no carbon required.

||NCU *abbr.* National Cyclists' Union.

-nd[1] *suf.* forming *ns.* & *adjs.* w. sense '(person or thing) to be treated in specified way' (*dividend, ordinand, reverend*). [f. or after L *-andus, -endus* of gerundives]

-nd[2] *suf.* forming *ns.* (*fiend, friend*). [OE *-ond,* orig. part. ending]

ND, N. Dak., *abbrs.* North Dakota.

n.d. *abbr.* no date.

Nd *symb.* neodymium.

né (nā) *a.* born (used in adding man's former name after his present name: *Lord Beaconsfield, né Benjamin Disraeli*). [F, p.p. of *naître* be born; cf. NÉE]

NE *abbr.* North-East(ern).

Ne *symb.* neon.

*NEA *abbr.* National Education Association.

Nĕǎ'nderthal (-tahl) *a.* of or belonging to the type of man widely distributed in palaeolithic Europe, with retreating forehead and massive brow-ridges. [f. ∿, valley in the Rhineland, Germany, where parts of a skeleton were found in 1857]

neap *a., n.,* & *v.* 1. *a.* ∿(-tide): see TIDE[1]. 2. *v.i.* (Of tide) tend towards neap, reach highest point of neap tide. 3. *v.t.* (In *pass.,* of ship) be kept aground, in harbour, etc., by neaping of tides. [OE *nēpflōd* (cf. FLOOD), of unkn. orig.]

Nĕǎpŏ'litan *a.* & *n.* (native or inhabitant) of Naples; ∿ ice, ice-cream made in layers of different colours and flavours, sweetmeat of similar appearance; ∿ violet, double sweet-scented kind of viola. [ME, f. L *Neapolitanus* (*Neapolites* n. f. L f. Gk *Neapolis* Naples f. *neos* new + *polis* city; see -AN)]

near[1] *adv.* & *prep.* (compar. & superl. also used as *preps.*). 1. *adv.* to or at a short distance (*to*), in(to) proximity in space or time; far and ∿, everywhere; ∿ at hand, within easy reach, not far in the future; ∿ by, not far off; ∿ upon, (arch.) not far in time from. 2. (arch.) almost, nearly, *not* nearly or anything like. 3. closely (*as near as one can guess; the nearer it resembles him the less I like it*); (arch.) parsimoniously (*lives very near*); go ∿ to do, come or go ∿ (to) doing, (narrowly escape or fail). 4. *prep.* near to or *to,* to or at a short distance (in space, time, condition, or resemblance) from (*occurs near the end; comes no nearer to the end; near one's* HEART; *the time draws near Christmas; sun is near setting; hope came near fulfilment; who comes nearest him in wit?*); *near the* KNUCKLE, *the* WIND[1]; NOWHERE *near.* 5. (in *comb.*) resembling, intended as a substitute for (*near-beer*); that is almost (*near-hysterical; a near--Communist.* |ME. f. ON *nær,* orig. compar. of *ná* = OE *nēah* NIGH]

near[2] *a.* (often governing *n.* like *prep.,* in *pred.* use; so also in compar. & superl.). 1. closely related (*near relation; near and dear*), intimate (*a near friend*). 2. (Of part of animal or vehicle ||or road, or horse etc. in team) left [orig. of side from which one mounted, opp. OFF] (*the near fore leg,* ||*near side front wheel*). 3. close at hand, close to, in place or time (*the nearest man; in the near future; the man near or nearest you; is nearer (to) us*); ∿'by *a.,* close in position; *Near* EAST(ERN); ∿ work (that must be done with the eye close to it). 4. (Of road or way) direct. 5. close, narrow, (*a near guess, resemblance, translation, race,* GO[2], *escape*); niggardly. 6. ∿ miss, (lit. or fig.) not a hit, but near enough to have effect (e.g. to damage target in bombing);

∿-sighted, short-sighted; ∿ thing, narrow escape. 7. Hence ∿'ISH[1] 2 *a.,* ∿'NESS *n.* [ME, f. prec.]

near[3] *v.i.* & *t.* draw near (to), approach. [f. NEAR[1,2]]

Nĕǎr'ctic *a.* (Zool.) of Arctic and temperate parts of N. America. [f. NEO- + ARCTIC]

near'ly *adv.* 1. closely (*nearly related; correspond, resemble, nearly*). 2. within a (very) little, almost; not ∿, nothing like, far from (*not nearly enough*). [f. NEAR[2] + -LY[2]]

neat[1] *n.* (*sing.,* or collect. as *pl.*; arch.) any bovine animal; (collect.) cattle; ∿'herd, cowherd; ∿-house, shed for cattle; ∿'s-foot, ∿'s-tongue, (used as food); ∿'s-leather (made from hide of ox). [OE *nēat,* = OS *nōt,* OHG *nōz,* ON *naut* f. Gmc *nautam (**naut-* make use of)]

neat[2] *a.* (Of liquor, esp. alcoholic) undiluted; of elegant simplicity in form or arrangement, nicely made or proportioned; (of language, style, sayings) brief, clear, and pointed, cleverly phrased, epigrammatic; deft, dextrous, cleverly done; tidy, methodical; *(sl.) excellent; ∿-handed, deft-handed; hence ∿'EN[6] *v.t.,* ∿'LY[2] *adv.,* ∿'NESS *n.* [f. F *net* f. L *nitidus* shining (*nitēre* shine)]

neath *prep.* (poet.) beneath. [f. BENEATH]

nĕb *n.* (Sc. & N. Engl.) beak or bill; nose; snout; tip, spout, point. [OE *nebb* = ON *nef,* rel. to MDu., MLG *nebbe* f. Gmc **nabhja-*; cf. NIB]

NEB *abbr.* ||National Enterprise Board; New English Bible.

Neb(r). *abbr.* Nebraska.

nĕ'bbish *n.* & *a.* (colloq.) submissive, timid, (person). [f. Yiddish *nebach* poor thing!]

nĕ'būla *n.* (*pl.* ∿e *or* ∿s). 1. (Astron.) bright or dark area due to reflection or absorption of light by cloud of dust or gas; bright area due to galaxy or large cloud of distant stars. 2. (Med.) clouded spot on cornea causing defective vision. [L, = mist]

nĕ'būlar *a.* of nebula(e); ∿ theory or hypothesis (that solar and stellar systems were developed from nebulae). [f. prec. + -AR[1]]

nĕ'būlous *a.* 1. (Astron.) of or like nebula(e); ∿ star, small cluster of indistinct stars, or star in luminous haze. 2. cloudlike; hazy, vague, indistinct, formless; clouded, turbid. 3. So nĕbūlo'sity *n.* [ME, f. F *nébuleux* or f. L *nebulosus* (as NEBULA; see -OUS)]

nĕ'būlý *a.* (Her.) of wavy form, represented as cloud. [f. F *nébulé* f. med. L *nebulatus* f. L NEBULA; see -Y[4]]

nĕcĕssār'ian *n.* & *a.* = NECESSITARIAN; hence ∿ISM (3) *n.* [f. NECESSARY + -ARIAN]

nĕcĕssǎr'ily (nĕ'-, -sĕ'r-) *adv.* as a necessary result, inevitably. [f. foll. + -LY[2]]

nĕ'cĕssarý *a.* & *n.* 1. *a.* indispensable, requisite, (*to or for* person etc.; *it is necessary that, to* do); requiring to, that must, be done. 2. determined by predestination or natural laws, not by free will; happening or existing by necessity (*necessary evil*); (of concept or mental process) inevitably resulting from nature of things or the mind, inevitably produced by previous state of things; (of agent) having no independent volition. 3. *n.* thing without which life cannot be maintained (*the necessaries of life*) or is unduly harsh; the ∿, (sl.) money or action needed for a purpose (*provide, do, the necessary*). [ME, f. AF **necessarie,* OF *necessarie* f. L *necessarius* (*necesse* needful; see -ARY[1])]

nĕcĕssitār'ian *n.* & *a.* (person) denying free will and maintaining that all action is determined by antecedent causes (opp. *libertarian*); hence ∿ISM (3) *n.* [f. NECESSITY + -ARIAN]

nĕcĕ'ssitāte *v.t.* 1. render necessary, involve as condition or accompaniment or result. 2. *force, compel, (person) *to* do. [f. med. L *necessitare* compel (as NECESSITY) + -ATE[3]]

nĕcĕ'ssitous *a.* poor, needy. [f. F *nécessiteux* or foll. + -OUS]

nĕcĕ'ssitý *n.* 1. constraint or compulsion regarded as a law prevailing through the material universe and governing all human action; logical ∿, compulsion to believe that of which the opposite is inconceivable. **2.** constraining power of circumstances, state of things compelling to certain course; LAY³ *under necessity*; **of ~,** unavoidably; **make a virtue of ~,** claim credit for alacrity or sense of duty when doing what one cannot avoid doing, do thing with a good grace; **~ knows no law** (absolves from any offence). **3.** imperative need (*for; necessity is the mother of invention*); indispensability (*of; the necessity of protecting life and property*); indispensable thing, necessary; (in *sing.* or *pl.*) want, poverty, hardship, pressing need. [ME, f. OF *necessité* f. L *necessitas -tatis* (*necesse* needful; see -ITY)]

nĕck¹ *n.* & *v.* **1.** *n.* part of body that connects head with shoulders; BREAK¹ one's *neck, neck of* task etc.; DEAD *from the neck up*; **get it in the ~,** (colloq.) suffer fatal or severe blow, have severe reprimand or punishment; **pain in the ~,** (colloq.) annoying or tiresome person or thing; **risk** one's **~,** take chance of being killed by falling etc.; **save** one's **~,** escape hanging; STICK¹ one's **neck out**; **talk through (the back of)** one's **~,** (sl.) talk foolishly or wildly; **up to** one's **~,** (colloq.) very deeply involved in; **~ and crop,** headlong, bodily; **~ and ~,** running level in race; **~ or nothing,** desperately, staking all on success. **2.** length of horse's head and neck as measure of its lead in race; flesh of animal's neck as food (esp. *neck of lamb* or *mutton*); part of shirt etc. around neck; (sl.) impudence (*you've got a neck asking that*). **3.** narrow part of cavity or vessel, esp. of bottle near mouth, or of passage, pass, or channel; pass, narrow channel, isthmus; part of violin etc. bearing finger-board; narrow connecting part between two parts of thing; (Geol.) solidified lava or igneous rock in old volcano crater or pipe; (Archit.) lower part of capital; **~ of the woods,** (colloq.) (remote) locality. **4. ~'band,** part of garment around neck; **~'cloth,** cravat; **~'erchief** (-chif), square of cloth worn round neck [f. KERCHIEF]; **~'lace** (-lis), ornament of precious stones or metal, or beads etc., worn round neck; **~'line,** outline of opening of garment at neck; **~'tie,** band of material (giving appearance of) securing shirt-collar when knotted in front (*~tie party,* (sl.) a hanging); **~-verse,** (Hist.) Latin words (usu. beginning of Ps. 51) printed in black letter, by reading which person claiming benefit of clergy might save his neck; **~'wear,** (Commerc.) collars and ties. **5.** Hence (-)**~ED²** (-kt) *a.* **6.** *v.i.* (sl.) (Of couple) clasp one another round the neck, engage in amorous fondling. **7.** *v.t.* (sl.) hug, embrace, (person). **8.** *v.t.* & *i.* form narrowed part (in). [OE *hnecca,* = MDu. *nac, necke,* OHG (*h*)*nac,* ON *hnakki* nape f. Gmc **hnak*(*ī*)- f. IE **knok-*]

||nĕck² *n.* (dial.) last sheaf of corn cut. [ME; orig. unkn.]

nĕ'cking *n.* (Archit.) = NECK¹ 3. [f. NECK¹ + -ING¹]

nĕ'cklet *n.* ornament or fur garment for neck. [f. NECK¹ + -LET]

nĕ'cro- *comb. form.* corpse, as: **~bio'sis,** decay in tissues of body; **~ge'nic,** produced by contact with dead bodies; **~LATRY** (-ŏ'l-); **~logy,** (-ŏ'l-), death-roll or obituary notice; **~phagous** (-ŏ'f-) that feeds on carrion; **~polis** (-ŏ'p-), (esp. ancient) cemetery; **ne'cropsy** [after AUTOPSY] or **~scopy** (-ŏ's-), post-mortem examination. [f. or after Gk *nekro-* (*nekros* corpse; see -o-)]

nĕ'cromăncy *n.* art of predicting by means of communicating with the dead; witchcraft; so **~ER¹** *n.,* **nĕcromă'ntic** *a.* [ME, f. OF *nigromancie* f. med. L *nigromantia* changed (by assoc. w. L *niger nigri* black) f. LL f. Gk *nekromanteia* (as prec.; see -MANCY)]

nĕcro'phĭl|y *n.* morbid (esp. erotic) attraction to corpses; so **nĕ'crophil(e), nĕcrophi'lia¹, ~ism** (1), *ns.* [f. as NECRO- + Gk *-philia* loving; see -y¹]

nĕcr|ō'sis *n.* (*pl.* **~ō'ses** *pr.* -ō'sēz). (Path.) death of circumscribed piece of tissue, esp. of bones; hence or cogn. **~o'TIC** *a.,* **~ō'se, nĕ'crotIZE** (3), *vbs. i.* [mod. L, f. Gk *nekrōsis* (*nekroō* kill; see NECRO-, -OSIS)]

nĕ'ctar *n.* **1.** (Gk & Rom. Myth.) drink of the gods; any delicious drink. **2.** sweet fluid produced by plants and made into honey by bees. **3.** Hence or cogn. **nĕctār'EAN, nĕctār'EOUS, ~ED²** (-erd), **~i'FEROUS, ~OUS,** *adjs.* [f. L f. Gk *nektar*]

nĕ'ctarine (-in, -ēn) *n.* kind of peach with thin downless skin and firm flesh. [n. use of arch. adj. f. NECTAR + -INE¹]

nĕ'ctarў *n.* flower's or plant's nectar-secreting organ. [f. mod. L *nectarium* (as NECTAR; see -ARY¹)]

NED *abbr.* (arch.) Oxford English Dictionary (orig. New English Dictionary).

||NEDC *abbr.* National Economic Development Council.

nĕ'ddў *n.* (colloq.) donkey; **||(N~)** = prec. [dim. of *Ned,* pet-form of man's Christian name *Edward*; see -y³]

||NEDO *abbr.* National Economic Development Office.

née, *nee, (nā) *a.* born (used in adding married woman's maiden name after her surname: *Mrs Ann Smith, née Jones*). [F, fem. p.p. of *naître* be born]

need¹ *n.* **1.** circumstances requiring some course of action (*if need arise* or *be* or *were; there is no* etc. *need, feel the need, have no need, to do* or *of doing* or abs.); **have ~,** *require to;* **had ~,** ought to (*had need remember*). **2.** necessity for presence or possession *of* (*the need of further securities*); **have ~ of,** require, want. **3.** emergency, crisis, time of difficulty, (*a friend in need is a friend indeed; failed him in his need;* **at ~,** in time of need); destitution, lack of necessaries, poverty. **4.** thing wanted, respect in which want is felt, requirement, (*my needs are few*). **5. ~'fire,** (1) fire got from dry wood by friction, and thought to have magical properties, (2) beacon, bonfire. [OE *nēd,* = OS *nōd,* OHG *nōt,* ON *nauth, neyth,* Goth. *nauths* f. Gmc **naudhiz, *nauthiz*]

need² *v.* **1.** *v.t.* stand in need of, require. **2.** be under necessity or obligation *to* or *to do* (*it needs to be done with care; need you ask?;* (ellipt.) *don't be away longer than you need*); (in 3 *sing. pres. neg.* or *interrog.* **need** without *to*: *he need not trouble himself; need she have come at all?;* (colloq.) *it needn't,* or *doesn't need to, be finished;* **~ not have done,** did not need to do). **3.** *v.i.* (arch.) be necessary; **it ~s not,** it is needless; *more* **than ~s,** than is necessary. [OE *nēodian* be necessary (*nēod* desire, var. of prec.)]

nee'dful *a.* requisite, necessary, indispensable, (*to, for,* or abs.; *it is needful to do,* or *that*); **the ~,** what is necessary, (sl.) money or action needed for a purpose; hence **~NESS** *n.* [ME, f. NEED¹ + -FUL]

nee'dle *n.,* & *v.t.* **1.** *n.* thin round long piece of smooth steel etc. pointed at one end and with eye for thread at other used in sewing; similar instrument without eye, used in KNITTING, crocheting, etc.; PIN¹*s and needles;* **sharp as a ~,** lit., or fig. acute, observant; **~ in a haystack,** thing so buried among or concealed by many others as to make search for it hopeless; **~'s eye,** least possible aperture, esp. w. ref. to Matt. 19:24. **2.** pointer on dial; (**magnetic**) **~,** piece of magnetized steel used as indicator on dial of compass and in magnetic and electric apparatus, esp. in telegraphy. **3.** pointed etching instrument; pointed surgical instrument; pointed end of hypodermic syringe; thin pointed piece of metal, wood, etc., that receives and transmits the vibrations set up by a revolving gramophone record; similar device used in making the record; steel pin exploding cartridge of breech-loader. **4.** obelisk (*Cleopatra's Needle*); sharp rock, peak. **5.** beam used as temporary support during underpinning. **6.** needle-shaped crystal. **7.** leaf of fir or pine. **8.** ||(sl.) fit of nervousness or bad temper (*got the needle while waiting*). **9. ~-bath,** shower-bath with fine strong spray; **~cord,** fine ribbed fabric; **~craft,** skill in needlework; **~fish,** garfish (*Belone belone*) or other long fish with slender jaws; **~ful,** length of thread etc. put into needle at one time; **||~ game, match,** etc., one closely contested or arousing exceptional personal feeling; ∾-lace (made with needles not bobbins); ∾-point, (1) fine sharp point, (2) = needle-lace, (3) gros or petit point; ∾ valve (closed by thin tapering part); ∾woman, (1) seamstress, (2) good or bad user of sewing-needle; ∾work, sewing or embroidery. 10. v.t. sew, pierce, or operate on, with needle; thread (one's way) between or through things; underpin with needle-beams; (colloq.) incite, irritate, prod into action. [OE nǣdl, = OS nādla, OHG nādala, ON nál, Goth. nēthla f. Gmc *nēthlō, *nētlā (*nē- sew)]

nee'dless a. unnecessary, uncalled for; ∾ to say, (parenth.) which I need not tell you; hence ∾LY² adv., ∾NESS n. [ME, f. NEED¹ + -LESS]

nee'dments n. pl. things needed, esp. personal necessaries carried on journey. [f. NEED¹,² + -MENT + -s¹]

needs (-z) adv. **1.** (arch.) of necessity. **2.** ∾ must (do, or ellipt.) cannot help or avoid or get out of doing; must ∾ do, (1) foolishly insists or insisted on doing, (2) = needs must do. [OE nēdes (as NEED¹, -s³)]

nee'd|ẏ a. (Of person) poor, destitute, without necessaries; (of circumstances) characterized by poverty; hence ∾iNESS n. [ME, f. NEED³ + -Y²]

neep n. (Sc. & N. Engl.) turnip. [OE nǣp f. L napus]

ne'er (nār) adv. **1.** (poet.) = NEVER 1. **2.** ∾ a, = NEVER a; ∾-do-well, (orig. Sc.) ∾-do-weel, good-for-nothing (person). [ME contr. of NEVER]

nefār'ious a. wicked, iniquitous; hence ∾LY² adv., ∾NESS n. [f. L nefarius (nefas wrong f. ne- not + fas divine law) + -OUS]

neg. abbr. negative.

nega'te v.t. nullify; deny existence of; imply or involve non-existence of; be the negation of. [f. L negare deny (neg- not) + -ATE³]

nega'tion n. denying; negative statement or doctrine; refusal, contradiction, denial of; (Logic) assertion that a certain proposition is false; absence or opposite of something actual or positive; negative or unreal thing, nonentity; so **ne'gat**ORY a. [F, or f. L negatio (as prec.; see -ATION)]

nega'tionist n. one who denies accepted beliefs without proposing substitutes. [f. prec. + -IST]

ne'gative¹ a. **1.** expressing or implying denial, prohibition, or refusal, (negative statute, vote, answer); ∾ proposition, (Logic) negation. **2.** lacking, or consisting in the lack of, positive attributes (∾ virtue, abstention from vice); marked by absence of qualities (negative reaction; test gave a negative result); ∾ evidence, instance, (of non-occurrence of something). **3.** (Alg., of quantity) less than zero, to be subtracted from others or from zero (∾ sign, -); in direction opposite that regarded as POSITIVE; negative FEEDBACK; ∾ quantity, (joc.) nothing. **4.** (Electr.) of the kind of charge carried by electrons (opp. POSITIVE); containing or producing such charge; ∾ pole, (of magnet) south-seeking pole. **5.** of opposite nature to thing regarded as positive (debt is negative capital); negative INCOME tax. **6.** (Photog.) having lights and shades of the actual object or scene reversed, or colours replaced by complementary ones. **7.** Hence ∾LY² (-vlĭ) adv., ∾NESS (-vn-), **negati'vity**, ns. [ME, f. OF negatif -ive or f. LL negativus (as NEGATE; see -IVE)]

ne'gative² n. **1.** negative statement, reply, or word (it is hard to prove a negative; two negatives make an affirmative); the ∾, position opposing the affirmative; in the ∾, negative(ly) (the answer is in the ∾, no), so as to reject proposal etc. **2.** negative quality, absence of something, (his character is made up of negatives). **3.** (Photog.) (developed film or plate bearing) negative image from which, positive pictures are obtained. [ME, = prohibition, f. F negative or LL negativa (sententia opinion, etc.) f. negativus (as prec.)]

ne'gative³ v.t. veto, reject, refuse to accept or countenance; disprove (inference, hypothesis); contradict (statement); neutralize (effect). [f. NEGATIVE¹]

ne'gativ|ism n. attitude of negationist; so ∾IST (2) n., ∾i'stIC a. [f. NEGATIVE¹ + -ISM]

negle'ct v.t., & n. **1.** v.t. disregard, not pay attention(s) to; leave uncared-for; leave undone, be remiss about; omit to do or doing. **2.** n. neglecting or being neglected; disregard of; negligence; hence ∾FUL a. [f. L neglegere -lect- (neg- not, legere choose, pick up)]

négligé, ne'gligee (ně'glĭzhā) n. free-and-easy or unceremonious attire; woman's loose informal garment(s), esp. (-ee) dressing-gown of thin fabric. [F, p.p. of négliger = prec.]

ne'glig|ence n. lack of proper care or attention, (piece of) carelessness, (CONTRIBUTORY negligence); freedom from restraint or artificiality in literature or art; so ∾ENT a. (of duty etc.), ∾entLY² adv. [ME f. OF, or f. L negligentia (negligere, = neglegere; see NEGLECT, -ENCE)]

ne'gligible a. that need not be considered (negligible QUANTITY). [obs. F (négliger NEGLECT; see -IBLE)]

nego'tiable (-sha-) a. that can be negotiated; open to discussion or modification. [f. foll. + -ABLE]

nego'ti|ate (-shǐ-) v. **1.** v.i. confer (with another) with view to compromise or agreement. **2.** v.t. arrange (affair), bring about (desired result), by negotiating. **3.** transfer (cheque etc.) to another for a consideration, convert into cash or notes, get or give value for (cheque etc.) in money. **4.** clear, get over or through, dispose of, (fence, obstacle, difficulty). **5.** Hence or cogn. ∾ANT, ∾A'TION (-shǐ-, -sǐ-), ∾ātOR, ns. [f. L negotiari (negotium business f. neg- not + otium leisure) + -ATE³]

Ne'gr|ess. See NEGRO.

Negri'llo n. (pl. ∾s). one of dwarf Negro people in Central and S. Africa. [Sp., dim. of NEGRO]

Negri'to (-rē'-) n. (pl. ∾s). one of small Negroid people in the Malayo-Polynesian region. [as prec.]

Ne'gritude n. quality of being a Negro; affirmation of the value of Negro culture. [f. F négritude NIGRITUDE]

Ne'gr|o n. (pl. ∾es; fem. Ne'gress) & a. **1.** n. member of black-skinned (orig.) African race of mankind. **2.** a. of this race, black-skinned, (Negro MINSTREL 2); occupied by or connected with Negroes (Negro SPIRITUAL); (of animals, n∾) black or dark (negro ant, bat, monkey). **3.** n∾-head, (1) strong black plug tobacco, (2) inferior indiarubber. **4.** Hence ∾HOOD n., ∾PHIL(E) a. & n., ∾PHO'BIA n. [Sp. & Port., f. L niger nigri black]

Ne'groid a. & n. (member) of division of mankind having characteristics typical of Negro race (esp. black skin, woolly hair, and flat nose); hence ∾AL (-oi'- a. [f. prec. + -OID]

Ne'gro|ism n. advancement of Negro interests and rights; idiom etc. used mainly by Negroes. [f. NEGRO + -ISM]

Ne'gus¹ n. (Hist.) ruler of Ethiopia. [f. Amh. n'gus king]

ne'gus² n. hot sweetened wine and water. [f. Col. F. Negus d. 1732, its inventor]

Neh. abbr. Nehemiah (OT).

neigh (nā) v.i., & n. (utter) prolonged cry (as) of horse. [OE hnǣgan, = MDu. neyen, MHG negen, of imit. orig.]

nei'ghbour, *-bor, (nā'ber) n. & v. **1.** n. dweller next door, near, in same street or village or district, or in adjacent country, (my neighbour Jones; are next-door neighbours; his nearest neighbour is 12 miles away; our neighbours across the Channel), esp. regarded as one who should be friendly (good, bad, neighbours) or as having claim on others' friendliness; duty to one's ∾ (to any fellow man). **2.** person or thing near or next to another (my neighbour at dinner; falling tree brought down its neighbour). **3.** (attrib.) neighbouring. **4.** Hence ∾LESS a., ∾SHIP n. **5.** v.t. & i. adjoin, border on or (up)on; hence ∾ING² a. [OE nēahgebūr (as NIGH; gebūr, cf. BOOR)]

nei'ghbourhood, *-bor-, (nā'ber-) n. **1.** neighbours, people of a district; district, esp. one forming a community within a town or city. **2.** nearness, vicinity *of* (**in the ∼ of** £*100*, about). **3.** neighbourly feeling or conduct. [ME, f. prec. +-HOOD]

nei′ghbourl|ў, *-bor-, (nā′ber-) *a.* characteristic of or befitting neighbour(s); friendly, kindly; hence **∼ĬNESS** *n.* [f. NEIGHBOUR +-LY¹]

nei′ther (nī′dh-, nē′dh-) *adv., conj., a.,* & *pron.* **1.** *adv.* (Introducing word, clause, etc., that is to be negatived equally with a following one(s) attached to it by *nor*) not either, not on the one hand, (*neither knowing nor caring; would neither come in nor go out; neither fish nor flesh nor fowl; neither* HERE *nor there*); (vulg., w. neg.) either (*I don't know that neither*); not either, also not, (*if you do not go, neither shall I; he did not go and neither did I; he should not have gone, (and) neither did he*). **2.** *conj.* (arch.) nor, nor yet, (*I know not, neither can I guess*). **3.** *a.* & *pron.* not either, not the one nor the other, (*neither accusation, neither of the accusations, is true; neither of them knows,* often also irreg. *know*); (loosely) none of any number of specified things. [ME *naither, neither,* f. OE *nōwther* contr. of *nōhwæther* (as NO², WHETHER); assim. to EITHER]

něk *n.* (S. Afr.) = COL 1. [Du., = NECK¹]

ně′kton *n.* group of free-swimming forms of organic life found at various depths in the ocean and in lakes, taken collectively. [G, f. Gk *nēkton* neut. of *nēktos* swimming (*nēkhō* swim)]

ně′llў *n.* **1.** largest species of petrel. **2.** ∥**not on your ∼,** (sl.) certainly not. **3.** effeminate person. [perh. f. woman's Christian name *Nelly;* sense 2 rhyming sl. f. *Nelly Duff* = puff = breath; cf. LIFE 1]

ně′lson *n.* wrestling-hold in which arm is passed under opponent's arm from behind and hand is applied to his neck. [app. f. name *Nelson*]

nělŭ′mbō *n.* (*pl.* **∼s**). plant of genus *Nelumbo,* Indian LOTUS. [mod. L, f. Sinh. *neḷum(bu)*]

ně′matocŷst *n.* cell in jellyfish etc. containing coiled thread that can be projected as sting. [f. as foll. + CYST]

ně′matōde *a.* & *n.* (worm) of slender unsegmented cylindrical shape. [f. Gk *nēma -matos* thread +-ODE]

Ně′mbŭtal, n-, *n.* (**P**) sodium salt of pentobarbitone, used as sedative and anticonvulsant. [f. *Na* (= sodium) + 5-ethyl-5-(1-methylbutyl) barbiturate + -AL; cf. BARBITAL]

nem. con. *abbr. nemine contradicente.*

Němě′an *a.* (Gk Ant.) **∼ games** (held at Nemea in alternate years); **∼ lion** (said to have been killed by Hercules). [f. L *Nem(a)eus* f. Gk *Nemeaios* (*Nemea* near Argos); see -AN]

němēr′tīne *a.* & *n.* (worm) of class Nemertea of marine flatworms, often brightly coloured. [f. mod. L *Nemertes* f. Gk *Nēmertēs* name of a sea nymph +-INE¹]

němě′sia (-zha) *n.* S. Afr. plant of genus *Nemesia,* cultivated for its variously coloured irregular flowers. [mod. L, f. Gk *nemesion,* name of a similar plant; see -IA¹]

ně′měs|ĭs *n.* (*pl.* **∼es** *pr.* -ēz). retributive justice; downfall caused by, agent of, this. [Gk, = righteous indignation, personified as goddess of retribution (*nemō* give what is due)]

nemine (ně′mĭnī, nā′-) *pron.* **∼ contradicente** or **dissentiente** (kŏntradĭsě′ntĭ, -kě′-; dĭsěntĭe′ntĭ), with no one dissenting. [abl. of L *nemo* nobody]

ne′ne (nā′nā) *n.* Hawaiian species of goose. [f. Hawaiian *nēnē*]

ně′nuphār *n.* water-lily. [med. L, f. Arab. & Pers. *nīnūfar, nīlūfar* f. Skr. *nīlōtpala* blue lotus (*nīla* blue, *utpala* lotus)]

nēō- *comb. form.* new, modern, later, or revived, as: **∼-Ca′mbrian,** (Geol.) of the later Cambrian period or system; **∼cla′ssic(al),** of a revival of classical style or treatment in art, literature, music, etc.; **∼-colo′nialism,** use of economic, political, or other means of obtaining or retaining influence over other countries, esp. former colonies; **∼-He′llenism,** revival of Greek ideals; **∼my′cin,** antibiotic related to streptomycin; **∼pe′ntane,** isomer of pentane, the

last to be discovered; **Neopla′tonism,** 3rd-c. mixture of Platonic ideas with Oriental mysticism, similar doctrine in medieval and later times; **∼-schola′sticism,** revival and restatement of teachings of medieval schoolmen; **∼tro′pical,** of tropical and S. America; **Neozo′ic,** (Geol.) of later period of geological history, post-Palaeozoic or post-Mesozoic. [Gk (*neos* new; see -o-)]

nēody′mium *n.* (Chem.) metallic element of lanthanide series. [f. NEO- + DIDYMIUM]

nēoli′thic *a.* of the later Stone Age, when ground or polished stone weapons and implements prevailed. [f. NEO- + Gk *lithos* stone +-IC]

nēolō′gian *a.* & *n.* **1.** *a.* of, inclined to, marked by, neologism in theology. **2.** *n.* neologist in theology. [f. NEOLOGY +-AN]

nēŏ′log|ism, nēŏ′log|ў, *ns.* coining or using of new words, new-coined word; tendency to or adoption of novel or rationalistic religious views; so **∼IST** (1) *n.,* **∼IZE** (2) *v.i.* [f. F *néologisme, néologie,* f. as NEO-, -LOGY, -ISM]

ne′ŏn *n.* (Chem.) inert gaseous element occurring in traces in the atmosphere and giving orange-red glow when electricity is passed through it in a sealed low-pressure tube, whence its use in lights and illuminated advertisements (*neon lamp, light, sign*). [Gk, neut. of *neos* new]

ně′onāte *n.* new-born child; so **nēonā′tAL** *a.* [f. mod. L *neonatus* (as NEO-, NATION)]

nēŏnto′log|ў *n.* study of organisms not yet extinct; hence **∼IST** (3) *n.* [f. NEO- + ONTOLOGY]

ně′ophrŏn *n.* white Egyptian vulture or other bird of genus *Neophron.* [name of man turned into vulture in *Metamorphoses* of Antoninus Liberalis (2nd c.)]

ně′ophŷte *n.* new convert esp. among primitive Christians or Roman Catholics; newly ordained RC priest; novice of religious order; beginner, novice, tiro. [f. eccl. L f. NT Gk *neophutos* newly planted (as NEO-, *phuton* plant)]

ně′oplăsm *n.* (Path.) new growth of tissue in animal part of body, esp. tumour; so **nēoplă′stIC** *a.* [f. NEO- + Gk PLASMA formation]

ně′oprēne *n.* synthetic rubberlike polymer. [f. NEO- + *chloroprene* etc. (perh. f. PROPYL +-ENE)]

nēŏ′těnў *n.* (Zool.) retention of juvenile features in adult animal; sexual maturity in larval form. [f. G *neotenie* f. as NEO- + Gk *teinō* extend]

nēotě′ric *a.* (literary) recent, newfangled, modern. [f. LL f. Gk *neōterikos* (*neōteros* compar. of *neos* new; see -IC)]

Něpalē′se (-z) *a.* & *n.* (*pl.* same). = foll. [f. *Nepal* (see foll.) + -ESE]

Nèpa′lī (-aw′-) *a.* & *n.* (native, inhabitant, or language) of Nepal. [f. *Nepal,* country NE of India, + -I]

něpě′nthe *n.* = foll. 1. [var. of foll., after It. *nepente*]

něpě′nthes (-z) *n.* **1.** (poet.) drug causing forgetfulness of grief. **2.** pitcher-plant of genus *Nepenthes.* [L, f. Gk *nēpenthes* (*pharmakon* drug), neut. of *nēpenthēs* (*nē-* not, *penthos* grief)]

něphelō′|měter *n.* instrument for measuring turbidity of liquid; so **∼phelomě′trIC** *a.,* **∼METRY** *n.* [f. Gk *nephelē* cloud + -o- +-METER]

ně′phew (-v-, -f-) *n.* brother(-in-law)'s or sister(-in-law)'s son; cf. NEPOTISM. [ME f. OF *neveu* f. L *nepos*]

nephŏ′logŷ *n.* study of the clouds. [f. Gk *nephos* cloud + -o- +-LOGY]

ně′phrīte *n.* = JADE² 1. [f. G *nephrit* f. Gk *nephros* kidney, w. ref. to its supposed efficacy in kidney disease; see -ITE¹ (2)]

nèphri′tic *a.* of or in the kidneys, renal; of nephritis. [LL f. Gk *nephritikos* (as foll.; see -IC)]

nèphri′tis *n.* inflammation of the kidneys. [LL, f. Gk (*nephros* kidney; see -ITIS)]

nèphr(o)- *comb. form.* kidney, as: **∼e′ctomy** *n.,* excision of kidney; **∼ŏ′loGY, ∼ŏ′tomY,** *ns.* [f. Gk (as prec.) + -o-]

ne plus ultra (nē plŭs ŭ'ltra, nā plo͞os o͞o'ltrah) *n.* prohibition of advance, impassable obstacle; furthest point attained or attainable; highest pitch or form *of*, acme, culmination. [L, = not further beyond, supposed inscription on Pillars of Hercules (Strait of Gibraltar) prohibiting passage by ships]

nĕ'pot|ism *n.* undue favour in appointing one's relatives to office (orig. by Popes for illegitimate sons called nephews); so ~IST (1) *n.* [f. F *népotisme* f. It. *nepotismo* (*nepote* NEPHEW; see -ISM)]

Nĕ'ptūne *n.* **1.** (Roman god of) the sea (~'s **cup**, sponge of genus *Poterion*). **2.** one of the farthest planets of the solar system, discovered in 1846 from mathematical computations. [ME f. F, or f. L *Neptunus*]

Nĕptū'nian *a.* & *n.* (Geol.) produced by water action; (person) maintaining aqueous origin of certain rocks, so **Nĕ'ptūn**IST (2) *n.* (opp. *Plutonist* or *Vulcanist*; of planet Neptune. [f. L *Neptunius* (as prec.) + -AN]

nĕptū'nium *n.* (Chem.) transuranic element produced when uranium atoms absorb bombarding neutrons. [f. NEPTUNE, planet next beyond Uranus, + -IUM]

||NERC *abbr.* Natural Environment Research Council.

nĕr'ĕid *n.* sea-nymph; (Zool.) long sea-worm or centipede. [f. L f. Gk *Nērēis -idos* daughter of sea-god Nereus; see -ID³ 2]

nĕrī'nē *n.* bulbous S. Afr. plant of genus *Nerine* with showy red or pink flowers, e.g. Guernsey lily. [mod. L, f. L name of water-nymph]

nĕr'ka *n.* sockeye salmon. [native name]

nero antico (nāro ahntē'ko) *n.* kind of black marble found in Roman ruins. [It.]

nĕr'oli *n.* essential oil from flowers of bitter orange, used in perfumery. [f. F *néroli* f. It. *neroli*, perh. f. name of Italian princess]

Nĕrō'nian *a.* (as) of Nero or his times; cruel, licentious, tyrannical. [f. L *Neronianus* f. C. C. *Nero -onis*, Rom. emperor d. AD 68; see -IAN]

nĕrts. See NUT 1.

nĕr'v|āte *a.* (Bot.) (Of leaf) having ribs; so ~A'TION *n.* [f. foll. + -ATE²]

nĕrve *n.*, & *v.t.* **1.** *n.* fibre or bundle of fibres connecting and conveying impulses of sensation and motion between brain or spinal cord or ganglionic organ and some part of the body; material constituting these. **2.** (in *pl.*) bodily state in regard to physical sensitiveness and interaction between brain and other parts, disordered state in these respects, exaggerated sensitiveness, nervousness; **does not know what ~s are,** has equable and confident temperament; **bundle of ~s,** very nervous person; **a fit of ~s,** nervous state; **get on** person's ~s, be a source of worry or irritation or annoyance to him; **has iron ~s, ~s of steel,** etc., is easily upset or frightened; ~ **war,** = WAR¹ *of* nerves. **3.** (poet. or arch.) sinew, tendon. **4. strain every ~,** make all possible efforts. **5.** vigour, energy. **6.** (Bot.) rib, esp. midrib, of leaf. **7.** coolness in danger, boldness, assurance, (lose one's ~, become timid or irresolute); (colloq.) audacity, impudence, (*had the nerve, has a nerve, to ask for more*). **8.** ~-**cell,** cell transmitting impulses in nerve tissue; ~-**centre,** group of closely connected ganglion-cells, (fig.) centre of control; ~ **gas,** poison gas that affects the nervous system; ~-**knot,** (arch.) ganglion; ~-**racking,** greatly straining the nerves. **9.** Hence (-)**nĕrv**ED² (-vd) *a.*, **nĕr'vo**- *comb. form.* **10.** *v.t.* give strength, vigour, or courage, to; brace one*self* to face danger or suffering. [ME, = sinew, f. L *nervus*, rel. to Gk *neuron*]

nĕr'velĕss *a.* inert, lacking vigour or spirit, listless; (of style) flabby, diffuse; (Bot. & Entom.) without nervures; (Anat. & Zool.) without nerves; confident, not nervous; hence ~LY² *adv.*, ~NESS *n.* [f. prec. + -LESS]

nĕr'vīne *a.* & *n.* (Med.) (medicine) relieving nerve--disorders. [f. F *nervin* (as NERVE; see -INE¹)]

nĕr'vous *a.* **1.** full of nerves; of the nerves (~ **system,** nerves and nerve-centres as a whole, allowing organism to co-ordinate its response to environment; **central ~ system,** brain and spinal cord); affecting, or acting on, the nerves (~ **breakdown,** severe weakness or disorder of nerves). **2.** having disordered or delicate nerves, excitable, highly strung, easily agitated, timid; ||~ **of** doing, afraid to do. **3.** (Of literary style) vigorous, terse. **4.** (arch.) sinewy, muscular. **5.** Hence ~LY² *adv.*, ~NESS *n.* [ME, f. L *nervosus* (as NERVE; see -OUS)]

nĕr'vure (-yer) *n.* one of the tubes forming framework of insect's wing, vein; principal vein of leaf. [F (*nerf* NERVE; see -URE)]

nĕr'vỹ *a.* **1.** (poet.) sinewy, strong. **2.** jerky, nervous. **3.** (sl.) cool, confident, impudent; trying to the nerves. [f. NERVE + -Y²]

nĕ'sci|ence *n.* (literary). not knowing, absence of knowledge *of*; so ~ENT *a.* & *n.*, ignorant (*of*), agnostic. [f. LL *nescientia* f. L *nescire* not know (*ne*- not, *scire* know); see -ENCE]

nĕss *n.* promontory, headland, cape. [OE *næs*, = ON *nes*, LG *nesse*, rel. to OE *nasu* NOSE]

-nĕss *suf.* forming *ns.* from *adjs.*, expr. state or condition (*bitterness, clearness, conceitedness, happiness, lovingness, up-to-date-ness*), instance of this (*a kindness*), or material in a state (*foulness*). [OE *-nes(s), -nis(s)*, = OS, OHG *-nessi, -nissi*, Goth. *-nassus* f. Gmc **n* in p.p. of strong vbs. + **-assus* (**-atjan* vbl suf.)]

nĕst *n.* & *v.* **1.** *n.* structure or place made or chosen by bird for laying eggs and sheltering young (**it's an ill bird that fouls its own ~,** one should not speak ill of home etc.; FEATHER² one's *nest*; animal's or insect's abode or spawning or breeding place. **2.** snug or secluded retreat, lodging, shelter, bed, receptacle; haunt *of* robbers etc.; fostering-place *of* vice etc. **3.** brood or swarm in same nest etc.; group of machine--guns; collection or series of similar objects; ~ of **tables** (fitting one under another when not in use). **4.** ~-**egg,** (1) real or imitation egg left in nest to induce hen to go on laying there, (2) sum of money kept as reserve or nucleus. **5.** Hence ~'FUL 2 *n.*, ~'LIKE *a.* **6.** *v.i.* make or have nest in specified place, take to nest--building; take wild birds' nests or eggs; fit together like nest of tables. **7.** *v.t.* (in *p.p.*) established (as) in nest; (of boxes etc.) packed one inside another. [OE, = OHG *nest* f. IE **nizdo-* (**ni* down, **sed-* sit)]

nĕ'stle (-sel) *v.* **1.** *v.i.* settle oneself, be settled, comfortably *down*, or *in*, *into*, *among*, etc., leaves, wraps, chair, etc.; press oneself affectionately (*close*) to or up to person; lie half-hidden or embedded. **2.** *v.t.* push (head, face, shoulder, etc.) affectionately or snugly in or *into*; (usu. in *p.p.*) hold as if in nest. [OE *nestlian*, = MDu., MLG *nestelen* (as prec.; see -LE 3)]

nĕ'stling (-sl-) *n.* bird too young to leave nest. [ME, f. NEST + -LING¹, or f. prec. + -ING³]

Nĕ'stor (-ŏr, -er) *n.* wise old man, senior of company etc. [name of character in Homer's *Iliad*]

Nĕstŏr'ian *a.* & *n.* (adherent) of doctrine of Nestorius, asserting that Christ embodied distinct divine and human persons; hence ~ISM (3) *n.* [f. LL *Nestorianus* (*Nestorius*, patriarch of Constantinople 428–31); see -IAN]

nĕt[1] *n.* & *v.* (-tt-). **1.** *n.* fabric of twine, cord, hair, etc., joined at intervals to form a set of meshes; piece of this used for catching fish, birds, etc., or for protecting fruit, confining hair, holding cargo, keeping away mosquitoes, dividing tennis-court, enclosing practice--ground for cricket batsmen, etc.; football or hockey or lacrosse goal-space enclosed by net. **2.** moral or mental snare; means of catching or entrapping a person; spider's web; reticulation, network. **3.** ~'**ball,** game in which ball has to be thrown so as to fall through an elevated horizontal ring from which net hangs; ~ **curtain** (of fine-meshed material); ~'**work,** (*n.*) arrangement with intersecting lines and interstices recalling those of net, complex system of railways, rivers, canals, etc., chain of interconnected persons or operations or electrical conductors, group of broadcasting stations connected for simultaneous broadcast of same programme, (v.t.) broadcast thus. **4.** Hence ∼'FUL 2 n. **5.** v.t. cover, confine, catch, with net(s); put (ball) in net or goal; fish (river etc.) with nets, set nets in (river); make (purse, hammock, etc.) by netting; (usu. in p.p.) mark with netlike pattern, reticulate. **6.** v.i. make netting. [OE net(t), = OS net(ti), OHG nezzi, ON net, Goth. nati]

nĕt², **nĕtt**, a., & v.t. (-tt-). **1.** a. free from deduction, remaining after necessary deductions (of), (∼ **profit**, true profit, actual gain after working expenses have been paid, opp. gross profit); (of price) off which discount is not allowed; (of weight) excluding that of container etc.; (of effect, result, etc.) ultimate, effective; net TON². **2.** v.t. gain or yield (sum) as net profit. [F; see NEAT²]

nĕ'ther (-dh-) a. (arch. or joc.) = LOWER³ 1 (nether lip, jaw); ∼ **garments** etc., trousers; ∼ **man** or **person**, legs etc.; nether MILL¹stone; ∼ **regions**, ∼ **world**, hell, underworld; hence ∼MOST a. [OE nithera etc., = OS nithiri, OHG nidari, ON nethri f. Gmc *nithar down(wards)]

Nĕ'therlander n., **Nĕ'therlandish** a., (-dh-). (native or inhabitant) of the Netherlands. [f. Du. Nederlander, Nederlands(ch) (Nederland; see foll.)]

Nĕ'therlands (-dh-; -z) n. **1.** kingdom of Holland in N. Europe. **2.** (Hist.) Low Countries. [f. Du. Nederland (as NETHER, LAND¹)]

nĕ'tsuke (-sōōkā) n. (pl. ∼s, or same). carved button-like ornament formerly worn by Japanese to suspend articles from girdle. [Jap.]

nĕtt. See NET².

nĕ'tting n. In vbl senses; netted string, thread, or wire; piece of this used for various purposes. [f. NET¹ + -ING¹]

nĕ'ttle n., & v.t. **1.** n. plant of genus Urtica, including two common species growing profusely on waste land and covered with stinging hairs; other plant resembling these, esp. DEAD nettle; GRASP the nettle; ∼-**rash**, eruption on skin in patches like those made by nettle stings. **2.** v.t. sting with nettles, irritate, provoke, annoy. [OE net(e)le, = OS netila, OHG nezzila, OSw. netla f. Gmc *natilōn; see -LE 1]

neume, **neum**, n. (Mus.) sign in plainsong indicating note or group of notes to be sung to a syllable. [ME f. OF neume, f. med. L neu(p)ma f. Gk pneuma breath]

neur'al (nūr'-) a. (Anat.) of the nerves; of the central nervous system; situated on same side of body as the central nervous system, dorsal. [f. Gk neuron nerve + -AL]

neurā'lg|ia (nūră'lja) n. intense intermittent pain due to affection of nerve(s) esp. of head or face; hence ∼IC a. [mod. L, f. as prec.; see -ALGIA]

neurăsth|ē'nia (nūr-) n. debility of nerves causing fatigue, listlessness, etc.; so ∼ĕ'nIC a. & n. [f. Gk neuron nerve + -ASTHENIA]

neurā'tion (nūr-) n. distribution of nervures, venation. [irreg. f. Gk neuron nerve + -ATION]

neur|ī'tis (nūr-) n. inflammation of nerve(s); hence ∼ī'tIC a. [as foll. + -ITIS]

neur'o- (nūr'ō) comb.form. nerve(s), as: ∼**glia** (-ŏ'glĭa, -oglī'a), non-nervous supporting tissue in nervous system; ∼**mu'scular**, of nerves and muscles; ∼**path**, person of abnormal nervous sensibility or affected by nervous disease; so ∼**pa'thic** a., ∼**pathy** (-ŏ'p-) n.; ∼**patho'logy**, pathology of nervous system; ∼**physio'logy**, physiology of nervous system; ∼**pterous** (-ŏ'p-), of the Neuroptera, order of insects having four membranous transparent wings with reticulate neuration; ∼**sur'gery** (performed on nervous system); ∼**tomy** (-ŏ't-), cutting of nerve esp. to produce sensory paralysis. [f. Gk neuron nerve + -o-]

neuro'log|y (nūr-) n. scientific study of nerve systems; hence **neurolo'g**ICAL (nūr-) a., ∼IST (3) n. [f. mod. L f. mod. Gk neurologia (as prec.; see -LOGY)]

neurō'ma (nūr-) n. (pl. ∼s or ∼ta). tumour on nerve or in nerve-tissue. [f. as foll. + -OMA]

neur'ōn, **neur'ōne**, (nūr'-) n. nerve-cell and its appendages; hence **neurō'n**AL, **neurō'n**IC, (nūr-) adjs. [Gk neuron nerve]

neurō's|is (nūr-) n. (pl. ∼es pr. -ēz). functional derangement due to disorders of nervous system, esp. without organic change; behaviour showing inability to take rationally objective view of life. [mod. L (as NEURO-; see -OSIS)]

neurō't|ic (nūr-) a. & n. **1.** (person) suffering from neurosis. **2.** of neurosis; (colloq.) showing undue adherence to unrealistic idea of things. **3.** Hence ∼ICALLY adv., ∼icISM (2) n. [f. prec.; see -OTIC]

neu'ter a., n., & v.t. **1.** a. (Gram.) (of noun etc.) neither masculine nor feminine; (of verb) intransitive. **2.** neutral in war, argument, opinion, etc.; **stand** ∼, remain neutral, declare neutrality. **3.** (Bot.) with neither pistils nor stamens, asexual; (Entom.) sexually undeveloped, sterile. **4.** n. neuter noun, adjective, pronoun, verb, or gender; sexually undeveloped female insect, esp. bee or ant; castrated animal; neutral person. **5.** v.t. castrate. [ME, = OF neutre or f. L. neuter neither (ne- not, uter either)]

neu'tral a. & n. **1.** a. not assisting either of two belligerent States, belonging to a State or group of States that thus stands aloof, exempted or excluded from active or passive hostilities; taking neither side in dispute or difference of opinions; indifferent, impartial. **2.** not distinctly marked or coloured, indefinite, vague, indeterminate; ∼ **tint**, grey or slate-colour; neutral VOWEL. **3.** (Chem.) neither acid nor alkaline; (Electr.) neither positive nor negative; (Entom. & Bot.) sexually undeveloped, asexual; neutral EQUILIBRIUM; ∼ **gear**, condition in which engine is disconnected from driven parts. **4.** Hence or cogn. ∼ITY (-ă'l-) n., ∼LY² adv. **5.** n. neutral State or person; subject of neutral State; neutral gear. [ME f. obs. F, or f. L neutralis of neuter gender (as prec.; see -AL)]

neu'traliz|e, **-is|e** (-īz), v.t. make neutral; counterbalance, render ineffective by opposite force or effect; exempt or exclude (place) from sphere of hostilities; hence ∼A'TION n. [f. F neutraliser f. med. L neutralizare (as prec.; see -IZE)]

neutri'nō (-ē'-) n. (pl. ∼s). (Phys.) either of two stable elementary particles with zero electric charge and probably zero mass, interacting only very slightly with matter. [It., dim. of neutro neutral (as NEUTER)]

neu'trōn n. elementary particle of about same mass as proton but without electric charge, present in all atomic nuclei except those of ordinary hydrogen; ∼ **bomb** (using neutrons to do harm to life rather than buildings etc.); ∼ **star**, hypothetical very dense star composed mainly of neutrons. [f. NEUTRAL + -ON]

Nev. abbr. Nevada.

névé (nĕ'vā) n. expanse of granular snow not yet compressed into ice at head of glacier. [Swiss F, = glacier, f. Rom. *nivatum f. L nix nivis snow]

nĕ'ver adv. **1.** at no time or moment, on no occasion, not ever, (have never been there; never even looked; never before, since, yet). **2.** ∼ **is a long time** or **word** or **day** (comment on rash renunciation or despair or negative prophecy); ∼, ∼ (emphat.); **it is** ∼ **too late to mend**, reformation is always possible; NOW or never; ∼ **say die**, do not despair. **3.** not . . . at any time, not . . . ever, (is never likely to succeed; I never remember her winning); not at all (never fear; never MIND²). **4.** (colloq., expr. surprise or incredulity, in sentence or ellipt.) surely not, you do not mean it, (you have never left the key in the lock!; 'He ate the whole turkey.'—'Never!'; I ∼ did!, well, I ∼!, i.e. heard of such a thing etc.). **5.** ∼ **a**, not a, no . . . at all; ∼ **a one**, none; ∼ **so**, (in concessive clause) to unlimited extent (task was beyond him, though he work never so hard); ∼ **the**, (w. compar.) = NONE the. **6.** (in comb. w. participles etc.) never-to-be-forgotten, -ending, -failing, etc. **7.** ∼**mor'e**, at no future time; N∼ N∼ (**Land**), imaginary Utopian place, (Austral.) remote parts of NT and northern Queensland; ‖**never-ne'ver**, (colloq.) hire-purchase; ∼**thele'ss** adv. & conj., despite that, but despite that, notwithstanding, all the same. [OE næfre (ne not, æfre EVER)]

***ne'vus.** See NAEVUS.

new[1] a. **1.** not existing before, now first made, brought into existence, invented, introduced, known or heard of, experienced, or discovered (a ∼ **one on**, (colloq.) story or situation not previously met by); unfamiliar or unaccustomed to. **2.** renewed, fresh, further, additional, different, changed, (a new morality; the new chairman; my new tailor); (in place-names) discovered or founded later than and named after (New Orleans; New Zealand); new BIRTH, BROOM, DEAL[2]; turn over a new LEAF; **a ∼ life**, living in conditions very different from previous ones; ∼ **man**, (Theol.) one converted to Christianity (put on the ∼ man, show conversion by reforming oneself); New MODEL[1]; new STYLE. **3.** **the ∼** (as distinctive epithet implying difference of character), later, modern, (derog.) newfangled, advanced in method or doctrine; **the ∼ mathematics** (using SET[2] theory etc. in elementary teaching); **the ∼ poor, rich**, classes recently impoverished, enriched, by social changes etc.; **the ∼ woman**, (derog.) woman who aspires to freedom and independence and rejects convention; the New TESTAMENT, WORLD. **4.** of recent origin, growth, arrival, or manufacture, now first used, not worn or exhausted, (new bread, wine; new furniture, clothes; new countries, soil; a heart, pleasures, ever new; fifteen new members); (of a language) modern, in use since medieval times; **as good as ∼**, not having been impaired (as) by wear and tear; **New Christian**, Marrano; new CHUM; ∼ **foundation**, cathedral etc. founded after Reformation; ∼ **look**, (colloq.) altered or renovated or up-to-date appearance; ∼ **potatoes** (first of new crop); ∼ **wave**, nouvelle vague. **5.** (Of family or person) lately risen to position. **6.** ∼'**comer**, person lately arrived; **New Englander**, inhabitant of **New England**, six NE states of USA or district in northern NSW; ∼-**fa'shioned**, made in or following a new fashion; ***New Left**, extremist radical movement among students etc.; ∼ **light**, (person accepting) modern or liberal views on religious matters; ∼ **moon**, moon when first seen as crescent after conjunction with sun, time of such appearance; **New'speak**, artificial official language in Orwell's 1984; ∼ **star**, nova; ‖∼ **town** (established as completely new settlement with government sponsorship); ∼ **year**, coming or lately begun year, first few days of year, esp. in civil calendar (**New Year's Day**, ***New Year's**, 1 Jan.; **New Year's Eve**, 31 Dec.) or religious calendar (e.g. Jewish, day or two days in Sept.–Oct.); **New Yorker**, native or inhabitant of New York; **New Zealander**, (1, Hist.) Maori, (2) inhabitant of New Zealand of European descent. **7.** Hence ∼'ISH[1] 2 a., ∼'NESS n. [OE nīwe, OS, OHG niuwi, ON nýr, Goth. niujis f. Gmc *neujaz f. IE *newjos]

new[2] adv. (preceding, and now usu. hyphened with, word it qualifies). **1.** newly, recently, just; ∼-**blown**, having just come into bloom (lit. or fig.); ∼-**born**, recently born (and see 2); ∼-**come**, lately arrived; ∼-**found**, recently discovered or disclosed; ∼-**laid**, (of egg) freshly laid; ∼-**mown**, (of hay etc.) freshly cut. **2.** anew, afresh, re-; ∼-**born**, regenerated (and see 1); ∼-**model**, rearrange, recast. [OE nīwe (as prec.)]

New'burg n. lobster ∼ (cooked in thick cream sauce with sherry or brandy). [19th c.; orig. unkn.]

New'castle (-ahsel) n. ∼ **disease**, serious respiratory disease of fowls, caused by virus; COALS to Newcastle. [f. ∼ upon Tyne, in NE England]

new'el n. centre pillar of winding stair (**open** or **hollow** ∼, central well of winding stair); post

supporting stair-handrail at top or bottom. [ME, f. OF no(u)el knob f. med. L nodellus dim. of L nodus knot; see -LE 2]

newfa'ngled (-nggeld) a. (derog.) different from the good old fashion, objectionably novel. [f. (now dial.) newfangle ME f. newe NEW[2]+-fangel f. OE *fangol inclined to take, +-ED[1]]

Newfou'ndland n. ∼ (**dog**), (dog of) large breed with thick coarse coat, noted for sagacity and swimming powers. [name of Canadian province, an island at mouth of St. Lawrence river]

new'ly adv. **1.** recently (usu. with p.p. = NEW[2] 1; the newly-discovered country; a guest newly arrived); ∼-**wed**, (person) recently married. **2.** in new manner. [OE nīwlīce (as NEW[1], -LY[2])]

New'märkèt n. **1.** ∼(**coat**), close-fitting overcoat for man or woman. **2.** card-game in which players seek to play cards corresponding to duplicates on table and thus win stakes on these. [∼ in Cambridgeshire, noted for horse-races]

news (-z) n. **1.** new or interesting information, fresh events reported, (have you heard the or this news?; was in the news last year; that is news to me); **bad ∼**, report of unwelcome events, (colloq.) unpleasant person or thing; **good ∼**, report of welcome events; that is **no ∼**, already well known; **no ∼ is good ∼**, absence of information justifies continued optimism. **2.** medium for transmitting news; (regular) broadcast report of fresh events; (N∼) part of newspaper title (Evening News, Wallasey News). **3.** ∼'**agent**, *∼ **dealer**, dealer in newspapers, etc.; ∼-**boy**, ∼-**girl**, (who delivers or sells newspapers); ∼ **bulletin**, collection of items of news, esp. for broadcasting; ∼'**cast**(er), radio or television broadcast(er) of news reports; ‖∼ **cinema**, = news theatre; ∼ **conference**, press conference; *∼'**hawk**, *∼'**hound**, reporter; ∼-**letter**, printed informal bulletin of club etc., (Hist.) letter sent out periodically to convey news to country towns etc.; ∼'**monger**, a gossip; ∼'**paper** (-s-), (1) printed publication usu. daily or weekly containing news, advertisements, literary matter, correspondence, etc., (2) material of this for wrapping etc.; ∼'**paperman** (-s-), journalist; ∼'**print**, paper for printing newspapers on; ∼-**reader**, = newscaster; ∼'**reel**, cinema film giving the news; ∼-**room**, (1) room reserved for newspaper-reading, (2) room where news is prepared for broadcasting etc.; ∼-**sheet**, simple form of newspaper, news-letter; ∼-**stand**, stall for sale of newspapers; ∼ **theatre**, cinema showing mainly newsreels; ∼-**vendor**, newspaper-seller; ∼'**worthy**, important or interesting enough to be mentioned as news. **4.** Hence ∼'LESS, ∼'Y[2], adjs. [ME, pl. of NEW[1] after OF noveles or med. L nova neut. pl. of L novus new]

newt n. small tailed amphibian esp. of genus Triturus, eft. [ME, for ewt (a newt = an ewt; cf. NICKNAME) var. of evet EFT]

new'ton n. **1.** (Phys.) unit of force, force that, acting for one second on a mass of one kilogram, gives it a velocity of one metre per second. **2.** N∼'s laws of **motion**, three propositions about the relations between forces acting and motions occurring. [f. Sir I. Newton, Engl. scientist d. 1727]

Newto'nian a. of Newton or his theory of the universe; devised etc. by Newton; classical (Newtonian mechanics); (of telescope) with oblique mirror to reflect image to side of tube. [f. as prec. +-IAN]

nèxt a., adv., prep., & n. **1.** a. lying, living, being, nearest or nearest to (in the next house; my next neighbour; the shop next to the corner; the chair next to the fire); next DOOR[1]; ∼ **friend**, (Law) person acting on behalf of a minor or other person legally incompetent; ∼ **but one**, with one other intervening; ∼ **to**, (fig.) almost (next to nothing; next to impossible), *(sl.) very friendly with. **2.** soonest come to, first ensuing, immediately following, coming nearest in order etc. to, immediately before, (will ask the next man I see, the next policeman; shall return *next week, next year, next Friday, on Friday next; she arrived (the) next day; the Sunday next before Easter; the next two letters are from the same person; the next town to London in size*); ∼**-best**, second-best; **the** ∼ **man,** any average person; *next* WORLD. **3.** *adv.* in the next place or degree, on the next occasion, (*in the week next ensuing; placed his chair next to hers; next came a strange figure; when I next saw him he was lame*); WHAT *next?.* **4.** *prep.* (arch.) in or into the next place to, on the next occasion to, in the next degree to, (*I was standing next him; placed his chair next hers; loves him next her own child*). **5.** *n.* next person or thing (∼ **of kin,** living person most closely related by kin to someone); next letter, issue, etc., (*will tell you in my next; to be continued in our next*); next week etc. (*the Friday, week, year,* etc., *after next*); ∼ **please,** ask your next question, let the next person come, etc. [OE *nēhsta,* = OS *na(h)isto,* OHG *nāhisto,* ON *næstr,* superl. (as NIGH; see -EST¹)]

ne′xus *n.* bond, link, connection, (usu. fig.); **the cash** ∼ (consisting in money payments). [L (*nectere nex- bind*)]

‖**NF** *abbr.* National Front.

NF, Nfld., *abbrs.* Newfoundland.

‖**NFU** *abbr.* National Farmers' Union.

n.g. *abbr.* no good.

‖**NGA** *abbr.* National Graphical Association.

ngai′o (nī′ō) *n.* (pl. ∼-**s**). small NZ tree (*Myoporum laetum*) with edible fruit and light white timber. [Maori]

NGO *abbr.* non-governmental organization.

NH *abbr.* New Hampshire.

‖**NHS** *abbr.* National Health Service.

‖**NI** *abbr.* National Insurance; Northern Ireland.

Ni *symb.* nickel.

ni′acin *n.* nicotinic acid. [f. NICOTINIC + ACID + -IN]

Niä′gara *n.* cataract, torrent, deluge. [f. ∼ Falls, famous N. Amer. waterfall]

nib *n.,* & *v.t.* (-**bb**-). **1.** *n.* point of quill pen; metal or quill pen-point; point of tool etc. **2.** (in *pl.*) coffee beans or cocoa beans removed from their shells. **3.** *v.t.* make, mend, insert nib of, (pen). [prob. f. MDu. *nib* or MLG *nibbe,* var. of *nebbe* NEB]

ni′bble *v.* & *n.* **1.** *v.t.* take small bites at; ∼ **off,** remove thus. **2.** *v.t.* & *i.* bite gently or cautiously or playfully (esp. of fish with bait, or rabbit); ∼ **at,** lit., and fig. of dallying with temptation, bargain, etc. **3.** *v.i.* carp at, make trifling criticisms. **4.** *n.* act of nibbling, esp. of fish at bait; enough (grass etc.) to nibble at; very small amount of food.) [prob. f. LDu. orig.; cf. LG *nibbeln* gnaw]

ni′blick *n.* (Golf). iron with large round heavy head, used esp. for playing out of bunkers. [19th c.; orig. unkn.]

nibs (-z) *n.* (sl.) **his** etc. ∼, burlesque title after *His Grace* etc. [19th c.; cf. earlier (cant) *nabs*]

nice *a.* **1.** fastidious, dainty, hard to please, of refined or critical tastes; precise, punctilious, scrupulous, particular, (*must not be too nice about the means*). **2.** requiring precision, care, tact, or discrimination, (*a nice experiment, question, problem, point, negotiation*). **3.** minute, subtle, (*a nice distinction, shade of meaning*). **4.** attentive, close, (*a nice inquiry, observer*). **5.** delicately sensitive, discriminative, or deft, (*a nice ear, judgement, hand*). **6.** (colloq.) agreeable, attractive, delightful, well-flavoured, satisfactory, kind, friendly, considerate, generally commendable, (iron.) disgraceful (*made a nice mess of it*); ∼ **work,** task well performed. **7.** ∼ (**and**), (colloq.) satisfactor(il)y in respect of specified quality (*house stands nice and high; car is going nice and fast; this is a nice long one*); ∼**-looking,** (colloq.) pretty or of engaging appearance; **not very** ∼, (colloq.) unpleasant. **8.** Hence ∼′LY² (-slī) *adv.,* ∼′NESS (-sn-) *n.,* nī′cɪsH¹ 2 *a.* [ME, = stupid, wanton; OF, = silly, simple, f. L *nescius* ignorant (as NESCIENCE)]

niceish. Var. of NICISH (see NICE 8).

Niçe′ne (*or* nī′-) *a.* of Nicaea in Bithynia; **first and** **second** ∼ **Councils,** held AD 325, 787, to settle the Arian controversy, the question of images; ∼ **Creed,** formal statement of Christian belief based on that adopted at first Nicene Council. [ME, f. LL *Nic(a)enus* (L f. Gk *Nikaia* Nicaea)]

nī′cety *n.* punctiliousness; precision, accuracy, (**to a** ∼, exactly); intricate or subtle quality (*a point of great nicety*); minute distinction, subtle or unimportant detail, (in *pl.*) minutiae. [ME, f. OF *niceté* (as NICE; see -TY¹)]

niche (nĭch, nēsh) *n.,* & *v.t.* **1.** *n.* shallow recess in wall to contain statue, vase, etc.; (fig.) place destined or suitable for person's occupation (∼ **in the temple of fame,** right to be remembered for one's achievements); (Ecol.) appropriate combination of conditions for a species to thrive. **2.** *v.t.* place (statue etc.) in niche (usu. in *p.p.*); ensconce, settle, (esp. one*self,* or in *p.p.*) in a recess or corner. [F (*nicher* make a nest, OF *nichier* f. Rom. *nidicare* f. L *nidus* nest)]

Ni′chrōme, n-, (-k-) *n.* (P) alloy of nickel and chromium used for electrical resistors. [f. NICKEL + CHROME]

ni′cish. See NICE 8.

nick¹ *n.* notch, esp. serving as catch, guide, mark, etc.; (Print.) groove on side of piece of type to ensure correct placing; (sl.) prison, police station; **in good** ∼, (colloq.) in good condition; **in the** ∼ **of time,** only just in time, just at the right moment. [ME, perh. f. foll.]

nick² *v.t.* **1.** *v.t.* make nick(s) in, indent; make incision at root of (horse's tail), cut (horse) thus, to make him carry tail higher; just catch (the right moment, a train, etc.); ‖(sl.) catch, arrest, (criminal etc.); ‖(sl.) steal. **2.** *v.i.* cut *in* by short cut, at corner, etc., in hunting or racing; (of breeding stock) mingle *well* etc. with others. [16th c.; orig. unkn.]

Nick³ *n.* **Old** ∼, the Devil. [prob. f. pet-form of man's Christian name *Nicholas*]

ni′ckel *n.,* & *v.t.* (-**ll**-). **1.** *n.* hard silver-white lustrous ductile metallic element much used esp. in alloys; US five-cent piece; ∼ **brass,** alloy of copper, nickel, and zinc; ∼**-plate** *v.t.,* coat with nickel by plating; ∼ **silver,** (alloy like) German silver; ∼ **steel,** alloy of steel with nickel; hence ∼IC, ∼OUS, *adjs.* **2.** *v.t.* coat with nickel. [abbr. of G *kupfernickel* copper-coloured ore f. which nickel was first got (*kupfer* copper, *nickel* demon, w. ref. to disappointing nature of ore, which yielded no copper)]

*nickelō′dēon *n.* (colloq.) juke-box. [f. prec. + MELODEON]

‖**ni′cker** *n.* (sl.; *pl.* same). one pound sterling. [20th c.; orig. unkn.]

ni′ck-nack. Var. of KNICK-KNACK.

ni′cknāme *n.,* & *v.t.* **1.** *n.* name jokingly or admiringly or contemptuously added to or substituted for person's, place's, or thing's proper name; abbreviation or familiar form of (esp. Christian) name. **2.** *v.t.* call (person or thing) by a nickname; give nickname to. [ME, f. *eke-name,* with *n* from *an* (cf. NEWT); *eke* = addition, f. OE *ēaca* (as EKE¹), NAME¹]

ni′col *n.* ∼ (**prism**), device formed of two pieces of calcite cemented together so as to polarize transmitted and reflected light. [f. W. *Nicol,* Sc. physicist d. 1851, its inventor]

nicō′tian (-shan) *a.* & *n.* (arch.) **1.** *a.* of tobacco. **2.** *n.* tobacco-smoker. [f. as foll. + -IAN]

ni′cotin|e (-tēn) *n.* poisonous alkaloid extracted as oily liquid from tobacco; hence ∼ISM (5) *n.,* ∼IZE (5) *v.t.* [F, f. mod. L *nicotiana* (*herba*) tobacco-plant, f. J. *Nicot,* Fr. diplomat & introducer of tobacco into France 1560; see -INE⁵]

nicoti′nic *a.* ∼ **acid,** vitamin of B group, white crystalline derivative of pyridine, formed by oxidation of nicotine and acting to prevent pellagra. [f. prec. + -IC]

ni′ctit|āte *v.i.* close and open the eyes, wink; ∼**ating membrane,** third or inner eyelid of many animals; hence ∼A′TION *n.* [f. med. L *nictitare* frequent. of L *nictare* blink + -ATE³]

nīdamĕ′ntal *a.* (Of gland etc.) serving as receptacle for ova in molluscs etc. [f. L *nidamentum* (as NIDUS; see -MENT) +-AL]

nī′d(d)ering *n.* & *a.* (pseudo-arch.) base or cowardly (person). [misreading of obs. *nithing* f. ON *nithingr*; given currency by Sir W. Scott]

nī′ddle-nŏddle *a.* & *v.* **1.** *a.* nodding, quivering, unsteady. **2.** *v.t.* & *i.* keep nodding, sway. [redupl. f. NOD; see -LE 3]

||**nide** *n.* brood of pheasants. [f. F *nid* or f. L NIDUS]

nī′dif|icāte, nī′dif|y̆, *vbs. i.* build nest(s); so **~icā′-TION** *n.* [f. L *nidificare* (NIDUS; see -FY, -ATE³)]

nī′d-nŏd *v.i.* & *t.* (-dd-). keep nodding. [redupl. f. NOD]

nī′d|us *n.* (*pl.* **~i** *pr.* -ī, *or* **~uses**). place in which insect etc. deposits eggs; place in which spores or seeds develop; place of origin or development *of* disease, or *for* quality, doctrine, etc.; natural receptacle; collection of eggs, tubercles, etc. [L, f. IE (as NEST)]

niece *n.* brother(-in-law)'s or sister(-in-law)'s daughter. [ME f. OF, f. pop. L **neptia* f. L *neptis* granddaughter]

niĕ′ll|ō *n.* (*pl.* **~i** *pr.* -ē, *or* **~os**). black composition of sulphur with silver, lead, or copper, for filling engraved lines in silver or other metal; (specimen of) such ornamental work; hence **~ōED²** (-ōd) *a.* [It., f. L *nigellus* dim. of *niger* black]

Nier′steiner (-tīn-) *n.* Rhenish wine from Nierstein. [G]

Nie′tzschė|an (nē′ch-) *a.* & *n.* (follower) of Nietzsche; (supporter) of his principles, esp. w. ref. to the possibility of a superman able to overcome unworthy desires and thus dominate other persons; hence **~an**ISM (3), **~**ISM (3), *ns.* [f. F. W. *Nietzsche*, Ger. philosopher d. 1900 +-AN]

||**niff** *n.,* & *v.i.* (sl.) smell, stink; hence **~′y²** *a.* [orig. dial.]

nī′fty *a.* (sl.) spruce, smart, stylish; excellent; clever. [19th c.; orig. uncert.]

nī′ggard *n.* & *a.* **1.** *n.* parsimonious person, grudging giver *of.* **2.** *a.* (rhet. or poet.) = foll. [ME, alt. f. earlier (obs.) *nigon,* prob. of Scand. orig.; cf. NIGGLE, -ARD]

nī′ggardl|y̆ *a.* & *adv.* **1.** *a.* parsimonious, miserly; sparing, scanty; giving or given grudgingly or in small amounts; hence **~i**NESS *n.* **2.** *adv.* in niggardly manner. [f. prec. +-LY¹,²]

nī′gger (-g-) *n.* **1.** (derog., **R**) Negro; dark-skinned person. **2. ~ in the woodpile** or ***fence,** (sl.) suspicious circumstance, something that spoils a good thing; **work like a ~,** toil very hard. **3. ~**(-**brown**), (arch. or colloq.) dark shade of brown; **~head,** = NEGRO-*head* (1); **nigger** MINSTREL 2. [18th c. alt. f. *neger* (16th c.) f. F *nègre* f. Sp. *negro* NEGRO]

nī′ggle *v.* **1.** *v.i.* spend time, be over-elaborate, on petty details; find fault in petty manner. **2.** *v.t.* cause minor irritation to. [app. of Scand. orig.; cf. Norw. *nigla*]

nī′ggl|ing *a.* trifling, petty; lacking in breadth of view or boldness of effect; (of handwriting) cramped; so **~y²** *a.,* niggling, irritable. [f. prec. +-ING²]

nigh (nī) *adv., prep.,* & *a.* (arch., literary, or dial.) = NEAR¹,². (w. same usage of compar. & superl.); WELL*nigh.* [OE *nē(a)h,* = OS, OHG *nāh,* ON *ná-,* Goth. *nēhwa*]

night (nīt) *n.* **1.** dark period between day and day, time from sunset to sunrise; darkness prevailing in the night (*black* or *dark as night; went forth into the night*); period of figurative darkness (*the night of ignorance* or *barbarism*); nightfall (*shall not reach home before night*); weather or experiences or occupation of a night (**have a good** or **bad ~,** sleep well or not, be comfortable during the night or not); evening on which performance etc. occurs (FIRST *night*); **all ~** (**long**), throughout the night; **at ~,** during the night, at nightfall, in the evening, in the period 6 p.m. to midnight (*ten o'clock at night*); **by ~,** during the night, under cover of darkness; GOOD, LAST³, *night;* **make a ~ of it,** spend night in festivity; **~ and day,** at all

times, without ceasing; **~ out,** (1) festive evening, (2) evening of the week on which servant is free to go out; OVERNIGHT¹,²; **spend the ~ with,** (esp.) be provided with sleeping-place by (often implying sexual intimacy); **stay the ~,** remain until next day; **turn ~ into day,** work etc. by night as if it were day (with necessary bright lights); **work ~s,** be on night shift. **2.** (in *comb.*) by, like, during, appropriate to, employed for, active in, the night (*night-veiled, -black, -flying, -attire, -porter, -moth*); ||**~-bell** (to summon person at night, esp. on street-door of doctor's house); **~-bird,** (esp.) owl or nightingale, person who goes about at night; **~-blindness,** nyctalopia; **~-boat,** passenger-boat crossing in a night; **~′cap,** (1) cap worn in bed, (2) drink (esp. alcoholic) taken before going to bed; **~-chair,** = *night-stool;* **~-clothes** (worn in bed); **~-club,** establishment open at night for refreshment and entertainment; *night*-COMMODE; **~-dress,** woman's or child's loose garment worn in bed; **~′fall,** end of daylight; **~ fighter,** aeroplane used for interception at night; **~-glass,** short telescope for use at night; **~-gown,** = *night-dress,* (Hist.) dressing-gown; **~-hag,** female demon supposedly riding in the air at night, nightmare; **~-hawk,** (1) nightjar or mopoke, (2) thieving or other nocturnal prowler; **~′jar,** harsh-voiced nocturnal bird of family Caprimulgidae; ***~ letter,** telegram sent cheaply at night; **~-life,** urban entertainment open at night; **~-light,** short thick candle, or electric bulb, giving dim light through night for child, invalid, etc.; **~-line** (left with baited hooks to catch fish by night); **~-long** *a.* & *adv.,* (lasting) for whole night; **~′man** (employed to remove night-soil); **~′mare,** (1) female monster supposedly sitting upon and seeming to suffocate sleeper, incubus, (2) oppressive or paralysing or terrifying or fantastically horrible dream or (colloq.) experience (whence **~′marish** *a.*), (3) haunting fear or thing vaguely dreaded, [OE *mære* incubus]; **~-ni′ght,** (colloq.) good night; **~ nurse** (employed to attend patient(s) during night); **~-owl,** owl flying by night, (colloq.) person active at night; **~-piece,** (painting of) night scene or landscape; **~-rail,** (Hist.) woman's loose dressing-gown etc.; ***~-robe,** = *night-dress;* **~ safe,** safe with opening in outer wall of bank for deposit of money etc. when bank is closed; **~-scented stock,** STOCK 6 with flowers open at night; **~-school** (providing evening instruction for those working by day); **~ shift,** shift of workers employed during night; **~-shirt,** boy's or man's long shirt for sleeping in; **~-soil,** contents of cesspools etc. removed at night, esp. for use as manure; **~-spot,** (colloq.) night-club; ***~′stick,** policeman's truncheon; **~-stool,** close-stool for use at night; **~-time,** night as a state of things or opportunity (*in the ~-time,* by night); **~-watch,** (person or party keeping) watch by night, Hebrew or Roman division (one of three or four) of the night (*in the ~-watches,* during the anxious, wearisome, wakeful, etc., night); **~-watchman,** person keeping watch by night, (Cricket) inferior batsman sent in near close of day to avoid dismissal of better one in adverse conditions; **~-work** (that is, or must be, done by night). **3.** Hence **~′LESS** *a.* [OE *neaht, niht,* = OS, OHG *naht,* ON *nátt,* Goth. *nahts* f. Gmc **naht-* f. IE **nokt-*]

nī′ghtie (nī′ti) *n.* (colloq.) night-dress. [abbr.; see -IE]

nī′ghtingāle (nī′tĭngg-) *n.* small reddish-brown migratory thrush of genus *Luscinia,* the male singing melodiously and powerfully both by night and in the day. [OE *nihtegala* (whence obs. *nightgale*), OS, OHG *nahta-, nahtigala,* ON *nætrgali* f. Gmc (as NIGHT, **galan* sing); for *-n-* cf. FARTHINGALE]

nī′ghtly¹ (nī′t-) *a.* happening, done, existing, etc., in the night; happening every night; (literary) of or suiting night. [OE *nihtlic* (as NIGHT, -LY¹)]

nī′ghtly² (nī′t-) *adv.* every night. [ME, f. NIGHT +-LY²]

nī′ghtshāde (nīt-) *n.* **1.** plant of genus *Solanum;* **black ~,** *S. nigrum,* with white flowers and black poisonous berries; **woody ~,** *S. dulcamara,* with purple flowers and bright red berries. **2. deadly ~,** belladonna plant; **enchanter's ~,** white-flowered plant of genus *Circaea.* [OE *nihtscada,* = OHG *nahtscato,* app. f. as NIGHT + SHADE¹, prob. w. ref. to poisonous properties]

nighty. Var. of NIGHTIE.

nigrě′sc|ent *a.* blackish; so **~ENCE** *n.* [f. L *nigrescere* grow black (*niger nigri* black); see -ENT]

ni′gritūde *n.* blackness (lit. or fig.). [f. L *nigritudo* (as prec.; see -TUDE)]

ni′gromǎncў. Var. of NECROMANCY.

nihil ad rem (nīhĭl ǎd rě′m) *pred. a.* irrelevant. [L, = nothing to the matter]

nī′hil|ism (nī′ĭ-, nī′hĭ-) *n.* negative doctrines, total rejection of current beliefs, in religion or morals; (Philos.) scepticism that denies all existence; doctrine of Russian extreme-revolutionary party in 19th–20th c. finding nothing to approve of in the established order; hence **~IST** (2) *n.,* **~i′st**IC *a.* [f. L *nihil* nothing + -ISM]

nīhi′litў *n.* non-existence, nothingness; mere nothing, trifle, nullity. [f. med. L *nihilitas* (as prec.; see -ITY)]

nihil obstat (nīhĭl ŏ′bstăt) *n.* (RC Ch.) certificate that book is not open to objection on religious grounds; (fig.) authorization, official approval. [L, = nothing hinders]

-nik *suf.* forming *ns.* denoting person associated with specified thing or quality (*beatnik, nogoodnik*). [f. Russ. (as SPUTNIK) & Yiddish]

nil *n.* nothing, no number or amount, (esp. in scoring at games etc.; *three goals to nil*). [L, = *nihil* nothing]

ni′lgai (-gī) *n.* large short-horned Indian antelope (*Boselaphus tragocamelus*). [f. Hindi *nīlgāī* (*nīl* blue, *gāī* cow)]

nill *v.t.* & *aux.* (arch.) = WILL¹ not; **will he ~ he,** = WILLY-NILLY. [OE *nyle* (*ne* not, *wile* WILL¹)]

Nīlŏ′mĕter *n.* graduated pillar etc. showing height to which Nile rose during annual floods. [f. Gk *Neilometrion* (see foll., -METER)]

Nīlŏ′tic *a.* of the Nile or Nile region or its inhabitants or languages. [f. L f. Gk *Neilōtikos* (*Neilos* Nile; see -OTIC)]

nim *n.* game in which two players must alternately take one or more objects from one of several heaps and seek to avoid taking (or to take) the last remaining object. [20th c., perh. f. arch. *nim* to take (as foll.), or G *nimm* imper. of *nehmen* take]

ni′mble *a.* quick in movement, agile, swift; (of mind etc.) versatile, clever, quick to apprehend; dextrous; hence **~NESS** (-beln-) *n.,* **ni′mbl**Y² *adv.* [OE *nǣmel* quick to seize (*nman* take f. Gmc *neman;* see -LE 1), with *-b-* as in THIMBLE]

nimbō-stra′t|us (-ā′-, -ah′-) *n.* (*pl.* **~i** *pr.* -ī). (Meteorol.) low dark-grey layer of cloud. [mod. L, f. foll. + -o- + STRATUS]

ni′mb|us *n.* (*pl.* **~i** *pr.* -ī, *or* **~uses**). bright cloud or halo investing deity or person or thing; halo of saint etc.; (Meteorol.) rain-cloud; hence **~used**² (-st) *a.* [L, = cloud, aureole]

nimi′etў *n.* (literary). excess, too much. [f. L *nimietas* (*nimis* too much; see -TY¹)]

niminў-pi′minў *a.* affected, mincing; spiritless. [cf. MIMINY-PIMINY and NAMBY-PAMBY]

Ni′mrōd *n.* great hunter or sportsman. [f. Heb. *Nimrōd* valiant; see Gen. 10: 8, 9]

ni′ncompoōp *n.* simpleton, foolish person. [17th c. *nicompoop,* of uncert. orig.; perh. f. man's name *Nicholas* + obs. *poop* to cheat]

nine *a.* & *n.* one more than eight; symbol for this (9, ix, IX); card with nine pips; time of nine o'clock; size etc. denoted by nine; set of nine; (in *pl.*) gloves, shoes, etc., of ninth size; *baseball team; **the N~,** the Muses; **dressed (up) to the ~s** (very elaborately); **~ day's wonder,** novelty that attracts much attention but is soon forgotten; **~-tenths,** (fig.) nearly all; **~ times**

out of ten, nearly always; **~ to five,** ordinary office hours; *possession is nine* POINT¹*s of the law; cat has nine lives* (see LIFE); ||**~′pins,** skittles with nine objects to be knocked down by throwing a ball; ||**999,** telephone number for emergency services; hence **~**FOLD (-nf-) *a.* & *adv.* [OE *nigon,* = OS *nigun, nigon* f. Gmc *nigun,* var. of *niwun* f. IE *(e)newņ*]

nīnetēen (-nt-; -ē′n, nī′-) *a.* & *n.* one more than eighteen; symbol for this (19, xix, XIX); **1984** (w. ref. to totalitarian State described in Orwell's novel so titled); ||*nineteen to the* DOZEN; so **~**TH² *a.* (**~th hole,** (joc.) golf-club's bar) & *n.* [OE *nigontýne,* OS *nigentein,* OHG *niunzehan,* ON *nitján;* see prec., -TEEN]

nī′net|ў (-ntĭ) *a.* & *n.* **1.** nine times ten; symbol for this (90, xc, XC); (in *pl.*) numbers etc., esp. years of a century or a life, from 90 to 99; hence **~i**ETH¹ *a.* & *n.* **2. ~y-one,** (arch.) **one and ~y,** etc., ninety plus one etc., w. corresp. ordinals **~y-first** etc.; **~y-nine out of a hundred,** (fig.) nearly all. [OE *nigontig* (as NINE, -TY²)]

Ni′nevīte *n.* inhabitant of Nineveh. [f. eccl. L *Ninivitae* pl. (*Ninive* Nineveh, ancient capital of Assyria; see -ITE¹ (1))]

ni′nnў *n.* simpleton, foolish person. [perh. for *innocent;* see -Y³]

ni′non (nē′nawn) *n.* lightweight silk dress fabric. [F]

ninth *a.* & *n.* **1.** *a.* next after eighth; **~ part,** one of nine equal parts into which thing is or may be divided. **2.** *n.* ninth part; (Mus.) interval of octave and second. **3.** Hence **~′**LY² *adv.,* in the ninth place. [f. NINE + -TH²]

Ni′obē′AN *a.* [f. Gk *Niobē,* legendary daughter of Tantalus turned to stone while weeping for her slain children]

niō′b|ium *n.* (Chem.) rare metallic element usu. found associated with tantalum; hence **~**IC, **~**OUS, *adjs.* [f. prec. + -IUM]

nip¹ *v.* (**-pp-**) *n.* **1.** *v.t.* pinch, squeeze sharply, bite; pinch *off* (bud etc.); check growth of (esp. *nip in the* BUD¹; lit. or fig.); (of cold) affect injuriously, pain, whence **~′p**ING² *a.;* take *up, out,* etc., hurriedly or unobserved. **2.** *v.i.* ||(sl.) step etc. nimbly *in*(*to*), *out, up.* **3.** *n.* pinch, sharp squeeze, bite; (check to vegetation caused by) coldness of air; ***~ and tuck,** neck and neck. [ME, prob. of LDu. orig.]

nip² *n.* & *v.* (**-pp-**). **1.** *n.* small quantity of spirits etc. as pick-me-up. **2.** *v.i.* & *t.* take nips (of). [prob. abbr. of *nipperkin* small measure, of LDu. orig.; cf. LG, Du. *nippen* to sip]

Nip³ *n.* & *a.* (sl., derog.; **R**) Japanese. [f. NIPPONESE]

ni′pa (nē′-) *n.* E. Ind. palm-tree (*Nipa fruticans*) with creeping trunk and large feathery leaves; alcoholic drink from its sap. [Sp. & Port., f. Malay *nīpah*]

ni′pper *n.* In vbl senses; *fish that nips bait or other fishes; ||(sl.) young boy or girl; (in *pl.*) implement with jaws for gripping or cutting, forceps, pincers, pliers; (in *pl.,* arch.) pince-nez; horse's incisor tooth; crustacean's claw. [t. NIP¹,², + -ER¹]

ni′pple *n.* **1.** small projection in which mammary ducts terminate in mammal of either sex, esp. of woman's breast; teat of feeding-bottle. **2.** nipple-like protuberance on skin, glass, metal, etc.; small rounded elevation on mountain; (Hist.) perforated projection of musket-lock on which percussion-cap was placed; *short section of pipe with screw-thread at each end for coupling. **3. ~-wort,** yellow-flowered weed (*Lapsana communis*). [16th c. also *neble, nible,* perh. dim. f. *neb* + -LE 1]

Ni′ppon *n.* Japan; hence **~**E′SE *n.* (*pl.* same) & *a.,* **Nippō′n**IAN *a.* [Jap., = Japan (lit. 'land of the rising sun'; cf. JAPAN¹)]

ni′pp|ў *a.* (colloq.) active, nimble; chillingly cold; hence **~i**LY² *adv.* [f. NIP¹ + -Y²]

nirva′na (nērvah′-, nēr-) *n.* (Buddhism & Hinduism). beatitude attained by extinction of individuality and desires, with release from effects of karma. [f. Skr. *nirvāṇa* (*nirvā* be extinguished f. *nis* out + *vā*- to blow)]

*nisei' (nēsā') *n.* person whose parents were immigrants from Japan. [Jap., lit. 'second generation']

ni'si *a.* (Law). subject to conditions as regards taking effect (DECREE nisi; rule nisi). [L, = 'unless']

nisi prius (nīsī prī'us) *n.* (Law). hearing of civil cases by judges in Crown Court or (Hist.) assize court. [L, = 'unless before', in writ directing sheriff to provide jury unless judges came before specified date]

Ni'ssen *n.* ~ **hut**, tunnel-shaped hut of corrugated iron with cement floor. [f. P. N. ~, Brit. engineer d. 1930, its inventor]

nit *n.* egg or young form of louse or other parasitic insect; (sl.) stupid person; ~**-picking** *n.* & *a.*, (colloq.) fault-finding in petty manner. [OE hnitu, = MDu., MLG nēte, OHG (h)niz f. WG *hnito f. IE *knidā]

*ni'ter. See NITRE.

*ni'tery *n.* (colloq.) night-club. [f. nite (phonet. sp. of NIGHT) + -ERY]

ni'tid *a.* (literary). bright, shining, (lit. or fig.). [f. L nitidus (nitēre shine; see -ID¹)]

ni'trāte¹ *n.* salt or ester of nitric acid; potassium or sodium nitrate as fertilizer. [F (as NITRE; see -ATE¹ (3))]

nitrĭā'te² *v.t.* treat, combine, or impregnate, with nitric acid; hence ~A'TION *n.* [f. foll. + -ATE³]

‖ni'tre (-er), ***ni'ter,** *n.* saltpetre, potassium nitrate; **Chile** ~, sodium nitrate. [ME f. OF, f. L f. Gk nitron, of Semitic orig.]

ni'tric *a.* of or containing nitrogen; ~ **acid**, clear colourless pungent highly corrosive and caustic liquid, HNO₃; ~ **oxide**, colourless gas (NO). [f. F nitrique (as prec.; see -IC)]

ni'tride *n.* (Chem.) binary compound of nitrogen. [f. NITRE + -IDE]

ni'tri‖fy *v.t.* impregnate with nitrogen; turn into nitrite or nitrate; hence ~FICA'TION *n.* [f. F nitrifier (as NITRE; see -FY)]

ni'trile *n.* (Chem.) compound of alkyl radical with cyanogen. [f. NITRE; see -IL]

ni'trite *n.* salt or ester of nitrous acid. [f. NITRE + -ITE¹ (2)]

ni'trō- comb. form. of, containing, made with or by use of, nitric acid or nitre or nitrogen, as: ~**-acid**, compound of nitric acid with organic acid; ~**be'nzene**, poisonous yellow oil used to make aniline etc.; ~**-ce'llulose**, cellulose nitrate used in lacquers etc.; **N**~**-chalk**, (P) fertilizer made of calcium carbonate and ammonium nitrate; ~**-compound** (made by action of nitric acid and containing a nitro-group); ~**-explosive** (prepared by means of nitric acid); ~**-gly'cerine**, yellowish oily violently explosive liquid made by adding glycerine to mixture of nitric and sulphuric acids; ~**-group**, NO₂; ~**-lime**, calcium cyanamide, used as fertilizer; ~**-powder**, gunpowder made with nitric acid. [Gk (as NITRE; see -O-)]

ni'trogen *n.* colourless tasteless odourless gaseous element forming four-fifths of atmosphere, and present in compounds such as nitrates, proteins, etc.; ~ **cycle**, continuous transfer of nitrogen in various forms from soil to plants to animals, and back by decay; ~ **fixation**, formation of compounds from atmospheric nitrogen; hence **nitrŏ'gĕn**ous *a.* [f. F nitrogène (as NITRO-, -GEN)]

ni'trous *a.* of, like, impregnated with, nitre; ~ **acid** (HNO₂, containing less oxygen than nitric acid); ~ **oxide**, colourless sweetish-smelling gas (N₂O) used as anaesthetic, laughing-gas. [f. L nitrosus (as NITRE; see -OUS), partly thr. F nitreux]

nitty-gri'tty *n.* (sl.) realities or basic facts of a matter. [20th c.; orig. uncert.]

ni'twit *n.* (colloq.) stupid person; hence ~TED² *a.*, stupid. [perh. f. NIT + WIT²]

‖nix¹ *int.* (sl.) giving warning to confederates etc. that person in authority is approaching. [19th c., perh. = NIX³]

nix² *n.* (fem. ~'ie). water-elf. [G (fem. nixe)]

nix³ *n.*, & *v.t.* (sl.) **1.** *n.* nothing; = NO¹. **2.** *v.t.* cancel; reject. [f. G nichts nothing (dial. & colloq. nix)]

NJ abbr. New Jersey.

‖NLC abbr. National Liberal Club.

*NLRB abbr. National Labor Relations Board.

NM, N. Mex., abbrs. New Mexico.

NNE, NNW, abbrs. north-north-east, -west.

nō¹ *a.* **1.** not any (no circumstances could justify it; no two of them are alike); no NEWS (is good news); (if) no bishop, (then) no king; **king or no king**, regardless of the king, his kingship, etc. **2.** not a, quite other than, (service of no honourable kind; is no part of my plan; is no genius; no LITTLE; no SMALL); hardly any (is no distance; did it in no time); **there is** etc. **no —ing**, none is etc. possible (there's no accounting for tastes; there was no mistaking what he meant). **3.** (ellipt. as slogan, notice, etc.) we will not have any, let there not be any, there is not any, no . . . is allowed, (no Popery, no surrender, no parking, etc.). **4. no-account**, unimportant, worthless; **no-ball**, (n.) unlawfully delivered ball in cricket (counting one to batting side if not otherwise scored from), umpire's announcement of this, (v.t.) pronounce (bowler) to have bowled no-ball; **no-being**, (arch.) non--existence; **no-clai'm(s) bonus**, reduction of insurance premium charged to one who has not claimed payment under the insurance in preceding period; **no date**, (of book etc.) not bearing a date of publication etc.; no dice (see DIE¹), DOUBT¹, END¹; **no entry** (notice prohibiting vehicles or persons from entering a road or place); ***no-fault**, (of insurance) valid regardless of allocation of blame for accident etc.; no FEAR¹, FLOWERs, GO², GOOD 16, 17; ***no--hi'tter**, baseball game in which team does not get a man to first base; **no-ho'per**, (Austral. sl.) useless person; no JOKE¹, JOY¹; **no man**, no person; **no man's land**, piece of waste, unowned, or debatable ground, (Mil.) space between opposed trenches, (fig.) area not clearly belonging to any one subject etc.; by no MEAN¹s; no MISTAKE¹; **no-no**, (colloq.) thing not possible or acceptable; no-NONSENSE; **no one**, (pron.) no person, (a.) no single (no one man could lift it); ***no show**, nowhere; **no-show**, person who has reserved a seat etc. but does not use it or cancel reservation; **no side**, (Rugby Footb.) referee's announcement of the) end of the game; **no thoroughfare** (notice that path, street, etc. is closed at other end, or that passage is not permitted); **no trump(s)**, (Bridge) declaration or bid involving playing without a trump suit; **no--tru'mper**, hand on which a no-trump bid can suitably be, or has been, made; no WAY 2; **no'way(s)**, **no'wise**, in no manner, not at all; **no'whence**, **no'whither**, from, to, no place; NOWHERE; no WHIT¹, WONDER¹. [ME, f. nän, nōn NONE, orig. only bef. consonants]

nō² *adv.* **1. or no**, or not (pleasant or no, it is true); **whether or no**, (1) in either case, (2) which of a case and its negative (tell me whether or no). **2. no can do**, (colloq.) I am unable to do it. **3.** (Sc.) not (will ye no come back again?). [OE nō, nā (ne not, ō, ā, ever)]

nō³ *adv.* **1.** (w. compar.) by no amount, not at all, (no better than before); **is no better than she should be**, is morally suspect; no LONG²er; no SOONer . . . than. **2. no less (than)**, as much (n., a., or adv.) or many or important (as) (gave me £50, no less, or no less than £50; no less than ten people have told me; is no less than a scandal, a no less fatal victory; no less a person than Gladstone). **3. no more**, (n.) nothing further (have no more to say; want no more of it), (a.) not any more (no more wine?), (adv.) no longer (**is no more**, is dead or passed away), never again, to no greater extent (is no more a lord than I am; could no more do it than fly in the air), just as little, neither, (could not, come, and no more did he). [OE nā; see prec.]

nō⁴ *adv.* equivalent to negative sentence, & *n.* (pl. noes pr. nōz). **1.** *adv.* the answer to your question is negative, your request or command will not be complied with, the statement made or course of action intended or conclusion arrived at is not correct or satisfactory, the negative statement made is correct; **no, no** (emphat.); **no, nor,** or **no, not,** (substituting stronger phrase: *a man could not lift it, no, nor half a dozen; have not found so great faith, no, not in Israel*); OH¹ *no.* **2.** *n.* the word or answer *no*, a denial or refusal, negative vote, (*two noes make a yes*; **say no,** refuse request, deny statement made; **will not take no for an answer,** persists in spite of refusals); **the noes have it,** negative voters are in majority. [ME, = prec.]

No⁵. See NOH.

No. *abbr.* *North; number [f. L *numero*, abl. of *numerus* number].

n.o. *abbr.* (Cricket). not out.

No *symb.* nobelium.

Nōā́chian, Nōā́chic, (-k-) *adjs.* of the patriarch Noah or his time. [f. *Noach* = NOAH + -IAN]

Nō'ah (-a) *n.* ~'s ark, (1) ship in which Noah, his family, and animals were saved, (2) imitation of it as child's plaything, (3) large or cumbrous or old-fashioned trunk or vehicle, (4) small bivalve (*Arca noae*) with boat-shaped shell. [name of Heb. patriarch in Gen. 6]

nōb¹ *n.,* & *v.t.* (-bb-). **1.** *n.* (sl.) head; **his** ~, (Cribbage) score of one point for holding jack of same suit as card turned up by dealer. **2.** *v.t.* (Boxing). hit on the head. [perh. var. of KNOB]

||**nōb²** *n.* (sl.) person of wealth or high social position. [orig. Sc. *knahb, nab*; 18th c., orig. unkn.]

||**nō'bble** *v.t.* (sl.) tamper with (racehorse) to prevent its winning; secure support of or weaken (person) by underhand means; get hold of (money etc.) dishonestly; catch (criminal). [prob. = dial. *knobble, knubble* knock, beat, f. KNOB + -LE 1]

nō'bbut *adv.* (dial.) only, no more than. [f. NO² + BUT¹]

nō'bbȳ *a.* (sl.) suitable for a NOB²; smart, elegant. [f. NOB² + -Y²]

Nōbĕl (nō'-, -ĕ'l) *n.* ~ **prize,** one of the annual prizes (for physics, chemistry, physiology or medicine, literature, economic sciences, and the promotion of peace) awarded from the bequest of Alfred *Nobel* (d. 1896), Sw. inventor of dynamite; hence *~IST *n.,* winner of Nobel prize.

nōbē'lium *n.* (Chem.) artificially produced transuranic element. [f. as prec. + -IUM]

nobi'liarȳ (-lyerĭ) *a.* of (the) nobility; ~ **particle,** preposition, as French *de*, German *von*, prefixed to title of nobility. [f. F *nobiliaire* (as NOBLE; see -ARY¹)]

nobi'litȳ *n.* noble character, mind, birth, or rank; *the* or *a* class of nobles. [ME, f. OF *nobilité* or f. L *nobilitas* (as foll.; see -ITY)]

nō'ble *a.* & *n.* **1.** *a.* illustrious by rank, title, or birth, belonging to the nobility; of lofty character or ideals; showing greatness of character, magnanimous, morally elevated; splendid, magnificent, stately, imposing, impressive, in appearance; excellent, admirable, (*a noble horse, cellar*, etc.); ~ **gas,** gaseous element of group that almost never combine with other elements; ~**man,** ~**woman,** member of the nobility, person of noble rank or birth, peer(ess); ~ **metal,** gold, silver, platinum, etc. (resisting chemical action, not corroding or tarnishing in air or water, not easily attacked by acids); ~**mi'nded,** honourable, magnanimous; ~ **savage,** idealized primitive man in Romantic literature; ~ **science,** boxing; hence ~NESS (-beln-) *n.,* **nō'blȳ²** *adv.* **2.** *n.* nobleman, noblewoman; former English gold coin usu. worth 6s. 8d. [ME f. OF, f. L (*g*)*nobilis* (*gnō-KNOW)]

noblesse (noblĕ's) *n.* the class of nobles (esp. of a foreign country); ~ *oblige* (ōblē'zh), privilege entails responsibility. [ME = nobility, f. OF (as prec.; see -ESS²)]

nō'bodȳ *pron.* & *n.* **1.** *pron.* no person; *nobody's* BUSINESS, FOOL¹. **2.** *n.* person of no importance, authority, or position. [ME, f. NO¹ + BODY¹ (= person)]

nŏck *n.,* & *v.t.* **1.** *n.* notch at either end of bow for holding string; notch(ed horn piece in butt) of arrow for receiving bowstring. **2.** *v.t.* set (arrow) on string. [ME, perh. = *nock* forward upper corner of some sails, f. MDu. *nocke*]

nŏctă'mbūl|ant, -l|ous, *adjs.* walking by night; so ~IST *n.,* sleep-walker. [f. L *nox noctis* night + *ambulare* walk; see -ANT, -OUS]

nŏcti'vagant, -vagous, *adjs.* wandering by night. [f. L *noctivagus* (as prec., *vagari* wander) + -ANT, -OUS]

nō'ctūle *n.* largest British species of bat, *Nyctalus noctula*. [F, f. It. *nottola* bat]

nō'ctŭrn *n.* (RC Ch.) part of matins orig. said at night. [ME, f. OF *nocturne* or f. eccl. L *nocturnum* neut. (as n.) of L *nocturnus* (see foll.)]

nŏctŭr'nal *a.* of, in, done by, active in, the night; ~ **emission,** involuntary emission of semen during sleep. [f. LL *nocturnalis* f. *nocturnus* of the night (*nox noctis* night)]

nō'ctŭrne *n.* dreamy musical piece; (Paint.) night-piece. [F (as NOCTURN)]

nō'cŭous *a.* noxious, harmful. [f. L *nocuus* (*nocēre* hurt) + -OUS]

nŏd *v.* (-dd-) & *n.* **1.** *v.i.* incline head slightly and briefly in salutation (~**ding acquaintance,** very slight one *with* person or subject), assent, or command; let head fall forward in drowsiness, be drowsy, make mistake due to drowsiness or momentary lack of attention (**Homer sometimes** ~**s,** the best of us may be dull or make a slip), (of building etc., or fig.) incline from perpendicular (*nodding to its fall*); (of plumes) dance up and down as a result of motion. **2.** *v.t.* incline (head); signify (assent etc.) by nod. **3.** *n.* nodding of the head; this as sign of absolute power, or *of approval; **land of Nod,** sleep (w. pun on phr. in Gen. 4:16); **on the** ~, (colloq.) (1) on credit, (2) with merely formal assent and no discussion. [ME *nodde*; orig. unkn.]

nō'ddle¹ *n.* (colloq.) head. [ME *nodle*; orig. unkn.]

nō'ddle² *v.t.* nod or wag (head) [f. NOD + -LE 3]

nō'ddȳ *n.* simpleton; tropical sea-bird of genus *Anous*, resembling tern. [prob. f. obs. *noddy* foolish, which is perh. f. NOD + -Y²]

nōde *n.* **1.** knob on root or branch; point at which leaves spring from stem; hard swelling esp. on gouty or rheumatic joint. **2.** (Astron.) intersection point of planet's orbit and ecliptic or of two great circles of celestial sphere; hence **nō'dɪCAL** *a.* **3.** (Phys.) point or line of rest in vibrating body; (Electr.) point of zero current or voltage. **4.** (Math.) point at which curve crosses itself. **5.** Hence **nō'dAL** *a.* [f. L *nodus* knot]

nod|ō'se *a.* knotty, knotted; so ~o'sɪTY *n.* [f. L *nodosus* (as prec.; see -OSE¹)]

nō'dūl|e *n.* small rounded lump of anything (e.g. carbon in cast iron, mineral on sea-bed); small node in plant, swelling on root of legume, containing bacteria; small knotty tumour, node, ganglion; hence ~AR¹, ~ātĕd [-ATE², -ED¹], ~OSE¹, ~OUS, *adjs.,* ~A'TION *n.* [f. L *nodulus* dim. of *nodus* (see foll., -ULE)]

nō'd|us *n.* (*pl.* ~**i** *pr.* -ī). knotty point, difficulty, complication in plot of story etc. [L, = knot]

Nōē'l *n.* Christmas (esp. as *int.* in carols). [F, f. L (as NATAL)]

nōē'tic *a.* & *n.* **1.** *a.* of the intellect; purely intellectual or abstract; given to intellectual speculation. **2.** *n.* (in *sing.* or *pl.*) science of the intellect. [f. Gk *noētikos* (*noētos* intellectual f. *noeō* apprehend; see -IC)]

nŏg¹ *n.,* & *v.t.* (-gg-). **1.** *n.* pin, peg, small block, of wood; snag or stump on tree; nogging. **2.** *v.t.* secure with nogs; build in form of (brick- etc.) ~**gING¹** (-g-) *n.,* i.e. brickwork etc. in timber frame. [17th c.; orig. unkn.]

nŏg² *n.* ||strong beer brewed in East Anglia; = EGG¹-*nog*. [17th c.; orig. unkn.]

nŏ'ggĭn (-g-) *n.* small mug; small measure, usu. ¼ pint, of liquor; *(sl.) head. [17th c.; orig. unkn.]

Noh (nō), **Nō⁵,** *n.* traditional Japanese drama with dance and song, evolved from Shinto rites. [Jap. *nō*]

nŏ′how adv. in no way, by no means; (dial.) out of order, out of sorts. [f. NO¹ + HOW]

noil n. (in sing. or pl.) short wool-combings. [prob. f. OF noel f. med. L nodellus dim. of L nodus knot]

noise (-z) n. & v. **1.** n. loud outcry, clamour, shouting, confused sound of voices and movements; any sound, esp. loud or harsh or undesired one; irregular fluctuations accompanying but not relevant to a transmitted signal; (in pl.) conventional remarks, or speechlike sounds without actual words, (made sympathetic noises); ~s off, sounds made off stage to be heard by audience of play; BIG noise; **make a** ~, lit., or fig. talk or complain much about, be much talked of, attain notoriety in the world; ~-**maker**, device for making loud noise at festivity etc. **2.** v.t. make public, spread abroad, (person's fame, fact; it was noised abroad that). **3.** v.i. (arch.) make (much) noise. [ME f. OF, = outcry, disturbance, f. L NAUSEA]

noi′sel̇ess (-zl-) a. silent; making no avoidable noise; hence ~LY² adv., ~NESS n. [f. prec. + -LESS]

noisĕ′tte¹ (nwahzĕ′t) n. kind of rose, cross between China and musk roses. [f. P. Noisette, Fr. rose-grower, 1817]

noisĕ′tte² (nwahzĕ′t) n. small round piece of meat etc. [F, dim. of noix nut; see -ETTE]

noi′some a. (literary). harmful, noxious; evil-smelling; objectionable, offensive; hence ~NESS (-mn-) n. [ME, f. obs. noy (f. ANNOY) + -SOME¹]

noi′s|y̆ (-zĭ) a. clamorous, turbulent; full of, making much, noise; (of colour, garment, etc.) loud, conspicuous; hence ~ĭLY² adv., ~ĭNESS n. [f. NOISE + -Y²]

nolens volens (nŏlĕnz vŏ′lĕnz) adv. (literary). willy-nilly, perforce. [L participles, = unwilling, willing]

noli me tangere (nŏlī mē tă′njeri, mā tă′nggeri) n. warning against meddling or approach; person or thing that must not be touched; picture of Christ as he appeared to Mary Magdalen at sepulchre (John 20:17); (arch.) lupus. [L, = do not touch me]

*nŏ′llĕ(-prŏs) v.t. = NOL-PROS.

nolle prosequi (nŏlī prŏ′sĭkwī) n. (Law). relinquishment by plaintiff or prosecutor of (part of) his suit, stay of proceedings, entry of it on record. [L, = to refuse to pursue]

*nolo contendere (nōlō kontĕ′nderi) n. (Law). plea acknowledging validity of conviction but not guilt. [L, = I do not wish to contend]

nolo episcopari (nōlō ĕpĭskopā′ī) n. (formula expressing) avoidance of responsible office. [LL, = I do not wish to be a bishop]

*nŏl-prŏ′s v.t. (-ss-). (Law). relinquish by nolle prosequi. [abbr.]

nom. abbr. nominal.

nŏ′mad n. & a. (member of tribe) roaming from place to place for pasture; wanderer, wandering; hence or cogn. **nomă′dic** a., **nomă′dically** adv., ~ISM (2) n., ~IZE (2) v.i. [f. F nomade f. L f. Gk nomas -ados (nemō to pasture)]

nŏ′mbril n. (Her.) point half-way between fess point and base of shield. [F, = navel]

nom de guerre (nŏm de gār′) n. (pl. -ms pr. same). assumed name under which person fights, plays, writes, etc. [F, = war-name]

nom de plume (nŏm de plōō′m) n. (pl. -ms pr. same). writer's pseudonym, title or initials or borrowed name under which he writes. [formed in E of F words = pen-name, after prec.]

nŏ′mĕn n. (Rom. Ant.) second or gentilitial name, e.g. Marcus Tullius Cicero. [L, = name]

nŏ′menclātor n. slave etc. orig. in ancient Rome with duty of announcing names of persons met, usher assigning places at banquet; giver or inventor of names, esp. in scientific classification. [L (nomen name, calare call; see -OR)]

nomencl|ature (nomĕ′n-kla-, nŏ′men-klā-) n. person's or community's system of names for things; terminology of a science etc.; systematic naming;

catalogue, register; so ~ATIVE a. [F, f. L nomenclatura (as prec.; see -URE)]

nŏ′minal a. **1.** of, as, like, a noun (nominal and verbal roots). **2.** of or in names (nominal and essential distinctions); ~ **definition,** statement of all that is connoted in name of concept. **3.** existing in name only, not real or actual, (nominal and real prices, rulers); (of sum of money, rent, etc.) virtually nothing, much below actual value of thing; ~ **value,** face value (of coin, shares, etc.); hence ~LY² adv. **4.** consisting of, giving, the names (nominal list of officers etc.; nominal roll). [ME f. F, or f. L nominalis (nomen -inis name; see -AL)]

nŏ′minal|ism n. (Philos.) doctrine that universals or general ideas are mere names (opp. realism); so ~IST (2) n., ~i′stic a. [f. F nominalisme (as prec.; see -ISM)]

nŏ′mināt|e v.t. **1.** call by name of, mention by name, name or appoint (date, place). **2.** appoint, or propose for election, to office (a board of six nominated and six elected members; the candidates were nominated today); hence or cogn. ~OR, **nŏminEE′,** ns. [f. L nominare (as NOMINAL) + -ATE³]

nŏminā′tion n. In vbl senses; right of nominating for appointment (have a nomination at your disposal). [ME f. OF, or f. L nominatio (as prec.; see -ATION)]

nŏ′minative a. & n. **1.** (Gram.) (case) used as, or in agreement with, subject of verb (nominative ABSOLUTE); word in this case; hence **nŏminati′val** a. **2.** a. (pr. -ātĭv). of, or appointed by, nomination (the nominative and the elective principles). [ME, f. OF nominatif -ive or f. L nominativus (as NOMINATE; see -IVE), transl. Gk onomastikē (ptōsis case)]

nŏ′mo|gram n. graphical presentation of relations between quantities whereby value of one may be found by simple geometrical construction (e.g. drawing a straight line) from those of others; hence ~GRA′PHIC a., **nomŏ′**GRAPHY n. [f. Gk nomo- (nomos law; see -O-) + -GRAM]

nŏmothĕ′tic a. legislative; stating laws. [f. obs. nomothete legislator f. Gk nomothetēs, + -IC]

nŏn- pref. freely usable to give negative sense: (1) with vbl n. = not doing, failure to do, abstention from doing, (non-acceptance, non-attendance, non-compliance, non-delivery, non-existence, non-fulfilment, non-observance, non-payment, non-smoking compartment), (2) with n. formed from adj. = failure to be, not being, (non-belligerency, non-violence), (3) with n. of designation = person, thing, or all, that is not of the kind designated (non-ego, non-member, non-starter; occas. w. implication of pretence: non-event), (4) with n. to form attrib. a. = not connected with or not involving the thing (non-party, non-union), (5) with adj. = failing to be, not being, one who is not, thing that is not, (non-alcoholic, non-communicant a. & n., non-essential a. & n., non-existent, non-operational, non-productive, non-professional, non-uniform, non-verbal), (6) with adj. = neither such nor its (usu. blameworthy) opposite (dist. from IN-², UN-²; non-moral), (7) with adv. = not thus (non-sexually, non-contentiously), (8) with v. to form adj. = not doing, not behaving in specified way, not to be treated in specified way, (non-skid, non-stick, non-iron), as: ~-**abstai′ner** (3), one who does not abstain (esp. from liquor); ~-**a′ccess** (1), impossibility of access for sexual intercourse (in questions of paternity etc.); ~-**aggre′ssion** (1), refraining from aggression; ~-**ali′gned** (5), ~-**ali′gnment** (1), (esp. Polit., of State) not being aligned with others; ~-**appear′ance** (1) (esp. in lawcourt as party or witness); ~-**belli′gerent** (5) a. & n., (State) taking no active or declared part in war; ~-**claim** (1), failure to make claim within legal time; ~-**colle′giate** (5), not attached to a college, not having colleges; ~-**co′mbatant** (5) a. & n., (person) not fighting (esp. in war as being civilian, army chaplain, etc.); ~-**commi′ssioned** (5), (esp. of officer) not holding commission; ~-**commi′ttal** (1) a. & n., avoiding committing oneself to definite course of action or side of question; ~-**condu′cting** (5), ~-**condu′ctor** (3), (substance) that does not conduct heat or electricity; ∿-**content** (5), negative voter in House of Lords; ∿-**contri′butory** (5), not involving contributions (e.g. to pension scheme); ∿-**co-opera′tion** (1) (esp. of civil disobedience under Gandhi in India); ∿-**denomina′tional** (5), not restricted as regards religious denomination; ∿-**dri′ver** (3), one who does not drive a vehicle; ∿-**effe′ctive** (6) *a. & n.*, (soldier etc.) not available for active service; ∿-**e′go** (3), (Philos.) all that is not the conscious self; ∿-**Eucli′dean** (5), denying or dispensing with assumption(s) of Euclidean geometry; ∿-**event** (3), occurrence that has no special significance (despite possible attempt to give it this); ∿-**fea′sance** (1) (-z-), (Law) omission of necessary action [as MISFEASANCE]; ∿-**fe′rrous** (5), (of metal) other than iron or steel; ∿-**fi′ction** (3), literary matter based directly on fact (opp. novels etc.); ∿-**fla′m**(**mable**) (5), not inflammable; ∿-**hu′man** (6), not of the human race; ∿-**interfer′ence**, ∿-**interve′ntion**, (1), principle or practice of keeping aloof from others' disputes (esp. Polit.); ∿-**i′ron** (8), (of fabric) that needs no ironing; ∿-**joi′nder** (1), (Law) omission of partner etc. to become party to suit; ∿-**jur′ing** (5), ∿-**jur′or** (3), (Hist.) (beneficed clergyman) refusing oath of allegiance in 1689; ∿-**jur′y** (4), tried without jury; ∿-**li′near** (5) (esp. Math.); ∿-**lo′gical** (6), proceeding by means other than logic; ∿-**metal** (3), ∿-**meta′llic** (5), (esp., Chem.) (element) that is not a metal; ∿-**mo′ral** (6), unconcerned with morality (cf. *amoral, immoral*); ∿-**na′tural** (6), not belonging to the natural order of things; ∿-**ne′t** (5), (of book) not subject to minimum selling price; ∿-**nu′clear** (5), not involving nuclei or nuclear energy, not having nuclear weapons; ∿-**par′ty** (4), independent of political parties; ∿-**person** (3), unperson; ∿-**playing** (5) (esp. of captain of sports team who does not himself take part); ∿-**pro′fit**(-**making**) (4, 5), (of enterprise) not conducted primarily with a view to gain; ∿-**prolifera′tion** (1) (esp. of nuclear weapons); ∿-**resi′stance** (1), refusal to resist even unjust commands; ∿-**retur′nable** (5) (esp. of container to seller); ∿-**ri′gid** (6) (esp. of airship kept inflated by pressure of gas within); ∿-**ski′d** (8), (of tyres) designed to prevent skidding; ∿-**sli′p** (8), designed to avoid slipping; ∿-**smo′ker** (3), person who does not smoke, train-compartment etc. where smoking is forbidden; ∿-**star′ter** (3), (fig., colloq.) person or idea not worth considering further; ∿-**stick** (8), (esp.) that food will not adhere to during cooking; ∿-**u′nion** (4), not belonging to trade union, not made by members of a trade union; ∿-**vi′olence** (2), ∿-**vi′olent** (5), abstaining from use of violence to gain one's ends; ∿-**vo′ting** (5), (of shares) not entitling holder to vote; ∿-**whi′te** (5) *a. & n.*, (person) belonging to other than white race. [f. or after ME *no*(*u*)*n*- f. AF *noun*-, OF *non*-, *nom*- f. L *non* not]

no′na- *pref.* nine, as: ∿**gon**, plane figure with nine sides and angles. [L (*nonus* ninth)]

no′nage *n.* being under age, minority; immaturity, early stage. [ME, f. AF *nounage*, OF *nonage* (as NON-, AGE[1])]

nonagenār′ian *a. & n.* (person) from 90 to 99 years old. [f. L *nonagenarius* (*nonageni* distrib. of *nonaginta* ninety; see -ARY[1]) +-AN]

no′nary *a. & n.* **1.** *a.* (Arith., of SCALE[3] of notation) having nine as basis. **2.** *n.* group of nine. [f. L *nonus* ninth +-ARY[1]]

no′nce *n.* **for the** ∿, for the time being or present occasion; ∿-**word** (coined for one occasion). [ME *for than anes* = for the one (occasion), alt. by wrong division (cf. NEWT)]

no′nchal|ant (-sh-) *a.* unexcited, unmoved, cool, indifferent; hence ∿**ANCE** *n.*, ∿**antLY**[2] *adv.* [F, part. of *nonchaloir* (as NON-, *chaloir* be concerned)]

non-com. *abbr.* non-commissioned (officer).

non compos (**mentis**) (nŏn kŏ′mpŏs mĕ′ntĭs) *a.* not

in one's right mind. [L, = not having control of one's mind]

nŏnconfŏr′mist (-n-k-) *n.* one who does not conform to doctrine or discipline of an established Church, esp. (N∿) member of (usu. Protestant) sect dissenting from Anglican Church; one who does not conform to a prevailing principle; so **nŏnconfŏr′m-ism** (3) *n.* [f. NON- (3) + CONFORMIST]

nŏnconfŏr′mity (-n-k-) *n.* principles, practice, the body, of nonconformists, Protestant dissent; failure to conform (*to* rule etc.); lack of correspondence between things. [f. NON- (1) + CONFORMITY]

no′nda *n.* (edible fruit of) rosaceous Queensland tree (*Parinarium nonda*). [Aboriginal]

no′ndescript *a. & n.* (person or thing) not easily classified, neither one thing nor another, hybrid. [f. NON- (5) + *descript* described f. L *descriptus* (as DESCRIBE)]

none (nŭn) *pron., a., & adv.* **1.** *pron.* not any (one) *of* (*none of them came; none of them is* (or *are*, acc. to sense) *required; none of this concerns me; none of your impudence!*); no person, no one, (*none can tell*); no persons (*none but fools have ever believed it*); ∿ **other**, no other person (*than*). **2.** *a.* (usu. ellipt. = *no* with reference defined by noun previously used or shortly to follow). no, not any, *not to be counted in specified class*, (*you have money and I have none; his understanding is none of the clearest; this is none other, but the house of God; seeking rest and finding none; if a linguist is wanted, I am none; would rather have a bad reputation than none at all, poetry we have almost none*); ∿-**so-pretty**, LONDON pride. **3.** *adv.* by no amount, not at all, (w. *the* and compar., *so*, or *too*: *am none the wiser, none the better for it; are none so fond of him; the pay is none too high*); ∿ **the less**, nevertheless. [OE *nān* (ne not, ān ONE)]

nŏně′ntity *n.* **1.** non-existence, non-existent thing, figment. **2.** person or thing of no importance. [f. med. L *nonentitas* non-existence (as NON- (1), ENTITY)]

nōnes (-nz) *n. pl.* **1.** ninth day by inclusive reckoning before ides in ancient-Roman calendar (7th day of March, May, July, October, 5th of other months). **2.** (Eccl.) (office of) fifth of the canonical hours of prayer, orig. said at ninth hour (3 p.m.). [sense 1 f. OF *nones* f. L *nonae* fem. pl., sense 2 pl. of *none* f. F f. L *nona* fem. sing. (*nonus* ninth); cf. NOON]

non est (nŏn ě′st) *a.* (colloq.) non-existent, absent. [f. foll.]

non est inventus (nŏn ěst invĕ′ntus) *n.* sheriff's statement, in returning writ, that defendant is not to be found within his jurisdiction. [L, = he was not found]

nonesuch. See NONSUCH.

nŏně′t *n.* **1.** (Mus.) (performers of) composition for nine voices or instruments. **2.** group of nine. [f. It. *nonetto* (*nono* ninth f. L *nonus*); see -ET[1]]

nonetheless. Var. of NONE *the less.*

no′nius *n.* contrivance for graduating mathematical instruments, of which the vernier is an improved form. [mod. L, f. P. *Nuñes*, Port. mathematician d 1577]

nŏ′npareil (-el) *a. & n.* unrivalled or unique (person or thing). [F (as NON-, *pareil* equal f. pop. L *pariculus* dim. of L *par*)]

non placet (nŏn plā′sět) *n.* negative vote in church or university assembly. [L, = it does not please]

nŏnplŭ′s *n., & v.t.* (-**ss**-). **1.** *n.* state of perplexity, standstill, (usu. *at* a ∿), perplexed; *reduce* etc. *to* a *nonplus*). **2.** *v.t.* reduce to hopeless perplexity. [f. L *non plus* not more]

non possumus (nŏn pŏ′sūmus) *n.* statement of inability to act in a matter. [L, = we cannot]

nŏn-rě′sid|ent (-z-) *a. & n.* (person) sojourning in place only for short time or residing elsewhere; (clergyman) not residing where his duties require him; (of post) not requiring holder to reside; so ∿**ENCE** *n.* [f. NON- (3, 5) + RESIDENT]

nŏ′nsense *n. & int.* **1.** *n.* absurd or meaningless words or ideas, foolish or extravagant conduct; instance of this; arrangement etc. that one disapproves of; **no-**∿

a., serious, without flippancy. **2.** *int.* you are talking or proposing nonsense, it surely cannot be true, etc. **3.** ∼-**book** (meant to amuse by absurdity); ∼ **verses** (having no sense or only an absurd one). **4.** Hence **nŏnsë'ns**ICAL *a.*, **nŏnsë'nsical**LY² *adv.* [f. NON-(3)+SENSE]

non sequitur (nŏn sĕ'kwĭter) *n.* conclusion that does not logically follow from the premisses. [L, = it does not follow]

nŏ'n-stŏp *a., n.*, & *adv.* **1.** *a.* & *n.* (train etc.) not stopping at intermediate places; (of journey, performance, etc.) done without stop or intermission. **2.** *adv.* (or -ŏ'p) without stopping or pausing. [f. NON-(8)+STOP¹]

no'n(e)sŭch (nŭ'ns-) *n.* person or thing that is unrivalled, paragon; plant (*Medicago lupulina*) like lucerne with black pods. [f. NONE+SUCH, usu. now assim. to NON-]

nŏ'nsuit (-ōōt, -ūt) *n.*, & *v.t.* (Law). **1.** *n.* stoppage of suit by judge when plaintiff fails to make out legal case or bring sufficient evidence. **2.** *v.t.* subject (plaintiff) to nonsuit. [ME, f. AF *no*(*u*)*nsuit* (as NON-(1), SUIT)]

nŏn-U' (-ū') *a.* (colloq.) not characteristic of the upper class. [f. NON- (5)+U³]

nŏn-ū'sage (-z-), **nŏn-ū'se,** *ns.* failure to use. [f. NON-(1)+USAGE, USE¹]

nŏn-ū'ser (-z-) *n.* (Law). neglect to use a right, whereby it may be lost. [f. AF *nounuser* (as NON- (1), USE², -ER⁴)]

noo'dle¹ *n.* simpleton, whence ∼DOM (-deld-) *n.*; (sl.) head. [18th c.; orig. unkn.]

noo'dle² *n.* strip of dough made of flour and eggs, dried and used in soups. [f. G *nudel*]

nook *n.* secluded corner or place, recess. [ME *nok(e)* corner, of unkn. orig.]

noon *n.* **1.** twelve o'clock in the day, midday; ∼'**day,** ∼'**tide,** *∗*∼'**time,** midday. **2.** culminating point; ∼ **of night,** (poet.) midnight. [OE *nōn,* = OS *nōn(e),* OHG *nona,* ON *nōn* f. L *nona* (*hora*) ninth hour; orig. = 3 p.m. (cf. NONES)]

no one. See NO¹.

noose *n.*, & *v.t.* **1.** *n.* loop with running knot, tightening as rope or wire is pulled, esp. in snare, lasso, or hangman's halter; the marriage tie; snare or bond; **put** one's **head in a** ∼, bring about one's own downfall. **2.** *v.t.* capture with noose, ensnare; make noose on (cord); arrange (cord) in noose *round* neck etc. [ME *nose,* perh. f. OF *no*(*u*)*s* f. L *nodus* knot]

nŏ'pal *n.* Amer. cactus of genus *Nopalea,* esp. a species grown in plantations for breeding cochineal; hence ∼RY (3) *n.* [F & Sp., f. Nahuatl *nopalli* cactus]

*∗***nŏpe.** Var. (colloq.) of NO⁴.

nor (*or, when stressed,* nŏr) *conj.* & *adv.* **1.** *conj.* and not, and no more, neither, and not either, (*had neither arms nor provisions; not a man nor a child was to be seen; I said I had not seen it, nor had I; 'I cannot go'—'Nor can I'; all that is true, nor must we forget . . .*); (poet. or arch. w. omission of preceding *neither: thou nor I have made the world*). **2.** *adv.* (poet. or arch.) **nor . . . nor . . .,** neither . . . nor . . . [ME, contr. f. obs. *nother* f. OE *nawther, nāhwæther* (as NO², WHETHER)]

nŏr' = NORTH, esp. in compds. *nor'ward, nor'wester*). [abbr.]

Nŏr'bertine *a.* & *n.* Premonstratensian. [f. St. *Norbert* d. 1134, founder of the order+-INE¹]

Nŏr'dic *a.* & *n.* (person) of the tall blond dolichocephalic Germanic people found in N. Europe esp. in Scandinavia; (native or inhabitant) of Scandinavia, Finland, or Iceland; (of skiing) with cross-country work and jumping. [f. F *nordique* (*nord* north; see -IC)]

Nŏr'folk (-ok) *n.* ∼ **jacket,** man's loose belted jacket, with box pleats. [∼ in England]

‖**nŏr'land** *n.* northern region. [contr. of NORTH*land*]

nŏrm *n.* standard, pattern, type; standard quantity to be produced or amount of work to be done;

customary behaviour etc. [f. L *norma* carpenter's square]

nŏr'mal *a.* & *n.* **1.** *a.* (Geom.) standing at right angles, perpendicular. **2.** conforming to standard, regular, usual, typical; free from mental or emotional disorder; (Chem., of solution) containing one gram-equivalent of solute per litre; ∼ **school** (in France etc., for training teachers); hence ∼CY, ∼ITY (-ă'l-), *ns.,* ∼IZE (3) *v.t.,* ∼LY² *adv.* **3.** *n.* (Geom.) normal line; normal value of temperature etc., esp. = BLOOD-*heat*; usual state, level, etc. [F, or f. L *normalis* (as prec.; see -AL)]

Nŏr'man *n.* & *a.* **1.** *n.* inhabitant or native of Normandy, descendant of mixed Scandinavian and Frankish people there established, who conquered England 1066; any of the English kings from William I to Stephen; Norman French; Norman style. **2.** *a.* of the Normans; *Norman* CONQUEST; ∼ **English,** English as spoken or influenced by Normans; ∼ **French,** French as spoken by Normans or later in English lawcourts; ∼ **style** (Archit., with round arches and heavy pillars, whence ∼E'SQUE *a.*). **3.** Hence ∼ISM (2, 4) *n.,* ∼IZE (3, 4) *v.t.* & *i.* [f. OF *Normans* pl. of *Normant* f. ON *Northmathr* (as NORTH, MAN¹)]

nŏr'mative *a.* of or establishing a norm. [f. F *normatif -ive* f. L NORMA; see -ATIVE]

Nŏrn *n.* any of the female Fates of Scandinavian mythology. [ON; orig. unkn.]

‖**Nŏ'rroy** *n.* ∼ **(and Ulster),** third KING¹ of Arms, with jurisdiction north of the Trent (and in N. Ireland). [ME, f. AF *∗norroi* (*nor-* north, *roi* king)]

Nŏrse *n.* & *a.* **1.** *n.* the Norwegian language; the Scandinavian language-group; **Old** ∼, Germanic language of Norway and its colonies, or of Scandinavia, down to 14th c. **2.** (as *pl.*) *the* Norwegians. **3.** *a.* of ancient Scandinavia, esp. of Norway; so ∼'**land,** ∼'**man.** [f. Du. *noor*(*d*)*sch* (*noord* north; see -ISH¹)]

nŏrth *adv., a., & n.* **1.** (towards, at, near) point of horizon to left of person facing east; (**to the**) ∼ (**of**), in a northward direction (from); ∼ **wind,** wind blowing from the north; *north* BY¹ *east* or *west; lie* ∼ **and south,** lengthwise along line from north to south. **2.** w. uses and derivs. like those of *north*) ∼-**east,** ∼-**west,** compass point midway between north and east or west; ∼-∼-**east,** ∼-∼-**west,** compass point midway between north and north-east or north-west; ∼-**east,** ∼-**west, passage,** passage for ships along northern coast of Europe and Asia, northern coast of America, formerly thought of as possible routes to the East and from Atlantic to Pacific; **the N∼-West,** north-western part of country (esp. of Canada). **3.** *n.* compass point lying north (**magnetic** ∼, point indicated by north end of compass-needle. **4.** (usu. *N*∼). part of world or country or town lying to the north, esp. ‖∼ (**country**), northern part of England (north of Humber; so ∼-*cou'*ntryman); *the* Arctic; *∗*the Northern STATE¹s; card-player occupying position designated 'north'. **5.** N∼ **American,** (native or inhabitant) of North America, esp. of US or Canada; ∼'**bound,** travelling northwards; N∼ **Briton,** (arch.) Scot; N∼'**land,** (poet.) northern lands, northern part of a country; ∼ **light,** (from the north, esp. as desired by painters and in factory design); N∼'**man,** native of Scandinavia, esp. of Norway; *North* POLE²; N∼ **Sea** (between Britain, Netherlands, Germany, and Scandinavia); N∼ **star,** = POLE²-*star.* **6.** Hence ∼'WARD *a.* & *n.,* ∼'WARD(s) *adv.* [OE, = OS *north,* OHG *nord,* ON *northr*]

Nŏrtha'nts. *abbr.* Northamptonshire.

nŏrthea'ster *n.* NE wind. [f. NORTH-*east*+-ER¹]

*∗***nŏr'ther** *n.* strong cold north wind blowing in autumn and winter over Texas, Florida, and Gulf of Mexico. [f. NORTH+-ER¹]

nŏr'therly (-dh-) *a., adv., & n.* in a northern position or direction; (wind) blowing (nearly) from the north. [f. NORTH, as *easterly* etc.]

nŏr'thern (-dh-) *a. & n.* **1.** *a.* of or (dwelling) in the north; lying or directed towards the north; *Northern* HEMISPHERE; ∼ **lights,** aurora borealis; *Northern* STATE[1]*s*; hence ∼ER[1] (4) *n.*, ∼MOST *a.* **2.** *n.* inhabitant of the north, esp. of the Northern States. [OE *northerne* (as NORTH, -ERN)]

nŏr'thing *n.* (Naut. etc.) distance travelled or measured northward; northerly direction. [f. NORTH + -ING[1]]

Northumb. *abbr.* Northumberland.

Nŏrthŭ'mbrian *a. & n.* (native or dialect) of ancient Northumbria (England N. of Humber) or modern Northumberland. [f. obs. *Northumber,* persons living beyond Humber, f. OE *Northhymbre,* + -IAN]

nŏrthwē'ster *n.* NW wind. [f. NORTH-*west* + -ER[1]]

Nŏr'way *n.* ∼ **lobster,** slender Eur. lobster (*Nephrops norvegicus*); ∼ **rat,** common brown rat (*Rattus norvegicus*). [∼ in N. Europe, OE *Norweg* f. ON *Norvegr* (as NORTH, WAY)]

Nŏrwē'gian (-jan) *a. & n.* (native, inhabitant, or language) of Norway. [f. med. L *Norvegia* f. ON (as prec.) + -AN, w. assim. to prec.]

nŏr'-wē'ster *n.* northwester; glass of strong liquor; oilskin hat, sou'wester. [f. NORTHWESTER]

Nos. *abbr.* numbers. [cf. No.]

nōse (-z) *n. & v.* **1.** *n.* organ of face or head of man or animal, placed above mouth, containing nostrils, and serving for breathing and smelling; **as plain as the ∼ on your face,** easily seen; **by a ∼,** (win in race etc.) by very narrow margin; **count ∼s,** count those present, one's supporters, etc., decide question by mere numbers; *cut off* one's *nose to* SPITE one's *face;* **follow** one's ∼, go straight forward, be guided by instinct; **get up** person's ∼, (sl.) annoy him; **hold** one's ∼, compress nostrils between fingers to avoid bad smell; **keep** one's ∼ **clean,** (sl.) behave properly, avoid trouble; *keep* one's *nose to the* GRINDSTONE; LEAD[2] *by the nose;* LOOK *down* one's *nose at; make a* LONG[1] *nose;* ∼ **of wax,** (arch.) person or thing easily influenced or moulded; ***on the ∼,** (sl.) precisely, (Austral. sl.) annoying; **parson's** or **pope's ∼,** rump of (cooked) fowl; **pay through the ∼,** be overcharged, have to pay exorbitant price; **poke, thrust,** etc., one's ∼, pry or intrude *into* something or *in;* **put** person's ∼ **out of joint,** supplant or disconcert or frustrate him; **rub** person's ∼ **in it,** remind him humiliatingly of his error; **see no further than** one's ∼, be short-sighted (lit. or fig.); *bite* or SNAP person's *nose off;* **speak through** one's ∼, pronounce words with nasal twang; THUMB one's *nose;* **turn up** one's ∼ **at,** show disdain for; **under** person's ∼, straight before him, regardless of his displeasure; with one's ∼ **in the air,** haughtily. **2.** sense of smell; **has a good ∼** (esp. of dog, and fig. of detective etc.). **3.** odour or perfume of hay, tea, wine, tobacco, etc. **4.** open end of nozzle of pipe, tube, bellows, retort, etc. **5.** prow, projecting part; = NOSING; front end of motor car, aircraft, etc. **6.** (sl.) informer of police. **7.** ∼-**ape,** proboscis monkey; ∼'**bag** (containing fodder, for hanging on horse's head); ∼'**band,** lower band of bridle passing over nose and attached to cheek-straps; ∼'**bleed,** instance of bleeding from the nose; ∼-**cone,** cone-shaped nose of rocket etc.; ∼'**dive,** (*v.i.*) (aeroplane's) downward plunge, (*v.i.*) make this; ∼-**flute,** musical instrument blown with nose in Fiji etc.; ∼'**gay** [*gay* in obs. n. use = ornament], bunch of (esp. sweet-scented) flowers; ∼-**monkey,** proboscis monkey; ∼-**piece,** (1) = *noseband,* (2) part of helmet etc. protecting nose, (3) part of microscope to which object-glass is attached; ∼'**pipe,** piece of piping used as nozzle; ∼-**rag,** (sl.) pocket handkerchief; ∼'**ring** (fixed in nose of bull etc. for leading, or of person for ornament); ∼-**wheel,** landing-wheel under nose of aircraft. **8.** Hence (-)**nōse**D[2] (-zd), ∼'LESS (-zl-), *adjs.* **9.** *v.t.* perceive smell of, discover by smell, (fig.) detect, smell *out;* smell at, rub with the nose, thrust nose against or into. **10.** *v.i.* sniff (*at, about* adv. or

prep.), pry or search (*after, for*). **11.** *v.i. & t.* push one's way, push (one's *way*), with the nose (esp. of ship). [OE *nosu,* = MDu. *nōse,* rel. to OE *nasu,* OHG *nasa,* ON *nös;* cf. NAZE, NESS]

nō'ser (-z-) *n.* strong head wind. [f. prec. + -ER[1]]

nosey. See NOSY.

nŏsh *v. & n.* (sl.) **1.** *v.t. & i.* eat or drink, esp. between meals; ∼-**up,** (large) meal; hence ∼'ERY (3) *n.* **2.** *n.* food or drink, esp. snack. [Yiddish]

nō'sing (-z-) *n.* rounded edge of step, moulding, etc., or metal shield for it. [f. NOSE + -ING[1]]

nosŏ'graphў *n.* systematic description of diseases; so **nosŏ'**LOGY *n.,* (branch of medical science dealing with) classification of diseases. [f. Gk *nosos* disease + -O- + -GRAPHY]

nŏstä'lgĭa (-ja) *n.* homesickness as a disease; regretful or wistful memory of an earlier time; sentimental yearning *for* (some period of) the past; hence ∼IC *a.,* ∼ICALLY *adv.* [mod. L, f. Gk *nostos* return home; see -ALGIA]

nŏ'stŏc *n.* gelatinous blue-green unicellular alga of genus *Nostoc.* [name invented by Paracelsus]

Nŏstradā'mus *n.* prediction-monger, professed seer. [Latinized f. M. de *Nostredame,* Fr. astrologer and physician d. 1566]

nŏ'stril *n.* either opening in nose admitting air to lungs and smells to olfactory nerves; **stink in the ∼s of,** be offensive to; hence (-)∼ED[2] (-ld) *a.* [OE *nosthyrl, nosterl* (*nosu* NOSE, *thȳr*(*e*)*l* hole, cf. THRILL)]

nŏ'strum *n.* medicine prepared by person recommending it, quack remedy, patent medicine; pet scheme for political or social reform, panacea. [L, neut. of *noster* our, used in sense 'of our own make']

nō'sў, nō'sey, (-zĭ) *a. & n.* large-nosed (person); having distinctive (good or bad) smell; (sl., derog.) inquisitive (N∼ **Parker,** busybody); hence **nō'si**LY[2] *adv.,* **nō'si**NESS *n.,* (-z-). [f. NOSE + -Y[2]]

nŏt *adv.* **1.** (arch.) Negativing and following ordinary verbs (*I know not,* I do not know; *I doubt not; say not so; fear not; know ye not me?*). **2.** (Often **n't** joined to word) negativing auxiliaries or BE and following them or (in questions having *not* in full) their subjects (*I cannot* or *can't say; he will not, he won't,* (arch.) *he'll not, come; she is not, isn't,* (vulg.) *ain't, here;* (*you*) *do not* or *don't worry; didn't you,* (formal) *did you not, tell me?; am I not, aren't I we, smart?*). **3.** Negativing and preceding participles and infinitives (*not knowing, I cannot say; asked him not to come; that is how not to do it*). **4.** Used elliptically for negative sentence or verb or phrase (*Are you ill? Not at all. Not so. If it clears we will go out; if not,* not. *Popular or not, it is right. I hope not. I would as soon do it as not*); *as* LIKELY *as not;* ∼ **at all,** (in polite reply to thanks) there is no need to thank me; ∼ **that,** it is not to be inferred, however, (*if he said so—not that he ever did—he lied*); ∼ **but what,** (formal) ∼ **but that,** (arch.) ∼ **but,** (1) all the same or nevertheless (*I cannot do it; not but what* etc. *a stronger man might*), (2) not (*such* etc. ...) that ..., not (*not such a fool but what,* etc. *he can see it*). **5.** Preceding a word etc. that is to be rejected for one that follows with *but* or to emphasize by contrast one already used (*He is not my son, but yours,* or *but my nephew. He is your son,* (*and*) *not mine*). **6.** Preceding emphatic appended pronoun after negative statement etc. (*they will not be fooled, not they*). **7.** Preceding with sense 'not even one' (*not a hair of your head shall be touched*); ∼ **a thing,** nothing at all. **8.** Preceding in litotes or periphrasis a word of opposite sense to that which is to be conveyed (*not a few; not unconnected with; not seldom*); ∼ **once or** (or **nor**) **twice,** many times; ∼ **so** (or **too**) **well,** somewhat badly or ill; ∼ **least,** with considerable importance; ∼ **quite,** (1) almost, (2) noticeably not (*not quite proper*), (3) ||(ellipt., colloq.) socially unacceptable; *not* HALF, MUCH, VERY[1]. **9.** ∼-**being,** non-existence; ∼-**self,** = NON-*ego;* ∼ **sufficient** (written by banker on dishonoured cheque). [ME contr. of NOUGHT]

nota bene (nōta bě'nā) *v. imper.* observe what follows, take notice, (usu. drawing attention to a following qualification of what has preceded). [L, = note well]

notabi′lity *n*. prominent person; being notable (*names of no historical notability*); ‖(arch.) housewifely skill. [ME, f. OF *notabilité* or f. LL & med. L *notabilitas* (as foll.; see -ITY)]

nō′table *a*. & *n*. **1.** *a*. worthy of note, remarkable, striking, eminent; (arch., of woman; occas. pr. nŏ′t-) capable, bustling, housewifely; hence **nō′tabL**Y² *adv*. **2.** *n*. eminent person; **Assembly of N∼s,** (Fr. Hist.) irregular council serving as temporary parliament in emergencies. [ME f. OF, f. L *notabilis* (as NOTE²; see -ABLE)]

*nō′tarīz|e, -īse (-īz), *v.t.* attest as notary. [f. foll. + -IZE]

nō′tarў *n*. ∼ **(public)**, person publicly authorized to draw up or attest contracts etc., protest bills of exchange, etc., and perform other formalities; hence **notār′IAL** *a*., **notār′ial**LY² *adv*. [ME, f. L *notarius* secretary (as NOTE¹; see -ARY¹)]

notā′te *v.t.* write in notation. [back-form. f. foll.]

notā′tion *n*. representing of numbers, quantities, pitch and duration of sound, etc., by symbols; any set of symbols used for this, esp. in Arith., Alg., and Mus.; set of symbols used to represent chess moves, dance steps, etc.; *note, annotation; SCALE³ of *notation*. [F, or f. L *notatio* (as NOTE²; see -ATION)]

nŏtch *n*., & *v.t.* **1.** *n*. V-shaped indentation in edge or on convex surface; nick made on stick etc. in order to keep count; (fig.) = STEP² 7; *defile, pass; hence ∼ED² (-cht), ∼′Y², *adjs*. **2.** *v.t.* make notches in; make *into* saw etc. by notching; score (items etc.; often *up, down*) by notches (lit. or fig.); secure or insert (steps in staircase etc.) by notches. [f. AF (*noche* n. perh. f.) *nocher v., of uncert. orig.]

nōte¹ *n*. **1.** written sign representing pitch and duration of a musical sound; key of pianoforte etc.; single tone of definite pitch made by musical instrument, voice, engine, etc.; (single tone in) bird's song or call; significant sound or way of expressing oneself (*must sound a note of warning; there is a note of optimism in his report*); **strike a false, the right,** ∼, act inappropriately, suitably. **2.** characteristic, distinguishing feature, proof of genuineness, guarantee consisting *of*, (*catholicity is one note of the true Church; has the note of catholicity*); (arch.) stigma, mark of censure, (*on which the law has set a note of infamy*); (arch.) = MARK¹ 6 (*of exclamation* or *interrogation*). **3.** brief record of facts, impressions, or topics for speech or lecture or article (usu. in *pl*.: *make* or *take a note of* or *notes*; COMPARE¹ *notes; preaches from notes; spoke for an hour without a note*); annotation appended to passage in book etc., footnote; short or informal letter or other writing; formal diplomatic communication; ∼ (of hand), written promise to pay sum by certain time; ‖ = BANK³*note* (*five-pound note*); DEMAND¹, PROMISSORY, *note*. **4.** eminence (*critic, philosopher, person,* **of** ∼, distinguished); notice, attention, (*worthy of note*; **take** ∼ **of,** observe), whence ∼′WORTHY (-twĕrdhi) *a*. **5.** ∼′**book** (for entering memoranda in); ∼′**case,** pocket wallet for holding banknotes; ∼′**paper** (of kind used for esp. (esp. private) correspondence); ∼-**-row,** = SERIES 8. **6.** Hence ∼′LESS (-tl-) *a*., ∼′LET (-tl-) *n*., (∼pl.) folded card or paper with design on first leaf, used for informal letter. [ME f. OF, f. L *nota* mark]

nōte² *v.t.* observe, notice, give or draw attention to; set down or *down* as thing to be remembered or observed; annotate (book etc.); (in *p.p.*) celebrated, well known *for*. [ME, f. OF *noter* f. L *notare* (as prec.)]

no′thing (nŭ′-) *n*., *a*., & *adv*. **1.** *n*. no thing (with *adj.* following; *nothing great is easy*). **2.** not anything (*nothing has been done; have nothing to do today*); *nothing* DO¹*ing*; ∼ **else than,** ∼ (else) but, merely, only, unmistakably (*force* etc.; *did nothing but grumble*); ∼ **for it,** no alternative *but to*; ∼ **if not,** primarily (*critical, thorough,* etc.); **has** ∼ **in him,** is insignificant or lacks

individuality; **there is** ∼ **in it** or **to it,** it is untrue or unimportant or straightforward (cf. also IN¹ 5); ∼ **less than,** (1) at least, not a matter less important than, (*expected nothing less than a riot; is nothing less than scandalous*), (2, occas.) the very opposite of, not . . . at all; *nothing like* LEATHER; **is** ∼ **to,** (1) does not concern or influence, (2) cannot compare with; ∼ **venture** ∼ **win** or **have** (excuse for or encouragement to bold action); **be** or **have** ∼ **to do with,** not be concerned with, have no relationship or dealings with; **come to** ∼, turn out useless, fail; **feel like** ∼ **on earth,** (colloq.) suffer severe indisposition or embarrassment; **for** ∼, without payment, to no purpose; **count** or **go for** ∼, be unappreciated or profitless; **have** ∼ **on,** (1) possess no advantage over, know of nothing discreditable about, (iron.) be much inferior to, (2) be naked, (3) be free of engagements; **like** ∼ **on earth,** (colloq.) (ugly etc.) to an extreme degree; **look like** ∼ **on earth,** (colloq.) be very ugly, garish, etc.; **make** ∼ **of,** do without hesitation, treat a trifle, be unable to understand or use or deal with; **mean** ∼ **to,** not be understood, admired, desired, etc., by; NECK¹ *or nothing*; **no** ∼ (as colloq. conclusion of list of negatives: *no bread, no butter, no cheese, no nothing*); **to say** ∼ **of,** = *not to* MENTION²; STOP¹ *at nothing*; THINK *nothing of*; **to** ∼, to complete disappearance; **with** ∼ **on,** naked or otherwise inadequately clothed. **3.** (Arith.) no amount, nought, (*multiply 6 by nothing, and the result is nothing*). **4.** non-existence, what does not exist. **5.** trifling thing, event, remark, or person, (*he is nothing without his money; the little nothings of life; whisper soft* or *sweet nothings; the new commander-in--chief was a nothing*). **6.** be ∼, belong to no religious denomination, be an atheist or agnostic. **7.** *a*. (colloq.) unimportant, trivial. **8.** *adv*. not at all, in no way, (*helps us, avails, nothing; is nothing* LIKE¹ *as* or *so good* etc.; *is nothing near so extensive; nothing daunted; nothing* LOATH); *(as *int.*, colloq.) not at all (*Is it gold? Good nothing; it's pinchbeck*). [OE *nān* thing (as NO¹, THING)]

no′thingnèss (nŭ′-) *n*. non-existence, the non--existent; worthlessness, triviality, unimportance, insignificance, trifles. [f. prec. + -NESS]

nō′tice *n*., & *v.t.* **1.** *n*. intimation, intelligence, warning, (*give, have, notice*; **at short, a moment's, ten minutes',** etc., ∼, with such time for preparation); information or directions posted on notice--board. **2.** formal intimation of something or instructions *to* do something (*notice to* QUIT²; *till* FURTHER *notice*); announcement by party to agreement that it is to terminate at specified time (esp. between landlord and tenant or employer and employed; *give a week's* etc. *notice*; *she is under notice*). **3.** heed, attention, cognizance, observation, (*brought it to his notice*); **come into** or **to** or **under** ∼, attract attention; **take no** ∼ **of,** (1) not observe, (2) take no action in consequence of; **take** ∼ **that,** I warn you that; **take** ∼, show signs of intelligence or interest (cf. SIT 7 *up*). **4.** paragraph or article (esp. review of book, play, etc.) in newspaper or magazine. **5.** ‖∼-**board** (bearing notice, or provided for notices to be posted on). **6.** *v.t.* remark upon, speak of. **7.** perceive (*that, how*), take notice of; treat with politeness or condescension. **8.** serve with notice, give notice to. [ME f. OF, f. L *notitia* being known (*notus* p.p. of *noscere* know; see -ICE)]

nō′ticeab|le (-sa-) *a*. capable or worthy of being noticed; hence ∼LY² *adv*. [f. prec. + -ABLE]

nō′tifiable *a*. (Of disease) that must be notified to public-health authorities. [f. foll. + -ABLE]

nō′ti|fў *v.t.* make known, announce, report; inform, give notice to, (person *of, that,* or abs.); so ∼FICA′TION *n*. [ME, f. OF *notifier* f. L *notificare* (*notus* known; see NOTICE, -FY)]

nō′tion *n*. **1.** general concept under which particular thing may be classed; **first, second,** ∼**s,** (Philos.) = *first,* second, INTENTIONS. **2.** idea, conception, (*the notion of my doing it is absurd; I have not the faintest notion what he means*); view, opinion, theory, vaguely held or insecurely based (*has a notion that; such is the common notion*). **3.** faculty, capability, or intention *of* (*has no notion of obeying, obedience, discipline, letting himself be made a fool of*). **4.** (in *pl.*) *miscellaneous small wares, esp. cheap useful ingenious articles or haberdashery. [f. L *notio* idea (*notus*; see NOTICE, -ION)]

nō′tional *a.* **1.** (Of knowledge etc.) speculative, not based on experiment or demonstration; hence ∼IST (2) *n.* **2.** (Of thing, relation, etc.) existing only in thought, imaginary. **3.** (Gram., of verb) conveying its own meaning, principal, not auxiliary. **4.** Hence ∼LY² *adv.* [obs. F, or f. med. L *notionalis* (as prec.; see -AL)]

nō′tochŏrd (-k-) *n.* rudimentary or embryonic spinal cord or column. [f. Gk *nōton* back + -o- + CHORD¹]

notōr′ious *a.* (Of fact) well or commonly known (*it is notorious that*); (with designations of persons, conduct, etc., that imply condemnation) undisguised, widely talked of, generally known to deserve the name, (*notorious smuggler, offender, vice*); unfavourably known (*for* some quality or conduct, or abs.; *a ship notorious for ill-luck; the notorious Titus Oates*); hence or cogn. **nōtori′ETY¹** *n.*, ∼LY² *adv.* [f. med. L *notorius* f. L *notus* known (see NOTICE, -ORY) + -OUS]

notŏr′nis *n.* rare flightless NZ bird of genus *Notornis*. [f. Gk *notos* south + *ornis* bird]

Nŏtts. *abbr.* Nottinghamshire.

nŏtwithstǎ′ndĭng (-th-, -dh-) *prep., adv., & conj.* **1.** *prep.* without regard to or prevention by, not the less for, (*notwithstanding his objections; this notwithstanding*). **2.** *adv.* nevertheless, all the same. **3.** *conj.* (arch.) although, in spite of the fact that or *that.* [ME, orig. abs. part. f. NOT + WITHSTAND + -ING²]

nou′gat (noo′gah) *n.* sweetmeat of sugar, honey, nuts, and egg-white. [F, f. Prov. *nogat* (*noga* nut; see -ATE¹)]

nought (nawt) *n.* **1.** (poet. or arch.) nothing (for phrs. cf. NAUGHT). **2.** figure 0, cipher; ‖∼s and crosses, game in which usu. nine spaces in square array are filled alternately with noughts and crosses by two players seeking or complete a row of three of either kind. [OE *nōwiht* (ne not, *ōwiht*, var. of *āwiht* AUGHT¹)]

nou′mĕn|on *n.* (*pl.* ∼a). object of intellectual intuition devoid of all phenomenal attributes; hence ∼AL *a.*, ∼alLY° *adv.* [G, f. Gk *nooumenon* neut. pres. part. pass. of *noeō* apprehend, taken by Kant as antithesis to PHENOMENON]

noun *n.* (Gram.) **1.** word or phrase used as name of person, place, or thing, substantive. **2.** (arch.) substantive (∼ **substantive**) or adjective (∼ **adjective**). **3.** Hence ∼′AL *a.* [ME f. AF, = OF *nun, num,* f. L *numen* name]

nou′rish (nŭ′-) *v.t.* **1.** sustain with food (lit. or fig.); hence ∼ING² *a.* **2.** foster, cherish, nurse, (feeling, hope, etc.) in one's heart. [ME, f. OF *norir* (-ISH²) f. L *nutrire*]

nou′rishment (nŭ′-) *n.* sustenance, food; nourishing. [ME, f. prec. + -MENT]

nous (nows) *n.* (Gk Philos.) mind, intellect; (colloq.) common sense, gumption. [Gk]

nouveau riche (noŏvō rē′sh) *n.* (*pl.* -ux -es *pr.* same). one who has recently acquired (usu. ostentatious) wealth. [F, = new rich]

nouvelle (noŏ′vĕl) *n.* short novel; ∼ **vague** (vahg), new trend (esp. in Fr. film-making of early 1960s). [F, fem. of *nouveau* new; *vague* wave]

Nov. *abbr.* November.

nō′va *n.* (*pl.* ∼e or ∼s). star showing sudden large increase of brightness and then subsiding. [L, fem. of *novus* new, since orig. thought to be new star]

novā′tion *n.* (Law). substitution of new debtor, contract, etc., for former one. [f. LL *novatio* f. L *novare* make new (*novus* new); see -ATION]

nŏ′vel¹ *n.* fictitious prose narrative of book length portraying characters and actions credibly representative of real life in continuous plot; **the** ∼, this type of literature; hence ∼E′SE *n.*, style characteristic of

inferior novels, ∼E′SQUE *a.* [f. It. *novella* (*storia* story) fem. of *novello* new f. L *novellus* (*novus*); see -LE 2]

nŏ′vel² *a.* of new kind or nature, strange, hitherto unknown. [ME f. OF, f. L *novellus* (see prec.)]

nŏvelĕ′tt|e *n.* short novel, story of moderate length, (‖freq. derog. of light romance, whence ∼ISH¹ *a.*); (Mus.) piano piece of free form with several themes. [f. NOVEL¹ + -ETTE]

nŏ′vel|ist *n.* novel-writer; hence ∼istic *a.* [f. NOVEL¹ + -IST]

nŏ′veliz|e, -īs|e (-īz), *v.t.* convert (drama, facts) into a novel; hence ∼A′TION *n.* [f. NOVEL¹ + -IZE]

nŏve′lla *n.* short novel or narrative; tale such as those in Boccaccio's *Decameron*. [It. (see NOVEL¹)]

nŏ′velty *n.* new or unusual thing or occurrence; novel character of something; small decoration or toy of novel design. [ME, f. OF *novelté* (as NOVEL²; see -TY¹)]

Novĕ′mber *n.* eleventh month of year. [ME f. OF *novembre* f. L *November* (*novem* nine; cf. DECEMBER, SEPTEMBER)]

novē′na *n.* (RC Ch.) devotion consisting of special prayers or service on nine successive days. [med. L, f. L *novem* nine]

novēr′cal *a.* (arch.) stepmotherly. [f. L *novercalis* (*noverca* stepmother; see -AL)]

nŏ′vice *n.* person received in religious house on probation before taking the vows; new convert; inexperienced person, beginner, tiro; animal that has not won major prize in competition. [ME f. OF, L *novicius* (*novus* new; see -ICE)]

novi′ciate, -tiate, (-shi-) *n.* novice's probationary period or initiation or apprenticeship; novice (esp. in religion); quarters assigned to novices. [f. F *noviciat* or f. med. L *noviciatus* (as prec.; see -ATE¹)]

Nŏ′vocaine, n-, *n.* (P) local anaesthetic derived from benzoic acid. [f. L *novus* new + COCAINE]

now *adv., conj., & n.* **1.** *adv.* at the time when, or of which, one is writing or speaking; by this time; under the present circumstances (*I cannot now ever believe you again*); immediately (*must go now*); in the immediate past (*just now*; (arch.) *even now, but now*); on this further occasion (*well, what do you want now?*); (in narrative or discourse) then, next, by that time, (*Caesar now marched east; now let us consider the second point; now to put the cap back on; it was now clear*); HOW *now?*; (every) ∼ and then, (every) ∼ and again, from time to time, intermittently; ∼ . . . ∼ . . ., ∼ . . . then . . ., ∼ . . . and again . . ., at one moment . . . at another moment . . .; ∼ for it!, ∼ or never!, this is the moment to act; ∼ that, = sense 3. **2.** (Without temporal force, exclaiming, reproving, explanatory, soothing, exclaiming, etc.) pray, I beg, I insist, I warn you, and yet, you must know, it must be admitted, surely, (*Now what do you mean by it?. Now why didn't I think of that?. Oh, come now!. No nonsense, now!. You have revealed the secret; now you were paid to keep it. Now Barabbas was a robber. Now this has bad enough, but—. Now then, what mischief are you up to?. Now then, don't cry. Now, now, behave yourself!. You don't mean it, now*). **3.** *conj.* ∼ (that), consequently upon or simultaneously with the fact that (*Now I am a man I think otherwise. Now (that) you mention it, I do remember. You ought to write, now that you know the address*). **4.** *n.* this time, the present (chiefly after *preps.*: *is there by, before, till, now*); **as of** ∼, at this time; **for** ∼, until a later time (*goodbye for now*). [OE *nū*, = OS, OHG, ON, Goth. *nū*, corresp. to L *nunc*, Gk *nun*, Skr. *nū*]

now′aday *a.* of nowadays. [f. foll.]

now′adays (-z) *adv. & n.* **1.** (at) the present day, (in) these (advanced or newfangled) times. [ME, f. NOW *adv.* + A³ + DAY + -S³]

Nowel(l). Vars. of NOEL.

nowhere, nowhither. See NO¹.

nō′where (nō′wār) *adv. & pron.* (in or to) no place; ∼ **near**, not nearly; **be, come** (**in**), ∼, not be placed in race or competition; **come from** ∼, be suddenly evident or successful; **get** ~, make no progress, give (person) no success; **in the middle of** ~, (colloq.) far from towns etc. [OE *nāhwǣr* (as NO¹, WHERE)]

nowt *n.* (colloq. or dial.) nothing. [var. of NOUGHT]

nŏ'xious (-kshŭs) *a.* harmful, unwholesome; hence ~LY² *adv.*, ~NESS *n.* [f. L *noxius* (*noxa* harm) + -OUS]

noyade (nwahyah'd) *n.* execution by drowning, esp. wholesale as in France in 1794. [F (*noyer* drown f. L *necare* f. *nex* slaughter; see -ADE)]

noyau (nwah'yō) *n.* (*pl.* ~**x** *pr.* -z). liqueur of brandy flavoured with fruit-kernels. [F, = kernel, f. Rom. **nucale* neut. (as n.) of LL *nucalis* f. L *nux nucis* nut]

nŏ'zzle *n.* spout, mouthpiece, end fitted to hose etc. to form jet. [f. NOSE + -LE 1]

NP *abbr.* Notary Public.

n.p. *abbr.* new paragraph; no place of publication.

Np *symb.* neptunium.

||**NPA** *abbr.* Newspaper Publishers' Association.

||**NPL** *abbr.* National Physical Laboratory.

NR *abbr.* North RIDING².

nr. *abbr.* near.

NRA *abbr.* *National Recovery Administration; National Rifle Association.

NS *abbr.* new series; new style; Nova Scotia.

||**NSB** *abbr.* National Savings Bank.

***NSC** *abbr.* National Security Council.

***NSF** *abbr.* National Science Foundation.

||**NSPCC** *abbr.* National Society for the Prevention of Cruelty to Children.

NSW *abbr.* New South Wales.

NT *abbr.* New Testament; (Austral.) Northern Territory; no trumps.

n't *adv.* = NOT 2 (*isn't, mustn't*). [abbr.]

nth. See N.

Nth. *abbr.* North.

NTP *abbr.* normal temperature and pressure.

nū *n.* thirteenth Greek letter (N, *ν*) = n. [Gk]

nūance (nū'ans, -ah'ñs) *n.*, & *v.t.* **1.** *n.* delicate difference in or shade of meaning, feeling, opinion, colour, etc. **2.** *v.t.* give nuance(s) to. [F (*nuer* to shade, ult. f. L *nubes* cloud; see -ANCE)]

nŭb *n.* small knob or lump, esp. of coal; small residue, stub; point or gist (*of* matter or story). [app. var. of *knub*, f. MLG *knubbe, knobbe,* KNOB]

***nŭ'bbin** *n.* dwarfed or imperfect maize ear or other vegetable; = NUB. [f. prec.]

nŭ'bbl|e *n.* small knob or lump; hence ~Y² *a.* [dim. of NUB; see -LE 1]

||**NUBE** *abbr.* National Union of Bank Employees.

nū'bīle *a.* marriageable or sexually attractive (esp. of woman); hence **nūbī'lITY** *n.* [f. L *nubilis* (*nubere* become wife of; see -IL)]

nū'chal (-k-) *a.* of nape of neck. [f. *nucha* nape, f. med. L *nucha* medulla oblongata f. Arab. *nuḵa'* spinal marrow]

nūci- *comb. form.* nut, as **nūcī'FEROUS, nūcī'VOROUS,** *adjs.* [f. L *nux nucis* nut]

nū'clēar *a.* of, relating to, constituting, a nucleus; using nuclear energy (*nuclear weapon*); having nuclear weapons; ~ **bomb,** = ATOMIC *bomb;* ~ **disarm-ament,** renunciation of nuclear weapons; ~ **energy** (released or absorbed during reactions taking place in atomic nuclei); ~ **family,** father, mother, and child(ren); ~ **fission,** = FISSION 2; ~ **fuel,** source of nuclear energy; *nuclear* FUSION; ~ **physics** (dealing with the atomic nucleus); ~ **power,** (1) power derived from nuclear energy, (2) country that has nuclear weapons; ~**(-powered)** *a.,* (of ship) using nuclear power; *nuclear* REACTOR; ~ **warfare,** = ATOMIC *warfare.* [f. NUCLEUS + -AR¹]

nū'clēase *n.* (Chem.) enzyme causing hydrolysis of nucleic acids. [f. NUCLEIC + -ASE]

nū'clē|āte *v.t.* & *i.* form (into) a nucleus; hence ~A'TION *n.* [f. LL *nucleare* form kernel (NUCLEUS) + -ATE³]

nūclē'ic *a.* ~ **acid,** one of two acids (DNA and RNA)

present in all cells and having many nucleotide molecules linked in long chain. [f. NUCLEUS + -IC]

nū'clēŏ-. See NUCLEUS.

nūcleŏl|us (-ē'o-, -īō'-) *n.* (*pl.* ~**i** *pr.* -ī). spherical body in nucleus of living cell in resting state; hence ~AR¹ *a.* [LL, dim. of L NUCLEUS]

nū'clēŏn *n.* (Phys.) proton or neutron; particle of which these are regarded as different states. [f. NUCLEUS + -ON]

nūclēŏ'n|ic *a.* of nucleons or nucleonics; so ~ICS *n. pl.* (treated as *sing.*), branch of science and technology concerned with atomic nuclei and nucleons, esp. practical use of nuclear phenomena. [f. NUCLEAR after *electronics,* & f. prec. + -IC]

nū'clēoside *n.* (Chem.) compound of a sugar with a heterocyclic base. [f. NUCLEO- + -OSE² + -IDE]

nū'clēotīde *n.* (Chem.) compound of phosphate group linked to sugar of nucleoside. [f. NUCLEO- + *t* + -IDE]

nū'clē|us *n.* (*pl.* ~**i** *pr.* -ī). **1.** central part or thing round which others are collected; kernel of aggregate or mass; beginning meant to receive additions. **2.** (Astron.) condensed part of comet's head. **3.** (Phys.) positively charged central portion constituting main mass of atom. **4.** (Biol.) dense central part of plant or animal cell, containing genetic material; central part of ovule or seed; group of nerve-cells. **5.** Hence ~o-*comb. form;* ~**o-pro'tein,** compound of protein with nucleic acid. [L, = kernel, inner part, dim. of *nux nucis* nut]

nū'clide *n.* (Phys.) particular kind of atom defined by composition of its nucleus; hence **nūclī'dIC** *a.* [f. NUCLEUS + Gk *eidos* form; cf. -IDE]

nūde *a.* & *n.* **1.** *a.* naked, bare, unclothed, undraped; ~ **contract,** (Law) contract lacking a consideration and therefore void unless under seal; so **nū'dī-** *comb. form* (Zool.), **nū'dITY** *n.* **2.** flesh-coloured. **3.** *n.* nude human figure in painting, sculpture, photography, etc.; such a painting etc.; nude person; **the** ~, the undraped figure, unclothed state. **4.** Hence **nū'dIST** *n.,* one who lives unclothed as much as possible (on grounds of health) or advocates doing so; so **nū'dISM** (3) *n.* [f. L *nudus*]

nŭdge *v.t.,* & *n.* **1.** *v.t.* push slightly with elbow to draw attention privately, (fig.) draw attention of; push gradually. **2.** *n.* such push. [17th c.; orig. unkn.; cf. Norw. dial. *nugga, nyggja* to push, rub]

nŭff *n.* (colloq.) = ENOUGH (esp. ~ **said,** that is agreed or fully explained). [abbr.]

nū'gatorÿ *a.* trifling, worthless, futile; inoperative, not valid. [f. L *nugatorius* (*nugari* trifle f. *nugae* jests; see -ORY)]

nū'ggar *n.* large broad-beamed boat used on upper Nile. [f. Arab. *nukḵār*]

nū'gget (-g-) *n.* rough lump of native gold, platinum, or (fig.) something valuable. [app. f. dial. *nug* lump etc. + -ET¹]

||**NUGMW** *abbr.* National Union of General and Municipal Workers.

nui'sance (nū's-) *n.* **1.** anything injurious or obnoxious to the community or member of it and for which legal remedy exists. **2.** obnoxious person, offensive object, annoying action, anything disagree-able or inconvenient (*what a nuisance!*); ~ **value** (resulting from capacity to harass or frustrate). [ME f. OF, = hurt (*nuire nuis-* f. L *nocēre* to hurt; see -ANCE)]

||**NUJ** *abbr.* National Union of Journalists.

***nūke** *n.* (sl.) nuclear bomb. [abbr.]

nŭll *a.* & *n.* **1.** *a.* ~ (**and void**), not binding, invalid. **2.** without character or expression. **3.** non-existent, amounting to nothing; of zero (~ **hypothesis,** that difference between statistical samples does not imply difference between populations); ~ **instrument,** used by adjustment to give reading of zero). **4.** *n.* dummy letter in a cipher. [f. F *nul nulle* f. L *nullus* none (*ne* not, *ullus* any)]

nŭ′lla(-nŭlla) *n.* (Austral.) hardwood club used by Aborigines. [Aboriginal]

nulla bona (nŭla bō′na) *n.* sheriff's return stating that party has no goods to be distrained upon. [L, = no goods]

nŭ′llah (*-a*) (Anglo-Ind.) stream, watercourse, ravine. [f. Hindi *nālā*]

nŭllifi′dian *n.* & *a.* (person) having no religious faith or belief. [f. med. L *nullifidius* f. L *nullus* none + *fides* faith; see -IAN]

nŭ′lli|fў *v.t.* cancel, neutralize; hence ∼FICA′TION *n.* [f. NULL + -I- + -FY]

nŭlli′par|a *n.* woman who has never borne a child; hence ∼OUS *a.* [mod. L, f. L *nullus* none + -I- + *-para* fem. of *-parus* (*parere* bear)]

nŭ′llipŏre *n.* form of marine vegetation able to secrete lime, like coral. [f. L *nullus* none + PORE[1]]

nŭ′llity *n.* being null, invalidity, (esp. of marriage; ∼ suit, to establish this); act, document, etc., that is null; nothingness; a mere nothing; a nonentity. [f. F *nullité* or f. med. L *nullitas* f. L *nullus* none; see -ITY]

‖NUM *abbr.* National Union of Mineworkers.

Num. *abbr.* Numbers (OT).

numb (-m) *a.*, & *v.t.* **1.** *a.* deprived of feeling or power of motion (*numb with cold, shock, etc.*); ∼-**fish**, the electric ray or torpedo; ∼′**skull**, numskull; hence ∼′LY[2] *adv.*, ∼′NESS *n.* **2.** *v.t.* make numb; (fig.) stupefy, paralyse. [ME *nome(n)* p.p. of NIM take; for *-b* cf. THUMB]

nŭ′mbat *n.* small Austral. marsupial of genus *Myrmecobius*. [Aboriginal]

nŭ′mber[1] *n.* **1.** count, sum, or aggregate, of or *of* persons or things or abstract units; count of things etc. up to a certain one, showing latter's position in series; symbol or figure representing such count, esp. as identifying one member of a series (e.g. registered vehicle, telephone); person or thing (esp. single issue of magazine, single song etc. in opera, concert, etc.) whose place in series is indicated by such figure; (colloq.) person, garment, job, etc.; (in *pl.*; N∼*s*) OT book containing census; BACK[1] *number*; **by ∼s**, following simple instructions identified by numbers; GOLDEN *number*; **have** person's ∼, (sl.) understand his motives etc.; **in ∼s**, (of publication) in successive numbered parts; **make** one's ∼ **with**, (sl.) contact (a person); ROUND[1] *numbers*; **to the ∼ of**, amounting to as many as (*80* etc.); one's ∼ **is up**, (colloq.) one is doomed (to die); ∼ **one**, (*n.*) oneself (*always takes care of number one*), (*a.*) first in rank or importance, first-rate; ∼-**plate** (bearing number, esp. of registered vehicle); ∼**s game**, action involving only arithmetical work, *lottery based on occurrence of unpredictable numbers in results of races etc.; ‖N∼ **Ten** (**Downing Street**), official London house of Prime Minister; ∼ **two**, second in command. **2.** company (**is of our ∼**, is included among us); (in *sing.* or *pl.*) large, small, etc., or (fairly) large, collection or group *of* or abs. (*were present in* (*great*) *numbers, only in small numbers; saw a* (*great*) *number of birds; a small number came; there are numbers who live by begging*). **3.** (in *pl.*) numerical preponderance (*won by* (*force of*) *numbers*). **4.** numerical reckoning; **without** ∼, **out of** ∼, ∼LESS *a.*, innumerable; **in** ∼, when counted or estimated, numerically, (*one people exceeds another in number*). **5.** (Gram.) class of word-forms including all singular, all plural, or all dual etc. words (*Greek has three numbers;* '*things' is of the plural number*). **6.** (arch.) rhythm; (in *pl.*) groups of musical notes, metrical feet, verses. [ME f. AF *numbre*, OF *nombre* f. L *numerus*]

nŭ′mber[2] *v.t.* **1.** count, ascertain number of; (in *pass.*) be restricted in number (**his days** or **years are** ∼**ed**, he has not long to live). **2.** include, regard as, among, in, or with some class. **3.** ∼ (**off**), assign number(s) to, distinguish with number(s). **4.** have lived, live, (so many years); be able to show (so many inhabitants etc.); amount to (specified number). [ME, f. OF *nombrer* f. L *numerare* (as prec.)]

‖nŭ′mbles (-belz) *n. pl.* (arch.) deer's entrails. [ME, f. OF *numbles, nombles* loin etc., f. L *lumbulus* dim. of *lumbus* loin; cf. UMBLES]

nŭ′mdah *n.* embroidered felt rug from India etc. [f. Urdu *namdā*; see NUMNAH]

nŭ′m|ĕn *n.* (*pl.* ∼**ina**). local or presiding deity. [L *numen -minis*]

nŭ′merable *a.* that can be numbered. [f. L *numerabilis* (as NUMBER[2]; see -ABLE)]

nŭ′meral *a.* & *n.* **1.** (word, figure, group of figures) denoting a number. **2.** *a.* of number. [f. LL *numeralis* f. L (as NUMBER[1]; see -AL)]

nŭ′mer|ate *a.* acquainted with basic principles of mathematics and science; hence ∼ACY *n.* [f. L *numerus* number + -ATE[2], after *literate*]

numera′tion *n.* method or process of numbering or computing; calculation; assigning of numbers; (Arith.) expression in words of number written in figures; ∼ **table** (showing value of figures according to their ∼ place in system of notation). [ME, f. L *numeratio* payment, in LL numbering (as NUMBER[2]; see -ATION)]

nŭ′merātor *n.* number above line in vulgar fraction showing how many of the parts indicated by the denominator are taken (e.g. 2 in ⅔); person who numbers. [f. F *numérateur* or f. LL *numerator* (as NUMBER[2]; see -OR)]

numĕ′rical *a.* of, in, denoting, etc., number(s); hence ∼LY[2] *adv.* [f. med. L *numericus* (as NUMBER[1]; see -IC) + -AL]

numerŏ′log|ў *n.* divination by numbers; study of occult meaning of numbers; hence **numerolŏ′g**ICAL *a.*, ∼IST (3) *n.* [f. L *numerus* number + -o- + -LOGY]

nŭ′merous *a.* comprising many units (*a numerous library, family, army, class*); (with *pl. n.*) many (*received numerous gifts*); (arch.) coming from or containing many individuals (*the numerous voice of the people*), (of verse or prose) rhythmic, harmonious; hence ∼LY[2] *adv.* [f. L *numerosus* (as prec.; see -OUS)]

nŭ′minous *a.* of a numen; spiritual, indicating presence of divinity; awe-inspiring. [f. L NUMEN + -OUS]

numismă′t|ic (-z-) *a.* of coins or coinage; of coins and related things (e.g. medals); hence ∼ICALLY *adv.*, ∼ICS, **nŭmi′smat**IST (3), **numismatŏ′**LOGY, (-z-) *ns.* [f. F *numismatique* f. L *numisma* f. Gk *nomisma -atos* current coin (*nomizō* use currently; see -ISM, -ATIC)]

nŭ′mmarў *a.* of or in coin(s). [f. L *nummarius* (*nummus* coin; see -ARY[1])]

nŭ′mmŭlite *n.* disc-shaped fossil shell of foraminiferous protozoan in Tertiary strata. [f. L *nummulus* dim. of *nummus* coin, + -ITE[1] (2)]

nŭ′mnah (*-a*) *n.* saddle-cloth, pad placed under saddle. [f. Urdu *namdā* f. Pers. *namad* carpet]

nŭ′mskŭll *n.* stupid person; head (esp. of stupid person). [f. NUMB + SKULL]

nŭn *n.* woman living in convent usu. under vows of poverty, chastity, and obedience; ‖blue tit; ‖smew; ∼**'s cloth**, ∼**'s veiling**, thin woollen material; hence ∼′HOOD, ∼′SHIP, *ns.*, ∼′LIKE, ∼′NISH[1], *adjs.* [ME, partly f. OE *nunne*, = OHG, ON *nunna*, f. eccl. L *nonna* fem. of *nonnus* monk, orig. title given to elderly person, partly f. OF *nonne*]

nŭ′natăk *n.* isolated peak of rock projecting above surface of land ice or snow e.g. in Greenland. [Eskimo]

nŭ′n-buoy (-boi) *n.* buoy circular in middle and tapering to each end. [f. obs. *nun* child's top + BUOY[1]]

nunc dimittis (nŭngk dĭ′mĭtĭs) *n.* **1.** canticle beginning *Nunc dimittis* from Luke 2:29. **2.** permission to depart; **sing** ∼, be willing to depart from life etc. [L, = now lettest thou depart]

nŭ′nciatūre (-shat-) *n.* (tenure of) office of nuncio. [f. It. *nunziatura* (as foll.); see -URE]

nŭ′nciŏ (-shiō) *n.* (*pl.* ∼**s**). Pope's permanent diplomatic representative in another country. [It., f. L *nuntius* messenger]

nŭ′ncŭp|āte *v.t.* declare (will, testament) orally, not in writing; so ∼A′TION *n.*, ∼ATIVE *a.* [f. L *nuncupare* name + -ATE³]

nŭ′nnerў *n.* religious house for nuns, convent. [ME, f. AF *nonnerie* (*nonne* NUN; see -ERY)]

||**NUPE** *abbr.* National Union of Public Employees.

nŭ′ptial (-shǎl) *a.* & *n.* **1.** *a.* of marriage or wedding; ∼ **flight** (of ants etc., with mating). **2.** *n.* (usu. in *pl.*) wedding. [F, or f. L *nuptialis* (*nuptiae* wedding f. *nubere nupt-* become wife)]

||**NUR** *abbr.* National Union of Railwaymen.

nûrse¹ *n.* **1.** (sick-)∼, person, usu. woman, employed in & usu. trained for care of the sick or infirm. **2.** (dry-) ∼, woman employed to take charge of (but not suckle) young children; WET-*nurse*. **3.** country etc. that fosters some quality etc. (*the nurse of liberty*). **4.** nursing or being nursed; **at** ∼, **put out to** ∼, (of child, or fig. of estate). **5.** (Forestry) tree planted as shelter to others; (Entom.) sexually imperfect bee, ant, etc., caring for young brood, worker. **6.** ∼-**child,** foster-child; ∼-**frog** (of which male carries eggs till hatched); ∼′**maid,** young woman employed to take charge of child(ren), (fig.) one who takes solicitous care of another. [reduced f. ME and OF *norice*, *nurice* f. LL *nutricia* fem. of L *nutricius* (*nutrix* -*icis* f. *nutrire* nourish)]

nûrs|e² *v.t.* & *i.* **1.** suckle (child), give suck, act as wet-nurse; act as nurse(maid) to, have charge of; (in *pass.*) be brought up (*in* luxury, certain place, etc.). **2.** foster, tend, promote development of, (the arts, hatred, etc.); manage (plants, estate) with solicitude; cherish (grievance etc.). **3.** tend (sick person); try to cure (sickness, injured part); be sick-nurse. **4.** hold or clasp (baby, one's knees or foot) carefully or caressingly; sit close over (fire); treat carefully. **5.** ||keep favour of (electoral constituency) by continued attentions. **6.** (Bill.) keep (balls) together for series of cannons. **7.** Hence ∼′ING¹ (1) *n.*; ||∼ing home, private hospital, house for surgical operations, reception of invalids, etc.; ∼**ing father,** foster-father; ∼**ing mother,** (1) suckling woman, (2) foster-mother. [later form of ME *nur(i)sh* f. NOURISH, assim. to prec.]

nûrse³ *n.* one of several large sharks; ∼-**hound,** a dogfish (*Scyliorhinus stellaris*). [ME, perh. var. of HUSS, w. *n-* as in NEWT, assim. to NURSE¹]

nûr′serў *n.* **1.** room or place for children and their nurses; DAY *nursery.* **2.** practice, institution, sphere, place, in or by which qualities or classes of people are fostered or bred. **3.** plot of ground in which young plants are reared for transplantation, esp. trees etc. for sale; fish-rearing pond; place where animal life is developed. **4.** (Bill.) grouped balls (see NURSE² 6; esp. *nursery cannon*). **5.** ∼**man,** owner of or worker in plant nursery; ∼ **nurse** (trained to look after young children); ∼ **rhyme,** simple traditional song or story in rhyme for children; ∼ (**school**) (for young children esp. under 5); ∼ **slopes,** part of skiing-resort slopes suitable for beginners; ∼ (**stakes**), race for two-year-old horses. [ME, prob. f. AF *noricerie* (as NURSE¹; see -ERY)]

nûr′s(e)ling (-sl-) *n.* infant, esp. in relation to its nurse; ∼ **of,** person or thing bred in or fostered by. [f. NURSE² + -LING¹]

nûr′ture *n.*, & *v.t.* **1.** *n.* bringing up, fostering care; nourishment. **2.** *v.t.* nourish, rear, foster, train, educate. [ME, f. OF *nour(e)ture* (as NOURISH; see -URE)]

||**NUS** *abbr.* National Union of Seamen; National Union of Students.

nŭt *n.*, & *v.i.* (-tt-). **1.** *n.* (fruit consisting of hard or leathery shell enclosing) edible kernel; pod containing hard seeds (EARTH¹-*nut*, PEA*nut*); (in *pl.*, vulg.) testicles; ||*can't crack* etc. **for** ∼**s,** (sl.) even tolerably well; HARD or *tough nut to crack*; ∼**s** (**to you**) (sl. excl. of derision; also **nerts**). **2.** (arch. sl.) showy young man. **3.** (sl.) head (**off** one's ∼, crazy; **do** one's ∼, go crazy); crazy or cranky person; (in *pl.*, as *a.*) crazy;

∼**s about** or **on,** enthusiastic about; skilful at. **4.** small usu. hexagonal metal block pierced with female screw-thread to adjust or fasten bolt etc. and operated by spanner; ∼**s and bolts,** (fig.) practical details. **5.** holder that tightens or relaxes horsehair of violin-bow etc.; fixed bridge at neck end of strings of violin etc. **6.** small lump of coal, butter, etc. **7.** ∼-**brown,** coloured like ripe hazel-nut (esp. of girl's complexion, or of ale); ∼-**butter,** food like butter made from nuts; ∼-**case,** (sl.) crazy person; ∼′**cracker,** (usu. in *pl.*) instrument for cracking nuts, prominent chin and nose with points naturally, or by loss of teeth, near each other (∼*cracker man,* nickname of fossil hominid with large teeth); ∼-**gall,** gall found on dyer's oak used as dyestuff; ∼′**hatch** (-t-h-), small climbing bird feeding on nuts, insects, etc. [rel. to HATCH²]; ∼-**house,** (sl.) mental home or hospital; *∼-**meat,** kernel of nut; ∼-**oil** (got from hazel-nuts and walnuts, and used in paints and varnishes); ∼-**palm,** Australian cycad bearing edible nuts; ∼-**pine,** N. Amer. pine with edible nutlike seeds; ∼′**shell,** hard exterior covering of nut, tiny receptacle or dwelling, brief(est possible) way of expressing (*can give it to you in a nutshell*); ∼-**tree,** tree bearing nuts, esp. hazel; ∼-**weevil,** beetle laying eggs in green hazel and filbert nuts. **8.** Hence ∼′LET *n.*, small nut or nutlike fruit. **9.** *v.i.* seek or gather nuts (*go nutting*). [OE *hnutu*, = MLG, MDu. *note,* OHG (*h*)*nuz,* ON *hnot* f. Gmc **hnut-*]

||**NUT** *abbr.* National Union of Teachers.

nŭtā′tion *a.* (Bot.) nodding, drooping. [f. L *nutare* frequent. of -*nuere* nod + -ATE³]

nūtā′tion *n.* nodding; (Astron.) oscillation of earth's axis making motion of pole of equator round pole of ecliptic wavy; oscillation of spinning top; curvature in stem of growing plant. [f. L *nutatio* (as prec.; see -ION)]

nŭt′mĕg *n.* hard aromatic spheroidal seed got from fruit of evergreen E. Ind. tree (*Myristica fragrans*) used as spice and in medicine; ∼-**apple,** fruit of nutmeg-tree yielding mace and nutmeg. [ME; partial transl. of AF **nois mugue,* OF *nois mug(u)ede* f. Rom. **nuce muscata* f. L *nux* nut + L *muscus* MUSK]

nū′tria *n.* skin or fur of coypu. [Sp., = otter]

nū′trient *a.* & *n.* (substance) serving as or providing nourishment. [f. L *nutrire* nourish; see -ENT]

nū′triment *n.* nourishing food (lit. or fig.); hence ∼AL (-ĕ′n-) *a.* [f. L *nutrimentum* (as prec.; see -MENT)]

nŭtri′tion *n.* (supplying or receiving of) nourishment, food; hence ∼AL *a.*, of or relating to nutrition, ∼IST (3) *n.*, one who studies human nourishment. [F, or f. LL *nutritio* (as NUTRIENT; see -ITION)]

nŭtri′tious (-shŭs) *a.* nourishing, efficient as food; hence ∼LY² *adv.*, ∼NESS *n.* [f. L *nutritius* (as NURSE¹; see -ITIOUS²)]

nū′tritive *a.* & *n.* **1.** *a.* serving as nutritious food; concerned in nutrition. **2.** *n.* nutritious article of food. [ME, f. F *nutritif -ive* f. med. L *nutritivus* (as NUTRIENT; see -IVE)]

nŭ′tter *n.* nut-gatherer; (sl.) crazy person. [f. NUT + -ER¹]

nŭ′ttў *a.* abounding in nuts; tasting like nuts, of rich mellow flavour; (sl.) crazy; ∼ **about** or **on,** (sl.) = NUTS *about.* [f. NUT + -Y²]

nŭx vŏ′mĭca *n.* seed of E. Ind. tree (*Strychnos nux-vomica*) yielding strychnine. [med. L, f. L *nux* nut + *vomicus* (*vomere* vomit; see -IC)]

nŭ′zzle *v.i.* & *t.* burrow or press or rub or sniff with the nose, press nose or press (nose) *into* or *against*; nestle, lie snug, (also *refl.*). [ME, f. NOSE¹ + -LE 3]

NV *abbr.* Nevada.

NW *abbr.* North-West(ern).

NY *abbr.* New York.

nyala. Var. of INYALA.

NYC *abbr.* New York City.

nўctalō′pia *n.* **1.** recurrent loss of vision in twilight and dark. **2.** inability to see clearly except at night. [LL, f. Gk *nuktalōps* (*nux nuktos* night, *alaos* blind, *ōps* eye; see -IA¹); incorrect second sense due to over-looking of -*al*-]

nyctitro′pic *a.* (Bot.) turning in certain direction at night. [f. Gk *nukti*- comb. form of *nux nuktos* night + *tropos* turn; see -IC]

||**nye.** Var. of NIDE.

ny′lghau (-gaw) *n.* = NILGAI. [f. Hind. f. Pers. *nīlgāw* (*nīl* blue, *gāw* cow)]

ny′lon *n.* synthetic polymer of great toughness, lightness, and elasticity, widely used in industry and in textile fabrics; nylon fabric; (in *pl.*) stockings made of nylon. [invented wd, after *cotton*, *rayon*]

nymph *n.* **1.** one of class of mythological semi-divine maidens inhabiting sea, rivers, fountains, hills, woods, or trees, or attending superior deities; hence or cogn. ∼ě′AN, ∼′LIKE, *adjs.* **2.** (poet.) young and beautiful woman. **3.** immature form of insect which resembles adult; young dragonfly or damselfly. **4.** So ∼′AL *a.* [ME, f. OF *nimphe* f. L f. Gk *numphē*]

nymphae *n. pl.* (Anat.) labia minora. [L, pl. of *nympha* (see prec.)]

nymphet (nĭ′-, -ě′t) *n.* young nymph; nymphlike or sexually attractive young girl. [f. NYMPH + -ET¹]

nympho *n.* (*pl.* ∼s). (colloq.) nymphomaniac. [abbr.]

nympholepsy *n.* ecstasy or frenzy caused by desire of the unattainable. [f. foll., after *epilepsy*]

nymphol|ept *n.* person inspired by violent enthusiasm esp. for an ideal; hence ∼ě′ptIC *a.* [f. Gk *numpholēptos* caught by nymphs (as NYMPH, *lambanō* take)]

nympho|mā′nĭa *n.* (Path.) excessive sexual desire in women; hence ∼MA′NIAC *n.* [mod. L (as NYMPH, -O-, -MANIA)]

nystä′gm|us *n.* (eye-disease common among miners, with) continual rapid oscillation of eyeballs; hence ∼IC *a.* [f. Gk *nustagmos* nodding (*nustazō* nod)]

NZ *abbr.* New Zealand.

O

O¹, o, (ō) *n.* (*pl.* **Os** *or* **O's**). **1.** fifteenth letter of alphabet. **2.** (*O*). (As numeral in telephone numbers etc.) nought, zero.

O² (ō) *int.* (arch., poet., or rhet.) prefixed to name in vocative (*O God our help*) or expr. wish, entreaty, etc., (*O for the touch of a vanish'd hand; O come, all ye faithful; O* THAT²). [ME; natural excl. of sudden feeling]

O'¹ (ō, *o*) *pref.* of Irish patronymic names (*O'Connor*). [Ir. *ó, ua*, descendant]

o'² (*o*) *prep.* of, on, (arch., poet., or dial., exc. in some phrs.): (= OF) *o'clock, Jack-o'-lantern, will-o'-the-wisp,* (colloq.) *cup o' tea,* (= ON¹) *cannot sleep o' nights.* [abbr.]

-ō *suf.* forming usu. sl. or colloq. variants or derivatives (*beano, smoko, wino*). [perh. f. OH as joc. suf.]

-o-, terminal vowel of combining forms of wds; prop. used in Gk compounds (-I- being usu. in L), but now extended to many scientific and other terms made wholly or partly f. non-Gk wds (*occipito-frontal, spectro-scope, serio-comic*) and, in meaning, expressing not merely modification of second element by first (*Franco-German* = essentially German with some French characteristics), but equal or any other relations (*Franco-German war*); available as general formative of combining forms (*socio-*), esp. for wds in *-ic(al)* (*chemico-, politico-*); often elided before vowel (*neuralgia*).

O. *abbr.* Ohio; Old.

O *symb.* oxygen.

oaf *n.* (*pl.* ∼**s,** *or* **oaves** *pr.* -vz). stupid person; awkward lout; hence ∼'ISH¹ *a.* [orig. = elf's child, var. of obs. *auf* f. ON *álfr* elf]

oak *n.* **1.** tree and shrub of genus *Quercus*, of which the best known species is a forest tree yielding hard timber and acorns and having irregularly lobed leaves; BUR, **dyer's,** HOLM², **scarlet, white,** etc., ∼, other species of *Quercus*; **dwarf, ground,** SHE-, etc., ∼, plants named from some resemblance to oak esp. in leaves. **2.** wood of the oak (HEART *of oak*); (poet.) wooden ships; ‖outer door of university college rooms (**sport** one's ∼, shut this to exclude visitors); leaves of oak esp. as formerly worn on 29 May (see sense 5); ‖**the Oaks,** annual race at Epsom for three-year-old fillies [f. name of estate]. **3.** (*attrib.,* = , but now more usual than) oaken. **4.** ∼**-apple,** -GALL⁴, **-spangle, -wart,** kinds of excrescence produced on oaks by gall-flies. **5.** ‖**Oak-apple Day,** 29 May (Charles II restored 1660), on which oak-apples or oak-leaves were worn in memory of the ROYAL-oak incident; ∼**-beauty, -iappet,** kinds of moth bred on or resembling leaf etc. of oak; ∼**-fern,** a polypody (*Gymnocarpium dryopteris*) with tripartite fronds having subdivisions shaped like oak-leaves; ∼**-tree,** = sense 1; ∼**-wood,** (1) forest, copse, etc., of oaks, (2) wood of the oak. **6.** Hence ∼'EN⁵ *a.,* ∼'LET, ∼'LING¹² *a, ns.* [OE *āc,* = OHG *eih,* ON *eik* f. Gmc **aiks*]

oa'kum *n.* loose fibre got by picking old rope to pieces and used esp. in caulking (**pick** ∼, make this, esp. as formerly common task of convicts and paupers). [OE *ǣ-, ācumbe,* lit. 'off-combings']

O. & M. *abbr.* organization and methods.

‖**OAP** *abbr.* old-age pension(er).

oar *n.* & *v.* **1.** *n.* pole with blade used (usu. in even numbers) to propel boat by leverage against water, esp. one worked by single rower (cf. SWEEP² 4) with both hands (cf. SCULL), or to steer; **chained to the** ∼, constrained to work hard and long [w. allus. to galley-slaves]; **have an** ∼ **in,** be (meddlesomely) concerned with; **pulls a good** ∼, is good at rowing; **put in** one's ∼ or **put** one's ∼ **in,** interfere; **rest on** one's ∼**s, lie** or ***lay on** one's ∼**s,** relax one's efforts.

2. oarsman, rower, (*good, practised,* etc., *oar*); (fig.) wing, fin, arm used in swimming, etc.; stirring implement used in brewing. **3.** ∼**-fish,** ribbon-fish of genus *Regalecus;* *∼'**lock,** rowlock; ∼'**sman,** ∼'**swoman,** (-z-) rower; ∼'**smanship** (-z-), art of rowing; ∼'**weed,** large littoral alga esp. of genus *Laminaria.* **4.** Hence ∼'AGE (1) *n.* (poet.), (-)∼ED² (ōrd), ∼'LESS, ∼'Y² (poet.), *adjs.* **5.** *v.t.* & *i.* (poet.) row (*boat, water, one's way*). [OE *ār,* = ON *ár* f. Gmc **airō,* perh. cogn. w. Gk *eretmos* oar]

OAS *abbr.* on active service; Organization of American States.

oā's‖is *n.* (*pl.* ∼**es** *pr.* -ēz). fertile spot in desert (lit. or fig.). [LL f. Gk, app. of Egypt. orig.]

oast *n.* hop-drying kiln; ∼**-house,** building containing this. [OE *āst,* = MLG *eist* f. Gmc **aistaz,* **aithtaz* f. IE **aidh-* burn]

oat *n.* **1.** (in *pl.*) (grain yielded by) hardy cereal (*Avena sativa*) grown in cool climates as food for humans and horses; **feel** one's ∼**s,** (colloq.) be lively or **self--important*; **off** one's ∼**s,** (colloq.) lacking appetite for food. **2.** oat-plant; variety of oats; **wild** ∼, tall grass (*Avena fatua*) resembling oats (**sow** one's **wild** ∼**s,** indulge in youthful follies before becoming steady). **3.** (poet.) oat-stem used as musical pipe by shepherds etc.; pastoral or bucolic poetry. **4.** ∼'**cake,** thin unleavened cake made of oatmeal, esp. in Scotland and N. England; ∼**-grass,** = wild oat (see sense 2); ∼'**meal,** meal from oats used esp. in oatcakes and porridge, greyish-fawn colour. **5.** Hence ∼'EN⁵ *a.* [OE *āte, pl. ātan,* of unkn. orig.]

oath *n.* (*pl. pr.* ōdhz). **1.** solemn appeal to God or revered or dreaded person or object, in witness that statement is true or promise shall be kept; **take an, make, swear an,** ∼, bind oneself thus; **on** or **under** ∼, having thus sworn, stated or given by sworn person; **on** one's ∼, with solemn assertion of truth. **2.** (form of words containing) statement or promise so corroborated (*oath of allegiance, office, supremacy,* etc.). **3.** name of God etc. used as expletive to give emphasis or express anger etc., piece of profanity in speech, curse. [OE *āth,* = OS *ēth,* OHG *eid,* ON *eithr,* Goth. *aiths* f. Gmc **aithaz*]

OAU *abbr.* Organization of African Unity.

ob- *pref.* (usu. assim. to **oc-, of-, op-,** before *c, f, p* respectively) occurring mainly in wds derived from L wds already containing it, w. senses: **1.** exposure, openness, (*object, obnoxious, obtrude, obverse*). **2.** meeting (*occasion, occur, offend*), facing (*observe, obstetric, obvious, opportune*), direction (*oblation, oblong, offer*), spontaneity or compliance (*obey, obsequious*). **3.** opposition or hostility (*obloquy, obstreperous, opponent, oppress*), resistance (*obdurate, obstinate*). **4.** hindrance, blocking, concealment, (*obese, obstacle, obstruct, occlude, occult*). **5.** finality or completeness (*obsolete, obtain, occident, occupy*). **6.** (In mod. sci. wds, perh. f. as OBVERSE) inversely, in direction or manner contrary to the usual, (*obconical, obovate*). [L (*ob* towards, against, in the way of)]

‖**OB.** *abbr.* Old Boy; outside broadcast.

ob. *abbr. obiit.*

Obad. *abbr.* Obadiah (OT).

ŏbbliga'tō (-ah'-) *a.* & *n.* (*pl.* ∼**s**). (Mus.) **1.** *a.* (of accompaniment or part) inseparable, forming integral part of the composition, (opp. *ad libitum*). **2.** *n.* such part or accompaniment. [It., = obligatory, f. L *obligatus* p.p. (as OBLIGE)]

ŏbcō'nical *a.* (Biol.) in form of inverted cone. [f. OB-6 + CONICAL]

For other words in *ob-* **see OB-.**

ŏbcŏr'dāte *a.* (Biol.) in heart shape attached at apex. [f. OB- 6 + CORDATE]

ŏbdurate (ŏ'bdūr-, ŏbdūr'-) *a.* hardened against moral influence or persuasion; impenitent, stubborn; hence **ŏ'bdur**ACY *n.*, ∼LY² (-tlĭ) *adv.* [ME, f. L *obduratus* p.p. of OB(*durare* harden f. *durus* hard); see -ATE²]

∥OBE *abbr.* Officer (of the Order) of the British Empire.

ō'bèah (*-a*), **ō'bi¹,** *n.* kind of sorcery practised by Negroes esp. in W. Indies. [W. Afr.]

ŏbē'chė *n.* (light-coloured timber of) W. Afr. tree (*Triplochiton scleroxylon*). [Nigerian name]

obē'dïence *n.* **1.** obeying as act or practice or quality; submission to another's rule; compliance with law or command; task or duty in monastery or convent; compliance with monastic rule; **in ∼ to,** actuated by or in accordance with; **passive ∼,** (1) surrender to another's will without co-operation, (2) compliance with commands irrespective of their nature. **2.** (Eccl., esp. RC). being obeyed, (sphere of) authority, district or body of persons bound to obedience, (*return to the obedience of Rome; not belonging to either the Roman or the Byzantine obedience*). [ME f. OF, f. L *obedientia* (as OBEY; see -ENCE)]

obē'dïent *a.* submissive to or complying with superior's will, dutiful; acting in obedience *to*; ∥*your obedient* SERVANT; hence ∼LY² *adv.* [ME f. OF, f. L *obediens -entis* (as OBEY; see -ENT)]

obēdïë'ntiary̆ (-shel̆) *n.* holder of any office under superior in monastery or convent. [f. med. L *obedientiarius* (as OBEDIENCE; see -ARY¹)]

obei's|ance (ŏbā's-) *n.* gesture, esp. bow or curtsy, expressing submission, respect, or salutation, (*make an, do, pay, obeisance*); deference, homage, submission, (*do, make, pay, obeisance*); so ∼ANT *a.*, showing deference, obsequious. [ME, f. OF *obeissance* (as OBEY; see -ANCE)]

ŏ'belisk (*-ěl-*, *-ĭl-*) *n.* **1.** tapering usu. monolithic shaft of stone square or rectangular in section with pyramidal apex; mountain, tree, etc., of similar shape. **2.** mark (− or ÷) used in ancient MSS to indicate that word or passage is spurious etc.; reference mark (†; **double ∼,** ‡). [f. L f. Gk *obeliskos* dim. of *obelos* SPIT¹]

ŏ'belīze (*-ĕl-*, *-ĭl-*), **-īse** (-īz), *v.t.* mark with obelisk as spurious etc. [f. Gk *obelizō* (*obelos*; see prec., -IZE)]

ŏ'bel|us *n.* (*pl.* ∼**i** *pr.* -ī). = OBELISK 2. [L, f. Gk *obelos* SPIT¹]

obē'se (*o-*, *ō-*) *a.* very fat, corpulent; so ∼ITY *n.* [f. L OB(*esus* p.p. of *edere* eat) having eaten oneself fat]

obey' (ŏbā') *v.* **1.** *v.t.* comply with bidding of, be obedient to; execute (command); be actuated by (force, impulse). **2.** *v.i.* do what one is told to do. [ME, f. OF *obeir* f. L OB(*edire* = *audire* hear)]

ŏ'bfusc|āte *v.t.* darken, obscure, confuse, (mind, judgement, topic, etc.); stupefy, bewilder; hence ∼A'TION *n.*, ∼ātORY *a.* [f. LL OB(*fuscare* f. *fuscus* dark) + -ATE³]

ō'bi¹. See OBEAH.

ō'bi² *n.* broad sash worn by Japanese with kimono. [f. Jap. *obi* belt]

obiit (ŏ'biĭt) *v.i.* 3 *sing. past.* died (with date of death). [L, f. OB(*ire* it- go) die]

ŏ'bit *n.* (Hist.) memorial service, esp. in institution on anniversary of founder's or benefactor's death; (record of) date of person's death; (colloq.) obituary. [ME f. OF, f. L *obitus* death (as prec.)]

obiter dict|um (ŏbĭter dĭ'ktum) *n.* (*pl.* ∼**a**). judge's expression of opinion uttered in arguing point or giving judgement but not essential to his decision and therefore without binding authority; incidental remark. [L (*obiter* by the way, *dictum* thing said)]

obi'tūar|y̆ *n.* & *a.* **1.** *n.* notice of death(s) esp. in newspaper, brief biography of deceased person; hence ∼IST (1) *n.* **2.** *a.* recording a death; concerning

decease of a person. [f. med. L *obituarius* f. L *obitus* death (as OBIIT; see -ARY¹)]

ŏ'bjèct¹ *n.* **1.** thing placed before eyes or presented to one of the senses; material thing; thing observed with optical instrument or represented in picture. **2.** person or thing of affecting, esp. pitiable or ridiculous, appearance. **3.** person or thing to which action or feeling is directed, subject *of* or *for*, (*the Bible had been the object of his study; he is a proper object of* or *for charity*). **4.** thing aimed at, end, purpose; **no ∼,** not an important matter (esp. implying that the other party may make his own terms in the specified respect: *money, time, distance,* etc. (*is*) *no object*). **5.** (Philos.) thing thought of or apprehended as correlative to the thinking mind or subject, external thing, *the* non- -ego. **6.** (Gram.) noun or noun-equivalent governed by active transitive verb or by preposition; DIRECT², INDIRECT, *object.* **7.** ∼-**ball** (at which player aims his own ball in billiards etc.); ∼-**glass,** lens in telescope etc. nearest the object; ∼ **language** (that is discussed by a metalanguage); ∼-**lesson,** instruction about a material object that is present for inspection, (fig.) striking practical illustration of some principle; ∼- -**object,** object of sense or thought as it is in fact. **8.** Hence ∼LESS *a.* [ME, f. med. L *objectum* thing presented to the mind, p.p. of L OB(*jicere ject-* throw)]

objĕ'ct² *v.* **1.** *v.t.* adduce (quality, fact, *that*) as objection (*to* or *against* theory etc.); state (usu. *that*) as damaging fact to or *against* person etc. **2.** *v.i.* state objection, feel or express disapproval, have objection or dislike *to* (*I object to being treated like this*). **3.** Hence ∼OR *n.* (CONSCIENTIOUS *objector*). [ME, f. L *object-* (see prec.)]

objĕ'cti|fy̆ *v.t.* present as object of perception; make objective, express in concrete form, embody; hence ∼FICA'TION *n.* [f. OBJECT¹ + -I- + -FY]

objĕ'ction *n.* objecting; thing objected; adverse reason or statement; expression or feeling of disapproval or dislike. [ME f. OF, or f. LL *objectio* (as OBJECT¹; see -ION)]

objĕ'ctionab|le *a.* open to objection; undesirable, unpleasant, offensive, disapproved of; hence ∼LY² *adv.* [f. prec. + -ABLE]

objĕ'ctive *a.* & *n.* **1.** *a.* (Philos.) belonging not to the consciousness or the perceiving or thinking SUBJECT², but to what is presented to this, external to the mind, real. **2.** (Of person, writing, picture, discussion, etc.) dealing with outward things, exhibiting actual facts uncoloured by exhibitor's feelings or opinions (∼ correlative, method of evoking an emotion by symbol or indication); (Med., of symptoms) observed by another and not only felt by patient; hence ∼NESS (-vn-), **objĕctī'vity,** *ns.* **3.** (Gram.) constructed as, appropriate to, the object (∼ **case** in English, that governed by transitive verb or preposition, distinguished in form from the subjective only in some personal pronouns, as *him,* cf. *he;* ∼ **genitive,** as in 'the fear *of God'*, 'timor *Dei'*, cf. SUBJECTIVE); hence **objĕctī'**VAL *a.* **4.** ∼ **point,** (Mil.) point towards which the advance of troops is directed, (transf.) point or thing aimed at, = OBJECT¹ 4. **5.** Hence ∼LY² (-vlĭ) *adv.* **6.** *n.* = OBJECT¹-*glass;* objective point. [f. med. L *objectivus* (as OBJECT¹; SEE -IVE)]

objĕ'ctiv|ism *n.* tendency to lay stress on what is objective; doctrine that knowledge of non-ego is prior and superior to that of ego; so ∼IST (2) *n.* [f. prec. + -ISM]

objet d'art (ŏbzhā dâr') *n.* (*pl. -ets pr.* same). small artistic object. [F, lit. 'object of art']

objet trouvé (ŏbzhā trōō'vā) *n.* (*pl. -ts -és pr.* same). object found or picked up at random and presented as rarity or work of art. [F, lit. 'found object']

ŏ'bjŭrg|āte *v.t.* (literary). chide, scold; hence ∼A'TION *n.*, ∼atORY (objĕr'ga-, ŏ'bjĕrgä-) *a.* [f. L OB(*jurgare* quarrel f. *jurgium* strife) + -ATE³]

ŏblă'ncéolate *a.* (Bot.) lanceolate with more pointed end at base. [f. OB- 6 + LANCEOLATE]

ŏ′blāte¹ *n.* person dedicated to monastic or religious life or work. [F, f. med. L n. sense of L *oblatus* p.p. of OF(*ferre* bring) offer]

oblāte² (ŏ′blăt, oblā′t) *a.* (Geom., of spheroid) flattened at poles (cf. PROLATE). [f. mod. L *oblatus* (as prec.; cf. PROLATE)]

oblā′tion *n.* (presenting of bread and wine to God in) Eucharist; thing offered to God, sacrifice, victim; donation for pious uses; hence ∿AL, **ŏ′blat**ORY, *adjs*. [ME f. OF, or f. LL *oblatio* (as OBLATE¹; see -ION)]

ŏ′blĭgāte¹ *v.t.* (usu. in *p.p.*) bind (person, legally or morally) *to* do. [f. L (as OBLIGE) + -ATE³]

ŏ′blĭgāte² *a.* (Biol.) that has to be such (*obligate parasite* etc.; opp. *facultative*). [ME, f. L *obligatus* p.p. (as OBLIGE; see -ATE²)]

ŏblĭgā′tion *n.* **1.** binding agreement, esp. one enforceable under legal penalty, written contract or bond; constraining power of a law, precept, duty, contract, etc.; **of** ∿, obligatory; **day of** ∿ (on which all are required to attend Mass or Communion). **2.** one's bounden duty, a duty, burdensome task; (indebtedness for) service or benefit (*be*, LAY³, *put*, *under* (*an*) *obligation*; *repay an obligation*). [ME f. OF, f. L *obligatio -onis* (as OBLIGE; see -ATION)]

obligatorÿ (oblĭ′ga-, ŏ′blĭgā-) *a.* legally or morally binding, compulsory and not merely permissive; constituting an obligation. [ME, f. LL *obligatorius* (as foll.; see -ORY)]

oblī′ge *v.* **1.** *v.t.* (arch. or Law). bind (person, one*self*) by oath, promise, contract, etc., *to* person or *to* do. **2.** be binding on; constrain, compel, *to* do; make indebted by conferring favour, gratify *by doing* or *with*, perform a service for (person requesting it, or abs.). **3.** *v.i.* (colloq.) make contribution to entertainment (*with* song etc., or abs.). **4.** *v.t.* (in *pass.*) bound (*to* person) by gratitude (*for* small service); **much ∿d**, thank you. [ME, f. OF *obliger* f. L OB- (*ligare* bind)]

ŏbligee′ *n.* (Law). person to whom another is bound by contract or to whom bond is given (cf. OBLIGOR). [f. prec. + -EE]

obli′ging *a.* courteous, accommodating, ready to do service or kindness, hence ∿LY² *adv.*, ∿NESS *n.* [f. OBLIGE + -ING²]

ŏ′bligŏr *n.* (Law). one who binds himself to another by contract or gives bond. [f. OBLIGE + -OR]

obli′que (-ē′k) *a.*, *n.*, & *v.i.* **1.** *a.* slanting, declining from the vertical or horizontal, diverging from straight line or course; *oblique* SPHERE. **2.** (Geom.) (of line, plane figure, surface) inclined at other than right angle, (of angle) acute or obtuse, (of cone, cylinder, etc.) with axis not perpendicular to plane of base; (Anat.) neither parallel nor perpendicular to body's or limb's long axis; (Bot., of leaf) with unequal sides. **3.** not going straight to the point, roundabout, indirect. **4.** (Gram.) ∿ **case** (other than nominative or vocative); ∿ **oration** or **speech**, = REPORT¹*ed speech*. **5.** Hence or cogn. ∿LY² *adv.*, ∿NESS, **obli′qu**ITY, *ns.* **6.** *n.* oblique muscle, stroke (/), etc. **7.** *v.i.* (esp. Mil.) advance obliquely. [ME f. F, f. L *obliquus*]

obli′ter|āte *v.t.* blot out, efface, erase, destroy, leave no clear traces of; deface (postage stamp etc.) to prevent further use; hence ∿A′TION *n.* [f. L OB- (*li*(*t*)*terare* f. *li*(*t*)*tera* LETTER) + -ATE³]

obli′vion *n.* having or being forgotten, disregard, unregarded state; amnesty (*Act* or *Bill of Oblivion*); **fall into** ∿, be forgotten or disused. [ME f. OF, f. L *oblivio -onis* (*oblivisci* forget; see -ION)]

obli′vious *a.* forgetful, unmindful, (*of*); ∿ **to** or **of**, unaware or unconscious of; hence ∿LY² *adv.*, ∿NESS *n.* [ME, f. L *obliviosus* (as prec.; see -OUS)]

ŏ′blŏng *a.* & *n.* **1.** *a.* deviating from square form by having one long axis, rectangular with adjacent sides unequal; (of paper, book, rectangular postage stamp or panel, etc.) greater in breadth than in height. **2.** *n.* oblong figure or object. [ME, f. L OB(*longus* long) longish]

ŏ′bloquÿ *n.* abuse, detraction; being generally unfavourably spoken of. [ME, f. LL *obloquium* contradiction f. L OB(*loqui* speak) deny]

ŏbmūtě′sc|ence *n.* (arch.) obstinate silence; so ∿ENT *a.* [f. L OB(*mutescere* f. *mutus* dumb; see -ESCENCE)]

obnŏ′xious (-kshus) *a.* **1.** (arch.) liable *to* harm or evil or attack. **2.** offensive, objectionable, disliked; hence ∿LY² *adv.* **3.** Hence ∿NESS *n.* [f. L *obnoxiosus* or OB(*noxius* f. *noxa* harm); assoc. w. NOXIOUS; see -OUS]

obnū′bil|āte *v.t.* (literary). darken (as) with cloud, obscure (lit. or fig.); hence ∿A′TION *n.* [f. L OB(*nubilare* f. *nubes* cloud) + -ATE³]

ō′bōe, (arch.) **hautboy** (hō′boi), *n.* wood-wind double-reed instrument of treble pitch and plaintive incisive tone; its player; organ reed-stop imitating it; hence **ō′bō**IST (3) *n.* [(It. *oboe*) f. F *hautbois* (*haut* high, *bois* wood)]

ŏ′bol *n.* ancient-Greek coin, one-sixth of drachma. [f. L *obolus* f. Gk *obolos*, var. of *obelos* OBELISK]

obŏ′vāte *a.* (Biol.) ovate with narrower end at base. [f. OB-+OVATE¹]

obscē′ne *a.* indecent, esp. grossly or repulsively so; lewd; ||(Law, of publication) tending to deprave or corrupt; (colloq.) highly offensive, morally repugnant; (arch.) repulsive, loathsome; hence ∿LY² (-nlī) *adv.*, ∿NESS (-n-n-) *n.* [f. F *obscène* or f. L *obsc*(*a*)*enus* ill-omened, abominable]

obscē′nitÿ *n.* being obscene; instance of this in action, speech, etc. [f. L *obscaenitas* (as prec.; see -ITY)]

obscū′rant *n.* opponent of inquiry, enlightenment, and reform; one who deliberately avoids clarity or withholds explanation; hence ∿ISM (3), ∿IST (2), *ns.*, (obskūr′a-, ŏbskūrā′-). [G, f. L *obscurans* (*obscurare*; see OBSCURE, -ANT)]

obscūr′e *a.*, & *v.t.* **1.** *a.* dark, dim; (of colour) dingy, dull, indefinite; indistinct, not clear; *obscure* (= neutral) VOWEL. **2.** hidden, remote from observation; unnoticed; unknown to fame, humble. **3.** unexplained, doubtful; not easily understood or clearly expressed. **4.** Hence or cogn. ∿LY² (-ūr′lī) *adv.*, **obscūr′**ITY *n.* **5.** *v.t.* make obscure, dark, indistinct, or unintelligible; dim glory of, outshine; conceal from sight; so **ŏbscūrA′TION** *n.* [ME; *a.* f. OF *obscur* f. L *obscurus* dark; v. f. *a.* or f. L *obscurare* (*obscurus*)]

obscūrum per obscurius (ŏbskūrum pēr ŏbskūr′ius) *n.* = IGNOTUM PER IGNOTIUS. [L, = the obscure by the still more obscure]

ŏbsĕcrā′tion *n.* earnest entreaty. [ME, f. L *obsecratio* f. OB(*secrare* = *sacrare* f. *sacer sacri* sacred) entreat]

ŏ′bsēquies (-ĭz) *n. pl.* funeral rites; a funeral; hence **obsē′qui**AL *a.* [ME, pl. of obs. *obsequy* f. AF *obsequie*, OF *obseque* f. med. L *obsequiae* f. L *exsequiae* funeral rites (see EXEQUIES), assoc. w. *obsequium* (see foll.)]

obsē′quious *a.* servile, fawning; (arch.) obedient, dutiful; hence ∿LY² *adv.*, ∿NESS *n.* [ME, f. L *obsequiosus* f. OB(*sequium* f. *sequi* follow) compliance]

obsĕr′vance (-z-) *n.* keeping or performance of or of law, duty, custom, ritual, etc.; act of religious or ceremonial character, customary rite; the rule of a religious order; (arch.) respect, deference. [ME f. OF, f. L *observantia* (as OBSERVE; see -ANCE)]

obsĕr′vant (-z-) *a.* & *n.* **1.** *a.* attentive in observance; acute or diligent in taking notice; hence ∿LY² *adv.* **2.** *n.* (O∿). member of branch of Franciscan order that observes the strict rule. [F (as OBSERVE; see -ANT)]

ŏbservā′tion (-z-) *n.* **1.** noticing or being noticed, perception, faculty of taking notice; *post*, *attitude*, of ∿, favourable for watching from or in; ∿ **car** (in train esp. in US, so built as to afford good views). **2.** (Mil.) watching of fortress or hostile position or movements; ∿ **post** (esp. for watching effect of artillery fire). **3.** accurate watching and noting of phenomena as they occur in nature (cf. *experiment*) with regard to cause and effect or mutual relations; noting of symptoms of patient, behaviour of suspect, etc., (**under** ∿, being watched thus). **4.** taking of sun's or other heavenly body's altitude to find latitude

For other words in *ob-* see OB-.

or longitude. **5.** remark or statement, esp. one that is of the nature of comment. **6.** Hence ~AL *a.*, ~ALLY *adv.* [ME, f. L *observatio* (as OBSERVE; see -ATION)]

obser'vatory (-z-) *n.* building etc. whence natural, esp. astronomical or meteorological, phenomena may be observed. [f. mod. L *observatorium* f. L *observare*; see foll., -ORY]

obser'v|e (-z-) *v.* **1.** *v.t.* keep, follow, adhere to, perform duly, (law, command, appointed time, method, principle, silence, rite, anniversary, etc.). **2.** perceive, mark, watch, take notice of, become conscious of, (person, thing, *that, how*); **the ~ed of all ~ers**, person etc. on whom etc. attention is concentrated. **3.** examine and note (phenomena) without aid of experiment. **4.** say, esp. by way of comment. **5.** *v.i.* make remark(s) *on*. **6.** Hence ~ABLE *a.* [ME, f. OF *observer* f. L OB(*servare* keep) watch, attend to]

obser'ver (-z-) *n.* In vbl senses; interested spectator; person who attends conference etc. to note proceedings but does not participate; person trained to notice and identify aircraft, or carried in aeroplane to note enemy's position etc.; (in newspaper titles, as *The Observer, Rochdale Observer*). [f. prec. +-ER¹]

obse'ss *v.t.* (Of evil spirit, delusion, or fixed idea) haunt, harass, preoccupy, fill mind of, (*obsessed by* or *with*); hence ~IVE *a.* [f. L OB(*sidere sess- = sedēre* sit) besiege]

obse'ssion *n.* obsessing or being obsessed; unreasonably persistent idea in the mind; condition in which such ideas are present; hence ~AL *a.* [f. L *obsessio* (as prec.; see -ION)]

obsi'dian *n.* dark vitreous lava or volcanic rock like bottle-glass. [f. L *obsidianus*, error for *obsianus* (*Obsius* name of finder of a similar stone, mentioned by Pliny; see -IAN)]

obsole'sc|ent *a.* becoming obsolete, going out of use or date; (Biol., of organ once developed more fully) gradually disappearing; so ~ENCE *n.* [f. L OB(*solescere* f. *solēre* be accustomed; see -ESCENT)]

o'bsolete *a.* disused, discarded, antiquated, (Biol.) less developed than formerly or in cognate species, rudimentary; hence ~NESS (-tn-), **o'bsoletism** (3, 4), *ns.* [f. L *obsoletus* p.p. (as prec.)]

o'bstacle *n.* thing that obstructs progress; ~-**race** (in which artificial or natural obstacles have to be passed). [ME f. OF, f. L *obstaculum* f. OB(*stare* stand) impede]

obste'tr|ic(al) *adjs.* of midwifery, of childbirth and the processes immediately preceding and following it, as branch of medicine and surgery; hence ~ICS, ~IST. [f. mod. L *obstetricus* for L *obstetricius* f. *obstetrix* midwife f. OB(*stare* stand) be present; see -TRIX]

o'bstin|ate *a.* firmly adhering to one's chosen course of action or opinion, not easily persuaded; inflexible, self-willed; unyielding, not readily responding to treatment etc.; hence ~ACY *n.*, ~**ately** (-tlĭ) *adv.* [ME, f. L *obstinatus* p.p. of OB(*stinare* deriv. of *stare* stand) persist]

obstre'perous *a.* noisy, vociferous; turbulent, unruly, noisily resisting control; hence ~LY² *adv.*, ~NESS *n.* [f. L *obstreperus* f. OB(*strepere* make noise) +-OUS]

obstru'ct *v.t.* close up, fill with impediments, make impassable or difficult of passage; prevent or retard progress of, impede. [f. L OB(*struere struct-* build)]

obstru'ction *n.* blocking or being blocked, making or becoming more or less impassable; retarding of progress, esp. of Parliamentary business by deliberate delays, whence ~ISM (3), ~IST (2), *ns.*, or as illegal act in some games; obstacle; (Path.) blockage in bodily passage, esp. in intestine. [f. L *obstructio* (as prec.; see -ION)]

obstru'ctive *a.* & *n.* **1.** *a.* causing, intended to produce, obstruction; hence ~LY² (-vlĭ) *adv.*, ~NESS (-vn-) *n.* **2.** *n.* obstructive person or thing. [f. OBSTRUCT +-IVE]

obstu'pĕfȳ *v.t.* stupefy, esp. mentally. [f. L OB(*stupefacere*; see STUPEFY)]

obtai'n *v.* **1.** *v.t.* acquire, have granted to one, get; hence or cogn. ~ABLE *a.*, ~MENT, **obtĕ'ntion**, *ns.* **2.** *v.i.* be prevalent or established or in vogue. [ME, f. OF *obtenir* f. L OB(*tinēre tent- = tenēre* hold) keep]

obtĕ'st *v.* (arch.) **1.** *v.t.* adjure, supplicate, call to witness. **2.** *v.i.* protest. **3.** So **obtĕstA'TION** *n.* [f. L OB(*testari* f. *testis* witness)]

obtru'de (-ōo'd) *v.* **1.** *v.t.* thrust forward (*upon* or *on* person or his attention) importunately. **2.** *v.i.* be or become obtrusive. **3.** So **obtru'sion** (-ōo'zhon) *n.* [f. L OB(*trudere trus-* push)]

obtrŭ'ncāte *v.t.* (literary). cut off top of. [f. L OB(*truncare* f. *truncus* maimed) +-ATE³]

obtru'sive (-ōo'-) *a.* obtruding oneself; unduly noticeable; hence ~LY² (-vlĭ) *adv.*, ~NESS (-vn-) *n.* [f. as OBTRUDE +-IVE]

obtŭ'nd *v.t.* (Med.) blunt, deaden, (sense or faculty). [ME, f. L OB(*tundere tus-* beat)]

o'btŭr|āte *v.t.* stop up, close, seal, (orifice in body, breech of gun, etc.); hence or cogn. ~A'TION, ~ātoR, *ns.* [f. L *obturare* +-ATE³]

obtū'se *a.* of blunt form, not sharp-pointed or sharp-edged; (of angle) greater than one and less than two right angles; (of pain, the senses) dull, not acute; stupid, slow of perception; hence ~LY² (-slĭ) *adv.*, ~NESS (-sn-), **obtū'sITY**, *ns.* [f. L *obtusus* p.p. (as OBTUND)]

o'bvĕrse *a.* & *n.* **1.** *a.* narrower at base or point of attachment than at apex or top (as general term for wds in OB- 6: obovate, oblanceolate, etc.); answering as counterpart to something else; hence ~LY² (-slĭ) *adv.* **2.** *n.* side of coin or medal bearing the head or principal design (cf. REVERSE³); face of anything meant to be presented to view, front; counterpart of a fact or truth. [f. L *obversus* p.p. (as foll.)]

obvĕ'rt *v.t.* (Logic). infer another proposition with contradictory predicate by changing quality of (proposition), e.g. from *no men are immortal* to *all men are mortal*; so **obvĕr'sion** (-shon) *n.* [f. L OB(*vertere versturn*)]

o'bviāte *v.t.* clear away, get rid of, get round, neutralize, (danger, inconvenience, etc.). [f. LL OB(*viare* f. *via* way) oppose +-ATE³]

o'bvious *a.* open to eye or mind, clearly perceptible, palpable, indubitable; hence ~LY² *adv.*, ~NESS *n.* [f. L *obvius* (*ob viam* in the way) +-OUS]

oc- *pref.*, assim. form of OB- before *c*.

OC *abbr.* Officer Commanding; Officer of the Order of Canada.

ŏcari'na (-rē'-) *n.* small egg-shaped terracotta or metal wind instrument. [It. (*oca* goose, from its shape; see -INA¹)]

O'ccam (ŏ'-) *n.* **~'s razor**, principle that the fewest possible assumptions are to be made in explaining a thing. [f. William of ~, Engl. philosopher d. *c.* 1350]

occa'sion (-zhon) *n.*, & *v.t.* **1.** *n.* juncture suitable for doing something, opportunity, (**take ~**, avail oneself of opportunity *to do*). **2.** reason, ground, justification, incitement, need, (*there is no occasion to be angry*). **3.** subsidiary, incidental, or immediate cause (*the cause of a revolution may be obscure while its occasion is obvious*). **4.** (in *pl.*) affairs, business, (esp. *go about one's lawful occasions*). **5.** (particular time marked by) special occurrence (*on this festive occasion; on the occasion of his marriage; celebrate the occasion; dressed, dismantled, for the occasion*); **rise to the ~**, show requisite ability, energy, etc.; (**up)on ~**, whenever need arises, now and then. **6.** *v.t.* be the occasion or cause of, bring about esp. incidentally, cause (action etc., or person or thing *to do*). [ME f. OF, or f. L *occasio* juncture, reason, f. OC(*cidere cas- = cadere* fall) go down; see -ION]

occā'sional (-zho-) *a.* arising out of, made or meant for, adapted for use on, acting on, special occasion(s); happening irregularly; as occasion presents itself; coming now and then, not regular or frequent; ~

cause, secondary cause, occasion; ||∼ **licence** (to sell liquor only at specified times and places); ∼ **table,** small table for use as required; hence ∼ITY (-ă′l-) *n.,* ∼LY² *adv.* [f. prec.+-AL]

occa′sional|ism (-zho-) *n.* doctrine of some Cartesians that volition and sensation are connected with the following and preceding material phenomena not causally but as separately produced by God on the same occasion; so ∼IST (2) *n.* [f. prec.+-ISM]

O′ccident (ŏ′ks-) *n.* (poet. or rhet.) **1.** *the* west; western Europe; Europe, America, or both, as opp. countries east of them. **2.** European in contrast to Oriental civilization. [ME f. OF, f. L *occidens -entis* setting, sunset, west (as OCCASION; see -ENT)]

ŏccide′ntal (ŏks-) *a.* & *n.* **1.** *a.* of the Occident; western; of Western nations, whence ∼ISM (2), ∼IST (2, 3), *ns.,* ∼IZE (3) *v.t.;* hence ∼LY² *adv.* **2.** *n.* (*O*∼). native or inhabitant of the Occident. [ME f. OF, or f. L *occidentalis* (as prec.; see -AL)]

o′cciput (ŏ′ks-) *n.* (Anat.) back of head; so **ŏcci′pĭt**AL *a.,* **ŏcci′pĭto-** *comb. form,* (ŏks-). [ME f. L OC(*ciput -pitis* = *caput* head)]

O′ccit|an (ŏ′ks-) *n.* Provençal language; so ∼**ā′n**IAN *n.* & *a.* [F; cf. LANGUE D′OC]

occlu′de (-lōō′d) *v.t.* stop up, close, obstruct, (pores, orifice); (Chem.) absorb and retain (gases); ∼**d front** (Meteorol., resulting from occlusion. [f. L OC(*cludere clus-* = *claudere* shut)]

occlu′s|ion (-lōō′zhon) *n.* occluding; (Meteorol.) overtaking of warm front of depression by cold front, with upward displacement of warm air between them; (Dent.) position of teeth when jaws are brought together; (Phonet.) momentary closure of vocal passage; so ∼IVE *a.* [f. as prec.+-ION]

occu′lt¹ (ŏ-, o-) *a.* kept secret, esoteric, recondite, mysterious, beyond the range of ordinary knowledge; involving the supernatural, mystical, magical, whence ∼ISM (3), ∼IST (2, 3), *ns.;* (Med.) not obvious on inspection; hence ∼LY² *adv.,* ∼NESS *n.* [f. L OC(*culere -cult-;* cf. *celare* hide)]

occu′lt² (ŏ-, o-) *v.* **1.** *v.t.* conceal, cut off from view by passing in front, (usu. Astron., of concealing body much greater in apparent size than concealed body). **2.** *v.i.* ∼**ing light** in lighthouses, one that is cut off at regular intervals. So **ŏcculta′tion** *n.* [f. L *occultare* frequent. of *occulere* (see prec.)]

o′ccup|ant *n.* person holding property, esp. land, in actual possession; one who occupies, or resides or is in, a place; one who establishes title to ownerless thing by taking possession; hence ∼ANCY *n.* [F, or f. L *occupans -antis* (as OCCUPY; see -ANT)]

ŏccupā′tion *n.* occupying or being occupied; taking or holding possession, esp. of country or district by military force (**army of** ∼, left to hold occupied region till regular government is set up); tenure, occupancy; what occupies one, means of passing one's time, temporary or regular employment, business, calling, pursuit; ∼ **bridge, road,** etc., (private for use of occupiers of land); ||∼ **franchise,** right to vote as tenant. [ME f. AF *ocupacioun,* OF *occupation* f. L *occupatio -onis* (as OCCUPY; see -ATION)]

ŏccupā′tional *a.* of occupation(s); ∼ **disease, hazard,** (to which a particular occupation renders one especially liable); ∼ **therapy,** mental or physical activity to assist recovery from disease or injury. [f. prec.+-AL]

||**ŏ′ccupīer** *n.* person in (esp. temporary or subordinate) possession esp. of land or house, holder, occupant. [ME, f. foll.+-ER¹, or f. AF *occupiour*]

o′ccupȳ *v.t.* take possession of (country, region, town, strategic position) by military force or settlement; hold (office), reside in, be tenant of; take up or fill (space, time), reside or be in (place, position); place oneself in (building etc.) esp. as political demonstration; (esp. in *pass.* or *refl.*) keep busy or engaged (*with* or *in* thing or doing). [ME, f. AF *occupier* OF *occuper* f. L OC(*cupare* = *capere* take) seize]

occur′ *v.i.* (-**rr**-). be met with, be found, exist, in some place or conditions; come into one's mind (esp. *it occurs to me that*); come into being as event or process at or during some time. [f. L OC(*currere* run) go to meet, present itself]

occu′rrence *n.* occurring (**is of frequent** ∼, often occurs); incident, event. [f. *occurrent* that occurs (F, f. L *occurrens -entis* f. as prec.; see -ENT)+-ENCE]

ō′cean (ō′shan) *n.* **1.** great body of water surrounding the land of the globe; one of the main areas into which geographers divide this (usu. reckoned as five, the *Atlantic, Pacific, Indian, Arctic,* and *Antarctic, Oceans*). **2.** the sea; (poet.) the sea (*the dark unfathom′d caves of ocean*); immense expanse or quantity of anything (*oceans of time*). **3.** ∼-**going,** (of ship) able to cross the oceans; ∼ **greyhound,** swift ship, esp. passenger liner; *ocean* LANE; *ocean* TRAMP. **4.** Hence ∼WARD(s) *adv.* [ME f. OF *ocean(e),* f. L f. Gk *ōkeanos* stream encircling earth's disc, Atlantic]

oceanār′i|um (-sha-) *n.* (*pl.* ∼**ums** *or* ∼**a**). (place with) large pool for keeping sea animals. [f. prec., after AQUARIUM]

Oceā′ni|a (ōshī-) *n.* islands of Pacific and adjacent seas; hence ∼AN *a.* & *n.* [mod. L, f. F *Océanie* f. L (as OCEAN; see -IA¹)]

ōceā′nic (ō′shī-, ō′sĭ-) *a.* of, like, or near the ocean; of the part of the ocean distant from the continents; (of climate) governed by the ocean; (*O*∼) of Oceania. [f. OCEAN+-IC]

Oce′anid (os-) *n.* (*pl.* ∼**s,** *or* ∼**es** *pr.* -ă′nĭdēz). (Gk Myth.) ocean nymph. [f. Gk *ōkeanis -idos* daughter of Oceanus; see -ID³ ²]

ōcean|o′graphȳ (ōsha-) *n.* study of the oceans; hence ∼ō′GRAPHER *n.,* ∼OGRA′PHIC(AL) *adjs.* [f. OCEAN+-O-+-GRAPHY]

oce′ll|us *n.* (*pl.* ∼**i** *pr.* -ī). one of simple as opposed to compound eyes of insects etc.; facet of compound eye; spot of colour surrounded by ring of other colour, whence **o′cell**ATE², **o′cell**āTED¹, *adjs.* [L, dim. of *oculus* eye]

o′celot *n.* leopard-like feline (*Felis pardalis*) of S. and Central America; its fur. [F, abridged by Buffon f. Nahuatl *tlal(ocelotl* jaguar) of the field, and applied to different animal]

ŏch (ŏχ) *int.* (Sc. & Ir.) expr. surprise or regret, = *oh, ah.* [Gael. & Ir.]

*****ocher.** See OCHRE.

ŏchlŏ′cracȳ (ŏkl-) *n.* mob rule; hence **ŏ′chlo**CRAT *n.,* **ŏchlo**CRA′TIC *a.,* (ŏkl-). [f. F *ochlocratie* f. Gk *okhlokratia* (*okhlos* mob; see -CRACY]

ŏchō′ne (ŏχ-) *int.* (Sc. & Ir.) expr. regret or lament, = *oh, alas.* [f. Gael. & Ir. *ochóin*]

ō′chre, *****ō′cher,** (ō′ker) *n.* mineral of clay and hydrated ferric oxide, used as pigment varying from light yellow to brown or red; pale brownish yellow; hence ∼ISH¹, *****ō′cher**OUS, **ō′chrē**OUS, **ō′chr**OUS, **ō′chry**², (ō′k-) *adjs.* [ME, f. OF *ocre* L f. Gk *ōkhra* yellow ochre (*ōkhros* pale yellow)]

-ock *suf.* forming *ns.* orig. w. dim. sense (*hillock, bullock*). [f. or after OE *-uc, -oc*]

o′cker *n.* (Austral. sl.) boorish or aggressively Australian person. [20th c.; orig. uncert.]

o′clŏ′ck. See o′², CLOCK¹.

OCR *abbr.* optical character recognition.

Oct. *abbr.* October.

oct. *abbr.* octavo.

ŏct- *comb. form.* = OCTA-, OCTO-, before vowel.

ŏcta- *comb. form.* eight, as **ŏctā′MEROUS** *a.;* ∼**va′lent** (Chem.) having a valence of eight. [f. Gk *okta-* (*oktō* eight)]

ŏ′ctachŏrd (-k-) *a.* & *n.* eight-stringed (musical instrument); series of eight notes, e.g. the diatonic scale; hence ∼AL (-kôr′d-) *a.* [f. L f. Gk *oktakhordos* (as prec.; see CHORD¹)]

ŏ′ctăd *n.* group of eight. [f. LL f. Gk *oktas -ados* (*oktō* eight; see A1)]

ŏ′ctagon *n.* plane figure with eight sides and angles;

object or building with this cross-section; so **ŏctă'-gon**AL *a*. [f. L f. Gk OCTA(*gōnos* f. *gōnia* angle)]

ŏctahē'dr|on *n*. (*pl*. ∿ons *or* ∿a). solid figure contained by eight plane faces, and usu. eight triangles (**regular** ∿on, by equal and equilateral triangles); body, esp. crystal, in form of regular octahedron; hence ∿AL *a*. [f. Gk *oktaedron* (see OCTA-, -HEDRON)]

ŏ'ctal *a*. reckoning or proceeding by eights (*octal scale*). [f. OCT-+-AL]

ŏctă'mĕter *n*. (Pros.) verse of eight measures. [f. OCTA- after *hexameter*]

ŏ'ctāne *n*. hydrocarbon of paraffin series, C_8H_{18}; **high-∿**, (of fuel used in internal combustion engines) having good antiknock properties, not detonating readily during the power stroke; ∿ **number** or **rating** (indicating antiknock properties of fuel, and equal to 100 for one type of octane). [f. OCT- + -ANE 2]

ŏ'ctant *n*. **1.** arc of circle = ⅛ of circumference; ⅛ of area of circle, contained within two radii and such arc; one of eight parts into which three planes intersecting (esp. at right angles) at point divide space or solid body round it. **2.** (Astron.) point in body's apparent course 45° distant from given point, esp. point at which moon is 45° from conjunction or opposition with sun. **3.** instrument in form of graduated eighth of circle used in astronomy and navigation. [f. L *octans -antis* half-quadrant (*octo* eight)]

ŏ'ctärchȳ (-kǐ) *n*. government by eight rulers; eight kingdoms reckoned by some historians as established by Angles and Saxons in Britain (cf. HEPTARCHY). [f. OCT- after *heptarchy*]

ŏctarŏŏ'n. See OCTOROON.

ŏ'ctastȳle *a*. & *n*. (portico or building) with eight columns at end or in front. [f. L f. Gk OCTA(*stulos* pillar)]

O'ctateuch (ŏ'-; -k) *n*. first eight books of Bible. [f. LL f. Gk OCTAteukhos; cf. PENTATEUCH]

ŏ'ctave (-ĭv) *n*. **1.** seventh day after a festival; period of eight days including festival and its octave. **2.** group or stanza of eight lines, octet. **3.** (Mus.) note having twice or half the frequency of vibration of given note and lying eight diatonic degrees (alphabetical notes, both extreme notes being counted) above or below it (**second** ∿, having four times or a quarter the frequency, fifteen degrees above or below; so **third** etc. ∿); interval between note and its octave; series of notes filling this; note and its octave sounding together. **4.** group of eight. **5.** last of eight parrying positions in fencing. **6.** ||wine-cask holding ⅛ pipe. **7.** ∿-**coupler**, device connecting organ keys or pedals an octave apart so that both notes are sounded by one key; ∿-**flute**, (1) piccolo, (2) organ flute-stop sounding an octave higher than the ordinary. [ME f. OF, f. L *octava* (*dies* day, reckoned inclusively) fem. of *octavus* eighth (*octo* eight)]

ŏctă'vō *n*. (*abbr.* 8vo; *pl.* ∿s). (size of) book or page given by folding sheet three times to form quire of eight leaves. [L, abl. of *octavus* (see prec.), in phr. *in octavo* in an eighth (of a sheet)]

ŏctĕ'nnial *a*. lasting, or recurring every, eight years. [f. LL OCT(*ennium* f. *annus* year) period of eight years + -AL]

ŏctĕ't, ŏctĕ'tte, *n*. **1.** (Mus.) (performers of) composition for eight voices or instruments. **2.** group of eight; first eight lines of sonnet; (Chem.) stable group of eight electrons. [f. It. *ottetto* or G *oktett*, assim. to OCT-, DUET, QUARTET(TE)]

ŏcto- *comb. form.* eight. [f. L *octo* or Gk *oktō* eight]

Octŏ'ber (ŏ-) *n.* tenth month of year; ||(arch.) beer brewed in October. [OE f. L (as prec.; cf. DECEMBER, SEPTEMBER)]

Octŏ'brist (ŏ-) *n.* member of moderate party in Russian Duma. [f. prec. + -IST, because supporter of Imperial Constitutional Manifesto of 30 Oct. 1905]

ŏctōcĕntenarȳ (-sĕntē'-, -sē'ntĭ-) *a*. & *n*. (festival) of the 800th anniversary. [f. OCTO-+CENTENARY]

ŏctŏdĕ'cimō *n*. (*pl*. ∿s). (size of) book or page given by folding sheet into eighteen leaves. [f. *in octodecimo* f. L OCTO(*decimus* tenth) eighteenth; cf. OCTAVO]

ŏctogĕnār'ian *a*. & *n*. (person) from 80 to 89 years old. [f. L *octogenarius* (*octogeni* distrib. of *octoginta* eighty; see -ARY¹)+-AN]

ŏctonār'i|us *n*. (*pl*. ∿i *pr*. -ī). (Pros.) verse of eight feet; hence ∿AN *a*. & *n*. [L (see foll.)]

ŏ'ctonarȳ *a*. & *n*. **1.** *a*. based on the number eight. **2.** *n*. group of eight; eight-line stanza (esp. of divisions of Ps. 119). [f. L *octonarius* containing eight (*octoni* eight each f. *octo* eight); see -ARY¹]

ŏ'ctopŏd *n*. eight-armed cephalopod of order Octopoda, e.g. octopus or argonaut. [f. Gk *oktōpous -podos* (*oktō* eight, *pous* foot)]

ŏ'ctopus *n*. (*pl*. ∿es, *or* **octo'podes** *pr*. -ŏ'podēz). cephalopod mollusc of family Octopodidae, with eight suckered arms round mouth; (fig.) organized and usu. harmful ramified power or influence. [f. Gk *oktōpous* (see prec.)]

ŏctorŏŏ'n, -tar-, *n*. offspring of quadroon and white, person of one-eighth Negro blood. [f. OCTO- after QUADROON]

ŏctosȳllă'bic *a*. & *n*. eight-syllabled (verse). [f. LL OCTO(*syllabus* f. L *syllaba* SYLLABLE) + -IC]

ŏctosȳ'llable *n*. & *a*. = prec.; word of eight syllables. [f. LL *octosyllabus* (see prec.), after *syllable*]

ŏ'ctroi (-rwah) *n*. duty levied in some European countries on goods entering town; place where, officials by whom, it is levied. [F (*octroyer* grant, f. Gallo-Rom. *auctoricare, med. L *auctorizare*; see AUTHORIZE)]

||OCTU (ŏ'ktŭ) *abbr*. Officer Cadets Training Unit.

ŏ'ctuple *a*., *n*., & *v*. **1.** *a*. & *n*. eightfold (amount). **2.** *v.t.* & *i*. multiply by eight. [F, or f. L *octuplus a*. (*octo* eight; cf. DOUBLE¹)]

ŏ'cular *a*. & *n*. **1.** *a*. of, for, by, with, etc., the eye(s) or sight, visual; ∿ **demonstration** or **proof** (perceived by the eyes); *ocular* SPECTRUM; hence ∿LY² *adv*. **2.** *n*. eyepiece of optical instrument. [f. F *oculaire* f. LL *ocularis* (*oculus* eye; see -AR¹)]

ŏ'cularist *n*. maker of artificial eyes. [f. F *oculariste* (as prec.; see -IST)]

ŏ'culate *a*. = OCELLATE. [f. L *oculatus* (*oculus* eye; see -ATE²)]

ŏ'cŭl|ist *n*. one who specializes in treatment of eye disorders or defects; hence ∿i'stIC *a*. [f. F *oculiste* f. L *oculus* eye; see -IST]

ŏcŭlō- *comb. form.* eye, as: ∿na'sal, of eye and nose. [f. L *oculus* eye + -o-]

ŏd¹ *n*. hypothetical power once thought to pervade nature and account for various scientific phenomena; hence **ŏ'dIC** *a*. [arbitrary term coined in G by Baron von Reichenbach, Ger. scientist d. 1869]

ŏd² *n*. (arch.) = GOD (as *int.* or in oaths: *od rot it, od(d)s bodikins,* etc.). [corrupt.]

OD *abbr*. ordnance datum.

o.d. *abbr*. outer diameter.

ŏ'dal. Var. of UDAL.

ŏ'dalisque (-k) *n*. (Hist.) Eastern female slave or concubine, esp. in Turkish Sultan's seraglio. [F, f. Turk. *odalık* (*oda* chamber, *lık* function)]

ŏdd *a*. & *n*. **1.** *a*. left over when the rest have been distributed or divided into pairs (∿ **socks** etc., pair that do not match). **2.** (Of number) not divisible by two (∿ **and even**, a game of chance); (of things or persons numbered consecutively) bearing such number (*no parking on odd dates*). **3.** (Appended to number, sum, weight, etc.) with something over of lower denomination etc. (**forty** ∿, between 40 and 50; **sixty thousand** ∿, with some extra hundreds, tens, or units; **sixty** ∿ **thousand**, between 60 and 70 thousand; **twelve pounds** ∿, between £12 and £13). **4.** by which round number, given sum etc., is exceeded (*There are 1006; what shall we do with the odd*

six?). **5.** additional, casual, beside the reckoning, unconnected, unoccupied, incalculable, unpredictable, (*picks up odd bargains*; *do it at odd moments*; *in some odd corner*); ∼ **numbers, volumes,** (belonging to incomplete sets of magazines, books). **6.** extraordinary, strange, queer, remarkable, eccentric; hence ∼'ISH¹ 2 *a.*, ∼'LY² *adv.* **7.** ∼'ball, ∼ fish, (colloq.) eccentric person; O'ddfellow, member of a fraternity similar to Freemasons; ∼ job, casual isolated piece of work; ∼ man, (1) person who has deciding vote in committee etc. with evenly divided members, (2) ‖man who does odd jobs; ∼ man out, (1) method of selecting one of three or more persons e.g. by tossing coins, (2) person or thing differing from all others of a group in some respect; ∼ trick, (1) thirteenth trick at whist when each side has won six, (2) trick at bridge won by a side that already has six or more. **8.** Hence ∼'NESS *n.* **9.** *n.* (Golf). *the* stroke which one side plays after the LIKE¹ 16; handicap of one stroke at each hole. **10.** See ODDS. [ME, f. ON *odda-* in *odda-mathr* third man, odd man, f. *oddi* angle]
o'ddity *n.* strangeness; peculiar trait; queer person; fantastic object, strange event. [f. prec. + -ITY]
o'ddment *n.* odd article, something left over; (in *pl.*) odds and ends, ‖(Print.) matter other than text. [f. ODD + -MENT]
odds (-z) *n. pl.* (sometimes treated as *sing.*). **1.** ratio between amounts staked by parties to bet; lay, give, ∼ *of three to one*, (said of party offering the higher amount); take ∼, offer the lower amount; ∼-on, state when (betting odds indicate that) success is more likely than failure; over the ∼, above generally agreed price etc. **2.** chances or balance of probability in favour of or against some result (*the odds are that he will do it*; *long odds against his doing it*); by all ∼, certainly. **3.** balance of advantage (*the odds are in your favour*; *won against (all) the odds*; *have fought against longer odds*). **4.** equalizing allowance to weaker competitor (*give, receive odds*). **5.** difference giving advantage (*it makes no odds*; what's the ∼?, what does it matter?). **6.** variance, strife, (*are at odds with fate, with their neighbours*). **7.** (arch.) inequalities (make ∼ even, do away with these). **8.** ∼ and ends, remnants, stray articles; ∼ and sods, (vulg.) odds and ends, unattached persons. [app. pl. of ODD *n.*; cf. NEWS]
ode *n.* **1.** (Hist.) poem meant to be sung (choral ∼, song of chorus in Greek play etc.). **2.** lyric, usu. rhymed, often in form of address, usu. of exalted style, often in varied or irregular metre, and usu. between about 50 and 200 lines in length. [f. F, f. LL *oda* f. Gk *ōidē* Attic form of *aoidē* song (*aeidō* sing)]
-ode *suf.* **1.** forming *ns.* w. sense 'thing of the nature of' (*geode, phyllode, trematode*). **2.** (Electr.) forming names of electrodes, or devices having them (*cathode, diode*). [sense 1 f. Gk -*ōdēs* adj. ending (see -O-, -*eidēs* -like); sense 2 f. Gk *hodos* way]
ode'um *n.* (*pl.* ∼s *or* ode'a). building for musical performances, esp. among ancient Greeks and Romans. [f. F *odéum* or f. L *odeum* f. Gk *ōideion* (as ODE)]
o'dic. See OD¹.
o'dious *a.* hateful, repulsive; hence ∼LY² *adv.*, ∼NESS *n.* [ME, f. OF *odieus* f. L *odiosus* (as foll.; see -OUS)]
o'dium *n.* general or widespread dislike or reprobation incurred by person or attaching to action (*exposed me to odium*; *the odium of the transaction*); ∼ theologicum (thēolŏ'jĭkŭm), bitterness proverbially characterizing theologians who disagree. [L, = hatred (*odi* to hate)]
odo'meter *n.* instrument for measuring distance travelled by wheeled vehicle. [f. F *odomètre* f. Gk *hodos* way; see -METER]
odo'nto- *comb. form.* tooth, as: ∼glo'ssum, orchid with large handsome flowers having toothlike process on lip; ∼LOGY (-ŏ'l-), scientific study of the teeth; ∼rhy'nchous (-rĭ'ngkŭs), (of bird) having toothlike serrations in the bill. [f. Gk *odous odont-* tooth + -o-]
odo'ntoid *a.* toothlike; ∼ process (projection from

second cervical vertebra). [f. Gk *odontoeidēs* (as prec.; see -OID)]
*o'dor. See ODOUR.
ŏdori'ferous *a.* diffusing (usu. agreeable) scent, fragrant; hence ∼LY² *adv.* [ME, f. L *odorifer* (as ODOUR; see -FEROUS)]
o'dorous *a.* having scent; = prec.; hence ∼LY² *adv.* [f. L *odorus* fragrant (as foll.) + -OUS]
‖o'dour, *o'dor, (ō'der) *n.* **1.** property of a substance that has pleasant or unpleasant or any effect on the nasal sense of smell; hence ∼LESS *a.* **2.** fragrance; (arch., usu. in *pl.*) substance(s) emitting sweet scent, perfume(s). **3.** (fig.) savour, trace, (*no odour of intolerance attaches to it*); *good or bad* or *ill* repute or favour (*is in bad odour with the authorities*); ∼ of sanctity, reputation for holiness (orig. lit., sweet odour exhaled by dying or exhumed saint). [ME f. AF *odour*, OF *odor* f. L *odor -oris* smell, scent]
o'dyssey *n.* series of wanderings, long adventurous journey. [title of epic poem attributed to Homer and describing adventures of Odysseus (Ulysses) returning to Ithaca from siege of Troy, f. L f. Gk *Odusseia* (*Odusseus* Odysseus; see -Y¹)]
OECD *abbr.* Organization for Economic Co-operation and Development.
oe'cist (ē's-) *n.* founder of (esp. ancient-Greek) colony. [f. Gk *oikistēs* (*oikizō* settle f. *oikos* house; see -IST)]
oecology. Var. of ECOLOGY.
oecumenical etc. Var. of ECUMENICAL etc.
OED *abbr.* Oxford English Dictionary.
oedē'ma, *edē'ma, (ēd-, ĭd-) *n.* (Path.) swollen state of tissue etc. with serous fluid, local dropsy; hence ∼TOSE¹, ∼TOUS, *adjs.* [LL, f. Gk *oidēma -atos* (*oideō* swell)]
Oe'dip|us (ē'd-) *n.* solver of riddles; ∼us complex, (Psych.) manifestation of infantile sexuality towards parents, with attraction to parent of opposite sex (esp. mother) and jealousy towards other parent; hence ∼AL *a.* [f. Gk *Oidipous*, who solved the Sphinx's riddle, and in ignorance married his mother]
OEEC *abbr.* (Hist.) Organization for European Economic Co-operation.
œillade (ēryah'd) *n.* (esp. amorous) glance of eye. [F *œil* eye; see -ADE]
oeno'log|y, *ēn-, (ēn-) *n.* knowledge or study of wines; hence ∼ICAL (ēnŏlŏ'j-) *a.*, ∼IST (3) *n.* [f. Gk *oinos* wine + -o- + -LOGY]
oe'nophil|e (ē'-) *n.* connoisseur of wines; so ∼IST (1) (ēnŏ'fĭl-) *n.* [f. as prec. + -PHIL(E)]
*OEO *abbr.* Office of Economic Opportunity.
*OEP *abbr.* Office of Emergency Preparedness.
o'er (ōr) *adv. & prep.* (poet.) = OVER; so o'er- (ōr) *pref.* [contr.]
oer'sted (ěr'-) *n.* unit of magnetic field strength. [f. H. C. Oersted, Da. physicist d. 1851]
oeso'phag|us, *ēs-, (ēs-) *n.* (*pl.* ∼i *pr.* -jī, *or* ∼uses). canal from mouth to stomach, gullet; hence ∼EAL (ēsŏfa'jĭal, ēsŏfajē'al) *a.* [ME, f. Gk *oisophagos*]
oe'strogen, *ē's-, (ē's-) *n.* sex hormone or other substance capable of developing and maintaining female characteristics of body; hence ∼IC (-jē'n-) *a.* [f. foll. + -o- + -GEN]
oe'str|um, oe'str|us, *ē's-, (ē's-) *n.* sexual HEAT of animals, rut; (arch.) stimulus; hence ∼OUS *a.* [f. Gk *oistros* gadfly, frenzy]
œuvre (ērvr) *n.* (totality of) works of an author, painter, composer, etc. [F, = work, f. L OPERA¹]
of (ov *or, when stressed,* ŏv) *prep.* connecting its *n.* or *pron.* w. preceding *n.*, *a.*, *adv.*, or *v.*, and indicating relations roughly classified as follows: **1.** Removal, separation, point of departure, privation, (*north, within a mile in, front, upwards, have the advantage, of*; *wide of the mark*; *heal, rid, ease, deliver, rob, of*; *destitute, empty, free, bare, of*; *take* LEAVE¹ *of*; *balk, cheat, defraud, deprive, disappoint, of*; *independently, guiltless, irrespective, of*); OUT *of*; *(of time) = to* (*a quarter of six* = 5.45). **2.** Origin, derivation,

cause, agency, authorship, (*be, come, descend, spring, born, of; borrow, buy, win, receive, hire,* thing *of; have comfort, wish* person *joy, of; ask, demand, learn, expect, of; of* one's *own* ACCORD²; *of* COURSE¹, *of* RIGHT³, *of* NECESSITY; **of itself,** = *by* or *in* ITSELF; *die of; smell, taste, of; tired, ashamed, afraid,* SICK¹, *glad, proud, of; it was kind, foolish, naughty, clever, cruel, of you to say so; has the approval of his master; the works of Shakespeare, the 'Iliad' of Homer*); (arch., w. *pass.*) by (*warned of God; rejected of men*). **3.** Material, substance, closer definition, identity, (*house of cards; built of brick; an inch of rain; make a* FOOL¹, *the* BEST¹, *of;* MAKE¹ *much of; a family of eight; the name of Jones; the class of idiots; city of Rome, Isle of Man, University of Oxford, Battle of Waterloo, vice of drunkenness; a fool of a man, her scamp of a husband, the worst liar of any man I know; your letter of 1 May; had a bad time, troublesome journey, of it*); **be of,** possess (*importance, interest, value, etc.*). **4.** Concern, reference, direction, respect, (*think well of him; never heard of it; was informed of the fact; is true of every case; what of it?; repent, beware, of; cannot conceive, approve, think, of; does not admit or allow of; accuse, convict, suspect, of; avail, bethink,* oneself *of; short, guilty, certain, sure, confident, fond, of; swift of foot, hard of heart, hard of hearing; on behalf of,* in respect *of; at 30 years of age*). **5.** Objective relation (*the levying of taxes; love of virtue; for* FEAR¹ *of; in* SPITE *of; in search of knowledge; great eaters of pork; redolent, productive, fruitful, lavish, prodigal, sparing, capable, sensible, careful, observant, desirous, impatient, characteristic, destructive, indicative, of*); (arch. or vulg.) *what are you a-doing of?* what are you doing?. **6.** Description, quality, condition, (*man of tact, person of consequence, case of measles, farm of 100 acres, the hour of prayer, coat of many colours; potatoes of our own growing; in the act of, on the point of, departing; girl of ten years,* or, with mixed construction, *of ten years old*). **7.** Partition, classification, inclusion, selection, (*no more of that; finished last of all;* **some,** or **five, of us,** (1) a portion, or five, of us (who are more numerous), (2) we, being several or five persons; *any part, the whole, of it; too much of a gentleman to do that; the most dangerous of enemies;* **he of all men,** he most or least of all; **here** (most surprisingly, distressingly, etc.) **of all places; on this night of nights** (most outstanding of all); **is the one thing of all others that,** (illogically, = out of all things that); **of all the impudence!** (that can be imagined); **song of songs, holy of holies,** (those best deserving the name); **a friend of mine, of the vicar's,** i.e. (orig.) in the number of my, the vicar's friends, but illogically extended, as *that long nose of his, this only son of the vicar's; drink deep of flattery, partake of food; was* **sworn of the Council,** admitted as member; *his temper is* **of the quickest,** belongs to the quickest class; *a sort of thud; comes in* **of an evening,** (colloq.) at some time in the evenings; **of old, yore, late years,** LATE¹ 8, somewhere in the specified periods). **8.** Belonging, connection, possession, (*we of the middle class; companions of his exile; articles of clothing; the manners of today; a thing of the past; the tip of the iceberg; the master of the house; the widow of the man who was killed; a topic of conversation; the cause, result, counterpart, opposite, image, of; for the sake of*). [OE, unaccented form of *æf,* = OS, ON, Goth. *af,* OHG *ab(a)* f. Gmc *abh(a)* f. IE *ap(o)*]

of- *pref.,* assim. form of OB- before *f.*

*ō'fay *n.* (esp. Black sl.; **R**) White person. [20th c.; orig. unkn.]

off (ŏf, awf) *adv., prep., a.,* & *n.* **1.** *adv.* away, at or to a distance, (*rode off; is far, three miles, two years, off; went off on a new line of thought; beat off the attack; keep assailant off; ward off disaster*); **take** oneself, **be,** MAKE¹ ~, depart (*to*); ~ **with you!,** go; ~ **with his head!,** behead him; FALL¹ *off;* GO¹ *off;* PUT¹ *off;* ~ **we go!,** (1) we are starting, (2) let us start; **they're** ~!, horse-race has started; RIGHT⁴ *off;* STRAIGHT *off.* **2.** (so as to be) out of position, not on or touching or dependent or attached, loose, separate, gone, got rid of, incorrect or insufficient, (*my hat is off; take his clothes off; cut, break,*

shake, throw, etc., *off;* DOZE, DROP², *off*); = *off colour;* (Theatr.), not on the stage (NOISES *off*); LAUGH, SLEEP², **walk,** etc., ~, get rid of by such action; **be ~ with the old love,** have severed connection; **get** one's *daughters, stock,* ~, dispose of by marriage, sale; **the gilt is** ~, disillusionment has come; **the meat** etc. **is** ~ (has begun to decay); ||**a bit** ~, (sl.) somewhat annoying or unfair. **3.** so as to break continuity or continuance or cease or not begin operation, discontinued, cancelled, stopped, not obtainable, (**broke** ~, ceased to speak; *turn off the gas, the water, the light, the radio; cut off supplies; fence off the paddock; leave off work; the engagement, bargain, strike, is off*); (of employee) not at work (*is off sick*); (of item on menu etc.) no longer available; ~ **and on,** intermittently, waveringly, now and again. **4.** to the end, entirely, so as to be clear, (*clear, drink, kill, pay, polish, sell,* TELL¹, TICK¹, *work, off*); to decide a tie etc. (*play-off,* JUMP²-*off,* etc.). **5.** situated as regards money, supplies, etc., (*well, better, badly, comfortably,* etc., *off; how are you off for sugar?*). **6.** *prep.* from, away or down or up from, disengaged or distant from, (so as to be) no longer on or not yet on, (*chased them off the grass; is off the beaten track; fell off a ladder; caught me off balance; take cover off dish; eats off silver plate;* (colloq.) *won a lot of money off him; lay some distance off shore; took something off the price; is off duty or work; cut a slice off, dine off, the joint; was only a yard off me; keep ship two points off the wind*); not quite (~ **white,** with grey or yellow tinge); (of garment) designed so as not to cover (*off the shoulders*); not attracted by for the time being (*off one's food, off smoking*); no longer obliged to use (*am off my diet*); leading from or not far from (*in a street off the Strand*); (Golf) with an official handicap of (*plays off three*); at sea opposite (*sank off Cape Horn*); *off* BEAM¹; ~ **colour,** not in good health, *somewhat indecent; *off the* CUFF¹; ~ **one's feet,** (colloq.) to a condition of no longer being able to stand (*I was run off my feet with jobs to do; carry or sweep* person *off his feet,* make him enthusiastic or excited); *off* FORM¹, ELSE'S GAME¹, one's HAND¹'s, one's HEAD¹, *LIMIT¹'s, *the* MAP¹; ~ **the peg,** (of clothes) ready-made; ~ **the point,** irrelevant(ly); *off the* RECORD¹, *the* REEL¹. **7.** ~**-beat,** (*n.,* Mus.) unaccented part of bar, (*a.*) not coinciding with the beat, (fig.) unusual or eccentric or unconventional; ~**-ce'ntre,** not quite coinciding with central position; ~**-cut,** remnant of paper, timber, etc., after cutting, usu. sold more cheaply; ~**-glide,** (Phonet.) glide made in leaving a sound; ~**-key,** out of tune (lit. or fig.); ~**-li'ne** *a.* & *adv.,* (Computers) not directly connected or on-line, operating non-simultaneously with the process for which the computation is done; ~**-load,** unload; ~**-peak,** (for use) away from the peak of electricity consumption, traffic, etc.; ||~**-putting,** (colloq.) repellent, disconcerting; ~**-scourings,** refuse, dregs, (*of;* lit. or fig.); ~'**shore,** situated at sea some distance from the shore, (of purchases etc.) made or registered abroad, (of wind) blowing seawards; ~**si'de,** (Footb. etc.) between ball and opponents' goal, esp. in situation where player may not play the ball; ~**si'der,** (Austral. colloq.) assistant, partner, deputy; ~**-sta'ge** *a.* & *adv.,* not on the stage, not visible to audience; ~**-street,** (esp. of parking of vehicles) not on the street. **8.** *a.* farther, far, (*on the off side of the wall*); (of part of animal or vehicle ||or road, or horse etc. in team) right [opp. NEAR², orig. w. ref. to side from which one mounted] (*the off front wheel, hind leg, side*); (Cricket) towards, in, or coming from, that half of the field (as divided by line through two middle stumps) in which playing batsman does not stand (opp. ON², LEG; *an off drive,* whence ~**dri've** *v.t.; off stump;* LONG¹ *off;* MID¹-*off;* ~ **break** etc., deviation of ball from off side); disengaged (*will do it when I have an off moment*); ~ **chance,** a slight possibility; ~**-day** (when one is not at one's best); ||~**-licence,** (place with) licence to sell beer etc. for consumption off the premises; ~'**print,** printed copy of article etc. that was orig. part of larger publication; ∼**-season**, ∼**-time**, (when business etc. is fairly slack); *∼**-year** (when no national elections take place). **9.** *n.* (Cricket). the off side. **10.** start of horse-race. [different. sp. of OF, since 15/16th c.]

Off. *abbr.* Office; Officer.

ŏ'ffal *n.* refuse, waste stuff, scraps, garbage; parts cut off as less valuable from carcass meant for food, esp. entrails, also head, tail, kidneys, heart, tongue, liver, etc.; carrion, putrid flesh; low-priced fish (e.g. cod as opp. to sole or other prime fish); bran or other by-product of grain (often in *pl.*); offscourings, dregs. [ME, f. MDu. *afval* (*af* OFF, *vallen* FALL[1])]

‖**offĕ'nce**, *****offĕ'nse**, *n.* attacking, aggressive action, taking the offensive, (*the best* DEFENCE *is offence*); wounding of the feelings, wounded feeling, annoyance, umbrage, (*no offence was meant; is quick to take offence; give offence to; cannot be done without offence*); transgression, misdemeanour, illegal act, (esp. *commit an offence against*); **no** ∼, (colloq.) I did not or do not intend to offend you; hence ∼LESS (-sl-) *a.* [orig. = stumbling(-block), ME & OF *offens* f. L *offensus* annoyance, and ME & F *offense* f. L *offensa* a striking against, hurt, displeasure, both f. OF(*fendere fens-* strike)]

offĕ'nd *v.* **1.** *v.i.* stumble morally, do wrong, transgress, (*against* law, decency, person, etc.), whence ∼ER[1] *n.* (FIRST *offender*), ∼ING[2] *a.* **2.** *v.t.* wound feelings of, anger, cause resentment or disgust in or through outrage, (*am sorry you are offended; offended at* or *by* thing, *with* or *by* person; *offends the eye, the taste, her delicacy, my sense of justice,* or abs.); hence ∼EDLY *adv.* [ME, f. OF *offendre* f. L (as prec.)]

*****offĕ'nse.** See OFFENCE.

offĕ'nsive *a.* & *n.* **1.** *a.* aggressive, intended for or used in attack, (*offensive weapon, movement;* opp. DEFENSIVE); giving or meant to give offence, insulting, (*offensive language*); disgusting, ill-smelling, nauseous, repulsive; hence ∼LY[2] (-vlĭ) *adv.*, ∼NESS (-vn-) *n.* **2.** *n.* attitude of assailant, aggressive action, (*take, act* or *be on, abandon, the offensive*); an attack, offensive campaign or stroke, (*the long-expected German offensive*); aggressive action for any purpose (*peace offensive*). [f. F *offensif-ive* or f. med. L *offensivus* (as OFFENCE; see -IVE)]

ŏ'ffer[1] *v.* **1.** *v.t.* present (victim, first-fruits, prayer) *to* deity, revered person, etc., by way of sacrifice, give in worship or devotion; hence ∼ING[1] (4) *n.* **2.** hold out in hand, or tender in words or otherwise, for acceptance or refusal or consideration (*offered me his flask to drink from; was offered £5, a lift, good prospects, a free pardon; offer oneself, one's services, an opinion, a few remarks,* etc.; *offer no apology*); hence ∼ING[1] (2) *n.* **3.** (arch., abs.) make proposal of marriage. **4.** show for sale. **5.** give opportunity to enemy for *battle.* **6.** express readiness *to do* or provide if desired; attempt, try to show, (violence, resistance, etc., often *to*); show an intention *to do* (*offered to strike me*). **7.** (Of thing) present to sight or notice (*each age offers its characteristic riddles*). **8.** *v.i.* present itself, occur, (*as opportunity offers; the first path that offered*). [OE *offrian* in religious sense, = OS *offron,* ON *offra,* f. L OF(*ferre* bring); other senses f. OF *offrir,* of same orig.]

ŏ'ffer[2] *n.* expression of readiness to give or do or pay or provide if desired, or to sell on terms (**on** ∼, for sale at certain, e.g. reduced, price), proposal esp. of marriage; bid. [ME, f. prec.]

ŏ'ffertory̆ *n.* (Eccl.) part of mass or communion service preceding canon, at which alms of congregation are usu. collected; anthem accompanying this; (by confus. w. OFFER[1]*ing*) the alms collected; collection of money at religious service. [ME, f. eccl. L *offertorium* (LL *offert-* for L *oblat-* p.p. st. of *offerre* OFFER[1]; see -ORY) offering]

offhă'nd (ŏf-, awf-) *adv.* & *a.* **1.** without preparation or premeditation. **2.** unceremonious(ly), informal(ly), curt(ly); so ∼ED[2] *a.*, ∼ĕdLY[2] *adv.* [f. OFF 6 + HAND[1]]

ŏ'ffice *n.* **1.** piece of kindness, attention, service, (**ill**

etc. ∼) disservice, (*owing to, by, through, the good* or *ill offices of*). **2.** duty attaching to one's position, task, function, (*it is my office, the office of the arteries, to*). **3.** position with duties attached to it, place of authority or trust or service, esp. of public kind (*was given an office under the Government*), tenure of official position esp. that of minister of State (*take, enter upon, hold, leave, resign, office;* JACK[1]*-in-office*) or party forming Government (*out of office for 13 years*). **4.** ceremonial duty (esp. *perform* **the last** ∼**s** *to*, rites due to the dead). **5.** (Eccl.) authorized form of worship, daily service of RC breviary (also **divine** ∼; **say** ∼, recite this), Anglican morning and evening prayer, (introit at beginning of) mass or communion service, any occasional service such as the **O**∼ **for the Dead. 6.** place for transacting business (*goes down to the office at 9 a.m.*); room etc. in which the clerks of an establishment work, counting-house; room in which any kind of administrative or clerical work is done; (with qualification) room etc. set apart for business of particular department of large concern (‖*booking, goods, lost-property, -office* in railway station) or local branch of an organization (*our Manchester office; a* POST[2] *office*) or company for specified purpose (*insurance, fire* or *fire-insurance, -office*); *consulting-room of doctor etc. **7.** (**O**∼). quarters or staff or collective authority of a Government department etc. (*the* ‖FOREIGN, ‖HOME[1], POST[2], *Office*) or part thereof (*Passport Office*); ∼ **of arms**, College of Arms, or similar body in another country. **8.** ‖(in *pl.*) parts of house devoted to household work, storage, etc. **9.** (sl.) hint, signal, (*give, take, the office*). **10.** Holy **O**∼, the Inquisition; ∼**-bearer**, official or officer; ∼**-block**, large building designed to contain business offices; ∼**-boy, -girl,** (employed to do minor jobs in business office); ∼ **hours** (during which business is regularly conducted); ∼**-worker**, employee in business office. [ME f. OF, f. L *officium* performance of a task (in med. L also office, divine service), for *opificium* (*opus* work, *facere -fic-* do)]

ŏ'fficer *n.,* & *v.t.* **1.** *n.* holder of public, civil, or ecclesiastical office, sovereign's servant or minister, appointed or elected functionary, (usu. w. qualifying word(s): *Officer of the Household; medical officer (of health); probation officer; returning officer; scientific officer*). **2.** president, treasurer, secretary, etc., of society. **3.** bailiff (*sheriff's officer*); constable (*police officer*). **4.** person holding authority in navy, army, air force, or mercantile marine, esp. with commission in army or navy or air force (GENERAL, STAFF[1], COMMISSION[1]*ed,* FIELD, COMPANY[1], WARRANT[1]-, NON-*commissioned,* FLAG[4]-, PETTY, AIR[1], *officer*); ∼ **of arms,** herald or pursuivant; ∼ **of the day** (responsible for guard and inspection on a particular day). **5.** member of grade below commander in Order of the British Empire etc. **6.** *v.t.* (usu. in *p.p.*). provide with officers; act as commander of. [ME, f. AF *officer,* OF *officier* f. med. L *officiarius* f. L *officium* (see prec., -ARY[1], -ER[2])]

offi'cial (-shăl) *a.* & *n.* **1.** *a.* of an office, the discharge of duties, or the tenure of an office; holding office, employed in public capacity (‖*Official* REFEREE); derived from or vouched for by person(s) in office, properly authorized (‖ ∼ **birthday**, day in June chosen for observance of sovereign's birthday); (Med.) according to the pharmacopoeia, officinal; usual with persons in office (*official solemnity, red tape,* etc.); hence ∼LY[2] *adv.* **2.** *n.* ∼ (**principal**), presiding officer or judge of archbishop's, bishop's, or esp. archdeacon's court. **3.** person holding public office or engaged in official duties; hence ∼DOM, ∼E'SE (= officials' jargon), ∼ISM (2), *ns.* [a. 16th c. f. L *officialis* (as OFFICE; see -AL); n. ME orig. f. OF f. L *officialis*]

offi'ci̱āte (-shī-) *v.i.* **1.** discharge priestly office, perform divine service; so ∼ANT (1) *n.* **2.** act in some official capacity, esp. on particular occasion (usu. *as* host, best man, etc.). [f. med. L *officiare* perform divine service (*officium;* see OFFICE) + -ATE[3]]

officinal (ŏfĭsĭ'-, ofĭ'sĭ-) *a.* (Of herb or drug) used in medicine or the arts; (of medical preparation) kept ready at druggists', made from pharmacopoeia recipe (cf. MAGISTRAL), (of name) adopted in pharmacopoeia; hence ∼LY² *adv.* [f. med. L *officinalis* f. L *officina* workshop; see -AL]

offi'cious (-shŭs) *a.* **1.** (given to) offering service that is not wanted, doing or undertaking more than is required, intrusive, meddlesome, whence ∼NESS *n.* **2.** (Diplom.), opp. *official)* informal, unofficially friendly or candid, not binding. **3.** Hence ∼LY² *adv.* [f. L *officiosus* obliging (*officium*; see OFFICE, -OUS)]

o'ffing (ŏ'-, aw'-) *n.* part of visible sea distant from shore or beyond anchoring-ground (*was seen in the offing*); position at distance from shore (*gain, keep,* etc., *an offing*); **in the** ∼, (fig.) not far away, likely to appear. [perh. f. OFF + -ING¹]

o'ffish (ŏ'-, aw'-) *a.* (colloq.) inclined to aloofness; hence ∼NESS *n.* [f. OFF + -ISH¹; cf. *uppish*]

o'ffset (ŏ'-, aw'-) *n.,* & *v.t.* (-tt-; offset). **1.** compensation, set-off, consideration or amount diminishing or neutralizing effect of contrary one. **2.** (Print.) transfer of ink to clean sheet laid on freshly-printed surface; ∼ (**process**), method of printing in which ink is transferred from plate or stone to uniform rubber surface and thence to paper etc. **3.** (Surv.) short distance measured perpendicularly from main line of measurement. **4.** (Archit.) sloping ledge in wall etc. where thickness of part above is diminished. **5.** bend made in pipe etc. to carry it past obstacle. **6.** short side-shoot from stem or root serving for propagation; offshoot, scion, mountain-spur. **7.** (arch.) start, set--off, outset. **8.** *v.t.* (or -ĕ't) counterbalance, compensate; (esp. in *p.p.*) place out of line; print by offset process. [f. OFF + SET¹]

o'ffshoot (ŏ'-, aw'-) *n.* side-shoot or branch (lit. or fig.), derivative. [f. OFF + SHOOT¹]

offspring (ŏ'-, aw'-) *n.* (*pl.* same). person's child(ren) or descendant(s); animal's young or descendant(s); (fig.) result. [OE *ofspring* (OF from, *springan* SPRING¹)]

OFM *abbr.* Order of Friars Minor.

OFS *abbr.* Orange Free State.

oft (ŏ-, aw-) *adv.* (arch. or literary) often (*oft-told, oft--recurring; many a time and oft*); ∼-times, often. [OE, = OS *oft(o)*, OHG *ofto*, ON *oft*, Goth. *ufta*]

often (ŏ'fen, ŏ'fien, aw'-) *adv.* & *a.* (∼er, ∼est). **1.** *adv.* frequently, many times, at short intervals, (with sing. generalized or pl. subj.) in a considerable proportion of the instances (*the victim often dies, the victims often die, of it*); **as** ∼ **as not,** in (about) half the instances; **every so** ∼, from time to time; **more** ∼ **than not,** in more than (about) half the instances; **once too** ∼ (w. ref. to discomfort after several successes); ∼ **and** ∼ (emphatic form); ∼times, (arch.) often. **2.** *a.* (arch.) frequent. [ME; extended f. prec., prob. after *selden* = SELDOM]

ŏ'gam. See OGHAM.

ŏ'gdoäd *n.* group of eight. [f. LL f. Gk *ogdoas -ados* (*ogdoos* eighth f. *oktō* eight; see -AD)]

ōgee (ō'-, -ē') *n.* & *a.* (moulding) showing in section a double continuous curve, concave below passing into convex above; S-shaped (line); ∼ **arch** etc. (with two ogee curves meeting at apex); hence ∼'d [-ED²] *a.* [app. f. OGIVE, as being the usu. moulding in groin--ribs]

ŏ'g(h)am (ŏ'gam) *n.* ancient British and Irish alphabet of twenty characters formed by parallel strokes on either side of or across a continuous line; inscription in this; one of the characters. [OIr. *ogam*, referred to *Ogma*, supposed inventor]

ogi'val *a.* of ogive arch; ogee-shaped. [F, or f. foll. + -AL]

ōgīve (ō'-, -ī'v) *n.* diagonal groin or rib of vault; pointed or Gothic arch, S-shaped line, whence **ogi'val** *a.* [ME f. F, of unkn. orig.]

ŏ'gle *v.* & *n.* **1.** *v.i.* cast amorous glances. **2.** *v.t.* eye amorously. **3.** *n.* amorous glance. [prob. f. LDu.; cf. LG *oegeln,* frequent. of *oegen* look at (-LE 3)]

O'gpu (ŏ'gpōō) *n.* former (1923–34) organization for combating counter-revolutionary activities in Soviet Russia. [initial letters of *Ob"edinennoe Gosudarstvennoe Politicheskoe Upravlenie,* United State Political Administration]

ō'gre (-ger) *n.* man-eating giant in folklore etc.; terrifying person; hence ∼ISH¹, **ō'grish¹,** *adjs.,* **ō'gress¹** *n.* [F, first used by Perrault 1697, of unkn. orig.]

Ogy̆'gian (o-) *a.* of obscure antiquity, prehistoric. [f. L f. Gk *Ōgugios* of Ogyges, mythical king of Attica or Boeotia]

oh¹ (ō) *int.* expr. surprise, pain, entreaty, etc., (*oh, what a lie! oh, how horrible! oh, do come; oh for wings! oh dear me! oh yes you wi'll*); *oh* BOY; **oh' no,** certainly not; **oh no'** (expr. horror); **oh-oh** (expr. disappointment); **oh well** (expr. resignation to thing); **oh' yes** (expr. firm assertion); **oh ye's?** (expr. scepticism). [var. of O²]

oh² (ō) *n.* = O¹ 2.

OH *abbr.* Ohio.

o.h.c. *abbr.* overhead camshaft.

ohm (ōm) *n.* (Electr.) **1.** unit of resistance, transmitting current of 1 ampere when subjected to potential difference of 1 volt; hence ∼'AGE *n.,* electrical resistance measured in ohms, ∼'IC *a.,* ∼'METER *n.* **2. Ohm's law** (stating that current is proportional to voltage and inversely proportional to resistance). [f. G. S. *Ohm,* Ger. physicist d. 1854]

OHMS *abbr.* On Her (or His) Majesty's Service.

ōhō' *int.* expr. surprise or exultation. [ME, f. O² + HO]

ōhō'ne. Var. of OCHONE.

o.h.v. *abbr.* overhead valve.

-oid *suf.* forming *adjs.* & *ns.* w. sense '(something) having the form of or resembling' (*asteroid, rhomboid, thyroid*); hence ∼'AL *adj. suf.,* ∼'ALLY *adv. suf.* [f. mod. L -*oides* f. Gk -*oeidēs* (as -o-, -*eidēs* having the form of, f *eidos* form)]

oï'di|um *n.* (*pl.* ∼a). (fungus of genus *Oidium* bearing) conidium forming part of a chain, plant-mildew caused by this fungus. [mod. L., f. Gk *ōion* egg + -*idion* dim. suf.]

oil¹ *n.* **1.** one of various liquid viscid unctuous usu. inflammable chemically neutral substances lighter than and insoluble in water but soluble in alcohol and ether, classified as non-volatile **fatty** or **fixed** ∼s of animal or vegetable origin, used as varnishes, lubricants, illuminants, soap constituents, etc., ESSENTIAL or **volatile** ∼s chiefly of vegetable origin, giving plants etc. their scent, used in medicine and perfumery, and MINERAL *oils* used as fuels and illuminants. **2.** *petroleum (Austral. & NZ sl.) news, facts; *oil of* VITRIOL; STRAP-*oil*; POUR *oil on the flames, on the waters* or *on troubled waters*; **burn the midnight** ∼, read or work far into the night; **strike** ∼, (lit.) find petroleum by sinking shaft, (fig.) attain prosperity or success; ∼ **and vinegar** or **water,** type of dissimilar or irreconcilable things. **3.** (often in *pl.*) = *oil-colour,* (colloq.) picture painted in oil-colours; (colloq., usu. in *pl.*) = *oilskin.* **4.** ∼-**bird, -nut, -palm, -plant, -seed, -tree,** species of bird etc. from which oil is got; ∼-**heater, -lamp, -stove,** (using oil as fuel etc.). **5.** ∼-**bomb,** incendiary bomb containing oil; ∼'**cake,** mass of compressed linseed etc. left when oil has been expressed, used as cattle food or manure; ∼'**can** (containing oil, esp. long-nozzled to oil machinery); ∼'**cloth,** (1) fabric waterproofed with oil, (2) oilskin, (3) canvas coated with linseed etc. oil and used to cover table or floor; ∼-**colour,** (usu. in *pl.*) paint made by grinding pigment in oil; ∼ **drum,** metal drum used for transporting oil; ∼ **engine,** (driven by explosion of vaporized oil mixed with air); ∼'**field,** district yielding petroleum; ∼-**fired,** using oil as fuel; ∼-**gauge,** (1) hydrometer measuring specific gravity of oils, (2) device for testing level of lubricant oil in engine etc.; ∼-**gland** (secreting oil); ∼-**hole** (in machinery to receive lubricating oil); ∼'**man**, maker or seller of oils, *operator of oil-well; ∼-**meal**, ground oilcake; ∼-**paint**, = *oil-colour*; ∼-**painting**, art of painting, picture painted, in oil-colours, (*she is no oil-painting*, (colloq.) she is ugly); ∼-**pan**, engine sump; ∼-**paper** (made transparent or waterproof by soaking in oil); ∼-**press**, apparatus for pressing oil from seeds etc.; *oil* RIG[1]; ∼-**shale** (yielding oil by distillation); ∼'**skin**, cloth waterproofed with oil, garment or (in *pl.*) suit of this; *oil*-SLICK; ∼'**stone**, (fine-grained stone used with oil as) whetstone; *oil*-TANKER; ∼ **well** (from which petroleum is drawn). **6.** Hence ∼'LESS (-l-l-) *a.* [ME *oli*, *oile* f. AF, ONF *olie* = OF *oile* etc. f. L *oleum* (olive) oil (*olea* OLIVE)]

oil[2] *v.* **1.** *v.t.* apply oil to, lubricate; ∼ **the wheels**, lit., or fig. make things go smoothly by courtesy, bribery, etc.; *go on oiled* WHEEL[1]*s*; ∼ person('s **hand** or **palm**), bribe him; ∼ one's **tongue**, say smooth things, flatter. **2.** *v.i.* & *t.* (with *butter*, *grease*, etc., as subj. or obj.) turn into oily liquid. **3.** *v.t.* impregnate or treat with oil; ∼**ed silk** (waterproofed with oil); (in *p.p.*, sl.) drunk (**well** ∼**ed**, very drunk). **4** *v.t.* & *i.* supply with oil; (of ship etc.) take oil on board as fuel. [ME, f. prec.]

oi'ler *n.* In vbl senses; oilcan for oiling machine; oil-tanker; *oil*-well; *(in *pl.*) oilskins. [f. prec. + -ER[1]]

oi'l|y̆ *a.* of, like, containing much, covered or soaked with, oil; (of manner etc.) fawning, insinuating, obsequious; hence ∼ĭLY[2] *adv.*, ∼ĭNESS *n.* [f. OIL[1] + -Y[2]]

oi'ntment *n.* unctuous preparation applied to skin to heal or beautify, unguent; FLY[1] *in the ointment.* [ME *oignement*, *ointment* f. OF *oignement* f. pop. L *unguimentum* f. L (as UNGUENT); forms *oint-* after obs. *oint* anoint (OF, p.p. of *oindre* ANOINT)]

Oir'eachtas (ĕr'ăχthăs) *n.* legislature of Irish Republic: the President, Dáil, and Seanad. [Ir.]

OK[1] (ōkā') , **ōkay'**, *a.* & *adv.*, *n.*, & *v.t.* (colloq.) **1.** *a.* & *adv.* all right, satisfactor(ily); (as int.) I agree. **2.** *n.* approval, sanction. **3.** *v.t.* mark 'OK'; approve, sanction. [orig. US, abbr. of 'oll korrect']

OK[2] *abbr.* Oklahoma.

oka'pi (-ah'-) *n.* bright-coloured partially striped Central-Afr. ruminant (*Okapia johnstoni*) discovered 1900, with likeness to giraffe, deer, and zebra. [Mbuba]

ōkay'. See OK[1].

ōkey-dō'ke(y) *a.* & *adv.* (sl.) = OK[1]. [redupl.]

Okla. *abbr.* Oklahoma.

ŏ'kra *n.* tall malvaceous orig. Afr. plant (*Hibiscus esculentus*) with mucilaginous seed-pods used as a vegetable and for thickening soups. [W. Afr. native name]

-ŏl *suf.* (Chem.) **1.** Termination of ALCOHOL, used in names of alcohols in the wider sense or analogous compounds (*methanol*, *phenol*). **2.** = L *oleum* oil (*benzol*, *menthol*).

ōld *a.* (cf. ELDER[1], ELDEST) & *n.* **1.** *a.* advanced in age, far on in natural period of existence, not young or near its beginning, (**the** ∼, old people; **young and** ∼, everyone); made long ago, long in use, worn or damaged in the passage of time, (*an old book*, *suit*, *teapot*). **2.** having characteristics, experience, feebleness, etc., of age (*old head on young* SHOULDERs; *child has an old face*; *old* BUFFER[2], *fogy*, etc.; *a man is as old as he feels*); worn, dilapidated, shabby. **3.** (Appended to period of time) of age (*is ten years old*; *could read Greek at ten years old*; cf. OF 6); *four* etc. *-year-*∼ (*pl.* ∼**s**), person or animal, esp. racehorse, of that age. **4.** practised or inveterate *in* action or quality or as agent etc. (*old in crime*, *folly*, *cunning*, *diplomacy*; *an old trooper*, CAMPAIGNer, *offender*). **5.** dating from far back, made long ago, long established or known or familiar or dear, ancient, not new or recent, primeval, (**of** ∼ **standing**, long established; *old as the hills*; *Old England*; *Old Night*; *old friends*; *the old* STORY[1]; *an old debt*, *grudge*, *old* SCOREs; *an old name*, *family*); (of wine)

matured with keeping; (w. description or name of person as playful or friendly mention): *you old rascal!*, *there's old George!*; (colloq.) ∼ **chap**, **fellow**, **son**, etc., (sl.) ∼ **bean**, **stick**, **thing**, ‖TOP[3], etc., = *old man* (6); **the** ∼ one or **gentleman**, **Old Harry**, **Nick**, SCRATCH[2], etc., the Devil; **good** ∼ (with name, sl. exclamation in real or iron. commendation of person's or thing's performance); **have a fine**, **good**, **HIGH**, etc., ∼ **time** etc., (sl.) be well amused or entertained; *little* ∼ (in affectionate or playful ref. to person or thing); **any** ∼ **thing**, (sl.) anything no matter what (so **any** ∼ **how** etc.). **6.** belonging only or chiefly to the past, obsolete or obsolescent, out of date, antiquated, antique, concerned with antiquity, not modern, bygone, only lingering on, former, quondam; **the good** ∼ **days** or **times**, customs etc. of earlier generations, regarded as better; ∼ **fashions** (that have gone or are going out); ∼ **London**, **Paris**, **England**, etc., London etc. as it once was, or the extant relics of its former state; (of language) as used in former or earliest times (*Old* ENGLISH[1], LATIN, NORSE, SAXON, SLAVONIC). **7.** *old* ADAM[1]; ∼ **age**, period of life from about 65 or 70 onwards; *old-age* PENSION(ER); ∼ **bachelor**, man confirmed in bachelorhood; *Old* BAILEY[1]; **Old Believer**, member of Russian sect, orig. protesting against 17th-c. liturgical reforms; ‖**Old Bill**, (sl.) police(man); ∼ **bird**, wary person; *my* etc. ∼ **bones**, I etc. who am old; ∼ **boy**, (1) former member of school (so *Old Etonian* etc.; ∼-*boy network*, supposed system of favouritism among those associated since school-days, (2, colloq.) elderly man, (as *voc.*) = *old man* (6); ∼ **clothes**, (1) worn or shabby clothes, (2) discarded clothes; ∼-**clo'thes-man**, dealer in discarded clothes; *Old* CONTEMPTIBLES; ∼ **country**, (1) country long inhabited or civilized, (2) *the* mother country of colonists etc.; *Old Dominion, Virginia; ∼-**established**, long established; ‖∼ **face**, style of type imitating 18th-c. designs; ∼-**fa'shioned**, (*a.*) in or according to old fashion(s), conservative, antiquated, (∼-*fashioned look*, of dignified reproof), (*n.*) *cocktail of whisky, bitters, etc.; ∼ **firm**, (colloq.) *the* established and reliable partnership; ∼ **foundation**, (cathedral etc. founded before Reformation; *Old French* (esp. of period before 1400); *old* FUSTIC; ∼ **girl**, fem. of *old boy*; *Old Glory*, US national flag; ∼ **gold**, colour of tarnished gold, dull brownish-golden colour; ∼ **guard**, original or past or conservative member(s) of party etc.; ∼ **hand**, practised workman, person with much experience (*at doing*), (Austral. Hist.) former convict; *old* HAT; *Old* HUNDREDTH; ∼ **lady** (lit., or colloq. to or of mother or elderly wife); ‖*Old Lady of Threadneedle Street*, Bank of England; *old* LAG[2]; ∼ **light** (opp. *new light*; see NEW[1] 6); *∼-**line**, established, conservative; ∼ **maid**, (1) elderly spinster, (2) precise tidy fidgety man, (3) round game at cards in which players try not to be left with unpaired queen; ∼-**mai'dish**, fussy and prim; ∼ **man**, (1) lit., (2) southernwood, (3, sl.) employer, manager, headmaster, (Naut. sl.) ship's captain, (4, colloq.) husband, (5, colloq.) father, (6, colloq., as *voc.*) male person or animal regarded with affection or intimacy, (7, Theol.) *the* unregenerate man, (8, Austral.) adult male kangaroo; ∼ *man of the sea*, person who cannot be shaken off [f. Arabian-Nights tale of Sindbad]; ∼ *man's beard*, (1) clematis, esp. traveller's joy, (2) *kind of moss (*Tillandsia usneoides*); ∼ **master**, (painting by) great painter of former times, esp. of 13th–17th c. in Europe; *old* MOON[1]; ∼ **one**, (1) *the* Devil, (2) familiar joke; ‖**Old Pals Act**, (joc.) doctrine that friends should help each other to the maximum extent; *Old* PRETENDER; *old* RETAINER; *old* SALT; ∼ **school**, one's former school; *of the old* SCHOOL[1]; ‖∼ **school tie**, necktie of characteristic pattern worn by former members of a particular (public) school, (fig.) mark of sentimental or excessive loyalty to traditional values and ideas; ~ **soldier,** former or long-serving soldier, (fig.) experienced person; *come the* ~ *soldier over,* seek to impose on esp. on grounds of greater experience; *old* STAGER; *old* STYLE; ‖*old* SWEAT; *Old* TESTAMENT; ~**-time,** belonging to old times, (of dancing) comprising kinds of dance known for many years; **~-ti'mer,* person with long experience or standing; *old wives' tale* (see WIFE); ~ **woman,** (1) fem. of *old man* (1, 4, 5), (2) fussy or timid man; ~**-wo'manish,** fussy and timid; *Old* WORLD; ~**-world,** belonging to old times (also joc. ~*e-worlde* pr. -dī; -dǐ); ~ **year,** year just ended or about to end. **8.** Hence ~'ISH[1] 2 *a.,* ~'NESS *n.* **9.** *n.* of ~ *a.* & *adv.,* (living) in the old time (*the men of old; of old there were giants*); *have heard it* **of** ~, since long ago. [OE *ald,* = OS *ald,* OHG *alt.* f. WG **aldha* (**al-* grow, nourish)]

o'lden[1] *a.* (literary). old-time, of a former age, (esp. *the olden time*). [ME, f. OLD + -EN[5]]
o'lden[2] *v.t.* & *i.* make or grow feeble etc. as with age. [f. OLD + -EN[6]]
o'ldie *n.* (colloq.) old person or thing. [f. OLD + -IE]
o'ldster *n.* old person. [f. OLD + -STER, after *youngster*]
-ōle *suf.* (Chem.) forming names of compounds esp. heterocyclic (*indole*). [f. L *oleum* oil; cf. -OL 2]
olēā'ceous (-shŭs) *a.* (Bot.) of the family Oleaceae, incl. olive and jasmine. [f. mod. L *Oleaceae* f. L *olea* olive-tree; see -ACEOUS]
olēā'ginous *a.* having properties of or producing oil; oily, greasy, (lit. or fig.). [f. F *oléagineux* f. L *oleaginus* (*oleum* oil)]
olēā'nder *n.* evergreen poisonous Mediterranean shrub (*Nerium oleander*) with leathery lanceolate leaves and fine red, white, or pink flowers. [med. L]
olēā'ster *n.* the wild olive (*Olea oleaster*); small yellow-flowered tree like it, of genus *Elaeagnus.* [ME f. L (*olea* olive-tree; see -ASTER)]
olēcrā'non *n.* (Anat.) bony prominence on upper end of ulna at elbow. [f. Gk *ōle(no)kranon* (*ōlenē* elbow, *kranion* head)]
o'lefin (-ine), *n.* (Chem.) hydrocarbon of series C_nH_{2n}. [f. F *oléfiant* oil-forming (w. ref. to oily ethylene dichloride) + -IN, -INE[5]]
olē'ic *a.* (Chem.) ~ **acid,** unsaturated fatty acid present in many fats and soaps; hence **o'lēATE**[1] (3) *n.* [f. as foll. + -IC]
olēī'ferous *a.* yielding oil. [f. L *oleum* oil + -I- + -FEROUS]
*o'leō *n.* (*pl.* ~s). oleomargarine. [abbr.]
o'lēo- *comb. form.* oil, as: ~**graph,** picture printed in oil-colours; ~**mar'garine** (*or* -ē'n), fatty substance extracted from beef fat and serving as constituent of margarine, *margarine made from vegetable oils; ~**meter** (-ŏ'm-), instrument for determining density and purity of oils; ~**-re'sin,** natural or artificial mixture of essential oil and resin, e.g. BALSAM 1. [f. L *oleum* oil + -o-]
o'leum *n.* concentrated sulphuric acid containing excess sulphur trioxide in solution as oily corrosive liquid. [L, = oil]
‖**O lével** (ō'-) *n.* = ORDINARY *level* (in GCE). [abbr.]
olfă'ct|ion *n.* (Med.) smelling, sense of smell; so ~IVE *a.* [f. L *olfactus* a smell (*olēre* to smell, *facere* fact- make); see -ION]
olfă'ctorỹ *a.* concerned with smelling (*olfactory nerves*). [f. L *olfactorius (*olfactare* frequent. of *olfacere,* as prec.)]
oli'banum *n.* aromatic gum resin from tree of genus *Boswellia,* used as incense. [ME, f. med. L, f. LL f. Gk *libanos* frankincense, of Semitic orig.]
o'lid *a.* (arch.) rank-smelling, fetid. [f. L *olidus* (*olēre* smell; see -ID[1])]
o'ligărch (-k) *n.* member of oligarchy. [f. Gk *oligarkhēs* (*oligoi* few, *arkhō* to rule)]
o'ligărchỹ (-kǐ) *n.* government, State governed, by small group of persons; members of such government; so **oligăr'ch**IC(AL) (-kǐ-) *adjs.* [f. F *oligarchie* or med. L f. Gk *oligarkhia* (as prec.; see -Y[1])]

o'ligo- *comb. form.* few, slight, as: ~**car'pous,** having few fruits; **O~cene,** (Geol.) between Miocene and Eocene; ~**mer** (-ǐ'-), (Chem.) polymer with up to 5 monomer units; ~**poly** (-ŏ'p-), state of limited competition between few producers or sellers (cf. MONOPOLY). [f. Gk *oligos* small, *oligoi* few + -o-]
o'liō *n.* (*pl.* ~s). mixed dish, hotchpotch, stew of various meats and vegetables; medley, farrago, miscellany. [f. Sp. *olla* stew f. L *olla* jar]
oliva'ceous (-shŭs) *a.* (Biol. etc.) olive-green, of dusky yellowish green. [f. OLIVE + -ACEOUS]
o'livarỹ *a.* (Anat.) olive-shaped, oval. [f. L *olivarius* (as foll.; see -ARY[1])]
o'live *n.* & *a.* **1.** ~(-**tree**), evergreen tree (*Olea europaea*) with narrow leaves hoary below and axillary clusters of small white flowers, bearing olives (sense 2). **2.** small oval drupe with hard stone and bitter pulp, of dusky yellowish green when unripe and bluish black when ripe, yielding oil, and pickled unripe for eating as relish. **3.** leaf, branch, or wreath of olive-tree as emblem of peace; ~**branch,** (fig.) something done to show disposition for reconciliation. **4.** ~(-**wood**), wood of the olive-tree. **5.** (shell of) olive-shaped gastropod of genus *Oliva;* olivary body in brain. **6.** (in *pl.*) slices of beef or veal rolled up with stuffing and stewed. **7.** olive-shaped bar or button for fastening garment by insertion in corresponding loop. **8.** olive colour (see sense 10). **9.** ~**-branch,** (1) see sense 3, (2, joc.) child (w. ref. to Ps. 128:3); ~ **crown,** garland of olive as sign of victory; ~ **drab,** (greyish olive colour of US army uniforms; ~ **oil** (extracted from olives). **10.** *a.* ~(-**green**), coloured like the unripe olive. **11.** (Of complexion) yellowish-brown. [ME f. OF f. L *oliva* f. Gk *elaia* (*elaion* oil)]
o'livine (-ī-, -ēn) *n.* magnesium iron silicate mineral, usu. olive-green. [f. L *oliva* OLIVE + -INE[5]]
ŏlla podri'da (-rē'-) *n.* = OLIO. [Sp., lit. 'rotten pot' (as OLIO, L *putridus;* cf. PUTRID)]
ŏlm *n.* cave-dwelling salamander of genus *Proteus.* [G]
o'logỹ *n.* (joc.) any science or theory. [f. foll.]
-ŏ'logỹ *suf.* See -LOGY.
oloro'sō *n.* (*pl.* ~s). heavy dark medium-sweet sherry. [Sp., lit. 'fragrant']
Olỹ'mpiăd (o-) *n.* period of four years between celebrations of Olympic games, used by ancient Greeks in dating events (776 BC being first year of first Olympiad); celebration of modern Olympic games; regular international contest in chess etc. [ME, f. F *Olympiade,* or f. L f. Gk *Olumpias -ad-* (*Olumpios;* see foll., -AD)]
Olỹ'mpian (o-) *a.* & *n.* **1.** *a.* of Olympus, celestial; (of manners etc.) magnificent, condescending, superior; = foll. **2.** *n.* dweller in Olympus, one of the greater ancient-Greek gods; person of great attainments; person of superhuman calmness and detachment. [f. L *Olympus* or foll. + -IAN]
Olỹ'mpic (o-) *a.* & *n.* **1.** *a.* of or at Olympia in Elis in the Peloponnese. **2.** of the ~ **games,** (1) games held at Olympia every four years by ancient Greeks with athletic, literary, and musical competitions, (2) modern international athletic and sports meeting at various places, held every four years since 1896, except in 1916, 1940, and 1944. **3.** *n.* (in *pl.*) Olympic games; **Winter** ~**s,** similar contest in winter sports etc. in same years. [f. L f. Gk *Olumpikos* of Olympus or Olympia (the latter being named from the games in honour of Zeus of *Olympus*)]
Olỹ'mpus (o-) *n.* mountain in N. Thessaly on which chief Greek gods were thought to dwell; divine abode, heaven. [L, f. Gk *Olumpos*]
‖**OM** *abbr.* (member of the) Order of Merit.
-ŏ'ma *suf.* forming *ns.* denoting tumours and other abnormal growths (*carcinoma*). [mod. L, f. Gk *-ōma suf.* denoting result of vbl action]
o'madhaun (-dawn) *n.* (Ir.) foolish person. [f. Ir. *amadán* fool]

omā's|um *n. (pl.* ∼a). third STOMACH of ruminant. [L, = bullock's tripe]

ŏ'mbre (-ber) *n.* card-game for three, popular in Europe in 17th-18th c. [f. Sp. *hombre* man, w. ref. to one player who seeks to win the pool]

ombré (aw'nbrā) *a.* (Of fabric etc.) having gradual shading of colour from light to dark. [F, p.p. of *ombrer* shadow (as UMBER)]

ŏ'mbro- *comb. form.* rain, as ∼LOGY (-ŏ'l-), ∼METER (-ŏ'm-), *ns.* [f. Gk *ombros* rain-shower + -o-]

ŏ'mbuds|män (-bŏŏdzm-) *n. (pl.* ∼men). official appointed to investigate individuals' complaints against public authorities. [Sw., = legal representative]

-ome *suf.* forming *ns.* denoting objects or parts of a specified nature (*rhizome, trichome*). [var. of -OMA]

ō'méga *n.* last letter (Ω, ω) of Greek alphabet, = ō (cf. OMICRON); last of series, final development etc., (ALPHA *and Omega*). [Gk, *ō mega* = great O]

ŏ'melĕtte, ŏ'melĕt (ŏ'ml-) *n.* beaten eggs cooked in melted butter and folded and often flavoured with or containing herbs, cheese, chopped ham, jam, etc. (**savoury** ∼, with herbs etc.; **sweet** ∼, with sugar or jam; **one cannot make an** ∼ **without breaking eggs,** something must be sacrificed in order to achieve one's purpose). [F *omelette,* obs. *amelette* by metath. f. *alumette* var. of *alumelle* (*lemele* knife-blade f. L LAMELLA)]

ō'mĕn *n.,* & *v.t.* **1.** *n.* occurrence or object (supposedly) portending good or evil, prognostic, presage; prophetic signification (*is of good omen*). **2.** *v.t.* foreshow, give presage of; ILL-omened. [L *omen ominis*]

omĕ'nt|um *n. (pl.* ∼a). fold of peritoneum connecting stomach with other viscera; hence ∼AL *a.* [L]

omi'cron *n.* (fifteenth Greek letter (O, ο) = ŏ (cf. OMEGA). [Gk, *o micron* = small O]

ŏ'minous *a.* giving or being an omen (*of* good or evil, or abs.), portentous; of evil omen, inauspicious, foreshowing disaster, threatening; hence ∼LY[2] *adv.* [f. L *ominosus* (OMEN; see -OUS)]

omi'ssion (-shon) *n.* omitting, non-inclusion; non--performance, neglect, duty not done; **sins of** ∼ **and commission,** leaving undone those things which ought to be done, and doing those things which ought not to be done; so **omi'ssIVE** *a.* [ME f. OF, or f. LL *omissio* (as foll.; see -ION)]

omi't *v.t.* (-tt-). leave out, not insert or include; leave undone, neglect doing, fail to do; so **omi'ssIBLE** *a.* [ME, f. L *omittere -iss-* (o- for OB-, *mittere* send)]

ŏmni- *comb. form.* all-, of all things, in all ways or places, (cf. PAN-), as: ∼co'mpetent, having jurisdiction in all cases, able to deal with all matters; ∼dire'ctional, (of aerial etc.) receiving or transmitting in all directions; ∼far'ious, of all sorts [cf. MULTIFARIOUS]; **omni'fic,** all-creating; **omni'genous,** of all kinds. [L (*omnis* all)]

ŏ'mnibus *n.* & *a.* **1.** *n.* bus; omnibus book. **2.** *a.* serving several purposes at once, comprising several items; ∼ **book** or **volume,** low-priced volume containing several stories, plays, etc. (freq. by one author); ∼ **box** (in theatre, holding a number of subscribers). [F, f. L dat. pl. of *omnis,* = for all]

ŏmni'pot|ent *a.* having infinite power (**the O∼ent,** God); having full or absolute power; having very great influence; hence or cogn. ∼ENCE *n.,* ∼entLY[2] *adv.* [ME f. OF, f. L *omnipotens* (as OMNI-, POTENT)]

ŏmniprĕ's|ent (-z-) *a.* present everywhere at same time; widely or constantly met with; so ∼ENCE *n.* [f. med. L OMNI(*presens* PRESENT[1])]

ŏmni'sci|ent (-sĭe-, -shye-) *a.* having infinite or very extensive knowledge; hence or cogn. ∼ENCE *n.,* ∼entLY[2] *adv.* [f. med. L *omnisciens -entis* (as OMNI-, *scire* know; see -ENT)]

ŏmnium gä'therum (-dh-) *n.* (colloq.) miscellaneous assemblage of persons or things, strange mixture. [mock L (L *omnium* of all, GATHER)]

ŏmni'vorous *a.* feeding on many kinds of food, esp.

on both plants and flesh; (fig.) reading, observing, etc., whatever comes one's way; hence ∼LY[2] *adv.,* ∼NESS *n.* [f. L *omnivorus* (as OMNI-, -VOROUS)]

ō'moplāte *n.* (arch.) shoulder-blade, scapula. [f. Gk *ōmoplatē* (*ōmos* shoulder, *platē* blade)]

ŏ'mphalo- *comb. form.* navel, as: ∼tomy (-ŏ't-), dividing of umbilical cord. [f. Gk (as foll.) + -o-]

ŏ'mphalŏs *n.* (Gk Ant.) boss on shield, conical stone at Delphi supposed to be central point of earth; centre, hub, (*the centre and omphalos of a world-wide empire*). [Gk, = navel, boss, hub]

ŏn[1] *prep.* (see UPON for idiomatic preference). **1.** (so as to be) supported by or attached to or covering or enclosing (*sat on the table; floats on the water; is on the horns of a dilemma; everywhere on earth; lives on the Continent, on an annuity; a scholar on the foundation; a colonel on half-pay; is, gets, falls, on his knees* etc.; *travels on foot, wheels, the wing, the wings of the wind; tread on air,* person's *toes; dropped it, threw him, on the floor; came on deck; standing on a ladder; put a notice on the board; hangs on the wall; walks on the ceiling; has a blister on his heel; went on board; is on the jury, committee, general staff,* * *team; a writer on the press, the 'Mail'; dog is on the chain*); **on** one, carried with one, about one's person, (*have you a match on you?; rings on her fingers*); *on one's* HAND[1]*s,* one's HEAD[1]. **2.** with axis, pivot, basis, motive, standard, conformation, or guarantee, consisting in (*turn on one's heel; works on a ratchet; based on fact; imprisonment on suspicion; swear on my honour, on the Bible; had it on good authority; decided on this evidence; did it on purpose; can be explained on your theory; heard it on the radio; spoke on the telephone; got it on good terms; on account of; on the average; on penalty of death;* * *ten cents on the dollar; a tax on petrol; borrowed money on (the security of) his house; interest on one's capital; profit on sales*). **3.** (so as to be) close to, in the direction of, touching, arrived at, against, just at, (*house is on the shore, road;* * *on Fifth Avenue; on the right, North, far side, both sides, of; Clacton--on-Sea; Abingdon-on-Thames; marched on London; hit him on the head; a box on the ear; serve a notice, writ, on; lay hold on; seize on; bowling is on the wicket (is straight); drew his knife on me; smile, frown, turn one's back, on; make an attack on; a curse, plague, etc., on him, it!; rose on their oppressors; ship is driving on the rocks, on shore*); (colloq.) in a position to get (*on a hat-trick, having already 2 of the* 3); *on* FORM[1]; *on* one's GAME[1]. **4.** (Of time) during, exactly at, contemporaneously with, immediately after or before, as a result of, (*happened on the morning* etc. *of 29 May, on Christmas Eve, on the next day; does not run on Sundays on a Sunday; on the* HOUR; *on the* INSTANT[2]; *on the stroke of midnight;* CASH[1] *on delivery;* **on time, schedule, the minute,** etc., punctual(ly); *on arriving, my return, examination, I found; the time is just on nine o'clock*). **5.** in manner specified by *the* + adjective (*on the cheap, sly,* SQUARE[1]); in state or action specified by noun (*on fire,* TAP[1]*, loan, lease, sale, strike, guard; on the look-out, move, run, wane, watch; on one's best behaviour*). **6.** concerning, about, (while) engaged with, so as to affect, (*keen, mad, bent, determined, set, on;* GONE *on; die, rat, walk out, on; court martial was held on him; my opinion on free trade; writes, speaks, lectures, on finance; a book, an essay, on grammar; serves on active service; serves on the committee; is here on business, duty, holiday, leave; is on antibiotics, heroin, the Pill; Armstrong on trumpet; meditating on vanity; take vengeance on person; have* NOTHING *on person; the laugh was, the drinks are, on* (colloq., = at the expense of) *me; the fire went out on* (colloq., = to the disadvantage of) *me; did it on my way there; went on an errand; is not binding on us; work tells severely on him; title was conferred on him; draw cheque on bank; condoled with him on his loss*). **7.** added to (*ruin on ruin; put twopence on the price*). **8. on-li'ne** *a.* & *adv.,* (Computers) (carried out while) directly connected to the central processing unit, directly controlled by the computer; **o'nshore,** (of wind) blowing landwards; **onsi'de,** (Footb. etc.) not OFFSIDE; **on-sta'ge** *a.* & *adv.,* on the stage, visible to audience; **on-street** (esp. of parking of vehicles, opp. *off-street*). [OE *on, an,* =

OS, OHG *an(a)*, ON *á*, Goth. *ana* f. Gmc, cogn. w. Gk *ana*]

ŏn[2] *adv., a., & n.* **1.** *adv.* (so as to be) supported by, attached to, covering, enclosing, or touching, something (*has, put, his hat on; put the table-cloth on; keep your* HAIR *on*). **2.** in some direction, towards something, farther forward, towards point of contact, in advanced position or state, with continued movement or action, in operation or activity, (LOOK, MOVE[2], *on; from that day on; was well on in the day; getting on for two o'clock*); **broadside, end,** etc., **on** (with that part forward); (ellipt., = imper. of *go* or *come on*) *on, Stanley, on!*; *happened earlier, early, late(r), on* (see EARLY, LATE[2]); **on and on,** continually on(wards); *and so*[1] *on*; **speak, wait, work,** etc., **on,** continue to do so; (Cricket, of bowler) bowling; (of play, film, broadcast programme, etc.) being performed; (of actor etc.) on the stage; (of gas, water, etc.) running or available; (of electric current etc.) in or into state of flowing or activation of equipment etc.; (of proposed event, strike, etc.) to take place, not cancelled; (of employee) on duty. **3.** CARRY[1], CATCH[1], COME, GET[1], GO[1], HOLD[1], KEEP[1], PUT[1], TAKE[1], TRY, *on*. **4.** be on, (colloq.) be willing to participate or approve, make bet, be practicable or acceptable; **be on about,** (colloq.) refer to, discuss (esp. persistently); **be on at,** (colloq.) nag or grumble at (person); **be on to** (person), be aware of his intentions etc., find fault with, nag (*he's always on to me*); **be on to** (thing), notice it, be able to make use of it, realize its importance; HAVE[1] *on*; **on and off,** = OFF *and on*; **on to, onto,** *compd. prep.* (corresponding to *on* as *into* to *in*, but often written as two words) to a position on (*ran on to the track*; cf. *ran on to the end,* = sense 2). **5.** **o'ncoming** *a. & n.,* approach(ing) from the front; ||**o'n-cost,** overhead expense; **o'nfall** *n.,* assault; **o'nflow,** onward flow; **on-glide,** (Phonet.) glide made in beginning a sound; **o'ngoing** (ŏ'n-gōing) *a.,* continuing to exist etc.; **o'nlooker,** = LOOKER-*on;* **on-o'ff** *a.,* (of switch etc.) having two positions, 'on' and 'off'; **o'nrush,** onward rush. **6.** *a.* (Cricket). towards or in part of field on playing batsman's side and in front of his wicket (opp. OFF; *an on drive,* whence **on-dri've** *v.t.;* LONG[1] *on;* MID[1]-*on*). **7.** ||**on-licence,** (place with) licence to sell beer etc. for consumption on the premises. **8.** *n.* the on side in cricket (*a fine drive to the on*). [OE, f. prec.]

-ŏn *suf.* (Phys. etc.) forming *ns.* denoting elementary particles (*meson, neutron*), quanta (*photon*), molecular units (*codon*), or substances (*interferon, parathion*). [f. ION, orig. in *electron*]

o'nager *n.* wild ass, esp. *Equus onager* of Central Asia; ancient military engine for throwing rocks. [ME f. L, f. Gk *onagros* (*onos* ass, *agrios* wild)]

o'nan|ism *n.* masturbation; coitus interruptus; hence **~i'stic** *a.* [f. F *onanisme* or mod. L *onanism,* f. *Onan* (Gen. 38:9); see -ISM]

||**ONC,** ||**OND,** *abbrs.* Ordinary National Certificate, Diploma.

once (wŭns) *adv., conj., & n.* **1.** *adv.* for one time or on one occasion only, multiplied by one, by one degree, (*have read it more than once; not once in a hundred times; shall die once*); **~ or twice, ~ and again,** a few times; **~ again, ~ more,** an additional time; **~ (and) for all,** in final manner, definitively; (**every**) **~ in a while** or ||**way,** from time to time; **~ and away,** (1) = *once for all,* (2) = *once in a way;* **~ bitten twice shy,** pain, loss, etc., teaches caution; **for** (**this, that**) **~,** ||**for ~ in a way,** on this or that one occasion, even if on no other. **2.** (In negative or conditional or indefinite clause etc.) ever, at all, even for one or the first time, (*if we once lose sight of him; when once he understands; have not seen him here once; once past the fence we are safe*). **3.** on a certain but unspecified past occasion (also **~ upon a time**), at some period in the past, former(ly), (*once there was a giant; a once-famous doctrine*). **4.** **at ~,** immediately, without delay, at the

same time, (*do it at once, please; don't all crowd in at once; at once stern and tender*); **all at ~,** (1) all together, (2) without warning. **5.** **~-over,** (colloq.) (preliminary) inspection (often with additional sense of cursoriness, also **~-over-lightly**). **6.** *conj.* as soon as, if once, when once, (*once he hesitates, we have him; once I can get this job done*). **7.** *n.* one time, performance, etc., (*once is enough for me; happened only that once;* cf. sense 1). [ME *ānes, ōnes,* f. ONE+-s[3]]

||**o'ncer** (wŭ'nser) *n.* (sl.) £1 note. [f. ONCE+-ER[1]]

ŏnco- *comb. form.* (Med.) tumour, as: **~ge'nic, ~genous** (-ŏ'j-), *adjs.,* tumour-producing; **~logy** (-ŏ'l-) *n.,* study of tumours. [f. Gk *ogkos* mass+-o-]

on dit (awn dē') *n.* (*pl. pr.* same). piece of gossip or hearsay. [F, = they say]

one (wŭn) *a., n., & pron.* **1.** *a.* single and integral in number, neither one none nor fractional nor plural, numbered by the first or lowest integer, half of two, a; **~ man, ~ vote,** opp. PLURAL *vote;* **~-third** etc., part that is of size such that three etc. make whole; **~-and--twenty** etc., = twenty etc. plus one, twenty etc. **-one; ~-and-twentieth** etc., twenty etc. -first; **~ dozen, hundred,** etc., (precise or formal for *a*); **~ man in ten, a thousand,** etc., relatively few; **for ~ thing** (not to mention others); **~ or two,** lit., or = a few. **2.** *the* only, single, forming a unity, united, identical, the same, unchanging, a particular but undefined, to be contrasted with another, (*the one way to succeed; no one man is equal to it; is one and undivided; all in one direction; liked her at one time; that is one way of doing it*); **be made ~,** be married to each other; **become ~,** coalesce; *one* WITH; **neither ~ thing nor the other,** of (undesirably) mixed nature; **~ and** (emphatically) **the same; ~ day,** (1) on a day unspecified, (2) at some unspecified future date. **3.** *n.* (often used as substitute for repetition of previously expressed or implied noun). the number 'one', thing numbered with it, written symbol (l, i, I) for it, a unit, unity, a single thing or person or example, (*one is half of two; write down a one, three ones; came in ones and twos; sell scores where they sold ones; this is the only one; I lose a neighbour and you gain one; the big book and the little one; pick me out a good one, some good ones; which one or ones, what kind of a one, do you like?; that one, the one in the window, will do*); (colloq.) story, joke, (*have you heard the one about the dog that could play poker?*), think (QUICK one; *one for the* ROAD[1]); (colloq.) ||pound note, *dollar bill; (**all**) **in ~,** combined; **at ~,** reconciled, in agreement; **book, part, volume,** etc., **~** (first in series); **in ~,** (colloq.) at first attempt; **make ~,** (arch.) be member of a group; **never a ~,** none; NUMBER[1] *one;* TEN *to one;* ||*in the* YEAR *one.* **4.** *a.* used ellipt. for *a,* or for sense 1, with noun often merely implied). single person or thing of the kind expressed or implied (*one of them lost his or her hat; just one of those* THINGS; *one of the richest men in England; shall see you again one of these fine days*); *at ~ o'clock, at ~,* (i.e. hour); *like ~ o'clock,* (colloq.) vigorously; **~ and sixpence** (Hist.; i.e. shilling); *gave him ~ in the eye, ~ in the eye for the Liberals,* (i.e. blow, lit. or fig.); **for ~,** being one, even if alone (*I for one do not believe it*); *go one* BETTER[1]; *is one too* MANY (*for*); ALL *one; one and* ALL; **~ by ~, ~ after another,** singly, successively; **~ with another,** on the average; (**the**) **~ . . . the other** (formula distinguishing two things: *one is good, the other bad; took* (*the*) *one and left the other*); **~ another** (formula of reciprocity with orig. subjective and *another* objective or possessive: *struck one another, write to one another, buy one another's goods*). **5.** *pron.* a person of specified kind (*little, dear, loved, ones; behaved like one frenzied*; (colloq.) *what a one he is to make excuses or for making excuses!, you are a* (remarkable) *one!; he was one who had an eye for such mysteries; bought it from one Stephens*); ANYONE, NO[1] *one,* etc.; **many a ~,** many people; **the Holy One, One above,** God; **the Evil One,** the Devil. **6.** (arch.) a particular but unspecified person (*one came running*). **7.** any person, esp.

the speaker or writer, as representing people in general (poss. *one's*, obj. *one*, reference-form *one*, refl. *oneself*; (arch. or US) *his*, *him*, *he* and *him*, *himself*, (colloq.) *their*, *them*, *they* and *them*, *themselves*: *if one cuts off one's nose, one hurts only oneself*; *it offends one to be told one is not wanted*); (colloq.) I (*one let it pass, for one did not want to seem mean*). **8.** ∼**-armed bandit,** (sl.) fruit- -machine etc. operated by pulling down armlike handle; ∼**-eyed,** having only, or blind in, one eye, (fig., sl.) petty; ∼**-handed,** having, done or used etc. with one hand only; ∼**-horse,** drawn or worked by single horse, (fig., sl.) petty, poorly equipped; ∼ **-idea'd,** ∼**-ideaed,** (-*ĭad*) possessed by single idea, narrow-minded; ∼**-legged,** having only one leg, (fig.) one-sided, unequal; ∼**-man,** requiring, consisting of, done or managed by, one man (*one-man band, bus, exhibition of paintings*); ∼**-night stand,** (colloq.) single performance of play, concert, etc., in a place, sexual liaison lasting only from one day to the next; ∼**-off,** made as one (article etc.) only, not repeated; ∼ **-piece,** (of bathing-suit etc.) made as a single connected garment, not two-piece; ∼**se'lf,** reflexive, and emphatic appositional, form of *one* (sense 7) (*to starve oneself is suicide*; *to do right oneself is the great thing*; cf. HERSELF); ∼**-shot,** (colloq.) involving a single action or effort; ∼**-sided,** having, occurring on, one side only (*a* ∼*-sided street*, with houses on one side only; *a* ∼*-sided plant*, with leaves or flowers all on one side of stem), larger etc. on one side, partial, unfair, prejudiced; ∼**'step,** vigorous kind of foxtrot in duple time; ∼**-time,** former; ∼**-time pad,** pad of ciphers each for use once only; ∼**-(to-)one,** with correspondence of one member of one group to one of another; ∼**-track,** (of mind etc.) able to think of only one topic; ∼**-two,** (colloq.) delivery of two punches in quick succession, passing of ball from one player to another and immediately back to the first; ∼**-up,** scoring one point more than opponent, (fig.) maintaining a psychological advantage, whence ∼- -*u'pmanship* (colloq.); ∼**-way,** operating or moving in only one direction, *(of ticket) single not return; ∼- -way street* (in which traffic may move in one direction only). **9.** Hence ∼'FOLD *a.* [OE *ān*, = OS *ēn*, OHG *ein*, ON *einn*, Goth. *ains* f. Gmc *∗ainaz* f. IE *∗oinos*]

-ōne *suf.* forming *ns.* (Chem.) denoting various compounds, esp. ketones (*acetone*). [f. Gk -*ōnē* fem. patronymic]

oneir'ic (-īr'-) *a.* of dreams. [f. Gk *oneiros* dream + -IC]
oneir'o- (onīr'-) *comb. form.* dream, as: ∼**cri'tic,** interpreter of dreams; ∼**logy** (onīrŏ'-), study and interpretation of dreams; ∼**MANCY** *n.* [f. as prec. + -o-]

o'neness (wŭ'n-n-) *n.* being one, singleness; singularity, uniqueness; wholeness, unity, union, agreement, concord; identity, sameness, changelessness. [f. ONE + -NESS]

||**o'ner** (wŭ'-) *n.* (sl.) remarkable or pre-eminent person or thing; severe blow. [f. ONE + -ER¹]

o'nerous *a.* burdensome, causing or requiring trouble; (Law) accompanied by obligations; hence ∼LY² *adv.*, ∼NESS *n.* [ME, f. OF *onereus* f. L *onerosus* (*onus oneris* burden; see -OUS]

oneself. See ONE 7, 8.

o'nion (ŭ'nyon) *n.* (plant *Allium cepa* with) edible rounded bulb of many concentric coats and pungent smell and flavour, much used in cooking or eaten pickled or in salad; **know** one's ∼**s,** (sl.) be good at one's job; **off** one's ∼, (sl.) crazy; ∼ **dome,** bulbous cupola as often found on churches in Russia etc.; ∼ **-skin,** (1) outermost or any outer coat of onion, (2) thin smooth translucent paper; hence ∼y² *a.* [ME, f. AF *union*, OF *oignon* f. Gallo-Rom. *∗unione* f. L *unio -onis*]

o'nly¹ *attrib. a.* that is (or are) the one (or all the) specimen(s) of the class, sole, (*the only way is to die*; *the only child of his parents*; *the only instances known*; *was an only son*; *only you can help me*; *my one and only hope*); best or

alone worth considering (*gliding is the only sport*); ∼ (or **onlie**) **begetter,** person solely responsible for originating something [w. allus. to dedication of Shak. *Sonnets* 1609]; ∼**-begotten,** begotten as the only child. [OE *ānlic*, *ǣnlic* (as ONE, -LY¹)]

o'nlỹ² *adv.* & *conj.* **1.** *adv.* solely, merely, exclusively, and no one or nothing more or besides or else, and that is all, (*is right only because it is customary*; *one and one only*; *it will only make matters worse*; *I can only guess what happened*; *has only just succeeded or arrived*; *I not only heard it, but saw it*); IF *only.* **2.** no longer ago than (*came only yesterday*); with no better result than (*picked it up, only to drop it again*). **3.** ∼ *too* glad, true, etc., glad etc. and not, as might be expected or desired, the opposite. **4.** *conj.* it must however be added that, but then, (*he makes good resolutions, only he never keeps them*); with the exception, were it not, that (*he does well, only that he is nervous at the start*; *I would describe it, only (that) you would be bored*). [ME *onliche*, partly f. prec., partly f. OE *ǣnlīce* after prec.; cf. ONE, -LY²]

||**o.n.o.** *abbr.* or near offer.

ŏnomă'stic *a.* relating to name(s). [f. Gk *onomastikos* (*onoma* name)]

onomato|poe'ia (onŏma-, ŏnomă-; -pē'*a*) *n.* formation of names or words from sounds that resemble those associated with the object or action to be named, or that seem naturally suggestive of its qualities; word so formed (e.g. *cuckoo, sizzle*); hence or cogn. ∼**poe'IC** (-pē'-), ∼**pŏē'tIC,** *adjs.* [LL, f. Gk *onomatopoiia* word- -making (*onoma -matos* name, *poieō* make)]

ŏ'nsĕt *n.* attack, assault, impetuous beginning, (esp. *at the first onset*). [f. ON¹ + SET² (cf. SET¹ *on*)]

ŏ'nslaught (-awt) *n.* onset, fierce attack. [earlier *anslaight* f. MDu. *aenslag* (*aen* on, *slag* blow) w. assim. to obs. *slaught* slaughter]

-ŏnt *suf.* (Biol.) denoting an individual of a specified type (*symbiont*). [f. Gk *ōn ont*- being]

Ont. *abbr.* Ontario.

onto *prep.* See ON² 4.

ŏntŏ|gĕ'nĕsis *n.* (Biol.) origin and development of an individual (cf. PHYLOGenesis); hence ∼**gĕnĕ'tIC** *a.* [f. as foll. + Gk *genesis* birth]

ŏntŏ'genỹ *n.* = prec. [f. Gk *ōn ont*- being, pres. part. of *eimi* be, + -o- + -GENY]

ŏntŏ'log|ỹ *n.* branch of metaphysics dealing with the nature of being; so **ŏntolŏ'gICAL** *a.*, ∼**IST** (3) *n.* [f. mod. L *ontologia* (as prec.; see -LOGY)]

ŏ'nus *n.* burden, duty, responsibility; ∼ *probandi* (*pr.* -ă'ndī), ∼ *burden³ of proof*. [L]

ŏ'nward *adv.* & *a.*, **ŏ'nwards** (-z) *adv.* **1.** *adv.* further on, towards the front, with advancing motion. **2.** *a.* directed onward. [f. ON² + -WARD(s)]

ŏ'nỹmous *a.* not anonymous. [back-form. f. ANONYMOUS; see AN- 4]

ŏ'nyx *n.* kind of chalcedony with different colours in layers; ∼ **marble** (with banded onyx-like structure). [ME f. OF *oniche, onix*, f. L f. Gk *onux* finger-nail, onyx]

ōŏ-, *∗**ŏŏ-,** *comb. form.* (Biol.) egg, ovum, as: **o'ocyte,** female gametocyte; **oo'gamous** (ŏŏ'g-), reproducing by union of mobile male and immobile female cells; **ooge'nesis,** production or development of ovum; **oo'logy** (ŏŏ'l-), study or collecting of birds' eggs; **oophore'ctomy,** ovariectomy; **o'osperm,** fertilized ovum. [f. Gk *ōion* egg + -o-]

ōō'dles (-dlz) *n.* (colloq., as *sing.* or *pl.*) great quantity, superabundance, (*oodles of money*). [19th c. US; orig. unkn.]

ōōf *n.* (sl.) money, cash; hence ∼'Y² *a.*, rich. [f. Yiddish *ooftisch*, G *auf dem tische* on the table (of money in gambling)]

ooh (ōō) *int.* expr. surprised pleasure, excitement, pain, etc. [natural excl.]

o'olite *n.* rock, esp. limestone, made up of rounded grains; (Geol.) series of fossiliferous Jurassic rocks of this type; hence **ōōli'tIC** *a.* [f. F *oŏlithe* (as OO-, see -LITE)]

oō′lŏng n. dark kind of cured China tea. [f. Chin. *wulong*, = black dragon]

oomiak. Var. of UMIAK.

oō′mpah n. rhythmical sound of deep-toned brass instruments in military band etc. [imit.]

oŏmph n. (sl.) attractiveness, esp. sex appeal; energy, enthusiasm. [20th c.; orig. uncert.]

-oōn suf. forming ns., orig. f. F wds in stressed *-on* (*dragoon*), esp. f. It. *-one* f. L *-o -onis* (*balloon, buffoon*); replaced by *-on* in recent borrowings and those with unstressed *-on* (*baron*).

oŏnt n. (Anglo-Ind.) camel. [f. Hindi *ūnt*]

oōps int. (colloq.) of surprise or on making obvious mistake. [natural excl.]

oōze¹ n. **1.** wet mud, slime, esp. in river-bed or estuary or on ocean bottom. **2.** tanning liquor, infusion of oak-bark etc. **3.** exudation, sluggish flow, something that oozes. **4.** Hence **oō′zY²** a. [sense 1 f. OE *wāse*, = ON *veisa* puddle; sense 2 f. OE *wōs* juice, sap, = ON *vás*; sense 3 f. foll.]

oōze² v. **1.** v.i. (Of moisture) pass slowly through the pores of a body, exude, percolate; (of substance) exude moisture; (fig.) leak *out* or *away* (*the secret oozed out; my courage is oozing away*). **2.** v.t. emit steadily (lit. or fig.; moisture, information, confidence, encouragement). [ME *wōsen*, f. prec. 2]

op- pref., assim. form of OB- before p.

OP abbr. Dominican [f. *Order of Preachers*, L *Ordo Praedicatorum*]; observation post; opposite prompt.

o.p. abbr. out of print; overproof.

op. abbr. & (colloq.) n. or a. = OPERATION 2, 3; operator; optical (*op art*); opus.

opă′city n. being opaque; obscurity of meaning, obtuseness of understanding. [f. F *opacité* f. L *opacitas -tatis* (as OPAQUE; see -ITY)]

o′pah (-a) n. rare brilliant-coloured large N. Atlantic fish (*Lampris regius*) of mackerel family. [W. Afr. name]

o′pal n. amorphous quartzlike form of hydrated silica, some kinds of which show changing colours (e.g. **common** ~, milk-white or bluish with green, yellow, and red reflections); ~ **glass,** semi- -translucent white glass. [f. F *opale* or f. L *opalus*, prob. ult. f. Skr. *upalas* precious stone]

ōpale′sc|ent a. showing changing colours like opal; so ~ENCE n. [f. prec. + -ESCENT]

o′palīne a. & n. **1.** a. opal-like, opalescent, iridescent. **2.** n. opal glass. [f. OPAL + -INE¹]

opā′que (-k) a. (~r, ~st) & n. **1.** a. not transmitting light, not transparent; impenetrable to sight; not lucid, obscure, dull-witted; hence ~LY² adv., ~NESS n. **2.** n. opaque thing or substance. [ME *opak*, f. L *opacus*, sp. now assim. to F]

op. cit. abbr. in the work already quoted. [f. L *opere citato*]

ōpe a., & v.t. & i. (poet.) = OPEN¹,². [ME, v. f. a., reduced f. OPEN¹ on anal. of p.p. (cf. *awake, wove,* f. *awaken, woven*)]

OPEC (ō′pĕk) abbr. Organization of Petroleum Exporting Countries.

o′pen¹ a. (~er, ~est) & n. **1.** a. not closed or blocked up, allowing entrance or passage or access, having gate or door or lid or part of boundary withdrawn, unenclosed, with ends not joined, unconfined, un- obstructed, uncovered, bare, exposed, undisguised, public, manifest, not exclusive or limited, (*open gate, passage, church, drawer, box, bottle, field, grave, drain, sore, road, sea,* SKY, *carriage, hostilities, scandal, contempt;* LAY³ *open; door flew open*); (of boat) undecked; (of ears) eagerly attentive; (of mouth) with lips apart in voracity, frankness, etc., or esp. in gaping stupidity or surprise; (of mind) accessible to new ideas, un- prejudiced or undecided; (of meeting) admitting all persons, not only members etc.; (of exhibition, building, shop, etc.) accessible to visitors or cus- tomers; (of race, championship, scholarship, etc.) unrestricted as to competitors, (of champion etc.)

having won such a contest; (of electrical circuit) not continuous; (of river, harbour) free of ice; (of weather, winter) not frosty; (of bowels) not con- stipated; (of return ticket) without specified date of travel; ||(of cheque) not crossed; ~ **to,** willing to receive (*offers, persuasion,* etc.), liable to (*attack, mis- interpretation, question,* etc.), available to (*there are three courses open to us*); **throw** ~, cause to be suddenly or widely open, make accessible to. **2.** expanded, unfolded, outspread, spread out, not close, with (wide) intervals, porous, communicative, frank, (*open book* lit. or fig.; *open flower*); (of eyes) watchful (**with** ~ **eyes,** (1) consciously, under no misapprehension, (2) in eager attention or surprise; (of face) ingenuous- -looking; **be** ~ **with,** speak frankly to. **3.** (Mus.) (Of note) (1) produced from unstopped pipe or string or without slide, key, or piston, (2) written with head as outline, e.g. minim. **4.** (Phonet.) (Of vowel) pro- duced with relatively wide opening of mouth (cf. CLOSE¹); (of syllable) ending in vowel. **5.** ||~ **access,** (in library) system whereby users themselves can take books from shelves; **in the** ~ **air,** not in building etc.; *with open* ARM¹*s,* whence ~-ar′med a.; O~ **Brethren,** less exclusive section of Plymouth Brethren; ~**cast,** (of mine or mining) with removal of surface layers and working from above, not from shafts; ~ **city** (that is not defended even if attacked); ~ **country,** (1) land affording wide views, (2) land free from houses or fences; ~ **court** (not *in camera,* or to which public are admitted); ~ **day** (when public may visit place normally closed to them); **the** ~ **door,** free admission of immigration or foreign trade; *force an* ~ *door,* demand from willing giver; ~**-ended,** having no predetermined limit or boundary; ~**-field system** (of medieval agriculture, with arable land of village apportioned in unenclosed strips to villagers); ~ **hand,** generosity, whence ~-ha′nded a.; ~ **harmony** (of chord with wide intervals); ~ **heart,** frankness, unsuspiciousness, kindliness, cordiality, whence ~-hear′ted a.; ~-heart, (of surgery) with heart exposed and no blood circulating through it; ~**-hearth process** (for making steel, in shallow reverberatory furnace); *keep open* HOUSE¹; ~ **ice** (through which navigation is possible); ~ **letter** (esp. of protest, printed in newspaper etc. but addressed to a person); ~ **market** (with free com- petition of buyers and of sellers); ~**-mi′nded,** with open mind, unprejudiced; ~**-mouthed** (-dhd), with mouth open esp. in surprise; ~ **order,** (Mil. etc.) formation with wide spaces between men, units, or ships; ~**-plan,** (of house, office, estate, etc.) with few interior walls; ~ **prison,** = PRISON *without bars;* ~ **question,** matter on which differences of opinion are legitimate; ~ **sandwich** (without bread on top); ~ **score** (Mus., with different staff for each part); ||~ **season** (opp. CLOSE¹ *season*); *open* SECRET; *~ **shelf,** = open access;* so ~ **shelves;** ~ **shop** (opp. CLOSED *shop*); ~**-and-shut case,** (colloq.) perfectly straight- forward matter; ~ **society** (without rigid structure or beliefs); ~ **space** (not obstructed by buildings etc.); ~ **town** (as *open city*); ||O~ **University** (teaching mainly by broadcasting and correspon- dence, and open even to those without scholastic qualifications); *open* VERDICT; ~ **weave** (of fabric with noticeable space between threads etc.); ~- **-work,** pattern with interstices in metal, leather, lace, etc. **6.** Hence ~NESS (-n-n-) n. **7.** n. the ~, open space or country or air, public notice or view. **8.** of open championship etc. [OE, = OS *opan,* OHG *offan,* ON *opinn* f. Gmc **upanaz* (as UP)]

o′pen² v. **1.** v.t. make (more) open; remove cork or cap of (bottle); start or establish or set going (business, shop, account, innings, bidding, debate, campaign, etc.); (abs.) = open a book (*I opened at p. 12*); cere- monially declare (building etc.) to be completed and in use; break up (ground) with plough etc.; cause evacuation of (bowels); bring (prospect, lit. or fig.) to view; reveal or communicate (intentions etc.); make (mind, heart, etc.) more sympathetic or enlightened; (of counsel in lawcourt) make preliminary statement in (case) before calling witnesses. **2.** *v.i.* become open or more open; (of door, room, etc.) give or have access *into* (passage), *on to* (lawn), etc.; (of prospect, lit. or fig.) be revealed; begin speaking, writing, etc., (*by mentioning, with compliment,* etc.); make a start (*session opened yesterday; story opens with a murder*); (of hounds) begin to give tongue; *the* HEAVENS *opened.* **3.** *v.t.* & *i.* (Naut.) get view of by change of position, come into full view, (*take care not to open the obelisk; the harbour light opened*). **4.** ～ **out,** unfold, develop, expand, accelerate, become communicative; ～ **up,** make accessible, bring to notice, reveal, accelerate, begin shooting or sounding. **5.** *open the* BALL[2]; *open the* DOOR *to*; ～ one's **eyes,** show surprise; ～ person's **eyes,** undeceive or enlighten him; ～ **fire,** begin shooting; **not** ～ one's **lips** or **mouth,** remain silent; *open* PARLIAMENT; *open* SESAME; ～ one's **shoulders,** (of batsman) hit freely. **6.** Hence ～ABLE *a.* [OE *openian,* = OS *opanon,* OHG *offanōn* (as prec.)]

ō'**pener** (ō'pn-) *n.* In vbl senses; device for opening bottles, tins, etc.; first item on programme etc.; opening batsman; (in *pl.*) cards entitling holder to open betting in poker etc. [f. prec. + -ER[1]]

ō'**pening**[1] (ō'pn-) *n.* In vbl senses; pair of facing pages in book; gap, passage, aperture; commencement, initial part; counsel's preliminary statement of case; (Chess) recognized sequence of moves for beginning of game; opportunity, favourable situation *for* (employment, transaction, etc.); ～ **time,** hour at which business begins, esp. in sale of alcoholic drinks. [ME, f. OPEN[2] + -ING[1]]

ō'**pening**[2] (ō'pn-) *a.* In vbl senses; initial, first, (*his opening remarks*); ～ **batsman,** one of two who begin the innings. [ME, f. OPEN[2] + -ING[2]]

ō'**penly** *adv.* without concealment, publicly, frankly. [OE *openlīce* (as OPEN[1], -LY[2])]

ō'**pera**[1] *n.* **1.** dramatic performance or composition of which music is an essential part, branch of art concerned with this, place where it is performed; performance humorously compared to opera (*＊*SOAP *opera*); GRAND *opera*; **comic** ～ (with much spoken dialogue, usu. with humorous treatment); **light** ～ (not on serious theme); *opéra comique* (ŏpāra kŏmē'k; with spoken dialogue, not necessarily humorous); *opéra bouffe,* ～ *buffa,* (bŏŏf, bŏŏ'fa; of farcical character); ～ *seria* (sĕr'ia, sār'-), 18th-c. opera on heroic theme with arias. **2.** ～**-cloak, -hood,** (lady's, for wearing at opera or to evening parties); ～**-glass(es),** small binoculars for use at opera or theatre; ～**-hat,** man's tall collapsible hat; ～**-house,** theatre for performance of opera; ||～ **top** (of petticoat etc., cut low with narrow straps orig. for wearing with evening dress). [It. f. L, = labour, work]

ō'**pera**[2]. See OPUS.

ō'**perable** *a.* that can be operated; (Surg.) that can be treated by operation. [f. LL *operabilis* f. L (as OPERATE; see -ABLE)]

ō'**perand** *n.* (Math.) quantity etc. to which an operation is applied. [f. L *operandum,* neut. gerundive of *operari*; see foll., -ND[1]]

ō'**perat|e** *v.* **1.** *v.i.* be in action, produce an effect, exercise influence, (*the tax operates to our disadvantage*); play (*up*)*on* person's fears etc., try to act (*up*)*on*; fulfil its function, (of medicines etc.) have desired effect. **2.** perform surgical or other operation (*on*); (try to) execute purpose; (Mil.) carry on strategic movements; (of stockbroker etc.) buy and sell esp. with view to influencing prices. **3.** *v.t.* bring about, accomplish; manage, work, conduct. **4.** ～**ing-room, -table,** (for use in surgery); ||～**ing-theatre,** room for surgical operations (orig. when done before students). [f. L *operari* work (*opus operis* work) + -ATE[3]]

ōperā't|ĭc *a.* of or like OPERA[1]; hence ～ICALLY *adv.* [irreg. f. OPERA[1], after *dramatic*]

ōperā'tion *n.* **1.** operating or being operated; working, action, way thing works, (time or range of) efficacy or validity, scope, (*is in, comes into, operation; its operation is easily explained*); active process, activity, performance, discharge of function, (*the operation of breathing, thinking, pruning,* etc.); financial transaction; ～(**s**) **research,** = OPERATIONAL *research.* **2.** (Surg.) act done with hand or instrument to some part of body to remedy deformity, injury, disease, pain, etc. **3.** strategic movement esp. of troops, ships, etc. (COMBINED *operation*); (as part of code-name for military or civil campaign: *Operation Overlord, Plowshare*); ～**s room** (from which operations are controlled). **4.** (Math.) subjection of number or quantity or function to process affecting its value or form, e.g. multiplication, differentiation. [ME f. OF, f. L *operatio -onis* (as OPERATE; see -ATION)]

ōperā'tional *a.* engaged in or on operation(s); used for operation(s); able to operate or function; ||～ **research,** scientific study of business and other operations, providing quantitative basis for management decisions. [f. prec. + -AL]

ō'perative *a.* & *n.* **1.** *a.* having effect, in operation, efficacious; (Law) expressing intent to perform a transaction; practical, not theoretical or contemplative; having principal relevance ('*may*' *is the operative word*); of surgical operations; hence ～LY[2] (-vlĭ) *adv.* **2.** *n.* worker, artisan, mechanic, mill-hand; *＊*private detective. [f. LL *operativus* f. L (as OPERATE; see -IVE)]

ō'peratīze (-īz), *v.t.* put (drama etc.) into operatic form. [irreg. after *dramatize*; cf. OPERATIC]

ō'perātor *n.* one who operates; one who makes connections of lines in telephone exchange; person who engages in business, esp. (colloq.) speculatively or shrewdly; (Math.) symbol or function denoting an operation. [LL, f. L (as OPERATE; see -OR)]

ope̅r'cūl|um *n.* (*pl.* ～**a**). fish's gill-cover; plate or flap closing aperture of mollusc's shell when animal is retracted; similar lidlike structure in plants, eggs of some insects, etc.; hence ～AR[1], ～ATE[2], *adjs.,* ～I- *comb. form.* [L (*operire* cover; see -CULE)]

ōpere̅'tta *n.* one-act or short opera; light opera; musical comedy. [It. (dim. of OPERA; cf. -ETTE)]

ō'perōse *a.* (arch.) requiring or showing or taking great pains, laborious; hence ～LY[2] (-slĭ) *adv.,* ～NESS (-sn-) *n.* [f. L *operosus* (*opus operis* work; see -OSE[1])]

ō'phicleide (-līd) *n.* obsolete wind instrument consisting of tapering brass tube bent double serving as bass or alto to key-bugle; powerful organ reed-stop. [f. F *ophicléide* f. Gk *ophis* serpent + *kleis kleidos* key]

ophĭ'dĭan *a.* & *n.* (member) of the Ophidia or Serpentes, suborder of reptiles including the snakes; snake(like). [f. mod. L *Ophidia* f. Gk *ophis* snake + -IA[2]; see -AN]

ō'phĭo- *comb. form.* snake, as ～LATRY (-ŏ'l-), serpent-worship, ～LOGY (-ŏ'l-), *ns.* [f. Gk *ophis* snake + -o-]

ō'phīte *n.* (Min.) serpentine, serpentine marble; hence **ophī'tĭc** *a.* [f. L f. Gk *ophitēs* (as prec.; see -ITE[1] (2))]

ŏphthǎ'lmĭa, ŏphthǎlmī'tĭs, *ns.* inflammation of the eye, esp. conjunctivitis. [LL, mod. L, f. Gk (*ophthalmos* eye); see -IA[1], -ITIS]

ŏphthǎ'lmĭc *a.* of the eye; affected with ophthalmia; good for eye-disease; ||～ **optician** (qualified to prescribe as well as dispense spectacle etc.). [f. L f. Gk *ophthalmikos* (as prec.; see -IC)]

ŏphthǎ'lmo- *comb. form.* eye, as ～LOGY (-ŏ'l-), scientific study of the eye; ～SCOPE, instrument for inspecting retina etc. [f. Gk *ophthalmos* eye + -o-]

ō'pĭate[1] *a.* & *n.* **1.** *a.* containing opium; narcotic, soporific. **2.** *n.* drug containing opium and easing pain or inducing sleep; (fig.) thing that causes inaction or soothes the feelings. [f. med. L *opiatus, -um* (as foll.; see -ATE[2])]

ō'pĭate[2] *v.t.* mix with opium; stupefy. [f. med. L *opiare* f. L OPIUM, + -ATE[3]]

opi'ne *v.t.* express or hold the opinion (*that*). [f. L *opinari* think, believe]

opi'nion (-yon) *n.* **1.** judgement or belief based on grounds short of proof, provisional conviction, view held as probable, (**in my** ~, as it seems to me; **be of** (the) ~ **that**, believe; **a matter of** ~, disputable point); (**public**) ~, views or sentiments, esp. on moral questions, prevalent among people in general; ~ **poll**, = GALLUP *poll*. **2.** what one thinks on or on a particular question, a belief, a conviction, (*the courage of, act up to,* one's *opinions*). **3.** formal statement by expert when consulted of what he holds to be the fact or the right course, professional advice, (*you had better have another, a second, opinion*); *(Law)* formal statement of reasons for judgement given. **4.** estimate (*have, formed, a very high, good, poor, low, favourable, opinion of him*); favourable estimate (*has a great opinion of himself*). [ME f. OF, f. L *opinio -onis* (as OPINE; see -ION)]

opi'nionātěd (-nyo-) *a.* obstinate in opinion, dogmatic; self-willed; hence ~NESS *n.* [f. obs. *opinionate* in same sense, f. prec. +-ATE²]

opi'nionātive (-nyo-) *a.* = prec. [f. OPINION +-ATIVE]

ŏpĭsŏ'mĕter *n.* instrument for measuring curved lines as on map, made of wheel running on screw and afterwards returned to original position by rolling along straight scale. [f. Gk *opisō* backwards + -METER]

opi'stho- *comb. form.* behind, as: ~GRAPH, (Gk & Rom. Ant.) parchment or slab with writing on both sides. [f. Gk *opisthen* behind + -O-]

ō'pĭum *n.* reddish-brown heavy-scented bitter drug prepared from juice of the opium POPPY (*Papaver somniferum*), smoked or eaten as stimulant, intoxicant, or narcotic, and used as sedative (LAUDANUM) in medicine; ~ **den**, haunt of opium-smokers; ~ **habit** (of taking opium); hence ~ISM (5) *n.*, ~IZE (5) *v.t.* [ME, f. L f. Gk *opion* poppy-juice (*opos* juice)]

ŏpodě'ldŏc *n.* liniment made with soap and camphor. [wd used and prob. made by Paracelsus (*c.* 1540) for kinds of medical plaster]

opō'panăx *n.* fetid gum resin formerly used in medicine, from root of *Opopanax chironium*; gum resin like myrrh, used in perfumery; ~ **tree**, sponge-tree. [ME f. L f. Gk (*opos* juice, *panax* f. as PANACEA)]

opŏ'ssum *n.* **1.** American small arboreal or aquatic nocturnal marsupial of family Didelphidae, with thumbed hind-foot (see also POSSUM). **2.** (Austral. & NZ). = POSSUM 2. [f. Virginian Ind. *āpassūm*]

opp. *abbr.* opposite.

ŏ'ppĭdan *a.* & *n.* **1.** (inhabitant) of a town. **2.** *n.* ‖non--colleger at Eton, living in boarding-house in town. [f. L *oppidanus* of town other than Rome (*oppidum* town; see -AN)]

ŏ'ppĭlāte *v.t.* (arch. Med.) block up, obstruct; so ~A'TION *n.* [f. L OP(*pilare* ram down)]

‖**ŏ'ppō** *n.* (*pl.* ~s). (sl.) colleague, friend. [f. OPPOSITE *number*]

oppŏ'nency̆ *n.* antagonism, opposition. [f. foll. + -ENCY]

oppŏ'nent *a.* & *n.* **1.** *a.* opposing, contrary, opposed; ~ **muscle** (opposing thumb or lateral digit to other digit). **2.** *n.* person opposed or on opposing side in contest etc. [f. L OP(*ponere* place); see -ENT]

ŏppŏrtūne (ŏ'-, -ū'n) *a.* (Of time) suitable, well--selected or as favourable as if chosen; (of action or event) well-timed, done or occurring by design or chance at favourable time; hence ~LY² (-nlĭ) *adv.*, ~NESS (-n-n-) *n.* [ME, f. OF *opportun -une* f. L OP(*portunus* f. *portus* harbour), orig. of wind driving towards harbour]

ŏppŏrtūn|ism (-ū'-, ŏ'-) *n.* allowing of due or undue weight to circumstances of the time in determining policy; grasping at opportunities when they occur; preference of what can to what should be done, compromise, practical politics, adaptation to circumstances; putting of expediency before principle; so ~IST (2) *n.* [f. prec. +-ISM, after It. (-*ismo*) and F (-*isme*), Polit. terms]

ŏppŏrtū'nitў̆ *n.* favourable occasion, good chance, (*of doing, to do, for* action, or abs.; *find, make, get, seize, give, afford, an opportunity; take the* (first) *opportunity of*); ~ **knocks**, an opportunity occurs. [ME, f. OF *opportunité* f. L *opportunitas -tatis* (as OPPORTUNE; see -ITY)]

oppŏ's|e (-z) *v.t.* **1.** place or produce or cite (thing, person) as obstacle, antagonist, counterpoise, or contrast, *to*, represent (things) as antithetical, (*to fury let us oppose patience; you are opposing things that are practically identical; to Plato I oppose Aristotle; opposed himself to it with all his power*); place (thumb or big toe) against finger(s) or other toe(s) front to front, whence ~ABLE (-z-) *a.* **2.** set oneself against (person, thing); withstand, resist, obstruct, propose the rejection of (resolution, motion, application, etc.); (abs.) act as opponent(s) or as check (*the duty of an Opposition is to oppose; the opposing team*). **3.** (in *p.p.*) contrary, opposite, contrasted, (*characters strongly opposed; black is opposed to white; a proper meal as opposed to just a snack; theories as opposed to facts*); (of person) hostile, adverse, (*is firmly opposed to the merger*). **4.** Hence ~eLESS (-zl-) *a.*, (poet. or rhet.) irresistible. [ME, f. OF *opposer* f. L *opponere* (see OPPONENT, POSE¹)]

ŏ'pposite (-z-) *a., n., adv.,* & *prep.* **1.** *a.* having position on the other or farther side, facing, front to front or back to back, (*on opposite sides of the square; came from, went in, opposite directions; the tree opposite to the house*); (of angles) between opposite directions of two intersecting lines; (of leaves etc.) placed at same height on opposite sides of stem, or placed straight in front of other organ, opp. ALTERNATE¹; ~ **number**, person or thing similarly placed in another set etc. to the given one. **2.** of contrary kind, diametrically different *to* or *from*, being the other of a contrasted pair, (*of an opposite kind to, from, what I expected*; **the** ~ **sex**, men in relation to women or vice versa. **3.** Hence ~LY² (-tlĭ) *adv.*, ~NESS (-tn-) *n.* **4.** *n.* opposite thing or term (*you are cold-blooded, she is the opposite; black is the opposite of white; the most extreme opposites have some qualities in common*). **5.** *adv.* & *prep.* in opposite place, position, or direction (to) (*tree stands opposite, opposite the house*); across the street (*there was an explosion opposite*); ~ **prompt**, side of theatre stage usu. to actor's right; **play** ~, (of lead in stage-play or film) have (specified actor or actress) as one's leading man or lady. [ME f. OF, f. L *oppositus* p.p. of *opponere*; see OPPONENT, -ITE¹]

ŏpposi'tion (-z-) *n.* **1.** placing opposite, opposing (of thumb); contrast, antithesis; diametrically opposite position (esp. Astrol. & Astron., of two heavenly bodies when their longitude differs by 180°, opp. *conjunction*); **in** ~, (of planet) opposite sun. **2.** (Logic). relation between two propositions with same subject and predicate but differing in quantity or quality or both. **3.** antagonism, resistance, being hostile, (*offer, meet with, determined opposition*; put it in opposition to public opinion). **4.** ‖**the O**~, **Her Majesty's O**~, chief parliamentary party opposed to that in office (*the Leader of the Opposition; from the Opposition benches*); **in** ~, occupying this position, esp. opp. *in office.* **5.** any party opposed to some proposal; one's competitors or rivals. **6.** Hence ~AL *a.* [ME f. OF, f. L OP(*positio -onis*; see POSITION)]

ŏppŏ'sitive (-z-) *a.* adversative, antithetic; fond of opposing. [f. med. L *oppositivus* (as prec.; see -IVE)]

opprě'ss *v.t.* lie heavy on, weigh down, (spirits, imagination, etc.); govern tyrannically, keep under by coercion, subject to continual cruelty or injustice; so ~ION (-shon), ~OR, *ns.* [ME, f. OF *oppresser* f. med. L OP(*pressare* f. L *premere* PRESS²)]

opprě'ssive *a.* oppressing; tyrannical; difficult to endure; (of weather etc., esp.) hot and close; hence ~LY² (-vlĭ) *adv.*, ~NESS (-vn-) *n.* [f. F *oppressif -ive* f. med. L *oppressivus* (as prec.; see -IVE)]

ŏpprō'brious *a.* conveying reproach; abusive, vituperative; hence ~LY² *adv.* [ME, f. LL *opprobriosus* (as foll.; see -OUS)]

ŏpprō'brium *n.* disgrace attaching to some act or

conduct, infamy; cause of this. [L, f. OP(*probrum* disgraceful act)]

oppŭ′gn (-ū′n) *v.t.* controvert, call in question. [ME, f. L OP(*pugnare* fight) attack, besiege]

oppŭ′gn|ant *a.* attacking, opposing; so ∽ANCE, ∽ANCY, **ŏppŭgnā′**TION, *ns.* [f. as prec.; see -ANT]

ŏ′psimäth *n.* (literary). one who learns only late in life; so **ŏpsi′math**Y[1] *n.* [f. Gk *opsimathēs* (*opse* late, *math-* learn)]

ŏ′psonin *n.* substance in blood serum assisting action of phagocytes; hence **ŏpsŏ′n**IC *a.* [f. Gk *opsōnion* victuals + -IN]

ŏpt *v.i.* exercise an option, make choice, (*between* alternatives or *for* alternative); ∽ **out** (**of**), choose not to participate (in); hence ∽′ANT *n.* (esp. person who may choose one of two nationalities). [f. F *opter* f. L *optare* choose, wish]

ŏptative (ŏ′pta-, ŏptā′-) *a.* & *n.* (Gram.) **1.** *a.* expressing wish; ∽ **mood**, set of verb-forms of this kind, distinct chiefly in Sanskrit and Greek; hence ∽LY[2] (-vlĭ) *adv.* **2.** *n.* optative mood. [f. F *optatif -ive* f. LL *optativus* (as prec.; see -ATIVE)]

ŏ′ptic *a.* & *n.* **1.** *a.* (Anat.) of the eye or sense of sight (*optic nerve, neuritis*, etc.); ∽ **angle** (between lines from extremities of object to eye, or from two eyes to one point); ∽ **axis**, (1) axis of eye, (2) direction in doubly refracting crystal for which no double refraction occurs; ∽ **lobe**, dorsal lobe of midbrain, from which optic nerves arise. **2.** *n.* lens etc. in optical instrument; (arch. or joc.) eye. **3.** ||(*O*∽; **P**). device fastened to neck of bottle for measuring out spirits. **4.** (in *pl.*, treated as *sing.*) science of sight and esp. of the laws of light as its medium; science of similar behaviour of other radiation or particles (*electron optics*); components of optical instrument. [f. F *optique* or f. med. L f. Gk *optikos* (*optos* seen f. *op-* see); sense 4 renders med. L f. Gk *optika* n. pl.; see -IC]

ŏ′ptical *a.* visual, ocular; ∽ **art** (giving illusions of movement by use of contrasting colours); ∽ **illusion**, (instance of) involuntary mental misinterpretation of thing seen, due to its deceptive appearance. **2.** of sight or light in relation to each other; belonging to optics; constructed to assist sight or on the principles of optics; ∽ **activity**, (Chem.) property of rotating plane of polarization of light; ∽ **glass** (very pure, for lenses etc.); ∽ **microscope** (using direct perception of light, opp. electron microscope etc.). **3.** Hence ∽LY[2] *adv.* [f. prec. + -AL; see -ICAL]

ŏpti′cian (-shan) *n.* maker or seller of optical instruments, esp. spectacles; person trained in provision of means to correct defects of eyesight (OPHTHALMIC *optician*). [f. F *opticien* f. med. L *optica* (see OPTIC, -ICIAN)]

ŏ′ptimal *a.* = OPTIMUM. [f. L *optimus* best + -AL]

ŏ′ptim|ism *n.* doctrine, esp. as set forth by Leibniz, that the actual world is the best of all possible worlds; view that good must ultimately prevail over evil in the universe; hopeful disposition, inclination to take favourable views (cf. PESSIMISM); so ∽IST (2) *n.*, ∽i′st**IC** *a.*, ∽i′st**ICALLY** *adv.* [f. F *optimisme* f. L OPTIMUM; see -ISM]

ŏ′ptimize, -ise (-īz), *v.* **1.** *v.t.* make optimum; make the most of. **2.** *v.i.* be optimist. [f. L *optimus* best + -IZE]

ŏ′ptim|um (*pl.* ∽a) & *a.* **1.** *n.* most favourable (natural) conditions (for growth, reproduction, etc.); best compromise between opposing tendencies. **2.** *a.* best or most favourable (*optimum temperature*). [L, neut. (as n.) of *optimus* best]

ŏ′ption *n.* choice, choosing, thing that is or may be chosen, (*make* one's *option*; SOFT *option*; *none of the options is satisfactory*); liberty of choosing, freedom of choice, (LOCAL[2] *option*; *imprisonment without the option* (*of a fine*); **have no** ∽ **but to**, must; **keep** or **leave** one's ∽**s open**, not commit oneself); (St. Exch. etc.) purchased right to call for, or make delivery, or either, within specified time of specified stocks etc. at specified rate. [F, or f. L *optio* (st. of *optare* choose; see -ION)]

ŏ′ptional *a.* not obligatory; hence ∽LY[2] *adv.* [f. prec. + -AL]

ŏptŏ′|mĕter *n.* instrument for testing the refractive power and visual range of the eye; hence ∽**mĕtr**IST (3) *n.*, sight-tester, *ophthalmic optician, ∽**METRY** *n.* [f. Gk *optos* seen + -METER]

ŏ′ptophōne *n.* instrument converting light into sound, and so enabling the blind to read print etc. by ear. [f. as prec. + -PHONE]

ŏ′pŭl|ent *a.* rich, wealthy; abounding, abundant, profuse; luxurious; hence or cogn. ∽ENCE *n.*, ∽ent**LY**[2] *adv.* [f. L *opulens, opulentus* (*opes* wealth; see -ULENT)]

ōpŭ′ntia (-sha) *n.* cactus of genus *Opuntia*; prickly pear. [L, name of a plant, f. *Opus -untis* in Locris in ancient Greece]

ŏ′pus *n.* (*pl.* o′**pera**). **1.** musician's separate composition or set of compositions of any kind (used esp. in citing it from among his works by number usu. indicating order of publication; abbr. *op.*: *Beethoven op.* 15). **2.** ∽ (**magnum**), **magnum opus**, great literary undertaking, writer's or other artist's chief production. [L, = work]

opŭ′scŭl|e, opŭ′scŭl|um (*pl.* ∽a), *ns.* minor musical or literary composition. [(*-ule* F) f. L *opusculum* dim. of prec.; see -CULE]

ōr[1] *n.* & *a.* (usu. placed after *n.*) (Her.) gold or yellow (colour). [F, f. L *aurum* gold]

ōr[2] *prep.* & *conj.* (arch.) before (in time), esp. (poet.) *or ever, or e'er.* [OE *ār* f. ON *ár*, = OE *ǣr* ERE]

or[3] (*when stressed*, ōr) *conj.* introducing second of two alternatives (*white or black*), all but the first of any number (*white or grey or black*), only the last of any number (*white, grey, or black*), the second of each of several pairs (*white or black, red or yellow, blue or green*), (poet.) each of two (*or in the heart or in the head*); or ELSE; *or* so[1] 11; **not A or B**, not A, and also not B. An alternative introduced by *or* may be (1) on equal footing with preceding (*will you be there or not?*; *any Tom, Dick, or Harry*); (2) as true as the preceding (*tomatoes are red or yellow*); (3) mere synonym (*common or garden heliotrope*); (4) indication that preceding is doubtfully accurate (**one or two, five or six**, etc., a few); (5) explanation of preceding (*saw a dug-out or hollowed-tree boat*); (6) statement of only remaining possibility or choice given (often after *either*; *a thing must surely be or not be*; *for goodness' sake either take it or leave it*); (7) statement of result of rejection etc. of preceding (often with *else*; *she must weep or she must die*; *run, or else you will be late*); (8) second etc. member of indirect question or conditional protasis after *whether* (*ask him whether he was there or not*; *must do it whether I like or dislike it*); (9) significant afterthought (*he obviously knows the reason—or is he bluffing?*). [reduced form of obs. *other conj.* (which superseded OE *oththe* or), of uncert. orig.]

-or *suf.* **1.** Forming *ns.* (1) denoting condition, f. or after OF *-or, -ur* or f. L *-or -oris* (*error, horror, tremor*), (2) denoting agent, f. or after AF *-eour*, OF *-ĕor, -ĕur* or f. L *-ator, -etor, -itor* (*donor, emperor, tailor, vendor*), (3) denoting agent, f. L *-or* (*actor, doctor, inventor; creator, creditor, equator, escalator*), (4) f. other *sufs.* (*bachelor, mirror, sailor*), (5) * = -OUR (*color*); in Law (often -ŏ′r) opp. -EE (*mortgagor, obligor*); of inanimate opp. personal agents (*conveyor, resistor, sensor*; cf. -ER[1]). **2.** Forming *adjs.* f. AF *-our* f. L *-or*, w. comparative sense (*major, senior*).

OR *abbr.* operational research; Oregon; other ranks.

ŏ′rache, ŏ′rach, *n.* wild or kitchen-garden plant of genus *Atriplex*, esp. species used instead of spinach. [ME *arage* f. AF *arasche* f. L *atriplex* f. Gk *atraphaxus*]

ŏ′racle *n.* **1.** place at which ancient Greeks etc. were accustomed to consult their deities for advice or prophecy; ||**work the ∽**, secure desired answer by secretly influencing priests etc., (fig.) bring secret influence to bear in one's favour. **2.** response, often ambiguous or obscure, given at such place. **3.**

(personal or other means of conveying) divine inspiration or revelation. **4.** person or thing (regarded as) serving as infallible though mysterious guide, test, or indicator; authoritative, profoundly wise, or mysterious adviser or advice, judge or judgement, prophet or prophecy. [ME f. OF, f. L *oraculum* (*orare* speak)]

orā′cūlar *a.* of oracle(s); mysterious or ambiguous like the ancient oracles; hence ~ITY (-ă′r-) *n.*, ~LY² *adv.* [f. L (as prec.) + -AR¹]

ōr′acў *n.* ability to express oneself fluently in speech. [f. L *os oris* mouth + -ACY, after *literacy*]

ōr′al *a.* & *n.* **1.** *a.* spoken, verbal, by word of mouth, not written, (*oral examination, tradition*); done or taken by the mouth (*oral contraceptive*); (Anat.) of the mouth; ~ **sex**, fellatio, cunnilingus, etc.; ~ **society** (that has not reached the stage of literacy); hence ~LY² *adv.* **2.** *n.* (colloq.) oral examination etc. [f. LL *oralis* f. L *os oris* mouth; see -AL]

ō′range¹ (-ĭnj) *n.* & *a.* **1.** *n.* (evergreen tree, *Citrus aurantium* or *C. sinensis*, bearing fragrant white flowers and) large roundish many-celled juicy acid or sweet fruit enclosed in bright reddish-yellow tough rind; fruit or plant resembling this; *bitter* or SEVILLE *orange*; BLENHEIM *Orange*; BLOOD¹, CHINA¹, MANDARIN², *orange*; **mock** ~, the shrub *Philadelphus coronarius*, with strong-scented white usu. clustered flowers; TANGERINE *orange*; hence **ō′rang**ERY (3) (-ĭnj-) *n.* **2.** ~(-colour), reddish yellow like colour of orange, between red and yellow in spectrum; orange pigment. **3.** ~-blossom, flowers of orange, often worn by bride at wedding; ~-**flower water**, solution of neroli in water; *orange* MARMALADE; ~-**peel**, (rough surface resembling) skin of orange; ~ **pekoe** (made from very small leaves); *orange* SQUASH¹; ~-**stick**, thin stick pointed at one end and usu. of orange-wood for manicuring finger-nails; ~-**tip**, butterfly having wings tipped with orange; ~-**wood** (of orange tree). **4.** *a.* orange-coloured, reddish-yellow. [ME f. OF *orenge*, ult. f. Arab. *nāranj* f. Pers *nārang*]

O′range² (ŏ′rĭnj) *a.* of the extreme Protestants in Ireland, esp. in Ulster, whence ~ISM (3) *n.*; ~**man**, member of political society formed 1795 to support Protestantism in Ireland; ~**man's Day**, 12 July in N. Ireland as holiday on anniversary of battles of 1690 and 1691. [prob. f. ~ Lodge of Belfast Freemasons, named after William of ~ (William III), member of princely house from ~ in S. France]

ŏrangeā′de (-ĭnjā′d) *n.* effervescent or still drink of orange juice etc.; synthetic substitute for this. [f. ORANGE¹ + -ADE l]

Orangism. Var. of ORANGE²*ism*.

ŏrāng-u′tăn, -ou′tăng (-ŏŏ′t-, -ută′-) *n.* large long-armed arboreal anthropoid ape (*Pongo pygmaeus*) of Borneo and Sumatra. [Malay *ōrang ūtan* wild man]

orā′te *v.i.* (joc. or derog.) make speech, hold forth, play the orator. [back-form. f. foll.]

orā′tion *n.* **1.** formal address or harangue or discourse esp. of ceremonial kind. **2.** (Gram.) language, way of speaking; **direct** ~, *oratio recta*, person's words as actually spoken; **indirect** or **oblique** ~, *oratio obliqua*, = REPORT*ed speech*. [ME, f. L *oratio* discourse, prayer (*orare* speak, pray; see -ATION)]

ŏ′rator *n.* **1.** maker of a speech; eloquent public speaker; ||(**public**) ~, official speaking for university on ceremonial occasions. **2.** *plaintiff in chancery. [ME, f. AF *oratour*, OF *orateur* f. L *orator -oris* speaker, pleader, (as prec.; see -OR)]

ŏratō′rĭō *n.* (*pl.* ~s). semi-dramatic musical composition usu. on sacred theme performed by soloists, chorus, and orchestra, without action, scenery, or costume. [It., f. eccl. L *oratorium*, orig. of musical services at church of ORATORY¹ of St. Philip Neri in Rome]

ŏ′ratorў¹ *n.* **1.** small chapel, place for private worship. **2.** (O~). RC religious society of simple priests without vows founded in Rome 1564 to give plain preaching and popular services; branch of this in England etc.;

hence **ŏratō′r′**IAN *a.* & *n.* [ME, f. AF *oratorie*, OF *oratoire* f. eccl. L *oratorium* neut. (as n.) of L *oratorius* (*orare* pray, speak; see -ORY)]

ŏ′ratorў² *n.* (art of making) speeches, rhetoric; highly coloured presentation of facts; eloquent or exaggerating language; hence **ŏratō′r**ICAL *a.* [f. L *oratoria* (*ars* art) of speaking, fem. of *oratorius* (see prec.)]

ôrb *n.* & *v.* **1.** *n.* sphere, globe; heavenly body; (poet.) eyeball, eye. **2.** globe surmounted by cross as part of regalia. **3.** *v.t.* & *i.* enclose in, form or gather into, orb. [f. L *orbis* ring]

ôrbi′cūl|ar *a.* circular, disc-shaped, ring-shaped (~**ar muscle**, sphincter); spherical, globular, rounded, (fig.) forming complete whole; hence or cogn. ~**ă′r**ITY *n.*, ~**ar**LY² *adv.*, ~**ATE²** *a.* (of leaf etc.). [ME, f. LL *orbicularis* f. L *orbiculus* dim. of *orbis* ring; see -CULE, -AR¹]

ôr′bĭt *n.* & *v.* **1.** *n.* eye-socket; border round eye of bird or insect. **2.** curved usu. closed course of planet, comet, satellite, spacecraft, etc.; path of electron round atomic nucleus; state of motion in an orbit (*in, into, orbit*); (fig.) range, sphere of action. **3.** *v.i.* (Of satellite etc.) move in an orbit; fly in a circle. **4.** *v.t.* move in orbit round (body etc.); put into orbit. **5.** Hence ~ER¹ *n.*, spacecraft (planned to be) in orbit. [f. L *orbita* track of wheel or moon, in med. L eye-cavity, fem. (as n.) of *orbitus* circular (*orbis* ring)]

ôr′bital *a.* & *n.* **1.** *a.* (Anat., Astron., & Phys.) of orbit(s). **2.** (Of road) passing round the outside of a city. **3.** *n.* (Phys.) state or function representing possible motion of electron round atomic nucleus. [f. prec. + -AL]

ôrc, ôr′ca, *n.* cetacean of genus *Orca*, esp. killer whale; sea or other monster. [f. F *orque* or f. L *orca* kind of whale]

Orcā′dian (ōr-) *a.* & *n.* (native or inhabitant) of Orkney. [f. L *Orcades* Orkney Islands + -IAN]

orch. *abbr.* orchestra; orchestrated by.

ôr′chard *n.* enclosure with fruit-trees, ~IST *n.*, ~**man**, fruit-grower; hence ~ING¹ *n.*, cultivation of fruit-trees. [OE *ortgeard* f. L *hortus* garden + YARD²]

ôrchě′st|ĭc (-k-) *a.* of dancing; hence ~ICS *n.* [f. Gk *orkhēstikos* (*orkhēstēs* dancer; see foll.)]

ôr′chěstra (-k-) *n.* **1.** semicircular space in front of ancient-Greek theatre-stage where chorus danced and sang. **2.** part of modern theatre or concert-room assigned to band or chorus; *theatre stalls; ~ **pit** (in front of stage and on lower level); ~ **stalls**, front rows of stalls. **3.** (Mus.) body of instrumental performers, usu. large combination of string, wood-wind, brass, and percussion instruments, esp. in theatre or concert-room; hence **ôrchě′str**AL (k) *a.* [L, f. Gk *orkhēstra* (*orkheomai* to dance)]

ôr′chestr|āte (-k-) *v.t.* compose, arrange, or score, for orchestral performance; (fig.) combine (elements of) harmoniously or for maximum effect; hence ~A′TION, ~**āt**or, *ns.* [f. prec. + -ATE³]

ôrchestri′na (-kĭstrē′-), *ôrchě′strion (-k-), *ns.* mechanical instrument meant to give orchestra-like effect. [f. ORCHESTRA + -INA¹; cf. *accordion*]

ôr′chid (-k-) *n.* member of large family Orchidaceae of monocotyledonous plants, often epiphytic, usu. with one petal much larger than the other two and in exotic kinds having fantastic shapes and brilliant colours; hence ~A′CEOUS *a.*, ~IST (3), ~ŏ′LOGY, *ns.* [f. mod. L *Orchid(ac)eae*, irreg. f. L ORCHIS; see -ID²]

ôr′chil, ôrchǐ′lla, *n.* red or violet dye from lichen, esp. *Roccella tinctoria*; lichen yielding it. [ME, f. OF *orcheil* etc., perh. ult. f. L *herba urceolaris* plant for polishing glass pitchers (*urceolus* pitcher); cf. ARCHIL]

ôr′chis (-k-) *n.* orchid, esp. wild kind, or of genus *Orchis* with tuberous root and erect fleshy stem having spike of usu. purple or red flowers. [L f. Gk *orkhis*, orig. = testicle (w. ref. to shape of tuber)]

ôrchī′tǐs (-k-) *n.* inflammation of the testicles. [mod. L, f. Gk *orkhis* testicle; see -ITIS]

ôr′cin(ōl) *n.* (Chem.) colourless crystalline substance extracted from lichens and yielding various dyes by chemical treatment. [f. mod. L *orcina* f. It. *orcello* orchil + -IN; see -OL]

ord. *abbr.* ordinary.

ŏrdai'n *v.t.* **1.** (Eccl.) appoint ceremonially to Christian ministry, confer holy orders (esp. those of deacon or priest) on, (*was ordained priest, elder,* etc., or abs.). **2.** (Of God, fate, etc.) destine, appoint, (*has ordained the time, death as our lot, us mortal, us to die, that we should live*). **3.** appoint authoritatively, decree, enact, (thing, *that; what the laws ordain*). **4.** So ~MENT *n.* [ME, f. AF *ordeiner*, OF *ordein*- stressed stem of *ordener* f. L *ordinare* (*ordo -inis* order)]

ŏrdeal (-ē'l, -ē'al) *n.* **1.** ancient Gmc etc. mode of deciding suspected person's guilt or innocence by subjecting him to physical test such as plunging hand in boiling water, safe endurance of which was taken as divine acquittal. **2.** experience that tests character or endurance, severe trial. **3.** ~ **bean,** Calabar bean; ~ **tree,** tanghin. [OE *ordāl, ordēl,* = OS *urdēli,* OHG *urteili* judgement f. Gmc **uzdailjam* (**uz-* out, **dailjan* DEAL²)]

ŏr'der[1] *n.* **1.** social class or rank, set of persons separate and homogeneous as regards social level, (*the higher, lower, orders; all orders and degrees of men; the order of baronets; the clerical, military, order*); kind, sort, (*talents of a high, considerations of quite another, order*). **2.** any of the nine grades of angelic beings (seraphim, cherubim, thrones, dominations, principalities, powers, virtues, archangels, angels); grade of Christian ministry (**holy** ~**s,** those of bishop, priest, and deacon; **minor** ~**s,** (RC Hist.) those of acolyte, exorcist, reader, and door-keeper); (**holy**) ~**s,** status of clergyman; **take** (**holy**) ~**s,** be ordained; **in** (**holy**) ~**s,** ordained. **3.** fraternity of monks and friars, or formerly of knights, bound by common rule of life (*the Franciscan order; the order of Templars*); Masonic or similar fraternity; company usu. instituted by sovereign to which distinguished persons are admitted by way of honour or reward (*Order of the* GARTER, *the* BATH¹, *Merit; Royal* VICTORIAN *Order*), insignia worn by members of this (*was wearing the order of the Golden Fleece*). **4.** (Archit.) mode of treatment with established proportions between parts, esp. one of the **five** (**classical**) ~**s,** Doric, Ionic, Corinthian, Tuscan, and Composite, of column and entablature, the first three being Greek in origin, the others Roman. **5.** (Math.) degree of complexity (*equation* **of the first** ~, involving only first derivative etc.); ~ (**of magnitude**), class in a system of classification determined by size, usu. by powers of 10; **of, in, on, the** ~ **of,** having the order of magnitude specified by (*errors of the order of one in a million*), approximately (*of the order of 7%*). **6.** (Biol.) classification-group below class and above family; NATURAL *order.* **7.** sequence, succession, manner of following, (*in alphabetical, chronological,* etc., *order; in order of merit; follow the order of events; inverts the natural order;* **in** ~, one after another according to some principle; **out of** ~, not systematically arranged); regular array, condition in which every part or unit is in its right place, tidiness, normal or healthy or efficient state, (*drew them up in order; are scattered without any order; love of order;* **in bad** ~, **out of** ~, not in ~, not working rightly; **in** ~, **in good** ~, **in working** etc. ~, ready or fit for use; OPEN¹ *order*); (Mil.) style of dress and equipment (REVIEW¹ *order*). **8.** (arch.) suitable action, measures, (*take order to do;* **take** ~ **with,** arrange, dispose of). **9.** constitution of the world, way things normally happen, collective manifestations of natural forces or laws, natural or moral or spiritual system with definite tendencies, (esp. *the order of nature* or *things* or *the world; the old order changeth; whether there is a moral order or not*). **10.** stated form of divine service (*the order of confirmation*). **11.** principles of decorum and rules of procedure accepted by legislative assembly or public meeting, or enforced by its president (*Speaker called him to order*);

O~! O~!, protest against infringement of it; **call to** ~, (of chairman) declare (meeting) open; **point of** ~, (interruption of debate etc. with) inquiry whether something being said or done is **in** or **out of** ~, i.e. according or not according to rules etc.; ~ **of the day,** programme, business set down for treatment, (fig.) prevailing state of things, principal topic of action, procedure decided upon; ~-**paper,** written or printed order of the day. **12.** prevalence of constituted authority, law-abiding state, absence of riot, turbulence, and violent crime, (LAW¹ *and order; order was restored;* **keep** ~, enforce it). **13.** (Mil.) the ~, position of company etc. with arms ordered (see ORDER²). **14. in** ~ **to** do, with a view to, for the purpose of, doing; **in** ~ **that,** with the intention or to the end that. **15.** (in *sing.* or *pl.*) command, injunction, authoritative direction or instruction, (*gave orders, an order, the order, for thing to be done, that it should be* done, etc.; *judge gave, made, refused, an order; obedient to orders*); ||O~ **in Council,** sovereign's order on some administrative matter given by advice of Privy Council; **by** ~, according to direction of the proper authority; *till* FURTHER *orders;* STANDING² *orders; under* STARTER'*s orders.* **16.** (**banker's**) ~, instruction (to bank) to pay money or deliver property, signed by owner or responsible agent; **money** ~ (for payment of specified sum, esp. issued by Post Office or bank for payment at another branch); ||**postal** ~, ||**post-office** ~, kinds of Post-Office money order, the latter payable only to a specified person; STANDING² *order.* **17.** (Commerc. etc.) direction to manufacturer, tradesman, waiter, etc., to supply something; quantity of goods thus supplied; **made to** ~, made according to special directions, to suit individual measurements, etc., (opp. *ready-made*), (fig.) exactly what is wanted; **is on** ~, has been ordered but not yet received; *a large or* TALL *order;* STANDING² *order;* ~-**book** (in which tradesman enters orders); ~-**form,** outline of order, in which details are to be filled in by customer. **18.** pass admitting bearer gratis, cheap, or as privilege, to theatre, museum, private house, etc.; ~ **to view,** house-agent's request for client to be allowed to inspect premises. [ME f. OF *ordre* f. L *ordo ordinis* row, array, degree, command, etc.]

ŏr'der² *v.t.* **1.** put in order, array, regulate, (*order* one's *affairs; they order this matter better in France*); ~ **arms,** (Mil.) stand rifle with butt on ground and hold it close to right side. **2.** (Of God, fate, etc.) ordain (*so we hoped, but it was otherwise ordered*); command, bid, prescribe, (*order a retreat,* thing *to be* done, *thing *done;* person *to do, that* person or thing *should*); command or direct (person etc.) to go *to, away, home,* etc., (~ **about,** send hither and thither, domineer over); direct manufacturer, tradesman, waiter, etc., to supply; tell waiter etc. what is to be served at (meal). [ME, f. prec.]

ŏr'derly *a.* & *n.* **1.** *a.* methodically arranged or inclined, regular, obedient to discipline, not unruly, well-behaved; hence **ŏr'derli**NESS *n.* **2.** (Mil.) of orders, charged with conveyance or execution of orders; ||~ **book,** regimental or company book for entry of orders; ||~ **officer,** officer of the day; ~ **room** (in barracks, for company's business). **3.** *n.* soldier in attendance on officer to carry orders etc.; attendant in (esp. military) hospital for cleaning etc. work; ||street cleaner. [f. ORDER¹ + -LY¹]

ŏr'dinal *a.* & *n.* **1.** (number) defining thing's position in series, ('*first*', '*twentieth*', etc., *are ordinals or ordinal numbers;* cf. CARDINAL). **2.** *a.* (Biol.) of an ORDER¹ (sense 6). **3.** *n.* (Eccl.) service-book, esp. one with forms of service used at ordinations. [ME, f. LL *ordinalis* a. med. L *ordinale* neut. (as n.), f. L (as ORDER¹; see -AL)]

ŏr'dinance *n.* authoritative direction, decree; enactment by local authority; religious rite; (arch.) ordonnance. [ME, f. OF *ordenance* f. med. L *ordinantia* f. L *ordinare* (see ORDAIN, -ANCE)]

ŏr'dĭnănd *n.* candidate for ordination. [f. L *ordinandus*, gerundive of *ordinare* ORDAIN; see -ND¹]

ŏr'dĭnarў *a.* & *n.* **1.** *a.* regular, normal, customary, usual, not exceptional, not above the usual, common-place; ‖(of shares, stock, etc.) not preference or deferred; ‖**in** ∾ appended to *physician* etc., by perma-nent appointment (esp. to the royal household), not temporary or extraordinary; **in the** ∾ **way** *I should refuse*, if the circumstances were not exceptional; **out of the** ∾, unusual; ‖∾**level,** GCE examination of basic standard; ∾ **seaman** (of lower rating than able seaman); hence **ŏr'dĭnari**LY² *adv.*, **ŏr'dĭnari**NESS *n.* **2.** *a.* & *n.* ‖(person) having immediate or *ex officio* and not deputed jurisdiction; **the O**∾, archbishop in province, bishop in diocese; (**Lord**) **O**∾ in Scotland, one of judges of Court of Session constituting Outer House. **3.** *n.* rule or book laying down order of divine service. **4.** ‖public meal provided at fixed time and price in inn etc.; ‖establishment providing this; *tavern. **5.** (Her.) charge of earliest, simplest, and commonest kind (esp. chief, pale, bend, fess, bar, chevron, cross, saltire). **6.** early type of bicycle, with one large and one very small wheel. [ME, f. L *ordinarius* orderly (as ORDER¹; see -ARY¹); n. thr. AF & OF *ordinarie*]

ŏr'dĭnate *n.* (Math.) straight line from any point drawn parallel to one coordinate axis and meeting the other, (usu.) coordinate measured parallel to *y*-axis; any of series of parallel chords of conic section in relation to bisecting diameter (esp. used of half the chord, from curve to diameter). [f. L (*linea*) *ordinate* (*applicata*) line applied parallel (*ordinare*; see ORDAIN)]

ŏrdĭnā'tion *n.* arrangement in ranks, classification; conferring of holy orders esp. as priest or deacon, admission to church ministry; decreeing, ordain-ment. [ME f. OF, or f. L *ordinatio* (as ORDAIN; see -ATION)]

ŏr'dnance *n.* mounted guns, cannon; branch of government service dealing esp. with military stores and materials; ‖∾ **datum,** mean sea level as defined for ‖∾ **survey** (Government survey of Great Britain and (formerly) Ireland, orig. under Master of the Ordnance, preparing accurate and detailed maps (∾ **maps**) of the whole country). [ME, var. of ORDINANCE]

ŏr'donnance *n.* systematic arrangement esp. of liter-ary or architectural work. [F, f. OF *ordenance* (see ORDINANCE)]

Ordŏvī'cian (ōr-; -shan) *a.* & *n.* (Geol.) (of) the second Palaeozoic period or system, below Silurian and above Cambrian. [f. L *Ordovices* ancient British tribe in N. Wales + -IAN]

ŏr'dūre *n.* excrement, dung; obscenity, foul language. [ME f. OF (*ord* foul f. L *horridus*; see HORRID, -URE)]

ore *n.* solid naturally-occurring mineral aggregate from which metal or other valuable constituent(s) may be usefully extracted; (poet.) metal, esp. gold. [in form repr. OE *ār* brass (= OS, OHG *ēr*, ON *eir*, Goth. *aiz* f. Gmc *aiz* f. IE *ajiz*); in sense repr. OE *ōra* unwrought metal = Du. *oer*, LG *ūr*, of unkn. orig.]

Ore. *abbr.* Oregon.

ŏr'ĕăd *n.* (Gk & Rom. Myth.) mountain nymph. [ME, f. L *oreas -ados* f. Gk *oreias* (*oros* mountain; see -AD l)]

orĕ'ctĭc *a.* (Philos. & Med.) of desire or appetite. [f. Gk *orektikos* (*oregō* stretch out; see -IC)]

Oreg. *abbr.* Oregon.

oreganō (ŏrĭgah'-, orĕ'ga-) *n.* dried wild marjoram (*Origanum vulgare*), used as seasoning. [Sp., = ORIGANUM]

O'rĕgon (ŏ'-) *n.* ∾ **pine,** Douglas fir. [∾ in US]

ŏr'ĕĭde. See OROIDE (etym.).

ŏrĕŏ'graphy, ŏrĕŏ'logў, etc. Vars. of OROGRAPHY, OROLOGY, etc.

ŏr'e-weed. Var. of OARweed.

ŏrfe *n.* golden-coloured IDE. [G & F; cf. L f. Gk *orphos* sea-perch]

ŏr'fray. See ORPHREY.

ŏr'gan *n.* **1.** musical instrument of pipes supplied with wind by bellows, sounded by keys, and distributed into sets or stops having special tone, which in turn form groups or partial organs (*great, choir, swell, solo, pedal, organ*) each with separate keyboard; device producing similar music electronically; hence ∾IST (3) *n.* **2.** = BARREL¹-*organ*; ∾-**grinder,** player of this. **3.** keyboard wind-instrument with metal reeds, harmonium; AMERICAN *organ*; MOUTH¹-*organ*. **4.** part of animal or vegetable body adapted for special vital function (*organs of speech, perception, digestion,* etc., *vocal, reproductive, organs; nasal organ; organ of* CORTI); (arch.) person's voice with reference to its quality or power; (Phren.) region of brain held to be seat of particular faculty. **5.** medium of communication, mouthpiece of opinion, esp. newspaper or magazine or review representing a party, cause, sect, pursuit, etc. **6.** ∾-**bird,** Tasmanian bird of shrike family with discordant note; ∾-**blower,** person or mechanism working bellows of musical organ; ∾-**builder** (of musical organs); ∾-**loft,** gallery in church or concert-room for organ; ∾-**pipe,** pipe of musical organ, natural formation (e.g. cactus or coral) with vertical parts like grouped pipes of organ; ∾-**screen,** ornamental screen often between choir and nave on which organ is placed in cathedral etc.; ∾-**stop,** set of pipes of similar tone in musical organ, handle of mechanism that brings it into action. [ME, f. OE *organa* & OF *organe*, f. L f. Gk *organon* tool, f. IE *tworgan-*WORK¹]

organdie, *-dў, (ŏrgă'-, ŏr'ga-) *n.* fine translucent cotton etc. muslin, usu. stiffened. [f. F *organdi*, of unkn. orig.]

ŏrganĕ'lle *n.* (Biol.) organized or specialized structure within a cell. [f. mod. L *organella* dim.; see ORGAN, -LE 2]

ŏrgă'nĭc *a.* **1.** (Physiol.) of the bodily organs, vital; (Path., of disease) affecting structure of an organ (opp. *functional*). **2.** having organs or organized physical structure, of animals or plants, (opp. *in organic*); (of food etc.) produced without artificial fertilizers or pesticides. **3.** (Chem.) (Of compound etc.) existing as constituent of organized bodies or formed from bodies so existing, containing carbon in its molecule; ∾ **chemistry,** that of carbon com-pounds. **4.** constitutional, inherent, fundamental, structural; ∾ **law** (stating formal constitution of a country). **5.** organized or systematic or co-ordinated (*organic unity; an organic whole*). **6.** Hence **ŏrgă'n-**ICALLY *adv.* [f. F *organique* f. L f. Gk *organikos* (as ORGAN; see -IC)]

ŏr'ganĭsm *n.* organized body with connected inter-dependent parts sharing common life; (material structure of) individual living animal or plant; whole with interdependent parts compared to living being. [f. F *organisme* (as ORGANIZE; see -ISM)]

ŏr'ganist. See ORGAN 1.

ŏrganĭzā'tion, -ĭs- (-īz-), *n.* organizing or being organized; organized body or system or society (∾ **man,** one who regards these as taking priority over individuals' needs); hence ∾AL *a.* [ME, f. med. L *organizatio*, or f. foll. + -ATION]

ŏr'ganīz|e, -īs|e (-īz), *v.t.* **1.** (usu. in *p.p.*) furnish with organs, make organic, make into living being or tissue. **2.** form into an organic whole, form (an organic whole); enrol as members of formal body, e.g. trade union; give orderly structure to, frame and put into working order, make arrangements for or initiate (undertaking involving co-operation). **3.** Hence ∾ABLE *a.*, ∾ER¹ *n.* [ME, f. OF *organiser* f. med. L *organizare* f. L (as ORGAN; see -IZE)]

ŏr'ganŏ- *comb. form.* **1.** (esp. Biol.) organ, as: ∾**le'ptic,** affecting the organs of sense; ∾**the'rapy,** treatment of disease with extracts of organs. **2.** (Chem.) organic, as: ∾**meta'llic,** (of compound) organic and con-taining a metal. [f. Gk (as ORGAN) + -o-]

ŏr'ganŏn, ŏr'ganum, *n.* instrument of thought,

means of reasoning, system of logic. [Gk (-*on*) & L (-*um*), see ORGAN; *Organon* was title of Aristotle's logical writings, and *Novum* (new) *Organum* that of Bacon's]

ŏrgă'nza *n.* thin stiff transparent dress-fabric of silk or synthetic fibre. [prob. f. *Lorganza* *P]

ŏr'ganzine (-ēn) *n.* silk thread in which the main twist is in contrary direction to that of the strands. [f. F *organsin* f. It. *organzino*, of unkn. orig.]

ŏr'găsm *n.* violent excitement, rage, paroxysm; culmination of sexual excitement esp. in coition; hence **ŏrgă'sm**IC (-z-), **ŏrgă'st**IC, *adjs.* [f. F *orgasme* or mod. L f. Gk *orgasmos* (*orgaō* swell, be excited)]

ŏr'geat (-jiăt, -zhah) *n.* cooling drink made from barley or almonds and orange-flower water. [F, f. Prov. *orjat* (*ordi* barley f. L *hordeum*)]

ŏrgia'stic *a.* of the nature of an orgy. [f. Gk *orgiastikos* (*orgiastēs* agent-n. f. *orgiazō* celebrate orgy)]

ŏr'gŭlous *a.* (arch.) haughty; splendid. [ME, f. OF *orguillus* (*orguill* pride f. Frank. *urgōli*)]

ŏr'gў *n.* **1.** drunken or licentious revel, (usu. in *pl.*) revelry or debauchery; excessive indulgence in an activity. **2.** (Gk & Rom. Ant.; usu. in *pl.*) secret rites in worship of various gods, esp. in that of Bacchus celebrated with wild dancing, drinking, and singing. [orig. pl., f. F *orgies* f. L f. Gk *orgia* secret rites pl. f. IE *worg-WORK[1]*]

-ŏr'ial. See -ORY.

ŏ'ribi *n.* small S. Afr. antelope of genus *Ourebia*. [Afrik., app. f. Hottentot]

ŏr'iel *n.* large windowed polygonal recess built out usu. from upper storey and supported from ground or on corbels; ∼ (**window**), window of oriel, projecting window of upper storey. [ME, f. OF *oriol* gallery, of unkn. orig.]

ŏr'ient[1] *n.* & *a.* **1.** *n.* (O∼). (poet. or rhet.) the east. **2.** (O∼). the East, the countries E. of Mediterranean, esp. E. Asia. **3.** orient pearl. **4.** *a.* (poet.) oriental. **5.** (Of precious stones and pearls of finest kinds, as coming anciently from the East) lustrous, sparkling, precious; (arch.) radiant, (of sun, daylight, etc., or fig.) rising, nascent. [ME f. OF, f. L *oriens -entis* rising, sunrise, east, (*oriri* rise; see -ENT)]

or'ĭĕnt[2] (ŏr'-, ŏ'r-) *v.* **1.** *v.t.* place (building etc.) so as to face E., build (church) with chancel end due E., bury with feet eastward; place or exactly determine position of with regard to points of compass, settle or find bearings of, (fig.) bring into clearly understood relations, direct *towards*; ∼ one**self**, determine how one stands in relation to one's surroundings. **2.** *v.i.* turn eastward or in specified direction. [f. F *orienter* (*orient*: see prec.)]

oriĕ'ntal (ŏr-, ŏr-) *a.* & *n.* **1.** *a.* of the Orient, of the East or countries E. of Mediterranean, esp. E. Asian; occurring in or coming from or characteristic of the civilization etc. of the East; hence ∼ISM (2, 4), ∼IST (3), *ns.*, ∼IZE (2, 3) *v.i.* & *t.* **2.** (arch.) easterly. **3.** (Of pearl etc.) orient. **4.** Hence ∼LY[2] *adv.* **5.** *n.* (O∼). native or inhabitant of the Orient. [ME f. OF, or f. L *orientalis* (as ORIENT[1]; see -AL)]

orientāte (ŏ'r-, ŏr'-) *v.t.* & *i.* = ORIENT[2]. [prob. back-form. f. foll.]

orientā'tion (ŏr-, ŏr-) *n.* orienting (oneself) or being oriented; relative position; faculty by which birds etc. find their way home from a distance; ∼ **course** (for information of newcomers to university etc.). [app. f. ORIENT[2] + -ATION]

orienteer'ing (ŏr-, ŏr-) *n.* competitive sport of finding one's way on foot across rough country with map and compass. [f. Sw. *orientering*]

ŏ'rifice *n.* aperture, mouth of cavity, perforation, vent. [F, f. LL *orificium* (*os oris* mouth, *-ficere* = *facere* make)]

ŏ'riflămme *n.* sacred banner of St. Denis, banderole of red silk on lance received by early French kings from abbot of St. Denis on starting for war; (fig.) anything material or ideal serving as rallying-point in

struggle; bright conspicuous object, blaze of colour, etc. [ME f. OF, f. L *aurum* gold + *flamma* flame]

ŏrĭga'mi (-ah'-) *n.* Japanese art of folding paper into intricate designs. [Jap. (*ori* fold, *kami* paper)]

ŏ'rigan, ori'ganum, *n.* wild marjoram or other plant of genus *Origanum*. [(ME. OF *origan*) f. L f. Gk *origanon*]

ŏ'rigin *n.* derivation, beginning or rising or coming from something, person's ancestry, source, starting-point, (*a word of Latin origin; country of origin; a man of humble origin*); (Anat.) place at which muscle is more firmly attached or nerve begins in brain etc.; (Math.) fixed point from which coordinates are measured. [f. F *origine* or f. L *origo -ginis* (*oriri* rise)]

ori'gĭnal *a.* & *n.* **1.** *a.* existing from the first, primitive, innate, initial, earliest; ∼ **sin**, innate depravity held to be common to all human beings in consequence of the Fall. **2.** that has served as pattern, of which copy or translation has been made, not derivative or dependent, first-hand, not imitative, novel in character or style, inventive, creative, thinking or acting for oneself, (*where is the original picture?; what does the original Greek say?; is it an original drawing or a woodcut?; made a very original remark; has an original mind*); ∼ **print** (made directly from artist's own work on wood, stone, etc., and printed by him or under his supervision). **3.** Hence or cogn. **origĭnă'l**ITY *n.*, ∼LY[2] *adv.* **4.** *n.* pattern, original model, thing from which another is copied or translated, (*several transcripts from the same original; the original is in the National Gallery; reads 'Don Quixote' in the original*); eccentric person; duplicate garment made by well-known designer. [ME f. OF, or f. L *originalis* (as prec.; see -AL)]

ori'gĭn|āte *v.* **1.** *v.t.* give origin to, initiate, cause to begin; hence ∼ATIVE *a.* **2.** *v.i.* have origin, begin, (usu. *from* or *in* thing or place, *with* or *from* person). **3.** So ∼A'TION, ∼ātOR, *ns.* [f. med. L *originare* (as ORIGIN) + -ATE[3]]

ŏrină'sal (-z-) *a.* of, sounded with, both mouth and nose (esp. of French nasalized vowels). [f. L *os oris* mouth + -I- + NASAL]

ŏr'ĭŏle *n.* bird of genus *Oriolus*, esp. **golden** ∼ with black and yellow plumage in male; Amer. bird of family Icteridae with similar coloration. [f. med. L *oriolus* f. OF *oriol* f. L *aureolus* dim. of *aureus* golden (*aurum* gold)]

Orī'on (o-) *n.* (Astron.) brilliant constellation on equator, figured as hunter with belt and sword; ∼'s **belt**, three bright stars in short line across middle of the constellation; ∼'s **hound**, Sirius. [ME f. L, f. Gk *Ōriōn*, name of legendary hunter]

-ŏr'ious. See -ORY.

ŏ'rison (-z-) *n.* (arch., usu. in *pl.*) a prayer. [ME, f. AF *ureison*, OF *oreison*, f. L (as ORATION); see -ISON]

-ŏr'ium *suf.* forming *ns.* denoting place (*auditorium, crematorium*). [L, neut. of adjs. in *-orius* (see -ORY)]

Ori'ya (ŏrē'a) *n.* (member or language of) Hindu people of Orissa. [Hindi]

ŏrle *n.* (Her.) narrow band, or border of charges, near edge of shield. [F *o*(*u*)*rle* (*ourler* to hem f. Rom. *orulare* f. *orula* dim. of L *ora* edge)]

ŏr'lop *n.* lowest deck of ship with three or more decks. [ME, f. MDu. *overloop* covering (*overloopen* run over; see OVER-, LEAP[1])]

ŏr'mer *n.* edible univalve mollusc of genus *Haliotis*, sea-ear. [Channel-Is. F, f. F *ormier* f. L *auris maris* ear of sea]

ŏr'molu (-lōō) *n.* gilded bronze used in decorating furniture; gold-coloured alloy of copper, zinc, and tin; articles made of or decorated with these; (fig.) showy trash. [f. F *or moulu* powdered gold (for use in gilding)]

ŏr'nament[1] *n.* **1.** (Eccl., usu. in *pl.*) accessories of worship (e.g. altar, chalice, sacred vessels, service-books); ∼(**s**) **rubric**, that immediately before Order for Morning and Evening Prayer in Book of Common Prayer. **2.** thing used or serving to adorn, quality or person whose existence or presence confers grace or honour, (*mantelpiece crowded with ornaments*; *was an ornament to his country* or *age*). **3.** (Mus., in *pl.*) grace-notes. **4.** adorning, being adorned, embellishment, features or work added for decorative purposes, (*a tower rich in ornament*; *more for ornament than for use*). [ME f. AF *urnement*, OF *o(u)rnement* f. L *ornamentum* equipment (*ornare* adorn; see -MENT)]

ōr'namĕnt² *v.t.* adorn, beautify; hence ∼A'TION *n.* [f. prec.]

ōrnamë'ntal *a.* & *n.* **1.** *a.* serving as or constituting ornament(s); hence ∼ISM (3), ∼IST (2, 3), *ns.*, ∼LY¹ *adv.* **2.** *n.* ornamental thing, esp. plant grown for its beauty. [f. ORNAMENT¹ + -AL]

ōrnā'te *a.* elaborately adorned; (of literary style) embellished with flowery language etc.; hence ∼LY² (-tlĭ) *adv.*, ∼NESS (-tn-) *n.* [ME, f. L *ornatus* p.p. of *ornare* adorn; see -ATE²]

ōr'ner|ў *a.* (colloq.) of poor quality; coarse, unpleasant, cantankerous; hence ∼iNESS *n.* [var. of ORDINARY]

ōrni'thic *a.* of or pertaining to birds. [f. Gk *ornithikos* birdlike (as foll.; see -IC)]

ōr'nitho- *comb. form.* bird, as: ∼**mancy,** divination by the flight and cries of birds; ∼**rhy'nchus** (-rĭ'ngk-), platypus [Gk *rhugkhos* bill]; ∼**scopy** (-ŏ's-), observation of birds esp. by augurs. [Gk (*ornis ornithos* bird)]

ōrnitho'log|ў *n.* study of birds; so **ōrnitholŏ'gICAL** *a.*, ∼IST (3) *n.* [f. mod. L *ornithologia* f. Gk *ornithologos* treating of birds (as prec.; see -LOGY)]

ōroge'nėsis, ōrō'genў, *ns.* (Geol.) process of formation of mountains; so **ōrogenE'TIC, ōroge'nIC,** *adjs.* [f. Gk *oros* mountain + GENESIS, -GENY]

orō'graphy (ŏr-, ōr-) *n.* branch of physical geography dealing with mountains; hence **oroGRA'PHIC(AL)** (ŏr-, ōr-) *adjs.* [f. Gk *oros oreos* mountain + -O- + -GRAPHY]

ōr'oide *n.* gold-coloured alloy of copper and zinc. [f. *oreide* a similar or identical alloy, f. F *oréide* (OR¹ gold); assim. to -OID]

orō'log|ў (ŏr-, ōī-) *n.* study of mountains; hence **ōrolŏ'gICAL** *a.*, ∼IST (3) *n.* [f. Gk *oros oreos* mountain + -O- + -LOGY]

orotŭnd (ŏ'r-, ōī'-) *a.* (Of utterance or phrasing) with full voice, imposing, dignified; pompous, magniloquent, pretentious. [f. L *ore rotundo* with well-turned speech, lit. with round mouth (Horace *Ars Poetica* 323)]

ōr'phan *n.*, & *a.*, & *v.t.* **1.** *n* & *a* (child) bereaved of parent(s); (fig.) (person) bereft of previous protection or advantages; hence ∼HOOD *n.*, ∼IZE (3) *v.t.* **2.** *v.t.* bereave of parent(s). [ME, f. LL f. Gk *orphanos* bereaved]

ōr'phanage *n.* orphanhood; institution for orphans' education etc. [f. prec. + -AGE]

Orphe'an (ōr-) *a.* like the music of Orpheus, melodious, entrancing. [f. L *Orpheus* a. f. Gk *Orpheios* (*Orpheus*; see foll.) + -AN]

Or'ph|ic (ōr'-) *a.* of Orpheus or the mysteries or doctrines associated with his name, oracular, mysterious; Orphean; so ∼ISM (3) *n.* [f. L f. Gk *Orphikos* (*Orpheus*, legendary Gk poet and lyre-player; see -IC)]

ōr'phrey, ōr'fray, *n.* ornamental often richly embroidered stripes and borders of ecclesiastical vestment. [ME *orfreis* (taken as pl.) (gold) embroidery f. OF, f. med. L *aurifrisium* etc. f. L *aurum* gold + *Phrygius* Phrygian, also 'embroidered']

ōr'piment *n.* arsenic trisulphide as mineral, formerly used as yellow dye and as artists' pigment; RED *orpiment*. [ME f. OF, f. L *auripigmentum* (*aurum* gold, *pigmentum* PIGMENT)]

ōr'pine, ōr'pĭn, *n.* succulent herbaceous purple-flowered plant (*Sedum telephium*). [ME, f. OF *orpine*, prob. alt. of prec., orig. of yellow-flowered species of same genus]

Or'pington (ōī'-) *n.* (bird of) breed of usu. buff white-legged poultry. [∼ in Kent]

ŏ'rra *a.* (Sc.) odd, not matched, occasional, extra. [18th c.; orig. unkn.]

ŏ'rrerў *n.* clockwork model of the planetary system. [named after 4th Earl of *Orrery*, for whom one was made]

ŏ'rris¹ *n.* iris plant, esp. *Iris florentina*; ∼(-**root**), fragrant root of this or other iris used in perfumery and medicine; ∼-**powder,** powdered orris-root. [16th c., app. an unexpl. alt. of IRIS]

ŏ'rris² *n.* gold or silver lace or embroidery. [*c.* 1700, perh. alt. of *orfreis* ORPHREY]

ōrt *n.* (arch.; usu. in *pl.*) refuse scrap(s), leavings. [ME, pl. f. MLG *orte*, perh. f. *o(o)r-* out (cf. ORDEAL) + *eten* EAT]

ōr'tho- *comb. form.* **1.** straight, rectangular, upright, right, correct, as: ∼**cepha'lic,** with breadth of skull from ⅘ to ⅘ of length, between mesocephalic and dolichocephalic; ∼**chroma'tic,** giving fairly correct relative intensity to colours in photography by being sensitive to all except red; ∼**clase,** common felspar in crystals with two cleavages at right angles [Gk *klasis* breaking]; ∼**do'ntia,** ∼**do'ntics,** correction of irregularities in teeth and jaws; so ∼**do'ntic** *a.*, ∼**do'ntist** *n.*; ∼**ge'nesis,** view of evolution according to which variations follow a defined direction and are not merely sporadic and fortuitous; ∼**gnathous** (-ŏ'g-), upright-jawed, not prognathous; ∼**gonal** (-ŏ'g-), of or involving right angles; ∼**pterous** (-ŏ'p-), of the insect order Orthoptera with straight narrow forewings, including cockroaches, crickets, grasshoppers, etc.; ∼**rho'mbic,** (Cryst.) having three unequal axes at right angles to each other; ∼**tone,** (word) having independent accent, not enclitic or proclitic. **2.** (Chem.) (1) relating to two adjacent carbon atoms in benzene ring, (2) relating to acids and salts (e.g. *orthophosphates*) giving *meta*- compounds on removal of water; ∼**hydrogen,** form of hydrogen molecule with nuclear spins in same direction. [f. Gk *orthos* straight + -O-]

ōr'thodŏx *a.* holding correct or currently accepted opinions esp. on religious doctrine, not heretical or independent-minded or original; generally accepted as right or true esp. in theology, in harmony with what is authoritatively established, approved, conventional; (of Judaism) with strict retention of traditional observances; **O∼ Church,** the Eastern or Greek Church separated from Western Church in 9th c., recognizing Patriarch of Constantinople as head, and the national Churches of Russia, Romania, Greece, etc., in communion with it; hence ∼LY² *adv.* [f. eccl. L f. Gk ORTHO(*doxos* f. *doxa* opinion) right in opinion]

ōr'thodoxў *n.* being orthodox. [f. LL f. late Gk *orthodoxia* sound doctrine (as prec.; see -Y¹)]

orthoep|y (ōr'thŏėpĭ, ōrthŏ'ĭpĭ) *n.* science of (correct) pronunciation of words; hence ∼IC (-ĕ'p-) *a.*, ∼IST (3) *n.* [f. Gk ORTHO(*epeia* f. *epos* word) correct speech; see -Y¹]

ōrthŏ'graphў *n.* **1.** correct or conventional spelling; spelling with reference to its correctness (*his orthography is shocking*). **2.** perspective projection used in maps and elevations in which the observer is supposed infinitely distant so that the projecting lines are parallel; map etc. so projected. **3.** So **ōrthogra'phIC(AL)** *adjs.*, **ōrthogra'phicALLY** *adv.* [ME, f. OF *ortografie* f. L f. Gk ORTHO(*graphia* -GRAPHY)]

ōrthopae'd|ics, *-pē'-, *n.* branch of medicine dealing with correction of deformities of bones or muscles, orig. in children; so ∼IC *a.*, ∼IST (3) *n.* [f. F ORTHO(*pédie* f. Gk *paideia* rearing of children) + -ICS]

ōrthŏ'pt|ic *a.* (Med.) relating to correct or normal use of eyes; hence ∼ICS *n.* (esp. of remedial treatment of eye-muscles); ∼IST (3) *n.* [f. ORTHO- + Gk *optikos* of sight (see OPTIC)]

ōr'tolan *n.* small Eur. bird (*Emberiza hortulana*) frequenting gardens, esteemed as table delicacy. [F f.

Prov., lit. gardener f. L *hortulanus* (*hortulus* dim. of *hortus* garden; see -AN)]

Orvie'tō (ōrviā'tō) *n.* (*pl.* ~s). white wine made near *Orvieto* in central Italy.

Orwĕ'lliăn (ōr-) *a.* of or characteristic of the writings of Orwell. [f. G. *Orwell*, pseudonym of E. A. Blair, Engl. writer of political satires (e.g. *1984*) d. 1950]

-orў *suf.* forming: **1.** *ns.* usu. denoting place (*dormitory, laboratory, oratory, refectory*) [f. ONF & AF -*orie*, OF -*oire* or f. L -*oria*, -ORIUM]. **2.** *adjs.* (& *ns.*) usu. w. sense of (person or thing) relating to or involving vbl action (*accessory, amatory, compulsory, inhibitory, perfunctory, predatory, promissory*). [f. AF -*ori(e)*, OF -*oir(e)* or f. L -*orius*]

o'rŷx *n.* large straight-horned African antelope of genus *Oryx*. [ME f. L f. Gk *orux* stonemason's pickaxe, f. its pointed horns]

OS *abbr.* old style; ordinary seaman; ordnance survey; outsize; out of stock.

Os *symb.* osmium.

OSA *abbr.* Order of St. Augustine.

O'sāge (ō'-) *n.* ~ **orange,** N. Amer. thorny tree (*Maclura pomifera*) with hard orange-coloured wood. [name of N. Amer. Indian tribe]

OSB *abbr.* Order of St. Benedict.

O'scan (ŏ'-) *a.* & *n.* (of or in) the ancient language of Campania, allied to Latin, surviving only in inscriptions. [f. L *Oscus*+-AN]

O'scar (ŏ'-) *n.* one of the statuettes awarded by the Academy of Motion Picture Arts & Sciences for excellence in film acting, directing, etc. [man's Christian name]

ŏ'scill|āte *v.* **1.** *v.i.* & *t.* (cause to) swing like pendulum; move to and fro between two points. **2.** *v.i.* vacillate, vary between extremes of opinion, action, condition, etc. **3.** (Electr., of current) undergo high-frequency alternations as across spark-gap or in valve-transmitter circuit; (of radio receiver) radiate electromagnetic waves owing to faulty operation. **4.** Hence or cogn. ~A'TION, ~ātoR, *ns.,* ~atORY (ŏ'sĭlă-, osī'la-) *a.* [f. L *oscillare* swing+-ATE³]

osci'llo- *comb. form.* oscillation esp. of electric current, as: ~**graph,** device for recording oscillations; ~**scope,** device for viewing oscillations, usu. by display on screen of cathode-ray tube. [f. as prec. +-o-]

ŏ'scǐne, ŏ'scǐnīne, *adjs.* (Of bird) passerine. [f. L *oscen -cinis* song-bird (as OB-, *canere* sing)+-INE¹]

ŏscĭtā'tion *n.* yawning, drowsiness; inattention, negligence. [f. L *oscitatio* (*oscitare* gape f. *os* mouth, *citare* move; see -ATION)]

ŏ'scŭlar *a.* of the mouth; (joc.) of kissing. [f. L *osculum* mouth, kiss, (dim. of *os* mouth; see -CULE)+-AR¹]

ŏ'scŭl|āte *v.* **1.** *v.i.* & *t.* (arch. or joc.) kiss. **2.** *v.i.* (Biol., of species etc.) be related through intermediate species etc., have common characters *with* another or with each other. **3.** *v.t.* (Math., of curve or surface) have contact of higher than first order with, meet at three or more coincident points. **4.** Hence or cogn. ~ANT *a.,* ~A'TION *n.* [f. L *osculari* kiss (as prec.) +-ATE³]

ŏ'scŭlatorў *a.* & *n.* **1.** *a.* of kissing or osculation. **2.** *n.* = PAX 1. [f. as prec.+-ORY]

ŏ'scŭl|um *n.* (*pl.* ~a). mouthlike aperture, esp. of sponge. [L; see OSCULAR]

-ōse¹ *suf.* forming *adjs.* denoting possession of a quality (*bellicose, grandiose, jocose, morose, verbose*); hence **-ōse**LY² (-slī) *adv. suf.,* **-ōse**NESS (-sn-) *n. suf.* (cf. -OSITY). [f. or after L -*osus*]

-ōse² *suf.* (Chem.) forming names of carbohydrates (*cellulose, sucrose*). [after GLUCOSE]

OSF *abbr.* Order of St. Francis.

ŏ'sier (-zher, -zier) *n.* (shoot of) species of willow, esp. *Salix viminalis,* used in basketwork; ~**-bed,** place where these are grown. [ME f. OF; cf. med. L *auseria* osier-bed]

-ō'sis *suf.* forming *ns.* (*pl.* ~o'ses *pr.* -ō'sēz) denoting

process or condition (*apotheosis, metamorphosis*), esp. pathological state (*acidosis, neurosis, thrombosis*). [f. L or f. Gk -ōsis suf. of vbl ns. (-oō vbl ending)]

-ŏ'sitў *suf.* forming *ns.* f. *adjs.* in -OSE¹ and -OUS (*verbosity, curiosity*). [f. F -*osité* or f. L -*ositas -ositatis*; see -ITY]

OSM *abbr.* Servite. [f. *Order of Servants of Mary*]

Osmă'nli (ŏz-, ŏs-) *a.* & *n.* = OTTOMAN¹. [Turk. (*Osman* f. Arab. *'uṭmān* (see OTTOMAN¹), -*lı* adj. suf.)]

ŏ'smĭum (ŏ'z-) *n.* hard bluish-white metal of the platinum group, the heaviest known metal. [f. Gk *osmē* smell (from the pungent smell of its tetroxide) +-IUM]

ŏsmŏ's|ĭs (ŏz-) *n.* (*pl.* ~es *pr.* -ēz). tendency of solvent to diffuse through porous partition into more concentrated solution; hence **ŏsmŏ'**TIC *a.,* **ŏsmŏ't**ICALLY *adv.,* (ŏz-). [orig. *osmose*, after F f. Gk *ōsmos* push; see -OSIS]

ŏ'smund (-z-) *n.* fern of genus *Osmunda,* esp. *O. regalis* with very large fronds. [ME, f. AF]

ŏ'sprey (-ĭ, -ā) *n.* **1.** large bird (*Pandion haliaetus*) preying on fish of inland waters. **2.** egret-plume on woman's hat. [ME, f. OF *ospres,* app. ult. repr. L *ossifraga* osprey (*os* bone, *frangere* break)]

ŏ'ssĕin *n.* organic substance of bones. [f. L (as foll.) +-IN]

ŏ'ssĕous *a.* consisting of bone, ossified; having bony skeleton (*osseous and cartilaginous fishes*). [f. L *osseus* (*os ossis* bone)+-OUS]

ŏ'ssia *conj.* (Mus.) or (indicating an alternative and usu. easier passage to be played). [It.]

Ossiă'nic (ŏ-) *a.* of the (bombastic) style used in Macpherson's 18th-c. purported translations of Ossian's poems. [f. *Ossian,* legendary Gaelic bard +-IC]

ŏ'ssicle *n.* (Anat.) small bone, e.g. of middle ear; (Zool.) small piece of bony or chitinous or calcareous substance in animal framework. [f. L *ossiculum* dim. (as OSSEOUS; see -CULE)]

O'ssie (ŏ'zĭ) *n.* & *a.* (sl.) Australian. [abbr.; see -IE]

ŏ'ssĭfrage *n.* osprey. [f. L *ossifraga*; see OSPREY]

ŏ'ssi|fŷ (ŏ'-) *v.i.* & *t.* turn into bone, harden; make or become rigid or callous or unprogressive; so **ŏssĭ'**FIC *a.,* ~FICA'TION *n.* [f. F *ossifier* f. L *os ossis* bone; see -FY]

ŏ'ssuarў *n.* receptacle for bones of dead, charnel-house, bone-urn; cave in which ancient bones are found. [f. LL *ossuarium* (irreg. f. *os*; see prec., -ARY¹)]

*OST *abbr.* Office of Science and Technology.

ŏstei'tis *n.* (Path.) inflammation of bone substance. [f. Gk *osteon* bone+-ITIS]

ŏstĕ'nsĭb|le *a.* professed, for show, put forward to conceal the real, (*his ostensible function was as interpreter*); hence ~LY² *adv.* [F, f. med. L *ostensibilis* f. L *ostendere -ens-* stretch out to view (as OB-, *tendere* stretch); see -IBLE]

ŏstĕ'nsĭve *a.* directly demonstrative; (of definition) indicating by direct demonstration that which is signified by a term. [f. LL *ostensivus* (as prec.; see -IVE)]

ŏstĕ'nsorў *n.* receptacle for displaying Host to congregation, monstrance. [f. med. L *ostensorium* (as OSTENSIBLE; see -ORY)]

ŏstĕntā't|ion *n.* pretentious display esp. of wealth or luxury, showing off, attempt or intention to attract notice; hence ~IOUS *a.,* ~iousLY² *adv.,* (-shus). [ME f. OF, f. L *ostentatio -onis* (*ostentare* frequent. of *ostendere*; see OSTENSIBLE, -ATION)]

ŏ'stĕŏ- *comb. form.* bone, as: ~**arthri'tis,** degenerative arthritis esp. in elderly persons; ~**ge'nesis,** formation of bone; ~**graphy** (-ŏ'g-), scientific description of the bones; ~**logy** (-ŏ'l-), anatomy dealing with skeleton and bones, animal's bony structure; ~**mala'cia,** softening of bone by loss of mineral substance; ~**myeli'tis,** inflammation of (esp. the marrow) of a bone; ~**phyte,** small outgrowth from bone; ~**poro'sis,** brittleness of bones due to porosity from loss of mineral substance. [f. Gk *osteon* bone + -o-]

ŏstĕŏ′pathў *n.* curative treatment aiming at correcting supposed deformation of skeleton as cause of many diseases; hence **ŏ′stĕo**PATH 1 *n.*, **ŏstĕopä′th**ıc *a.* [f. prec. + -PATHY]

ŏstĭna′tō (-ah′-) *n.* (*pl.* ∼s) & *a.* (Mus.) (melodic figure) repeated through all or part of a piece. [It., = OBSTINATE]

‖**ŏ′stler** (ŏ′sl-) *n.* stableman at inn. [f. earlier HOSTLER, *hosteler* f. AF; OF (*h*)*ostelier* f. as HOSTEL; see -ER²]

O′stmĕn (ŏ′-) *n. pl.* (Ir. Hist.) Scandinavian settlers. [ME, f. ON *Austmenn* (as EAST, MAN¹)]

Ostpolitik (ŏstpōlĭtē′k) *n.* politics of a Eur. country w. ref. to Communist countries of E. Europe. [G (*ost* east, *politik* politics)]

ŏ′strac|īze, -|īse (-ĭz), *v.t.* **1.** (In ancient Athens etc.) banish (dangerously powerful or unpopular citizen) for ten or five years by voting-system in which name of person to be ostracized was written on potsherd. **2.** exclude from society, favour, or common privileges, refuse to associate with. **3.** So ∼ISM (1) *n.* [f. Gk *ostrakizō* (*ostrakon* shell, potsherd)]

ŏ′strac|ŏn *n.* (*pl.* ∼a). potsherd used in ostracizing or for inscribing. [f. Gk *ostrakon* (see prec.)]

ŏ′strich *n.* swift-running flightless African and formerly Arabian bird *Struthio camelus*, largest living bird, with wing and tail feathers valued as ornaments, swallowing hard substances to assist working of gizzard, and reputed to bury its head in sand when pursued, in the belief that it cannot be seen (*has the digestion of an ostrich*, can digest any food; *is following an ostrich policy*); (fig.) person who refuses to accept facts; ∼-**farm** (breeding ostriches for feathers); ∼-**plume**, feather or bunched feathers of ostrich. [ME, f. OF *ostric*(*h*)*e* f. Rom. *avistruthius f. L *avis* bird, LL f. Gk *strouthiōn* ostrich (*strouthos* sparrow, ostrich)]

O′strogŏth (ŏ′-) *n.* member of Eastern branch of Goths, who conquered Italy in 5th–6th c.; hence ∼IC (-ŏ′th-) *a.* [f. LL *Ostrogothi* pl. f. Gmc *austro-EAST + LL *Gothi* GOTHS]

-ot¹ *suf.* forming *ns.* (orig. dim.; *ballot*, *chariot*, *parrot*). [F]

-ot², **-ote**, *sufs.* forming *ns.* denoting persons (*idiot*, *patriot*, *zealot*), e.g. natives etc. of a place (*Cypriot*). [f. F -*ote*, L -*ota*, Gk -*ōtēs*]

OT *abbr.* Old Testament.

ŏ′tarў *n.* eared SEAL¹. [f. mod. L *otaria* f. Gk *ous ōtos* ear]

‖**OTC** *abbr.* Officers' Training Corps.

-ote. See -OT².

o′ther (ŭ′dh-) *a.*, *n.* or *pron.*, & *adv.* **1.** *a.* not the same as one or more or some already mentioned or implied, separate in identity, distinct in kind, alternative or further or additional, *the* etc. only remaining, (*we have other evidence*; *other people think otherwise*; *have no other place to go to*; *must leave it till some other time*; *on the other side of the river*; *a few other examples would be useful*; *give me some other ones*; *now open the*, *your*, *other eye*); **the** ∼ **day, night, week,** etc., (*adv.*) a few days etc. ago; *on the other* HAND¹; *other* RANK¹*s*; ∼ **than** or (arch.) **from,** different from (*any person other than yourself*; *do not wish her other than she is*); ‖*the other* PLACE¹; **the** ∼ **thing,** an unexpressed alternative; ∼ **things being equal,** if conditions are or were alike in everything but the point in question; *the other* WOMAN, WORLD; ANOTHER (‖*A. N. Other*); EVERY *other*; NONE *other*; **someone, something, some time, some way,** etc., **or** ∼, some unspecified or unknown person, thing, (at) some unspecified time, (in) some unspecified way, etc. **2.** (Often ellipt. with numerals, as) ANOTHER; **the** ∼ **two** etc., the other two etc. persons or things, of kind not needing specification. **3.** ∼-**directed,** governed by external circumstances and trends; ∼**guess** *a.* [corrupt. of ∼*gates* adv. & *a.* (GATE², -s³)] in another way], (arch.) of very different kind; ∼**where**(**s**), (arch. or poet.) elsewhere; ∼-**wor′ldly,** concerned with the future life or some imagined

world to the neglect of the present or real one. **4.** *n.* or *pron.* (orig. ellipt. use of *a.*, but now w. pl. usu. ∼s). other person, thing, specimen, etc. (*give me one other,* ANOTHER, *some others*, *the two others*; *do good to others*; *if this soap is*, *these pillows are*, *too soft*, *have you any other*, *others?*; *one or other of us will be there*; *he acts while others talk*; *where have the others got to?*; (arch.) *in other of his sermons*; *one or each neutralizes the other*); *they neutralize* EACH *other* or ONE *another*; *I can do* **no** ∼, (arch.) nothing else; **of all** ∼s (see OF 7). **5.** *adv.* otherwise (*other than cursorily*, *than by repeating it*). [OE *ōther*, = OS *ōthar*, *andar*, OHG *andar*, ON *annarr*, Goth. *anthar* f. Gmc *antheraz f. IE *ánteros]

o′thernĕss (ŭ′dh-) *n.* being other, diversity, difference; thing or existence that is not the thing mentioned or the thinking subject. [f. prec. + -NESS]

o′therwīse (ŭ′dherwīz) *adv.* & *a.* **1.** *adv.* in a different way (*could not have acted otherwise*; *am otherwise engaged that day*; *Judas*, *otherwise* (*called or known as*) *Iscariot*; occas. preceded by *any* or *no* with reminiscence of its etym.: *could do it no otherwise*; *does not influence him any otherwise than by example*); if circumstances are or were or had been different, else, or else (*seize the chance*, *otherwise you will regret it*); in other respects (*he is unruly*, *but not otherwise blameworthy*); **and** ∼, **or** ∼, = *and* or *or* followed by the negation or opposite of a preceding *n.* or *a.* (*the merits or otherwise of the Bill*, i.e. or demerits; *additions automatic and otherwise*, i.e. and not automatic); ∼-**minded,** having different, or jarring, inclinations or views, averse to current opinions. **2.** *a.* in a different state (*the matter is quite otherwise*; *a sentence I could wish otherwise*; *how can it be otherwise than useless?*); that would otherwise exist (*their otherwise dullness*). [OE *on ōthre wisan* (as OTHER, WISE²)]

ŏ′tic *a.* of or relating to the ear. [f. Gk *ōtikos* (*ous ōtos* ear; see -IC)]

-ŏ′tic *suf.* forming *adjs.* (& *ns.*) corresp. to *ns.* in -OSIS, in sense '(person or thing) affected with or producing or resembling -OSIS' (*hypnotic*, *narcotic*, *neurotic*, *osmotic*); hence **-ŏ′tic**ALLY or *a.* after F -*otique* f. L f. Gk -*ōtikos* (-*ōtēs* n. suf.; -*otos* a. suf.; see -IC)]

ŏ′tiōse (-shĭ-, -tĭ-) *a.* not required, serving no practical purpose, functionless; (arch.) indolent or futile; hence ∼LY² (-slĭ) *adv.*, ∼NESS (-sn-) *n.* [f. L *otiosus* (*otium* leisure; see -OSE¹)]

oti′tis *n.* inflammation of the ear; ∼ **media** (of the middle ear). [mod. L (as OTO-, -ITIS)]

ŏ′to- *comb. form.* ear, as: ∼**lith,** particle or larger body of calcareous matter in ear; ∼**logy** (-ŏ′l-), science of ear diseases, anatomy of the ear, etc.; ∼(**rhino**)-**laryngo′logy,** study of the ears (and nose) and larynx; ∼**scope,** instrument for examining cavity of ear, or for auscultation of sounds in it. [Gk *ōto-* (*ous ōtos* ear; see -O-)]

ottava rima (otahva rē′ma) *n.* stanza of eight lines, 11-syllabled in Italian, 10-syllabled in English, with rhymes *abababcc* (as in Byron's *Don Juan*). [It., lit. eighth rhyme]

ŏ′tter *n.* **1.** furred aquatic fish-eating mammal of genus *Lutra* etc. with short legs, round feet, and webbed toes; its fur; SEA *otter*. **2.** piece of board used to carry fishing-bait in water; type of paravane esp. as used on non-naval craft. **3.** ∼-**board,** device for keeping mouth of trawl open; ∼-**dog, -hound,** (of breed used in otter-hunting); ∼-**spear** (used in otter-hunting). [OE *otr*, *ot*(*t*)*or*, = MDu., MLG *otter*, OHG *ottar*, ON *otr* f. Gmc *otraz f. IE *udros]

ŏ′ttō¹. See ATTAR.

O′ttō² (ŏ′-) *n.* ∼ **engine,** type of internal combustion engine with four piston-strokes in cycle, as in most motor vehicles. [f. N. A. ∼, Ger. engineer d. 1891]

O′ttoman¹ (ŏ′-) *a.* & *n.* **1.** *a.* of the dynasty of Osman or Othman I, his branch of the Turks, or the empire ruled by his descendants; Turkish; *Ottoman* PORTE. **2.** *n.* Ottoman person, Turk. [F, f. Arab. '*uṭmānī* adj. of Othman ('*uṭmān*)]

ŏ′ttoman² *n.* cushioned seat like sofa or chair without back or arms, often a box with cushioned top; footstool of similar design; heavy fabric of silk with cotton or wool. [f. F *ottomane* fem. (as prec.)]

OU *abbr.* ||Open University; Oxford University.

oubliĕ'tte (ōō-) *n.* secret dungeon with entrance only by trapdoor. [F (*oublier* forget); see -ETTE]

ouch[1] *n.* (arch.) clasp or buckle, often jewelled; setting of precious stone. [ME *ouche* f. *nouche*, OF *nouche*, *nosche*, f. OFrank. *nuskja* buckle, clasp; for loss of *n-* cf. ADDER]

ouch[2] *int.* of pain or annoyance. [imit.; cf. G *autsch*]

OUDS *abbr.* Oxford University Dramatic Society.

ouf (ōōf) *int.* expr. stifling, alarm, or relief. [natural excl.]

ought[1], **aught**[2], (awt) *n.* (colloq.) figure denoting nothing, nought. [perh. f. *an ought* for a NOUGHT; cf. ADDER]

ought[2] (awt) *v. aux.* (the only form in use, except arch. ~'est or ~st, is **ought** serving as present or past finite) expr. duty, rightness, shortcoming, advisability, or strong probability; *neg.* ~ **not**, (colloq.) ~n't *pr.* aw'tent, (vulg.) **didn't** or **hadn't** ~; the past sense (except when merely due to sequence of tenses in reporting etc.) is indicated by a following perf. inf.: *we ought to love our neighbours; I said it, and still think I ought to have said it; it ought not to be allowed; he ought to have been a lawyer, not a don; you ought to know, to have known, better; you ought to have seen his face when he realized; it ought to be done at once, to have been done long ago; I told you it ought to be, to have been, done; he ought to be there by now; Cambridge ought to win.* [OE *āhte*, past of *āgan* OWE]

ought[3] Var. of AUGHT[1].

Ouija, **o-**, (wē'jah, -a) *n.* ~(-**board**), (**P**) board lettered with alphabet and other signs, used with planchette or movable pointer to obtain messages in spiritualistic seances. [f. F *oui* yes + G *ja* yes]

ounce[1] *n.* measure of weight, 1/16 lb. avoirdupois, 1/12 lb. (480 grains) in troy and apothecaries' weight; (fig.) small quantity (*an ounce of practice is worth a pound of theory*); ||**fluid** ~, 8 drachms, 1/20 pint, 1·734 cu. in.; *fluid~*, 1/16 pint, 1·804 cu. in. [ME & OF *unce*, f. L *uncia* twelfth part of pound or foot (cf. INCH[1])]

ounce[2] *n.* Asian feline (*Panthera uncia*), the mountain panther or snow-leopard, smaller than leopard but marked like it. [ME, f. AF **unce*, OF *once* for earlier *lonce* (*l* mistaken for def. art.), = It. *lonza* f. Rom. **luncia* f. L LYNX]

OUP *abbr.* Oxford University Press.

our *poss. pron. attrib.* of us, of ourselves, that we are thinking of, (*is in our midst; our friend will have to watch his step; for all our sakes; acting on our behalf; have done our share*). **2.** of all people; **Our Father**, (1) the creator of us human beings, (2) the LORD's Prayer; *Our* LADY, LORD, SAVIOUR. **3.** of Us the king or queen, emperor or empress (*given under Our seal*); of us the present spokesman of a newspaper etc. (*a worthless book in our opinion*). [OE *ūre* orig. gen. pl. of 1st pers. pron. = of us (thus OS *ūser*, OHG *unsēr*, ON *vár*, Goth. *unsara*), later treated as possessive adj. (= OS *unsa*, OHG *unsēr*, ON *várr*, Goth. *unsar*)]

-our (er) *suf.*, = -OR in sense (1) (*colour*) or (arch.) other senses (*tenour*).

ours (-z) *poss. pron. pred.* (& abs.) = OUR; for phrs. see HERS. [ME, f. OUR + -s[3]]

oursĕ'lf *pron.* replacing MYSELF when used by sovereign, newspaper-writer, etc., who uses *we* instead of *I* (cf. OUR 3); = ONE*self* after *we* = ONE (*can we imagine a world in which ourself does not exist?*). [ME, f. as foll. + SELF]

oursĕ'lves (-vz) *pron.* Emphat. & refl. form corresp. to WE or US (for uses cf. HERSELF). [ME *our(e) selfs*; cf. OUR, YOURSELVES]

-ous *suf.* forming *adjs.* meaning 'abounding in, characterized by, of the nature of' (*envious, fabulous, glorious, grievous, hazardous, mountainous, murderous,*

poisonous); cf. -ACIOUS, -EOUS, -FEROUS, -IOUS, -VOROUS, etc.; (Chem.) denoting state of lower valence than -IC (*ferrous*); hence -OUSLY[2] *adv. suf.*, -OUSNESS *n. suf.* (cf. -OSITY). [f. or after AF *-ous*, OF *-eus*, cf. L *-osus*; cf. -OSE[1]]

ousel. See OUZEL.

oust *v.t.* put out of possession, eject, deprive *of*, expel *from*, drive out, force oneself or be put into the place of; *so* ~ER[4] *n.*, (Law & US) ejection. [f. AF *ouster*, OF *oster* take away, f. L OB(*stare* stand) oppose, hinder]

out *adv., prep., n., a., int.,* & *v.t.* **1.** *adv.* away from or not in or at a place, the right or normal state, the fashion, etc., (*keep him out; get out* (*of here*)*!;* TIDE[1] *is out; her son is out in Canada; anchored some way out; on the voyage out; crinolines are out*); with attentiveness (LOOK, WATCH[2], *out*); with distribution from a centre (DOLE[1], SHARE[2], *out*); not in one's house, office, etc., (*an evening* or *night out; go out for a walk, for a meal*); (of tooth) extracted; (of joint etc.) dislocated (*put his shoulder out*); (Polit., of party etc.) not in office; (of batsman, batter, etc.) no longer taking part as such because of having been caught etc. (*side was all out for 51;* **not** ~, not having been dismissed thus); away from centre of operations (*boarded out, contracted out*); (of time) not spent in working; (of workers) on strike; (of jury) considering verdict in private; (of fire, candle, etc.) no longer burning; no longer visible (*cannot get the stain out; inscription has been painted out*); in error (*was 3% out in my calculations; your guess was not far out*); not worth considering (*that idea is out*); no longer on friendly terms (*with*); unconscious, (Boxing) unable to defend oneself (*out for the* COUNT[1]). **2.** in(to) the open, publicity, existence, notice, hearing (*called out to warn me*), view (*woolly,* WRONG, *side out*), or clearness; so as to be clearly heard (*call out*); (of book etc.) published; (of star etc.) visible at nightfall; (of flowers etc.) no longer in bud, open; (of chicken etc.) hatched; (of rash etc.) visible; (of secret) revealed; (of young woman, arch.) introduced to society; (w. superl.) known to exist (*is the best game out*); *out and* ABOUT; *out at* ELBOW[1]*s;* ~ **for**, having one's interest or effort directed to, intent on; ~ **to**, keenly striving to (do); ALL *out;* STRAIGHT *out;* WAY *out; murder, truth,* etc., **will** ~, is sure to be discovered. **3.** to or at an end, completely, (*she had her cry* or *sleep out; tired out; sold out; storm blew itself out; hear me out; die out;* FIGHT[1] *it out; before the week is out*); in finished form (*have not typed it out yet*); (in radio conversation etc.) transmission ends; ~ **and away,** by far; ~ **and** ~, thorough(ly), surpassing(ly). **4.** ~ **of** *prep.*, from within, not within, from among, beyond range of, (so as to be) without, from, owing to, by use of (material), at specified distance from (town, port, etc.), beyond, (*come out of the house; I was never out of England; nine people out of ten know that; must choose out of these; is out of sight; was swindled out of his money; is out of breath, work, spades and hearts, sugar,* etc.; *get money out of him; got value out of the treatment; asked out of curiosity; what did you make it out of?; is seven miles out of Liverpool; something out of the ordinary*); *out of* (animal) having as dam (*filly out of Lutetia*); *out of* DATE[2], DOORS, DRAWING, HAND[1]; ~ **of it**, not included, forlorn; *out of* KEEPING, NUMBER[1], ORDER[1], POCKET[1], *the* QUESTION[1], SORT[1]*s, the* WAY, *this* WORLD. **5.** *prep.* out of (FROM 13 *out*); **out* at (*looked out the window*). **6.** *n.* way of escape; **at** ~**s**, at variance or enmity (*the* ~**s**, the party out of office; *the* IN[4]*s and* outs. **7.** *a.* (Of match) played away; (of island) away from the mainland); ~ **size** (beyond the ordinary; see OUTSIZE) **8.** *int.* = *get* etc. *out!;* (arch.) expr. abhorrence, reproach, etc., (*out upon you!*). **9.** *v.i.* come or go out (*murder will out*); ~ **with**, let us eject, dismiss, etc., (unwanted person); ~ **with it**, say what you are thinking. **10.** *v.t.* put out; (sl. or colloq.) eject forcibly; (Boxing) knock out. [OE (= OS, ON, Goth.) *ūt,* OHG *ūz,* cogn. w. Skr. *ud-*]

out- *pref.* = prec. *adv.* or *a.* or *prep.*, to *vbs.* or *ns.* **1.** To *vbs.*, w. sense of outward action, manifestation, completion, etc., (*outblaze, outspread*). **2.** To participles and gerunds as in 1, but often with specialized sense (*outcast, outstanding*). **3.** To *ns.* as in 1, giving sense of (a) vbl action (*outbreak, outburst*), (b) that which acts (*outcrop, outgrowth*), (c) that which is acted upon, made, done, etc., (*outcry, outlook*), (d) place or time of action (*outlet, outset*). **4.** To *ns.*, w. sense (a) external (*outline, outside*), (b) separate, away from the centre or main body, (*outhouse, outpost*). **5.** To *ns.*, forming *adjs.* & *advs.* w. sense '(that is) out of' (*outdoors, outlaw*). **6.** With general sense of excess, (a) to *vbs.*, w. idea of acting successfully or to a greater extent (*outface*), (b) to *vbs.* or *ns.*, forming *v.t.* whose obj. is a person or thing surpassed or defeated by more, better, or longer action (or action as) (*outvote, outrun, outgeneral*), (c) to *vbs.*, forming *v.t.* whose obj. is person or thing exceeded by continued action (*outgrow, outlive, outstay*), (d) to *ns.* or *adjs.*, forming *v.t.* whose obj. is person or thing surpassed in some respect (*outclass, outnumber, outwit*), (e) to name of person noted for some quality, forming *v.t.* (usu. w. name repeated as obj.) indicating that even he is surpassed in that quality (*out-herod*).

out-a'ct *v.t.* surpass in acting or performing. [f. OUT-6(b) + ACT²]

ou'tage *n.* period of non-operation of power-supply etc. [f. OUT- + -AGE]

out-and-ou'ter *n.* (sl.) thorough or supreme person or thing; extremist. [f. OUT *and out* + -ER¹]

ou'tback *n.* (esp. Austral.) remote inland districts; hence ~ER¹ *n.* [f. OUT + BACK³]

outbă'lance *v.t.* outweigh (lit. or fig.). [f. OUT-6(a) + BALANCE²]

outbi'd *v.t.* (-dd-; outbi'd). bid higher than (other person) at auction; offer more than; surpass in exaggeration etc. [f. OUT- 6(b) + BID¹]

outblă'ze *v.* **1.** *v.i.* blaze out(wards). **2.** *v.t.* blaze more brightly than. [f. OUT- 1, 6(b) + BLAZE²]

ou'tboard *a.* & *adv.* on or towards, or nearer than something else to, outside of ship, aircraft, or vehicle; (of motor) attached externally to stern of boat; (of boat) having outboard motor. [f. OUT- 5 + BOARD¹]

ou'tbound *a.* outward bound. [f. OUT- 2 + BOUND⁵]

outbră've *v.t.* face defiantly; outdo in bravery. [f. OUT- 6(a, b) + BRAVE²]

ou'tbreak (-āk) *n.* breaking out (esp. fig. of anger, war, disease, volcano, etc.); outcrop; insurrection. [f. OUT- 3(a) + BREAK³]

ou'tbreeding *n.* breeding from animals not closely related. [f. OUT- 2 + BREEDING]

ou'tbuilding (-bi-) *n.* detached subordinate building, outhouse. [f. OUT- 4(b) + BUILDING]

ou'tburst *n.* bursting out; explosion of feeling esp. in angry words; outcrop. [f. OUT- 3(a) + BURST³]

ou'tcast (-kah-) *a.* & *n.* (person) cast out from home and friends; homeless and friendless (vagabond). [ME, f. OUT- 2 + p.p. of CAST¹]

ou'tcaste¹ (-kah-) *n.* & *a.* (Ind.) (person) who has lost his caste or has no caste. [f. OUT- 5 + CASTE]

outca'ste² (-kah'-) *v.t.* (Ind.) cause (person) to lose his caste. [f. prec.]

outcla'ss (-ah's) *v.t.* belong to higher class than; defeat easily. [f. OUT- 6(d) + CLASS]

||**ou't-cŏllège** *a.* belonging to college but not residing there. [f. OUT- 5 + COLLEGE]

ou'tcome (-ŭm) *n.* result, visible effect. [f. OUT- 3(b) + obs. *come* n. (as COME)]

ou'tcrŏp *n.*, & *v.i.* (-pp-). **1.** *n.* emergence of stratum, vein, or rock, at surface; stratum etc. thus emerging; (fig.) noticeable manifestation. **2.** *v.i.* crop out, appear as outcrop. [f. OUT- 3(a, b) + CROP¹]

ou'tcrȳ *n.* crying out; clamour, uproar. [ME, f. OUT- 3(a, c) + CRY¹]

outda'nce (-ah'ns) *v.t.* surpass in dancing. [f. OUT- 6(b) + DANCE¹]

outdā're *v.t.* overcome by daring; outdo in daring. [f. OUT- 6(a, b) + DARE]

outdā'tĕd *a.* out of date; obsolete. [p.p. of *outdate* v. f. OUT- 1 + DATE³]

outdi'stance *v.t.* get far ahead of, leave (competitor) behind completely. [f. OUT- 6(d) + DISTANCE]

outdo' (-ōō') *v.t.* (outdi'd; outdo'ne *pr.* -dŭ'n; cf. DO¹). exceed or excel in doing or performance, be superior to, surpass. [f. OUT- 6(b) + DO¹]

ou'tdoor (-ŏr) *a.* done or existing or used out of DOORS; ||~ **relief,** (Hist.) = OUT-RELIEF. [f. OUT- 5 + DOOR]

outdoor's (-ŏr'z) *adv.* & *n.* **1.** *adv.* outside buildings, out of doors, in or into the open air. **2.** *n.* the world outside buildings, the open air. [f. as prec. + -s¹]

ou'ter *a.* & *n.* **1.** *a.* farther from centre or inside, relatively far out, external, of the outside; objective, physical, not subjective or psychical; *outer* BAR¹; ~ **garments,** ~**wear,** (worn over other clothes, or worn outdoors); **O~ House** (of Sc. Court of Session, where judges sit singly); ~ **man** or **woman,** personal appearance, dress; ~ **space,** universe beyond earth's atmosphere; **the ~ world,** people outside one's own circle; hence ~MOST *a.* **2.** *n.* division of target farthest from bull's-eye; shot that strikes this. [ME, f. OUT, replacing UTTER¹]

outfā'ce *v.t.* abash by staring or by confident demeanour; defy. [f. OUT- 6(a) + FACE²]

ou'tfall (-awl) *n.* mouth of river, drain, etc., where it empties into sea etc. [f. OUT- 3(d) + FALL²]

ou'tfield *n.* **1.** outer part of cricket or baseball field; hence ~ER¹ *n.* **2.** outlying land. [f. OUT- 4(b) + FIELD]

ou'tfighting (-fīt-) *n.* fighting other than at close range. [f. OUT- 4(b) + FIGHT¹ + -ING¹]

ou'tfit *n.* complete equipment or set of things for a purpose; set of clothes to be worn together; (colloq.) group of persons regarded as a unit, organization. [f. OUT- 3(b) + FIT⁴]

ou'tfitter *n.* supplier of equipment, esp. men's clothing. [f. prec. + -ER¹]

outflă'nk *v.t.* have flank extending beyond that of (enemy); outmanœuvre (thus, or fig.). [f. OUT- 6(d) + FLANK]

ou'tflow (-ō) *n.* outward flow; amount that flows out. [f. OUT- 3(a, b) + FLOW]

outflȳ' *v.t.* (-flew'; -flow'n). surpass in flying; fly farther or faster than. [f. OUT- 6(b) + FLY²]

outfŏ'x *v.t.* (colloq.) outwit. [f. OUT- 6(b) + FOX²]

outgĕ'neral *v.t.* (||-ll-). outdo in generalship; get the better of by superior strategy or tactics. [f. OUT- 6(b) + GENERAL]

outgō'¹ *v.t.* (outwe'nt; outgo'ne *pr.* -gŏ'n, -gaw'n; cf. GO¹). (arch.) go faster than; surpass. [f. OUT- 6(b) + GO¹]

ou'tgō² *n.* (*pl.* ~es *pr.* -ōz). expenditure. [f. OUT- 3(b) + GO²]

ou'tgŏing *a.* & *n.* **1.** *a.* going out; retiring from office; friendly, sociable. **2.** *n.* going out; (in *pl.*) expenditure. [f. OUT- 2, 3(a, b) + GOING¹,²]

outgrow' (-ō') *v.t.* (-grew'; -grow'n). grow faster than; become taller than (person) or too big for (clothes, one's strength); leave behind (childish ailment or habit or taste) as one grows or develops. [f. OUT- 6(b, c) + GROW]

ou'tgrowth (-ōth) *n.* process of growing out; that which grows out; offshoot, natural product. [f. OUT- 3(a, b) + GROWTH]

outguĕ'ss (-gĕ's) *v.t.* guess correctly what is intended by (another). [f. OUT- 6(a) + GUESS]

outgŭ'n (-nn-). surpass in power of guns (lit. or fig.). [f. OUT- 6(d) + GUN]

out-hĕ'rod *v.t.* exceed in evil or extravagance (usu. *out-herod Herod*). [f. OUT- 6(e) + *Herod,* blustering tyrant in miracle-plays, representing Herod (ruler of Judaea at birth of Christ)]

ou'thouse (-t-h-) *n.* (*pl. loc. pr.* -zĭz). house or building or shed belonging to main house and built near or against it; *outdoor lavatory. [ME, f. OUT- 4(b) + HOUSE¹]

ou'ting *n.* pleasure-trip, holiday away from home; appearance in outdoor contest etc. [f. OUT *v.* = put out, go out + -ING¹]

outjo'ckey *v.t.* outwit by adroitness or trickery. [f. OUT- 6(b) + JOCKEY²]

outju'mp *v.t.* surpass in jumping. [f. OUT- 6(b) + JUMP²]

outlä'ndish *a.* looking or sounding foreign; unfamiliar, bizarre, uncouth. [OE *ūtlendisc* (*ūtland* foreign country f. OUT + LAND¹; see -ISH¹)]

outla'st (-lah'-) *v.t.* last longer than (person, thing, or duration). [f. OUT- 6(a, b) + LAST⁴]

ou'tlaw *n.,* & *v.t.* **1.** *n.* person deprived of protection of law; banished or exiled person; lawless violent person. **2.** *v.t.* declare (person) outlaw; make illegal, proscribe. **3.** So ~RY *n.,* condition of or condemnation as outlaw. [OE (*ūtlagian* v. f.) *ūtlaga* f. ON *útlagi* (*útlagr* outlawed f. *út* OUT + **lagu* LAW¹)]

ou'tlay *n.* what is spent on something. [f. OUT- 3(c) + LAY³]

ou'tlet (-ĭt, -ĕt) *n.* place or means of exit or escape or expression; market for goods; *(Electr.) power point. [ME, f. OUT- 3(d) + LET²]

ou'tlĭer *n.* outlying part or member; (Geol.) minor part of formation separated from main body by denudation. [f. OUT- 3(b) + LIE³ + -ER¹]

ou'tlïne *n.,* & *v.t.* **1.** *n.* (in *sing.* or *pl.*) line(s) enclosing the apparently plane figure presented by any object to sight, contour, external boundary; sketch containing only contour lines and no shading (**in** ~, so sketched); form representing word in shorthand; rough draft, verbal description of essential parts only, summary; (in *pl.*) main features, general principles. **2.** *v.t.* draw or describe in outline; mark outline of in decorating etc. [f. OUT- 4(a) + LINE²]

outli've *v.t.* live longer than; live beyond (specified period or date); live through (an experience); = LIVE² *down.* [ME, f. OUT- 6(b, c) + LIVE²]

ou'tlŏok *n.* looking out; what is seen on looking out, view, prospect (esp. fig.); mental attitude. [f. OUT- 3(a, c) + LOOK]

ou'tlỹing *a.* situated far from a centre, remote. [f. OUT- 2 + LYING²]

‖outmanœu'vre, *-maneu'ver, (-nōō'ver) *v.t.* outdo in manœuvring; outgeneral. [f. OUT- 6(b) + MANŒUVRE²]

outmä'tch *v.t.* be more than a match for, surpass. [f. OUT- 6(a) + MATCH²]

outmea'sure (-ĕ'zher) *v.t.* exceed in quantity or extent. [f. OUT- 6(a) + MEASURE²]

outmŏ'dĕd *a.* no longer in fashion; obsolete. [f. OUT + MODE + -ED¹]

ou'tmŏst *a.* outermost; uttermost. [ME, var. of *utmest* UTMOST]

ou'tnĕss *n.* externality, objectivity. [f. OUT + -NESS]

outnŭ'mber *v.t.* exceed in number. [f. OUT- 6(d) + NUMBER¹]

outpä'ce *v.t.* go faster than, outdo in contest. [f. OUT- 6(d) + PACE¹]

ou't-pätient (-shĕnt) *n.* hospital patient who is not in the hospital except briefly from time to time when receiving treatment. [f. OUT 7 + PATIENT]

ou't-pĕnsioner (-sho-) *n.* one who receives a pension from an institution without having to live there. [f. OUT 7 + PENSIONER]

outplay' *v.t.* surpass in playing; play better than. [f. OUT- 6(b) + PLAY¹]

outpoi'nt *v.t.* score more points than. [f. OUT- 6(d) + POINT¹]

ou'tpŏst *n.* post or detachment set at a distance from main body of army esp. to prevent surprise; distant branch or settlement. [f. OUT- 4(b) + POST²]

ou'tpouring (-pôr-) *n.* what is poured out; (usu. in *pl.*) spoken or written expression of emotion. [f. OUT- 3(c) + POUR + -ING¹]

ou'tput (-ŏŏt) *n.,* & *v.t.* (**-tt-**; *p.t.* & *p.p.* **ou'tput** or **ou'tputted**). **1.** *n.* (quantity or amount of) product of a process, esp. of manufacture, or of mental or artistic work; (Electr.) power etc. delivered by an apparatus; place where energy, information, etc., leaves a system. **2.** *v.t.*

put or send out; (of computer) supply (results etc.). [f. OUT- 3(c) + PUT²]

ou'träge *n.,* & *v.t.* **1.** *n.* forcible violation of others' rights, sentiments, etc. (*never safe from outrage*); deed of violence, gross or wanton offence or indignity (*an outrage upon decency, justice,* etc.); strong resentment (*at*). **2.** *v.t.* do violence to, subject to outrage, injure, insult, violate, ravish; infringe (law, morality, etc.) flagrantly; cause to feel strong resentment. [ME, f. OF *outrage* (*outrer* exceed f. *outre* f. L *ultra* beyond; see -AGE)]

outrä'geous (-jus) *a.* immoderate, extravagant, extraordinary; violent, furious; grossly cruel, immoral, offensive, or abusive; hence ~LY² *adv.,* ~NESS *n.* [ME, f. OF *outrageus* (as prec.; see -OUS)]

outrä'nge (-nj) *v.t.* (Of gun or its user) have longer range than. [f. OUT- 6(d) + RANGE²]

outrä'nk *v.t.* be superior in rank to. [f. OUT- 6(d) + RANK¹]

outré (ōō'trā) *a.* outside the bounds of what is usual or proper; eccentric or indecorous. [F, p.p. of *outrer* (see OUTRAGE)]

outrea'ch *v.t.* reach farther than; surpass; (poet.) stretch out (arm etc.). [f. OUT- 1, 6(b) + REACH¹]

‖ou't-relief *n.* (Hist.) assistance given to poor persons not living in workhouse etc. [f. OUT 7 + RELIEF¹]

outrï'de *v.t.* (-ro'de; -rï'dden). ride better, faster, or farther than; (of ship) come safely through (storm etc.). [f. OUT- 6(b, c) + RIDE]

ou'trïder *n.* mounted attendant riding ahead of, or with, carriage; motor-cyclist acting as guard in similar manner; *herdsman keeping cattle within bounds. [f. OUT- 4(b) + RIDER]

ou'trĭgged (-gd) *a.* (Of boat etc.) having outriggers. [f. OUT- 2 + RIG¹ + -ED¹, after foll.]

ou'trigger (-g-) *n.* beam, spar, or framework, rigged out and projecting from or over ship's side for various purposes; similar projecting beam etc. in building; log etc. fixed parallel to canoe to stabilize it; extension of splinter-bar enabling extra horse to be harnessed outside shafts, such horse; iron bracket bearing rowlock attached horizontally to boat's side to increase leverage of oar, boat with these. [f. OUT- 4(b) + RIG¹ + -ER¹; perh. partly after obs. (Naut.) *outligger*]

outright (-rīt) *adv.* & *a.* **1.** *adv.* (-ï't). altogether, entirely, once for all, not by degrees or instalments or half and half, (*kill, buy, outright*); without reservation, openly. **2.** *a.* (ow'-) downright, direct, thorough; hence ~NESS *n.* [ME, f. OUT + RIGHT⁴]

outrī'val *v.t.* (‖-ll-). outdo as rival. [f. OUT- 6(a) + RIVAL]

outrŭ'n *v.t.* (-nn-; -ra'n; -ru'n). run faster or farther than; escape; go beyond (specified point or limit). [f. OUT- 6(b, c) + RUN¹]

ou'trŭsh *n.* rushing out; violent overflow. [f. OUT- 3(a, b) + RUSH²]

outse'll *v.t.* (-so'ld). sell more than; be sold in greater quantities than. [f. OUT- 6(b) + SELL]

ou'tsĕt *n.* start, commencement, (*at* or *from the outset*). [f. OUT- 3(d) + SET²]

outshï'ne *v.t.* (-sho'ne). shine brighter than; (fig.) surpass in splendour or excellence. [f. OUT- 6(b) + SHINE¹]

outsïde *n., a., adv.,* & *prep.* **1.** *n.* (-ï'd, ow'-). external side or surface, outer parts, (*knows only the outsides of books*); (of path) side away from wall or next to road; external appearance, outward aspect; all that is without, the world as distinguished from the thinking subject, (*impressions from the outside*); position on outer side (*open the door from the outside; on the outside looking in*); (colloq.) highest computation (*there were a hundred, it is a mile, at the outside*); (in *pl.*) outer sheets of ream of paper; ‖(Hist.) passenger travelling on outside of coach etc.; outside player in football etc.; ~ **in,** = INSIDE *out.* **2.** *a.* (ow'-). of, on, nearer, the outside, outer; ‖~ **broadcast** (not made from studio); ~

edge, progression on outer edge of one skate, (Cricket) edge of bat away from batsman; ∼ **seat** (nearer the end); ∼ **track** (longer because of curve); ∼ **work** (done off the premises). **3.** (Of a chance) remote, very unlikely; (of player in football etc.) positioned nearest to edge of field (*outside forward, left, three-quarter,* etc.); not belonging to some circle or institution; (of broker) not member of Stock Exchange; greatest existent or possible or probable (*quote the outside prices*). **4.** *adv.* (-ī'd). on or to the outside, the open air, open sea, etc., not within or enclosed or included; (sl.) not in prison; **come** or **step** ∼, come out from room or house (esp. said as challenge to fight). **5.** ∼ **and in,** outside and inside; ∼ **of,** = sense 6; **get** ∼ **of,** (sl.) eat or drink. **6.** *prep.* (-ī'd). external to, not included in, beyond the limits of, other than, not in, to or at the outside of, at or to the exterior of, (*natural forces are outside morality; cannot go outside the evidence; has few interests outside his work; met her outside the post office*). [f. OUT- 4(a) +SIDE¹]

outsī'der *n.* non-member of some circle, party, profession, etc., uninitiated person, layman; person without special knowledge, breeding, etc., or not fit to mix with good society (RANK³ *outsider*); competitor thought to have no chance in race or competition. [f. prec. + -ER¹]

ou'tsīght (-īt) *n.* sight of what is external (opp, *insight*). [f. OUT- 3(a) +SIGHT¹]

outsī't *v.t.* (-tt-; -sa't). sit beyond duration of; sit longer than (another). [f OUT-6(b) +SIT]

ou'tsīze *a.* & *n.* (of) exceptionally large size (in garments, measurements, etc.) or (fig.) exceptionally great development; outsize person or thing. [f. OUT 7 +SIZE¹]

ou'tskīrts *n. pl.* outer border or fringe of town, district, subject, etc. [f. OUT- 4(b) +SKIRT + -s¹]

outsmā'rt *v.t.* (colloq.) outwit, be cleverer than. [f. OUT- 6(d) +SMART²]

outspā'n *v.* (-nn-) & *n.* (S. Afr.) **1.** *v.i.* & *t.* unyoke, unharness. **2.** *n.* act, time, or place of outspanning. [f. Du. *uitspannen* (as OUT, SPAN²); cf. INSPAN]

outspe'nd *v.t.* (-spe'nt). spend more than (resources etc., or another). [f. OUT- 6(b) +SPEND]

outspō'ken *a.* given to or involving plain speaking, frank; hence ∼LY² *adv.,* ∼NESS (-n-n-) *n.* [f. OUT- 2 +SPOKEN]

outsprea'd (-ě'd) *v.t.* (**outsprea'd**), & *a.* (*pr. ow'-when attrib.*) **1.** *v.t.* spread out, expand. **2.** *a.* spread out, fully extended or expanded. [ME, f. OUT- 1, 2 +SPREAD¹]

outstā'nding *a.* conspicuous, eminent, esp. by excellence (*at, in*), whence ∼LY² *adv.*; that is not yet determined or settled. [f. OUT- 2 +STANDING²]

outstā'r'e *v.t.* outdo in staring; abash by staring. [f. OUT- 6(b) +STARE]

ou'tstātion *n.* station (sense 2 or 7) at a distance from headquarters or from populous areas. [f. OUT- 4(b) +STATION]

outstay' *v.t.* stay longer than (another); stay beyond the limit of (one's invitation etc.; *outstay* one's WELCOME). [f. OUT- 6(b, c) +STAY¹]

outstě'p *v.t.* (-pp-). step outside or beyond. [f. OUT- 6(c) +STEP¹]

ou'tstrětched (-cht) *a.* stretched out or forth (esp. of person's arms). [f. OUT- 2 +STRETCH + -ED¹]

outstri'p *v.t.* (-pp-). pass in running etc.; surpass in competition or relative progress or ability. [f. OUT- 6(b) +obs. *strip* run fast]

ou't-swinger *n.* (Cricket). ball that swings away from batsman. [f. OUT- 3(b) +SWINGer]

out-ta'lk (-aw'k) *v.t.* outdo or overcome in talking. [f. OUT- 6(b) +TALK]

out-tö'p *v.t.* (-pp-). surmount, surpass in height (lit. or fig.). [f. OUT- 6(d) +TOP¹]

ou't-tray *n.* tray for documents etc. dealt with and to be taken elsewhere. [f. OUT- 3(c) +TRAY]

ou't-tūrn *n.* quantity produced; result of a process or sequence of events. [f. OUT- 3(c) +TURN²]

outvǎ'lūe *v.t.* be of greater value than. [f. OUT- 6(d) +VALUE]

outvīe' *v.t.* (-vy'ing). outdo in contest or rivalry. [f. OUT- 6(b) +VIE]

outvō'te *v.t.* defeat by majority of votes. [f. OUT- 6(b) +VOTE]

outwa'lk (-aw'k) *v.t.* outdo in walking; walk beyond. [f. OUT- 6(b) +WALK¹]

ou'tward *a., adv.,* & *n.* **1.** *a.* (arch.) outer. **2.** directed towards the outside; going out; bodily, external, material, visible, apparent, superficial; **the** ∼ **eye** (opp. *mind's eye*); ∼ **form,** appearance; ∼ **man,** (Theol.) body as opp. soul, (joc.) clothing etc. (cf. OUTER *man*); **to** ∼ **seeming,** apparently; ∼ **things,** the world around us; hence ∼LY² *adv.* **3.** *adv.* outwards; ∼ **bound,** (of ship or passenger) going away from home. **4.** *n.* outward appearance. [OE *ūtweard* (as OUT, -WARD)]

ou'twardněss *n.* external existence, objectivity; interest or belief in outward things, objective-mindedness. [f. prec. + -NESS]

ou'twards (-z) *adv.* in an outward direction; towards what is outside. [OE *ūtweardes* (as OUTWARD, -s³)]

ou'twash (-wǒ-) *n.* material carried from glacier by melt-water and deposited beyond moraine. [f. OUT- 3(c) +WASH²]

outwa'tch (-ǒ'ch) *v.t.* keep awake longer than; keep awake beyond end of (night etc.). [f. OUT- 6(b, c) +WATCH²]

outwear' (-ār') *v.t.* (-wor'e; -wor'n). wear out or away; pass (time) by endurance; live beyond duration of (undesirable state). [f. OUT- 1, 6(c) +WEAR¹]

outwei'gh (-wā') *v.t.* exceed in weight, value, importance, or influence. [f. OUT- 6(b) +WEIGH]

outwi't *v.t.* (-tt-). be too clever or crafty for, deceive by greater ingenuity. [f. OUT- 6(d) +WIT²]

ou'twith (-dh) *prep.* (Sc.) outside. [ME, f. OUT adv. + WITH]

ou'twork (-ērk) *n.* **1.** advanced or detached part of fortification. **2.** work done outside shop or factory that arranges it; hence ∼ER¹ *n.* [f. OUT- 4(b) +WORK¹]

outwō'rn *a.* out of date, obsolete; worn out, exhausted. [f. OUT- 2 +WORN]

ou'zel, ou'sel, (ōō'zel) *n.* = RING¹ *ouzel;* **water** ∼, diving bird of genus *Cinclus;* (arch.) blackbird. [OE *ōsle* blackbird = OHG *amsala;* orig. unkn.]

ou'zō (ōō'-) *n.* (*pl.* ∼s). Greek spirituous drink flavoured with aniseed. [mod. Gk]

ō'va. See OVUM.

ō'val *a* & *n.* **1.** *a.* egg-shaped or ellipsoidal, having the outline of an egg or elliptical; hence ∼ITY (-ǎ'l-) *n.,* ∼LY² *adv.,* ∼NESS *n.* **2.** *n.* closed curve with one axis considerably longer than the other, like ellipse or outline of egg; thing with oval outline. [f. med. L *ovalis* (as OVUM; see -AL)]

ō'var̆ỷ *n.* **1.** either of two reproductive organs in which ova are produced in female animals; hence ∼IE'CTOMY, ∼IǑ'TOMY, ∼I'TIS, *ns.* **2.** lower part of pistil, consisting of one or more carpels, from which fruit is formed. **3.** Hence **ovār'IAN** *a.* [f. mod. L *ovarium* (as OVUM; see -ARY¹)]

ō'vāte¹ *a.* (Biol.) egg-shaped as solid or in outline, oval. [f. L *ovatus* (as OVUM; see -ATE²)]

ō'vate² *n.* member of third class of Welsh bards. [f. assumed L *Ovates* pl., Gk *Ouateis*]

ovā'tion *n.* enthusiastic reception, spontaneous applause; (Rom. Ant.) lesser form of TRIUMPH. [f. L *ovatio* (*ovare* exult; see -ATION)]

o'ven (ŭ'-) *n.* **1.** brick or stone or iron receptacle for baking bread or other food in; **Dutch** ∼, (1) metal box of which open side is turned towards ordinary fire, (2) covered cooking-pot for braising etc. **2.** chamber for heating or drying; small furnace or kiln used in chemistry, metallurgy, etc. **3.** ∼-**bird,** S. Amer. bird of genus *Furnarius* making domed nests; ∼-**ready,** (of food) prepared before sale so as to be ready for immediate cooking in oven; ∼**ware,** dishes that can be used for cooking food in oven. [OE *ofen,* = OHG *ovan,* ON *ofn,* Goth. **auhns* f. Gmc **ohwnaz* f. IE **ukw(h)nos*]

ō′ver *adv., n., a.,* & *prep.* **1.** *adv.* outward and downward from brink or from erect position (*lean, fall, jump, knock,* etc., *over*). **2.** so as to cover or touch whole surface (*brush, paint, it over*); ONCE*-over.* **3.** with motion above something, so as to pass across something, (*climb, look, boil, over*). **4.** so as to produce fold or reverse position, upside down, (*bend it over*; TURN[1] *over*); overleaf (*see* over); (Cricket, as umpire's call) change to bowling from opposite end; *roll* ∼ **and** ∼, so that same point comes uppermost repeatedly. **5.** across a street or other space or distance (*take this over to the post office; is over in, am going over to, has come over here from, America*); ∼ **against,** in opposite situation to, adjacent to, in contrast with; **asked him** ∼ (to come as visitor from place not far off). **6.** with transference or change from one hand, party, etc., to another (*went over to the enemy; handed over the tickets;* GIVE[1] *over*); ∼ (**to you,**) (in radio conversation etc.) I await your reply, action, etc. **7.** too, in excess, in addition, besides, more, apart, till later time, more (*anxious* etc.) than is right (*see* OVER- 6), (*shall have something over; £20 and over*); HOLD[1], STAND[1], *over,* **not** ∼ **well** etc., fairly badly etc.; ∼ **and above,** moreover, into the bargain. **8.** from beginning to end, with repetition, with detailed consideration, (*read, count, over; did it six times over; talk or think the matter over*); (**all**) ∼ **again,** **∼,* (*begin* etc.) a second time (from the beginning); ∼ **and** ∼, many times. **9.** at an end, settled, (*the struggle is over; get it over (and done) with*). **10. all** ∼, (1) completely finished, (2) in or on one's whole body etc. (*went hot and cold all over; is all over mud*), (3) in characteristic attitude, behaviour, etc. (*that is Jones all* ∼, that is what one would expect of Jones). **11.** *n.* (Cricket). number of balls (orig. 4 or 5, later 6 or 8) bowled between two calls of 'over' (sense 4); the play that results; MAIDEN *over.* **12.** *a.* upper, outer, superior, extra, (usu. as pref.; see OVER- 1). **13.** *prep.* above, in or to position higher than, on, at all or various points upon, to and fro upon, all through, round about, concerning, engaged with, (*an umbrella over his head; bridge over the Thames; projects over the street; doubt hangs over the question; writing over the signature 'Disgusted'; with his hat over his eyes; draw a veil over it; a change came over him; blush spread over his face; rice is grown all over India; you may travel over Europe or Europe over and not find it; the* WORLD *over; sitting over the fire, lunch, a glass of wine,* etc.; *heard it over the radio; spoke over the telephone; pause over the details; laugh over the absurdity of it; go to sleep over one's work*); (Math.) divided by (*a over b* = *a/b*); ∼ **all,** from end to end (see OVERALL); **all** ∼, in or on all parts of, (sl.) very attentive or effusive to (person); HAND[1] *over hand; over* one's HEAD[1]; *over head and* EAR[1]*s.* **14.** with or so as to get or give superiority or preference to, beyond, more than, in comparison with, (*is king, reigns, has jurisdiction, over; was victor, won the victory, was victorious, over; set him over the rest; has no control over herself; give me the preference over him; cost over £50; decrease of 25 over last year*); ∼ **and above,** besides, not to mention. **15.** out and down from, down from edge of, so as to clear, across, on or to the other side of, throughout, through duration of, till end of, during, (*fell over the edge, the precipice; stumbled over a tree-root; jumped over the brook; looking over the hedge; spoke over her shoulder; running over the meadow; if we can tide over the next month; has deteriorated over the years; will not live over today; can you stay over Wednesday?; will go there some time over the weekend*); ∼ **the way,** facing on opposite side of street. **16.** Hence ∼LY[2] *adv.* (chiefly US & Sc.), excessively, too. [OE *ofer,* = OS *obar,* OHG *ubar,* ON *yfir,* Goth. *ufar,* f. Gmc **ubheri* f. IE **uperi* compar. of **upó* from under towards]

ō′ver- *pref.* = prec. *a.* or *prep.* or *adv.* **1.** To *ns.,* w. sense 'upper, outer, of higher kind, upside down, extra, to

or in higher position', (*overcoat, overlord, overtime*). **2.** As *prep.* to *ns.,* forming *n., a.,* or *adv.,* (*overall, overboard, overtime*). **3.** As *prep.* to *vbs.,* forming *v.t.* whose obj. is that of *over* following the original *v.* in an equivalent phrase, & similarly to vbl derivs., (*overhang*[1] a thing, = *hang over* it; *overcome, override, oversight*). **4.** As *adv.* in local senses (above, by way of cover, down from above or from erectness, past, beyond, in addition) to *vbs.* or vbl derivs. (*overshadow, overbalance*[1], *overwhelm, overtake, overhear*). **5.** As *adv.* in sense of completely, effectually, into submission, to *vbs.* or vbl derivs. (*overawe, overjoyed*). **6.** As *adv.* or *a.* to *vbs.,* *adjs., advs.,* or *ns.,* with sense of excess over what is desirable or suitable or true, or over a definite limit, (*overdo, overpay, overwork*). **7.** As *adv.* to *vbs.,* with sense of harming oneself by doing action to excess (*overeat, oversleep*). **8.** As *adv.* to *vbs.* or vbl derivs. or *adjs.,* with sense of 'more than' (*overdue, overfill*). **9.** As *prep.* to *n., v.i.,* etc. forming *v.t.* usu. with sense of 'exceeding' (*overpower, overtop*).

ōver-abou′nd *v.i.,* **-abŭ′ndance** *n.,* **-abŭ′ndant** *a.,* **-abŭ′ndantly** *adv.* See OVER- 6.

ōverǎ′ct *v.t.* & *i.* act (part, emotion, etc.), act part, with exaggeration. [f. OVER- 6 + ACT[2]]

ōver-ǎ′ctive *a.,* **-ǎctī′vitў** *n.* See OVER- 6.

ō′verall (-awl) *n., a.,* & *adv.* **1.** *n.* ‖garment worn over others as protection from wet, dirt, etc. while working; (in *pl.*) outer trousers or leggings or combination suit as protection from dirt in work or (child's) playing, ‖close-fitting cavalry trousers. **2.** *a.* from end to end (*overall length*); total, inclusive of all; taking into account all aspects. **3.** *adv.* (or -aw′l). in all parts (*ship dressed* ∼, from end to end); taken as a whole. [f. OVER- 2 + ALL]

ōver-ănxī′etў (-ngz-) *n.,* **-ă′nxious** *a.,* **-ă′nxiously** *adv.,* (-ngkshu-). See OVER- 6.

ōverǎr′ch *v.t.* form arch over; hence ∼ING[2] *a.* [f. OVER- 4 + ARCH[2]]

ō′verārm *a.* & *adv.* (Cricket etc.) with hand above shoulder (*overarm bowling, service*); (Swimming) with one or both arms lifted out of water during stroke. [f. OVER- 1 + ARM[1]]

ōverawe′ *v.t.* restrain by awe; keep in awe. [f. OVER- 5 + AWE]

ōverbă′lance[1] *v.* **1.** *v.t.* & *i.* (cause to) lose balance and fall; capsize. **2.** *v.t.* outweigh (lit. or fig.). [f. OVER- 4, 8 + BALANCE[2]]

ō′verbălance[2] *n.* (amount of) excess. [f. prec.]

ōverbear′ (-ār′) *v.t.* (-bor′e; -bor′ne). bear down or upset by weight or force; put down or repress by power or authority; surpass in importance etc.; outweigh; hence ∼ING[2] *a.,* domineering, masterful. [f. OVER- 4 + BEAR[3]]

ōverbĭ′d[1] *v.t.* (-dd-; overbi′d). make higher bid than; (Bridge) (1) bid more on (one's hand, or abs.) than its strength warrants, (2) overcall. [f. OVER- 9, 6 + BID[1]]

ō′verbĭd[2] *n.* bid that is higher than another or higher than is justified. [f. as prec. + BID[2]]

ō′verblouse (-z) *n.* garment like BLOUSE 2 but worn without tucking into skirt or trousers. [f. OVER- 1 + BLOUSE]

ōverblow′ (-ō′) *v.t.* (-blew′; -blow′n). (Mus.) blow (pipe etc.) so strongly as to produce harmonic instead of fundamental note. [f. OVER- 6 + BLOW[1]]

ōverblow′n (-ō′n) *a.* **1.** (Of storm etc.) passed over; excessively inflated or pretentious. **2.** (Of flower, or fig. of woman's beauty) too fully open, past its prime. [sense 1 p.p. of *overblow* f. OVER- 4, 6 + BLOW[1]; sense 2 f. OVER- 6 + p.p. of BLOW[3]]

ō′verboard *adv.* from within ship into water (*fall overboard*); **go** ∼, (colloq.) be highly enthusiastic; **throw** ∼, lit., or fig. = abandon, discard. [f. OVER- 2 + BOARD[1]]

ōverbō′ld *a.* See OVER- 6.

ōverboo′k *v.t.* make too many bookings for (aircraft flight etc., or abs.). [f. OVER- 8 + BOOK[2]]

For other words in *over-* **see** OVER-.

ō'verbōot *n.* boot worn over another boot or shoe. [f. OVER- 1 + BOOT¹]

ōverbrī'm *v.* (-mm-). **1.** *v.t.* flow over brim of (*the liquor that o'erbrims the cup*). **2.** *v.i.* (Of vessel or liquid) overflow at the brim. [f. OVER- 3 + BRIM²]

ōverbuī'ld (-bǐ'-) *v.t.* (-buī'lt). build over or upon; place too many buildings on (land). [f. OVER- 3, 9 + BUILD¹]

ō'verbūr'den¹ *v.t.,* -**bûr'densome** *a.* See OVER- 6.

ō'verbūrden² *n.* excessive burden; (Mining etc.) rock etc. that is to be removed in order to expose the deposit sought. [f. OVER- 4, 1 + BURDEN¹]

ōverbu'sy̆ (-bǐ'zǐ) *a.,* -**buy'** (-bǐ') *v.t.* & *i.* See OVER- 6.

ōverca'll¹ (-aw'l) *v.t.* (Bridge). make higher bid than (previous bid, opponent, or abs.); || = OVERBID¹ (1). [f. OVER- 9, 6 + CALL¹]

ō'vercall² (-awl) *n.* (Bridge). act or instance of overcalling. [f. as prec. + CALL²]

ōvercă'nopy̆ *v.t.* (literary). form canopy over. [f. OVER- 4 + CANOPY]

ōvercă'pitalīze, -īse (-īz), *v.t.* fix or estimate capital of (company etc.) too high. [f. OVER- 6 + CAPITALIZE]

ōver-cār'eful (-ār'f-) *a.* See OVER- 6.

ōverca'st¹ (-ah'-) *v.t.* (overca'st). **1.** (esp. in *p.p.*) cover (sky etc.) with clouds or darkness. **2.** stitch over (edge) to prevent unravelling. [ME, f. OVER- 9 + CAST¹]

ō'vercast² (-ah-) *n.* cloud covering (part of) sky. [f. prec.]

ōver-cau'tion *n.,* -**cau'tious** (-shŭs) *a.* See OVER- 6.

ōverchār'ge¹ *v.t.* put too much (explosive, electric, etc.) charge into; put exaggerated or excessive detail into (description, picture, etc.); charge too high a price for (thing) or to (person); charge (specified sum) beyond right price. [ME, f. OVER- 6 + CHARGE²]

ō'verchārge² *n.* excessive charge (of explosive etc. or of money; see prec.). [f. OVER- 6 + CHARGE¹]

ō'vercheck *n.* (cloth with) combination of two different-sized check patterns. [f. OVER- 1 + CHECK³]

ōverclou'd *v.t.* cover (as) with cloud(s); make obscure. [f. OVER- 4 + CLOUD]

ō'vercoat *n.* coat worn outside another, esp. over indoor clothes for warmth in cold weather; protective coat of paint etc. [f. OVER- 1 + COAT]

ōvercō'me (-ŭ'm) *v.* (-cā'me; -co'me). **1.** *v.t.* prevail over, master; (in *p.p.*) exhausted, made helpless, affected with great emotion (*with* or *by*); ~ **with liquor**, drunk. **2.** *v.i.* be victorious. [OE *ofercuman* (as OVER- 3, COME)]

ōver-cŏmpēnsā'tion *n.* (Psych.) exaggerated correction of real or fancied defect of character. [f. OVER- 6 + COMPENSATION]

ōver-cŏ'nfidence *n.,* -**cŏ'nfident** *a.,* -**cŏ'nfidently̆** *adv.,* -**cŏŏ'ked** (-kt) *a.,* -**crĕdū'lity̆** *n.,* -**crĕ'dulous** *a.* See OVER- 6.

ōvercrŏ'p *v.t.* (-pp-). exhaust (land) by continuous cropping. [f. OVER- 6 + CROP²]

ōvercrow' (-ō) *v.t.* exult or triumph over. [f. OVER- 3 + CROW³]

ōvercrow'd *v.t.,* -**cūriŏ'sity̆** *n.,* -**cūr'ious** *a.,* -**cūr'iously̆** *adv.,* -**dĕ'licacy̆** *n.,* -**dĕ'licate** *a.* See OVER- 6.

ōverdĕvĕ'lop *v.t.* develop too greatly; (Photog.) treat with developer for too long or otherwise excessively. [f. OVER- 6 + DEVELOP]

ōverdō' (-ōō') *v.t.* (overdi'd; overdo'ne *pr* -dŭ'n; cf. DO¹). carry to excess, go too far in; (esp. in *p.p.*) cook too much; fatigue, exhaust; ~ **it** or **things**, (1) work too hard, (2) exaggerate, carry an action too far. [OE *oferdōn* (as OVER- 6, DO¹)]

ō'verdōse¹ *n.* excessive dose (of drug etc.). [f. OVER- 6 + DOSE]

ōverdō'se² *v.t.* give excessive dose of or to. [f. OVER- 6 + DOSE]

ō'verdraft (-ahft) *n.* overdrawing of bank account; amount by which sums drawn exceed credit balance. [f. OVER- 6 + DRAFT¹]

ōverdraw' *v.* (-drew'; -draw'n). **1.** *v.t.* draw cheque in excess of the amount credited to (one's account); (in *p.p.*) having overdrawn one's account; exaggerate in describing or depicting. **2.** *v.i.* overdraw one's account. [f. OVER- 6 + DRAW¹]

ōverdrĕ'ss *v.* **1.** *v.t.* dress with too much display or formality. **2.** *v.i.* overdress oneself. [f. OVER- 6 + DRESS¹]

ō'verdrĕss² *n.* dress worn over another dress or a blouse etc. [f. OVER- 1 + DRESS²]

ōverdrĭ'nk *v.i.* & *refl.* (-dra'nk; -dru'nk). drink too much. [f. OVER- 7 + DRINK¹]

ōverdrī've¹ *v.t.* (-dro've; -dri'ven). drive (horse etc.), work (person), to exhaustion. [f. OVER- 6 + DRIVE¹]

ō'verdrīve² *n.* mechanism in motor vehicle providing gear ratio higher than that of usual gear. [f. OVER- 1 + DRIVE²]

ōverdūe' *a.* past the time when due or ready; not yet paid, arrived, born, etc., though after the expected time. [f. OVER- 8 + DUE¹]

ōver-ea'ger *a.,* -**ea'gerly̆** *adv.,* -**ea'gernĕss** *n.,* (-g-), -**ear'nĕst** (-ēr'-) *a.* See OVER- 6.

ōverea't *v.i.* & *refl.* (-a'te; -ea'ten). eat too much. [f. OVER- 7 + EAT]

ōver-ĕ'mphasis *n.,* -**ĕ'mphasīze** *v.t.* See OVER- 6

ōverĕ'stimāte¹ *v.t.* form too high an estimate of; hence ~A'TION *n.* [f. OVER- 6 + ESTIMATE²]

ōverĕ'stimate² *n.* too high an estimate. [f. OVER- 6 | ESTIMATE¹]

ōver-excī'te *v.t.,* -**exēr'tion** (-g-) *n.,* -**expō'se** (-z) *v.t.,* -**expō'sure** (-zher) *n.* See OVER- 6.

ō'verfall (-awl) *n.* turbulent stretch of sea etc. caused by strong current or tide over submarine ridge, or by meeting of currents; structure for overflow of water from canal or lock. [f. OVER- 4 + FALL²]

ōver-fati'gue (-ē'g) *v.t.,* & *n.* See OVER- 6.

ōverfee'd *v.i.* & *t.* (-fe'd). feed to much. [f. OVER- 7 + FEED¹]

ōverfi'll *v.t.* & *i.* fill to overflowing. [OE *oferfyllan* (as OVER- 8, FILL)]

ōverfi'sh *v.t.* fish (stream etc.) too much and thus deplete it. [f. OVER- 6 + FISH²]

ōverflow'¹ (-ō') *v.* **1.** *v.t.* flow over (brim etc.); flow over brim of; flood (surface); (of crowd etc.) extend beyond limits of (room etc.). **2.** *v.i.* (Of receptacle) be so full that contents overflow it, (of contents) overflow container; (of kindness, harvest, etc.) be very abundant. [f. OE *oferflōwan* (as OVER- 3, FLOW)]

ō'verflow² (-ō) *n.* what overflows or is superfluous; outlet for excess liquid; ~ **meeting** (for those who cannot find room at principal meeting, and therefore meet elsewhere). [f. (as) prec.]

ōverfly̆' *v.t.* (-flew'; -flow'n). fly over or beyond (place or territory); so **ō'verFLIGHT¹** *n.* [f. OVER- 3 + FLY²]

ō'verfōld *n.* (Geol.) fold of strata such that middle part is upside down. [f. OVER- 4 + FOLD²]

ōverfŏ'nd *a.* ~ **of**, having too great an affection or liking for; hence ~LY² *adv.,* ~NESS *n.* [f. OVER- 6 + FOND]

ōverfulfi'l, *-ll, (-fōōl-) *v.t.* (-ll-). fulfil (plan etc.) before appointed time; hence ~MENT *n.* [f. OVER- 6 + FULFIL]

ōverfu'll (-ōō'l) *a.* filled to overflowing or excessively. [f. OVER- 8 + FULL¹]

ō'verglāze *n.* & *a.* **1.** *n.* second glaze applied to pottery. **2.** *a.* (Of painting etc.) done on glazed surface. [f. OVER- 1, 2 + GLAZE]

ō'verground *a.* raised above the ground; not underground. [f. OVER- 2 + GROUND¹]

ōvergrow' (-ō') *v.t.* (-grew'; -grow'n; esp. in *p.p.,* of plants, lit. or fig.). grow over, overspread; grow over so as to choke; grow too big for (one's strength etc.); so **ō'verGROWTH** *n.* [ME, f. OVER- 3, 6, 7 + GROW]

ō'verhănd *a.* & *adv.* with hand above object held; with hand above shoulder; with palm of hand downward or inward; (Swimming) = OVERARM; ~**knot,** simple knot made by forming loop and passing free end through it. [f. OVER- 1 + HAND¹]

ōverhă′ng¹ v.t. & i. (-hu′ng). jut out (over); (fig.) impend (over). [f. OVER- 3 + HANG¹]

ō′verhăng² n. fact or amount of overhanging; overhanging part. [f. prec.]

ōver-hā′ste n., **-hā′stily** adv., **-hā′sty** a. See OVER- 6.

ōverhau′l¹ v.t. take to pieces in order to examine; examine condition of (and repair if necessary); overtake. [orig. Naut., = release (rope-tackle) by slackening, f. OVER- 4 + HAUL]

ō′verhaul² n. thorough examination (with repairs if necessary). [f. prec.]

ōverhea′d¹ (-ĕ′d) above one's head; in the sky or in the storey above. [f. OVER- 2 + HEAD¹]

ō′verhead² (-ĕd) a. & n. **1.** a. placed overhead (overhead wires); (of driving mechanism) above the object driven; (of expenses) arising from management, office supplies, interest on borrowed capital, etc., as distinct from business transactions. **2.** n. (in pl. or *sing.) overhead expenses. [f. prec.]

ōverhear′ v.t. (-hear′d). hear as eavesdropper or as unperceived or unintentional listener. [f. OVER- 4 + HEAR]

ōverhea′t v.t. heat to excess, make too hot (lit. or fig.); (in p.p.) too passionate about a matter. [ME, f. OVER- 6 + HEAT²]

ōver-indŭ′lge v.t. & i., **-indŭ′lgence** n., **-indŭ′lgent** a. See OVER- 6.

ōver-i′ssue (-shōō, -sū) v.t., & n. **1.** v.t. issue (notes, shares, etc.) beyond authorized amount or ability to pay. **2.** n. things or amount so issued. [f. OVER- 6 + ISSUE²]

ōverjoy′ed (-oi′d) a. filled with extreme joy (at, to hear etc.). [p.p. of overjoy, f. OVER- 5 + JOY²]

ō′verkill n. amount by which (capacity for) destruction (lit. or fig.) exceeds what is necessary for victory over or annihilation of enemy. [f. OVER- 6 + KILL²]

‖ōver-lā′bour (-er), ***-lā′bor,** v.t., **-lā′den** a. See OVER- 6.

ōverlă′nd¹ adv. by land, not by sea. [f. OVER- 2 + LAND¹]

ō′verländ² a. & v. **1.** a. (proceeding) entirely or partly by land. **2.** v.t. & i. (Austral.) drive (livestock) or go long distance overland; hence ~ER¹ n. [f. prec.]

ōverlă′p¹ v. (-pp-). **1.** v.t. partly cover; cover and extend beyond. **2.** v.i. (Of two or more things) partly coincide, not be completely separate. [f. OVER- 3 + LAP²]

ō′verlăp² n. fact or process or amount of overlapping; overlapping part. [f. prec.]

ōver-lā′rge a. See OVER- 6.

ōverlay′¹ v.t. (-lai′d). **1.** cover surface of with coating etc. **2.** overlie. [ME, f. OVER- 4 + LAY³]

ō′verlay² n. thing laid over another; coverlet, small tablecloth, etc.; transparent sheet to be superimposed on another sheet. [f. prec.]

ōverlay′³. See OVERLIE.

ōverlea′f adv. on other side of leaf (of book). [f. OVER- 2 + LEAF]

ōverlea′p v.t. (for forms see LEAP¹). leap over, surmount; omit, ignore. [OE oferhlēapan (as OVER- 3, LEAP¹)]

ōverlie′ v.t. (-ly′ing; -lay′; -lai′n). lie on top of; smother (child) thus. [ME, f. OVER- 3 + LIE³]

ōverli′ve v.t. live beyond (specified age, another, or abs.). [OE oferlibban (as OVER- 9, LIVE²)]

ōverloa′d¹ v.t., **ō′verload²** n., **ōver-lŏ′ng** a. See OVER- 6.

ōverlŏŏ′k v.t. **1.** have prospect of or over from above; be higher than. **2.** fail to observe; take no notice of, allow (offence) to go unpunished. **3.** superintend, oversee; hence ~ER¹ (ō′-) n. **4.** bewitch with the evil eye. [ME, f. OVER- 3 + LOOK]

ō′verlŏrd n. supreme lord; hence ~SHIP n. [ME, f. OVER- 1 + LORD]

ō′verlȳ. See OVER 16.

ō′ver|măn¹ n. (pl. ~men). overseer in colliery; (Philos.) = SUPERMAN. [f. OVER- 1 + MAN¹]

ōvermă′n² v.t. (-nn-). provide with too many men as crew, staff, etc. [f. OVER- 6 + MAN²]

ō′vermăntel n. ornamental shelves etc. over mantelpiece. [f. OVER- 2 + MANTEL]

ōver-ma′nў (-ĕ′-) a. See OVER- 6.

ōverma′ster (-ah′-) v.t. (usu. fig.) master completely, conquer; hence ~ING² a. [ME, f. OVER- 5 + MASTER²]

ōvermă′tch v.t. be more than a match for, defeat by superior strength etc. [f. OVER- 8 + MATCH²]

ō′ver-measure (-ĕ′zher) n. amount beyond what is proper or sufficient. [f. OVER- 6 + MEASURE¹]

ōver-mŏ′dest a., **-mŏ′dĕstly** adv., **-mŭ′ch** a., n., & adv., **-nī′ce** a., **-nī′ceness** (-sn-), **-nī′cetў,** ns. See OVER- 6.

ōverni′ght¹ (-ī′t) adv. on the preceding evening with a view to, or as regarded from, the next day; from one day to the next (stayed overnight; cannot change one's habits overnight). [ME, f. OVER- 2 + NIGHT]

ō′vernīght² (-īt) a. done etc. overnight; for use etc. overnight. [f. prec.]

ōverpa′ss¹ (-ah′s) v.t. pass over or across or beyond; get to the end of, surmount. [ME, f. OVER- 3 + PASS¹]

ō′verpass² (-ahs) n. road that crosses another by means of bridge. [f. OVER- 4 + PASS¹]

ōverpa′ssed, ōverpa′st, (-ah′st) a. that has gone by, past. [p.p. of OVERPASS¹; cf. PAST¹]

ōverpay′ v.t. (-pai′d). recompense (person, service) too highly; hence ~MENT n. [f. OVER- 6 + PAY²]

ōver-peo′pled (-ēpeld) a. containing too many people. [f. OVER- 6 + PEOPLE + -ED¹]

ōverpersuā′de (-sw-) v.t. persuade (person) in spite of his contrary judgement or inclination. [f. OVER- 5 + PERSUADE]

ōverpi′tch v.t. (Cricket). bowl (ball) so that it pitches or would pitch too near the stumps; (fig.) exaggerate. [f. OVER- 6 + PITCH²]

ōverplay′ v.t. play (part) to excess; give undue importance to; ~ one's **hand,** (Cards, or fig.) be unduly optimistic as to one's capabilities. [f. OVER- 6 + PLAY¹]

ō′verplŭs n. surplus, superabundance. [ME, partial transl. of AF SURPLUS or med. L su(pe)rplus]

ōverpoi′se (-z) v.t. (arch.) outweigh. [f. OVER- 8 + POISE¹]

ōver-pŏ′pŭlātĕd a. over-peopled; hence ~A′TION n. [f. OVER- 6 + POPULATE + -ED¹]

ōverpow′er v.t. reduce to submission, subdue; make (thing) ineffective or imperceptible by greater intensity; (of heat, emotion, etc.) be too intense for, overwhelm; hence ~ING² a. [f. OVER- 9 + POWER]

ōverpra′ise (-z) v.t., & n., **-prĕ′ssure** (-sher) n. See OVER- 6.

ōverpri′nt¹ v.t. **1.** (Photog.) print (positive) darker than was intended. **2.** print too many copies (of work, or abs.). **3.** print further matter on (already printed surface, esp. postage stamp); print (further matter) thus. [f. OVER- 6, 3 + PRINT²]

ō′verprĭnt² n. words etc. overprinted; postage stamp having these. [f. prec.]

ōver-produ′ce v.t. produce more of (commodity; usu. abs.) than is wanted; so **ōver-**PRODU′CTION n. [f. OVER- 6 + PRODUCE²]

ō′verprōof a. containing more alcohol than proof spirit does. [f. OVER- 2 + PROOF¹ 5]

ōverrā′te v.t. have too high an opinion of; ‖give too high assessment for rates. [f. OVER- 6 + RATE²]

ōverrea′ch v.t. circumvent, outwit, get the better of by cunning or artifice; ~ one**self,** strain oneself by reaching too far, defeat one's object by going too far. [f. OVER- 9, 7 + REACH¹]

ōver-reā′ct v.i. respond more violently etc. than is justified. [f. OVER- 6 + REACT]

ōver-refī′ne v.t. refine too much, make too subtle distinctions in (matter, or abs.). [f. OVER- 6 + REFINE]

For other words in over- **see** OVER-.

ōverrī′de *v.t.* (-ro′de; -ri′dden). **1.** ride over (enemy country) with armed force; trample (person) under one's horse's hoofs; (fig.) trample underfoot, supersede arrogantly, refuse to comply with, have or claim superior authority or precedence over, make ineffective; move so as to extend over; (of part of fractured bone) overlap another part. **2.** exhaust (horse etc.) by riding. [f. OVER- 3, 6 + RIDE]

||ō′verrīder *n.* vertical attachment on motor-car bumper to prevent another bumper from becoming locked behind it. [f. prec. + -ER¹]

ōverrī′pe *a.* See OVER- 6.

ōverrū′ff *v.t.* overtrump. [f. OVER- 9 + RUFF⁴]

ōverru′le (-ōō′l) *v.t.* set aside (decision, argument, proposal) by virtue of superior authority; annul decision by or reject proposal of (person) thus. [f. OVER- 9 + RULE]

ōverrū′n¹ *v.t.* (-nn-; -ra′n; -ru′n). flood (land); ravage (country) with hostile force; (of vermin, weeds, etc.) swarm or spread over; exceed (limit, due time, etc.); (Print.) carry over (word etc.) to next line or page. [OE *oferyrnan* (as OVER- 3, RUN¹)]

ō′verrūn² *n.* (amount of) overrunning; movement of vehicle at speed greater than is imparted by engine. [f. prec.]

ōversai′ling *a.* (Of part of building) projecting beyond what is below. [f. OVER- 3 + F *saillir* SALLY¹ + -ING²]

over-scru′pūlous (-ōō′-) *a.* See OVER- 6.

ōversea′¹, ōversea′s¹ (-z), *advs.* across or beyond the sea. [ME, f. OVER- 2 + SEA (+ -s¹)]

ō′versea², o′verseas² (-z), *adjs.* lying beyond the sea, foreign; pertaining to transport, countries, etc., across the sea. [f. prec.]

ōversee′ *v.t.* (-saw′; -see′n). superintend (workers, doing of work, etc.); hence **ō′verseeER¹** (-sēr) *n.* (||*overseer of the poor*, (Hist.) parish officer with duty of assisting the poor from public funds). [OE *oferséon* look at from above (as OVER- 3, SEE¹)]

ōversĕ′ll *v.t.* (-so′ld). sell more of (commodity etc., or abs.) than one can deliver; (fig.) exaggerate merits of. [f. OVER- 6 + SELL]

over-sĕ′nsĭtive *a.*, **-sĕ′nsĭtivenĕss** (-vn-) *n.* See OVER- 6.

ōversĕ′t *v.t.* (-tt-; overse′t). overturn, upset; set up (type) in excess. [f. OVER- 8 + SET¹]

ō′versew (-sō) *v.t.* (*p.p.* ∼n *or* ∼ed). sew (two edges) with every stitch in same direction through both edges and thread between stitches passing across and outside the join; join sections of (book) by stitch of this type. [f. OVER- 4 + SEW]

over-sĕ′xed (-kst) *a.* having unusually great sexual desires. [f. OVER- 6 + SEX + -ED²]

ōvershā′dow (-dō) *v.t.* shelter from sun; cast into the shade; make apparently less important by one's own brilliance. [OE *ofersceadwian* (as OVER- 4, SHADOW²)]

ō′vershoe (-ōō) *n.* shoe of rubber, felt, etc., worn over another as protection from wet, cold, etc. [f. OVER- 1 + SHOE¹]

ōvershōō′t¹ *v.t.* (-sho′t). send missile, travel, beyond (*mark* etc.; lit., or fig. of exaggeration, excess, etc.); (of aircraft) pass beyond limit of (runway etc.) when landing; **o′vershot wheel** (turned by water flowing above it). [ME, f. OVER- 4 + SHOOT¹]

ō′vershōōt² *n.* act or amount of overshooting. [f. prec.]

ōversī′de *adv.* over side of ship (into smaller boat, or into sea). [f. OVER- 2 + SIDE¹]

ō′versĭght (-īt) *n.* supervision; omission to notice, mistake due to inadvertence. [ME, f. OVER- 3 + SIGHT¹]

over-sī′mplify *v.t.* distort (problem, or abs.) by stating it in too simple terms; so **over-SIMPLIFICA′TION** *n.* [f. OVER- 6 + SIMPLIFY]

ō′versīze, -zed (-zd), *adjs.* of more than the usual size. [f. OVER- 6 + SIZE¹ (+ -ED²)]

ōverskīrt *n.* outer or second skirt. [f. OVER- 1 + SKIRT]

ō′verslaugh (-aw) *n.*, & *v.t.* **1.** ||(Mil.) passing over of one's turn of duty, pass over (duty), in consideration

of another duty that takes precedence of it. **2.** *v.t.* *pass over in favour of another; *omit to consider. [f. Du. (*overslag* n. f.) *overslaan* omit (as OVER, *slaan* strike)]

ōverslee′p *v.i.* & *refl.* (-sle′pt). sleep too long; continue sleeping after intended time of waking. [ME, f. OVER- 7 + SLEEP²]

ō′versleeve *n.* separate sleeve covering ordinary sleeve to protect it etc. [f. OVER- 1 + SLEEVE¹]

over-soli′citous *a.*, **-soli′citūde** *n.* See OVER- 6.

ō′versoul (-ōl) *n.* God as spirit animating the universe and including all human souls. [f. OVER- 1 + SOUL]

ōverspĕ′nd *v.* (-spe′nt). **1.** *v.t.* spend more than (specified amount). **2.** *v.i.* & *refl.* spend too much. [f. OVER- 6, 7 + SPEND]

ō′verspill *n.* what is spilt over or overflows; (fig.) surplus population leaving a country or city to live elsewhere. [f. OVER- 4 + SPILL¹]

ōversprea′d (-ĕ′d) *v.t.* (-sprea′d). become spread or diffused over; cover or occupy surface of; (esp. in *pass.*) cover *with* (*high mountains overspread with trees*). [OE *ofersprǽdan* (as OVER- 3, 4, SPREAD¹)]

ōversta′ff (-ah′f) *v.t.* provide too many persons as staff for. [f. OVER- 6 + STAFF¹]

ōverstā′te *v.t.* state too strongly; exaggerate; hence ∼MENT (-tm-) *n.* [f. OVER- 6 + STATE²]

ōverstay′ *v.t.* stay longer than (time, one's WELCOME, etc.). [f. OVER- 9 + STAY¹]

ō′versteer *v.i.*, & *n.* (Of motor vehicle) (have) tendency to turn more sharply than was intended. [f. OVER- 6 + STEER¹]

ōverstĕ′p *v.t.* (-pp-). pass beyond (boundary, lit. or fig.). [f. OVER- 3 + STEP¹]

ōverstŏ′ck (-ō, -strai′n *v.t.*, & *n.*, -strĕ′ss *v.t.*, & *n.*, -stre′tch *v.t.* See OVER- 6.

ōverstrūng *a.* **1.** (ō′-). (Of piano) with strings in sets crossing each other obliquely. **2.** (-ŭ′ng). (Of person, his nerves, etc.) (too) highly strung or intensely strained. [f. OVER- 4, 6 + STRUNG]

ōverstŭ′dy *v.t.*, & *n.* See OVER- 6.

ōverstŭ′ff *v.t.* stuff more than is necessary; (in *p.p.*, of furniture) made soft and comfortable by thick upholstery. [f. OVER- 6 + STUFF]

over-subscrī′be *v.t.* (usu. in *p.p.*). subscribe more than amount of (shares offered for sale, etc.). [f. OVER- 8 + SUBSCRIBE]

ōversŭ′btle (-ŭ′tel) *a.*, **-supplȳ′** *v.t.*, & *n.*, **-swĕ′ll** *v.t.* See OVER- 6.

ōvert (ō′vert, ōvĕ′rt) *a.* openly done, unconcealed, patent; **market** ∼, OPEN¹ market; hence ∼LY² *adv.* [ME f. OF, p.p. of *ovrir* open f. L *aperire*]

ōvertā′ke *v.t.* (-too′k; -ta′ken) come abreast with, by faster movement reach same point at same time as, (person or thing moving ahead of one in same direction); pass (such person or thing, or abs.) by faster movement; (of storm, misfortune, etc.) come suddenly or unexpectedly upon (person etc.); become level with or exceed (compared value etc.). [ME, f. OVER- 4 + TAKE¹]

ōverta′sk (-ah′-) *v.t.* give or be too heavy a task to or for. [f. OVER- 6 + TASK]

ōvertā′x *v.t.* make excessive demand on (person for tax, or as regards his strength etc.). [f. OVER- 6 + TAX¹]

ōverthrow′¹ (-ō′) *v.t.* (-threw′; -throw′n). upset, knock down; cast out from power, vanquish; subvert, put an end to, (institution etc.). [ME, f. OVER- 4 + THROW¹]

ō′verthrow² (-ō) *n.* **1.** defeat, subversion. **2.** (Cricket). fielder's return of ball, not stopped near wicket and thus allowing further run(s); such run. [sense 1 f. prec.; sense 2 f. OVER- 6 + THROW²]

ō′verthrŭst *n.* (Geol.) thrust of (esp. lower) strata on one side of fault over those on other side. [f. OVER- 3 + THRUST]

ō′vertīme *n.* & *adv.* (time during which person works) in addition to regular hours; payment for this. [f. OVER- 1, 2 + TIME¹]

ŏvertīr′e *v.t.* See OVER- 6, TIRE¹.

ŏ′vertŏne *n.* (Mus.) = *upper* PARTIAL; (fig.) (subtle or elusive) secondary quality or implication. [f. OVER-1 + TONE¹, after G *oberton*]

ŏvertŏ′p *v.t.* (-pp-). be or become higher than; surpass. [f. OVER- 9 + TOP¹]

ŏvertrai′n *v.t.* & *i.* subject to or undergo too much (esp. athletic) training, with consequent loss of proficiency. [f. OVER- 6, 7 + TRAIN]

ŏ′vertrick *n.* (Bridge). trick taken in excess of one's contract. [f. OVER- 6 + TRICK]

ŏvertrŭ′mp *v.t.* play higher trump than (another player, or abs.). [f. OVER- 9 + TRUMP²]

ŏ′verture *n.* **1.** opening of negotiations with another, formal proposal or offer, (usu. in *pl.*, esp. *make overtures to*). **2.** (Mus.) orchestral piece opening opera, oratorio, etc. (**concert** ∼, one-movement composition in same style). **3.** beginning of poem etc. [ME f. OF, f. L *apertura* APERTURE]

ŏvertŭr′n¹ *v.t.* & *i.* (cause to) fall down or over, upset; overthrow, subvert, abolish, invalidate. [ME, f. OVER- 4 + TURN¹]

ŏ′vertŭrn² *n.* upsetting, subversion. [f. OVER- 4 + TURN²]

ŏver-ū′se¹ (-z) *v.t.*, **ŏver-ū′se²** *n.*, **-vă′lūe** *v.t.* See OVER- 6.

ŏ′verview (-vū) *n.* general survey. [f. OVER- 3 + VIEW]

ŏverwee′ning *a.* arrogant, presumptuous, conceited, self-confident. [ME, f. OVER- 6 + WEEN + -ING²]

ŏ′verweight (-wāt) *n.* & *a.* **1.** *n.* preponderance; excessive or extra weight. **2.** *a.* (-wā′t). beyond allowed or suitable weight (*luggage*, *person*, *is overweight*). [f. OVER- 1, 2 + WEIGHT¹]

ŏverwei′ght² (-wā′t) *v.t.* load unduly (*with*). [f. OVER- 6 + WEIGHT²]

ŏverwhĕ′lm *v.t.* bury or drown beneath superincumbent mass, submerge utterly; crush; bring to sudden ruin or destruction; overpower with emotion or *with* excess of business etc.; hence ∼ING² *a.*, irresistible by force of numbers, influence, amount, etc. [f. OVER- 4 + WHELM]

ŏverwi′nd *v.t.* (-wou′nd). wind (watch etc.) beyond proper stopping-point. [f. OVER- 6 + WIND³]

ŏverwi′nter *v.* spend the winter (*at, in*, etc.). [f. OVER- 3 + WINTER]

ŏverwor′k (-êr′k) *v.* & *n.* **1.** *v.t.* & *i.* (cause to) work too hard. **2.** *v.t.* weary or exhaust with too much work; (fig.) make excessive use of. **3.** *n.* excessive work. [f. OVER- 6 + WORK¹,²]

overwrī′te (ŏvêr′t) *v.* (-wro′te; -wri′tten). **1.** *v.t.* write on top of (other writing); write too much about. **2.** *v.i.* & *refl.* write too much or too elaborately. [f. OVER- 3, 7 + WRITE]

ŏverwrou′ght (ŏveraw′t) *a.* over-excited; suffering reaction from over-excitement. [f. OVER- 6 + WROUGHT]

ŏver-zea′l *n.*, **-zea′lous** (-ĕ′-) *a.* See OVER- 6.

ŏ′vĭ-¹ *comb. form.* egg, ovum, as: ∼**duct**, canal through which ova pass from ovary esp. in oviparous animals; ∼**form**, egg-shaped; ∼**parous** (-ĭ′-), (Zool.) producing young by means of eggs expelled from body before they are hatched (cf. VIVIPAROUS), whence ∼**pa′rity** *n.*; ∼**po′sit** (-ŏ′z-), lay egg(s), esp. with ∼**po′sitor**, pointed tubular organ with which female insect deposits eggs, whence ∼**posi′tion** *n.* [f. L OVUM + -I-]

ŏ′vĭ-² *comb. form.* sheep, as: ∼**bo′vine** *a.* & *n.*, (animal) having character intermediate between sheep and ox, musk-ox; ∼**CIDE** *n.*, (joc.) sheep-killing. [f. L *ovis* sheep + -I-]

Ovi′dian (o-) *a.* of or like (the poems of) Ovid. [f. P. *Ovidius* Naso (Ovid), Roman poet d. AD 17 + -IAN]

ŏ′vine *a.* of or like sheep. [f. LL *ovinus* f. L *ovis* sheep; see -INE¹]

ŏ′void *a.* & *n.* **1.** *a.* egg-shaped as solid or as surface; oval with one end more pointed than the other. **2.** *n.* ovoid body or surface. [f. F *ovoïde* f. mod. L *ovoides* (as OVUM; see -OID)]

ŏ′vŏl|ō *n.* (*pl.* ∼**i** *pr.* ∼ē). (Archit.) convex moulding of quarter-circle or quarter-ellipse section, receding downwards. [It., dim. of *ovo* egg f. L OVUM]

ŏvotĕ′st|is *n.* (*pl.* ∼**es** *pr.* -ēz). (Zool.) organ producing both ova and spermatozoa. [f. as foll. + TESTIS]

ŏvŏvivi′parous *a.* (Zool.) producing young by means of eggs hatched within the body. [f. OVUM + -O- + VIVIPAROUS]

ŏ′vŭl|āte *v.i.* produce ovule(s) or ovum or ova; discharge ova from ovary; so ∼A′TION *n.*, ∼**ātory** *a.* [f. mod. L *ovulum* (as foll.) + -ATE³]

ŏ′vŭl|e *n.* rudimentary seed, female germ-cell of seed-plants; unfertilized ovum; hence ∼AR¹ *a.* [F, f. med. L *ovulum*, dim. of foll.]

ŏ′vum *n.* (*pl.* **o′va**). female germ-cell in animals, capable of developing into new individual when fertilized by male sperm; egg esp. of mammal, fish, or insect. [L, = egg]

ow *int.* expr. sudden pain. [natural excl.]

owe (ō) *v.t.* (OWING). **1.** be under obligation to (re)pay (person money, money to person, money) or render (person honour etc., gratitude etc. *to* person; ∼ **it to** one**self to** do, need to do in order to avoid unfairness to oneself); (abs.) be in debt (*for* thing, with creditor in dat.: *I owe you for your services, owed for all my clothes*); ∼ person **a grudge**, cherish resentment against him. **2.** be indebted for *to* person or thing (*we owe to Newton the principle of gravitation; he owes his success to good luck*; *I owe him much*). [a pret.-pres. v. like CAN², DARE, MAY¹: OE *āgan* (see OUGHT²), = OS *ēgan*, OHG *eigan*, ON *eiga*, Goth. *aigan* f. Gmc **aig-* f. IE **(o)ik-*]

Ow′en|ism (ō′ĭ-) *n.* communistic co-operation advocated by Robert Owen; so ∼ITE¹ (1) *n.* [f. R. *Owen*, Welsh social reformer d. 1858 + -ISM]

ow′ing (ō′ĭ-) *pred. a.* yet to be paid, owed, due, (*paid all that was owing*); ∼ **to**, attributable to, caused by, (*all this was owing merely to ill luck*), (as *prep.*) on account of (*owing to the drought, crops are short*). [ME, f. OWE + -ING²]

owl *n.* **1.** large-headed hook-beaked large-eyed soft-plumaged usu. nocturnal bird of prey of order Strigiformes (BARN¹-*owl*, HORN¹*ed* or LONG¹-*eared owl*, *tawny owl*, etc.); ∼**s to Athens** = COAL¹s *to Newcastle* [the owl being an emblem on Athenian coins]. **2.** solemn person, wise-looking dullard, [f. owl's reputed appearance]; hence ∼*ISH¹* *a.* **3.** ∼ (pigeon), variety of pigeon with owl-like head. **4.** ∼-**light**, dusk, twilight; ∼-**monkey**, douroucouli; ∼-**parrot**, (arch.) kakapo. **5.** Hence ∼′ERY (3) *n.* [OE *ūle*, = OLG **ūla*, ON *ugla* f. Gmc **uwwalōn*]

ow′lĕt *n.* small or young owl. [earlier *howlet*, dim. of OWL, assim. to HOWL]

own¹ (ōn) *a.* **1.** (Appended to possessive adj. or case) in full ownership, proper, peculiar, individual, and not another's, (*saw it with my own eyes; has a value all its own; let person* STEW² *in his own juice; loves truth for its own sake; be one's own* MAN¹; *may I have it for my* (*very*) *own?*; **my** ∼ (*sweetheart etc.*) (expr. affection, esp. in voc.)); ∼ **goal** (scored against one's own side)); (often also used to emphasize not the ownership, but the identity of the subject etc.): *cooks her own meals, every man his own lawyer, am my own master*; (abs.) private property, kindred, etc., (*may I not do what I will with my own?; came unto his own, and his own received him not*); **of** one's ∼, belonging to one (exclusively) (*I have nothing of my own; will give you one of my own; has a way of her own in such matters*); **come into** one's ∼, get possession of one's rightful property, be properly esteemed etc.; **get** one's ∼ **back**, (colloq.) get even, revenge oneself (*on*); **hold** one's ∼, maintain position, not be defeated or lose strength; **on** one's ∼, independent(ly), on one's own account or responsibility or resources, alone, unrivalled; *in a* CLASS *of* or *on* one's *or its own*. **2.** (Without preceding possessive) ∼ **brother, sister,** (with

both parents the same); ~ **cousin,** first cousin.
[OE *ǣgen, āgen,* = OS *ēgan,* OHG *eigan,* ON *eiginn*
f. Gmc **aiganaz* f. p.p. of **aigan* possess; see OWE]
own² (ōn) *v.* **1.** *v.t.* have as property, possess; (in *p.p.,* in
comb.) held as property by (*State-owned*); acknowledge
authorship, paternity, or possession, of (*child,
pamphlet, hat, that nobody will own*); admit as existent,
valid, true, etc.,(*owns his deficiencies, himself indebted,
(that) he did not know*); submit to (person's dominance
etc.) without protest. **2.** *v.i.* confess to (*owns to a sense of
shame, to having* done); ~ **up,** (colloq.) make frank
confession. [OE *āgnian* (*āgen* OWN¹)]
ow′ner (ō′-) *n.* one who owns as property; (sl.) captain
of ship; ||~**-driver, -occupier,** etc., one who both
owns and drives vehicle, occupies house, etc.; hence
~LESS *a.,* ~SHIP (1) *n.* [ME, f. OWN² + -ER¹]
ŏx (*pl.* o′**xen**). **1.** any bovine animal, individual of
kinds of large usu. horned cloven-footed ruminant
used when domesticated for draught, for supplying
milk, and for eating as meat. **2.** castrated male of
domestic species (*Bos taurus*) of this; **the black ox has
trod on** one's **foot,** misfortune or old age has come
upon one; *play the* GIDDY *ox.* **3.** ox-bird, dunlin; **ox-
-bow,** (1) U-shaped collar of ox-yoke, (2) horseshoe
bend in river, (3) lake formed from this when river
cuts across narrow end; **ox-fence,** strong cattle-fence
or jumping-obstacle of railing(s), hedge, and often
ditch; **ox-gall** (used for cleansing, and in painting
and pharmacy); o′**xherd,** cowherd; o′**xhide,**
(leather from) hide of ox; o′**xlip,** primula, (pop.)
hybrid of primrose and cowslip [f. as COWSLIP];
ox-pecker, Afr. bird feeding on ticks on animals;
o′**xtail,** tail of ox, much used for soup-making;
ox-tongue, (1) tongue of ox, esp. for cooking, (2)
bugloss; **ox-wagon** (drawn by ox(en)). [OE *oxa,* =
OS, OHG *ohso,* ON *uxi, oxi,* Goth. *auhsa* f. Gmc **ohson*
f. IE **uksin-*]
ŏx- *comb. form.* (Chem.) = OXY- (2) (*oxazole*) or OXALIC
(*oxamide*). [abbr.]
ŏxǎ′lic *a.* (Chem.) ~ **acid,** highly poisonous and sour
acid, (COOH)₂, found in wood sorrel and other
plants; so o′**xal**ATE¹ (3) *n.* [f. F *oxalique* f. L f. Gk *oxalis*
wood sorrel; see -IC]
||**O′xbridge** (ō′-) *n.* (characteristics of) Oxford and
Cambridge universities, esp. in contrast to newer
ones. [portmanteau wd f. *Ox(ford)* + (*Cam*)*bridge*]
o′**xer** *n.* ox-fence. [f. OX + -ER¹]
ŏ′**x-eye** (-ī) *n.* **1.** eye of ox; large human eye, whence
ŏ′**x-eye**D (-īd) *a.* **2.** plant with flower like eye of ox;
white ~, a ~ **daisy,** *Chrysanthemum leucanthemum*;
yellow ~, corn marigold. [ME, f. OX + EYE¹]
Oxf. *abbr.* Oxford.
O′xfăm (ō′-) *abbr.* Oxford Committee for Famine
Relief.
O′xford (ŏ′-) *n.* ~ **accent,** style of pronouncing
English in manner supposed affected and character-
istic of members of Oxford University; ||~ **bags,** very
wide trousers; ~ **blue** (dark, sometimes with purple
tinge); ~ **clay,** deposit of stiff blue clay underlying
coral rag in English Midland counties; ~ **frame,**
picture-frame of which sides cross each other at
corners and project; ~ **Group** (**Movement**),
religious movement founded at Oxford 1921, with
discussion of personal problems by groups; ~
Movement, Tractarianism, ~ **shoe,** o′**xford,** low
shoe lacing over instep; ~ **Tracts,** the 'TRACT²s for
the Times'. [~ in England]
o′**xid|ant** *n.* oxidizing agent; so ~ATE³ *v.t.* (arch.),
~A′TION *n.,* ~ATIVE *a.* [F, part. of *oxider* (as foll.); see
-ANT]
o′**xide** *n.* binary compound of oxygen. [F (*oxygène*
OXYGEN, *-ide* after *acide* ACID¹)]
ŏ′**xidīz|e, -īs|e** (-īz), *v.* **1.** *v.t.* cause to combine with
oxygen; cover (metal) with coating of oxide, make
rusty. **2.** *v.i.* take up, or enter into combination with,
oxygen; rust. **3.** ~ed **silver,** (incorrect name for)
silver with dark coat of silver sulphide. **4.** Hence
~ABLE *a.,* ~A′TION, ~ER¹ (2), *ns.* [f. prec. + -IZE]

O′xon. (ŏ′-) *abbr.* Oxfordshire; of Oxford (University
or diocese). [f. L *Oxoniensis;* see foll.]
Oxō′nian (ŏ-) *a.* & *n.* (member) of Oxford University;
(native or citizen) of Oxford. [f. *Oxonia* Latinized
name of *Ox(en)ford* + -AN]
ŏ′**xter** *n.,* & *v.t.* (Sc. & N. Engl.) **1.** *n.* armpit; inner side
of upper arm. **2.** *v.t.* support with or by taking the
arm, put under the arm; hug. [f. OE *ōhsta, ōxta*]
ŏ′**xy̆-** *comb. form.* (1) sharp, as: ~**car′pous,** with
pointed fruit; ~o′**pia,** abnormal keenness of vision.
(2, Chem.) oxygen, as: ~**-ace′tylene,** consisting of,
involving use of, a mixture of oxygen and acetylene
(~*-acetylene blowpipe,* for producing intensely hot
flame for welding etc.); so ~**-hy′drogen** *blowpipe,
flame, light,* etc.; ~**acid,** ~**salt,** (containing oxygen);
~**haemoglo′bin,** bright red compound of oxygen
and haemoglobin in arteries etc. [f. Gk *oxu- (oxus*
sharp, acid)]
ŏ′**xy̆gen** *n.* colourless tasteless odourless gas, most
abundant of all elements, existing in air and combined in water and most minerals and organic
substances, and essential to animal and vegetable life;
~ **mask** (placed over nose and mouth to supply
oxygen for breathing); ~ **tent,** enclosure to allow
patient to breathe air with increased oxygen
content; hence ŏxy̆′gĕnOUS *a.* [f. F *oxygène* acidifying
principle (as OXY- (2), -GEN); it was at first held to be
the essential principle in formation of acids]
ŏxy̆′gen|āte (ŏ′kŏī , ŏksī′-) *v.t.* supply, treat, or mix,
with oxygen, oxidize; charge (blood) with oxygen by
respiration; so ~A′TION *n.* [f. F *oxygéner* (as prec.) +
-ATE³]
ŏxy̆′genīze (ŏ′ksī-, ŏksī′-), -īse (-īz), *v.t.* = prec. [f.
OXYGEN + -IZE]
ŏxy̆mŏr′on *n.* (Rhet.) figure of speech with pointed
conjunction of seemingly contradictory expressions
(e.g. *faith unfaithful kept him falsely true*). [f. Gk *oxumōron*
neut. (as n.) of *oxumōros* pointedly foolish (*oxus* sharp,
mōros foolish)]
ŏxy̆tō′cin *n.* pituitary hormone controlling uterine
contraction and release of milk, used in synthetic
form to induce labour etc. [f. *oxytocic* accelerating
parturition f. Gk *oxutokia* sudden delivery (as OXY-
(1), *tokos* childbirth), + -IN]
ŏ′**xy̆tōne** *a.* & *n.* (Gk Gram.) (word) with acute accent
on last syllable. [f. Gk *oxutonos* (as OXY- (1), *tonos*
tone)]
oy′er *n.* criminal trial under the writ of ~ **and
terminer** or commission to judges on circuit to hold
courts. [ME, f. AF *oyer et terminer* f. L *audire* hear, *et*
and, *terminare* determine; see -ER⁴]
ōye′z, ōye′s, *int.* uttered, usu. thrice, by public crier or
court officer to command silence and attention. [ME,
f. AF, OF *oiez, oyez* imper. pl. of *oïr* hear f.L *audire*]
oy′ster *n.* edible bivalve mollusc of genus *Ostrea* or
family Ostreidae, usu. eaten uncooked; oyster-
-shaped morsel of meat in fowl's back; something
regarded as containing all that one desires (*the world's
my oyster*); (sl.) taciturn person; **vegetable** ~, salsify;
~**-bank, -bed,** part of sea-bottom where oysters
breed or are bred; ~**-catcher,** coastal wading bird
of genus *Haematopus;* ~**-farm,** sea-bottom used for
breeding oysters; ~**-knife** (of shape adapted for
opening oysters); ~**-park,** oyster-bed or -farm;
~**-plant,** salsify; ~(**-white**), white with pale
grey tinge. [ME & OF *oistre* f. L *ostrea, ostreum* f. Gk
ostreon]
Oz (ŏz) *n.* (Austral. sl.) Australia. [abbr.]
oz. *abbr.* ounce(s). [It. (*onza* ounce)]
ŏzō′**cerite, -ker-,** *n.* waxlike fossil paraffin used for
candles, insulating, etc. [f. G *ozokerit* f. Gk *ozō*
smell + *kēros* wax; see -ITE¹]
ŏzōn|e (ō′-, -ō′n) *n.* form of oxygen with three atoms in
molecule, having pungent and supposedly refreshing
odour; (pop.) invigorating air at seaside etc.; (fig.) exhilarating influence; hence ozō′nIC *a.,* ~IZE (3, 5) *v.t.*
[f. G *ozon* f. Gk, neut. pres. part. of *ozō* smell; see -ONE]
*ozt., ||**oztr.,** *abbrs.* troy ounce(s).

P

P, p, (pē) *n.* (*pl.* **Ps** *or* **P's**). sixteenth letter of alphabet; MIND² one's *P's and Q's.*

P *abbr.* (Chess) pawn; POISE².

p. *abbr.* page; (decimal) pence or penny; PIANO¹; pico-.

P *symb.* phosphorus.

pa¹ (pah) *n.* (vulg.) father. [abbr. of PAPA]

pa² (pah), **pah²,** *n.* Maori camp or village (formerly fortified). [Maori *pà* (*pà* block up)]

PA *abbr.* Pennsylvania; personal assistant; Press Association; public address.

p.a. *abbr.* per annum.

Pa. *abbr.* pascal; Pennsylvania.

Pa *symb.* protactinium.

pǎ'būlum *n.* food (esp. fig., *mental pabulum*). [L (*pascere* feed)]

PABX *abbr.* private automatic branch (telephone) exchange.

pǎ'ca *n.* rodent of genus *Cuniculus*, esp. spotted cavy of S. & Central America. [Sp. & Port., f. Tupi]

pāce¹ *n.* **1.** single step in walking or running; space traversed in this (about 30 in.); space between successive stationary positions of same foot in walking (about 60 in.). **2.** mode of walking or running; gait; any of various (esp. ambling or racking) gaits of (esp. trained) horse etc.; (fig.) put person **through his ∼s,** test his qualities in action etc. **3.** speed in walking or running; rate of progression (lit. or fig.); **go the ∼,** go at great speed, (fig.) indulge in dissipation; **keep ∼,** advance at equal rate (*with*); **set the ∼,** regulate the speed or rate of progress; **stand** or **stay the ∼,** be able to keep up with others. **4. ∼-maker,** (1) rider, runner, etc., who sets pace for another in race etc., (2) region of vertebrate heart initiating contraction in each beat, or electrical device performing same function; **∼-setter,** = *pace-maker* (1). **5.** Hence **-pācED²** (-st) *a.* [ME, f. OF *pas* f. L *passus* (*pandere* pass-stretch)]

pāce² *v.* **1.** *v.i.* walk with slow or regular pace; (of horse) = AMBLE; hence **pā'cING¹** *n.*, harness-racing for pacing horses. **2.** *v.t.* traverse by pacing; measure (distance *out*) by pacing; set pace for (rider, runner, etc.). **3.** Hence **pā'cER¹** *n.* [f. prec.]

pace³ (pā'sĭ, pah'chā) *prep.* (In announcing contrary opinion) with all due respect or deference to (person named). [L, abl. of *pax* peace]

pacha etc. See PASHA etc.

pachi'nkō *n.* Japanese form of pin-ball. [Jap.]

pachi'si (-chē'-) *n.* four-handed Indian game with six cowries used like dice. [Hindi, = of 25, the highest throw]

pǎ'chy̆dérm (-k-) *n.* thick-skinned mammal, esp. elephant or rhinoceros; (fig.) thick-skinned person; so **pǎchy̆dér'matOUS** (-k-) *a.* [f. F *pachyderme* f. Gk *pakhudermos* (*pakhus* thick, *derma* -matos skin)]

paci'fic *a.* & *n.* **1.** *a.* tending to peace; of peaceful disposition; characterized by peace, tranquil; hence **paci'fICALLY** *adv.* **2.** *a.* & *n.* (*P∼*). (of or adjoining) the ocean between America to the east and Asia to the west; **P∼ Time,** standard time used in Pacific region of Canada and US. [f. F *pacifique* or f. L *pacificus* (*pax pacis* peace; see -FIC)]

pǎcĭfĭcā'tion *n.* pacifying; being pacified; treaty of peace; so **paci'fĭcatORY** *a.* [F, f. L *pacificatio -onis* (as PACIFY; see -FICATION)]

pǎ'cĭf|ĭsm *n.* doctrine that the abolition of war or violence is desirable and possible; (support of) policy of arbitration in international disputes; so **∼IST** (2) *n.* [f. F *pacifisme* (*pacifier*; see foll.)]

pǎ'cĭf|y̆ *v.t.* appease (person, anger, excitement, etc.); bring (country etc.) to state of peace; hence **∼ĪER¹** *n.*,

(*esp.*) baby's dummy. [ME, f. OF *pacifier* or f. L *pacificare* (as PACIFIC; see -FY)]

pǎck¹ *n.* **1.** bundle of things wrapped up or tied together for carrying, esp. on shoulder or back, e.g. pedlar's bundle, soldier's or walker's knapsack. **2.** a measure of various goods, e.g. 500 sheets of gold leaf. **3.** (usu. derog.) lot or set (*pack of fools, lies, nonsense, thieves*). **4.** number of hounds kept together for hunting or of animals (esp. wolves) or birds (esp. grouse) naturally associating; organized group of Cub Scouts or Brownies, or of submarines etc. **5.** (Rugby Footb.) team's forwards. **6.** ||set of playing-cards. **7.** large area of large crowded pieces of floating ice in sea. **8.** quantity of fish, fruit, etc., packed in a season etc.; method of packing, or set of things packed, for selling (*pack of cigarettes*). **9.** (Med.) wrapping of (part of) body in wet sheet etc.; sheet etc. so used. **10.** application of medicinal or cosmetic substance to skin etc.; substance so applied; MUD *pack*. **11. ∼-drill,** military punishment of walking up and down in full marching equipment (*no names no ∼-drill,* discretion will prevent punishment); **∼-horse** (for carrying packs); **∼-ice,** = sense 7; **∼'man,** (arch.) pedlar; ***∼-rat,** large hoarding rodent; **∼-saddle** (adapted for supporting packs); **∼'thread,** stout thread for sewing or tying up packs. [ME f. MDu., MLG *pak*, of unkn. orig.]

pǎck² *v.* **1.** *v.t.* put (things) together into bundle, box, bag, etc., for transport or storing (often **∼ up,** esp. abs.); **∼ed meal** etc. (prepared earlier and put in container for one to carry to place of eating). **2.** put closely together; crowd together; (Naut.) **∼ on** (hoist) **all sail; form** (hounds etc.) into pack; place (cards) together in pack. **3.** cover (thing) with something pressed tightly round; (Med.) wrap (body or part of it) in wet sheet etc. **4.** (sl.) carry or possess (gun etc.); be capable of delivering (a punch) with skill or force. **5.** fill (bag, box, case, etc.) with clothes etc. (**∼** one's **bags,** prepare to depart); cram (space etc. *with*); load (animal) with pack; fill (theatre etc.) with spectators. **6. ∼ off,** send or drive (person) away, esp. summarily; **∼ed out,** (colloq.) crowded. **7.** (sl.) **∼ it in,** end it, finish; **∼ it up,** desist. **8.** *v.i.* crowd together (of animals or Rugby forwards) form pack. **9.** depart with one's belongings; **send ∼ing,** dismiss (person) abruptly. **10.** (sl.) **∼ up,** retire from contest, activity, etc.; (of machine etc.) cease to function, break down. **11.** Hence **∼'ER¹** *n.* [ME, f. MDu., MLG *pakken*; cf. prec.]

pǎck³ *v.t.* select (jury etc.) so as to secure biased decision in one's favour. [prob. f. obs. v. *pact,* f. PACT]

pǎ'ckage *n.,* & *v.t.* **1.** *n.* bundle of things packed, parcel; box etc. in which goods are packed; **∼** (**deal**), transaction agreed to as a whole, the less favourable items as well as the more favourable; **∼ holiday, tour,** etc., (with fixed route etc. at fixed inclusive price). **2.** *v.t.* make up into or enclose in a package; hence **pǎ'ckagING¹** (-kĭj-) *n.*, (making of) wrapper(s) or container(s) for goods. [f. PACK² + -AGE]

pǎ'ckèt *n.* **1.** small package; (colloq.) considerable sum of money won or lost; ||**catch, cop, stop, a ∼,** (sl.) be (severely) injured etc.; ||PAY¹-*packet.* **2. ∼**(-**boat**), mail-boat. [f. PACK¹ + -ET¹]

pǎ'ckĭng *n.* In vbl senses; (oil-absorbing) material closing a joint or assisting in lubrication of an axle; substance used to fill gaps in order to protect fragile objects, etc.; **∼-box, ∼-gland,** = STUFFING-*box*; **∼-case,** (usu. wooden) case or framework for packing goods in; **∼-needle,** large needle for sewing up packages; **∼-sheet,** sheet for packing goods in,

(Med.) wet sheet used in hydropathy. [ME, f. PACK² + -ING¹]

păct *n.* agreement, treaty. [ME, f. OF *pact(e)* f. L *pactum*, neut. p.p. (as n.) of *pacisci* agree]

păd¹ *n.* **1.** (arch., sl.) road (**gentleman, knight, squire, of the** ∼, highwayman); = FOOT¹*pad*. **2.** (arch.) ∼ (**-nag**), easy-paced horse. **3.** (Austral.) track, path. [16th c. cant, f. Du., LG *pad* PATH]

păd² *v.* (**-dd-**). **1.** *v.t.* tramp along (road etc.) on foot; ∥∼ **it**, ∥∼ **the hoof**, (sl.) go on foot. **2.** *v.i.* travel on foot; walk with soft dull steady sound of steps. [f. prec., or LG *padden* tread]

păd³ *n.* **1.** cushion or soft stuffing used to diminish jarring, fill out hollows, absorb fluid, etc.; guard for leg and ankle in cricket etc. (SHIN-*pad*); = INK-*pad*; **2.** number of sheets of blotting-, writing-, or drawing--paper held together at edge. **3.** soft stuffed saddle without frame. **4.** fleshy cushion forming sole of foot in some quadrupeds; paw of fox, hare, etc. **5.** *floating leaf of water-lily. **6.** (sl.) bed, lodging; house. **7.** flat surface for helicopter take-off, rocket launching, etc. **8.** handle to which various tools can be fitted (∼-saw, small compass-saw). [prob. of Du. or LG orig.]

păd⁴ *v.t.* (**-dd-**). furnish with a pad, stuff; fill out or *out* (sentence, publication, etc.) with superfluous matter; ∼ded cell, room with padded walls in mental hospital; hence ∼'d**ING¹** (4) *n.* [f. prec.]

pă'ddle¹ *n.* **1.** small spadelike implement with long handle; short broad-bladed oar used without rowlock; **double** ∼ (with blade at each end); *∼ **ball**, game like squash played with wooden paddle. **2.** one of the boards fitted round circumference of paddle--wheel or mill-wheel; paddle-shaped instrument; (Zool.) fin or flipper. **3.** ∼-**wheel**, wheel for propelling ship (∼-**boat**, ∼-**steamer**, etc.), with boards round circumference so as to press backward against water. [15th c., of unkn. orig.; cf. syn. (Sc. & N. Engl.) *pattle*]

pă'ddle² *v.* & *n.* **1.** *v.i.* & *t.* move on water, propel canoe, by means of paddles (∼ one's **own canoe,** (fig.) depend on oneself alone); row gently. **2.** *v.t.* *spank, thrash. **3.** *n.* action or spell of paddling. [f. prec.]

pă'ddle³ *v.i.*, & *n.* **1.** *v.i.* dabble with the feet or wade about in shallow water; (arch.) toy with the fingers (*in, on, about,* thing); (of child) toddle. **2.** *n.* spell of paddling. [prob. of LDu. orig.; cf. LG *paddeln* tramp about]

pă'ddock¹ *n.* small field, esp. near stable or as part of stud farm; turf enclosure adjoining racecourse, where horses or cars are brought together before race; (Austral. & NZ) field, plot of land. [app. var. of (now dial.) *parrock* (OE *pearruc*; see PARK¹)]

∥**pă'ddock²** *n.* (arch. or dial.) frog or toad. [f. ME *padde* (= ON *padda*, MDu., MLG *padde*) toad, + -OCK]

Pă'ddy¹ *n.* (Nickname for) Irishman. [pet-form of Ir. man's Christian *Padraig* = Patrick; see -Y³]

pă'ddy² *n.* rice before threshing or in the husk; ∼(-**field**), field where rice is grown. [f. Malay *pādī*]

∥**pă'ddy³**, ∥**pă'ddywhăck,** *ns.* (colloq.) rage, fit of temper. [f. PADDY¹]

pă'ddymĕlon. Var. of foll.

pă'dĕmĕlon *n.* small wallaby of coastal scrub. [corrupt. of Aboriginal name]

Pa'dishah (pah-') *n.* Shah of Iran; (Hist.) Sultan of Turkey; *(colloq.; *p*∼) important or influential person. [f. Pers. *pād(i)šāh* (*pati* lord; see SHAH)]

pă'dlŏck *n.*, & *v.t.* **1.** *n.* detachable lock hanging by pivoted hook or by chain etc. on object fastened. **2.** *v.t.* secure with padlock. [ME, f. LOCK²; first elem. unexpl.]

padou'k *n.* timber-tree of genus *Pterocarpus*; its wood, resembling rosewood. [Burm.]

pa'dre (pah'drĭ, -drā) *n.* (colloq.) chaplain in army etc. [It., Sp., & Port., = father, priest, f. L *pater patris* father]

pă'dŭasoy *n.* strong corded silk fabric much worn in 18th c. (cf. POULT-DE-SOIE). [earlier *poudesoy* f. F *pou--de-soie,* of unkn. orig.; assoc. w. *Padua* in Italy]

pae'an *n.* chant of thanksgiving for deliverance (orig. addressed to Apollo or Artemis); song of praise or triumph. [L, f. Doric Gk *paian* hymn to Apollo under name of *Paian,* orig. physician of the gods]

pae'derăst(y). See PEDERAST(Y).

paediă'tr|ĭc, *pĕdiă'tr|ĭc, *a.* relating to children and their diseases; hence ∼i'CIAN, ∼ICS, ∼IST (3), *ns.* [f. foll. + Gk *iatros* physician + -IC]

pae'do-, *pĕ'dō-, *comb. form.* child, as: ∼-**baptism,** infant baptism; ∼**phile,** person displaying paedophilia; ∼**phi'lia,** sexual love directed towards children. [f. Gk *pais paidos* boy, child + -O-]

paĕ'lla (pah-) *n.* Spanish dish of rice, saffron, chicken, seafood, etc., cooked and served in large shallow pan. [Cat., f. OF *paele* f. L *patella* pan]

pae'on *n.* metrical foot of one long syllable placed first, second, third, or fourth (**first** etc. ∼) and three short; hence **paeŏ'nĭc** *a.* [L, f. Gk *paiōn,* Attic form of *paian* PAEAN]

pae'onỹ. See PEONY.

pā'gan *n.* & *a.* heathen; unenlightened or irreligious (person); hence ∼DOM, ∼ISM (2), *ns.,* ∼ISH¹ *a.,* ∼IZE (3) *v.t.* & *i.* [ME, f. L *paganus* civilian (*pagus* country district; see -AN); sense 'heathen' in Christian L (Tertullian, Augustine)]

pāge¹ *n.,* & *v.t.* **1.** *n.* boy or man, usu. in livery, employed to attend to door, go on errands, etc.; boy employed as personal attendant of person of rank, bride, etc.; (Hist.) boy in training for knighthood and attached to knight's service; ∼-**boy,** (1) = *page,* (2) woman's hair-style with hair long and rolled under at the ends; hence ∼'HOOD (-jh-), ∼'SHIP (-jsh-), *ns.* **2.** *v.t.* summon by means of or as by a page, calling out name of wanted person until he is found. [ME f. OF, perh. f. It. *paggio* f. Gk *paidion,* dim. of *pais paidos* boy]

pāge² *n.* (one side of) leaf of book, periodical, etc.; what is printed etc. on this; (fig.) episode that might fill page in written history etc.; (in *pl.*) passage in book etc. (*his finest pages*). [F, f. L *pagina* (*pangere* fasten)]

pāge³ *v.t.* put consecutive numbers on pages of (book etc.) for use in reference. [f. prec.]

pă'geant (-jant) *n.* brilliant spectacle, esp. procession, arranged for effect; spectacular procession, or play performed in the open, illustrating historical events; tableau, allegorical device, etc., on fixed stage or moving vehicle; (fig.) empty or specious show; hence ∼RY (5) *n.* [ME *pagyn,* of unkn. orig.]

pă'ginal *a.* of pages; corresponding page for page; so **pă'ginARY¹** *a.* [f. LL *paginalis* (as PAGE²; 3CC -AL)]

pă'gin|āte *v.t.* page (book etc.), hence ∼A'TION *n.* [f. F *paginer* f. L *pagina* PAGE² + -ATE³]

pagō'da *n.* **1.** sacred building, esp. tower usu. of pyramidal form, in India, China, etc.; ornamental imitation of this. **2.** ∼-**tree,** tree of various species resembling pagoda in shape; *shake the* ∼-*tree,* (Hist.) make one's fortune quickly in India (w. ref. to ∼ as name of gold coin). [f. Port. *pagode,* prob. ult. f. Pers. *butkada* idol temple]

pagū'r|ian *a.* & *n.* (of) the hermit-crab. [f. L f. Gk *pagouros* kind of crab + -IAN]

pah¹ *int.* expr. disgust or contempt. [natural utterance]

pah². See PA²

Pah'lavi *n.* language of Persia under Sassanian kings. [f. Pers. *pahlawī* (*pahlav* f. *parthava* Parthia)]

paid. See PAY².

pail *n.* vessel, usu. round, of wood or metal or plastic for carrying liquids etc.; amount contained in this (*half a pail of milk*); hence ∼'FUL 2 *n.* [OE *pægel* gill; cf. MDu. *pegel* gauge; assoc. w. OF *paelle* (see PAELLA)]

paillasse. Var. of PALLIASSE.

paille'tte (pīyě't, pălyě't) *n.* piece of bright metal used in enamel painting; spangle. [F, dim. of *paille* f. *palea* straw, chaff]

pain[1] *n.* **1.** suffering or distress of body (from injury or disease) or mind; *a* particular occurrence of this (*pain in the* NECK[1]); **in** ～, undergoing this. **2.** (in *pl.*) throes of childbirth; trouble taken (*take pains; be at pains to* do; *get* a thrashing etc. *for* one's *pains*). **3.** punishment (*pains and penalties*); **on** or **under** ～ **of** (death or other punishment that would be incurred). **4.** ～**-killer**, medicine for alleviating pain. [ME, f. OF *peine* f. L *poena* penalty]

pain[2] *v.t.* & *i.* **1.** *v.t.* inflict pain upon; (in *p.p.*) expressing pain (*pained look*). **2.** *v.i.* give rise to pain, ache (*my arm is paining*). [ME, f. OF *pener* f. LL *poenare* (as prec.)]

pai'nful *a.* **1.** causing pain; grievous, vexatious; (esp. of part of body) suffering pain. **2.** causing trouble or difficulty; laborious. **3.** Hence ～LY[2] *adv.*, ～NESS *n.* [ME, f. PAIN[1] + -FUL]

pai'nless *a.* not suffering or causing pain; hence ～LY[2] *adv.*, ～NESS *n.* [f. PAIN[1] + -LESS]

pai'nstaking (-z-) *a.* careful, industrious. [f. PAIN[1] + -s[1] + TAKING[2]]

paint[1] *n.* colouring-matter, esp. when suspended in liquid in order to impart colour to a surface; LUMINOUS *paint*; colouring-matter to adorn face etc., rouge etc.; **as pretty** etc. **as** ～, very pretty etc.; ～'**box**, box containing dry paints before use; ～'**brush**, house--painter's or artist's brush; ～'**work**, work of painting, painted surface. [f. foll.]

paint[2] *v.t.* **1.** portray, represent, (object, or abs.) by using paints, make (picture) thus; adorn (wall etc.) with painting; (fig.) represent (incident etc.) in words vividly as by painting; *not so* BLACK[1] *as* one *is painted*. **2.** cover surface of (object) with paint; apply paint of specified colour to (*paint the door green*); ～ one**self into a corner**, (colloq.) get into difficult position of one's own making; *paint the* LILY; ～ **out**, efface with paint; ～ **the town red**, (sl.) cause commotion by riotous spree etc.; ～**ed lady**, orange-red butterfly with black and white spots. **3.** apply liquid or cosmetic to (face etc., or abs.); apply (liquid to skin etc.; *paint iodine on the cut*). [ME, f. *peint* p.p. of OF *peindre* f. L *pingere pict-* paint]

pai'nter[1] *n.* one who paints pictures; one who colours woodwork etc. with paint; ～'**s colic**, form of colic to which painters who work with lead are liable; so **pai'ntress**[1] *n.* [ME, f. OF *peintour* f. Rom. **pinctor -oris* f. L *pictor* (as prec.; see -ER[2])]

pai'nter[2] *n.* rope attached to bow of boat for making it fast to ship, stake, etc.; **cut the** ～, (fig.) effect a separation. [ME, prob. f. OF *penteur* rope from mast--head; cf. G *pentertakel* (*pentern* fish the anchor)]

pai'nterly *a.* characteristic of a painter, artistic; characteristic of paintings; (of a painting) not using clearly defined outlines. [f. PAINTER[1] + -LY[1]]

pai'nting *n.* In vbl senses; art of representing or depicting by colours on surface; product of this. [ME, f. PAINT[2] + -ING[1]]

pai'nty *a.* of paint; (of picture etc.) overcharged with paint. [f. PAINT[1] + -Y[2]]

pair[1] *n.* **1.** set of two persons or things, couple, (esp. of things that usu. exist or are used in couples, as gloves, SHOE[1]s, sculls, heels, eyes); two playing-cards of same denomination; (Cricket) = *pair of* SPECTACLES. **2.** article consisting of two corresponding parts not used separately (*pair of scissors, tongs, trousers, pyjamas*). **3.** engaged or married couple; mated couple of animals; ～ (**of horses**), two horses harnessed side by side; (Parl. etc.) two voters on opposite sides absenting themselves from division by mutual arrangement, person willing to act thus (*cannot find a pair*). **4.** the other member of a pair (*where is the pair to this sock?*). **5.** flight *of stairs* or (fixed or portable) *steps*. **6.** ～**-horse** *a.*, for a pair of horses; ～**-oar**, boat rowed by two oarsmen; ～ **production**, (Phys.) conversion of radiation quantum into electron and positron; ～ **royal**, set of three cards of same denomination. [ME, f. OF *paire* f. L *paria* neut. pl. of *par* equal]

pair[2] *v.t.* & *i.* arrange (persons, things), be arranged, in couples; unite in love or marriage; (of animals) mate; unite (*with* one of opposite sex); ～ **off**, arrange or go off in pairs, (Parl. etc.) make a pair, (colloq.) marry (*with*). [f. prec.]

pai's|a (pī'-) *n.* (*pl.* ～**e** *pr.* -ā, or ～**a**). coin of India, Pakistan, Nepal, and Bangladesh, one-hundredth of rupee or taka. [Hindi]

Pai'sley (-z-) *a.* (Of garment) made of soft wool woven or printed with bright coloured design (～ **pattern**) of usu. curved abstract figures. [～ in Strathclyde, Scotland]

*pajamas. See PYJAMAS.

||**Pǎk,** ||**Pǎ'kǐ,** *ns.* (sl.) Pakistani. [abbr.]

pa'kéha (pah'kǐhah) *n.* (NZ) white man; ～ **Maori,** white man living as Maori. [Maori]

Pakista'nǐ (pah-; -ah'-) *a.* & *n.* (native) of Pakistan. [Hind.; see -I]

pǎl *n.,* & *v.i.* (**-ll-**). (colloq.) **1.** *n.* comrade, mate; ||OLD *Pals Act.* **2.** *v.i.* ～ (**up**), associate (*with*). [E Gypsy, = brother, mate, ult. f. Skr. *bhrātr* BROTHER]

pǎ'lace *n.* official residence of sovereign, president, archbishop, or bishop; stately mansion; spacious building for entertainment, refreshment, etc.; ||GIN[2]--*palace*; ～ **revolution,** overthrow of sovereign etc. without civil war. [ME, f. OF *palais* f. L *Palatium,* hill in Rome, house of emperor Augustus built on this]

pǎ'ladǐn *n.* any of the Twelve Peers of Charlemagne's court, of whom the Count Palatine was the chief; knight errant, champion. [f. F *paladin* f. It. *paladino* f. L *palatinus* (see PALATINE[1])]

Pǎlaeǎr'ctǐc *a.* (Zool.) of Arctic and temperate parts of Old World. [f. foll. + ARCTIC]

pǎ'laeo-, *pǎ'lēo-, *comb. form.* ancient, old, (esp.) of ancient times, as : ～**anthropo'logy,** study of fossil man; ～**bo'tany,** study of fossil plants; ～**climato'-logy,** study of climate in past times; ～**ma'gnetism,** (study of) magnetism remaining in rocks from past times. [f. Gk *palaios* ancient]

Pǎ'laeocēne, *Pǎ'lēocēne, *a.* & *n.* (Geol.) (of) lowest division of Tertiary period or system. [f. prec. + Gk *kainos* new]

pǎlaeǒ'|graphý, *pǎlēǒ'|graphý, *n.* study of ancient writing and inscriptions; hence ～**GRAPHER** *n.,* **pǎlaeo**GRA'PHIC(AL) *adjs.* [*f.* F *paléographie* f. mod. L *palaeographia* (as PALAEO-, -GRAPHY)]

pǎlaeoli'thǐc, *pǎlēoli'thǐc, *a.* (Archaeol.) of a period in which primitive stone implements were used. [f. PALAEO- + Gk *lithos* stone + -IC]

pǎlaeǒntǒ'|logý, *pǎlēǒntǒ'|logý, *n.* study of life in the geological past; hence **pǎlaeǒnto**LO'GICAL *a.,* ～**LOGIST** *n.* [f. PALAEO- + Gk *onta* neut. pl. of *eimi* be, + -O- + -LOGY]

Pǎlaeozō'ǐc, *Pǎlēozō'ǐc, *a.* & *n.* (Geol.) (of the) geological era containing the oldest forms of highly organized life (reptiles, seed-bearing plants, etc.). [f. PALAEO- + Gk *zōē* life, *zōos* living + -IC]

palae'stra, palē'stra, *n.* (esp. Gk & Rom. Ant.) wrestling-school, gymnasium. [ME f. L *palaestra,* f. Gk *palaistra* (*palaiō* wrestle)]

pǎ'lafitte *n.* prehistoric hut on piles over lake in Switzerland or N. Italy. [F, f. It. *palafitta* pile-fence (*palo* stake, *fitto* fixed)]

pǎ'lais (-lā) *n.* ～ (**de danse**) (-dedah'ńs), public hall for dancing. [F, = (dancing) hall]

pǎlanqui'n, pǎlankee'n, (-n-kē'n) *n.* covered litter for one, in India and the East, carried usu. by four or six men. [f. Port. *palanquim;* cf. Hindi *pālki,* f. Skr. *palyanka, paryanka* bed, couch (*pari* around)]

pǎ'lat|able *a.* pleasant to the taste; (fig.) agreeable to the mind; hence ～**ABI'LITY** *n.,* ～**ABLY** *adv.* [f. PALATE + -ABLE]

pǎ'latal *a.* & *n.* **1.** *a.* of the palate; (Phonet., of sound) made by placing tongue against (usu. hard) palate, e.g. *y* in *yes,* whence ～**IZE** (3) *v.t.* **2.** *n.* palatal sound. [F (as foll.; see -AL)]

pă'late *n.* **1.** structure closing upper part of mouth cavity in vertebrates; **hard, soft, ∼,** its front, back, part; *cleft palate* (see CLEAVE[1]). **2.** sense of taste; mental taste, liking. [ME, f. L *palatum*]

palā'tial (-shal) *a.* like a palace; (of building) splendid; hence ∼LY[2] *adv.* [f. L (as PALACE) +-AL]

pală'tinate *n.* **1.** territory under a Count Palatine. **2.** ||(Durham Univ.) light shade of purple or lavender; blazer of this colour as sports distinction. [f. foll. +-ATE[1]]

Pă'latīne[1] *a.* (Count) ∼, count having within his territory jurisdiction such as elsewhere belongs only to sovereign (in Engl. Hist. also **Earl** ∼); **County p∼,** his territory (still in England of Lancashire and Cheshire). [ME, f. F *palatin* -*ine* f. L *palatinus* of the PALACE; see -INE[1]]

pă'latīne[2] *a.* & *n.* **1.** *a.* of the palate; ∼ **bones,** two bones forming hard palate. **2.** *n.* palatine bone. [f. F *palatin* -*ine* (as PALATE; see -INE[1])]

pă'latogrăm *n.* record of areas of contact between tongue and palate in producing a sound. [f. L *palatum* PALATE +-O- +-GRAM]

pala'ver (-lah'-) *n.* & *v.* **1.** *n.* conference, (prolonged) discussion, esp. (Hist.) between African or other natives and traders etc.; profuse or idle talk; cajolery; (sl.) affair, business. **2.** *v.i.* talk profusely. **3.** *v.t.* flatter, wheedle. [f. Port. *palavra* word f. L (as PARABLE)]

pāle[1] *n.* **1.** pointed piece of wood for fence etc., stake; boundary (esp. fig.); **beyond the ∼,** outside bounds of civilized behaviour etc.). **2.** (Hist.) the **(English) P∼,** part of Ireland under English rule; **the P∼,** part of Russia to which Jews were confined. **3.** (Her.) vertical stripe in middle of shield; **in ∼,** arranged vertically. [ME, f. OF *pal* f. L *palus* stake]

pāle[2] *a.* (Of person or complexion) of whitish or ashen appearance; (of colour) faint, not dark or deep; faintly coloured; (of faint lustre, dim; ∼**-face,** supposed N. Amer. Ind. name for white man; hence ∼'LY[2] (-l-lĭ) *adv.,* ∼'NESS (-ln-) *n.* [ME, f. OF *pal(l)e* f. L *pallidus* (*pallēre* be pale)]

pāle[3] *v.* **1.** *v.i.* grow pale; (fig.) become feeble in comparison (*before* or *beside*). **2.** *v.t.* make pale. [ME, f. OF *palir* (as prec.)]

pā'lea *n.* (*pl.* ∼e). (Bot.) chafflike bract, esp. in flower of grasses. [L, = chaff]

pāled (-ld) *a.* having palings. [f. PALE[1] +-ED[2]]

*pā'lēo-. See PALAEO-.

Pălĕstī'nian *n.* & *a.* **1.** *n.* native or inhabitant of Palestine. **2.** *a.* of, pertaining to, or connected with, Palestine. [f. *Palestine* in SW Asia +-IAN]

pălē'stra. See PALAESTRA.

pă'letŏt (-etō) *n.* loose cloak for man or woman; 19th-c. woman's fitted jacket. [F]

pă'lette *n.* artist's thin usu. wooden slab held in hand and used for holding and mixing colours when painting; colours used by particular artist or on particular occasion; ∼**-knife,** thin steel blade with handle for mixing or applying colours or for use in kitchen etc. [F, dim. of *pale* shovel f. L *pala* spade]

pa'lfrey (pawl'-, pă'-) *n.* (arch. or poet.) saddle-horse for ordinary riding, esp. for ladies. [ME, f. OF *palefrei* f. med. L *palefredus*, LL *paraveredus* f. Gk *para* beside, extra, + L *veredus* light horse, of Gaulish orig.]

Pā'li (pah'-) *n.* Indic language used in canonical books of Buddhists. [f. Skr. *pāli-bhāsā* (*pāli* canon, *bhāsā* language)]

pă'limpsĕst *n.* & *a.* **1.** *n.* writing-material or manuscript on which the original writing has been effaced to make room for a second writing; monumental brass turned and re-engraved on reverse side. **2.** *a.* (Of document or brass) so treated. [f. L f. Gk *palimpsēstos* (*palin* again, *psaō* rub smooth)]

pā'lindrōme *n.* & *a.* (word, verse, etc.) that reads the same backwards as forwards (e.g. *rotator*); hence **pălindrŏ'mic** *a.* [f. Gk *palindromos* running back again (*palin* again, *drom-* run)]

pā'ling *n.* pale; fence of pales. [f. PALE[1] +-ING[1]]

pălin|gĕ'nĕsĭs (-nj-) *n.* regeneration (lit. or fig.); revival; (Biol.) exact reproduction of ancestral character in ontogenesis, whence ∼**gĕnĕ'tĭc** *a.* [f. Gk *palin* again + *genesis* birth, GENESIS]

pă'linōde *n.* poem in which author retracts thing said in former poem; recantation. [F, or f. LL *palinodia* f. Gk *palinōidia* (*palin* again, *ōidē* song)]

pălisā'de *n.,* & *v.t.* **1.** *n.* fence of pales or of iron railings; (Mil.) strong pointed wooden stake used in close defensive row; *∼(in pl.)* line of high cliffs; ∼ **layer** (Bot., of elongated cells below epidermis). **2.** *v.t.* furnish or enclose with palisade. [f. F *palissade* f. Prov. *palissada* (*palissa* paling f. Gallo-Rom. *palicea f. L *palus* stake)]

pā'lish *a.* somewhat pale. [ME, f. PALE[2] +-ISH[1]]

pall[1] (pawl) *n.* cloth, usu. of black or purple or white velvet, spread over coffin, hearse, or tomb; woollen shoulder-band with front and back pendants, worn by Pope and some metropolitans and archbishops; (Her.) Y-shaped charge representing front of this; (fig.) mantle, cloak, (*pall of darkness, of smoke*); ∼'**bearer,** person helping to carry or accompany coffin at funeral. [OE *pæll,* f. L *pallium* cloak]

pall[2] (pawl) *v.* **1.** *v.i.* become uninteresting, ∼ **on,** cease to interest or attract (person, mind, taste). **2.** *v.t.* satiate, cloy. [ME, f. APPAL]

Pallā'dian *a.* (Archit.) in the neoclassical style of Palladio; ∼ **window,** = VENETIAN *window.* [f. A. *Palladio,* It. architect d. 1580 +-AN]

palla'dium[1] *n.* (*pl.* ∼a). image of Pallas on which safety of Troy was held to depend; safeguard. [ME, f. L f. Gk *palladion* (*Pallas Pallados* epithet of Athene)]

pallā'dium[2] *n.* rare hard white metallic element of platinum group. [mod. L, f. *Pallas,* an asteroid discovered (1803) just previously, +-IUM; cf. CERIUM]

pă'llĕt[1] *n.* straw bed; mattress. [ME *pail(l)et* f. AF *paillete* straw, f. OF *paille* f. L *palea*]

pă'llĕt[2] *n.* flat wooden blade with handle, used by potters etc., artist's palette; projection on part of machine, serving to change mode of motion of wheel; projection transmitting motion from escapement to pendulum etc.; valve under each pipe in wind-chest of organ; portable platform for transporting and storing loads, whence ∼IZE (1, 5) *v.t.* [f. F PALETTE]

pălliasse (pă'-, -ă's) *n.* straw mattress. [f. F *paillasse* f. It. *pagliaccio* f. Rom. *paleaceum f. L *palea* straw]

pă'lliāte *v.t.* alleviate (disease) without curing; extenuate, excuse; so ∼A'TION *n.* [f. LL *palliare* cloak (*pallium*) +-ATE[3]]

pă'lliative *a.* & *n.* (thing) that serves to palliate. [f. F *palliatif -ive* or f. med. L *palliativus* (as prec.; see -IVE)]

pă'llid *a.* pale, esp. from sickness etc.; hence ∼LY[2] *adv.,* ∼ITY (-ĭ'd-), ∼NESS, *ns.* [L *pallidus* (as PALE[2])]

pă'llium *n.* (*pl.* ∼a or ∼ums). man's large rectangular cloak esp. as worn by ancient Greeks; Pope's etc. PALL[1]; mantle of mollusc, whence ∼AL *a.* [L]

pall-ma'll (pălmă'l, pĕlmĕ'l) *n.* (Hist.) game in which ball was driven through iron ring suspended in long alley. [f. obs. F *pallemaille* f. It. *pallamaglio* (*palla* ball, *maglio* mallet)]

pă'llor *n.* pallidness, paleness. [L (*pallēre* be pale; see -OR)]

pă'lly *a.* (colloq.) friendly. [f. PAL +-Y[2]]

palm[1] (pahm) *n.* **1.** tree of family Palmae (chiefly tropical, usu. with upright unbranched stem and head of large pinnate or fan-shaped leaves); leaf of palm-tree as symbol of victory; supreme excellence, prize for this, (esp. *bear* or *yield the palm*); branch of various trees substituted for palm in northern countries, esp. in celebrating Palm Sunday. **2.** ∼ **civet,** paradoxure; ∼**-honey,** refined sap of coquito palm; ∼**-oil,** (1) oil got from various palms, (2) (with pun on PALM[2]) bribe-money; **P∼ Sunday,** Sunday before Easter, on which Christ's entry into Jerusalem is celebrated by processions in which branches of palm are carried; ∼ **wine,** alcoholic drink from fermented palm-sap. **3.** So **pălma′ceous** *a.* [OE *palm(a)*, = OS, OHG *palma*, ON *pálmr*, Gmc f. L *palma* PALM², its leaf being likened to a spread hand]

palm² (pahm) *n.* inner surface of hand between wrist and fingers; part of glove that covers this; breadth (about 4 in.) or length (about 8 in.) of hand as measure; palmate part of antler; CROSS², GREASE², person's *palm*; **in the ~** (= HOLLOW²) **of** one's **hand; ~-oil** (see prec.); hence (-)′ED² (pahmd) *a.*, ~′FUL 2 *n.* [ME f. OF *paume*, f. L *palma*; later assim. to L]

palm³ (pahm) *v.t.* **1. ~** (**off**), impose or thrust fraudulently (*on* person; **~** person **off with**, cause him to accept thus). **2.** conceal (cards, dice, etc.) in hand; touch or strike with palm; bribe. [f. prec.]

pă′lmar *a.* of or in the palm of the hand. [f. L *palmaris* (as PALM²; see -AR¹)]

pă′lmary *a.* bearing the palm, pre-eminent. [f. L *palmarius* (as PALM¹; see -ARY¹)]

pă′lmāte *a.* PALM²-shaped; having lobes etc. like spread fingers. [f. L *palmatus* (as PALM²; SEE -ATE²)]

pa′lmer (pah′m-) *n.* **1.** (Hist.) pilgrim returning from Holy Land with palm branch or leaf; itinerant monk under vow of poverty. **2. ~**(**-worm**), destructive hairy caterpillar. **3.** hairy artificial fly in angling. [ME f. AF, = OF *palmier* f. med. L *palmarius* pilgrim (as PALMARY); cf. -ER²]

pălme′tte *n.* (Archaeol.) ornament of radiating petals like palm-leaf. [F, dim. of *palme* PALM¹; see -ETTE]

pălme′ttŏ *n.* (*pl.* **~s**). palm-tree esp. of small size, e.g. dwarf fan-palm (*Chamaerops humilis*). [f. Sp. *palmito*, dim. of *palma* PALM¹, assim. to It. wds in -*etto*)]

pă′lmĭpĕd, -pēde, *a.* & *n.* web-footed (bird). [f. L *palmipes -pedis* (as PALM², *pes pedis* foot)]

pa′lmistry (pah′m-) *n.* supposed divination from lines etc. in palm of hand; so [as back-form.] **pa′lmist** (3) (pah′m-) *n.* [ME, f. PALM² + second element (orig. *-estry*) unexpl.]

pa′lmy (pah′mĭ) *a.* of, like, abounding in, palms; triumphant, flourishing, (*palmy days*). [f. PALM¹ + -Y²]

pălmȳr′a *n.* palm (*Borassus flabellifer*) grown in India and Sri Lanka, with fan-shaped leaves used for matting etc. [f. Port. *palmeira* palm-tree, assim. to *Palmyra* in Syria]

palŏ′lō *n.* (*pl.* **~s**). worm living in Pacific reefs and caught as delicacy on coming to sea-surface for breeding. [native name in Samoa and Tonga]

pălomi′nō (-mē′-) *n.* (*pl.* **~s**). golden or cream-coloured horse with light-coloured mane and tail, orig. bred in south-western US. [Amer. Sp., f. Sp. *palomino* young pigeon (*paloma* dove f. L *palumba*)]

***palŏŏ′ka** *n.* (sl.) poor performer at sport; lout. [20th c.; orig. unkn.]

pălŏvĕr′dĕ *n.* yellow-flowered thorny tree of genus *Cercidium* in Arizona etc. [Amer. Sp., = green tree]

pălp¹. Var. of PALPUS.

pălp² *v.t.* feel, handle. [f. L *palpare*]

pă′lp|able *a.* that can be touched or felt; readily perceived by senses or mind; hence **~abi′lity** *n.*, **~ably** *adv.* [ME, f. LL *palpabilis* (as PALPATE; see -ABLE)]

pă′lpal *a.* of palpus or palpi. [f. mod. L *palpalis* (PALPUS; see -AL)]

pălp|ā′te *v.t.* examine by touch (esp. in medical examination); so **~a′tion** *n.* [f. L *palpare* touch gently + -ATE³]

pă′lpebral *a.* of the eyelids. [f. LL *palpebralis* (*palpebra* eyelid; see -AL)]

pă′lpĭtāte *v.i.* pulsate, throb; tremble (*with* fear, pleasure, etc.). [f. L *palpitare* frequent. of *palpare* touch gently + -ATE³]

pălpĭtā′tion *n.* throbbing, trembling; increased activity of heart due to exertion, agitation, or disease. [f. L *palpitatio* (as prec.; see -ATION)]

pă′lp|us *n.* (*pl.* **~i** *pr.* -ī). segmented sense-organ at mouth of insect, feeler. [L (*palpare* feel)]

pa′lsgrāve (pawl′z-) *n.* Count PALATINE¹. [f. Du. *paltsgrave* (*palts* palatinate, *grave* count)]

pa′lstāve (paw′l-) *n.* celt of bronze etc. shaped to fit into split handle. [f. Da. *paalstav* f. ON *pálstavr* (*páll* hoe f. L *palus* stake, *stafr* STAFF¹)]

pa′lsỹ (paw′lzī, pŏ′lzĭ) *n.*, & *v.t.* **1.** *n.* paralysis, esp. with involuntary tremors; (fig.) cause or condition of utter helplessness. **2.** *v.t.* affect with palsy, paralyse (usu. fig.). [ME *pa(r)lesi* f. OF *paralisie* f. Rom. **paralisia* f. L (PARALYSIS)]

pa′lter (pawl′-, pŏ′l-) *v.i.* shuffle, equivocate, (*with* person); haggle (*with* person *about* thing); trifle (*with* subject). [16th c.; orig. unkn.]

pa′ltr|ỹ (pawl′-, pŏ′l-) *a.* worthless, petty, contemptible; hence **~iness** *n.* [16th c., f. *paltry* trash, app. f. *palt, pelt,* rubbish + -RY (cf. *trumpery*); cf. LG *paltrig* ragged]

palūdal (palū′-, pă′l-) *a.* of a marsh; malarial. [f. L *palus -udis* marsh + -AL]

pā′lỹ¹ *a.* (poet.) somewhat pale. [f. PALE² + -Y²]

pā′lỹ² *a.* (Her.) divided into equal vertical stripes. [f. OF *palé* (*pal* PALE¹; see -Y⁴)]

pălȳnŏ′|logỹ *n.* study of pollen in connection with plant geography, dating of fossils, allergies, etc.; hence **pălȳnolo′gical** *a.*, **~logist** *n.* [f. Gk *palunō* sprinkle + -o- + -LOGY]

pă′mpa *n.* (usu. in *pl., pr. -az or -as*). large treeless plain in S. America south of the Amazon, esp. in Argentina, **~s-grass,** large ornamental grass orig. from S. America. [Sp., f. Quechua *pampa* plain]

pă′mper *v.t.* over-indulge (person, tastes, etc.), spoil (person) with luxury. [ME, frequent. of obs. *pamp* cram; cf. -ER³]

pămper′ō (-ār′ō-) *n.* (*pl.* **~s**). strong cold SW wind blowing from Andes to Atlantic. [Sp., f. as PAMPA]

pă′mphlĕt *n.* small usu. unbound treatise, esp. in prose on subject of current interest. [ME, f. *Pamphilet,* familiar name of 12th-c. L amatory poem *Pamphilus seu de Amore*; see -ET¹]

pămphlēteer′ *n.*, & *v.i.* **1.** *n.* writer of pamphlets. **2.** *v.i.* write pamphlets. [f. prec. + -EER]

păn¹ *n.* **1.** metal or earthenware or plastic vessel, usu. shallow, for domestic purposes, (BED¹*pan,* FRY²*ing-pan,* SAUCE*pan,* WARM²*ing-pan*). **2.** panlike vessel in which substances are heated etc.; bowl of pair of scales; bowl of water-closet; part of lock that held the priming in obsolete types of gun; hollow in ground (SALT-*pan*); hard substratum of soil; ***(sl.) face. **3.** contents of pan. **4.** Hence **~′FUL** 2 *n.* [OE *panne,* = OS *panna,* OHG *phanna,* f. WG **panna,* perh. ult. f. L *patina* dish]

păn² *v.* (**-nn-**). **1.** *v.t.* (colloq.) criticize severely. **2. ~ off, out,** wash (gold-bearing gravel) in pan. **3.** *v.i.* search for gold thus; **~ out,** yield gold, (fig., of actions etc.) succeed, work, (*well* etc.). [f. prec.]

păn³ *v.* (**-nn-**) & *n.* **1.** *v.t.* swing (cine-camera) horizontally to give panoramic effect or follow moving object. **2.** *v.i.* (Of cine-camera) be moved thus. **3.** *n.* panning movement. [f. PANORAMA]

pan⁴ (pahn) *n.* leaf of the betel; this enclosing lime and areca-nut parings, chewed by Asians. [Hindi, f. Skr. *parna* feather, leaf]

păn- *comb. form.* all, as: (1) relating to the whole universe (**panco′smism,** doctrine that material universe is all that exists); (2) relating to the whole of a continent, racial group, religion, etc., (*pan-American, pan-Hellenism, pan-Anglican*). [Gk *pan,* neut. of *pas* all)]

pănacē′a *n.* universal remedy. [L, f. Gk *panakeia* (*pan,* akēs remedy) all-healing]

pana′che (-ah′sh, -ă′sh) *n.* tuft or plume of feathers, esp. as head-dress or on helmet; (fig.) display, swagger, verve. [F, f. It. *pennacchio* f. LL *pinnaculum* dim. of *pinna* feather]

pana′da (-nah′-) *n.* bread boiled to pulp and flavoured; thick paste of flour etc. [Sp., f. Rom. **panata* f. L *panis* bread; see -ADE]

pănama′ (-ah′) *n.* **~** (**hat**), hat of fine pliant straw like

material made (orig. in Ecuador) from leaves of the screw-pine. [f. P∼ in Central America]
Pănamā'nian *a.* & *n.* (native or inhabitant) of Panama. [f. as prec. +euphonic -*n*- + -IAN]
pănatĕ'lla *n.* long thin cigar. [f. Sp. *panatela* long thin biscuit f. It. *panatella* dim. of *panata* (as PANADA)]
pă'ncāke (-n-k-) *n.*, & *v.i.* **1.** *n.* thin flat batter-cake cooked esp. in pan (**flat as a** ∼, completely flat), sometimes rolled up with filling; flat cake (e.g. of make-up); **P∼ Day,** Shrove Tuesday (on which pancakes are traditionally eaten); ∼ **landing** (of aircraft descending vertically in level position). **2.** *v.i.* make pancake landing. [ME, f. PAN[1] + CAKE]
panchay'at (pŭnchī'at *n.* (Ind.) village council. [Hindi, f. Skr. *pancha* five]
pănchromă'tic (-n-kr-) *a.* (Photog.) (of film etc.) sensitive to all visible spectrum colours. [f. PAN- + CHROMATIC]
păncrā'tium (-n-k-) *n.* (Gk Ant.) athletic contest in wrestling and boxing; hence **păncrā'tic** (-n-k-) *a.* [L, f. Gk *pagkration* (as PAN-, *kratos* bodily strength)]
pă'ncre|as *n.* **1.** gland near stomach discharging a digestive secretion (*pancreatic juice*) into duodenum and insulin into blood. **2.** Hence ∼ă'tic *a.*, ∼ati'tis *n.* [mod. L., f. Gk *pagkreas* (as PAN-, *kreas -atos* flesh)]
pă'ncrèatin *n.* enzyme(s) present in pancreatic juice; digestive extract prepared from animal pancreases. [f. as prec. + -IN]
pă'nda *n.* **1.** Indian racoon-like animal, with reddish--brown fur and long bushy tail. **2.** (**giant**) ∼, large rare bearlike black-and-white mammal of E. Tibet and W. China. **3.** ||∼ **car,** police patrol car (orig. with broad white stripe over body). [Nepali name]
pănda'nus *n.* screw-pine. [mod. L, f. Malay *pandan*]
Pănde'an *a.* of the god Pan; ∼ **pipe,** = PAN-PIPE. [irreg. f. Gk *Pan* (cf. PANIC[2]) + -EAN]
pă'ndĕct *n.* (usu. in *pl.*) compendium in 50 books of Roman civil law made by order of Justinian in 6th c.; complete body of laws. [f. F *pandecte,* or f. L f. Gk PAN(*dektēs* f. *dekhomai* receive) all-receiver]
pănde'mĭc *a.* & *n.* (disease) prevalent over the whole of a country or over the whole world. [f. Gk PAN(*dēmos* people) + -IC]
păndĕmō'nium *n.* abode of all demons; (place of) lawless violence or uproar; utter confusion. [mod. L (Milton) f. PAN- + Gk *daimōn* DEMON; see -IUM]
pă'nder *n.,* & *v.t.* **1.** go-between in clandestine amours, procurer; one who ministers to evil designs. **2.** *v.i.* minister (*to* base passions or evil designs, or person having these). [f. *Pandare,* character in Boccaccio and in Chaucer's 'Troilus and Criseyde', f. L f. Gk *Pandaros*]
pa'ndĭt (pŭ'-) *n.* = PUNDIT 1. [Hindi, as PUNDIT]
P. & O. *abbr.* Peninsular and Oriental Steamship Company.
Păndŏr'a[1] *n.* ∼'s **box,** (Gk Myth.) box in which Hope alone remained when by its rash opening all other blessings were lost to (or all ills were let loose upon) mankind, (fig.) thing from which unmanageable problems are rashly generated. [f. Gk *Pandōra* all-gifted (as PAN-, *dōron* gift)]
păndŏr'a[2], **păndŏr'e,** *n.* stringed instrument like cithern. [f. It. *pandora* etc. f. LL f. Gk *pandoura* three--stringed lute]
||**p. & p.** *abbr.* postage and packing.
pāne[1] *n.* single sheet of glass in (compartment of) window; rectangular division of chequered pattern etc. [ME, f. OF *pan* f. L *pannus* piece of cloth]
pāne[2]. Var. of PEEN.
pănĕgy'ric *n.* & *a.* laudatory (discourse); so ∼AL *a.* [f. F *panégyrique* f. L f. Gk *panēgurikos* of public assembly, f. PAN(*ēguris* = *agora* assembly); see -IC]
pă'nĕgyrīze, -īse (-īz), *v.t.* speak or write in praise of, eulogize; so **pănĕgy'rIST** (1) *n.* [f. Gk *panēgurizō* (as prec.; see -IZE)]
pă'nel[1] *n.* **1.** distinct compartment of surface, esp. of wainscot, door, etc., often sunk below or raised above

general level; CONTROL[1] *panel;* INSTRUMENT panel. **2.** piece of material esp. of different kind or colour inserted in woman's dress etc. **3.** team in broadcast or public quiz programme etc.; body of experts assembled for discussion or consultation; hence ∼lIST, *∼IST, *n.*, member of this. **4.** ||(Hist.) list of doctors registered in a district as accepting patients under National Insurance Act. **5.** slip of parchment; list of jury; jury; ||(Sc. Law) person(s) on trial, the accused. **6.** ∼-**beater,** workman who beats out metal panels of motor vehicles; ∼ **game,** quiz etc. played by panel (sense 3); ∼ **heating** (of rooms by panels in wall etc. containing sources of heat); ∼-**pin,** thin nail with very small head; ∼-**saw** (with small teeth for cutting thin wood for panels). [ME & OF, = piece of cloth, saddle-cushion, f. Rom. *pannellus* dim. of L *pannus;* cf. PANE[1]]
pă'nel[2] *v.t.* (||-ll-). fit (wall, door, etc.) with panels; ornament (dress etc.) with panel(s); hence ∼lING[1] (2),*∼ING[1] (2), *n.* [f. prec.]
păng *n.* shooting pain; sudden sharp mental pain. [16th c.; var. of earlier *pronge, prange,* MLG *prange* pinching, Goth. *anapraggan* oppress]
pă'nga (-ngga) *n.* African tool like machete. [native name in E. Africa]
Pănglŏ'ssian (-ngg-) *a.* excessively optimistic. [f. *Pangloss,* character in Voltaire's 'Candide' + -IAN]
păngo'lin (-ngg-) *n.* scaly ant-eater of Asia and Africa. [f. Malay *peng-gōling* roller (from habit of rolling itself up)]
*****pă'nhăndle** *n.* & *v.* **1.** *n.* narrow strip of one political division of a country extending between two others. **2.** *v.t.* & *i.* (sl.) beg (from) in street. [f. PAN[1] + HANDLE[1]]
pă'nĭc[1] *n.* grass of genus *Panicum,* e.g. Italian millet and other cereals. [OE, f. L *panicum* (*panus* thread on bobbin, millet-ear f. Gk *pēnos* web)]
pă'nĭc[2] *a.,n.,* & *v.* (-ck-). **1.** *a.* (Of terror) unreasoning, excessive; excessively hasty through fear; for use in emergency (*panic bolt, button, stations*). **2.** *n.* infectious fright, sudden alarm (e.g., in commerce) leading to hasty measures; ∼-**monger,** one who fosters a panic; ∼-**stricken,** ∼-**struck,** affected with panic; hence ∼kY[2] **3.** *v.t.* & *i.* affect or be affected with panic; ***amuse** (audience etc.) greatly. [f. F *panique* f. mod. L f. Gk *panikos* (*Pan* rural god causing terror)]
pă'nĭcle *n.* (Bot.) loose irregular type of compound inflorescence, as in oats. [f. L *paniculum* dim. of *panus* thread]
pănjă'ndrum *n.* (Mock title of) exalted personage; pompous official or pretender. [app. invented in nonsense verse by S. Foote 1755]
||**pă'nnage** *n.* (right of or payment for) pasturage of pigs; acorns, beech-mast, etc., as food for pigs. [ME, f. OF *pasnage, pannage* f. med. L *pastionaticum* (L *pastio* pasture f. *pascere past-* feed; see -AGE)]
pănne *n.* ∼ (**velvet**), velvet-like fabric of silk or rayon with flattened pile. [F]
pă'nnier *n.* **1.** basket, esp. one carried, usu. in pairs, by beast of burden or on bicycle or on the shoulders; bag similarly carried on bicycle or motor cycle; covered basket for surgical instruments and medicines for ambulance. **2.** (Hist.) (frame supporting) part of skirt looped up round hips. [ME, f. OF *panier* f. L *panarium* bread-basket (*panis* bread; see -ARY[1])]
pă'nnikin *n.* small metal drinking-vessel; its contents. [f. PAN[1] + -KIN, after *cannikin*]
pă'noplỹ *n.* complete suit of armour; (fig.) complete or splendid array; hence ∼iED[2] (-lĭd) *a.* [f. F *panoplie* or f. mod. L f. Gk PAN(*oplia* f. *hopla* arms) full armour of hoplite]
pănŏ'ptic *a.* showing or seeing the whole at one view. [f. Gk *panoptos* seen by all, *panoptēs* all-seeing + -IC]
*****pănŏ'pticon** *n.* circular prison with cells round warders' well in centre. [f. PAN- + Gk *optikos* of sight, OPTIC]
pănora'ma (-rah'-) *n.* picture of landscape etc.

arranged on inside of cylindrical surface or successively rolled out before spectator; photograph containing wide view, esp. one made with rotating camera; continuous passing scene; unbroken view of surrounding region (lit. or fig.); hence **pănorǎ′m**IC *a*. [f. PAN- +Gk *horama* view (*horaō* see)]

pă′n-pīpe(s) *n*. musical instrument made of series of reeds or pipes fixed together with mouthpieces in line. [f. *Pan*, Greek rural god, + PIPE[1]]

pă′nsÿ (-zĭ) *n*. **1.** garden plant (*Viola tricolor*) with flowers of various rich colours. **2.** ~ (**boy**), (colloq.) effeminate man, male homosexual. [f. F *pensée* thought, pansy (*penser* think f. L *pensare* frequent. of *pendere pens-* weigh)]

pănt[1] *v*. & *n*. **1.** *v.i.* gasp for breath; (fig.) yearn (*for* or *after* thing; *to* do); (of heart etc.) throb violently. **2.** *v.t.* utter gaspingly (*out*). **3.** *n*. gasp; throb. [ME, f. AF **panter* f. OF *pantaisier* pant, f. Rom. **pantasiare* for **phantasiare* f. Gk *phantasioō* cause to imagine (as FANTASY)]

pănt[2]. See PANTS.

păntagru′el|ism (-ŏŏ′-) *n*. extravagant coarse satirical humour; so **păntagruĕ′l**IAN (-ŏŏ-) *a*., ~IST (1) *n*. [f. *Pantagruel*, character in Rabelais + -ISM]

păntalĕ′t(te)s (-ts) *n*. *pl*. (Hist.) woman's long drawers esp. with frill at ankle; woman's cycling trousers. [dim. of foll.; see -ET[1], -ETTE]

păntalŏŏ′n *n*. **1.** character in Italian comedy wearing pantaloons (sense 2); clown's butt and abettor in pantomime. **2.** (Hist.; usu. in *pl*.) garment of breeches and stockings in one piece, close-fitting breeches down to ankle as transition from knee-breeches to trousers. **3.** *(in *pl*., arch.) trousers. [f. F *pantalon* f. It. *pantalone*, Venetian character in Italian comedy, perh. f. *San Pantaleone*, favourite Venetian saint in former times]

‖**păntĕ′chnicon** (-kn-) *n*. **1.** (arch.) furniture warehouse (orig. name of a bazaar). **2.** ~ (**van**), large van for removing furniture. [f. PAN- +Gk *tekhnikon* (neut.) of art (*tekhnē*; see -IC)]

pă′nthe|ism *n*. doctrine that God is everything and everything God; worship of all gods; so ~IST (2) *n*., ~**i′st**IC(AL) *adjs*. [f. PAN- +Gk *theos* god + -ISM]

păntheon (pă′nthĭon, -ē′on) *n*. temple dedicated to all the gods, esp. circular one at Rome; deities of a people collectively; building in which illustrious dead are buried or have memorials. [ME, f. L f. Gk PAN(*theion* holy f. *theos* god)]

pă′nther *n*. leopard; *puma; hence ~ESS[1] *n*. [ME f. OF *pantere* f. L *panthera* f. Gk *panthēr*]

pă′ntie|s (-tĭz) *n*. *pl*. (colloq.) short trousers worn by children; short-legged or legless knickers worn by women and girls; ~**-belt**, *~**-girdle**, woman's very light corset made in this shape. [dim. of PANTS; see -IE]

pă′ntihōse (-z) *n*. woman's tights (TIGHT 9). [f. prec. + HOSE]

pă′ntīle *n*. roof tile transversely curved to ogee shape, one curve being much larger than the other. [f. PAN[1] + TILE]

păntisŏ′cracÿ *n*. (Hist.) Utopian community in which all are equal and all rule. [f. Gk *pas pantos* all + *isokratia* ISOCRACY]

‖**pă′ntŏ** *n*. (*pl*. ~s). (colloq.) = PANTOMIME 1. [abbr.]

pănto- *comb. form*. all, as: ~**lo′gic, panto′logy** (-ŏ′l-), (of) universal knowledge; ~**mor′phic**, taking all shapes; ~**sco′pic**, having wide range of vision. [f. Gk *pas pantos* all + -O-]

pă′nto|graph (-ahf) *n*. **1.** instrument with jointed rods for copying plan etc. on any scale; hence ~**GRA′PHIC** *a*. **2.** jointed framework conveying current to electric vehicle from overhead wires. [f. prec. + Gk *-graphos* writing]

pă′ntomīm|e *n*. & *v*. **1.** ‖dramatic entertainment usu. produced about Christmas and based on fairy-tale, with singing, dancing, clowning, topical jokes, transformation scene, and stock roles. **2.** dumb show. **3.** (Rom. Hist.) actor performing in dumb show. **4.**

Hence or cogn. **păntomī′m**IC *a*., ~IST (3) *n*. **5.** *v.t.* & *i.* express (thing), express oneself, by dumb show. [F, or f. L f. Gk PANTO(*mimos* MIME)]

păntothĕ′nic *a*. ~ **acid**, vitamin of B group essential to growth, found in liver etc. [f. Gk *pantothen* from all sides (as PANTO-) + -IC]

pă′ntrÿ *n*. room or cupboard in which bread and other provisions or (*butler's, housemaid's, pantry*) plate, table-linen, etc., are kept; ~**man**, butler or his assistant. [ME, f. AF *panetrie*, OF *paneterie* (*panetier* baker f. Rom. **panatarius* f. LL *panarius* bread-seller f. L *panis* bread); see -ERY]

pănts *n*. *pl*. (colloq.) **1.** trousers or slacks; **pant**(**s**) **suit**, trouser suit; (*bore, scare, talk*, etc.) **the ~ off,** (sl.) bring thus to a state of extremity; **with** one's ~ **down,** (sl.) in state of embarrassing unpreparedness etc. **2.** ‖underpants. **3.** panties. [abbr. of PANTALOONS]

panty-hose. Var. of PANTIHOSE.

***pă′ntÿwaist** *n*. & *a*. **1.** *n*. child's garment of short trousers buttoned to bodice. **2.** *n*. & *a*. effeminate (person). [f. PANTIES + WAIST]

pă′nzer (-tser) *a*. & *n*. **1.** *a*. armoured (*panzer division, troops*). **2.** *n*. (in *pl*.) armoured troops. [G, = coat of mail]

păp[1] *n*. (arch. or dial.) nipple esp. of woman; (in *pl*.) conical hilltops side by side. [ME, of Scand. orig., ult. imit. of sucking]

păp[2] *n*. soft or semi-liquid food for infants or invalids; mash, pulp; undemanding reading-matter; hence ~**p**Y[2] *a*. [ME, prob. f. MLG, MDu. *pappe*, prob. f. med. L **pappa* f. L *pappare* eat]

papa′ (-ah′) *n*. (arch., esp. childish). father. [F f. LL, f. Gk *pap(p)as*]

pă′pacÿ *n*. Pope's (tenure of) office; papal system. [ME, f. med. L *papatia* (*papa* pope; see -ACY)]

papā′in *n*. enzyme got from unripe papaws, used to tenderize meat. [f. PAPAYA + -IN]

pā′pal *a*. of the Pope or his office; P~ **States,** (Hist.) Pope's temporal dominions esp. in central Italy; hence ~ISM (3), ~IST (2), *ns*., ~IZE (3) *v.t.* & *i.*, ~LY[2] *adv*. [ME f. OF, f. med. L *papalis* f. eccl. L *papa* POPE[1]; see -AL]

papā′verous *a*. like or allied to the poppy; so **papāver**A′CEOUS *a*. [f. L *papaver* poppy + -OUS]

papaw′, pawpaw′, *n*. **1.** (oblong orange edible fruit of) palmlike tropical Amer. tree of which stem, leaves, and fruit contain a milky juice that makes meat tender. **2.** *N. Amer. tree with purple flowers and oblong edible fruit. [earlier *papay*(*a*) f. Sp. & Port. *papaya*, of Carib orig.]

papay′a (-pī′a) *n*. = PAPAW 1. [var. of PAPAW]

pā′per[1] *n*. & *a*. **1.** *n*. substance used for writing, printing, drawing, wrapping up parcels, etc., made of compactly interlaced fibres of rags, straw, wood, etc., in thin sheet; SILVER[1] *paper*; **commit to ~,** write down; on ~, in theory, judging from statistics, etc., (*on paper he is the better man*), in writing; **put pen to ~,** begin writing. **2.** negotiable documents, e.g. bills of exchange; = *paper money*; (sl.) free passes to theatre etc. **3.** (in *pl*.) documents proving person's or ship's identity, standing, etc.; documents belonging to or relating to a person or matter. **4.** set of questions to be answered at one session in examination; written answers to these. **5.** = NEWS*paper*, WALL*paper*. **6.** piece of paper, esp. as wrapper etc. **7.** document printed on paper (‖GREEN *Paper*, ‖WHITE[1] *Paper*); essay or dissertation, esp. one read to learned society. **8.** *a*. made of paper; flimsy like paper; conducted by means of writings (*paper warfare*); written on paper but not really existing (*paper profits*). **9.** ~**back** *n*. & *a*., (book) bound in paper (often as cheap version or reprint); ~**-boy, -girl,** (who delivers or sells newspapers); ~**-chase,** cross-country run in which a trail of torn-up paper is laid by one or more runners to set a course for the rest; ~**-clip,** piece of bent wire by which a few sheets of paper may be held together; ~**-hanger,** one whose business it is to cover walls with wallpaper, (sl.) forger esp. of cheques; ∼**-knife**, blunt knife of ivory, wood, etc., for opening sealed envelopes, leaves of book, etc.; ∼**-mill** (in which paper is made); ∼ **money**, banknotes etc. used as currency; *paper* MULBERRY, NAUTILUS, TIGER; ∼**weight**, small heavy object for preventing loose papers from being displaced; ∼**work**, office administration and record-keeping. **10**. Hence ∼Y² *a*. [ME f. AF *papir*, = OF *papier* f. L PAPYRUS]

pā′per² *v.t.* enclose in paper; decorate (wall etc.) with paper (∼ **over the cracks**, seek to disguise flaws or dissension); furnish with paper; (sl.) fill (theatre etc.) by giving free passes. [f. prec.]

Pā′phian *a*. of (esp. illicit) sexual love. [f. L *Paphius* (*Paphos*, city in Cyprus sacred to Aphrodite or Venus) + -AN]

papier mâché (păpyā mă′shā, mah′-) *n*. moulded paper pulp used for boxes, trays, etc. [F, = chewed paper]

papiliona′ceous (-yonā′shŭs) *a*. (Bot.) with corolla like a butterfly. [f. mod. L *papilionaceus* f. L *papilio -onis* butterfly; see -ACEOUS]

papi′lla *n*. (*pl.* ∼e). small nipple-like protuberance in a part or organ of the body, e.g. from dermis into epidermis; (Bot.) small fleshy projection on plant; hence or cogn. **pă′pill**ARY¹, **pă′pill**ATE² (2), **pă′pill**OSE¹, *adjs.* [L, = nipple, dim. of PAPULA]

păpillo′ma *n*. wartlike tumour, often arising from papilla(e). [f. prec. + -OMA]

papi′llon (-lyon) *n*. (breed of) toy dog with ears suggesting form of butterfly. [F, = butterfly, f. as PAPILIONACEOUS]

pā′pist *n*. advocate of papal supremacy; (usu. derog.) Roman Catholic; hence **papi′st**IC(AL) *adjs.*, ∼RY (5) *n*. [f. F *papiste* or mod. L *papista* f. eccl. L *papa* POPE¹; see -IST]

papoo′se *n*. N. Amer. Indian young child. [Algonquin]

pă′pp|**us** *n*. (*pl.* ∼i *pr.* -ī). (Bot.) downy appendage on fruit of thistles, dandelions, etc.; hence ∼OSE¹ *a*. [L, f. Gk *pappos*]

paprika (pă′prī-, paprē′-) *n*. ripe (red) PEPPER¹; red condiment made from it. [Magyar]

pă′pūl|**a** (*pl.* ∼ae), **pă′pūle**, *n*. pimple; small fleshy projection on plant; hence ∼AR¹, ∼OSE¹, ∼OUS, *adjs*. [f. L *papula*; see -ULE]

păpyrā′ceous (-shŭs) *a*. (Biol.) of the nature of, or as thin as, paper. [f. L PAPYRUS + -ACEOUS]

păpyrŏ′|logy *n*. study of ancient papyri; hence **păpyro**LO′GICAL *a*., ∼LOGIST *n*. [f. as foll. + -O- + -LOGY]

papyr′|us *n* (*pl.* ∼i *pr.* -ī). aquatic plant of sedge family, paper reed; ancient writing-material prepared by Egyptians etc. from stem of this; MS written on this. [ME f. L, f. Gk *papuros*]

păr¹ *n*. **1**. equality, equal footing, esp. *on a par* (*with*); ∼ **of exchange**, recognized value of one country's currency in terms of another's; (of stocks, shares, etc.) at ∼, at face value, **above** ∼, at a premium, **below** ∼, at a discount. **2**. average or normal amount, degree, health, or condition, (*above*, *below*, *up to*, *par*). **3**. number of strokes a first-class golfer should normally require for a hole or course (calculated according to a formula and usu. less than the BOGEY¹ figures); ∼ **for the course**, (colloq.) normal or expected event. [L, *a*. & *n*., = equal, equality]

|**păr²** *n*. (colloq.) paragraph. [abbr.]

par- *pref.* See PARA-¹.

par., para., *abbrs.* paragraph.

pă′ra *n*. (colloq.) parachutist; paragraph. [abbr.]

păra-¹ *pref.* (usu. **par-** bef. vowel or *h*) meaning: **1**. beside (*parabola*, *paramilitary*, *parathyroid*). **2**. beyond (*paradox*, *paranormal*). **3**. (Chem.) modification of (*paraldehyde*). **4**. (Chem.) relating to diametrically opposite carbon atoms in a benzene ring (*paradichlorobenzene*). [f. or after Gk *para-* (*para* beside, past, beyond)]

păra-² *comb. form*. protect, ward off, (*parachute*, *parasol*). [F f. It. (*para* imper. of *parare* defend)]

parā′bas|**is** *n*. (*pl.* ∼es *pr.* -ēz). chorus's address to audience in ancient Greek comedy. [Gk, f. PARA-¹ (*bainō* go) step forward]

părabī|ō′sis *n*. (*pl.* ∼oses *pr.* -ō′sēz). (Biol.) natural or artificial joining of two individuals; hence ∼o′TIC *a*. [mod. L, f. as PARA-¹ + Gk *biōsis* mode of life (*bios* life; see -OSIS)]

pă′rable *n*. narrative of imagined events used to typify moral or spiritual relations (*the parables of Christ in the Gospels*); allegory. [ME, f. OF *parabole*, f. LL sense 'allegory, discourse' of L *parabola* comparison (as foll.)]

parā′bola *n*. open plane curve formed by intersection of cone with plane parallel to its side, resembling path of projectile under action of gravity. [mod. L, f. Gk PARA¹(*bolē* a throw f. *ballō*) placing side by side, comparison]

părabŏ′l|**ic** *a*. **1**. of or expressed in a parable. **2**. of or like a parabola. **3**. Hence ∼ICALLY *adv*. [f. LL f. Gk *parabolikos* (as prec.; see -IC)]

părabŏ′lical *a*. = prec. 1. [f. as prec. + -AL]

parā′boloid *n*. ∼ (**of revolution**), solid generated by rotation of parabola about its axis of symmetry; solid having two or more non-parallel parabolic cross-sections; hence ∼AL *a*. [f. PARABOLA + -OID]

părace′tamŏl *n*. (tablet of) compound forming white crystalline powder, a mild analgesic and antipyretic. [f. *para-acetylaminophenol*]

parā′chronism (-k-) *n*. error in chronology, esp. assignment of too late date. [f. PARA-¹ + Gk *khronos* time + -ISM, perh. after *anachronism*]

pă′rachut|**e** (-shoot) *n*., *a*., & *v*. **1**. *n*. umbrella-shaped apparatus of silk etc. allowing person or heavy object to descend safely from a height, esp. from aircraft; similar natural or artificial device, e.g. one that opens behind aircraft to retard its motion when landing. **2**. *a*. (to be) dropped by parachute (*parachute flare*, *troops*). **3**. *v.t.* & *i*. convey or descend (as if) by means of parachute. **4**. Hence ∼IST *n.*, uscr of parachute, (in *pl.*) parachute troops. [F (as PARA-², CHUTE)]

pă′raclēte *n*. advocate; (*P*∼) the Holy Spirit as advocate or counsellor (John 14:16, 26, etc.). [ME, f. OF *paraclet* f. LL f. Gk PARA¹(*klētos* f. *kaleō* call) call in aid]

parā′de *n*. **1**. display, ostentation, esp. *make a parade of* (one's virtue etc.). **2**. muster of troops for inspection, esp. one held regularly at set hours; ∼(**-ground**) (used for this); **on** ∼, mustering thus, (fig.) displaying oneself in a formal or purposeful manner. **3**. public square or promenade. **4**. public procession; group of persons or things passed in review. [F, = show, f. Sp. *parada* and It. *parata* f. Rom. *parare* prepare, furnish; see -ADE]

parā′de² *v*. **1**. *v.t.* assemble (troops) for review or other purpose; display ostentatiously; march through (streets etc.) with display. **2**. *v.i.* march in procession with display. [f. prec.]

părǎdichlŏrobě′nzēne (-k-) *n*. white crystalline readily subliming compound used esp. against moths. [f. PARA-¹ + DI-² + CHLORO-² + BENZENE]

părǎdi′ddle *n*. drum roll with alternate beating of sticks. [imit.]

pă′radigm (-īm) *n*. example or pattern, esp. of inflexion of noun, verb, etc.; hence **părǎdig′m**IC *a*. [f. LL f. Gk *paradeigma* f. PARA¹- (*deiknumi* show) show side by side]

pă′radise *n*. **1**. (earthly) ∼, garden of Eden. **2**. abode of God and of the righteous after death, heaven; region or state of supreme bliss; BIRD *of paradise*; FOOL¹'*s paradise*. **3**. park in which animals are kept. **4**. Hence or cogn. **pă′radis**AL, **părǎdisā′**IC(AL) [irreg. after *Mosaic* etc.], **părǎdi′sē**AN, **părǎdisī**AC(AL), **părǎdi′sī**AL, **părǎdi′sī**AN, **părǎdi′s**IC(AL), *adjs*. [ME, f. OF *paradis* f. LL f. Gk *paradeisos* f. Avestan *pairidaēza* park (*pairi* around, *diz* shape); cf. PARVIS]

pă′rados (-dŏs, -dō) *n.* elevation of earth behind fortified place to secure from rearward attack, esp. mound along back of trench. [F (PARA-², *dos* back f. L *dorsum*)]

pă′radŏx *n.* seemingly absurd though perhaps actually well-founded statement (HYDROSTATIC *paradox*); self-contradictory or essentially absurd statement; person or thing conflicting with preconceived notions of what is reasonable or possible; paradoxical quality or character; hence or cogn. ∼ER¹ (3), ∼IST (3), ∼Y¹, *ns.* [orig. = statement contrary to accepted opinion, f. LL f. Gk *paradoxon* neut. adj. (PARA-¹, *doxa* opinion)]

păradŏ′xical *a.* of, like, involving, or fond of, paradox; hence ∼ITY (-ă′l-) *n.*, ∼LY² *adv.* [f. prec. +-ICAL]

păradŏ′xūre *n.* palm civet, animal of genus *Paradoxurus* with remarkably long curving tail. [f. mod. L *paradoxurus* f. Gk *paradoxos* (see PARADOX) + *oura* tail]

pă′raffin *n.*, & *v.t.* **1.** *n.* colourless tasteless odourless inflammable oily or waxy substance got by distillation from petroleum or shale and used for making candles etc. (∼ **wax**, solid paraffin obtained by distillation from shale or petroleum; ‖**liquid** ∼, odourless tasteless mild laxative); ‖∼ (**oil**), oil so obtained and used as fuel or illuminant or lubricant. **2.** (Chem.) hydrocarbon belonging to methane series, with general formula C$_n$H$_{2n+2}$. **3.** *v.t.* treat with paraffin. [G (1830), f. L *parum* little + *affinis* related, from small affinity it has for other substances]

pă′ragōge *n.* (Gram. & Philol.) addition of letter or syllable to a word in some contexts or as a language develops; hence **păragŏ′gIc** *a.* (*the t* in '*peasant*' *is paragogic*). [LL, f. Gk *paragōgē* derivation (as PARA-¹, *agōgē* f. *agō* lead)]

pă′ragon *n.*, & *v.t.* **1.** *n.* model of excellence; supremely excellent person or thing, model (*of* virtue etc.); perfect diamond of 100 carats or more. **2.** *v.t.* (poet.) compare (thing *with*). [obs. F, f. It. *paragone* touchstone, f. med. Gk *parakonē* whetstone]

pă′ragraph (-ahf) *n.*, & *v.t.* **1.** *n.* distinct passage or section in book etc., usu. marked by indentation of first line (HANGING² *paragraph*); symbol (usu. ¶) formerly used to mark new paragraph, now as reference mark; detached item of news etc. in newspaper, freq. without heading, whence ∼ER¹ (3), ∼IST (3), *ns.* **2.** Hence **păragră′phIC** *a.* **3.** *v.t.* write paragraph about (person, thing); arrange (article etc.) in paragraphs. [f. F *paragraphe* or f. med. L f. Gk PARA¹(*graphos* f. *graphō* write) short stroke marking break in sense]

pă′ra-hȳdrogĕn *n.* form of hydrogen molecule with spins of nuclei in opposite directions. [f. PARA-¹ + HYDROGEN]

pă′rakeet, *pă′rrakeet, pă′roquĕt (-kĕt), *n.* small (esp. long-tailed) parrot. [f. OF *paroquet*, It. *parrocchetto*, *perrochetto*, Sp. *periquito*, perh. ult. f. dims. of *Pierre* etc. Peter; cf. PARROT]

părä′ldĕhȳde *n.* polymer of ALDEHYDE 1, used as narcotic and sedative. [f. PARA-¹ + ALDEHYDE]

părălĭpŏ′mĕna, -leip- (-līp-), *n. pl.* things omitted from work and added as supplement; books of Chronicles in OT, containing particulars omitted from Kings. [ME, f. eccl. L f. Gk *paraleipomena* f. PARA¹(*leipō* leave) omit]

părali′ps|is, păralei′ps|is (-lī′-), *n.* (*pl.* ∼**es** *pr.* -ēz) trick of securing emphasis by professing to say little or nothing of subject, e.g. *I say nothing of his antecedents, how from youth upwards* etc. [f. LL f. Gk PARA¹(*leipsis* f. *leipō* leave) passing over]

pă′rall|ax *n.* (angular amount of) apparent displacement of object, caused by actual change of point of observation; hence ∼ă′ctIC *a.* [f. F *parallaxe* f. mod. L f. Gk *parallaxis* change (*parallassō* to alternate f. as PARA-¹, *allassō* exchange f. *allos* other)]

pă′rallĕl¹ *a.* & *n.* **1.** *a.* (Of lines etc.) continuously equidistant, (of line) having this relation *to*; ∼ **bars,** pair of parallel rails supported on posts for gymnastic exercises; ∼ **ruler,** two rulers connected by pivoted cross-pieces, for drawing parallel lines; *parallel* SPHERE. **2.** (fig.) precisely similar, analogous, or corresponding. **3.** *n.* ∼ (**of latitude**), each of the parallel circles of constant latitude on earth's surface (*the 49th parallel*), or corresponding line on map; similar circle on celestial sphere; person or thing precisely analogous to another; comparison (*draw a parallel between two things*); two parallel lines (‖) as reference mark; **in** ∼, (Electr., of conductors etc.) arranged so as to join at common points at each end. [f. F *parallèle* f. L f. Gk *parallēlos* (PARA-¹, *allēlos* one another)]

pă′rallĕl² *v.t.* represent as similar, compare, (things, one *with* another); find or mention something parallel or corresponding to; be parallel to, correspond to. [f. prec.]

părallĕlepiped (-ĕ′pīpĕd, -epī′pĭd) *n.* (Geom.) solid bounded by parallelograms. [f. Gk *parallēlepipedon* (as PARALLEL¹, EPI(*pedon* ground) plane surface)]

pă′rallĕlism *n.* being parallel (lit. or fig.); comparison or correspondence of successive passages, esp. in Hebrew poetry. [f. Gk *parallēlismos* f. *parallēlizō* place side by side (as PARALLEL¹; see -IZE, -ISM)]

părallĕ′logrăm *n.* four-sided plane rectilinear figure whose opposite sides are parallel; ∼ **of forces,** (parallelogram illustrating) theorem that if two forces acting at a point be represented in magnitude and direction by two sides of a parallelogram meeting at that point, their resultant is represented by the diagonal drawn from that point. [f. F *parallélogramme* f. LL f. Gk *parallēlogrammon* (as PARALLEL¹, *grammē* line)]

pară′log|ism *n.* illogical reasoning (esp. of which reasoner is unconscious, cf. SOPHISM); fallacy; so ∼IST (1) *n.*, ∼IZE (2) *v.i.* [f. F *paralogisme* f. LL f. Gk *paralogismos* f. *paralogizomai* reason falsely f. PARA¹(*logos* reason) contrary to reason]

pă′ralȳs|e (-z), ***pă′ralȳz|e,** *v.t.* affect with paralysis; (fig.) render powerless, cripple; hence ∼A′TION *n.* F *paralyser* (*paralysie*; cf. PALSY)]

pară′lȳs|is *n.* (*pl.* ∼**es** *pr.* -ēz). nervous disease with impairment or loss of motor or sensory function of nerves; (fig.) state of utter powerlessness. [L, f. Gk *paralusis* f. PARA¹(*luō* loosen) disable]

părylȳ′t|ic *a.* & *n.* (person) affected with paralysis (lit. or fig.); ‖(sl.) very drunk; hence ∼ICALLY *adv.* [ME, f. OF *paralytique* f. L f. Gk *paralutikos* (as prec.; see -IC)]

păramăgnĕ′tic *a.* & *n.* (body or substance) tending to become weakly magnetized so as to lie parallel to a magnetic field force; hence **păramă′gnĕt**ISM (3) *n.* [f. PARA-¹ + MAGNETIC]

păramă′tta. Var. of PARRAMATTA.

păramē′cium, -moe′cium (-mē′-), *n.* ciliated slipper-shaped protozoan of genus *Paramecium.* [mod. L, f. Gk PARA¹(*mēkĕs* f. *mēkos* length) oval]

păramĕ′dical *a.* (Of services etc.) supplementing and supporting medical work. [f. PARA-¹ + MEDICAL]

pară′mĕter *n.* (Math.) quantity constant in case considered, but varying in different cases; (esp. measurable or quantifiable) characteristic or feature; hence **păramĕ′tr**IC *a.*, **pară′mĕtr**IZE (3) *v.t.* [mod. L, f. Gk *para* beside + *metron* measure]

părami′litarȳ *a.* ancillary to and similarly organized to military forces. [f. PARA-¹ + MILITARY]

păramnē′sia (-z-) *n.* (Psych.) = DÉJÀ VU. [f. PARA-¹ + AMNESIA]

pă′ramō *n.* (*pl.* ∼**s**). high treeless plateau in tropical S. America. [Sp. & Port., f. L *paramus*]

paramoecium. See PARAMECIUM.

pă′ramount *a.* supreme; in supreme authority; pre-eminent (*of paramount importance*); hence ∼CY *n.*, ∼LY² *adv.* [f. AF *paramont* f. OF *par* by + *amont* above (cf. AMOUNT¹)]

pă′ramour (-oor) *n.* (arch. or rhet.) illicit lover of married man or woman. [ME, f. OF *par amour* by love]

păr'äng n. Malay heavy sheath-knife. [Malay]

păranoi'a n. mental derangement with delusions of grandeur, persecution, etc.; abnormal tendency to suspect and mistrust others; hence **păranoi'**AC, **pǎranō'**IC, **pǎ'ran**OID, adjs. & ns. [mod. L f. Gk, f. PARA¹(noos mind) distracted]

păranōr'mal a. lying ouside the range of normal scientific investigations etc.; hence ∼LY² adv. [f. PARA-¹+NORMAL]

pǎ'rapet (-ĭt, -ĕt) n. low wall at edge of balcony, roof, etc., or along sides of bridge etc.; (Mil.) defence of earth or stone to conceal and protect troops, esp. mound along front of trench; hence ∼ED² a. [F, or f. It. PARA²(petto breast f. L pectus) breast-high wall]

pǎ'raph n. flourish after signature, orig. as precaution against forgery. [ME, f. F paraphe f. med. L paraphus for paragraphus PARAGRAPH]

păraphernā'lia n. pl. (sometimes treated as sing). personal belongings; equipment, accessories, appurtenances, etc.; (Hist.) articles of personal property that law allowed married woman to keep and treat as her own. [med. L, n. f. neut. pl. a. f. LL f. Gk PARA¹(pherna f. phernē dower); cf. -AL, -IA²]

pǎ'raphrāse (-z) n., & v.t. 1. n. free rendering or amplification of a passage, expression of its sense in other words; one of a collection of metrical para phrases of passages of Scripture used in Church of Scotland etc.; so **păraphrā'stic** a. 2. v.t. express meaning of (passage) in other words. [F, or f. L f. Gk paraphrasis f. PARA¹(phrazo tell)]

păraplē'g|ia n. (Path.) paralysis of legs and part of whole of trunk; so ∼IC a. & n. [mod. L, f. Gk paraplēgia f. PARA¹(plēssō strike)]

părapsȳchō'log|ȳ (-rasĭk-) n. study of mental phenomena outside sphere of ordinary psychology (hypnosis, telepathy, etc.); so **părapsȳcho**LO'GICAL (-rasĭk-) a., ∼IST (3) n. [f. PARA-¹+PSYCHOLOGY]

pǎ'raquat (-ŏt) n. quick-acting herbicide, becoming inactive on contact with soil. [f. PARA-¹+QUATERNARY (f. position of bond between two parts of molecule rel. to quaternary nitrogen atom)]

pǎ'rasäng n. ancient-Persian measure of length, about 3¾ miles. [f. L f. Gk parasaggēs, of Pers. orig.]

părasēlē'n|ē n. (pl. ∼ae), bright spot on lunar halo, mock moon. [mod. L, f. as PARA-¹+Gk selēnē moon]

pǎ'rasīt|e n. self-seeking hanger-on, toady; animal or plant living in or on another and drawing nutriment directly from it; plant that climbs about another plant, wall, etc.; unprofitable dependent person or thing; (Philol.) inorganic sound or letter developing from an adjacent one; hence or cogn. **părasī'tic**(AL) adjs., **părasī'tic**IDE (1), ∼ISM (2), ∼ō'LOGY, ns. [f. L f. Gk PARA¹(sitos food) one who eats at another's table]

pǎ'rasītīze, -īse (-īz), v.t. (usu. in p.p.) infest as a parasite. [f. prec.+-IZE]

pǎrasōl (pǎ'-, -ō'l) n. light umbrella used to give protection from sunlight. [F, f. It. PARA²(sole sun f. L sol)]

părasȳmpathĕ'tic a. (Anat.) relating to the part of the nervous system that connects with nerve cells in or near viscera. [f. PARA-¹+SYMPATHETIC, because some of these nerves run alongside sympathetic nerves]

părasȳ'nthēsis n. (Philol.) derivation from a compound, as black-eyed from black eye(s)+-ed; so **părasȳnthĕ'tic** a. [f. Gk parasunthesis (as PARA-¹, SYNTHESIS)]

părătā'xis n. (Gram.) placing of clauses etc. one after another, without words to indicate co-ordination or subordination, as Tell me, how are you?; so **părătă'ctic** a. [f. Gk PARA¹(taxis arrangement f. tassō arrange)]

ărathi'on n. agricultural insecticide of high toxicity. [f. PARA-¹+THIO-+-ON]

ărathȳr'oid a. & n. (Anat.) (gland) adjacent to thyroid, secreting hormone that regulates calcium levels in body. [f. PARA-¹+THYROID]

ǎ'ratrōōp|s n. pl. parachute troops; hence ∼ER¹ n., member of these. [f. PARACHUTE+TROOP+-s¹]

păratȳ'phoid n. & a. (one of numerous kinds) of fever resembling typhoid, but caused by different bacteria. [f. PARA-¹+TYPHOID]

pǎ'ravāne n. torpedo-shaped device towed at a depth regulated by its vanes or planes to cut the moorings of submerged mines. [f. PARA-¹+VANE]

pǎr'boil v.t. boil and partly cook; (fig.) overheat (person). [ME, f. OF parbo(u)illir f. LL PER(bullire boil) boil thoroughly, confus. w. PART¹]

păr'bŭckle n., & v.t. 1. n. rope for raising or lowering casks and cylindrical objects, the middle being secured at the upper level, and both ends passed under and round the object and then hauled or let slowly out. 2. v.t. raise (up) or lower (down) thus. [earlier parbunkle, of unkn. orig.; assoc. w. BUCKLE¹]

păr'cel n. & adv. 1. n. part (arch.); PART¹ and parcel. 2. piece of land, esp. as part of estate. 3. goods etc. wrapped up in single package; bundle of thing(s) so wrapped, usu. in paper; ∼ post, branch of postal service concerned with parcels. 4. (Commerc.) quantity dealt with in one transaction. 5. adv. (arch.) partly (parcel blind, drunk). 6. ∼ gilt, partly gilded, esp. (of cup etc.) with inner surface gilt. [ME f. OF parcelle f. Rom. *particella f. L particula (as PART¹; see -CULE)]

păr'cel² v.t. (∥-ll-). divide (out) into portions; wrap (up) as parcel; (Naut.) cover (caulked seam) with canvas strips and pitch, wrap (rope) with canvas strips, whence ∼lING³ (4) n. [f. prec.]

păr'cēnary n. joint heirship. [f. AF parcenarie = OF parçonerie (as foll.; see -ERY)]

păr'cēner n. joint heir. [ME f. AF, = OF parçonier f. Rom. *parti(ti)onarius (as PARTITION; see -ER²)]

părch v. 1. v.t. (Of sun, thirst, etc.) make (earth, person, etc.) hot and dry; roast (corn, peas, etc.) slightly. 2. v.i. become hot and dry. [ME parch, parche, of unkn. orig.]

păr'chment n. skin, esp. of sheep or goat, prepared for writing, painting, etc.; manuscript written on this; (vegetable) ∼, high-grade paper made to resemble parchment; parchment-like skin, esp. husk of coffee-bean; hence ∼Y² a. [ME f. OF parchemin f. Rom. *particaminum, blending LL pergamina of Pergamum (Bergama in Turkey) w. Parthica pellis Parthian skin, scarlet-dyed leather]

păr'clōse (-z) n. screen or railing in church to separate chapel etc. [ME, f. OF parclos -ose p.p. (as n.) of parclore (par- PER-; see CLOSE²)]

pǎrd¹ n. (arch.) leopard. [ME f. OF, f. L f. Gk pardos, pardalis]

***părd²**, ***păr'dner**, ns. (sl.) partner, comrade. [corrupt.]

păr'dalōte n. small brightly-coloured Austral. bird of genus Pardalotus, with spotted plumage. [f. mod. L f. Gk pardalōtos spotted like a leopard (as PARD¹)]

păr'don¹ n. 1. forgiveness; (RC Ch.) = INDULGENCE, festival at which this is granted; (free) ∼, (Law) remission of legal consequences of crime or conviction; general ∼ (for offences generally, or to number of persons not named individually). 2. courteous forebearance; (I beg your) ∼, beg ∼, (formula of apology for thing done, for dissent or contradiction, or for not hearing or understanding what was said). [ME f. OF perdun, pardun f. pardoner (see foll.]

păr'don² v.t. forgive (person, offence, person his offence); make (esp. courteous) allowances for, excuse (person, fault, person for doing); ∼ me, = I beg your PARDON¹); so ∼ABLE a., ∼ABLY adv. [ME, f. OF pardoner, perduner f. med. L PER(donare give) concede, remit]

păr'doner n. (Hist.) person licensed to sell papal pardons or indulgences. [ME f. AF (as PARDON¹; see -ER²)]

pāre v.t. trim (thing) by cutting away irregular parts etc.; cut away skin, rind, etc., of (fruit etc.); (fig.) diminish little by little (away, down); shave, cut, (edges etc.) *off*, *away*; hence **par̄'ER**[1] (2), **par̄'ING**[1] (1, 2), *ns*. [ME, f. OF *parer* adorn, peel (fruit), f. L *parare* prepare]

părėgŏ'ric *a*. & *n*. ∼ (**elixir**), camphorated tincture of opium used as analgesic. [f. LL f. Gk *parēgorikos* soothing (as PARA-[1], *-agoros* speaking f. *agora* assembly)]

pareir'a (-ār'*a*) *n*. drug from root of Brazilian shrub, used as diuretic etc. [f. Port. *parreira* vine trained against wall]

parĕ'nchy̆m|a (-ngk-) *n*. **1**. (Anat.) essential substance of gland, organ, etc., as distinguished from flesh and connective tissue. **2**. (Bot.) cellular material, usu. soft and succulent, found esp. in softer parts of leaves, pulp of fruits, bark and pith of stems, etc. **3**. Hence ∼AL, **părĕnchy̆'mat**ous (-ngk-), *adjs*. [f. Gk *paregkhuma* something poured in besides (as PARA-[1], *egkhuma* infusion f. *egkheō* pour in f. *en* in + *kheō* pour)]

par̄'ent *n*. one who has begotten or borne offspring, father or mother; forefather (**our first** ∼**s**, Adam and Eve); one who has adopted a child; animal or plant from which others are derived; (fig.) source, origin, (*of* evils etc.); initiating organization etc.; ∼-**tea'cher association**, organization consisting of, and promoting good relations between, teachers and their pupils' parents; hence or cogn. **parĕ'nt**AL *a*., ∼HOOD (-t-h-) *n*. ∼ING[1] *n*., being a parent. [ME f. OF, f. L *parens parentis* (*parere* bring forth; see -ENT)]

par̄'entage *n*. descent from parents, lineage, (*his parentage is unknown*). [ME f. OF (as prec.; see -AGE)]

parĕ'nteral *a*. (Med.) administered or occurring elsewhere than in the alimentary canal. [f. PARA-[1] + Gk *enteron* intestine + -AL]

parĕ'nthĕs|is *n*. (*pl.* ∼es *pr.* -ēz). word, clause, or sentence, inserted into a passage to which it is not grammatically essential, and usu. marked off by brackets, dashes, or commas (**in** ∼, thus inserted, lit. or fig.); (pair of) round bracket(s) ( ) used for this; (fig.) interlude, interval. [LL, f. Gk *parenthesis* f. *parentithēmi* put in beside (as PARA-[1], EN-[2], *tithēmi* place)]

parĕ'nthĕsīze, -ise (-īz), *v.t*. insert (words etc., or abs.) as parenthesis; put between marks of parenthesis. [f. prec. + -IZE]

părenthĕ'tic *a*. of, or inserted as a, parenthesis; (fig.) interposed; so ∼AL *a*., ∼ALLY *adv*. [f. PARENTHESIS, after *synthesis*, *synthetic*, etc.]

parĕr'g|on *n*. (*pl*. ∼a). subsidiary work, work apart from one's main employment; ornamental accessory. [L, f. Gk *parergon* (as PARA-[1], *ergon* work)]

pă'rĕs|is *n*. (*pl*. ∼es *pr*. -ēz). (Med.) partial paralysis, affecting muscular motion but not sensation; so **pare**TIC *a*. [mod. L, f. Gk, f. *pariēmi* let go (as PARA-[1], *hiēmi* let go)]

par excellence (pär ĕ'ksɛlahṅs) *adv*. by virtue of special excellence, above all others that may be so called, (*Mayfair was the fashionable quarter par excellence*). [F, f. L *per excellentiam*]

par̄'fait (-fā) *n*. rich iced pudding of whipped cream, eggs, etc.; layers of ice cream, fruit, etc., served in tall glass. [F (*parfait* PERFECT[1])]

pargana. Var. of PERGUNNAH.

par̄'gĕt *v.t*., & *n*. **1**. *v.t*. plaster (wall etc.), esp. with ornamental pattern; roughcast. **2**. *n*. plaster thus applied; roughcast. [ME, f. OF *pargeter*, *parjeter* (*par* all over, *jeter* throw; cf. JET[3])]

par̄hē'l|ion (-lyon, -lĭon) *n*. (*pl*. ∼ia). bright spot on solar halo, mock sun; (hence ∼i'ACAL, ∼IC, *adjs*. [f. L f. Gk *parēlion* (as PARA-[1], *hēlios* sun)]

pariah (pă'rĭa, parī'*a*) *n*. member of a low caste in S. India; member of low or no caste; (fig.) social outcast; ∼-**dog**, = PYE-DOG. [f. Tamil *paṛaiyar* pl. of *paṛaiyan* hereditary drummer (*paṛai* drum)]

Pār'ian *a*. & *n*. **1**. *a*. of the island of Paros in the Aegean, famed for white marble. **2**. *n*. fine white kind of porcelain. [f. L *Parius* of Paros + -AN]

parī'etal *a*. **1**. (Anat.) of the wall of the body or of any

of its cavities; ∼ **bone**, one of pair forming part of sides and top of skull. **2**. (Bot.) of the wall of a hollow structure etc. **3**. *pertaining to residence within a college. [f. F *pariétal* or f. LL *parietalis* (*paries -etis* wall; see -AL)]

pari mutuel (pahrē mū'tŭĕl) *n*. form of betting in which winners divide losers' stakes (less a percentage for management); totalizator. [F, = mutual stake]

pari passu (pārī pă'sōō, pārī) *adv*. with equal pace; simultaneously and equally. [L]

Pă'ris *n*. ∼ **green**, poisonous chemical used as pigment and insecticide; ∼ **white**, fine WHITING[1] used in polishing; PLASTER[1] *of* Paris. [∼ in France]

pă'rish *n*. **1**. (**ecclesiastical**) ∼, area having its own church and clergyman. **2**. ‖(**civil**) ∼, district constituted for purposes of civil government, orig. (Hist.) for poor-law administration; **go on the** ∼, (Hist.) receive parochial relief. **3**. inhabitants of a parish. **4**. *chiefly in Louisiana. **5**. ∼ **clerk**, official performing various duties connected with the church, esp. (formerly) leading the responses; ‖*parish* LANTERN; ∼ **council**, administrative body in civil parish; ‖*parish* LANTERN; ∼ **pump** (fig., w. ref. to purely parochial or restricted outlook); ∼ **register**, book recording christenings, marriages, and burials, at parish church. [ME *paroche*, *parosse* f. OF *paroche*, *paroisse* f. eccl. L *parochia*, *paroechia* f. Gk *paroikia* sojourning f. *paroikos* (PARA-[1], *-oikos* -dwelling f. *oikeō* dwell)]

parĭ'shioner (-sho-) *n*. inhabitant of parish. [f. obs. *parishen* (ME f. OF *parossien*; as prec., -IAN) + -ER[1]]

Parī'sĭan (-z-) *a*. & *n*. (native or inhabitant) of Paris in France. [f. F *parisien* (*Paris*; see -IAN)]

pă'rison *n*. rounded mass of glass formed by rolling immediately after taking from furnace. [f. F *paraison* (*parer* prepare f. L *parare*; see -ISON)]

părĭsy̆llă'bic *a*. & *n*. (Gram.) (noun) that has same number of syllables in all cases (e.g. L *aedes aedis*). [f. L *par* equal + -I- + SYLLABIC]

pă'rity[1] *n*. equality, esp. among members or ministers of church, or among occupational groups as regards pay etc.; parallelism, analogy, (*parity of reasoning*); (Commerc.) equivalence in another currency, being at PAR[1]; (of number) fact of being even or odd; (Phys., of quantity) fact of changing its sign or remaining unaltered under a given transformation of coordinates etc. [f. F *parité* or f. LL *paritas* (as PAR[1], -ITY)]

pă'rity[2] *n*. (Med.) fact of having borne children; number of children previously borne. [f. as -PAROUS + -ITY]

pärk[1] *n*. **1**. large enclosed piece of ground, usu. with woodland and pasture, attached to country house etc.; enclosure in town ornamentally laid out for public recreation; sports ground; large tract of land kept in natural state for public benefit (*national park*). **2**. (space occupied by) artillery, stores, etc., in encampment; area assigned for motor cars etc. to be left in; = OYSTER-*park*. **3**. ∼**land**, open grassland with tree-clumps etc.; ∼**way**, highway in park etc. prohibited to heavy vehicles. **4**. Hence ∼**ISH**[1] *a*. [ME, f. OF *parc* f. med. L *parricus* f. Gmc orig., cogn. w. OE *pearruc* (see PADDOCK[1])]

pärk[2] *v.t*. **1**. enclose (ground) in or as park; (Mil.) arrange (artillery etc.) compactly in a park; place or leave (vehicle, or abs.), usu. temporarily, in park or elsewhere; (colloq.) deposit and leave, usu. temporarily; ∼ **one**self, (sl.) sit down. **2**. ∼**'ing-lot**, outdoor area for parking vehicles; ∼**'ing-meter**, coin-operated meter receiving fees for parking vehicle in street, and indicating time allowed; ∼**'ing-ticket**, notice of fine etc. imposed for parking vehicle illegally. [f. prec.]

pär'ka *n*. skin jacket with hood attached, worn by Eskimos; similar garment worn by mountaineers etc. [Aleutian]

‖**pär'kin** *n*. (dial.) gingerbread made with oatmeal and treacle. [perh. f. name *Parkin*, dim. of PETER[1]]

Pār′kĭnson[1] *n.* ~'s **disease,** progressive disease of nervous system, with tremor, muscular rigidity, and emaciation; hence ~ISM (5) *n.* [f. J. ~, Engl. surgeon d. 1824]

Pār′kĭnson[2] *n.* ~'s **law,** (joc.) fact that work will always last as long as the time available for it. [f. C. N. ~, Engl. writer b. 1909]

||**pär′kў** *a.* (sl. or dial.) (Of air, morning, etc.) chilly. [19th c.; orig. unkn.]

||**Parl.** *abbr.* Parliament(ary).

pär′lance *n.* (particular) way of speaking as regards choice of words (*in common, legal,* etc., *parlance*). [OF (*parler* speak f. Rom. **paraulare* f. **paraula* f. L *parabola* (see PARABLE), in LL 'speech'; see -ANCE)]

*pär′lay *v.t. & n.* **1.** *v.t.* use (money won on bet) as further stake; increase in value (as if) by parlaying **2.** *n.* act of parlaying; bet so made. [f. *paroli* such action in faro (F f. It., f. *paro* like f. L *par* equal)]

pär′ley[1] *n.* conference for debating of points in dispute, esp. (Mil.) discussion of terms for armistice etc.; **beat** or **sound a** ~, call for it by drum or trumpet. [perh. f. OF *parlee,* fem. p.p. (as n.) of *parler* speak; see PARLANCE]

pär′ley[2] *v.* **1.** *v.i.* discuss terms (of armistice *with* enemy etc.). **2.** *v.t.* speak (esp. foreign language) [f. prec.]

pärleyvōō′ (-lĭv-) *n.,* & *v.i.* (joc.) **1,** *n,* French language; Frenchman. **2.** *v.i.* speak French. [f. F *parlez-vous (français)?* do you speak (French)?]

pär′liament (-lam-) *n.* **1.** (*P*~). council forming with the Sovereign the supreme legislature of United Kingdom, consisting of House of Lords (Spiritual and Temporal) and House of Commons (representatives of towns etc.); **Houses of P**~, these jointly or the buildings where they meet; MEMBER *of Parliament;* **open P**~, (of Sovereign) declare its session open with ceremonial. **2.** body of persons belonging to Parliament for period between successive dissolutions. **3.** corresponding legislative assembly in other countries. [ME f. OF *parlement* speaking (as PARLANCE, see -MENT)]

pärliamentār′ian (-lam-) *n. & a.* **1.** *n.* skilled debater in parliament; adherent of Parliament in Civil War of 17th c. **2.** *a.* = foll. [f. prec. + -ARIAN]

pärliamĕ′ntarў (-lam-) *a.* **1.** of parliament; ||~ **agent** (charged with interests of party concerned in private legislation of Parliament). **2.** ||(*P*~). enacted or established by Parliament; **P**~ **Commissioner for Administration,** ombudsman in United Kingdom; *Parliamentary* (*Private* or *Under-*)SECRETARY. **3.** (Of language) admissible in Parliament, (colloq.) civil. [f. PARLIAMENT + -ARY[1]]

||**pär′lour** (-ler), ***pär′lor,** *n* ordinary sitting-room of family in private house; room in mansion, convent, inn, etc., for private conversation; **shop* etc. providing specified goods or services (*beauty parlour, ice cream parlour*); place for milking cows; ***~ **car,** luxuriously fitted railway coach; ~ **game,** indoor game, esp. word-game; ~**maid,** maid who waits at table; ~ **socialist** etc., one who advocates doctrines without trying to put them into effect; ~ **tricks,** (usu. derog.) social accomplishments. [ME f. AF *parlur,* OF *parleor, parleur* f. Rom. **paraulare* (see PARLANCE)]

pär′lous *a. & adv.* (arch. or joc.) **1.** *a.* perilous; hard to deal with; surprisingly clever etc. **2.** *adv.* extremely. [ME, = PERILOUS]

Pär′ma *n.* ~ **violet,** sweet-scented violet with lavender-coloured flowers. [~ in Italy]

Pärmésăn (-zăn, pär′-) *a. & n.* ~ (**cheese**), kind of hard cheese made at Parma and elsewhere, used esp. in grated form. [F, f. It. *parmegiano* of Parma in Italy]

Pärnä′ssian *a. & n.* **1.** *a.* of Parnassus; poetic. **2.** *a. & n.* (member) of group of French poets in late 19th c., emphasizing strictness of form, named from anthology *Le Parnasse contemporain* (1866). [f. Mount *Parnassus* in Greece, anciently sacred to Muses + -IAN]

paro′chial (-k-) *a.* of a parish; ***(of school) denomin-ational; (fig., of affairs, opinions, etc.) confined to narrow area; hence ~ISM (2), ~ITY (-ă′l-), *ns.,* ~IZE (3) *v.t.,* ~LY[2] *adv.* [ME, f. AF *parochiel,* OF *parochial* f. eccl. L *parochialis* (as PARISH; see -AL)]

pä′rod|ў *n.,* & *v.t.* **1.** *n.* composition in which an author's characteristics are humorously imitated; feeble imitation, travesty. **2.** *v.t.* compose parody of (literary work, manner, etc.). **3.** So **parŏ′d**IC *a.,* ~IST (3) *n.* [f. LL *parodia* or f. Gk *parōidia* burlesque poem (as PARA-[1], *ōidē* ode)]

parō′l *a. & n.* (Law.) oral (declaration); (of document) not given under seal. [f. OF *parole* (as foll.)]

parō′le *n.,* & *v.t.* **1.** *n.* word of honour; prisoner's promise that he will not attempt escape, or will return if conditionally liberated; liberation on these terms; **on** ~, liberated on this understanding. **2.** (Mil.) password used only by officers of guard (cf. COUNTERSIGN[1]). **3.** *v.t.* put (prisoner) on parole; hence **parōl**EE′ *n.* [F, = word, f. Rom. **paraula;* see PARLANCE]

păronomā′sia (-z-) *n.* play(ing) on words, pun. [L, f. Gk *paronomasia* (as PARA-[1], *onomasia* naming f. *onomazō* to name f. *onoma* name)]

pä′ronўm *n.* word cognate with another; word formed from a foreign word, so **parŏ′nўm**OUS *a.* [f. Gk *parōnumon,* neut. (as n.) of *parōnumos* (as PARA-[1], *onuma* name)]

paroquet. See PARAKEET.

parŏ′tĭd *a. & n.* **1.** *a.* situated near the ear; ~ **gland** (salivary, in front of ear, with ~ **duct,** opening into mouth). **2.** *n.* parotid gland. [f. F *parotide* or f. L f. Gk *parōtis -idos* (as PARA-[1], *ous ōtos* ear)]

părotī′tis *n.* inflammation of parotid gland; mumps. [f. prec. + -ITIS]

-parous *suf.* bearing offspring of specified number or kind (*multiparous, viviparous*). [f. L *-parus* -bearing (*parere* bring forth) + -OUS]

Parou′sia *n.* (Theol.) second advent of Christ. [Gk, = presence, advent]

pä′roxўsm *n.* fit of disease; fit (*of* rage, laughter, etc.); hence **parŏxў′sm**AL (-zm-) *a* [f. F *paroxysme* f. med. L f. Gk *paroxusmos* f. *paroxunō* exasperate (as PARA-[1], *oxunō* sharpen f. *oxus* sharp)]

parŏ′xўtōne *a. & n.* (in Gk Gram.) (word) with acute accent on last syllable but one. [f. mod. L f. Gk *paroxutonos* (as PARA-[1], OXYTONE)]

pär′pen *n.* stone passing through wall from side to side, with two smooth vertical faces. [ME, f. OF *parpain,* prob. f. Rom. **perpannius* f. L *per* through, *pannus* piece of cloth, in Rom. 'piece of wall']

pär′quet (-kī, -kā) *n.,* & *v.t.* **1.** *n.* wooden flooring of pieces of wood, often of different kinds, arranged in pattern; ***theatre stalls; so ~RY (1) (-kĭt-) *n.* **2.** *v.t.* floor (room) thus. [F, = small compartment, floor, dim. of *parc* PARK[1]; see -ET[1]]

pärr *n.* salmon with dark bands on sides, younger than smolt. [18th c., of unkn. orig.]

pärramä′tta *n.* light dress fabric of wool and silk or cotton. [f. *P*~ in New South Wales]

pä′rri|cīde *n.* **1.** one who kills his father or near relative; one who kills person regarded as sacred; person guilty of treason against his country. **2.** any of these crimes. **3.** So ~**cī′d**AL *a.* [F, or f. L (1) *par(r)icida* (2) *-cidium,* of uncert. orig., assoc. in L w. *pater* father and *parens* parent; see -CIDE]

pä′rrot *n.,* & *v.t.* **1.** *n.* bird with short hooked bill, of order Psittaciformes, mainly tropical, of which many species have beautiful plumage, and some can be taught to repeat words; person who repeats another's words or imitates his actions unintelligently, whence ~RY (4) *n.;* ~**-fashion** *a. & adv.,* repeating or imitating thus; ~**-fish,** scarus, with mouth like parrot's bill; hence ~LET *n.,* small S. Amer. parrot of genus *Forpus.* **2.** *v.t.* repeat (words, or abs.) mechanically, drill (person etc.) to do this. [prob. f. obs. or dial. F *perrot* parrot, dim. of *Pierre* PETER[1]; cf. PARAKEET]

pa′rry v.t., & n. **1.** v.t. turn aside, ward off, avert, (weapon, blow, awkward question), esp. with one's own weapon etc. **2.** n. act of parrying. [prob. repr. F *parez* imper. of *parer* f. It. *parare* ward off]

parse (-z) v.t. describe (word in context) in terms of grammar, stating inflexion, relation to sentence, etc.; resolve (sentence) into its component parts and describe them in terms of grammar. [perh. f. ME *pars* parts of speech f. OF *pars*, pl. of *part* PART[1], infl. by L *pars* part]

par′sec n. unit of stellar distance, about 3¼ light--years, the distance at which a star would have a parallax of one second of arc, i.e. at which the mean radius of the earth's orbit subtends this angle. [f. PARALLAX + SECOND]

Parsee′ n. **1.** adherent of Zoroastrianism, descendant of Persians who fled to India from Muslim persecution in 7th–8th c.; hence ~ISM (3) n. **2.** = PAHLAVI. [f. Pers. *pārsī* Persian (*pārs* Persia)]

par′sim|ony n. carefulness in employment of money etc. or (fig.) of immaterial things; excessive carefulness with money, meanness; **law of ~ony** (that no more causes or forces should be assumed than are necessary to account for the facts); hence ~o′niOUS a. [ME, f. L *parsimonia, parcimonia* (*parcere pars-* spare; see -MONY)]

par′sley n. biennial umbelliferous plant (*Petroselinum crispum*) with white flowers and aromatic leaves, used for seasoning and garnishing dishes; ~ **fern** (with leaves like parsley); ~**-piert**, dwarf annual herb (*Alchemilla arvensis*) [prob. corrupt. of F *perce-pierre* pierce stone]; *parsley* SAUCE. [ME *persil* etc. f. OF *peresil* f. Rom. *petrosilium f. L f. Gk *petroselinon* (*petra* rock, *selinon* parsley), & ME *petrosilye* f. OE *petersilie*, f. Rom. as above]

par′snip n. (biennial umbelliferous plant, *Pastinaca sativa*, with yellow flowers and) large pale yellow tapering root used as culinary vegetable; *fine words* BUTTER[2] *no parsnips*. [ME *pas(se)nep* (w. assim. to *nep* turnip) f. OF *pasnaie* f. L *pastinaca*]

par′son n. rector; vicar or any beneficed clergyman; (colloq.) any (esp. Protestant) clergyman; ~**-bird**, (NZ) = TUI; *parson's* NOSE; hence or cogn. ~AGE (5) n., **parso′nic**(AL) adjs. [ME *person(e)*, *parson* f. OF *persone* f. L *persona* PERSON (in med. L rector)]

part[1] n. & adv. **1.** n. some but not all of a thing or number of things; (*a*) *part of it was spoilt, parts of it are excellent,* (*a*) *part of them have arrived,* (*a*) *great part of this is true, the most* or *greater part* (the majority) *of them failed.* **2.** division of book, broadcast serial, etc., esp. as much as is issued etc. at one time. **3.** portion of human or animal body (**the ~s**, genitals); component of machine etc. **4.** each of several equal portions of a whole; **three ~s** (quarters); *gold content is five parts per million; take 3 parts of sugar, 5 of flour,* etc. **5.** portion allotted, share, (**have neither ~ nor lot in,** (arch.) not be concerned in; ART[2] *and part*); person's share in action, his duty, (*I have done my part; it was not my part to interfere*). **6.** character assigned to actor on stage; words spoken by actor on stage; copy of these; (fig.) **play a** *noble, an unworthy*, ~, behave nobly etc.; **play a** ~, (1) contribute by action etc., (2) act deceitfully. **7.** (Mus.) melody or other constituent of harmony assigned to particular voice or instrument. **8.** (in *pl.*) abilities; *a man of (good, many) parts.* **9.** (in *pl.*) region (*a stranger in these parts; from foreign parts*). **10.** side in agreement or dispute. **11.** *parting of hair. **12. for the most** ~, in most cases, mostly; **for my** ~, so far as I am concerned; **in ~(s)**, partly; **on the ~ of**, proceeding from (*there was no objection on my part*), done etc. by; ~ **and parcel**, essential part *of*; ~ **of speech**, each of the grammatical classes of words (in English usu. noun, adjective, pronoun, verb, adverb, preposition, conjunction, interjection); **take ~**, assist (*in doing, in* discussion etc.); **take the ~ of**, support, back up; **take** (words, action) **in good** ~, not be offended at. **13.** ~**-exchange** n., & v.t., (give in)

transaction in which article is given as part of payment for more expensive one; ~**-owner,** one who owns in common with others; ~**-song,** song with three or more voice-parts, freq. without accompaniment, and harmonic rather than contrapuntal in character; ~ **time,** less than FULL[1] *time* (so ~*-time* a., occupying or using only part of one's working time, ~*-timER*[1] (1) n.); ~**-work,** publication appearing in several parts at different times. **14.** adv. in part, partly (*made part of iron and part of wood; is part iron part wood; a lie that is part truth*). [ME f. OF, f. L *pars partis*]

part[2] v. **1.** v.t. & i. divide into parts (*the crowd parted and let him through; the cord parted* (broke)). **2.** v.t. separate (hair of head on either side of parting) with comb; separate (combatants, friends, fool and his money, etc.; *till death us do part*); *part* BRASS *rags with; part* COMPANY. **3.** v.i. quit one another's company (*let us part friends; the best of friends must part*); (arch.) depart (*the curfew tolls the knell of parting day*); ~ **from,** say goodbye to; ~ **with,** give up, surrender, (property etc.). **4.** (colloq.) part with one's money, pay, (*if I know him, he won't part*). **5.** (arch.) distribute in shares. [ME, f. OF *partir* f. L *partire, partiri* (as prec.)]

partā′k|e v. (**partoo′k;** **parta′ken**). **1.** v.i. take a share or part (*in* or *of* thing, *with* person); take, esp. eat or drink some or (colloq.) all *of* (*he partook of our lowly fare, partook of a bun*); have some (*of* quality etc.; *his manner partakes of insolence*). **2.** v.t. (arch.) take a share in. **3.** Hence ~ABLE a. [16th c., back-form. f. *partaker, partaking = part-taker* etc.]

par′tan n. (Sc.) crab. [ME, app. f. Celt.]

par′ter′re (-tār′) n. level space in garden occupied by flower-beds; * = PIT[1] 3. [F, = *par terre* on the ground]

partheno|ge′nesis n. (Biol.) reproduction from gametes but without fertilization, esp. as normal process in invertebrates and lower plants; so ~**gene′tic** a. [mod. L, f. Gk *parthenos* virgin + as GENESIS]

Par′thian a. of Parthia, ancient kingdom of W. Asia; ~ **shot** etc., remark, glance, etc., reserved for moment of departure, like missile shot backwards by retreating Parthian horseman. [f. *Parthia* + -AN]

parti (pärtē′) n. person regarded as eligible etc. in the marriage market (*is quite a parti*); ~ **pris** (-prē′), preconceived view, bias. [F, = party, side]

par′tial (-shăl) a. & n. **1.** a. biased, unfair; ~ **to,** having a liking for (person or thing). **2.** forming only a part, not complete, (*a partial success*); ~ **eclipse** (in which part only of the luminary is covered or darkened); ~ **tone,** (Mus.) any constituent of a complex tone; *partial* VERDICT. **3.** Hence ~LY[2] adv. **4.** n. (Mus.) partial tone; **upper ~s,** those higher than main note produced from string, pipe, etc., harmonics, overtones. [ME, f. OF *parcial* f. LL *partialis* (as PART[1]; see -AL)]

partia′lity (-shi-) n. bias, favouritism; fondness (*for*). [ME, f. OF *parcial(i)té* f. med. L *partialitas* (as prec.; see -ITY)]

par′tible a. that can or must be divided (*among*; esp. of heritable property). [f. LL *partibilis* f. L (as PART[2]; see -IBLE)]

parti′cip|ate v.i. have share, take part, (*in* thing, *with* person); have something *of* (*his poems participate of the nature of satire*); so ~ANT, ~ATION, ~ATOR, ins., ~ATORY a.; ~ATING[2] a., *(of insurance etc.) entitling to share of company's additional profits. [f. L *participare* (*particeps -cipis* taking part f. as PART[1] + *-cip- = cap-* st. of *capere* take) + -ATE[3]]

par′ticiple n. verbal adjective qualifying noun but retaining some properties of verb, e.g. tense and government of object, as *qualifying* here (also used in compound verb-forms; *is going, has gone*); so **partici′piAL** a. [ME f. OF, by-form of *participe* f. L *participium* (as prec.)]

par′ticle n. minute portion of matter (ELEMENTARY *particle*); smallest possible amount (*has not a particle of sense*); minor part of speech, esp. short indeclinable one; common prefix or suffix such as *un-, out-, -ness, -ship*. [ME, f. L *particula* (as PART¹; see -CULE)]

parti'coloured (-ŭlerd) *a.* partly of one colour, partly of another or others. [f. PARTY² + COLOURED]

parti'cular *a. & n.* **1.** *a.* relating to one as distinguished from others, special; ||P∼ **Baptists,** (Hist.) body holding doctrines of *particular election* and *particular redemption* (i.e. of only some of the human race); *particular* INTENTION. **2.** (Logic). (Of proposition) in which something is predicated of some, not all, of a class (opp. *universal*). **3.** one considered apart from others, individual, (*this particular tax is no worse than others*; *particular* AVERAGE¹). **4.** worth notice, special, more than ordinary, (*took particular trouble*; *for no particular reason*). **5.** detailed (*full and particular account*); scrupulously exact, fastidious (*about, what or as to what one eats* etc.). **6.** Hence or cogn. ∼ITY (-ă'r-) *n.*, ∼LY² *adv.* **7.** *n.* detail, item; **in** ∼, especially (*mentioned one case in particular*), specifically (*did nothing in particular*); (in *pl.*) detailed account or information. [ME f. OF *particuler* f. L *particularis* (as PARTICLE; see -AR¹)]

parti'cular|ism *n.* doctrine of particular election or redemption; exclusive devotion to a party, sect, etc.; principle of leaving political independence to each State in an empire etc.; so ∼IST (2) *n.* [f. F (*-isme*), mod. L (*-ismus*), & G *partikularismus* (as prec.; see -ISM)]

parti'culariz|e, -ıs|e (-īz), *v.t.* name specially or one by one, specify, (items, or abs); hence ∼A'TION *n.* [f. F *particulariser* (as PARTICULAR; see -IZE)]

parti'culate (-ăt, -at) *a. & n.* (matter) in the form of separate particles. [f. L *particula* PARTICLE + -ATE²]

partie carrée (pārtē kărā') *n.* party of four persons, esp. two men and two women. [F, = square party]

par'ting *n.* In vbl senses; leave-taking (often *attrib.*: *parting injunctions*; ∼ **shot,** = PARTHIAN *shot*); dividing line of combed hair; ∼ **of the ways,** point at which road divides into two or more, (fig.) point at which choice must be made between courses of action. [f. PART²+ -ING¹]

pārtĭsăn¹ (-z-), **-zăn**¹, (-ă'n, pār't-) *n.* **1.** adherent of party, cause, etc., esp. unreasoning adherent (often *attrib.*: *in a partisan spirit*). **2.** (Mil.) guerrilla; (Hist.) member of light irregular troops employed in special enterprises. **3.** Hence ∼SHIP *n.* [F, f. It. dial. *partigiano* etc. (*parte* PART¹; see -AN)]

pār'tisan² (-z-), **-zan**², *n.* (Hist.) long-handled spear like halberd. [f. obs. F *partizane* f. obs. It. *partesana, partigiana* (as prec.)]

pār'ti'ta (-ē'-) *n.* (*pl.* ∼e *pr.* -ā). (Mus.) suite; air and set of variations on it. [It., fem. p.p. of *partire* divide f. as PART²]

pār'tite *a.* divided (esp. in *comb.*, as *tripartite*); (Bot. & Entom.) divided (nearly) to the base. [f. L *partitus* p.p. of *partiri* PART²]

pār'ti'tion *n.*, & *v.t.* **1.** *n.* division into parts; such part; structure separating two such parts, esp. slight wall, whence ∼ED² (-shond) *a.*; (Polit.) division of country into separately governed parts; (Law) division of real property between joint tenants etc. **2.** *v.t.* divide into parts; ∼ **off,** separate (part of room etc.) by a partition. [ME f. OF, f. L *partitio -onis* (as prec.; see -ION)]

pār'titive *a. & n.* (Gram.) (word) denoting part of a collective whole (e.g. *some, any*); ∼ **genitive,** that used to indicate a whole divided into parts, expressed in English by *of*, as in *most of us*; hence ∼LY² (-vlĭ) *adv.* [f. F *partitif -ive* or f. med. L *partitivus* (as PARTITE; see -IVE)]

partizan¹,². See PARTISAN¹,².

Pār'tlĕt *n.* (arch.) (Personal name for) hen. [f. OF *Pertelote*, proper name, of unkn. orig.]

pār'tly *adv.* with respect to a part or some parts; in some degree. [f. PART¹ + -LY²]

pār'tner *n.*, & *v.t.* **1.** *n.* sharer (*with* person, *in* or *of* thing). **2.** person associated with others in business of which he shares risks and profits; ∼ (one who

engages jointly) **in** crime (lit. or fig.); SLEEP²*ing partner.* **3.** wife or husband. **4.** companion in dance (esp. *dancing partner*); player associated with another in game and scoring jointly with him. **5.** (Naut., in *pl.*) timber framework round hole in deck through which mast, pump, etc., passes. **6.** Hence ∼LESS *a.*, ∼SHIP *n.*, state of being a partner, persons who are partners, joint business. **7.** *v.t.* associate (persons, one *with* another) as partners; be partner of. [ME, alt. of PARCENER, after PART¹]

pār'tridge *n.* (*pl.* ∼ *or* ∼s). game-bird of genus *Perdix* etc., esp. **common** or **grey** ∼ (*Perdix perdix*); ∼-**berry,** N. Amer. trailing evergreen (*Mitchella repens*) with edible but insipid scarlet berries; ∼-**wood,** (1) dark-striped hard red wood used for cabinet work etc., (2) speckled effect produced on wood by a certain fungus. [ME *partrich* etc. f. OF *perdriz* etc. f. L *perdix -dicis*; for *-dge* cf. CABBAGE]

pārtŭr'ient *a.* about to give birth (lit., or fig. of the mind etc.). [f. L *parturire* be in labour (incept. f. *parere* part-* bring forth); see -ENT]

pārtūri'tion *n.* act of bringing forth young, child-birth, (lit. or fig.) [f. LL *parturitio*, f. as prec.; see -ION]

pār'ty¹ *n* **1.** body of persons united in a cause, opinion, etc.; attachment to such body, taking of sides on public questions; **the P∼,** (esp.) the Communist party; ∼ **line,** policy adopted by a party (and see sense 4); ∼ **politics** (governed by rivalry between parties); ∼ **spirit,** (usu. derog.) zeal for a party (and see sense 2). **2.** body of persons travelling or working together (*fishing, reading, -party*); social gathering, esp. of invited guests at private house, (*birthday, dinner, tea, -party*); ∼ **spirit,** enthusiasm for taking part in such gatherings (and see sense 1). **3.** each of two or more persons making the two sides in legal action, contract, marriage, etc., (THIRD *party*); accessory (*to* action); (vulg. or joc.) person (*an old party with spectacles*). **4.** ∼-**coloured,** = PARTICOLOURED; ∼ **line,** telephone line shared by two or more subscribers (and see sense 1); ∼-**wall,** wall shared by each of the occupiers of the two buildings etc. that it separates. [ME, f. OF *partie*, f. Rom. *partita* fem p.p. (as n.) of L *partire* (see PART²) f. *parti*, f. L (as prec.)]

pār'ty² *a.* (Her.) divided into parts of different tinctures. [ME, f. OF *parti*, f. L (as prec.)]

pār'venu (-ōō) *n. & a.* (person) of obscure origin but having gained wealth or position, upstart. [F, p.p. of *parvenir* arrive f. L PER(*venire* come)]

pār'vis, pār'vise, *n.* enclosed area in front of cathedral, church, etc.; room over church-porch. [ME, f. OF *parvis, pare(v)is,* f. Rom. *paravisus* f. LL *paradisus* PARADISE, court in front of St. Peter's, Rome]

pas (pah) *n.* (*pl.* same). precedence (*dispute, give, take, the pas*). **2.** step in dancing; ∼ **de chat** (pah de shah'), leap in which each foot in turn is raised to opposite knee; ∼ **de deux** (pah de dē'r'), dance for two persons; *pas* GLISSÉ; ∼ **seul** (pah sēr'l), solo dance. [F, = step]

pă'scal *n.* unit of pressure, one newton per square metre; (P∼) computer language used in training. [f. B. *Pascal*, Fr. scientist d. 1662]

pă'schal (-k-) *a.* **1.** of the Jewish Passover; ∼ **lamb,** lamb sacrificed at Passover, (fig.) Christ. **2.** of Easter. [ME, f. OF *pascal* f. eccl. L *paschalis* (*pascha* f. Gk *paskha* f. Aram. *pasha*, rel. to Heb. *pesah* PASSOVER; see -AL)]

păsh *n.* (sl.) passion (*for*). [abbr.]

pa'sha, pa'cha, (pah'sha) *n.* (Hist.) (Title placed after name of) Turkish officer of high rank, e.g. military commander, governor of province, etc.; ∼**lĭc** *n.*, pasha's province or jurisdiction. [f. Turk. *paşa*, prob. = *başa* (*baş* head, chief)]

păshm *n.* under-fur of hairy quadrupeds in Tibet etc., esp. that of goats as used for Cashmere shawls. [f. Pers. *pašm* wool]

Pa′shtō (pŭ′-) *n. & a.* (of) the Iranian language of the Pathans. [Pashto]

paso doble (pahsō dō′blā) *n.* (ballroom dance based on) Latin-American style of marching. [Sp., = double step]

på′sque-flower (-skf-) *n.* anemone with bell-shaped purple flowers. [earlier *passe-flower*, f. F *passe-fleur*; assim. to *pasque* = obs. *pasch* (as PASCHAL), Easter]

påsquinā′de *n.* lampoon, satire, orig. one exhibited in public place. [f. It. *pasquinata* (*Pasquino*, statue at Rome on which Latin verses were annually posted; see -ADE)]

pass[1] (pahs) *v.* (*p.p.* ∿ed *or as adj.* PAST[1], *both pr.* pahst). **1.** *v.i.* move onward, proceed, (*along, down, over, on*, etc.); circulate, be current; be accepted *as*; be currently known *by or under the name of*; *(of person with some Black ancestry) be accepted as White. **2.** be transported *from* place *to* place; change (*into* something, *from* one state *to* another); die (usu. *pass hence, pass from among us*, etc., and see sense 15); go by (*saw the procession pass*; *time passes rapidly*; *remarks pass unnoticed*); come to an end (*kingdoms and nations pass*; *paroxysm has passed*). **3.** get through, effect a passage (∿ed **pawn**, chess pawn with no opposing pawn ahead on its own or adjacent files); go uncensured, be accepted as adequate, (*let the matter pass*); (of bill in Parliament, proposal, etc.) be sanctioned; (of candidate) satisfy examiner. **4.** happen, be done or said, (*I saw or heard what passed or was passing*). **5.** adjudicate (*upon*); (of judgement) be given (*for* plaintiff etc.) **6.** (Cards). forgo one's opportunity, e.g. of making a bid; throw up one's hand. **7.** *v.t.* leave (thing etc.) on one side or behind, as one goes (**has** ∿**ed the chair**, has been chairman, president, mayor, etc.); overtake; not declare or pay (dividend); go across (sea, frontier, mountain range). **8.** (Of bill) be examined and approved by (House of Commons etc.); reach standard required by (examiner, examination); *pass* MUSTER[1]. **9.** outstrip; surpass; be too great for (*it passes my comprehension*). **10.** transport (usu. w. *prep.* or *adv.*; cf. sense 15); move, cause to go, (*passed his hand across his forehead*; *pass flour through a sieve*; *pass a rope round it*; *pass in* one's CHECK[1]*s*; ∿ one's **eye over**, read (document) cursorily); (Footb., Hockey, etc.) kick or throw or hit (ball, or abs.) to or *to* another player of one's own side. **11.** cause to go by (*pass troops etc. in review*); cause or allow (bill in Parliament, candidate for examination, etc.) to proceed as being found satisfactory after scrutiny; ∿ed **master**, = PAST[1] *master* (2). **12.** spend (*time, the winter*, etc.). **13.** hand, transfer, (*read this and pass it round, to Bob*; *please pass the salt*); cause (coin, esp. base coin) to circulate; (arch.) pledge (one's *word, oath*, etc.). **14.** utter (criticism, judicial sentence, *on or upon*); *pass the* TIME[1] *of day*; discharge from body as or with excreta (∿ **water**, urinate). **15.** (w. *advs.*): ∿ **away**, (fig.) die, cease to exist, come to an end; ∿ **by**, walk etc. past; ∿ **off**, (of feelings etc.) disappear gradually, (of proceedings) be carried through (*smoothly* etc.), palm off (thing or person *on* person *for or as* what it is not), evade or lightly dismiss (awkward remark etc.); ∿ **on**, proceed on one's way, (fig.) die, transmit to next person in series; ∿ **out**, depart, (of cadet) complete military training, (fig.) die, distribute as largess, (colloq.) become unconscious; ∿ **over**, (fig.) die, or as in sense 16 (*pass it over in silence*); ∿ **up**, (colloq.) refuse or neglect (opportunity etc.). **16.** (w. *preps.*): ∿ **by**, omit, disregard, walk etc. past; ∿ **for**, be accepted as; ∿ **over**, omit, disregard, ignore claims of (person) to promotion etc., make no remark on (*pass over his subsequent conduct*); ∿ **through**, experience. [ME, f. OF *passer* f. Rom. **passare* f. L *passus* PACE[1]]

pass[2] (pahs) *n.* **1.** passing, esp. of examination or at cards; ||attainment of standard that satisfies university examiners and entitles to ∿ **degree** but not to honours degree. **2.** BRING *to pass*; *come to pass* (COME 8). **3.** critical position (*things have come to a* (*strange*,

pretty) *pass*). **4.** written permission to pass into or out of a place, or to be absent from quarters; = FREE[1] *pass*. **5.** thrust in fencing; juggling trick; passing of hands over anything, as in conjuring or hypnotism; **make a** ∿ **at**, (colloq.) make amorous advances to. **6.** (Footb. etc.) transference of ball to another player of one's own side. **7.** ∿′**book**, (1) book supplied by bank etc. to person having current or deposit account, which shows all sums deposited and drawn, (2) (S. Afr.) document to be carried by non-White persons; ∿′**key**, (1) private key to gate etc. for special purposes, (2) master-key; ||∿′**man**, one who takes pass degree at university; ∿-**mark**, minimum mark needed to pass examination; ∿′**word**, selected word or phrase known only to one's own side and used to distinguish friend from enemy. [partly f. prec., partly f. F *passe* (*passer* as prec.)]

pass[3] (pahs) *n.* **1.** narrow passage through mountains; this as commanding access to a country; **sell the** ∿, (fig.) betray cause. **2.** navigable channel, esp. at river's mouth; passage for fish over weir. [ME, var. of PACE[1], infl. by F *pas* and by PASS[1]]

pa′ssab|le (pah′-) *a.* In vbl senses; that can pass muster, fairly good, whence ∿**LY**[2] *adv.* [ME f. OF (as PASS[1]; see -ABLE)]

påssaca′glia (-ah′lya) *n.* (Mus.) instrumental piece usu. with ground bass, derived from old dance. [It., f. Sp. *pasacalle* (*pasar* pass, *calle* street; because often played in streets)]

på′ssage[1] *n.* **1.** passing, transit (BIRD *of passage*); transition from one state to another; voyage or crossing from port to port. **2.** liberty or right to pass through; right of conveyance as passenger by sea or air; **work** one's ∿, earn this right by labour (lit. or fig.). **3.** passing of a bill etc. into law. **4.** ∿(**way**), way by which one passes, esp. narrow way between buildings, corridor etc. giving communication between different rooms in house. **5.** duct etc. in the body; **back** ∿, (colloq.) rectum; **front** ∿, (colloq.) vagina. **6.** (in *pl.*) what passes between two persons mutually, interchange of confidences etc. **7.** ∿ **of or at arms**, fight (lit. or fig.). **8.** short part of book etc. (*famous, difficult, corrupt*, PURPLE, *passage*); particular phrase or short section in a piece of music. [ME f. OF (as PASS[1]; see -AGE)]

på′ssage[2] *v.* **1.** *v.i.* (Of horse or rider) move sideways, by pressure of rein on horse's neck and of rider's leg on opposite side. **2.** *v.t.* make (horse) do this. [f. F *passager*, earlier *passéger* f. It. *passeggiare* to walk, pace (*passeggio* walk f. L *passus* PACE[1])]

på′ssant *a.* (Her.) (Of animal) walking and looking to dexter side, with three paws on ground and right fore--paw raised. [ME f. OF, part. of *passer* PASS[1]; see -ANT]

passé (på′sā) *a.* (*fem.* ∿**e** *pr.* same). past the prime, esp. (of woman) past the period of greatest beauty; behind the times, out of date. [F, p.p. of *passer* PASS[1]]

*på′ssel *n.* (large) group *of* (persons etc.). [alt. of PARCEL[1]]

passementerie (på′smentrĭ) *n.* trimming of gold or silver lace, braid, beads, etc. [F (*passement* gold lace etc. f. *passer* PASS[1]; see -MENT, -ERY)]

på′ssènger (-nj-) *n.* traveller in or on public or private conveyance by land or water or air (other than driver, pilot, etc.); FOOT[1]-*passenger*; (colloq.) member of team, crew, etc., who does, or can do, no effective work; ∿-**mile**, one mile travelled by one passenger, as unit of traffic; ∿-**pigeon**, extinct wild pigeon of N. America, capable of long flight; ∿ **seat** (esp. in motor vehicle next to driver's seat); ∿ **train** (opp. goods train). [ME f. OF *passager* n., f. OF adj. *passager* passing (as PASSAGE[1], -ER[2]); *-n-* as in *messenger* etc.]

passe-partou′t (påspårtōō′, pah-) *n.* master-key; picture-frame (esp. for mounted photographs) consisting of two pieces of glass fastened together at edges with adhesive tape; adhesive tape or paper used thus. [F, = passes everywhere]

pa′sser (pah′-) *n.* In vbl senses; ∼**-by,** one who goes past, esp. casually. [ME, f. PASS[1] + -ER[1]]

pä′sserine *a.* & *n.* **1.** (bird) of the order Passeriformes, perching (esp. song)bird. **2.** *a.* of the size of a sparrow. [f. L *passer* sparrow + -INE[1]]

pä′ss|ible *a.* (Theol.) capable of feeling or suffering; so ∼IBI′LITY *n.* [ME f. OF, or f. LL *passibilis* f. L *pati* pass- suffer; see -IBLE]

passim (pä′sim) *adv.* (Of allusions, phrases, etc., to be found in specified author or book) in many places, here and there throughout (*this occurs in Milton passim*). [L (*passus* scattered f. *pandere* spread)]

pa′ssing[1] (pah′-) *n.* In vbl senses; **in** ∼, by the way, in the course of a speech etc.; ∼**-bell** (rung to announce person's death); ∼**-note,** *∼**-tone,** (Mus., not belonging to the harmony but interposed to secure smooth transition). [ME, f. PASS[1] + -ING[1]]

pa′ssing[2] (pah′-) *a.* & *adv.* **1.** *a.* In vbl senses; transient, fleeting; cursory, incidental; ∼ **shot,** (Tennis) stroke intended to place ball beyond and out of reach of opponent. **2.** *adv.* (arch.) very (*passing strange, rich*). [ME, f. PASS[1] + -ING[2]]

pä′ssion (-shon) *n.* **1.** strong emotion; outburst of anger (*flew into a passion*); sexual love; strong enthusiasm (*for thing, for doing*), object arousing this. **2.** (*P*∼). *the* sufferings of Christ on the Cross, (musical setting of) narrative of this from Gospels. **3.** ∼**-flower,** plant of genus *Passiflora* [flower of which was supposed to suggest instruments of the Crucifixion]; ∼**-fruit,** edible fruit of some species of passion-flower; ∼**-play,** miracle play representing Christ's Passion; **P**∼ **Sunday,** fifth Sunday in Lent; **P**∼**tide,** last two weeks of Lent; **P**∼ **Week,** (1) week between Passion Sunday and Palm Sunday, (2) = HOLY *Week*. **4.** Hence ∼LESS *a.* [ME f. OF, f. LL *passio -onis* f. L *pati* pass- suffer; see -ION]

pä′ssion[2] (-shon) *v.i.* (poet.) feel or express passion. [f. OF *passioner* (as prec.)]

pä′ssional[1] (-sho-) *n.* book of the sufferings of saints and martyrs. [f. med. L *passionale* neut. adj. (as n.) f. L *passio* PASSION[1]]

pä′ssional[2] (-sho-) *a.* of, or marked by, passion. [f. PASSION[1] + -AL]

pä′ssionate (-sho-) *a.* dominated by or easily moved to strong feeling, esp. love or anger; due to passion; (of language etc.) showing passion; hence ∼LY[2] (-tlĭ) *adv.,* ∼NESS (-tn-) *n.* [ME, f. med. L *passionatus* (as PASSION[1]; see -ATE[2])]

Pä′ssionist (-sho-) *n.* member of a RC order pledged to do their utmost to keep alive the memory of Christ's Passion. [f. PASSION[1] + IST]

pä′ssiv|āte *v.t.* make passive; hence ∼A′TION *n.* [f. foll. + -ATE[3]]

pä′ssive *a.* & *n.* **1.** *a.* suffering action, acted upon. **2.** (Gram.) ∼ **voice,** that comprising those forms of transitive verbs that attribute the verbal action to the person etc. to whom it is directed (the logical object), as *He was seen by us*; (of verb etc.) in passive voice; INDIRECT *passive*; cf. ACTIVE, MIDDLE[1]. **3.** offering no opposition, submissive; *passive* OBEDIENCE; ∼ **resistance,** non-violent refusal to co-operate. **4.** not active, inert; (of debt) incurring no interest-payment; (of metal etc.) abnormally unreactive. **5.** Hence ∼LY[2] (-vlĭ) *adv.,* ∼NESS (-vn-), **pässĭ′vITY,** *ns.* **6.** *n.* (Gram.) passive voice or form of verb. [ME, f. OF *passif -ive,* or f. L *passivus* (as PASSION[1]; see -IVE)]

Pa′ssŏver (pah′-) *n.* Jewish spring festival commemorating liberation of Israelites from Egyptian bondage, held from 14th to 21st day of seventh month of Jewish year; = PASCHAL *lamb.* [f. *pass over,* pass without touching, w. ref. to exemption of Israelites from death of first-born (Exod. 12)]

pa′sspŏrt (pah′-) *n.* official document certifying identity and citizenship, permitting person(s) specified in it to travel to and from foreign country, establishing identity and nationality, and entitling to protection; (fig.) thing that ensures admission to or

attainment of (*flattery is the sole passport to his favour*). [f. F *passeport* (*passer* PASS[1], PORT[1])]

past[1] (pah-) *a.* & *n.* **1.** *a.* having passed (PASS[1]); gone by in time (*his prime is past; our past years; in times past*); just gone by (*the past month; for some time past*); (Gram.) expressing past action or state (*past tense, participle*); relating to a former time (*past president*); ∼ **definite,** ∼ **historic,** (Gram.) tense expressing completed action in the past; ∼ **master,** (1) one who has been master in guild, Freemason's lodge, etc., (2, fig.) thorough master (*in or of a subject*); *past* PERFECT[1]. **2.** *n.* past time, esp. *the past*; what has happened in past time (*cannot undo the past*); person's past life or career, esp. one that is not creditable (*a woman with a past*); past tense. [p.p. of PASS[1]]

past[2] (pah-) *prep.* & *adv.* **1.** *prep.* beyond in time or place (*stayed till past two o'clock; half past three; old man past seventy; ran past the house*); (beyond the range or duration or compass of (*past belief, endurance, bearing, caring,* PRAYING *for*); ∼ **it,** (sl.) incompetent through senility etc., ineffective after long use; **not put it** ∼ person (*to do*), (colloq.) regard him as (esp. morally) capable (of doing). **2.** *adv.* so as to pass by (*hasten past*). [ME, f. prec. as in *is past* = 'has passed' w. obj.]

pa′sta (pä′-, pah′-) *n.* (dish made from cooked) dried flour paste used in Italian cooking in various shapes (macaroni, spaghetti, vermicelli, etc.). [It., = PASTE[1]]

päste[1] *n.* **1.** flour moistened and kneaded, with butter, suet, lard, etc., as cooking material. **2.** sweet doughy confection (*almond paste*). **3.** easily spread preparation of ground meat, fish, etc., (*anchovy paste*). **4.** cement of flour or starch and water. **5.** soft plastic mixture for any purpose (*toothpaste*). **6.** hard vitreous composition used in making imitation gems. **7.** mixture of clay, water, etc., used in making pottery. **8.** ∼′**board,** stiff substance made by pasting together sheets of paper, (*attrib.,* fig.) unsubstantial, flimsy. [ME f. OF, f. LL *pasta* small square medicinal lozenge f. Gk *pastē* (*pastos* sprinkled)]

päste[2] *v.t.* fasten with paste; stick up (playbill etc.) on wall with paste; cover (thing *with* paper etc.) by pasting; (sl.) beat, thrash, bomb etc. heavily; ∼′**down,** outer blank leaf of book pasted on inside of cover; ∼**-up,** document prepared for copying etc. by pasting various materials on a backing. [f. prec.]

pä′stel *n.* artists' crayon made of dried paste compounded of pigments with gum solution; drawing in pastel, whence ∼(**l**)IST (3) *n.;* ∼ **colour** etc. (light and subdued). [F, or f. It. *pastello,* dim. of *pasta* PASTE[1]]

pä′stern *n.* part of horse's foot between fetlock and hoof; corresponding part in other animals. [ME *pastron* f. OF *pasturon* (*pasture* hobble f. *pastoire* f. med. L *pastoria* f. L *pastorius* of a shepherd; see PASTOR]

pa′steurīz|e (pä′ster-, pah′-, -scher-), **-īs|e** (-ĭz), *v.t.* subject (milk etc.) to Pasteur's method of partial sterilization by heating; hence ∼A′TION *n.* [f. L. *Pasteur,* Fr. chemist d. 1895 + -IZE]

pästĭ′cciŏ (-ĭ′chō) *n.* (*pl.* ∼s). = foll. [It. (see foll.)]

pästi′che (-ē′sh) *n.* medley, esp. musical composition, or picture, made up from various sources; literary or other work of art composed in the style of a well-known author. [F, f. It. *pasticcio* f. Rom. **pasticius* f. LL *pasta* PASTE[1]]

pä′stille (-ĭl, -ēl) *n.* small roll of aromatic paste burnt as fumigator etc.; = LOZENGE 2. [F, f. L *pastillus* little loaf, lozenge (*panis* loaf)]

pa′stĭme (pah′-) *n.* recreation; game, sport. [f. PASS[1] + TIME[1]]

pa′stor (pah′-) *n.* **1.** minister in charge of church or congregation, whence ∼SHIP *n.;* person exercising spiritual guidance. **2.** pink species of starling. [ME f. AF & OF *pastour* f. L *pastor -oris* shepherd (*pascere* past-feed, graze; see -OR)]

pa′storal (pah′-) *a.* & *n.* **1.** *a.* of shepherds; relating to flocks and herds; (of land) used for pasture; (of poem, picture, etc.) portraying country life, whence ∼ISM

(2) *n.* **2.** of a pastor; concerned with spiritual guidance of a body of Christians; ~ **epistles** (of Paul to Timothy and Titus, dealing with pastor's work); ~ **staff,** crosier; ~ **theology** (considering religious truth in relation to spiritual needs). **3.** Hence ~ITY (-ă′l-) *n.*, ~LY² *adv.* **4.** *n.* pastoral play, poem, poetry, or picture; letter from pastor, esp. bishop, to clergy or people. [ME, f. L *pastoralis* (as prec.; see -AL)]

păstora′l|ē (-ah′-) *n.* (*pl.* ~i *pr.* -ē, *or* ~es). simple opera etc. with rural subject; slow quiet instrumental composition with notes flowing in groups of three and usu. with drone notes in bass suggesting bagpipes. [It., f. as prec.]

pa′storalist (pah′-) *n.* (Austral.) sheep- or cattle-farmer. [f. PASTORAL + -IST]

pa′storate (pah′-) *n.* pastor's (tenure of) office; body of pastors; *parsonage. [f. PASTOR + -ATE¹]

***păstra′mǐ** (-ah′-) *n.* seasoned smoked beef. [Yiddish]

pā′strÿ *n.* (baked) flour-paste; article(s) of food made wholly or partly of this; ~-cook, one who makes pastry, esp. for public sale. [f. PASTE¹ after OF *pastaierie; see -ERY]

pa′sturage (pah′scher-, -tūr-) *n.* pasturing; herbage for cattle etc.; pasture-land. [OF (as foll.; see -AGE)]

pa′sture (pah′-) *n.* & *v.* **1.** *n.* herbage for cattle, sheep, etc.; (piece of) land covered with this; **common** ~, use of herbage by cattle of several owners. **2.** *v.t.* lead or put (cattle etc.) to pasture; (of sheep etc.) eat down (grassland); put sheep etc. on (land) to graze. **3.** *v.i.* graze. [ME f. OF, f. LL *pastura* (as PASTOR; see -URE)]

pa′stÿ¹ (pă′-, pah′-) *n.* pie of meat, fruit, jam, etc., enclosed in paste and baked without dish. [ME, f. OF *pasté(e)* f. med. L *pastata* f. LL *pasta* PASTE¹; see -Y⁴]

pā′stÿ² *a.* of or like paste; ~(-faced), of (unhealthily) pale complexion. [f. PASTE¹ + -Y²]

păt¹ *n.* **1.** light stroke or tap, esp. with hand as caress etc.; ~ **on the back** (fig., as token of approbation). **2.** small mass (esp. of butter) formed by patting. **3.** sound made by striking lightly with something flat. [ME; prob. imit.]

păt² *v.* (-tt-). **1.** *v.t.* strike (thing) gently with flat surface (~′**ball,** poor or feeble cricket or lawn tennis); flatten thus (~-a-cake [first words of a nursery rhyme] child's game with patting of hands); strike gently with inner surface of hand or fingers, esp. to mark sympathy, approbation, etc.; ~ (person, oneself) **on the back,** (fig.) express approbation of, congratulate. **2.** *v.i.* beat lightly *upon*. [16th c., f. (or rel. to) prec.]

păt³ *adv.* & *a.* apposite(ly), opportune(ly), (*story came pat to his purpose*); (known thoroughly and) ready for any occasion (*has the story (off) pat*); **stand** ~, (Poker) retain hand dealt to one, not draw other cards, (fig.) refuse to change, stick to one's decision etc.; hence ~′LY² *adv.* [16th c., rel. to PAT¹,².]

Păt⁴ *n.* (Nickname for) Irishman. [abbr. of man's Christian name *Patrick*]

Pat. *abbr.* Patent.

păta̅gi′|um *n.* (*pl.* ~a). (Zool.) wing-membrane of bat or similar animal; scale covering wing-joint in Lepidoptera. [med. L use of L f. Gk *patageion* gold edging on tunic]

păta̅vi′nitÿ *n.* dialectal characteristics of Patavium (Padua) as seen in Livy's Latin; provincialism. [f. L *patavinitas* (*Patavinus* of Padua; see -INE¹, -ITY)]

pătch¹ *n.* **1.** piece of cloth, metal, etc., put on to mend hole or rent; piece of plaster etc. put over wound; pad worn to protect injured eye; (Mil.) piece of cloth on uniform as badge of unit; **not a** ~ **on,** (colloq.) not comparable to, very much inferior to. **2.** (Hist.) small disc etc. of black silk stuck on either side of face, worn esp. by women in 17th–18th c. for adornment. **3.** large or irregular distinguishable area on surface; in ~es, in isolated areas or periods of time; ||**strike a bad** ~, go through a period of bad luck or difficulty. **4.** piece of ground; number of plants growing in one

place (*brier-patch*); area patrolled by police etc. **5.** scrap, remnant. **6.** ~-**pocket** (consisting of piece of cloth sewn on garment); ~ **test,** test for allergy by applying to the skin patches containing allergenic substances; ~′**work,** work made up of fragments of different kinds and colours (lit. or fig.; often *attrib.*). **7.** Hence ~′ERY (1) *n.* [ME *pacche, patche,* perh. var. of *peche* f. AF **peche,* OF *piece* dial. var. of *piece* PIECE¹]

pătch² *v.t.* put patch(es) on; ~ (**up**), repair with patches; (of material) serve as patch to; ~ (**up**), (fig.) repair, set to rights (matter, trouble, quarrel), esp. hastily or temporarily; ~ (**up**), put together hastily; piece (things) together (lit. or fig.); appear as patches on (surface). [f. prec.]

patchouli (pă′chŏŏli̅, pachŏŏ′-) *n.* odoriferous E. Ind. plant; perfume got from it. [native name in Madras]

pă′tch|ÿ *a.* having patches; irregular, uneven in quality; hence ~iLY² *adv.*, ~iNESS *n.* [f. PATCH¹ + -Y²]

pāte *n.* (arch. or colloq.) head, often as representing seat of intellect; (hence -pā′tED² *a.* [ME, of unkn. orig.]

pâté (pă′tā, pah′-) *n.* pie, patty; paste of meat etc.; ~ **de foie gras** (de fwah grah), paste or pie of fatted goose liver. [F, f. OF *pasté* (as PASTY¹)]

patĕ′lla *n.* (*pl.* ~e). kneecap, whence **patĕ′llAR¹, patĕ′ll**ATE², *adjs.*; (Rom. Ant.) small pan. [L, dim. of *patina* (see foll.)]

pă′ten *n.* shallow dish used for bread at Eucharist; circular plate of metal. [ME, f. AF **pateine,* OF *patene* or f. L *patena, -ina* shallow dish f. Gk *patanē* plate]

pă′tent¹ *a.* **1.** ||**letters** ~ [OF *lettres patentes,* med. L *litterae patentes*], = PATENT² **1. 2.** conferred or protected by PATENT²; (of food, medicine, etc.) proprietary; *patent* LEATHER; ~ **log,** elaborated rotary form of ship's log, recording speed on dial fixed on taffrail; ~ **still** (allowing continuous distillation). **3.** (fig.) to which one has proprietary claim; (colloq.) such as might be patented, ingenious, well-contrived. **4.** (Of door etc.) open; (fig.) plain, obvious; hence **pă′t**ENCY *n.*, ~LY² *adv.* [ME f. OF, and f. L *patēre* lie open; see -ENT]

pă′tent² *n.* **1.** open letter from sovereign etc. conferring right, title, etc., esp. sole right for a period to make, use, or sell, some invention. **2.** government grant of exclusive privilege of making or selling new invention; invention or process so protected; (fig.) sign that one is entitled to something, possesses a quality, etc., (*a patent of gentility*). **3.** ~ **agent,** *attorney,** (specializing in procurement of patents); ~ **office** (from which patents are issued); ||~-**roll** (recording patents issued in UK in a year). [abbr. of *letters* PATENT¹]

pă′tent³ *v.t.* obtain patent for (invention); hence ~ABLE *a.* [f. prec.]

pătentee′ *n.* taker-out or holder of a patent; person for the time being entitled to the benefit of a patent. [PATENT² + -EE]

||**pā′ter** *n.* (sl.) father. [L]

păterfami′li̅as *n.* (Rom. Law, or joc.) head of family or household. [L]

pater′nal *a.* **1.** of or like a father; fatherly; related through the father (~ **grandmother,** father's mother). **2.** (Of government, legislation, etc.) limiting the freedom of the subject by well-meant regulations, whence ~ISM (3), ~IST (2), *ns.*, ~i′stIC *a.* **3.** Hence ~LY² *adv.* [f. LL *paternalis* f. L *paternus* (*pater* father); see -AL]

pater′nitÿ *n.* fatherhood (~ **test,** test to determine from blood samples whether a man may be or cannot be father of a particular child); one's paternal origin; (fig.) authorship, source. [ME, f. OF *paternité* or f. LL *paternitas* (as prec.; see -ITY)]

păternŏ′ster *n.* **1.** the Lord's Prayer, esp. in Latin; **devil's** ~, (1) this said backwards, (2) muttered imprecation. **2.** bead in rosary indicating that paternoster is to be said; series of like things, e.g. moving compartments serving as lift; ~ (**line**), weighted fishing-tackle with hooks at intervals. [OE, f. L *pater noster* our father]

path *n.* (pahth; *pl. pr.* pahdhz). **1.** way made for foot-passengers, esp. one merely made by walking, not specially constructed. **2.** track laid for foot or cycle racing. **3.** line along which person or thing moves; (fig.) course of action, line of conduct. **4.** ∼'**finder,** explorer, aircraft (or its pilot) sent ahead of bombers to guide them whon to their objective and mark out their targets; ∼'**way,** = sense l, (Biochem. etc.) sequence of reactions by which energy is made available. **5.** Hence ∼'LESS *a.* [OE *pæth,* = OLG *pad,* OHG *pfad* f. WG **path-*]

-päth *suf.* forming *ns.* denoting: **1.** practitioner of curative treatment (*homoeopath, osteopath.*) **2.** sufferer from a disease (*psychopath*). [sense l back-form. f. -PATHY; sense 2 f. Gk *-pathēs* -sufferer (as PATHOS)]

Patha'n (-tah'n) *n.* member of a people inhabiting NW Pakistan and SE Afghanistan. [Hindi]

pathĕt'ic *a.* **1.** exciting pity or sadness or contempt; of the emotions; ∼ic **fallacy,** crediting inanimate things with human emotions. **2.** Hence ∼ICS *n. pl.,* study of, indulgence in, or demonstration of, emotions; ∼ICALLY *adv.* [f. F *pathétique,* f. LL f. Gk *pathētikos* (as PATHOS; see -ETIC)]

pä'thic *n.* victim; catamite. [f. L f. Gk *pathikos* passive (as PATHOS; see -IC)]

pătho- *comb. form.* disease, as: ∼**gnomo'nic,** characteristic of a particular disease; ∼**gnomy** (-ŏ'g-), study of the emotions. [f. Gk *pathos* suffering (see PATHOS)]

pä'thogen *n.* agent causing disease; so **păthoGE'NIC, pathŏ'GENOUS,** *adjs.* [f. prec. + -GEN]

păthogĕ'nĕsis, pathŏ'gĕnў, *ns.* mode of development of a disease; so **păthogĕnĕ'tIC** *a.* [f. PATHO- + GENESIS, -GENY]

păthŏlŏ'gical *a.* of pathology; (apparently) morbid (*a pathological dislike of dogs*); hence ∼LY² *adv.* [f. foll. + -ICAL]

pathŏ'logЈў *n.* science of bodily diseases; symptoms of a disease; hence ∼IST (3) *n.* [f. F *pathologie* or mod. L *pathologia* (as PATHO-, -LOGY)]

pä'thŏs *n.* quality in speech, writing, events, etc., that excites pity or sadness. [f. Gk *pathos* suffering, rel. to *paskhō* suffer, *penthos* grief]

-pathy *suf.* forming *ns.* denoting curative treatment (*allopathy, homoeopathy, hydropathy*), or feeling (*telepathy*). [f. Gk *patheia* suffering; see -Y¹]

pä'tience (-shens) *n.* **1.** calm endurance of pain or of any provocation; perseverance; forbearance; quiet and self-possessed waiting for something; **have no** ∼ **with,** be irritated by, be unable to bear patiently (person, his conduct, etc.); **lose** (one's) ∼, become impatient (*with*); **out of** ∼ **with,** no longer able to endure; *the patience of* JOB⁴. **2.** ‖game of cards, usu. for one player, in which cards are to be brought into specified arrangement. [ME f. OF, f. L *patientia* (as foll.; see -ENCE)]

pä'tient (-shent) *a.* & *n.* **1.** *a.* having or showing patience; ∼ **of,** (arch.) (1) enduring with patience, (2) admitting of or compatible with (*the facts are patient of two interpretations*); hence ∼LY² *adv.* **2.** *n.* person under medical or dental or psychiatric treatment; person accepted by doctor etc. for treatment if this is needed in future. **3.** person undergoing action (opp. *agent*). [ME f. OF, f. L *patiens -entis* (*pati* suffer; see -ENT)]

pä'tin⎸a *n.* incrustation, usu. green, on surface of old bronze, esteemed as ornament; similar alteration on other surfaces; gloss produced by age on woodwork; hence ∼**ätēd** [-ATE²], ∼OUS, *adjs.,* ∼A'TION *n.* [It., f. L *patina* dish]

pati'ne (-ē'n) *n.* = prec. [F, f. L (as prec.)]

pä'tiŏ *n.* (*pl.* ∼s). inner court open to sky in Spanish or Sp.-Amer. house; paved usu. roofless area adjoining and belonging to house. [Sp.]

pătĭ'sserie *n.* pastry-cook's shop or wares. [f. F

pâtisserie f. med. L *pasticium* pastry (*pasta* PASTE¹); see -ERY]

Pă'tna *n.* ∼ **rice,** variety of rice with long firm grains. [∼ in India, where orig. grown]

pă'tois (-twah) *n.* (*pl.* same *pr.* -z). dialect of common people in a region, differing materially from the literary language; jargon. [F, = rough speech, perh. f. OF *patoier* treat roughly (*patte* paw)]

‖**pä'trial** *a.* & *n.* (person) having right of abode in UK through British birth of parent; hence **pä'triä'lITY** *n.* [obs. F, or f. med. L *patrialis* f. L *patria* fatherland (*pater* father); see -AL]

pä'triărch (-k) *n.* **1.** father and ruler of family or tribe; (Bibl., in *pl.*) (1) sons of Jacob, (2) Abraham, Isaac, and Jacob, and their forefathers. **2.** (In early and Orthodox Churches) bishop, esp. of Antioch, Alexandria, Constantinople, Jerusalem, or Rome, or head of autocephalous church; (RC Ch.) bishop ranking next above primates and metropolitans, and immediately below the Pope; head of a Uniat community. **3.** founder of an order, science, etc.; venerable old man; oldest member of a group. **4.** So **pä'triăr'chAL** (-k-) *a.* [ME, f. OF *patriarche* f. eccl. L f. Gk *patriarkhēs* (*patria* family f. *patēr* father, *-arkhēs* -ruler)]

pä'triărchate (-k-) *n.* office, see, or residence, of ecclesiastical patriarch; rank of tribal patriarch. [f. med. L *patriarchatus* (as prec.; see -ATE¹)]

pä'triărchЈў (-kī) *n.* patriarchal system of society, government, etc.; so ∼ISM (3) *n.* [f. med. L f. Gk *patriarkhia* (as PATRIARCH; see -Y¹)]

patri'cian (-shan) *n.* & *a.* **1.** *n.* (Hist.) ancient Roman noble (cf. PLEBEIAN); member of a noble order in later Roman Empire; officer representing Roman emperor in provinces of Italy and Africa; nobleman in some Italian republics. **2.** *a.* noble, aristocratic; of the ancient Roman nobility. [ME, f. OF *patricien* f. L *patricius* having noble father (*pater patris* father; see -ICIAN)]

patri'ciate (-shi-) *n.* patrician order, aristocracy; rank of patrician. [f. L *patriciatus* (as prec.; see -ATE¹)]

pä'tricid⎸e *n.* = PARRICIDE (esp. w. ref. to killing of one's father); hence ∼AL *a.* [f. LL *patricida, patricidium,* alt. of L *parricida, parricidium,* (see PARRICIDE), after *pater* father]

pătrĭli'nĕal *a.* of or based on (kinship with) father or descent through male line. [f. L *pater patris* father + LINEAL]

pătrĭlŏ'cal *a.* of system of marriage where wife goes to live with husband's group. [f. as prec. + LOCAL²]

pä'trimonў *n.* property inherited from one's father or ancestors, heritage (lit. or fig.), endowment of church etc.; hence **pätrimŏ'niAL** *a.* [ME *patrimoine* f. OF *patrimoine* f. L *patrimonium* (*pater patris* father; see -MONY)]

pä'triot *n.* one who defends or is zealous for his country's prosperity, freedom, or rights; hence or cogn. **pätriŏ'tIC** *a.,* ∼ISM (3) *n.* [f. F *patriote* f. LL f. Gk *patriōtēs* (*patrios* of one's fathers f. *patēr patros* father; see -OT²)]

patri'st⎸ic *a.* of (the study of the writings of) the Fathers of the Church; hence ∼ICS *n.,* such study. [f. G *patristisch* f. L *pater patris* father; see -IST, -IC]

patrŏ'l *n.* & *v.* (-ll-). **1.** *n.* going the ROUND²s of garrison, camp, etc.; perambulation of town etc. by police (∼ **car,** car used for this; *** ∼ **wagon,** police van for prisoners); routine operational voyage of ship or of aircraft; routine monitoring of astronomical etc. phenomena. **2.** detachment of guard, police constable(s), etc., assigned for patrol (∼**man,** ***patrol constable); detachment of troops sent out to reconnoitre, such reconnaissance; ‖official controlling traffic where children cross road; unit of usu. six in Scout troop or Guide company. **3.** *v.i.* act as patrol. **4.** *v.t.* go round (camp, town, etc.) as patrol. [(f. G *patrolle* f. F *patrouille*) f. F *patrouiller* paddle in mud (*patte* paw)]

patrŏ'log|ў n. study, or a collection, of writings of the Fathers of the Church; hence **pătro**LO'GICAL a., ∼IST (3) n. [f. Gk patēr patros father + -o- + -LOGY]

pā'tron n. one who countenances, protects, or gives influential support to (person, cause, art, etc.); (esp. regular) customer of shop etc.; ∼ (saint), tutelary saint of person, place, etc.; (Rom. Ant.) (1) former owner of manumitted slave, (2) protector of a CLIENT; ‖one who has right of presenting to benefice; so **pā'tron**ESS[1] n. [ME f. OF, f. L patronus protector of clients, defender (pater patris father)]

pă'tronage n. support or encouragement given by patron; ‖right of presenting to benefice or office; patronizing airs; customer's support. [ME f. OF (as prec.; see -AGE)]

patronal (pā'tro-, patrō'-) a. of a patron saint (the patronal festival etc.). [F, or f. LL patronalis (as PATRON; see -AL)]

pă'troniz|e, -īs|e (-īz), v.t. act as patron towards, support, encourage, (person, practice, shop, etc.); treat condescendingly, whence ∼INGLY adv. [f. obs. F patroniser or f. med. L patronizare (as PATRON; see -IZE)]

pătronў'mic a. & n. (name) derived from name of a father or ancestor. [f. LL f. Gk patrōnumikos f. patrōnumos (patēr patros father, onuma, onoma name); see -IC]

***patrōō'n** n. (Hist.) possessor of landed estate with manorial privileges (finally abolished c. 1850) under Dutch governments of New York and New Jersey. [Du., = PATRON]

***pă'tsў** n. (sl.) person who is ridiculed, deceived, or victimized. [20th c.; orig. unkn.]

pă'ttée (-tā, -tī) a. (of cross) having almost triangular arms becoming very broad towards their ends. [F (patte paw; see -Y[4])]

pă'tten n. shoe with sole made thick or set on iron ring etc., for raising wearer's foot out of mud etc. [ME, f. OF patin (patte paw, -in -INE[1])]

pă'tter[1] n. language of a profession or class; deceptive speech of salesman etc.; rapid speech used by comedian or introduced into song; words of comic song. [f. foll.]

pă'tter[2] v.t. & i. repeat (prayers etc.) in rapid mechanical way; talk glibly. [ME, f. pater = PATERNOSTER]

pă'tter[3] v. & n. 1. v.i. make rapid succession of taps, as rain on window-pane; run with short quick steps. 2. v.t. cause (water etc.) to patter. 3. n. rapid succession of taps or short light steps. [f. PAT[2] + -ER[5]]

pă'ttern n., & v.t. 1. n. excellent or ideal example (she is a pattern of domestic virtues). 2. model or design or working instructions from which thing is to be made; sample (of tailor's cloth, wallpaper, etc.). 3. (decorative) design as executed on carpet, wallpaper, cloth, etc.; regular form or order (behaviour pattern; pattern of one's daily life); marks made by shots, bombs, etc., on area of target; ∼ bombing (on large area, not single target); ∼-room, -shop, part of foundry etc. in which patterns are prepared. 4. v.t. model (thing after or on design etc.). 5. decorate with pattern. [ME patron (see PATRON); different. in sense and sp. since 16th–17th c.]

pă'tty n. 1. little pie or pastry; ∼pan (for baking patty in). 2. *small flat cake of minced meat etc. [f. F pâté PASTY[1]]

pă'tūlous a. open, expanded; (of boughs etc.) spreading; hence ∼LY adv., ∼NESS n. [f. L patulus (patēre be open) + -OUS]

pau'a (pow'a) n. large edible NZ shellfish of genus Haliotis; its ornamental shell; fish-hook made from this. [Maori]

pau'c-ity n. smallness of number or quantity. [ME, f. OF paucité or f. L paucitas (paucus few; see -ITY)]

Paul n. rob PETER[1] to pay Paul; ∼ Jones, (dance in which there is) exchange of dance-partners according to prescribed movement [Amer. naval officer d. 1792]; ∼ Pry, inquisitive person [character in

comedy by J. Poole 1825]. [man's Christian name; ME, f. OF Pol f. L Paulus]

Pau'line a. & n. 1. a. of St. Paul (the Pauline epistles). 2. n. past or present member of St. Paul's School in London. [ME, f. med. L Paulinus (as prec.; see -INE[1])]

paulow'nia (-ō'-) n. Chinese tree of genus Paulownia, with fragrant purple flowers. [f. Anna Paulovna, Russ. princess d. 1865 + -IA[1]]

paunch n., & v.t. 1. n. belly, stomach; protruding abdomen, whence ∼'Y[2] a.; ruminant's first STOMACH, rumen; (Naut.) thick strong mat, (rubbing ∼) wooden shield on mast, to prevent chafing. 2. v.t. disembowel (animal). [ME, f. AF pa(u)nche, ONF panche f. Rom. *pantice f. L pantex panticis bowels]

pau'per n. person without means of livelihood, beggar; (Hist.) recipient of poor-law relief; person who may sue in forma pauperis; hence ∼DOM, ∼ISM (2), ns., ∼IZE (3) v.t. [L, = poor]

pause (-z) n., & v.i. 1. n. interval of inaction or silence, esp. due to hesitation; temporary stop; give ∼ to, cause (person) to hesitate. 2. break made in speaking or reading; (Mus.) mark (⌒) over note or rest that is to be lengthened by some unspecified amount. 3. v.i. make a pause, wait; linger upon (word etc.). [ME f. OF, or f. L pausa f Gk pausis (pauō stop); v. f. n. or f. F pauser or f. L pausare]

pā'vage n. paving; tax or toll towards paving of streets. [ME f. OF (paver PAVE; see -AGE)]

pă'van, pava'ne (-ah'n), n. (Hist.) stately dance in which dancers were elaborately dressed; music for this. [f. F pavane f. Sp. pavana, poss. f. pavon peacock]

pāve v.t. cover (street, floor, etc.) with or (fig.) as with pavement (paved with stone, flowers, good intentions); (fig.) prepare the way (for or to changes, reform, etc.); hence **pā'ver**[1], **pā'ving**[1] (1, 2, 3), **pā'vior** or **pā'viour** (-vyer), ns. [ME, f. OF, f. L paver, back-form. f. as PAVEMENT]

pavé (pă'vā) n. pavement; setting of jewels placed close together. [F, p.p. of paver (see prec.)]

pā'vement (-vm-) n. 1. covering of street, floor, etc., made of stones, tiles, wooden blocks, asphalt, etc., ‖esp. paved footway at side of road, *esp. roadway; ∼ artist, ‖one who draws with chalks on pavement to get money from passers-by, *one who displays paintings etc. on pavement. 2. (Zool.) pavement-like formation of close-set teeth etc. [ME f. OF, f. L pavimentum (pavire beat, ram; see -MENT)]

pavi'lion (-lyon) n., & v.t. 1. n. tent, esp. large peaked one; light ornamental building; building used for entertainments; ‖building adjacent to cricket or other ground for players and spectators; detached building at hospital; projecting (usu. highly decorated) subdivision of building; temporary stand at exhibition; part of cut gem-stone below girdle. 2. v.t. enclose in or furnish with pavilion. [ME, f. OF, f. L papilio -onis butterfly, tent]

pavio(u)r. See PAVE.

pā'vis(e) n. (Hist.) convex shield covering whole body used in sieges etc. [ME, f. OF *paveis, pavais f. It. pavese f. med. L pavense (scutum shield) of Pavia in Italy, where orig. made]

pavlō'va n. meringue cake, usu. served with cream etc. [f. A. Pavlova, Russ. ballerina d. 1931]

pā'vonīne a. of or like a peacock. [f. L pavoninus (pavo -onis peacock; see -INE[1])]

paw[1] n. foot of animal having claws or nails, opp. hoof; (colloq.) person's hand. [ME pawe, powe f. OF poue etc. f. Rom. f. Frank. *pauta]

paw[2] v.t. & i. strike with paw: (of horse) strike (ground), strike ground, with hoofs; (colloq.) handle awkwardly or rudely or indecently. [f. prec.]

‖**paw'k|ў** a. (Sc. & dial.) drily humorous; shrewd; hence ∼ĭLY[2] adv., ĭNESS n. [f. Sc. & N. Engl. dial. pawk trick, of unkn. orig. + -Y[2]]

pawl n., & v.t. 1. n. lever with catch for teeth of wheel or bar; (Naut.) short bar used to lock capstan, windlass, etc., and prevent it from recoiling. 2. v.t.

secure (capstan etc.) with pawl. [perh. f. LG & Du. *pal*, rel. to *pal* fixed]

pawn[1] *n.* chess-man of smallest size and value; (fig.) unimportant person subservient to others' plans. [ME, f. AF *poun*, OF *peon* f. med. L *pedo -onis* foot--soldier f. L *pes pedis* foot; cf. PEON]

pawn[2] *n.* **1.** (usu. fig.) thing left in another's keeping as security, pledge. **2.** state of being pledged (*in* or *at pawn*); ~'broker, one who lends money at interest on security of personal property pawned; ~'broking, his occupation; ~'shop, his place of business; ~-ticket, his receipt for thing pledged. [ME, f. OF *pan, pand, pant* pledge, security f. WG **panda*]

pawn[3] *v.t.* deposit (thing) as security for payment of money or performance of action; (fig.) pledge (one's life, honour, word). [f. prec.]

pawpaw'. See PAPAW.

päx *n.* **1.** tablet with representation of Crucifixion etc. formerly kissed at Mass by priest and people. **2.** kiss of peace. **3.** ||(school sl., as *int.*). peace!, truce!. [ME f. L, = peace]

PAX *abbr.* private automatic (telephone) exchange.

pay[1] *n.* **1.** payment; wages; **in the** ~ (employment) **of.** **2.** ~-bed, hospital bed whose use is paid for by user; ~-claim, demand for increase of pay; ~-day, day on which payment is (to be) made, ||(Stock Exch.) day on which transfer of stock has to be paid for; ***~ dirt, ~ gravel, ground worth working for ore (lit. or fig.); ***~ envelope, = *pay-packet*; ~'load, productive or useful part of load of aircraft, rocket, etc.; ~'master, official who pays troops, workmen, etc. (often fig.); ||**Paymaster General,** minister at head of department of Treasury through which payments are made; ||~-packet (containing employee's wages); ~ phone, ***~ station, coin-box telephone; ~'roll, list of employees receiving regular pay. [ME, f. OF *paie* (*payer*; see foll.)]

pay[2] *v.* (**paid**). **1.** *v.t.* give (person) what is due in discharge of debt or for services done or goods received; (fig.) reward, recompense; *pay him in his own* COIN[1]; *the* DEUCE[2] *or devil to pay;* ~ **off,** pay in full and discharge or be quit of (ship's crew, creditor, debt, etc.); ~ (person) **out** or **back,** punish him or be revenged on him; *pay the* PIPER; **put paid to,** (colloq.) deal effectually with (person), terminate (hopes etc.). **2.** recompense (work); **paid holidays** (during which normal wages continue to be paid). **3.** hand over (money owed *to* person; *paid the fee to the clerk, paid him his fee*); hand over the amount of (debt, wages, ransom); undergo (penalty); (esp. Naut.) let rope *out* or *away* by slackening it. **4.** ~ **in,** pay to one's own or another's banking account; *pay its* or one's WAY 9; ~ **up,** pay full amount of (arrears, or abs.); **paid-up member** (who has made all necessary payments for membership). **5.** render, bestow, (attention, respect, court, compliment, visit, *to;* CALL[2] *on*). **6.** (Of business etc.) yield adequate return to (person). **7.** *v.i.* hand over money to discharge debt etc.; (of business etc.) yield adequate return, be profitable or advantageous; ~ing guest, boarder. **8.** ~ **for,** hand over the price of, bear the cost of, (fig.) suffer or be punished for (fault etc.); *pay through the* NOSE; ~ **off,** (colloq.) yield good results or succeed, (of ship) turn to leeward through movement of helm; ~-off n., (sl.) act of payment, climax, final reckoning. **9.** ||~-as-you--earn, method of collecting income tax by deducting at source as income is earned. **10.** Hence ~EE', ~'ER[1], ns. [ME, f. OF *payer* f. L *pacare* appease (*pax pacis* peace)]

pay[3] *v.t.* (Naut.) smear with pitch, tar, etc., as defence against wet. [f. OF *peier* f. L *picare* (*pix picis* PITCH[1])]

pay'able *a.* that must be paid, due; that may be paid; (of mine etc.) profitable. [ME, f. PAY[2] + -ABLE]

||**PAYE** *abbr.* pay-as-you-earn.

pay'ment *n.* paying; amount paid; (fig.) recompense. [ME, f. OF *paiement* (as PAY[2]; see -MENT)]

pay'nim *n.* (arch.) pagan; non-Christian, esp.

Muslim. [ME, f. OF *pai(e)nime* f. eccl. L *paganismus* heathenism (as PAGAN; see -ISM)]

payō'la *n.* bribe(ry) offered in return for deliberate help in promoting a commercial product by unsanctioned means. [f. PAY[1] + *-ola* as in *Victrola,* make of gramophone]

paysage (pāzah'zh) *n.* rural scene, landscape; landscape painting, whence **pay'sag**IST (3) *n.* [F (*pays* country; see PEASANT, -AGE)]

Pb *symb.* lead. [f. L *plumbum*]

||**PBI** *abbr.* (colloq.) poor bloody infantry.

PBX *abbr.* private branch exchange (private telephone switchboard).

PC *abbr.* police constable; Privy Counsellor.

p.c. *abbr.* per cent; postcard.

*****pct.** *abbr.* per cent.

*****PD** *abbr.* Police Department.

pd. *abbr.* paid.

Pd *symb.* palladium.

p.d.q. *abbr.* (sl.) pretty damn quick.

*****PDT** *abbr.* Pacific Daylight Time.

PE *abbr.* physical education.

p/e *abbr.* price/earnings (ratio).

pea *n.* **1.** hardy climbing leguminous plant (*Pisum sativum*) whose seeds grow in pods and are used for food; its seed (**green** ~s, the seeds gathered unripe for food); SPLIT[1] *peas*; **as like as two** ~s, indistinguishable. **2.** similar plant (CHICK-PEA, EVERLASTING *pea,* SWEET *pea*). **3.** ~-green, colour of green peas; ~'nut, (plant *Arachis hypogaea,* whose fruit is a pod containing) seed used as food and yielding oil (~*nut butter,* paste of ground roasted peanuts; ~*nuts,* (sl.) paltry thing, esp. small amount of money); ~-shooter, toy tube from which dried peas are shot by blowing; ~ soup (made from sep. dried peas); ~-sou'per, (colloq.), thick yellow fog; ~-stick (on which pea-plant is trained in garden). [back-form. f. PEASE taken as *pl.*; cf. CHERRY]

peace *n.* **1.** freedom from or cessation of war (*peace with honour; peace at any price,* **make** (bring about) ~); *a* treaty of peace between two powers at war. **2.** freedom from civil disorder; **the** (**queen's**) ~, general peace of the realm as secured by law; BREACH[1] *of the peace;* JUSTICE *of the Peace.* **3.** quiet, tranquillity; (in and after Bibl. use) *peace be with you, peace to his ashes!; mental calm* (*peace of mind*). **4. at** ~, in state of friendliness or quietness, not at strife (*with*); **hold** one's ~, keep silence; **keep the** ~, prevent, or refrain from, strife; **make** one's ~, bring oneself back into friendly relations (*with*). **5.** ***P~ **Corps,** organization of young people to work in developing countries; ~'maker, one who brings about peace; ~-offering, propitiatory or conciliatory gift, (Bibl.) offering presented as thanksgiving to God; ~-pipe, calumet, tobacco-pipe as token of peace among N. Amer. Indians; ~'time, period when a country is not at war. [ME f. AF *pes,* OF *pais* f. L *pax pacis*]

pea'ceab|le (-sa-) *a.* disposed or tending to peace; free from disturbance, peaceful; hence ~leNESS (-bəln-) *n.,* ~LY[2] *adv.* [ME f. OF *peisible, plaisible* f. LL *placibilis* pleasing f. L *placēre* please; see -IBLE]

pea'ceful (-sf-) *a.* characterized by peace; belonging to a state of peace; not violating or infringing peace (*peaceful* COEXISTENCE); hence ~LY[2] *adv.,* ~NESS *n.* [ME, f. PEACE + -FUL]

peach[1] *n.* **1.** large fruit, usu. round, with downy white or yellow skin flushed with red, highly flavoured sweet pulp, and rough stone; ~(-tree), tree (*Prunus persica*) bearing this; (sl.) person or thing of superlative merit, attractive young woman. **2.** ~-blow, (Oriental porcelain-glaze of) delicate purplish-pink colour; ~ **brandy,** spirituous liquor from peach juice; ~-colour(ed), (of) yellowish pink; ~ **Melba,** confection of ice cream and peaches with liqueur etc. [f. Dame N. *Melba,* Austral. soprano d. 1931]; ~es and cream, (fig. of complexion) creamy skin with downy pink cheeks. **3.** Hence ~'Y[2] *a.* [ME, f. OF *peche, pesche,* f. med. L *persica* f. L *persicum (malum)*, lit. Persian apple]

peach² *v.* (colloq. or arch.) **1.** *v.i.* turn informer; inform (*against* or *on* accomplice). **2.** *v.t.* inform against. [ME, f. *appeach* f. AF *enpecher*, OF *empechier* IMPEACH]

pea'-chick *n.* young peafowl. [f. as PEACOCK + CHICK¹]

pea'cŏck *n.* & *v.* **1.** *n.* male peafowl, bird with splendid plumage and tail-coverts that can be expanded erect like fan (often as the type of ostentatious display; *proud as a peacock*). **2.** ∼ (**blue**), lustrous blue of peacock's neck; ∼ **butterfly** (with ocellated wings); ∼ **coal** (iridescent). **3.** *v.t.* plume one*self*. **4.** *v.i.* make display; strut about ostentatiously, whence ∼ERY (4) *n.*; (Austral. sl.) acquire best land in a district. **5.** Hence ∼ISH¹, ∼LIKE, *adjs.* [ME *pecock* f. OE *pēa* f. L *pavo*, + COCK¹]

pea'fowl *n.* peacock or peahen, pheasant of genus *Pavo.* [f. as prec. + FOWL]

pea'hĕn *n.* female peafowl. [ME, f. as PEACOCK + HEN]

pea'-jăckĕt *n.* sailor's short double-breasted overcoat of coarse woollen cloth. [prob. f. Du. *pijjakker (pij* coat of coarse cloth, *jekker* jacket), assim. to JACKET]

peak¹ *n.,* & *v.i.* **1.** *n.* projecting part (usu. at front) of cap. **2.** (Naut.) narrow part of ship's hold esp. at bow (*forepeak*) or stern (*after-peak*); upper outer corner of sail extended by gaff. **3.** pointed top, esp. of mountain; point e.g. of beard or hair (WIDOW'*s peak*). **4.** highest point in curve or record of fluctuations or in career etc.; ∼ **hour,** time of most intense traffic etc.; ∼**-load,** maximum of electric power demand etc. **5.** Hence ∼ED² (-kt), ∼'Y², *adjs.* **6.** *v.i.* reach highest value, quality, etc. [prob. back-form f. *peaked* var. of dial. *picked* pointed (PICK¹, -ED²)]

peak² *v.i.* waste away, esp. *peak and pine; (in p.p.)* sharp--featured, pinched; so ∼'Y² *a.,* sickly, puny. [16th c.; of unkn. orig.]

peak³ *v.t.* & *i.* (Naut.) tilt (yard) vertically; place (oars) apeak; (of whale) raise (tail, flukes), raise tail or flukes, straight up in diving vertically. [prob. f. APEAK]

pea'kỹ¹·². See PEAK¹, PEAK².

peal¹ *n.* & *v.* **1.** *n.* loud ringing of bell(s), esp. series of changes on set of bells; set of bells; loud volley of sound, esp. of thunder or laughter. **2.** *v.i.* sound forth in a peal. **3.** *v.t.* utter sonorously; ring (bells) in peals. [ME *pele* f. *apele* APPEAL²]

peal² *n.* salmon grilse. [16th c.; orig. unkn.]

pean¹ *n.* (Her.) fur represented as sable spotted with or. [16th c.; orig. unkn.]

*pē'an². Var. of PAEAN.

pear (pār) *n.* fleshy fruit usu. with brown or yellow skin, tapering towards stalk; ∼(-**tree**), tree (*Pyrus communis*) bearing this; *alligator* or AVOCADO *pear;* ANCHOVY *pear;* PRICKLY *pear;* ∼**-drop,** small sweetmeat with shape and flavour of pear. [OE *pere, peru,* = MDu., MLG *pere* f. pop. L **pira* f. L *pirum*]

pearl¹ *n.* **1.** concretion, usu. white or bluish--grey, formed within shell of ∼**-oyster** or other bivalve mollusc, having beautiful lustre and highly prized as gem; imitation of this; (in *pl.*) necklace of pearls; MOTHER¹-*of-pearl;* SEED-*pearl.* **2.** precious thing, finest example (*of*) its kind); **cast** ∼**s before swine,** offer good thing to one incapable of appreciating it. **3.** pearl-like thing, e.g. dew-drop, tear, tooth. **4.** ∼ **ash,** commercial potassium carbonate; ∼ **barley** (reduced by attrition to small rounded grains); ∼ **bulb** (translucent electric-light); ∼ **button** (of mother-of-pearl or imitation thereof); ∼**-diver,** one who dives for pearl-oysters; ∼**-fisher,** one who fishes for pearl-oysters; ∼ **millet,** tall cereal (*Pennisetum glaucum*); ∼ **onion,** very small onion used in pickles; ∼'**wort,** weed of genus *Sagina.* **5.** Hence ∼ED² (-ld) *a.,* adorned with pearls, formed into pearl-like drops or grains, like pearl in colour etc. [ME f. OF *perle,* f. Rom. **perla,* prob. f. **pernula* dim. of L *perna* leg (applied to leg-of-mutton-shaped bivalve)]

pearl² (pêrl) *v.* **1.** *v.t.* sprinkle with pearly drops; make pearly in colour etc.; reduce (barley etc.) to small rounded grains. **2.** *v.i.* form pearl-like drops; fish for pearl-oysters, whence ∼'ER¹ *n.* [ME, f. prec.]

||**pearl³** (pêrl) *n.* picot. [var. of PURL¹]

pearl'ỹ (pêr-) *a.* & *n.* **1.** *a.* resembling a pearl; containing pearls or mother-of-pearl; adorned with pearls; **P∼ Gates** (of Heaven); ||∼ **king, queen,** costermonger, his wife, wearing pearlies; *pearly* NAUTILUS. **2.** *n.* (in *pl.*) ||costermongers' clothes decorated with pearl buttons; pearly kings and queens. [ME, f. PEARL¹ + -Y²]

||**pear'main** (pār'-, pêr'-) *n.* variety of apple with firm white flesh. [ME, = warden pear, f. OF *parmain, permain,* prob. f. Rom. **Parmanus of Parma* in Italy]

*peart (pêrt) *a.* lively; cheerful. [var. of PERT]

pea'sant (pĕ′z-) *n.* countryman, rustic; worker on the land, esp. labourer or small farmer; hence ∼RY (1) *n.* [ME, f. AF *paisant,* OF *païsent,* earlier *païsence (païs* country f. Rom. **pagensis* f. L *pagus* canton; see -ING³)]

pea'scŏd (-z-). Var. of PEASECod.

pease (-z) *n.* peas (esp. ∼**-pudding,** pudding of boiled peas, eggs, etc.); ∼'**cod,** (arch.) pea-pod. [OE *pise* pea, pl. *pisan,* f. LL *pisa* f. L *pisum* f. Gk *pison;* cf. PEA]

peat¹ *n.* **1.** (cut piece of) vegetable matter decomposed in water and partly carbonized, used for fuel etc.; ∼'**bog,** ∼'**moss,** bog composed of peat; ∼'**reek,** smoke of, or whisky distilled over, peat-fire. **2.** Hence ∼'ERY (3) *n.,* ∼'Y² *a.* [ME, f. AL *peta,* perh. f. Celt. **pett-;* cf. PIECE¹]

peat² *n.* (arch., derog.) person, esp. woman, (*proud peat*). [16th c.; orig. unkn.]

peau-de-soie (pōdəswah') *n.* smooth finely-ribbed satiny fabric of silk or rayon. [F, = skin of silk]

*pea'vey *n.* lumberjack's cant-hook with projecting spike near end. [f. *Peavey,* surname of inventor]

pĕ'bble *n.* small stone worn and rounded by action of water (**not the only** ∼ **on the beach,** not without competitors to be reckoned with); colourless transparent rock-crystal used for spectacles, lens of this, (colloq.) thick spectacle-lens; agate or other gem, esp. found as pebble in streams; ∼**-dash,** mortar with pebbles in it as coating for wall; hence **pĕ'bblỹ²** *a.* [OE *papel-stān* pebble-stone, *pyppelrīpig* pebble--stream; orig. unkn.]

pébrine (pābrē′n) *n.* epidemic disease of silkworms, characterized by black spots. [F, f. Prov. *pebrino (pebre* PEPPER¹)]

p.e.c. *abbr.* photoelectric cell.

pĕcă'n *n.* (pinkish-brown smooth nut of) a hickory (*Carya illinoensis*) of the Mississippi region. [f. earlier *paccan,* of Algonquian orig.]

pĕ'ccable *a.* liable to sin; hence ∼ABI′LITY *n.* [F, f. med. L *peccabilis (peccare* sin; see -ABLE)]

pĕccadi'llō *n.* (*pl.* ∼es or ∼s). trifling offence, venial sin. [f. Sp. *pecadillo,* dim. of *pecado* sin, f. L (as foll.)]

pĕ'ccant *a.* sinning; morbid, inducing disease; so ∼ANCY *n.* [F, or f. L *peccare* sin; see -ANT]

pĕ'ccarỹ *n.* American gregarious wild pig of genus *Tayassu.* [f. Carib *pakira*]

pĕcca'vi (-ah′-) *int.* & *n.* (expr.) confession of guilt. [L, = I have sinned]

pêche Mĕ'lba (pāsh-, pĕsh-) *n.* = PEACH¹ *Melba.* [F]

pĕck¹ *n.* measure of capacity for dry goods, = 2 gallons or 8 quarts; vessel used for this; **a** ∼ (large number, amount) *of troubles, of dirt.* [ME f. AF *pek,* of unkn. orig.]

pĕck² *v.* & *n.* **1.** *v.t.* strike (thing) with beak (∼'**ing order,** social hierarchy, orig. as observed among domestic fowls; ∼ **out,** pluck out by pecking); make (hole etc.) thus; ∼ kiss (person's cheek etc.) hastily or perfunctorily; (colloq.) eat (food, or abs.), esp. in nibbling or listless fashion; mark with short strokes; break (*up, down,* etc.) with pick etc. **2.** *v.i.* strike *at* (thing) with beak, (fig.) carp *at.* **3.** *n.* stroke with beak, mark made with this; hasty or perfunctory kiss;

∼**order,** = *pecking order*. **4.** (sl.) food [ME, prob. f. MLG *pekken*, of unkn. orig.]

pe′cker *n.* bird that pecks (*flower-pecker, woodpecker*); **(sl.) penis; ||**keep your** ∼ **up,** (sl.) maintain your courage. [f. prec. + -ER¹]

pe′ckish *a.* (colloq.) hungry; **irritable. [f. PECK² + -ISH¹]

Pe′cksniff *n.* unctuous hypocrite talking much of benevolence etc.; hence **Pe′cksni′ff**IAN *a.* [character in Dickens's *Martin Chuzzlewit*]

pecori′nō (-ē′-) *n.* (*pl.* ∼s). Italian ewe-milk cheese. [It. (*pecorino* a. of ewes f. *pecora* sheep)]

pe′ct|ĕn *n.* (*pl.* ∼ens, *or* ∼ines *pr.* -ĭnēz). **1.** (Zool.) comblike structure of various kinds in animal bodies; so ∼**in**ATE², ∼**inā**tED¹, *adjs.,* ∼**ina′**TION *n.,* (Zool. & Bot.). **2.** scallop of genus Pecten. [f. L *pecten pectinis* comb]

pe′ct|in *n.* (Chem.) soluble gelatinous carbohydrate derivative acting as setting agent in jams and jellies; so ∼IC *a.* [f. Gk *pēktos* congealed (*pēgnumi* make solid) + -IN]

pe′ctoral *n.* & *a.* **1.** *n.* ornamental breastplate esp. of Jewish high priest; pectoral fin, medicine, etc. **2.** *a.* of or for the breast or chest; good for chest disease; worn on the breast; ∼ **cross,** cross so worn by bishops etc.; ∼ **fin** (on side of fish). [ME f. OF, f. L *pectorale* n., *pectoralis* a. (*pectus pectoris* breast, chest; see -AL)]

pe′ctōse *n.* (Chem.) insoluble carbohydrate derivative found in unripe fruits etc. and converted into pectin by ripening, heating, etc. [f. PECTIC + -OSE²]

pe′cŭlāte *v.t.* & *i.* embezzle (money); so ∼A′TION, ∼ātOR, *ns.* [f. L *peculari* rel. to *peculium* (see foll.) + -ATE³]

pecū′liar *a.* & *n.* **1.** *a.* belonging exclusively *to*; belonging to the individual, esp. one's *own peculiar* (character etc.); particular, special, (*a point of peculiar interest*). **2.** strange, odd, (*a peculiar flavour; he has always been a little peculiar*). **3.** ∼ **people,** (1) the Jews, (2) God's elect, (3) (**P**∼ **People**) evangelical fundamentalist Christian denomination founded 1838 relying on divine healing for cure of disease. **4.** *n.* peculiar property, privilege, etc.; parish or church exempt from jurisdiction of diocese in which it lies; (*P*∼) one of the *Peculiar People* (3). [ME, f. L *peculiaris* of private property (*peculium* f. *pecu* cattle; see -AR¹)]

pecūliā′rity *n.* being peculiar; characteristic; (instance of) unusualness. [f. prec. + -ITY]

pecū′liarly *adv.* as regards oneself alone, individually (*does not affect him peculiarly*); especially, more than usually, (*peculiarly annoying*); oddly (*they dress peculiarly*). [f. PECULIAR + -LY²]

pecū′niar|y̆ *a.* (consisting) of money (*pecuniary aid, considerations*); (of offence) having money penalty; hence ∼ILY² *adv.* [f. L *pecuniarius* (*pecunia* money f. *pecu* cattle; see -ARY¹)]

pe′dagōgue (-g) *n.* (arch. or derog.) schoolmaster, teacher; hence or cogn. **pĕdagŏ′g**IC(AL) (-ŏ′g-, -ŏ′j-) *adjs.,* **pĕ′dagŏg(u)**ISM (1) (-gĭ-) *n.* [ME, f. L f. Gk *paidagōgos* (*pais paidos* boy, *agōgos* guide)]

pe′dagōg|y̆ (-jĭ, -gĭ) *n.* science of teaching; so ∼ICS *n.* [f. F *pédagogie* f. Gk *paidagōgia* (as prec.; see -Y¹)]

pe′dal¹ *n.* & *v.* (||-ll-). **1.** *n.* (Mus., in organ) (1) any of wooden keys played upon by the feet, (2) foot-lever for drawing out several stops at once or other purposes; (in piano) foot-lever for making the tone more sustained and fuller (**loud** ∼) or softer (**soft** ∼); (in harp) foot-lever for altering pitch of strings; foot-lever in various machines, esp. for transmitting power to wheel of bicycle (∼ **cycle**) or tricycle; (Mus.) note sustained in one part, usu. bass, through successive harmonies some of which are independent of it; ∼**pushers,** women's sports trousers reaching to calf. **2.** *v.i.* play on organ pedals. work cycle pedals; ride bicycle. **3.** *v.t.* work (bicycle) by pedals. [f. F *pédale* f. It. *pedale* f. L (as foll.)]

pe′dal² *a.* **1.** (Zool.) of the feet or foot (esp. of mollusc).

2. (Math.) ∼ **triangle** (formed by feet of perpendiculars or other concurrent lines from vertices of a triangle). [f. L *pedalis* (*pes pedis* foot; see -AL)]

pĕ′dalō *n.* (*pl.* ∼s). pedal-operated pleasure-boat. [f. PEDAL¹]

pĕ′dant *n.* one who overrates or parades book-learning or technical knowledge or insists on strict adherence to formal rules; one who is obsessed by a theory; doctrinaire; hence or cogn. **pĕdă′nt**IC *a.,* ∼IZE (2, 3) *v.t.* & *i.,* ∼RY (1, 4, 5) *n.* [f. F *pédant* f. It. *pedante*; app. f. as PEDAGOGUE + -ANT]

pĕ′date *a.* (Zool.) footed; (Bot., of leaf) having divisions like toes or bird's claws. [f. L *pedatus* (*pes pedis* foot; see -ATE²)]

pĕ′ddle *v.* **1.** *v.i.* follow occupation of pedlar; busy oneself with trifles. **2.** *v.t.* sell as pedlar; (fig.) deal out in small quantities, retail. [back-form. f. PEDLAR; in sense 'trifle' orig. var. of PIDDLE]

****pĕ′ddler.** Var. of PEDLAR.

pĕ′deră′sty̆, pae′d-, *n.* sodomy with a boy; so **pĕ′derăst, pae′d-,** *n.,* one who commits pederasty. [f. mod. L f. Gk *paiderastia* (*pais paidos* boy, *erastēs* lover); see -Y¹]

pĕ′dĕstal *n.,* & *v.t.* (||-ll-). **1.** *n.* base supporting column or pillar; base of statue etc. (**put** or **set on a** ∼, (fig.) regard as highly admirable or important); each of two supports of knee-hole table; foundation (lit. or fig.); ∼ **table** etc. (with single central support). **2.** *v.t.* set or support on pedestal. [f. F *piédestal* f. It. *piedestallo* (*piè* foot f. L *pes pedis, di* of, *stallo* STALL¹)]

pĕdĕ′strian *a.* & *n.* **1.** *a.* going or performed on foot; of walking; for walkers (∼ **crossing,** part of road where pedestrians going across have priority over traffic; *pedestrian* PRECINCT); prosaic, dull, uninspired. **2.** *n.* one who walks in street etc.; one who walks as athletic performance, whence ∼ISM (2) *n.;* hence ∼IZE (2, 3) *v.i.* & *t.* [f. F *pédestre* or f. L *pedester -tris* + -IAN]

*****pēdiă′tric** etc. See PAEDIATRIC etc.

pĕ′dicăb *n.* rickshaw pulled by cyclist. [f. PEDAL¹ + -I- + CAB]

pĕ′dicel, pĕ′dicle, *ns.* small (esp. subordinate, cf. PEDUNCLE) stalklike structure in plant or animal; (Surg.) part of graft left temporarily attached to original site; hence **pĕ′dicell**ATE², **pĕdĭ′cūl**ATE², *adjs.* [f. mod. L *pedicellus* & L *pediculus* dim. of *pes pedis* foot; see -CULE]

pĕdĭ′cūlar, pĕdĭ′cūlous, *adjs.* louse-infested; so **pĕdĭcūlo′sis** *n.* [f. L *pedicularis, -losus* (*pediculus* louse; see -AR¹, -OUS)]

pĕ′dicūre *n.,* & *v.t.* **1.** *n.* care or treatment of feet, esp. of toe-nails; person who practises this. **2.** *v.t.* treat (feet) by removing corns etc. [f. F *pédicure* f. L *pes pedis* foot + *curare* (see CURE²)]

pĕ′digree *n.* & *a.* **1.** *n.* genealogical table; ancestral line (of man or animal); derivation (of word); ancient descent; hence **pĕ′digre**ED² *a.* **2.** *a.* having a recorded line of descent, esp. one showing pure breeding (*pedigree cattle*). [ME *pedegru* etc., f. AF **pe de gru*, OF **pie de grue* crane's foot, mark denoting succession in pedigrees]

pĕ′diment *n.* triangular part crowning front of building in Grecian style, esp. over portico; similarly placed member of same or other form in Roman and Renaissance styles; (Geol.) broad flattish rock surface at foot of mountain slope; hence **pĕdĭmĕ′nt**AL, ∼ED², *adjs.* [earlier *pedament, periment,* perh. corrupt. of PYRAMID]

pĕ′dlar *n.* travelling vendor of small wares usu. carried in pack; (fig.) retailer (*of gossip etc.); ∼'s French,* (arch.) thieves' cant, gibberish; hence **pĕ′dla**RY (5) *n.* [ME *pedlere* alt. of *pedder* f. *ped* pannier, of unkn. orig.]

*****pēdō-.** See PAEDO-.

pēdŏ′|logy *n.* science of natural soils; hence **pĕdo-lo′gical** *a.,* ∼LOGIST *n.* [f. Russ. *pedologiya,* f. Gk *pedon* ground; see -LOGY]

pĕdŏ′mĕter n. instrument for estimating distance travelled on foot by recording number of steps taken. [f. F *pédomètre* f. L *pes pedis* foot; see -O-, -METER]

pĕdŭ′ncle (-ŭ′ngkel) n. (Bot.) stalk of flower, fruit, or cluster, esp. main stalk bearing solitary flower or subordinate stalks (*pedicels*); (Zool.) stalklike process in animal body; hence ∼ŭlAR¹, ∼ŭlATE², adjs. [f. mod. L *pedunculus* f. L *pes pedis* foot; see -UNCLE]

pee v.i., & n. (colloq.) **1.** v.i. urinate. **2.** n. urination; urine. [f. *piss*]

peek v.i., & n. peep (*in*, *out*, etc.); (take) quick or sly look. [ME *pike*, *pyke*, of unkn. orig.]

pee′kabōō n. & a. **1.** n. * = BO-PEEP. **2.** a. (Of garment etc.) transparent or with pattern of small holes. [f. prec. + BOO]

peel¹ n. (Hist.) small square tower built in 16th c. in border counties of England and Scotland for defence against forays. [ME *pel* stake, palisade, f. AF & OF *pel* f. L *palus* stake; cf. PALE¹]

peel² n. shovel, esp. baker's shovel for bringing loaves etc. into or out of oven. [ME & OF *pele* f. L *pala*, rel. to *pangere* fix]

peel³ v. & n. **1.** v.t. strip the peel (sense 4), rind, bark, etc., from (orange, potato, tree, etc.); take *off* (skin, peel, etc.); (Croquet) send (another player's ball) through hoop; **keep** one's **eyes** ∼ed, (sl.) watch carefully (*for*). **2.** v.i. (Of tree, animal body, etc.) become bare of bark, skin, etc.; (of bar, surface, skin, etc.) come off or *off* like peel; (sl., of person) strip for exercise etc.; ∼ **off,** veer away and detach oneself from group of marchers etc. **3.** Hence ∼′er¹ [-ER¹ (1, 2)] n., ∼′ING¹ (2) n. (*potato peelings*). **4.** n. rind, outer coating, of fruit, potato, prawn, etc.; **candied** ∼ (usu. of citrus fruits, used in cookery etc.). [in 17th c. different. f. PILL²]

pee′ler² n. **1.** ‖(arch. sl.) policeman. **2.** (P∼; Hist.) member of Irish constabulary, founded under Peel's secretaryship. [f. Sir Robert *Peel*, Engl. statesman d. 1850 + -ER¹]

Pee′līte n. (Polit. Hist.) conservative supporting Peel, esp. w. ref. to repeal of corn-laws (1846). [f. as prec. + -ITE¹]

peen n., & v.t. **1.** n. wedge-shaped or thin end of a hammer-head (opp. *face*). **2.** v.t. hammer with peen; treat with stream of metal shot. [17th c.; also *pane*, app. f. F *panne* f. Du. *pen* f. L *pinna* point]

peep¹ v.i., & n. (imit.) feeble shrill sound (as) of young birds, mice, etc., chirp, squeak. [imit.; cf. CHEEP]

peep² v.i. look through narrow aperture (*at*, *into*, etc.); look furtively (∼ing Tom, furtive voyeur [f. name of Coventry tailor in story of Lady Godiva]); (of daylight, flower, distant object) come (*out*) slowly or partly into view, emerge, (fig., of quality etc.) show itself unconsciously; ∼-bo, = BO-PEEP; ∼-toe(d) a., (of shoe) leaving toes partly bare. [ME; cf. PEEK, PEER³]

peep³ n. furtive or peering glance; first appearance, esp. *of dawn*, *of day* (∼-of-day boys, Protestant organization in Ireland (1784–95) searching opponents' houses at daybreak for arms); ∼-hole, small hole to peep through; ∼-show, small exhibition of pictures etc. viewed through lens in small orifice; ∼-sight, aperture backsight of some rifles. [f. prec.]

pee′per n. one who peeps; (sl.) eye; *(sl.) private detective. [f. PEEP² + -ER¹]

pee′pul. Var. of PIPAL.

peer¹ n. **1.** equal in civil standing or rank (*jury of his peers*); equal in any respect (*you will not easily find his peer*), whence ∼′LESS a.; ∼ **group,** those of the same status as, and associated with, a person. **2.** member of one of the degrees (duke, marquis, earl, viscount, baron) of nobility in UK, whence ∼′ESS¹ n.; LIFE *peer*; ∼ **of the realm,** one of class of peers whose adult members may all sit in House of Lords. **3.** noble of any country. [ME, f. AF & OF *pe(e)r* f. L *par* equal]

peer² v.t. & i. (cause to) rank equally *with*. [ME, f. OF *perer* f. LL *pariare* f. L *par* equal]

peer³ v.i. look searchingly or with difficulty (*into*, *at*, etc.); appear, peep out; (arch.) come into view. [var. of *pire*, LG *pīren*; perh. partly f. APPEAR]

peer′age n. the peers (PEER¹ 2); nobility, aristocracy; rank of peer or peeress (LIFE *peerage*); book containing list of peers with genealogy etc. [ME, f. PEER¹ + -AGE]

peeve n. (sl.) cause of annoyance; mood of vexation. [back-form. f. PEEVISH]

peeved (-vd) a. (sl.) irritated, annoyed. [f. foll. + -ED¹]

pee′vish a. querulous, irritable; hence ∼LY² adv., ∼NESS n. [ME, = foolish, mad, spiteful, etc., of unkn. orig.]

pee′wit, pē′wit, n. lapwing; its cry; ∼ (gull), black-headed gull. [imit.]

pĕg¹ n. **1.** pin or bolt of wood, metal, etc., usu. round and slightly tapering, for holding together parts of framework etc., stopping up vent of cask, hanging hat etc. on, holding rope of tent, tightening or loosening string of violin etc., marking cribbage score, etc.; ‖CLOTHES-*peg*. **2.** a ∼ to hang (discourse etc.) on, suitable occasion, pretext, or theme, for; off the ∼, (of clothes) ready-made; *square peg in round* HOLE¹; take person down a ∼ (or two), humble him. **3.** ‖a drink, esp. of spirits. **4.** ∼-board, board with holes and pegs, esp. for game, as toy, or for commercial displays; ∼-leg, (wearer of) artificial leg; ∼′top, pear-shaped spinning-top with metal peg; ∼*top skirt* or *trousers* (wide at hips, narrow below). [ME, prob. of LDu. orig.; cf. MDu. *pegge*, Du. dial. *peg*, LG *pigge*]

pĕg² v. (-gg-). **1.** v.t. fix (thing *down*, *in*, *out*, etc.) with peg; ∼ **down,** restrict (*to* rules etc.). **2.** prevent price of (stock etc.) from falling (or rising) by freely buying (or selling) at given price; stabilize (prices, wages, exchange rates, etc.). **3.** mark (score) with pegs on cribbage-board (level ∼ging, even scores, lit. or fig.); mark *out* boundaries of (mining claim etc.). **4.** v.i. (away), work persistently (*at*); ∼ **out,** (Croquet) hit peg with ball as final stroke in game, (Cribbage) score winning point, (sl.) die, be ruined. [f. prec.]

Pē′gasus n. (Gk Myth.) winged horse that with stroke of hoof caused fountain Hippocrene to flow on Mt. Helicon; (fig.) poetic genius; hence **Pegase**AN (pĕgasē′an, pǐgā′sian) a. [L, f. Gk *Pēgasos* (*pēgē spring*)]

pĕg′matīte n. coarsely crystalline type of granite. [f. Gk *pēgma* -*atos* thing joined together (*pēgnuō* fasten) + -ITE¹]

Peh′levi (pā′-). Var. of PAHLAVI.

PEI abbr. Prince Edward Island.

pei′gnoir (pā′nwär) n. woman's loose dressing-gown. [F (*peigner* to comb)]

peine forte et dure (pān fōrt ä dūr′) n. (Hist.) pressing to death, inflicted on person charged with felony who refused to plead. [F, = severe and hard punishment]

pejorative (pē′jer-, pĭjŏ′r-) a. & n. depreciatory (word) (*the pejorative suffix* -*aster*). [f. F *péjoratif* -*ive* f. LL *pejorare* make worse (*pejor*); see -ATIVE]

pĕ′kan n. N. Amer. carnivorous mammal of weasel family, valued for fur. [Can. F, f. Abnaki *pékané*]

pēke n. (colloq.) Pekingese dog. [abbr.]

Pēkingē′se, Pēkinē′se, (-z) n. (*pl.* same) & a. (inhabitant) of Pekin(g); small short-legged snub-nosed dog with long silky hair. [f. *Pekin(g)* (now *Beijing*) in China + -ESE]

pē′kōe n. superior kind of black tea. [f. Chin. dial. *pek-ho* (*pek* white, *ho* down), leaves being picked young with down on them]

pĕ′lage n. fur, hair, wool, etc., of quadruped. [F (*poil* hair; see -AGE)]

Pēlā′gian¹ n. & a. (follower) of the monk Pelagius (4th–5th c.), who denied doctrine of original sin; hence ∼ISM (3) n. [f. eccl. L *Pelagianus* (*Pelagius*; see -AN)]

pēlā′gian² a. of, or inhabiting, inhabitant of, the open sea. [f. L f. Gk *pelagios* of the sea (*pelagos*) + -AN]

pēlā′gic a. of, or performed on, the open sea (*pelagic sealing*, *whaling*); (of marine life) belonging to the upper layers of the open sea. [f. L f. Gk *pelagikos* (as prec.; see -IC)]

pĕlargō'nĭum *n.* plant of genus *Pelargonium*, with showy flowers and usu. fragrant leaves (in cultivation pop. called *geranium*). [mod. L, f. Gk *pelargos* stork; cf. GERANIUM]

Pĕlă'sgĭc (-zj-, -zg-) *a.* of the Pelasgians, an ancient people inhabiting coasts and islands of E. Mediterranean and Aegean. [f. Gk *Pelasgikos* (*Pelasgoi* Pelasgians; see -IC)]

pēle. Var. of PEEL[1].

pĕlerine (pĕ'l-, -ē'n) *n.* woman's long narrow cape or tippet. [f. F *pèlerine*, fem. of *pèlerin* PILGRIM]

pĕlf *n.* (usu. derog. or joc.) money, wealth. [ME, f. ONF *pelfe*, var. of OF *pelfre, peufre* spoils, of unkn. orig.; cf. PILFER]

pĕ'lham (-ləm) *n.* bridle combining curb and snaffle. [f. surname *Pelham*]

pĕ'lican *n.* large gregarious water-fowl of genus *Pelecanus*, with pouch in bill for storing fish, fabled to feed its young with its own blood; ||~ **crossing**, pedestrian crossing with traffic lights operated by pedestrians; *P~ **State**, Louisiana. [OE *pellican* & OF *pelican*, f. LL *pelicanus* f. Gk *pelekan* prob. f. *pelekus* axe w. ref. to its bill]

pĕli'sse (-ē's) *n.* woman's mantle with armholes or sleeves, reaching to ankles; fur-lined mantle or cloak, esp. as part of hussar's uniform. [F, f. med. L *pellicia* (*vestis* garment) of fur (*pellis* skin)]

pĕllă'grĭa *n.* deficiency disease characterized by cracking of skin and often ending in insanity; hence ~ous *a.* [It., f. *pelle* skin, after *podagra*]

pĕ'llĕt *n.,* & *v.t.* **1.** *n.* small ball of paper, bread, etc.; pill; small mass of material regurgitated by bird of prey or excreted by rodent etc.; small shot; hence ~IZE (3) *v.t.* **2.** *v.t.* make into pellet(s); hit with (esp. paper) pellets. [ME f. OF *pelote*, f. Rom. *pilotta* dim. of L *pila* ball]

pĕ'llĭcle *n.* thin skin; membrane; film; so **pelli'culAR**[1] *a.* [f. F *pellicule* f. L *pellicula*, dim. of *pellis* skin]

pĕ'llĭtory *n.* **1.** ~ **of Spain**, plant with pungent-flavoured root, used as local irritant etc. **2.** ~ **of the wall**, low bushy plant with greenish flowers growing on or at foot of walls. [sense 1 alt. f. ME f. OF *peletre, peretre*, f. L f. Gk *purethron* feverfew; sense 2 f. earlier *peritorie, paretorie* f. AF *paritarie*, OF *paritaire* f. LL *parietaria* (*paries -etis* wall)]

pĕll-mĕ'll *adv., a.,* & *n.* **1.** *adv.* in disorder, promiscuously; headlong, recklessly. **2.** *a.* confused, tumultuous. **3.** *n.* confusion, medley, mêlée. [f. F *pêle-mêle*, OF *pesle mesle, mesle pesle*, etc., redupl. of *mesle* (*mesler* mix)]

pĕllu'cĭd (-ōō'-, -ū'-) *a.* transparent, clear, not distorting images or diffusing light; clear in style or expression; mentally clear; hence **pĕllucĭ'dĭTY** (-ōō-, -ū-) *n.*, ~LY[2] *adv.* [f. L *pellucidus* f. PER(*lucēre* shine); see -ID[1]]

Pĕ'lmanĭsm *n.* system of memory-training, orig. that devised by the *Pelman* Institute; card-game based on this; hence ~IZE *v.t.* learn or memorize by Pelmanism. [-ISM]

pĕ'lmĕt *n.* valance or narrow pendent border (esp. over window or door to conceal curtain rods). [prob. f. F PALMETTE]

pĕlŏr'us *n.* sighting device like ship's compass for taking bearings. [perh. f. *Pelorus*, reputed name of Hannibal's pilot]

pĕlō'ta *n.* Basque or Spanish game played in walled court with ball and wicker baskets. [Sp., = ball, augment. of *pella* f. L *pila*]

pĕlt[1] *n.* **1.** skin of sheep or goat with short wool on; undressed skin of fur-bearing animal; raw skin of sheep etc. stripped of wool or fur; so **pĕ'ltRY** (1) *n.* **2.** (joc.) human skin. [ME, f. obs. *pellet* skin dim. of *pel* f. AF *pell*, OF *pel*, or back-form. f. *peltry*, AF *pelterie*, OF *peleterie* (*peletier* furrier), ult. f. L *pellis* skin]

pĕlt[2] *v.* & *n.* **1.** *v.t.* assail with missiles (lit. or fig.); strike repeatedly with missiles. **2.** *v.i.* (Of rain etc.) beat

with violence; fire repeatedly *at*; run fast. **3.** *n.* pelting; (at) full ~, as fast as possible. [16th c., of unkn. orig.]

pĕ'lt|a *n.* (*pl.* ~ae). small light shield of ancient Greeks, Romans, etc.; (Bot.) shieldlike structure, whence ~ATE[2] *a.* [L, f. Gk *peltē*]

pĕ'lv|ĭs *n.* (*pl.* ~es *pr.* -ēz, *or* ~ises). (Anat.) basin-shaped cavity formed in most vertebrates by innominate bone with sacrum and other vertebrae, whence ~IC *a.*; basin-like cavity of kidney. [L, = basin]

Pĕ'mbroke (-ŏŏk) *n.* variety of Welsh corgi with short tail; ~ (**table**), table on four fixed legs with hinged flaps that can be raised and supported. [~ in Dyfed, Wales]

Pembs. *abbr.* Pembrokeshire (former county in Wales).

pĕ'mmĭcan *n.* N. Amer. Ind. cake of dried and pounded meat mixed with melted fat; beef so treated and flavoured with currants etc. for travellers in Arctic etc. [f. Cree *pimecan* (*pime* fat)]

pĕ'mphĭg|us *n.* (Path.) formation of watery vesicles or eruptions on skin of body; hence ~OID, ~OUS, *adjs.* [mod. L, f. Gk *pemphix -igos* bubble]

pĕn[1] *n.* small enclosure for cows, sheep, poultry, etc., or for other purposes; (Jamaica) farm, plantation; enclosure (often with concrete roof) for sheltering submarines. [OE *penn*, of unkn. orig.]

pĕn[2] *v.t.* (-nn-). enclose, shut *up*, shut *in*; shut up (cattle etc.) in pen. [ME *pennen*, app. f. OE *pennian* (as prec.)]

pĕn[3] *n.,* & *v.t.* (-nn-). **1.** *n.* quill-feather with quill pointed and split in two, for writing with ink; similar instrument of steel, gold, etc., fitted into rod of wood, plastic, etc. (~'holder); FOUNTAIN-pen; *put pen to* PAPER[1]. **2.** writing, style of writing, (*made a living with his pen*; *wields a formidable pen*; *the pen is mightier than the sword*). **3.** ~ **and ink**, instruments of writing, writing; ~-**and-ink** *a.,* drawn or written with these; ~-**feather**, quill-feather of bird's wing; ~-**friend**, friend with whom one corresponds without meeting; ~'**knife**, small folding knife usu. carried in pocket; ~-**light**, small electric torch shaped like fountain-pen; ~'**man**, (1) one who writes a (*good, bad,* etc.) hand, (2) author; ~'**manship**, skill in writing, style of handwriting, action or style of literary composition; ~-**name**, literary pseudonym; ~-**pal**, (colloq.) = *pen-friend;* ~-**pusher**, ~-**pushing**, (colloq.) clerical work(er); ~'**wiper**, appliance usu. of small pieces of cloth for wiping pen after use. **4.** *v.t.* write, compose and write, (letter etc.). [ME f. OF *penne*, f. L *penna* feather]

pĕn[4] *n.* female swan. [16th c.; orig. unkn.]

*pĕn[5] *n.* (sl.) penitentiary. [abbr.]

PEN *abbr.* International Association of Poets, Playwrights, Editors, Essayists, and Novelists.

Pen. *abbr.* Peninsula.

pĕ'nal *a.* of punishment; concerned with inflicting this (*penal laws*); (of offence) punishable, esp. by law; inflicted as punishment (~ **servitude**, (Hist.) imprisonment with compulsory labour); inflicted as if by way of punishment (*penal taxation*); used as place of punishment (*a penal colony*); hence ~LY[2] *adv.* [ME f. OF, or f. L *poenalis* (*poena* PAIN[1]; see -AL]

pĕ'nalize, -ise (-īz) *v.t.* make or declare (action) penal; subject to penalty or comparative disadvantage. [f. prec. + -IZE]

pĕ'naltŷ *n.* **1.** punishment, esp. payment of sum of money, for breach of law, rule, or contract, (*on or under penalty of* dismissal etc.); money thus paid; **the ~ of**, disadvantage resulting from (quality etc.). **2.** disadvantage imposed on competitor in sports etc. who has broken rule or won previous contest; (Bridge etc.) points gained by opponents when contract is not fulfilled; ~ (**bully, corner, kick, shot,** etc.), action in various games allowed as redress to side against which foul has been committed; ~ **area**, (Assoc. Footb.) part of ground in front of goal in which foul by defenders involves award of penalty kick; ~ **box,**

(Ice Hockey) place for penalized players and some officials; ∼ **goal** (scored from penalty kick or bully). [f. AF *penalte, F *pénalité* f. med. L *penalitas* (as PENAL; see -ITY)]

pĕ′nance *n.*, & *v.t.* **1.** *n.* (RC & Orthodox Ch.) sacrament including contrition, confession, satisfaction, and absolution. **2.** act of self-mortification as expression of penitence, esp. one imposed by priest; **do** ∼, perform such act. **3.** *v.t.* impose penance on. [ME f. OF, f. L *poenitentia* (as PENITENT; see -ANCE)]

pĕnă′nnūlar *a.* almost ringlike. [f. L *paene* almost + ANNULAR]

pēnă′tes (-ah′tēz, -āz) *n. pl.* (Rom. Myth.) household gods, esp. of the store-room; see LAR. [L (*penus* provision of food)]

pĕnce. See PENNY.

pe′nchant (pah′nshahn) *n.* inclination, liking, (*for*). [F, pres. part. of *pencher* incline]

pĕ′ncil [1] *n.* **1.** instrument for drawing or writing, esp. of graphite, chalk, etc., enclosed in cylinder of wood or in metal or plastic case with tapering end; similarly shaped device used as cosmetic etc. **2.** (Optics) set of rays meeting at a point; (Geom.) figure formed by set of straight lines meeting at a point. **3.** (fig.) draughtsman's art or style. **4.** (arch. or tech.) artist's paint-brush. **5.** ∼-**case,** holder for pencil(s) etc.; ∼- **-sharpener,** device with cutting edge for sharpening pencil by rotation. [ME, f. OF *pincel* f. Gallo-Rom. *penicellum f. L *penicillum* paintbrush dim. of *peniculus* brush dim. of *penis* tail]

pĕ′ncil [2] *v.t.* (‖-ll-). tint or mark (as) with lead pencil; write with pencil; write tentatively; (esp. in *p.p.*) mark delicately with thin parallel or concentric lines of colour or shading; hence ∼lER [1] *n.*, (‖esp., sl.) bookmaker. [f. prec.]

pĕ′ndant [1], **pĕ′ndent** [1], *n.* **1.** hanging ornament, esp. one attached to necklace, bracelet, etc. **2.** (Naut.) short rope hanging from head of mast etc. with eye at lower end for receiving hooks of tackles. **3.** = PENNANT 1. **4.** shank and ring of pocket-watch by which it is suspended. **5.** (or *pr.* pah′ndahn). match, parallel, companion, complement, (*to*). [ME, f. OF (*-ant*), f. *pendre* hang f. L *pendere*; see -ANT]

pĕ′ndent [2], **pĕ′ndant** [2], *a.* hanging; overhanging; undecided, pending, whence **pĕ′nd**ENCY *n.*; (Gram.) of which the construction is incomplete, esp. ∼ **nominative** (with no verb). [ME, f. as prec.]

pĕ′ndente lite (pĕndĕ′ntī lī′tī) *adv.* (Law). during the progress of a suit. [L]

pĕndĕ′ntīve *n.* (Archit.) spherical triangle formed by intersection of dome with two adjacent arches springing from supporting columns. [f. F *pendentif -ive* adj. (as PENDANT [1]; see -IVE)]

pĕ′nding *a.* & *prep.* **1.** *a.* undecided, awaiting decision or settlement, (*a suit, a treaty, was then pending*); about to come into existence (*patent pending*); ∼-**tray** (to contain documents awaiting decision). **2.** *prep.* during (*pending these negotiations*, orig. = while these negotiations are pending); until (*pending his return*). [after F *pendant* (see PENDANT [2], -ING [2])]

pĕndră′gon *n.* (Title of) ancient British or Welsh prince. [W, = chief war-leader (*pen* head, *dragon* standard)]

pĕ′ndūlāte *v.i.* swing like pendulum; (fig.) be undecided. [f. PENDULUM + -ATE [3]]

pĕ′ndūlīne *a.* (Of nest) suspended; (of bird) building such nest. [F (as foll.; see -INE [1])]

pĕ′ndūlous *a.* (Of ears, breasts, bird's nest, flower, etc.) suspended, drooping, hanging down; oscillating; hence ∼LY [2] *adv.* [f. L *pendulus* (*pendēre* hang) + -OUS]

pĕ′ndūlum *n.* body suspended so as to be free to swing, esp. rod with weighted end regulating movement of clock's works; **swing of the** ∼, tendency to alternation of power between political parties, or to oscillation of public opinion between extremes; COMPENSATION *pendulum*. [f. L neut. adj. (as prec.)]

pē′nĕplain *n.* (Geol.) region that is almost a plain, in consequence of erosion. [f. L *paene* almost + PLAIN [1]]

pĕnĕträ′lia *n. pl.* innermost shrine or recesses. [L, neut. pl. of *penetralis* interior (as foll.; see -AL)]

pĕ′nĕtr|āte *v.* **1.** *v.t.* find access into or through, pass through; (of man) bring penis into vagina of (woman); permeate; imbue (person, thing, *with*); (fig.) see into, find out, discern, (person's mind, meaning, design, the truth); (of sight) pierce through (darkness, thicket, etc.). **2.** *v.i.* make a way (*into, through, to*); be absorbed by the mind (*my hint did not penetrate*); (in *pres. part.*) gifted with or suggestive of insight, (of voice etc.) easily heard through or above other sounds. **3.** Hence or cogn. ∼ABI′LITY, ∼A′TION, ∼ātOR, *ns.*, ∼ABLE, ∼ATIVE, *adjs.* [f. L *penetrare* place or enter within (*penitus* interior) + -ATE [3]]

pē′nguin (-nggwĭn) *n.* sea-fowl of southern hemisphere with wings developed into scaly flippers with which it swims under water. [16th. c., orig. = great auk; of uncert. orig.]

pē′nial *a.* of the penis. [f. PENIS + -AL [1]]

pĕ′nicillate *a.* (Biol.) having or forming small tuft(s); marked with streaks as of pencil or brush. [f. L *penicillum* (PENCIL [1]) + -ATE [2]]

pĕnicī′llin *n.* antibiotic of group produced naturally on moulds, able to prevent growth of certain disease-causing bacteria. [f. mod. L *Penicillium* genus of tufted moulds f. L *penicillum* (PENCIL [1]), + -IN]

pē′nīle *a.* of the penis. [f. mod. L *penilis* (PENIS); see -IL]

pĕnī′nsūla *n.* piece of land almost surrounded by water or projecting far into the sea. [f. L *paeninsula* (*paene* almost, *insula* island)]

pĕnī′nsūlar *a.* & *n.* **1.** *a.* of (the nature of) a peninsula; (Hist.) of Spain and Portugal, or of the war there in 1808–14. **2.** *n.* inhabitant of a peninsula. [f. prec. + -AR [1]]

pĕnī′nsūlāte *v.t.* make (land) into a peninsula. [f. PENINSULA + -ATE [3]]

pē′nĭs *n.* (*pl.* ∼es or pe′nes *pr.* -ēz). copulatory and (in mammals) urinary organ of male animal; ∼ **envy,** (Psych.) woman's or girl's subconscious desire to be male. [L, = tail, penis]

pĕ′nit|ent *a.* & *n.* **1.** that repents; hence or cogn. ∼ENCE *n.*, ∼ent LY [2] *adv.* **2.** *n.* repentant sinner, person doing penance under direction of confessor; (in *pl.*) various RC orders associated for mutual discipline etc. [ME f. OF, f. L *paenitens* (*paenitēre* repent; see -ENT)]

pĕnitĕ′ntial (-nshal) *a.* of penitence or penance; ∼ **psalms,** seven psalms (6, 32, 38, 51, 102, 130, 143) with especial expression of penitence; hence ∼LY [2] *adv.* [f. OF *penitencial* f. LL *paenitentialis* (*paenitentia* penitence f. as prec.; see -ENCE, -AL)]

pĕnitĕ′ntiarȳ (-sherĭ) *n.* & *a.* **1.** *n.* office in papal court deciding questions of penance, dispensations, etc., (**Grand P**∼, cardinal presiding over this); *reformatory prison. **2.** *a.* of penance; of reformatory treatment; *(of offence) making culprit liable to prison sentence. [ME f. med. L *paenitentiarius* a. & n. (as PENITENCE; see -ARY [1])]

Penn(a). *abbr.* Pennsylvania.

pĕ′nnant *n.* **1.** (Naut.) tapering flag, esp. that flown at mast-head of vessel in commission; **broad** ∼, short swallow-tailed pennant distinguishing commodore's ship in squadron. **2.** = PENNANT [1] 2. **3.** = PENNON. **4.** *flag denoting sports championship etc. [blend of PENNANT [1] and PENNON]

pĕ′nnĭless *a.* having no money; poor, destitute. [ME, f. PENNY + -LESS]

pĕ′nnĭll *n.* (*pl.* ∼ion *pr.* -ĭ′lyon). (stanza of) improvised verse sung to harp at eisteddfod etc. [W (*penn* head)]

pĕ′nnon *n.* long narrow flag, triangular or swallow-tailed, esp. as military ensign of lancer regiments; long pointed streamer of ship; flag; hence ∼ED [2] (-nd) *a.* [ME f. OF, f. L *penna* feather; see -OON]

pĕ′nn′orth. See PENNYWORTH.

Pĕnnsylvā′nĭ|a *n.* ∼**a Dutch,** (dialect of High

German spoken by) descendants of 17th–18th c. German and Swiss immigrants to Pennsylvania etc.; hence ∼AN *a.*, (*esp., Geol.) upper Carboniferous period or system. [∼ in US]

pĕ′nnỹ *n.* (*pl.* usu. **pe′nnies** for separate coins, **pence** for sum of money). **1.** British bronze coin worth 1/100 of pound; monetary unit represented by this, abbr. *p.* **2.** (Hist.) British bronze coin worth 1/240 of pound; monetary unit represented by this, abbr. *d.* **3.** *(colloq.) one-cent coin. **4.** (Bibl.) denarius. **5. like a bad** ∼, repeatedly present when not desired; **the** ∼ **drops**, understanding dawns; **pennies from heaven**, unexpected benefits; *an* HONEST *penny*; **in for a** ∼, **in for a pound**, thing once begun must be concluded at all costs; **in** ∼ **numbers**, in small quantities at a time; PETER′*s pence*; ∼ **plain, twopence coloured** (mocking cheap showiness); **a pretty** ∼, a large sum of money; SPEND *a penny*; **take care of the pence**, be economical in small outlays; **a** ∼ **for your thoughts** (said to person deep in thought); **two a** ∼, almost worthless though readily obtainable. **6.** ∼**-a-line** *a.*, (of writing) cheap and superficial; ∼**-a-li′ner**, hack writer; ∼ **black**, first adhesive postage stamp (UK, 1840, value one penny, printed in black); ||∼ **blood**, (sl.) = *penny* DREADFUL; ∼**-cress**, plant *Thlaspi arvense* with flat round pods; ||∼ **farthing**, (colloq.) old type of high bicycle; ||*penny* GAFF³; ∼**-in-the-slot**, (of machine) actuated by dropping small coin into slot; ∼ **pinching**, (*n.*) niggardliness, (*a.*) niggardly; ||∼ **post** (for conveyance of letters at former ordinary charge of 1d. irrespective of distance); ∼**weight**, unit of weight, 24 grains, 1/20 of an ounce troy; *penny* WHISTLE; ∼ **wise**, (over-)careful in small expenditures, esp. *penny wise and pound foolish*, careful in small but wasteful in large matters; ∼**worth**, **penn′orth**, (pĕ′nĭwĕrth, pĕ′nerth), as much as can be bought for a penny (*not a pennyworth*, not the least bit), a bargain (*a good or bad pennyworth*). [OE. *penig*, *penning*, – OS *penning*, OHG *pfenning*, ON *penningr*, f. Gmc **panningaz*, **pandingaz*, perh. rel. to PAWN²]

-pennỹ *suf.* forming *adjs.* w. sense 'costing . . . pence' (*fivepenny*, *twopenny-halfpenny*). [f. prec.]

pĕ′nnỹroyal *n.* creeping species of mint (*Mentha pulegium*) cultivated for supposed medicinal virtues; *aromatic herb of genus *Hedeoma* or *Monardella*. [app. f. earlier *puliol(e) ryall* f. AF *puliol*, OF *pouliol* f. Rom. *pulegeolum f. L *pulegium* + as ROYAL]

pĕ′nnỹwort (-ĕrt) *n.* plant with rounded leaves (**wall** ∼, *Umbilicus rupestris*, growing in crevices; **marsh** or **water** ∼, *Hydrocotyle vulgaris*, growing in marshy places). [ME. f. PENNY + WORT]

pēnŏ′log│ỹ *n.* study of punishment of crime and of prison management; hence **pēnolŏ′g**ICAL *a.*, ∼IST (3) *n.* [f. L *poena* penalty + -o- + -LOGY]

pensée (pahňsā′) *n.* a thought or reflection put into literary form. [F]

pĕ′nsīle *a.* hanging down, pendulous; (of bird etc.) building pensile nest. [f. L *pensilis* (*pendēre pens-* hang; see -IL)]

pĕ′nsion (-shon) *n.*, & *v.t.* **1.** *n.* periodic payment made esp. by government, company, or employer, in consideration of past service or on retirement etc.; similar payment to person who is not a professed servant for good will, secret service, etc., or to artist, scientist, etc., to enable him to carry on work of public interest; periodic payment by government to persons above specified age (*old-age pension*) or disabled or widowed; hence ∼LESS *a.* **2.** (*pr.* pah′ńs-yawň). European boarding-house providing all or some meals at fixed rate; *live* **en** ∼, as boarder. **3.** *v.t.* grant pension to; bribe with pension; ∼ **off**, dismiss with pension, cease to employ or use. [ME f. OF, f. L *pensio -onis* payment (*pendere pens-* pay; see -ION)]

pĕ′nsionable (-sho-) *a.* entitled (of services etc.) entitling person, to pension. [f. prec. + -ABLE]

pĕ′nsionarỹ (-sho-) *a.* & *n.* (recipient) of a pension;

creature, hireling; **Grand P**∼, (Hist.) first minister of Holland and Zealand (1619-1794). [f. med. L *pensionarius* (as PENSION; see -ARY¹)]

pĕ′nsioner (-sho-) *n.* recipient of pension, esp. old-age pension; ||(Camb. Univ.) undergraduate without financial support from college. [ME f. AF; OF *pensionier*, f. as prec.]

pĕ′nsĭve *a.* plunged in thought; sorrowfully thoughtful; hence ∼LY² (-vlĭ) *adv.*, ∼NESS (-vn-) *n.* [ME, f. OF *pensif -ive* (*penser* think f. L *pensare* frequent. of *pendere pens-* weigh)]

pĕnstē′mon. Var. of PENTSTEMON.

pĕ′nstŏck *n.* sluice, flood-gate; *channel for conveyance of water to water-wheel. [f. PEN¹ in sense 'mill-dam' + STOCK]

pĕnt *a.* closely confined, shut *in or up*. [p.p. of *pend* var. of PEN²]

pĕ′nta- *comb. form.* **1.** five, as: ∼**chord** (-k-), musical instrument with five strings, series of five musical notes; ∼**gynous** (-tă′jĭ-), having five pistils; ∼HE′DRON, solid figure with five faces; ∼**merous** (-tă′m-), (Bot.) having five parts in flower-whorl, (Zool.) having five joints; **penta′ndrous**, having five stamens; ∼**prism**, pentagonal prism used in viewfinder to get constant deviation of all rays of light through 90°; **pentato′mic**, (Chem.) having five atoms (of a specified kind) in the molecule; ∼**va′lent**, (Chem.) having a valence of five. **2.** (Chem.), forming names of compounds) containing five atoms or groups of a specified kind (*pentachloride*, *pentoxide*). [Gk (*pente* five)]

pĕ′ntacle *n.* figure used as symbol, esp. in magic, e.g. pentagram. [f. med. L *pentaculum* (as PENTA-; see -CULE)]

pĕ′ntăd *n.* the number five; group of five. [f. Gk *pentas -ados* (*pente* five; see -AD 1)]

pĕ′ntagon *n.* plane figure with five sides and angles; ***the P**∼, (pentagonal Washington headquarters of) leaders of US defence forces; so **pĕntă′gon**AL *a.* [f. F *pentagone* or f. LL f. Gk *pentagonon* (as PENTA-, -GON)]

pĕ′ntagrăm *n.* five-pointed star formed by producing sides of pentagon both ways till they intersect, formerly used as mystic symbol. [f. Gk *pentagrammon* (as PENTA-, -GRAM)]

pĕntă′mĕter *n.* **1.** (Gk & L Pros.) form of dactylic verse composed of two halves each of two feet (dactyls in second half, dactyls or spondees in first) and long syllable, chiefly used alternately with hexameters to form elegiac verse. **2.** verse of five feet, e.g. English iambic verse of ten syllables. [L, f. Gk *pentametros* (as PENTA-, -METER)]

pĕ′ntāne *n.* (Chem.) hydrocarbon of the paraffin series, C_5H_{12}. [f. Gk *pente* five + -ANE (2)]

pĕ′ntăngle (-nggel) *n.* pentagram. [ME, perh. f. med. L *pentangulum, *pentaculum* PENTACLE, assim. to L *angulus* ANGLE¹]

Pĕ′ntateuch (-k) *n.* first five books of OT, traditionally ascribed to Moses; hence **pĕntateu′ch**AL (-kal) *a.* f. eccl. L f. eccl. Gk PENTA(*teukhos* implement, book) of five books]

pĕnt│ă′thlon *n.* athletic contest comprising five different events for competitor; hence ∼A′THLETE *n.* [Gk (*pente* five, *athlon* contest)]

pĕntatŏ′nic *n.* (Mus.) consisting of five notes; relating to such a scale. [f. PENTA- + TONE¹ + -IC]

Pĕ′ntĕcŏst *n.* **1.** Jewish harvest festival, on fiftieth day after the second day of Passover (Lev. 23:15, 16); synagogue ceremony on anniversary of giving of Law on Mount Sinai. **2.** Whit Sunday. **3.** Hence **pĕntĕcŏ′st**AL *a.* (∼**al Church**, one emphasizing gifts of Holy Spirit). [OE *pentecosten* & OF *pentecoste*, f. eccl. L f. Gk *pentēkostē* (*hēmera*) fiftieth (day)]

pĕ′nthouse (-t-h-) *n.* (*pl. -ses* -zĭz). sloping roof, esp. as subsidiary structure attached to wall of main building; house or flat on roof of tall building; awning, canopy, etc. [ME *pentis*, AF *pentis f. OF apentis, -dis, f. med. L appendicium, in LL = append-age, f. L (as APPEND); infl. by HOUSE[1]]

pĕntimĕ'nt|ō n. (pl. **~i**). reappearance of earlier underlying painting when layer added later becomes transparent, revealing artist's change of mind etc. [It., = repentance]

*pĕntobā̆r'bităl, ||pĕntobā̆r'bitōne, ns. narcotic and sedative barbiturate drug. [f. PENTA- + -O- + BARBITAL, BARBITONE]

pĕ'ntōde n. thermionic valve having five electrodes. [f. Gk pente five + hodos way]

pĕ'nt-rōōf n. roof sloping in one direction only. [f. PENTHOUSE + ROOF]

pĕntstemon (pĕntstē'-, pĕ'ntstĕ-) n. Amer. herbaceous plant of genus Penstemon, with showy flowers and five stamens, one sterile. [mod. L, irreg. f. PENTA- + Gk stēmōn warp, used for 'stamen']

pĕ'ntȳl n. = AMYL. [f. PENTANE + -YL]

penŭlt (pĭnŭ'-, pĕ'-) a. & n. last but one (esp. of syllable). [abbr. of L paenultimus (see foll.) or of foll.]

penŭ'ltimate a. & n. **1.** a. last but one. **2.** n. last syllable but one. [f. L paenultimus (paene almost, ultimus last), after ultimate]

penŭ'mbr|a n. (pl. **~ae** or **~as**). partly shaded region around shadow of opaque body, esp. around total shadow of moon or earth in eclipse; less dark outer part of sunspot; partial shadow; hence **~AL** a. [mod. L, f. L paene almost + UMBRA shadow]

penŭr'ious a. poor, scanty; stingy, grudging, whence **~LY**[2] adv., **~NESS** n. [f. med. L penuriosus (as foll.; see -OUS)]

pĕ'nŭrȳ n. destitution, poverty; lack, scarcity, (of). [ME, f. L penuria, perh. rel. to paene almost; see -Y[1]]

peon (pĕ'on, pūn) n. (Ind. etc.) office-messenger, attendant, orderly; (Sp. Amer.) day-labourer; bull-fighter's assistant; (Hist.) worker held in servitude in southern US. [f. Port. peão & Sp. peon, f. med. L pedo -onis walker f. L pes pedis foot; cf. PAWN[1]]

pĕ'onage n. employment or service of peons. [f. prec. + -AGE]

pĕ'onȳ, pae'onȳ, n. plant with large globular red, pink, or white flowers, in cultivation often double. [OE peonie f. L f. Gk paiōnia (Paiōn, physician of the gods; cf. PAEAN)]

peo'ple (pē'pel) n., & v.t. **1.** n. persons composing community, tribe, race, or nation, (the English people; English-speaking peoples; a warlike people). **2.** (as pl.) persons belonging to a place or forming a company or class etc. (chosen people (see CHOOSE); PECULIAR people; the people here are furious); subjects of king etc.; congregation of parish priest etc.; armed followers, retinue, workpeople, etc.; parents or other relatives (his people are sure to hear of it); the persons not having special rank or position in a country etc.; persons in general (people don't like to be kept waiting). **3.** (as sing. or pl.) the body of enfranchised or qualified citizens. **4.** v.t. fill with people, populate, fill (place with animals etc.); (of persons, animals, etc.) inhabit, occupy, fill, (esp. in p.p.; a thickly peopled country). [ME, f. AF poeple, people, OF pople, peuple, f. L populus]

pĕp n., & v.t. (-pp-). (sl.) **1.** n. vigour, go, spirit; **~ pill** (containing stimulant drug); **~ talk,** exhortation to activity or courage; hence **~ PY**[2] a., (sl.) full of pep. **2.** v.t. fill with vigour, ginger up. [abbr. of PEPPER[1]]

||PEP abbr. Political and Economic Planning.

pĕperi'nō (-rē'-) n. light porous (usu. brown) volcanic rock formed of small grains of sand, cinders, etc. [It. (pepere pepper)]

pĕ'plum n. short flounce of blouse etc. worn over skirt; (Gk Ant.) woman's outer garment. [L, f. Gk peplos]

pĕ'pō n. (pl. **~s**). fleshy fruit of melon or cucumber type, with numerous seeds. [L, = pumpkin, f. Gk pepōn abbr. of pepōn sikuos ripe gourd]

pĕ'pper[1] n. **1.** pungent aromatic condiment got from dried berries of certain plants (esp. Piper nigrum) used whole or ground into powder when unripe (**black ~**) or when either ripe or husked (**white ~**); (fig.) anything pungent. **2.** plant of genus Capsicum; its fruit, used unripe (**green ~**) or ripe (**red or yellow ~**) as vegetable or source of condiment; CAYENNE pepper; **sweet ~,** pepper with relatively mild taste. **3.** **~-and-salt,** cloth of dark and light threads woven together, showing small dots of dark and light intermingled; **~box,** (1) small usu. round container with perforated lid for sprinkling pepper, (2) ||irregular buttress in Eton fives-court; **~corn,** dried berry of Piper nigrum, esp. as nominal rent; **~-mill** (for grinding peppercorns by hand); **~-pot,** (1) = pepperbox (1), (2) W. Ind. dish of meat etc. stewed with cayenne pepper etc., (3, colloq.) Jamaican; **~wort,** cress of genus Lepidium. [OE piper, pipor, = OS pipari, pepar, OHG pfeffar, f. L piper f. Gk peperi f. Skr. pippalī- berry, peppercorn]

pĕ'pper[2] v.t. sprinkle or treat with pepper; besprinkle as with pepper; pelt with missiles (lit. or fig.); punish severely. [f. prec.]

pĕ'ppermint n. species of mint (Mentha piperita) grown for its essential oil; (Austral.) eucalyptus yielding similar oil; oil of peppermint; lozenge or sweetmeat flavoured with this. [f. PEPPER[1] + MINT[3]]

pĕ'pperȳ a. of, like, abounding in, pepper; (fig.) pungent, stinging, hot-tempered. [f. PEPPER[1] + -Y[2]]

pĕ'ppȳ. See PEP.

pĕ'psin n. enzyme contained in gastric juice, converting proteins into peptones in presence of weak acid. [G, f. Gk pepsis digestion (*pep- cook) + -IN]

pĕ'ptic a. & n. digestive; **~ glands** (secreting gastric juice); **~ ulcer** (in stomach or duodenum). [f. Gk peptikos able to digest (as PEPTONE; see -IC)]

pĕ'ptīde n. (Chem.) compound with two or more amino-acids linked in sequence with elimination of water molecules. [f. G peptid, back-form. f. as POLYPEPTIDE]

pĕ'pt|ōne n. protein derivative soluble in water and non-coagulable by heat, formed from protein by action of pepsin in the process of digestion; hence **~onIZE** (3) v.t. [f. G pepton f. Gk peptos, neut. pepton cooked]

pêr prep. **1.** through, by, by means or instrumentality of, (per post, rail, steamer, bearer); (**as**) **~,** in accordance with (as per instructions); **as ~ usual,** (joc.) as usual. **2.** for each (two pounds per man; five miles per hour). **3.** (Her.) in the direction of (party per pale, divided in a vertical direction). [L]

per- pref. **1.** through, all over, (perforate, pervade); completely, very, (pervervid, perturb); to destruction, to the bad, (pervert, perdition). **2.** (Chem.) having maximum of some element in combination: (1) in names of binary compounds -ide (peroxide), (2) in names of oxides, acids, etc., in -ic (perchloric, per-manganic); (3) in names of salts of these acids (per-chlorate, permanganate). [f. L per- (as prec.)]

peradvĕ'nture (per-, pĕr-) adv. & n. (arch. or joc.) **1.** adv. perhaps; **if, lest, ~,** if, lest, it chance that. **2.** n. uncertainty, chance, conjecture; doubt (beyond or without (all or a) peradventure). [ME, f. OF per or par auenture by chance (as PER, ADVENTURE[1])]

perai. See PIRANHA.

perā'mbŭl|āte v. **1.** v.t. walk through, over, or about, (streets, country, etc.); travel through and inspect (territory); formally establish boundaries of (parish etc.) by walking round them. **2.** v.i. walk from place to place. **3.** Hence or cogn. **~A'TION** n., **~ātorY** a. [f. L PER(ambulare walk) + -ATE[3]]

||perā'mbŭlātor n. = PRAM[2]. [f. prec + -OR]

pêr ā'nnum adv. for each year. [L]

percā'le n. closely woven cotton fabric like calico. [F, of uncert. orig.]

pêr că'put, pêr că'pita, adv. & a. for each person. [L, = by head]

percei'v|e (-sē'v) v.t. apprehend with the mind, observe, understand, (circumstance, that, how, etc.); apprehend through one of the senses, esp. sight;

regard mentally in specified manner; hence ⌒ABLE *a.*
[ME, f. AF *perceiver, OF *perceivre, perçoivre, f. L
PER(cipere cept- = capere take)]

pēr cĕ'nt(.), ***percĕ'nt**, *adv.* & *n.* **1.** *adv.* in every
hundred; **cent** ⌒, (arch.) interest equal to principal;
‖**three** etc. ⌒**s**, public securities yielding interest of
3 etc. per cent. **2.** *n.* percentage; one part in every
hundred (*half a per cent*). [f PER + CENT]

percĕ'ntage *n.* rate or proportion per cent; proportion (*only a small percentage of books are worth reading*). [f.
prec. + -AGE]

percĕ'ntile *n.* (Statistics). one of 99 values of a variable dividing a population into 100 equal groups as regards the value of that variable. [f. PER CENT; see -IL]

pēr'cĕpt *n.* (Philos.) object of perception; mental
product, as opp. to action, of perceiving. [f. L
perceptum perceived (thing), neut. p.p. of percipere
PERCEIVE, after concept]

percĕ'pt‖ible *a.* that can be perceived by senses or
intellect; hence ⌒IBI'LITY *n.*, ⌒IBLY *adv.* [OF, or f. LL
perceptibilis f. L (as PERCEIVE; see -IBLE)]

percĕ'ption *n.* act or faculty of perceiving; intuitive
recognition (*of* truth, aesthetic quality, etc.);
(Philos.) action by which the mind refers its sensations to external object as cause; hence ⌒AL *a.* [ME, f.
L perceptio (as PERCEIVE; see -ION)]

percĕ'ptive *a.* having perception; discerning, sensitive; hence ⌒LY[2] (-vlĭ) *adv.*, ⌒NESS (-vn-), **pĕrcĕp-
tĭ'vITY**, *ns.* [f. med. L perceptivus (as PERCEIVE; see
-IVE)]

pĕrch[1] *n.* (*pl.* ⌒ or ⌒'**es**). spiny-finned freshwater
food-fish of genus *Perca*. [ME, f. OF perche f. L f. Gk
perkē]

pĕrch[2] *n.* **1.** horizontal bar for bird to rest upon;
anything serving for bird etc. to rest upon; (fig.)
elevated or secure position; **knock** (person) **off his**
⌒, vanquish, destroy, make less confident or condescending. **2.** measure of length esp. for land, 5½ yds.;
(**square**) ⌒, 30¼ sq. yds. [ME, f. OF perche f. L pertica
pole]

pĕrch[3] *v.* **1.** *v.i.* alight or rest as or like bird (*on* bough
etc.); (of person or thing) settle, alight, rest, (*on*);
hence ⌒'ER[1] *n.*, one of large class of passerine birds
with feet adapted for perching. **2.** *v.t.* (esp. in *p.p.*)
place (as) on perch (*town perched on a hill*). [ME, f. OF
percher (as prec.)]

percha'nce (-ah'-) *adv.* (arch.) by chance; possibly,
maybe. [ME, f. AF par chance (par by, CHANCE[1])]

percheron (pār'sherawn) *n.* strong and swift horse
orig. bred in le *Perche*, district of N. France. [F]

perchlŏr'‖ic (-k-) *a.* (Chem.) containing chlorine in
maximum valence (*perchloric acid*); hence ⌒ATE[1] (3)
n. [f. PER- 2 + CHLORIC]

perci'pi‖ent *a.* & *n.* **1.** *a.* perceiving, conscious;
discerning; hence ⌒ENCE *n.* **2.** *n.* one who perceives
esp. something outside range of senses. [f. L (as
PERCEIVE; see -ENT)]

pēr'col‖āte *v.* **1.** *v.i.* (Of liquid, or fig.) filter, ooze,
through. **2.** *v.t.* ooze through, permeate; (of person or
strainer) strain (liquid, powder) through pores etc.;
prepare (coffee) by repeated downward passage of
boiling water through ground beans. **3.** Hence or
cogn. ⌒A'TION, ⌒ātOR, *ns.* [f. L PER(colare strain f.
colum strainer) + -ATE[3]]

per contra (pēr kŏ'ntra) *adv.* on the opposite side of
account, assessment, etc. [It.]

percŭ'ss *v.t.* (Med.) tap gently with finger or
instrument for purposes of diagnosis etc. [f. L PER-
(cutere cuss- = quatere shake) strike]

percŭ'ssion (-shon) *n.* forcible striking of one (usu.
solid) body against another; (Med.) percussing;
(Mus.) playing by striking (*percussion band, instrument*),
group of such instruments in orchestra; ⌒ **cap**, small
metal or paper device in (real or toy) firearm,
containing explosive powder and exploded by fall of a
hammer; hence or cogn. **percŭ'ss**IVE *a.* [F, or f. L
percussio (as prec.; see -ION)]

percūtā'nèous *a.* made or done through the skin. [f.
L per cutem through the skin + -ANEOUS, after cutaneous]

pēr di'ĕm (-dī'-, -dē'-) *adv.*, *a.*, & *n.* **1.** *adv.* & *a.* for
each day. **2.** *n.* allowance or payment for each day.
[L]

perdi'tion *n.* eternal death, damnation. [ME, f. OF
perdiciun or f. eccl. L perditio f. L PER(dere dit- = dare
give) destroy; see -ITION]

pĕrdū(e)' *a.* **1.** (Mil.) placed as an outpost in hiding
(*lie perdu*). **2.** (**perdue** esp. *fem.*) hidden (*information,
spy, had remained perdu*). [F, p.p. of perdre lose (as prec.)]

perdūr'‖able *a.* permanent; eternal; durable; hence
⌒ABI'LITY *n.*, ⌒ABLY *adv.* [ME f. OF, f. LL PER-
(durabilis DURABLE)]

père (pār) *n.* the father, senior, (appended to name to
distinguish between father and son of same names; cf.
FILS); **Père David deer**, large grey slender-antlered
deer named after Father A. David, Fr. missionary d.
1900. [F, = father]

pĕ'regrin‖āte *v.i.* (arch. or joc.) travel, journey; so
⌒A'TION, ⌒ātOR, *ns.* [f. L peregrinari (as foll.) + -ATE[3]]

pĕ'regrine *a.* & *n.* **1.** *a.* (arch.) foreign, imported from
abroad, outlandish. **2.** ⌒ (**falcon**), kind of falcon
much used for hawking. [f. L peregrinus (peregre
abroad, f. per through + ager field; scc -INE[1])]

peremptor‖ȳ (perĕ'm-, pĕ'rĭm) *a.* **1.** (Law). final, not
open to appeal or challenge (⌒**y challenge**,
prisoner's objection to proposed juror by right
without need to give reason). **2.** (Of statement or
command) admitting no denial or refusal; absolutely
fixed, essential; (of person etc.) dogmatic, imperious,
dictatorial. **3.** Hence ⌒ILY[2] *adv.*, ⌒INESS *n.* [f. AF
peremptorie, OF peremptoire f. L peremptorius deadly,
decisive, f. PER(imere empt- = emere take, buy) destroy,
cut off; see -ORY]

perĕ'nnial (-nyal) *a.* & *n.* **1.** *a.* lasting through, (of
stream) flowing through all seasons of, the year;
lasting long or for ever; (of plant) living several years
(cf. ANNUAL); hence **perennia'lITY** *n.*, ⌒LY[2] *adv.* **2.** *n.*
perennial plant; HERBACEOUS perennial. [f. L PER(ennis
f. annus year) + -AL]

pēr'fĕct[1] *a.* & *n.* **1.** *a.* complete, not deficient; faultless;
(Mus., of pitch) absolute; thoroughly trained or
skilled (*in* duties etc.); (colloq.) exceedingly satisfactory. **2.** exact, precise, (*a perfect square, circle*; see
SQUARE[1] 6); entire, unqualified, (*a perfect stranger*;
perfect nonsense). **3.** (Math., of number) equal to sum of
its divisors; (Gram., of tense) denoting completed
event or action viewed in relation to the present
(**future** ⌒, tense giving sense *will have done*; **past** ⌒,
pluperfect); (Bot.) having all four whorls of the
flower, (of fungus) in stage where sexual spores are
formed; ⌒ **interval**, (Mus.) fourth or fifth as it would
occur in major or minor scale starting on the lower
note of the interval, or octave. **4.** Hence ⌒LY[2] *adv.*,
(esp.) quite, quite well, completely, ⌒NESS *n.* **5.** *n.*
perfect tense. [ME and OF parfit, perfet f. L perfectus
p.p. of PER(ficere fect- = facere do) complete]

perfect[2] (pēr'fĕkt, pēr'fĭkt) *v.t.* complete, carry
through; make perfect; improve; complete printing
of (sheet) by printing second side; so ⌒IBI'LITY *n.*,
perfĕ'ctIBLE *a.* [f. prec.]

perfĕ'ction *n.* completion; making perfect; full
development; faultlessness (**to** ⌒, exactly, completely); comparative excellence; perfect person or
thing; highest pitch, extreme, perfect specimen or
manifestation, (*of* quality etc.); an accomplishment.
[ME f. OF f. L perfectio -onis (as PERFECT[1]; see -ION)]

perfĕ'ction‖ist *n.* one who holds that religious or
moral perfection may be attained; (usu. derog.) one
who aims at perfection in his work; (*P-*; Hist.)
member of communistic community of Oneida
Creek, NY; hence ⌒ISM (3) *n.* [f. prec. + -IST]

perfĕ'ctive *a.* & *n.* (Gram.) **1.** *a.* (Of verb aspect etc.)
expressing completion of action (opp. *imperfective*). **2.**
n. perfective aspect or form of verb. [f. med. L
perfectivus (as PERFECT[1]; see -IVE)]

*perfe′ctŏ *n.* (*pl.* ~s). large thick cigar pointed at each end. [Sp., = perfect]

perfer′vid *a.* very fervid. [f. mod. L *perfervidus* (as PER-, *fervidus* FERVID)]

per′fidy *n.* breach of faith, treachery; so **perfi′diOUS** *a.* (*perfidious* ALBION). [f. L *perfidia* f. PER(*fidus* f. *fides* faith) treacherous]

perfo′liate *a.* (Bot.) having the stalk apparently passing through the leaf. [f. mod. L *perfoliatus* (as PER-, FOLIATE¹)]

per′for|āte¹ *v.* **1.** *v.t.* make hole(s) through, pierce, esp. make rows of holes in (sheet) to assist in separating stamps, coupons, etc.; make an opening into; pass or extend through. **2.** *v.i.* penetrate (*into, through,* etc.). **3.** Hence or cogn. ~A′TION, ~ātOR, *ns.,* ~ATIVE *a.* [f. L PER(*forare* pierce) + -ATE³]

per′forate² *a.* perforated. [f. L *perforatus* p.p. of *perforare* (see prec.)]

perfor′ce *adv.* unavoidably, necessarily. [ME, f. OF *par force* by FORCE¹]

perfor′m *v.* **1.** *v.t.* carry into effect, be agent of, (command, promise, task, operation, etc.); go through, execute, (public function, play, piece of music, etc.). **2.** *v.i.* act in play; play, sing, etc.; (of trained animal) execute tricks etc. at public show etc.; hence ~ING² *a.* (~**ing arts**, those, such as drama, that require public performance). **3.** Hence ~ABLE, ~ATIVE, *adjs.,* ~ER¹ *n.* [ME, f. AF *parfourmer,* f. OF *parfournir* (assim. to *forme* FORM¹), f. *par* PER- + *fournir* FURNISH]

perfor′mance *n.* execution (*of* command etc.); carrying out, doing; notable feat; performing of play, piece of music, or public exhibition (*there are two performances a day; the afternoon performance*); achievement under test; (colloq.) action resembling a public exhibition, ridiculous or contemptible behaviour. [f. prec. + -ANCE, perh. thr. AF]

per′fūme¹ *n.* sweet smell; fluid containing essence of flowers etc., scent. [f. F *parfum* (as foll.)]

perfūme² (perfū′m, per′fūm) *v.t.* (esp. in *p.p.*) impart sweet scent to; impregnate with sweet smell. [f. F *parfumer* f. obs. It. *parfumare, perfumare* (as PER-, *fumare* smoke, FUME); orig. of smoke from burning substance]

perfū′m|er *n.* maker or seller of perfumes; hence ~ERY (1, 2, 3) *n.* [f. prec. + -ER¹]

perfū′nctor|y̆ *a.* done merely for sake of getting through a duty; acting thus, superficial, mechanical, (*a perfunctory inspection, inquirer*); hence ~iLY² *adv.,* ~iNESS *n.* [f. LL *perfunctorius* careless f. L PER(*fungi funct-* perform); see -ORY]

perfū′s|e (-z) *v.t.* besprinkle (*with* water etc.); cover, suffuse, (*with* radiance etc.); pour or diffuse (water etc.) through or over; (Med.) cause a fluid to pass through (organ etc.); so ~ION (-zhon) *n.,* ~IVE (-s-) *a.* [f. L PER(*fundere fus-* pour)]

per′gola *n.* arbour or covered walk, formed of growing plants trained over trellis-work. [It., f. L *pergula* projecting roof (*pergere* proceed)]

pergŭ′nnah (-a), **perga′na** (-gŭ′-), *n.* division of territory in India, group of villages. [f. Urdu *pargana* district]

perhăps (perhă′ps, prăps) *adv.* it may be, possibly, (*perhaps he has lost it; he has perhaps lost it; perhaps you would like to see it?*). [f. PER + HAP¹ + -s¹]

pēr′i¹ *n.* (Pers. Myth.) fairy, good (orig. evil) genius; beautiful or graceful being. [f. Pers. *parī*]

pĕ′ri- *pref.* **1.** round, about, as: ~**cho′ndrium** (-k-), membrane enveloping cartilages (except at joints); ~**cli′nal,** (Geol.) sloping down in all directions from central point; ~**gynous** (perī′jĭ-), (of stamens) situated around pistil or ovary; ~**lymph,** fluid in labyrinth of ear; ~**pteral** (perī′p-), (of temple) surrounded by single row of pillars; ~**stome,** (Bot.) fringe of small teeth around mouth of capsule in mosses, (Zool.) parts around mouth in various invertebrates. **2.** (Astron. etc.) point nearest to (*perigee,* (*perihelion*). [f. Gk *peri* around, about]

pĕ′riănth *n.* (Bot.) outer part of flower. [f. F *périanthe* f. mod. L *perianthium* f. as prec. + Gk *anthos* flower]

pĕ′riăpt *n.* thing worn about the person as charm, amulet. [f. F *périapte* f. Gk PERI(*apton* f. *haptō* fasten)]

pĕricar′d|ium *n.* (*pl.* ~ia). membranous sac enclosing the heart; hence ~iAC, ~iAL, *adjs.,* ~i′TIS *n.* [mod. L, f. Gk *perikardion* (as PERI-, *kardia* heart; see -IUM)]

pĕ′ricarp *n.* (Bot.) vessel containing seed, with pulp if present, formed from wall of ripened ovary. [f. F *péricarpe* or f. mod. L f. Gk PERI-(*karpion* f. *karpos* fruit) pod, shell]

pĕ′riclāse *n.* mineral consisting mainly of magnesia. [f. mod. L *periclasia,* erron. f. Gk *peri* exceedingly + *klasis* breaking, from its perfect cleavage]

peri′copē *n.* short passage, paragraph; portion of Scripture read in public worship. [f. LL f. Gk PERI(*kopē* cutting f. *koptō* cut)]

pĕricrā′nium *n.* membrane enveloping skull; (arch., joc.) skull, brain, intellect. [mod. L, f. Gk PERI(*kranion* skull)]

pĕ′ridŏt *n.* green variety of olivine, esp. as precious stone. [ME f. OF *peritot,* of unkn. orig.]

pĕ′rigee *n.* point (in orbit of moon, planet, or artificial satellite) nearest to earth; hence **perigē′AN** *a.* [f. F *périgée* f. mod. L f. Gk PERI(*geion* f. *gē* earth)]

pĕriglā′cial (-sīal, -shal) *a.* of a region adjoining a glacier. [f. PERI- + GLACIAL]

pĕrihē′li|on (-lyon, -līon) *n.* (*pl.* ~a). point (of planet's or comet's orbit) nearest to sun. [Graecized f. mod. L *perihelium* f. as PERI- + Gk *hēlios* sun]

pĕ′ril *n.,* & *v.t.* (||-ll-). **1.** *n.* danger; **in** ~ **of** (in danger of losing) one's *life* etc.; **you do it at your** ~, if you do it you take the risk; *keep off* **at your** ~ (take the risk if you do not). **2.** *v.t.* expose to danger, imperil. [ME f. OF, f. L *peric(u)lum* (**per-* try; see -CULE)]

pĕ′rilous *a.* full of risk, dangerous, hazardous; exposed to imminent risk of destruction etc.; hence ~LY² *adv.,* ~NESS *n.* [ME, f. OF *perillous* f. L *periculosus* (*periculum;* see prec.)]

pĕ′rilune (-ōōn, -ūn) *n.* point in body's orbit about moon where it is closest to moon's centre. [f. PERI- + *luna* moon, after *perigee*]

peri′meter *n.* circumference or outline of closed figure; length of this; outer boundary of camp, fortification, airfield, etc.; instrument for measuring field of vision. [f. F *périmètre* or f. L f. Gk PERI(*metros* f. *metron* measure)]

per impossibile (per impŏsi′bĭlā) *adv.* by means of something that is in fact impossible. [L]

pĕ′rinā′tal *a.* of the time immediately before and after birth. [f. PERI- + NATAL]

per incuriam (per inkūr′iam) *adv.* (Law). by oversight (of judge etc.). [L]

pĕrinē′|um *n.* (Anat.) region of the body between anus and scrotum or vulva; hence ~AL *a.* [f. LL f. Gk *perinaion*]

pēr′iod *n.* & *a.* **1.** *n.* amount of time between recurrences of astronomical or other phenomena; time of planet's revolution. **2.** time during which disease runs its course. **3.** (time of) occurrence of menstruation. **4.** distinct portion of history, life, etc.; any portion of time (*showers and bright periods; spread the work over a period*); time allocated for lesson in school; (Geol.) time forming part of era; **the** ~, the part of history under discussion, esp. the present day (*the girl, costume, catchwords, of the period*). **5.** complete sentence, esp. one consisting of several clauses; (in *pl.*) rhetorical language. **6.** full pause at end of sentence; = FULL¹ *stop* (**put a** ~ **to,** bring to an end); (appended to statement, stressing its completeness; *we want the best, period*). **7.** set of figures marked off in large number to assist in reading; set of figures repeated in recurring decimal; (Chem.) sequence of elements between two noble gases in periodic table. **8.** *a.* (Esp. of furniture, dress, and architecture) belonging to or characteristic of a particular (past) period. [ME, f. OF *periode* f. L f. Gk PERI(*odos* = *hodos* way)]

pĕrĭŏ'dĭc[1] *a.* **1.** of revolution of heavenly body, (*periodic motion*, VARIATION); recurring at regular intervals, so **pĕrĭodĭ'c**ITY *n.*; recurring at intervals; ∼ **function**, (Math.) function returning to same value at regular intervals; ∼ **table**, (Chem.) arrangement of elements in order of atomic numbers and in which elements of similar chemical properties appear at regular intervals. **2.** (Of diction etc.) expressed in PERIODS (sense 5). [f. F *périodique* or f. L f. Gk *periodikos* (as prec.; see -IC)]

pĕrĭŏ'dĭc[2] *a.* (Chem.) containing maximum proportion of iodine (*periodic acid*); hence **pĕrĭ'od**ATE[1] (3) *n.* [f. PER- 2 + IODIC]

pĕrĭŏ'dĭcal *a. & n.* **1.** *a.* = PERIODIC[1] 1; hence ∼LY[2] *adv.* **2.** *a. & n.* (magazine etc.) published at regular intervals, e.g. monthly. [f. PERIODIC[1] + -AL]

periodīzā'tion *n.* dividing of history into periods. [f. PERIOD + -IZE + -ATION]

pĕrĭodŏnt|al *a.* (Med.) of the tissues surrounding the teeth; hence ∼ICS, ∼IST (3), *ns.* [f. PERI- + Gk *odous odontos* tooth + -AL]

pĕrĭodŏntŏ'logў *n.* study of structures surrounding and supporting teeth. [f. PERI- + Gk *odous odontos* tooth + -O- + -LOGY]

pĕrĭŏ'stē|um *n.* (*pl.* ∼a). membrane enveloping the bones where no cartilage is present; hence ∼AL *a.*, **pĕrĭōstī'**TIS *n.* [mod. L f. Gk PERI(*osteon* bone)]

pĕripatĕ't|ĭc *a. & n.* **1.** (*P*-). Aristotelian [from Aristotle's custom of walking in Lyceum while teaching]. **2.** *a.* going from place to place on one's business, itinerant; hence ∼ICALLY *adv.* **3.** Hence ∼ĬCISM (2, 3) *n.* **4.** *n.* (usu. joc.) traveller; itinerant dealer; (in *pl.*) journeyings to and fro. [ME, f. OF *peripatetique* or f. L f. Gk *peripatētikos* f. PERI(*pateō* walk); see -IC]

pĕripetei'a (-ī'a, -ē'a) *n.* sudden change of fortune in drama or in life. [Gk (as PERI-, *pet*- f. *piptō* fall)]

peri'pheral *a. & n.* **1.** *a.* of the periphery; (Anat.) near the surface of the body; of minor importance; (of equipment etc.) used with a computer but not an integral part of it; hence ∼LY[2] *adv.* **2.** *n.* piece of peripheral equipment etc. [f. foll. + -AL]

pĕri'pherў *n.* bounding line esp. of round surface; external boundary or surface; outer or surrounding region. [f. LL f. Gk PERI(*phereia* f. *pherō* bear) circumference; see -Y[1]]

peri'phras|is *n.* (*pl.* ∼es *pr.* -ēz). roundabout way of speaking, circumlocution; roundabout phrase; so **pĕriphră'st**IC *a.* (∼*tic conjugation*, *genitive*, one formed analytically w. aux. v., w. prep., instead of by inflexion; *did go* = *went*, *of Caesar* = *Caesar's*). [L f. Gk, f. PERI(*phrazō* declare)]

peri'que (-ē'k) *n.* dark strong-flavoured Louisiana tobacco. [Louisiana F]

pĕ'riscōpe *n.* apparatus with tube and mirrors by which observer in trench, submerged submarine, rear of crowd, etc., can see things otherwise out of sight. [f. PERI- + -SCOPE]

pĕriscŏ'pic *a.* of periscope(s); (of lens) allowing distinct vision over wide angle. [f. prec. + -IC]

pĕ'rish *v.* **1.** *v.i.* suffer destruction, lose life or normal qualities, come to untimely end (*by the sword* etc.); ∼ **the thought!**, I sincerely hope it will not be so. **2.** *v.t.* (Of cold or exposure) reduce to distress or inefficiency or moribund state (*we were perished with cold*; *in perishing cold*; *the heat had perished all vegetation*), whence ∼INGLY *adv.* **3.** Hence ‖∼ER[1] *n.*, (sl.) annoying person, ‖∼ING[2] *a. & adv.*, (sl.) confounded(ly). [ME, f. OF *perir* (see -ISH[2]) f. L PER(*ire* go) pass away]

pĕ'rishable *a. & n.* **1.** *a.* liable to perish; subject to speedy decay; hence ∼NESS (-beln-) *n.* **2.** *n.* (in *pl.*) things (esp. foodstuffs in transit) subject to speedy decay. [f. prec. + -ABLE]

pĕ'rispĕrm *n.* mass of albumen outside embryo-sac in some seeds. [f. PERI- + Gk *sperma* seed]

pĕrispŏ'mĕn|on *a. & n.* (*pl.* ∼a). (Gk Gram.) (word) with circumflex accent on last syllable. [Gk, neut. pres. part. pass.; cf. CIRCUMFLEX]

peri'stalĭth *n.* (Archaeol.) ring of standing stones round burial-mound etc. [irreg. f. Gk PERI(*statos* standing) + -LITH]

pĕristă'l|tĭc *a.* **1.** (Physiol.) of the automatic muscular movement consisting of successive wavelike contractions and relaxations, by which contents of alimentary canal etc. are propelled along it. **2.** of a pump operating by similar action. **3.** So ∼sis *n.*, peristaltic movement, ∼tICALLY *adv.* [f. Gk *peristaltikos* (as PERI-, *stellō* place); see -IC]

pĕ'ristўle *n.* row of columns surrounding temple, court, cloister, etc.; space so surrounded. [f. F *péristyle* f. L f. Gk PERI(*stulon* f. *stulos* pillar)]

pĕriton|ē'um *n.* (*pl.* ∼e'ums *or* ∼e'a). (Anat.) double serous membrane lining cavity of abdomen; hence ∼ē'AL *a.*, ∼ī'TIS *n.* [LL, f. Gk PERI(*tonaion* f. -*tonos* stretched)]

pĕ'riwig *n.* (esp. Hist.) wig; hence ∼gED[2] (-gd) *a.* [alt. of PERUKE, w. -*wi*- for F -*u*- sound]

pĕ'riwinkle[1] *n.* plant of genus *Vinca*, esp. evergreen trailing plant with blue or white flowers; ∼ (**blue**), colour of blue periwinkles. [ME f. AF *pervenke*, OF *pervenche* f. LL *pervinca*, w. assim. to foll.]

pĕ'riwinkle[2] *n.* winkle. [16th c., of unkn. orig.]

pĕr'jur|e *v. refl.* ∼e oneself, swear falsely; (in *p.p.*) guilty of or involving perjury; so ∼ER[1] *n.* [ME, f. OF *parjurer* f. L PER(*jurare* swear)]

pĕr'jurў *n.* swearing to statement that one knows to be false; wilful utterance of false evidence while on oath; breach of oath; hence **perjur'ious** (-joor'-) *a.* [ME, f. AF *perjurie*, f. OF *parjurie* f. L *perjurium* (as prec.)]

pĕrk[1] *v. & a.* (colloq.) **1.** *v.i.* ∼ (**up**), recover confidence or courage or liveliness. **2.** *v.t.* raise (head etc.) briskly; smarten *up*; ∼ (**up**), restore confidence or courage or liveliness of. **3.** *a.* perky. [ME, perh. f. var. of PERCH[2]]

‖pĕrk[2] *n.* (colloq., usu. in *pl.*) perquisite. [abbr.]

pĕrk[3] *v.* (colloq.). **1.** *v.i.* (Of coffee) make bubbling sound in percolator. **2.** *v.t.* percolate (coffee). [abbr. of PERCOLATE]

pĕr'k|ў *a.* self-assertive, saucy, pert, lively, cheerful; hence ∼ILY[2] *adv.*, ∼INESS *n.* [f. PERK[1] + -Y[2]]

pĕr'lite *n.* obsidian or other vitreous rock with concentric structure, expandable by heating. [F (*perle* PEARL[1]; see -ITE[1])]

pĕrm[1] *n.*, & *v.t.* (give) permanent wave (to). [abbr.]

pĕrm[2] *n.*, & *v.t.* (colloq.) (make) permutation (of). [abbr.]

pĕr'mafrost (-ŏst, -awst) *n.* subsoil remaining below freezing point throughout the year in polar regions. [f. PERMANENT + FROST]

pĕr'malloy *n.* alloy of nickel and iron that is easily magnetized and demagnetized. [f. PERMEABLE + ALLOY[1]]

pĕr'manent *a.* lasting, or intended to last or function, indefinitely (opp. *temporary*); ∼ **gas**, substance remaining gaseous under all normal conditions; ∼ **magnet** (retaining its power without continued excitation); ∼ **set**, (amount of) irreversible deformation of substance after being subjected to stress; ‖*Permanent* (*Under*-)SECRETARY; ∼ **tooth** (following milk-tooth in mammal and lasting most of life); ∼ **wave**, artificial wave in the hair intended to last for some time, produced by one of several processes; ‖∼ **way**, finished road-bed of railway; hence or cogn. **pĕr'man**ENCE, **pĕr'man**ENCY (esp. = permanent thing or arrangement), *ns.*, ∼LY[2] *adv.* [ME f. OF, or f. L PER(*manēre* remain); see -ENT]

permă'nganate (-nggānāt, -at) *n.* (Chem.) salt of permanganic acid, esp. **potassium** ∼ (used in solution as disinfectant and oxidizer). [f. foll. + -ATE[1] (3)]

pĕrmăngă'nĭc (-ngg-) *a.* (Chem.) containing manganese in maximum valence (*permanganic acid*). [f. PER- 2 + MANGANIC]

pĕrmèabi'litў *n.* ability to be permeated; (Phys.)

quantity measuring substance's influence on magnetic flux in region it occupies. [f. PERMEABLE +-ITY]

pẽr'mĕ|āte v. **1.** v.i. penetrate throughout, pervade, saturate. **2.** v.i. diffuse itself *through, among*, etc. **3.** Hence or cogn. ∽ANCE, ∽A'TION, ns., ∽ABLE, ∽ANT, adjs. [f. L PER(*meare* pass, go) +-ATE³]

pẽr mĕ'nsĕm adv. for each month. [L]

Pẽr'mian a. & n. (Geol.) (of) latest Palaeozoic period or system, above Carboniferous. [f. *Perm* in Russia +-IAN]

permi'ss|ible a. allowable; hence ∽IBI'LITY n., ∽IBLY adv. [ME f. F, or f. med. L *permissibilis* (as PERMIT¹; see -IBLE)]

permi'ssion (-shon) n. consent or liberty (*to* do). [ME f. OF, or f. L *permissio* (as PERMIT¹; see -ION)]

permi'ssive a. **1.** giving permission; ∽ **legislation** (giving powers, but not enjoining their use). **2.** tolerant, liberal, esp. in sexual matters, (*the permissive society*). **3.** Hence ∽LY² (-vlĭ) adv., ∽NESS (-vn-) n. [ME, f. OF (-*if -ive*), or f. med. L *permissivus* (as foll.; see -IVE)]

permi't¹ v. (-tt-). **1.** v.t. give consent or opportunity (for) (*permit me to say; appeals are permitted; permit him access to it; will not permit it to be altered; hole to permit escape of steam*). **2.** v.i. give opportunity (*weather permitting*); admit *of* (alteration, delay, etc.) [f. L PER(*mittere miss-* let go)]

pẽr'mĭt² n. written order giving permission to act, esp. for entry into a place, landing or removal of dutiable goods, etc.; permission. [f. prec.]

*****pẽr'mĭt³** n. large W. Ind. sea game-fish of genus *Trachinotus*. [f. Sp. *palometa*]

pẽrmitti'vitỹ n. (Electr.) quantity measuring substance's ability to store electrical energy in electric field. [f. PERMIT¹ + -IVE + -ITY]

pẽrmūtā'tion n. **1.** variation of the order of a set of things; any one such arrangement. **2.** (pop.) combination or selection of specified number of items from larger group (esp. of matches in football pool). [ME f. OF, or f. L *permutatio* (as foll.; see -ATION)]

permū'te v.t. alter the sequence or arrangement of. [ME, f. L PER(*mutare* change)]

pẽrn n. honey-buzzard. [f. mod. L *pernis*, erron. f. Gk *pternis* a kind of hawk]

perni'cious (-shŭs) a. destructive, ruinous, fatal; ∽ **anaemia**, severe progressive form of anaemia; hence ∽LY² adv., ∽NESS n. [f. L *perniciosus* (*pernicies* ruin f. *nex necis* death; see -OUS)]

perni'ckety a. (colloq.) fastidious; (over-)precise; ticklish, requiring tact or careful handling. [19th c. Sc., of unkn. orig.]

pẽrnŏctā'tion n. passing the night; (Eccl.) all-night vigil; so **pẽrnŏ'ctATE³** v.i. [f. LL *pernoctatio* f. L PER(*noctare* f. *nox noctis* night); see -ATION]

pĕron̂e'al a. (Anat.) of or near the fibula. [f. mod. L *peronaeus* peroneal muscle (*perone* fibula f. Gk *perone* pin, fibula)]

pẽ'ror|āte v.i. sum up and conclude speech, so ∽A'TION n.; speak at length. [f. L PER(*orare* speak)]

perŏ'xide n., & v.t. **1.** n. (Chem.) compound of oxygen with another element containing the greatest possible proportion of oxygen; (**hydrogen**) ∽, (1) colourless viscid liquid, H_2O_2, (2) aqueous solution of this, used as antiseptic and (esp.) to bleach hair; ∽ **blonde**, (usu. derog.) woman with hair bleached thus. **2.** v.t. bleach (hair) with peroxide. [f. PER- 2 + OXIDE]

perpĕ'nd¹ v.t. (arch.) ponder, consider, (matter, or abs.). [f. L PER(*pendere* weigh)]

pẽr'pend². Var. of PARPEN.

pẽrpend'cular a. & n. **1.** a. at right angles to plane of horizon; (of ascent, cliff, etc.) very steep; erect, upright; (joc.) in standing position; (Geom.) at right angles (*to* given line, plane, or surface); **P∽ style**, (Archit.) third stage of English Gothic (15th–16th c.), with vertical tracery in large windows; hence ∽ITY (-ă'r-) n., ∽LY² adv. **2.** n. perpendicular line;

plumb-rule or other instrument for showing perpendicular line; **the ∽**, perpendicular line or direction; *is out of* (*the*) ∽, is not straight up and down. [ME, f. L *perpendicularis* (*perpendiculum* plumb-line f. PER- + *pendēre* hang); see -AR¹]

pẽr'pĕtr|āte v.t. perform, commit, (crime, blunder, pun or other thing viewed as outrageous); hence ∽ABLE a., ∽A'TION, ∽ātor, ns. [f. L PER(*petrare* = *patrare* effect) +-ATE³]

perpĕ'tūal a. **1.** eternal; permanent during life; applicable or valid for ever or for indefinite time; continuous; (colloq.) frequent, repeated (*this perpetual nagging*). **2.** ∽ **calendar** (that can be used for any year or over a long period of time); ∽ **check**, (Chess) position where draw is obtained by repeated checking of king; ∽ **curate**, (Hist.) clergyman of new church, or appointed at instance of lay rector of benefice to execute spiritual duties of benefice (now called *vicar*); ∽ **motion** (of hypothetical machine running for ever unless subject to external forces or wear); ∽ **screw**, ENDLESS screw. **3.** Hence ∽LY² adv. [ME f. OF *perpetuel* f. L *perpetualis* (*perpetuus* f. *perpes -etis* continuous; see -AL)]

perpĕ'tū|āte v.t. make perpetual; preserve from oblivion; hence or cogn. ∽ANCE, ∽A'TION, ∽ātor, ns. [f. L *perpetuare* (as prec.) +-ATE³]

pẽrpĕtū'itỹ n. quality of being perpetual (**in, to, for,** ∽, for ever); perpetual possession or position; perpetual annuity. [ME, f. OF *perpetuité* f. L *perpetuitas -tatis* (as PERPETUAL; see -ITY)]

perplĕ'x v.t. bewilder, puzzle, (person, his mind); complicate, confuse, (matter); (arch., esp. in *p.p.*) entangle, intertwine; hence ∽ĕdLY², ∽INGLY, advs. [back-form. f. *perplexed* f. obs. *perplex* a. f. OF *perplexe* or f. L PER(*plexus* p.p. of *plectere* plait) +-ED¹]

perplĕ'xitỹ n. bewilderment; thing that bewilders; (arch.) entangled state. [ME, f. OF *perplexité* f. LL *perplexitas* (as prec.; see -ITY)]

per pro(c). abbr. = foll.

per procurationem (pẽr prŏkūrātiō'nĕm) adv. by proxy; through an agent. [L]

pẽr'quĭsite (-z-) n. casual profit additional to normal revenue or emolument; thing that has served its primary use and to which subordinate or servant has then a customary right; incidental benefit attaching to employment etc.; customary gratuity; (fig.) thing to which person has sole right. [ME, f. med. L *perquisitum* f. L PER(*quirere quisit-* = *quaerere* seek) search diligently for]

Pĕ'rrier (-iā) n. (P) an effervescent natural mineral water freq. bottled. [name of spring at Vergèze, France]

pĕ'rron n. (steps leading up to) platform in front of door of church or other large building. [ME f. OF, f. Rom. *****petro petron-* augment. of L *petra* stone; see -OON]

‖pẽ'rrỹ n. drink like cider, made from juice of pears fermented. [ME *pereye* etc. f. OF *peré* f. Rom. *****piratum* f. L *pirum* pear; see -Y⁴]

pẽrse a. & n. (arch.) bluish-grey (colour). [ME, f. OF *pers*, f. med. L *persus*, of unkn. orig.]

per se (pẽr sē', -sā') adv. by or in itself, intrinsically. [L]

pẽr'sĕc|ūte v.t. pursue with enmity and ill-treatment; subject to penalties on grounds of religious or political beliefs; harass, worry; importune (person *with* questions etc.); so ∽ū'TION n. (∽ution complex or **mania**, insane delusion that one is persecuted), ∽ūtor n. [ME, f. OF *persecuter* back-form. f. *persecuteur* persecutor f. LL *persecutor* f. L PER(*sequi secut-* follow) pursue]

pẽrsĕvēr'|ance n. steadfast pursuit of an aim, constant persistence; (Theol.) continuance in state of grace. [ME f. OF, f. L *perseverantia* (as PERSEVERE; see -ANCE)]

persĕ'ver|āte v.i. continue action etc. for unusually or excessively long time; (Psych., of action or mental state) tend to be spontaneously repeated; so ∼A'TION *n*. [f. L *perseverare* (see foll.) +-ATE³]

persevēr'e *v.i.* continue steadfastly, persist, (*in course of action, in do*ing, *at* or *with* task etc., or abs.). [ME, f. OF *perseverer* f. L *perseverare* persist f. PER(*severus* severe) very strict]

Pēr'sian (-shan) *a.* & *n.* (native or language) of Persia (Iran); ∼ **carpet** or **rug** (made in Persia with fine skilful weave and traditional patterns); ∼ (**cat**), cat of breed with long silky hair and thick tail; ∼ **lamb,** silky tightly-curled fur of young caracul. [ME f. OF *persien* f. med. L **Persianus* (*Persia*; see -AN)]

pērsiĕ'nnes (-nz) *n. pl.* window shutters, or outside blinds, with louvers. [F, fem. pl. (as n.) of obs. *persien* Persian (see prec.)]

pēr'siflage (-ahzh) *n.* light raillery, banter. [F (*persifler* banter f. as PER-+ *siffler* whistle; see -AGE)]

persĭ'mmon *n.* (edible fruit of) American or E. Asian tree of genus *Diospyros*. [corrupt. of Algonquian wd]

persi'st *v.i.* continue firmly or obstinately (*in* opinion, course of action, do*ing*) esp. against obstacles, remonstrance, etc.; (of institution, custom, phenomenon, etc.) continue in existence, survive. [f. L PER(*sistere* stand)]

persi'st|**ent** *a.* persisting (*in*); enduring; constantly repeated; (Biol., of horns, leaves, etc.) remaining, instead of falling off in the normal manner; hence or cogn. ∼ENCE, ∼ENCY, *ns.*, ∼entLY² *adv.* [f. prec., or back-form. f. *persistence*, after *insistent*]

pēr'son *n.* **1.** individual human being (*a cheerful and forthright person; found a friend in the person of his landlord*). **2.** living body of human being (*he had a fine person; attracted by her fortune, not her person*); *acting, appearing,* **in his own** (**proper**) ∼ or **in** ∼ (himself, personally); (euphem.) genitals (*expose one's person*). **3.** (Law). human being (**natural** ∼) or body corporate (**artificial** ∼) with recognized rights and duties. **4.** character in play or story. **5.** one of three modes of being of the Godhead; Father (First P∼), Son (Second P∼), and Holy Spirit (Third P∼). **6.** (Gram.) one of three classes of personal pronouns, verb-forms, etc., denoting respectively the person etc. writing or speaking (**first** ∼), written or spoken to (**second** ∼), or written or spoken of (**third** ∼). [ME, f. OF *persone* f. L *persona* actor's mask, character in play, human being]

persō'na *n.* (*pl.* ∼e). aspect of personality as shown to or perceived by others (opp. *anima*); ∼ **grata** (grah'ta), person (esp. diplomat) acceptable to certain others; ∼ **non grata** (nŏn), person not acceptable. [L, as prec.]

pēr'sonable *a.* handsome, comely; pleasing by one's appearance and demeanour. [ME, f. PERSON + -ABLE]

pēr'sonage *n.* person of rank or importance; person; character in play etc. [ME, f. PERSON + -AGE, infl. by med. L *personagium* effigy & F *personnage*]

pēr'sonal *a.* **1.** one's own, individual, private, (*to suit his personal convenience; personal EQUATION, TOUCH*²; *this is personal to myself*); of the body and clothing (one's *personal appearance; personal hygiene*). **2.** done, made, etc., in person (*personal SERVICE*¹ 7, *acquaintance, interview; made a personal appearance at the meeting*). **3.** directed or referring to an individual (*personal call, letter*); directed hostilely to an individual (*personal abuse, remarks*); (given to) making personal remarks (*do not let us become personal*); ∼ **column,** part of newspaper devoted to short advertisements of personal or semi-personal nature. **4.** of, or existing as, a person, not an abstraction or a thing (*a personal God*). **5.** (Law). ∼ **property** or **estate,** chattels or chattel interests in land, all property except land and those interests in land that pass to one's heir; cf. REAL². **6.** (Gram.) of or denoting one of the three persons; *personal* PRONOUN. [ME f. OF, f. L *personalis* (as PERSON; see -AL)]

pērsonă'lity *n.* **1.** being a person; personal existence

or identity; ∼ **cult,** extreme adulation of an individual; **multiple** ∼, (Psych.) the apparent existence of two or more distinct personalities alternating in one individual; SPLIT¹ *personality.* **2.** distinctive personal character. **3.** person, esp. a celebrity (*television personality*). **4.** (Of remark) fact of being aimed at an individual, (usu. in *pl.*) such remark. [ME, f. OF *personalité* f. LL *personalitas -tatis* (as prec.; see -ITY)]

pēr'sonalĭz|**e, -ĭs**|**e** (-īz), *v.t.* personify; make personal, esp. by marking with owner's name etc.; hence ∼A'TION *n.* [f. PERSONAL + -IZE]

pēr'sonally *adv.* In adj. senses; in person, in one's own person, (*he conducted them personally; writ was served on them personally*); as a person (*a God existing personally*); for one's own part (*personally, I see no objection*). [f. PERSONAL + -LY²]

pēr'sonaltў *n.* personal estate (opp. *realty*). [f. AF *personalté* (as PERSONAL; see -TY¹)]

pēr'sonate¹ *a.* (Bot., of corolla) having the opening of the lips closed by upward projection of the lower, as in snapdragon. [f. L *personatus* masked (as foll.; see -ATE²)]

pēr'son|**āte**² *v.t.* play the part of (character in drama, also fig.); pretend to be (person) esp. for fraudulent purpose, impersonate; hence ∼A'TION, ∼ātor, *ns.* [f. LL *personare* (as PERSON) + -ATE²]

personĭfĭca'tion *n.* personifying; person or thing viewed as striking example or embodiment of (quality etc.). [f. foll.; see -FICATION]

persō'nĭfy *v.t.* attribute personal nature to (abstraction or thing); symbolize (quality) by figure in human form; (esp. in *p.p.*) embody (quality) in one's own person, exemplify typically. [f. F *personnifier* (as PERSON; see -FY)]

pērsonnĕ'l *n.* body of persons employed in public undertaking, armed forces, factory, office, etc.; ∼ **carrier,** armoured vehicle for transporting troops; ∼ **department, manager,** etc., (concerned with appointment, advising, training, etc., of employees). [F, = personal, as n.]

perspĕ'ctive *n.* & *a.* **1.** *n.* art of delineating solid objects on plane surface so as to give same impression of relative positions, magnitudes, etc., as the actual objects do when viewed from particular point; picture so drawn; apparent relation between visible objects as to position, distance, etc.; (fig.) aspect of a subject and its parts as viewed by the mind, view, prospect, (lit. or fig.); **in** ∼, drawn or viewed (lit. or fig.) according to rules of perspective; hence **pērspĕcti'**vAL *a.* **2.** *a.* of or in perspective; hence ∼LY² (-vlĭ) *adv.* [ME, f. med. L *perspectiva* (*ars* art) f. PER(*spicere spect-* look); see -IVE]

Pēr'spĕx, p-, *n.* (P) tough unsplinterable transparent acrylic thermoplastic, much lighter than glass. [f. L PER(*spicere spect-* look)]

pērspĭca'cious (-shŭs) *a* having mental penetration or discernment; hence or cogn. ∼LY² *adv.,* ∼NESS, **pērspĭca'**cITY, *ns.* [f. L *perspicax -acis* (as prec.; see -ACIOUS)]

perspĭ'cūous *a.* easily understood, clearly expressed; (of person) expressing things clearly; hence or cogn. **pērspĭcū'**ITY, ∼NESS, *ns.,* ∼LY² *adv.* [ME, = transparent, f. L *perspicuus* (as PERSPECTIVE) + -OUS]

pērspĭra'tion *n.* perspiring; = SWEAT 1, 2; hence **perspi'ratory** *a.* [F (as foll.; see -ATION)]

perspīr'e *v.i.* & *t.* = SWEAT 7, 8. [f. F *perspirer* f. L PER(*spirare* breathe)]

persuā'd|**e** (-sw-) *v.t.* cause (person, one*self*) to have belief (*of* fact, *that* thing is so); induce (person *to* do, *into* action); (in *p.p.*) convinced (*of* thing, *that*); hence or cogn. ∼ABLE *a.,* ∼ER¹,² *n.,* (esp., sl.) gun etc. [f. L PER(*suadēre suas-* advise)]

persuā'sible (-sw-) *a.* [f. L PER(*suadēre suas-* advise)]

persuā'sion (-swā'zhon) *n.* **1.** persuading, persuasiveness. **2.** belief, conviction, (*it is my private persuasion that he is mad*); religious belief, sect holding this, (*he is of the Roman Catholic persuasion*); (joc.) kind, sort, (*no one of* *the male persuasion was present*). [ME, f. L *persuasio* (as prec.; see -ION)]

persuā′sive (-sw-) *a.* & *n.* **1.** *a.* able to persuade; hence ∼LY² (-vlĭ) *adv.*, ∼NESS (-vn-) *n.* **2.** *n.* motive, inducement. [f. F *persuasif* *-ive* or f. med. L *persuasivus* (as PERSUADE; see -IVE)]

pĕrt *a.* saucy or impudent in speech or conduct; (of clothes etc.) neat and suggestive of jauntiness; = PEART; hence ∼′LY² *adv.*, ∼′NESS *n.* [ME, f. OF *apert* f. L *apertus* p.p. of *aperire* open, & f. OF *aspert* f. L *expertus* EXPERT¹]

PERT *abbr.* programme evaluation and review technique.

pertai′n *v.i.* belong as part, appendage, or accessory, *to*; be appropriate (*to*); have reference or relate *to*. [ME, f. OF *partenir* f. L PER(*tinēre* = *tenēre* hold)]

pĕrtinā′cious (-shəs) *a.* stubborn, persistent, obstinate, (in a course of action etc.); hence or cogn. ∼LY² *adv.*, ∼NESS, **pĕrtină′city**, *ns.* [f. L PER(*tinax* = *tenax* TENACIOUS)]

pĕr′tin|ent *a.* pertaining, relevant, apposite, (*to* matter being considered etc.); to the point; hence or cogn. ∼ENCE, ∼ENCY, *ns.*, ∼entLY² *adv.* [ME f. OF, or f. L (as PERTAIN; see -ENT)]

pertŭr′b *v.t.* throw into confusion or disorder; disturb mentally, agitate; (Phys. etc.) cause deviation of motion or of other behaviour of (body etc.); so **pĕrturbA′TION** *n.*, ∼ATIVE (pertĕr′bat-, pĕr′terbāt-) *a.* [ME, f. OF *pertourber* f. L PER(*turbare* disturb)]

pertŭ′ssis *n.* (Path.) whooping cough. [mod. L, f. PER-+L *tussis* cough]

peru′ke (-ōō′k) *n.* (esp. Hist.) wig. [f. F *perruque* f. It. *perrucca, parrucca*, of unkn. orig.]

peru′se (-ōō′z) *v.t.* read, esp. thoroughly or carefully; (fig.) examine (person's face etc.) carefully; hence **peru′sAL** 2 (-ōō′zəl) *n.* [ME, prob. f. AL *PER(*usare* f. Rom. **usare* USE²) use up]

Peru′vian (-ōō′-) *a.* & *n.* **1.** *a.* of Peru; ∼ **bark** (of cinchona tree). **2.** *n.* native or inhabitant of Peru. [f. mod. L *Peruvia* Peru + -AN]

pervā′de *v.t.* spread throughout, permeate, saturate, (lit., or fig. of influences etc.); be rife among or through; hence **pervā′sion** (-zhən) *n.* [f. L PER(*vadere* *vas-* go)]

pervā′sive *a.* pervading; able to pervade; hence ∼LY² (-vlĭ) *adv.*, ∼NESS (-vn-) *n.* [f. as prec. + -IVE]

pervĕr′se *a.* persistent in error; different from what is reasonable or required; wayward; peevish; perverted, wicked; (of verdict) against weight of evidence or judge's direction; hence or cogn. ∼LY² (-slĭ) *adv.*, ∼NESS (-sn-), **pervĕr′sity**, *ns.* [ME, f. OF *pervers* perverse, f. L *perversus* (as PERVERT¹)]

pervĕr′sion (-shən) *n.* perverting, being perverted; perverted form of a thing; preference for a form of sexual activity other than normal intercourse. [ME, f. L *perversio* (as foll.; see -ION)]

pervĕr′t¹ *v.t.* turn aside (thing) from its proper use or nature; misconstrue, misapply, (words etc.); lead astray (person, mind) from right opinion or conduct or esp. religious belief; (in *p.p.*) showing perversion; hence **pervĕr′sIVE** *a.* [ME, f. OF *pervertir* or f. L PER(*vertere vers-* turn)]

pĕr′vĕrt² *n.* perverted person, apostate; person showing perversion of sexual instincts. [f. prec.; cf. CONVERT²]

pĕr′vious *a.* affording passage (*to*); permeable; (fig.) accessible (*to* reason etc.); hence ∼NESS *n.* [f. L PER(*vius* f. *via* way) + -OUS]

Pe′sach (pā′sahχ) *n.* Passover festival. [f. Heb. *Pesaḥ*]

pese′ta (-sā′-) *n.* Spanish orig. silver coin and monetary unit. [Sp., dim. of *pesa* weight f. L *pensa* pl. of *pensum* (see POISE¹)]

Peshi′tō, Peshi′tta, (-shĕ′-) *n.* principal ancient Syriac version of OT and NT. [f. Syriac *p'šīttâ* simple, plain]

***pĕ′skў** *a.* (colloq.) troublesome, confounded, annoying. [18th c., perh. f. **pesty* (PEST, -Y²)]

pe′sō (pā′-) *n.* (*pl.* ∼s). silver coin and monetary unit in several Latin-American countries and in Philippines. [Sp., = weight, f. L *pensum* (see POISE¹)]

pĕ′ssarỹ *n.* (Med.) instrument worn in vagina to prevent uterine displacements or as contraceptive; vaginal suppository. [ME, f. LL *pessarium, pessulum* (*pessum, pessus* f. Gk *pessos* oval stone)]

pĕ′ssim|ism *n.* tendency to look at the worst aspect of things or expect bad results (cf. OPTIMISM); doctrine that this world is the worst possible, or that all things tend to evil; so ∼IST (2) *n.*, ∼i′stIC *a.*, ∼i′stICALLY *adv.* [f. L *pessimus* worst + -ISM, after *optimism*]

pĕst *n.* troublesome, annoying, or destructive person, animal, or thing; (arch.) pestilence, plague; ∼**-house,** hospital for sufferers from plague etc. [f. F *peste* or f. L *pestis* plague]

pĕ′ster *v.t.* trouble, annoy; importune (*kept pestering me for an interview*). [prob. f. *impester* f. F *empestrer* encumber; infl. by PEST]

pĕ′sticide *n.* substance for destroying pests, esp. insects. [f. PEST + -I- + -CIDE (1)]

pĕstī′ferous *a.* noxious, pestilential; (fig.) bearing moral contagion, pernicious. [f. L *pestifer, -ferus* (as PEST; see -FEROUS)]

pĕ′stilence *n.* fatal epidemic disease, esp. bubonic plague. [ME f. OF, f. L *pestilentia* (as foll.; see -ENCE)]

pĕ′stilent *a.* destructive to life, deadly; (fig.) injurious to morals etc.; (colloq.) troublesome, annoying; hence ∼LY² *adv.* [f. L *pestilens, pestilentus* (*pestis* plague; see -LENT)]

pĕstilĕ′ntial (-shəl) *a.* of pestilence; pestilent; hence ∼LY² *adv.* [ME, f. med. L *pestilentialis* f. L *pestilentia* (as prec.) see -IAL]

pĕ′stle (-səl) *n.* & *v.* **1.** *n.* club-shaped instrument for pounding substances in a mortar; appliance for pounding etc. **2.** *v.t.* pound (as) with pestle. **3.** *v.i.* use pestle. [ME, f. OF *pestel* f. L *pistillum* dim. of **pistrum* (*pinsare pist-* pound)]

pĕsto′log|ỹ *n.* scientific study of pests (esp. harmful insects) and of methods of dealing with them; hence **pĕstolŏ′gICAL** *a.*, ∼IST (3) *n.* [f. PEST + -O- + -LOGY]

pĕt¹ *n.*, *a.*, & *v.t.* (-tt-). **1.** *n.* animal tamed and kept as favourite or treated with fondness; darling, favourite; ∼**-cock,** small stop-cock for draining, letting out steam, etc. **2.** *a.* kept as pet (*pet lamb*); of or for pet animals (*pet food, shop*); favourite (∼ **aversion** etc., (joc.) thing or person particularly disliked); expressing fondness or familiarity (*pet-form* of name etc., *pet name*). **3.** *v.t.* treat as a pet; fondle (esp. person of opposite sex erotically; or abs.). [16th c. Sc. & N. Engl. dial.; orig. unkn.]

pĕt² *n.* offence at being slighted, ill-humour, (*be in a pet*). [16th c., of unkn. orig.]

Pet. *abbr.* Peter (NT).

pĕ′ta- *pref.* denoting factor of 10¹⁵. [perh. f. PENTA-]

pĕ′tal *n.* each of the divisions of the corolla of a flower; hence ∼INE (-ĭn), (-)∼(1)ED² (-ld), ∼OID, *adjs.* [f. mod. L *petalum*, in LL metal plate f. Gk *petalon* leaf (*petalos* outspread)]

pĕ′talŏn *n.* gold plate on mitre of Jewish high priest. [Gk; see prec.]

pĕtăr′d *n.* (Hist.) small bomb used to break down door etc. by explosion (HOIST² *with his own petard*); kind of firework, cracker. [f. F *pétard* (*péter* break wind; see -ARD)]

pĕ′tasus *n.* ancient Greek low-crowned broad-brimmed hat, esp. as worn by Hermes; winged hat of Hermes. [L, f. Gk *petasos*]

pĕtaur′ist *n.* marsupial of genus *Petaurista*, with patagium enabling it to take flying leaps. [f. Gk *petauristēs* performer on springboard (*petauron*); see -IST]

Pēte *n.* for *Pete's* SAKE¹. [abbr. of foll.]

Pē′ter¹ *n.* **1.** BLUE¹ Peter; ∼ **Pan,** person who retains youthful features etc. and seems not to age; ∼ *Pan collar* (flat, with rounded ends); **rob** ∼ **to pay Paul,** take away from one to give to another, discharge one debt by incurring another. **2.** ~**'s fish,** haddock or other fish with marks supposed to have been made by St. Peter's thumb and finger; ~**-penny,** ~**'s penny** or **pence,** (Hist.) annual tax of penny paid to papal see, (since 1860) voluntary payment to papal treasury. [man's Christian name, f. eccl. L f. eccl. Gk *Petros,* lit. 'stone', transl. Aram. *kēpā* surname given to St. Peter by Jesus (Matt. 16:17); ~ *Pan* hero of play by Barrie (1904)]

pe'ter[2] *v.i.,* & *n.* **1.** *v.i.* ~ **out,** (of stream, vein of ore, or fig.) give out, come to an end. **2.** (Bridge). play an echo. **3.** *n.* (Bridge). = ECHO[1]. [19th c.; orig. unkn.]

pe'ter[3] *n.* (sl.) prison cell; safe; ~**'man,** safe-breaker. [perh. f. PETER[1]]

pe'tersham *n.* thick corded silk ribbon. [f. Lord *Petersham,* Engl. army officer d. 1851]

pe'thidine (-ēn) *n.* synthetic soluble analgesic derived from piperidine. [perh. f. PIPERIDINE + ETHYL]

pe'tiol|e *n.* (Bot.) slender stalk joining leaf-blade to stem; hence ~AR[1], ~ATE[2], *adjs.* [f. F *pétiole* f. L *petiolus* little foot, stalk]

pe'tit[1] (-tǐ) *a.* (Law). = PETTY. [ME f. OF, = small, f. Rom. *pittittus, perh. imit. of child's speech]

petit[2] (petē') *a.* ~ **bourgeois** (boor'zhwah), member of lower middle classes; ~ **four** (foor), very small fancy cake etc.; ~**-maître** (-mā'tr), dandy, coxcomb; ~ **mal** (mahl), mild form of epilepsy without loss of consciousness; ~ **point** (pwăn), (1) embroidery on canvas using small stitches, (2) tent-stitch; ~**s pois** (pwah), small green peas; ~ **verre** (vār), glass of liqueur. [F, = small (as prec.)]

petite (petē't) *a.* (Of woman) of small dainty build; ~ **bourgeoisie** (boorzhwahzē'), lower middle classes. [F, fem. of prec.]

peti'tion *n.* & *v.* **1.** *n.* asking, supplication, request; formal written supplication from one or more persons to sovereign etc.; (Law) formal written application to court for writ, order, etc.; P~ **of Right,** (Hist.) parliamentary declaration of rights and liberties of the people assented to by Charles 1 in 1628, (Law) common-law remedy against Crown for recovery of property. **2.** *v.t.* make petition to (sovereign etc. *for* thing, *to do*). **3.** *v.i.* ask humbly (*for* thing, *to be* allowed to do etc.). **4.** Hence ~ARY[1] *a.,* ~ER[1] *n.* [ME f. OF, f. L *petitio -onis* (*petere petit-* seek; see -ION)]

petitio principii (pǐtǐshiō prǐnsǐ'pǐī) *n.* begging the question (see BEG 4). [L, = assuming a principle (see prec.)]

pe'trel *n.* sea-bird of family Procellariidae or Hydrobatidae, usu. flying far from land; **storm(y)** ~, small petrel of N. Atlantic with black and white plumage and long wings, (fig.) person causing unrest. [17th c., also *pitteral,* of uncert. orig.; later assoc. w. St. Peter (Matt. 14:30; see -REL)]

Pe'tri *n.* ~ **dish,** shallow covered dish for culture of bacteria etc. [f. J. R. ~, Ger. bacteriologist d. 1921]

petrifa'ction *n.* petrifying; petrified substance or mass. [f. foll. after *stupefaction;* see -FACTION]

pe'trify *v.* **1.** *v.t.* change into stone; (fig.) paralyse or stupefy with astonishment, terror, etc., (*petrified with fear* etc.); deprive (mind, doctrine, etc.) of vitality. **2.** *v.i.* turn into stone (lit. or fig.). [f. F *pétrifier* f. med. L *petrificare* f. L f. Gk *petra* rock; see -FY]

Pe'trine *a.* of St. Peter. [f. eccl. L *Petrus* PETER[1] + -INE[1]]

pe'tro- *comb. form.* **1.** rock: as *petro*GE'NESIS, ~**glyph,** (esp. prehistoric) rock-carving. **2.** petroleum, as PETROCHEMISTRY; ~**dollar,** dollar available in petroleum-exporting country. [f. Gk *petros* stone or *petra* rock + -O-]

petroche'mical (-k-) *a.* & *n.* **1.** *a.* of petrochemistry or petrochemicals. **2.** *n.* substance industrially obtained from petroleum or natural gas. [f. foll. + CHEMICAL]

petroche'mistry (-k-) *n.* chemistry of rocks; chemistry of petroleum. [f. PETRO- + CHEMISTRY]

petro'|graphy *n.* scientific description of composition and formation of rocks; hence ~GRAPHER *n.,* *petro*GRA'PHIC(AL) *adjs.* [f. PETRO- + -GRAPHY]

||**pe'trol** *n.* refined petroleum used as fuel in motor vehicles, aircraft, etc.; ~**-pump,** machine for transferring this esp. from underground reservoir to tank in motor vehicle; ~ **station,** filling-station. [f. F *pétrole* f. med. L PETROLEUM]

***petrola'tum** *n.* petroleum jelly. [mod. L, f. prec. + -atum; see -ATE[1]]

petro'leum *n.* hydrocarbon oil found in upper strata of earth, refined for use as fuel for heating and in internal-combustion engines, as illuminant, as dry-cleaning agent, etc.; ~ **ether,** volatile liquid distilled from petroleum; ~ **jelly,** translucent solid mixture of hydrocarbons got from petroleum and used as lubricant etc. [med. L, f. L f. Gk *petra* rock + L *oleum* oil]

petro'lic *a.* of petrol or petroleum. [f. PETROL + -IC]

petro'log|y *n.* study of origin, structure, etc., of rocks; so *petrolo'*gIC(AL) *adjs.,* ~IST (3) *n.* [f. PETRO- + -LOGY]

pe'tronel *n.* (Hist.) large pistol used esp. by horse-soldiers in 16th–17th c. [f. F *petrinal,* var. of *poitrinal* n. f. a. (*poitrine* chest f. Rom. *pectorina f. L *pectus -oris;* see -AL); the butt end rested against the chest in firing]

pe'trous *a.* of or like rock, (Anat.) hard (part of the temporal bone, protecting the inner ear). [f. L *petrosus* (L f. Gk *petra* rock, see -OUS)]

pe'tticoat *n.* **1.** woman's or child's undergarment hanging from waist or shoulders, or (Hist.) outer skirt, (*have known him since he was in* ~s, a young child; *a Cromwell in* ~s, in all but her sex). **2.** woman or girl; (in *pl.*) the female sex; (*attrib.*) feminine; ~ **government,** dominance of women in the home or in politics. **3.** Hence ~ED[2], ~LESS, *adjs.* [ME, f. *petty coat*]

pe'ttifog *v.i.* (-gg-). practise legal chicanery; quibble or wrangle about petty points. [back-form. f. foll.]

pe'ttifogg|er (-g-) *n.* inferior legal practitioner; rascally lawyer; petty practitioner in any activity; hence ~ERY (4) *n.,* ~ING[2] *a.,* (-g-). [f. PETTY + *fogger* underhand dealer, prob. f. *Fugger* family of merchants in Augsburg (15th–16th c.)]

pe'ttish *a.* peevish, petulant, easily put out; hence ~LY[2] *adv.,* ~NESS *n.* [f. PET[2] + -ISH[1]]

pe'ttitoes (-ōz) *n. pl.* pig's trotters, esp. as food. [orig. = offal, f. F *petite oie* giblets of a goose, w. assim. to PETTY, TOEs]

pe'tt|y *a.* unimportant, trivial; contemptible; minor, inferior, on a small scale, (*petty princes, farmers*); (Law) of lesser importance (cf. GRAND; *petty* JURY, LARCENY, SESSIONS, TREASON); ~**y bourgeois,** ~ PETIT[2] *bourgeois,* ~**y cash,** (money from or for) small cash items of receipt or expenditure; ~**y officer,** naval NCO; hence ~ILY[2] *adv.,* ~INESS *n.* [ME *pety,* var. of PETIT[1]]

pe'tul|ant *a.* peevishly impatient or irritable; hence or cogn. ~ANCE *n.,* ~antLY[2] *adv.* [f. F *pétulant* f. L *petulans -antis* (*petulare f. *petere* seek; see -ANT)]

petu'nia *n.* plant of genus *Petunia* with white, purple, red, etc., funnel-shaped flowers; dark violet or purple colour. [mod. L, f. F *petun* f. Guarani *petý* tobacco; see -IA[1]]

petu'ntse (-ōō'-, -ū'-) *n.* white powdered granite used in China for making porcelain. [f. Chin. *baidunzi* (*bai* white, *dun* stone + suf. -zi)]

pew *n.,* & *v.t.* **1.** *n.* (In church) enclosed compartment or fixed bench with back; (colloq.) seat (*find, take, a pew*); ~**-rent** (for pew or seats in church); hence ~'AGE (4) *n.,* ~'LESS *a.* **2.** *v.t.* furnish with pews; enclose in pew. [ME *pywe, puwe* f. OF *puye* balcony f. L *podia* pl. of PODIUM]

pe'wit. See PEEWIT.

pew'ter *n.* grey alloy of tin with lead or other metal; utensil(s) of this; ||(sl.) tankard etc. as prize; hence ~ER[1] *n.,* worker in pewter. [ME f. OF *peutre, peualtre* f. Rom. *peltrum, of unkn. orig.]

peyō′t|e (pāō′-) *n.* **1.** Mexican cactus of genus *Lophophora.* **2.** hallucinogenic drug prepared from this plant. **3.** Hence ⁓ISM (3) *n.,* Amer. Ind. religion using peyote sacramentally. [Amer. Sp., f. Nahuatl *peyotl*]

PF *abbr.* Patriotic Front.

Pf. *abbr.* pfennig.

***Pfc** *abbr.* Private First Class.

pfe′nnig *n.* small German copper coin, worth ₁₀₀ of a mark. [G, cogn. w. PENNY]

PG *abbr.* paying guest.

pH (pēā′ch) *n.* (Chem.) negative decimal logarithm of hydrogen-ion concentration in moles per litre, giving measure of acidity or alkalinity of a solution. [G, f. *potenz* power + *H* symbol for hydrogen]

phae′ton (fā′-) *n.* light open four-wheeled carriage usu. drawn by pair of horses; *touring-car. [f. F *phaéton* f. L f. Gk *Phaethōn,* son of Helios the sun god and famous for bad driving of sun-chariot (*phaethōn* shining)]

phage (fāj, fahzh) *n.* = BACTERIOPHAGE. [abbr.]

phägedae′n|a, *-dē′n|a, *n.* spreading ulcer; so ⁓IC *a.* [L, f. Gk *phagedaina* (*phag-* eat)]

phä′go|cyte *n.* leucocyte etc. capable of absorbing foreign matter, esp. bacteria, in the body; hence ⁓cy′tIC *a.* [f. Gk *phag-* eat + -o- + -CYTE]

phä′gocytīze, -īse (-īz), **-ōse,** *v.t.* consume by phagocytosis. [f. prec. + -IZE, & back-form. f. foll.]

phägocytō′s|is *n.* (*pl.* ⁓es *pr.* ⁓ēz). consumption of bacteria etc. by phagocytes. [f. PHAGOCYTE + -OSIS]

-phagous *comb. form.* eating (*ichthyophagous*). [f. L f. Gk *-phagos* + -OUS]

-phagy *comb. form.* eating (*ichthyophagy*). [f. Gk *-phagia* + -Y¹]

phä′lange (-nj) *n.* = PHALANX 3. [F, f. L PHALANX]

phalä′ngeal (-nj-) *a.* (Anat.) of a phalanx. [f. prec. + -AL]

phalä′nger (-nj-) *n.* (Austral. & NZ). arboreal thick-furred marsupial, e.g. flying squirrel or possum. [F, f. Gk *phalaggion* spider's web, f. webbed toes of its hind feet]

phä′lanst|erȳ *n.* (buildings of) socialistic PHALANX; so ⁓ēr′IAN *a.* & *n.* [f. F *phalanstère* (f. foll. after *monastère* monastery)]

phä′län|x *n.* (*pl.* ⁓xes, *or* ⁓ges *pr.* -njĕz). **1.** (Gk Ant.) line of battle, esp. body of Macedonian infantry drawn up in close order. **2.** set of persons etc. forming compact mass, or banded together for common purpose; (Hist.) socialistic community of about 1800 persons as proposed by Fourier. **3.** (Anat.) bone of finger or toe; (Bot.) bundle of stamens united by filaments. [L, f. Gk *phalagx -ggos*]

phä′larōpe *n.* small wading and swimming bird of family Phalaropodidae, noted for tameness. [F, f. mod. L *Phalaropus,* irreg. f. Gk *phalaris* coot + *pous podos* foot]

phä′ll|us *n.* (*pl.* ⁓i *pr.* -ī, *or* ⁓uses). image of the (usu. erect) penis, venerated in some religious systems as symbolizing generative power in nature; penis or clitoris; so ⁓IC *a.,* ⁓(ic)ISM (3) *ns.* [LL, f. Gk *phallos*]

phanä′riot *n.* member of class of Greek officials in Constantinople under Ottoman Empire. [f. mod. Gk *phanariōtēs* f. Phanar part of city where they lived, f. Gk *phanarion* lighthouse (on the Golden Horn); see -OT²]

phä′nerogăm *n.* (Bot.) plant that has stamens and pistils, flowering plant, (cf. CRYPTOGAM); so ⁓IC (-ă′m-), **phänerō′gam**OUS, *adjs.* [f. F *phanérogame* f. Gk *phaneros* visible + *gamos* marriage]

phä′ntasīze, phä′ntast. Vars. of FANTASIZE, FANTAST.

phä′ntāsm *n.* illusion, phantom; illusive likeness (*of*); supposed vision of absent (living or dead) person; hence **phäntä′sm**AL, **phäntä′sm**IC, (-z-) *adjs.* [ME, f. OF *fantasme* f. L f. Gk *phantasma* (*phantazō* make visible f. *phainō* show)]

phäntäsmag|or′ia (-z-) *n.* optical device for rapidly varying size of images on screen; shifting scene of real or imagined figures; hence ⁓o′rIC *a.* [prob. f. F *fantasmagorie* (as prec. + fanciful ending)]

phä′ntasȳ. See FANTASY.

phä′ntom *n.* & *a.* **1.** *n.* (mere) apparition, spectre; image (*of*); vain show, form without substance or reality; mental illusion. **2.** *a.* merely apparent, illusive; ⁓ circuit, arrangement of telegraph etc. wires equivalent to an extra circuit; ⁓ limb, sensation apparently coming from limb previously removed by amputation. [ME f. OF *fantosme* f. pop. L *fantauma* f. Gk (as PHANTASM)]

Phār′aoh (fār′ō) *n.* (Title of) ruler of ancient Egypt; ⁓'s serpent, chemical toy burning and uncoiling in serpentine form; hence **Phāraō′n**IC *a.* [OE, f. eccl. L f. Gk *Pharaō* f. Heb. *par′ōh* f. Egypt. *pr-′o* great house]

Phä′risee *n.* one of ancient Jewish sect (cf. SADDUCEE, ESSENE) distinguished by strict observance of traditional and written law, held to have pretensions to superior sanctity; self-righteous person, formalist, hypocrite; so **Phärisā′IC**(AL) *adjs.,* **Phä′risā**ISM (3) *n.* [OE *fariseus* & OF *pharise* f. eccl. L *pharisaeus* f. Gk *Pharisaios* f. Aram. *p'rišayyâ* pl. f. Heb. *pārûš* separated]

phärmaceu′t|ical (-sū′-, -kū′-) *a.* of or engaged in pharmacy; of the use or sale of medicinal drugs; hence or cogn. ⁓ICALLY *adv.,* ⁓ICS *n.* [f. LL f. Gk *pharmakeutikos* (*pharmakeutēs* druggist f. *pharmakon* drug) + -AL]

phär′macist *n.* person skilled in or practising pharmacy; pharmaceutical chemist. [f. PHARMACY + -IST]

phärmacō′log|ȳ *n.* science of action of drugs on the body; hence **phärmaco**LO′GICAL *a.,* ⁓IST (3) *n.* [f. mod. L *pharmacologia* f. Gk *pharmakon* drug; see -LOGY]

phärmacopœ′i|a (-pē′a) *n.* book (esp. one officially published) containing list of drugs with directions for use; stock of drugs; hence ⁓AL (-pē′al) *a.* [mod. L, f. Gk *pharmakopoiia* (*pharmakopoios* drug-maker f. as prec. + *-poios* making)]

phär′macȳ *n.* preparation and (esp. medicinal) dispensing of drugs; pharmacist's shop, dispensary. [ME, f. OF *farmacie* f. med. L f. Gk *pharmakeia* practice of the druggist (*pharmakeus* f. *pharmakon* drug)]

phär′ös *n.* lighthouse or beacon to guide mariners. [L, f. Gk *Pharos* island off Alexandria, lighthouse on this]

pharȳ′ngo- (-ngg-) *comb. form.* pharynx, as: ⁓cele, abnormal enlargement at base of pharynx; ⁓scope, instrument for inspecting pharynx; ⁓tomy (fărĭng-gŏ′t-), incision into pharynx. [f. as foll. + -o-]

phä′rynx *n.* cavity, with enclosing muscles and mucous membrane, behind nose and mouth, and connecting them to oesophagus; hence **pharȳ′ng**AL (-ngg-), **phärȳnge′**AL (-nj-), *adjs.,* **phärȳngi′**TIS (-nj-) *n.* [mod. L, f. Gk *pharugx -ggos*]

phāse (-z) *n.,* & *v.t.* **1.** *n.* stage of change or development; aspect of moon or planet, according to amount of illumination (esp. applied to new moon, first quarter, full moon, last quarter); aspect (of situation or question); genetic or seasonal variety of animal's coloration etc. **2.** (Phys.) particular stage in periodically recurring sequence of movements or changes (esp. of alternating electric currents); **in** ⁓, having same phase at same time; **out of** ⁓, not in phase; **three-**⁓, (of electric generator, motor, etc.) designed to supply or use simultaneously three separate alternating currents of the same voltage, but with phases differing by ⅓ of a period. **3.** (Chem.) physically distinct form of matter that can be present in a system; ⁓ rule (relating numbers of phases, constituents, and degrees of freedom). **4.** Hence **phä′s**IC (-z-) *a.* **5.** *v.t.* carry out (programme etc.) in phases or stages; ⁓ **in** or **out**, bring gradually into or out of use. [f. F phase & f. earlier *phasis,* f. Gk *phasis* appearance (*phan-* show)]

phä′tic *a.* (Of speech etc.) used to convey general sociability rather than to communicate specific meaning, e.g. *nice morning, isn't it?.* [f. Gk *phatos* spoken (*phan-* speak) + -IC]

Ph.D. *abbr.* Doctor of Philosophy. [f. L *philosophiae doctor*]

phea′sant (fĕ′z-) *n.* long-tailed game-bird of genus *Phasianus* etc., orig. Asian; ∼-**eyed**, (of flower) marked like eye of pheasant; ∼′**s-eye**, (1) plant of genus *Adonis*, with dark centre, (2) common narcissus; hence ∼RY (3) *n.* [ME, f. AF *fesaunt* f. OF *faisan* f. L f. Gk *phasianos* (bird) of river *Phasis* in Asia Minor]

phĕnă′cĕtĭn *n.* antipyretic acetyl derivative of phenol. [f. foll. + ACETYL + -IN]

phēno- *comb. form.* **1.** (Chem.) derived from benzene (*phenol, phenyl*). **2.** showing (*phenocryst*). [f. Gk *phainō* shine (w. ref. to substances used for illumination), show + -o-]

*∗**phēnobâr′bĭtăl,** ‖**phēnobâr′bĭtōne,** *ns.* narcotic and sedative barbiturate drug used esp. in epilepsy. [f. prec. 1 + BARBITAL, BARBITONE]

phē′nocrȳst *n.* large or conspicuous crystal in porphyritic rock. [f. F *phénocryste* (as PHENO- 2, CRYSTAL)]

phē′nŏl *n.* (Chem.) hydroxyl derivative of aromatic hydrocarbon, esp. monohydroxybenzene (C_6H_5OH), used in dilute form as antiseptic and disinfectant. [f. F *phénole* (*phène* benzene f. as PHENO-; see -OL)]

phĕnō′log‖ȳ *n.* study of the times of recurring natural phenomena esp. in relation to climatic conditions; so **phĕnolŏ′g**ICAL *a.*, ∼IST (3) *n.* [f. PHENOMENON + -LOGY]

phĕnŏ′mĕnal *a.* of the nature of a phenomenon; perceptible by, or evidenced only by, the senses; concerned with phenomena; remarkable, prodigious; hence ∼LY[2] *adv.*, ∼IZE *v.t.*, make, or represent as, phenomenal. [f. PHENOMENON + -AL]

phĕnŏ′mĕnal‖ism *n.* doctrine that phenomena are the only objects of knowledge; so ∼IST (2) *n.*, ∼ĭ′stIC *a.* [f. prec. + -ISM]

phĕnŏmĕn‖ŏ′logȳ *n.* science of phenomena; description and classification of phenomena; hence ∼olŏ′gICAL *a.* [f. foll. + -O- + -LOGY]

phĕnŏ′mĕn‖on *n.* (*pl.* ∼a). thing that appears or is perceived, esp. thing the cause of which is in question; (Philos.) that of which a sense or the mind directly takes note, immediate object of perception; remarkable person, thing, occurrence, etc. [f. LL f. Gk *phainomenon* neut. pres. part. (as *n.*) of *phainomai* appear (*phainō* show)]

phē′no‖type *n.* (Biol.) set of observable characteristics of individual or group as determined by genotype and environment; hence ∼tȳ′pIC *a.* [f. G *phaenotypus* (as PHENO- 2, TYPE[1])]

phē′nȳl *n.* (Chem.) radical formed from benzene by removal of hydrogen atom. [f. PHENO- + -YL]

phē′ro‖mōne *n.* (Biol.) substance secreted and released by animal for detection and response to another of same species; hence ∼mō′nAL *a.* [f. Gk *pherō* convey + -o- + HORMONE]

phew *int.* expr. impatience, discomfort, relief, astonishment, or disgust. [imit. of puffing]

phi *n.* twenty-first Greek letter (Φ, φ) = ph; *∗**Phi Beta Kappa,** (member of) oldest Amer. college fraternity, named from initial letters of its Gk motto, = 'philosophy the guide to life'. [Gk]

phi′al *n.* small glass bottle, esp. for liquid medicine. [ME, f. OF *fiole* f. L *phiola, phiala* f. Gk *phialē* broad flat vessel; cf. VIAL]

phil-. See PHILO-.

-phil, -phile, *suf.* forming *ns.* & *adjs.* w. sense '(one who is) fond of', as *bibliophil(e), Russophil(e).* [f. Gk *philos* dear, loving]

Phil. *abbr.* Philadelphia; Philharmonic; Philippians (NT); Philosophy.

phi′labĕg. Var. of FILIBEG.

philadĕ′lphus *n.* deciduous shrub of genus *Philadelphus*, esp. mock orange. [mod. L, f. Gk *philadelphon*]

philă′nder *v.i.* flirt with or *with* woman; be one who flirts habitually; hence ∼ER[1] *n.* [f. *philander n.* f. Gk *phil*(*andros* f. *anēr* male person) fond of men, taken as name of lover]

phi′lanthrōpe *n.* = PHILANTHROPIST. [f. Gk PHIL- (*anthrōpos* human being)]

philanthrŏ′p‖ic *a.* loving one's fellow men, benevolent, humane; hence ∼ICALLY *adv.* [f. F *philanthropique* (as prec.; see -IC)]

philă′nthrop‖ȳ *n.* love of mankind; practical benevolence; hence ∼ISM (3), ∼IST (2), *ns.*, ∼IZE (1, 2) *v.t.* & *i.* [f. LL f. Gk *philanthrōpia* (as PHILANTHROPE; see -Y[1])]

philă′tel‖ȳ *n.* collection and study of postage stamps; hence **philatĕ′l**IC *a.*, ∼IST (3) *n.* [f. F PHIL(*atélie* f. Gk *ateleia* exemption from payment f. *a-* not + *telos* toll, tax)]

-phile. See -PHIL.

Philem. *abbr.* Philemon (NT).

philhârmŏ′nic (-lhâr-, -lär-) *a.* fond of music (*philharmonic society*). [f. F *philharmonique* f. It. *filarmonico* (as PHIL-, HARMONIC)]

philhĕllēne (fĭ′-, -hĕ′-) *a.* & *n.* (person) friendly to the Greeks or (Hist.) supporting the cause of Greek independence; hence **philhĕllē′n**IC *a.*, **philhĕ′llĕn**ISM (3), **philhĕ′llĕn**IST (2), *ns.* [f. Gk PHIL(*ellēn* HELLENE)]

-phi′lia *suf.* forming *ns.* w. sense 'love of, fondness for' (*coprophilia*); hence ∼**phi′l**IC *adj. suf.* (*bibliophilic*). [Gk (*philos* loving; see -IA[1])]

Phili′ppic *n.* **1.** (in *pl.*) orations of Demosthenes against Philip of Macedon; Cicero's orations against Antony. **2.** (*p∼*). bitter invective. [f. L f. Gk *philippikos* (*Philippos* Philip; see -IC)]

philippi′na (-pē′-), **philippi′ne**[1] (-ē′n), **philopoe′na** (-pē′-), *∗**opē′na,** *n.* almond or other nut with double kernel, the finding of which at dessert etc. and sharing it with person of the opposite sex involves giving or receiving of a present at next meeting; the present; the custom. [f. G *Philippchen* little Philip alt. of *vielliebchen* darling dim. of *viellieb* very dear]

Phi′lippine[2] (-ēn) *a.* of the Philippine Islands; Filipino. [f. *Philip* II of Spain + -INE[1]]

Phi′listine *n.* & *a.* **1.** *n.* member of a people opposing Israelites in ancient Palestine; uncultured person, one whose interests are material and commonplace, lacking in culture; so **phi′listin**ISM (2) *n.* **2.** *a.* uncultured, commonplace, prosaic. [ME, f. F *Philistin* or LL f. Gk *Philistinos* = *Palaistinos* f. Heb. *pelištī*]

phillu′men|ist (-lōō′-, -lū′-) *n.* collector of matchbox labels; so ∼Y[1] *n.* [f. PHIL- + L *lumen* light + -IST]

*∗**Phi′llȳ** *n.* (sl.) Philadelphia. [abbr.; see -Y[3]]

philo- *comb. form.* (**phil-** bef. vowel or *h*). liking, fond of, as: ∼**bib′lic,** fond of books; ∼**de′ndron,** tropical Amer. climbing plant; ∼**gynist** (-ŏ′j-), lover of women; ∼**proge′nitive,** prolific, loving one's offspring; ∼**te′chnic** (-tĕ′k-), fond of (esp. the industrial) arts. [f. or after Gk *philo-* (*phileō* to love, *philos* friend)]

philŏ′log‖ȳ *n.* science (esp. historical and comparative) of language(s); *∗*study of literature; love of learning and literature; hence ∼ER[1] (arch.), **philolŏ′g**IAN, ∼IST (3), *ns.*, **philolŏ′g**ICAL *a.*, ∼IZE (2) *v.i.* [f. F *philologie* f. L f. Gk PHILO(*logia* = -LOGY) of learning]

Phi′lomĕl, Philomē′la, *ns.* (poet.) the nightingale. [*earlier philomene* f. med. L *philomena* f. L f. Gk *philomēla* nightingale; cap. w. ref. to myth of Philomela]

philop(o)ena. See PHILIPPINA.

philŏ′soph‖er *n.* seeker after wisdom; person skilled in philosophy or in one of its branches; one who regulates his life by the light of philosophy; one who shows philosophic calmness in trying circumstances; ∼**ers′** (or ∼**er′s**) **stone,** supreme object of alchemy, substance supposed to change other metals into gold or silver; so ∼ASTER *n.* [ME, f. AF *philosofre* var. of OF *philosophe* f. L f. Gk *philosophos* (as PHILO-, SOPHIST)]

philŏsŏ′ph‖ic(al) *adjs.* of, or consonant with, philosophy; skilled in or devoted to philosophy (*philosophical* *society*); wise; calm under adverse but irremediable circumstances; temperate; hence ∼ICALLY *adv*. [f. LL *philosophicus* f. L *philosophia* (see PHILOSOPHY, -IC, -ICAL)]

philŏ'sophīze, -īse (-īz), *v*. **1.** *v.i.* play the philosopher; speculate, theorize; moralize. **2.** *v.t.* render philosophic. [app. f. F *philosopher* + -IZE]

philŏ'sophў *n.* seeking after wisdom or knowledge, esp. that which deals with ultimate reality, or with the most general causes and principles of things and ideas and human perception and knowledge of them, physical phenomena (*natural philosophy*), and ethics (*moral philosophy*); advanced learning in general (*doctor of philosophy*); philosophical system; system of principles for conduct of life; serenity, calmness. [ME f. OF *filosofie* f. L f. Gk PHILO(*sophia* wisdom f. *sophos* wise)]

-philous *suf.* = -PHILIC. [f. med. L f. Gk *-philos* + -OUS]

‖**phi'ltre** (-ter), ***phi'lter**, *n.* drink supposed to be able to excite sexual love in drinker. [f. F *philtre* f. L f. Gk *philtron* (*phileō* to love)]

-philў *suf.* = -PHILIA. [f. as -PHILIA + -Y¹]

phīm|ō'sis *n.* (*pl.* ∼oses *pr.* -ō'sēz). constriction and non-retractability of foreskin; hence ∼o'TIC *a.* [mod. L, f. Gk, = muzzling]

phiz *n.* (arch., colloq.) face; expression of face. [abbr. of *phiznomy* = PHYSIOGNOMY]

phlĕb|ī'tĭs *n.* inflammation of walls of vein; hence ∼ī'TIC *a.* [mod. L, f. Gk (as foll.) + -ITIS]

phlĕbŏ'tom|īze, -īse (-īz), *v.* **1.** *v.i.* practise phlebotomy. **2.** *v.t.* bleed (person, part of body). **3.** So ∼IST (3) *n.* [f. F *phlébotomiser* (*phlébotomie*, as foll.; see -IZE)]

phlĕbŏ'tomў *n.* (esp. Hist.) blood-letting as medical operation. [ME, f. OF *flebothomi* f. LL f. Gk *phlebotomia* (*phleps phlebos* vein; see -TOMY)]

phlĕgm (flĕm) *n.* **1.** thick viscous (semi-)fluid substance secreted by mucous membranes of respiratory passages, esp. when morbid or excessive and discharged by cough etc., whence ∼'Y² (flĕ'mĭ) *a.* **2.** (Hist.) this substance regarded as a HUMOUR¹. **3.** coolness, calmness, sluggishness, apathy, (supposed to result from predominance of phlegm in constitution). **4.** Hence **phlĕgmă'tĭc** *a.*, **phlĕgmă'tĭcally** *adv.* [ME & OF *fleume* f. LL f. Gk *phlegma -atos* inflammation (*phlegō* burn)]

phlŏ'ĕm *n.* (Bot.) soft tissue of stems (opp. XYLEM). [f. Gk *phloos* bark]

phlogi'stĭc (-j-, -g-) *a.* of phlogiston; (Med.) inflammatory. [f. as foll. or f. Gk *phlogistos* inflammable + -IC]

phlogi'ston (-j-, -g-) *n.* substance formerly supposed to exist in all combustible bodies, and to be released in combustion. [mod. L, f. Gk (*phlogizō* set on fire f. *phlox phlogos* flame; see -IZE)]

phlŏx *n.* plant of genus *Phlox*, with clusters of flowers of various colours. [L, f. Gk name of a plant (lit. flame)]

-phōbe *suf.* forming *ns.* & *adjs.* w. sense '(one who is) not fond of, (person) disliking or fearing' (*Gallophobe, Russophobe, xenophobe*). [F, f. L f. Gk *-phobos*, adj. suf. f. *phobos* fear]

phŏ'b|ĭa *n.* (morbid) fear or aversion; hence ∼IC *a.* & *n.* [foll. used as separate wd]

-phō'bĭa *suf.* forming abstract *ns.* corresp. to *adjs.* in -PHOBE (*Gallophobia, Russophobia, xenophobia*); hence **-phō'bĭc** *suf.* forming *adjs.* [L f. Gk]

phoe'bē (fē'-) *n.* Amer. flycatcher of genus *Sayornis*. [imit.; infl. by woman's Christian name *Phoebe*]

Phoe'bus (fē'b-) *n.* (poet.) the sun. [L, f. Gk *Phoibos* sun-god]

Phoeni'cian (fĭnĭ'shăn, -nē'-) *a.* & *n.* (inhabitant) of Phoenicia (ancient name for part of coast of Syria etc.) or its colonies. [ME, f. OF *phenicien* f. L f. *Phoenicia* f. L f. Gk *Phoinikē* Phoenicia (*Phoinix -ikos* Phoenician); see -AN]

phoe'nix (fē'-) *n.* **1.** (Myth.) bird, the only one of its kind, that after living five or six centuries in Arabian

desert burnt itself on funeral pile and rose from the ashes with renewed youth to live through another cycle. **2.** unique person or thing. [OE & OF *fenix* f. L f. Gk *phoinix* Phoenician, purple, phoenix]

phō'las *n.* = PIDDOCK. [mod. L, f. Gk *phōlas* that lurks in a hole (*phōleos*)]

phŏn *n.* (Phys.) unit of perceived loudness of sounds. [f. Gk *phōnē* sound]

phō'n|āte *v.i.* utter vocal sound; hence **phonA'TION** *n.*, ∼atory *a.* [f. Gk *phōnē* voice + -ATE³]

phonau'tograph (-ahf) *n.* apparatus for automatic visible recording of vibrations of sound. [f. F *phonautographe* (as prec., AUTO-, -GRAPH)]

phōne¹ *n.*, & *v.i.* & *t.* (colloq.) telephone; ∼-in *n.*, broadcast programme during which listeners or viewers telephone to the studio etc. and participate. [abbr.]

phōne² *n.* (Phonet.) simple vowel or consonant sound. [f. as foll.]

-phōne *suf.* forming *ns.* & *adjs.* meaning (1) instrument using sound (*dictaphone, xylophone*), (2) that uses a specified language (*anglophone*). [f. Gk *phōnē* voice, sound]

phō'nēme *n.* (Phonet.) unit of significant sound in a specified language; hence **phōnē'mic** *a.* **phōnē'mics** *n.* [f. F *phonème* f. Gk *phōnēma* sound, speech (*phōneō* speak)]

phonē'ndoscōpe *n.* apparatus for making small sounds (esp. in human body) distinctly audible. [f. as -PHONE + Gk *endon* within + -o- + -SCOPE]

phonē'tĭc *a.* representing vocal sounds (*phonetic* ALPHABET), esp. (of system of spelling) using always same symbol for same sound, whence ∼ISM (3), ∼IST (2), *ns.*, ∼IZE (3) *v.t.*; of vocal sounds; hence **phonē't-ICALLY** *adv.* [f. mod. L f. Gk *phōnētikos* (*phōneō* speak; see -ETIC)]

phonē'tics *n. pl.* (usu. treated as *sing.*) (study of) phonetic phenomena; hence **phōnēti'cian** *n.* [f. prec. + -ICS]

phō'nētist *n.* person skilled in phonetics; advocate of phonetic spelling. [f. PHONETICIST]

phō'n|ey, phō'n|ў, *a.* (∼ier, ∼iest) & *n.* (sl.) **1.** *a.* sham, counterfeit; fictitious; fraudulent; hence ∼iLY² *adv.*, ∼iNESS *n.* **2.** *n.* phoney person or thing. [20th c.; orig. unkn.]

phō'nĭc *a.* of sound, acoustic; of vocal sounds. [f. Gk *phōnē* voice + -IC]

phō'no- *comb. form.* sound, as: ∼lite, clinkstone; ∼meter (-ŏ'm-), instrument recording number or force of sound-waves; ∼scope, (1) apparatus for testing musical strings, (2) instrument for representing sound-vibrations in visible form. [f. Gk *phōnē* voice, sound + -o-]

phō'nogrăm *n.* symbol representing spoken sound. [f. PHONO- + -GRAM]

phō'nograph (-ahf) *n.*, & *v.t.* **1.** ‖earlier form of gramophone using cylinders and able to record as well as reproduce sound; *gramophone. **2.** *v.t.* record or reproduce by phonograph. [f. as PHONO- + -GRAPH]

phono'graphў *n.* writing in (esp. shorthand) symbols corresponding to sounds of speech; recording of sounds by phonograph; hence **phōnogră'phic** *a.* [f. as PHONO- + -GRAPHY]

phono'log|ў *n.* study of sounds in a language; hence **phōnolŏ'gical**, ∼IST (3) *n.* [f. PHONO- + -LOGY]

phō'nŏn *n.* (Phys.) quantum of sound or elastic vibrations. [f. Gk *phōnē* sound + -ON]

phō'nў. See PHONEY.

phō'ŏ'ey *int.* expr. disgust. [imit.]

-phōre *suf.* forming *ns.* w. sense 'bearer' (*ctenophore, semaphore*); so **-phorous** *adj. suf.* [f. mod. L f. Gk *-phoros -phoron* bearing, bearer (*pherō* bear)]

phŏr'mium *n.* liliaceous plant of genus *Phormium* whose fibre is used commercially; New Zealand flax. [mod. L, f. Gk *phormion* a species of plant]

phŏ'sgēne *n.* colourless poisonous gas, carbon

oxychloride. [f. Gk *phōs* light + -GEN (1), w. ref. to its orig. production by action of sunlight on chlorine and carbon monoxide]

phŏ'sphāte *n.* salt or ester of phosphoric acid, esp. used as fertilizer; effervescent drink containing small amount of phosphate; hence **phŏsphā'tIC** *a.* [F (*phosphore* PHOSPHORUS; see -ATE¹ (3))]

phŏ'sphēne *n.* appearance of rings of light produced by pressure on eyeball, due to irritation of retina. [irreg. f. Gk *phōs* light + *phainō* show]

phŏ'sphīde *n.* (Chem.) binary compound of phosphorus with other element or radical. [f. PHOSPHO- + -IDE]

phŏ'sphine (-ēn) *n.* (Chem.) colourless ill-smelling gas, phosphorus trihydride; hence **phŏsphi'nIC** *a.* [f. PHOSPHO- + -INE⁵, after *amine*]

phŏ'sphīte *n.* (Chem.) salt or ester of phosphorous acid. [F (as PHOSPHO-, -ITE¹)]

phŏspho- *comb. form.* phosphorus. [abbr.]

phŏ'sphor¹ *n.* synthetic fluorescent or phosphorescent substance. [G, f. L PHOSPHORUS]

phŏ'sphor² *n.* = PHOSPHORUS; ∼ **bronze,** tough hard bronze alloy containing a small proportion of phosphorus, used (esp.) for bearings. [abbr.]

phŏ'sphorāte *v.t.* combine or impregnate with phosphorus. [f. PHOSPHORUS + -ATE³]

phŏsphor|ĕ'scence *n.* radiation similar to fluorescence but detectable after excitation ceases; emission of light without combustion or perceptible heat; so ∼E'SCE *v.i.*, ∼E'SCENT *a.* [f. PHOSPHORUS + -ESCENCE]

phŏspho'ric. See PHOSPHORUS.

phŏ'sphorīte *n.* non-crystalline form of apatite. [f. PHOSPHORUS + -ITE¹]

phŏ'sphor|us *n.* non-metallic element existing in allotropic forms, incl. a yellowish waxlike substance undergoing slow combustion at ordinary temperatures and hence appearing luminous in the dark; hence or cogn. **phŏsphŏ'rIC,** ∼OUS, *adjs.,* ∼ISM (5) *n.* [L, = morning star, f. Gk *phōsphoros* (*phōs* light, -*phoros* -bringing)]

phŏ'ssỹ *a.* ∼ jaw, (colloq.) gangrene of jawbone caused by phosphorus poisoning. [abbr.; see -Y³]

phŏt *n.* (Phys.) unit of illumination, one lumen per square centimetre. [f. Gk *phōs phōtos* light]

phŏ'tic *a.* of light; (of ocean layers) reached by sunlight. [f. as prec. + -IC]

phŏ'tism *n.* hallucinatory sensation or vision of light. [f. Gk *phōtismos* (*phōtizō* shine f. *phōs phōtos* light; see -ISM)]

phŏ'tō *n.* (*pl.* ∼s), & *v.t.* = PHOTOGRAPH; ∼ **finish,** close finish of race (photographed to enable judge to decide winner etc.), or of any contest. [abbr.]

phŏ'tō- (-*o*, -ō) *comb. form.* **1.** light, as: ∼**cell,** photoelectric cell; ∼**che'mistry,** study of chemical effects of light; ∼*che'mical* *a.*; ∼**conducti'vity,** conductivity due to action of light; ∼**di'ode,** semiconductor diode responding electrically to illumination; ∼**ele'ctric,** marked by or utilizing emission of electrons from substances exposed to light (∼*electric cell,* device using this effect to generate current; ∼*electri'city* n.); ∼**meter** (-ō'm-), instrument for measuring light; ∼*me'tric* *a.*, ∼*metry* (-ō'm-) n.; ∼**phobia,** (Path.) dread of light; ∼**se'nsitive,** reacting chemically etc. to light; ∼**sphere,** luminous envelope of sun or star from which its light and heat radiate; ∼*sphe'ric* a.; ∼**sy'nthesis,** process in which energy of sunlight is used by green plants to build up complex substances from carbon dioxide and water; ∼*synthe'tic* a.; ∼**tropism** (-ō'tr-), tendency of plant etc. to bend or turn towards or away from source of light; ∼*tro'pic* a.; ∼**volta'ic,** relating to production of electric current at junction of two substances exposed to light. **2.** photography, as: ∼**composi'tion,** filmsetting; ∼**copier,** machine for photocopying documents; ∼**copy** *n.,* & *v.t.,* (make) photograph or xerograph of document for use as copy of that document; ∼**fit,** Identikit picture made from photographs;

∼**ge'nic** (-jĕ'-), (1) producing or emitting light, (2) apt to be a good subject for photographs; ∼**gram,** photograph; ∼**gra'mmetry,** use of photography for surveying; ∼**li'tho** (colloq.), ∼**litho'graphy,** lithography with plates made photographically; ∼**mi'crograph,** photograph of object enlarged by microscope; ∼*micro'graphy* n.; ∼**-o'ffset,** offset printing with plates made photographically; ∼**setting,** filmsetting; ∼**stat** (||P; *n.,* & *v.t.*) = *photocopy.* [f. Gk *phōs phōtos* light, or f. as prec.]

phŏ'tograph (-ahf) *n.,* & *v.t.* **1.** *n.* picture taken by means of chemical action of light or other radiation on sensitive film. **2.** *v.t.* take photograph of (person etc., or abs.). **3.** Hence **photo'graphER¹, photŏ'graphY¹,** *ns.,* **phŏtoGRA'PHIC** *a.* [f. PHOTO- + -GRAPH]

phŏtogravŭr'e *n.* picture produced from photographic negative transferred to metal plate and etched in; this process. [F (as PHOTO-, *gravure* engraving)]

phŏ'tŏn *n.* quantum of electromagnetic radiation energy, proportional to frequency of radiation. [f. Gk *phōs phōtos* light, after *electron*; see -ON]

phrā'sal (-z-) *a.* (Gram.) consisting of a phrase; ∼ **verb,** idiomatic phrase of verb and adverb (and preposition) (*break down, look forward to*). [f. foll. + -AL]

phrāse (-z) *n.,* & *v.t.* **1.** *n.* mode of expression, diction, (*felicity of phrase; in Eliot's phrase, 'not with a bang but a whimper'*); an idiomatic expression; small group of words usu. without predicate, esp. preposition with the word(s) it governs, equivalent to adjective, adverb, or noun (e.g. the house on the hill, I refuse to do it); short pithy expression; (Mus.) short and more or less distinct passage of about four bars ending in cadence, forming part of longer passage or of whole piece; ∼**book** (listing frequent expressions with equivalents in foreign language, for use by tourists etc.). **2.** *v.t.* express in words; divide (music) into phrases, esp. in performance, whence **phrā'sING¹** (-z-) *n.* [f. earlier *phrasis,* f. L f. Gk (*phrazō* declare, tell)]

phrā'sēogrăm (-z-) *n.* written symbol representing a phrase, esp. in shorthand. [f. as prec. + -o- + -GRAM]

phrā'sĕ|ŏlogy (-z-) *n.* choice or arrangement of words; mode of expression; hence ∼**olŏ'gICAL** *a.* [f. mod. L *phraseologia* f. Gk *phraseōn* gen. pl. of *phrasis* PHRASE; see -LOGY]

phrā'trỹ *n.* unit of kinship in ancient Greece; tribal division among primitive peoples. [f. Gk *phratria* (*phratēr* clansman, cogn. w. BROTHER)]

phrĕă'tic *a.* (Geol., of water) situated underground but reachable by wells. [f. Gk *phrear phreatos* well + -IC]

phrĕnĕ't|ic *a.* frantic; fanatic; hence ∼ICALLY *adv.* [ME, var. of FRENETIC]

phrĕ'nic *a.* (Anat.) of the diaphragm. [f. F *phrénique* f. Gk *phrēn phrenos* diaphragm, mind; see -IC]

phrĕnŏ'log|ỹ *n.* study of external conformation of cranium as supposed index to development and position of organs belonging to the various mental faculties; hence **phrĕnolŏ'gICAL** *a.,* ∼IST (3) *n.* [f. as prec. + -o- + -LOGY]

Phrỹ'gian (-z-) *n.* **1.** *a.* of Phrygia, ancient country in Asia Minor, or its people or language; ∼ bonnet or **cap,** ancient conical cap with top bent forwards, now identified with cap of liberty; ∼ **mode,** (Mus.) (1) ancient Greek MODE, reputedly warlike in character, (2) third of church modes (with E as final and C as dominant). **2.** *n.* Phrygian person or language. [f. L *Phrygianus* (*Phrygia*; see -AN)]

phthă'l|ic *a.* (Chem.) derived from naphthalene; ∼**ic acid,** one of three isomeric dicarboxylic acids derived from benzene; hence ∼ATE¹ (3) *n.* [abbr. of NAPHTHALIC]

phthĭ'sĭc(al) (thĭ'z-, fthĭ'-, tĭ'-) *a.* of or having phthisis. [f. *phthisic* phthisis f. OF *tisike* f. Rom. **(ph)thisica* f. L *phthisicus* a. (as foll.); see -IC, -ICAL]

phthĭ'sĭs (thĭ'-, fthĭ'-, tĭ'-) *n.* progressive wasting disease, now esp. pulmonary tuberculosis. [L f. Gk (*phthinō* to decay)]

phŭt *n. & adv.* **1.** *n.* dull sound of impact, or of collapse of inflated object, etc. **2.** *adv.* **go** ~, (colloq.) collapse (lit. or fig.). [f. Hindi *phạṭnā* to burst]

phỹlă'cterỹ *n.* small leather box containing Hebrew texts on vellum, worn by Jews at morning weekday prayer to remind them to keep the law (**make broad the** ~, make a display of righteousness); (usu. ostentatious) religious observance; amulet, charm; fringe, border. [ME, f. OF **filaterie* f. LL f. Gk *phulaktērion* amulet (*phulassō* guard)]

phỹlĕ'tĭc *a.* (Biol.) of a phylum; racial. [f. Gk *phuletikos* (*phuletēs* tribesman f. *phulē* tribe; see -IC)]

phỹ'llo- *comb. form.* leaf, as: ~**phagous** (-ŏ'f-), feeding on leaves; ~**pod** *a.* & *n.*, leaf-footed (crustacean); ~**stome**, leaf-nosed bat; ~**taxis**, ~**taxy**, arrangement of leaves on axis or stem. [f. Gk *phullo-* (*phullon* leaf)]

phỹ'llōde *n.* flattened petiole resembling a leaf. [f. mod. L *phyllodium* f. Gk *phullōdēs* leaflike (as prec.)]

phỹlloxēr'a *n.* plant-louse of genus *Phylloxera*, esp. of species attacking vines. [mod. L, f. Gk *phullon* leaf + *xēros* dry]

phỹlo- *comb. form.* (Biol.) race, tribe, as: ~**ge'nesis**, ~**geny** (-ŏ'j-), (history of) evolution of animal or plant type; ~**gene'tic**, ~**ge'nic**, adjs. [f. Gk *phulon*, *phulē*]

phỹ'l|um *n.* (*pl.* ~**a**). (Biol.) major division of animal or plant kingdom, containing species having same general form. [mod. L, f. Gk *phulon* race]

phỹ'sĭc (-z-) *n.*, & *v.t.* (**-ck-**). **1.** *n.* art of healing; medical profession; (arch.) medicine (*a dose of physic*); ~ **garden** (for cultivation of medicinal plants). **2.** *v.t.* dose with physic (lit. or fig.). [ME, f. OF *fisique* medicine f. L f. Gk *phusikē* (*epistēmē* knowledge) of nature (*phusis*; see -IC)]

phỹ'sĭcal (-z-) *a.* **1.** of matter, material, (*physical force*, opp. to *moral*); of, or according to the laws of, nature (*physical explanations of miracles*; *a physical impossibility*); belonging to physics; bodily (*physical examination*, *exercise, strength, love, beauty, education*). **2.** ~ **chemistry** (applying physics to study chemical behaviour); ~ **geography** (dealing with natural features); ~ **jerks**, (colloq.) physical exercises; ~ **science,** study of inanimate natural objects; ~ **training,** exercise to promote health and strength. **3.** Hence ~LY² *adv.* [ME, f. med. L *physicalis* f. L *physica* (as prec.; see -AL)]

physí'cian (-zǐ'shan) *n.* one who practises the healing art including medicine and surgery; one legally qualified in both medicine and surgery; (esp.) specialist in medical diagnosis and treatment; (fig.) healer. [ME f. OF *fisicien* (as PHYSIC; see -ICIAN)]

phỹ'sĭcist (-ĭ'z-) *n.* person skilled in physics. [f. PHYSICS + -IST]

phỹ'sĭckỹ (-z-) *a.* suggestive of physic. [f. PHYSIC + -Y²]

phỹ'sĭcō- (-z-) *comb. form.* physical, of physics (and), as: ~**-chemical**, pertaining to physics and chemistry or to physical chemistry. [f. Gk *phusikos* (see PHYSIC) + -O-]

phỹ'sĭcs (-z-) *n.* science dealing with properties and interactions of matter and energy. [f. pl. of *physic* a. (as in n.) physical, after L *physica*, Gk *phusika* natural things]

phỹsĭŏ'cracỹ (-z-) *n.* government according to natural order esp. as advocated by 18th-c. economists; so **phỹ'sĭo**CRAT (-z-) *n.* [f. F *physiocratie* f. Gk *phusio-* (*phusis* nature; see -O-, -CRACY)]

phỹsĭŏ'gnom|ỹ (-zĭŏ'n-) *n.* art of judging character from features of face or form of body, whence ~IST (3) *n.*; cast of features, type of face; external features of country etc.; characteristic (moral or other) aspect; hence **phỹsĭognŏ'm**IC(AL) (-zĭŏn-) *adjs.* [ME *fisnomie* etc. f. OF *phisonomie* f. med. L *phisonomia* f. Gk *phusiognōmonia* judging of a man's nature (by his features) (*phusis* nature, *gnōmōn* judge f. **gnō-* know)]

phỹsĭŏ'graph|ỹ (-z-) *n.* description of nature, of natural phenomena, or of a class of objects; physical geography; hence ~ER¹ *n.*, **phỹsĭŏgrä'ph**IC(AL) (-z-) *adjs.* [f. F *physiographie* (as foll; see -GRAPHY)]

phỹsĭŏlŏ'gĭc|(al) (-z-) *a.* pertaining to physiology; ~**al salt solution** (with concentration about equal to that of body fluids); hence ~ALLY *adv.* [f. foll. + -IC, -ICAL]

phỹsĭŏ'log|ỹ (-z-) *n.* science of functions and phenomena of living organisms and their parts; these functions; hence ~IST (3) *n.* [f. F *physiologie* or f. L f. Gk *phusiologia* (*phusis* nature; see -LOGY)]

phỹ'sĭŏ *n.* (*pl.* ~**s**). (colloq.) physiotherapist. [abbr.]

phỹsĭothĕ'rap|ỹ (-zĭo-, -ō-) *n.* treatment of disease or injury or deformity by massage, heat, exercises, etc., not by drugs; hence ~IST (3) *n.* [f. Gk *phusio-* (as PHYSIOLOGY) + THERAPY]

phỹsĭ'que (-zē'k-) *n.* bodily structure, organization, and development. [F, *n. f. a.* (as PHYSIC)]

-phỹte *suf.* forming *ns.* denoting a vegetable or plantlike organism (*saprophyte*, *zoophyte*); hence **-phỹ'tĭc** *adj. suf.* [f. Gk *phuton* plant (*phuō* come into being)]

phỹto- *comb. form.* plant, as: ~**ge'nesis**, ~**geny** (-ŏ'j-), generation or evolution of plants; ~**graphy** (-ŏ'g-), descriptive botany; ~**mer**, structural unit in plant; ~**patho'logy**, pathology of plants; ~**phagous** (-ŏ'f-), feeding on plants; ~**plan'kton**, plankton consisting of plants; ~**tomy** (-ŏ't-), dissection of plants; ~**to'xic**, poisonous to plants; ~**zo'on**, zoophyte. [f. as prec. + -O-]

pī¹ *n.* sixteenth Greek letter (Π, π) = p; (Math., *n.*) symbol of ratio of circumference (Gk *periphereia*) of circle to diameter (approx. 3.14159); **pi-meson,** = PION. [Gk]

||**pī²** *a.* (school etc. sl.) pious; **pi jaw,** sermonizing, long dull moral lecture. [abbr.]

*pī³. See PIE³.

piä'cŭlar *a.* expiatory; needing expiation. [f. L *piacularis* (*piaculum* expiation f. *piare* appease; see -AR¹)]

piä'ffe *v.i.* (Of horse etc.) move as in trot, but slower. [f. F *piaffer* to strut]

piä'ffer *n.* movement of piaffing. [f. as prec.]

pīa mā'ter *n.* (Anat.) delicate inner membrane enveloping brain and spinal cord. [med. L, = tender mother, transl. of Arab. *al-'umm al-rakīka*; cf. DURA MATER]

pi'anism (pē'a-) *n.* art or technique of piano-playing. [f. PIANO² + -ISM]

piani'ssim|ō *a.*, *adv.*, & *n.* (*pl.* ~**os**, or ~**i** *pr.* -ē). (Mus.) (passage to be) performed very softly. [It., superl. of PIANO¹]

pi'anist (pē'a-) *n.* player of piano; hence **pianĭ'st**IC *a.* [f. F *pianiste* (as PIANO²; see -IST)]

pia'n|ō¹ (-ah'-) *a.*, *adv.*, & *n.* (*pl.* ~**os**, or ~**i** *pr.* -ē). (Mus.) (passage to be) performed softly; (fig.) subdued(ly). [It., f. L *planus* flat, (of sound) soft]

piä'nō² *n.* (*pl.* ~**s**). musical instrument with metal strings struck by hammers worked by levers from a keyboard (vibration being stopped by dampers when keys are released), and with PEDAL¹s regulating character of tone; GRAND, UPRIGHT, *piano*; PLAYER*-piano*; ~**-accordion**, accordion with melody played on small piano-like keyboard; ~ **organ**, mechanical piano constructed like barrel-organ; ~**-player**, (1) pianist, (2) contrivance for playing piano automatically; ~**-stool** (to provide seat for player and hold esp. sheet music). [It., abbr. of foll.]

piänofŏr'tè *n.* (Formal or arch. name for) PIANO². [It., earlier *piano e forte* soft and loud, expressing its gradation of tone]

Piano'la (pēa-) *n.* (**P**) make of automatic piano-player; (*p*~) easy task, esp. bridge hand needing no skill. [app. dim. of PIANO²]

piano nobile (pyahnō nō'bīlă) *n.* (Archit.) main storey of large house. [It., = noble floor]

piassa'va (pēasah'va) *n.* stout fibre from leaf-stalks of various Amer. and Afr. palm-trees. [Port., f. Tupi *piaçába*]

||**piä'stre** (-ter), ***piä'ster**, *n.* small coin of Middle Eastern countries. [f. F *piastre* f. It. *piastra* (*d'argento*) plate (of silver), f. as PLASTER[1]]

piä'zza (-tsa) *n.* public square or market-place esp. in Italian town; *veranda of house. [It., f. as PLACE[1]]

pi'broch (pē'brŏk, -χ) *n.* series of variations on a theme for bagpipe, esp. martial or funerary. [f. Gael. *piobaireachd* art of piping (*piobair* piper f. *piob* f. E PIPE[1])]

pi'ca[1] *n.* unit of type-size (⅙ inch); size of letters in typewriting (10 per inch). [f. AL *pica* 15th-c. book of rules about church feasts, perh. f. as PIE[1]]

pi'ca[2] *n.* (Path.) eating of substances other than normal food. [mod. or med. L, = magpie]

pi'cadōr *n.* mounted man with lance in bullfight. [Sp. (*picar* prick)]

picarě'sque (-k) *a.* (Of a style of fiction) dealing with adventures of rogues. [F, f. Sp. *picaresco* (*pícaro* rogue; see -ESQUE)]

picaröo'n *n.* rogue; thief; pirate; pirate ship. [f. Sp. *picarón* (as prec.; see -OON)]

***picayu'ne** (-yōō'n) *n.* & *a.* **1.** *n.* small coin, esp. 5-cent piece; (colloq.) insignificant person or thing. **2.** *a.* (colloq.) mean, contemptible; trifling, petty. [f. F *picaillon* Piedmontese coin, cash, f. Prov. *picaioun*, of unkn. orig.]

piccali'lli *n.* pickle of chopped vegetables, mustard, and hot spices. [18th c., perh. f. PICKLE +CHILLI]

||**pi'ccaninny**, ***pi'ck-**, *n.* & *a.* **1.** *n.* small Black or Australian Aboriginal child. **2.** *a.* (arch.) very small; baby. [W. Ind. Negro, f. Sp. *pequeño* or Port. *pequeno* little]

pi'ccolŏ *n.* (*pl.* ~s). small flute, sounding an octave higher than the ordinary; its player. [It., = small (flute)]

pichiciä'gō *n.* (*pl.* ~s). small S. Amer. burrowing animal allied to armadillos. [f. Sp. *pichiciego* perh. f. Guarani *pichey* armadillo + Sp. *ciego* blind f. L *caecus*]

pick[1] *n.* **1.** tool consisting of iron bar usu. curved with point at one end and point or chisel-edge at other, with wooden handle passing through middle perpendicularly, used for breaking up hard ground, masonry, etc., and in quarries etc. **2.** instrument for picking; plectrum. [ME, app. var. of PIKE[1]]

pick[2] *v.* **1.** *v.t.* break surface of (ground etc.) with or as with pick; make (HOLE[1]s etc.) thus. **2.** probe (teeth with toothpick, nostril with finger, etc.) to remove extraneous or unwanted matter; *pluck strings of (banjo etc.) **3.** clear (BONE[1], carcass) of adherent flesh; detach (flower, fruit, etc.) from place where it grew. **4.** (Of bird) take up (grains etc.) in bill; (of person) eat (food, or meal, or abs.) in small bits. **5.** select carefully (*pick* one's *words*, *way*, *steps*; *picked men*). **6.** pull apart (*pick oakum*); ~ **to pieces,** (fig.) criticize hostilely. **7.** *v.t.* & *i.* ~ **and choose,** select carefully or fastidiously; ~ person's **brains,** extract his ideas or information for one's own use; ~ **a lock,** open it (esp. with intent to rob) with pointed instrument, skeleton key, etc.; ~ person's **pocket,** steal its contents from him while he is wearing the garment etc.; *pick a* QUARREL[2]; ~ **and steal,** pilfer. **8.** ~ **at,** (1) = *pick on* (1), (2) eat without interest; ~ **off,** pluck off, shoot (persons etc.) without haste one by one; ~ **on,** (1) nag at, find fault with, (2) select; ~ **out,** take from among larger number, distinguish from surrounding objects, relieve (ground colour *in* or *with* another), make out (meaning of passage etc.), play (tune) by ear on piano etc.; ~ **over,** select best from; ~ **up,** lay hold of and take up from ground etc., accept responsibility for paying (bill etc.), raise (feet) clear of ground, (Golf, ellipt.) pick up one's ball esp. when conceding hole, raise one*self* after a fall etc., gain, acquire (livelihood, germ, knowledge of language, profit, tricks, information), succeed in seeing with

telescope or searchlight, hearing with radio, etc., take (person, or thing overtaken) along with one, make acquaintance of (person) casually, (of police etc.) find and take into custody, regain (lost path etc., flesh, spirit), recover health, (of weather, share-prices, etc.) improve, make acquaintance *with*, (of motor engine) recover speed or accelerate quickly etc., (in games) select sides by alternate choosing; ~-**up** *n.,* picking up, person met casually, small open motor truck, part of record-player carrying stylus, detector of vibrations etc. **9.** ~'**lock,** person who picks locks, instrument used for this; ~-**me-up,** tonic (lit. or fig.) to relieve depression; ~'**pocket,** one who steals from pockets (see sense 7); ||~'**thank,** (arch.) sycophant. **10.** Hence ~ABLE *a.* [ME, earlier *pike*, of unkn. orig.]

pick[3] *n.* picking; selection (**take your** ~, choose whichever you prefer); right to select (*he had first pick of their father's collection*); the best part *of* (**the** ~ **of the bunch,** the best of the lot). [f. prec.]

pi'ck-a-băck, pi'ggyback (-g-), *adv.* & *n.* **1.** *adv.* (Of way person or thing is carried) on shoulders or back like a bundle; on the back or top of a larger object. **2.** *n.* ride thus given. [16th c.; orig. unkn.]

***pi'ckaninny.** See PICCANINNY.

pi'ckăxe, *pi'ckăx, *n.* & *v.* **1.** *n.* − PICK[1] 1. **2.** *v.t.* break (ground etc.) with pickaxe. **3.** *v.i.* work with pickaxe. [ME *pikois* f. OF *picois*, rel. to PIKE[1]; assim. to AXE]

pi'ckelhaube (-howbe) *n.* (Hist.) German soldier's spiked helmet. [G]

pi'cker *n.* in vbl senses; one who gathers or collects (*hop-picker, rag-picker*). [f. PICK[2] +-ER[1]]

pi'ckerel *n.* (*pl.* ~ or ~s). young pike. [ME, dim. of PIKE[3]; see -REL]

pi'ckět *n.* & *v.* **1.** *n.* pointed stake or peg driven into ground to form palisade, tether horse, etc.; (Hist.) (stake with pointed top on which person stood on one foot as) form of military punishment. **2.** (Mil.) small body of troops sent out to watch for enemy etc., or held ready in quarters, party of sentries, outpost; camp-guard doing police duty in garrison town etc. **3.** person(s) stationed by trade union etc. to dissuade workers from working during strike etc.; such action. **4.** *v.t.* secure (place) with stakes; tether (animal); station as picket; beset (factory, workers) with pickets. **5.** *v.i.* act as picket. [f. F *piquet* pointed stake (*piquer* prick); f. *pic* PICK[1]; see -ET[1]]

pi'cking *n.* In vbl senses; (in *pl.*) gleanings, remaining scraps; (in *pl.*) perquisites, pilferings. [ME, f. PICK[2] +-ING[1]]

pi'ckle *n.,* & *v.t.* **1.** *n.* brine, vinegar, or similar liquor in which meat, fish, vegetables, etc., are preserved (ROD *in pickle*); food, esp. (in *pl.*) vegetables, preserved in pickle; acid solution for cleaning metal etc.; (colloq.) plight (*sad, sorry,* iron. *nice,* etc., pickle); (colloq.) mischievous child. **2.** *v.t.* preserve in pickle; treat with pickle; (in *p.p.,* sl.) drunk. [ME *pekille, pykyl,* f. MDu., MLG *pekel* of unkn. orig.]

Pickwi'ckian *a.* (joc.) (Of words or their sense) not in accordance with their usual meaning, conveniently understood so as to avoid offence etc. [f. *Pickwick* (character in Dickens's 'Pickwick Papers') +-IAN]

***pi'cky** *a.* (colloq.) excessively fastidious. [f. PICK[2] +-Y[2]]

pi'cnic *n.,* & *v.i.* (-ck-). **1.** *n.* pleasure outing including meal out of doors; (colloq.) something especially agreeable or easily accomplished (**no** ~, not an easy job). **2.** *v.i.* take part in picnic. **3.** Hence ~KER[1] *n.,* ~**ky**[2] *a.* (colloq.). [f. F *pique-nique,* of unkn. orig.]

pi'cō- (pī'-, pē'-) *pref.* denoting factor of 10^{-12} (*picometre*). [f. Sp. *pico* beak, peak, little bit]

pi'cot (pē'kō) *n.* small loop of twisted thread in edging to lace etc. [F, dim. of *pic* peak, point]

picotee' *n.* carnation of which flowers have light ground with darker edging to petals. [f. F *picoté -ée* p.p. of *picoter* prick (as prec.)]

pi'cquět (pī'kĭt). Var. of PICKET 2.

pi'cr|ic *a.* ∼ **acid,** yellow very bitter substance used in dyeing and surgery, and in explosives; hence ∼ATE[1] (3) *n.* [f. Gk *pikros* bitter + -IC]

Pict *n.* one of an ancient people in N. Britain; hence ∼'ISH[1] *a.* [ME, f. LL *Picti* perh. f. *pingere pict-* paint, tattoo]

pi'ctograph (-ahf), **pi'ctogrăm,** *ns.* pictorial symbol; primitive record consisting of these; pictorial representation of statistics; hence **pictográ'phic** *a.,* **pictó'graph**Y[1] *n.* [f. L *pingere pict-* paint + -O- + -GRAPH, -GRAM]

pictōr'ial *a.* & *n.* **1.** *a.* of, or expressed in, picture(s); illustrated; picturesque; hence ∼LY[2] *adv.* **2.** *n.* journal, postage stamp, etc., with picture(s) as main feature. [f. LL *pictorius* f. L *pictor* painter (as foll.) + -AL]

pi'cture *n.,* & *v.t.* **1.** *n.* painting or drawing of person(s) or object(s) real or imagined, esp. as work of art; portrait; beautiful object (*her hat is a picture*). **2.** scene, total visual or mental impression produced, (fig.) conjuncture or affair (**in the** ∼, fully informed or noticed; **out of the** ∼, irrelevant); *she looks* **the very picture** (a perfect example) *of health, of misery*. **3.** = FILM 3; visible presentation of this; image on television screen; ||(in *pl.*) cinema (performance). **4.** ∼-**book** (consisting chiefly or wholly of pictures); ∼-**card,** court-card; ∼-**gallery,** (hall etc. containing) collection of pictures; ∼-**goer,** one who frequents the cinema; ∼ **hat,** lady's wide-brimmed and highly decorated hat as in pictures by Reynolds and Gainsborough; *picture*-MOULDING; ||∼-**palace,** cinema; ∼ **postcard** (with picture on one side); ||∼-**theatre,** (arch.) cinema; ∼ **window,** large window facing attractive view; ∼-**writing,** mode of recording events etc. by pictures as in early hieroglyphs etc. **5.** *v.t.* represent in picture; describe graphically; imagine (*to oneself*). [ME, f. L *pictura* (*pingere pict-* paint; see -URE)]

picturĕ'sque (-kcherĕ'sk) *a.* like, or fit to be the subject of, a striking picture; (of language etc.) strikingly graphic, vivid; hence ∼LY[2] *adv.,* ∼NESS *n.* [f. F *pittoresque* f. It. *pittoresco* (*pittore* painter f. L as PICTORIAL; see -ESQUE); assim. to prec.]

pi'cturize, -ise, (pi'kcheriz) *v.t.* make into picture, esp. into cinema film. [f. PICTURE + -IZE]

pi'cul *n.* Chinese weight (133⅓ lb.). [f. Malay *pikul* man's load]

pi'ddl|e *v.i.,* & *n.* **1.** *v.i.* work or act in trifling way; hence ∼ING[2] *a.,* (colloq.) trifling, trivial. **2.** (colloq. or childish). urinate. **3.** *n.* (colloq. or childish). urination; urine. [in sense 1 perh. f. PEDDLE, in sense 2 prob. f. PISS + PUDDLE[1]]

pi'ddock *n.* bivalve mollusc of genus *Pholas* used for bait. [18th c.; orig. unkn.]

pi'dgin *a.* & *n.* **1.** *a.* ∼ **English,** jargon chiefly of English words used orig. between Chinese and Europeans. **2.** *n.* simplified English or other language used for communication between persons of different nationality etc.; = PIGEON[2]. [corrupt. of *business*]

pī'-dŏg. See PYE-DOG.

pie[1] *n.* magpie; other bird (||RAIN[1]-*pie,* SEA *pie*); pied animal. [ME f. OF, f. L *pica*]

pie[2] *n.* **1.** dish of meat, fish, fruit, etc., enclosed in or covered with paste etc. and baked (*easy, nice,* etc., as ∼, very easy etc.; **have a finger in the** ∼, be (esp. officiously) concerned in the matter; ∼ **in the sky,** delusive prospect of future happiness after present suffering); similar object (MUD *pie*). **2.** ∼ **chart** (representing relative quantities by areas of sectors of circle); ∼'**crust,** baked paste of pie; (*promises are*) *like* ∼*crust,* made to be broken; ∼*crust table* (with ornamental edge like piecrust); ∼-**eyed,** (sl.) drunk; ∼'**man,** vendor of pies. [ME, perh. = prec., f. miscellaneous contents compared to objects collected by magpie]

pie[3], ***pī**[3], *n.,* & *v.t.* **1.** *n.* confused mass of printers' type; (fig.) chaos. **2.** *v.t.* mix (type). [perh. transl. F PÂTÉ = prec.]

pie'bald (pī'bawld) *a.* & *n.* **1.** *a.* (Usu. of animal, esp. horse) of two colours irregularly arranged, esp. black and white; (fig.) motley, mongrel. **2.** *n.* piebald animal. [f. PIE[1] + BALD]

piece[1] *n.* **1.** one of the distinct portions into which thing is composed or into which it is divided or broken (**in one** ∼, unbroken, (fig.) unharmed; **in** ∼**s,** broken; **break to** ∼**s,** break into fragments; **go to** ∼**s,** (fig.) collapse; PICK[2], PULL[1], TAKE[1], *to pieces*); one of the things of which a set is composed (*piece of furniture; 21- -piece tea-set; five-piece band*). **2.** enclosed portion *of* (land); ∼ **of water,** small lake etc. **3.** detached portion (*of* a substance); *a piece of* one's MIND[1]. **4.** definite quantity (e.g. of wallpaper = 12 yds.) in which thing is made up for sale etc. **5.** ∼ **of work,** thing made by working (lit. or fig.; NASTY *piece of work*). **6.** example, specimen, (*a piece of impudence; fine piece of painting, cricket*); item (*piece of news*); (derog.) person, esp. woman; *piece of* GOODS. **7.** firearm; artillery weapon. **8.** man (esp. other than pawn) at chess; man at draughts etc. **9.** coin (*penny, ten-cent, piece*); ∼ **of eight** (i.e. REAL[1]s), Spanish dollar. **10.** picture; literary or musical composition, usu. short; drama. **11.** *paid* **by the** ∼ (according to amount done); **of a** ∼, uniform, consistent, in keeping (*with*); **say** one's ∼, (fig.) give one's opinion, make prepared statement. **12.** ∼-**goods,** textile fabrics (esp. Lancashire cotton goods) woven in standard lengths; ∼-**rates,** ∼-**work,** (paid by the piece). [ME f. AF *pece,* OF *piece* f. Rom. **pettia,* prob. of Gaulish orig.; cf. PEAT[1]]

piece[2] *v.t.* put together, form into a whole; join threads in spinning, whence **pie'cer**[1] *n.;* eke *out;* make *out* (story, theory, chain of evidence) by combination of parts; join *together;* patch *up.* [ME, f. prec.]

pièce de résistance (pēās de rāzē'stahñs) *n.* (*pl.* **pièces** *pr.* same). most substantial dish at meal; most important or remarkable item. [F]

pie'cemeal (-sm-) *adv.* & *a.* **1.** *adv.* piece by piece, part at a time. **2.** *a.* done etc. piecemeal. [ME, f. PIECE[1] + -*meal* f. OE *mǣlum* (instr. dat. pl. of *mǣl* MEAL[2])]

pīed (pīd) *a.* particoloured: **Pied Piper,** delusive enticer [f. Browning's poem]. [ME, f. PIE[1] + -ED[2], orig. of friars]

pied-à-terre (pyādahtār') *n.* (*pl.* **pieds-à-terre** *pr.* same). place kept available as temporary quarters when needed. [F, lit. 'foot to earth']

pie'dmŏnt *n.* region at foot of mountains. [f. P∼ in Italy, region at foot of Alps]

pie-dog. See PYE-DOG.

pier *n.* breakwater, mole; structure of iron or wood open below running out into sea and used as promenade and landing-stage; support of arch or of span of bridge, pillar; solid masonry between windows etc.; ∼-**glass,** large mirror (orig. used to fill up this). [ME *per,* f. AL *pera,* of unkn. orig.]

pierce *v.* **1.** *v.t.* (Of sharp instrument etc., or fig. of cold, pain, grief, glance, discernment, discerning person, shriek, etc.) penetrate; prick (substance *with* pin etc.); make hole in (cask, ear-lobe for ear-ring, etc.); force one's way through or into. **2.** *v.i.* penetrate *through, into,* etc. [ME, f. OF *percer,* f. Rom. *pertusiare f. L PER(*tundere tus-* thrust) bore through]

Piērian (-ēr'i-, -ē'ri-) *a.* (of Pieria in N. Thessaly, reputed home) of the Muses. [f. L *Pierius* + -AN]

pier'rōt (pēr'ō) *n.* (*fem.* **pierre'tte**). French pantomime character; itinerant minstrel with whitened face and loose white costume. [F, dim. of *Pierre* PETER[1]]

pietà (pyātah') *n.* picture or sculpture of Virgin Mary holding dead body of Christ on her lap. [It., f. L (as PIETY)]

pietas (pī'etahs) *n.* respect due to ancestor, forerunner, etc. [L; see PIETY]

pī'et|ism *n.* Spener's movement for revival of piety in Lutheran Church in 17th c.; pious sentiment; exaggeration or affectation of this; so ∼IST (2) *n.,* ∼ī'st**ic**(AL) *adjs.* [f. G *pietismus* (as PIETY; see -ISM)]

pī′etý n. quality of being pious; act etc. showing this. [ME, f. OF *piété* f. L *pietas -tatis* dutifulness (as PIOUS; see -TY¹); cf. PITY]

pīēzō|-ĕlĕ′ctrĭc a. becoming electrically polarized under pressure; so ∼-ELECTRI′CITY n. [f. Gk *piezō* press + -O- + ELECTRIC]

pīēzŏ′mĕter n. instrument for measuring magnitude or direction of pressure. [f. as prec. + -METER]

pī′ffl|e v.i., & n. (sl.) **1.** v.i. talk or act feebly, trifle; hence ∼ER¹ n., ∼ING² a., trivial, worthless. **2.** n. nonsense; empty discourse. [imit.]

pig n. & v. (-gg-). **1.** n. non-ruminant omnivorous ungulate bristly mammal of family Suidae; *young pig; flesh of (usu. young or sucking) domesticated pig as food, esp. *roast pig*; (esp. in *comb.*) similar animal (GUINEA-*pig*); **in** ∼, (of sow) pregnant. **2.** (colloq.) greedy, dirty, sulky, obstinate, or annoying person, unpleasant thing, whence ∼′gISH¹ a. (-g-); (sl., derog.) policeman; **make a** ∼ **of** oneself, overeat etc. **3.** oblong mass of metal (esp. iron or lead) from smelting-furnace. **4. bleed like a (stuck)** ∼ (copiously); **buy a** ∼ **in a poke**, buy thing without seeing it or knowing its value; ∼**s might fly**, (iron.) that is unlikely. **5.** ∼′**headed**, obstinate; ∼-**iron**, crude iron from smelting-furnace; ∼-**jump** n , & v.i., (Austral. sl., of horse) jump (made) sportively from all four legs; ∼ **Latin**, made-up jargon; ||∼-**meat**, pork, ham, or bacon; ∼′**nut**, = EARTH¹-*nut* (1); *∼′**pen**, = STY¹; ∼′**skin**, (leather made of) pig's skin, *a football; ∼-**sticker**, long sharp knife; ∼′**sticking**, hunting of wild boar with spear on horseback, butchering of pigs; ∼′**sty**, = STY¹; **in a** ∼′s **eye**, (sl.) certainly not; ∼′s **wash**, ∼′**swill**, ∼′**wash**, swill of brewery or kitchen given to pigs; ∼′**weed**, herb (esp. of genus *Amaranthus*) eaten by pigs. **6.** Hence ∼′LET, ∼′LING¹, ns., ∼′LIKE a. **7.** v.t. (Of sow) bring forth (piglets, or abs.); ∼ **it**, live in disorderly or untidy fashion. **8.** v.i. herd together like pigs; behave like pig. [ME *pigge*, f. OE **picga*, **pigga*, cf. *dog*, *frog*]

pī′geon¹ (-jĭn, -jon) n. **1.** bird of family Columbidae, esp. variety of *Columba livia*, wild or domesticated, produced by breeding, trained to carry missives, etc., dove; **carrier** ∼, HOMING *pigeon*, (trained to carry home messages tied to its neck or leg, or to fly home quickly from a distance). **2.** simpleton, person easily swindled. **3. clay** ∼, clay saucer thrown into air from trap as mark for shooting; ∼-**breast**, deformed human chest with breastbone projecting; ∼-**hawk**, sparrow-hawk; ∼-**hearted**, cowardly; ∼-**hole**, (n.) small recess for pigeon to nest in, one of set of compartments for papers etc. in cabinet etc., (v.t.) deposit (document) in this, put aside (matter) for future consideration or neglect, assign (thing) to definite place in memory; ||∼ **pair**, (1) boy and girl twins, (2) boy and girl as sole children; ∼′s **milk**, partly-digested food with which pigeons feed their young, ||imaginary article for which children are sent on fool's errand; ∼-**toed**, having the toes turned inwards. **4.** Hence ∼RY (3) n. [ME, f. OF *pijon* f. Rom. **pibio* f. LL *pipio -onis* (**pip-*, imit.)]

pigeon² (-jĭn, -jon) a. & n. = PIDGIN; (colloq.) (a person's) business, job, or particular concern.

pī′ggerý (-g-) n. pig-breeding establishment; = STY¹; piggishness. [f. PIG + -ERY]

pī′ggȳ¹, pī′ggie, (-gĭ) n. little pig; ||game of tipcat; ∼**back**, = PICK-A-BACK; ∼ **bank**, pig-shaped hollow pot for saving money in. [f. PIG + -Y³]

pī′ggȳ² (-gĭ) a. like (that of) a pig. [f. PIG + -Y³]

pī′gment n., & v.t. **1.** n. colouring-matter used as paint or dye, usu. as insoluble suspension; natural colouring-matter of animal or plant tissue; hence ∼AL (-ĕ′n-), ∼ARY¹, adjs., ∼A′TION n., (esp.) excessive colouring of tissue by deposition of pigment. **2.** v.t. colour (as) with pigment. [ME, f. L *pigmentum* (**pig-* root of *pingere* paint; see -MENT)]

pī′gmȳ. See PYGMY.

pī′gtail n. tobacco twisted into thin roll; plait of hair hanging from back of head, esp. as worn by Chinese under the Manchus, by young girls, and formerly by soldiers and sailors; hence ∼ED² (-ld) a. [f. PIG + TAIL¹, w. ref. to shape]

pī′ka n. small mammal of family Ochotonidae, akin to rabbit but small-eared. [f. Tungus *piika*]

pīke¹ n., & v.t. **1.** n. (Hist.) long wooden shaft with pointed steel or iron head, infantry weapon superseded by the bayonet. **2.** [perh. diff. wd, of Norse orig.] ||peaked top of hill (esp. in names of hills in Lake District). **3.** v.t. thrust through or kill with pike. [OE *pīc* point, prick]

pīke² n. toll-bar; toll; turnpike road; ∼′**man**, keeper of turnpike. [abbr. of TURN¹*pike*]

pīke³ n. (pl. same). large voracious freshwater fish (*Esox lucius*) with long narrow snout; other fish of same family; ∼-**perch**, pikelike perch of genus *Lucioperca* or *Stizostedion*. [ME, = PIKE¹, f. its pointed jaw]

pīke⁴ v.i. (colloq.) ∼ **on**, withdraw timidly from; hence pī′kER¹ n., cautious or timid or mean person. [ME, perh. f. PIKE¹]

pī′kelet (-kl-) n. small round teacake; crumpet. [f. W. (*bara*) *pyglyd* pitchy (bread)]

pī′kestaff (-kstahf) n. wooden shaft of pike, walking-stick with metal point; **plain as a** ∼ [orig. *packstaff*], smooth staff used by pedlar], quite plain or obvious. [f. PIKE¹ + STAFF¹]

pilä′ff n. oriental dish of rice or wheat with meat, spices, etc. [f. Turk. *pilâv*]

pilä′ster n. rectangular column, esp. one engaged in wall. [f. F *pilastre* f. It. *pilastro* f. med. L *pilastrum* f. L *pila* pillar]

pilau′, pilaw′. Vars. of PILAFF.

pilch n. infant's garment or wrapper worn over napkin. [OE *pyl(e)ce*, **pilece* f. LL *pellicia*; see PELISSE]

pī′lchard n. small sea-fish (*Sardinia pilchardus*) allied to herring. [16th c. *pilcher* etc., of unkn. orig.]

pīle¹ n., & v.t. **1.** n. pointed stake or post; heavy beam driven vertically into bed of river, soft ground, etc. as support for bridge etc.; (Her.) wedge-shaped charge; ∼-**driver**, machine for driving piles into ground; ∼-**dwelling**, dwelling built on piles esp. in lake. **2.** v.t. furnish with piles; drive piles into. [OE *pīl*, = OHG *pfīl*, f. L *pilum* javelin]

pīle² n. **1.** heap of things laid more or less regularly upon one another; = FUNERAL *pile*; (colloq.) large quantity; (colloq.) heap of money, fortune, (*make a pile*; **make** one's ∼, amass as much money as one wants). **2.** lofty mass of buildings; large building. **3.** series of plates of dissimilar metals laid one upon another alternately to produce electric current; (**atomic**) ∼, nuclear REACTOR. [ME f. OF, f. L *pila* pillar, pier, mole]

pīle³ v. **1.** v.t. ∼ (**up, on**), heap up; load (table etc. *with*); ∼ **arms**, (Hist.) place (usu. four) rifles with butts on ground and muzzles supporting one another; ∼ **on the agony**, (colloq.) intensify painful description etc.; ∼ **it on**, (colloq.) exaggerate; ∼ **up**, run (ship) on rocks or aground, cause (vehicle or aircraft) to crash; ∼-**up** n., collision of several motor vehicles. **2.** v.i. crowd *in, into*, or *on* vehicle, *out of* place, etc.; ∼ **up**, accumulate. [f. prec.]

||**pīle⁴** n. (arch.) reverse of coin; **cross or** ∼, heads or tails. [ME, as PILE², orig. = lower die of minting apparatus]

pīle⁵ n. soft hair, down, wool of sheep; soft surface on cloth, esp. on velvet, plush, etc., or on carpet. [ME, prob. f. AF *pyle*, *peile*, OF *poil* f. L *pilus* hair]

pīle⁶ n. (usu. in *pl.*) haemorrhoid; ∼′**wort**, lesser celandine (from reputed efficacy against piles). [ME, prob. f. L *pila* ball, f. globular form of external pile]

pī′lĕ|us n. (pl. ∼i pr. -ī). (Bot.) caplike part of mushroom or other fungus; hence ∼ATE² a. [L, = felt cap]

pī′lfer v.t. steal (thing, or abs.) esp. in small quantities;

hence ∼AGE (3), ∼ER¹, ns. [ME, f. AF & OF *pelfrer*
pillage, of unkn. orig.; assoc. w. PILL²; cf. PELF]
pilgar'lic n. (arch.) bald head; bald-headed man;
poor creature. [= *pilled* or *peeled garlic*]
pi'lgrim n., & v.i. **1.** n. one who journeys to sacred
place as act of religious devotion; person regarded as
journeying to a future life (*The Pilgrim's Progress*);
traveller; P∼ **Fathers,** English Puritans who
founded colony of Plymouth, Massachusetts, in 1620;
hence ∼IZE (2) v.i. **2.** v.i. wander like pilgrim. [ME
pilegrim f. Prov. *pelegrin* f. L *peregrinus* stranger; see
PEREGRINE]
pi'lgrimage n., & v.i. **1.** n. pilgrim's journey, esp. *go on
(a) pilgrimage*; (fig.) mortal life viewed as a journey. **2.**
v.i. go on a pilgrimage. [ME, f. Prov. *pilgrinatge* (as
prec.; see -AGE)]
pili'ferous a. (esp. Bot.) having hair; so **pi'li**FORM a.
[f. L *pilus* hair + -I- + -FEROUS]
pill¹ n. **1.** small ball or flat round piece of medicinal
substance for swallowing whole (**the** ∼, (colloq.) oral
contraceptive; GILD¹ *the pill*); (fig.) something that has
to be done willy-nilly, a humiliation etc., (*swallow* or
sweeten the pill, a bitter pill, etc.); ∼'**box,** shallow
cylindrical box for holding pills, hat of similar shape,
(Mil.) small isolated chiefly underground concrete
fort; ∼'**wort,** fern with small globular involucres. **2.**
(sl. or joc.) ball, e.g. cannon-ball, tennis-ball, ||(in *pl.*)
billiards. [f. MDu., MLG *pille* prob. f. L *pilula* dim. of
pila ball]
||**pill²** v.t. (arch.) pillage, plunder; (arch. or dial.) =
PEEL³. [ME *pile, pyle,* perh. f. OE **pilian, pylan* f. L
pilare (*pilus* hair), infl. by F *piller* plunder; in sense
'remove the bark etc. from', different. as PEEL³]
pi'llag|e n., & v.t. **1.** n. plundering, esp. as practised in
war. **2.** v.t. sack, plunder, (place, person, or abs.);
hence ∼ER¹ (-ij-) n. [ME f. OF (*piller* plunder; see
-AGE)]
pi'llar n. vertical structure of stone, wood, metal, etc.,
slender in proportion to height, used as support or
ornament; post supporting a structure; (fig.) person
who is a main supporter (*a pillar of the faith*); upright
mass of air, water, rock, etc.; (Mining) solid mass of
coal etc. left to support roof of the working; *Pillars of
HERCULES*; **from** ∼ **to post,** (driven etc.) to and fro,
from one resource to another; ||∼-**box,** hollow pillar
about 5 ft. high in which letters may be posted (∼-*box
red,* bright red colour of this); hence ∼ED² (-erd) a.,
∼ET¹ n. [ME & AF *piler,* OF *pilier* f. Rom. *pilare f. L
pila pillar; see -AR¹]
pi'llion (-lyon) n. seating for passenger behind motor-
-cyclist etc. (ride ∼, be such passenger); (Hist.)
woman's light saddle, cushion attached to hinder
part of saddle for second rider, usu. woman. [f. Gael.
pillean, pillin dim. of *pell* cushion f. L *pellis* skin]
pi'lliwinks n. (Hist.) instrument of torture for
squeezing fingers. [ME *pyrwykes, pyrewinkes,* of unkn.
orig.]
pi'llory n., & v.t. **1.** n. (Hist.) wooden framework with
holes for head and hands of offender exposed to
public ridicule etc. **2.** v.t. put in the pillory; (fig.)
expose to ridicule. [ME, f. AL *pillorium* f. OF *pilori*
etc., prob. f. Prov. *espilori,* of uncert. orig.]
pi'llow (-ō) n., & v.t. **1.** n. cushion of linen etc. stuffed
with feathers etc. as (usu. oblong) support for head in
reclining esp. in bed (**take counsel of** one's ∼, not
decide until next day); pillow-shaped block or
support. **2.** ∼**case,** ∼**slip,** washable case of linen etc.
for pillow; ∼**fight,** children's mock fight with
pillows in bedroom; ∼**lace** (made on padded
support); ∼ **lava** (forming rounded masses); hence
∼Y² a. **3.** v.t. rest, or prop up, on pillow(s). [OE **pylw-
st. of *pyle, pylu,* = OHG *pfuliwī, pfulwo* f. WG **pulwī(n)*
f. L *pulvinus* cushion]
pi'llule. See PILULE.
pi'lose, pi'lous, adjs. covered with hair; so **pilo's**ITY
n. [f. L *pilosus* (*pilus* hair; see -OSE¹)]
pi'lot n., a., & v.t. **1.** n. person qualified to take charge

of ships entering or leaving a harbour (**drop the** ∼,
(fig.) dismiss trusted adviser); person who operates
the flying controls of an aircraft; *cowcatcher; (fig.)
guide; (arch.) steersman. **2.** ∼ **balloon,** small
balloon whose movements are observed as it rises in
the air, used to ascertain direction and velocity of
currents at various heights; ∼-**bird,** rare dark-brown
Austral. babbler with distinctive loud cry; ∼ **chute,**
small parachute serving to bring main one into
operation; ∼-**cloth,** thick blue woollen cloth for
seamen's coats etc.; ∼ **engine** (clearing the way for
another and testing the safety of the permanent way);
∼-**fish,** small fish said to act as pilot to food for
shark; ∼-**house,** = WHEEL¹-*house*; ∼-**jacket,** = PEA-
-JACKET; ∼-**light,** (1) small gas-burner kept alight to
light another, (2) electric indicator light or control
light; ||∼ **officer,** lowest commissioned rank in RAF;
hence or cogn. ∼AGE (3, 4) n., ∼LESS a. **3.** a.
experimental, small-scale, (*pilot plant, scheme*). **4.** v.t.
conduct as pilot (lit. or fig.); act as pilot on (way,
piece of water); act as pilot of (aircraft). [f. F *pilote* f.
med. L *pilotus, pedot(t)a* f. med. Gk *pēdótēs f. Gk *pēdon*
oar]
Pi'ls(e)ner (-z-, -s-) n. lager beer (like that) brewed at
Pilsen (Plzeň) in Czechoslovakia.
pi'lule, pi'llule, n. pill; small pill; hence **pi'lul**AR¹,
pi'lulOUS, adjs. [F, f. L *pilula* (see PILL¹)]
pime'ntó n. (pl. ∼s). allspice (tree); pimiento. [f. Sp.
pimiento (as foll.)]
pimie'ntō n. (pl. ∼s). sweet pepper. [Sp., f. L
pigmentum PIGMENT, in med. L = spice]
pimp n., & v.i. (act as) one who solicits clients for
prostitute or brothel, pander; ponce. [17th c., of
unkn. orig.]
pi'mpernel n. (**scarlet**) ∼, small annual plant found
in cornfields and on waste ground, with scarlet (or
blue or white) flowers closing in cloudy or rainy
weather. [ME, f. OF *pimpernelle, piprenelle* f. Rom.
*piperinella (*piperinus pepper-like f. L *piper* PEPPER¹)]
pi'mping a. small, mean; sickly. [17th c., of unkn.
orig.]
pi'mpl|e n. small hard inflamed spot on skin; similar
slight swelling on a surface; hence ∼ED² (-pěld), ∼Y²,
adjs. [ME, nasalized f. OE *piplian* break out in
pustules]
pin¹ n. **1.** thin usu. cylindrical piece of (usu. tinned
brass or iron) wire with sharp point and round
broadened head for fastening together parts of dress,
papers, etc.; thing of small value (*don't care a pin; for
two pins I'd resign*). **2.** peg of wood or metal for various
purposes (**split** ∼, metal cotter to be passed through
hole and held there by the gaping of its split end);
(Golf) stick with flag placed in hole to mark its
position (∼-**high,** (of ball) at same distance ahead as
pin); peg round which one string of musical instrument is fastened; half-firkin cask; BELAYing-*pin,*
||DRAWING-*pin,* HAIR*pin,* ||NINE*pins,* ROLL²ing-*pin,*
THOLE²-*pin*. **3.** (in *pl.*, colloq.) legs (*quick on his pins*). **4.**
(Chess.) pinning of man. **5.** ∼**s and needles,**
tingling sensation in limb recovering from numbness;
on ∼**s and needles,** in state of mental agitation due
to suspense. **6.** ∼-**ball,** game in which small metal
balls are shot across sloping board and strike against
pins etc. with lights to indicate scoring; ∼'**cushion,**
small cushion for sticking pins in to keep them ready
for use; ∼-**feather,** ungrown feather; ∼-**fire,** (of
cartridge) exploded by means of pin attached to it;
∼-**head,** (fig.) minute thing, (colloq.) stupid person;
∼-**headed,** (colloq.) stupid; ∼-**hole** (made by pin or
into which peg fits); ∼-*hole camera* (with pin-hole
aperture and no lens); ∼-**money,** annual allowance
to woman for dress expenses etc., allowance settled on
wife, or money earned by her, for private expenditure, (colloq.) very small sum of money; ∼-**point,**
(n.) point of pin, (fig.) something very small or sharp,
(a., of target) small and requiring very accurate and
precise bombing and shelling, (v.t.) locate with high

precision, designate precisely; ~'**prick,** (fig.) trifling irritation; ~**-stripe,** very narrow stripe in cloth; ~-**table,** table used in playing pin-ball; ~'**tail,** duck or grouse with pointed tail; ~**-tuck,** very narrow ornamental tuck; ~**-wheel,** small Catherine wheel; ~**-worm,** small intestinal nematode worm of which female has pointed tail. [OE *pinn,* = MDu., MLG *pinne,* OHG *pfinn,* Icel. *pinni* f. L *pinna* point etc., assoc. w. *penna* PEN³]

pin² *v.t.* (-**nn-**). fasten (thing *to* another, *up,* etc., things *together*) with pin(s); (fig.) fix (blame or responsibility for deed), fix blame for, *on* (person); transfix with pin, lance, etc.; ~ one's **faith** or **hopes** (rely implicitly) *on* or *to* (person etc.); seize and hold fast (*against* wall etc.); (Chess) prevent (opposing man) from moving except by exposing more valuable man to capture; ~ **down,** bind (person etc.) *to* (promise, arrangement), force (person) to declare his intentions, restrict actions of (enemy etc.), specify (thing) precisely; ~-**up** n., (colloq.) picture of attractive or famous person, pinned up on wall etc., such person. [ME, f. prec.]

pi'nafore *n.* child's or woman's washable covering worn over dress etc. to protect it from dirt; ~ **dress** (without collar and sleeves, for wearing over blouse or jumper). [f. PIN² + AFORE (orig. pinned on front of dress)]

pina'ster *n.* = CLUSTER *pine.* [L, = wild pine (*pinus* PINE¹; see -ASTER)]

pi'nce-nez (pă'nsnā) *n* (*pl* same). pair of eyeglasses with spring to clip nose. [F, lit. = pinch-nose]

pi'ncer|s (-z) *n. pl.* (**pair of**) ~**s,** gripping-tool made of two limbs pivoted together forming pair of jaws with pair of handles to press them together with; similar organ of crustaceans etc.; ~ **movement,** (Mil.) converging movement against enemy position. [ME *pinsers, pinsours,* f. AF f. OF *pincier* PINCH²]

pince'tte (pănsè't) *n.* small pincers, tweezers. [F]

pinch¹ *n.* **1.** pinching, squeezing; (fig.) stress (*of* poverty etc.; *feel the pinch*); **at** or **in a** ~, in an emergency, if necessary; *~-hitter,* baseball player who bats instead of another in emergency, (fig.) person acting as substitute. **2.** as much as can be taken up with tips of finger and thumb (*a pinch of snuff, of salt*). [ME, f. foll.]

pinch² *v.* **1.** *v.t.* grip tightly between two surfaces, esp. between tips of finger and thumb, (lit., or fig. of cold, hunger, etc., esp. *pinched with cold*; **where the shoe** ~**es,** where one's difficulty or trouble is); (Hort.) shorten back or down by pinching; stint (person etc. *in, of, for,* food etc.); (sl.) steal (thing), rob (person), arrest. **2.** *v.i.* be niggardly; sail (purposely or not) very close to wind. [ME, f. AF & ONF **pinchier* = OF *pincier,* f. Rom. **pinctiare, *punctiare* f. L *pungere punct-* prick]

pi'nchbeck *n. & a.* **1.** *n.* goldlike alloy of copper and zinc used in cheap jewellery etc. **2.** *a.* counterfeit, sham. [f. C. *Pinchbeck,* Engl. watchmaker d. 1732]

Pinda'ric *a. & n.* **1.** *a.* of, or supposedly like the style of, the Greek poet Pindar. **2.** *n.* (usu. in *pl.*) Pindaric ode, metre, or verse. [f. L f. Gk *Pindarikos (Pindaros* Pindar; see -IC)]

pine¹ *n.* **1.** tree of genus *Pinus* with evergreen needle-shaped leaves growing in sheathed clusters of two or more (cf. FIR), many species of which afford timber, tar, and turpentine; its wood; = *pineapple*; **Chile** ~, monkey-puzzle; hence **pi'nery** (3) *n.* **2.** ~'**apple,** (large juicy edible collective fruit of) stiff-leaved tropical plant (*Ananas comosus*) [from fruit's resemblance to pine-cone], (sl.) hand-grenade; ~**-beauty,** ~ **carpet,** moths whose larvae feed on pine-trees; ~-**cone,** fruit of the pine; ~ **marten,** dark-brown European or Amer. marten. [ME, f. OE *pín* & OF *pin* f. L *pinus*]

pine² *v.i.* languish, waste *away,* from grief, disease, etc.; long eagerly (*for, after,* to do). [OE *pinian,* = OHG *pínón,* ON *pína,* rel. to obs. E *pine* punishment, f. Gmc f. med. L *pena,* L *poena*]

pi'neal *a.* (Anat.) shaped like a pine-cone; ~ **body** or **gland,** eyelike conical gland of unknown function behind third ventricle of brain. [f. F *pinéal* f. L *pinea* PINE¹-cone; see -AL]

pine'tum *n.* (*pl.* ~**a**). plantation of pine-trees or other conifers. [L (*pinus* pine)]

pi'nfold *n.,* & *v.t.* (confine in) pound for stray cattle etc. [OE *pundfald* (**pund* POUND², *fald* FOLD¹)]

ping *n.,* & *v.i.* (make) abrupt single ringing sound as of rifle bullet in flight, desk-bell, etc.; hence ~'ER¹ (2) *n.,* (esp.) device to ring bell after pre-set time. [imit.]

Pi'ng-Pŏng, pi'ng-pŏng, *n.* (*P) table tennis. [imit. f. sound of bat striking ball]

pi'nguid (-nggwĭd) *a.* (usu. joc.) fat, oily, greasy. [f. L *pinguis* fat + -ID¹]

pi'nguin (-nggwĭn) *n.* (fruit of) tropical Amer. plant (*Bromelia pinguin*) allied to pineapple. [17th c.; orig. unkn.]

pi'nion¹ (-nyon) *n.* terminal segment of bird's wing; (poet.) wing; any flight-feather of wing. [ME, f. OF *pignon* f. Rom. **pinnio -on-* augment. of L *pinna*; see PIN¹, -OON]

pi'nion² (-nyon) *v.t.* cut off pinion of (wing, bird) to prevent flight; bind the arms of (person), bind (arms); bind (person etc.) fast *to* (thing). [f. prec.]

pi'nion³ (-nyon) *n.* small cog-wheel engaging with larger one; cogged spindle engaging with wheel. [f. F *pignon* alt. f. obs. *pignol* f. Rom **pineolus* f. L *pinea* PINE¹-cone]

pink¹ *n. & a.* **1.** *n.* garden plant of genus *Dianthus* with sweet-smelling white, pink, crimson, or variegated flowers. **2.** the ~ (embodied perfection) *of elegance* etc.; **the** ~ (most perfect condition) *of health* etc.; **in the** ~, (sl.) in very good health. **3.** pale red colour slightly inclining to purple. **4.** (hunting-)~, fox-hunter's red coat, cloth for this, fox-hunter. **5.** *a.* of pale red colour of various kinds (ROSE¹-*pink,* SALMON-*pink*), whence ~'ISH¹ 2, ~'Y², *adjs.,* ~'LY² *adv.,* ~'NESS *n* ; (Polit. sl.) mildly communist. **6.** ~ **disease** (of young children, with pink discoloration of extremities); *pink* ELEPHANTS; ~-**eye,** contagious fever of horse, contagious ophthalmia in man; *pink* GIN³. [perh. f. dial. *pink-eyed* having small eyes]

pink² *n.* yellowish lake pigment made by combining vegetable colouring matter with a white base (*brown, French, pink*). [17th c.; orig. unkn.]

pink³ *n.* (Hist.) sailing-vessel, esp. with narrow stern (orig. small and flat-bottomed). [ME, f. MDu. *pin(c)ke,* of unkn. orig.]

pink⁴ *v.t.* pierce slightly with sword etc.; ~ (**out**), ornament (leather etc.) with perforations; cut scalloped or zigzag edge on; adorn, deck; ~'**ing scissors** or **shears,** dressmaker's serrated shears for cutting zigzag edge. [ME perh. f. LDu.; cf. LG *pinken* strike, peck]

||**pink⁵** *n.* young salmon; (dial.) minnow. [15th c. *penk,* of unkn. orig.]

pink⁶ *v.i.* (Of vehicle engine) emit series of high-pitched explosive sounds caused by detonation of mixture. [imit.]

pi'nkie *n.* (US & Sc.) little finger. [cf. dial. *pink* small, half-shut (eye), -IE]

pi'nkō *n.* (pl. ~**s**). (sl.) politically 'pink' person. [f. PINK¹+-O]

*Pi'nkster *n.* Whitsuntide; **p**~ **flower,** pink azalea. [Du., = Pentecost]

pi'nna *n.* (*pl.* ~**e**). broad upper part of external ear; primary division of pinnate leaf; fin or finlike structure. [L, = *penna* feather, wing, fin]

pi'nnace *n.* warship's or other ship's small boat usu. motor-driven (orig. schooner-rigged or eight-oared). [f. F *pinnace,* perh. f. Rom. **pinacea (navis* ship) f. L *pinus* PINE¹]

pi'nnacle *n.,* & *v.t.* **1.** *n.* small ornamental turret usu. ending in pyramid or cone, crowning a buttress, roof, etc.; natural peak; (fig.) culmination, climax. **2.** *v.t.* set (as) on pinnacle; form the pinnacle of; furnish with

pinnacles. [ME *pinacle* f. OF *pin(n)acle* f. LL *pinnaculum* (*pinna* wing, point; see PIN¹, -CULE)]

pi′nnate *a.* (Bot., of compound leaf) with series of leaflets on each side of common petiole; (Zool.) with branches, tentacles, etc., on each side of an axis; hence or cogn. **pi′nnāt**ED¹ *a.*, ∼LY² (-tlǐ) *adv.* [f. L *pinnatus* feathered (PINNA; see -ATE²)]

pi′nni- *comb. form.* wing, fin, as: ∼grade, ∼ped, *adjs.* & *ns.*, fin-footed (animal). [f. L PINNA + -I-]

pi′nnūl|e *n.* (Bot.) secondary division of pinnate leaf; (Zool.) part or organ like small wing or fin; sight at end of index of astrolabe etc.; hence ∼AR¹ *a.* [f. L *pinnula* dim. of PINNA; see -ULE]

pi′nny *n.* (childish or colloq.) pinafore. [abbr.; see -Y³]

*****pi′nochle** (pē′*nokel*) *n.* card-game with double pack of 48 cards (ace to nine only); combination of queen of spades and jack of diamonds in this game. [19th c.; orig. unkn.]

*****pinō′le** *n.* flour made from parched cornflour, esp. mixed with sweet flour of mesquite beans, sugar, etc. [Amer. Sp., f. Aztec *pinolli*]

piñon (pēnyō′n) *n.* nut-pine tree; its fruit. [Sp., f. L *pinea* PINE¹-cone]

pīnt *n.* measure of capacity for liquids etc., ⅛ of gallon; ‖this quantity of a liquid, esp. milk or beer; ∼-pot, (pewter) pot holding one pint; ∼-sized, (colloq.) diminutive. [ME, f. OF *pinte*, of unkn. orig.]

‖**pi′nta** *n.* (colloq.) pint of milk, beer, etc. [corrupt. of *pint of*]

pinta′dō (-ah′-) *n.* (*pl.* ∼s). pigeon-sized petrel of southern seas; W. Ind. mackerel-like fish. [f. Port. *pintado* guinea-fowl, p.p. (as n.) of *pintar* f. Rom. **pinctare* (**pinctus* f. L *pictus* p.p. of *pingere* paint)]

pi′ntle *n.* pin or bolt, esp. one on which some other part turns. [OE *pintel* penis, of unkn. orig.; cf. OFris. etc. *pint*]

*****pi′ntō** (pī′-, pē′-) *a. & n.* (*pl.* ∼s). piebald (horse). [Sp., = mottled, f. Rom. **pinctus*; see PINTADO]

pi′ny *a.* of, like, or abounding in, pines. [f. PINE¹ + -Y²]

piolet (pyōlā′) *n.* Alpinist's two-headed ice-axe. [F]

pī′ŏn (Phys.) meson having mass about 270 times that of electron; hence **pīŏ′n**ɪc *a.* [f. PI¹ (letter used as symbol for the particle) + -ON]

pioneer′ *n. & v.* **1.** *n.* (Mil.) member of infantry group serving to prepare road for main body of troops. **2.** initiator of enterprise, original explorer, settler, etc. **3.** *v.i.* act as pioneer. **4.** *v.t.* open up (road etc.) as pioneer; act as pioneer to, conduct; originate (course of action etc. followed later by others). [f. F *pionnier* foot-soldier, pioneer, OF *paonier*, *peon(n)ier* (as PEON, -IER)]

pi′ous *a.* devout, religious (*pious* FRAUD); hypocritically virtuous; dutiful; hence ∼LY² *adv.* [f. L *pius* dutiful, pious + -OUS]

pīp¹ *n.* disease of poultry, hawks, etc., marked by thick mucus in throat and often by white scale on tip of tongue; (sl.) fit of disgust, depression, or bad temper, (*he gives me the* pip). [ME, f. MDu. *pippe*, MLG *pip* f. WG **pipit* f. med. L **pip(p)ita*, prob. corrupt. of L *pituita* slime]

pip² *n.* each spot on playing-cards, dice, or dominoes; ‖star (1–3 acc. to rank) on shoulder of army officer's uniform; single blossom of clustered inflorescence; rhomboidal segment of surface of pineapple; image of object on radar screen. [16th c. *peep*, of unkn. orig.]

‖**pip³** *v.* (-pp-) (colloq.) **1.** *v.t.* blackball; hit with shot; defeat (∼ *at the* post, defeat at the last moment). **2.** *v.i.* ∼ out, die. [f. prec. or foll.]

pip⁴ *n.*, & *v.t.* (-pp-). **1.** *n.* seed of apple, pear, orange, grape, etc., whence ∼LESS *a.*; ***(sl.) excellent person or thing. **2.** *v.t.* remove pips from (fruit). [abbr. of PIPPIN]

‖**pip⁵** *n.* short high-pitched sound, usu. mechanically produced (*the six pips of the time-signal*). [imit.]

pi′pa (pē′-) *n.* toad of genus *Pipa*, female of which carries eggs and tadpoles on her back. [f. Surinam Negro *pipál* masc., *pipá* fem.]

pi′pal (pē′-) *n.* large Indian fig-tree (*Ficus religiosa*) allied to banyan, bo-tree. [f. Hindi *pīpal* f. Skr. *pippala*]

pīpe¹ *n.* **1.** tube of wood, metal, etc., esp. for conveying water, gas, etc. **2.** (Mus.) wind-instrument consisting of single tube, each of the tubes by which sound is produced in organ; (in *pl.*) = BAG¹*pipes*; boatswain's whistle, sounding of this. **3.** (arch.) voice, esp. in singing; song or note of bird. **4.** tubular organ, vessel, etc. in animal body. **5.** cylindrical vein of ore. **6.** cavity in cast metal. **7.** (tobacco-)∼, narrow tube of clay, wood, etc., with bowl at one end for drawing in smoke of burning tobacco; quantity of tobacco held by this (*light, smoke, a pipe*); PEACE-*pipe*; **put that in your** ∼ **and smoke it,** (colloq.) consider that fact etc. and accept it if you can. **8.** cask for wine, esp. as measure of two hogsheads, usu. = 105 gal. **9.** ∼′clay, (*n.*) fine white clay used for tobacco pipes and for whitening leather etc., (*v.t.*) whiten with this, (fig.) put in order; ∼-cleaner, piece of flexible fabric-covered wire used to clean inside of tobacco-pipe; ∼-dream, groundless hope or scheme, as indulged in when smoking a pipe (orig. of opium-smoker's fantasies); ∼-fish, long slender fish of genus *Syngnatha* etc. with elongated snout; ∼-light, spill for lighting pipe; ∼′line (esp. for conveying petroleum to a distance), (fig.) channel of supply of goods, information, etc. (*in the* ∼line, awaiting completion or processing); ∼ **major,** NCO commanding regimental pipers; ∼-organ, (Mus.) organ using pipes not (only) reeds; ∼-rack (for tobacco-pipes); ∼-rolls, (Hist.) annual 12th–19th-c. records of British Exchequer [prob. because subsidiary documents were rolled in pipe form]; ∼-stem, shaft of tobacco-pipe; ∼-stone, hard red clay used by Amer. Indians for tobacco-pipes. **10.** Hence ∼′FUL 2 (-pf-) *n.*, ∼′LESS (-pl-), **pī′py²**, *adjs.* [OE *pīpe*, = OHG *pfīfa*, ON *pīpa*, f. Gmc f. Rom. **pīpa* f. L *pipare* peep, chirp]

pīpe² *v.* **1.** *v.t.* play (tune, etc., or abs.) on pipe(s); lead or bring (person etc.) by sound of pipe; summon (crew *up*, to meal, work, etc.) by sounding whistle; whistle; utter in shrill voice; ∼ down, (Naut.) dismiss from duty; ‖∼ one's eye(s), (colloq.) weep. **2.** propagate (pinks etc.) by cuttings taken off at joint of stem. **3.** trim (dress etc.), ornament (cake etc.), with PIPING¹. **4.** furnish with pipes; convey (oil, water, gas, etc.) by pipes; transmit (music, broadcast programme, etc.) by wire or cable for hearing elsewhere. **5.** ∼ away, give signal for (boat) to start; ∼ down, (colloq.) be quiet, be less insistent or confident; ∼ up, begin to play, sing, speak, etc. [OE *pīpian* & OF *piper* f. L *pipare* (as prec.); in senses 2–4 f. prec.]

‖**pip e′mma** *adv. & n.* (colloq.) = PM. [formerly signallers' names for letters *PM*]

pi′per *n.* one who plays on pipe, esp. itinerant musician; bagpipe-player; **pay the** ∼ (**and call the tune,** bear the cost (and have control) of a proceeding etc.; kind of gurnard whistling when caught. [OE *pīpere* (as PIPE¹, -ER¹)]

pīpe′ridine (-ēn) *n.* (Chem.) peppery-smelling liquid formed by reduction of pyridine. [f. L *piper* pepper + -IDE + -INE⁵]

pīpe′tte *n.* slender tube for transferring or measuring small quantities of liquids, esp. in chemistry. [F, dim. of *pipe* PIPE¹; see -ETTE]

pī′ping¹ *n.* In vbl senses; ornamentation of dress, upholstery, etc., usu. as edging by means of (cord enclosed in) pipelike fold; ornamental cordlike lines of sugar on cake. [f. PIPE¹,² + -ING¹]

pī′ping² *n.* In vbl senses; **the** ∼ **time(s) of peace** (marked by pastoral piping as opp. to martial music); ∼ (hissing or very) **hot.** [ME, f. PIPE² + -ING²]

pīpistrĕ′lle *n.* small bat of genus *Pipistrellus.* [F, f. It. *pipistrello*, *vip-*, f. L *vespertilio* bat (*vesper* evening)]

pi′pit *n.* bird of family Motacillidae, esp. of genus *Anthus*, superficially resembling lark; MEADOW *pipit.* [prob. imit.]

pi′pkin *n.* small earthenware pot or pan. [16th c.; orig. unkn.]

pi′ppin *n.* apple grown from seed; red and yellow dessert apple; (sl.) excellent person or thing. [ME f. OF *pepin*, of uncert. orig.]

pi′p-squeak *n.* (sl.) insignificant or contemptible person or thing. [imit.]

pi′qu|ant (pē′kănt) *a.* agreeably pungent, sharp, appetizing; (fig.) pleasantly stimulating, or disturbing, to the mind; hence ∼ANCY *n.*, ∼antLY² *adv.* [F, pres. part. of *piquer* (as foll.; see -ANT)]

pique¹ (pēk) *v.t.*, & *n.* **1.** *v.t.* irritate, wound the pride of; arouse (curiosity, interest); plume one*self* on. **2.** *n.* ill-feeling, enmity, resentment, (*in a fit of pique*; *took a pique against me*). [f. F (*pique* n. f.) *piquer* v. prick, irritate, *se piquer* take offence, f. Rom. **piccare*]

pique² (pēk) *n.* & *v.* **1.** *n.* winning of 30 points on cards and play in piquet before opponent scores anything. **2.** *v.t.* & *i.* score pique (against). [f. F *pic*, of unkn. orig.]

piqué (pē′kā) *n.* stiff ribbed cotton etc. fabric. [F, p.p. (as n.) of *piquer*; see PIQUE¹]

piquě′t¹ (-kē′t) *n.* card-game for two players with pack of 32 cards (ace to seven only). [F, of unkn. orig.]

pi′quet² (pī′kĭt). Var. of PICKET 2.

pir′acy. See PIRATE.

pira′gua (-gwa) *n.* long narrow canoe made from single tree-trunk; two-masted sailing-barge. [Sp. f. Carib, = dug-out]

pira′nha (-ah′nya), **pira′ya** (-ah′ya), **pėrai′** (-rī′), *n.* voracious S. Amer. freshwater fish of genus *Serrasalmus*. [Port. f. Tupi, var. of *piraya* scissors]

pirarucú (-rōōkōō′) *n.* = ARAPAIMA. [Port. f. Tupi, = red fish]

pir′ate *n.*, & *v.t.* **1.** *n.* (ship used by) one who robs at sea; marauder; one who infringes another's copyright or other business rights; one who broadcasts without official authorization (freq. *attrib.*: *pirate radio station*). **2.** *v.t.* plunder; reproduce (book etc.) without permission, for one's own benefit. **3.** Hence or cogn. **pir′acy** *n.*, **pirā′tic**(AL) *adjs.* [ME, f. L *pirata* f. Gk *peiratēs* (*peiraō* attempt, assault)]

piraya. See PIRANHA.

piripi′ri *n.* (NZ) weed (*Acaena sanguisorbae*) having prickly burs. [Maori]

pirō′gue (-ō′g) *n.* = PIRAGUA. [F, prob. f. Galibi]

pirouě′tte (-rōō-) *n.*, & *v.i.* **1.** *n.* ballet-dancer's spin round on one foot or on point of toe. **2.** *v.i.* dance thus. [F, = spinning-top]

pis aller (pēz ălā′) *n.* course of action etc. followed for want of a better. [F (*pis* worse, *aller* go)]

pi′scary *n.* common of ∼, right of fishing in another's water in common with owner (and others). [ME, f. med. L *piscaria* neut. pl. (as n.) of L *piscarius* (*piscis* fish; see -ARY¹)]

pi′scatory *a.* of fishermen or fishing, whence **piscatōr′ial** *a.*; addicted to fishing. [f. L *piscatorius* (*piscator* fisherman f. *piscis* fish)]

Pi′sce|s (-sēz, -skēz) *n.* (*pl.* same). (person born under) sign of the ZODIAC, the Fishes; hence ∼AN *a.* & *n.*, (person) born under Pisces. [ME f. L, pl. of *piscis* fish]

pi′sciculture *n.* artificial rearing of fish; hence **pisciculturAL** *n.*, **piscicu′lturIST** (3) *n.*, (-cher-). [f. L *piscis* fish, after *agriculture* etc.]

pisci′na (-sē′-, -sī′-) *n.* (*pl.* ∼e or ∼s). fish-pond; ancient-Roman bathing-pond; (Eccl.) perforated stone basin near altar in church for carrying away water used in rinsing chalice etc. [L (*piscis* fish)]

pisci′ne¹ (-ē′n) *n.* bathing-pool. [F, f. as prec.]

pi′scine² *a.* of fish [f. L *piscis* fish + -INE¹]

pisci′vorous *a.* fish-eating. [f. as prec. + -i- + -VOROUS]

pisé (pē′zā) *n.* rammed clay or earth (and gravel) as building-material. [F, p.p. (as n.) of *piser* pound f. L *pinsare*]

Pi′sgah (-zga) *n.* ∼ **sight** etc., distant view of

unattainable object. [name of mountain whence Moses viewed the Promised Land (Deut. 3:27)]

pish *int.* expr. contempt, impatience, or disgust. [imit.]

pishō′gue (-ō′g) *n.* (Ir.) sorcery; charm, spell. [f. Ir. *pis*(*r*)*eog* witchcraft]

pi′siform (pī′s-, pī′z-) *a.* pea-shaped; ∼ **bone**, small bone of upper row of carpus. [f. mod. L *pisiformis* (*pisum* pea; see -FORM)]

pi′smire *n.* (dial.) ant. [ME, f. foll. (from smell of anthill) + obs. *mire* ant]

piss *v.* & *n.* (vulg.) **1.** *v.i.* urinate; ∼ **off**, (sl.) go away. **2.** *v.t.* discharge (blood etc.) with the urine; wet with urine; ∼ **off**, (sl., usu. in *p.p.*) annoy; (in *p.p.*, sl.) drunk. **3.** *n.* urine; act of urinating; (sl.) = MICKEY¹; ∼**-pot**, chamber-pot. [ME, f. OF *pisser* f. Rom. **pišare* (imit.)]

pissoir (pēswăr′) *n.* public urinal. [F]

pista′chio (-tah′sh-, -tă′-) *n.* (*pl.* ∼s). (tree, *Pistacia vera*, yielding) nut with greenish edible kernel; colour of this kernel. [f. It. *pistaccio* and Sp. *pistacho* f. L f. Gk *pistakion* f. Pers. *pistah*]

piste (pēst) *n.* ski-track of compacted snow. [F, = racetrack]

pi′stil *n.* female organ of flower, comprising ovary, style, and stigma; hence ∼LARY¹, ∼li′ferous, ∼line¹, *adjs.* [f. F *pistile* or f. L *pistillum* PESTLE]

pi′stillate *a.* having pistils but no stamens; having pistils. [f. prec. + -ATE²]

pi′stol *n.*, & *v.t.* (||-ll-). **1.** *n.* small firearm held and fired by one hand (**hold** ∼ **to** person's **head**, coerce him by threats); implement of similar shape; ∼**-grip**, handle of pistol-butt shape; ∼**-shot**, range of, or shot fired from, pistol; ∼**-whip** *v.t.* (*-pp-*), beat with pistol; hence ∼EER² *n.*, soldier armed with pistol. **2.** *v.t.* shoot with pistol. [f. obs. F f. G *pistole* f. Czech *pišťal*]

pistō′le *n.* (Hist.) foreign gold coin, esp. Spanish coin. [f. F *pistole* abbr. of *pistolet*, of uncert. orig.]

pi′ston *n.* disc or short cylinder of wood, metal, etc., fitting closely within tube in which it moves up and down, used in cylinder of steam or petrol engine to impart motion by means of ∼**-rod**, or in pump to receive motion; ∼**-ring** (sealing gap between piston and cylinder-wall); sliding valve in cornet etc. [F, f. It. *pistone* var. of *pestone* augment. of *pestello* PESTLE]

pit¹ *n.* **1.** natural hole in ground; hole made in digging for mineral etc. or for industrial purposes, (*chalk*, *clay*, *gravel*, *coal*, *saw*, *tan*, *-pit*); covered hole as trap for wild beasts or (esp. Bibl.) for enemies (**dig a** ∼ **for**, (fig.) try to ensnare); **the** (**bottomless**) ∼ (**of hell**), hell; = COCKPIT 2. hollow in animal or plant body or on any surface (∼ **of the stomach**, depression below bottom of breastbone); depressed scar, e.g. after smallpox. **3.** ||that part of auditorium of theatre which is on floor of house, esp. rear part of this, whence ∼′TITE¹ (1) *n.*; ||people occupying this. **4.** sunken area in workshop floor for access to underside of motor vehicles; place at which racing cars are refuelled, given fresh tyres, etc., during race. **5.** *part of floor of an exchange allotted to special trading (*wheat-pit*). **6.** ∼′**fall**, covered pit as trap for animals etc., (fig.) unsuspected snare or danger; ∼**-head**, (area surrounding) top of coal-mine shaft; ∼′**man**, collier, (pl. *-ns*) *connecting rod in machinery; ||∼ **pony** (kept underground for haulage in coal-mines); ∼**-prop**, balk of wood used as temporary support in a mine; ∼**-saw**, large saw working in saw-pit; ∼ **viper**, Amer. snake of family Crotalidae, with pit between eye and nostril. [OE *pytt*, = OS *putti*, OHG *pfuzzi*, f. WG **putti*, **putja* f. L *puteus* well]

pit² *v.t.* (*-tt-*). **1.** *v.t.* put into a pit (esp. vegetables etc. for storage); set (cock, dog, etc.) to fight (orig. in pit; *against* another), (fig.) match (person, one's wits, *against*); (esp. in *p.p.*) make pits, esp. scars, in. **2.** *v.i.* (Path., of flesh etc.) retain impression of finger etc. when touched. [ME, f. prec.]

*pĭt³ *n.*, & *v.t.* (-tt-). **1.** *n.* stone (of fruit). **2.** *v.t.* remove pits from. [perh. Du., cogn. w. PITH]

pĭ't-a-păt *adv.* & *n.* (with) sound as of light quick steps, (with) faltering sound, (*his feet, heart, went pit-a--pat*). [imit.]

pitch¹ *n.*, & *v.t.* **1.** *n.* black or dark-brown tenacious resinous substance, semi-liquid when hot, hard when cold, got from distillation of tar or turpentine, used for caulking seams of ships etc.; TOUCH¹ *pitch*. **2.** ~-black, ~-darkness, (with no light at all); ~-pine, pine-tree of species yielding much resin, esp. *Pinus rigida*; ~'stone, obsidian etc. looking like pitch. **3.** *v.t.* cover, coat, smear, with pitch. [OE *pic* (*pician* v.), = OS *pik*, OHG *peh*, ON *bik*, Gmc f. L *pix picis*]

pitch² *v.* **1.** *v.t.* erect and fix (tent, camp); (abs.) encamp. **2.** fix or plant (thing) in definite position; ~ wickets, (Cricket) fix stumps in ground and place bails. **3.** pave (road) with set stones. **4.** ~ed **battle,** battle planned beforehand and fought on chosen ground, not casual skirmish, (fig.) vigorous argument etc. **5.** (Mus. etc.) set at particular pitch, (fig.) express in particular style or at particular level. **6.** throw, fling; (in games) throw (flat object) towards a mark; (Cricket) cause (bowled ball) to strike ground (at specified point etc.); (sl.) tell (tale, yarn). **7.** (Golf). play (ball) with PITCH³ shot. **8.** *v.i.* fall heavily (on one's head, *into*, etc.); (of ship, vehicle, etc.) plunge in longitudinal direction (cf. ROLL² 4); (of bowled cricket-ball) strike the ground. **9.** ~ **in,** (colloq.) set to work vigorously; ~ **into,** (colloq.) assail forcibly with blows, words, etc., make vigorous attack on, (person, food, etc.); ~ (**up**)**on,** happen to select; ~-and-toss, game of skill and chance in which coins are pitched at a mark and then tossed. [ME *pic(c)he*, perh. f. OE **picc(e)an* (cf. *picung* stigmata)]

pitch³ *n.* **1.** pitching (e.g. of ship). **2.** mode of delivering cricket-ball in bowling; delivery of base-ball by pitcher; ~ (**shot**), (Golf) lofted approach shot with ball not running far after alighting. **3.** advertising or recommendation by salesman etc. **4.** ||place at which street performer, bookmaker, etc., is stationed (QUEER *the pitch*); (Cricket) area between or near wickets; area for playing football etc. on. **5.** height to which falcon etc. soars before swooping on prey (*fly a high pitch*; lit. or fig.). **6.** height, degree, intensity, (*of* quality etc.; *affairs reached such a pitch that* etc.); (Mus.) quality of sound governed by rate of vibration of string etc., degree of acuteness or graveness of tone, (*high pitch, low pitch*); CONCERT¹ *pitch*. **7.** degree of slope; steepness of slope of roof, stratum, etc., (~ed **roof,** not flat); (Mech.) distance between successive corresponding points or lines, e.g. between successive teeth of cog-wheel, ridges of screw, or positions of propeller before and after one rotation. **8.** ~-pipe, small pipe blown by mouth to set pitch for singing or tuning. [f. prec.]

pĭ'tchblĕnde *n.* uranium oxide ore found in pitchlike masses and yielding radium. [f. G *pechblende* (as PITCH¹, BLENDE)]

pĭ'tcher¹ *n.* **1.** large usu. earthenware vessel with handle or two ears and usu. a lip shaped for pouring, for holding liquids; jug; **little ~s have long ears,** children are apt to overhear. **2.** (Bot.) modified leaf in pitcher form; ~-plant (with such leaves, which often hold liquid secretion). **3.** Hence ~FUL 2 *n.* [ME, f. OF *pichier, pechier* f. Frank. *bikari BEAKER]

pĭ'tcher² *n.* In vbl senses; player who delivers ball, esp. in baseball; stone used for paving. [f. PITCH² + -ER¹]

pĭ'tchförk *n.*, & *v.t.* **1.** *n.* long-handled fork with two prongs for pitching hay etc. **2.** *v.t.* cast (as) with pitchfork; (fig.) thrust (person) forcibly (*into* position, office, etc.). [in ME *pickfork*, prob. f. PICK¹ + FORK, assoc. w. PITCH²]

pĭ'tchў *a.* of, like, dark etc. as, pitch. [f. PITCH¹ + -Y²]

pĭ'téous *a.* deserving or causing pity, deplorable; hence ~LY² *adv.*, ~NESS *n.* [ME *pito(u)s* etc. f. AF *pitous*, OF *pitos* f. Rom. *pietosus (as PIETY; see -OUS)]

pĭth *n.*, & *v.t.* **1.** *n.* spongy cellular tissue in stems and branches of dicotyledonous plants; similar tissue lining rind of orange etc.; (arch.) spinal marrow; ~ **helmet** (made from dried pith of sola etc.). **2.** (fig.) essential part, quintessence, (*pith and marrow of*); physical strength, vigour; force, energy; of ~ (importance) **and moment** (Shak. *Hamlet* III. i. 86). **3.** Hence ~LESS *a.* **4.** *v.t.* slaughter or immobilize (animal) by severing spinal cord; remove pith or marrow from. [OE *pitha*, = MDu., MLG *pitte, pit* f. WG *pith(*th*)*on*, of unkn. orig.]

pĭthĕcă'nthrōpe *n.* member of extinct genus *Pithec-anthropus* of apelike men, now included in genus *Homo*. [f. Gk *pithēkos* ape + *anthrōpos* man]

pĭthecoid (pĭ'thī-, -thē'-) *a.* like an (esp. anthropoid) ape. [f. F *pithécoïde* (as prec.; see -OID)]

pĭ'th|os *n.* (*pl.* ~oi). (Archaeol.) large storage-jar. [Gk]

pĭ'th|ў *a.* of, like, abounding in, pith; (fig.) condensed and forcible, terse; hence ~ĭLY² *adv.*, ~ĭNESS *n.* [ME, f. PITH + -Y²]

pĭ'tiab|le *a.* deserving or causing pity or contempt; hence ~leNESS (-bln-) *n.*, ~LY² *adv.* [ME, f. OF *piteable, pitoiable* (as PITY; see -ABLE)]

pĭ'tiful *a.* (Of thing) causing pity; contemptible; (arch.) compassionate; hence ~LY² *adv.*, ~NESS *n.* [ME, f. PITY + -FUL]

pĭ'tiléss *a.* showing no pity (lit. or fig.); hence ~LY² *adv.*, ~NESS *n.* [ME, f. PITY + -LESS]

pĭ'tŏn (pē'-) *n.* peg or spike driven into rock or crack to support climber or rope. [F, = eye-bolt]

Pĭ'tŏt (pē'tō) *n.* ~ **tube** (bent at right angles and used to measure speed of flow or of aircraft etc.). [f. H. ~, Fr. physicist d. 1771]

pĭ'tpăn *n.* Central-Amer. dug-out boat. [Miskito]

pĭ'ttance *n.* allowance or remuneration, esp. scanty one (*a mere pittance*); small number or amount; (Hist.) pious bequest to religious house for extra food etc. [ME f. OF *pitance*, f. med. L *pi(e)tantia* f. L *pietas* PITY; see -ANCE]

pĭ'tter-pătter. Var. of PIT-A-PAT.

pĭ'ttīte. See PIT¹.

pĭttŏ'sporum *n.* evergreen shrub of genus *Pittosporum* with fragrant flowers and seeds embedded in viscous pulp. [f. Gk *pitta* PITCH¹ + -o- + *sporos* seed]

pĭtū'itarў *a.* & *n.* **1.** *a.* (arch.) of or secreting phlegm, mucous. **2.** ~ **gland** or **body,** small ductless gland at base of brain which has important influence on growth and bodily functions, and was once thought to secrete nasal mucus. **3.** *n.* pituitary gland. [f. L *pituitarius* (*pituita* slime; see -ARY¹)]

pĭ'turi *n.* (Austral.) (narcotic drug got from) shrub *Duboisia hopwoodii*. [Aboriginal]

pĭ'tў *n.*, & *v.t.* **1.** feeling of sorrow aroused by person's distress or suffering (*cannot help feeling pity for him*); **take ~ on,** feel or act compassionately towards; **for ~'s sake,** = for God's sake (GOD 7). **2.** regrettable fact, regrettableness, ground for regret, (*what a pity!*; *it is a thousand pities you did not mention it*); **more's the ~,** so much the worse; **it is** or **was ~ of them,** (arch.) one feels sorry for them. **3.** *v.t.* feel (often contemptuous) pity for (*he is much to be pitied*; *I pity you if you think that*); hence ~INGLY *adv.* [ME, f. OF *pité* f. L (as PIETY)]

pityrĭ'as|is *n.* (*pl.* ~es *pr.* -ēz). (Path.) skin disease characterized by shedding of branlike scales. [mod. L, f. Gk *pityriasis* (*pituron* bran; see -ASIS)]

pĭ'vot *n.* & *v.* **1.** *n.* short shaft or pin on which something turns or oscillates; man or men about whom body of troops wheels; (fig.) cardinal or crucial person or point; hence ~AL *a.* **2.** *v.t.* furnish with or attach by pivot. **3.** *v.t.* & *i.* turn as on pivot. **4.** *v.i.* hinge (*up*)*on* (lit. or fig.). [F, of uncert. orig.]

pix¹. Var. of PYX.

pix² *n. pl.* (colloq.) pictures. [abbr.]

pĭ'xie, pĭ'xў, *n.* supernatural being akin to fairy; ~ **hat, hood,** (with pointed crown). [17th c.; orig. unkn.]

pi'xĭl(l)ātèd *a.* bewildered; crazy; drunk. [var. of *pixie-led* (prec., LED) + -ATE³ + -ED¹]

pi'zza (pē'tsa) *n.* open pie containing spiced tomatoes, cheese, etc. [It., = pie]

pizzeri'a (pētserē'a) *n.* place where pizzas are made or sold. [It. (as prec.; cf. -ERY)]

pizzica't|ō (pītsĭkah'tō) *adv., a.,* & *n.* (*pl.* ~os or ~i *pr.* -ē). (Mus.) (note or passage performed by) plucking string of violin etc. with finger instead of using bow. [It., p.p. of *pizzicare* twitch (*pizzare* f. *pizza* edge)]

pi'zzle *n.* (vulg.) penis of animal, esp. that of bull formerly used as flogging instrument. [f. LG *pesel*, dim. of MLG *pēse*, MDu. *pēze*]

pk. *abbr.* park; peak; peck(s).

pl. *abbr.* place; plate; (esp. Mil.) platoon; plural.

||PLA *abbr.* Port of London Authority.

plă'c|able *a.* easily appeased, mild, forgiving; hence or cogn. ~ABI'LITY *n.*, ~ABLY *adv.* [ME f. OF, or f. L *placabilis* (*placare* appease; see -ABLE)]

plă'cărd *n.*, & *v.t.* **1.** document printed on one side of single sheet for posting up or otherwise displaying. **2.** *v.t.* (or plakăr'd). set up placards on (wall etc.); advertise (wares etc.) by placards; display (poster etc.) as placard. [ME f. OF *placquart* (*plaquier* to plaster f. MDu. *placken*; see -ARD)]

placāte (plakă't, plă'kāt) *v.t.* pacify, conciliate; hence **placā'tORY** *a.*, propitiatory. [f. L *placare* + -ATE³]

plăce¹ *n.* **1.** particular part of space; part of space occupied by person or thing (*it has changed its place*); *ANYPLACE, *EVERYplace, *NO¹ place, *SOMEPLACE; in *~US, at some places but not at others*. **2.** city, town, village, etc.; group of houses in town etc.; residence, dwelling, (*he has a place in the country; come round to my place*); country house with surroundings; go ~s, (colloq.) be successful. **3.** building or area devoted to specified purpose (*place of amusement, worship; bathing- -place*); ||ANOTHER place; ||the other ~, (joc., in Cambridge Univ.) Oxford (and vice versa). **4.** particular spot on surface etc. (*a sore place on his wrist*). **5.** particular passage, or point reached, in book etc. **6.** rank, station, (*servants must know their place*); keep person in his place, squash his pretensions; PRIDE of place. **7.** (Racing). position among placed competitors, esp. other than that of winner. **8.** position of figure in series as indicating its value in decimal or similar notation (*calculated to 50 decimal places*). **9.** step in progression of argument, statement, etc., (*in the first, second, place*). **10.** proper or natural position (*take your places; there is no place for doubt; is in or out of its or his place*); space, seat, accommodation, for person etc. at table, in conveyance, etc., (*take two places in the coach; always a place for you at our table*); fall into ~, begin to show intelligible relationship; in ~ of, in exchange or substitution for, instead of; *place in the* SUN; take the ~ of, be substituted for. **11.** office, employment, esp. government appointment; duties or entitlements of office etc. (*it is not my place to inquire into that*); position as chosen member of team etc. **12.** all over the ~, in disorder (lit. or fig.); give ~ to, make room for, yield precedence to, be succeeded by; in ~, in the right position, suitable; out of ~, in the wrong position, unsuitable; take ~, (esp. of prearranged event) occur. **13.** ~-bet (that horse etc. will be among first ||3 or *2 in race); ~-brick (imperfectly burnt from being on windward side of kiln); ~ card (marking place to be occupied by person, esp. at table); ~ -kick, (Footb.) kick made when ball is previously placed for that purpose on ground; ||~'man, holder of public office, esp. one appointed from motives of self-interest rather than suitability; ~-mat, small mat on table at person's place; ~-name, name of town, village, hill, field, lake, etc.; ~-setting, set of dishes and implements for one person to eat with. [ME f. OF, f. Rom. *plattja f. L f. Gk *plateia* (*hodos*) broad (way)]

plăce² *v.t.* **1.** put (thing etc.) in particular place or state; arrange (set of things) in their proper places. **2.**

appoint (person, esp. clergyman) to post; find situation, living, etc., for. **3.** invest (money); dispose of (goods) to customer; put (order for goods etc.) into hands of firm etc. **4.** have (confidence etc. *in* or *on*). **5.** assign rank to; locate; fully identify, remember circumstances of previous meeting with, assign to a class or identify (*I know that man's face but I can't place him*). **6.** state position of (usu. any of first 3 horses or runners) in race; be ~d, ||be among first three or *be second. **7.** get (goal) by PLACE¹-*kick*. **8.** Hence ~'MENT (-sm-) *n.* [f. prec.]

placĕ'bō *n.* (*pl.* ~s). **1.** (RC Ch.) opening antiphon of the vespers for the dead. **2.** (Med.) medicine given to humour, rather than cure, the patient; dummy pill etc. used as control; blank sample in test. [L, = I shall be acceptable or pleasing (*placēre* please), first word of Ps. 114:9 in Vulgate]

placĕ'nt|a *n.* (*pl.* ~ae or ~as). flattened circular spongy vascular organ in uterus of pregnant mammals (expelled after parturition) and helping to nourish foetus, which is attached to it by umbilical cord; (Bot.) part of carpel to which ovules are attached; hence ~AL *a.* (~al mammal, mammal other than marsupial or monotreme). [L, f. Gk *plakous -ountos* flat cake f. root of *plax plakos* flat plate]

plă'cer *n.* deposit of sand, gravel, etc., in bed of stream etc. containing valuable minerals in particles. [Amer. Sp., cogn. w. *placel* sandbank f. *plaza* PLACE¹]

placet (plā'sĕt) *n.* affirmative vote in church or university assembly. [L, = it pleases]

plă'cid *a.* mild; peaceful; serene, not easily disturbed; hence **placi'dITY** *n.*, ~LY² *adv.* [f. F *placide* or f. L *placidus* (*placēre* please; see -ID¹)]

plă'ckĕt *n.* opening or slit esp. in woman's skirt, for fastenings or access to pocket. [var. of PLACARD, assoc. w. -ET¹]

plă'coid *a.* & *n.* **1.** *a.* (Of fish-scale) plate-shaped; having placoid scales. **2.** *n.* placoid fish. [f. Gk *plax plakos* flat plate + -OID]

plafond (plăfaw'n) *n.* **1.** ceiling, esp. one enriched with paintings; such painting. **2.** early form of contract bridge. [F (*plat* flat, *fond* bottom)]

plă'gal *a.* (Mus.) (Of church mode) having sounds comprised between dominant and its octave (cf. AUTHENTIC); ~ cadence or close (in which chord of subdominant immediately precedes that of the tonic). [f. med. L *plagalis* f. *plaga* plagal mode, f. L f. Gk *plagios* oblique, (in med. Gk) plagal, f. *plagos* side; see -AL]

plage (plahzh) *n.* sea beach (esp. at fashionable resort); (Astron.) unusually bright region on sun. [F]

plā'giar|ize, ~ise (-īz), *v.t.* take and use another person's (thoughts, writings, inventions, etc.) as one's own; so ~ISM (1), ~IST (1), *ns.* [f. foll. + -IZE]

plā'giary *n.* (arch.) plagiarism; plagiarist. [f. L *plagiarius* kidnapper (*plagium* a kidnapping f. Gk *plagion*; see -ARY¹)]

plā'gio- *comb. form.* oblique, as: ~cepha'lic, having anterior part of skull more developed on one side, posterior on the other; ~clase, triclinic feldspar; ~cla'stic, (Min.) having oblique cleavage; ~stome, fish with mouth placed transversely beneath snout, e.g. shark or ray. [f. Gk *plagios* oblique (*plagos* side) + -o-]

plăgue (-g) *n.*, & *v.t.* **1.** affliction, esp. as divine punishment; (colloq.) unusual infestation *of* (cater-pillars etc.); (colloq.) nuisance, trouble; pestilence (**the** ~ = BUBONIC *plague*, PNEUMONIC *plague*); (arch., as imprecation) *plague on it!* etc.; ~-spot, spot on skin characteristic of plague, locality infected with plague, (fig.) source or symptom of moral corruption. **2.** *v.t.* afflict with plague; (colloq.) annoy, bother, whence ~SOME¹ (-gs-) *a.* (colloq.). [ME, f. L *plaga* stroke, wound, prob. f. Gk *plaga, plēgē* (**plag-* strike)]

plā'gu|ў, *plā'gu|ey, (-gĭ) *a.* & *adv.* (arch.) annoying(ly); exceeding(ly) (*was plaguy glad to get back again*); hence ~iLY² (-gĭ-) *adv.* [f. prec. + -Y²]

plaice *n.* (*pl.* same). European flat-fish, *Pleuronectes platessa*, much used as food; similar Amer. fish. [ME, f. OF *plaïz* f. LL *platessa* app. f. Gk *platus* broad]

plaid (plăd) *n.* & *a.* **1.** *n.* long piece of twilled woollen cloth, usu. with chequered or tartan pattern, outer article of Highland costume, worn over the shoulder; cloth used for this; hence ∼'ED² *a.* **2.** *a.* made of plaid; having plaidlike pattern. [f. Gael. *plaide*, of unkn. orig.]

plain¹ *a.*, *adv.*, & *n.* **1.** *a.* clear, evident; simple, readily understood, (*plain words, English*; *plain as a* PIKESTAFF); not in code. **2.** not intricate (*plain cooking, sewing*); unembellished, (of drawings etc.) not coloured; (of food) not rich or elaborate or highly seasoned; not luxurious (*plain* LIVING¹). **3.** outspoken, straightforward, (**be** ∼ **with,** tell home truths to); unsophisticated (*I am a plain man*); of homely manners, dress, or appearance; ugly (*a pity the poor girl is so plain*). **4.** Hence ∼'LY² *adv.*, ∼'NESS (-n-n-) *n.* **5.** *adv.* clearly (*learn to speak plain*; *ah, did you once see Shelley plain?*); simply (*that is plain stupid*). **6.** ∼ **card** (not trump, or not court-card); ∼'**chant,** = *plainsong*; ∼ **chocolate** (without milk added in manufacture); ∼ **clothes,** unofficial dress, esp. of policeman on duty but not in uniform; ∼ **cook,** person able to do plain cooking; ∼ **dealing,** candour, straightforwardness; ∼ **sailing,** sailing in a straightforward course, (fig.) simple situation or course of action; *plain* SERVICE¹ 6; ∼'**song,** traditional church music in medieval modes and in free rhythm depending on accentuation of the words, and sung in unison; ∼**-spoken,** outspoken; ∼ **suit** (not trumps); ∼ **time** (not paid for at overtime rates); ∼ **weaving** (with weft alternately over and under warp). **7.** *n.* level tract of country; ∼'**sman** (-z-), inhabitant of a plain. **8.** ordinary stitch in knitting (opp. PURL¹). [ME f. OF *plain* a. & n., f. L *planus* a., *planum* n.]

plain² *v.i.* (arch. or poet.) mourn; complain; emit plaintive sound. [ME, f. OF *plaindre* (st. *plaign*-) f. L *plangere planct*- lament]

plaint *n.* ‖(Law) accusation, charge; (literary) lamentation, complaint. [ME, f. OF *plainte* fem. p.p. (as n.) of *plaindre*, and OF *plaint* f. L *planctus* (as prec.)]

plai'ntiff *n.* party who brings suit into court of law (opp. *defendant*). [ME, f. OF *plaintif* a. (as foll.)]

plai'ntive *a.* expressive of sorrow; mournful- (-sounding); hence ∼LY² (-vlĭ) *adv.*, ∼NESS (-vn-) *n.* [ME, f. OF (-*if*, -*ive*) f. *plainte* (as PLAINT; see -IVE)]

plai'ster¹·². Var. of PLASTER¹·².

plait (plăt) *n.*, & *v.t.* **1.** = PLEAT. **2.** *n.* interlacing of three or more strands of hair, ribbon, straw, etc.; material thus interlaced. **3.** *v.t.* form (hair, straw, etc.) into plait. [ME f. OF *pleit* fold, f. Rom. *plic(i)tum* p.p. (as n.) of L *plicare* fold]

plan *n.* & *v.* (-nn-). **1.** *n.* drawing or diagram made by projection on horizontal plane (cf. ELEVATION), esp. one showing relative position of parts of (one floor of) building; large-scale detailed map of town or district. **2.** table indicating times, places, etc., of intended proceedings etc.; scheme of arrangement. **3.** formulated or organized method by which thing is to be done (FIVE-*year plan*), project, design; way of proceeding (*the better plan is to peel them after boiling*; *plan of campaign*); imaginary plane perpendicular to line of vision and containing objects shown in picture. **4.** *v.t.* make plan of (ground, existing building); design (building to be constructed etc.); scheme, arrange beforehand, (procedure etc.); (esp. in *p.p.*) conduct in accordance with plan. **5.** *v.i.* make plans; ∼ **on,** (colloq.) aim at do*ing.* **6.** Hence ∼'**nER¹,** ∼'**nING¹** (1), *ns.* (esp. w. ref. to controlled designing of buildings and development of land). [F, f. earlier *plant*, f. It. *pianta* plan of building; cf. PLANT¹]

plā'nar *a.* (Math.) of or relating to, in the form of, a plane. [f. PLANE³ + -AR¹]

planār'ian *n.* flatworm of family Planariidae, usu.

living in fresh water. [f. mod. L *Planaria* genus-name, fem. (as n.) of L *planarius* lying flat]

plă'nchet (-sh-) *n.* plain disc of metal from which coin is made. [dim. of *planch* slab of metal f. OF *planche* (see PLANK¹)]

plănchě'tte (-sh-) *n.* small usu. heart-shaped board supported by two castors and vertical pencil, which when person's fingers rest lightly on board is said to trace letters etc. without conscious direction. [F, dim. of *planche* PLANK¹]

Plănck *n.* ∼('s) **constant,** (Phys.) fundamental constant of proportionality between energy and frequency of quanta of electromagnetic radiation. [f. M. ∼, Ger. physicist d. 1947]

plāne¹ *n.* tall spreading tree of genus *Platanus* with broad angular palmately-lobed leaves. [ME & OF, f. L f. Gk *platanos* (*platus* broad)]

plāne² *n.*, & *v.t.* **1.** *n.* tool for smoothing surface of woodwork by paring shavings from it, consisting of wooden or metal stock from smooth bottom of which a steel blade projects; similar tool for smoothing metal. **2.** *v.t.* smooth (wood, metal) with plane; pare away or down (irregularities) with plane; (arch.) level (*plane the way*). [n. ME & OF, f. LL *plana*, v. ME f. OF *planer*, f. L *planare* (*planus* PLAIN¹)]

plāne³ *n.*, & *v.i.* **1.** *n.* surface such that the straight line joining any two points in it lies wholly in it; imaginary surface of this kind in which points or lines in material bodies lie; level surface. **2.** flat thin object such as table-top; main supporting surface of aeroplane; aeroplane. **3.** (fig.) level (*of* thought, attainment, knowledge, etc.; *his superstition places him on the same plane as the savage*). **4.** ∼ **sailing,** art of determining ship's position on the theory that she is moving on a plane, (fig.) = PLAIN¹ *sailing*. **5.** *v.i.* travel, glide (*down* etc.), in aeroplane; soar; (of speedboat etc.) skim over water. [f. L *planum* flat surface, neut. (as n.) of *planus* PLAIN¹; different. f. PLAIN¹ in 17th c.]

plāne⁴ *a.* (Of surface etc.) perfectly level, as a PLANE³; (of angle, figure, etc.) lying in a plane; ∼ **chart** on which meridians and parallels of latitude are represented by equidistant straight lines, used in PLANE³ sailing); ∼**-table,** surveying instrument used for direct plotting in the field, with circular table and pivoted alidade. [var. of PLAIN¹, after F *plan plane*]

plă'nět¹ *n.* **1.** (Astron.) heavenly body revolving in approximately circular orbit round sun; the earth; **major** ∼, (1) Jupiter, Saturn, Uranus, or Neptune, (2) planet other than asteroids; **minor** ∼, asteroid; hence ∼**ŏ'**LOGY *n.* **2.** (Hist.) heavenly body distinguished from fixed stars by having apparent motion of its own (including moon and sun), esp. (Astrol.) with reference to its supposed influence on persons and events; ∼**-stricken,** ∼**-struck,** (arch.) bewildered, terrified. [ME, f. OF *planete* f. LL f. Gk *planētēs* wanderer, planet, (*planaomai* wander)]

plă'nět² *n.* chasuble. [f. med. L *planeta*, perh. f. LL *planetica* (*vestis*) traveller's (cloak) (*planeticus* f. as prec.; see -IC)]

plănetār'i|um *n.* (*pl.* ∼**ums** or ∼**a**). orrery; device for projecting image of night sky as seen at various times and places; building containing this. [mod. L, f. as prec.]

plă'nětary *a.* of or like planets (*planetary influence, motions, system*); terrestrial, mundane; wandering, erratic; ∼ **nebula,** ring-shaped nebula formed by shell of gas round star. [f. LL *planetarius* (as PLANET¹; see -ARY¹)]

plănětě'simal *n.* one of a vast number of minute planetary bodies, esp. those which, according to the ∼ **hypothesis,** formed the planets by accretion in a cold state. [f. PLANET¹, after *infinitesimal*]

plă'nětoid *n.* asteroid. [f. PLANET¹ + -OID]

plă'ng|ent (-nj-) *a.* (Of sound) loud and reverberating; plaintive; hence ∼ENCY *n.* [f. L *plangere* lament; see -ENT]

plani'|mĕter *n.* instrument for mechanically

measuring the area of a plane figure; so **plăni-mĕ'tri̇c**(AL) *adjs.*, ~METRY *n.* [f. F *planimètre* f. L *planus* level; see -METER]

plă'nish *v.t.* flatten (sheet metal etc.) with smooth--faced hammer or otherwise; flatten out (coining--metal) between rollers; hence ~ER¹ (1, 2) *n.* [ME, f. OF *planir* smooth (*plain* PLANE⁴; see -ISH²)]

plă'ni̇|sphēre *n.* map formed by projection of (part of) sphere on plane, esp. to show appearance of heavens at particular time and place; hence ~SPHĔ'RIC *a.* [ME, f. med. L *planisphaeri∷m* (as PLANE⁴, SPHERE); infl. by F *planisphère*]

plănk¹ *n.* long wide piece of timber, a few inches thick; item of political or other programme (cf. PLATFORM); **walk the** ~, (Hist., of pirates' captive etc.) be made to walk blindfold into sea along plank laid over side of ship; ~ed (of boards, without mattress, in prison etc.). [ME f. ONF *planke* = OF *planche* f. LL *planca* board (*plancus* flat-footed)]

plănk² *v.t.* furnish, cover, or floor, with planks, whence ~'ING¹ (2, 3) *n.*; (colloq.) put *down* roughly or violently, esp. pay (money, or abs.) *down* on the spot; *cook and serve (food) on plank with garnish. [ME, f. prec.]

plă'nktŏn *n.* (chiefly microscopic) drifting or floating forms of organic life found at various depths in seas, lakes, rivers, etc., taken collectively (cf. BENTHOS, NEKTON); hence ~IC (-ŏ'n-) *a.* [G, f. Gk *plagktos* wandering (*plazomai* wander)]

plă'nner, plă'nning. See PLAN 6.

plănō- *comb. form.* level, flat, as. ~co'ncave, ~co'nvex, (of lens etc.) with one surface plane and the other concave, convex; ~meter (-ŏ'm-), flat plate as gauge for plane surfaces. [f. L *planus* flat + -O-]

plant¹ (-ah-) *n.* **1.** living organism having neither power of locomotion nor special organs of sensation or usu. digestion, member of the vegetable kingdom; small plant (other than trees and shrubs). **2.** fixtures, implements, machinery, etc., used in industrial processes; factory. **3.** (sl.) planned swindle or burglary, hoax, thing deliberately placed for discovery by others. **4.** ~louse, small insect that infests plants, esp. aphis. **5.** Hence ~'LET *n.*, ~'LIKE *a.* [f. OE *plante* & F *plante* f. L *planta* sprout, slip, cutting, or f. foll.]

plant² (-ah-) *v.t.* **1.** place (tree, shoot, bulb, seed, crop, etc.) into ground or soil so that it may take root and grow; deposit (young fish, spawn, oysters) in river etc.; ~ **out**, transfer (plant) from pot or frame to open ground, set out (seedlings) at intervals. **2.** fix (stake, feet, etc.) firmly (*in*, *on*, ground etc.); station (person), esp. as spy; ~ one**self**, take up a position. **3.** establish, found, (community, city, church); settle (person) in a place as colonist etc.; cause (idea etc.) to take root *in* (mind); furnish (land *with* plants, district *with* settlers etc.). **4.** deliver (blow, thrust) with definite aim. **5.** (sl.) conceal (stolen goods etc.), esp. with view to misleading a later discoverer; abandon. **6.** *bury. **7.** Hence ~'ABLE *a.* [OE *plantian* & OF *planter*, f. L *plantare*]

Plăntă'gĕnĕt *n.* & *a.* (member) of the family founded by Geoffrey of Anjou, esp. any of the English kings from Henry II to Richard II. [surname, orig. nickname, f. sprig of broom (L *planta* plant, *genista* broom) worn as cognizance]

pla'ntain¹ (-ă'ntĭn, -ah'-) *n.* plant of genus *Plantago*, esp. low herb with broad flat leaves spread out close to ground and seeds much used as food for cage-birds; ~ **lily**, hosta. [ME & OF, f. L *plantago* -*ginis* (*planta* sole of foot, from its broad prostrate leaves)]

pla'ntain² (-ă'ntĭn, -ah'-) *n.* (fruit of) treelike tropical herbaceous plant allied to banana and bearing similar fruit. [earlier *platan*, f. Sp. *plá(n)tano* plane--tree, prob. assim. f. Galibi *palatana* etc.]

plă'ntar *a.* (Anat.) of the sole of the foot. [f. L *plantaris* (*planta* sole; see -AR¹)]

plantă'tion (plă-, plah-) *n.* assemblage of planted

growing plants, esp. trees; estate on which cotton, tobacco, etc., is cultivated (formerly by slave labour; ~ **song**, song of the kind sung by Blacks on American plantations); (Hist.) colonization, colony. [ME f. OF, or f. L *plantatio* (as PLANT²; see -ATION)]

pla'nter (-ah-) *n.* cultivator of soil; (Ir. Hist.) English settler on forfeited lands in 17th c., person settled in evicted tenant's holding in 19th c.; occupier of plantation, esp. in (sub-)tropical countries, (*coffee*, *cotton*, *sugar*, *tobacco*, *-planter*); machine for planting (*corn*, *potato*, *-planter*); container for decorative plants. [ME, f. PLANT² + -ER¹]

plă'ntigrāde *a.* & *n.* (animal) that walks on its soles, e.g. bear (cf. DIGITIGRADE). [F, f. mod. L *plantigradus* f. L *planta* sole + -I- + -*gradus* -walking]

plantŏ'cracy̆ (plah-) *n.* ruling class of planters. [f. PLANTER + -O- + -CRACY]

plă'nxty̆ *n.* (Ir.) (dance to) animated harp-tune in triplets. [18th c.; orig. unkn.]

plaqu|e (-ahk, -ăk) *n.* ornamental tablet of metal, porcelain, etc., plain or decorated; small badge of rank in honorary order; (Path.) patch of eruption etc., fibrous lesion in atherosclerosis; film on teeth where bacteria proliferate; so ~E'TTE (-ăkĕ't) *n.* [F, f. Du. *plak* tablet (*plakken* stick)]

plăsh¹ *n.* marshy pool; puddle; hence ~'Y² *a.* [OE *plæsc*, = MDu *plasch*, imit.; cf. foll.]

plăsh² *v.* & *n.* **1.** *v.i.* & *i.* splash; strike surface of (water) so as to break it up. **2.** *n.* splash, plunge; hence ~'Y² *a.* [cf. Du. *plassen*, LG *plaschen*; prob. imit.]

plăsh⁶ *v.t.* bend down and interweave (branches, twigs) to form hedge; make, renew, (hedge) thus. [ME, f. OF *pla(i)ssier* f. Rom. **plectiare* f. L *plectere* plait; cf. PLEACH]

plă'sm. Var. of foll.

plă'sm|a (-z-) *n.* **1.** green variety of quartz. **2.** colourless coagulable part of blood, lymph, or milk, in which the corpuscles or fat-globules float; so ~A'TIC *a.* **3.** = PROTOPLASM. **4.** (Phys.) gas of positive ions and free electrons with approximately equal positive and negative charge, and so usu. in approximately equal numbers. [LL, = mould, f. Gk *plasma -atos* (*plassō* 'to shape)]

plăsmŏ'di|um (-z-) *n.* (*pl.* ~**a**). mass of naked protoplasm formed by fusion or aggregation of amoeboid bodies without fusion of their nuclei; parasitic protozoan of genus *Plasmodium*, causing malaria in man. [mod. L, f. PLASMA + -*odium* (see -ODE)]

plăsmŏ'lȳsi̇s (-zm-) *n.* contraction of protoplasm of plant cell due to immersion in a solution stronger than the cell fluid; hence **plăsmŏ'lȳse**, **-lȳze*, (-zm-) *v.t.*, subject to plasmolysis. [mod. L, f. as PLASMA + -O- + -LYSIS]

pla'ster¹ (-ah'-) *n.* **1.** curative or protective application consisting of some substance spread on linen etc. and capable of adhering at the temperature of the body (COURT¹, MUSTARD, *plaster*); = STICK¹*ing-plaster*. **2.** soft plastic mixture, esp. of lime, sand, and hair, for spreading on walls etc. to form smooth surface and harden by drying; ~ **of Paris**, fine white plaster of gypsum used for making moulds or casts, in bandages for immobilizing limbs etc., or as cement etc. [prepared from gypsums of Montmartre, Paris]. **3.** ~**board**, board with core of plaster for walls etc.; ~ **saint**, person regarded as being without moral faults and human frailty. **4.** Hence ~Y² *a.* [OE & OF *plastre*, f. med. L *plastrum* f. L f. Gk *emplastron*]

pla'ster² (-ah'-) *v.t.* **1.** cover (wall etc.) with plaster or the like, whence ~ER¹ *n.*; coat, bedaub; (fig.) load to excess (*with* praise etc.); (sl.) bomb or shell heavily; (in *p.p.*, sl.) drunk. **2.** apply medical plaster to; stick or fix (thing) like plaster on surface; make smooth with fixative etc. (*hair plastered down*). [ME, f. prec. or f. F *plastrer* (*plastre*, as prec.)]

pla'stic¹ (-ă'-, -ah'-) *a.* **1.** moulding, giving form to clay, wax, or other yielding solid; ~ **arts**, those concerned with modelling (e.g. sculpture, ceramics) or with representation of solid objects; ∼ **surgery** (repairing or replacing deficient structure esp. by transfer of tissue), so ∼ **surgeon. 2.** causing growth of natural forms, formative of immaterial things; (Biol.) capable of forming living tissue. **3.** produced by moulding; capable of being (easily) moulded; ∼ **bomb,** one containing putty-like explosive capable of being moulded by hand. **4.** (fig.) pliant, supple. **5.** Hence **pla′sti**CALLY (-ă′-, -ah′-) adv., **plăsti′ci**TY n., ∼IZE (3) v.t., ∼**īz**ER¹ (2) n. [f. F plastique or f. L f. Gk plastikos (plassō to mould; see -IC)]

plä′stic² n. & a. **1.** n. synthetic resinous etc. polymeric substance that can be given any permanent shape; (in pl., attrib., esp.) = sense 2. **2.** a. made of plastic (plastic bag, flowers). [f. prec.]

Plä′stĭcine (-ēn) n. (**P**) plastic substance used for modelling. [f. PLASTIC¹ + -INE⁴]

plä′stid n. small body in cytoplasm of plañt cell, containing pigment or food. [G, f. Gk plastos shaped + -ID²]

plä′stron n. fencer's leather-covered breastplate; breast-covering of facings-cloth worn by lancers; ornamental front on woman's bodice; man's starched shirt-front; ventral part of shell of tortoise or turtle, corresponding part in other animals; (Hist.) steel breastplate. [F, f. It. piastrone augment. of piastra breastplate, f. L emplastrum PLASTER¹]

plät¹ n. *plan of land ownership etc.; (arch.) patch or plot of ground. [16th c., collat. form of PLOT¹]

plät² n., & v.t. (-tt-). Var. of PLAIT 2, 3.

plat³ (plah) n. dish of food; ∼ **du jour** (dū zhoor′; lit. 'of the day'), dish given special prominence on day's menu. [F, = dish, flat surface, f. plat flat f. pop. L *plattus f. Gk platus]

plä′tan n. plane-tree. [ME, f. L (see PLANE¹)]

pläte¹ n. **1.** flat thin usu. rigid sheet of metal etc. with even surface and more or less uniform thickness; this as part of mechanism; *anode of thermionic valve; (Geol.) rigid sheet of rock in earth's outer crust. **2.** smooth piece of metal etc. for engraving; impression from this; illustration on special paper in book. **3.** piece of metal with name or inscription for affixing to something (coffin, door, name, -plate; **put up** one's ∼, begin practice as doctor etc.). **4.** thin sheet of metal, glass, etc., coated with sensitive film for photography. **5.** stereotype, electrotype, or plastic cast of page of composed movable types, or metal or plastic copy of filmset matter, from which sheets are printed. **6.** horizontal timber laid along top of wall to support ends of joists or rafters (roof, WALL, window, -plate). **7.** (Biol.) thin flat organic structure or formation. **8.** (collect. sing.) ‖table and domestic utensils of silver, gold, or other metal, (pewter plate); (objects of) plated metal (electroplate). **9.** silver or gold cup as prize for (orig. horse-)race; such race; SELLing plate. **10.** shallow usu. circular vessel, now usu. of earthenware or china, from which food is eaten or served (cake, dessert, dinner, soup, -plate; **on a** ∼, (colloq.) to be taken without need of effort; **on one's plate,** (colloq.) for one to deal with or consider); contents of this (a plate of strawberries); *main course of meal, served on one plate; *food for one person esp. at meal to raise funds; shallow vessel used for collection in churches etc. (put a coin in the plate). **11.** thin piece of plastic material, moulded to shape of gums etc., to which artificial teeth are attached; (colloq.) denture. **12.** (Baseball). flat piece of whitened rubber marking station of batter (**home** ∼) or pitcher. **13.** light shoe for racehorse. **14.** ∼ **armour** (of metal plates, for man, ship, etc.); ‖∼**-basket** (for spoons, forks, etc.); ∼ **clutch** (with engagement by metal plates); ∼ **glass,** glass of fine quality orig. cast in plates, for shop windows etc.; ∼**-holder,** light-proof container for photographic plate; ‖∼**′layer,** man employed in fixing and repairing railway rails [f. flanged strip used as track in early colliery railways]; ∼**-mark,**

(1) = HALLmark, (2) impression left on margin of engraving by pressure of the plate; ∼**-powder** (for cleaning silver); ‖∼**-rack** (in which plates are kept or placed to drain); plate TRACERY. **15.** Hence ∼′FUL 2 (-tf-) n. (lit. or fig.), ∼′LESS a., ∼′LET n. (esp. thrombocyte), (-tl-). [ME f. OF, f. med. L plata plate armour (platus a. f. pop. L *plattus; see PLAT³)]

pläte² v.t. cover (esp. ship) with plates of metal for protection, ornament, etc.; cover (other metal) with thin coat of silver, gold, or tin; make plate of (type etc.) for printing. [ME, f. prec.]

plä′teau (-tō) n. (pl. ∼x or ∼s, pr. -z). tableland; ornamented tray or dish; decorative plaque; woman's hat with level top; state of little variation following an increase. [F, f. OF platel dim. of PLAT³]

plä′ten n. plate in printing-press by which paper is pressed against type; corresponding part, e.g. roller carrying paper in typewriter etc. [f. OF platine flat piece (plat flat; see PLAT³)]

plä′ter n. one who plates with silver etc.; one who makes or applies plates in shipbuilding; inferior racehorse, competing chiefly for plates (sense 9). [f. PLATE¹,² + -ER¹]

plätere′sque (-sk) a. richly ornamented in style suggesting silverware. [f. Sp. plateresco (platero silversmith f. plata silver); cf. -ESQUE]

plä′tform n., & v.t. **1.** n. raised level surface, natural or artificial terrace; thick sole of shoe; floor area for conductor etc. at entrance to bus or tram; ‖raised surface along side of line at railway station; ∼ **ticket** (for access to this by non-traveller). **2.** raised flooring in hall or open air from which speaker addresses audience (**the** ∼, (fig.) oratory suitable to this); (fig.) political basis of party etc., declared policy of political party. **3.** v.t. place (as) on platform. [f. F plateforme ground-plan (PLAT³ plate flat, forme FORM¹)]

plä′ting n. In vbl senses; coating of gold, silver, etc.; plate-racing. [f. PLATE² + -ING¹]

plati′nic a. of platinum, esp. (Chem.) in tetravalent form. [f. PLATINUM + -IC]

plä′tinĭze, -īse (-īz), v.t. coat with platinum. [f. PLATINUM + -IZE]

plä′tinoid n. alloy of copper, zinc, nickel, etc.; a platinum metal. [f. PLATINUM + -OID]

plä′tinotype n. (print made by) process of photographic printing in platinum black. [f. foll. + -O- + TYPE¹]

plä′tinum n. white heavy ductile malleable metallic element unaffected by simple acids and fusible only at very high temperature; ∼ **black,** platinum in form of powder like lampblack; ∼ **blonde,** (woman with) silvery-blonde (hair); ∼ **metal,** metallic element (osmium, iridium, palladium, etc.) found with and resembling platinum. [mod. L (see -IUM) f. earlier platina f. Sp., dim. of plata silver; see -INE⁴]

plä′tit|ude n. commonplaceness; commonplace remark, esp. one solemnly delivered; hence ∼**ū′din**IZE (2) v.i., ∼**ū′din**ous a. [F (PLAT³), after certitude, multitudinous, etc.]

plätitūdinā′r′ian n. & a. **1.** n. one who uses platitudes. **2.** a. characterized by or fond of using platitudes. [f. prec., after latitudinarian]

Plato′nic a. of Plato the Greek philosopher (d. 347 BC) or his doctrines; confined to words or theory, not leading to action, harmless; ∼ **body** or **solid,** (Geom.) one of five REGULAR solids (tetrahedron, cube, octahedron, dodecahedron, icosahedron); ∼ **love,** purely spiritual love usu. for one of opposite sex; ∼ **year,** cycle in which heavenly bodies were supposed to go through all their possible movements and return to original positions; hence or cogn. **Plato′ni**CALLY adv., **Plä′ton**ISM (3), **Plä′ton**IST (2), ns., **Plä′ton**IZE (2, 3) v.i. & t. [f. L f. Gk Platōnikos (Platōn Plato; see -IC)]

platoo′n n. **1.** (Mil.) subdivision of a company, a tactical unit commanded by a lieutenant and usu. divided into three sections. **2.** group of persons acting together. **3.** (Hist.) small infantry detachment, esp. a unit for volley-firing etc., volley fired by it. [f. F *peloton* small ball, dim. of *pelote*; see PELLET, -OON]

pla'tteland (plah'telahnt) *n.* (S. Afr.) = BACK[1]*veld*. [Afrik., = flat land]

plä'tter *n.* **1.** (US or arch.) (*large) flat dish or plate esp. for food. **2. on a** ∼, = *on a* PLATE[1] 10. **3.** (sl.) *gramophone record. [ME & AF *plater*, f. AF *plat* PLATE[1]]

plä'tÿ- *comb. form.* broad, flat, as: ∼he'lminth, flatworm; ∼pus, Australian egg-laying aquatic and burrowing mammal with ducklike beak and flat tail; ∼rrhine (-rīn), (of monkey) with nostrils far apart and directed forwards or sideways, (of person) having broad nose with flat bridge. [f. Gk *platu-* (*platus* broad, flat)]

plau'dït *n.* (usu. in *pl.*) round of applause; emphatic expression of approval. [shortened f. L *plaudite* applaud, imper. pl. of *plaudere plaus-* applaud, said by Roman actors at end of play]

plau's|ïble (-z-) *a.* (Of argument, statement, etc.) specious, seeming reasonable or probable; (of person) persuasive but deceptive; hence or cogn. ∼IBI'LITY *n.*, ∼IBLY *adv.* [f. L *plausibilis* (as prec.; see -IBLE)]

play[1] *v.* **1.** *v.i.* move about in lively or unrestrained or capricious manner, frisk, flutter, pass gently (*around, about, etc.*), strike lightly (*on etc.*), (*bees play about flowers, tresses play on her neck; smile played on his lips; wind plays on water; his fancy played round the idea*). **2.** emit light, water, cannonade, etc., (*fountains play from 10 till 4*). **3.** amuse oneself, sport, frolic, trifle, pass time pleasantly, *with*; (sl.) act as required (*he wouldn't play*); (prov.) be away from work or on strike; ∼ **about** or **around**, behave irresponsibly (*with*); ∼(**up)on words**, make pun. **4.** employ oneself in a game; gamble; ∼ **at**, engage in (game), (fig.) engage in (*fighting* etc.) in trivial or half-hearted way; ∼ **fair**, play or (fig.) act fairly; ∼ **false**, act deceitfully or treacherously; *play with* FIRE[1]; ∼ **into** person's **hands**, act so as to give him the advantage; ∼ **off**, play extra match to decide draw or tie; ∼ *off n.*, such extra game; ∼**ed out**, exhausted of energy or vitality or usefulness; ∼ **safe**, ∼ **for safety**, act with caution; *play on the* SQUARE[1], *for* TIME[1] 9; ∼ **up**, put all one's energy into game, (colloq.) behave annoyingly. **5.** (Of cricket-ground, tennis-court, etc.) be in (specified) condition. **6.** perform *on* (musical instrument etc.); ∼ **by ear**, (1) perform without aid of written music, (2) proceed instinctively or step by step according to results; ∼ (**up)on**, make use of (person's fears, credulity, etc.). **7.** perform role on stage (*in drama*); *play to the* GALLERY; ∼ **up to**, act so as to support (another actor), (fig.) flatter. **8.** *v.t.* allow (fish) to exhaust itself by pulling against line; allow (light, water, etc.) to fall *on, over,* etc. **9.** perform, execute, (trick, prank, joke, *on* person; stroke etc. in game). **10.** employ oneself in game of (cricket, bridge, etc., or abs.); ∼ **it cool**, (colloq.) be relaxed or unemotional); gamble on (∼ **both ends against the middle**, support each side to ensure one's own gain; ∼ **the market**, speculate in stocks etc.; *play the races); pretend for fun (*that we are gypsies* etc.); *play* BALL[1], DUCK[1]*s and drakes*, FAST[3] *and loose*, the GAME[1], HELL *with*, *HOOK(E)Y; ∼ **off**, complete (game etc. that is to be played). **11.** contend against (other person or team) in game; include (person) in team for game; occupy (specified position) in team at football etc.; ∼ **for**, (colloq.) regard (person) as being or having; ∼ one**self in**, become accustomed to prevailing conditions (in game, or fig.); ∼ **off**, oppose (person etc. *against* another) esp. for one's own advantage; ∼ **up**, (colloq.) annoy, tease. **12.** (Cricket etc.) strike (ball, or abs.) in specified (esp. defensive) manner; *play* BACK[3]; ∼ **on**, (abs., Cricket) be out by playing ball on to one's own wicket. **13.** move (chess-man etc.); take (playing-card) from one's hand and lay it face upwards on table in one's turn; (fig.) make

use of (advantage available; *play* one's *ace*, one's *trump card*); ∼ one's **cards right** or **well**, (fig.) make good use of one's opportunities. **14.** perform on (musical instrument, or abs.); perform (piece of music etc. *on* instrument); accompany going *in, out,* etc., (of person) with music; ∼ **by ear** (cf. sense 6). **15.** cause (gramophone, tape recorder, recording, etc.) to produce music or other sound; ∼ **back**, make audible (what has previously been recorded); ∼*-back n.*, (device for) such reproduction of sound; ∼ **down**, minimize; ∼ **up**, make the most of, exploit. **16.** perform (drama, role, etc.) on stage; (fig.) act in real life the part of (*play the fool*, GOD, *the* MAN[1], *truant*, etc.; *play* one's *part well*); give dramatic performance at (theatre etc.). **17.** Hence ∼'ABLE *a.* [OE *pleg(i)an, plægian* exercise, = MDu. *pleien* dance, perh. rel. to OS *plegan*, OHG *pflegan* attend to]

play[2] *n.* **1.** brisk, light, or fitful movement. **2.** activity, operation, (*lively play of fancy; other forces come into play, are in full play, are brought or called into play*); **in** ∼, engaged or occupied (*hold* one's *attackers in play*); **make** ∼, act effectively; **make** ∼ **with**, use ostentatiously. **3.** freedom of movement, space for this, scope for activity, (*bolts should have half an inch of play; allow full play to curiosity*). **4.** recreation, amusement, esp. as spontaneous activity of children or young animals; **at** ∼, engaged in playing; *said it only* **in** ∼, not seriously; ∼ **of words**, (arch.) trifling with words; ∼ **on words**, pun. **5.** playing of game; manner or style of this; action in game (**make a** ∼ **for**, *(sl.) seek to acquire); *ball is* **in** ∼ (being used in ordinary course of game), *is* **out of** ∼ (temporarily out of use according to rules); CHILD'*s*, FAIR[2], FOUL, *play.* **6.** (prov.) being away from work (of workers on strike etc.). **7.** story to be acted on stage etc.; **as good as a** ∼, very amusing or interesting; hence ∼'LET *n.* **8.** gaming, gambling. **9.** ∼-**acting** (lit. or fig.); ∼-**actor** (usu. derog.); ∼'**bill**, bill or placard announcing theatrical play, *theatre programme; ∼'**buy**, irresponsible pleasure-loving usu. rich man; ∼'**fellow**, companion in (usu. children's) play; ∼'**goer**, frequenter of theatre; ∼'**ground**, piece of ground used for playing esp. at school, place for recreation (*playground of the idle rich*); ∼ **group**, group of young children who play together regularly under supervision; ∼'**house**, (1) theatre, (2) *toy house; ∼'**mate**, playfellow; ∼-**pen**, ∼-**suit**, portable enclosure, garment, for young child to play in; ∼'**thing**, toy, (fig.) person etc. treated as mere toy; ∼'**time**, time assigned for playing or recreation; ∼'**wright**, dramatist. [OE *plega, plæga* exercise (as prec.)]

play'a (-ī'a) *n.* (Geog.) flat salt area flooded with weather. [Sp., = beach, f. LL *plagia*]

play'er *n.* In vbl senses; person engaged in or skilful in a game; performer on musical instrument; ||(Hist.) professional cricketer etc.; actor; = RECORD-*player*; ∼-**piano** (fitted with apparatus enabling it to be played automatically). [OE *plegere* (as PLAY[1], -ER[1])]

play'ful *a.* frolicsome, sportive; humorous, jocular; hence ∼LY[2] *adv.*, ∼NESS *n.* [ME, f. PLAY[2] + -FUL]

play'ing *n.* In vbl senses; ∼-**card**, oblong piece of pasteboard used in games, usu. in pack of 52, identical on one side and marked on the other side to show one of thirteen ranks in one of four suits; ∼-**field**, field used in outdoor games. [ME, f. PLAY[1] + -ING[1]]

pla'za (-ah'-) *n.* market-place, open square (esp. in Spanish town). [Sp., = PLACE[1]]

plea *n.* pleading, argument, excuse; appeal, entreaty, (*make a plea for*); (Law) formal statement by or on behalf of defendant, defence, (**special** ∼, alleging new fact); (Hist.) action at law (*Court of Common Pleas*); ∼ **bargaining**, practice of agreeing to drop charge(s) or to sentence leniently, if accused pleads guilty to other charge(s). [ME & AF *ple, plai*, OF *plait, plaid* agreement, discussion f. L *placitum* decree, neut. p.p. (as n.) of *placēre* please]

pleach *v.t.* entwine, interlace; esp. = PLASH³. [ME *pleche* f. OF **plechier* var. of *ple(i)ssier, pla(i)ssier*; see PLASH³]

plead *v.* (∼'ed, *or* (esp. US, Sc., dial.) pled). **1.** *v.i.* address court as advocate on behalf of either party, whence ∼'ER¹ *n.* (SPECIAL *pleader*); put forward a plea; make appeal or entreaty; ∼ **with**, make earnest appeal to, whence ∼'INGLY *adv.* **2.** *v.t.* maintain (cause) in court; allege formally as plea, (fig.) allege as excuse etc. (*I can only plead inexperience, a previous engagement*), whence ∼'ABLE *a.*; ∼ **guilty**, confess liability or guilt; ∼ **not guilty**, deny liability or guilt. [ME, f. AF *pleder*, OF *plaidier* (as PLEA)]

plea'ding *n.* In vbl senses; (usu. in *pl.*) formal (now usu. written) statement of cause of action or defence; SPECIAL *pleading*. [ME, f. prec. + -ING¹]

plea'sance (plĕ'z-) *n.* (arch.) pleasure, enjoyment; pleasure-ground, esp. one attached to mansion. [ME, f. OF *plaisance* (as foll.; see -ANCE)]

plea'sant (plĕ'z-) *a.* (∼er, ∼est). agreeable to mind, feelings, or senses; ‖(arch.) jocular, facetious; hence ∼LY² *adv.*, ∼NESS *n.* [ME, f. OF *plaisant* (as PLEASE; see -ANT)]

plea'santry̆ (plĕ'z-) *n.* humorous behaviour in conversation etc., jocularity; humorous speech, joking remark. [f. F *plaisanterie* (as prec.; see -ERY)]

please (-z) *v.* **1.** *v.t.* give pleasure to (*meant only to please the eye; this book will please you*); ∼ one**self**, do as one likes; **be ∼d at, about, with**, derive pleasure or satisfaction from; **be ∼d** (glad) **to** (do; esp. as polite form of consent or offer); **be ∼d** (graciously willing) **to** (do; in formal or iron. deference, *Her Majesty has been graciously pleased to confer* etc., *your lordship was pleased to doubt my veracity*); (with *it* as subject, expressed or omitted, representing a prec. or foll. infinitive, clause, or sentence, now chiefly as in last use) *it has never pleased him to explain*; (*may it*) *please your honour, there was no moon that night; the matter will be cleared up some day, please God.* **2.** *v.i.* think fit, have will or desire, (*take as many as you please*); give pleasure (*he was anxious to please*). **3. if you ∼**, with your permission (polite form of request esp. for trifling services; *I will take another cup, if you please*), if I may say so and be believed (iron., with implication that nothing could be more unreasonable; *and now, if you please, he expects me to pay for it!*). **4.** (in *imper.*, orig. = *may it please you*) ring the bell, please; *may I come in, please?; won't you please come in?; coffee for two, please; please return it soon; please don't forget the key.* **5.** Hence **please**D¹ (-zd), **plea'**SING² (-z-), *adjs.* [ME *plaise* f. OF *plaisir* f. L *placēre*]

plea'surab|le (plĕ'zher-) *a.* causing pleasure; hence ∼leNESS (-beln-) *n.*, ∼LY² *adv.* [f. foll. + -ABLE, after *comfortable*]

plea'sure (plĕ'zher) *n. & v.* **1.** *n.* feeling of satisfaction or joy; sensuous enjoyment as an object of life (*a life given up to pleasure; man of ∼*, profligate); source of pleasure (*it is a pleasure to talk to him*); gratification (*do me the pleasure of dining with me*); **take** (**a**) ∼ **in**, like doing; **take** one's ∼, (arch.) enjoy oneself (esp. sensually); **with** ∼, gladly, certainly. **2.** will, desire, (*shall consult his pleasure; can be altered at pleasure*); gracious wish (of monarch etc.). **3.** ∼**-boat** etc. (used for pleasure, not business); ∼**-ground** (laid out for pleasure). **4.** *v.t.* give (esp. sexual) pleasure to. **5.** *v.i.* take pleasure (*in* thing, *in* doing). [ME & OF *plesir, plaisir* PLEASE, used as n.; see -URE]

pleat *n., & v.t.* **1.** *n.* fold or crease, esp. flattened fold in cloth doubled upon itself; BOX²-*pleat*; **inverted ∼**, box-pleat formed on inside of material; KNIFE-*pleat*. **2.** *v.t.* fold (cloth etc.) thus. [ME, var. of PLAIT]

plĕb *n.* (sl.) plebeian, person of lower classes. [abbr.]

*plēbe *n.* (colloq.) member of lowest class at US Naval or Military Academy. [shortened f. PLEBEIAN]

plēbē'ian (-bē'an) *n. & a.* **1.** *n.* commoner in ancient Rome (cf. PATRICIAN); commoner. **2.** *a.* of low birth, of the common people, uncultured; coarse, base, ignoble; hence ∼IZE (3) *v.t.*, ∼NESS (-n-n-) *n.* [f. L *plebeius* (*plebs plebis* common people) + -AN]

plĕ'biscite *n.* direct vote of all electors of State on important public question, e.g. change in the constitution; public expression of community's opinion, with or without binding force; (Rom. Hist.) law enacted by plebeians' assembly; hence **plĕbi'scit**-ARY¹ *a.* [f. F *plébiscite* f. L *plebiscitum* (*plebs plebis* commons, *scitum* decree f. *sciscere* vote for)]

plĕ'ctr|um *n.* (*pl.* ∼**a** *or* ∼**ums**). small pointed piece of ivory, quill, etc., for plucking strings of guitar, zither, etc.; corresponding part of harpsichord etc. [L, f. Gk *plēktron* (*plēssō* strike)]

plĕd. See PLEAD.

plĕdge¹ *n.* **1.** thing handed over to person as security for fulfilment of debt, payment of debt, etc., and liable to forfeiture in case of failure; thing put in pawn; (fig.) child as token of mutual love; thing given as token of favour etc. or of something to come. **2.** drinking of a health, toast. **3.** promise (*under pledge of secrecy*); solemn engagement to abstain from intoxicants (*take, sign, keep, the pledge*); (Polit.) leader's public promise to adopt or not adopt some course; *(person making) promise to join fraternity etc. **4.** state of being pledged (*goods lying in pledge, taken out of pledge*). [ME & OF *plege* f. Frank. L *plebium* (*plebire* assure), perh. f. Gmc *pleg-; cf. PLIGHT]

plĕdge² *v.t.* deposit as security, pawn; promise solemnly by pledge of (one's honour, word, etc.); bind (person, one*self*) by solemn promise; drink to the health of; hence ∼'ABLE (-ja-) *a.*, **plĕdgEE'** *n.*, one who receives a pledge, **plĕ'dgER¹, plĕ'dgOR**, (-jer) *ns.* [f. prec.]

plĕ'dgĕt *n.* small wad of lint etc. [16th c., of unkn. orig.]

Plei'ad (plī'-) *n.* (*pl.* ∼**es** *pr.* -dēz, *or* ∼**s**). **1.** (in *pl.*) cluster of stars in constellation Taurus, usu. spoken of as 7. **2.** (fig.) brilliant group of (usu. 7) persons or things, esp. French poets of the latter part of 16th c. [ME, f. L *Plēias* f. Gk *Pleias -ados*]

plein air (plĕnār') *a.* (Paint.) representing effects of atmosphere and light not observable in studio; hence **pleinair'ist(e)** (plĕ-) *n.*, painter using this style. [F, = open air, orig. of Fr. impressionists *c.* 1870]

Plei'stocēne (plī's-) *a. & n.* (Geol.) (of) division immediately above Pliocene, and forming lower part of Quaternary period or system. [f. Gk *pleistos* most + *kainos* new]

plē'nary̆ *a.* entire, absolute, unqualified, (*plenary* INSPIRATION, *indulgence*); (of assembly) to be attended by all members. [f. LL *plenarius* (*plenus* full; see -ARY¹)]

plĕnipotĕ'ntiary̆ (-sheř̆) *a. & n.* (person, esp. diplomatic envoy) invested with full power of independent action; (of power) absolute. [f. med. L *plenipotentiarius* (*plenus* full, *potentia* power); see -ARY¹]

plē'nitude *n.* fullness, completeness; abundance. [ME f. OF, f. LL *plenitudo* (*plenus* full; see -TUDE)]

plē'ntēous *a.* (rhet.) plentiful; hence ∼LY² *adv.*, ∼NESS *n.* [ME f. OF *plentivous* (*plentif -ive* f. *plenté* PLENTY; see -IVE, -EOUS; cf. *bounteous*)]

plē'ntiful *a.* abundant, copious; hence ∼LY² *adv.*, ∼NESS *n.* [ME, f. foll. + -FUL]

plē'nty̆ *n., a., & adv.* **1.** *n.* abundance, quite enough, as much as one could desire, (*of* thing, *or* abs.; *plenty of cake, there are plenty of apples; here is cake in plenty; we are in plenty of time*); **horn of ∼**, cornucopia. **2.** *a.* (colloq.) existing in ample quantity. **3.** *adv.* (colloq.) fully (*it is plenty large enough*). [ME *plenteth, plente* f. OF *plentet* f. L *plenitas -tatis* (*plenus* full; see -TY¹)]

plē'num *n.* space filled with matter (∼ **system**, method of ventilation by forcing air in and out); full assembly. [L, neut. of *plenus* full]

plēochrō'|ic (-k-) *a.* showing different colours when

viewed in different directions; so ∼ISM (2) *n*. [f. Gk *pleiōn* more + -*khroos* f. *khrōs* colour + -IC]

plĕomŏr′ph|ic *a*. (Biol., Chem., & Min.) exhibiting, or occurring in, more than one distinct form; so ∼ISM (2) *n*. [f. as prec. + Gk *morphē* form + -IC]

plĕ′on|ăsm *n*. use of more words than are needed to give the sense (*hear with* one's *ears*; *preceded his successor*); hence ∼ă′stIC *a*. [f. LL f. Gk *pleonasmos* (*pleonazō* be superfluous f. *pleon* more)]

plĕ′siosaur. Var. of foll.

plĕsiosaur′us *n*. extinct marine reptile with long neck, short tail, and four large paddles. [mod. L, f. Gk *plēsios* near + *sauros* lizard]

plĕ′thor|a *n*. morbid condition marked by excess of red corpuscles in the blood; (fig.) over-supply, glut; hence or cogn. ∼IC *a*., **plĕthŏ′rICALLY** *adv*. [LL, f. Gk *plēthōrē* (*plēthō* be full)]

pleur′|a (ploor′*a*) (*pl.* ∼ae). either of the two serous membranes lining the thorax and enveloping the lungs in mammals; (also *pleuron*) lateral part of the body-wall in arthropods; hence ∼AL *a*. [med. L f. Gk, = side of body, rib]

pleur′|isў (ploor′-) *n*. inflammation of the pleura, marked by pain in chest or side, fever, etc.; so ∼i′tIC *a*. [ME, f. OF *pleurisie* f. LL *pleurisis* alt. f. L f. Gk *pleuritis* (as prec., see -ITIS)]

pleuro- (ploor-) *comb. form*. pleura, side of body, as. ∼**dy′nia,** pain in side usu. in intercostal muscles; ∼**-pneumo′nia,** pneumonia complicated with pleurisy, esp. contagious disease of cattle etc. [f. as PLEURA + -O-]

pleur′|on (ploor′-) *n*. (*pl.* ∼a). See PLEURA. [Gk, = side of body, rib]

Plĕ′xiglas, plĕ′xiglass, (-ahs) *n*. (*P) = PERSPEX. [f. as foll. + GLASS[1]]

plĕ′xor *n*. (Med.) small hammer used in percussion. [irreg. f. Gk *plēxis* percussion + -OR (cf. *flexor* etc.)]

plĕ′xus *n*. network, complication; (Anat.) network of nerves or vessels in animal body (*gastric, pulmonary,* SOLAR, *plexus*); hence **plĕ′xIFORM** *a*. [L (*plectere plex-* plait)]

pli′able *a*. = foll.; hence **pliABI′LITY** *n*., **pli′abLY[2]** *adv*. [F (*plier* bend; see PLY[1], -ABLE)]

pli′ant *a*. bending easily, supple; (fig.) yielding, compliant; hence **pli′ANCY** *n*., ∼LY[2] *adv*. [ME, f. OF (as prec.; see -ANT)]

pli′cate *a*. (Biol. & Geol.) folded; so **plica′tED[1]** *a*. [f. L *plicatus*, p.p. of *plicare* fold; see -ATE[2]]

plica′tion *n*. folding; fold, folded condition. [ME, f. med. L *plicatio* (see -ATION) or f. L *plicare* fold, after *complication*]

plié (plē′ā) *n*. (Ballet). bending of knees. [F, p.p. of *plier* bend (see PLY[1])]

pli′ers (-z) *n. pl.* (*pair of*) pincers having long jaws with parallel surfaces, for holding small objects, bending wire, etc. [f. (dial.) *ply* bend (as PLIABLE) + -ER[1] + -S[1]]

plight[1] (plīt) *v.t.*, & *n.*, (arch.) **1.** *n t* (esp. in *p.p.*) pledge (one's TROTH, faith, promise); engage one*self* (*to* person; *plighted lovers*). **2.** *n*. engagement, pledging. [v. f. n., f. OE *pliht* danger, = MDu. *plicht*, OHG *pfliht* duty, f. Gmc *pleh-*; cf. PLEDGE[1]]

plight[2] (plīt) *n*. condition, state, esp. unfortunate one (*sorry, evil, hopeless, plight*). [ME & AF *plit* = OF *pleit* fold; see PLAIT; -*gh*- by confus. w. prec.]

Plimsoll *a*. & *n*. ∼ **line,** ∼ **mark,** marking on ship's side showing limit of legal submersion in summer or under various conditions; ‖(*p*∼) rubber-soled canvas sports shoe. [f. S. ∼, Engl. politician d. 1898, promoter of Merchant Shipping Act of 1876]

plinth *n*. lower square member of base of column; projecting part of wall immediately above ground; base supporting a vase, statue, etc. [f. F *plinthe* or L *plinthus*, f. Gk *plinthos* tile, brick, squared stone]

Pli′ocēne *a*. & *n*. (Geol.) (of) highest division of Tertiary period or system. [f. Gk *pleiōn* more + *kainos* new]

plissé (plē′sā) *a*. & *n*. (material) treated so as to cause permanent puckering. [F, p.p. of *plisser* pleat]

PLO *abbr*. Palestine Liberation Organization.

plŏd *v*. (-dd-) & *n*. **1.** *v.i.* walk doggedly or laboriously, trudge, (*on, along,* etc.); work steadily, drudge, slave, (*at* etc.). **2.** *v.t.* make (one's *way*) or tread laboriously. **3.** Hence ∼′dER[1] *n*. **4.** *n*. laborious walk or work. [16th c., prob. imit.]

-ploid *suf*. (Biol.) forming *adjs*. denoting number of sets of chromosomes in a cell (*diploid, polyploid*). [after HAPLOID]

ploi′dў *n*. (Biol.) degree of multiplicity of chromosomes in a cell. [after DIPLOIDY, POLYPLOIDY, etc.]

plŏnk[1]. See PLUNK.

plŏnk[2] *n*. (sl.) cheap or inferior wine. [orig. Austral., perh. f. prec. or f. F *vin blanc* white wine]

plŏp *n*., *adv.*, & *v*. (-pp-). **1.** *n*. sound as of smooth object dropping into water without splash; act of falling with this sound. **2.** *adv*. with a plop. **3.** *v.t.* & *i*. (cause to) fall thus. [19th c.; imit.]

plŏ′sion (-zhon) *n*. (Phonet.) sudden release of breath in pronunciation of stop consonant (STOP[2] 5). [f. EXPLOSION]

plŏ′sive (-s-, -z-) *a*. & *n*. (Phonet.) (of) stop consonant (STOP[2] 5). [f. EXPLOSIVE]

plŏt[1] *n*. piece (usu. small) of ground; *plan of land ownership etc.; plan of main events or topics in play, poem, novel, etc., whence ∼LESS *a*.; conspiracy (*Gunpowder Plot*); secret plan; curve etc. found by plotting. [OE, & f *complot* (OF, = secret plan), both of unkn. orig.]

plŏt[2] *v.t.* (-tt-). make plan or map of (existing object, place or thing to be laid out, constructed, etc.); mark (point etc.), mark value of (quantity), on diagram; make (curve etc.) by marking out a number of points; plan, contrive, (crime etc., or abs.); plan secretly; hence ∼′tER[1] (1, 2) *n*. [f. prec.]

plough[1] (plow), (US or arch.) **plow[1],** *n*. **1.** implement for cutting furrows in soil and turning it up, consisting of cutting blade (∼′share) and mould-board fixed in frame drawn by tractor, horses, etc., and guided by ∼′man; **the P**∼, constellation Ursa Major or its seven bright stars; **put one's hand to the ∼,** undertake task (Luke 9:62). **2.** ploughed land. **3.** implement or device resembling plough (SNOW[1]- -*plough*). **4.** ‖(sl.) rejection of candidate in examination [f. foll.]. **5.** ∼**-beam,** central beam of plough; ∼**-boy,** boy who leads plough-horses etc.; ∼**-land,** (Hist.) as much land as could be ploughed by one team of 8 oxen in the year, unit of assessment in N. & E. counties of England; ∼**′man** (see sense 1; ∼**man's lunch,** meal of bread and cheese etc.; *ploughman's* SPIKENARD); **P**∼ **Monday** (first after Epiphany); ∼**′share** (see sense 1); ∼**-shoe,** appliance for protecting or supporting ploughshare; ∼**-staff** (ending in small spade, used to clear earth etc. from coulter etc.); ∼**-tail,** rear of plough, (fig.) farm-labour (*at the plough tail*). [OE *plōh* f. ON *plógr*, - OFris. *plōch*, OS *plōg*, OHG *pfluoc* f. Gmc **plōgaz* f. N. Italic **plog-*]

plough[2] (plow), (US or arch.) **plow[2],** *v*. **1.** *v.t.* turn up (earth, or abs.) with plough, esp. before sowing (∼ **the sand**(**s**), labour uselessly); ∼ **back,** turn (grass etc.) with plough into soil to enrich it, (fig.) reinvest (profits) in same business etc. **2.** root *out*, cast *up*, thrust *down*, (roots, weeds) with plough; furrow, scratch, (surface) as with plough; produce (furrow, line) thus (∼ **a lonely furrow,** carry on without help; (of ship etc.) cleave (surface of water etc.); ‖(sl.) reject (candidate) in examination. **3.** *v.i.* move like plough violently *through* or *into* obstacles; advance laboriously (*through* snow etc., *through* book etc.); ‖(sl.) fail in examination. [ME, f. prec.]

plo′ver (plŭ′-) *n*. gregarious medium-sized wading bird of family Charadriidae, incl. lapwing. [ME & AF; OF *plo*(*u*)*vier*, f. Rom. **ploviarius* f. L *pluvia* rain]

plow[1,2]. See PLOUGH[1,2].

ploy *n.* (colloq.) expedition, undertaking; occupation, job; manœuvre to frustrate opponent etc. [orig. Sc., 18th c.; orig. unkn.]

||**PLP** *abbr.* Parliamentary Labour Party.

||**PLR** *abbr.* Public Lending Right.

plŭck[1] *n.* plucking, twitch; ||(arch.) rejection or failure in examination; heart, liver, and lungs, of animal as food; courage, spirit, whence (-)∿ED[2] (-kt), ∿'LESS, ∿'Y[2], *adjs.*, ∿'ĭLY[2] *adv.*, ∿'ĭNESS *n.* [ME, f. foll.]

plŭck[2] *v.* **1.** *v.t.* pull off, pick, (flower, feather, hair); (arch.) pull, drag, snatch, (*away, off, out,* etc.); pull at, twitch; sound (string of musical instrument) thus; strip (bird) of feathers (CROW[1] *to pluck*); plunder, swindle, (*pluck a pigeon*); ||(arch.) reject (candidate) in examination; ∿ **up** one's **heart, spirits, courage,** take courage. **2.** *v.i.* tug or snatch *at.* **3.** Hence ∿'ER[1] *n.* [OE *ploccian, pluccian,* cogn. w. MLG *plucken,* MDu. *plocken,* ON *plokka, plukka,* f. Gmc **plukkōn* etc., ult. f. Rom. **piluccare*]

plŭg[1] *n.* piece of solid material fitting tightly into hole, used to fill gap or cavity or act as wedge; natural or morbid concretion acting thus; stopper for vessel or pipe; device of metal pins in insulated casing, fitting into holes in socket for making electrical connection; (colloq.) electric socket; (colloq.) release-mechanism of water-closet flushing-apparatus (*pull the plug*); = FIRE[1]-*plug*; = SPARK[2]*ing-plug*; tobacco pressed into cake or stick, piece of this cut off for chewing; *inferior horse etc.; (colloq.) favourable reference to commercial product etc.; *∿-**hat,** (colloq.) top hat; *∿-**ugly,** (sl.) ruffian. [f. MDu. & MLG *plugge,* of unkn. orig.]

plŭg[2] *v.* (**-gg-**). **1.** *v.t.* stop (hole etc. *up*) with plug; (sl.) shoot (person etc.); (sl.) strike (person etc.) with fist; (colloq.) seek to popularize (song, theory, policy, etc.) by constant repetition and favourable mention; ∿ **in,** connect electrically by inserting plug into socket; ∿-**in** *a.* & *n.,* (appliance) able to be connected thus. **2.** *v.i.* (colloq.) plod (*away at* work etc.). [f. prec.]

plŭm *n.* **1.** (tree of genus *Prunus* bearing) roundish fleshy fruit with sweet pulp and flattish pointed stone; reddish-purple colour; dried grape or raisin as used for *plum-cake* etc.; (fig.) good thing, best of a collection, prize in life etc., well-paid position. **2.** ∿-**cake** (containing raisins, currants, etc.); ∿ **duff,** plain flour pudding with raisins or currants; ∿ **pudding,** (1) rich boiled pudding of flour, breadcrumbs, suet, raisins, currants, eggs, spices, etc., eaten esp. at Christmas, (2) ordinary suet-pudding with raisins; ∿-**pudding dog,** Dalmatian; ∿-**pudding stone,** (Geol.) conglomerate of flint or other pebbles. [OE *plūme,* = MLG *plūme,* MHG *pflūme,* ON *plóma,* f. med. L *pruna* f. L *prunum*]

plu′mag|e (-ōō′-) *n.* bird's feathers; hence (-)∿ED[2] (-ĭjd) *a.* [ME f. OF (as PLUME[1]; see -AGE)]

plumassier′ (ploō-) *n.* one who trades or works in ornamental feathers. [F (*plumasse* augment. of PLUME[1]; see -IER)]

plŭmb[1] (-m) *n., a., & adv.* **1.** *n.* ball of lead, esp. that attached to mason's ∿-**line** (string for testing perpendicularity of wall etc.; also fig.); **out of** ∿, not vertical; ∿-**rule,** mason's plumb-line attached to board. **2.** sounding-lead, plummet. **3.** *a.* vertical; (fig.) downright, sheer, (*plumb nonsense*); (Cricket of wicket) level, true. **4.** *adv.* vertically; (fig.) exactly (*points plumb in the same direction*); *(sl.) quite, utterly, (*plumb crazy*). [ME, prob. f. OF *plombe f. Rom. *plumba f. L *plumbum* lead; assim. to OF *plomb* lead]

plŭmb[2] (-m) *v.t.* sound (depth, lit. or fig.) with plummet, whence ∿'LESS (-ml-) *a.*; make vertical. [f. prec.]

plŭmb[3] (-m) *v.* **1.** *v.i.* work as plumber. **2.** *v.t.* provide with, fit as part of, plumbing system. [back-form. f. PLUMBER]

plŭmbā′gō (*pl.* ∿s). **1.** graphite; hence **plŭmbā′gĭn-** ous *a.* **2.** leadwort, plant of genus *Plumbago* with greyish-blue etc. flowers. [L *plumbago -aginis* (*plumbum* LEAD[1])]

plŭ′mbāte. See PLUMBIC.

plŭ′mbèous *a.* of or like lead; lead-glazed. [f. L *plumbeus* (as PLUMBAGO) + -OUS]

plŭ′mb|er (-mer) *n.* workman who fits and repairs water-pipes, cisterns, etc.; so ∿ERY (2, 3) (-merĭ) *n.* [ME *plummer* etc., f. OF *plommier* f. L *plumbarius* (*plumbum* LEAD[1]; see -ARY[1])]

plŭ′mb|ic *a.* **1.** (Chem.) containing lead, esp. in tetravalent form, whence ∿ATE[1] (3) *n.*; so ∿ĭ′FEROUS *a.* **2.** (Path.) due to presence of lead; so ∿ISM (5) *n.,* lead-poisoning. [f. L *plumbum* lead + -IC]

plŭ′mbĭng (-mĭ-) *n.* plumber's work; system of water--pipes etc. constructed by plumber; (colloq.) *the* lavatory. [f. PLUMBER + -ING[1]]

plume[1] (-ōōm) *n.* feather, esp. large one used for ornament (**borrowed** ∿s, pretentious display not of one's own making); ornamental feather or bunch of feathers or horsehair, esp. as attached to helmet or hat, or worn in hair; trail of smoke from chimney, blown snow from mountain, etc.; (Zool.) feather-like part or formation; hence **plu′mERY** (1) (-ōō′-) *n.,* ∿'LESS, ∿'LIKE, *adjs.,* ∿'LET *n.,* (-ōō′ml-). [ME f. OF, f. L *pluma* DOWN[2]]

plume[2] (-ōōm) *v.t.* furnish with plume(s); dress one*self* with borrowed PLUME[1]s; pride one*self* (*on* esp. something trivial or to which one has no claim); (of bird) trim, dress, preen, (it*self,* its feathers). [f. prec. or L *plumare* cover with feathers]

plu′micŏrn (-ōō′-) *n.* ear-tuft of owl. [f. L *pluma* plume + *cornu* horn]

plŭ′mmer-blŏck *n.* (Mech.) metal case to support revolving shaft, with movable cover giving access to bearings. [perh. f. surname *Plummer* + BLOCK[1]]

plŭ′mmèt *n., & v.i.* **1.** *n.* (weight attached to) plumb--line; sounding-lead; weight attached to fishing-line to keep float upright. **2.** *v.i.* fall rapidly. [ME f. OF *plommet* dim. (as PLUMB[1])]

plŭ′mmy *a.* of, or abounding in, plums; (colloq.) good, desirable, (of voice) rich in tone. [f. PLUM + -Y[2]]

plu′mōse (-ōō′-) *a.* feathered; feather-like. [f. L *plumosus* (as PLUME[1]; see -OSE[1])]

plŭmp[1] *a.* & *v.* **1.** *a.* (Esp. of person or animal or part of body) full, rounded, fleshy, filled out; hence ∿'LY[2] *adv.,* ∿'NESS *n.,* ∿'Y[2] *a.* **2.** *v.t.* make plump; fatten *up.* **3.** *v.i.* become plump; swell *out* or *up.* [ME *plompe,* f. MDu. *plomp* blunt, MLG *plump, plomp* shapeless etc.]

plŭmp[2] *v., n., adv.,* & *a.* **1.** *v.t.* & *i.* drop or plunge with abrupt descent (*down upon* etc.); (colloq.) utter abruptly, blurt *out.* **2.** *v.i.* ||vote *for* (one candidate alone, when one might vote for two); (fig.) go whole--heartedly *for* one of alternative choices; *come or go abruptly. **3.** *n.* abrupt plunge, heavy fall. **4.** *adv.* (colloq.) with sudden or heavy fall; directly, bluntly, (*I told him plump*). **5.** *a.* (colloq.) direct, unqualified, (*answer with a plump 'No'*). [ME, f. MLG *plumpen,* MDu. *plompen;* of imit. orig.]

plŭmp[3] *n.* (arch.) company, troop; cluster. [ME, of unkn. orig.]

plu′mūl|e (ploō′-) *n.* **1.** rudimentary stem of embryo plant; hence ∿AR[1] *a.* **2.** little feather of down; hence ∿A′CEOUS *a.* [F, or f. L *plumula,* dim. (as PLUME[1])]

plu′my (-ōō′-) *a.* plumelike; feathery; adorned with plumes. [f. PLUME[1] + -Y[2]]

plŭ′nder *v.t.,* & *n.* **1.** *v.t.* rob (place, person) forcibly of goods, esp. as in war; rob systematically; steal, embezzle, (goods, or abs.); hence ∿AGE (3), ∿ER[1], *ns.* **2.** *n.* violent or dishonest acquisition of property; property so acquired; (sl.) profit, gain. [f. LG *plündern,* lit. 'rob of household goods' f. MHG *plunder* clothing etc.]

plŭnge (-nj) *v.* & *n.* **1.** *v.t.* thrust violently (*into* liquid, cavity, etc.); (fig.) thrust (person etc. *into, in,* condition, action, etc.; esp. in p.p.p.: *plunged in gloom*); immerse completely, sink entirely (pot containing plant) in ground. **2.** *v.i.* throw oneself, dive, (*into*

water, difficulty, discussion, etc., or *in*); enter
impetuously (*into* room, *up*, *down*, stairs, etc.); descend
violently or suddenly; (of horse) start violently
forward; (of ship) pitch; (sl.) gamble deeply, run into
debt; **plunging fire** (from guns at higher level);
plunging neckline (cut low). **3.** *n.* plunging, dive,
(∿-**bath**, bath large enough to dive into; ∿ **neckline,** = *plunging neckline*); (fig.) decisive step (*take the
plunge*); ∿ **basin** or **pool** (in hollow formed at foot of
waterfall). [ME, f. OF *plungier* f. Rom. *plumbicare
sound with plummet (L *plumbum*)]

plŭ'nger (-nj-) *n.* In vbl senses; part of mechanism
that works with plunging or thrusting motion; rubber
cup on handle for removal of blockages by suction;
(sl.) reckless gambler, speculator. [f. prec.+-ER¹]

plŭnk, plŏnk, *v.* & *n.* **1.** *v.t.* & *i.* throw or fall or put
down heavily or suddenly; *hit unexpectedly; (cause
to) sound with plunk. **2.** *n.* sound made by sharply
plucked string of harp, banjo, etc.; *(colloq.) heavy
blow; *(sl.) dollar. [imit.]

plupĕrfĕct (-ōōpĕr'-, -ōō'-) *a.* & *n.* (Gram.) (tense)
denoting action completed prior to some past point of
time specified or implied (expr. in E by *had* with *p.p.*:
he had called). [f. mod. L *plusperfectum* f. L *plus quam
perfectum* more than perfect, transl. Gk *hupersuntelikos*]

plur'al (-oor'-) *a.* & *n.* **1.** (Gram.) ∿ (**number**),
(form or class of forms of noun, verb, etc.) denoting
more than one (or, in languages with dual, more than
two). **2.** *a.* more than one in number; ∿ **society**
(containing members of more than one race); ∿
vote, voter, voting, (of one person in more than one
constituency). **3.** Hence ∿LY² *adv.* [ME, f. OF *plurel* f.
L *pluralis* (*plus pluris* more; see -AL)]

plur'al|ism (-oor'-) *n.* holding of more than one
office, esp. benefice, at a time; (Philos.) system that
recognizes more than one ultimate principle (cf.
MONISM); form of society in which members of
minority groups maintain independent traditions; so
∿IST (2) *n.*, ∿I'STIC *a.* [f. prec+-ISM]

plura'litў (-oor-) *n.* state of being plural; large
number, multitude; holding of two or more benefices
or offices; benefice or office held with another;
majority (of votes etc.); *majority over each other
candidate etc. but not over all together. [ME, f. OF
pluralité f. LL *pluralitas* (as PLURAL; see -ITY)]

plur'alīze (-oor'-), **-īse** (-īz), *v.* **1.** *v.t.* make plural;
express in the plural. **2.** *v.i.* hold more than one
benefice. [f. PLURAL+-IZE]

pluri- (-oori) *comb. form.* several, as: ∿li'teral, (Heb.
Gram.) having more than 3 letters in the root;
∿pre'sence, (Theol.) presence in more than one
place at the same time. [f. L *plus pluris* more, *plures*
several+-I-]

plŭs (prep., a., & n. **1.** *prep.* with the addition of
(symbol+; *3 plus 4 equals 7*); above zero (*temperatures
between minus ten and plus ten degrees*); (colloq.) with,
having gained, possessing; ∿ **one** etc., adverse
handicap assigned to golfer etc. (added to his score);
∿-**fours,** long wide knickerbockers worn esp. by
golfers [so named because, to produce the overhang,
the length is normally increased by four inches]. **2.** *a.*
additional, extra; (after number etc.) at least (*fifteen
plus*); ALPHA etc. *plus*; (Math.) positive; (Electr.)
having positive charge; *plus* SIGN¹. **3.** *n.* the symbol
(+); additional quantity, positive quantity; advantage. [L, = more]

plŭsh *n.* & *a.* **1.** *n.* cloth of silk, cotton, etc., with nap
longer and softer than that of velvet; hence ∿'y² *a.*,
stylish, luxurious. **2.** *a.* made of plush; plushy; hence
∿'LY² *adv.* [f. obs. F *pluche* contr. f. *peluche* f. OF
peluchier f. It. *peluzzo* dim. of *pelo* f. L *pilus* hair]

plu'tărchў (plōō'tärkĭ) *n.* plutocracy. [f. Gk *ploutos*
wealth+-*arkhia* -rule]

Plu'tō (-ōō'-) *n.* farthest known planet of solar system.
[L, f. Gk *Ploutōn* god of the underworld]

plutŏ'cracў (-ōō-) *n.* rule of the wealthy; State ruled
by the wealthy; (ruling class of) wealthy persons; so

plu'toCRAT *n.*, **plutocră'tic** *a.*, (-ōō-). [f. Gk
ploutokratia (as foll.; see -CRACY)]

plutŏ'latrў (-ōō-) *n.* worship of wealth. [f. Gk *ploutos*
wealth; see -LATRY]

plu'ton (-ōō'-) *n.* (Geol.) body of rock exposed after
solidification at great depth. [back-form. f.
PLUTONIC]

Plutō'nian (-ōō-) *a.* infernal; of the infernal regions.
[f. L f. Gk *Ploutōnios* (*Ploutōn* god of the underworld)
+-AN]

plutŏ'nic (-ōō-) *a.* & *n.* **1.** *a.* (P∿) = prec. **2.** (Geol., of
rock) formed as igneous rock by solidification at great
depth; ∿ **theory** (attributing most geological
phenomena to action of internal heat, whence
Plu'tonISM (3), **Plu'ton**IST (2), (-ōō'-) *ns.*). **3.** *n.*
plutonic rock. [f. as prec.+-IC]

plutō'nium (-ōō-) *n.* (Chem.) radioactive metallic
element formed from neptunium, used in nuclear
weapons and reactors. [f. PLUTO (next planet after
Neptune)+-IUM]

plu'vi|al (-ōō'-) *a.* & *n.* **1.** *a.* of rain, rainy; so ∿ous *a.*
2. (Geol.) caused by rain. **3.** *n.* period of prolonged
rainfall; (Hist.) long cloak as ecclesiastical vestment.
[f. L *pluvialis* (*pluvia* rain; see -AL); n. also f. med. L
pluviale rain-cloak]

pluvi|ŏ'mĕter (-ōō-) *n.* rain-gauge; hence ∿omĕ'-
tric(AL) *adjs.* [f. L *pluvia* rain+-O-+-METER]

plȳ¹ *n.* fold, thickness, layer, of cloth etc., strand of
rope, yarn, etc., (TWO, THREE, etc., -*ply*); (fig.) turn,
tendency, (*take a ply*); ∿('wood), strong thin board
made by gluing layers with the grains crosswise.
[ME, f. F *pli* (*plier*, *pleier* f. L *plicare* fold)]

plȳ² *v.* **1.** *v.t.* use, wield vigorously, (tool, weapon);
work at (one's business, task, trade); supply (person
etc.) persistently *with* (food etc.); assail vigorously
(person *with* questions, arguments). **2.** *v.i.* work
steadily; (Naut.) sail to windward; (of vessel or its
master, bus, etc.) go to and fro *between* (places); (of
boatman, porter, cabman) attend regularly for
custom (*at* place, *for* hire). [ME *plye*, f. APPLY]

Plў'mouth (-muth) *n.* ∿ **Brethren,** Calvinistic
religious body formed at Plymouth c. 1830, with no
formal creed and no official order of ministers; ∿
Rock, medium-sized breed of domestic fowl of Amer.
origin. [∿ in Devon and in Massachusetts]

PM *abbr.* post-mortem; Prime Minister; Provost
Marshal.

p.m. *abbr.* after noon. [f. L *post meridiem*]

Pm *symb.* promethium.

PMG *abbr.* Paymaster (or Postmaster) General.

PMRAFNS *abbr.* Princess Mary's Royal Air Force
Nursing Service.

PNdB *abbr.* perceived noise decibel(s).

||**PNEU** *abbr.* Parents' National Educational Union.

pneumă'tic (n-) *a.* & *n.* **1.** *a.* of, or acting by means of,
wind or (esp. compressed) air; ∿ **dispatch,** conveyance of parcels etc. along tubes by compression or
exhaustion of air; ∿ **drill,** machine for breaking up
road surface etc. and driven by force of compressed
air; ∿ **trough** (for collecting gases in jars over surface
of water or mercury); ∿ **tube** (for pneumatic
dispatch); ∿ **tyre** (inflated with air). **2.** containing or
connected with air-cavities esp. in fish or in bones of
birds; spiritual. **3.** Hence **pneumă'ti**CALLY *adv.*,
pneumati'CITY *n.*, (n-). **4.** *n.* pneumatic tyre; (arch.)
cycle with such tyres; (in *pl.*, treated as *sing.*) science
of mechanical properties of gases. [f. F *pneumatique* or
f. L f. Gk *pneumatikos* (*pneuma* wind f. *pneō* breathe; see
-IC)]

pneu'mato- (n-) *comb. form.* air, breath, spirit, as:
∿cyst, air-sac in body of bird etc.; **pneumato'logy**
(n-;-ŏ'-), theory of spiritual beings, doctrine of the
Holy Spirit, (arch.) psychology, whence ∿lo'gical
a.; ∿phore, part of some compound hydrozoa
containing air-cavity. [Gk, f. *pneuma* (as prec.)]

pneumō- (n-) *comb. form.* lungs, as: ∿conio'sis, lung
disease due to inhalation of dust etc. [Gk *konis* dust];

∼**ga′stric**, of lungs and stomach (esp. = VAGUS); ∼**thor′ax**, presence of air or gas in cavity between lung and chest-wall. [abbr. of *pneumono*- f. Gk *pneumōn* lung + -O-]

pneumonĕ′ctomў (n-) *n*. (Surg.) excision of (part of) lung. [f. as prec. + -ECTOMY]

pneumō′nia (n-) *n*. inflammation of the substance of one (**single** ∼) or both (**double** ∼) lungs; so **pneumō′nic** *a*. (**pneumonic plague**, virulent contagious bacterial disease affecting lungs), **pneumoni′tis** *n*., (n-). [L f. Gk (*pneumōn* lung; see -IA[1])]

PNG *abbr*. Papua New Guinea.

pō *n*. (*pl*. **pos**). (colloq.) chamber-pot; **po-faced**, solemn-faced, humourless. [var. of POT[1], after F pr.]

PO *abbr*. Petty Officer; Pilot Officer; postal order; Post Office.

Po *symb*. polonium.

poach[1] *v.t.* cook (egg) without shell in or with boiling water; cook (fish etc.) by simmering in water or milk; hence ∼′ER[1] (2) *n*. [ME, f. OF *pochier* (*poche* POKE[1])]

poach[2] *v*. **1.** *v.t.* trample, cut up (turf etc.) with hoofs; trespass on (land etc.), capture (game, fish) by illicit or unsportsmanlike methods; obtain (advantage, start in race) by unfair means; (Tennis etc.) strike (ball, or abs.) in partner's court. **2.** *v.i.* (Of land) become sodden by being trampled; encroach, trespass, (*on* person's *preserves* etc., lit. or fig.). **3.** Hence ∼′ER[1] *n*. [earlier *poche*, perh. f. F *pocher* put in pocket (as prec.)]

pŏ′chard (-ch-, -k-) *n*. diving duck esp. of genus *Aythya*, esp. European species with bright reddish-brown head and neck. [16th c.; orig. unkn.]

pŏchĕ′tte (-sh-) *n*. woman's envelope-shaped handbag. [F, dim. of *poche* pocket; see POKE[1]]

pŏck *n*. eruptive spot esp. in smallpox; mark resembling this; ∼-**marked**, bearing marks (like those) left by smallpox. [OE *poc*, = MDu., MLG *pocke* f. Gmc *pukno*-]

pŏ′ckĕt[1] *n*. & *a*. **1.** *n*. small bag inserted in or attached to coat, trousers, etc., for carrying small articles (*watch, ticket, -pocket*); **in** person's ∼, (1) close to or intimate with him, (2) completely under his control; **put** one's **pride in** one's ∼, accept humiliation to achieve one's aim. **2.** bag, sack, (esp. of hops); pouchlike compartment in suitcase, on interior surface of door of motor car, etc. **3.** (fig.) pecuniary resources (*it is beyond my pocket; he will suffer in his pocket*); **put** one's **hand in** one's ∼, spend or give money; **in** ∼, having gained in a transaction, (of money) available; **out of** ∼, having lost in a transaction; **out-of-**∼ **expenses**, actual outlay of cash incurred. **4.** pouch at each corner and on each longer side of billiard-table into which balls are driven; cavity in earth filled with gold or other ore, whence ∼Y[2] *a*.; cavity in rock esp. (Geol.) filled with foreign matter; closed side-branch in passage etc.; (Mil.) (troops occupying) isolated area in battle (*mopping up enemy pockets; pockets of resistance*); isolated group (of unemployed persons etc.); = AIR[1] *pocket*. **5.** *a*. of suitable size or shape for carrying in pocket (*pocket calculator, dictionary, -watch*). **6.** ∼ **battleship**, ship armoured and equipped like, but smaller than, a battleship; ∼-**book**, (1) notebook, (2) booklike case for papers or paper money carried in pocket, (fig.) = sense 3 (*hurt one's pocket-book*), (3) *pocket-size book, usu. paperback, (4) *large handbag; ||*pocket BOROUGH; ∼ **handkerchief** (carried in pocket; fig. of small lawn etc.); ∼-**knife**, knife with folding blade(s) to be carried in pocket; ∼-**money** (for occasional expenses, esp. that allowed regularly to children); ∼-**piece**, lucky coin or token carried in pocket as charm; ∼-**pistol**, (joc.) pocket spirit-flask; *∼ **veto**, indirect veto of bill by retention in hands of President etc. until adjournment of legislature. **7.** Hence ∼FUL (2) *n*., ∼LESS *a*. [ME f. AF *poket(e)* dim. of *poke* POKE[1]]

pŏ′ckĕt[2] *v.t.* put into one's pocket; confine as in pocket; appropriate, usu. dishonestly; submit to (affront, injury); conceal, suppress, (feelings); (Bill.) drive (ball) into pocket; *veto (bill) indirectly by retaining it; hence ∼ABLE *a*. [f. prec.]

pōcōcūră′nt|ē *a*. & *n*. uncaring, indifferent, (person); hence ∼(**ē**)ISM (2) *n*. [It., = caring little]

pŏd[1] *n*. socket of brace and bit. [16th c., of unkn. orig.; perh. cogn. w. PAD[3]]

pŏd[2] *n*. & *v*. (**-dd-**). **1.** *n*. long seed-vessel esp. of leguminous plants; cocoon of silkworm; case of locust's eggs; narrow-necked eel-net; compartment suspended under aircraft etc. **2.** *v.i.* bear or form pods. **3.** *v.t.* remove (peas etc.) from pods. [back-form. f. dial. *podware, podder* field crops, of unkn. orig.]

pŏd[3] *n*., & *v.t.* (**-dd-**). **1.** *n*. small herd of seals or whales. **2.** *v.t.* drive (seals) into a pod. [19th c. US of unkn. orig.]

podagr|a (pŏdă′g-, pŏ′dag-) *n*. (Med.) gout, esp. in feet; hence ∼AL, ∼IC, ∼OUS, adjs. [L, f. Gk *podagra* (*pous podos* foot, *agra* seizure)]

pŏ′ddĕd *a*. bearing pods; growing in pod; (fig.) well-off, snug. [f. POD[2] + -ED[2]]

pŏ′ddў *n*. (Austral.) hand-fed calf. [E dial. wd, of unkn. orig.]

podestà (pŏdĕstah′) *n*. (Hist.) magistrate in Italian municipalities; chief magistrate in medieval Italian towns. [It., f. L *potestas -tatis* power]

pŏ′dgў *a*. (Of person) short and fat; (of face etc.) soft and fat. [f. *podge* short fat person (cf. PUDGE) + -Y[2]]

***podī′atr|ў** *n*. chiropody; so ∼IST (3) *n*. [f. Gk *pous podos* foot + *iatros* physician + -Y[1]]

pŏ′di|um *n*. (*pl*. ∼**a**). continuous projecting base or pedestal round room, house, etc.; raised platform round arena of amphitheatre; continuous bench round room; conductor's or speaker's rostrum. [L, f. Gk *podion* dim. of *pous podos* foot]

pŏdophy′llin *n*. yellow bitter cathartic resin got from root of may-apple. [f. mod. L *podophyllum* May-apple f. Gk *pous podos* foot + *phullon* leaf, + -IN]

pŏ′dzŏl, pŏ′dsŏl, *n*. soil with certain materials leached from surface layers into a lower stratum; hence ∼IZE (3) *v.t.* [Russ. (*zola* ashes)]

pō′e *n*. = PARSON-bird. [Tahitian, = 'ear-rings', from curled tufts under throat]

***POE** *abbr*. port of entry.

pō′ĕm *n*. a metrical composition, esp. of elevated character; elevated composition in verse or prose (*prose poem*); (fig.) something not in words but akin or compared to a poem (*their lives are a poem*). [f. F *poème* or L f. Gk *poēma* = *poiēma* (*poieō* make)]

pō′esў (-sĭ, -zĭ) *n*. (arch. or poet.) art or composition of poetry; poems collectively. [ME, f. OF *poesie* f. Rom. **poesia* f. L f. Gk *poēsis* = *poiēsis* making, poetry, (as prec.)]

pō′ĕt *n*. writer of poems; writer in verse, esp. one possessing high powers of imagination, expression, etc.; **Poet LAUREATE**; **Poets' Corner,** part of Westminster Abbey containing graves and monuments of several poets; hence ∼ESS[1] *n*. [ME, f. OF *poete* f. L f. Gk *poētēs* = *poiētēs* maker, poet, (as POEM; see -ET[2])]

pŏĕtă′ster *n*. paltry or inferior poet. [mod. L (as prec.; see -ASTER)]

pŏĕ′t|ic *a*. **1.** of, or proper to, poets or poetry (*poetic JUSTICE, LICENCE[1]*). **2.** having the good qualities of poetry. **3.** Hence ∼ICALLY *adv*., ∼ICS *n*. [f. F *poétique* f. L *poeticus* f. Gk *po(i)ētikos* (as POET; see -IC, -AL)]

pŏĕ′tical *a*. = prec.; written in verse (*poetical works*). [ME, f. as prec. + -ICAL]

pŏĕ′ticīze, -īse (-īz), *v.t.* make (theme) poetic. [f. POETIC + -IZE]

pŏ′etīze, -īse (-īz), *v*. **1.** *v.i.* play the poet, compose poetry. **2.** *v.t.* treat poetically; celebrate in poetry. [f. F *poétiser* (as POET; see -IZE)]

pō′etrў *n*. art or work of the poet; elevated expression of elevated thought or feeling in metrical or rhythmical form; quality (in any thing) that calls for poetical expression; **prose** ~, prose having all the qualities of poetry except metre. [ME, f. med. L *poetria* f. L *poeta* POET, prob. after *geometry*]

po-faced. See PO.

pŏ′gŏ *n.* *(pl.* ~s). stiltlike toy with cross-piece for feet, spring, and handles, used to jump about on. [20th c.; orig. uncert.]

pŏgono- *comb. form.* beard, as: ~**logy** (-ŏ′l-), study of beards; ~**tomy** (-ŏ′t-), shaving; ~**trophy** (-ŏ′t-), beard-growing. [f. Gk *pōgōn* beard + -o-]

pŏ′grom *n.* organized massacre (orig. and esp. of Jews in Russia). [Russ., = devastation *(gromit'* destroy)]

pōhutuka′wa (-hōōtukah′-) *n.* (NZ) evergreen tree with brilliant crimson flowers. [Maori]

poi′gn|ant (poi′na-, poi′nya-) *a.* sharp or pungent in taste or smell; painfully sharp *(poignant hunger, regret, sarcasm);* pleasantly piquant; causing sympathy; hence ~ANCY *n.,* ~ant**LY²** *adv.* [ME f. OF, pres. part. of *poindre* prick f. L *pungere;* see -ANT]

poi′kilothĕrm *n.* cold-blooded animal; hence ~AL, ~IC, (-ĕr′-) *adjs.* [f. Gk *poikilos* multicoloured, changeable + *thermē* heat]

poilu (pwah′lōō) *n.* (arch.) (Nickname for) French private soldier. [F, lit. hairy *(poil* hair)]

poincia′na (-ah′-) *n.* tropical tree with bright red flowers [mod. L, f. M. de Poinci, 17th-c. governor in West Indies + -ana fem. suf. (cf. -AN)]

poind (pēnd, pīnd) *v.t.,* & *n.* (Sc.) 1. *v.t.* distrain upon, impound. 2. *n.* act of poinding; animal or chattel poinded. [ME, f. OE *pyndan* impound]

poinsĕ′ttia *n.* plant of genus *Euphorbia* with large scarlet bracts surrounding small yellowish flowers. [mod. L, f. J. R. *Poinsett,* Amer. diplomat d. 1851 + -IA¹]

point¹ *n.* 1. very small mark on a surface. 2. stop or punctuation-mark (esp. FULL¹ *point);* dot, small stroke, used in Semitic languages to indicate vowels or distinguish consonants; = DECIMAL *point (four* ~ *six,* 4.6, ~ *one,* 0.1). 3. single item, detail, particular, *(we differ on these points; it is a point of conscience; point of* ORDER¹ 11; STRETCH *a point);* **possession is nine** ~**s of the law** (nine-tenths, almost the whole). 4. unit of scoring in games etc., or fig. in debate; **give** ~**s to,** allow handicap to (opponent), (fig.) be superior to; **score** ~**s off,** (fig.) worst in argument or repartee; **win on** ~**s,** (of boxer) win by scoring more points, not by knock-out. 5. unit in appraising value of bridge hand or of exhibit in show; unit of value in rationing; unit of weight (2 mg.) for diamonds; unit (of varying value) in quoting price of stocks etc.; *unit of credit for academic work. 6. (Print.) unit of measurement for type bodies (UK & US 0.0138 in., European 0.0148 in.). 7. (Geom.) that which has position but not magnitude, e.g. intersection of two lines. 8. precise place or spot *(point of contact; Bombay and points east;* ~ **of no return,** point in a long--distance journey at which supplies become insufficient to return to starting-place and one must continue onwards, or in action after which one cannot withdraw); (Hunting) spot to which straight run is made, such run, (~**-to-**~ *race,* horse-race over course defined only by certain landmarks); (Her.) any of nine particular spots on shield used for specifying position of charges etc.; || = POWER *point.* 9. stage or degree in progress or increase *(abrupt to the point of rudeness; full to bursting-point; decided to give up at this point);* level of temperature *(boiling, freezing, melting, -point,* temperature at which liquid boils etc.). 10. precise moment for action etc. *(when it came to the point, he declined);* exact moment *(of death etc.).* 11. distinctive trait, characteristic *(it has its points; singing is not his strong point);* feature of animal by which its quality is judged; *the* essential thing, *the* thing under discussion, *(that is just the point; come to the point);* **beside the** ~, irrelevant(ly); **carry** or **gain** or **make** one's ~, secure agreement to one's object; **in**

~, apposite, relevant; **make** ~ **of,** regard or treat as essential, insist on; **make** or **prove a** ~, establish proposition, prove contention; **to the** ~, relevant(ly); **you have a** ~ **there,** your contention is valid and relevant; *I* TAKE¹ *your point.* 12. ~ (**lace**), thread lace made wholly with needle, (improp.) pillow-lace imitating this. 13. sharp or operative end of tool, weapon, pin, pen, etc., **(not to put too fine a** ~ **on it,** to speak bluntly); electrical contact device in distributor of motor vehicle. 14. tip, extreme end; ~ (of the jaw), (Boxing) tip of chin as spot for knock--out blow; (Ballet etc.) tip of toe; promontory; (Mil.) small leading party of advanced guard; (in *pl.*) extremities of horse, dog, etc., *(bay has black points).* 15. sharp-pointed tool, e.g. etching-needle; tine of deer's horn. 16. (Railways, usu. in *pl.*) ||tapering movable rail by which train is directed from one line to another; tapered division on backgammon board. 17. (Hist.) tagged lace for lacing bodice, attaching hose to doublet, etc. 18. (Naut.) short piece of cord at lower edge of sail for tying up a reef. 19. one of 32 directions marked as equidistant points on compass; corresponding direction towards horizon; CARDINAL *points.* 20. salient feature of story, joke, remark, etc., *(don't see the point);* pungency, effectiveness, *(his remarks lack point);* purpose, value, *(there is no point in wasting time).* 21. (Cricket) (position of) fieldsman placed more or less in line with popping-crease a short distance on the off side of batsman; (Lacrosse) defender's position to right of and in front of goal-keeper. 22. (Of dog) act of pointing. 23. **at all** ~**s,** in every part or respect; **at the** ~ (on the verge) **of** death etc.; **in** ~ (as a matter) **of fact;** (up)**on the** ~ **of,** on the very verge of (action, doing); ~ **of** (thing that vitally affects one's) **honour;** ~ **of view,** position from which thing is viewed, (fig.) way of looking at a matter; **up to a** ~, by no means wholly. 24. ||~**-duty** (of constable or traffic warden stationed at particular point to regulate traffic etc.); ~ **lace** (see sense 12); ||~′**sman,** man in charge of railway points, constable on point-duty. [ME, f. F *point* f. L *punctum,* & F *pointe* f. L *puncta,* neut. & fem. p.p. (as *n.*) of *pungere* prick; in sense 22 perh. f. foll.]

point² *v.* 1. *v.t.* sharpen (pencil etc.). 2. punctuate; insert points in (written Hebrew etc.); mark (Psalms etc.) with signs for chanting. 3. give point or force to (words, actions) *(pointing his remarks with apt illustrations; to point a* MORAL). 4. fill in joints of (brickwork etc.) with mortar or cement smoothed with trowel. 5. (Of dog) indicate presence of (game, or abs.) by acting as pointer. 6. direct (finger, weapon, etc., *at* or *towards;* person etc. *to);* ~ **out,** indicate, show, draw attention to (thing, fact, *that* etc.); ~ **up,** emphasize. 7. *v.i.* direct attention (*to, at;* lit. or fig.); aim or be directed *at* or *towards;* tend *towards;* ~ **to,** be evidence of. [ME, f. prec. & f. OF *pointer* (as prec.)]

point-blä′nk *a.* & *adv.* 1. with arm or weapon level, at very close range; ~ **distance, range,** (within which gun may be aimed horizontally). 2. (fig.) direct(ly), flat(ly), *(point-blank refusal; told him point-blank it would not do).* [prob. f. prec. + BLANK², i.e. white spot in centre of target]

point d'appui (pwăn dăpwē′) *n. (pl. -ts pr.* same). (Mil.) point of support, base, rallying-place; (fig.) basis of argument etc. [F]

point-dĕvi′ce *a.* & *adv.* (arch.) 1. *a.* perfectly correct, extremely neat or precise. 2. *adv.* in point-device manner. [ME *at point devis* app. f. OF or AF **à point devis* to the point arranged, or arranged to the proper point (see POINT¹, DEVICE)]

poi′ntĕd *a.* having or sharpened to, a point; (of remark etc.) having point, penetrating, cutting; emphasized, made evident; hence ~**LY²** *adv.,* ~**NESS** *n.* [ME, f. POINT¹ + -ED², or p.p. of POINT²]

poi′nter *n.* in vbl senses; index hand of clock, balance, etc.; rod used for pointing to words etc. on black-board, map, etc.; (colloq.) hint, suggestion; dog of breed that on scenting game stands rigidly, with muzzle stretched towards it and usu. one foot raised; (in *pl.*) two stars in Great Bear, straight line through which points nearly to pole-star. [f. POINT² + -ER¹]

pointillé (pwă'ntīlā) *a.* (Of bound book) decorated with gilt dots; (of picture) painted by pointillism. [F, p.p. of *pointiller* mark with dots (as POINT¹)]

poi'ntill|ism (pwă'n-) *n.* (Art). method of producing light effects by crowding a surface with small spots of various colours, which are blended by the spectator's eye; so ∼IST (3) *n.* [f. F *pointillisme* (as prec.; see -ISM)]

poi'nting *n.* In vbl senses; punctuation; filling up joints of brickwork etc. with cement, facing thus given to the joints; system of signs for chanting psalms etc. [ME, f. POINT² + -ING¹]

poi'ntless *a.* without a point, blunt; without point or force, meaningless; not having scored a point; hence ∼LY² *adv.*, ∼NESS *n.* [ME, f. POINT¹ + -LESS]

poi'nty *a.* having noticeable sharp end; *∼-head, (derog.) would-be expert. [f. POINT¹ + -Y²]

poise¹ (-z) *v.* & *n.* **1.** *v.t.* balance; hold suspended or supported; carry (one's head etc., in specified way). **2.** *v.i.* be balanced; hover in air etc. **3.** *n.* equilibrium (lit. or fig.), composure, self-possession; carriage (*of* head etc.). [v. ME f. OF *peser* (st. *pois*-) f. Rom. **pesare* f. L *pensare* frequent. of *pendere pens-* weigh; n. f. OF *pois, peis* f. Rom. **pesum* f. L *pensum* weight, p.p. (as n.) of *pendere*]

poise² (-z) *n.* unit of dynamic viscosity, such that shear of one dyne per sq. cm. causes velocity change of 1 cm. per sec. for each centimetre transverse to plane of shear. [f. J. L. M. *Poiseuille*, Fr. physician d. 1869]

poi'son (-z-) *n.*, & *v.t.* **1.** *n.* substance that when introduced into or absorbed by a living organism may destroy life or injure health, esp. one that destroys life by rapid action even when taken in small quantity; **slow** ∼ (of which repeated doses are eventually injurious); **hate** person like ∼ (bitterly); **what's your** ∼?, (colloq.) what would you like to drink?. **2.** (fig.) baneful principle, doctrine, etc.; (Phys. & Chem.) substance interfering with normal progress of chain reaction, catalytic reaction, etc. **3.** *poison* GAS¹; ∼ ivy, N. Amer. climbing plant or shrub of genus *Rhus*, secreting irritant oil from leaves; ∼ pen, (practice of) anonymous writer of libellous or scurrilous letters. **4.** Hence ∼OUS *a.* **5.** *v.t.* administer poison to (person, animal), kill or injure thus, whence ∼ER¹ *n.*; produce morbid effects in (blood etc.); infect (air, water, etc.) with poison, (esp. in *p.p.*) smear (weapon) with poison; corrupt, pervert, (person, mind); destroy, spoil, (person's pleasure etc.); render (land, furnace, etc.) foul and unfit for its purpose by noxious application etc.; (Phys. & Chem.) act as poison on (catalyst etc.). [n. ME f. OF *puison, poison* (as POTION); v. f. OF *poisonner* (*poison*)]

poke¹ *n.* bag, sack, (usu. dial., exc. *buy a* PIG *in a poke*). [ME, f. ONF *poke, poque,* = OF *poche*; cf. POUCH¹]

poke² *v.* **1.** *v.t.* thrust or push (thing *in, up, down,* etc.) with hand, arm, point of stick, etc.; thrust end of finger etc. against, stir (fire) with poker; (colloq.) shut (one*self* etc.) *up* in poky place; produce (hole etc. *in* thing) by poking; thrust forward, esp. obtrusively, (lit., or fig.: *don't poke your nose into my affairs*); (sl.) copulate with (woman); ∼ **fun at,** assail with ridicule; ∼ one's **head,** (1) carry head thrust forward, (2) cause head to project (*through* window etc.); ∼ **in the ribs,** nudge with finger or elbows in friendly manner. **2.** *v.i.* make thrusts with stick etc. (*at* etc.); be thrust forward *through* opening, *up, down,* etc.; pry (*about, into*); move or act slowly or ineffectively, potter *about* or *around*. [ME, f. MDu., MLG *poken,* of unkn. orig.]

poke³ *n.* poking; thrust, nudge; device fastened on cattle etc. to prevent their breaking through fences; projecting brim or front of woman's bonnet or hat; ∼(-bonnet), bonnet with this. [f. prec.]

po'ker¹ *n.*, & *v.t.* **1.** *n.* stiff metal rod with handle, for

stirring fire; **as stiff as a** ∼ (esp. of person's bearing); **red-hot** ∼, plant of genus *Kniphofia* with spikes of scarlet or yellow flowers. **2.** implement used in ∼-work, (design made by) burning white wood etc. with heated metal rod. [f. POKE² + -ER¹]

po'ker² *n.* card-game for two or more persons, each of whom bets on the value of his hand and may win by holding strongest hand on agreed system of ranking, or by bluffing others into ceasing to compete; ∼ dice (with card designs from ace to nine instead of spots); ∼-face, (person with) impassive countenance appropriate to player of this game; so ∼-*faced a.* [19th c., orig. unkn.; cf. G *pochen* to brag, *pochspiel* bragging game]

po'keweed (-kw-) *n.* tall Amer. plant of genus *Phytolacca* with purple berries yielding emetic and purgative. [f. *poke,* Amer. Ind. word + WEED]

*po'key *n.* (sl.) prison. [perh. f. foll.]

po'ky *a.* (Of place, room, etc.) confined, mean, shabby; (of occupation etc.) pottering, petty. [f. POKE² + -Y²]

*pol *n.* (colloq., derog.) politician. [abbr.]

*po'lack *n.* (sl., derog.) person of Polish origin. [f. F *Polaque* & G *Polack* f. Pol. *Polak*]

pola'cre (-ah'ker), **pola'cca,** *n.* three-masted Mediterranean merchant vessel. [f. F *polacre, polaque,* It. *polacca* = Polish, Pole, as prec.; reason for name unkn.]

po'lar *a.* & *n.* **1.** *a.* of or near either pole of the earth or celestial body or of the celestial sphere; of species or variety living in north polar regions (*polar bear, hare);* ∼ circles (parallel to equator at distance of 23° 27′ from the poles); ∼ distance, angular distance of point on sphere from nearer pole; ∼ star, = POLE²--*star.* **2.** having polarity, magnetic; having electric charges; (of molecule) having opposite properties at its ends. **3.** (Geom. etc.) relating to a POLE²; ∼ curve (related in particular way to given curve and to fixed point called *pole*). **4.** (fig.) analogous to the pole of the earth or to the pole-star; directly opposite in character or tendency. **5.** Hence ∼LY² *adv.* **6.** *n.* polar curve. [f. F *polaire* or mod. L *polaris* (as POLE²; see -AR¹)]

pōlari- *comb. form* = prec., as: **polari'meter, pola'riscope** (-lă'r-), instruments for measuring, showing, the polarization of light; so **polarime'tric, polarisco'pic,** *adjs.*, **polari'metry** *n.* [f. mod. L *polaris* (as prec.) + -I-]

polă'rity *n.* tendency of loadstone, magnetized bar, etc., to point with its extremities to the magnetic poles of the earth; tendency of a body to lie with its mathematical axis in particular direction; possession of two poles having contrary qualities (lit. or fig.); electrical condition of body (positive or negative); (fig.) magnetic attraction towards an object. [f. POLAR + -ITY]

po'lariz|e, -is|e (-īz), *v.* **1.** *v.t.* restrict vibrations of (transverse waves, esp. light) so that they have different amplitudes in different planes through their line of propagation; give magnetic or electric polarity to; reduce voltage of (electric cell) by action of electrolysis products. **2.** *v.t.* & *i.* (fig.) divide into two groups at opposite extremes of opinion etc. **3.** Hence or cogn. ∼ABLE *a.,* ∼A'TION, ∼ER¹ (2), *ns.* [(partly thr. F.) f. POLAR + -IZE]

pōlaro'graph|y *n.* (Chem.) analysis by measurement of current-voltage relationships in electrolysis between mercury electrodes; hence **pōlarogra'ph**IC *a.* [f. POLAR + -O- + -GRAPHY]

pōlatou'che (-ōō'ch) *n.* small flying squirrel. [F, f. Russ. *poletuchii* flying]

pō'lder *n.* piece of low-lying land reclaimed from sea or river, esp. in Netherlands. [prob. f. MDu. *polre, polder*]

pole¹ *n.*, & *v.t.* **1.** *n.* long slender rounded piece of wood or metal esp. as support for tent, telegraph wires, bean-plants, etc., or propulsion of barge, punt, etc., wooden shaft fitted to front of vehicle and attached to yokes or collars of the horses etc.; **under bare ~s**, (Naut.) with no sail set; **up the ~**, (sl.) in a difficulty, crazy, drunk; **~-jump(ing)**, **~-vault(ing)**, (over high crossbar with help of pole held in hands); **~ position**, most favourable position at start of motor race [orig. next to inside boundary-fence]. **2.** (As measure) rod, perch, 5½ yds. or 30¼ sq. yds. **3.** *v.t.* furnish with poles; push, move, (*off* etc.) with pole. [OE *pāl*, = MDu. *pael*, OHG *pfāl*, ON *páll*, Gmc f. L *palus* stake]

pōle² *n.* **1. North** and **South P~s**, (1) the two points in the celestial sphere about which the stars appear to revolve, (2) extremities of the earth's or other body's axis of rotation, whence **~'**WARD *a.*, **~'**WARD(s) *adv.*, (-lw-), (3) **magnetic ~s**, points near these extremities where magnetic needle dips vertically; **from ~ to ~**, throughout the world. **2.** (Geom.) each of two points in which axis of circle cuts surface of sphere; fixed point to which others are referred. **3.** each of the two opposite points on surface of magnet at which magnetic forces are concentrated; each of two terminals (**positive** and **negative ~**) of electric cell, battery, etc.; (Biol.) extremity of main axis of any spherical or oval organ; (fig.) each of two opposed principles etc. (**be ~s apart** or **asunder**, differ greatly). **4. ~-star**, star in Little Bear, now about 1° distant from north pole of heavens, (fig.) thing serving as guide, lodestar, centre of attraction. [ME, f. L f. Gk *polos* pivot, axis, sky]

Pōle³ *n.* native or inhabitant of Poland. [G, f. Pol. *Polanie* lit. field-dwellers (*pole* field)]

po'le-axe, *-äx, (-lă-) *n.*, & *v.t.* **1.** *n.* battleaxe; axe formerly used in naval warfare as weapon and for cutting ropes etc.; halberd; butcher's axe for slaughtering, with hammer at back. **2.** *v.t.* slaughter or strike (as if) with pole-axe. [ME *pol(l)ax*, *-ex* f. MDu. *pol(l)aex*, MLG *-exe* (as POLL¹, AXE)]

pō'lecăt (-lk-) *n.* ‖small brownish-black fetid carnivorous mammal of weasel family, native of Europe; *skunk. [f. CAT¹; orig. of first syl. unkn.]

polē'mic *a.* & *n.* **1.** *a.* controversial, disputatious, hence **~AL** *a.*, **~ALLY** *adv.*, **pŏ'lěm**IZE (2) *v.i.* **2.** *n.* controversial discussion, (in *pl.*) practice of this, esp. in theology; controversialist. [f. med. L f. Gk *polemikos* (*polemos* war; see -IC)]

polē'nta *n.* porridge made of maize meal etc. [It., f. L, = pearl barley]

poli'ce (-ē's) *n.*, & *v.t.* **1.** *n.* civil force responsible for maintaining public order; (as *pl.*) members of this (*several hundred police; the police are on his track*); force with similar functions of enforcing regulations (*military, railway, *KITCHEN, police*); (Hist.) civil administration. **2.** ‖*police* CONSTABLE; **~ dog** (trained and used by police to track criminals etc.); **~man**, member of police force; **~-officer**, policeman or policewoman; **~ state**, totalitarian State controlled by esp. secret police supervising citizens' activities; **~ station**, office of local police force; **~woman**, woman member of police force. **3.** *v.t.* control (country etc.) by means of police; furnish with police; (fig.) keep order in, control; *~ (**up**), clean (barracks etc.). [F, f. med. L *politia* POLICY¹]

pōliclī'nic *n.* out-patients' department of hospital. [f. G *poliklinik* f. Gk *polis* city + *klinik* CLINIC]

pŏ'licy¹ *n.* prudent conduct, sagacity; course or general plan of action (to be) adopted by government, party, person, etc., (*honesty is the best policy*); (arch.) craftiness; (Sc.) park round country seat etc. [ME f. OF *policie* f. L f. Gk *politeia* citizenship (*politēs* citizen f. *polis* city); in Sc. sense (earlier = improvement of estate) confused w. L *politus* polished]

pŏ'licy² *n.* (document containing) contract of insurance. [f. F *police* bill of lading, contract of insurance, f. Prov. *polis(s)a* prob. f. med. L *apodissa*, *apodixa*, f. L f. Gk *apodeixis* evidence, proof, f. APO(*deiknumi* show)]

pō'liō *n.* (*pl.* **~s**). (colloq.) = foll. [abbr.]

pōliōmyēlī'tis *n.* (Path.) infectious viral inflammation of nerve cells in grey matter of spinal cord, with temporary or permanent paralysis. [mod. L, f. Gk *polios* grey + as MYELITIS]

pŏ'lish¹ *v.t.* & *i.* make or become smooth and glossy by friction; (fig. esp. in *p.p.*) make elegant or cultured, refine; smarten *up*; **~ off**, finish off quickly; hence **~ABLE** *a.*, **~ER¹** (1, 2) *n.* [ME, f. OF *polir* (see -ISH²) f. L *polite polit-*]

pŏ'lish² *n.* smoothness or glossiness produced by friction; friction applied for this purpose; substance used to produce smooth glossy surface; (fig.) refinement, high degree of elegance. [f. prec.]

Pō'lish³ *a.* & *n.* **1.** *a.* of Poland or the Poles. **2.** *n.* the language of Poland. [POLE³ + -ISH¹]

pŏ'litbūrō *n.* (*pl.* **~s**). principal committee of a Communist party; (fig.) similar body with controlling power. [f. Russ. *politbyuro* (*politicheskiĭ* political, *byuro* bureau)]

polī'te *a.* (**~r**, **~st**). having refined manners, courteous; cultivated; cultured; well-bred; (of literature etc.) refined, elegant, (*polite letters*); hence **~LY²** (-tlī) *adv.*, **~NESS** (-tn-) *n.* [f. L *politus* (as POLISH¹)]

politesse (pŏlītě's) *n.* formal politeness. [F, f. It. *politezza*, *pulitezza* (*pulito* POLITE)]

pŏ'litic *a.*, & *v.i.* (**-ck-**). **1.** *a.* (Of person) sagacious, prudent, (of action etc.) judicious, expedient; scheming, crafty; **body ~**, State, or similarly organized system; hence **~LY²** *adv.* **2.** *v.i.* engage in politics. [ME, f. OF *politique* f. L f. Gk *politikos* (*politēs* citizen f. *polis* city; see -IC)]

polī'tical *a.* **1.** of or affecting the State or its government; of public affairs; of politics. **2.** (Of person) engaged in civil administration. **3.** having an organized form of society or government. **4.** belonging to, or taking, a side in politics; relating to person's or organization's status or influence (*a political decision*). **5.** *political* ASYLUM, ECONOMY; **~ geography** (dealing with boundaries and possessions of States); **~ prisoner**, person imprisoned for political offence; *political* SCIENCE; **~ verse**, Byzantine and modern Greek verse composed by accent, not quantity, [f. Gk *politikos* popular). **6.** Hence **~LY²** *adv.* [f. L *politicus* (see prec.) + -AL]

pŏlitī'cian (-shan) *n.* one skilled in politics, statesman; one interested or engaged in politics, esp. as profession; *one who makes a trade of politics. [f. as POLITIC; see -ICIAN]

polī'ticīze, **-īse** (-īz), *v.* **1.** *v.i.* act the politician; engage in or talk politics. **2.** *v.t.* give political character to. **3.** Hence **~A'TION** *n.* [f. as POLITIC + -IZE]

polī'ticō *n.* (*pl.* **~s**). one interested or engaged in politics, esp. as profession or trade. [Sp., = POLITIC (as *n.*)]

polī'ticō- *comb. form.* politically, political and, as: **~-economical**, **~-geographical**, **~-moral**, **~-social**. [f. Gk *politikos* (see POLITIC) + -O-]

pŏ'litics *n. pl.* (also treated as *sing.*). science and art of government; political affairs or life (*politics is a dirty business*); political principles (*what are his politics?*; the *politics of the decision is not clear*); **not practical ~**, (1) not likely enough to be worth discussing, (2) liable to meet practical difficulties. [f. POLITIC; see -ICS]

pŏ'lity *n.* form or process of civil government; organized society, State; (arch.) condition of civil order. [f. L *politia* POLICY¹]

pŏ'lka *n.*, & *v.i.* (**~ed** or **~'d**, *pr.* -ad). **1.** *n.* lively dance of Bohemian origin in duple time; music for this; **~ dot**, round dot as one of many forming regular pattern on textile fabric etc. **2.** *v.i.* dance the polka. [F & G, f. Czech *půlka* half-step (*půl* half)]

pŏll¹ *n.* **1.** human head; part of this on which hair grows (*grey, flaxen, poll*); **~-tax** (levied on every person). **2.** counting of voters esp. at parliamentary or other election; voting at election (*exclusion of Blacks from the poll*); result of voting; number of votes recorded (*heavy, light, poll*). **3.** = GALLUP *poll*; hence ~'STER *n*. [ME, perh. f. LDu.]

pōll[2] *v*. **1.** *v.t.* (arch.) crop hair of. **2.** cut off top of (tree, plant), esp. make a pollard of; (esp. in *p.p.*) cut off horns of (cattle); cut evenly edge of (sheet). **3.** take the vote(s) of, (in *pass.*) have one's vote taken; (of candidate) receive (so many votes); give (vote). **4.** *v.i.* give one's vote. [ME, f. prec.]

pōll[3] *a*. & *n*. **1.** *a*. polled, cut evenly. **2.** *n*. hornless animal, esp. one of a breed of hornless oxen. [abbr. of p.p. of prec.]

pōll[4] *n*. ~ **parrot**, (1) tame parrot, (2) user of conventional or unoriginal phrases and arguments. [f. *Poll*, conventional name for parrot, alt. f. *Moll*, familiar form of *Mary*]

pŏ'llack, pŏ'llock, *n*. marine food-fish of genus *Pollachius*, allied to cod, but with protruding lower jaw. [earlier (Sc.) *podlock*; orig. unkn.]

pŏ'llan *n*. Irish lake fish, allied to trout. [perh. f. Ir. *poll* deep water]

pŏ'llard *n*., & *v.t.* **1.** *n*. animal that has cast or lost its horns; ox, sheep, or goat, of hornless breed; tree polled so as to produce close rounded head of young branches; bran sifted from flour; fine bran containing some flour. **2.** *v.t.* make (tree) a pollard. [f. POLL[2] + -ARD]

pŏ'llen *n*. fine powdery substance discharged from anther of flower, male element that fertilizes ovules; ~ **analysis,** palynology; ~ **count,** index of amount of pollen in air published as warning to those allergic to it; hence ~LESS, **polli'nic, pŏllini'**FEROUS, *adjs.* [L *pollen pollinis* fine flour, dust]

pŏ'll|ĕx *n*. (*pl.* ~ices *pr.* -īsēz). innermost digit of fore-limb, thumb. [L, = thumb or big toe]

pollicitā'tion *n*. (Civil Law). promise not yet formally accepted, and therefore revocable. [F, or f. L *pollicitatio* (*pollicitari* bid at auction, frequent. of *polliceri* promise; see -ATION)]

pŏ'llin|āte *v.t.* fertilize or sprinkle with pollen, shed pollen upon; hence ~A'TION *n*. [f. as POLLEN + -ATE[3]]

polli'nic, pŏllini'ferous. See POLLEN.

pŏ'lliwŏg *n*. (dial. & US). tadpole. [earlier *polwigge, polwygle,* f. POLL[1] + WIGGLE]

pŏ'llock. See POLLACK.

pollu't|e (-ōō't) *v.t.* destroy the purity or sanctity of; make foul or filthy; contaminate or defile (man's environment); hence or cogn. ~ANT *a*. & *n*., **pollu'tion** (-ōō'-) *n*. [ME, f. L *polluere -lut-*]

pŏ'llỹ *n*. (colloq.) Apollinaris. [abbr.; see -Y[3]]

Pŏllyă'nna *n*. cheerful optimist; hence ~ISH[1] *a*., ~ISM (2) *n*., (-aĭ-). [character in novel (1913) by E. Porter]

pŏ'llywŏg. Var. of POLLIWOG.

po'lō *n*. game of Eastern origin like hockey played on horseback with long-handled mallet (~-**stick**); ~-**neck,** high round turned-over collar; WATER[1] *polo*. [Balti, = ball]

pŏ'lōcrŏsse *n*. game played on horseback with long-handled stick having net at end. [f. prec. + LACROSSE]

pŏlonai'se (-z) *n*. **1.** woman's dress consisting of bodice with skirt open over petticoat from waist downwards. **2.** (music for or in style of) slow processional dance of Polish origin in triple time. [F, fem. (as n.) of *polonais* Polish f. med. L *Polonia* Poland]

polō'nium *n*. radioactive metallic element forming the last stage before lead in the decay of radium. [F & mod. L, f. med. L *Polonia* Poland (discoverer's native country) + -IUM]

||**polō'nỹ** *n*. sausage of partly cooked pork etc. [app. replacing *Bologna* or *Bolognian sausage*]

pŏ'ltergeist (-gīst) *n*. noisy mischievous ghost, esp. one manifesting itself by physical damage. [G (*poltern* create disturbance, *geist* GHOST)]

pŏ'lt-fŏŏt *n*. (*pl.* -feet) & *a*. (arch.) club-foot(ed). [f. obs. *polt* pestle, club, (17th c.; orig. unkn.) + FOOT[1]]

pŏltrōō'n *n*. spiritless coward; so ~ERY (4) *n*. [f. F *poltron* f. It. *poltrone* (perh. f. *poltro* sluggard); see -OON]

pŏ'lỹ *n*. (*pl.* ~s). (colloq.) polytechnic. [abbr.]

pŏ'lỹ- *pref.* **1.** many, much, as: ~**ade'lphous,** (Bot.) with stamens united in 3 or more bundles; ~**a'ndrous,** of or practising polyandry, (Bot.) having numerous stamens; ~**andry,** polygamy in which woman has more than one husband; ~**ato'mic,** (Chem.) consisting of many atoms, having many replaceable atoms or radicals; ~**ba'sic,** (Chem.) having more than two replaceable hydrogen atoms; ~**chaete** (-kēt) *a*. & *n*., **chae'tan,** ~**chae'tous,** (-kē't-) *adjs.,* (annelid worm) with many bristles on the foot-stumps; ~**cry'stal**(**line**), (body) consisting of several or many crystals with various orientations; ~**da'ctyl** *a*. & *n*., (animal) with more than normal number of fingers or toes; ~**dae'monism,** belief in many supernatural powers; ~**gene,** ~**gene'tic,** ~**ge'nic,** (Geol.) composed of rock formed in several ways; ~**ge'nesis,** (theoretical) origination of a race or species from several independent stocks; ~**graph,** (1) lie-detector, (2) writer of many or various works; ~**gynous** (-ĭ'g-, -ĭ'j-), of or practising polygyny, (Bot.) having numerous pistils, styles, or stigmas; ~**gyny** (-ĭ'g-, -ĭ'j-), polygamy in which man has more than one wife; ~**mor'phic,** ~**mor'phous,** multiform, esp. (Biol.) varying in individuals, passing through successive variations, so ~**mor'phism** *n*.; ~**o'nymous,** called by several different names; ~**o'pia,** disorder of the eyes in which one object appears as two or more; ~**phagous** (-ĭ'f-), (Zool.) feeding on various kinds of food; ~**phone,** letter or symbol standing for different sounds; ~**phyle'tic,** formed by polygenesis; ~**ptych** (-k), painting etc. with four or more folding leaves; ~**sa'ccharide,** carbohydrate resolvable into two or more monosaccharides; ~**synthe'tic,** (of languages) combining several or all parts of a sentence into one word; ~**to'nal,** (Mus.) using more than one key; ~**va'lent,** (Chem.) having a valence of more than two, or several valences; ~**zo'an,** (= BRYOZOAN. **2.** polymerized, as: ~**e'ster** (esp. as synthetic resin or fibre), ~**e'thylene** (esp. = POLYTHENE); ~**styr'ene,** hard colourless thermoplastic styrene polymer; ~**unsa'turated,** (of chem. compound) containing several double or triple bonds, and therefore reactive; ~**urethane** (-ĕ'-, -ūr'-), synthetic resin or plastic used esp. as foam; ~**vinyl chlor'ide,** tough resistant colourless thermoplastic consisting of or made from polymer of vinyl chloride. [sense 1 f. Gk *polu-* (*polus* much, *polloi* many); sense 2 f. POLYMER]

pŏlỹ'anthus *n*. cultivated primrose from hybridized primulas. [mod. L, f. as POLY- + Gk *anthos* flower]

pŏlỹchromā'tic (-kr-) *a*. many-coloured; (of radiation) containing more than one wavelength. [f. POLY- + CHROMATIC]

pŏ'lỹchrōme (-kr-) *a*. & *n*. **1.** *a*. painted, printed, or decorated, in many colours. **2.** *n*. work of art in several colours, esp. coloured statue; varied colouring. **3.** Hence **pŏlỹchrō'm**IC, **pŏlỹchrŏm**OUS, (-kr-) *adjs.* [F, f. Gk *polukhrōmos* (as POLY-, *khrōma* colour)]

pŏ'lỹchromỹ (-kr-) *n*. art of painting in several colours, esp. as applied to ancient pottery etc. [f. F *polychromie* (as prec.; see -Y[1])]

pŏ'lỹclinic *n*. clinic devoted to various diseases; general hosital. [f. POLY- + CLINIC]

pŏlỹ'gam|ous *a*. **1.** having more than one wife or (less usu.) husband at once; so **pŏlỹgă'm**IC *a*., ~IST (1), ~Y[1], *ns*. (2). (Zool.) having more than one mate. **3.** (Bot.) bearing some flowers with stamens only, some with pistils only, some with both, on same or different plants. [f. Gk *polugamos* (as POLY-, *-gamos* marrying) + -OUS]

pŏlỹ'gĕn|ỹ *n*. (theoretical) origination of mankind from several independent pairs of ancestors; so ~ISM (3) *n*., doctrine of polygeny; so ~IST (2) *n*. [f. POLY- + -GENY]

pŏ'lỹglŏt *a*. & *n*. of many languages; (person)

speaking or writing several languages; (book, esp. Bible) with text and translation into several languages; hence **polyglŏ′ttal, polyglŏ′ttic**, *adjs.*, ∼ism (1) *n.* [f. F *polyglotte* f. Gk *poluglōttos* (as POLY-, *glōtta* tongue)]

pŏ′lygon *n.* figure (usu. plane rectilinear) with many (usu. more than four) angles and sides; ∼ **of forces**, polygon illustrating theorem relating to several forces acting at a point; hence **poly′gonal** *a.* [f. LL f. Gk *polugōnon* neut. a. as n. (*polu-* POLY-, *-gōnos* angled)]

pŏlyhē′dr|on *n.* (*pl.* ∼a). solid figure with many (usu. more than six) faces; hence ∼al, ∼ic, *adjs.* [f. Gk *poluedron*, neut. (as n.) of *poluedros* (*polu-* POLY-, *hedra* base; cf. -HEDRON)]

pŏlyhi′stor *n.* = foll. [f. Gk *poluistōr* (*polu-* POLY- + *histōr*; see HISTORY)]

pŏ′lymath *n.* person of varied learning; great scholar; so **poly′mathy[1]** *n.* [f. Gk *polumathēs* (as POLY-, *math-* st. of *manthanō* learn)]

pŏ′lymer *n.* (Chem.) compound whose molecule is formed from a number of repeated units of one or more compounds of low molecular weight (*monomers*); hence **pŏlyme′ric** *a.*, ∼ism (2) *n.*, ∼ize (2, 3) *v.i.* & *t.* [G, f. Gk *polumeros* having many parts (as POLY-, *meros* share)]

poly′merous *a.* (Biol.) having many parts. [f. as prec. + -OUS]

Pŏlynē′sian (-shan) *a.* & *n.* (inhabitant or language) of Polynesia. [f. *Polynesia*, island-group including New Zealand, Hawaii, Samoa, etc. (f. as POLY- + Gk *nēsos* island + -IA[1]) + -AN]

pŏlyneur|ī′tis (-nūr-) *n.* inflammation of several nerves at same time; hence ∼i′tic *a.* [f. POLY- + NEURITIS]

pŏlynō′mial *a.* & *n.* (Alg.) (expression) of more than two terms, esp. (sum) of terms containing different powers of the same variable(s). [f. POLY-, after MULTInomial]

poly′nya *n.* space of open water in midst of ice, esp. in Arctic seas. [Russ. (*pole* field)]

pŏ′lyp *n.* **1.** (Zool.) individual member of coelenterate colony etc. **2.** (Path.) small tumour of mucous membrane, with tentacle-like ramifications. [f. F *polype* f. as POLYPUS]

pŏ′lypary *n.* common stem or supporting structure of a colony of polyps. [f. mod. L *polyparium* (as POLYPUS; see -ARIUM)]

pŏlypĕ′ptīde *n.* (Chem.) peptide formed by combination of many aminoacids. [f. G *polypeptid* (as POLY- 2, PEPTONE, -IDE)]

pŏ′lyphāse (-z) *a.* (Electr.) designed to supply or use simultaneously several alternating currents of the same voltage but with different phases. [f. POLY- + PHASE]

pŏlyphŏ′nic, poly′phonous, *adjs.* having many voices; (Philol., of letter etc.) representing more than one sound; (Mus.) contrapuntal; so **poly′phony[1]** *n.* [f. Gk *poluphōnos* (as POLY-, *phōnē* voice, sound) + -IC, -OUS]

pŏ′lyploid *a.* & *n.* (Biol.) (organism or cell) having more than two haploid sets of chromosomes; hence ∼y[1] *n.*, condition of being polyploid. [G (as POLY-, -PLOID)]

pŏ′lypŏd *a.* & *n.* (animal) with many feet. [f. F *polypode* a. f. Gk (as POLYPUS)]

pŏ′lypŏdy *n.* fern of genus *Polypodium* or family Polypodiaceae, esp. common species growing on moist rocks, walls, trees, etc. [ME, f. L f. Gk *polupodion* (as POLYPUS)]

pŏ′lyp|oid *a.* of or like a polyp; so ∼ous *a.* [f. POLYP + -OID]

pŏ′lyp|us *n.* (*pl.* ∼i *pr.* -ī, *or* ∼uses). (Path.) = POLYP 2. [ME f. L, f. Gk *pōlupos, polupous* cuttlefish, polyp in nose (*polu-* POLY-, *pous podos* foot)]

pŏ′lysēm|y *n.* (Philol.) existence of many meanings (of word etc.); hence ∼ic, ∼ous, *adjs.* [f. POLY- + Gk *sēma* sign + -Y[1]]

pŏlysyllā′b|ic *a.* (Of word) having many syllables; marked by polysyllables; hence ∼ically *adv.* [f. med. L f. Gk *polusullabos* (as foll.) + -IC]

pŏ′lysyllable *n.* polysyllabic word. [f. med. L *polysyllaba* (vox word) (as POLY-, SYLLABLE)]

pŏlytĕ′chnic (-k-) *a.* & *n.* (institution, esp. college) dealing with or devoted to various esp. technical subjects. [f. F *polytechnique* f. Gk *polutekhnos* (as POLY-, *tekhnē* art); see -IC]

pŏ′lythē|ism *n.* belief in, or worship of, many gods or more than one god; so ∼ist (2) *n.*, ∼i′stic *a.* [f. F *polythéisme* f. Gk *polutheos* of many gods (as POLY-, *theos* god); see -ISM]

pŏ′lythēne *n.* tough light translucent thermoplastic polymer of ethylene. [f. POLYethylene]

pŏm *n.* Pomeranian dog; (Austral. & NZ sl.) = POMMY. [abbr.]

po′mace (pŭ′mĭs) *n.* mass of crushed apples in cider-making before or after juice is pressed out; refuse of fish etc. after oil has been extracted, used as fertilizer. [ME, f. med. L *pomacium* cider f. L *pomum* apple]

poma′de (-ah′d) *n.*, & *v.t.* **1.** *n.* scented ointment for hair and skin of head. **2.** *v.t.* anoint with pomade. [f. F *pommade* f. It. *pomata* f. med. L *pomata* f. L *pomum* apple (see -ADE); perh. orig. made f. apples]

pomā′nder (po-, pō-) *n.* ball of mixed aromatic substances placed in cupboard etc. or (Hist.) carried in box, bag, etc., as preservative against infection; (usu. spherical) container for this; spiced orange etc. similarly used. [earlier *pom(e)amber* f. AF *pome ambre, OF *pome d'embre* f. L *pomum de ambra* apple of ambergris]

pomā′tum *n.*, & *v.t.* = POMADE. [mod. L, f. L *pomum* apple + *-atum* -ATE[1]]

pŏ′mbe *n.* intoxicating drink made in Central and E. Africa from millet etc. [Swahili]

pōme *n.* **1.** (Bot.) succulent fruit with firm fleshy body enclosing carpels forming the core, e.g. apple, pear, quince; so **pomi′ferous** *a.* **2.** metal ball; (poet.) apple. [ME f. OF, f. Rom. *poma orig. pl. of *pomum* fruit, apple]

pŏ′megranate (-mĭg-, -mg-) *n.* tropical tree (*Punica granatum*) native to N. Africa and W. Asia; its fruit, about size of orange with tough golden or orange rind and acid reddish pulp enclosing many seeds; ornamental representation of this. [ME, f. OF *pome grenate* etc. (see prec.) f. Rom. *granata f. L (*malum*) *granatum* many-seeded (*granum* seed; see -ATE[2])]

po′melo (pŭ′m-) *n.* (*pl.* ∼s). shaddock or grapefruit. [19th c.; orig. unkn.]

Pŏmerā′nian *a.* & *n.* ∼ (**dog**), small dog with long silky hair, pointed muzzle, and pricked ears. [f. *Pomerania* in Germany & Poland + -AN]

pŏ′mfret *n.* food-fish of family Stromateidae, found in Indian and Pacific Oceans. **2.** black food-fish (*Brama raii*) of northern seas. [app. f. Port. *pampo*]

‖**po′mfrĕt-cāke** (pŭ′-, pŏ′-) *n.* small round flat liquorice sweetmeat made at Pontefract (earlier *Pomfret*) in West Yorkshire.

pŏ′miculture *n.* fruit-growing. [f. L *pomum* fruit + -I- + CULTURE]

Pommār′d (-ār′) *n.* a red burgundy wine. [∼ in E. France]

po′mmel (pŭ′m-) *n.*, & *v.t.* (‖-ll-). **1.** *n.* knob esp. at end of sword-hilt; upward projecting front part of saddle. **2.** *v.t.* = PUMMEL. [ME, f. OF *pomel* f. Rom. *pomellum dim. of L *pomum* fruit, apple]

pŏ′mmy, pŏ′mmie, *n.* (Austral. & NZ sl.) British person, esp. recent immigrant. [20th c.; orig. uncert.]

pomŏ′log|y *n.* science of fruit-growing; hence **pōmo-lŏ′gical** *a.*, ∼ist (3) *n.* [f. L *pomum* fruit + -o- + -LOGY]

pŏmp *n.* splendid display, splendour; specious glory (esp. in *pl.*; *the pomps and vanities of this wicked world*). [ME, f. OF *pompe* f. L f. Gk *pompē* procession, pomp (*pempō* send)]

pŏ′mpadour (-oor) *n.* woman's hair-style with hair

in high turned-back roll round face. [f. Marquise de *Pompadour*, mistress of Louis XV of France d. 1764].

pŏ'mpanō *n.* (*pl.* ~**s**). W. Ind. and N. Amer. food--fish esp. of genus *Trachinotus*. [f. Sp. *pámpano*]

||**Pŏ'mpey** *n.* (sl.) Portsmouth. [corrupt.; cf. *Pompey*, Roman general d. 48 BC]

pŏ'm-pŏm¹ *n.* automatic quick-firing gun esp. on ship. [imit.]

pŏ'm-pŏm². Var. of foll.

pŏ'mpŏn *n.* ornamental tuft or bunch of ribbon, flowers, etc., on women's or children's hats and shoes; round tuft on soldier's cap, front of shako, etc.; dahlia etc. with small tightly-clustered petals. [F, of unkn. orig.]

pŏ'mpous *a.* **1.** self-important, consequential; (of language) pretentious, unduly grand in style; so **pŏmpo'sity** *n.* **2.** (arch.) magnificent, splendid. **3.** Hence ~**LY²** *adv.*, ~**NESS** *n.* [ME, f. OF *pompeux* f. LL *pomposus* (as POMP; see -OUS)]

'pŏn *prep.* = UPON ('*pon my word*). [abbr.]

pŏnce *n.*, & *v.i.* **1.** *n.* man who lives off prostitute's earnings. **2.** *v.i.* act as ponce; move *about* effeminately etc. [perh. f. POUNCE¹]

pŏ'nceau (-sō) *n.* poppy-colour, bright red; red dye. [F]

pŏ'nchō *n.* (*pl.* ~**s**). S. Amer. cloak of oblong piece of cloth with slit in middle for head; cycling-cape or other garment made to similar design. [S. Amer. Sp., f. Araucanian]

pŏnd *n.* & *v.* **1.** *n.* fairly small body of still water formed naturally or by hollowing or embanking; (joc.) the sea (cf. HERRING-*pond*); ~**-life**, animals (esp. invertebrates) that live in ponds; ~'**weed**, aquatic herb (esp. of genus *Potamogeton*) growing in still water. **2.** *v.t.* hold back, dam up, (stream). **3.** *v.i.* form pond. [ME, var. of POUND²]

pŏ'ndage *n.* capacity of pond; storage of water. [f. prec. + -AGE]

pŏ'nder *v.* **1.** *v.t.* weigh mentally, think over, (matter, how, etc.). **2.** *v.i.* think *on*, muse *over*. [ME, f. OF *ponderer* f. L *ponderare* (*pondus -eris* weight)]

pŏ'nder|able *a.* having appreciable weight (lit. or fig.); hence ~ABI'LITY *n.* [f. LL *ponderabilis* (as prec.; see -ABLE)]

pŏnderā'tion *n.* weighing, balancing, (lit. or fig.). [f. L *ponderatio* (as PONDER; see -ATION)]

*pŏnderŏ'sa *n.* (red timber of) N. Amer. pine-tree (*Pinus ponderosa*). [mod. L, fem. of L *ponderosus* (see foll.)]

pŏ'nderous *a.* heavy; unwieldy; laborious; (of style) dull, tedious; hence or cogn. **pŏndero'sity**, ~**NESS**, *ns.*, ~**LY²** *adv.* [ME, f. L *ponderosus* (*pondus -eris* weight; see -OUS)]

pŏ'nè¹ *n.* dealer's opponent in two-handed card--games. [L, 2 sing. imper. of *ponere* place]

*pŏne² *n.* maize bread, esp. as made by N. Amer. Indians; fine light bread made with milk, eggs, etc.; cake or loaf of this. [Algonquian, = bread].

pŏng *n.*, & *v.i.* (colloq.) stink. [20th c.; orig. unkn.]

pongee' (pŭnjē') *n.* soft usu. unbleached kind of Chinese silk fabric; imitation of this in cotton etc. [perh. f. Chin. dial. *pun-chī* own loom, i.e. home--made]

pŏ'ngid (-nj-) *a.* & *n.* (anthropoid ape) of family Pongidae. [f. mod. L *Pongidae* (*Pongo*, genus-name; see foll., -ID²)]

pŏ'ngo (-nggō) *n.* (*pl.* ~**s**). ape of genus *Pongo*, orang--utan; (Naut.) soldier. [f. Congolese *mpongo*, orig. of African apes]

pŏ'niard (-yerd) *n.*, & *v.t.* (literary). (pierce or stab with) dagger. [f. F *poignard* f. OF *poignal* f. med. L *pugnale* f. L *pugnus* fist; see -ARD]

pons (pŏnz) *n.* ~ (**Varolii**), band of nerve-fibres in brain [f. C. *Varoli*, It. anatomist d. 1575]; **pons asinor'um**, bridge of asses, i.e. (1) 5th proposition of 1st book of Euclid ('the angles at the base of an isosceles triangle are equal to one another'), (2) anything found difficult by beginners. [L, = bridge]

pŏnt *n.* (S. Afr.) ferry-boat moved by rope or cable. [Du.]

||**Pŏ'ntéfräct-cäke.** Var. of POMFRET-CAKE.

pŏ'nti|fex *n.* (*pl.* ~**fices** *pr.* -ĭ'fĭsēz). (Rom. Ant.) member of principal college of priests in Rome (**Pontifex Maximus,** head of this); = foll. [L *pontifex -ficis* (perh. *pons pontis* bridge, *-fex* f. *facere* make)]

pŏ'ntiff *n.* **1.** (**sovereign** or **supreme**) ~, the Pope. **2.** bishop; chief priest. [f. F *pontife* f. as prec.]

pŏntĭ'fical *a.* & *n.* **1.** *a.* of or befitting a pontiff; pretending to infallibility, pompously dogmatic; ~ **Mass** (celebrated by bishop in full vestments); hence ~**LY²** *adv.* **2.** *n.* office-book of Western Church containing forms for rites to be performed by bishops; (in *pl.*) vestments and insignia of bishop. [ME f. F, or f. L *pontificalis* (as PONTIFEX; see -AL)]

pŏntĭfĭca'lia *n. pl.* pontificals. [L, neut. pl. of *pontificalis* (see prec.)]

pŏntĭ'ficate¹ *n.* office of pontifex, bishop, or pope; period of this. [f. L *pontificatus* (as PONTIFEX; see -ATE¹)]

pŏntĭ'ficāte² *v.i.* **1.** play the pontiff, pretend to infallibility; be pompously dogmatic. **2.** officiate as bishop, esp. at Mass. [f. med. L *pontificare* (as PONTIFEX) + -ATE³]

pŏ'ntify *v.i.* = prec. 1. [f. F *pontifier* f. med. L *pontificare* (see prec., -FY)]

pŏntoneer', -nier', *n.* one who has charge of pontoons or of construction of a pontoon-bridge. [f. F *pontonnier* f. med. L *pontonarius* ferryman f. L *ponto* (see foll., -ARY¹)]

pŏntoō'n¹ *n.*, & *v.t.* **1.** *n.* flat-bottomed boat used as ferry-boat or to carry lifting-gear etc.; one of several boats, hollow metal cylinders, etc., used to support temporary bridge; = CAISSON 2. **2.** *v.t.* cross (river) by means of pontoons. [f. F *ponton* f. L *ponto -onis* (*pons pontis* bridge; see -OON)]

||**pŏntoō'n²** *n.* vingt-et-un; hand at this, = NATURAL 19. [prob. corrupt.]

pō'ny *n.*, & *v.t.* **1.** *n.* horse of any small breed; small--sized *motor car, drinking-glass, etc.; *crib for translation; ||(sl.) £25; (in *pl.*, sl.) racehorses. **2.** ~ **express,** rapid postal system using ponies; ~**-tail,** woman's or girl's hair drawn back, tied, and hanging behind like pony's tail; ~**-trekking,** travelling across country on ponies for pleasure. **3.** *v.t.* *(sl.) pay *up*. [perh. f. *poulney f. F *poulenet* dim. of *poulain* foal]

*poōch *n.* (sl.) dog. [20th c.; orig. unkn.]

poōd *n.* Russian weight, 36 lb. avoirdupois. [f. Russ. *pud* f. LG or ON *pund* POUND¹]

poō'dle *n.*, & *v.t.* **1.** *n.* breed of dog with long curling hair often clipped and shaved in elaborate pattern. **2.** *v.t.* clip and shave (dog) thus. [f. G *pudel*(*hund*) f. LG *pud*(*d*)*eln* splash in water; cf. PUDDLE²]

poōf (*pl.* **pooves**), (Austral.) **poō'fter,** *ns.* (colloq., derog.) effeminate man; male homosexual. [19th c.; cf. PUFF¹ in sense 'braggart']

poōh (poō) *int.* expr. impatience or contempt. [imit.]

Pōōh-Bah' (poōb-) *n.* holder of many offices at once. [character in W. S. Gilbert's *The Mikado*]

poōh-poō'h (poōpoō') *v.t.* express contempt for, ridicule, dismiss (idea etc.) scornfully. [redupl. of POOH]

poō'ja. See PUJA.

poō'ka *n.* (Ir.) hobgoblin. [f. Ir. *púca*]

poōl¹ *n.* & *v.* **1.** *n.* small body of still water, usu. of natural formation; small shallow body of any liquid; deep still place in river; = SWIMMING-*pool*; ||**the P~** (**of London**), part of Thames just below London Bridge. **2.** *v.t.* form into pool. **3.** *v.i.* form pool; (of blood) become static. [f. OE *pōl*, MLG, MDu *pōl*, OHG *pfuol* f. WG **pōl-*]

poōl² *n.*, & *v.t.* **1.** *n.* (Cards) collective amount of players' stakes and fines; receptacle for these. **2.**

||game on billiard-table in which each player has ball of different colour with which he tries to pocket the others in fixed order, winner taking the whole stakes; *game on billiard-table with usu. 16 balls; *~'room, place for playing this, betting, etc. **3.** (collective stakes in) joint gambling venture; **football** ~, form of gambling in which a proportion of the entry money for the competition is awarded in prizes to those who (most) correctly forecast the results of certain football matches; **the ~s,** various such competitions conducted week by week. **4.** arrangement between competing parties by which prices are fixed and business shared to do away with competition. **5.** common fund, e.g. of the profits of separate firms; common supply of persons, services, commodities, etc.; group of persons sharing duties etc. **6.** fencing competition between two teams in which each member of one team fights each member of the other. **7.** *v.t.* throw into common fund; share in common; (of transport organizations etc.) share (traffic, receipts). [f. F *poule* (= hen) in same sense; assoc. w. prec.]

poon *n.* E. Ind. tree of genus *Calophyllum*; ~ **oil** (from seeds of this, used in medicine and for lamps). [f. Sinh. *pūna*]

*****poo'ntäng** *n.* (sl.) sexual intercourse [f F *putain* prostitute]

poop[1] *n.*, & *v.t.* **1.** *n.* stern of ship; aftermost and highest deck. **2.** *v.t.* (Of wave) break over stern of (ship); (of ship) receive (wave) over stern. [ME, f. OF *pupe*, *pope* f. Rom. **puppa* f. L *puppis*]

poop[2] *v.t.* (esp. in *p.p.*; colloq.) exhaust; tire out. [20th c.; orig. unkn.]

||**poop**[3] *n.* (sl.) foolish insignificant person. [abbr. of *nincompoop*]

poop[4] *n.* (sl.) wind from anus; defecation; faeces. [imit.]

poor *a.* **1.** not having means to procure comforts or necessaries of life (*poor in* SPIRIT[1]); ill supplied, deficient, (*in a possession or quality*); (of soil) unproductive. **2.** scanty, inadequate, less or less good than is expected, (*the crop, visibility, was poor; had a poor night; is a poor driver; came* **a** ~ **second,** far behind winner; *in poor* SPIRIT[1]*s*); paltry, sorry, (*that is a poor consolation; it is a poor look-out if that happens*); spiritless, despicable, (*he is a poor creature*); humble, insignificant, (often iron. or joc.; *in my poor opinion*); **take a** ~ **view of,** regard with disfavour or pessimism. **3.** (Expr. pity or sympathy) unfortunate, hapless, (*poor fellow!; the poor child is inconsolable*). **4.** ~**-box,** money-box esp. in church for relief of the poor; ~**-house,** (Hist.) workhouse; ~**-law,** (Hist.) law relating to support of paupers; ~ **man's,** cheaper or cheaper substitute for (*cabbage* etc.); ~ **man's weather-glass,** pimpernel; ||~**-rate,** (Hist.) rate or assessment for relief or support of the poor; ~ **relation,** (fig.) inferior or subordinate member of group; ~**-spirited,** timid, cowardly; *~ **white,** (esp. Black derog.; **R**) member of socially inferior group of white people. [ME & OF *pov(e)re, poure,* f. L *pauper*]

poor'ly *adv.* & *pred. a.* **1.** *adv.* scantily, defectively; with no great success; meanly, contemptibly. **2.** *a.* unwell (*he is (looking) very poorly*). [ME, f. prec. + -LY[2]]

poor'ness *n.* defectiveness; lack of some good quality or constituent. [f. POOR + -NESS]

||**poort** (pōrt) *n.* (S. Afr.) pass, narrower than a nek. [Du., = gate(way)]

poöve. Var. of POOF.

pop[1] *v.* (-pp-). **1.** *v.i.* make small quick explosive sound(s) as of cork when drawn; fire gun (*at bird* etc.); move, go, come, (*in, out, up,* etc.) unexpectedly or quickly or suddenly; (of cricket-ball) rise sharply from pitch; ~ **off,** (colloq.) die. **2.** *v.t.* put (thing *in, out, down,* etc.) unexpectedly or quickly or suddenly; (sl.) inject (drug etc.). **3.** put (question) abruptly; ~ **the question,** (colloq.) propose marriage. **4.** cause to burst with a pop; ||(sl.) pawn; *parch (maize) till it

bursts open. **5.** ~**'corn,** maize so parched; ~**'gun,** child's toy gun shooting pellet etc. by compression of air with piston, (derog.) inefficient firearm; *~**'over,** cake made from thin batter as hollow shell; ||~**-shop,** (sl.) pawnbroker's shop; ~**-up** *a.,* (of toaster etc.) operating so as to move object (toast when ready etc.) quickly upwards. [ME; imit.]

pop[2] *n.* & *adv.* **1.** *n.* abrupt explosive sound; (colloq.) effervescing drink; ||(sl.) pawning (**in** ~, in pawn); (sl.) attempt, turn. **2.** *adv.* with sound of pop (*heard it go pop*); ~ **goes the weasel,** 19th-c. country dance in which dancer darted under arms of others to his partner. [as prec.]

pop[3] *n.* & *a.* (colloq.) **1.** *n.* popular concert, record, music, etc. **2.** *a.* popular; performing popular music etc. (*pop group*); ~ **art** (based on modern popular culture and mass media); ~ **festival** (at which popular music etc. is performed). [abbr.]

||**Pop**[4] *n.* social and debating club at Eton. [perh. f. L *popina* cookshop, or E *lollipop shop* (orig. meeting-place)]

pop[5] *n.* (colloq., esp. as *voc.*) father; any older man. [f. PAPA]

pop. *abbr.* population.

po'padam. Var. of POPPADAM.

pope[1] *n.* **1.** Bishop of Rome as head of Roman Catholic Church; head of Coptic Church; (fig.) person pretending to or credited with infallibility etc.; = RUFF[3]. **2.** P~ **Joan,** card-game using compartmented tray [f. name of mythical female pope]; ~**'s eye,** lymphatic gland surrounded with fat in middle of sheep's leg.; ~**'s head,** (arch.) round long-handled broom; *pope's* NOSE. **3.** Hence ~'DOM (-pd-) *n.,* ~'LESS (-pl-) *a.* [OE f. eccl. L *pāpa* bishop, pope, f. eccl. Gk *papas* = Gk *pappas* father; cf. PAPA]

pope[2] *n.* parish priest of Orthodox Church in Russia etc. [f. Russ. *pop* f. OSlav. *popŭ* f. WG **papo* f. eccl. Gk (as prec.)]

po'pery *n.* (derog.) papal system, Roman Catholic religion. [f. POPE[1] + -ERY]

po'p-eyed (-īd) *a.* (colloq.) having bulging eyes; open-eyed (with surprise etc.). [f. POP[1] + EYE[1] + -ED[2]]

po'pinjay *n.* **1.** (arch.) parrot. **2.** (Hist.) figure of parrot on pole as mark to shoot at. **3.** conceited person; fop, coxcomb. [ME, f. AF *papejaio,* OF *papingay* etc., f. Sp. *papagayo* f. Arab. *babaḡā*; assim. to JAY]

po'pish *a.* (derog.) of popery, papistical; hence ~LY[2] *adv.* [f. POPE[1] + -ISH[1]]

po'plar *n.* tree of genus *Populus,* of rapid growth (often w. allus. to straightness of trunk and freq. tremulous leaves; * = TULIP-*tree* (1); **trembling** ~, aspen. [ME, f. AF *poplier,* OF *poplier (pople* f. L *populus*)]

po'plin *n.* plain-woven fabric usu. of cotton, with corded surface. [f. obs. F *papeline* perh. f. It. *papalina* (fem.) PAPAL, f. the papal town Avignon where it was made]

popli'teal *a.* of the hollow at back of knee. [f. mod. L *popliteus* f. L *poples -itis* this hollow; see -AL]

*****po'ppa.** Var. of POP[5].

po'ppadam *n.* (Ind.) small fried cake eaten with curry. [f. Tamil *pappaḍam*]

po'pper *n.* In vbl senses; ||(colloq.) press-stud. [f. POP[1] + -ER[1]]

po'ppet *n.* **1.** ||(colloq.) small or dainty person, esp. as term of endearment. **2.** lathe-head; (Naut.) short piece of wood for various purposes. **3.** ~**-head,** lathe-head; ||(Mining) frame at top of shaft supporting pulleys for ropes used in hoisting; ~**-valve** (mushroom-shaped and lifted bodily from seat, not hinged). [ME *popet(te),* ult. f. L *pu(p)pa;* cf. PUPPET]

po'pping *n.* In vbl senses; ~**-crease,** (Cricket) [perh. = striking-crease] line 4 ft. in front of and parallel to wicket, within which batsman must keep bat or one foot grounded to avoid risk of being stumped. [f. POP[1] + -ING[1]]

po'pple *v.i.,* & *n.* **1.** *v.i.* (Of water) tumble about, toss to and fro. **2.** *n.* rolling, tossing, ripple, (of water); hence **pŏ'pplў²** *a.* [ME, prob. f. MDu. *popelen* murmur, quiver, of imit. orig.]

pŏ'pp̄y *n.* herb of genus *Papaver* having milky juice with narcotic properties and showy esp. scarlet flowers; **Californian** ∼, eschscholtzia; || **(Flanders)** ∼, emblem of dead in World Wars, esp. artificial red poppy worn on **P**∼ **Day** (= Remembrance Sunday) [f. *Flanders* as scene of fighting 1914–18]; **opium** ∼, usu. white-flowered poppy (*Papaver somniferum*) from which opium is obtained; ∼-**head**, seed capsule of poppy, ornamental top to end of church seat; PRICKLY *poppy*; SHIRLEY *poppy*; **Welsh** ∼, yellow-flowered plant (*Meconopsis cambrica*); hence **pŏ'ppiED²** (-pĭd) *a.* [OE *popig, papæg*, *papāg, *pāpau f. med. L *papauum* f. L *papaver*]

pŏ'ppỹcŏck *n.* (sl.) nonsense. [f. Du. dial. *pappekak*] ***Pŏ'psicle** *n.* (P) ice lolly. [fanciful form.]

pŏ'psỹ, pŏ'psie, *n.* (colloq., esp. as term of endearment for) young woman. [f. POPPET + -Y³, -IE]

pŏ'pŭlace *n.* the common people; (derog.) the rabble. [F, f. It. *popolaccio* (*popolo* people + -*accio* pejorative suf.)]

pŏ'pŭlar *a.* **1.** of, or carried on by, the people (*popular election, etymology, meetings, tumult*). **2.** adapted to the understanding, taste, or means, of the people, (*in popular language; popular science*); ∼ **music,** songs, folk-tunes, etc., not seeking to appeal to refined or classical taste. **3.** liked or admired by the people or by people generally or by specified class, (*popular teachers; the popular hero; is popular with his men*); so **pŏpŭlă'rITY** *n.* **4.** prevalent among the people (*popular fallacies,* LATIN). **5.** ∼ **front,** (Polit.) party or coalition representing left-wing elements. **6.** Hence ∼LY² *adv.* [ME, f. AF *populer*, OF *populeir*, or f. L *popularis* (*populus* people; see -AR¹)]

pŏ'pŭlariz|e, -īs|e (-īz), *v.t.* make popular; cause (person, principle, etc.) to be generally known or liked; present (technical subject etc.) in popular form; hence ∼A'TION *n.* [f. prec. + -IZE]

pŏ'pŭlāte *v.t.* inhabit, form the population of, (country, town, etc.); supply with inhabitants (*a densely populated district*). [f. med. L *populare* (as PEOPLE) + -ATE³]

pŏpŭlā'tion *n.* **1.** degree to which place is populated; act or process of supplying with inhabitants. **2.** total number of inhabitants of a town, country, etc.; the inhabitants of a place (*the population turned out to welcome him*). **3.** total number or quantity of things in a given place or region; (Statistics) total group of items under consideration. **4.** ∼ **explosion,** sudden large increase of population of world or country. [f. LL *populatio* (as PEOPLE; see -ATION)]

pŏ'pŭl|ist *n.* & *a.* (adherent) of political party seeking to represent the whole of the people (orig. in US 1892–1904, aiming at public control of railways, graduated income tax, etc.); so ∼ISM (3) *n.*, ∼ī'stIC *a.* [f. L *populus* people + -IST]

pŏ'pŭlous *a.* thickly inhabited; hence ∼NESS *n.* [ME, f. LL *populosus* (as PEOPLE; see -OUS)]

pŏ'rbea'gle *n.* shark of genus *Lamna*, with pointed snout. [18th c.; Corn. dial., of unkn. orig.]

pŏr'celain (-slĭn) *n.* fine kind of earthenware with translucent body and transparent glaze; thing(s) made of this; ∼ **clay,** kaolin; ∼-**shell,** cowrie; hence or cogn. ∼IZE (3) *v.t.*, ∼OUS, **pŏrcĕllā'nEOUS, pŏr-cĕllā'nIC, pŏrce'llanOUS,** *adjs.* [f. F *porcelaine* cowrie, porcelain, f. It. *porcellana* (*porcella* dim. of *porca* sow (cowrie being perh. likened to sow's vulva) f. L *porca* fem. of *porcus* pig)]

pŏrch *n.* covered approach to entrance of building; *veranda (∼ **climber,** cat burglar); **the P**∼, colonnade at Athens to which Zeno and his disciples resorted, (hence) Stoic school or philosophy (cf. ACADEMY, GARDEN, LYCEUM); hence -ED² (-cht), ∼'LESS, *adjs.* [ME, f. OF *porche* f. L *porticus* (transl. Gk *stoa*) f. *porta* passage]

pŏr'cīne *a.* of or like pigs. [f. F *porcin* or f. L *porcinus* (*porcus* pig; see -INE¹)]

pŏr'cŭpĭn|e *n.* **1.** ||rodent of family Hystricidae with body and tail covered with erectile spines; *similar arboreal rodent of family Erethizontidae. **2.** machine with many spikes or teeth, e.g. for hackling flax etc. **3.** (*attrib.*, applied to animals with spines, etc.) *porcupine ant-eater, crab, fish, grass.* **4.** Hence ∼ISH¹, ∼Y², *adjs.* [ME, f. OF *porc espin*, f. Prov. *porc espi*(*n*) f. Rom. *porcospinus f. L *porcus* pig + *spina* thorn]

pŏre¹ *n.* minute opening in surface, through which fluids may pass. [ME f. OF, f. L f. Gk *poros* passage, pore]

pŏre² *v.i.* **1.** ∼ **over,** be absorbed in studying (book etc.), (fig.) meditate, think intently upon, (subject). **2.** (arch.) look intently *at*, (*up*)*on, over.* [ME *pure* etc., perh. f. OE *pūrian; cf. PEER³]

***pŏr'gỹ** (-gĭ) *n.* perchlike sea fish of family Sparidae. [18th c.; orig. uncert. and app. various; cf. Sp. & Port. *pargo*]

pŏr'ifer *n.* animal of phylum Porifera, sponge. [f. mod. L *Porifera* f. L *porus* PORE¹ + -I- + -*fer* bearing + -A 2]

porism (pŏr'-, pŏ'r-) *n.* (Math.) proposition concerned with the conditions that will render a given problem capable of innumerable solutions; corollary; so **pŏrismă'tIC** (-z-), **pŏrī'stIC,** *adjs.* [f. LL f. Gk *porisma -matos* (*porizō* deduce f. *poros* way)]

pŏrk *n.* flesh (esp. unsalted) of pig used as food; *∼-**barrel,** (colloq.) government funds as source of political benefit; ∼-**butcher,** one who slaughters pigs for sale, or sells pork rather than other meats; *∼-**fish,** yellow-striped black Atlantic fish; ∼ **pie** (minced etc. pork); ∼-**pie hat** (with flat rimmed crown and brim turned up all round). [ME & OF *porc* f. L *porcus* pig]

pŏr'ker *n.* pig raised for food; young fattened pig. [f. prec. + -ER¹]

pŏr'kling *n.* young or small pig. [f. PORK + -LING¹]

pŏr'kỹ¹ *a.* of or like pork, esp. (colloq.) fleshy, fat. [f. PORK + -Y²]

***pŏr'kỹ²** *n.* (colloq.) porcupine. [abbr.; see -Y³]

pŏrn *n.* (colloq.) pornography. [abbr.]

pŏr'nō *n.* & *a.* (colloq.) **1.** *n.* pornography. **2.** *a.* pornographic. [abbr.]

pŏrnŏ'cracỹ *n.* dominance of prostitutes, esp. in 10th-c. Rome. [f. Gk *pornē* prostitute + -O- + -CRACY]

pŏrnŏ'graph|y *n.* explicit description or exhibition of sexual activity in literature, films, etc., intended to stimulate erotic rather than aesthetic feelings; literature etc. containing this; hence or cogn. ∼ER¹ *n.*, **pŏrnogră'phIC** *a.* [f. Gk *pornographos* (*pornē* prostitute, *graphō* write) + -Y¹]

poroplă'stic (pŏr-, pŏr-) *a.* (Surg.) (Of felt for splints etc.) both porous and plastic. [f. as PORE¹ + -O- + PLASTIC¹]

pŏr'ous *a.* full of pores (lit. or fig.); hence or cogn. **pŏrŏ'sITY,** ∼NESS, *ns.* [ME, f. OF *poreux* f. med. L *porosus* f. L *porus* PORE¹; see -OUS]

pŏrphỹ'ria *n.* disease with abnormal metabolism, sometimes genetically caused, with symptoms suggesting insanity. [mod. L, f. *porphyrin* (purple substance excreted by porphyria patients; cf. foll.) + -IA¹]

pŏrphỹrŏ'gĕnīte *n.* person born in the PURPLE. [f. med. L *porphyrogenitus* f. late Gk *porphurogennētos* (Gk *porphura* purple, *gennētos* born)]

pŏr'phỹrỹ *n.* hard rock anciently quarried in Egypt, composed of crystals of white or red felspar in red matrix; (Geol.) unstratified or igneous rock having homogeneous base in which crystals of one or more minerals are disseminated; so **pŏrphỹrī'tIC** *a.* [ME, ult. f. med. L *porphyreum*, L f. Gk *porphurītēs* (*porphura* purple)]

pŏr'poise (-pŭs) *n.* small whale of genus *Phocaena*, with blunt rounded snout. [ME *porpays* etc. f. OF *po*(*u*)*rpois* etc. f. Rom. *porcopiscis f. L *porcus* pig + *piscis* fish]

pŏrră′ceous (-shŭs) *a.* (arch.) leek-green. [f. L *porraceus* (*porrum* leek; see -ACEOUS)]

porrĕ′ct *v.t.* (Zool.) stretch out (part of body); (Eccl. Law) tender, submit, (document). [ME, f. L *porrigere -rect-* (*por-* PRO-¹, *regere* direct)]

pŏ′rridge *n.* soft food of oatmeal or other meal or cereal boiled in water or milk; (sl.) imprisonment; **save** one's **breath to cool** one's ~, keep one's advice etc. for one's own use. [16th c., alt. f. POTTAGE]

pŏ′rringer (-nj-) *n.* small basin from which soup etc. is eaten esp. by children. [earlier *pottinger* f. OF *potager* (*potage*; see POTTAGE, -ER¹); *-n-* as in *messenger* etc.]

pŏrt¹ *n.* harbour (lit. or fig.); town or place possessing harbour, esp. one where customs officers are stationed; FREE¹ *port*; ~ **of call**, place where ship or (fig.) person stops during journey; **P~ of London Authority,** corporate body controlling London harbour and docks. [OE, f. L *portus*, & ME prob. f. OF f. L *portus*]

pŏrt² *n.* **1.** (esp. Sc.) gate, gateway, esp. of walled town. **2.** (Naut.) opening in side of ship for entrance, loading etc.; porthole. **3.** aperture for passage of steam, water, etc.; aperture in wall etc. for gun to be fired through. **4.** ~**hole** (-t-h-), (esp. glazed) aperture in ship's or aircraft's side for admission of light and air, or (formerly) for pointing cannon through. [ME & OF *porte* f. L *porta*]

pŏrt³ *n.* external deportment, carriage, bearing; (Mil.) position taken in porting arms. [ME f. OF *port*, f. as foll.]

pŏrt⁴ *v.t.* (Mil.) carry (rifle, or other weapon) diagonally across and close to the body, with barrel etc. opposite middle of left shoulder (esp. command *port arms!*). [f. F *porter* f. L *portare* carry]

pŏrt⁵ *n.*, & *v.i.* (Naut. & Aeron.) **1.** *n.* left-hand side of ship or boat or aircraft looking forward (cf. STAR-BOARD); *port* TACK¹, WATCH¹. **2.** *v.i.* turn (helm, or abs.) to port. [prob. orig. side turned towards PORT¹]

pŏrt⁶ *n.* ~ (**wine**), strong sweet dark-red (occas. brown or white) fortified wine of Portugal. [shortened f. *Oporto*, city of Portugal, whence shipped]

pŏrt⁷ *n.* (Austral.) portmanteau. [abbr.]

pŏr′t|able *a.* & *n.* **1.** *a.* easily movable, convenient for carrying, (*portable furnace*, *radio*); hence ~ABI′LITY *n.* **2.** *n.* portable object, esp. radio, typewriter, etc. [ME f., or f. LL *portabilis* f. L *portare* carry; see -ABLE]

pŏr′tage *n.*, & *v.t.* **1.** *n.* carrying, carriage; cost of this. **2.** carrying of boats or goods between two navigable waters; place at which this is necessary. **3.** *v.t.* convey (boat, goods) over portage. [ME f. OF (*porter*; see PORT⁴, -AGE)]

pŏr′tal¹ *n.* door(way), gate(way), esp. elaborate one; point of entry (*~-to-~*, of time spent by workman between entrance to factory etc. and place of actual working). [ME f. OF, f. med. L *portale* neut. adj. as n. (see foll.)]

pŏr′tal² *a.* (Anat.) of the porta or transverse fissure of the liver; ~ **vein** (conveying blood to liver or other organ exc. heart). [f. mod. L *portalis* f. L *porta* gate; see -AL]

pŏrtamĕ′nt|o *n.* (*pl.* ~**i** *pr.* -ē). (Mus.) gliding continuously from one pitch to another in singing, playing violin, etc.; piano-playing in a manner intermediate between legato and staccato. [It., = carrying]

pŏr′tative *a.* serving to carry or support; (Hist.) portable (esp. of a small pipe-organ). [ME, f. OF *portatif*, app. alt. of *portatil* f. med. L *portatilis* f. L *portare* carry; see -IVE, -IL]

pŏrtcŭ′llis *n.* strong heavy grating sliding up and down in vertical grooves, lowered to block gateway in fortress etc.; (**P~**) a pursuivant of English College of Arms, with this as badge; hence ~ED² (-st) *a.* [ME, f. OF *porte coleïce* sliding door (*porte* door f. L *porta*, *col*(*e*)*ice* fem. of *couleïs* sliding f. Rom. **colaticius* f. L *colare* filter)]

Pŏrte *n.* the (**Sublime** or **Ottoman**) ~, (Hist.)

Ottoman court at Constantinople, Turkish government until 1923. [F. (*la Sublime* ~ = the exalted gate), transl. of Turk. title of central office of Ottoman government]

porte-cochère (pŏrtkŏshār′) *n.* gateway and passage for vehicles through house into courtyard; *structure extending from entrance of building over place where vehicles stop to discharge passengers. [F (*porte* PORT², *cochère* fem. adj. f. *coche* COACH)]

pŏrtĕ′nd *v.t.* foreshow, foreshadow, as an omen; give warning of (*this portends a renewal of the conflict*). [ME, f. L *portendere -tent-* (*por-* PRO-¹, *tendere* stretch)]

pŏr′tĕnt *n.* omen, significant sign of something to come; prodigy, marvellous thing; so **pŏrtĕ′ntous** *a.* like a portent, (joc.) pompously solemn. [f. L *portentum* (as prec.)]

||pŏr′ter¹ *n.* gatekeeper, door-keeper, esp. of large building etc. [ME & AF, OF *portier* f. LL *portarius* (*porta* door; see -ER²)]

pŏr′ter² *n.* **1.** person employed to carry burdens, esp. railway or airport or hotel employee who handles luggage, or hospital employee, whence ~AGE (4) *n.* **2.** *sleeping-car attendant. **3.** (US or Hist.) dark-brown bitter beer brewed from charred or browned malt [app. orig. made esp. for porters]. **4.** *~**house,** (1) house at which porter and other liquors were retailed, (2) house where steaks, chops, etc., were served; ~**house steak,** choice cut of beef from between sirloin and tenderloin; ||*porter's* KNOT¹. [ME, f. OF *port*(*e*)*our* f. med. L *portator -oris* (*portare* carry; see -ER²)]

pŏr′tfire *n.* device for firing rockets, igniting explosives in mining, etc. [after F. *porte-feu* (*porter* as PORT⁴, *feu* fire)]

pŏrtfo′lio *n.* (*pl.* ~s). case for keeping loose sheets of paper, drawings, etc.; list of investments held by person, company, etc.; (fig.) office of minister of State; **Minister without** ~, Cabinet Minister who is not in charge of any department of State. [earlier *porto folio*, f. It. *portafogli* (*porta* imper. of *portare* carry, *fogli* pl. of *foglio* leaf f. L *folium*)]

pŏr′tico *n.* (*pl.* ~es *or* ~s). colonnade, roof supported by columns at regular intervals, usu. attached as porch to building. [It., f. L *porticus* PORCH]

portière (pŏrtyār′) *n.* curtain hung over door(way). [F (*porte* door f. L *porta*)]

pŏr′tion *n.*, & *v.t.* **1.** *n.* part, share; amount of food allotted to one person; dowry, whence ~LESS *a.*; one's destiny, one's lot; *a* (limited) quantity. **2.** *v.t.* divide (thing) into shares, distribute *out*, assign (thing *to* person) as share; give dowry to. [ME f. OF (*portionner* v. f.) *porcion*, *portion* n. f. L *portio -onis*]

Pŏr′tland *n.* ~ **cement,** hydraulic cement manufactured from chalk and clay, whose colour when set is similar to that of ~ **stone,** valuable building limestone. [f. Isle of ~ in Dorset, peninsula whence the stone is obtained]

pŏr′t|ly *a.* bulky, corpulent; (arch.) of stately appearance; hence ~INESS *n.* [f. PORT³ + -LY¹]

pŏrtmă′nteau (-tō) *n.* (*pl.* ~s *or* ~x, *pr.* -z). leather trunk for clothes etc., opening into two equal parts; ~ **word,** factitious word blending the sounds and combining the meanings of two others (*motel*, *Oxbridge*). [f. F *portmanteau* (*porter* carry f. L *portare*, *manteau* MANTLE¹)]

pŏrtola′nō (-lah′-) *n.* (*pl.* ~s). (Hist.) book of sailing directions with charts, description of harbours, etc. [It. (*porto* PORT¹)]

pŏr′trait (-rĭt) *n.* likeness of person or animal made by drawing, painting, photography, etc.; person etc. resembling or typifying another; verbal picture, graphic description. [F, p.p. (as n.) of OF *portraire* PORTRAY]

pŏr′traitist (-rĭt-) *n.* one who paints or takes portraits. [f. prec. + -IST]

pŏr′traiture (-rĭcher) *n.* portraying; portrait; graphic description. [ME f. OF (as PORTRAIT; see -URE)]

portray' v.t. make likeness of; describe graphically; hence ~AL 2 n. [ME, f. OF portraire (por- f. L PRO-[1], traire draw f. Rom. *tragere f. L trahere)]

por'treeve n. (Hist.) chief officer of town or borough. [OE portgerēfa (port town = PORT[1] or PORT[2], gerēfa REEVE[1])]

por'tress n. female porter. [ME, f. PORTER[1] + -ESS]

Port Salu't (pōr sälū') n. pale mild type of cheese. [f. name of Trappist abbey in France]

Portugue'se (-gē'z) a. & n. (pl. same). (native, inhabitant, or language) of Portugal; ~ man-of--war, dangerous (sub)tropical hydrozoan of genus Physalia, with sail-shaped crest and poisonous sting. [f. Port. portuguez f. med. L portugalensis (see -ESE)]

pōse[1] (-z) v. & n. 1. v.t. formulate (assertion, claim, etc.; propound (question, problem); place (artist's model etc.) in certain attitude. 2. v.i. assume an attitude, esp. for artistic purposes, or to impress others; set up, give oneself out, as (connoisseur etc.); ~ as, pretend to be. 3. n. attitude of body or mind, esp. one assumed for effect (his philanthropy is a mere pose). [(n. f. F pose) f. F poser f. LL pausare PAUSE; some senses by confus. w. L ponere place, cf. COMPOSE]

pōse[2] (-z) v.t. puzzle (person) with question or problem. [f. obs. appose f. OF aposer var. of oposer OPPOSE]

po'ser (-z-) n. In vbl senses; puzzling question or problem. [f. POSE[1,2] + -ER[1]]

pōseur (-zēr') n. (fem. poseuse pr. -zēr'z). person who poses for effect or behaves affectedly. [F (poser POSE[1])]

pŏsh a., & v.t. (sl.) 1. a. smart; stylish; first-rate. 2. v.t. smarten up. [orig. uncertain; perh. f. sl. posh money, a dandy]

pŏ'sit (-z-) v.t. assume as fact, postulate; put in position, place, (posited by natural agency). [f. L ponere posit- place]

posi'tion (-z-) n., & v.t. 1. n. way in which thing or its parts are placed or arranged; configuration of chess--men etc. during game. 2. mental attitude, way of looking at question. 3. (Logic etc.) proposition; statement of proposition. 4. place occupied by a person or thing; proper place (in or out of position); (Mil.) place where troops are posted for strategical purposes (the position was stormed); being advantageously placed (manœuvring for position); in a ~ to, enabled by circumstances or resources or information to do, state, etc.; ~ vector (Math., defining position of point). 5. situation of vowel in syllable, esp. (Gk & L Pros.) of short vowel before two consonants, making the syllable metrically long. 6. (fig.) situation in relation to other persons or things (difficult for a person in my position). 7. rank, status, (high) social standing; paid (official or domestic) employment. 8. Hence ~AL a. 9. v.t. place in position; (Mil.) place or post (troops). [ME f. OF, or f. L positio -onis (as prec.; see -ITION)]

pŏ'sitive (-z-) a. & n. 1. a. formally or explicitly stated, definite, unquestionable, (positive assertion; have no positive proof; here is proof positive). 2. (Of person) convinced, confident in opinion, cocksure. 3. (Gram.) ~ (degree of) adjective, adverb, primary form expressing simple quality without comparison (cf. COMPARATIVE, SUPERLATIVE). 4. absolute, not relative; (colloq.) downright, out-and--out, (it would be a positive miracle). 5. dealing only with matters of fact, practical, (positive philosophy); constructive (a positive suggestion). 6. marked by presence, not absence, of qualities (positive reaction; cf. NEGATIVE[1]). 7. (Alg., of quantity) greater than zero (cf. NEGATIVE[1]); positive FEEDBACK; ~ sign (+). 8. tending in the direction naturally or arbitrarily taken as that of increase or progress (clockwise rotation is positive). 9. containing or producing ~ charge, electricity, (of the kind produced by rubbing glass with silk; cf. NEGATIVE[1]); ~ pole, (of magnet) north--seeking pole; ~ ray, canal ray. 10. (Photog.)

showing lights and shades or colours as in original image cast on film etc. (opp. NEGATIVE[1]). 11. Hence ~LY[2] (-vlǐ) adv., ~NESS (-vn-), pŏsiti'vITY (-z-), ns. 12. n. positive degree, adjective, photograph, quantity, etc. [ME f. OF positif -ive or f. L positivus (as POSIT; see -ITIVE)]

pŏ'sitiv|ism (pŏ'z-) n. philosophical system of Auguste Comte, recognizing only positive facts and observable phenomena, and rejecting metaphysics and theism; religious system founded on this; LOGICAL positivism; so ~IST (2) n., ~ĭ'stIC a. [f. F positivisme (as prec.; see -ISM)]

pŏ'sitr|ŏn (-z-) n. (Phys.) elementary particle with mass of electron and charge of same amount as electron's but positive; hence ~ō'nIUM n., (Phys.) system comprising positron and electron. [f. POSITIVE + -TRON]

posŏ'logy̆ n. study of the quantities in which drugs should be administered; hence pŏsolŏ'gICAL a. [f. F posologie f. Gk posos how much; see -LOGY]

pŏ'sse n. body (of constables); strong force or company; ~ comitatus (kŏmĭtā'tus), (Hist.) body of men above age of 15 in a county, summoned by sheriff to repress riot etc. [med. L, = power f. L posse be able; comitatus = of the county]

possë'ss (-z-) v.t. 1. hold as property, own; have (faculty, quality, etc.; they possess a special value for us). 2. maintain (oneself, one's mind, soul, in patience etc.). 3. (Of demon etc. or cause of infatuation) occupy, dominate, (person etc.) (possessed by a devil, by or with an idea; like one ~ed, with great energy; what ~ed you?, how could you be so foolish?); copulate with (woman). 4. ~ oneself of, take or get for one's own; be ~ed of, own, have. 5. So ~OR n., ~ORY a. [f. OF possesser f. L possidēre -sess- (potis able, sedēre sit)]

possë'ssion (-zĕ'shon) n. 1. possessing or being possessed; actual holding or occupancy; (Law) visible power of exercising such control as attaches to (but may exist apart from) lawful ownership (possession is nine POINT[1]s of the law); (Footb. etc.) temporary control of ball etc. by a particular player; in ~, (of thing) possessed, (of person) possessing; in ~ of, having in one's possession; in the ~ of, held or owned by; take ~, become owner or possessor of. 2. thing possessed; (in pl.) property, wealth; subject territory, esp. foreign dominion. [ME f. OF, or f. L possessio -onis (as prec.; see -ION)]

possë'ssive (poz-) a. & n. 1. a. of possession; showing a desire to possess, or to retain what one possesses. 2. (Gram.) indicating possession; ~ case (e.g. John's, the baker's); possessive PRONOUN. 3. Hence ~LY[2] (-vlǐ) adv., ~NESS (-vn-) n. 4. n. possessive case or word. [f. L possessivus (as POSSESS; see -IVE), transl. Gk ktētikē (ptōsis case)]

pŏ'ssĕt n. (Hist.) drink made of hot milk curdled with ale, wine, etc., often flavoured with spices etc., formerly much used as remedy for colds etc. [ME poshote; orig. unkn.]

pŏssibi'lit̆y n. state or fact of being possible (the possibility of miracles; cannot by any possibility be in time; there is no possibility of his coming; it is within the range of possibility); capability of being used, improved, etc.; thing that may exist or happen (what are the possibilities?; there are three possibilities). [ME, f. OF possibilité or f. LL possibilitas -tatis (as foll.; see -ITY)]

pŏ'ssible a. & n. 1. a. that can exist, be done, or happen; that is quite possible; it is scarcely possible to say; it is possible (that) he knows or may know; there are three possible excuses (that may be made); provide against a possible loss of men (that may occur); get the greatest possible assistance; get all the assistance possible; come if possible (if you can); come as early as possible (as you can). 2. that is likely to happen etc. (few thought his election possible); that is acceptable for want of better (here is a possible way of doing it). 3. n. highest possible score esp. in shooting (scored a possible at 800 yards);

possible candidate, member of team, etc., (**Possibles and Probables,** teams for football etc. trial match). [ME f. OF, or f. L *possibilis* (*posse* be able; see -IBLE)]

po'ssibly *adv.* in accordance with possibility (*cannot possibly do it; how can I possibly?*); perhaps, maybe, for all one knows to the contrary. [ME, f. prec. + -LY²]

po'ssum *n.* (colloq.) **1.** = OPOSSUM | **play ~,** (1) pretend to be unconscious [from opossum's habit of seeming to feign death if attacked], (2) feign ignorance. **2.** (Austral. & NZ). phalanger resembling Amer. opossum. [abbr.]

post¹ *n.,* & *v.t.* **1.** *n.* stout piece of timber or metal usu. cylindrical or square and of considerable length, placed vertically as support in building; stake or stout pole to mark boundary, carry notices, etc. (**deaf as a ~,** completely deaf; *from* PILLAR *to post*); pole etc. marking point in race, esp. STARTING-*post* (**left at the ~,** outdistanced from the start) or WINNING¹-*post* (**beaten at** or **on the ~,** defeated at the last moment); (Mining) vertical mass of coal left to support roof. **2. ~-mill,** windmill pivoted on post and turning to catch the wind; **~-oak,* oak with hard durable wood used for posts etc. **3.** *v.t.* ~ (**up**), attach (paper etc.) to post or in prominent place, advertise (fact, thing, person) by placard or in published list; publish name of (ship) as overdue or missing; placard (wall etc.) with bills; **achieve* (score in game etc.). [OE, f. L *postis*; in ME, also f. OF etc.]

post² *n.* & *adv.* **1.** *n.* (Hist.) one of a series of men stationed with horses along roads at intervals, the duty of each being to ride forward with letters to next stage; courier, letter-carrier, mail-cart. **2.** ||single dispatch of letters, letters so dispatched; letters taken from post office or postal letter-box on one occasion (*I missed the morning post*); letters etc. delivered at one place on one occasion (*the post has come; had a heavy post today*); official conveying of letters, parcels, etc., (*send it by post;* GENERAL *post*); post office or postal letter-box (*take it to the post*); **by return of ~,** by next mail in opposite direction, (Hist.) by same courier who brought the dispatch. **3.** (As name of newspaper) *Evening Post* etc. **4.** size of paper, about 500 × 400 mm. **5.** *adv.* (arch.) with post-horses, express, with haste, (*ride post*). **6.** ||**~-bag,** mail-bag; **~-box,** postal letter-box; ||**~-boy,** (1) boy or man who carries letters, (2) postilion; **card,* card for conveyance by post without envelope, or similar card for various purposes; **~-chaise,** (Hist.) travelling carriage hired from stage to stage or drawn by horses so hired; ||**~-code,** group of (letters and) figures included in postal address to assist sorting; **~ exchange,* (Mil.) camp shop; ||**~-free,** carried free of charge by post, or with postage prepaid; **~-ha'ste** *n.* (arch.) & *adv.,* (with) great speed or haste; **~-horn** (Hist., blown to announce arrival of the post); **~-horse** (Hist., kept at inns etc. for use of post or travellers); **'man,* one who delivers or collects letters etc.; ||*~man's knock,* parlour game in which pretended letters are delivered in exchange for kisses; **~'mark,** (*n.*) official mark stamped on letter, esp. one giving place, date, etc., of dispatch or arrival, and serving to cancel stamp, (*v.t.*) mark (envelope etc.) with this; **~'master**¹, official in charge of post office; *P~master General,* minister at head of country's postal service; **~'mistress,** woman in charge of a post office; **P~ Office,** public department or corporation responsible for postal and telecommunication services; **~ office,** room or building where postal business is carried on (||GENERAL *Post Office;* **~-office box,** numbered place in post office where letters are kept until called for; ||*post-office* ORDER¹ 16), **postman's knock;* **~-paid,** on which postage has been paid; **~-town** (with post office, esp. one that is not sub-office of another). [f. F *poste* (fem.) f. It. *posta* f. Rom. **posta = posita* fem. p.p. of L *ponere posit-* place]

post³ *v.* **1.** *v.i.* travel with haste, hurry; ||(Hist.) travel

with relays of horses. **2.** *v.t.* put (letter etc.) into post office or letter-box for transmission. **3.** (Bookk.) carry (entry) from auxiliary book to more formal one (esp. from day-book to journal or ledger), or from one account to another; **~** (**up**), complete (ledger etc.) thus, (fig., esp. in *p.p.*) supply (person) with full information. [f. prec., or f. obs. F *poster*]

post⁴ *n.,* & *v.t.* **1.** *n.* place where soldier is stationed or which he patrols, (fig.) place of duty; position taken by body of soldiers, force occupying this; fort. **2.** (**trading-**)**~,** place occupied for purposes of trade (esp. in region not yet fully settled). **3.** situation, paid employment. **4.** (Naval Hist.) commission as officer in command of vessel of 20 guns or more; ||**~ captain,** holder of such commission (not of courtesy title or inferior command). **5.** ||(Mil.) **first, last, ~,** bugle-call giving notice of hour of retiring for night (*last post* also blown at mil. funerals etc.). **6.** *v.t.* place, station, (soldiers etc.); appoint to post or command. [f. F *poste* (masc.) f. It. *posto* f. Rom. **postum* f. L neut. p.p. (as POST²)]

post- *pref.* after, behind, as: **~cla'ssic(al),** later than the classical period (usu. of Greek and Roman literature); **~co'ital,** occurring or existing after coitus; **~-commu'nion,** part of Eucharistic office following act of communion; **~da'te,** affix or assign a date later than the actual one to (document, event, etc.); **~-date,** such date; **~dilu'vian** *a.* & *n.,* (person) existing, occurring, after the Flood; **~-e'ntry,** late or subsequent entry (for race, in bookkeeping, etc.); **~exi'lic,** subsequent to the Jews' exile in Babylon; **~fi'x,** append (letters) at end of word; **~'fix,** suffix; **~-gla'cial** *a.* & *n.,* (period) subsequent to a glacial period; **~gra'duate,** (*a.*) (of a course of study) carried on after taking first degree, (*n.*) student taking such course; **P~Impre'ssionism,** artistic aims and methods [so named as a reaction from impressionism] directed to expressing rather the individual artist's than the ordinary observer's presumable conception of the objects represented; so *P~Impre'ssionist* n., *~impressioni'stic* a.; **~lude,** (Mus.) concluding voluntary [after PRELUDE¹]; **~-mille'nnial,** following the millennium; **~-mille'nnialism,** doctrine that second Advent will follow the millennium; so *~-mille'nnialist* n.; **~-na'tal,** existing or occurring after (child)birth; **~nu'ptial,** subsequent to marriage; **~-par'tum,** following parturition; **~-tax,** (of income) after deduction of taxes; **~-war,** occurring or existing after a war (||*~-war credits,* credits resulting from reduced income-tax allowances at time of 1939–45 war). [f. after L *post* adv. & prep.]

po'stage *n.* amount charged for carriage of letter etc. by post, now usu. prepaid by **~ stamp,** small adhesive label to be affixed, or stamp embossed or impressed on envelope etc., having specified value; **~ due,** postage not prepaid and usu. demanded by special postage stamp; **~ meter,* franking-machine. [f. POST² + -AGE]

po'stal *a.* & *n.* **1.** *a.* of the POST²; by post (*postal vote*); **~ card,* = POST²*card;* **~ code,** = POST²-*code;* **~ meter,* franking-machine; ||*postal* ORDER¹ 16; **P~ Union,** union of governments of various countries for regulation of international postage. **2.** *n.* **postcard. [F (*poste* POST² + -AL)]

po'stee'n *n.* Afghan sheepskin greatcoat. [f. Pers. *postīn* of leather]

po'ster *n.* In vbl senses; billposter; placard (as) displayed in public place; **~ paint** (gummy opaque kind). [f. POST¹ + -ER¹]

po'ste re'sta'nte (-ah'nt) *n.* department in post office in which letters are kept until called for. [F, = letter(s) remaining (i.e., at the post office)]

poste'rior *a.* & *n.* **1.** *a.* later, coming after in series, order, or time; so **~ITY** (-ŏ'r-) *n.* **2.** hinder; hence **~LY**² *adv.,* as viewed from behind. **3.** *n.* (in *sing.* or *pl.*) buttocks. [L, compar. of *posterus* following (*post* after)]

For other words in *post-* **see** POST-.

pŏstĕ'rĭtў *n.* descendants of a person; all succeeding generations (*deserves the gratitude of posterity*). [ME, f. OF *posterité* f. L *posteritas -tatis* (*posterus*; see prec., -ITY)]

pŏ'stern *n.* back door; side way or entrance. [ME, f. OF *posterne, posterle*, f. LL *posterula* dim. f. *posterus* (see POSTERIOR)]

pŏ'stface *n.* brief explanatory note or comments at end of book. [F (as POST-, PREFACE)]

pŏ'sthūmous (-tū-) *a.* (Of child) born after death of its father; (of book etc.) published after author's death; occurring after death; hence ∿LY² *adv.* [f. L *postumus* last (superl. f. *post* after), in LL *posth-* by assoc. w. *humus* ground, + -OUS]

pŏsti'che (-ē'sh) *n.* coil of false hair, worn as adornment. [F, = false, f. It. *posticcio*]

pŏ'stil *n.* (Hist.) marginal note, comment, esp. on text of Scripture; commentary. [ME, f. OF *postille* f. med. L *postilla*, of uncert. orig.]

posti'lion, postillion, (-lyon) *n.* rider on near horse drawing coach etc. without coachman. [f. F *postillon* f. It. *postiglione* post-boy (*posta* POST²)]

pŏstli'minў *n.* **1.** (Rom. Law). right of banished person or captive to resume civic privileges on return. **2.** (Internat. Law). restoration to their former status of persons and things taken in war, when they come again into the power of the nation they originally belonged to. [f. L POST(*liminium* f. *limen liminis* threshold)]

pŏ'stmaster¹ (-mah-) *n.* See POST².

‖**pŏ'stmaster²** (-mah-) *n.* scholar of Merton College, Oxford; hence ∿SHIP (1, 2) *n.* [16th c.; orig. unkn.]

pŏst-mŏr'tĕm¹ *adv.* after death. [L]

pŏst-mŏr'tem² *a.* & *n.* (examination) made after death, esp. to determine its cause; (colloq.) (discussion) after conclusion (of game, election, etc.). [f. prec.]

pŏst-ŏ'bit *a.* & *n.* **1.** *a.* taking effect after death. **2.** *n.* bond securing to lender a sum to be paid on death of specified person from whom borrower has expectations. [f. L *post obitum* (*post* after, *obitus* decease f. *obire* die)]

postpō'ne (pō-, po-; -stp-, -sp-) *v.t.* cause to take place at later time; treat (thing) as inferior in importance (*to* another); hence ∿MENT (-nm-) *n.* [f. L POST(*ponere posit-* place)]

pŏstposi'tion (-zǐ'-) *n.* particle or word placed after another, usu. as enclitic, (e.g. -WARDS); hence or cogn. ∿AL, **pŏstpŏ'sǐtive** (-zǐ-), *adjs.* [f. LL *postpositio* (as prec.; see -ION)]

pŏstprӑ'ndial *a.* (usu. joc.) after-lunch or -dinner (*postprandial nap, eloquence*). [f. POST- + L *prandium* a meal + -AL]

pŏ'stscrĭpt (pō'stsk-, pō'sk-) *n.* additional paragraph esp. at end of letter after signature. [f. L *postscriptum* neut. p.p. (as n.) of POST(*scribere* write)]

pŏ'stŭlant *n.* candidate esp. for admission into religious order. [F, or f. L *postulans -antis* (as foll.; see -ANT)]

pŏ'stŭlate¹ *n.* thing claimed or assumed as basis of reasoning, fundamental condition; prerequisite; (Math.) claim to take for granted the possibility of simple operation, e.g. of drawing straight line between any two points. [f. L *postulatum*, neut. p.p. (as n.) of *postulare* demand; see -ATE¹]

pŏ'stŭl|ate² *v.t.* demand, require as a necessary condition, claim, take for granted (thing, *that*, *to* do); (Eccl. Law) nominate or elect subject to superior sanction; so ∿A'TION *n.*, ∿ātoR *n.*, (esp. RC Ch.) one who presents case for canonization or beatification. [f. L *postulare* demand + -ATE³]

pŏ'stur|e *n.* & *v.* **1.** *n.* relative position of parts esp. of body, attitude of body or mind; condition, state, (*of* affairs etc.). **2.** *v.t.* dispose limbs of (person) in particular way. **3.** *v.i.* assume posture (lit. or fig.), esp. for effect. **4.** Hence ∿AL *a.*, ∿ER¹ *n.*, (-cher-). [F, f. It. *postura* f. L *positura* (*ponere posit-* place; see -URE)]

pŏ'sў (-zǐ) *n.* **1.** (arch.) short motto, line of verse etc., inscribed within ring (∿-**ring**) etc. **2.** small bunch of flowers. [f. POESY]

pŏt¹ *n.* **1.** rounded vessel of earthenware, metal, or glass, for holding liquids or solids; = CHAMBER-*pot*, COFFEE-*pot*, FLOWER*pot*, GLUE-*pot*, *jam-pot*, TEA*pot*; such vessel for cooking; drinking-vessel of pewter etc.; contents of pot (*a pot of tea, of honey*). **2.** vessel, usu. of silver, as prize in athletic sports, (sl.) any prize in these; CHIMNEY-*pot*; LOBSTER-*pot*; (colloq.) = *pot-belly*. **3.** size of paper, 375 × 312 mm. [from the orig. watermark of a pot]. **4.** (colloq.) large sum (*made a pot* or *pots of money*); total amount bet by all players. **5.** BIG *pot*; **the** ∿ **calls the kettle black,** person blames another for fault he too has; **go to** ∿, (colloq.) be ruined or destroyed (orig. of meat cut up for cooking); *keep the pot* BOIL²*ing.* **6.** ∿-**ale,** refuse from distillation, used as pig-food; ∿-**belly,** (person with) protuberant belly; ∿-**boiler,** work of literature or art done merely to make a living, writer or artist who does this; ∿-**bound,** (of plant) whose roots fill flowerpot and lack room to expand; ∿-**boy,** publican's assistant; *∿ **cheese,** cottage cheese; ∿ **hat,** bowler; ∿-**herb,** any of those grown in kitchen garden; POT--HOLE; ∿-**hook,** hook over fireplace for hanging pot etc. on or for hot pot, curved stroke in handwriting esp. as made in learning to write; ∿--**house,** (derog.) public house; ∿-**hunter,** sportsman who shoots anything he comes across, person who takes part in contest merely for sake of prize; so ∿-*hunting n.* & *a.*; ∿ **luck,** whatever is to be had (for a meal, or fig.; *come and take pot luck with us*); ∿'**man,** publican's assistant; ∿ **pie,** meat or fruit pie baked in a pot; ∿ **plant** (grown in flowerpot); ∿-**roast,** (*n.*) piece of meat cooked slowly in covered dish, (*v.t.*) cook thus; ∿-**shot,** shot at game-bird etc. merely to provide a meal, shot aimed at animal etc. within easy range, random shot; ∿-**still,** kind of STILL² in which heat is applied directly and not by steam-jacket; ∿'**stone,** granular variety of soapstone; ∿-**valiant,** valiant because drunk; so ∿ **valour;** ‖∿'**wall(op)er,** householder voter (before 1832) [f. *wall(op)* boil]. **7.** Hence ∿'FUL 2 *n.* [OE *pott*, corresp. to OFris., MDu., MLG *pot*, f. pop. L **pottus*]

pŏt² *v.* (**-tt-**). **1.** *v.t.* (esp. in *p.p.*) place (butter, fish, minced meat, etc., usu. salted or seasoned) in pot or other vessel to preserve it. **2.** place (plant) in soil in pot; (Bill.) pocket; abridge, epitomize; bag (game), kill (animal) by pot-shot; seize, secure; (colloq.) make (esp. child) sit on chamber-pot. **3.** *v.i.* shoot (*at*, or abs.). [f. prec.]

pŏt³ *n.* (sl.) marijuana; ∿-**head,** one who smokes this. [prob. f. Mex. Sp. *potiguaya*]

pŏt'|able *a.* drinkable; hence ∿ABI'LITY *n.* [F, or f. LL *potabilis* f. L *potare* drink; see -ABLE]

pŏta'ge (-ah'zh) *n.* thick soup. [F, as POTTAGE]

potӑ'mic *a.* of rivers; so **pŏtamŏ'LOGY** *n.* [f. Gk *potamos* river + -IC]

pŏ'tăsh *n.* alkaline substance (crude potassium carbonate) orig. got by leaching vegetable ashes and evaporating the solution in iron pots; **caustic** ∿, potassium hydroxide. [17th c. *pot-ashes* f. Du. *pot--asschen* (as POT¹, ASH²)]

potӑ'ss|ium *n.* soft silver-white metallic element, one of the alkali metals; *potassium* PERMANGANATE; hence ∿IC *a.* [f. prec. + -IUM]

potӑ'tion *n.* drinking; (usu. in *pl.*) tippling; a drink; hence **pŏ'tatory** *a.* [ME f. OF, or f. L *potatio* (*potare* drink; see -ATION)]

potā'tō *n.* (*pl.* ∿**es**). **1.** plant (*Solanum tuberosum*) with farinaceous tubers much used for food; its tuber; (colloq.) hole in stocking. **2. hot** ∿, (sl.) thing awkward to deal with; **small** ∿**es,** insignificant person or thing; **Spanish** or **sweet** ∿, (root of) tropical climbing plant (*Ipomoea batatas*) with sweet tuberous roots used for food. **3.** *potato* CHIP¹; ‖*potato* CRISP; ∿-**ring,** (Hist.) Irish (usu. silver) ring used as stand for bowl etc. [f. Sp. *patata* var. of Taino *batata*]

For other words in *post-* **see POST-.**

pŏtee'n, pŏthee'n, *n.* (Ir.) whisky from illicit still. [f. Ir. *poitín* dim. of *pota* POT¹]

pō't|ent¹ *a.* (Of reason etc.) cogent; (of drug etc.) strong; (of male) not impotent; (literary) powerful, mighty; hence or cogn. ∼ENCE, ∼ENCY, *ns.*, ∼ent·LY² *adv.* [f. L *potens -entis* part. of *posse* be able; see -ENT]

pō'tent² *a.* & *n.* (Her.) with crutch-head shape; (fur) formed by series of such shapes. [a. f. n., ME, f. OF *potence* crutch f. L *potentia* power (as prec.)]

pō'tentāte *n.* monarch, ruler. [ME, f. OF *potentat* or f. L *potentatus* dominion (as prec.; see -ATE¹)]

pote'ntial (-shǎl) *a.* & *n.* **1.** *a.* capable of coming into being or action, latent; *potential* ENERGY; ∼ **mood**, (Gram.) subjunctive expressing possibility; hence or cogn. ∼ITY (-shǐǎ'l-) *n.*, ∼IZE (3) *v.t.*, ∼LY² *adv.* **2.** *n.* (Phys.) quantity determining energy of mass in gravitational field, of charge in electric field, etc.; ∼ **barrier,** region of high potential impeding movement of particles etc.; ∼ **difference,** (esp.) difference of electric potential between points. **3.** possibility (*reached its highest potential*); resources that can be used; (Gram.) potential mood. [ME, f. OF *potencial* or f. LL *potentialis* (*potentia*; as POTENT¹, see -AL)]

pote'ntiāte (-shǐ-) *v.t.* endow (esp. drug) with (more) power; make possible. [f. POTENCY, POTENCE + -ATE³, after *substantiate*]

pŏtenti'lla *n.* herb or shrub of genus *Potentilla*, cinquefoil. [med. L, dim. of L *potens* POTENT¹]

potĕntiŏ'|mĕter (-shǐ-) *n.* instrument for measuring or adjusting electrical potential; hence **potĕntio-mĕ'tr**IC (-shǐ-) *a.*, ∼METRY *n.* [f. POTENTIAL + -O- + -METER]

pŏthee'n. See POTEEN.

pō'ther (-dh-) *n.* & *v.* (literary). **1.** *n.* choking smoke or cloud of dust; noise, din; verbal commotion (*made a pother about it*); display of sorrow. **2.** *v.t.* fluster, worry. **3.** *v.i.* make a fuss. [16th c.; orig. unkn.]

pŏ't-hōl|e *n.*, & *v.i.* **1.** *n.* (Geol.) deep cylindrical hole formed esp. by wearing away of rock. **2.** deep hole in ground or river-bed; depression in road surface caused by traffic etc. **3.** *v.i.* explore pot-holes; hence ∼ER¹ *n.* [f. POT¹ + HOLE¹]

pō'tion *n.* dose or draught of liquid medicine or of drug or poison. [ME f. OF, f. L *potio -onis* (*potus* having drunk; see -ION)]

pŏ'tlătch *n.* tribal feast of N. Amer. Indians given by aspirant to high social standing. [Chinook, f. Nootka *patlatsh* gift]

pŏtoroō' *n.* (Austral.) long-nosed rat-kangaroo. [Aboriginal]

pot-pourri (pōpoorē', pōpoor'ī) *n.* mixture of dried petals and spices kept in jar for its perfume; musical or literary medley. [F, = rotten pot]

pŏ'shĕrd *n.* (esp. Archaeol.) broken piece of earthenware. [ME, f. POT¹ + SHERD]

Pŏtt¹ *n.* ∼**'s fracture,** (Med.) fracture of lower end of fibula usu. with dislocation of ankle. [f. P. ∼, Engl. surgeon d. 1788]

pŏtt². Var. of POT¹.

pŏ'ttage *n.* (arch.) soup, stew; MESS¹ *of pottage*. [ME f. OF *potage* (as POT¹; see -AGE)]

pŏ'tter¹ *n.* maker of earthenware vessels; ∼**'s field,** burial place for paupers, strangers, etc., [after Matt. 27:7]; ∼**'s wheel,** horizontal revolving disc to carry clay during moulding. [OE *pottere* (as POT¹, -ER¹)]

pŏ'tter² *v.* **1.** *v.i.* work in feeble or desultory manner (*at* or *in* subject or occupation); dawdle, loiter, (*about* etc.). **2.** *v.t.* trifle *away* (one's time etc.). **3.** Hence ∼ER¹ *n.* [frequent. of dial. *pote* push f. OE *potian*; see -ER⁵]

pŏ'tter|ў *n.* vessels etc. made of baked clay; potter's work or workshop; ||**the P∼ies,** district in N. Staffordshire, seat of English pottery industry. [ME f. OF *poterie* (*potier* POTTER¹; see -Y¹)]

pŏ'tt-. In vbl senses; ∼**-shed** (in which delicate plants are grown in pots for later planting out). [f. POT² + -ING¹]

pŏ'ttle *n.* **1.** ||(arch.) measure for liquids, half gallon; pot etc. containing this. **2.** small wicker or chip basket for strawberries etc. [ME f. OF *potel* (as POT¹; see -LE 2)]

pŏ'ttō *n.* (*pl.* ∼s). W. Afr. lemur (*Perodicticus potto*); kinkajou. [perh. f. Guinea dial.]

||**pŏ'ttў¹** *a.* (sl.) **1.** ∼ (little), insignificant, trivial. **2.** foolish or crazy (*about* someone or something). [19th c.; orig. unkn.]

pŏ'ttў² *n.* (colloq.) chamber-pot, esp. for child. [f. POT¹ + -Y³]

pouch¹ *n.* small bag or detachable outside pocket; baggy area of skin (under eyes etc.); soldier's leather ammunition-bag; lockable bag for mail or dispatches; pocket-like receptacle in which marsupials carry young during lactation; baglike cavity, esp. seed-vessel, in plant; hence ∼ED² (-cht), ∼'Y², *adjs.* [ME, f. ONF *pouche* = OF *poche*; cf. POKE¹]

pouch² *v.t.* put into pouch; take possession of, pocket; make (part of dress) hang like pouch. [f. prec.]

pouf. Var. of POOF, POUFFE.

pouffe (pōof) *n.* large cushion used as low seat; soft stuffed couch; = PUFF¹ 2. [F; ult. imit.]

poulā'rd (pōo-) *n.* domestic hen spayed and fattened for eating. [F *poularde* (*poule* hen)]

poult¹ (pōlt) *n.* young of domestic fowl, turkey, pheasant, etc. [ME, contr. f. PULLET]

poult² (pōō) *n.* = foll. [abbr.]

poult-de-soie (pōōdĕswah') *n.* fine corded (usu. coloured) silk or taffeta. [F, of unkn. orig.]

pou'lter¹ (pōl'-) *n.* = foll. (now only as guild-name); ∼**'s measure,** (Pros.) metre with alternate lines of 12 and 14 syllables [perh. f. occasional selling of 14 instead of 12 eggs as a dozen]. [ME, f. OF *pouletier* (as PULLET; see -ER²)]

pou'lterer (pōl'-) *n.* dealer in poultry and usu. game. [f. prec. + -ER¹]

pou'ltice (pōl'-) *n.*, & *v.t.* **1.** *n.* soft mass of bread, bran, kaolin, etc., usu. made with boiling water and spread on muslin etc. and applied to sore or inflamed part. **2.** *v.t.* apply poultice to. [orig. *pultes* pl. f. L *puls pultis* pottage, pap, etc.]

pou'ltrў (pōl'-) *n.* domestic fowls (FOWL 1), ducks, geese, turkeys, etc., esp. as source of food. [ME, f. OF *pouletrie* (as POULTERER; see -RY)]

pounce¹ *n.*, & *v.i.* **1.** *n.* claw or talon of bird of prey; pouncing, sudden swoop, (*make a pounce*). **2.** *v.i.* make sudden attack (*up*)*on*, (fig.) seize eagerly (*up*)*on* (blunder etc.). [perh. f. PUNCHEON¹]

pounce² *n.*, & *v.t.* **1.** *n.* fine powder formerly used to prevent ink from spreading on unsized paper etc.; powdered charcoal etc. dusted over perforated pattern to transfer design to object beneath. **2.** *v.t.* smooth (paper, surface of hat, etc.) with pounce or pumice; transfer (design) by use of pounce; dust (pattern) with pounce. [(v. f. F *poncer*) f. F *ponce* f. pop. L **pomice* f. L *pumex* PUMICE]

pou'ncĕt-bŏx *n.* (arch.) small box with perforated lid for perfumes. [16th c.; perh. orig. error f. *pounced* (= perforated) *box*]

pound¹ *n.*, & *v.i.* **1.** *n.* measure of weight, 16 oz. avoirdupois (0.4536 kilogram), 12 oz. troy (0.3732 kilogram); ∼**-cake,** rich cake containing a pound (or equal weights) of each chief ingredient; ∼ **of flesh,** [see Shak. *Merchant of Venice* IV. i] (fig.) any legal but unconscionable demand. **2.** ∼ (**sterling**) (*pl.* also same), monetary unit of United Kingdom, formerly represented by gold sovereign, abbr. £ (*five pounds* or *pound* = £5); monetary unit of some other countries; PENNY *wise and pound foolish*; ∼ **note,** banknote for £1; ∼ **Scots,** (Hist.) is. 8d. **3.** *v.i.* ||test weight of coins by weighing number that ought to weigh one pound. [OE *pund* = OS, ON, Goth. *pund*, OHG *pfunt* f. Gmc **pundo* f. L *pondo* Roman pound weight of 12 ounces]

pound² *n.*, & *v.t.* **1.** *n.* enclosure for detention of stray cattle, distrained cattle or goods, officially removed vehicles, etc., till redeemed; enclosure for animals;

(fig.) place of confinement; ∼-**lock** (with two gates to confine water). **2.** *v.t.* shut (cattle etc.) in pound. [ME, f. OE **pund* (in *pundfald*; cf. PINFOLD); cf. POND]

pound[3] *v.* **1.** *v.t.* crush or bruise with repeated strokes; thump, pummel, with fists etc.; knock, beat, (thing *to* pieces, *into* a jelly, etc.); ∼ **out,** produce (as if) with heavy blows. **2.** *v.i.* deliver heavy blows, fire heavy shot, (*at, on, away at*); walk, run, ride, make one's way, heavily (*along* etc.); (of heart) beat heavily. [OE *pūnian*, cogn. w. Du. *puin*, LG *pün* rubbish]

pou′ndage *n.* commission or fee of so much per pound sterling; percentage of total earnings of a business, paid as wages; payment of so much per pound weight; charge on postal order etc.; TONNAGE *and poundage*. [ME, f. POUND[1] + -AGE]

pou′ndal *n.* (Phys.) unit of force, the force that, acting for one second on one-pound mass, gives it velocity of one foot per second. [f. POUND[1] + -*al* perh. after *quintal*]

pou′nder[1] *n.* In vbl senses; instrument for pounding with or in, pestle or mortar. [f. POUND[3] + -ER[1]]

pou′nder[2] *n.* thing that, or gun carrying shell that, weighs a pound or (-∼) so many pounds (*a three- -pounder*); (-∼) thing worth, or person possessing, so many pounds sterling. [f. POUND[1] + -ER[1]]

pour (por) *v.* & *n.* **1.** *v.t.* cause (liquid, granular substance, light, etc.) to flow esp. downwards, discharge copiously, (*pour hot water over it; pour out the tea*; ∼ **oil on the flames,** aggravate passion etc.; ∼ **oil on the waters, or on troubled waters,** (fig.) calm a disturbance with soothing words etc.; *pour cold* WATER[1] *on*); discharge (missiles, crowd from building, etc.; *forth, out*) copiously or in rapid succession; send *forth* or *out* (words, music, etc.). **2.** *v.i.* (of liquid etc.) flow (*forth, out, down*) in stream, (of rain) descend heavily, whence ∼′ING[2] *a.*, (**it never rains but it** ∼**s,** (fig.) events esp. misfortunes always come several together or in quick succession; pour tea into cups; (fig.) come in, out, etc., abundantly (*letters poured in from all quarters*). **3.** Hence ∼′ER[1] (1, 2) *n.* **4.** *n.* pouring; heavy fall of rain, downpour; amount of molten metal etc. poured at a time. [ME, of unkn. orig.]

pourboire (poorbwär′) *n.* gratuity, tip. [F, = *pour boire* (money) for drinking]

pourparler (poorpär′lā) *n.* (usu. in *pl.*) informal discussion preliminary to negotiation. [F, f. OF *po(u)rparler* discuss]

pour′point (poor-) *n.* (Hist.) stuffed and quilted doublet. [ME, f. OF p.p. of *pourpoindre* perforate, quilt (*pour* PRO-[1] for *par* PER-, *poindre* prick f. L *pungere*]

pousse-café (pōōskäfā′) *n.* drink of liqueur(s) taken esp. with coffee after dinner. [F, = push-coffee]

poussette (pōō-) *v.i.,* & *n.* **1.** *v.i.* dance round one another with hands joined, as couple in country dance. **2.** *n.* this action. [F, dim. of *pousse* push (*pousser* PUSH[1])]

pou′ssin (pōō′săn) *n.* young chicken bred for eating. [F]

pou sto (pōō stō′) *n.* standing-place, basis of operation, fulcrum. [f. Gk *pou stō* where I may stand, f. Archimedes' claim to be able to move the earth if given somewhere to stand while doing so]

pout[1] *n.* = BIB[1]; eel-pout. [OE **puta* in *ælepūta* eel- -pout, app. f. WG **pūt*- inflate; cf. foll.]

pout[2] *v.* & *n.* **1.** *v.t.* protrude (lips), protrude lips, (of lips) protrude, esp. as sign of (mock) displeasure; **sulk. **2.** *n.* such protrusion; **the** ∼**s,** fit of sulking. [ME, perh. f. OE **pūtian* f. WG **pūt*- be inflated; cf. prec.]

pou′ter *n.* In vbl senses; kind of pigeon with great power of inflating crop. [f. prec.[2] + -ER[1]]

||**pou′ting** *n.* = BIB[1]. [f. POUT[2] + -ING[3]]

po′verty *n.* being poor (POOR 1), indigence, want, (Eccl.) renunciation of right to individual ownership of property; scarcity, deficiency, (*in, of*); inferiority, poorness, meanness; ∼ **line,** minimum income level

needed to get necessities of life; ∼-**stricken,** poor (lit., or fig., *a poverty-stricken language*); ∼ **trap,** situation in which increase of pay leads to no greater total income, because of loss of benefits. [ME, f. OF *poverte, poverté* f. L *paupertas -tatis* (*pauper* poor; see -TY[1])]

pow *int.* expr. sound of blow or explosion. [imit.]

POW *abbr.* prisoner of war.

pow′an (pō′-) *n.* fish of British lakes, allied to trout. [Sc. form of POLLAN]

pow′der *n.,* & *v.t.* **1.** *n.* mass of dry particles or granules, dust; medicine in the form of powder (**take a** ∼, (sl.) depart quickly); cosmetic powder applied to face, skin, or hair. **2.** = GUNpowder (FOOD *for powder*; **keep** one's ∼ **dry,** be cautious and alert; **smell of** ∼, experience of fighting; **not worth** ∼ **and shot,** not worth shooting, or fighting or striving for). **3.** ∼ **blue,** pale blue orig. of powdered smalt for laundry use; *powder* COMPACT[3]; ∼-**down,** down-feathers found in definite patches on some birds; ∼-**flask,** (Hist.) case for carrying gunpowder; ∼-**horn,** (Hist.) powder- -flask orig. and esp. of horn; ∼-**keg,** (fig.) thing that may explode; ∼-**magazine,** place where gunpowder is stored; ∼ **metallurgy,** use of metal powders to form shaped objects; ∼-**monkey,** (Hist.) boy employed on board ship to carry powder to guns; ∼- -**puff,** soft pad for applying powder to skin; ∼-**room,** ladies' cloakroom; ∼ **snow,** loose dry snow on ski- -run etc. **4.** Hence ∼Y[2] *a.* **5.** *v.t.* sprinkle powder on, cover (*with* powder etc.); apply powder to (nose, hair, or abs.); decorate (surface) with spots or small ornamental figures (esp. in *p.p.*) reduce to (fine) powder (*powdered milk, sugar*). [ME, f. OF (*poudrer* v. f.) *poudre, pol(d)r* e f. L *pulvis pulveris* dust]

pow′er *n.,* & *v.t.* **1.** *n.* ability to do or act (*will do all in my power*; has the power of changing its colour); particular faculty of body or mind (*taxes his powers to the utmost; man of varied powers*). **2.** vigour, energy; **more** ∼ **to you, to your elbow!,** (expr. encouragement or approval). **3.** active property (*has a high heating power*). **4.** government, influence, authority, (*over*; **in** person's ∼, under his control); personal ascendancy (*over*); political or social ascendancy (*the party now in power*; BLACK[1] *Power*; ∼ **politics,** political action based on threats to use force). **5.** authorization, delegated authority, (*a bill to extend and define their powers; power of* ATTORNEY). **6.** influential person, body, or thing, (*the press had not become a power in the State*; **the** ∼**s that be,** constituted authorities [Rom. 13:1]); State having international influence (GREAT *Power*). **7.** deity (*merciful powers!*); (in *pl.*) sixth ORDER[1] of ninefold celestial hierarchy. **8.** (colloq.) large number or amount (*has done me a power of good*). **9.** (Math.) third, **tenth,** etc., ∼ of a number, product obtained from three, ten, etc., factors equal to that number (*the third power of 2, or 2*[3], *is 8; the sixth power of 1,000 is 1,000,000,000,000,000,000*). **10.** instrument for applying energy to mechanical purposes (cf. LEVER; **the mechanical** ∼**s,** simple machines (lever, inclined plane, etc.). **11.** mechanical or electrical energy as opp. to hand-labour; (*attrib.*) operated by this (*power lathe, shovel*); ∼ **cut,** temporary withdrawal or failure of electric power-supply; ∼-**dive** *n.,* & *v.i.,* (of aircraft) dive without shutting off engine power; ∼- **house,** = *power-station,* (fig.) source of drive or influence; ∼ **pack,** equipment for converting alter- nating current (from mains) to direct current; ||∼ **point,** socket for connection of electrical apparatus to mains; ∼-**station,** building etc. where electric power is generated for distribution; ∼ **stroke** (during which piston is moved by expansion of gases in internal combustion engine). **12.** capacity for exerting mechanical force, power. Hence HORSE[1]*power.* **13.** magnifying capacity of lens. **14.** *v.t.* supply (vehicle, vessel, etc.) with mechanical or electrical energy; HIGH, LOW[1], *-powered.* [ME & AF *poer* etc., OF *poeir* f. Rom. **potēre* be able]

pow'erful *a.* having great (physical or other) power or influence (*powerful grasp, horse, mind, ally, book, speech, odour*); hence ∿LY² *adv.* [ME, f. prec. + -FUL]

pow'erless *a.* without power (to act etc.); wholly unable (*to help* etc.); hence ∿LY² *adv.*, ∿NESS *n.* [f. POWER + -LESS]

pow'wow *n.* & *v.* **1.** *n.* N. Amer. Ind. medicine-man or sorcerer; magic ceremonial, conference, of N. Amer. Indians; political or other meeting esp. for discussion. **2.** *v.i.* act as powwow; hold powwow; confer, discuss, (*about* etc.). **3.** *v.t.* doctor, treat with magic. [f. Algonquian *powah, powwaw* magician (lit. 'he dreams')]

pöx *n.* **1.** virus disease with pocks (usu. in *comb.*, as CHICKEN-*pox,* COW¹*pox,* SMALL*pox*); (arch.) **a** ∿ **on him** etc. (excl. of impatience). **2.** (colloq.) syphilis. **3.** plant disease causing pocklike spots. **4.** Hence ∿'Y² *a.,* (sl.) infested by pox, worthless. [alt. sp. of POCKS]

pözzola'na (pŏtsolah'na) *n.* volcanic ash used for mortar or hydraulic cement. [It., f. *pozz(u)olano a.* of *Pozzuoli* near Naples]

p.p. *abbr. per procurationem.*

pp. *abbr.* pages.

pp *abbr.* pianissimo.

‖**PPE** *abbr.* philosophy, politics, and economics.

p.p.m. *abbr.* parts per million.

‖**PPS** *abbr.* Parliamentary Private Secretary; additional postscript [f. POST- + POSTSCRIPT].

PQ *abbr.* Province of Quebec; Quebec Party [f. F *Parti Québécois*].

PR *abbr.* proportional representation; public relations; *Puerto Rico.

pr. *abbr.* pair.

Pr *symb.* praseodymium.

PRA *abbr.* President of the Royal Academy.

praam. See PRAM¹.

prä'ctic|able *a.* that can be done, feasible; (of road, passage, ford) that can be used or traversed; (Theatr., of window etc.) real, that can be used as such; hence ∿ABI'LITY, ∿ableNESS (-beln-), *ns.,* ∿ABLY *adv.* [f. F *praticable* (*pratiquer* put into practice f. as foll.); see -ABLE]

prä'ctical *a.* & *n.* **1.** *a.* of, concerned with, shown in, practice (opp. *theoretical; practical agriculture, examination, philosophy; practical* JOKE¹); available or useful in practice; engaged in practice, practising; inclined or suited to action rather than speculation (*does not appeal to practical minds; a practical man good at improvising; is true for all practical purposes*); that is such in effect though not nominally, virtual, (*a practical atheist; has practical control*); feasible (*practical* POLITICS); *∿ **nurse** (trained in routine nursing but not registered); hence ∿ITY (-ă'l-), ∿NESS, *ns.* **2.** *n.* practical examination or study. [f. earlier *practic* f. obs. F *practique* or f. LL f. Gk *praktikos* (*prassō* do, act; see -IC) + -AL]

prä'ctically *adv.* in a practical manner; virtually, almost, (*practically nothing*). [f. prec. + -LY²]

prä'ctice¹ *n.* **1.** habitual action or carrying on (*the practice of advertising; makes a practice of saving*); action as opp. to theory; method of legal procedure; habit, custom, (*has been the regular practice*). **2.** repeated exercise in an art, handicraft, etc., (*practice makes perfect*); spell of this (*ball, target, practice*). **3.** professional work, business, or connection, of lawyer, doctor, etc., (*has a large practice; sold his practice*). **4.** (arch., esp. in *pl.*) scheming, (usu. underhand) contrivance, artifice; SHARP¹ *practice.* **5.** (Arith.) mode of finding value of given number of articles, or of quantity of commodity at given price, when quantity or price or both are in several denominations. **6. good** ∿, (1) satisfactory procedure, (2) means of improving one's skill; **in** ∿, (1) in the realm of action (*quite useless, would never work, in practice*); **put** (plan, method) **in**(to) ∿, actually apply it), (2) skilled through having recently had practice (sense 2); **out of** ∿, no

longer possessing former skill. [ME, f. PRACTISE, after *advice, device*]

*****prä'ctice²**. See PRACTISE.

prä'cti'cian (-shan) *n.* worker, practitioner. [f. obs. F *practicien* (*pratique* f. med. L *practica* f. Gk *praktikē* fem. (as *n.*) of *praktikos;* see PRACTICAL)]

prä'ctis|e, *prä'ctic|e², *v.* **1.** *v.t.* perform habitually, apply in action, (*practise the same method; practise what you preach*); exercise, pursue, (profession or activity; ∿ing Catholic etc., active in religion; ∿ing doctor, barrister, etc., engaged in actual practice, not retired nor merely qualified); exercise oneself in or on (art, instrument, or abs.; *practise the flute, the piano, music, running*); (esp. in *p.p.*) exercise (person, one*self, in* action or subject). **2.** *v.i.* (arch.) scheme, contrive, (*when first we practise to deceive*); ∿e (up)on, impose upon, take advantage of, (person, his credulity, etc.). **3.** So ∿ER¹ *n.* [ME, f. OF *pra(c)tiser* or f. med. L *practizare* alt. f. *practicare* (*practica* prec.)]

prä'cti'tioner *n.* professional or practical worker, esp. in medicine (GENERAL *practitioner*). [f. obs. *practitian* = PRACTICIAN + -ER¹]

prae- *pref.* = PRE- (esp. in wds regarded as L or relating to Rom. Ant.). [L; see PRE-]

prae'cipe (prē'sĭpĭ) *n.* (Law). writ demanding action or explanation of non-action; order requesting writ. [L (first wd of writ), imper. of *praecipere* enjoin (see PRECEPT)]

praeco'cial, *prēco'cial, (-shal) *a.* (of bird) whose young can feed themselves as soon as hatched. [f. as PRECOCIOUS; see -AL]

praelē'ctor. Var. of PRELECTOR.

praemūnī're *n.* (Hist.) writ charging sheriff to summon person accused of asserting or maintaining papal jurisdiction in England. [med. L, = forewarn, for L PRAE(*monēre* warn), the wds *praemunire facias* that you warn (so-and-so to appear) occurring in the writ]

praeno'men *n.* (Rom. Ant.) first or personal name (e.g. *Marcus Tullius Cicero*). [L (*prae* before, *nomen* name)]

‖**praepo'stor,** ‖**prepo'stor,** (prĭp-) *n.* (At some public schools) prefect, monitor. [f. *praepositor* alt. of L *praepositus* p.p. (as *n.*) of PRAE(*ponere posit-* place) set over; see -OR]

praesidium. Var. of PRESIDIUM.

prae'tor, *prē'tor, *n.* (Rom. Hist.) annually elected magistrate performing some duties of consul (orig. consul as leader of army); hence **praetōr'IAL** *a.,* ∿SHIP *n.* [ME, f. F *préteur* or f. L *praetor,* perh. f. as PRAE- + *ire* it- go; see -OR]

praetōr'ian, *prē-, (prīt-) *a.* & *n.* **1.** *a.* of a praetor; of bodyguard of Roman general or emperor. **2.** *n.* man of praetorian rank; soldier of praetorian guard. [ME, f. L *praetorianus* (as prec.; see -IAN)]

prägmä't|ic *a.* **1.** meddlesome; dogmatic. **2.** of pragmatism. **3.** treating facts of history with reference to their practical lessons; dealing with matters according to their practical significance or immediate importance. **4.** of the affairs of a State (∿ic **sanction,** imperial or royal ordinance issued as fundamental law, esp. that of Emperor Charles VI in 1713 settling Austrian succession). **5.** Hence ∿icä'lITY *n.,* ∿ICALLY *adv.* [f. LL f. Gk *pragmatikos* (*pragma -matos* deed; see -IC)]

prägmä'tical *a.* = prec. 1, 2. [f. as prec. + -AL]

prä'gmat|ism *n.* officiousness; pedantry; matter-of-fact treatment of things; (Philos.) doctrine that evaluates any assertion solely by its practical consequences and its bearing on human interests; so ∿IST (2) *n.,* ∿i'stIC *a.* [f. Gk *pragma* (see PRAGMATIC) + -ISM]

prä'gmatīze, -ïse (-īz) *v.t.* represent as real; rationalize (myth). [f. as prec. + -IZE]

prahu. See PROA.

prair'ie *n.* large treeless tract of level or undulating grassland esp. in N. America; ∿-**chicken,** ∿-**hen,**

N. Amer. grouse of genus *Tympanuchus*; ∼-**dog**, N. Amer. rodent of genus *Cynomys*, with bark like dog's; ∼ **fire**, (fig.) thing that spreads rapidly; ∼ **oyster**, raw egg seasoned and swallowed whole; *∼ **schooner**, covered wagon used by pioneers in crossing the prairies; *P∼ **State**, Illinois; ∼ **wolf**, coyote. [F, f. OF *praerie* f. Rom. **prataria* f. L *pratum* meadow; see -ARY¹]

praise (-z) *v.t.*, & *n*. **1.** *v.t.* express warm approbation of, commend the merits of, (person, thing); glorify, extol the attributes of, (God etc.). **2.** *n.* praising, commendation, (*won high praise*; *was loud in his praises*); ∼ **be!** (excl. of pious gratitude); **sing** person's ∼**s**, (fig.) commend him highly; hence ∼'FUL (-zf-) *a.* [ME, f. OF *preisier* price, prize, praise, f. LL *pretiare* f. L *pretium* price; cf. PRIZE¹]

prai'seworth|y (prā'zwērdhĭ) *a.* worthy of praise, commendable; hence ∼ĭLY² *adv.*, ∼ĭNESS *n.* [f. prec. +-WORTHY]

Pra'krĭt (prah'-) *n.* any of the dialects of N. and Central India anciently existing alongside Sanskrit, or derived from such. [f. Skr. *prākṛta* unrefined; cf. SANSKRIT]

pra'line (prah'lēn) *n.* sweet made by browning nuts in boiling sugar. [F, f. Marshal de Plessis-*Praslin*, Fr. soldier d. 1675, whose cook invented it]

pra'lltrĭller (-ah'-) *n.* (Mus.) grace consisting in one rapid alternation of written note with note immediately above it. [G (*prallen* rebound, *triller* TRILL)]

pram¹, praam, (prahm) *n.* flat-bottomed boat used in Baltic etc. for shipping cargo etc.; flat-bottomed boat equipped with guns; Scandinavian ship's boat corresp. to dinghy. [f. MDu. *prame, praem,* MLG *prām(e)* f. OSlav. *pramŭ*]

‖**prăm²** *n.* carriage for one or two young children, with three or usu. four wheels, pushed by person on foot; milkman's delivery cart. [abbr. of PERAMBULATOR]

prance (-ah-) *v.i.*, & *n.* **1.** *v.i.* (Of horse) raise forelegs and spring from hind legs; (fig.) walk or behave in elated or arrogant manner. **2.** *n.* prancing (movement). [ME, of unkn. orig.]

prā'ndĭal *a.* (joc.) of dinner. [f. L *prandium* a meal +-AL]

‖**prăng** *v.* & *n.* (sl.) **1.** *v.t.* bomb (target) successfully; crash (aircraft or vehicle); damage by impact. **2.** *v.i.* crash aircraft or vehicle. **3.** *n.* act or instance of pranging. [imit.]

prănk¹ *n.* mad frolic, practical joke; hence ∼'FUL, ∼'ISH¹, ∼'SOME¹, *adjs.*, ∼'STER *n.* [16th c., of unkn. orig.]

prănk² *v.* (literary). **1.** *v.t.* dress, deck, (person, one*self*, thing, often *out* or *up*); adorn, spangle, (field *with* flowers etc.). **2.** *v.i.* show oneself off. [rel. to MLG *prank* pomp, Du. *pronk* finery]

prāse (-z) *n.* kind of leek-green translucent quartz. [F, f. L f. Gk *prasios* a. leek-green (*prason* leek)]

prāsèody'mium (-z-) *n.* (Chem.) metallic element of lanthanide series. [f. G *praseodym* f. Gk *prasios* (see prec.) from its green salts, +G *didym* DIDYMIUM]

prăt *n.* (vulg.) buttocks; (sl.) fool; ∼'**fall**, (sl.) fall on buttocks, humiliating failure.

prăt|e *v.* & *n.* **1.** *v.i.* chatter; talk too much; talk foolishly or irrelevantly. **2.** *v.t.* tell or say (thing) in prating manner. **3.** Hence ∼'ER¹ *n.*, ∼'ING² *a.* **4.** *n.* prating; idle talk. [ME, f. MDu., MLG *praten*, prob. imit.]

prā'tie *n.* (dial., esp. Ir.) potato. [corrupt.]

prā'tincōle *n.* bird of genus *Glareola*, like swallow in appearance and habits, allied to plover. [f. mod. L *pratincola* f. L *pratum* meadow +*incola* inhabitant]

prătique (-ă'tēk, -ē'k) *n.* licence to have dealings with a port, granted to ship after quarantine or on showing clean bill of health. [F, = practice, intercourse, f. It. *pratica* f. med. L *practica* (see PRACTICIAN)]

prā'ttl|e *v.* & *n.* **1.** *v.i.* talk in childish or artless fashion. **2.** *v.t.* say (thing) thus. **3.** Hence ∼'ER¹ *n.*, ∼'ING² *a.*

4. *n.* childish chatter; inconsequential talk. [f. MLG *pratelen* (as PRATE; see -LE 3)]

prau. See PROA.

prawn *n.*, & *v.i.* **1.** *n.* marine crustacean like large shrimp. **2.** *v.i.* fish for prawns. [ME *pra(y)ne,* of unkn. orig.]

prā'xis *n.* accepted practice, custom; practising of an art etc. [med. L f. Gk, = doing (*prassō* do)]

pray *v.* **1.** *v.t.* make devout supplication to (God, object of worship); beseech earnestly (God, person, *for* thing, to do, *that*); ask earnestly for (permission etc.). **2.** *v.i.* engage in prayer, make entreaty, (*to* God, to person, *for* thing, for or on *behalf of* person, *to* do, *that*); *praying* MANTIS; **past** ∼**ing for**, hopeless. **3.** = *I pray* (*pray God she is safe*); ∼ (I beg or urge you to) consider etc.; *what is the use of that*, ∼ (tell me)?. **4.** ∼ **in aid** (arch. ∼ *in aid of*: in orig. adv., not prep.), summon to one's support. [ME, f. OF *preier* f. LL *precare* f. L *precari* entreat]

prayer¹ (prār) *n.* **1.** solemn request or thanksgiving to God or object of worship; formula used in praying, e.g. *the* LORD'*s Prayer*; form of divine service consisting largely of prayers (*morning, evening, prayer; family prayers*); action or practice of praying; entreaty to a person; thing prayed for; *(colloq.) a* slight chance of success etc. **2.** ∼-**book**, book of forms of prayer, esp. Book of COMMON¹ Prayer; ∼-**mat**, small carpet used by Muslims when praying; ∼-**meeting**, religious meeting at which several persons offer prayer; ∼-**wheel**, revolving cylindrical box inscribed with or containing prayers, used esp. by Buddhists of Tibet. **3.** Hence ∼'FUL, ∼'LESS, *adjs.* [ME f. OF *preiere* f. Gallo-Rom. **precaria* fem. (as *n.*) of L *precarius* obtained by entreaty (*prex precis* prayer; see -ARY¹)]

pray'er² *n.* one who prays. [ME, f. PRAY +-ER¹]

PRB *abbr.* Pre-Raphaelite Brotherhood.

prē- *pref.* before (in time, place, order, degree, of importance). **1.** Forming *vbs.* & *vbl ns.* w. sense 'do, doing, thing done, beforehand', as: ∼-**arra'nge(ment)**; ∼-**au'dience**, right (of lawyer at Bar) to be heard before another; ∼-**ca'st**, (esp. in *p.p.*) cast (concrete) in blocks before use; ∼-**conce'rt**; ∼-**condi'tion**, (*n.*) prior condition, one that must be fulfilled beforehand, (*v.t.*) bring into desired condition beforehand; ∼-**coo'k**; ∼-**da'te**, antedate; ∼-**dige'st**, render (food) easily digestible before ingestion, (fig.) make (reading matter) easily assimilable; ∼-**doo'm** *v.t.*; ∼-**ele'ct**, ∼-**ele'ction** (see also sense 2); ∼-**enga'ge(ment)**; ∼-**esta'blish**; ∼-**exi'st(ence)**; ∼-**hea't** *v.t.*; ∼-**medica'tion**, (colloq.) ∼-**me'd**, treatment with medicines to prepare for operation etc.; ∼-**mo'tion**, motion given beforehand, esp. divine act as determining the will of the creature; ∼-**ordai'n**, appoint beforehand; ∼-**pa'ck(age)** *v.t.*, pack (goods) ready for sale before distributing them; ∼-**recor'd**; ∼-**sele'ct**; ∼-**se't**; ∼-**shri'nk**, (esp. in *p.p.*) treat (fabric, garment) so that it shrinks during manufacture, not after; ∼-**stre'ss**, (esp. in *p.p.*) strengthen (concrete) by means of stretched wires etc. in it. **2.** Forming *adjs.* & *ns.* w. sense '(person etc.) existing, dating from, before the time of', as: ∼-**ada'mic** *a.*, ∼-**ada'mite** *n.* & *a.*, (of supposed race) existing before the time of Adam; ∼-**Ca'mbrian**, (Geol.) (of) period or system prior to Cambrian; ∼-**Chri'stian**, before Christ(ianity); ∼-**cla'ssic(al)**, before the classical period (usu. of Greek and Roman literature); ∼-**Colu'mbian**, before discovery of America by Columbus; ∼-**co'nscious**, (*a.*) antecedent to consciousness, (*n.*) = FORECONSCIOUS; ∼-**dyna'stic**, of period before dynasties (esp. of Egypt); ∼-**ele'ction**, (of act, promise) done or given before election (see also sense 1); ∼-**exi'lic**, before the Jews' exile in Babylon; ∼-**gla'cial**, before a glacial period; ∼-**hu'man**, existing before man existed; ∼-**lapsar'ian**, before the Fall of man; ∼-**ma'rital**, of the time before marriage; ∼-**me'nstrual**, immediately before menstruation; ∿-**mille′nnial**(**ism**), (belief that Christ's Second Advent will occur) before the millennium; so ∿-**mille′nnialist** *n.*; ∿-**na′tal,** existing or occurring before (child)birth; ∿**pra′ndial,** before--dinner; ∿-**school,** of time before child is old enough to attend school; ∿-**scienti′fic,** before the rise of modern science; ∿-**Socra′tic,** (philosopher) of the time before Socrates; ∿-**ta′x,** (of income) before deduction of taxes; ∿-**war′** *a.* & *adv.*, (occurring or existing) before a war. **3.** Forming *adjs.* (esp. Anat. & Zool.) *w.* sense 'situated in front of', as: ∿-**cor′dial,** in front of or about the heart; ∿-**co′stal,** in front of the ribs; ∿-**dor′sal,** anterior to the dorsal region; ∿--**fro′ntal,** in front of frontal bone of skull, in forepart of frontal lobe of brain; ∿-**maxi′llary,** in front of the upper jaw; ∿-**o′cular,** in front of the eye. [f. or after L *prae-* (*prae* adv. & prep.)]

preach *v.* & *n.* **1.** *v.i.* deliver sermon or religious address; give moral advice in obtrusive way. **2.** *v.t.* deliver (sermon); proclaim, expound, (the Gospel, Christ, *that*, etc.) in public discourse; advocate, inculcate, (quality, conduct, principle, etc.) thus. **3.** Hence or cogn. ∿**ABLE** *a.*, ∿′**MENT** (usu. derog.) *n.* & *n.* (colloq.) preaching, sermon, lecture. [ME, f. OF *prechier* f. L. PRAE(*dicare* declare) proclaim, in eccl. L 'preach']

prea′cher *n.* one who preaches; minister of religion; Dominican friar; **the P**∿, Solomon as supposed speaker in Ecclesiastes. [ME. f. AF *prech*(*o*)*ur*, OF *proch*(*e*)*or* f. eccl. L *praedicator* (*praedicare*, as prec.; see -ER²)]

prea′chify *v.i.* (colloq.) preach, moralize, or hold forth, tediously. [f. PREACH + -I- + -FY; cf. *speechify*]

prea′ch|y *a.* (colloq.) fond of preaching or moralizing or holding forth; hence ∿**iNESS** *n.* [f. PREACH + -Y²]

preă′mble *n.*, & *v.i.* **1.** *n.* preliminary statement in speech or writing; introductory part of statute, deed, etc. **2.** *v.i.* make preamble. [ME, f. OF *preambule* f. med. L *praeambulum* f. LL *praeambulus* (a.) going before (as PRE-, AMBLE)]

Preb. *abbr.* Prebendary.

pre′bend *n.* part of estate revenue of cathedral or collegiate church granted to canon or member of chapter as stipend; portion of land or tithe from which this stipend is drawn; = foll.; so ∿**AL** *a.* [ME, f. OF *prebende* f. LL *praebenda* pension, neut. pl. gerundive of L *praebēre* grant (*prae* forth, *habēre* hold)]

pre′bendary *n.* holder of prebend; honorary canon; hence ∿**SHIP** *n.* [ME, f. med. L *praebendarius* (as prec.; see -ARY¹)]

precā′rious *a.* dependent on chance, uncertain, (*makes a precarious living*); insecure, perilous, (*precarious health; the precarious life of a fisherman*); (arch.) held during the pleasure of another (*precarious tenure*); (arch.) doubtful (assumption etc.); hence ∿**LY²** *adv.*, ∿**NESS** *n.* [f. L *precarius* (see PRAYER¹)]

pre′cative *a.* = foll. **1.** [f. LL *precativus* f. as foll.; see -IVE]

pre′catory *a.* **1.** (esp. Gram., of word or form) expressing request. **2.** ∿ **words** (in a will, requesting that a thing be done); ∿ **trust,** precatory words that are held to be binding. [f. LL *precatorius* f. L *precari* pray; see -ORY]

precau′tion *n.* prudent foresight; action taken beforehand to avoid evil or ensure good result; hence ∿**ARY¹** *a.* [f. F *précaution* f. LL *praecautio -onis* f. L PRAE(*cavēre caut-* beware of); see -ION]

precē′de *v.t.* (Of person or thing) go before in rank or importance (*such duties precede all others; sons of barons precede baronets*); come before (thing etc., or abs.) in order (*the words that precede, that precede this paragraph*); walk etc. in front of (*preceded by our guide*); come before in time (*in the years preceding his accession*); cause (thing) to be preceded *by* (*must precede this measure by milder ones*). [f. OF *preceder* f. L PRAE(*cedere cess-* go)]

precedence, precedency, (prē′sĭ-, prĭsē′-) *ns.* priority in time or succession; superiority, higher

position; right of preceding others in ceremonies and social formalities; **takes** ∿ **of,** has or claims right to precede, is recognized as superior to. [ME, f. PRECEDENT²; see -ENCE, -ENCY]

pre′cedent¹ *n.* previous case taken as example for subsequent cases or as justification (*there is no precedent for this; it is without precedent; do not take this as a precedent; that would create a precedent*); (Law) decision, procedure, etc., serving as rule or pattern. [ME, f. OF n., as foll.]

precedent² (prĭsē′-, prē′sĭ-) *a.* preceding in time, order, rank, etc.; hence ∿**LY²** *adv.* [ME, f. OF a. & n. f. as PRECEDE; see -ENT]

pre′cedènted *a.* having, or supported by, precedent. [f. PRECEDENT¹ + -ED²]

precē′nt *v.* **1.** *v.i.* act as precentor. **2.** *v.t.* lead singing of (psalm etc.). [back-form. f. foll.]

precē′ntor *n.* one who leads singing of congregation; (in Engl. cathedrals) member of clergy in general control of musical arrangements, in old foundations ranking next to dean and having succentor as his deputy, and in new foundations being a minor canon; (in synagogue) one who leads congregation in prayer; hence or cogn. ∿**SHIP, precē′n**TRIX, *ns.* [f. F *précenteur* or f. L *praecentor* f. PRAE(*cinere cent-* = *canere* sing); see -OR]

prē′cept *n.* command, maxim; so **prēcō′pt**IVE *a.* **2.** moral instruction (*example is better than precept*); divine command. **3.** writ, warrant; written order from sheriff to arrange and hold election; ||order for collection or payment of money under a RATE¹ **2.** [ME, f. L *praeceptum* neut. p.p. (as n.) of PRAE(*cipere cept-* = *capere* take) warn, instruct]

precē′pt|or *n.* teacher, instructor; hence or cogn. **precēptōr′IAL** *a.*, ∿**ORSHIP,** ∿**RESS**¹, *ns.* [f. L *praeceptor* (as prec.; see -OR)]

precē′ptory *n.* (Hist.) subordinate community of Knights Templars; estate or buildings of this. [f. med. L *praeceptoria* fem. (as n.) of *praeceptorius* a. (as prec.; see -ORY)]

precē′ssion (-shən) *n.* (Phys.) slow movement of axis of spinning body, gyroscope, etc., around another axis; ∿ **of the equinoxes,** (Astron.) (earlier occurrence of the equinoxes in each successive sidereal year, due to) slow retrograde motion of equinoctial points along ecliptic; hence ∿**AL** *a.* [f. LL *praecessio* (as PRECEDE; see -ION)]

pre′cinct *n.* **1.** space enclosed by walls or other boundaries of a place or building, esp. around place of worship; (in *pl.*) environs. **2.** boundary. **3.** *subdivision of county or city or ward for election and police purposes. **4.** district in town where traffic is prohibited, esp. *pedestrian precinct.* [ME, f. med. L *praecinctum* neut. p.p. (as n.) of PRAE(*cingere* gird) encircle]

pre′cious (-shus) *a.* & *adv.* **1.** *a.* of great price, costly; ∿ **metals,** gold, silver, or platinum metals; ∿ **stone,** piece of mineral having great value, esp. as used in jewellery. **2.** of great non-material worth (*precious words, privilege, knowledge, blood of Christ*); beloved (person, or abs.). **3.** affectedly refined in language, workmanship, etc.; so **prēcio′si**TY (-shĭŏ′s-) *n.* **4.** (colloq.) very bad, considerable, (*made a precious mess of it; a precious sight more than you think*); worth little (*you can keep your precious raffle-tickets*). **5.** Hence ∿**LY²** *adv.*, ∿**NESS** *n.* **6.** *adv.* (colloq.) extremely, very, (*took precious good care of that; precious little of it*). [ME, f. OF *precios* f. L *pretiosus* (*pretium* price; see -OUS)]

pre′cipice *n.* vertical or steep face of rock, cliff, mountain, etc. [f. F *précipice* or f. L *praecipitium* falling headlong, precipice (as PRECIPITATE; see -ICE)]

precī′pit|ant¹ *a.* = PRECIPITATE²; hence ∿**ANCE,** ∿**ANCY,** *ns.* [f. obs. F *précipitant* pres. part. of *précipiter* (as PRECIPITATE³; see -ANT)]

precī′pitant². See PRECIPITATE³.

precī′pitate¹ *n.* **1.** (Chem.) substance precipitated from solution. **2.** (Phys.) moisture condensed from vapour by cooling and deposited, e.g. rain, dew. [f. mod. L *praecipitatum* neut. p.p. (as n.) of L *praecipitare* (see PRECIPITATE³, -ATE¹)]

prĕcī'pĭtate² *a.* headlong, violently hurried, (*precipitate departure*); (of person or act) hasty, rash, inconsiderate; hence ∿LY² (-tlĭ) *adv.*, ∿NESS (-tn-) *n.* [f. L *praecipitatus* p.p. of *praecipitare* (see foll., -ATE²)]

prĕcī'pĭt|āte³ *v.t.* **1.** throw down headlong; (fig.) hurl or fling (person etc. *into* condition etc.). **2.** hurry, urge on, (course of events etc.); hasten occurrence of (*served to precipitate his ruin*). **3.** (Chem.) cause (substance) to be deposited in solid form from solution; (Phys.) cause (dust etc.) to be deposited from air on surface, condense (vapour) into drops and so deposit; hence ∿ABLE *a.*, ∿ABI'LITY, ∿ANT, ∿ātOR, *ns.* [f. L *praecipitare* f. PRAE(*ceps -cipitis* f. *caput* head) headlong, + -ATE³]

prĕcĭpĭtā'tion *n.* precipitating, being precipitated; precipitateness; (Meteorol.) (quantity of) rain, snow, etc., falling to ground. [f. F *précipitation* or f. L *praecipitatio* (as prec.; see -ATION)]

prĕcī'pĭtous *a.* of or like a precipice; dangerously steep; = PRECIPITATE²; hence ∿LY² *adv.*, ∿NESS *n.* [f. obs. F *précipiteux* f. L *praeceps* (see PRECIPITATE³, -OUS)]

précis (prā'sē) *n.* (*pl.* same *pr.* -ēz), & *v.t.* **1.** *n.* summary, abstract, esp. of speech or written work. **2.** *v.t.* make précis of. [F, = foll. (as n.)]

prĕcī'se *a.* accurately expressed, definite, exact; punctilious, scrupulous in observance of rules etc.; **the** ∿ (exact, identical) *moment* etc.; hence ∿NESS (-sn-) *n.* [f. F *précis -ise* f. L *praecisus* p.p. of PRAE(*cidere cis-* = *caedere* cut) cut short]

prĕcī'selў (-slĭ) *adv.* in precise manner; in exact terms; (in emphatic or formal assent) quite so. [f. prec. + -LY²]

prĕcī'sian (-zhan) *n.* one who is rigidly precise or punctilious, esp. in religious observance; hence ∿ISM (3) *n.* [f. PRECISE + -IAN]

prĕcī'sion (-zhon) *n.* & *a.* **1.** *n.* accuracy; degree of refinement in measurement etc. **2.** Hence ∿IST (2) *n.* **3.** *a.* marked by or adapted for precision (*precision bombing, instruments, tools*). [f. F *précision* or f. L *praecisio* (as PRECISE; see -ION)]

prĕclu'de (-ōō'd) *v.t.* exclude, prevent, make impracticable, (*so as to preclude all doubt*); so **prĕclu'sIVE** (-lōō'-) *a.* [f. L PRAE(*cludere clus-* = *claudere* shut)]

*precocial. See PRAECOCIAL.

prĕcō'cious (-shus) *a.* (Of plant) flowering or fruiting early; (of person) prematurely developed in some faculty or characteristic; (of action etc.) indicating such development; hence or cogn. ∿LY² *adv.*, ∿NESS, **prĕcō'cITY**, *ns.* [f. L *praecox -cocis* f. PRAE(*coquere* cook) ripen fully + -OUS]

prĕcŏgnĭ'tion *n.* (esp. supernatural) foreknowledge; (Sc. Law) preliminary examination of witnesses etc., esp. in order to know whether there is ground for trial. [f. LL *praecognitio* f. as PRE-, COGNITION]

prĕconcei've (-sē'v) *v.t.* form (idea, opinion, etc.) beforehand; anticipate in thought; so **prēCONCE'P-TION** *n.* (esp. = prejudice). [f. PRE- + CONCEIVE]

prĕ'conīz|e, -īs|e (-īz), *v.t.* proclaim publicly; commend publicly; summon by name; (RC Ch., of Pope) approve publicly the appointment of (bishop); so ∿A'TION *n.* [ME, f. med. L *praeconizare* f. L *praeco -onis* herald; see -IZE]

prĕcŭr'sor *n.* forerunner, harbinger, esp. John the Baptist in relation to Christ; one who precedes in office etc.; substance from which another is formed by decay, chemical transformation, etc. [f. L *praecursor* f. PRAE(*currere curs-* run); see -OR]

prĕcŭr's|orў *a.* preliminary, introductory, serving as harbinger (*of*); so ∿IVE *a.* [f. L *praecursorius* (as prec.; see -ORY)]

*prĕdā'ceous (-shus) *a.* (Of animal) predatory. [f. as foll. + -ACEOUS]

prĕdā'cious (-shus) *a.* (Of animal) predatory; per-

taining to such animals (*predacious instincts*); hence **prĕdA'CITY** *n.* [f. L *praeda* booty + -ACIOUS; cf. *audacious*]

prĕ'dator *n.* predatory animal. [f. L *praedator* plunderer (*praedari* seize as plunder f. *praeda* booty; see -OR)]

prĕ'datorў *a.* of or addicted to plunder or robbery; (of animal) preying naturally upon others. [f. L *praedatorius* (as prec.; see -ORY)]

prēdĕcea'se *v.t.*, & *n.* **1.** *v.t.* die earlier than (another person). **2.** *n.* death preceding that of another. [f. PRE- + DECEASE]

prē'dĕcĕssor *n.* former holder of office or position, with respect to a later holder, (*my, William's, predecessors*; *his immediate predecessor*); thing to which another has succeeded (*will share the fate of its predecessor*); forefather. [ME, f. OF *predecesseur* f. LL PRAE(*decessor* retiring officer f. as DECEASE); see -OR]

prēdĕ'lla *n.* (painting on vertical face of) altar-step; (painting or sculpture on) raised shelf at back of altar. [It., = stool]

prēdĕstĭnār'ian *n.* & *a.* (holder of the doctrine) of predestination. [f. PREDESTINATION + -ARIAN]

prēdĕ'stĭnate¹ *a.* predestined. [ME, f. as foll.; see -ATE²]

prēdĕ'stĭnate² *v.t.* (Of God) ordain (person) in advance to salvation or to (any fate), to (do); determine beforehand. [f. eccl. L PRAE(*destinare* establish) + -ATE³]

prēdĕstĭnā'tion *n.* God's appointment from eternity of some of mankind to salvation and eternal life; God's foreordaining of all that comes to pass; fate, destiny. [ME, f. eccl. L *praedestinatio* (as prec.; see -ATION)]

prēdĕ'stĭne *v.t.* determine beforehand, appoint as if by fate; (Theol.) predestinate. [ME, f. OF *predestiner* or f. eccl. L *praedestinare* PREDESTINATE²]

prēdētĕr'min|e *v.t.* decree beforehand, predestine, so ∿ATE² *a.*; (of motive etc.) impel (person etc. *to* thing, *to* do) beforehand; so ∿A'TION *n.* [f. LL PRAE(*determinare* DETERMINE)]

prē'dĭal *a.* & *n.* **1.** *a.* of land or farms; rural, agrarian; (of slave, tenant, etc.) attached to farms or the land; (of tithe) consisting of agricultural produce. **2.** *n.* predial slave. [f. med. L *praedialis* f. L *praedium* farm; see -AL]

prē'dĭc|able *a.* & *n.* **1.** *a.* that may be predicated or affirmed; hence ∿ABI'LITY *n.* **2.** *n.* predicable thing, esp. (in *pl.*) Aristotle's classes of predicates viewed relatively to their subjects (viz. genus, species, difference, property, accident). [f. med. L *praedicabilis* a., *praedicabile* n., (thing) that may be affirmed (as PREDICATE²; see -ABLE)]

prēdĭ'cament *n.* **1.** thing predicated, esp. (in *pl.*, Philos.) Aristotle's ten categories, whence ∿AL (-ĕ'n-) *a.* **2.** unpleasant, trying, or dangerous situation. [ME, f. LL *praedicamentum* (as PREDICATE²; see -MENT)]

prē'dĭcant *a.* & *n.* **1.** *a.* (Of religious order, esp. Dominicans) engaged in preaching. **2.** *n.* predicant person, esp. Dominican friar; *predikant*. [f. L *praedicans* part. of *praedicare* (see PREDICATE², -ANT)]

prē'dĭcate¹ *v.t.* (Logic). what is predicated, what is affirmed or denied of the subject by means of the copula (e.g. *mortal* in *all men are mortal*). **2.** (Gram.) what is said of the subject, including the copula (e.g. *are mortal* in above ex.) or other verb and its adjuncts. [f. LL *praedicatum* (transl. Gk *katēgoreumenon*), neut. p.p. of L *praedicare* (as foll.; see -ATE³)]

prē'dĭc|āte² *v.t.* assert or affirm as true or existent (*many truths may be predicated about humanity; we predicate goodness or badness of a motive; predicate of a motive that it is good or bad*); (Logic) assert (thing) about subject; *found or base (statement etc.) *on*; so ∿A'TION *n.* [f. L PRAE(*dicare* declare) proclaim + -ATE³]

prēdĭ'cative *a.* making a predication; (Gram., of *a.* or *n.*, opp. *attributive*) forming part or the whole of the predicate (e.g. *old* in *the dog is old* but not in *the old*

For other words in *pre-* **see PRE-.**

dog); hence ~LY² (-vlĭ) *adv*. [f. L *praedicativus* (as prec.; see -IVE)]

prĕ'dicatory *a*. of, given to, marked by, preaching. [f. LL *praedicatorius* (as PREDICATE²; see -ORY)]

prĕdi'ct *v.t.* foretell, prophesy, (thing, *that, who*, etc.); hence or cogn. ~ABI'LITY, **prĕdi'ct**ION, *ns*., ~ABLE, ~IVE, *adjs*., ~ABLY, ~IVELY (-vlĭ), *advs*. [f. L PRAE(*dicere dict-* say)]

prĕdi'ctor *n*. In vbl senses; instrument for determining height, direction, speed, and range of hostile aircraft to be attacked with anti-aircraft fire. [f. prec. + -OR]

predikant (prädĕkah'nt) *n*. minister of Dutch Protestant church, esp. in S. Africa. [Du. (as PREDICANT)]

prĕdilĕ'ction *n*. mental preference, liking, (*for*). [f. F *prédilection* f. med. L **praedilectio -onis* f. PRAE(*diligere*) prefer; see DILIGENT, -ION]

prĕdispō'se (-z) *v.t.* render liable, subject, or inclined (*to* feeling, disease, etc., *to* do). [f. PRE- + DISPOSE]

prĕdisposi'tion (-zĭ'-) *n*. state of mind or body favourable *to* (mercy, bronchitis, etc.). [f. PRE- + DISPOSITION]

prĕ'dnisŏne (-z-) *n*. drug similar to cortisone but more active. [perh. f. *pregnant* + *diene* + *cortisone*]

prĕdŏ'min|āte *v.i.* have or exert control (*over* person etc.), be superior; be the stronger or main element, preponderate, (*garden in which dahlias predominate*); hence or cogn. ~ANCE *n*., ~ANT, ~ATE², *adjs*. [f. med. L **PRAE(dominari* DOMINATE)]

prĕ-ĕ'min|ent *a*. excelling others; distinguished beyond others in some quality; hence or cogn. ~ENCE *n*., ~entLY² *adv*. [ME f. L PRAE(*eminens* EMINENT)]

prĕ-ĕ'mpt *v*. **1.** *v.t.* obtain by pre-emption; *occupy (public land) so as to have right of pre-emption, (fig.) appropriate beforehand, forestall. **2.** *v.i.* (Bridge). make pre-emptive bid. [back-form. f. foll.]

prĕ-ĕ'mpt|ion *n*. purchase by one person etc. before opportunity is offered to others; right so to purchase (esp. public land); (fig.) prior appropriation. [f. med. L PRAE(*emptio* f. *emere empt-* buy); see -ION]

prĕ-ĕ'mptive *a*. relating to pre-emption; (Mil.) intended to prevent attack by disabling threatening enemy; (Bridge, of bid) intended to be high enough to impede further bidding esp. by opponents. [f. as prec. + -IVE]

preen *v.t.* (Of bird) tidy (feathers) with beak; (of person) smarten (one*self*, one's clothes, etc.); ~ one*self*, congratulate oneself, show self-satisfaction; ~ **gland** (at base of bird's tail, secreting oil used in preening). [ME, app. var. of PRUNE³, assoc. w. Sc. & dial. *preen* pierce, pin]

pref. *abbr*. preface; preference; preferred; prefix.

prĕ'făb *n*. (colloq.) prefabricated building. [abbr.]

prĕfă'bric|āte *v.t.* manufacture sections of (building etc.) prior to their assembly on a site; produce in artificially standardized way; so ~A'TION *n*. [f. PRE- + FABRICATE]

prĕ'face *n*., & *v.t.* **1.** *n.* introduction to book stating subject, scope, etc.; preliminary part of a speech; introduction to central part of Eucharistic service. **2.** *v.t.* furnish (book etc.) with preface; introduce (act, speech, *with*); (of event etc.) lead up to (another). **3.** So **prĕfatŏr'ial, prĕ'fatory** *adjs*. [ME f. OF, f. med. L *praefatia* for L *praefatio* f. PRAE(*fari* speak)]

prĕ'fĕct *n*. **1.** (Rom. Ant.) chief magistrate; governor; military or naval commander. **2.** chief administrative officer of French, Japanese, etc., department; ~ of **police**, head of Paris police. **3.** (In some schools) senior pupil authorized to maintain discipline. **4.** So **prĕfe'ctor**AL, ~ŏr'IAL, *adjs*. [ME f. OF, f. L *praefectus* p.p. (as n.) of PRAE(*ficere fect-* = *facere* make) set in authority over]

prĕ'fĕctūre *n*. (period of) office, official residence, district under government, of a prefect; hence **prĕfĕ'ctur**AL (-kcher-) *a*. [f. F *préfecture* or f. L *praefectura* (as prec.; see -URE)]

prĕfĕr' *v.t.* (-rr-). **1.** promote (person *to* office); hence ~MENT *n*. **2.** bring forward, submit, (statement, information, accusation, etc., *to* person in authority etc., *against* offender, etc.). **3.** choose rather, like better, (*gentlemen prefer blondes*; *prefer water to wine*; *prefer to leave it alone*; *prefer that it should be left*; *prefer to go to prison rather than pay*); hence **prĕ'fer**ABLE *a*., **prĕ'fer**ABLY *adv*. [ME, f. OF *preferer* f. L PRAE(*ferre lat-* bear)]

prĕ'ference *n*. liking *of* or *for* one thing better than (*to* or *over*) another (*do this in preference to that*); thing one prefers; prior right esp. to receive payment of debts; ||~ **bond, share, stock,** (on which dividend is paid before any is paid on ordinary stock); favouring of one person or country before others in business relations, esp. favouring of a country by admitting its products at lower import duty. [f. F *préférence* f. med. L *praeferentia* (as prec.; see -ENCE)]

prĕferĕ'ntial (-shal) *a*. of, giving, receiving, preference; (of customs tariff etc.) favouring particular countries, whence ~ISM (3), ~IST (2), *ns*.; hence ~LY² *adv*. [as prec., after *differential*; see -IAL]

prĕfĕr'red (-ĕr'd) *a*. In vbl senses; (of shares etc.) = PREFERENCE *shares* etc. [p.p. of PREFER]

prĕfĭ'gure (-ger) *v.t.* represent beforehand by figure or type, picture to oneself beforehand; hence or cogn. **prĕfigūra'TION, ~MENT, *ns*., **prĕfĭ'gūrat**IVE *a*. [ME, f. eccl. L PRAE(*figurare* FIGURE²)]

prĕ'fix² *n*. verbal element placed at beginning of word to qualify meaning (e.g. *be-, ex-, re-*) or (in some languages) as inflexional formative; title placed before name, e.g. *Mr*. [f. mod. L *praefixum*, p.p. (as n.) of L PRAE(*figere* FIX¹)]

prĕfi'x² (-ks) *v.t.* add (chapter, paragraph, etc., *to* book etc.) as introduction; join (word, verbal element) as prefix (*to* word); hence or cogn. ~A'TION, **prĕfi'x**ION (-kshon), **prĕfi'x**TURE, *ns*. [ME, f. OF PRE(*fixer* FIX¹)]

prĕfŏr'm *v.t.* form beforehand; so ~A'TION *n*. [f. PRE- + FORM²]

prĕfŏr'mative *a*. & *n*. **1.** *a*. forming beforehand; prefixed as formative element of word. **2.** *n*. preformative syllable or letter. [f. PRE- + FORMATIVE]

prĕ'gnable *a*. able to be captured etc., not impregnable. [ME f. OF *prenable* takable; see IMPREGNABLE¹]

prĕ'gnant *a*. (Of woman or female animal) having developing child(ren) or young in the womb; teeming with ideas; imaginative, inventive; fruitful in results, plentifully furnished *with* (consequences etc.); (of words or acts) having a hidden meaning, significant, suggestive, whence ~LY² *adv*.; ~ **construction** (Gram.) in which more is implied than the words express, e.g. *not have a chance* implying *of success* etc.; hence **prĕ'gn**ANCY *n*. [ME, f. F *prégnant* or f. L *praegnans -ntis*, earlier *praegnas* (prob. as PRAE- + (*g)nasci* be born)]

prĕhĕ'nsile *a*. (Zool.) (Of tail or limb) capable of grasping; hence **prĕhĕnsi'l**ITY *n*. [f. F *préhensile* f. L PRE(*hendere hens-* grasp); see -IL]

prĕhĕ'nsion (-shon) *n*. grasping, seizing; mental apprehension. [f. L *prehensio* (as prec.; see -ION)]

prĕhistŏ'r|ic *a*. of the period antecedent to written history; (colloq.) utterly out of date; hence ~ICALLY *adv*. [f. F *préhistorique* (as PRE-, HISTORIC)]

prĕhi'story *n*. prehistoric matters or times; study of these; history (of a situation etc.) to this point; so **prĕ**HISTOR'IAN *n*. [f. PRE- + HISTORY, after prec.]

prĕ-igni'tion *n*. premature firing of explosive mixture in internal combustion engine. [f. PRE- + IGNITION]

prĕjŭ'dge *v.t.* pass judgement on (person) before trial or proper inquiry; form premature judgement on (person, cause, action, etc.); so ~MENT (-jm-), **prĕjudic**A'TION (-jōō-), *ns*. [f. PRE- + JUDGE²; after F *préjuger* or L PRAE(*judicare* JUDGE²)]

prĕ'judice (-jōō-) *n*., & *v.t.* **1.** *n.* preconceived opinion, bias, (*against*, etc., *in favour of*, person or thing; *divest your* *mind of prejudice*; *has a prejudice against foreigners*; *has a prejudice in our favour*; *this is mere prejudice*); injury that results or may result from some action or judgement (*to the prejudice of*); **without** ∼, without detriment to or *to* any existing right or claim. **2.** *v.t.* impair validity or strength of (right, claim, statement, one's chances, etc.); (esp. in *p.p.*) cause (person) to have a prejudice (*against* or *in favour of*). [ME, f. OF (*prejudicier* v. f.) *prejudice* n. f. L PRAE(*judicium* judgement)]

prèjudi'cial (-jŏŏdi'shǎl) *a.* causing prejudice, detrimental, (*to* rights, interests, etc.); hence ∼LY[2] *adv.* [ME, f. OF *prejudiciel* (as prec.; see -IAL)]

prē'lacў *n.* office, rank, see, of a prelate; *the* prelates; church government by prelates (usu. derog. for *episcopacy*). [ME, f. AF *prelacie* f. med. L *prelatia* (as foll.; see -ACY)]

prē'lat|e *n.* high ecclesiastical dignitary, e.g. (arch)-bishop, metropolitan, patriarch, (Hist.) abbot or prior; chaplain of an order; hence ∼ESS[1] *n.*, **prè-lă'tic**(AL) *adjs.* [ME, f. OF *prelat* f. med. L *praelatus* p.p. (as n.); see PREFER]

prē'latīze, -īse (-īz), *v.t.* bring (church) under prelatical government. [f. prec. + -IZE]

prē'lature *n.* office of prelate; *the* prelates. [f. F *prélature* f. med. L *praelatura* (as PRELATE; see -URE)]

prēlē'ct *v.i.* discourse, lecture, (*to* audience, *on* subject); so **prēlē'ct**ION, **prēlē'ct**OR, *ns.* (praelector, Camb. Univ. college fellow presenting candidates for degrees etc.). [f. L PRAE(*legere lect-* read)]

prēlībā'tion *n.* foretaste (usu. fig.). [f. LL PRAE(*libatio* LIBATION)]

prēli'm *n.* (colloq.) preliminary examination; (Print., in *pl.*; *or* prē'līmz) front matter, pages preceding text of book. [abbr.]

prēli'minar|ў *a.*, *adv.*, & *n.* **1.** *a.* introductory, preparatory; hence ∼ĭLY[2] *adv.* **2.** *adv.* = PREPARATORY 2. **3.** *n.* (usu. in *pl.*) preliminary action or arrangement. [f. mod. L *praeliminaris* or F *préliminaire* f. as PRE- + L *limen liminis* threshold; see -ARY[1]]

prē'lūde[1] *n.* **1.** performance, action, event, condition, serving as introduction (*to* another); introductory part of poem etc. **2.** (Mus.) introductory movement esp. one preceding fugue or forming first piece of suite; short piece of music of similar type and on one theme. **3.** Hence or cogn. **prēlū'd**IAL *a.*, **prē'lūd**IZE (2) *v.i.* [f. F *prélude* f. med. L *praeludium* (as foll.)]

prē'lūde[2] *v.* **1.** *v.t.* serve as prelude to, introduce, foreshadow; introduce with a prelude. **2.** *v.i.* give prelude (*to*). **3.** So **prèlu'sion** (-zhon) *n.*, **prèlu's**IVE *a.*, (-lū'-, -lŏŏ'-). [f. L PRAE(*ludere lus-* play)]

prē'matūre *a.* & *n.* occurring or done before the usual or proper time, too early, hasty, (*premature decision, decay*); ∼ **baby** (born 3 to 12 weeks before the expected time; cf. *miscarriage*); hence ∼LY[2] (-ūrlĭ) *adv.*, ∼NESS (-ūrn-), **prèmatūr'**ITY, *ns.* [f. L PRAE(*maturus* MATURE[1]) very early]

prēmĕ'dit|āte *v.t.* (esp. in *p.p.*) think out, design, (action etc.) beforehand; so ∼A'TION *n.* [f. L PRAE(*meditari* MEDITATE) + -ATE[3]]

prē'mier *a.* & *n.* **1.** *a.* first in position, importance, order, or time; of earliest creation (*premier earl*). **2.** *n.* prime minister, esp. in Great Britain and in provinces etc. of Commonwealth countries. **3.** Hence ∼SHIP *n.* [ME, f. OF = first, f. L (as PRIMARY)]

première (prĕ'myar) *n.*, & *v.t.* **1.** *n.* first performance of or in play, film, etc. **2.** *v.t.* give *première* of. [F, fem. of *premier* a. (as prec.)]

prē'mise[1] *n.* **1.** (Logic). = PREMISS. **2.** (in *pl.*) aforesaid or foregoing matters, esp. (Law) *the* aforesaid houses, lands, or tenements; introductory statement in deed of conveyance. **3.** (in *pl.*) house or building with grounds and appurtenances; **on the** ∼**s**, in the house etc. concerned. [ME, f. OF *premisse* f. med. L *praemissa* (*propositio* proposition) set in front f. L PRAE(*mittere miss-* send)]

prēmi'se[2] (-z) *v.t.* say or write (thing, *that*) by way of introduction. [f. prec.]

prē'miss *n.* (Logic). previous statement from which another is inferred, esp. MAJOR[2] and MINOR premisses in syllogism. [var. of PREMISE[1]]

prē'mium *n.* **1.** reward, prize, (**put a** ∼ **on**, provide, or act as, incentive to, attach especial value to); ||P∼ (**Savings**) **Bond**, government security with chances of cash prizes but zero interest. **2.** amount to be paid in consideration of contract of insurance. **3.** sum additional to interest, wages, etc., a bonus; fee for instruction in profession etc.; *charge for loan (additional to normal interest); **at a** ∼, above nominal or usual price (cf. DISCOUNT[1]), (fig.) in high esteem. [f. L *praemium* booty, reward, (as PRAE-, *emere* buy, take)]

prēmō'lar *a.* & *n.* (tooth) in front of true molars (in man, bicuspid). [f. PRE- + MOLAR[1]]

prēmoni'tion *n.* forewarning; presentiment; so **prēmŏ'nit**OR n., **prēmŏ'nit**ORY *a.* [f. F *prémonition* or f. LL *praemonitio* f. L PRAE(*monēre monit-* warn); see -ION]

Prēmŏnstratĕ'nsïan *a.* & *n.* (member) of order of regular canons founded at *Prémontré* in 1119, or of corresponding order of nuns. [f. med. L *Praemonstratensis* (*Praemonstratus* abbey of Prémontré, lit. foreshown, as having been prophetically indicated by St. Norbert; see -ESE) + -IAN]

prēmŏr'se *a.* (Bot. & Entom.) with the end abruptly terminated. [f. L PRAE(*mordēre mors-* bite) bite off]

prē'ntice *n.*, & *v.t.* (arch.) = APPRENTICE, esp. ∼ (inexperienced) **hand**; hence ∼SHIP (-s-sh-) *n.* (arch.). [ME, f. APPRENTICE]

prēŏccūpā'tion *n.* prepossession, prejudice; occupation of a place beforehand; occupation, business, that takes precedence of all others; mental absorption. [f. F *préoccupation* or f. L *praeoccupatio* (as foll.; see -ATION)]

prēŏ'ccūpў *v.t.* engage beforehand, engross (mind etc.); appropriate beforehand; (in *p.p.*) distrait, with thoughts elsewhere. [f. PRE- + OCCUPY, after L *praeoccupare* seize beforehand]

prēp *n.*, *a.*, & *v.* (-pp-). (colloq.) **1.** *n.* ||preparation of school work; time during which this is done. **2.** *a.* preparatory (*prep school*). **3.** *v.t.* & *i.* *prepare. [abbr.]

prēparā'tion *n.* **1.** preparing; being prepared; (usu. in *pl.*) thing done to make ready (*for*); in ∼, to get ready *for*; **make** ∼**s**, prepare (*for*). **2.** ||work done by pupils to prepare for lessons, as part of school routine. **3.** substance, e.g. food or medicine, specially prepared; (Mus.) (note sounded in) preparing of a discord. [ME f. OF, f. L *praeparatio -onis* (as PREPARE; see -ION)]

prēpa'rative *a.* & *n.* **1.** *a.* preparatory; hence ∼LY[2] (-vlĭ) *adv.* **2.** *n.* preparatory act; (Mil. & Naut.) signal on drum, bugle, etc., as order to make ready. [ME, f. OF *preparatif -ive*, f. med. L *praeparativus* (as PREPARE; see -IVE)]

prēpa'rator|ў *a.* & *adv.* **1.** *a.* serving to prepare, introductory (*to*); ∼**y school** (where pupils are prepared ||for higher school, *for college or university); hence ∼ĭLY[2] *adv.* **2.** *adv.* in a preparatory manner (*am packing it up preparatory to sending it by post*). [ME, f. LL *praeparatorius* (as foll.; see -ORY)]

prēpār'e *v.* **1.** *v.t.* make (person, one*self*, thing) ready (*for*); make ready (food, meal) for eating; make (person) mentally ready or fit (*for* news, *to* hear, etc.); **be** ∼**d**, be ready or willing (*to* do). **2.** get (lesson, speech, sermon) ready by previous study; make (person) ready by teaching (*for* college, examination, the army, etc.). **3.** make (chemical product etc.) by regular process. **4.** (Mus.) lead up to (discord) by sounding the dissonant note in it as consonant note in preceding chord. **5.** *v.i.* prepare oneself or things (*for*, *to* do, etc.). **6.** Hence **prēpār'ĕd**NESS *n.*, readiness (esp. of preparations for possible hostilities). [ME, f. F *préparer* or f. L PRAE(*parare* make ready)]

prēpay' *v.t.* (**prepai'd**). pay (charge) beforehand; pay (postage), pay postage of (letter, parcel, etc.)

For other words in *pre-* **see** PRE-.

name

prepense | 811 | **present**

beforehand, e.g. by affixing stamp; hence ~ABLE a., ~MENT n. [f. PRE- + PAY²]

prēpē'nse a. (usu. placed after n.) deliberate, intentional; **malice** ~, intention to injure; hence ~LY² (-slĭ) adv. [earlier prepensed p.p. of obs. prepense v. alt. f. earlier purpense f. AF & OF PUR(penser; see PENSIVE)]

prepŏ'nder|ant a. surpassing in influence, power, number, or importance, predominant; hence ~ANCE n., ~antLY² adv. [f. as foll.; see -ANT]

prepŏ'nder|āte v.i. weigh more, be heavier, (~ate over, exceed in number, quantity, etc.); be of greater moral or intellectual weight; be the chief element, predominate. [f. L PRAE(ponderare PONDER) + -ATE³]

prepŏsi'tion (-z-) n. word governing (and normally preceding) noun or pronoun, expressing latter's relation to another word (e.g. the italic wds in: found him at home, wait in the hall, what did you do it for?, the bed (that) he slept on, won by waiting, came through the roof, that is what I was thinking of); hence ~AL a. [ME, f. L praepositio (transl. Gk prothesis) f. PRAE(ponere posit- place); see -ION]

prepŏ'sitive (-z-) a. (Gram.) (of word, particle, etc.) proper to be placed before or prefixed. [f. LL praepositivus (as prec.; see -IVE)]

prepossě'ss (-z-) v.t. imbue, inspire, (person with notion, feeling, etc.); (usu. in pass., of idea etc.) take possession of (person); prejudice (usu. favourably and at first sight), whence ~ING² a., **prepossě'ssion** (-zĕ'shon) n. [f. PRE- + POSSESS]

prepŏ'sterous a. contrary to nature, reason, or common sense; perverse, foolish; utterly absurd; hence ~LY² adv., ~NESS n. [f. L PRAE(posterus coming after) reversed, absurd + -OUS]

||**prepŏ'stor.** See PRAEPOSTOR.

prepŏ't|ent a. very powerful; more powerful than others; (Biol.) having stronger fertilizing influence or power of transmitting hereditary qualities; so ~ENCE, ~ENCY, ns. [ME, f. L praepotens -entis part. of PRAE-(posse be able)]

||**prē-prě'ference** a. (Of shares, claims, etc.) ranking before preference shares etc. [f. PRE- + PREFERENCE]

prē'print n. printed document issued in advance of general publication. [f. PRE- + PRINT¹]

prē'pūce n. foreskin; similar structure of clitoris; so **prepū'tIAL** (-shal) a. [ME, f. L praeputium]

Prē-Rǎ'phael|ite (-fĕl-) n. artist or writer who aims at producing work in the spirit that prevailed before the time of Raphael; ~ite **Brotherhood**, group of English artists including Holman Hunt, Millais, D. G. Rossetti; so ~(ĭt)ISM (3) n. [f. PRE- + Raphael, It. painter d. 1520 + -ITE¹]

prěrě'quisite (-z-) a. & n. (thing) required as previous condition (for, of, to). [f. PRE- + REQUISITE]

prěrŏ'gative n. & a. 1. n. (royal) ~, right of the sovereign, theoretically subject to no restriction. 2. exclusive right or privilege (it is our prerogative to ride; we have the prerogative of riding); **the** ~ **of**, right to show (mercy etc.). 3. natural or divinely-given advantage, privilege, or faculty (reason and conscience are man's prerogatives). 4. ~ **court**, (Hist.) archbishop's court for probate of wills etc. 5. a. privileged, enjoyed by privilege; (Rom. Hist.) having the right to vote first. [n. ME f. OF or f. L praerogativa privilege, orig. tribe or century that voted first by lot; a. ME; both f. L PRAE(rogativus f. rogare ask; see -IVE) asked first]

Pres. abbr. President.

prě'sage¹ n. omen, portent; presentiment, foreboding; hence **presā'geful** (-jf-) a. [ME, f. F présage f. L praesagium f. PRAE(sagire perceive keenly) forebode]

presage² (prě'sij, prisā'j) v.t. portend, foreshadow; give warning of (event etc.) by natural means (such ideas are held to presage insanity); (of person) predict, or have presentiment of. [f. F présager f. L praesagire (as prec.)]

prěsbý|ō'pia (-z-, -s-) n. long-sightedness incident to old age, caused by loss of power of accommodation;

hence ~ŏ'pic a. [mod. L, f. Gk presbus old man + ōps ōpos eye; see also -IA¹]

prě'sbýter (-z-, -s-) n. 1. (In early Christian Church) one of several officers managing affairs of local church. 2. (In Episcopal church) minister of second order, priest. 3. (In Presbyterian church). elder. 4. Hence or cogn. **prěsbý'terAL**, **prěsbýtē'rIAL**, adjs., **prěsbý'terATE¹**, ~SHIP, ns., (-z-, -s-). [eccl. L, f. Gk presbuteros elder (compar. as n. of presbus old)]

Prěsbýtē'rian (-z-, -s-) a. & n. 1. a. ~ **Church**, one governed by elders, all (including ministers) of equal rank, esp. national Church of Scotland, (in England & Wales part of UNITED Reformed Church from 1972); hence ~ISM (3) n., ~IZE (3) v.t. 2. n. adherent of Presbyterian system; member of Presbyterian Church. [f. eccl. L presbyterium (as foll.) + -AN]

prě'sbýterý (-z-, -s-) n. eastern part of chancel beyond choir, sanctuary; body of presbyters, esp. court next above kirk-session, district represented by this; (RC Ch.) priest's house. [ME, f. OF presbiterie f. eccl. L f. Gk presbuterion (as PRESBYTER; see -Y¹)]

prě'sci|ent (-sī-, -shī-) a. having foreknowledge or foresight; hence or cogn. ~ENCE n., ~entLY² adv. [f. L PRAE(scire know); see -ENT]

prěsci'nd v. 1. v.t. cut off (part from whole) esp. prematurely or abruptly. 2. v.i. ~ **from**, leave out of consideration. [f. L PRAE(scindere cut)]

prěscri'be v. 1. v.t. lay down or impose authoritatively (prescribe to him what he is to do or how to do it; the statutes prescribe the practice); (Med.) advise use of (medicine etc., or abs.; to or for patient, for complaint; lit. or fig.); ~**d** book, — SET³ book. 2. v.i. assert prescriptive right or claim (to or for thing). [f. L PRAE(scribere script-write) direct in writing]

prě'script n. ordinance, law, command. [f. L praescriptum neut. p.p. (as n.); see prec.]

prěscri'ption n. 1. prescribing; physician's (usu. written) direction for composition and use of medicine; medicine thus prescribed. 2. (Law). (**positive**) ~, uninterrupted use or possession from time immemorial or for period fixed by law as giving title or right; **negative** ~, limitation of time within which action or claim can be raised. 3. (fig.) ancient custom viewed as authoritative, claim founded on long use. [ME f. OF, f. L praescriptio -onis (as PRESCRIBE; see -ION)]

prěscri'ptive a. prescribing; (Ling.) laying down rules of usage; based on prescription (prescriptive right); prescribed by custom; hence ~LY² (-vlĭ) adv. [f. LL praescriptivus (as PRESCRIBE; see -IVE)]

prěsělě'ctive a. (Of motor-car gear) that can be selected and set in advance; so **prěsele'ctor** n. [f. PRE- + SELECTIVE]

prě'sence (-z-) n. 1. being present (your presence is requested; in the presence of a large company; REAL² presence); place where person is (admitted to, banished from, his presence); **in this** (august etc.) ~, in the presence of this (etc.). person; ||**the** ~, ceremonial attendance on person of high (esp. royal) rank (remained in, retired from, the presence). 2. personal appearance, (esp. imposing) bearing, (a man of fine presence); bodily presence with view to influence (the British presence east of Suez). 3. person or thing that is present. 4. ~ **of mind**, calmness and self-command in sudden emergencies; ~-**chamber** (in which great personage receives guests etc.). [ME f. OF, f. L praesentia (as foll.; see -ENCE)]

prě'sent¹ (-z-) a. 1. (usu. pred.) being in the place in question (no one else was present in place, at proceedings etc.); ~ **company excepted**, excluding those who are here now; ~ **to**, felt or remembered by (mind, imagination). 2. being dealt with, discussed, etc., (no excuse in the present case). 3. existing, occurring, being such, now (the present Duke of Fife; in the present fashion; during the present month); **the** ~, the author, writer, etc., I who am writing; ~-**day** a., of this time, modern; ~ **value** or **worth**, sum that with compound interest dating from now will amount to given sum in given time. **4.** (Gram.) ∿ **participle, tense,** etc., (denoting action etc. now going on or habitually performed in past and future). **5.** (arch.) ready to hand, ready with assistance, (*a very present help in trouble*). [ME f. OF, f. L *praesens -entis* part. of PRAE(*esse* be) be at hand]

prĕ'sent² (-z-) *n.* **1.** *the* present time, the time now passing; **at** ∿, now (*do not want any more at present; is at present in Egypt*); **for the** ∿, just now, as far as the present is concerned, (*that will do for the present*); (**there is**) **no time like the** ∿ (urging immediate action). **2.** (Gram.) present tense. **3.** (Law or joc.) (*know all men* etc. *by*) **these** ∿**s,** this document. [ME, f. prec.]

prĕ'sent³ (-z-) *n.* gift; **make a** ∿ **of,** present (thing *to* person). [ME, f. OF (as prec.), orig. in phr. *mettre une chose en present à quelqu'un,* put a thing into the presence of a person]

prĕse'nt⁴ (-z-) *v.t.,* & *n.* **1.** *v.t.* introduce (person *to* another); introduce (person) to sovereign at court; ∿ one**self,** appear esp. as candidate for examination etc.; (Med., *refl.* or *abs.,* of patient or disease etc.) be the subject of initial investigation of condition. **2.** bring or offer (actor, play or other entertainment, new product, theory, etc.) to the public. **3.** recommend (clergyman) to bishop for institution (*to* benefice). **4.** exhibit (thing *to* person etc.; *present a ragged appearance; presented its front to me*); show (quality etc.; *cases that present some difficulty*); (abs., of part of foetus) be directed towards cervix at time of delivery. **5.** (Mil.) ∿ (**arms**), hold (rifle etc.) vertically as deferential position in saluting. **6.** (Of idea etc.) offer or suggest *itself.* **7.** (Law). bring formally under notice, submit, (complaint, offence, *to* authority). **8.** aim (weapon *at*), hold out (weapon) in position for aiming. **9.** offer or give (thing *to* person) as gift; offer (compliments, regards, *to*); deliver (cheque, bill, etc., *to* person etc.) for acceptance etc.; ∿ person **with** thing, present it to him, cause him to have it (*this presented me with a problem*). **10.** *n.* act of aiming weapon esp. firearm, position of weapon when aimed, position of 'present arms' in salute. [ME, f. OF *presenter* f. L *praesentare* (as PRESENT¹)]

prĕse'nt|able (-z-) *a.* of decent appearance, fit to be introduced or go into company; suitable for presentation (as a gift etc.); hence ∿**ABI'LITY** *n.,* ∿**ABLY** *adv.* [f. prec. + -ABLE]

prĕsentā'tion (-z-) *n.* **1.** presenting or being presented; ∿ (gratis) **copy** of book etc. **2.** exhibition, theatrical representation, etc. **3.** formal introduction esp. at royal court. **4.** (Philos.) modification of consciousness due to direct cognition; hence ∿**AL** *a.* **5.** attitude of foetus towards cervix at time of delivery. [ME f. OF, f. LL *praesentatio -onis* (as PRESENT⁴; see -ATION)]

prĕsentā'tion|ism (-ĕz-) *n.* (Philos.) doctrine that in perception the mind has immediate cognition of the object; so ∿IST (2) *n.* [f. prec. + -ISM]

prĕse'ntative (-z-) *a.* (Of benefice) to which patron has right of presentation; serving to present an idea to the mind; (Philos.) of (the nature of) presentation. [prob. f. med. L **praesentativus* (as PRESENTATION; see -IVE)]

prĕsentee' (-z-) *n.* person presented; recipient of present. [ME f. AF (as PRESENT⁴; see -EE)]

prĕse'ntient (-shĕnt) *a.* having a presentiment (*of* event etc., or abs.). [f. L PRAE(*sentiens* SENTIENT)]

prĕse'ntiment (-z-, -s-) *n.* vague expectation, foreboding, (*of* coming event, esp. evil). [f. obs. F *présentiment* (as PRE-, SENTIMENT)]

prĕ'sently (-z-) *adv.* soon, after a short time; (US, Sc., etc.) at the present time, now. [ME, f. PRESENT¹ + -LY²]

prĕse'ntment (-z-) *n.* **1.** (Law). statement on oath by jury of fact within their knowledge. **2.** formal complaint of offence made by parish authorities to

bishop or archdeacon at his visitation. **3.** theatrical representation; delineation; portrait; statement, description, (*of*); act or mode of presenting to the mind. [ME, f. OF *presentement* (as PRESENT⁴; see -MENT)]

prĕservā'tion (-z-) *n.* preserving or being preserved; state of being well or ill preserved (*in an excellent state of preservation*). [ME f. OF, f. med. L *praeservatio -onis* (as PRESERVE²; see -ATION)]

prĕsēr'vative (-z-) *a.* & *n.* (quality, course of action, etc.) tending to preserve; (substance) for preserving perishable foodstuffs. [ME, f. OF *preservatif -ive* f. med. L *praeservativus -um* (as PRESERVE²; see -ATIVE)]

prĕsēr've¹ (-z-) *n.* **1.** (in *sing.* or *pl.*) preserved fruit; jam. **2.** ground set apart for protection of game or *natural resources; piece of water for fish; (fig.) sphere regarded by person as being for him alone. [f. foll.]

prĕsēr'v|e² (-z-) *v.t.* **1.** keep safe (*from* harm, decay, etc.); keep alive (name, memory, etc.); (Heaven) ∿ **us!** (excl. of dismay or deprecation). **2.** maintain (state of things); retain (quality, condition); **well** ∿**ed,** (of elderly person) showing little sign of ageing. **3.** prepare (fruit, meat, etc.) by boiling with sugar, pickling, etc., to prevent decomposition or fermentation; keep from decomposition, by refrigeration, chemical treatment, etc. **4.** keep (game, river, or abs.) undisturbed for private use. **5.** Hence ∿**ABLE** *a.,* ∿**ER¹** *n.* [ME, f. OF *preserver* f. LL PRAE(*servare* keep)]

prĕ'sès (-z) *n.* (*pl.* same). (Sc.) president, chairman. [f. L *praeses* (as PRESIDE)]

prĕsī'de (-z-) *v.i.* occupy chair of authority (*at* or *over* meeting of society or company); sit at head of table; exercise control, sit or reign supreme, (lit. or fig.); ∿ **at** the organ, piano, etc., (colloq.) act as organist etc. [f. F *présider* f. L PRAE(*sidēre = sedēre* sit)]

prĕ'sidency (-z-) *n.* (period of) office of president; district administered by president, esp. (Hist.) one of three divisions of E. India Company's territory. [f. Sp. & Port. *presidencia,* It. *presidenza* f. med. L *praesidentia* (as prec.; see -ENCY)]

prĕ'sident (-z-) *n.* head of temporary or permanent body of persons, presiding over their meetings and proceedings; elected head of republican State; presiding officer of legislative body; head of some colleges and US universities; person presiding over meetings of academy, literary or scientific society, etc.; *person directing general policy of bank or company; head of advisory council, board, etc., (||**Lord P**∿ **of the Council,** Cabinet Minister presiding at meetings of Privy Council; ||**Lord P**∿, chief judge of Court of Session); (Hist.) governor of province, colony, etc.; hence or cogn. **prĕsidĕ'nt**IAL (-z-; -shal) *a.,* ∿**SHIP** *n.* [ME f. OF, f. L (as PRESIDE; see -ENT)]

prĕsi'diary *a.* of, having, serving as, a garrison. [f. L *praesidiarius* (*praesidium* garrison f. as PRESIDE; see -ARY¹)]

prĕsi'dio *n.* (*pl.* ∿**s**). (In Spain and Sp. America) fort, garrison town. [Sp., as foll.]

prĕsi'dium (-s-, -z-) *n.* standing committee in a Communist organization, esp. in Supreme SOVIET. [f. Russ. *prezidium* f. L (as PRESIDIARY)]

prĕss¹ *n.* **1.** crowding; crowd (*of* people etc.); throng, crush, in battle; hurry, pressure of affairs, (*the press of modern life*). **2.** pressing (*give it a slight press*). **3.** (Naut.) ∿ **of sail, canvas,** (as much as wind etc. will allow). **4.** instrument for compressing, flattening, or shaping, or for extracting juice etc. **5.** = PRINTING-*press*; printing-house or establishment; publishing firm etc. (*Oxford University Press*); the art, practice, of printing; **at** or **in** (**the**) ∿, being printed; *send, go, come,* **to** (**the**) ∿ (to be printed); ||CORRECTOR *of the press*; **freedom** or **liberty of the** ∿, right to print and publish anything without censorship (but still with liability for libel etc.; now often assoc. w. sense 6). **6.** the newspapers and periodicals generally (*favourably noticed by the press*); **get** or **have a good** etc. ∿, receive good etc. notice; *the* GUTTER, UNDERGROUND², YELLOW, *press*; (as name of newspaper) *Aberdeen Press and Journal, Bucks Free Press*. **7**. large usu. shelved cupboard for clothes, books, etc., esp. standing in recess in wall. **8**. ~ **agent**, person employed by theatre, actor, etc., to attend to advertising and press--publicity; *press* ATTACHÉ; ~**-box**, reporters' enclosure esp. at sports event; ~ **campaign** (by letters and articles in newspapers); ~ **conference**, interview given to journalists by some person to make announcement or answer questions; *~ **clipping**, = ||*press* CUTTING; ~**-gallery** (for reporters esp. in legislative assembly); ~'**man**, (1) ||journalist, (2) operator of printing-press; ~'**mark**, library shelf--mark showing location; *press* RELEASE². [ME f. OF *presse* (*presser*, as foll.)]

press² *v*. **1**. *v.t.* exert steady force against (thing in contact; *let a heavy weight press it*; *press it under or with a stone*; *press the two plates together*); do this as sign of affection etc. (*he pressed my hand, pressed her to his side*); move (thing *up, down, against*, etc.) by pressing; (of weight-lifter) raise (weight) to shoulders and then above head; ~ **the button**, set electric machinery etc. in motion, (colloq.) take decisive initial step. **2**. squeeze (juice etc. *out of, from*, etc.); compress or squeeze (thing) to flatten or shape or smooth it, or to extract juice etc.; make (gramophone record) thus; *pressed* STEEL. **3**. (Of enemy, attacking force, etc.) bear heavily on (esp. in p.p.; *hard pressed*); weigh down, oppress, (feelings, mind, spirits); **be ~ed for** (have barely enough) *space, time, money*, etc. **4**. urge, entreat, (person *to do*; person, or abs., *for* answer etc.). **5**. use strict or strained interpretation of (words, metaphor). **6**. urge (course of action, opinion, *upon* person); force (offer, gift, etc., *upon*); insist on (*did not press the point*). **7**. *v.i.* exert pressure, bear with weight or force, (*on, against*, etc.); (Golf) strive too hard for long hit etc. and so strike ball imperfectly. **8**. produce strong mental or moral impression, esp. weigh heavily, (*up*)*on* (mind, person). **9**. be urgent, demand immediate action, (*time presses*; *no business that presses*); make insistent demand *for*. **10**. crowd, throng, (*up, round*, etc.); hasten, urge one's way, *on, forward*, etc. **11**. ~**-button** *a.* = PUSH¹*-button*; ||~**-stud**, small device fastened by pressing to engage two parts; ~**-up**, (usu. in *pl.*) exercise in which prone body is raised by pressing down on hands to straighten arms. [ME, f. OF *presser* f. L *pressare* frequent. of *premere press*-]

press³ *v.t.*, & *n*. (Hist. or fig.) **1**. *v.t.* force (man, or abs.) to serve in army or navy; (fig.) bring into use as makeshift (*was pressed into service*). **2**. *n*. compulsory enlistment esp. in navy; ~**-gang**, (*n.*) body of men employed to press men, (fig.) group using similar coercive methods, (*v.t.*) force into service (as if) by press-gang. [alt. (by assoc. w. PRESS¹,²) of obs. *prest* v. & n. f. OF (*prest* loan, advance pay f.) *prester* f. L PRAE(*stare* stand) furnish]

pré'ssing¹ *a*. In vbl senses; urgent (*pressing need, danger*); importunate, persistent, (*a pressing invitation*; *since you are so pressing*); hence ~LY² *adv*. [f. PRESS² + -ING²]

pré'ssing² *n*. In vbl senses; thing made by pressing (esp. part of vehicle, gramophone record or series of these made at one time). [f. PRESS² + -ING¹]

pré'ssure (-sher) *n.*, & *v.t.* **1**. *n*. exertion of continuous force, force so exerted, upon or against a body by another in contact with it. **2**. amount of this, expressed by the force on a unit area, esp. that of the atmosphere (*atmospheric pressure*); **blood** ~, varying pressure, measured for diagnosis etc., of blood in vessels, (colloq.) abnormally high value of this (*suffers from blood pressure*). **3**. affliction, oppression; trouble, embarrassment, (*under financial pressure*). **4**. urgency (*wrote hastily and under pressure*); constraining influence (*pressure must be brought to bear on him*). **5**. **high** ~, (1) condition of atmosphere with pressure above

average, (2) pressure in engines higher than atmospheric, (3) pressure in engines higher than in other parts of the same machine, (4) (fig.) high degree of activity, speed, etc., (*working at high pressure*; *high--pressure work*); **high-~** *v.t.* (colloq.) coerce by insistence; **low ~**, (1) condition of atmosphere with pressure below average, (2) (fig.) low degree of activity, speed, etc. **6**. ~**-cooker**, apparatus for cooking quickly under high pressure; ~ **gauge** (for showing pressure of steam etc.; ~ **group**, group of persons seeking to coerce legislature etc. by concerted action, propaganda, and like methods; ~ **mine** (detonated by pressure); ~ **suit**, inflatable suit for person flying at high altitude. **7**. *v.t.* apply pressure to; coerce, persuade. [ME, f. L *pressura* (as PRESS²; see -URE)]

pré'ssuriz|e, **-īs|e**, (-sherīz) *v.t.* = prec. 7; raise to high pressure; (esp. in *p.p.*) maintain normal atmospheric pressure in (aircraft cabin etc.) at high altitude; hence ~A'TION *n*. [f. prec. + -IZE]

préstidi'git|ātor *n*. conjurer; so ~A'TION *n*. [f. F *prestidigitateur* (*preste* nimble, as PRESTO¹, + L *digitus* finger; see -OR)]

préstí'ge (-ē'zh) *n*. & *a*. **1**. *n*. influence or good reputation derived from past achievements, associations, etc.; hence ~FUL *a*. **2**. *a*. having or conferring prestige. [F, – illusion, glamour, f. LL *praestigium* f. as foll.]

préstí'gious (-jus) *a*. having or showing prestige; hence ~LY² *adv*., ~NESS *n*. [orig. = deceptive, f. L *praestigiosus* (*praestigiae* juggler's tricks; see -OUS)]

préstí'ssimō *adv.*, *a.*, & *n*. (*pl.* ~s). (Mus.) very quick (movement or passage). [It., superl. (as foll.)]

pré'stō¹ *adv.*, *a.*, & *n*. (*pl.* ~s). (Mus.) quick (movement). [It., f. LL *praestus* f. L *praesto* ready]

pré'stō² *adv*. (In conjurer's formulae at moment of sudden change etc.) quickly (*hey presto!*). [= prec.]

présŭ'm|e (-z-) *v*. **1**. *v.t.* take the liberty, be impudent enough, venture, (*to do*). **2**. suppose to be undoubtedly true, take for granted, (*I presume that he has seen them*; *I presume this decision to be final*; *you had better presume no such thing*); hence ~ABLE *a.*, ~ABLY *adv*. **3**. *v.i.* be impudent, take liberties; ~e (**up**)**on**, take advantage of, make unscrupulous use of (person's good nature, one's acquaintance with him, etc.); hence ~INGLY *adv*. [ME, f. OF *presumer* f. L PRAE-(*sumere sumpt*- take) anticipate, venture]

présŭ'mption (-z-) *n*. **1**. arrogance, assurance. **2**. taking for granted, thing that is or may reasonably be taken for granted (*this was a mere presumption*; *the presumption is that he had lost it*); ground for presuming (*there is a strong presumption against its truth*). **3**. (Law). ~ **of fact**, inference of fact from known facts; ~ **of law**, (1) assumption of truth of thing until the contrary is proved, (2) inference established by law as universally applicable to certain circumstances. [ME, f. OF *presumpcion* f. L *praesumptio -onis* (as prec.; see -ION)]

présŭ'mptive (-z-) *a*. **1**. giving grounds for presumption (*presumptive evidence*); hence ~LY² (-vlǐ) *adv*. **2**. **heir** ~ (whose right of inheritance is liable to be superseded by birth of another heir; cf. APPARENT). [f. F *présomptif -ive* f. LL *praesumptivus* (as PRESUME; see -IVE)]

présŭ'mptuous (-z-) *a*. unduly confident, presuming, forward; hence ~LY² *adv.*, ~NESS *n*. [ME, f. OF *presumptueux* f. LL *praesumptuosus, -tiosus* (as PRESUME; see -IOUS)]

présuppó'se (-z) *v.t.* assume beforehand (thing, *that*); involve, imply, (*effects presuppose causes*). [ME, f. OF *presupposer*, after med. L *praesupponere* (as PRE-, SUPPOSE)]

présŭpposi'tion (-zǐ'-) *n*. presupposing; thing assumed beforehand as basis of argument etc. [f. med. L PRAE(*suppositio* f. *suppositus*; as SUPPOSE; see -TION)]

||**prétê'nce**, ***prétê'nse**, *n*. **1**. claim (to merit etc.); **in ~**, (Her.) borne on an inescutcheon to indicate pretension or claim. **2**. ostentation, display, (*devoid of*

all *pretence*); false profession of purpose, pretext, (*under the pretence of helping*; *on the slightest pretence*; FALSE *pretences*). **3.** pretending, make-believe. [ME, f. AF *pretense*, f. AL **pretensa* fem. sing. or neut. pl. (as n.) of med. L *pretensus* pretended (as foll.)]

prětě'nd *v.* **1.** *v.t.* feign, give oneself out, (*to* be or do; *does not pretend to be a scholar*). **2.** make oneself seem (*to* do), make it seem (*that*), in play. **3.** profess falsely to have (*you should pretend illness*); allege falsely (*that*); (in *p.p.*) falsely avowed as such (*a pretended friend*). **4.** *v.i.* venture, aspire, presume, (*to* do); lay claim *to* (right, title, etc.); ~ **to**, profess to have (quality etc.), (arch.) try to win (person, person's hand) in marriage. [ME, f. F *prétendre* or f. L PRAE(*tendere tent-*, later *tens-* stretch)]

prětě'nder *n.* one who makes (esp. baseless) pretensions (*to* title etc., or abs.); **Old, Young, P~,** son, grandson, of James II as claimants to British throne; hence ~SHIP *n.* [f. prec. + -ER[1]]

*prětě'nse. See PRETENCE.

prětě'nsion (-shon) *n.* assertion of a claim (*to* thing, or abs.); justifiable claim (*to* thing, *to* be or do; *he has no pretensions to the name*; *has some pretensions to be chosen as the site*); pretentiousness. [f. med. L *praetensio, -tio,* (as PRETEND; see -ION)]

prětě'ntious (-shŭs) *a.* (Of person, book, speech, etc.) making claim to great merit or importance; ostentatious; hence ~LY[2] *adv.,* ~NESS *n.* [f. F *prétentieux* (as prec.; see -IOUS)]

prēter- *pref.* beyond, outside the range of, more than, as: ~**hu'man,** beyond what is human, superhuman; ~**na'tural,** outside the ordinary course of nature, supernatural; ~**na'turalism,** system or doctrine of the preternatural. [f. L *praeter* adv. & prep. past, beyond, compar. of *prae* before]

prē'terite, *prē'terit, *a.* & *n.* (Gram.) ~ (**tense**), tense expressing past action or state; ~**-present** (**tense**), tense originally preterite but now used as present (e.g. *can, may, shall*). [ME f. OF, or f. L *praeteritus* p.p. of *praeterire* pass (as prec., *ire it-* go)]

prēterī'tion *n.* omission, disregard, (*of*); (Theol.) passing over of the non-elect. [f. LL *praeteritio* (as prec.; see -ION)]

prēter|mi't *v.t.* (-tt-). omit to mention (fact etc.); omit to do or perform, neglect; leave off (custom, continuous action) for a time; so ~**mi'ssion** (-shon) *n.* [f. L *praetermittere* (as PRETER-, *mittere miss-* let go)]

pre'těxt[1] *n.* ostensible reason, excuse; (**up**)**on** or **under the** ~ *of* or *that*, professing as one's object etc. [f. L *praetextus* outward display f. PRAE(*texere text-* weave)]

prětě'xt[2] *v.t.* allege (thing, *that*) as pretext. [f. F *prétexter* (*pretexte,* = prec.)]

prē'tōne *n.* syllable or vowel preceding the stressed syllable; so prēTŌ'NIC *a.* [f. PRE- + TONE[1]]

*prē'tor etc. See PRAETOR etc.

prē'tti|fÿ *v.t.* make pretty; represent with finical prettiness; hence ~FICA'TION *n.* [f. PRETTY + -FY]

prě'ttilÿ *adv.* in a way that pleases the eye, ear, or aesthetic sense, (*prettily dressed*). [ME, f. PRETTY + -LY[2]]

prě'ttiněss *n.* **1.** beauty of a dainty or graceful kind; pretty thing, ornament, etc. **2.** affected or trivial beauty of style in literature or art; so **prě'ttÿism** (2) *n.* [f. foll. + -NESS]

prě'ttÿ *a.* & *adv.* **1.** *a.* (Of woman or child) attractive in dainty or graceful way; attractive to eye, ear, or aesthetic sense, (*pretty cottage, song, scene, story*); fine, good of its kind, (*has a pretty wit*; *very pretty sport*); (iron.) considerable (*cost me a pretty penny*; *a pretty mess you have made*); (arch.) fine, stout, (*a pretty fellow*) (ellipt.) **my** ~ (one, child); hence ~ISH[1] 2 *a.* **2.** *adv.* fairly, moderately, (*am pretty well*; *find it pretty difficult*); ~ **much** or **well,** very nearly (*the same thing* etc.); **sitting** ~, (colloq.) advantageously placed. **3.** ~~~, overdoing the prettiness, aiming too much at pretti-

ness. [OE *prættig,* corresp. to MLG *prattich* capricious, obs. Du. *prettig* sportive; f. WG **pratt-* trick]

prē'tzel *n.* crisp knot-shaped biscuit flavoured with salt, used esp. by Germans as relish with beer. [G]

preux chevalier (prĕr shĕvălyā') *n.* (*pl.* ~**s** pr. same). gallant knight. [F]

prēvai'l *v.i.* **1.** gain the mastery, be victorious, (*against, over*); ~ (**up**)**on,** persuade (*to* do). **2.** be the more usual or prominent, predominate; exist or occur in general use or experience, be current; ~**ing wind** (that most frequently occurs at a place). [ME, f. L PRAE(*valēre* have power), infl. by AVAIL[1]]

prē'val|ent *a.* generally existing or occurring; predominant; hence or cogn. ~ENCE *n.,* ~**ent**LY[2] *adv.* [f. as prec.; see -ENT]

prēvă'ric|āte *v.i.* speak or act evasively or misleadingly; quibble, equivocate; so ~**ātion,** ~**ātor,** *ns.* [f. L PRAE(*varicari* straddle f. *varus* bent, knock-kneed) walk crookedly, practise collusion, in eccl. L transgress, + -ATE[3]]

prēvě'nient *a.* preceding something else; having in view the prevention (*of*); ~ **grace** (Theol., preceding repentance and predisposing the heart to seek God). [f. L *praevenire* (see foll., -ENT)]

prēvě'nt *v.t.* **1.** hinder, stop, (*this may prevent him from writing, his* or (colloq.) *him writing*; *wish to prevent all dispute*). **2.** (arch.) meet, deal with, (wish, question, etc.) before it is expressed etc.; precede, arrive before. **3.** (Theol.) **God ~s** (goes before, guides) *us with His grace.* **4.** Hence or cogn. ~**ABLE,** ~**IBLE,** *adjs.,* **prēvě'nt**ION *n.* [ME = anticipate, f. L PRAE(*venire, vent-* come) come before, hinder]

prēvě'ntīve *a.* & *n.* **1.** *a.* serving to prevent, esp. (Med.) to keep off disease; ||~ **detention,** imprisonment of habitual criminal for corrective training etc.; ~ **medicine** (seeking to prevent disease rather than cure it); ||P~ **Service,** department of Customs concerned with prevention of smuggling. **2.** *n.* preventive agent, measure, drug, etc. **3.** Hence or cogn. **prēvě'nt**ATIVE *a.* & *n.,* ~LY[2] (-vlĭ) *adv.* [f. prec. + -IVE]

prē'view (-vū) *n.,* & *v.t.* **1.** *n.* view or examination of a film, play, book, etc., before it is seen by the general public; *trailer of film. **2.** *v.t.* view in advance of public presentation. [f. PRE- + VIEW]

prē'vious *a.* & *adv.* **1.** *a.* coming before in time or order; prior *to*; done or acting hastily (*you have been a little too previous*), whence ~NESS *n.;* ~ **question,** (Parl. etc.) question whether vote shall be taken on main question (put to avoid putting of main question or * to close debate on it); hence ~LY[2] *adv.* **2.** *adv.* ~ **to,** before (*had called previous to writing*). [f. L PRAE(*vius* f. *via* way) + -OUS]

prēvi'se (-z) *v.t.* (literary). foresee, forecast, (event etc., or abs.); so **prēvi'sion** *n.,* **prēvi'sion**AL *a.,* (-zho-). [f. L PRAE(*vidēre vis-* see)]

prē'vūe. Var. of PREVIEW.

*prě'x(ÿ) *n.* (sl.) president (esp. of college). [abbr.]

prey[1] (prā) *n.* animal(s) hunted or killed by other animal for food (**beast** or **bird of** ~, one that kills and devours flesh of other animals); (Bibl.) what one brings away safe from contest etc. (Jer. 21:9); person or thing that falls a victim (*to* enemy, disease, fear, etc.). [ME, f. OF *preie* f. L *praeda* booty]

prey[2] (prā) *v.i.* **1.** ~ (**up**)**on,** seek or take (animal etc.) as prey, plunder (person). **2.** Of disease, emotion, etc.) exert harmful or destructive influence (*up*)*on.* [ME, f. OF *pre*(*i*)*er* f. LL *praedare* f. L *praedari* (as prec.)]

prī'apism *n.* licentiousness; (Path.) persistent erection of penis; so **prīă'pIC** *a.,* phallic. [f. F *priapisme* f. LL f. Gk *priapizō* (*priapizō* be lewd f. *Priapos* god of procreation; see -ISM)]

prīce *n.,* & *v.t.* **1.** *n.* money or other consideration for which thing is bought or sold (*what is the price of this?*; *price £5 each*; *offered at reduced prices*); odds in betting (*the STARTING price of a horse*); ~ **current,** ~**-list,** list of current prices of commodities; ~**-fixing,**

For other words in *pre-* **see** PRE-.

determination of prices by agreement between sellers; ~-ring, RING[1] 5 of traders to maintain prices of goods; ~-tag, cost (lit. or fig.); above, beyond, without, ~, so valuable that no price can be stated; at a ~, at a relatively high price; of (great) ~, valuable; set a ~ on, announce amount for which thing will be bought or sold; set a ~ on person's head or life, offer specified reward for his capture or death. 2. (fig.) what must be given, done, sacrificed, etc., to obtain a thing (*must be done at any price*; *peace at any price*; *every man has his* ~, can be won over by some inducement); (*would not have it, do it*, etc.) at any ~, on any terms, for any sacrifice or consideration; ||what ~ . . .?, (sl.) (1) what is the chance of . . .?, (2) the vaunted . . . has failed. 3. *v.t.* fix or find the price of (thing for sale); (fig.) estimate the value of; ~ oneself out of the market, charge a prohibitive price. [n. ME f. OF *pris* f. L *pretium* (cf. PRAISE, PRIZE[1]); v. var. of *prise* = PRIZE[1]]

priced (-īst) *a.* to which a price is assigned (esp. in comb.: high, low, -priced); (of catalogue etc.) in which prices are named. [f. prec. + -ED[1,2]]

pri'celess (-sl-) *a.* invaluable; (sl.) most amusing, incredibly absurd; hence ~NESS *n.* [f. PRICE + -LESS]

pri'c|ey *a.* (~ier, ~iest). (colloq.) expensive. [f. PRICE | -Y[2]]

prick[1] *n.* pricking, puncture, (~s of conscience, remorse); mark made by pricking; (arch.) goad for oxen, esp. (fig.) kick against the ~s, hurt oneself by useless resistance (Acts 9:5); (vulg.) penis, (vulg., derog.) man; ~-ears, erect pointed ears of some dogs etc., conspicuous ears of person, esp. of Roundheads; ~-eared, having such ears. [OE *pric(c)a*, = MLG *pricke*; cf. foll.]

prick[2] *v.* 1. *v.t.* pierce slightly, make minute hole in, (~ a or the bladder or bubble, show the emptiness of a person or thing that has seemed important); (fig.) cause pain to (*my conscience pricked me*); (arch.) spur, urge on, (horse). 2. mark off (name etc. in list) by pricking, ||select (sheriff) thus; mark (pattern *off, out*) with pricks or dots. 3. ~ in, off, out, plant (seedlings etc.) in small holes pricked in earth; ~ up one's ears, (of dog) erect the ears when on the alert, (fig., of person) become suddenly attentive. 4. *v.i.* feel pricking sensation; make thrust (*at, into*, etc.) as if to prick; (arch.) advance on horseback. [OE *prician*, = MLG, MDu. *prikken*]

pri'cker *n.* In vbl senses; pricking instrument, e.g. awl or stitch-wheel. [f. prec. + -ER[1]]

pri'cket (-kĕt) *n.* ||male fallow deer in second year, with straight unbranched horns; spike to stick candle on. [ME, f. AL *prikettus, -um* dim. f. PRICK[1]; see -ET[1]]

pri'ckle[1] *n.* & *v.* 1. *n.* small thorn; (Bot.) thornlike process developed from, and capable of being peeled off with, epidermis of plant; hard-pointed spine of hedgehog etc. 2. *v.t.* & *i.* affect or be affected with sensation as of pricks. [n. f. OE *pricel*, = MDu., MLG *prickel*, cogn. w. PRICK[1]; v. also dim. of PRICK[2], = MDu. *prickelen*]

pri'ckle[2] *n.* wicker basket for fruit etc. [17th c., of unkn. orig.]

pri'ckly *a.* armed with prickles (esp. in names of plants and animals); (fig., of person) ready to take offence; tingling; ~ heat, inflammation of skin near sweat glands with eruption of vesicles and prickly sensation, common in hot countries; ~ pear, (1) cactus of genus *Opuntia*, (2) its usu. pear-shaped edible fruit; ~ poppy, yellow-flowered plant (*Argemone mexicana*) with prickly leaves; ~ rhubarb, gunnera; hence pri'ckliNESS *n.* [f. PRICKLE[1] + -Y[2]]

pri'cy. Var. of PRICEY.

pride *n.*, & *v.* *refl.* 1. *n.* (unduly) high opinion of one's own qualities, merits, etc.; arrogant bearing or conduct; ~ of place, exalted position, consciousness of this, arrogance. 2. (proper) ~, sense of what befits one's position, preventing one from doing unworthy thing; false ~, mistaken feeling of this kind; put one's

pride in one's POCKET[1]. 3. feeling of elation and pleasure due to action or circumstance that does one credit; take a ~ in, be proud of (person, thing, doing). 4. object of this feeling (*he is his mother's pride*; esp. in names of plants, as LONDON *pride*); best of a class etc. 5. (Her.) peacock in his ~ (with tail expanded and wings drooping). 6. company (of lions etc.). 7. best condition, prime (esp. *pride of* GREASE[1]); ~ of the morning, mist or shower at sunrise, indicating fine day to come. 8. Hence ~'FUL (-df-; chiefly Sc.), ~'LESS (-dl-), *adjs.* 9. *v.* *refl.* ~ oneself (up)on, be proud of (thing, quality, doing). [OE *prȳtu, prȳte, prȳde* f. *prūd* PROUD]

prie-dieu' (prēdyẽr') *n.* kneeling-desk esp. for prayer; ~ (chair), chair with tall sloping back for use in praying. [F, lit. 'pray God']

priest *n.*, & *v.t.* 1. *n.* ordained minister of RC, Anglican, or Orthodox Church (in Anglican Church, one above deacon and below bishop with authority to administer sacraments and pronounce absolution); minister of the altar, esp. officiant at Eucharist; official minister of non-Christian religion, whence ~'ESS[1] *n.*; HIGH *priest*; ~'craft, ambitious or worldly policy of priests; ~-ridden, held in subjection by priests; ~'s hole, (Hist.) secret hiding-place for RC priest; ||~-vicar, minor canon in some cathedrals. 2. Hence ~'HOOD (-t-h-), ~'LING[1] *ns.*, ~'LESS, ~'LIKE, *adjs.* *v.t.* make (person) a priest. [OE *prēost*, = OHG *priast, prēst*, ON *prestr*, ult. f. eccl. L PRESBYTER]

prie'stl|y *a.* of, like, befitting, a priest; P~y code, one of the constituent elements in the Hexateuch; hence ~iNESS *n.* [OE *prēostlic* (as prec., -LY[1])]

prig *n.* precisian in speech or morals or manners, conceited or didactic person; hence ~'gERY (2), ~'gISM (2), *ns.*, ~'gISH[1] *a.*, (-g-). [16th c. cant, of unkn. orig.]

prim *a.* & *v.* (-mm-). 1. *a.* (Of person, manner, speech, etc.) formal and precise, demure; (esp. of woman) prudish; hence ~'LY[2] *adv.*, ~'NESS *n.* 2. *v.i.* assume prim air. 3. *v.t.* form (face, lips, etc.) into prim expression; make prim. [17th c., prob. orig. cant f. OF *prin* prime excellent f. L *primus* first]

pri'ma (prē'-) *fem. a.* first, chief; ~ balleri'na, chief female performer in ballet; ~ do'nna (pr. -prē'-; *pl.* ~ donnas, *or* prime donne *pr.* prema dō'nă), chief female singer in opera, (transf.) temperamental person. [It.]

pri'macy *n.* office of a primate; pre-eminence. [ME, f. OF *primatie* or f. med. L *primatia* (as PRIMATE; see -ACY)]

primae'val. See PRIMEVAL.

prima fā'cie (-shē) *adv.* & *a.* (arising) at first sight, (based) on the first impression, (*has prima facie a good case*; *see a prima facie reason for it*). [ME f. L, abl. of *primus* first, *facies* FACE[1]]

pri'mal *a.* primitive, primeval; chief, fundamental; hence ~'LY[2] *adv.* [f. med. L *primalis* f. L *primus* first; see -AL]

pri'mary *a.* & *n.* 1. *a.* earliest, original; of the first rank in a series, not derived, (*the primary vowel sounds*; *the primary meaning of a word*). 2. of the first importance, chief. 3. (Geol.; P~) of the lowest series of strata; (Biol.) belonging to first stage of development. 4. ~ amputation (performed before inflammation supervenes); ~ battery, cell, (generating electricity by irreversible chemical reaction); ~ coil (to which current is supplied in transformer; *primary* COLOUR[1]; ~ education, that which begins with the rudiments of knowledge (cf. SECONDARY); *~ election (to appoint party conference delegates or to select candidates for principal election); ~ feather, large flight-feather of bird's wing; ~ planet (revolving directly round sun as centre; not a satellite); ~ school (where primary education is given); ~ tense, (L & Gk Gram.) present, future, perfect, or future perfect (cf. HISTORIC). 5. Hence pri'mariLY[2] *adv.* **6.** *n.* primary planet, period, coil, feather, election, etc. [ME, f. L *primarius* (*primus* first; see -ARY¹)]

pri'mate (-at, -āt) *n.* **1.** archbishop (**P~ of England**, Archbishop of York; **P~ of all England**, Archbishop of Canterbury). **2.** (Zool.) member of order Primates; hence **primato'LOGY** *n.* **3.** Hence **prīmā'-tIAL** (-shǎl) *a.* [ME, f. OF *primat* f. L *primas -atis* a. 'of first rank' (*primus* first), in med. L = primate]

Prīmātes (prīmā'tēz, prī'māts) *n. pl.* (Zool.) highest order of mammals, including man, apes, monkeys, tarsiers, and lemurs. [mod. L, f. as prec.]

primavě'ra (prē-) *n.* (hard light timber of) Central Amer. yellow-flowered tree (*Cybistax donnellsmithii*). [Sp., = spring, f. L *prima* first +*ver* SPRING² 2]

prime¹ *n.* **1.** state of highest perfection (*in the prime of life, manhood,* etc.; *prime of* GREASE¹); *the* best part (*of thing*). **2.** beginning or first age of anything; (Eccl.) (office of) second canonical hour of prayer, appointed for first hour of day (i.e. 6 a.m.); (arch.) this time. **3.** prime number. **4.** (Print.) symbol ' added to letter etc. as distinguishing mark, or to figure as symbol for minutes or feet. **5.** first of eight parrying positions in fencing. [OE *prīm* f. L *prima* (*hora*) first (hour), & MF f. OF *prime* (as foll.), or f. foll.]

prime² *a.* **1.** chief, most important, (*prime agent, motive*), first-rate (esp. of cattle and provisions), excellent, whence ~'LY² (-mlǐ) *adv.*, ~'NESS (-mn-) *n.* **2.** primary, fundamental; (Arith., of a number) divisible only by itself and unity (e.g. 2, 3, 5, 7, 11), (of numbers) having no common factor but unity. **3.** prime COST¹, MERIDIAN; ~ **minister**, principal minister of sovereign or State; *prime* MOVER; ~ **rate**, lowest rate at which money can be borrowed commercially; ~ **time** (at which highest rates are charged, esp. to advertisers on television); ~ **vertical**, great circle of the heavens passing through zenith and E. and W. points of horizon. [ME f. OF, f. L *primus* first]

prime³ *v.t.* **1.** prepare (explosive) for detonation; (Hist.) supply (firearm, or abs.) with gunpowder for firing charge. **2.** pour liquid into (pump) to make it start working; inject petrol into (cylinder or carburettor of internal combustion engine). **3.** equip (person *with* information etc.); ply (person *with* liquor). **4.** cover (wood etc.) with first coat of paint or with oil etc. to prevent paint from being absorbed. [16th c.; orig. unkn.]

pri'mer¹ *n.* elementary school-book for teaching children to read; small introductory book. [ME f. AF, f. med. L *primarius*, *-arium*, f. L *primus* first; see -ER² (2)]

pri'mer² *n.* In vbl senses; cap, cylinder, etc., used to ignite powder of cartridge etc.; substance used to prime wood etc. [f. PRIME³+-ER¹]

primer̄'ō *n.* (*pl.* ~s). (Hist.) gambling card-game fashionable in 16th–17th c. [f. Sp. *primera* fem. of *primero* first, f. as PRIMARY]

prīmě'val, prīmae'val, *a.* of the first age of the world; ancient, primitive; hence ~LY² *adv.* [f. L *primaevus* (*primus* first, *aevum* age) +-AL]

prīmigrǎ'vida *n.* (*pl.* ~e). woman pregnant for the first time. [mod. L, fem. f. L *primus* first + *gravidus* GRAVID]

prī'ming¹ *n.* In vbl senses; gunpowder placed in pan of firearm; train of powder connecting fuse with charge in blasting etc.; mixture used by painters for preparatory coat; preparation of sugar added to beer. [f. PRIME³ +-ING¹]

prī'ming² *n.* acceleration of the tides taking place from neap to spring tides (cf. LAG¹). [f. *prime* v. f. PRIME¹,² +-ING¹]

primi'par|a *n.* (*pl.* ~ae). woman bearing child for the first time; hence ~OUS *a.* [L (*primus* first, *-parus* f. *parere* bring forth)]

pri'mitive *a.* & *n.* **1.** *a.* early, ancient, (**the P~ Church**, Christian Church in its earliest times); old--fashioned, undeveloped, uncultured; at an early

stage of civilization. **2.** original, primary; (Gram., of words; Philol., of language) radical, not derivative; (Math., of line, figure, etc.) from which another is derived, from which some construction begins, etc.; (of colour) primary; (Geol.) of the earliest period; (Biol.) appearing in earliest or very early stage of growth or evolution; **P~ Methodist**, member of society of Methodists founded 1810 by Hugh Bourne by secession from main body, joined with other Methodists 1932. **3.** Hence ~LY² (-vlǐ) *adv.*, ~NESS (-vn-) *n.* **4.** *n.* painter of period before Renaissance, or modern imitator of such, or untutored painter with direct naïve style; picture by such painter; primitive word, line, etc.; (*P~*) Primitive Methodist. [ME f. OF *primitif -ive* or f. L *primitivus* first of its kind (*primitus* in the first place f. *primus* first; see -IVE)]

pri'mitivism *n.* primitive behaviour; belief in superiority of what is primitive. [f. prec. +-ISM]

pri'mō (-ē'-) *n.* (*pl.* ~s). (Mus.) leading or upper part in duet etc. [It.]

primogě'nitor *n.* earliest ancestor; ancestor. [var. of *progenitor*, after foll.]

primogě'nit|ure *n.* fact of being first-born child; (**right of**) ~**ure**, right of succession belonging to the first-born, esp. feudal rule by which whole real estate of intestate passes to eldest son; so ~AL, ~ARY¹, *adjs.* [f. med. L *primogenitura* f. L *primo* first + *genitura* (*gignere genit-* beget; see -URE)]

primŏr'dial *a.* existing at or from the beginning, primeval; original, fundamental; hence ~ITY (-ā'l-) *n.*, ~LY² *adv.* [ME, f. LL *primordialis* (as foll.; see -AL)]

primŏr'di|um *n.* (*pl.* ~a). (Biol.) rudiment of part or organ. [L, neut. (as n.) of *primordius* original (*primus* first, *ordiri* begin)]

primp *v.t.* make (hair, clothes, etc.) tidy; make (one*self*) smart. [dial. var. of PRIM]

pri'mrōse (-z) *n.* plant of genus *Primula* (esp. *P. vulgaris*) bearing pale yellow flowers in early spring; flower of this; the colour of this flower; EVENING primrose; **the ~ path**, unjustified (esp. disastrous) pursuit of ease or pleasure (w. ref. to Shak. *Hamlet* I. iii. 50); ||P~ **Day, League**, anniversary of the death (19 Apr. 1881) of, Conservative association formed in memory of, Benjamin Disraeli Earl of Beaconsfield; ~ **peerless**, twin-flowered European narcissus. [ME *primerose*, corresp. to OF *primerose* and med. L *prima rosa* lit. first rose; sense unexpl.]

pri'mŭla *n.* herbaceous perennial of genus *Primula* with flowers of various colours. [med. L, fem. (as n.) of *primulus* dim. of *primus* first]

prīmum mŏ'bile *n.* outermost sphere added in Middle Ages to Ptolemaic system, supposed to revolve round earth in 24 hours carrying with it the contained spheres; (fig.) prime source of motion or action. [med. L, lit. first moving thing, transl. Arab. *al-muḥarrik al-awwal*]

pri'mus *n.* presiding bishop of Scottish Episcopal Church; ~ **inter pares** (ĭnter pār'ēz), first among equals, senior or spokesman member of a group; (P~, P) brand of portable stove burning vaporized oil for cooking etc. [L, = first]

prince *n.* **1.** (rhet.) sovereign ruler; **the P~ of Peace**, Christ; ~ **of darkness, the air, this** or **the world,** etc., *the* Devil. **2.** ruler of small State, actually or nominally feudatory to king or emperor. **3.** male member of royal family, esp. ~ (**of the blood**), son or grandson of British king or queen; ~ **consort**, (title conferred on) husband of reigning female sovereign being himself a prince; **P~ of Denmark,** Hamlet (*Hamlet without the P~ of Denmark,* thing robbed of its essence); **P~ of Wales,** (title usu. conferred on) heir apparent to British throne. **4.** (As English rendering of foreign titles) noble usu. ranking next below duke; (as courtesy title in some connections) duke, marquis, earl; (as title of cardinal) ~ **of the (Holy Roman) Church. 5.** (fig.) the chief, the greatest, (*of* novelists, liars, etc.). **6.** **P~ **Albert,** (colloq.) frock-coat; ~

bishop, bishop who is also a prince; P∼ **Regent**, prince who acts as regent, esp. George (afterwards IV) as regent 1811-20; ∼ **royal**, eldest son of reigning monarch; (P∼) **Rupert's drops**, pear--shaped lumps of glass bursting to pieces when thin ends are broken off; P∼ **Rupert's metal**, = *prince's metal*; ∼'s **feather**, tall plant (*Amaranthus hypochondriacus*) with feathery spikes of small red flowers; ∼'s **metal**, brasslike alloy of copper and zinc. **7.** Hence ∼'DOM (-sd-), ∼'KIN (-sk-), ∼'LET, ∼'LING¹ 2, (-sl-), ∼'SHIP (-s-sh-), *ns.*, ∼'LIKE (-sl-) *a.* [ME f. OF, f. L *princeps principis* first, chief, sovereign (*primus* first, *cipere* = *capere* take)]

pri'ncelў (-slĭ) *a.* (worthy) of a prince; held by a prince; sumptuous, splendid; hence ∼iNESS *n.* [f. prec. + -LY¹]

pri'ncèss (*or* -ĕ's exc. when attrib.) *n.* **1.** wife of prince; female member of royal family, esp. ∼ (**of the blood**), daughter or granddaughter of British king or queen; P∼ **Regent**, (1) princess who acts as regent, (2) wife of Prince Regent; ∼ **royal**, (title conferrable on) sovereign's eldest daughter. **2.** (arch.) queen. **3.** (fig.) pre-eminent woman or thing personified as woman. **4.** ∼ **dress, petticoat, slip,** (made in panels with flared skirt and without seam at waist). [ME f. OF *princesse* (as PRINCE; see -ESS¹)]

pri'ncipal *a.* & *n.* **1.** *a.* (usu. *attrib.*) first in rank or importance, chief, (*their principal food is potatoes; the principal town of the district; the principal persons concerned*); main, leading, (*a principal cause of his failure*); ∼ **boy, girl,** actress who takes leading male, female, part in pantomime. **2.** (Of money) constituting the original sum invested or lent. **3.** (Gram.) ∼ **sentence, clause,** one to which another is subordinate; ∼ **parts** of verb, those from which all others can be deduced. **4.** *n.* head, ruler, superior; head of some schools, colleges, and universities, whence ∼SHIP *n.*; leading performer in concert, play, etc.; ‖civil servant of grade below Secretaries. **5.** person for whom another acts as agent etc. (*I must consult my principal*); person directly responsible for crime, either (∼ **in the first degree**) as actual perpetrator or (∼ **in the second degree**) as aiding; person for whom another is surety; combatant in duel (opp. *second*). **6.** main rafter supporting purlins; main girder. **7.** capital sum as distinguished from interest or from income. **8.** organ stop sounding octave above diapason. [ME f. OF, f. L *principalis* first, original (as PRINCE; see -AL)]

principa'litў *n.* **1.** government of a prince; State ruled by a prince; ‖**the P∼**, Wales. **2.** (in *pl.*) fifth ORDER¹ of ninefold celestial hierarchy. [ME, f. OF *principalité* f. LL *principalitas -tatis* (as prec.; see -ITY)]

pri'ncipallў *adv.* for the most part, chiefly. [f. PRINCIPAL + -LY²]

pri'ncipate *n.* **1.** (Rom. Hist.) rule of early emperors while some republican forms were retained. **2.** State ruled by a prince. [ME, f. OF *principat* or f. L *principatus* first place (as PRINCE; see -ATE¹)]

pri'nciple *n.* **1.** fundamental source, primary element, (*held water to be the first principle of all things*). **2.** fundamental truth as basis of reasoning etc. (*arguing from first principles*); (Phys. etc.) general law (*Archimedes' principle; principle of relativity*); general law as guide to action (*moral, conservative, principles; a dangerous principle*); **in** ∼, as regards fundamentals but not necessarily in detail. **3.** (in *pl.* or collect. *sing.*) personal code of right conduct (*a man of high principle; has ability but no principles; principle is everything*); **on** ∼, from settled moral motive (*I refuse on principle*). **4.** law of nature forming basis for construction or working of machine etc. (*in all these instruments the principle is the same*). **5.** (Chem.) constituent of a substance, esp. one giving rise to some quality etc., (*bitter principle of cinchona bark*). [ME, f. AF *principle, OF principe f. L principium* source, in pl. foundations (as PRINCE)]

pri'ncipled (-pĕld) *a.* based on or having (esp. praiseworthy) principles of behaviour. [f. prec. + -ED²]

prink *v.* **1.** *v.t.* make (one*self* etc.) smart; dress or smarten one*self up*; (of bird) preen. **2.** *v.i.* dress oneself up. [16th c.; cf. PRANK²]

print¹ *n.* **1.** indentation in or mark on surface preserving the form left by pressure of some body (*fingerprint; footprint*); hence ∼'LESS *a.* **2.** printed cotton fabric. **3.** language embodied in printed form; printed lettering (*large*, SMALL, *clear, print*). **4.** state of being printed (*book is in* ∼, (1) in printed form, (2) available from the publisher, not **out of print** (all copies sold); **appear in** ∼, have one's work published; RUSH² *into print*); printed publication, esp. newspaper; quantity of a book etc. printed at one time. **5.** picture or design printed from block or plate; (Photog.) picture produced from negative. **6.** ∼ **-seller**, dealer in engravings etc.; ∼**-shop**, his shop; ∼**works**, factory where cotton fabrics are printed. [ME, f. OF *priente, preinte*, fem. p.p. (as n.) of *preindre* press f. L *premere*]

print² *v.t.* **1.** impress, stamp, (surface, e.g. of butter or wax, *with* seal, die, etc.; a mark or figure *on* or *in* yielding or other surface); (fig.) impress (idea, scene, etc., *on* mind, memory). **2.** produce (book, picture, etc., or abs.) by applying inked types, blocks, or plates, to paper, vellum, etc.; (of author or editor) cause (book, MS) to be thus produced; express or publish in print (*not bound to print every opinion you hold*); write (words, letters, or abs.) without joining, in imitation of typography; ∼ **out**, (of computer etc.) produce output in printed form, ∼**-out**, (production of) such output. **3.** mark (textile fabric) with decorative design in colours; transfer (coloured design) from paper etc. to unglazed surface of pottery. **4.** (Photog.) ∼ (**out, off**), produce (picture) by transmission of light through negative. **5.** ∼**ed circuit**, electric circuit with thin strips of conductor on flat insulating sheet, usu. made by printing-like process. **6.** Hence ∼'ABLE *a.*, able or fit to be printed. [ME *prente, printe*, f. prec.]

pri'nter *n.* In vbl senses; one who prints books, magazines, advertising matter, etc.; owner of printing business; printing instrument; P∼s' **Bible** (with *Printers for Princes*, Ps. 119:161); *printer's* DEVIL¹; ∼'s **mark**, printer's device used as trade mark; ∼'s **pie**, = PIE³ *n.*; *printers'* REAM¹; so **pri'ntERY (3) *n.* [f. prec. + -ER¹]

pri'nting *n.* In vbl senses; impression of a book; ∼**-ink**, ∼**-press**, (for printing on paper etc. from types etc.). [ME, f. PRINT² + -ING¹]

pri'or¹ *n.* **1.** superior officer of religious house or order, (in abbey) officer next under abbot; so ∼Ess³ *n.* **2.** Hence or congr. ∼ATE¹ (1), ∼SHIP, *ns.* [OE, & ME f. OF *pri(o)ur*, f. L *prior* (see foll.), as n.]

pri'or² *a.* & *adv.* **1.** *a.* earlier; coming before in time, order, or importance, (*to*); ∼ **art**, (Patents) relevant methods etc. known before the disclosure of an invention. **2.** *adv.* ∼ **to**, before (*existing prior to his appointment*). [L, = former, elder, compar. of OL *pri* (L *prae*) before]

prio'ritў *n.* being earlier or antecedent; precedence in rank etc.; an interest having prior claim to consideration. [ME, f. OF *priorité* f. med. L *prioritas -tatis* f. L *prior* (as prec.); see -ITY]

pri'orў *n.* monastery or nunnery governed by prior(ess); *alien* ∼, ∼ *alien*, (dependent on abbey in another country). [ME, f. AF *priorie*, med. L *prioria* (as PRIOR; see -Y¹)]

‖**prise**. See PRIZE³.

pri'sm *n.* solid figure whose two ends are similar, equal, and parallel rectilinear figures, and whose sides are parallelograms (**pentagonal** etc. ∼, with five etc. sides); transparent body of this form, usu. triangular, with refracting surfaces at acute angle with each other; ∼ **binoculars** (in which triangular prisms are used to shorten the instrument); PRUNE¹*s and prism(s)*; hence **pri'sm**AL (-z-) *a.* [f. LL f. Gk *prisma prismatos* thing sawn (*prizō* to saw)]

prismă′t|ic (-z-) *a.* **1.** of or like a prism; ∿**ic binoculars,** = PRISM *binoculars;* ∿**ic compass,** hand-compass used in survey work, with attached prism enabling the dial to be read while the sight is taken. **2.** (Of colours) formed, distributed, etc., (as if) by transparent prism. **3.** Hence ∿ICALLY *adv.* [f. F *prismatique* f. Gk *prisma* (see prec., -IC)]

pri′smoid (-z-) *n.* body like prism, with similar but unequal parallel polygonal ends; hence ∿AL (-oi′-) *a.* [f. PRISM + -OID]

pri′son (-z-) *n.,* & *v.t.* **1.** *n.* place in which person is kept in captivity, esp. building to which person is legally committed while awaiting trial or for punishment; custody, confinement, (*in prison*); ∿-**bird,** = GAOL*bird;* ∿-**breaking,** escape from prison; ∿ **camp** (for prisoners of war or of State); ∿-**house,** (usu. rhet.) prison; ∿ **without bars,** area to which offenders are confined although without physical restraints. **2.** *v.t.* (poet. or dial.) imprison. [ME f. OF *prisun, -on,* f. L *prensio -onis* (*prehensio* f. *prehendere -hens-* lay hold of; see -ION]

pri′soner (-zn-) *n.* person kept in prison; (fig.) person or thing confined by illness, another's grasp, etc.; ∿ (**at the bar**), person in custody on criminal charge and on trial; *prisoner of* CONSCIENCE; ∿ **of State, state** ∿, (confined for political reasons); ∿ (**of war**), one who has been captured in war; **take** (person) ∿, seize and hold as prisoner; ∿**s′ base,** game played by two parties of boys etc., each occupying distinct base or home. [ME, f. AF; = OF *prisonier* (as prec.; see -ER² (2))]

pri′ss|y *a.* prim, prudish; hence ∿iLY² *adv.* [perh. f. PRIM + SISSY]

pri′stine (-īn, -ēn) *a.* ancient, primitive, old and unspoiled; fresh as if new. [f. L *pristinus* former; see -INE²]

pri′thee (-dhī) *int.* (arch.) pray, please, (*tell me, prithee*). [= (*I*) *pray thee*]

pri′vacy *n.* being withdrawn from society or public interest (*lived in absolute privacy*); being alone and undisturbed; avoidance of publicity (*in such matters privacy is impossible*). [ME, f. PRIVATE + -ACY]

privat-docent, -dozent, (prĕvaht dōtsĕ′nt) *n.* (In German university) private teacher or lecturer recognized by university but not on salaried staff. [G]

pri′vate *a.* & *n.* **1.** *a.* (Of person) not holding public office or official position. **2.** kept or removed from public knowledge or observation (*the matter was kept private; had private reasons; we are quite private here*). **3.** not open to the public (*private carriage, door; news came through private channels*). **4.** one's own (*my private property*); individual, personal, not affecting the community, (*motives of private malice*). **5.** confidential (*asked for some private conversation; this is for your private ear*). **6.** (Of place) retired, secluded. **7. in** ∿, privately, in private company or life. **8.** ∿ **act,** ∿ **bill,** ∿ **statute,** (of legislation affecting individual or corporation only); ||∿ **company** (with restricted membership and limited transfer of shares); *private* DETECTIVE; ∿ **enterprise,** business(es) not under State control, (fig.) individual initiative; ∿ **eye,** (colloq.) private detective; ∿ **hotel** (not necessarily accepting all comers); ∿ **house,** dwelling-house of private person (opp. shop, office, or public building); ∿ **law** (relating to private persons and property); ∿ **life** (as private person, not as official, public performer, etc.); ∿ **means,** income from investments etc., not earned as salary or wages; ∿ **member,** (in House of Commons etc.) one not holding Government appointment; ∿ **parts,** genitals; ||∿ **patient,** patient treated by doctor otherwise than under National Health Service; ∿ **practice** (of doctor etc. who is not only an employee); ∿ **press,** printing establishment operated by private person(s) not primarily for profit and usu. on small scale; ∿ **school,** ||school supported wholly by payment of fees, usu. for owner's profit, *school not supported

mainly by State; *private* SECRETARY; ∿ **soldier,** ordinary soldier other than officers (*and recruits); ∿ **view** (of picture etc. exhibition before it is opened to the public); *private* WAR¹, WIRE; ∿ **wrong,** offence against individual but not against society as a whole. **9.** Hence ∿LY² (-tlī) *adv.* **10.** *n.* private soldier (*∿ **first class,** soldier ranking above ordinary private but below officers); (in *pl.*) genitals. [ME, f. L *privatus,* orig. p.p. of *privare* deprive; see -ATE²]

privateer′ *n.* armed vessel owned and officered by private persons holding commission from government (*letters of* MARQUE¹) and authorized to use it against hostile nation esp. in capture of merchant shipping, whence ∿ING¹ (1) *n.*; ∿(**sman**), commander or (in *pl.*) crew of this. [f. prec. + -EER, after *volunteer*]

privā′tion *n.* loss or absence (*of quality; cold is the privation of heat*); lack of the comforts or necessaries of life (*died of privation; suffered many privations*). [ME, f. L *privatio* (as PRIVATE; see -ATION)]

pri′vative *a.* consisting in or marked by the loss or removal or absence of some quality or attribute; (of term) denoting privation or absence of quality etc.; (Gram., of particle etc.) expressing privation, as Gk *a-* = 'not-'; hence ∿LY² (-vlī) *adv.* [f. F *privatif -ive* or f. L *privativus* (as prec.; see -IVE)]

pri′vet *n.* plant of genus *Ligustrum,* esp. bushy evergreen shrub (*Ligustrum vulgare*) with smooth dark-green leaves, small white flowers, and small shining black berries, much used for hedges; ∿-**hawk,** large species of moth depositing eggs on privet. [16th c., of unkn. orig.]

pri′vileg|e *n.,* & *v.t.* **1.** *n.* right, advantage, or immunity, belonging to person, class, or office, esp. freedom of members of legislative assembly when speaking therein; special advantage or benefit (*to converse with him was a privilege*); monopoly or patent granted to individual, corporation, etc.; *(St. Exch.) option. **2.** *v.t.* invest with privilege; allow (person *to do*) as privilege; exempt (person *from* liability etc.). **3.** Hence ∿ED¹ (-ijd) *a.* [ME; n. f. AF *privilege,* OF *privilege* f. L *privilegium* bill or law affecting an individual (*privus* private, *lex legis* law); v. f. OF *privilegier* f. med. L *privilegiare* f. L *privilegium*]

pri′vity *n.* **1.** (Law). relation between two parties that is recognized by law, e.g. that of blood, lease, service. **2.** being privy (*to* plans etc.). [ME, f. OF *priveté* f. med. L *privitas -tatis* f. L *privus* private; see -ITY]

pri′vy *a.* & *n.* **1.** *a.* (Of thing, place, etc.) hidden, secluded; (of action) secret, whence **pri′vi**LY² *adv.;* ∿ **to,** in the secret of (person's plans etc.). **2.** **P**∿ **Council,** sovereign's or governor-general's private counsellors, (in UK) body of advisers chosen by sovereign (now chiefly as personal honour, most functions being performed by Cabinet, committees, etc.) together with princes of the blood, archbishops, etc.; ∿ **counsellor, councillor,** private adviser, esp. member of Privy Council; ∿ **parts,** (arch.) genitals; ||∿ **purse,** allowance from public revenue for monarch's private expenses, keeper of this; ||∿ **seal,** seal formerly affixed to documents that are afterwards to pass, or that do not require, the Great Seal; ||**Lord P**∿ **Seal,** senior Cabinet Minister without official duties (formerly keeper of privy seal). **3.** *n.* (arch. or US). lavatory. **4.** (Law). person having a part or interest in any action, matter, or thing. [ME, f. OF *privé* f. L *privatus* PRIVATE]

prize¹ *n., a.,* & *v.t.* **1.** *n.* reward given as symbol of victory or superiority to student in school or college who excels in attainments, to successful competitor in athletic contest, to exhibitor of best specimen of manufactured products, works of art, etc., in exhibition; (fig.) anything striven for or worth striving for (*many prizes in the Church; missed all the great prizes of life*); money or money's worth offered for competition in lottery etc. **2.** *a.* to which prize is adjudged in show, competition, etc. (*prize bull, poem,* etc.); supremely excellent or outstanding of its kind. **3.** ||~ **fellow-ship** (given as reward for eminence in examination), ~ **fellow,** holder of this; ~**-fight,** boxing-match for money; ~**-fighter,** ~**-fighting,** (one who engages in) professional boxing; ~**'man,** winner of (often specified academic) prize; ~**-money** (offered as prize); ~**-ring,** enclosed area (now usu. square) for, or (fig.) practice of, prize-fighting. **4.** *v.t.* value highly (*we prize liberty more than life*). [n. ME, var. of PRICE; v. ME, f. OF *pris-* st. of *preisier* PRAISE]

prize² *n.,* & *v.t.* **1.** *n.* ship or property captured at sea in virtue of rights of war; ~**-court,** department of admiralty court concerned with prizes; ~**-money** (realized by sale of prize, esp. Hist., such money as awarded to crew of capturing ship); **make** ~ **of,** seize (cargo, ship, etc.) thus; **become** (*lawful* etc.) ~, be thus seized. **2.** (fig.) find, windfall, (*see what a prize I have found!*). **3.** *v.t.* make prize of. [ME f. OF *prise* taking, booty, fem. p.p. (as n.) of *prendre* f. L *prehendere* -*hens-* seize; later identified w. PRIZE¹]

prize³, prīse (-z), *v.t.,* & *n.* **1.** *v.t.* force (lid etc. *up, out,* box etc. *open*) by leverage. **2.** *n.* leverage, purchase. [v. f. n., ME & OF *prise* levering instrument (as prec.)]

prō¹ *a., n.,* & *prep.* **1.** *a.* ~ **and con**(tra), (of arguments or reasons) for and against, on both sides. **2.** *n.* (in *pl.*) ~s and con(tra)s, reasons for and against. **3.** *prep.* ~ **and con**(tra), for and against. [L, = for, on behalf of]

prō² *n.* (*pl.* ~s) & *a.* (colloq.) professional; ~**-am,** involving professionals and amateurs. [abbr.]

prō-¹ *pref.* denoting: **1.** substitute(d) for, as: ~**-cathe'dral** *a.* & *n.,* (church) used as substitute for cathedral; ||~**-pro'ctor,** university proctor's assistant or deputy. **2.** (person) favouring or siding with (opp. ANTI-), as: *pro-Communist, pro-Market.* **3.** forwards (*proclaim, produce*). **4.** forwards and down-wards (*prolapse, prostrate*). **5.** onwards (*proceed, progress*). **6.** in front of (*prohibit, protect*). [f. L *pro* in front (of), for, on behalf of, instead of, on account of] **pro-²** *pref.* before (in time, place, order, etc.) (*problem, proboscis, prodrome, prognathous, prophet, protasis*). [f. Gk *pro* before]

PRO *abbr.* Public RECORD² Office; public relations officer.

prō'a, pra(h)u (prah'ōō), *n.* Malay boat, esp. with large triangular sail and with canoe-like outrigger. [f. Malay *prā(h)ū*]

probabi'lior|ism *n.* ethical doctrine that the side on which evidence preponderates ought to be followed (cf. foll.); so ~IST (2) *n.* [f. L *probabilior* more PROBABLE + -ISM]

prō'babil|ism *n.* ethical doctrine that where authorities differ any course may be followed for which a recognized Doctor of the Church can be cited (cf. prec.); theory that there is no certain knowledge, but may be grounds of belief sufficient for practical life; so ~IST (2) *n.* [f. as PROBABLE + -ISM]

probabi'lity *n.* **1.** quality of being probable; **in all** ~, most probably. **2.** likelihood (*there is no probability of his coming*). **3.** (most) probable event (*what are the probabilities?; the probability is that he will come*). **4.** (Math.) extent to which an event is likely to occur, measured by the ratio of the favourable cases to the whole number of cases possible (*from a bag containing 3 red balls and 7 white balls, the probability of a red ball's being drawn first is 3/10*). [f. F *probabilité* or f. L *probabilitas* (as foll.; see -ITY)]

prō'bab|le *a.* & *n.* **1.** *a.* that may be expected to happen or prove true, likely, (*reckon the probable cost; it is probable that he forgot; gives a probable account of the matter*); hence ~LY² *adv.* **2.** *n.* a probable candidate, member of team, etc. (cf. POSSIBLE 3). [ME f. OF, or f. L *probabilis* (*probare* prove; see -ABLE)]

prō'bănd *n.* person forming starting-point for genetic study of family etc. [f. L *probandus,* gerundive of *probare* test]

prō'băng *n.* surgeon's flexible strip of whalebone etc.

with sponge, button, etc., at end for introducing into throat. [17th c., named *provang* by inventor; orig. unkn., perh. alt. after *probe*]

prō'bate (-āt, -at) *n.,* & *v.t.* **1.** *n.* official proving of will; verified copy of will with certificate as handed to executors; ~ **duty,** (US or Hist.) tax on personal property of deceased testator. **2.** *v.t.* *obtain probate of (will). [ME, f. L *probatum* neut. p.p. (as n.) of *probare* PROVE]

proba'tion *n.* testing of conduct or character of person, esp. of candidate for membership in religious body etc. or for employment (on ~, undergoing this before full admission etc.); moral trial or discipline; (Law) system of suspending sentence on selected offenders during good behaviour under supervision of person (~ **officer**) acting as friend and adviser (*was put on probation*). [ME f. OF, or f. L *probatio* (as PROVE; see -ATION)]

proba'tion|ary *a.* **1.** of, serving for, done in the way of, probation; so ~AL *a.* **2.** undergoing probation. [f. prec. + -ARY¹]

proba'tioner *n.* person on probation, e.g. hospital nurse at early stage of training; offender under probation; hence ~SHIP (1) *n.* [f. PROBATION + -ER¹]

prō'bative *a.* affording proof, evidential. [f. L *probativus* (as PROVE; see -IVE)]

probe *n.,* & *v.t.* **1.** *n.* blunt-ended surgical instrument usu. of metal for exploring wound etc.; (**space**) ~, unmanned exploratory spacecraft transmitting information about its environment; (fig., f. v.) pene-trating investigation. **2.** *v.t.* explore (wound, part of body) with probe; penetrate (thing) with sharp instrument; (fig.) examine closely, sound, (person, motive, report, etc.); hence ~'ABLE (-ba-) *a.* [f. LL *proba* proof, in med. L = examination. L *probare* test]

prō'bit *n.* (Statistics) unit of probability based on deviation from mean of standard distribution. [f. *probability unit*]

prō'bity *n.* uprightness, honesty. [f. F *probité* or f. L *probitas* (*probus* good; see -ITY)]

prō'blem *n.* **1.** doubtful or difficult question or task (*how to prevent it is a problem; the problem of ventilation*); (*attrib.*) causing problems; ~ **child** (difficult to control, unruly), ~ **play, novel,** etc., (in which social or other problem is treated). **2.** thing hard to understand (*his whole conduct is a problem to me*). **3.** (Geom.) proposition in which something has to be constructed (cf. THEOREM); (Phys. & Math.) inquiry starting from given conditions to investigate a fact, result, or law; (Chess, Bridge, etc.) arrangement of men, cards, etc., in which solver is challenged to accomplish specified result, often under prescribed conditions. [ME, f. OF *probleme* or f. L f. Gk *problēma -matos* f. PRO²(*ballō* throw)]

problemă't|ic(al) *adjs.* doubtful, questionable, (*its success is problematical; the whole question is problematical*); (Logic) enunciating or supporting what is possible but not necessarily true; hence ~ICALLY *adv.* [f. F *problématique* or f. LL f. Gk *problēmatikos* (as prec.; see -IC)]

prō'blemist *n.* one who studies or composes (esp. chess) problems. [f. PROBLEM + -IST]

prōbŏscĭ'dēan *a.* & *n.* **1.** *a.* having a proboscis; of or like a proboscis. **2.** *a.* & *n.* (mammal) of the order Proboscidea, containing elephants and their extinct allies. [f. mod. L *Proboscidea* (as PROBOSCIS; see -A 2) +-AN]

prōbŏscĭ'dĭan *a.* & *n.* = prec. [f. foll. + -AN]

probŏ'scĭs *n.* elephant's trunk; long flexible snout of tapir etc.; elongated part of mouth of some insects; sucking organ in some worms; (joc.) human nose; ~ **monkey** (with nose projecting far beyond mouth); ~ **prŏbŏscĭ'ferous, prŏbŏscĭ'dĭform,** *adjs.* [L *proboscis -cidis* f. Gk *proboskis* f. PRO²(*boskō* feed)]

procē'dur|e (-dyer) *n.* proceeding; mode of conduct-ing business (esp. in parliament) or legal action;

mode of performing task; hence ∼AL *a.*, of or relating to procedure. [f. F *procédure* (as foll.; see -URE)]

procee'd *v.i.* **1.** go on, make one's way, (*to* place); go on (*with* or *in* action, investigation, remarks, etc.; *to* another subject, *to* do); adopt course of action (*how shall we proceed?*); (abs.) go on to say ('*in either case*', he *proceeded*, '*our course is clear*'). **2.** take legal proceedings *against* person; ||∼ **to** (take) *the degree of MA*, ∼ (take degree of) *MA*; (of action) be carried on (further), take place, (*the case, the play, will now proceed*). **3.** come forth, issue, originate, (*sobs heard to proceed from her bed; volumes proceed from the Press; exertions proceed from a false hope*). [ME, f. OF *proceder* f. L PRO¹(*cedere cess-* go)]

procee'ding *n.* In vbl senses; action, piece of conduct, (*a high-handed proceeding*); **legal** ∼**s**, (steps taken in) legal action; (in *pl.*) published report of discussions or conference (*Proceedings of the Royal Society*). [f. prec. + -ING¹]

prō'ceeds (-z) *n. pl.* money produced by sale, performance, etc., (*the proceeds will be devoted to charity*). [pl. of obs. *proceed* n. f. PROCEED]

prŏcĕleusmă'tĭc *a.* & *n.* (Pros.) (foot) of four short syllables. [f. LL f. Gk *prokeleusmatikos* f. *prokeleusma* exhortation f. PRO²(*keleuō* command) incite; see -IC]

prō'cĕss¹ *n.*, & *v.t.* **1.** *n.* progress, course; **in** ∼ **of** *construction* etc., being constructed etc.; **in** ∼ **of time**, as time goes on. **2.** course of action, proceeding, esp. series of operations in manufacture, printing, photography, etc. (∼ **heat, steam,** etc., those got as by-products of manufacturing processes); natural or involuntary operation, series of changes. **3.** action at law, formal commencement of this, summons or writ (∼**-server,** sheriff's officer). **4.** (Anat., Zool., & Bot.) natural appendage, outgrowth, protuberance. **5.** *v.t.* treat (material, food esp. to prevent decay) by particular process. **6.** Hence ∼ER¹, ∼OR, *ns.* (FOOD, WORD¹, *processor*). [ME f. OF *proces* f. L *processus* (as PROCEED)]

prŏcĕ'ss² *v.i.* (colloq.) walk in procession. [back-form. f. foll.]

procĕ'ssion (-shŏn) *n.* & *v.* **1.** *n.* proceeding of body of persons (or of boats etc.) in orderly succession, esp. as religious ceremony or political demonstration or on festive occasion, (*go, walk, in procession*); body of persons doing this; (fig.) race in which no competitor is able to overtake another; (Theol.) emanation of the Holy Spirit; ∼ **moth** (of genus *Thaumetopoea*, with caterpillars that go in processions, whence ∼ARY¹ *a.*). **2.** *v.i.* go in procession; hence ∼IST (1) *n.* **3.** *v.t.* walk along (street) or around (land) in procession. [ME f. OF, f. L *processio -onis* (as PROCEED; see -ION)]

procĕ'ssional (-shŏ-) *a.* & *n.* **1.** *a.* of processions; used, carried, sung, in processions. **2.** *n.* processional hymn; (Eccl.) office-book of processional hymns etc. [f. med. L *processionalis* a., *-ale* n., (as prec.; see -AL)]

procès-verb|al (prŏsăvărbah'l) *n.* (*pl.* ∼**aux** *pr.* -bō'), written report of proceedings, minutes; (Fr. Law) written statement of facts in support of charge. [F]

prō'chronism (-k-) *n.* referring of event etc. to an earlier than the true date (*races held in June and called by a prochronism the Mays*). [f. PRO-² + Gk *khronos* time + -ISM]

proclai'm *v.t.* announce officially (thing, *that*); declare (war, peace); announce officially the accession of (sovereign); declare (person, thing) officially to be (a traitor etc.); declare publicly or openly (thing, *that*); make known as being (*his accent proclaimed him a Scot*); (arch.) place (district etc.) under legal restrictions, prohibit (meeting etc.), by declaration; so **prŏclamA'TION** *n.*, **proclă'matory** *a.* [ME *proclame* f. L PRO¹*clamare* cry out; cf. CLAIM¹]

procli't|ic *a.* & *n.* (Gram.) (monosyllable) closely attached in pronunciation to following word and having itself no accent, e.g. *at* in *at home*; hence ∼ICALLY *adv.* [f. mod. L *procliticus* f. Gk PRO²*klinō* lean forward, after LL *encliticus* (see ENCLITIC)]

procli'vĭtȳ *n.* tendency (*to* or *towards* action or habit, esp. bad one; *to* do). [f. L *proclivitas* f. PRO¹(*clivis* f. *clivus* slope) inclined; see -ITY]

prōcŏ'nsul *n.* **1.** (Rom. Hist.) governor of province, in later republic usu. an ex-consul. **2.** ||(rhet.) governor of modern colony etc. **3.** deputy consul. **4.** Hence or cogn. ∼AR¹ *a.*, ∼ATE¹ (1) *n.*, (-ŭl-), ∼SHIP *n.* [ME f. L, earlier *pro consule* (one acting) for consul]

procră'stin|āte *v.i.* defer action, be dilatory; hence or cogn. ∼A'TION, ∼ātOR, *ns.*, ∼ATIVE, ∼ātORY, *adjs.* [f. L PRO¹(*crastinare* f. *crastinus* of tomorrow f. *cras* tomorrow) + -ATE³]

prō'crĕ|āte *v.t.* bring into existence by natural process of reproduction, generate, (offspring, or abs.); hence or cogn. ∼ANT, ∼ātIVE, *adjs.*, ∼A'TION *n.* [f. L PRO¹(*creare* CREATE) + -ATE³]

Procrŭ'stĕan *a.* seeking to enforce uniformity by violent methods. [f. Gk *Prokroustēs*, lit. stretcher (*prokrouō* beat out), name of legendary robber who fitted victims to his bed by stretching or lopping; see -AN]

prŏ'cto- *comb. form.* rectum, as *procto*SCOPE. [f. Gk *prōktos* anus + -O-]

prŏ'ctor *n.* **1.** ||(At Oxford & Cambridge) each of two university officers (**senior, junior,** ∼) appointed annually and having various functions esp. discipline of persons *in statu pupillari*; *supervisor of students in examination etc. **2.** (Law.) person managing causes in court (now chiefly Eccl.) that administers civil or canon law; ||Queen's or King's P∼, official who has right to intervene in probate, divorce, and nullity cases when collusion or suppression of facts is alleged. **3.** representative of clergy in Church of England convocation. **4.** Hence **prŏctōr'**IAL *a.*, ∼IZE (1) *v.t.*, ∼SHIP *n.* [ME, syncopation of PROCURATOR]

procŭ'mbent *a.* lying on the face, prostrate; (Bot.) growing along the ground. [f. L PRO¹(*cumbere* lay oneself) fall forwards; see -ENT]

prŏcūrā'tion *n.* **1.** procuring, obtaining, bringing about; so **procūr'**AL 2, **procūr'**ANCE, *ns.* **2.** function or authorized action of attorney; ||(Eccl.) provision of entertainment for bishop or other visitor by incumbent etc., now commuted to money payment; (fee for) negotiation of loan. **3.** procurer's trade or offence. [ME f. OF, or f. L *procuratio* (as PROCURE; see -ATION)]

prŏ'cūrātor *n.* **1.** (Rom. Hist.) treasury officer in imperial province. **2.** agent, proxy, esp. one who has power of attorney; ∼ **fiscal,** coroner and public prosecutor of district in Scotland; ∼ **general,** high-ranking procurator, esp. ||head of law department of Treasury. **3.** Hence **procurātōr'**IAL *a.*, ∼SHIP *n.* [ME, f. OF *procurateur* or f. L *procurator* agent, collector in province (as PROCURE; see -OR)]

prŏ'cūratorȳ *n.* (Law.) authorization to act for another (*letters of procuratory*). [f. med. L *procuratorium* neut. (as n.) of LL *procuratorius* (as prec.; see -ORY)]

procūr'e *v.* **1.** *v.t.* (formal). obtain by care or effort, acquire, (*must procure you a copy; will procure a copy for you; cannot procure employment*); bring about (*procured his dismissal*). **2.** *v.i.* & *t.* act as procurer or procuress (of). **3.** Hence **procūr'**ABLE *a.*, ∼MENT (-ūr'm-) *n.* [ME, f. OF *procurer* f. L PRO¹(*curare* see to) take care of, manage]

procūr'|er *n.* In vbl senses; man or woman who obtains women for gratification of another's lust, whence ∼ESS¹ *n.* [ME f. AF *procurour*, OF *procureur* f. L PROCURATOR]

prŏd *v.* (-dd-) & *n.* **1.** *v.t.* poke with finger, pointed instrument, end of stick, etc.; (fig.) stimulate to action. **2.** *v.i.* make prodding motion *at*. **3.** *n.* poke, thrust; stimulus to action; pointed instrument. [16th c., perh. imit.]

prŏdĕ'li'sion (-zhŏn) *n.* elision of initial vowel (as in *I'm* for *I am*). [f. L *prod-* = PRO-¹ + ELISION]

prŏ'digal *a.* & *n.* recklessly wasteful (person); lavish *of;* ∼ (**son**), repentant wastrel, returned wanderer, etc. (Luke 15:11–32); hence or cogn. ∼ITY (-ă'l-) *n.*, ∼IZE *v.t.*, spend lavishly, ∼LY² *adv.* [f. LL **prodigalis* f. L *prodigus* lavish; see -AL]

prodi′gious (-*jus*) *a.* marvellous, amazing; enormous; abnormal; hence ∼LY² *adv.*, ∼NESS *n.* [f. L *prodigiosus* (as foll.; see -OUS)]

pro̅′dĭgy̆ *n.* marvellous thing, esp. one out of the ordinary course of nature; wonderful example *of* (some quality); person endowed with surprising qualities or abilities, esp. precocious child. [f. L *prodigium* portent]

pro̅′drŏme *n.* preliminary book or treatise (*to* another); (Path.) premonitory symptom (*of*), whence **prŏ′drom**AL, **prodrŏ′mic**, *adjs.* [F, f. mod. L f. Gk PRO²(*dromos* running) precursor]

prŏ′du̅ce¹ *n.* amount produced, yield, esp. in assay of ore; what is produced, esp. agricultural and natural products collectively (*dairy produce*); result (*of* labour, efforts, etc.). [f. foll.]

produ̅′ce² *v.t.* **1.** bring forward for inspection or consideration (*will produce evidence, witnesses, reasons; produce your tickets*). **2.** bring (play, performer, book, etc.) before the public. **3.** (Geom.) extend, continue, (line *to* a point). **4.** manufacture (goods) from raw materials etc. **5.** bring about, cause, (a reaction, a sensation, etc.); bring into existence; (of land etc.) yield (agricultural etc. produce); (of animal or plant, joc. of person) bear, yield, (offspring, fruit). **6.** So **produ̅′cible** *a.* [ME, f. L PRO¹(*ducere duct-* lead)]

produ̅′cer *n.* In vbl senses; (Econ.) one who produces article for use (opp. *consumer*); person generally responsible for production of a film or play (apart from direction of the acting); ‖director of play or broadcast programme; ∼ **gas**, combustible gas formed by passing air, or air and steam, through red-hot carbon. [f. prec. + -ER¹]

prŏ′duct *n.* thing or substance produced by natural process or manufacture; result (*the product of his labours*); (Math.) quantity obtained by multiplying quantities together. [ME, f. L *productum*, neut. p.p. (as n.) of *producere* PRODUCE²]

produ̅′ction *n.* **1.** producing; being produced; being manufactured, esp. in large quantities (*go into production*); ∼ **line**, group of machines and workers progressively making some product. **2.** total yield; thing produced, esp. literary or artistic work. [ME f. OF, f. L *productio -onis* (as prec.; see -ION)]

produ̅′ctive *a.* producing, tending to produce, (*productive of figs, of great annoyance*); (Econ.) producing commodities of exchangeable value (*productive labour*); producing abundantly (*a productive soil, mine, writer*); hence ∼LY² (-vlĭ) *adv.*, ∼NESS (-vli-) *n.* [f. F *productif -ive* or f. LL *productivus* (as PRODUCT, see -IVE)]

productı̆′vity *n.* capacity to produce; quality or state of being productive; production per unit of effort; effectiveness of productive effort, esp. in industry. [f. prec. + -ITY]

prŏ′em *n.* preface or preamble to book or speech; beginning, prelude; hence **proē′mIAL** *a.* [ME, f. OF *pro(h)eme* or f. L f. Gk *prooimion* prelude (as PRO-², *oimē* song)]

prŏf *n.* (colloq.) professor. [abbr.]

Prof. *abbr.* Professor.

profa̅′ne¹ *v.t.* treat (sacred thing) with irreverence or disregard; violate, pollute, (what is entitled to respect); so **prŏfan**A′TION *n.* [ME *prophane* f. L *profanare* (as foll.)]

profa̅′ne² *a.* **1.** not belonging to what is sacred or biblical (*profane history, literature, writer*); not initiated into religious rites or any esoteric knowledge; (of rite etc.) heathen. **2.** irreverent, blasphemous; so **profa̅′nIty** *n.* **3.** Hence ∼LY² (-nlĭ) *adv.*, ∼NESS (-n-n-) *n.* [ME f. OF *prophane* or f. med. L *prophanus* f. L PRO¹(*fanus* f. *fanum* temple) before (i.e. outside) the temple, not sacred]

profe̅′ss *v.* **1.** *v.t.* lay claim to (quality, feeling), pretend (*to* be or do), (*they profess extreme regret; does not*

profess to be a scholar). **2.** openly declare (*they profess themselves quite content*). **3.** affirm one's faith in or allegiance to (religion, God, Christ); receive into religious order under vows. **4.** make (law, medicine, flute-playing, the flute, etc.) one's profession or business. **5.** teach (subject) as professor. **6.** *v.i.* perform duties of a professor. [ME, f. L PRO¹(*fĭtēri fess-* = *fatēri* confess) declare publicly]

profe̅′ss|ed (-st) *a.* self-acknowledged (*a professed Christian*); alleged, ostensible, whence ∼**ĕd**LY² *adv.*; claiming to be duly qualified (*a professed anatomist*); ∼**ed monk, nun**, (who has taken vows of religious order). [ME, p.p. of prec.]

profe̅′ssion (-shŏn) *n.* **1.** declaration, avowal, (*accept my sincere professions of regard*); declaration of belief in a religion; vow made on entering, fact of being in, a religious order. **2.** vocation or calling, esp. one that involves some branch of advanced learning or science (*the military profession; a carpenter by profession*); **the learned** ∼**s** (divinity, law, medicine); **the oldest** ∼, prostitution; hence ∼LESS *a.* **3.** body of persons engaged in a profession; **the** ∼, (Theatr. sl.) actors and actresses. [ME f. OF, f. L *professio -onis* (as PROFESS; see -ION)]

profe̅′ssional (-sho-) *a.* & *n.* **1.** *a.* of, belonging to, connected with, a profession, (*professional men, etiquette, jealousy*); ∼ *politician, agitator*, etc., (making a trade of politics etc.); ∼ *boxer, golfer, boxing, golf*, etc., (for monetary reward; opp. *amateur*); hence ∼LY² *adv.* **2.** *n.* professional person, esp. professional golfer etc. [f. prec. + -AL]

profe̅′ssional|ism (-sho-) *n.* qualities or typical features of a profession or professionals; so ∼IZE (3) *v.t.* [f. prec. + -ISM]

profe̅′ssor *n.* **1.** one who makes profession (esp. of a religion). **2.** teacher of high rank, esp. holder of a highest-rank or *senior teaching appointment in university (often as title: *Professor Smith*), whence ∼ATE¹ (1), ∼ESS¹ (arch.), **prŏfessŏr′iATE** (1), ∼SHIP, *ns.*, **prŏfessōr′IAL** *a.* **3.** professional teacher, sportsman, etc. [ME, f. OF *professeur* or f. L *professor* (as PROFESS; see -OR)]

prŏ′ffer *v.t.*, & *n.* **1.** *v.t.* (esp. in *p.p.*) offer (gift, services, hand, etc., arch. *to* do). **2.** *n.* (literary) offer, proposal. [ME; (n. f. AF *profre*) f. AF & OF *proffrir* f. PRO-¹, *offrir* OFFER¹)]

profı̆′cient (-shĕnt) *a.* & *n.* adept, expert, (*in* or *at* an art etc.; *in* doing); hence **profı̆′cien**CY (-shĕn-) *n.*, ∼LY² *adv.* [f. L (as PROFIT¹; see -ENT)]

prŏ′fı̆le *n.*, & *v.t.* **1.** *n.* drawing, silhouette, or other representation, of side view esp. of human face, whence **pro′fı̆l**IST (3) *n.*; *drawn* etc. **in** ∼, as seen from one side; outline (esp. of the human face) as seen from the side. **2.** short printed or broadcast biographical or character sketch; schematic description of person's interests for use in information retrieval etc. **3.** vertical cross-section of structure; curve of variation of a quantity along a cross-section (**keep a low** ∼, remain inconspicuous); flat outline piece of scenery on stage. **4.** *v.t.* represent in profile; give profile to. [(n. f. obs. It. *profilo*) f. obs. It. PRO¹(*filare* spin f. L *filare* f. *filum* thread)]

prŏ′fĭt¹ *n.* **1.** advantage, benefit, (*have studied it to my profit; no profit in such pursuits*). **2.** pecuniary gain, excess of returns over outlay, (*sold* **at a** ∼, for more than one paid to get it); ∼ **and loss account**, account in which gains are credited and losses debited so as to show net profit or loss at any time; ∼-**sharing** (of profits esp. between employer and employed); ∼-**taking**, sale of shares etc. at time when profit will accrue. **3.** Hence ∼LESS *a.* [ME f. OF, f. L *profectus* progress, profit f. PRO¹(*facere fect-* = *facere* do) advance]

prŏ′fĭt² *v.* **1.** *v.t.* (Of thing) bring advantage to (person etc.; *it will not profit him to act thus*). **2.** *v.i.* be of advantage; (of person etc.) be benefited or assisted (*hope to profit from your advice; profited by the confusion to make my escape*). [ME, f. OF *profiter* (as prec.)]

prŏ′fit|able *a.* beneficial, useful; yielding profit, lucrative, (*a profitable speculation*); hence ⌒ABI′LITY, ⌒able NESS (-beln-), *ns.,* ⌒ABLY *adv.* [ME f. OF (as prec.; see -ABLE)]

prŏfiteer′ *v.i.,* & *n.* **1.** *v.i.* (seek to) make excessive profits out of others' needs, esp. in times of scarcity. **2.** *n.* person who profiteers. [f. PROFIT¹ + -EER]

profi′terōle *n.* small hollow cake of choux pastry that may have sweet or savoury filling. [F, dim. of *profit* PROFIT¹]

prŏ′flig|ate *a.* & *n.* **1.** *a.* licentious, dissolute; recklessly extravagant; hence ⌒ACY *n.,* ⌒ately² (-tlĭ) *adv.* **2.** *n.* profligate person. [f. L *profligatus* dissolute, p.p. of PRO¹(*fligare = fligere* strike down) overthrow, ruin; see -ATE²]

prō fŏr′ma *adv., a.,* & *n.* **1.** *adv.* & *a.* (done) for form's sake. **2.** *a.* & *n.* ⌒ (**invoice**), invoice sent to purchaser in advance of goods, for completion of business formalities. [L]

profou′nd *a.* (⌒er, ⌒est) & *n.* **1.** *a.* having or showing great knowledge or insight (*profound statesman, inquiry, treatise*); demanding deep study or thought (*profound doctrines*). **2.** (Of state or quality) deep, intense, unqualified, (*fell into a profound sleep; take a profound interest; simulated a profound indifference*); (rhet.) having, coming from, extending to, a great depth, (*profound crevasses*); (of sigh) deep-drawn; (of disease) deep-seated. **3.** Hence or cogn. ⌒LY² *adv.,* ⌒NESS, **profŭ′nd**ITY, *ns.* **4.** *n.* (poet.) *the* vast depth (*of* ocean, futurity, the soul, etc.). [ME, f. AF, OF *profund, profond* f. L PRO¹(*fundus* bottom) deep]

profŭ′se *a.* lavish, extravagant, (*in* or *of* gifts, promises, expenditure, etc.); (of thing) exuberantly plentiful (*profuse bleeding, variety*); hence or cogn. ⌒LY² (-slĭ) *adv.,* ⌒NESS (-sn-), **profŭ′sION** (-zhon), *ns.* [ME, f. L *profusus* p.p. of PRO¹(*fundere fus-* pour)]

∥prŏg *n.,* & *v.t.* (-**gg**-). (sl.) **1.** *n.* proctor at Oxford or Cambridge. **2.** *v.t.* subject (undergraduate) to exercise of proctor's authority. [abbr.]

proge′nitive *a.* capable of or connected with the production of offspring. [as foll.; see -IVE]

proge′nit|or *n.* ancestor of person, animal, or plant; (fig.) political or intellectual predecessor, original of a copy; hence ⌒ŏr′IAL *a.,* ⌒orSHIP, ⌒rESS¹, **prŏge′ni**TRIX, *ns.* [ME, f. OF *progeniteur* f. L *progenitor -oris* f. PRO¹(*gignere genit-* beget); see -OR]

proge′niture *n.* (begetting of) offspring. [f. L as prec.; see -URE]

prŏ′genў *n.* offspring of person, animal, or plant; descendants; (fig.) issue, outcome. [ME, f. OF *progenie* f. L *progenies* f. PRO¹(*gignere* beget)]

proge′st|erōne *n.* (Physiol.) steroid sex hormone inhibiting ovulation during pregnancy; so ⌒oGEN *n.,* substance having physiological effects similar to those of progesterone. [f. *progestin* (PRO-² before, GESTATION, -IN) + *luteosterone* (CORPUS *luteum,* STEROL, -ONE)]

proglŏ′tt|is *n.* (*pl.* ⌒ides *pr.* -ĭdēz). propagative segment of tapeworm. [mod. L, f. Gk PRO²(*glōssis* f. *glōssa, glōtta* tongue), from its shape]

prŏgnath|ous (-ŏ′gna-, -nā′-) *a.* with projecting jaws; (of jaws) projecting; so **prŏgnă′th**IC *a.,* ⌒ISM (2) *n.* [f. PRO-² + Gk *gnathos* jaw + -OUS]

prŏgnō′s|is *n.* (*pl.* ⌒es *pr.* -ēz). prognostication, esp. (Med.) forecast of course of disease. [LL, f. Gk PRO²(*gnōsis* f. *gignōskō* know)]

prŏgnŏ′stic *n.* & *a.* **1.** *n.* advance indication, omen, (*of*); prediction, forecast. **2.** *a.* foretelling, predictive, (*of*). [n. ME, f. OF *pronostique* f. L f. Gk *prognōstikon* neut. (as n.) of *prognōstikos* f. PRO²(*gignōskō* learn), see -IC; a. f. med. L f. Gk *prognōstikos*]

prŏgnŏ′stic|āte *v.t.* foretell, foresee, (event, *that*); (of thing) betoken; hence or cogn. ⌒ABLE, ⌒atIVE, ⌒ātORY, *adjs.,* ⌒A′TION, ⌒ātOR, *ns.* [f. med. L *prognosticare* (as prec.) + -ATE³]

∥prŏ′grămme, (US & Computers) **prŏ′grăm,** *n.,* & *v.t.* **1.** *n.* descriptive notice of series of events, e.g. of course of study, play, concert, etc.; such series of

events (*a programme of lectures*); broadcast performance; definite plan of intended proceedings; ⌒ **music** (intended to suggest scenes or events). **2.** series of (coded) instructions to control operation of computer or other machine. **3.** Hence **prŏgrăm′mä′t**IC *a.* **4.** *v.t.* make programme or definite plan of; (-**mm**-, *-**m**-) express (problem) or instruct (computer) by means of program, whence ⌒m**ER**¹ *n.* [f. LL f. Gk *programma -atos* f. PRO²(*graphō* write) write publicly; sp. after F *programme*]

prŏ′grĕss¹ *n.,* & *v.t.* **1.** *n.* forward or onward movement in space (*made slow progress; continued his progress*); **in** ⌒, in course of occurrence, going on. **2.** advance or development esp. to better state (*made no progress in his studies; the progress of civilization; disease made rapid progress*); ⌒**-chaser**, person employed to check regular progress of manufacturing work; ⌒ **report**, account of progress made. **3.** ∥(arch.) State journey, official tour, esp. by royal person. **4.** *v.t.* cause (work etc.) to make regular progress. [ME, f. L *progressus* f. PRO¹(*gredi gress-* = *gradi* walk)]

progrĕ′ss² *v.i.* move forward or onward; be carried on (*the controversy, the building of the house, is progressing*); advance or develop esp. to better state (*we progress in knowledge; science progresses*). [f. prec.; readopted from US after becoming obs. in England in 17th c.]

progrĕ′ssion (-shon) *n.* progressing (*mode of progression*); succession, series; (Math.) ARITHMETICAL, GEOMETRICAL, HARMONIC, *progression*; (Mus.) passing from one note or chord to another; hence ⌒AL *a.* [ME f. OF, or f. L *progressio* (as PROGRESS¹; see -ION)]

progrĕ′ssionist (-sho-) *n.* advocate of or believer in progress e.g. in political or social matters; one who holds that life on earth has been marked by gradual progression to higher forms. [f. prec. + -IST]

progrĕ′ssive *a.* & *n.* **1.** *a.* moving forward (*progressive motion*); proceeding step by step, successive; (of card-game, dance, etc.) with periodic change of partners; (of taxation) at rates increasing with the sum taxed; (Gram., of tense) expressing action in progress (*am writing, was writing*). **2.** advancing in social conditions, character, efficiency, etc., (*a progressive nation*); (of disease, violence, etc.) continuously increasing in severity or extent; favouring rapid progress or reform (*progressive principles, party*), whence **progrĕ′ssiv**ISM (3) *n.*; (of education etc.) informal and without strict discipline, stressing individualism. **3.** Hence ⌒LY² (-vlĭ) *adv.,* ⌒NESS (-vn-) *n.* **4.** *n.* advocate of progressive policy. [f. F *progressif -ive* or f. med. L *progressivus* (as PROGRESS¹; see -IVE)]

pro hac vice (prō hahk vī′sĭ, vē′sĭ, vē′chĭ) *adv.* for this occasion (only). [L]

prohi′bit *v.t.* forbid, debar, (action, thing, person's doing, person *from* doing); prohibited DEGREES; hence ⌒ER¹, ⌒OR, *ns.* [ME, f. L PRO¹(*hibēre hibit-* = *habēre* hold)]

prōhibi′tion (-ōhĭb-, -ōĭb-) *n.* forbidding, being forbidden; edict or order that forbids; (esp. US Hist., **P**⌒) forbidding by law of the manufacture and sale of intoxicants, whence ⌒IST (2) *n.*; (Law) writ from superior court forbidding inferior court to proceed in suit deemed to be beyond its cognizance. [ME f. OF, or f. L *prohibitio* (as prec.; see -ION)]

prohi′bitive *a.* prohibiting; such as to prevent the use or abuse or purchase of a thing (*prohibitive tax; published at a prohibitive price*); hence or cogn. ⌒LY² (-vlĭ) *adv.,* ⌒NESS (-vn-) *n.,* **prohi′bit**ORY *a.* [f. F *prohibitif -ive* or f. L *prohibitivus* (as PROHIBIT; see -IVE), & f. PROHIBIT + -IVE]

projĕ′ct¹ *v.* **1.** *v.t.* plan, contrive, (scheme, course of action, etc.). **2.** cast, throw, impel, (body *into* space etc.); extrapolate (results *to* future time etc.); (Psych.) form projection of; go out of one*self into* another's feelings, the future, etc. **3.** cause (light, shadow) to fall on surface etc.; cause (image) to be visible *on* screen etc.; (fig.) cause (idea etc.) to take shape or become known. **4.** (Geom.) draw straight lines from a centre or parallel lines through every point of (given figure) to produce corresponding figure on a surface or line by intersecting it, draw (such lines), produce (such corresponding figure); make projection (sense 6) of (earth, sky, etc.). **5.** *v.i.* protrude, jut out. [ME, f. L PRO¹(*jicere ject-* = *jacĕre* throw)]

prŏ'jĕct² *n.* plan, scheme; planned undertaking, esp. by student(s) for presentation of results at specified time. [ME, f. L *projectum* neut. p.p. (as n.) of *projicere* (see prec.)]

projĕ'ctīle *a.* & *n.* **1.** *a.* impelling (*projectile force*); capable of being projected by force, esp. from gun. **2.** *n.* (*or* prŏ'jĭktīl). projectile missile. [f. mod. L *projectilis* a., *-ile* n., (as PROJECT¹; see -IL)]

projĕ'ction *n.* **1.** throwing; being thrown. **2.** presentation of image on screen etc.; hence ∾IST (3) *n.* **3.** planning; thing planned. **4.** protruding; thing that protrudes; thrusting forward. **5.** (Geom.) projecting of a figure (see PROJECT¹ 4); ∾ **of a point**, point in derived figure corresponding to point in original figure. **6.** representation on plane surface of (any part of) surface of earth or of celestial sphere, e.g. MERCATOR'S *projection*; **conical, cylindrical,** ∾ (with meridians first projected on cone, cylinder). **7.** mental image viewed as objective reality; (Psych.) unconscious transfer of one's own impressions or feelings to external objects or persons. [f. L *projectio* (as PROJECT¹; see -ION)]

projĕ'ctive *a.* **1.** (Geom.) of or derived by projection; (of a property of a figure) unchanged by projection; ∾ **geometry** (dealing with projective properties). **2.** mentally projecting or projected (*projective imagination*). **3.** Hence ∾LY² (-vlǐ) *adv.* [f. PROJECT¹ + -IVE]

projĕ'ctor *n.* **1.** one who forms a project; (arch.) promoter of speculative companies. **2.** apparatus for projecting rays of light or projecting image on screen. [f. PROJECT¹ + -OR]

prolă'pse¹ *v.i.* (Path.) slip forward or down out of place. [f. L PRO¹(*labi laps-* slip)]

prō'lăpse² *n.* (Path.) prolapsing of part or organ (esp womb or rectum). [f. foll.]

prolă'psus *n.* = prec. [mod. L, f. LL = fall (as PROLAPSE¹)]

prō'lāte *a.* (Geom., of spheroid) lengthened in direction of polar diameter (cf. OBLATE²); growing or extending in width; (fig.) widely spread; (Gram.) = foll.; hence ∾LY² (-tlǐ) *adv.* [L *prolatus* p.p. of PRO¹(*ferre* carry) prolong; see -ATE²]

prolă'tive *a.* (Gram.) serving to continue or complete predication, e.g. *go* (prolative infinitive) in *you may go.* [f. as prec. + -IVE]

prōle *a.* & *n.* (colloq.) proletarian. [abbr.]

prō'lĕg *n.* fleshy abdominal limb of caterpillar or other larva. [f. PRO-¹ + LEG]

prŏlĕgŏ'mĕn|on *n.* (usu. in *pl.* ∾a). preliminary discourse or matter prefixed to book etc., introduction; hence ∾ARY¹, ∾OUS, *adjs.* [L f. Gk, neut. pass. pres. part. of PRO²(*legō* say)]

prolĕ'ps|is *n.* (*pl.* ∾es *pr.* -ēz). anticipation; representation of thing as existing before it actually does or did so; (Gram.) anticipatory use of adjectives, as in *paint the town red*; so **prolĕ'ptic** *a.* [LL f. Gk *prolēpsis* f. PRO²(*lambanō* take) anticipate]

prŏlētā'r|ian *a.* & *n.* (member) of the proletariat; hence ∾ISM (2) *n.,* ∾IZE (3) *v.t.* [f. L *proletarius* one who served the State not with property but with offspring (*proles*); see -ARY¹, -AN]

prŏlētā'r'iat, -ate, *n.* (Rom. Hist., or derog.) of modern society) lowest class of community; (Econ.) wage-earners, esp. those without capital and dependent on daily labour for subsistence; **dictatorship of the** ∾, Communist ideal of domination by the proletariat after the suppression of capitalism and the bourgeoisie. [f. F *prolétariat* (as prec.; cf. -ATE¹)]

prŏli'fer|āte *v.* **1.** *v.i.* reproduce itself, grow, by multiplication of elementary parts; increase rapidly in numbers etc. **2.** *v.t.* produce (cells etc.) thus. **3.** So ∾A'TION *n.,* ∾ATIVE *a.* [back-form. (see -ATE³) f. *proliferation* f. F *prolifération* (*prolifère* as foll.; see -ATION)]

prŏli'ferous *a.* **1.** (Bot.) producing leaf or flower buds from leaf or flower; producing new individuals from buds etc. **2.** (Zool.) multiplying by budding. **3.** (Path.) spreading by proliferation. [f. L *proles* offspring + -I- + -FEROUS]

prŏli'fic *a.* producing (much) offspring; abundantly productive (*of*), abounding *in*; hence ∾ACY [irreg.], **prōlifi'cITY,** ∾NESS, *ns.* [f. med. L *prolificus* (as prec.; see -FIC)]

prolix (prō'lĭks, prolĭ'ks) *a.* lengthy, tediously wordy, (*prolix speech, writer*); hence *or* cogn. **prŏli'xITY** *n.,* ∾LY² *adv.* [ME, f. OF *prolixe* or f. L *prolixus* (as PRO-¹, *liquēre* be liquid) poured forth, extended]

prolŏcūtor (prō'lo-, prolŏ'-) *n.* chairman esp. of lower house of convocation of either province of Church of England; spokesman; hence ∾SHIP *n.* [ME f. L, f. PRO¹(*loqui locut-* speak); see -OR]

prŏ'logīze, -guīze (-gīz), **-īse** (-īz), *v.i.* write or speak a prologue. [f. med. L *prologizare* f. Gk *prologizō* speak prologue (as foll.), or f. foll. + -IZE]

prŏ'lŏgue (-g) *n.,* & *v.t.* **1.** *n.* preliminary discourse, poem, etc., esp. introducing play (cf. EPILOGUE); (fig.) act or event serving as introduction (*to*). **2.** *v.t.* introduce or furnish with a prologue. [ME *prolog* f. OF *prologue,* f. L f. Gk PRO²(*logos* speech)]

prolŏ'ng *v.t.* extend (action, condition, etc.) in duration; extend in spatial length; lengthen pronunciation of (syllable etc.); (in *p.p.*) lengthy, long continued; so **prōlŏnga'TION** (-ngg-) *n.* [ME, f. OF *prolonger* & f. LL PRO¹(*longare* f. *longus* long)]

prolu'|sion (-ū'zhon, -ōō'-) *n.* preliminary essay, article, or attempt; so ∾SORY *a.* [f. L *prolusio* f. PRO¹(*ludere lus-* play) practise beforehand; see -ION]

prŏm *n.* (colloq.) promenade (||concert). [abbr.]

prŏmena'd|e (-ah'd) *n.* & *v.* **1.** *n.* walk, ride, drive, taken for exercise, amusement, or display, or as social ceremony; place, esp. paved public walk (||at seaside), for this; *school or university ball or dance; ∾e **concert,** one at which (part of) audience is not seated and can move about; ∾e **deck,** an upper deck on a passenger ship, where passengers may promenade. **2.** *v.i.* make a promenade; hence ∾ER¹ *n.* (esp. at promenade concert). **3.** *v.t.* make a promenade through (place); lead (person) about a place esp. for display. [F (*se promener* walk, refl. of *promener* take for a walk; see -ADE)]

prōmē'thazine (-ēn) *n.* drug of antihistamine type. [f. PROPYL + dimethylamine + phenothiazine]

Promē'thēan *a.* of or like Prometheus in his skill or punishment. [f. Gk *Promētheus* (demigod in myth who stole fire from Olympus and taught men the use of it and various arts, and was punished by being chained to rock in Caucasus and preyed on by vulture) + -AN]

promē'thium *n.* (Chem.) radioactive metallic element of lanthanide series, artificially made. [f. Prometheus (as prec.) + -IUM]

prŏ'minence *n.* being prominent; prominent thing; (Astron.) cloud of incandescent gas projecting above sun's chromosphere. [obs. F, f. L *prominentia* jutting out (as foll.; see -ENCE)]

prŏ'min|ent *a.* jutting out, projecting; conspicuous; distinguished; hence *or* cogn. ∾ENCY *n.,* ∾entLY² *adv.* [f. L PRO¹(*minēre;* cf. EMINENT) jut out; see -ENT]

promi'scūous *a.* of mixed and indiscriminate composition or kinds; indiscriminate (*promiscuous massacre, hospitality*); (of person) having sexual relations not limited by marriage or cohabitation, (of sexual relations) of this kind; (colloq.) casual, carelessly irregular; hence **prŏmiscū'ITY** *n.,* ∾LY² *adv.* [f. L PRO¹(*miscuus* f. *miscēre* mix) + -OUS]

prŏ'mise¹ *n.* **1.** assurance given that one will do or not do something or will give or procure something (*a promise of help, to help*); BREACH¹ *of promise;* BREAK¹ one's *promise;* KEEP¹ one's *promise;* **land of** ∾, =

PROMISE²*d land*. **2.** (fig.) ground of expectation of future achievements or good results (*a book, writer, of great promise*). [ME, f. L *promissum* neut. p.p. (as n.) of PRO¹(*mittere* send) put forth, promise]

prŏ'mǐse² *v*. **1.** *v.t.* make (person) a promise to give or procure him (thing) (*I promise you a fair hearing*); make (person, or abs.) a promise (*to do, that* thing shall be done etc.; *cannot positively promise*); ∼ one**self**, look forward to (a pleasant time etc.); (colloq.) assure (*I promise you, it will not be so easy*); (fig.) afford expectation of (*these discussions promise future storms*), seem likely (*to do*). **2.** *v.i.* ∼ **well** etc., hold out good etc. prospect. **3.** ∼**d land,** Canaan (Gen. 12:7 etc.), heaven, any place of expected felicity. **4.** Hence **prŏ'mǐsER¹** *n.*, (esp. Law) **prŏmǐsEE´, prŏ'mǐsOR,** *ns.* [ME, f. prec.]

prŏ'mǐsing *a.* likely to turn out well, hopeful, full of promise, (*promising boy, sky, beginning*); hence ∼LY² *adv.* [f. prec. + -ING²]

prŏ'mǐssŏry *a.* conveying or implying a promise; full of promise (*of*); ∼ **note,** signed document containing written promise to pay stated sum to specified person or to bearer at specified date or on demand. [f. med. L *promissorius* f. L *promissor* (as PROMISE¹; see -ORY)]

prŏ'montŏry *n.* point of high land jutting out into sea etc., headland; (Anat.) prominence or protuberance in the body. [f. med. L *promontorium* alt. (after *mons montis* mountain) f. L *promunturium* (perh. f. PRO-¹, *mons*); see -ORY]

promō'te *v.t.* advance (person *to* position or higher office); help forward, encourage, (process, result), support actively the passing of (law); initiate (project), take necessary steps for passing of (private act of parliament); publicize and sell (product); (Chess) raise (pawn) to rank of queen etc. when it reaches opponent's end of board; hence or cogn. **promō'tiON** *n.*, **promō'tionAL, promō'tiVE,** *adjs.* [ME, f. L PRO¹(*movēre* mot- move)]

promō'ter *n.* In vbl senses; (**company**) ∼, one who promotes formation of joint-stock company; one who is financially responsible for sporting event, theatrical production, etc. [earlier *promotour* f. AF, f. med. L *promotor* (as prec.; see -OR)]

prŏmpt¹ *a., adv., & n.* **1.** *a.* ready in action, acting with alacrity; made, done, etc., readily or at once (*prompt reply, decision, payment*); hence or cogn. **∼'ĭTUDE, ∼'NESS,** *ns.,* **∼'LY²** *adv.* **2.** (Of payment) made forthwith; (of goods) for immediate delivery and payment (*prompt iron*). **3.** *adv.* punctually (*at six o'clock prompt*). **4.** *n.* time limit for payment of account, stated on ∼**-note.** [ME f. OF, or f. L *promptus* p.p. of *promere* prompt- produce (PRO-¹, *emere* take)]

prŏmpt² *v.t., & n.* **1.** *v.t.* incite, move, (person etc. *to* action, *to* do); help (actor, reciter, or abs.) by supplying the words that come next, assist (hesitating speaker) with suggestion; inspire, give rise to, (feeling, thought, action); hence ∼'ING¹ *n.* **2.** *n.* thing said to help the memory esp. of actor; ∼**-book,** copy of play for prompter's use; ∼**-box** (on stage, occupied by prompter); ∼ **side** of stage (usu. to actor's left). [ME, f. med. L *promptare, f. L promptus (see prec.)]

prŏ'mpter *n.* one who prompts, esp. (Theatr.) person placed out of sight of audience who prompts actors. [ME (as prec., -ER¹)]

prŏ'mulg|āte *v.t.* make known to the public, disseminate (creed etc.), proclaim (decree, news); hence or cogn. ∼A´TION, ∼ātOR, *ns.* [f. L *promulgare* (as PRO-¹, *mulgēre* milk, cause to come forth) + -ATE²]

prŏmŭ'lge *v.t.* (arch.) = prec. [f. as prec.]

pronā'|ŏs *n.* (pl. ∼oi). (Gk Ant.) space in front of body of temple, enclosed by portico and projecting side walls. [L, f. Gk PRO²(NAOS) hall of a temple]

prŏ'n|āte *v.t.* put (hand, foreleg) into prone position (cf. SUPINATE); so ∼A´TION *n.*, ∼ā'tOR *n.* (esp. muscle effecting this). [back-form. f. *pronation* (as foll.; see -ATION); see -ATE³]

prōne *a.* **1.** having front or ventral part downwards,

(of hand) with palm downwards, lying face downwards (cf. SUPINE); lying flat, prostrate; (arch.) with downward slope or direction; hence ∼'LY² (-nlĭ) *adv.* **2.** disposed, liable, (*to* usu. bad quality, action, or condition; *to* do); (in *comb.*) more than usually likely to suffer (*accident-prone person; strike-prone industries*). **3.** Hence ∼'NESS (-n-n-) *n.* [ME, f. L *pronus* (*pro* forwards)]

proneur (prōnēr´) *n.* extoller, flatterer. [f. F *prôneur* (*prôner* eulogize f. *prône* place in church where addresses were delivered)]

prŏng *n., & v.t.* **1.** *n.* each of two or more projecting pointed parts at end of fork, whence (-)∼ED² (-ngd) *a.* (**three-∼ed attack**, on three separate points at once); ∼**-buck, -horn, -horn(ed) antelope,** N. Amer. deerlike ruminant (*Antilocapra americana*). **2.** *v.t.* pierce, stab, turn up (soil etc.), with fork. [ME; also *prang*, perh. rel. to MLG *prange* pinching instrument]

pronŏ'minal *a.* of (the nature of) a pronoun; hence ∼IZE (3) *v.t.*, ∼LY² *adv.* [f. LL *pronominalis* f. L PRO¹(*nomen nominis* noun); see -AL]

prŏ'noun *n.* **1.** word used instead of (proper or other) noun to designate (without naming) person or thing already mentioned or known from context or forming the subject of inquiry; pronominal adjective. **2.** **demonstrative ∼** (*this, that*); **distributive ∼** (*each, either,* etc.); **impersonal** or **indefinite ∼** (*any, some, anyone, something,* etc.); **interrogative ∼** (*who?, what?, which?*); **personal ∼** (*I, we, thou, you, he, she, it, they; me us,* etc.); **possessive ∼,** adjective representing possessive case (*my, her, our,* etc.), with absolute forms *mine, hers, ours,* etc.); **reciprocal ∼** (*one another,* etc.); **reflexive ∼** (*myself, oneself,* etc.); **relative ∼** (*who, what, which, that*). [f. PRO-¹ + NOUN, after F *pronom,* L *pronomen* transl. Gk *antōnumia* (as ANTI-, *onuma* name)]

pronou'nce *v.* **1.** *v.t.* utter, deliver, (judgement, sentence, curse, etc.) formally or solemnly; state, declare, as being in one's opinion, (*apples were pronounced excellent; cannot pronounce him (or that he is) out of danger*); hence ∼MENT (-sm-) *n.* **2.** utter, speak, (words, or abs.; *pronounce more distinctly*), esp. with reference to different ways (*how do you pronounce 'fulsome'?; cannot pronounce French*); hence ∼ABLE (-sa-) *a.* **3.** *v.i.* pass judgement, give one's opinion, (*on, for, against, in favour of*). [ME, f. OF *pronuncier* f. L PRO¹-(*nuntiare* announce f. *nuntius* messenger)]

pronou'nced (-st) *a.* In vbl senses; strongly marked, decided, (*pronounced tendency, flavour*); hence **pronou'ncèd**LY² *adv.* [p.p. of prec.]

pronou'ncing *n.* In vbl senses; ∼ **dictionary** (in which pronunciation is the thing chiefly indicated). [f. PRONOUNCE + -ING¹]

prŏ'nto *adv.* (sl.) promptly, quickly. [Sp., f. L (as PROMPT¹)]

pronŭnciamě'nto *n.* (*pl.* ∼s). proclamation, manifesto, esp. (in Spanish-speaking countries) one issued by insurrectionists; pronouncement. [f. Sp. *pronunciamiento* (*pronunciar* f. L as PRONOUNCE; see -MENT)]

pronŭncĭā'tion *n.* way in which a word is pronounced; a person's way of pronouncing words (*his pronunciation is often faulty*). [ME, f. OF *prononciation* or f. L *pronuntiatio* (as PRONOUNCE; see -ATION)]

proof¹ *n., & v.t.* **1.** *n.* fact or evidence or argument sufficing or helping to establish a fact (*this requires no proof; as (a) proof of his esteem; proof POSITIVE of his intention or that he intended*), whence ∼LESS *a.*; spoken or written legal evidence. **2.** proving, demonstration, (*not capable of proof; in proof of my assertion*). **3.** (Sc. Law). trial before judge instead of by jury. **4.** test, trial, (*must be brought to the proof; will stand a severe proof; the proof of the pudding is in the eating*); ∼**-plane,** small flat conductor on insulating handle for measuring electrification of a body. **5.** standard of strength of distilled alcoholic liquors (∼ **spirit,** alcohol-water mixture having this standard strength; **above ∼,**

For other words in *pro-* **see** PRO-.

stronger than this). **6.** (Print.) trial impression taken from type or film, for making corrections etc.; ∼--reader, -reading, (person employed in) reading and correcting proofs; so ∼-*read* v.t.; ∼-**sheet,** sheet of proof. **7.** photographic print made for selection etc. **8.** each of a limited number of careful impressions made from engraved plate before printing of ordinary issue and usu. (also ∼ *before letters*) before inscription is added; **artist's, engraver's,** ∼ (taken for examination or alteration by him); **signed** ∼, early proof signed by artist. **9.** v.t. make proof of (printed work, engraving, etc.). [ME *prōf prōve,* earlier *prēf* etc. f. OF *proeve, prueve* f. LL *proba* f. L *probare* (see PROVE)]
prōof[2] a., & v.t. **1.** a. (Of armour) of tried strength; impervious to penetration or undesired action (*proof against the severest weather, the pricks of conscience*); able to resist or withstand damage or destruction (esp. in comb.: *bomb, bullet, burglar,* CHILD, *pilfer, sound, splinter, -proof;* FOOL[1]*proof,* WATER[1]*proof*). **2.** v.t. make (thing) proof, esp. make (fabric etc.) waterproof, (also in comb.: *sound-proof,* WATER[1]*proof*). [a. f. prec., app. by ellipsis f. phr. *of proof* = proved to be impenetrable; v. f. a., or f. prec.]
prŏp[1] n. & v. (-**pp**-). **1.** n. rigid support, esp. one not forming structural part of thing supported, e.g. pole; = CLOTHES-*prop;* (fig.) person etc. who upholds institution etc., (Rugby Footb.) forward at either end of front row of scrum; (esp. Austral., of horse) action of propping. **2.** v.t. support (as) by prop (lit. or fig.); hold *up* thus. **3.** v.i. (Esp. Austral., of horse etc.) come to a dead stop with forelegs rigid. [ME, prob. f. MDu. *proppe;* v. f. n., or f. MLG, MDu. *proppen*]
prŏp[2] n. (colloq.) = PROPERTY 2; (in *pl.*) property--man. [abbr.]
prŏp[3] n. (colloq.) aircraft propeller; ∼-*jet,* turbo--prop. [abbr.]
prop. abbr. proposition.
prōpaedeu′tic a. & n. (subject or study) serving as introduction to higher study; (in *pl.*) preliminary learning; hence ∼AL a. [f. PRO-[2]+*paedeutics* science of education (f. Gk *paideutikos* of teaching), after Gk *propaideuō* teach beforehand]
prōpagā′nda n. **1.** association or organized scheme for propagation of a doctrine or practice; (usu. derog.) doctrines, information, etc., thus propagated. **2.** (RC Ch.) (**Congregation** or **College of) the P**∼, committee of cardinals in charge of foreign missions. [It., f. mod. L *congregatio de propaganda fide* congregation for propagation of the faith]
prōpagā′nd∥ist n. member or agent of a propaganda; one who disseminates propaganda; so ∼ISM (1) n., ∼i′stic a., ∼IZE (2, 4) v.i. & t. [f. prec.+-IST]
prō′pag∥āte v. **1.** v.t. multiply specimens of (plant, animal, disease, etc.) by natural process from parent stock; (of plant, animal, etc.) reproduce (it*self*). **2.** hand down (quality etc.) from one generation to another. **3.** disseminate, diffuse, (statement, belief, practice). **4.** extend the operation of, transmit, (vibration, earthquake, etc.). **5.** v.i. undergo propagation. **6.** Hence or cogn. ∼A′TION, ∼ātor, n., ∼ātive a. [f. L *propagare* multiply plants from layers, f. PRO[1](*pago* f. root of *pangere* fix, layer)+-ATE[3]]
prō′pāne n. (Chem.) hydrocarbon of the paraffin series, C₃H₈. [f. PROPIONIC+-ANE]
prōparŏ′xȳtŏne a. & n. (Gk Gram.) (word) with acute accent on last syllable but two. [f. Gk PRO[2]-(*paroxutonos* PAROXYTONE)]
propĕ′l v.t. (-**ll**-). drive or push forward, give onward motion to, (lit. or fig.); ∼**ling pencil** (with lead moved forward by turning outer case). [ME, = 'expel', f. L PRO[1](*pellere puls-* drive)]
propĕ′llant n. propelling agent; explosive that propels bullet or shell from firearm; substance used as reagent in rocket engine to provide thrust. [f. prec. +-ANT]
propĕ′llent a. propelling, propulsive. [f. PROPEL +-ENT]

propĕ′ller n. In vbl senses; revolving shaft with blades (usu. SCREW-*propeller*), for propelling ship or aircraft; ∼ **shaft** (transmitting power from engine to propeller or to driven wheels of motor vehicle); ∼ **turbine,** turbo-propeller. [f. PROPEL+-ER[1]]
propĕ′nsitȳ n. inclination or tendency (*to* condition, quality, thing, *to* do, *for* doing). [f. *propense* f. L *propensus* inclined, p.p. of PRO[1](*pendēre* hang)+-ITY]
prō′per a. & n. **1.** a. (arch., usu. w. possessive pron.) own (*with my* (*own*) *proper eyes*). **2.** ∼ **motion,** (Astron.) the part of the apparent motion of a fixed star etc. that is due to its actual movement in space relative to the sun. **3.** belonging or relating exclusively or distinctively (*to*); ∼ **psalms, lessons,** (appointed for particular day). **4.** ∼ **noun** or **name,** (Gram.) name used to designate an individual person, animal, town, ship, etc. (e.g. *Jane, Neddy, London, Victory*). **5.** accurate, correct, (*in the proper sense of the word*). **6.** (usu. placed after n.) strictly so called, real, genuine, (*within the sphere of architecture proper*); ∼ **fraction** (less than unity, with numerator less than denominator). **7.** (colloq.) thorough, complete, (*there will be a proper row about this*). **8.** (arch., of person). handsome, comely. **9.** fit, suitable, right, (*choose the proper time; do it the proper way*). **10.** in conformity with demands of society, decent, respectable, (*she is so distressingly proper; would it be quite proper?*). **11.** (Her.) in the natural, not conventional, colours (*a peacock proper*). **12.** n. (Eccl.) service used for one particular occasion. [ME f. OF *propre* f. L *proprius* one's own, special]
prōpĕrĭspō′mĕn∥on a. & n. (*pl.* ∼a). (Gk Gram.) (word) with circumflex accent on last syllable but one. [Gk (as PRO-[2], PERISPOMENON]
prō′perlȳ adv. fittingly, suitably, (*do it properly or not at all*); accurately, correctly, (*properly speaking*); rightly, duly, (*he very properly refused*); with decency or good manners (*behave properly*); (colloq.) thoroughly (*puzzled him properly*). [f. PROPER+-LY[2]]
prō′pertied (-ĭd) a. having a (landed) property. [f. foll. +-ED[2]]
prō′pertȳ n. **1.** owning, being owned, (*property has its duties*); thing owned, possession(s), esp. real estate, (*the book is his property; regards him as her exclusive property; a man of* (*great*) *property*); **common** ∼, (fig.) = COMMON[1] *knowledge;* PERSONAL, REAL[2], *property;* ∼ **qualification** (based on possession of property); ∼ **tax** (levied directly on property). **2.** article other than costume, furniture, etc., used on theatre stage or in film; ∼-**man, -master,** man in charge of such articles. **3.** attribute, quality, characteristic, (*the properties of soda; has the property of dissolving grease*); (Logic) quality common to a whole class but not necessary to distinguish it from others. [ME, f. AF *propreté,* OF *proprieté* f. L *proprietas -tatis* (as PROPER; see -TY[1])]
prō′phecȳ n. faculty of a prophet (*the gift of prophecy*); prophetic utterance; foretelling of future events. [ME, f. OF *profecie* f. LL f. Gk *prophēteia* (as PROPHET; see -CY)]
prō′phes∥ȳ v. **1.** v.i. speak as a prophet; foretell future events; (arch.) expound the Scriptures. **2.** v.t. foretell (event, *that, who,* etc.). **3.** Hence ∼ĬER[1] n. [ME, f. OF *profecier* (as prec.)]
prō′phĕt n. **1.** inspired teacher, revealer or interpreter of God's will; prophetical writer or writing in OT (**major** ∼s, Isaiah, Jeremiah, Ezekiel, Daniel; **minor** ∼s, Hosea to Malachi, whose surviving writings are not lengthy), whence ∼ISM (3) n.; **the P**∼, (1) Muhammad, (2) Joseph Smith, founder of Mormons, or one of his successors. **2.** spokesman, advocate, (*of* principle etc.); one who foretells events (*am no weather-prophet*); (sl.) tipster. **3.** Hence ∼ESS[1], ∼HOOD (-t-h-), ∼SHIP, n. [ME, f. OF *prophete* f. L *propheta, prophetes* f. Gk PRO[2](*phētēs* speaker f. *phēmi* speak) spokesman]
prophĕ′tic a. of a prophet; predicting, containing a prediction *of* (event etc.); hence ∼AL a., ∼ALLY adv.,

∼ism (2, 4) *n.* [f. F *prophétique* or f. LL f. Gk *prophētikos* (as prec.; see -IC)]

prŏphўlǎc'tĭc *a.* & *n.* (medicine or course of action) tending to prevent disease or other misfortune. [f. F *prophylactique* f. Gk *prophulaktikos* f. PRO²(*phulassō* guard)]

prŏphўlǎ'xĭs *n.* (*pl.* ∼es *pr.* -ēz). preventive treatment against disease etc. [mod. L, f. PRO-²+Gk *phulaxis* a guarding, after prec.]

propĭ'nquitў *n.* nearness in place; close kinship; similarity. [ME f. OF *propinquité* or f. L *propinquitas* (*propinquus* near f. *prope* near to; see -ITY)]

prōpĭŏ'nĭc *a.* ∼ acid, colourless sharp-smelling liquid (C₂H₅COOH) found in wood-distillation products; hence PRO-²+Gk *piōn* fat, as being first in series of 'true' fatty acids]

propĭ'tiāte (-shĭ-) *v.t.* appease (offended person etc.). [f. L *propitiare* (as PROPITIOUS)+-ATE³]

propĭtiā'tion (-shĭ-) *n.* appeasement; (esp. Christ's) atonement; (arch.) gift etc. meant to propitiate (*Christ is the propitiation for our sins*). [ME, f. LL *propitiatio* (as prec.; see -ATION)]

propĭ'tiator|ў (-sha-) *a.* & *n.* 1. *a.* serving or intended to propitiate (*a propitiatory smile*); hence ∼ĭLY² *adv.* 2. *n.* the mercy-seat (esp. fig. of Christ). [ME, f. eccl. L *propitiatorius* (as PROPITIATE; see -ORY)]

propĭ'tious (-shŭs) *a.* well-disposed, favourable, (*the fates were propitious*); (of omen etc.) favourable; (of weather, occasion, etc.) suitable *for*, favourable *to*, (purpose); hence ∼LY² *adv.* [ME, f. OF *propicieus* or f. L *propitius*; see -OUS]

prŏ'polis *n.* red or brown resinous substance got by bees from buds for use as glue etc. [L, f. Gk PRO²(*polis* city) suburb, bee-glue]

propō'nent *a.* & *n.* (person) that puts forward a motion, theory, or proposal. [f. L *proponere* (as PROPOUND; see -ENT)]

propôr'tion *n.*, & *v.t.* 1. *n.* comparative part, share, (*a large proportion of the earth's surface, of the profits*); comparative relation, ratio, (*the proportion of births to the population*); *price will be raised in* ∼ (*to the cost* etc., or abs.), by the same factor. 2. correct relation of one thing to another or between parts of a thing (*windows are in admirable proportion*; *his success bore no proportion to his abilities*; *exaggerated out of all proportion*); hence ∼LESS *a.* 3. (in *pl.*) dimensions, size, (*athlete, building, of magnificent proportions*). 4. (Math.) equality of ratios between two pairs of quantities (*3, 5, 9, and 15 are in proportion*; set of such quantities, (Arith.) RULE of three; DIRECT², INVERSE, *proportion.* 5. *v.t.* make (thing etc.) proportionate *to* (*must proportion the punishment to the crime*); hence (-)∼ED¹ (-shond) *a.*, ∼MENT *n.* [ME; n. f. OF, or f. L PRO¹(*portio* portion), v. f. OF *proporcioner* or f. med. L *proportionare* f. L *proportio*]

propôr'tion|al *a.* & *n.* 1. *a.* in due proportion, corresponding in degree or amount, (*a proportional increase in the expense*; *resentment proportional to his injuries*); ∼al representation, electoral system such that all parties are represented in proportion to their voting strength; hence or cogn. ∼ABLE, ∼ATE², *adjs.*, ∼ABLY, ∼ALLY, ∼ateLY² (-tlĭ), *advs.*, ∼ǎ'ITY *n.* 2. *n.* one of the terms of a proportion (*5, 3, 10, 6 are proportionals*; *6 is a mean proportional between 3 and 12*). [ME, f. LL *proportionalis* (as prec.; see -AL)]

propôr'tionalist *n.* advocate of proportional representation. [f. prec.+-IST]

propō'sal (-z-) *n.* act of proposing something; offer of oneself as partner in marriage (*have had a proposal*); course of action etc. proposed (*the proposal was never carried out*). [f. foll.+-AL]

propō's|e (-z) *v.* 1. *v.t.* put forward for consideration, propound; set up as an aim (*the object I propose to myself*); nominate (person) as member of society etc.; offer (person's health, person) as subject for drinking of toast; put forward as a plan (*we propose* (the making of) *a change, that a change should be made*); intend,

purpose, (*to do, doing*). 2. *v.i.* make proposal (*man proposes, God disposes*); offer oneself as partner in marriage (*to*). 3. Hence ∼ER¹ *n.* [ME, f. OF *proposer* f. L *proponere* (as PROPOUND)]

propŏsĭ'tion (-z-) *n.*, & *v.t.* 1. *n.* statement, assertion; (Logic) form of words consisting of subject and predicate; (Math.) formal statement of theorem or problem, often including the demonstration; hence ∼AL *a.* 2. proposal, scheme proposed; (sl.) problem, undertaking, opponent, prospect, etc., that is to be dealt with (*a difficult, a paying, proposition*; not a ∼, unlikely to succeed). 3. *v.t.* (colloq.) make proposal (esp. of sexual intercourse) to. [ME f. OF, or f. L *propositio* (as foll.; see -ITION)]

propou'nd *v.t.* offer for consideration, propose, (question, problem, scheme, matter, etc., *to* person); produce (will etc.) before proper authority so as to establish its legality; hence ∼ER¹ *n.* [earlier *propoune*, *propone* f. L PRO¹(*ponere posit-* place); cf. *compound*, *expound*]

prōprae'tor, *prōprē'tor, *n.* (Rom. Hist.) ex-praetor with authority of praetor in province not under military control. [L, earlier *pro praetore* (one acting) for praetor]

proprī'etary *a.* of a proprietor (*proprietary rights*); holding property (*the proprietary classes*); held in private ownership; ∼ colony, (Hist.) N. Amer. colony granted by Crown to particular person; ∼ medicines (manufacture and sale of which is restricted by patent etc.); ∼ name or term (use of which is restricted by being trade mark etc.). [f. LL *proprietarius* (as PROPERTY; see -ARY¹)]

proprī'et|or *n.* holder of property, owner esp. of a business; hence ∼ôr'IAL *a.*, ∼orSHIP, ∼rESS¹, *ns.* *proprietary* n. f. as prec.]

proprī'etў *n.* fitness, rightness, (*doubt the propriety of the term, of refusing him*); correctness of behaviour or morals; (in *pl.*) details of correct conduct (*must observe the proprieties*). [ME, = 'ownership, peculiarity', f. OF *propriété* PROPERTY]

prōprioce'ptive *a.* (Biol.) relating to stimuli produced and perceived within an organism. [f. L *proprius* own+-o-+RECEPTIVE]

prŏptō's|is *n.* (*pl.* ∼es *pr.* -ēz). (Path.) prolapse, protrusion, esp. of eye. [LL, f. Gk *proptōsis* f. PRO²-(*piptō* fall)]

propŭ'ls|ion (-shon) *n.* driving or pushing forward; (fig.) impelling influence; so ∼IVE *a.* [f. obs. *propulse* v. f. L *propulsare* frequent. of *propellere* PROPEL]

prŏ'pўl *n.* (Chem.) radical, C₃H₇, derived from propane. [f. PROPIONIC+-YL]

prŏpўlae'|um *n.* (*pl.* ∼a). entrance to temple; the P∼a, entrance to Acropolis at Athens. [L, f. Gk PRO²(*pulaion* f. *pulē* gate)]

prŏ'pўl|ŏn *n.* (*pl.* ∼ons or ∼a). = prec. [L, f. Gk PRO²(*pulon* f. *pulē* gate)]

pro rata (prō rah'ta, rā'-) *adv.* & *a.* proportional(ly). [L, = according to the rate]

prōrā'te *v.t.* allocate or distribute *pro rata*. [f. prec.]

pro re nata (prō rē nā'ta, rā nah'-) *adv.* & *a.* for an occasion that has arisen. [L, = for the affair born]

prorŏ'gue (-g) *v.* 1. *v.t.* discontinue meetings of (parliament etc.) without dissolving it. 2. *v.i.* (Of parliament etc.) be prorogued. 3. So **prōroga'TION** *n.* [ME *proroge* f. OF *proroger, -guer* f. L PRO¹(*rogare* ask) prolong]

pros- *pref.* to, towards, in addition. [Gk (*pros* prep.)]

prosā'ĭc (proz-, prō-) *a.* like prose, lacking poetic beauty; unromantic, commonplace, dull, (*a prosaic life, person, view of things*); hence **prosā'ICALLY** (-z-) *adv.*, ∼NESS *n.* [f. F *prosaïque* or f. LL *prosaicus* (as PROSE; see -IC)]

prŏ'sā|ist (-zā-) *n.* prose-writer; prosaic person; so ∼ISM (4) *n.* [f. F *prosaïste* f. L *prosa* PROSE; see -IST]

prosce'ni|um (prō-, pro-) *n.* (*pl.* ∼ums or ∼a). (Theatr.) part of stage in front of drop or curtain, esp. with the enclosing arch; stage of ancient theatre. [L, f. Gk PRO²(*skēnion* f. *skēnē* stage)]

For other words in *pro-* see PRO-.

prŏsciu'ttō (-shoō'-) *n.* (*pl.* ~**s**). spiced ham. [It.]

proscrī'be *v.t.* put (person) outside protection of law; banish, exile, (esp. fig.); reject, denounce, (practice etc.) as dangerous etc.; so **proscri'ption** *n.*, **pro-scri'ptive** *a.* [f. L PRO¹(*scribere script-* write)]

prōse (-z) *n.* **1.** *n.* ordinary non-metrical form of written or spoken language (*Milton's prose works*); passage of this for translation etc.; (Eccl.) = SEQUENCE 5; *prose* IDYLL, POEM, POETRY. **2.** plain matter-of-fact quality (*the prose of existence*); tedious discourse. **3.** *v.i.* talk tediously (*about* etc.); hence **prō'sER¹** (-z-) *n.* **4.** *v.t.* turn (poem etc.) into prose. [ME f. OF, f. L *prosa* (*oratio*) straightforward (discourse), fem. of *prosus*, earlier *prorsus* direct]

prosĕ'ctor *n.* one who dissects dead bodies in preparation for anatomical lecture etc. [LL, = anatomist, f. PRO¹(*secare sect-* cut), perh. after F *prosecteur*]

prŏ'sécūte *v.t.* follow up, pursue, (inquiry, studies); carry on (trade, pursuit); institute legal proceedings against (person) or with reference to (claim, crime, etc.), or abs., (*trespassers will be prosecuted*; *shall not prosecute*). [ME, f. L PRO¹(*sequi secut-* follow)]

prŏsĕcū'tion *n.* prosecuting (*of* pursuit etc.); (Law) institution and carrying on of criminal charge before court; carrying on of legal proceedings against person; prosecuting party (*the prosecution denied this*); ‖**director of public** ~**s**, public PROSECUTOR. [OF, or f. LL *prosecutio* (as prec.; see -ION)]

prŏ'sécūtor *n.* one who prosecutes esp. in criminal court; **public** ~, law officer conducting criminal proceedings on behalf of State or in public interest; so **prŏ'sécū'trix** *n.* [f. PROSECUTE or f. med. L *prosecutor* (as PROSECUTE); see -OR]

prŏ'selÿt|e *n.*, & *v.t.* **1.** *n.* person converted from one opinion, creed, or party, to another; Gentile convert to Jewish faith. **2.** *v.t.* *make a proselyte of (person, or abs.). **3.** Hence ~ISM (1, 2) *n.*, ~IZE (3) (-lī-) *v.t.* (often abs.). [ME, f. LL *proselytus* f. Gk PROS(*ēluthos* f. st. *ēluth-* of *erkhomai* come) stranger, convert]

prŏsĕ'nchým|a (-ngk-) *n.* (Bot.) tissue of elongated cells placed with their ends interpenetrating, esp. fibro-vascular tissue; hence ~AL, ~atous (-ngkī'm-), *adjs.* [f. Gk *pros* toward + *egkhuma* infusion, after *parenchyma*]

prŏ'sĭfÿ (-z-) *v.* **1.** *v.t.* turn into prose; make prosaic. **2.** *v.i.* write prose. [f. PROSE + -I- + -FY]

prosit (prō'sĭt) *int.* in drinking person's health etc. [G f. L, = may it benefit]

prŏ'sod|ÿ *n.* science of versification, laws of METRE¹; study of speech-rhythms; hence **prosŏ'dıc** *a.*, ~IST (3) *n.* [ME, f. L *prosodia* accent f. Gk PROS(*ōidia* as ODE)]

prŏsōpō'graph|ÿ (-so-, -so-) *n.* description of person's appearance, personality, social and family connections, and career; study of such descriptions; hence ~ER¹ *n.*, **prŏsōpŏgrä'ph|ıc**(AL) *adjs.* [f. mod. L *prosopographia* f. Gk *prosōpon* face, person (see -GRAPHY)]

prŏsōpopoe'ia (-pē'a) *n.* rhetorical introduction of pretended speaker or personification of abstract thing. [L, f. Gk *prosōpopoiia* (*prosōpon* person, *poieō* make)]

prŏ'spĕct¹ *n.* **1.** extensive view of landscape etc. (*a fine, striking, prospect*); mental view of matters (*opened a new prospect to his mind*). **2.** expectation, what one expects, (*offers a gloomy prospect*; *his prospects were brilliant*; *no developments in prospect*); hence ~LESS *a.* **3.** (Mining). place giving expectations of mineral deposit; sample of ore for testing; resulting yield. **4.** possible or probable customer, subscriber, etc. [ME, f. L PRO-SPECTUS]

prospĕ'ct² *v.* **1.** *v.i.* explore region (*for* gold etc.), whence ~OR *n.*; (fig.) look out *for*, (of mine) promise (*well, ill*). **2.** *v.t.* explore (region) for gold etc., work (mine) experimentally; (of mine) promise (specified yield). [f. prec.]

prospĕ'ctive *a.* concerned with or applying to the

future (cf. RETROSPECTIVE; *the law was held to be exclusively prospective, implies a prospective obligation*); expected, future, some day to be, (*prospective peer, bridegroom, profit*); hence ~LY² (-vlǐ) *adv.*, ~NESS (-vn-) *n.* [f. obs. F *prospectif -ive* or f. LL *prospectivus* (as foll.; see -IVE)]

prospĕ'ctus *n.* printed document describing chief features of school, commercial enterprise, forthcoming book, etc. [L, = prospect, f. PRO¹(*spicere spect-* = *specere* look)]

prŏ'sper *v.* **1.** *v.i.* succeed, thrive, (*cheats never prosper*; *nothing will ever prosper in his hands*). **2.** *v.t.* make successful (*Heaven prosper our attempt*). [ME, f. OF *prosperer* or f. L *prosperare* (as foll.)]

prŏ'sperous *a.* flourishing, successful, thriving, (*a prosperous merchant, enterprise*); hence or cogn. **prŏspĕ'rıty** *n.*, ~LY² *adv.* **2.** auspicious (*a prosperous wind*; *in a prosperous hour*). [ME, f. obs. F *prospereus* f. L *prosper(us)*; see -OUS]

prŏstaglă'ndin *n.* any of a group of fatty acids causing contraction of muscles in mammalian (esp. uterine) tissues. [G, f. foll. + GLAND¹ + -IN]

prŏ'stāte *n.* ~ (**gland**), large gland round neck of bladder, accessory to male genital organs, or one of several similar glands in other mammals; hence **prostā'tıc** *a.* [F, f. mod. L *prostata* f. Gk PRO²(*states* f. *states* standing) one that stands before]

prŏ'sthĕs|ĭs *n.* (*pl.* ~**es** *pr.* -ēz). **1.** (Gram.) addition of letter or syllable at beginning of word, e.g. *be-* in *beloved*. **2.** (Surg.) making up of deficiencies (e.g. by false teeth or artificial limb) as a branch of surgery. **3.** part thus supplied. **4.** Hence **prŏsthĕ'tıc** *a.*; **prŏs-thĕ'tıcs** *n. pl.* (usu. treated as *sing.*) = sense 2. [LL, f. Gk *prosthesis* f. PROS(*tithēmi* place)]

prŏ'stitūte *n.*, & *v.t.* **1.** *n.* woman who offers her body to promiscuous sexual intercourse esp. for payment or as religious rite; man who undertakes sexual actions for payment. **2.** *v.t.* make a prostitute of (esp. one*self*); (fig.) sell (one's honour etc.) unworthily, put (abilities etc.) to wrong use, debase. **3.** So **prŏstĭ-tū'tion** *n.* [(n. f. L *prostituta*) f. L PRO¹(*stituere stitut-* = *statuere* set up, place) offer for sale]

prŏ'strate¹ *a.* lying with face to ground, esp. as token of submission or humility; lying in horizontal position; overcome, overthrown, (*prostrate with grief*); physically exhausted; (Bot.) growing along the ground. [ME, f. L *prostratus p.p.* (as foll.)]

prostrā'te² (-ŏs-, -os-) *v.t.* lay (person etc.) flat on ground; throw one*self* down prostrate (*at* shrine, *before* person etc.); (fig.) overcome, make submissive; (of fatigue etc.) reduce to extreme physical weakness; hence **prŏstrā'tıon** (*or* pros-) *n.* [ME, f. L PRO¹-(*sternere strat-* lay flat)]

prŏ'stýle *n.* & *a.* (that has) portico with not more than four columns. [f. L *prostylos* having pillars in front (as PRO-², STYLE)]

prŏ's|ÿ (-zī) *a.* commonplace, tedious, wearisomely dull, (*prosy talk, talker*); hence ~ILY² *adv.*, ~INESS *n.* [f. PROSE + -Y²]

Prot. *abbr.* Protectorate; Protestant.

prŏtácti'nium *n.* (Chem.) radioactive metallic element whose chief isotope yields actinium by decay. [G, f. as PROTO- + ACTINIUM]

prōtă'gonist *n.* chief person in drama or plot of story; leading person in contest, principal performer; advocate or champion of course of action, method, etc. [f. Gk *prōtagōnistēs* (as PROTO-, *agōnistēs* actor)]

prŏ'tamine (-ēn) *n.* any of a group of simple proteins found esp. in fish sperm. [f. PROTO- + AMINE]

pro tanto (prō tă'ntō) *adv.* so far; to that extent. [L, = for so much]

prŏ'tas|ĭs *n.* (*pl.* ~**es** *pr.* ~ēz). clause expressing condition in conditional sentence; so **protă'tıc** *a.* [L, f. Gk PRO²(*tasis* f. *teinō* stretch) proposition]

prō'tēa *n.* S. Afr. shrub of genus *Protea*, with conelike flower-heads. [mod. L, f. PROTEUS, w. ref. to the many species]

prŏ′tean (-ĭan, -ē′an) *a.* variable, versatile; taking many forms. [f. PROTEUS + -AN]

prŏ′tēase *n.* (Chem.) enzyme able to decompose proteins and peptides. [f. PROTEIN + -ASE]

protĕ′ct *v.t.* keep safe, defend, guard, (person or thing *from* or *against* danger, injury, disadvantage etc.); (Econ.) guard (home industry) against competition by import duties on foreign goods; ||provide funds to meet (bill, draft); provide (machinery etc.) with appliances to prevent injury from it. [f. L PRO¹(*tegere tect-* cover)]

protĕ′ction *n.* protecting, defence, (*is safe under your protection*; *affords protection against weather*; ||**Court of P**~, department of Supreme Court attending to affairs of the mentally unfit); protecting person or thing (*a dog is a great protection against burglars*); (arch.) keeping of woman as mistress. **2.** = SAFE² *conduct*. **3.** (Econ.) system of protecting home industries; hence ~ISM (3), ~IST (2), *ns.* **4.** immunity from molestation, obtained by payment under threat of violence; ~ (money), money so paid. [ME f. OF, or f. LL *protectio* (as prec.; see -ION)]

protĕ′ctive *a.* serving or seeking or intended to protect; (of food) protecting against deficiency diseases; ~ **clothing** (against burns, radiation, etc.); ~ **colouring** (making animal or plant less likely to be seen or attacked by predator); ~ **custody,** detention of person actually or allegedly for his own protection; hence ~LY² (-vlĭ) *adv.*, ~NESS (-vn-) *n.* [f. PROTECT + -IVE]

protĕ′ctor *n.* **1.** person who protects; regent in charge of kingdom during minority, absence, etc., of sovereign (**Lord P**~ **of the Commonwealth,** title of Oliver Cromwell 1653–8 and Richard Cromwell 1658–9), whence ~AL *a.*, ~SHIP *n.*; hence **protĕ′ctress¹** *n.* **2.** thing or device that protects (*chest-protector*). [ME, f. OF *protecteur* f. LL *protector* (as PROTECT; see -OR)]

protĕ′ctorate *n.* office of protector of kingdom or State; period of this, esp. under the Cromwells 1653–9; protectorship of weak or underdeveloped State by stronger one; State thus protected. [f. prec. + -ATE¹]

protĕ′ctory *n.* institution for care of destitute or delinquent children. [f. PROTECT + -ORY]

protégé (prŏ′tĕzhā) *n.* (*fem.* ~**e** *pr.* same). person to whom another is (usu. permanent) protector or patron. [F, p.p. of *protéger* f. L *protegere* PROTECT]

prŏ′tëifŏrm *a.* very changeable in form. [f. PROTEUS + -I- + -FORM]

prŏ′tein (-tēn) *n.* (Chem.) one of a class of organic compounds (containing carbon, hydrogen, oxygen, and nitrogen, freq. also sulphur, occas. phosphorus, iron, etc.) forming an important part of all living organisms, and the essential nitrogenous constituent of the food of animals; hence ~A′CEOUS, **prōtei′n**IC (-tē′n-), **prōtë′in**OUS, *adjs.* [f. F *protéine*, G *protein*, f. Gk *prōteios* primary; see -IN]

prŏ′te′m *a.* & *adv.* (colloq.) = foll. [abbr.]

pro tempore (prŏ tĕ′mperĭ) *a.* & *adv.* for the time being (esp. of appointment to office). [L]

prŏtĕŏ′lysis *n.* hydrolysis of proteins or peptides; hence **prŏtĕoly′t**IC *a.* [mod. L, f. PROTEIN + -O- + -LYSIS]

Prŏterozō′ic *a.* & *n.* (Geol.) (of the) geological era containing the oldest forms of life. [f. Gk *proteros* former + *zōē* life, *zōos* living + -IC]

prŏ′tĕst¹ *n.* formal statement or action of dissent or disapproval, remonstrance, (*made a protest; paid it under protest*); written declaration usu. by notary public that bill has been duly presented and payment or acceptance refused; solemn declaration; demonstration of objection to official policy (*marched in protest*). [ME f. OF (*protester*; see foll.)]

protĕ′st² *v.* **1.** *v.t.* affirm solemnly (one's innocence etc., *that*, or abs.) esp. in reply to accusation etc.; write or obtain PROTEST¹ in regard to (bill); *object to

(decision etc.). **2.** *v.i.* make (often written) protest *against* (action, proposal). **3.** Hence ~ER¹, ~OR, *ns.* [ME, f. OF *protester* f. L PRO¹(*testari* assert f. *testis* witness)]

Prŏ′tĕstant *n.* & *a.* **1.** (member or adherent) of any of the Christian bodies that separated from the Roman communion in the Reformation (16th c.), or their offshoots; hence ~ISM (3) *n.*, ~IZE (3) *v.t.* & *i.* **2.** *n.* (Hist., in *pl.*) those who dissented from decision of Diet of Spires (1529), adherents of Reformed doctrines in Germany. **3.** *n.* & *a.* (*p*~; *or* protĕ′s-) protesting (person). [f. mod. L *protestans*, part. of L *protestari* (see prec., -ANT)]

prŏtĕstā′tion *n.* solemn affirmation (*of*, *that*); protest (*against*). [ME f. OF, or f. LL *protestatio* (as prec.; see -ATION)]

Prŏ′teus (-tūs, -tĭus) *n.* **1.** changing or inconstant person or thing. **2.** (*p*~). bacterium of genus *Proteus*; olm. [L, f. Gk *Prōteus* sea-god fabled to take various shapes]

prŏthalā′mi|**um, -ĭŏn,** *n.* (*pl.* ~**a**). song to celebrate forthcoming wedding. [made by Spenser on *epithalamium* (cf. PRO-²)]

prŏthă′lli|**um** *n.* (*pl.* ~**a**). = foll. [mod. L, f. PRO-² + Gk *thallion* dim. of *thallos*; see THALLUS, -IUM]

prŏthă′ll|**us** *n.* (*pl.* ~**i** *pr.* -ī). (Bot.) gametophyte of fern etc.; corresponding structure in higher plant. [mod. L, f. PRO-² + as THALLUS]

prŏ′thĕs|**is** *n.* (*pl.* ~**es** *pr.* -ēz). (Eccl.) (placing of Eucharistic elements on) credence table, part of church where this stands; (Gram.) = PROSTHESIS, whence **prothĕ′t**IC *a.* [Gk, f. PRO²(*tithēmi* place)]

prothonotary. See PROTONOTARY.

Protī′sta *n. pl.* kingdom of organisms (bacteria, protozoa, etc.) not distinguished as animals or plants; hence **prŏ′tist** *n.*, member of this kingdom, **prōtistŏ′LOGY** *n.* [mod. L, f. Gk *prōtista*, neut. pl. superl. f. *prōtos* first]

prŏ′tium *n.* (Chem.) ordinary isotope of hydrogen as dist. from heavy hydrogen (deuterium or tritium). [mod. L, f. PROTO- + -IUM]

prŏ′to- *comb. form.* **1.** original, primitive (*proto-Germanic*, *proto-Slavic*). **2.** first, original, as: ~**hi′ppus,** extinct Pliocene quadruped related to horse; ~**mar′tyr,** first martyr (esp. St. Stephen, first Christian martyr); ~**pe′ctin,** pectose; ~**phyte,** unicellular plant; ~**ther′ia,** monotremes; ~**zo′ic,** (1) (of strata) containing earliest traces of living beings, (2) protozoan. [f. Gk *prōto-* (*prōtos* first)]

prŏ′tocŏl *n.* & *v.* (-ll-). **1.** *n.* original draft of diplomatic document, esp. of terms of treaty agreed to in conference and signed by the parties; formal statement of transaction; (observance of) official formality and etiquette; official formulae at beginning and end of charter, papal bull, etc.; *record of experimental observations etc. **2.** *v.i.* draw up protocol(s). **3.** *v.t.* record in protocol. [orig. Sc. *prothocoll* f. OF *-cole* f. med. L f. late Gk PROTO(*kollon* f. *kolla* glue) flyleaf glued to binding of book]

prŏ′tŏn *n.* (Phys.) elementary particle with unit positive electric charge, forming part (or, in hydrogen, whole) of atomic nucleus; hence **protŏ′n**IC *a.* [Gk, neut. of *prōtos* first]

protonotary, protho-, (prŏt(h)onŏ′-, prot(h)ŏ′no-) *n.* chief clerk in some law courts (orig. in Byzantine court); **P**~ **Apostolic(al),** member of college of prelates who register papal acts, direct the canonization of saints, etc. [f. med. L f. late Gk PROTO(*notarios* NOTARY)]

prŏ′toplăsm *n.* viscous translucent colourless substance forming main constituent of cells in organisms, the basis of life in plants and animals; hence **prŏtoplă′sm**AL, **prŏtoplăsmă′t**IC, **prŏtoplă′sm**IC, (-z-) *adjs.* [f. Gk *protoplasma* (as PROTO-, PLASMA)]

prŏ′toplăst *n.* mass of protoplasm within one cell; hence **prŏtoplă′st**IC *a.* [F *protoplaste* or f. LL f. Gk PROTO(*plastos* moulded f. *plassō* mould)]

For other words in *pro*- see PRO-.

prŏ′to|týpe n. an original thing or person in relation to a copy, imitation, representation, later specimen, improved form, etc.; trial model, preliminary version, esp. of aeroplane etc.; hence ∼týpAL, ∼tý′pIC(AL), adjs. [F, or f. LL f. Gk PROTO(tupos TYPE¹)]

prŏtŏzŏ′|on n. (pl. ∼a). animal of subkingdom or phylum Protozoa, usu. unicellular and microscopic; hence ∼AL a., ∼AN a. & n., ∼ŏ′LOGY n. [mod. L, f. as PROTO- + Gk zōion animal; see -A 2]

protrǎ′ct v.t. 1. prolong, lengthen, make last longer, (protracted their stay for some weeks); hence ∼èdLY² adv. 2. draw (plan of ground etc.) to scale. [f. L PRO¹- (trahere tract- draw)]

protrǎ′ctíle a. (Zool.) (Of organ etc.) capable of being extended. [f. prec.; see -IL]

protrǎ′ction n. protracting or being protracted; action of protractor muscle; drawing to scale. [F, or f. LL protractio (as PROTRACT; see -ION)]

protrǎ′ctor n. instrument for measuring angles, usu. in form of graduated semicircle; muscle serving to extend limb etc. [f. PROTRACT + -OR]

protru′de (-ōō′d) v. 1. v.t. thrust forth, cause to project; (fig.) obtrude. 2. v.i. extend beyond or above the surrounding surface, project. 3. Hence **protru′dENT, protru′sIBLE, protru′sIVE**, (-ōō′-) adjs., **protru′sION** (-ōō′zhon) n [f L PRO¹(trudere trusthrust)]

protru′síle (-ōō′-) a. (Of limb etc.) capable of being thrust forth. [f. PRO-¹ + EXTRUSILE]

protū′ber|ant a. bulging out, prominent (lit. or fig.), hence ∼ANCE n. [f. LL PRO¹(tuberare f. tuber bump); see -ANT]

proud a. & adv. 1. a. valuing oneself highly or too highly, esp. on the ground of (qualities, rank, possessions, etc.); ∼(-hearted), haughty, arrogant; PURSE¹-proud. 2. feeling oneself greatly honoured (am proud of his acquaintance, of knowing him, to know him, that I know him). 3. having a proper pride (too proud to complain; HOUSE¹-proud). 4. (Of action etc.) showing pride; of which one is or may be justly proud (a proud day for us; a proud sight). 5. (Of thing) imposing, splendid; (of waters) swollen, in flood; slightly projecting, (of flesh) overgrown round healing wound. 6. Hence ∼LY² adv. 7. adv. (colloq.) do (person, oneself) ∼, treat with great generosity or honour. [OE prūt, prūd, = ON prūthr f. OF prud, prod obl. case of pruz etc. valiant, f. Rom. *prodis f. LL prode, f. L prodesse be of value (PRO-¹, esse be)]

Prov. abbr. Proverbs (OT); Province.

prov|e (prōōv) v. (p.p. ∼ed or, esp. US, Sc., & literary, ∼′en). 1. v.t. (arch.) test qualities of, try. 2. subject (gun etc.) to testing process; cause (dough) to rise in bread-making. 3. (Arith.) test accuracy of (calculation); the EXCEPTION proves the rule. 4. = PROOF¹ 9. 5. make certain, demonstrate by evidence or argument, (fact, the truth of, thing etc. to be, that), whence ∼′ABLE a.; ∼e oneself, show one's abilities etc.; (Sc. Law, as verdict in criminal trial) not proven, the evidence is insufficient to establish either guilt or innocence. 6. be found (to be, to do); be found to be (will prove the winner). [ME, f. OF prover f. L probare test, approve, demonstrate (probus good)]

prŏ′vènance n. (place of) origin. [F, f. provenir f. L PRO¹(venire come); see -ANCE]

Provençal (prŏvahńsah′l) a. & n. (inhabitant or native or language) of Provence. [F (as PROVINCIAL, f. provincia as L colloq. name for southern Gaul under Roman rule)]

prŏ′vènder n. fodder; (joc.) food for human beings. [ME, f. OF provendre, provende f. Rom. *probenda f. L praebenda (see PREBEND)]

*prŏ′vènience n. = PROVENANCE. [f. L PRO¹(venire come); see -ENCE]

prŏ′vèrb n. short pithy saying in general use; person or thing that is notorious (their fickleness is a proverb; he is a proverb for inaccuracy); (Book of) P∼s, didactic

poetical OT book of maxims ascribed to Solomon and others. [ME, f. OF proverbe or f. L PRO¹(verbium f. verbum word)]

provêr′bial a. of or expressed in proverbs (proverbial wisdom; the proverbial ill wind); that has become a proverb, notorious; hence ∼ITY (-ǎ′l-) n., ∼LY² adv. [ME, f. L proverbialis (as prec.; see -AL)]

provī′d|e v. 1. v.i. make due preparation (for possible event, person's safety, entertainment, etc.; against attack etc.); make due preparation of maintenance (for person). 2. v.t. (Of person, law, etc.) stipulate (that); supply, furnish, (person with thing, thing for or to person); equip with necessaries (you must provide yourselves). 3. (Hist.) appoint (incumbent to benefice); (of Pope) appoint (successor to benefice not yet vacant). 4. ∼ing (that) conj. = foll. 2. [ME, f. L PRO¹(vidēre vis- see)]

provī′dèd a. & conj. 1. a. In vbl senses. 2. conj. ∼ (that), on the condition or understanding that, only if. [p.p. of prec.]

prŏ′vidence n. foresight, timely care; thrift; beneficent care of God or nature (special ∼, particular instance of this); (P∼) God in this aspect. [ME f. OF, or f. L providentia (as PROVIDE; see -ENCE)]

prŏ′vident a. having or showing foresight, thrifty (‖P∼ Society, = FRIENDLY Society); hence ∼LY² adv [ME, f. L (as PROVIDE; see -ENT)]

prŏvidě′ntial (-shal) a. of or by divine foresight or interposition; opportune, lucky; hence ∼LY² adv. [f. PROVIDENCE + -AL, after evidential etc.]

provī′der n. In vbl senses; breadwinner of family etc. [f. PROVIDE + -ER¹]

prŏ′vince n. 1. principal administrative division of country etc.; (Eccl.) district under archbishop or metropolitan; (Rom. Hist.) territory outside Italy under Roman governor; the ∼s, whole of a country outside capital. 2. sphere of action, business, (is not within my province); branch of learning etc. (in the province of aesthetics). [ME f. OF, f. L provincia charge, province]

provī′ncial (-shal) a. & n. 1. a. of a province; of the provinces; having the manners, speech, narrow views, etc., associated with or attributed to inhabitants of the provinces, whence ∼ITY (-shĭǎ′l-) n.; hence ∼IZE (3) v.t., ∼LY² adv. 2. n. inhabitant of a province or the provinces; countrified person; (Eccl.) head of, chief of religious order in a province. [ME f. OF, f. L provincialis (as prec.; see -AL)]

provī′ncial|ism (-sha-) n. provincial manner, fashion, mode of thought, etc.; word or phrase peculiar to provincial region; attachment to one's province rather than country; so ∼IST (2, 3) n. [f. prec. + -ISM]

provī′sion (-zhon) n., & v.t. 1. n. providing (for, against; esp. make provision); provided amount of something. 2. (in pl.) supply of food, eatables and drinkables; hence ∼LESS a. 3. legal or formal statement providing for something; clause of this. 4. (Hist.) appointment to benefice not yet vacant (cf. PROVIDE 3). 5. v.t. supply with provisions (sense 2); hence ∼MENT n. [ME f. OF, f. L provisio -onis (as PROVIDE; see -ION)]

provī′sional (-zho-) a. providing for immediate needs only, temporary; hence ∼ITY (-ǎ′l-), ∼NESS, ns., ∼LY² adv. [f. prec. + -AL]

provī′sō (-zō) n. (pl. ∼s). stipulation; clause of stipulation or limitation in document. [L, neut. abl. p.p. of providēre PROVIDE, in med. L phr. proviso quod it being provided that]

provī′sor (-z-) n. 1. (Hist.) holder of a provision (sense 4). 2. (Eccl.) deputy of (arch)bishop. [ME, f. AF provisour f. L provisor -oris (as PROVIDE; see -OR)]

provī′sor|ỹ (-z-) a. conditional; making provision (provisory care); hence ∼iLY² adv. [f. F provisoire or f. med. L provisorius (as prec.; see -ORY)]

Prŏ′vō′ n. (pl. ∼s). member of Dutch anarchist group seeking to provoke the authorities. [f. F provocateur provoker]

Prŏ'vō² n. (pl. ~s). (colloq.) member of Provisional wing of IRA. [abbr.; see -O]

prŏvocā'tion n. incitement esp. to anger etc., instigation, irritation, (did it under severe provocation; downs tools at or on the slightest provocation); cause of annoyance. [ME f. OF, or f. L provocatio (as PROVOKE; see -ATION)]

provŏ'cative a. & n. (thing) tending to cause provocation (of curiosity, anger, lust, etc.); intentionally annoying. [ME, f. obs. F provocatif -ive, f. LL provocativus (as foll.; see -IVE)]

provō'k|e v.t. rouse, incite, (person to anger, to do); irritate (person into doing); instigate, tempt, allure; call forth (indignation, inquiry, a storm, etc.); cause (will provoke fermentation); hence ~ING² a. [ME, f. OF provoquer f. L PRO¹(vocare call)]

prŏ'vost (in sense 4 provō') n. **1.** ‖head of some colleges at Oxford, Cambridge, etc.; *high administrative officer in university; head of chapter in modern cathedral or of religious community. **2.** (Sc.) head of municipal corporation or burgh (in four cities, **Lord P~**). **3.** Protestant clergyman in charge of principal church of town etc. in Germany etc. **4.** ~ **(marshal)**, head of military police in camp or on active service, master-at-arms of ship on which court martial is to be held; *~ **guard**, body of soldiers under provost marshal. **5.** Hence ~SHIP n. [ME, f. OE profost & f. AF provost, prevost f. med. L propositus for praepositus; see PRAEPOSTOR]

prow¹ n. fore-part adjoining stem of boat or ship; pointed projecting front part. [f. F proue f. Prov. proa or It. dial. prua f. L prora f. Gk prōira]

prow² a. (arch.) worthy, gallant. [ME, f. OF prou, prod, f. Rom. *prodis (see PROUD)]

prow'ĕss n. valour, gallantry; skill, expertness. [ME, f. OF proesce (as prec.; see -ESS²)]

prowl v. & n. **1.** v.i. go about in search of plunder or prey (lit. or fig.). **2.** v.t. traverse (streets, place) thus. **3.** Hence ~ER¹ n. **4.** n. prowling (on the prowl; *~ **car**, police squad car). [ME prolle, of unkn. orig.]

prox. abbr. proximo.

prox. acc. abbr. proxime accessit.

prŏ'ximal a. (Anat.) situated towards centre of body or point of attachment; hence ~LY² adv. [f. L proximus nearest + -AL]

prŏ'ximate a. nearest, next before or after (in place, order, time, connection of thought, causation, etc.); approximate; hence ~LY² (-tlĭ) adv. [f. L proximatus p.p. of proximare draw near (as prec.); see -ATE²]

‖**proxime accessit** (prŏksĭmĭ aksĕ'sĭt) n. (person gaining) next place in merit to prize-winner(s) in examination etc. [L, = came very near]

prŏxi'mĭtў n. nearness in space, time, etc. (to); ~ **of blood**, kinship; ~ **fuse**, radio device causing projectile to explode when near target. [ME, f. F proximité or f. L proximitas (as PROXIMAL; see -ITY)]

prŏ'ximō a. (Commerc.) of next month (the 3rd proximo). [L, = in the next (mense month)]

prŏ'xў n. agency of substitute or deputy (voted, was married, by proxy); person authorized to act for another (made me his proxy; stood proxy for the godmother); document authorizing person to vote on behalf of another, vote so given. [ME, f. obs. procuracy f. med. L procuratia (as PROCURATION; see -ACY)]

PRS abbr. President of the Royal Society.

prud|e (prood) n. person of extreme (esp. affected) propriety in conduct or speech, esp. as regards sexual matters; hence or cogn. ~'ERY (4) n., ~'ISH¹ a. [F, back-form. f. prudefemme fem. of prud'homme good man and true (as PROW², homme f. L homo hominis man)]

pru'd|ent (-ŏŏ'-) a. (Of person or conduct) careful to avoid undesired consequences; circumspect, discreet; hence or cogn. ~ENCE n., ~entLY² adv. [ME f. OF, or f. L prudens = providens PROVIDENT]

prudĕ'ntial (-ŏōdĕ'nshǎl) a. & n. **1.** a. of, involving, marked by, prudence, (prudential motives, policy); hence ~ISM (2), ~IST (2), ns., ~LY² adv. **2.** n. (in pl.) prudential considerations or matters, esp. *minor

administrative or financial matters. [f. prec. + -IAL, after evidential etc.]

pru'inōse (-ŏŏ'-) a. (Biol.) covered with white powdery substance, frosted. [f. L pruinosus (pruina hoar-frost; see -OSE¹)]

prune¹ (proon) n. dried plum; (colloq.) disliked person; ~s **and prism(s)** (of mincing way of speaking etc.; see Dickens's Little Dorrit II. v). [ME f. OF, f. Rom. *pruna f. L prunum f. Gk prou(m)non plum]

prun|e² (proon) v.t. trim (tree etc., often down) by cutting away dead or overgrown branches etc. with ~'ing-hook etc., esp. to promote growth; lop (branches etc.) off, away; (fig.) remove (superfluities), reduce (costs etc.), clear (book etc. of what is superfluous). [ME prowyne f. OF pro(o)ignier f. Rom. *PRO¹(rotundiare cut to round shape f. rotundus ROUND¹)]

prune³ (proon) v.t. (arch.) = PREEN. [ME prune, pruyne, proyne, f. OF poroign- st. of poroindre f. as PRO- + L ungere anoint]

prunĕ'lla¹ (proo-) n. strong silk or worsted fabric used formerly for barristers' gowns etc. and for uppers of women's shoes; LEATHER and prunella. [perh. f. F prunelle, of uncert. orig.]

prunĕ'lla² (proo-) n. plant of genus Prunella, esp. self-heal (formerly thought to cure quinsy). [mod. L, = quinsy; earlier brunella dim. of med. L brunus brown]

prur'i|ent (-oor'-) a. given to or arising from indulgence of lewd ideas; hence ~ENCE, ~ENCY, ns., ~entLY² adv. [f. L prurire itch, be wanton; see -ENT]

prurī'gō (-oor-) n. disease of skin with violent itching; so **pruri'gin**OUS (-oor-) a. [L prurigo -ginis (prurire to itch)]

prurī'tus (-oor-) n. violent itching of skin. [L, = itching (as prec.)]

Prŭ'ssian (-shan) a. & n. (native or inhabitant) of Prussia; **Old** ~, language spoken in Prussia until 17th c.; ~ **blue**, deep blue pigment got from ferrocyanides by treatment with ferric salt; ~ **carp**, crucian; hence ~IZE (3) v.t. (esp. w. ref. to rigid discipline). [f. Prussi a Balto-Slavic people + -IAN]

prŭ'ssic a. of, or got from, Prussian blue; ~ **acid**, hydrocyanic acid. [f. F prussique (Prusse Prussia; see -IC)]

prӯ¹ v.i. look or peer inquisitively (into, about adv.); inquire impertinently into (person's affairs, conduct, etc.); hence ~'ING² a. [ME prie, of unkn. orig.]

***prӯ²** v.t. **1.** = PRIZE³. **2.** get (out of, open, etc.) with effort. [f. PRIZE³ taken as pries 3 sing.]

PS abbr. Police Sergeant; postscript; private secretary; prompt side.

Ps(s). abbr. Psalm(s) (OT).

psalm (sahm) n. sacred song, hymn; **the (Book of) P~s**, book of these in OT; ~**-book**, book containing the Psalms, esp. metrical version of these for public worship. [OE (p)sealm f. LL f. Gk psalmos song sung to harp (psallō pluck, sing to harp)]

psa'lmĭst (sah'm-) n. author of a psalm; **the P~**, David or author of any of the Psalms. [f. LL psalmista (as prec.; see -IST)]

psa'lmod|ў (sah'm-, să'lm-) n. practice or art of singing psalms, hymns, anthems, etc. esp. in public worship, whence **psalmŏ'd**IC (săl-) a., ~IST (3) n., ~IZE (2) v.i.; arrangement of psalms for singing, psalms so arranged. [ME, f. LL psalmodia f. Gk psalmōidia song sung to harp (as PSALM, ōidē song)]

psa'lter (saw'l-, sŏ'l-) n. the Book of Psalms; version of this (Latin, English, Prayer-Book, Scottish Metrical, Psalter); copy of the Psalms esp. for liturgical use. [ME f. AF sauter, OF sautier, & f. OE (p)saltere, f. LL f. Gk psaltērion stringed instrument (psallō pluck), in eccl. L Book of Psalms]

psaltĕr'ium (sawl-, sŏl-) n. third STOMACH of ruminant. [L (see prec.); named from likeness to book]

psa'ltery (saw'l-, sŏ'l-) n. ancient and medieval

For other words in pro- see PRO-.

instrument like dulcimer but played by plucking strings with fingers or plectrum. [ME, f. OF *sauterie* etc. f. L (as PSALTER)]

psĕphŏ′|logy (ps-, s-) *n.* study of trends in elections and voting; hence ∿LOGIST *n.*, ∿lŏ′gICAL (-fo-) *a.* [f. Gk *psēphos* pebble, vote + -o- + -LOGY]

pseud (s-) *a.* & *n.* (colloq.) **1.** *a.* not genuine; pretentious, esp. in intellectual or social matters. **2.** *n.* such person. [abbr. of PSEUDO]

pseud-. See PSEUDO-.

pseudĕpī′graph|a (s-) *n. pl.* spurious writings, esp. Jewish writings ascribed to various OT prophets etc. but written in or somewhat before the early Christian period; hence ∿AL, **pseudĕpīgră′ph**IC(AL) (s-), *adjs.* [neut. pl. of Gk PSEUD(*epigraphos*; see EPIGRAPH) with false title]

pseu′dō (s-) *a.* & *n.* (*pl.* ∿s). sham, spurious, insincere, (person). [f. foll.]

pseu′dō- (s-) *comb. form.* (usu. **pseud-** bef. vowel). false, apparent, supposed but not real, as: ∿- -archa′ic, artificially archaic in style etc.; ∿carp, (Bot.) fruit formed other than from ovary, e.g. strawberry, fig; ∿science, pretended science. [Gk, f. st. of *pseudēs* false, *pseudos* falsehood]

pseu′dograph (s-; -ahf) *n.* a spurious literary work. [f. LL f. Gk PSEUDO(*graphos*; see GRAPH)]

pseu′do|mŏrph (s-) *n.* false form, esp. crystal etc. consisting of one mineral with form proper to another; hence ∿mŏr′phIC, ∿mŏr′phous, *adjs.*, ∿mŏr′phISM (2) *n.* [f. PSEUDO- + Gk *morphē* form]

pseu′donym (s-) *n.* fictitious name, esp. one assumed by author. [f. F *pseudonyme* f. Gk neut. adj. (as foll.)]

pseud|ŏ′nymous (s-) *a.* writing, written, under a fictitious name; hence ∿onÿ′mITY *n.* [f. Gk PSEUD-(*ōnumos* f. *onuma, onoma* name) + -OUS]

pseu′dopŏd (s-) *n.* = foll. [f. mod. L (as foll.)]

pseudopŏ′di|um (s-) *n.* (*pl.* ∿a). temporary protrusion of protoplasm from cell for movement, feeding, etc. [mod. L (as PSEUDO-, PODIUM)]

pshaw (*or* sh-) *int.* expr. contempt or impatience. [imit.]

psi *n.* twenty-third Greek letter (Ψ, ψ) = ps; parapsychological factors or faculties collectively. [Gk]

p.s.i.(g.) *abbr.* pounds per square inch (gauge).

psīlă′nthrop|ism (s-) *n.* doctrine that Christ was a mere man; so **psīlanthrŏ′p**IC (s-) *a.*, ∿IST (2) *n.* [f. eccl. Gk *psīlanthrōpos* merely human (*psilos* bare, mere, *anthrōpos* man) + -ISM]

psīlocÿ′bīn (s-) *n.* hallucinogen found in Mexican mushrooms of genus *Psilocybe*. [f. *Psilocybe* (f. Gk *psilos* bald + *kubē* head) + -IN]

psīlŏ′s|īs (s-) *n.* (*pl.* ∿es *pr.* -ēz). (Path.) stripping bare, e.g. of hair or flesh; = SPRUE[2]. [f. Gk *psilōsis* (*psilos* bare; see -OSIS)]

psī′ttacīne (s-) *a.* of parrots; parrot-like. [f. L *psittacinus* (*psittacus* f. Gk *psittakos* parrot; see -INE[1])]

psittacŏ′s|īs (s-) *n.* (*pl.* ∿es *pr.* -ēz). contagious disease of birds transmissible (esp. from parrots) to human beings as form of pneumonia. [mod. L, f. L *psittacus* (as prec.) + -OSIS]

psŏ′as (s-) *n.* ∿ **magnus** or **major, parvus** or **minor,** two hip-muscles. [Gk, acc. pl. of *psoa*, taken as sing.]

psŏrī′as|īs (s-) *n.* (*pl.* ∿es *pr.* -ēz). skin disease marked by red scaly patches. [mod. L f. Gk *psōriasis* (*psōriaō* have itch f. *psōra* itch)]

ps(s)t *int.* seeking to attract person's attention surreptitiously. [imit.]

*PST *abbr.* Pacific Standard Time.

‖PSV *abbr.* public service vehicle.

*psych (sīk) *v.t.* (sl.) psychoanalyse; analyse (problem etc.) in psychological terms. [abbr.]

psÿ′chĕ (sī′kǐ) *n.* soul, spirit; mind. [L, f. Gk *psukhē* breath, life, soul, in Gk Myth. personified as beloved of Eros]

psÿchĕd|ĕ′lic (sīk-) *a.* & *n.* (hallucinogenic drug) expanding the mind's awareness; having similar effect to such experiences; hence ∿ē′lIA[2] *n. pl.*, psychedelic drugs, articles, etc. [irreg. f. Gk (as prec.) + *dēlos* clear, manifest + -IC]

psÿchī′atr|ÿ (sīk-) *n.* study and treatment of mental disease; hence or cogn. **psÿchiă′tr**IC(AL) (sīk-) *adjs.*, ∿IST (2) *n.* [f. as PSYCHE + *iatreia* healing (*iatros* healer)]

psÿ′chic (sī′k-) *a.* & *n.* **1.** *a.* = foll. (∿ **force,** non- -physical force assumed to explain spiritualistic phenomena); able to exercise psychical or occult powers; (Bridge, of bid) made by player whose hand does not have the strength normally implied by his bid. **2.** *n.* person susceptible to psychic influence, medium; psychic bid; (in *pl.*) study of psychical phenomena. [f. Gk *psukhikos* (as PSYCHE; see -IC)]

psÿ′chical (sī′k-) *a.* of the soul or mind, whence ∿LY[2] *adv.*; of phenomena and conditions apparently outside domain of physical law (*psychical research*), so **psÿ′chic**ISM (3), **psÿ′chic**IST (3), (sī′k-) *ns.* [f. as prec. + -AL]

psÿ′chō (sī′kō) *a.* & *n.* (*pl.* ∿s). (colloq.) psychotic (person). [abbr.]

psÿ′chō- (sī′kō) *comb. form.* mind, soul, as: ∿-a′ctive, affecting the mind; ∿dyna′mic(s), (science) of the mental powers; ∿ge′nesis, origin of the soul or mind; ∿graph, instrument for supposed writing by spirits; ∿kine′sis, movement of objects by mental influence without physical contact; ∿lingui′stics, study of interrelation between use of language and speaker's and hearer's minds; ∿mo′tor, of motion resulting from mental activity; ∿neuro′sis, neurosis esp. with indirect expression of emotional feelings; ∿phy′sics, science of general relations between mind and body; ∿physio′logy, branch of physiology dealing with mental phenomena; ∿sur′gery, brain surgery as means of treating mental disorder; ∿the′rapy, treatment of mental disorder by psychological means; ∿tro′pic, (of drug) acting on the mind. [f. Gk *psukho-* (as PSYCHE, -O-)]

psÿchō|aná′lÿsis (sīk) *n.* therapeutic method for treating mental disorders by investigating interaction of conscious and unconscious elements in the mind and bringing the latter into consciousness; so ∿A′NALYSE *v.t.*, ∿A′NALYST *n.*, ∿ANALY′TIC(AL) *adjs.* [f. prec. + ANALYSIS]

psÿchŏlŏ′gical (sīk-) *a.* of the mind; of psychology; *psychological* BLOCK[1]; ∿ **moment** [f. F mistransl. of G *das moment* 'potent element' as *der moment* 'moment of time'], the psychologically appropriate moment, (colloq.) the most appropriate time; ∿ **warfare** (achieving aims by acting on enemy's minds); hence ∿LY[2] *adv.* [f. as foll. + -ICAL]

psÿchŏ′log|ÿ (sīk-) *n.* science of the nature, functions, and phenomena, of human mind; treatise on or system of this; (colloq.) mental characteristics; hence ∿IST (3) *n.*, ∿IZE (2, 3) *v.t.* & *i.* [f. mod. L *psychologia* (as PSYCHO-, -LOGY)]

psÿchŏ′mĕtr|ÿ (sīk-) *n.* **1.** divination of facts concerning an object from contact with it. **2.** measurement of mental abilities; hence **psÿchomĕ′tr**IC (sīk-) *a.*, ∿IST (3) *n.* [f. PSYCHO- + -METRY]

psÿ′chopăth (sīk-) *n.* person suffering chronic mental disorder esp. with abnormal social behaviour; mentally or emotionally unstable person; hence or cogn. **psÿchopă′th**IC, **psÿchopathŏ′**LOGY, psÿchŏ′pathÿ[1], *ns.*, (sīk-). [f. PSYCHO- + -PATH]

psÿch|ŏ′sis (sīk-) *n.* (*pl.* ∿oses *pr.* -ō′sēz). severe mental derangement involving the whole personality; hence ∿o′TIC *a.* & *n.* of or relating to, (person) suffering from, a psychosis. [f. Gk *psukhōsis* (*psukhoō* give life to; see PSYCHE, see -OSIS)]

psÿchōsomă′tic (sīk-) *a.* of mind and body; (of disorders etc.) caused or aggravated by mental stress. [f. PSYCHO- + SOMATIC]

psÿchrŏ′mĕter (sīk-) *n.* wet-and-dry-bulb thermometer for measurement of atmospheric humidity. [f. Gk *psukhros* cold + -o- + -METER]

PT *abbr.* physical training; *****PT boat,** motor torpedo--boat [f. *P*atrol *T*orpedo].

pt. *abbr.* part; pint; point; port.

Pt *symb.* platinum.

PTA *abbr.* parent-teacher association.

ptăr'mĭgan (t-) *n.* bird of grouse family, with black or grey plumage in summer and white in winter. [= Gael. *tàrmachan*; *p*- is pseudo-etym. after Gk wds in *pt*-]

Pte. *abbr.* Private (soldier).

ptĕrĭd|ŏ'logў (t-) *n.* study of ferns; so **∼olŏ'gICAL** *a.*, **∼ŏ'log**IST (3) *n.* [f. Gk *pteris -idos* fern + -o- + -LOGY]

ptĕ'ridophȳte (t-) *n.* fern or similar plant (e.g. club--moss, horse-tail). [f. as prec. + Gk *phuton* plant]

ptĕ'ro- (t-) *comb. form.* wing, as: **∼da'ctyl, ∼saur,** kinds of extinct winged reptile; **∼pod,** mollusc with middle part of foot expanded into pair of winglike lobes. [f. Gk *pteron* wing + -O-]

ptĕ'rȳgoid (t-) *a.* **∼ process,** each of two processes descending from sphenoid bone. [f. Gk *pterux -ugos* wing + -OID]

ptīsan (tī'zan, tĭză'n) *n.* nourishing decoction, esp. barley-water. [ME & OF *tizanne* etc. f. L f. Gk *ptisanē* peeled barley]

PTO *abbr.* please turn over.

Ptŏlĕmā'ĭc (t-) *a.* **1.** of Ptolemy, 2nd-c. astronomer of Alexandria, esp. **∼ system** (of astronomy, in which earth was held to be the stationary centre round which sun and stars revolved; cf. COPERNICAN). **2.** of the Ptolemies, rulers of Egypt from death of Alexander the Great to Cleopatra. [f. L f. Gk *Ptolemaios* + -IC]

ptomaine (tō'mān, tomā'n) *n.* any of various amine compounds (some toxic) in putrefying animal and vegetable matter; **∼ poisoning,** (arch.) food poisoning. [f. F *ptomaïne* f. It. *ptomaina* irreg. f. Gk *ptōma* corpse; see -INE⁵]

ptō'sĭis (t-) *n.* (*pl.* **∼es** *pr.* -ēz). drooping of upper eyelid from paralysis of a muscle; downward displacement of an organ. [Gk *ptōsis* (*piptō* fall)]

Pty. *abbr.* (Austral., NZ, & S. Afr.) proprietary.

ptȳ'alĭn (t-) *n.* enzyme found in saliva of man and some animals. [f. Gk *ptualon* spittle + -IN]

Pu *symb.* plutonium.

||pŭb *n.* (colloq.) public house; **∼-crawl,** a journey to several pubs with one or more drinks at each. [abbr.]

pŭ'bertў *n.* being or becoming functionally capable of procreation through natural development of repro-ductive organs; **age of ∼** (at which puberty begins; in law usu. 14 in boys, 12 in girls); hence **pŭ'bertAL** *a.* [ME, f. F *puberté* or f. L *pubertas* (*puber* adult; see -TY¹)]

pū'bēs (-z) *n.* lower part of abdomen, covered with hair at and after puberty. [L]

pūbĕ'sc|ence *n.* arrival at puberty; soft down on leaves and stems of plants, downiness; soft down on parts of animals esp. insects; so **∼ENT** *a.* [F, or f. med. L *pubescentia* f. L *pubescere* reach puberty (incept. f. prec.); see -ESCENCE]

pū'bĭc *a.* of the pubes or pubis. [f. PUBES + -IC]

pū'b|ĭs *n.* (*pl.* **∼es** *pr.* -ēz). bone forming front of each half of pelvis. [f. L *os pubis* bone of the PUBES]

pŭ'blĭc *a.* & *n.* **1.** *a.* of or concerning the people as a whole (*public holiday, interest*). **2.** done by or for, representing, the people (*public assembly, expenditure*). **3.** ||of, for, acting for, a university (*public orator, lecture, examination*). **4.** open to or shared by all the people (*public baths, lavatory,* LIBRARY, *meeting, road*). **5.** open to general observation, done or existing in public, (*made his views public; made a public protest; gave it public utterance*); **go ∼,** become public company; hence **∼LY²** *adv.* **6.** of or engaged in the affairs or service of the people (*public life; a public man; public money; public records;* NOTARY *public*). **7.** **∼ act,** **∼ bill,** (of legislation affecting the people as a whole); **∼-address system,** equipment of loudspeakers etc. to enable speaker, musician, etc., to be heard by many; ||**∼**

bar, least expensive bar in public house; ||**∼ com-pany** (with shares available to all buyers); **in the ∼ domain,** belonging to the community as a whole, esp. no longer copyright; **∼ enemy,** criminal whom special efforts are made to apprehend; **in the ∼ eye,** receiving much publicity; *public* FIGURE¹; **∼ health,** protection of the public from disease by adequate sanitation, hygiene, etc.; **∼ house,** inn, esp. ||pro-viding alcoholic liquor for consumption on the premises; **∼ law,** (1) law of relations between persons and State, (2) = *public act;* **∼ lending right,** right of authors to payment when their books etc. are lent by public libraries; *public* LIBEL; **∼ nuisance,** (Law) illegal act harming community rather than an indi-vidual, (colloq.) person who is obnoxious to many members of community; *public* OPINION, ||ORATOR; **∼ ownership** (by the State); *public* PROSECUTOR; *Public* RECORD² *Office;* **∼ relations,** (esp. good) relations between organization etc. and the general public (**∼** *relations officer,* employee concerned with public rela-tions and issuing information to newspapers etc.); **∼ school,** ||endowed grammar (usu. boarding-) school preparing pupils esp. for universities or public ser-vices, (Sc., US, etc.) school managed by public authorities; **∼ servant,** State official; **∼ spirit, ∼-spi'rited,** (being) ready to do things for the benefit of people in general; **∼ transport,** buses, trains, etc., available to public and having fixed routes, as opp. to hired or private vehicles; **∼ utility,** organization supplying water, gas, electricity, etc., and regarded as a public service; *public* WORK¹*s;* **∼ wrong,** offence against society as a whole. **8.** *n.* the (members of the) community in general (*the public is the best judge, are the best judges*); section of the community (*the reading public*); ||(colloq.) public house; **in ∼,** openly, publicly. [ME f. OF, or f. L *publicus* (*pubes* adult; see -IC)]

pŭ'blĭcan *n.* **1.** ||keeper of public house. **2.** (Rom. Hist., and in NT) tax-farmer, tax-collector. [ME f. OF *publican* f. L *publicanus* (*publicum* public revenue f. as prec.; see -AN)]

publĭcā'tion *n.* making publicly known; issuing of book, engraving, music, etc., to the public; book etc. so issued. [ME f. OF, f. L *publicatio -onis* (as PUBLISH; see -ATION)]

pŭ'blĭc|ist *n.* writer on or person skilled in inter-national law; writer on current public topics, esp. journalist; publicity agent; so **∼ISM** (2) *n.,* **∼ĭ'st**IC *a.* [f. F *publiciste* f. L (*jus*) *publicum* public law; see -IST]

publĭ'cĭtў *n.* being open to general observation, notoriety; the business of advertising (goods or persons); **∼ agent,** person employed to keep the name of an actor etc. well known to the public. [f. F *publicité* (as PUBLIC; see -ITY)]

pŭ'blĭcize, -ise (-īz), *v.t.* make publicly known, esp. by advertisement. [f. PUBLIC + -IZE]

pŭ'blĭsh *v.t.* **1.** make generally known; (Law) make (libel etc.) known to third party. **2.** announce formally, promulgate (edict etc.); read (banns of marriage). **3.** (Of author, editor, or publisher) issue copies of (book, engraving, etc., or abs.) for sale to the public. **4.** Hence **∼ABLE** *a.* [ME *publise* etc. f. *publier, publ'ier* f. L *publicare* (as PUBLIC); see -ISH²]

pŭ'blĭsher *n.* In vbl senses; one who produces copies of book, newspaper, etc., and distributes them to booksellers or to the public; *****proprietor of newspaper etc. [ME, f. prec. + -ER¹]

pŭccoō'n *n.* N. Amer. plant yielding red or yellow dye. [Algonquian]

pūce *a.* flea-colour, purple-brown. [F, = flea (-colour), f. L *pulex -icis*]

pŭck¹ *n.* mischievous or (arch.) evil sprite; (fig.) mischievous child; hence **∼'ISH¹, ∼'LIKE,** *adjs.* [OE *pūca* = ON *púci* mischievous demon; ult. orig. unkn.; cf. W *pwca,* Ir. *púca*]

pŭck² *n.* rubber disc used in ice hockey. [19th c.; orig. unkn.]

pŭ'cka. Var. of PUKKA.
pŭ'cker v. & n. 1. v.t. & i. ~ (**up**), contract, gather, (of brow, seam, material) into wrinkles, folds, or bulges, intentionally or as fault e.g. in sewing. **2.** n. such bulge etc.; hence ~Y² a. [prob. frequent. f. as POKE¹, POCKET¹ (cf. PURSE²); see -ER⁵]
pŭd¹ n. child's hand; forefoot of some animals. [17th c.; orig. unkn.]
pud² (pŏŏd) n. (colloq.) = foll. [abbr.]
pu'dding (pŏŏ'-) n. **1.** soft or fairly firm food consisting of ingredients mixed with or enclosed in flour or other farinaceous or cereal substance and cooked by boiling, steaming, or baking, (HASTY, MILK¹, PLUM, YORKSHIRE, *pudding*); sweet (course of meal); *the* PROOF¹ *of the pudding*. **2.** intestine of pig etc. stuffed with oatmeal, blood, etc., (BLACK¹ *pudding*). **3.** person or thing of pudding-like appearance etc. **4.** (Naut.) also **puddening**). pad, tow binding, to prevent chafing etc. **5.** ~-**cloth,** (in which some puddings are tied up for boiling); **in the ~ club,** (sl.) pregnant; ~ **face,** large fat face; ~-**head,** stupid person; ~-**stone,** conglomerate rock of rounded pebbles in siliceous matrix. **6.** Hence ~Y² a. [ME *poding*, f. OF *boudin* black pudding f. Gallo-Rom. **botellinus* f. L *botellus* sausage; see BOWEL]
pŭ'ddle¹ n. small dirty pool esp. of rain on road etc.; clay (and sand) mixed with water as watertight covering for embankments etc., hence **pŭ'ddly²** a. [ME. *podel, puddel, puddle*, dim. of OE *pudd* ditch; see -LE 1; cf. G dial. *p(f)udel* pool]
pŭ'ddle² v. **1.** v.i. dabble or wallow in mud or shallow water; make PUDDLE¹ from clay etc.; busy oneself in untidy way. **2.** v.t. make (water etc.) muddy; knead (clay and sand) into, line (canal etc.) with, PUDDLE¹; stir about (molten iron) to produce wrought iron by expelling carbon. **3.** Hence **pŭ'ddl**ER (1, 2) n. [ME, f. prec.; cf. POODLE, Du. *poedelen*, LG *pud(d)eln* splash in water]
pu'dency n. modesty. [f. LL *pudentia* (as foll.; see -ENCY)]
pŭdĕ'nd|um n. (usu. in pl. ~a). genitals, esp. of woman; hence or cogn. **pŭdĕ'nd**AL, **pŭ'd**IC, adjs. [f. L *pudenda* (*membra* parts), neut. pl. of gerundive of *pudēre* be ashamed]
pŭdge n. (colloq.) short thick or fat person, animal, or thing; hence **pŭ'dg**Y² a. [cf. PODGY]
puĕ'blŏ (pwĕ'-) n. (pl. ~s). town or village in Latin America, esp. settlement of Indians. [Sp., = people f. L *populus*]
pŭ'erĭle a. boyish, childish; suitable only for children, trivial, whence or cogn. ~LY² (-l-lĭ) adv., **pŭerĭ'l**ITY n.; ~ **breathing** (with loud pulmonary murmur as in children, usu. sign of disease in adult). [f. F *puéril* or f. L *puerilis* (*puer* boy; see -IL)]
pŭĕr'peral a. of or due to childbirth; ~ **fever** (following childbirth and caused by uterine infection). [f. L *puerperus* (*puer* child, *-parus* bearing) + -AL]
pŭff¹ n. **1.** short quick blast of breath or wind; sound (as) of this, small quantity of vapour, smoke, etc., emitted at one puff. **2.** round soft protuberant mass of material in dress (*puff sleeve*), of hair of head, etc.; *eiderdown; = POWDER-*puff*. **3.** piece, cake, etc., of light pastry esp. of puff pastry. **4.** unduly or extravagantly laudatory review of book, advertisement of tradesman's goods, etc., esp. in newspaper. **5.** ~-**adder,** large venomous Afr. viper inflating upper part of body when excited; ~-**ball,** fungus with ball-shaped spore-case; ~ **pastry** (light and flaky); ||**puff-puff,** (childish for) steam-engine, train. [ME *puf*, imit.; see IL]
pŭff² v. **1.** v.i. emit puff of air or breath; (of air etc.) come *out* or *up* in puffs; ~ (**and blow**), breathe hard, pant; (of person smoking, steam-engine, etc.) emit puffs, move with puffs, (*puffed away at his cigar*; *train puffed out of the station*); become inflated, swell, (*up*, *out*). **2.** v.t. ~ (**out**), put out of breath (*arrived somewhat puffed*), utter pantingly. **3.** blow (dust, smoke, light

object, *out*, *up*, *away*, etc.) with puff; smoke (pipe) in puffs. **4.** blow *out*, *up*, inflate; ~ **up,** elate, make proud, (esp. in *p.p.*, *with* pride etc.). **5.** advertise (goods) with exaggerated or false praise. **6.** Hence ~'ER n. (also in childish use, = PUFF¹-*puff*). [ME *puffe*, perh. f. OE **puffan*, imit. of sound of breath]
pŭ'fferẎ n. advertisement, puffing. [f. prec. + -ERY]
pŭ'ffin n. N. Atlantic auk with large furrowed particoloured bill. [ME *poffin*, *pophyn*, of unkn. orig.]
pŭff|ỹ a. gusty; short-winded; puffed out, swollen; corpulent; hence ~iNESS n. [f. PUFF¹,² + -Y²]
pŭg¹ n. **1.** ~(-**dog**), dwarf breed of dog like bulldog, with broad flat nose and deeply wrinkled face, whence ~'gISH¹, ~'gY², (-g-) adjs.; ~-**nose**(d), (with) short squat or snub nose. **2.** (Quasi-proper name for) fox. **3.** ||small locomotive for shunting etc. [16th c., perh. f. LDu.]
pŭg² n., & v.t. (-**gg**-). **1.** n. loam or clay mixed and prepared for making bricks, pottery, etc.; ~-**mill** (for preparing pug). **2.** v.t. prepare (clay) thus; pack (space esp. under floor, to deaden sound) with pug, sawdust, etc.; hence ~'gING² (3) (-g-) n. [19th c.; orig. unkn.]
pŭg³ n., & v.t. (-**gg**-). **1.** n. footprint of animal. **2.** v.t. track by pugs. [f. Hindi *pag* footprint]
pŭg⁴ n. (sl.) pugilist. [abbr.]
pŭ'ggaree (-rĭ) n. Indian's light turban; thin scarf of muslin etc. worn round hat and sometimes hanging down behind as protection against sun. [f. Hindi *pagrī* turban]
pŭ'gil|ist n. (esp. professional) boxer; so ~ISM (2) n., ~i'stIC a. [f. L *pugil* boxer + -IST]
pŭgnā'cious (-shus) a. disposed to fight, quarrelsome; hence or cogn. ~LY² adv., **pŭgnā'cITY** n. [f. L *pugnax -acis* (*pugnare* fight, f. *pugnus* fist); see -ACIOUS]
Pŭ'gwash (-ŏsh) n. ~ **conferences,** regularly held international conferences of eminent scientists to discuss world problems. [~ in Nova Scotia, where first held]
puǐ'snĕ (pū'nǐ) a. & n. ~ (**judge**), judge of superior court inferior in rank to chief justices; (Law) later, subsequent (*to*), (*puisne mortgagees*; *mortgagees puisne to the plaintiff*). [OF (*puis* after f. L *postea*, *né* born f. L *natus*); cf. PUNY]
puissance (pū'ĭs-, pwĭ's-) n. **1.** (*or* pwĭsah'ns). (In show-jumping) test of horse's ability to jump high obstacles. **2.** (arch.) great power, might, or influence. [ME in sense 2, f. OF (as foll.; see -ANCE)]
pu'issant (pū'ĭs-, pwĭ's-) a. (literary). having great power or influence, mighty; hence ~LY² adv. [ME f. OF, f. Gallo-Rom. **possiantem* f. L *posse* be able; cf. POTENT¹]
pu'ja (pŏŏ'-), **pŏŏ'ja,** n. Hindu religious rite. [Skr.]
pūke v.i. & t., & n. vomit. [16th c.; prob. imit.]
pukĕ'kō (pŏŏk-) n. (pl. ~s). (Austral. & NZ). gallinule (*Porphyrio melanotus*) with blue, black, and white plumage. [Maori]
pŭ'kka, -ah (-a), a. (Anglo-Ind.) of full weight; genuine; permanent, solidly built. [f. Hindi *pakkā* cooked, ripe, substantial]
pu'ku (pŏŏ'kŏŏ) n. red African antelope (*Adenota vardoni*). [f. Zulu *mpuku*]
pŭ'lchri|tūde (-kr-) n. (literary). beauty; hence ~**tū'din**OUS a. [ME, f. L *pulchritudo -dinis* (*pulcher -chri* beautiful; see -TUDE)]
pūle v.i. cry querulously or weakly, whine, whimper. [16th c., prob. imit.; cf. F *piauler*]
Pu'litzer (pŏŏ'lĭtser, pū'-) n. ~ **prize,** one of 13 annual awards for achievements in American journalism, literature, and music. [f. J. ~, Amer. newspaper-publisher d. 1911]
pull¹ (pŏŏl) v. **1.** v.t. exert upon (thing etc.) force tending to move it to oneself (*don't pull my hair*; *pull his sleeve* or *him by the sleeve*; *pull person's* LEG; *pull* RANK¹, the STRINGS, WIRES); damage (muscle etc.) by abnormal strain. **2.** cause (thing etc.) to move towards oneself or in direction so regarded (*pull it nearer*; *pull*

him into the room; *pull your cap over your ears*; *pull the trigger*); draw (knife, gun, etc.) out of its sheath etc. in order to use it (*on* person); ~ **caps**, (arch.) scuffle, quarrel. **3.** attract or secure (support, custom). **4.** ~ (thing) **apart or to pieces**, separate its parts forcibly, (fig.) criticize (person, thing) unfavourably. **5.** remove (cork, tooth, etc.) by pulling; draw (quantity of liquor) from barrel etc.; pluck (plant, often *up*) by root; (colloq.) accomplish, pull off, (*pull a* FAST³ *one*). **6.** ~**ed bread**, pieces from inside of new loaf, rebaked till crisp; ~**ed figs** (flattened before being packed). **7.** print upon (sheet), print (copy, proof), orig. in old hand-press by pulling bar towards one. **8.** move (boat etc., or abs.) by pulling; ~ one's **weight**, row with effect in proportion to one's weight, (fig.) do one's fair share of work. **9.** check (horse) esp. so as to make him lose race; ~ one's **punches**, fail to give full force to one's blows in boxing (lit. or fig.). **10.** (Cricket). strike (ball, or abs.), strike ball bowled by (bowler), to leg side. **11.** (Golf). drive (ball, or abs.) widely to left (of right-handed player). **12.** *pull a* FACE¹; ~ **a** *sanctimonious* etc. **face**, assume such expression. **13.** *v.i.* exert pulling force (*horse pulls well*; *engine will not pull*); tear or pluck *at* (thing). **14.** proceed with effort (*up* hill etc.); (of horse) strain, esp. habitually, against bit. **15.** draw or suck *at* (pipe, tankard, etc.). **16.** (Of boat, vehicle, etc.) be caused to move esp. in specified direction. **17.** ~ **about**, pull from side to side, treat roughly; ~ **back**, (cause to) retreat; ~**-back** *n.*, retarding influence, *withdrawal of troops; ~ **down**, demolish (building etc.), lower in health, spirits, price, etc.; ~ **in**, acquire (profit, payment, etc.), (colloq.) arrest (person), (of train) enter station, (of vehicle) move to side of road or off road, whence ~*-in n.*, place for doing this, ||esp. lorry-drivers' café; ~ **off**, remove garment etc. by pulling (opp. ~ **on**), succeed in winning or achieving; ~ **out**, depart, withdraw from an undertaking, (of train) move out of station, (of vehicle) move away from side of road, or from behind another to overtake it; ~ *out of the fire*, save (game etc.) when the situation seems hopeless; ~*-out n.*, (1) page or plate in book that folds out from front edge of leaves to facilitate reference, (2) middle section of magazine etc. removable by pulling; *~ **over**, (of vehicle) pull in; ~ **round**, (cause to) recover from illness etc.; ~ **through** *adv. & prep.*, get (person), get oneself, safely through (danger, illness, etc.); ~*-through n.*, cord with which cleaning-rag is drawn through rifle; ~ **together**, work in harmony; ~ one**self together**, rally, recover oneself, esp. recover one's self-control; ~ **up**, cause (person, horse, vehicle) to stop, reprimand, check oneself, improve one's relative position in race etc. (and cf. sense 5); ~*-up n.*, house of call for travellers, *exercise of pulling oneself up to an overhead bar. **18.** Hence ~´ER¹ *n.* [OE (*ā*)*pullian*, perh. rel. to LG *pūlen*, MDu. *polen* to shell]

pull² (pŏŏl) *n.* **1.** act of pulling, wrench, tug; force thus exerted; (fig.) advantage, means of exerting influence, interest with the powerful. **2.** (Print.) rough proof. **3.** pulling at bridle to check horse esp. in racing. **4.** spell of rowing. **5.** (Cricket & Golf). pulling stroke. **6.** deep draught of liquor; suck at cigarette, cigar, or pipe. **7.** handle etc. by which pull is applied, e.g. BELL¹-*pull*. [ME, f. prec.]

pu´llet (pŏŏ´-) *n.* young domestic fowl, esp. hen from time she begins to lay till first moult. [ME, f. OF *poulet* dim. of *poule* f. Rom. **pulla* fem. of L *pullus* chicken]

pu´lley (pŏŏ´-) *n.*, & *v.t.* **1.** *n.* grooved wheel(s) for cord etc. to pass over, mounted and used for changing direction of power; wheel or drum fixed on shaft and turned by belt, used esp. to increase power or speed. **2.** *v.t.* hoist, furnish, work, with pulley. [ME, f. OF *polie* prob. ult. f. med. Gk **polidion* pivot dim. of *polos* POLE²]

Pu´llman (pŏŏ´-) *a. & n.* ~ (**car** or **coach**), railway carriage or motor coach with especially comfortable seats etc.; sleeping-car. [f. G. M. ~, Amer. designer d. 1897]

pu´llover (pŏŏ´-) *n.* (usu. knitted) outer garment for upper part of body, put on by being pulled over head. [f. PULL¹+OVER]

pŭ´llŭl|āte *v.i.* (Of shoot or bud) sprout out, bud; (of seed) sprout; (fig., of doctrine etc.) develop, spring up; abound *with*; hence or cogn. ~ANT *a.*, ~A´TION *n.* [f. L *pullulare* sprout (*pullulus* dim. of *pullus* young of animal)+-ATE³]

pŭ´lmonarў *a.* **1.** of, in, connected with, the lungs (*pulmonary diseases*); ~ **artery**, main artery conveying blood from heart to lungs; ~ **vein** (returning this blood to heart). **2.** having lungs or lunglike organs; so **pŭ´lmon**ATE² *a.* **3.** affected with or subject to lung-disease. [f. L *pulmonarius* (*pulmo -onis* lung; see -ARY¹)]

pulmo´nic *a.* = prec. **1.** [f. F *pulmonique* or f. mod. L *pulmonicus* f. L *pulmo* (as prec.)]

pŭlp *n. & v.* **1.** *n.* soft moist part of fruit; any fleshy soft part of animal body, e.g. nervous substance in interior cavity of tooth; soft shapeless mass, e.g. that of rags, wood, etc., from which paper is made (~ **magazine** etc., publication printed (orig.) on rough paper made from wood-pulp, often containing sensational or poor-quality writing; ~´**wood**, timber suitable for making pulp); ore pulverized and mixed with water; hence ~´LESS, ~´OUS, ~´Y², *adjs.* **2.** *v.t.* reduce to pulp; remove pulp from (coffee-beans etc.), whence ~´ER¹ (2) *n.* **3.** *v.i.* become pulpy. [f. L *pulpa*]

pu´lpit (pŏŏ´-) *n.* raised enclosed platform usu. with desk from which preacher in church or chapel delivers sermon; *the* profession of preaching; *the* preachers. [ME, f. L *pulpitum* scaffold, platform]

pulpiteer´ (pŏŏ-) *n.*, & *v.i.* **1.** *n.* (usu. derog.) professional preacher. **2.** *v.i.* preach. [f. prec.+-EER]

pu´lque (pŏŏ´lkĕ, -kā) *n.* Mexican fermented drink from sap of maguey; ~ **brandy**, strong intoxicant made from pulque. [17th c.; Amer. Sp., of unkn. orig.]

pŭ´lsăr *n.* cosmic source of regularly and rapidly pulsating radio signals. [f. *pulsating star*, after *quasar*]

pŭlsāte´ (-ā´t, pŭ´l-) *v.i.* expand and contract rhythmically, beat, throb (lit. or fig.); vibrate, quiver, thrill; hence or cogn. **pŭlsA´**TION, **pŭlsā´**TOR, *ns.*, **pŭ´lsat**ORY *a.* [f. L *pulsare* frequent. of *pellere puls*-drive, beat+-ATE³]

pŭ´lsatĭle *a.* of, or having the property of, pulsation; (of musical instrument) played by percussion. [f. med. L *pulsatilis* (as prec.; see -IL)]

pŭlsatĭ´lla *n.* pasque-flower; its extract, used in pharmacy. [mod. L, dim. of *pulsata* fem. p.p. (as PULSATE), because quivering in wind]

pŭlse¹ *n. & v.* **1.** *n.* rhythmical throbbing of arteries as blood is propelled along them esp. as felt in wrists, temples, etc. (FEEL person's *pulse*; *has a rapid, strong, pulse*); each successive beat of arteries or heart; (fig.) throb or thrill of life or emotion, latent sentiment. **2.** rhythmical recurrence of strokes e.g. of oars; (Mus.) beat; single vibration of sound, light, etc.; brief variation of electric current etc. esp. as signal. **3.** Hence ~´LESS (-sl-) *a.* **4.** *v.i.* pulsate (lit. or fig.). **5.** *v.t.* send *out*, in etc., by pulses or rhythmic beats. [n. ME f. OF *pous* f. L *pulsus* (*pellere puls*- drive, beat); v. f. L *pulsare* (as PULSATE)]

pŭlse² *n.* **1.** (as *sing.* or *pl.*) edible seeds of leguminous plants, e.g. peas, beans, lentils. **2.** any kind of these. [ME f. OF *pols* f. L *puls pultis* porridge of meal etc.]

pŭlsi´meter *n.* instrument for measuring rate or force of pulse. [f. PULSE¹+-I-+-METER]

Pŭlso´meter *n.* (P) steam-condensing vacuum pump. [f. PULSE¹+-O-+-METER, from pulsatory action of steam]

pŭ´lveriz|e,-ĭs|e (-īz) *v.* **1.** *v.t.* reduce to powder or dust, divide (liquid) into spray, whence ~**ātor**, ~**ER¹** (2), *ns.*; (fig.) demolish, crush, smash. **2.** *v.i.* crumble to dust. **3.** Hence ~**ABLE** *a.*, ~**A´TION** *n.* [ME, f. LL *pulverizare* (*pulvis pulveris* dust; see -IZE)]

pŭlvĕ′rulent (-rōō-) *a.* powdery, of dust; covered with powder; (of rock etc.) having only slight cohesion, apt to crumble. [f. L *pulverulentus* (as prec.; see -ULENT)]

pŭ′lvinate, -ātĕd, *adjs.* (Archit.) swelling, esp. (of frieze) with convex face; (Bot. & Entom.) cushion--like, having cushion-like swelling. [f. L *pulvinatus* (*pulvinus* cushion); see -ATE², -ED¹]

pŭ′ma *n.* large Amer. feline (*Felis concolor*). [Sp., f. Quechua]

pŭ′mice *n.*, & *v.t.* **1.** *n.* ～(-stone), (piece of) light porous kind of lava used for removing stains from skin etc., as powder for polishing, etc.; so **pŭmi′ceous** (-shŭs) *a.* **2.** *v.t.* rub or clean with pumice; (in *p.p.*), of horse's hoof) made spongy by disease. [ME f. OF *pomis* f. L *pumex pumicis* (dial. *pom*-); cf. POUNCE²]

pŭ′mmel *v.t.* (‖l-ll-). strike repeatedly esp. with fist. [altered f. POMMEL]

pŭmp¹ *n.* **1.** machine, usu. cylinder in which piston etc. is moved up and down by rod, for raising water; machine of this kind or with rotary action etc. for raising or moving liquids, compressing or rarefying gases, inflating tyres, etc. (fig. of heart, insect's suckers, etc.); pumping, stroke of pump. **2.** ～-brake, handle of pump esp. with transverse bar for several persons to work at; ～-handle *v.t.*, (colloq.) shake (person's hand) effusively; ～-priming, (fig.) stimulation of commerce etc. by investment; ～-room, building where pump is worked, esp. at spa where medicinal water is dispensed. [ME *pumpe, pompe*, orig. Naut., = MDu. *pompe*, LG *pump*(*e*); prob. imit.]

pŭmp² *v.* **1.** *v.i.* work a pump. **2.** *v.t.* raise or move (water, air, etc., esp. *in, into, out, up*) with pump; make (ship, well, etc.) *dry* by pumping; ～ **up**, inflate (pneumatic tyre), inflate tyres of (bicycle etc.). **3.** cause to move, pour forth, be sent *out*, etc., as if by pumping; elicit information from (person) by persistent questioning. **4.** *v.t.* & *i.* move vigorously up and down as if pumping. [f. prec.]

pŭmp³ *n.* light shoe usu. without fastening, worn esp. for dancing, tennis, etc.; *court shoe. [16th c.; orig. unkn.]

pu′mpernickel (pŭ′-, pōō′-) *n.* German wholemeal rye bread. [G, f. earlier sense 'lout', 'stinker' (*pumpe*(*r*)*n* break wind, *Nickel* Nicholas)]

pŭ′mpkin *n.* (plant of genus *Cucurbita* bearing) large egg-shaped or globular orange-coloured fruit with edible layer next to rind, used in cookery and as food for cattle; *some ～s, (colloq.) important person or thing. [alt. (after -KIN) f. earlier *pompon, pumpion*, f. obs. F *po*(*m*)*pon* f. L *pepo -onis* f. Gk *pepōn* large melon (see PEPO)]

pŭn¹ *n.*, & *v.i.* (-nn-). **1.** *n.* humorous use of word to suggest different meanings, or of words of same or similar sound with different meanings (e.g. *gout had taken him in toe*); play on words. **2.** *v.i.* make pun(s) (on word or subject); hence ～′**ningLY²** *adv.* [17th c., perh. f. obs. *pundigrion*, a fanciful formation]

‖**pŭn²** *v.t.* (-nn-). consolidate (earth, rubble) by pounding or ramming. [dial. var. of POUND³]

pu′na (pōō′-) *n.* high bleak plateau in Peruvian Andes; = MOUNTAIN sickness. [Quechua, in first sense]

pŭnch¹ *n.* **1.** instrument or machine for cutting holes in leather, metal, paper, etc., driving bolt etc. out of hole (**starting**-～), enlarging hole, etc.; NAIL¹-*punch*. **2.** tool or machine for impressing design or stamping die on material. [f. foll., or abbr. of PUNCHEON¹]

pŭnch² *v.t.*, & *n.* **1.** *v.t.* strike esp. with closed fist; ‖～-ball, *～′ing-bag, inflated ball or bag held by elastic bands etc. and punched as form of exercise; ～-up, (colloq.) fist-fight, brawl. **2.** prod with stick etc., esp. *drive (cattle) thus. **3.** pierce (metal, leather, bus-ticket, etc.) as or with punch; pierce (hole) thus; ～(ed) **card, tape,** etc., (perforated according to specified code, for conveying instructions to computer etc.). **4.** Hence ～′ER (1, 2) *n.* **5.** *n.* blow with fist (*a punch on the head*; PULL¹ one's *punches*);

ability to deliver this; ～**-drunk,** stupefied through having been severely or repeatedly punched (lit. or fig.). **6.** (sl.) vigour, momentum, effective force; ～ **line,** words giving point of joke etc. **7.** Hence ～′Y² *a.*, (1) having force or vigour, (2) (colloq.) punch--drunk. [ME, var. of POUNCE¹]

pŭnch³ *n.* drink usu. of wine or spirits mixed with hot or cold water or milk, sugar, lemons, spice, etc.; ～-bowl, (1) bowl in which punch is mixed, (2) round deep hollow in hill(s). [17th c.; orig. unkn.]

pŭnch⁴ *n.* **1.** ‖(**Suffolk**) ～, short-legged thickset draught horse. **2.** (P～). grotesque humpbacked figure in puppet-show called *Punch and Judy*, esp. as title of a London weekly comic paper; **as pleased** or **as proud as P～,** showing great pleasure or pride. [abbr. of PUNCHINELLO]

pŭ′ncheon¹ (-nshŏn) *n.* short post, esp. one supporting roof in coal-mine; = PUNCH¹. [ME, f. OF *poinson, po*(*i*)*nchon*, f. Rom. **punctio -onis* or **punctiare* (L *pungere punct-* prick); see -ION]

pŭ′ncheon² (-nshŏn) *n.* (Hist.) large cask for liquids etc. holding from 72 to 120 gal. [ME, f. OF *poinson, po*(*i*)*nchon*, of unkn. orig.]

Pŭnchĭně′llŏ *n.* (*pl.* ～s). chief character in Italian puppet-show; short stout person of comical appearance. [17th c., perh. assim. form of *Polichinello* f. Neapolitan dial. *Polecenella*, It. *Pulcinella*, perh. dim. of *pollecena* young turkey-cock with hooked beak (*pulcino* chicken f. Rom. **pullicinus* f. L *pullus*)]

pŭ′nct|āte *a.* (Biol. & Path.) marked or studded with points, dots, or spots; hence ～A′TION *n.* [f. L (as POINT¹; see -ATE⁷)]

pŭnctǐ′lĭŏ (-lyŏ) *n.* (*pl.* ～s). delicate point of ceremony or honour; etiquette of such points; petty formality. [f. It. *puntiglio* & Sp. *puntillo* dim. of *punto* POINT¹]

pŭnctǐ′lious (-lyŭs) *a.* attentive to punctilio(s) or to details of conduct, duties, etc.; hence ～LY² *adv.*, ～NESS *n.* [f. F *pointilleux* (*pointille* f. It. as prec.; see -OUS)]

pŭ′nctual *a.* observant of appointed time, neither early nor late; (arch.) punctilious; (Geom.) of a point; hence ～ITY (-ă′l-) *n.*, ～LY² *adv.* [ME, f. med. L *punctualis* f. L *punctum* POINT¹; see -AL]

pŭ′nctuāte *v.t.* insert stops in (writing), mark or divide with stops; (fig.) interrupt at intervals (speech with exclamations etc.); emphasize, accentuate. [f. med. L *punctuare* (as prec.) + -ATE³]

pŭnctuā′tion *n.* insertion of vowel and other points in Hebrew etc., practice or art of punctuating; ～ **mark,** = STOP² 2. [f. med. L *punctuatio* (as prec.); see -ATION)]

pŭ′nct|um *n.* (*pl.* ～·a). (Biol. & Path.) speck, dot, spot of colour or elevation or depression on surface [L, = POINT¹]

pŭ′ncture *n.* & *v.* **1.** *n.* pricking, prick, esp. accidental piercing of pneumatic tyre; hole thus made. **2.** *v.t.* prick, pierce, (lit. or fig.). **3.** *v.i.* undergo puncture. [ME, f. L *punctura* (*pungere punct*- prick; see -URE)]

pŭ′ndit *n.* **1.** Hindu learned in Sanskrit and in philosophy, religion, and jurisprudence, of India. **2.** learned expert or teacher; hence ～RY (5) *n.* [f. Hind. *pandit* f. Skr. *pandita* learned]

pŭ′ng|ent (-nj-) *a.* **1.** (Of reproof, satire, etc.) biting, caustic; mentally stimulating, piquant. **2.** affecting organs of smell or taste, or skin etc., with pricking sensation (*pungent gas, smoke, sauce*). **3.** (Biol.) sharp--pointed. **4.** Hence ～ENCY *n.*, ～entLY² *adv.* [f. L *pungere* prick; see -ENT]

Pū′nic *a.* & *n.* Carthaginian (language); *Punic* FAITH. [f. L *Punicus, Poenicus* (*Poenus* f. Gk *Phoinix* Phoenician; see -IC)]

pŭ′nish *v.t.* **1.** cause (offender) to suffer (*by* or *with* penalty, *for* offence), inflict penalty on (offender); inflict penalty for (offence). **2.** (colloq.) inflict severe blows on (opponent in boxing); (of race, competitor) tax severely the powers of (competitor); take full advantage of (weak bowling, bowler, stroke at tennis, etc.); subject to severe stress or depletion; hence ᴧING² *a*. **3.** Hence ᴧER¹ *n*., ᴧABLE *a*. [ME, f. OF *punir* (-ISH²) f. L *punire* (*poenire* f. *poena* penalty)]

pŭ′nishment *n*. punishing or being punished; penalty inflicted on offender; (colloq.) severe treatment by opponent. [ME, f. AF & OF *punissement* (*punir*; see prec., -MENT)]

pū′nitive *a*. inflicting or intended to inflict punishment (*punitive justice, expedition*); (of damages) = VINDICTIVE; (of taxation etc.) extremely severe; so **pū′nitory** *a*. [f. F *punitif* -*ive* or f. med. L *punitivus* (as prec.; see -IVE)]

Pŭnja′bi (-ah′-) *a*. & *n*. (native or language) of the Punjab in India. [f. Hindi *pañjābī* (*Pañjāb* Punjab; see -I)]

∥**pŭnk¹** *n*. (arch.) prostitute. [16th c., of unkn. orig.]

pŭnk² *n*. & *a*. **1.** *n*. rotten wood, fungus growing on wood, used as tinder. **2.** (colloq.) worthless stuff, nonsense; worthless person; novice; young ruffian. **3.** *a*. (colloq.) worthless, rotten; ᴧ **rock,** style of simple rock music played with great vigour but lacking polish. [18th c., of unkn. orig.; cf. SPUNK]

pŭ′nkah (-ka) *n*. (Ind.) portable fan usu. of leaf of palmyra; large swinging cloth fan on frame worked by cord or electrically. [f. Hindi *pankhā* fan f. Skr. *pakṣaka* (*pakṣa* wing)]

pŭ′nner *n*. tool for ramming earth round post etc. to make it firm. [f. PUN² + -ER¹]

∥**pŭ′nnet** *n*. small chip or plastic basket for fruit or vegetables. [19th c., perh. dim. of dial. *pun* POUND¹; see -ET¹]

pŭ′nster *n*. (esp. inveterate) maker of puns. [f. PUN¹ + -STER]

pŭnt¹ *n*. & *v*. **1.** *n*. flat-bottomed shallow boat, broad and square at both ends, propelled by long pole thrust against bottom of river etc. **2.** *v.t*. propel with such pole; convey in punt. **3.** *v.i*. use punt-pole; travel in punt. [ME, f. MLG *punte, punto*, MDu. *ponte* ferry--boat, f. L *ponto* Gaulish transport vessel]

pŭnt² *v.t*., & *n*. **1.** *v.t*. kick (football) after it has been dropped from the hands and before it reaches ground; ᴧ**-about,** kicking about of football for practice, ball so used. **2.** *n*. such kick. [prob. f. dial. *punt* push forcibly (cf. BUNT³)]

pŭnt³ *v.i*., & *n*. **1.** *v.i*. (At faro and other card-games) lay stake against bank; ∥(colloq.) bet on horse etc., speculate in shares etc. **2.** *n*. player who punts; point in faro. [f. F *ponter* (*ponte* player against bank f. Sp. *punto* POINT¹)]

pŭ′nter¹ *n*. In vbl senses. [f. PUNT¹ + -ER¹]
pŭ′nter² *n*. In vbl senses. [f. PUNT² + -ER¹]
pŭ′nter³ *n*. In vbl senses; prostitute's client. [f. PUNT³ + -ER¹]

pū′n|y̆ *a*. undersized; weak, feeble; petty; hence ᴧiNESS *n*. [phonetic sp. of PUISNE]

pŭp *n*., & *v.t*. (-pp-). **1.** young dog; **in** ᴧ, (of bitch) pregnant; **sell** person **a** ᴧ, swindle him esp. by selling thing on prospective value. **2.** young wolf, rat, seal, etc. **3.** objectionable young man. **4.** ᴧ **tent,** small tent of simple design. **5.** *v.t*. (Of bitch etc.) bring forth (young, or abs.). [back-form. f. PUPPY as if dim. in -Y³]

pŭ′p|a *n*. (pl. ᴧae). form taken by insect in torpid stage of passive development between larva and imago; hence ᴧAL *a*. [mod. L; in L, = girl, doll]

pŭ′p|āte *v.i*. become a pupa; hence ᴧA′TION *n*. [f. prec. + -ATE³]

pū′pil *n*. **1.** one who is taught by another, schoolchild, disciple; (Law) person below age of puberty and under care of guardian; ᴧ**-teacher,** (Hist.) boy or girl teaching in elementary school under head teacher and concurrently receiving general education from him or elsewhere. **2.** circular opening in centre of iris of eye, varying in size to regulate passage of light to the retina. **3.** Hence or cogn. ᴧ(l)AR¹, ᴧ(l)ARY², *adjs*., ᴧ(l)ă′rITY, ᴧSHIP, *ns*. [ME, f. OF *pupille* or f. L *pupillus, pupilla* ward, orphan, *pupilla* pupil of eye, dims. of *pupus* boy, *pupa* girl]

pū′pillage, pū′pilage, *n*. nonage, minority (fig. of country, language, etc.); being a pupil. [f. prec. + -AGE]

pūpi′parous *a*. (Entom.) bringing forth young already advanced to pupal state. [f. mod. L *Pupipara*, neut. pl. (as *n*.) of *pupiparus* (as PUPA, *parere* bring forth)]

pŭ′ppet *n*. figure, usu. small, representing human being or animal and moved by various means as entertainment in ᴧ**-show;** person whose acts are controlled by another; ᴧ **state,** country professing to be independent but actually under the control of some greater power; ᴧ**-valve,** = POPPET-*valve*; hence ᴧEER, ᴧRY (4, 5), *ns*. [later form of POPPET]

pŭ′ppy *n*. young dog; vain empty-headed young man, coxcomb, = PUP 3; ᴧ**-dog,** (childish) = *puppy*; ᴧ **fat,** temporary fatness of child or adolescent; ᴧ **love,** = CALF¹-*love*; hence ᴧDOM, ᴧHOOD, *ns*., ᴧISH¹ *a*. [ME, perh. f. OF *po(u)pee* doll, plaything, toy f. Rom. *puppata* (as POPPET)]

pur- *pref*. = PRO-¹ (*purchase, purport, pursue*). [AF, f. OF *por-, pur-, pour-* f. L *por-, pro-*]

Purā′n|a (poorah′-) *n*. any of a class of Sanskrit sacred poems of Hindu mythology; hence ᴧIC *a*. [f. Skr. *purāṇa* ancient legend, ancient (*purā* formerly)]

∥**Pŭr′beck** *n*. ᴧ **stone,** hard limestone used in building etc. [ᴧ in Dorset]

pŭr′blind *a*., & *v.t*. **1.** *a*. partly blind, dim-sighted; (fig.) obtuse, dull; hence ᴧNESS *n*. **2.** *v.t*. make purblind. [ME *pur(e) blind* f. PURE orig. in sense 'utterly', w. assim. to PUR-]

pŭr′chase¹ *n*. **1.** buying; ᴧ**-money,** price (to be) paid; ᴧ **tax,** (Hist.) tax on goods bought, at rate increasing with decreasing necessity of the goods. **2.** (Hist.) practice of buying commissions in army. **3.** thing bought. **4.** annual rent or return from land (*sold at 20 years' purchase*); (fig.) **is not worth an hour's** ᴧ, (of person's life etc.) cannot be trusted to last an hour longer. **5.** (Law). acquisition of property by one's personal action, not by inheritance. **6.** mechanical advantage, leverage, (lit. or fig.); appliance for gaining this, esp. (Naut.) rope, windlass, pulley, etc. [ME, f. AF *purchas*, OF *porchas* (as foll.)]

pŭr′chas|e² *v.t*. **1.** buy; acquire (victory, freedom, etc., *with* one's blood, toil, etc.). **2.** (Naut.) haul up (anchor etc.) by means of pulley, lever, etc. **3.** Hence or cogn. ᴧABLE *a*., ᴧER¹ *n*. [ME, f. AF PUR(*chacer* CHASE²) procure, seek]

pŭr′dah (-da) *n*. (Ind. etc.) curtain, esp. one serving to screen Muslim or Hindu women from being seen by men or strangers; (fig.) Indian system of secluding women of rank from public view. [f. Urdu & Pers. *pardah* veil, curtain]

pūre *a*. **1.** unmixed, unadulterated (*pure white, air, alcohol, water*); (of sound) not discordant, esp. (Mus.) perfectly in tune; (of vowel) not joined with another in diphthong, (Gk Gram.) preceded by another vowel; (of consonant) not accompanied by another. **2.** of unmixed descent (*pure-blooded, -bred*); pure MATHEMATICS, SCIENCE. **3.** mere, simple, nothing but, sheer, (*knowledge pure and simple; pure nonsense, prejudice*). **4.** not corrupt (*his taste was severe and pure*); morally undefiled, guiltless, sincere; sexually undefiled, chaste. **5.** Hence ᴧLY² (pūr′lǐ) *adv*., (esp.) merely, exclusively, solely, entirely; ᴧ′NESS (pūr′n-) *n*. [ME, f. OF *pur* pure f. L *purus*]

purée (pūr′ā) *n*. pulp of vegetables, meat, fruit, etc., (boiled and) passed through sieve or otherwise reduced to a uniform mass. [F]

pŭr′fle *n*., & *v.t*. **1.** *n*. ornamental border esp. of violin etc.; (arch.) embroidered edge of garment. **2.** *v.t*. adorn with purfle; ornament (edge of building *with* crockets etc.); beautify; hence **pŭr′flıng¹** *n*., (esp.) inlaid bordering on back and belly of violin etc. [ME, f. OF *porfil(er)* f. Rom. *PRO*¹(*filare* f. L *filum* thread)]

pŭrgā′tion *n*. purification; purging of bowels; spiritual cleansing, esp. (RC Ch.) of soul in purgatory.

(Hist.) clearing of oneself from accusation or suspicion by oath or ordeal. [ME f. OF or f. L *purgatio* (as PURGE; see -ATION)]

pŭr'gative *a.* & *n.* strongly laxative (medicine); (thing) serving to purify. [ME, f. OF *purgatif* -*ive* or f. LL *purgatiuus* (as PURGE; see -ATIVE)]

pŭr'gatorȳ *n.* & *a.* **1.** *n.* condition or place of spiritual purging, esp. (RC Ch.) of souls departing this life in grace of God but having to expiate venial sins etc.; place or state of temporary suffering or expiation. **2.** *a.* purifying; so **pŭrgatŏr'IAL** *a.* [ME, f. AF *purgatorie*, OF -*oire* f. med. L *purgatorium*, neut. (as n.) of LL *purgatorius* (as foll.; see -ORY)]

pŭrge *v.t.*, & *n.* **1.** *v.t.* make physically or spiritually clean (*of* or *from* impurities, sin, etc.); remove by cleansing process (lit. or fig.), clear *away*, *off*, *out*; (of medicine or person) clear (bowels, person, or abs.) by evacuation (**purging agaric, flax,** etc., plants yielding purgatives); clear (person, one*self*, *of* charge, suspicion); (Law) atone for, wipe out, (offence, esp. contempt of court, or sentence) by expiation and submission; rid (political party, army, etc.) of persons regarded as undesirable. **2.** *n.* such clearance, purgation; purgative. [ME, f. OF *purg(i)er* f. L *purgare* purify (*purus* pure)]

purificā'tion *n.* purifying or being purified; ritual cleansing, esp. that of woman after childbirth enjoined by Jewish law; **the P~** (**of the Virgin Mary**), presentation of Christ in Temple on completion of Mary's purification (Luke 2:22), least in honour of this (2 Feb.); so **pŭr'ificātorY** *a.* [ME f. OF, or f. L *purificatio* (as PURIFY; see -FICATION)]

pŭr'ificātor *n.* (Eccl.) cloth used at Eucharist for wiping chalice and paten, and fingers and lips of celebrant. [mod. var. of *purificatory* n. f. med. L *purificatorium* (as PURIFICATORY; see prec.)]

pŭr'if̄ȳ *v.t.* make pure (*of* or *from* impurities, sin, etc.); make ceremonially clean; clear of extraneous elements; hence **~īER**[1] (2) *n.* [ME, f. OF *purifier* f. L *purificare* (as PURE; see -FY)]

Pŭr'im *n.* Jewish festival commemorating defeat of Haman's plot (Esth. 9). [Heb., pl. of *pūr*, perh. = LOT 1]

pŭr'ine (-ēn) *n.* (Chem.) white crystalline base forming uric acid on oxidation. [f. G *purin* f. L *purus* pure + *uricum* uric; see -INE[5]]

pŭr'ist *n.* stickler for or affecter of scrupulous purity esp. in language or art; so **~ism** (3) *n.*, **~i'stic(al)** *adjs.* [f. F *puriste* (*pur* PURE; see -IST)]

pŭr'itan *n.* & *a.* **1.** *n.* (Hist.; *P~*). member of the party of English Protestants who regarded reformation of Church under Elizabeth as incomplete and sought to abolish unscriptural and corrupt ceremonies etc. **2.** purist member of any non-religious party; person practising or affecting extreme strictness in religion or morals. **3.** Hence **pŭrità'nic(al)** *adjs.*, **~ism** (3) *n.*, **~ize** (2, 3) *v.i.* & *t.* **4.** *a.* of the Puritans; puristic; scrupulous in religion or morals. [f. LL *puritas* (as foll.) after earlier *Cutharan* (as CATHAR; see -AN)]

pŭr'itȳ *n.* pureness, cleanness, freedom from physical or moral pollution. [ME, f. OF *pureté*, w. assim. to LL *puritas* -*tatis* f. L *purus* pure; see -ITY]

pŭrl[1] *n.*, & *v.t.* **1.** *n.* cord of twisted gold or silver wire for bordering; ||chain of minute loops, picot, ornamenting edges of lace, ribbon, etc.; stitch in knitting with needle put into stitch in opposite to normal (PLAIN[1]) direction. **2.** *v.t.* border (material, or abs.) with purl; make (stitch, or abs.) purl; make stitches of (stockings etc.) purls. [orig. *pyrle*, *pirle* f. Sc. *pirl* twist; later senses perh. f. different wds]

pŭrl[2] *v.i.*, & *n.* **1.** *v.i.* (Of brook etc.) flow with swirling motion and babbling sound. **2.** *n.* such motion or sound. [16th c., prob. imit.; cf. Norw. *purla* bubble up]

pŭrl[3] *n.* (Hist.) ale or beer with wormwood infused; ||hot beer mixed with gin as tonic. [17th c.; orig. unkn.]

pŭrl[4] *v.* & *n.* (colloq.) **1.** *v.t.* & *i.* turn upside down, upset. **2.** *n.* cropper, heavy fall. [prob. var. of *pirl* (see PURL[1])]

||**pŭr'ler** *n.* (colloq.) throw or blow that hurls one head foremost; **come** or **take a ~**, fall headlong. [f. prec. + -ER[1]]

pŭr'lieu (-lū) *n.* **1.** ||(Hist.) tract on border of forest, esp. one earlier included in it and still partly subject to forest laws. **2.** one's bounds, limits; one's usual haunts; (in *pl.*) outskirts, outlying region (lit. or fig.). [ME *purlew*, prob. alt. after LIEU f. AF *purale(e)*, OF *pouralle* perambulation to settle boundaries (*po(u)raler* traverse f. *po(u)r*- PUR- + *aller* go; see ALLEY[1])]

pŭr'lin *n.* horizontal beam running along length of roof, resting on principals and supporting common rafters or boards. [ME; AL *perlio* -*onis* perh. f. as PER- + L *ligare* bind]

purloi'n *v.t.* (formal or joc.) steal, pilfer; hence **~ER**[1] *n.* [ME, f. AF PUR(*loigner* f. *loign* far f. L *longe*) put away, do away with]

pŭr'ple *n.*, *a.*, & *v.* **1.** *n.* & *a.* (of) a colour that is intermediate between red and blue; (**Tyrian**) **~**, (of) the crimson colour got from molluscs of genera *Thais*, *Purpura*, and *Murex*. **2.** *n.* purple robe, esp. as dress of emperor, king, consul, etc.; **born in the ~**, born in reigning family, (fig.) situated in most privileged class. **3.** scarlet official dress of cardinal. **4.** **~ emperor**, large butterfly with purple wings; ||**~ heart**, purple heart-shaped tablet of drug Drinamyl; **P~ Heart**, US decoration for those wounded in action; **~heart**, purplish veneering wood from tropical Amer. tree; **~ passage** or **patch**, ornate passage in literary composition. **5.** Hence **pŭr'plIsh**[1], **pŭr'plȳ**[2], *adjs.* **6.** *v.t.* & *i.* make or become purple. [OE alt. f. *purpure purpuran* f. L PURPURA]

pŭr'point. Var. of POURPOINT.

pŭr'pŏrt[1] *n.* ostensible meaning; sense or tenor of document or statement. [ME, f. AF & OF *purport*, *porport* (*purporter*; see foll.)]

purpŏr't[2] *v.t.* (Of document or speech) have as its meaning, convey, state, (fact, *that*); profess, be intended to seem (*to do*; *a letter purporting to be written by you*, *to contain your decision*); hence **~EDLY** *adv.*, professedly. [f. AF & OF *purporter* f. med. L PRO[1](*portare* carry)]

pŭr'pose[1] *n.* **1.** object to be attained, thing intended, (*could not effect my purpose*; *this will answer* or *serve our* or *the purpose*; *what was the purpose of this law?*; *for the purpose of easier access*); **~-built, -made,** etc., built etc. for a specific purpose; **on ~**, in order (*to do, that*); **on ~, of set ~**, **~LY**[2] (-slĭ) *adv.*, designedly, not by accident; **serve no ~**, be useless; **to the ~**, relevant, useful for one's purpose; **to little, some, no, ~**, with little etc. result or effect. **2.** intention to act; resolution, determination. **3.** Hence **~LESS** (-sl-), *a.* [ME, f. OF *porpos*, *purpos*, (*porposer*, *purposer*; see foll.)]

pŭr'pose[2] *v.t.* have as one's purpose, design, intend; **am ~d,** (arch.) intend (*to do*, *doing*, *that*). [ME, f. OF *porposer*, *purposer* f. L *proponere* (as PROPOUND)]

pŭr'poseful (-sf-) *a.* having or indicating (conscious) purpose; intentional; hence **~LY**[2] *adv.*, **~NESS** *n.* [f. PURPOSE[1] + -FUL]

pŭr'posive *a.* having, serving, done with a purpose; (of person or conduct) having purpose and resolution, purposeful. [f. PURPOSE[1,2] + -IVE]

pŭr'pūra *n.* disease marked by purple or livid spots on skin; mollusc of genus *Purpura*, including some that yield purple dye. [L, f. Gk *porphura* (shellfish yielding) purple]

pŭr'pūre *n.*, & *a.* (usu. placed after *n.*) (Her.) purple. [OE, & f. OF *purpre*, f. L *purpura* (as prec.)]

purpur'ic *a.* of purpura (*purpuric fever*); **~ acid**, organic acid forming purple or red salts. [f. L PURPURA + -IC]

pŭr'purin *n.* red colouring-matter got esp. from madder. [f. L PURPURA + -IN]

purr v. & n. **1.** v.i. (Of cat or other feline animal, fig. of person) make low vibratory sound expressing pleasure; (of machine etc.) make similar sound. **2.** v.t. utter, express, (words, contentment) thus. **3.** n. such sound. [imit.]

pur sang (pür sah´ṅ) a. or adv. (placed after n. or a.) of the full blood, without admixture, through and through, genuine, (is Welsh or a Welshman, militarist, a cynic, pur sang). [F, = thoroughbred animal (pur pure, sang blood)]

purse[1] n. **1.** small pouch of leather etc. for carrying money on the person, orig. closed by drawing strings together; *handbag. **2.** (fig.) money, funds; **heavy** or **long** ∼, wealth; **light** ∼, poverty; ‖PRIVY purse; **the public** ∼, national treasury. **3.** sum collected, subscribed, or given, as present or as prize for contest. **4.** baglike natural or other receptacle, pouch, cyst, etc. **5.** ∼**-bearer,** one who has charge of another's or a company's money, ‖official carrying Great Seal before Lord Chancellor in purse; ∼**-net,** bag-shaped net for catching rabbits etc., opening of which can be closed with cords; ∼**-proud,** arrogant through wealth; ∼**-seine,** purse-net for fishing; ∼**-strings,** strings for closing mouth of purse (hold the ∼-strings, have control of expenditure; tighten, loosen, the ∼-strings, reduce, increase, expenditure). **6.** Hence ∼´FUL 2 (-sf-) n., ∼´LESS (-sl-) a. [OE purs f. med. L bursa, byrsa purse f. Gk bursa hide, leather]

purse[2] v. **1.** v.t. ∼ (**up**), contract (lips, brow) in wrinkles. **2.** v.i. become wrinkled. [ME, f. prec.]

pur´ser n. officer on ship who keeps accounts, esp. head steward in passenger vessel; hence ∼SHIP n. [ME, f. PURSE[1] + -ER[1]]

pur´slane (-ĭn) n. low succulent herb (Portulaca oleracea) formerly much used in salads and pickled. [ME, f. OF porcelaine (cf. PORCELAIN) alt. f. L porcil(l)aca, portulaca]

pursu´ance n. carrying out, pursuing, (of plan, object, idea, etc.; in pursuance of the regulations). [f. as foll; see -ANCE]

pursu´ant a. & adv. **1.** a. pursuing. **2.** adv. conformably to (the Act etc.); so ∼LY[2] adv. [ME, = prosecuting, f. OF po(u)rsuiant part. of po(u)rsu(iv)ir (as foll.), see -ANT; assim. to AF pursuer and foll.]

pursue´ v. **1.** v.t. follow with intent to overtake or attract or capture or kill; (fig., of consequences, penalty, disease, etc.) persistently attend, stick to; seek after, aim at, (pleasure etc., one's object); proceed in compliance with (plan etc.); proceed along, continue, (road, inquiry, conduct); continue to investigate or discuss (topic); follow (studies, recreation, profession); hence pursu´ABLE a. **2.** v.i. go in pursuit (after, or abs.). [ME, f. AF pursiwer, -suer, = OF porsivre etc., f. Rom. *PRO[1]-, *PER(sequere f. L sequi follow); cf. SUE]

pursu´er n. In vbl senses; ‖(Civil & Sc. Law) prosecutor or plaintiff. [ME, f. prec. + -ER[1]]

pursui´t (-sū´t, -sōō´t) n. **1.** pursuing, esp. **in** ∼ (of animal, person, one's object); ∼ **plane,** fighter aircraft; ∼ **race,** cycle race where riders start at intervals along track and seek to overtake others. **2.** profession, employment, recreation, action that one follows. [ME, f. OF poursuite (as PUR-, SUIT)]

‖**pur´suivant** (-sĭ-, -swĭ-) n. officer of College of Arms below herald; (arch.) follower, attendant. [ME, f. OF pursivant pres. part. (as n.) of pursivre (as PURSUE; see -ANT)]

pur´s|y[1] a. short-winded, puffy; corpulent; hence ∼INESS n. [ME, earlier pursive f. AF porsif f. OF polsif (polser breathe with difficulty f. L pulsare, as PULSATE; see -IVE)]

pur´sy[2] a. puckered. [f. PURSE[1] + -Y[2]]

pur´tenance n. (arch.) entrails of animal. [ME, f. AF *purtinaunce f. OF pertinance; cf. PERTINENCE, APPURTENANCE]

pur´ul|ent (-ōōl-) a. of, full of, discharging, pus; hence or cogn. ∼ENCE, ∼ENCY, ns., ∼entLY[2] adv. [F, or f. L purulentus (as PUS; see -ULENT)]

purvey´ (-vā´) v. **1.** v.t. provide or supply (articles of food) as one's business. **2.** v.i. make provision, act as purveyor, (for person, army, etc.). [ME, f. AF purveier, OF porveïr f. L providēre PROVIDE]

purvey´ance (-ā´a-) n. purveying; ‖(Hist.) right of sovereign to provisions etc. at fixed price. [ME f. OF porveance, f. L providentia PROVIDENCE]

purvey´or (-vā´-) n. one whose business it is to supply articles of food, esp. on large scale; (Hist.) officer exercising purveyance for sovereign. [ME, f. AF purveour, OF porveour (as PURVEY; see -OR)]

pur´view (-vū) n. enacting-clauses of statute; scope, intention, range, (of act, document, scheme, book, occupation, etc.); range of physical or mental vision. [ME, f. AF purveü, OF porveü p.p. of porveïr (as PURVEY)]

pus n. (Med.) yellowish viscous matter produced from inflamed or infected tissue. [L pus puris]

Pu´sey|ism (-zĭ-) n. (Hist.) (Hostile term for) Tractarianism; so ∼ITE[1] (-zĭ¯īt) n. [f. E. B. Pusey, Engl. theologian d. 1882 + -ISM]

push[1] (pŏosh) v. **1.** v.t. exert upon (thing etc.) force tending to move it away from oneself. **2.** cause (thing etc.) to move (up, down, away, back, etc.) thus (lit. or fig.); thrust forward or upward; make (one's way) by force or persistence; push the BOAT[1] out; ∼ **the button** = PRESS[2] the button. **3.** urge, impel, (on, to do, to effort, into action, etc.). **4.** follow up, prosecute (claim etc.); engage actively in making (one's fortune); extend (one's conquests etc.). **5.** press the adoption, use, sale, etc., of (goods etc.) esp. by advertisement; sell (drug) illegally. **6.** press (person) hard (do not wish to push him for payment); tax abilities or tolerance of; ∼ed for, (colloq.) scarcely able to find enough (time, money, etc.); ∼ one's **luck,** (colloq.) take undue risks. **7.** v.t. & i. (cause to) project, thrust out, forth, etc., (plants push out new roots; cape pushes out into sea). **8.** v.i. exert pushing force (do not push against the fence); make persistent demands for. **9.** make one's way (ahead, on, etc.) forcibly or persistently. **10.** exert oneself esp. to surpass others or succeed in business etc. **11.** ∼ **along,** (colloq.) depart; ∼ **around,** bully, treat with contempt; ∼**-button** a., operated by pushing a button, (of warfare) conducted by guided missiles whose flight is controlled thus; ∼ **off,** (of person in boat) push with oar etc. against bank etc. to get boat out into stream etc., (sl.) go away; ∼**-over,** (colloq.) opponent or difficulty easily overcome; ∼**-pull,** operating by pushing and pulling, (Electr.) consisting of two valves etc. operated alternately by alternating current; ∼ **through,** bring (matter) to a conclusion, compel acceptance of (proposal etc.); ∼**-up,** = PRESS[2]-up. [ME, f. AF *pusser, OF pousser, pou(l)ser f. L pulsare (as PULSATE)]

push[2] (pŏosh) n. **1.** act of pushing, shove, thrust; force thus exerted; (Bill.) stroke in which ball is pushed, not struck; exertion of influence to promote person's advancement. **2.** vigorous effort (must make a push to get it done, for home); (Mil.) attack in force. **3.** continuous pressure of arch etc.; pressure of affairs, crisis, pinch. **4.** enterprise, determination to get on, self-assertion; hence ∼´FUL a. **5.** (sl., esp. Austral.) gang of thieves, ruffians, etc. **6.** ‖(sl.) **give, get, the** ∼, dismiss, be dismissed. **7.** ∼**-ball,** game played with enormous ball pushed, not kicked, towards opponents' goal; ‖∼**-bike,** (sl.) bicycle worked by pedalling (opp. motor bike); ∼(-**button**), button to be pushed to operate electric circuit etc.; ∼**-cart,** handcart; ‖∼**-chair,** child's folding chair on wheels; ∼**-rod** (opening and closing valves in internal combustion engine); ∼**-start** n., & v.t., start(ing of) motor vehicle by pushing it along to turn engine. [f. prec.]

pu´sher (pŏo´-) n. In vbl senses; illegal seller of drugs; pushing person; child's utensil for pushing food on to spoon etc. [f. PUSH[1] + -ER[1]]

pu'shing (pŏŏ'-) *a*. In vbl senses; making (unduly) vigorous efforts to advance oneself in business etc.; (colloq.) having nearly reached age of (*forty* etc.); hence ∼LY² *adv*. [f. PUSH¹ + -ING²]

Pŭ'shtu (-ōō) *n*. & *a*. = PASHTO. [f. Pers. *puštū*]

pu'shy (pŏŏ-) *a*. (colloq.) (unpleasantly) pushing or self-assertive. [f. PUSH¹,² + -Y²]

pŭsillá'nimous (-s-, -z-) *a*. lacking courage, timid; hence or cogn. **pŭsillani'mity** *n*., ∼LY² *adv*. [f. eccl. L *pusillanimis* (*pusillus* very small, *animus* mind) + -OUS]

puss (pŏŏs) *n*. cat (esp. as *voc.*); (quasi-proper name for) hare; (colloq.) playful or coquettish girl; ∼ **in the corner,** game in which central person tries to occupy position left vacant by others changing places; ∼ **moth,** large European moth (*Cerura vinula*). [prob. f. MLG *pūs*, Du. *poes*, of unkn. orig.]

*pŭ'ssley, -lȳ, *n*. purslane. [corrupt.]

pu'ssȳ (pŏŏ'-) *n*. ∼(-cat), (childish name for) cat; (vulg.) vulva; ∼foot, (*n*., *pl*. ∼*foots*) **liquor--prohibition(ist) [f. nickname of W. E. Johnson, Amer. prohibitionist d. 1945], (*v.i.*) move stealthily, act (over-)cautiously or non-committally; ∼ willow, willow with silky catkins. [f. PUSS + -Y²]

pŭ'stŭl|āte *v.t.* & *i.* form into pustules; hence or cogn. ∼ATE² *a.*, ∼A'TION *n*. [f. LL *pustulare* (*pustula*; see foll.) + -ATE³]

pŭ'stŭl|e *n*. pimple; **malignant** ∼e, form of anthrax; (Bot. & Zool.) wart, wartlike excrescence; hence or cogn. ∼AR¹, ∼OUS, *adjs*. [ME f. OF, or f. L *pustula*; see -ULE]

put¹ (pŏŏt) *v.* (-tt-; put). **1.** *v.t.* move (thing etc.; lit. or fig.) so that it comes into some situation (*put it in your pocket, on the table, up the chimney, down the well; put children to* BED¹, *convict in prison; put matter before adviser, new life into invalid*); **not know where to** ∼ one*self*, be much embarrassed or uncomfortable; hurl (*the shot* or *the weight*) from hand as athletic exercise; thrust (weapon) *into*, send (missile) *through*; propel (tram of coal); harness (horse etc.) *to* (cart etc.); bring (animal) *to* one of opposite sex for breeding, *to* or *at* fence etc. for jumping, *to* a pace; substitute (one thing *for* another); impose (*in* another's *place* etc.); *put the* BOOT¹ *in*, one's FOOT¹ *down, in it,* ‖*the* LID *on it, words into* person's MOUTH¹, one's *hand to the* PLOUGH¹, one's SHOULDER *to the wheel,* ‖*a* SOCK¹ *in it, a* SPOKE¹ *in* person's *wheel;* STAY¹ *put.* **2.** bring into specified relation or state (*put machine out of action, goods on the market, the matter right, proposal into shape; put out of* COUNTENANCE¹, *out of* COURT¹, *a good* or *bold* FACE¹ *on it,* one's MIND¹ *to,* person *in* MIND¹ *of,* person's NOSE *out of joint,* STORE *by* or *on, the* WIND¹ *up,* person *in* WISE¹); write (words etc.) in specified position (*put your signature to it, a tick against his name*); impose the existence of (*put an* END¹ *or* STOP² *to it, a* VETO *on it*); cause (person) to go or be, habitually or temporarily, (*put one's child to school,* one's *daughter on the stage; put him at his ease, on his guard, on the right track, on antibiotics, off smoking, out of temper, to mind the sheep, through his* PACE¹*s*); estimate (price etc.) *at*; express (thought etc.) in specified way; convert (thought etc.) *into* words, translate *into* (language); make investment of (money *into* land etc.); impose (tax etc.), lay (blame etc.), *on*; stake (money *on* horse etc.); apply *to* (use etc.); submit (cause, question, etc.) *to* (person, vote, etc.; *I* ∼ *it to you,* I appeal to you; *I* ∼ *it to you that,* I challenge you to deny that); subject (person etc.) *to* (DEATH, expense, SHAME¹, *the* TEST¹, torture, etc.); drive (person) *to* (FLIGHT² etc.); HARD *put to it;* ∼ **it across,** (sl.) get even with or deceive (person); *not put it* PAST² person. **3.** *v.i.* (Naut.) proceed, take one's course, *back, forth, in* (*to* harbour etc.), *off* (*from* shore etc.), *out, to* sea, in ship. **4.** ***(Of river etc.) flow *into* or *out of.* **5.** ∼ **and take,** gambling game played with special top that decides whether player puts money into or takes it from pool; ∼ (**up**)**on,** deceive, victimize, play joke on, (person); ∼- **on** *n.*, (colloq.) deception, hoax. **6.** (w. *advs.*): ∼

about, lay (sailing vessel) on opposite tack, (of vessel) go about; cause (horse, body of men) to turn round; trouble, distress; disseminate (rumour etc.). **7.** ∼ **across,** make acceptable or effective; convey significance of; ***achieve by deceit. **8.** ∼ **away,** lay (money etc.) aside for future use; (colloq.) put into confinement, kill (injured, old, etc. animal), consume (food or drink); (arch.) divorce (wife). **9.** ∼ **back,** check advance of; move back the hands of (clock); restore to former place; change (planned event) to later date or time. **10.** ∼ **by,** lay (money etc.) aside for future use. **11.** ∼ **down,** suppress by force or authority; snub; write down, make a note of; enter name of (person) on list, esp. as subscriber etc.; account, reckon, (*I put him down as* or *for a fool*); attribute (*put it down to his nervousness*); preserve (eggs etc.) for future use; cease to read (book); put (baby) to bed; kill (injured, old, etc. animal); land (aircraft); allow (passenger) to alight; ∼-**down** *n.*, a snub. **12.** ∼ **forth,** exert (effort, eloquence); bring into circulation; (of plant) send out (buds, leaves, or abs.). **13.** ∼ **forward,** thrust (one*self* etc.) into prominence; advance, set forth, (theory etc.); advance hands of (clock). **14.** ∼ **in,** install in office etc.; formally present (document etc.) in lawcourt etc.; *put in an* APPEARANCE; make a claim *for,* be candidate *for,* (election, appointment, etc.); interpose (remark, blow, etc.); perform (spell of work) as part of a whole; (colloq.) spend (time). **15.** ∼ **off,** postpone; postpone engagement with (person); evade (person etc. *with* excuse etc.); hinder or dissuade *from,* offend, disconcert; remove (clothes one is wearing), etc. **16.** ∼ **on,** clothe oneself or another with; assume, take on, (character, appearance); develop additional (flesh, weight); stage (a play etc.); add (speed, amount *to* price, runs etc. *to* score); advance hands of (clock); bring into action (pressure, SCREW¹); cause (cricketer) to bowl, (electric light) to shine, (electrical device) to operate, (train) to run, etc.; ∼ **it on,** (colloq.) overcharge, simulate emotion, etc. **17.** ∼ **out,** dislocate (joint); cause (batsman, batter, etc.) to be out; extinguish (light, fire, etc.), disconcert, confuse; annoy, irritate, inconvenience; exert (strength etc.); lend (money) at interest; give (work) to be done off the premises; blind (person's eyes). **18.** ∼ **over,** make acceptable or effective; convey significance of; ***postpone; ***achieve by deceit. **19.** ∼ **through,** carry out (task); connect (person) by telephone to another via exchange(s); make (telephone call); complete (business transaction). **20.** ∼ **together,** form (whole) by combination of parts, combine (parts) into whole; *put* TWO *and two together.* **21.** ∼ **under,** render unconscious by anaesthetic etc. **22.** ∼ **up,** construct, build; raise (price etc.); offer (prayer), present (petition, proposal), provide (money as backer etc.); propose, as candidate, for election; cause (game) to rise from cover; publish (banns); display (notice); offer for sale or competition; pack up in parcel or receptacle; sheathe (sword); lodge (guest), be or become lodger *at;* concoct (∼-**up** *a.*, fraudulently concocted); *put* person's BACK¹ *up; put up a* FIGHT²; *put* one's HAIR *up;* ∼ **up to,** inform (person) of, instruct (person) in, instigate (person) in (doing etc.); ∼ **up with,** submit to, tolerate, (annoyance, insult, etc.). [ME, f. OE **putian* or **pūtian, potian, pȳtan,* of unkn. orig.]

put² (pŏŏt) *n.* **1.** throw of the shot or weight. **2.** (St. Exch.) option of selling stock at fixed price at given date. [ME, f. prec.]

pŭt³. See PUTT.

pū'tative *a.* reputed, supposed (*his putative father*); hence ∼LY² (-vlǐ) *adv.* [ME, f. OF *putatif -ive* or f. LL *putativus* f. L *putare* think; see -ATIVE]

pŭ'tlŏg, pŭ'tlŏck, *n.* short horizontal timber projecting from wall, on which scaffold floor-boards rest. [17th c.; orig. uncert.]

pŭ't-pŭt *n.*, & *v.i.* (-tt-). (make) rapid intermittent sound of small petrol engine. [imit.]

pŭ'tre|fȳ *v.* **1.** *v.i.* become putrid, rot, go bad; fester, suppurate; become morally corrupt. **2.** *v.t.* cause to putrefy. **3.** So ∿FA'CTION *n.*, ∿FA'CIENT, ∿fā'ctIVE, *adjs.* [ME, f. L *putrefacere* (*puter putris* rotten; see -FY)]

pŭtrĕ'sc|ent *a.* in process of rotting; of or accompanying this process; so ∿ENCE *n.*, ∿IBLE *a.* [f. L *putrescere* incept. of *putrēre* (see foll., -ESCENT)]

pŭ'trid *a.* decomposed, rotten; foul, noxious; (fig.) corrupt; (sl.) of poor quality, very unpleasant; hence ∿ITY (-ĭ'd-), ∿NESS, *ns.*, ∿LY² *adv.* [f. L *putridus* (*putrēre* to rot f. *puter putris* rotten; see -ID¹)]

putsch (pŏŏch) *n.* attempt at a political revolution. [Swiss G, = thrust, blow]

pŭtt, pŭt³, *v.* (-tt-) & *n.* **1.** *v.i.* & *t.* strike (golf-ball) gently with club to get it into or nearer to hole on smooth grass area (∿'ing-green). **2.** *n.* such stroke. [different. f. PUT¹,²]

pŭ'ttee (-ĭ) *n.* long strip of cloth wound spirally round leg from ankle to knee for protection and support; *leather legging. [f. Hindi *paṭṭī* band, bandage]

pu'tter¹ (pŏŏ'-) *n.* In vbl senses; miner who moves loads of coal etc. into position for raising to surface. [ME, f. PUT¹ + -ER¹]

pŭ'tter² *n.* In vbl sense; golf-club used in putting. [f. PUTT + -ER¹]

pŭ'tter³ *n.*, & *v.i.* = PUT-PUT. [imit.]

***pŭ'tter⁴.** Var. of POTTER².

pu'tt|ō (pŏŏ-) *n.* (*pl.* ∿i). figure of child (esp. cherub- or Cupid-like) in Renaissance painting or sculpture. [It., = boy, f. L *putus*]

pŭ'tty *n.*, & *v.t.* **1.** *n.* (jewellers') ∿, powder of tin (and lead) oxide for polishing glass or metal; (plasterers') ∿, fine mortar of lime and water without sand. **2.** (glaziers') ∿, cement of whiting, raw linseed oil, etc., for fixing panes of glass, filling up holes in woodwork, etc. **3.** (fig.) compliant person; ||∿ medal, (joc.) fit reward for small service (*you deserve a putty medal*). **4.** *v.t.* cover, fix, join, fill up, with putty. [f. F *potée*, lit. POT¹ful; see -Y⁴]

puy (pwē) *n.* small volcanic cone esp. in Auvergne, France. [F, = hill, f. L PODIUM]

pŭ'zzle¹ *n.* bewilderment, perplexity; perplexing question, enigma; problem or toy designed to test knowledge, ingenuity, or patience; ∿-head(ed), -pate(d), (person) with confused ideas. [f. foll.]

pŭ'zzle² *v.* **1.** *v.t.* perplex (*puzzled at, that, to find* etc.); find *out* by patience and ingenuity (solution of problem etc.). **2.** *v.i.* be perplexed (*about* or *over* problem etc.). **3.** Hence ∿MENT (-zelm-), **pŭ'zzlER¹** (1, 2), *ns.* [16th c.; orig. unkn.]

puzzolana. Var. of POZZOLANA.

PVC *abbr.* polyvinyl chloride.

Pvt. *abbr.* Private (*soldier).

||**PW** *abbr.* Policewoman.

PWR *abbr.* pressurized water reactor.

***PX** *abbr.* post exchange.

pȳae'm|ia, *pȳē'm|ia, *n.* blood-poisoning marked by formation of abscesses in viscera; hence ∿IC *a.* [mod. L, f. Gk *puon* pus + *haima* blood + -IA¹]

pȳ'cnic. Var. of PYKNIC.

pȳ'e-dŏg, pī'(e)-dŏg, (pī'd-) *n.* ownerless mongrel of the East. [f. Anglo-Ind. *pye, paĕ,* Hindi *pāhī* outsider, + DOG¹]

pȳĕlo- *comb. form.* pelvis (of skeleton or kidney), as: **py'elogram,** X-ray picture of renal pelvis; **pyeli'tis,** inflammation of renal pelvis. [f. Gk *puelos* trough]

pȳ'gmȳ, pī'gmȳ, *n.* & *a.* **1.** *n.* one of a diminutive race of men said to have inhabited parts of Ethiopia or India; one of a group of very short people in equatorial Africa; dwarf (fig. of intellectual inferiority etc.); elf, pixie; so **pȳgm(a)e'AN** (-ē'an) *a.* **2.** *a.* of the pygmies; (of person or animal) dwarf. [ME, f. L f. Gk *pugmaios* dwarf(ish) (*pugmē* length from elbow to knuckles, fist)]

||**pȳja'ma|s, *paja'ma|s,** (-ah'maz) *n. pl.* loose trousers tied round waist, worn by both sexes in the East; suit of loose trousers and jacket for sleeping etc. (∿ jacket, trousers, etc., garments forming part of this). [f. Urdu *pā(ĕ)jāma* f. Pers. *pae, pay,* leg + Hindi *jāma* clothing]

pȳ'knic *a.* & *n.* (Anthrop.) (person) characterized by thick neck, large abdomen, and relatively short limbs. [f. Gk *puknos* thick + -IC]

pȳ'lon *n.* gateway esp. of Egyptian temple; tall structure erected as support (esp. for electric-power cables) or boundary or decoration; structure marking path for aircraft; structure supporting aircraft engine. [f. Gk *pulōn* (*pulē* gate)]

pȳlōr'|us *n.* (*pl.* ∿i *pr.* -ī). (Anat.) opening from stomach into duodenum; part of stomach where this is; hence **pȳlō'rIC** *a.* [LL, f. Gk *pulōros, pulouros* gatekeeper (*pulē* gate, *ouros* warder)]

||**pȳorrhoe'a, *pȳorrhē'a,** (-rē'a) *n.* discharge of pus, esp. in disease of tooth-sockets; this disease. [f. Gk *puo-* (*puon* pus) + *rhoia* flux (*rheō* flow)]

pȳraca'ntha *n.* evergreen thorny shrub of genus *Pyracantha* with white flowers and scarlet berries. [L, f. Gk *purakantha*]

pȳ'ramĭd *n.* **1.** monumental (esp. ancient Egyptian) structure of stone etc. with polygonal or (usu.) square base, and sloping sides meeting at apex. **2.** solid of this shape with base of three or more sides (**pentagonal** etc. ∿, with five etc. sides). **3.** pyramid-shaped thing or pile of things; fruit-tree trained in pyramid shape; ∿ selling, form of financial trickery where agents are recruited in increasing numbers at successively lower levels. **4.** ||(in *pl.*) game played on billiard-table with (usu. 15) coloured balls and one cue-ball. **5.** Hence or cogn. **pȳrā'mĭdAL** *a.*, ∿WISE *adv.* [ME, f. L f. Gk *puramis -idos*]

pȳre *n.* heap of combustible material, esp. funeral pile for burning corpse. [f. L f. Gk *pura* (*pur* fire)]

pȳrē'thrum *n.* chrysanthemum with finely divided leaves; insecticide made from dried flowers of this. [L, f. Gk *purethron* feverfew]

pȳrĕ'tic (pīr-, pĭr-) *a.* of, for, or producing, fever. [f. mod. L *pyreticus* f. Gk *puretos* fever; see -IC]

pȳrĕ'x|ia (pīr-, pĭr-) *n.* (Path.) fever; hence ∿ĬAL, ∿IC(AL), *adjs.* [mod. L, f. Gk *purexis* (*puressō* be feverish f. *pur* fire); see -IA¹]

pyrhĕliŏ'mĕter *n.* instrument for measuring heat radiated by sun. [f. Gk *pur* fire + *hēlios* sun + -O- + -METER]

pȳ'ridine (-ēn) *n.* (Chem.) colourless volatile odorous liquid base got from dry distillation of bone-oil and coal-tar, used as solvent and in chemical manufacture. [f. Gk *pur* fire + -ID⁴ + -INE⁵]

pȳr'īte *n.* = *iron* PYRITES. [F, or f. L (as foll.)]

pȳrī'tēs (-z) *n.* (*iron*) ∿, yellow lustrous iron sulphide mineral; **copper** ∿, double sulphide of copper and iron; hence **pȳrī'tIC, pȳrĭtī'FEROUS, pȳr'ĭtOUS,** *adjs.* **pȳr'ĭtIZE** (3) *v.t.* [L, f. Gk *puritēs* of fire (*pur*; see -ITE¹)]

pȳr'ō *n.* (colloq.) = PYROGALLIC *acid.* [abbr.]

pȳrō- *comb. form.* **1.** fire, as: ∿ele'ctric, ∿electri'city, (property of) becoming electrically charged when heated; ∿ga'llic acid, ∿llol, weak acid used as developer in photography etc.; ∿ge'nic, ∿genous (-ŏ'j-), productive of heat, esp. in the body, or of fever, (of rock) igneous, (of substance) produced by combustion of another; ∿latry (-ŏ'l-), fire-worship; ∿li'gneous, produced by action of fire or heat on wood; **pyr'omancy,** divination by fire; ∿ma'nia, ∿ma'niac, (person suffering from) incendiary mania; ∿pho'ric, (of substance) that takes fire spontaneously on exposure to air. **2.** (Chem.) new substance formed from another by destructive distillation etc. (*pyrophosphate*); (Min.) mineral etc. showing some property or change under action of heat, or having fiery red or yellow colour. [f. Gk *puro-* (*pur* fire)]

pȳrŏ'graphȳ *n.* = POKER¹-*work.* [f. prec. + -GRAPHY]

pȳr′olȳse, *pȳr′olȳze, *v.t.* decompose by pyrolysis. [f. foll. after *analyse*]

pȳrŏ′lȳs|ĭs *n.* (*pl.* ∼es *pr.* -ēz). chemical decomposition by action of heat; so **pȳrolȳ′tĭc** *a.* [f. PYRO- +-LYSIS]

pȳrŏ′mĕter *n.* instrument for measuring high temperatures; so **pȳromĕ′trĭc** *a.*, **pȳrŏ′METRY** *n.* [f. PYRO- + -METER]

pȳr′ōpe *n.* deep-red garnet. [ME, f. OF *pirope* f. L f. Gk *purōpos* gold-bronze, lit. fiery-eyed (*pur* fire, *ōps* eye)]

pȳrŏ′sĭs *n.* (Med.) burning sensation in lower part of chest with eructation of watery fluid. [mod. L, f. Gk *purōsis* (*puroō* set on fire f. *pur* fire)]

pȳrotĕ′chn|ĭc (-tĕ′k-) *a.* & *n.* **1.** *a.* of (the nature of) fireworks (*pyrotechnic display*); (fig., of wit etc.) brilliant, sensational; hence or cogn. ∼ĭcAL *a.*, ∼ĭST (3), **pȳr′otĕchnv**[1] (-tĕk-), *ns.* **2.** *n.* (in *pl.*) art of making, or display of, fireworks (lit. or fig.). [f. *pyrotechny* (PYRO-, Gk *tekhnē* art) + -ɪC]

pȳrŏ′xēne *n.* mineral composed of silicates esp. of calcium and magnesium, a common component of igneous rocks. [f. PYRO- + Gk *xenos* stranger (because supposed alien to igneous rocks)]

pȳrŏ′xȳlĭn *n.* cellulose nitrate soluble in ether and alcohol to form collodion and used as basis of lacquers, artificial leather, etc. [f. F *pyroxyline* f. as PYRO- + Gk *xulon* wood + -ɪN]

pȳ′rrhĭc[1] (-rĭk) *n.* & *a.* **1.** ∼ (dance), war-dance of ancient Greeks. **2.** (based on) metrical foot consisting of two short syllables. [sense 1 f. L or Gk *purrhikhē*, said to be named from one *Purrhikhos*, the inventor; sense 2 f. L f. Gk *purrhikhios* (*pous*) pyrrhic (foot)]

Pȳ′rrhĭc[2] (-rĭk) *a.* ∼ **victory** (gained at too great cost, like that of Pyrrhus king of Epirus over the Romans at Asculum in 279 BC). [f. Gk *purrhikos* (*Purrhos* Pyrrhus; see -ɪC)]

Pȳ′rrhon|ism (-rɒ-) *n.* philosophy of Pyrrho of Elis (*c.* 300 BC), doctine that certainty of knowledge is unattainable; scepticism, philosophic doubt; so **Pȳrrhŏ′nɪAN** (-rŏ′-), **Pȳrrhŏ′nɪC** (-rŏ′-), *adjs.* & *ns.*, ∼ɪST (2) *n.* [f. Gk *Purrhōn* Pyrrho + -ɪSM]

pȳru′vĭc (-ōō′-) *a.* ∼ **acid,** organic acid important in making available energy from food in the body. [f. as PYRO- + L *uva* grape + -ɪC]

Pythăgorĕ′an *a.* & *n.* (follower) of Pythagoras, philosopher of Samos (6th c. BC) said to have believed in transmigration of souls and explanation of the universe in terms of numbers; **Pytha′goras′ theorem,** ∼ **theorem** or **proposition,** (that square on hypotenuse of right-angled triangle is equal to sum of squares on other two sides). [f. L f. Gk *Puthagoreios* +-AN]

Pȳ′thian *a.* & *n.* **1.** *a.* of (Apollo's oracle and priestess at) Delphi; ∼ **games** (celebrated by ancient Greeks every four years near Delphi). **2.** *n.* Apollo or his priestess at Delphi; frenzied person. [f. L f. Gk *Puthios* (*Puthō,* older name of Delphi) + -AN]

pȳ′thon *n.* large snake (esp. of genus *Python*) killing by compression; hence **pȳthŏ′nĭc** *a.* [L, f. Gk *Puthōn* huge serpent or monster slain near Delphi by Apollo in myth]

pȳ′thonèss *n.* Pythian priestess; witch. [ME, f. OF *phitonise* f. med. L *phitonissa* f. LL *pythonissa* fem. of *pytho* f. Gk *puthōn* soothsaying demon (cf. prec., -ESS[1])]

pȳūr′ia *n.* (Path.) presence of pus in urine. [f. Gk *puon* pus + -URIA]

pȳx *n.* **1.** (Eccl.) vessel in which consecrated bread is kept. **2.** ||box at Royal Mint in which specimen gold and silver coins are deposited to be tested at the annual **trial of the** ∼ by jury of Goldsmiths′ Company. [ME, f. L (see PYXIS)]

pȳxĭ′di|um *n.* (*pl.* ∼a). (Bot.) seed-capsule of which the top comes off like lid of box. [mod. L, f. Gk *puxidion,* dim. (as foll.)]

pȳ′x|ĭs *n.* (*pl.* ∼ides *pr.* -ĭdēz). small box, casket; = prec. [ME f. L, f. Gk *puxis* (*puxos* BOX[1])]

Q

Q, q, (kū) *n.* (*pl.* **Qs** *or* **Q's**). seventeenth letter of alphabet; MIND[2] one's *P's and Q's*; **Q-boat, Q-ship,** = MYSTERY[1] *ship*; **Q department** etc. (of quartermaster).

Q. *abbr.* Queen('s); question.

QARANC *abbr.* Queen Alexandra's Royal Army Nursing Corps.

QARNNS *abbr.* Queen Alexandra's Royal Naval Nursing Service.

QB *abbr.* Queen's Bench.

QC *abbr.* Queen's Counsel.

QED, QEF, QEI, *abbrs.* QUOD[2] *erat demonstrandum, faciendum, inveniendum.*

QF *abbr.* quick-firing.

Q fever (kū'-) *n.* mild febrile disease caused by rickettsiae. [f. initial letter of QUERY]

qibla. Var. of KIBLAH.

Qld. *abbr.* Queensland.

QM *abbr.* quartermaster.

QMG *abbr.* Quartermaster General.

QMS *abbr.* Quartermaster Sergeant.

||QPM *abbr.* Queen's Police Medal.

qr. *abbr.* quarter(s).

QSO *abbr.* quasi-stellar object, quasar.

q.t. *n.* (sl.) quiet (*on the q.t.*). [abbr.]

qt. *abbr.* quart(s).

qu. *abbr.* query.

qua (kwā, kwah) *conj.* as, in the capacity of, (*objects to the Church not qua Church, but qua Establishment*). [L, abl. fem. sing. of *qui* who (rel. pron.)]

quäck[1] *v.i.,* & *n.* (utter) harsh sound made by ducks; talk loudly and foolishly; **quack-quack,** (childish name for) duck. [imit.; cf. Du. *kwakken,* G *quacken* croak, quack]

quäck[2] *n., a.,* & *v.* **1.** *n.* ignorant pretender to skill esp. in medicine or surgery; one who offers wonderful remedies or devices, charlatan; hence ∼'ERY (4) *n.,* ∼'ISH[1] *a.* **2.** *a.* being a quack (*quack doctor*); characteristic of or used by a quack (*quack remedies*). **3.** *v.i.* play the quack; talk pretentiously. **4.** *v.t.* puff or advertise extravagantly (cure etc.). [abbr. of *quacksalver* f. Du. (prob. f. obs. *quacken* prattle, *salf* SALVE[1]; see -ER[1])]

quad (kwŏd) *n.* (colloq.) quadrangle; quadraphonic; quadrat; quadruple; QUADRUPLET 1. [abbr.]

quadragēnār'ian (-ŏd-) *a.* & *n.* (person) from 40 to 49 years old. [f. LL *quadragenarius* (*quadrageni* distrib. of *quadraginta* forty; see -ARY[1]) + -AN]

Quadragē'sima (-ŏd-) *n.* ∼ (**Sunday**), first Sunday in Lent. [LL, fem. (as n.) of L *quadragesimus* fortieth (*quadraginta* forty, Lent having 40 days]

quadragē'simal (-ŏd-) *a.* (Of fast, esp. Lent) lasting forty days; Lenten. [f. prec. + -AL]

qua'dr|ängle (kwŏ'drănggel) *n.* **1.** four-cornered figure, esp. square or rectangle; so ∼ä'ngūlAR[1] (-ngg-) *a.* **2.** four-sided court wholly or mainly enclosed by parts of large buildings; such court with buildings round it. [ME f. OF, f. LL *quadrangulum* square, neut. (as n.) of *quadrangulus* (as QUADRI-, ANGLE[1])]

qua'drant (-ŏ'd-) *n.* **1.** quarter of circle's circumference; plane figure enclosed by two radii of circle at right angles and arc cut off by them; quarter of sphere etc. **2.** thing, esp. graduated strip of metal, shaped like quarter-circle; instrument graduated (esp. through an arc of 90°) for taking angular measurements. **3.** Hence **quadrä'ntAL** *a.* [ME, f. L *quadrans -antis* quarter (*quattuor* four)]

quadraphō'n|ic (-ŏd-) *a.* (Of sound-reproduction) using four transmission channels; hence ∼ICALLY *adv.,* ∼Y[1] (-ŏ'fonĭ) *n.* [f. QUADRI- + STEREOPHONIC]

qua'drat (-ŏ'd-) *n.* (Print.) small metal block used in spacing (**em** ∼, **en** ∼, broader, narrower, size); (Biol.) small area marked out for study. [var. of foll.]

qua'drate[1] (-ŏ'd-) *a.* & *n.* **1.** *a.* (esp. Anat. & Zool.) square, rectangular, (*quadrate bone, muscle*). **2.** *n.* rectangular object; quadrate bone or muscle. [ME, f. L *quadratus* (as foll.; see -ATE[2])]

quadrā'te[2] (kwa-, kwŏ-) *v.* **1.** *v.t.* make square; make conform (*with, to,* or abs.). **2.** *v.i.* correspond or conform (*with,* or abs.). [f. L *quadrare* (as QUADRI-) + -ATE[3]]

quadrä'tic *a.* & *n.* **1.** *a.* square; (Math.) involving second and no higher power of unknown quantity or variable (*quadratic equation*). **2.** *n.* quadratic equation; (in *pl.*) branch of algebra dealing with these. [f. F *quadratique* or f. mod. L *quadraticus* (as QUADRATE[1]; see -IC)]

qua'drature (-ŏ'd-) *n.* (Math.) finding of square with area equal to that of figure bounded by curve (*quadrature of the circle*); (Astron.) one of two points at which moon is 90° from sun, position of heavenly body in relation to another 90° away; (Electr.) phase difference of 90°. [F, or f. L *quadratura* (as QUADRATE[2]; see -URE)]

quadrĕ'nnial (-ŏd-) *a.* lasting, recurring, every four years; hence ∼LY[2] *adv.* [f. as foll. + -AL]

quadrĕ'nni|um (-ŏd-) *n.* (*pl.* ∼ums *or* ∼a). period of four years. [f. L *quadriennium* (as foll., *annus* year)]

qua'dri- (-ŏ'd-) *comb. form.* four, as: ∼fid *a.,* cleft into four divisions or lobes; ∼li'ngual, using, or in, four languages; ∼no'mial, consisting of four algebraic terms; ∼par'tite, consisting of four parts, shared by or involving four parties; ∼pole, = QUADRUPOLE; ∼reme, ancient galley with four banks of oars; ∼sylla'bic, four-syllabled; ∼sy'llable, word of four syllables; ∼va'lent, (Chem.) having a valence of four. [L (*quattuor* four)]

qua'dric (-ŏ'd-) *a.* & *n.* (Geom.) (surface) described by equation of second degree. [f. L *quadra* square + -IC]

qua'dricĕps (-ŏ'd-) *n.* (Anat.) four-headed muscle at front of thigh. [mod. L (as QUADRI-, BICEPS)]

quadri'ga (-ē'-, -ī'-) *n.* (*pl.* ∼e). ancient chariot with four horses abreast. [L (as QUADRI-, *jugum* yoke)]

quadrilä'teral (-ŏd-) *a.* & *n.* four-sided (figure); area defended by four fortresses (esp. Hist., one in N. Italy). [f. LL *quadrilaterus* (as QUADRI-, *latus lateris* side) + -AL]

quadri'lle[1] *n.* fashionable 18th-c. game for four persons with forty cards. [F, perh. f. Sp. *cuartillo* (*cuarto* fourth), w. assim. to foll.]

quadri'lle[2] *n.* square dance containing usu. five figures; music for it. [F, f. Sp. *cuadrilla* troop, company (*cuadra* square) or f. It. *quadriglia* (*quadra* square)]

quadri'llion (-yon) *n.* (for *pl.* usage see HUNDRED). a million raised to the fourth power; *a thousand raised to the fifth power. [F (as QUADRI-, MILLION)]

quadriplē'g|ia (-ŏd-) *n.* (Path.) paralysis of both arms and both legs; hence ∼IC *a.* & *n.* [mod. L, f. as QUADRI- + Gk *plēgē* blow, stroke + -IA[1]; cf. PARAPLEGIA]

quadri'vium *n.* (Hist.) medieval university course of arithmetic, geometry, astronomy, and music. [L, = place where four roads meet (as QUADRI-, *via* road)]

quadroō'n *n.* offspring of white and mulatto, person of quarter-Negro blood; hybrid of similarly proportioned descent between other human, animal, or plant stocks. [f. Sp. *cuarterón* (*cuarto* fourth), w. assim. to QUADRI-]

quadrophonic. Var. of QUADRAPHONIC.

quadru'manous (-rōō'-) *a.* four-handed; belonging to the group Quadrumana of mammals with opposable digit on all four limbs (primates other than man). [f. mod. L *quadrumana* neut. pl. (as n.) of *quadrumanus* (as foll., L *manus* hand)]

qua'druped (-ŏ'drōō-) *n.* & *a.* **1.** *n.* four-footed animal, esp. four-footed mammal; hence **quadru'pedAL** (-rōō'-) *a.* **2.** *a.* four-footed. [f. F *quadrupède* or f. L *quadrupes -pedis* a. & n. (*quadru-* form of QUADRI-occas. used before *p-*, *pes* foot)]

qua'druple (-ŏ'drōō-) *a.*, *n.*, & *v.* **1.** *a.* fourfold, consisting of four parts or involving four parties (*quadruple alliance*); ∼ **time** (Mus., with four beats to the bar). **2.** amounting or equivalent to four times the amount or number of (*has a light and heat quadruple that of the earth*); hence **qua'drupLY²** (-ŏ'drōō-) *adv.* **3.** *n.* number or amount four times greater than another. **4.** *v.t.* & *i.* multiply by four. [F, f. L *quadruplus* (as prec., *-plus* as in *duplus* DUPLE)]

quadruplet (-ŏ'drōō-, -ŏdrōō'-) *n.* **1.** one of four children born at a birth; set of four things working together. **2.** bicycle for four; (Mus.) group of four notes to be performed in the time of three. [f. prec., after *triplet*]

quadru'plicate¹ (-ŏdrōō'-) *a.* & *n.* **1.** *a.* fourfold; (esp.) of which four copies are made. **2.** *n.* **in** ∼, in four exactly similar examples or copies. [f. L *quadruplicare* (*quadruplex -plicis* fourfold; cf. QUADRUPED, DUPLEX); see -ATE⁸,¹]

quadru'plic|āte² (-ŏdrōō'-) *v.t.* multiply by four; make four copies of; hence ∼A'TION *n.* [f. as prec. + -ATE⁸]

quadrupli'cit̄y (-ŏdrōō-) *n.* state of being fourfold. [f. L *quadruplex -plicis* (see QUADRUPLICATE¹), after *duplicity*]

qua'drupōle (-ŏ'drōō-) *n.* (Phys.) system of two equal and opposite dipoles. [f. as QUADRUPED + POLE²]

quaer'e (kwēr'ĭ) *v.t.*, & *n.* (arch.) **1.** *v.t.* (in *imper.*) inquire, it is a question, I should like to know, (*most interesting, no doubt; but quaere, is it true?*). **2.** *n.* question, query. [L, imper. of *quaerere* ask]

quae'stor *n* (Rom. Hist.) magistrate acting as State treasurer, paymaster, etc.; treasurer; hence **quaestōr'IAL** *a.*, ∼SHIP *n.* [ME f. L (*quaerere quaesit-* seek; see -OR)]

quaff (-ahf, -ŏf) *v.i.* & *t.* (literary). drink deeply; drain (cup etc.) in copious or long draughts. [16th c.; perh. imit.]

quag (kwăg, kwŏg) *n.* marshy or boggy spot; quaking bog; hence ∼'gy² (-gĭ) *a.* [rel. to dial. *quag* v. 'shake', prob. imit.]

qua'gga *n.* extinct S. Afr. quadruped related to ass and zebra, less striped than latter. [f. Xhosa-Kaffir *iqwara*]

qua'gmīre (kwă'-, kwŏ'-) *n.* quaking bog, fen, marsh, slough (lit. or fig.). [f. QUAG + MIRE¹]

*qua'hŏg, ***qua'haug**, (kwaw'-) *n.* edible round clam of Atlantic coast of N. America. [Narraganset Indian]

quaich, quaigh, (kwāχ) *n.* (Sc.) kind of drinking-cup, usu. of wood and having two handles. [f. Gael. *cuach* cup, prob. f. L *caucus*]

quail¹ *n.* (pl. ∼ or ∼s). migratory bird of genus *Coturnix* etc. allied to partridge and esteemed as food; ∼-call, ∼-pipe, whistle with note like quail's for luring these birds; hence ∼'ERY (3) *n.* [ME, f. OF *quaille* f. med. L *coacula* (prob. imit.); cf. MDu., MLG *quackele*, OHG *wahtala*]

quail² *v.i.* (Of person, his heart, courage, spirit, or eyes) flinch, be cowed, give way, *before* or *at* or *to*. [ME, of unkn. orig.]

quaint *a.* attractive or piquant in virtue of unfamiliar, esp. old-fashioned, appearance, ornamentation, manners, etc., daintily odd; hence ∼'LY² *adv.*, ∼'NESS *n.* [earlier senses 'wise, cunning'; ME f. OF *cointe* f. L *cognitus* p.p.p. of *cognoscere* ascertain]

quāk|e *v.i.*, & *n.* **1.** *v.i.* shake, tremble, rock to and fro,

(of earth with earthquake, person usu. *for* or *with* fear or cold, bog when trodden on, etc.); ∼'ing-grass, grass of genus *Briza* with slender stalks trembling in wind; hence ∼'y² *a.* **2.** *n.* act of quaking; (colloq.) earthquake. [OE *cwacian*]

Quā'ker *n.* **1.** (Pop. name for) member of the (Religious) Society of Friends, Christian movement without written creed or ordained ministers, devoted to peaceful principles, and formerly noted for plainness of dress and simplicity of living. **2.** *∼ (gun), dummy gun in ship or fort. **3.** ∼-bird, sooty albatross; ∼(s') meeting, religious meeting of Friends, silent till some member is moved by the Holy Spirit, (fig.) silent meeting, company in which conversation flags. [Hence ∼DOM, ∼ESS¹, ∼ISM (3, 4), *ns.*, ∼ISH¹, ∼LY¹, *adjs.* [f. prec. + -ER¹]

qualificā'tion (-ŏl-) *n.* **1.** modification, recognition of contingency (*statement with many qualifications*), restricting or limiting circumstance (*hedged with qualifications*), detraction from completeness or absoluteness (*his delight had one qualification*). **2.** quality or accomplishment fitting person or thing (*for* post etc., or abs.); condition that must be fulfilled before right can be acquired or office held (*the qualification for citizenship may be a specified income*); document attesting such fulfilment. **3.** attribution of quality (*the qualification of his policy as opportunist is unfair*). **4.** Hence **qua'lificātory** (-ŏ'l-) *a.* [F, or f. med. L *qualificatio* (as prec.; see -FICATION)]

qua'lify (-ŏ'l-) *v.* **1.** *v.t.* attribute some quality to, describe *as*, (*qualify documents as heretical, person as a scoundrel, proposal as iniquitous; adjectives qualify nouns*). **2.** invest or provide with the necessary qualities, make competent, fit, or legally entitled, (*for being or doing, to be or do, for* post or sphere, or abs.); ∼ing examination, round, etc., (to ensure that candidates are not below a fixed standard or that competitors do not exceed a fixed number). **3.** modify (statement, opinion), make less absolute or sweeping, subject to reservations or limitation. **4.** moderate, mitigate, make less complete or pleasing or unpleasing; alter strength or flavour of (spirit etc. with water, or vice versa). **5.** *v.i.* fulfil a condition, esp. pass test or take oath, to make oneself eligible (*for* post, competition, etc., or abs.). **6.** Hence **qua'lifiER¹** (-ŏ'l-) *n.* [f. F *qualifier* f. med. L *qualificare* f. L *qualis* such as; see -FY]

qua'litative (-ŏ'lĭta-, -tā-) *a.* concerned with or depending on quality (esp. Chem. of analysis, opp. *quantitative*); hence ∼LY² (-vlĭ) *adv.* [f. LL *qualitativus* (as foll.; see -ATIVE)]

qua'lit̄y (-ŏ'l-) *n.* & *a.* **1.** *n.* degree of excellence, relative nature or kind or character, (opp. *quantity*; *of good, high, poor, quality; is made in three qualities; quality matters more than quantity*; **in the** ∼ **of**, as); general excellence (**has** ∼, is excellent). **2.** faculty, skill, accomplishment, characteristic trait, mental or moral attribute, (**give a taste of** one's ∼, show what one can do; *has many good qualities, the DEFECTS of his qualities, the qualities of a ruler, the quality of inspiring confidence* or *of courage*). **3.** (arch.) high rank or social standing (**people of** ∼, **the** ∼, the upper classes). **4.** (Logic). (Of proposition) being affirmative or negative. **5.** (Of sound, voice, etc.) distinctive character apart from pitch and loudness, timbre. **6.** *a.* possessing high degree of excellence; concerned with maintenance of high quality (*quality control*). [ME, f. OF *qualité* f. L *qualitas -tatis* (*qualis* of what kind; see -ITY)]

qualm (-ahm, -awm) *n.* momentary faint or sick feeling, queasiness; misgiving, sinking of heart; scruple of conscience, doubt of one's own rectitude in some matter; hence ∼'ISH¹ *a.* [16th c., of uncert. orig.]

qua'ndar̆y (-ŏ'n-) *n.* state of perplexity, difficult situation, practical dilemma. [16th c., of uncert. orig.]

quand même (kahṅ mäm) *adv.* despite any consequences, even so, all the same. [F]

quă′ngō (-nggō) n. (pl. ∾s). semi-public body with financial support from and senior appointments made by Government. [abbr. of *quasi-autonomous non-governmental organization*]

‖**quant** (kwŏnt) n. & v. **1.** n. punting-pole with projection to prevent its sinking in mud, used by Norfolk bargemen etc. **2.** v.t. & i. propel (boat) with quant. [15th c., perh. f. L f. Gk *kontos* boat-pole]

quanta. See QUANTUM.

qua′ntic (-ŏ′n-) n. (Math.) rational integral homogeneous function of two or more variables. [f. L *quantus* how much + -IC]

qua′nti∣fy (-ŏ′n-) v.t. determine quantity of; measure or express as quantity; (Logic) define application of (term, proposition) by use of *all, some,* etc.; hence ∾**fi**ABLE a., ∾**fi**CA′TION, ∾**fi**ER¹, ns. [f. med. L *quantificare* (as prec.; see -FY)]

qua′ntitative (-ŏ′ntĭta-, -tā-) a. measured or measurable by, or concerned with, quantity (esp. Chem. of analysis, opp. *qualitative*); of or based on the quantity of syllables (*quantitative scansion, verse,* etc.); hence ∾LY² (-vlĭ) adv. [f. med. L *quantitativus* (as QUANTITY; see -ATIVE)]

qua′ntitive (-ŏ′n-) a. = prec. [as foll.; see -IVE]

qua′ntity (-ŏ′n-) n. **1.** property of things that is estimable by some sort of measure, the having of size, extension, weight, amount, or number. **2.** portion, sum, (of electricity, money, etc.). **3.** specified or considerable portion or number or amount of something, *the* amount of something present, (*a small quantity of blood; a quantity of baskets; buys in quantity, in large quantities; the quantity of heat in a body*); (in pl.) large amounts or numbers, abundance, (*is found in quantities on the shore*); ‖BILL⁴ *of quantities;* ∾ **surveyor,** person who measures and prices work of builders. **4.** (Pros.) length or shortness of vowel sounds or syllables (see LONG¹ 9); FALSE *quantity*; ∾**-mark** (put over vowel to indicate quantity). **5.** (Logic). extension given to subject of proposition. **6.** (Math.) thing having quantity; figure or symbol representing it; negligible ∾, (fig.) person etc. that need not be reckoned with; unknown ∾, (fig.) person or thing whose action or effect cannot be foreseen. [ME, f. OF *quantité* f. L *quantitas -tatis* (*quantus* how much; see -ITY)]

qua′ntiz∣e, -is∣e, (kwŏ′ntīz) v.t. form into quanta; apply quantum mechanics to; hence ∾A′TION n. [f. foll. + -IZE]

qua′nt∣um (-ŏ′n-) n. (pl. ∾a). **1.** amount; share, portion; required, desired, or allowed amount. **2.** (Phys.) discrete unit quantity of energy proportional to frequency of radiation; ∾**um mechanics, theory,** etc., (making use of assumption that energy exists in this form). [L, neut. of *quantus* how much]

quăquăvêr′sal a. (Geol.) pointing in every direction. [f. LL *quaquaversus* (*quaqua* wheresoever, *versus* towards) + -AL]

qua′rantine (kwŏ′rantēn) n., & v.t. **1.** n. (period of) isolation imposed on persons or animals that have arrived from elsewhere or been exposed to, and might spread, infectious or contagious disease. **2.** v.t. impose such isolation on, put in quarantine. [f. It. *quarantina* forty days (*quaranta* forty; see -INE¹)]

‖**quare impedit** (kwârĭ ĭ′mpedĭt) n. writ issued against objector in case of disputed presentation to benefice. [ME f. L, = why does he hinder?]

‖**qua′renden, -der,** (kwŏ′-) n. deep red Devon and Somerset apple. [ME, of unkn. orig.]

quărk (*or* -ōrk) n. (Phys.) one of several (orig. three) hypothetical components of elementary particles. [f. 'Three quarks for Muster Mark' in Joyce's *Finnegans Wake*]

qua′rrel¹ (kwŏ′-) n. (Hist.) short heavy arrow or bolt used in crossbow or arbalest. [ME, f. OF *quar*(*r*)*el*, f. Rom. **quadrellus* dim. of LL *quadrus* square]

qua′rrel² (kwŏ′-) n. **1.** occasion of complaint against person or his actions (*have no quarrel against* or *with him*); pick a ∾, contrive or eagerly accept such

occasion to begin contention. **2.** violent contention or altercation (*between* persons, of person *with* another); rupture of friendly relations; hence ∾SOME¹ a. [ME f. OF *querele,* f. L *querel*(*l*)*a* complaint (*queri* complain)]

qua′rrel³ (kwŏ′-) v.i. (‖-ll-). **1.** take exception, find fault *with* (*I never quarrel with Providence*); ∾ **with** one's **bread and butter,** abandon employment by which one lives. **2.** contend violently (*with* person, *about* or *for* or *over* thing); fall out, have dispute, break off friendly relations. [ME, f. prec. & f. OF *quereler* (*querele;* see prec.)]

qua′rry¹ (kwŏ′-) n. object of pursuit by bird of prey, hounds, hunters, etc.; intended victim or prey. [ME, f. AF **quire, quere* f. OF *cuiree, couree* (assim. to *cuir* leather and *curer* disembowel) f. Rom. **corata* entrails f. L *cor* heart (see -EE, -Y⁴); orig. = parts of deer placed on hide and given to hounds]

qua′rry² (kwŏ′-) n. & v. **1.** n. excavation made by taking stone for building etc. from its bed; place whence stone or (fig.) information etc. may be extracted; ∾**man,** worker in quarry. **2.** v.t. extract (stone) from quarry; extract (facts etc.) laboriously from books etc. **3.** v.i. laboriously search documents etc. [ME, f. med. L *quare*(*r*)*ia* f. OF *quarriere* (**carre* f. L *quadrum* square)]

qua′rry³ (kwŏ′-) n. diamond-shaped pane of glass as used in lattice windows; ∾ (**tile**), unglazed floor-tile. [later form of QUARREL¹ in same sense]

quart¹ (kwôrt) n. measure of capacity, quarter of gallon or two pints (**put ∾ into pint pot,** make less contain greater, (fig.) do what is impossible); vessel containing this amount; *unit of dry measure, 1/32 bushel, 1101 c.c.; ∾ **bottle** of wine or spirit, ⅕ gal. [ME, f. OF *quarte* f. L *quarta* fem. of *quartus* fourth (*quattuor* four)]

quart² (kârt) n. fourth of eight parrying positions in fencing; sequence of four cards of same suit in piquet etc. (∾ **major,** quart headed by ace). [f. F *quarte* f. as prec.]

quar′tan (kwôr′-) a. & n. (fever) recurring every third (by inclusive reckoning fourth) day. [ME f. OF *quartaine* f. L (*febris* fever) *quartana* (*quartus* fourth; see -AN)]

quartā′tion (kwôr-) n. combining of three parts of silver with one of gold as preliminary in purifying gold. [f. L *quartus* fourth + -ATION]

quarte. Var. of QUART².

quar′ter¹ (-ôr′-) n. **1.** one of four equal parts into which thing is or might be divided (*cut apple into quarters; can get it elsewhere for a quarter* (*of*) *the price*); ∾ **of a century,** any period of 25 years; *second* etc. ∾ **of the century,** 26th to 50th etc. years of it; ∾ **of an hour,** any consecutive 15 minutes; **bad** ∾ **of an hour,** *mauvais quart d'heure;* ∾ **mile,** quarter of a mile etc. **2.** (US & Can.) 25 cents or quarter dollar, as amount or coin. **3.** one of four parts, each including leg or wing, into which animal's or bird's.carcass is divided; (in pl.) similar parts of traitor quartered after execution; (in *pl.*) = HIND³*quarters*. **4.** either side of ship abaft the beam; **on the** ∾, between astern and abeam. **5.** (Her.) one of four divisions of quartered shield; charge occupying this, placed in chief. **6.** ‖grain-measure of eight bushels, used in stating large quantities, prices, etc.; quarter of hundredweight, ‖28 lb. or *25 lb. **7.** side of boot or shoe from back to vamp. **8.** fourth part of year, for which payments become due on quarter-day; school or *university term. **9.** fourth part of lunar month; moon's position between first and second (**first** ∾) or third and fourth (**last** ∾) of these; (Amer. & Austral. Footb.) one of four equal periods constituting match. **10.** point of time 15 minutes before or after any hour o'clock (*at a quarter to* or *past six; it is not the quarter yet; strikes the hours, half-hours, and quarters*). **11.** (race over) distance of quarter mile. **12.** (region lying about) point of compass, direction, district, locality, source of supply or help or information, (*wind blows from all quarters;*

flocked in from all quarters; no help to be looked for in that quarter). **13.** division of town, esp. one appropriated to or occupied by special class (*the Chinese*, LATIN, *manufacturing, residential, quarter*). **14.** (in *pl.*) lodgings, abode, esp. place where troops are lodged or stationed; **beat to ~s,** (Naut.) summon crew to appointed stations as for action; CLOSE¹ *quarters*; **take up** one's **~s,** go to lodge *in, with*, etc. **15.** exemption from death offered or granted to enemy in battle who will surrender (*give or receive quarter; ask for or cry quarter*); **give no ~ to,** (fig.) attack relentlessly. **16.** **~-back,* football player directing attacking play; **~-bell** (sounding the quarter-hours); **~-binding** of book (with narrow leather at back and none at corners); **~-day** on which quarterly payments are due, tenancies begin and end, etc.: ||Lady Day 25 Mar., Midsummer Day 24 June, Michaelmas 29 Sept., and Christmas 25 Dec., or in Scotland Candlemas 2 Feb., Whitsunday 15 May, Lammas 1 Aug., Martinmas 11 Nov.; **1 Jan.*, 1 Apr., 1 July, 1 Oct.); **~deck,** (1) part of upper deck between stern and after-mast, (2) the officers (cf. LOWER³ *deck*) of ship or navy; **~-final,** match or round preceding semi-final; **~-horse,* strong horse of breed able to run quarter mile at high speed; **~-hour,** (1) fifteen minutes, (2) = sense 10; **~ ill,** cattle and sheep disease causing putrefaction in one or more of the quarters; **~-jack,** (1) clock jack striking quarters, (2) (Mil. sl.) = *quartermaster*; ||**~-light,** (1) window in body of closed carriage apart from door-window, (2) window in side of motor vehicle other than main door-window; **~master,** (Naut.) petty officer or rating in charge of steering, binnacle, signals, hold-stowing, etc., (Mil.) regimental officer with duties of assigning quarters, laying out camp, and looking after rations, clothing, etc.; **Q~master General,** head of army department controlling quartering, equipment, etc.; **~master sergeant,** sergeant assisting army quartermaster; **~-miler,** runner whose distance is the quarter mile; **~-note,* (Mus.) crotchet; **~-plate,** photographic plate or film 8.3 × 10.8 cm, photograph reproduced from it; **~ sessions,** (||Hist.) court of limited criminal and civil jurisdiction and of appeal held usu. quarterly; **~staff,** stout pole 6–8 ft. long formerly used by peasantry as weapon; **~-tone,** (Mus.) half a semitone. [ME f. AF, OF *quartier* f. L *quartarius* fourth part (of a measure) f. *quartus* fourth; see -ER² (2)]

quar'ter² (-ôr'-) *v.t.* **1.** divide into four equal parts; (Hist.) divide (traitor's body) into quarters. **2.** (Her.) place or bear (charges or coats of arms) quarterly on shield; add (another's coat) to one's hereditary arms, place in alternate quarters *with*; divide (shield) into four or more parts by vertical and horizontal lines. **3.** put (esp. soldiers) into quarters, station or lodge in specified place; impose (person *on* another) as lodger. **4.** (Of dog etc.) range or traverse (ground) in every direction. **5.** cut (log) into quarters and these into planks so as to show the grain well. [ME, f. prec.]

quar'terage (-ôr'-) *n.* quarterly payment; a quarter's wages, allowance, pension, etc. [ME, f. QUARTER¹ +-AGE]

quar'tering (-ôr'-) *n.* In vbl senses; (Her., in *pl.*) coats marshalled on shield to denote alliances of family with heiresses of others; square lengths of timber made by sawing planks into four lengths. [f. QUARTER² +-ING¹]

quar'terly (-ôr'-) *a., n., & adv.* **1.** *a.* produced or occurring once every quarter of a year; (Her., of shield) quartered. **2.** *n.* quarterly review or magazine. **3.** *adv.* once every quarter of a year; (Her.) in the four, or in two diagonally opposite, quarters of shield. [f. QUARTER¹ +-LY¹,²]

||**quar'tern** (-ôr'-) *n.* (arch.) **~(-loaf),** four-pound loaf; quarter of a pint. [ME = quarter, f. AF *quartrun*, OF *quart(e)ron* (QUART¹(*e*) fourth or *quartier* QUARTER¹)]

quartě't, -ě'tte, (-ôr-) *n.* **1.** (Mus.) (performers of) composition for four voices or instruments; **piano ~,** 3 stringed instruments with piano. **2.** set of four. [f. F *quartette* f. It. *quartetto* (*quarto* fourth f. L *quartus*); see -ET¹]

quar'tic (-ôr'-) *a. & n.* (Math.) (equation) involving fourth and no higher power of unknown quantity or variable. [f. L *quartus* fourth +-IC]

quar'tile (-ôr'-) *a. & n.* **1.** *a.* (Astrol.) of aspect of two heavenly bodies 90° apart. **2.** *n.* quartile aspect; (Statistics) one of 3 values of a variable dividing a population into 4 equal groups as regards the value of that variable. [f. med. L **quartilis* f. L *quartus* fourth; see -IL]

quar'tō (-ôr'-) *n.* (*abbr.* 4to; *pl.* **~s**). size given by folding sheet of paper twice; book consisting of sheets so folded; **~ paper** (so folded, and cut). [f. L (*in*) *quarto* (in fourth (of sheet), abl. of *quartus* fourth]

quartz (kwôrts) *n.* mineral form of silica, massive or crystallizing in hexagonal prisms; **~ clock** (operated by electric vibrations of quartz crystal); **~ lamp,** quartz tube containing mercury vapour as light source. [f. G *quarz* f. WSlav. *kwardy*]

quar'tzite (-ôr'ts-) *n.* compact granular quartz rock. [f. prec. +-ITE¹]

quā'sar (-s-, -z-) *n.* (Astron.) starlike object having spectrum with large red-shift. [f. *quasi*-stellar]

quash (kwŏsh) *v.t.* annul, make void, reject as not valid, put an end to, (esp. by legal procedure or authority); suppress, crush, (rebellion etc.). [ME, f. OF *quasser, casser* annul f. LL *cassare* (*cassus* null, void, or f. L *cassare* frequent. of *quatere* shake)]

qua'si (kwā'zī, -ah'zī, -s-) *adv.* (introducing explanation) that is to say, as if it were. [L, = as if, almost]

qua'si- (kwā'zī, -ah'zī, -s) *pref.* seeming(ly), not real(ly); half-, almost; **~stellar object,** quasar. [f. prec.]

qua'ssia (kwŏ'sha) *n.* S. Amer., esp. Surinam, tree (*Quassia amara*); (wood, bark, or root of this or similar tree, yielding) bitter medicinal tonic and insecticide. [f. G. *Quassi*, 18th c. Surinam Negro, who discovered its medicinal properties; see -IA¹]

quatercenten'ary (kwă-, kwŏ-, -sentē'-, -sě'ntĭ-) *a. & n.* (festival) of the four-hundredth anniversary. [f. L *quater* four times +CENTENARY]

quatěr'narў *a. & n.* **1.** *a.* having four parts, esp. (Chem.) compounded of or linked with four elements or radicals; concerned with the number four; (Geol., Q~) belonging to most recent period or system, subsequent to Tertiary. **2.** *n.* set of four things; (Geol., Q~) Quaternary period or system. [ME, f. L *quaternarius* (*quaterni* distrib. of *quattuor* four; see -ARY¹)]

quater'nion *n.* set of four; (Math.) operator that changes one vector into another and depends on four geometrical elements. [ME, f. LL *quaternio -onis* (as prec.)]

quater'nitў *n.* being four; set of four persons (esp. of the Godhead in contrast to *Trinity*). [f. LL *quaternitas* (as QUATERNARY; see -ITY)]

quā'torzain (kă'-) *n.* fourteen-line poem, irregular sonnet. [f. F *quatorzaine* (*quatorze* fourteen f. L *quattuordecim*)]

quator'ze (k-) *n.* set of four aces, kings, queens, or jacks, in one hand at piquet, scoring 14. [F; see prec.]

qua'train (-ŏ't-) *n.* stanza of four lines usu. with alternate rhymes. [F (*quatre* four f. L *quattuor*)]

quatre. Var. of CATER¹.

quā'trefoil (k-) *n.* four-cusped figure, esp. as ornament in architectural tracery, resembling symmetrical four-lobed leaf or flower. [ME, f. AF **quatrefoil* (*quatre* four; see FOIL¹)]

quattrŏcě'nt|ō (-ahtrōchě'-) *n.* Italian style of art of the 15th c.; hence **~IST** (2, 3) *n.* [It., = 400, used w. ref. to years 14—]

quā'ver¹ *v.* **1.** *v.i.* (esp. of voice or musical sound) vibrate, shake, tremble; use trills or shakes in singing. **2.** *v.t.* sing (note, song) with quavering; say (*out*) in trembling tones. [ME, frequent. of obs. *quave*, perh. f. OE *cwafian* of imit. orig.; see -ER⁵]

quā'ver² *n*. **1.** trill in singing; tremulousness in speech, whence ~y². *a*. **2.** ||(Mus.) note with one-hooked symbol, equal to half crotchet. [f. prec.]

quay (kē) *n*. solid stationary artificial landing-place lying alongside or projecting into water for (un)-loading ships; ~'side, land forming or near quay; hence ~ AGE (1, 4) (kē'ij) *n*. [ME *key(e)*, *kay* f. OF *kay* f. Gaulish *caio* f. OCelt. *kagio*-]

Que. *abbr.* Quebec.

quean *n*. (arch.) impudent or ill-behaved girl or woman. [OE *cwene* woman, = OS *cwena*, OHG *quena*, ON *kvenna* gen. pl., Goth. *qino* f. Gmc *kwenōn; cf. QUEEN¹]

quea'sı|̌y (-zĭ) *a*. (Of food) unsettling the stomach, causing nausea; (of person or his stomach) (1) feeling nausea, (2) easily upset, weak of digestion; (of conscience etc.) over-scrupulous, tender; hence ~ĭLY² *adv.*, ~ĭNESS *n*. [ME *queysy*, *coisy*, perh. f. AF & OF *coisir* hurt]

quebra'chō (käbrah'-) *n*. (*pl.* ~s). S. Amer. tree (esp. *Aspidosperma quebracho*) yielding very hard timber and medicinal bark; bark of this tree, used as tonic to aid respiration. [Sp. (*quebrar* break, *hacha* axe)]

Quě'chu|a (kě'chwa) *n*. member or language of Peruvian Indian tribe that was dominant in Inca empire; hence ~AN *a*. [Sp., f. Quechua]

queen¹ *n*. **1.** ~ (**consort**), king's wife. **2.** female sovereign of kingdom; Q~ Anne is dead (retort to stale news); *Queen Anne's* BOUNTY; Q~ Anne's lace, wild carrot; Q~-Anne, in the style of English architecture, furniture, etc., in or about Queen Anne's time, early 18th c. **3.** worshipped female, e.g. the Virgin Mary (*Queen of grace* etc.); ancient goddess (Q~ of heaven, Juno, of love, Venus, of night, Diana, etc.); person's sweetheart or wife or mistress; majestic woman; great woman player etc. (*tennis queen*); belle or mock sovereign on some occasion (*Queen of the* MAY³). **4.** personified best example of anything that can be regarded as fem. (*the queen of watering-places, roses, nurses*); ~ of puddings (made with breadcrumbs and meringue); ~ of the meadows, meadowsweet). **6.** ~ (bee, wasp, ant), perfect fertile female of bee etc.; adult female cat. **7.** most powerful piece in chess (~'s bishop, knight, pawn, rook, those placed nearest queen at start). **8.** court-card bearing representation of queen and usu. ranking next below king. **9.** (sl.) male homosexual. **10.** ~-cake, small soft currant cake often heart-shaped; ~ dowager, widow of king; ~ mother, queen dowager who is mother of sovereign; ~-post, one of two upright timbers between tie--beam and principal rafters of roof-truss; ||*Queen's* BENCH, BOUNTY, COLOUR¹, COUNSEL¹, ENGLISH¹, EVIDENCE, GUIDE¹, HIGHWAY, MESSENGER, PROCTOR, SCOUT¹, SHILLING, SPEECH; ~'s-ware, cream-coloured Wedgwood. **11.** Hence ~'DOM, ~'HOOD, *ns.*, ~'LESS, ~'LIKE, *adjs.* [OE *cwēn*, = OS *quān*, ON *kvæn*, *kván*, Goth. *qēns* wife f. Gmc *kwæniz*; cf. QUEAN]

queen² *v*. **1.** *v.t.* make (woman) queen; ~ it, play the queen; (Chess) convert (pawn) to queen when it reaches opponent's end of board. **2.** *v.i.* (Of pawn) be converted thus. [f. prec.]

quee'nie *n*. (sl.) = QUEEN¹ 9. [f. QUEEN¹ + -IE]

quee'nl|ȳ *a*. fit for or appropriate to a queen; majestic, queenlike; hence ~ĭNESS *n*. [f. QUEEN¹ + -LY¹]

Quee'nsberry (-z-) *n*. ~ Rules, standard rules esp. of boxing. [f. 8th Marquis of ~, Engl. nobleman d. 1900, who supervised preparation of boxing laws 1867]

queer *a.*, *n.*, & *v.t.* **1.** *a.* strange, odd, eccentric; of questionable character, shady, suspect; out of sorts, giddy, faint, (*feel queer*); ||(sl.) drunk; (sl., esp. of man) homosexual; in Q~ Street, (sl.) in a difficulty, in

debt or trouble or disrepute; hence ~'ISH¹ (2) *a.*, ~'LY² *adv.*, ~'NESS *n*. **2.** *n*. (sl.) (Esp. male) homosexual. **3.** *v.t.* (sl.) spoil, put out of order; ~ the pitch for person, ~ person's pitch, spoil his chances beforehand. [perh. f. G *quer* oblique (as THWART)]

quell *v.t.* (literary). suppress, forcibly put an end to, crush, overcome, reduce to submission, (fear, opposition, rebellion, rebels, etc.); hence (-)~'ER¹ *n*. [OE *cwellan* kill, = OS *quellian*, OHG *quellen*, ON *kvelja* f. Gmc *kwaljan*]

quench *v.t.* **1.** cause (fire, light, etc.) to cease burning (lit. or fig.). **2.** cool, esp. with water (heat, heated thing); cool (hot metal or coke, etc.) rapidly in cold water, oil, air, etc. **3.** stifle, suppress, (desire, speed, motion, electric spark or discharge); slake (thirst); (sl.) reduce (opponent) to silence. **4.** Hence ~'ABLE, ~'LESS, *adjs.*, ~'ER¹ (1, 2) *n*. [ME, f. OE *-cwencan* causative f. *-cwincan* be extinguished]

queně'lle (k-) *n*. seasoned ball or roll of pounded fish or meat. [F; orig. unkn.]

quer'ist *n*. (literary). person who asks questions. [f. L *quaerere* ask + -IST]

quern *n*. hand-mill for grinding corn; small hand-mill for pepper etc., ~-stone, millstone. [OE *cweorn(e)*, = OS *quern*, OHG *quirn(a)*, ON *kvern*, Goth. *-qairnus* f. Gmc *kwern*-]

quě'rulous (-rŏŏ-) *a*. complaining, peevish; hence ~'LY² *adv.*, ~'NESS *n*. [f. LL *querulosus* or L *querulus* (*queri* complain; see -OSE¹, -OUS)]

quer'ȳ *n*. & *v*. **1.** *n*. = QUAERE 1. **2.** a question, esp. expressing doubt or objection (*was prepared to suppress all queries*); question mark or the word *query* or *qu.* or *qy*. written against statement, or the word *query* interjected in speech, to question accuracy. **3.** *v.t.* ask, inquire, (*whether, if,* etc.); call (thing) in question in speech or writing, question accuracy of; *question (person). **4.** *v.i.* put a question. [Anglicized form of QUAERE, after *inquiry*]

quest¹ *n*. seeking or thing sought by inquiry or search, esp. object of medieval knight's pursuit; in ~ of, seeking. [ME, f. OF *queste* f. Rom. *quaesita* fem. p.p. (as n.) of L *quaerere* seek]

quest² *v*. **1.** *v.i.* (Of dog etc.) search (*about*) for game; go (*about*) in search of or for something. **2.** *v.t.* (poet.) search for, seek out. [ME, f. OF *quester* (as prec.)]

quě'stion¹ (-schon) *n*. **1.** sentence adapted by order of words, use of interrogative pronoun or question mark, or other means, to elicit information, (*put a question to, ask a question of*); POP¹ the question; ~ and answer, alternation of questions and answers, as in catechism; LEADING², RHETORICAL, *question*; indirect or oblique ~, question made into dependent clause; ~ mark, punctuation mark (?) indicating question; ~-master, chairman of broadcast quiz etc.; ||~ time, (Parl.) period when members may question ministers. **2.** (raising of) doubt about or objection to thing's truth, credibility, advisability, etc. (*allowed it without question*); beyond all ~, certainly, undoubtedly; CALL¹ in question; make no ~ of fact etc., but that it is so etc., be certain of it; hence ~LESS *a*. & (arch.) *adv*. **3.** problem requiring solution, matter or concern depending on conditions of; BEG the question; *success* is (merely) a ~ of time, will certainly come sooner or later; it is (only) a ~ of, what is required or involved is (merely). **4.** subject being discussed or for discussion, thing to be voted on; *the person in* ~, that we are referring to or discussing; come into ~, be discussed, become of practical importance; *that* is not the ~, is irrelevant; the ~ is (introducing or recalling exact matter of debate); Q~! (in public assemblies, used to recall speaker from digression); OPEN¹ *question*; out of the ~, too impracticable to be worth discussing; *the* PREVIOUS *question*; put the ~, require supporters and opponents of proposal to record their votes, divide meeting etc. **5.** (arch.) torture to elicit confession (*was put to the question*).

[ME, f. AF *questiun*, OF *question* f. L *quaestio -onis* (*quaerere quaest-* seek; see -ION)]

que′stion² (-schọn) *v.t.* ask questions of, interrogate, subject to examination, (person); seek information from study of (phenomena, facts); call in question, throw doubt upon, raise objections to, (*question the honesty, accuracy, fitness, of*); **it cannot be ~ed but** (**that**), it is certain that. [ME, f. OF *questionner* (as prec.)]

que′stionab|le (-schọn-) *a.* doubtful as regards its truth or quality; not clearly in accordance with honesty, honour, wisdom, etc.; hence **~LY²** *adv.* [f. prec. + -ABLE]

que′stionary (-schọn-) *n.* = foll. [f. med. L *quaestionarium* or f. F (as foll.); see -ARY¹]

quĕstionnair′e (kwĕ′schọn-, kĕstĭo-) *n.* formulated series of questions esp. for statistical study; document containing these. [F (*questionner* QUESTION², -*aire* -ARY¹)]

que′tzal *n.* beautiful Central Amer. bird (*Pharomachrus mocino*), the male with long green tail-coverts; monetary unit of Guatemala. [Sp., f. Aztec; *quetzalli* the bird's tail-feather]

queue (kū) *n.*, & *v.i.* **1.** *n.* hanging plaited tail of hair or wig, pigtail. **2.** line or sequence of persons, vehicles, etc., awaiting their turn to be attended to or proceed. **3.** *v.t.* (Of persons etc.) form *up* in queue; take one's place in a queue. [F, f. L *cauda* tail]

qui′bbl|e, *n.*, & *v.i.* **1.** *n.* play on words, pun; equivocation, evasion, unsubstantial or purely verbal argument etc. esp. one depending on ambiguity of words; petty objection. **2.** *v.i.* use quibbles; hence **~ER¹** *n.*, **~ING²** *a.* [dim. of obs. *quib* prob. f. L *quibus* dat. & abl. pl. of *qui* who (familiar f. use in legal documents); see -LE 1]

quiche (kēsh) *n.* open tart with sweet or (usu.) savoury filling. [F]

Quichua. Var. of QUECHUA.

quick *a.*, *n.*, & *adv.* **1.** *a.* taking only a short time to traverse a distance or do a thing, rapid, swift, done or obtained in short time or with little interval, (*in quick succession; at a quick trot; a quick way of doing it*); (of fire) burning strongly; (of oven) hot; **be ~**, act in quick manner; hence **~LY²** *adv.* **2.** vigorous, lively; ready, sensitive, (*quick to take offence*); prompt to act, perceive, be affected, learn, think, or invent; **~ ear, eye, sight,** (acute, alert); **~ temper,** tendency to be easily irritated; **has ~ wits**, is ready at grasping situation, making repartees, etc., whence **~-witt**ED² *a.* **3.** (arch.) living, alive, (*the quick and the dead*); **~ with child**, at stage of pregnancy when movements of foetus have been felt. **4.** **~-change**, (of actor etc.) quickly changing costume or appearance to play another part; **~ fire**, firing of shots in quick succession; *quick*LIME¹; **~ march**, (Mil.) march in quick time (esp. as word of command for starting at usual pace); **~ one**, (colloq.) a quickly taken drink; **~′sand**, (bed of) loose wet sand readily swallowing up heavy objects placed on it; **~′set**, (hedge) formed of live (slips of) plants esp. hawthorn set in ground to grow, such slips; **~′silver**, (*n.*) mercury, (fig.) mobility of temperament or mood, (*v.t.*) coat (mirror-glass) with amalgam of tin; **~ step**, step used in quick time; **~′step**, a fast foxtrot; **~′thorn**, hawthorn (*Crataegus oxyacantha*); **~ time**, marching at about 120 paces per minute; **~ trick**, (Bridge) (card that should win) trick in first two rounds of suit. **5.** Hence **~′**NESS *n.* **6.** *n.* tender or sensitive flesh below skin or esp. nails (*bites his nails to the quick*); tender part of wound or sore where healthy tissue begins (*probed it to the quick*); seat of feeling or emotion (*the insult stung him to the quick*); *mercury. **7.** *adv.* quickly, at rapid rate, in comparatively short time, (*ran as quick as I could; who will be there quickest?; quick-drying, -fading, -forgotten*, etc.); (ellipt. for *imper.* of *go, come, be, quick*) act quickly; **~-firing**, (of gun) with special mechanism for firing shots in quick succession;

~-freeze *v.t.*, & *n.*, freeze (food), freezing of food, rapidly so as to preserve its natural qualities. [OE *cwic*(*u*) alive, = OS *quik*, OHG *quek*, ON *kvikr*, f. Gmc *kwikwaz f. IE **qwej-*]

qui′cken *v.* **1.** *v.t.* give or restore natural or spiritual life or vigour to, animate; stimulate, rouse, inspire; (arch.) kindle, make (fire) burn brighter. **2.** *v.i.* receive or come to life; (of woman or foetus) reach quick stage in pregnancy (see QUICK 3). **3.** *v.t.* & *i.* accelerate, make or (of pace, motion, etc.) become quicker. [ME, f. prec. + -EN⁶]

qui′ckie *n.* (colloq.) thing done or made quickly or hastily. [f. QUICK + -IE]

||**quid¹** *n.* (*pl.* same). (sl.) one pound sterling (*at ten quid a week*); **~s in**, in a position of profit. [prob. f. *quid* nature of a thing, f. L *quid* what, something]

quid² *n.* lump of tobacco etc. for chewing. [dial. var. of CUD]

qui′ddity *n.* essence of a person or thing, what makes a thing what it is; quibble, captious subtlety. [f. med. L *quidditas* f. L *quid* what; see -ITY]

qui′dnunc *n.* newsmonger, person given to gossip. [f. L *quid* what + *nunc* now]

quid prō quō′ *n.* (thing given as) compensation, return made, consideration, (*must get, must find him, a quid pro quo*). [L, = something for something]

quie′sc|ent *a.* motionless, inert; silent, dormant; hence or cogn. **~**ENCE, **~**ENCY *n.*, **~**entLY² *adv.* [f. L *quiescere* (*quies* QUIET¹; see -ESCENT)]

qui′et¹ *n.* silence, stillness; being free from disturbance or agitation or urgent tasks; peaceful state of social or political affairs; rest, repose, peace of mind; unruffled deportment, calm. [ME, f. AF *quiete* f. OF *quieté* (*quiet*; see foll.)]

qui′et² *a.* (**~er**, **~est**). **1.** with no or slight or gentle sound or motion; of peaceful or peaceful disposition; (of colour, dress, etc.) unobtrusive, not showy; **keep ~**, say nothing (*about*); **be ~**, (colloq., esp. in *imper.*) cease talk etc. **2.** not overt, private, disguised, (*quiet resentment; had a quiet dig at him*); **on the ~**, unobtrusively, secretly. **3.** undisturbed, not interfered with or interrupted, free or far from strife or uproar or vigorous action; not formal (*a quiet dinner-party, wedding*). **4.** enjoyed in quiet, tranquil, not anxious or remorseful. **5.** Hence **~LY²** *adv.*, **~**NESS, **qui′ĕ**TUDE, *ns.* [ME, f. OF *quiet*(*e*) f. L *quietus* p.p. of *quiescere* (see QUIESCENT)]

qui′et³ *v.* **1.** *v.t.* reduce to quietness, soothe, calm. **2.** *v.i.* **~** (**down**), become quiet. [f. prec. & f. LL *quietare* f. L *quietus* QUIET²]

||**qui′eten** *v.t.* & *i.* = prec. [f. QUIET² + -EN⁶]

qui′et|ism *n.* passive attitude towards life with devotional contemplation and abandonment of the will, as form of religious mysticism; non-resistance principles; so **~**IST (2) *n.* & *a.*, **~′**ISTIC *a.* [f. It. *quietismo* (as QUIET² see -ISM)]

quiē′tus *n.* **1.** acquittance or receipt given on payment of account etc. **2.** release from life; death, extinction, final riddance, (*got, gave him, his quietus; have given the quietus to it*). [f. med. L *quietus* (*est* he is) quit (QUIET²) used as receipt form]

||**quiff** *n.* curl plastered down on the forehead; man's tuft of hair brushed upwards over forehead. [20th c.; orig. unkn.]

quill¹ *n.* **1.** hollow stem of feather; plectrum, fishing-float, or toothpick, made of this. **2.** **~**(**-feather**), whole large feather of wing or tail; **~**(**-pen**), pen made from this. **3.** one of porcupine's spines; bobbin esp. of hollow reed; musical pipe made of hollow stem; curled-up piece of cinnamon or cinchona bark. **4.** **~-coverts**, feathers covering base of quill-feathers; **~-driver**, (arch., derog.) clerk or journalist or author. [ME, prob. f. (M)LG *quiele*]

quill² *v.* **1.** *v.t.* form into cylindrical quill-like folds, goffer; hence **~′**ING (2) *n.* **2.** *v.i.* wind thread or yarn on bobbin. [f. prec.]

qui′llêt n. (arch.) quibble, fine distinction. [perh. abbr. of obs. *quillity*, app. alt. of QUIDDITY]

quilt n., & v.t. **1.** n. bed-coverlet made of padding enclosed between two layers of cloth etc. and kept in place by cross lines of stitching; bedspread of similar design (CRAZY or PATCH¹*work quilt*). **2.** v.t. cover or line with padded material; make or join together (pieces of cloth with padding between) after the manner of a quilt; sew up (coin, letter, etc.) between two layers of garment etc.; compile (literary work) out of extracts or borrowed ideas; hence ∼ING¹ (1, 3) n. [ME, f. OF *coilte, cuilte* f. L *culcita* mattress, cushion]

quĭn n. (colloq.) quintuplet. [abbr.]

qui′nacrine (-ĭn, -ēn) n. anti-malarial drug derived from acridine. [f. *quinine + acridine*]

qui′narў a. of the number five; having five parts. [f. L *quinarius* (*quini* distrib. of *quinque* five; see -ARY¹)]

qui′nate a. (Bot.) (Of leaf) having five leaflets. [f. L *quini* (as prec.) + -ATE²]

quince n. hard acid yellowish pear-shaped fruit used as preserve or as flavouring; tree (*Cydonia oblonga*) bearing it; JAPANESE quince. [ME, orig. collect. pl. of obs. *quoyn, coyn*, f. OF *cooin* f. L *cotoneum* var. of *cydoneum* (apple) of *Cydonia* in Crete]

quincĕntenary (-sĕntē′-, -sĕ′ntĭ-) a. & n. (festival) of the five-hundredth anniversary. [irreg. f. L *quinque* five + CENTENARY]

qui′ncŭnx n. (arrangement of) five objects set so that four are at corners of square or rectangle and the other at its centre (e.g. the five on dice or cards; esp. as basis of arrangement in planting trees etc.); so **quincŭ′ncIAL** (-shal) a. [L, = five-twelfths (*quinque* five, *uncia* twelfth, OUNCE¹)]

quingĕntē′narў (-nj-) a. & n. = QUINCENTENARY. [f. L *quingenti* 500, after CENTENARY]

quinine (-ĭ′nēn, -ē′n) n. alkaloid found esp. in cinchona bark; salt of this, used as febrifuge and tonic. [f. *quina* cinchona bark (Sp. f. Quechua *kina* bark) + -INE⁵]

qui′nŏl n. = HYDROquinone. [f. as prec. + -OL]

qui′noline (-ēn) n. oily amine got from distillation of coal tar or by synthesis and used in preparation of drugs etc. [f. prec. + -INE⁵]

quinquagenā̆r′ian a. & n. (person) from 50 to 59 years old. [f. L *quinquagenarius* (*quinquageni* distrib. of *quinquaginta* fifty; see -ARY¹) + -AN]

quinquagenarў (-kwajē′-, -kwā′je′-) a. & n. **1.** = prec. **2.** (festival) of the fiftieth anniversary. [as prec.]

Quinquagē′sima n. ∼ (**Sunday**), Sunday before Lent. [med. L fem. (as n.) of L *quinquagesimus* fiftieth (*quinquaginta* fifty), after QUADRAGESIMA]

qui′nque- comb. form. five, as: ∼cente′nnial a. & n., = QUINCENTENARY; ∼la′teral, five-sided; ∼va′lent, (Chem.) having a valence of five. [L (*quinque* five)]

quinque′nnial a. lasting, recurring every, five years; hence ∼LY² adv. [f. L *quinquennis* (as foll.) + -AL]

quinquē′nni|um n. (pl. ∼ums or ∼a). period of five years. [L (*quinque* five, *annus* year)]

qui′nquĕrēme n. ancient galley with five banks of oars. [f. L *quinqueremis* (*quinque* five, *remus* oar)]

qui′ns|ў n. inflammation of throat with abscess on, or suppuration of region around, tonsils; hence ∼ĭED² (-ĭd) a. [ME, f. OF *quinencie* f. med. L *quinancia* f. Gk *kunagkhē* (*kun-* dog, *agkhō* throttle)]

quint (kĭnt) n. sequence of five cards of same suit in ·piquet etc. (∼ **major**, quint headed by ace). [f. F *quinte* f. L *quinta* fem. of *quintus* fifth (*quinque* five)]

quinta (kwī′nta) n. country house with vineyard etc. [Sp. & Port., orig. of house and farm let at charge of one-fifth (*quinta parte*) of produce]

qui′ntain (-tĭn) n. (Hist.) (medieval military exercise of tilting at) post set up as mark and often provided with sandbag to swing round and strike unskilful tilter. [ME, f. OF *quintaine* perh. ult. f. L *quintana* camp market f. *quintus* (*manipulus*) fifth (maniple)]

qui′ntal n. weight of about 100 lb.; weight of 100 kg. [ME f. OF; med. L *quintale*, f. Arab. *ḳinṭār*]

qui′ntan a. & n. (fever) recurring every fourth (by inclusive reckoning fifth) day. [f. L (*febris* fever) *quintana* (*quintus* fifth; see -AN)]

quinte (kănt) n. fifth of eight parrying positions in fencing. [F; see QUINT]

quintĕ′ssence n. **1.** most essential part of any substance, refined extract; purest and most perfect form, manifestation, or embodiment, *of* some quality or class. **2.** (Ancient Philos.) fifth substance (beside the four elements) forming heavenly bodies and pervading all things. **3.** Hence **quintĕssĕ′nt**IAL (-shal) a. [ME in sense 2, f. F, f. med. L *quinta essentia* fifth ESSENCE]

quintĕ′t, -ĕ′tte, n. **1.** (Mus.) (performers of) composition for five voices or instruments; **piano**, **clarinet**, etc., ∼, 4 stringed instruments plus instrument named. **2.** set of five. [f. F *quintette* f. It. *quintetto* (*quinto* fifth f. L *quintus*); see -ET¹]

quinti′llion (-yon) n. (for pl. usage see HUNDRED). ||a million raised to fifth power; *a thousand raised to sixth power. [f. L *quintus* fifth + MILLION]

qui′ntūp|le a., n., & v., ∼lĕt (-ĭ′-, -ū′-) n., ∼lў adv., **quintŭ′plicate**, (-at) a. & n., (-āt) v.t., **quintŭpli-cā′tion** n. fivefold etc. (for detailed senses see QUADRUPLE etc., substituting *five* for *four*). [f. F *quintuple* f. L *quintus* fifth, after QUADRUPLE]

quip n., & v.i. (-pp-). **1.** n. sarcastic remark; clever saying; equivocation, quibble. **2.** v.i. make quips. [abbr. of obs. *quippy* perh. f. L *quippe* forsooth]

qui′pu (kē′pōō, kwē′-) n. ancient Peruvians' substitute for writing by variously knotting threads of various colours. [Quechua, = knot]

quīre¹ n. four sheets of paper etc. folded to form eight leaves as often in medieval MSS; any collection of leaves one within another in MS or book (**in** ∼s, unbound, in sheets); 25 (formerly 24) sheets of paper. [ME, f. OF *qua(i)er* f. Rom. *quaternum* f. L *quaterni* set of four (as QUATERNARY)]

quīre². See CHOIR.

quirk n. **1.** quibble, quip; trick of action or behaviour; twist or flourish in drawing or writing; hence ∼Y² a. **2.** (Archit.) acute hollow between convex part of moulding and soffit or fillet. [16th c., of unkn. orig.]

***quĭrt** n., & v.t. (strike with) short-handled riding-whip with braided leather lash. [f. Sp. *cuerda* CORD]

qui′sle (-z-) v.i. (colloq.) be a quisling. [back-form. f. foll.]

qui′sling (-z-) n. person co-operating with an enemy who has occupied his country; traitor; hence ∼ITE¹ a. & n. [f. V. *Quisling*, renegade Norwegian Army officer d. 1945]

quit¹ pred. a. **1.** (arch.) free, clear, absolved. **2.** rid of (*glad to be quit of the trouble*). **3.** ∼**claim**, (n.) renunciation of right esp. to land, (v.t.) renounce claim to, give up (thing) *to*; ∼**rent**, (usu. small) rent paid by freeholder or copyholder in lieu of service. [ME, f. OF *quitte* f. med. L *quittus* f. L *quietus* QUIET²]

quit² v.t. (-tt-; ||∼′ted, *quit). **1.** give up, let go, abandon (task etc., or abs.; ∼ **hold of,** loose); cease, stop, (quit grumbling); hence ∼′TER¹ n., one who deserts task or post, shirker. **2.** depart from, leave, (place, person, etc.; quitted Paris at midnight; quitted him in anger); (abs.; of tenant) leave occupied premises (esp. give, have etc., notice to quit). **3.** behave, acquit, conduct, oneself well etc. (quit yourselves, arch.; you, like men). **4.** (arch.) rid oneself of. **5.** (poet.) requite, repay, clear off, (quit love with hate; death quits all scores). [ME, = release, f. OF *quit(t)er* f. L *quietus* QUIET², QUIT¹]

quitch n. ∼(-**grass**), = COUCH³-grass. [OE *cwice*, = MLG *kweke*, perh. cogn. w. QUICK]

quīte adv. **1.** completely, wholly, entirely, altogether, to the utmost extent, nothing short of, in the fullest sense, positively, absolutely, (quite covers it; is quite a hero; was quite by myself); NOT quite; ∼ **other,** very different; ∿ **another,** a very different; ∿ **(so),** I grant the truth of that; ∿ **something,** a remarkable thing; *quite the* THING 2. **2.** somewhat, to some extent, (*it took quite a long time*); ∿ **a few,** a considerable number. [ME, f. obs. *quite* a. = QUIT¹]

quïts *pred. a.* on even terms by retaliation or repayment (*will be quits with him yet*; *now we are quits*); **call it** ∿, **cry** ∿, acknowledge that things are now even, agree not to proceed further in quarrel etc.; DOUBLE² *or quits.* [perh. colloq. abbr. of med. L *quittus* (see QUIT¹)]

quï'ttance *n.* (arch. or poet.) release *from* something; acknowledgement of payment, receipt; requital. [ME, f. OF *quitance* (*quiter* QUIT²; see -ANCE)]

quï'ver¹ *n.* case for holding arrows; **have an arrow** or **shaft left in** one's ∿, not be resourceless; ∿ **full of children,** large family (Ps. 127:5); hence ∿FUL (2) *n.* [ME, f. AF *quive(i)r*, OF *quivre* f. WG (OE *cocor*, OS *kokar(i)*, OHG *kohhar(i)*)]

quï'ver² *v. & n.* **1.** *v.i.* tremble or vibrate with slight rapid motion (of person, leaf, wing, voice, light, etc.; *with* emotion, *in* the wind etc.). **2.** *v.t.* (Of bird, esp. skylark) make (wings) quiver. **3.** *n.* quivering motion or sound. [ME, f. obs. *quiver* nimble; cf. QUAVER¹]

qui vive (kē vē'v) *n.* **on the** ∿, on the alert, watching for something to happen. [F, = lit. (long) live who?, i.e. on whose side are you?, as sentry's challenge]

Quï'xote *n.* enthusiastic visionary, pursuer of lofty but impractical ideals, person utterly regardless of his material interests in comparison with honour or devotion; hence **quixŏ'tic** *a.,* **quixŏ'tically** *adv.,* **quï'xot**ISM (2), **quï'xot**RY (4), *ns.* **quï'xot**IZE (2, 3) *v.t. & i.* [f. Don ∿, hero of Cervantes' romance, f. Sp. *quixote* thigh armour]

quiz¹ *n.* (*pl.* ∿'zes), & *v.t.* (-zz-). **1.** (arch.) odd or eccentric person, person of ridiculous appearance; person given to quizzing. **2.** hoax, ridicule, thing done to expose or burlesque another's oddities. **3.** Hence ∿'zIcAL *a.* **4.** *v.t.* (arch.) make sport of (person or his ways), regard with mocking air; look curiously at, observe the ways or oddities of, survey through an eyeglass. [18th c., of unkn. orig.]

quiz² *v.t.* (-zz-), & *n.* (*pl.* ∿'zes). **1.** *v.t.* examine by questioning. **2.** *n.* interrogation, questionnaire, examination; test of knowledge in radio or television or other entertainment programme. [19th c. dial, of unkn. orig.]

∥**quŏd**¹ *n.,* & *v.t.* (-dd-). (sl.) **1.** *n.* prison (*in, out of, quod*). **2.** *v.t.* imprison. [17th c.; orig. unkn.]

quod² (kwŏd) *pron.* ∿ **erat demonstrandum, faciendum, inveniendum,** (ĕrăt dĕmonstră'ndum, făshiĕ'ndum, ĭnvĕnĭĕ'ndum), which was the thing to be proved, made or done, found (formulae in geometrical demonstrations, and, esp. in abbr. *QED*, in gen. use); ∿ *vide* (vï'dĭ, vē'dā), which see (in cross and other references). [L, = which, neut. of *qui* who]

quŏd'lĭbĕt *n.* (Hist.) (exercise on) topic of philosophical or theological disputation. [ME, f. L *(quod what, libet* it pleases one)]

quoin (koin) *n.,* & *v.t.* **1.** *n.* external angle of building; stone or brick forming angle, corner-stone, whence ∿'ING¹ (3) *n.*; internal corner of room; wedge for locking type in forme, raising level of gun, keeping barrel from rolling, etc. **2.** *v.t.* secure or raise with quoins. [var. of COIN¹]

quoit (koit, kwoit) *n.,* & *v.t.* **1.** *n.* heavy flattish sharp-edged iron ring thrown to encircle iron peg or to fix itself in ground near it in game of ∿s; ring of rope, rubber, etc., for use in similar game; (flat stone of) dolmen. **2.** *v.t.* fling like a quoit. [ME, of unkn. orig.]

quŏ'ndăm *a.* that once had but no longer has the specified character, sometime, former, (*a quondam friend of mine*). [L adv., = formerly]

****Quŏ'nsĕt** *n.* ∿ **hut, (P)** building similar to Nissen hut. [∿ in Rhode Island, US]

quŏr'|um *n.* fixed number of members that must be present to make proceedings of assembly or society or board valid; hence ∿ATE² *a.,* constituting a quorum. [L, = of whom (we will that you etc. be one etc.), in wording of commissions]

quŏ'ta *n.* **1.** share that individual person or company is bound to contribute to or entitled to receive from a total. **2.** quantity of goods etc. which under government controls must be manufactured, exported, imported, etc.; maximum quantity which may similarly be manufactured etc.; number of yearly immigrants allowed to enter a country, students allowed to enrol for a course, etc. [f. med. L *quota* (*pars*) how great (a part), fem. of *quotus* (*quot* how many)]

quŏtā'tion *n.* **1.** quoting or being quoted; passage quoted. **2.** amount stated as current price of stocks or commodities; contractor's estimate. **3.** (Print.) quadrat etc. used for filling up blanks. **4.** ∿**-marks,** inverted commas and apostrophes, single (' ') or double (" "), used to mark beginning and end of quoted passage, or book etc. title, or word(s) regarded as slang, jargon, etc. [f. med. L *quotatio* (as QUOTE; see -ATION)]

quŏ'tative *a.* of quoting; given to quotation. [as foll.; see -ATIVE]

quŏte *v.t.,* & *n.* **1.** *v.t.* cite or appeal to (author, book) in confirmation of some view; repeat or copy out passage(s) from. **2.** repeat or copy out (borrowed passage) usu. with indication that it is borrowed, (abs.) make quotations, (*from* author, book, speech, etc.). **3.** enclose (words) within quotation-marks (esp. in *imper.* in dictation etc.). **4.** adduce or cite *as*; state price of (usu. *at* figure); (St. Exch.) regularly list price of. **5.** Hence **quŏ't**ABLE *a.* **6.** *n.* (colloq.) passage quoted; commercial quotation; (usu. in *pl.*) quotation-mark. [ME, earlier 'mark with numbers', f. med. L *quotare* (*quot* how many, or as QUOTA)]

quŏth *v.t.* 1st & 3rd pers. past ind. (arch.) said *I, he, she,* rarely *we* or *they;* ∿'**a,** quoth he (used in quoting contemptuously, = *forsooth*). [OE *cwæth* past of *cwethan* say, = OS *quethan,* OHG *quedan,* ON *kuetha,* Goth. *qithan* f. Gmc *kwethan]

quoti'dian *a. & n.* **1.** *a.* daily, of every day; ∿ **fever** (recurring every day). **2.** commonplace, trivial. **3.** *n.* quotidian fever. [ME f. OF *cotidien* & f. L *cotidianus, quotidianus* (*cotidie* daily; see AN)]

quŏ'tient (-shent) *n.* (Arith.) result given by dividing one quantity by another; INTELLIGENCE *quotient.* [ME, f. L *quotiens* how many times (*quot* how many), by confusion w. -ENT]

Qur'an (kŭrah'n). Var. of KORAN.

q.v. *abbr.* = QUOD² *vide.*

qy. *abbr.* query.

R

R, r (är) *n.* (*pl.* **Rs** *or* **R's**). eighteenth letter of alphabet; **the r months,** those with *r* in their names (Sept.–Apr.) as season for oysters; **the three Rs,** reading (w)riting, and (a)rithmetic, as basis of elementary education.

R. *abbr.* Railway; rand; Réaumur; Regiment; *Regina*; registered as trademark; *Republican; Rex; River; (Chess) rook; Royal.

r. *abbr.* recto; right; röntgen(s); run(s).

RA *abbr.* right ASCENSION; Royal Academician; Royal Academy; Royal Artillery.

Ra *symb.* radium.

RAAF *abbr.* Royal Australian Air Force.

ră′bbĕt *n.,* & *v.t.* **1.** *n.* step-shaped channel etc. cut along edge or face or projecting angle of wood etc. usu. to receive edge or tongue of another piece; ∿ **plane** (for cutting groove along an edge). **2.** *v.t.* join or fix with rabbet; make rabbet in. [ME, f. OF *rab*(*b*)*at* abatement, recess (*rabattre* REBATE[1]); assim. to -ET[1]]

ră′bbi *n.* Jewish scholar or teacher esp. of the law; person appointed as Jewish religious leader; **Chief R∿,** religious head of British Jewish communities. [ME & OE f. eccl. L, f. Gk *rhabbi* f. Heb. *rabbī* my master (*raḇ* master + pronominal suf.)]

ră′bbin *n.* Jewish scholar or teacher of the law (**the ∿s,** chief Jewish authorities on law and doctrine, most important of them 2nd–13th c.); hence ∿ATE[1], ∿ISM (3), ∿IST (2, 3), *ns.,* **rabbi′**NICAL *a.* [F, or f. mod. L *rabbinus* (as prec.); -*n* perh. f. Semitic pl.]

ră′bbĭt *n.,* & *v.i.* **1.** *n.* burrowing gregarious herbivorous mammal (*Oryctolagus cuniculus*) of hare family, brownish grey in natural state, also black or white or pied in domestication; *hare; ‖(colloq.) poor performer at any game (esp. cricket, golf, or lawn tennis); ∿ **punch,** short chop with edge of hand to opponent's nape; *rabbit*-WARREN; WELSH[1] *rabbit*; hence ∿Y[2] *a.* **2.** *v.i.* hunt rabbits; ∿ **on,** (sl.) talk pointlessly, waffle. [ME, perh. f. OF; cf. F dial. *rabotte,* Walloon *robète,* Flem. *robbe*]

ră′bbĭt[2] *v.t.* (vulg.) ∿ **it** etc. (form of imprecation). [prob. alt. of RAT[2]]

ră′bble[1] *n.* disorderly crowd, mob; contemptible or inferior set of people; *the* lower or disorderly classes of the populace; ∿**-rouser,** one who stirs up the rabble in agitation for social or political change. [ME; orig. uncert.]

ră′bble[2] *n.* iron bar with bent end for stirring molten metal etc. [f. F *râble* f. med. L *rotabulum,* L *rutabulum* (*ruere rut-* rake up) fire-shovel]

Răbelai′sian (-zyan) *a.* & *n.* **1.** *a.* of or like Rabelais or his writings; marked by exuberant imagination and language and coarse humour and satire. **2.** *n.* admirer or student of Rabelais. [f. F. *Rabelais,* Fr. satirist d. 1553 + -IAN]

ra′bi (rŭ′bē) *n.* (Ind.) principal grain harvest. [f. Urdu *rabī* spring crop]

ră′bid *a.* furious, violent, (*rabid hate*); unreasoning, insensate, headstrong, (*rabid segregationist*); (esp. of dog) affected with rabies, mad; of rabies; hence **rabi′d**ITY, ∿NESS, *ns.,* ∿LY[2] *adv.* [f. L *rabidus* (*rabere* rave; see -ID[1])]

ră′bies (-z) *n.* contagious virus disease of dogs etc.; hydrophobia. [L (*rabere* rave)]

‖RAC *abbr.* Royal Armoured Corps; Royal Automobile Club.

raccoo′n. See RACOON.

răce[1] *n.* **1.** contest of speed between runners, ships, vehicles, horses, etc., or persons etc. doing anything; (in *pl.*) series of these for horses, dogs, etc., at fixed time on regular course; ∿**card,** programme of races; ∿**course,** ground for horse-racing; ∿**goer,** one who frequents horse-races; ∿**horse** (bred or kept for racing); ‖∿**-meeting,** sequence of horse-races at a place; ∿**-track,** (usu. oval) track for horse or vehicle races; *∿**way,** track for trotting or pacing. **2.** channel of stream (MILL[1]-*race*); channel for balls in ball-bearing; channel along which shuttle moves; (Austral.) fenced passageway for drafting sheep. **3.** onward sweep or movement, esp. strong current in sea or river (*tide set with a strong race*). **4.** (arch.) course of sun or moon, course of life, (*ere he had run half his race*). [ME, = running, f. ON *rás,* = OE *rǣs*]

răce[2] *v.* **1.** *v.i.* compete in speed *with*; indulge in horse-racing (*a racing man;* **the racing world,** the turf); go at full speed or (of propeller, paddle-wheel, vehicle engine, etc.) at excessive speed because of diminished resistance or load. **2.** *v.t.* have race with, try to surpass in speed; cause (horse etc.) to race (*raced his car against a train*); make (person or thing) move or work at full or excessive speed (*raced me along at five miles an hour; raced the Bill through the House*). [f. prec.]

răce[3] *n.* **1.** group of persons or animals or plants connected by common descent, posterity of (person); house, family, tribe, or nation regarded as of common stock; distinct ethnical stock (*the Caucasian, Mongolian, etc., race*); genus or species or breed or variety of animals or plants, any great division of living creatures (*the human, feathered, four-footed, etc., race*). **2.** descent, kindred, (*of noble, Oriental, etc., race; separate in language and race*). **3.** class of persons etc. with some common feature (*the race of poets, dandies,* etc.). **4.** ∿ **relations** (between members of different races in same country); ∿**-riot,** outbreak of violence due to racial antagonism; ∿ **suicide,** gradual disappearance of a race through voluntary limitation of reproduction. [F, f. It. *razza,* of unkn. orig.]

răce[4] *n.* root (of ginger). [f. OF *rais, raiz* f. L. *radix radicis* root]

ră′cĕmāte *n.* (Chem.) racemic mixture. [f. RACEMIC + -ATE[1] (3)]

racĕ′me *n.* (Bot.) flower-cluster with the separate flowers attached by short equal stalks at equal distances along central stem. [f. L *racemus* grape-bunch]

racĕ′m|ĭc *a.* (Chem.) composed of equal numbers of dextrorotatory and laevorotatory molecules of a compound; hence **ră′cĕm**IZE (3) *v.t.* & *i.* [f. prec. + -IC, orig. of tartaric acid in grape-juice]

ră′cĕmōse *a.* (Bot.) in form of raceme; (Anat., of gland etc.) clustered. [f. L *racemosus* (as RACEME; see -OSE[1])]

ră′cer *n.* In vbl senses; horse, yacht, bicycle, etc., (of kind) used for racing; circular horizontal rail along which the traversing-platform of a heavy gun moves. [f. RACE[2] + -ER[1]]

rachĕ′l (-sh-) *a.* & *n.* (of) pale fawn colour used in cosmetics. [f. *Rachel,* Fr. actress d. 1858]

ră′ch|ĭs (-k-) *n.* (*pl.* ∿**ides** *pr.* -īdēz). stem of grass etc. bearing flower-stalks at short intervals; axis of pinnately compound leaf or frond; vertebral column or cord from which it develops; feather-shaft, esp. the part that bears the barbs. [mod. L, f. Gk *rhakhis* spine; the E pl. -*ides* is erron.]

rach|ī′tĭs (-k-) *n.* rickets; hence ∿ī′tIC *a.* [mod. L, f. Gk *rhakhitis* (as -ITIS)]

‖Ră′chmanĭsm (-k-) *n.* exploitation of slum tenants by unscrupulous landlords. [f. P. *Rachman,* London landlord of early 1960s + -ISM]

ră′cial (-shal) *a.* of, in regard to, due to, characteristic of, race; hence ∿LY[2] *adv.* [f. RACE[3] + -IAL]

rā′cial|ism (-sha-) *n.* belief in superiority of a particular race; antagonism between different races; hence ∿IST (2) *n.* [f. prec. + -ISM]

rā′c|ism *n.* **1.** = prec. **2.** theory that human abilities etc. are determined by race. **3.** Hence ∿IST (2) *n.* [f. RACE³ + -ISM]

răck¹ *n.*, & *v.i.* **1.** *n.* driving clouds. **2.** *v.i.* (of clouds) be driven before wind. [ME, prob. of Scand. orig.; cf. Norw. and Sw. dial. *rak* wreckage etc. (*reka* drive)]

răck² *n.*, & *v.t.* **1.** *n.* fixed or movable frame of wooden or metal bars for holding fodder; framework with rails, bars, pegs, or shelves, for keeping or placing articles on or in (*plate, luggage, hat, tool, pipe, -rack*); instrument of torture stretching victim's joints by turning of rollers to which wrists and ankles were tied; **on the** ∿, (fig.) in distress or under strain. **2.** cogged or indented bar or rail engaging with wheel or pinion or worm, or serving with pegs etc. to adjust position of something; ∿-**railway** (with cogged rail between bearing rails); ∿-**wheel,** cog-wheel. **3.** *v.t.* ‖fill *up* (stable-rack) with hay or straw; fasten (horse) up to rack. **4.** place in or on rack. **5.** *∿ up,* achieve (score etc.). [ME, f. Du. *rak, rek,* MLG *rek(ke)* rail etc., prob. f. *recken* (see foll.)]

răck³ *v.t.* **1.** stretch joints of (person) by pulling esp. with rack; (of disease or bodily or mental agony) inflict torture on (*a racking headache; racked with pain*); shake violently, injure by straining, task severely, (*cough that seemed to rack his whole body*); ∿ one's **brain**(s), make great mental effort (*for* something to say, a plan, etc.). **2.** exact utmost possible amount of (rent), oppress (tenants) by exacting excessive rent, exhaust (land) with excessive use; ∿-**rent,** (*n.*) (1) rent equal to full annual value of property, (2) excessive rent, (*v.t.*) exact this from (tenant) or for (land); ∿-**renter,** tenant paying or landlord exacting rack-rent. [ME, f. MDu., MLG *racken, recken* stretch, = OE *reccan,* OS *rekkian,* OHG *recchan,* ON *rekja,* Goth. *ufrakjan* f. Gmc **rakjan*]

răck⁴ *n.* arrack (esp. *rack punch*). [f. ARRACK]

răck⁵ *n.,* & *v.i.* **1.** *n.* horse's gait between trot and canter, both legs of one side being lifted almost at once, and all four feet being sometimes off ground together. **2.** *v.i.* progress thus. [perh. ult. rel. to Arab. *faras rikwa* easy-paced horse]

răck⁶ *v.t.* ∿ (**off**), draw off (wine, beer, etc.) from the lees. [ME, f. Prov. *arracar* (*raca* stems and husks of grapes, dregs)]

răck⁷ *n.* destruction (*go to rack and ruin*). [var. of WRACK, WRECK]

răck⁸ *n.* joint of lamb etc. including front ribs. [perh. f. RACK²]

rā′cket¹, rā′cquet (-kit), *n.* **1.** bat having frame strung with catgut, nylon, etc., used in tennis, rackets, etc.; (in *pl.,* usu. treated as *sing.*) ball-game for two or four persons played with rackets in plain four-walled court. **2.** snow-shoe resembling racket. **3.** ∿ **ball,** small hard kid-covered ball of cork and string; ∿-**press** (for keeping rackets taut and in shape); ∿-**tail,** humming-bird with racket-shaped tail. [f. F *racquette* f. It. *racchetta* f. Arab. *rāḥa* palm of hand]

rā′cket² *n.,* & *v.i.* **1.** *n.* disturbance, uproar, din; busy activity, social excitement, gaiety; hence ∿Y² *a.* **2.** (sl.) dodge, game, line of business. **3.** scheme for obtaining money, or effecting some other object, by fraudulent (and often violent) means. **4.** ordeal, trying experience; **stand the** ∿, (1) come successfully through test, (2) face costs or other consequences of action. **5.** *v.i.* ∿ (**about**), live gay life, move *about* noisily. [16th c., perh. imit.]

răckéteer′ *n.* one who operates a racket (see prec. 3); hence ∿ING¹ *n.* [f. prec. + -EER]

***rā′con** *n.* radar beacon that can be identified and located by its response to radar signal from ship, etc. [f. radar + beacon]

răcŏnt|eur′ (-tēr′) *n.* (*fem.* ∿**euse** *pr.* -ēr′z). teller of

anecdotes (*good, skilful,* etc., *raconteur*). [F (*raconter* relate, RECOUNT¹)]

rac(c)ōō′n *n.* greyish-brown furry bushy-tailed sharp-snouted N. Amer. nocturnal carnivore. [Algonquian dial.]

racquet. See RACKET¹.

rā′c| y *a.* having in high degree the qualities that characterize its kind (*racy flavour*); of distinctive quality or vigour, not smoothed into sameness or commonness, retaining traces of origin (∿**y of the soil,** of homely directness, spirited, lively, piquant); **risqué;* hence ∿ILY² *adv.,* ∿INESS *n.* [f. RACE³ + -Y²]

rad. *abbr.* radian(s); radical.

‖**RADA** (colloq. rah′da) *abbr.* Royal Academy of Dramatic Art.

rā′dăr *n.* system for ascertaining direction and range, or presence, of aircraft, ships, coasts, and other objects, by sending out short radio waves which they reflect; apparatus used for this; ∿ **trap,** arrangement using radar to detect vehicles etc. travelling faster than speed limit. [f. *radio detection and ranging*]

‖**RADC** *abbr.* Royal Army Dental Corps.

rā′ddle *n.,* & *v.t.* **1.** *n.* red ochre. **2.** *v.t.* colour with raddle, or with much rouge crudely used; (in *p.p.*) dilapidated. [var. of RUDDLE]

rā′dial *a.* & *n.* **1.** *a.* of or in rays. **2.** arranged like rays or radii, having position or direction of a radius; ∿ **engine** (having cylinders arranged along radii); ∿ (**-ply**), (of tyre) having fabric layers parallel and tread strengthened. **3.** having spokes or radiating lines. **4.** acting or moving along lines that diverge from a centre; ∿ **symmetry,** symmetry about every line or plane through a centre; ∿ **velocity,** speed of motion along such line, esp. between star etc. and observer. **5.** relating to the radius (sense 1) (*radial artery, vein, nerve*). **6.** Hence ∿LY² *adv.* **7.** *n.* radial nerve or artery; radial-ply tyre. [f. med. L *radialis* (as RADIUS; see -AL)]

rā′dian *n.* unit of angle, equal to angle at centre of circle subtended by arc whose length is equal to radius. [f. RADIUS + -AN]

rā′diant *a.* & *n.* **1.** *a.* emitting rays of light; (of eyes or looks) beaming with joy or hope or love; (of light) issuing in rays; (of beauty) splendid or dazzling; hence or cogn. **rā′diance, rā′diancy,** *ns.,* ∿LY² *adv.* **2.** operating radially ; (Bot. etc.) extending radially, radiating; ∿ **heat** (transmitted by radiation, not by conduction or convection); ∿ **heater** (emitting radiant heat; ∿ **point,** point from which rays or radii proceed, (Astron.) apparent focal point of meteor shower. **3.** *n.* point or object from which light or heat radiates, esp. in electric or gas heater; (Astron.) radiant point. [ME, f. L *radiare* (as RADIUS); see -ANT]

rā′diate¹ *a.* having divergent rays or parts radially arranged; hence ∿LY² (-tlī) *adv.* [as foll.; see -ATE²]

rā′diāt|e² *v.* **1.** *v.i.* emit rays of light, heat, or other electromagnetic waves; (of light or heat) issue in rays; diverge or spread from central point. **2.** *v.t.* emit (light or heat or sound) from centre; disseminate as from a centre; give manifest evidence of (life, love, joy, etc.); (in *p.p.*) with parts arranged in rays. **3.** Hence ∿IVE *a.* [f. L *radiare* (as RADIUS) + -ATE³]

rădiā′tion *n.* radiating; emission of energy as electromagnetic waves or as moving particles; energy thus transmitted, esp. invisibly; ∿ **chemistry,** study of chemical effects of this on matter; ∿ **sickness** (caused by exposure to excessive radiation). [f. L *radiatio* (as prec.; see -ATION)]

rā′diātor *n.* In vbl senses; apparatus for heating room etc., consisting of metal case containing winding pipe through which steam or hot water circulates; oil or electric heater, usu. portable; engine-cooling apparatus in motor vehicle or aeroplane, with large surface for cooling circulating water; ∿ **grille,** mascot, etc., (at front end of motor car, where radiator is usu. placed). [f. prec. + -OR]

ră′dical *a. & n.* **1.** *a.* of the root(s). **2.** naturally inherent, essential, fundamental, (*a radical error*; *the radical rottenness of human nature*). **3.** forming the basis, primary, (*the radical idea* or *principles of a system*). **4.** affecting the foundation, going to the root, (*radical change, cure, reform*); (of surgery etc.) seeking to ensure removal of all diseased tissue (opp. CONSERVATIVE); (of politician) desiring radical reforms, (Hist.) ||belonging to extreme section of Liberal party, *seeking extreme anti-South action at time of Civil War; (of measure etc.) advanced by or according to principles of radical politicians, whence ∿ISM (2) *n.*, ∿IZE (3) *v.t. & i.* **5.** (Math.) of the root of a number or quantity (∿ **sign**, √, ∛, ∜, etc., indicating that square, cube, fourth, etc., root of number following is to be taken). **6.** (Philol.) of the roots of words. **7.** (Mus.) belonging to the root of a chord. **8.** (Bot.) of, or springing direct from, the root or the main stem close to it. **9.** Hence ∿LY² *adv.* **10.** *n.* (Philol.) root; fundamental principle; (Math.) (1) quantity forming or expressed as root of another, (2) radical sign; (Chem.) element or atom, or group of these, normally forming part of compound and remaining unaltered during compound's ordinary chemical changes; (Polit.) person holding radical views or belonging to radical party. [ME, f. LL *radicalis* f. L *radix radicis* root; see -AL]

radices. See RADIX.

ră′dicle *n.* part of plant embryo that develops into primary root; rootlet; (Anat.) rootlike subdivision of nerve or vein; (Chem.) radical; so **radi′cŭl**AR¹ *a.* [f. L *radicula* (as prec.; see -ULE)]

ră′dii. See RADIUS.

ră′diŏ *n.* (*pl.* ∿s), *a.*, & *v.* **1.** *n.* transmission and reception of messages etc. by electromagnetic waves of radio-frequency, without connecting wire; message so sent; (esp. sound) broadcasting; apparatus for receiving signals by radio; broadcasting station (*Radio Luxembourg*). **2.** *a.* of or relating to, sent by, used in or using, radio; ∿ **cab, car,** (equipped with radio for communication); *radio* FIX²; *radio* HAM¹. **3.** of or concerned with stars or other celestial bodies from which radio waves are received or reflected (*radio astronomy, galaxy,* TELESCOPE); ∿ **star,** small celestial object emitting strong radio waves. **4.** *v.t.* send (message), send message to (person), by radio. **5.** *v.i.* communicate or broadcast by radio. [short for *radio-telegraphy* etc.]

ră′diŏ- *comb. form.* **1.** (Anat.) belonging to the radius in conjunction with some other part, as: ∿-**car′pal,** of radius and wrist. **2.** (Phys.) connected with rays or radiation, as: ∿-**assay′** (based on radiation from sample etc.); ∿-**bio′logy** (concerned with effects of radiation on organisms); ∿**meter** (-ŏ′m-), (1) instrument illustrating conversion of radiant energy into mechanical force, (2) instrument for measuring intensity of radiation; **radiopa′que,** opaque to X-rays or similar radiation; ∿**scopy** (-ŏ′s-), examination by X-rays etc. of objects opaque to light; ∿-**the′rapy,** treatment of disease by X-rays or other forms of radiation. **3.** connected with radioactivity, as: ∿-**cae′sium,** ∿-**co′balt,** etc., artificially prepared radioisotopes of these elements; ∿-**car′bon,** radioisotope of carbon, esp. carbon 14; ∿-**che′mistry,** chemistry of radioactive materials; ∿-**element,** natural or artificial radioisotope; ∿**i′sotope,** radioactive isotope; ∿-**nu′clide,** radioactive nuclide. **4.** connected with radio, as: ∿-**controlled,** controlled from a distance by radio; ∿-**frequency,** (of) the frequency of radio waves, between about 10 kilohertz and 0.1 terahertz; ∿-**gonio′meter,** direction-finder; ∿**loca′tion,** = RADAR; ∿**pho′nic,** pertaining to synthetic sound produced by electronic means etc.; ∿**sonde,** miniature radio transmitter e.g. carried up in balloon to broadcast information about pressure, temperature, etc., at various levels [f. G *sonde* probe]; ∿-**te′legram** (sent by radio); ∿-**tele′graphy,** ∿-**tele′phony,** (using radio). [f. RADIUS + -O-]

rădĭŏǎ′ctĭve *a.* of or exhibiting radioactivity. [f. prec. + ACTIVE]

rădĭŏǎcti′vitў *n.* (Phys.) property of spontaneous disintegration of atomic nuclei usu. with emission of penetrating radiation or particles. [f. RADIO- + ACTIVITY]

rădiogĕ′n|ic *a.* **1.** produced by radioactivity. **2.** suitable for broadcasting by radio. **3.** Hence ∿ICALLY *adv.* [f. RADIO- 3, 4 + -GENIC]

ră′diogrăm *n.* **1.** picture obtained by X-rays, gamma rays, etc. **2.** radio-telegram. **3.** ||combined radio and electric gramophone. [f. RADIO- 3, 4 + -GRAM, GRAMOPHONE]

ră′diograph (-ahf) *n.*, & *v.t.* **1.** *n.* instrument recording intensity of radiation. **2.** = prec. **1.** **3.** *v.t.* obtain X-ray, gamma-ray, etc., picture of. **4.** Hence **rădiŏ′graph**ER¹ *n.*, **rădiogră′ph**IC *a.*, **rădiŏ′graph**Y *n.* [f. RADIO- + -GRAPH]

rădiolār′ian *n.* protozoan of order Radiolaria, with siliceous skeleton and radiating pseudopodia. [f. mod. L *radiolaria* f. L *radiolus* dim. of RADIUS, + -AN]

rădiŏ′log|ў *n.* scientific study of X-rays and other high-energy radiation, esp. as used in medicine; hence **rădiolŏ′g**IC(AL) *adjs.*, ∿IST (3) *n.* [f. RADIO- + -LOGY]

ră′dish *n.* (cruciferous plant, *Raphanus sativus*, with) fleshy pungent root often eaten raw as relish in salads. [OE *rædic* f. L *radix radicis* root]

ră′dium *n.* (Chem.) radioactive metallic element obtained from pitchblende etc., used esp. in luminous materials and in radio-therapy; ∿ **emanation,** radon; ∿ **therapy,** treatment of disease by the use of radium. [f. L *radius* ray + -IUM]

ră′di|us *n.* (*pl.* ∿i *pr.* -ī, or ∿uses), & *v.t.* **1.** *n.* thicker and shorter bone of forearm in man (cf. ULNA); corresponding bone in animal's foreleg or bird's wing. **2.** (Math.) straight line from centre to circumference of circle or sphere; radial line from focus to any point of curve (∿ **vector,** variable line drawn from fixed point to orbit or other curve, or to any point as indication of latter's position). **3.** length of radius of circle etc.; (fig.) distance from a centre (*all within a radius of 20 miles; has a large radius of action*). **4.** any of a set of lines diverging from a point like radii of circle; object of this kind, e.g. spoke. **5.** (Bot.) outer rim of composite flower-head, e.g. daisy, also radiating branch of umbel. **6.** *v.t.* give rounded form to (edge etc.). [L, = staff, spoke, ray]

ră′d|ix *n.* (*pl.* ∿ices *pr.* -īsēz) number or symbol used as basis of numeration scale (*ten is the radix of decimal numeration and of common logarithms*); source or origin *of.* [L, = root]

ră′dŏme *n.* dome or covering protecting radar equipment, esp. on outer surface of aircraft. [f. radar + *dome*]

ră′dŏn *n.* (Chem.) gaseous radioactive inert element arising from the disintegration of radium. [f. RADIUM after *argon* etc.]

ră′dŭla *n.* (*pl.* ∿e). filelike structure in molluscs for scraping off food particles and drawing them into mouth. [L, = scraper (*radere* scrape; see -ULE)]

||**RAF** (colloq. răf) *abbr.* Royal Air Force.

ră′ffia *n.* palm-tree (*Raphia ruffia*) orig. of Madagascar; fibre from its leaves used for tying up plants and for making hats, baskets, mats, etc. [Malagasy]

ră′ffināte *n.* product of extraction of liquid with solvent. [f. F *raffiner* + -ATE¹ (5)]

ră′ffish *a.* disreputable, dissipated, tawdry; hence ∿LY² *adv.*, ∿NESS *n.* [f. as RAFT² + -ISH¹]

ră′ffle¹ *n. & v.* **1.** *n.* sale of article, esp. for charity, by taking entry fee from any number of persons and assigning the article by lot to one of them. **2.** *v.i.* enter one's name in raffle *for* article. **3.** *v.t.* sell by raffle. [ME, kind of dice-game, f. OF *raf(f)le*, of unkn. orig.]

ră′ffle² *n.* rubbish, refuse; lumber, debris. [ME, perh. f. OF *ne rifle, ne rafle* nothing at all]

raft¹ (rah-) *n. & v.* **1.** *n.* collection of logs, casks, etc., fastened together in the water for transportation. **2.** flat floating structure of timber or other materials for conveying persons or things, esp. as substitute for boat in emergencies; floating accumulation of trees, ice, etc. **3.** ∼**'sman,** worker on raft. **4.** *v.t.* transport as or on raft; form into a raft; cross (water) on raft(s). **5.** *v.i.* work raft (*across* water etc.). [ME, f. ON raptr RAFTER²]

raft² (rah-) *n.* (colloq.) large collection, crowd, *of.* [f. *raff* rubbish, perh. of Scand. orig.]

ra'fter¹ (rah'-) *n.* man who rafts timber. [f. RAFT¹ + -ER¹]

ra'fter² (rah'-) *n.*, & *v.t.* **1.** *n.* one of the sloping beams forming framework of a roof; **principal** ∼, strong beam in truss, underlying **common** ∼**s.** **2.** *v.t.* (usu. in *p.p.*) provide with rafters. [OE *ræfter,* = OS *rehter,* MLG *rafter,* rel. to RAFT]

||**RAFVR** *abbr.* Royal Air Force Volunteer Reserve.

răg¹ *n.* **1.** torn or frayed piece of woven material, one of the irregular scraps to which cloth etc. is reduced by wear and tear; CHEW *the rag;* in ∼**s,** much torn; RED *rag.* **2.** (in *pl.*) old and torn clothes; GLAD¹ *rags;* in ∼**s,** in old clothes; ∼**s to riches,** poverty to affluence. **3.** (usu. w. neg.) smallest scrap of cloth or sail (*not a rag to cover him; spread every rag of sail*). **4.** (collect.) rags used as material for paper, stuffing, etc. **5.** remnant, odd scrap, irregular piece, (*flying rags of cloud; cooked to* ∼**s,** till it falls to pieces; *not a rag of evidence*). **6.** (derog.) flag, handkerchief, curtain, newspaper, etc. **7.** jagged projection esp. on metal. **8.** ||∼ **and bone man,** itinerant dealer in old clothes etc.; ∼**-bag,** bag in which scraps of fabric etc., are kept for use, (fig.) miscellaneous collection; ∼**-bolt** (with barbs to keep it tight when driven in); ∼ **book,** child's book of untearable cloth; ∼ **doll,** stuffed cloth doll; ∼ **paper** (made from rags); ∼**-picker,** collector and seller of rags; ∼**'tag** (**and bobtail**), the riff-raff, ragged or low or disreputable people; ∼**'time,** (*n.*) popular music of US black origin with much syncopation, (*a.*) farcical (*a ragtime army*); ∼ **trade,** (colloq.) business of designing, making, and selling women's clothes; ∼**'weed,** (1) = *ragwort,* (2) *plant of genus *Ambrosia* with allergenic pollen; ∼**-wheel,** sprocket-wheel (with projections catching in links of chain that passes over it); ∼**'wort,** yellow-flowered ragged-leaved plant of genus *Senecio.* [ME, prob. back-form. f. RAGGED, *raggy*]

răg² *n.* large coarse roofing-slate; ∼(**'stone**), hard coarse stone breaking up in thick slabs (CORAL *rag*). [ME, of unkn. orig., but assoc. w. prec.]

răg³ *v.* (-gg-) & *n.* (sl.) *v.t.* scold, reprove severely; tease, torment, play rough jokes on, disarrange (person's room etc.) by way of practical joke. **2.** *v.i.* ||engage in rough play; be noisy and riotous. **3.** *n.* ||noisy disorderly conduct or scene; rowdy celebration; annual comic parade etc. of students esp. to collect money for charity; prank. [18th c., of unkn. orig., cf. BALLYRAG]

răg⁴ *n.* = (piece of) RAG¹*time.* [abbr.]

rag⁵ (rahg). Var. of foll.

ra'ga (rah'-) *n.* (Ind. Mus.) pattern of notes used as basis for improvisation; piece using a particular raga. [Skr., = colour, musical tone]

rä'gamŭffĭn *n.* person in ragged dirty clothes; hence ∼LY¹ *a.* [prob. f. RAG¹ w. fanciful termination]

räge¹ *n.* **1.** (fit of) violent anger; violent operation of some natural force or some sentiment (*the rage of the wind, of faction*). **2.** vehement desire or passion (*for*); object of widespread temporary enthusiasm or fashion (*the open-air cure was the,* or *all the, rage*). **3.** (poet.) poetic or prophetic or martial ardour. [ME f. OF, f. Rom. *rabia* f. L RABIES]

räge² *v.i.* rave, storm, speak madly or furiously, (*at, against,* or abs.), be full of anger; (of wind, sea, passion, feeling, battle, pain, disease, etc.) be violent, be at its height, operate unchecked, prevail. [ME, f. OF *rager* (as prec.)]

ra'g(g)ee, ra'gi, (rah'gē) *n.* coarse cereal (*Eleusine coracana*) forming staple food in parts of India etc. [f. Hindi *rāgī*]

ră'gged (-g-) *a.* rough, shaggy, hanging in tufts; having broken jagged outline or surface, full of rough or sharp projections; faulty, imperfect, lacking finish or smoothness or uniformity, (*ragged rhymes, time* in rowing, etc.); rent, torn, frayed; (of person) (1) in ragged clothes, (2) almost exhausted (*was run ragged*); ∼ **robin,** crimson-flowered campion (*Lychnis floscuculi*) with tattered petals; ||∼ **school,** (Hist.) free school for poor children; hence ∼LY² *adv.,* ∼NESS *n.,* ∼Y² *a.* [ME, f. ON *roggvathr* tufted]

ragi. See RAGEE.

rä'glan *n.* overcoat without shoulder seams, the sleeve running up to the neck; ∼ **sleeve** (of this kind). [f. Lord *Raglan,* Brit. commander d. 1855]

rä'gout (-ōō) *n.,* & *v.t.* **1.** *n.* meat in small pieces stewed with vegetables and highly seasoned. **2.** *v.t.* cook thus. [f. F *ragoût* (*ragoûter* revive taste of; see RE-, GUST²)]

rä'gŭly̆ *a.* (Her.) like row of sawn-off branches. [perh. f. RAGGED after *nebuly*]

***rah** *int.* expr. encouragement, approval, etc. [f. HURRAH]

raid *n.* & *v.* **1.** *n.* sudden attack made by military party, ship(s), or aircraft; predatory incursion in which surprise and rapidity are usu. relied upon, foray, inroad; surprise visit by police etc. to arrest suspected persons or seize illicit goods; (St. Exch.) attempt to lower price by concerted selling of shares. **2.** *v.i.* make raid *into* etc. **3.** *v.t.* make raid on (person, place, cattle). **4.** Hence ∼'ER¹ *n.* [ME, Sc. form of OE *rād* ROAD¹]

rail¹ *n.* & *v.* **1.** *n.* horizontal or inclined bar or continuous series of bars of wood or metal used to hang things on, as top of banisters, as part of fence, as protection against contact or falling over, or for similar purpose; **over the** ∼, over side of ship; **the** ∼**s,** inside boundary fence of racecourse. **2.** horizontal piece (cf. STILE²) in frame of panelled door etc. **3.** steel bar or continuous line of bars laid on ground usu. as one of two forming railway track (**off the** ∼**s,** disorganized, out of order, not working right); railway (*send it by rail; free on rail; rail travel, unions*). **4.** ∼**'car,** self-propelled railway coach; *∼ **fence** (made of posts and rails); ∼**'head,** (1) farthest point reached by railway under construction, (2) point on railway at which road transport of goods begins; ∼**'man,** (1) railwayman, (2) ||lowest grade of staff in BR; *∼**'road,** (*n.*) railway, (*v.t.*) rush (person, thing) *to, into, through,* etc., send (person) to prison by fraud. **5.** Hence ∼'AGE (4) *n.,* ∼'LESS (-l-l-) *a.* **6.** *v.t.* furnish or enclose (place) with rail(s) (*in, off*); provide (bench etc.) with rail(s); hence ∼'ing² [-ING¹ (3, 4)] *n.* **7.** lay (railway route) with rails; convey (goods) by rail. **8.** *v.i.* travel by rail. [ME, f. OF *reille* iron rod f. L *regula* RULE]

rail² *n.* small wading bird of family Rallidae, esp. LAND¹*rail,* WATER¹-*rail.* [ME, f. ONF *raille* f. Rom. **rasc(u)la,* perh. imit.]

rail³ *v.i.* use abusive language (*at* or *against,* arch. *on* or *upon*); hence ∼'ER¹ *n.,* ∼'ing² [-ING¹ (1)] *n.,* ∼'ing³ [-ING²] *a.* [ME, f. F *railler* f. Prov. *ralhar* jest f. Rom. **ragulare* (*ragere* roar, bray, f. L *rugire* bellow & Rom. **bragere* BRAY¹)]

rai'llery *n.* (piece of) good-humoured ridicule, rallying. [f. F *raillerie* (as prec.; see -ERY)]

rai'lway *n.* **1.** track or set of tracks of steel rails for passage of trains of carriages or trucks drawn by locomotive engine and conveying passengers and goods. **2.** tracks of this kind worked by single company; organization and persons required for their working. **3.** track on which wheels run (*cable railway*). **4.** (Hist.) road laid with rails for carts etc. **5.** ∼**man,** railway employee; ∼**yard,** area where rolling-stock is kept and made up into trains. [f. RAIL¹ + WAY]

rai′ment n. (arch. or literary). clothing. [ME, f. obs. *arrayment* (as ARRAY¹, -MENT)]

rain¹ n. **1.** condensed moisture of atmosphere falling visibly in separate drops; fall of such drops; *as* RIGHT¹ *as rain;* ∼ **or shine,** whether it rains or not. **2.** (in *pl.*) falls of rain; **the** ∼**s,** rainy season in tropical countries. **3.** (rainlike descent of) falling liquid or solid particles or objects (lit. or fig.; *a rain of ashes, frogs, pearls, rice, fire, of melody, kisses, congratulations*). **4.** ∼**-bird,** bird said to foretell rain by its cry, esp. green woodpecker; ∼**-check,** ticket given for later use when baseball match etc. is interrupted by rain, (fig.) promise that an offer will be maintained though deferred; ∼′**coat,** waterproof or water-resistant coat; ∼**-doctor,** sorcerer seeking to produce rain by magic; ∼′**drop,** single drop of rain; ∼′**fall,** (1) shower, (2) quantity of rain falling within given area in given time; ∼ **forest,** luxuriant tropical forest with heavy rainfall; ∼**-gauge,** instrument measuring rainfall; ∼**-maker,** Amer. Ind. rain-doctor; ∼**-making,** attempt to increase rainfall by artificial means; ‖∼**-pie,** green woodpecker; ∼**-shadow,** region shielded from rain by mountains etc.; ∼**-wash,** (movement of) loose material carried away by rain; ∼**-water** (collected from rain, not got from wells etc.); ∼**-worm,** common earthworm. **5.** Hence ∼′LESS, ∼′PROOF², ∼′TIGHT, *adjs.* [OE *regn, rēn,* = OS, OHG *regan,* ON *regn,* Goth. *rign*]

rain² v. **1.** *v. impers.* it ∼s or is ∼ing, rain comes down; it ∼ed *blood, frogs, invitations,* etc., there was a rain of them; *it rains* CAT¹s *and dogs; it never rains but it* POURS; it ∼s in, rain penetrates house etc.; *it has rained itself* OUT 3. **2.** *v.i.* (Of the sky, the clouds, etc.) send down rain; fall in showers or like rain (*flowers rained from their hands; tears rained down her cheeks; blows rain upon him*). **3.** *v.t.* send down like rain, lavishly bestow, (*he rained benefits, blows, on* or *upon us*); ∼ **off** or **out,* (esp. in *p.p.*) prevent or stop (event etc.) by rain. [OE *regnian* (as prec.)]

rai′nbow (-ō) n. & a. **1.** n. arch showing sequence of colours (conventionally red, orange, yellow, green, blue, indigo, violet) formed in sky (or across cataract etc.) opposite sun by reflection, twofold refraction, and dispersion of sun's rays in falling raindrops etc.; similar effect from moon, fog, sea spray, etc.; **secondary** ∼, additional arch with colours in reverse order formed inside or outside rainbow by twofold reflection and twofold refraction; **all the colours of the** ∼, many colours. **2.** a. many-coloured; ∼ **trout,** large trout (*Salmo gairdnerii*) orig. of Pacific coast of N. Amer. [OE *regnboga* (as RAIN¹, BOW¹)]

rai′n|ȳ a. **1.** (Of weather, climate, day, month, season, region, etc.) in or on which rain is falling or much rain usually falls; ∼**y day,** (fig.) time of esp. pecuniary need. **2.** (Of cloud, wind, etc.) laden with or bringing rain. **3.** Hence ∼iLY² *adv.,* ∼iNESS n. [OE *rēnig* (as RAIN¹, -Y²)]

raise (-z) v.t., & n. **1.** v.t. set upright, cause to stand up or *up,* restore to or towards vertical position, rouse, (*raised him from his knees, the standard of revolt, the country against the invader*); ∼ **from the dead,** restore to life; ∼ **a dust,** (fig.) cause turmoil, obscure the truth; ∼d **pastry** etc. (standing without support); ∼ person's **spirits,** give him new courage or cheerfulness; ∼ **the wind,** (fig.) procure money for some purpose. **2.** build up or *up,* construct, create, produce, breed, educate, utter, make audible, start, give occasion for, elicit, set up, advance, (*raise palace, large family, blister,* one's *own vegetables, storm, shout, hymn, controversy, prejudice, claim, demand, objection, question, false hopes*); *a deliverer was* ∼d **up,** caused by Providence to appear; ∼ **a laugh,** cause others to laugh; ∼ one's **voice,** speak (see also sense 3). **3.** put or take into higher position, extract from earth, direct upwards, promote to higher rank, make higher or nobler, cause to ascend, increase amount of, heighten level of, (Naut.) come in sight of (land, ship); cause (bread) to rise

with yeast; make nap on (cloth); increase (stake), bet more than (another player), at poker etc.; make bid contracting for more tricks in same suit as (partner), increase (bid) thus, at bridge etc.; (Math.) multiply (quantity) *to* a power; ∼d **beach,** (Geol.) beach lying above water level owing to changes since its formation; ∼ one's **eyebrows,** look supercilious or shocked; ∼ one's **eyes,** look upwards; ∼ one's **glass to,** drink health of; ∼ one's **hand to,** make as if to strike (person); ∼ one's **hat,** remove it momentarily as gesture of courtesy or respect (*to*); ∼ one's **voice,** speak louder (see also sense 2). **4.** levy, collect, bring together, procure, manage to get, (*raise tax, loan, subscription, money, army, fleet*). **5.** relinquish, cause enemy to relinquish, (SIEGE, blockade); remove (barrier, embargo). **6.** cause (ghost etc.) to appear (opp. LAY³); (colloq.) find (person etc. wanted); ∼ **Cain, the devil, hell,** etc., (colloq.) make disturbance. **7.** n. **increase in salary.* **8.** (Cards). increase in stake or bid (cf. sense 3). [ME, f. ON *reisa* = OE *rǣran* REAR²]

rai′sin (-z-) n. partially dried grape. [ME f. OF, f. Rom. **racimus* f. L. *racemus* grape-bunch]

raison d′état (rāzawn dātah′) n. (*pl.* **-ns** *pr.* same). = REASON¹ *of State.* [F]

raison d′être (rāzawn dā′tr, -ě′-) n. (*pl.* **-ns** *pr.* same). purpose etc. that accounts for or justifies or originally caused thing's existence. [F, = reason for being]

raj (rahj) n. (Ind. Hist.) sovereignty (*the British raj in India*). [Hindi *rāj* reign]

ra′ja, ra′jah, (rah′ja) n. (Hist.) Indian king or prince; petty dignitary or noble in India; Malay or Javanese chief; hence ∼SHIP n. [f. Hindi *rājā* f. Skr. *rājan* king]

Ra′jput, Ra′jpŏŏt, (rah′jpŏŏt) n. member of Hindu soldier caste claiming descent from Kshatriyas. [f. Hindi *rājpūt* f. Skr. *rājan* king + *putrá* son]

rāke¹ n. implement consisting of pole with cross-bar toothed like comb at end, or with several tines held together by cross-piece, for drawing together hay etc. or smoothing loose soil or gravel; wheeled implement for same purpose; implement resembling rake used for other purposes, e.g. by croupier drawing in money at gaming-table. [OE *raca, racu,* = MLG, MDu. *rāke,* cogn. w. MLG *rēke,* OHG *rehho,* ON *reka*]

rāke² v. **1.** v.t. collect, draw *together,* gather *in* or *up,* pull *out,* clear *off,* (as) with rake (*rake out the fire; rake up* or *together all possible charges; rake off the leaves*); clean or smooth with rake; search (as) with rake, ransack; make *level, clean,* etc., with rake; scratch, scrape; ∼ **over** or *up,* revive memory of (past quarrels, grievances, etc.). **2.** sweep with shot, enfilade, send shot along (ship) from stem to stern, sweep with the eyes, (of window etc.) have commanding view of. **3.** v.i. rake, search as with rake (*have been raking among* or in or *into old records*). **4.** ∼**-off,** (colloq., usu. derog.) commission, share of profits. [ME, f. ON *raka* scrape, rake, & f. prec.]

rāke³ n. dissipated or immoral man of fashion; ∼'s **progress,** continuous deterioration through vicious indulgence [title of series of engravings by Hogarth 1735]. [f. *rakel* dial. var. of RAKEHELL]

rāke⁴ v. & n. **1.** v.i. (Of ship or its bow or stern) project at upper part of bow or stern beyond keel; (of mast or funnel) incline from perpendicular towards stern. **2.** v.t. give backward inclination to (back of seat etc.). **3.** n. amount by which thing rakes; raking position or build; slope of stage or auditorium in theatre; slope of seat-back etc.; angle of surface of cutting tool. [17th c., prob. rel. to G *ragen* project, of unkn. orig.]

rā′kehĕll (-kh-) n. (arch.). = RAKE³; hence ∼Y² a. [f. RAKE² + HELL]

rā′kish¹ a. (as) of or like a RAKE³; jaunty, casual; hence ∼LY² *adv.,* ∼NESS n. [f. RAKE³ + -ISH¹]

rā′kish² a. (Of ship) smart and fast-looking, seeming built for speed and therefore open to suspicion of piracy. [f. RAKE⁴ + -ISH¹, assoc. w. RAKE³]

râle (rahl) n. (Path.) sound additional to that of

respiration heard in auscultation of unhealthy lungs. [F (*râler* to rattle)]

rällentä′nd|ō *adv.*, *a.*, & *n.* (*pl.* ∼os *or* ∼i). (Mus.) (passage performed) with gradual decrease of speed. [It.]

rä′lli cär(t) *n.* light two-wheeled horse-drawn vehicle for four persons. [f. *Ralli*, name of first purchaser 1885, +CAR, CART]

rä′lline *a.* of the bird-family Rallidae (see RAIL²). [f. mod. L *rallus* RAIL²; see -INE¹]

rä′llÿ¹ *v.* & *n.* **1.** *v.t.* & *i.* reassemble, get together again, after rout or dispersion; (cause to) renew conflict. **2.** bring or come together as support or for concentrated action (*rallied his party, his party rallied, round* or *behind* or *to him*). **3.** revive (faculty etc.) by effort of will, pull oneself together, assume or rouse to fresh energy; throw off prostration or illness or fear, regain health or consciousness, revive; (of share--prices etc.) increase after fall. **4.** *n.* act of reassembling forces or renewing conflict, reunion for fresh effort; recovery of energy after or in the middle of exhaustion or illness; (Tennis etc.) series of strokes before point is decided; competition for motor vehicles over public roads; mass meeting of supporters or persons having a common interest; ∼--cross, motor racing over roads and cross-country. [f. F *rallier* (as RE, ALLY¹)]

rä′llÿ² *v.t.* subject to good-humoured ridicule, banter. [f. F *railler* (see RAIL³)]

räm¹ *n.* **1.** uncastrated male sheep, tup. **2.** (*R*∼). the zodiacal sign Aries. **3.** = BATTER¹*ing-ram*; (battleship with) projecting beak at bow for piercing sides of other ships. **4.** falling weight of pile-driving machine; rammer; hydraulic water-raising or lifting machine; piston of hydrostatic press; plunger of force-pump; ∼-jet, type of jet engine in which air is drawn in and compressed by motion through the air. [OE *ram(m)*, = MDu, MLG, OHG *ram*, perh. rel. to ON *rammr* strong]

räm² *v.t.* (-mm-). **1.** beat down (soil etc., or abs.) into solidity with wooden block etc.; make (post, plant, etc.) firm by ramming soil round it. **2.** drive (pile etc.) *down, in, into,* by heavy blows; force (charge) home, pack (gun) tight with charge, by pushing with ramrod; squeeze or force into place by pressure (*rammed his clothes into a bag, his hat down on his head; had the list rammed into me by repetition*; ∼ **the argument home,** lay sufficient stress on it); cram with stuffing etc. **3.** (Of ship, vehicle, etc.) strike (as) with ram, dash or violently impel (thing) *against, at, on, into,* (*rammed his head against the wall, his horse at a fence*). **4.** Hence ∼′**mER**¹ (2) *n.* [ME, f. prec.]

‖**RAM** *abbr.* Royal Academy of Music.

Ramada′n (-ah′n) *n.* ninth month of Muslim year, during all daylight hours of which rigid fasting is observed. [f. Arab. *ramaḍān* (*ramaḍa* be hot; reason for name uncert.)]

rä′mal *a.* (Bot.) of or proceeding from a branch. [f. L *ramus* branch +-AL]

Ra′man (rah′-) *n.* (Phys.) ∼ **effect** etc. (involving change of frequency in scattering of radiation in a medium). [f. Sir C. V. ∼, Ind. physicist d. 1970]

rä′mble *v.i.*, & *n.* **1.** walk for pleasure, with or without definite route. **2.** *v.i.* wander in discourse, talk or write disconnectedly. [prob. f. MDu. *rammelen* (of animal) wander about in sexual excitement, frequent. of *rammen* copulate with, cogn. w. RAM¹; see -LE 3]

rä′mbler *n.* In vbl senses; straggling or climbing rose, esp. red-flowered kind called **crimson** ∼. [f. prec. +-ER¹]

rä′mbling *a.* peripatetic, wandering, disconnected, desultory, incoherent; (of plant) straggling, climbing; (of house, street, etc.) irregularly arranged; hence ∼LY *adv.* [f. n. RAMBLE +-ING²]

*∗**rämbu′nctious** (-shŭs) *a.* unruly; uncontrollably exuberant; hence ∼LY *adv.*, ∼NESS *n.* [19th c., of unkn. orig.]

rämbu′tan (-ōō′-) *n.* red plum-sized fruit of an E. Ind. tree, covered with prickles and with pleasant subacid pulp; tree (*Nephelium lappaceum*) that bears this. [Malay *rambūtan* (*rambut* hair, in allusion to spines)]

‖**RAMC** *abbr.* Royal Army Medical Corps.

rä′mĕkin *n.* small quantity of cheese with breadcrumbs, eggs, etc., baked and served in small mould (∼ **case, dish**); (small ovenware mould for) food thus served. [f. F *ramequin*, of LDu. orig.]

rä′mie *n.* tall E. Asian etc. plant (*Boehmeria nivea*); strong fibre from its bast, woven into durable material. [f. Malay *rāmī*]

rämĭfĭcä′tion *n.* ramifying, (arrangement of) tree's branches; subdivision of complex structure comparable to tree's branches (*the ramifications of a river, society, trade, lot, inquiry*). [F (*ramifier*; see foll., -ATION)]

rä′mĭfÿ *v.* **1.** *v.i.* form branches or subdivisions or offshoots, branch out. **2.** *v.t.* (usu. in *pass.*) cause to branch out, arrange in branching manner (*railways were ramified over the country*). [f. F *ramifier* f. med. L *ramificare* f. L *ramus* branch; see -FY]

rä′mmer. See RAM².

rä′mōse *a.* branched, branching. [f. L *ramosus* (*ramus* branch; see -OSE¹)]

rämp¹ *n.* slope, inclined plane joining two levels of ground, floor, etc.; stairs for entering or leaving aircraft; difference in level between opposite abutments of rampant arch; upward bend in stair-rail. [f. F *rampe* (*ramper*; see foll.)]

rämp² *v.* **1.** *v.i.* (Of lion etc.) stand on left hind foot with fore-paws in air, or assume or be in threatening posture; storm, rage, rush *about*. **2.** (Archit., of wall) ascend or descend to different level. **3.** *v.t.* furnish or build with ramp. [ME, f. OF *ramper* creep]

‖**rämp³** *n.* & *v.* (sl.) **1.** *n.* swindle, racket, esp. conducted by levying of exorbitant prices. **2.** *v.i.* engage in ramp. **3.** *v.t.* subject (person etc.) to ramp. [n. f. v., 16th c.; orig. unkn.]

rämpä′ge *v.i.*, & *n.* **1.** *v.i.* behave violently, storm, rage, rush *about*. **2.** *n.* (or rä′-). violent behaviour; **on the** ∼, rampaging; hence ∼OUS (-jŭs) *a.* [18th c., perh. f. RAMP²]

rä′mpant *a.* **1.** (Her., esp. of lion; after *n.*) ramping. **2.** violent or extravagant in action or opinion, arrant, aggressive, unchecked, prevailing, (*rampant theorists, violence*); rank, luxuriant, (*a rich soil makes nasturtiums too rampant*); (of arch etc.) having one abutment higher than the other, climbing. **3.** Hence **rä′mp-**ANCY *n.*, ∼LY² *adv.* [ME f. OF, part. of *ramper* (see RAMP², -ANT)]

rä′mpärt *n.*, & *v.t.* **1.** *n.* broad-topped and usu. stone--parapeted walk on top of defensive wall; (fig.) defence, protection. **2.** *v.t.* fortify or protect (as) with rampart. [f. F *rempart, rempar* f. *remparer* fortify (as RE-, *emparer* take possession of f. Prov. *amparer* f. Rom. *∗anteparare* place before another f. L *ante* before + *parare* prepare)]

rä′mpion *n.* bell-flower (*Campanula rapunculus*) with white tuberous roots used as salad. [f. med. L *rapuncium, rapontium*, prob. f. L *rapum* RAPE³]

rä′mröd *a.* rod for ramming down charge of muzzle--loaded firearm; (fig.) thing that is very straight or rigid. [f. RAM² +ROD]

rä′mshǎckle *a.* (Usu. of house or vehicle) tumble-down, crazy, rickety. [earlier *ramshackled* p.p. of obs. *ransackle* RANSACK]

rä′mson *n.* (esp. in *pl.*) (root, eaten as relish, of) broad-leaved garlic (*Allium ursinum*). [OE *hramsan* pl. of *hramsa* wild garlic, later taken as sing.]

rän. See RUN¹.

RAN *abbr.* Royal Australian Navy.

ranch (rah-) *n.*, & *v.i.* **1.** *n.* cattle-breeding establishment esp. in US and Canada; farm where other animals are bred (*mink ranch*); *∗***DUDE** RANCH. **2.** *v.i.* conduct ranch; hence ∼′ER¹ *n.* [f. Sp. *rancho* group of persons eating together]

ră′ncĭd *a.* smelling or tasting like rank stale fat; hence ∼ITY (-ĭ′d-), ∼NESS, *ns.* [f. L *rancidus* stinking (**rancēre* be putrid; see -ID[1])]

ră′ncour (-ker), ***ră′ncor,** *n.* inveterate bitterness, malignant hate, spitefulness; hence **ră′ncor**ous *a.* [ME f. OF, f. LL *rancor -oris* (as prec.; see -OR)]

rănd[1] *n.* levelling-strip of leather between heel and sides of shoe or boot. [OE, = OS *rand*, OHG *rant*, ON *rönd* edge, rim f. Gmc *rand-]

rand[2] (rahnt) *n.* (S. Afr.) **1.** ridge of high ground on either side of river. **2.** (*or* rănd). monetary unit of S. Afr. countries. [Afrik., = edge, cogn. w. prec.; sense 2 f. *the R*∼, gold-field district near Johannesburg]

R. and A. *abbr.* Royal and Ancient (Golf Club, St. Andrews).

răndă′n[1] *n.* style of rowing for three men, the middle using pair of sculls and the others oars; boat for such use. [19th c.; orig. uncert.]

răndă′n[2] *n.* spree (*on the randan*). [perh. var. of RANDOM]

R. & B. *abbr.* rhythm and blues.

R. & D. *abbr.* research and development.

ră′ndem *adv.* & *n.* **1.** *adv.* with three horses harnessed tandem. **2.** *n.* carriage or team so driven. [prob. formed on *random* and *tandem*]

ră′ndom *n.* & *a.* **1.** *n.* **at** ∼, at haphazard, without aim or purpose or principle, heedlessly. **2.** *a.* made, done, etc., at random (*random sample, selection*); (Statistics) with equal chances for each item, given by random process, whence ∼IZE (3) *v.t.*; (of masonry) with stones of irregular size and shape; hence ∼LY[2] *adv.*, ∼NESS *n.* [ME, f. OF *randon* great speed (*randir* gallop)]

ră′ndĭ̆y *a.* lustful, eager for sexual gratification; (Sc.) loud-tongued, boisterous, lusty; hence ∼ĬNESS *n.* [perh. f. obs. *rand* f. obs. Du. *randen, ranten* RANT + -Y[2]]

ra′nee, ra′nĭ, (rah′nĭ) *n.* (Hist.) Hindu queen; raja's wife or widow. [f. Hindi *rānī* = Skr. *rājnī* fem. of *rājan* king]

răng. See RING[2].

răngati′ra (-nggatē′-) *n.* (NZ). Maori chief or noble. [Maori]

rănge[1] (-nj) *v.* **1.** *v.t.* place or arrange in a row or ranks or in specified situation or order or company (usu. in *pass.* or *refl.*: *ranged their troops; ranged themselves on each side; range oneself with the majority party; was ranged against, among, on the side of, with,* etc.; *trees ranged in ascending order of height*); **ra′nging-pole, -rod,** (for setting straight line in surveying); ∼ one**self,** (arch.; imit. F) take up definite position in society, settle down, e.g. by marrying. **2.** ‖(Print.) make (type) lie flush at ends of successive lines. **3.** traverse in all directions (*ranging the woods*). **4.** *v.i.* run in a line, reach, lie spread out, extend, be found or occur over specified district, vary between limits (*ranges north and south, along the sea; nightingale ranges from the Channel to Warwickshire*). **5.** be level (*with*); (Print., of type) lie flush (see sense 2); rank or find right place *with* or *among* (*ranges with the great writers*). **6.** rove, wander, (*over, along, through,* etc., district or region; *his thoughts range over past, present, and future*); **ranging fancy,** inconstant affections. **7.** (Of gun) throw projectile over, (of projectile) traverse, specified distance (*ranges over a mile*); obtain range of target by adjustment after firing past it or short of it. [ME, f. F *ranger* (*rang* RANK[1])]

rănge[2] (-nj) *n.* **1.** row, line, tier, or series, of things, esp. of buildings or mountains. **2.** lie, direction, (*the range of the strata is east and west*). **3.** large open stretch of grazing or hunting ground; tract over which one ranges. **4.** piece of ground or enclosure with targets for shooting. **5.** area over which plant, animal, etc., is distributed, area included in or concerned with something, (region between) limits of variation, limited scale or series, distance attainable by gun or projectile, distance between gun etc. and objective, distance that can be traversed without refuelling etc., extent of time covered by forecast etc., (*gives the ranges of all species; the thorniest question in the whole range of* *politics; the range of her voice is astonishing; his reading is of very wide range; the range of the thermometer readings is about 10 degrees; Hebrew is out of my range; the enemy are out of range, have found the range of our camp*). **6.** cooking fireplace usu. with oven(s), boiler(s), and iron top plate with openings for saucepans etc.; *electric or gas cooker. **7.** ∼**-finder,** instrument for estimating distance of object, esp. one to be shot at or photographed. [ME f. OF, = row, rank (*ranger*; see prec.)]

ră′nger (-nj-) *n.* In vbl senses; keeper of a royal park, forest, etc., whence ∼SHIP *n.*; *commando; member of body of mounted troops or other armed men; ‖senior Guide. [ME, f. RANGE[1] + -ER[1]]

ră′ngy̆ (-njĭ) *a.* (Of person) tall and slim. [f. RANGE[1,2] + -Y[2]]

rani. See RANEE.

rănk[1] *n.* **1.** row, line, queue; ‖place where taxis stand to await customers; (Chess) row of squares across board (cf. FILE[3]). **2.** number of soldiers drawn up in single line abreast; **the** ∼**s,** or **the** ∼ **and file,** common soldiers, i.e. privates and corporals, (fig.) ordinary undistinguished people; **close** ∼**s,** maintain solidarity; **other** ∼**s,** soldiers other than commissioned officers; **rise from the** ∼**s,** advance by one's own exertions (of common soldier or sergeant who is given commission, or of self-made man). **3.** order, array, (**keep** ∼, **break** ∼, remain, fail to remain, in line). **4.** place in a scale; position in a hierarchy, grade of advancement; distinct social class, grade of dignity, (high) social position, (*people of all ranks; in the front* or *top rank of performers*); **persons of** ∼, members of nobility or gentry; **pull** ∼, make unfair use of one's seniority etc.; ∼ **and fashion,** high society. [f. OF *ranc, renc,* f. Gmc *hrengaz RING[1]]

rănk[2] *v.* **1.** *v.t.* arrange (esp. soldiers) in rank; classify, give certain grade to; *take precedence of (person) in respect to rank. **2.** *v.i.* have rank or place (*ranks among the Great Powers, next to the king,* etc.); *have senior position among members of hierarchy etc. [f. prec.]

rănk[3] *a.* **1.** too luxuriant, coarse, over-productive, choked with or apt to produce weeds or excessive foliage. **2.** foul-smelling, offensive; loathsome, indecent, corrupt. **3.** strongly marked, unmistakable, flagrant, virulent, gross, complete, (*rank treason, pedantry, poison, nonsense, outsider*). **4.** Hence ∼LY[2] *adv.*, ∼NESS *n.* [OE *ranc,* = MLG *rank* long and thin, ON *rakkr* erect, f. Gmc *rankaz]

ră′nker *n.* (commissioned officer who has been) a soldier in the ranks. [f. RANK[1] + -ER[1]]

ră′nkle *v.i.* (Of envy, disappointment, etc., or their cause) be bitter, give intermittent or constant pain; (arch., of wound, sore, etc.) fester, continue painful. [ME in last sense, f. OF *rancler* (*rancle, raoncle, draoncle,* festering sore f. med. L *dranculus, dracunculus* dim. of *draco* serpent)]

ră′nsăck *v.t.* thoroughly search (place, receptacle, person's pockets, one's conscience, etc.); pillage, plunder, (house, country, etc.). [ME, f. ON *rannsaka* (*rann* house, *-saka* f. *sækja* seek)]

ră′nsom *n.,* & *v.t.* **1.** *n.* (liberation of prisoner in consideration of) sum of money or value paid for release; **hold** person **to** ∼, be willing to release him for such consideration, (fig.) demand concessions from by threat of damaging action; **worth a king's** ∼, of immense value. **2.** *v.t.* redeem, buy freedom or restoration of; atone for, expiate; hold to ransom, release for a ransom; exact ransom from. [ME, f. OF *ransoun(er)* f. L *redemptio -onis* REDEMPTION]

rănt *v.* & *n.* **1.** *v.i.* use bombastic language. **2.** *v.t.* & *i.* declaim, recite theatrically; preach noisily, whence (esp. arch. derog. of Primitive Methodist, and Hist. of sect of 17th-c. English antinomians) ∼′ER[1] *n.* **3.** *n.* piece of ranting, tirade; empty turgid talk. [f. Du. *ranten* rave]

ră′ntĭpōle *n.* & *a.* wild, reckless, (person). [18th c., of unkn. orig.]

ranŭ′ncŭl|us *n.* (*pl.* ∼**uses,** *or* ∼**i** *pr.* -ī). plant of genus *Ranunculus*, e.g. buttercup; hence ∿A'CEOUS *a.*, of family Ranunculaceae. [L, orig. dim. of *rana* frog]

ranz-des-vaches (rahnsdävah'sh) *n.* Swiss herdsmen's melody played on alpenhorn or sung. [Swiss F]

||**RAOC** *abbr.* Royal Army Ordnance Corps.

răp¹ *n.* & *v.* (**-pp-**). **1.** smart slight blow; ∿ **on** or **over the knuckles**, punishment inflicted on child, (fig.) reproof. **2.** (sl.) blame, censure, punishment, etc.; **take the ∿,** suffer the consequences. **3.** sound made by knocker on door etc., or (Spiritualism) by some agency on table or floor. **4.** (sl.) a conversation. **5.** *v.t.* strike (esp. person's knuckles) smartly; criticize adversely; ∿ **out,** utter (oath, pun, etc.) abruptly or on the spur of the moment, (Spiritualism) express (message, word) by raps. **6.** *v.i.* make sound called rap (*rapped at the door, on the table,* etc.); (sl.) talk. [ME, prob. imit.]

răp² *n.* a small amount, the least bit, (*don't care a rap*). [earlier sense 18th-c. Irish counterfeit halfpenny, abbr. of Ir. *ropaire*]

rapā'cious (-shus) *a.* grasping, extortionate, predatory; hence or cogn. ∿LY² *adv.*, **rapā'city** *n.* [f. L *rapax -acis* (*rapere* snatch; see -ACIOUS)]

||**RAPC** *abbr.* Royal Army Pay Corps.

rāpe¹ *v.t.* & *n.* **1.** *v.t.* (poet.) take by force. **2.** commit rape on (woman); hence **rā'pist** (1) *n.* **3.** *n.* (poet.) carrying off (esp. of woman) by force. **4.** forcible or fraudulent sexual intercourse esp. imposed on woman (***statutory ∿,** sexual intercourse with girl below age of consent); forcible sodomy; (fig.) forcible interference with institution, country, etc., violation *of.* [ME, f. AF *rap*(*er*) f. L *rapere* seize]

||**rāpe²** *n.* (Hist.) any of six divisions of Sussex. [OE, var. of *rāp* ROPE, w. ref. to fencing-off of land]

rāpe³ *n.* plant (*Brassica napus*) grown as food for sheep and for its seed from which oil is made, cole-seed; ∿**-cake,** rape-seed pressed into flat shape after extraction of oil and used as manure; ∿**-oil** (made from rape-seed and used as lubricant and in foodstuffs). [ME, f. L *rapum, rapa* turnip]

rāpe⁴ *n.* refuse of grapes after wine-making, used in making vinegar; vessel used in vinegar-making. [f. F *râpe*, med. L *raspa*]

ră'phia *n.* Var. of RAFFIA.

ră'phĭde *n.* (Bot.) needle-shaped crystal of irritant substance formed in plant. [back-form. f. *raphides* pl. of *raphis* f. Gk *rhaphis -idos* needle]

ră'pĭd *a.* (∿er, ∿est) & *n.* **1.** *a.* quick, swift; acting or completed in short time; (of slope) descending steeply; (Photogr.) fast; ∿ **eye-movement** (esp. jerky kind during periods of dreaming); ∿**-fire,** firing shots, asking questions, etc., in quick succession; *∿ **transit,** (1) high-speed urban transport of passengers, (2) lightning (chess); hence or cogn. **rapi'dity** *n.,* ∿LY² *adv.* **2.** *n.* (usu. in *pl.*) steep descent in river-bed, with consequently swift current. [f. L *rapidus* (*rapere* seize; see -ID¹)]

ră'pier *n.* light slender sword for thrusting only; ∿**-thrust,** (fig.) delicate or witty repartee. [prob. f. Du. *rapier* or LG *rappir,* f. F *rapière,* of unkn. orig.]

ră'pĭne *n.* (rhet.) plundering, robbery. [ME f. OF, or f. L *rapina* (*rapere* seize; see -INE⁴)]

ră'pist. See RAPE¹.

răpparee' *n.* 17th-c. Irish irregular soldier or freebooter. [f. Ir. *rapaire* short pike]

răppee' *n.* coarse kind of snuff. [f. F. (*tabac*) *râpé* RASPED (tobacco)]

răppĕ'l *n.,* & *v.i.* (||**-ll-**). (make) descent of steep rock-face by using doubled rope fixed at higher point. [F, = recall (*rappeler* f. as RE-, APPEAL¹)]

rappŏ'rt (-ŏr') *n.* (esp. useful) communication, (harmonious) relationship, or connection, (*in rapport with*); (Spiritualism) communication through medium. [F (*rapporter* f. as RE-, AP-, *porter* f. L *portare* carry)]

răppŏrteur' (- êr') *n.* person who prepares account of proceedings of committee etc. for higher body. [F. (as prec.)]

rapprochement (răprŏ'shmahṅ) *n.* re-establishment or recommencement of harmonious relations, esp. between States. [F (*rapprocher* f. as RE- + APPROACH¹; see -MENT)]

răpscă'llion (-lyon) *n.* (arch. or joc.) rascal, scamp, rogue. [earlier *rascallion,* perh. f. RASCAL]

răpt *p.p., & a.* **1.** *p.p.* carried away bodily or in spirit from earth, from life, from consciousness, or from ordinary thoughts and perceptions (*away, up,* etc.). **2.** *a.* absorbed, enraptured, intent, (*listen with rapt attention*); hence ∿LY² *adv.* [ME, f. L *raptus* p.p. of *rapere* seize]

ră'ptor *n.* bird of prey (see foll.), of order Raptores. [L, = ravisher, plunderer, (*rapere rapt-* seize; see -OR)]

răptŏr'ĭal *n.* & *a.* (Zool.) **1.** *n.* bird (usu. large) which preys on other birds, mammals, etc.; bird of prey (eagle, falcon, owl, etc.); predatory animal or bird. **2.** *a.* predatory; adapted for seizing prey. [f. L *raptor* (see prec.) + -IAL]

ră'pture *n.* **1.** mental transport, ecstatic delight; (in *pl.*) vehement pleasure or the expression of it; **be in** or **go into ∿s,** be enthusiastic, talk enthusiastically. **2.** (arch.) act of transporting a person from one place to another. **3.** Hence **ră'pturous** (-cher-) *a.* [obs. F, or f. med. L *raptura* (as RAPT; see -URE)]

ră'ptured (-cherd) *a.* (arch.) enraptured, in ecstasy. [p.p. of obs. *rapture* v. (as prec.)]

rara avis (rāra ā'vis, rāra ā'vis) *n.* rarity, kind of person or thing rarely encountered. [L, = rare bird]

rāre¹ *a.* **1.** with only loosely packed substance, of less than usual density (*the rare atmosphere of the mountain tops*). **2.** few and far between, uncommon, unusual, exceptional, seldom found or occurring, (*it is rare for person etc. to do; it is rarely that person etc. does*). **3.** of uncommon excellence, remarkably good, very amusing, (*a miracle of rare device; had rare fun with him*). **4.** ∿ **bird,** *rara avis;* ∿ **earth,** (oxide of) lanthanide element; ∿ **gas,** = NOBLE *gas.* **5.** Hence ∿LY² (rār'li) *adv.,* (esp.) seldom, not often, finely, in an unusual degree, ∿'NESS (rār'n-) *n.* [ME, f. L *rarus*]

rāre² *a.* (Of meat) underdone. [var. of obs. *rear* half-cooked (of eggs), f. OE *hrēr*]

rār'ebit (rār'b-) *n.* See WELSH¹.

rār'ee-show (-ō) *n.* show carried about in a box, peep-show; any show or spectacle. [app. = *rare show* as pronounced by Savoyard showmen]

rār'e|fȳ *v.* **1.** *v.t.* lessen density or solidity of (esp. gas); purify, refine, (person's nature etc.); make (idea etc.) subtle. **2.** *v.i.* become less dense. **3.** So ∿FA'CTION, ∿FICA'TION, *ns.,* ∿fā'ctIVE *a.* [ME, f. OF *rarefier* or med. L *rarificare* f. L *rarefacere* (*rarus* rare, *facere* make); see -FY]

rār'ing *a.* (colloq.) enthusiastic, eager, (*to go* etc.). [part. of *rare,* dial. var. of ROAR or REAR²]

rār'itȳ *n.* rareness (see RARE¹); uncommon thing, thing valued as being rare. [f. F *rareté,* or f. L *raritas* (as RARE¹; see -ITY)]

||**RASC** *abbr.* (Hist.) Royal Army Service Corps.

ra'scal (rah'-) *n.* & *a.* **1.** *n.* rogue, knave, scamp, (often joc., esp. to child: *you lucky rascal!*). **2.** *a.* (arch.) belonging to the rabble; **the ∿ rout,** the common people. **3.** Hence ∿DOM, ∿ISM (2), **răscă'lity** *ns.,* ∿LY¹ *a.* [ME, f. OF *rascaille* rabble, prob. f. ONF *rasque f. Rom. *rasica (*rasicare f. L *radere* ras- scrape)]

rasche'l (-sh-) *n.* fabric like tricot but more loosely knitted. [f. G. *Raschelmaschine,* kind of knitting-machine f. as RACHEL]

rase. See RAZE.

răsh¹ *n.* eruption of the skin in spots or patches; (fig.) sudden widespread onset of (*a rash of strikes*). [cf. OF *ra*(*s*)*che* eruptive sores, = It. *raschia* itch]

răsh² *a.* hasty, impetuous, overbold, reckless, acting or done without due consideration; hence ∿LY² *adv.,* ∿'NESS *n.* [ME, f. OE **ræsc,* = MDu. *rasch,* OHG *rasc,* ON *röskr* f. Gmc **raskuz,* perh. cogn. w. RATHE]

ră'sher *n.* thin slice of bacon or ham. [16th c., of unkn. orig.]

rasp (rah-) *n.* & *v.* **1.** *n.* coarse kind of file having separate teeth. **2.** *v.t.* scrape with rasp; scrape roughly; grate upon (person or his feelings), irritate; scrape *off* or *away*; say gratingly. **3.** *v.i.* make grating sound. **4.** Hence ∼'ER¹ *n.*, (esp., Hunting) high difficult fence. [ME, f. OF *raspe*(*r*) f. Rom. **raspare* f. WG **raspōn* scrape together]

ra'spatory (rah'-) *n.* rasp used in surgery. [f. F *raspatoire* or f. med. L **raspatorium* (*raspare* RASP; see -ORY)]

ra'spberry (rah'zb-) *n.* **1.** (bramble *Rubus idaeus* bearing) usu. red berry of numerous drupels on conical receptacle. **2.** (sl.) sound, gesture, or sign expressing dislike, derision, or disapproval; dismissal [f. *raspberry tart*, rhyming sl. = *fart*]. **3.** ∼-cane, raspberry plant; ∼ vinegar, kind of syrup made from raspberries. [f. 16th c. *rasp* (now dial.) f. obs. *raspis*, of unkn. orig., + BERRY¹]

ra'ssè *n.* small civet. [f. Jav. *rase*]

Rǎstafār'ian *a.* & *n.* (member) of an orig. Jamaican sect regarding Blacks as a chosen people. [f. *Ras Tafari*, title of Emperor Haile Selassie of Ethiopia d. 1975, venerated by the sect as a god, + -AN]

rǎ'ster *n.* pattern of scanning lines for cathode-ray tube picture. [G, = screen, f. L *rastrum* rake (*radere rasscrape*)]

rǎt¹ *n.*, & *v.i.* (-tt-). **1.** *n.* rodent of genus *Rattus* (**like a drowned** ∼, (of person) wet through; **rats!**, (sl.) (1) nonsense!, incredible!, (2) drat it!; **smell a** ∼, have suspicions of foul play etc.); similar rodent (MUSK-*rat*, WATER¹-*rat*). **2.** (colloq.) unpleasant person; (Polit.) person who deserts his party in difficulties as rats are said to desert a doomed house or ship, turncoat. **3.** workman who refuses to join strike, takes striker's place, or accepts less than trade-union wages. **4.** ∼'bag, (Austral. & NZ sl.) unpleasant or eccentric person; ∼-catcher (who rids houses of rats), (sl.) informal hunting dress; *∼'fink, (sl.) = FINK²; ∼ kangaroo, (Austral.) small ratlike marsupial; ∼ race, fiercely competitive struggle, struggle to maintain one's position in work or life; ∼'sbane, thing (esp. plant) poisonous to rats; ∼'s-tail, thing shaped like a rat's tail, e.g. kind of file; ∼-tail, (1) grenadier fish, (2) (horse with) hairless horse's tail; ∼-tail(*ed*) spoon (with tail-like prolongation of handle along back of bowl). **5.** *v.i.* (Of person or dog) hunt or kill rats; play the rat in politics; ∼ on, desert (person), break *(promise)*; hence ∼'tER¹ *n.* [OE *ræt* & OF *rat* f. Rom. **rattus*]

rǎt² *v.t.* (-tt-; esp. in 3 sing. pres. subj.; arch., vulg.) = DRAT. [corrupt. of ROT²]

ra'ta (rah'-) *n.* large handsome NZ tree with crimson flowers and hard red wood. [Maori]

rǎ'table. Var. of RATEABLE.

rǎtafi'a (-ĕ'*a*) *n.* liqueur flavoured with almonds or kernels of peach, apricot, or cherry; kind of biscuit similarly flavoured. [F, prob. rel. to TAFIA (Creole)]

ratǎ'n. Var. of RATTAN.

rǎtaplǎ'n *n.* & *v.* (-nn-). **1.** *n.* drumming sound. **2.** *v.t.* play (as) on drum. **3.** *v.i.* make rataplan. [F; imit.]

rǎtatǎ't. Var. of RAT-TAT.

ratatouille (rahtahtōō'ĭ) *n.* Provençal stew of vegetables. [F dial.]

rǎtch *n.* ratchet(-wheel). [perh. f. G *ratsche*; cf. foll.]

rǎ'tchèt *n.*, & *v.t.* (-tt-). **1.** *n.* set of teeth on edge of bar or wheel in which pawl etc. engages to ensure motion in one direction only; ∼(-wheel), wheel with rim so toothed. **2.** *v.t.* provide with ratchet; make into ratchet. [f. F *rochet* blunt lance-head, bobbin, ratchet, etc.; cf. It. *rocchetto* spool, ratchet, dim. f. Rom. **rokk*-f. Gmc **rukkon*]

rǎte¹ *n.* **1.** stated value of numerical proportion prevailing or to prevail between two sets of things (*moving at a rate of ten miles per hour; watch loses at the rate of two minutes a day*; BIRTH *rate*, DEATH *rate*); amount etc. mentioned for application to all compatible cases; standard or way of reckoning; (measure of) value, tariff charge, (*rate of exchange, of interest*); speed (*travelling at a great rate; prices increasing at a dreadful rate*); **at that** or **this** ∼, (colloq.) if this is a fair specimen, if this assumption is true, etc.; **at any** ∼, in each or any possible case, even if a stronger statement is doubtfully true, etc. **2.** ‖assessment levied by local authorities for local purposes at so much per pound of assessed value of buildings and land owned; (in *pl.*) amount thus paid by householder etc. **3.** class (*first-rate*; often derog. *second, third*, etc., *-rate*). **4.** ‖∼'payer, person liable to pay RATE¹s (sense 2). [ME f. OF, f. med. L *rata* (L *pro rata parte* or *portione* according to the proportional share), f. *ratus* p.p. of *rēri* reckon]

rǎte² *v.* **1.** *v.t.* estimate worth or value of (*I do not rate his merits high; each offence is rated at a fixed penalty*; OVERRATE, UNDERRATE); assign fixed value to (coin, metal) in relation to monetary standard (*the copper coinage is rated much above its real value*); assign value to (work, power of machine, etc.). **2.** consider, regard as, (*I rate him among my benefactors*). **3.** ‖subject to payment of a local rate; value for purpose of assessing rates on. **4.** (Naut.) class under a certain RATING¹. **5.** *be worthy of, deserve. **6.** *v.i.* rank or be rated *as.* [ME, f. prec.]

rǎte³ *v.t.* scold angrily. [ME, of unkn. orig.]

rǎte⁴. Var. of RET.

rǎ'te|able (-ta-) *a.* **1.** ‖liable to payment of RATE¹s (sense 2) (∼able value, value at which house etc. is assessed for this); hence ∼ABI'LITY (-ta-) *n.* **2.** (arch.) proportional. **3.** Hence ∼ably² (-ta-) *adv.* [f. RATE² + -ABLE]

ra'tel (rā'-, rah'-) *n.* African and Indian nocturnal carnivorous burrowing mammal of genus *Mellivora*. [Afrik.; orig. unkn.]

rath (rah-) *n.* (Ir. etc. Ant.) prehistoric hill-fort. [Ir.]

rǎthe (-dh) *a.* (poet.) coming, blooming, etc., early in the year or day; ∼-ripe, ripening early, precocious. [OE *hræth, hræd*, = OHG (*h*)*rad*, ON *hrathr*, Goth. **raths* f. Gmc **hrathaz*; cf. RASH²]

ra'ther (rah'dh-) *adv.* **1.** more truly, to a greater extent, as a more accurate description or preferable account of the matter, or to be more precise, (*is rather good than bad; derived rather from imagination than from reason; orderliness is not the result of law, rather is it the cause of it; late last night, or rather, early this morning*); the ∼ that, so much the more because. **2.** in a modified way, to some extent, slightly, somewhat, (*I rather think you know him; the performance was rather a failure, was rather good, was rather a good one, was rather better than I expected, fell rather flat*). **3.** by preference, for choice, sooner, as an alternative chosen sooner *than* another (of same grammatical form, or inf. after finite v.; *would much rather not go; he would rather have died than refused; use soft water rather than hard; the desire to seem clever rather than honest; he resigned rather than act dishonestly*); **had** ∼, would rather (*I had rather err with Plato than be right with Horace*). **4.** ‖(colloq.) (In answer) most emphatically, yes without doubt, assuredly, (*Have you been here before?—R∼!*). [ME, f. OE *hrathor*, compar. of *hræthe* adv. f. *hræth* a.; see prec.]

***ra'thskěller** (rah'ts-) *n.* beer-saloon or restaurant in basement. [G, = (restaurant in) town-hall cellar]

rǎ'ti|fy² *v.t.* confirm or accept (agreement made in one's name) by formal consent, signature, etc.; so ∼FICA'TION *n.* [ME, f. OF *ratifier* f. med. L *ratificare* (as RATE¹; see -FY)]

rā'ting¹ *n.* In vbl senses; ‖amount fixed as local rate; (Naut.) person's position or class on ship's books, ‖non-commissioned sailor; any of the classes into which racing yachts are distributed by tonnage; estimated number of audience as index of popularity of a broadcast; estimated standing etc. of person (CREDIT¹ *rating*). [f. RATE² + -ING¹]

rā'ting² *n.* angry reprimand. [f. RATE³ + -ING¹]

rā'tio (-shiō) *n.* (*pl.* ∼s) quantitative relation between two similar magnitudes determined by the number of times one contains the other integrally or fractionally (*are in the ratio of three to two* or *3:2*; *the ratios 1:5 and 20:100 are the same*; INVERSE *ratio*). [L (as RATE[1]; see -ION)]

rătiŏ′cin|āte (rătĭ-, răshĭ-) *v.i.* go through logical processes, reason formally, use syllogisms; so ~A′TION *n.*, ~ATIVE *a.* [f. L *ratiocinari* (as prec.) + -ATE[3]]

ră′tion *n.*, & *v.t.* **1.** *n.* (usu. in *pl.*) fixed daily allowance of food served out esp. for members of Services (and formerly of forage for animals). **2.** fixed allowance of food etc. for civilians in time of shortage (~ **book, card,** document entitling holder to a ration); single portion *of* provisions, fuel, clothing, etc.; (in *pl.*) provisions; **given out with the** ~**s,** (sl.) awarded without regard to merit. **3.** *v.t.* limit (persons, food, clothing) to fixed ration; ~ (**out**), share (food etc.) in fixed quantities. [F, f. It. *razione* or Sp. *ración* f. L *ratio -onis* reckoning, RATIO]

ră′tional *a.* **1.** endowed with reason, reasoning; sensible, sane, moderate, not foolish or absurd or extreme; of or based on reasoning or reason, rejecting what is unreasonable or cannot be tested by reason in religion or custom; ~ **dress,** (Hist., esp.) knicker-bockers worn by women instead of skirts; ~ **leanings,** doubts about the truth of divine revela-tion, the possibility of miracles, etc. **2.** (Math.) (of quantity) expressible as ratio of whole numbers. **3.** Hence or cogn. ~ITY (-ă′l-) *n* , ~l Y[2] *adv.* [ME, f. L *rationalis* (as prec.; see -AL.)]

rătiona′le (-ah′l, -ah′lĭ) *n.* reasoned exposition, state-ment of reasons; fundamental reason, logical basis, *of.* [mod. L, neut. (as n.) of L *ratonals* (see prec.)]

ră′tional|ism *n.* practice of explaining the super-natural in religion in a way consonant with reason, or of treating reason as the ultimate authority in religion as elsewhere; theory that reason is the foundation of certainty in knowledge (opp. *empiricism, sensational-ism*); so ~IST (2) *n.*, ~i′stIC *a.* [f. RATIONAL + -ISM]

ră′tionaliz|e, -is|e (-īz), *v.* *v.t.* explain (*away*) by rationalism, bring into conformity with reason; (Math.) clear of surds; make (an industry) more efficient by scientifically reducing or eliminating waste of labour, time, or materials. **2.** *v.i.* be or act as rationalist; (colloq.) find 'reasons' for irrational or unworthy behaviour. **3.** Hence ~A′TION *n.* [f. RATIONAL + -IZE]

ră′tīte *a.* (Of bird) having keelless breastbone, e.g. ostrich, emu, cassowary, (opp. *carinate*). [f. L *ratis* raft + -ITE[2]]

ră′tline, -lin, -ling, *n.* (usu. in *pl.*) one of the small lines fastened across ship's shrouds like ladder-rungs. [ME; orig. unkn.]

ratoo′n *n.*, & *v.i.* **1.** new shoot springing from sugar--cane etc. root after cropping. **2.** *v.i.* send up ratoons. [f. Sp. *retoño* sprout]

ratta′n *n.* E. Ind. climbing palm of genus *Calamus* etc. with long thin many-jointed pliable stems; piece of rattan stem used as cane etc. [earlier *rot(t)ang* f. Malay *rōtan* (prob. f. *raut* pare)]

răt-tă′t, răt-tăt-tă′t, *n.* rapping sound, esp. of knocker. [imit.]

ră′ttle[1] *v.* **1.** *v.i.* give out rapid succession of short sharp hard sounds, cause such sounds by shaking something (*he rattled at the door*); talk in lively thoughtless way (*on, away, along*); move or fall with rattling noise, drive vehicle or ride or run briskly, (*down, along, past,* etc.). **2.** *v.t.* make (chain, window, crockery, etc.) rattle (~ **the sabre,** threaten war); say or recite (verses, stories, lists, oaths) rapidly (*off, out, over, away,* etc.); (sl.) excite, agitate, fluster, make nervous, frighten; make move quickly. [ME, prob. f. MDu. & LG *ratelen* (imit.)]

ră′ttle[2] *n.* **1.** instrument or plaything made to rattle esp. in order to give alarm or to amuse babies; set of horny rings in rattlesnake's tail; plant with seeds that rattle in their cases when ripe (**red** ~, pink-flowered marsh plant *Pedicularis palustris*; **yellow** ~, yellow--flowered plant of genus *Rhinanthus*); rattling sound

(DEATH-*rattle*); uproar, bustle, noisy gaiety, racket; noisy flow of words, empty chatter, trivial talk; lively incessant talker. **2.** ~-**bag, -bladder, -box,** rattle constructed of bag etc. with objects inside; ~-**brain, -head, -pate,** (person with) frivolous mind; ~**snake,** venomous Amer. snake with rattling struc-ture in tail; ~**trap** *n.* & *a.*, rickety (vehicle etc.), (in *pl.*) curiosities, odds and ends. [f. prec.]

ră′ttler *n.* In vbl senses; remarkably good specimen of anything; *rattlesnake; *goods train. [ME. f. RATTLE[1] + -ER[1]]

ră′ttling *n.* In vbl senses; brisk, vigorous, (a *rattling wind, pace*); (as *adv.*) ~ **good** etc., remarkably good etc. [f. RATTLE[1] + -ING[2]]

ră′tty *a.* relating to or infested with rats; (sl.) irritable, touchy. [f. RAT[1] + -Y[2]]

rau′cous *a.* hoarse, harsh-sounding; hence ~LY[2] *adv.*, ~NESS *n.* [f. L *raucus* + -OUS]

rau′nch|y *a.* slovenly; coarsely outspoken; hence ~ĭLY[2] *adv.*, ~iNESS *n.* [20th c.; orig. unkn.]

ră′vage *v.* & *n.* **1.** *v.t.* & *i.* devastate, plunder, make havoc (in). **2.** *n.* devastation, damage; (esp. in *pl.*) destructive effect *of.* [f. F. *ravage(r)* alt. f. *ravine* rush of water; see -AGE]

||**RAVC** *abbr.* Royal Army Veterinary Corps.

răve′l *n.* rail of cart, (in *pl.*) permanent or removable framework added to sides of cart to increase capacity. [var. of dial *rathe* (15th c., of unkn. orig.)]

răve′ *v.* & *n.* **1.** *v.i.* talk wildly or furiously (as) in delirium (*about, against, at, of, over, for*); **raving mad,** uncontrollably mad so as to rave. **2.** (Of sea, wind, etc.) howl, roar. **3.** speak with rapturous admiration *about, of, over*; go into raptures; **raving beauty,** notably beautiful person. **4.** *v.t.* utter with ravings (*rave one's grief* etc.); make one*self* hoarse etc. by raving. **5.** Hence ră′vER[1] *n.*, (esp. colloq.) wild pleasure-loving person, ră′vING[1] (1) *n.* (usu. in *pl.*). **6.** *n.* raving sound of wind etc.; (colloq.) highly enthusi-astic review (of film, play etc.); (sl.) infatuation; ~(-**up**), (sl.) lively party. [ME, prob. f. ONF *raver,* rel. to (M)LG *reven* be senseless, rave]

ră′vel *v.* (||-ll-) *v.* **1.** *v.t.* & *i.* entangle or become entangled or knotted, confuse, complicate, (thread etc.; (fig.) question, problem; *the ravelled skein of life*); fray out, whence ~lING[1] (2) *n.* **2.** *v.t.* ~(**out**), disentangle, unravel, distinguish the separate threads or subdivisions of. **3.** *n.* tangle, knot, complication; frayed or loose end. [perh. f. Du. *ravelen,* tangle, fray out, unweave, LG *rabbeln* to ripple flax]

ră′velin (-vl-) *n.* (Hist.) outwork of fortifications, with two faces forming salient angle. [F, f. obs. It. *ravellino,* of unkn. orig.]

rā′ven[1] *n.* & *a.* **1.** *n.* large glossy blue-black hoarse--voiced bird (*Corvus corax*) feeding chiefly on flesh, often kept tame, sometimes thought to be of evil omen. **2.** *a.* glossy black (~ **locks,** black hair). [OE *hræfn,* = OS *-hraban,* OHG (*h*)*raban,* ON *hrafn* f. Gmc *hrabhnaz,* *hrabhan*]

ră′ven[2] *v.* **1.** *v.i.* plunder, go plundering *about,* seek *after* prey or booty, prowl for prey; have ravenous appetite (*for*). **2.** *v.t.* devour (food, or abs.) voraciously. [f. OF *raviner* ravage f. Rom. *rapinare* f. L *rapina* RAPINE]

ră′venous *a.* rapacious; voracious (*ravenous hunger, eagerness,* etc.); famished, very hungry; hence ~LY[2] *adv.*, ~NESS *n.* [ME, f. OF *ravineus* (as prec.; see -OUS]

ră′vin *n.* (poet. or rhet.) robbery, rapine; (seizing and devouring of) prey (**beast of** ~, beast of prey). [ME f. OF *ravine* f. L *rapina* RAPINE]

ravi′n|e (-ē′n) *n.* deep narrow gorge, mountain cleft; hence ~ED[2] (-ē′nd) *a.* [F (as prec.)]

răviō′li *n.* small pasta cases containing meat etc. [It.]

ră′vish *v.t.* **1.** (arch.) carry off (person, thing) by force; (of death, circumstances, etc.) take from life or from sight. **2.** commit rape on (woman); hence ~ER[1] *n.* **3.** enrapture, charm, entrance, fill with delight; hence or cogn. ~ING[2] *a.*, ~MENT *n.* [ME, f. OF *ravir* f. Rom. *rapire* f. L *rapere* seize; see -ISH[2]]

raw *a.* & *n.* **1.** *a.* uncooked; (of brick) not hardened by fire; not roasted (*raw* SIENNA, *raw* UMBER); unripe; in unwrought state, not or not completely manufactured; (of silk) as reeled from cocoons; (of cloth) unfulled; (of alcoholic spirit) undiluted; (of grain) unmalted; (of statistics etc.) not analysed or corrected. **2.** crude in artistic quality, lacking finish. **3.** inexperienced, untrained, fresh to a thing, (*is a raw lad*; *raw recruits*). **4.** stripped of skin, having the flesh exposed, sensitive to touch from being so exposed; (of edge of cloth) without hem or selvage. **5.** (Of atmosphere, day, etc.) damp and chilly. **6.** ~-boned, with bones almost exposed, gaunt; *raw* DEAL²; ~'hide, (rope or whip of) untanned leather; ~ material, that out of which any process of manufacture makes the articles it produces (*the finished product of one industry is the raw material of another*; *the raw material of an army is men*). **7.** Hence ~ISH¹ 2 *a.*, ~'NESS *n.* **8.** *n.* raw place on person's or esp. horse's skin; **in the ~**, (1) in its natural state without mitigation (*life in the raw*), (2) naked; **touch** person **on the ~**, wound his feelings on the point(s) on which he is sensitive. [OE *hrēaw*, = OS, OHG (*h*)*rāo*, ON *hrár* f. Gmc *hrawaz f. IE *krowos]

ray¹ *n.* **1.** single line or narrow beam of light from small or distant source; straight line in which radiation is propagated to given point; (in *pl.*) radiation of specified type (COSMIC, GAMMA, *rays*; X-RAYS); ~ **gun**, imaginary weapon causing injury by emission of rays. **2.** (fig.) fragment or remnant or beginning of enlightening or cheering influence (*a ray of hope, truth, genius*). **3.** any of a set of straight lines passing through one point; any of a set of radiating lines or parts or things. **4.** (Bot.) marginal part of composite flower, e.g. daisy; (Zool.) one of set of bones etc. supporting fish's fin, radial division of starfish. **5.** Hence ~ED² (rād), ~'LESS, *adjs.*, ~'LET *n.* [ME, f. OF *rai* f. L RADIUS]

ray² *v.* **1.** *v.i.* (Of light etc., or fig. of thought, hope, etc.) issue, come *forth*, *off*, or *out*, in rays. **2.** *v.t.* & *i.* radiate. [f. prec., or F *rayer*, OF *raier* f. L *radiare* (RADIUS)]

ray³ *n.* large sea-fish of order Hypotremata, allied to shark, with broad flat body, used as food, esp. the skate. [ME, f. OF *raie* f. L *raia*]

ray⁴, re¹ (rā), *n.* (Mus.) second note of scale in movable-doh system; the note D in fixed-doh system. [ME *re* f. L *resonare*; see GAMUT]

ray'ah (rī'a) *n.* (Hist.) non-Muslim subject of Ottoman empire. [f. Turk. *rāya* pl. of *raiyye* f. Arab. *ra'īya* flock, subjects (*ra'ā* to pasture)]

ray'ŏn *n.* textile fibre or fabric made from cellulose. [orig. P; arbitr. f. RAY¹]

răze, răse (-z), *v.t.* **1.** completely destroy, level with the ground, (town, house, walls, etc.; usu. *raze to the ground*). **2.** erase, scratch out, (esp. fig.; *raze* person's *name from remembrance*). **3.** (arch.) wound slightly, graze. [ME *rase* in sense 3 f. OF *raser* shave close f. Rom. *rasare f. L *radere ras-* scrape]

razee' *n.*, & *v.t.* (Hist.) **1.** *n.* ship reduced in height by removal of upper deck(s). **2.** *v.t.* turn into a razee; make smaller by cutting. [f. F *rasé(e)* (fem.) p.p. of *raser* (see prec.)]

ră'zor *n.*, & *v.t.* **1.** *n.* instrument with sharp edge(s) used in cutting hair esp. from skin; SAFETY *razor*. **2.** ~-**back**, back sharp as razor's edge (~-*back whale*, rorqual); ~-**bill**, auk (*Alca torda*) with sharp-edged black-and-white bill; *razor*-BLADE; ~-**edge**, keen edge, sharp mountain ridge, critical situation, sharp line of division (*keep on the razor-edge of orthodoxy*; *on a* ~-*edge* or ~'*s edge*, in great danger; ~-**fish, -shell**, bivalve of family Solenidae with shell like handle of cutthroat razor; ~-**slasher**, criminal who attacks victims with razor. **3.** *v.t.* use razor on; shave, cut down close. [ME, f. OF *rasor* (as RAZE; see -OR)]

*răzz *n.*, & *v.t.* **1.** *n.* = RASPBERRY 2. **2.** *v.t.* tease, ridicule. [f. *razzberry*, corrupt. of RASPBERRY]

ră'zzĭa *n.* raid, plundering or slave-collecting expedition, orig. as carried out by African Muslims. [F, f. Algerian Arab. *ġazīa*, Arab. *ġazwa* (*ġazw* make raids); Arab. *ġ* pr. like F velar *r*]

ră'zzle(-dăzzle) *n.* (sl.) excitement, bustle, stir, spree (*on the razzle*); noisy advertising. [redupl. of DAZZLE]

răzz(a)mată'zz *n.* (colloq.) = prec.; old-fashioned sentimental, or insincere actions; humbug. [prob. alt. f. prec.]

Rb *symb.* rubidium.

RC *abbr.* Red Cross; reinforced concrete; Roman Catholic.

RCA *abbr.* *Radio Corporation of America; ‖Royal College of Art.

RCAF *abbr.* Royal Canadian Air Force.

‖RCM *abbr.* Royal College of Music.

RCMP *abbr.* Royal Canadian Mounted Police.

RCN *abbr.* Royal Canadian Navy; ‖Royal College of Nursing.

‖RCO *abbr.* Royal College of Organists.

‖RCOG *abbr.* Royal College of Obstetricians and Gynaecologists.

‖RCP *abbr.* Royal College of Physicians.

‖RCS *abbr.* Royal College of Science; Royal College of Surgeons; Royal Corps of Signals.

‖RCT *abbr.* Royal Corps of Transport.

‖RCVS *abbr.* Royal College of Veterinary Surgeons.

RD *abbr.* refer to drawer; ‖Royal Naval Reserve Decoration.

Rd. *abbr.* road.

‖RDC *abbr.* (Hist.) Rural District Council.

RDF *abbr.* radio direction-finder.

re¹. See RAY⁴

rē² *prep.* **1.** (Law etc.) in the matter of (as first word of headline stating matter to be dealt with). **2.** (colloq.) about, concerning. [L, abl. of *res* thing]

're *v.* (colloq., chiefly after pronouns) = *are* (see BE). [abbr.]

re- (rī *or* rē, esp. in senses 8 & 9, *or* rě) *pref.* in vbs. and vbl derivatives (sometimes *red-* before vowels: *redeem, redolent, redound*), denoting: **1.** in return, mutual(ly), (*react, rebound, remunerate, resemble, respond, revenge*). **2.** opposition (*rebel, rebuff, reluctant, repel, resist*). **3.** behind, after, (*relic, remain, repent, retain, retard*). **4.** retirement, secrecy, (*recluse, recondite, refuge, reticence*). **5.** off, away, down, (*rebuke, recede, relegate, renounce, repress, resolve*). **6.** frequentative or intensive force (*redouble, refine, regard, remark, research, resonant, revile*). **7.** negative force (*recant, reprobate, resign*).

In senses 8 & 9 (which are not always distinguishable) *re-* can be prefixed to almost any E vb. or vbl derivative; it is often hyphenated in British use in wds made for the occasion, in wds having homonyms, and before *e* (*re-contravention, re-pair* = pair again, *re-entry*).

8. once more, again, afresh, (esp. in order to alter or improve or renew): *readjust, reaffirm, reapply, reappraise, rearrange, reassert, reassess, reassign, rebaptize, rebroadcast, rebuild, recapitulate, recite, recoin, recolonize, recolour, recombine, recommence, recompose, redecorate, redesign, redistribute, redivide, redress, redye, re-edit, refashion, refectory, refurnish, regenerate, regenesis, regrind, regroup, rehear, rehouse, reimpose, reinter, relabel, remint, rename, reorder, reorganize, repack, repaper, repartition, repeat, replant, represent, repressurize, reprovision, republish, reread, rerun, resettle, reshape, resole, restart, restock, resurface, resurvey, retell, retim, returf, retype, reuse, revaccinate, revictual, revise, revisit, rewind, rework.* **9.** back, with return to previous state after lapse or cessation or occurrence of opposite state: *reabsorb, readmit, reafforest, reanimate, reappear, reappoint, reascend, reassemble, reassume, recalesce, recall, receive, recidivist, recombine, reconquer, reconvert, recross, recumbent, recur, redescend, rediscover, redissolve, reduce, re-elect, re-embark, re-emerge, re-enact, re-engage, re-enter, re-establish, re-export, reforest, refresh, refurbish, regain, regerminate, regild, regress, reheat, rehumanize, reignite, reimport, reimpose, reincorporate, reinsert, reintroduce, reinvigorate, reject, rekindle,* *relax, remilitarize, renationalize, renew, renovate, reoccupy, reopen, repatriate, repeople, replace, replenish, repolish, repopulate, repurchase, repurify, requicken, resilient, resuscitate, retort, retract, retrieve, reverse, revitalize, revive.* [f. L *re-, red-,* again, back, etc.]

||**RE** *abbr.* Royal Engineers; Royal Society of Painter-Etchers and Engravers.

Re *symb.* rhenium.

reach[1] *v.* **1.** *v.t.* & *i.* stretch out, extend, (*out* etc.; *reached out his hand, its branches; a dominion reaching from the Ebro to the Carpathians*). **2.** *v.i.* stretch out the hand etc., make reaching motion or effort (lit. or fig.; *you must reach out further; mind reaches forward to an ideal; ship reaches ahead in race*). **3.** (Naut.) sail with wind abeam or abaft the beam. **4.** *v.t.* & *i.* get as far as, attain to or to, arrive at, (specified point or object of destination, or abs.), succeed in affecting with the hand or instrument or missile or influence, (*reach* BOTTOM[1] 2; *reached land; could not reach his enemy,* esp. in fencing, boxing; *how is her conscience to be reached?*; *the steps by which you reach the entrance; your letter reached me today; every syllable reached the audience; has reached agreement with them, a decision, middle age, its seventh edition; cannot reach so high, far enough, down, up to it,* etc.; *number of applications reached 200; as far as the eye could reach,* to the greatest distance visible; *my income will not reach to it*); establish communication with (*reached him by radio*). **5.** hand, pass or take with outstretched hand, (*reached him the book; reached down his hat*). **6.** ||**~-me-down** *a.* & *n.,* (sl.) ready-made (garment). **7.** Hence ~'ABLE *a.* [f. OE *rǣcan,* MDu., MLG *reiken,* OHG *reichen* f. WG **raikjan*]

reach[2] *n.* **1.** act of reaching out. **2.** extent to which hand etc. can be reached out, influence be exerted, motion be carried out, or mental powers be used, range, scope, compass, (**within** one's ~, **above, out of, beyond,** one's ~, possible, impossible, of being grasped by stretching out the hand or (fig.) of attainment or performance; *has a wide reach; within easy reach of the airport; no help was within reach*). **3.** continuous extent, esp. part of river that can be looked along at once between two bends, or part of canal between locks. **4.** (Naut.) distance traversed in reaching [f. prec.]

reä'ct[1] *v.* **1.** *v.i.* produce reciprocal or responsive effect, act upon the agent, (*they react upon each other*); (Chem. of substance, Phys. of particle etc.) be the cause of activity or interaction with another (*nitrous oxide reacts with the metal*), whence ~ANT *a.* **2.** respond to stimulus, undergo change or show behaviour due to some influence. **3.** (Mil.) make counter-attack(s). **4.** be actuated by repulsion *against,* tend in reverse or backward direction. **5.** *v.t.* (Chem.) cause (substance etc.) to react with another. [f. RE- 1 + ACT[2], & f. med. L RE(*agere* act, do)]

rē-ä'ct[2] *v.t.* act again. [f. RE- 8 + ACT[2]]

reä'ctance *n.* (Electr.) component of impedance of alternating-current circuit etc. due to capacitance or inductance or both. [f. REACT[1] + -ANCE]

reä'ction *n.* **1.** responsive or reciprocal action (esp. *action and reaction*); (Chem. & Phys.) reacting of one substance etc. with another; CHAIN *reaction.* **2.** response of organ etc. to external stimulus; responsive feeling (*what was his reaction to this news?*); immediate or first impression. **3.** occurrence of condition after interval of opposite (e.g. glow felt after cold bath, depression after excitement). **4.** (Mil.) counter-stroke. **5.** tendency to oppose change or to return to former system esp. in politics, whence ~IST (2) *n.* **6.** propulsion by emitting jet of particles etc. in direction opposite to that of desired motion. [f. REACT[1] + -ION, & f. med. L RE(*actio* ACTION)]

reä'ctionarÿ *a.* & *n.* (Polit.) (person) tending to oppose change or seeking to return to former system. [f. prec. + -ARY[1]]

reä'ctivāte *v.t.* restore to a state of activity; hence ~A'TION *n.* [f. RE- 9 + ACTIVATE]

reä'ctive *a.* showing reaction; pertaining to reactance; hence **reäcti'vITY** *n.* [f. REACT[1] + -IVE]

reä'ctor *n.* In vbl senses; (Med.) patient etc. reacting positively to foreign substance; (**nuclear**) ~, assembly of materials in which controlled nuclear chain reaction takes place; (Electr.) component used to provide reactance, esp. inductance; apparatus for chemical reaction of substances. [f. REACT[1] + -OR]

read *v.* (**read** *pr.* rĕd) & *n.* **1.** *v.t.* interpret mentally, declare interpretation or coming development of, (*read dream, riddle, omen, men's hearts or thoughts or faces*); ~ **cards,** person's **hand,** etc., (as fortune-teller); ~ **the sky** (as astrologer or meteorologist). **2.** (be able to) convert into the intended words or meaning (written or printed or other symbols or things expressed by such symbols, or abs.; *reads or can read hieroglyphics, shorthand, Braille, Morse, music, several languages; cannot or does not read or write*); understand words intended by (person); (of computer) copy or transfer (data) from (~ **in**) or to (~ **out**) magnetic tape etc., whence ~**-in,** ~**-out,** *ns.* **3.** reproduce mentally or (often *aloud, out, off,* etc., or w. ind. obj.) vocally, while following their symbols, with eyes or fingers, the words of (author, book, letter, etc., or abs.; *read the letter over or through; was reading Plato; read it to me; have no time to read; the Bible is the most read of all books*); ~ person **a lecture** or **a lesson,** reprove him; *the Bill was* ~ **for the first** etc. **time,** allowed its first etc. READING; TAKE[1] *as read;* ~ **proof,** (Print.) check its correctness and mark changes needed; **seldom ~s French** (anything written in it); **~s well,** has good intonation etc., reads expressively. **4.** study by reading (esp. subject at university); (in *p.p.* in act. sense as *a.*) WELL-, *deeply, slightly, little,* etc. *versed* in subject by reading, acquainted with literature; ~ **up,** make special study of (subject). **5.** find (thing) recorded, find statement, in print etc. (*revenge, we read, is a kind of wild justice; I have read somewhere that . . .; have read of it*). **6.** interpret (statement, action) in certain sense (*may be read several ways; my silence is not to be read as consent*). **7.** assume to be intended in or deducible from writer's words, find implications, (*you read too much into the text*); ~ **between the lines,** search for or discover hidden meaning in document, speech, etc. **8.** (Of editor or text) give as the word(s) probably used or intended by author (*Bentley reads 'peraeque'*); (in correcting statements) *for 'white'* read *'black',* 'black' should replace 'white'. **9.** bring into specified state by reading (*read myself to sleep*); ||~ one**self in,** (of incumbent) enter upon office by public reading of the 39 Articles etc.; *~ **out,** expel (from political party etc.) (as if) by reading form of dismissal. **10.** (Of recording instrument) present (figure etc.) to person reading it (*thermometer reads 20°*). **11.** *v.i.* carry out course of study by reading (*is reading for the Bar; shall not read for honours*). **12.** convey meaning when read (*name reads from left to right*); sound or affect hearer or reader *well, ill,* etc., when read (*play reads better than it acts; reads like a threat, translation,* etc.). **13.** *n.* time spent in reading (*have a quiet read*); (colloq.) book etc. as regards readability (*is a good read*). [OE *rǣdan* advise, consider, discern, = OS *rādan,* OHG *rātan,* ON *rátha,* Goth. *-rēdan* f. Gmc **rēdhan*]

rea'd|able *a.* capable of being read with pleasure or interest; legible; hence ~ABI'LITY, ~**able**NESS (-beln-), *ns.,* ~**ably** *adv.* [f. prec. + -ABLE]

rĕaddrĕ'ss *v.t.* change address of (letter). [f. RE- 8 + ADDRESS[1]]

rea'der *n.* In vbl senses; person employed by publisher to read and report on offered MSS; printer's proof-corrector; person appointed to read aloud, esp. parts of service in church (LAY[2] *reader*); ||higher grade of lecturer in some universities etc. (*reader in Roman law*); book of selections for use by students of a language etc.; device for producing image that can be read from microfilm etc.; hence ~SHIP *n.,* esp. (number of) readers of newspaper etc. [OE (as READ, -ER[1])]

For other words in *re-* **see** RE-.

rea′dil̆y (rĕ′-) *adv.* without showing reluctance, willingly; without difficulty (*the facts may be readily ascertained*). [ME, f. READY + -LY²]

rea′diness (rĕ′-) *n.* prompt compliance, willingness; facility, prompt resourcefulness, quickness in argument or action; ready or prepared state (*all is in readiness*). [ME, f. READY + -NESS]

rea′ding *n.* In vbl senses; literary knowledge (*a man of vast reading*); **first, second, third,** ∼, successive occasions on which Bill must have been presented for acceptance to legislature before it becomes law (*first* ∼, permitting introduction, *second,* ‖approving general principle, *general debate on committee report, *third,* ‖accepting details as amended in committee, *prior to final vote); entertainment at which something is read to audience (*poetry reading*); word(s) read or given by an editor or found in text of a passage (*the right, true, best, MS,* etc., *reading*); (specified quality of) matter to be read (*is good, dull, reading; there is plenty of reading in it*); figure etc. shown by recording instrument (*40° difference between day and night readings*); interpretation, view taken, rendering, (*what is your reading of the facts?; his reading of Iago was generally condemned*); ∼ **age** of child, age of average child with same reading ability; ∼**-desk** (for supporting book etc., lectern); **-lamp, -light,** (arranged to give light for reading by); ∼ **matter,** books etc. as providing something to read; ∼**-room** (in club, library, etc., for persons wishing to read). [OE (as READ, -ING¹)]

rĕadjŭ′st *v.t.,* **rĕadjŭ′st**MENT *n.* See RE- 8.

rea′dy̆ (rĕ′-) *a., adv., n.,* & *v.t.* **1.** *a.* with preparations complete (*dinner is ready*); in fit state (*are ready to march*); with resolution nerved (*am ready to risk my life*); willing, apt, inclined, (*is too ready to suspect; was ready to swear with rage*); about *to* (*a bud just ready to burst*); prompt, quick, facile, (*is very ready with excuses; has a ready pen, wit*); provided beforehand; within reach, easily secured, (*a ready source of revenue*); fit for immediate use (*found an instrument ready to hand*); unreluctant (*gave a ready consent; found ready acceptance*); easy (*its ready solubility in water; the readiest way to do it*); **make** ∼, prepare (*they made ready for the attempt or to fight, or made everything ready*); ∼ **money,** (1) actual coin or notes, (2) payment on the spot; ∼ **reckoner,** book or table of results of arithmetical computations of kind commonly wanted in business etc.; ∼, **steady, go!** (formula for starting race). **2.** *adv.* (usu. with *p.p.* & often hyphened). beforehand, so as not to require doing when the time comes, (*please pack everything ready; boxes are ready packed or packed ready*). **3.** ∼**-made,** ∼**-to-wear,** (of clothes) made in standard shapes and sizes, not to customer's individual measure, (fig.) unoriginal, commonplace, available without special effort; ∼**-to-eat,** (of food) not needing to be cooked. **4.** *n.* position in which rifle is held before the PRESENT⁴ (*come to the ready*); (sl.) ready money (*planked down the ready*); **at the** ∼, ready for action. **5.** *v.t.* make ready, prepare. [ME *rædi*(*g*), *re*(*a*)*di,* f. OE *rǣde,* OHG *reiti,* ON *reithr,* Goth. *garaiths* f. Gmc **raidh-* put in order, prepare, + -Y²]

rĕaffi̅r′m *v.t.,* **rĕaffirm**A′TION *n.* See RE- 8.

rĕaffo̅′rest *v.t.,* **rĕafforest**A′TION *n.* See RE- 9.

rĕa′gency̆ *n.* reactive power or operation. [f. RE- 1 + AGENCY; cf. REACT¹]

rĕa′gent *n.* (Chem.) substance used to cause reaction, esp. to detect another substance; reactive substance or force. [f. RE- 1 + AGENT; cf. REACT¹]

real¹ (rĕ′al, rā′-, rääh′l) *n.* former silver coin and money of account in Spain and Spanish-speaking countries. [Sp., n. use of *real a.* (as ROYAL)]

rĕ′al² *a.* & *adv.* **1.** *a.* actually existing as a thing or occurring in fact, objective, genuine, rightly so called, natural, sincere, not merely apparent or nominal or supposed or pretended or artificial or hypocritical or affected; ∼ **life,** that lived by actual people, opp. fiction, drama, etc.; **a** ∼ **man** etc. (worthy of the name); ∼ **money,** current coin or notes, cash; **the** ∼

presence (of Christ's body and blood in Eucharist); **the** ∼ **thing,** not a makeshift or inferior article; *real* TENNIS; ∼ **time,** actual time in process analysed by computer; **for** ∼, (sl.) genuine(ly). **2.** (Law). consisting of or relating to immovable property such as land or houses (esp. *real property* or *estate*; cf. PERSONAL). **3.** (Philos.) having an absolute and necessary and not merely contingent existence. **4.** (Econ.) valued by purchasing power, adjusted for changes in value of money, (*real income, values, wages*). **5.** (Math., of quantity) not having any IMAGINARY part; (Opt., of image etc.) such that light actually passes through it. **6.** *adv.* (Sc. & US colloq.) really, very. [AF, = OF *reel,* & f. LL *realis* (*res* thing; see -AL)]

rĕä′lgar *n.* arsenic sulphide mineral used as pigment and in fireworks. [ME f. med. L, f. Arab. *rahj al-gār* dust of the cave]

rĕali̅′gn (-ī′n) *v.t.* put into new or former alignment; (fig.) regroup (in politics etc.); hence ∼MENT *n.* [f. RE- 8, 9 + ALIGN]

rĕ′allism *n.* **1.** scholastic doctrine that universals or general ideas have objective existence (cf. *nominalism, conceptualism*). **2.** belief that matter as object of perception has real existence (cf. *idealism*). **3.** practice of regarding things in their true nature and dealing with them as they are, freedom from prejudice and convention, practical views and policy (cf. *idealism*). **4.** fidelity of representation, truth to nature, insistence upon details; showing of life etc. as it is without glossing over what is ugly or painful (cf. *idealism*). **5.** So ∼IST (2) *n.,* ∼i̅′stic *a.* [f. REAL² + -ISM]

rĕä′lity̆ *n.* property of being real, resemblance to original (*reproduced with startling reality*); real existence, what is real, what underlies appearances, (**in** ∼, in fact, opp. *in words, in appearance,* etc.); existent thing (*did not grasp the realities of the situation*); real nature *of.* [f. med. L *realitas,* or F *réalité* (as REAL²; see -ITY)]

rĕ′ali̅z̆|e, -i̅s|e (-ī̆z), *v.t.* **1.** (usu. in *pass.*) convert (hope, plan, etc.) into fact; (Mus.) reconstruct (part) in full from figured bass. **2.** give apparent reality to, make realistic, present as real, (*these details help to realize the scene*). **3.** conceive as real, apprehend clearly or in detail (fact, *that, how,* etc.). **4.** convert (securities, property, or abs.) into money; amass (fortune, specified profit); fetch as price. **5.** Hence ∼ABLE *a.,* ∼A′TION *n.* [f. REAL² + -IZE, after F *réaliser*]

rĕ′ally̆ *adv.* ∼ (**and truly**), in fact, in reality; positively, indeed, I assure you, I mean what I say, I protest; **not** ∼, (euphem.) no, not in fact; ∼**!** (expr. surprise or censure); ∼**?,** do you mean it?, is that so?. [ME, f. REAL² + -LY²]

realm (rĕlm) *n.* **1.** (rhet. or Law). kingdom (*coin, peer, the laws, of the realm*). **2.** sphere, province, domain, (*the realm(s) of fancy, poetry,* etc.). [ME f. OF *realme, reaume,* f. L REGIMEN *regiminis*; infl. by OF *reiel* ROYAL]

realpolitik (räählpŏlite̅′k) *n.* politics based on realities and material needs, rather than on morals or ideals. [G]

*re̅′altor *n.* real-estate agent (prop. *R*∼, person in real-estate business who is a member of the National Association of Realtors). [f. foll. + -OR]

rĕ′alty̆ *n.* real estate (opp. *personalty*). [f. REAL² + -TY¹]

ream¹ *n.* twenty quires or 500 (formerly 480) sheets of paper (or larger number, to allow for waste). **2.** (usu. in *pl.*) large quantity (*wrote reams and reams of verse*). [ME *rēm, ri̅m,* f. OF *raime,* ult. f. Arab. *rizma* bundle]

ream² *v.t.* **1.** widen (hole in metal etc.) with borer; *squeeze juice from (fruit); hence ∼ER (2) *n.* **2.** turn over edge of (cartridge-case etc.) (Naut.) open (seam) for caulking. [19th c., of uncert. orig.]

rĕä′nimate *v.t.,* **rĕanima**′TION *n.* See RE- 9.

reap *v.t.* **1.** cut (grain or similar crop, or abs.) with sickle in harvest; gather in thus or with machine as harvest; (fig.) receive as consequence of one's own or others' actions (*reap as one has sown; sow wind and reap*

WHIRL*wind*; *reap the fruits of* one's *forethought*); ~ **where one has not sown**, profit by others' toil. **2.** harvest crop of (field etc.). **3.** ~**'ing-hook**, sickle; ~**'ing-machine** (for cutting grain and often binding sheaves without manual labour). **4.** hence ~*ER*[1] (1, 2) *n.* (fig. of death personified). [OE *ripan, reopan*, *riopan, *repan, of unkn. orig.]

rĕappear' *v.i.*, **rĕappear'**ANCE *n.*, see RE- 9; **rĕapplý'** *v.t.* & *i.*, see RE- 8; **rĕappoi'nt** *v.t.*, **rĕappoi'nt**MENT *n.*, see RE- 9; **rĕapprai'se** (-z) *v.t.*, **rĕapprai'**SAL (-z-) *n.*, see RE- 8.

rear[1] *n.* **1.** hindmost part of army or fleet (**hang on the ~ of**, follow with view to attacking); back of, space behind, position at back of, army or camp or person (**bring up the ~**, come last; **in the ~**, behind; **take in the ~**, attack from behind); back part of anything (**at the ~ of**, behind); (colloq.) buttocks; ‖(colloq.) water-closet or latrine. **2.** *a.* hinder, back-; so ~'MOST *a.* **3.** ~**-admiral**, flag-officer below vice-admiral; ~**-commodore**, yacht-club officer below vice-commodore; ~'**guard** [f. OF *rereguarde* f. L RETRO-; cf. GUARD[1]], body of troops detached to protect rear esp. in retreats (~*guard action*, engagement between rearguard and enemy, lit. or fig.); ~**-lamp**, ~**-light**, (usu. red, at rear of motor vehicle or bicycle); *rear* VASSAL; ~**-view mirror** (enabling driver of vehicle to see traffic etc. behind); ~'**ward** *n.* [f. AF *rerewarde* = rearguard], rear (esp. in prep. phrs.; *to rearward of, in the rearward*); ~'WARD *a.* & *adv.*, ~'WARDS *adv.*, towards the rear. [prob. f. (*in the*) *rearward* or rearguard (see above); cf. VAN[2]]

rear[2] *v.* **1.** *v.t.* (rhet.) raise, set upright, build, hold upwards, (*rear a monument, cathedral*, etc.; *reared his mighty stature; rear* one's *head,* one's *voice*). **2.** bring up, breed, foster, educate, cultivate, (cattle, game, children, crops, etc.). **3.** *v.i.* (Of horse etc.) raise itself on hind legs; (rhet.) extend to great height. **4.** Hence ~'ER[1] *n.* [OE *rǣran*, = OE *reisa*, Goth. *-raisjan* f. Gmc *raizjan causative of *reisan raise]

rear'-arch *n.* inner arch of window or door opening different in size or shape from the outer. [f. REAR[1] + ARCH[1]]

rĕar'm *v.t.* provide (troops, one*self*, or abs.) with weapons again after disarming, or with weapons of more modern type; restore military strength of (country); so **rĕar'mament** *n.* [f. RE- 8 + ARM[3]]

rĕarra'nge (-nj) *v.t.*, **rĕarra'nge**MENT (-njm-) *n.* See RE- 8.

rear'-vault (-awlt, -ōlt) *n.* vault between arched window or door head and arch in inner face of wall. [f. REAR[1] + VAULT[1]]

rĕasce'nd *v.i.* & *t.* See RE- 9.

rea'son[1] (-z-) *n.* **1.** (fact adduced or serving as) motive, cause, or justification, (*give reasons for; prove with reasons; the reason of* or *for his conduct; failed by reason of bad management; I saw reason to be suspicious; for no other reason than that I forgot, but this; there is no reason to suppose*); ~ **of State**, political justification esp. for immoral proceeding; **with ~**, not unjustifiably. **2.** (Logic). premiss of syllogism, esp. minor premiss when given after conclusion. **3.** intellectual faculty characteristic esp. of human beings by which conclusions are drawn from premisses (*whether dogs have reason is really a question of definition; there can be no opposition between reason and common sense*). **4.** intellect personified (*God and Reason are identical*); (as transl. of G *vernunft* in Kant) faculty transcending the understanding (G *verstand*) and providing a priori principles, intuition. **5.** sanity (*has lost his,* is restored to, *reason*). **6.** sense, sensible conduct, what is right or practical or practicable, moderation; **Age of R~**, 18th c. in England and France; **bring to ~**, induce to cease vain resistance; **in ~**, within the bounds of moderation; *without* RHYME[1] *or reason*; **it stands to ~**, it can be logically proved that, it cannot be denied without paradox, it would be generally admitted;

listen to ~, allow oneself to be persuaded; **see ~**, (1) regard it as justifiable (*to do*, etc.), (2) be brought to reason; **within ~**, = *in reason*. **7.** Hence ~LESS *a.* [ME, f. OF *reisun, res(o)un* f. Rom. *ratione f. L *ratio, -onis (rēri rat-* consider; see -ION)]

rea'son[2] (-z-) *v.* **1.** *v.i.* form or try to reach conclusions by connected thought silent or expressed (*from* premisses; *about*, (arch.) *of* or *upon,* subject); hence ~ER[1], ~ING[1], *ns.* **2.** use reasoning *with* person by way of persuasion. **3.** *v.t.* discuss *what, whether, why,* etc.; conclude, assume as step in reasoning, say by way of reasoning, *that.* **4.** express in logical form (*a reasoned exposition*), embody reasons in (amendment etc.). **5.** persuade or bring by reasoning *out of* or *into* (tried to *reason him out of his fears; reasoned himself into perplexity*). **6.** think *out* (consequences etc.). **7.** Hence ~ING[1] (1) *n.* [ME, = question, converse, f. OF *raisoner* (as prec.)]

rea'sonab|le (-z-) *a.* **1.** having sound judgement, sensible, moderate, not expecting too much, ready to listen to reason. **2.** in accordance with reason, not absurd; within the limits of reason, not greatly less or more than might be expected; inexpensive, not extortionate; tolerable, fair. **3.** (arch.) endowed with faculty of reason. **4.** Hence ~leNESS (-bln-) *n.*, ~LY[2] *adv.* [ME, f. OF *raisonable* (as REASON[1]; see -ABLE), after L *rationabilis*]

rĕasse'mble *v.i.* & *t.*, **rĕasse'mbly**[1] *n.*, see RE- 9; **rĕasser't** *v.t.*, **rĕasser'tion** *n.*, **rĕasse'ss** *v.t.*, (-i'n) see RE- 8, **rĕassu'me** *v.t.*, **rĕassu'mp**TION *n.*, see RE- 9.

rĕassur'|e (-ashoor') *v.t.* **1.** restore confidence to, dispel apprehensions of; confirm in opinion or impression; hence ~INGLY *adv.* **2.** reinsure. **3.** So ~ANCE *n.* [f. RE- 9 & 8 + ASSURE]

Réaumur (rā'ōmūr) *a.* pertaining to the ~ **scale** of temperature, on which water freezes at 0° and boils at 80° under standard conditions. [f. R. de ~, Fr. physicist d. 1757]

‖**reave** (rēft). (arch. or poet.) **1.** *v.t.* (esp. in *p.p.*) forcibly deprive *of.* **2.** take by force, carry off, (*away, from*). **3.** *v.i.* = REIVE. [OE *rēafian*, = OS *rōbon*, OHG *roubōn*, Goth. *-raubōn* f. Gmc *raubhōjan (**raubh-*; cf. ROB)]

rĕbapti'ze *v.t.* See RE- 8.

rĕbar'bative *a.* (literary). repellant, unattractive. [f. F *rébarbatif -ive* (*barbe* beard)]

rĕba'te[1] *v.t.* (arch.) diminish, reduce force or effect of; blunt, dull. [ME, f. OF *rabattre* (as RE- 5, ABATE)]

rĕbate[2] (rē'bāt, rĭba't) *n.* deduction from sum to be paid, discount; partial refund. [f. prec.]

rebate[3] (ră'bĭt) *n.*, & *v.t.* = RABBET. [respelling of RABBET, after prec.]

rĕ'bĕc, rĕ'bĕck, *n.* medieval usu. three-stringed instrument played with bow. [f. F *rebec* var. of OF *rebebe, rubebe* f. Arab. *rabāb*]

rĕ'bel[1] *n.* & *a.* **1.** *n.* person who rises in arms against, resists, or refuses allegiance to, the established government; person or thing that resists authority or control. **2.** *attrib. a.* rebellious; of rebels; in rebellion. [ME, f. OF *rebelle* f. L *rebellis* (as RE- 2, *bellum* war); orig. of renewed warfare by conquered]

rĕbě'l[2] *v.i.* (-ll-). act as rebel (*against*); feel or manifest repugnance (*against* custom etc.). [ME, f. OF *rebeller* f. L RE(*bellare* make war) revolt]

rĕbě'llion (-lyon) *n.* organized armed resistance to established government (**the Great R~**, period of English history 1642-51); open resistance to any authority. [ME f. OF, f. L *rebellio -onis* (as REBEL[1]; see -ION)]

rĕbě'llious (-lyus) *a.* in rebellion; disposed to rebel, insubordinate, defying lawful authority; (of disease) difficult to treat; (of thing) unmanageable, refractory; hence ~LY[2] *adv.*, ~NESS *n.* [ME, f. prec. + -OUS or f. earlier *rebellous* + -IOUS]

rĕbě'llow (-ō) *v.i.* & *t.* (poet.) re-echo loudly. [RE- 6, after L RE(*boare* bellow)]

rē′bid v. (-dd-; re′bid) & n. (Cards). **1.** v.i. bid after having previously bid. **2.** v.t. bid (suit) again at higher level. **3.** n. act of rebidding; bid thus made. [f. RE- 8+BID[1,2]]

rēbī′nd v.t. (re-bou′nd). bind (esp. book) again. [f. RE- 9+BIND[1]]

rēbī′rth n. fresh incarnation; spiritual enlightenment; revival (the rebirth of learning); so **rēBOR′N** a. [f. RE- 8+BIRTH]

rē′bŏant a. (poet.) rebellowing, resounding, re--echoing. [f. L reboare rebellow; see -ANT]

rēbŏ′re v.t. make new boring in, esp. widen bore of (cylinder in internal-combustion engine). [f. RE- 8+BORE[1]]

rēbŏ′rn. See REBIRTH.

rēbou′nd[1] v.i. spring back after impact; have reactive effect, recoil upon agent, (their evil example will rebound upon themselves). [ME, f. OF rebonder, rebondir (as RE-1, BOUND[3])]

rē′bound[2] n. act of rebounding, recoil; reaction after emotion (**take** person **on** or **at the ∼**, utilize such reaction to persuade him to contrary of previously intended action etc.); (Basketball, Football, etc.) (getting possession of) ball rebounding from wall, goal-post, etc. [f. prec. or F rebond]

rē-bou′nd[3]. See REBIND.

rēbroa′dcast (-aw′dkah-) v.t., & n. See RE-8.

rēbŭ′ff n., & v.t. **1.** n. rejection of one who makes advances, proffers help or sympathy, shows interest or curiosity, makes request, etc.; repulse, snub. **2.** v.t. give rebuff to. [f. obs. F rebuffe(r) f. It. ribuffo, ribuffare, rabbuffo, rabbuffare, (as RE-8, buffo puff)]

rēbui′ld (-bi′-) v.t. See RE-8.

rēbŭ′ke v.t., & n. **1.** v.t. subject to protest or censure (for fault etc.); reprove. **2.** n. rebuking or being rebuked; reproof. [ME, f. AF & ONF re(buker = OF buchier beat, orig. cut down wood f. busche log; see RE-5)]

rē′bus n. enigmatic representation of name, word, etc., by pictures etc. suggesting its syllables; (Her.) device suggesting name of its bearer. [f. F rébus f. L rebus, abl. pl. of res thing, in phr. de rebus quae geruntur concerning the things that are taking place, title in 16th-c. Picardy of satirical pieces containing such riddles]

rēbū′t v.t. (-tt-). force or turn back, check; refute, disprove, (evidence, charge), whence ∼tABLE a., ∼tAL 2, ∼MENT, ns. [ME, f. AF rebuter, OF rebo(u)ter (as RE-9, BUTT[4])]

rēbŭ′tter n. refutation; (Law) defendant's reply to plaintiff's surrejoinder. [f. AF rebuter (as prec.; see -ER[4])]

rēcă′lcĭtr|ant a. & n. (person) objecting to restraint or obstinately disobedient; hence ∼ANCE n. [f. L re(calcitrare kick out with heels f. calx calcis heel); see RE-2, -ANT]

rēcalÉ′sce v.i. grow hot again (esp. of iron allowed to cool from white heat, whose temperature rises at certain point for short time); hence ∼E′SCENCE n. [f. L re(calescere grow hot); see RE-9, -ESCE]

rēca′ll[1] (-aw′l) v.t. summon to return from a place or from different occupation, inattention, digression, etc.; cancel or suspend appointment of (official sent to distance, esp. overseas); bring back to or to memory, serve as reminder of; recollect, remember; revive, resuscitate; revoke, annul, (action, decision), take back (gift); hence ∼ABLE a. [f. RE-9+CALL[1]]

rēca′ll[2] (-aw′l) n. summons to come back; cancelling or suspension of appointment abroad; signal to ship etc. to return to base; possibility of recalling esp. in sense of annulling (beyond or past recall); act of remembering; ability to remember; TOTAL recall. [f. RE-9+CALL[2], after prec.]

rēcă′nt v. **1.** v.t. withdraw and renounce (opinion, statement, etc.) as erroneous or heretical. **2.** v.i. disavow former opinion, esp. with public confession of error. **3.** Hence **rēcănta′TION** n. [f. L re(cantare sing, CHANT) revoke; see RE-7]

*rēcă′p v.t. (-pp-). put another cap on; partially replace worn tread of (tyre). [f. RE-8+CAP[2]]

rē′căp[2] v.t. (-pp-), & n. (colloq.) **1.** v.t. = foll. **2.** n. recapitulation. [abbr.]

rēcapi′tŭl|āte v.t. go over main points or headings of, summarize; go briefly through again; hence ∼atIVE, ∼atORY, adjs. [f. L re(capitulare f. capitulum CHAPTER); see RE-8, -ATE[3]]

rēcapitūlā′tion n. recapitulating; (Biol.) re-appearance in embryos of successive type-forms in line of development; (Mus.) passage repeating exposition. [ME f. OF, or f. LL recapitulatio (as prec.; see -ATION)]

rēcă′pture v. & n. **1.** v.t. & i. capture (what has been lost); (Chess) capture a man that has just captured; re-experience (past emotion etc.). **2.** n. act of re-capturing. [f. RE-9+CAPTURE]

rēca′st[1] (-kah′-) v.t. (**reca′st**). put into new form; improve arrangement of; change cast of (play etc.). [f. RE-8+CAST[1]]

rēca′st[2] (-kah′-) n. recasting; recast form. [f. RE-8+CAST[2]]

rē′ccé (rē′kĭ) n. & v. (sl.) **1.** n. reconnaissance. **2.** v.t. & i. reconnoitre. [abbr.]

recd. abbr. received.

rēcē′de[1] v.i. go or shrink back or farther off; be left at increasing distance by observer's motion; slope backwards; withdraw (from engagement, opinion, etc.), decline in character or value. [ME, f. L re(cedere cessgo); see RE-5]

rē-cē′de[2] v.t. cede back to former owner. [f. RE-9+CEDE]

rēcei′pt (-sē′t) n., & v.t. **1.** n. fact or action of receiving or being received into person's hands or possession (goods will be sent on receipt of remittance; am in receipt of your order; entrusted with the receipt of subscriptions); written acknowledgement of this, esp. of payment of sum due. **2.** (usu. in pl.) amount of money etc. received. **3.** (arch.) recipe. **4.** (arch.) place where money is officially received, esp. ∼ of custom, custom-house. **5.** v.t. place written receipt on (bill). [ME receit(e) f. AF & ONF receite, OF reçoite, recete f. med. L recepta fem. p.p. (as n.) of L recipere RECEIVE; -p- inserted after L]

rēcei′v|e (-sē′v) v.t. **1.** accept delivery of, take (proffered thing) into one's hands or possession; accept (stolen goods though knowing of the theft, or abs.); consent to hear (confession, oath) or consider (petition); ∼e **the sacraments**, eat and drink Eucharistic bread and wine; ∼ing-order (see foll.). **2.** urge up against, stand force or weight of, encounter with opposition, (received his body in their hands; arch receives weight of roof; received the sword-point with his shield); (Tennis) be required to play against (service, or abs.). **3.** admit, consent or prove able to hold, provide accommodation for, submit to, serve as receptacle of, (had to receive the visits, attentions, etc., of); admit to membership of church etc.; be marked (lit. or fig.) more or less permanently with (impression etc.); convert (broadcast signals) into sound or picture. **4.** entertain (person as guest, company at formal reception or abs.); greet, welcome, esp. in specified manner, (you stay here and receive him; how did she receive his offer?; was received with cries of 'Traitor'; news was received with horror). **5.** (esp. in p.p.) give credit to, accept as authoritative or true, (an axiom universally received); (in p.p.) generally accepted thus (received opinions); ∼ed **pronunciation**, ***R∼d Standard**, form of English speech used, with local variations, by majority of educated English-speaking people. **6.** acquire, get, be given, be provided with, have sent to or conferred or inflicted on one, (have not yet received my fee; receive a letter, news, a report; received the name of John; pleasant to receive sympathy; deserves more attention than it receives; receive orders to march; received many insults, a thrust, a broken jaw, the contents of his pistol); (abs.) partake of; be at or on the ∼ing end, (colloq.)

bear the brunt of something unpleasant. **7.** Hence ∼ABLE *a.* [ME, f. OF *receivre, reçoivre* f. L *re(cipere cept-* = *capere* take) recover; see RE- 9]

recei′ver (-sē′v-) *n.* In vbl senses; (**official**) ∼, person appointed by court's **receiving-order** to administer property of bankrupt or insane person or property under litigation, whence ∼SHIP *n.* (**in** ∼**ship,** having one's property thus administered); person who receives stolen goods; receptacle etc. for receiving something in machine or instrument, esp. part of telephone that contains ear-piece; vessel for collecting products of distillation; radio or television receiving apparatus. [ME, f. AF **receivere, -our* f. OF *recevere, -our,* & f. prec. + -ER¹]

recē′nsion (-shon) *n.* revision of text; revised text. [f. L *recensio* f. *re(censēre* review) revise; see RE- 8, -ION]

rē′cent *a.* not long past, that happened or began to exist or existed lately; not long established, lately begun, modern; (Geol., *R*∼) of the latter part of the Quaternary period or system, including the present time; hence **rē′cency** *n.*, ∼LY² *adv.,* ∼NESS *n.* [f. L *recens recentis* or F *récent*]

recē′ptacle *n.* containing vessel, place, or space; (Bot.) common base of floral organs, axis of cluster. [ME, f. OF, or f. L *receptaculum* (as foll.)]

recē′ption *n.* **1.** receiving or being received, esp. of person into a place or company (*the rooms were prepared for his reception; was honoured by reception into the Academy*); ‖place where guests register on arriving at hotel etc., or where firm's clients etc. are welcomed; ‖∼ **order** (authorizing entry of patient into mental hospital). **2.** formal or ceremonious welcome (*the reception of the delegates is arranged for Monday next*); occasion of receiving guests, assembly held for this purpose, (*after the review, conference, wedding, there will be a reception*); ∼**-room** (available or suitable for receiving company or visitors). **3.** receiving of ideas or impressions into the mind. **4.** welcome or greeting of specified kind, demonstration of feeling towards person or project; **warm** ∼, hostile response or enthusiastic welcome. **5.** receiving of broadcast signals; efficiency with which these are received. **6.** Hence ∼IST (3) *n.,* person employed by hotel, photographer, doctor, dentist, etc., to receive clients. [ME f. OF, or f. L *receptio* (as RECEIVE; see -ION)]

recē′ptive *a.* able or quick to receive impressions or ideas (*a mind more receptive than retentive or creative*); concerned with receiving stimuli etc.; hence ∼LY² (-vlī) *adv.,* ∼NESS (-vn-), **recepti′vity,** *ns.* [f. F *réceptif -ive* or f. med. L *receptivus* (as prec.; see -IVE)]

recē′ptor *n.* & *a.* (Biol.) (organ) able to respond to light, heat, drug, etc., and transmit signal to sensory nerve. [f. OF *receptour* or f. L *receptor* (as prec.; see -OR)]

recē′ss *n.* & *v.* **1.** *n.* temporary cessation from work, vacation, esp. of Parliament or *lawcourt or *during school day; (arch.) receding of water, land, glacier, etc., from previous limit, amount by which it recedes. **2.** remote or secret place (*in the inmost recesses of the Alps, of the heart*); receding part of mountain chain etc., space set back from line of wall; (Anat.) fold or indentation in organ. **3.** *v.t.* place in a recess, set back; provide with recess(es); *order temporary cessation from work of (court etc.). **4.** *v.i.* *take recess, adjourn. [f. L *recessus* (as RECEDE¹)]

recē′ssion (-shon) *n.* receding or withdrawal from a place or point; receding part of object, recess; temporary decline in economic activity or prosperity; hence ∼ARY¹ *a.* [f. L *recessio* (as prec.; see -ION)]

recē′ssional (-sho-) *a.* & *n.* ∼(**hymn**), hymn sung while clergy and choir withdraw after service. [f. prec. + -AL]

recē′ssive *a.* tending to recede; (Phonet., of accent) falling near beginning of word; (Genetics, of characteristic) found in second and later generations of hybrids, but not in first generation because there masked by dominant characteristic inherited from one parent; hence ∼LY² (-vlī) *adv.* [f. RECESS after *excessive*]

Rě′chabīte (-k-) *n.* total abstainer, esp. member of a benefit society (*Independent Order of Rechabites*). [f. eccl. L *Rechabita* f. Heb. *rēkābîm* pl. (Jer. 35:6); see -ITE¹ (1)]

rē′charge¹ *n.* renewed charge; material etc. used for this. [f. RE- 9 + CHARGE¹]

rechar′ge² *v.t.* charge again; reload; ∼ one's **batteries,** (fig.) have period of rest and recuperation. [f. RE- 9 + CHARGE²]

réchauffé (rishō′fā) *n.* warmed-up dish; rehash. [F, p.p. of *réchauffer* (as RE-, CHAFE)]

recher′ché (reshār′shā) *a.* devised or got with care or difficulty, (excessively) far-fetched or thought out. [F, p.p. of *rechercher* (as RE-, *chercher* seek)]

rēchri′sten (-krī′sen) *v.t.* christen again; (fig.) give new name to. [f. RE- 8 + CHRISTEN]

recī′div|ist *n.* one who relapses into crime; so ∼ISM (2) *n.* [f. F *récidiviste* f. *récidiver* f. med. L *recidivare* f. L *recidivus* f. RE(*cidere* = *cadere* fall); see RE- 9, -IVE, -IST]

rē′cipē *n.* medical prescription, remedy prepared from it; statement of ingredients and procedure for preparing dish etc. in cookery; expedient, device for effecting something. [2nd sing. imper. (as used in prescriptions) of L *recipere* take, RECEIVE]

recī′pi|ent *a.* & *n.* **1.** *a.* receiving; receptive; hence ∼ENCY. **2.** *n.* person who receives something. [f. F *récipient* f. It. *recipiente* or l. *recipiens* (*recipere* RECEIVE; see -ENT)]

reci′procal *a.* & *n.* **1.** in return (*I helped him, and had reciprocal help from him*); mutual (*reciprocal love, protection, injuries*); inversely correspondent, complementary, (*I took the chamois for a man, and it made the reciprocal mistake*); (Gram.) expressing mutual action or relation ('*each other*' *is a reciprocal pronoun*); hence ∼LY² *adv.* **2.** *n.* (Math.) function or expression so related to another that their product is unity (*1/5 is the reciprocal of 5*). [f. L *reciprocus* (ult. f. *re-* back, *pro* forward) + -AL]

reci′proc|āte *v.t.* & *i.* **1.** (Mech.) go with alternate backward and forward motion (∼**ating engine** etc., one in which work is done by part that moves thus); give such motion to. **2.** give and receive mutually, interchange, (influence etc.); return, requite, (affection etc.), make a return (*with* thing given in return). **3.** So ∼A′TION *n.* [f. L *reciprocare* (as prec.) + -ATE³]

reciprō′city *n.* reciprocal condition, mutual action; principle or practice of give-and-take, esp. interchange of privileges between States, clubs, etc., as basis of commercial etc. relations. [f. F *réciprocité* (*réciproque* f. L *reciprocus;* see RECIPROCATE, ITY)]

reci′tal *n.* **1.** detailed account of a number of connected things or facts, relation *of* the facts of an incident etc., a narrative. **2.** part of document stating facts. **3.** act of reciting; performance of programme by one musician with or without accompanist (*vocal, piano,* etc., *recital*) or by small group of musicians or by solo dancer; hence ∼IST (1) *n.* [f. RECITE + -AL]

recitati′ve (-ē′v) *n.* musical declamation of kind usual in narrative and dialogue parts of opera and oratorio; words or part given in recitative. [f. It. *recitativo* (as foll.; see -IVE)]

recī′te *v.t.* & *i.* repeat aloud or declaim (poem, passage) from memory esp. before audience, give recitation (∼**reciting-note,** that held for indefinite number of syllables in chanting); (Law) rehearse (facts) in document; mention in order, enumerate; so **recitA′TION, recī′tER¹,** *ns.* [ME, f. OF *reciter* or f. L *re(citare* CITE); see RE- 8]

reck *v.* (rhet. or poet., in neg. & interrog. sents. only). **1.** *v.i.* ∼ **of,** pay heed to, take account of, care about. **2.** care, be troubled, concern oneself, (*if, though, that, how, whether,* etc., or abs.; or impers. w. ind. obj. and same construction following, *what recks it him that . . .?*); (impers.) be of importance (*it recks little*). **3.** *v.t.* pay heed to, care about, (*recks not his own rede*). [OE *reccan,* of uncert. orig., & **rēcan,* = OS *rōkjan,* OHG *ruohhen,* ON *rœkja* f. Gmc *rōkjan]

rĕ′cklèss *a.* lacking caution, regardless of consequences, rash; heedless *of* danger etc.; hence ∼LY² *adv.*, ∼NESS *n.* [OE *recelēas* (as prec., -LESS)]

rĕ′ckon *v.* 1. *v.t.* ascertain (number, amount), ascertain number or amount of, by counting or usu. by calculation, compute; start *from*, go on *to*, in counting (things, or abs.); count *up*, sum *up* character of; arrive at as total (*I reckon 53 of them*). 2. include in computation, count *in*, place in class *among* or *with* or *in*, take *for*, regard *as*, consider (*to be*) (*reckon him wise, beyond redemption*). 3. conclude after calculation, be of the confident opinion, (*that*). 4. *v.i.* make calculations, cast up account or sum, (∼ **with**, take into account; **to be** ∼**ed with**, not negligible; *reckon without* one's HOST²); settle accounts *with* person. 5. rely or count or base plans (*up*)*on.* 6. Hence ∼ER¹ (1, 2) *n.* [OE (*ge*)*recenian*, = MDu., MLG *rekenen*, OHG *rehhanōn* f. WG *rekenōjan]

rĕ′ckoning (-kn-) *n.* In vbl senses; bill in public house etc.; **day of** ∼, time when something must be atoned for or avenged; DEAD *reckoning*; **out in** one's ∼, mistaken in a calculation or expectation. [ME, f. prec. +-ING¹]

rĕclai′m *v.* & *n.* 1. *v.t.* win back or away from vice or error or savagery or waste condition, reform; tame, civilize; (demand to) recover possession of; bring under cultivation esp. from state of being flooded by sea or marsh, whence ∼ABLE *a.* 2. *v.i.* (arch.) make protest. 3. So **rĕclamA′TION** *n.* 4. *n.* reclaiming or being reclaimed. [ME, f. OF *reclamer reclaim-* f. L *re*(*clamare* shout) cry out against; see RE- 2]

réclame (rā′klahm) *n.* notoriety; art or practice by which notoriety is secured. [F (as prec.)]

rĕ′clinate *a.* (Bot.) bending downwards. [f. L *reclinatus* p.p. of *reclinare* (as foll.; see -ATE²)]

rĕcli′ne *v.* 1. *v.t.* lay (esp. one's head, body, or limbs) in more or less horizontal or leaning position; (in *p.p.*, of person) lying thus. 2. *v.i.* assume, or be in, horizontal or leaning position; sit with back or side supported at considerable inclination to vertical. [ME, f. OF *recliner* or f. L *reclinare* bend back, recline; see RE- 9, DECLINE¹]

rĕclu′s|e (-lō̄o′s) *a.* & *n.* (person) given to or living in seclusion or isolation, esp. as religious discipline, hermit; hence ∼IVE *a.* [ME, f. OF *reclus recluse* p.p. of *reclure* f. L *re*(*cludere clus-* = *claudere* shut); see RE- 4]

rĕcogni′tion *n.* recognizing or being recognized (*honour given in recognition of services; was changed out of all recognition*); hence **rĕcŏ′gniTORY** *a.* [f. L *recognitio* (as RECOGNIZE; see -ITION)]

rĕcŏ′gnizance (-kŏ′gn-, -kŏ′n-) *n.* bond by which person engages before court or magistrate to observe some condition, e.g. to keep the peace, pay a debt, or appear when summoned; sum pledged as surety for such observance. [ME, f. OF *recon*(*n*)*issance* (as RE-, COGNIZANCE)]

rĕcŏ′gnizant (-kŏ′gn-, -kŏ′n-) *a.* showing recognition (*of* favour etc.); conscious or showing consciousness of something. [f. foll. +-ANT]

rĕ′cogniz|e, -is|e (-īz), *v.t.* 1. acknowledge validity or genuineness or character or claims of, accord notice or consideration or reward to; (of chairman etc.) allow to speak in debate; discover or realize nature of; treat *as*, acknowledge *for*, realize or admit *that.* 2. know again, identify as known before. 3. Hence ∼ABLE *a.*, ∼ABI′LITY *n.*, ∼ABLY *adv.* [f. OF *recon*(*n*)*iss-*st. of *reconnaistre* f. L *re*(*cognoscere cognitum* learn), see RE- 8; assim. to -IZE]

rĕcoi′l *v.i.*, & *n.* 1. *v.i.* retreat under enemy's attack; suddenly move or spring back, shrink mentally, in fear or horror or disgust; rebound after impact, (of gun) be driven backwards by discharge, spring back; (Phys., of atom etc.) move backwards by conservation of momentum on emission of particle; ∼ (**up**)**on**, have adverse reactive effect upon (its source etc.; *their treason recoiled on their own heads*). 2. *n.* (or rē′-) act or fact or sensation of recoiling. [ME, f. OF *reculer* f. Rom. *reculare (as RE- 5, L *culus* buttocks)]

rĕcoi′n *v.t.* See RE- 8.

rĕcollĕ′ct¹ *v.t.* succeed in remembering, recall to mind, remember. [f. L *re*(*colligere collect-* COLLECT²); see RE- 8]

rē-collĕ′ct² *v.t.* collect again; recover control of (oneself). [f. as prec., or f. RE- 9 + COLLECT²]

rĕcollĕ′ct|ion *n.* act or power of recollecting; thing recollected, reminiscence; person's memory, time over which it extends, (*happened within my recollection*); so ∼IVE *a.* [F, or f. med. L *recollectio* (as RECOLLECT¹; see -ION)]

rĕcŏ′lonize *v.t.*, **rĕcŏlonizA′TION** *n.*, **rēco′lour** (-kŭ′ler) *v.t.* See RE- 8.

rĕcŏ′mbinant *a.* (Biol., of gene etc.) incorporated into chromosome other than its original one. [f. foll. +-ANT]

rĕcombi′ne *v.t.* & *i.*, **rĕcŏmbinA′TION** *n.*, see RE- 8, 9; **rĕcomme′nce**MENT (-sm-) *n.*, see RE- 8.

rĕcomme′nd *v.t.* 1. speak or write of or suggest as fit for employment or favour or trial (*to* person, *for* post, promotion, decoration, *as* remedy, etc.). 2. (Of qualities, conduct, etc.) make acceptable, serve as recommendation of. 3. advise (course of action or treatment, person *to do*, *that* thing should be done). 4. give (one*self*, one's spirit, a child, etc.) in charge *to* God or a person or his care etc. 5. Hence or cogn. ∼A′TION *n.*, ∼ABLE, ∼atORY, *adjs.* [ME in sense 4, f. med. L *re*(*commendare* COMMEND); see RE- 5]

rĕcommi′t *v.t.* (-**tt**-). commit again, esp. return (bill etc.) to committee for further consideration; hence ∼TAL 2, ∼MENT, *ns.* [f. RE- 8 + COMMIT]

rĕ′compĕnse *v.t.* & *n.* 1. *v.t.* requite, reward or punish, (person, action, person *for* action, action *to* person); make amends to (person) or for (another's loss, injury, etc.). 2. *n.* reward, requital; atonement or satisfaction given for injury; retribution. [ME, f. OF *recompense*(*r*) f. LL *re*(*compensare* COMPENSATE); see RE- 1]

rĕcompŏ′se (-z) *v.t.* See RE- 8.

rĕ′concil|e *v.t.* 1. make friendly after estrangement (persons to one another, person *to* or *with* another, person to oneself). 2. purify (consecrated place etc.) by special service after profanation or desecration. 3. (usu. in *refl.* or *pass.*) make acquiescent or contentedly submissive (*to* what is disagreeable, *to* doing, or abs.). 4. heal, settle, (quarrel etc.). 5. harmonize, make compatible, show compatibility of by argument or in practice, (apparently conflicting facts, statements, qualities, actions, or one such *with* another). 6. Hence or cogn. ∼ABLE *a.*, ∼ABI′LITY, ∼eMENT (-lm-), **rĕconciliA′TION**, *ns.* [ME, f. OF *reconcilier* or f. L *re*(*conciliare* CONCILIATE); see RE- 9]

recondi′te (rĕ′kon-, rikŏ′n-) *a.* (Of subject or knowledge) abstruse, out of the way, little known; (of author or style) dealing in recondite knowledge or allusion, obscure; hence ∼LY² (-tlī) *adv.*, ∼NESS (-tn-) *n.* [f. L (*conditus* p.p. of *condere* hide); see RE- 4]

rĕcondi′tion *v.t.* overhaul and refit, rehabilitate, renovate; make habitable or usable again. [f. RE- 8 + CONDITION²]

rĕcŏ′nnaissance (-nĭs-) *n.* military, naval, etc., examination of region by detachment to locate enemy or ascertain strategic features; reconnoitring party; preliminary survey. [F (earlier -*oissance*) f. st. of *reconnaître* (as foll.; see -ANCE)]

‖**rĕconnoi′tre** (-ter), ***-ter,** *v.* & *n.* 1. *v.t.* make reconnaissance of (enemy, district); approach and try to learn position and condition etc. of. 2. *v.i.* make reconnaissance. 3. *n.* reconnaissance. [f. obs. F *reconnoître* f. L *recognoscere* RECOGNIZE]

rĕcŏ′nquer (-ker) *v.t.*, **rĕco′NQUEST** *n.* See RE- 9.

rĕconsi′der *v.t.* consider again, esp. as regards possible change of decision; hence ∼A′TION *n.* [f. RE- 8 + CONSIDER]

rĕconsŏ′lidate *v.t.* & *i.*, **rĕconsŏlidA′TION** *n.* See RE- 8.

For other words in *re-* see RE-.

rĕcŏ'nstĭtūte v.t. build up again from parts; restore previous constitution of (dried food etc.) by adding water; piece together (past events) into intelligible whole; reorganize; so **rĕ**CONSTITU'TION n. [f. RE-8 + CONSTITUTE]

rĕconstrŭ'ct v.t. build again; restore (past event) mentally; reorganize; so **rĕ**CONSTRU'CTION n. (R∿ion, *reincorporation of seceded states into US after Civil War). [f. RE- 8 + CONSTRUCT¹]

rĕconvē'ne v.t. & i., **rĕconvēr't** v.t., **rĕconvēr'sION** (-shon) n. See RE- 9.

rĕcŏr'd¹ v.t. register, set down for remembrance or reference, put in writing or other legible shape, represent in some permanent form, (his thoughts have been recorded for us by himself, his features by Watts, and his voice by the gramophone); ∿ing angel (who registers men's good and bad actions). 2. convert (sound, broadcast programme, etc.) to permanent form for later reproduction. 3. Hence ∿ABLE a., ∿IST n., person who records sound. [ME, f. OF recorder f. L recordari remember (as RE- 9, cor cordis heart)]

rĕ'cŏrd² n. & a. 1. n. state of being recorded or preserved in writing etc.; on ∿, in legal or other record; go on ∿, act so that one's words etc. are recorded; court of ∿ (whose proceedings are recorded and valid as evidence of fact); matter of ∿, thing established as fact by being recorded. 2. official report of proceedings and judgement in cause before court of record, copy of pleadings etc. constituting case to be decided by court; travel out of, keep to, the ∿, introduce, abstain from introducing, irrelevant matter. 3. piece of recorded evidence or information, account of fact preserved in permanent form, document or monument preserving it; for the ∿, official(ly), for sake of recording facts; off the ∿, unofficial(ly), secret(ly); get, keep, put, set, the ∿ straight, correct a misapprehension; (Public) R∿ Office, institution keeping official archives for public inspection. 4. object serving as memorial of something, portrait etc. 5. trace made by recording instrument on disc or cylinder for subsequent reproduction by gramophone; similar trace on magnetic tape etc.; disc etc. bearing such trace; ∿-player, apparatus for reproducing sound from gramophone records. 6. facts known about person's past (has an honourable record of service; his record is against him); have a ∿, have been convicted on previous occasion. 7. best performance or most remarkable event of its kind on record; break or beat the ∿, outdo all predecessors. 8. a. best or highest or most extreme hitherto recorded. [ME f. OF record remembrance (recorder; see prec.)]

rĕcŏr'der n. In vbl senses; judge, esp. ||presiding at Crown Court or sitting as circuit judge at Central Criminal Court, judge in County Court of N. Ireland, whence ∿SHIP n.; recording instrument; recording-apparatus in instrument or machine; – TAPE recorder; (Mus.) vertical instrument like flute, one of family with various ranges. [ME f. AF recordour, OF recordeur (as RECORD¹, -ER²), & f. RECORD¹ (incl. obs. sense 'practise tune') + -ER¹]

rĕcŏr'ding n. In vbl senses; process of recording sound etc. for later reproduction; sound etc. thus recorded, television programme recorded on film, material on which it has been recorded. [f. RECORD¹ + -ING¹]

rĕcou'nt¹ v.t. narrate, tell in detail. [f. ONF & AF re(conter COUNT²); see RE- 8]

rē-cou'nt² v.t. count again. [f. RE- 8 + COUNT²]

rē'-count³ n. recounting, esp. of election votes to preclude error. [f. RE- 8 + COUNT¹]

rĕcou'p (-ōō'p) v.t. & i. 1. (Law). 2. deduct, keep back, (part of sum due), make such deduction. 2. compensate (person loss, person for loss, loss); ∿(oneself), recover what one has expended or lost. 3. Hence ∿MENT n. [f. F re(couper cut); see RE- 5]

rĕcour'se (-ōr's) n. resorting or betaking of oneself to

possible source of help (have ∿ to, adopt as adviser, helper, or expedient); person or thing resorted to; without ∿ (formula used by endorser of bill etc. to disclaim responsibility for non-payment). [ME, f. OF recours f. L re(cursus COURSE¹); see RE- 9]

rĕco'ver¹ (-kŭ'-) v. & n. 1. v.t. regain possession or use or control of, acquire or find (out) again, reclaim, (has recovered his kingdom, his friends' affection, the meaning of the hieroglyphics, the track, health, his appetite, his voice, metal from scrap, much land from the sea); ∿ oneself, regain consciousness, calmness, control of limbs, senses, (horse recovers itself after stumble); ∿ one's feet or legs, stand up after fall. 2. secure (restitution, compensation, damages, or abs.) by legal process (plaintiff shall recover according to verdict; his remedy is to recover in a court of law; action to recover damages for illegal imprisonment). 3. retrieve, make up for, cease to feel effects of, (must try to recover lost time). 4. Hence ∿ABLE a. 5. v.i. & t. come or (arch.) bring back to consciousness, health, or normal state or position (have or am quite recovered from my illness; sat down to recover from his agitation). 6. n. recovery of normal position in fencing etc. [ME, f. AF recoverer, OF recoverer f. L recuperare RECUPERATE]

rē-co'ver² (-kŭ'-) v.t. cover again (esp. umbrella etc.). [f. RE- 8 + COVER¹]

rĕco'verỹ (-kŭ'-) n. act or process of RECOVER¹ing or being recovered; (Golf) stroke bringing ball out of bunker etc. [ME, f. AF recoverie, OF reco(u)vree (as RECOVER¹; see -Y⁴)]

rĕ'cre|ant a. & n. (rhet. or poet.) craven, coward(ly), apostate; hence ∿ANCY n., ∿antLY² adv. [ME f. OF, part of recroire f. med. L (se) re(credere entrust) yield in trial by combat; see RE- 6, -ANT]

rĕ'cre|āte v. 1. v.t. (Of pastime, relaxation, holiday, employment, etc., or refl. of person indulging in them) refresh, entertain, agreeably occupy. 2. v.i. amuse oneself, indulge in recreation. 3. Hence ∿ATIVE a. [f. L re(creare create); see RE 8, -ATE³]

rē-crea'te² v.t. create over again. [f. RE- 8 + CREATE]

rĕcrea'tion n. (means of) recreating oneself, pleasurable exercise or employment; ∿ ground, public land for games etc.; hence ∿AL a. [ME f. OF, f. L recreatio -onis (as RECREATE¹; see -ATION)]

rĕcri'min|āte v.i. retort accusation, indulge in mutual or counter charges; hence or cogn. ∿A'TION n., ∿ATIVE, ∿ATORY, adjs. [f. med. L re(criminare accuse f. crimen CRIME); see RE- 1)]

rĕcro'ss (-ŏ's, -aw's) v.t. See RE- 9.

rĕcrud|ĕ'sce (-ōō-) v.i. (Of sore, disease, etc., or fig. of discontent etc.) break out again; so ∿E'SCENCE a., ∿E'SCENCE n. [back-form. f. recrudescent, -ence f L re(crudescere f. crudus raw); see RE- 8, -ESCENT]

rĕcrui't¹ (-rōō't) n. newly enlisted and not yet trained soldier, *soldier or sailor of lowest rank; person who joins a society etc.; (raw) ∿, tiro. [earlier sense 'reinforcement', f. obs. F dial. recrute = F recrue fem. p.p. (as n.) of recroître, f. L re(crescere grow); see RE- 8]

rĕcrui't² (-rōō't) v. 1. v.t. enlist recruits for (army, regiment, crew, society, party); enlist (person) as recruit. 2. replenish, fill up deficiencies or compensate wear and tear in; refresh, reinvigorate. 3. v.i. get or seek recruits. 4. (arch.) (seek to) recover health etc. (has gone into the country to recruit); hence ∿AL 2 n. 5. Hence ∿MENT n. [f. F recruter (recrute; see prec.)]

rĕ'ctal a. of or by means of the rectum. [f. RECTUM + -AL]

rĕ'ctăngle (-nggel) n. four-sided plane rectilinear figure with four right angles, esp. one with adjacent sides unequal. [F, or f. med. L rectangulum f. LL rectiangulum f. L rectus straight + angulus ANGLE¹]

rĕctă'ngular (-ngg-) a. shaped, or having base or sides or section shaped, like rectangle; placed, or having parts or lines placed, at right angles; ∿ co-ordinates (measured along axes at right angles); ∿ hyperbola (with perpendicular asymptotes); hence ∿ITY (-ă'r-) n., ∿LY² adv. [f. prec. + ANGULAR]

rĕ′ctĭ|fŷ *v.t.* **1.** make right, correct, amend, reform, adjust, (method, calculation, statement, position, instrument). **2.** abolish, get rid of, exchange for what is right, (abuse, anomaly, error, omission, grievance). **3.** (Chem.) purify or refine by repeated distillation or other process. **4.** (Geom.) find straight line equal in length to (curve). **5.** (Electr.) convert (alternating current) to direct current. **6.** Hence or cogn. ∼fīABLE *a.*, ∼FICA′TION, ∼fīER¹ (1, 2), *ns.* [ME, f. OF *rectifier* f. med. L *rectificare* f. L *rectus* right; see -FY]

rĕctĭlī′nĕal *a.* = foll. [f. as foll. + -AL]

rĕctĭlī′nĕar *a.* in or forming a straight line; bounded or characterized by straight lines; hence ∼ITY (-ă′r-) *n.*, ∼LY² *adv.* [f. LL *rectilineus* f. L *rectus* straight + *linea* LINE¹; see -AR¹]

rĕ′ctĭtūde *n.* moral uprightness, righteousness; correctness, rightness. [ME f. OF, or f. LL *rectitudo* f. L *rectus* right; see -TUDE]

rĕ′ctō *n.* (*pl.* ∼s). right-hand page of open book; front of leaf (opp. VERSO). [f. L *recto* (*folio*) on the right (leaf)]

rĕ′ctor *n.* **1.** (In Ch. of England) incumbent of parish where all tithes formerly passed to incumbent (cf. VICAR); (in RC Ch.) head priest of church etc.; LAY² *rector*. **2.** head of university, college, school, or religious institution; (**Lord**) **R**∼, elected representative of students on governing body of Scottish university. **3.** Hence ∼ATE¹, ∼SHIP, *ns.* [ME, f. OF *rectour* or f. L *rector* ruler (*regere rect-* rule; see -OR)]

rĕctŏr′ial *a.* & *n.* **1.** *a.* pertaining to a rector. **2.** *n.* election of Scottish university Rector. [f. prec. + -IAL]

rĕ′ctory *n.* ‖rector's benefice; rector's house. [f. AF & OF *rectorie* or med. L *rectoria* (as RECTOR; see -Y¹)]

rĕ′ctr|ix *n.* (*pl.* ∼ices *pr.* -isēz). bird's strong tail-feather directing flight. [L, fem. of RECTOR]

rĕ′ct|um *n.* (*pl.* ∼ums or ∼a). final section of large intestine, terminating at anus. [f. L *rectum* (*intestinum*) straight (intestine)]

rĕ′ct|us *n.* (*pl.* ∼i *pr.* -ī). (Anat.) straight muscle. [L, = straight]

rĕcŭ′mb|ent *a.* lying down, reclining; hence ∼ENCY *n.*, ∼entLY² *adv.* [f. L *re*(*cumbere* lie) recline; see RE- 9, -ENT]

rĕcu′per|āte (-kū′-, -kōō′-) *v.t.* & *i.* restore, be restored or recover, from exhaustion, illness, loss, etc.; so ∼A′TION *n.*, ∼ATIVE *a.* [f. L *recuperare* recover (as RE- 9, **cup-* = **cap-* take) + -ATE³]

rĕcū′r *v.i.* (-rr-; *part. pr.* -ēr′ing, -ŭ′rǐng). go back in thought or speech *to*; (of idea etc.) come back to one's mind etc., return to mind; (of problem etc.) present itself again; occur again, be repeated, (∼**ring decimal,** decimal fraction in which same figures are repeated indefinitely). [f. L *re*(*currere curs-* run); see RE- 9]

rĕcū′rrent *a.* (Of nerve, vein, branch, etc.) turning back so as to reverse direction; occurring again or often or periodically; hence **rĕcū′rr**ENCE *n.*, ∼LY² *adv.* [f. as prec.; see -ENT]

rĕcū′r′sion *n.* return; ∼ **formula,** (Math.) expression giving successive terms of series etc.; hence **rĕcū′r′s**-IVE *a.* [f. LL *recursio* (as RECUR; see -ION)]

rĕcū′rv|e *v.t.* & *i.* bend backwards; hence or cogn. ∼ATE² *a.*, ∼ATURE *n.* [f. L *re*(*curvare* -at- bend); see RE- 9]

rĕ′cūs|ant (-z-) *n.* & *a.* (Hist.) (person) who refused to attend Church of England services; (person) refusing submission to authority or compliance with regulation (*against*); so ∼ANCE, ∼ANCY, *ns.* [f. L *recusare* refuse (as RE- 2, CAUSE¹); see -ANT]

rēcy′cle *v.t.* return to previous stage of cyclic process, esp. convert (waste) to reusable material. [f. RE- 8 + CYCLE]

rĕd *a.* & *n.* **1.** *a.* of or approaching the colour seen at least-refracted end of spectrum, of shades varying from crimson to bright brown and orange, esp. those seen in blood, rubies, glowing coals, human lips, and fox's hair, (*red as a rose* etc.; *blood, fiery, yellowish, deep,*

etc., -*red*); flushed in face with shame, anger, etc.; (of hands) blood-stained; (of eyes) bloodshot, or sore with weeping; (of hair or animal's coat) reddish-brown, tawny, ALL-*red*; (as distinguishing epithet) *red deer, ant, cabbage,* etc. **2.** having to do with bloodshed, burning, violence, or revolution (*red battle, ruin;* SEE¹ *red; a red republican*); anarchistic or communistic. **3.** (*R*∼). Russian, Soviet, (*the Red Army, Air Force*); Communist (*Red China*). **4.** *red* ADMIRAL; ∼ **arsenic,** realgar; ∼ **bark,** red kind of cinchona; ∼ **biddy,** mixture of cheap red wine and methylated spirits; ∼**blind,** having retina insensitive to red rays; ∼**blooded,** virile, vigorous; ∼′**breast,** robin; ‖∼′**brick,** (of university) of modern foundation; ∼′**bud,** Amer. tree of Judas-tree genus; ∼′**cap,** ‖military policeman, *railway porter; ∼ **cedar,** an Amer. juniper (*Juniperus virginiana*); ∼ **cell,** erythrocyte; *∼ **cent,** smallest (orig. copper) coin; ∼′**coat,** (Hist.) British soldier (from former scarlet uniform of most regiments); ∼ **corpuscle,** erythrocyte; **Red Crescent,** organization like Red Cross in Muslim countries; ∼ **cross,** (1) St. George's cross, national emblem of England, (2) Christian side in crusades; **Red Cross,** (emblem of) ambulance etc. service organized according to Geneva Convention of 1864 for treatment of sick and wounded in war and those suffering by large-scale natural disasters; *red* CURRANT; ‖∼ **duster,** (sl.) = *red* ENSIGN; ∼**eye,** rudd; ‖∼**fish,** (1) male salmon in spawning season, (2) rose-fish; *red* FLAG⁴; ∼ **gold,** (arch. or poet.) real gold, money; ‖*red* GROUSE¹; **Red Guard,** young activist in Communist China; ∼ **gum,** (1) teething-rash in children, (2) (kinds of eucalyptus yielding) reddish resin; ∼-**ha′nded,** in the act of crime (*caught red-handed*); ∼ **hat,** (Hist.) cardinal's hat, (symbol of) cardinal's rank; ∼′**head,** person with red hair; ∼ **heat,** being red-hot (lit. or fig.), temperature of red-hot thing; ∼ **herring,** (1) herring(s) reddened by being cured in smoke (*neither fish, flesh, nor good* ∼ *herring,* of indefinite character), (fig.) irrelevant diversion [f. use of red herring in exercising hounds]; ∼-**hot,** heated to redness, highly exciting or excited, enthusiastic, furious; *red-hot* POKER¹; ‖**Red Indian,** N. Amer. Indian, with reddish skin; *red* JASMINE; ‖∼ **lane,** (sl.) throat; ∼ **lead,** pigment made from red oxide of lead; ∼**legs,** redshank, red-stemmed plant; ∼**letter,** (of day) marked with red letter(s) in calendar as saint's day or festival, (fig.) memorable as date of joyful occurrence; ∼ **light,** red lamp as danger-signal on road, railway, etc. (*see the* ∼ *light,* (fig.) realize approach of disaster) ∼-**light district** (containing many brothels); *red* MAGGOT; ∼ **man,** = *Red Indian;* ∼ **meat,** beef, lamb, mutton, etc., (opp. *white meat*); ∼ **orpiment,** realgar; ∼ **pepper,** (1) CAYENNE pepper, (2) ripe fruit of PEPPER¹ 2; ∼′**poll,** red-crested bird similar to linnet, (in *pl.*) red-haired polled cattle; ∼ **rag,** thing that excites person's rage as red object allegedly enrages bull; *red* RATTLE²; ∼ **ribbon,** ribbon of the Order of the Bath; *red* ROAN¹; ∼ **rose,** emblem of Lancashire, or of House of Lancaster in Wars of the Roses; ∼ **sanders,** red SANDAL²WOOD; ∼′**shank,** large kind of sandpiper; ∼**shift,** (Astron.) displacement of spectral lines to longer wavelengths in radiation from distant galaxies etc.; ∼**short,** (of iron) brittle while red-hot; ∼′**skin,** = *Red Indian;* ∼ **snow** (reddened by snow-plant and common in Arctic and Alpine regions); ∼ **spider,** mite infesting hothouse plants esp. vines; ∼ **squirrel,** native English squirrel (*Sciurus leucourus*); **Red Star,** emblem of some Communist countries; ∼′**start,** red-tailed song-bird of genus *Phoenicurus* [OE *steort* tail]; ∼ **tape,** excessive use of or adherence to formalities esp. in public business; *red* TERROR; ∼**water,** malarial cattle and sheep disease with red urine; ∼ **wine** (coloured by grape-skins); ∼′**wing,** thrush with red wing-coverts; ∼′**wood,** tree yielding red wood, esp. Californian *Sequoia sempervirens*. **5.** Hence ~'**den**[6] *v.t. & i.*, ~'**dish**[1] 2, ~'**dv**[2], *adjs.*, ~'**ly**[2] *adv.*, ~'**ness** *n.* **6.** *n.* red colour; red pigment; red clothes or material (*dressed in red*); the red colour in roulette and rouge-et-noir; red light; red ball in billiards etc.; debtor side of account (**in the** ~, in debt); revolutionary radical or republican; anarchist; communist. [OE *rēad*, = OS *rōd*, OHG *rōt*, ON *rauthr*, Goth. *rauths* f. Gmc **raudhaz* f. IE **roudhos*]

rĕdǎ'ct *v.t.* put into literary form, arrange for publication, edit; so ~**or** *n.* [f. L *red*(*igere act-* = *agere* drive, bring); see re- 8]

rĕdǎ'ction *n.* preparing or being prepared for publication, revision, editing, rearrangement; new edition. [f. F *rédaction* f. L (as prec.; see -ion)]

rĕdǎ'n *n.* field-work with two faces forming salient angle. [F, f. *redent* notching (as re-, *dent* tooth)]

rĕdd *v.t.* (**redd**). (esp. Sc.) clear up; arrange, tidy; put right, settle, compose. [ME, = MLG, Du. *redden*]

rĕ'ddle *n.* red ochre, ruddle. [var. of RUDDLE]

rēde[1] *n.* (arch.) counsel, advice, whence ~**less** (-dl-) *a.*; resolve, design; narrative. [OE *rǣd*, = OS *rād*, OHG *rāt*, ON *ráth* f. Gmc **rǣdhaz* (**rǣdhan* READ)]

rēde[2] *v.t.* (arch.) advise (person (*to*) do; read (riddle, dream). [var. of READ, common ME sp. retained for arch. senses]

rēde'corāte *v.t.*, **rēdĕcorā'tion** *n.* See re- 8.

rēdee'm *v.t.* **1.** buy back, recover by expenditure of effort or by stipulated payment, (*redeem one's rights, position, honour, mortgaged land, pawned goods*); compound for, buy off, (charge or obligation) by payment; convert (tokens etc.) into goods or cash. **2.** fulfil (promise). **3.** purchase the freedom of (another, oneself); save (person's life) by ransom. **4.** save, rescue, reclaim; (of God or Christ) deliver from sin and damnation. **5.** make amends for, compensate, counterbalance, (fault, defect; *has one redeeming feature*); save *from* a defect (*the eyes redeem the face from ugliness*) or *oneself from* blame. **6.** Hence ~**able** *a.*, ~**er**[1] *n.* (of Christ; see sense 4). [ME, f. OF *redimer* or L *red*(*imere -empt-* = *emere* buy); see re- 8]

rēde'mpt|ion *n.* **1.** redeeming or being redeemed (**past or beyond** ~**ion**, such that there is no hope of redemption); deliverance from sin and damnation wrought by Christ's atonement (**in the year of our** ~**ion** *1973* etc., AD 1973 etc.). **2.** thing that redeems (*that blow was or proved his redemption*). **3.** Hence ~**ive** *a.* [ME f. OF, f. L *redemptio* (as prec.; see -ion)]

Rēdē'mptorist *n.* (*fem.* ~**ine**). member of RC Congregation of the Redeemer. [f. F *rédemptoriste* f. OF & L *redemptor* redeemer (as REDEEM, -OR); see -ist]

rēdēploy' *v.t.* send (troops, workers, etc.) to new place or task; hence ~**ment** *n.* [f re- 8 + DEPLOY]

rēdescĕ'nd *v.i. & t.*, see re- 9; **rēdēsī'gn** (-zī'n) *v.t.*, **rēdēvĕ'lop** *v.t.*, **rēdēvĕ'lopment** *n.*, see re- 8.

rēdī'al *v.t.* (||-ll-||). dial again. [f. re- 8 + DIAL]

rēdiffū'sion (-zhon) *n.* relaying of broadcast programmes, esp. by wire from central receiver. [f. re- 8 + DIFFUSION]

rē'dingōte (-ngg-) *n.* woman's long coat with cut-away front or contrasting piece on breast. [F, f. E *riding-coat*]

rēdi'ntĕgr|āte *v.t.* restore to wholeness or unity; renew or re-establish in entirety or perfect state; so ~**a'tion** *n.* [ME, f. L *red*(*integrare* INTEGRATE[2]); see re- 9, -ate[3]]

rēdirĕ'ct *v.t.* direct again, esp. change address of (letter); hence ~**ion** *n.* [f. re- 8 + DIRECT[1]]

rēdisco'ver (-kŭ'-) *v.t.*, **rēdisco'very** *n.*, **rēdissŏ'lve** (-z-) *v.t. & i.*, **rēdissolu'tion** *n.*, see re- 8; **rēdistri'bute** *v.t.*, **rēdistribū'tion** *n.*, **rēdistri'butive** *a.*, see re- 8.

rēdivi'de *v.t.*, **rēdivi'sion** *n.*, see re- 8.

rēdivi'vus (-ē'-) *a.* (placed after *n.*) come back to life. [L (as re-, *vivus* living)]

rēdo' (-ōō') *v.t.* (**redi'd**; **redo'ne** *pr.* -dŭ'n; cf. DO[1]). do again; redecorate. [f. re- 8 + DO[1]]

rē'dol|ent *a.* fragrant; having a strong smell, odorous,

(fig.) strongly suggestive or reminiscent or mentally associated, *of or with*; so ~**ence** *n.* [ME f. OF, or f. L *red*(*olēre* smell); see re- 6, -ent]

rēdou'ble (-dŭ'-) *v. & n.* **1.** *v.t. & i.* intensify, increase, make or grow greater or more intense or numerous, (*redouble* one's *efforts; the clamour redoubled*). **2.** *v.t.* (Bridge.) double again a bid already doubled by opponent. **3.** *n.* (Bridge). redoubling of a bid. [f. F *re*(*doubler* DOUBLE[3]); see re- 6]

rēdou'bt (-ow't) *n.* outwork or field-work usu. square or polygonal and without flanking defences. [f. F *redoute* f. obs. It. *ridotta* f. med. L *reductus* refuge f. p.p. of L *reducere* withdraw (see REDUCE); -*b*- after DOUBT[1] (cf. foll.)]

rēdou'btable (-ow't-) *a.* (Of opponent, warrior, controversialist, etc.) formidable. [ME, f. OF *redoutable* f. *re*(*douter* DOUBT[2]) fear; see re- 6]

rēdou'btĕd (-ow't-) *a.* (arch.) dreaded, redoubtable. [p.p. of obs. *redoubt* f. OF *redouter* (see prec.)]

rēdou'nd *v.i.* result in contributing, make great contribution, *to* one's advantage, credit, etc., (*this procedure will redound to our advantage; the tale* or *fact redounds to their credit*); come as final result *to*, come back or recoil *upon*, person (*the benefits that redound to us from his self-sacrifice*). [ME, orig. − overflow, f. OF *redonder* f. L *red*(*undare* surge f. *unda* wave); see re- 6]

rē'dŏx *n. & a.* (Chem.) (of) oxidation and reduction. [f. *reduction* + *oxidation*]

rēdraw' *v.t.* (**redrew'**; ~**n**). draw again or differently. [f. re- 8 + DRAW[1]]

rēdrĕ'ss *v.t.*, & *n.* **1.** *v.t.* readjust, set straight again, (~ **the balance**, restore equality); set right, remedy, make up for, get rid of, rectify, (distress, wrong, damage, grievance, abuse); hence ~**al**, 2, ~**ment**, *ns.* **2.** *n.* reparation for wrong, redressing of grievances etc. [ME, f. OF *redresse*(*r*), *redrecier* (as re- 8, DRESS[1])]

rēdū'ce *v.* **1.** convert physically or mentally *to* other (esp. simpler or more general) form (*reduce fraction to its lowest terms, oral traditions to writing*, compound *of* components), subject to such conversion (*reduce fractions, compound*), make suitable or conformable or adapted *to*, bring by classification or analysis *to* (*reduce observations to formula*; *the facts may all be reduced to three heads*). **2.** bring by force or necessity *to* some state or action, subdue, bring back to obedience, (*reduce person to discipline, the Crown to submission, besieged fortress, rebels*; *reduced him to asserting an absurdity; was reduced to despair, to weakness, to borrowing clothes, to borrowing*). **3.** bring lower (~ **to the ranks**, make (guilty NCO) a private again); weaken (*is in a very reduced state*); diminish (*reduce liquid to two-thirds of its bulk; reduce the prices of the goods, the temperature of the mixture*); convert to smaller number by omission, reclassification, etc.; impoverish (~**d circumstances**, poverty after prosperity); (Photog.) make (negative) less dense. **4.** (Surg.) restore (dislocated etc. part) to original or proper position, remedy (dislocation etc.) thus. **5.** (Chem.) convert (oxide etc.) to metal; remove oxygen from or add hydrogen or electrons to. **6.** *v.i.* lessen one's weight or size. **7.** Hence **rēdū'cer**[1] (1, 2) *n.*, **rēdū'cible** *a.* [ME in sense 'restore to original or proper position', f. L *re*(*ducere duct-* bring); see re- 9]

reductio ad absurdum (ridŭktiō ăd absĕr'dum) *n.* proof of falsity by showing absurd logical consequence; proof of truth by thus proving falsity of alternative(s); carrying of principle to unpractical lengths. [L, = reduction to the absurd]

rēdū'ction *n.* reducing or being reduced; amount by which prices etc. are reduced; reduced copy of picture, map, etc.; ~ **to absurdity**, = prec.; so **rēdū'ctive** *a.* [ME f. OF, or f. L *reductio* (as REDUCE; see -ion)]

rēdū'ction|ism *n.* analysis of complex things into simple constituents; view that a system can be fully understood in terms of its isolated parts, or an idea in terms of simple concepts; hence ~**ist** (2) *n.*, ~**i'stic** *a.* [f. prec. + -ism]

rēdŭ'nd|ant *a.* **1.** superfluous; ||(of industrial worker) liable to dismissal as being no longer needed for any available job. **2.** excessive, pleonastic; that can be omitted without loss of significance. **3.** copious, luxuriant. **4.** Hence or cogn. ∼ANCE, ∼ANCY, *ns.* (‖∼ancy payment, by employer to redundant worker according to length of service etc.), ∼antLY[2] *adv.* [f. L (as REDOUND; see -ANT)]

rĕdū′plic|āte *v.t.* make double, repeat; (Philol. & Gram.) repeat (letter, syllable), form (tense) by reduplication; so ∼ATIVE *a.* [f. LL *re(duplicare* DUPLICATE[2]); see RE- 8, -ATE[3]]

rĕdŭplǐcā′tion *n.* doubling, repetition; counterpart; (Philol. & Gram.) repetition of syllable (exactly or with change of vowel etc.: *hurly-burly, see-saw*) or letter in word-formation (esp. in perf. in Gk and L, as *leluka* from *luō, pependi* from *pendere*), part so repeated. [f. LL *reduplicatio* (as prec.; see -ATION)]

rēdȳe′ *v.t.* (∼**ing**). See RE- 8.

ree. See REEVE[2].

ree′bok *n.* small S. Afr. antelope with sharp horns. [Du., = roebuck]

rē-ĕ′chō (-kō) *v.i. & t.* echo; echo again and again, resound. [f. RE- 6 + ECHO[2]]

reed[1] *n.*, & *v.t.* **1.** *n.* (tall straight stalk of) firm-stemmed water or marsh plant esp. of genus *Phragmites*; **broken** or (arch.) **bruised**∼, unreliable person or thing; **lean on a** ∼, put trust in weak thing or person. **2.** (collect.) reeds growing in a mass or used as material esp. for thatching, ‖wheat-straw prepared for thatching. **3.** (poet.) arrow; musical pipe of reed or straw; pastoral poetry. **4.** vibrating part, of varying shape and material, used in some musical wind-instruments (∼ **instruments**, esp. oboe, bassoon, clarinet, bagpipe, and some organ-pipes) to produce the sound; (usu. in *pl.*) reed instrument. **5.** weaver's comblike implement for separating warp-threads and bringing weft into proper position; (in *pl.*) set of semicylindrical adjacent mouldings like reeds laid together. **6.** ∼-**babbler** or -**bird** or -**warbler** or -**wren**, bird frequenting reed-beds, esp. *Acrocephalus scirpaceus*; ∼-**bunting**, bunting frequenting reed-beds; ‖∼-**mace**, cat's-tail; ∼-**organ**, (Mus.) harmonium etc. with wind operating metal reeds; ∼-**pheasant**, bearded TIT[1]; ∼-**pipe**, (1) musical pipe of reed, (2) reeded organ-pipe; ∼-**stop**, organ-stop consisting of reed-pipes. **7.** *v.t.* thatch with reed; make (straw) into reed; decorate with moulding of reeds (see sense 5), whence ∼′ING[1] (2) *n.*; fit (musical instrument or organ-pipe) with reed. [OE *hrēod*, = OS *hriod*, OHG *(h)riot* f. WG **hreudha*]

reed[2] *n.* fourth STOMACH of ruminant. [OE *rēada*]

rē-ĕ′dit *v.t.*, **rē-**EDITION *n.* See RE- 8.

ree′dling *n.* bearded TIT[1]. [f. REED[1] + -LING[1]]

rē-ĕ′ducāte *v.t.*, **rē-ĕducā′TION** *n.* See RE- 8.

ree′d|ȳ *a.* **1.** full of reeds; (poet.) made of reed. **2.** like a reed in weakness, slenderness, or (of grass etc.) thickness; (of voice) like reed instrument in tone, scratchy, not round and clear. **3.** Hence ∼**ɪNESS** *n.* [ME, f. REED[1] + -Y[2]]

reef[1] *n.*, & *v.t.* **1.** *n.* one of several strips across top of square sail or bottom of fore-and-aft sail that can be taken in or rolled up to reduce sail's surface in high wind; **take in a** ∼, lit., or fig. proceed cautiously. **2.** ∼-**knot**, double knot made symmetrically for secure holding and easy casting off; ∼-**point**, one of short pieces of rope attached to sail to secure it when reefed. **3.** *v.t.* take in reef(s) of (sail); shorten (topmast, bowsprit; paddles of paddle-wheel by shifting them nearer centre); ∼′**ing-jacket**, thick close-fitting double-breasted jacket. [ME *riff, refe* f. Du. *reef, rif,* f. ON *rif* RIB, in same sense (cf. foll.)]

reef[2] *n.* **1.** ridge of rock or shingle or sand at or just above or below surface of water; (fig.) hazardous obstacle. **2.** lode of ore; bedrock surrounding this. [earlier *riff(e)* f. MDu., MLG *rif, ref,* f. ON *rif* (as prec.)]

ree′fer[1] *n.* one who reefs; (sl.) midshipman; REEF[1]-knot; reefing-jacket. [f. REEF[1] + -ER[1]]

ree′fer[2] *n.* marijuana cigarette. [f. REEF[1] thing rolled + ER[1]]

***ree′fer**[3] *n.* (colloq.) refrigerator. [abbr.]

reek[1] *n.* **1.** foul or stale smell (*the reek of tobacco*); fetid atmosphere (*amid reek and squalor*). **2.** (Sc. or literary). smoke; vapour, visible exhalation; hence ∼′y[2] *a.* (**Auld Reekie,** Edinburgh). [OE *rēc, *rīec,* = OS *rōk,* OHG *rouh,* ON *reykr* f. Gmc **raukiz* (**rauk-, *reuk-; cf. foll.)]

reek[2] *v.i.* **1.** smell unpleasantly (*of* garlic, tobacco, blood; (fig.) *of* corruption, affectation, etc.). **2.** emit smoke, vapour, steam, etc. [OE *rēocan,* = MDu. *rieken,* OHG *riohhan,* ON *rjúka* f. Gmc **reuk-;* cf. prec.]

reel[1] *n.*, & *v.t.* **1.** *n.* rotatory device on which thread, silk, yarn, paper, film, magnetic tape, wire, etc., are wound; quantity of thread etc. thus wound; contrivance for winding and unwinding line as required, esp. in fishing (**off the** ∼, (fig.) straight off, without hitch or pause, in rapid succession); ‖small cylinder with rimmed ends on which sewing-cotton etc. is wound for convenience; revolving part in various machines. **2.** *v.t.* wind (thread, fishing-line, etc.) on reel; take (cocoon silk etc.) *off,* draw (fish, log-line, etc.) *in* or *up,* by use of reel; rattle (story, list, verses) *off* without pause or apparent effort. [OE *hrēol,* of unkn. orig.]

reel[2] *v.i.*, & *n.* **1.** *v.i.* (Of eyes, mind, head) be in a whirl, be dizzy, swim; sway, stagger, stand or walk or run unsteadily, be shaken physically or mentally, rock from side to side, swing violently, (*his mind, the front rank, the ship, the tower, reeled under the shock; reel to and fro like a drunken man*); seem to shake (*the mountains reeled before his eyes*). **2.** *n.* reeling motion (lit. or fig.). [ME, f. prec.]

reel[3] *n.*, & *v.i.* **1.** *n.* lively esp. Scottish dance, usu. of two couples in line and describing circular figures; music for this. **2.** *v.i.* dance reel. [perh. f. prec. 2]

rē-ĕlĕ′ct *v.t.*, **rē-**ELE′CTION *n.*, **rē-ĕ′ligible** *a.*, **rē-ĕmbā′rk** *v.i. & t.*, **rē-ĕmbā′rkА**′TION *n.*, **rē-ĕmĕr′ge** *v.i.*, **rē-ĕmĕr′gENCE** *n.*, **rē-ĕmĕr′gENT** *a.*, **rē-ĕnā′ctMENT** *n.* See RE- 9.

***rē-ĕnfōr′ce.** Var. of REINFORCE.

rē-ĕ′nter *v.i. & t.*, **rē-ĕ′nTRANCE** *n.* See RE- 9, and cf. foll. and RE-ENTRY.

rē-ĕ′ntrant *a. & n.* (angle) pointing inwards (opp. *salient;* esp. in Fortif.); reflex (angle). [f. RE- 9 + ENTRANT]

rē-ĕ′ntrȳ *n.* act of entering again, esp. (of spacecraft, missile, etc.) or re-entering earth's atmosphere; (Law) a retaking, possession; (**card of**) ∼, card that can be relied on to give holder the lead again by winning a trick. [f. RE- 9 + ENTRY]

rē-ĕstă′blish *v.t.*, **rē-ĕstă′blishMENT** *n.* See RE- 9.

reeve[1] *n.* **1.** (Hist.) chief magistrate of town or district; manorial supervisor of villeins. **2.** minor local official; (Can.) president of village or town council. [OE *(ge)rēfa, girāfa* (as Y-, *rōf* assembly)]

reeve[2], **ree,** *n.* female of RUFF[2]. [17th c. & 16th c., of unkn. orig.]

reeve[3] *v.t.* (**rove** or ∼**d**). (Naut.) thread (rope, rod, etc.) *through* ring or other aperture; pass rope through (block etc.); fasten (rope, block, or other object) *in, on, round, to,* something by reeving; (of ship) thread (shoals, ice-pack). [prob. f. Du. *rēven* REEF[1]]

rē-ĕxă′mine (-gz-) *v.t.* examine again (esp. one's witness after cross-examination by opponents); so **rē-ĕxāminА**′TION (-gz-) *n.* [f. RE- 8 + EXAMINE]

rē-ĕxpōr′t[1] *v.t.*, **rē-ĕ′xpORT**[2] *n.* See RE- 9.

***rĕf** *n.* (colloq.) referee in sports. [abbr.]

ref. *abbr.* reference.

rēfă′ce *v.t.* put new facing on (building). [f. RE- 8 + FACE[2]]

rēfă′shion (-shon) *v.t.* See RE- 8.

rĕfĕ′ction *n.* refreshment by food or drink (*milk and eggs were offered for our refection*); slight meal, repast. [ME, f. OF, f. L *refectio -onis* f. *reficere* as foll.); see RE-, -ION]

For other words in *re-* **see** RE-.

refe'ctory (*or in monastic use* rĕ'fĭ-) *n*. room used for meals in monasteries, colleges, etc.; ∼ **table** (long and narrow). [f. LL *refectorium* f. L *re(ficere fect-* = *facere* make) refresh; see RE- 8, -ORY]

refer' *v*. (-rr-). 1. *v.t.* trace or ascribe *to* person or thing as cause or source, consider as belonging *to* certain date or place or class, (*refer one's victories to Providence, miraculous tales to ignorance, ill temper to indigestion, the lake-dwellings to the sixth century, the origins of sculpture to Egypt, barnacles to the molluscs*); ∼**red pain** (felt in part of body other than its true source); hence ∼ABLE (rĭfĕr'-, rĕ'fer-) *a*. 2. commit, hand over, (one*self*, question for decision) *to* person etc. (*I refer myself to your generosity; let us refer the dispute to arbitration*); ∼ **to drawer** (banker's note suspending payment etc. of cheque). 3. *v.t.* & *i.* send on or direct (person), make appeal or have recourse, *to* some authority or source of information, (abs.) cite authority or passage, (*for proof I refer to your report, to the facts of human nature, to Proverbs 10:19; referred to his watch for the exact time*); send (person) to medical specialist etc., whence ∼RAL 2 *n*.; send (proposal etc.) *back to* lower body, court, etc.; fail (examination candidate). 4. *v.t.* interpret (statement etc.) as being directed *to*. 5. *v.i.* (Of statement etc.) have relation, be directed, *to* (*these remarks refer only to deliberate offences*). 6. (Of person speaking etc.) make allusion, draw attention, *to* (*he several times referred to the increase in expenditure; found myself on the peak referred to*). [ME, f. OF *referer* f. L *re(ferre latum* bring) carry back; see RE- 9]

referee' *n*. & *v*. 1. *n*. arbitrator, person to whom dispute is to be or is referred for decision; ||**Official R**∼, person attached to Supreme Court, to whom questions arising in an action may be referred for inquiry and report or for trial where parties consent; umpire esp. in football or boxing; ||person willing to testify to character of applicant for employment; person who assesses value of scientific paper etc. sent for publication. 2. *v.i.* & *t.* act as referee (for). [f. prec.+-EE]

re'ference (-fr-) *n*., & *v.t.* 1. *n*. referring of matter for decision or settlement or consideration to some authority, scope given to such authority, (*the peerage was allowed without reference to the House of Lords; the Commission must confine itself to, that is a question outside, the terms of reference*). 2. relation, respect, correspondence, *to* (*the parts of a machine all have reference to each other; success seems to have little reference to merit*); **in** or **with** ∼ **to**, regarding, as regards, about; **without** ∼ **to**, not taking account of. 3. allusion *to* (*made reference, a* or *no reference, several references, to our previous conversation*). 4. direction more or less precise *to* (page etc. of) book, file, etc. where information may be found (*gives many, verify your, does not give, references*); book, passage, etc., so cited; ∼ **mark** (used to refer reader of text to note or to part of diagram, esp. asterisk *, obelisk or dagger †, double obelisk ‡, section §, parallel ||, paragraph ¶). 5. act of looking up passage etc., or of referring another or applying to person, for information (*reference to the dictionary would have enlightened him; please give me a reference, apply to, supply a reference from, your last employer*); ∼ (**book**) (to be used not for continuous reading but to consult on occasion); *reference* LIBRARY. 6. person willing to testify to character of applicant for employment or of would-be credit-account customer etc.; testimonial; thing taken to have standard value etc. 7. Hence **refere'ntIAL** (-shal) *a*. 8. *v.t.* provide (book etc.) with references to authorities. [f. REFER+-ENCE]

refere'nd|um *n*. (*pl.* ∼**ums** or ∼**a**). referring of political question to electorate for direct decision by general vote; vote thus taken. [L, gerund and neut. of *referre* of *referre* (REFER)]

re'ferent *n*. what is symbolized by word etc. [f. L *referens* (as prec.; see -ENT)]

refĕr'ral. See REFER 3.

rĕ'ffo *n*. (*pl.* ∼**s**). (Austral. sl.) European refugee. [abbr.+-o]

refi'll[1] *v.t.* fill again; provide new filling for. [f. RE- 9+FILL]

rē'fill[2] *n*. renewed filling; material etc. used for this. [f. prec.]

refi'ne *v*. 1. *v.t.* free from dross or impurities or defects, purify, clarify; make elegant or cultured, imbue with delicacy of feeling or taste, polish manners or appearance of; improve (up)on by refinements. 2. *v.i.* become pure or clear or improved in polish or delicacy; employ subtlety of thought or language, make fine distinctions. [f. RE- 6+FINE[2] *v*., & F *raffiner*]

refi'nement (-nm-) *n*. refining or being refined; fineness of feeling or taste, polished manners etc.; subtle or ingenious manifestation *of*, piece of elaborate arrangement, (*all the refinements of reasoning, torture*; *a countermine was a refinement beyond their skill*); instance of improvement (*up*)*on*; piece of subtle reasoning, fine distinction. [f. prec.+-MENT, after F *raffinement*]

refi'n|er *n*. In vbl senses; person whose business is to refine crude oil, metal, sugar, etc., whence ∼ERY (3) *n*. [f. REFINE+-ER[1]]

refi't[1] *v.t.* & *i.* (-tt-). make or become fit again (esp. of ship undergoing renewal and repairs); hence ∼MENT *n*. [f. RE- 8+FIT[4]]

rē'fit[2] *n*. refitting. [f. prec.]

refla'te *v.t.* (Econ.) cause reflation of (currency, economy, etc.). [f. RE- 9, after *inflate, deflate*]

rēflā'tion *n*. (Econ.) inflation following deflation, to restore system to its previous condition. [f. RE- 9, after *inflation, deflation*]

reflĕ'ct *v*. 1. *v.t.* (Of surface or body) throw back (heat, light, sound, object, etc.), cause to rebound, (**shine with** ∼**ed light**, be noticeable only because of another's brilliance). 2. (Of mirror etc., or transf.) show image of, reproduce to eye or mind, exactly correspond in appearance or effect to, (*laws reflect the average moral attitude of half a century earlier*); ∼**ing telescope**, = REFLECTOR 2. 3. (Of action, result, etc.) bring back or cause to redound (credit, discredit, etc.), (abs.) bring discredit, (*up*)*on* person or method responsible. 4. *v.i.* & *t.* go back in thought, meditate, or consult with oneself (*on, upon,* or abs.), remind oneself or consider (*that, how,* etc.). 5. *v.i.* make disparaging remarks (*up*)*on*. [ME, f. OF *reflecter* or f. L *re(flectere flex-* bend); see RE- 9]

reflĕ'ction, ||**reflĕ'xion**, (-kshon) *n*. 1. reflecting or being reflected (**angle of** ∼, angle made by reflected ray with perpendicular to surface); reflected light, heat, colour, or image. 2. (piece of) censure (*on* or *upon*; thing bringing discredit (*up*)*on*. 3. reconsideration (*on reflection, I doubt whether I was right*). 4. mental faculty dealing with products of sensation and perception. 5. idea arising in the mind, mental or verbal; comment, apophthegm, (*on* or *upon*). 6. Hence ∼AL, ∼LESS, *adjs*. [ME, f. OF *reflexion* or f. LL *reflexio* (as prec.; see -ION), w. assim. to *reflect*]

reflĕ'ctive *a*. 1. (Of surface etc.) giving back reflection or image; (of light etc.) reflected. 2. (Of mental faculties) concerned in reflection or thought; (of person, mood, etc.) thoughtful, given to meditation. 3. Hence ∼LY[2] (-vlĭ) *adv*., ∼NESS (-vn-) *n*. [f. REFLECT +-IVE]

reflĕ'ctor *n*. body or surface reflecting rays, particles, objects, etc., esp. piece of glass or metal (usu. concave) for reflecting light in required direction, e.g. red one on back of vehicle. 2. (telescope etc. provided with) mirror to produce images. [f. REFLECT +-OR]

reflet (reflĕ') *n*. lustre or iridescence, esp. on pottery. [F, f. It. *riflesso* reflection, REFLEX[1]]

rē'flĕx[1] *n*. 1. reflected light or colour or glory (*the fame of Greece was a reflex from the glory of Athens*); (Paint.) part of picture represented as affected by the light or colour of another part. 2. image or reflection in mirror etc. 3. reproduction, secondary manifestation, corresponding result, (*legislation should be a reflex of public opinion*). 4. (Philol.) word etc. formed by development from earlier stage of language. **5.** a reflex action (*doctor tested patient's reflexes*); CON-DITION²ed *reflex*; hence ∿ŏ′LOGY *n*. [f. L *reflexus* (as REFLECT)]

rĕ′flĕx² *a.* **1.** bent backwards; (of light etc.) reflected; ∿ **angle** (exceeding 180°). **2.** (Of thought etc.) introspective, directed back upon itself or its own operations; (of effect or influence) reactive, coming back upon its author or source; (Radio etc.) using same amplifier for both radio-frequency and audio-frequency signal; copying by reflection from object to be copied. **3.** (Physiol.) ∿ **action** (independent of the will, caused as automatic response to nerve-stimulation); ∿ **arc**, sequence of nerves involved in this. **4.** ∿ (**camera**), camera in which image is reflected by mirror(s) to allow focusing up to moment of exposure. **5.** Hence ∿LY² *adv.* [f. L *reflexus* p.p. of *reflectere* REFLECT]

rĕflĕ′xed (-kst) *a.* (Bot.) bent back. [p.p. of obs. *reflex* v. = REFLECT]

rĕflĕ′x|ible *a.* capable of being reflected; hence ∿IBI′LITY *n.* [f. as prec. + -IBLE]

reflexion. See REFLEXION.

rĕflĕ′xive *a.* & *n.* (Gram.) (word or form) implying subject's action on himself or itself (*pride oneself, wash oneself, suggest itself, bethought me*); (adjective) referring to subject of sentence; (verb) indicating that subject is same as object; *reflexive* PRONOUN; hence ∿LY² (-vlĭ) *adv.* [f. as REFLEXED + -IVE]

rĕfloa′t *v.t.* set (stranded ship) afloat again. [f. RE-9 + FLOAT²]

rĕ′flu|ent (-ŏŏ-) *a.* flowing back (*refluent tide, blood*); hence ∿ENCE *n.* [ME, f. L *re(fluere* flow); see RE-9, -ENT]

rĕ′flŭx *n.* backward flow; (Chem.) method of boiling in which vapour is liquefied and returned to boiler. [ME, f. RE-9 + FLUX]

rĕfŏ′rĕst *v.t.*, **rĕfŏrĕstā′TION** *n.* See RE-9.

rĕfŏ′rm¹ *v.* **1.** *v.t.* & *i.* make (person, institution, procedure, conduct, one*self*), or (of person or body of persons) become, better by removal or abandonment of imperfections, faults, or errors; *correct (legal document); R∿ed, of Reform Judaism; R∿ed **Church**, one that has accepted the principles of the Reformation, esp. Calvinist opp. Lutheran. **2.** *v.t.* abolish, cure, (abuse, malpractice). **3.** Hence ∿ABLE *a.* [ME, f. OF *reformer* or f. L *re(formare* FORM²); see RE-8]

rĕfŏ′rm² *n.* removal of abuse(s) esp. in politics (R∿ **Bill, Act**, those of 1831-2 etc. amending parliamentary representation); improvement made or suggested; (R∿) simplified and rationalized form of Judaism; ∿ **school**, reformatory for young persons. [f. prec. or f. F *réforme*]

rĕ-fŏ′rm³ *v.t.* & *i.* form again. [f. RE-8 + FORM²]

rĕ-fŏrmā′tion¹ *n.* forming or being formed again. [f. RE-8 + FORMATION]

rĕformā′tion² *n.* reforming or being reformed, esp. radical change for the better in political, religious, or social affairs; **the R∿**, 16th-c. movement for reform of doctrines and practices of Roman Church ending in establishment of Reformed or Protestant Churches, whence ∿AL *a.* [ME f. OF, or f. L *reformatio* (as REFORM¹; see -ATION)]

rĕfŏ′rmative *a.* = foll. [f. OF *reformatif -ive* or med. L *reformativus* (as REFORM¹; see -ATIVE)]

rĕfŏ′rmatory *a.* & *n.* **1.** *a.* tending or intended to produce reform. **2.** *n.* (US or Hist.) institution to which juvenile or female offenders are sent to be reformed. [f. REFORMATION + -ORY]

rĕfŏ′rmer *n.* In vbl senses; leader in the Reformation; advocate of reform. [f. REFORM¹ + -ER¹]

rĕfŏ′rm|ism *n.* policy of reform rather than abolition; hence ∿IST (2) *n.* [f. REFORM² + -ISM]

rĕfrā′ct *v.t.* (Of water, air, glass, etc.) deflect (ray of light etc.) at certain angle when it enters obliquely from another medium of different density; determine

refractive condition of (eye); hence or cogn. ∿ION *n.* (**angle of** ∿**ion**, angle made by refracted ray with perpendicular to surface; **double** ∿**ion**, refraction forming two rays in different directions), ∿IVE *a.* (∿**ive index**, ratio of velocity of light in two adjacent media). [f. L *re(fringere fract-* = *frangere* break); see RE-5]

rĕfrăctŏ′mĕter *n.* instrument for measuring refractive index. [f. prec. + -O- + -METER]

rĕfrā′ctor *n.* refracting medium or lens; telescope using lens to produce image. [f. REFRACT + -OR]

rĕfrā′ctor|y *a.* & *n.* **1.** *a.* stubborn, unmanageable, rebellious; (of wound, disease, etc.) not yielding to treatment; (of person etc.) resistant to infection; (of substance) hard to fuse or work. **2.** Hence ∿ILY² *adv.*, ∿INESS *n.* **3.** *n.* substance especially resistant to heat, corrosion, etc. [alt. of obs. *refractary* f. L *refractarius* (as REFRACT, -ARY¹); see -ORY]

rĕfrai′n *n.* recurring phrase or line(s) esp. at end of stanzas; music accompanying this. [ME f. OF, earlier *refrait*, prob. f. Prov. *refranh*, bird song (*refranhar* f. Rom. **refrangere*, L *refringere*; see REFRACT)]

rĕfrai′n² *v.* **1.** *v.t.* (arch.) put restraint upon, curb, (oneself, one's tears, soul, etc.). **2.** *v.i.* abstain from doing something; abstain *from* act or do*ing*. [ME, f. OF *refrener* f. L *re(frenare* f. *frenum* bridle); see RE-9]

rĕfră′ng|ible (-nj-) *a.* that can be refracted; hence ∿IBI′LITY *n.* [f. mod. L *refrangibilis* (*refrangere* = L *refringere*; see REFRACT, -IBLE)]

rĕfrĕ′sh *v.* **1.** *v.t.* (Of food, drink, rest, amusement, etc., or person providing these, esp. in ∿ one**self**) reanimate, reinvigorate; ∿*ing innocence* etc., interesting to blasé observer. **2.** freshen up (memory, esp. by consulting source of information); restore (fire etc.) with fresh supply; make cool again. **3.** *v.i.* take esp. liquid refreshment. [ME, f. OF *refreschi(e)r* (*fres fresche* FRESH; see RE-9)]

rĕfrĕ′sher *n.* In vbl senses; extra fee to counsel in prolonged case; (colloq.) a drink; ∿ **course** (reviewing previous studies, or giving instruction in modern methods etc.). [ME, f. prec. + -ER¹]

rĕfrĕ′shment *n.* refreshing or being refreshed in mind or body; thing, esp. (usu. in *pl.*) drink or food, that refreshes (*the sight was a refreshment to him*; *take some refreshment(s)*); ∿ **room** (where food and drink are available at railway station etc.); R∿ **Sunday** (4th in Lent, with gospel f. John 6). [ME, f. OF *refreschement* (as REFRESH; see -MENT)]

rĕfri′gerant *a.* & *n.* (substance) that cools, or (Med.) allays fever. [f. F *réfrigérant* or f. L (as foll.; see -ANT)]

rĕfri′ger|āte *v.* **1.** *v.t.* & *i.* make or become cool or cold. **2.** subject (food etc.) to cold in order to freeze or preserve. **3.** So ∿A′TION *n.* [f. L *re(frigerare* f. *frigus frigoris* cold); see RE-9, -ATE³]

rĕfri′gerātor *n.* cabinet or room in which food etc. is refrigerated. [f. prec. + -OR]

rĕfri′geratory *n.* & *a.* **1.** *n.* cold-water vessel attached to still for condensing vapour. **2.** *a.* cooling. [f. mod. L *refrigeratorium* n., L *refrigeratorius* a. (as REFRIGERATE; see -ORY)]

rĕfri′ng|ent (-nj-) *a.* (Phys.) refracting; hence ∿ENCE, ∿ENCY, *ns.* [f. L *refringere*; see REFRACT, -ENT]

rĕft. See REAVE.

rĕfu′el *v.t.* & *i.* (||-ll-). replenish fuel supply (of). [f. RE-9 + FUEL]

rĕ′fūge *n.* **1.** (place of) shelter from pursuit or danger or trouble (*has found (a) refuge*; *take refuge in a cave, in lying*); **city of** ∿ (for those guilty of manslaughter in ancient Israel); (**house of**) ∿, institution for the homeless etc. **2.** person, thing, course, that gives shelter or is resorted to in difficulties (*he is the refuge of the distressed*; *books are the refuge of the destitute*); traffic island. [ME f. OF, f. L *re(fugium* f. *fugere* flee); see RE-4]

rĕfūgee′ *n.* person taking refuge, esp. in foreign country from religious or political persecution, or from war, earthquake, etc. [f. F *réfugié* p.p. (as n.) of (*se*) *réfugier* (as prec.)]

For other words in *re-* **see** RE-.

refu'lg|ent *a.* shining, gloriously bright; hence or cogn. ∼ENCE *n.*, ∼ent̄LY² *adv.* [f. L *re(fulgēre* shine); see RE- 6, -ENT]

refu'nd¹ *v.t.* pay back (money received or taken, expenses incurred by another, or abs.); reimburse; hence ∼MENT *n.* [ME, in sense 'pour back', f. OF *refonder* or f. L *re(fundere fus-* pour; see RE- 9); later assoc. w. FUND]

re'fund² *n.* refunding; repayment. [f. prec.]

re-fu'nd³ *v.t.* fund (debt etc.) afresh. [f. RE- 8 + FUND]

refur'bish *v.t.*, see RE- 9; **refur'nish** *v.t.*, see RE- 8.

refu'sal (-z-) *n.* **1.** refusing or being refused; **will take no** ∼, is importunate. **2.** (first) ∼, right or privilege of deciding to accept or reject a thing before it is offered to others. [f. foll. +-AL 2]

refu's|e¹ (-z) *v.* **1.** *v.t.* say or convey by action that one will not accept or submit to or give or grant or gratify or consent *(refuse offer, gift, chance, office, candidate, person as husband etc.; refuse orders, control, etc.; refuse obedience, compliance; refused me satisfaction, my request; refuse to do; car refuses to start)*; not grant request made by (person); (of horse) be unwilling to jump (fence etc., or abs.); hence ∼ABLE *a.* **2.** *v.i.* make refusal; (Cards) not follow suit. [ME, f. OF *refuser* f. Rom. *refusare* prob. f. L *recusare* (see RECUSANT) after *refutare* REFUTE]

re'fuse² *n.* & *a.* (what is) rejected as worthless or left over after use, esp. in household. [ME, perh. f. OF *refusé* p.p. (as prec.)]

re-fu'se³ (-z) *v.t,* fuse again. [f. RF- 9 + FUSF¹,³]

refu't|e *v.t.* prove falsity or error of (statement, opinion, argument, person advancing it), rebut or repel by argument; hence or cogn. ∼ABLE *a.*, ∼AL 2, **refuta'TION**, *ns.* [f. L *re(futare;* cf. CONFUTE; see RE- 9]

regai'n *v.t.* recover possession of *(regain confidence, consciousness)*; reach (place) again; recover (one's *balance or feet or footing or legs).* [f. F *re(gagner* GAIN²); see RE- 9]

re'gal¹ *a.* of or by kings *(regal government, title, office)*; fit for a king, magnificent, *(lives in regal splendour)*; hence ∼LY² *adv.* [ME f. OF, or f. L *regalis (rex regis* king; see -AL)]

re'gal² *n.* (Hist.) small portable reed-organ. [f. F *régale]*

rega'le¹ *n.* (arch.) choice repast (lit. or fig.), feast of some dainty; a dainty; choice flavour. [obs. F, f. OF *gale* pleasure]

rega'le² *v.* **1.** *v.t.* entertain choicely (often iron.) with food or *with* talk etc., (of beauty, flowers, etc.) give delight to. **2.** *v.i.* feed oneself choicely *(on).* **3.** Hence ∼MENT (-lm-) *n.* [f. F *régaler* (as prec.)]

rega'lia¹ (-lya) *n. pl.* insignia of royalty used at coronations, insignia of an order, e.g. of Freemasons, or of civic dignity. [med. L, = royal privileges, f. L, neut. pl. of *regalis* REGAL¹; see -IA²]

rega'lia² (-lya) *n.* large cigar of especially good quality. [f. Sp. *regalia* royal privilege (cf. prec.)]

re'galism *n.* doctrine of sovereign's ecclesiastical supremacy. [f. REGAL¹ + -ISM]

rega'lity *n.* attribute of kingly power, being king; royal privilege. [ME, f. OF *regalité* or f. med. L *regalitas* (as REGAL¹; see -ITY)]

regar'd¹ *v.t.* **1.** gaze upon (usu. w. adv. phr. or adv.; *found him regarding me with curiosity, intently).* **2.** give heed to, take into account, let one's course be affected by, (esp. w. neg.; person, advice, etc., or abs.). **3.** look upon or contemplate mentally *with* reverence, horror, etc., or in specified manner *(regard it in that light)* or with specified sentiment *(I still regard him kindly)*, or as being *(is to be regarded as a wild beast; regard it as madness* or *indispensable, him as among my friends).* **4.** (Of thing) concern, have relation to, have some connection with; **as** ∼**s,** ∼**ing** *(part. or prep.)*, about, concerning, in respect of, so far as it concerns, *(considerations regarding peace; am innocent as regards or regarding the former).* [ME, f. F *re(garder* GUARD²); see RE- 6; cf. REWARD]

regar'd² *n.* **1.** gaze, steady or significant look. **2.** respect, point attended to, *(in this* etc. *regard;* **in** ∼ **to** or **of, with** ∼ **to,** regarding, in respect of; **in** person's ∼, concerning or about or towards him. **3.** attention, heed, care, *(to* or *for; regard must be had* or *paid to general principles; the next object of regard is his conduct; act without regard to* or *for decency; pays no regard to expostulations* or *adviser)*; hence ∼FUL *a. (of).* **4.** esteem, kindly feeling or respectful opinion, *(for; have little* or *a great regard for him, no* or *a high regard for his judgement* or *advice)*; (in *pl.)* expression of friendliness in letter etc., compliments, *(kind regards to you all; give him my (best* etc.*) regards).* [ME f. OF *regard (regarder;* see prec.)]

regar'dant *a.* (Her.) looking backwards; (arch.) observant, with steady or intent gaze. [AF & OF (as REGARD¹; see -ANT)]

regar'dless *a.* & *adv.* without paying attention; without regard or consideration *(of* expense etc.; *or* abs.); hence ∼LY² *adv.*, ∼NESS *n.* [f. REGARD² + -LESS]

rega'tta *n.* meeting for boat or yacht races. [It. (Venetian)]

regd. *abbr.* registered.

regel|ā'te *v.i.* freeze again (esp. of pieces of ice etc. frozen together after temporary thawing of surfaces); hence ∼A'TION *n.* [f. RE- 9 + L *gelare* freeze + -ATE³]

re'gency *n.* office of regent; commission acting as regent; regent's or regency-commission's period of office (the R∼, 1810–20 in England, 1715–23 in France; R∼ dress, furniture, etc., of the style characteristic of the Regency in England, R∼ stripes, broad coloured stripes of equal width on fabric etc.). [ME, f. med. L *regentia* (as REGENT; see -ENCY)]

rege'ner|āte *v.* **1.** *v.t.* invest with new and higher spiritual nature; improve moral condition of, breathe new and more vigorous and spiritually higher life into, (person, institution, etc.). **2.** generate again, bring into renewed existence, *(must regenerate his self--respect)*; form afresh (lost etc. part of body); (Electr.) increase (current) by feedback. **3.** *v.i.* reform oneself **4.** come into renewed existence. **5.** Hence or cogn. ∼ATE², ∼ATIVE, *adjs.*, ∼A'TION, ∼ātor, *ns.* [f. L *re(generare* GENERATE); see RE- 8]

rege'nēsis *n.* See RE- 8.

re'gent *n.* & *a.* **1.** *n.* person appointed to administer State, esp. kingdom during minority, absence, or incapacity of monarch. **2.** *member of the governing body of a State University. **3.** (arch.) ruler, ruling principle. **4.** ∼**-bird,** Austral. bower-bird; ∥R∼ **House,** (Cambridge Univ.) general assembly of resident senior members. **5.** *a.* (placed after *n.*) acting as regent *(Queen, Prince,* etc., *Regent).* [ME f. OF, or f. L *regere* rule; see -ENT]

reger'minate *v.i.*, **regermina'TION** *n.* See RE- 9.

re'ggae (-ā) *n.* W. Ind. style of music with strongly accented subsidiary beat. [W. Ind.]

re'gicide *n.* killer or participator in killing of a king (the R∼s, those concerned in trying and executing Charles I of England or Louis XVI of France); killing of a king; hence **regici'd**AL *a.* [f. L *rex regis* king + -I- + -CIDE]

régie (rāzhē') *n.* State monopoly or control of tobacco, salt, etc. [F, fem. p.p. of *régir* rule]

regī'ld (-g-) *v.t.* See RE- 9.

regime, régi'me, (rāzhē'm) *n.* **1.** method or system of government, prevailing system of things; ANCIEN RÉGIME. **2.** condition(s) under which scientific, industrial, etc., process occurs. [f. F *régime* f. as foll.]

re'gimen *n.* (Med.) prescribed course of exercise, way of life, and esp. diet; (Gram.) relation of syntactic dependence between words, government; (arch.) system of government. [L *(regere* rule)]

re'giment (-jĭm-, -jm-) *n.*, & *v.t.* **1.** *n.* permanent recruiting and training unit of army usu. commanded by (Lieutenant-)Colonel and divided into several companies or troops or batteries and often into two or more battalions; operational unit of artillery, tanks, armoured cars, etc.; **Royal R~ (of Artillery**), Royal Artillery. **2.** large array or number, legion, (usu. *of*). **3.** (arch.) rule, government, (*monstrous regiment of women*). **4.** (*or* -ĕnt) *v.t.* form (men) into regiment(s); organize (workers, labour, data, etc., esp. oppressively) in groups or according to a system, whence **regiment**A'TION (*or* -ĕn-) *n.* [ME in sense 3, f. OF, f. LL *regimentum* (as prec.; see -MENT)]

regime'ntal *a.* & *n.* **1.** *a.* of a regiment; *regimental* COLOUR[1]; hence **~**LY[2] *adv.* **2.** *n.* (in *pl.*) dress worn by regiment, military uniform. [f. prec.+-AL]

Regina (rijī'na) *n.* reigning queen (abbr. *R.*, in signatures to proclamations: *Elizabeth R.*; in titles of Crown lawsuits: **~ v. Jones**, the Crown versus Jones; etc.). [L (*rex regis* king; see -INA)]

re'gion (-jon) *n.* **1.** tract of land, space, place, having more or less definitely marked boundaries or characteristics (*a desert, fertile, region; the region between the Elbe and the Rhine*). **2.** separate part of world or universe; layer of atmosphere or sea according to height or depth; LOWER[3], UPPER, regions. **3.** department of country etc. (*the North-East, Strathclyde, Region*); sphere or realm of (*you are getting into the region of metaphysics*); **in the ~ of**, approximately. **4.** part of the body round or near some organ etc. (*the lumbar, abdominal*, etc., *region; the region of the eyes*). **5.** Hence **~**AL *a.*, **~**alISM (2, 4) *n.*, **~**alIZE (3) *v.t.* [ME f. OF, f. L *regio -onis* direction, district (*regere* direct; see -ION)]

regisseur' (rāzhisēr') *n.* director of ballet; ||director or *producer of stage-play. [f. F *régisseur* stage--manager]

re'gister[1] *n.* **1.** book etc. in which entries are made of details to be recorded for reference; official or authoritative list kept e.g. of births, marriages, and burials or deaths, of shipping, of professionally qualified persons, of qualified voters in constituency, (**~ office**, a registry). **2.** (Mus.) sliding part in organ controlling set of pipes; set of pipes thus controlled; compass of voice or instrument, part of voice-compass (*head, lower*, etc., *register*). **3.** form of language (colloquial, literary, etc.) customarily used in particular circumstances. **4.** adjustable plate for widening or narrowing an opening and regulating draught esp. in fire-grate; indicator recording speed, force, etc.; CASH[1] *register.* **5.** (Print.) exact correspondence of position of printed matter on two sides of leaf (**in ~**, so corresponding); (Photog.) correspondence of position of colour--components of printed picture. **6.** certificate of ship's ownership (*register* TON[1]). [ME & OF *regestre, registre*, or f. med. L *regestrum, registrum* alt. of *regestum* (LL *regesta* pl. things recorded f. as RE- 8, L *gerere gest-* carry)]

re'gister[2] *v.* **1.** *v.t.* set down (name, fact, etc.) formally, record in writing; (fig.) make mental note of. **2.** enter or cause to be entered in particular register; **~ letter**, entrust it to post office for transmission as **~ed post** with special precautions for safety and for compensation in case of loss; **~ed nurse** (with State certificate of competence in nursing); **~** one**self** (or abs.), put one's name on electoral etc. register, or as guest in register kept by hotel, as participant at conference, etc. **3.** (Of instrument) record automatically, indicate; express (emotion) facially or by gesture. **4.** *v.i.* & *t.* (Print. etc.) correspond, make correspond, exactly in position. **5.** *v.i.* make impression on person's mind (*name did not register with me*). **6.** Hence **re'gister**ABLE *a.* [ME, f. OF *registrer*, or f. med. L *registrare* (as prec.)]

re'gister[3] *n.* registrar; **Lord Clerk R~**, State archivist in Scotland. [prob. f. foll.]

registrar (rĕ'-, -ār') *n.* official recorder, person charged with keeping register, esp. in university; ||judicial and administrative officer of High Court etc.; doctor undergoing hospital training as specialist; **R~ General**, head of office conducting population census; hence **~**SHIP *n.* [f. med. L *registrarius* (*registrum* REGISTER[1]; see -AR[2])]

||**re'gistrary** *n.* registrar of Cambridge University. [f. as prec.; see -ARY[1]]

registra'tion *n.* registering or being registered; **~ mark, number**, combination of letters and figures identifying motor vehicle. [f. obs. F *régistration* or f. med. L *registratio* (as prec.; see -ATION)]

re'gistry *n.* registration; place or office where registers or records are kept; **~ (office**), place where marriages are conducted without religious ceremony, or (arch.) where lists of vacant situations and of persons seeking them are kept. [f. obs. *registery* f. med. L *registerium* (as REGISTER[1])]

||**Re'gius** *a.* **~ professor**, holder of chair founded by sovereign (esp. one at Oxf. or Camb. instituted by Henry VIII) or filled by Crown appointment. [L, = royal (*rex regis* king)]

re'glet *n.* (Archit.) narrow strip separating mouldings; (Print.) thin strip of wood or metal separating type. [f. F *réglet* dim. of *règle* (as RULE)]

re'gnal *a.* of a reign (**~ year**, beginning with sovereign's accession or an anniversary of it). [f. AL *regnalis* (as REIGN[1]; see -AL)]

re'gnant *a.* reigning (**Queen R~**, queen ruling in her own right and not as consort); (of things, qualities, opinions, etc.) predominant, prevalent. [f. L *regnare* REIGN[2]; see -ANT]

regor'ge *v.* **1.** *v.t.* bring or cast up again after swallowing. **2.** *v.i.* gush or flow back from pit, channel, etc. [f. F *regorger*, or f. RE- 9+GORGE[2]]

regra't|e *v.t.* (Hist.) buy up (goods) to retail at profit in same or neighbouring place; hence **~**ER[1] *n.* [f. OF *regrater* (perh. as RE-, *grater* to scratch, of Gmc orig.)]

re'gress[1] *n.* going back; declension, backward tendency; reasoning from effect to cause. [ME, f. L *regressus* (as foll.)]

regre'ss[2] *v.i.* move backwards (lit. or fig.). [f. L *re(gredi gress- = gradi* step); see RE- 9]

regre'ssion (-shon) *n.* backward movement, retreat; (Geom.) return of curve; relapse, reversion; return to earlier stage of development; **~ curve** (giving best fit to inexact data); so **regre'ss**IVE *a.* [f. L *regressio* (as prec.; see -ION)]

regre't *v.t.* (-**tt**-), & *n.* **1.** *v.t.* feel sorrow for loss of, wish one could have again; be distressed about or sorry for (event, fact), grieve at, repent (action etc.); be sorry to say etc. or *that* (esp. in polite refusal of invitation etc.); hence **~**TABLE *a.*, **~**TABLY *adv.* **2.** *n.* sorrow for loss of person or thing; repentance or annoyance concerning thing done or not done (*has no regrets; expressed regret for his misbehaviour*); (real or politely simulated) vexation or disappointment caused by occurrence or situation (*hear with regret of* or *that; refuse with much regret or many regrets*); hence (of person or feeling) **~**FUL *a.*, **~**FULLY *adv.* [ME, perh. f. F, f. OF *regreter* bewail, perh. f. as RE- 3+Gmc *grētan*; cf. GREET[2]]

regrou'p, *v.t.* & *i.*, **regrou'p**MENT *n.*, (-ōō'-). See RE-8.

Regt. *abbr.* Regiment.

re'gulable *a.* admitting of regulation. [f. REGULATE +-ABLE]

re'gular *a.* & *n.* **1.** *a.* (Eccl.) bound by religious rule, belonging to religious or monastic order, (opp. *secular; regular canon, clerk*, or *clerk, canon, regular*). **2.** (Of shape, structure, arrangement, or of objects in these respects) following or exhibiting a principle, harmonious, consistent, systematic, symmetrical, (*regular nomenclature, formation, features, curve*); (of flower) having radial symmetry; (Geom., of figure) having all sides and all angles equal; **the five ~ solids**, tetrahedron or triangular pyramid bounded by 4 equal triangles, hexahedron or cube by 6 equal squares, octahedron by 8 equal triangles, dodecahedron by 12 equal pentagons, and icosahedron by 20 equal triangles. **3.** acting, done, recurring, uniformly or calculably in time or manner, habitual, constant, not capricious or casual, orderly, (*regular working, footsteps, procedure, sequence, pulse, bowels, customer, salary, orbit, bedtime, employment*); (of person) defecating or menstruating at predictable times; **keep ~ hours,** do same thing at same time daily; **a ~ life** (lived in orderly manner, esp. without excesses). **4.** conforming to a standard of etiquette etc., not transgressing conventions, correct, (*had no regular introduction; the attitude of the Government has been quite regular*). **5.** (Gram.) (Of verb, noun, etc.) following a normal type of inflexion. **6.** properly constituted or qualified, not defective or amateur, devoted exclusively or primarily to its nominal function, (*cooks as well as a regular cook; has no regular profession*); **~ army** or **soldiers** (opp. volunteers or militia or conscripts). **7.** (colloq.) complete, thorough, indubitable, (*he is a regular rascal, brick, hero; had a regular smash, overhauling,* etc.). **8.** Hence **~ITY** (-ă'r-) *n.,* **~IZE** (3) *v.t.,* **~LY²** *adv.* **9.** *n.* one of the regular clergy; regular soldier; (colloq.) regular customer, visitor, etc.; (colloq.) person permanently employed. [ME f. OF *reguler,* & f. L *regularis* (*regula* RULE); see -AR¹]

rĕ′gŭl|āte *v.t.* control by rule, subject to restrictions; moderate, adapt to requirements; alter speed of (machine, clock) so that it may work accurately; hence **~ātor** *n.,* **~ATIVE** *a.* [f. LL *regulare* f. L *regula* RULE + -ATE³]

rĕgŭlā′tion *n.* & *a.* **1.** *n.* regulating or being regulated; prescribed rule, authoritative direction. **2.** *a.* in accordance with regulations, of correct pattern etc., ordinary, usual, formal, (*of the regulation size; exceed the regulation speed; a regulation sword, cap; the regulation mourning*). [f. prec. + -ATION]

rĕ′gŭl|us *n.* (*pl.* **~i** *pr.* -ī, *or* **~uses**). **1.** (Chem.) purer or metallic part of mineral separated by sinking to bottom in crucible on reduction; impure metallic product of smelting various ores; hence **~INE¹** *a.* **2.** goldcrest. [L, dim. of *rex regis* king; sense 1 orig. of metallic form of antimony, perh. as title of honour due to its readiness to combine with gold]

rēgûr′git|āte *v.* **1.** *v.i.* gush back. **2.** *v.t.* (Of person, animal, stomach, crop, or receptacle) cast or pour out again. **3.** Hence **~A′TION** *n.* [f. med. L *re(gurgitare* f. L *gurges gurgitis* whirlpool); see RE- 9, -ATE³]

rĕhabi′lit|āte *v.t.* restore to privileges, reputation, or proper condition; restore to effectiveness or normal life by training (esp. after imprisonment or illness); hence **~A′TION** *n.* [f. med. L *re(habilitare,* see HABILI-TATE); see RE- 9]

rēhā′ndle *v.t.* handle again, esp. give new form or arrangement to. [f. RE- 8 + HANDLE²]

rēhă′ng *v.t.* (rehu′ng). hang (esp. picture or curtain) again or differently. [f. RE- 8 + HANG¹]

rēhă′sh¹ *v.t.* put (old material) into new form without significant change or improvement. [f. RE- 8 + HASH¹]

rē′hăsh² *n.* rehashing; material rehashed. [f. RE- 8 + HASH²]

rēhear′ *v.t.* See RE- 8.

rēhear′sal (-hẽr′-) *n.* rehearsing; performance of play or other entertainment or important event preparatory to public performance; DRESS² *rehearsal.* [ME, f. foll. + -AL 2]

rēhear′se (-hẽr′s) *v.t.* recite, say over, repeat from beginning to end, give list of, recount, enumerate; have rehearsal of (play etc., part in it, or abs.), practise for later public performance; train (person) by rehearsal. [ME, f. AF *rehearser,* OF *reherc(i)er,* perh. f. as RE- + *hercer* to harrow (*herse* a harrow; see HEARSE)]

rē-hea′t *n.,* & *v.t.* **1.** *n.* obtaining of extra power by using hot exhaust to burn extra fuel in engine. **2.** *v.t.* heat again. [f. RE- 9 + HEAT¹,²]

rēhobō′ăm *n.* large winebottle, twice size of jeroboam. [f. *Rehoboam* (1 Kgs. 11-14)]

Reich (rīk, rīχ) *n.* the German commonwealth as a whole (**First ~,** Holy Roman Empire, 962-1806; **Second ~,** 1871-1918; **Third ~,** Nazi regime, 1933-45). [G, = empire]

Rei′chstag (rī′kstahg) *n.* (Hist.) the German parliament. [G]

rē′i|fȳ *v.t.* convert (person, abstract concept mentally) into thing, materialize; hence **~FICA′TION** *n.,* **~ficātory** *a.* [f. L *res* thing + -I- + -FY]

reign¹ (rān) *n.* sovereignty, rule, sway, (*under the reign of Queen Victoria; his reign was a gentle one; the reign of law in nature; democracy resumed her reign; Reign of* TERROR); (poet.) realm, sphere; period during which sovereign, champion, etc., reigns (*in the reign of John; during five successive reigns*). [ME, f. OF *re(i)gne* kingdom f. L *regnum* (*rex regis* king)]

reign² (rān) *v.i.* **1.** hold royal office, be king or queen (lit. or fig.; *reigned over Great Britain for 60 years; a king who desired to rule as well as reign; better to reign in hell than serve in heaven*); **~ing beauty,** woman acknowledged as supreme beauty for the time being; **~ing champion** etc. (who most recently won the title). **2.** hold sway, prevail, (*dissension and improvidence reigned*); **silence ~s,** all is quiet. [ME, f. OF *reignier* f. L *regnare* (as prec.)]

rēigni′te *v.t.* & *i.* See RE- 9.

Reilly. See RILEY.

rēimbûr′se *v.t.* repay (person who has expended money, person's expenses, person expenses); hence **~MENT** (-sm-) *n.* [f. RE- 9 + obs. *imburse* put in purse f. med. L *imbursare* (as IM-¹, PURSE¹)]

rēimpôr′t¹ *v.t.,* **rēi′mpôrt²** *n.,* see RE- 9; **rēimpō′se** (-z) *v.t.,* **rēimposi′TION** (-z-) *n.,* see RE- 8, 9.

rein (rān) *n.,* & *v.t.* **1.** *n.* (in *sing* or *pl.*) long narrow strap with each end attached to bit used to guide or check horse etc. in riding or driving, similar device to restrain child etc.; (*fig.*) means of control; **draw ~,** stop one's horse, pull up, abandon effort, retrench expenditure, etc.; **give horse the ~(s),** let it go its own way; **give (free) ~(s) to,** let (one's imagination etc.) have free scope; **keep a tight ~ on,** allow little freedom to; **assume, drop, the ~s of government,** enter upon, resign, office; hence **~′LESS** *a.* **2.** *v.t.* check or manage with reins; (fig.) govern, restrain, control; pull *up* or *back* with reins, hold *in* with reins, (horse, or abs.; lit. or fig.). [ME, f. OF *rene, reigne,* earlier *resne,* f. Rom. *retina f. L *retinēre* RETAIN]

rēincar′n|āte *v.t.* bring soul of (person) into another body after death; so **~ATE⁹** *a.,* **~A′TION** *n.* [f. RE-8 + INCARNATE²]

rēincor′porāte *v.t.,* **rēincorpora′TION** *n.,* (-n-k-). See RE- 9.

rei′ndeer (rā′n-) *n.* (*pl.* usu. same). subarctic deer (*Rangifer tarandus*), with large antlers in both sexes, used for drawing sledges and kept in herds for its milk, flesh, and hide; **~ moss,** lichen of genus *Cladonia* much eaten by reindeer. [ME, f. ON *hreindýri* (*hreinn* reindeer, *dýr* DEER)]

rēinfôr′ce *v.t.* strengthen or support by additional men or material or by increase of numbers, quantity, size, thickness, importance, etc., (*reinforce fortress, army, provisions, party, the basses* etc. in band or chorus, *person's health* etc. with food etc., one's *argument* with fresh points); **~d concrete** (with metal bars, gratings, or wire, embedded in it to increase its strength). [f. earlier *renforce* f. F *renforcer,* after RE- 6, *inforce =* ENFORCE]

rēinfôr′cement (-sm-) *n.* reinforcing or being reinforced; (in *pl.*) additional men, ships, etc., for military or naval force; anything that reinforces. [f. prec. + -MENT]

reins (rānz) *n. pl.* (arch.) the kidneys; the loins. [ME f. OF, f. L *renes* pl.]

rēinser′t *v.t.,* **rēinser′TION** *n.* See RE- 9.

rēinstā′te *v.t.* restore to or replace in lost position, privileges, etc.; restore to health or proper order; hence **~MENT** (-tm-) *n.* [f. RE- 9; cf. INSTATE]

rēinsur′e (-shoor′) *v.i.* & *t.* insure again (esp. of insurer securing himself by transferring risk to another insurer); so **rēinsur′ANCE** *n.* [f. RE- 8 + INSURE]

rëïnter′ *v.t.*, **rëïntér′prèt** *v.t.* See RE- 8.

rëïnvĕ′st *v.t.* invest again (esp. money *in* other property, or person *with* privilege or *in* office); hence ∿MENT *n.* [f. RE- 8, 9 + INVEST]

rëïnvi′gorāte *v.t.*, **rëïnvigorA′TION** *n.* See RE- 9.

rëï′ssūe¹ (-shōō, -sū) *v.t.* issue again. [f. RE- 8 + ISSUE²]

rëï′ssūe² (-shōō, -sū) *n.* new issue, esp. of previously published book etc. [f. RE- 8 + ISSUE¹]

rëï′ter|āte *v.t.* say or do again or repeatedly; so ∿A′TION *n.*, ∿ATIVE *a.* [f. L re(*iterare* ITERATE); see RE- 8]

∥**reiv|e** (rēv) *v.i.* make raids, plunder; hence ∿ER¹ *n.* [var. of REAVE]

rèjě′ct¹ *v.t.* put aside or send back as not to be accepted, practised, believed, chosen, used, complied with, etc., (*reject doctrine, custom, evidence, candidate, literary contribution, food, request, suitor, vote*; *sorting- -machine rejects all defective specimens*); refuse acceptance of; cast up again, vomit, evacuate; hence or cogn. ∿ABLE *a.*, ∿ER¹, ∿OR, *ns.* [ME, f. L re(*jicere ject-* = *jacère* throw); see RE- 9]

rē′jĕct² *n.* person or thing rejected as unfit or below standard. [f. prec.]

rějĕctamĕ′nta *n. pl.* refuse, waste matters; things cast up by the sea. [mod. L (as REJECT¹; see -MENT)]

rějĕ′ction *n.* rejecting or being rejected; ∿ **slip**, formal notice from editor or publisher accompanying rejected MS. [f. F *réjection* or f. L *rejectio* (as REJECT¹; see -ION)]

rějĭ′g *v.t.* (-gg-). re-equip (factory etc.) for new type of work. [f. RE- 8 + JIG¹]

rèjoi′ce *v.* **1.** *v.t.* cause joy to, make glad, (*the news rejoiced him; I am rejoiced to hear it, that it should be so, at it,* etc.). **2.** *v.i.* feel great joy; be glad *that* or *to* do, take delight *in* or *at*; ∿ **in**, be blessed in the possession of, (joc.) have. **3.** make merry, celebrate some event; hence **rèjoi′cings** (-z) [-ING¹] *n. pl.* [ME, f. OF re(*joir joiss-* JOY²); see RE- 6]

rèjoi′n¹ *v.* **1.** *v.i.* (Law). reply to charge or pleading, esp. to plaintiff's replication. **2.** *v.t.* say in answer, retort. [ME, f. OF *rejoindre rejoign-* (as RE- 9, JOIN)]

rèjoi′n² *v.t.* & *i.* join together again, reunite; join (companion, company, etc.) again. [f. as prec. or RE- 9 + JOIN]

rèjoi′nder *n.* what is REJOIN¹ed or said in reply, retort; (Law) reply by rejoining. [f. AF *rejoinder* v. (as n.); see REJOIN¹, -ER⁴]

rèju′ven|āte (-ōō′-) *v.t.* & *i.* make or become young again; hence ∿A′TION, ∿ātOR, *ns.* [f. RE- 9 + L *juvenis* young + -ATE³]

rèjuven|ě′sce (-ōō-) *v.i.* & *t.* become young again; (Biol.) (of cells) gain, fill (cells) with, fresh vitality; so ∿E′SCENT *a.*, ∿E′SCENCE *n.* [f. LL re(*juvenescere* f. L *juvenis* young); see -ESCENT, RE- 9]

rēki′ndle *v.t.* & *i.* See RE- 9.

-rel *suf.* w. dim. or derog. force (*cockerel, doggerel, mongrel, scoundrel*). [f. or after OF *-erel(le)*]

rèlā′bel *v.t.* See RE- 8.

rèlă′pse *v.i.*, & *n.* **1.** *v.i.* fall back, sink again, (*into wrongdoing, error, heresy, weakness or illness, quiescence or indolence*); **relapsing fever,** bacterial infectious disease with recurrent periods of fever. **2.** *n.* act or fact of relapsing, esp. deterioration in patient's condition after partial recovery. [f. L re(*labi laps-* slip); see RE- 9]

rèlā′t|e *v.* **1.** *v.t.* narrate, recount, whence ∿ER¹ *n.* **2.** bring into relation (*to, with,* or abs.; *cannot relate the phenomena with* or *to anything we know* or *to each other*); establish relation between; (in *p.p.*) connected, allied, akin by blood or marriage, (*the law extends to several related groups; is related to the royal family*), whence ∿ědNESS *n.* **3.** *v.i.* have reference to, stand in some relation *to*, (*notices nothing but what relates to himself; how parts relate to parts*); (of person) bring oneself into relation *to*. [f. L *relat-* (see REFER)]

rèlā′tion *n.* **1.** narration, a narrative; (Law) laying of information. **2.** what one person or thing has to do with another, way in which one stands or is related to

another, kind of connection or correspondence or contrast or feeling that prevails between persons or things, (*the relations primarily expressed by prepositions are those of place and time; the outlay seems to bear no relation, is out of all relation, to the object aimed at; the relation between them is that of guardian and ward; the report has relation to a state of things now past*); (in *pl.*) dealings *with* others (PUBLIC *relations*), sexual intercourse; **in** ∿ **to,** as regards; hence ∿AL *a.* **3.** = foll. **4.** kinsman, kins- woman, relative, (*the squire and his relations; is he any relation, what relation is he, to you?; he is no relation*). [ME f. OF, or f. L *relatio* (as prec.; see -ION)]

rèlā′tionship *n.* state of being related; condition or character due to being related; kinship (lit. or fig.). [f. prec. + -SHIP]

rĕ′lative *a.* & *n.* **1.** *a.* (Gram.) (Of adjective, adverb, or PRONOUN) referring, and attaching a subordinate clause, to an expressed or implied antecedent; (of clause) attached to antecedent by relative word. **2.** having mutual relations, corresponding in some way, related to each other; (Mus.), of major and minor keys) having same signature; (of rank) corresponding in grade to another in a different service etc. **3.** pertinent, relevant, related to the subject, (*without some more relative proof*). **4.** comparative (*what are the relative merits of the two?; made the next attempt with relative coolness*); in relation to something else (*their relative positions are the same though they are miles apart; relative density, humidity, pitch*); proportioned to some- thing else (*supply is relative to demand*); implying comparison ('*heat*', '*speed*', '*strength*', *are relative words*); correlative or essentially involving a different but corresponding idea (*the concepts of husband and wife are relative to each other*); not having absolute existence but conditioned by relation to (*she is beautiful to me, but beauty is relative to the beholder's eye*). **5.** having reference, relating, *to* (*detailed the facts relative to the matter*). **6.** Hence ∿LY² (-vlĭ) *adv.* **7.** *n.* (Gram.) relative word, esp. pronoun, whence **rèlătĭ′vAL** *a.*; (Philos.) relative thing or term. **8.** kinsman, kinswoman; relation by blood or by marriage; species related to another by common origin (*the apes, man's closest relatives*). [ME, f. OF *relatif -ive* or f. LL *relativus* having reference or relation (as RELATE, -IVE)]

rĕ′lativ|ism *n.* doctrine that knowledge is relative, not absolute; so ∿IST (2) *n.* [f. prec. + -ISM]

rělatĭ′vĭty *n.* relativeness; (Econ., often in *pl.*) relative grading of jobs and pay; (Phys.) (**special**) ∿, theory based on the principle that all uniform motion is relative and that light has constant velocity in vacuum, regarding space-time as four-dimensional continuum, and modifying previous conceptions of geometry; **general** ∿, theory extending this to gravi- tation and accelerated motion; hence **rèlativĭ′stIC** *a.*, (of phenomena etc.) accurately described only by relative theories. [f. RELATIVE + -ITY]

rĕ′lativīz|e, -īs|e (-īz) *v.t.* make relative; apply relativity theory to; hence ∿A′TION *n.* [f. RELATIVE + -IZE]

rèlā′tor *n.* relater; (Law) maker of relation (sense 1). [L (as RELATE; see -OR)]

rèlă′x *v.* **1.** *v.t.* cause or allow to become loose or slack or limp, enfeeble, enervate, mitigate, abate, (*relax the bowels, the muscles, one's grasp, discipline, a rule, one's attention, one's efforts*); (in *p.p.*) at ease, unperturbed; ∿ed **throat,** form of sore throat; ∿ing **climate** (causing sluggish feeling, opp. *bracing*); hence ∿ANT *a.* & *n.*, (drug etc.) that relaxes. **2.** *v.i.* grow less tense or rigid or stern or ceremonious or energetic or zealous (*his hold, hands, severity, features, manner, en- deavours, relaxed*; *must not relax in one's efforts*); cease work or effort (*take one's coat off and relax*). [ME, f. L re(*laxare* f. *laxus* LAX¹); see RE- 9]

rèlăxā′tion *n.* partial remission of penalty, duty, etc.; cessation from work; recreation, amusements; dimi- nution of tension, severity, precision, etc.; (Phys.) restoration of equilibrium following disturbance. [f. L *relaxatio* (as prec.; see -ATION)]

rē′lay¹ *n.* **1.** set of fresh horses substituted for tired ones; gang of men, supply of material, etc., similarly used (*operated in relays*); ∼ (**race**), race between teams of which each person does part of the distance, the 2nd etc. members of the teams starting when the 1st etc. finish. **2.** relayed message etc. **3.** (Electr.) device actuating changes in circuit etc. in response to other changes affecting itself; device to receive, reinforce, and transmit telegraph message, broadcast programme, etc. [ME, f. OF *relai* (*relayer*; see foll.)]

rēlay² (rēlā′, rē′lā) *v.t.* **1.** arrange in, provide with, replace by, relay(s). **2.** receive (message etc. esp. by radio) and transmit to others. [f. prec. or f. OF *relayer* (as RE-, *laier* ult. f. L *laxare*; cf. RELAX)]

rē-lay′³ *v.t.* (**re-lai′d**). lay again. [f. RE- 8 + LAY³]

rēleas′e¹ *v.t.* **1.** set free, liberate, deliver, unfasten, (*from*); allow to move from fixed position; (Cinemat.) issue (film etc.) for (esp. general) exhibition; make (information, gramophone record, etc.) publicly or generally available. **2.** (Law). remit (debt), surrender (right), make over (property) to another; hence ∼EE′, ∼OR, *ns.* **3.** Hence ∼ABLE *a.* [ME, f. OF *relesser*, *relaiss(i)er* f. L *relaxare* (see RELAX)]

rēlea′se² *n.* **1.** deliverance, liberation, from trouble, sorrow, life, duty, restriction, or fixed position. **2.** handle, catch, etc., that releases part of machine etc. **3.** document etc. made available for publication (*news*, *press*, *release*); film, record, etc. that is released; releasing of document, film, etc., thus. **4.** (Law). conveyance of right or estate to another; document effecting this. [ME, f. OF *reles* (*relesser*; see prec.)]

rē′lēg|ate *v.t.* banish to place of exile; consign or dismiss to some usu. inferior position, sphere, etc.; (Sport) transfer (team) to lower division of league etc.; transfer (matter) for decision or execution, refer (person) for information etc., *to*; hence ∼ABLE *a.*, ∼A′TION *n.* [f. L *re(legare* send); see RE- 5, -ATE³]

rēlē′nt *v.i.* relax severity, become less stern, abandon harsh intention, yield to compassion; hence ∼LESS *a.* [ME, f. med. L *relentare* f. as RE- 9 + L *lentare* bend (*lentus* flexible)]

rē′lēv|ant *a.* bearing on or pertinent *to* the matter in hand; hence ∼ANCE, ∼ANCY, *ns.*, ∼antLY² *adv.* [f. med. L *relevans*, part. of L *relevare* RELIEVE; see -ANT]

rēli′|able *a.* that may be relied on; of sound and consistent character or quality; hence ∼ABI′LITY, ∼ableNESS (-bəln-), *ns.*, ∼ABLY *adv.* [f. RELY + -ABLE]

rēli′ance *n.* trust, confidence, (*upon*, *on*, *in*; *have*, *place*, *feel*, *reliance upon* etc.); thing depended upon (*the well is our chief reliance*); so **rēli′ANT** *a.* [f. RELY + -ANCE]

rē′lic *n.* **1.** part of holy person's body or belongings kept after his death as object of reverence; memento, souvenir. **2.** (in *pl.*) dead body, remains, of person; what has survived destruction or wasting, remnant, residue, scraps. **3.** surviving trace or memorial *of* a custom, belief, period, people, etc.; object interesting because of age or associations. [ME *relike*, *relique*, etc., f. OF *relique*, f. L RELIQUIAE]

rē′lict *n.* widow *of*; geological or other object which has survived in primitive form; animal or plant known to have existed in same form in previous geological ages. [(in 1st sense f. OF *relicte* f. LL *relicta*) f. p.p. of L *re(linquere lict-* leave); see RE- 3]

rēlie′f¹ *n.* **1.** alleviation of or deliverance from pain, distress, anxiety, etc., (*the medicine brought relief*; *gave a sigh of relief*; *it is a relief to come across an optimist*); ∼ (**bus** etc.) (supplementing ordinary service); ∼ **road**, road (esp. bypass) by which traffic can avoid congested area. **2.** feature etc. that diversifies monotony or relaxes tension (*a blank wall without relief*; *a comic scene follows by way of relief*). **3.** assistance given to the poor (esp. ||Hist. under the Poor Law) or to persons in special danger or need or difficulty (*a relief fund for the earthquake victims*; *income-tax relief*). **4.** reinforcement (esp. raising of siege) *of* besieged town. **5.** (replacing of person or persons on duty by) person(s) appointed to take turn of duty. **6.** (esp. Law). redress

of hardship or grievance (*sought relief of the nuisance*). [ME, f. AF *relef*, OF *relief*, (*relever reliev-* RELIEVE)]

rēlie′f² *n.* **1.** method of moulding or carving or stamping in which design stands out from plane or curved surface with projections proportioned and more (**high** ∼) or less (**low** ∼) closely approximating to those of objects imitated; piece of sculpture etc. in relief. **2.** appearance of being done in relief given by arrangement of line or colour or shading, distinctness of outline (lit. or fig.), vividness, (*stands out in relief*; *bring out the facts in full relief*); ∼ **map**, (1) map-model showing elevations and depressions of area dealt with, usu. on exaggerated relative scale, (2) ordinary map indicating hills and valleys by shading, colouring, or hachures, rather than by contour lines alone; ∼ **printing**, letterpress printing. [F, f. It. *rilievo* (*rilevare* raise f. L, as foll.)]

rēlie′v|e *v.t.* **1.** bring, give, be a, RELIEF¹ to (*besieged town was relieved*; *medicine relieves pain*; *am much relieved to hear it*; *devotes himself to relieving distress* or *the distressed*; *black dress relieved with white lace*); release (person) from duty or task by taking his place or providing a substitute. **2.** ∼e one's **feelings**, use strong language or vigorous behaviour when annoyed etc.; ∼e **nature** or one**self**, urinate or defecate; ∼e person **of**, take (load, duties, restriction, etc. or (joc.) purse, watch, etc.) from him. **3.** ∼**ing arch** (built into wall to relieve pressure); ||∼**ing officer**, (Hist.) official who took charge of poor or insane persons not otherwise cared for. **4.** bring into RELIEF², make appear solid or detached. **5.** Hence ∼ABLE *a.* [ME, f. OF *relever* f. L *re(levare* f. *levis* light); see RE- 9]

rēlie′vō *n.* (*pl.* ∼s). = RELIEF² (esp. in It. forms of combs.; ALTO, BASSO, MEZZO, -RELIEVO). [f. It. *rilievo* RELIEF² w. Anglicized spelling and pronunc.]

rēli′giŏ- *comb. form.* religion; religious. [f. foll.]

rēli′gion (-jŏn) *n.* **1.** particular system of faith and worship (*the Christian, Muslim, Buddhist, religion*; *established* ∼, that of Established CHURCH¹; **freedom of** ∼, right to follow whatever religion one chooses; NATURAL, REVEAL¹ed, *religion*; *all religions are the same to him*). **2.** human recognition of superhuman controlling power and esp. of a personal God or gods entitled to obedience and worship; effect of such recognition on conduct and mental attitude; **get** ∼, (vulg. or joc.) be converted to such recognition. **3.** thing that one is devoted to or is bound to do (*make a religion of football, of doing physical exercises*). **4.** life under monastic conditions (*enter into, be in, religion*; *her name in religion is Sister Mary*). **5.** Hence ∼LESS *a.* [ME, f. AF *religiun*, OF *religion* f. L *religio -onis* obligation, bond, reverence]

rēli′gioner (-jŏn-) *n.* member of monastic order; person zealous for religion. [f. prec. + -ER¹]

rēli′gion|ism (-jŏn-) *n.* excessive religious zeal; so ∼IST (2) *n.*, person (excessively) zealous for religion. [f. RELIGION + -ISM]

rēli′gionize (-jŏn-), **-ise** (-īz), *v.t.* convert to or imbue with religion. [f. RELIGION + -IZE]

rēli′giōse *a.* excessively religious. [f. L *religiosus* (as RELIGIOUS; see -OSE¹)]

rēligiō′sity *n.* being religious or religiose. [ME, f. L *religiositas* (as foll.; see -ITY)]

rēli′gious (-jŭs) *a.* & *n.* **1.** *a.* imbued with religion, pious, devout; of or belonging to a monastic order; of or concerned with religion; scrupulous, conscientious, (*with religious care, exactitude*, etc.); hence ∼LY² *adv.*, ∼NESS *n.* **2.** *n.* (*pl.* same). person bound by monastic vows. [ME, f. AF *religius*, OF *religious* f. L *religiosus* (as RELIGION; see -IOUS)]

rēli′ne *v.t.* renew lining of (esp. garment). [f. RE- 9 + LINE⁴]

rēli′nquish *v.t.* give up, abandon, cease from, (habit, plan, hope, belief); resign, surrender, (right, possession); relax hold of (object held); hence ∼MENT *n.* [ME, f. OF *relinquir* f. L *re(linquere* leave); see RE- 3, -ISH²]

rĕ'liquarў *n.* receptacle for relic(s). [f. F *reliquaire* (as RELIC; see -ARY[1])]

relique (rĕ'lĭk, rĕlē'k) *n.* (arch.) relic. [F (as RELIC)]

reliquiae (rĭlĭ'kwĭē) *n. pl.* remains; (Geol.) fossil remains of animals or plants. [L (*reliquus* remaining, f. as RE- 3 + *linquere liq-* leave)]

rĕ'lish[1] *n.* **1.** flavour, distinctive taste *of*; slight dash or tinge *of* some quality. **2.** appetizing flavour, attractive quality, (*meat has no relish when one is ill*; *horseplay loses its relish after childhood*); thing eaten with plainer food to add flavour. **3.** enjoyment of food or other things, zest, liking *for*, (*eat, read, appreciate jest*, etc., *with great relish*; *has no relish for poetry*). [alt. (w. assim. to -ISH[2]) of obs. *reles* f. OF *reles, relais* remainder (*relaisser*; see RELEASE[1])]

rĕ'lish[2] *v.* **1.** *v.t.* serve as relish to, make piquant etc. **2.** get pleasure out of, like, be pleased with, (*thought he could relish a lobster*; *does not relish the prospect*); whence ~ABLE *a.* **3.** *v.i.* taste, savour, smack, suggest presence, *of*; affect the (lit. or fig.) taste *well, badly*, etc. [f. prec.]

rĕlĭ've *v.* **1.** *v.i.* (arch.) come to life again. **2.** *v.t.* live (period, experience) over again (esp. in imagination). [f. RE- 8 + LIVE[2]]

rĕloa'd *v.t.* load again (esp. firearm, or abs.). [f. RE- 9 + LOAD[2]]

rĕloc'āte *v.t. & i.* locate again; move to a new district of work or residence; so ~A'TION *n.* [f. RE- 8 + LOCATE]

rĕlu'cent (-ōō'-, -ū'-) *a.* shining, bright. [f. L *re(lucēre* shine); see RE- 6, -ENT]

rĕlŭ'ct *v.i.* (arch.) show reluctance; struggle *against*. [f. L *reluctari* (see foll.)]

rĕlŭ'ct|ant *a.* unwilling, disinclined, (*to* do, or abs.; *am very reluctant to admit*; *gave me reluctant assistance*); hence ~ANCE *n.,* ~antLY[2] *adv.* [f. L *re(luctari* struggle); see RE- 2, -ANT]

rĕlu'me (-ū'm, -ōō'm) *v.t.* (poet.) rekindle (light or flame; lit. or fig.); make (eyes etc.) bright again; light (sky etc.) up again. [f. RE- 9, after *illume*]

rĕlŷ' *v.i.* depend with confidence or assurance (*up*)*on* person or thing (*is relying upon a broken reed*; *I rely on you to do it, its being done, today*; *you may rely upon it that he will be here*; *I was relying on getting there by midnight*). [ME (earlier senses 'rally, be vassal of'), f. OF *relier* bind together f. L *re(ligare* bind); see RE- 9]

rĕm *n.* unit of effective absorbed dose of ionizing radiation in human tissue, equivalent to one roentgen of X-rays. [f. roentgen equivalent *man*]

REM (rĕm) *abbr.* rapid eye-movement.

rĕmai'n *v.i.* **1.** be left over after removal of or use of or dealing with the other part(s) etc. (*the few pleasures that remain to an old man*; *worse things remain to be told*; *outcome remains to be seen*; *nothing remains but to draw the moral*). **2.** be in same place or condition during further time, continue to exist, be extant, be left behind, (*remain in London till Easter*; *let it remain as it is*; *as things are they remain*; *the Parthenon remains to attest to us or as a proof of*; *this visit will always remain in my memory*; *the luggage unfortunately remained on the platform*; *victory remained with the Thebans*). **3.** (w. compl.) continue to be (*one thing remains certain*; *remain faithful* etc.); **I** ~ *yours truly* etc. (formula concluding letter). [ME, f. OF *remain-* stressed st. of *remanoir* (or f. OF *remaindre* f. Rom. **remanere*) f. L *re(manēre* stay); see RE- 3]

rĕmai'nder *n., & v.t.* **1.** *n.* residue, remaining persons or things; (Arith.) number left after subtraction or division; copies of book left unsold when demand has almost ceased, often offered at reduced price. **2.** (Law). residual interest in estate when devised to another simultaneously with creation of estate (~ **man**, devisee of this); right of succession to title or position on holder's decease; hence ~SHIP *n.* **3.** *v.t.* treat or dispose of copies of (book) as remainder. [ME in sense 2, f. AF, = OF *remaindre*; see prec., -ER[4]]

rĕmai'ns (-z) *n. pl.* **1.** what remains over, surviving members or parts or amount, (*the remains of a nation, family, meal, stock, building*, of one's *conscience* or *strength*,

etc.). **2.** relic(s) of obsolete custom or of antiquity (*Roman remains*). **3.** works, esp. those not before or yet published, left by author (*literary remains*). **4.** dead body, corpse. [ME f. OF (as REMAIN), & f. REMAIN]

rĕmā'ke[1] *v.t.* (**rema'de**). make again or differently. [f. RE- 8 + MAKE[1]]

rĕ'māke[2] *n.* thing that has been remade, esp. a cinema film. [f. prec.]

rĕmā'n *v.t.* (-nn-). **1.** equip (fleet etc.) with fresh men. **2.** make courageous again. [f. RE- 8, 9 + MAN[2]]

rĕma'nd (-ah'-) *v.t., & n.* **1.** *v.t.* send back *to*, reconsign, (esp. prisoner into custody to allow of further inquiry). **2.** *n.* recommittal to custody; **on** ~, in state of being remanded; ||~ **centre** or **home**, institution for temporary detention of juvenile offenders. [ME, f. LL *re(mandare* commit); see RE- 9]

rĕ'man|ent *a.* remaining, residual; ~ent **magnetism**, magnetization remaining after removal of source of excitation; so ~ENCE *n.* [ME, f. L *remanēre* REMAIN; see -ENT]

rĕmār'k[1] *v.* **1.** *v.t.* take notice of, perceive, regard with attention, observe, (person, thing, fact, *that* etc.); say by way of comment (*that*). **2.** *v.i.* make comment (*up*)*on*. [f. F *re(marquer* MARK[2]); see RE- 6]

rĕmār'k[2] *n.* noticing, observing, (**worthy of** ~, remarkable), commenting (*is the subject of general remark*; *let it pass without remark*); a written or spoken comment, anything said, (*his remarks are often interesting*; **make a** ~, utter a comment). [f. F *remarque* (as prec.)]

rĕmār'kab|le *a.* worth notice, exceptional; striking, conspicuous; hence ~leNESS (-beln-) *n.,* ~LY[2] *adv.* [f. F *remarquable* (as REMARK[1]; see -ABLE)]

rĕmā'rrÿ *v.i. & t.,* **rēMA'RRIAGE** *n.* See RE- 8.

re'mblai (rah'nblā) *n.* earth used to form ramparts, parapets, etc.; earth brought to form railway embankments etc. [F, f. *remblayer* embank (as RE-, *emblayer* heap up)]

Rĕmbrandtĕ'sque (-ntĕ'sk) *a.* after the style of Rembrandt, with marked effects of light and shade. [f. *Rembrandt* van Rijn, Du. painter d. 1669 + -ESQUE]

||**REME** (rĕ'mē) *abbr.* Royal Electrical and Mechanical Engineers.

rĕmē'dial *a.* affording a remedy; intended to remedy disease, deficiency, etc., (*remedial measures, therapy*); hence ~LY[2] *adv.* [f. LL *remedialis* f. L *remedium* (as foll.); see -AL]

rĕ'mĕd|ў *n., & v.t.* **1.** *n.* cure *for* or *against* disease, healing medicine or treatment; means of removing or counteracting or relieving anything undesirable (*the only remedy for superstition is knowledge*); redress, legal or other reparation; hence ~iLESS *a.* (poet. or rhet.). **2.** margin within which coins as minted may differ from the standard fineness and weight. **3.** *v.t.* rectify, make good; so **rĕmē'diABLE** *a.* [ME; n. f. AF *remedie*, OF *remede*, v. f. OF *remedier* or L *remediare*, f. L *re(medium* f. *medēri* heal); see RE- 1, -Y[1]]

rĕmĕ'mber *v.t.* **1.** keep in the memory, not forget, bring back into one's thoughts, know by heart, (person, thing, fact, *that, to* do, *how to* do, *when, why*, etc., or abs.); ~ one**self**, remember one's manners or intentions after a lapse; hence ~ABLE *a.* **2.** make present to, tip, (*remembered me in his will*; *remember the waiter*). **3.** mention in one's prayers. **4.** convey greetings from (person) *to* another (*remember me kindly to them*; *asked to be remembered to you*). [ME, f. OF *remembrer* f. LL *re(memorari* f. L *memor* mindful); see RE- 9]

rĕmĕ'mbrance *n.* **1.** remembering or being remembered, memory, recollection, (*has escaped my remembrance*; *put in remembrance of*; *more than once within my remembrance*; *a pillar in remembrance of the exploit*); ||**R~ Day**, (Hist.) Armistice Day; ||**R~ Sunday** (nearest 11 Nov., when those who were killed in the wars of 1914–18 and 1939–45 are commemorated). **2.** keepsake, souvenir, memorial. **3.** (in *pl.*) greetings conveyed through third person. [ME f. OF (as prec.); see -ANCE)]

For other words in *re-* **see** RE-.

rèmě'mbrancer *n.* **1.** ‖King's or Queen's R∼, officer collecting debts due to sovereign; ‖City R∼, official representing Corporation of City of London before parliamentary committees etc. **2.** reminder, memento, (*of*). [ME, f. AF *remembrauncer* (*remembraunce*, as prec.; see -ER¹)]

rĕ'mĕx *n.* (*pl.* **remiges** *pr.* rĕ'mǐjēz). primary or secondary quill in bird's wing. [L, = rower (*remus* oar)]

rĕmǐ'lǐtarīze *v.t.*, **rĕmǐlǐtarīzA'TION** *n.* See RE- 9.

rĕmǐ'nd *v.t.* make (person) have recollection (*of, about, to* do, *that, how,* etc., or abs.). [f. RE- 8 + MIND²]

rĕmǐ'nder *n.* thing that reminds or is memento (*of*). [f. prec. + -ER¹]

rĕmǐ'ndful *a.* acting as a reminder, reviving the memory, (*of*). [f. REMIND + -FUL]

rĕmǐni'sce *v.i.* (colloq.) indulge in reminiscence(s). [back-form. f. foll.]

rĕmǐni'scence *n.* **1.** remembering, recovery of knowledge by mental effort; (Platonic Philos.) recovery of things known to the soul in previous existences. **2.** remembered (and related) fact or incident; relating of this; (in *pl.*) collection in literary form of incidents that person remembers. **3.** feature of a thing reminding or suggestive of other thing (*there is a reminiscence of the Greek type in her face*). **4.** Hence **rĕmǐni'sce'ntIAL** (-shal) *a.* [f. LL *reminiscentia* f. L. *reminisci* remember; see RE- 9, -ENCE]

rĕmǐni'scent *a.* recalling past things, given to or concerned with retrospection, mindful or having memories *of*; reminding or suggestive *of*; hence ∼LY² *adv.* [as prec.; see -ENT]

rĕmǐ'nt *v.t.* See RE- 8.

rĕmǐ'se¹ (-ē'z) *n.*, & *v.i.* **1.** (arch.) coach-house; carriage hired from livery-stable. **2.** (Fenc.) second thrust made for recovery from first. **3.** *v.i.* (Fenc.) make remise. [F, f. *remis remise* p.p. of *remettre* put back; cf. REMIT¹]

rĕmǐ'se² (-z) *v.t.* (Law). surrender, make over, (right, property). [f. F *remis(e)* (as prec.)]

rĕmǐ'ss *a.* careless of duty, lax, negligent, (arch.) lacking force or energy; hence ∼LY² *adv.*, ∼NESS *n.* [ME, f. L *remissus* p.p. of *remittere* slacken; see REMIT¹]

rĕmǐ'ssible *a.* that may be remitted. [f. F *rémissible* or f. LL *remissibilis* (as REMIT¹; see -IBLE)]

rĕmǐ'ss|ion (-shon) *n.* **1.** forgiveness (*of* sins etc.), forgiveness of sins; remitting of debt, penalty, etc.; shortening of convict's prison sentence on account of his good behaviour. **2.** diminution of force, effect, degree, violence (esp. of disease or pain), etc. **3.** So ∼IVE *a.* [ME f. OF, or f. L *remissio* (as foll.; see -ION)]

rĕmǐ't¹ *v.* (-tt-). **1.** *v.t.* (Usu. of God) pardon (sins etc.); refrain from exacting or inflicting or executing (debt, punishment, sentence). **2.** *v.t.* & *i.* abate, slacken, mitigate, partly or entirely cease from or cease, (*remit* one's *anger to efforts, the siege; pain, enthusiasm, begins to remit*). **3.** *v.t.* refer (matter for decision etc.) *to* some authority, send back (case) to lower court. **4.** send or put back (*in*)*to* previous state; postpone, defer, *to* or *till*. **5.** transmit (money etc.), get conveyed by post etc.; hence ∼TEE' *n.* **6.** Hence ∼TAL 2 *n.* [ME, f. L *re*(*mittere miss-* send); see RE- 5]

rĕmǐt² (rē'mǐt, rǐmǐ't) *n.* item remitted for consideration; terms of reference of committee etc. [f. prec.]

rĕmǐ'ttance *n.* money sent to person; sending of money; ‖∼ **man**, emigrant subsisting on remittances from home. [f. REMIT¹ + -ANCE]

rĕmǐ'ttent *a.* & *n.* (fever etc.) that abates at intervals. [f. as REMIT¹; see -ENT]

rĕmǐ'tter¹ *n.* In vbl senses. [f. REMIT¹ + -ER¹]

rĕmǐ'tter² *n.* (Law). substitution, in favour of holder of two titles to estate, of the more valid for the other by which he entered on possession; remitting of case to other court. [f. REMIT¹ + -ER⁴]

rĕ'mnant *n.* the little or few that remain(s), small remaining quantity or piece or number of persons or things; surviving trace *of*; fragment, scrap, esp. piece of cloth etc. left when greater part has been used or sold. [ME, f. obs. & OF *remenant* (*remenoir* REMAIN; see -ANT)]

rĕmō'del *v.t.* (‖-ll-). model again or differently, reconstruct. [f. RE- 8 + MODEL²]

*remold¹,². See REMOULD¹,².

rĕmō'nĕtīz|e (-mŭ'n-), **-īs|e** (-īz), *v.t.* restore (metal etc.) to former position as legal tender; hence ∼A'TION *n.* [f. RE- 9 + MONETIZE]

rĕmō'nstrance *n.* (Hist.) formal statement of public grievances (**the Grand R∼**, from House of Commons to Crown 1641); remonstrating, expostulation, a protest. [ME f. obs. F, or f. med. L *remonstrantia* (as foll.; see -ANCE)]

remonstr|āte (rĕ'mon-, rǐmŏ'n-) *v.* **1.** *v.i.* make protest, expostulate, (*against* course of action, *with* person, *on* or *upon* matter, or abs.). **2.** *v.t.* urge in remonstrance (*that*). **3.** Hence or cogn. ∼ANT *a.* & *n.*, ∼A'TION, ∼ātOR (rĕ'mon-) *ns.*, ∼ative *a.* [f. med. L *re*(*monstrare* show); see RE- 2, -ATE³]

rĕmŏ'ntant *a.* & *n.* (rose) blooming more than once in year. [F (*remonter* REMOUNT²; see -ANT)]

rĕ'mora *n.* fish of genus *Echeneis* etc., attaching itself to ships, sharks, etc., and formerly supposed to retard motion of ship to which it adhered; (arch.) obstruction, impediment. [L, = hindrance (as RE- 2, *mora* delay)]

rĕmŏ'r'se *n.* **1.** bitter regret for wrong committed; hence ∼FUL (-sf-) *a.* **2.** compunction, compassionate reluctance to inflict pain or be cruel, (esp. *without remorse*); hence ∼LESS (-sl-) *a.* [ME, f. OF *remors* f. med. L *remorsus* f. L *re*(*mordere mors-* bite) vex; see RE- 3]

rĕmō'te *a.* (∼r, ∼st). **1.** far apart. **2.** far away or off in place or time (*lies remote from the road; came from the remotest parts of the earth; memorials of remote ages*); not closely related (*a remote ancestor, descendant, kinsman*); distant or widely different or by nature separate *from* (*remote causes, effects; introduces considerations remote from the subject*); ∼ **control**, control of apparatus etc. from a distance by means of electrically operated device, radio, etc. **3.** out-of-the-way, secluded, (*a remote village*); aloof, not friendly. **4.** (Esp. in *superl.*, of idea etc.) slight(est), faint(est), least, (*have not the remotest, have only a very remote, conception of what he means*). **5.** Hence ∼LY² (-tlǐ) *adv.*, ∼NESS (-tn-) *n.* [ME, f. L *remotus* (as REMOVE¹)]

rĕmou'ld¹ (-mō'-), ***rĕmō'ld¹**, *v.t.* mould again, refashion; reconstruct tread of (tyre). [f. RE- 8 + MOULD²]

rĕ'mould² (-mō-), ***rĕ'mōld²**, *n.* remoulded tyre. [f. prec.]

rĕ'mount¹ *n.* fresh horse for rider, supply of fresh horses for regiment etc. [f. foll.]

rĕmou'nt² *v.* **1.** *v.t.* go up, get on to, (hill, ladder, horse, etc. again); furnish (person) with fresh horse etc.; put (picture etc.) in fresh mount. **2.** *v.i.* go up again, get on horseback again, make fresh ascent; go back *to* specified date, period, source. [ME, f. OF *re*(*monter* MOUNT²; see RE- 9) & f. MOUNT²]

rĕmo'v|able (-mōō'-) *a.* In vbl senses; subject to removal from office; hence ∼ABI'LITY *n.* [f. REMOVE¹ + -ABLE]

rĕmo'val (-mōō'-) *n.* act of removing or being removed; transfer of furniture etc. to different house, whence ∼IST (3) *n.* (Austral.). [f. foll. + -AL 2]

rĕmo've¹ (-ōō'v) *v.* **1.** *v.t.* take off or away from place occupied, convey to another place, change situation of, get rid of, dismiss, (*remove* one's *hat, the tea-things, all traces, superfluous hair, magistrate from office; this will remove all apprehension, the last doubts*); conduct removal of (furniture etc., as special trade); *remove* MOUNTAINs; hence **rĕmo'vER¹** (1, 2) (-mōō'-) *n.* **2.** ‖(arch., in *pass.*, of dish at dinner etc.) be succeeded by (*boiled haddock removed by hashed mutton*). **3.** *v.i.* change one's place of residence, go away *from*, go *to* (another place), (*am removing from London to Oxford; truth has *removed from earth*). **4.** (in *p.p.*) distant or remote *from* (*is not many degrees removed from the brute*); **once, twice,** etc., ~**d** (of COUSINS). [ME, f. OF *removeir* f. L *re*(*movēre* *mot-* move); see RE- 5]

rĕmo've² (-ōo'v) *n.* **1.** stage in gradation, degree, (*is but one remove, a few removes, from*). **2.** distance, degree of remoteness, (*at a certain remove its shape seems to change*). **3.** ||promotion to higher form at school (*has not got his remove*); ||a form or division in some schools. **4.** ||(arch.) dish that succeeds another at table. **5.** (arch.) change of residence, departure, removal. [f. prec.]

rĕmū'ner|āte *v.t.* reward, pay for service rendered; serve as or provide recompense for (toil etc.) or to (person); hence or cogn. ~A'TION *n.*, ~ATIVE, ~ATORY, *adjs.* [f. L *re*(*munerari* f. *munus muneris* gift); see RE- 1, -ATE³]

Renai'ssance (re-, rĭ-; -*sans*, -sahns) *n.* revival of art and letters under influence of classical models in 14th–16th c., period of its progress, style of art and architecture developed by it; (*r~*) any similar revival. [F (*r~*) (as RE- 8, *naissance* birth f. L *nascentia* or *naître naiss-* be born f. Rom. *nascere; cf. NASCENT, -ANCE)]

rĕ'nal *a.* of the kidneys. [f. F *rénal* f. LL *renalis* f. L *renes* kidneys; see -AL]

rĕnā'me *v.t.* See RE- 8.

rĕnä'scence *n.* rebirth, renewal; = RENAISSANCE. [f. foll. +-ENCE]

rĕnä'scent *a.* springing up anew, being reborn. [f. L *re*(*nasci* be born); see RE- 8, -ENT]

rĕncŏ'ntre (-*ter*) *n.* (arch.) = foll. [F (as foll.)]

rĕncou'nter *n.*, & *v.t.* (arch.) (have) encounter, battle, skirmish, duel; meet(ing) by chance. [f. F *rencontre*(*r*) (as RE-, ENCOUNTER)]

rĕnd *v.* (**rent**). (arch. or rhet.) **1.** *v.t.* tear or wrench (*off, away, out of, from, asunder, apart,* etc., or abs.; *a province rent from the empire*; ~ one's **garments** or **hair** (in grief etc.); **turn and** ~, (fig.) abuse (person) unexpectedly. **2.** *v.t.* & *i.* split or divide in two or in pieces or into factions (lit. or fig.: *heart is rent by contending emotions*); ~ **the air,** sound piercingly. [OE *rendan,* = OFris. *renda,* cogn. w. MLG *rende*]

rĕ'nder *v.t.* **1.** give in return (*render thanks, good for evil*). **2.** (arch.) give back; hand over, deliver, give up, surrender, (*render to Caesar the things that are Caesar's*). **3.** pay (tribute etc.), show (obedience etc.), give (assistance etc.), do (service etc.), (*to*). **4.** produce for inspection, submit, present, send in, (account, reason, etc.); **account** ~**ed,** bill previously sent in and not yet paid (phr. used as substitute for repetition of items). **5.** reproduce, portray, give representation or performance or effect of, execute, translate, (*painter has hardly rendered the expression; the quartet, Iago, the dramatist's conception, was well rendered; how would you render 'solvitur ambulando'?; poetry can never be adequately rendered in another language*); hence ~ING¹ (1, 2) *n.* **6.** (w. obj. & compl.) make, cause to be, convert into, (*age had rendered him peevish; the tone rendered it an insult*). **7.** ~ (**down**), melt (fat) down, extract by melting, clarify. **8.** cover (stone, brick) with first coat of plaster; hence ~ING¹ (2) *n.* **9.** ~-**set,** (*v.t.*) plaster (wall etc.) with two coats, (*n.* & *a.*) (plastering) of two coats. [ME f. AF; OF *rendre* f. Rom. *rendere f. L *reddere reddit-* (as RE- 1, *dare* give)]

re'ndezvous (rŏ'ndivōo, -dā-) *n.* (*pl.* same *pr.* -ōoz), & *v.i.* (~**es,** ~**ed,** ~**ing,** *pr.* -ōoz, -ōod, -ōoing). **1.** *n.* place appointed for assembling of troops or ships; place where people often meet; meeting-place agreed on, meeting by agreement. **2.** *v.i.* meet at rendezvous. [F, f. *rendez-vous* present yourselves (*rendre*; see prec.)]

rĕndi'tion *n.* interpretation, rendering, *of* dramatic role, musical piece, etc. (see RENDER 5). [obs. F (*rendre* RENDER; see -ITION)]

rĕ'nĕgāde *n.*, & *v.i.* **1.** *n.* apostate, esp. from Christianity to Islam; deserter of party or principles, turncoat. **2.** *v.i.* be renegade. [f. Sp. *renegado* f. med. L *re*(*negatus* f. *negare* deny); see RE- 9]

rĕnĕgā'dō *n.* (*pl.* ~**es**). (arch.) = prec. [Sp., as prec.]

rĕnē'ge, -gue, (-g) *v.* **1.** *v.i.* (Cards) *revoke; ~ **on,** fail to keep (promise etc.), disappoint (person, or abs.). **2.** *v.t.* deny, renounce, abandon. [f. med. L *renegare* (as RE-, *negare* deny)]

rĕnew' *v.t.* **1.** restore to original state, make (as good as) new, revive, regenerate, (*nature dies and is renewed*; *renew* person's *life, sorrow, energy; renew the golden age*; *rose from her knees renewed by the Holy Spirit*). **2.** patch, fill up, reinforce, replace, (*coat renewed in places; renew the water in the bowl; renew garrison, tyres,* etc.). **3.** get, begin, make, say, or give, anew, continue after intermission, (*renew attack, acquaintance, correspondence, speech, game, efforts; renew one's vows, statements,* etc.); grant or be granted continuation of (subscription, agreement, lease, bill, or abs.); grant or be granted continued validity of (licence etc.); recover (one's youth, strength, etc.). **4.** Hence ~ABLE *a.*, ~AL 2 *n.* [ME, f. RE- 9 + NEW¹]

rē'nifŏrm *a.* kidney-shaped. [f. L *ren* kidney + -I- + -FORM]

renit|ent (rĕ'ni-, rinī'-) *a.* resistant to force; recalcitrant; so ~ENCE, ~ENCY, *ns.* [f. F *rénitent* & L *renitens* (*reniti* resist; see -ENT)]

rĕ'nnĕt *n.* curdled milk found in stomach of unweaned calf, or preparation of stomach-membrane or of plant, used in curdling milk for cheese, junket, etc. [ME, prob. f. OE **rynet,* cogn. w. RUN¹]

rĕnou'nce *v.* & *n.* **1.** *v.t.* consent formally to abandon, surrender, give up, (claim, right, peerage, possession). **2.** repudiate, refuse to recognize any longer, decline association or disclaim relationship with, withdraw from, discontinue, forsake, (*renounce treaty, principles,* person's *authority, all thought of, design, attempt, son* etc., *friend, friendship*); ~ **the world,** abandon society or temporal affairs. **3.** *v.i.* (Law). refuse or resign right or position esp. as heir or trustee. **4.** (Cards). follow with card of another suit when having no card of suit led (cf. REVOKE). **5.** Hence ~MENT (-sm-) *n.* **6.** *n.* (opportunity of) renouncing at cards. [ME, f. OF *renoncer* f. L *re*(*nuntiare* announce); see RE- 5]

rē'novāte *v.t.* make new again, repair, restore to good condition or vigour; so ~A'TION, ~ātor, *ns.* [f. L *re*(*novare* f. *novus* new); see RE- 8, -ATE³]

rĕnow'n *n.* celebrity, fame, high distinction, (*man, town,* etc., *of renown or great* etc. *renown*). [ME, f. AF *ren*(*o*)*un,* OF *renon, renom* (*renomer* make famous f. as RE- 8 + *nomer* f. L *nominare* NOMINATE)]

rĕnow'ned (-nd) *a.* famous, celebrated. [ME, f. OF *reno*(*u*)*mer* (as prec.) + -ED¹]

rĕnt¹. See REND.

rĕnt² *n.* large tear in garment etc.; opening in clouds etc. as if torn; cleft, fissure, gorge. [f. obs. *rent* var. of REND]

rĕnt³ *n.* & *v.* **1.** *n.* tenant's periodical payment to owner or landlord for use of land or premises; payment for availability of telephone service, machinery, etc.; ***for** ~, available to be rented; ~**-free** *a.* & *adv.*, with exemption from rent; ~**-roll,** register of person's lands etc. with rents due from them, sum of one's income from rent; ||~**-service,** (tenure by) personal service in lieu of or in addition to rent. **2.** *v.t.* take, occupy, use, at a rent (*from*); let or hire (*out*) for rent (*to*); ~**-a-** (*van, crowd,* etc., with often joc. ref. to availability on hire). **3.** *v.i.* be let *at* specified rent. [ME, f. OF *rente* f. Rom. *rendita fem. p.p. of *rendere (see RENDER)]

rĕ'nt|able *a.* In vbl senses; giving adequate ratio of profit to capital; hence ~ABI'LITY *n.* [f. prec. + -ABLE]

rĕ'ntal *n.* income from rents; amount paid or received as rent; act of renting; *rented house etc.; *~ **library** (lending books for a fee). [ME f. AF, or f. AL *rentale* (as RENT³; see AL 2)]

rĕ'nter *n.* In vbl senses; ||distributor of cinema films. [f. RENT³ + -ER¹]

For other words in *re-* **see** RE-.

rentier (rah'ntiā) *n.* person living on dividends from property, investments, etc. [F (*rente* dividend)]

rēnŭ'mber *v.t.* change number(s) of. [f. RE- 8 + NUMBER²]

rĕnŭnciā'tion *n.* renouncing, document expressing it; self-denial, giving up of things; so **rĕnŭ'nci**ANT *n.* & *a.*, **rĕnŭ'nci**ATIVE (-sha-), **rĕnŭ'nci**ATORY (-shaterĭ), *adjs.* [ME, f. OF *renonciation* or f. LL *renuntiatio* (as RENOUNCE; see -ATION)]

rēō'ccŭpȳ *v.t.*, **rēŏccŭp**A'TION *n.*, **rēō'pen** *v.t.* & *i.*, see RE- 9; **rēōr'der** *v.t.*, & *n.*, **rēōr'ganīze** *v.t.*, **rēōrganīz**A'TION *n.*, see RE- 8.

rēorĭĕnt (-ōr'-, -ō'r-) *v.t.* give new orientation to; readjust, change outlook of (person). [f. RE- 8 + ORIENT²]

rēorient|āte (-ŏ'r-, -ōr'-) *v.t.* = prec.; hence ~A'TION *n.* [f. RE- 8 + ORIENTATE]

rĕp¹, **rĕpp**, *n.* textile fabric with corded surface used in curtains and upholstery. [f. F *reps*, of unkn. orig.]

rĕp² *n.* (colloq.) representative, esp. commercial traveller. [abbr.]

rĕp³ *n.* (sl.) person of immoral character. [perh. for REPROBATE²; cf. RIP¹]

rĕp⁴ *n.* (colloq.) repertory (theatre or company). [abbr.]

rĕp⁵ *n.* (sl.) reputation. [abbr.]

*Rep. *abbr.* Representative (in Congress); Republican.

rēpai'nt¹ *v.t.* paint again or differently; restore paint or colouring of. [f. RE- 8, 9 + PAINT²]

rē'paint² *n.* act of repainting; repainted thing, e.g. golf-ball. [f. prec.]

rĕpair'¹ *v.i.*, & *n.* **1.** *v.i.* resort, have recourse, go often or in great numbers or for a specific purpose, *to*. **2.** *n.* (arch.) resort (*have repair to*); place of frequent resort; being visited by numbers (*a place of great, little, repair*). [ME, f. OF *repaire*(*r*) f. LL *repatriare* REPATRIATE]

rĕpair'² *v.t.* **1.** restore (building, machine, garment, tissue, strength, etc.) to good condition; renovate or mend by replacing or refixing parts or compensating loss or exhaustion; hence ~ABLE *a.*, ~ER¹ *n.* **2.** remedy, set right again, make amends for, (loss, wrong, error). [ME, f. OF *reparer* f. L re(*parare* make ready); see RE- 9]

rĕpair'³ *n.* **1.** restoring to sound condition (*health, bicycle, house, shoe, is beyond* or *in need of repair*); act or result of doing this (*shop is closed during repairs; repairs done while you wait; the repair is barely visible*); hence ***~man** (esp. for motor vehicles etc.). **2.** good condition, relative condition, for working or using (*is in, out of, repair; must be kept in good, is in bad, repair*). [f. prec.]

rĕpă'nd *a.* (Bot. & Zool.) with undulating margin, wavy. [f. L re(*pandus* bent); see RE- 9]

rĕpa'per *v.t.* See RE- 8.

rĕ'parable *a.* (Of loss etc.) that can be made good. [F, f. L *reparabilis* (as REPAIR²; see -ABLE)]

rĕparā'tion *n.* **1.** repairing or being repaired. **2.** making of amends; compensation, (esp. in *pl.*, for war damage by defeated State). **3.** Hence **reparat**IVE (rĕ'per-, ripă'r-) *a.* [ME f. OF f. LL *reparatio -onis* (as REPAIR²; see -ATION)]

rĕpartee' *n.* witty retort; (making of) witty retorts (*a great master, a storehouse, of repartee*). [f. F *repartie* fem. p.p. (as *n.*) of re(*partir* PART²) start again, reply promptly; see RE- 8]

rĕpartī'tion *v.t.* See RE- 8.

rēpa'ss (-ah's) *v.t.* & *i.* pass again, esp. on the way back. [ME, f. OF *repasser* (as RE- 9, PASS¹)]

rĕpa'st (-ah'-) *n.* (formal). (food supplied for or eaten at) meal (esp. of specified kind; *rich, slight, luxurious,* etc., *repast*). [ME f. OF (*repaistre* f. LL *repascere repast*-feed; see RE- 8, PASTOR)]

rēpă'trī|āte *v.t.* & *i.* restore or return to native land; hence ~ATE¹ *n.*, one who has been repatriated, ~A'TION *n.* [f. LL re(*patriare* f. L *patria* native land); see RE- 9]

rēpay' *v.* (repai'd). **1.** *v.t.* pay back (money); return

(blow, visit, service, etc.); give in recompense *for*; make repayment to (person); make return for, requite, (action). **2.** *v.i.* make repayment. **3.** Hence ~ABLE *a.*, **rēpay'ment** *n.* [f. OF re(*paier* PAY²); see RE- 9]

rēpea'l *v.t.*, & *n.* **1.** *v.t.* revoke, rescind, annul, (law etc.); hence ~ABLE *a.* **2.** *n.* abrogation, repealing. [ME, f. AF *repeler*, OF *rapeler* (as RE- 9, APPEAL¹)]

rĕpea't *v.* & *n.* **1.** *v.t.* say or do over again, recite, rehearse, report, reproduce, give imitation of, (*repeat action, statement, poem, conversation, attempt, pattern, signal,* etc.; *action was repeated several times,* whence ~ĕdLY² *adv.*); **not,** ~ **not,** emphatically not; *language* **will not bear** ~**ing,** is too foul etc. to repeat; ~ **itself,** recur in same form; ~**oneself,** say or do same thing over again; hence ~ABLE *a.* **2.** *v.i.* (Of watch etc.) strike last quarter etc. over again when required; (of firearm) fire several shots without reloading. **3.** recur, appear again or repeatedly (*the last three figures repeat;* ~**ing decimal,** recurring decimal); (of food) be tasted intermittently for some time after being swallowed; ***illegally vote more than once in election. 4.** *n.* repeating, esp. of item in programme in response to encore; repeated broadcast programme; (Mus.) passage intended to be repeated, mark indicating this; pattern repeated in wallpaper etc.; (Commerc.) fresh consignment similar to previous one, order given for this. [ME, f. OF *repeter* f. L re(*petere* seek); see RE- 8]

rēpea'ter *n.* In vbl senses; firearm or watch that repeats; device for automatic re-transmission or amplification of electrically transmitted message; signal lamp indicating the state of another that is invisible. [f. prec. + -ER¹]

rĕpêchage (rĕ'peshahzh) *n.* (Rowing etc.) extra contest in which runners-up in the eliminating contests compete for a place in the final. [F (*repêcher* fish out, rescue; see -AGE)]

rēpĕ'l *v.t.* (-ll-). **1.** drive back, repulse, ward off, refuse admission or acceptance or approach to, (*repel assailant, attack, temptation, weapon, blow, moisture, suggestion, plea, offer,* person's *advances, electric charge with same sign*). **2.** be repulsive or distasteful to. [ME, f. L re(*pellere puls*- drive); see RE- 2]

rēpĕ'llent *a.* & *n.* (substance) that repels (esp. insects etc.). [f. L *repellere* as prec.; see -ENT]

rē'pent¹ *a.* (Bot.) creeping, esp. growing along or just under surface of ground. [f. L *repere* creep; see -ENT]

rēpĕ'nt² *v.* **1.** *v.t.* & *i.* think with contrition of or *of*, be regretful about or *of*, wish one had not done, resolve not to continue wrongdoing in, (action etc., or abs.; *you shall repent, repent this, repent of this*). **2.** (arch., *refl.*) feel regret or penitence about something or *of* (*I now repent me*). **3.** (arch., *impers.*) affect with penitence or regret (*it repents me that I did it*). **4.** So ~ANCE *n.*, ~ANT *a.* [ME, f. OF *repentir* (as RE- 3, *pentir* f. Rom. *paenitire f. L *paenitēre*)]

rēpeo'ple (-pē'-) *v.t.* See RE- 9.

rēpercŭ'ss|ion (-shon) *n.* echo; recoil after impact; indirect effect or reaction of event or act; so ~IVE *a.* [ME f. OF, or f. L *repercussio* (as RE-, PERCUSSION)]

rē'pertoire (-twār) *n.* stock of pieces etc. that company or performer knows or is prepared to give; totality of regularly performed pieces, regularly used techniques, etc. [f. F *répertoire* f. LL (as foll.)]

rē'pertorȳ *n.* **1.** place for finding something, store or collection, esp. of information, instances, facts, etc. **2.** = prec.; theatrical performance of various plays for short periods by one ~ **company.** [f. LL *repertorium* f. L *reperire repert*- find; see -ORY]

rē'pĕtĕnd *n.* recurring figures of decimal; recurring word or phrase, refrain. [f. L (as REPEAT; see -ND¹)]

répétiteur (rĕpĕt1tĕr') *n.* tutor or coach of musicians, esp. opera-singers. [F]

rĕpĕti'ti|on *n.* repeating or being repeated; piece set to be learnt by heart; copy, replica; ability of musical instrument to repeat note quickly; hence or cogn.

∼ionAL, ∼ionARY¹, ∼ious (-shŭs), rĕpĕ′tĭtive, *adjs.*
[f. F *répétition* or f. L *repetitio* (as REPEAT; see -ITION)]
rĕpī′ne *v.i.* fret, be discontented, (*at, against,* or abs.).
[f. RE- 6 + PINE², after *repent*]
rĕpī′que (-ē′k) *n. & v.* **1.** *n.* winning of 30 points on
cards alone before beginning to play in piquet. **2.** *v.t.
& i.* score repique (against). [f. F *repic* (as RE-,
PIQUE²)]
rĕplā′ce *v.t.* put back in place; take place of, succeed,
be substituted for; (in *pass.*) be succeeded or have
one's or its place filled *by*, be superseded; fill up place
of (*with, by*), find or provide substitute for; hence
∼ABLE (-sa-) *a.* [f. RE- 9 + PLACE²]
rĕplā′cement (-sm-) *n.* replacing or being replaced;
person or thing that takes the place of another. [f.
prec. + -MENT]
rĕplă′nt (-ah′-) *v.t.* See RE- 8.
rĕplay′¹ *v.t.* play (match, recording, etc.) over again.
[f. RE- 8 + PLAY¹]
rē′play² *n.* replaying (of match, recording of incident
in game, etc.). [f. prec.]
rĕplĕ′nish *v.t.* fill up again (*with,* or abs.); (in *p.p.*)
filled, fully stored, full, (*with,* or abs.); renew (supply
etc.); hence ∼MENT *n.* [ME, f. OF *re(plenir* f. *plein* full f.
L *plenus*); see RE- 9, -ISH²]
rĕplē′ite *a.* filled, stuffed, fully imbued, well stocked,
with; gorged, sated, (*with*); hence or cogn. ∼teNESS
(-tn-), ∼tion, *ns.* [ME, f. OF *replet* replete or f. L *repletus*
p.p. of *re(plēre plet-* fill); see RE- 6]
rĕplĕ′vin *n.* restoration or recovery of distrained
goods on security given for submission to trial and
judgement; writ granting replevin; action arising out
of replevin. [ME f. AF, f. OF (as foll.)]
rĕplĕ′vy *v.t.* recover by replevin. [f. OF *re(plevir* f.
Gmc **pleg jan*; cf. PLEDGE¹) recover; see RE- 9]
rĕ′plica *n.* duplicate made by original artist of his
picture etc.; facsimile, exact copy; copy, model, esp.
on smaller scale. [It. (*replicare* REPLY)]
rĕ′plicate¹ *n.* (Mus.) tone one or more octaves above
or below given tone. [as foll.]
rĕ′plicate² *a.* (Bot.) folded back on itself. [as foll.;
see -ATE²]
rĕ′plic|āte³ *v.t.* repeat; make replica of; fold back;
hence ∼ABLE *a.* [f. L *re(plicare* fold); see RE- 9, -ATE³]
rĕplicā′tion *n.* **1.** replying, rejoinder, answer, esp.
reply to answer; (Law) plaintiff's reply to defendant's
plea. **2.** copy, copying; repetition. [ME, f. OF
replicacion f. L *replicatio -onis* (as prec.; see -ATION)]
rĕplȳ′ *v. & n.* **1.** *v.i.* make answer, respond, in word or
action (*to*). **2.** *v.t.* say in answer (*he replied that I must
please myself*; *'Please yourself'*, *he replied*). **3.** *n.* act of
replying (*what he says in reply*); what is replied,
response; (Law) = prec.; ∼ **coupon** (for prepaying
reply to letter, exchangeable for stamps in any
country); ∼ **paid**, (of telegram) with cost of reply
prepaid by sender, (of envelope etc.) for which
addressee undertakes to pay postage. [ME, f. OF
replier f. L (as REPLICATE³)]
rēpoi′nt *v.t.* point (esp. brickwork) again. [f. RE-
9 + POINT²]
rēpŏ′lish *v.t.*, rēpŏ′pūlāte *v.t.* See RE- 9.
rēpŏ′rt¹ *v.* **1.** *v.t.* bring back or give account of, state as
ascertained fact, tell as news, narrate or describe or
repeat esp. as eye-witness or hearer etc. (*to*), relate as
spoken by another, make official or formal statement
about, name (offence, offender) *to* authorities or abs.,
present (oneself) as returned or arrived, (*reports open
water at the pole, the pole to be accessible, that he reached the
pole*; *reported all details of the scene to me*; *my actual words
and those reported to you were quite different*; *was reported (to
the police) for speeding*); ||(Parl., of committee chairman)
announce that committee has dealt with (bill); ||∼
progress, state what has been done so far; ∼**ed
speech,** speaker's words with changes of person,
tense, etc., usual in reports; hence ∼**ed**LY² *adv.* **2.** take
down word for word or epitomize or write description
of for publication (*report law case, proceedings, meeting,*
or abs.). **3.** *v.i.* make, draw up, or send in report. **4.**

present oneself *to* (person) as returned or arrived or
sick etc.; be responsible *to* (superior, supervisor, etc.).
5. give report *of* to convey that one is *well* or *badly*
impressed (*reports well of the prospects*; *is badly reported
of*). **6.** Hence ∼ABLE *a.* [ME, f. OF *reporter* f. L
re(portare bring); see RE- 9]
rēpŏ′rt² *n.* **1.** common talk, rumour, (*mere report is not
enough to go upon*; *the report goes that*); way person or
thing is spoken of, repute, (*things of good report*; *faithful
through good and evil report*). **2.** account given or
opinion formally expressed after investigation or
consideration or collation of information, description
or epitome or reproduction of scene or speech or law
case esp. for newspaper publication, (||∼ **stage,**
House of Commons debate on bill when reported);
periodical statement on pupil's work, conduct, etc.,
at school. **3.** sound of explosion (*went off with a loud
report*). [ME f. OF (*reporter*; see prec.)]
rēpŏrta′ge (-ah′zh) *n.* (typical style of) reporting
events for press etc.; factual presentation in book etc.
[f. REPORT¹ + -AGE, after F]
rēpŏ′rter *n.* one who reports; person employed to
report news etc. for newspaper or broadcast. [ME, f.
AF **reportour*, OF *reporteur* (as REPORT¹, -ER²), & f.
REPORT¹ + -ER¹]
**rēpŏrtŏr′ial *a.* of newspaper reporter(s); hence
∼LY² *adv.* [f. prec., after *editorial*]
rēpŏ′s|e¹ (-z) *v.t.* place (trust etc.) *in*; hence ∼AL 2 *n.*
[f. RE- 4 + POSE¹, after L *re(ponere posit-* place)]
rēpŏ′se² (-z) *v. & n.* **1.** *v.t.* rest (oneself, or abs.); lay
(one's head etc.) to rest (*on* pillow etc.); give rest to,
refresh with rest. **2.** *v.i.* lie, be lying or laid, esp. in sleep
or death (*in, on,* or abs.); be supported or based *on
(the whole system reposes on fear*); (of memory etc.) dwell
on. **3.** *n.* cessation of activity or excitement, respite
from toil, sleep, peaceful or quiescent state, stillness,
tranquillity; restful effect, harmonious combination
in art, composure or ease of manner, (*lacks repose*);
angle of ∼ (beyond which inclined body will not
support another on its surface by friction); hence
∼FUL (-zf-) *a.* [ME, f. OF *repos(er* f. LL *re(pausare
PAUSE*); see RE- 5]
rēpŏ′sitory (-z-) *n.* **1.** receptacle; place where things
are stored or may be found, museum, warehouse,
store, shop, (*book, person, etc., is a repository of curious
information*); burial-place. **2.** recipient of confidences
or secrets. [f. obs. F *repositoire* or f. L *repositorium* (as
REPOSE¹; see -ORY)]
rēpossĕ′ss (-z-) *v.t.* regain possession of (esp. forfeited
hire-purchase goods); so ∼ION (-shŏn) *n.* [f.
RE- 9 + POSSESS]
rēpŏ′t *v.t.* (-tt-). put (plant) in another (esp. larger)
pot. [f. RE- 8 + POT²]
repou′ssé (repōō′sā) *a. & n.* (ornamental metalwork)
hammered into relief from reverse side. [F, p.p. of
re(pousser PUSH¹); see RE- 3]
rĕpp. See REP¹.
rĕpped (-pt) *a.* having surface like rep. [f. REP¹ + -ED²]
repr. *abbr.* represent etc.; reprint(ed).
rēprĕhĕ′n|d *v.t.* rebuke, blame, find fault with; so
∼SIBLE *a.,* ∼SION (-shŏn) *n.* [ME, f. L *re(prehendere*
seize); see RE- 2]
rĕprĕsĕ′nt (-z-) *v.t.* **1.** call up in the mind by
description or portrayal or imagination, place likeness before mind or senses, serve or be meant as
likeness of, (*can you represent infinity to yourself?*; *can only
represent it to you by metaphors*; *picture represents murder of
Abel*; *is represented in hunting costume*). **2.** try to bring
(facts influencing conduct) home (*to*), state by way of
expostulation or incentive, (*represented the rashness of it,
that it could not succeed, that it must succeed*). **3.** make out to
be etc., allege that, describe or depict as, (*am not what
you represent me to be or as*; *in the corner is the Pope
represented as a beggar*; *represents that he has, himself to have,
seen service*). **4.** act (play etc.), play part of on stage. **5.**
symbolize, act as embodiment of, stand for, corres-
pond to, be specimen of, (*sovereign represents majesty of
State*; *inch of rain represents 100 tons to acre*; *by-election result*

For other words in *re-* see RE-.

does not represent country's views; *symbol* χ *represents guttural sound*; *camels are represented in the New World by llamas*; *Welsh football is represented in the team by Morgan*). **6.** fill place of, be substitute or deputy for, be entitled to act or speak for, be sent as member to legislature or delegate to meeting etc. by, (*Queen was represented by the Duke*; *members representing urban constituencies*). **7.** Hence ~ABLE *a*. [ME, f. OF *representer* or f. L *re*(*praesentare* PRESENT[4]); see RE- 8]

rĕprĕsĕntā'tion (-z-) *n*. representing or being represented; thing (esp. painting etc.) that represents another; (esp. in *pl*.) statement made by way of allegation or to convey opinion; PROPORTIONAL *representation*. [ME f. OF, or f. L *repraesentatio* (as prec.; see -ATION)]

rĕprĕsĕntā'tional (-z-) *a*. of representation; ~ **art** (seeking to portray reality). [f. prec. + -AL]

rĕprĕsĕntā'tion|ism (-zĕ-) *n*. (Philos.) doctrine that perceived objects are only a representation of real external objects; so ~IST (2) *n*. [f. REPRESENTA-TION + -ISM]

rĕprĕsĕ'ntative (-z-) *a*. & *n*. **1.** *a*. serving as portrayal or symbol *of* (*a group representative of the theological virtues*); that presents or can present ideas to the mind (*imagination is a representative faculty*); (of art) representational; typical of a class or classes, containing typical specimens of all or many classes, (*the truth of an allegory is representative, not literal*; *call a meeting of representative men*; *a very representative selection, collection*); consisting of elected deputies or representatives; based on representation of nation etc. by such deputies (*representative government, institutions*); hence ~LY[2] (-vlĭ) *adv*., ~NESS (-vn-) *n*. **2.** *n*. sample, specimen, typical embodiment, analogue, *of*; person's or firm's agent; delegate, substitute, successor, heir; deputy in representative legislature (**House of R~s,** lower house of US Congress and other national Parliaments). [ME, f. OF *representatif -ive* or f. med. L *repraesentativus* (as REPRESENT; see -ATIVE)]

rĕprĕ'ss *v.t.* **1.** check, restrain; keep under, quell; suppress, prevent from sounding or bursting out or rioting. **2.** (Psych.) actively exclude (unpleasant or unwelcome thought) from conscious awareness, (usu. in *pass.*) subject (person) to repression of his thoughts. **3.** Hence or cogn. ~ION (-shŏn) *n*., ~IVE *a*. [ME, f. L *re*(*primere = premere* PRESS[2]); see RE- 5]

rĕpriĕ've *v.t.*, & *n*. **1.** *v.t.* postpone or remit execution of (condemned person); (fig.) give respite to. **2.** *n*. reprieving or being reprieved; (warrant for) remission or commutation of capital sentence; respite. [ME as p.p. *repryed*, f. AF & OF *repris* p.p. of *re*(*prendre* f. L *prehendere* take; see RE- 8; 16th-c. *-v-* uncxpl.]

rĕ'primand (-ah-) *n*., & *v.t.* official(ly) or sharp(ly) rebuke (*for* fault). [f. F *réprimande*(*r*) f. Sp. f. L *reprimenda* neut. pl. gerundive of *reprimere* REPRESS]

rĕpri'nt[1] *v.t.* print again; make reprint of. [f. RE- 8 + PRINT[2]]

rĕ'print[2] *n*. book reprinted, reprinting of book, in same or new form; quantity thus reprinted; article reprinted after separation from accompanying articles, = SEPARATE[1] 2. [f. prec.]

rĕpri'sal (-z-) *n*. **1.** act of retaliation. **2.** (Hist.) forcible seizure of foreign subjects' persons or property in retaliation (**letters of ~,** official warrant authorizing this). [ME in sense 2, f. AF *reprisaille* f. med. L *reprisalia* f. *repraehensalia* (as REPREHEND; see -AL 2)]

rĕpri'se (-ē'z) *n*. repeated passage in music; repeated song etc. in musical programme. [F, fem. p.p. (as n.) of *reprendre* (see REPRIEVE)]

rĕproa'ch *v.t.*, & *n*. **1.** *v.t.* scold, censure, express disapproval to (person; *with* his offence or *for* fault); (of look etc.) convey protest or censure to (*his eyes reproach me*); (arch.) rebuke (offence). **2.** *n*. thing that brings disgrace or discredit (*to*; *the state of the roads is a reproach to civilization*); opprobrium, disgraced or discredited state, (*live in reproach and ignominy*; *the things*

that had brought reproach upon him); **above** or **beyond** ~, perfect. **3.** scolding, rebuke, censure, (*heap reproaches on*; *the mute reproach in his eyes*); **term of** ~, word implying censure; hence ~FUL *a*. **4.** (in *pl*.) (chiefly RC) set of antiphons and responses for Good Friday, representing reproaches of Christ to his people. [ME, f. OF *reproche*(*r*) f. Rom. **repropiare* f. as RE- 7 + L *prope* near]

rĕ'prob|āte[1] *v.t.* express or feel disapproval of, censure; (of God) reject, exclude from salvation; so ~A'TION *n*. [ME, f. L *re*(*probare* approve) disapprove; see RE- 7, -ATE[3]]

rĕ'probāte[2] *a*. & *n*. (person who is) rejected by God, hardened in sin, of highly immoral character, or unprincipled. [f. LL *reprobatus* p.p. of L *reprobare* (see prec., -ATE[2])]

rĕprodŭ'c|e *v*. **1.** *v.t.* produce copy or representation of; cause to be seen, heard, etc., again; produce offspring of (one*self, itself*); form afresh (lost etc. part of body). **2.** *v.i.* produce further members of same species by natural means; give specified quality of result when copied (*picture does not reproduce well*). **3.** Hence ~IBI'LITY *n*., ~IBLE *a*., ~**ibLY**[2] *adv*. [f. RE- 8 + PRODUCE[2]]

rĕprodŭ'ct|ion *n*. reproducing; copy of painting etc.; (*attrib*. of furniture etc.) made in imitation of earlier style; so ~IVE *a*. [f. prec., after *production*]

rĕpro'graphў *n*. science and practice of copying documents by photography, xerography, etc.; hence **rĕprogrā'phic** *a*. [f. REPRODUCE + -GRAPHY]

rĕproō'f[1] *n*. blame (*a word, glance, of reproof*); rebuke, words expressing blame. [ME f. OF *reprove* (*reprover* REPROVE)]

rĕproō'f[2] *v.t.* make fresh proof of (printed matter etc.); render (coat etc.) waterproof again. [f. RE- 8, 9 + PROOF[1,2]]

rĕpro've (-ōō'v) *v.t.* rebuke, scold, (person, conduct, etc.). [ME, f. OF *reprover* f. LL *reprobare* disapprove; see REPROBATE[1]]

rĕprovi'sion (-zhŏn) *v.t.* See RE- 8.

rĕ'ptant *a*. (Biol.) creeping. [f. L *reptare* frequent. of *repere* crawl; see -ANT]

rĕ'ptile *n*. & *a*. **1.** *n*. member of the Reptilia or class of animals including snakes, lizards, crocodiles, turtles, and tortoises, whence **rĕpti'lian** (-lyan) *a*. & *n*.; mean, grovelling, or repulsive person. **2.** *a*. (Of animal) creeping; mean and grovelling. [ME, (n. f. OF or LL *reptile* neut.) f. LL *reptilis* f. L *repere* rept-crawl; see -IL]

rĕpŭ'blic *n*. a State in which supreme power is held by the people or its elected representatives or by elected or nominated president, not by monarch etc.; (fig.) society of persons or animals with equality between members (*the republic of* LETTERS); **R~ Day** (commemorating foundation of republic; in India 26 Jan.). [f. F *république* f. L *respublica* (*res* concern, *publicus* PUBLIC)]

rĕpŭ'blican *a*. & *n*. **1.** *a*. of, constituted as, characterizing, republic(s). **2.** *a*. & *n*. (person) advocating or supporting republican government. **3.** (*R~*). *** (member) of political party opposed to Democratic Party and favouring only moderate degree of central power. **4.** (Of birds) social, living in large communities. **5.** Hence ~ISM (3) *n*., ~IZE (3) *v.t.* [f. prec. + -AN]

rĕpŭ'blish *v.t.*, **rĕpUBLICA'TION** *n*. See RE- 8.

rĕpŭ'di|āte *v.t.* **1.** divorce (one's wife; esp. of the ancients or non-Christians). **2.** disown, disavow, reject; refuse dealings with, deny. **3.** refuse to recognize or obey (authority, treaty) or discharge (obligation, debt). **4.** Hence or cogn. ~A'TION *n*., ~ātor, *ns*. [f. L *repudiare* (*repudium* divorce) + -ATE[3]]

rĕpŭ'gn (-ū'n) *v*. (arch.) **1.** *v.i.* offer opposition; strive *against*. **2.** *v.t.* strive against; affect disagreeably, be repugnant to (ME, f. L *re*(*pugnare* fight) oppose; see RE- 2]

rĕpŭ'gnance *n*. antipathy, aversion, (*to*, *against*);

inconsistency, incompatibility, of ideas, statements, tempers, etc., (*of, between, to, with*). [ME, in second sense, f. F *répugnance* or f. L *repugnantia* (as prec.; see -ANCE)]

repŭ'gn|ant *a.* distasteful (*to*); contradictory (*to*), incompatible (*with*); (poet.) refractory, resisting. [ME, f. F *répugnant* or f. L (as REPUGN; see -ANT)]

repŭ'lse *v.t.*, & *n.* **1.** *v.t.* drive back (attack, attacking enemy) by force of arms, (fig.) foil in controversy; rebuff (friendly advances or their maker), refuse (request, offer, or its maker); = REPEL 2. **2.** *n.* repulsing or being repulsed, rebuff, (*inflict, meet with, suffer*, etc., *a repulse*). [(n. f. L *repulsus* or -*sa*) f. L *repellere* (see REPEL)]

repŭ'lsion (-shon) *n.* aversion, disgust; (Phys., or fig.) tendency of bodies to repel each other or increase their mutual distance (opp. *attraction*). [f. LL *repulsio* (as REPEL; see -ION)]

repŭ'lsĭve *a.* **1.** causing aversion or loathing, loathsome, disgusting; hence ∼LY² (-vlĭ) *adv.*, ∼NESS (-vn-) *n.* **2.** (Phys.) exerting repulsion. **3.** (arch.) (Of behaviour etc.) repellent, cold, unsympathetic. [f. F *répulsif -ive* or REPULSE 1 + -IVE]

repŭr'chase *v.t.*, & *n.*, **repŭr'ĭfy** *v.t.* See RE- 9.

rē'pŭtab|le *a.* of good repute, respectable; hence ∼LY² *adv.* [obs. F, or f. med. L *reputabilis* (as REPUTE; see -ABLE)]

rēpŭtā'tion *n.* what is generally said or believed about person's or thing's character (*has not justified his reputation; has a reputation for integrity, for stealing; place has a bad reputation*); state of being well reported of, credit, distinction, respectability, good report, (*persons of reputation*); the credit or discredit *of* doing or of being (*has the reputation of swindling his customers, of being the best shot in England*). [ME, f. L *reputatio* (as foll.; see -ATION)]

repū'te *v.t.*, & *n.* **1.** *v.t.* (usu. in *pass.*) consider, reckon. **2.** (in *pass.*) be generally considered or reported of, (with compl. or *to* be or do; *is reputed the best doctor* or *to be the best*); be generally *well, ill*, etc., thought or spoken of. **3.** (in *p.p.* as *a.*) passing as being but probably or possibly not being (*his reputed father, clemency*); ‖∼d pint etc., bottle of beer etc. sold as pint etc. but not guaranteed as imperial pint etc.; hence **repū'tĕd**LY² *adv.* **4.** *n.* reputation (*a philosopher of repute; know him by repute*). [ME, f. OF *reputer* or f. L *re(putare* think); see RE- 6]

rĕquĕ'st *n.*, & *v.t.* **1.** *n.* act of asking for something, petition made, thing asked for, (*came at his request; made two requests; you shall have your request*); **by** or **on** ∼, in response to expressed wish; ∼ **programme** etc. (composed of items requested by audience etc.); ∼ **stop** (where bus etc. stops only on passenger's request). **2.** state of being sought after, demand, (*is now in great request*). **3.** *v.t.* (arch.) seek permission to do. **4.** ask to be given or allowed or favoured with (*request candid consideration*, person's *presence*, etc.); ask *that*; ask (person) *to* do. [ME, f. OF *requeste*(*r*) f. Rom. **requaesita* fem. p.p. (as n.) of L *requaerere* (see REQUIRE)]

rĕquī'cken *v.t.* See RE- 9.

rĕ'quiĕm *n.* special Mass for repose of souls of the dead; musical setting for this; dirge. [ME f. L (acc. of *requies* repose), initial wd of the Mass]

rĕquiĕ'scăt *n.* wish for dead person's repose. [L, = may he or she rest (in peace)]

rĕquī're *v.t.* order (person), demand (*of* or *from* person), *to* do (*they require me* or *of me to appear*); demand or ask in words (person's action, act or thing *of* person, thing *at* person's *hands, that*, etc.) esp. as of right (*they require my appearance, an oath of me, a gift at my hands* or *from* or *of me, that I should appear*). **2.** lay down as imperative (*had done all that was required by the Act; Gray's 'Anatomy' is required reading for nurses*). **3.** need, depend for success, fulfilment, etc., on, (*the emergency requires it, that it should be done; irony requires care in its use, to be used with care; place would require an army to take it;*

machine requires no attention; it required all his authority to keep them under control); wish to have (*do you require tea?*). **4.** Hence ∼MENT (-īt′m-) *n.* [ME, f. OF *requere* f. Rom. **requaerere* f. L *re(quirere quisit-* = *quaerere* seek); see RE- 6]

rĕ'quisite (-z-) *a.* & *n.* **1.** *a.* required by circumstances, necessary to success etc.; hence ∼NESS (-tn-) *n.* **2.** *n.* thing needed (*for* some purpose). [ME, f. L *requisitus* p.p. (as prec.)]

rĕquĭsĭ'tion (-z-) *n.*, & *v.t.* **1.** *n.* requiring, demand made, esp. formal and usu. written demand that some duty should be performed; order given by authorities laying claim to use of property or materials; being called or put into service (**under** or **in** ∼, being used or applied). **2.** *v.t.* demand use or supply of esp. by requisition order. [f. F *réquisition* or f. L *requisitio* (as REQUIRE; see -ITION)]

rĕquī't|e *v.t.* make return for, reward or avenge, (service, wrong, injury, treatment; *with* what is given etc. thus); make return to, repay with good or evil, (person; *for* treatment received, *with* treatment given); give in return (*requite* person's *love, like for like*); hence ∼AL 2 *n.* [f. RE- 1 + *quite* var. of QUIT²]

rēreā'd *v.t.* (rereā'd *pr.* -rĕ'd). See RE- 8.

rēr'e-ărch *n.* Var. of REAR-ARCH.

rēr'e-dŏrter *n.* latrine behind dormitory of convent or monastery. [f. *rere* var. of REAR¹ + DORTER]

rēr'edŏs (rēr'd-) *n.* ornamental screen covering wall at back of altar. [ME, f. AF **reredos* f. OF *areredos* (*arere* behind, *dos* back); cf. ARREAR]

rē-rou'te (-ōo't) *v.t.* (∼ing *pr.* -tĭ-). send or carry by different route. [f. RE- 8 + ROUTE]

rērŭ'n *v.t.* (-nn-; -ra'n; -ru'n), & *n.* **1.** *v.t.* run (race, film, etc.) again. **2.** *n.* act of rerunning. [f. RE- 8 + RUN¹]

rēsā'le *n.* sale of thing bought. [f. RE- 9 + SALE]

rĕscī'nd *v.t.* abrogate, annul, revoke, cancel; so **rĕscī'ss**ION (-zhon) *n.* [f. L *re(scindere sciss-* cut); see RE- 5]

rē'script *n.* **1.** Roman emperor's written reply to appeal for guidance esp. from magistrate on legal point; Pope's decretal in reply to question, any papal decision. **2.** ruler's or government's or official edict or announcement. **3.** thing rewritten, rewriting; palimpsest. [f. L *rescriptum*, neut. p.p. (as n.) of *re(scribere script-* write); see RE- 1]

rĕ'scū|e *v.t.*, & *n.* **1.** *v.t.* set free or bring away from or *from* attack, custody, danger, or harm; (Law) unlawfully liberate (person), forcibly recover (property); hence ∼ER¹ *n.* **2.** *n.* rescuing or being rescued (*come* or *go to* person's or *the rescue*); succour, deliverance; illegal liberation, forcible recovery; ∼**e bid,** (Bridge) bid made to get one's partner out of difficult situation. [ME *rescowe* f. OF *rescoure* f. Rom. **reexcutere* f. as RE- 6 + L EX¹(*cutere* = *quatere* shake)]

research (rĭsĕr'-, rē'-) *n.* & *v.* **1.** *n.* careful search or inquiry *after* or *for* or *into*; endeavour to discover new or collate old facts etc. by scientific study of a subject, course of critical investigation, (*his researches have been fruitful; is engaged in research*). **2.** *v.i.* make researches; hence ∼ER¹ *n.* **3.** *v.t.* make researches into or for. [f. obs. F *recerche*(*r*) (as RE- 6, SEARCH)]

rēsea't *v.t.* provide (church, hall, valve, etc.) with fresh seat(s); seat (person, one*self*) again. [f. RE- 8 + SEAT]

rĕsĕ'ct *v.t.* (Surg.) cut out part of (lung etc.); pare down (bone, cartilage, etc.); so ∼ION *n.* [f. L *re(secare sect-* cut); see RE- 5]

rĕ'sĕda *n.* **1.** herbaceous plant of genus *Reseda*, e.g. mignonette. **2.** (or -z- or rĭsē'da). pale green colour as of mignonette flowers. [L, perh. f. imper. of *resedare* assuage, used in curative charm]

rēsĕ'll *v.t.* (resō'ld). sell after buying. [f. RE- 9 + SELL]

rĕsĕ'mbl|e (-z-) *v.t.* **1.** be like, have similarity to or feature(s) in common with or same appearance as; so ∼ANCE (*to, between, of*) *n.*, ∼ANT (*to*) *a.* **2.** (arch.) liken (*to*). [ME, f. OF *re(sembler* f. L *similare*, f. *similis* like); see RE- 1]

For other words in *re-* **see RE-.**

rĕsĕ'nt (-z-) *v.t.* show or feel indignation at or retain bitter feelings about (do*ing*, insult or injury sustained); hence or cogn. ∼FUL *a.*, ∼MENT *n.*, (*at, of*). [f. obs. F *resentir* (as RE- 1, L *sentire* feel)]

rĕsĕr'pine (-ēn) *n.* alkaloid from plants of genus *Rauwolfia*, used as tranquillizer and in treatment of hypertension. [f. G *reserpin* f. mod. L *Rauwolfia* (f. L. *Rauwolf*, Ger. botanist d. 1596) *serp*entina; see -INE⁵]

rĕservā'tion (-z-) *n.* **1.** reserving or being reserved. **2.** (Eccl.) right reserved to Pope of nomination to vacant benefice; power of absolution reserved to superior; practice of retaining for some purpose a portion of the Eucharistic elements (esp. the bread) after celebration. **3.** (Law). (clause reserving) right or interest retained in estate being conveyed. **4.** strip of land between carriageways of road; *tract of land reserved esp. for exclusive occupation by Indian tribe. **5.** express or tacit limitation or exception made about something (**mental** ∼, qualification tacitly added in making statement, oath, etc.). **6.** booking (of berth on ship, room in hotel, seat in train, etc.); place so booked. [ME f. OF, or f. LL *reservatio* (as foll.; see -ATION)]

rĕsẽr've¹ (-z-) *v.t.* **1.** postpone use or enjoyment or treatment of, keep back for later occasion, (∼e oneself for, not expend one's energies till); postpone delivery of (judgement). **2.** secure or retain possession or control or use of esp. by legal or formal stipulation (*for* or to one*self* or another; *management reserves the right to refuse admission*); ||∼ed list, (Hist.) list of naval officers retired from active service but liable to be called out in emergency; ∼ed occupation (from which person will not be taken for military service); ∼ed seat, (at entertainment etc.) that has been or may be booked; hence ∼ABLE *n.* **3.** set apart, destine, *for* some use or fate; (in *pass.*) be left by fate *for*, fall first or only *to*. **4.** (in *p.p.* as *a.*) reticent, slow to reveal emotions or opinions, uncommunicative; hence ∼edLY² *adv.* [ME, f. OF *reserver* f. L *re*(*servare* keep); see RE- 3]

rĕsẽr've³ (z-) *n.* **1.** thing reserved for future use, extra stock or amount, (*has a great reserve of energy, great reserves of strength*); (Banking, in *sing.* or *pl.*) assets kept readily available as cash or at central bank, or as gold or foreign exchange (∼ **currency**); company's profit added to capital. **2.** (Mil., in *sing.* or *pl.*) troops withheld from action to reinforce others or to cover retreat; forces outside regular army and navy and air force liable to be called out in emergency; reservist. **3.** extra player chosen in case substitute should be needed to make up team for game. **4.** state of being kept unused but available (*has it in reserve*). **5.** place reserved for some special use (*game reserve; nature reserve*), esp. for exclusive occupation by native tribe. **6.** limitation, exception, restriction, or qualification, attached to something; *I accept your statement* **without** ∼, fully; *sale* or *auction* **without** ∼, not subject to a fixed price being reached; ∼ (**price**), lowest price that will be accepted; *we publish this* **with all** ∼, **all proper** ∼s, without endorsing it. **7.** self-restraint, abstinence from exaggeration or ill-proportioned effects, in artistic or literary expression; reticence, avoidance of plain speaking, coolness of manner, lack of cordiality; intentional suppression of truth. [f. prec.]

rĕ-sẽr've³ *v.t.* See RE- 8.

rĕsẽr'vist (rĭz-) *n.* (Mil. etc.) member of reserve forces. [f. prec. +-IST]

rĕ'servoir (-zervwär) *n.* **1.** receptacle constructed usu. of earthwork or masonry in which large quantity of water is stored. **2.** any natural or artificial receptacle esp. for or of fluid, place where fluid etc. collects; part of machine or organ of body holding fluid; reserve supply or collection *of* knowledge, facts, etc. [f. F *réservoir* (*réserver* RESERVE³; see -ORY)]

rĕsĕ't *v.t.* (-tt-; rese't). set (gems, printing type, etc.) again or differently. [f. RE- 8 +SET¹]

rĕsĕ'ttle *v.t.*, **rĕsĕ'ttle**MENT (-telm-) *n.*, **rĕshä'pe** *v.t.*, **rĕshĭ'p** *v.t.* See RE- 8.

rĕshŭ'ffle *v.t.*, & *n.* **1.** *v.t.* shuffle (cards) again; interchange posts of (Government ministers etc.). **2.** *n.* reshuffling. [f. RE- 8 +SHUFFLE]

rĕsī'de (-z-) *v.i.* (Of person) have one's home, dwell permanently, *at, in, abroad*, etc.; (of incumbent official) be in residence; (of power, right, etc.) rest or be vested *in* person etc.; (of quality) be present or inherent *in*. [ME, prob. back-form. f. RESIDENT, infl. by F *résider* or L *re*(*sidēre* = *sedēre* sit); see RE- 3]

rĕ'sidence (-z-) *n.* **1.** residing (**have, take up**, (one's) ∼, dwell, begin to dwell; **in** ∼, dwelling at specified place esp. for performance of duties etc.). **2.** place where one resides, abode *of*; house esp. of considerable pretension, mansion, (*desirable residence for sale*). [ME f. OF, or f. med. L *residentia* f. L *residēre* (see prec., -ENCE)]

rĕ'sidency (-z-) *n.* (Hist.) official residence of, territory supervised by, Governor-General's representative at Indian native court, or other government agent (see RESIDENT); *period of specialized medical training. [f. as prec.; see -ENCY]

rĕ'sident (-z-) *a.* & *n.* **1.** *a.* residing (*whether resident at home or abroad; the resident population*); (of birds etc.) non-migratory; dwelling in a place in fulfilment of duty; having quarters on the spot (*resident housekeeper, surgeon, tutor*); inherent, located, *in* (*a right resident in the nation; powers of sensation resident in the nerves*). **2.** *n.* permanent inhabitant of town or neighbourhood (opp. *visitor*); (Hist.) Indian Governor-General's political agent residing at native court, British government agent in other semi-dependent State, whence ∼SHIP *n.*; *person undergoing specialized medical training. [ME f. OF, or f. L (see RESIDE, -ENT)]

rĕsidĕ'ntial (-z-; -shal) *a.* suitable for or occupied by private houses (*residential area, estate, street*); used as residence (*residential hotel*); connected with residence (*a residential course of study; the residential qualification for voters*). [f. RESIDENCE +-IAL]

rĕsidĕ'ntiary (-z-; -sherī) *n.* & *a.* **1.** *n.* ecclesiastic who must officially reside in a place. **2.** *a.* subject to, requiring, of or for, official residence (usu. after *n.*; *Canon, Canonry, Residentiary; at his residentiary house*). [f. med. L *residentiarius* (as RESIDENCE; see -ARY¹)]

rĕsĭ'dūal (-z-) *a.* & *n.* **1.** (quantity) remaining, left over, left as residue or residuum. **2.** (Math.) (quantity) resulting from subtraction. **3.** (error in calculation) still unaccounted for or not eliminated. [f. RESIDUE +-AL]

rĕsĭ'dūarȳ (-z-) *a.* of the residue of an estate (*residuary bequest, clause, legatee*); of or being a residuum, residual, still remaining. [f. RESIDUUM +-ARY¹]

rĕ'sĭdūe (-z-) *n.* remainder, rest, what is left or remains over; what remains of estate after payment of charges, debts, and bequests; (Chem. etc.) residuum. [ME, f. OF *residu* f. L *residuum* (see foll.)]

rĕsĭ'dū|um (-z-) *n.* (pl. ∼a). what remains, esp. (Chem. etc.) substance left after combustion or evaporation; residual; residue. [L, neut. (as n.) of *residuus* remaining (*residēre*; see RESIDE)]

rĕsĭ'gn (-zī'n) *v.* **1.** *v.t.* relinquish, surrender, hand over, (office, right, claim, property, charge, task, life, hope; to person, *into* person's hands etc.; one*self* to another's guidance etc.). **2.** reconcile one*self*, one's mind, etc. (to one's *fate* etc., to *doing*). **3.** *v.i.* accept the inevitable without repining; hence ∼ED¹ (2) (-zī'nd) *a.*, ∼ĕdLY² *adv.* **4.** give up office, retire, (*as chairman* etc., *from* chairmanship etc.); (Chess) discontinue play and admit defeat. [ME, f. OF *resigner* f. L *re*(*signare* SIGN², seal) unseal, cancel; see RE- 7]

rĕ-sĭ'gn² (-sī'n) *v.t.* & *i.* sign again. [f. RE- 8 +SIGN²]

rĕsĭgnā'tion (-z-) *n.* resigning esp. of a document conveying it (*give, send in, tender*, one's *resignation*); being resigned, uncomplaining endurance of sorrow or other evil. [ME f. OF, f. med. L *resignatio* (as RESIGN¹; see -ATION)]

rĕsī'le (-z-) *v.i.* (Of elastic body) recoil, rebound, resume shape and size after stretching or compression; have or show elasticity or buoyancy or recuperative power; withdraw *from* course of action. [f. obs. F *resilir* or f. L *re*(*silire* = *salire* jump); see RE- 9]

rĕsī'li|ent (-zī'lye-) *a.* recoiling, springing back; resuming original form after stretching, bending, etc.; (of person) readily recovering from depression etc., buoyant; so ᴖENCE, ᴖENCY, *ns.* [f. L (as prec.; see -ENT)]

rĕ'sĭn (-z-) *n.*, & *v.t.* **1.** *n.* adhesive inflammable substance insoluble in water (cf. GUM²) secreted by most plants and exuding naturally or upon incision esp. from fir and pine; (**synthetic**) ᴖ, solid or liquid organic compound made by polymerization etc. and used esp. as or in plastics. **2.** Hence or cogn. ᴖATE¹ (3) *n.*, ᴖATE³ *v.t.*, ᴖī'FEROUS, ᴖīFORM, *adjs.*, ᴖīFICA'TION *n.*, ᴖīFY *v.t.*, ᴖOID *a.* & *n.*, ᴖOUS *a.* **3.** *v.t.* rub or treat with resin. [ME *resyn, rosyn*, f. L *resina* & med. L *rosina, rosinum*]

rĕsĭpi'sc|ence *n.* (arch.) recognition of error, return to good sense; so ᴖENT *a.* [f. F *résipiscence* or f. LL *respiscentia* f. *re*(*sipiscere* f. *sapere* know); see RE- 9]

rĕsī'st (-zī'-) *v.* & *n.* **1.** *v.t.* stop course of, withstand action or effect of, prevent from reaching or penetrating, repel, abstain from, (*projectile, weapon, cutting edge, frost, heat, moisture, attack, temptation, power, infection, disease, influence, suggestion,* etc., *doing*); **cannot** ᴖ *a joke* etc., (1) feels obliged to make it if it suggests itself, (2) is certain to be amused, attracted, etc., by it; hence ᴖIBLE *a.* **2.** strive against, oppose, try to impede, refuse to comply with, (*resist arrest*). **3.** *v.i.* offer resistance, make opposition; hence or cogn. ᴖANT *a.*, ᴖER¹ *n.* **4.** *n.* composition applied to surfaces for protection from some agent employed on them, esp. to parts of calico that are not to take dye. [ME, f. OF *resister* or f. L *re*(*sistere* stop, redupl. of *stare* stand); see RE- 2]

rĕsī'stance (-zī'-) *n.* **1.** (power of) resisting (*showed resistance to complying, to wear and tear*); (Biol.) ability to resist adverse conditions; PASSIVE *resistance*; ᴖ (**movement**), secret organization resisting authority, esp. in a conquered country. **2.** hindrance, impeding or stopping effect, exerted by material thing on another (*overcome the resistance of the air*); **line of** ᴖ, direction in which it acts; **take line of least** ᴖ, (fig.) adopt easiest method or course. **3.** (Phys.) property of failing to conduct (electricity, heat, etc.); amount of this property in a body; (Electr.) resistor. [ME, f. F *résistance, résistence* f. LL *resistentia* (as prec.; see -ANCE)]

rĕsĭstibi'lity (-zī-) *n.* being resistible; power of offering resistance. [f. RESIST + -IBILITY]

rĕsī'stive (-zī'-) *a.* able to resist; (Electr.) pertaining to resistance. [f. med. L *resistivus*, or f. RESIST + -IVE]

rĕsĭsti'vity (-zī-) *n.* (Electr.) resisting power of specified material. [f. prec. + -ITY]

rĕsī'stless (-zī'-) *a.* (arch.) irresistible; unresisting; hence ᴖLY² *adv.* [f. RESIST + -LESS]

rĕsī'stor (-zī'-) *n.* (Electr.) device having resistance to passage of current. [f. RESIST + -OR]

rĕsī't *v.t.* (-tt-; **resa't**). sit (examination) a second time after failing. [f. RE- 8 + SIT]

rĕsō'le *v.t.* See RE- 8.

rĕsō'lŭble¹ (-z-) *a.* that can be resolved; analysable *into*, resolvable. [f. F *résoluble* or f. LL *resolubilis* (as RESOLVE, after *soluble*)]

rē-sō'lŭble² *a.* that can be dissolved again. [f. RE- 9 + SOLUBLE]

rĕ'solute (-zŏlōōt, -ūt) *a.* (Of person or his mind or action) determined, decided, bold, not vacillating, unshrinking, firm of purpose; hence ᴖLY² (-tlĭ) *adv.*, ᴖNESS (-tn-) *n.* [f. L *resolutus* p.p. of *resolvere* (see RESOLVE)]

rĕsolu'tion (-zŏlōō'-, -ū'-) *n.* **1.** separation into components, decomposition; analysis, conversion *into* other form; (Med.) disappearance of inflammation etc. without suppuration; (Pros.) substitution of two

short syllables for one long; (Mus.) causing discord to pass into concord; (Mech. etc.) replacing of single force etc. by two or more jointly equivalent to it; (Phys. etc.) resolving power, smallest interval measurable by an instrument. **2.** solving *of* doubt, problem, question, etc. **3.** formal expression of opinion by legislative body or public meeting; form proposed for this. **4.** resolve, thing resolved on; **good** ᴖs, intentions that one formulates mentally for virtuous conduct. **5.** resolute temper or character, boldness and firmness of purpose. [ME, f. L *resolutio* (as RESOLVE; see -ION)]

rĕ'solutive (-zŏlōō-, -ū-) *a.* & *n.* **1.** (Med.) having dissolving power, disintegrating. **2.** (Law). ᴖ **condition**, one whose fulfilment terminates contract etc. [f. med. L *resolutivus* (as RESOLVE; see -IVE)]

rĕsŏ'lv|e (-z-) *v.* & *n.* **1.** *v.t.* & *i.* dissolve (*into*), disintegrate, analyse, break up or separate into parts, dissipate, convert or be converted *into*, reduce by mental analysis *into*, (*resolve thing, thing is resolved*, or *resolves itself*, or *resolves, into its elements; telescope resolves nebula into stars; inflammation or tumour resolves*, or *is resolved, without suppuration*); (Pros.) replace (long syllable) by two short syllables; (Mech. etc.) replace (force etc.) by two or more jointly equivalent to it; (Mus.) convert (discord) or be converted into concord; ᴖ**ing power**, instrument's ability to distinguish very small or very close objects. **2.** *v.t.* solve, explain, clear up, settle, (*all doubts were resolved; the problem of its origin has not yet been resolved*). **3.** *v.t.* & *i.* decide upon, make up one's mind (*up*)on action or doing *to* do, form mentally or (of legislative body or public meeting) pass by vote the resolution *that,* (of circumstances etc.) bring (person) to resolution *to* do or (*up*)*on* action or doing, (*resolved that nothing should induce him, that he would* do, *on* or *upon doing; this discovery resolved us on going* or *to go*); (in *p.p.* as *a.*) resolute. **4.** Hence ᴖABLE *a.* **5.** *n.* decision come to in the mind (*and she kept her resolve*); * = RESOLUTION 3; (poet.) resoluteness, steadfastness, (*a mind, deeds, of high resolve*). [ME, f. L *re*(*solvere solut-* solve); see RE- 5]

rĕsŏ'lvent (-z-) *a.* & *n.* (Med. etc.) (drug, application, substance) effecting resolution of tumour etc. [f. as prec.; see -ENT]

rĕ'son|ant (-z-) *a.* & *n.* **1.** *a.* (Of sound) echoing, resounding, continuing to sound, reinforced or prolonged by vibration or reflection; (of body, room, etc.) tending to reinforce or prolong sounds esp. by vibration; (of place) resounding *with*; (Phys.) responding to vibrations of a particular frequency esp. by itself strongly vibrating; hence or cogn. ᴖANCE *n.*, ᴖantLY² *adv.* **2.** *n.* (Phonet.) sound involving resonance, esp. vowel or nasal. [f. F *résonnant* or f. L *re*(*sonare* sound); see RE- 6, -ANT]

rĕ'sonate (-z-) *v.i.* produce or show resonance, resound. [f. L (as prec.) + -ATE³]

rĕ'sonātor (-z-) *n.* instrument responding to single note and used for detecting it in combinations; appliance for giving resonance to sounds or other vibrations. [f. prec. + -OR]

rĕsŏr'b *v.t.* absorb again; hence ᴖENCE *n.*, ᴖENT *n.* [f. L *re*(*sorbēre sorpt-* absorb); see RE- 9]

rĕsŏr'cĭn (-z-) *n.* = foll. [f. RESIN + ORCIN]

rĕsŏr'cĭnŏl (-z-) *n.* (Chem.) crystalline organic compound usu. made by synthesis and used in production of dyes, drugs, resins, etc. [f. prec. + -OL]

rĕsŏr'ption (-z-) *n.* resorbing or being resorbed; (Path.) absorption of tissue within the body. [f. RESORB, after *absorption*]

rĕsŏr't¹ (-z-) *v.i.* **1.** turn for aid, have recourse, *to* (*resort to force, fighting, experiment,* etc.). **2.** go in large numbers or often *to* (*visitors resorted to him,* or *to the shrine, by the hundred; watched the inn to which he was known to resort*). [ME, f. OF *re*(*sortir* come or go out); see RE- 8]

rĕsŏr't² (-z-) *n.* **1.** thing to which recourse is had, what is turned to for aid, expedient, (*a taxi, repetition of the experiment, was the only resort*). **2.** recourse (*cannot be* *done without resort to compulsion*); **in the last ~**, when all else has failed, as final attempt. **3.** frequenting or being frequented (*encouraged the resort of scholars; a place of great resort*). **4.** place frequented usu. for specified purpose (esp. holidays) or quality (*health, holiday, resort; mountain, seaside, resort*). [ME f. OF (*resortir*; see prec.)]

rē-sŏr′t³ *v.t.* sort again. [f. RE- 8 + SORT²]

rĕsou′nd (-z-) *v.* **1.** *v.i.* (Of place) ring or echo (*with*); (of voice, instrument, sound, etc.) produce echoes, go on sounding, fill place with sound. **2.** (Of fame, event, etc.) be much talked of, produce sensation, (*through* Europe etc.). **3.** *v.t.* repeat loudly (the praises etc. *of*); (of place) re-echo (sound). [ME (RE- 9, SOUND² v., after OF *resoner* or L *resonare* (see RESONANT)]

rĕsou′nding (-z-) *a.* In vbl senses; unmistakable, emphatic, (*was a resounding success*); hence ~LY² *adv.* [f. prec. + -ING²]

rĕsour′ce (-sŏr′s, -z-) *n.* **1.** (usu. in *pl.*) means of supplying what is needed, stock that can be drawn on, *available assets; (in *pl.*) country's collective means for support and defence. **2.** (arch.) possibility of aid (*lost without resource*). **3.** expedient, device, shift, (*flight was his only resource; am at the end of my resources*). **4.** leisure occupation (*reading is a great resource*); **left to one's own ~s**, given no help in passing time or dealing with problems. **5.** skill in devising expedients, practical ingenuity, quick wit, (*is full of resource*). **6.** Hence ~FUL (-sf-), ~LESS (-sl-), *adjs.* [f. F *ressource*, *ressourse*, fem. p.p. (as n.) of OF dial. *resourdre* f. as RE- 9 + L *surgere* rise]

rĕspĕ′ct¹ *n.* **1.** reference, relation, (*to; the terms have respect to position alone; is true with respect to the French; with respect to possible routes, there are three*). **2.** heed or regard *to* or *of*, attention *to*, (*have not had* or *paid respect to anything but colour; did it quite without respect to the results*); **~ of persons** (cf. foll. 2). **3.** particular, detail, point, aspect, (*of; is admirable in respect of style; in all, many, some, respects; in one, this, respect*). **4.** (arch.) consideration *that*; **in ~ that**, because. **5.** deferential esteem felt or shown towards person or quality (*has won the respect of all; have the greatest respect for him; with respect, I suggest you are quite wrong*). **6.** (in *pl.*) one's polite messages or attentions (*give him my, sends his, respects*); **pay** one's **~s**, make polite visit; **pay** one's **last ~s** (to dead person, e.g. by attending funeral). [ME f. OF, or f. L *respectus* (*respicere*; see foll.)]

rĕspĕ′ct² *v.t.* **1.** regard with deference, esteem, or honour; avoid degrading or insulting or injuring or interfering with or interrupting, treat with consideration, spare, refrain from offending or corrupting or tempting, (*respect person's feelings or innocence, the rule of the road; respect neutrality, privileges, property*); **~ one**self, have self-respect. **2.** (arch.) pay heed to; **~ persons**, discriminate unfairly between them under influence of wealth or status. **3.** (arch.) relate to, be directed to or concerned with. [f. L *re(spicere spect- = specere* look at), or f. *respectare* frequent. of *respicere*; see RE- 6]

rĕspĕctabi′lĭty *n.* being, those who are, socially respectable. [f. foll. + -ITY]

rĕspĕ′ctab|**le** *a.* **1.** deserving respect (*did it from respectable motives*). **2.** considerable in number, size, amount, etc., of some merit or importance, fairly good or many or much, tolerable, passable, (*a respectable hill, antiquity, painter, score, minority; respectable talents*). **3.** of fair social standing, having the qualities necessary for such standing, not disreputable, honest and decent in conduct; (of activity, clothes, etc.) befitting respectable persons; hence ~LY² *adv.* [f. RESPECT¹ + -ABLE]

rĕspĕ′cter *n.* In vbl senses (*is no respecter of persons*). [f. RESPECT² + -ER¹]

rĕspĕ′ctful *a.* showing deference (*respectful behaviour; stood at a respectful distance*); hence ~LY² *adv.*, ~NESS *n.* [f. RESPECT¹ + -FUL]

rĕspĕ′cting *a.* & *prep.* **1.** *a.* having reference to (*legislation respecting property*). **2.** *prep.* in respect of (*am at a loss respecting his whereabouts*). [f. RESPECT² + -ING²]

rĕspĕ′ctive *a.* pertaining or proper to each, individual, several, comparative, (*go to your, put them in their, respective places; were given places according to their respective rank or ranks; he and I contributed respective amounts of £10 and £1; the election result depends on the respective popularity of the candidates*); hence ~LY² (-vlĭ) *adv.*, (esp.) for each separately or in turn, and in the order mentioned (*he and I contributed £10 and £1 respectively*). [f. F *respectif -ive* or f. med. L *respectivus* (as RESPECT²; see -IVE)]

rĕspĕ′ll *v.t.* (**respe′lt** or **~ed** *pr.* -lt). spell again or differently, esp. phonetically. [f. RE- 8 + SPELL²]

respirable (rĕ′sper-, rĭspīr′-) *a.* (Of air, gas, etc.) that can, or is fit to, be breathed. [F, or f. LL *respirabilis* (as RESPIRE; see -ABLE)]

rĕspirā′tion *n.* breathing; single inspiration and expiration, a breath; plant's absorption of oxygen and emission of carbon dioxide; ARTIFICIAL *respiration*. [ME f. F, or f. L *respiratio* (as RESPIRE; see -ATION)]

rĕ′spirātor *n.* apparatus worn over the mouth and nose to warm or filter inhaled air or to prevent inhalation of poison gas etc.; apparatus for maintaining artificial respiration. [f. as foll. + -OR]

rĕspīr′e *v.* **1.** *v.i.* breathe air, inhale and exhale air, whence **respirat**ORY (rĕ′sperăt-, rĭspī′rat-, rĭspīr′at-) *a.*; breathe again, take breath, recover hope or spirit, get rest or respite. **2.** *v.t.* breathe (air etc.); (arch.) exhale (perfume, amiability, etc.). [ME, f. OF *respirer* or f. L *re(spirare* breathe); see RE- 9]

rĕ′spīte *n.*, & *v.t.* **1.** *n.* delay permitted in the discharge of an obligation or suffering of a penalty; interval of rest or relief. **2.** *v.t.* grant respite to, reprieve, (condemned person); postpone execution or exaction of (sentence, obligation); give temporary relief from (pain, care) or to (sufferer). [ME, f. OF *respit* f. L *respectus* RESPECT¹]

rĕsplĕ′nd|**ent** *a.* brilliant, dazzlingly or gloriously bright; hence or cogn. ~ENCE, ~ENCY, *ns.*, ~ent**LY²** *adv.* [ME, f. L *re(splendēre* glitter); see RE- 6, ENT]

rĕspŏ′nd¹ *n., v.i.* make answer; (of congregation) make set answers to priest etc.; act or behave in answering or corresponding manner (*responded with a drop-kick, left-hander, etc.; horse responds to bridle, vehicle to controls, illness to treatment*); (Bridge) make bid on basis of partner's preceding bid. **2.** show sensitiveness *to* by behaviour or change (*does not respond to kindness, to treatment; nerve responds to stimulus, string to note, etc.*). **3.** (arch.) correspond, be analogous; so ~ENCE, ~ENCY, *ns.* **4.** *v.t.* say in answer. [f. L *re(spondēre spons-* pledge) answer; see RE- 1]

rĕspŏ′nd² *n.* **1.** (Eccl.) responsory; response to versicle. **2.** (Archit.) half-pillar or half-pier attached to wall to support arch, esp. at end of arcade. [ME f. OF (*respondre* answer f. Rom. *respondere* f. as prec.)]

rĕspŏ′ndent *a.* & *n.* **1.** *a.* making answer; responsive *to*; in position of defendant. **2.** *n.* one who makes answer, defends thesis, etc.; defendant esp. in appeal or divorce case. [as RESPOND¹; see -ENT]

rĕspŏ′nse *n.* **1.** answer given in word or act, reply, retort, (*in response to; made no response*); action, feeling, movement, change, etc., elicited by stimulus or influence (*his response was to resign; called forth no response in his breast*); (Bridge) bid made in responding. **2.** (Eccl.) responsory; any part of the liturgy said or sung in answer to priest. [ME, f. OF *respons(e)* or f. L *responsum* neut. p.p. (as n.) of *respondēre* RESPOND¹]

rĕspŏnsĭbi′lĭty *n.* **1.** being responsible (*refuses all responsibility for it; will take the responsibility of doing it*); **on** one's **own ~**, without authorization. **2.** charge for which one is responsible (*a family is a great responsibility*). [f. foll. + -ITY]

rĕspŏ′nsĭb|**le** *a.* **1.** liable to be called to account (*to person, for thing, or abs.*); (of ruler, government) not autocratic; morally accountable for actions, capable of rational conduct; of good credit or position or repute, respectable, evidently trustworthy. **2.** being the primary cause *for* (result etc.); involving responsibility (*a responsible task*). **3.** Hence ∼LY² *adv.* [obs. F, f. L *respondēre* (see RESPOND¹, -IBLE)]

respŏ'nsive *a.* answering, by way of answer; (of liturgy etc.) using responses; responding readily to or *to* some influence, impressionable, sympathetic; hence ∼LY² (-vlĭ) *adv.*, ∼NESS (-vn-) *n.* [f. F *responsif* -*ive* or f. LL *responsivus* (as RESPOND¹; see -IVE)]

respŏ'nsory *n.* anthem said or sung by soloist and choir after lesson. [ME, f. LL *responsorium* (as RESPOND¹; SEE -ORY)]

rēspray' *v.t.* spray again (esp. to change colour of paint on vehicle). [f. RE- 8 + SPRAY²]

rest¹ *v.* **1.** *v.i.* be still, cease or abstain or be relieved from exertion or action or movement or employment, lie in sleep or death, lie buried (*in* churchyard etc.), be tranquil, be let alone, (*waves that never rest; never let your enemy rest; rest from one's labours; let her rest in peace; is too feverish to rest; could not rest under the imputation, till he got his wish*); *rest on* one's OARS; *conclude calling of witnesses in law case; (of land) lie fallow; (of matter under discussion) be left without further investigation; ‖be ∼ing, (of actor) be out of work; *∼ up, rest oneself thoroughly. **2.** lie, be spread out, be supported or based, depend, rely, (of look etc.) alight or be steadily directed, (*up*)*on*, (*shadow, light, rests on his face; roof rests on four arches; hand resting on the table; science rests on observation; I rest upon your promise; his gaze rested on a strange object*); be propped *against*; repose trust *in* (*be content to rest in God*). **3.** *v.t.* give relief or repose to, allow to rest, (*stayed a day to rest myself; rest your men for an hour; says the goggles rest his eyes; must rest the ground*); ∼ one's **case,** conclude presentation of it; (God) ∼ **his soul,** may God give his soul repose; (in *p.p.*) refreshed or reinvigorated by resting. **4.** place for support or foundation (*up*)*on* (*rest one's elbow, load, on the table; rest* one's *case on equity, unimpeachable evidence*). **5.** ∼'ing-place, place provided or used for resting (*last ∼ing-place,* the grave). [OE *ræstan, restan,* = OHG *restan*]

rest² *n.* **1.** repose or sleep esp. in bed at night (*go, retire, to rest; take* one's *rest; get a good night's rest*). **2.** abstinence or freedom from or absence of exertion or activity or movement or worry or molestation, a period of such abstinence etc., (*a rest from work* etc.; *give* person, horse, machine, (fig.) topic of discussion, etc., *a rest; take a short rest*); **at** ∼, not moving, not agitated or troubled (esp. of the dead); **set** *question,* person's *mind* or *fears,* **at** ∼ (settle, relieve); DAY *of rest;* **come to** ∼, cease moving; **lay to** ∼, bury in grave. **3.** place of resting or abiding; lodging-place or shelter provided for sailors, cabmen, or other class. **4.** prop or support or steadying-piece for resting thing on, e.g. for gun in aiming, telephone-receiver, billiard-cue, cutting-tool in lathe, foot. **5.** (Mus.) interval of silence or sign denoting it; pause in elocution, caesura in verse. **6.** ∼-balk, ridge left unploughed between furrows; ∼-cure, some weeks in bed as medical treatment; ∼-day, (1) day spent in rest, (2) = DAY *of rest;* ∼-home, place where old or frail people can be cared for; ∼-house, (Ind.) house for travellers to rest at; ∼ mass, (Phys.) mass of a body when at rest; ∼-room, public lavatory in factory, shop, etc. [OE *ræst, rest,* = OS, OHG *rasta,* ON *röst,* Goth. *rasta* mile (as distance after which one rests)]

rest³ *v.i.* **1.** (arch.) remain over (*whatever rests of hope*). **2.** ∼ **with,** be left in the hands or charge of (*it rests with you to propose terms; the management of affairs rested with Wolsey*). **3.** remain in specified state (*rest assured, satisfied,* etc.). [ME, f. OF *rester* f. L *re*(*stare* stand); see RE- 3]

rest⁴ *n.* **1.** *the* remaining part(s) or individuals *of, the* remainder of some quantity or number, *the* others; **and the** or **all the** ∼ **of it,** and all else that might be mentioned; **for the** ∼, as regards anything beyond what has been specially mentioned. **2.** ‖(Banking) reserve fund; (Tennis etc.) = RALLY¹. [ME, f. OF *reste* (*rester;* see prec.)]

rest⁵ *n.* (Hist.) check holding butt of medieval tilter's spear when couched for charging (*with, lay* or *set* one's, *lance in rest*). [ME, f. ARREST²]

rēstār't *v. & n.* See RE- 8.

rēstā'te *v.t.* express again or differently, esp. more clearly or convincingly; hence ∼MENT (-tm-) *n.* [f. RE- 8 + STATE²]

rĕ'staurant (-torawṅ, -torŏnt) *n.* public premises where meals or refreshments may be had; ‖∼ car, dining-car. [F (*restaurer* RESTORE; see -ANT)]

rĕstaurateur' (-toratēr') *n.* restaurant-keeper. [F (*restaurer* RESTORE)]

rĕ'stful *a.* favourable to repose, free from disturbing influences, soothing; hence ∼LY² *adv.*, ∼NESS *n.* [ME, f. REST² + -FUL]

rĕ'st-härrow (-ō) *n.* tough-rooted herb of genus *Ononis.* [f. obs. *rest* v. or REST⁵ + HARROW¹]

rĕ'stiff. See RESTIVE.

rĕstitū'tion *n.* restoring of or *of* thing to proper owner, reparation for injury, (esp. *make restitution*); restoring of thing to its original state, repr. (Theol.) *the restitution of all things;* resumption of original shape or position because of elasticity. [ME f. OF or f. L *restitutio* f. *re*(*stituere stitut- = statuere* establish) restore; see RE- 8, -ION]

rĕ'stive, (arch.) **rĕ'stiff,** *a.* (Of horse) refusing to advance, stubbornly standing still or moving backwards or sideways, jibbing, refractory; (of person) unmanageable, rejecting control, fidgety, restless; hence **rĕ'stive**LY² (-vlĭ) *adv.*, **rĕ'stive**NESS (-vn-) *n.* [ME f. OF *restif -ive* f. Rom. *restivus inclined not to move (as REST³; see -IVE)]

rĕ'stless *a.* finding or affording no rest; uneasy, agitated; constantly in motion, fidgeting, etc.; ∼ **flycatcher,** small Austral. bird (*Seisura inquieta*); hence ∼LY² *adv.*, ∼NESS *n.* [OE *restlēas* (as REST², -LESS)]

rēstŏ'ck *v.t. & i.* See RE- 8.

rĕstorā'tion *n.* restoring or being restored; (period of) re-establishment of monarch etc. (**the R**∼, return of Charles II of England in 1660); model or drawing representing supposed original form of extinct animal, ruined building, etc. [17th c. alt. (after RESTORE) of *restauration,* ME f. OF, or f. LL *restauratio* (as RESTORE; see -ION)]

rĕstorā'tion|ism *n.* doctrine that all men will ultimately be restored to happiness in the future life; so ∼IST (2) *n.* [f. prec. + -ISM]

rĕstŏ'rative *a. & n.* **1.** *a.* tending to restore health or strength; hence ∼LY² (-vlĭ) *adv.* **2.** *n.* restorative food, medicine, etc. [ME, var. of obs. *restaurative* f. OF *restauratif -ive* (as foll.; see -ATIVE)]

rĕstŏr'|e *v.t.* **1.** give back, make restitution of. **2.** (attempt to) bring back to original state by rebuilding, repairing, repainting, emending, etc., (*church, picture, text, has been restored, restored out of all recognition,* etc.); make representation of supposed original state of (extinct animal, ruin, etc.). **3.** reinstate, bring back to dignity or right; bring back to or *to* health etc., cure (person). **4.** re-establish, renew, bring back into use. **5.** reinsert by conjecture (missing words in text, parts of extinct animal, etc.). **6.** replace, put back, bring to former place or condition. **7.** Hence ∼ABLE *a.*, ∼ER² *n.* [ME, f. OF *restorer* f. L *restaurare*]

rĕstrai'n¹ *v.t.* check or hold in *from,* keep in check or under control or within bounds, repress, keep down; confine, imprison; hence ∼ABLE *a.*, ∼ĕdLY² *adv.* (*with self-restraint*). [ME, f. OF *restrei*(*g*)*n-* st. of *restreindre* f. L *re*(*stringere strict-* tie); see RE- 2]

rē-strai'n² *v.t.* strain again. [f. RE- 8 + STRAIN¹]

rĕstrai'nt *n.* **1.** restraining or being restrained, stoppage, check, controlling agency or influence, confinement esp. because of insanity; **in** ∼ **of,** in order to restrain; ∼ **of trade,** action seeking to interfere with free-market conditions; **without** ∼, freely, copiously. **2.** constraint or reserve of manner; self-control, avoidance of excess or exaggeration, austerity of literary expression. [ME, f. OF *restreinte* fem. p.p. of *restreindre* (see RESTRAIN¹)]

rĕstri′ct *v.t.* confine, bound, limit, (*to, within; has a very restricted application; am restricted to advising; is restricted within narrow limits*); subject to restriction; designate as not for general disclosure; ~ed **area** (‖in which there is a special speed limit for vehicles, *which military personnel are not allowed to enter*); hence ~ĕdLY² *adv.* [f. L *restringere* (see RESTRAIN¹)]

rĕstri′ction *n.* restricting or being restricted; thing that restricts; limitation placed on action. [ME f. OF, or f. L *restrictio* (as prec.; see -ION)]

rĕstri′ctive *a.* imposing restrictions; ~ **practice**, agreement to limit competition or output in industry; hence ~LY² (-vlĭ) *adv.*, ~NESS (-vn-) *n.* [ME, f. OF *restrictif -ive* or f. med. L *restrictivus* (as RESTRICT; see -IVE)]

rĕstrŭ′cture *v.t.* give new structure to; rebuild, rearrange. [f. RE- 8 + STRUCTURE]

rĕstŭ′dy̆ *v.t.* See RE- 8.

rĕstȳ′le *v.t.* remake in new style. [f. RE- 8 + STYLE]

rĕsŭ′lt (-z-) *v.i.*, & *n.* **1.** *v.i.* arise as actual or follow as logical consequence (*from* conditions, causes, premisses, etc., or abs.); have outcome or end in specified manner esp. *in* failure, success, etc. (*resulted badly, in a large profit*). **2.** *n.* consequence, issue, or outcome of something, satisfactory outcome (*knows how to get results*; **without** ~, in vain, fruitless); (in *pl.*) list of scores, winners, etc., in sporting events or competitions; hence ~FUL, ~LESS, *adjs.* **3.** quantity, formula etc., obtained by calculation. [ME, f. med. L f. L *re*(*sultare* = *saltare* frequent. of *salire* jump; see RE- 9]

rĕsŭ′ltant (-z-) *a.* & *n.* **1.** *a.* resulting, esp. as total outcome of more or less opposed forces. **2.** *n.* force etc. equivalent to two or more acting in different directions at same point. [f. as prec.; see -ANT]

rĕsŭ′me (-z-) *v.* **1.** *v.t.* get or take again or back, recover, reoccupy, (*resume* one's *spirits, sway, liberty, seat; resume gift, grant, territory*). **2.** *v.t.* & *i.* begin again (upon), go on (with) after interruption, begin to speak or work or use again, recommence, (*the House resumed its labours* or *resumed; resume the thread of one's discourse; resumed her maiden name*). **3.** make résumé of, recapitulate, summarize. [ME, f. OF *resumer*, or f. L *re*(*sumere sumpt-* take); see RE- 8]

résumé (rĕ′zŏōmā) *n.* summary, *curriculum vitae. [F, p.p. of *résumer* (as prec.)]

rĕsŭ′mpt|ion (-z-) *n.* resuming; hence ~IVE *a.* [ME f. OF, or f LL *resumptio* (as RESUME; see -ION)]

rĕsŭ′pinate *a.* (Bot., of leaf etc.) upside down. [f. L *resupinatus* p.p. of *resupinare* bend back; see RE- 1, SUPINE¹, -ATE²]

rĕsŭr′face (-ĭs) *v.t.* See RE- 8.

rĕsŭr′g|ent *a.* rising or arising again; tending to rise again; hence ~ENCE *n.* [f. L *re*(*surgere surrect-* rise); see RE- 9, -ENT]

rĕsurre′ct (-z-) *v.t.* (colloq.) revive practice or memory of; take from grave, exhume; dig up. [back-form. f. foll.]

rĕsurre′ction (-z-) *n.* **1.** (*R*~). rising of Christ from the grave; rising again of dead at the Last Judgement. **2.** exhumation (lit. or fig.), resurrecting, (~ **man**, (Hist.) body-snatcher; ~IST (1) *n.*; ~ **plant**, club-moss of genus *Selaginella* of Egypt, Jericho, unfolding when moistened after being dried. **3.** revival after disuse or inactivity or decay, restoration to vogue or memory. **4.** Hence ~AL *a.* [ME f. OF, f. LL *resurrectio -onis* (as RESURGENT; see -ION)]

rĕsŭrvey′ (-ā′) *v.t.*, **rĕsŭr′vey** (-ā) *n.* See RE- 8.

rĕsŭ′scit|āte *v.t.* & *i.* revive from unconsciousness or apparent death, return or restore to vogue, vigour, or vividness; hence or cogn. ~A′TION, ~ātor, *ns.*, ~ATIVE *a.* [f. L *re*(*suscitare* raise); see RE- 9, -ATE³]

rĕt *v.* (-tt-). **1.** *v.t.* soften (flax, hemp) by soaking or exposing to moisture; (in *pass.*) = sense 2. **2.** *v.i.* (Of hay etc.) be spoilt by wet, rot. [ME, = MDu. *re*(*e*)*ten, ro*(*o*)*ten*; cogn. w. ROT²]

ret. *abbr.* retired; returned.

rĕtā′ble *n.* shelf, or frame enclosing decorated panels, above back of altar. [f. F *rétable, retable* f. Sp. *retablo* f. med. L *retabulum* f. *retrotabulum* rear table (as RETRO-, TABLE)]

rē′tail¹ *n.*, *a.*, & *adv.* **1.** *n.* sale of goods in small quantities at a time and usu. not for resale. **2.** *a.* & *adv.* in retail trade (*do you buy wholesale or retail?*). [ME, f. AF *retaille* f. OF *retaille* piece cut off (*retaillier*; see RE- 5, TAIL²)]

retail² (rē′-, -ā′l) *v.* **1.** *v.t.* sell (goods) in retail trade. **2.** recount, relate details of. **3.** Hence ~ER¹ *n.* **4.** *v.i.* (Of goods) be retailed (esp. *at* or *for* specified price). [ME, f. prec.]

rĕtai′n *v.t.* **1.** keep in place, hold fixed; ~ing **wall**, wall supporting and confining mass of earth or water. **2.** secure services of (esp. barrister) by engagement and preliminary payment; ~ing **fee** (paid to secure services thus). **3.** keep possession of, not lose, continue to have; continue to practise or recognize, allow to remain or prevail, not abolish or discard or alter. **4.** succeed in remembering, not forget. **5.** Hence ~ABLE *a.* [ME, f. AF *retei*(*g*)*n-* f. st. of OF *retenir* f. Rom. **retenēre* f. L *re*(*tinēre tent-* = *tenēre* hold); see RE- 3]

rĕtai′ner *n.* **1.** (Law) formal retention of something as one's own, authorization to retain thus; being retained to serve in some capacity, authorization to serve thus; retaining fee. **2.** In vbl senses; (Hist.) dependant or follower of person of rank; **old** ~, (joc.) old and faithful servant. [f. RETAIN + (sense 1) ER⁴, (sense 2) -ER¹]

rĕtā′ke¹ *v.t.* (retoo′k; reta′ken). take again; recapture. [f. RE- 8, 9 + TAKE¹]

rē′tāke² *n.* act of retaking; second or subsequent filming of a scene. [f. prec.]

rĕtā′li|āte *v.* **1.** *v.t.* repay (injury, insult, etc.) in kind; cast (accusation) back *upon* person. **2.** *v.i.* do as one is done by, esp. return evil, make reprisals. **3.** Hence ~A′TION *n.*, ~ATIVE, ~atORY, (-lya-) *adjs.* retaliatory TARIFF). [f. L *re*(*taliare* f. *talis* such); see RE- 1, -ATE³]

rĕtar′d *v.t.*, & *n.* **1.** *v.t.* make slow or late, delay progress or development or arrival or accomplishment or happening of; (in *p.p.*, esp.) backward in mental or physical development. **2.** Hence or cogn. ~ANT *a.* & *n.*, **rĕtar′da**′TION, ~ER¹, ~MENT, *ns.*, ~ATIVE, ~atORY, *adjs.* **3.** *n.* retardation. [f. L *re*(*tardare* f. *tardus* slow); see RE- 3]

rĕtar′date *a.* *n.* mentally retarded (person). [f. L *retardare* (see prec., -ATE²)]

rĕtch *v.i.*, & *n.* **1.** *v.i.* make motion of vomiting esp. ineffectually and involuntarily. **2.** *n.* such motion or sound of it. [var. of (now dial.) *reach,* f. OE *hrǣcan* spit, ON *hrækja* f. Gmc *hraik-, of imit. orig.]

retd. *abbr.* retired; returned.

rĕtĕ′ll *v.t.* (reto′ld). tell again in same or another form. [f. RE- 8 + TELL¹]

rĕtĕ′ntion *n.* retaining or being retained (Med.) failure to evacuate urine or other secretion; hence ~IST *n.*, one who favours retention of a policy (esp. of capital punishment). [ME f. OF, or f. L *retentio* (as RETAIN; see -ION)]

rĕtĕ′ntive *a.* tending to retain; (of memory) tenacious, not forgetful; (Surg., of ligature etc.) serving to keep something in place; ~ **of**, (of substance) apt to retain (moisture etc.); hence ~LY² (-vlĭ) *adv.*, ~NESS (-vn-) *n.* [ME, f. OF *retentif -ive* or f. med. L *retentivus* (as RETAIN; see -IVE)]

rē′think *v.t.* (re′thought), & *n.* **1.** *v.t.* consider afresh, esp. with view to making changes. **2.** *n.* rethinking, reassessment. [f. RE- 8 + THINK]

rĕtiā′r|ius *n.* (*pl.* ~i pr. -ī). Roman gladiator using net to trap opponent. [L (*rete* net)]

rē′tiary (-sheri) *n.* net-making or geometrical spider. [f. L (as prec.; see -ARY¹)]

rē′tic|ence *n.* reserve in speech, avoidance of saying all one knows or feels or more than is necessary; abstinence from over-emphasis in art; holding back of some fact; disposition to silence, taciturnity; so ∼ENT a. (on, upon, about). [f. L reticentia f. re(ticēre = tacēre be silent); see RE- 4, -ENCE]

rĕ'ticle n. network of fine threads or lines in focal plane of optical instrument to help accurate observation. [f. L RETICULUM]

rĕtĭ'cŭl|āte v.t. & i. divide or be divided in fact or appearance into a network; arrange or be arranged in small squares or with intersecting lines; so ∼ATE² a., ∼A'TION n. [back-form. f. reticulated f. reticulate a. f. L reticulatus (as RETICULUM; see -ATE²)]

rĕ'ticŭle n. 1. = RETICLE. 2. (arch.) woman's netted or other bag carried or worn to serve purpose of pocket. [f. F réticule f. L (as foll.)]

rĕtĭ'cŭl|um n. (pl. ∼a). 1. ruminant's second STOMACH. 2. netlike structure, fine network in cytoplasm, reticulated membrane etc.; hence ∼AR¹, ∼OSE¹, adjs., ∼ŎCYTE n., immature erythrocyte containing reticulum. [L, dim. of rete net; see -CULE]

rĕ'tĭfŏrm a. netlike, reticulated. [f. L rete net + -I- + -FORM]

rĕ'tĭn|a n. (pl. ∼as or ∼ae). layer at back of eyeball sensitive to light; hence ∼AL a., ∼I'TIS n., ∼OL n., vitamin A. [ME f. med. L, f. L rete net]

rĕ'tĭnūe n. suite or train of persons in attendance upon great personage. [ME, f. OF retenue fem. p.p. (as n.) of retenir RETAIN]

*rĕtĭr'acў n. retirement, seclusion. [f. RETIRE + -ACY, after privacy]

rĕtĭr'al n. (Sc.) retirement from office etc. [f. foll. + -AL 2]

rĕtĭr'e v. 1. v.i. withdraw, go away, retreat, seek seclusion or shelter, recede, go (as) to bed; ∼ from the world, become recluse; into oneself, become uncommunicative or unsociable, whence rĕtĭr'ING² a.; retiring collection (taken at end of service or concert). 2. cease from or give up office or profession or employment (esp. on completion of normal time of serving), (Cricket) voluntarily terminate or be compelled to suspend one's innings, (retire from the army, from the presidency, on a pension; batsman retired hurt); retiring age, age at which persons normally retire. 3. v.t. compel (employee etc.) to retire; (Mil.) order (troops) to retire; (Finance) withdraw (bill, note) from circulation or currency. [f. F retirer (as RE- 9, tirer draw)]

rĕtĭr'ed (-ĭr'd) a. withdrawn from society or observation, secluded, (lives a retired life; in a retired valley); who has retired (a retired general, grocer); ∼ list (of retired officers); ∼ pay, pension of former officer or official; hence ∼NESS n. [f. prec. + -ED¹ (2)]

*rĕtĭr'ee' n. person who retires from employment etc. [f. RETIRE + -EE]

rĕtĭr'ement (-ĭr'm-) n. In vbl senses; seclusion, privacy; secluded place; condition of having retired; ∼ pension (received by person who retires from employment etc., or = old-age PENSION). [f. RETIRE + -MENT]

rĕtōō'l v.t. equip (factory etc.) with new tools. [f. RE- 8 + TOOL¹]

rĕtŏr't¹ v. & n. 1. v.t. repay (humiliation, insult, attack) in kind; send (mischief etc., charge, sarcasm, jest), back (on or upon originator or aggressor); make (argument) tell against or against its user; say by way of witty reply, or counter-charge or counter-argument; (in p.p.) recurved, twisted or bent backwards. 2. v.i. make retort. 3. n. incisive reply, repartee; turning of charge or argument against its originator; piece of retaliation. [f. L re(torquēre tort- twist); see RE- 9]

rĕtŏr't² n., & v.t. 1. n. vessel usu. of glass with long downward-bent neck used in distilling liquids; vessel for heating mercury for purification, coal to generate gas, or iron and carbon to make steel. 2. v.t. purify (mercury) by heating in retort. [f. F retorte f. med. L retorta fem. p.p. (as n.) of retorquēre (see prec.)]

rĕtŏr'tion n. bending back (lit. or fig.); retaliation by State upon subjects of another. [f. RETORT¹ + -ION, perh. after contortion]

rĕtou'ch (-ŭ'-) v.t. improve (composition, picture, photographic negative or print, etc.) by fresh touches or alterations. [prob. f. F retoucher (as RE- 8, TOUCH¹)]

rĕträ'ce v.t. trace back to source or beginning; (arch.) look over again; recall the course of in memory; go back over (one's steps or way; lit., or fig. of undoing or reconsidering actions). [f. F retracer (as RE- 8, TRACE¹)]

rĕträ'ct¹ v.t. & i. draw (esp. part of one's body) or be drawn back or in (snail retracts its horns; surgeon retracts skin with instrument; organ is retracted by muscle); draw (undercarriage etc.) into body of aircraft; hence or cogn. ∼ABLE, ∼IVE, adjs. [f. L re(trahere tract- draw); see RE- 4]

rĕträ'ct² v.t. withdraw, revoke, cancel, refuse to abide by, acknowledge falsity or error of, expressly abandon, (statement, promise, opinion, chess move, or abs.); hence rĕträctA'TION n. [f. OF retracter or f. L re(tractare draw, frequent. of trahere draw); see RE- 9]

rĕträ'ct|ĭle (ĭle a.) retractable; capable of being retracted; hence ∼ĭ'lity n. [f. RETRACT¹, after contractile]

rĕträ'ction n. retracting or being retracted. [f. RETRACT¹,² + -ION]

rĕträ'ctor n. device or muscle for retracting. [f. RETRACT¹ + -OR]

rĕtrai'n v.t. & i. See RE- 8.

rĕ'tral a. (Biol. etc.) hinder, posterior, at the back. [f. RETRO- + -AL]

rĕtransl|ā'te (-trä-, -trah-; -s-, -z-) v.t. translate again, esp. back into the original language; so ∼A'TION n. [f. RE- 8, 9 + TRANSLATE]

rĕtrea'd¹ (-ĕ'd) v.t. (retro'd; retro'dden). tread again (path etc.). [f. RE- 8, 9 + TREAD]

rĕtrea'd² (-ĕ'd) v.t. put fresh tread on (tyre). [f. RE- 8 + TREAD n.]

rĕ'tread³ (-ĕd) n. retreaded tyre. [f. prec.]

rĕtrea't v. & n. 1. v.i. go back, retire, relinquish a position, (esp. of army etc.); recede (retreating chin, forehead). 2. v.t. (Chess). move (piece) back from forward or threatened position. 3. n. act of, (Mil.) signal for, retreating (beat a ∼, retreat, abandon undertaking; make good one's ∼, get safely away); (Mil.) bugle-call at sunset. 4. withdrawing into privacy or security, (place of) seclusion; temporary retirement for religious exercises or meditation; place for reception of pensioners or alcoholics or others in need of care; lurking-place; (place of) shelter. [v. ME, f. OF retraiter; n. ME f. OF retret(e) f. retraite fem. p.p. (as n.) of retraire f. L retrahere (see RETRACT¹)]

rĕtrĕ'nch v. 1. v.t. cut down, reduce amount of, (expenses, things causing outlay); cut off, deduct, (retrenched a year from the established period); make excisions in or of, shorten or remove, (literary work or passages in it). 2. v.i. cut down expenses, introduce economies. 3. Hence ∼MENT n. [f. obs. F retrencher (as RE-, TRENCH)]

rĕtri'al. See RETRY.

rĕtrĭbū'tion n. recompense usu. for evil done, vengeance, requital; so rĕtrĭ'bŭtIVE a. [ME, f. LL re(tributio f. tribuere tribut- assign; see RE-, -ION)]

rĕtrie've|v.t., & n. 1. v.t. (esp. of dog of special breed) find and bring in (killed or wounded game etc., or abs.); hence ∼ER¹ n. 2. recover by investigation or effort of memory; find again (stored information etc.); restore to knowledge or recall to mind. 3. regain possession of. 4. rescue from bad state etc.; restore to flourishing state, revive, (esp. one's fortunes etc.). 5. make good, repair, set right, (loss, disaster, error, situation). 6. Hence ∼ABLE a., ∼AL 2 n. 7. n. possibility of recovery (beyond or past retrieve). [ME, f. OF retroeve- stressed st. of re(trover find); see RE- 9]

rĕtri'al. v.t. See RE- 8.

rĕ'trō- pref. (1) backwards, back again, in return, (retroact, retroflex); (2) (Anat. & Path.) behind (∼ster'nal a., behind the breastbone), situated behind. [f. L retro backwards]

rĕtrŏä'ct v.i. react; operate in backward direction;

For other words in re- see RE-.

have retrospective effect; so ∼IVE a., ∼ION n. [f. prec. +ACT²]

rĕ′tro|cēde¹ v.i. move back, recede; so ∼cē′dENCE n., ∼cē′dENT a. [f. L RETRO(cedere cess- go)]

rĕtrocē′de² v.t. cede (territory) back again. [f. F rétrocéder (as RETRO-, CEDE)]

rĕtrocē′ss|ion (-shon) n. In vbl senses; so ∼IVE a. [f. as RETROCEDE¹,²; see -ION]

rĕ′trōchoir (-kwī̄r) n. part of cathedral or large church behind high altar. [f. med. L RETRO(chorus CHOIR)]

rĕ′troflĕx, -flĕxed (-kst), adjs. (Anat., Path., Bot., etc.) turned backwards; (Phonet.) cacuminal; so rĕtroflĕ′xION (-kshon) n. [f. L RETRO(flectere flex- bend)]

rĕtrogradā′tion n. (Astron.) apparent backward motion of planet in zodiac, motion of heavenly body from E. to W., backward movement of lunar nodes on ecliptic; (arch.) retrogression. [f. LL RETROgradatio (see GRADATION)]

rĕ′trogrāde a., n., & v.i. 1. a. directed backwards (retrograde motion), retreating; reverting esp. to inferior state, declining; inverse, reversed, (in retrograde order); (Astron.) in or showing retrogradation; hence ∼LY² (-dlĭ) adv. 2. n. degenerate person. 3. v.i. move backwards, recede, retire; decline, revert; (Astron.) show retrogradation. [a. ME, f. L RETROgradus (gradus step), v. f. L retrogradi or LL retrogradare (gradi walk)]

rĕtrogrĕ′ss v.i. go back, move backwards, deteriorate; so ∼IVE a. [f. RETRO-, after PROGRESS²]

rĕtrogrĕ′ssion (-shon) n. backward or reversed movement; return to less advanced state, reversal of development, decline, deterioration; (Astron.) retrogradation. [f. RETRO-, after progression]

rĕ′trojĕct v.t. throw back (usu. as opp. project). [f. RETRO-, after PROJECT¹]

rĕ′tro-rŏckĕt n. auxiliary rocket for slowing down spacecraft etc., e.g. when re-entering earth's atmosphere. [f. RETRO-+ROCKET²]

rĕtrŏr′se a. (Biol.) turned back or down; hence ∼LY² (-slĭ) adv. [f. L retrorsus = RETRO(versus p.p. of vertere turn)]

rĕ′trospĕct n. regard or reference to precedent or authority or previous conditions, survey of past time or events (in ∼, when looked back on). [f. RETRO-, after PROSPECT¹]

rĕtrospĕ′ction n. action of looking back esp. into the past; indulgence or engagement in retrospect. [prob. f. retrospect v. (as prec.)+-ION]

rĕtrospĕ′ctive a. of, in, proceeding by, retrospection (retrospective exhibition of his paintings); (of statute, award, etc.) not restricted to the future, licensing or punishing etc. past actions, having application to the past, retroactive; (of view) lying to the rear; hence ∼LY² (-vlĭ) adv. [f. RETROSPECT+-IVE]

retroussé (retrōō′sā) a. (Of nose) turned up at tip. [F, p.p. of retrousser tuck up (as RE-, TRUSS)]

rĕ′trovĕrt v.t. turn backwards (esp. Path. in p.p., of womb); so rĕtrovĕr′sION (-shon) n. [f. LL RETRO(vertere vers- turn)]

rĕtry′ v.t. try (defendant, law case) again; so rĕtrī′AL n. [f. RE-8+TRY]

rĕtsī′na (-ē′-) n. resin-flavoured Greek wine. [mod. Gk]

rĕ′ttery n. flax-retting place. [f. RET+-ERY]

rĕtū̆r′f v.t. See RE-8.

rĕtū̆r′n¹ v. 1. v.i. come or go back (gone never to return; return home, by the way one came; they have returned, (arch.) they are returned, cf. -ED¹ (2)); (in p.p.) that has come or gone back. 2. recur, go back, to (shall return to the subject; unto dust shalt thou return; return to one's old habits). 3. v.t. bring, convey, give, yield, put, send, or pay, back or in return or requital (fish must be returned to the water; return borrowed book or money, undelivered letter to sender; investments return a profit; return sword to scabbard; return the COMPLIMENT¹, a blow, a visit, an answer; return

person's greeting, love, gun-fire, etc.); throw, strike, etc., (ball) back in cricket, tennis, etc.; (Cards) lead (suit) previously led or bid by partner, lead (suit or card) after taking trick; ∼ thanks, express thanks esp. in grace at meals or in response to toast or condolence. 4. say in reply, retort. 5. state, mention, or describe, officially esp. in answer to writ or formal demand (liabilities were returned at £50,000; were all returned guilty, unfit for work); (of constituency) elect as MP etc.; ||∼ing officer, official conducting election in constituency and announcing name of person elected. 6. (Archit.) continue (wall etc.) in changed direction, esp. at right angles. 7. Hence ∼ABLE a. [ME, f. retorner, returner f. Rom. re(tornare TURN¹); see RE- 9]

rĕtū̆r′n² n. 1. coming or going back (his return was the signal for riots; POINT¹ of no return; have had a return of the symptoms, died on the return voyage); = return of POST²; ||∼ (ticket), ticket for journey to place and back to starting-point (so return fare); many happy ∼s (of the day) (birthday or festival greeting). 2. (Archit.) part receding from line of front, e.g. side of house or of window-opening (return angle, side, wall, etc.); termination of dripstone; ∼ crease, (Cricket) line at right angles at each end of bowling and popping creases. 3. (in sing. or pl.) (coming in of) proceeds or profit of undertaking (the returns were large; brings an adequate return); small profits and quick ∼s, motto of cheap shop etc. relying on large trade. 4. giving, sending, putting, or paying, back, thing so given etc., returning (of ball, suit at cards, etc.), (must ask for the return of the book or loan; received a ticket in return for his fare, neglect in return for attention); SALE or return; ∼ (match or game), second match etc. between same opponents; (Electr.) conductor bringing current back to source. 5. formal report compiled or submitted by order (income-tax return); ||sheriff's report on writ, (returning officer's announcement of) election as MP etc. 6. Hence ∼LESS a. [ME, f. AF retorn, return (retorner; see prec.)]

rĕtū̆′se a. (Bot. etc.) having broad end with central depression. [f. L re(tundere tus- beat); see RE- 9]

rĕtȳ′pe v.t. See RE- 8.

rēū′nion (-nyon) n. 1. reuniting or being reunited; reunited state. 2. social gathering, esp. of intimates or persons with common interest. [f. F réunion (réunir) or AL reunio (reunire unite); see RE- 9, UNION]

rēūnī′te v.t. & i., see RE- 9; rēū̆r′ge v.t., rēū′sable (-z-) a., rēū′se¹ (-z) v.t., rēū′se² n., see RE- 8.

rĕv n. & v. (-vv-). (colloq.) 1. n. revolution (of engine). 2. v.i. (Of engine) revolve; ∼ up, increase in speed of revolution. 3. v.t. ∼ (up), cause (engine) to run quickly (esp. when first starting). [abbr.|

Rev. abbr. Revelation (NT); Reverend.

rĕvă′ccināte v.t., rĕvă′ccinā′TION n., (-ks-). See RE- 8.

rĕvă′lorīz|e, -īs|e (-īz), v.t. establish new value of (currency etc.); hence ∼A′TION n. [back-form. f. revalorization f. F révalorisation (as RE- 8, VALORIZA-TION)]

rĕvă′lū|e v.t. give different value to (esp. currency, in sense opp. devalue); hence ∼A′TION n. [f. RE- 8+VALUE]

rĕvă′mp v.t. vamp or patch up again; renovate, revise, improve. [f. RE- 8+VAMP¹]

reva′nch|ism (-ah′-) n. (Polit.) policy of seeking to recover lost territory etc.; hence ∼IST (2) n. [f. F revanche (as REVENGE²)+-ISM]

Revd abbr. Reverend.

rĕvea′l¹ v.t. 1. disclose, divulge, betray; display, show, let appear; ∼ itself, come to sight or knowledge. 2. (Esp. of God) make known by inspiration or supernatural means; ∼ed religion (opp. natural religion). 3. Hence ∼ABLE a. [ME, f. OF reveler or f. L re(velare f. velum veil); see RE- 7]

rĕvea′l² n. internal side surface of opening or recess, esp. of doorway or window-aperture. [f. obs. revale v. lower f. OF re(valer f. avaler); see RE- 4, VAIL¹]

rĕveiˊllĕ (-vă'lǐ, -vĕ'lǐ) n. military waking-signal sounded in morning on bugle or drums etc. [f. F *réveillez* imper. pl. of *réveiller* awaken (as RE-, *veiller* f. L *vigilare* keep watch)]

rĕˊvel v. (||-ll-) & n. **1.** v.i. make merry, be riotously festive, feast, carouse, whence ∼lER¹ n.; take keen delight *in*. **2.** v.t. throw *away* (money, time) in revelry. **3.** n. revelling; (in *sing.* or *pl.*) (occasion of indulgence in) merry-making (*the revels began*); MASTER¹ *of the Revels*; ∼ rout, (arch.) party of revellers; hence ∼RY (4, 5) n. [ME, f. OF *revel(er)* riot f. L *rebellare* REBEL²]

rĕvelaˊtion n. **1.** disclosing of knowledge, or knowledge disclosed, to man by divine or supernatural agency; **the R∼** (of **St. John the Divine**), (colloq.) (**the**) **R∼s**, last book of NT, Apocalypse; hence ∼AL a. **2.** striking disclosure (*it was a revelation to me*; *what a revelation!*); revealing *of* some fact. [ME f. OF, or f. LL *revelatio* (as REVEAL¹; see -ATION)]

rĕvelaˊtionist n. believer in divine revelation; **The R∼**, author of the Revelation. [f. prec. + -IST]

revenant (rĕ'venant, re'venahṅ) n. one returned from the dead or from exile etc. [F, part. of *revenir* (see REVENUE)]

rĕvĕndicaˊtion n. formal claiming back, or recovery by such claim, of lost goods, territory, etc. [F (*revendiquer* claim back; see -ATION)]

rĕvĕˊnge¹ (-nj) v. **1.** v.t. satisfy one*self*, (in *pass.*) be satisfied, with retaliation (*for* offence, *on*, *upon*, *of*, offender); retaliate, requite, exact retribution for, (offence to oneself or another; *on*, *upon*, offender); avenge (person). **2.** v.i. take vengeance. [ME, f. OF *revenger*, *revencher* f. LL *re(vindicare* lay claim to); see RE- 1]

rĕvĕˊnge² (-nj) n. **1.** revenging, act done in revenging; desire to revenge, vindictive feeling, whence ∼FUL (-njf-) a. **2.** (In games) opportunity given for reversing former result by return game (*give person his revenge*). [f. prec.]

rĕˊvenūe n. **1.** income, esp. of large amount, from any source; (in *pl.*) items constituting this. **2.** State's annual income from which public expenses are met (||INLAND or *INTERNAL *revenue*); department of civil service collecting this; ∼ cutter, officer, etc. (employed against smugglers); ∼ tax (imposed to raise revenue, not to affect trade). [ME, f. OF *revenu(e)* masc. or fem. p.p. (as n.) of *revenir* f. L *re(venire* come) return; see RE- 9]

rĕvĕˊrˈberˈāte v.t. & i. (Of sound, light, heat) be returned or echoed or reflected, return (sound etc.) thus; ∼ating furnace etc. (constructed to throw heat back on substance dealt with), so ∼atory a. & n.; hence or cogn. ∼Aˊtion, ∼ātor, ns., ∼ant, ∼ative, adjs. [f. L *re(verberare* lash f. *verbera* pl. scourge); see RE- 9, -ATE³]

rĕvēˊreˊ v.t. regard as sacred or exalted, hold in deep and usu. affectionate or religious respect, venerate. [f. F *révérer* or L *re(verēri* fear); see RE- 6]

rĕˊverence n., & v.t. **1.** n. revering (*hold in, regard with, reverence*; *feel reverence for, pay reverence to*); capacity for this (*the younger generation lacks reverence*); (arch.) gesture showing that one reveres, bow, curtsy, obeisance; so **rĕverĕˊnt**IAL (-shal) a. **2.** being revered; **saving your** ∼ (arch., apology for use of coarse term); **your** or **his** ∼ (arch. or Ir. or joc., title used to or of clergyman). **3.** v.t. regard with reverence, venerate. [ME f. OF, f. L *reverentia* (as prec.; see -ENCE)]

rĕverˊend a. & n. **1.** a. deserving reverence, revered, (esp. as title of clergyman; **Very R∼**, of dean etc.; **Right R∼**, of bishop; **Most R∼**, of archbishop or Irish RC bishop; *Revd* or *Rev.* or *the Revd John or J. Smith*, or *the Revd Mr Smith*); **the** ∼ **gentleman**, the clergyman in question; **R∼ Mother**, Mother Superior of convent. **2.** n. (colloq., usu. in *pl.*) clergyman. [ME f. OF, or f. L *reverendus* gerundive of *reverēri* (see REVERE, -ND¹)]

rĕˊverent a. feeling or showing reverence; hence ∼LY² adv. [ME, f. L *reverens* (as REVERE; see -ENT)]

rĕˊverie n. (fit of) abstracted musing (*was lost in* (a) *reverie*); (arch.) fantastic notion or theory, delusion; (Mus.) instrumental piece suggesting dreamy or musing state. [f. obs. F *resverie* f. OF *reverie* rejoicing, revelry (*rever* be delirious, of unkn. orig.; see -ERY)]

rĕverˊs (-vēr') n. (*pl.* same *pr.* -z). turned-back edge of garment revealing under-surface; material on this surface. [F, = REVERSE³]

rĕvĕrˊseˊ¹ a. opposite or contrary (*to*, or abs.) in character or order, inverted, back or backward, upside down, (*in the reverse direction to the time before*; *the reverse side* etc. of a coin, picture, etc., cf. REVERSE³); ∼ battery, fire, etc., (playing on enemy's rear or into works from rear); ∼ gear (used to make vehicle etc. travel backwards); hence ∼LY² (-slǐ) adv. [ME, f. OF *revers(e)* f. L *reversus* p.p. of *re(vertere* vers- turn); see RE- 9]

rĕvĕrˊseˊ² v. **1.** v.t. turn the other way round or up or inside-out, invert, transpose, convert to opposite character or effect, (*reverse motion, policy, order,* etc.); make (vehicle) travel backwards; make (engine etc.) work in contrary direction; ∼e arms, hold rifle(s) butt upwards; ||∼e the charge(s), make recipient of telephone call responsible for payment. **2.** revoke, annul, (decree, act, etc.); *∼e oneself, change one's mind. **3.** v.i. (Of dancer, esp. in waltz) revolve in opposite direction; (of vehicle etc.) travel backwards; ∼ing light (operated when vehicle is travelling backwards). **4.** Hence ∼AL 2, ∼IBIˊLITY, ns., ∼IBLE a., ∼IBLY adv. [ME, f. OF *reverser* f. LL *re(versare* frequent. of *vertere* turn)]

rĕvĕrˊseˊ³ n. **1.** *the* contrary (*of*, or abs.; *with others the reverse (of this) happens*); contrary of usual manner (*name printed in reverse*); reverse gear or motion; **the** ∼ **of**, far from (*complimentary* etc.). **2.** (device on) subordinate side of coin etc. (lit. or fig.; opp. *obverse*). **3.** reverse side; verso of leaf. **4.** piece of misfortune, disaster, esp. defeat in battle, (*the reverses of fortune*; *suffered a reverse*). [ME, f. OF *revers(e)* f. L *reversus* (as REVERSE¹)]

rĕvĕrˊsion (-shon) n. **1.** (return to grantor or his heirs or passing to ultimate grantee of, right of ultimate succession to) estate granted till specified date or event, esp. death of original grantee (**in** ∼, on such conditions); hence ∼ER¹ n., beneficiary of return by reversion. **2.** sum payable on person's death esp. by way of life-insurance. **3.** thing to which one has a right, or expects to succeed, when relinquished by another; such right. **4.** return to a previous state, habit, etc., esp. (Biol.) to ancestral type. **5.** Hence ∼AL, ∼ARY¹, adjs. [ME f. OF, or f. L *reversio* (as REVERSE¹; see -ION)]

rĕvĕrˊt v. **1.** v.i. (Of property, office, etc.) return by reversion; hence ∼ER⁴ n. (Law). **2.** return *to* former state etc. (cf. prec.); (abs.) fall back into wild state. **3.** recur *to* subject in talk or thought. **4.** v.t. turn (eyes, steps) back. [ME, f. OF *revertir* or f. L (as REVERSE¹)]

rĕvĕrˊtible a. (Of property) subject to reversion. [ME, f. prec. + -IBLE]

rĕvĕˊt v.t. (-tt-). face (rampart, wall, etc.) with masonry esp. in fortification. [f. F *revêtir* f. OF *revestir* f. LL *re(vestire* clothe f. *vestis*); see RE- 8]

rĕvĕˊtment n. retaining-wall or facing (as prec.). [f. F *revêtement* (as prec.; see -MENT)]

rĕvīˊctual (-vǐ'tel) v.t. See RE- 8.

rĕviewˊ¹ (-vū') n. **1.** (esp. Law). revision (*is not subject to review*); **court of** ∼ (before which sentences etc. come for revision). **2.** display and formal inspection of troops, fleet, etc.; ∼ order, dress and arrangement usu. at reviews; **pass in** ∼, (lit. or fig.) examine or be examined. **3.** retrospect, survey of the past; general survey or reconsideration of subject or thing. **4.** published account or criticism of book etc.; periodical publication with articles on current events, new books, art, etc. **5.** second view. [f. obs. F *reveue* (*revoir* f. *re(voir* see); cf. VIEW]

rĕviewˊ² (-vū') v.t. **1.** (or rē-) view again. **2.** subject to esp. legal review. **3.** survey, glance over, look back on.

4. hold review of (troops etc.). **5.** write review of (book etc., or abs.); hence ~ER¹ *n.* **6.** Hence ~ABLE *a.*, ~AL 2 *n.* [f. RE- 9 + VIEW, or f. prec.]

revī'le *v.* **1.** *v.t.* call by ill names, abuse, rail at. **2.** *v.i.* talk abusively, rail. **3.** Hence ~EMENT (-lm-), ~ER¹, ~ING¹ (1), *ns.* [ME, f. OF *reviler* (as RE- 6, VILE)]

revī's|e (-z) *v.t.*, & *n.* **1.** *v.t.* read or look over or re--examine or reconsider and correct, improve, or amend (literary matter, printer's proofs, law, constitution, etc.); R~ed Version, R~ed Standard Version, revisions 1881–95, 1946–57, of Authorized Version of Bible. **2.** re-read (work learnt or done, or abs.) to improve one's familiarity with it, its quality, etc. **3.** Hence or cogn. ~ABLE, ~ORY, *adjs.*, ~AL 2, ~ER¹, **revī'sion** (-zhon), *ns.* **4.** *n.* (Print.) proof-sheet embodying corrections made in earlier proof. [f. F *réviser* look at, or f. L *revisere* (as RE- 8, *visere* intensive of *vidēre vis-* see)]

revī'sion|ism (-zhon-) *n.* policy of revision or modification, esp. of Marxist-Leninist doctrine; hence ~IST (2) *n.* [f. REVISION + -ISM]

revī'sit (-z-) *v.t.*, see RE- 8; **revī'talīze** *v.t.*, see RE- 9.

revī'val *n.* **1.** bringing or coming back into use or vogue (~ **of learning, letters,** etc., at Renaissance); GOTHIC *Revival*; new production of old play etc. **2.** (special effort with meetings etc. to promote) reawakening of religious fervour; hence ~ISM (3), ~IST (2), *ns.* **3.** restoration to bodily or mental vigour or to life or consciousness. [f. foll. + -AL 2]

revī'v|e *v.i.* & *t.* come or bring back to consciousness, life, existence, vigour, notice, use, activity, validity, or vogue; hence ~ABLE *a.* [ME, f. OF *revivre* or f. LL RE(*vivere* live); see RE- 9]

revī'ver *n.* In vbl senses; (sl.) stimulating drink; preparation used for restoring faded colour etc. [f. prec. + -ER¹]

revī'vi|fy *v.t.* restore to animation, activity, vigour, or life; hence ~FICA'TION *n.* [f. F *revivifier* or f. LL *re(vivificare* VIVIFY); see RE- 8]

revivi'scence *n.*, **revivi'scent** *a.* returning to life or vigour. [(f. LL *reviviscentia*) f. L *re(viviscere* incept. of *vivere* live); see RE- 8, -ENCE, -ENT]

‖revī'vor *n.* (Law). proceeding for revival of suit after death of party etc. [f. REVIVE + -OR]

revō'ke *v.* & *n.* **1.** *v.t.* repeal, annul, withdraw, rescind, cancel, (decree, consent, promise, permission); (arch.) call back, so **re'vocABLE**, **re'vocatORY**, *adjs.*, **revoca'TION** *n.* **2.** *v.i.* (Cards). make revoke. **3.** *n.* card-player's failure to follow suit when able to do so. [ME, f. OF *revoquer* or f. L *re(vocare* call); see RE- 9]

revō'lt *v.* & *n.* **1.** *v.i.* cast off allegiance, make rising or rebellion, fall away *from* or rise *against* ruler, go over to rival power; (in *p.p.*) having revolted (*his revolted subjects*; see -ED¹ (2)). **2.** feel revulsion or disgust *at*, rise in repugnance *against*, turn in loathing *from*, (common sense, nature, one's *heart*, revolts at or against or from it). **3.** *v.t.* affect with strong disgust, nauseate; hence ~ING² *a.* **4.** *n.* act of rebelling; rising, insurrection; **in** ~, having revolted. **5.** sense of loathing; mood of protest or defiance. [f. F *révolte(r)* f. It. *rivolta(re)* f. Rom. **revolvitare* intensive of L *revolvere* (see REVOLVE)]

re'volute¹ (-ōōt) *a.* (Bot. etc.) with rolled-back edge. [f. L *revolutus* p.p. of *revolvere* (see REVOLVE)]

revolu'te² (-ōō't) *v.i.* (sl.) engage in political revolution. [back-form. f. foll.]

revolu'tion (-lōō'-) *n.* **1.** revolving, motion in orbit or circular course or round axis or centre, rotation, (time taken for) single completion of orbit or rotation, cyclic recurrence; ~ **counter,** device for indicating number or rate of revolutions of engine etc. **2.** complete change, turning upside down, great reversal of conditions (INDUSTRIAL *Revolution*); fundamental reconstruction, esp. forcible action by nation etc. to substitute new ruler or system of government (**the R~,** expulsion of James II of England 1688; **American R~,** overthrow of British rule 1775 etc.; **French R~,** overthrow of monarchy

1789 etc.; **Russian R~,** overthrow of monarchy 1917); hence ~IZE (1, 3) *v.t.*, ~ISM (3), ~IST (2), *ns.* [ME f. OF, or f. LL *revolutio* (as REVOLVE; see -ION)]

revolu'tionary (-ōō'-) *a.* & *n.* (instigator or supporter) of political revolution; (*R~*) of the American etc. Revolution; involving great and usu. violent changes. [f. prec. + -ARY¹]

revō'lv|e *v.* **1.** *v.t.* & *i.* turn round, turn round and round, rotate, move in circular orbit, (*mechanism for revolving the turntable*; *Earth revolves both round* or *about sun and on its axis*; *seasons, years, revolve*); ~**ing credit** (automatically renewed as debts are paid off); ~**ing door** (with several partitions turning round central axis, to exclude draughts of air). **2.** *v.t.* ponder (problem etc.) in the mind. [ME, f. L *re(volvere* roll); see RE- 6]

revō'lver *n.* pistol with revolving chambers enabling user to fire several shots without reloading. [f. prec. + -ER¹]

revūe' *n.* theatrical entertainment reviewing (esp. satirically) current events etc. or comprising many unrelated episodes. [F, = REVIEW¹]

revū'lsion (-shon) *n.* **1.** sudden violent change of feeling, sudden reaction in taste, fortune, trade, etc.; sense of loathing. **2.** (Med.) counter-irritation, treatment of one disordered organ etc. by acting upon another. [F, or f. L *re(vulsio* f. *vellere vuls-* pull); see RE- 9]

revū'lsive *a.* & *n.* (Med.) (substance) producing revulsion. [f. prec. + -IVE]

rewar'd (-wör'd) *n.*, & *v.t.* **1.** *n.* return or recompense for service or merit (**gone to his** ~, dead and in Heaven), requital for good or evil, retribution; sum offered for detection of criminal, restoration of lost property, etc.; hence ~LESS *a.* **2.** *v.t.* repay, requite, recompense (service or doer of it, offender, offence); hence ~ING² *a.*, (of task, book, etc.) well worth doing, reading, etc. [ME, f. AF, ONF *reward(er)* = OF *reguard(er)* REGARD¹,²]

rē'wa-rēwa *n.* (NZ). tall handsome timber tree (*Knightia excelsa*) [Maori]

rēwī'nd *v.t.* See RE- 8.

rēwīr'e *v.t.* (esp. Electr.) wire again or differently. [f. RE- 8 + WIRE]

rēwor'd (-er'd) *v.t.* change wording of. [f. RE- 8 + WORD²]

rēwrī'te¹ (rērī't) *v.t.* (rewro'te; rewri'tten). write again or differently. [f. RE- 8 + WRITE]

rē'write² (rē'rīt) *n.* rewriting; thing rewritten; **~* **man,** journalist employed to put incoming material into form suitable for publication. [f. prec.]

Rex (rēks) *n.* reigning king (in use as REGINA). [L]

Rē'xine (-ēn) *n.* (P) artificial leather used in upholstery, bookbinding, etc. [20th c.; orig. unkn.]

Rey'nard (rē'n-, rā'n-) *n.* (Proper name for) the fox; a fox. [ME, f. OF *Renart* name of fox in the *Roman de Renart*]

Rey'nolds (rē'-; -z) *n.* ~ **number,** (Phys.) quantity indicating degree of turbulence of flow past obstacle etc. [f. O. ~, Engl. physicist d. 1912]

r.f. *abbr.* radio frequency.

‖RFA *abbr.* Royal Fleet Auxiliary.

‖RFC *abbr.* Rugby Football Club.

*RFD *abbr.* rural free delivery.

RGS *abbr.* Royal Geographical Society.

Rh *abbr.* Rhesus (factor).

r.h. *abbr.* right hand.

Rh *symb.* rhodium.

‖RHA *abbr.* Royal Horse Artillery.

rha'bdomancy *n.* use of divining-rod, esp. for discovering subterranean water or ore. [f. Gk *rhabdomanteia* (*rhabdos* rod; see -MANCY)]

Rhadamā'nth|us *n.* stern and incorruptible judge; hence ~INE² *a.* [f.*Gk*, name of judge in underworld]

Rhae'tian (-shan) *a.* & *n.* = RHAETO-ROMANIC. [f. L *Rhaetia* a district of the Alps + -IAN]

Rhae'tic *a.* & *n.* (of) the set of strata intermediate between Lias and Trias in Europe. [f. L *Rhaeticus* (as prec.; see -IC)]

Rhaeto-Romā'nce *a.* & *n.* = foll. [f. as foll. + ROMANCE]

Rhaeto-Romā'nic *a.* & *n.* (of or in) any of the Romance dialects of SE Switzerland and Tyrol, esp. Romansh and Ladin. [f. L *Rhaetus* of Rhaetia in the Alps + -O- + ROMANIC]

rhă'psŏde *n.* reciter of epic poems, esp. of Homer, in ancient Greece. [f. Gk *rhapsōidos* (*rhaptō* stitch, *ōidē* song, ODE)]

rhă'psodĭst *n.* one who rhapsodizes; = prec. [f. RHAPSODY + -IST]

rhă'psodize, -īse (-īz), *v.i.* talk or write rhapsodies (*about, on*, etc.). [f. foll. + -IZE]

rhă'psodў *n.* **1.** enthusiastic extravagant utterance or composition; emotional irregular piece of music; hence **rhăpsŏ'dɪCAL** *a.* **2.** (Gk Ant.) epic poem, or part of it, of length for one recitation. **3.** Hence **rhăpsŏ'dɪc** *a.* [f. L *rhapsodia* f. Gk *rhapsōidia* (as RHAPSODE; see -Y[1])]

rhă'tanў *n.* (astringent dried root of) S. Amer. shrub of genus *Krameria*. [f. mod. L *rhatania* f. Port. *ratanha*, Sp. *ratania*, f. Quechua *rataña*]

rhe'a (rē'a, rī'a) *n.* S. Amer. flightless bird like ostrich. [mod. L genus-name, f. L f. Gk *Rhea* mother of Zeus]

rhē'bok. Var. of REEBOK.

Rhē'mĭsh *a.* of Rheims (~ **Bible, Testament,** etc., NT translated by Roman Catholics of English College at Rheims 1582). [f. obs. E *Rhemes* Rheims + -ISH[1]]

Rhē'nĭsh *a.* & *n.* (arch.) **1.** *a.* of the Rhine and districts on its banks. **2.** *n.* Rhine wine. [ME *rynis*(*ch*) etc., f. AF *reneis*, OF *r*(*a*)*inois* f. med. L *Rhenanus* (*Rhenus* Rhine), assim. to L sp.; see -ISH[1]]

rhē'nĭum *n.* (Chem.) rare metallic element of manganese group. [mod. L, f. L *Rhenus* Rhine + IUM]

rhēŏ'log|ў *n.* science dealing with flow and deformation of matter; hence **rhēolŏ'gɪCAL** *a.*, ~IST (3) *n.* [f. Gk *rheos* stream + -O- + -LOGY]

rhē'ostăt *n.* (Electr.) instrument used to control current by varying resistance. [f. as prec. + -STAT]

rhēŏ'tropĭsm *n.* tendency to be oriented in accordance with flow of water etc.; so **rhēotrŏ'pɪc** *a.* [f. as RHEOLOGY + Gk *tropikos* (*tropē* a turning f. *trepō* turn, -IC) + -ISM]

rhē'sus *n.* small catarrhine monkey (*Macaca mulatta*) common in N. India; ~ **baby,** infant with haemolytic disorder from its blood being rhesus-positive and its mother's rhesus-negative; ~ **factor,** antigen occurring in red blood cells of most persons and some animals (as in the rhesus monkey, in which it was first observed); **~-positive, ~-negative,** having, not having, the rhesus factor. [mod. L, arbitr. use of L f. Gk *Rhēsos*, mythical king of Thrace]

rhē'tor *n.* ancient Greek or Roman teacher or professor of rhetoric; (mere) orator. [ME f. LL *rethor*, f. L f. Gk *rhētōr*]

rhē'toric *n.* (treatise on) art of persuasive or impressive speaking or writing; language designed to persuade or impress (but perhaps insincere or exaggerated); persuasiveness of or looks or acts. [ME, f. OF *rethorique* f. L f. Gk *rhētorikē* (*tekhnē* art) (as foll.; see -IC)]

rhetŏ'rical *a.* **1.** expressed with a view to persuasive or impressive effect, artificial or extravagant in language, of the nature of rhetoric; ~ **question** (asked not for information but to produce effect, as *who cares?* for *nobody cares*). **2.** of the art of rhetoric; given to rhetoric, oratorical. **3.** Hence ~LY[2] *adv.* [ME, f. L f. Gk *rhētorikos* (as RHETOR; see -IC) + -AL]

rhĕtori'cian (-shan) *n.* rhetor; rhetorical speaker or writer. [ME, f. OF *rethoricien* (as prec.; see -ICIAN)]

rheum (rōŏm) *n.* (arch.) watery secretion or discharge of mucous membrane such as tears, saliva, or mucus; catarrh. [ME f. OF *reume*, f. LL f. Gk *rheuma* -*atos* stream (*rheō* flow)]

rheumă't|ic (rōŏ-) *a.* & *n.* **1.** *a.* of, suffering from, subject to, producing, or produced by, rheumatism;

~ic fever, non-infectious fever with inflammation and pain in joints; hence **~ICALLY** *adv.*, **~ickY[2]** *a.* (colloq.), **rheu'mato-** (-ōō'-) *comb. form.* **2.** *n.* (in *pl.*, colloq.) rheumatism. [ME, f. OF *reumatique* or f. L f. Gk *rheumatikos* (as prec.; see -IC)]

rheu'matism (rōō'-) *n.* disease marked by inflammation and pain in joints, muscles, or fibrous tissue, esp. rheumatoid arthritis; **acute ~,** rheumatic fever; **muscular ~,** myalgia. [f. F *rhumatisme* or f. L f. Gk *rheumatismos* (*rheumatizō* f. RHEUMA; see -IZE, -ISM)]

rheu'matoid (rōō'-) *a.* having the character of rheumatism; **~ arthritis,** chronic progressive disease causing inflammation and stiffening of joints. [f. prec. + -OID]

rheumatŏ'log|ў (rōō-) *n.* study of rheumatic diseases; hence **rheumatolŏ'gɪCAL** (rōō-) *a.*, ~IST (3) *n.* [f. RHEUMATISM + -O- + -LOGY]

rheu'mў (rōō'-) *a.* (arch.) consisting of or flowing with rheum; (of air) damp, raw. [f. RHEUM + -Y[2]]

‖RHG *abbr.* Royal Horse Guards.

rhī'nal *a.* (Anat. etc.) of nostril or nose. [f. Gk *rhis* RHINO-) + -AL]

‖rhine[1] (rēn) *n.* (dial.) large open ditch. [app. repr. OE *ryne* stream]

Rhīne[2] *n.* ~'land, region adjoining the Rhine; **r~'stone,** imitation diamond; ~ **wine,** (usu. white) wine from Rhine vineyards. [f. river ~ in Germany]

rhīnī'tĭs *n.* inflammation of (mucous membrane of) nose. [f. RHINO- + -ITIS]

rhī'nō[1] *n.* (*sl.*) money. [17th c.; orig. unkn.]

rhī'nō[2] *n.* (*pl.* same or **~s**). (*sl.*) rhinoceros. [abbr.]

rhī'no- *comb. form.* nose, as: **~phary'ngeal,** of nose and pharynx; **~pla'stic, ~plasty,** (of) plastic surgery of the nose; **~scoPE.** [f. Gk *rhis rhinos* nostril, nose + -O-]

rhīnŏ'ceros *n.* (*pl.* **~es** or same). large pachydermatous African and S. Asian quadruped with horn or two horns on nose and thick folded and plated skin; ~ **bird,** ox-pecker; so **rhīnŏcerŏ'tɪc** *a.* [ME, f. L f. Gk RHINO-(*kerōs* f. *keras* horn)]

rhī'zo- *comb. form.* root, as: **~carp,** plant with perennial root but perishing stems; **~pod,** protozoan with rootlike pseudopodia. [f. Gk *rhiza* root + -O-]

rhī'zoid *a.* & *n.* (Bot.) **1.** *a.* rootlike. **2.** *n.* root-hair or filament of fern etc. [f. as prec. + -OID]

rhī'zōme *n.* prostrate or subterranean rootlike stem emitting both roots and shoots. [f. Gk *rhizoma* (*rhizoō* take root, f. as RHIZO-)]

rhō *n.* seventeenth Greek letter (P, ρ) = r. [Gk]

rhŏ'damine (-ēn) *n.* brilliant red synthetic basic dye. [f. RHODO- + AMINE]

Rhōde I'sland (ī'l-) *n.* ~ **Red,** Amer. breed of reddish-black domestic fowl. [~ in US]

Rhŏ'des (-dz) *n.* ~ **Scholar,** holder of any of a number of ~ **Scholarships** awarded annually and tenable at Oxford Univ. by students from certain Commonwealth countries, South Africa, the United States, and W. Germany. [f. C. J. ~, Brit. statesman d. 1902]

Rhŏ'dian *a.* & *n.* (native or inhabitant) of Rhodes. [f. L *Rhodius* (*Rhodus* f. Gk *Rhodos* Rhodes, island in Aegean Sea) + -AN]

rhŏ'dium[1] *n.* ~ (**wood**), scented wood of Canary convolvulus; ~ **oil** (got from this). [mod. L *rhodium* (*lignum* wood), neut. of *rhodius* roselike f. Gk *rhodon* rose]

rhŏ'dium[2] *n.* hard white metallic element of platinum group. [f. Gk *rhodon* rose (from colour of solution of its salts) + -IUM]

rhŏ'do- *comb. form.* (esp. Min. & Chem.) rose-coloured, as: **~chro'site** (-krŏ'sīt), manganese carbonate occurring in rose-red crystals. [f. Gk *rhodon* rose + -O-]

rhōdodĕ'ndron *n.* evergreen shrub of genus *Rhododendron*, with large clusters of trumpet-shaped flowers. [L, = oleander, f. Gk (as prec., *dendron* tree)]

rhŏdŏ'psin *n.* visual purple. [f. as RHODO- + Gk *opsis* sight + -IN]

rhodŏr′a n. N. Amer. pink-flowered shrub of genus *Rhodora*. [mod. L, f. L plant-name f. Gk *rhodon* rose]

rhŏmb (-m) n. rhombus; object or part with such outline; (Cryst.) rhombohedron; hence **rhŏ′mb**IC a., **rhŏ′mb**O- *comb. form.* [f. F *rhombe*, or f. L RHOMBUS]

rhŏmbohē′dr|on n. (*pl.* ~a or ~ons). (crystal in shape of) solid bounded by six equal rhombuses; hence ~AL a. [f. RHOMBO- (see prec.) after *polyhedron* etc.]

rhŏ′mboid a. & n. **1.** a. having or nearly having the shape of a rhombus. **2.** n. quadrilateral of which only opposite sides and angles are equal. [f. F *rhomboïde* or f. LL f. Gk *rhomboeidēs* (as RHOMB; see -OID)]

rhŏmboi′dal a. = prec.; having the shape of a rhomboid; hence ~LY² adv. [f. prec. + -AL]

rhŏmboi′dė|us n. (*pl.* ~i pr. -ī). (Anat.) muscle connecting shoulder-blade to vertebrae. [mod. L *rhomboideus* (*musculus* muscle) f. *rhomboides* (as RHOMBOID)]

rhŏ′mb|us n. (*pl.* ~uses, or ~i pr. -ī). (Geom.) oblique equilateral parallelogram, e.g. diamond on playing-cards. [L f. Gk *rhombos*]

RHS abbr. Royal Historical, Horticultural, or Humane Society.

rhu′bårb (roo′-) n. **1.** (purgative made from) root of Chinese and Tibetan plant of genus *Rheum*. **2.** (fleshy leaf-stalks, used like fruit, of) garden plant of genus *Rheum*. **3.** yellowish-brown colour like that of medicinal rhubarb. **4.** (colloq.) murmurous hubbub or conversation (from crowd actors' repetition of the word). **5.** *(sl.) heated dispute. [ME, f. OF *r(e)ubarbe* f. Rom. **r(h)eubarbum* f. med. L *r(h)eubarbarum*, *rhabarbarum* f. LL f. Gk *rha* + as BARBAROUS; assoc. w. L f. Gk *rhēon* rhubarb]

rhŭmb (-m) n. (Naut.) any of 32 points of compass; angle between two successive compass-points; ~(-line), line cutting all meridians at same angle, line followed by ship sailing in fixed direction. [f. F *rumb* prob. f. Du. *ruim* room, assoc. w. L RHOMBUS]

rhŭ′mba. Var. of RUMBA.

rhyme¹, rime¹, n. **1.** identity of sound between words or verse-lines extending from end to last fully accentuated vowel and (in E Pros., strictly) not further (*greet/deceit, shepherd/leopard, quality/frivolity, stationary/probationary, is it/visit,* give rhymes, but *seat/deceit, station/crustacean, visible/invisible,* strictly do not); *single* or *male* or MASCULINE, *double* or *female* or FEMININE, *treble* or *triple,* ~ (according to number of syllables included); **imperfect** ~ (as in *love/move, phase/race*); **internal** ~ (involving word within verse-line); **neither** ~ **nor reason, without** ~ **or reason,** (with) no reasonable character; ~-scheme, arrangement of rhymes in piece of verse. **2.** poem with rhymes, (in *pl.* or *sing.*) verse having rhymes, use of rhyme, (NURSERY rhyme; *prefer blank verse to rhyme; am sending you some rhymes*); ~ **royal,** stanzas of seven ten-syllable lines with rhyme-scheme *ababbcc,* as in Shakespeare's *Rape of Lucrece.* **3.** word providing a rhyme (*to* another; *can't find a rhyme to 'teacups'; English is badly off for double rhymes*). **4.** Hence ~′LESS (-ml-) a. [(*rhyme* 17th c. var., w. assim. to RHYTHM, of) ME f. OF *rime* f. med. L *rithmus, rythmus* f. L f. Gk *rhuthmos* RHYTHM]

rhyme², rime², v. **1.** v.i. write rhymes, versify; choose rhymes; **rhyming dictionary** (listing words by their terminal sounds); hence **rhy̆′me**R¹, **rhy̆′me**STER (-ms-), **rhy̆′mi**ST (3) ns. **2.** (Of words or lines) exhibit rhyme; (of word) supply or act as rhyme *to* or *with*; **rhyming slang** (replacing words by rhyming words or phrases, e.g. *stairs* by *apples and pears*). **3.** v.t. put or make (story etc.) into rhyme (~d **verse,** opp. *blank verse*); while (time) *away* in rhyming; treat (word) as rhyming *with.* [(*rhyme* 17th c. var. of) ME *rime* f. OF *rimer* (see prec.)]

rhy̆′olite n. fine-grained granite rock. [f. G *rhyolit* f. Gk *rhuax* lava-stream + *lithos* stone; see -LITE]

rhy̆′thm (-dhem, +them) n. **1.** metrical movement determined by various relations of long and short or accented and unaccented syllables; measured flow of words and phrases in verse or prose. **2.** aspect of musical composition concerned with periodical accent and the duration of notes; ~ **and blues,** popular music with blues themes and strong rhythm; ~ **section,** part of dance band or jazz band mainly supplying rhythm. **3.** (Art etc.) harmonious correlation of parts; regular succession of opposites. **4.** (Phys., Physiol., etc.) movement with regular succession of strong and weak elements. **5.** regularly recurring sequence of events; ~ **method,** contraception by avoiding sexual intercourse near times of ovulation. **6.** Hence or cogn. **rhy̆′thm**IC(AL) adjs., ~LESS a., **rhy̆′thm**IST (3) n., (-dh-, -th-). [f. F *rhythme* or L f. Gk *rhuthmos* (cf. *rheō* flow)]

RI abbr. King and Emperor [f. L *Rex et Imperator*]; Queen and Empress [f. L *Regina et Imperatrix*]; Rhode Island; Royal Institute (of Painters in Water Colours); Royal Institution.

ri′a (rē′a) n. (Geog.) long narrow inlet formed by partial submergence of river valley. [f. Sp. *ría* estuary]

ri′ant a. (Of face, eyes, etc., and esp. of landscape) smiling, cheerful. [F, part. of *rire* f. L *ridēre* laugh; see -ANT]

rib n., & v.t. (-bb-). **1.** n. one of curved bones articulated in pairs to spine and protecting thoracic cavity and its organs; **true** or **sternal** ~ (joined also to breastbone, opp. **false, floating,** or **short** ~); **poke** or **dig** person in the ~s (to draw his attention good-naturedly); **smite under the fifth** ~, (Bibl.) stab mortally. **2.** ~(s) *of beef* etc. (as joint of meat); SPARE-RIB. **3.** (joc. w. ref. to Gen. 2:21) wife, woman. **4.** ridge or long raised piece often of stronger or thicker material across surface or through structure, serving to support as part of framework or strengthen or adorn, e.g. vein of leaf or insect's wing, shaft of feather, spur of mountain, vein of ore, ridge between furrows, wave-mark on sand, raised pattern of lines or bands along or across rows in knitting (made by alternation of plain and purl stitches), similar line in woven fabric formed by coarser yarn, one of ship's curved timbers to which planks are nailed or corresponding ironwork, arch supporting vault, groin, raised moulding on groin or across ceiling etc., wooden or iron beam helping to carry bridge, hinged rod of umbrella frame. **5.** ~-cage, bones of thorax; ~-grass, ~′wort, PLANTAIN¹ with long narrow leaves. **6.** Hence (-)~bED² (-bd), ~′LESS, adjs. **7.** v.t. provide with ribs, act as ribs of, whence ~′bING¹ (3, 6) n.; mark with ridges; plough with spaces between furrows; (colloq.) make fun of, tease. [OE *rib(b),* = OS *ribbi,* OHG *rippi, rippa,* ON *rif* f. Gmc **rebhja, rebhjō*]

RIBA abbr. Royal Institute of British Architects.

ri′bald n. & a. **1.** n. irreverent jester, user of scurrilous, blasphemous, or indecent language; so ~RY (4, 5) n. **2.** a. (Of language or its user) scurrilous, obscene, irreverent, coarsely humorous. [ME, earlier sense 'low-born retainer', f. OF *ribau(l)t, ribau(l)d* (*riber* pursue licentious pleasures f. Gmc, cogn. w. OHG *hriba* whore)]

ri′band n. = foll. [ME, f. OF *riban, r(e)uban,* prob. f. Gmc compd. of BAND¹]

ri′bbon n. **1.** (piece or length of) silk or other material woven into narrow band esp. for adorning hair or costume or for tying round a package; ribbon of special colour etc. worn to indicate award of medal etc. or membership of knightly order, club, college, athletic team, etc., (BLUE¹, RED, *ribbon*); **R**~ **Society,** (Hist.) Irish RC secret society formed in early 19th c. and associated with agrarian crime, whence **R**~ISM (3) n. **2.** long narrow strip of anything, e.g. inked material struck by typewriter types to print on paper; ribbon-like object or mark, (in *pl.*) driving-reins; (in *pl.*) ragged strips (*hang in, torn to, ribbons*). **3.** ~ **building,** ~ **development,** the building of houses along main road, extending outwards from a town or village; ∼-**fish**, long slender flat fish of various species; ∼-**grass**, slender-leaved grass with white--striped leaves; **R**∼-**man**, member of Ribbon Society; ∼ **microphone** (in which signal is produced by metal strip); ∼-**worm**, nemertine. **4.** Hence (-)∼ED² (-nd) a. [var. of prec.]

ribofla'vin n. vitamin B₂. [f. RIBOSE + L *flavus* yellow + -IN]

ribonucle'ic a. ∼ **acid,** nucleic acid yielding ribose on hydrolysis, present in cytoplasm and controlling synthesis of proteins. [f. foll. + NUCLEIC]

ri'bose n. sugar found in many nucleosides and in several vitamins and enzymes. [G (*ribon* by rearrangement f. related sugar *arabinose*; see -OSE²)]

ri'bosom|e n. minute particle in cytoplasm concerned with formation of proteins from amino-acids; hence ∼AL a. [f. RIBONUCLEIC + -SOME³]

‖**RIC** abbr. Royal Institute of Chemistry.

Ricar'dian a. & n. (adherent) of Ricardo; according to his views. [f. D. *Ricardo*, Engl. economist d. 1823 + -IAN]

rice n., & v.t. **1.** n. (pearl-white seeds, used as staple food in many Eastern countries, and elsewhere in puddings, cakes, etc., and savoury dishes, of) chiefly oriental grass (*Oryza sativa*) grown in marshes. **2.** ∼-bird, (1) Java sparrow, (2) bobolink; ∼-**bowl,** (fig.) area producing much rice; ∼-**paper,** paper made from pith of oriental tree (*Tetrapanax papyriferum*), resembling rice-straw paper and used for painting and in cookery as base for macaroons etc. **3.** v.t. *pass (cooked potatoes etc.) through device to form thin strings; hence **ri'cer**¹ (2) n. [ME, f. OF *ris* f. It. *riso* f. Rom. *orizum* f. L f. Gk *oruza*, of Oriental orig.]

ricercar' (rēchär-) n. (Mus.) instrumental composition of study or fugue type, esp. of 16th–18th c. [It., = to seek out]

rich a. **1.** (Of person, society, State, etc.) having riches. **2.** (Of country, period, soil, etc.) abounding in or *in* natural resources or some valuable possession or production, fertile; **strike it** ∼, find source of prosperity. **3.** valuable (*rich offerings; a rich harvest*). **4.** (Of dress, furniture, building, banquet, etc.) splendid, costly, elaborate, (*with* lace, sculpture, etc.). **5.** (Of food or diet) containing or involving large proportion of fat, oil, butter, eggs, spice, etc. **6.** (Of colour, voice, sound, smell) mellow, deep, full, not thin. **7.** abundant, ample, (*a rich supply of ideas*). **8.** (Of incident, assertion, etc.) highly amusing or ludicrous, full of entertainment or material for humour. **9.** (Of mixture in internal combustion engine) highly combustible, containing more than normal proportion of fuel. **10.** Hence ∼'EN⁶ v.i. & t., ∼'NESS n. [OE *rīce*, os *rīki*, OHG *rīchi*, ON *rīkr*, Goth. *reiks*, f. an early Gmc adoption of Celt. *rīx* = L *rex* king, & f. OF *riche* rich, powerful, of Gmc orig.]

Ri'chard n. ∼ **Roe,** fictitious character in law (cf. JOHN *Doe*). [man's Christian name]

ri'chès (-z) n. (usu. as *pl.*) abundant means, valuable possessions; ownership of these. [ME *richesse* f. OF *richeise* (*riche* RICH; see -ESS²), taken as pl.]

ri'chly adv. In adj. senses; fully, thoroughly, (*richly deserves a thrashing, to succeed*). [f. RICH + -LY²]

Ri'chter (-k-) n. ∼ **scale** (for stating strength of earthquake). [f. C. F. ∼, Amer. seismologist b. 1900]

rick¹ n., & v.t. **1.** n. stack of hay, corn, peas, etc., esp. one regularly built and thatched; ∼-**stand,** short wooden or stone pillars bearing joists to raise rick from ground; ∼-**yard,** enclosure for ricks. **2.** v.t. form into rick(s). [OE *hrēac*, = MDu. *rooc*, ON *hraukr*, of unkn. orig.]

‖**rick²,** ‖**wrick,** n., & v.t. slight(ly) sprain or strain (*have a rick in my neck; ricked his back when digging*). [ME *wricke*, f. MLG *wricken* move about, sprain]

ri'ckèt|s n. (as *sing.* or *pl.*) children's disease with softening of bones, esp. of spine, and bow-legs etc., assoc. w. deficiency of vitamin D; ∼-*comb. form* (ricket-

-*producing*). [17th c., of uncert. orig.; assoc. w. Gk *rhakhitis* RACHITIS, adopted as its scientific name]

rickě'ttsi|a n. parasitic micro-organism of genus *Rickettsia* causing typhus etc.; hence ∼AL a. [mod. L, f. H. T. *Ricketts*, Amer. pathologist d. 1910 + -IA¹]

ri'ckèt|y̆ a. **1.** suffering from, or of (the nature of), rickets. **2.** feeble, weak-jointed; shaky, insecure. **3.** Hence ∼iNESS n. [f. RICKETS + -Y²]

ri'ckey n. drink of spirit (esp. gin), lime-juice, etc. [20th c.; orig. uncert.]

ri'ckrack. See RICRAC.

ri'ckshaw, -sha, n. light two-wheeled hooded vehicle drawn by one or more persons. [abbr. of *jinricksha(w)* f. Jap. *jinrikisha* (*jin* person, *riki* power, *sha* vehicle)]

ri'cochet (-shā, -shět) n., & v.i. (-t- or -tt-, *pr.* -shād *or* -shětid, -shāing *or* -shěting, etc.). **1.** n. skipping or rebounding of projectile esp. shell or bullet on water, ground, wall, etc.; hit made after this. **2.** v.i. (Of projectile) skip or rebound once or more on water etc. [F, of unkn. orig.]

ri'crăc, ri'ckrăck, n. zigzag braid trimming for garments. [redupl. of RACK³]

‖**RICS** abbr. Royal Institution of Chartered Surveyors.

ri'ct|us n. (Anat. & Zool.) expanse or gape of mouth or beak; hence ∼AL a. [L, = open mouth (*ringi rict-* gape)]

rid¹ v.t. (-dd-; rid, arch. **ri'dded**). make (person or place) free, disencumber, *of* (esp. in *p.p.* with *be* or *get*; *glad to be, must get, rid of him*); (arch.) abolish, clear away, get rid of, (pest); hence ∼'d**ANCE** n. (**good** ∼**dance,** thing or person one is glad to be rid of; cf. RUBBISH). [ME, earlier sense 'clear (land etc.)', f. ON *rythja*]

rid², **ri'dden.** See RIDE.

ri'ddle¹ n. & v. **1.** n. question, statement, or description, designed or serving to test ingenuity or give amusement in divining its answer or meaning or reference, conundrum, enigma; puzzling or mysterious fact, thing, or person. **2.** v.i. speak in or propound riddles. **3.** v.t. solve (riddle); ∼ **me,** (arch.) solve my riddle (if you can). [OE *rǣdels(e)* opinion, riddle, (= os *rādisli*, -*lo*, OHG *rātisli*) f. *rǣdan* READ; cf. BURIAL]

ri'ddle² n. & v.t. **1.** n. coarse sieve for corn, gravel, cinders, etc. **2.** v.t. pass (corn etc.) through riddle, sift, (fig.) test searchingly (evidence, truth); fill (ship, person) with holes esp. of gunshot, (fig.) pelt with questions, refute (person, theory) with facts; (in *p.p.*) filled *with* (faults etc.). [OE *hriddel*, earlier *hrīder*; cf. *hrīdrian* sift]

ri'ddling a. expressed in riddles; puzzling; hence ∼LY² adv. [f. RIDDLE¹ + -ING²]

ride v. (**rode,** arch. **rid; ri'dden,** arch. **rid**) & n. **1.** v.i. sit on and be carried by horse etc., go on horseback etc. or on bicycle etc. or in train or other esp. public conveyance (cf. DRIVE¹), sit or go or be *on* something as on horse etc. astride, sit on and manage horse, lie at anchor, float buoyantly, (of moon etc.) seem to float, (of thing normally level or even) project or overlap, rest *in* or *on* while moving, (*ride at full speed; riding on his father's shoulders, back, knee, foot; rides well, cannot ride, learn to ride, riding-lessons or -school; bird or ship rides on the wind* or *waves; ship rode at anchor*). **2.** ∼ **again,** (fig.) return to vigour; *ride-a-*COCK*-HORSE;* ∼ **for a fall,** ride or (fig.) act recklessly, risk defeat; ∼ **high,** (fig.) be successful; *ride to* HOUND¹*s*; **let** thing ∼, leave it undisturbed; ∼ **off on,** use (side-issue) to evade main point; ∼ **over,** = WALK¹ *over* (2) in horse-race; *ride* ROUGHSHOD; ∼ **and tie,** (arch.) method of travel by two or more with one horse, each riding ahead in turn and leaving it tied to await other(s); ∼ **up,** (of garment) work upwards when worn. **3.** v.t. traverse on horseback etc., ride over or through, (*ride 50 miles, a race, a desert, a ford*); ride on, sit heavily on, oppress, haunt, dominate, tyrannize over, (*ride a horse, a bicycle; ship* *rides the waves; nightmare rides sleeper; ridden by fears, prejudices,* etc.; *cliché,* HAG¹, *priest,* etc. *-ridden*); be carried by, travel on; *(seek to) annoy; mount (female) in copulation; yield to (blow) so as to reduce its impact. **4.** give ride to, cause to ride, (*ride child on one's back*); (of rider) cause (horse etc.) to move forward (*at fence* etc.). **5.** ~ **down,** overtake or trample on horseback; *ride* HERD¹; ~ **off,** (Polo) edge (opponent) away from ball; ~ **out,** come safely through (storm; lit. or fig.). **6.** Hence **ri'd**ABLE *a.* **7.** *n.* journey in esp. public conveyance, spell of riding on horse, bicycle, person's back, etc.; **take for a** ~, (sl.) (1) drive (person) away in motor vehicle prior to murdering him, (2) deceive, hoax. **8.** path (esp. through woods) for riding on. **9.** quality of sensations when riding (*gives a bumpy ride*). [OE *rīdan,* = OS *-rīdan,* OHG *rītan,* ON *rítha*]

ri'der *n.* **1.** In vbl senses. **2.** (Naut., in *pl.*) additional set of timbers or iron plates strengthening ship's frame. **3.** additional clause amending or supplementing document, esp. ‖parliamentary Bill at third reading; corollary, naturally arising supplement; ‖expression of opinion, recommendation etc., added to verdict. **4.** (Math.) problem arising as corollary of theorem etc. **5.** piece in machine etc. that surmounts or bridges or works on or over others. **6.** Hence ~LESS *a.* [OE *rīdere* (as prec., -ER¹)]

ridge *n.* & *v.* **1.** *n.* line of junction of two surfaces sloping upwards towards each other (*ridge of roof, nose,* etc.); long narrow hill-top, mountain range, watershed; (Agric.) one of set of raised strips separated by furrows; (Hort.) raised hotbed for melons etc.; (Meteorol.) elongated region of high barometric pressure; any narrow elevation across surface. **2.** ~-**piece,** beam along ridge of roof; ~-**pole,** (1) horizontal pole of long tent, (2) = *ridge-piece;* ~-**tile** (used for roof-ridge); ~-**tree,** = *ridge-piece;* ~'**way,** road along ridge. **3.** Hence **ri'dgy**² *a.* **4.** *v.t.* break up (land) into ridges; mark with ridges; plant (cucumbers etc.) in ridges. **5.** *v.t.* & *i.* gather into ridges. [OE *hrycg,* = OS *hruggi,* OHG *hrucki,* ON *hryggr* f. Gmc **hrugjaz*]

ri'dicule *n.,* & *v.t.* **1.** *n.* holding or being held up as object of derision or mockery; (arch.) ridiculous thing or person. **2.** *v.t.* make fun of, subject to ridicule, laugh at. [F, or f. L *ridiculum* neut. of *ridiculus* laughable (*ridēre* laugh)]

ridi'culous *a.* deserving to be laughed at, absurd, unreasonable; hence ~LY² *adv.,* ~NESS *n.* [f. as prec. + -OUS, or L *ridiculosus*]

ri'ding¹ *n.* In vbl senses; road for riders, esp. green track through or beside wood; *riding-*HABIT¹; ~-**lamp, -light,** (borne by ship at anchor); ~-**school** (where horsemanship is taught). [ME, f. RIDE + -ING¹]

‖**ri'ding**² *n.* **1.** (Hist.) division (**East, North,** or **West R**~) of Yorkshire. **2.** similar division of other county; (Can.) electoral division. [OE **thriding, *thrithing* f. ON *thrithjungr* (*thrithi* THIRD; see -ING³) third part, w. loss of *th-* owing to preceding *-t(h)* of *east* etc.]

Rie'sling (-z-, -s-) *n.* (dry white wine made from) European variety of grape. [G]

rifaciment|o (rĭfahchĭmĕ'ntō) *n.* (*pl.* ~**i** *pr.* -ē). remodelled form of a literary or musical work. [It. (*rifare* remake)]

rife *pred. a.* of common occurrence, met with in large numbers or quantities, prevailing, current, numerous; well provided *with;* hence ~'NESS (-fn-) *n.* [OE *rȳfe, *rīfe,* prob. f. ON *rífr* acceptable (*reifa* enrich, *reifr* cheerful)]

riff *n.* short repeated phrase in jazz and similar music. [20th c.; orig. unkn.]

ri'ffle *n.* & *v.* **1.** *n.* (In gold-washing) groove or slat set in trough or sluice to catch gold particles; *shallow part of stream where water flows brokenly; *patch of waves or ripples on water. **2.** *v.t.* ruffle (water etc.); turn (pages) in quick succession; shuffle (playing-cards) rapidly, esp. by flexing and combining two halves of pack. **3.** *v.i.* leaf (*through* pages). [perh. var. of RUFFLE¹]

ri'ff-räff *n.* the rabble, disreputable or undesirable persons. [ME *riff and raff* f. OF *rif et raf*]

ri'fle¹ *v.t.* **1.** search and rob, esp. of all that can be found in various pockets or storing-places; carry off as booty. **2.** make spiral grooves in (gun or its barrel or bore) to produce rotatory motion of projectile; hence **ri'fling**¹ (1, 2) *n.* [sense 1 ME, f. OF *rifler* graze, scratch, plunder f. ODu. *riffelen;* sense 2 ult. f. OF *rifler*]

ri'fle² *n.* **1.** ~ (**gun** arch.), firearm with rifled barrel esp. one fired from shoulder-level; (in *pl.*) troops armed with rifles. **2.** (arch.) groove made in rifling a gun. **3.** ~-**bird,** dark-green Australian bird of paradise; ~-**green** *n.* & *a.,* (of) dark green as in rifleman's uniform; *rifle-*GRENADE; ~-**man,** (1) soldier armed with rifle, esp. private or other soldier in some regiments, (2) = *rifle-bird,* (3) small yellow and green NZ bird; ~-**pit,** excavation as cover for riflemen firing at enemy; ~-**range,** (1) distance coverable by shot from rifle, (2) place for rifle-practice; *~-**scope,** telescopic sight for rifle; ~-**shot,** (1) = *rifle-range* (1), (2) good etc. marksman with rifle, (3) shot fired with rifle. [f. prec.]

rift *n.,* & *v.t.* **1.** *n.* cleft, fissure, chasm, in earth or rock; rent, crack, split in an object, opening in cloud etc.; disagreement, dispute; ~-**valley,** steep-sided valley formed by subsidence of earth's crust; hence ~'LESS, ~'Y² *adj.* **2.** *v.t.* (esp. in *p.p.*) rend apart, cleave. [ME, of Scand. orig. (cf. Da., Norw. *rift* cleft, Icel. *ript* breach of contract); cogn. w. RIVE]

rig¹ *v.t.* (-**gg**-) & *n.* **1.** *v.t.* provide (ship) with necessary spars, ropes, etc., or ~'GING¹ (3) (-g-) *n.,* prepare for sea in this respect; assemble and adjust parts of (aircraft); fit (*out, up,* or abs.) with or *with* or in clothes or other equipment; ‖~-**out** *n.,* (colloq.) such clothes etc. **2.** set *up* (structure) hastily or as makeshift or by utilizing odd materials. **3.** ~'**ging-loft,** gallery in dockyard for fitting rigging, (Theatr.) space over stage from which scenery is manipulated. **4.** *n.* way ship's masts, sails, etc., are arranged, whence ~GED² (-ged) *a.* (*ketch-, sloop-, rigged*); person's or thing's look as determined by clothes etc.; **in full** ~, (colloq.) smartly or ceremonially dressed. **5.** equipment for constructing oil-well. [ME, perh. of Scand. orig. (cf. Norw. *rigga* bind or wrap up)]

rig² *n.,* & *v.t.* (-**gg**-). **1.** *n.* trick, dodge, way of swindling. **2.** *v.t.* manage or conduct fraudulently (*a rigged election;* ~ **the market,** cause artificial rise or fall in prices). [19th c.; orig. unkn.]

rigadoo'n *n.* lively dance for two persons; music for this. [f. F *rigodon, rigaudon,* perh. f. inventor *Rigaud*]

‖**rigg** *n.* dogfish. [19th c. dial., of uncert. orig.]

ri'gger (-g-) *n.* In vbl senses; one who attends to rigging of aircraft; (of rowing-boat) = OUTRIGGER; = THIMBLE*rigger;* ship rigged in specified way. [f. RIG¹,² + -ER¹]

right¹ (rīt) *a.* **1.** (arch., of line) straight. **2.** (Of angle) neither acute nor obtuse, of 90°, made by lines meeting not obliquely but perpendicularly with equal angles on either side, (**at** ~ **angles,** turning or placed with such angle; ~-**angled,** containing or making a right angle; involving right angle(s), not oblique, (*right* ASCENSION; ~ **sailing,** sailing due N., S., E., or W.; *right* SPHERE); (of cone, cylinder, prism, etc.) with base or ends perpendicular to axis. **3.** (Of conduct etc.) just, morally good, required by equity or duty, proper, (opp. *wrong; it is only right to tell you, that you should know*); ~-**minded,** having natural inclination to favour what is right. **4.** correct, true, (opp. *wrong; right use of words; did not give a right account of the matter; your opinions are right enough*); the preferable or most suitable, *the* less wrong or not wrong, (*which is the right way to proceed?; the right man in the right place; does not do it the right way; a fault on the right side; hold it right side up*); MR *Right;* ~ **side,** (of fabric etc.) side meant for show or use; **on the** ~ **side of,** in favour with (person); **on the** ~ **side of** *forty* etc., not yet 40 etc. years old. **5.** in good or normal condition, sound, sane, satisfactory, well-advised, not mistaken, (opp. *wrong*; *all's right with the world*; *is not quite right in the head*); **are you ∼?**, are you satisfied, comfortable, etc.?; **as ∼ as rain, as a trivet,** etc., entirely normal; **get ∼,** bring or come into right state; **in** one's **∼ mind,** not mad etc.; **put or set ∼,** restore to order, health, etc., correct mistaken ideas of (person), justify one*self* (*with* person); **she'll be ∼,** (Austral. colloq.) that will be all right; **∼ (you are)!,** ||**∼ oh!,** (colloq. excl. of assent to order or proposal); hence **∼'EN**[6] *v.t.* **6.** (arch. or colloq.) rightful, real, veritable, properly so called (*right* WHALE; *made a right mess of it*). **7.** (Of position, opp. LEFT[1]) on or towards that side of human body of which the hand is normally more used, on or towards that part of an object which is analogous to person's right side or (with opposite sense) which is nearer to spectator's right hand, (*right side, eye,* etc.; *right flank* of army etc.); **∼ about** (**turn** or **face**), right turn continued to face rear, reversal of policy, hasty retreat; **∼ arm,** (fig.) one's most reliable helper; *right* BANK[1], BOWER[3]; **∼ field,** (Baseball) part of field on first-base side, to catcher's right; **∼ hand,** hand of right side, this as the better hand (*put one's right hand to the work*) or w. ref. to shaking of hands (*give the right hand of fellowship*), region or direction on right side of person (*at, on, to* one's *right hand*), indispensable or chief assistant; **∼-hand,** placed on the right hand; **∼-hand man,** (1) soldier on one's right hand in line, (2) indispensable or chief assistant; **∼-hand screw,** = right-handed screw; **∼-handed,** using right hand more than left, turning to right, (of blow etc.) struck with right hand, (of tool etc.) made to suit use of right hand, (of screw) advanced by turning to right; **∼-hander,** right-handed blow or person; **∼-and-left,** (of screw etc.) having right-handed and left-handed parts at opposite ends; **∼ turn** (that brings one's front to face as one's right side did before); **∼ wing** (of army, football etc. team, or political party, cf. RIGHT[3] 4), **∼-wi′nger,** member of this. **8.** Hence **∼'ISH**[1] 2 *a.*, **∼'LY**[2] *adv.*, **∼'MOST** *a.*, **∼'NESS** *n.*, **∼'WARD** *a.* & *adv.*, **∼'WARDS** *adv.* [OE *riht,* = OS, OHG *reht,* ON *réttr,* Goth. *raihts* f. Gmc **rehtaz*]

right[2] (rīt) *v.t.* **1.** restore to proper or straight or vertical position (*boat righted herself*; *could not right the boat, car*; **∼** one*self,* recover one's balance); put (helm) amidships. **2.** make reparation for or to, avenge, (wrong, wronged person); vindicate, justify, rehabilitate. **3.** correct (mistakes etc.), correct mistakes in; (*refl.*) come to proper state (*that is a fault that will right itself*). **4.** Hence **∼'ABLE** *a.* [OE *rihtan* (*riht;* see prec.)]

right[3] (rīt) *n.* **1.** what is just, fair treatment; **by ∼(s),** if right were done; **do** person **∼, do ∼ by** person, treat or think of him fairly; **the ∼,** what is RIGHT[1] 3, the juster cause; **in the ∼,** having justice or truth on one's side. **2.** justification, fair claim, being entitled to privilege or immunity, thing one is entitled to, (*has a, the, no, right* to thing, to do, of doing, etc.; *belongs to him of* or *as of* or *by right*; *rights and duties*); (in *pl.*) authority to act in specified way; **in** one's **own ∼,** not through marriage, adherence, etc.; *right of* SEARCH; *rights of* WAR[1]; **∼ of way,** right established by usage to pass over another's ground, path subject to such right, precedence in passing granted to one vehicle etc. with regard to another, *land acquired for public use or service; **Bill of R∼s,** (1) ||constitutional settlement of 1689, (2) *constitutional amendments of 1791, (3) statement of rights of a class of persons; **∼s issue,** offer of new shares at reduced price in proportion to holdings of old shares; **within** one's **∼s,** not exceeding one's authority or entitlement; hence **∼'LESS** *a.* **3.** (in *pl.*) right condition, true state, (**set** or **put to ∼s,** arrange properly); true statement (*have not heard, do not know, the rights of the case*); ||**bang to** or ***dead to ∼s,** (sl.) red-handed. **4.** right-hand part or region or direction (*is on your, to the, right; to* or *from right and left*); (*R∼;* Polit.) conservative members of (orig. continental) parliament etc. or other conservatives,

whence **∼'ISM** (3), **∼'IST** (2), *ns.*; right-hand side of stage when facing audience; (Boxing) (blow with) right hand; (in marching etc.) right foot; right wing of army. [OE *riht* (as RIGHT[1])]

right[4] (rīt) *adv.* **1.** straight (*go right on*; *wind was right behind us*); (colloq.) immediately (*I'll be right back*); **∼ away, off,** immediately, without pausing. **2.** all the way *to, round, through,* etc., completely *off, out,* etc., (*sank right to the bottom; veranda right round house; took gate right off hinges; turned right round*). **3.** exactly, quite, (*right here, now; right in the middle*); **∼ on!** (colloq. excl. of approval). **4.** very, to the full, (*know right well; banqueted right royally; was right glad to hear*); **∼-down,** thorough(ly); ||*Right* HONOURABLE, *Right* REVEREND. **5.** justly, properly, correctly, aright, truly, satisfactorily, (*whether they act right or wrong; does not hold his pen, do the sum, right; nothing goes right with me; if I remember right; guessed right*). **6.** on or to the right side; **∼ and left,** to or on both sides, on all sides, (*he was abused right and left*); **∼, left, and centre,** on all sides. [OE *rihte* (*riht;* see RIGHT[1])]

ri′ghteous (rī′chus) *a.* (Of person, life, action) morally right, just, upright, virtuous, law-abiding; hence **∼LY** *adv.,* **∼NESS** *n.* [OE *rihtwīs* (as RIGHT[3] + -WISE or RIGHT[1] + WISE[2]), w. assim. to *bounteous* etc.]

ri′ghtful (rī′t-) *a.* (Of action etc.) equitable, fair; (of person) legitimately entitled to position etc. (*the rightful king, heir, owner*); (of office, property, etc.) that one is entitled to; hence **∼LY**[2] *adv.,* **∼NESS** *n.* [OE *rihtful* (as RIGHT[3], -FUL)]

||**rightō** (rī′tō, -ō′) *int.* (colloq.) expr. assent to order or proposal. [f. RIGHT[1] + O[2]]

ri′gid *a.* not flexible, stiff, unyielding, (*a rigid bar, stem, frame, airship*); inflexible, harsh, strict, precise, punctilious, (*rigid justice, principles, Catholics, adherence to rules, economy*); hence or cogn. **rigi′diFY** *v.t.* & *i.,* **rigi′dITY** *n.,* **∼LY**[2] *adv.* [f. F *rigide* or f. L *rigidus* (as RIGOR[1])]

ri′gmarōle *n.* & *a.* **1.** *n.* rambling or meaningless talk or tale. **2.** *a.* incoherent, rambling. [alt. f. obs. *ragman roll* = catalogue, orig. unkn.]

ri′gor[1] (rī′gŏr, rī′ger) *n.* (Path.) sudden chill with shivering before fever etc.; rigidity of body caused by shock, poisoning, etc.; **∼ mor′tis,** stiffening of body after death. [ME f. L (*rigēre* be stiff; see -OR)]

||**ri′gour** (-ger), ***ri′gor**[2], *n.* severity, strictness, harshness, (in *pl.*) harsh measures; strict enforcement of rules etc. (*with the utmost rigour of the law*); extremity or excess of weather, hardship, famine, etc., great distress; austerity of life, Puritanic strictness of observance or doctrine, whence **ri′gor**ISM (3), **ri′gor**IST (2), *ns.*; logical accuracy, exactitude; so **ri′gor**OUS *a.* [ME, f. OF *rigour* f. L RIGOR[1]]

Rig-Ve′da (-vä′-, -vē′-) *n.* the oldest and chief VEDA. [f. Skr. *r̥gveda* (*r̥c* praise, *vēda* VEDA)]

rīle *v.t.* **1.** (colloq.) anger, irritate. **2.** *make (water) turbulent or muddy. [var. of ROIL]

Ri′ley, Rei′lly, (rī′-) *n.* the life of **∼,** (sl.) a carefree existence. [20th c.; orig. unkn.]

rilie′vo (rēlyā′vō) *n.* (*pl.* **∼s**) = RELIEF[2], RELIEVO. [It., = RELIEF[2]]

rill *n.* small stream, runnel, rivulet; hence **∼'ET**[1] *n.* [prob. f. LDu. orig.; cf. LG *ril(le)*]

rille *n.* (Astron.) trench or narrow valley on moon's surface. [G, as prec.]

rim[1] *n.,* & *v.t.* (**-mm-**). **1.** *n.* outer ring of wheel's framework, not including tyre; (poet.) circular object (**golden ∼,** crown); (Naut.) surface of the water. **2.** raised edge or border, margin, verge, esp. of something more or less circular; **∼-brake** (acting on rim of wheel); ***∼-rock,** outcrop with steep face; hence **∼'LESS,** (-)**∼**MED[2] (-md), *adjs.* **3.** *v.t.* furnish with rim, serve as rim to, edge, border. [OE *rima,* = ON *rimi* ridge]

||**rim**[2] *n.* (arch.) **∼ (of the belly),** peritoneum. [OE *rēoma,* = OS, OHG *riomo* strap]

rime[1,2] *n.* & *v.t.* & *v.* See RHYME[1,2].

rime[3] *n.,* & *v.t.* **1.** *n.* frost, esp. formed from cloud or fog; hence **ri′m**Y[2] *a.* **2.** (poet.) hoar-frost. **3.** *v.t.* cover with rime. [OE *hrīm,* = MDu. *rijm,* ON *hrím*]

Ri'mmon *n.* **bow down in the house of** ∼, compromise one's convictions. [name of deity in ancient Damascus, 2 Kings 5:18]

ri'mōse, ri'mous, *adjs.* (Bot. etc.) full of chinks or fissures. [f. L *rimosus* (*rima* chink; see -OSE¹, -OUS)]

ri'mu (rē'mŏo) *n.* (NZ). principal indigenous softwood (tree, *Dacrydium cupressinum*). [Maori]

rind *n.*, & *v.t.* **1.** *n.* bark of tree or plant; peel of fruit or vegetable; harder outer layer of cheese or other substance; skin of bacon etc.; external aspect, surface; hence -∼ED² *a.* **2.** *v.t.* strip bark from. [OE *rind(e)*, = OS, OHG *rinda*]

ri'nderpëst *n.* virulent infectious disease of ruminants (esp. cattle). [G (*rinder* cattle, *pest* PEST)]

ring¹ *n.*, & *v.t.* **1.** *n.* circlet usu. of precious metal and often set with gem(s) worn round finger as ornament or token (esp. of betrothal or marriage) or signet, or hung from or encircling other part of body. **2.** circular band of any material and usu. small size. **3.** raised or sunk or otherwise distinguishable line or band round, or rim of, cylindrical or circular object. **4.** fold, coil, bend, piece, structure, part, or mark, having form of circular band, (*has livid rings round his eyes*; *puffing out rings of smoke*; ANNUAL, FAIRY, *ring*); halo round moon etc.; (Chem.) group of atoms representable as closed sequence. **5.** persons, trees, etc., disposed in a circle, such disposition; combination of traders, politicians, spies, etc., acting together for control of operations; PRICE-*ring*; hence ∼'STER *n.* **6.** circular or other enclosure or space for circus, boxing (PRIZE¹-*ring*; HATS *in the ring*), betting at races (**the** ∼, bookmakers), showing of cattle, etc. **7.** circular or spiral course (**make** or **run** ∼**s round,** go or do things very much better or quicker than). **8.** ∼**-bark** *v.t.*, cutting in bark of (tree) to kill it or to retard its growth and improve fruit production; ∼**-bolt,** bolt with ring attached for fastening rope to etc.; ∼**-bone,** (horse-disease with) deposit of bony matter on pastern--bones; ∼**-cartilage,** cricoid; ∼ **circuit** (Electr., serving many power points with one fuse in supply to ring); ∼**-cut,** remove ring of (bark; see *ring-bark*); ∼**-dove,** large species of pigeon (*Columba palumbus*); ∼**-fence** (completely enclosing estate etc.); ∼**-finger,** third finger esp. of left hand, on which wedding-ring is worn, ∼**'leader,** (one of) chief instigator(s) in mutiny, riot, etc.; ∼**-lock** (opened by right adjustment of several grooved rings); ∼ **main,** electrical supply through cable in closed ring providing alternative paths; ∼**'master,** director of circus performance; ∼**-neck,** ring-necked pheasant, plover, duck, or (Austral.) parrot; ∼**-necked,** with band(s) of colour round neck; ∼ **ouzel,** thrush (*Turdus torquatus*) allied to blackbird; ∼**-plover,** small plover of genus *Charadrius*; ∼**-pull,** (of tin) with seal broken by pulling a ring; ∼ **road,** bypass encircling town; ∼**'side** *a.*, (of seat, view, etc.) close to scene of action; ∼**-snake,** ‖common European grass-snake (from its coiling), *small snake of genus Diadophis* with ring round neck; ∼**-straked,** (arch.) with bands of colour round body; ∼**'tail,** (1) female hen-harrier, (2) golden eagle till its third year, (3) ring-tailed opossum, lemur, or phalanger; ∼**-tailed,** (1) with tail ringed in alternate colours, (2) with tail curled at end; ∼**-taw,** game with marbles in ring; ∼**-wall** (completely enclosing estate etc.); ∼**'worm,** contagious fungous disease of skin, appearing in circular patches esp. on child's scalp. **9.** Hence (-)∼ED² (-ngd), ∼'LESS, *adjs.* **10.** *v.t.* encompass (*round, about, in*), hem in (*game, cattle*) by riding or beating in circle round them. **11.** put ring on (bird etc.; cf. BAND¹ 2); put ring in nose of (pig, bull). **12.** = *ring-bark*. **13.** cut (onions, apples) into rings. [OE *hring,* = OS, OHG *hring,* ON *hringr,* f. Gmc *hrengaz*]

ring² *v.* (**rang,** arch. **rung; rung**) & *n.* **1.** *v.i.* give forth clear resonant sound (as) of vibrating metal (*bell, trumpet, coin, sound, rings,* often *out* etc.; *with a ringing laugh*; *a shot rang out*); (of bell) be sounded for

specified or implied purpose; sound in specified way; ∼ **true, false,** (of coin tested by throwing on counter, (fig.) of sentiments etc.). **2.** (Of place) resound, re-echo, (*with sound, to* sound or its cause, *with* fame etc. or its theme, *with* talk of). **3.** (Of utterance or other sound) ∼ in one's **ears, heart,** etc., linger in one's hearing, haunt the memory. **4.** (Of ears) be filled with sensation as of bell-ringing or with sound. **5.** ring bell as summons; ‖∼ (**up**), make telephone call (∼ **off,** end telephone conversation). **6.** *v.t.* make (bell) ring; ∼ **a bell,** (colloq.) begin to revive a memory; ∼ **the bell,** (colloq.) be successful [from use of bell in machines for testing strength or skill], strike sympathetic or responsive note; ∼ **up,** raise (church bell) over beam and ring it there; ∼'**ing engine,** pile-driver worked by ropes like peal of bells. **7.** sound (peal, KNELL¹, *the* CHANGE¹s) on bells (or with *bell* or *bells* as subj.). **8.** announce (hour etc.) by sound of bell(s). **9.** summon (*up* etc.) by ringing bell, ‖esp. by telephone; ∼ **back,** make telephone call to (person who has telephoned one earlier, or abs.); ∼ **up,** record (sale etc.) on cash register; ∼ **curtain up** or **down** in theatre, direct it by bell to be raised or lowered, (fig.) mark beginning or end of an enterprise etc. **10.** usher *in* or *out* with bell-ringing (esp. new or old year). **11.** *n.* set of (church) bells. **12.** ringing sound, ringing tone in voice etc., resonance of coin or vessel; specified feeling conveyed by utterance etc. (*has a melancholy ring*). **13.** act of ringing bell, sound so produced; (colloq.) call on the telephone (*give me a ring*). [OE *hringan,* = ON *hringja*]

ri'ngent (-nj-) *a.* gaping, grinning, (esp. Bot., of wide labiate corolla). [as RICTUS; see -ENT]

ri'nger *n.* **1.** quoit that falls round peg; fox that runs in ring when hunted; *substituted racehorse etc.; person's double. **2.** bell-ringer; device for ringing bell; (Austral.) fastest shearer in shed. [f. RING¹,² +-ER¹]

ri'nghäls *n.* (S. Afr.) snake akin to cobra with coloured ring round neck, spitting venom at victim. [Afrik. (*ring* RING¹, *hals* neck)]

ri'nglêt *n.* **1.** curly lock of hair, long curl; hence ∼ED², ∼Y², *adjs.* **2.** butterfly of family Satyridae. **3.** (arch.) small ring, fairy ring on grass, ring-shaped mark etc. [f. RING¹ +-LET]

rink *n.* stretch of ice used for game of curling; sheet of natural or artificial ice, floor, for (roller-)skating; strip of bowling green used for a match; team of four players in bowls or curling. [ME, orig. Sc.; = jousting-ground; perh. orig. *renk f. OF *renc* RANK¹]

rinse *v.t.*, & *n.* **1.** *v.t.* wash out or *out* (vessel, mouth) by filling with clean water etc., moving about or shaking, and emptying; pour liquid over or wash lightly; put (clothes) through clean water to remove soap etc.; clear (impurities) *out* or *away* by rinsing. **2.** *n.* rinsing (*give it a rinse*); solution for temporary tinting of hair. [ME, f. OF *rincer, raincier,* of unkn. orig.]

ri'ot *n.*, & *v.i.* **1.** *n.* disorder, tumult, disturbance of the peace, outbreak of lawlessness, on part of a crowd (in Law, by three or more); ‖R∼ Act (by which persons not dispersing after official reading of part of it incur guilt of felony) (*read the R*∼ *Act,* (joc.) insist that noise, disobedience, etc., is to cease); ∼ **gun, shield,** (for use in dealing with riots). **2.** loud revelry, a revel; unrestrained indulgence in or display or enjoyment of something (*a riot of emotion, colour, sound*); (colloq.) very amusing thing or person. **3.** (Hunt.) following of any scent indiscriminately; **run** ∼ (orig. of hounds doing this, now usu. fig. of person or his tongue or fancy throwing off all restraint, or of luxuriant vegetation etc.). **4.** (arch.) loose living, debauchery. **5.** *v.i.* live wantonly, revel. **6.** make or engage in a political riot or offence against the Riot Act; so ∼ER² (4) *n.* [ME, f. OF *riote(r), rihoter;* orig. unkn.]

ri'otous *a.* marked by rioting or by dissolute conduct; wildly profuse; hence ∼LY² *adv.*, ∼NESS *n.* [ME f. OF (as RIOT, -OUS)]

rip¹ *n.* worthless horse; dissolute person, rake; rascal. [perh. var. of REP³]

rip² *v.* (**-pp-**) & *n.* **1.** *v.t.* cut or tear (thing) quickly or forcibly away from something (*rip out the lining*; *rip the boards off*); make long cut or tear in, cut or tear vigorously apart; ∼ **off**, (sl.) defraud, steal, whence ∼-*off* n. **2.** split (wood, rock), saw (wood) along the grain. **3.** strip (roof) of tiles or slates and laths. **4.** make (fissure, passage) by ripping. **5.** open *up* (wound, quarrel, sorrow, the past) again. **6.** *v.i.* come violently asunder, split. **7.** rush along (of ship, or transf.); let ∼, (colloq.) not check speed of or interfere with; ∼ **into**, attack verbally. **8.** ||(in *pres. part.*, arch. sl.) fine, splendid, enjoyable, first-rate. **9.** ∼-**cord**, cord for releasing parachute from its pack or opening balloon gasbag; ∼-**roaring**, wildly noisy; ∼-**saw**, coarse saw used for ripping wood; ∼-**snorter**, (sl.) energetic person or thing. **10.** *n.* act of ripping; long tear or cut. [ME, of unkn. orig.]

rip³ *n.* stretch of broken water in sea or river, overfall; ∼ **current**, ∼-**tide**, strong surface current from shore, (fig.) conflicting psychological forces. [perh. rel. to prec.]

RIP *abbr.* (may he or she or they) rest in peace. [f. L *requiesca(n)t in pace*]

ripār'ian *a.* & *n.* **1.** *a.* of or on river-bank (*riparian proprietor, rights*). **2.** *n.* riparian proprietor. [f. L *riparius* (*ripa* bank; see -ARY¹) +-AN]

ripe *a.* & *v.* **1.** *a.* ready to be reaped, gathered, eaten, drunk, used, or dealt with, fully developed, mellow, mature, prepared or able *to* undergo something, in fit state *for*, (*ripe corn, fruit, cheese, wine, seed*; *ripe scholar, scholarship, judgement, experience, understanding*; *opportunity ripe to be seized*; *time is ripe for speaking the truth*; *mood or person, plan, land, disease, ripe for mischief, execution, development, treatment*); (of person's age) advanced; (of age, beauty, etc.) mature; (of lips) red and full like ripe fruit; hence **ri'pEN⁶** *v.t.* & *i.*, ∼'**LY²** (-plĭ) *adv.*, ∼'**NESS** (-pn-) *n.* **2.** *v.i.* & *i.* (esp. poet.) ripen. [OE *rīpe*, = OS *rīpi*, OHG *rīfi* f. WG]

ripie'n|ō (-pyä´-) *n.* (*pl.* ∼**os** or ∼**i**). (Mus.) supplementary player or instrument. [It. (as RE-, *pieno* full!)]

ripo'ste *n.*, & *v.i.* **1.** *n.* quick return thrust in fencing, (fig.) quick counterstroke, retort. **2.** *v.i.* deliver riposte. [f. F *ri(s)poste(r)* f. It. *risposta* RESPONSE]

ri'pper *n.* In vbl senses; tool for ripping roof; rip-saw; (arch. sl.) 'ripping' person or thing. [f. RIP² +-ER¹]

ri'pple¹ *n.*, & *v.t.* **1.** *n.* toothed implement used to remove seeds from flax. **2.** *v.t.* treat with ripple. [corresp. to MDu., MLG *repel(en)*, OHG *riffila, rifilōn*]

ri'pple² *n.* & *v.* **1.** *n.* ruffling of water's surface, small wave(s); wavy or crinkled appearance in hair, ribbons, etc.; gentle lively sound that rises and falls (*ripple of applause, conversation, laughter*); (Electr.) slight variation in strength of current etc.; *riffle in stream; ∼-**mark**, ridge or ridged surface left on sand or mud or rock by water or wind; hence **ripplET¹** *n.*, **ri'pplY²** *a.* **2.** *v.i.* & *t.* form, flow in, show, agitate or mark with, sound like, ripples. [n. 18th c., f. v. 17th c., of unkn. orig.]

*ri'p-răp** *n.* loose stone as foundation for structure. [redupl. of RAP¹]

Ripuār'ian *a.* of the ancient Franks living on Rhine between Meuse and Moselle; ∼ **law**, code observed by them. [f. med. L *Ripuarius* +-AN]

Rip văn Wi'nkle *n.* person with utterly antiquated ideas or information. [hero of tale (by W. Irving, 1820), who slept 20 years]

rise¹ (-z) *v.i.* (**rose** pr. rōz; ∼**n** pr. ri'zen). **1.** get up from lying or sitting or kneeling position, get out of bed, (of meeting etc.) cease to sit for business, recover standing or upright position, become erect, leave ground, (*all rose when he entered*; *found he could not, was too weak to, rise*; *rise at 5 a.m., with the lark, with the SUN, rise up early*; *Parliament will rise next week*; *fell never to rise again*; *the hair rose on his head*; *horse rises on its hind legs*); come to life again or *again* or *from the dead* (*Christ is risen*); stand after receiving accolade (*rise, Sir Thomas*); depart *from* (table, meal) on finishing

eating; ∼ **and shine**, (joc.) get out of bed etc. smartly. **2.** cease to be quiet or submissive, rebel, (*rise in arms, rebellion*, etc., *against oppression, oppressor*); (of wind) begin to blow (more strongly); **gorge** or **stomach rises**, indignation or disgust is felt; *my whole soul* **rises against it**, finds it intolerable. **3.** come or go up, grow upwards, ascend, mount, soar, project or swell upwards, become higher, reach higher position or level or amount, increase, incline upwards, come to surface, become or be visible above or *above* surroundings or horizon, develop greater energy or intensity, be progressive, (*sun, star, morning, dawn, rises; the risen sun; smoke rises straight up; balloon rises from the ground; picture or idea rises before the mind; river, tide, flood, level, has risen considerably, is rising; temperatures, prices, demands, rise; a man likely to rise in his profession, to greatness; rises in a gentle curve; followed its progress with rising interest; bubbles rise; castle rises in the foreground; does not rise above mediocrity*); (of tree etc.) attain specified height; (of blister etc.) form; (of bread etc.) swell by action of yeast etc.; (of person's spirits) become more cheerful; (of barometer etc.) show higher atmospheric pressure; (of fish) come to surface to feed; (of person's facial colour) become brighter or deeper; (of theatre curtain) be moved away to reveal scene; ∼ **above**, be superior to (petty feelings etc.); *rise from the* RANK's; ∼ **in the world**, attain higher social position; ∼ **to**, develop powers equal to (occasion etc.) **4.** have origin, begin to be or flow *from, in, at*, etc., (*river rises from a spring, in the Grampians*, etc.; *earth and heaven rose at His word; the difficulty rises from misapprehension*). **5.** (poet.) arise (*a feud, rumour, rose*). [OE *rīsan*, = OS, OHG *rīsan*, ON *rísa*, Goth. *-reisan* f. Gmc]

rise² (-z) *n.* **1.** act or manner of rising; *going up of theatre curtain. **2.** ascent, upward slope, knoll, hill, (*came to a rise in the road; chapel stands on a rise*). **3.** social advancement, upward progress, increase in power, rank, value, price, amount, height, pitch, ||wages, etc., (*the rise and fall of statesmen; the rise of the tide is 30 ft.*); **on the** ∼, increasing. **4.** movement of fish to surface (*not a sign of a rise*); **get** or **take a** ∼ **out of**, (fig.) draw (person) into display of temper or characteristic behaviour. **5.** vertical height of step, arch, incline, etc.; = foll. **2.** **6.** origin, start, (*has or takes its rise in or from*; **give** ∼ **to**, cause, induce, suggest). [f. prec.]

ri'ser (-z-) *n.* **1.** In vbl senses. **2.** vertical piece between treads of staircase. **3.** vertical pipe for flow of liquid or gas. [ME, f. RISE¹ +-ER¹]

ri'shi *n.* Hindu sage or saint. [f. Skr. *riṣi*]

ri'sible (-z-) *a.* **1.** inclined to laugh; hence **risiBI'LITY** (-z-) *n.* **2.** of laughter (*risible nerves, faculties*, etc.). **3.** laughable, ludicrous. [f. LL *risibilis* f. L *rīdēre rislaugh*; see -IBLE]

ri'sing¹ (-z-) *n.* In vbl senses; resurrection; insurrection, revolt. [f. RISE¹ +-ING¹]

ri'sing² (-z-) *a.* In vbl senses; advancing to maturity (*the rising generation*) or high standing (*a rising young lawyer*); approaching specified age; (of ground) sloping upwards; ∼ **butt** or **hinge** (raising door as it opens). [f. RISE¹ +-ING²]

risk *n.*, & *v.t.* **1.** *n.* hazard, chance of or *of* bad consequences, loss, etc., exposure to mischance, (*there is the risk of his catching cold; at the risk of his life*); **at** ∼, exposed to danger; **at** person's ∼, with him to bear any loss etc. resulting; **put at** ∼, expose to danger; **run** ∼**s, a** ∼, **the** ∼, expose oneself or be exposed to loss etc. (*of*); **take** ∼**s** etc., expose oneself so. **2.** amount of insurance; person or thing insured or otherwise representing source of risk; ∼-**money**, allowance to cashier to cover accidental deficits. **3.** Hence ∼'**FUL**, ∼'**LESS**, *adjs.* **4.** *v.t.* expose to chance of injury or loss; venture on, accept the chance of, (*risk the jump, a battle, a sprained ankle*). [f. F *risque(r)* f. It. *risco* danger, *riscare* run into danger]

ri'sk|ў *a.* **1.** fraught with or full of risk. **2.** risqué. **3.** Hence ∼iLY² *adv.*, ∼iNESS *n.* [f. prec. +-Y²]

Risōrgĭmĕ′ntō *n.* movement in mid 19th c. to unite and liberate Italy. [It., = resurrection]

risŏ′ttō (-z-) *n.* (*pl.* ∼**s**). Italian dish of rice with stock, meat, onions, etc. [It.]

risqué (rĭ′skā) *a.* (Of story etc.) slightly indecent. [F, p.p. of *risquer* RISK]

rĭ′ssōle *n.* fried ball or cake of meat or fish mixed with bread-crumbs etc. or enclosed in pastry. [F, f. OF *ruissole, roussole* f. Rom. **russeola* (*pasta* paste) fem. of LL *russeolus* reddish f. L *russus* red]

rit. *abbr.* ritardando.

ritār̄dă′nd|ō (rē-) *adv., a.,* & *n.* (*pl.* ∼**os** or ∼**i**). (Mus.) = RALLENTANDO. [It.]

rite *n.* (form of procedure, action required or usual, in) a religious or solemn observance (*the rites of hospitality; the rite of confirmation; burial* or *funeral rites*; **conjugal** or **nuptial** ∼**s**, (arch.) sexual intercourse between husband and wife; (body of usages characteristic of) part of a Church (LATIN *rite*); ∼ **of passage** (used when person reaches new status in life, e.g. adolescence or marriage); hence ∼′LESS (-tl-) *a.* [ME, f. OF *rit(e)* or f. L *ritus* (religious) usage]

rĭtĕnu′t|ō (rētĕnōō′tō) *adv., a.,* & *n.* (*pl.* ∼**os** or ∼**i**). (Mus.) (passage performed) with immediate reduction of speed. [It.]

ritōr̄nĕ′ll|ō *n.* (*pl.* ∼**os**, or ∼**i** *pr.* -ē). (Mus.) short instrumental refrain, interlude, etc., in vocal work. [It., dim. of *ritorno* RETURN²]

rĭ′tūal *a.* & *n.* **1.** *a.* of, with, consisting in, involving, religious or other rites; ∼ **murder**, sacrifice of person to god(s); hence ∼LY² *adv.* **2.** *n.* prescribed order of performing religious etc. rites; book containing this; performance of ritual acts, whence (w. implication of excess) ∼ISM (3), ∼IST (2), *ns.* ∼ĭ′stIC *a.,* ∼IZE (2, 3) *v.i.* & *t.* [f. L *ritualis* (as RITE; see -AL)]

rĭ′tzy (-tsĭ) *a.* (colloq.) high-class, luxurious; ostentatiously smart. [f. *Ritz*, name of luxurious hotels f. C. *Ritz*, Swiss hotel-owner d. 1918 + -Y²]

rĭ′vage *n.* (poet.) coast, shore, bank. [ME f. OF (*rive* f. L *ripa* bank; see -AGE)]

rĭ′val *n., attrib. a.,* & *v.* (||-ll-). **1.** *n.* person's competitor for some prize (esp. another's love) or in some activity or quality; thing that equals another in quality; hence ∼RY (2, 4), ∼SHIP, *ns.* **2.** *a.* that is a rival or are rivals. **3.** *v.t.* vie with, be comparable to, seem or claim to be as good etc. as. **4.** *v.i.* (arch.) be in rivalry. [f. L *rivalis* (*rivus* stream; see -AL), orig. = using same stream]

rīve *v.* (∼**d**; ∼′**n** *pr.* rĭ′ven). **1.** *v.t.* (arch. or poet.) rend, cleave, wrench *away* or *off* or *from*, strike asunder, tear with hands or claws. **2.** (Of workman) split (wood, stone), make (laths etc.) by splitting. **3.** *v.i.* be split, gape under blow etc.; (of wood etc.) admit of being split. [ME, f. ON *rífa*]

rĭ′vel *v.i.* & *t.* (||-ll-). (arch.) wrinkle, crumple, shrivel. [ME, back-form. f. *rivelled*, OE *rifelede* app. f. **rifel* a wrinkle + -ED²]

rĭ′ven. See RIVE.

rĭ′ver¹ *n.* In vbl senses. [f. RIVE + -ER¹ (1)]

rĭ′ver² *n.* & *a.* **1.** *n.* copious stream of water flowing in channel to sea or lake or marsh or another river (||*the river Thames*, **the Thames river*); copious flow or stream *of* (*a river of* lava; ∼**s of blood**, much bloodshed); **sell down the** ∼, (colloq.) defraud or betray; *****up the** ∼, (colloq.) in(to) prison. **2.** *a.* (In names of animals, plants, and things) living in, situated or used on, river(s). **3.** ***∼ **bottom**, low-lying land beside river; ∼**god**, mythological being dwelling in and personifying a river; ∼**head**, source of river; ∼**horse**, hippopotamus; ∼**side**, ground along bank of river. **4.** Hence (-)∼ED² (-erd), ∼LESS, *adjs.* [ME, f. AF *river(e)*, OF *riviere* river (bank) f. Rom. **riparia* (*terra* land) fem. of L *riparius* (see RIPARIAN)]

rĭ′verain *a.* & *n.* **1.** *a.* of river or its neighbourhood; situated or dwelling by river. **2.** *n.* person dwelling by river. [F (*rivière*, as prec.)]

rĭ′verīne *a.* of or on river or its banks, riparian. [f. RIVER² + -INE¹]

rĭ′vĕt *n.,* & *v.t.* **1.** *n.* nail or bolt for holding together metal plates etc., its headless end being beaten out or pressed down after passing through two holes. **2.** *v.t.* clench (bolt etc.); join or fasten with rivets (*together, down,* etc.); fix, make immovable; concentrate, direct intently, (eyes, attention, etc., *on* or *upon*); engross (attention), engross attention of; hence ∼ER¹ (1, 2) *n.* [ME f. OF (*river* clench, of unkn. orig.)]

rĭvier′a (-ār̄′*a*) *n.* region with climate and scenery like that of the Riviera region on coast of SE France, Monaco, and NW Italy. [It., = sea-shore]

rĭvière (rĭ′vĭār̄, rēvyār̄′) *n.* gem necklace, esp. of more than one string. [F, = RIVER²]

rĭ′vūlĕt *n.* small stream. [f. obs. *riveret* (F, dim. of *rivière* RIVER²), perh. after It. *rivoletto* dim. of *rivolo* dim. of *rivo* f. L *rivus* stream; see -LET]

||**RL** *abbr.* Rugby League.

rly. *abbr.* railway.

RM *abbr.* Resident Magistrate; ||Royal Mail; ||Royal Marines.

rm. *abbr.* room.

||**RMA** *abbr.* Royal Military Academy.

||**RMS** *abbr.* Royal Mail Steamer; Royal Society of Miniature Painters.

r.m.s. *abbr.* root-mean-square.

RN *abbr.* ***registered nurse; ||Royal Navy.

Rn *symb.* radon.

RNA *abbr.* ribonucleic acid.

||**RNAS** *abbr.* Royal Naval Air Service, Station.

||**RNLI** *abbr.* Royal National Lifeboat Institution.

||**RN(V)R** *abbr.* Royal Naval (Volunteer) Reserve.

RNZAF *abbr.* Royal New Zealand Air Force.

RNZN *abbr.* Royal New Zealand Navy.

roach¹ *n.* (*pl.* same). small freshwater fish (esp. *Rutilus rutilus*) allied to carp (**sound as a** ∼, in first-rate health etc.); ∼**-backed,** ∼**-bellied,** (convex in profile). [ME, f. OF *roc(h)e,* of unkn. orig.]

roach² *n.* (Naut.) upward curve in foot of square sail. [18th c.; orig. unkn.]

roach³ *n.* ***cockroach; (sl.) marijuana cigarette-butt. [abbr.]

road¹ *n.* **1.** (usu. in *pl.*) piece of water near shore in which ships can ride at anchor. **2.** line of communication, esp. specially prepared track, between places for use of pedestrians, riders, and vehicles (**by** ∼, using transport along roads; **one for the** ∼, (colloq.) final drink before departure; **on the** ∼, travelling, esp. as a commercial traveller, itinerant performer, or vagrant; **take the** ∼, set out; ||**take to the** ∼, (arch.) become highwayman); **rule of the** ∼, custom regulating side to be taken by vehicles, riders, or ships, meeting or passing each other. **3.** way of getting to (*the road to* York, ruin, success); (as name of thoroughfare) *York Road, Graham Road; royal* ∼ **to,** way of attaining without trouble. **4.** underground passage in mine; ***railway. **5.** one's way or route; **in the, my,** etc., ∼, (colloq.) obstructing someone or something; **get out of the, my,** etc., ∼, (colloq.) cease to obstruct. **6.** ∼**-bed,** (1) foundation structure of a railway, (2) whole material laid down of an ordinary road, (3) ***part of road on which vehicles travel; ∼**-block,** obstruction on road set up by army or police to stop traffic for questioning etc.; ∼**book** (describing roads of country etc.); ||∼ **fund** (Hist., for construction and maintenance of roads and bridges); ||∼ **fund licence,** (colloq.) vehicle excise tax certificate; ∼**-hog,** reckless or inconsiderate (***esp. obstructive) motorist or cyclist; ∼**-holding,** stability of moving vehicle; ∼**-house,** inn or club on main road in country district; ∼′**man** (repairing roads); ∼**-map** (showing roads of a country or area); ∼**-metal,** broken stone for road-making or railway ballast; ∼′**runner,** bird of New Mexico etc. like cuckoo, able to run quickly; ∼ **sense,** capacity for safe behaviour on the road, esp. in traffic; ∼ **show,** theatrical performance by company on tour; ∼'side, border of road; ∼ sign (giving information to drivers etc.); ∼'stead (= sense 1); ∼ test (of vehicle by use on road); ∼'way, road, central part of road (opp. footpath at side), part of bridge or railway used for traffic; ∼-works, construction or repair of roads; ∼'worthy, fit to be used on the road, (of person) fit to travel. 7. Hence ∼'LESS a. [OE rād (rīdan RIDE), = MDu. rēd, ON reith]

road[2] v.t. (Of dog) follow up (game-bird, or abs.) by scent of trail. [19th c.; orig. unkn.]

roa'die n. (colloq.) manager of itinerant musicians. [f. ROAD¹ + -IE]

roa'dster n. open car without rear seats; horse or bicycle for use on the road. [f. ROAD¹ + -STER]

roam v. & n. **1.** v.i. ramble, wander. **2.** v.t. walk or travel unsystematically over or through or about (country, seas). **3.** n. act of roaming, ramble. [ME; orig. unkn.]

roan[1] a. & n. **1.** a. (Of animal) with coat of which the prevailing colour is thickly interspersed with another, esp. bay or sorrel or chestnut mixed with white or grey (red roan; blue ∼, black mixed with white; strawberry ∼, red mixed with white or grey). **2.** n. roan horse or cow. [OF, of unkn. orig.]

roan[2] n. soft sheepskin leather used in bookbinding as substitute for morocco. [ME, perh. f. Roan, old name of Rouen in N. France]

roar v. & n. **1.** v.i., & n. (utter, send forth) loud deep hoarse sound (as) of lion, person(s) in pain or rage or excitement, the sea, thunder, cannon, engine, furnace, etc., (the roar of the waves; lions roaring after their prey; roared with pain or for mercy); (utter) loud laughter (set table in a ∼, make company laugh loud). **2.** v.i. (Of horse) make loud noise in breathing due to disease; travel in vehicle at high speed with engine roaring. **3.** v.t. say, sing, utter, (words, chorus, oath, etc., out) in loud tone. **4.** Hence ∼'ER¹ n. [OE rārian, = MDu. reeren, MLG rāren, rēren, OHG rērēn, of imit. orig.]

roar'ing a. & adv. **1.** a. In vbl senses; riotous, noisy; boisterous, brisk, (do a roaring business or trade); ∼ forties (see FORTY); the ∼ game, curling. **2.** adv. ∼ (very) drunk. [f. prec. + -ING²]

roast v., attrib. a., & n. **1.** v.t. cook (esp. meat) by exposure to open fire or in oven; heat or calcine (ore) in furnace; heat (coffee-beans) in preparation for grinding; expose (victim for torture, oneself or some part for warmth) to fire or great heat; (in part.) very hot; ridicule, banter, chaff; *censure. **2.** v.i. undergo roasting. **3.** a. (Of meat, potato, chestnut, etc.) roasted. **4.** n. roast meat or a dish of it (RULE the roast); piece of meat for roasting; operation of roasting; *party where roasted food is eaten. [ME; n. partly f. OF rost, partly f. a. f. obs. p.p. of v., partly f. v. f. OF rostir f. WG *raustjan (*raust(a) gridiron)]

roa'ster n. In vbl senses; oven or dish for roasting food in; ore-roasting furnace; coffee-roasting apparatus; pig, potato, fowl, etc., fit for roasting. [ME, f. prec. + -ER¹]

rob v.t. (-bb-). deprive (person etc.) of or of property by (threat of) violence, feloniously plunder (person or place, of), deprive of what is due or normal; rob PETER¹ to pay Paul; (abs.) commit robbery; so ∼'ber², ∼'bery (2, 4), ns. [ME, f. OF rob(b)er f. Gmc *raubh-; cf. REAVE]

robe n. & v. **1.** n. long loose outer garment; dressing-gown; baby's outer garment esp. for christening etc.; (often in pl.) longer outer garment worn as indication of wearer's rank, office, profession, etc., gown, vestment; *blanket or wrap of fur etc.; *wardrobe; ∼-de-chambre (rŏbdǝshah'ńbr), dressing-gown, wrapper. **2.** v.t. clothe (person) in robe; dress. **3.** v.i. assume one's robes or vestments; ro'bing-room (in which these are donned). [ME f. OF, f. Rom. *rauba f. Gmc (as prec., orig. sense 'booty')]

ro'bin n. **1.** ∼ (redbreast), small brown red-breasted European bird (Erithacus rubecola); *red-breasted thrush (Turdus migratorius); bird of similar appearance etc. to either of these. **2.** R∼ Goodfellow, a mischievous sportive sprite in English folklore; R∼ Hood, (type of) medieval forest outlaw; ROUND¹ robin. [ME f. OF, fam. var. of man's Christian name Robert]

robi'nia n. N. Amer. tree or shrub of genus Robinia, e.g. locust-tree. [mod. L, f. J. Robin, 17th-c. Fr. gardener; see -IA¹]

ro'borant a. & n. (Med.) strengthening (drug). [f. L roborare (robur -oris strength); see -ANT]

rŏ'bŏt n. apparently human automaton, intelligent and obedient but impersonal machine; machine-like person; (S. Afr.) automatic traffic-signal. [Czech (in K. Čapek's play R.U.R. (Rossum's Universal Robots) 1920), f. robota forced labour]

robŭ'st a. (∼er, ∼est). (Of person) having strong health and physique; (of animal, plant, body, health, etc.) not slender or delicate or weakly; (of exercise, discipline, etc.) tending to or requiring strength, invigorating, vigorous; (of wine etc.) full-bodied; (of equipment etc.) strongly built; (of intellect etc.) sensible, straightforward, not given to nor confused by subtleties; hence ∼LY² adv., ∼NESS n. [f. F robuste, or f. L robustus firm and hard (robur, robur oak, strength)]

robŭ'stious (-schǝs) a. boisterous, self-assertive, noisy; (arch.) robust. [f. prec. + -IOUS]

roc n. gigantic bird of Eastern legend. [f. Sp. rocho, ruc f. Arab. ruḵ]

||**ROC** abbr. Royal Observer Corps.

rŏcai'lle (-kī') n. 18th-c. style of ornamentation resembling artificial rocks or shells. [F (roc, f. as ROCK¹)]

rŏ'cambōle n. species of leek used for seasoning. [F, f. G rockenbolle]

rŏche moutŏ'nnée (rŏsh mŏŏtŏ'nā) n. (Geol.) small mass of rock shaped by glacial action. [F, = fleecy rock]

rŏ'chĕt n. surplice-like vestment used chiefly by bishops and abbots. [ME f. OF, dim. f. WG (cf. OE rocc, OS rok, OHG roch, ON rokkr); see -ET¹]

rŏck[1] n. **1.** solid part of earth's crust underlying soil; sure foundation, support, or protection; mass of rock projecting and forming hill, cliff, etc., or standing up into or out of sea etc. from bottom (the R∼, Gibraltar); (fig.) source of danger or destruction; on the ∼s, (colloq.) (1) short of money, (2) broken down, (3, of drink) served with ice cubes only. **2.** hard compact material of which rock consists (a mass, needle, of rock); large detached stone, boulder; (Geol.) any particular igneous or stratified mineral constituent of earth's crust, including sands, clays, etc.; *stone of any size; *(sl., in pl.) money; (sl.) gem, esp. diamond. **3.** hard usu. cylindrical sweetmeat made from sugar with flavouring esp. of peppermint. **4.** (blue) ∼, = rock-pigeon. **5.** ∼-badger, S. Afr. hyrax; ∼-bed, base of rock, rocky bottom; ∼-bird, bird frequenting rocks, esp. puffin; ∼-bottom, (colloq., of prices etc.) very lowest (level); ∼-bound, (of coast) abounding in rocks; ∼-cake, bun with rugged surface; *∼ candy (= sense 3); ∼-cork, light variety of asbestos; ∼-crystal, transparent colourless quartz usu. in hexagonal prisms; ∼-dove, = rock-pigeon; ∼-drill, rock-boring tool or machine; ∼-fish, rock-frequenting goby, bass, wrasse, catfish, etc.; ∼-garden, artificial mound or bank of stones with rock-plants etc. planted in the interstices, garden in which rockeries are the chief feature; ∼-goat, ibex; ∼-hewn, cut out of the rock; ∼-hopper, small penguin of genus Eudyptes; ∼-kangaroo, wallaroo; ∼'ling [-LING¹], small fish of cod family found in pools among rocks; ∼ lobster, crawfish; ∼-oil, petroleum; ∼-pigeon, wild dove frequenting rocks, supposed source of domestic pigeon; ∼-plant (growing on or among rocks); ∼-rabbit, Syrian hyrax; ∼-ribbed, (fig.) uncompromising; ∼-rose, plant of genus Cistus, Helianthemum, etc.; ∼ salmon, ||(trade name for) dogfish, *amberjack; ∼-salt, common salt as solid mineral; ∿-**snake**, large python; ∿-**sucker**, sea lamprey; ∿-**tar**, petroleum; ∿-**tripe**, = *tripe-de-roche*; ∿-**whistler**, Alpine marmot; ∿-**wool**, mineral wool made from limestone etc.; ∿-**work**, rockery or rock-garden. **6.** Hence ∿'LESS, ∿'LIKE, *adjs.*, ∿'LET *n.* [ME, f. OF *ro*(*c*)*que*, *roche*, med. L *rocca*, of unkn. orig.]

röck² *n.* (Hist.) distaff. [ME, f. MDu. *rocke*, MLG *rocken*, OHG *rocko* or f. ON *rokkr*, f. Gmc **rukkon*]

röck³ *v.* & *n.* **1.** *v.t.* & *i.* move gently to and fro (as) in cradle, set or keep or be in such motion,(*rock him to sleep*; *ship rocking on, rocked by, the waves*; *sat rocking* (*himself*) *in his chair*); distress, perturb. **2.** sway from side to side, shake, oscillate, reel, (*earthquake rocks house*; *house rocks*); dance to rock music; ∿ **the boat,** (colloq.) disturb equilibrium of situation. **3.** ∿'**ing** -**chair** (mounted on rockers, or with seat arranged to rock); ∿'**ing-horse,** wooden horse on rockers for child; ∿'**ing-stone,** poised boulder easily rocked; ∿'**ing-turn,** (Skating) turn from any edge to same in opposite direction with body revolving away from convex of first curve (**counter-**∿'**ing-turn,** same turn with body revolving away from concave); ∿- -**shaft** (that oscillates about axis without making complete revolutions); ∿-**staff,** part of apparatus working smith's bellows. **4.** *n.* rocking motion; spell of rocking; rocking or swinging music; ∿ (**and** or '**n**' **roll**), (popular dance to) music with heavy beat and simple melody, often with blues element. [OE *roccian*, prob. f. Gmc **rukk-* move, remove]

rö'cker *n.* In vbl senses; one of the curved bars on which cradle etc. rocks (**off** one's ∿, (sl.) crazy); rocking-chair; skate with highly curved blade; switch pivoting between 'on' and 'off' positions; = ROCK³*ing* -*turn*; ‖‖leather-jacketed teenage motor-cyclist. [f. prec. + -ER¹]

rö'ckerў *n.* pile of rough stones with soil between them for growing rock-plants on. [f. ROCK¹ + -ERY]

rö'ckét¹ *n* (**sweet**) ∿, plant of genus *Hesperis* grown for flowers; cruciferous annual plant (*Eruca sativa*) grown for salad; **dyer's** ∿, = WELD¹; **wall-**∿, yellow-flowered weed stinking when crushed; **yellow** ∿, winter-cress. [f. *roquette* f. It. *rochetta*, *ruchetta* dim. of *ruca* f. L *eruca* downy-stemmed plant]

rö'ckét² *n.* & *v.* **1.** *n.* cylindrical paper or metal case that can be projected to height or distance by ignition of contents, used in firework displays, for signalling, to carry line to ship in distress, etc.; engine containing its own propellant and depending for its operation on reaction due to continuous jet of rapidly expanding gases released in combustion of propellant, used to propel military warhead or spacecraft, whence ∿EER', ∿RY (5), *ns.*; rocket-propelled bomb etc. **2.** ‖‖(sl.) reprimand. **3.** *v.t.* bombard with rockets. **4.** *v.i.* move rapidly upwards or away. [f. F *roquette* f. It. *rocchetto* dim. of *rocca* ROCK², w. ref. to cylindrical shape; see -ET¹]

rö'ckling *n.* see ROCK¹ 5.

rö'ckĺў *a.* & *n.* **1.** *a.* of rock; full of or abounding in rocks (*a rocky shore*); **the R**∿**y Mountains,** range in western N. Amer.); like rock in ruggedness, firmness, solidity, etc. **2.** (colloq.) unsteady, tottering. **3.** Hence ∿ĭLY² *adv.*, ∿ĭNESS *n.* **4.** *n.* (in *pl.*) **the R**∿**ies,** the Rocky Mountains. [f. ROCK¹ or (sense 2) ROCK³ + -Y²]

rocŏ'cŏ *a.* & *n.* (*pl.* ∿**s**). **1.** *a.* of a style of decoration prevalent in 18th-c. Europe, with scroll-work, shell motifs, etc. **2.** (Of furniture, architecture, etc., also of literary style) highly ornamented, florid. **3.** *n.* rococo style. [F, joc. alt. f. ROCAILLE]

röd *n.* **1.** slender straight round stick growing as shoot on tree or cut from it or made from wood, switch, wand, (occas. as symbol of office etc.); **divining, dowsing,** -∿ (see DOWSE²). **2.** such stick, or bundle of twigs, for use in caning or flogging (**the** ∿, use of this; **make** etc. **a** ∿ **for** one's own back, prepare trouble for oneself; **kiss the** ∿, take punishment meekly or gladly; **have a** ∿ **in pickle for,** be ready to punish

when time comes). **3.** = FISH²*ing-rod*; angler using this. **4.** (As measure) = PERCH² or square perch. **5.** slender metal bar, connecting bar, shaft, (*curtain*, *piston*, etc., *-rod*); **ride the** ∿**s,** *(sl.) travel illicitly under railway carriage or wagon. **6.** (sl.) penis;* = HOT¹ *rod*; *pistol or revolver. **7.** (Anat.) rod-shaped structure in retina etc. **8.** Hence ∿'LESS, ∿'LIKE, *adjs.*, ∿'LET *n.* [OE *rodd*, prob. rel. to ON *rudda* club]

röde¹. See RIDE.

röde² *v.i.* (Of wildfowl) fly landwards in the evening; (of woodcock) fly in the evening during breeding season. [18th c.; orig. unkn.]

rö'dent *a.* & *n.* **1.** (mammal) of the order Rodentia with strong incisors and no canine teeth (e.g. rat, mouse, squirrel, beaver, porcupine); ‖∿ **officer,** official rat-catcher; hence **rodĕ'nt**IAL (-shal) *a.*), rodent. **2.** *v.t.* gnawing (esp. Path. of slow- -growing ulcers). [f. L *rodere ros-* gnaw; see -ENT]

rodeo (rö'dĭō, -dā'ō) *n.* (*pl.* ∿**s**). round-up of cattle on ranch for branding etc., enclosure for this; exhibition of cowboys' skill in handling animals etc.; exhibition of motor-cycle feats etc. [Sp. (*rodear* go round ult. f. L *rotare* ROTATE)].

** rŏdomontä'de** *n.*, *a.*, & *v.i.* **1.** *n.* & *a.* boastful, bragging, (saying or talk). **2.** *v.i.* brag, talk big. [F, f. obs. It. *rodomontada* f. *rodomont* It. *rodomonte* f. name of boastful character in *Orlando* epics]

röe¹ *n.* (*pl.* ∿**s** or same). ∿(-**deer**), small European and Asian deer (*Capreolus capreolus*); ∿'**buck,** male roe. [OE *ra*(*ha*), = OS, OHG *rēho*, ON *rá* f. Gmc **raih-*]

röe² *n.* (**hard**) ∿, mass of eggs in female fish's ovary; (**soft**) ∿, male fish's milt; ∿-**stone,** oolite; hence (-)**röED²** (röd) *n.* [ME *row*(*e*), *rough*, f. MLG, MDu. *roge*(*n*), OHG *rogo*, *rogan*, ON *hrogn*]

roe'ntgen (rŭ'ntyen) *n.* unit of ionizing radiation, amount producing one electrostatic unit of positive or negative ionic charge in one c.c. of air under standard conditions. [f. W. C. *Röntgen*, Ger. physicist d. 1923, discoverer of X-rays]

roentgenö'graphў (rŭntyen-) *n.* photography using X-rays; so ∿LOGY *n.*, radiology. [f. as prec. + -O- + -GRAPHY]

roga'tion *n.* **1.** (Eccl.) (usu. in *pl.*) litany of the saints chanted on the three days (**R**∿ **days**) in **R**∿ **Week** before Ascension Day and following **R**∿ **Sunday;** ∿ **flower,** milkwort of genus *Polygala*; hence ∿AL *a.* **2.** (Rom. Ant.) law proposed before the people by consul or tribune. [ME, f. L *rogatio* (*rogare* ask; see -ATION)]

rö'ger *n.*, *v.*, & *int.* **1.** *n.* (sl.) copulation. **2.** JOLLY¹ *Roger.* **3.** *v.t.* & *i* (sl.) copulate (with). **4.** *int.* (In signalling etc.) your message has been received and understood; (sl.) I agree. [man's Christian name *Roger*, used in signalling code for letter *R*]

rögue (-g) *n.*, & *v.t.* **1.** *n.* dishonest or unprincipled person; (joc.) mischievous child or waggish or arch person; ∿**s' gallery,** collection of photographs of known criminals etc. **2.** inferior or defective specimen among many that are acceptable. **3.** ∿ (**buffalo, elephant,** etc.) wild animal driven or living apart from the herd and of savage temper. **4.** Hence **rö'gu**ERY (4) (-gerĭ) *n.*, **rö'gu**ISH¹ (-gĭ-) *a.*, (esp.) playfully mischievous. **5.** *v.t.* remove rogues (sense 2) from. [16th-c. cant wd, of unkn. orig.]

ROI *abbr.* Royal Institute of Oil Painters.

roil *v.t.* make (water etc.) turbid by stirring; perturb; vex, annoy. [perh. f. OF *ruiler* mix mortar f. LL *regulare* REGULATE]

roi'ster *v.i.* revel noisily, be uproarious, (esp. in *part.* as *a.*); hence ∿ER¹, ∿ING¹, *ns.* [f. obs. *roister* roisterer f. F *rustre* ruffian var. of *ruste* f. L *rusticus* RUSTIC]

Rö'land *n.* **a** ∿ **for an Oliver,** effective retort, well- -balanced combat or exchange. [name of legendary nephew of Charlemagne celebrated with his comrade Oliver in the *Chanson de Roland*]

röle, rôle, (röl) *n.* actor's part; one's function, what

person or thing is appointed or expected to do; ∼-
-**playing,** behaving in accordance with specified
function etc. [f. F *rôle* and obs. F *roule, rolle* = foll.]

rōll[1] *n.* **1.** cylinder formed by turning flexible fabric
such as paper or cloth over and over upon itself
without folding (*rolls of carpet, paper, film,* etc.); similar
structure of pastry etc. (SAUSAGE, SWISS, *roll*). **2.**
document, esp. official record, in this form (‖**Master
of the R∼s,** one of the judges of the Court of Appeal
and Keeper of the Records at the Public Record
Office); register or catalogue (*in the roll of saints; a long
roll of heroes; on the rolls of fame;* ∼ **of honour,** esp. list
of those who have died for their country in war); ‖the
official list of qualified solicitors (**strike off the ∼s,**
debar from practising after dishonesty etc.); list of
persons esp. soldiers or schoolchildren (∼-**call,**
calling over of this to detect absentees; so **call the ∼**).
3. more or less (semi)cylindrical straight or curved
mass of anything however formed (*a roll of butter, hair,
straw, tobacco; has rolls of fat on him*); *money,* esp. as
banknotes rolled together; (Archit.) moulding of
convex section; (in Ionic capital) volute. **4.** turned-
-back edge of something, e.g. coat-collar. **5.** cylinder
or roller, esp. to shape metal in rolling-mill. **6.** ∼ (of
bread), **bread** ∼, small loaf esp. for one person at
one meal; **egg, ham,** etc., ∼ (cut open and stuffed
with specified food). [ME, f. OF *ro(u)lle* f. L *rotulus,
rotula* dim. of *rota* wheel]

rōll[2] *v. & n.* **1.** *v.t. & i.* move or send or go in some
direction by turning over and over on axis (cf. SLIDE[1])
esp. to lower level (*roll barrel; barrel started rolling; ball
or coin rolled under the table* or *into a hole; river rolls stones
down; rolling stone gathers no* MOSS; hence ∼**ing stone,**
person of unsettled habits); (cause to) start moving
(as if) in this manner; (make) revolve between two
surfaces (*rolling a marble between his palms*); *throw
(dice); *rob with violence. **2.** change direction (of)
with rotatory motion (*his eyes roll strangely; rolled his
eyes on us*); ∼-**top desk** (with flexible cover sliding
in curved grooves). **3.** *v.i.* wallow, turn about in fluid
or loose medium, (of horse etc.) lie on back and kick
about, esp. to dislodge rider etc.; ∼'**ing in,** (colloq.)
plentifully supplied with (money etc.); ∼'**ing,**
(colloq.) very rich. **4.** *v.t. & i.* sway or rock; walk with
swaying gait as of sailor, reel; (of ship, vehicle, etc.)
sway to and fro about axis in direction of travel. **5.**
undulate, show undulating surface or motion, go or
propel or carry with such motion, (*sea, river, rolls; river
rolls its waters to sea; waves roll in, smoke rolls up; chimney
rolls up smoke; the mist rolled away; a rolling expanse* or
plain). **6.** utter or be uttered, sound, with vibratory or
undulating or trilling effect (*roll out verses, song,* etc.;
thunder, drum, organ, echo, rolls; roll one's *rs*). **7.** (Of
vehicle or furniture) advance or convey on wheels
etc. usu. *along, by,* etc., (of person) be so conveyed,
(*carriage rolled along, rolled them by; he rolled past in his
carriage*); (of time) elapse as if on wheels etc. (*the years
roll by, roll on*); *∼'**away,** bed that can be folded up
and moved away on wheels; ∼'**ing barrage,** =
CREEPING *barrage;* ∼'**ing-stock,** railway or *road
vehicles of a company. **8.** *v.t.* flatten by passing roller
over or by passing between rollers (*roll lawn, metal,
pastry for pies,* etc.); ∼**ed gold,** thin coating so applied
on base metal; ∼**ed oats** (husked and crushed);
∼'**ing-mill** (for rolling metal into various shapes);
∼'**ing-pin,** roller for pastry; ∼'**ing-press,** (1)
copperplate-printer's press with revolving cylinder,
(2) press with rollers for various purposes. **9.** *v.t. & i.*
∼ (**up**), turn over and over upon itself into more
or less cylindrical shape (*hedgehog rolls itself into a ball*
or *rolls up*); *roll up* one's SLEEVES. **10.** form in(to)
cylindrical or spherical shape, or accumulate into
mass, by rolling (*roll a cigarette, a huge snowball, snow
into a ball*); ∼**ed into one,** combined in one person
etc.; ∼'**mop(s),** rolled flavoured pickled herring
fillet; ∼-**neck,** loosely turned-over neck of garment.
11. ∼ **back,** cause to retreat or decrease; ∼ **in,** arrive

in great numbers or quantities; ∼ **on,** put on or apply
by rolling, (colloq. in *imper.,* of a time) come quickly
(*roll on Saturday!*); ∼-*on* n., (1) light elastic corset, (2)
liquid deodorant etc. applied by means of rotating
ball in neck of container; ∼-**on** ∼-**off,** (of ferry) that
vehicles can be driven on and off; ∼ **over,** send
(person) rolling or sprawling; ∼ **up,** (Mil.) drive
flank of (enemy line) back and round so that line is
shortened or surrounded, (colloq.) arrive in vehicle,
(colloq.) appear on the scene, and see sense 9. **12.**
Hence ∼'ABLE *a.* **13.** *n.* rolling motion (*the roll of the
sea, ship*); (Aeron.) complete revolution about longitudinal axis; spell of rolling (*a roll on the grass*); rolling
gait; ∼-**bar,** metal bar strengthening motor-car roof
or acting as protection in open-top car. **14.** quick
continuous-sounding beating of drum; long peal of
thunder, prolonged shout; rhythmic flow of words.
[ME, f. OF *rol(l)er, rouler* f. Rom. **rotulare* f. L *rotulus*
(as prec.)]

rō'ller *n.* **1.** In vbl senses; cylinder of wood, stone,
metal, etc., and of various proportions used alone or
as rotating part of machine for lessening friction,
smoothing ground, pressing, stamping, crushing,
spreading ink or paint, rolling up cloth on, etc.;
∼(**bandage**), long surgical bandage rolled up for
convenience of applying; small cylinder on which
hair is rolled for setting; kind of tumbler-pigeon; long
swelling wave; brilliant-plumaged bird allied to
hoopoe, breed of canary with trilling song, [G (*rollen*
to roll)]. **2.** ∼ **bearing,** bearing like ball-bearing but
with small cylinders instead of balls; ∼-**coaster,**
switchback at fair etc.; *roller*-SKATE[2]; ∼ **towel,** towel
with ends joined, hung on roller. [ME, f. prec. +-ER[1]]

rō'llick *v.i., & n.* **1.** *v.i.* be jovial, indulge in high
spirits, enjoy life boisterously, revel, (esp. in *pres. part.*
as *a.*). **2.** *n.* exuberant gaiety; frolic, spree, escapade.
[19th c., prob. dial.; perh. f. ROMP + FROLIC]

rōly-pō'ly *n. & a.* **1.** ∼ (**pudding**), pudding made of
sheet of paste covered with jam etc., formed into roll,
and boiled or baked; *tumbler toy; (Austral.) bushy
plant that breaks off and is rolled by wind. **2.** *a.* (Usu.
of child) podgy, plump. [prob. formed on ROLL[2]]

Rŏm *n.* (*pl.* ∼'**a**). male gypsy. [Romany, = man,
husband]

Rom. *abbr.* Romans (NT).

rom. *abbr.* roman (type).

Romā'ic *a. & n.* (of) the vernacular language of
modern Greece. [f. Gk *Rhōmaikos* Roman (used esp. of
Eastern Empire) f. *Rhōmē* Rome]

*romai'ne *n.* cos lettuce. [F, fem. of *romain* (see
ROMAN[1])]

rō'maji *n.* Roman alphabet used to transliterate
Japanese. [Jap.]

Rō'man[1] *n.* **1.** citizen, soldier, native, or inhabitant, of
ancient Rome, member of ancient-Roman State;
inhabitant of medieval or modern Rome. **2.** (in *pl.*)
Christians of ancient Rome. **3.** (Print.; *r∼*). roman
type. **4.** = ROMAN CATHOLIC. [ME, f. OF *Romain* n. &
a. f. L *Romanus* (*Roma* Rome); see -AN]

Rō'man[2] *a.* **1.** of ancient Rome or its territory, people,
or (arch.) language; surviving from period of Roman
rule (*Roman road*); ∼ **alphabet,** letters A–Z as in W.
European languages; *Roman candle,* = ∼ **Empire,**
that established by Augustus 27 BC and divided by
Theodosius AD 395 into Western or Latin and
Eastern or Greek Empire, of which the Eastern lasted
till 1453, and the Western, after lapsing in 476, was
revived 800 by Charlemagne and continued to exist
as the **Holy** ∼ **Empire** till 1806; ∼ **holiday,**
enjoyment provided by others' discomfiture, (orig.
code developed by ancient Romans and forming
basis of many modern codes; ∼ **nose** (with high
bridge, aquiline; ∼ **numerals,** letters I = 1, V = 5,
X = 10, L = 50, C = 100, D = 500, M = 1000 used
in writing numbers (opp. *arabic numerals*); *Roman
snail; r∼* **type,** plain upright type used in ordinary
print, opp. *Gothic* or *black letter* and *italic.* **2.** of papal

Rome, esp. = ROMAN CATHOLIC, whence ∿ISH[1] 2 *a*. **3.** of medieval or modern Rome. **4.** of kind ascribed to Romans of early times (*Roman honesty, virtue*). [ME, f. as prec.]

roman-à-clef (rōmahnahklā′) *n.* (*pl.* **-ns-** *pr.* same). novel in which real persons or events appear in disguise. [F, = novel with a key]

Rōman Că′tholĭc *a.* & *n.* (member) of part of Christian Church acknowledging the Pope as its head; hence **Rōman Cathŏ′licĭsm** (3) *n.* [17th c., transl. L (*Ecclesia*) *Romana Catholica* (*et Apostolica*), app. orig. as conciliatory term; see ROMAN[2], CATHOLIC]

romă′nce *n.*, & *v.i.* **1.** *n.* R∿ (**languages**), the languages descended from Latin (French, Spanish, Italian, etc.); (*R∿*) vernacular language of old France mainly developed but distinguished from Latin, corresponding language of Italy, Spain, Provence, etc. **2.** medieval tale usu. in verse of some hero of chivalry [named as being written in Romance]. **3.** prose or rarely verse tale with scene and incidents remote from everyday life, class of literature consisting of such tales; set of facts, episode, suggesting such tales by its strangeness or emotional effect; atmosphere characterizing such tales, mental tendency to be influenced by it, sympathetic imaginativeness. **4.** love affair viewed as resembling tale of romance; love-story. **5.** (an) exaggeration, (a) picturesque falsehood. **6.** (Mus.) short simple or informal piece. **7.** *v.i.* exaggerate or distort the truth, esp. fantastically. [ME, f. OF *romanz, -ans, -ance* f. pop. L **romanice* in the vernacular (opp. *Latine* in Latin) adv. f. L *Romanicus* ROMANIC]

romă′ncer *n.* medieval or other writer of romances; fantastic liar. [ME, f. *romance* v. (f. prec.) + -ER[1]]

Rŏ′manĕs *n.* gypsy language, Romany. [Romany (adv.), f. as ROMANY]

Rōmanĕ′sque (-k) *n.* **1.** = ROMANCE 1. **2.** (Archit.) style of art and architecture prevalent in Romanized Europe between the classical and Gothic periods, esp. in period 1050–1200, with massive vaulting and round arches. [F (*roman* ROMANCE); see -ESQUE]

roman-fleuve (rōmahnflĕr′v) *n.* (*pl.* **-ns-** **-es** *pr* same). novel with leisurely description of lives of members of family etc. [F, = river novel]

Rōmā′nian, Rumā′nian (rōō-), *n.* & *a.* (native, inhabitant, or language) of Romania. [f. *Romania, Rumania* in E. Europe + -AN]

Romă′nic *a.* & *n.* **1.** (of) ROMANCE 1. **2.** *a.* descended from, inheriting civilization etc. of, the ancient Romans; Romance-speaking. [f. L *Romanicus* (as ROMAN[1]; see -IC]

Rŏ′manĭsm *n.* Roman Catholicism; (partiality for) things pertaining to the Romans. [f. ROMAN[1] + -ISM]

Rŏ′manĭst *n.* **1.** (usu. derog.) Roman Catholic. **2.** student of Roman history or law or of Romance languages. [f. mod. L *Romanista* (as ROMAN[1]; see -IST)]

rŏ′manĭz|e, -īs|e (-īz), *v.t.* make Roman or Roman Catholic in character; put into Roman alphabet or roman type; hence ∿A′TION *n.* [f. ROMAN[1] + -IZE, or f. F *romaniser*]

Rōmā′nō- *comb. form.* Roman (and) (*Romano-British*). [f. ROMAN[1] + -O-]

Roma′nsh, Rou-, Ru-, (ro-, rōō-; -ă′-, -ah′-) *n.* & *a.* (of) the Rhaeto-Romanic dialects, esp. that spoken in the Grisons, E. Switzerland. [f. Romansh *Ruman(t)sch, Roman(t)sch* f. med. L *romanice* adv. (as ROMANCE)]

romă′ntic *a.* & *n.* **1.** *a.* characterized by or suggestive of or given to romance, imaginative, emotional, remote from experience, visionary, (*a romantic story, scene, adventure, girl*). **2.** (Of music) subordinating form to theme, imaginative, passionate. **3.** (Of project etc.) fantastic, unpractical, quixotic, dreamy. **4.** (Of literary or artistic method etc.) preferring grandeur or picturesqueness or passion or irregular beauty to finish and proportion, subordinating whole to parts or form to matter, (opp. *classic, classical*); hence ∿IST (2) *n.* **5.** Hence **romă′nt**ICALLY *adv.*, ∿ISM (2, 3) *n.*,

∿IZE (2, 3) *v.i.* & *t.* **6.** *n.* romanticist; (in *pl.*) romantic ideas or talk. [f. *romant* var. of ROMAUNT f. OF (*romanz* ROMANCE) + -IC]

Rŏ′manȳ *n.* & *a.* gypsy; (of) the Indo-European language of the gypsies. [f. Romany *Romani* fem. and pl. of *Romano* a. (ROM)]

romau′nt *n.* (arch.) tale of chivalry etc. [OF (see ROMANTIC)]

Rōme *n.* **1.** Roman Empire. **2.** Roman Catholicism; hence ∿′WARD (-mw-) *adv.* & *a.*, ∿′WARDS (-mw-) *adv.*, **Rŏ′mĬSH**[1] *a.* (usu. derog.). **3. all roads lead to** ∿, the place finally reached does not depend on the route chosen; ∿ **was not built in a day,** achievements take time; **when in** ∿ **do as** ∿ **does,** one should conform to others' practices when visiting them. [OE, f. OF & f. L *Roma* Rome in Italy]

rŏ′mneya (-nǐa) *n.* shrub of genus *Romneya*, akin to poppy. [f. T. *Romney* Robinson, Brit. astronomer d. 1882 + -A]

rŏmp *v.i.*, & *n.* **1.** *v.i.* (Of children etc.) play about together, chase each other, wrestle, etc.; (colloq.) get along, past, etc., without effort, come in or home as easy winner. **2.** *n.* child or (arch.) woman fond of romping, tomboy; spell of romping, boisterous play; hence ∿′Y[2] *a.* [perh. var. of RAMP[2]]

rŏ′mper *n.* (in *sing.* or *pl.*) young child's play-garment usu. covering trunk only. [f. prec. + -ER[1]]

rŏ′ndeau (-dō) *n.* ten-line or thirteen-line poem with only two rhymes throughout and opening words used twice as refrain. [F, earlier *rondel* (see foll.)]

rŏ′ndel *n.* = prec., esp. of specialized form. [ME f. OF (*rond* ROUND[1]; see -LE 2); cf. ROUNDEL]

rŏ′ndō *n.* (*pl.* ∿s). piece of music with leading theme which returns from time to time. [It., f. F RONDEAU]

rŏ′ndure (-dyer) *n.* (literary). round outline or object. [f. F *rondeur* (as ROUND[1]; see -URE)]

rōne *n.* (Sc.) gutter to carry off rain from roof. [19th c.; orig. unkn.]

Rŏ′nĕŏ *n.* (*pl.* ∿s), & *v.t.* **1.** *n.* (P) machine for duplicating documents from stencils. **2.** *v.t.* (r∿). reproduce on Roneo. [20th c.; orig. unkn.]

rŏ′nggĕng (-ŭg-g-) *n.* popular dancing and singing in Malaysia. [Malay]

rō′nin *n.* (Hist.) lordless wandering samurai. [Jap.]

Rŏ′ntgen (rŭ′ntyen) *n.* **1.** ∿ **rays,** X-rays. **2.** (r∿), = ROENTGEN. [f. as ROENTGEN]

röntgenography etc. Var. of ROENTGENOGRAPHY etc.

rōō *n.* (Austral. colloq.) kangaroo. [abbr.]

rōōd *n.* **1.** (arch.) the Cross of Christ (often in oaths, as *by the Rood*). **2.** crucifix, esp. one raised on middle of rood-screen; HOLY *Rood* Day. **3.** ∿**-arch** (between nave and choir); ∿**-beam,** cross-beam, usu. as head of rood-screen, supporting rood; ∿**-cloth** (veiling rood in Lent); ∿**-loft,** gallery on top of rood-screen; ∿**-screen,** wooden or stone carved screen separating nave and choir. **4.** quarter of an acre. [OE *rōd*, = OS *rōda*, cross, de OE *rōd*, = OS *rōda*, OHG *ruota* rod]

roof *n.*, & *v.t.* **1.** *n.* upper covering of house or building or room usu. supported by its walls (**under one** ∿, in same building; **under** person's ∿, in his house, esp. w. ref. to hospitality; **go through, hit,** or **raise the** ∿, (colloq.) become very angry; **a** ∿ **over** one's **head,** somewhere to live); overhead rock in cave, mine, etc.; branches, sky, etc., overhead; top of covered vehicle; ∿ **of the mouth,** palate; ∿**-garden** (on flat roof of building); ∿**-rack,** framework to carry luggage etc. on motor-car roof; ∿**-top,** outer surface of roof; ∿**-tree,** ridge-piece of roof; hence ∿′AGE (1) *n.*, (-)∿ED[2] (-ft), ∿′LESS, *adjs.* **2.** *v.t.* cover (in, over) with roof, be roof of; hence ∿′ING[1] (3) *n.* [OE *hrōf*, = OFris. *hrōf*, MLG *rōf*, MDu. *roof*, ON *hróf* boat-shed]

rōō′fer *n.* In vbl senses: maker or mender of roofs; ||(colloq.) = COLLINS[1]. [f. prec. + -ER[1]]

rōō′inĕk (rō′-) *n.* newcomer, esp. British immigrant, in S. Africa. [Afrik.; = red-neck]

rŏŏk[1] *n.*, & *v.t.* **1.** *n.* black hoarse-voiced European and

Asiatic crow, nesting in colonies; sharper, esp. at dice or cards, person who lives off inexperienced gamblers etc.; ∼**-rifle** (of small bore for rook-shooting); hence ∼'LET, ∼'LING¹, *ns.*, ∼'Y² *a*. 2. *v.t.* win money from at cards etc. esp. by swindling; charge (customer) extortionately. [OE *hrōc*, = MDu. *roec*, MLG *rōk*, OHG *hruoh*, ON *hrókr* f. Gmc *hrokaz, prob. imit.]

rook² *n.* chess piece with battlement-shaped top. [ME, f. OF *roc*(*k*) ult. f. Arab. *rukk*, orig. sense uncert.]

roo'kerў *n.* **1.** (clump of trees with) colony of rooks. **2.** colony of penguins etc. or seals. **3.** (Hist.) crowded cluster of mean houses or tenements.[f. ROOK¹ + -ERY]

roo'kie *n.* (sl.) new recruit in army etc.; *new member of team etc. [corrupt. of *recruit*, after ROOK¹ + -IE]

room (rŏŏm, rŏŏm) *n.* & *v.i.* **1.** *n.* space that is or might be occupied by something, capaciousness or ability to accommodate contents, (*takes up too much room*; *there is plenty of room*; *we have no room here for idlers*; *not room to swing a* CAT¹); space in or on (*house-room*, *shelf-room*); **would rather have his** ∼ **than his company,**wish he was elsewhere; **make** ∼, vacate standing-ground etc. or post etc. for or *for* another, clear a space *for* person or thing by removal of others; ∼ **for,** (arch. *imper.*) make way for (person); in person's ∼, **in the** ∼ **of,** (arch.) instead of, in succession to, as substitute for. **2.** opportunity, scope, *to do* or *for* (*room to deny ourselves*; *no room for dispute*; *leave room for evasion*); **there is** ∼ **for improvement,** things are not as good as they should or could be. **3.** part of building enclosed by walls or partitions, floor, and ceiling; (in *pl.*) set of these occupied by person or family, apartments or lodgings; persons present in a room; **leave the** ∼, (colloq.) go to lavatory; ∼ **and board,** = BOARD¹ and lodging; ∼**-divider,** piece of furniture used to divide room into separate parts; ∼**-mate,** person occupying same room as another; ∼ **service** (of food etc. to hotel guest in his room); ∼ **temperature,** normal temperature of a room, about 20°C. **4.** Hence *∼'E'TTE *n.*, private single compartment in sleeping--car; ∼'FUL 2 *n.*, ∼ED² (-md) *a*. **5.** *v.i.* *have room(s), lodge, board; ∼'**ing-house,** lodging-house; hence ∼'ER¹ *n*. [OE *rūm*, = OS, OHG, ON, Goth. *rūm* f. Gmc *rūmaz spacious]

roo'm|ў *a.* capacious, of ample size to contain; hence ∼ILY² *adv.*, ∼INESS *n*. [f. ROOM + -Y²]

roost¹ *n.* & *v.* **1.** *n.* bird's perching or resting place, esp. hen-house or part of it in which fowls sleep; (fig.) sleeping-accommodation; **come home to** ∼, recoil upon originator; RULE the roost. **2.** *v.i.* (Of bird or person) settle for sleep, be perched or lodged for the night. **3.** *v.t.* provide with sleeping-place. [OE *hrōst*, = MDu. *roest*; cf. OS *hrōst* roof-spars]

roost² *n.* tidal race in Orkneys and Shetlands. [f. ON *rōst*]

***roo'ster** *n.* domestic cock. [f. ROOST¹ + -ER¹]

root¹ *n.* **1.** part of plant normally below earth's surface and serving to attach it to earth and convey nourishment from soil to it, (in *pl.*) such part divided into branches or fibres; corresponding organ of epiphyte, part attaching ivy to its support, permanent underground stock of plant, small plant with root for transplanting; (in *pl.*, fig.) what attaches one emotionally to a place etc.; **pull up by the** ∼s, uproot (lit. or fig.); **put down** ∼s, **strike** or **take** ∼, begin to draw nourishment from soil, (fig.) become established; ∼ **and branch,** thorough(ly), radical(ly); **strike at the** ∼(s) **of,** set about destroying; hence ∼'LET *n*. **2.** (plant, e.g. turnip or carrot, with) edible root. **3.** (Bibl.) scion, offshoot, (*there shall be a root of Jesse*). **4.** embedded part of bodily organ or structure (*root of hair, tongue, tooth, nail*, etc.); part of thing attaching it to a greater or more fundamental whole; (in *pl.*) base (of mountain etc.). **5.** source or origin (*of*; *love of money is the root of all evil*; *has its roots in the distant past*); ∼ **fallacy, idea,** etc., the one from which the rest originated. **6.** basis, dependence, means of continuance or growth, (*has its*

root(*s*) *in selfishness*; *has no root in the nature of things*). **7.** bottom, essential substance or nature, (*get at* or *to the root*(*s*) *of things*); **has the** ∼ **of the matter in him,** is essentially sound, w. ref. to Job 19:28. **8.** (Math.) value of unknown quantity satisfying given equation; ∼ **of,** number or quantity that when multiplied by itself a usu. specified number of times gives (specified number etc.; CUBE root, SQUARE² root); square root; ∼**-mean-square,** square root of arithmetic mean of squares of a set of numbers; ∼ **sign,** = RADICAL *sign*. **9.** (Philol.) ultimate unanalysable ¹element of language, basis (whether itself surviving as a word or not) on which words are made by addition of prefixes or suffixes or by other modification. **10.** (Mus.) fundamental note of chord. **11.** *∼ **beer,** effervescent drink made from extract of roots etc.; ∼**-stock,** (1) rhizome, (2) plant into which graft is inserted, (3) primary form whence offshoots have arisen. **12.** Hence ∼'AGE (1, 3) *n.*, ∼'LESS (esp. fig.), ∼'Y², *adjs.* [OE *rōt* f. ON *rót* f. Scand. *wrōt- cogn. w. WORT and L RADIX]

root² *v.* **1.** *v.t.* & *i.* (cause to) take root or grow roots, fix firmly to the spot, establish, (*some kinds root freely*; *take care to root them firmly*; *fear rooted him to the spot*); (in *p.p.*) firmly established (*her affection was deeply rooted*; *rooted objection to*). **2.** *v.t.* drag or dig up by the roots; ∼ **out,** exterminate. **3.** (poet.) uproot, tear away, *from*. [ME, f. prec.]

root³, **rout**², *v.* **1.** *v.i.* (Of pig etc.) turn up ground with snout, beak, etc., in search of food; rummage (*among, in*). **2.** *(sl.) be active *for* another by giving encouraging applause or support; hence ∼'ER¹ *n*. **3.** *v.t.* turn up (ground) by rooting; gouge *out*; search *out*, hunt *up*. [earlier *wroot* f. OE *wrōtan* & ON *róta*; MLG *wrōten*, MDu. *wroeten*, OHG *ruozzen*]

‖**roo'tle** *v.i.* & *t.* = prec. 1, 3. [f. ROOT³ + -LE 3]

rōpe *n.* & *v.* **1.** *n.* (piece of) stout cord made by twisting together strands of hemp, sisal, flax, cotton, nylon, wire, etc.; *lasso; the ∼, (esp.) halter for hanging a person; **the** ∼s, (1) those enclosing boxing-ring etc. (*on the* ∼s, near defeat), (2) the conditions in some sphere of action (*know, show person, the ropes*); **give** person ∼, ∼ **enough to hang himself, plenty of** ∼, etc., not check him, leave him to bring about his own discomfiture; **on the** ∼, (Mount.) roped together; ∼ **of onions, ova, pearls,** quantity of these strung together; ∼ **of sand,** delusive security. **2.** ∼**-dancer, -dancing,** performer, performing, on tightrope; ∼**-ladder,** two long ropes connected by short cross--pieces as ladder; ∼'**manship,** skill in rope-dancing or rope-climbing; ∼**-moulding** (cut spirally in imitation of rope-strands); ∼**-quoit,** ring of rope used in quoits played on board ship; ∼'**s end,** short piece of rope used to flog (esp. sailor) with; INDIAN *rope-trick*; ∼**-walk,** long piece of ground used for twisting rope; ∼**-walker, -walking,** = *rope-dancer, -dancing*; ∼'**way,** cable railway; ∼**-yard,** rope--making establishment; ∼**-yarn,** (piece of the) material (esp. after unpicking) of which rope-strands consist, (fig.) mere trifle. **3.** Hence **rō'pING¹** (6) *n*. **4.** *v.t.* fasten or secure or catch with rope; (Mount.) connect (party) with rope, attach (person) to rope, (abs.) put on rope; enclose, close *in* or *off*, (space) with rope; ∼ **in,** persuade to take part, decoy; hence **rō'pABLE,** ∼ABLE, (-pa-) *a.*, (esp., Austral. sl.) angry. **5.** *v.i.* (Mount.) climb *down* or *up* using rope. [OE *rāp*, = MDu. *reep*, MLG *rēp*, OHG *reif*, ON *reip*, Goth. *-raip* f. Gmc *raipaz, *raipam]

rō'pey. Var. of foll.

rō'p|ў *a.* **1.** (Of wine, bread, etc.) forming viscous or gelatinous threads; like a rope. **2.** (colloq.) poor in quality. **3.** Hence ∼INESS *n*. [ME, f. ROPE + -Y²]

***rōque** (-k) *n.* croquet played on hard court surrounded by bank. [alt. f. ROQUET]

Rŏ'quefŏrt (-kfōr) *n.* blue cheese orig. made from ewes' milk. [∼ in S. France]

rŏ'quelaure (-kelōr) *n.* (Hist.) man's cloak

reaching to knees. [F (Duc de *Roquelaure*, Fr. commander d. 1738)]

rŏ′quet (-kā, -kĭ) *v.* & *n.* **1.** *v.t.* cause one's ball to strike, (of ball) strike, (another ball at croquet). **2.** *v.i.* strike another ball thus. **3.** *n.* act or fact of roqueting. [app. arbitr. f. CROQUET²; orig. used in same sense]

rŏ-rŏ *a.* roll-on roll-off. [abbr.]

rŏr′qual *n.* whale of genus *Balaenoptera*, with dorsal fin. [F, f. Norw. *røyrkval*, f. OIcel. *reythr* the specific name + *hvalr* WHALE]

Rŏr′schach (-shahk) *n.* (Psych.) ∼ **test** (in which standard ink-blots are successively presented to subject for statement of what they suggest to him). [f. H. ∼, Swiss psychiatrist d. 1922]

||**rŏr′tў** *a.* (sl.) enjoyable (*had a rorty time*); fond of amusement and excitement. [19th c.; orig. unkn.]

rŏ′săce (-z-) *n.* rose-window; rose-shaped ornament or design. [F, f. L *rosaceus* (see foll.)]

rosā′ceous (-zā′shŭs) *a.* (Bot.) of the large family Rosaceae, of which the rose is the type. [f. L *rosaceus* (*rosa* rose; see -ACEOUS)]

rŏsā′niline (-z-; -ēn, -ĭn) *n.* (red dye obtained from) organic base derived from aniline; fuchsine. [f. ROSE¹ + ANILINE]

rosār′ian (-z-) *n.* **1.** rose-fancier. **2.** (RCCh.) member of a Confraternity of the Rosary. [f. L *rosarium* ROSARY + -AN]

rosār′ium (-z-) *n.* rose-garden. [L (as foll.)]

rŏ′sarў (-z-) *n.* **1.** rose-garden; rose-bed. **2.** (RCCh) form of devotion in which five or fifteen decades of Aves are repeated, each decade preceded by Paternoster and followed by Gloria; book containing this; string of 55 or 165 beads for keeping count in this. **3.** similar form of bead-string used in other religions. [ME, f. L *rosarium* rose-garden, neut. (as n.) of *rosarius* (as ROSE¹; see -ARY²)]

Rŏ′scian (-shĭ-) *a.* like Roscius; eminent as an actor. [f. L *Roscianus* (Q. *Roscius* Gallus, Roman actor d. 62 BC; see -AN)]

rŏse¹ (-z) *n.*, *a.*, & *v.t.* **1.** *n.* (prickly bush or shrub bearing) a beautiful and usu. fragrant flower usu. of red or pink or yellow or white colour (BRIER¹-, CABBAGE-, DAMASK, MONTHLY, MOSS-, MUSK-, TEA-, etc., *rose*), whence **rŏ′sery** (3) (-z-) *n.*; flowering plant resembling this (CHRISTMAS *rose*, ROCK¹-*rose*); ∼ **of Jericho**, a resurrection plant (*Anastatica hierochuntica*); ∼ **of May**, white narcissus; ∼ **of Sharon**, St. John's wort, (Bibl.) flowering plant of unknown identity. **2.** ATTAR or *otto of roses*; **no bed of** ∼**s**, difficult task or condition; **gather** (life's) ∼**s**, seek pleasure; **path strewn with** ∼**s**, life of delights; *∼ **without a thorn**, impossible happiness, unalloyed delight. **3.** rose-flower as emblem of innocence, beauty, etc.; **under the** ∼, in confidence, under pledge of secrecy; **Wars of the R**∼**s**, 15th-c. civil wars between Yorkists with white and Lancastrians with red rose as emblem. **4.** representation of the flower in heraldry or decoration (esp. as national emblem of England); **golden** ∼, ornament blessed by Pope on 4th Sunday in Lent and sent as compliment to some RC sovereign, city, etc. **5.** rose-shaped design, e.g. on compass card or on sound-hole of lute etc. **6.** rosette worn on shoe or clerical hat. **7.** sprinkling-nozzle of watering-can or hose. **8.** = *rose diamond*; = *rose-window*. **9.** light crimson colour, pink; (usu. in *pl.*) rosy complexion (*roses in her cheeks*). **10** ∼-**apple**, tropical tree of genus *Eugenia*, cultivated for foliage and fragrant fruit, its fruit; ∼-**bay**, oleander, rhododendron, or a willow-herb (*Epilobium angustifolium*); ∼-**bowl** (for displaying cut roses); ∼-**bud**, bud of rose, thing resembling it (*rosebud mouth*), pretty girl; ∼-**bush**, rose plant; ∼-**chafer**, green or copper-coloured beetle frequenting roses; ∼-**colour**, rosy red, pink; ∼-**coloured**, rosy, (fig.) optimistic, sanguine, cheerful, (*takes rose-coloured views*; *see things through rose-coloured spectacles*); ∼ **comb**, flat fleshy comb of fowl; ∼-**cut**, cut as a ∼ **diamond** (hemi-

spherical with curved part in triangular facets); ∼-**engine**, appendage to lathe for engraving curved patterns; ∼-**fish**, bright red food-fish of northern coasts; ∼-**gall**, excrescence of dog-rose etc. made by insect; ∼ **geranium**, pink-flowered species of *Pelargonium*; rose-HIP²; ∼-**leaf**, leaf or usu. petal of rose (*crumpled* ∼-*leaf*, slight vexation alloying general felicity); ∼-**lipped**, with rosy lips; ∼ **madder**, pale pink pigment; ∼-**mallow**, hibiscus or hollyhock; ∼(-**head**) **nail** (with head shaped like rose diamond); ∼ **noble**, 15th–16th c. English gold coin of varying value stamped with rose; ∼-**pink**, = *rose-colour(ed)* (lit. or fig.); ∼-**point**, point lace with design of roses; ∼-**red** *a.* & *n.*, red as (of) a rose; ∼-**root**, plant (esp. *Sedum rosea*) with root smelling like rose when dried or bruised; ∼-**tree**, rose plant, esp. standard rose; ∼-**water**, perfume made from roses, (fig.) compliments, gentle handling, etc.; ∼-**window** (circular, usu. with roselike or spokelike tracery); ∼′**wood**, valuable close-grained cabinet wood of one of various kinds named from their fragrance. **11.** Hence ∼ LESS, ∼ LIKE, (-zl-) *adjs.* **12.** *a.* coloured like a pale red rose, of warm pink. **13.** *v.t.* (esp. in *p.p.*) make (face, snow-slope, etc.) rosy. [ME f. OE *rōse*, MDu. *rōse*, OHG *rōsa*, ON *rása*, & f OF *rose*, f. L *rosa*]

rose². See RISE¹.

rosé² (rōzā′) *n.* light pink wine, coloured by only brief contact with grape-skins. [F, = pink]

rŏ′séate (-z-) *a.* rose-coloured (lit. or fig.); ∼ **spoonbill, tern**, (with partly pink plumage); hence ∼LY² (-tlĭ) *adv.* [f. L *roseus* (as ROSE¹) rosy + -ATE²]

rosĕ′lla (-z-) *n.* brightly coloured Austral. parakeet of genus *Platycercus*. [corrupt. of *Rosehill*, NSW, where first found]

rŏ′semarў (-zm-) *n.* evergreen fragrant shrub with leaves used as culinary herb, in perfumery, etc., and taken as emblem of remembrance. [ME, earlier *rosmarine* f. OF *rosmarin* or MDu. *rosemarine* or f. L *ros marinus* (*ros* dew, *marinus* MARINE), w. assim. to ROSE¹ and *Mary* name of the Virgin)]

rosĕ′ola (-z-) *n.* rosy rash in measles etc.; German measles; mild febrile disease of infants; hence ∼AR¹, ∼ous, *adjs.* [mod. var. of RUBEOLA f. L *roseus* ROSE¹-coloured]

rosery. See ROSE¹ 1.

rosĕ′tt|e (-z-) *n.* rose-shaped ornament for dress or harness made of ribbons, leather strips, etc., esp. as supporter's badge or (symbol of) award; (Archit.) (1) carved or moulded conventional rose on wall etc., (2) rose-window; (Biol.) roselike cluster of parts, markings resembling rose; = ROSE¹ *diamond*; roselike object or symbol or arrangement of parts; hence ∼ED² *a.* [F, dim. of *rose* ROSE¹; see -ETTE]

Rŏsh Hasha′nah (-ah′na) *n.* Jewish New Year. [Heb., = beginning of the year]

Rŏsicru′cian (-zĭkrōō′shan) *n.* & *a.* (member) of 17th–18th-c. society devoted to occult lore (said to have been founded 1484 by Christian Rosenkreuz); (member) of later organization deriving from this; hence ∼ISM (3) *n.* [f. mod. L *rosa crucis* (or *crux*), as Latinization of G *Rosenkreuz*, + -IAN]

rŏ′sin (-z-) *n.*, & *v.t.* **1.** *n.* resin: solid residue after distillation of oil of turpentine from crude turpentine); hence ∼Y² *a.* **2.** *v.t.* smear, seal up, rub (esp. bow of violin etc.), with rosin. [ME, alt. f. RESIN]

Rŏsină′ntè (-z-) *n.* worn-out horse. [f. Sp. *Rocinante* (*rocin* worn-out horse), name of Don Quixote's horse]

rosō′liŏ (-z-) *n.* (*pl.* ∼**s**). sweet cordial of spirits, sugar, and flavouring. [It., f. mod. L *ros solis* sundew]

||**RoSPA** (rŏ′spa) *abbr.* Royal Society for the Prevention of Accidents.

rŏ′ster *n.*, & *v.t.* **1.** *n.* list or plan showing turns of duty or leave for individuals or companies esp. of a military force. **2.** *v.t.* place on roster. [f. Du. *rooster* list, orig. gridiron (*roosten* ROAST), w. ref. to parallel lines]

rŏ′stral *a.* (Of column etc.) adorned with beaks actual or sculptured etc. of ancient war-galleys; (Zool.

etc.) of or on the rostrum. [f. *rostr*ATE² or f. ROSTRUM+-AL]

rŏstrā′tĕd *a.* (Of column etc.) = prec.; (Zool. etc.) having, or ending in, a rostrum. [f. L *rostratus* (as foll.; see -ATE²)+-ED¹]

rŏ′str|um *n.* (*pl.* ~a *or* ~ums). **1.** platform for public speaking (orig. *rostra* in Roman forum adorned with beaks of captured galleys) or for orchestral conductor; pulpit, office, etc., that enables one to be heard by the public. **2.** (Rom. Ant.) beak of war-galley. **3.** (Zool. & Bot.) beak, stiff snout, beaklike part, esp. of insect or arachnid; hence ~ATE², ~i′FEROUS, ~i′FORM, *adjs.* [L, = beak (*rodere ros-* gnaw)]

rŏ′sў (-zĭ) *a.* coloured like a pink or red rose (esp. of complexion as indicating health, of blush, wine, sky, light, etc.), (fig.) = ROSE¹-*coloured*; (arch.) smelling like a rose, made of or covered or strewn with roses; ~ **cross,** supposed emblem of Rosicrucians; ~ **-fingered** (Homeric epithet of dawn etc.); hence **rŏ′sǏLY²** *adv.,* **rŏ′sǏNESS** *n.,* (-z-). [ME, f. ROSE¹+-Y²]

rŏt¹ *n.* & *int.* **1.** *n.* decay, putrefaction, rottenness; DRY¹ *rot*; hence *rot*-PROOF² *a.,* & *v.t.* **2.** (**the**) ~, virulent liver-disease of sheep. **3.** (sl.) nonsense, absurd statement or argument or proposal, foolish course, undesirable state of things, (*don't talk rot; it is perfect rot to trust him*). **4.** sudden series of (freq. unaccountable) failures (*a rot set in; must try to stop the rot*). **5.** *int.* expr. incredulity or ridicule. [ME, perh. f. Scand.; cf. Icel., Norw. *rot*]

rŏt² *v.* (**-tt-**). **1.** *v.i.* undergo natural decomposition, decay, putrefy, (~ **off,** drop from stem etc. through rottenness); (fig., of society, institutions, etc.) gradually waste away from lack of vigour or use, (of prisoner) waste away (*left to rot in gaol*). **2.** *v.t.* cause to rot, make rotten; ||(sl.) chaff, banter, tease. **3.** ~-**gut** *a.* & *n.,* (liquor) injurious to stomach etc. [OE *rotian,* = MDu. *roten,* MLG *röten,* OS *roton,* OHG *rōzzēn;* cf. RET, ROTTEN]

rŏ′ta *n.* **1.** list of persons acting, or duties to be done, in rotation; roster. **2.** (RC Ch.; **R**~). supreme ecclesiastical and secular court. [L, = wheel]

rŏ′tarў *a.* & *n.* **1.** *a.* acting by rotation (*rotary drill, pump*). **2.** *n.* rotary machine; *traffic roundabout. **3.** *a.* & *n.* (**the**) **R**~, **R**~ **International,** world-wide society of business men with many branches (**R**~ **Clubs**) for international service to humanity, orig. named from members entertaining in rotation; hence **Rotār′IAN** *a.* & *n.,* (member) of Rotary. [f. med. L *rotarius* (as prec.; see -ARY¹)]

rŏ′tate¹ *a.* (Bot.) wheel-shaped. [f. as ROTA+ -ATE²]

rŏtā′t|e² *v.i.* & *t.* move round axis or centre, revolve; arrange (esp. crops) or take in rotation; hence ~ABLE, **rŏ′tative, rŏ′tat**ORY, *adjs.* [f. L *rotare* (*rota* wheel)+-ATE³]

rŏtā′tion *n.* rotating or being rotated; recurrence, recurrent series or period, regular succession of various members of a group in office etc., (*take office in* or *by rotation*); ~ **of crops,** growing of different crops in regular order to avoid exhausting soil; hence ~AL *a.* [f. L *rotatio* (as prec.; see -ATION)]

rŏtā′tor *n.* (Anat.) muscle that rotates a limb etc.; revolving apparatus or part. [L (as ROTATE²; see -OR)]

Rŏ′tavātor *n.* (P) machine with rotating blade to turn soil over; hence [as back-form.] **rŏ′tav**ATE³ *v.t.,* treat with Rotavator. [f. ROTARY+CULTIVATOR]

***ROTC** *abbr.* Reserve Officers' Training Corps.

rŏtch(e) *n.* the little AUK. [later form of 17th-c. Du., Fris. *rotge,* of unkn. orig.]

rŏte *n.* **by** ~, by mere habituation, as knowledge got by repetition, from unintelligent memory. [ME, of unkn. orig.]

rŏ′tifer *n.* minute aquatic animal of phylum Rotifera, with rotatory organs used in swimming. [f. mod. L *rotiferus* f. L *rota* wheel+-I-+-*fer* bearing]

roti′sserie *n.* establishment where roast meat is sold;

cooking-device for roasting meat on revolving spit. [f. F *rôtisserie* (as ROAST; see -ERY)]

rŏtogravūr′e *n.* photogravure printed on rotary machine. [f. ROTARY+PHOTOGRAVURE]

rŏ′tor *n.* rotary part of machine; horizontally--rotating vane of helicopter. [irreg. for ROTATOR]

rŏ′tten *a.* (~**er,** ~**est**). **1.** decomposed or decomposing, putrid, perishing from decay, falling to pieces or friable or easily breakable or tearable from age or use. **2.** (Of sheep) affected with the rot. **3.** morally, socially, or politically corrupt, effete; ||*rotten* BOROUGH; **something is** ~ **in the state of Denmark,** (Shak. *Hamlet* I. iv. 90) things are unsatisfactory. **4.** inefficient, worthless; (sl., of state of things, plan, etc.) disagreeable, regrettable, ill--advised, disagreeably ill (*I feel rotten today*). **5.** ~- **stone,** decomposed siliceous limestone used as polishing-powder. **6.** Hence ~LY² *adv.,* ~NESS (-n-n-) *n.* [ME, f. ON *rotinn,* cogn. w. ROT², RET]

rŏ′tter *n.* (sl.) one who is objectionable on moral or other grounds; useless or inefficient or undesirable person. [f. ROT²+-ER¹]

Rŏ′ttweiler (-wī-) *n.* dog of tall black breed. [G (*Rottweil* in SW Germany)]

rotū′nd (rō-, rŏ-) *a.* circular, round; (of mouth) rounded in speaking etc., (of speech, literary style, etc.) as from rotund mouth, sonorous, grandiloquent; (of person) plump, podgy; hence or cogn. ~ITY *n.,* ~LY² *adv.* [f. L *rotundus* (*rotare* ROTATE²)]

rotū′nda *n.* building with circular ground-plan, esp. one with dome; circular hall or room. [earlier *rotonda,* f. It. *rotonda* (*camera*) round (chamber), fem. of *rotondo* round f. as prec.]

roturier (rŏtūr′ĭā) *n.* plebeian. [F (*roture* newly broken ground, plebeian tenure, f. med. L *ruptura;* see RUPTURE, -IER)]

rou′ble, ru′ble, (rōō′-) *n.* Russian monetary unit. [F, f. Russ. *rubl'*]

roucou′ (rōōkōō′) *n.* annatto. [f. F *ro(u)cou* f. Tupi *rucu, urucú*]

roué (rōō′ā) *n.* (esp. elderly) debauchee, rake. [F, p.p. of *rouer* break on wheel, = one deserving this]

rouge (rōōzh) *a., n.,* & *v.* **1.** *a.* **R**~ **Croix** (krwah), **R**~ **Dragon,** two pursuivants of English College of Arms; ~**-et-noir** (-ānwâr′), gambling game with red and black marks on table for placing of stakes; ~**-royal marble** (reddish Belgian kind). **2.** *n.* fine red substance made orig. from safflower and used for colouring cheeks and lips; powdered ferric oxide etc. as polishing agent for metal etc.; JEWELLER'S *rouge.* **3.** *v.t.* & *i.* colour, adorn oneself, with rouge. [F, = red, f. L *rubeus* cogn. w. RED]

rough (rŭf) *a., adv., n.,* & *v.t.* **1.** *a.* having uneven or irregular surface, not smooth or level or polished, diversified or broken by prominences, hairy, shaggy, coarse in texture, rugged, (*rough skin, hands, paper, bark, road, cloth, country*); ~ **edges,** edges of original sheets in book left untrimmed; ~ **rice,** = PADDY². **2.** not mild or quiet or gentle, unrestrained, violent, stormy, boisterous, disorderly, riotous, inconsiderate, harsh, unfeeling, unpleasant, severe, grating, taxing, astringent, (*rough manners, soldier, play; rough water, sea, weather, wind; rough words; rough element of the population, quarter of the town; rough usage, handling; rough remedies; rough baritone voice*); (of wine etc.) sharp or harsh in taste; *rough* BREATHING; *rough* DEAL²; ~ **luck,** worse than one deserves; *rough* MUSIC; ~ **passage,** crossing over rough sea (lit. or fig.); ~ **stuff,** (sl.) boisterous or violent behaviour; ~ **tongue,** habit of rudeness in speech (~ **edge** or **side of** one's **tongue,** severe or harsh words); ~ **work,** violence, task requiring use of force, (and in sense 3). **3.** deficient in finish or elaboration or delicacy, incomplete, rudimentary, entirely or partly unwrought, merely passable, inexact, approximate, preliminary, (*rough nursing, style, welcome, kindness, accommodation, sketch; rough state, attempt, makeshift, circle; rough draft, estimate, translation*);

~ **coat,** first coat of plaster applied; ~ **copy,** (1) original draft, (2) copy of picture etc. showing only essential features; *rough* DIAMOND; ||~ **grazing,** pasture in natural state; ~ **justice,** treatment approximating to fairness; ~ **shooting** (without help of beaters etc.). **4.** ~**-and-ready,** not elaborate, just good enough, not over-particular, roughly efficient or effective; ~**-and-tumble,** (*a.*) irregular, scrambling, disorderly, regardless of procedure-rules, (*n.*) haphazard fight, scuffle; ~'**cast,** (*a.*, of wall etc.) coated with mixture of lime and gravel, (of plan etc.) imperfectly elaborated, (*n.*) plaster of lime and gravel for walls, (*v.t.*) coat (wall) with roughcast, prepare (plan, essay, etc.) in outline; ~**-dry,** dry (clothes) but not iron them etc.; ~**-footed,** (of bird) having feathered feet; ~**-grind,** give preliminary grinding to (edged tool etc.); ~**-hew,** shape out roughly, give crude form to, (in *p.p.*) uncouth, unrefined; ~ **house,** (sl.) disturbance, row, horseplay; ~**-house,** (*v.t.*) handle (person) roughly, (*v.i.*) make a disturbance, act violently; ~**-legged,** (of horse or bird) having hairy or feathered legs; ~'**neck,** (colloq.) driller on oil rig, *(sl.) a rowdy; ~**-rider,** horse-breaker, man who can ride unbroken horses, (Mil.) irregular cavalryman; ~'**shod,** (of horse) having shoes with the nail-heads projecting (*ride* ~*shod over,* treat inconsiderately or arrogantly); *rough-spoken* (SEE SPEAK), ~**-wrought,** with the earlier processes of preparation done. **5.** Hence ~'EN⁶ *v.t. & i.,* ~'ISH¹ 2 *a.,* ~'LY² *adv.* (roughly SPEAKING²), ~'NESS *n.* **6.** *adv.* in rough manner (*land should be ploughed rough; play rough; see also sense* 4); **sleep** ~ (not in proper bed etc., esp. out of doors). **7.** *n.* rough ground (*over rough and smooth*); (Golf) rough ground off the fairway between tee and green; spike etc. used to rough a horse; hard part of life, piece of hardship, (*take the rough with the smooth*); rowdy, hooligan; *the* unfinished or natural state, *the* general way, (*shape it from the rough; have seen it only in* (*the*) *rough; is true in the rough*). **8.** *v.t.* turn *up* (feathers, hair, etc.) by rubbing against the grain (~ person **up the wrong way,** irritate him), secure (horse or its shoes) against slipping by insertion of spikes or projecting nails in shoes; break in (horse); shape or plan *out* roughly; sketch in roughly; give first shaping to (gem, lens, etc.); ~ **it,** do without ordinary conveniences of life; ~ **up,** (sl.) treat (person) with violence, attack violently. [OE *rūh,* = MLG, MDu. *rū*(*ch*), OHG *rūh* f. WG *~rūh*(*w*)*a*]

rou′ghage (rŭ′fij) *n.* coarse fodder; indigestible material eaten in food to stimulate action of intestines. [f. prec. +-AGE]

roula′de (rōōlah′d) *n.* florid passage of runs etc. in solo vocal music, usu. sung to one syllable. [F (*rouler* ROLL², see -ADE)]

rouleau′ (rōōlō′) *n.* (*pl.* ~**x** or ~**s,** *pr.* -z). cylindrical packet of coins; coil or roll, esp. as trimming. [F (*rôle* ROLL¹)]

roulĕ′tt|e (rōō-) *n.* **1.** gambling game on table with revolving compartmented wheel in which ball rolls randomly; RUSSIAN *roulette.* **2.** (Math.) curve generated by point on curve rolling on another. **3.** revolving toothed wheel used in engraving; similar wheel for making slits between postage stamps in sheet, whence ~ED¹ *a.,* divided thus. [F, dim. of *rouelle* f. LL *rotella* dim. of L *rota* wheel]

Roumansh. See ROMANSH.

rou′ncy̆ *n.* (arch.) riding-horse. [ME, f. OF *ronci*(*n*), med. L *roncinus, runcinus,* of unkn. orig.]

round¹ *a.* **1.** spherical or circular or cylindrical or approaching these forms, presenting convex or circular outline or surface, (*the round world; round limbs, post, tower; round hole, mat, shield, table*); (of face) as broad as long; (of jacket) cut level and short, without skirts; (of arch) semicircular, not pointed; (of cheeks) plump, not hollow; (Phonet., of vowel) pronounced with rounded lips. **2.** done with or involving circular motion. **3.** entire, continuous, all together, not broken or defective or scanty, sound, smooth, plain, genuine, candid, outspoken, (~ **dozen, score,** etc., that and no less, so many together; ~ **unvarnished tale,** the plain truth); (of sum of money) considerable; (of style) flowing; (of voice) not harsh; (of statement etc.) categorical, unmistakable. **4.** ~**-arm,** (Cricket, of bowling) with arm swung horizontally; ~ **brackets,** of ( ) shape; ~ **dance,** (1) dance in which couples circulate round ballroom, (2) dance in which participants form ring; ~ **figure**(**s**), (1) round number, (2) figure given as estimate; ~ **game** (for any number of players, with no teams or partners); ~ **hand,** writing with bold curves; ~**-hand,** = *round-arm;* R~'**head,** member of Parliament party in English Civil War [from custom of wearing hair close-cut]; ~**-house,** (Hist.) lock-up or place of detention, (Naut.) cabin or set of cabins on after part of quarterdeck esp. in sailing-ship, locomotive repair-shed, *blow given with wide swing of arm; ~ **number,** number stated without odd units etc.; *round peg in square* HOLE¹; ~ **robin,** (1) petition esp. with signatures written in circle to conceal order of writing, (2) *tournament in which each competitor plays against every other; ~ **shot,** (Hist.) spherical ball for smooth-bore cannon; ~**-shouldered,** with shoulders bent forward so that back is convex; R~ **Table** (at which King Arthur and his knights sat so that none might have precedence); ~**-table conference** (at which all present are on equal footing); ~**-top,** (orig. circular) platform round mast-head; ~ **towel,** roller towel; ~ **trip,** circular tour or trip, *esp. by same route out and back; ~ **turn,** (Naut.) single turn of rope round post etc.; ~'**worm** (of rounded form, opp. *flatworm*). **5.** Hence ~'ISH 2 *a.,* ~'NESS *n.* [ME, f. OF *ro*(*u*)*nd-* st. of *ro*(*o*)*nt,* reont f. Rom. *retundus* f. L *rotundus* ROTUND]

round² *n.* **1.** round object (**this earthly** ~, the earth); rung of ladder; sandwich made from whole slices of bread; ~ **of beef,** thick disc from haunch as joint; ~ **of bread** or **toast,** slice cut across loaf. **2.** solid form of sculpture etc. (opp. *relief*); **in the** ~, (fig.) with all the features etc. fully shown, all things considered, (Theatr.) with audience all round stage. **3.** circumference, bounds, extent, *of* (*in all the round of Nature*). **4.** revolving motion, circular or circuitous or recurring course, circuit, cycle, series, (*the earth in its daily* or *yearly round; a continuous round of pleasure*); group of houses etc. to which goods are regularly delivered; **the daily** ~, ordinary occupations of the day; **make** or **go** one's ~**s,** take customary route for inspection etc.; **make the** ~ **of,** go round; **go the** ~(**s**), (of news etc.) be passed on from person to person. **5.** (Mil., in *pl.*) watch that goes round inspecting sentries, circuit it makes. **6.** (Golf). playing of all holes in course once. **7.** (Mus.) canon for three or more voices singing at same pitch or in octaves. **8.** allowance of something distributed or measured out esp. to each member of a group, (ammunition for) one shot from (each) gun, sequence of actions by each member of a group in turn, one of set or series, one spell of play etc., one stage in competition, (*serve out a round of drinks; fired several rounds at us; round after round of cheers; a fight of ten rounds; knocked out in the third round; the winners in the first round are paired for the second*); (Archery) fixed number of arrows shot from fixed distance. **9.** ~'**sman** (-z-), ||tradesman's employee going round for orders and esp. with goods, *police officer in charge of patrol. [ME, f. prec.]

round³ *adv. & prep.* **1.** *adv.* with more or less circular motion, with return to starting-point after such motion, with rotation, with change to opposite position, (lit. or fig.; *sun goes, summer comes, round; brings us round to winter;* GET¹ *round to; the* CLOCK¹ *round, all the year round; wheels go round; he turned* or *looked round when I shouted; soon won him round*); measuring (specified distance) in girth. **2.** to or at or affecting all or many points of a circumference or area or members of a

round company etc., in every direction from a centre or within a radius, (*tea was served* or *handed round*; *pass* or *send the* HAT *round*; *head goes round with giddiness*; *room hung round with portraits*; *spread destruction round*; *all the neighbours for a mile round*); ALL *round*; GET¹ *round*; SHOW¹ *round*. **3.** by circuitous way (*will you jump over or go round?*; *go a long way round*); **ask** person ∼ (out of his house into one's own); BRING *round*; COME *round*; *order car* etc. ∼, from garage to front door etc. **4.** ∼ **and** ∼, several times round; ∼ **about**, in a ring (about), all round, on all sides (of), with change to opposite position, circuitously, approximately (*it will cost round about £10*); ∼'**about**, (*n.*) circuitous way, ‖road junction where all traffic has to follow a curved course in one direction round a central area, piece of circumlocution, ‖merry-go-round (‖*lose on the swings what you make on the roundabouts*, end without net profit or loss), (*a.*) circuitous, circumlocutory, plump or stout. **5.** *prep.* so as to encircle or enclose (*tour round the world*; *has a blanket round her*; *round the* CLOCK¹). **6.** with successive visits to, at or to points on the circumference of, (*hawks them round the cafés*; *station them round the field*; *seated round the table*). **7.** in various directions from or with regard to (*diffuses cheerfulness round her*; *the fields round Oxford*; *shells bursting round me*). **8.** having as axis of revolution or central point (*turns round its centre of gravity*; *write book round an event*); so as to come close from various sides but not into contact (lit. or fig.; *argue round and round a matter*). **9.** so as to double or pass in curved course, having thus passed, in the position that would result from thus passing, (*go*, *be*, *find* person, *round the corner*); ∼ **and** ∼, several times round. [ME, f. ROUND¹, as prep. perh. f. AROUND]

round⁴ *v.* **1.** *v.t. & i.* give or assume round shape (*rounded eyes*, *mouth*); pronounce (vowel) with rounded lips; crop (ears of dog etc.); make (angle) less sharp; make (number etc.) round by omitting units etc. (∼ **down**, **up**, do so by subtracting, adding, small amount). **2.** *v.t.* ∼ (**off** or **out**), bring to complete or symmetrical or well-ordered state. **3.** gather *up* (cattle, or transf.) by riding round, gather *up* (stragglers, criminals, etc.); hence ∼-**up** *n.* (lit., or fig. summary of events etc.). **4.** pass round, double, (cape, corner, etc.). **5.** ∼ **off**, (1) = sense 2, (2) blunt the angles of; ∼ **on**, make unexpected retort to (friend etc.), inform against. [f. ROUND¹; in ME perh. after OF *rondir*]

round⁵ *v.i. & t.* (arch.) whisper (*rounded him in the ear*). [OE *rūnian* (= OS *rūnon*, OHG *rūnēn*) f. *rūn* RUNE; *-d* as in SOUND²]

rou'ndel *n.* small disc, esp. decorative medallion etc.; circular identifying mark on aircraft etc.; rondeau or rondel. [ME, f. OF *rondel(le)* (as ROUND¹; see -LE 2)]

rou'ndelay *n.* short simple song with refrain; (arch.) bird's song. [f. F *rondelet* (as RONDEL; see -ET¹), w. ASSIM. TO LAY¹ or *virelay*]

rou'nder *n.* In vbl senses; complete run of player through all the bases arranged in a round as unit of scoring in rounders; ‖(in *pl.*, treated as *sing.*) game thus played with bat and ball between two sides. [f. ROUND¹·² + -ER¹]

rou'ndly *adv.* in thoroughgoing manner (*go roundly to work*); bluntly, with plain speech, without qualification, severely, (*told them roundly that he would not*; *roundly asserts that it is true*; *was roundly abused*); in circular way (*swells out roundly*). [f. ROUND¹ + -LY²]

roup¹ *v.t., & n.* (Sc. & N. Engl.) (sell by) auction. [ME 'to shout', of Scand. orig.; cf. Icel. *raupa* boast]

roup² (roop) *n.* infectious poultry-disease, esp. advanced coryza, or fowl pox; hence ∼'Y² *a.* [16th c.; orig. unkn.]

rouse¹ (-z) *n.* (arch.) draught of liquor, bumper, toast, revel, drinking-bout; **take** one's ∼, carouse; **give a** ∼, propose or drink toast. [prob. for *carouse*, perh. f. wrong division of *drink carouse*]

rouse² (-z) *v.* **1.** *v.t.* startle (game) from lair or cover. **2.** bring out of sleep, stir up or *up*, startle from or *from* or *out of* sleep or inactivity or confidence or carelessness (*to* action, *to* energy, *to* do, etc.); ∼ one**self**, overcome one's indolence. **3.** provoke temper of, inflame with passion, (*is terrible when roused*). **4.** evoke (feelings). **5.** stir (liquid, esp. beer while brewing). **6.** (Naut.) haul vigorously *in*, *out*, *up*. **7.** *v.i.* ∼ (**up**), cease to sleep, become active. [orig. as hawking and hunting term, so prob. f. AF; orig. unkn.]

rou'seabout (-za-) *n.* = ROUSTABOUT 2. [f. prec. + ABOUT]

rou'sing (-z-) *a.* exciting, stirring, (*a rousing cheer*, *sermon*, *song*); (of fire) blazing strongly. [f. ROUSE² + -ING²]

Rousseau'|ism (rōōsō'-) *n.* (adherence to) views of Rousseau regarding supremacy of the popular will and degrading effects of civilization; so ∼IST (2) *n.* J. J. *Rousseau*, Fr. philosopher d. 1778 + -ISM]

rou'stabout *n.* **1.** *dock labourer, deck hand; labourer on oil rig; *unskilled labourer. **2.** (Austral.) odd-job man on farm etc. [f. dial. and US *roust* rout out + ABOUT]

rout¹ *n., & v.t.* **1.** *n.* assemblage or company esp. of revellers or rioters, (Law) assemblage of three or more persons proceeding to unlawful act; riot, tumult, disturbance, clamour, fuss. **2.** disorderly retreat of defeated army or troops (**put to** ∼, utterly defeat). **3.** (arch.) ‖large evening party or reception (∼-**seat**, light bench hired for use at this). **4.** *v.t.* put to rout. [ME, f. AF *rute*, OF *route* f. Rom. *rupta* (*turba*) broken (company); see ROUTE]

rout² *v.i. & t.* = ROOT³; force or fetch *out* (*of bed* or from bed or house or hiding-place); hence ∼'ER¹ *n.*, type of plane with two handles used to cut grooves etc. [var. of ROOT³]

route (rōōt, Mil. freq. rowt) *n., & v.t.* (*part.* ∼**ing** *pr.* -tī-). **1.** *n.* course or way taken (esp. regularly) in getting from starting-point to destination; (Mil., arch.) marching orders; *delivery etc. round; *∼ **man**, roundsman; ∼ **march**, training march of battalion etc.; EN ROUTE. **2.** *v.t.* send, forward, direct to be sent, by a certain route. [ME, f. OF *r(o)ute* road f. Rom. *rupta* (*via*) fem. p.p. (as n.) of L *rumpere* break]

routi'n|e (rōōtē'n) *n. & a.* **1.** *n.* regular course of procedure, unvarying performance of certain acts; (Theatr.) set sequence in dance or other performance; (Computers) sequence of instructions for performing a task; hence ∼ISM (3), ∼IST (2), *ns.* **2.** *a.* performed by rule (*routine duties* etc.); hence ∼eLY² (-nli) *adv.* [F (as prec.; see -INE⁴)]

roux (rōō) *n.* (*pl.* same. mixture of fat (esp. butter) and flour used in making sauces etc. [F, = browned (butter); see RUSSET]

rōv|e¹ *v. & n.* **1.** *v.i.* wander without settled destination, roam, ramble; (of eyes) look in changing directions (∼**ing eye**, person's tendency to ogle); ∼**ing commission**, authority given to person(s) conducting an inquiry to travel as may be necessary. **2.** *v.t.* wander over or through. **3.** *n.* act of roving (*on the rove*); ∼-**beetle**, long-bodied beetle of family Staphylinidae. [ME, orig. term in archery = shoot at casual mark with range not determined, perh. f. dial. *rave* stray, prob. of Scand. orig.]

rōve² *n., & v.t.* **1.** *n.* sliver of cotton, wool, etc., drawn out and slightly twisted. **2.** *v.t.* form into roves. [18th c.; orig. unkn.]

rōve³ *n.* small metal plate or ring for rivet to pass through and be clenched over. [f. ON *ró*, w. excrescent *v*]

rōve⁴. See REEVE³.

rō'ver¹ *n.* In vbl senses. [f. ROVE² + -ER¹]

rō'ver² *n.* **1.** archery mark chosen at undetermined range; mark for long-distance shooting. **2.** wanderer; (Croquet) (player of) ball that has passed all hoops but not pegged out; (*R~*) senior Scout (now *Venture Scout*). [ME, f. ROVE[1] + -ER[1]]

rō'ver² *n.* sea robber, pirate. [ME, f. MLG, MDu. *rōver* (*rōven* rob cogn. w. REAVE; SEE -ER[1])]

row¹ (rō) *n.* **1.** number of persons or things in a more or less straight line; **in a ~**, so arranged, (colloq.) in succession (*two Sundays in a row*). **2.** ~ (**of houses**), street with houses along one or each side; **~-house*, terrace-house. **3.** line of seats across theatre etc. (*in the front, third*, etc., *row*); row of plants in garden (**hard ~ to hoe**, difficult task); horizontal line of entries in table etc. [ME *raw, row,* f. OE **rāw, rǣw* f. Gmc **rai(g)wa*]

row² (rō) *v. & n.* **1.** *v.i. & t.* propel boat, propel (boat), convey (passenger) in boat, with oars etc. (~ **over**, = WALK¹ *over* (2) in boat-race; w. cogn. obj., *row a race, a few strokes, a fast stroke, 30 to the minute*); row race with; ~ **down**, overtake in rowing, esp. bumping, race; ~ **out**, exhaust by rowing (*the crew were completely rowed out at the finish*); *~-boat*, ||*~'ing-boat*, boat propelled by oars; *~'ing-machine*, device for exercising muscles used in rowing; hence ~*'ER¹ n.* **2.** *n.* spell of rowing; excursion in rowing-boat. [OE *rōwan,* = MLG *rojen,* ON *róa;* cogn. w. RUDDER, L *remus* oar]

row² *n. & v.* (colloq.) **1.** *n.* disturbance, commotion, noise, dispute, **make, kick up, a ~**, (1) raise noise, (2) make vigorous protest. **2.** shindy, free fight, (*town-and-gown row*). **3.** condition of being reprimanded (*shall get into a row*). **4.** *v.t.* reprimand. **5.** *v.i.* make, engage in, row. [18th-c. sl., of unkn. orig.]

row'an (row'-, rō'-) *n.* (Sc. & N. Engl.) *~(-tree)*, mountain ash (*Sorbus aucuparia*); **~(-tree)*, *S. americana;* *~(-berry)*, scarlet berry of these. [f. Scand., corresp. to Norw. *rogn, raun,* Icel. *reynir*]

row'd|y *n. & a.* rough and disorderly and noisy (person); hence *~iNESS, ~yISM* (2), *ns.* [19th c. US, orig. sense lawless backwoodsman; orig. unkn.]

row'el *n., & v.t.* (||-ll-). **1.** *n.* spiked revolving disc at end of spur. **2.** circular piece of leather etc. with hole in centre inserted between horse's skin and flesh to discharge exudate. **3.** *v.t.* urge with rowel; insert rowel in. [ME, f. OF *roel(e)* f. LL *rotella* dim. of L *rota* wheel]

*row'en *n.* (in *sing.* or *pl.*) aftermath. [ME, f. ONF **rowain,* OF *regain* (as RE-, GAIN¹)]

row'lock (rŏ'-, rŭ'-) *n.* pair of thole-pins or other contrivance on boat's gunwale serving as fulcrum for oar and keeping it in place. [alt. of earlier OARlock, OE *ārloc* (OAR, LOCK²), after ROW²]

||**Row'ton** *n.* ~ **house**, type of lodging-house for poor men, providing better conditions than common lodging-house. [f. Lord ~, Engl. social reformer d. 1903]

roy'al *a. & n.* **1.** *a.* of, from, suited to, worthy of, in service or under patronage of, a king or queen (*after n.* in some phrs.: BLOOD¹ *royal,* PRINCE(SS) *royal,* RHYME¹ *royal*); belonging to the king or queen (*the royal anger, hands,* etc.); of family of king or queen. **2.** *Royal* ACADEMY (*of Arts*); **R~ Air Force,** air force of Britain or Commonwealth country; *royal* ASSENT²; ||~ **blue,** deep pure vivid blue; ~ **burgh** (holding charter from Crown); ||*Royal* COMMISSION¹; *royal* DUKE; **R~ Engineers,** engineering branch of British army; ~ **family** (to which sovereign belongs); *Royal* HIGHNESS; **R~ Institution,** British society founded 1799 for diffusion of scientific knowledge; ||**R~ Marine,** British or Commonwealth MARINE 4; **R~ Navy,** navy of Britain or Commonwealth country; ~ **oak,** sprig of oak worn on 29 May to commemorate restoration of Charles II (1660), who hid in oak after battle of Worcester (1651); *Royal* REGIMENT; *royal* ROAD¹; *Royal* SOCIETY; ~ **standard,** banner bearing royal heraldic arms; ||*Royal* VICTORIAN *Chain, Order;* ~ **warrant** (authorizing tradesman to supply goods to royal person). **3.** kingly, majestic, stately, splendid;

first-rate, on great scale, of exceptional size etc., (*royal magnanimity; gave us royal entertainment; in royal spirits; had a royal time*); BATTLE¹ *royal;* ~ **fern,** osmund; *royal* FLUSH⁵; ~ **jelly,** substance secreted by honey-bee workers and fed to future queen bees; ~ **mast, sail,** (above topgallant mast and sail); ~ **stag** (with head of 12 or more points); *royal* TENNIS. **4.** Hence *~LY² adv.* **5.** *n.* royal stag, sail, or mast; size of paper about 620 × 500 mm.; (colloq.) member of royal family; **the R~s,** (1) the Royal Scots Regiment, (2) the Royal Marines. [ME, f. OF *roial* f. L *regalis* REGAL¹]

roy'al|ist *n.* **1.** monarchist, supporter of monarch as an institution or of the royal side in civil war etc. **2.** **die-hard, reactionary,* (esp. *economic royalist*). **3.** So *~ISM* (3) *n., ~i'stIC a.* [f. prec. + -IST]

roy'alt|y *n.* **1.** office or dignity or power of king or queen, sovereignty; royal persons; member of royal family. **2.** royal right (now esp. over minerals) granted by sovereign to individual or corporation; sum paid to patentee for use of patent or to author etc. for each copy of his book etc. sold or for each public performance of his work. [ME, f. OF *roialté* (as ROYAL; see -TY¹)]

||**Roy'ston** *n.* ~ **crow,** hooded or grey crow. [~ in Herts.]

||**rŏ'zzer** *n.* (sl.) policeman. [19th c.; orig. unkn.]

RP *abbr.* Royal Society of Portrait Painters.

||**RPC** *abbr.* Royal Pioneer Corps.

RPI *abbr.* retail price index.

r.p.m. *abbr.* resale price maintenance; revolutions per minute.

RPS *abbr.* Royal Photographic Society.

*RR *abbr.* railroad; rural route.

||**RRC** *abbr.* (Lady of the) Royal Red Cross.

RS *abbr.* Royal Scots; Royal Society.

Rs. *abbr.* rupees.

RSA *abbr.* Royal Scottish Academician, Academy; Royal Society of Arts.

RSC *abbr.* Royal Society of Chemistry.

RSD *abbr.* Royal Society of Dublin.

RSE *abbr.* Royal Society of Edinburgh.

RSFSR *abbr.* Russian Soviet Federative Socialist Republic.

||**R.Sigs.** *abbr.* Royal Corps of Signals.

RSM *abbr.* Regimental SERGEANT-Major.

||**RSPCA** *abbr.* Royal Society for the Prevention of Cruelty to Animals.

RSV *abbr.* Revised Standard Version (of Bible).

RSVP *abbr.* (In invitation etc.) please answer. [f. F *répondez s'il vous plaît*]

RT *abbr.* radio telegraphy; radio telephony.

rt. *abbr.* right.

||**Rt. Hon.** *abbr.* Right Honourable.

Rt. Rev(d). *abbr.* Right Reverend.

||**RU** *abbr.* Rugby Union.

Ru *symb.* ruthenium.

rŭb¹ *v.* (**-bb-**) *& n.* **1.** *v.t.* press one's hand or an object on and slide it along over or up and down the surface of; ~ one's **hands** (each with the other usu. in sign of keen satisfaction, or for warmth); ~ **noses,** rub one's nose against another's as primitive or animal greeting; *rub* person's NOSE *in it;* ~ **shoulders** or **elbows,** come into contact (lit. or fig.) *with* other people; ~ (**up**) **the wrong way,** stroke against the grain, irritate or repel as by stroking cat thus. **2.** polish, clean, abrade, chafe, make dry, sore, bare, etc., by rubbing. **3.** reproduce design of (sepulchral brass or stone) by rubbing paper laid on it with heelball or coloured chalk etc.; hence *~'bING¹* (2) *n.* **4.** slide (hand, object) *against* or *in* or *on* or *over* something; (objects) together or *together,* with friction. **5.** bring (stain etc.) *out,* (nap etc., or fig. novelty, shyness, etc.) *off* or *away,* force (liniment etc., or fig. lesson, humiliating fact, etc.) *in* or *into,* reduce to powder etc., force *through* sieve, bring size or level of *down,* spread (ointment etc.) *over,* dry (horse, one*self*) *down,* polish or brush (tarnished object, or fig. one's memory, Greek, etc.) *up*, mix (pigment, etc.) *up* into paste, by rubbing (lit. or fig.); ∼ **it in**, (fig.) continue to refer to person's failure etc.; ∼ **out**, erase with rubber, (sl.) kill. **6.** *v.i.* come into or be in sliding contact, exercise friction, *against* or *on*; ∼ **off**, be transferred or removed by contact (lit. or fig.). **7.** (Of BOWL²) be retarded or diverted by unevenness of ground, (fig., of person, process, etc.) go *on, along, through*, with more or less restraint or difficulty. **8.** (Of cloth, skin, etc.) get frayed or worn or sore or bare with friction. **9.** ∼-**stone**, (piece of) stone used for sharpening, smoothing, etc. **10.** *n.* spell of rubbing (*give it a rub, rub-up, rub--down*). **11.** (Bowls). inequality of ground impeding or diverting bowl, diversion etc. of bowl by this; (fig.) impediment or difficulty (**there's the** ∼, that is the point at which doubt or difficulty arises). **12.** ∼ **of** or **on the green**, (Golf) accidental interference with course or position of ball. [ME *rubben*, perh. f. LG *rubben*; orig. unkn.]

rŭb² *n.* = RUBBER³. [abbr.]

rŭ'b-a-dŭb *n.*, & *v.i.* (-bb-). (make) rolling sound of drum. [imit.]

ruba't|ō (roōbah'-) *a.* & *n.* (*pl.* ∼os, *or* ∼i *pr.* -ē). (Mus.) (performed at) speed momentarily varied for sake of expression. [It., = robbed]

rŭ'bber¹ *n.*, & *v.t.* In vbl senses; masseur or masseuse; Turkish-bath attendant; implement used for, part of machine operating by, rubbing. [f. RUB¹+-ER¹]

rŭ'bber² *n.* **1.** elastic solid made from latex of tropical plants or synthetically and used in pneumatic tyres etc.; piece of this or other substance for erasing pencil--marks; (sl.) rubber condom; *(in pl.)* galoshes. **2.** ∼ **band**, loop of rubber to hold papers etc. together; ∼ **cheque**, (joc., cf. BOUNCE¹) cheque refused by bank because of insufficiency of money in account; ∼ **goods**, (esp.) contraceptives; *∼-**neck** *n.*, & *v.i.*, (be) gaping sightseer or inquisitive person; ∼ **plant**, plant yielding rubber, esp. *Ficus elastica* grown as ornamental dwarf; ∼ **solution**, liquid drying to rubber-like material, used for mending rubber articles; ∼ **stamp**, device for inking and imprinting on surface, (fig.) one who mechanically copies or agrees to others' actions, indication of such agreement; ∼-**stamp** *v.t.*, (fig.) approve automatically without proper consideration. **3.** Hence ∼IZE *v.t.*, treat or coat with rubber, ∼Y² *a.* [f. prec., through its use in rubbing out pencil-marks]

rŭ'bber³ *n.* match of three or five successive games between same sides or persons at whist, bridge, cricket, lawn tennis, etc.; **the** ∼, winning of two games in rubber, third game when each side has won one. [orig. unkn.; as term in bowls from *c.* 1600]

rŭ'bbish *n.*, *int.*, & *v.t.* **1.** *n.* waste material, debris, refuse, litter; worthless material or articles, trash; **good riddance** (**to bad** ∼), (said esp. at departure of person one dislikes). **2.** *n.* & *int.* absurd ideas or suggestions, nonsense (often as excl. of contempt). **3.** Hence ∼Y² *a.* **4.** *v.t.* (Austral.) reject as worthless; criticize severely. [ME, f. AF *rubbous* etc., perh. f. *robeus* pl. of *robel* = foll.]

rŭ'bble *n.* waste fragments of stone, brick, etc., from old houses; pieces of undressed stone used, esp. as filling-in, for walls; (Geol.) loose angular stones etc. as covering of some rocks; water-worn stones; hence **rŭ'bbl**Y² *a.* [ME *robyl, rubel*, perh. f. AF *robel* f. OF *robe* spoils; see ROBE]

***rube** (roōb) *n.* (colloq.) country bumpkin. [abbr. of *Reuben*]

ru'bef̄y, -ifȳ, (roō'-) *v.t.* make red; (Med., of counter--irritant) stimulate (skin etc.) to redness, so **rubė**FA'CIENT *a.* & *n.*, **rubė**FA'CTION *n.*, (roō-). [ME, f. OF *rubifier, rubefier* f. med. L *rubificare* f. L *rubefacere* (*rubeus* red; see -FY)]

rubė'lla (roō-) *n.* (Path.) acute infectious virus disease with red rash, German measles. [mod. L, neut. pl. (as n.) of L *rubellus* reddish]

ru'bellīte (roō-) *n.* red variety of tourmaline. [f. L *rubellus* reddish+-ITE¹ (2)]

rubė'ola (roō-) *n.* (Path.) measles. [f. med. L *rubeola* dim. (as n.) of L *rubeus* red]

Ru'bicon (roō'-) *n.*, & *v.t.* **1.** *n. the* boundary by passing which one becomes committed to an enterprise (*cross the Rubicon*). **2.** (*r*∼). winning of game in piquet before opponent has scored 100. **3.** *v.t.* (*r*∼). defeat (opponent) thus. [ancient name of stream limiting Julius Caesar's province and crossed by him in 49 BC as start of war with Pompey]

ru'bicŭnd (roō'-) *a.* (Of face, complexion, or person in these respects) ruddy, high-coloured; hence ∼ITY (-ŭ'n-) *n.* [f. F *rubicond* or f. L *rubicundus* (*rubēre* be red)]

rubi'dium (roō'-) *n.* soft silvery element of alkali--metal group. [f. L *rubidus* red (w. ref. to spectrum lines)+-IUM]

rubify. See RUBEFY.

rubi'ginous (roō-) *a.* rust-coloured. [f. L *rubigo -inis* rust+-OUS]

ru'bious (roō'-) *a.* (poet.) ruby-coloured. [f. RUBY+-OUS]

ruble. See ROUBLE.

ru'bric (roō'-) *n.* **1.** heading of chapter, section, etc., special passage, or sentence, written or printed in red or in special lettering. **2.** direction for conduct of divine service (prop. in red) inserted in liturgical book; hence ∼AL *a.*, **rubrī'CIAN** (roō-), ∼ISM (3), ∼IST (2), *ns.* **3.** explanatory words; established custom. [ME, f. OF *rubrique, rubric(h)e*, or f. L *rubrica* (*terra*) red (earth, ochre) as writing-material, cogn. w. *rubeus* red]

ru'bric|āte (roō'-) *v.t.* mark with, print or write in, red; furnish with rubrics; hence ∼A'TION, ∼ātor, *ns.* [f. L *rubricare* (*rubrica*; see prec.)+-ATE³]

ru'bȳ (roō'-) *n.* & *a.*, & *v.t.* **1.** *n.* rare precious stone consisting of corundum with colour varying from deep crimson or purple to pale rose (**above rubies**, of inestimable value). **2.** *a.* & *n.* (of) glowing purple--tinged red colour. **3.** ∼ **glass** (coloured with oxides of copper, iron, lead, tin, etc.); ∼-**tail**, insect with ruby--coloured hinder part; ∼ **wedding** (fortieth anniversary). **4.** *v.t.* dye or tinge ruby-colour. [ME, f. OF *rubi* f. med. L *rubinus* (*lapis* stone), cogn. w. L *rubeus* red]

RUC *abbr.* Royal Ulster Constabulary.

ruche (roōsh) *n.* frill or gathering of lace etc. as trimming; hence **ruch**ED² (roōsht) *a.*, **ru'ch**ING¹ (2) (roō'sh-) *n.* [F, f. med. L *rusca* tree-bark, of Celt. orig.]

rŭck¹ *n.* main body of competitors not likely to overtake leaders; (fig.) undistinguished crowd of persons or things; (Rugby Footb.) loose scrum with ball on ground; (Austral. Footb.) group of three mobile players. [ME 'stack of fuel, heap, rick'; app. Scand., = Norw. *ruka* w. same meanings]

rŭck² *n.* & *v.* **1.** *n.* crease, wrinkle. **2.** *v.i.* & *t.* ∼ (**up**), form ruck. [f. ON *hrukka* (**hrunka*)]

‖rŭ'ckle *n.* & *v.* = prec. [f. prec.+-LE³]

ru'cksăck (rŭ'-, roō'-) *n.* bag slung by straps from both shoulders and carried on back for carrying walker's or climber's necessaries. [G (*rucken* dial. var. of *rücken* back, *sack* SACK¹)]

rŭ'ckus *n.* = foll. [cf. foll. and RUMPUS]

rŭ'ction *n.* (colloq.) disturbance, tumult, row. [19th c., of unkn. orig.]

rŭdbě'ckia *n.* composite garden plant of genus *Rudbeckia*, native to N. America. [mod. L, f. O. *Rudbeck*, Sw. botanist d. 1740+-IA¹]

rŭdd *n.* (*pl.* same). red-eyed freshwater fish resembling roach. [app. rel. to *rud* red colour f. OE *rudu*, cogn. w. RED]

rŭ'dder *n.* broad flat wooden or metal piece hinged to vessel's stern-post or rear of aeroplane for steering with; (fig.) guiding principle etc.; ∼-**fish** (of kind that follows ships); hence ∼LESS *a.* [OE *rōther*, =

MDu., MLG *rōder*, OHG *ruodar* f. WG *rōthra-* f. st. of ROW²]

rŭ'ddle *n.*, & *v.t.* **1.** *n.* red ochre, esp. of kind used for marking sheep. **2.** *v.t.* mark or colour (as) with ruddle. [rel. to obs. *rud* (see RUDD)]

rŭ'ddock *n.* robin redbreast. [OE *rudduc* (as prec.; see -OCK)]

rŭ'dd|ў *a.* & *v.* **1.** *a.* (Of face or its owner) freshly or healthily red, rosy; (of health, youth, etc.) marked by ruddiness; (of light, fire, sky, object lighted up, etc., or in animal name) reddish (*ruddy duck, plover, squirrel*); ||(sl.) bloody, damnable; hence ∼ĭLY² *adv.*, ∼ĭNESS *n.* **2.** *v.t.* & *i.* make or grow ruddy. [OE *rudig* (as RUDD, -Y²)]

rude (rōōd) *a.* **1.** primitive, simple, in natural state, uncivilized, uneducated, roughly made or contrived or executed, coarse, lacking subtlety or accuracy, (*rude times, men, simplicity, ignorance, chaos; rude plough, beginnings, methods; rude path, verses, drawing; rude fare, plenty; rude writer, style; rude observer, version, classification*). **2.** violent, not gentle, unrestrained, startling, sudden, abrupt, (*rude passions, blast, shock, awakening, reminder*). **3.** vigorous, hearty, (*rude health*). **4.** insolent, impertinent, offensive, (*rude remarks; say rude things*); be ∼ to, insult. **5.** Hence ∼'LY² (-dlĭ) *adv.*, ∼'NESS (-dn-), (colloq.) **ru'dery** (4), *ns.*, **ru'dish**¹ 2 *a.*, (rōō'-). [ME f. OF, f. L *rudis* unwrought]

Rü'desheimer (rōō'dĕs-hī-) *n.* a white Rhine wine. [f. G *Rüdesheimer* (*wein*) (*Rüdesheim* on the Rhine)]

ru'diment (rōō'-) *n.* **1.** (in *pl.*) elements or first principles or of of knowledge or some subject. **2.** (in *pl.*) imperfect beginning of or of something that will develop or might under other conditions have developed. **3.** part or organ imperfectly developed as being vestigial or having no function (e.g. the breast in males). **4.** Hence ∼ARY¹ (-ĕ'n-) *a.* [F, or f. L *rudimentum* (as RUDE, after *elementum* ELEMENT)]

rue¹ (rōō) *v.t.* (∼'ing or **ru'ing**, *pr.* rōō'-), & *n.* **1.** *v.t.* repent of, bitterly feel the consequences of, wish undone or non-existent, (*you shall rue it; rue the day, hour, etc., when one did thing etc.*) **2.** *n.* (arch.) repentance, dejection at some occurrence. **3.** *n.* (arch.) compassion, pity. [OE *hrēow*(*an*), = OS *hreuwan*, OHG (*h*)*riuwa*(*n*)]

rue² (rōō) *n.* perennial evergreen shrub (*Ruta graveolens*) with bitter strong-scented leaves formerly used in medicine. [ME f. OF, f. L *ruta* f. Gk *rhutē*]

rue'ful (rōō'f-) *a.* expressing or causing (mock) sorrow or compassion; **Knight of the R∼ Countenance,** Don Quixote; hence ∼LY² *adv.*, ∼NESS *n.* [ME, f. RUE¹ + -FUL]

rufe'sc|ent (rōō-) *a.* (Zool. etc.) reddish, hence ∼ENCE *n.* [f. L *rufescere* (*rufus* reddish; see -ESCENT)]

rŭff¹ *n.* deep projecting frill of several folds of linen or muslin starched and separately goffered worn round neck esp. in 16th c.; projecting or conspicuously coloured ring of feathers or hair round bird's or animal's neck; domestic pigeon like jacobin. [perh. f. *ruff* = ROUGH]

rŭff² *n.* (*fem.* reeve). bird of sandpiper family of which male has RUFF¹ and ear-tufts in breeding season. [f. prec.]

rŭff³, **rŭffe,** *n.* small freshwater fish of perch family, with prickly scales. [ME, prob. f. ROUGH]

ruff⁴ *n.*, & *v.i.* & *t.* trump(ing) at cards; CROSS-*ruff.* [orig. name of card-game f. OF *ro*(*u*)*ffle* = It. *ronfa* (perh. alt. of *trionfo* TRUMP²)]

rŭ'ffian *n.* brutal violent lawless turbulent person, desperado, bully, rough; hence ∼ISM (2) *n.*, ∼LY¹ *a.* [f. F *ruf*(*f*)*ian* f. It. *ruffiano,* perh. f. dial. *rofia* scurf]

rŭffl|e¹ *v.* & *n.* **1.** *v.t.* disturb smoothness or tranquillity of (feathers, hair, water, composure or temper or person in regard to it, brow); *bird* ∼*es up its feathers* (in anger or to keep out the cold); gather (lace etc.) into ruffle. **2.** *v.i.* (Of sea, hair, temper, etc.) undergo ruffling, lose smoothness or calmness. **3.** *n.* perturbation, bustle; rippling effect on water; ornamental

gathered or goffered frill of lace etc. worn at opening of garment esp. about wrist or breast or neck; RUFF¹ of bird etc.; (Mil.) vibrating drum-beat. [ME, of unkn. orig.]

rŭ'ffl|e² *v.i.* (arch.) swagger about, behave arrogantly or quarrelsomely; hence ∼ER¹ *n.* [ME, of unkn. orig.]

ru'fous (rōō'-) *a.* (Esp. of animals) reddish-brown. [f. L *rufus* red(dish) + -OUS]

rŭg *n.* **1.** large wrap or coverlet of thick woollen stuff. **2.** floor-mat of shaggy material or thick pile; **pull the** ∼ **(out) from under,** (fig.) remove support or concealment of (person). [prob. f. Scand. (Norw. dial. *rugga* coverlet, Sw. *rugg* ruffled hair) & cogn. w. RAG²]

Rŭgbei'an (-bē'an) *n* & *a.* (past or present member) of Rugby School. [f. *Rugby* after L adjs. in *-eius*]

Rŭ'gbў *n.* *Rugby* FIVES; ∼ (**football**), game played with oval ball (∼ **ball**) which may be kicked or carried; ||∼ **League,** partly professional Rugby football with teams of 13; ||∼ **Union,** amateur Rugby football with teams of 15. [f. ∼ School in Warwickshire (where first played)]

rŭ'gg|ed (-g-) *a.* **1.** having rough uneven surface (*rugged bark*); (of ground or country) full of abrupt ups and downs, craggy, wooded, etc.; (of features) strongly marked, irregular in outline. **2.** unsoftened, unpolished, lacking gentleness or refinement, harsh in sound, austere, unbending, involving hardship, (*rugged manners, grandeur, individualist, kindness, honesty, character, verse, times, life*); robust, sturdy, (esp. of machine etc., whence *∗∼*IZE (3) *v.t.*). **3.** Hence ∼LY² *adv.*, ∼NESS *n.* [ME, prob. f. Scand.; cf. RUG, and Sw. *rugga* roughen]

||**rŭ'gger** (-g-) *n.* (colloq.) Rugby football. [f. RUGBY + -ER¹ (5)]

ru'gōse (rōō'-) *a.* (esp. Biol.) wrinkled, corrugated; hence or cogn. ∼LY² (-slĭ) *adv.*, **rugo'sity** (rōō-) *n.* [f. L *rugosus* (*ruga* wrinkle; see -OSE¹)]

ru'in (rōō'-) *n.* & *v.* **1.** *n.* downfall, fallen or wrecked or impaired state, lit. (of building or structure) or fig. (*the ruin of my hopes*); complete loss of property or position (*bring to ruin*); RACK⁷ and ruin. **2.** (in *sing.* or *pl.*) what remains of building, town, structure, etc., or fig. of person, that has suffered ruin (*the ruins of Baalbek; is but the ruin of what he was; lies in ruins; lives in an old ruin*). **3.** what causes ruin, destroying agency, havoc, (*will be the ruin of us*). **4.** So [f. obs. *ruinate* v.] **ruinA'TION** (rōō-) *n.* **5.** *v.t.* (esp. in *p.p.*) reduce (place) to ruins. **6.** bring to ruin (*her extravagance ruined him*); utterly impair or wreck (*ruin one's new hat, one's prospects*). **7.** *v.i.* (poet.) fall headlong or with a crash. [n. ME f. OF *ruine,* v. f. F *ruiner* or med. L *ruinare,* f. L *ruina* (*ruere* fall)]

ru'inous (rōō'-) *a.* in ruins, dilapidated; bringing ruin, disastrous, (*ruinous folly, expense*), whence ∼LY² *adv.*; hence ∼NESS *n.* [ME, f. L *ruinosus* (as prec.)]

rule (rōōl) *n.* & *v.* **1.** *n.* principle to which action or procedure conforms or is adapted or intended to conform, dominant custom, canon, test, standard, normal state of things, (*deduce rules of action; the rules of decorum, cricket; rule of the* ROAD¹); R∼s, (Austral.) = Australian Rules (football); **as a** ∼, usually, more often than not; **by** ∼, in regulation manner, mechanically; EXCEPTION *proves rule*; GOLDEN *rule;* ∼ **of three,** method of finding number in same ratio to one given as exists between two others given; ∼ **of thumb** (based on experience or practice, not theory); WORK² *to rule.* **2.** government, dominion, (*under British rule; the rule of force, of law; entrusted with the rule of half the tribe*). **3.** (Eccl.) code of discipline observed by religious order. **4.** (Law.) order made by judge or court w. ref. to particular case only (*rule* NISI); ∼ **absolute** (making rule nisi no longer contingent). **5. the ∼s,** (Hist.) limited area outside Fleet and King's Bench prisons in London where prisoners were allowed to live on certain terms. **6.** graduated often jointed straight measure used by carpenters etc.; *by rule and* LINE²; **run the ~ over,** (fig.) examine cursorily for correctness or adequacy; SLIDE²-*rule*. **7.** (Print.) thin slip of metal for separating headings, columns, etc.; ||short (**en ~**) or long (**em ~**) dash in punctuation etc. **8.** Hence ~'LESS (-l-l-) *a*. **9.** *v.t.* exercise sway or decisive influence over, keep under control, curb, (person, conduct, one's passions; **ruling passion,** motive that habitually directs one's actions); (arch. in *pass.*) consent to follow advice, be guided *by*. **10.** *v.t.* & *i.* be the ruler(s) or have the sovereign control of or *over*, (*rules over many millions*; *kings should rule by love*); **~ the roast** or **roost,** be in control. **11.** *v.t.* (Of prices, or goods etc. in regard to them or to quality etc.) have a specified general level, be for the most part, (*corn, prices, the market, ruled high* etc.; **ruling prices,** those current). **12.** *v.t.* give judicial or authoritative decision (*that*; *rule* person or thing *out of order*); **~ out,** exclude, pronounce irrelevant or ineligible; hence **ru'**LING¹ (2) (rōō'-) *n*. **13.** make parallel lines across (paper), make (straight line), with ruler or mechanical help; hence **ru'**LING¹ (2) (rōō'-) *n*. OF *reule*(*r*) f. Rom. *regula & LL *regulare* f. L *regula* straight stick]

ru'ler (rōō'-) *n*. **1.** person or thing bearing (esp. sovereign) rule (*of*); hence ~SHIP². **2.** straight strip or cylinder of wood, metal, etc., used in ruling paper or lines. [ME, f. prec.+-ER¹]

rŭm¹ *n*. **1.** spirit distilled from sugar-cane residues or molasses; *rum* BABA; *rum*-SHRUB². **2.** *~intoxicating liquor; *~-**runner,** (colloq.) smuggler of intoxicants; *~-**shop,** (colloq.) place where intoxicants are sold. [17th c., perh. abbr. of contemporary forms *rumbullion, rumbustion*; orig. unkn.]

||**rŭm²** *a*. (colloq.) odd, strange, queer; difficult, dangerous; *rum* GO² or START²; hence **rŭ'm**LY² *adv.*, **rŭ'm**NESS *n*. [16th-c. cant, orig. = fine, spirited, perh. var. of ROM]

Rumanian. See ROMANIAN.

Rumansh. See ROMANSH.

rŭ'mba *n*., & *v.i.* (~ed or ~'d, *pr.* -ad). **1.** *n.* Cuban Negro dance; ballroom dance imitative of this; music for it. **2.** *v.i.* dance rumba. [Amer. Sp.]

rŭ'mble¹ *v.* & *n.* **1.** *v.i.* make deep continuous sound (as) of thunder, earthquake, heavy machinery, gas in the bowels, etc.; go *along, by,* etc., making or in vehicle making such sound. **2.** *v.t.* utter, say *out,* give *forth,* with such sound. **3.** *n.* rumbling sound; *(sl.) gang-fight; hind part of carriage arranged as extra seat or for luggage; *~ **seat,** uncovered folding seat in rear of motor car; ~-**tumble,** lumbering vehicle, rough motion. [ME *romble,* prob. f. MDu. *rommelen, rummelen,* (imit.)]

rŭ'mble² *v.t.* (sl.) understand fully, see through, detect. [19th c.; orig. unkn.]

rŭmbŭ'stious (-schus) *a.* (colloq.) boisterous, uproarious. [prob. var. of ROBUSTIOUS]

ru'm|**ĕn** (rōō'-) *n*. (*pl.* **~ens** or **~ina**). ruminant's first STOMACH. [L *rumen ruminis* throat]

ru'minant (rōō'-) *n*. & *a*. **1.** *n.* animal that chews the cud. **2.** *a.* belonging to the ruminants; contemplative, given to or engaged in meditation. [as foll.; see -ANT]

ru'min|**āte** (rōō'-) *v.* **1.** *v.i.* chew the cud. **2.** *v.i.* & *t.* meditate, ponder, (*over, about, of, on*); hence or cogn. ~ATIVE *a.*, ~**ātor** *n.* **3.** So ~A'TION *n*. [f. L *ruminari* (as RUMEN) + -ATE³]

rŭ'mmage *v.* & *n.* **1.** *v.t.* & *i.* make thorough search in or in, make search (*through* or *among*). **2.** *v.t.* bring *out* or *up* from among other things; disarrange, throw *about,* in searching. **3.** *n.* things got by rummaging, miscellaneous accumulation; thorough search (esp. of ship by Customs officer); **~ sale,** (1) clearance sale of unclaimed articles at docks etc., (2) = JUMBLE³ *sale*. [v. f. n. in obs. sense arranging of casks etc. in hold, f. AF *rumage f. OF *arrumage* (arrumer stow f. a- AD-, *run* ship's hold f. MDu. *ruim* ROOM; see -AGE)]

rŭ'mmer *n.* large drinking-glass. [cf. Du. *roemer,* LG *römer,* (*roemen* praise, boast; see -ER¹)]

rŭ'mmy¹ *a.* (colloq.) = RUM². [f. RUM² + -Y²]

rŭ'mmy² *n.* card-game played usu. with two packs, each player seeking to dispose of his cards by forming sequences or sets of cards of same rank. [20th c., of unkn. orig.]

||**ru'mour,** ***ru'mor,** (rōō'mer) *n.*, & *v.t.* **1.** *n.* general talk, report, or hearsay, of doubtful accuracy; *a* or *the* current but unverified statement or assertion (*that, of*). **2.** *v.t.* (usu. in *pass.*) report by way of rumour (*it is rumoured that he will come; he is rumoured to be coming; the rumoured disaster*). [ME, f. OF *rumur, rumor* f. L *rumor -oris* noise]

rŭmp *n.* **1.** tail-end, posterior, buttocks, of animal or bird or person; hence ~'LESS *a.,* (of fowl) tailless. **2.** small or contemptible remnant of a parliament or similar body; **the R~,** (Hist.) remnant of Long Parliament either after its restoration 1659 or from Pride's Purge 1648 to its first dissolution 1653. **3.** ~ **steak** (cut from ox's rump). [ME, prob. f. Scand.; cf. MDa. *rumpe,* MSw. *rumpa,* Icel. *rumpr*]

rŭ'mple *v.t.* wrinkle, crease, tousle, ruffle, disorder, (fabric, leaves, garment, hair, etc.). [f. obs. *rumple* n. f. MDu. *rompel*(*en*) (*rompe* wrinkle)]

rŭ'mpus *n.* (colloq.) disturbance, brawl, row, uproar; *~ **room** (esp. in basement of house for hobbies, games, etc.). [18th c.; prob. fanciful]

rŭ'mpў *n.* Manx tailless cat. [f. RUMP + -Y³]

rŭn¹ *v.* (**-nn-; ran; run**). **1.** *v.i.* (Of person) progress at pace faster than walk by advancing each foot alternately, never having both feet on ground at once; (of animal) go at quicker than its walking pace, amble, trot, canter, gallop, etc. **2.** (Cricket). (start to) traverse length of pitch to score run. **3.** flee, abscond, (*run for it;* CUT² *and run*). **4.** go or travel hurriedly, precipitately, briefly, etc.; **~ to meet,** anticipate (one's troubles etc.); *run* RIOT; **~ over** or **down** or *up* or **across** (*to* place by brief journey or for flying visit; **he who ~s may read** (said of easily intelligible exposition etc.; cf. Hab. 2:2). **5.** *run* WILD. **6.** compete in or *in* race (ALSO-*ran*); finish race in specified position (*ran third in the mile*); seek election etc. (*for parliament, the presidency, president,* etc.). **7.** (Of ship etc.) go straight and fast (*ship runs before the wind, into port, ashore, aground, on the rocks, foul of* another); (of salmon) go up river from sea. **8.** advance (as) by rolling or on wheels, spin round or along, revolve (as) on axle, go with sliding or smooth or continuous or easy motion, be in action, work freely, be current or operative, have duration, (*ball, carriage, wheel, spindle, sledge, time, runs; rope runs in pulley; his life runs smoothly; kept the engine running while waiting; lease runs for 99 years;* WRIT¹ *runs*); (of play etc.) be presented (*for* specified number of performances etc.); **~ in the family,** (of trait etc.) be found in all or many members of it; **~ in** one's **head,** (of tune etc.) seem to be heard repeatedly, (of idea etc.) constantly recur to one. **9.** (Of public conveyance by land or water) ply (*from, to, between*), be in course of plying (*train is running late*); (of fire, news, enthusiasm, etc.) spread rapidly from point to point (*news ran like wildfire; a cheer ran down the line; a shiver ran down my spine*). **10.** (Of colour in fabric) spread from dyed parts, (of ink) spread beyond proper place. **11.** (Of thought, eye, memory, etc.) pass in transitory or cursory way (*thoughts run through one's head; eyes run over object*); **~ back over the past,** survey it summarily. **12.** (Of liquid, grain, sand, etc., of vessel containing or object emitting etc., or fig.) flow, be wet, drip, flow with, (*till the blood ran; ran blood; fountains run wine; is running with oil; heavy sea is running; tide runs strong; river runs clear, thick; feeling ran* HIGH; one's **blood ~s cold,** one is horrified; SANDS *are running out*); *(of stocking) ladder; (of candle) gutter; (of nose, eyes) drop mucus or tears, so *run at the nose, run with sweat;* **~ dry,** cease to flow, be exhausted; **~ low, short,** become or have too little (*our tea ran short;*

we ran short of tea). **13.** extend, be continuous, have a certain course or order, progress, proceed, have a tendency or common characteristic or average price or level, (*fence runs round the house; road runs at right angles to, along, the ridge; story, title, document, runs as follows; must not run to extremes; runs to sentiment; my inclination does not run that way; inflation is running at 15%; prices ran high*). **14.** *v.t.* (w. cogn. obj.) pursue, follow, traverse, cover, make way (esp. swiftly) through or over, wander about in, perform, attempt or be exposed or submit to, (*course, way, race, a mile, run at cricket*); *run* BLOCKADE[1]; ~s **a chance of being,** may be; ~ **its course,** follow natural progress, be left to itself; ~ **errands, messages,** be a messenger; *run the* GAUNTLET[2]; *run* RISK(*s*). **15.** sew (fabric) loosely or hastily with running stitches. **16.** chase, hunt, have running race with, (*run fox five miles*); ~ **to earth,** chase to its lair, (fig.) discover after long search; *run into the* GROUND[1] 5; ~ person **hard** or **close,** press him severely in race, competition, or comparative merit etc.; ~ **off** one's **feet,** very busy; *run* RAGGED. **17.** make run or go (*run ship aground* or *to New York, boat down to water, car into garage, train or road through,* person *out of town,* one's *head against, cart into wall, sword or pin into,* one's *hand or eye along, down,* or *over* thing, *rope through eyelet, metal into mould, water into bath, fingers or comb through hair*); turn (cattle etc.) out to graze; smuggle (brandy, guns, etc.); enter (horse *for* race, candidate *for* election etc.); cause (machine etc.) to operate, (experiment etc.) to be conducted; own and use (vehicle etc.); *publish (article or advertisement *in* newspaper etc.); take (person) for journey in motor car etc.; keep going, manage, conduct operation(s) of, (coach, steamer, business, person, etc.); *run it* FINE[2]; ~ **the show,** (colloq.) dominate in an undertaking etc.; ~ **a temperature,** be feverish. **18.** allow (account, bill) to accumulate for some time before paying. **19.** (w. *preps.*): ~ **across,** happen to meet; ~ **after,** pursue with attentions, seek society of, give much time to (pursuit etc.); ~ **against,** happen to meet; ~ **at,** assail by charging or rushing; ~ **in,** incur (debt); ~ **into,** fall into (practice, absurdity, etc.), incur (debt), be continuous or coalesce with, have collision or chance meeting with, reach or attain (*some length, five editions,* etc.); ~ **on,** be concerned (continually) with (*talk or mind runs on a subject*), use as fuel (*runs on diesel oil*); ~ **over,** review, glance over, touch (notes of piano etc.) in quick succession, (of vehicle) pass over (animal, prostrate person); ~ **through,** examine or rehearse cursorily, peruse, review, deal successively with, consume (estate etc.) by reckless or quick spending, traverse, pervade; ~ **to,** reach (amount, number, etc.), have money or ability or (of money etc.) be enough for (some expense or undertaking), fall into (ruin), (of person) indulge or show inclination towards (coarseness, fat, etc.); *run to* SEED; ~ **upon,** (of thoughts etc.) be engrossed by, dwell on. **20.** (w. *advs.*); ~ **about,** bustle, hurry from one person etc. to another, (esp. of children) play or wander without restraint; ~'**about** *n.*, light motor car or aircraft; ~ **along,** (colloq.) depart; ~ **around,** ||take from place to place by car etc., fob off at successive places (so ~-*around* n.); ~ **away,** flee, abscond, elope, (of horse) bolt, (of horse or person) get clear away *from* competitors in race; ~'**away** *n.* & *a.,* fugitive (~*away marriage* etc., wedding after elopement); ~ **away with,** carry off (person, stolen property, etc.), win (prize etc.) easily, accept (notion) hastily, (of expense etc.) consume (money etc.), (of horse etc.) bolt with (rider, carriage or its occupants); ~ **down,** (of clock etc.) stop for want of winding, (of person or his health etc.) become enfeebled from overwork, poor feeding, etc., (*had, was much, run down*), reduce numbers of (staff etc.), knock down or collide with (person, ship, etc.), overtake (game, person) in pursuit, discover after search, disparage; ~-**down,** (*n.*) reduction in numbers, detailed analysis, (*a.*) de-

cayed, declined from prosperity; ~ **in,** (of combatant) rush to close quarters, (colloq.) arrest and take into custody, bring (new machinery, esp. car engine) into good working order by carefully running it; ~-**in** *n.,* approach to action or event, quarrel; ~ **off,** flee, flow away, digress suddenly, write or recite (poem, list, etc.) fluently, drain (liquid) off, produce (copies etc.) on machine, decide (race) after tie or trial heats; ~ **on,** (of written characters) be joined together, continue in operation, elapse, speak volubly, talk incessantly, (Print.) continue in same line as what precedes; ~ **out,** come to an end (of period, of stock of something, or of its owner; ~ *out of,* exhaust one's stock of), escape from containing vessel, (of rope) pass or be paid out, jut out, come out of contest in specified position etc. or complete required score etc., complete (race), advance (gun etc.) so as to project, put down wicket of (batsman while he is running), exhaust one*self* by running; ~ **over,** (of vessel or contents) overflow, review, glance over; ~ **through,** pierce with sword etc., draw line through (written words); ~ **up,** grow quickly, rise in price, amount *to,* be runner-up, accumulate (number, sum, debt) quickly, force (rival bidder) to bid higher, force up (price, or commodity in regard to price), erect or construct (wall, house, garment, etc.) to great height or in unsubstantial or hurried way, raise (flag) on mast etc., add up (column of figures); ~ **up against,** meet with (difficulty etc.); ~-**up** *n.,* approach to action or event, (Golf) long approach shot. [OE *rinnan, =* OS, OHG *rinnan,* ON *rinna,* Goth. *rinnan*]

run[2] *n.* **1.** act or spell of running; **at a** or **the** ~, running; **go and have a** ~!, (sl.) begone; **have a (good)** ~ **for** one's **money,** get some enjoyment etc. out of expenditure or effort [orig. w. ref. to horse's not being scratched after placing of bets]; **had a good** ~ (esp. in hunting or on ship, train, etc.); **on the** ~, (1) fleeing, (2) bustling about. **2.** short excursion or visit; distance travelled by ship in specific time (usu. 24 hours). **3.** (Cricket). traversing of length of pitch by both batsmen without either's being run out; (Baseball etc.) return of batter to plate after touching the other bases; point scored thus or otherwise. **4.** rhythmical motion, way things tend to move, direction, general tendency of development, regular route. **5.** rapid motion (**come down with a** ~, fall quickly); ladder in stocking etc. **6.** (Mus.) rapid scale passage. **7.** continuous stretch or spell or course, long series or succession, general demand, (*a 500 ft. run of pipe; a long run of success, of power; play had a long run; a run of luck; in the* LONG[1] *or* SHORT *run*); quantity produced in one period of operation (*print run, production run*); ~ **on,** great demand for (commodity etc.), repeated occurrence of (red in rouge-et-noir etc.); ~ **on the bank,** sudden demand from many customers for immediate repayment. **8.** common, general, average, or ordinary type or class; the **common** or **general** or **ordinary** ~ **of men,** average men; ~ **of the mill** or **mine,** ordinary or average product or specimen, not specially selected or distributed. **9.** class or line of goods; batch or drove of animals born or reared together; shoal of fish in motion. **10.** regular track of some animals, enclosure for fowls etc., range of pasture (*sheep-run*); SKI-*run*. **11.** trough for water to run in; *small stream, brook. **12.** permission to make unrestricted use of (*gave me the run of their books, house*). **13.** (Of aircraft) flight on straight and even course at constant speed before or while dropping bombs. [f. prec.]

ru'nagate *n.* (arch.) vagabond. [assim. of obs. *renegate* 'renegade' to RUN[1] and obs. *agate* away]

ru'ncible *a.* ~ **spoon,** fork curved like spoon, with three broad prongs, one edged. [nonsense word used by E. Lear, Engl. humorist d. 1888, perh. after *rouncival* large pea]

ru'ncinate *a.* (Bot.) saw-toothed, with lobes curved towards base. [f. mod. L *runcinatus* f. L *runcina* PLANE[2] (formerly taken to mean saw); see -ATE[2]]

||**rŭ′ndāle** n. joint occupation of (esp. Irish, earlier Scottish) land, each holder having several strips not contiguous. [f. Sc. *ryndale* (*rin* RUN¹, *dale* DOLE¹)]

rune (rōōn) n. **1.** any letter of earliest Gmc alphabet used esp. by Scandinavians and Anglo-Saxons from *c.* 3rd c. and formed by modifying Roman or Greek characters to suit carving; letter of similar alphabet of 8th-c. Mongolian Turks; similar mark of mysterious or magic significance. **2.** (division of) Finnish poem. **3.** ~-**staff,** (1) magic wand inscribed with runes, (2) runic calendar. [f. ON *rún,* pl. *rúnar* magic signs, cogn. w. OE *rūn,* OS, OHG, Goth. *rūna*; see ROUND⁵]

rŭng¹ n. short stick attached at each end as rail, spoke, or crossbar in chair etc.; this or corresponding piece of rope etc. in ladder (lit. or fig.; *lowest, topmost, rung of life's ladder*); hence ~ED² (-ngd), ~′LESS, *adjs.* [OE *hrung,* = MLG *runge,* OHG *runga,* Goth. *hrugga* rod]

rŭng². See RING².

ru′nic (rōō′-) a. of, in, marked with, runes; (of poetry etc.) of the ancient-Scandinavian type; (of ornament) interlacing as on runic monuments and metal-work. [f. mod. L *runicus* f. ON *rún* RUNE; see -IC]

rŭ′nlĕt² n. (arch.) cask of varying size for wine etc. [ME, f. OF *rondelet* dim. of *rondelle* dim. of *ronde* (ROUND¹)]

rŭ′nlĕt² n. small stream. [f. RUN² + -LET]

rŭ′nnable a. suitable for being hunted (*runnable stag*). [f. RUN¹ + -ABLE]

rŭ′nnel n. brook, rill; gutter. [later form (assim. to RUN¹) of *rinel* f. OE *rynel* (as RUN¹; see -LE 1)]

rŭ′nner n. **1.** In vbl senses. **2.** messenger, scout, collector, or agent for bank etc., tout; (Hist.) police-officer (Bow STREET *runner*). **3.** running bird, esp. water-rail. **4.** smuggler; one who runs a blockade. **5.** revolving millstone. **6.** (Naut.) rope in single block with one end round tackle-block and other having hook. **7.** creeping stem that issues from main stem of strawberry etc. and takes root, stolon; twining plant; ||~ (**bean**), twining bean, esp. SCARLET runner. **8.** ring etc. that slides on rod, strap, etc.; one of the long pieces of wood etc. on which sledge etc. slides; groove or rod for thing to slide along; roller for moving heavy article; long narrow ornamental cloth for table etc. **9.** ~-**u′p,** competitor or team taking second place. [ME, f. RUN¹ + -ER¹]

rŭ′nning¹ n. In vbl senses; **make, take up, the** ~, take the lead, set the pace, (lit. in race, or fig. of talk etc.); **in, out of, the** ~, (of competitor) with good, no, chance of winning; ~-**board,** footboard on either side of a locomotive, motor car, etc. [OE (as RUN¹, -ING¹)]

rŭ′nning² a. In vbl senses; (after *pl. n.*) following each other without interval, in succession, (*happened three days running*); ~ **account,** current ACCOUNT²; ~ **battle** (continuing but with constant change of location); ~ **bowsprit** (that can be drawn in when not needed to carry sails); ~ **commentary,** oral description of events in progress; ~-**dog,** (Polit., derog.) subservient follower; *running* FIGHT², FIRE¹; ~ **hand,** writing in which pen etc. is not lifted after each letter; ~ **headline** etc., repeated or varying heading of page; ~ **jump** (in which jumper runs to take-off); *take a* ~ *jump at yourself!*, (sl.) begone; ~ **knot** (that slips along rope etc. and changes size of noose); *~ **mate,** candidate for secondary position in election, horse from same stable as pace-setter; ~ **postman,** (Austral.) vine of genus *Kennedya*; ~ **repairs,** minor repairs and replacements; ~ **rope** (freely movable through pulley etc.); ~ **sore** (suppurating); ~ **stitch,** (one of) line of small non-overlapping stitches for gathering etc.; ~ **water** (flowing in stream or from taps etc.). [ME, f. RUN¹ + -ING²]

rŭ′nnÿ a. tending to run or flow; excessively fluid. [f. RUN¹ + -Y²]

rŭ′nrig n. (Sc.) = RUNDALE. [f. RUN¹ + Sc. & N. Engl. *rig* ridge]

rŭnt n. ox or cow of small esp. Scottish-Highland or Welsh breed; large breed of domestic pigeon; small pig; weakling or undersized person. [16th c.; orig. unkn.]

rŭ′nway n. **1.** trail to animals' watering-place. **2.** incline down which logs are slid. **3.** gangway (usu. of special kind). **4.** specially prepared surface on airfield, for taking off and landing of aircraft. [f. RUN¹ + WAY]

rupee′ (rōō-) n. monetary unit of India, Pakistan, Sri Lanka, Nepal, Mauritius, and Seychelles. [f. Hind. *rūpiyah* f. Skr. *rūpya* wrought silver]

rupi′ah (rōōpē′a) n. monetary unit of Indonesia. [f. as prec.]

rŭ′pture n. & v. **1.** n. breach of harmonious relations, disagreement and parting; (Path.) abdominal hernia; breaking, breach. **2.** v.t. burst, break, (cell, vessel, membrane); sever (connection, marriage, etc.); affect with hernia. **3.** v.i. undergo rupture. [ME f. OF, or f. L *ruptura* (*rumpere rupt-* break; see -URE)]

rur′al (roor′-) a. in, of, suggesting, the country (opp. *urban*), pastoral or agricultural, (*in rural seclusion; rural policeman, constituency, sports,* etc.); ||*rural* DEAN¹; ~ **district** (||Hist.) group of country parishes governed by elected council; hence ~ITY (-ă′l-) n., ~IZE (2, 3) v.i. & t., ~LY² adv. [ME f. OF, or f. LL *ruralis* (*rus ruris* the country; see -AL)]

ruridecanal (roorĭdĭkā′-, -dĕ′ka-) a. of rural DEAN¹ or deanery. [f. L *ruri-* (as prec., -I-) + DECANAL]

Ruritā′n|ia (roor-) n. imaginary Central-European kingdom, the novelist's and dramatist's locale for court romances in a modern setting; hence ~IAN a. & after *Lusitania*] [n. [scene of Anthony Hope's novels *The Prisoner of Zenda* (1894) & *Rupert of Hentzau* (1898), f. as prec. after *Lusitania*]

ru′sa (rōō′-) n. large E. Ind. deer, esp. sambur. [mod. L f. Malay]

ruse (rōōz) n. stratagem, feint, trick. [ME f. OF (*ruser* drive back, perh. f. Rom. **ru(r)sare* f. L *rursus* backwards; cf. RUSH²)]

rŭsh¹ n. **1.** marsh or waterside plant with naked slender tapering pith-filled stems (prop. leaves) formerly used for strewing floors and still for making chair-bottoms and plaiting baskets etc., a stem of this, (collect.) rushes as a material; (arch.) thing of no value (*don't care, not worth, a rush*). **2.** ||~-**bearing,** annual N. Engl. festival on occasion of carrying rushes and garlands to strew floor and decorate walls of church; ~ **candle** (made by dipping pith of a rush in tallow); ~′**light,** rush candle (usu. fig. of feeble glimmer of intelligence, scanty information, etc.). **3.** Hence ~′LIKE, ~′Y², *adjs.* [OE *rysc(e)*, corresp. to MLG, MHG *rusch*]

rŭsh² v. & n. **1.** v.t. impel, drag, force, carry along forcefully and rapidly, (*rushed them into danger, round the sights; patient was rushed to hospital; bull is rushed down the field; emergency legislation was rushed through Parliament*); ~ **person** (**off his feet**), force him to act hastily; **pay attentions* to (person) with view to securing acceptance of proposal. **2.** capture by sudden vehement assault; swarm upon and take possession of (gold-field, platform at meeting, etc.). **3.** pass (obstacle, stream, fence, etc.) with a rapid dash; ~ one's **fences,** act with undue haste. **4.** (sl.) charge (customer) exorbitant price. **5.** v.i. rush precipitately, violently, with great speed, go or resort without proper consideration (*in*) *to,* (*rush into* or *out of the room; dark horse rushed past the favourite; rush to extremes*); ~ **at,** attack impetuously; ~ **into print,** write to newspaper, publish book, etc. without proper consideration. **6.** flow, fall, spread, roll, impetuously or fast (*river rushes past; a rushing mighty wind; avalanches rush down; blood rushed to his face; his past life rushed into his memory*). **7.** n. act of rushing, violent or tumultuous advance, spurt, charge, onslaught, period of great activity, (*the rush of the tide; carry the citadel with a rush; a rush of blood to the head; a sudden rush of business*); (Cinemat., colloq.) first print or preliminary showing of film before cutting; (Footb.) combined dash or several players with the ball, *carrying of ball; sudden migration of large numbers esp. to new gold-field; strong run *on* or *for* some commodity; ∼**-hour** (at which traffic is busiest); ∼ **job** etc. (done with minimum delay). [ME, f. AF *russher*, = OF *rus(s)er* (see RUSE)]

rŭsk *n.* piece of bread pulled or cut from loaf and rebaked usu. as light biscuit. [f. Sp. or Port. *rosca* twist, coil, roll of bread]

Rŭss *n. & a.* (arch.) = RUSSIAN. [f. Russ. *Rus*' early name of Russia and Russian people]

Rŭ'ssell *n.* ∼ **cord**, ribbed fabric of cotton and wool used for academic gowns etc. [19th c.; orig. unkn.]

rŭ'ssèt *n. & a.* **1.** *n.* (Hist.) coarse homespun reddish-brown or grey cloth worn by peasants; reddish brown; kind of rough-skinned russet-coloured apple. **2.** *a.* reddish-brown, whence ∼Y² *a.*; (arch.) rustic, homely, simple. [ME f. AF, f. OF *ro(u)sset* dim. of *roux* red f. Prov. *ros*, It. *rosso* f. L *russus* red; see -ET¹]

Rŭ'ssia (-sha) *n.* ∼ (**leather**), durable bookbinding leather from skins impregnated with birch-bark oil. [∼ in E. Europe]

Rŭ'ssian (-shan) *n. & a.* **1.** *n.* native, inhabitant, or language of Russia (**Little** ∼, Ukrainian); GREAT *Russian* **2.** *a.* of or from Russia; ∼ **boot** (loosely enclosing calf); ∼ **roulette**, firing of revolver held to one's head with one chamber loaded; ∼ **salad** (of mixed diced vegetables with mayonnaise). **3.** of or in Russian. **4.** Hence ∼IZE (3) *v.t.* [f. med. L *Russianus* (as prec.; see -AN)]

Rŭ'ssi|fy *v.t.* make Russian in character; hence ∼FICA'TION *n.* [f. RUSS + -I- + -FY]

Rŭ'sski *n.* (joc. or derog.) Russian person. [f. RUSSIAN after Russ. surnames ending in -*ski*]

Rŭ'ssō- *comb. form.* Russian (and); hence ∼PHIL(E) *n. & a.*, ∼PHOBE *n. & a.*, ∼PHO'BIA *n.* [f. RUSS + -O-]

rŭst *n. & v.* **1.** *n.* reddish or yellowish-brown coating formed on iron or steel by oxidation esp. as effect of moisture and gradually corroding the metal; similar coating on other metals; (fig.) impaired state due to disuse or inactivity, inaction as deteriorating influence. **2.** (plant-disease with rust-coloured spots caused by) fungus of order Uredinales. **3.** Hence ∼'LESS *a.* (esp. of chrome steel), ∼-PROOF² *a.*, & *v.t.* **4.** *v.i.* become rusty; undergo oxidation; (of plant) be attacked by rust; (of bracken etc.) become rust-coloured; lose quality or efficiency by disuse or inactivity. **5.** *v.t.* affect with rust, corrode. [OE *rūst*, = OS, OHG *rost* f. Gmc *rudh-*, cogn. w. RED]

rŭ'stic *a. & n.* **1.** *a.* having the appearance or manners of country people, characteristic of peasants, unsophisticated, unpolished, unrefined, uncouth. **2.** of rude or country workmanship (∼ **seat, bridge, work**, structure of untrimmed branches or rough timber; (of lettering) freely formed; (Archit.) with rough-hewn or roughened surface or with sunk joints (∼-**work**, such masonry). **3.** (arch.) rural. **4.** Hence or cogn. **rŭ'sti**CALLY *adv.*, **rŭsti'**CITY *n.* **5.** *n.* countryman, peasant. [ME, f. L *rusticus* (*rus* the country)]

rŭ'stic|āte *v.* **1.** *v.i.* retire to or sojourn in the country,

lead a rural life. **2.** *v.t.* send down temporarily from university as punishment; make rural; mark (masonry) with sunk joints or roughened surface. **3.** Hence ∼A'TION *n.* [f. L *rusticari* live in the country (as prec.) + -ATE³]

rŭ'stl|e (-sĕl) *v. & n.* **1.** *v.i.*, & *n.* (give forth) sound (as) of dry leaves blown, rain pattering, or silk garments in motion; go with rustle (*along* etc.); be finely clad *in* (silk etc.); *(colloq.)* hustle, move energetically. **2.** *v.t.* cause to rustle by shaking etc.; *(colloq.)* acquire or deal with by exerting efforts; *(steal (cattle or horses); ∼e up, (colloq.) forage for, produce when needed. **3.** Hence ∼ER¹ (-sl-) *n.* [ME *rustel* etc., imit.; cf. obs. Flem. *ruysselen*, Du. *ritselen*]

rŭ'stre (-ter) *n.* (Her.) lozenge with round hole. [F]

rŭ'st|ỹ *a.* rusted, affected with rust; of antiquated appearance; (of voice) croaking, creaking; stiff with age or disuse, antiquated, behind the times; impaired by neglect, in need of furbishing, (*his Greek is a little rusty*); (of black clothes) discoloured by age; rust-coloured; hence ∼iLY² *adv.*, ∼iNESS *n.* [OE *rūstig* (as RUST, -Y²)]

rŭt¹ *n.*, & *v.t.* (-tt-). **1.** *n.* track sunk by passage of wheels; established mode of procedure, beaten track, groove, (**in a** ∼, following a fixed pattern of behaviour difficult to change); hence ∼'tv² *a.* **2.** *v.t.* (esp. in *p.p.*) mark with ruts. [prob. f. OF *rote* (as ROUTE)]

rŭt² *n.*, & *v.i.* (-tt-). **1.** *n.* periodic sexual excitement of male deer, goat, ram, etc. **2.** *v.i.* be affected with rut; hence ∼'tiSH¹ *a.* [ME, f. OF *ru(i)t* f. L *rugitus* (*rugire* roar)]

rutabā'ga (rŏŏ-) *n.* swede turnip. [f. Sw. dial. *rotabagge*]

ruth (rŏŏth) *n.* (arch.) pity, compassion; hence ∼'FUL *a.* [ME, f. RUE¹ + -TH¹]

ruthē'nium (rŏŏ-) *n.* rare hard white metallic element of platinum group. [f. med. L *Ruthenia* Russia (from its discovery in ores from the Urals) + -IUM]

rŭtherfŏr'dium (-dh-) *n.* (Chem.) kurchatovium [f E. *Rutherford*, Engl. physicist d. 1937 + -IUM]

ru'thless (rŏŏ-) *a.* having no pity or compassion; hence ∼LY² *adv.*, ∼NESS *n.* [ME, f. RUTH + -LESS]

ru'tile (rŏŏ'-) *n.* titanium dioxide as mineral. [F, or G *rutil*, f. L *rutilus* reddish]

RV *abbr.* Revised Version (of Bible).

RWS *abbr.* Royal Society of Painters in Water Colours.

-rỹ *suf.*, = -ERY (which see for numbered meanings; *chantry, infantry, Jewry; gadgetry, rivalry, rocketry*). [shortened f. -ERY, or by anal.]

Ry. *abbr.* Railway.

rỹe *n.* (grain of) a N. European cereal (*Secale cereale*) used for bread in northern countries and for fodder elsewhere; ∼ (**whisky**), whisky distilled from rye. [OE *ryge*, = ON *rugr* f. Gmc *rugiz*]

rỹ'e-grass (rī'grahs) *n.* fodder grass of genus *Lolium*. [f. obs. *ray-grass*; orig. unkn.]

ryō'kăn *n.* traditional Japanese inn. [Jap.]

rỹ'ot *n.* Indian peasant. [f. Urdu *ra'īyat* f. Arab. (as RAYAH)]

S

S, s, (ĕs) *n.* (*pl.* **Ss** *or* **S's,** *pr.* ĕ′sĭz). nineteenth letter of alphabet; S-shaped object or curve.

-s¹ (*pr.* -z after vowel or voiced consonant; see notes on Plurals, p. xvi.) *suf.* denoting *pl.* of *ns.*; w. *adv.* force in *evenings* (= in the evenings), *Mondays* (= on Mondays), etc. [OE *-as* pl. ending]

-s² (*pr.* -z after vowel or voiced consonant; see notes on Verb forms, p. xvii.) *suf.* denoting 3 pers. sing. pres. ind. of vbs. [OE dial., prob. f. OE 3 pers. sing. pres. ending *-es, -as*]

-s³ (*pr.* -z after vowel or voiced consonant) *suf.* forming *advs.* (*besides, eftsoons, needs,* -WARDS, & w. changed sp. *once*), and abs. poss. *adjs.* (*hers, ours*). [f. as -'s 1]

-s⁴ (*pr.* -z after vowel or voiced consonant) *suf.* forming nicknames (*Carrots, Fats*) or pet names (*Pops, ducks*). [after -s¹]

's- (s-, z-) *pref.* (chiefly arch., in oaths). God's ('*sblood,* '*sdeath,* '*struth*). [abbr.]

-'s *suf.* denoting: **1.** Possessive case of *sing. ns.* etc. **2.** Plural of letter (*S's*) or symbol (*8's*). **3.** (colloq.) *is* or *has* (*he's, she's, who's, it's, Smith's*). **4.** (colloq.) *us* in *let's.* **5.** (colloq.) *does* (*what's* he say?). [sense 1 f. OE gen. sing. ending; sense 2 as -s¹; senses 3–5 abbr.]

S. *abbr.* Saint; siemens; Society; South(ern).

s. *abbr.* second(s); shilling(s) [orig. f. L SOLIDUS]; singular; son; succeeded.

S *symb.* sulphur.

SA *abbr.* Salvation Army; sex appeal; South Africa; South America; South Australia; (Hist.) *Sturmabteilung* (political militia of Nazi party).

sabadi′lla *n.* Mexican plant (*Schoenocaulon officinale*) whose seeds yield veratrine. [f. Sp. *cebadilla* dim. of *cebada* barley]

Sabae′an, Sabē′an, *a.* & *n.* (native) of ancient Yemen; (erron.) = SABIAN. [f. L f. Gk *Sabaios* (*Saba* f. Arab. *sabā* = Heb. *š^e bā* people of Yemen) + -AN]

Sā′baïsm *n.* worship of stars or of spirits in them, in ancient Arabia and Mesopotamia. [f. F *sabaïsme* f. Heb. *ṣābā* host of heaven); see -ISM]

Sā̆bāŏth (să̆′-, -bā′-) *n. pl.* **Lord** (**God**) **of** ∼ (in NT and *Te Deum*), Lord of HOST's. [ME f. LL f. Gk *Sabaōth* f. Heb. *ṣ^e bāōṯ* pl. of *ṣābā* (see prec.)]

Săbbatār′ian *n.* & *a.* **1.** *n.* strict sabbath-keeping Jew. **2.** Christian who favours observing Sunday strictly as sabbath. **3.** Christian who observes Saturday as sabbath. **4.** Hence ∼ISM (3) *n.* **5.** *a.* holding, or relating to, tenets of Sabbatarians. [f. LL *sabbatarius* f. L *sabbatum* (see foll., -ARY¹) + -AN; see -ARIAN]

să′bbath *n.* **1.** ∼ (**day**), seventh day of week as day of religious rest appointed for Israelites; ∼ **day's journey,** distance Israelite might travel on sabbath, about ⅞ mile, (fig.) easy journey. **2.** ∼ (**day**), Christian Sunday esp. as day of obligatory abstinence from work and play (esp. in Presbyterian use, or joc.); hence ∼′LESS *a.* **3.** period of rest. **4.** (**witches'**) ∼, supposed general midnight meeting of the Devil and witches. [OE *sabat,* L *sabbatum,* & OF *sab(b)at,* f. Gk *sabbaton* f. Heb. *šabbāṯ* (*šābaṯ* to rest)]

sabbă′tic|(al) *adjs.* of or appropriate to the sabbath; ∼al **year,** (1) seventh year in which Israelites were to cease tilling and release debtors and Israelite slaves, (2) period of leave granted at intervals to university professor, missionary, etc. for study, travel, etc., (so ∼al *term* etc., or as *n.*); hence ∼al LY² *adv.* [f. LL f. Gk *sabbatikos* of sabbath (as prec.; see -IC) + -AL]

să′bbatize, -īse (-īz), *v.* **1.** *v.i.* keep the, have a, sabbath. **2.** *v.t.* make (day) into, keep as, a sabbath. [ME, f. LL *sabbatizare* f. Gk *sabbatizō* (as SABBATH; see -IZE)]

SABC *abbr.* South African Broadcasting Corporation.

Săbĕ′llĭan¹ *a.* & *n.* (Rom. Hist.) (member) of group of tribes in ancient Italy including Sabines, Samnites, Campanians, etc. [f. L *Sabellus* + -IAN]

Săbĕ′llĭan² *a.* & *n.* (holder) of the doctrine of Sabellius that the three Divine persons are merely aspects of one. [f. LL *Sabellianus* (*Sabellius* 3rd-c. African heresiarch); see -AN]

*sā′ber. See SABRE.

Sā′bĭan *a.* & *n.* **1.** (member) of a sect classed in Koran with Muslims, Jews, and Christians, as believers in the true God. **2.** (erron.) (adherent) of Sabaism. [f. Arab. *ṣābī* + -AN]

să′bĭcu (-kōō) *n.* W. Ind. timber-tree (*Lysiloma sabicu*); its mahogany-like wood. [Cuban Sp. *sabicú*]

Sā′bĭne *a.* & *n.* (one) of a people of central Apennines in ancient Italy. [f. L *Sabinus*]

sā′ble¹ *n.* small brown-furred Arctic and sub-arctic carnivorous quadruped allied to marten; its skin or fur; fine paint-brush made of sable's hair; (**American**) ∼, Amer. pine marten. [ME f. OF, f. med. L *sabelum* f. Slav.]

sā′ble² *n.* & *a.* **1.** *n.* (poet. or rhet.) black; (in *pl.*) mourning garments, whence **sā′bl**ED² (-bĕld) *a.* **2.** ∼ (**antelope**), large stout-horned Afr. antelope of which male is mostly black. **3.** *a.* (poet. or rhet.) black, dusky, gloomy, dread; **his** ∼ **Majesty,** the Devil; hence **sā′bl**Y² *adv.* **4.** *n.,* & *a.* (usu. after *n.*) (Her.) black. [ME f. OF (Her.), perh. f. prec.]

sā′bŏt (-ō) *n.* shoe hollowed out from one piece of wood, worn by French peasants etc.; wooden-soled shoe; hence ∼ED² (-bŏd) *a.* [F, blend of *savate* shoe + *botte* boot]

să′botage (-ahzh) *n.,* & *v.t.* **1.** *n.* malicious or wanton destruction, esp. doing of damage to equipment etc. by dissatisfied workmen or by hostile agents. **2.** *v.t.* commit sabotage on; (fig.) destroy, render useless, (*sabotaged my plans*). [F (*saboter* make noise with sabots, bungle, wilfully destroy, f. as prec.; see -AGE)]

săboteur (-tēr′) *n.* one who commits sabotage. [F]

să′bra *n.* native-born Israeli. [f. mod. Heb. *sābrāh* opuntia fruit]

sā′bre (-er), ***sā′ber,** *n.,* & *v.t.* **1.** *n.* cavalry sword with curved blade; cavalry soldier and horse; light fencing-sword with tapering blade; ∼-**bill,** S. Amer. bird with curved bill; ∼-**cut,** (1) blow with sabre, (2) wound made or scar left by it; ∼-**rattling,** display or threats of military force (cf. RATTLE¹); ∼-**toothed lion** or **tiger,** extinct mammal with long sabre-shaped upper canines; ∼-**wing,** S. Amer. humming-bird with curved wings. **2.** *v.t.* cut down or wound with sabre. [F, earlier *sable* f. G *sabel, säbel, schabel* f. Pol. *szabla* or Magyar *szablya*]

să′bretăche (-ertăsh) *n.* cavalry officer's flat satchel on long straps from left of waist-belt. [F, f. G *säbeltasche* (as prec., *tasche* pocket)]

sabreur (-ēr′) *n.* user of sabre, esp. cavalryman. [F (*sabrer* SABRE 2)]

săc *n.* baglike membrane-enclosed cavity in animal or vegetable organism; membranous envelope of hernia, cyst, tumour, etc.; = SACK¹ 2. [F, or f. L *saccus* SACK¹]

‖SAC *abbr.* Senior Aircraftman.

săcca′de (-ah′d) *n.* brief rapid movement of eye between fixation points; hence **saccă′d**IC *a.* [F, = violent pull, f. OF *saquer, sachier* pull]

sa′ccate *a.* (Bot.) dilated into bag; contained in sac. [f. SAC + -ATE²]

să′ccharĭde (-ker-) *n.* (Chem.) = SUGAR 3. [f. mod. L *saccharum* sugar + -IDE]

săcchari′|mĕter (-ker-) *n.* instrument for measurement of sugar content of a solution by means of polarized light; so ∼METRY n. [f. F saccharimètre (as prec., -I-, -METER)]

sǎ'ccharin (-ker-) n. very sweet substance used as substitute for sugar by diabetics, slimmers, etc. [G (as SACCHARIDE; see -IN)]

sǎ'ccharine (-kerēn) a. sugary; of, containing, like, sugar; unpleasantly over-polite etc. [f. as SACCHARIDE + -INE¹]

sǎ'ccharō- (-kerō) comb. form. sugar (and), as ∼GE'NIC (1) a. [f. Gk sakkharon sugar + -O-]

sǎcchorō'|mèter (-ker-) n. instrument for measurement of sugar content of a solution; so ∼METRY n. [f. as prec. + -METER]

sǎ'ccharōse (-ker-) n. sucrose. [f. mod. L saccharum sugar + -OSE]

sǎ'cciform (-ks-) a. sac-shaped. [f. L saccus sac + -i- + -FORM]

sǎ'ccūl|ar a. of or like a sac; so ∼ATE² a., ∼A'TION n. [f. L (as foll.) + -AR¹]

sǎ'ccūle n. small sac or cyst. [f. L sacculus (as SAC; see -ULE)]

sǎ'cerdōtage n. (joc.) sacerdotalism; priest-ridden state. [as foll. w. ref. to dotage]

sǎcerdō'tal a. of priest(s) or priesthood, priestly; (of doctrine etc.) ascribing sacrificial functions and supernatural powers to ordained priests, claiming excessive authority for the priesthood; hence ∼ISM (3), ∼IST (2), ns., ∼IZE (3) v.t., ∼LY² adv. [ME f. OF, or f. L sacerdotalis (sacerdos -dotis priest; see -AL)]

sǎ'chem n. **1.** supreme chief of some Amer. Ind. tribes. **2.** *political leader. [Narraganset, = SAGAMORE]

sǎ'chet (-shā) n. small perfumed bag; (packet of) dry perfume for laying among clothes etc.; packet for small quantity of shampoo etc. [F, dim. of sac f. L saccus]

sǎck¹ n., & v.t. **1.** n. large usu. oblong bag for storing and conveying goods, usu. open at one end and made of coarse flax or hemp, whence ∼ING¹ (3) n.; ∼('FUL 2 n.), sack with contents (usu. of); amount (of corn, coal, flour, wool, potatoes, etc.) usu. put in sack, as unit of measure or weight; *(sl.) bed (hit the ∼, go to bed); the ∼, (colloq.) dismissal (get, give person, the sack). **2.** woman's short loose dress with sacklike appearance; (arch. or Hist.) woman's loose gown, or silk train attached to shoulders of this. **3.** man's or woman's loose-hanging coat not shaped to back. **4.** ∼'cloth, coarse fabric of flax or hemp, sacking, (fig.) mourning or penitential garb, esp. sackcloth and ashes (orig. Bibl.); ∼ race (between competitors in sacks up to waist or neck). **5.** v.t. put into sack(s); (colloq.) dismiss from service etc. [OE sacc f. L f. Gk sakkos, of Semitic orig.]

sǎck² v.t., & n. **1.** v.t. (Of victorious army or its commander) plunder, give over to plunder, (captured town etc.); (of burglar etc.) carry off valuable contents of. **2.** n. sacking of captured place. [v. f. n., f. F. sac in phr. mettre à sac put to sack, f. It. sacco SACK¹]

sǎck³ n. (Hist.) white wine formerly imported into Britain from Spain and the Canaries (sherry, Canary, etc., sack). [16th c. wyne seck, f. F vin sec dry wine]

sǎ'ckbut n. Renaissance kind of trombone; (Bibl., as wrong transl.) triangular harp. [f. F saquebute, earlier saqueboute hook for pulling man off horse (saquer pull, boute as BUTT⁴)]

sǎ'ckless a. (arch. or Sc.) innocent (of); harmless, feeble-minded. [OE sacléas f. ON saklauss (as SAKE¹, -LESS)]

sǎcque (sǎk) n. = SACK¹ 2. [var. of SACK¹, w. pseudo-F sp.]

sǎ'cral a. (Anat.) of the sacrum; (Anthrop.) of or for sacred rites. [f. E or L SACRUM + -AL]

sǎ'crament n., & v.t. **1.** n. religious ceremony or act regarded as outward and visible sign of inward and spiritual grace (applied by the Eastern, pre--Reformation Western, and RC Churches to the seven rites of baptism, confirmation, the Eucharist,

penance, extreme unction, ordination, and matrimony; restricted by most Protestants to baptism and the Eucharist); the ∼, the ∼ of the altar, the Blessed or Holy S∼, (1) the Eucharist, (2) the consecrated elements esp. the bread or Host; **take, receive, the** ∼ to do or upon (as confirmation of some promise or oath). **2.** thing of mysterious and sacred significance, sacred influence, symbol, etc. **3.** oath or solemn engagement taken. **4.** v.t. (esp. in p.p.) bind by oath. [ME f. OF sacrement f. L sacramentum solemn oath etc. (sacrare hallow f. sacer SACRED; see -MENT), used in Christian L as transl. of Gk mustērion MYSTERY¹]

sǎcramĕ'ntal a. & n. **1.** a. of (the nature of) a or the sacrament, whence ∼ITY (-ă'l-) n.; (of doctrine etc.) attaching great importance to the sacraments, whence ∼ISM (3), ∼IST (2), ns.; hence ∼LY⁸ adv. **2.** n. observance analogous to but not reckoned among the sacraments, e.g. use of holy water or sign of the cross. [ME f. F, or f. LL sacramentalis (as prec.; see -AL)]

sǎcramentār'ian a. & n. **1.** (Hist.) denying, one who denies, the Real Presence (holding that 'body and blood of Christ' was used only in sacramental, i.e. symbolic, sense). **2.** holding or involving, holder of, sacramental doctrine, whence ∼ISM (3) n. [f. mod. L sacramentarius (as prec.; see -ARY¹) + -AN; see -ARIAN]

sacrār'i|um n. (pl. ∼a). sanctuary of church; (RC) piscina; (Rom. Ant.) shrine, room of penates in house. [L (sacer sacri holy; see -ARIUM)]

sǎ'cred a. **1.** devoted or held especially acceptable to a deity, dedicated or reserved or appropriated to some person or purpose; made holy by religious association, hallowed; ∼ book, writings, (embodying laws etc. of a religion); Sacred COLLEGE; S∼ Heart, the heart of Jesus (or of Mary) as object of devotion; ∼ number (associated with religious symbolism, e.g. 7); ∼ poetry, music, (on religious themes); S∼ (= HOLY) Writ; (as specific epithet of animal etc.) now or formerly sacred to some god (sacred IBIS, monkey, beetle). **2.** safeguarded or required by religion or reverence or tradition, indefeasible, inviolable, sacrosanct, (His Most Sacred Majesty the King; regards it as a sacred duty; their property or persons will be held sacred; no place was sacred from him, from outrage); ∼ cow, (fig.) idea or institution unreasonably held to be immune from questioning or criticism [w. ref. to Hindus' respect for cow as holy animal]. **3.** Hence ∼LY² adv., ∼NESS n. [ME, p.p. of obs. sacre consecrate f. OF sacrer f. L sacrare (sacer sacri holy)]

sǎ'crifice n. & v. **1.** n. slaughter of animal or person, surrender of a possession, as offering to a deity, (fig.) act of prayer or thanksgiving or penitence as propitiation; what is thus slaughtered or presented or done, victim, offering; (Theol.) Christ's offering of himself in the Crucifixion, the Eucharist as either a propitiatory offering of the body and blood of Christ or an act of thanksgiving. **2.** giving up of valued thing for the sake of another that is more worthy or more important or more urgent, thing thus given up, loss thus entailed; (will gain nothing by the sacrifice of your principles; at some sacrifice of regularity; surplus stock for sale at a sacrifice; made sacrifices so that her son could go to university); (in games) loss incurred deliberately to avoid greater loss or to obtain compensating advantage; SELF-sacrifice. **3.** So **sǎcrifi'cial** (-shǎl) a. **4.** v.t. & i. offer (as) sacrifice (to, or abs.); give up, treat as secondary or of inferior importance, devote, to (has sacrificed herself, her whole life, her pleasures, to his interest; sacrifice accuracy to vividness); sell at a loss. [ME f. OF, f. L sacrificium (sacrificus as prec.; see -FIC)]

sǎ'crilège n. robbery or profanation of sacred building, outrage on consecrated person or thing, violation of what is sacred; so **sǎcrilē'gious** (-jus) a. [ME f. OF, f. L sacrilegium (sacrilegus stealer of sacred things, f. sacer sacri sacred + legere take possession of)]

sǎ'cring n. (arch.) consecration of Eucharistic elements; ordination and consecration of bishop, sovereign, etc.; ∿-**bell** (rung at elevation of elements in Eucharist). [ME, f. obs. *sacre* (see SACRED) +-ING¹].

sä′crist *n.* official keeping sacred vessels etc. of religious house or church. [f. OF *sacriste* or f. med. L *sacrista* (as SACRED; see -IST)]

sä′cristan *n.* = prec.; (arch.) sexton of parish church. [ME, f. med. L *sacristanus* (as prec.; see -AN)]

sä′cristy̆ *n.* repository for vestments, vessels, etc., of a church. [f. F *sacristie* or It. *sacrestia* or f. med. L *sacristia* (as SACRIST; see -Y¹)]

sä′crō- *comb. form.* of sacrum and (*sacro-iliac*). [f. SACRUM +-O-]

sä′crosănct *a.* (Of person, place, law, etc.) secured by religious sanction against outrage, inviolable; hence **săcrosä′nct**ITY *n.* [f. L *sacrosanctus* (*sacro* abl. of *sacrum* SACRED rite, *sanctus* as SAINT)]

sä′cr|um *n.* composite triangular bone of ankylosed vertebrae forming back of pelvis. [f. L *os sacrum* transl. Gk *hieron osteon* sacred bone (from sacrificial use)]

‖**SACW** *abbr.* Senior Aircraftwoman.

săd *a.* **1.** sorrowful, mournful, showing or causing sorrow; **a ∿der and a wiser man,** one who has had a distressing but instructive experience; **in ∿ earnest,** (arch.) seriously. **2.** (derog., usu. joc.) shocking, deplorably bad, incorrigible, (*is a sad slut, coward; writes sad stuff*); ∿ **dog,** rake, scapegrace. **3.** (Of colour) dull, neutral-tinted; (of pastry etc.) heavy. **4.** ∿-**iron,** solid flat-iron; *∿* **sack,** (colloq.) very inept person. **5.** Hence ∿′**dEN**⁶ *v.t.* & *i.*, ∿′**dISH**¹ 2 *a.*, ∿′**LY**² *adv.*, ∿′**NESS** *n.* [OE *sæd*, = OS *sad*, OHG *sat*, ON *sathr*, Goth. *saths* f. Gmc **sadhaz* full, cogn. w. L *satis*]

sä′ddle *n.*, & *v.t.* **1.** *n.* seat for rider, placed on back of horse etc. (usu. raised at front and rear, and leather-covered with side-flaps and girths and stirrups) or forming part of bicycle etc. or of agricultural machine; **in the ∿,** mounted, (fig.) in office or control. **2.** part of shaft-horse's harness that bears shafts. **3.** part of animal's back resembling saddle in shape or marking; rear part of male fowl's back. **4.** saddle-shaped thing, e.g. ridge between two summits, support for cable or wire on top of suspension-bridge pier or telegraph-pole, joint *of* mutton or venison consisting of the two loins. **5.** ∿**back,** (Archit.) tower-roof with two opposite gables, saddlebacked hill, bird with saddle-like marking (esp. the grey crow or a black NZ bird), black pig with white stripe across back; ∿**backed,** with upper outline concave, (Archit.) having saddleback; ∿-**bag,** one of pair of bags laid across horse etc. behind saddle, bag attached behind saddle of bicycle or motor cycle; ∿-**bow** (-bō), arched front or rear of saddle [BOW¹]; ∿-**cloth** (laid on horse's back under saddle); ∿**fast,** (arch.) firmly seated in saddle; ∿-**horse** (for riding); *∿* **shoe** (with contrasting band across upper); ∿-**sore,** chafed by riding on saddle; ∿-**stitch** (of wire staple through centre of magazine etc.); ∿-**tree,** (1) frame of saddle, (2) tulip-tree (with saddle-shaped leaves). **6.** Hence ∿LESS (-del-l-) *a.* **7.** *v.t.* put saddle on (horse etc.); (of trainer) enter (horse) for race; burden (person) *with* task, responsibility, etc.; put (burden) *on* or *upon* (person). [(v. f. OE *sadolian*) f. OE *sadol*, *sadl*, MDu. *sadel*, OHG *satal*, *satul*, ON *söthull* f. Gmc **sadhulaz*]

sä′ddl|er *n.* maker of or dealer in saddles and other equipment for horses; (Mil.) man in charge of cavalry regiment's saddlery; hence ∿ERY (1, 2, 3) *n.* [ME, f. prec. +-ER¹]

Să′ddŭcee *n.* member of Jewish sect or party (cf. PHARISEE, ESSENE) of time of Christ that denied resurrection of the dead, existence of spirits, and obligation of the traditional oral law; hence *n.* or cogn. **Săddŭce′AN** *a.*, ∿ISM (3) *n.* [OE *sad(d)ucēas* f. LL f. Gk *Saddoukaios* f. Heb. *sᵉdûḳî*, prob. = descendant of Zadok (2 Sam. 8: 17)]

sa′dhu (sah′dōō) *n.* (Ind.) holy man, sage, or ascetic. [Skr., = holy man]

sa′d|ism (sä′-, sah′-) *n.* form of sexual perversion

marked by love of cruelty to others (opp. MASOCHISM); deriving of pleasure from inflicting or watching cruelty; so ∿IST (2) *n.*, **sadi′st**IC *a.* [f. F *sadisme* (Count or 'Marquis' de Sade, Fr. author d. 1814; see -ISM)]

sadō-mă′soch|ism (sä-, sah-; -k-) *n.* combination of sadism and masochism in one person; hence ∿IST (2) *n.*, ∿**i′st**IC *a.* [f. prec. +-O-+MASOCHISM]

s.a.e. *abbr.* stamped addressed envelope.

sae′ter (sä′-) *n.* high summer-pasture in Scandinavia. [Norw., f. ON *setr* SEAT]

safär′i *n.* journey or (esp. scientific or hunting) expedition esp. in E. Africa (*go on safari*); ∿ **park,** area where lions etc. are kept in the open for viewing. [Swahili, f. Arab. *safara* to travel]

safe¹ *n.* strong locked repository or receptacle for valuables; ***condom;** = MEAT-*safe*; ∿-**blower,** ∿-**cracker,** criminal who breaks safes open. [orig. *save*, f. SAVE¹, assim. to foll.]

safe² *a.* **1.** (*pred.*, after *come*, *arrive*, *bring*, *keep*, etc.). ∿ (**and sound**), uninjured (*parcel came safe*; *saw them safe home*); secure, out of or not exposed to danger (*from*), (*now we are, can feel, safe*; *is safe from his enemies*); (Baseball) having reached a base successfully. **2.** affording security or not involving danger (*put it in a safe place*; *is it safe to leave him?*; *maximum safe load 10 tons*; *safe custody, convoy,* etc.; *dog is not safe to touch*); **it is ∿ to say,** it may be said without risk of exaggeration or falsehood; **on the ∿ side,** with margin of security against risks; PLAY¹ *safe*. **3.** debarred from escaping or doing harm (*have got him safe*). **4.** cautious and unenterprising, consistently moderate, that can be reckoned on, unfailing, certain *to do* or *be*, sure to become, (*a safe critic, statesman; safe methods; a safe* CATCH², *winner; better to be safe than sorry; is safe to win, be there*); ∿ **bet** (that is certain to succeed); ∿ **seat** (in Parliament etc., that is sure to be won by a particular party). **5.** ∿ **conduct,** (document conveying) privilege granted by sovereign, commander, etc., of immunity from arrest or harm on particular occasion or in district; ∿ **deposit,** building containing strong-rooms and safes let separately; ∿ **keeping,** preservation in safe place; ∿ **period,** time during and near menstrual period (when conception is least likely). **6.** Hence ∿LY² [-flī] *adv.*, ∿′NESS (-fn-) *n.* [ME f. AF *saf*, OF *sauf* f. L *salvus* uninjured]

sä′feguärd (-fgärd) *n.*, & *v.t.* **1.** *n.* safe conduct; proviso, stipulation, quality, or circumstance, that tends to prevent something undesired. **2.** *v.t.* guard or protect (rights etc.) by precaution or stipulation. [ME, f. AF *salve garde*, OF *sauve garde* (as prec., GUARD¹)]

sä′fety̆ (-ftǐ) *n.* **1.** being safe, freedom from danger or risks, (*there is safety in numbers; cannot do it with safety*); PLAY¹ *for safety;* ∿ **first,** motto inculcating caution. **2.** safeness, being sure or likely to bring no danger, (*is the safety of the experiment certain?*). **3.** ∿(-**catch**), contrivance for locking gun-trigger, preventing fall of lift, etc. **4.** ∿(-**bicycle**), (arch.) bicycle of usual low-saddled modern form (opp. *ordinary*). **5.** (Amer. Footb.) rearmost defensive player; touchdown behind one's own goal-line. **6.** ∿-**belt,** strap securing occupant of seat in aircraft, motor car, etc., or person standing at a height; ∿ **curtain,** fireproof curtain that can be lowered to cut off the auditorium in a theatre from the stage; ∿ **factor** or **factor of** ∿, ratio of material's strength to expected strain, (fig.) margin of security against risks; ∿ **film,** cinematographic film on slow-burning or non-inflammable base; ∿ **fuse,** FUSE² containing a slow-burning composition for firing detonators from a distance, (Electr.) protective FUSE³; ∿-**glass** (that will not splinter when broken); ∿ **lamp,** miner's lamp so protected as not to ignite firedamp; ∿ **match** (igniting only on specially prepared surface); ∿ **net** (placed to catch acrobat etc. in case he falls); ∿-**pin** (with point that is bent back to head and can be held in guard so that user may not be pricked nor pin come out); ~ **play,** (Bridge) play designed to give best chance of making one's contract even at cost of overtrick; ~ **razor** (with guard to prevent blade from cutting skin); ~**-valve,** (in steam-boiler) valve opening automatically to relieve excessive pressure, (fig.) means of giving harmless vent to excitement etc. (*sit on the* ~*-valve,* follow policy of repression); **~* **zone,** area of road marked off for pedestrians etc. to wait safely. [ME *sauwete,* f. OF *sauveté* f. med. L *salvitas -tatis* f. L *salvus* (as SAFE²); see -TY¹]

sä′fflower *n.* thistle-like plant (*Carthamus tinctorius*) yielding red dye used in rouge etc.; its dried petals; dye made from them. [f. Du. *saffloer* or G *safflor* f. OF *saffleur* f. obs. It. *saffiore*; orig. unkn.]

sä′ffron *n.* & *a.* **1.** *n.* orange-coloured stigmas of a crocus (*Crocus sativus*), used for colouring and flavouring confectionery, liquors, rice, etc.; MEADOW *saffron.* **2.** *a.* & *n.* saffron-colour(ed), whence ~v² *a.*; ~ **cake** (flavoured with saffron). [ME, f. OF *safran* f. Arab. *za'farān*]

sä′franin *n.* colouring-matter of saffron; yellowish--red synthetic dyestuff. [f. F *safranine* (as prec.; see -IN)]

säg *v.i.* (-gg-), & *n.* **1.** *v.i.* sink or subside under weight or pressure; hang sideways, be lopsided, (*gate, bridge, sags*); have downward bulge or curve in middle (*ceiling, slackened rope, sags*); (Commerc.) fall in price; (of ship) drift from course (esp. to leeward); hence ~′gy² (gī) *a.* **2.** *n.* amount that rope etc. sags, distance from middle of its curve to straight line between supports; sinking, subsidence; fall in price; (Naut.) tendency to leeward. [ME, f. MLG *sacken,* Du. *zakken* subside]

sa′ga (sah′-) *n.* medieval Icelandic or Norwegian prose narrative, esp. one embodying history of Icelandic family or Norwegian king; story of heroic achievement or adventure; series of connected books giving history of a family etc.; long involved story. [ON, = narrative, cogn. w SAW²]

sagā′cious (-shŭs) *a.* mentally penetrating, gifted with discernment, having practical wisdom; acute--minded, shrewd; (of saying, plan, etc.) showing sagacity; (of animal) exceptionally intelligent, seeming to reason or deliberate; hence or cogn. ~LY² *adv.,* **sagā′city** *n.* [f. L *sagax sagacis* +-OUS]

sä′gamŏre *n.* = SACHEM 1. [f. Penobscot *sagamo*]

säge¹ *n.* **1.** aromatic herb (*Salvia officinalis*) with dull greyish-green leaves; its leaves used in cookery (~ **and onions,** stuffing used for goose, duck, pork, etc.). **2.** ~**-brush,** growth of plants (esp. of genus *Artemisia*) characterizing some sterile alkaline regions of US; ~ **cheese** or ~ **Derby** (flavoured and mottled by addition of sage-infusion to the curd); ~**-green,** colour of sage-leaves; ~**-grouse,** large grouse of sage-brush regions; ~ **tea,** medicinal infusion of sage-leaves. **3.** Hence **sä′gy²** *a.* [ME f. OF *sauge* f. L *salvia* healing plant (*salvus* safe)]

sage² *a.* & *n.* **1.** *a.* wise, discreet, judicious, having the wisdom of experience, of or indicating profound wisdom, (often iron.) wise-looking, solemn-faced; hence ~LY² (-jlǐ) *adv.,* ~′NESS (-jn-) *n.* **2.** *n.* profoundly wise man (often iron.), esp. any of the ancients traditionally reputed wisest of their time (**the Seven S~s,** 7 Greeks each credited with a notable saying); hence ~′SHIP (-jsh-) *n.* [ME f. OF, f. Gallo-Rom. *sapius (L *sapere* be wise)]

sä′ggar *n.* case of baked fireproof clay enclosing pottery while it is baked. [prob. contr. of SAFEGUARD]

sä′gitta *n.* (Geom.) greatest distance of arc from its chord, measured perpendicular to the chord. [L, = arrow]

sä′gittal *a.* (Anat.) of suture between parietal bones; in same plane as this. [F, f. med. L *sagittalis* (as prec.; see -AL)]

Săgittār′ı̆us *n.* sign of the ZODIAC, the Archer; hence ~AN *a.* & *n.,* (person) born under Sagittarius. [L, = archer (as SAGITTA; see -ARY¹)]

sä′gittāte *a.* (Bot. & Zool.) shaped like arrowhead. [f. as SAGITTA + -ATE²]

sä′gŏ *n.* (*pl.* ~s). (palm esp. of genus *Metroxylon,* with pith yielding) kind of starch used as food in puddings etc. [f. Malay *sāgū* (orig. thr. Port.)]

saguăr′ō (-gw-) *n.* (*pl.* ~s). giant cactus of SW United States & Mexico. [Mex. Sp.]

Sahăr′|a (sa-h-) *n.* arid region (lit. or fig.); hence ~AN, ~IAN, ~IC, *adjs.* [f. ~ desert in N. Africa, f. Arab. *ṣaḥrā'* desert]

sahib (sahb, sah′ĭb) *n.* **1.** (arch.) European or other superior as spoken of or to by Indians (also used as honorific affix; *Colonel Sahib, Jones Sahib*). **2.** (colloq.) gentleman (*pukka sahib*). [Urdu, f. Arab. *ṣāḥib* friend, lord]

said. See SAY².

sai′ga (sā′-, sī′-) *n.* antelope (*Saiga tartarica*) of steppes. [Russ.]

sail¹ *n.* **1.** piece of canvas or other textile material extended on rigging to catch wind and propel vessel, (collect.) some or all of ship's sails (CARRY¹, CROWD², hoist, lower, MAKE¹, SET¹, SHORTEN, STRIKE, *sail*); **take in** ~, furl it, (fig.) moderate one's ambitions; *take* WIND¹ *out of* person's *sails*; **under** ~, with sails set. **2.** (collect.) ships in squadron or company (*a fleet of twenty sail*). **3.** ship (esp. as discerned from its sails). **4.** (in *pl.,* Naut. *sl.*) maker or repairer of sails; ||(Hist.) chief petty officer in charge of rigging. **5.** wind--catching apparatus, usu. set of boards, attached to arm of windmill. **6.** sail-fish's dorsal fin; tentacle of nautilus; float of Portuguese man-of-war. **7.** ~**-arm,** arm of windmill; **~***′boat** (propelled by sail); ~**′cloth,** (1) canvas for sails, (2) canvas-like dress--material; ~**-fish,** (1) fish of genus *Istiophorus* with large dorsal fin, (2) basking shark; ~**′plane,** glider designed for soaring. **8.** Hence (-)~ED² (-ld), ~′LESS (-l-l-), *adjs.* [OE *segel,* = OS *segel,* OHG *segal,* ON *segl* f. Gmc *seglam]

sail² *v.* & *n.* **1.** *v.i.* (Of vessel, or person on board) travel on water by use of sails (~**′ing-ship, -vessel,** opp. *steamer; sail close to or near the* WIND¹) or engine-power; start on such voyage (*we sail next week;* ~**′ing orders,** instructions to captain for departure, destination, etc.). **2.** (Of bird, cloud, moon, etc.) glide in air; (esp. of woman) walk in stately manner; move smoothly; (fig.) pass easily (*sailed through the examination*); ~ **in** (*adv.*), **into,** (colloq.) attack physically or verbally. **3.** *v.t.* travel over or along, navigate, glide through, (*the sea, Spanish main, sky,* etc.). **4.** control navigation of (ship; PLAIN¹, PLANE³, *sailing;* ~**′ing-master,** officer navigating ship, ||esp. yacht); set (toy boat) afloat. **5.** *n.* voyage or excursion in sailing-vessel (*go for a sail*); voyage of specified duration (*is ten days' sail from Plymouth*). [OE *segl(i)an* f. Gmc *segljan (as prec.)]

sai′ler *n.* ship of specified sailing-power (*fast, good, bad, sailer*). [f. prec. + -ER¹]

sai′lor *n.* seaman, esp. one below rank of officer; **good, bad,** ~, person not liable, very liable, to sea--sickness; ~ **hat** (of straw with straight narrow brim and flat top, or with turned-up brim in imitation of sailor's worn by women or children); ~**-man,** (vulg. or joc.) sailor; ~**s' home,** institution for lodging sailors cheaply ashore; hence ~ING¹ (1) *n.,* ~LESS, ~LY¹, *adjs.* [var. of prec.; see -OR]

||**sain** *v.t.* (arch.) make sign of the cross on, bless, protect by divine power or enchantment. [OE *segnian,* = OS *segnon,* OHG *seganōn,* ON *signa,* f. L *signare* mark (*signum* SIGN¹)]

sai′nfoin (sā′-) *n.* pink-flowered herb (*Onobrychis viciaefolia*) grown for fodder. [f. obs. F *saintfoin,* orig. lucerne, f. mod. L *sanctum foenum* holy hay alt. of *sanum foenum* wholesome hay, based on L *herba medica* healing plant alt. of *herba Medica* grass from Media; cf. MEDICK]

saint *n.* (or, when unstressed, sent) usu. *abbr.* **St., S.,** in *pl.* **Sts., SS**) *n.,* & *v.t.* **1.** *a.* holy, canonized or officially recognized by the Church as having won by exceptional holiness a high place in heaven and veneration on earth, (usu. as prefix to name of person or archangel: *St. Paul, St. Michael*; hence ellipt. names of churches as *St. Peter's*, and of towns called after their churches often with loss of possessive sign as *St. Andrews* and *St. Albans*, and some Christian and family names taken either from patron saint or from local names as above; also in some names of churches not called after saints: *St. Saviour's, Sepulchre's, Faith, Cross*); **St. —'s Day**, Church festival in memory of particular saint. **2. St. Andrew**, patron saint of Scotland; **St. Andrew's cross** (X-shaped); **St. Andrew's day**, 30 Nov.; **St. Anthony('s) cross** (T--shaped); **St. Anthony's fire**, erysipelas or ergotism; **St. Bartholomew's day**, 24 Aug.; **St. Bernard (dog)**, very large dog of breed orig. kept by monks of Hospice on Great St. Bernard pass in Alps for rescue of travellers; **St. David**, patron saint of Wales; **St. David's day**, 1 Mar.; **St. Denis**, patron saint of France; **St. Elmo**, patron saint of seamen; **St. Elmo's fire**, corposant; **St. George**, patron saint of England; **St. George's cross** (+-shaped, red on white ground); **St. George's day**, 23 Apr.; (**Court of**) **St. James's**, the British Court; **St. John's wort**, yellow-flowered plant of genus *Hypericum*; ||**St. Leger**, horse-race at Doncaster for three-year-olds [f. founder's name]; ||*St. Luke's*, ||*St. Martin's*, SUMMER[1]; **St. Martin's day**, 11 Nov.; ||**St. Michael and St. George**, order of knighthood esp. for distinguished service as diplomat etc.; **St. MONDAY**; **St. Patrick**, patron saint of Ireland; **St. Patrick's day**, 17 Mar.; **Order of St. Patrick**, Irish order of knighthood; *St. Peter's* KEY[1]s; ||**St. Stephen's**, House of Commons [w. ref. to former use of St. Stephen's chapel, Westminster, for its meetings]; **St. Swithin's day**, 15 July, on which rain or absence of rain is said to presage the same for 40 days; *St.* VALENTINE'*s day*; *St. Vitus's* DANCE[2]. **3.** *n.* one of the blessed dead or other member of the company of heaven; canonized person (see sense 1; PATRON *saint*); (Bibl., arch., and by Puritans, Mormons, etc.) one of God's chosen people, member of the Christian Church or one's own branch of it (**communion of** ∼s, fellowship of Christians past and present); person of great real or affected holiness (*would provoke, try the patience of, a saint*); ∼'s **day**, Church festival in memory of a saint, often observed as holiday at schools etc.; ALL *Saints' Day*. **4.** Hence ∼'DOM, ∼'HOOD (-t-h-), ∼'LING[1], ∼'SHIP, *ns.*, ∼'LIKE, ∼'LY[1], *adjs.* **5.** *v.t.* canonize, admit to the calendar of saints; call or regard as a saint; (in *p.p.*) worthy to be so regarded, of saintly life, (of place etc.) sacred; *my sainted* AUNT. [ME, f. OF *seint, saint* f. L *sanctus* holy, p.p. of *sancire* consecrate]

saintpau'lia (sen-) *n.* blue-flowered E. Afr. herb of genus *Saintpaulia*, African violet. [mod. L, f. Baron W. von *Saint Paul*, Ger. soldier d. 1910, its discoverer +-IA[1]]

Saint-Sīmō'nian *a.* & *n.* (advocate) of socialism in which State controls property and distributes profits according to value of work; hence ∼ISM (3), **Saint--Sī'mon**ISM (3), *ns.* [f. C. de *Saint-Simon*, Fr. socialist d. 1825]

saith. See SAY[2].

saithe *n.* fish akin to cod, with skin which soils fingers like wet coal. [f. ON *seithr*]

sāke[1] *n.* **for the** ∼ **of, for my** etc. ∼, out of consideration for, in the interest of, because of, owing to, in order to please or honour or get or keep, (*for the sake of uniformity; for conscience' sake; for my own sake as well as yours; for both our sakes*); **for Christ's, God's, goodness', Heaven's**, (sl.) **Pete's**, etc., ∼ (excl. of urgent supplication); **for his name's** ∼, (1) because he bears the name he does, (2) in the interest of his reputation; **for old times'** ∼, (arch.) **for old** ∼'s ∼, in memory of old days. [OE *sacu* contention, charge, fault, sake, = OS *saka*, OHG *sahha*, ON *sǫk* f. Gmc *sakō* affair, accusation, (*sak-*, cogn. w. SEEK)]

sa'kè[2] (sah'-) *n.* Japanese fermented liquor made from rice. [Jap.]

sā'ker *n.* **1.** large falcon (*Falco sacer*) used in hawking, esp. the female (larger than the male or ∼ET[1] *n.*). **2.** (Hist.) old form of cannon. [ME, f. OF *sacre* (in both senses), f. Arab. *ṣaḳr*]

sa'kī (sah'-) *n.* S. Amer. monkey with long non--prehensile tail, and neck-ruff. [F, f. Tupi *çahy*]

sal (sahl) *n.* Indian tree (*Shorea robusta*), yielding timber and dammar resin. [f. Hindi *sāl*]

salaa'm (-lah'm) *n.* & *v.* **1.** *n.* oriental salutation 'Peace'; Indian obeisance with or without this, low bow of head and body with right palm on forehead; (in *pl.*) respectful compliments. **2.** *v.t.* & *i.* make salaam (to). [f. Arab. *salām*]

sā'lable. Var. of SALEABLE.

salā'cious (-shus) *a.* lustful, lecherous; (of writings, pictures, talk, etc.) tending to cause sexual desire; hence or cogn. ∼LY[2] *adv.*, ∼NESS, **salā'cITY**, *ns.* [f. L *salax salacis* (*salire* leap) +-OUS]

sā'lad *n.* cold dish of various mixtures of raw or cooked vegetables or herbs usu. seasoned with oil, vinegar, etc., and eaten with or including cold meat, fish, hard-boiled eggs, etc.; vegetable or herb suitable for eating raw; FRUIT *salad*; ∼ **cream**, creamy salad--dressing; ∼ **days**, period of youthful inexperience; ∼**-dressing**, mixture of oil, vinegar, etc., used with salad; ∼**-oil**, olive or other vegetable oil for salad--dressing. [ME, f. OF *salade* f. Prov. *salada* f. Rom. **salata* (*herba* herb), fem. p.p. (as n.) of **salare* f. L *sal* salt]

salā'de. Var. of SALLET.

sā'lamänder *n.* **1.** lizard-like animal supposed to live in fire; elemental spirit living in fire; (Zool.) tailed amphibian of order Caudata, whence **sălamā'ndroID** *a.* & *n.*; * = GOPHER[2] 1. **2.** red-hot iron for firing gunpowder; hot iron plate for browning top of pudding etc. **3.** Hence **sălamā'ndr**IAN, **sălamā'ndr**INE[1], *adjs.* [ME, f. OF *salamandre*, f. L f. Gk *salamandra*]

salā'mi (-lah'-) *n.* Italian sausage highly salted and flavoured often with garlic. [It., pl. of *salame*, f. pop. L **salamen* (**salare* to salt)]

săl ammō'niäc *n.* ammonium chloride, hard white crystalline salt, said to have been made from camels' dung near temple of Jupiter Ammon. [f. L *sal ammoniacus* (*sal* salt; see AMMONIACAL)]

sä'langäne (-ngg-) *n.* swift that makes edible nest. [F, f. *salanga* name in Luzon, Philippines]

salā'r'iät *n.* the salaried class. [F (*salaire*, see foll.; after *prolétariat*)]

sä'lary *n.*, & *v.t.* **1.** *n.* fixed payment made by employer at regular intervals, usu. monthly or quarterly, to person doing other than manual or mechanical work (cf. WAGE[1]s). **2.** *v.t.* (esp. in *p.p.*) pay salary to. [ME, f. AF *salarie*, OF *salaire* f. L *salarium* orig. soldier's salt-money (*sal* salt; see foll.)]

sāle *n.* **1.** exchange of a commodity for money or other consideration, selling; BILL[4] *of sale*; **on** or **for** ∼, offered for purchase; ∼ **and**, or **or, return**, arrangement by which retailer takes quantity of goods with right of returning without payment all that he fails to sell. **2.** instance of this (*made a sale*); amount sold (*the sale was, sales were, enormous*). **3.** event at which goods are sold (∼ **of work**, selling of goods made by parishioners etc. for charity; ||JUMBLE[3], RUMMAGE, WHITE[1], *sale*); public auction (**put up for** ∼, offer at auction); rapid disposal at reduced prices of shop's stock at end of season etc. **4.** ∼**-ring**, circle of buyers at auction; ∼**-room** (in which auctions are held); ***∼s **clerk**, salesman in shop; ∼s **department** (of a firm, concerned with making sales as opp. manufacturing or dispatching goods); ∼s **engineer**, salesman with technical knowledge of his goods and their market; ∼'s**girl**, ∼'s**lady**, (-z-) saleswoman; ∼s **resistance**, opposition or apathy of prospective customer etc., to be overcome by salesmanship; ∼s

talk, persuasive talk to promote sale of goods or (fig.) acceptance of an idea; ~s **tax,** tax on (receipts from) sales. [OE *sala,* f. ON, cogn. w. Gmc **saljan* SELL]

sā'le|able (-*la*-) *a.* fit for sale, finding purchasers; hence ~ABI'LITY *n.* [f. prec. + -ABLE]

sä'lep *n.* nutritive flour or starch from dried tubers of orchidaceous plants esp. of genus *Orchis.* [F, f. Turk. *sālep* f. Arab. (*ḵuṣa-'l-*) *ta'lab* fox('s testicles)]

***sälerā'tus** *n.* impure potassium or sodium bicarbonate as ingredient in baking-powder. [f. mod. L *sal aeratus* aerated salt]

Salē'sian (-zhan) *a.* & *n.* (member) of an educational RC religious order. [f. St. François de *Sales,* Fr. RC bishop d. 1622 + -IAN]

sā'les|man (*fem.* ~**woman**; *pl.* ~**men**), **sā'les|- pèrson,** (-lz-) *ns.* person employed to sell goods in shop or as middleman between producer and retailer or *as commercial traveller; hence ~**man**SHIP (3) *n.* [f. SALE + 's l + MAN[1], PERSON]

Sā'lian[1] *a.* (Rom. Ant.) of the Salii or priests of Mars. [f. L *Salii* n. pl. (*salire* leap) + -AN]

Sā'lian[2] *a.* & *n.* (member) of 4th-c. Frankish tribe near R. Ijssel, from which Merovingians were descended. [f. LL *Salii* the tribe + -AN]

Sā'lic *a.* = prec., ~ **law,** (1) Frankish law-book extant in Merovingian and Carolingian times, (2) law excluding females from dynastic succession, esp. as alleged fundamental law of French monarchy (based on a quotation, not referring to such succession, from the law-book). [f. F *Salique* or f. med. L *Salicus* f. *Salii* (as prec.; see -IC)]

sä'licèt *n.* organ stop like salicional but one octave higher. [f. as SALICIONAL]

sä'licin *n.* bitter crystalline substance got from willow-bark etc. and used medicinally. [f. F *salicine* f. L *salix -icis* willow; see -IN]

sali'cional (-shon-) *n.* organ stop with soft reedy tone as of willow-pipe. [G, f. L *salix* (as prec.) w. suf.]

sälicy'lic *a.* ~ **acid,** benzene derivative used as antiseptic and to treat rheumatism; hence **sali'cyl**ATE[1] (3) *n.* [f. *salicyl* its radical (f. F *salicyle* f. as SALICIN; see -YL) + -IC]

sä'lient *a.* & *n.* **1.** *a.* (Of angle, esp. in Fortif., opp. *re-entrant*) pointing outwards; jutting out, prominent, conspicuous, most noticeable, (*salient points, features, characteristics*); (Her., of lion etc.) standing on hind legs with fore-paws raised. **2.** (arch.) leaping or dancing; (of water etc.) jetting forth; ~ **point,** (arch.) initial stage or origin or first beginning. **3.** *n.* salient angle or part in fortification or line of attack or defence. **4.** Hence **sā'li**ENCE, **sä'li**ENCY, *ns.,* ~LY[2] *adv.* [f. L *salire* leap; see -ENT]

sälič'ntian (-shən) *a.* & *n.* (member) of the order Salientia of amphibians, incl. frogs and toads. [f. mod. L *Salientia* (as prec.; see -IA[2])]

sali'ferous *a.* (Geol.) (Of strata) containing much salt. [f. L *sal* salt + -I- + -FEROUS]

sali'na *n.* salt lake. [Sp., f. med. L, – salt-pit]

saline (sā'-, sali'n) *a.* & *n.* **1.** *a.* (Of natural waters, springs, etc.) impregnated with salt or salts; containing salt; (of taste) salt; of chemical salts, of the nature of a salt; (of medicine) containing salt(s) of alkaline metals or magnesium; hence **sali'ni**TY, **sälinō'-**METER, *ns.* **2.** *n.* salt lake, spring, marsh, etc.; salt-pan, salt-works; saline substance, esp. medicine; solution of salt in water. [ME; a. f. L *sal* salt + -INE[1], n. f. as prec. or f. a.]

sali'va *n.* colourless liquid given by mixed secretions of salivary and mucous glands discharged into mouth and assisting mastication, spittle; ~ **test** (e.g. of racehorse's saliva to determine whether the horse has been doped); so ~ARY[1] (sä'lĭ-, sali'-) *a.* [ME f. L]

sä'liv|āte *v.* **1.** *v.t.* produce unusual secretion of saliva in (person) usu. with mercury. **2.** *v.i.* secrete or discharge saliva esp. in excess. **3.** So ~A'TION *n.* [f. L *salivare* (as prec.) + -ATE[3]]

Salk (sawlk) *n.* ~ **vaccine,** first vaccine developed against poliomyelitis. [f. J.E. ~, Amer. scientist b. 1914]

sä'llee *n.* (Austral.) acacia of various species. [Aboriginal]

sä'llenders, së'llanders, (-z) *n. pl.* dry eruption on front of hock of horse's hind leg. [16th c.; orig. unkn.]

sä'llèt *n.* (Hist.) light helmet with outward-curving rear part. [f. F *salade* ult. f. Rom. **caelata* fem. p.p. (as n.) of L *caelare* engrave (*caelum* chisel)]

sä'llow[1] (-ō) *n.* willow-tree, esp. of low-growing or shrubby kind, whence ~Y[2] *a.*; a shoot, or the wood, of this. [OE *salh* salg- f. Gmc **salhaz,* cogn. w. OHG *salaha,* ON *selja,* L *salix*]

sä'llow[2] (-ō) *a.* & *v.* **1.** *a.* (Of skin or complexion, or person in these respects) of sickly yellow or pale brown; hence ~ISH[1] *a.,* ~NESS *n.* **2.** *v.t.* & *i.* make or grow sallow. [OE *salo* dusky, = MDu. *salu* dirty, OHG *salo* dark, ON *sölr* yellow, f. Gmc **salwa*-]

sä'llý[1] *n.,* & *v.i.* **1.** *n.* rush of besieged upon besiegers, sortie; a going forth, excursion; sudden start into activity, outburst; (arch.) escapade; witticism, piece of banter, lively remark esp. by way of attack upon person or thing or of diversion in argument; ~**port,** opening in fortification for making sally from. **2.** *v.i.* make military sally (*out*); go *forth* or *out* on a journey, for a walk, etc.; (arch.) issue or come out suddenly. [f. F *saillie* fem. p.p. (as n.) of *saillir* issue, f. OF *salir* f. L *salire* leap]

sä'llý[2] *n.* first movement of bell when set for ringing; bell's position when set; part of bell-rope prepared with inwoven wool for holding; ~**hole** (through which bell-rope passes). [perh. f. prec. in sense 'leaping motion']

Sä'llý[3] *n.* AUNT *Sally;* ‖~ **Lunn,** sweet light teacake served hot [perh. f. name of girl hawking them at Bath *c.* 1800]. [fam. form of woman's name *Sarah;* see -Y[3]]

sälmagŭ'ndi *n.* dish of chopped meat, anchovies, eggs, onions, etc., and seasoning; general mixture, miscellaneous collection, of articles, subjects, qualities, etc. [f. F *salmigondis,* of unkn. orig.]

sä'lmi (-ē) *n.* ragout or casserole esp. of partly roasted game-birds. [F, abbr. f. as prec.]

sä'lmon (sä'mon) *n.* (*pl.* usu. same) & *a.* **1.** *n.* large silver-scaled pink-fleshed anadromous fish of genus *Salmo* etc., much prized for food and sport; (Austral. & NZ) barramundi or other fish resembling this; ~**-colour(ed),** (of) the orange-pink colour of salmon-flesh; ~**ladder, -leap, -pass, -stair,** series of steps or other arrangement for allowing salmon to pass dam and ascend stream; ~**pink,** salmon-colour(ed); ~ **trout,** trout resembling salmon; hence **sä'lmon**OID *a.* & *n.* **2.** *a.* salmon-coloured, orange-pink. [ME; f. AF *sa(u)moun,* OF *saumon* f. L *salmo -onis*]

sälmonë'll|a *n.* pathogenic bacterium of genus *Salmonella,* esp. of species causing food poisoning; hence ~O'SIS *n.* [mod. L, f. D.E. *Salmon,* Amer. veterinary surgeon d. 1914 + dim. suf.]

Sälomŏ'nic, Sälomŏ'nian, *adjs.* of or as of SOLOMON. [f. LL *Salomon* Solomon + -IC, -IAN]

sä'lon (-awn) *n.* reception-room in continental, esp. French, great house; (Hist.) (meeting of notabilities in) reception-room of (esp. Parisian) lady of fashion; room or establishment where hairdresser, couturier, etc., receives clients; (S~) annual exhibition of living artists' pictures; ~ **music,** light music for drawing-room. [F; see foll.]

saloō'n *n.* **1.** hall or large room, esp. in hotel or place of public resort, fit for assemblies, exhibitions, etc. **2.** public room for first-class or for all passengers on ship. **3.** ‖luxurious railway carriage without compartments, serving as lounge etc. **4.** ‖public room(s) or gallery for specified purpose (*billiard, dancing, hairdressing, shooting,* etc. *-saloon*). **5.** * = BAR[1] 7; ‖ = *saloon bar.* **6.** ‖ = *saloon car.* **7.** ‖~ **bar,** first-class bar in public house; ‖~ **car,** (1) motor car with closed body and no partition behind driver, (2) = sense 3;

∼ **deck** (for passengers using saloon); *∼-**keeper** (of bar); ||∼ **pistol, rifle,** (adapted for short-range practice in shooting-saloon). [f. F *salon,* f. It. *salone* augment. of *sala* hall; see -OON]

Salō′pian *a.* & *n.* (native) of Shropshire; (past or present member) of Shrewsbury School. [f. AF *Salopesberia* f. ME, f. OE *Scrobbesbyrig* Shrewsbury, + -IAN]

sălpiglō′ssĭs *n.* herbaceous garden-plant allied to petunia, with trumpet-shaped flowers. [mod. L, irreg. f. Gk *salpigx* trumpet + *glōssa* tongue]

să′lpĭng- (-nj) *comb. form.* (Med.) of Fallopian tubes, as: ∼E′CTOMY, ∼I′TIS, *ns.* [f. Gk *salpigx salpiggos,* lit. 'trumpet']

sälse *n.* mud volcano. [F, f. It. *salsa* f. name of one near Modena]

să′lsĭfy *n.* European plant (*Tragopogon porrifolius*) with long cylindrical fleshy root cooked as vegetable; **black** ∼, scorzonera. [f. F *salsifis* f. obs. It. *salsefica,* of unkn. orig.]

salt (sawlt, sŏlt) *n., a.,* & *v.t.* **1.** *n.* (**common**) ∼, substance that gives sea-water its characteristic taste, got in crystalline forms from strata consisting of it or by evaporation of brine pumped from these or of sea- -water, and used for seasoning or preserving food and other purposes, sodium chloride, (BAY² *salt,* ROCK¹- -*salt,* SEA-*salt*); **table** ∼ (powdered or easy to powder for the salt-cellar); **in** ∼, sprinkled with salt or immersed in brine as preservative. **2. eat** ∼ **with,** be guest of; **eat** person's ∼, be his guest or dependant; **not made of** ∼, not disconcerted by wet weather; **put** ∼ **on tail of,** capture, [w. ref. to joc. directions given children for catching bird]; **rub** ∼ **into wound,** exacerbate humiliation etc.; **take with a grain** or **pinch of** ∼, regard as exaggerated, be incredulous about, believe only part of; **the** ∼ **of the earth,** people or classes for whose existence the world is better, those whose qualities are a model for the rest, [Matt. 5: 13]; **worth** one's ∼, efficient, capable, having merit. **3.** sting, piquancy, pungency, wit, (ATTIC¹ *salt*). **4.** (in *sing.* or *pl.*) substance resembling salt in taste, form, etc., (BATH¹ *salts,* EPSOM *salt*(*s*), GLAUBER's *salt*(*s*), *salt*(*s*) *of* LEMON¹, SMELL*ing-salts*); (in *pl.,* esp.) such substance used as laxative; **like a dose of** ∼**s,** (sl.) very fast. **5.** (Chem.) compound of basic and acid radicals, acid with whole or part of its hydrogen replaced by a metal or metal-like radical. **6.** = *salt-cellar;* **above, below,** etc., **the** ∼, (Hist.) seated at table among the family and their equals, among the servants and dependants. **7.** marsh over- flowed by sea, often used as pasture or for collecting water for salt-making. **8.** (in *pl.*) exceptional rush of sea-water up river. **9.** (old) ∼, experienced sailor. **10.** ∼'**bush,** orache; ∼-**cat** [*cat* unexpl.], mass of salt mixed with gravel, urine, etc., to attract pigeons and keep them at home; ∼-**cellar** [assim. of obs. *saler* (f. AF **saler,* OF *salier* salt-box f. L as SALARY) to CELLAR], vessel holding salt for table use, (colloq.) unusually deep hollow above collar-bone in (esp. woman's) neck; ∼-**dome,** mass of salt forced up into sedimentary rocks; ∼-**glaze,** glaze on stoneware made by throwing salt into hot kiln containing the ware; *∼-**grass** (growing in salt meadows or alka- line regions); ∼ **lake,** lake of salt water; ∼-**lick,** place to which animals resort to lick earth impreg- nated with salt; ∼-**marsh,** = sense 7; ∼-**mine,** mine yielding rock-salt, (fig.) place of unremitting toil; ∼-**pan,** depression near sea, or vessel, used for getting salt by evaporation; *∼-**shaker,** container of salt for sprinkling on food; ∼-**spoon** (usu. with short handle and roundish deep bowl for taking table salt); ∼- -**well,** bored well yielding brine; ∼-**works,** place where salt is made; ∼'**wort,** (1) plant of genus *Salsola,* (2) glasswort. **11.** Hence ∼'LESS *a.* **12.** *a.* impregnated with, containing, tasting of, cured or preserved or seasoned with, salt (cf. FRESH); (of plant) growing in sea or salt-marshes; (of tears etc.) bitter,

afflicting; (of wit etc.) pungent; (of story, jest, etc.) indecent, spicy; ∼ **fish,** (W. Ind.) preserved cod; ∼ **horse,** (Naut. sl.) salt beef; *salt* JUNK¹; ∼ **meadow** (subject to flooding with salt water); ∼ **water,** sea- -water etc., (sl.) tears; ∼-**water,** of, or living in, the sea. **13.** Hence ∼'ISH¹ 2 *a.,* ∼'LY² *adv.,* ∼'NESS *n.* **14.** *v.t.* cure or preserve with salt or brine; ∼ **away** or **down,** (sl.) put (money etc.) by. **15.** sprinkle (road, snow to melt it in street) with salt. **16.** make salt or piquant, season, (lit. or fig.); (in *p.p.,* of horse or person) proof against diseases incident to climate or special conditions by habituation, hardened. **17.** treat with solution of salt or mixture of salts. **18.** (Commerc. sl.) ∼ **an account** etc., put extremely high or low price for articles, ∼ **the books,** show receipts as larger than they have really been; ∼ **a mine,** (sl., lit. or fig.) introduce extraneous ore etc. to make it seem rich. [(v. f. OE *s*(*e*)*altan*) f. OE *s*(*e*)*alt,* OS, ON, Goth. *salt,* OHG *salz* f. Gmc **saltam,* n. f. *saltaz a., f. IE **sal-*]

SALT (sawlt, sŏlt) *abbr.* Strategic Arms Limitation Talks.

sältarĕ′llō *n.* (*pl.* ∼**s**). Italian and Spanish dance for one couple, with sudden skips. [f. It. *salterello,* Sp. *saltarelo* rel. to It. *saltare,* Sp. *saltar* leap, dance f. L *saltare* (as foll.)]

sältā′tion *n.* leaping, dancing; a jump; sudden transition or movement; so **să′ltat**ORY, **sältatō̄r′**IAL, *adjs.* [f. L *saltatio* (*saltare* frequent. of *salire salt*- leap; see -ATION)]

sa′lter (saw′l-, sŏ′l-) *n.* manufacturer of or dealer in salt; = DRY¹-*salter;* workman at salt-works; person who salts fish etc. [OE *sealtere* (as SALT v., -ER¹)]

sa′ltern (saw′l-, sŏ′l-) *n.* salt-works; set of pools for natural evaporation of sea-water. [OE *sealtærn* (as SALT, *ærn* building)]

să′ltigrāde *a.* & *n.* (spider) with legs adapted for jumping. [f. mod. L *Saltigradae* f. L *saltus* leap (*salire salt*-) + -*gradus* walking]

săltimbă′ncō *n.* (*pl.* ∼**s**). (arch.) mountebank, quack. [It. (*saltare* leap, *in* on, *banco* bench)]

sa′lting (saw′l-, sŏ′l-) *n.* in vbl senses; (esp. in *pl.*) = SALT 7. [ME, f. SALT + -ING¹]

să′ltīre *n.* (Her.) ordinary formed by bend and bend sinister crossing like a St. Andrew's cross (**in** ∼, so arranged); hence ∼WISE (-īrwīz) *adv.* [ME, f. OF *sau*(*l*)*toir* etc. stirrup-cord, stile, saltire, f. med. L *saltatorium* (as SALTATION; see -ORY)]

||**saltpē′tre, *saltpē′ter,** (sawl-, sŏl-; -ter) *n.* potas- sium nitrate, white crystalline salty substance used as constituent of gunpowder, in preserving meat, and medicinally; **Chile** ∼, sodium nitrate; ∼-**paper,** touchpaper. [ME f. OF *salpetre,* f. med. L *salpetra* prob. for *sal petrae salt of rock (i.e. found as incrustation), w. assim. to SALT; *petrae* f. LL f. Gk *petra* rock]

să′ltus *n.* sudden transition, breach of continuity. [L, = leap]

sa′lt|** y̆** (saw′l-, sŏ′l-) *a.* = SALT 12; hence ∼ĭNESS *n.* [ME, f. SALT + -Y²]

salu′br|**ious** (-lōō′-, -lū′-) *a.* (Esp. of climate, air, etc.) healthy; hence or cogn. ∼**ious**LY² *adv.,* ∼ITY *n.* [f. L *salubris* (*salus* health) + -OUS]

salu′ki (-lōō′-) *n.* tall swift slender silky-coated dog, Arabian gazelle-hound. [f. Arab. *salūkī*]

să′lūtary *a.* producing good effects, beneficial; (arch.) salubrious. [ME, f. F *salutaire* or f. L *salutaris* (*salus -utis* health; see -ARY²)]

sălūtā′tion *n.* (use of) words spoken or written or gesture to convey interest in another's health etc., pleasure at sight of or communication with him, or courteous recognition of his arrival or departure; **the Angelic S**∼, the AVE Maria; hence or cogn. ∼AL *a.* [ME f. OF, or f. L *salutatio* (as SALUTE; see -ATION)]

salu′tat|**ory** (-lōō′-, -lū′-) *a.* & *n.* **1.** *a.* of salutation. **2.** *n.* *salutatory oration, esp. as given by (usu. second- -ranking) member of graduating class (the ∼ō̄r′ĭAN *n.*). [f. L *salutatorius* (as foll.; see -ORY)]

salu'te (-ōō't, -ū't) v. & n. **1.** v.t. make salutation to, greet; (arch.) hail as (king etc.). **2.** v.t. & i. perform salute to or to, perform salute; (arch.) kiss (person, cheek, hand) esp. at meeting or parting. **3.** v.t. accost or receive with smile, oath, etc.; (arch.) become perceptible to (eye, ear, person arriving). **4.** n. gesture expressing respect, homage, or courteous recognition, to person esp. when arriving or departing; (arch. or joc.) kiss esp. as greeting; (Mil., Naut.) prescribed movement or position of body (esp. raising hand to cap) or weapon, or use of flag(s) or discharge of gun(s), in sign of respect (a salute of 7 guns was fired); **the ~**, attitude taken by individual soldier, sailor, policeman, etc., in saluting; **take the ~**, (1, of highest officer present) acknowledge it by gesture as meant for him, (2) be recipient of ceremonial salutes by members of procession. **5.** (Fenc.) formal performance of certain guards etc. by fencers before engaging. [ME, f. L salutare (salus -utis health); n. partly f. OF salut (saluer f. L salutare)]

salūti'ferous a. (arch.) promoting health or safety. [f. L salutifer (as prec.; see -FEROUS)]

sa'lvage n., & v.t. **1.** n. (payment made or due for) saving of a ship or its cargo from loss by wreck or capture, rescue of property from fire, wreckage, etc.; property salvaged. **2.** saving and utilization of waste paper, scrap-metal, etc.; materials salvaged. **3.** v.t. make salvage of; save from wreck, fire, etc.; hence **~ABLE** (-ja-) a. [F, f. med. L salvagium f. L salvare SAVE¹; see -AGE]

salvā'tion n. **1.** saving of the soul; deliverance from sin and its consequences and admission to heaven brought about by Christ (find ~, be converted; **work out** one's **own ~**, find unaided how to avoid disaster). **2.** preservation from loss, calamity, etc.; person or thing that preserves from these (be the salvation of). **3.** S~ **Army**, world-wide missionary organization on military model for charity and revival of Christianity among the destitute. **4.** Hence **~ISM** (3), **~IST** (2), ns. (esp. w. ref. to Salvation Army). [ME, f. OF sauuacion, salvacion, f. eccl. L salvatio -onis (salvare SAVE¹; see -ATION), transl. Gk sōtēria]

salve¹ (sǎlv, sahv) n., & v.t. **1.** n. (poet.) healing ointment for sores or wounds. **2.** See LIPsalve. **3.** thing that is soothing for wounded feelings or uneasy conscience or (arch.) explains away discrepancy or palliates fault. **4.** v.t. (arch.) anoint (wound etc.). **5.** (arch.) smooth over or make good (defect, disgrace, etc.). **6.** soothe (pride, self-love, conscience, etc.). **7.** (arch.) account for, dispose of, harmonize, vindicate, (difficulty, doubt, discrepancy, person's honour). [n. f. OE s(e)alf(e), OS OHG salba f. Gmc *salbhō, v. f. OE s(e)alfian, in senses 5 to 7 partly f. L salvare SAVE¹]

Sā'lve² n. ~ (Regina), RC antiphon (beginning thus) recited after Divine Office from Trinity Sunday to Advent, music for it. [ME f. L, imper. of salvēre = hail(, queen)]

salv|e³ v.t. save (ship, cargo) from loss at sea; save (property) from fire; hence **~ABLE** a. [back-form. f. SALVAGE]

sā'lver n. tray usu. of gold, silver, brass, or electroplate, on which refreshments, letters, cards, etc., are handed. [f. F salve tray for presenting certain things to king f. Sp. salva assaying of food (salvar SAVE¹); assoc. w. platter]

sā'lvia n. plant of genus Salvia, esp. cultivated species with blue or usu. red flowers. [L, = SAGE¹]

sā'lvo¹ n. (pl. ~s). saving clause, reservation, (with an express salvo of their rights); tacit reservation, quibbling evasion, bad excuse; expedient for saving reputation or soothing pride or conscience. [L, abl. of salvus SAFE² as used in salvo jure without prejudice to the right of (person)]

sā'lvo² n. (pl. ~es or ~s). simultaneous firing of artillery or other guns esp. as salute, or in sea-fight; number of bombs released from aircraft at same moment; round or volley of applause. [f. earlier salve, F f. It. salva salutation (as SAVE²)]

săl volā'tile n. (flavoured alcoholic solution, used as restorative in faintness etc., of) ammonium carbonate. [mod. L, = volatile salt]

sā'lvor n. person or ship making or assisting in salvage. [f. SALVE³ + -OR]

||**Săm** n. (sl.) **stand ~**, bear the expense esp. of drink; **upon my ~** (excl. of asseveration). [19th c.; in second phr. prob. f. obs. cant sal(o)mon the Mass, perh. f. LL Salomon Solomon]

SAM abbr. surface-to-air missile.

Sam. abbr. Samuel (OT).

sama'dhi (-ah'dī) n. (Buddhism & Hinduism). state of concentration induced by meditation. [f. Skr. samādhi contemplation]

sā'mara n. (Bot.) winged fruit of sycamore, ash, etc. [mod. L, f. L, = elm-seed]

Samă'ritan n. & a. **1.** n. native or language of Samaria (**good ~**, genuinely charitable person, w. ref. to Luke 10: 33 etc.); adherent of the Samaritan religious system, accepting only the (Samaritan) Pentateuch; member of an organization offering help and friendship to those in despair. **2.** a. of Samaria or the Samaritans; ~ **Pentateuch**, recension used by Samaritans of which MSS are in archaic characters. **3.** Hence **~ISM** (2, 3, 4) n. [f. LL Samaritanus f. Gk Samareitēs (Samareia Samaria); see -AN]

samār'ium n. (Chem.) metallic element of lanthanide series. [f. samarskite mineral in which its spectrum was first observed (Samarski 19th-c. Russ. official, -ITE¹ (2)) + -IUM]

să'mba n., & v.i. (~ed or ~'d, pr. -ad). **1.** n. Brazilian Negro dance; ballroom dance imitative of this; music for it. **2.** v.i. dance samba. [Port., of Afr. orig.]

samb(h)ar. Var. of SAMBUR.

să'mbo n. (pl. ~s or ~es). **1.** half-breed esp. of Negro and Indian or European blood. **2.** (S~). (derog.) Negro. [f. Sp. zambo, perh. = zambo bandy-legged; sense 2 perh. a diff. wd]

Sam Brow'ne n. army officer's belt and strap supporting it. [f. Sir Samuel J. Browne, Brit. mil. commander d. 1901]

să'mbur n. SE Asian elk (Rusa unicolor). [f. Hindi sā(m)bur]

sāme a., pron., & adv. **1.** a. monotonous, uniform, unvarying (the same old story); hence **~'NESS** (-mn-) n. **2. this, these, that, those, ~**, the aforesaid, the person(s) or thing(s) previously alluded to or thought of, (this same man was later my tutor; what is the use of this same patience?; (derog.) these same politicians would now have us believe etc.). **3. the ~ a.**, (or an) identical, not different, unchanged, unvarying, (the same causes produce the same effects; the same car was later used in another crime; the difference between a body in motion and the same body at rest; the same observations are true of the others also; all planets travel in the same direction; either method comes or amounts to the same thing; say the same thing twice over, bigotry is the same in every age; she was always the same to me; he was not the same man after his illness; just the ~, one and the ~, the very ~, emphatically the same; much the ~, not appreciably different; at the same TIME¹; by the same TOKEN), (arch.) identical with (words of the same nature with those he had first heard), (emphatic substitute—before full or ellipt. rel. clause with that, where, etc., or esp. as which often replaces that under its influence—for) the, that, those, (at the same time that I am trying to stop it; to the same place where I had found it; on the same grounds that he would defend suicide; I have the same Bible my mother gave me; sailors received the same pay as soldiers; gave the same answer as before). **4. the ~ pron.**, the same thing (we must all say it or do the same; would do the same again; **and the ~ to you!**, I wish you may have the same thing; **it is all** or **just the ~**, it makes no difference), (arch.) the same person (**from the ~, to the ~**, heading of poem or letter coming from or addressed to same person as previous one), (arch., colloq., or Law) the aforesaid thing or person (*he that shall endure unto the end, the same shall be saved*). **5. the ∿** *adv.*, in the same manner (*we take what pleasure we can get, the same as you do, the same as in the past*; ALL *the same*; **just the ∿**, in spite of changed conditions; **think the ∿ of, feel the ∿ to**, remain in the same mind regarding). **6.** *pron.* (colloq.) = *the same* (see sense 4); **∿ here**, the same thing applies to me. **7.** *adv.* (colloq.) = *the same* (see sense 5). [ME f. ON, = OHG, Goth. *sama* f. Gmc **samaz* f. IE **somós*]

sā′mel *a.* (Of brick or tile) imperfectly baked, soft, from being outermost in the kiln. [17th c., perh. f. OE **saméled* half-burnt]

sā′mfu (-ōō) *n.* Chinese woman's suit of jacket and trousers. [Cantonese]

Sā′mian *a. & n.* (native) of Samos; **∿ ware**, fine Gaulish pottery found on Roman sites in Britain. [f. L f. Gk *Samios* (island of *Samos* in the Aegean Sea) + -AN]

sā′misĕn *n.* long three-stringed Japanese guitar, played with plectrum. [Jap., f. Chin. *san-hsien* (*san* three, *hsien* string)]

sā′mīte *n.* (Hist.) rich medieval dress-fabric of silk occas. interwoven with gold. [ME, f. OF *samit* f. med. L *examitum* f. med. Gk *hexamiton* f. Gk *hexa-* six- + *mitos* thread]

sā′mizdăt *n.* system of clandestine publication of banned literature in USSR. [Russ.]

sā′mlĕt *n.* young salmon. [f. earlier *salmonet* (SALMON, -ET[1]), after -LET]

Sā′mnīte *n. & a.* (member) of a people of ancient Italy often at war with republican Rome; their language. [ME, f. L *Samnites* pl., cogn. w. *Sabinus* SABINE; see -ITE[1]]

Samō′an *a. & n.* (native or language) of Samoa. [f. *Samoa* in the Pacific + -AN]

sā′movâr *n.* apparatus with interior heating tube to keep water at boiling-point for making tea. [Russ., = self-boiler]

Sā′moy|ĕd (-mo-) *n.* **1.** member of a people of northern Siberia; their language. **2.** dog of white Arctic breed. **3.** Hence **∿ĕ′dIC**, *a. & n.*, (language) of the Samoyeds. [f. Russ. *samoed*]

*sămp *n.* (porridge of) coarsely-ground maize. [f. Algonquin *nasamp* softened by water]

sā′mpăn *n.* small boat usu. with stern-oar(s), used in Far East. [f. Chin. *san-ban* (*san* three, *ban* board)]

sā′mphīre *n.* cliff plant with aromatic saline fleshy leaves used in pickles; glasswort. [earlier *samp(i)ere* f. F (*herbe de*) *Saint Pierre* St. Peter('s herb)]

sa′mple (sah′-) *n., & v.t.* **1.** *n.* small separated part of something illustrating the qualities of the mass etc. it is taken from, specimen, pattern, (esp. as offered by dealer in commodities sold by weight or measure); illustrative or typical example (*that is a fair sample of his methods*). **2.** *v.t.* take or give samples, try the qualities, get a representative experience, of. [ME, f. AF *assample*, OF *essample* EXAMPLE]

sa′mpler[1] (sah′-) *n.* In vbl senses; *a collection of samples. [f. prec. + -ER[1]]

sa′mpler[2] (sah′-) *n.* piece of embroidery worked in various stitches as specimen of proficiency (often preserved and displayed on wall etc.). [f. OF *es-samplaire* (as EXEMPLAR)]

Sā′mson *n.* person of great strength or resembling Samson in some respect; **∿(′s)-post**, (Naut.) strong pillar passing through hold or between decks, post in whale-boat to which harpoon rope is attached. [LL, f. Gk *Sampsōn* f. Heb. *šimšôn* (Judg. 13–16)]

sā′murai (-oorī) *n.* (*pl.* same). Japanese army officer; (Hist.) military retainer of daimios, member of military caste in Japan. [Jap.]

sā′native, sā′natory, *adjs.* healing, of or tending to physical or moral health, curative. [ME, f. OF *sanatif* or f. LL *sanativus* (*sanare* cure; see -IVE), w. mod. var. in -ORY]

sănatōr′i|um *n.* (*pl.* ∿ums *or* ∿a). establishment for

treatment of invalids, esp. of convalescents and the chronically sick; room or building for sick persons in school etc. [mod. L (as prec.; see -ORY)]

sănbeni′tō (-nē′-) *n.* (*pl.* ∿s). penitential yellow garment shaped like monk's scapular with red St. Andrew's cross before and behind worn by confessed and penitent heretic under Spanish Inquisition; similar black garment painted with flames and devils worn by impenitent heretic at auto-da-fé. [f. Sp. *sambenito* (*San Benito* St. Benedict, as shaped like scapular introduced by him)]

sā′ncti|fȳ *v.t.* consecrate, set apart or observe as holy; purify or free from sin, (in *p.p.*) sanctimonious; impart sanctity to, make legitimate or binding by religious sanction, give colour of morality or innocence to, justify, sanction (*the end sanctifies the means*); make productive of or conducive to holiness; hence or cogn. ∿FICA′TION *n.*, ∿fīER[1] *n.* (esp. Holy Spirit). [ME, f. OF *saintifier* f. eccl. L *sanctificare* f. L *sanctus* holy; see -FY]

sănctimō′nious *a.* making a show of sanctity or piety; hence ∿LY[2] *adv.*, ∿NESS *n.* [as foll. + -OUS]

sā′nctimony *n.* sanctimoniousness. [f. L *sanctimonia* sanctity (as SAINT; see -MONY)]

sā′nction *n., & v.t.* **1.** *n.* (Hist.) law, decree; PRAGMATIC *sanction*. **2.** penalty for disobedience or reward for obedience attached to a law, clause containing this; (Eth.) consideration operating to enforce obedience to any rule of conduct; (Polit., esp. in *pl.*) economic or military action by State(s) to coerce another into conformity with international norms of conduct. **3.** confirmation or ratification of law etc. by supreme authority, express authoritative permission, countenance or encouragement given to action etc. by custom etc. **4.** *v.t.* ratify, invest with authority, make binding; authorize; countenance (action etc.); attach penalty or reward to (law). [F, f. L *sanctio -onis* (*sancire sanct-* make sacred; see -ION)]

sā′nctitūde *n.* (arch.) saintliness. [ME, f. L *sanctitudo* (as SAINT; see -TUDE)]

sā′nctitȳ *n.* holiness of life, saintliness, (ODOUR *of sanctity*); sacredness, being hallowed, right to reverence, inviolability; (in *pl.*) sacred obligations, feelings, etc. [ME, f. OF *sain(c)tité* or f. L *sanctitas* (as SAINT; see -ITY)]

sā′nctuarȳ *n.* **1.** place recognized as holy; church, temple, tabernacle, HOLY place, HOLY of holies; penetralia, inmost recess, (lit. or fig.); part of chancel between altar rails and east window or screen, containing high altar. **2.** (Hist.) sacred place where fugitive from law, or debtor, was secured by medieval Church law against arrest or violence; place in which similar immunity was established by custom or law. **3.** place of refuge (*London, the sanctuary of political refugees*); (right of affording) immunity from arrest etc.; **take ∿**, resort to place of refuge. **4.** place or time for preservation and protection of birds and wild animals. [ME, f. AF *sanctuarie*, OF *sanctuaire* f. L *sanctuarium* (as SAINT; see -ARY[1])]

sā′nctum *n.* **1.** holy place; **∿ sanctor′um**, holy of holies in Jewish temple, (fig.) inner retreat, esoteric doctrine, etc. **2.** ∿ (**sanctor′um**), (joc.) person's private room, study, den. [L, neut. of *sanctus* holy, p.p. of *sancire* consecrate; *sanctorum* gen. pl. in transl. of Heb. *ḳōdeš haḳḳŏdāšīm* holy of holies]

sā′nctus *n.* the hymn 'Holy, holy, holy' closing the Eucharistic preface; music for this; **∿ bell**, bell in turret at junction of nave and chancel, or handbell, rung at the sanctus or at elevation. [ME f. L, = holy]

sănd *n., & v.t.* **1.** *n.* minute fragments resulting from wearing down of esp. siliceous rocks and found covering parts of the sea-shore, river-beds, deserts, etc.; (in *sing.* or *pl.*) shoal or submarine bank of sand; (usu. in *pl.*) grain of sand; (in *pl.*) expanse or tracts of sand; **built** etc. **on ∿**, unstable; **head in the ∿**, refusal to acknowledge obvious danger; PLOUGH[2] *the sand(s)*; ROPE *of sand*; **the ∿s are running out** etc., time of grace etc. is nearly at end [w. ref. to hour-glass etc.]. **2.** light brown colour like that of sand. **3.** *(colloq.)* firmness of purpose, grit. **4.** ~'**bag**, (*n.*) bag filled with sand for use (a) in fortification for making temporary defences, or for protection of building etc. against blast and splinters, (b) as ballast esp. for boat or balloon, (c) as ruffian's weapon inflicting heavy blow without leaving mark, (d) to stop draught from window or door, (*v.t.*; *-gg-*) barricade or defend, provide (window, chink), with sandbag(s), fell with blow from sandbag, *persuade by harsh means; ~'**bank**, deposit of sand forming shallow place in sea or river; ~-**bar**, sandbank at mouth of harbour or river or *on coast; ~-**bath**, (Chem.) vessel of heated sand to provide uniform heating; ~-**bed**, stratum of sand; ~-**blast** *n.*, & *v.t.* (treat with) jet of sand driven by compressed air or steam for cleaning or roughening glass etc.; ~-**box**, mould of sand used in founding, box of sand on locomotive for sprinkling slippery rails, (Golf) container for sand used in teeing, (Hist.) device for sprinkling sand to dry ink, *sand-pit enclosed in box; ~'**boy**, (prob.) boy hawking sand for sale (*happy as a ~boy*, in high spirits); ~-**castle**, structure of sand made usu. by child on sea-shore; ~-**cloud**, driving sand in simoom; ~-**crack**, disease of horses' hoofs, crack in human foot from walking on hot sand, crack in brick due to imperfect mixing; *~-**dollar**, round flat sea-urchin; *sand*-DUNE; ~-**eel**, eel-like fish of genus *Ammodytes*; ~-**flea**, (1) chigoe, (2) = *sand*-*hopper*; ~-**fly**, (1) midge of genus *Simulium*, (2) biting fly of genus *Phlebotomus* transmitting a virus disease; ~-**glass**, wasp-waisted reversible glass with two bulbs containing enough sand to take a definite time in passing from upper to lower bulb; ~-**groper**, (Austral.) gold-rush pioneer, (joc.) Western Australian; ~-**hill**, dune; *~'**hog**, workman under water making tunnel etc.; ~-**hopper**, small jumping crustacean burrowing on sea-shore; *~'**lot**, unoccupied sandy ground used for children's games; ~'**man**, personification of tiredness causing children's eyes to smart towards bedtime; ||~-**martin**, bird (*Riparia riparia*) nesting in side of sand-pit or sandy bank; ~-**painting**, Amer. Ind. ceremonial design made with coloured sands; ~'**paper**, (*n.*) paper with sand or other abrasive stuck to it for smoothing or polishing, (*v.t.*) polish with sandpaper; ~'**piper**, bird of family Scolopacidae haunting open wet sandy places; ~-**pit**, (esp.) partly sand-filled hollow for children to play in; ~-**pump** (for clearing drill-hole, caisson, etc., of wet sand); ~-**shoe**, (esp. of canvas with rubber or hemp sole for use on sand); ~-**skipper**, = *sand-hopper*; ~-**spout**, pillar of sand raised by desert whirlwind; ~'**stone**, sedimentary rock of compressed sand (*old red, new red*, ~*stone*, (Geol.) series of rocks below, above, Carboniferous); ~-**storm**, desert storm of wind with clouds of sand; ~-**table**, (Mil.) relief model in sand for explanation of tactics etc.; ~'**wort**, plant of genus *Arenaria* etc. growing in sand; ~-**yacht**, boat on wheels propelled over sand by wind. **5.** *v.t.* sprinkle with sand; overlay with, bury under, sand; adulterate (sugar etc.) with sand; polish with sand or sandpaper, whence ~ER[1] (2) *n.* [OE, = OS *sand*, OHG *sant*, ON *sandr* f. Gmc *sandam*, *sandaz*]

să'ndal[1] *n.*, & *v.t.* (||-ll-). **1.** *n.* sole with open-work (or no) upper, attached to foot by thongs passing over instep and around ankle; strap for fastening low shoe, passing over instep or around ankle. **2.** *v.t.* (esp. in *p.p.*) put sandals on (feet, person); fasten or provide (shoe) with sandal. [ME, f. L f. Gk *sandalion* dim. of *sandalon* wooden shoe, prob. of Asiatic orig.]

să'ndal[2] *n.* ~(**wood**), scented wood esp. from E. Ind. or Australian ~-**tree** of genus *Santalum*; red ~**wood**, red timber or dyewood from E. Ind. tree (*Pterocarpus santalinus*); ~**wood oil**, yellow aromatic

oil from sandal-tree. [ME, f. med. L *sandalum*, ult. f. Skr. *candana*]

să'ndarăc, -ăch, (-k) *n.* **1.** realgar. **2.** resin of N. Afr. conifer (*Tetraclinis articulata*), used in making varnish. [f. L f. Gk *sandarakē*, of Asiatic orig.]

să'nd-blind *a.* (arch.) dim-sighted, purblind. [ME, prob. f. OE *samblind* (sam- half f. WG *sami-*, BLIND[1]), assim. to SAND]

să'nderling *n.* small wading bird of sandpiper family. [perh. f. OE *sandyrthling* (as SAND, *yrthling* ploughman, also name of some bird)]

să'nders, sau'nders, (-z) *n.* SANDAL[2] wood, esp. red sandalwood. [ME, f. OF *sandre* var. of *sandle* SANDAL[2]]

să'ndhi (-dī) *n.* (Gram.) change in form of word determined by its position in an utterance (e.g. change of *a* to *an* before vowel). [f. Skr. *saṃdhi* putting together]

să'ndiver *n.* liquid scum formed in glass-making. [ME, app. f. F *suin de verre* exhalation (*suer* to sweat) of glass]

să'ndwich (-ch, -j) *n.*, & *v.t.* **1.** *n.* two or more slices of (usu. buttered) bread with meat or other relish between (ham, egg, jam, cucumber, etc., *sandwich*); cake of two or more layers with jam etc. between. **2.** ~-**board**, one of two advertisement boards carried by sandwich-man; ||~-**boat**, boat in bumping race rowing first in lower and last in higher division on same day; ~ **course** (of training with alternate periods of practical and theoretical instruction); ~-**man** (walking in street with sandwich-boards hanging before and behind). **3.** *v.t.* insert (thing, statement, etc.) between two of another character; squeeze (*in*) between others. [f. 4th Earl of *Sandwich*, Engl. nobleman d. 1792, said to have eaten only slices of bread and meat while gaming for 24 hours]

să'nd|ў[1] *a.* In *n.* senses; (of hair) yellowish-red, (of person) having sandy hair; ~**y blight**, (Austral.) ophthalmia with sandlike grains in eye; hence ~**iNESS** *n.*, ~**ўish**[1] 2 *a.* [OE *sandig* (as SAND, -Y[2])]

Să'ndy[2] *n.* (Nickname for) Scotsman. [usual Sc. pet-form of man's name *Alexander*]

săne *a.* of sound mind, not mad; (of views etc.) moderate, sensible; hence ~LY[2] (-nlī) *adv.* [f. L *sanus* healthy]

săng. See SING.

să'nga(r) (-ngg-) *n.* stone breastwork round hollow. [f. Pashto *sangar*]

săngaree' (-ngg-) *n.* cold drink of wine diluted and spiced. [f. Sp. SANGRÍA]

sang-de-bœuf (sahňdeběf') *n.* & *a.* (of) a deep red colour found on old Chinese porcelain. [F, = ox's blood]

sang-froi'd (sahňfrwah') *n.* composure, coolness, in danger or under agitating circumstances. [F, = cold blood]

să'ngrail (-ngg-) *n.* = GRAIL[2]. [ME, f. OF *saint graal* (as SAINT, GRAIL[2])]

sangrí'a (sănggrē'a) *n.* Spanish drink of red wine with lemonade etc. [Sp., = bleeding; cf. SANGAREE]

sănguifica'tion (-nggwī-) *n.* formation of, or conversion of food into, blood. [f. mod. L *sanguificatio* (*sanguificare* form blood f. L *sanguis* blood; see -FICATION)]

să'nguinar|ў (-nggwī-) *a.* accompanied by or delighting in bloodshed or slaughter; bloody, bloodthirsty, (of laws) inflicting death freely; hence ~iLY[2] *adv.*, ~iNESS *n.* [f. L *sanguinarius* (*sanguis -inis* blood; see -ARY[1])]

să'nguine (-nggwin) *a.*, *n.*, & *v.t.* **1.** *a.* habitually hopeful, confident, expecting things to go well, whence ~LY[2] (-nlī) *adv.*, ~NESS (-n-n-) *n.* **2.** (Hist.) of the TEMPERAMENT in which the blood predominates over the other HUMOUR[1]s, with ruddy complexion and courageous hopeful amorous disposition; (of complexion) bright, ruddy, florid. **3.** (Her. or literary). blood-red; (arch.) of blood, sanguinary. **4.** *n.* blood-red colour; crayon coloured red with iron oxide; a drawing in red chalk. **5.** *v.t.* (poet.) stain with blood, stain red. [ME, f. OF *sanguin -ine* blood-red f. L *sanguineus* (as prec.)]

sắngui′néous (-nggwĭ′-) *a.* sanguinary; (Med.) of blood; blood-red; full-blooded, plethoric. [f. L (as prec.) + -ous]

Sa′nhĕdrĭn, Sä′nhĕdrĭm, (-nĭ-) *n.* highest court of justice and supreme council in ancient Jerusalem, with 71 members. [f. late Heb. *sanhedrīn* f. Gk *sunedrion* (as syn-, *hedra* seat)]

sä′nĭcle *n.* umbelliferous plant of genus *Sanicula*, formerly believed to have healing properties. [ME f. OF, f. med. L *sanicula* perh. f. L *sanus* healthy]

sä′nĭ|ēs (-z) *n.* (*pl.* same). (Med.) thin discharge from wound or ulcer; hence ∼ous *a.* [L]

sä′nĭfy *v.t.* make healthy, improve sanitary state of, (place). [f. L *sanus* healthy + -i- + -fy]

*sănĭtăr′ium *n.* sanatorium. [pseudo-L f. L *sanitas* health (see foll., -arium)]

sä′nĭtar|ў *a.* of the conditions that affect health esp. with regard to dirt and infection; free from or designed to obviate influences deleterious to health; ∼y **engineer** (dealing with systems needed to maintain public health); *∼y **napkin,** ||∼y **towel,** absorbent pad used during menstruation; ∼y **ware,** porcelain for lavatories etc.; hence **sănĭtar′ian** *n.* & *a.,* ∼ıly² *adv.,* ∼ıness *n.* [f. F *sanitaire* f. L *sanitas* (see sanity, -ary¹)]

sănĭtā′tion *n.* (maintaining or improving of) sanitary conditions; drainage and disposal of sewage and refuse from houses etc.; hence ∼ıst (2) *n.*, [by back-form.] **sä′nĭtate³** *v.t.* & *i.* [irreg. f. sanitary + -ation]

sä′nĭtīze, -īse (-īz) *v.t.* make sanitary. [f. sanitary + -ize]

sä′nĭtý *n.* being sane, mental health; tendency to avoid extreme views. [ME, f. L *sanitas* (as sane; see -ity)]

sănk. See sink¹.

sannya′sī (sŭnyah′sī) *n.* Hindu religious mendicant. [Hindi & Urdu *sannyāsī* f. Skr. *saṃnyāsin* laying aside (*saṃ* together, *ni* down, *as* throw)]

săns¹ (-z) *prep.* (arch. or joc.) without (esp. w. ref. to *sans teeth, sans eyes, sans taste, sans everything,* Shak. *As You Like It* II. vii. 166). [ME, f. OF *san*(z), *sen*(s) f. Rom. *sene f. L *sine*; infl. by L *absentia* in the absence of]

sans² (sahn) *prep.* ∼-*gêne* (-zhĕ′n), absence of constraint, familiarity, making oneself at home; ∼ *peur et* ∼ *reproche* (sahn pēr à sahn reprō′sh) *a.*, chivalrous in character. [F, as prec.; *gêne* constraint, *peur* fear, *reproche* reproach]

sănsculō′tt|e (sănzk-, sahnk-) *n.* extreme republican or revolutionary; hence ∼ism (3) *n.* [F, lit. = without knee-breeches, orig. of lower-class Parisian republicans in French Revolution]

sănsĕ′rĭf *n.* & *a.* (Print.) (form of type) without serifs. [app. f. sans¹ + serif]

Sä′nskrĭt *n.* & *a.* (of or in) the ancient and sacred language of Hindus in India; hence **Sänskrĭ′tıc** *a.*, ∼ıst (3) *n.* [f. Skr. *saṃskṛta* composed, elaborated, (*saṃ* together, *kṛ* make, -*to* p.p. ending)]

sans-serif. Var. of sanserif.

Sä′nta Claus (-z), (colloq.) **Sä′nta,** *n.* person said to fill children's stockings with presents on the night before Christmas. [orig. US, f. Du. dial. *Sante Klaas* St. Nicholas]

săntolī′na *n.* aromatic shrub of genus *Santolina.* [mod. L, var. of foll.]

săntō′nĭca *n.* species of wormwood (*Artemisia pauciflora*); drug made from its dried buds. [L (*Santones* Aquitanian tribe; see -ıc)]

sä′ntonĭn *n.* extract of santonica used as anthelmintic. [f. prec. + -ın]

sanyasi. Var. of sannyasi.

săp¹ *n.,* & *v.t.* (-pp-). **1.** *n.* vital juice circulating in plants; (fig.) vital spirit (*the sap of youth*); ∼-**green** *n.* & *a.,* pigment made from buckthorn berries, (of)

colour of this; ∼('**wood**), soft outer layers of recently formed wood between heartwood and bark; hence ∼'ful, ∼'less, ∼'py², *adjs.* **2.** *(sl.) bludgeon (orig. one made from sapling). **3.** *v.t.* drain or dry (wood) of sap; (fig.) exhaust vigour of (*his energy, constitution, belief, had been sapped by adversity*; cf. foll.); remove sapwood from (log); *(sl.) hit with sap (sense 2). [OE *sæp,* = MDu., MLG *sap,* OHG *saf,* prob. f. Gmc *sap(*p*)*am*]

săp² *n.* & *v.* (-pp-). **1.** *n.* making of trenches to cover assailants' approach to besieged place, (fig.) insidious or slow undermining of belief, resolution, etc.; covered siege-trench. **2.** *v.i.* dig sap; approach by sap. **3.** *v.t.* undermine, make insecure by removing foundations, (fig.) destroy insidiously (cf. prec.), (*cliffs sapped by the tide; health sapped by the damp climate; science was sapping old beliefs*). [n. f. F *sappe* or f. It. *zappa* spade(work), v. f. F *sap*(*p*)*er* f. It. *zappare* (*zappa*), prob. of Arab. orig.]

săp³ *n.* (sl.) foolish person. [abbr. of *sapskull* (sap¹ = *sapwood,* skull)]

sä′pajou (-jōō) *n.* capuchin or spider monkey. [F, said to be Cayenne wd]

sä′pan *n.* ∼-**wood,** red dyewood obtained from E. Ind. tree (*Caesalpinia sappan*). [f. Du. *sapan* f. Malay *sapang,* of S. Ind. orig.]

sapē′lè *n.* (mahogany-like hard wood of) W. Afr. tree of genus *Entandrophragma.* [W. Afr. name]

sä′pĭd *a.* having (esp. agreeable) flavour, savoury, palatable, not insipid; (literary; of talk, writing, etc.) not vapid or uninteresting; hence **sapĭ′dıty** *n.* [f. L *sapidus* (*sapere* taste; see -ıd¹)]

sä′pĭent *a.* (literary). would-be wise, of fancied sagacity, aping wisdom; (poet.) wise; hence or cogn. **sä′pĭence** *n.,* ∼ly² *adv.* [ME f. OF, or L part. st. of *sapere* be wise; see -ent]

säpiĕ′ntial (-shal) *a.* of wisdom; ∼ **books,** Prov., Eccles., Ecclus., Cant., Wisd., etc. [ME f. F, or f. eccl. L *sapientialis* (L *sapientia* wisdom, as prec.; see -al)]

sä′pling *n.* young tree; (fig.) a youth, greyhound in first year. [ME, f. sap¹ + -ling¹]

säpodi′lla *n.* large evergreen tropical Amer. tree with durable wood and edible fruit (∼ **plum**) and sap yielding chicle. [f. Sp. *zapotillo* dim. of *zapote* f. Aztec *tzápotl*]

sāponā′ceous (-shus) *a.* of, like, containing, soap, soapy (lit., or joc. fig.). [f. mod. L *saponaceus* f. L *sapo -onis* soap; see -aceous]

sapō′nĭ|fy *v.* (Chem.) **1.** *v.t.* turn (fat or oil) into soap by decomposition with alkali; convert (ester) to acid and alcohol. **2.** *v.i.* be saponified. **3.** Hence or cogn. ∼fıable *a.,* ∼fıcā′tion *n.* [f. F *saponifier* (as prec.; see -fy)]

sä′ponĭn *n.* plant glycoside causing foaming in solutions. [f. F *saponine* f. L *sapo -onis* soap; see -ın]

sä′pŏr *n.* quality perceptible by taste, e.g. sweetness; distinctive taste of substance; sensation of taste. [ME f. L (*sapere* taste; see -or)]

sä′ppan *n.* Var. of sapan.

sä′pper *n.* In vbl senses; ||soldier of Royal Engineers (esp. as official term for private). [f. sap¹,² + -er¹]

Sä′pph|ĭc (să′fĭk) *a.* & *n.* **1.** *a.* of Sappho or Sapphism; ∼ıc **verse, stanza,** (in Gk metres invented by Sappho and imitated in L by Horace, esp. four-line stanza with short fourth line copied in E light verse); hence ∼ısm *n.,* homosexual relations between women. **2.** *n.* (in *pl.*), ∼ıcs). verse in sapphic stanzas. [f. F *sa*(*p*)*phique* L f. Gk *Sapphikos* (*Sapphō* poetess of Lesbos c. 600 BC, suspected of Sapphism; see -ıc)]

sä′pphīr|e (să′fīr) *n.* & *a.* **1.** *n.* transparent blue precious stone consisting of corundum; precious transparent corundum of any colour; bright blue of sapphire, azure; humming-bird with bright blue colouring; so ∼ıne² (să′fīrīn) *a.* **2.** of sapphire blue; ∼e **wedding** (45th anniversary). [ME, f. OF *safir* f. L f. Gk *sappheiros* prob. 'lapis lazuli']

sä′ppý. See sap¹.

să'pro- comb. form. (Biol.) rotten, putrefying, as: ~GE'NIC, causing or produced by putrefaction; ~phagous (-ŏ'f-), living on decaying matter; ~PHILE a. & n., (bacterium) inhabiting putrid matter; ~PHYTE, vegetable organism living on dead or decayed organic matter, whence ~phy'tIC a. [f. Gk sapros putrid +-o-]

să'rabănd n. stately old Spanish dance; music for this or in its rhythm, in triple time freq. with long note on second beat of bar. [f. F sarabande f. Sp. & It. zarabanda]

Să'racen n. & a. 1. n. (Hist.) nomad of Syrian and Arabian desert; Arab or Muslim of time of Crusades. 2. ||~ corn, (arch.) buckwheat; ~'s head (as heraldic charge or inn-sign). 3. So (esp. Islamic Archit.) **Săracĕ'n**IC a. 4. a. of Saracens. [ME, f. OF Sar(r)azin, Sar(r)acin f. LL f. late Gk Sarakēnos perh. f. Arab. šarḳī eastern]

sară'ngi (-nggī) n. Indian stringed instrument played with bow. [f. Hindi sārangī]

sarape. See SERAPE.

săr'căsm n. bitter or wounding remark; taunt, esp. one ironically worded; language consisting of, faculty of uttering, use of, such remarks; so **sărcă'stic** a., **sărcă'stically** adv. [f. F sarcasme or f. LL f. late Gk sarkasmos f. Gk sarkazō tear flesh, in late Gk gnash the teeth, speak bitterly (sarx sarkos flesh; cf. -ISM)]

sărcě'lle n. teal or similar duck. [ME f. OF cercelle f. L querquedula]

sarcenet. Var. of SARSENET.

sărcō'ma n. (pl. ~ta). malignant tumour of connective tissue; hence ~to'sis n., ~tous a. [mod. L f. Gk sarkōma (sarkoō become fleshy f. sarx sarkos flesh; see -OMA)]

sărcŏ'phag|us n. (pl. ~i pr. -gī, -jī). stone coffin esp. adorned with sculpture or inscription; [L, f. Gk sarkophagos a. (as n.) flesh-consuming (as prec., -phagos -eating)]

săr'coplăsm n. (Anat.) interfibrillar substance of muscle. [f. Gk sarx sarkos flesh +-o- + PLASM]

săr'cous a. consisting of flesh or muscle. [f. as prec. +-ous]

sărd n. yellow or orange-red cornelian. [ME, f. F sarde or f. L sarda = LL sardius f. Gk sardios prob. f. Sardō Sardinia]

Sărdanapā'lian a. as of, like, Sardanapalus. [f. Sardanapalus, legendary last king of Nineveh, notorious for effeminate luxury, +-IAN]

sărdĕ'lle n. sardine or similar fish. [f. It. sardella dim. of sarda f. L (as SARDINE²)]

săr'dine¹ n. precious stone mentioned in Rev. 4:3. [ME, f. LL f. Gk sardinos var. of sardios SARDIUS]

sărdi'ne² (-ē'n) n. young pilchard, or similar young or small fish allied to herring, often tinned tightly packed in oil; like ~s, crowded close together. [ME f. OF, = It. f. L sardina (sarda f. Gk, perh. f. Sardō Sardinia)]

Sărdi'nian a. & n. (native or inhabitant or language) of the island or of the kingdom (1720-1861, including also Piedmont etc.) of Sardinia. [f. Sardinia island W. of Italy +-AN]

săr'dius n. (Bibl. etc.) a precious stone. [ME f. LL f. Gk sardios SARD]

sărdŏ'n|ic a. bitterly mocking, cynical, (laugh, laughter, humour, affected merriment, etc.); hence ~ICALLY adv. [f. F sardonique (see -IC), earlier sardonien f. L f. Gk sardonios (= Sardinian) alt. of sardanios, Homeric epithet of bitter or scornful laughter]

săr'donyx n. onyx in which white layers alternate with sard. [ME, f. L f. Gk sardonux (prob. as SARD, ONYX)]

săr'ee. See SARI.

sărgă'ssō n. (pl. ~s or ~es). seaweed of genus Sargassum with berry-like air-vessels found floating in island-like masses in Sargasso Sea etc. of N. Atlantic. [f. Port. sargaço, of unkn. orig.]

sărge n. (sl.) sergeant. [abbr.]

săr'i, săr'ee, n. length of cotton or silk draped round body, worn as main garment by Hindu women. [f. Hindi sāṛ(h)ī]

sărk n. (Sc. & N. Engl.) shirt or chemise; hence ~'ING¹ n., boarding between rafters and roof. [ME serk f. ON serkr f. Gmc *sarkiz]

Sărmă'tian (-shan) a. & n. (inhabitant) of ancient Sarmatia (Russia and Poland); (poet.) Pole, Polish. [f. L Sarmatia (Sarmatae its inhabitants f. Gk Sarmatai) +-AN]

sằr'mentōse, sằrmě'ntous, adjs. (Bot.) with long thin trailing shoots. [f. L sarmentosus (sarmenta pl. twigs, brushwood, f. sarpere to prune; see -MENT, -OSE¹, -OUS)]

săr'nie n. (colloq.) sandwich. [abbr.; see -IE]

sarŏ'ng n. Malay & Javanese garment, long strip of (often striped) cloth worn by both sexes tucked round waist or under armpits; woman's garment imitating this. [Malay, lit. 'sheath']

săr'ŏs n. (Astron.) period of about 18 years between repetitions of eclipses. [Gk, f. Babylonian šār(u) 3600 (years)]

sarrŭ'sophōne n. metal wind instrument played with double reed like oboe. [f. Sarrus, 19th-c. Fr. inventor, +-o-+-PHONE]

sărsaparī'lla n. tropical Amer. smilax esp. Smilax ornata (Jamaica ~ [f. place whence its dried roots etc. were shipped]); dried roots, or extract of these used as tonic etc., of (esp. Jamaica) sarsaparilla. Sp. zarzaparilla (zarza bramble, prob. +dim. of parra vine)]

săr'sen n. sandstone etc. boulder, relict carried by ice in glacial period. [prob. var. of SARACEN]

săr'senět (-sn-) n. fine soft silk material used esp. for linings. [ME, f. AF sarzinett perh. dim. of sarzin SARACEN (see -ET¹) after OF drap sarrasinois Saracen cloth]

sărtōr'ial a. of tailor, tailoring, or men's clothes. [f. L sartor tailor (sarcire sart- patch; see -OR) +-IAL]

sărtōr'ius n. (Anat.) long narrow muscle across front of thigh. [mod. L, f. as prec. (being used in adopting tailor's cross-legged position)]

Săr'um n. (Eccl.) Salisbury; ~ use, order of divine service used in diocese of Salisbury from 11th c. to Reformation. [med. L, prob. f. misread abbr. of L Sarisburia Salisbury]

*s.a.s.e. abbr. self-addressed stamped envelope.

săsh¹ n. ornamental strip of material worn usu. as part of uniform or insignia over one shoulder or round waist, or by woman or child round waist. [earlier shash f. Arab. šāš muslin, turban]

săsh² n. 1. frame usu. of wood holding pane(s) of glass and usu. made to slide up and down in grooves of window aperture; glazed sliding light of glasshouse or garden-frame. 2. ~-cord, ~-line, strong cord attaching sash-weights to sash; ~-tool, glazier's or painter's brush for work on sash-window; ~-weight (attached to each end of sash to balance it at any height); ~-window (with one or usu. two sashes of which one or each can be slid over the other to make opening). [f. sashes, corrupt. of CHASSIS, mistaken for pl.]

*săshay' v.i. walk or move ostentatiously, casually, or diagonally. [corrupt. of CHASSÉ]

săshed (-sht) a. In adj. senses. [f. SASH¹,² +-ED²]

să'shimi n. Japanese dish of garnished raw fish in thin slices. [Jap.]

să'sin n. common Indian antelope (Antilope cervicapra). [Nepali]

să'sine n. (Sc. Law). possession of feudal property; act or document granting this. [var. of SEISIN]

Sask. abbr. Saskatchewan.

să'squătch n. supposed yeti-like animal of NW America. [Amer. Ind.]

*săss. Var. of SAUCE.

să'ssaby n. large S. Afr. antelope (Damaliscus lunatus) like hartebeest. [f. Tswana tsessébe, -dbi]

să'ssafrăs n. (small tree of genus Sassafras, esp. N. Amer. species yielding) bark used medicinally or in perfumery. [f. Sp. *sasafrás* or Port. *sassafraz*, of unkn. orig.]

Sassā'nian, Sā'ssanid, *ns.* & *adjs.* (member, esp. a king) of dynasty ruling Persian empire AD 211–651. [f. *Sasan* founder of dynasty + -IAN, -ID³]

Sa'ssenäch (-χ, -k) *n.* & *a.* (Sc. & Ir., usu. derog.) English(man). [f. Gael. *Sasunnoch*, Ir. *Sasanach* f. L *Saxones* Saxons]

*sa'ssy̆. Var. of SAUCY.

sāstru'gi (-ōō'gī) *n. pl.* wavelike irregularities on the surface of hard polar snow, caused by winds. [f. Russ. *zastrugi* small ridges]

sät. See SIT.

SAT *abbr.* South Australian Time.

Sat. *abbr.* Saturday.

Sā'tan *n.* the Devil, Lucifer. [OE f. LL f. Gk, f. Heb. *śāṭān,* lit. 'adversary' (*śaṭan* oppose)]

satä'n|ic *a.* of, like, or befitting Satan; diabolical, hellish; hence ∼ICALLY *adv.* [f. prec. + -IC]

Sā'tan|ism *n.* **1.** deliberate wickedness, pursuit of evil for its own sake, diabolical disposition; so ∼IZE (3) *v.t.* **2.** worship of Satan, with travesty of Christian forms; so ∼IST (2) *n.* [f. SATAN + -ISM]

Sātanŏ'logy̆ *n.* (history or collection of) beliefs concerning the Devil. [f. SATAN + -O- + -LOGY]

SATB *abbr.* (Mus.) soprano, alto, tenor, bass.

sä'tchel *n.* small bag (usu. of leather and hung from shoulder with strap, for carrying books etc. esp. to and from school). [ME, f. OF *sachel* f. L *saccellus* (as SACK¹; see -LE 2)]

sāte¹ *v.t.* gratify (desire, desirous person) to the full; cloy, surfeit, weary with over-abundance (*sated with pleasure*); hence ∼'LESS (-tl-) *a.* (poet.). [prob. f. dial. *sade*, OE *sadian* (as SAD), assim. to SATIATE²]

sāte². See SIT.

satee'n *n.* cotton fabric woven like satin, with glossy surface. [f. *satin* after *velveteen*]

sä'tellite *n.* & *a.* **1.** *n.* person's follower or henchman or hanger-on; member of great man's retinue; underling. **2.** heavenly body revolving round planet (lit. or fig.), whence **sätelli'tic** *a.*; artificial body placed in orbit round earth or other planet. **3.** *a.* minor, secondary; ∼ (**state**), country nominally independent but controlled by a greater power; ∼ **town,** smaller town dependent on a larger town near it. [F, or f. L *satelles satellitis* attendant]

sati. See SUTTEE.

sä'tiate¹ (-shyat) *a.* (arch.) satiated. [f. L *satiatus* p.p. of *satiare* (*satis* enough); see -ATE²]

sä'ti|āte² (-shǐ-) *v.t.* = SATE¹; hence **sä'tiABLE** (-sha-) *a.* (arch.), ∼A'TION *n.* [f. as prec. + -ATE³]

satī'ety̆ *n.* glutted or satiated state, feeling of having had too much of something, cloyed dislike *of*; **to ∼,** to extent beyond what is desired. [f. obs. F *societé* f. L *satietas -tatis* (*satis* enough); see -TY¹)]

sä'tin *n.*, *a.*, & *v.t.* **1.** *n.* silk etc. fabric with glossy surface on one side got by twill weave with weft--threads almost hidden. **2.** *a.* smooth as satin. **3.** ∼ --**bird,** glossy Austral. bower-bird; ∼ **finish,** polish given to silver etc. with metallic brush; ∼**-flower,** (1) honesty, (2) chickweed, (3) (Austral.) a glossy--flowered umbellifer; ∼ **paper,** fine glossy writing--paper; ∼**-spar,** fibrous calcium carbonate; ∼**-stitch,** long straight embroidery stitch giving appearance of satin; ∼ **white,** white pigment of calcium sulphate and alumina; ∼**wood,** (choice glossy timber of) Ind. tree (*Chloroxylon swietenia*) or one of several Austral. etc. trees. **4.** Hence ∼y̆² *a.* **5.** *v.t.* give glossy surface to (paper). [ME f. OF, f. Arab. *zaytūnī* of Tseutung in China]

sätine't, sätine'tte, *n.* satin-like fabric made partly or wholly of cotton or synthetic fibre. [f. prec. + -ET¹, -ETTE]

sä'tīre *n.* **1.** composition in verse or prose ridiculing vice or folly or lampooning individual(s), this branch of literature; thing that brings ridicule upon something (*our lives are a satire upon our religion*); use of

ridicule, irony, sarcasm, etc., in speech or writing to expose and discourage vice or folly. **2.** (Rom. Ant.) poetic medley, esp. poem ridiculing prevalent vices or follies. [F, or f. L *satira* later form of *satura* medley]

satī'ric *a.* of satires or satire, containing satire, writing satires, (*satiric verse, poem, poet, writer, intent*). [f. F *satirique* or f. LL *satiricus* (as prec.; see -IC)]

satī'rical *a.* = prec.; given to the use of satire in speech or writing or to cynical observation of others, sarcastic, humorously critical; hence ∼LY² *adv.* [as prec.; see -ICAL]

sä'tirist *n.* writer of satires; satirical person. [f. SATIRE + -IST]

sä'tirīze, -īse (-īz), *v.t.* assail with satire; write satire(s) upon; describe satirically. [f. F *satiriser* (as SATIRE; see -IZE)]

sätisfä'ction *n.* **1.** payment of debt, fulfilment of obligation, atonement (*for*); thing accepted by way of satisfaction; (Eccl.) performance of penance; (Theol.) atonement by Christ for sins of mankind; **enter ∼,** (Law) place on record of court that payment ordered has been made. **2.** satisfying or being satisfied in regard to desire or want or doubt, thing that satisfies desire or gratifies feeling, (*find satisfaction in; give satisfaction; heard it with great satisfaction; their satisfaction at or with the results; if you can prove it to my satisfaction; the satisfaction of not having to do it; would be a satisfaction to me; thinks only of present satisfaction*). **3.** opportunity of fighting duel with person by whom one feels insulted (*give, demand, satisfaction*). [ME f. OF, f. L *satisfactio -onis* (as SATISFY; see -ION)]

sätisfä'ctor|y̆ *a.* **1.** satisfying expectations or needs, leaving no room for complaint, causing satisfaction, adequate, (*satisfactory proof, method, result, pupil, pair of shoes, marriage, compromise*). **2.** (Theol.) serving as atonement for sin. **3.** Hence ∼ILY² *adv.,* ∼INESS *n.* [f. F *satisfactoire* or f. med. L *satisfactorius* (as SATISFY; see -ORY)]

sä'tisf|y̆ *v.* **1.** *v.t.* pay (debt, creditor), fulfil (obligation), comply with (demand), (Math., of quantity) make (equation) true. **2.** meet the expectations or desires of, be equal to (notion, preconception, etc.), be accepted by (person, his taste, etc.) as adequate, content; ∼**y̆ the examiners,** reach minimum standard to succeed in university examination. **3.** (in *pass.*) be content or pleased (*with*), demand no more than or consider it enough *to* do; REST³ *satisfied.* **4.** put an end to (an appetite or want), rid (person) of an appetite or want, by sufficient supply. **5.** furnish with adequate proof, convince, make confident, (*of fact, that* it is so; ∼**y̆** one*self,* attain to practical certainty). **6.** adequately meet (objection, doubt, request, conditions). **7.** *v.i.* give satisfaction, leave nothing to be desired; (of Christ) make atonement for sins of mankind. **8.** Hence ∼IABLE, ∼YING², *adjs.* [ME, f. OF *satisfier* f. L *satisfacere -fact-* (*satis* enough; see -FY)]

satŏ'ri *n.* (Buddhism). sudden enlightenment. [Jap.]

satra'ngi (-ŭ'njī) *n.* Indian cotton carpet. [Bengali, f. Skr. *catúranga* chess for four players]

sä'träp *n.* holder of provincial governorship or ∼y̆¹ *n.,* in ancient Persian empire, viceroy; (rhet.) subordinate ruler, colonial governor, etc. [ME, f. OF *satrape,* or f. L f. Gk *satrapēs* f. OPers. *xšaθra-pāvan* country-protector]

Sä'tsuma *n.* **1.** ∼ (**ware**), cream-coloured Japanese pottery. **2.** (*s*∼). kind of mandarin orange orig. grown in Japan. [∼ province in Japan]

sä'tur|āte (-cher-, -tūr-) *v.t.* fill with moisture, soak thoroughly; imbue *with,* steep *in,* (learning, tradition, prejudice, etc.); fill to capacity (*with*); overwhelm (defences, target area) by concentrated bombing; (Phys. etc.) cause (substance, solution, air, vapour, metal) to absorb or hold greatest amount possible of another substance, moisture (*saturated* STEAM); magnetism, electricity, etc.; (Chem.) cause (substance) to combine with maximum amount of another substance, esp. hydrogen in fats; (in *p.p.*, of colour) free from admixture of white, full, rich; hence or cogn. ∼ATE² *a.* (literary), ∼ABLE *a.*, ∼ANT *a.* & *n.* [f. L *saturare* (*satur* full) + -ATE³]

satura'tion (-cher-, -tūr-) *n.* saturating or being saturated; ∼ **point**, stage beyond which no more can be absorbed or accepted. [f. LL *saturatio* or f. prec.; see -ATION]

Sa'turday (-dā, -dǐ) *n.* & *adv.* **1.** *n.* day of week, following Friday; HOLY *Saturday.* **2.** *adv.* (cf. FRIDAY 2). [OE *Sætern(es)dæg* transl. of L *Saturni dies* day of Saturn]

Sa'turn *n.* **1.** (Rom. Ant.) Italic god of agriculture later identified with Greek Kronos, father of Zeus, ruler of the world in a golden age of innocence and plenty. **2.** planet of solar system, most distant of the 5 anciently known, with broad flat rings, credited in astrology with producing cold sluggish gloomy temperament in those born under its influence. **3.** (Alch.) the metal lead. [f. L *Saturnus*, perh. f. Etruscan]

saturnā'l|ia *n.* **1.** *pl.* (*S*∼*ia*). ancient-Roman festival of Saturn in December observed as time of unrestrained merry-making extending even to slaves, predecessor of modern Christmas-tide. **2.** (as *sing.* or *pl.*) scene or time of wild revelry or tumult (*a saturnalia of crime*); hence ∼IAN *a.* [L, neut. pl. (as n.) of *Saturnalis* (as prec.; see -AL)]

Satūr'nian *a.* & *n.* **1.** *a.* of the god or the planet Saturn; ∼ **age**, golden age; ∼ **metre**, **verse**, metre used in early Latin poetry before introduction of Greek metres. **2.** *n.* (in *pl.*) Saturnian verse. [f. L *Saturnius* (as SATURN) + -AN]

satūr'nic *a.* (Path.) affected with lead-poisoning; so **sä'turn**ISM (5) *n.* [f. SATURN 3 + -IC]

sä'turnīne *a.* **1.** of sluggish gloomy temperament, (of looks etc.) suggestive of or produced by such temperament; hence ∼LY² (-nlĭ) *adv.* **2.** of the metal lead; of or affected by lead-poisoning. [ME, f. OF *saturnin* f. med. L *Saturninus* (as SATURN; see -INE¹)]

satya'graha (sahtyah'grah-hah) *n.* (Ind.) passive resistance esp. as advocated by Gandhi. [Skr. (*satya* truth, *āgraha* obstinacy)]

sä'tyr *n.* one of a class of Greek woodland deities in human form with horse's ears and tail (or, as represented by Romans, with goat's ears, tail, legs, and budding horns); lustful or sensual-minded man; satyrid butterfly. [ME, f. OF *satyre* or f. L f. Gk *saturos*]

satyri'as|is *n.* (*pl.* ∼es *pr.* -ēz). (Path.) excessive sexual desire in men. [LL, f. Gk *saturiasis* (as prec.; see -ASIS)]

saty'ric *a.* of satyrs; ∼ **drama**, kind of ancient-Greek comic play with chorus of satyrs. [f. L f. Gk *saturikos* (as SATYR; see -IC)]

sä'tyrid *n.* butterfly of family Satyridae. [f. mod. L *Satyridae* f. genus *Satyrus* (as SATYR); see -ID³]

sauce *n.*, & *v.t.* **1.** *n.* liquid or soft preparation taken as relish with some article of food; BREAD, **egg**, MINT³, **parsley**, **tomato**, etc., ∼ (with these as prominent ingredient); **white** ∼ (of melted butter, flour, etc.); *sauce for the* GANDER; **serve with the same** ∼, subject to same usage. **2.** (fig.) something that adds piquancy (*is taste without the sauce of danger*). **3.** *stewed etc. fruit eaten as dessert or used as garnish; *vegetables eaten with meat etc. **4.** impudence, impertinent speech, cheek, (*none of your sauce!*). **5.** ∼-**alone**, hedge-weed formerly used to flavour salads and sauces; ∼-**boat**, vessel in which sauce is served; ∼'**box**, (colloq.) impudent person; ∼'**pan** (-an), metal cooking-vessel, usu. cylindrical with long side-handle, for use on top of stove etc. **6.** Hence ∼'LESS (-sl-) *a.* **7.** *v.t.* (arch.) season with sauces or condiments (lit. or fig.). **8.** (colloq.) be impudent to, cheek, (person). [ME f. OF f. Rom. *salsa fem. (as n.) of L *salsus* (*salere sals*- to salt f. *sal* salt)]

sau'cer *n.* **1.** shallow vessel for standing cup on to catch spilt tea etc.; FLYING² *saucer*; ∼ **eye** (large and

round as a saucer, or wide open in surprise etc.). **2.** vessel placed under flowerpot to prevent water from running away at once; any small shallow round vessel resembling tea-saucer. **3.** Hence ∼FUL 2 *n.*, ∼LESS *a.* [ME = condiment-dish, f. OF *saussier(e)* sauce-boat, prob. f. LL *salsarium* (as SAUCE; see -ER² (2))]

sau'c|y *a.* impudent to superiors, cheeky; (colloq.) smart-looking; hence ∼ILY² *adv.*, ∼INESS *n.* [earlier sense 'savoury', f. SAUCE + -Y²]

Sau'di (sow'-) *n.* & *a.* (native or inhabitant) of Saudi Arabia; (member) of dynasty founded by Saud. [f. A. Ibn-*Saud*, Arab. king d. 1953 + -I]

sauer'kraut (sowr'krowt) *n.* German dish of chopped pickled cabbage. [G (*sauer* SOUR, *kraut* vegetable)]

***sau'ger** (-g-) *n.* small pike-perch. [19th c.; orig. unkn.]

Sau'mūr (sō-) *n.* white wine produced near Saumur. [∼ in W. France]

sau'na (saw'-, sow'-) *n.* (building for) Finnish-style steam-bath. [Finn.]

saunders. See SANDERS.

sau'nter *v.i.*, & *n.* **1.** *v.i.* walk in leisurely way or without destination, stroll, (lit., or fig., *saunter through life*); hence ∼ER¹ *n.* **2.** *n.* leisurely ramble or gait. [ME, = muse; orig. unkn.]

saur'ian *a.* & *n.* (of or like) a lizard. [f. mod. L *Sauria* f. Gk *saura* lizard + -AN]

saur'y *n.* long-beaked sea-fish (*Scombresox saurus*) of temperate waters. [perh. f. LL f. Gk *sauros* horse--mackerel]

sau'sage (sŏ's-) *n.* **1.** pork or other meat minced, seasoned, and stuffed into long cylindrical cases prepared from entrails or synthetic material and divided when full into lengths of a few inches by twisting or tying; a length of this; **Bologna** ∼, large kind made of bacon, veal, pork-suet, etc., and sold ready for eating cold; **not a** ∼, (sl.) nothing at all; ‖∼-**dog**, (colloq.) dachshund; ∼-**machine**, sausage-making appliance (also fig. of relentlessly uniform process); ∼-**meat**, meat and bread etc. minced and seasoned for use in sausages or as a stuffing etc.; ∼-**roll**, sausage-meat enclosed in pastry and baked. **2.** (colloq.) sausage-shaped object; *(derog.) a German. [ME, f. ONF *saussiche* f. med. L *salsicia* f. *salsus* (as SAUCE)]

sauté (sō'tā) *a.*, *n.*, & *v.t.* (∼**d** or ∼**ed** *pr.* -ād). **1.** *a.* & *n.* (food) quickly fried in hot pan with little fat. **2.** *v.t.* cook thus. [F, p.p. of *sauter* jump]

Sauter'ne(s) (sōtēr'n, -ār'n) *n.* light sweet white wine from Bordeaux region of France. [f. *Sauternes* district of Gironde]

sauve qui peut (sōv kē pēr') *n.* precipitate flight in various directions. [F, lit. 'save (himself) who can']

sä'vage *a.*, *n.*, & *v.t.* **1.** *a.* uncivilized, in primitive state, (*savage tribes, life*). **2.** fierce, cruel, furious, (*savage persecution, persecutor, revenge, criticism, blow*); (colloq.) angry, out of temper. **3.** (arch.) uncultivated, wild, (*a savage animal, scene*). **4.** (Her.) (Of human figure) naked. **5.** Hence or cogn. ∼LY² (-ĭjlĭ) *adv.*, ∼NESS (-ĭjn-), **sä'vag**ERY (2, 4) (-ĭjrĭ), *ns.* **6.** *n.* member of savage tribe esp. of one living by hunting and fishing, whence ∼DOM (-ĭjd-) *n.*; brutally cruel or barbarous person. **7.** *v.t.* (Of horse, dog) attack and bite or trample; (of critic etc.) attack fiercely. [ME f. OF *sauvage* wild f. Rom. *salvaticus* f. L *silvaticus* (*silva* a wood; see -ATIC)]

savă'nnah (-na), **-nna**, *n.* grassy plain with few or no trees in tropical and subtropical regions. [f. Sp. *zavana*, perh. of Carib orig.]

sä'vant (-ahn) *n.* (*fem.* ∼**e** *pr.* -ahnt). learned person, esp. distinguished scientist. [F, part. (as n.) of *savoir* know (as SAPIENT)]

sava'te (-ah't) *n.* form of boxing in which feet as well as fists are used. [F, orig. a kind of shoe; cf. SABOT]

sāve¹ *v.* & *n.* **1.** *v.t.* rescue, preserve, protect, deliver, from or *from* danger or misfortune or harm or discredit (*saved my* LIFE, *me from drowning*; *save*

APPEARANCES, one's BACON, *the* DAY, one's or person's FACE[1], one's SKIN[1]; ～ **the situation,** find or provide way out of difficulty, avert disaster); keep in specified state (*save us alive; save* HARMLESS). **2.** (**God**) ～, may God preserve or protect (*God save the Queen*); (**God**) ～ **me from** *my friends* etc. (comment on well-meant but inopportune interference); (*God*) *save the* MARK[1]; (**God**) ～ **us!** (excl. of surprise). **3.** bring about spiritual salvation of, preserve from damnation, (*who then can be saved?*). **4.** keep for future use or enjoyment; husband, reserve, abstain from expending; ～ one's **breath,** be silent; *save one's breath to cool one's* PORRIDGE; **you may** ～ **your pains** or **trouble** (need not take, will take in vain); ～ one*self*, not use up one's strength. **5.** relieve (person, one*self*, or abs.) from need of expending (money, trouble, etc.) or from exposure to (annoyance etc.); obviate need of, reduce requisite amount of, (*that will save me, I saved myself, £50; his secretary saved him much time or labour, many interviews; a stitch in time saves nine; soap saves rubbing*); ～ **the follow-on,** (Cricket) get enough runs to prevent it; ～**-all,** device to prevent waste, esp. (Hist.) pan with spike for burning-up candle-ends. **6.** avoid losing, be in time for, succeed in catching, (*batted stubbornly and saved the game; write hurriedly to save the post*); ～ **the tide,** get in or out while it serves. **7.** make reservation concerning, make reservation. **8.** Hence **sā′vABLE** *a.* **9.** *v.i.* save (*up*) money for future use; (Footb. etc.) prevent opponent from scoring; ||～**-as-you-earn,** method of saving by regular deduction from earnings. **10.** *n.* (Footb. etc.) act of preventing opponent from scoring; (Bridge) sacrifice-bid to prevent unnecessary losses. [ME, f. AF *sa*(*u*)*ver*, OF *salver, sauver* f. LL *salvare* f. L *salvus* SAFE[2]]

sāve[2] *prep.* & *conj.* **1.** *prep.* (arch., poet., or rhet.) except, but, (w. n. etc. in obj. case; *forty stripes save one; all save him*). **2.** *conj.* (arch.) unless, but, except, (*all the conspirators save only he; save where the beetle wheels his droning flight; I am well save that I have a cold; happy save for one want*). [ME f. OF *sauf sauve* f. L *salvo, salva*, abl. sing. of *salvus* SAFE[2]]

sä′veloy *n.* highly seasoned dried sausage. [corrupt. of F *cervelas, -at*, f. It. *cervellata* (*cervello* brain)]

sä′ver *n.* In vbl senses; person who saves money; device for economical use (of soap, time, etc.); (sl.) hedging bet. [f. SAVE[1] + -ER[1]]

sä′vin, sä′vine, *n.* (kind of juniper with) tips of shoots yielding a volatile oil used medicinally; *red cedar. [OE, f. OF *savine* f. L *sabina* (*herba*) Sabine (herb)]

sä′ving[1] *a.* & *prep.* **1.** *a.* In vbl senses; making economical use of (*labour-saving*); ～ **clause** (containing stipulation of exemption etc.); ～ **grace,** redeeming grace (of God, or fig.). **2.** *prep.* except, with the exception of; without offence to (*saving your presence, your* REVERENCE). [ME, f. SAVE[1] + -ING[2]; in sense 2 prob. f. SAVE[2] after *touching*]

sä′ving[2] *n.* In vbl senses; (usu. in *pl.*) money saved; *～s account,** deposit account; ～**s bank** (receiving small deposits at interest and devoting profits to benefit of depositors); ||～**s certificate,** interest-bearing document issued by Government for benefit of savers. [ME, f. SAVE[1] + -ING[1]]

sä′viour *n.* (-vyer) *n.* deliverer, redeemer (**the** or **our S**～, Christ); person who saves a State etc. from destruction etc. [ME, f. OF *sauvëour* f. eccl. L *salvator -oris* (transl. Gk *sōtēr*) f. LL *salvare* SAVE[1]]

savoir-faire (sǎvwǎrfār′) *n.* quickness to know and do the right thing, tact. [F, = know how to do]

savoir-vivre (sǎvwǎrvē′vr) *n.* good breeding, being at home in society. [F, = know how to live]

***sä′vor,** *sä′vory*[1]. See SAVOUR, SAVOURY.

sä′vory[2] *n.* herb of genus *Satureia* of mint family, used in cookery. [ME *saverey*, perh. f. OE *sætherie* f. L *satureia*]

||**sä′vour** (-ver), ***sä′vor,** *n.* & *v.* **1.** *n.* characteristic taste, flavour, relish, or (arch.) smell, power to affect the taste (lit. or fig.); quality suggestive, perceptible

admixture, *of*; hence ～LESS *a.* **2.** *v.t.* appreciate or perceive the (lit. or fig.) taste of, enjoy esp. lingeringly or with deliberation. **3.** *v.i.* suggest by taste, smell, or otherwise the presence *of* (*the offer savours of impertinence*). [ME; n. f. OF, f. L *sapor -oris* (*sapere* taste; see -OR); v. f. OF *savourer* f. LL *saporare* f. L *sapor*]

||**sä′vour|ȳ** (-verĭ), ***sä′vor|ȳ**[1], *a.* & *n.* **1.** *a.* with appetizing taste or smell; (fig.) pleasant, acceptable; (of food) having salt or piquant and not sweet flavour (*sweet or savoury omelette*); hence ～iLY[2] *adv.,* ～iNESS *n.* **2.** *n.* ||savoury dish, esp. one served at beginning or usu. end of dinner as stimulant or digestive. [ME, f. OF *savouré* p.p. (as prec.); see -Y[4]]

savoy′ *n.* hardy cabbage with wrinkled leaves. [f. *Savoy* in SE France]

Savoy′ard *n.* & *a.* **1.** (native) of Savoy. **2.** *n.* devotee or performer of Gilbert and Sullivan operas (orig. produced at Savoy Theatre). [F (*Savoie* Savoy; see -ARD)]

sä′vvȳ *v., n.,* & *a.* (sl.) **1.** *v.i.* & *t.* know; **no** ～, I do, he etc. does, not know or understand. **2.** *n.* knowingness, understanding. **3.** *a.* *knowing, wise. [orig. Black & Pidgin E after Sp. *sabe usted* you know]

saw[1] *n.* & *v.* (*p.p.* ～*n* or ～*ed*). **1.** *n.* tool worked by hand or mechanically and with variously shaped usu. steel blade or edge having teeth of various forms cut in or attached to it for dividing wood, metal, stone, bone, etc., by to-and-fro or rotatory motion; BAND[1]-*-saw,* BOW[1]-*saw,* CIRCULAR *saw,* CROWN[1] *saw,* FRAME[2]-*-saw,* FRET[1]*saw,* HACK[2]-*saw,* HAND[1]*saw,* JIG[2]*saw,* PIT[1]-*saw,* RIP[2]-*saw,* STONE-*saw.* **2.** (Zool. etc.) serrated organ or part. **3.** ～**-bill,** merganser; *～**′buck,** saw-horse, (sl.) $10 note; ～**-doctor,** machine for making teeth of saw; ～**′dust,** tiny wood fragments produced in sawing used in packing, pugging, stuffing, drying moisture, etc.; ～**-edged,** with jagged edge like saw; ～**′fish,** large sea-fish of family Pristidae with toothed flat end of snout used as weapon; ～**-fly,** insect of family Tenthredinidae, injurious to plants, with serrated ovipositor; ～**-frame** (in which saw-blade is held taut); ～**-gate,** saw-frame; ～**-gin,** cotton-GIN[1] with saw-teeth; ～**-horse,** rack supporting wood for sawing; ～**′mill** (driven by water or steam for mechanical sawing of wood); ～**-pit** (in which lower of two men working pit-saw stands); ～**-set,** tool for wrenching saw-teeth in alternate directions to give kerf wider than blade and let saw work freely; ～**′tooth(ed)** *a.,* shaped like teeth of saw, esp. of roof, wave, etc., with one steep and one slanting side; ～**-wort,** plant (*Serratula tinctoria*) yielding yellow dye from its serrated leaves. **4.** *v.t.* cut (wood etc.) with, make (boards etc.) with, saw; ～**′bones,** (sl.) surgeon; ～**ed-off,** ||～**-n-off,** (of gun) with part of barrel removed by sawing, (of person, colloq.) undersized. **5.** *v.i.* use saw. **6.** *v.t.* & *i.* move backward and forward, divide (the air etc.), with motion as of saw or person sawing. [OE *sagu, saga,* = OHG *saga,* ON *sög* f. Gmc *sagō,* *sagon*]

saw[2] *n.* proverbial saying, old maxim, (esp. *old* or *wise saw*). [OE *sagu,* = OHG, ON *saga,* f. Gmc *sagō* cogn. with SAY[2]; cf. SAGA]

saw[3]. See SEE[1].

saw′der *n.,* & *v.t.* (colloq.) **1.** *n.* **soft** ～, compliments, flattering speeches, blarney. **2.** *v.t.* flatter. [fig. use of var. of SOLDER]

sawn. See SAW[1].

Saw′ney *n.* **1.** (derog.) Scotsman. **2.** (colloq.) simpleton. [Sc. var. of SANDY[2]]

saw′yer *n.* **1.** man employed in sawing timber; TOP[1]-*-sawyer.* **2.** *uprooted tree held fast by one end in river (and sawing up and down). **3.** (NZ). weta. [ME, earlier *sawer* (saw, -ER[1]); see -YER]

sǎx[1], **zǎx,** *n.* slater's chopper, with point for making nail-holes; **sa′xboard,** uppermost strake of open boat. [OE *seax* knife, = OS, OHG *sahs,* ON *sax* f. Gmc *sahsam* f. IE *sok-, sek-*]

sǎx[2] *n.* (colloq.) saxophone. [abbr.]

sǎ′xatǐle *a.* (Biol.) living or growing on or among rocks. [F, or f. L *saxatilis* (*saxum* rock)]

sǎxe *n.* ~ (**blue**), light blue with greyish tinge. [F, = Saxony, source of dye so coloured]

sǎ′xhŏrn *n.* brass wind instrument of trumpet family made in several sizes, usu. held either with mouth upwards or with tube encircling player's body. [f. C. J. & A. Sax, Belgian instrument-makers d. 1865 & 1894, +HORN¹]

sǎxi′colǐne, -lous, *adjs.* (Biol.) = SAXATILE. [f. mod. L *saxicolus* (*saxum* rock, *colere* inhabit) +-INE¹, -OUS]

sǎ′xifrage (-ǐj, -āj) *n.* Alpine or rock plant of genus *Saxifraga* etc., with tufted foliage and panicles of white or yellow or red flowers. [ME f. OF, or f. LL *saxifraga* (*herba*) f. L *saxum* rock +*frangere* break]

Sǎ′xon *n.* & *a.* **1.** *n.* member, language (usu. **Old** ~), of Germanic people that conquered parts of England in 5th–6th c.; = ANGLO-SAXON, whence ~DOM *n.* **2.** native of modern Saxony. **3.** Germanic (opp. Latin or Romance) elements of English. **4.** *a.* of the Saxons (~ **architecture,** form of Romanesque preceding Norman in England); belonging to or originating from the Saxon language or Old English, whence ~ISM (2, 4), ~IST (2), *ns.*; ~ **blue,** solution of indigo in sulphuric acid as dye; hence ~IZE (2, 3) *v.i.* & *t.* [ME f. OF, f. LL *Saxo -onis* f. Gk *Saxones* pl. f. WG *Saxon-* (OE *Seaxan, Seaxe*, pl., OS, OHG *Sahso*)]

sǎ′xony *n.* fine kind of wool; cloth made from it. [f. *S*~ in Germany, f. LL *Saxonia* (as prec.)]

sǎ′xophōne *n.* keyed brass wind instrument made in several sizes, having reed like that of clarinet; hence ~IST (3) (-ofŏn-, -ŏ′fon-) *n.* [f. as SAXHORN +-O-+ -PHONE]

sǎ′xtūba *n.* large saxhorn. [f. SAXHORN + TUBA]

say¹ *n.* (arch.) fine cloth like serge. [ME, f. OF *saie* f. L *saga* pl. of *sagum* military cloak]

say² *v.* (**said** *pr.* sĕd; 3 *sing. pres.* **says** *pr.* sĕz, (arch.) **saith** *pr.* sĕth; 2 *sing. pres.* (arch.) ~st or ~est, *past* **saidst** or **saidest**) & *n.* **1.** *v.t.* utter, make (specified remark), recite, rehearse, in ordinary speaking voice; repeat (lesson) to teacher; speak words of (prayers, grace, Mass, etc.); (ellipt.) = *that is to say* (1) (£50 *say fifty pounds*); ||**1** ~ (excl. drawing attention, opening conversation, or expressing surprise); **not to** ~, and indeed (*his language was irreverent, not to say blasphemous*); ~ **much, something, for,** indicate high quality of; ~ **for** oneself, utter (*something* etc.) by way of conversation or oratory (and cf. sense 4); *say* person NAY; *say* NO⁴; ~ **no more,** cease speaking on a particular topic or at all; **to** ~ **nothing of,** even disregarding; ~ **nothing to,** (fig.) leave (person) unmoved; ~ **out,** express fully or candidly; ~**s** or **said he** etc., **said I,** (colloq.) ~**s I,** (used in reporting conversation); ~**s you,** (vulg. *int.*) I disagree; ~ **something,** make a short speech; *say* WHEN; *say the word, a few words, a good word for,* (see WORD¹); *say* YES; so¹ *to say*; **that is to** ~, (1) in other words, more explicitly, (2) or at least (*he never went, that is to say it is not recorded that he did*); **when all is said and done,** after all, in the long run; **you can** ~ **that** (again), **you said it,** (colloq.) I agree emphatically; **you don't** ~ (**so**), (colloq.) that is incredible. **2.** state, promise, prophesy, (*that*); have specified wording or reading (*the Bible says that thou shalt not steal*; *it says here that he was killed*; *the clock says ten to six*); (in *pass.*) be asserted (*tree is said to be six hundred years old*), be described by a term (*in that case the loser is said to be rubiconed*); DARE *say*; HEAR *say*; **I'll** ~, (colloq.) yes indeed; **I'm not** ~**ing,** I refuse to answer the question; **the said,** (Law or joc.) the previously mentioned; **it is said,** the rumour is (*that*); **it** ~**s in the Bible,** the Bible says; ~ **so,** say the thing in question; **they** ~, the rumour is (*that*). **3.** put into words, express (*that was well said*; *no* SOONER *said than done*); convey information (*spoke for an hour but didn't say much*). **4.** adduce or allege in argument or excuse (*there is much to be said on both sides*; *have you anything to say for yourself?*).

5. form and give opinion or decision as to, or abs., (*there is no saying, it is hard to say, who it was*; *do say which you will have*); **I cannot** or **could not** ~, I do not know (*whether* etc., or abs.); **and so** ~ **all of us,** and that is our opinion too; **what do you** ~ **to?**, would you like?; **how** ~ **you?** (asking jury for verdict); ~- -**so** *n.*, (1) power of decision, (2) mere assertion. **6.** select as example, assume, take (specified number etc.) as near enough, (*let us say, shall we say,* or usu. ellipt. *say; any country, let us say Sweden, might do the same*; *well, say it were true, what then?*; *a few of them, say a dozen or so*). **7.** *v.i.* speak, talk; (in *imper.,* poet.) tell me; * = I *say*; ~ **away,** ~ **on,** say what you have to say. **8.** *n.* (opportunity of saying) what one has to say (*said his say*; *let him have his say*); share in decision (*had no say in the matter*); power of (final) decision. [OE *secgan*, = OS *seggian,* OHG *sagēn,* ON *segja,* f. Gmc **sagjan,* **sagæjan*]

||**SAYE** *abbr.* save-as-you-earn.

say′ǐng *n.* In vbl senses; sententious remark, maxim, adage; **as the** ~ **is** or **goes** (form used in quoting proverb or phrase); **go without** ~, be too well known or obvious to need mention; ~ **and doing,** speech and action; **there is no** ~, it is impossible to know. [ME, f. SAY² + -ING¹]

Sb *symb.* antimony [f L *stibium*]

SBN *abbr.* Standard Book Number.

S. by E., S. by W., *abbrs.* South by East, West.

SC *abbr.* small capitals; South Carolina; special constable.

sc. *abbr.* scilicet.

Sc *symb.* scandium.

scǎb *n.,* & *v.i.* (-bb-). **1.** *n.* dry rough incrustation formed over sore in healing; mange, itch, or similar skin-disease; fungous plant-disease causing scablike roughness. **2.** (arch.) mean low fellow. **3.** person who refuses to join strike or trade union or takes striker's place or breaks rules of his trade or group. **4.** Hence ~**bED²** (-bd), ~**bY²,** *adjs.* **5.** *v.i.* (Of sore) form scab, heal over; act as scab. [ME, f. ON **skabbr* = OE *sceabb* (cf. SHABBY)]

scǎ′bbard *n.* sheath of sword, bayonet, etc., (**throw away the** ~, commit oneself to fighting a matter out to the end); ***sheath for revolver etc.; ~-**fish,** silvery-white sea-fish shaped like sword-scabbard. [ME *sca(u)berc* etc., f. AF **escauberc, escauberge* prob. f. Frank. **skār(a)* (cf. SHEAR²) +**berg-* protect]

scǎ′bies (bǐēs, bǐēz) *n.* contagious disease, the ITCH¹. [ME f. L (*scabere* scratch)]

scǎ′bious *a.* & *n.* **1.** *a.* scabby, affected with mange, itch, etc. **2.** *n.* wild or cultivated annual or perennial herb of genus *Scabiosa* with blue, pink, or white, pincushion-shaped flowers. [n. ME f. med. L *scabiosa* (*herba*) named as specific against itch, a. f. F *scabieux* or f. L *scabiosus* (as prec.; see -OUS)]

scǎ′brous *a.* **1.** (Zool., Bot., etc.) having rough surface, scurfy. **2.** (Of subject, situation, etc.) requiring tactful treatment, hard to handle with decency. **3.** indecent, salacious; behaving licentiously. **4.** Hence ~LY² *adv.,* ~NESS *n.* [f. F *scabreux* or f. LL *scabrosus* f. L *scaber* rough; see -OUS]

scǎd *n.* fish of family Carangidae, like large mackerel. [17th c.; orig. unkn.]

*scǎds (-z) *n. pl.* (colloq.) large quantities *of.* [19th c.; orig. unkn.]

scǎ′ffold *n.,* & *v.t.* **1.** *n.* elevated platform of timber for execution of criminals (the ~, death by execution), for drying tobacco, etc.; scaffolding. **2.** *v.t.* attach scaffolding to (building); hence ~ER¹ *n.* [ME, f. AF **scaffaut,* OF (*e*)*schaffaut,* earlier *escadafaut* f. Rom. **EX¹*(*catafalcum*; cf. CATAFALQUE)]

scǎ′ffolding *n.* temporary structure of poles or tubes and planks providing workmen with platform(s) to stand on while building or repairing house etc.; materials for this; temporary framework (lit. or fig.) for other purposes; ~-**pole,** mastlike pole helping to support scaffolding. [ME, f. prec. + -ING¹]

scăgliŏ′la (-lyŏ′-) *n.* imitation stone of plaster mixed with glue. [f. It. *scagliuola* dim. of *scaglia* SCALE¹]

scā′lable *a.* In vbl senses. [f. SCALE¹,²,³ + -ABLE]

scā′lar *a.* & *n.* (Math.) (quantity) having only magnitude, not direction (cf. VECTOR). [f. L *scalaris* (*scala* ladder; see SCALE³, -AR¹)]

scală′rifŏrm *a.* (Bot. & Zool.) (of veins in insect's wings, or of alternating thick and thin strips in structure) ladder-shaped. [f. prec. in sense 'ladder--like' + -I- + -FORM]

scalawag. See SCALLYWAG.

scald¹ (-aw-, -ŏ-) *v.t.,* & *n.* **1.** *v.t.* injure or pain (skin, or person or animal or part in regard to skin) with hot liquid or vapour (*was scalded to death by the steam*); **like a ∼ed cat,** moving unusually fast; **∼ing tears,** tears of bitter grief. **2.** heat (milk) to near boiling-point; **∼ed cream** (from milk scalded and allowed to stand); hence **∼′ER¹** (2) *n.* **3.** cleanse (vessel *out*) by rinsing with boiling water; treat (poultry etc.) with boiling water to remove feathers etc. **4.** *n.* injury to skin by scalding. [ME, f. AF, ONF *escalder*, OF *eschalder* f. LL EX¹(*caldare* f. L *calidus* hot)]

scald². See SKALD.

scā′ld-head (-aw′ld-hĕd) *n.* scalp-disease, e.g. ringworm. [f. p.p. of SCALL + HEAD¹]

scāle¹ *n.* & *v.* **1.** *n.* one of the small thin bony or horny overlapping plates protecting the skin of many fishes and reptiles. **2.** plate or thin outer piece with some resemblance to fish-scale in organic or other object, e.g. pod, husk, rudimentary leaf or feather, bract, metamorphosed hair of Lepidoptera, bulb-layer, flake of skin, scab, lamina on surface of rusty iron; **the ∼s fall from** person's **eyes,** he is no longer deceived. **3.** incrustation inside boiler etc.; tartar on teeth. **4.** **∼- -armour** (of metal scales attached to leather etc.); **∼-board,** very thin wood for back of mirror, picture, etc.; **∼-bug,** = *scale-insect*; **∼-fern,** ceterach; **∼-insect** (of family Coccidae, clinging to plants and secreting a shieldlike scale as covering); **∼-leaf,** modified leaf resembling scale; **∼-moss,** liverwort with scalelike leaves; **∼-winged,** lepidopterous; **∼-work,** overlapping arrangement. **5.** Hence **(-)scāled** (-ld), **∼′LESS** (-l-l-), **scā′lÿ²,** *adjs.* **6.** *v.t.* take away scale(s) from (fish, almonds, teeth, iron, etc.). **7.** *v.i.* (Of skin, metal, etc.) form, come off in, drop, scales; (of scales) come *off.* [ME, f. OF *escale* f. Gmc *skalō* (cf. foll.)]

scāle² *n.,* & *v.t.* **1.** *n.* ∼(-pan), dish of simple balance; **throw into the ∼,** cause to be factor in contest or debate; **tip** or **turn the ∼(s),** outweigh opposite scale (*at-* specified weight), (of motive or circumstance) be decisive. **2.** (in *sing.* or *pl.*) weighing--instrument (**hold the ∼s even,** be impartial judge); (*S∼s*) the zodiacal sign Libra; **pair of ∼s,** simple balance. **3.** *v.t.* (Of thing weighed) show (specified weight) in the scales. [ME, f. ON *skál* bowl = OHG *scāla* f. Gmc *skēlō,* cogn. w. *skalō* whence OE *scealu* SHELL¹; cf. SHALE]

scāle³ *n.* & *v.* **1.** *n.* series of degrees, ladder-like arrangement or classification, graded system, (*is high in the scale of creation* or *the social, intellectual,* etc., *scale*; *at the top, bottom, of the scale*; *fees according to a prescribed scale*); SLIDING *scale.* **2.** (Mus.) arrangement by pitch of all notes used in any system of music (CHROMATIC, DIATONIC, MAJOR², MINOR, PENTATONIC, *scale*); **play, sing, ∼s,** perform notes in such sequence as exercise for fingers, voice, etc. **3.** ∼(**of notation**), (Arith.) basis of numerical system as shown by ratio between units in adjacent places of number; **ordinary** or **denary** or **decimal ∼** (with successive places denoting units, tens, hundreds, etc.); **binary ∼** (denoting units, twos, fours, etc.); **ternary ∼** (denoting units, threes, nines, etc.). **4.** relative dimensions, ratio of reduction or enlargement in picture, map, etc., (*philanthropy, armies, on a large* or *grand scale*; *a building of small scale but fine proportions*; *large, small, -scale map*; *on a scale of one to fifty thousand, an inch to the mile,* etc.); (*attrib.*) made to scale (*scale model*); **economies of ∼,**

proportionate savings got by using larger quantities; **in ∼,** in proportion to surroundings etc.; **to ∼,** with uniform reduction or enlargement. **5.** set of marks at measured distances on line for use in measuring or making proportional reductions and enlargements; rule determining intervals between these; piece of metal etc. or apparatus on which they are marked. **6.** *v.t.* climb (wall, steep place, or abs.) with ladder (**scaling-ladder**) or by clambering. **7.** represent in dimensions proportional to the actual ones, reduce to common scale; **∼ up, down,** make larger, smaller, in due proportion, increase, reduce, in size. **8.** *v.i.* (Of quantities etc.) have common scale, be commensurable. [n. ME (= ladder), v. ME f. OF *escaler* or f. med. L *scalare,* f. L *scala* (*scandere* climb)]

scā′lēne *a.* & *n.* **1.** *a.* unequal-sided; ∼ **cone, cylinder,** (with axis not perpendicular to base); ∼ **muscle,** any of several muscles connecting spine and ribs; ∼ **triangle** (with no two sides equal). **2.** *n.* scalene triangle or muscle. [f. LL f. Gk *skalēnos* unequal, cogn. w. *skolios* bent]

scale′n|us *n.* (*pl.* ∼i *pr.* ∼ī). scalene muscle. [mod. L, f. as prec.]

scā′ler *n.* In vbl senses; electronic instrument registering a fixed number of events as one unit of counting. [f. SCALE¹,²,³ + -ER¹]

scall (-awl) *n.* (arch.) scaly eruption on skin (**dry ∼,** the itch; **moist ∼,** eczema). [ME, f. ON *skalli* bald head, f. Gmc *skal-* (as SHALE, SHELL¹)]

scallawag. See SCALLYWAG.

scā′llion (-yon) *n.* shallot; long-necked onion without normal bulb. [ME, f. AF *scal(o)un* = OF *escalo(i)gne* f. Rom. *escalonia f. L *Ascalonia* (*caepa*) (onion) of *Ascalon* in Palestine]

scā′llop (-ă′-, -ŏ′-), **scŏ′llop,** *n.,* & *v.t.* **1.** *n.* bivalve mollusc with shell divided into grooves and ridges radiating from middle of hinge and edged with small rounded lobes. **2.** ∼(-**shell**), one valve of scallop used for cooking and serving various kinds of food or (Hist.) as pilgrim's badge. **3.** small pan used like scallop-shell to hold food. **4.** (in *pl.*) ornamental edging cut in material in imitation of scallop-edge. **5.** *v.t.* cook in scallop; ornament (edge, material) with scallops or **∼ING¹** (6) *n.* [ME, f. OF *escalope,* prob. f. Gmc]

scă′llÿwăg, scă′l(l)awăg (-a-w-), *n.* undersized or ill-fed animal; good-for-nothing person, scamp, scapegrace. [19th c. US sl., of unkn. orig.]

scălp *n.,* & *v.t.* **1.** *n.* skin with hair etc. of head excluding face; this or part of it cut or torn as trophy from enemy's head by Amer. Indian (**out for ∼s,** on the warpath, (fig.) in aggressive or pugnacious or savagely critical mood); **∼-lock,** single lock on Amer. Indian's shaven head left as challenge to enemies; hence **∼′LESS** *a.* **2.** (Sc.) bare rock projecting above water etc. **3.** *v.t.* take scalp of; criticize savagely; *defeat, humiliate; *(colloq.) resell (shares, tickets, etc.) at high or quick profit, whence **∼′er¹** [-ER¹] *n.* [north. ME, prob. of Scand. orig.]

scă′lpel *n.* surgeon's small light straight knife shaped for holding like pen. [F, or f. L *scalpellum* dim. of *scalprum* chisel (*scalpere* scratch); see -LE 2]

scă′lper² *n.* engraver's tool for hollowing out the bottom of sunken designs. [f. SCALP + -ER¹ & f. L *scalper* cutting tool (*scalpere* carve)]

scă′lpriform *a.* (Of incisor teeth) chisel-shaped. [f. L *scalprum* (as prec.) + -I- + -FORM]

scā′lÿ. See SCALE¹.

scă′mmonÿ *n.* (W. Asian plant, *Convolvulus scammonia,* yielding) a gum resin used as drastic purgative. [ME, f. OF *scamonee, escamonie* or f. L f. Gk *skammōnia*]

scămp¹ *n.* (derog. or joc.) rascal, knave, rogue; hence **∼′ISH¹** *a.* [f. *scamp* rob on highway, prob. f. MDu. *schampen* decamp f. OF *esc(h)amper* f. Rom. *EX¹- (*compare* f. L *campus* field)]

scămp² *v.t.* do (work etc.) in perfunctory or inadequate way. [perh. f. as prec.; cf. SKIMP]

scǎ'mper *v.i.*, & *n.* **1.** *v.i.* run impulsively (*about*) like excited or frightened animal or playing child; take scamper *through*. **2.** *n.* hasty run; gallop on horseback for pleasure; rapid tour or course of reading. [prob. f. as SCAMP¹ + -ER⁵]

scǎ'mpi *n. pl.* (dish of) large prawns. [It.]

scǎn *v.* (-nn-) & *n.* **1.** *v.t.* test metre of (line etc. of verse) by examining number and prosodic quantity of feet and syllables; read over with emphasis on rhythm. **2.** *v.i.* be metrically correct (*line does not scan*); admit of rhythmic reading (*line will not scan*). **3.** *v.t.* look at all parts successively of (face, horizon, etc.), intently or quickly; examine all parts of to detect radioactivity; cause (particular region) to be traversed by controlled (radar etc.) beam. **4.** resolve (picture) into its elements of light and shade in prearranged pattern for purposes of television transmission. **5.** Hence ∼'ner¹ (1, 2) *n.* **6.** *n.* act or process of scanning. [ME, f. L *scandere* climb, in LL scan verses, f. raising of one's foot in marking rhythm]

scǎ'ndal *n.* (thing that occasions) general feeling of outrage or indignation esp. as expressed in common talk, opprobrium; malicious gossip, backbiting, whence ∼MONGER *n.*; (Law) public affront, irrelevant abusive statement in court; ∼ sheet, newspaper etc giving prominence to (malicious) gossip; so ∼OUS *a.* [ME, f. OF *scandale* f. eccl. L f. Gk *skandalon* snare, stumbling-block]

scǎ'ndalīze¹, -īse¹ (-īz), *v.t.* offend moral feelings, sense of propriety, or ideas of etiquette, etc; shock. [ME in sense 'make scandal of', f. F *scandaliser* or f. eccl. L f. Gk *skandalizō* (as prec.; see -IZE)]

scǎ'ndalīze², -īse² (-īz), *v.t.* (Naut.) reduce area of (fore-and-aft sail). [alt. f. obs. *scantelize* = obs. *scantle* (SCANT V.; see -LE 3)]

scǎndalum mǎgnā'tum *n.* (Hist.) defamation of magnates. [med. L]

Scǎndinā'vian *a.* & *n.* (native, inhabitant, family of languages) of Scandinavia (Denmark, Norway, Sweden, and Iceland). [f. L *Scandinavia* + -AN]

scǎ'ndium *n.* (Chem.) trivalent metallic element resembling those of lanthanide series. [mod. L, f. *Scandia* Scandinavia (source of minerals containing it) + -IUM]

scǎ'nsion (-shon) *n.* metrical scanning; way verse scans. [f. L *scansio* (LL of metre) f. *scandere* scans-climb; see SCAN, -ION]

scǎnsō̄'rial *a.* (Of birds etc or their feet) habitually climbing, adapted for climbing. [L *scansorius* (as prec.; see -ORY) + -AL]

scǎnt *a.*, & *v.t.* **1.** *a.* (arch. or literary). barely sufficient, deficient, with scanty supply *of*, (*with scant regard for my feelings; scant of breath*); hence ∼LY² *adv.* **2.** *v.t.* (arch.) skimp, stint, provide grudgingly, (supply, material, person). [ME, f. ON *skamt* neut. of *skammr* short]

scǎ'nties (-īz) *n. pl.* (colloq.) women's short panties. [f. prec., after *panties*]

scǎ'ntling *n.* **1.** (arch.) specimen, sample; modicum, small amount, one's necessary supply *of*. **2.** timber beam of small cross-section; size to which stone or timber is to be cut. **3.** set of standard dimensions for parts of structure esp. in shipbuilding. [alt. after -LING¹ f. obs. *scantlon* f. OF *escantillon* sample]

scǎ'nt|ȳ *a.* of small extent or amount; barely sufficient; hence ∼ILY² *adv.*, ∼INESS *n.* [f. obs. *scant* scanty supply f. ON *skamt* neut. a. (as n.; see SCANT) + -Y²]

scāpe¹ *n.*, & *v.t.* **1.** (arch.) escape. [ME, f. ESCAPE¹,²]

scāpe² *n.* (Bot.) long flower-stalk coming directly from root; (Entom.) base of antenna; shaft of column. [f. L f. Gk *skapos*, cogn. w. SCEPTRE]

-scāpe *suf.* forming *ns.* w. sense (representation of) view of (*seascape, wirescape*). [after LANDSCAPE]

scā'pegoat (-pg-) *n.*, & *v.t.* **1.** *n.* goat allowed to escape when Jewish chief priest had laid sins of people upon it (Lev. 16). **2.** person bearing blame that should fall on others. **3.** *v.t.* make scapegoat of. [f. SCAPE¹ + GOAT]

scā'pegrāce (-pg-) *n.* hare-brained person, esp. young person or child who constantly gets into trouble. [f. SCAPE¹ + GRACE = one who escapes the grace of God]

scā'phoid *a.* & *n.* (Anat.) boat-shaped (bone in foot or usu. hand). [mod. L, f. Gk *skaphoeidēs* (*skaphos* boat; see -OID)]

scǎ'pūla *n.* (*pl.* ∼e). shoulder-blade. [LL, sing. of L *scapulae*]

scǎ'pūlar *a.* & *n.* **1.** *a.* of shoulder or shoulder-blade; ∼ arch, = shoulder GIRDLE¹; ∼ feathers (growing near insertion of wing). **2.** *n.* monastic short cloak covering shoulders; badge of affiliation to an ecclesiastical order, consisting of two strips of cloth hanging down breast and back and joined across shoulders. **3.** bandage for or over shoulders. **4.** scapular feather. [a. f. prec. + -AR¹, n. f. LL *scapulare* (as prec.; see -AR¹)]

scǎ'pūlarȳ *n.* = prec. 2, 4. [ME, f. AF *scapelorie*, OF *eschapeloyre* f. med. L *scapelorium, scapularium* (as SCAPULA; see -ARY¹)]

scār¹ *n.* & *v.* (-rr-). **1.** *n.* mark left after healing of wound or burn or sore, (fig.) abiding effect of grief etc.; mark left by damage; mark on plant left by fall of leaf etc.; hence ∼'LESS *a.* **2.** *v.t.* (esp. in *p.p.*) mark with scar(s). **3.** *v.i.* & *t.* heal over, form scar (*on*). [ME, f. OF *eschar(r)e* f. LL f. Gk *eskhara* scab]

scār², **scaur**, *n.* precipitous craggy part of mountain-side or cliff. [ME, f. ON *sker* low reef in sea]

scǎ'rab *n.* sacred dung-beetle of ancient Egypt; foll.; ancient-Egyptian etc. gem cut in form of beetle and engraved with symbols on flat side as signet etc. [f. L *scarabaeus* f. Gk *skarabeios*]

scǎrabae'id *n.* member of Scarabaeidae family of beetles, incl. dung-beetle, cockchafer, etc. [f. mod. L *Scarabaeidae* (as prec.; see -ID³)]

scǎ'ramouch *n.* (arch.) boastful poltroon, braggart. [f. It. *Scaramuccia* stock character in Italian farce (*scaramuccia* = SKIRMISH), infl. by F form *Scaramouche*]

scārce *a.* & *adv.* **1.** *a.* (usu. *pred.*) (Esp. of food, money, or other necessaries of life) insufficient for the demand or need, not plentiful, scanty; hence **scār'city** *n.* (*of*, or abs. = dearth of food). **2.** seldom met with, rare, hard to find, (*a scarce book, moth*); **make** oneself ∼, (colloq.) make off, esp. surreptitiously, keep out of the way; hence ∼'NESS (-sn-) *n.* **3.** *adv.* (arch. or literary). scarcely. [ME f. AF & ONF (*e*)*scars*, OF *eschars* f. Rom. **excarpsus* p.p. of **excarpere* f. L *excerpere* (see EXCERPT²)]

scār'cely (-slī) *adv.* **1.** hardly, barely, only just, (*is scarcely seventeen years old; had scarcely arrived when my friend left; I scarcely know him*). **2.** surely not, not unless the unlikely happens or is true, (*you will scarcely maintain that; he can scarcely have said so*); (mild or apologetic or ironical substitute for) not (*I scarcely think so, know what to say, expected to be insulted*). [ME, f. prec. + -LY²]

scāre *v.* & *n.* **1.** *v.t.* strike with sudden terror, frighten (as) with something feared; (in *p.p.*) frightened *of*, *to* do, (of expression etc.) betraying terror; drive *away*, *off*, *up*, etc., by fright; ***∼ **out** or **up**, frighten (game) out of cover, (fig.) discover, manage to find; ∼'dy-cat (-ār'dī-), (colloq.) timid person. **2.** keep (birds) away from sown land etc.; ∼'crow, figure of man hung with old clothes and set up in field to keep birds away, object of baseless fear, badly dressed or grotesque-looking or skinny person. **3.** *v.i.* become scared. **4.** *n.* unreasoning terror, esp. baseless general apprehension of war, invasion, epidemic, etc., whence ∼'MONGER (-ār'm-) *n.*; commercial panic; ∼-**head**(ing), extravagantly sensational newspaper headline; hence **scār'y** *a.* (colloq.). [ME *skerre*, f. ON *skirra* frighten (*skjarr* timid)]

scārf¹ *n.* (*pl.* **scarves** *pr.* -vz, *or* ∼s). long narrow strip of material worn for ornament or warmth round neck, over shoulders, or baldric-wise; square piece of material worn round neck or over woman's hair (||∼-**pin, -ring**, ornamental device for fastening this);

∽-**skin,** outermost layer of skin constantly scaling off (esp. of that adhering to base of nails); ∽-**wise,** baldric-wise; hence ∽ED² (-ft) *a.* [prob. f. ONF *escarpe* = OF *escherpe* sash etc., prob. same wd as *esc*(*h*)*arpe* SCRIP¹; infl. by foll.]

scarf² *v.t.,* & *n.* **1.** *v.t.* join ends of (pieces of timber, metal, or leather) by bevelling or notching so that they overlap without increase of thickness and then bolting, brazing, or sewing them together; cut blubber of (whale). **2.** *n.* joint made by scarfing. [v. f. n., ME prob. f. OF *escarf (*escarver v. perh. f. ON)]

sca'rificātor *n.* surgical instrument for scarifying, in which several lancet-points protrude at once from plane surface on touching of trigger. [mod. L, f. F *scarificateur* (as SCARIFY; see -OR)]

scarifier (-ă'r-, -ār'-) *n.* In vbl senses; = prec.; agricultural machine with prongs for loosening without turning soil; spiked road-breaking machine. [f. foll. + -ER¹]

scari'fȳ¹ (-ă'r-, -ār'-) *v.t.* (Surg.) make superficial incisions in, cut off skin from; (fig.) pain by severe criticism etc.; loosen (soil) with scarifier; so ∽FICA'-TION *n.* [ME, f. F *scarifier* f. LL *scarificare* f. L *scarifare* f. Gk *skariphaomai* (*skariphos* stylus); see -FY]

scar'ify² *v.* scare, terrify. [f. SCARE + -I- + -FY]

scar'ious *a.* (Bot., of bract etc.) thin, dry, and membranous. [f. F *scarieux* or mod. L *scariosus*; see -OUS]

scarlati'na (-tē'-) *n.* scarlet fever. [mod. L, f. It. *scarlattina* (*febbre* fever), dim. of *scarlatto* SCARLET]

scar'lĕt *n.* & *a.* (of) brilliant red colour inclining to orange; scarlet clothes or material (*dressed in scarlet*); ∽ **fever,** infectious bacterial fever with scarlet rash; ∽ **hat,** cardinal's hat, (symbol of) cardinal's rank; *scarlet* PIMPERNEL; ∽ **rash,** roseola; ∽ **runner,** (scarlet-flowered climbing plant bearing) kind of bean; ∽ **woman,** (1) prostitute, (2) (derog.) RC Church. [ME, f. OF *escarlate*; ult. orig. unkn.]

scaroid (-ă'r-, -ār'-) *a.* & *n.* (fish) of family Scaridae, incl. scarus. [f. SCARUS + -OID]

scarp *n.,* & *v.t.* **1.** *n.* inner wall or slope (cf. COUNTER-SCARP) of ditch in fortification; steep slope. **2.** *v.t.* make (slope) perpendicular or steep; provide (ditch) with steep scarp and counterscarp; (in *p.p.,* of hillside etc.) steep, precipitous. [f. It. *scarpa*]

scar'per *v.i.* (sl.) escape, run away. [prob. f. It. *scappare* escape, infl. by rhyming sl. *Scapa Flow* go]

scar'us *n.* bright-coloured fish with beaklike jaws, allied to wrasse family. [L, f. Gk *skaros*]

scar'y. See SCARE.

scăt¹ *v.i.* (-tt-), & *int.* (colloq.) depart quickly. [perh. abbr. of SCATTER]

scăt² *n.,* & *v.i.* (-tt-). (sing) wordless jazz song using voice as instrument. [prob. imit.]

scāthe (-dh) *v.t.,* & *n.* **1.** *v.t.* (poet.) injure esp. by blasting or withering up. **2.** (esp. in *pres. part.*) wither with severe speech (*scathing sarcasm, ridicule, remarks*). **3.** (w. neg.) do the least harm to (*shall not be scathed*; cf. UNSCATHED). **4.** *n.* (arch., usu. w. neg.) harm, injury, (*without scathe*); hence ∽'LESS (-dhl-) *a.* (usu. *pred.*). [v. ME f. ON *skatha* = OE *sceathian,* n. OE f. ON *skathi* = OE *sceatha* malefactor, injury, f. Gmc **skathōjan,* *skathon]

scăto'logȳ *n.* **1.** study of coprolites. **2.** preoccupation with excrement. **3.** preoccupation with obscene literature. **4.** Hence **scăto**LO'GICAL *a.* [f. Gk *skōr skatos* dung + -O- + -LOGY]

scato'phagous *a.* feeding on dung. [as prec. + Gk -*phagos* -eating + -OUS]

scă'tter *v.* & *n.* **1.** *v.t.* throw here and there (*scatter seed*; *scatter gravel on road*); cover by scattering (*scatter road with gravel*). **2.** *v.t.* & *i.* disperse, turn in dispersed flight, rout or be routed. **3.** *v.t.* dissipate (cloud, hopes); (Phys.) deflect or diffuse (light, particles, etc.). **4.** *v.i.* & *t.* (Of gun) send charge, send (charge), in spreading manner. **5.** (in *p.p.*) not situated together, wide apart, sporadic, (*scattered villages,*

garrisons, instances). **6.** ∽-**brain,** flighty person; ∽--**brained,** heedless, desultory; *∽-**shot** *n.* & *a.,* firing at random. **7.** *n.* act of scattering; extent of distribution esp. of shot; small amount scattered; ∽ **cushions, rugs,** etc., (to be placed here and there in room). [ME, prob. var. of SHATTER]

‖**scă'ttĭly̆** *a.* (sl.) feeble-minded; hare-brained; hence ∽ILY² *adv.,* ∽INESS *n.* [f. SCATTER-*brained* + -Y²]

scaup *n.* diving duck of genus *Aythya*. [f. *scaup,* Sc. var. of *scalp* mussel-bed, wh. it frequents]

scau'per. Var. of SCALPER².

scaur. See SCAR².

scă'venge (-nj) *v.t.* & *i.* be, or act as, scavenger (of); remove unwanted products from (internal-combustion engine cylinder etc.); make search for or *for* (thing) among what is unwanted by others. [back-form. f. foll.]

scă'venger (-nj-) *n.,* & *v.i.* **1.** *n.* ‖person employed to keep streets clean by carrying away refuse; hence ∽ERY (2, 5) *n.* **2.** animal, esp. beetle, feeding on carrion. **3.** *v.i.* = prec. [ME *scavager* (cf. *messenger*) inspector of imports f. AF *scawager* (*scawage* f. ONF *escauwer* inspect f. Flem. *scauwen* cogn. w. SHOW¹)]

scă'zon *n.* (Pros.) Greek or Latin metre of limping character, esp. trimeter of two iambuses and spondee or trochee. [L f. Gk *skazōn* (*skazō* limp)]

Sc.D. *abbr.* Doctor of Science. [f. L *scientiae doctor*]

SCE *abbr.* Scottish Certificate of Education.

scena (shā'nah) *n.* (Mus.) scene or portion of opera; elaborate dramatic solo usu. including recitative. [It. f. L (see SCENE)]

scēnar'|iō (-ār'-, -ar'-) *n.* (*pl.* -ios). **1.** (table of) scene-distribution, appearances of characters, etc., in dramatic work, outline libretto. **2.** complete plot of film play with details of scenes etc.; imagined sequence of future events. **3.** Hence ∽IST (3) *n.* [It. (as prec.)]

scĕnd. See SEND².

scēne *n.* **1.** (arch.) stage of theatre. **2.** place of action (**come on the** ∽, arrive; **quit the** ∽, (esp.) die); place on which something is exhibited as on the stage (*this world is a scene of strife*); (sl.) area of action or interest (*poetry is not my scene*), way of life. **3.** place in which events set forth in drama or tale are supposed to occur, locality of event, (*the scene is laid in India*; *the scene of the disaster was the North Sea*). **4.** portion of a play during which action is continuous or in which no intermediate entries or exits occur, subdivision of an act, (*in the third scene of Act II*; *the famous duel scene*); similar portion of film, book, etc. **5.** description with more or less abrupt beginning and end of an incident or part of person's life etc. (*scenes of clerical life, from a goldfield,* etc.); actual incident that might occasion such description (*distressing scenes occurred*), agitated conversation esp. with display of temper, stormy encounter or interview. **6.** any of the pieces of painted canvas, woodwork, etc., used to help in representing scene of action on stage; whole of these together; **behind the** ∽**s,** among the stage machinery or the actors off the stage, (fig.) not known to the public, using information of this kind; **set the** ∽, (fig.) describe location of events, give preliminary information; SET³ *scene.* **7.** landscape or view spread before spectator like scene in theatre (*a silvan, desolate, scene*; *a scene of destruction*); **change of** ∽, variety of surroundings esp. secured by travel. **8.** ∽-**dock,** space near stage where scenes are stored; ∽-**painter, -painting,** (of theatre scenes); ∽-**shifter,** ∽--**shifting,** (person engaged in) changing scenes in theatre. [f. L f. Gk *skēnē* tent, stage]

scē'nery *n.* accessories used in drama to give resemblance to supposed scene of action; general appearance of natural features of a district (*the scenery is imposing*); picturesque features of landscape; **change of** ∽, = *change of scene.* [earlier *scenary* f. It. SCENARIO (cf. -ARY¹); assim. to -ERY]

scē'nic *a.* of or on the stage (*scenic performances*); of the nature of a show, picturesque in grouping; (of picture etc.) telling a tale, representing an incident; having fine natural scenery; ~ **railway**, miniature railway running through artificial picturesque scenery at fairs etc.; hence **scě′nICALLY** adv. [f. L f. Gk skēnikos of the stage (as SCENE; see -IC)]

scěnt v. & n. **1.** v.t. discern by smell (scent game etc.), (fig.) begin to suspect presence or existence of (scent treachery); ~ **out**, discover by smelling about or search. **2.** make fragrant or rank (rose, carrion, scents the air); apply perfume to (handkerchief etc.; scented soap, tobacco). **3.** v.i. & t. exercise sense of smell (goes scenting about); apply this to (lifts its head and scents the air). **4.** n. odour, esp. of agreeable kind, proceeding from or belonging to something (the scent of hay); hence (-)~′ED[2], ~′LESS, adjs. **5.** (Hunt.) trail perceptible to hounds' sense of smell left by animal, (fig.) indications that can be followed thus, (follow up, lose, recover, etc., the scent; **on the (right)** ~, having clue; **put** or **throw off the** ~, deceive by false indications; COLD[1], HOT[1], scent); trail laid in paper-chase; **false** ~ (laid to deceive as to course, lit. or fig.). **6.** power of detecting or distinguishing smells or of discovering presence of something, (some dogs have practically no scent; keen--scented; has a wonderful scent for talent). **7.** ||liquid perfume distilled from flowers etc **8.** ~**-bag**, (1) pouch containing special odoriferous substance in some animals, (2) bag of aniseed etc. as substitute for fox in hunting; ~**-bottle** (for perfume); ~**-gland** (secreting musk, civet, etc.); ~**-organ**, scent-bag (1) or scent-gland. [ME sent f. OF sentir perceive, smell, f. L sentire; -c- (17th c.) unexpl.]

scě′psĭs (sk-), *ske′psĭs, n. philosophic doubt; sceptical philosophy. [f. Gk skepsis inquiry, doubt (skeptomai consider)]

*scě′pter. See SCEPTRE.

scě′ptic (sk-), *skě′ptĭc, n. **1.** ancient or modern adherent of Pyrrhonism. **2.** person who doubts truth of the Christian or of all religious doctrines. **3.** person of sceptical habit of mind, or unconvinced of truth of particular fact or theory, or who takes cynical views. **4.** Hence ~ISM (3) n. [f. F sceptique or L f. Gk skeptikos (as SCEPSIS; see -IC)]

scě′ptical (sk-), *skě′ptical, a. **1.** inclined to suspend judgement, given to questioning truth of fact(s) and soundness of inference(s), critical, incredulous. **2.** accepting Pyrrhonism, denying possibility of knowledge. **3.** holding, designed to support, inspired by, the ideas of sceptics. **4.** Hence ~LY[2] adv. [f. as prec.; see -ICAL]

||**scě′ptr|e** (-ter), *scě′pter, n. staff borne as symbol of personal sovereignty; royal or imperial authority; hence ~ED[2] (-terd) a. [ME, f. OF (s)ceptre f. L f. Gk skēptron (skēptō lean on)]

sch. abbr. scholar; school; schooner.

schadenfreude (shah′denfroide) n. malicious enjoyment of others' misfortunes. [G (schade harm, freude joy)]

schăppe (sh-) n. fabric or yarn made from waste silk. [G, = waste silk]

schě′dŭle (sh-) n., & v.t. **1.** n. tabulated statement of details, inventory, etc., esp. as appendix or annex to principal document; list of events, rates, etc.; *time-table; time stated in timetable or plan (behind, on, schedule); **according to** ~, as planned. **2.** v.t. make schedule of; include in schedule, esp. ||include (building) in list of those to be preserved and protected; ~**d flight, service**, etc., (according to regular time-table); ~**d territories**, (Hist.) = STERLING area. [ME f. OF cedule f. LL schedula slip of paper, dim. of scheda f. Gk skhedē papyrus-leaf; see -ULE]

schee′lite (sh-) n. (Min.) calcium tungstate in native crystalline form. [f. K. W. Scheele, Sw. chemist d. 1786 + -ITE[1] (2)]

schě′ma (sk-) n. (pl. ~ta). synopsis, outline, diagram; proposed arrangement; (Logic) syllogistic figure; (Kantian Philos.) general type, essential form,

conception of what is common to all members of a class. [f. Gk skhēma -atos form, figure]

schemǎ′t|ic (skī-, -ē-) a. & n. **1.** a. of a schema or scheme; representing objects by symbols etc.; hence ~ICALLY adv. **2.** n. schematic diagram. [f. as prec. + -IC]

schě′matism (sk-) n. schematic arrangement or presentation. [f. mod. L f. Gk skhēmatismos (as foll.; see -ISM)]

schě′matīz|e, -īs|e, (sk-; -īz) v.t. represent by schema or scheme; put in schematic form; hence ~A′TION n. [f. Gk skhēmatizō assume a form, or f. as SCHEMA + -IZE]

schěm|e (sk-) n. & v. **1.** n. systematic arrangement proposed or in operation (COLOUR[1] scheme); table of classification or of appointed times, outline, syllabus; plan of construction, work, action, etc.; artful or underhand design. **2.** v.i. make plans, plan esp. in secret or underhand or artful way (to do, for, or abs.), intrigue; hence ~ER[1], ~ING[1] (1), ns., ~ING[2] a. **3.** v.t. plan to bring about. [f. L f. Gk (as SCHEMA)]

schemozzle. Var. of SHEMOZZLE.

scherzǎ′nd|ō (skārts-) adv., a., & n. (pl. ~os or ~i). (Mus.) (passage performed) in playful manner. [It., gerund of scherzare to jest (as foll.)]

scher′zō (skār′tsō) n. (pl. ~s). vigorous (prop. light and playful) composition, independent or as movement in works of symphony or sonata type. [It., lit. 'jest']

Schiedǎ′m (sk-) n. Hollands gin. [~ in Holland]

schi′lling (sh-) n. Austrian monetary unit and coin. [G (as SHILLING)]

schi′pperke (sk-, sh-) n. small black tailless breed of dog. [Du. dial., = little boatman, f. its use as watch--dog on barges]

schi′sm (sĭ′-, skĭ′-) n. separation of a Church into two Churches or secession of part of a Church owing to difference of opinion on doctrine or discipline; offence of causing or promoting such separation; dividing of a group into mutually opposing parties. [ME f. OF s(c)isme f. eccl. L f. Gk skhisma -atos cleft (skhizō to split)]

schismǎ′tic (sĭz-, skĭz-) a. & n., -ic|al a. **1.** a. tending or inclined to, guilty of, schism; hence ~ALLY adv. **2.** n. holder of schismatic opinions; member of schismatic faction or seceded branch of a Church. [ME, f. OF scismatique f. eccl. L f. eccl. Gk skhismatikos (as prec.; see -IC, -AL)]

schist (sh-) n. foliated metamorphic rock presenting layers of different minerals and splitting into thin irregular plates; hence ~′OSE[1] a. [f. F schiste f. L f. Gk skhistos split (as SCHISM)]

schi′stosōme (sh-, sk-) n. bilharzia worm. [f. Gk skhistos divided (as SCHISM) + -o- + sōma body]

schistosomi′as|is (sh-, sk-) n. (pl. ~es pr. -ēz). bilharziasis. [f. mod. L Schistosoma (genus-name; as prec.) + -ASIS]

schizǎ′nthus (sk-) n. flowering annual plant of genus Schizanthus, with showy white, violet, or crimson flowers and finely-divided leaves. [mod. L, f. Gk skhizō to split + anthos flower]

schi′zō (skĭ′tsō) a. & n. (pl. ~s). (colloq.) schizophrenic. [abbr.]

schi′zocǎrp (sk-) n. (Bot.) dry fruit that splits into single-seeded parts when ripe. [f. Gk skhizō to split + karpos fruit]

schi′zoid (skĭ′ts-, skĭ′z-) a. & n. **1.** a. tending to or resembling schizophrenia or a schizophrenic, but usu. without delusions. **2.** n. schizoid person. [f. SCHIZOPHRENIA + -OID]

schizomy′cēte (sk-) n. member of a class of minute often single-cell vegetable organisms intermediate between algae and fungi and multiplying by fission, including bacteria etc. [f. Gk skhizō to split + mukēs -ētos mushroom]

schizophr|ē′nia (skĭts-, skĭz-) n. mental disease marked by disconnection between thoughts, feelings, and actions, freq. with delusions and retreat from social life; hence ~ĕ′nɪc a. & n. [mod. L, f. Gk skhizō to split + phrēn mind; see -ɪᴀ¹]

schizothy′m|ia (skits-, skiz-) n. (Psych.) introvert character with tendency to schizophrenia; hence ~ɪc a. [mod. L, f. as prec. + Gk thumos temper; see -ɪᴀ¹]

*schlemie′l (shl-) n. (colloq.) foolish or unlucky person. [f. Yiddish shlumiel]

schlier′en (shlēr′-) a. (Of apparatus etc.) producing light-patterns representing variations in physical properties of gas or other transparent medium. [G, pl. of schliere streak]

*schlöck (shl-) a. & n. poor-quality or second-hand (material). [f. Yiddish shlak a blow]

schmaltz (shmawlts) n. sugary sentimentalism in music etc.; hence ~′ʏ² a. [Yiddish, f. G schmalz dripping, lard]

schmück (shm-) n. (sl.) foolish or contemptible person. [Yiddish]

schnäpps (shn-) n. strong Hollands gin. [G, = dram of liquor, f. LG & Du. snaps mouthful (as sɴᴀᴘ)]

schnau′zer (shnow′tser) n. German breed of house-dog with close wiry coat. [G (schnauze muzzle, sɴᴏᴜᴛ)]

schni′tzel (shni′ts-) n. veal cutlet; Wiener or Vienna ~, one breaded, fried, and garnished. [G, = slice]

schnorkel. See sɴᴏʀᴋᴇʟ.

schnŏr′rer (shn-) n. (sl.) beggar. [Yiddish, f. G schnurrer]

schŏ′lar (sk-) n. 1. learned person, person versed in language or literature (is something of a Russian scholar); (vulg. or dial.) person able to read and write; a ~ and a gentleman, person of good education and breeding; hence ~ʟʏ¹ a. 2. holder of scholarship (sense 2). 3. person who learns (proved an apt, dull, scholar; at 90 he was still a scholar); scholar's ᴍᴀᴛᴇ¹. 4. (arch.) schoolboy or schoolgirl. 5. (rhet.) person's disciple. [ME, f. OE scol(i)ere & OF escol(i)er, f. LL scholaris f. L schola sᴄʜᴏᴏʟ¹; see -ᴀʀ¹]

schŏ′larship (sk-) n. 1. quality of having attained learning; methods and achievements characteristic of scholars. 2. (right to) payment from funds of school, university, etc., for education there, or from other funds for education, usu. gained by competitive examination. [f. prec. + -sʜɪᴘ]

scholă′stic (sk-) a. & n. 1. a. of universities, schools, schooling, dons, or schoolmasters, educational, academic, pedantic, formal, (a scholastic education, post; scholastic attire, manners, precision, life); ~ agent (finding posts for teachers). 2. (as) of the schoolmen, dealing in logical subtleties; ~ theology (much concerned with precise definition of and deduction from dogma). 3. Hence or cogn. scholă′stɪcᴀʟʟʏ (sk-) adv., ~ɪsᴍ (2, 3) n. 4. n. schoolman; modern theologian of scholastic tendencies; Jesuit between novitiate and priesthood. [f. L f. Gk skholastikos studious (skholazō be at leisure f. as sᴄʜᴏᴏʟ¹; see -ɪᴄ)]

schŏ′li|ăst (sk-) n. commentator, esp. ancient grammarian who wrote scholia on the classics; hence ~ă′stɪc a. [f. med. Gk skholiastēs (skholiazō write scholia; see foll.)]

schŏ′li|um (sk-) n. (pl. ~a). marginal note, explanatory comment, esp. one by ancient grammarian on passage in classical author. [mod. L, f. Gk skholion (skholē disputation; see foll.)]

schŏōl¹ (sk-) n., & v.t. 1. n. institution for educating children or giving instruction ‖usu. of more elementary or more technical kinds than that given at universities (ᴀᴘᴘʀᴏᴠᴇᴅ, ʙᴏᴀʀᴅɪɴɢ-, ᴄᴏᴍᴘʀᴇʜᴇɴsɪᴠᴇ, ᴄᴏɴᴛɪɴᴜᴀᴛɪᴏɴ, ᴅᴀᴍᴇ-, ᴅᴀʏ-, ᴇʟᴇᴍᴇɴᴛᴀʀʏ, ғʀᴇᴇ¹, *ɢʀᴀᴅᴇ, ɢʀᴀᴍᴍᴀʀ, ʜɪɢʜ, ‖ɪɴ ᴀ ɴ ᴛ, ᴍᴇᴅɪᴄᴀʟ, ᴍɪxᴇᴅ, ‖ᴍᴏᴅᴇʀɴ, ɴɪɢʜᴛ-, ɴᴏʀᴍᴀʟ, ᴘʀɪᴍᴀʀʏ, ᴘʀɪᴠᴀᴛᴇ, ᴘᴜʙʟɪᴄ, sᴇᴄᴏɴᴅᴀʀʏ, sᴜᴍᴍᴇʀ¹, sᴜɴᴅᴀʏ, ᴛᴇᴄʜɴɪᴄᴀʟ, school; ‖ᴏʟᴅ school tie); *university, or department thereof; centre for archaeological research (British School at Athens, Rome); keep a ~, manage private school. 2. buildings of such institution (at ~, attending lessons), any of its rooms used for teaching in (the fifth-form, chemistry, school); its pupils (the whole

school knows); time during which teaching is done (there will be no school today); go to ~, attend lessons in a school (need not go to school today). 3. being educated in a school (at ~, *in ~, in course of this; go to, leave, ~, begin, cease, this; go to ~ to, (fig.) imitate or learn from); (fig.) circumstances or occupation serving to discipline or instruct (in the school of adversity; learnt his generalship in a severe school). 4. medieval lecture-room (the ~s, medieval universities and their professors and teaching and disputations); ‖branch of study with separate examinations at university (the history, mathematical, Greats, school); hall in which university examinations are held; (in pl.) such examinations. 5. disciples or imitators or followers of philosopher, artist, etc., band or succession of persons devoted to some cause or principle or agreeing in typical characteristics, (left no school behind him; school of Epicurus, Raphael, etc.; British school of painters; Lake school of literature; peripatetic school of philosophy; laissez-faire school of economics; belonged to a different school of thought); ‖group of gamblers; a gentleman etc. of the old ~, according to the older acceptation of the word. 6. (Mus.) handbook (of counterpoint etc.). 7. ~ age, age-range in which children normally attend school; ~-bag (for carrying books etc. to or from school); ~-board, (US or Hist.) local education authority; ~-book (for use in schools); ~′boy, boy attending school; ~ bus (taking children to or from school); ~′child, child attending school; ‖~-dame, keeper of dame-school; ~-days, time of being at school esp. as looked back upon; ~ divine, (arch.) scholastic theologian; ~ fee(s), amount periodically paid by parent etc. to school for teaching of pupil(s); ~′fellow, past or present member of same school; ~′girl, girl attending school; ‖~′house, building of esp. village school; ‖~ house, (orig.) headmaster's house at boarding-school; ~-inspector (officially reporting on efficiency of schools); ~-kid, (colloq.) schoolchild; ‖~-leaver, boy or girl leaving school on reaching specified age (esp. the minimum ‖~-leaving age) or stage; *~-ma′m, *~-marm, (colloq.) schoolmistress; ~′man, (1) teacher in medieval European university, theologian seeking to deal with religious doctrines by rules of Aristotelian logic, (2) *teacher; ~-marmish, (colloq.) prim and fussy; ~′master, head or assistant male teacher in school; ~′master-ing, teaching for one's living; ~′mate, = schoolfellow; ~′mistress, head or assistant female teacher in school; ~′mistressy, (colloq.) prim and fussy; ~′room (used for lessons in school or private house); ~-ship, training-ship; ~′teacher, master or mistress in (esp. infant or primary) school; ~-time, (1) lesson-time at school or home, (2) school-days; school ʏᴇᴀʀ. 8. v.t. send to school, provide for education of; hence ~′ɪɴɢ¹ n. 9. discipline, bring under control, deliberately train or accustom to, induce to follow advice, (must school his temper; school oneself to patience, to take an interest); (in p.p.) educated or trained in (habit etc.). [ME, f. OE scōl, scolu, & f. OF escole f. Rom. scola, f. L schola school f. Gk skholē leisure, disputation, philosophy, lecture-place]

schŏōl² (sk-) n., & v.i. 1. n. shoal of or of fish, porpoises, whales, etc.; ~-fish, fish that forms school, esp. the menhaden. 2. v.i. form schools. [ME, f. MLG, MDu. schōle, = OS scola, OE scolu troop f. WG *skula]

schŏō′lable (sk-) a. liable by age etc. to compulsory education. [f. sᴄʜᴏᴏʟ¹ + -ᴀʙʟᴇ]

schŏō′ner (sk-) n. 1. fore-and-aft-rigged vessel with two or more masts; *ᴘʀᴀɪʀɪᴇ schooner. 2. *tall beer-glass; ‖measure for beer, sherry, etc. [18th c.; orig. uncert.]

schŏrl (sh-) n. black tourmaline. [f. G schörl]

schötti′sche (shŏtē′sh) n. (music for) kind of slower polka. [f. G der schottische tanz the Scottish dance]

schuss (shŏōs) n., & v.i. (make) straight downhill run on skis. [G, lit. 'shot']

schwa (shwah, shvah) *n.* (Phonet.) indistinct vowel sound as in second syllable of *common* or *comma*; symbol (ə) representing this. [G, f. Heb. *š*^e*wā*, app. f. *šaw* emptiness]

sciä´graphy̆, skī-, *n.* art of shading in drawing etc.; X-ray radiography; hence **sci´a**GRAM (2) *n.*, **sci´a**GRAPH (1, 2, 3) *n.*, & *v.t.*, **sciä**GRA´PHIC *a.*, (or **skī-**). [f. F *sciagraphie* f. L f. Gk *skiagraphia* (*skia* shadow; see -GRAPHY)]

sciä´machy̆, skī-, (-kī) *n.* fighting with shadows; imaginary or futile combat. [f. Gk *skiamakhia* (as prec., *-makhia* -fighting; see -Y¹)]

sciä´tic *a.* **1.** of the hip; ∼ **nerve** (from pelvis to thigh, largest nerve in human body). **2.** of or affecting the sciatic nerve; suffering from or liable to sciatica. **3.** Hence **sciä´**TICALLY *adv.* [f. F *sciatique* f. LL *sciaticus* f. L f. Gk *iskhiadikos* subject to sciatica (*iskhion* hip-joint)]

sciä´tica *n.* neuralgia of hip and thigh, pain in sciatic nerve. [ME, f. LL *sciatica* (*passio*), fem. of *sciaticus* (see prec.)]

sci´ence *n.* **1.** (arch.) knowledge. **2.** systematic and formulated knowledge (**moral, political, natural,** etc., ∼, such knowledge in reference to morals etc.); pursuit of this or principles regulating such pursuit (*man of science*). **3.** (**natural**) ∼, physical or natural sciences collectively. **4.** branch of knowledge (esp. one that can be conducted on scientific principles), organized body of the knowledge that has been accumulated on a subject, (*the science of optics, ethics, philology*); **applied** ∼ (studied for practical purposes); DISMAL *science*; EXACT *science*; **natural** ∼, one dealing with material phenomena and based mainly on observation, experiment, and induction, as chemistry, biology; PHYSICAL *science*; **pure** ∼, one depending on deductions from self-evident truths, as mathematics, logic, or one studied without practical applications; SOCIAL *science*. **5.** expert's skill as opp. strength or natural ability esp. in boxing or other sport. **6.** ∼ **fiction,** fanciful fiction based on postulated scientific discoveries or environmental changes, freq. dealing with space travel, life on other planets, etc. [ME f. OF, f. L *scientia* (*scire* know; see -ENCE)]

scie´nter *adv.* (Law). intentionally, knowingly. [L (*scire* know; cf. -ENT)]

scie´ntial (-shal) *a.* pertaining to or having knowledge. [f. LL *scientialis* (as SCIENCE; see -AL)]

scienti´f|ic *a.* (Of investigation etc.) according to rules laid down in exact science for performing observations and testing soundness of conclusions, systematic, accurate; of, used or engaged in, (esp. natural) science (*scientific discoveries, instruments, books, terminology, men*); (of act or agent) assisted by expert knowledge (*a scientific boxer, game; scientific cruelty*); hence ∼ICALLY *adv.* [f. F *scientifique* or f. LL *scientificus* (as SCIENCE; see -FIC)]

sci´ent|ism *n.* (use of) method or doctrine (deemed) characteristic of scientists; so ∼i´stic *a.* [f. as foll. + -ISM]

sci´entist *n.* person with expert knowledge of a (usu. physical or natural) science; person using scientific methods. [f. SCIENCE, SCIENTIFIC + -IST]

scientó´log|y̆ *n.* religious system based on study of knowledge and seeking to develop the highest potentialities of mankind; hence ∼IST (2) *n.* [f. L *scientia* knowledge + -O- + -LOGY]

sci´-fi *n.* (colloq.) science fiction. [abbr.; cf. HI-FI]

sci´licĕt (sī´lisĕt, skē´likĕt) *adv.* to wit, that is to say, namely, (introducing word to be supplied or explanation of ambiguous one). [ME f. L, = *scire licet* one is permitted to know]

sci´lla *n.* bulbous plant of genus *Scilla*, esp. blue-flowered cultivated species. [L f. Gk *skilla*]

Scillō´nian *a.* & *n.* (native or inhabitant) of Scilly Isles. [f. *Scilly*, perh. after *Devonian*]

sci´mitar *n.* oriental curved sword usu. broadening towards point. [f. F *cimeterre*, It. *scimitarra*, etc., of unkn. orig.]

scĭntĭ´graphy̆ *n.* use of a radioisotope and scintillation counter to get picture of bodily organ etc. [f. SCINTILLATION + -GRAPHY]

scĭntĭ´lla *n.* spark (esp. fig.; *not a scintilla of evidence* etc.). [L]

scĭ´ntĭll|āte *v.i.* sparkle, twinkle, emit sparks; (fig.) talk etc. cleverly or wittily; so ∼ANT, ∼ĀTING², *adjs.* [f. L *scintillare* (as prec.) + -ATE³]

scĭntĭllā´tion *n.* scintillating; twinkling of star; (Phys.) flash produced in material by ionizing particle etc. (∼ **counter,** device for detecting and recording such events). [f. as prec. + -ATION]

sci´ol|ist *n.* superficial pretender to knowledge; hence ∼ISM (2) *n.*, ∼i´stic *a.* [f. LL *sciolus* smatterer (*scire* know) + -IST]

sci´on *n.* **1.** shoot of plant, esp. one cut for grafting or planting. **2.** descendant, younger member of (esp. noble) family. [ME, f. OF *ciun, cion, sion,* shoot, twig, of unkn. orig.]

scire facias (sīrī fā´shiăs) *n.* writ to enforce or annul judgement, patent, etc. [L, = let (him) know]

scirŏ´ccō. Var. of SIROCCO.

sci´rrh|us (sĭ´rus, skĭ´-) *n.* (*pl.* ∼i *pr.* -ī). (Path.) hard carcinoma; hence or cogn. ∼OID, ∼OUS, *adjs.*, ∼O´SITY *n.* [mod L., f. Gk *skir(r)os* (*skiros* hard)]

sci´ssel *n.* waste clippings of metal or remainder of metal plate from which discs have been punched in coining. [f. F *cisaille* (*cisailler* clip with shears)]

sci´ssile *a.* able to be cut or divided. [f. L *scissilis* (*scindere* sciss- cut; see -IL)]

sci´ssion (-shŏn) *n.* cutting, being cut; division, split. [ME f. OF, or f. LL *scissio* (as prec.; see -ION)]

sci´ssor (-z-) *v.t.* cut (*off, up, into,* etc.) with scissors; clip out or *out* (cutting from newspaper, book, etc.). [f. foll.]

sci´ssor|s (sĭ´zerz) *n. pl.* **1.** (**pair of**) ∼**s,** instrument for cutting fabrics etc., made of two blades with handles for thumb and one finger or the fingers and so pivoted that their cutting edges close on what is to be cut (*I want a pair of, some, scissors; where are my scissors?*; NAIL¹-*scissors*); ∼**s and paste,** compiling of books merely out of excerpts from others, or without independent research. **2.** (Gymnastics) forward and backward movement of legs in manner of scissors; (Wrestling) holding of opponent's head or body with one's legs. **3.** ∼**-bill,** = SKIMMER 3; ∼**-bird, -tail,** (esp.) fork-tailed flycatcher; ∼**-tooth,** in Carnivora acting like scissors against one in other jaw. **4.** Hence ∼WISE *adv.* [ME *sisoures* f. OF *cisoires* f. LL *cisoria* pl. of *cisorium* cutting instrument (as CHISEL; see -ORY); assoc. w. L *scindere sciss-* cut]

sci´ur|ine *a.* of the squirrel family; squirrel-like; so ∼OID *a.* [f. L f. Gk *skiouros* squirrel (*skia* shadow, *oura* tail) + -INE¹]

sclēr´|a *n.* = SCLEROTIC 2; hence ∼I´TIS, ∼ŏ´TOMY, *ns.* [mod. L, f. fem. of Gk *sklēros* hard]

sclērĕ´nchy̆ma (-ngk-) *n.* (Zool.) hard tissue of coral; (Bot.) tissue of cells with thick woody walls. [mod. L, f. Gk *sklēros* hard + *egkhuma* infusion, after *parenchyma*]

sclēr´oid *a.* (Bot. & Zool.) of hard texture. [f. Gk *sklēros* hard + -OID]

sclērō´ma *n.* (*pl.* ∼**ta**). morbid hardening of tissue. [f. mod. L f. Gk *sklērōma* (as SCLEROSIS; see -OMA)]

sclērō´meter *n.* instrument for determining hardness of materials. [f. Gk *sklēros* hard + -O- + -METER]

sclēr´ophy̆ll, sclēr´ophy̆te, *ns.* plant with large amount of sclerenchyma, preventing loss of water. [f. as prec. + Gk *phullon* leaf, -PHYTE]

sclēr´ōsed (-st, -zd) *a.* affected by sclerosis. [f. foll. + -ED¹]

sclerō´s|is (-ēr-, -er-) *n.* (*pl.* ∼**es** *pr.* -ēz). **1.** scleroma; ARTERIOSCLEROSIS; ATHEROSCLEROSIS; **disseminated** or **multiple** ∼, chronic progressive sclerosis of brain and spinal cord. **2.** (Bot.) hardening of cell-wall with lignified matter. [ME f. med. L f. Gk *sklērōsis* (*sklēro* harden; see -OSIS)]

sclerō´tic (-ēr-, -er-) *a.* & *n.* **1.** *a.* of or having sclerosis; of the sclerotic. **2.** *n.* membrane coating eye round iris, white of eye; hence **sclĕroti'tis** *n.* [f. med. L *sclerotica* (as prec.)]

sclēr'ous *a.* (Path., Anat., & Bot.) indurated, bony. [f. Gk *sklēros* hard + -OUS]

SCM *abbr.* State Certified Midwife; Student Christian Movement.

scŏff¹ *n.*, & *v.i.* **1.** *n.* mocking words, taunt, gibe; object of ridicule, laughing-stock. **2.** *v.i.* speak derisively esp. of religion or object of respect; aim scoffs or mockery *at*; hence ∼'ER¹ *n.* [perh. f. Scand.; cf. early mod. Da. *skuf, skof* jest, mockery]

scŏff² *n.* & *v.* (sl.) **1.** *n.* food, meal. **2.** *v.t.* & *i.* eat greedily. [n. f. Afrik. *schoff* repr. Du. *schoft* quarter of a day (hence, meal); v. orig. var. of dial. *scaff*, assoc. w. n.]

scŏld *v.* & *n.* **1.** *v.i.* find fault noisily, rail. **2.** *v.t.* (esp. of parent, employer, mistress to child, servant) rebuke, whence ∼'ING¹ (1) *n.* **3.** *n.* railing or nagging woman. [v. f. n., ME, prob. f. ON *skáld* SCALD²]

scō'l|ĕx *n.* (*pl.* ∼eces *pr.* -ē'sēz, or ∼ices *pr.* -ĭsēz). head of larval or adult tapeworm. [mod. L, f. Gk *skōlēx* worm]

scŏli|ō'sis *n.* (*pl.* ∼o'ses *pr.* -ō'sēz). lateral curvature of spine; hence ∼o'TIC *a.* [mod. L f. Gk (*skolios* bent; see -OSIS)]

scŏ'llop. See SCALLOP.

scŏlopĕ'ndrium *n.* hart's-tongue fern. [mod. L f. Gk *skolopendrion* (*skolopendra* millepede, f. fancied resemblance)]

scŏ'mb|er *n.* mackerel or other fish of family Scombridae; so ∼rɪD³ *n.*, ∼roɪD *a.* & *n.* [L, f. Gk *skombros*]

scŏnce¹ *n.* flat candlestick with handle; bracket candlestick to hang on wall. [ME, f. OF *esconse* lantern or f. med. L *sconsa* f. L *absconsa* fem. p.p. (as n.) of *abscondere* hide; see ABSCOND]

scŏnce² *n.* (arch. joc.) head, crown of head. [perh. f. prec.]

scŏnce³ *n.* small fort or earthwork, usu. defending a ford, pass, etc.; (arch.) shelter, screen. [f. Du. *schans* brushwood f. MHG *schanze*]

‖**scŏnce**⁴ *v.t.*, & *n.* (Oxf. Univ.) **1.** *v.t.* inflict forfeit (or penalty involving drinking) of beer etc. for offence against table etiquette upon (member of company or his offence); (Hist., of university official etc.) fine for breach of discipline. **2.** *n.* such forfeit. [17th c., perh. f. SCONCE²]

scŏne *n.* soft cake of barley-meal or oatmeal or wheat-flour of size for single portion usu. baked quickly in oven or on griddle; DROP¹ *scone*. [orig. Sc., perh. f. MDu. *schoon(broot)*, MLG *schon(brot)* fine (bread)]

scoōp *n.*, & *v.t.* **1.** *n.* short-handled deep shovel for taking up and transferring grain, sugar, coal, coins, etc.; large long-handled ladle-shaped dipping-vessel for liquids; excavating part of digging-machine etc.; gougelike or spoonlike instrument e.g. for surgical use or for serving ice cream, mashed potatoes, etc.; quantity taken with scoop. **2.** motion as of, act of, scooping; (Mus.) singer's exaggerated portamento; large profit made quickly or by anticipating one's competitors; piece of news published by newspaper in advance of its rivals. **3.** ∼-neck, rounded low-cut neck of garment; ∼-net (for sweeping river-bottom, or for catching bait). **4.** *v.t.* lift (*up*), hollow (*out*), (as) with scoop; secure (large profit etc.) by sudden action or stroke of luck; forestall (rival newspaper, reporter, etc.) with news scoop. [ME, f. MDu., MLG *schōpe* bucket etc., WG f. **skōp-*, cogn. w. SHAPE¹]

scoōt *v.i.* (colloq.) run, dart, make off esp. hastily. [19th c. US; earlier *scout*, of unkn. orig.]

scoō'ter *n.* child's toy propelled by foot and consisting of footboard with wheel at front and back and long steering-handle; (**motor**) ∼, light motor vehicle of similar design for seated adults with protective front section, whence ∼ɪsT (3) *n.*; *sail-boat able to travel on both water and ice. [f. prec. + -ER¹]

scō'pa *n.* (*pl.* ∼e). small brushlike tuft of hairs esp. on bee's leg. [sing. of L *scopae* = twigs, broom]

scōpe¹ *n.* **1.** outlook, purview, sweep or reach or sphere of observation or action, extent to which it is permissible or possible to range, opportunity, outlet, vent, (*mind, undertaking, of wide scope; is beyond my scope; give no, ample, scope for expatiating, to ability; seeks scope for his energies*). **2.** (arch.) end aimed at, purpose, intention. **3.** (Naut.) length of cable out when ship rides at anchor. [f. It. *scopo* aim f. Gk *skopos* target (*skeptomai* look at)]

scōpe² *n.* (colloq.) instrument etc. whose name ends in -SCOPE. [abbr.]

-scōpe *suf.* forming *ns.* denoting (1) thing looked at or through (*kaleidoscope, telescope*), (2) instrument for observing or showing (*gyroscope, oscilloscope*). [f. or after mod. L *-scopium* f. Gk *skopeō* look at]

-scŏpic *suf.* forming *adjs.* w. sense 'looking at' (*macroscopic*) or 'pertaining or similar to an instrument whose name ends in -SCOPE' (*gyroscopic, oscilloscopic, telescopic*). [f. as prec. + -IC]

scopŏ'lamine (-ĭn, -ēn) *n.* = HYOSCINE. [f. *Scopolia* genus-name of plants yielding it, f. G. A. *Scopoli*, It. naturalist d. 1788 + AMINE]

scō'pŭla *n.* (*pl.* ∼e). = SCOPA, esp. on bee's or spider's leg. [LL, dim. of L SCOPA; see -ULE]

-scopy *suf.* forming *ns.* w. sense 'looking at' (*necroscopy*) or 'use of an instrument whose name ends in -SCOPE' (*microscopy*). [f. as -SCOPE + -Y¹]

scŏrbū't|ic *a.* & *n.* of or like, (person) affected with, scurvy; hence ∼ICALLY *adv.* [f. mod. L *scorbuticus* f. med. L *scorbutus* scurvy, perh. f. MLG *schorbūk* (*schoren* break, *būk* belly) + -IC]

scŏrch *v.* & *n.* **1.** *v.t.* burn surface of with flame or heat so as to discolour or injure or pain; affect with sensation of burning; hence ∼'ING² *a.*, ∼ed earth **policy,** burning crops etc. and removing or destroying anything that might be of use to an enemy occupying the country. **2.** *v.i.* become discoloured etc. with heat. **3.** (sl.) (Of motorist or cyclist) go at very high or excessive speed. **4.** *n.* (sl.) spell of such driving or riding. **5.** mark made by scorching. [ME, perh. rel. to *skorkle* in same sense]

scŏr'cher *n.* In vbl senses; (colloq.) very hot day; (sl.) fine specimen of its kind. [f. prec. + -ER¹]

scōre *n.* & *v.* **1.** *n.* notch cut or line cut or scratched or drawn; (arch.) mark showing starting-point in race or standing-place in shooting-match (**go off at** ∼, start off vigorously); (Naut.) groove in block or dead-eye to hold rope. **2.** running account kept by scores against customer's name esp. formerly for drink in inns, reckoning esp. for entertainment; **pay** one's ∼, settle reckoning; **pay off old** ∼**s,** (fig.) pay person out for past offence. **3.** number of points made by player or side in some games or awarded to competitor etc., list or total of items of this for each player etc., (*make a good score; what is the score now?*); ∼**-board** (for publicly displaying score); ∼**-book, -card, -sheet,** (prepared for entering esp. cricket scores in); **keep** (**the**) ∼, register it as it is made; **know the** ∼, (fig., colloq.) be aware of the essential facts. **4.** (Mus.) copy of a composition on set of staves braced and barred together (named from bar drawn through all staves); CLOSE¹, FULL¹, OPEN¹, SHORT, VOCAL, *score*; **in** ∼, with parts arranged below each other and corresponding. **5.** (*pl.* ∼ or ∼s; for pl. usage see HUNDRED). twenty, set of twenty, (esp. FOURscore, THREEscore); (in *pl.*) great numbers; (arch.) weight of twenty (or twenty-one) pounds, esp. in weighing pigs or oxen. **6.** reason, motive, (*rejected* **on the score of absurdity** etc., as being absurd etc.; **on that** ∼, so far as that matter is concerned); topic, subject, (*no speculations on that score*). **7.** (colloq.) remark or act by which person scores off another; piece of good fortune. **8.** *v.t.* mark with notches or incisions or lines, slash, furrow, make (line etc.) with something that marks; ∼ **out,** draw line through (words etc.); ∼

under, underline. **9.** *criticize (person) severely. **10.** mark *up* in score (sense 2), enter (item of debt *against* or *to* customer); (fig.) mentally record (offence *against* or *to* offender); make record of (point in cricket etc. score, or abs., keep the score, whence **scōr′ER**[1] *n.*). **11.** win and be credited with (*has scored a success, a goal, a century at cricket*); count for score of (points in game; *a goal scores six points*); allot score to (competitor etc.); ~ **points off,** (colloq.) = *score off* (see sense 13). **12.** (Mus.) orchestrate, whence **scōr′ING**[1] (6) *n.*; arrange *for* instrument(s); write out in score. **13.** *v.i.* make score in game (*failed to score*); secure an advantage or have good luck (*that is where he scores*); (sl.) obtain drugs illegally; ~ **off,** (colloq.) worst in argument or repartee, inflict some humiliation on. [n. f. OE **scoru,* v. partly f. ON *skora,* f. ON *skor* notch, tally, twenty, f. GMC *skurō (**skur-,* **sker-,* cut; see SHEAR)]

scōr′i|a *n.* (*pl.* ~ae). cellular lava or fragments of it; slag or dross of metals; hence ~A′CEOUS *a.* [L, f. Gk *skōria* refuse (*skōr* dung)]

scōr′i|fy *v.t.* reduce to dross, assay (precious metal) by thus treating a portion of its ore fused with lead and borax; hence ~FICA′TION, ~fIER[1] (2), *ns.* [f. prec. + -FY]

scorn *n.,* & *v.t.* **1.** *n.* disdain, contempt, derision, (**think** ~ **of,** despise; LAUGH *to* scorn). **2.** object of contempt (*a scorn to or the scorn of all onlookers*). **3.** *v.t.* hold in contempt, consider beneath notice, abstain from or refuse *to* do as unworthy (*scorns lying, a lie, to lie*); hence ~′ER[1] *n.* (esp. *of*). [ME, f. OF *esc(h)arn(ir)* f. Rom. **escarnire,* *eskernire f. Gmc **skarnjan,* *skernjan; cf. OS *skern* mockery)]

scōr′nful *a.* full of scorn, contemptuous (*of*); hence ~LY[2] *adv.,* ~NESS *n.* [ME, f. prec. + -FUL]

scōr′per. Var. of SCALPER[2].

Scōr′pi|ō *n.* (*pl.* ~os). (person born under) sign of the ZODIAC, the Scorpion; hence ~AN *a.* & *n.,* (person) born under Scorpio. [ME f. L (*scorpius* f. Gk *skorpios* scorpion)]

scor′pioid *n.* & *a.* (Bot.) (inflorescence) curled up at end like scorpion's tail and uncurling as flowers develop. [f. Gk *skorpioeidēs* (as prec.; see -OID)]

scor′pion *n.* **1.** arachnid with lobster-like claws and jointed tail that can be bent over to inflict poisoned sting on prey held in claws; (**false**) ~, similar arachnid without tail. **2.** (Bibl.) whip armed with metal points (1 Kgs. 12:11). **3.** (*S*~). *the* zodiacal sign Scorpio. **4.** (Hist.) kind of ballista. **5.** (sl.) native of Gibraltar. **6.** ~**-fish** (of family Scorpaenidae, with spines on head and on fins); ~**-fly** (of order Mecoptera, with curled abdomen); ~**-grass,** forget-me-not; ~**-shell,** gastropod with long spines fringing outer lip of aperture. [ME f. OF, f. L SCORPIO *-onis*]

scorzonēr′a *n.* plant of genus *Scorzonera,* esp. species with white parsnip-like root used as vegetable. [It. (*scorzone* venomous snake f. Rom. *scurtione f. med. L *curtio*)]

scōt[1] *n.* **1.** (Hist.) payment corresponding to modern tax, rate, or other assessed contribution (**pay** ~ **and lot,** share pecuniary burdens of borough etc.). **2.** ~**-free,** unharmed, unpunished, safe. [ME, f. ON *skot* & f. OF *escot,* of Gmc orig.; cf. SHOT[3]]

Scot[2] *n.* **1.** native of Scotland. **2.** (Hist.) member of Gaelic tribe that migrated from Ireland to Scotland about 6th c. [OE *Scottas* pl., f. LL *Scottus*]

Scotch[1] *a.* & *n.* **1.** *a.* of Scotland or its inhabitants; in the form of English used in (esp. Lowlands of) Scotland; ~ **broth,** soup made from beef or mutton with pearl barley and vegetables; ~ **cap** (of shapes worn in Highland costume, glengarry, tam-o′-shanter, etc.); ~ **catch,** (Mus.) short note on the beat followed by long one; ~ **collops,** (1) beef cut small and stewed, (2) steak and onions; ~ **egg,** hard-boiled egg enclosed in sausage-meat; *Scotch* FIR (*Pinus sylvestris*), KALE, MIST; ~ **pebble,** agate, jasper, cairngorm, etc., found in Scotland; ~ **pine,** = *Scotch fir*; ~ **snap,** = *Scotch catch*; *~ **tape** (*P), adhesive usu. transparent

cellulose or plastic tape; ~ **terrier** (small rough-haired short-legged kind); ~ **whisky,** kind distilled in Scotland esp. from malted barley; ~ **woodcock,** scrambled eggs on anchovy toast. **2.** ~**′man,** ~**′woman,** native of Scotland. **3.** *n.* form of English used in (esp. Lowlands of) Scotland; **the** ~, (*pl.*) the people of Scotland. **4.** Scotch whisky. [contr. of SCOTTISH]

scotch[2] *v.t.,* & *n.* **1.** *v.t.* (arch.) make incisions in, score; wound without killing, slightly disable. **2.** decisively put an end to; frustrate (plan etc.). **3.** *n.* slash; line on ground for HOP[2]scotch. [ME; orig. unkn.]

scotch[3] *n.* & *v.t.* **1.** ~*n.* wedge or block placed against wheel etc. to prevent motion downhill. **2.** *v.t.* hold up (wheel, barrel) with scotch. [17th c., perh. = *scatch* stilt f. OF *escache*]

scō′ter *n.* large sea-duck of genus *Oidemia* or *Melanitta.* [17th c.; orig. unkn.]

scō′tia (-sha) *n.* concave moulding esp. in base of column. [L, f. Gk *skotia* (*skotos* darkness, w. ref. to shadow produced)]

scō′ticē etc. See SCOTTICE etc.

Scō′t|ism *n.* (Hist.) metaphysical doctrines of Duns Scotus; so ~IST (2) *n.* [f. John Duns *Scotus,* Sc. schoolman d. 1308 (L *Scotus* Scot) + -ISM]

Scŏtland Yǎr′d *n.* headquarters of London Metropolitan Police; its Criminal Investigation Department. [f. Great & New ~, streets where it was successively situated until 1967]

scōtodi′nia *n.* (Med.) giddiness. [f. Gk *skotos* darkness + *dinē* whirl + -IA[1]]

scotō′ma *n.* (*pl.* ~ta). (Path.) obscuration of part of the field of vision. [LL, f. Gk *skotōma* (*skotoō* darken f. as prec.; see -OMA)]

Scŏts *a.* & *n.* (esp. Sc.) = SCOTCH[1] 3; POUND[1] *Scots*; ||*Scots* GREYS; *Scots Guards*; ~**′man,** = SCOTCH[1]*man*; ~**′woman,** = SCOTCH[1]*woman.* [ME, orig. *Scottis,* north. var. of SCOTTISH]

scŏ′t(t)icē *adv.* in Scotch. [med. L, f. LL *Scot(t)icus*]

Scŏ′t(t)icism *n.* Scotch phrase, word, or idiom. [f. LL as prec. + -ISM (4)]

Scŏ′t(t)icīze, -ise (-īz), *v.* **1.** *v.i.* imitate the Scotch in idiom or habits. **2.** *v.t.* imbue with, model on, Scotch ways. [f. LL as SCOTTICE) + -IZE]

Scŏ′ttie *n.* (colloq.) Scotchman; Scotch terrier. [f. SCOT[2] + -IE]

Scŏ′ttish *a.* (esp. Sc. or literary). of Scotland or its inhabitants (*Scottish dancing, Gaelic, islands, Nationalist*); ~ **Certificate of Education** (corresponding to GENERAL Certificate of Education). [ME, f. SCOT[2] + -REL]

scou′ndrel *n.* unscrupulous person, villain, rogue; hence ~DOM, ~ISM (3), *ns.,* ~LY[1] *a.* [16th c., of unkn. orig.; cf. -REL]

scour[1] *v.t.,* & *n.* **1.** *v.t.* cleanse or brighten by friction (metal with sand etc., cloth etc. with soap or chemicals); (of water, of person with water) clear out (channel, harbour, pipe, etc.) by flushing or flowing through or over; purge (bowels) drastically; clear (rust, stain, etc.) *away, off,* by rubbing etc. (lit. or fig.); ~**′ing-rush,** kind of horse-tail plant with siliceous coating used for polishing wood etc.; hence (-)~′ER[1] (1, 2) *n.* **2.** *n.* clearing action of swift current on channel etc. (*the scour of the tide*); diarrhoea in cattle; substance used for scouring fabrics; act of scouring. [ME, f. MDu., MLG *schüren* f. F *escurer* f. LL EX[1]*curare* clean (off) f. L *curare* (see CURE[2])]

scour[2] *v.* **1.** *v.i.* rove, range, go along hastily, esp. in search or pursuit. **2.** *v.t.* hasten over or along, search rapidly or thoroughly. [ME, of unkn. orig.]

scourge (skerj) *n.,* & *v.t.* **1.** *n.* whip for chastising persons; person or thing regarded as instrument or manifestation of divine or other vengeance or punishment (e.g. barbarian conqueror, pestilence, war). **2.** *v.t.* use whip on; chastise, afflict, oppress, harass. [ME, f. OF *escorge* n., *escorgier* v., f. Rom. EX[1]*corrigiare* f. L *corrigia* thong, whip]

‖**scouse** *n.* & *a.* lobscouse; (sl.) (native) of Liverpool; Liverpool dialect. [f. LOBSCOUSE]

scout[1] *n.*, & *v.i.* **1.** *n.* person sent out to get information (esp. Mil., about enemy or surroundings); (colloq.) fellow, person, (*a good scout*); ∼ **car,** fast armoured vehicle for reconnaissance etc.; TALENT-*scout*. **2.** (*S*∼). member of boys' organization (**S**∼ **Association**) intended to develop character by esp. open-air activities; **King's** or **Queen's S**∼ (who has reached highest rank of proficiency). **3.** ‖patrolman of motoring organization. **4.** ship or aircraft designed for reconnoitring, esp. small fast aircraft. **5.** college servant at Oxford Univ. (cf. GYP[1]). **6.** act of seeking (esp. Mil.) information (*on the scout*). **7.** ∼'**master,** officer in charge of scouts or Scouts. **8.** *v.i.* act as scout; ∼ **about** or **around,** make search (*for*); hence ∼'ER[1] *n.* (esp. **S**∼**er,** adult member of Scout Association), ∼'ING[1] (1) *n.* [ME, f. OF *escoute*(*r*) listen(ing), earlier *ascolter* f. Rom. **ascultare* f. L *auscultare*]

scout[2] *v.t.* reject (proposal, notion) with scorn or ridicule. [f. Scand.; cf. ON *skúta*, *skúti* taunt]

scow *n.* (esp. US) flat-bottomed boat used as lighter etc. [f. Du. *schouw* ferry-boat]

scowl *v.i.*, & *n.* **1.** *v.i.* wear sullen look, look sour, frown ill-temperedly. **2.** *n.* scowling aspect, angry frown. [ME, prob. f. Scand.; cf. Da. *skule* look down or sidelong]

‖**SCR** *abbr.* Senior Combination Room; Senior Common Room.

scr. *abbr.* scruple(s).

scra'bble *v.i.*, & *n.* **1.** *v.i.* scrawl, scribble; scratch or grope *about* to find or collect something. **2.** *n.* (*S*∼; **P**) game in which players build up words from letter-blocks on a board. [f. MDu. *schrabbelen* frequent. of *schrabben* SCRAPE]

scräg *n.*, & *v.t.* (**-gg-**). **1.** *n.* lean and skinny person, animal, plant, etc., whence ∼'**gy**[2] (-gĭ) *a.*; bony part of animal's carcass as food, esp. neck of mutton or inferior part (∼**-end**) of it; (sl.) person's neck. **2.** *v.t.* (sl.) put to death by hanging, garotte, wring neck of; seize roughly by the neck; handle roughly. [perh. alt. f. dial. *crag* neck, rel. to MDu. *crāghe*, MLG *krage*]

scräm *v.i.* (**-mm-**). (sl.) go away, (in *imper.*) be off! [perh. f. foll.]

scrä'mble *v.* & *n.* **1.** *v.i.* make way as best one can over steep or rough ground by clambering, crawling, etc.; move hastily and anxiously; take part in physical or other struggle with competitors *for* as much as possible of something; (of aircraft or pilots) take off quickly in emergency. **2.** *v.t.* mix together indiscriminately; deal with hastily or awkwardly (*away, through,* etc.); cook (eggs) by breaking into pan with butter, milk, etc., stirring slightly, and heating (∼**d egg,** (joc.) gold braid on officer's cap); alter frequencies of transmitted speech of (telephone conversation etc.) so as to make it unintelligible except to recipient using similar process, whence **scrä'mbl**ER[1] (2) *n.*; cause (aircraft, pilots) to scramble. **3.** *n.* climb or walk over rough ground etc.; motor-cycle race over rough ground; eager struggle or competition for or *for* something. [16th c., imit.; cf. dial. synonyms *scamble, cramble*]

scrän *n.* (sl.) food, eatables; remains of food; **bad** ∼, (Ir.) bad luck (*to*). [18th c., of unkn. orig.]

scrä'nnel *a.* (arch.) (Of sound) weak, reedy, feeble; harsh, unmelodious (usu. w. allus. to Milton's *Lycidas* 124). [17th c.; cf. dial. synonyms *scrank*(*y*) & Norw. *skran* shrivelled]

scräp[1] *n.*, & *v.t.* (**-pp-**). **1.** *n.* small detached piece of something, fragment, remnant, (∼ **of paper,** (fig.) treaty etc. one does not intend to honour); (w. neg.) the least piece or amount; (in *pl.*) odds and ends, fragments of uneaten food, useless remains; hence ∼'**py**[2] *a.* **2.** picture, paragraph, etc., cut from book or newspaper for keeping in a collection; ∼**-book** (for pasting these into). **3.** rubbish, waste material; ∼(**-metal, -iron,** etc.), metal collected for reworking; ∼**-heap,** collection of waste material (lit.

or fig.); ∼**-merchant,** dealer in scrap; ∼**-yard,** place where scrap is collected. **4.** (in *sing.* or *pl.*) residuum of melted fat or of fish with the oil expressed; ∼**-cake,** compressed fish scrap. **5.** *v.t.* consign to scrap-heap, condemn as now useless, discard. [ME, f. ON *skrap* rel. to *skrapa* SCRAPE]

scräp[2] *n.*, & *v.i.* (**-pp-**). (colloq.) **1.** *n.* fight, scrimmage, esp. of unpremeditated kind; hence ∼'**py**[2] *a.*, quarrelsome, aggressive. **2.** *v.i.* have scrap (*with*). [perh. f. foll.]

scräpe *v.* & *n.* **1.** *v.t.* level surface of, clear of projections, abrade, smooth, polish, shave, or graze, by drawing sharp or angular edge breadthwise over or by causing to pass over such edge; clear (ship's bottom) of barnacles etc.; remove dirt from soles of (boots etc.) by drawing over scraper; leave no food on (plate); draw (hair) tightly *back* from forehead; ∼ **away,** reduce by scraping; *scrape* the BARREL[1]. **2.** take (projection, surface layer, stain, etc.) *off, out, away,* by scraping. **3.** excavate (hollow) by scraping. **4.** *v.t.* & *i.* draw or pass along with sound (as) of scraping, produce such sound from, emit such sound; draw back foot in making clumsy formal bow (**bow and** ∼, behave obsequiously); (derog.) play on violin. **5.** *v.i.* pass along something so as to graze or be grazed by it or just avoid doing so (*scraped against, along, the wall*); get *through* (adv. or prep.) etc. with a squeeze or narrow shave (lit., or fig. of passing examination etc.). **6.** *v.t.* amass by scraping or with difficulty or by parsimony, contrive to bring (*together, up*; ∼ **acquaintance with,** force oneself as an acquaintance on); (abs.) practise economy (*work and scrape as one may*). **7.** Hence **scrä'p**ING[1] (esp. 2), **scrä'p**ER[1] (1, 2), *ns.* (‖∼**rboard,** cardboard with blackened surface removable by scraping for making white-line drawings). **8.** *n.* act or sound of scraping; scraped place; ‖thinly applied layer of butter etc. on bread; scraping of foot in bowing; awkward predicament esp. resulting from escapade. [ME, f. ON *skrapa* or MDu. *schrapen*]

scrä'pie *n.* virus disease of sheep with severe itching causing animals to rub against trees etc. [f. SCRAPE. + -IE]

***scrä'pple** *n.* food made from stewed meat scraps and flour pressed into cakes. [f. SCRAP[1] + -LE 1]

scrä'ppy. See SCRAP[1] 1, SCRAP[2] 1.

scrätch[1] *v.t.*, *n.*, & *a.* **1.** *v.t.* score surface of, make long narrow superficial wounds in, with nail, claw, or something more or less pointed; ∼ **the surface (of),** not penetrate far in (to; lit. or fig.). **2.** get (some part of one) scratched (*have scratched my hands badly*); form (letters, representation), excavate (hole), by scratching; scribble (*a few lines* etc.). **3.** scrape without marking esp. with finger-nails to relieve itching; (abs.) scratch oneself, scratch ground etc. in search (*scratch about for stray seeds, for evidence*); ∼ one's **head** (esp. as sign of perplexity); ∼ **my back and I will** ∼ **yours** (of mutual aid or flattery). **4.** bring *together* or *up* by scraping or with difficulty; ∼ **along,** (abs.) make a living etc. with difficulty. **5.** score (written words etc.) *out* or *through,* strike *off* with pencil etc., erase (horse's name in list of entries for race, competitor's or *election candidate's name*), withdraw (horse, candidate, or abs. for *refl.*) from competition. **6.** *n.* mark or wound or sound made by scratching (**a** ∼ **of the pen,** signature or written order easily given); spell of scratching oneself; (colloq.) trifling wound; (sl.) money; (in *pl.*) horse-disease in which pastern appears scratched. **7.** line from which competitors not receiving handicap in race start; **start from** ∼, begin from the very beginning or without advantage or preparation; (**come**) **up to** ∼, be present at the right time, do(ing) what is required. **8.** ∼'**board,** scraperboard; ∼**-dial,** simple sundial scratched on church wall etc.; ∼ **pad** (of paper for jotting or scribbling); ∼(**-wig**), wig covering only part of head; ∼**-work,** graffito decoration. **9.** *a.* collected haphazardly, scratched together, heterogeneous, (*a scratch crew, meal, team*); with no handicap given (*scratch player, race*). [ME, prob. f. synonymous ME *scrat* & *cratch*, both of uncert. orig.; cf. MLG *kratsen*, OHG *krazzōn*]

Scrätch[2] *n.* (colloq.) **Old** ∽, the Devil. [f. obs. *scrat* hermaphrodite f. ON *skrat(t)i* goblin, OHG *scrato* sprite]

scrä'tch|ў *a.* (Of drawing etc.) done in scratches, careless or unskilful; making sound of scratching; tending to cattishness or irritability; tending to cause itching; hence ∽**ILY**[2] *adv.*, ∽**iNESS** *n.* [f. SCRATCH[1] + -Y[2]]

scrawl *v.* & *n.* **1.** *v.i.* & *t.* write in hurried more or less illegible way; mark (paper etc.) *over* with bad writing or lines like writing, cross (word etc.) *out* thus. **2.** *n.* piece of hasty or illegible writing; hurried note or letter. [perh. f. obs. *scrawl* sprawl alt. of CRAWL]

scraw'nў *a.* lean, scraggy. [var. of dial. *scranny*; cf. SCRANNEL]

‖**scray** *n.* common tern. [17th c., of unkn. orig.]

scream *v.* & *n.* **1.** *v.i.* utter piercing cry expressing terror, pain, vexation, or pretence of these, (of siren etc.) whistle or hoot shrilly; (of machine etc.) make shrill sound like scream, (of animal etc.) give shrill cry; speak or write angrily or excitedly; laugh uncontrollably; be blatantly obvious; (in *pres. part.*, of farce, fun etc.) causing spectators to scream, intensely funny. **2.** *v.t.* utter, say, in screaming tone (*screamed that she did not dare jump; scream out a curse, order,* etc.). **3.** *n.* screaming cry or sound (*screams of pain, laughter*); (sl.) irresistibly comical affair or person. [OE *scrǣman* or MDu. *schreemen*]

screa'mer *n.* In vbl senses; S. Amer. bird of family Anhimidae; *large exclamatory headline; (sl.) tale that raises screams of laughter, extraordinarily fine specimen of anything, exclamation mark. [f. prec. + -ER[1]]

scree *n.* (in *sing.*) or *pl.*) (mountain slope covered with) small stones that slide down when trodden on. [prob. back-form. f. *screes* pl. f. *screethes* f. ON *skritha* landslip rel. to *skritha* glide]

screech *v.i.* & *t.*, & *n.* scream with or of fright or pain or anger, or in harsh or uncanny tones; ∽**-owl**, owl that screeches instead of hooting, esp. barn-owl or *small owl of genus *Otus*. [16th-c. var. of ME *scritch* (imit.)]

screed *n.* unduly long harangue (esp. list of grievances) or writing; strip of plaster as guide to thickness; piece of wood or board for levelling concrete. [ME, prob. var. of SHRED]

screen *n.*, & *v.t.* **1.** *n.* partition of wood or stone separating without completely cutting off one part of church (esp. ROOD-*screen*), room, etc., from another. **2.** movable piece of furniture designed to shelter from excess of heat, light, draught, etc., or from observation; = SIGHT[1]-*screen*. **3.** thing utilized as shelter esp. from observation (*prepared the attack behind a screen of trees*), expression of face or measure adopted for concealment, protection afforded by these, (*under screen of night*); body of cavalry detached to keep enemy's scouts from getting in touch with main body; = WIND[1]*screen*. **4.** vertical surface for display of exhibits, notices, etc. **5.** blank surface on which moving or televised pictures or lantern-slides or radar images are projected; piece of ground glass in camera for focusing; ∽**'play**, script of a film; ∽ **test** (of would-be film actor's suitability); ∽**-writer**, writer of film-scripts; **the** ∽, moving pictures collectively. **6.** body intercepting light, heat, electric or magnetic induction, etc., in physical apparatus; ∽**-grid** (protecting control grid from influence of anode in thermionic valve). **7.** large sieve or riddle esp. for sorting grain, coal, etc., into sizes; *wire netting or perforated sheet in door etc. allowing flow of air; ∽**-printing**, process like stencilling with ink forced through prepared sheet of fine material (orig. silk). **8.** (Print.) transparent finely-ruled plate or film used in process of half-tone reproduction. **9.** *v.t.* afford shelter to, hide partly or completely, (*from*); (fig.) protect

another from deserved censure etc. by taking blame upon oneself or diverting it; ∽ **off**, shut off by or hide behind screen. **10.** show (object, scene, film, slide, etc.) on screen. **11.** pass (grain, coal, etc.) through screen; ∽**ed coal** (from which dust etc. has been removed); hence ∽**'ING**[1] (2) *n.*, (in *pl.*) refuse separated by sifting. **12.** test (person) to determine presence or absence of a quality (esp. reliability or loyalty), disease, weapon, etc. **13.** prevent from causing electrical interference. [ME, f. ONF *escren, escran* f. OFrank. *skrank*, OHG *skrank* barrier]

screw (-ōō) *n.* & *v.* **1.** *n.* cylinder or cone with spiral ridge called THREAD[1], running round it outside (MALE or *exterior screw*) or inside (FEMALE or *interior screw*); (**wood-**)∽, metal male screw with slotted head and sharp point for fastening things together with more security than nail; ∽**(-bolt)**, metal male screw with blunt end to receive nut and bolt things together; GRUB[1]-*screw*, wooden or metal male or female screw as part of appliance or machine acting to exert pressure in various ways; (in *sing.* or *pl.*) instrument of torture operating thus; ENDLESS, INTERRUPTED, RIGHT[1]-*and*-*left, screw*; **have a** ∽ **loose**, (colloq.) be slightly mad; **put the** ∽(s) on, exert pressure esp. to extort or intimidate. **2.** ∽**(-propeller)**, revolving shaft with twisted blades projecting from ship, boat, or aircraft, and propelling it by acting on screw principle upon water or air. **3.** one turn of a screw (*give it another screw*). **4.** ‖(Bill. etc.) oblique curling motion or tendency of ball struck below and to one side of centre. **5.** ‖small twisted-up paper *of* tobacco etc. **6.** (colloq.) miser, stingy or extortionate person. **7.** ‖(sl.) amount of salary or wages. **8.** (sl.) prison warder. **9.** (vulg.) (partner in) copulation. **10.** worn-out horse. **11.** *∽'ball* a. & *n.*, (sl.) mad, crazy, (person); ∽**-bean**, mesquite bean; ∽**-bolt** (see sense 1); ∽**-cap**, cap screwing on to thread of container aperture; ∽**-coupling**, right-and-left female screw for joining ends of pipes or rods; ∽**-cutter**, hand-tool for cutting screws; ∽**'driver**, tool like narrow blunt chisel for turning screws by the slot; ∽**-eye**, screw with loop for passing cord etc. through instead of slotted head; ∽ **gear**, endless screw with cogwheel or pinion; ∽**-hook**, hook to hang things on with screw at end of shank to fasten it in with; ∽**-jack**, (1) dentist's implement for regulating distance between crowded teeth, (2) vehicle JACK[1] worked by screw; ∽**-pile** (with screw at lower end and sunk by rotation); ∽**-pine**, plant of genus *Pandanus* with leaves arranged spirally and resembling those of pineapple; ∽**-plate**, steel plate with threaded holes for making male screws; ∽**-pod**, species of mesquite with spirally twisted pods; ∽**-press**, press worked by simple screw used esp. by printers and binders; ∽**-propeller** (see sense 2); ∽ **steamer** (propelled by one or more screws); ∽**-tap**, tool for making female screws; ∽**-top**, = *screw-cap*; ∽ **valve**, stopcock opened and shut by screw; ∽**-wheel** (worked by endless screw); ∽**-wrench** (for turning screws with angular head or nuts). **12.** *v.t.* fasten, tighten, etc., by use of screw(s); **his head is** ∽**ed on the right way or straight**, he has SENSE 6. **13.** turn (screw), twist round like screw; ∽ (**up**), make tenser or more efficient (∽ one's **courage to the sticking-place,** ∽ up one's **courage,** gather resolution); ∽ **up,** (sl.) bungle. **14.** put the screw upon, press hard on, oppress; squeeze, extort, (consent, money, etc.) *out of*; contort, distort, contract, (*screw* one's *face into wrinkles; screw up* one's *eyes*); (in *p.p.*, sl.) drunk(en). **15.** (sl.) burgle. **16.** *v.t.* & *i.* (vulg.) copulate (with). **17.** *v.i.* be miserly. **18.** (Of screw) revolve (*stiffly, to the right,* etc.); twist *round*. **19.** (Of rolling ball, or of person etc.) take curling course, swerve. **20.** Hence ∽**'ABLE** *a.* [ME, f. OF *escroue* female screw, nut, (f. WG *scrūva* or) f. L *scrofa* sow]

screw'ў (-ōō'ĭ) *a.* (Of horse) worn out; (sl.) crazy or eccentric or drunk. [f. SCREW + -Y[2]]

scri'bal. See SCRIBE.

scri′bble[1] *v.* & *n.* **1.** *v.t.* & *i.* write hurriedly or carelessly in regard to either handwriting or composition, or simply to obliterate (*scribble out the old address*); draw carelessly or meaninglessly; (joc. or derog.) be journalist, author, poet, etc., whence **scri′bbl**ER[1] *n.*; ‖**scri′bbling-pad, -paper,** (for casual jottings). **2.** *n.* careless handwriting or thing written in it; scrawl, hasty note, etc.; hence **scri′bbl**Y[2] *a.* [ME, f. med. L *scribillare* dim. of L *scribere* write; see -LE 3]

scri′bble[2] *v.t.* card (wool, cotton) coarsely. [prob. f. LG; cf. syn. G *schrubbeln*, frequent. f. LG *schrubben* (see SCRUB[2])]

scribe *n.*, & *v.t.* **1.** *n.* person who writes or can write; **am no great** ∼, do not write well. **2.** ancient or medieval copyist of manuscripts. **3.** (Bibl.) ancient--Jewish maker and keeper of records etc.; ancient--Jewish professional theologian and jurist. **4.** Hence **scri′b**AL *a.* **5.** ∼(-awl), pointed instrument for marking lines on wood, bricks, etc., to guide saw etc., or for writing words on barrel etc. **6.** *v.t.* mark with scribe; hence **scri′b**ER[1] (2) *n.* [n. ME, f. L *scriba* (*scribere* write); in sense 5 f. v. perh. f. DESCRIBE]

scrim *n.* open-weave esp. cotton fabric for lining, upholstery, *theatre-curtain, etc. [18th c., of unkn. orig.]

scri′mmage *n.* & *v.* **1.** *n.* tussle, confused struggle, row, brawl, skirmish. **2.** (Amer. Footb.) sequence of play beginning with placing of ball on ground with its longest axis at right angles to goal-line. **3.** *v.i.* engage in scrimmage. **4.** *v.t.* put (ball) into scrimmage. [var. of SKIRMISH]

scrimp *v.t.* & *i.* skimp; hence ∼′Y[2] *a.* [18th c., orig. Sc.; perh. cogn. w. SHRIMP]

‖**scri′mshänk** *v.i.* (sl., esp. Mil.) shirk duty; hence ∼ER[1] *n.* [19th c.; orig. unkn.]

scri′mshaw *v.* & *n.* **1.** *v.t.* & *i.* adorn (shells, ivory, etc.), adorn shells etc., with carved or coloured designs (as sailors' amusement at sea). **2.** *n.* (piece of) such work. [19th c.; perh. f. surname]

scrip[1] *n.* (arch.) beggar's or traveller's or pilgrim's wallet, satchel. [ME, f. OF *escrep*(*p*)*e* wallet, var. of *escherpe* SCARF[1], or f. ON *skreppa*]

scrip[2] *n.* **1.** provisional certificate of money subscribed to bank or company entitling holder to formal certificate in due time and to dividends etc.; (collect.) such certificates. **2.** extra share(s) issued in place of dividend. [abbr. of *subscription receipt*]

script *n.*, & *v.t.* **1.** *n.* handwriting, written characters (opp. *print*); printed cursive characters, imitation of handwriting in type; system of writing (*cannot read Russian script*). **2.** text of broadcaster's announcement or talk; text of play, film, etc., ∼-**writer,** writer for films, broadcasting, etc. **3.** ‖examinee's written answer. **4.** (Law). original document (opp. *copy*). **5.** *v.t.* write script for (film etc.). [ME, = thing written, f. OF *escri*(*p*)*t* f. L *scriptum*, neut. p.p. (as n.) of *scribere* write]

scriptor′i′um *n.* (*pl.* ∼a or ∼ums). room set apart for writing esp. in monastery; so ∼AL *a.*, of or for writing. [med. L (as prec.; see -ORY)]

scri′ptural (-cher-, -choor-) *a.* founded on, reconcilable with, laying stress on, appealing to, doctrines contained in the Bible, whence ∼ISM (3), ∼IST (2), *ns.*; of or taken from the Bible; hence ∼LY[2] *adv.*, ∼NESS *n.* [f. LL *scripturalis* f. L *scriptura* (see foll., -AL)]

scri′pture *n.* **1.** (*S*∼; in *sing.* or *pl.*), the Bible with or without the Apocrypha (*a doctrine not found in* (*Holy*) *Scripture* or *the Scriptures*; *a Scripture text*); *a* or *the* quotation from the Bible. **2.** sacred book of non--Christian religion. **3.** (arch.) inscription. [ME, f. L *scriptura* (as SCRIPT; see -URE)]

scri′vener *n.* **1.** (Hist.) copyist, drafter of documents, notary, broker, money-lender. **2.** (arch. or derog.) writer, author; ∼'s palsy, writer's cramp. [ME, f. obs. *scrivener* f. OF *escrivein* f. Rom. *scribano* f. L (as SCRIBE; see -AN) + -ER[1]]

scrobi′culate *a.* (Bot. & Zool.) pitted, furrowed. [f. L *scrobiculus* (*scrobis* trench; see -CULE) + -ATE[2]]

*scröd *n.* young cod. [19th c., of unkn. orig.]

scro′fül‖a *n.* disease with glandular swellings, prob. a form of tuberculosis; hence ∼OUS *a.* [ME, f. med. L sing. f. LL *scrofulae* pl. scrofulous swelling, dim. of L *scrofa* a sow]

scröll *n.* & *v.* **1.** *n.* roll of parchment or paper esp. written on; book or volume of the ancient roll form; (arch.) schedule or list. **2.** ornamental design esp. in architecture carved or drawn or otherwise made to imitate scroll of parchment more or less exactly, scroll-shaped ornament of Ionic capital or of chair etc., head of violin etc., flourish in writing, ribbon bearing heraldic motto, etc. **3.** ∼-**head,** volute at ship's bow; ∼-**lathe** (for spiral work); ∼-**saw,** (1) fretsaw, (2) saw for cutting along curved lines; ∼-**work,** ornament of spiral lines esp. as cut by scroll--saw. **4.** *v.t.* & *i.* curl up like paper. **5.** *v.t.* inscribe (as) in scroll; (esp. in *p.p.*) adorn with scrolls. [ME *scrowle* alt. f. *rowle* ROLL[1], perh. after syn. *scrow* f. as ESCROW]

Scröoge *n.* miser. [character in Dickens's *Christmas Carol*]

scrööp *n.*, & *v.i.* (make) grating noise or crisp rustle of silk. [imit.]

scrö′t‖um *n.* (*pl.* ∼a or ∼ums). (Anat.) pouch of skin containing testicles; hence ∼AL *a.*, ∼I′TIS, ∼OCELE, *ns.* [L]

scroung‖e (-nj) *v.* (sl.) **1.** *v.t.* collect by foraging; take illicitly; cadge. **2.** *v.i.* search about; obtain things by scrounging them. **3.** Hence ∼ER[1] *n.* [var. of dial. *scrunge* steal]

scrub[1] *n.* (ground or region covered with) brushwood or stunted forest growth; stunted or insignificant person, animal, or plant; ∼-**fowl,** ∼-**hen,** ∼-**turkey,** megapode; ∼-**oak,** ∼-**pine,** (dwarf kinds); ∼ **typhus,** rickettsial disease of W. Pacific; ∼ **wallaby,** pademelon; hence ∼'**by**[2] *a.* [ME, var. of SHRUB[1]]

scrub[2] *v.* (-bb-) & *v.* **1.** *v.t.* rub hard to clean or brighten esp. with soap and water applied with hard--bristled brush (∼'**bing-** or *∼-**brush**); (sl.) cancel, scrap; remove impurities etc. from (gas) in scrubber; ∼ **round,** (sl.) circumvent. **2.** *v.i.* use scrubbing--brush or other means of cleaning by hard rubbing; ∼ (**up**), (of surgeon etc.) clean hands and arms by scrubbing, before operation; *∼'**woman,** charwoman. **3.** *n.* scrubbing or being scrubbed; short--bristled brush or moustache. **4.** *(colloq.) player not belonging to regular team; second or weaker team; game of baseball with less than full complement of players. [ME, prob. f. MLG, MDu. *schrobben*, *schrubben*]

scru′bber *n.* In vbl senses: apparatus for purifying gases by passing them through a body or stream of water; (sl.) immoral or sluttish woman. [f. prec. + -ER[1]]

scrüff *n.* back of the neck as used to grasp and lift or drag animal or person by (*take by the scruff of the neck*). [alt. of *scuff*, perh. f. ON *skoft* hair]

scru′ff‖ÿ (-colloq.) scurfy; shabby, slovenly, unkempt, untidy; hence ∼ĭLY[2] *adv.*, ∼ĭNESS *n.* [f. *scruff* var. of SCURF + -Y[2]]

scrüm *n.* = foll.; (colloq.) milling crowd; ∼-**half,** half-back who puts ball into scrum. [abbr.]

scrü′mmage *n.* (Rugby Footb.) grouping of all forwards on each side to push against the other and seek possession of ball on ground between them. [as SCRIMMAGE]

scrump *v.i.* & *t.* steal (esp. fruit). [cf. SCRUMPY]

scru′mptious (-pshus) *a.* (colloq.) delightful, delicious; hence ∼LY[2] *adv.*, ∼NESS *n.* [19th c.; orig. unkn.]

scrü′mpÿ *n.* (esp. dial.) rough cider. [f. dial. *scrump* small apple + -Y[3]]

scrünch *v.* & *n.* = CRUNCH. [var. of CRUNCH]

scru′ple (-ōō'-) *n.* & *v.* **1.** *n.* (‖Hist.) apothecaries' weight-unit of 20 grains; (arch.) very small quantity.

2. (in *sing.* or *pl.*) feeling of doubt or hesitation on grounds of morality or propriety about acting or approving of action, conscientious objection, (**make no ∼ to do**, do without such hesitation or with easy conscience). **3.** *v.i.* feel or be influenced by scruples; (esp. w. neg.) hesitate owing to scruples *to do* **4.** *v.t.* (arch.) be deterred from or hindered in (doing, action) by scruples. [f. F *scrupule* or f. L *scrupulus* (*scrupus* rough pebble, anxiety; see -ULE)]

scru'pulous (-ŏŏ'-) *a.* **1.** careful to avoid doing wrong, conscientious even in small matters, not neglectful of details, punctilious, marked by extreme thoroughness, unfailing, (*a scrupulous person*; *scrupulous honesty, cleanliness, care, methods, respect, attention,* etc.). **2.** over-attentive to details, esp. to small points of conscience. **3.** Hence **scrupulo'sity** (-ŏŏp-) *n.*, ∼LY² *adv.*, ∼NESS *n.* [ME, f. F *scrupuleux* or f. L *scrupulosus* (as prec.; see -OUS)]

scruta'tor (-ŏŏ-) *n.* examiner, scrutineer; person given to scrutiny. [L (as SCRUTINY; see -OR)]

scrutineer' (-ŏŏ-) *n.* person checking ballot papers and counting votes. [f. SCRUTINY + -EER]

scru'tinize, -ise, (-ŏŏ'tĭnīz) *v.t.* look closely at, examine in detail. [f. foll. + -IZE]

scru'tiny (-ŏŏ'-) *n.* critical gaze, close investigation, examination into details; official examination of votes cast in election to check their validity or accuracy of counting. [ME, f. L *scrutinium* (*scrutari* search f. *scruta* rubbish; orig. of rag-pickers)]

scry *v.i.* use the crystal in crystal-gazing: hence ∼'ER¹ *n.* [f. DESCRY]

scu'ba (-ū'-, -ŏŏ'-) *n.* self-contained underwater breathing apparatus; aqualung. [acronym]

scud *v.i.* (-dd-), & *n.* **1.** *v.i.* run or fly straight and fast esp. with smooth easy motion, skim along; (Naut.) run before the wind. **2.** *n.* spell of scudding; vapoury driving clouds; driving shower; gust; wind-blown spray. [perh. alt. of SCUT]

scuff *v.* & *n.* **1.** *v.i.* walk with dragging feet, shuffle with the feet; *poke at* with foot. **2.** *v.t.* graze or brush or scrape against; wear away or mark thus. **3.** *n.* mark of scuffing; backless slipper. [imit.]

scu'ffle *v.i.* & *n.* (engage in) confused struggle or disorderly fight at close quarters. [prob. f. Scand.; cf. Sw. *skuffa* to push, cogn. w. SHOVE]

sculdu'ddery, sculdu'ggery (-g-), Vars. of SKULDUGGERY.

scull *n.* & *v.* **1.** *n.* one of pair of small oars used by single rower each with one hand; oar resting on boat's stern and worked with twisting strokes to propel like ship's screw; (in *pl.*) sculling-race. **2.** *v.t.* & *i.* propel (boat), propel boat, with sculls; (colloq.) lie or move aimlessly *about*. [ME, of unkn. orig.]

scu'ller *n.* user of scull(s); boat intended for sculling. [f. prec. + -ER¹]

scu'llery *n.* back kitchen, room for washing up dishes etc. [ME, f. AF *squillerie,* OF *escuelerie* (*escuele* dish f. L *scutella* salver dim. of *scutra* wooden platter; see -ERY)]

scu'llion (-yon) *n.* (arch.) cook's boy, washer of dishes and pots. [ME, of unkn. orig.]

sculp *v.t.* & *i.* (colloq.) sculpture. [f. L *sculpere;* now regarded as abbr.]

scu'lpin *n.* small American fish of family Cottidae, with large spiny head. [perh. f. obs. *scorpene* f. L f. Gk *skorpaina* a fish]

sculpt *v.t.* & *i.* (colloq.) sculpture. [f. F *sculpter* (*sculpteur* = foll.); now regarded as abbr.]

scu'lpt|or *n.* one who sculptures; hence ∼rESS¹ *n.* [L (as foll.; see -OR)]

scu'lptur|e *n.* & *v.* **1.** *n.* art of forming representations of objects etc. or abstract designs in the round or in relief by chiselling stone, carving wood, modelling clay, casting metal, or similar processes; a work of sculpture; (Zool. & Bot.) raised or sunk markings on shell etc.; hence ∼AL, ∼E'SQUE, (-cher-) *adjs.* **2.** *v.t.* represent in sculpture; shape like sculpture; adorn with sculpture; (in *p.p.,* Zool. & Bot.) having sculp-

ture. **3.** *v.i.* practise sculpture. [ME, f. L *sculptura* (*sculpere sculpt-* carve; see -URE)]

scum *n.* & *v.* (-mm-). **1.** *n.* impurities that rise to surface of liquid esp. in boiling or fermentation, floating film; (fig.) worst part, refuse, offscourings, (*of*), worthless person(s); hence ∼'my² *a.* **2.** *v.t.* take scum from, skim; be or form a scum on. **3.** *v.i.* (Of liquid) develop scum. [ME, f. MLG, MDu. *schūm,* OHG *scūm* f. Gmc *skūma-* (*skū-* cover)]

scu'mble *v.t.,* & *n.* **1.** *v.t.* modify (painting) by applying thin opaque coat to give softer or duller effect; modify (drawing) similarly with light pencilling etc. **2.** *n.* scumbling material or effect produced by it. [perh. frequent. of prec. 2; cf. -LE 3]

scu'ncheon (-nchon) *n.* inside face of door-jamb, window-frame, etc. [ME, f. OF *escoinson* (as EX-¹, COIN¹)]

scu'nner *n.,* & *v.i.* **1.** *n.* strong dislike (*take a scunner at, against*); object of loathing. **2.** *v.i.* (Sc.) feel sick, be nauseated. [n. f. v., ME, of unkn. orig.]

scup *n.* E. Amer. fish of genus *Stenostomus,* kind of porgy. [f. Narraganset *mishcup* thick-scaled (*mishe* large, *cuppi* scale)]

scu'pper¹ *n.* hole in ship's side to carry off water off deck. [ME, perh. f. AF, f. OF *escopir* f. Rom. *skuppire to spit, orig. imit.]

||**scu'pper²** *v.t.* (sl.) surprise and massacre; sink (ship, crew); defeat, discomfit. [19th c. Mil.; orig. unkn.]

***scu'ppernong** *n.* muscadine grape; wine from it. [f. river S∼ in N. Carolina]

scurf *n.* flakes on surface of skin cast off as fresh skin develops below, esp. those of head, dandruff; any scaly matter on a surface; ∼ **pea,** plant of genus *Psoralea* used against itch etc.; hence ∼'y² *a.* [OE, prob. f. ON *skurfr & earlier OE *sceorf* cogn. w. *sceorfan* gnaw, *sceorfian* cut to shreds]

scu'rrile *a.* (arch.) = foll. [F, or f. L *scurrilis* (*scurra* buffoon; see -IL)]

scu'rril|ous *a.* (Of person or language) grossly or obscenely abusive; given to or expressed with low buffoonery; hence or cogn. ∼OUSLY⁷ *adv.,* ∼ITY (-ĭl'-) *n.* [f. prec. + -OUS]

scu'rry *v.i.,* & *n.* **1.** *v.i.* run or move hurriedly esp. with short quick steps, scamper, (*the scurrying mice*). **2.** *n.* act or sound of scurrying; haste, bustle; flurry of rain or snow. [abbr. of *hurry-scurry* redupl. of HURRY²]

scu'rv|y *a.* & *n.* **1.** *a.* paltry, low, mean, dishonourable, contemptible, (*a scurvy trick, fellow*); hence ∼iLY² *adv.* **2.** *n.* deficiency disease from lack of vitamin C, with swollen gums, livid spots, and prostration, attacking those (esp. formerly sailors etc.) who live without fresh vegetables; ∼**y-grass,** kind of cress used against scurvy or as salad; hence ∼iED² (-vĭd) *a.* [f. SCURF + -Y²; n. sense by assoc. w. F *scorbut* (cf. SCORBUTIC)]

scut *n.* short tail esp. of hare, rabbit, or deer. [ME, orig. unkn.; cf. obs. *scut* short(en)]

scu'tage *n.* (Hist.) money paid by feudal land-owner in lieu of personal service. [ME, f. med. L *scutagium* f. L *scutum* shield; see -AGE]

scutch *v.t.,* & *n.* **1.** *v.t.* dress (fibrous material, esp. retted flax) by beating; ∼**-blade,** ∼'ER¹ (2) *ns.,* implements for scutching. **2.** *n.* scutcher. [f. OF *escouche, escoucher* (dial.), *escousser,* f. Rom. *excussare f. L EX¹(*cutere cuss-* = *quatere* shake)]

scu'tcheon (-chon) *n.* **1.** = ESCUTCHEON. **2.** ornamented brass etc. plate round or over keyhole; plate for name or inscription. [ME, f. ESCUTCHEON]

scute *n.* = SCUTUM. [f. L (as SCUTUM)]

scute'll|um *n.* (*pl.* ∼a). (Bot. & Zool.) shield, plate, or scale, in plant, insect, bird, etc., esp. one of the horny scales on birds' feet; hence **scu'tell**ATE² *a.,* ∼A'TION *n.* [mod. L, dim. of L *scutum*]

scu'tter *v.i.,* & *n.* (colloq.) scurry. [perh. alt. of SCUTTLE³; cf. -ER⁵]

scu'ttle¹ *n.* coal-box; ||part of motor-car body immediately behind bonnet. [ME, f. ON *skutill,* OHG *scuzzila* f. L *scutella* dish]

scu'ttle[2] *n.*, & *v.t.* **1.** *n.* hole with lid in wall or roof of house or ship's deck, side, or hatchway-covering; **~-butt,** water-butt usu. on deck with hole in top for dipping from, (sl.) rumour, gossip. **2.** *v.t.* make hole(s) in (ship), open sea-cocks of (ship), esp. for purpose of sinking. [ME, perh. f. obs. F *escoutille* f. Sp. *escotilla* hatchway dim. of *escota* cutting out cloth (*escotar* f. as EX-[1] + Gmc **skaut-*; cf. SHEET[1])]

scu'ttle[3] *v.i.*, & *n.* **1.** *v.i.* hurry along, scurry; run away, flee from danger or difficulty. **2.** *n.* hurried gait; precipitate flight or departure. [cf. dial. *scuddle* frequent. of SCUD; see -LE 3]

scu't|um *n.* (*pl.* **~a**). (Zool. etc.) shieldlike plate or scale, piece of bony armour in crocodile, sturgeon, turtle, armadillo, etc.; hence **~AL, ~ATE**[2], **~iFORM,** *adjs.* [L, = oblong shield]

Scy'lla *n.* **~ and Charybdis,** two dangers such that to avoid one increases the risk from the other. [f. names of sea-monster and whirlpool in Gk Myth.]

scÿphozö'an *a.* & *n.* (member) of class of coelenterates comprising true marine jellyfishes. [f. as foll. + -o- + Gk *zōion* animal +-AN]

scÿ'ph|us *n.* (*pl.* **~i** *pr.* -ī). **1.** (Gk Ant.) footless drinking-cup with two handles not higher than rim. **2.** (Bot.) cup-shaped part as in narcissus flower or in lichens, whence **~OSE**[1] *a.* **3.** Hence **~iFORM** *a.* [mod. L, Gk *skuphos*]

scythe (-dh) *n.*, & *v.t.* **1.** *n.* mowing and reaping implement of long slightly curved blade swung over ground by long usu. crooked pole with two short handles projecting at right angles from it; blade continuing axle of ancient war-chariot at each end, whence **scÿthED**[2] (-dhd) *a.* **2.** *v.t.* cut with scythe. [OE *sīthe,* = MLG *segede,* ON *sigthr* f. Gmc **segithō* (**seg-* cut), w. sp. prob. after *scissors*]

Scÿ'thian (-dh-, -th-) *a.* & *n.* (inhabitant or language) of ancient Scythia, region north of Black Sea. [f. L f. Gk *Skuthia* Scythia + -AN]

SD, S.Dak., *abbrs.* South Dakota.

SDR *abbr.* special drawing right (from International Monetary Fund).

se- *pref.* denoting 'apart, without' (*seclude, secure*). [L, f. OL *se* prep. & adv.]

SE *abbr.* South-East(ern).

Se *symb.* selenium.

sea *n.* **1.** expanse of salt water that covers most of earth's surface and encloses its continents and islands, the ocean, any part of this as opposed to dry land or fresh water, (*by sea and land; at the bottom of the sea; jumped into the sea*); **at ~,** away from (esp. out of sight of) land; (**all**) **at ~,** (fig.) perplexed, not knowing how to proceed; **beyond ~(s),** = OVERSEA(s)[1,2]; **by ~,** in ship(s); **follow the ~,** be sailor; **go to ~,** become sailor; **HIGH** *seas;* **on the ~,** (1) in ship etc., (2) situated on coast; **put (out) to ~,** leave land or port. **2.** particular tract of sea partly or sometimes wholly enclosed by land and usu. distinguished by special name (*the North, Mediterranean, Caspian, Dead, Sea*); freshwater lake (*Sea of Galilee*); **inland ~** (entirely land-locked); **the seven ~s,** Arctic, Antarctic, N. Pacific, S. Pacific, N. Atlantic, S. Atlantic, and Indian, Oceans. **3.** local motion or state of the sea; swell, great billow (*seas mountains high*); HALF-*seas-over;* **heavy ~** (with great waves); **long ~** (with long regular waves); SHIP[2] *a sea;* **short ~** (choppy and irregularly agitated). **4.** vast quantity or expanse of (*a sea of troubles, care, flame, upturned faces*); **~s of blood,** ruthless bloodshed. **5.** (Bibl.) = LAVER[2] 1. **6.** (*attrib.* and in *comb.*) living or used in or on, of, near, like, the sea (often prefixed to name of animal, fruit, etc., to form name of marine thing with merely superficial resemblance to what it is named after, as *sea canary, cucumber, -fox, raven*); **~ acorn,** barnacle; **~ air,** air at seaside esp. as recommended for invalids etc.; **~ anchor,** baglike contrivance to retard drifting and maintain direction of ship or seaplane; *sea* ANEMONE; **~-angel,** angel-fish; **~-arrow,** flying

squid; **~-bank,** = *sea-wall;* **~ bass,** sea-fish like bass, esp. *Centropristis striatus;* **~ bear,** (1) polar bear, (2) fur-seal; ***~bee,** member of naval construction battalion [f. *CB*]; **~-bells,** seashore bindweed; **~-belt,** seaweed with belt-like fronds; **~-bird** (frequenting sea or land near sea); **~ blubber,** jellyfish; **~'board,** seashore, coast region, line of coast; **~-boat,** (1) ship etc. having (specified) sea-going qualities, (2) boat which can be lowered quickly in emergency at sea; **~-boot,** sailor's high waterproof boot; **~-born,** (poet., esp. of Aphrodite) born in the sea; **~-borne,** conveyed by sea (*sea-borne commerce, goods*); **~-bow,** rainbow effect in sea-spray; *sea*-BREAM[1]; **~-breeze** (blowing landward from sea esp. during day in alternation with land-breeze at night); **~ breeze,** any breeze at sea; **~ buckthorn,** maritime shrub (*Hippophaë rhamnoides*) with orange berries; **~ butterfly,** pteropod; **~ cabbage,** sea-kale; **~-calf,** common seal; **~ canary,** white whale (from its whistling); **~ captain,** past or present captain of ship in navy or merchant service, (poet. or rhet.) great sailor or commander at sea; **~ change,** (unexpected or notable) transformation (w. ref. to Shak. *Tempest* I. ii. 400); **~-chest,** sailor's storage-chest; **~-cloth** (used in theatre to represent waves); **~ coal,** (arch.) coal (opp. *charcoal* etc.); *sea*-COAST[1]; **~-cock,** (1) grey plover, (2) valve by which sea-water can be let into ship's interior; **~ cook,** cook on board ship (esp. *son of a ~ cook* as Naut. term of abuse); **~-cow,** (1) sirenian, (2) walrus, (3) hippopotamus; **~ cucumber,** holothurian, esp. *bêche-de-mer;* **~-devil,** (1) devil inhabiting sea, (2) devil-fish or other ugly fish; **~-dog,** (1) common seal, (2) old sailor (esp. of the Elizabethan sea captains), (3) light near horizon thought to presage bad weather; **~ eagle,** fish-eating eagle esp. of genus *Haliaëtus;* **~-ear,** abalone; **~ elephant,** large seal of genus *Mirounga,* with proboscis in male; **~-fan,** fanlike polyp; **~'farer,** sailor; **~'faring** & *n.* traversing the seas, esp. habitually; **~ fennel,** samphire; **~-fight** (between warships); **~-fish** (opp. freshwater fish); **~-flower,** sea ANEMONE; **~ fog** (caused by difference of land and sea temperatures and extending only short way inland); **~'food,** edible salt-water (shell)fish; **~-fowl,** sea-bird; **~-fox,** thresher shark; **~ front,** part of town facing sea; **~ furbelow,** a brown seaweed (*Laminaria bulbosa*); **~ gherkin,** small sea cucumber; **~-girdle,** sea-belt; **~-girt,** (poet. or rhet., of island etc.) surrounded by sea; **~'going,** (of ship) for crossing sea, not coasting or river use, (of person) seafaring; **~ gooseberry,** ctenophore; **~ grape,** (1) glasswort, (2) sargasso, (3) W. Ind. tree with grapelike fruit, (4) (in *pl.*) cuttlefish eggs; **~-grass,** grasslike plant growing in or near sea; **~-green** *a.* & *n.*, (of) bluish green as of sea; **~-gull,** = GULL[1]; **~-hare,** mollusc of genus *Tethys* with tentacles like projecting ears; **~ hedgehog,** sea-urchin; **~-hog,** porpoise; **~ holly,** spiny-leaved blue-flowered evergreen plant; **~-horse,** (1) mythical creature harnessed to sea-god's chariot having horse's head and fish's tail, (2) walrus, (3) hippocampus; **~-island (cotton),** fine quality of long-stapled cotton orig. grown on islands off Georgia and S. Carolina; **~-kale,** perennial herb (*Crambe maritima*) with young shoots used as table vegetable; **~-kale beet,** chard; **~ kidney,** kidney-shaped coelenterate; **~-king,** medieval Scandinavian pirate chief; **~ lace,** kind of seaweed with long cordlike fronds; **~ lane,** lane (sense 4) for sea traffic; **~ lavender,** lavender-like orig. maritime shrub or rock-plant; **~ lawyer,** (1) shark, (2) (Naut. term of contempt for) captious person; **~-legs,** ability to walk on deck of rolling ship (*has not yet got his sea-legs*); **~ lemon,** yellow oval mollusc of family Dorididae; **~ leopard,** spotted species of seal; **~-letter,** official protective letter carried by neutral ship in wartime, describing her cargo, crew, etc.;

∼-**level,** level continuous with that of sea half-way between high and low water, used in reckoning height of hills etc. and as a barometric standard; ∼-**lift,** transport of supplies etc. by sea; ∼ **lily,** crinoid; ∼-**line,** (1) coastline, (2) horizon at sea; ∼-**lion,** large eared seal of Pacific esp. of genus *Zalophus* or *Otaria;* ∼ **lizard,** gastropod of genus *Glaucus;* ∼ **loch,** = LOCH 2; ||**Sea Lord,** naval member of Admiralty Board; ∼-**mark,** beacon, lighthouse, etc., or elevated conspicuous object, used to direct course at sea; ∼-**mat,** bryozoan forming flat matted crust; ∼ **melon,** holothurian of family Pentactidae; ∼-**mew,** GULL¹; *sea* MILE; ∼ **monster,** any huge, terrible, or strange (esp. mythical) sea-animal; ∼ **moss,** mosslike bryozoan or seaweed; ∼'**mount,** underwater mountain; ∼-**mouse,** iridescent sea-worm of genus *Aphrodite;* ∼-**mud,** saline deposit of salt marshes etc. used as manure; ∼ **necklace,** string of whelk egg-cases; ∼ **nettle,** stinging jellyfish; ∼ **oak,** seaweed of genus *Fucus;* ∼-**onion,** = SQUILL 2; ∼ **orange,** globose orange-coloured holothurian; ∼ **otter,** Pacific otter with very valuable fur; ∼ **parrot,** puffin; ∼-**pass,** = *sea-letter;* ∼-**pay** (for active service at sea); ∼-**pea,** purple-flowered plant (*Lathyrus maritimus*) growing on shore; ∼ **peach, pear,** ascidians resembling these fruits; ∼-**pen,** feather shaped polyp; ∼ **pie,** (1) sailors' pie of salt meat etc., (2) ||oyster-catcher; ∼-**piece,** picture of scene at sea; ∼-**pig,** (1) porpoise, (2) dugong; ∼-**pike,** sea-fish like pike, e.g. garfish, hake; ∼ **pilot,** oyster-catcher; ∼ **pincushion,** skate's egg-case; ∼-**pink,** seashore or Alpine plant with bright pink flowers, species of thrift; ∼'**plane,** aeroplane constructed for rising from and alighting on water; ∼'**port,** town with harbour; ∼ **power,** (1) ability to control and make successful use of the sea, esp. in maritime warfare, (2) State having this; ∼ **pumpkin,** = *sea melon;* ∼-**purse,** egg-case of skate or shark; ∼'**quake,** submarine earthquake; ∼ **raven,** species of sculpin (*Hemitripterus americanus*); *∼-**robin,** red gurnard; ∼-**room,** clear space at sea allowing ship to turn etc.; ∼ **rover,** pirate (ship); ∼-**salt** (got by evaporating sea-water); ∼'**scape,** picture or view of sea; **Sea Scout,** member of maritime branch of SCOUT¹s; ∼ **serpent,** (1) snake of family Hydrophidae living in sea, (2) enormous serpentine sea monster often reported as seen but never identified with known species; *sea-*SHANTY²; ∼ **shell,** shell of any salt-water mollusc; ∼-**shore,** land close to sea, (Law) area between high and low water marks; ∼'**sick,** vomiting or inclined to vomit from motion of ship etc., whence ∼'**sickness;** ∼'**side,** edge of sea, (place or places on) sea-coast esp. as holiday resort (*do you like the seaside?; must go to the seaside*); ∼ **slug,** (1) sea cucumber, (2) marine gastropod with internal or no shell; ∼ **snail,** (1) small slimy fish with ventral sucker, of family Liparididae, (2) spiral-shelled mollusc, e.g. whelk; ∼ **snake,** = *sea serpent;* ∼ **snipe,** (1) sandpiper, (2) snipe-fish; ∼-**squirt,** ascidian (squirting water when touched); ∼ **swallow,** tern; *sea-*TANG²(*le*); ∼-**thrift,** = *sea-pink;* ∼-**toad,** the angler-fish; ∼ **trout,** salmon trout; *sea-*UNICORN; ∼-**urchin,** marine animal of order Echinoidea, esp. globular sharp-spined kind; ∼-**wall,** wall or embankment made to prevent encroachment by the sea; ∼-**ware,** seaweed collected for manure or other uses; ∼-**way,** (1) ship's progress, (2) place where ship lies in open water, (3) inland waterway open to seagoing ships; ∼'**weed,** any alga growing in sea; ∼'**whip,** = *sea-fan;* ∼-**wife,** species of wrasse; ∼-**wind,** = *sea-breeze;* ∼-**wolf,** (1) sea elephant, (2) bass or wolf-fish, (3) pirate; ∼'**worthy,** (of ship) in fit state to put to sea, strong and well rigged etc.; *sea-*WRACK. **7.** Hence ∼'WARD *a., adv., & n.,* ∼'WARDS *adv.* [OE *sǣ,* = OS, OHG *sēo,* ON *sær,* Goth. *saiws* f. Gmc **saiwiz*]

seal¹ *n., & v.i.* **1.** *n.* fish-eating amphibious marine mammal of family Phocidae or Otariidae, with short limbs modified to serve chiefly for swimming but having fur or bristles; **eared** ∼ (of Otariidae, distinguished from **common** ∼, *Phoca vitulina,* and other Phocidae by larger size and visible external ears, e.g. sea-lion, sea elephant, and fur-seals); sealskin; ∼-**fishery,** ∼'ERY *n.,* (place for) hunting of seals; *seal-*ROOKERY; ∼'**skin,** skin of seal or usu. (garment made from) prepared fur of seals as clothing material. **3.** *v.i.* hunt seals. [OE *seolh seol-,* = MLG *sēl,* OHG *selah,* ON *selr* f. Gmc **selhaz*]

seal² *n. & v.t.* **1.** *n.* piece of wax, lead, or other such material, impressed with device and attached in some way to document usu. in addition to signature as guarantee of authenticity (**given under my hand and** ∼, signed and sealed by me; **set** one's ∼ **to, set the** ∼ **on,** authorize or confirm) or to envelope or to any receptacle such as box or room or house to prevent its being opened unknown to owner etc. (**leaden** ∼, stamped piece of lead holding ends of a wire used as fastening; **under** ∼ **of** *confession, confidence,* etc., subject to secrecy on stated grounds); impression stamped on or paper disc stuck to document as symbol equivalent to wax seal; adhesive stamp symbolizing a charity etc. **2.** (fig.) significant or prophetic mark (*has the seal of death in his face*). **3.** gem, engraved piece of metal, etc., serving as stamp to produce seal on wax etc. or paper (∼-**ring,** finger-ring with seal); ||∼**s of office,** those held during tenure esp. by Lord Chancellor or Secretary of State; ||**Great S**∼, seal in charge of Lord Chancellor or Lord Keeper used in sealing Parliament-writs, treaties, and important State papers; ||PRIVY *seal.* **4.** act done, thing given, event regarded, as confirmation or guarantee *of* (∼ **of love,** kiss, birth of child, etc.). **5.** substance used to close aperture etc., esp. water standing in drain-trap to prevent ascent of foul air. **6.** ∼-**wort,** (1) SOLOMON's seal, (2) pearlwort. **7.** *v.t.* affix seal to; stamp or fasten with seal; certify as correct with seal or stamp (**S**∼**ed Book,** one of the presumed perfect copies of Book of Common Prayer certified by Great Seal in 1662 and deposited in cathedrals etc.); show genuineness of (devotion etc.) *with* one's life etc. **8.** close securely or hermetically, stop up or *up,* (**my lips are** ∼**ed,** the matter is a secret and I must not speak of it; **is a** ∼**ed book to me,** is something of which I have and can get no knowledge; ∼**ed orders,** orders for procedure, not to be examined before specified time; *sealed* VERDICT); provide (pipe etc.) with water-seal by means of trap etc.; provide (road) with smooth surface of tar macadam etc.; record (chess move to be made after adjournment period); ∼**off,** cut off (an area) to prevent entry or exit; hence ∼'ANT *n.* **9.** set significant mark on, set apart, destine, decide irrevocably, (*death has sealed her for his own; is sealed to* or *for salvation* etc.; *his fate is sealed*); ||∼**ed pattern,** standard pattern of equipment, clothing, etc., approved for use by armed forces etc. **10.** ∼ (up), confine securely. **11.** ∼'**ing-wax,** mixture of shellac and rosin with turpentine and pigment, softened by heating and used for seals. [ME, f. AF *seal,* OF *seel*(*er*) f. L *sigillum* dim. of *signum* SIGN¹]

sea'ler *n.* In vbl senses; ship or person engaged in seal-hunting; inspector of weights and measures. [f. SEAL¹,², & -ER¹]

Sea'lyham (-liam) *n.* ∼ (**terrier**), breed of wire-haired short-legged terrier. [∼ in Dyfed, Wales]

seam *n., & v.t.* **1.** *n.* line of junction between two edges esp. those of two pieces of cloth, leather, etc., turned back and sewn together or of boards fitted edge to edge; fissure left by gaping of parallel edges (*ship's seams need caulking*); scar or wrinkle; **bursting** etc. **at the** ∼**s,** full to overflowing. **2.** line of separation between two strata; stratum of coal etc. **3.** ∼ **bowler,** ∼'ER¹ *n.,* (Cricket) one who makes the ball move off its seam when it bounces. **4.** Hence ∼'LESS *a.* **5.** *v.t.* unite with seam; (esp. in *p.p.*) mark or score with seam, fissure, or scar; ∼'**ing-lace,** galloon or other trimming sewn over seams in upholstery etc. [OE *sēam*, = MDu. *sōm*, OHG *soum*, ON *saumr* f. Gmc **saumaz* (**sau-*, **su-* SEW)]

sea′man *n.* (*pl.* **sea′men**). one whose occupation is on the sea, esp. if below rank of officer (ABLE-*bodied*, ‖LEADING², °ORDINARY, *seaman*); person skilled in navigation etc.; hence ∼LIKE, ∼LY¹, *adjs.*, ∼SHIP (3) *n.* [OE *sēman(n)* (as SEA, MAN¹)]

sea′mstress, sĕ′mpstress, (sĕ′ms-) *n.* sewing-woman. [OE *sēamestre* fem. (*sēamere* tailor, f. as SEAM +-ER¹, +-STER) +-ESS¹]

sea′mÿ *a.* showing seams; ∼ **side,** inside of garment etc. where rough edges of seams are visible, (esp., fig.) less presentable or attractive aspect *of life* etc. [f. SEAM +-Y²]

Sea′nad (shă′nadh) *n.* upper house of Parliament in the Republic of Ireland. [Ir., = senate]

se′ance (sā′-), **séance** (sā′ahṅs), *n.* session of a society or deliberative body; meeting for exhibition or investigation of spiritualistic phenomena. [f. F *séance* f. OF *seoir* f. L *sedēre* sit; see -ANCE]

sear¹ *a.,* & *v.t.,* **sēre²** *a.* **1.** *a.* (literary). (Of leaf, flower, etc., and fig. of age etc.) withered, dried up (**the ∼, the yellow leaf,** old age). **2.** *v.t.* scorch esp. with hot iron, cauterize, brand; make callous (*a seared conscience*); (arch.) blast, wither; ∼′**ing-iron** (for cauterizing). [OE *sēar* a., *sēarian* v., f. Gmc **sauraz, *saurōjan*]

sear². See SERE¹.

search (sĕr-) *v.* & *n.* **1.** *v.t.* look or feel or go over (person or his face or pockets, place, receptacle, book) for what may be found or to find something of which presence is suspected, probe (lit. or fig.; *search a wound,* one's *conscience*); ∼ **me!** *int.* (colloq., implying that the speaker does not know the answer to some inquiry, what to do, etc.). **2.** cover (area) with gun-fire. **3.** ∼ **out,** (arch.) ∼, look for, seek out. **4.** *v.i.* make search or investigation (*for,* or abs.); (in *pres. part.,* of examination etc.) thorough, leaving no loopholes, whence ∼′**ingLY**² *adv.* **5.** Hence ∼′ER¹ (1, 2) *n.* **6.** *n.* act of searching, investigation, quest, (*after* or *for*); **in** ∼ **of,** trying to find; **right of** ∼, belligerent's right to scour neutral vessel and search it for contraband. **7.** ∼′**light,** (1) outdoor electric lamp with concentrated powerful beam that can be turned in any direction for use during darkness esp. for discovering hostile aircraft, lost person, etc., (2) light from this (lit. or fig.; cf. LIME¹*light*); ∼-**party,** persons going out to look for lost or concealed person or thing; ∼-**warrant** (granted by Justice of the Peace etc. to enter premises of person suspected of concealing stolen property etc.). **8.** Hence ∼′LESS *a.,* (poet.) inscrutable. [ME, f. AF *sercher,* OF *cerchier* f. LL *circare* go round (as CIRCUS)]

sea′son (-z-) *n.* & *v.* **1.** *n.* proper time, favourable opportunity, time at which something is plentiful or in vogue or active; time of year when plant flourishes, or animal breeds or is hunted (‖CLOSE¹, ‖OPEN¹, *season*); time of year regularly devoted to an activity (*cricket season*) or to social activities generally (*London in the season*); time of year when a place is most frequented (HIGH, LOW¹, OFF-, *season*); **compliments of the** ∼ (esp. w. ref. to Christmas); **in** ∼, (of foodstuff) available in good condition and plentifully, (of animal) on heat, (of advice etc.) given when likely to be taken or needed (*a word in season*); **in and out of** ∼, at all times indiscriminately. **2.** period of indefinite or various length (*may endure for a season*); ∼(-**ticket**) (issued at fixed charge for any number of specified journeys taken, performances attended, etc., within a specified period). **3.** division of the year with distinguishable characteristics of temperature, rainfall, vegetation, etc. (**the four ∼s,** spring, summer, autumn, winter); **dry, rainy,** ∼, two seasons recognized in the tropics instead of the four of temperate countries. **4.** Hence ∼AL, ∼LESS, *adjs.* **5.** *v.t.* bring into efficient or sound condition by habitua-

tion, acclimatization, exposure, special preparation, use, or lapse of time, inure, mature, (*seasoned soldiers, timber*). **6.** make palatable or piquant by introduction of salt, condiments, wit, jests, etc., give zest to, flavour, (*highly seasoned dishes; conversation seasoned with humour*), whence ∼ER¹ (2), ∼ING¹ (4), *ns.*; temper, moderate, (*let mercy season justice*). **7.** *v.i.* become fit for use by being seasoned. [ME f. OF (*saisonner* f.) *seson* f. L *satio -onis* (*serere sat-* sow; see -ION) in Rom. sense seed-time]

sea′sonab|le (-z-) *a.* suitable to, of the kind usual at, the season (esp. of weather, frost etc. in winter); opportune, meeting the needs of the occasion, (*seasonable aid, caution,* etc.; *the seasonable arrival of*); hence ∼**le**NESS (-beln-) *n.,* ∼LY² *adv.* [ME, f. prec. +-ABLE]

seat *n.,* & *v.t.* **1.** *n.* thing used, esp. one made, for sitting on, chair, throne, stool, bench, bicycle-saddle, or other sitting-accommodation; place for one person in theatre, vehicle, etc.; occupation of a seat (*took his seat on the throne, a rock*); **take a** ∼, sit down; ∼-**belt,** safety belt for seated person in vehicle or aircraft; *∼-**mate,** person occupying seat paired with one's own in vehicle etc.; ∼-**mile,** distance of one mile travelled by one passenger; hence ∼′ING¹ (6) *n.,* ∼′ER¹ *n.,* motor car, aeroplane, etc., with seats for specified number. **2.** part of chair etc. on which sitter's weight directly rests, part of machine that supports another part (∼ **of valve,** surface etc. on which it slides or works). **3.** buttocks, part of trousers etc. covering them; *drive* etc. **by the** ∼ **of** one's **pants,** (colloq.) by instinct rather than rule. **4.** site or location, temporary or permanent scene, abiding-place, *of* (*the liver is the seat of the disease; the seat of war is mountainous; an ancient seat of learning*); ∼-**earth,** stratum underlying coal-seam. **5.** country mansion esp. with park or large grounds (*has a seat in Norfolk; the country seats of England*). **6.** right to sitting-accommodation or to sit as member of board or esp. House of Commons (**lose** one's ∼, fail to secure re-election to Parliament); authority or dignity symbolized by sitting in particular chair or throne. **7.** manner of sitting on horse etc. (*has a good, firm, graceful,* etc., *seat*). **8.** Hence ∼′LESS *a.* **9.** *v.t.* make sit, place or establish in seat, place one*self* in sitting posture, (in *p.p.*) sitting, (*took up the child and seated him on the bookcase; seated himself in state; found him seated on an inverted bucket*); **be** ∼**ed,** sit down. **10.** fit or provide (church, room, etc.) with seats; (of room etc.) have seats for (specified number). **11.** mend seat of (chair, trousers). **12.** establish in position, fix in particular place; put (machinery) on its supports; DEEP³-*seated*. [ME, f. ON *sæti* = OE *gesete,* MDu. *gesæte,* OHG *gasāzi* f. Gmc **gasætjam* (**sæt-, *set-* SIT)]

SEATO (sē′tō) *abbr.* South-East Asia Treaty Organization.

sĕbā′ceous (-shus) *a.* of tallow or fat, fatty; ∼ **gland, follicle, duct,** (secreting or conveying oily matter to lubricate skin and hair). [f. L *sebaceus* (*sebum* tallow); see -ACEOUS]

sĕbĕ′sten *n.* (plumlike fruit of) an E. Ind. tree (*Cordia myxa*). [ME f. med. L, f. Arab. *sabastān* f. Pers. *sapistān*]

‖**sĕborrhoe′|a, *sĕborrhē′|a,** (-rē′a) *n.* (Path.) excessive discharge from sebaceous glands; hence ∼IC *a.* [f. foll. after *gonorrhoea* etc.]

sē′bum *n.* secretion of sebaceous glands. [mod. L, f. L *sebum* grease]

sec (sĕk) *a.* (Of wine) dry. [F, f. L *siccus*]

SEC *abbr.* Securities & Exchange Commission.

Sec. *abbr.* Secretary.

sec *abbr.* secant.

sec. *abbr.* second(s); secondary.

sĕ′cant *a.* & *n.* (Math.) **1.** *a.* cutting (*secant line*). **2.** *n.* secant line, esp. radius of circle produced through one end of arc to meet tangent to other end; ratio of this to radius; ∼ **of angle,** ratio of greater to less of its containing lines as bounded by a perpendicular to either. [f. F *sécant(e)* f. L *secare* cut; see -ANT]

‖**sěcateurs** (sĕkatēr'z, sē'-) *n.* pair of pruning clippers used with one hand. [f. F *sécateur* cutter, irreg. f. L *secare* cut]

sě'cco *n.* (*pl.* ~**s**). painting on dry plaster with pigments suspended in water. [It., = dry, f. L *siccus*]

sěcě'd|e *v.i.* withdraw formally from membership of some body, esp. a Church or federation of States; hence ~ER[1] *n.* [f. L SE(*cedere cess-* go)]

sěcě'ssion (-shon) *n.* act of seceding (**War of S~**, American civil war of 1861-5, caused by secession of eleven Southern States); hence ~AL *a.*, -ISM (3), ~IST (2), *ns.* [f. F *sécession* or f. L *secessio* (as prec.; see -ION)]

sěclu'de (-ōō'd) *v.t.* keep (person, place, esp. one*self*) retired or away from company, screen from view, (*seclude* one*self from society; a secluded spot, life*, etc.). [ME, f. L SE(*cludere clus-* = *claudere* shut)]

sěclu'sion (-ōō'zhon) *n.* **1.** secluding or being secluded; retirement, privacy; hence ~IST (2) *n.* **2.** secluded place. [f. med. L *seclusio* (as prec.; see -ION)]

sěclu'sive (-lōō'-) *a.* serving or tending to seclude (oneself). [f. SECLUDE after *inclusive* etc.]

sě'cond *a.*, *n.*, & *v.t.* **1.** *a.* next after first (*the second man; the second man you meet; was the second to come; the world's second largest city*); *second* BASE[1] 9, -CHOP[5]; ~ **class**, set of persons or things ranking after others, next-to-best accommodation in train, ship, etc., mail delivered less quickly than first class, (place in) next to highest division in examination-list, and cf. sense 4; **come in** ~, be next to winner in race; ~ **day**, Monday; *second* FLOOR; ~ **gear**, next-to-lowest gear in motor vehicle or bicycle; ~ **master** or **mistress**, deputy to head teacher; ~ **to none**, surpassed by no other; *second* PERSON 5, 6; **in the** ~ **place**, secondly; *second* READING. **2.** other besides one or the first (*a second man now arrived*), additional, supplementary; ~ **advent**, return of Christ, esp. as preliminary to his expected personal reign on earth; ~ **ballot**, electoral method by which, if winner on first ballot has not polled more than half the votes cast, a second ballot is taken in which only he and the next candidate are eligible; ~ **chamber**, upper house in bicameral parliament; ~ **coming**, = *second advent*; ~ **home**, subsidiary place of residence; *second* HONEYMOON, LESSON; ~ **name**, surname; ~ **nature**, acquired tendency that has become instinctive (*habit is second nature; self-sacrifice is now second nature with him*); *second* SELF, SIGHT[1], STRING; ~ **teeth**, those of adults (cf. MILK[1]-*teeth*); ~ **thoughts**, opinion or resolution formed on reconsideration; *second* WIND[1]. **3.** of secondary kind, subordinate, derived, unoriginal, imitative, metaphorical; such as to be comparable to (*a second Daniel, Solomon*, etc.); (Mus., of instrument or voice) performing next to highest part or part subordinate to principal one; ~ **cause** (that is itself caused); *second* CHILDHOOD, COUSIN, FIDDLE; **at** ~ **hand**, by hearsay, not actual observation etc.; *second* INTENTION; ~ **lieutenant**, army officer below (*first) lieutenant; ~ **officer**, assistant mate on merchant ship; **the** ~ **sex**, women. **4.** ~-**best**, (what is) of second quality (*come off* ~-*best*, get the worst of it); ~-**class**, (*a.*) of second or of inferior class or position or quality, (of passenger, ticket) using, entitling to use of, second-class railway-carriage etc., (*adv.*; -ah's) by the second class (*travels second-class*); ~-**generation**, having parents belonging to first GENERATION; *~-**guess**, know only by hindsight; ~-**hand**, (*a.*) (of clothes, books, furniture, etc.) bought after use by a previous owner, (of shop etc.) where such goods can be bought, (of information etc.) taken on another's authority and not got by original observation or research, (*adv.*) at second hand; ~-**rate**, not of superior quality, rated in second class; *~-**storey man**, cat burglar. **5.** *n.* second person etc. in race etc. (**a good** ~, close to winner); second gear; (person having) place in second class in examination (**upper, lower, ~,** in upper, lower, division of second class). **6.** another person or thing besides the previously mentioned or

principal, whether regarded as next, inferior, or equal. **7.** (Mus.) (note at) interval of which the span involves two alphabetical notes, harmonic combination of notes thus separated. **8.** (in *pl.*) goods of second quality, esp. coarse flour or bread made from it; second helping of food; second course of meal. **9.** supporter chosen to assist principal in duelling, boxing, or wrestling. **10.** sixtieth part of a minute of time or angular measurement [see etym.]; (colloq.) short time (*wait a second*). **11.** ~ **in command**, officer next in rank to commanding or chief officer; ~(**s**) **hand**, extra hand in some watches and clocks recording seconds; ~-**mark**, mark (″) used with figures denoting seconds in statements of angular measurement or time (*1° 6′ 40″; 1h. 35′ 15″*), or denoting linear inches. **12.** *v.t.* supplement, support, back up, (*second words with deeds; will you second me if I ask him?*). **13.** (Of member of society or debating body) give the necessary formal support to (nomination, motion, etc., or its proposer) by rising with or without speech or otherwise acting to show that move is not isolated; hence ~ER[1] *n.* **14.** (*pr.* sǐkŏ'nd). ‖(Mil.) put (officer) into temporary retirement with a view to staff or other extra-regimental appointment; ‖transfer (official) temporarily to another department; hence ~MENT *n.* [a. ME f. OF, f. L *secundus* (*sequi* follow); *n.* (time etc.) ME f. OF *seconde* f. med. L *secunda* (*minuta*) secondary (minute), i.e. minute of a minute; *v.t.* F *seconder* f. L *secundare*]

sě'condarў *a.* & *n.* **1.** *a.* next below, coming in place or time after, depending on or derived from, of less importance or originality than, what is primary; of the second or inferior rank or class etc. (*to*), supplementary, indirectly caused; (Geol., S~) Mesozoic. **2.** ~ **battery, cell**, storage cell; ~ **coil** (from which current is taken in transformer); *secondary* COLOUR[1]; ~ **education** (for those who have received primary education but not yet proceeded to university or occupation); ~ **feather** (growing from second joint of bird's wing); ~ **planet**, planet's satellite; ~ **school** (where secondary education is given); ~ **sexual characteristics** (distinctive of one sex but not directly related to reproduction). **3.** Hence **sě'condariLY**[2] *adv.*, **sě'condariNESS** *n.* **4.** *n.* deputy or delegate; ‖minor cathedral dignitary; secondary planet, period, coil, feather, etc. [ME, f. L *secundarius* (as prec.; see -ARY[1])]

seco'nde (-aw'nd) *n.* second of eight parrying positions in fencing. [F, fem. of *second* SECOND]

sě'condlў *adv.* in the second place, as second item, (in enumerating topics, arguments, etc.). [ME, f. SECOND | -LY[2]]

sěcŏ'nd|o *n.* (*pl.* ~**i** *pr.* -ē). (Mus.) second or lower part in duet etc. [It.]

sě'crecў *n.* keeping of, ability to keep or habit of keeping, secrets (*he promised secrecy; can rely on his secrecy; done with great secrecy*); tendency to concealment, secretiveness; unrevealed state, being kept secret, (*there can be no secrecy about it*; **in** ~, secretly). [ME, f. *secretie* (obs. *secre* or SECRET adjs.; see -TY[1], -Y[1])]

sě'crět *a.* & *n.* **1.** *a.* (to be) kept private, not (to be) made known or exposed to view, (*secret treaty, understanding, errand, door, sin, process, influence*); ~ **ballot** (in which voters' choices are not made public); ~ **parts**, (arch.) genitals; ~ **service** (done to Government by securing information etc. without public disclosure); hence ~LY[2] *adv.* **2.** given to or having faculty of secrecy; ~ **agent**, spy; ~ **ink**, invisible ink; ~ **police** (operating in secret esp. for political purposes); **S~ Service**, Government intelligence department; ~ **society** (whose members are sworn to secrecy about it). **3.** secretive, close, reticent; (of place etc.) secluded, retired. **4.** *n.* thing (to be) kept secret (**keep a** ~ or **the** ~, not reveal it); thing known only to a limited number (**in the** ~, among the number of those allowed to know it; **open** ~, thing secret only to those who do not trouble to learn it); mystery, thing of which explanation is sought in vain, (*the secrets of nature*); true but not generally understood method for attainment *of* (*the secret of health, success, happiness, salvation, is temperance, to try again*, etc.); (RC Ch.) celebrant's private prayer in Mass; **in** ~, secretly. [ME f. OF, f. L *secretus* f. SE(*cernere cret-* sift) separate, set apart]

sècrètair'e *n.* escritoire. [F, as SECRETARY]

sècretār'iat *n.* office of secretary; members of a government administrative office collectively; (premises of) administrative office or department headed by Secretary(-General). [f. F *secrétariat* f. med. L *secretariatus* (as foll.; see -ATE¹)]

sè'cretarȳ *n.* **1.** (private) ~, person employed by another to assist him in correspondence, literary work, getting information, and other confidential matters. **2.** official appointed by society or company or corporation to conduct its correspondence, keep its records, and deal in the first instance with its business; HONORARY *secretary.* **3.** principal assistant of government minister or ambassador etc.; **S~-Ge'neral,** principal administrator of an organization; **S~ of State,** ‖head of a major government department, *=* FOREIGN Secretary, *head of general records department in a state; ‖**Parliamentary Private S~,** ‖**Parliamentary (Under-)S~,** members of parliament assisting head of government department; ‖**Permanent (Under-)S~,** ‖**Assistant (Under-)S~,** senior civil servants in government department. **4.** escritoire. **5.** (Print.) type-fount imitating secretary-hand. **6.** ~-**bird,** long-legged African raptorial bird, with crest likened to quill-pens stuck over writer's ear; ~-**hand,** 15th–17th-c. style of handwriting esp. in legal documents. **7.** Hence **sècretār'IAL** *a.,* ~SHIP (1, 2) *n.* [ME, f. LL *secretarius* (as SECRET; see -ARY¹)]

sècrè't|e *v.t.* **1.** put (object, person, one*self*) into place of concealment. **2.** (Physiol., of gland or organ or the person etc. of which it is part) produce by secretion, whence ~OR *n.,* ~ORY *a.* [sense 1 f. obs. *secret* v. f. SECRET; sense 2 f. as SECRET or by back-form. f. foll.]

sècrē'tion *n.* **1.** act of concealing (*the secretion of stolen goods*). **2.** (Physiol.) process by which substances are separated in gland etc. from blood or sap for function in the organism or for excretion; substance produced by such process, e.g. saliva, urine, resin. [f. F *sécrétion* or f. L *secretio* separation (as SECRET; see -ION)]

secretive (sē'krĭ-, sĭkrē'-) *a.* inclined to make secrets, intentionally uncommunicative, needlessly reserved; hence or cogn. ~LY² (-vlĭ) *adv.,* ~NESS (-vn-) *n.* [back-form. f. *secretiveness* after F *secrétivité* (as SECRET; see -IVE)]

sèct *n.* body of persons agreed upon religious doctrines usu. different from those of an established or orthodox Church from which they have separated and usu. having distinctive common worship; nonconformist or other Church as described by opponents; party or faction in a religious body; religious denomination; followers of a particular philosopher or philosophy or school of thought in politics etc. [ME, f. OF *secte* or f. L *secta* f. stem of *sequi secut-* follow]

sect. *abbr.* section.

sèctār'ian *a.* & *n.* (person) adhering to a sect, esp. in bigoted fashion; hence ~ISM (3) *n.,* ~IZE (3) *v.t.* [f. foll. + -AN; see -ARIAN]

sè'ctarȳ *n.* member of a sect, esp. (Hist.) of the Independents, Presbyterians, etc., at time of the English Civil War. [f. med. L *sectarius* adherent (as SECT; see -ARY¹)]

sè'ction *n.,* & *v.t.* **1.** *n.* part cut off from something; one of the parts into which something is divided arbitrarily or may naturally be considered as divided (e.g. length of cane-stem between two rings; *subject falls into five sections; last section of the journey*); one part of structure such as boat or wooden house that is made in parts for transportation; minor subdivision of book, statute, etc.; *one square mile of land; *area of

land, region; (Mil.) subdivision of platoon; part of the community or of a society etc. having separate interests or functions or characteristics; *particular district of a town (*residential section*); *division of sleeping-car; **microscopic** ~, thin slice cut from something for examination with microscope. **2.** (Surg.) separation by cutting. **3.** cutting of solid by plane (CONIC *section*); (area of) resulting figure; (CROSS-)~, representation of internal structure of something supposed to be cut thus (**vertical, horizontal, longitudinal, oblique,** etc., ~, according to position chosen for plane). **4.** (Biol.) group, esp. subgenus. **5.** ~(-**mark**), sign (§) used as reference mark or (with or without number) to indicate beginning of section of book etc. **6.** *v.t.* arrange in or divide into sections. [F, or f. L *sectio (secare sect-* cut; see -ION)]

sè'ctional *a.* **1.** pertaining to a section, esp. of the community; hence ~ISM (3) *n.,* (undue) limitation to one section, ~IZE (3) *v.t.,* ~LY² *adv.* **2.** made in parts for transportation. [f. prec. + -AL]

sè'ctor *n.* **1.** (Geom.) plane figure enclosed between two radii of circle, ellipse, etc., and the arc cut off by them (~ **of sphere,** solid generated by revolution of sector of circle round one radius). **2.** (Mil.) portion of a front controlled by one commander or headquarters; similar portion of any activity (*the private sector of industry*). **3.** mathematical instrument of two stiffly-hinged flat pieces with lines representing sines, tangents, etc., radiating from centre of joint for use in making diagrams etc. **4.** Hence ~AL *a.* [LL, = sector f. L = cutter (as prec.; see -OR)]

sèctōr'ial *a.* & *n.* **1.** *a.* of or like sector(s). **2.** (Of carnivore's premolar teeth) adapted for cutting. **3.** *n.* sectorial tooth. [sense 1 f. prec. + -IAL; sense 2 f. mod. L *sectorius* (as prec.) + -AL]

sè'cūlar *a.* & *n.* **1.** *a.* occurring once in or lasting for an age or a century; ~ **games,** ancient-Roman festival held at long intervals. **2.** lasting or going on for ages, occurring over an indefinitely long time (opp. *periodical, short-term*); ~ **change** (going on slowly but persistently); ~ **fame** (enduring); *secular* VARIATION (Astron.). **3.** concerned with the affairs of this world, not sacred or monastic or ecclesiastical, (*secular affairs, education, music*); **the** ~ **arm,** (Hist.) civil jurisdiction to which criminal was transferred by ecclesiastical courts for severer punishment; ~ **clergy,** parish priests etc. (opp. *regular clergy*). **4.** sceptical of religious truth or opposed to religious education etc.; hence ~ISM (3), ~IST (2), *ns.,* ~IZE (3) *v.t.* **5.** Hence **sècūlā'rITY** *n.,* ~LY² *adv.* **6.** *n.* secular priest. [ME (in senses 3 & 4 f. OF *seculer*) f. L *saecularis* (*saeculum* generation, age)]

sècū'nd *a.* (Bot. & Zool.) arranged on one side only (as flowers in lily-of-the-valley); hence ~LY² *adv.* [f. L (as SECOND)]

sècūr'e *a.,* & *v.t.* **1.** *a.* untroubled by danger or apprehension (*a quiet secure existence; dwell secure*); (arch.) confident or unsuspecting (*the secure hope of salvation*). **2.** safe against attack, impregnable; reliable, certain not to fail or give way, (*a secure foundation, fastening, foothold, grasp*); (usu. *pred.*) in safe keeping, firmly fastened, (*have got him secure; are you sure it is secure?*). **3.** having sure prospect *of,* safe *against* or *from,* (*secure of victory, against assault, from interruption*). **4.** Hence ~LY² (-ūr'lĭ) *adv.* **5.** *v.t.* fortify (town, harbour, etc., usu. *with* wall etc.); confine, enclose, fasten, or close, securely (*secure prisoner, valuables, buckle, window*); compress (blood-vessel) to prevent bleeding; ~ **arms,** (Mil.) hold rifle's muzzle down with lock in armpit to guard from rain. **6.** guarantee, make safe against loss, (*loan secured on landed property* etc.; *how can I secure myself against the consequences?*). **7.** succeed in getting, obtain, (esp. something coveted or competed for; *have secured front seats, a first-class cook, the prize, my ends*). **8.** Hence **sècūr'ABLE** *a.,* ~MENT (-ūr'm-) *n.* [f. L SE(*curus* f. *cura* care)]

secŭr′ĭtў n. In adj. senses; confidence; thing that guards or guarantees (**in ~ for,** as guarantee for); (organization for ensuring) safety of State, company, etc., against espionage, theft, or other danger (**~ risk,** person of doubtful loyalty); thing deposited or pledged as guarantee of fulfilment of undertaking or repayment of loan, to be forfeited in case of failure (**on ~ of,** using as guarantee); document as evidence of loan, certificate of stock, bond, etc.; **S~ Council,** permanent body of United Nations seeking to maintain peace and security. [ME, f. OF *securité* or f. L *securitas* (as prec.; see -ITY)]

sedă′n n. **1. ~**(-chair), 17th–18th-c. vehicle seating one and carried by two chairmen with poles. **2.** *enclosed motor car for four or more persons including driver. [perh. f. It. dial., ult. f. L *sella* saddle (see sit)]

sedā′te[1] a. (of person or his manner, look, speech, or writing) tranquil, equable, composed, settled, not impulsive or lively or agitated; hence **~LY**[2] (-tlĭ) adv., **~NESS** (-tn-) n. [f. L *sedatus* p.p. of *sedare* settle (*sedēre* sit); see -ATE[2]]

sedā′te[2] v.t. (Med.) put under sedation. [back-form. f. foll.]

sedā′tion n. (Med.) calming esp. by use of sedative drug. [f. F *sédation* or f. L *sedatio* (as SEDATE[1]; see -ATION)]

se′dative a. & n. (drug, influence, etc.) tending to calm or soothe. [ME, f. OF *sedatif* or f. med. L *sedativus* (as SEDATE[1]; see -IVE)]

se′dentar|ў a. sitting (*sedentary posture, statue*); (of person) inclined by nature or driven by occupation to, (of occupation) involving, (of life etc.) characterized by, much sitting and little physical exercise, whence **~ĭLY**[2] adv., **~ĭNESS** n.; (Zool. etc.) not migratory or free-swimming etc., (of spider) lying in wait till prey is in web. [f. F *sédentaire* or f. L *sedentarius* (*sedēre* sit; see -ENT, -ARY[1])]

Se′der (sā′-) n. ritual for the first night or first two nights of the Passover. [f. Heb. *sēḏer* order]

sedēr′unt n. (Sc.) sitting of ecclesiastical assembly or other body, or of a company over the wine or in talk (*had a long sederunt*). [L, = (the following persons) sat (*sedēre* sit)]

sedge n. grasslike plant of genus *Carex* with jointless stems growing in marshes or by waterside; bed of such plants; **~-warbler, -wren,** small warbler breeding among sedge; hence **se′dgy**[2] a. [OE, *secg* f. Gmc *sagjaz* (*sag-*; cf. SAW[1])]

sedī′l|e n. (pl. **~ia** pr. -ĭ′lĭa) (usu. in pl.) one of usu. three stone seats for priests in S. wall of chancel, often canopied and otherwise decorated. [L, = seat (*sedēre* sit)]

se′diment n. matter that settles to bottom of liquid; lees, dregs; (Geol.) water-borne or wind-borne matter that settles and may become consolidated into rock; hence **~ARY**[1] (-č′n-) a., **~A′TION** n. [f. F *sédiment* or f. L *sedimentum* (as prec.; see -MENT)]

sedī′ti|on n. agitation against the authority of a State; conduct or speech tending to rebellion or breach of public order; so **~ous** (-shus) a. [ME f. OF, or f. L *seditio* (*sed-* = SE-, *ire* it- go; see -ION)]

sedŭ′c|e v.t. lead astray, tempt into sin or crime, corrupt; persuade (person) into abandonment of principles, esp. chastity or allegiance; persuade by temptingness or attractiveness; hence **~ER**[1] n., **~IBLE** a. [f. L SE(*ducere* duct- lead)]

sedŭ′ction n. seducing or being seduced; thing that tends to seduce; tempting or attractive quality *of*. [f. F *séduction* or f. L *seductio* (as prec.; see -ION)]

sedŭ′ctive a. alluring, enticing; hence **~LY**[2] (-vlĭ) adv., **~NESS** (-vn-) n. [f. prec. after *inductive* etc.]

sedŭ′ctrĕss n. female seducer. [f. obs. *seductor* male seducer (as SEDUCE; see -OR) + -ESS[1]]

se′dŭlous a. diligent, persevering, assiduous, (*with sedulous care*); (of action etc.) deliberately and consciously continued, painstaking, (*sedulous flattery,*

attentions); **play the ~ ape,** acquire literary style by imitation; hence or cogn. **~LY**[2] adv., **sedŭ′lĭTY, ~NESS,** ns. [f. L *sedulus* zealous + -OUS]

se′dum n. fleshy-leaved plant of genus *Sedum,* with pink, white, or yellow flowers, e.g. stonecrop. [L, = houseleek]

see[1] v. (**saw; seen**). **1.** v.i. have or exercise the power of discerning objects with the eyes (*sees best at night; cannot see till the ninth day*); **~'ing** n., (Astron.) quality of observed images as determined by atmospheric conditions; **~ing eye,** dog trained to guide blind person; **~ing is believing,** one's own observation is the best evidence; *see* DOUBLE[1] 5; **~ over,** tour and examine (house etc.); **~ red,** see things as blood-coloured, be filled with fury; **~ through,** (fig.) not be deceived by, penetrate, detect nature of; **~-through** a., (esp. of clothing) transparent; **~ through a brick wall** etc., have superhuman acuteness. **2.** v.t. descry, discern by sight, observe, look at or over, (*come where we cannot be seen; children should be seen and not heard; please see whether it is there, where it is; was seen to fall or falling; saw him fall or falling; cannot see my way*); **~ the back of** (visitor, invader, etc.); **~ the light (of day),** be born or (fig.) published; **~ the light,** (fig.) undergo conversion etc., realize one's errors etc.; **~ the sights, town,** etc., be SIGHT'seer; *see* SOMETHING *of*, **~ stars,** have dancing lights before eyes from blow on head; **~ things,** have hallucinations; **things ~n** (not imaginary etc.); **~ visions,** be seer etc.; **~ one's way (clear) to** do or to doing, manage or feel able or entitled to do; **worth ~ing,** notable. **3.** look at for information (usu. in imper.: *see page 15*); watch, be spectator of, (film, game, etc.); meet (or be near) and recognize (person; *saw her in church today*); **see you (later)!, (I'll) be seeing you!,** colloq.) *au revoir.* **4.** learn from newspaper etc. (*I see that another speed record was broken yesterday*). **5.** discern mentally, attain to comprehension of, apprehend, ascertain by search or inquiry or reflection, consider, foresee, (*cannot see a man at the joke, the point; see* REASON[1]; *do you see what I mean?; justice is seen to be done; can't think what he sees* (finds attractive) *in her; must see what can be done; do not see the good, fun, advantage, etc., of doing; do not see how to do it; you see what it is to have faith; saw myself obliged to resign; saw myself having to continue indefinitely*); **~?,** (colloq.) do you understand what I mean?; **as far as I can ~,** to the best of my understanding or belief; **I ~,** I understand your explanation; **you ~,** (1) you understand, (2) you will understand when I explain. **6.** experience, go through more or less observantly, have presented to one's attention, (*shall never see death; have seen five reigns; see little of them now; never saw such a mess; 1839 saw him in Mesopotamia*); **we shall ~** (the outcome etc.); **will never ~** 50 etc. **again,** is over that age; **have ~n the day when** (in drawing attention to past state of affairs); **has ~n better** or **its** etc. **best days,** has declined from former prosperity etc.; **~ life,** mix freely with others, gain experience of men and manners esp. by dissipation etc.; *see* SERVICE[1] 2, 4. **7.** grant interview or be at home to, pay visit to, have meeting with, secure interview with, (*refused to see me; can I see you on business?, for lunch?; when will you come and see us?; must see the lawyer, doctor,* etc.; *can see you for five minutes*); (in gambling, esp. poker) accept (challenge to bet etc.), accept challenge of (person). **8.** call up picture of, imagine, (*cannot see him agreeing to it*). **9.** recognize as tolerable, consent willingly to, (*do not see going all that way for nothing*). **10.** escort, conduct, (*may I see you home?; mind you see him off the premises; saw him off* (attended his departure) *at Southampton; will you see me through* or *through the difficulty?*); be witness of (event etc.) (*see the New Year in; has seen his income gradually decrease*); supervise (action etc.) (*stay and see the doors locked; saw the book through the press*); contemplate without interfering (*are you going to see me treated like this?*; **~ person**

blowed, damned, further, etc., (first), refuse categorically to do what he asks or trouble about it); ∼ person out, be present at, or last until, his death, escort him from premises; ∼ thing out or through, not abandon it or depart before its completion; ∼ person right, make sure that he is safe, rewarded, etc. 11. take view of, have opinion of, (*I see life, things, it, differently now*; *I see it as being quite possible*; *see* EYE[1] *to eye*; *see* FIT[3] *to*); as I ∼ it, in my opinion. 12. *v.t.* & *i.* make provision, take care, give attention, make sure, (*see that it is done*; *see* (*that*) *you don't catch your foot*; *see to* one's *business*); ∼ about, ∼ after, take care of; ∼ here!, = LOOK *here!*; ∼ into, investigate; ∼ to it that, take care that. 13. *v.i.* reflect, take time to consider; let me ∼ (appeal for time to think before making answer or giving particulars, or confession that coming statement may need reconsideration); will ∼ about it (form for declining to act at once). [OE *sēon*, = OS, OHG *sehan*, ON *séa*, Goth. *saihwan* f. Gmc **sehwan* f. IE **seq^w-*]

see² *n.* what is committed to (arch)bishop, (archi-) episcopal unit, (*fill a vacant see*; *the see of Norwich, Canterbury*, etc.; **Holy See, See of Rome,** the papacy or papal court). [ME, f. AF *se*(*d*) = OF *sie*(*d*) f. Rom. **sede* f. L *sedes* seat (*sedēre* sit)]

seed *n.* & *v.* 1. *n.* flowering plant's unit of reproduction (esp. in form of grain) capable of developing into another such plant, (collect.) seeds in any quantity esp. as collected for sowing, (*its seeds are or seed is black*; *is full of seed*; *to be kept for or as seed*); go *or* run to ∼, cease flowering as seed develops, (fig.) become habitually unkempt, ineffective, etc. 2. semen; milt. 3. (Bibl.) offspring, progeny, descendants; raise up ∼, beget children; the ∼ of Abraham, Hebrews. 4. germ, prime cause, beginning, *of* (*seeds of doubt, strife, vice*; sow the ∼(s) of, first give rise to). 5. (colloq.) seeded player. 6. small seedlike container for application of radium etc. 7. ∼-bed, (fig.) place of development; ∼-cake (containing whole seeds esp. of caraway as flavouring); ∼-coat, outer integument of seed; ∼-corn (kept for seed); ∼ crystal (used to initiate crystallization); ∼-eater, bird (esp. finch) living mainly on seeds; ∼-fish (ready to spawn); ∼-leaf, ∼-lobe, cotyledon; ∼-lip, basket for seed in sowing by hand [OE *lēap* basket]; ∼ money (to initiate a project); ∼-oysters, young oysters for planting; ∼-pearl (very small); ∼-plot, = *seed-bed*; ∼-potato (kept for seed); ∼'sman (-z-), dealer in seeds; ∼-time, sowing season; ∼-vessel, pericarp. 8. Hence ∼LESS *a.* 9. *v.i.* go to seed; produce or let fall seed; sow seeds. 10. *v.t.* place seed(s) in; sprinkle (as) with seed; place crystal etc. in (solution etc.) to cause crystallization or condensation (esp. in cloud to produce rain). 11. remove seeds from (fruit etc.). 12. (Sport). designate stronger among (competitors in knock-out tournament), arrange (order of play) thus, so that they are not matched against one another till later rounds; designate (competitor) thus. [OE *sǣd*, = OS *sād*, OHG *sāt*, ON *sáth*, Goth. *-seths* f. Gmc **sǣdh-* (**sǣ-* sow¹)]

see'der *n.* In vbl senses; = DRILL² 2; apparatus for seeding raisins etc.; ‖spawning fish. [f. prec.+-ER¹]

see'dling *n.* plant raised from seed and not from cutting etc.; young tender plant. [f. SEED+-LING¹]

see'dly *a.* full of seed, going to seed; shabby-looking, in worn clothes; (colloq.) out of sorts, feeling ill, whence ∼ILY² *adv.*; hence ∼INESS *n.* [f. SEED+-Y²]

see'ing¹ *conj.* ∼ (that), considering that, inasmuch as, (*seeing that you do not know it yourself*; *seeing no other course is open to us*). [f. SEE¹+-ING²]

see'ing². See SEE¹ 1.

seek *v.* (sought *pr.* sawt). 1. *v.t.* make search or inquiry for, try or be anxious to find or get, ask (thing *of* person), aim at, pursue as object, endeavour *to* do, make for or resort to (place, person, for advice, health, etc.), (*seeks a situation as cook, wealth, scope for his energies*; *sought help from him*; *seeks my aid*; *sought his bed*,

a fortune-teller, the shore); ∼ dead (order to retriever to find killed game); ∼ out, single out for pursuit etc. (esp. make special efforts to secure society of), search for and find. 2. *v.i.* make search or inquiry (*after or for*); sought-after, much in demand, generally desired or courted. 3. (arch.) resort *to* (person, place). 4. is etc. to ∼ or much to ∼, is deficient, lacking, or not yet found (*an efficient leader is yet to seek*); not far to ∼, readily found. 5. Hence (-)∼ER¹ *n.* [OE *sēcan*, = OS *sokian*, OHG *suohhan*, ON *sækja*, Goth. *sōkjan* f. Gmc **sōk-*]

seel *v.t.* (arch.) close (person's eyes). [f. obs. *sile* f. F *ciller*, *siller* or f. med. L *ciliare* f. L *cilium* eyelid]

seem *v.i.* 1. give the impression or sensation of being, appear or be apparently perceived or ascertained *to* do or have done, (*be what you seem to be or seem*; *the man who seemed* (*to be*) *the ringleader*; *seems to be tired, a hopeless absurdity, a good fellow*; *seems certain to win*; *not the angel she seems to be*; *I seem* (*to be*) *deaf today*; *I seem to see him still*; *seems to have died at 35*); can't ∼ to, (colloq.) seem(s) unable to; do not ∼ to, (colloq.) somehow do not (*I do not seem to like him, to fancy it*); ∼ good to, be adopted as best course of action by. 2. (w. anticipatory *it* and following *that*-clause, or parenth. with *it* only, often with implication of anger or remonstrance). appear to be true or the fact (*it seems to me* = I think) that it will rain, that such talk is absurd, *that we had better make up our minds to do it*; *so we are to get nothing, it seems*; *it seems you were lying*); it would or (arch.) should ∼ (in guarded or ironical statement); MESEEMS. [ME, f. ON *sœma* honour (*sœmr* fitting)]

see'ming¹ *a.* ostensible, apparent only, apparent but perhaps not real, apparent and perhaps real, (*the seeming and the real*; *a seeming friend*; *with seeming sincerity*); ∼-virtuous etc. (usu. w. suggestion of falsity); hence ∼LY² *adv.* [ME, f. prec. +-ING²]

see'ming² *n.* appearance, aspect (*to* OUTWARD *seeming*); deceptive appearance. [ME, f. SEEM+-ING¹]

see'mly *a.* & *adv.* 1. *a.* conforming to propriety or good taste, suitable; hence ∼INESS *n.* 2. *adv.* (arch.) decorously. [ME, f. ON *sœmiligr* (as SEEM, -LY¹)]

seen. See SEE¹.

seep *v.i.* ooze out, percolate slowly, (lit. or fig.); hence ∼'AGE (3, 6) *n.* [perh. dial. form of OE *sipian* to soak]

seer¹ *n.* In vbl senses; (esp.) prophet, person who sees visions, person of preternatural insight esp. as regards the future. [ME, f. SEE¹+-ER¹]

seer² *n.* Indian (varying) measure of weight (about one kilogram) or liquid measure (about one litre). [f. Hindi *ser*]

seer³, seir (sēr), *n.* large Indian scombroid fish of genus *Cybium*. [corruption of Port. *serra* SAW¹]

seer'sucker *n.* striped material of linen, cotton, etc., with puckered surface. [f. Pers. *šir o šakar*, lit. 'milk and sugar']

see-saw *a.*, *adv.*, *n.*, & *v.i.* 1. *a.* & *adv.* with backward--and-forward or up-and-down motion as of a saw (*see-saw motion*; go ∼, vacillate or alternate). 2. *n.* game in which persons sit at each end of long board balanced on central support and move up and down alternately; board thus balanced; (fig.) contest in which the advantage repeatedly changes from one side to the other. 3. *v.i.* play at see-saw; move up and down as in see-saw; vacillate in policy etc. [redupl. of SAW¹]

seethe (-dh) *v.* (∼d; arch. *past* sod & *p.p.* SODDEN). *v.t.* & *i.* (arch.) cook by boiling. 2. *v.i.* (fig.) boil, bubble over, be agitated, (*the seething waters*; *seething with discontent*; *I was seething inwardly*; *madness, enthusiasm, seething in his brain*). [OE *sēothan*, = OS **siothan*, OHG *siodan*, ON *sjótha* f. Gmc **seuth-*]

se'gment *n.* 1. part cut off or separable or marked off as though separable from the other parts of some-thing (e.g. one ring of worm, one division of limb or skull, one wedge of orange-pulp); smallest distinct part of a spoken utterance. 2. (Geom.) part cut off by line or plane from any figure (∼ of circle, part enclosed between arc and chord; ∿ **of sphere,** part cut off by any plane not passing through centre); ∿ **of line,** part included between two points. **3.** ∿- **-gear, -rack, -wheel,** (with cogs occupying arc of circle only). **4.** Hence -AL (-ĕ'n-), ∿ARY[1], adjs. [f. L *segmentum* (*secare* cut; see -MENT)]

sĕgmĕnt[2] (-mĕ'-, sĕ'-) v. **1.** v.i. & t. divide into segments. **2.** v.i. (Biol., of cell) undergo cleavage or divide into many cells. **3.** Hence ∿A'TION n. [f. prec.]

sē'gō n. (pl. ∿s). ∿ (**lily**), N. Amer. plant (*Calochortus nuttallii*) with green and white campanulate flowers. [Paiute]

sĕ'grĕg|āte[1] v. **1.** v.t. put apart from the rest, isolate; enforce racial segregation on (persons) or in (community etc.). **2.** v.i. separate from a mass and collect together; (Biol., of genes) separate into dominant and recessive groups. **3.** So ∿ABLE, ∿ATIVE, adjs. [f. L SE(*gregare* f. *grex gregis* flock) +-ATE[3]]

sĕ'grĕgate[2] a. **1.** (arch.) set apart, separate. **2.** (Zool.) simple or solitary, not compound. [f. L *segregatus* p.p. (as prec.); see -ATE[2]]

sĕgrĕga'tion n. segregating or being segregated; enforced separation of different racial groups in a community etc., whence ∿IST (2) n. [f. LL *segregatio* (as SEGREGATE[1]; see -ATION)]

sē'gue (-gwā) v.i. (Mus.) go on without pause into. [It., – follows]

sĕguidi'lla (-gĭdi'lya) n. Spanish dance in triple time; music for it. [Sp. (*seguida* following f. *seguir* follow)]

sei (sa) n. small rorqual (*Balaenoptera borealis*). [f. Norw. *sejhval* sei whale]

seicĕ'nt|ō (sāchĕ'-) n. Italian style of art of the 17th c.; hence ∿(ō)IST (2, 3) n. [It., = 600, used w. ref. to years 16—]

seiche (sāsh) n. oscillation of lake etc. waters due usu. to changes in barometric pressure. [Swiss F]

Sei'dlitz (sĕ'dlĭts) n. ∿ **powder,** *∿ **powders,** aperient medicine of two powders mixed separately with water and then poured together to effervesce. [named w. ref. to mineral water of *Seidlitz* in Bohemia]

seigneur (sānyĕr'), **sei'gnior** (sā'nyer), n. feudal lord, lord of manor, whence **seigneur'IAL** (sānyĕr'-), **seigniŏr'IAL** (sānyŏr'-), adjs.; **grand seigneur** (grahn-), person of high rank or whose demeanour etc. correspond to popular ideal of great nobleman. [ME, f. OF *seigneur, seignor* f. L SENIOR -*oris*]

sei'gn(i)orage (sā'nyerĭj) n. **1.** (Hist.) something claimed by sovereign or feudal superior as prerogative. **2.** Crown's right to percentage on bullion brought to mint for coining; profit made by issue of coins rated above intrinsic value. [ME, f. OF *seignorage, seigneurage* (as prec.; see -AGE)]

sei'gniorỳ (sā'nyerĭ) n. lordship, sovereign authority; seigneur's domain. [ME, f. OF *seignorie* (as SEIGNEUR; see -Y[1])]

seine (sān) n. & v. n. ∿(-**net**), fishing-net for encircling fish, with floats at top and weights at bottom edge, and usu. hauled ashore. **2.** v.i. & t. fish or catch with seine; hence **sei'nER**[1] (sā'-) n. [ME, f. OF *saine*, & f. OE *segne*, OS, OHG *segina* f. WG *sagina*, f. L f. Gk *sagēnē*]

seir. See SEER[3].

seise. See SEIZE.

sei'sin (sĕ'z-) n. (Law). possession of land by freehold; act of taking such possession; what is so held. [ME, f. AF *sesine*, OF *seisine, saisine* (as SEIZE; see -INE[4])]

sei'sm|ic (sī'z-) a. of earthquake(s); hence or cogn. ∿(IC)AL adjs., ∿ICALLY adv. [f. Gk *seismos* earthquake +-IC]

sei'smo- (sī'z-) comb. form. earthquake, as: ∿gram, record given by ∿**graph** or ∿**meter** (-ŏ'm-) or ∿**scope,** instruments showing force, direction, etc., of earthquake; so ∿GRAPHY, ∿GRAPHER, (-ŏ'g-) ns., ∿GRA'PHIC(AL) adjs., ∿METRY (-ŏ'm-) n., ∿ME'TRIC(AL), ∿SCO'PIC, adjs., ∿LOGY, ∿LOGIST, (-ŏ'l-) ns., ∿LO'GICAL a. [f. as prec. +-O-]

seize (sēz) v. **1.** v.t. (Law; or **seise** pr. same). put in possession of (esp. in p.p.; ∿d or **seised of,** having in legal possession, (fig.) aware or informed of). **2.** take possession of (contraband goods, documents, etc.) by warrant or legal right, confiscate, impound, attach; hence **sei'zABLE** (sē'-) a. **3.** lay hold of forcibly or suddenly, snatch, grasp with hand or mind, comprehend quickly or clearly, (*seize fortress, power,* person *by the neck* etc., person's *hand, opportunity* or *occasion, an idea, a distinction, the essence of the matter*; *was seized by apoplexy, with remorse* or *panic*); (Naut.) fasten or attach by binding with turns of yarn etc., whence **sei'zING**[1] (4) (sē'-) n. **4.** v.i. lay hold eagerly (*up*)on (*seize upon a chance* or *pretext*). **5.** ∿ (**up**), (of moving part in machine) become stuck, jam, from undue heat or friction. [ME, f. OF *seizir, saisir* give seisin f. Frank. L *sacire* f. Gmc *sakjan* quarrel, claim at law, (*sak*-process, perh. infl. by *satjan* SET[1])]

seizin. Var. of SEISIN.

sei'zure (sē'zher) n. In vbl senses; (esp.) sudden attack of apoplexy etc., stroke. [ME, f. SEIZE +-URE]

sĕ'jant a. (Her.) (Of animal) sitting upright on haunches. [prop. *seiant* f. OF var. of *seant* sitting (*seoir* f. L *sedēre* sit; see -ANT)]

sĕlā'chian (-k-) n. & a. (fish) of order Selachii, including sharks and dogfishes. [f. mod. L *Selachii* f. Gk *selakhos* shark +-IAN]

sela'dang (-ah'-) n. Malayan gaur. [Malay]

sĕ'lah int. (In Psalms and Habakkuk, at end of verse; supposed to be a musical direction.) [f. Heb. *se·lāh*]

sĕ'ldom adv. & a. (occas. ∿er, ∿est). **1.** adv. rarely, not often, (*seldom* or *never*; *seldom, if ever*; *very seldom*). **2.** a. rare, uncommon. [OE *seldan* (OHG *seltan,* ON *sjaldan*), dat. f. Gmc *selda-*]

sĕlĕ'ct a., & v.t. **1.** a. chosen for excellence or suitability, choice, picked, got by rejection or exclusion of what is inferior; (of society etc.) exclusive, cautious in admitting members; hence ∿NESS n. **2.** ∿ **committee,** small parliamentary committee appointed to conduct some special investigation, *∿**man,** elected councillor in New England town. **3.** v.t. pick out as best or most suitable; hence *∿EE' n., conscript. [f. L SE(*ligere lect-* = *legere* pick)]

sĕlĕ'ction n. **1.** selecting, choice; being selected; what is selected (*a fine selection of summer goods*; *what is your selection for the Derby?*; *the new headmaster is a good selection*). **2.** (Biol.) sorting out in various ways (*natural, physical, artificial,* etc., *selection*) of the types of animal or plant better fitted to survive or multiply, regarded as a factor in evolution. [f. L *selectio* (as prec.; see -ION)]

sĕlĕ'ctive a. using selection; characterized by selecting, (Electr.) able to respond to one particular frequency; *∿ **service,** service in armed forces under conscription; hence ∿LY[2] (-vlĭ) adv., ∿NESS (-vn-) n. [f. SELECT 2 +-IVE]

selĕcti'vitỳ (sĭ-, sĕ-) n. quality of being selective; (esp., of radio receiver) ability to respond to a chosen frequency without interference from others. [f. prec. +-ITY]

sĕlĕ'ctor n. person who selects, esp. representative team; device that selects appropriate material, vehicle-gear, etc. [f. SELECT 2 +-OR]

sĕ'lĕnite n. **1.** gypsum occurring as transparent crystals or thin plates; hence **sĕlĕni'tic** a. **2.** (Chem.) salt of selenious acid. [sense 1 f. L f. Gk *selēnītēs* (*lithos*) moon(-stone) f. *selēnē* moon; sense 2 f. SELENIUM + -ITE[1]]

sĕlē'nium n. (Chem.) non-metallic element of sulphur group, characterized by variation of its electrical resistivity with intensity of illumination; ∿ **cell,** piece of this used as photoelectric device; hence **sĕlĕnATE**[1] (3) n., **sĕlĕ'nic,** **sĕlĕ'nious,** adjs. [mod. L, f. Gk *selēnē* moon +-IUM]

sĕlē'no- comb. form. moon, as: ∿**ce'ntric,** as seen etc. from centre of moon; ∿**dont** n. & a., (mammal) with crescent-ridges on crowns of teeth; ∿**graphy**

(sĕlĭnŏ´g-), study of or mapping of the moon, whence ∿GRAPHER (sĕlĭnŏ´g-) *n.*, ∿GRA´PHIC *a.*; ∿logy (sĕlĭnŏ´l-), science of the moon, whence ∿LOGIST (sĕlĭnŏ´l-) *n.* [f. Gk *selēnē* moon + -o-]

sĕlf *n.* (*pl.* selves *pr.* sĕlvz), *a.*, & *pron.* **1.** *n.* person's or thing's own individuality or essence, person or thing as object of introspection or reflexive action, (*the study of the self*; *showed his true self*; *the consciousness of self*); one's **former, better**, etc., ∿, oneself as one formerly was, one's nobler impulses, etc.; one's **second** ∿, intimate friend, right-hand man; **my humble** ∿, **your good selves, our noble selves** (as joc. toast), etc., **his, its,** etc., **own** or **very** ∿ (forms of *myself, himself* etc. when divided); **Caesar's, pity's,** etc., ∿, (rhet.) Caesar himself, pity itself. **2.** one's own interests or pleasure, concentration on these, (*cares for nothing but, refers everything to, self; self is a bad guide to happiness*). **3.** (*pl.* ∿s). flower of uniform, or of the natural wild, colour. **4.** (Commerc., vulg., or joc.) myself, yourself, himself, etc., (*cheque drawn to self; ticket admitting self and friend*). **5.** *a.* (Of colour) uniform, the same throughout, (of flower) self-coloured. **6.** *pron.* See HERSELF, HIMSELF, ITSELF, MYSELF, ONE*self*, OURSELF, OURSELVES, THEM-SELVES, THYSELF, YOURSELF. [OE. = OS *self*, OHG *selb*, ON *sjálfr*, Goth. *silba* f. Gmc *selbha*-]

sĕlf- *pref.* **1.** Expr. direct reflexive action, (w. *pres. part.*) acting on oneself or itself (*self-accusing, self-closing*), (w. *p.p.*) acted on by oneself or itself (*self-accused, self-propelled*), (w. vbl derivs.) of oneself or itself (*self-accuser, self-accusation, self-fertilization, self-explanatory*). **2.** Expr. action or condition (a) occurring without external agency or assistance (*self-acting, self-evident*), (b) relating to oneself or itself (*self-confident, self-inflicted, self-righteous*). **3.** Denoting 'uniform' or 'natural' (*self-coloured, self-faced*). **4.** ∿-**aba´ndonment, -aba´sement, -abho´rrence,** -ABNEGA´TION, sense 1; ∿-**absor´bed** 2b; ∿-**absor´ption** 2b, (1) absorption in oneself, (2) (Phys.) absorption, by a body, of radiation emitted within it; ∿-**abu´se** 1, (1) reviling of oneself, (2) masturbation; ∿-**accusa´tion, -accu´satory,** etc., 1; ∿-**a´cting, -a´ction, -acti´vity,** 2a, automatic (action); ∿-**addre´ssed** 2b, (of envelope for return communication); ∿-**adhe´sive** 2b; ∿-**adju´sting, -adju´stment,** 1, (of machinery etc.); ∿-**admira´tion, -adver´tisement,** 1; ∿-**affirma´tion** 1, (Psych.) recognition and assertion of the existence of the conscious self; ∿-**aggra´ndizement, -ana´lysis, -appoi´nted, -apprecia´tion, -approba´tion, -appro´val,** 1; ∿-ASSER´TING, **-asser´tion, -asser´tive,** etc., 1; ∿-**assur´ance, -assur´ed,** 2b; ∿-**bego´tten** 2a; ∿-**betray´al** 1; ∿-**bi´nder** 2a, reaping-machine with automatic arrangement for binding sheaves; ∿-**born** 1; ∿-**ca´tering** *a.* & *n.* 2a, occupying rented accommodation on holiday etc. but providing one's own food; ∿-**ce´ntred** 2b, preoccupied with one's own personality or affairs; ∿-**clea´ning, -clo´sing,** 1; ∿-**co´cking** 1, (of gun) with hammer raised by trigger, not by hand; ∿-**colle´cted** 2b, having or showing presence of mind or composure; ∿-**co´lour**(ed) 3, (of flower or material whose colour is uniform throughout, or flower whose colour has not been changed by cultivation etc.); ∿-**comma´nd** 1, power of controlling one's emotions; ∿-**commu´nion** 2b, meditation esp. upon one's own character or conduct; ∿-**compla´cent, -compla´cency,** 2b, (of person too easily pleased with himself); ∿-**concei´t**(ed) 2b; ∿-**condemna´tion, -conde´mned,** 1; ∿-**confe´ssed** 1, openly admitting oneself to be; ∿-**co´nfidence, -co´nfident**(ly), 2b; ∿-**congratula´tion, -co´nquest,** 1; ∿-**co´nscious**(ness) 2b, (esp. of person embarrassed or unnatural in manner from knowing he is observed by others, or (Philos. etc.) of man as having faculty of self-contemplation); ∿-**consi´stency,**

-**consi´stent,** 2b; ∿-**co´nstituted** 1, (esp. of person who or body which assumes function without right to it); ∿-**consu´ming** 1; ∿-**contai´ned** 1, (1) not communicative or dependent on others, (2) (‖esp. of living accommodation) complete in itself; ∿-**conte´mpt, -conte´mptuous**(ly), 1; ∿-**conte´nt** *n.,* **-conte´nted,** 2b; ∿-**contradi´ction, -contradi´ctory, -contro´l, -convi´cted, -crea´ted, -crea´tion, -cri´tical, -cri´ticism, -cu´lture, -decei´ving, -decei´ver, -decei´t, -dece´ption, -defea´ting,** 1; ∿-**defe´nce** 1, (esp. of judo etc.; *in ∿-defence,* not by way of aggression; *noble art of ∿-defence,* boxing); ∿-**delu´sion, -deni´al,** 1; ∿-DENY´ing 1 (∿-*denying ordinance,* (w. allus. to) resolution of Long Parliament 1645 depriving members of Parliament of civil and military office); ∿-**depe´ndence, -depe´ndent,** 2b; ∿-**deprecia´tion, -depre´ciative,** 1; ∿-**despair´** 2b; ∿-**destroy´ing,** *-destru´ct, -destru´ction, etc., 1; ∿-**determina´tion** etc., 1, (esp. w. ref. to free will as opp. fatalism etc., or (Polit.) a nation's right to determine its own allegiance or form of government); ∿-**deve´lopment** 1; ∿-**devo´tion** 1, devoting of oneself to person or cause; ∿-**di´scipline, -dispa´ragement, -display´, -disprai´se, -distru´st**(ful), -dou´bt, 1; ∿-**dri´ve** 1, (of hired vehicle) driven by hirer; ∿-**-e´ducated, -educa´tion, -effa´cement, -effa´cing,** 1; ∿-**ele´ctive** 1, (esp.) proceeding etc. by co-optation; ∿-**employ´ed** 1, working as owner of business etc.; ∿-**exi´dent**(ly) 2a, without need of demonstration; ∿-**examina´tion** 1; ∿-**e´xecuting** 1, not needing legislation etc. to enforce it; ∿-**exi´stent** 2a; ∿-**explai´ning, -expla´natory, -expre´ssion,** 1; ∿-**fa´ced** 3, (of stone) unhewn, undressed; ∿-**fee´ding, -fee´der,** 1, (furnace, machine, etc.) that renews its own fuel or material automatically; ∿-**fertiliza´tion, -fer´tilized, -fer´tilizing,** 1, ∿-**fer´tile, -ferti´lity,** 2a, (of plants fertilized by their own pollen, not from others); ∿-**fla´ttering, -fla´ttery,** 1; ∿-**forge´tful**(ness) 1, unselfish(ness); ∿-**fulfi´lling, -fulfi´lment, -ge´nerating,** 1; ∿-**gla´zed** 3, (of porcelain) covered with glaze of one tint; ∿-**glorifica´tion** 1; ∿-**go´verning, -go´vernment,** 1, (esp. of colony etc.); ∿-**heal** 1, plant (esp. *Prunella vulgaris*) believed to have great healing properties; ∿-**he´lp** 1, providing for oneself without waiting for external aid; ∿-**humilia´tion** 1; ∿-**i´mage** 2b, one's idea of what one is; ∿-**immola´tion** 1; ∿-**impor´tance, -impor´tant,** having high opinion of oneself, pompous(ness); ∿-**impo´sed** 2b, (of task etc.); ∿-**-i´mpotent** 2a, = *self-sterile*; ∿-**impro´vement** 1; ∿-**indu´ced** 2b; ∿-**indu´ctive, -indu´ction,** 2a, (Electr.) (capable of) production of electromotive force in circuit when current in that circuit is varied; ∿-**indu´lgence, -indu´lgent,** etc., 1, yielding to temptations of ease or pleasure; ∿-**infli´cted** 2b; ∿-**-i´nterest**(ed) 2b, (actuated by or absorbed in) what one conceives to be for one's own interests; ∿-**-invi´ted** 1, having had to ask for, having come without, an invitation; ∿-**invo´lved** 2b, wrapped up in oneself; ∿-**justifica´tion, -ki´ndled, -know´ledge, -loa´ding, -lo´cking,** 1; ∿-**-lo´ve** 1, selfishness, impulse towards self-indulgence; ∿-**lu´minous** 2a; ∿-**made** 1, (of person who has risen from poverty or obscurity by his own exertions); ∿-**-ma´stery,** -MATE¹, **-mortifica´tion, -mo´tion, -mo´ving, -mur´der**(er), 1; ∿-**opi´nion, -opi´nionated,** 2b, (of stubborn adherence to one's own opinions); ∿-**par´tial, -partia´lity,** 2b; ∿-**-perpe´tuating, -pi´ty, -plea´sing** *a.* & *n.*, 1; ∿-**poi´sed** 2a; ∿-**pollu´tion** 1, masturbation; ∿-**por´trait** 2a, portrait (literary or pictorial) made by a person of himself; ∿-**posse´ssed, -posse´ssion,** 1, cool(ness), composed, composure, in agitating circumstances etc.; ∿-**prai´se** 1; ∿-**preserva´tion** 1, (esp.) the primary instinct impelling conscious being to go on living and avoid injury; ∼-**pro'fit** 2b; ∼-**pro'pagating**, -**prope'lled**, 1; ||∼-**rai'sing** 1, (of flour) not needing addition of baking-powder etc.; ∼-**realiza'tion** 1, development of one's faculties esp. as ethical first principle; ∼-**recor'ding** 2a, (of scientific instrument etc.); ∼-**regar'd** 1, (proper) regard for oneself (opp. *altruism*); ∼-**re'gistering** 2a, (of scientific instrument etc.); ∼-**re'gulating** 1, (of machinery); ∼-**reli'ance**, -**reli'ant**, 2b; ∼-**renuncia'tion** 1, unselfishness; ∼-**repre'ssion**, -**reproa'ch(ful)**, 1; ∼-**repu'gnant** 2b, inconsistent; ∼-**respe'ct**, -**respe'ctful**, -**respe'cting**, 1, (of person who has, and adheres to, a standard of dignity and worthy conduct); ∼-**restrai'ned**, -**restrai'nt**, -**revea'ling** *a.*, -**revela'tion**, 1; ∼-**ri'ghteous(ness)** 2b, (being) righteous in one's own estimation; ∼-**ri'ghting** *a.* 1, (of boat); *∼-**ri'sing** 2a, = *self--raising*; ∼-**sa'crifice**, -**sa'crificing**, 1, subordinating one's own interests and desires to those of others; ∼'**same** 3, (emphatic form of *same*); ∼-**satisfa'ction**, -**sa'tisfied**, 2b, showing (undue) satisfaction with oneself or one's achievements; ∼-**sea'ling** *a.* 1, (of pneumatic tyre, fuel tank, etc.) having means of automatically sealing small punctures, (of envelope) self-adhesive for sealing; ∼-**seeking** *a.* & *n.* 2b, seeking one's own welfare before that of others; ∼-**ser'vice** 1, (esp. *attrib.*) system by which customers serve themselves with food or goods and pay a cashier or put money into and take food or goods from a machine, (colloq.) shop etc. using this system; ∼-**ser'ving** *a.* 1, placing one's own interests before others'; ∼-**slau'ghter** 1; ∼-**sow'n** 1, grown from seed that has dropped by chance; ∼-**star'ter** 2a, electric appliance for starting engine of motor vehicle without use of crank; ∼-**ste'rile**, -**steri'lity**, 2a, not being self-fertile; ∼-**styled** 1, having taken the name or description without right etc., pretended, would--be; ∼-**suffi'cient**, -**suffi'cing**, 2b, (1) requiring nothing from outside, independent, (2) sufficient in one's own opinion, presumptuous; ∼-**sugge'stion** 2b, reflexive suggestion of the mesmeric or hypnotic kind; ∼-**suppor't(ing)**, -**surre'nder**, -**sustai'ning**, -**sustai'ned**, -**tau'ght**, -**torme'nting** etc., -**tor'ture** etc., 1; ∼-**vi'olence** 2b, (esp.) suicide; ∼-**wi'll(ed)** 2b, (of obstinate pursuit of one's own desires or opinions); ∼-**wi'nding** 1, (of watch etc. with automatic winding apparatus); ∼-**wor'ship** 1. [f. prec.]

se'lfhood *n.* personality, separate and conscious existence. [f. SELF + -HOOD]

se'lfish *a.* deficient in consideration for others, thinking chiefly of one's own personal profit or pleasure, actuated by self-interest, (of motive etc.) appealing to self-interest; ∼ **theory of morals** (that pursuit of personal profit or pleasure is the ultimate motive of every action); hence ∼LY[2] *adv.*, ∼NESS *n.* [f. SELF + -ISH[1]]

se'lfless *a.* oblivious of oneself, incapable of or resisting selfishness; hence ∼LY[2] *adv.*, ∼NESS *n.* [f. SELF + -LESS]

se'lfness *n.* selfishness; self-regard. [f. SELF + -NESS]

Se'ljuk (-ŏŏk) *a.* & *n.* (member) of 11th–13th-c. Turkish dynasties in central and Western Asia; hence ∼IAN (-jŏŏ'k-) *a.* & *n.* [f. Turk. *seljūq* name of reputed ancestor)]

sell *v.* (**sold** *pr.* sō-) & *n.* **1.** *v.t.* make over or dispose of in exchange for money; *sell the* DUMMY, *the* PASS[3], *a* PUP, *down the* RIVER[2], SHORT 7; ∼ *one's* **life** etc. **dear(ly)**, (fig.) do great injury before being killed etc.; ∼*'ing--race* etc. (in which winning horse must be auctioned); hence ∼'ABLE *a.* **2.** cause to be sold (*the author's name alone will sell many copies*); keep stock of for sale or be a dealer in (*do you sell candles?*; *bookselling* etc.). **3.** betray for money or other reward (*sell one's country* etc.). **4.** offer dishonourably for money or other consideration, make a matter of corrupt bargaining, (*sell justice*, *oneself*, *one's honour* or *chastity*).

5. (sl.) disappoint by not keeping engagement etc., by failing in some way, or by trickery; **sold again!** (excl. used by or to disappointed person). **6.** advertise or publish merits of; give (person) information on value of something, inspire with desire to buy or acquire or agree to something; ∼**'ing point**, advantageous feature; **sold on**, (colloq.) enthusiastic about. **7.** *v.i.* (Of goods) find purchasers (*will never sell*; *selling like wildfire*, *hot* CAKES), have specified price (*it sells at* or *for £5*). **8.** ∼ **off**, sell remainder of (goods), clear out (stock), at reduced prices; ∼ **out**, (1) sell (all or some of one's shares in company, whole stock-in-trade, etc., or abs.), (2) cause betrayal (of); ∼*-out n.*, (1) selling of all tickets etc. for a show etc., commercial success, (2) betrayal; ||∼ **up**, sell one's business, house, etc., sell goods of (debtor) by distress or legal process. **9.** Hence (-)∼'ER[1] *n.*; ∼**er's** or ∼**ers' market**, one in which goods are scarce and expensive. **10.** *n.* (colloq.) deception, disappointment; manner of selling (HARD, SOFT, *sell*). [OE *sellan*, = OS *sellian*, OHG *sellen*, ON *selja*, Goth. *saljan* offer sacrifice f. Gmc **saljan*]

sellanders. See SALLENDERS.

Se'llōtāpe, s-, *n.*, & *v.t.* (fix with) adhesive usu. transparent cellulose or plastic tape. [P as noun]

se'ltzer (-ts-) *n.* ∼ **(water)**, medicinal mineral water from Nieder-Selters in Germany; artificial substitute for this, soda-water. [f. G *Selterser* a. (*Selters*)]

se'lvage, se'lvedge, *n.* edge of cloth so woven that it cannot unravel; border of different material or finish along edge of cloth intended to be removed or hidden; edge-plate of lock with opening for the bolt. [ME, f. SELF + EDGE[1], after Du. *selfegghe*]

selves. See SELF.

semä'ntème *n.* (Ling.) element expressing image or idea. [f. F *sémantème* (as foll.; see -EME)]

semä'nt|ic *a.* & *n.* **1.** *a.* relating to meaning in language; relating to connotations of words; hence ∼ICALLY *adv.* **2.** *n.* (in *pl.*, usu. treated as *sing.*) branch of philology concerned with meanings; hence ∼ICIST [f. F *sémantique* f. Gk *sēmantikos* significant (*sēmainō* signify f. *sēma* sign; see IO)]

se'maphore *n.* & *v.* **1.** *n.* signalling apparatus of post with movable arm(s), arrangement of lanterns, etc., for use (esp. on railways) by day or night; military etc. signalling by operator's two arms or by flag in each hand according to alphabetic code; hence **ssemapho'ric** *a.* **2.** *v.i.* & *t.* signal or send by semaphore. [f. F *sémaphore*, irreg. f. Gk *sēma* sign + *-phoros* -PHORE]

semäsi|o'logy *n.* semantics; hence ∼olo'gical *a.* [f. G *semasiologie* f. Gk *sēmasia* meaning (*sēmainō* signify); see -LOGY]

semä'tic *a.* (Zool.) (Of coloration, markings, etc.) significant, serving to warn off enemies or attract attention. [f. Gk *sēma sēmatos* sign + -IC]

se'mblable *a.* (arch.) having semblance of something, seeming. [ME f. OF (as foll.; see -ABLE)]

se'mblance *n.* what looks like, the outward appearance of, something (*put on a semblance of anger*; *bears the semblance of an angel and the heart of a devil*); resemblance. [ME f. OF *sembler* f. L *similare*, *simulare* SIMULATE)]

semée, semé, (sě'mī) *a.* (Her.) covered with small bearings of indefinite number (e.g. stars, fleurs-de-lis) arranged all over field. [F, fem. or masc. p.p. of *semer* to sow)]

semeiology, semeiotics. See SEMIOLOGY.

se'mème *n.* (Ling.) unit of meaning carried by morpheme. [f. SEMANTIC + -EME]

se'měn *n.* generative fluid of male animals, containing spermatozoa in suspension. [ME f. L *semen seminis* seed (*serere* to sow)]

semě'ster *n.* half-year course or term in (esp. German and US) universities. [G, f. L *semestris* six-monthly (*sex* six, *mensis* month)]

se'mi *n.* (colloq.) ||semi-detached house; *semi--trailer. [abbr.]

sě′mĭ- *pref.* denoting: **1.** a half of (*semicircle*). **2.** on one of two sides (*semi-detached*); in one of two directions (*semi-infinite*); in some particular (*semivowel*). **3.** little more or better than (*semi-barbarism*). **4.** rather less than (*semi-official*); in low degree (*semi-civilized*); not quite deserving the description (*semi-smile*). **5.** imperfect(ly) (*semi-bull, semi-double*). **6.** occurring, published, etc., twice in a specified period (*semi-annual*; cf. BI- 1(e)). **7.** ~a′nnual(ly), sense 6; ~auto-ma′tic 2; ~barbar′ian, -bar′barism, 3; ~-ba′sement 4, inhabited storey partly below ground level; ~bo′ld 4, (Print.; cf. BOLD 3); ||~breve 1, (Mus.) longest note in common use, = two minims (see BREVE); ~bull 5, (issued by pope after election and before coronation with one side of seal left blank); ~chor′us 1, part of chorus, passage performed by it; ~circle, ~cir′cular *a.*, 1, (amounting to, arranged as or in, shaped like) half of a circle or of its circumference, set of objects ranged in or object forming a semicircle, (~*circular canal*, one of three fluid-filled channels in ear giving information to brain to help maintain balance); ~ci′vilized 4; ~co′lon 4, punctuation-mark (;) of intermediate value between comma and full stop; ~condu′cting *a.*, ~condu′ctor, 4, (solid substance) that is non--conductor when pure or at low temperature but has conductivity between that of insulators and that of most metals when containing suitable impurity or at higher temperature; ~co′nscious 5; ~cy′linder, ~cyli′ndrical, 1, (of, forming, etc.) half of a cylinder cut longitudinally; ||~demisemiquaver 1; ~-depo′nent 4, (L Gram.) having active forms in present tenses and passive forms with active sense in perfect tenses; ~-deta′ched 2, (of house) joined to another by party-wall on one side only; ~dia′meter 1; ~-docume′ntary *a.* & *n.* 4, (cinema film) having a factual background and a fictitious story; ~-dome 1, 4, half-dome formed by vertical section, part of structure more or less resembling dome; ~-dou′ble 5, (Bot.) having only outer stamens converted to petals; ~fi′nal 4, match or round preceding the final (~*fi′nalist*, competitor in this); ~-fi′nished 4, prepared for final stage of manufacture; ~-fi′tted 4, (of garment) shaped to the body but not closely fitted; ~flu′id *a.* & *n.* 4, (fluid) of consistency between solid and liquid; ~i′nfidel 3; ~i′nfinite 4, limited in one direction and stretching to infinity in the other; ~i′nvalid 4; ~li′quid *a.* & *n.* 4, = *semi-fluid*; ~lu′nar 1, 4, half-moon-shaped, crescent--shaped, (esp. Anat., as ~*lunar bone* in carpus, *cartilage* in knee, *valve* in heart); ~me′tal, substance with some of the properties of metals; ~mo′nthly 6; ~offi′cial(ly) 4, (esp. of communications made to newspapers by official with stipulation that they shall not be formally attributed to him); ~opa′que, ~-per′manent, 4; ~per′meable 4, (esp. of membrane allowing small molecules to pass through but not large molecules); ~plume 2, feather with firm stem but downy web; ~pre′cious 4, (of gems less valuable than precious stones); ||~quaver 1, (Mus.) note with two-hooked symbol, equal to half a quaver; ~ri′gid 4, (of airship) having stiffened keel attached to flexible gas container; ~ski′lled 4, having or requiring some training but less than skilled work(er); ~-smile, ~so′lid, 4; ~sweet 4, (of biscuit etc.) slightly sweetened; ~tone 1, (Mus.) smallest interval used in classical European music, half of tone; ~-trai′ler 4, trailer having wheels at back but supported by towing vehicle at front; ~transpar′ent 4; ~tro′pical 4, subtropical; ~u′ncial 5, between uncial and minuscule; ~vowel 2, sound, or letter representing sound, intermediate between vowel and consonant (e.g. y, w); ~wee′kly 6. [F etc. or L, corresp. to Gk HEMI-, Skr. *sámi*]

sě′minal *a.* of seed or semen or reproduction, germinal, reproductive, propagative, (~ **fluid,** semen; **in the** ~ **state,** rudimentary, still undeveloped); providing a basis for future development (*seminal ideas, mind*); hence ~LY² *adv.* [ME f. OF, or f. L *seminalis* (as SEMEN; see -AL)]

sě′minar *n.* small class at university for discussion and research; *conference of specialists; short intensive course of study. [G, f. as foll.]

sě′minar|ў *n.* **1.** (arch. or fig.) place of education or development. **2.** training college for priests, rabbis, etc.; hence ~IST (3) *n.* [ME, f. L *seminarium* seed-plot neut. (as n.) of *seminarius* a. (as SEMEN; see -ARY¹)]

sēmini′ferous *a.* bearing seed; conveying semen. [f. SEMEN +-I-+-FEROUS]

sēmiŏ′logў, sēmiŏ′tics, sēmeiŏ′- (-mĭŏ′-), *ns.* branch of linguistics concerned with signs and symbols; (Path.) symptomatology; hence **sēmiolo′GI-CAL, sēmiŏ′tic**(AL), *adjs.* [f. Gk *sēmeion* sign (*sēma* mark), *sēmeiōtikos* of signs + -LOGY, -ICS]

Sě′m|ite *n.* & *a.* (member) of any of the races supposed to be descended from Shem, son of Noah (Gen. 10:21 ff.), including esp. the Jews, Phoenicians, Arabs, and Assyrians; so **Sěmi′tIC** *a.* (esp. of (1) languages of family including Hebrew and Arabic, (2) the Jews), ~itISM (2, 4), ~itIST (3) *ns.*, ~itIZE (3) *v.t.* [f. mod. L *Semita*, f. LL f. Gk *Sēm* Shem; see -ITE¹]

sě′mmit *n.* (Sc.) undershirt. [ME; orig. unkn.]

sēmoli′na (-lē′-) *n.* hard grains left after milling of flour, used in puddings etc. and in pasta; pudding etc. made of this. [f. It. *semolino* dim. of *semola* bran f. L *simila* flour]

sěmpiter′nal *a.* (rhet.) eternal, everlasting. [ME, f. OF *sempiternel* f. LL *sempiternalis* f. L *sempiternus* (*semper* always, *aeternus* eternal); see -AL]

semplice (sě′mplĭchä) *adv.* (Mus.) in a simple style of performance. [It., = SIMPLE]

sempre (sě′mprä) *adv.* (Mus.) throughout, always, (*sempre forte, rallentando*). [It.]

sempstress. See SEAMSTRESS.

||**SEN** *abbr.* State Enrolled Nurse.

Sen. *abbr.* Senate; Senator; Senior.

sěnā′r′i|us *n.* (*pl.* ~*i pr.* -ī). (L Pros.) verse of six feet, esp. iambic trimeter. [L (see foll.)]

sě′narў *a.* of six, by sixes. [f. L *senarius* (*seni* distrib. of *sex* six; see -ARY¹)]

sě′nate *n.* **1.** (Rom. Hist.) State council of the republic and empire sharing legislation with the popular assemblies, administration with the magistrates, and judicial power with the knights. **2.** upper and less numerous branch of the legislative assembly in US, France, and other countries, in states of US, etc.; (rhet.) any legislature or its proceedings or members. **3.** governing (academic) body of university or *college. [ME, f. OF *senat* f. L *scnatus* (*senex* old man; see -ATE¹)]

sě′nator *n.* member of senate; Lord of Session; hence or cogn. **sēnatō′r′IAL** *a.*, ~SHIP *n.* [ME, f. OF *senateur* f. L *senator -oris* (as prec.; see -OR)]

sēnā′tus *n.* ~ (acade′micus), senate of Scottish university; ~ **consu′ltum,** decree of ancient Roman senate, or of French senate under Napoleon I or III. [L (see SENATE)]

sěnd¹ *v.* (**sent**). **1.** *v.t.* order or cause to go, bring about conveyance of, (*to some destination, into place, out, away,* etc.; *send message* or *messenger* to; *sent me a book; will send an army; send goods all over the world*); ~ **in,** enter for competition etc.; ~ **on,** transmit to further destination or in advance of one's own arrival; ~ **up,** transmit to higher authority (see also sense 4); *send* WORD¹ 4. **2.** (Of God, providence, etc.) grant, bestow, inflict, bring about, cause to be, (*send rain, a judgement, pestilence; God send it may not be so!; send her victorious!*). **3.** propel, cause to move, (*send bullet; send person flying* (FLY² 5, PACK²ing); *sent his temperature up; send out* or *forth leaves, steam, odour*); cause to go (*mad, into raptures* etc., *to sleep* etc.). **4.** dismiss with or without force (*sent him away, about his business*); *send to* COVENTRY; ||~ **down,** rusticate or expel from university, put in prison, (Cricket) bowl (ball, over); ~ **off,** get (letter, parcel, etc.) dispatched, attend departure of (person) as sign of respect etc., (Footb. etc., of referee) order (player) to take no further part in a game; ∼-*off* n.; ∼ **up**, ‖(colloq.) satirize, ridicule by mimicking, *(sl.) put in prison, (see also sense 1); ∼-*up* n., ‖(colloq.) a satire. **5.** (sl.) affect emotionally, put into ecstasy. **6.** *v.i.* send message or letter (*sent to warn me*); ∼ **for,** tell (person) to come, order (book etc.) from elsewhere. **7.** Hence ∼'ER[1] n. [OE *sendan*, = OS *sendian*, OHG *sendan, senten,* ON *senda,* Goth. *sandjan* f. Gmc *sandhjan (**sandh-,* *santh causative of *senth)]

sĕnd[2], scĕnd, n., & *v.i.* (Naut.) **1.** n. impulse given by wave(s) (*scend of the sea*); plunge of vessel. **2.** *v.i.* (Of vessel) plunge or pitch owing to impulse of wave. [f. prec. or f. DESCEND]

sĕ'ndal n. (Hist.) (garment of) thin rich silk material. [ME, f. OF *cendal,* ult. f. Gk *sindon*]

Sĕnĕgalĕ'se (-z) a. & n. (*pl.* same). (native or inhabitant) of Senegal. [f. *Senegal* in W. Africa + -ESE]

sĕnĕ'sc|ent a. growing old; hence ∼ENCE n. [f. L *senescere* (*senex* old; see -ESCENT)]

sĕ'neschal (-shal) n. steward or major-domo of medieval great house; ‖cathedral official; judge in Sark. [ME f. OF, f. med. L *seniscalus* f. Gmc *siniskalkaz (**seni-* old, *skalkaz servant; cf. MARSHAL[1])]

senhor, senhora, senhorita, (sānyōr', -ōr'a, -erē'ta) ns. (used of or to Portuguese or Brazilians as SIGNOR etc.). [Port., f. L SENIOR]

sĕ'nīle a. showing the feebleness etc. of, incident to, old age (*senile apathy, decay, garrulity,* etc.), hence **sĕnī'lĭty** n. [f. F *sénile* or f. L *senilis* (*senex* old man; see -IL)]

sĕ'nior a. & n. **1.** a. more advanced in age, older or oldest in standing, superior in age or standing to, of higher or highest position, (opp. JUNIOR); (of school) having pupils in an older age-range; *of final year at university, high school, etc.; ∼ **citizen,** old person (above specified age); *∼ **college** (offering four-year course for baccalaureate); ‖∼ **combination** or **common room** (for use by senior members of college); ∼ **officer** (esp. one to whom a junior is responsible); ∼ **partner,** head of firm; ‖∼ **service,** Navy as opp. Army; ‖∼ **tutor,** college tutor in charge of the teaching arrangements; *senior* WRANGLER; so **sĕnĭō'rĬTY** n. **2.** (Appended to name for distinction, opp. JUNIOR) senior to another of same name. **3.** n. person of advanced age or comparatively long service etc.; one's elder or superior in length of service, membership, etc., (*is my senior*); senior student. [ME f. L, = older, old(ish) man, compar. of *senex senis* old (man)]

sĕ'nna n. (dried pods or leaflets, used as laxative, of) cassia plant. [f. med. L *sena* f. Arab. *sanā*]

sĕ'nnĕt n. (Hist.) signal call on trumpet or cornet (in stage-directions of Elizabethan plays). [perh. var. of SIGNET]

sĕ'nnĭght (-īt) n. (arch.) week. [OE *seofon nihta* seven nights]

sĕ'nnĭt, sĕ'nnĕt, n. (Naut.) braided cordage made in flat or round or square form from 3–9 cords. [17th c., of unkn. orig.]

señor (*pl.* ***señores***), ***señora, señorita,*** (sĕnyōr', -ōr'ĕz; -ōr'a; -erē'ta) ns. (used of or to Spaniards or Spanish-speakers as SIGNOR etc.). [Sp., f. L SENIOR]

Senr. *abbr.* Senior.

sĕ'nsāte a. perceived by the senses. [f. LL *sensatus* having senses (as SENSE; see -ATE[2])]

sĕnsā'tion n. **1.** consciousness of perceiving or seeming to perceive some state or condition of one's body or its parts or senses or of one's mind or its emotions, contents of such consciousness, (*had a sensation of giddiness, comfort, thirst, falling, pride; in search of a new sensation*). **2.** stirring of the emotions of many people or of eager interest among them, display of intense common emotion or interest, literary or other use of material calculated to cause such effect; event, person, etc., causing such effect. **3.** Hence ∼AL a., ∼alLY[2] adv. [f. med. L *sensatio* f. L *sensus* SENSE; see -ATION]

sĕnsā'tional‖ism n. **1.** (Philos.) theory that ideas are derived solely from sensation (opp. *rationalism*). **2.** pursuit of the sensational in literature, political agitation, etc. **3.** So ∼IST (2) n. [f. SENSATIONAL + -ISM]

sĕnse n., & *v.t.* **1.** n. any of the special bodily faculties by which sensation is roused (*has quick, keen, senses, a dull sense of smell*); **the five ∼s,** sight, hearing, smell, taste, and touch, by which the external world is perceived; **sixth ∼,** (supposed faculty giving) intuitive or extra-sensory knowledge; ∼**-datum,** element of experience received through the senses; ∼**-organ,** bodily organ conveying external stimuli to the sensory system. **2.** (in *pl.*) sanity or ordinary state of mind regarded as attested by possession of senses; **in** one's ∼**s,** sane; **has taken leave of, is out of, his** ∼**s,** has gone mad; **frightened out of his** ∼**s** (into loss of faculties); **come, bring** (person), **to his** ∼**s** (out of unconsciousness or folly). **3.** ability to perceive or feel or to be conscious of the presence or properties of things, sensitiveness of all or any of the senses; **errors of** ∼, mistakes in perception; **the pleasures of** ∼, those depending on sensation. **4.** consciousness of (a or *the sense of pleasure, having done well,* one's *own importance, shame, responsibility*); **under a** ∼ **of wrong,** feeling wronged. **5.** quick or accurate appreciation *of,* instinct regarding or insight into specified matter, habit of basing one's conduct on such instinct, (*sense of locality,* DIRECTION, *the ridiculous,* HUMOUR[1], *duty, gratitude; a keen sense of honour;* ROAD[1] *sense, the religious, moral, aesthetic, sense*). **6.** practical wisdom, judgement, COMMON[1] *sense,* conformity to these, (*sound, good, sense; had not the sense to do; has plenty of sense; what is the sense of talking like that?; has more sense to do; now you are talking sense*); **a man of** ∼ (sagacious). **7.** meaning, way in which a word etc. is to be understood, intelligibility or coherence or possession of a meaning, (*in what exact sense we shall rise again is doubtful; the sense of the word is clear; in the strict, literal, metaphorical, legal, proper, sense; in a vague, in every, sense*); **in a** or **one** ∼, provided that the statement is taken in a particular way, under limitations, (*what you say is true in a sense*); **make** ∼, be intelligible or practicable; **make** ∼ **of,** show to have a meaning. **8.** prevailing sentiment among a number of people (**take the** ∼ **of the meeting,** ascertain this by putting question etc.). **9.** (Math. etc.) direction of movement; position of line etc. in one of two opposite directions. **10.** *v.t.* perceive by sense; be vaguely aware of; *understand; (of machine etc.) detect. [ME, f. L *sensus* faculty of feeling, thought, meaning (*sentire sens-* feel)]

sĕ'nselĕss (-sl-) a. unconscious; incapable of sensation; wholly foolish; meaningless, purposeless; hence ∼LY[2] adv., ∼NESS n. [f. prec. + -LESS]

sĕnsĭbĭ'lĭty n. **1.** capacity to feel (*skin lost its sensibility*). **2.** exceptional openness to emotional impressions (*sense and sensibility*); delicacy of feeling, susceptibility (*sensibility to kindness* etc.); (over-)sensitiveness. **3.** (in *pl.*) susceptibility, tendency to feel offended etc. [ME, f. LL *sensibilitas* (as foll.; see -ITY)]

sĕ'nsĭble a. **1.** perceptible by the senses (*sensible phenomena, things*); great enough to be perceived, appreciable, (*a sensible difference, increase*). **2.** (arch.) aware, not unmindful, *of,* (*was sensible of his peril*). **3.** having or showing good sense, reasonable, judicious, moderate, practical, (*a sensible man, course of action, compromise; that is very sensible of him*); (of clothing) unpretentiously practical. **4.** Hence **sĕnsĭbLY**[2] adv., ∼NESS (-bln-) n. [ME f. OF, or f. L *sensibilis* (as SENSE; see -IBLE)]

sĕ'nsĭtive a. & n. **1.** a. having sensibility *to,* very open to or acutely affected by external stimuli or mental impressions; (of person) quick to take offence or have the feelings hurt; (of topic etc.) subject to restriction of discussion because of embarrassment, to ensure security, etc. **2.** (Of instrument etc.) readily responding *to* or recording slight changes of condition; ∼ **market** (liable to quick changes of price). **3.** (Of material) readily affected by or responsive *to* external action; ~ **paper,** (Photog.) paper prepared to respond to action of light; ~ **plant,** mimosa or other plant whose leaves curve downwards and leaflets fold together when touched, (fig.) sensitive person. **4.** Hence ~LY² (-vlĭ) *adv.,* ~NESS (-vn-), **sěnsǐtī'vǐTY** *ns.,* **sěnsǐtǒ'METER** *n.,* device for measuring sensitivity. **5.** *n.* person who is sensitive (esp. to occult influences). [ME, = sensory, f. OF *sensitif -ive* or f. med. L *sensitivus,* irreg. f. L *sentire sens-* feel; see -IVE]

sě'nsǐtīz|e, -īs|e (-īz), *v.t.* make sensitive; (Photog.) make sensitive to light; make (organism etc.) abnormally sensitive to foreign substance; hence ~A'TION, ~ER¹ (2), *ns.* [f. prec. + -IZE]

sě'nsor *n.* device giving signal for detection or measurement of a physical property to which it responds. [f. SENSORY, after *motor*]

sěnsō'r'ǐ|um *n.* (*pl.* ~**a** *or* ~**ums**). the seat of sensation, the brain, brain and spinal cord, or grey matter of these; (Biol.) whole sensory apparatus including nerve-system etc.; hence ~AL *a.* [LL, f. L *sentire sens-* feel; see -ORY]

sě'nsorȳ *a.* of sensation or the senses. [f. as prec. + -ORY]

sě'nsual (-sū-, -shōō-) *a.* **1.** of sense or sensation, = prec. **2.** of or depending on the senses only and not on the intellect or spirit, carnal, fleshly, (*sensual pleasures*); given to the pursuit of sensual pleasures or gratification of the appetites, self-indulgent in regard to food and drink and sexual enjoyment, voluptuous, licentious; indicative of sensual nature (*sensual lips, mouth*). **3.** (Philos.) holding the doctrine of, according to, of, sensationalism. **3.** Hence or cogn. ~ISM (2, 3), ~IST (1, 2), ~ITY (-ă'l-), *ns.,* ~IZE (3) *v.t.,* ~LY² *adv.* [ME, f. LL *sensualis* (as SENSE; see -AL)]

sě'ns|um *n.* (*pl.* ~**a**). (Philos.) sense-datum. [mod. L, neut. p.p. (as n.) of L *sentire* feel]

sě'nsŭous *a.* of, derived from, affecting, the senses esp. in neutral or aesthetic manner (opp. SENSUAL 2); hence ~LY² *adv.,* ~NESS *n.* [f. L *sensus* sense + -OUS]

sěnt. See SEND¹.

sě'ntence *n.,* & *v.t.* **1.** *n.* decision of lawcourt, esp. (declaration of) punishment allotted to person convicted in criminal trial (lit. or fig.); **under ~ of,** having been condemned to (death etc.). **2.** (Gram.) set of words complete in itself as expression of thought, containing subject and predicate (either, or part of either or both, of which may be omitted by ellipsis), and conveying a statement, question, exclamation, or command (e.g. *I go, will you go?, go* = go thou or you, *what?* = what did you say?, *fire!* = there is a fire; *hearts trumps* = hearts are trumps); **simple ~** (with single subject and predicate); **compound ~** (with more than one of either or (*usu.) both; **complex ~** (with subordinate clause or clauses); so **sěntě'ntIAL** (-shal) *a.* **3.** part of writing or speech between two full stops or equivalent pauses and often including several grammatical sentences (e.g. *I went, he came*); (Mus.) unit of two or more phrases. **4.** (arch.) opinion for or against some course or conclusion (*my sentence is for war*). **5.** (arch.) pithy or pointed saying, briefly expressed thought, maxim, proverb. **6.** *v.t.* announce sentence of (convicted criminal or transf.), declare condemned *to.* [ME f. OF, f. L *sententia* opinion (*sentire* be of opinion; see -ENCE)]

sěntě'ntious (-shŭs) *a.* aphoristic, pithy, given to the use of maxims, affecting a concise impressive style; (of style) affectedly formal; (of person) fond of pompous moralizing; hence ~LY² *adv.,* ~NESS *n.* [f. L *sententiosus* (as prec.; see -OUS)]

sě'nti|ent (-shent) *a.* having the power of perception by the senses; hence ~ENCE, ~ENCY, *ns.,* ~entLY² *adv.* [f. L *sentire* feel; see -ENT]

sě'ntiment *n.* **1.** a mental feeling, the sum of what one feels on some subject, a tendency or view based on or coloured with emotion, such feelings collectively as an influence, (*the sentiment of pity, patriotism; my* sentiment towards him is one of respect; animated by noble sentiments; sentiment unchecked by reason is a bad guide); **those are,** (joc.) **them's, my ~s,** that is what I think about it. **2.** emotional feeling conveyed in literature or art. **3.** tendency to be swayed by feeling rather than by reason, emotional weakness, false or unworthy tenderness or the display of it, nursing of the emotions. **4.** (sense intended to be conveyed by) the expression of some desire or view esp. as formulated for a toast etc. (*the sentiment is good though the words are injudicious; conclude* one's *speech with a sentiment*). [ME, f. OF *sentement,* f. med. L *sentimentum* (L *sentire* feel; see -MENT)]

sěntimě'ntal *a.* (Of person or action) characterized by sentiment (esp. sense 3); pertaining to sentiment; appealing to sentiment (~ **value,** value of a thing to particular person because of its associations); hence ~ISM (3), ~IST (2), ~ITY (-ă'l-), *ns.,* ~IZE (2, 3) *v.i.* & *t.,* ~LY² *adv.* [f. prec. + -AL]

sě'ntinel *n.,* & *v.t.* (||-ll-). **1.** *n.* soldier etc. posted to keep guard (lit. or fig.). **2.** ~ (**crab**), Indian-Ocean crab with long eye-stalks. **3.** *v.t.* (poet.) keep guard over or in. **4.** station sentinels at or in. [f. F *sentinelle* f. It. *sentinella,* of unkn. orig.]

sě'ntry *n.* **1.** (esp. Mil.) = prec. 1. **2.** ~-**box,** wooden cabin large enough to hold sentry standing; ~-**go,** duty of pacing up and down as sentry. [perh. f. obs. *centrinel,* var. of prec.]

Sěnu'ssi (-ōō'-) *n.* (*pl.* usu. same). member of N. Afr. Muslim sect noted for fanaticism and belligerence. [f. Sidi Muhammad ibn 'Alī *as-Sanūsī,* founder of the sect d. 1859]

sě'pal *n.* (Bot.) one of the divisions or leaves of the calyx. [f. F *sépale,* mod. L *sepalum,* formed by N. J. de Necker 1790, perh. as SEPARATE¹ + PETAL]

sě'par|able. able to be separated; (Gram., of prefix, or verb in respect of it) written as separate word in some collocations; hence ~ABI'LITY, ~**able**NESS (-beln-), *ns.,* ~**ab**LY² *adv.* [f. F *séparable* or f. L *separabilis* (as SEPARATE²; see -ABLE)]

sě'parate¹ *a.* & *n.* **1.** *a.* physically disconnected, forming a unit that is or may be regarded as apart or by itself, distinct, individual, of individuals, (*from,* or abs.; *the separate volumes may be had singly; live in separate rooms; the two questions are essentially separate; one is quite separate from the other*); ~ **estate,** married woman's property when not subject to husband's control; ~ **maintenance,** husband's allowance to wife from whom he lives separate by consent (cf. ALIMONY); hence ~LY² (-tlǐ) *adv.,* ~NESS (-tn-) *n.* **2.** *n.* copy of single article etc. reprinted from proceedings of society, magazine, etc., for separate distribution. **3.** (in *pl.*) separate articles of dress suitable for wearing together in various combinations. [f. L *separatus* p.p. (as foll.); see -ATE²]

sě'par|āte² *v.* **1.** *v.t.* make separate, sever, disunite, keep from union or contact; *discharge, dismiss. **2.** sort or divide (milk, ore, fruit, light, etc.) into constituent parts or sizes, get (*out*) (cream, waste product, etc.) by such process for use or rejection, whence ~**āt**OR *n.* **3.** *v.i.* secede *from,* go different ways, disperse; cease to live together as married couple. **4.** Hence ~ATIVE, ~atory, *adjs.* [ME, f. L SE(*parare* make ready) + -ATE³]

sěpara'tion *n.* separating or being separated; **judicial** or **legal ~** (of man and wife under ~ **order** made by court). [ME f. OF, f. L *separatio -onis* (as prec.; see -ATION)]

sě'parat|ist *n.* one who favours separation, esp. for political or ecclesiastical independence (opp. *unionist*); so ~ISM (3) *n.* [f. SEPARATE¹ + -IST]

Sěphăr'd|ī *n.* (*pl.* ~**im**). Jew of Spanish or Portuguese descent (cf. ASHKENAZI); hence ~IC *a.* [LHeb., f. *sᵉp̄āraḏ,* country mentioned in Obad. 20 and taken to be Spain]

sē'pia *n.* black fluid of cuttlefish; brown pigment prepared from this used in monochrome drawing and in water-colours; rich reddish-brown colour; drawing done in sepia. [L, f. Gk *sēpia* cuttlefish]

se′poy *n.* (Hist.) native Indian soldier under European, esp. British, discipline; *Sepoy* MUTINY. [f. Urdu & Pers. *sipāhī* soldier (*sipāh* army)]

sĕppu′ku (-ōō′kōō) *n.* hara-kiri. [Jap.]

sĕps *n.* skink of genus *Chalcides*, with serpent-like body. [L, f. Gk *sēps* (*sēpō* make rotten)]

sĕ′ps|is *n.* (*pl.* ∼es *pr.* -ēz). bacterial contamination from festering wound etc., blood-poisoning. [mod. L, f. Gk *sēpsis* (as prec.)]

sĕpt *n.* clan, esp. in Ireland. [prob. alt. of SECT]

sĕpt-, sĕ′pt|i-, *comb. forms.* seven, as: ∼**centenary,** (-tē′-, -sē′-) *a.* & *n.* (festival) of the 700th anniversary; ∼**e′nnial,** lasting, recurring every, seven years; ∼**e′nnium** (pl. *-iums* or *-ia*), period of seven years; ∼**ila′teral,** seven-sided; ∼**iva′lent,** (Chem.) having a valence of seven. [L (*septem* seven)]

Sept. *abbr.* September; Septuagint.

sĕ′pta. See SEPTUM.

sĕ′ptal *a.* of sept(s); of septum or septa. [f. SEPT, SEPTUM + -AL]

sĕ′pt|āte *a.* (Bot., Zool., & Anat.) having septum or septa, partitioned; hence ∼A′TION *n.* [f. SEPTUM + -ATE²]

Sĕpte′mber *n.* ninth month of year. [ME, f. L *September* (*septem* seven; orig. seventh month of Roman year)]

sĕptēnār′i|us *n.* (*pl.* ∼i *pr.* -ī). (Pros.) verse of seven feet, esp. trochaic or iambic tetrameter catalectic. [L (*septeni* distrib. of *septem* seven; see -ARY¹)]

sĕptēnary (sĕptē′n-, sĕ′ptĭn-) *a.* & *n.* **1.** *a.* of seven, by sevens, on basis of seven. **2.** *n.* group or set of seven (esp. years); septenarius. [f. L (as prec.; see -ARY¹)]

sĕ′ptēnate *a.* (Bot.) growing in sevens; having seven divisions. [f. L *septeni* (as SEPTENARIUS) + -ATE²]

sĕptĕ′t, -ĕ′tte, *n.* **1.** (Mus.) (performers of) composition for seven voices or instruments. **2.** set of seven. [f. G *septett* f. L *septem* seven; see -ET¹, -ETTE]

sĕ′ptfoil (sĕ′t-) *n.* **1.** (arch.) tormentil. **2.** seven-lobed ornamental figure. [f. LL *septifolium* after *cinquefoil, trefoil*]

sĕ′pti-. See SEPT-.

sĕ′pt|ic *a.* of or involving sepsis, putrefying; ∼**ic tank** (in which organic matter in sewage is disintegrated through bacterial activity); hence ∼ICALLY *adv.,* ∼i′cITY *n.* [f. L f. Gk *sēptikos* (*sēpō* make rotten; see -IC)]

sĕpticae′m|ia (-sē′m-), ***-cē′m|ia,** *n.* (Path.) blood-poisoning; hence ∼IC *a.* [mod. L, f. Gk *sēptikos* + *haima* blood + -IA¹; see prec., -AEMIA]

sĕpti′llion (-yon) *n.* (for *pl.* usage see HUNDRED). ‖a million raised to seventh power; *a thousand raised to eighth power. [F (*sept* seven, after *billion* etc.)]

sĕ′ptimal *a.* of the number seven. [f. L *septimus* seventh (*septem* seven) + -AL]

sĕ′ptime (-ēm) *n.* seventh of eight parrying positions in fencing. [f. L *septimus* (as prec.)]

sĕptūagĕnār′ian *a.* & *n.* (person) from 70 to 79 years old. [f. L *septuagenarius* (*septuageni* distrib. of *septuaginta* seventy; see -ARY¹) + -AN]

sĕptūagĕ′nary *a.* & *n.* of seventy; = prec. [as prec.]

Sĕptūagĕ′sima *n.* ∼ **(Sunday),** Sunday before Sexagesima. [ME f. L, = seventieth (day), f. as foll. (w. ref. to period of 70 days from Septuagesima to Saturday after Easter)]

Sĕ′ptūagint *n.* Greek version of OT including the Apocrypha, said to have been made about 270 BC by seventy-two translators. [f. L *septuaginta* seventy]

sĕ′pt|um *n.* (*pl.* ∼a). (Anat., Bot., & Zool.) partition such as that between the nostrils or the chambers of a poppy-fruit or shell. [f. L *s(a)eptum* (*saepire saept-* enclose f. *saepes* hedge)]

sĕ′ptŭple *a., n.,* & *v.* **1.** *a.* & *n.* sevenfold (amount). **2.** *v.t.* & *i.* multiply by seven. [f. LL *septuplus* f. L *septem* seven]

sĕptŭplĕt (sĕ′-, -ū′-) *n.* **1.** one of seven children born at a birth. **2.** (Mus.) group of seven notes to be played in the time of four or six. [f. as prec., after *triplet* etc.]

sĕpŭ′lchral (-kral) *a.* of sepulchre(s) or sepulture (*sepulchral mound, customs*); suggestive of the tomb, funereal, gloomy, dismal, (*a sepulchral look, voice*); hence ∼LY² *adv.* [f. F *sépulchral* or f. L *sepulchralis* (as foll.; see -AL)]

‖**sĕ′pulchre, *sĕ′pulcher,** (-ker) *n.,* & *v.t.* **1.** *n.* tomb esp. cut in rock or built of stone or brick, burial vault or cave; **the Holy S**∼ (in which Christ was laid); **whited** ∼, hypocrite (w. ref. to Matt. 23:27). **2.** *v.t.* lay in sepulchre; serve as sepulchre for. [ME f. OF, f. L *sepulc(h)rum* (*sepelire sepult-* bury)]

sĕ′pulture *n.* burying, putting in the grave. [ME f. OF, f. L *sepultura* (as prec.; see -URE)]

seq(q). *abbr.* the following. [f. L *sequens* etc.]

sĕquā′cious (-shus) *a.* (arch.) inclined to follow, lacking independence or originality, servile; (of reasoning or reasoner) not inconsequent, coherent; hence ∼LY² *adv.,* **sĕquā′ciTY** *n.* [f. L *sequax* (*sequi* follow); see -ACIOUS]

sĕ′quel *n.* what follows (esp. as result); continuation or resumption of a story or process or the like after a pause or intended or provisional ending (**in the ∼,** as things developed afterwards). [ME, f. OF *sequelle* or f. L *sequel(l)a* (*sequi* follow)]

sĕquē′la *n.* (*pl.* ∼e). (Path., esp. in *pl.*) morbid condition or symptom following upon some disease. [L (*sequi* follow)]

sĕ′quence *n.* **1.** (order of) succession, coming after or next, set of things that belong next to each other on some principle of order, series without gaps, (*shall follow the sequence of events; give the facts in historical sequence; calamities in rapid sequence*); set of poems on one theme; part of cinema film dealing with one scene or topic; set of three or more playing-cards next to each other in value. **2.** succession without implication of causality (opp. *consequence*). **3.** (Mus.) repetition of phrase or melody at higher or lower pitch. **4.** (Gram.) ∼ **of tenses,** dependence of subordinate verb tense according to certain rules on tense of principal verb (e.g. *I think you are, thought you were, wrong*). **5.** (Eccl.) hymn said or sung after the Gradual or Alleluia that precedes the Gospel. [ME, f. LL *sequentia* f. part. of *sequi* follow; see -ENCE]

sĕ′quent *a.* Following as sequence or consequence; consecutive. [OF, or f. L *sequens* (*sequi* follow; see -ENT)]

sĕquĕ′ntial (-shal) *a.* forming a sequence or consequence or sequela; hence ∼ITY (-shiă′l-) *n.,* ∼LY² *adv.* [f. SEQUENCE after *consequential*]

sĕquĕ′ster *v.t.* **1.** *v.t.* seclude, isolate, set apart, (*sequester oneself from the world*); esp. in *p.p.*: *a.* sequestered life, *retreat, cottage*); (Chem.) bind (metal ion) so that it cannot react. **2.** (Law) seize temporary possession of (debtor's estate etc.); (Eccl.) apply (income of benefice) to clearing of incumbent's debts or accumulating fund for next incumbent. **3.** confiscate, appropriate. [ME, f. OF *sequestrer* or f. LL *sequestrare* commit for safe keeping f. L *sequester* trustee]

sĕquestr|āte (sĭkwĕ′s-, sē′kwis-) *v.t.* = prec. 2, 3; hence or cogn. ∼ABLE *a.,* **sĕquĕstrā′TION, sĕ′quĕs-trātOR, ns.** [f. LL *sequestrare* (as prec.) + -ATE³]

sĕquĕ′str|um *n.* (*pl.* ∼a). piece of dead bone or other tissue detached from surrounding parts; hence ∼AL *a.,* **sĕquĕstrō′TOMY** *n.* [mod. L, neut. (as n.) of L *sequester* standing apart]

sĕ′quin *n.* **1.** circular spangle on dress; hence ∼**(n)**ED² (-nd) *a.* **2.** (Hist.) Venetian gold coin. [F, f. It. *zecchino* (*zecca* a mint f. Arab. *sikka* die)]

sĕquoi′a *n.* Californian coniferous tree of great height. [mod. L genus-name, f. *Sequoiah,* name of a Cherokee]

sĕr′a. See SERUM.

sĕră′c *n.* one of the castellated masses into which a glacier is divided at steep points by the crossing of crevasses. [f. Swiss F *sérac,* orig. name of a compact white cheese]

sera′glio (-ah′lyō) *n.* (*pl.* ∼s). harem; (Hist.) Turkish palace, esp. that of Sultan with government offices etc. at Constantinople. [f. It. *serraglio* f. Turk. f. Pers. *sarāy* palace; cf. foll.]

serai (-rī′, -rah′ī) *n.* = CARAVANSERAI. [f. Turk. f. Pers. (as prec.)]

sera′ng *n.* (Anglo-Ind.) native head of Lascar crew. [Hindi & Hind., f. Pers. *sarhang* commander]

săra′pe, săra′pe, zăra′pe, (-ah′pā) *n.* shawl or blanket worn as cloak by Spanish-Americans. [Mexican Sp.]

sĕ′raph *n.* (*pl.* ∼im *or* ∼s). celestial being, one of the highest ORDER[1] of ninefold celestial hierarchy gifted esp. with love and associated with light, ardour, and purity. [back-formation f. *seraphim* (cf. CHERUB) pl. f. LL f. Gk *seraphim* f. Heb. *ś·rāpīm*]

sĕra′ph|ic *a.* of or like seraphim; ecstatically adoring or fervent; S∼ic **Doctor,** St. Bonaventura; hence ∼ICALLY *adv.* [f. med. L *seraphicus* f. LL (as prec.; see -IC)]

sĕraskier′ *n.* (Hist.) Turkish commander-in-chief and minister of war. [Turk., f. Pers. *sar′askar* head of army]

Sĕrb, Sĕr′bĭan, *adjs.* & *ns.* (native, inhabitant, or language) of Serbia. [f. Serbo-Croatian *Srb* Serb + -IAN]

Sĕr′bŏ- *comb. form.* Serbian, as: ∼**-Cro′at,** ∼**-Croa′tian,** (of the) Slavonic language of the Serbs and Croats. [f. prec. + -o-]

Sĕrbō′nĭan *a.* ∼ **bog,** difficult position with no way of escape. [f. Gk *Serbōnis* (*limnē* lake) in Nile delta, in which whole armies were said to have disappeared (Milton *Paradise Lost* ii. 592)]

sĕre[1], sear[2], *n.* catch of gun-lock holding hammer at half or full cock. [prob. f. OF *serre* lock, bolt, grasp (*serrer*; see SERRIED)]

sĕre[2]. See SEAR[1].

sĕre[3] *n.* (Ecol.) sequence of animal or plant communities. [f. SERIES]

serein (serǎ′n̄) *n.* fine rain falling at evening in tropical situations from cloudless sky. [F, f. OF *serain* f. Gallo-Rom. **seranum* f. L *serum* evening (*serus* late)]

sĕrenā′d|e *n.*, & *v.t.* **1.** *n.* evening song or instrumental piece sung or played esp. by lover at his lady's window, or suitable for this; = foll. **2.** *v.t.* sing or play serenade to; hence ∼ER[1] *n.* [f. F *sérénade* f. It. *serenata* (*sereno* SERENE; see -ADE]

sĕrena′ta (-nah′-) *n.* (Mus.) cantata with pastoral subject; simple form of orchestral or wind-band suite. [It. (as prec.)]

sĕrendī′pĭt|y̆ *n.* the faculty of making happy and unexpected discoveries by accident; hence ∼OUS *a.* [coined by Horace Walpole (1754) after *The Three Princes of Serendip* (Sri Lanka), a fairy-tale]

serē′ne (sĭr-, ser-) *a.* (-**er,** -**est**), *n.*, & *v.t.* **1.** *a.* (of sky, air, etc.) clear and calm, (of sea etc.) unruffled; placid, tranquil, unperturbed, (*a serene temper, look, life*); **all** ∼, ||(sl.) all right; **His, Her, Their, Your, S∼ Highness(es)** (titles used of or to members of some European royal families); hence or cogn. ∼LY[2] (-nlī) *adv.,* **serē′nĭty** (sĭr-, ser-) *n.* (**your** etc. **Serenity,** title of reigning prince or similar dignitary). **2.** *n.* (poet.) serene expanse of sky, sea, etc. **3.** *v.t.* (poet.) make (sky, brow, etc.) serene. [f. L *serenus*]

sĕrf *n.* villein, person whose service is attached to the soil and transferred with it (cf. SLAVE); oppressed person, drudge; hence ∼′AGE, ∼′DOM, ∼′HOOD, *ns.* [OF, f. L *servus* slave]

sĕrge *n.* durable twilled worsted etc. fabric. [ME f. OF *sarge, serge* f. Rom. **sarica* f. L *serica* (*lana*); see SILK]

ser′geant (sär′jant) *n.* **1.** (Mil.) non-commissioned officer next below warrant officer; ∼**-major,** **highest-ranking non-commissioned officer;* ||(**regimental**) ∼**-major,** warrant officer assisting adjutant of regiment or battalion; **company** ∼**-major,** highest non-commissioned officer of company. **2.** police officer ranking below ||inspector or **captain. **3.** S∼ **Baker,** (Austral.) large brightly-coloured sea-fish; ∼**-fish,** sea-fish with lateral stripes

suggesting chevron. **4.** Hence ∼SHIP *n.* [ME, f. OF *sergent* f. L *serviens -entis* servant (*servire* SERVE; see -ENT)]

Sergt. *abbr.* Sergeant.

sĕr′ial *a.* & *n.* **1.** *a.* of, in, forming, a series, whence ∼ITY (-ǎ′l-) *n.*; (of story etc.) issued in instalments (∼ **rights,** copyright in regard to story etc. so issued), whence ∼IST (1) *n.*; (of publication) appearing in successive parts published usu. at regular intervals, periodical; (Mus.) of composition using transformations of a fixed SERIES of notes, whence ∼ISM (3), ∼IST (2), *ns.*; ∼ **number** (showing position in a series); hence ∼LY[2] *adv.* **2.** *n.* serial story; a serial publication, periodical. **3.** Hence ∼IZE *v.t.* [f. SERIES + -AL]

sĕr′iate[1] *a.*, **sĕr′iăte[2]** *v.t.* (arrange) in the form of a series, in orderly sequence; so **sēriA′TION** *n.* [f. SERIES + -ATE[2,3]]

seriă′tim (sēr-, sĕr-) *adv.* point by point, taking one subject etc. after another in regular order, (*consider seriatim*). [med. L f. L *series*, after LITERATIM etc.]

Sēr′ic *a.* (rhet. etc.) Chinese. [f. L *sericus*; see SILK]

sĕri′ceous (-shus) *a.* (Bot. & Zool.) covered with glossy down. [f. as prec.; see -EOUS]

sĕ′ricŭltur|e *n.* silkworm-breeding; production of raw silk; hence ∼AL *a.,* ∼IST (3) *n.,* (-ŭ′lcher-). [f. F *sériciculture* f. LL *sericum*; see SILK, -I-, CULTURE]

sĕriĕ′ma *n.* long-legged loud-voiced crested Brazilian or Argentinian bird. [mod. L, f. Tupi *siriema* etc. crested]

sĕr′ies (-ēz, -ĭz) *n.* (*pl.* same). **1.** number of things of which each is similar to the preceding or in which each successive pair are similarly related, sequence, succession, order, row, set, (*a series of kings, misfortunes*; **in** ∼, in ordered succession); group of stamps, coins, etc., of different denominations but issued at one time, in one reign, etc.; group of successive games between same teams, programmes with same actors etc. but each complete in itself, lectures by same speaker or on same subject, etc. **2.** set of successive issues of a periodical, of articles on one subject or by one writer, etc., esp. (*first, second,* etc., *series*) when numbered separately from a preceding or following set; set of independent books in common format or under common title or supervised by common general editor. **3.** (Geol.) set of strata with common characteristic. **4.** (Chem.) set of elements with common properties or of compounds related in composition or structure. **5.** (Math.) set of quantities constituting a progression or having the several values determined by a common relation (**arithmetical, geometrical,** ∼, one in ARITHMETICAL, GEOMETRICAL, progression). **6.** (Electr.) set of batteries etc. having positive electrode of each connected with negative electrode of next; set of circuits arranged **in** ∼, so that same current passes through each circuit. **7.** (Zool.) number of connected genera, families, etc. **8.** (Mus.) arrangement of twelve chromatic notes as basis for serial music. [L, = row, chain (*serere* join, connect)]

sĕ′rif *n.* (Typogr.) cross-line finishing off a stroke of a letter as in T (compare SANSERIF **T**). [perh. f. Du. *schreef* dash, line f. Gmc **skrebh-*]

seri′graph|y̆ *n.* art or process of printing designs by means of a silk screen; so **sĕ′rigraph,** ∼ER[1], *ns.* [irreg. f. L *sericum* SILK + -GRAPHY]

sĕ′rin *n.* small green Mediterranean finch of genus *Serinus,* esp. the wild canary. [F, of uncert. orig.]

sĕrinĕ′tte *n.* instrument for teaching cage-birds to sing. [F (as prec.; see -ETTE)]

seri′nga (-ngga) *n.* **1.** syringa. **2.** Brazilian rubber-tree. [F, f. as SYRINGA]

sĕriō-cŏ′m|ic *a.* combining the serious and the comic, jocular in intention but simulating seriousness or vice versa; hence ∼ICALLY *adv.* [f. foll. + -O- + COMIC]

sēr′ious *a.* **1.** thoughtful, earnest, sober, sedate, responsible, not frivolous or reckless or given to trifling, (*has a serious look, air*; *a serious young person*);

∼ **music, play,** etc., (not merely for amusement); ∼ **thought,** real deliberation. **2.** important, demanding consideration, not to be trifled with, not slight, (*this is a serious matter, question, step; make a serious alteration; have a serious rival in her affections; serious illness, danger, damage, accident, defeat*); ∼ **charge, offence,** (esp. of rape etc.) **3.** sincere, not ironical or jesting or perfunctory, in earnest, (*are you serious?; and now to be serious*). **4.** concerned with religion or ethics, not worldly or secular, (*serious subjects* etc.); (joc. or arch.) religious-minded, with thoughts concentrated on salvation. **5.** Hence ∼LY² *adv.* (esp. as preface to sentence implying that irony etc. is now to cease), ∼NESS *n.* [ME, f. OF *serieux* or LL *seriosus* (L *serius*; see -OUS)]

sĕ′riph. Var. of SERIF.

ser′jeant (sär′jant) *n.* **1.** ∼(**-at-law**), (Hist.) barrister of highest rank. **2.** ∼**-at-arms,** court, parliamentary, or city official with ceremonial duties. **3.** ‖**Common S**∼, circuit judge of Central Criminal Court with duties in City of London. **4.** ‖ = SERGEANT 1 (in official lists). **5.** Hence ∼SHIP *n.* [var. of SERGEANT]

sĕr′mon *n.* **1.** discourse usu. based on Scripture text and delivered from pulpit by way of religious instruction or exhortation; similar discourse on religious or moral subject delivered elsewhere or published; **S**∼ **on the Mount,** discourse of Christ recorded in Matt. 5–7. **2.** moral reflection suggested by natural objects etc. (esp. *sermons in stones*); piece of admonition or reproof, lecture. **3.** Hence ∼IZE (1, 2) *v.t.* & *i.* [ME, f. AF *sermun,* OF *sermon* f. L *sermo -onis* discourse, talk]

sērŏ′log|ў *n.* scientific study of sera and their effects; hence **sēro**LO′GICAL *a.,* ∼IST (3) *n.* [f. SERUM+-O- +-LOGY]

serŏ′sa *n.* (Med.) serous membrane. [mod. L, fem. of med. L *serosus* SEROUS]

sĕ′rotine *n.* chestnut-coloured European bat (*Eptesicus serotinus*). [f. F *sérotine* f. L *serotinus* late, of the evening (*serus* late)]

sēroto′nin *n.* compound present in blood serum, with vaso-constrictive action. [f. SERUM+-O-+TONIC +-IN]

sēr′ous *a.* of or like serum, watery; ∼ **gland, membrane,** (with serous secretion); so **sēro′**SITY *n.* [f. F *séreux* or f. med. L *serosus* (as SERUM; see -OUS)]

sĕr′pent *n.* **1.** scaly limbless reptile, snake esp. of large kind, or in rhet. use (**the, the old, S**∼, the Devil, w. ref. to Gen. 3 & Rev. 20); (fig.) treacherous person esp. one who worms himself into favour for base ends; kind of firework with serpentine motion; PHARAOH'*s serpent.* **2.** (Mus.) old wind instrument of long leather-covered wooden tube with several bends, giving powerful deep note. **3.** ∼**-charmer,** snake-charmer; ∼**-eater,** (1) secretary-bird, (2) markhor; ∼**-grass,** Alpine bistort; ∼ **lizard,** seps; ∼**'s-tongue,** adder's-tongue. **4.** Hence **serpĕ′nti**FORM, ∼**-LIKE,** *adjs.* [ME f. OF, f. L *serpens -entis* part. of *serpere* creep; see -ENT]

sĕr′pentine *a., n.,* & *v.i.* **1.** *a.* of or like a serpent (lit. or fig.), writhing, coiling, tortuous, sinuous, meandering, cunning, subtle, treacherous, (*serpentine windings* of stream, road, etc., or of insinuation); ∼ **verse,** metrical line beginning and ending with same word; ∼ **wisdom** (profound, w. ref. to Matt. 10:16). **2.** *n.* soft rock mainly of hydrated magnesium silicate, usu. dark green and sometimes mottled or spotted like serpent's skin, taking high polish and used as decorative material; (Skating) figure of three circles in line. **3.** *v.i.* move sinuously, meander. [v. f. a., ME, f. OF *serpentin* f. LL *serpentinus* (as prec.; see -INE¹); n. f. med. L *serpentina, -um* abs. use of a.]

serpi′ginous *a.* (Of skin-disease etc.) creeping from one part to another. [f. med. L *serpigo -ginis* ringworm f. L *serpere* creep, +-OUS]

sĕr′pŭla *n.* (*pl.* ∼e). marine worm of genus *Serpula,* inhabiting tortuous calcareous tubes. [LL, = small serpent, f. L *serpere* creep]

sĕ′rra *n.* (*pl.* ∼e). (Anat., Bot., & Zool.) serrated organ, structure, or edge. [L, = saw]

sĕrradi′lla *n.* clover of genus *Ornithopus,* grown as fodder. [Port., dim. of *serrado* serrated]

sĕ′rran *n.* carnivorous sea-fish of family Serranidae. [f. mod. L *serranus* f. L *serra* saw; see -AN]

sĕ′rrāte¹ *a.* (esp. Anat., Bot., & Zool.) notched like saw. [f. L *serratus* (as prec.; see -ATE²)]

sĕrr|ā′te² *v.t.* (esp. in *p.p.* as *a.*) provide with sawlike edge; hence ∼A′TION *n.* [f. LL *serrare* f. L *serra* saw, +-ATE³]

sĕ′rried (-rĭd) *a.* (Of ranks of soldiers, rows of trees, etc.) pressed together, without gaps, close. [f. p.p. of *serry* press close prob. f. F *serré* p.p. of *serrer* close f. Rom. **serrare* f. L *-serare* (*sera* lock), or f. p.p. of obs. *serr* f. OF *serrer*]

sĕ′rrul|āte (-rŏo-) *a.* finely serrate, with series of small notches; hence ∼A′TION *n.* [f. mod. L *serrulatus* f. L *serrula* (SERRA; see -ULE); see -ATE²]

sēr′|um *n.* (*pl.* ∼a or ∼ums). whey; amber-coloured liquid which separates from clot when blood coagulates; blood serum as antitoxin or therapeutic agent; watery animal fluid; ∼**um sickness** etc., skin eruption, fever, etc., sometimes following injections of scrum. [L, = whey]

sĕr′val *n.* tawny black-spotted long-legged African tiger-cat (*Felis serval*). [F, f. Port. *cerval* deerlike (*cervo* deer f. L *cervus*)]

sĕr′vant *n.* **1.** person who has undertaken usu. in return for stipulated pay to carry out the orders of an individual or corporate employer; (esp.) one who lives in house of master or mistress, receiving board and lodging and wages and performing domestic duties; CIVIL, PUBLIC, *servant;* ∼*s′* **hall,** room in which servants of large household have meals etc.; ∼ **of** ∼**s,** lowest of dependants, esp. ∼ *of the* ∼*s of God,* title assumed by popes, *servant.* of L *servus servorum Dei*; **a good** ∼ **but a bad master** (of things that should be treated as means and not ends). **2.** devoted follower, person willing to serve another, (*a servant of Jesus Christ*); ‖**your humble** ∼ (arch., in subscription of letter or as form of ironical courtesy); ‖**your obedient** ∼ (epistolary form preceding signature, now used only in letters of official type). [ME f. OF (as foll.; see -ANT)]

sĕrve *v.* & *n.* **1.** *v.t.* & *i.* be servant (to), do service (to), be useful (to); render obedience to (deity etc.); be employed *in* (organization, esp. armed forces, or country etc., esp. abroad); be soldier etc. (in war, *against* enemy, *under* commander); ∼ **at table,** act as waiter; ∼ **two masters,** seek to obey two conflicting principles. **2.** meet needs (of), avail, suffice, satisfy, perform function, be suitable, do what is required for, (*serve a purpose; to serve some private ends; that excuse will not serve you; his attempt served only to postpone the inevitable; it serves to show the folly of; one packet serves him for a week; nothing would serve (him) but absolute submission; a sofa serving (him) as or for (a) bed; buses serve the area; one curate serves two parishes*); go through due period of (office, apprenticeship, prison sentence, etc.); (Mil.) keep (gun, battery, etc.) firing; copulate with (mare etc.; esp. of stallion etc. hired for purpose); (Naut.) bind (rope etc.) with small cord to strengthen it; (of tide) be suitable for getting out of harbour etc.; **it will** ∼ (do what is absolutely necessary); **as memory** ∼**s,** whenever one remembers; ∼ **the** or one's **need(s)** or **turn,** be adequate; **as occasion** ∼**s,** when circumstances are favourable; ∼ **the purpose of,** take the place of, be used as; ∼ (one's) **time,** undergo imprisonment, apprenticeship, etc.; ∼ one's **time,** hold office for normal period. **3.** dish *up,* set (food) on table, set out ready, distribute, attend in shop etc., supply (person *with*), make legal delivery of (writ etc.), (Eccl.) act as server (at), (Tennis etc.) set ball etc. or set (ball) in play, produce (fault etc.) thus, (*asparagus served with butter; serve up dinner; ladies and gentlemen, dinner is served;*

ammunition, rations, etc., *out* or *round*; *was serving a customer* (*with stockings*), *serving in the shop*; *serve* person, *town*, etc., *with gas, water*); *serve with the same* SAUCE; ~ person **with** (warrant, writ, notice, process, attachment, etc.), ~ (writ etc.) **on** person, deliver document to person concerned in legally formal manner. **4.** treat, treat to, pay (person) out, (*has served me shamefully*; *you may serve me as you will*); play (trick etc.) on; ~ **out**, retaliate on; ~(**s**) **him right!** (excl. of satisfaction at sight of offender getting his deserts). **5.** Hence (**-**)**sĕr'ver**[1] (1, 2) *n.*, (esp., Eccl.) celebrant's assistant, **sĕr'very** (3) *n.*, room from which meals etc. are served and in which utensils are kept, **sĕr'ving**[2] *a.* (*serving-man*, male servant). **6.** *n.* (Tennis etc.) = SERVICE[1] 10. [ME, f. OF *servir* f. L *servire -it-* (*servus* slave)]

Sĕr'vian[1]. Var. of SERBIAN.

Sĕr'vian[2] *a.* ~ **wall** (built by Servius Tullius, king of Rome in 6th c. BC). [f. *Servius* + -AN]

sĕr'vice[1] *n.*, & *v.t.* **1.** *n.* being servant, servant's status; master's or mistress's employ; **be in** or **go into** (esp. domestic) ~; **take** ~ **with,** become servant to; **take into** one's ~, employ (person) as servant. **2.** department of royal or public employ or of work done to meet some general need, persons engaged in it, employment in it, (*the* CIVIL, *consular,* DIPLOMATIC, ||PREVENTIVE, SECRET, *service; the bus, railway, telephone,* etc., *service; BBC World Service; the public services*); ||(in *pl.*) public supply of water, electricity, etc.; **the** (armed or fighting) ~**s,** navy, army, and air force; **on** (active) ~, employed in the armed services; **see** ~, have experience esp. in the armed services; (*attrib.*) of the kind issued to the services (*service rifle*). **3.** person's control or behalf; **at your** etc. ~, ready to obey orders or be used; ||**on His** or **Her Majesty's** ~ (frank stamped on official envelopes etc.). **4.** what employee or subordinate or vassal is bound to, work done, or doing of work, on behalf of employer, benefit conferred on or exertion made on behalf of someone, expression of willingness to confer or make these, performance of functions by machine etc., (*has a right to my service; asks for my services; will you do me a service?; typewriter, typist, has given good service*); = *service charge;* **has seen** ~, has been much used, shows signs of wear; **my** ~ **to him** (arch. form of respectful message); YEOMAN *service.* **5.** use, assistance, (*can I, will it, be of service to you?*). **6.** liturgical form or office appointed for use on some occasion, (whole proceedings, usu. including one such service or more, of) single meeting of congregation for worship, musical setting of all or several of the invariable parts of a liturgy adapted for such treatment (*the communion, burial,* etc., *service; special services were held; holds four services every Sunday*); DIVINE *service;* **full** ~ (performed by choir without solos, or performed with music wherever possible); **plain** ~ (read or monotoned). **7.** legal serving of or *of* writ etc.; **personal** ~, delivery with announcement of contents to person affected; ~ **by publication, substitution,** publishing of writ etc. by posting up or insertion in newspaper or by handing to neighbour etc., recognized as sufficient under some conditions. **8.** serving of food etc.; set of dishes, plates, etc., required for serving meal (*dinner, dessert, tea,* etc., *service*). **9.** system of trains, steamers, buses, etc., plying at stated times; transport thus provided (*a fast service to London*). **10.** (single act of) serving in tennis etc., manner of serving, person's turn to serve, game in which one serves, (*his service is weak, terrific; whose service is it?; he lost his service*). **11.** provision of what is necessary for due maintenance of thing or operation; assistance or advice given to customers after sale by manufacturers or vendors of goods. **12.** serving of mare etc. **13.** ~ **area,** (1) area for supply of petrol, refreshments, etc., near road, (2) area round broadcasting station where reception is normally satisfactory; ~**book,** book of offices of a Church; ~ **bus** or **car,** (Austral. & NZ) motor coach;

~ **charge,** additional charge for service rendered; ~**-court,** (Tennis etc.) area within which validly served ball must fall; ~ **dress,** ordinary military etc. uniform; ~ **engineer** (who maintains and services equipment already in use); ||~ **flat** (in which domestic service and sometimes meals are provided by the management); ~ **industry** (providing services, not goods; e.g. tourism); ~**-line** (bounding service-court); ~**man** (-sm-), (1) man in armed services, (2) man providing service (sense 11); ~ **module** (containing main engine and power supplies of spacecraft); ~ **pipe** (conveying water or gas from main to building); ~ **road** (to serve houses lying back from main road, not for through traffic); ~ **station,** place where service (esp. of petrol etc.) is available; ~**woman** (-sw-), woman in armed services. **14.** *v.t.* provide service (sense 11) for (machine etc.); supply with service; pay interest on (debt etc.). [ME f. OF, or f. L *servitium* (*servus* slave; see -ICE)]

sĕr'vice[2] *n.* ~ (**tree**), European tree of genus *Sorbus,* esp. *S. domestica* with leaves like those of mountain ash, cream-coloured flowers, and small round or pear-shaped fruit eaten when overripe; ~**-berry,** (1) fruit of service tree, (2) (edible fruit of) Amer. shrub of genus *Amelanchier.* [earlier *serves,* pl. of obs. *serve* f. OE *syrfe* f. Gmc *surbhjōn* f. pop. L **sorbea* f. L *sorbus*]

sĕr'vice|able (-sa-) *a.* of use, useful or usable, willing and able to render or capable of rendering service, (*a serviceable person, reminder, instrument*); durable, suited for rough use or ordinary wear rather than for ornament; hence ~ABI'LITY, ~**able**NESS (-beln-), *ns.,* ~ABLY *adv.* [ME, f. OF *servisable* (as SERVICE[1], -ABLE)]

sĕrviĕ'tte *n.* table-napkin. [ME f. OF (*servir* SERVE; see -ETTE)]

sĕr'vile *a.* **1.** of or being a slave or slaves; ~ **war** (between slaves in revolt and their owners). **2.** as of a slave, slavish, cringing, fawning, menial, completely dependent, (*servile spirit, creature, submission, flattery, fear, imitation*); hence **sĕrvi'l**ITY *n.* **3.** ~ **works,** (Eccl.) menial or mechanical work forbidden on Sundays and major Church festivals. **4.** Hence ~LY[2] (-l-lī) *adv.* [ME, f. L *servilis* (*servus* slave; see -IL)]

sĕr'ving *n.* In vbl senses; quantity of food served to one person, helping. [f. SERVE + -ING[1]]

Sĕr'vite *a.* & *n.* (friar or nun) of Order of Servants of Mary. [f. med. L *Servitae* pl. f. L *servus* servant]

sĕr'vitor *n.* **1.** (arch. or poet.) attendant, henchman, servant. **2.** (Hist.) Oxford undergraduate assisted from college funds and performing menial duties in return; hence ~SHIP *n.* [ME f. OF f. LL (as SERVE; see -OR)]

sĕr'vitūde *n.* **1.** slavery (lit. or fig.); subjection (esp. involuntary) to a master, bondage; PENAL *servitude.* **2.** (Law). subjection of property to an easement. [ME f. OF, f. L *servitudo -inis* (*servus* slave; see -TUDE)]

sĕr'vo *n.* (*pl.* ~**s**) servo-motor or servo-mechanism. [abbr.]

sĕr'vo- *comb. form* denoting means of powered automatic control of a larger system (*servo-assisted, -mechanism, -motor*). [f. *servo-motor* f. F *servo-moteur* f. L *servus* slave + F *moteur* MOTOR]

sĕ'samĕ *n.* annual E. Ind. herbaceous plant (*Sesamum indicum*) with seeds used in various ways as food and yielding an edible oil; its seeds; (**open**) ~, [w. ref. to Arabian-Nights tale] magical or mysterious means of commanding access to what is usu. inaccessible. [f. L f. Gk *sēsamon, sēsamē,* of Oriental orig.]

sĕ'samoid *a.* & *n.* **1.** *a.* shaped like a sesame-seed, nodular, (esp. of small independent bones developed in tendons passing over angular structure such as the kneecap and the navicular bone). **2.** *n.* sesamoid bone. [f. prec. + -OID]

sĕ'squi- *pref.* denoting one and a half. **1.** (Chem.) (Of compound) in which there are three equivalents of a named element or radical to two others (*sesquioxide, sesquisulphide*). **2.** ~**centenary** (-tē'-, -sĕ'-),

∼cente'nnial, (festival) of the one-hundred-and-
-fiftieth anniversary; ∼peda'lian (-ā′l-), (of word)
many-syllabled [f. L *sesquipedalis* (Horace), lit. 1½ feet
long], cumbrous and pedantic; **sesqui'plicate,** in
ratio of square roots of cubes. [L, f. *semis-que* a half in
addition]

sess. Var. of CESS[1].

sĕ'ssīle *a.* (Bot. & Zool.) (Of flower, leaf, eye, etc.)
attached directly by the base without stalk or
peduncle; fixed in one position, immobile; ∼ **oak,**
durmast. [f. L *sessilis* (*sedēre sess-* sit; see -IL)]

sĕ'ssion (-shǒn) *n.* **1.** (arch.) being seated, sitting
posture. **2.** being assembled esp. for transaction of
deliberative or judicial business; single uninterrupted
meeting for such purpose; period during which such
meetings are held daily or at short or regular
intervals; period between meeting and prorogation
or final adjournment of legislative body; period spent
continuously in an activity; **in** ∼, sitting or assembled
for business, not on vacation. **3.** ∥academic year;
*university term. **4.** governing body of a Presbyterian
church. **5. Court of S**∼, supreme civil court in
Scotland; ∥KIRK-*session*; LORDS *of Session*; **petty** ∼**s,**
meeting of two or more magistrates for summary
trying of certain offences; QUARTER[1] *sessions*. **6.** Hence
∼AL *a.* (∼**al order,** one valid only for, renewable
each, session of Parliament). [MF. f. OF, or f. L *sessio
-onis* (as prec.; see -ION)]

sĕ'stĕrce, sĕstĕr'tius (-shǔs, *pl.* -tii *pr.* -shĭi), *ns.*
ancient-Roman silver (and later bronze) coin and
money of account = ¼ denarius or 2½ (later 4) asses.
[f. L *sestertius* (*nummus* coin) = 2½ (*semis* half, *tertius*
third)]

sĕstĕr't|ium (-shǔm) *n.* (*pl.* ∼**ia**). ancient-Roman
money of account = 1,000 sesterces. [L, orig. gen. pl.
of prec., w. ellipsis of *mille* thousand]

sĕstĕ't *n.* sextet; last six lines of sonnet. [f. It. *sestetto*
(*sesto* f. L *sextus* sixth; see -ET[1])]

sĕsti'na (-tē′-) *n.* form of rhymed or unrhymed poem
with six stanzas of six lines and final triplet, each
stanza having same words to end its lines but in
different order. [It. (as prec.; cf. -INE[4])]

sĕt[1] *v.* (-tt-; set). **1.** *v.t.* put, lay, stand, (usu. w. *adv.* or
adv. phr.: *set load* or *passenger down, ashore,* etc., *statue up,
food before person, flowers in water, one brick on another*); ∼
(thing) **against** another, balance, reckon as counterpoise or compensation for it; ∼ **apart,** reserve,
separate; ∼ **aside,** reserve, reject, disregard, annul;
∼ **by,** (arch.) reserve, save for future use; *set* FOOT[1] 12,
SEAL[2], *on*; ∼ **stone out,** lay with edge projecting
beyond one below; ∼ person **over** others or thing,
put in authority. **2.** apply (thing) *to* (*set pen to paper,
bugle to one's lips, spurs to horse*); *set* FIRE[1] *to*; ∼ one's **hand
to,** sign (document), begin (task); *set* SEAL[2] *to*; *set* one's
SHOULDER *to the wheel*; ∼ one's **wits to,** try to solve
(problem); ∼ one's **wits to** another's, argue with
him. **3.** station, place ready, place or turn in right or
specified position or direction, dispose suitably for use
or action or display; put hands of (clock or watch) to
right time; arrange for (alarm-clock) to sound at
desired time; cause (hen) to sit on eggs; place (eggs)
for hen to sit on; put (seed, plant, etc.) in ground to
grow (QUICK*set*); arrange (butterfly etc.) as specimen;
make (trap) ready to catch victim; *start (a fire);
(Bridge) defeat (contract); give sharp edge to (razor);
give teeth of (saw) alternate outward inclination; lay
(table) for meal; place (chairs etc.) for visitors etc.; *set*
one's CAP[1] *at*; ∼ **sail,** (1) hoist sail, (2) begin voyage;
set the SCENE; ∼ **a** or (Naut.) **the watch,** station
sentinels etc.; SHARP[1]-*set*. **4.** join, attach, fasten; fix,
determine, decide; appoint, settle, establish; put parts
of (bone, limb, etc.) into right relative position for
healing after fracture or dislocation, deal thus with
(fracture or dislocation); give (person, one*self*) permanent feeling *against* person or thing; fix (hair) while
damp so that it dries in desired style; insert (jewel) in
gold etc. as frame or foil; ∼ **eyes on,** catch sight of; ∼

one's **face against,** steadfastly oppose; ∼ one's
heart, hopes, etc., **on,** long for, be resolved to get; ∼
one's **life on a chance** etc., risk it [metaph. from
gambling]; *set a* PRICE *on*; ∼ (STORE, **little, much,**
etc.) **by,** estimate at specified value; ∼ one's **teeth,**
clench them, (fig.) make up one's mind inflexibly. **5.**
(Print.) ∼ (**up**), arrange (type) in words etc., construct words of (book etc.) in type; print in specified
manner (∼ **close,** print with small spaces between
words or letters; ∼ **out** or **wide,** print with these
spaces large). **6.** bring by placing, arranging, impelling, or other means, into specified state (*set things
right, to* RIGHT[3]*s, in order, in motion; set* PERSON *on his feet*
(lit. or fig.), *box on its end; set machine going, person
laughing*); *set* persons *by the* EAR[1]*s*; *set* person *at* EASE; *set
on* FIRE[1], *on* FOOT[1] 12; *set* one's HOUSE[1] *in order*; *set
question,* person's *mind* or *heart, at* REST[2]; *set* person
RIGHT[1] 5; *set* person's *teeth on* EDGE[1]; *set at* DEFIANCE, *at*
NAUGHT; ∼ **free,** release, liberate. **7.** make sit down *to*
task, order to apply energies *to doing,* cause *to* WORK[1],
apply oneself *to* WORK[1], (*set him to dictation, wood-
-chopping, work at his Greek*); ∼ one**self** *to do,* make up
one's mind, resolve or undertake. **8.** exhibit or
arrange as pattern or as material to be dealt with
(often w. ind. obj.; *set, set person, an example, task,
problem,* etc., to be followed, done, solved, by him);
compose (puzzle, questions, etc.) to be answered;
*establish (a record etc.); ∼ **the fashion, the pace,**
determine it by leading. **9.** ∼ (**to music**), provide
(poem, words) with music usu. composed for the
purpose. **10.** ornament or provide (surface) *with* (*gold,
field, sky, set with gems, daisies, stars; shall set top of wall
with broken glass, this bed with geraniums*). **11.** *v.t.* & *i.*
turn to solid or hard or rigid from liquid or soft or
mobile state; curdle, solidify, harden, (*cement, jelly, has
or is set*); take shape, develop into definiteness or
maturity; (of egg) become solid by cooking or
incubation; (of blossom) form into fruit, (of fruit)
develop out of blossom, (of tree) develop fruit, (of
face) take hard expression; (of eyes) become motionless in death, swoon, etc. **12.** *v.i.* be brought towards
or below horizon by earth's rotation (*sun, moon, sets*);
one's **star** ∼**s,** greatness departs. **13.** (Of tide,
current, etc., and fig. of feeling, custom, etc.) have
motion, gather force, sweep along, show or feel
tendency, (*tide sets in, out; current sets strongly, eastwards;
opinion is setting against it; his soul set to grief*). **14.** (Of
hunting dog) take rigid attitude indicating presence
of game; ∼ (**to partner,** (of dancer) take position
facing partner. **15.** (dial. or vulg.) sit. **16.** (w. *preps.*):
∼ **about,** begin, take steps towards, (task, doing),
(colloq.) attack; ∼ (**up**)**on,** urge (dog etc.) to attack
(person etc.), attack. **17.** (w. *advs.*): ∼ **back,** place
farther back in space or time, impede or reverse
advance of, (sl.) cost (person) specified amount; ∼-
-*back* n., reversal or arrest of progress, relapse, placing
of building etc. farther back than it might have been;
∼ **down,** put in writing, record, allow (passenger) to
alight, attribute *to,* explain or describe to oneself *as;*
∼-*down* n., rebuff; ∼ **forth,** make known, declare,
expound, adorn, begin journey or expedition; ∼
forward, (arch.) assist progress of, begin going
forward; ∼ **in,** arise, come into vogue, become
established, (*reaction, rain, set in; it set in to rain*), fit
(part of garment) into remaining part; ∼ **off,** act as
adornment or foil to, enhance, make more striking,
detonate, use as compensating item *against,* cause to
begin, start (person) laughing or talking on pet
subject, begin journey; ∼-*off* n., thing set off against
another, thing of which the amount or effect may be
deducted from that of another of opposite tendency,
counterpoise, counter-claim, thing that embellishes,
adornment to something, (Archit. & Print.) = OFF-
SET; ∼ **on,** instigate, advance to the assault; ∼ **out,**
embellish, demonstrate, exhibit, declare, begin
journey, begin with intent *to* do, mark out design of
(work to be done); ∼-*out* n., commencement, things

set out, equipment, display; ~ **to,** begin doing something vigorously, esp. (usu. w. pl. subj.) fighting or arguing; ~-*to* n. (pl. ~-*tos*), combat esp. conducted with fists or verbally; ~ **up,** develop figure of by physical training (esp. WELL *set up*), start (institution, HOUSE[1], business, SHOP, etc.), cause (soreness etc.), establish (new record), establish (person) or provide with means of establishment or establish oneself in some capacity (*his father, £5000, set him up as a tobacconist* or *in the tobacco trade; shall set up as a dentist*), provide adequately *in* or *with* some article (*am set up with novels for the winter*), place (standard, notice, etc.) in view, prepare (task etc. for another; type etc., see sense 5), begin uttering (protest, shriek, etc.) loudly, propound (theory), restore after ill-health or depression; ~-*up* n., manner or position of setting up, erectness of carriage of body, (colloq.) (structure or arrangement of) an organization etc., *artificially easy task etc.; ~ (one**self**) **up as** or **for,** (colloq.) make pretensions to being (scholar, moralist, etc.). [OE *settan*, = OS *settian*, OHG *sezzan*, ON *setja*, Goth. *satjan* f. Gmc *satjan* causative of *setjan* SIT]

sĕt[2] *n.* **1.** number of things or persons that belong together as essentially similar or as complementary to each other, group, collection, (*set of studs, chairs, stamps, novels by Dickens, golf-clubs, lectures; a fine set of players, officers*); = SERVICE[1] 8 (*dinner etc. set*); TOILET--*set*; section of society consorting together (*the fast, jet, racing, smart, set*); ~ (**of quadrilles**), figures that make up a quadrille; ~ (**of dancers**), number needed to make up square dance; ~ (**of teeth**), person's or animal's natural or artificial teeth collectively; radio or television receiver; (Tennis etc.) group of games counting as unit towards match for side that wins greater number of games in it (~ **point,** state of a set in lawn tennis when one side needs only one more point to win it, this point); (Math. etc.) collection of things having a specified common property (~ **theory,** study of sets without regard to nature of their individual constituents). **2.** slip or shoot or bulb or tuber for planting; young fruit just set. **3.** (poet.) setting *of* sun. **4.** way current or wind or opinion etc. sets, drift or tendency *of*, (*the set of the current, of public feeling; the set of his mind is towards intolerance*); (Psych.) predisposition to a response etc. **5.** configuration, conformation, habitual posture, way head etc. is set on or carried, way dress etc. sits or flows, (*the set of the hills, his head, the drapery*); warp or bend or displacement caused by continued pressure or position (*has got a set to the right*); setting of damp hair; (Austral. & NZ colloq.) grudge. **6.** (amount of) alternate deflection of saw-teeth. **7.** last coat of plaster on wall. **8.** adjustment of reeds in weaving; (square in) tartan pattern. **9.** amount of spacing in type causing letters to be close or wide set; width of piece of type. **10.** number of eggs in nest, or number laid before bird sits, clutch. **11.** (**dead**) ~, setter's pointing in presence of game; **make a dead ~ at,** attack esp. by argument or ridicule, (esp. of woman) try to win affections of. **12.** badger's burrow. **13.** granite paving-block. **14.** (Theatr.) set scene; setting, stage furniture, etc., in production of film or play. [sense 1 f. OF *sette* f. L *secta* SECT; other senses f. prec.]

sĕt[3] *a.* In vbl senses; unmoving, fixed (*set smile, eyes, look, purpose*); (Cricket, of batsman) fully accustomed to prevailing type of bowling, light, etc.; (of book etc.) specified for reading in preparation for examination; (of meal) served according to fixed menu; ready for action (*to* do); **all** ~, (colloq.) ready to start; **close-**~, placed with only small intervals between; ~ **fair,** (of weather etc.) fine without sign of breaking; ~ **form** *of prayer* etc. (not extempore); *~ **line,** trawl-line; ~ (**up**)**on,** determined to get etc., absorbed in; ~ **phrase,** invariable or customary arrangement of words; ~ **piece,** (1) fireworks arranged on scaffolding etc., (2) formal or elaborate arrangement esp. in art or literature; **of ~ purpose,**

intentionally, deliberately; ~ **scene** (built up of more or less solid material); ~ **screw** (for adjusting or clamping parts of machine); ~ **scrum** (in Rugby Footb., ordered by referee); ~ **speech** (composed beforehand); ~ **square,** draughtsman's right--angled triangular plate for drawing lines esp. at 90°, 60°, 45°, or 30°; ~ **time** (prearranged). [p.p. of SET[1]]

sĕt'|a *n.* (*pl.* ~**ae**). (Bot. & Zool.) stiff hair, bristle; so ~**A′CEOUS** *a.* [L, = bristle]

sētī′ferous, sētī′gerous, sē′tōse, *adjs.* having bristles. [f. L *seta* bristle, *setiger, setosus,* bristly; see -FEROUS, -GEROUS, -OSE[1]]

sē′ton *n.* (Surg.) skein of cotton etc. passed below skin and left with ends protruding to promote drainage etc. [ME, f. med. L *seto, seta*, silk, app. f. L *seta* bristle]

sĕtt. Var. of SET[2] (esp. in senses 2, 8, 12, 13).

sĕttee′[1] *n.* long seat for more than one person, with back and usu. with arms. [18th c., perh. fanciful var. of SETTLE[1]; see -EE]

sĕttee′[2] *n.* (Hist.) Mediterranean sharp-prowed lateen-sailed vessel with two or three masts. [f. It. *saettia* (*saetta* arrow f. L *sagitta*)]

sē′tter *n.* In vbl senses; (one of) breed (*English, Irish, Gordon,* etc., *setter*) of long-haired dog trained to stand rigid on scenting game (cf. SET[1] 14). [ME, f. SET[1] + -ER[1]]

sĕ′tterwort (-wêrt) *n.* bear's-foot plant. [f. MLG *siterwort* etc. (see WORT); first element of unkn. orig.]

sĕ′tting *n.* **1.** In vbl senses. **2.** music to which words of a song etc. are set. **3.** metal or other frame in which jewel is set; surroundings of any object regarded as its framework or as accessories setting it off, environment, (Theatr.) way a play is put on the stage, scenery, properties, costumes, etc.; cutlery etc. for one person at table. **4.** ~-**board** (on which entomological specimens are set); ~-**lotion** (used to prepare hair for being set); ~-**needle,** needle in wooden handle used in setting specimens; ~-**rule,** brass rule or steel plate with which type is kept temporarily in place as it is set up in the stick; ~-**stick,** compositor's STICK[2]. [ME, f. SET[1] + -ING]

sĕ′ttle[1] *n.* bench with high back and arms and often with chest from seat to floor. [OE *setl* place to sit, = OHG *sezzal*, Goth. *sitls* f. Gmc *setlaz, *setlam*]

sĕ′ttle[2] *v.* **1.** *v.t.* & *i.* ~ (**down**), establish or become established in more or less permanent abode or place or way of life (*shall settle in London, Australia; settle feet in stirrups, plant's roots well down in ground, invalid among pillows, oneself in chair*); ~ **in,** become established in a place. **2.** (cause to) sit down or *down* to stay for some time (*settle down to dinner, a game of chess, reading*); (of bird, fog, darkness, etc.) come down and remain for some time; (of disease etc.) establish itself *in* or *on* specified part; **cannot ~ to work, to anything,** (of restless or excited or desultory person). **3.** ~ (**down**), (cause to) cease from wandering or motion or change or disturbance or turbidity (*things will soon settle into shape; marry and settle down; settle down to married life, to defensive play; let excitement settle down; settle beer by leaving to stand*); aid digestion of (meal); remedy disordered state of (nerves, stomach, etc.). **4.** bring to or attain fixity or composure or certainty or clarity or decision; (in *p.p.*) fixed, not rapidly changing, (*man of settled convictions; settled habitation,* (esp. fine) *weather*); ~ **up,** finally arrange (a matter). **5.** determine, agree upon, decide, appoint; resolve (quarrel, question, doubts, etc.); terminate (lawsuit) by mutual agreement; ~ one's **affairs,** (esp.) make will etc. when death is imminent; ~ **the day,** fix date; ~ **for** etc., agree on, accept; ~ **the matter** or **it,** leave no more to be discussed. **6.** *v.t.* colonize, establish colonists in, become dwellers in, people, (country etc.). **7.** *v.i.* subside, come down to the bottom or on a surface, (*dust, solid matter, soon settles*); (of soil, house, foundation, etc.) come gradually to lower level; (of ship) show loss of buoyancy, begin to sink. **8.** *v.t.* deal effectually with, dispose of, get rid of; get rid of importunity or obstruction of (person) by argument or conflict or killing; *settle* person's HASH². **9.** *v.t.* & *i.* pay money owed according to (account, bill, etc.); pay (money owed); ~ **up**, draw up and settle (account etc.); ~ **with**, pay (agreed proportion of) bills of (creditor etc.), (fig.) get revenge on; ||se'ttling day, (St. Exch.) day of settlement. **10.** *v.t.* bestow legally for life *on* (*settled an annuity on him*; *settled all his property on his wife*); ~d estate (held by tenant for life under specified conditions). [OE *setlan* (as prec.)]

se'ttlement (-t·lm-) *n.* In vbl senses; ||(St. Exch.) regular settling of accounts; (Law) conveyance of, or creation of estate(s) in, property to make provision for one or more beneficiaries differing from what would result from simple conveyance or statutory inheritance (**marriage** ~, usu. made at time of marriage and in favour of wife, her children, etc.); group of social workers from a college etc. who establish themselves in poor or crowded district to provide education, recreation, etc., for the inhabitants; newly settled tract of country, colony; subsidence of wall, house, soil, etc.; **Act of S~**, statute of 1701 vesting British crown in Sophia of Hanover and her heirs. [f. prec. +-MENT]

se'ttler *n.* In vbl senses; one who settles in new colony, early colonist; (sl.) decisive blow, argument, or event; ~'s clock, (Austral.) laughing JACK¹ass. [f. SETTLE² + -ER¹]

se'ttlor *n.* (Law). one who makes a settlement esp. of property. [f. prec.; see -OR]

se'twall (-awl) *n.* valerian plant, *Valeriana officinalis*. [ME f. AF *zedewal*, OF *citoual* f. med. L *zedoale*, var. of *zedoarium* ZEDOARY]

se'ven *a.* & *n.* **1.** one more than six; symbol for this (7, vii, VII); card with seven pips; time of seven o'clock; size etc. denoted by seven; set of seven; (in *pl.*) gloves, shoes, etc., of seventh size; ||(in *pl.*) Rugby Football matches with seven players on each side. **2.** ~**league boots** (in fairy-tale, giving wearer the power of going seven leagues at each stride); *the Seven* SAGE²*s*, or *Wise Men*; *the seven* SEAS, *deadly* SIN¹*s*, *cardinal* VIRTUES, WONDER¹*s of the world*; ~**year itch**, alleged tendency to infidelity after seven years of marriage; **S~ Years War** (of France, Austria, and Russia against Britain and Prussia, 1756–63). **3.** Hence ~FOLD *a.* & *adv.* [OE *seofon,* = OS, OHG *sibun,* ON *sjau,* Goth. *sibun* f. Gmc *sebhun* f. IE *septm*]

se'venteen (-ē'n, sē'-) *a.* & *n.* one more than sixteen; symbol for this (17, xvii, XVII); **sweet** ~, age of girlish beauty; so ~TH² *a.* & *n.* [OE *seofontīene,* = OHG *sibunzehan,* ON *sjautján* (as prec., -TEEN)]

se'venth *a.* & *n.* **1.** *a.* next after sixth; ~ **part,** one of seven equal parts into which thing is or may be divided. **2.** *n.* seventh part, thing, etc.; (Mus.) (note at) interval of which the span involves seven alphabetical notes, harmonic combination of notes thus separated. **3.** ~ **day,** Saturday (esp. when kept as sabbath); **S~-day Adventists**, millenarian and Sabbatarian sect; *seventh* *GRADE 1; *seventh* HEAVEN. **4.** Hence ~LY² *adv.*, in the seventh place. [f. SEVEN + -TH²]

se'venty *a.* & *n.* **1.** seven times ten; symbol for this (70, lxx, LXX); set of seventy persons or things (**the** ~, (1) the disciples in Luke 10, (2) the Sanhedrin, (3) the Septuagint translators); ~ **times seven**, large indefinite number (Matt. 18:22); (in *pl.*) numbers etc., esp. years of a century or a life, from 70 to 79; hence ~FOLD *a.* & *adv.*, **se'venti**ETH¹ *a.* & *n.* **2.** ~-**one** etc. (arch.) **one-and-**~ etc., seventy plus one etc., w. corresp. ordinals ~**-first** etc. [OE -*seofontig,* = OS *sivuntig,* OHG *sibunzug,* ON *sjautigr* (as SEVEN, -TY²)]

se'ver *v.* **1.** *v.t.* & *i.* separate, divide, part, disunite, (*sever friends* or *friendship, rope, connection*; *sea severs England and* or *from France*; *the rope severed under the strain*); (Law) make (oneself) separate party in suit. **2.** *v.t.* cut or break off, take away, (part) from or *from*

whole (*severed his head, his head from his body*; *sever* one*self from the Church*). **3.** terminate employment contract of (person). **4.** Hence or cogn. ~ABLE *a.*, ~ANCE *n.* (~**ance pay**, amount paid to employee on termination of contract). [ME, f. AF *severer,* OF *sevrer* f. Rom. *seperare f. L *separare* SEPARATE²]

se'veral (-vr-) *a.* & *pron.* **1.** *a.* separate, diverse, distinct, individual, respective, (*all of us in our, went their, several ways; indicted on three several counts; the several members of the Board*); **collective and** ~ **responsibility** (of persons as a body and as individuals); **joint and** ~, (of bond etc.) signed by more than one person, of whom each is liable for whole sum; hence ~LY² *adv.* **2.** a few, more than two but not many, (*have called several times; myself and several others*). **3.** *pron.* a moderate number, more than two but not many, of mentioned or implied persons or things (*several of you have seen him; went salmon-fishing and caught several*). [ME f. AF, f. AL *separalis* f. L *separ* SEPARATE¹; see -AL]

se'veralty (-vr-) *n.* separateness; individual or un-shared tenure of estate etc. (esp. *in severalty*). [ME, f. AF *severalte* (as prec.; see -TY¹)]

sevēr'e *a.* (~**r,** ~**st**). **1.** austere, strict, harsh, rigorous, unsparing, (*severe look, discipline, critic, sentence, inspection*), ~ (**up**)**on**, harsh in judgement of. **2.** violent, vehement, extreme, (*a severe winter, attack of influenza*); (of weather) very cold or stormy. **3.** making great demands on endurance, energy, skill, or other quality, (*severe test, pain, competition, requirements*); serious, not slight, (*severe haemorrhage, shortage*). **4.** unadorned, stripped of all that is unessential, without redundancy, restrained, terse, (*severe architecture, beauty, simplicity, style*). **5.** Hence or cogn. ~LY² (-ēr'li) *adv.* (**leave** or **let** ~**ly alone**, abstain from dealing with as mark of disapproval, (joc.) avoid meddling with as too formidable or difficult); **sevē'rity** *n.* [f. F *sévère* or f. L *severus*]

se'very *n.* (Archit.) compartment of vaulted ceiling. [ME, f. AF **civorie,* OF *civoire* (as CIBORIUM)]

Sē'ville *n.* ~ **orange**, small bitter orange used for marmalade. [~ in S. Spain]

Sèvres (sāvr) *n.* fine porcelain made at Sèvres. [~ in N. France]

sew (sō) *v.* (*p.p.* ~n *pr.* sōn, *or* ~ed *pr.* sōd). **1.** *v.t.* fasten (material, pieces) by passing thread again and again through holes made with threaded needle or with awl etc. (*sew cloth, leather, pieces together, sheets of book*); hence ~'ING¹ (5) *n.* **2.** make by sewing (*sew seam, pleat, shirt, book, boot, buttonhole*); fasten *on* or *in,* attach, by sewing (*sew on a button; can you sew buttons?; sew in a patch*), close *up* (hole, rent, wound, bag) by sewing. **3.** enclose, fasten *up,* by sewing receptacle (*sew up money in a bag; sew money into one's belt*); ~ **up,** (colloq., esp. in *p.p.*) ||utterly exhaust, ||intoxicate, finish dealing with (a matter), *obtain exclusive use of. **4.** *v.i.* use needle and thread or sewing-machine. **5.** ~'**ing-machine,** machine for sewing or stitching; ~'**ing-press,** apparatus for sewing books. [OE *si(o)wan,* = OHG *siuwen,* ON *sýja,* Goth. *siujan* f. Gmc *siwjan f. IE **siw-,* **sju-*]

sew'age (sū'-, sōō'-) *n.* matter conveyed in SEWER³s; ~**-farm** (on which sewage is treated and used as manure, esp. one that utilizes and disposes of a town's sewage); ~**-works** (for artificial purification of sewage before discharge to river etc.). [formed f. SEWER³ by change of (supposed) -ER¹ to -AGE]

sewě'llel *n.* small burrowing rodent of the W. coast of US. [Amer. Ind.]

sew'er¹ (sō'-) *n.* In vbl senses. [f. SEW + -ER¹]

sew'er² *n.* (Hist.) person who set out table, placed guests, carried and tasted dishes, etc. [ME, f. AF *asseour* f. OF *asseoir* to seat, set, f. LL AS(*sidēre = sedēre* sit) sit beside]

sew'er³ (sū'-) *n.* & *v.t.* **1.** *n.* conduit or channel usu. covered over for carrying off the drainage waters and excrementitious matter of a town, factory, house, etc., public drain; ~**-gas,** foul air of sewers; ~ **rat,** common brown rat; hence ∼AGE (1) *n*. **2.** *v.t.* drain with sewers; provide with sewers. [ME, f. AF *sever(e)*, ONF *se(u)wiere* channel to carry off overflow from a fish-pond f. Rom. *EX¹*aquaria* (*aqua* water; see -ARY¹); cf. EWER]

sew′in *n*. salmon trout of Welsh etc. rivers. [16th c., of unkn. orig.]

sewn. See SEW.

sex *n*., *a*., & *v.t.* **1.** *n.* being male or female or hermaphrodite (*what is its sex?*; *my sex does not matter*; *without distinction of age or sex*); hence ∼′ISM *n*., prejudice or discrimination against people (esp. women) because of their sex, ∼′IST (2) *n*., ∼′LESS *a*. (lit. or fig.). **2.** males or females collectively (*all ranks and both sexes*); **the fair, gentle, second, softer, weaker,** ∼, (arch. joc.) **the** ∼, women; **the sterner** ∼, men. **3.** sexual instincts, desires, etc., or their manifestation; (colloq.) sexual intercourse (*have sex with*). **4.** *a.* pertaining to sex (*sex education*); arising from difference or consciousness of sex (*sex antagonism, instinct, urge*); ∼ **act,** sexual intercourse; ∼ **appeal,** attractiveness arising from difference of sex; ∼ **change,** (esp.) apparent change of sex by surgical means; ∼ **chromosome** (concerned in determining the sex of an organism); ∼ **kitten,** young woman mischievously exploiting her sex appeal; ∼ **life,** person's activities relating to sex (sense 3); ∼**-limited,** (Genetics) appearing only in one sex; ∼**-linked,** (Genetics) carried on or by a sex chromosome; ∼ **maniac,** person needing excessive gratification of sex instincts; ∼′**pot,** (colloq.) sexy person (esp. woman); ∼**-starved,** deprived of sexual gratification. **5.** *v.t.* determine sex of, whence ∼′ER¹ *n*.; (in *p.p.*) equipped with sexual characteristics (esp. *highly* etc. *sexed*). [ME, f. OF *sexe* or f. L *sexus*]

sex-, sē′x|ĭ-, *comb. forms.* six, as: ∼a′**ngular**(**ly**), hexagonal(ly); ∼**centenary** (-tē′-, -sĕ′-) *a*. & *n*., (festival) of the six-hundredth anniversary; ∼**di′gi-tate,** six-fingered; ∼**e′nnial,** lasting, recurring every, six years; ∼′**foil,** six-lobed ornamental figure; ∼**isylla′bic,** ∼**isy′llable,** (word) of 6 syllables; ∼(**i**)**va′lent,** (Chem.) having a valence of six; ∼**par′tite,** divided into six. [f. L *sex* six, -I-]

sexagenār′ian *a*. & *n*. (person) from 60 to 69 years old. [f. L *sexagenarius* (*sexageni* distrib. of *sexaginta* sixty; see -ARY¹) +-AN]

sexage′narȳ *a*. & *n*. of sixty; = prec. [as prec.]

Sexage′sima *n*. ∼ (**Sunday**), Sunday before Quinquagesima. [ME f. eccl. L, = sixtieth (day), prob. named loosely as preceding QUINQUAGESIMA]

sexage′simal *a*. & *n*. of sixtieths or sixty; reckoning or reckoned by sixtieths; ∼ (**fraction**) (with denominator equal to power of 60 as in the divisions of the degree and hour); hence ∼LY² *adv*. [f. L *sexagesimus* (as prec.) +-AL]

sexŏ′log|ȳ *n*. study of sexual life or relationships, esp. in human beings; hence **sexolŏ′g**ICAL *a*., ∼IST (3) *n*. [f. SEX +-O-+-LOGY]

sext *n*. (Eccl.) (office of) canonical hour of prayer appointed for sixth daytime hour (i.e. noon). [ME, f. L *sexta* (*hora* hour) fem. of *sextus* sixth]

se′xtain *n*. sestina. [perh. alt. f. obs. F *sestine*, after *quatrain, sixain*]

se′xtant *n*. instrument with graduated arc of 60° used in navigation and surveying for measuring the angular distance of objects by means of mirrors. [f. L *sextans -ntis* sixth part (*sextus* sixth; see -ANT)]

sextĕ′t, -ĕ′tte, *n*. **1.** (Mus.) (performers of) composition for six voices or instruments. **2.** set of six. [alt. of SESTET after L *sex* six]

sexti′llion (-lyon) *n*. (for *pl.* usage see HUNDRED). ||a million raised to the sixth power; *a thousand raised to the seventh power. [F, f. L *sex* six, after *septillion* etc.]

se′xtō *n*. (*pl.* ∼s). book-size in which each leaf is ⅙ of printing-sheet; book of this size. [f. L *sextus* sixth, as QUARTO]

sextŏdĕ′cĭmō *n*. (*pl.* ∼s). book-size in which each leaf is 1/16 of printing-sheet; book of this size. [f. L *sextus decimus* 16th, as QUARTO]

se′xton *n*. officer charged with care of church and churchyard, and often with duties of bell-ringer and grave-digger; ∼ **beetle** (of genus *Necrophorus*, burying carrion to serve as nidus for eggs). [ME *segerstane* etc., f. AF, OF *segerstein, secrestein* f. med. L *sacristanus* SACRISTAN]

se′xtŭple *a*., *n*., & *v.* **1.** *a.* & *n.* sixfold (amount). **2.** *v.t.* & *i.* multiply by six. [f. med. L *sextuplus*, irreg. f. L *sex* six, after LL *quintuplus* QUINTUPLE]

sextŭplĕt (sĕ′-, -ū′-) *n*. **1.** one of six children born at a birth. **2.** (Mus.) group of six notes to be played in the time of four. [f. prec., after *triplet* etc.]

se′xual (-ksŭ-, -kshŏō-) *a*. **1.** of sex, a sex, or the sexes; pertaining to relations between the sexes, esp. w. ref. to mutual attraction and to gratification of resulting desires; ∼ **intercourse** or (arch.) **commerce,** copulation esp. of man and woman; ∼ **organs,** reproductive organs, esp. genitals. **2.** (Bot., of classification) based on the distinction of sexes in plants; hence ∼IST (2) *n*. **3.** (Biol.) having sex; (of reproduction) occurring by fusion of male and female gametes. **4.** Hence ∼ITY (-ă′l-) *n*., ∼IZE (3) *v.t.*, ∼LY² *adv*. [f. LL *sexualis* (as SEX; see -AL)]

se′x|ȳ *a*. unduly engrossed in or concerned with sex; sexually stimulating, attractive, or provocative; hence ∼INESS *n*. [f. SEX +-Y²]

sĕz *v.i.* = SAY²s; ∼ **you** (see SAY²). [phonetic repr.]

SF *abbr.* science fiction.

sf *abbr.* sforzando.

s.f. *abbr. sub finem.*

SFA *abbr.* Scottish Football Association.

sfŏrză′ndō (-ts-), **sfŏrza′tō** (-tsah′-), *adjs.* & *advs.* (Mus.) with sudden emphasis. [It., gerund & p.p. of *sforzare* use force]

sfumato (sfŏōmah′tō) *a*. (Paint.) with indistinct outlines. [It., p.p. of *sfumare* shade off (*s-* = EX-¹, *fumare* smoke)]

sfz *abbr.* sforzando.

SG *abbr.* *senior grade; Solicitor-General; specific gravity.

sgd. *abbr.* signed.

sgraffi′t|ō (-ahfĕ′-) *n*. (*pl.* ∼**i** *pr.* -ē). = GRAFFITO 2. [It., pp. of *sgraffire* scratch (*s-* = EX-¹, *graffio* scratching)]

Sgt. *abbr.* Sergeant.

sh. Var. of HUSH² *int.*

||**sh.** *abbr.* shilling(s).

shă′bb|ȳ *a*. contemptible, paltry, dishonourable, (*played me a shabby trick*); niggardly, mean; faded, worn, threadbare, dilapidated, poorly dressed; of poor quality, in bad repair or condition; ∼**y-gentee′l,** showing signs of shabbiness but attempting to keep up genteel appearances (so ∼**y-genti′lity**); hence ∼ILY² *adv*., ∼INESS *n*., ∼ȲISH¹ 2 *a*. [f. *shab* scab f. OE *sceabb* f. ON *skabbr (cf. SCAB) +-Y²]

shă′brăck *n*. (Hist.) cavalry saddle-cloth. [f. G *schabracke*, of E. Eur. orig. (cf. Russ. *shabrak*)]

Shabu′ōt(h), Shevu′ōt(h), (-vŏō′-) *n*. = PENTECOST 1. [f. Heb. *šāḇūʻ ōt*, = weeks, w. ref. to weeks between Passover and Pentecost]

shăck *n*., & *v.i.* **1.** *n.* roughly built cabin etc. **2.** *v.i.* (sl.) ∼ **up,** cohabit *with* or *together*. [perh. f. Mex. *jacal*, Aztec *xacatli* wooden hut]

shă′ckle *n*., & *v.t.* **1.** *n.* metal loop or staple, link closed by bolt for connecting chains etc., coupling link; long link joining pair of wrist or ankle rings; (in *pl.*) fetters, (fig.) impediments or restraints (*the shackles of convention*). **2.** ∼**-bolt,** (1) bolt for closing shackle, (2) bolt with shackle at its end; ∼**-joint** (in some fishes, formed by bony ring passing through hole in another bone). **3.** *v.t.* fetter, impede, trammel. [OE *sc(e)acul* fetter, corresp. to LG *shäkel* link, coupling, ON *skökull* wagon-pole f. Gmc **skak-*]

shăd *n*. (*pl.* ∼s or ∼). anadromous deep-bodied fish of genus *Alosa*, much esteemed as food; *~'**berry,** *~'**bush,** = SERVICE²-*berry* (2). [f. OE *sceadd*, of unkn. orig.]

shă'ddock n. (tree, *Citrus grandis*, bearing) largest citrus fruit, of which small round varieties are called grapefruit. [f. Capt. *Shaddock*, introducer to W. Indies in 17th c.]

shāde¹ n. **1.** comparative darkness (and usu. coolness) caused by interception of light (and usu. heat) rays; (fig.) comparative obscurity (**put in**(to) **the ~, throw into the ~,** outshine); (in *pl.*) darkness *of* night or evening; **~ tree** (grown mainly to give shade). **2.** (in *sing.* or *pl.*) place sheltered from sun, cool or sequestered retreat; ||(in *pl.*) wine-vaults; **in the ~,** (of temperature) measured at position not directly exposed to sun. **3.** darker part of picture; **without light and ~,** (of painting, or fig. of description or character) monotonous, uniformly glaring or sombre. **4.** a colour esp. with regard to its depth, or as distinguished from one nearly like it, or made darker by admixture of black, gradation of colour, material so coloured, (*in all shades of purple*; *I want the same colour in a lighter shade*; *all the newest shades in stock*); (fig.) slightly differing variety (*people of all shades of opinion*; *delicate shades of meaning*). **5.** slight difference, small amount, (*am a shade better today*) **6.** unsubstantial or unreal thing; **is the shadow of a ~,** (rhet.) is delusive. **7.** ghost of person after death (*spoke with the shade of Homer*); **the ~s,** Hades; **S~** of *Fowler* etc.! (excl. at stylistic blunder etc., that would have outraged person invoked). **8.** screen excluding or moderating light, heat, etc.; eye-shield; translucent cover for lamp etc.; *window-blind; *(in *pl.*) sun-glasses. **9.** Hence ~LESS (-dl-) *a.* [OE *sc*(*e*)*adu*, = OS *scado*, OHG *scato*, Goth. *skadus* f. Gmc *skadhw- f. IE *skotw- or *skatw-]

shād|e² v. **1.** v.t. screen from excessive light (*shaded his eyes with his hand*; *trees shade the street*). **2.** cover, keep off, or moderate power of (luminous object, light) with or as intervening object. **3.** make dark or gloomy (*a sullen look shaded his face*). **4.** darken (parts of drawing etc.) esp. with parallel pencil lines to give effects of light and shade or gradations of colour, whence ~ING¹ (6) *n.* **5.** v.i. & t. (Of colour or light, and fig. of opinion, practice, etc.) pass off by degrees into (or *into*) other colour or variety; make (colour etc.) pass thus into another; reduce (prices etc.) slightly. [ME, f. prec.]

shadoo'f n. pole with bucket and counterpoise used esp. in Egypt for raising water. [f. Egypt. Arab. *šādūf*]

shă'dow¹ (-dō) n. **1.** = SHADE¹ 1, 2, 3 (*sitting in the shadow*; *the shadow of death is on his face*; VALLEY *of the shadow of death*; *the shadows of night*; *under the shadow of misfortune*); substance used to darken painting, eyes, etc. **2.** patch of shade, region not reached by light, sound, etc., because of intervening object; dark figure projected by body that intercepts light rays, this regarded as person's or thing's appendage (**afraid of** one's **own ~,** very timid; **may your ~ never grow less,** wish for person's increasing prosperity); (fig.) one's inseparable attendant or companion; **cast a long ~,** (fig.) be significant. **3.** reflected image. **4.** type, faint representation, foreshadowing, premonition, (*coming events cast their shadows before*). **5.** slightest trace (*without a shadow of* (*a*) *doubt*). **6.** unsubstantial or unreal thing or counterfeit (*catch at shadows*; *having only the shadow of freedom*); phantom, ghost, (lit., or fig.: *worn to a shadow*); **the ~ of** one's **former self,** much weakened or emaciated. **7.** shelter, protection, (*under the shadow of the Almighty*). **8.** ~**bird,** = HAMMER¹-*head* (3); ~**boxing** (against imaginary opponent as form of training); ||**S~ Cabinet, Chancellor,** etc., (of members of Opposition party who would probably be Cabinet ministers if that party became the Government); ~ **factory,** one planned or built for possible reserve production against the emergency of war; ~**graph,** shadow-like picture made esp. with

X-rays; ~ **roll,** thick piece of material on horse's head to prevent seeing shadow on ground. **9.** Hence ~LESS, ~Y², *adjs.* [repr. OE *scead*(*u*)*we*, obl. case of *sceadu* SHADE¹]

shă'dow² (-dō) v.t. cast shadow over; set *forth* dimly, in outline, allegorically, or prophetically; secretly follow and watch all movements of. [OE *sceadwian* (as prec.)]

shā'd|ỹ *a.* giving, situated in, shade; (of action, conduct, etc.) avoiding the light, disreputable, of dubious honesty; **on the ~y side of** *forty* etc., more than; hence ~ILY² *adv.*, ~INESS *n.* [f. SHADE¹ + -Y²]

shaft (-ah-) n. **1.** (slender pole of) lance or spear. **2.** arrow, esp. of longbow; (fig.) remark aimed like arrow (*shafts of satire, envy*). **3.** ray *of* light; bolt or stroke *of* lightning. **4.** stem, stalk; column between base and capital, one of group of clustered columns; spire; part of chimney above roof; central stem of feather; part more or less long and narrow and straight supporting or connecting part(s) of greater thickness etc.; part of golf-club between handle and head. **5.** (Mech.) large axle, revolving bar transferring force by belts or cogs; hence ~ING¹ (3, 6) *n.* **6.** handle of tool etc. **7.** one of pair of bars between which horse of vehicle is harnessed. **8.** vertical or inclined excavation giving access to mine; tunnel of blast-furnace; upward vent for smoke or foul air from tunnel, drain, etc.; vertical passage for movement of lift etc.; ~**grave** (in deep rectangular pit). [OE *scæft, sceaft,* = OS, OHG *scaft,* ON *skapt* f. Gmc *skaft-]

shăg¹ n. **1.** rough growth or mass of hair etc.; (arch.) long-napped rough cloth. **2.** coarse kind of cut tobacco. **3.** cormorant, esp. crested cormorant (*Phalacrocorax aristotelis*). [OE *sceacga,* cogn. w. ON *skegg* beard, OE *sceaga* coppice, SHAW¹ f. Gmc *skag-]

shăg² v.t. (-gg-). (sl.) copulate with; (in *p.p.*) exhausted, tired *out.* [18th c.; orig. unkn.]

***shă'gbȧrk** n. (wood of) hickory with thick curling bark. [f. *shag* a. = full. + BARK¹]

shă'gg|ỹ (-gī) *a.* hairy, rough-haired; (of hair) coarse and abundant, unkempt; (of land etc.) overgrown with forest or rough vegetation; (of tree etc.) having rough branches or twigs; (Biol.) having hairlike covering; ~**y-do'g story,** long detailed inconsequential narrative amusing only to its teller or by its pointlessness; hence ~ILY² *adv.*, ~INESS *n.*, (-g-). [f. SHAG¹ + -Y²]

shagree'n n. kind of untanned leather with artificially granulated surface made from skin of horse, ass, shark, etc., and usu. dyed green; shark-skin rough with natural papillae used for rasping and polishing. [var. of CHAGRIN in sense 'rough skin']

shah n. monarch of Iran. [f. Pers. *šāh* f. OPers. *ḳšāyṯiya* king]

shaik(h). See SHEIKH.

shāke¹ v. (shook *pr.* -ŏŏk; **sha'ken,** arch. or colloq. **shook**). **1.** v.t. move (thing, person) violently or quickly up and down or to and fro with the hand(s) etc. (*like a terrier shaking a rat*; *shook the mat to get the dust out*; *deserves a good shaking*); ~ **hands,** ~ **person by the hand,** clasp right hands with or without shaking at meeting or parting, in reconciliation or congratulation, or over concluded bargain. **2.** v.t. & i. (cause to) tremble or rock or quiver or vibrate or wave, jolt, jar, brandish, (*explosion shook the house*; *the earth shook*); tremble violently (*with* cold, fear, etc.); **hand ~s** (is unsteady); *shake* one's FINGER *at*; ~ one's **fist, stick,** etc., **at,** threaten with fist etc.; ~ one's **head,** move it from side to side in refusal, denial, disapproval, or concern (*over* or *at*, or abs.); *shake a* LEG; ~ **in** one's **shoes,** tremble with apprehension. **3.** v.t. agitate, shock, disturb, (*was much shaken by, with, at, the news*; *shake him out of his lethargy*; *shaken but unhurt in the accident*; *shook my composure*); (colloq.) upset composure of (person); (Austral. sl.) steal, rob. **4.** weaken, impair, make less convincing or firm or stable or courageous, (*the firm's credit was shaken*; *could not shake the witness's evidence*; *his faith in Providence was greatly shaken*; *the ranks were shaken but not broken*). **5.** *v.i.* (Of voice, musical note, singer, etc.) make tremulous sounds, change pitch or power with rapid alternations, trill, (*his voice shook with emotion*). **6.** (colloq.) shake hands (*we shook on the bargain*). **7.** ~ **down**, fetch or send down by shaking (fruit from tree; straw or blankets etc. on floor for bed, whence ~'*down* n.; grain etc. in vessel into least volume), become compact, get comfortably settled or into harmony with associates or circumstances (~*down cruise* of new ship, to run the engines in and accustom the crew to the ship), *(sl.) extort money from; ~ **off**, get rid of (dust etc.; fig., illness, bad habit, undesirable companion, worry) by shaking (*shake the* DUST[1] *off* one's *feet*; ~ **out**, empty (vessel, garment, etc.) of contents or dust, (contents) from vessel etc., spread or open (sail, flag, reef) by shaking; ~-*out* n., radical upheaval or reorganization; ~ **up**, mix (ingredients), restore (pillow etc.) to shape, discompose (person), by shaking, rouse from stagnant or lethargic or convention-ridden state, whence ~-*up* n. **8.** Hence ~ABLE (-ka-), **shā′kABLE**, *adjs.* [OE *sc(e)acan*, = OS *skakan*, ON *skaka* f. Gmc *skakan*]

shāke[2] *n.* **1.** shaking or being shaken (*with a shake of the head*; *give it, had, a shake*); **all of a** ~, trembling; **no great** ~**s**, (sl.) not very good or efficient; **the** ~**s**, fit of trembling or shivering. **2.** jolt, jerk, shock; = MILK[1] shake; (US & NZ) earthquake. **3.** (Mus.) trill. **4.** (colloq.) moment; **in two** etc. ~**s** (**of a lamb's tail** etc.), **in a brace of** ~**s**, very quickly, in no time. **5.** crack in growing timber. [f. prec.]

shā′ken. See SHAKE[1].

shā′ker *n.* In vbl senses; vessel for shaking together ingredients of cocktails etc.; SUGAR-*shaker*; (*S*~) member of Amer. religious sect with simple life in celibate mixed communities [named from religious dances], whence **Shā′ker**ESS[1], **Shā′ker**ISM (3), *ns.* [ME, f. SHAKE[1] + -ER[1]]

Shākespear′i‖an, -ks-, -ēr′-, -ėan, (-kspēr′-) *a.* & *n.* **1.** *a.* (in the style) of Shakespeare. **2.** *n.* student of Shakespeare's works. **3.** So ~A′NA *n. pl.* [f. W. *Shakespeare*, Engl. dramatist d. 1616 + -IAN]

shā′kō *n.* (*pl.* ~**s**). form of military hat, more or less cylindrical with peak and upright plume or tuft. [f. F *schako* f. Magyar *csákó* (*süveg*) peaked (cap) f. *csák* peak f. G *zacken* spike]

shā′k‖y̌ *a.* unsteady, apt to shake, trembling, unsound, infirm, (*a shaky hand, table, old man, house*); unreliable, wavering, (*shaky credit, voters, courage*); (of timber) containing shakes; hence ~ILY[2] *adv.*, ~INESS *n.* [f. SHAKE[1,2] + -Y[2]]

shāle *n.* finely stratified stone splitting readily into thin plates and resembling slate but softer and less solid, consisting of consolidated mud or clay; ~-**oil** (got from bituminous shale); hence **shā′ly**[2] *a.* [prob. f. G *schale* f. OE *sc(e)alu* cogn. w. ON *skál* SCALE[2]]

shall (shal or, when stressed, shăl) *v. aux.* (*pres.* **shall**, or **'ll** (after *I* or *we*), exc. 2 *sing.* (arch.) **shalt**, *neg.* **shall not**, (colloq.) **shan't** *pr.* shahnt; *past should* *pr.* shŏŏd or shud, *or* **'d** (after *I* or *we*), exc. 2 *sing.* (arch.) **shouldst** *pr.* shŏŏdst, *or* **shouldest** *pr.* shŏŏ′dist, *neg.* **should not**, (colloq.) **shouldn't** *pr.* shŏŏ′dėnt; no other parts used). **1.** In first person (the others having *will, would*) forming simple future or conditional statement or question (*we shall hear about it tomorrow*; *I should have been killed if I had let go*; *shall I hear from you soon?*; *should I hear from you in that case?*) or emphatic intention (*I shall return*). **2.** In 2nd and 3rd persons (1st having *will, would*) forming future or conditional statement expressing speaker's will or intention (*you shall not catch me again*; *he should not have gone if I could have prevented it*). **3.** (Less often than *will, would*) in sentences of type 1 changed in reporting from 1st to other person (*he says or said, you say or said, that he, you, shall or should never manage it*). **4.** Replacing *will* or

would in sentences of type 1 changed in reporting from 2nd or 3rd person to 1st (*he says I shall never manage it*, reporting *you will never*). **5.** In reporting sentences of type 2 that contained *shall* or *should* (*you promised I, he, should not catch you at it again*). **6.** In 2nd-person questions corresponding to type 1, by attraction to expected answer (*shall you be going to church?*) or to avoid implication of request in *will*. **7.** In any person to form statements or questions involving the notions of command and future or conditional duty, obligation, likelihood, etc., (*thou shalt not steal*; *any person failing to display the licence shall be guilty of an offence*; *I, you, he, should really have been more careful*; *shall I, he, open the door?*; *we should be safe now*; *why should I, you, he, obey?*; (iron.) *I should* WORRY). **8.** In any person to form conditional protasis or indefinite clause (*if, when, we shall be defeated or defeat shall overtake us*; *anyone who should say*; *it is surprising that I, you, they, should be or have been so foolish*; *if you should happen to be there*; *should I, she, be there I will tell her*; (in tentative or modest expression) *I should like to disagree, I should say it is time*). **9.** Alternatively with *may, might*, in any person in purpose-clause (*in order that I, you, he, shall or should not be able*). **10.** *it should* SEEM; **you** ~ **find,** (arch.) be sure you will find. [OE *sceal*, = OHG *scal*, OS, ON, Goth. *skal*, preterite-present v. f. Gmc *skal-*, *skul-* owe f. IE *skel-* etc.]

shalloo′n *n.* light twilled woollen cloth for coat-linings etc. [f. *Châlons-sur-Marne* in NE France]

shā′llop *n.* light open boat for shallow water. [f. F *chaloupe* f. Du *sloep* SLOOP]

shallo′t *n.* onion-like plant (*Allium ascalonicum*) with cloves like, but of milder flavour than, those of garlic. [f. *eschalot* f. F *eschalotte* alt. of OF *escaloigne* (see SCALLION)]

shā′llow (-ō) *a.*, *n.*, & *v.* **1.** *a.* of little depth (*shallow water*, *a shallow stream, dish*); (fig.) superficial, trivial, (*a shallow mind, argument, man*); hence ~LY[2] *adv.*, ~NESS *n.* **2.** *n.* shallow place, shoal. **3.** *v.i.* & *t.* become or make shallow. [ME, prob. rel. to *schald*, OE *sceald* SHOAL[1]]

shalō′m *n.* & *int.* (excl. of) salutation at meeting or parting, used among Jews. [f. Heb. *šālôm* peace]

shălt. See SHALL.

shā′lwār (-ŭ′lv-) *n.* loose trousers worn by both sexes in some S. Asian countries. [f. Pers. *šalwār*]

shăm *v.* (-mm-), *n.*, & *a.* **1.** *v.t.* & *i.* feign, simulate, (*sham illness, sleep, fear*; *is only shamming*); pretend to be (*shammed ill, dead, asleep*); hence ~**mer**[1] *n.* **2.** *n.* imposture, pretence, humbug, (*this age of shams*); person or thing pretending or pretended to be something that he or it is not; (arch.) embroidered linen laid on bed in day for show. **3.** *a.* pretended, counterfeit; ~ **fight,** imitation battle for training troops or for display; ~ **plea,** (Law, advanced only to gain time); ~-**Tudor** etc. (simulating an architectural or other style). [perh. north. dial. var. of SHAME[1,2]]

shā′man *n.* priest or witch-doctor of class claiming to have sole contact with gods etc.; hence ~ISM (3) *n.*, ~**i′stic** *a.* [f. G *schamane* & Russ. *shaman* f. Tungusian *samán*]

shă′mateur (-tūr, -tér) *n.* sports player classed as amateur though often profiting like professional; hence ~ISM (3) *n.* [f. SHAM + AMATEUR]

shă′mbl‖e *v.i.*, & *n.* **1.** *v.i.* walk or run in shuffling or awkward or decrepit way; ~**ing gait** (of person who shambles). **2.** *n.* shambling gait. [prob. f. dial. *shamble* a. ungainly, perh. f. *shamble legs* w. ref. to straddling trestles (see foll.)]

shā′mbles (-belz) *n. pl.* (usu. treated as *sing.*) butcher's slaughter-house; scene of carnage (*the place became a shambles*); (colloq.) mess, muddle. [pl. of *shamble* stool, stall f. OE *sc(e)amul*, = OS *skamel*, OHG *scamil* f. WG f. L *scamellum* dim. of *scamnum* bench]

shămbŏ′lic *a.* (colloq.) chaotic, disorganized. [f. prec. after SYMBOLIC]

shāme[1] *n.* **1.** feeling of humiliation excited by consciousness of (esp. one's own) guilt or shortcoming, of having made oneself or been made ridiculous, or of having offended against propriety, modesty, or decency, (*flushed with shame*; *begin with shame to take the lowest room*). **2.** restraint imposed by, desire to avoid, such humiliation (*cannot do it for very shame*; *has no sense of shame, is quite without* or *dead to* or *lost to shame*); **for** ∼! (appeal to person not to disregard, or reproof for disregarding, this restraint or desire). **3.** state of disgrace or regret or ignominy or discredit (∼ **on you!**, you should be ashamed; **put** person **to** ∼, disgrace him esp. by exhibiting one's superior qualities etc.); person or thing that brings disgrace etc.; **what a** ∼!, (1) that is disgraceful!, (2) how unlucky!. [OE *sc(e)amu*, ◼ OS, OHG *skama*, ON *skömm* f. Gmc **skamō*]

shāme[2] *v.t.* bring shame on, be a shame to, make ashamed; put to shame by outdoing (*a sanctity which shames our religions*); force by shame *into* or *out of* doing, conduct, etc. [OE *sc(e)amian*, = OS *skamon*, OHG *skamōn*, Goth. *skaman* (as prec.)]

shā′mefāced (-mfăst) *a.* displaying shame; modest, shy, diffident; hence ∼LY[2] (-sĭd-) *adv.*, ∼NESS *n.* [16th c. etym. misinterpretation of *shamefast* f. OE *sc(e)amfæst* (as SHAME[1], FAST[3]), after FACE[1]]

shā′meful (-mf-) *a.* that causes or ought to cause shame (sense 1); disgraceful, degrading; hence ∼LY[2] *adv.*, ∼NESS *n.* [OE *sc(e)amful* (as SHAME[1], -FUL)]

shā′melèss (-ml-) *a.* having or showing no sense of shame, impudent; hence ∼LY[2] *adv.*, ∼NESS *n.* [OE *sc(e)amlēas* (as SHAME[1], -LESS)]

shā′mmȳ *n.* = CHAMOIS 2. [repr. corrupted pronunc.]

shămpōō′ *v.t.*, & *n.* **1.** *v.t.* lather, wash, and rub (head, hair); clean (hair) with dry shampoo; clean surface of (carpet, car, etc.) with soap or chemical. **2.** shampooing; substance used for this; DRY[1] *shampoo*. [f. Hind. *chhāmpo*, imper. of *chhāmpnā* to press]

shă′mrŏck *n.* trefoil (esp. *Trifolium minus*) used as national emblem of Ireland. [f. Ir. *seamrōg* trefoil, dim. of *seamar* clover]

Shă′ndèan *a.* having characteristics of (the family portrayed in) Sterne's novel *Tristram Shandy*. [f. *Shandy* + -AN]

shă′ndrȳdăn *n.* chaise with hood; old rickety vehicle. [19th c.; orig. unkn.]

shă′ndȳ(găff) *n.* mixed drink of beer and ginger-beer or lemonade. [19th c.; orig. unkn.]

shăngāi′ (-hī′) *v.t.* (Naut. sl.) ship as sailor while unconscious from drugs etc.; (sl.) trick into awkward situation. [f. S∼ in China]

Shăngri-La′ (-nggrĭlah′) *n.* imaginary paradise on earth. [name of hidden valley in J. Hilton's *Lost Horizon*]

shănk *n.* & *v.* **1.** *n.* leg (**on** S∼**s's mare** or **pony**, walking as opp. riding etc.); lower part of leg, leg from knee to ankle; lower part of animal's foreleg, esp. as cut of meat; shin-bone; upright part of bird's foot; footstalk of flower; ‖leg of stocking. **2.** shaft of pillar etc., shaft of tool between head etc. and handle, stem of key, spoon, anchor, etc., straight part of nail or fish-hook, narrow middle of sole of shoe etc., whence (-)∼ED[2] (-kt) *a.*; *first or last part of* (afternoon etc.). **3.** *v.i.* ∼ **off**, (of flower) fall off by decay of shank. **4.** *v.t.* (Golf) strike (ball) with heel of club. [OE *sceanca*, = LG *schanke* f. WG **skanka*, cogn. w. MHG *schenkel* thigh]

shă′nnȳ *n.* oblong olive-green European sea-fish, the smooth blenny. [19th c., of unkn. orig.; cf. 18th c. *shan*]

shan't. See SHALL.

shăntŭ′ng *n.* soft undressed Chinese silk (usu. undyed). [f. S∼, Chin. province]

shă′ntȳ[1] *n.* hut, cabin; mean roughly-built dwelling; ∼ **town** (consisting of shanties). [19th c., orig. N. Amer., of uncert. orig.]

shă′ntȳ[2] *n.* (sea-)∼, sailor's song (with alternating solo by ∼**man**, and chorus) sung while pulling etc. [prob. F *chantez*, imper. pl. of *chanter* sing; see CHANT]

shāpe[1] *v.* (arch. *p.p.* **sha′pen**). **1.** *v.t.* create, form, construct; model, mould, fashion, bring into desired or definite figure or form; (in *p.p.*) having such figure (*shaped like a pear*); hence **shā′pER**[1] (1, 2) *n.* **2.** adapt, make conform, *to*; plan, devise; direct, aim, (one's course etc.); frame mentally, imagine, call up image of. **3.** Hence ∼ABLE (-pa-), **shā′pABLE**, *adjs.* **4.** *v.i.* assume form, develop into shape, give signs of future shape (∼ (**up**) **well**, be promising); ∼ **up**, take (specified) form. [ME, back-form. f. p.p.; orig. f. OE *sceppan*, Goth. *gaskapjan* create, f. Gmc **skap-*]

shāpe[2] *n.* **1.** configuration, external form, total effect produced by thing's outlines, (*spherical in shape*; *has the shape of a boat*). **2.** appearance, guise, (*monster in human shape*). **3.** specific form, embodiment, (*intention took shape in action*; *showed me politeness in the shape of an invitation*). **4.** kind, description, sort, (*made no approach in any shape or form*). **5.** symmetrical or definite form, orderly arrangement, proper form or condition, (*get one's ideas into shape*; *knock* or LICK *into shape*; *give shape to*); **in bad, good, poor,** etc., ∼ (condition); hence ∼′LESS (-pl-) *a.* **6.** person considered as impressing the sight, and esp. as indistinctly seen or imagined, apparition, ghost, (*a shape loomed through the mist*; *a grim mysterious shape stalked towards me*). **7.** pattern for working from, mould for shaping hat, jelly, etc.; untrimmed hat; jelly, blancmange, etc., shaped in mould; piece of material made in a particular form. **8.** Hence (-)**shāpED**[2] (-pt) *a.* [OE *gesceap* creation, = OS *giskapu* creatures, ON *skap* condition f. as prec.]

SHAPE (shāp) *abbr.* Supreme Headquarters Allied Powers Europe.

shā′pell̄ȳ (-plĭ) *a.* well formed or proportioned, of the right or a pleasing shape; hence ∼iNESS *n.* [ME, f. SHAPE[2] + -LY[1]]

shărd[1]. Var. of SHERD, = potsherd. [OE *sceard*, = MLG *skart* crack, ON *skarthr* notch f. Gmc **skardaz* notched (**skar-*, **sker-* SHEAR[1])]

shărd[2] *n.* beetle's wing-case. [back-form. f. *shard-borne* (Shak.) = born in shard (dial. = cow-dung), misinterpreted as 'borne on shards']

shāre[1] *n.* **1.** portion detached for individual from jointly owned amount (*must get a share of the plunder*); part one gets or contributes (*had a large share in bringing it about, but no share of the credit*; *has his share of conceit*). **2.** part one is entitled to have or bound to contribute, equitable portion, (*that is your fair share*; LION's *share*; *took my, more* or *less than my*, (*fair*) *share of the burden*; *gets more than its* (*due*) *share of attention*); **go ∼s**, make equitable division (*with others*); ∼ **and** ∼ **alike**, with equal division. **3.** part-proprietorship of property held by joint owners (*has a share in the bank, estate*, etc.), esp. one of the equal parts into which company's capital is divided entitling owner to proportion of profits; DEFER[1]*red*, ‖ORDINARY, ‖PREFERENCE or *preferred*, *shares*; ∼′**holder**, owner of shares; ∼ **index**, number showing how prices of shares have fluctuated; ∼**-pusher**, (colloq.) one who peddles shares by circular or advertisement. [ME, OE *sceáru* division, OS, OHG *scara* troop, cogn. w. SHEAR[1]]

shāre[2] *v.* **1.** *v.t.* apportion (food, property, task, etc.) among others, give each a share of; give away part of (*would share his last crust*); get or have share of, benefit from or possess or use or endure jointly with others. **2.** *v.i.* have share (*in*), be sharer(s), (*will share with you in the undertaking*); ∼ **and** ∼ **alike**, make equal division; ∼**-cropper**, tenant farmer who pays part of crop as rent, whence ∼*-crop* *v.i.* & *t.*; ∼ **out**, distribute, whence ∼*-out* *n.*, distribution esp. of profits, booty, etc., in shares. **3.** Hence **shā′r′ER**[1] *n.* [f. prec.]

shāre[3] *n.* ploughshare; blade of seeding-machine or cultivator; ∼**-beam**, part of plough in which share is fixed. [OE *scear*, *scær*, = OHG *scar(o)*, WG f. Gmc **skar-*, **sker-* SHEAR[1]]

shari'ah (-ē'a) n. Muslim code of religious law. [f. Arab. *šarī'a*]

sharif. Var. of SHERIF.

shark n. long-bodied lateral-gilled inferior-mouthed elasmobranch sea-fish, esp. if large and voracious; rapacious person, swindler; *(sl.) brilliant student; ∼-skin, (1) skin of shark, shagreen, (2) dull-surfaced smooth usu. heavy fabric; ∼'s-mouth, opening in awning for mast etc. [16th c., of unkn. orig.]

sharp¹ a., n., & adv. **1.** a. having edge or point able to cut or pierce, not blunt; peaked, pointed, edged, *(sharp gable, summit, ridge)*; (of sand etc.) composed of angular grains; ∼ end, (colloq.) bow of ship, place of direct action or decision. **2.** well-defined, clean-cut, *(sharp outline, distinction, contrast, impression, features)*. **3.** abrupt, angular, *(sharp fall, turn, incline)*. **4.** keen, pungent, acid, tart, shrill, piercing, biting, harsh, acrimonious, severe, intense, painful, *(sharp appetite, flavour, wine, sauce, voice, cry, frost, air, words, tongue, temper, reproof, contest, attack of cramp)*. **5.** acute, sensitive, quick to see or hear or notice, keen-witted, vigilant, clever, *(sharp eyes, ears, intelligence, wits, attention; sharp-eyed, -witted, etc.; keep a sharp look-out; a sharp remark, child)*; (sl.) stylish or flashy with regard to dress; **as ∼ as a needle,** very intelligent; ∼'shooter, skilled marksman. **6.** quick to take advantage, bent on winning, artful, unscrupulous, dishonest; **be too ∼ for,** outwit; ∼ **practice,** dishonest or barely honest dealings. **7.** vigorous, brisk, speedy, not loitering, impetuous, *(take a sharp walk)*; ∼'s **the word** (exhortation to be quick); ∼ **work,** matter quickly dispatched, fight etc. that takes all one's energy. **8.** (Mus.) above true pitch (**C, F,** etc., ∼, a semitone higher than C, F, etc.); (of key) having sharp(s) in signature. **9.** Hence ∼'LY² adv., ∼'NESS n. **10.** n. sewing-needle of slender make; (Mus.) note raised a semitone above natural pitch, sign indicating this raising; (colloq.) swindler, cheat; *(joc.) expert; ||(in pl.) middlings (between flour and bran). **11.** adv. punctually *(at six o'clock sharp)*; suddenly *(pulled up sharp)*; at a sharp angle *(turn sharp right)*; (Mus.) above true pitch *(sings sharp)*; LOOK *sharp*; ∼-**set,** (1) set with sharp edge, (2) hungry; ∼-**shod,** shod with sharp iron to prevent slipping. [OE *sc(e)arp*, = OS *skarp*, OHG *skarf, scarpf*, ON *skarpr* f. Gmc **skarpaz*]

sharp² v. **1.** v.t. *(Mus.) make sharp. **2.** v.i. (arch.) play unfairly, swindle, at cards etc. [f. OE **scierpan* sharpen f. Gmc **skarpjan*, & prob. partly f. prec.]

shar'pen v.t. & i. make or become sharp; hence (-)∼'ER¹ (1, 2) n. [ME, f. SHARP¹ + -EN⁶]

shar'per n. swindler, esp. at cards etc. [f. SHARP² + -ER¹]

shar'pish a. & adv. (colloq.) somewhat or fairly sharp(ly). [f. SHARP¹ + -ISH¹]

Shā'sta n. ∼ **daisy,** large-flowered daisy (*Chrysanthemum maximum*) like ox-eye. [∼ in California]

Sha'stra (-ah'-) n. Hindu sacred writings. [f. Hindi *šāstr*, Skr. *šāstra*]

shā'tter v.t. & i. **1.** break suddenly and violently in pieces; hence ∼-PROOF² a. **2.** v.t. utterly destroy, dissipate, *(shattered nerves, health, hopes)*; (colloq.) severely discompose. [ME, rel. to SCATTER]

shāve¹ v. (p.p. ∼d or, exc. as a., sha'ven). **1.** v.t. remove (hair), free (chin etc.) of hair, remove hair from chin etc. of (person), with razor *(has shaved off or shaved his beard; a shaven chin)*. **2.** pare surface of (wood etc.) with spokeshave, plane, etc., whence shā'VING¹ (2) n.; (fig.) reduce amount of, reduce by (amount). **3.** pass close to without touching, skirt, miss narrowly, nearly graze. **4.** v.i. shave oneself *(he does not shave every day)*. **5.** ∼-**hook,** tool for scraping surface of metal before soldering; *∼-**tail,** newly broken-in mule, (fig.) newly commissioned officer; **sha'ving-brush** (for lathering chin etc. before shaving); **sha'ving--cream** (for applying to chin etc. with or without brush, to assist shaving); **sha'ving-soap** for making

lather to assist shaving); **sha'ving-stick,** cylindrical piece of shaving-soap. [OE *sc(e)afan,* = OS **scaban,* OHG *scaban,* ON *skafa,* Goth. *skaban* f. Gmc **skabhan*]

shāve² n. **1.** having one's beard etc. shaved *(must have a shave)*. **2.** close approach without contact, narrow miss or escape or failure (CLOSE¹ *shave*). **3.** tool (e.g. knife-blade with handle at each end) for shaving wood etc. **4.** ||(arch.) trick, deception, hoax. [f. prec.; sense 3 f. OE *sceafa,* = OHG *scaba,* ON *skafa* f. Gmc **skabhōn* (as prec.)]

sha'veling (-vl-) n. (arch.) shaven person; monk, friar, priest. [f. SHAVE¹ + -LING¹]

shā'ven. See SHAVE¹.

shā'ver n. In vbl senses; electrically driven razor; (colloq.), lad, youngster, *(young shaver)*. [ME, f. SHAVE¹ + -ER¹]

Shā'vian a. & n. (in the manner, admirer) of G. B. Shaw, Brit. dramatist etc. d. 1950. [f. *Shavius* L form of *Shaw* + -IAN]

Shavuot(h). Var. of SHABUOT(H).

||**shaw¹** n. (arch. or dial.) thicket, wood. [OE *sceaga,* = ON *skagi* promontory; cf. SHAG¹]

||**shaw²** n. stalks and leaves of potatoes, turnips, etc. [perh. = SHOW²]

shawl n., & v.t. **1.** n. (usu. rectangular) piece of fabric often folded into triangle, worn over shoulders, round neck, etc., or wrapped round baby; ∼ **collar,** rolled collar extended downwards to meet or cross at waist; ∼-**pattern,** variegated design like that of Oriental shawl. **2.** v.t. (esp. in p.p.) put shawl on (person). [f. Urdu etc. f. Pers. *šāl,* prob. f. *Shāliāt* in India]

shawm n. obsolete musical instrument of oboe type. [ME, f. OF *chalemie, chalemel, chalemeaus* pl., f. Rom. **calamellus* dim. of L f. Gk *kalamos* reed]

shay n. (arch. or dial.) = CHAISE 1. [back-form. f. CHAISE taken as pl.]

shē (or, when unstressed, shǐ) pron. (obj. HER¹, refl. HERSELF or arch. HER¹, poss. HER², HERS, pl. THEY etc.), n., & a. **1.** pron. the female (or thing personified as female, e.g. the moon, nation, ship, motor vehicle) previously mentioned or implied as easily identified; the or any female person *who*; (Austral. colloq.) it, the state of affairs *(she'll be* RIGHT¹ 5). **2.** n. female, woman, **(the not impossible ∼,** woman one might love; *is the child, the puppy, a he or a she?*). **3.** a. (usu. w. hyphen). female *(she-goat, -ass, -bear, etc.)*; ∼-**cat,** ∼-**devil,** malignant or spiteful woman; ∼-**oak,** Australian casuarina tree; ∼-**pine,** Australian evergreen tree yielding yellow timber. [ME *sce, sche,* etc., f. OE fem. demonstr. pron. & a. *sīo, sēo,* acc. *sīe*]

shea n. W. Afr. tree whose fatty nut yields a vegetable butter (∼-**butter**). [f. Mandingo *si, se, sye*]

shea'ding n. any of the six administrative divisions of the Isle of Man. [f. SHED¹ + -ING¹]

sheaf n. (pl. **sheaves** pr. -vz), & v.t. **1.** n. cluster of things laid lengthwise together and usu. tied *(sheaf of papers, arrows,* etc.), esp. armful of corn-stalks tied after reaping (∼-**binder,** tool for tying these). **2.** v.t. make into sheaves. [OE *scēaf,* = OS *skōf,* OHG *scoub,* ON *skauf* fox's brush, f. Gmc **skaubhaz* (as SHOVE)]

shea'ling. Var. of SHIELING.

shear¹ v. (*past* ∼ed, arch. exc. Austral. & NZ **shore;** *p.p.* **shorn** or ∼ed). **1.** v.t. & i. (arch. or poet.) cut with sword etc. *(shore off his plume; shore through the bone)*. **2.** v.t. clip, cut with scissors or shears; clip wool off (sheep, or abs.); remove or reduce nap of (cloth) by clipping; (fig.) fleece, strip bare, *(come home shorn; shorn of his glory* etc.); hence ∼'ER¹ n. **3.** distort or break by SHEAR² (sense 2). **4.** v.i. (Of structure, material, etc.) be distorted or broken by SHEAR² (sense 2). [OE *sceran,* = OS, OHG *sceran,* ON *skera* f. Gmc **sker-, *skar-, *skār-, *skur-,* cut, shear]

shear² n. **1.** (in pl.) clipping or cutting instrument with two meeting blades pivoted as in scissors or connected by spring and passing close over each other edge to edge *(a pair of shears)*; ∼'**bill,** = SKIMMER 3; ∼-**grass** (with sharp-edged leaves); ∼-**legs,** SHEER⁴s; ∼ **steel**

(of special quality for shears and other cutting tools); ∼'**tail,** humming-bird with tail like shears. **2.** (Mech. & Geol.) strain produced by pressure in structure of a substance, its successive layers being shifted laterally over each other. [OE *scērero* & *scēara* pl., = OHG *skari*, ON *skæri* f. Gmc **skær-* (as prec.)]

shear'ling *n.* (wool from) sheep shorn once. [ME, f. SHEAR¹ +-LING¹]

shear'water (-waw-) *n.* long-winged sea-bird of genus *Puffinus*, usu. flying close to surface of water; = SKIMMER 3. [f. SHEAR¹ + WATER¹]

shea't-fish *n.* (*pl.* usu. same). large catfish (*Silurus glanis*), largest European freshwater fish. [earlier SHEATH-*fish*, prob. after G *scheid*]

sheath *n.* (*pl. pr.* -dhz, -ths). close-fitting cover esp. for blade of weapon or tool; (Bot., Zool., & Anat.) investing membrane, tissue, skin, horny case, etc.; sheathing of cable etc.; condom; woman's close--fitting dress; ∼-**bill,** Antarctic sea-bird with horny sheath at base of bill; ∼-**knife** (dagger-like, carried in sheath); hence ∼'LESS *a.* [OE *scǣth, scēath,* = OS *skēthia*, OHG *sceida*, ON *skeithir* pl. f. Gmc *skaithiz, *skaithjo, prob. cogn. w. SHED¹]

sheathe (-dh) *v.t.* put into sheath (∼ **the sword,** cease from war, lit. or fig.); encase, protect with casing or **shea'th**ING¹ (3) (-dh-, -th-) *n.* [ME, f. prec.]

sheave¹ *n.* grooved wheel in pulley-block etc. for rope to run on. [ME, f. OE **scife, scīfe,* = OS, OHG *scība* f. Gmc *skibh disc, quoit, wheel, pane, slice of bread]

sheave² *v.t.* gather (corn etc.) into sheaves. [f. SHEAF]

sheaves. See SHEAF.

***shēbā'ng** *n.* (sl.) shed, hut; matter, affair, business (*the whole shebang*). [19th c.; orig. unkn.]

shèbee'n *n.* (Ir.) unlicensed house selling alcoholic liquor. [f. Anglo-Ir. *síbín* (*séibe* mugful; see -EEN)]

Shechinah. Var. of SHEKINAH.

shěd¹ *v.t.* (-dd-; shed). part with, let fall off, (*tree sheds leaves*; *stag sheds horns*; *snake sheds skin*; *bather sheds clothes*); reduce (electrical power load) by disconnection etc.; drop (∼ *tears,* weep; ∼ one's **blood,** be wounded or killed *for* one's *country* etc.); cause (blood) to flow by injury, disperse, diffuse, spread abroad, (*shed* LIGHT¹ *on*; *shed love, radiance, perfume,* etc., *around* one); hence ∼'**dER**¹ *n.,* (esp.) female salmon after spawning. [OE *sc(e)adan,* = OS *skēdan, skēthan,* OHG *sceidan,* Goth. *skaidan* f. Gmc **skaithan,* *skaidhan]

shěd² *n.* one-storeyed building for storing goods or vehicles or keeping cattle etc. or for use as workshop etc. and consisting of roof with some or all or no sides open; hence ∼'**d**ING¹ (3) *n.* [app. var. of SHADE¹]

sheen *n.* splendour, radiance, brightness; gloss etc. on surface. [f. obs. *sheen* beautiful, resplendent, f. OE *scēne,* = OS, OHG *scōni,* Goth. *skauns* f. Gmc **skau-* behold (cf. SHOW¹); sense assim. to SHINE²]

shee'nӯ *a.* covered with sheen; bright and shiny. [f. prec. + -Y²]

shee'nӯ *n.* (sl., derog.; **R**) Jew. [19th c.; orig. unkn.]

sheep *n.* (*pl.* same). **1.** wild or domesticated (for its meat, wool, and leather) timid gregarious woolly often horned ruminant of genus *Ovis*; ∼ **and goats,** the good and the wicked (Matt. 25:33); BLACK¹ *sheep*; *cast* or *make sheep's* EYE¹*s*; *like* ∼ (of person(s) with no initiative or independence); *as well be hanged for a sheep as a* LAMB¹; WOLF *in sheep's clothing.* **2.** bashful or docile person; (usu. in *pl.*) member of minister's flock, parishioner etc. **3.** sheepskin leather. **4.** ∼-**bot,** fly and larva injurious to sheep; ∼-**cote,** (arch.) = *sheep-fold*; ∼-**dip,** preparation for cleansing sheep of vermin or preserving their wool, place where this is used; ∼-**dog,** dog trained to guard and herd sheep, esp. (1) collie, (2) (*Old English*) ∼-**dog,** breed of rough-coated short-tailed dog used by shepherds; ||∼-**farmer,** breeder of sheep; ∼-**fold,** enclosure for penning sheep; *∼-**herder,** shepherd; ∼-**hook,** shepherd's crook; *∼'**man,** (*pl.* -men) breeder of sheep; ||∼'**meat,** mutton or lamb; ∼-**pen** = *sheep--fold*; ∼-**pox,** sheep-disease akin to smallpox; ∼-**run,**

extensive sheep-walk, esp. in Australia; ∼'**s-bit,** plant (*Jasione montana*) resembling scabious; ∼'**s fescue,** a pasture grass (*Festuca ovina*); ∼'**shank,** bight and hitches used to shorten rope's length temporarily; ∼'**s-head,** (1) head of sheep (esp. as food), (2) large marine food-fish with sheeplike head; ∼-**shearing,** (festival at) shearing of sheep; ∼'**skin,** (1) garment or rug of sheep's skin with wool on, (2) leather of sheep's skin used in bookbinding etc., (3) *parchment of it or deed or diploma engrossed on this; ||∼-**walk,** tract of land on which sheep are pastured; ∼-**wash,** lotion for killing vermin or preserving wool on sheep, place where this is used. **5.** Hence ∼'LIKE *a.* [OE *scēp, scæp, scēap,* = OS *scāp,* OHG *scāf* f. WG *skǣpa]

shee'pish *a.* shy, diffident; embarrassed through shame; hence ∼LY² *adv.,* ∼NESS *n.* [f. prec. + -ISH¹]

sheer¹ *a.* & *adv.* **1.** *a.* mere, simple, unassisted, undiluted, uncompounded, neither more nor less than, absolute, (*did it by sheer force, through sheer bad luck; is sheer waste, nonsense; a sheer impossibility*); (of rock, fall, ascent, etc.) perpendicular, unrelieved by more gradual slope; (of textile) diaphanous. **2.** *adv.* plumb, perpendicularly, outright, (*fell sheer downward 3000 ft; torn sheer out by the roots; rises sheer from the water*). [ME *schere* prob. f. dial. *shire* pure, clear f. OE *scīr,* = OS *skīr(i),* ON *skírr,* Goth. *skeirs* f. Gmc *skīraz etc. (**skī-;* see SHINE¹)]

sheer² *v.i.* & *n.* **1.** *v.i.* (Naut.) deviate from course. **2.** ∼ **away** or **off,** part company, depart, esp. from person or topic one dislikes or fears or is offended by. **3.** *n.* (Naut.) deviation from course. [perh. f. MLG *scheren* = SHEAR¹]

sheer³ *n.* upward slope of ship's lines towards bow and stern. [prob. f. SHEAR²]

sheer⁴ *n.* ∼**s,** ∼-**legs,** hoisting-apparatus of two (or more) poles attached at or near top and separated at bottom for masting ships or putting in engines etc., used in dockyards or on ∼-**lulk,** dismasted ship used for the purpose. [var. of SHEAR²]

sheet¹ *n.* **1.** rectangular piece of linen, cotton, etc. used generally in pairs as inner bedclothes (**between the** ∼**s,** in bed), whence ∼'ING¹ (3) *n.*; WHITE¹ (*as a*) *sheet.* **2.** broad more or less flat piece of thin material (*a sheet of iron, glass, paper,* etc.); set of postage stamps printed on one piece of paper for later division into units; CLEAN¹ *sheet.* **3.** wide expanse of water, snow, ice, flame, colour, etc. **4.** complete piece of paper of the size in which it was made; (Print.) such piece before or after printing and folding (**in** ∼**s,** printed and folded but not bound); (esp. scurrilous etc.) news paper. **5.** ∼ **copper, iron, metal,** etc., (spread by rolling, hammering, etc., into thin sheets), ∼ **glass** (made by drawing and cutting into sheets when cool); *sheet* LIGHTNING; ∼ **music** (published in sheets, not bound). [OE *scēte, scīete* f. Gmc *skautjōn (**skaut-*SHOOT¹)]

sheet² *v.* **1.** *v.t.* furnish with sheets; cover with sheet (*the sheeted dead*); form into sheets (*sheeted rain*). **2.** *v.i.* (Of rain etc.) move in sheets. [f. prec.]

sheet³ *n.,* & *v.t.* **1.** *n.* rope or chain at lower corner of sail for regulating its position etc.; (in *pl.*) space at bow or stern of open boat; **flowing** ∼ (not close--hauled, eased for free wind); **a** ∼, **three** ∼**s in the wind,** (sl.) rather, very, drunk; ∼-**anchor,** second anchor orig. carried outside waist of ship for use in emergencies, (fig.) thing depended on for ultimate security, one's best or only hope or expedient; ∼-**bend,** method of temporarily fastening rope in bight of another. **2.** *v.t.* ∼ **home,** extend (sail) fully with sheet. [ME f. OE *scēata,* ON *skaut* (as SHEET¹)]

sheikh, sheik, shaik(h), (-āk, -ēk) *n.* chief, head of Arab tribe, family, or village; Muslim leader; (colloq.) romantic lover; hence ∼'DOM *n.* [ult. f. Arab. *šayk* old man, sheikh (*šāka* be or grow old)]

shei'la (-ē'-) *n.* (Austral. & NZ sl.) young woman; girl. [orig. *shaler,* of unkn. orig.; assim. to name *Sheila*]

shĕkă′rrў. See SHIKAREE.

shĕ′kel *n*. Israeli monetary unit; ancient-Jewish etc. weight and silver coin; (in *pl*., colloq.) money, riches. [f. Heb. *šeḳel* (*šāḳal* weigh)]

Shĕkī′nah (*-a*) *n*. visible glory of God resting over mercy-seat, or seen in other natural or supernatural phenomena. [f. Heb. *š*ᵉ*ḳīnāh* (*šāḳan* rest, dwell)]

shĕ′ldrāke *n*. (*fem*. & *pl*. **she′lduck** *or* **sheld duck**). bright-plumaged coastal wild duck of genus *Tadorna*. [ME, prob. f. dial. *sheld* pied, cogn. w. MDu. *schillede* variegated, + DRAKE²]

shĕlf *n*. (*pl*. **shelves** *pr*. shĕlvz). **1.** projecting slab of stone or board or other rigid material let into or hung on wall to support things, one of the boards in cabinet, bookcase, etc., on which books etc. stand; **on the ~**, put aside, done with, (esp. of person past work or of unmarried woman now growing old and regarded as unlikely to be married). **2.** ledge, horizontal steplike projection in cliff face etc.; reef or sandbank under water; CONTINENTAL *shelf*. **3.** ~-**life**, time for which stored thing remains usable; ~**-mark**, mark etc. on book showing its place in library; ~-**room**, available space on shelf. **4.** Hence **shĕlvED²** (-vd) *a*., ~-**FUL** 2 *n*. [ME, f. (M)LG *schelf*, cogn. w. OE *scylfe* partition, *scylf* crag]

shĕll¹ *n*. **1.** hard outer case enclosing nut-kernel, seed, fruit, egg, animal (esp. marine mollusc) or part of it; husk, crust, pod, carapace, scale, conch, wing-case, pupa-case; **come out of** one's ~, throw off reserve, become communicative. **2.** walls of unfinished or gutted building, ship, etc. **3.** inner or roughly-made coffin; light racing-boat; hollow case of pastry etc.; metal framework of vehicle body etc. **4.** hollow metal or paper case to contain explosives for fireworks, cartridges, etc.; explosive projectile or bomb for use in big gun or mortar, whence ~′PROOF² *a*.; *cartridge. **5.** handguard of sword. **6.** building shaped like conch; ‖intermediate form in school [f. such building at Westminster School]. **7.** outward show, mere semblance. **8.** (Phys.) group of electrons with almost equal energy in atom. **9.** ~′**back**, (Naut. sl.) old sailor; ~-**bark**, hickory with bark in long narrow plates; ~-**bit**, gouge-shaped boring-bit; ~ **company**, unimportant firm made subject of take-over bid because of its status on Stock Exchange etc.; ~ **egg** (still in its shell, not dried etc.); ~′**fish**, aquatic shelled mollusc (oyster etc.) or crustacean (crab, shrimp, etc.); *~ **game**, thimblerig; ~-**heap**, ~-**mound**, kitchen MIDDEN; ~-**jacket**, army officer's tight-fitting undress jacket reaching only to waist behind; ~-**lime**, fine quality lime produced by burning sea-shells; ~-**money**, shells as medium of exchange (wampum etc.); ~-**pink**, delicate pale pink; ~-**shock**, nervous breakdown resulting from exposure to bombardment and other battle conditions; ~-**work**, ornamentation of shells cemented on wood etc. **10.** Hence (-)~ED² (-ld), ~-LESS, ~′Y², *adjs*. [OE *sc(i)ell*, = MDu., MLG *schelle*, ON *skel*, Goth. *skalja* f. Gmc *skaljō* (*skal*- SCALE¹,²)]

shĕll² *v*. **1.** *v.t.* take out of shell, remove shell or pod from, (*shell peas*). **3.** provide or cover with shell(s). **3.** bombard (town etc.), fire at (troops), with shells. **4.** *v.i.* (Of metal etc.) come *off* in scales; (of seed etc.) be released from shell. **5.** ~ **out**, (sl.) pay up (money or abs.), hand over (required sum); ~-*out* *n*., (1) act of shelling out, (2) snooker etc. played by three or more persons. [f. prec.]

shella′c *n*., & *v.t.* (-ck-). **1.** LAC¹ melted into thin flakes, used for making varnish. **2.** *v.t.* varnish with shellac; *(sl.) defeat or thrash soundly. [f. SHELL¹ + LAC¹, transl. F *laque en écailles* lac in thin plates]

Shĕ′lta *n*. ancient hybrid cant language of Irish gypsies and pipers, Irish and Welsh travelling tinkers, etc. [19th c.; orig. unkn.]

shĕ′lter¹ *n*. thing serving as shield or barrier against attack, danger, heat, wind, etc.; screen or cabin built to keep wind and rain off persons (*bus, cabman's,*

shelter); place of safety or immunity esp. as provided for the homeless, *animals, etc.; shielded condition (*find, take, shelter*); ~-**belt**, line of trees etc. to protect crops from wind; hence ~LESS *a*. [16th c., perh. f. obs. *sheltron* phalanx f. OE *scieldtruma* (as SHIELD, *truma* troop)]

shĕ′lter² *v*. **1.** *v.t.* act or serve as shelter to, protect, conceal, harbour; defend *from* blame, trouble, etc.; protect (industry, trade, etc.) from competition; ~ oneself *under, beneath, behind,* etc., use the protection available. **2.** *v.i.* take shelter *under, in, from*, etc. [f. prec.]

shĕ′ltie, **shĕ′ltў**, *n*. Shetland pony. [prob. repr. ON *Hjalti* Shetlander as pr. in Orkney]

shĕlve¹ *v.t.* put (books etc.) on shelf, (fig.) abandon or defer consideration of (plan etc.), remove (person) from active work etc.; fit (cupboard etc.) with shelves, whence **shĕ′lvING¹** (3) *n*. [f. *shelves* pl. of SHELF]

shĕlve² *v.i.* (Of ground etc.) slope in specified direction (*away, off*). [perh. f. *shelvy* a. having underwater reefs f. *shelve* n. ledge, f. prec.]

shelves. See SHELF.

shĕmŏ′zzle *n*. (sl.) rumpus, brawl; muddle. [f. Yiddish, after LHeb. *šel-lō′-mazzāl* of no luck]

shĕnă′nigan *n*. (colloq.) nonsense; trickery; high-spirited behaviour. [19th c.; orig. unkn.]

Shĕ′ōl *n*. Hebrew underworld abode of the dead. [f. Heb. *š*ᵉ*′ōl*]

shĕ′pherd (-perd) *n*., & *v.t.* **1.** *n*. man who tends sheep esp. at pasture (lit., or fig. esp. of minister in relation to his flock; **the Good S~**, Christ); ~ **dog**, sheep-dog; ~'**s crook**, staff with hook at one end used by shepherds; ~'**s needle**, white-flowered common weed with spiny fruit; ~'**s pie**, minced meat baked under mashed potatoes; ~'**s plaid**, (woollen cloth with) small black and white check pattern; ~'**s purse**, white-flowered hairy cornfield weed with triangular or cordate pods; hence ~ESS¹ *n*. **2.** *v.t.* tend (sheep, lit. or fig.) as shepherd; marshal or conduct or drive (crowd etc.) like sheep. [OE *scēaphierde* (as SHEEP, HERD²)]

shĕ′rardīze, **-īse** (-īz), *v.t.* coat (iron or steel) with zinc by heating in contact with zinc dust. [f. *Sherard* Cowper-Coles, Engl. inventor d. 1936 + -IZE]

Shĕ′raton *n*. style of furniture introduced in England *c.* 1790, with delicate and graceful forms. [f. T. ~, Engl. furniture-maker d. 1806]

shĕr′bet *n*. oriental cooling drink of sweetened diluted fruit-juices; effervescing sweet flavoured drink or powder; *water-ice. [f. Turk. *şerbet*, Pers. *šerbet* f. Arab. *šarba* drink (*šariba* to drink); cf. SHRUB², SYRUP]

shĕrd *n*. potsherd. [var. of SHARD]

sheri′f (-ē′f), **-ee′f**, *n*. descendant of Muhammad through his daughter Fatima, entitled to wear green turban or veil; Muslim leader. [f. Arab. *šarīf* noble (*šarafa* be exalted)]

shĕ′riff *n*. ‖(High) ~, chief executive officer of Crown in county, charged with keeping the peace, administering justice under direction of the courts, executing writs by deputy, presiding over elections, etc.; ‖honorary officer elected annually in some towns; ~ (-**depute**), (in Scotland) chief judge of county or district; *elective officer responsible for keeping the peace in his county, executing court orders, and supervising county jail; ~ **court**, (Sc.) county court; hence ~altY¹, ~DOM, ~HOOD, ~SHIP, *ns*. [OE *scīr-gerēfa* (as SHIRE, REEVE¹)]

Shĕr′lŏck *n*. ~ (Holmes) (hōmz), skilful detective, acute reasoner. [f. *Sherlock Holmes*, character in stories by Sir A. Conan Doyle]

Shĕr′pa *n*. (one of) a Himalayan people living on the borders of Nepal and Tibet. [native name]

shĕ′rrў *n*. white usu. fortified wine orig. from S. Spain; glass of this; *sherry* COBBLER; ~-**glass**, small wineglass for sherry; *sherry* SACK³. [earlier *sherris* f. Sp. (*vino de*) *Xeres* (now Jerez de la Frontera) in Andalusia]

Shĕ′tland *a*. ~ **lace**, open-work woollen trimming; ~

pony (small hardy rough-coated breed); ~ **sheep-
-dog**, (one of a) breed of dog like small collie; ~ **wool**,
fine loosely twisted wool from Shetland sheep; hence
~ER¹ (4) n. [f. ~ Islands NNE of Scotland]
sheva. Var. of SCHWA.
Shevuot(h). See SHABUOT(H).
shew, shewbread. See SHOW¹.
shh. Var. of HUSH² int.
Shi'ah (shē′a) n. Muslim branch esp. in Iran that
regards Ali as first successor of Muhammad and
rejects first three Sunnite Caliphs; hence **Shi'ITE¹** (1)
(shē′-) n. [f. Arab. šī′a party (of Ali, Muhammad's
cousin and son-in-law)]
shi'bboleth n. test word or principle or behaviour or
opinion, the use of or inability to use which reveals
one's party, nationality, orthodoxy, etc. (see Judg.
12:6); catchword, esp. old-fashioned and generally
abandoned doctrine or formula of a party or sect.
[ME, f. Heb. šibbōlet ear of corn]
shield n., & v.t. **1.** n. variously shaped and sized
detached piece of armour made of leather, wood, or
metal, for carrying in hand or on arm to receive
thrust or stroke, esp. one of elongated form large
enough to cover most of body. **2.** protective plate or
screen in machinery etc.; person or thing that
protects one; shieldlike part in animal or plant;
(Geol.) mass of ancient rock under land area; (Her.)
drawing etc. of shield used for displaying person's
coat of arms; trophy in form of shield; *policeman's
shield-shaped badge. **3.** ~**'bug**, flat insect with large
scutellum; ~**-fern**, common handsome fern with
buckler-shaped indusia. **4.** Hence ~'LESS a. **5.** v.t.
protect, screen, esp. from censure or punishment
(often with implication of illegitimate concealment of
facts). [(v. f. OE sceldan) f. OE sc(i)eld, = OS, OHG
scild, ON skjöldr, Goth. skildus f. Gmc *skelduz, prob.
orig. = board, cogn. w. SCALE¹]
shie'ling n. (Sc.) grazing-ground for cattle; roughly
constructed hut for shepherds or sportsmen. [f. Sc.
shiel hut, ME, of unkn. orig., + -ING¹]
shi'er, shi'est. See SHY¹.
shift¹ v. **1.** v.t. & i. change or move from one position to
another, (of cargo) get shaken out of place; change
form or character; *change gear in vehicle; ~ one's
ground, take up new position in argument etc.; ~
the scene, the scene ~**s**, (in drama, novel, etc.); ~
(off), get rid of (responsibility etc.) to another. **2.** (sl.)
move quickly; consume (food or drink). **3.** v.i. use
expedients, take whatever course is available, contrive to do something, manage or get along or make a
livelihood; ~ **for** oneself, depend on one's own
efforts. **4.** (arch.) be evasive or indirect. [OE sciftan
arrange, divide, etc., = MLG schiften, schichten, ON
skipta f. Gmc *skip-]
shift² n. **1.** change of position or form or character,
substitution of one thing for another, vicissitude,
rotation. **2.** relay of workers (night shift); time for
which they work. **3.** new device, expedient, stratagem, resource. **4.** dodge, trick, artifice, piece of
evasion or equivocation. **5. make** ~, manage or
contrive (to do, or abs.), get along somehow (must
make shift without it). **6.** woman's dress of oblong form;
(arch.) chemise. **7.** arrangement by which joints of
successive rows in brickwork etc. do not coincide. **8.**
displacement of spectral lines (RED-shift); (sound) ~,
systematic change in pronunciation as a language
evolves; (Bridge) change of suit in bidding or *play;
change of position of typewriter type-bars to type
capitals etc.; *(mechanism for) gear-change in motor
vehicle. [ME, f. prec.]
shi'ftless a. lacking resourcefulness; lazy, inefficient;
hence ~LY² adv., ~NESS n. [f. prec. + -LESS]
shi'ft|y a. not straightforward, evasive; deceitful;
hence ~iLY² adv., ~iNESS n. [f. SHIFT² + -Y²]
shige'lla (-g-) n. aerobic bacterium of genus Shigella,
causing dysentery. [mod. L, f. K. Shiga, Jap. bacteriologist d. 1957 + dim. suf.]

shih-tzu' (shētsoō′) n. (animal of) long-haired short-
-legged breed of dog. [f. Chin. shizi lion]
Shiite. See SHIAH.
shikar' n. (Ind.) hunting. [f. Urdu f. Pers. šikār]
shikar'ee (-rī), **shikar'i, shekā'rry**, n. (Ind.)
hunter, esp. native professional hunter or guide. [f. as
prec.]
***shill** n. person employed to decoy or entice others.
[prob. f. earlier shillaber, of unkn. orig.]
shille'lagh (-ā′la, -ā′lī) n. Irish cudgel of blackthorn
or oak. [f. S~ in Co. Wicklow, Ireland]
shi'lling n. **1.** former British monetary unit and coin
= 1/20 of pound or twelve pence; **take the King's** or
Queen's ~, enlist as soldier [w. ref. to now obs.
method of recruiting]; CUT² off one's heir etc. with a
shilling; ~**-mark**, solidus; ~**sworth** (z-), as much as
can be bought for a shilling. **2.** monetary unit in E.
Afr. countries. [OE scilling, = OS, OHG scilling, ON
skillingr, Goth. skilliggs f. Gmc *skillingaz]
shi'lly-shally n., a., & v.i. **1.** n. inability to make up
one's mind, indecision, vacillation. **2.** a. vacillating. **3.**
v.i. vacillate, be undecided, hesitate to act or choose
one's course of action. [orig. shill I, shall I, redupl. of
SHALL I²]
shi'ly. Var. of shyly (see SHY¹).
shim n., & v.t. (-mm-). **1.** n. thin slip or wedge used in
machinery etc. to make parts fit. **2.** v.t. fit or fill up
thus. [18th c.; orig. unkn.]
shi'mmer v.i., & n. (shine with) tremulous or faint
diffused light; hence ~Y² a. [OE scymrian, = MDu.,
MLG schēmeren, f. Gmc *skim-, *ski- SHINE¹; cf. -ER⁵]
***shi'mmy** n., & v.i. **1.** n. kind of foxtrot accompanied
by oscillation of body; abnormal vibration of (front)
wheels of motor car. **2.** v.i. dance a shimmy; move in
similar manner; vibrate abnormally. [20th c.; orig.
unkn.]
shin n. & v. (-nn-). **1.** n. front of leg below knee; ~ of
beef, ox's (esp. fore-)shank; ~**-bone**, tibia; ~-
-guard, ~**-pad**, protective pad worn at football etc.
2. v.i. climb up or down (tree, wall, etc.) by using arms
and legs, not on ladder etc. **3.** v.t. kick on shin. [OE
sinu, = MLG, MDu. schēne, OHG scina]
shi'ndig n. (colloq.) festive gathering (esp. boisterous
one); = foll. [prob. f. foll.]
shi'ndy n. brawl, disturbance, row, noise, (KICK² up a
shindy); = prec. [perh. alt. f. SHINTY]
shine¹ v. (in sense 1 **shone** pr. shŏn; in other senses or
arch. ~**d**). **1.** v.i. emit or reflect light, be bright, glow,
(lit. or fig.; lamp was shining; face shone with soap or with
gratitude etc.); (of sun, star, etc.) be visible, not be
obscured by clouds etc.; be brilliant, be a luminary,
excel, in some respect or sphere (does not shine in
conversation; is a shining example). **2.** *~ up to, seek to
ingratiate oneself with. **3.** v.t. cause to shine; (colloq.)
make bright, polish, (shoes, brass, etc.). [OE scīnan, =
OS skīnan, OHG scīnan, ON skína, Goth. skeinan f.
Gmc *skīnan f. *skī-, *ski-]
shine² n. **1.** light, brightness, (RAIN¹ or shine); *polishing (of shoes etc.); high degree of polish; **take the** ~
out of, (1) impair brilliance or newness of, (2) throw
into the shade by surpassing. **2.** (sl.) disturbance,
shindy, sensation; *(R) Negro; **take a** ~ **to,** take a
fancy to. [f. prec.]
shi'ner n. **1.** (sl.) black eye; (in pl.) money. **2.** *small
silvery freshwater fish of genus Notropis etc. [f. SHINE¹
+ -ER¹]
shi'ngle¹ (-nggel) n., & v.t. **1.** n. rectangular slip of
wood used like roof-tile on roofs, spires, etc.; *small
signboard esp. of doctor, lawyer, etc.; shingled hair,
shingling of hair. **2.** v.t. roof with shingles; cut (hair of
head) so that all ends are exposed like roof-shingles,
cut hair of (head, person) thus. [ME, app. f. L
scindula, earlier scandula]
shi'ngle² (-nggel) n. (in sing. or pl.) small rounded
pebbles, esp. lying on sea-shore; hence **shi'nglY²**
(-ngg-) a. [16th c., of uncert. orig.]
shi'ngles (-nggelz) n. pl. (usu. treated as sing.) acute

painful viral inflammation of nerve ganglia, with skin eruption often forming girdle round middle of body. [ME, f. med. L *cingulus* f. L *cingulum* girdle (*cingere* gird)]

shi′nny [1] *v.i.* (colloq.) shin *up* tree etc. [f. SHIN]

shi′nny [2]. Var. of SHINTY.

Shi′ntō *n.* Japanese religion revering ancestors and nature-spirits; hence ∼ISM (3), ∼IST (2), *ns.* [Jap., f. Chin. *shen dao* way of the gods]

||**shi′nty** *n.* game like hockey played with ball and curved sticks, and taller goal-posts; stick or ball used in it. [earlier *shinny*, app. f. cry used in the game *shin ye, shin you, shin t' ye*, of unkn. orig.]

shi′n|y *a.* glistening, polished, rubbed bright; (of coat, trousers, etc.) with nap worn off; hence ∼iNESS *n.* [f. SHINE[2] + -Y[2]]

ship [1] *n.* **1.** vessel with bowsprit and three, four, or five square-rigged masts; any large seagoing vessel; *air-craft; SPACE*ship*; (sl.) boat, esp. racing-boat. **2.** BREAK[1] *ship; when my* etc. ∼ **comes home** or **in**, fortune is made; ∼ **of the desert,** camel; *ship of the* LINE[2] 19; **take** ∼, embark. **3.** ∼('s) **biscuit,** hard coarse kind made for keeping, formerly used on board ship; ∼**′board,** used or occurring on board ship; **on** ∼**′board,** on board ship; ∼**-breaker,** contractor who breaks up old ships; ∼**-broker,** agent in shipping goods and insuring ships; ∼**′builder,** ∼**′building,** (person engaged in) business of con-structing ships; ∼ **burial** (Archaeol., in ships under mound); ∼**-canal** (to allow ships to go inland); *ship('s)*-CHANDLER(*y*); ∼**-fever,** typhus; ∼**′lap,** fit (boards) together for cladding etc. by rabbeting so that each overlaps the one below; ∼**′load,** quantity of something forming whole cargo; ∼**′master,** captain of ship; ∼**′mate,** person belonging to or sailing on same ship as another, esp. fellow sailor; ∼**-money,** (Hist.) impost for providing ships for navy (revival of which by Charles I was a cause of Civil War); ∼**′owner,** person owning (shares in) ship(s); ∼**-railway** (for transportation of ships overland from water to water); ∼**-rigged,** square-rigged; ∼**′s articles,** terms on which seamen take service on ship; *ship's* COMPANY, ||CORPORAL[3]; ∼**′shape** *adv.* or *pred. a.*, in good order, trim and neat; ∼**′s husband,** agent appointed by owners to see that ship in port is well provided in all respects; ∼**′s papers,** documents establishing ownership, nationality, nature of cargo, etc., of ship; ∼**-way,** inclined structure on which ship is built and down which it slides to be launched; ∼**-worm,** worm-shaped mollusc boring into ship timbers; ∼**′wreck,** (*n.*) destruction of ship by storm, foundering, stranding, striking rock, etc., (fig.) ruin *of one's hopes* etc., (*v.t.*) inflict shipwreck (lit. or fig.) on (person, hopes, etc.), (*v.i.*) suffer shipwreck; ∼**′wright,** shipbuilder, ship's carpenter; ∼**′yard,** shipbuilding establishment. **4.** Hence ∼LESS *a.* [OE *scip,* = OHG *skif,* OS, ON, Goth. *skip,* f. Gmc **skipam*]

ship [2] *v.* (-pp-). **1.** *v.t.* put, take, or send away (goods, passengers, sailors) on board ship; (Commerc.) deliver (goods) to forwarding agent for conveyance by land or water or air; step (mast), fix (rudder etc.), in its place on ship; take (oars) from rowlocks and lay inside boat; (of ship or boat) take in (water) over side (∼ **a sea,** be flooded by wave). **2.** *v.i.* take ship, embark; (of sailor) take service on ship. [OE *scipian* (as prec.)]

-ship *suf.* forming abstract *ns.* f. *adjs.* (*hardship*) or *ns.* (*courtship, friendship, scholarship*), w. senses (1) being so-and-so, status, office, honour, (2) tenure of office, (3) skill in certain capacity, (4) (number of) those who are. [OE *-scipe* etc.; = OS *-scipi,* OHG *-scaf(t),* ON *-skap* f. Gmc *skapiz* (*skap-*; see SHAPE[1])]

shi′pment *n.* shipping of goods etc.; amount shipped, consignment. [f. SHIP[2] + -MENT]

||**shi′ppen, -on,** *n.* (dial.) cow-house, cattle-shed. [OE *scypen* f. Gmc *skupinī* (*skup-*; cf. SHOP, -EN[2])]

shi′pper *n.* merchant etc. who sends or receives goods by ship, or *by land or air. [OE *scipere* (as SHIP[1], -ER[1])]

shi′pping *n.* In vbl senses; ships, esp. the ships of a country, port, etc.; ∼**-agent,** person acting for ship or line of ships at a port etc.; ∼**-articles,** = SHIP[1]'s *articles*; ||∼**-bill,** manifest of goods shipped; ||∼**-master,** official in whose presence ship's articles are signed, paying off is done, etc.; ∼**-office** (of shipping--agent or -master). [ME, f. SHIP[2] + -ING[1]]

shi′ralee *n.* (Austral.) tramp's swag. [20th c.; orig. unkn.]

||**shire** *n.* county; (Austral.) rural area with its own elected council; KNIGHT *of the shire*; **the** ∼**s,** (1) band of English counties with names (formerly) in *-shire* extending NE from Hampshire and Devon, (2) midland counties of England, (3) fox-hunting district of England comprising mainly Leics. and Northants. ∼(**-horse**), heavy powerful breed of draught-horse bred chiefly in midland counties of England. [OE *scīr,* OHG *scīra* care, official charge; orig. unkn.]

||**-shire** (-sher, -shīer) *suf.* forming names of counties and districts (*Derbyshire, Hallamshire, Hampshire*). [f. prec.]

shirk *v.t.,* & *n.* **1.** *v.t.* avoid meanly, get out of, shrink selfishly from, (duty, responsibility, fighting, etc., or abs.); hence ∼ER[1] *n.* **2.** *n.* shirker. [f. obs. *shirk n.* sponger, perh. f. G *schurke* scoundrel]

Shir′ley *n.* ∼ **poppy,** cultivated variety of common corn poppy with various coloured single or double flowers. [f. ∼ Vicarage, Croydon, Surrey, where first produced]

shirr *n.,* & *v.t.* **1.** *n.* elastic webbing; elastic thread woven into fabric; gathered trimming, gathering in garment etc. **2.** *v.t.* gather (material) with parallel threads run through; hence **shir′r**ING[1] *n.* **3.** *bake (eggs) without shells. [19th c., of unkn. orig.]

shirt *n.* **1.** man's loose sleeved garment of linen, silk, etc., for upper part of body, usu. worn inside jacket and trousers; NIGHT-*shirt*; **in** one's ∼**-sleeves,** only wearing jacket (∼**-sleeve** *a.*, informal, direct); **keep** one's ∼ **on,** (sl.) keep one's temper; **the** ∼ **off** one's **back,** one's last remaining possessions; **put** one's ∼ **on,** (sl.) bet all one has upon, be sure of; ∼**-front,** breast of shirt esp. if stiffened and starched (∼**-front** *wicket,* absolutely true and smooth cricket pitch). **2.** ∼ (**blouse**), *∼**waist,** woman's blouse resembling man's shirt; ∼ **dress,** *∼**maker,** *∼**waister,** woman's dress with bodice like shirt; *shirt*-TAIL[1] 2. **3.** Hence ∼′ED[2], ∼′LESS, *adjs.,* ∼′ING[1] (3) *n.* [OE *scyrte,* corresp. to ON *skyrta* (cf. SKIRT), f. Gmc *skurt-SHORT*]

shir′t| y *a.* (sl.) angry, annoyed; hence ∼iLY[2] *adv.,* ∼iNESS *n.* [f. prec. + -Y[2]]

shi′sh kebāb *n.* pieces of marinated meat and vegetable cooked on skewers. [f. Turk. *şiş kebabi* (*şiş* skewer, KEBAB roast meat)]

shit *v.i.* (-tt-; shit), & *n.* (vulg.) **1.** *v.i.* defecate. **2.** *n.* faeces; act of defecating; nonsense; contemptible person; worthless thing. [OE *scītan* f. Gmc *skīt-,* *skīt-*]

Shiva. Var. of SIVA.

shi′ver [1] *v.i.,* & *n.* **1.** *v.i.* experience or show quick slight vibrating movement (such as is) caused by sensation of cold, tremble with cold or fear. **2.** *n.* momentary shivering movement; (in *pl.*) attack of shivering, feeling of fear or horror (*gave me the cold shivers*); hence ∼Y[2] *a.* [ME *chivere,* perh. f. *chavele* chatter (f. as JOWL) + -ER[5]]

shi′ver [2] *n.* (usu. in *pl.*) & *v.* **1.** *n.* (one of) the many small pieces into which thing is shattered by blow or fall. **2.** *v.t.* & *i.* break into shivers; ∼ **my timbers** (reputed naut. imprecation). [ME *scifre,* cogn. w. OHG *scivaro* splinter f. Gmc *skif-,* *skīf-* split]

shoal *a., n.,* & *v.* **1.** *a.* (arch.) (of water) shallow, not deep. **2.** *n.* shallow place, submerged sandbank esp. one that shows at low water; (fig., usu. in *pl.*) hidden danger(s) or impediment(s); hence ∼´Y² a. **3.** v.i. get shallower. **4.** v.t. (Of ship) come into shallower part of (water). [OE *sceald* f. Gmc **skaldaz*, rel. to SHALLOW]

shoal² n., & v.i. **1.** n. multitude, crowd, great number, esp. of fish swimming in company (cf. SCHOOL²), (*shoals of people*; *gets letters in shoals*). **2.** v.i. (Of fish) form shoals. [prob. re-adoption of MDu. *schōle* SCHOOL²]

*shoat n. young (esp. weanling) pig. [ME; cf. W. Flem. *schote*]

shŏck¹ n. **1.** violent collision, concussion, or impact (*clashed with a mighty shock*); violent shake or tremor of earth's surface as part of earthquake; ∼ **absorber,** device on vehicle etc. for absorbing shocks, vibrations, etc.; ∼ **tactics,** (Mil.) use of cavalry to charge in masses, (fig.) sudden and violent action; ∼ **troops,** troops specially trained for assault. **2.** sudden and disturbing physical or mental impression (*news came upon me with a shock, was a great shock*; ELECTRIC *shock*); (Path.) acute state of prostration following over-stimulation of nerves by sudden pain as of wound etc. or violent emotion (*died of shock*; *the shock is more dangerous than the loss of blood*); ∼ **therapy, treatment,** method of treating psychiatric patients by means of an electric shock or powerful drug inducing coma or convulsions. **3.** injury inflicted on credit, stability, etc., great disturbance of organization or system. **4.** ∼**-brigade, -workers,** (in USSR) body of workers engaged in especially arduous task; shock-PROOF²; ∼ **stall,** excessive strain produced by air resistance on aircraft when speed approximates to that of sound; ∼ **wave,** sharp change of pressure in narrow region travelling through air etc., caused by explosion or by body moving faster than sound. [f. F *choc* (*choquer*; see foll.)]

shŏck² v. **1.** v.t. affect with indignation, sorrow, disgust, or horror, appear improper or outrageous or scandalous to (*was shocked at, by, that, to hear,* etc.); affect with electric or pathological shock. **2.** v.i. cause shock; (arch.) collide violently. [f. F *choquer,* of unkn. orig.]

shŏck³ n., & v.t. **1.** n. group of usu. twelve corn sheaves stood up close together in field. **2.** v.t. arrange (corn) in shocks. [ME, = OS *scok,* MDu., MLG *schok* shock of corn, SIXTY]

shŏck⁴ n. unkempt or shaggy mass of hair; ∼ **head,** rough head of hair; ∼**-headed,** having a shock of hair. [cf. obs. *shock*(*-dog*), earlier *shough,* shaggy--haired poodle]

shŏ´cker n. (colloq.) shocking or very bad specimen of anything; sordid or sensational novel etc.; shock absorber. [f. SHOCK² + -ER¹]

shŏ´cking a. & adv. **1.** a. causing indignation or disgust; (colloq.) very bad (*shocking weather*); hence ∼LY² adv., ∼NESS n. **2.** adv. (colloq.) shockingly. [f. SHOCK² + -ING²]

shŏd. See SHOE².

shŏ´ddy n. & a. **1.** n. fibre made from old cloth etc. shredded; inferior cloth made partly of such fibre; anything of worse quality than it claims or seems to have. **2.** a. counterfeit, pretentious, trashy, shabby, poorly done; hence ∼ILY² adv., ∼INESS n. [19th c., of unkn. (dial.) orig.]

shoe¹ (-ōō) n. (arch. pl. **shoon**). **1.** outer foot-covering of leather etc. with fairly stiff sole and ∥not reaching above ankle; another pair of ∼s, a different matter; **dead men's** ∼s, property or position as looked forward to by expectant successor; ***if the** ∼ **fits,** if the CAP¹ fits; **be in** person's ∼s, be in his situation or plight; DIE² in one's shoes; *where the shoe* PINCH²*es*; **put the** ∼ **on the right foot,** apportion blame etc. truly; **shake in** one's ∼s, be filled with apprehension. **2.** metal rim nailed to hoof of horse etc., horseshoe. **3.** thing like shoe in shape or use, e.g. wheel-drag, BRAKE⁵-shoe, socket, ferrule, mast-step. **4.** ∼´black, person who cleans shoes of passers-by for payment; ∼**-buckle** (for fastening shoe over instep, or worn

only as ornament); ∼´**horn,** curved piece of horn, metal, etc., for helping heel into shoe; ∼**-lace,** cord for lacing shoes; ∼**-leather,** leather for shoes, wearing-out of shoes by walking (*save shoe-leather*); ∼´**maker,** maker or mender of boots and shoes; ∼´**making** n.; *∼´**shine,** polishing of shoes; ∼**-string,** (1) shoe-lace, (2, colloq.) a small or inadequate amount of money, (attrib.) precarious, just adequate, (*a shoe-string majority*); ∼**-tree,** shaped block for keeping shoe in shape. **5.** Hence ∼´LESS a. [OE *scōh,* = OS *scōh,* OHG *scuoh,* ON *skór,* Goth. *skōhs* f. Gmc **skōh(w)az*]

shoe² (-ōō-) v.t. (**shod,** ∼´**ing**). fit (esp. horse etc.) with shoe(s); protect (end of pole etc.) with metal shoe; (in p.p.) having shoes etc. of specified kind (DRY¹*-shod,* ROUGH*shod,* SLIP¹*shod*; *car shod with radial tyres*). [OE *scōg(e)an,* = OHG *scuohōn,* ON *skúa* (as prec.)]

shŏ´far n. (pl. **sho´froth** pr. -rōt). ram's-horn trumpet used by Jews in religious ceremonies and as ancient battle-signal. [f. Heb. *šōpār,* pl. *šōpārôt*]

shō´gun (-ōōn) n. (Hist.) Japanese hereditary commander-in-chief and virtual ruler before 1868; hence ∼ATE² n. [Jap., = general, f. Chin. *jiang jun*]

shŏne. See SHINE¹.

shoō int., & v.i. & t. (utter) excl. used to frighten birds etc. away; drive away thus; *∼´**fly,** temporary road or railway, policeman etc. detailed to watch others; *∼´**fly pie,** very sweet treacly dessert; ⁺∼**-in,** something easy or certain to succeed. [imit.]

shoŏk¹. See SHAKE¹.

*shoŏk² n., & v.t. **1.** n. set of staves and headings for cask ready for putting together. **2.** v.t. pack in shooks. [18th c., of unkn. orig.]

shoŏn. See SHOE¹.

shoōt¹ v. (**shot²**). **1.** v.i. come or go vigorously or swiftly out, forth, along, etc., or abs., (*boat shot out from the creek*; *flash shoots across sky*); (of plant) put forth buds, (of bud) appear; (of cricket-ball) dart along ground after pitching; (of pain) pass with stabbing sensation (*through, up,* arm etc.), (of part of body) be intermittently painful; ∼ **ahead,** come quickly to front of competitors etc.; ∼ **up,** rise suddenly, (of person) grow rapidly; ∼´**ing star,** small meteor appearing like star, moving rapidly and disappearing. **2.** project abruptly out (*mountain-spur, cape, shoots out*). **3.** v.t. send out, discharge, propel, emit, violently or swiftly (*bow shoots arrow*; *have shot my* BOLT¹; *gun shoots missile,* or abs. *shoots, shoots straight*; *coaches collided and passengers were shot out*; *sun shoots its rays*; *tree shoots out branches*; *shot a glance at his neighbour*); let (rubbish etc.) fall or slide from container; move (door-bolt) so as to fasten or unfasten door; ∼ one's **cuffs** or **linen,** display shirt-cuffs by shaking or pulling them down; ∼ **out,** (arch.) protrude (lips etc.) esp. in mockery. **4.** v.t. & i. discharge (bullet etc.) from gun etc., (fig., sl.) inject (drug); cause (bow, gun, etc.) to discharge missile; discharge gun etc., make use of gun etc. (*shoots well, straight*); kill or wound (person, animal) with missile from gun etc.; kill (person) thus as punishment; hunt game etc. habitually or on one occasion with gun, shoot the game *over* estate etc., shoot game in or on (coverts, estate, etc.); (Footb. etc.) score (goal), take shot at goal; (Golf, Cinemat.) make (specified score) for round; (esp. Cinemat.) photograph; *(colloq.) play game of (craps etc.); *∼!, (sl.) say what you have to say; ∼ **the cat,** (sl.) vomit; ∼ **down,** kill (person) cold-bloodedly by shooting, cause (aircraft or its pilot) to fall to ground by shooting, (fig.) argue effectively against (proposal etc.); ∼ **it out,** (sl.) engage in decisive gun-battle or ∼**-out** n.; ∼ **a line,** (sl.) talk pretentiously; ∥∼ **the moon,** (sl.) remove one's goods by night to avoid paying rent; *∼ **off** one's **mouth,** (sl.) talk freely; *shoot the* SUN; ∼ **up,** terrorize (district) by indiscriminate shooting. **5.** v.t. be, have one's boat, swept swiftly under or down (bridge, rapids, falls); (sl.) pass (traffic-lights at red). **6.** plane (edge of board) accurately. **7.** Hence ∼'ABLE *a*. [OE *scēotan*, = OS *skietan*, OHG *sciozzan*, ON *skjóta* f. Gmc *skeut-, *skaut-, *skut-; cf. SHEET¹, SHOT¹, SHUT]

shoot² *n*. young branch or sucker, new growth of plant; rapid in stream; = CHUTE 1; shooting-party or -expedition or -practice or -land; **the whole** ∼, (sl.) everything. [f. prec.]

shoo'ter *n*. In vbl senses; (Cricket) ball that shoots; shooting-implement (esp. in comb.: PEA-, SIX-, *shooter*). [ME, f. SHOOT¹ +-ER¹]

shoo'ting *n*. In vbl senses; right of shooting over particular land; estate etc. rented to shoot over; ||∼-**box,** sportsman's lodge for use in shooting-season; ||∼-**brake** or -**break,** estate car; ∼-**coat, -jacket,** (as worn when shooting game); ∼-**gallery,** place for shooting at targets with rifles etc.; ∼-**iron,** (sl.) firearm; ∼-**range,** ground with butts for rifle practice; ∼-**stick,** walking-stick which may be adapted to form a seat; ∼ **war,** one in which there is shooting (opp. *cold war* or *war of nerves*). [f. SHOOT¹ +-ING¹]

shop *n*. & *v*. (-pp-). **1.** *n*. building, room, etc., for retail sale of some commodity or service (*chemist's, butcher's, fruit-, betting-, shop*; **come to the wrong** ∼, (sl.) apply to wrong person etc.), or in which manufacture or repairing is done (*engineering-shop; fitting, pattern,* etc., *-shop*; CLOSED *shop*). **2.** (sl.) institution, establishment, place of business, etc. **3.** one's profession, trade, or business, things connected with it, or talk of it esp. when inopportune; **set up** ∼, establish oneself in business; **shut up** ∼, cease business for the day or permanently; hence ∼'**py²** *a*. **4. all over the** ∼, (sl.) in disorder (*my books are all over the shop*), in every place (*have looked for it all over the shop*), wildly (*hitting, steering,* etc., *all over the shop*). **5.** ||∼ **assistant** (in retail shop); ∼-**bell** (on door of shop, to give notice of customer's entrance); ∼-**boy, -girl,** assistant in shop; ∼-**floor,** (fig.) workers as dist. from management; ∼'**keeper,** owner and manager of shop (*nation of* ∼*keepers,* the English); ∼-**lifter,** ∼-**lifting,** (ostensible customer) stealing goods in shop; ∼'**man,** ||shopkeeper or his assistant, *workman in repair-shop; ||∼-**soiled,** soiled or faded by display in shop (lit. or fig.); ∼ **steward,** person elected by fellow-workers in a factory etc. as their spokesman in dealings with employer; ||∼'**walker,** attendant in large shop who directs customers, supervises assistants, etc.; *shop*-WINDOW; ∼-**worn,** = *shop-soiled*. **6.** *v.i.* go to shop(s) to make purchases (*or inspect goods); ∼ **around,** look for best bargain; hence ∼'**per¹,** ∼'**ping¹** (1, 2), *ns.* (∼*ping centre, street,* one with many shops). **7.** *v.t.* (sl.) imprison; inform against. [ME, f. AF & OF *eschoppe* booth f. MLG *schoppe,* OHG *scopf* porch, rel. to SHIPPEN]

shor'an *n*. system of aircraft navigation using return of two radar signals by two ground stations. [f. *short range navigation*]

shore¹ *n*. land that adjoins sea or large body of water (**in** ∼, on the water near or nearer to shore, cf. INSHORE; **on** ∼, ashore; **these** ∼**s,** the island where one is); (Law) land between ordinary high and low water marks; ∼-**based,** operating from a base on shore; ∼ **leave,** (Naut.) permission to go ashore, period of this; ∼'**weed,** stoloniferous plant (*Littorella uniflora*) growing in shallow water; hence ∼'LESS (-ōr'l-) *a.,* ∼'WARD *a.* & *adv.,* ∼'WARDS *adv.,* (-ōr'w-). [ME, f. MDu., MLG *schōre,* perh. f. root of SHEAR¹]

shore² *n.,* & *v.t.* **1.** *n*. prop, beam set obliquely against ship, wall, tree, etc., as support. **2.** *v.t.* support, hold *up,* (as) with shore(s); hence **shōr'ING¹** (3) *n*. [ME, f. MDu., MLG *schōre* prop, of unkn. orig.]

shore³, shorn. See SHEAR¹.

short *a., adv., n.,* & *v.t.* **1.** *a*. measuring little from end to end in space or time, soon traversed or finished, (*a short line, journey, way off; a short time ago; he, his joy etc., had but a short life*). **2.** of small stature, not tall, (usu. of

human being, or of upright thing, as chimney, tower, tree). **3.** not far-reaching, acting near at hand; deficient, scanty, having partial or total lack *of,* below the degree of (*nothing short of miraculous*), abruptly finished; (seemingly) less than the stated amount etc. (*after a few short years of happiness*); (of bill of exchange) maturing at early date; (Cricket; of ball) pitching relatively near bowler, (of fieldsman or his position) relatively near batsman; (of person's memory) retaining only things from the immediate past; ∼ **of breath,** panting, short-winded; **come** ∼, be inadequate or disappointing; **come** ∼ **of,** fail to reach or amount to; CUT², FALL¹, *short;* **go** ∼, not have enough (*of*); *run short* (RUN¹ 12). **4.** concise, brief, curt, sullenly or snappishly reticent, uncivil; **in** ∼, to use few words, without circumlocution, to give conclusion briefly; *is called Bob* **for** ∼, by way of short name; **something** ∼, drink of spirits etc. **5.** (Phonet. & Pros.) (of vowel or syllable) (1) having the less of the two recognized durations, (2) unstressed; (of Engl. vowel) having sound other than that called LONG¹ 9. **6.** (Of pastry, clay, etc.) friable, crumbling, not tenacious; COLD-SHORT. **7.** (St. Exch. etc.; of stocks, stockbroker, crops, etc.) sold, selling, etc., when the amount is not in hand, with reliance on getting the deficit in time for delivery; **sell** ∼, (fig.) disparage. **8.** ∼-**arm,** (of blow etc.) delivered with arm not fully extended; ∼'**bread,** crisp dry crumbly cake made with flour, butter, and sugar; ∼'**cake,** (1) shortbread, (2) cake of short pastry usu. served with fruit; ∼ **change,** insufficient money given as change; ∼-*change* v.t., rob by giving short change, cheat; ∼ **circuit,** electric circuit through small resistance, esp. instead of resistance of normal circuit; ∼-*circuit* v.t. & i., cause short circuit (in), (fig.) shorten or avoid by taking more direct route; ∼'**coming,** failure to come up to a standard, deficiency, defect; *short* COMMONS; ∼-**coupled,** (of animal) having short body between fore and hind legs; *short* CUT¹; ∼ **date,** early date for maturing of bill etc.; ∼-**dated,** due for early payment or redemption; ∼-**day,** (of plant) needing regular cycle of light and dark to cause flowering; *short* DIVISION; ∼ **drink,** cocktail etc., e.g. before meal; ∼'**fall,** deficit below what was expected; ∼ **for,** an abbreviation of ('*Bob' is short for 'Robert'*); ∼ **game,** (Golf) approaching and putting; **get** or **have by the** ∼ **hairs,** be in complete control of (person); ∼'**hand,** method of rapid writing for keeping pace with speaker etc., (fig.) abbreviated or symbolic mode of expression; *shorthand* TYPIST; ∼-**ha'nded,** undermanned or understaffed; ∼ **haul,** transport of goods, or other effort made, over a short distance; ∼ **head,** (Racing) distance less than length of horse's head; ∼-*head* v.t., beat by a short head; ∼'**horn,** one of a breed of cattle with short horns; *short* HUNDRED-WEIGHT; ||∼ **list** (of selected candidates, from which final choice will be made); ||∼-*list* v.t., put on short list; ∼-**lived** (-īvd), having a short life, ephemeral; ∼ **mark,** = BREVE 3; *short* MEASURE¹; ∼ **metre,** hymn stanza of four lines with 6, 6, 8, and 6 syllables; *at short* NOTICE; ∼ **odds,** nearly equal stakes or chances in betting; ∼ **on,** (colloq.) having partial or total lack of; *∼ **order** (for food quickly prepared, at lunch-room etc.); *in ∼ *order,* immediately; ∼-**pitched,** (Cricket; of ball) pitching relatively near bowler; ∼-**range,** having a short range, relating to a short period of future time; *short* RIB; **in the** ∼ **run,** over a short period of time; ∼ **score,** (Mus.) one not giving all parts; *short* SEA; ∼ **story,** very brief story with immediate point; *short* SHRIFT; ∼ **sight,** ability to see clearly only what is comparatively near; ∼-**sighted,** having short sight, (fig.) lacking imagination or foresight; ∼-**sleeved,** with sleeves not reaching below elbow; ∼-**sta'ffed,** not adequately provided with staff; ∼'**stop,** (Baseball) fielder near second base; ∼ **story** (with fully developed theme but shorter than novel); ∼ **suit** (of less than four cards);

in ~ **supply**, scarce; ~ **and sweet**, brief and pleasant (usu. iron.); ~ **temper**, self-control soon or easily lost; **in the** ~ **term**, over a short period of time; ~**-term**, occurring in or relating to a short period of time; ~ **time**, condition of working fewer than the regular hours per day or days per week; ~ **title**, abbreviated form of title; *short* TON¹; ~ **view**, consideration of the present time only, not the future; ~ **waist**, high or shallow waist of dress or body; ~ **wave**, radio wave of about 10 to 100 metres wavelength; ~ **weight** (less than it is alleged to be); *short* WHIST³; ~ **wind**, easily exhausted breathing-power; ~**-winded**, having short wind, (fig.) unable or unwilling to discourse or perform at length; **make** ~ **work of**, accomplish, dispose of, destroy, consume, etc., quickly. **9.** Hence ~'ISH¹ 2 *a.*, ~'NESS *n.* **10.** *adv.* abruptly, before the natural or expected time or place, in short manner; **bring or pull up** ~, check or pause abruptly; **stop** ~, suddenly cease, not go on to the end; **take up** ~, interrupt (person); **be caught or taken** ~, be put at disadvantage, esp. (colloq.) by sudden desire to defecate; ~ **of**, without going so far as, except, putting out of the question, (*all aid short of war; short of an earthquake, they are bound to win*). **11.** *n.* short syllable or vowel; mark indicating that vowel is short; short film; (St. Exch. etc.) person who sells short; (colloq.) short circuit, short drink esp. of neat spirits; (in *pl.*) trousers reaching only to knees or higher, *underpants; (in *pl.*) short-dated stocks; (in *pl.*) mixture of bran and coarse flour; see also LONG¹ 14, 15. **12.** *v.t.* & *i.* (colloq.) short-circuit. [OE *sceort*, = OHG *scurz* f. Gmc *skurtaz*; cf. SHIRT, SKIRT]

shor'tage *n.* (amount of) deficiency (*there is no shortage; a shortage of 100 tons*). [f. prec. 11 + -AGE]

shor'ten *v.i.* & *t.* become or make actually or apparently shorter or short, curtail; reduce the amount of (sail spread); (of prices, odds, etc.) become shorter, decrease; hence ~ING¹ (3) *n.*, fat used for making pastry (short). [f. SHORT + -EN⁶]

shor'tly *adv.* before long, a short time or after; in few words, briefly; curtly. [OE *scortlice* (as SHORT, LY²)]

shor'ty, **-ie**, *n.* (colloq.) person or garment shorter than the average. [f. SHORT + -Y³, -IE]

shŏt¹ *n.* (*pl.* in sense 2 usu. same). **1.** single missile for cannon or gun, non-explosive projectile, (CHAIN-*shot*, GRAPE-*shot*, ROUND¹ *shot*, etc.); heavy ball thrown by athletes; *not a shot in* one's or the LOCKER. **2.** small lead pellet of which several are used for single charge or cartridge, esp. in sporting guns; such pellets collectively. **3.** discharge of cannon or gun (*several shots were fired, heard*), firing of space-rocket (MOON¹-*shot*); remark aimed at a person; stroke in golf, tennis, cricket, billiards, etc.; attempt to hit with projectile or missile or fig. to make stroke in game or guess or do something (*at each shot he was nearer the bull's-eye; a beautiful shot from cover-point took off the bails; a lucky shot at goal; had a shot at learning Greek*); **like a** ~, willingly, without hesitation; **make a bad** ~, guess wrong; LONG¹, PARTHIAN or *parting*, SNAP, *shot*; ~ **in the dark**, a mere guess. **4.** range, reach, distance to or at which thing will carry or act, (*within* EAR¹*shot*). **5.** possessor of specified skill with rifle, gun, pistol, etc., (*is a good, bad, crack* or *first-class*, or *no, shot*); BIG *shot*. **6.** hypodermic injection of drug, vaccine, etc. (~ **in the arm**, (fig.) stimulus or encouragement); (colloq.) dram of spirits. **7.** photograph; film sequence photographed continuously by one camera. **8.** ~**-blasting**, cleaning of metal etc. by impact of stream of shot; ~**-firer** (who fires blasting-charge in mine etc.); ~**'gun**, smooth-bore gun for firing small shot at short range (~*gun marriage* or *wedding*, wedding enforced esp. because of bride's pregnancy); ~**-tower** (in which shot was made from molten lead poured through sieves at top and falling into water at bottom). **9.** Hence ~'PROOF² *a.* [OE *sc(e)ot*, *gesc(e)ot*, = OS -*scot*, OHG *scoz*, ON *skot* f. Gmc *skutaz* (*skut-* SHOOT¹)]

shŏt² *v.* & *a.* **1.** *v.t.* & *i.* Past tense of SHOOT¹. **2.** *a.* In vbl senses; (of coloured material) woven or dyed so as to show different colours at different angles; (of board-edge) accurately planed; (sl.) exhausted, finished, drunk; ~ **through**, permeated or suffused (*with*); FOOL¹'s *bolt is soon shot*; **get** ~ **of**, (sl.) = *get shut of* (SHUT 5); **I'll be** ~ **if** (form of neg. asseveration). [sense 2 p.p. of SHOOT¹]

shŏt³ *n.* reckoning, (one's share of) bill at inn etc., (*pay* one's *shot*). [ME, = SHOT¹ (cf. OE *scēotan* shoot, pay, contribute); cf. SCOT¹]

shŏ'tten *a.* ~ **herring**, one that has spawned, (fig., arch.) weakened or dispirited person. [ME, arch. p.p. of SHOOT¹]

should. See SHALL.

shou'lder (shō'l-) *n.* & *v.* **1.** *n.* part of body at which arm or foreleg or wing is attached, either lateral projection below or behind neck; ~**(-joint)**, combination of end of upper arm with those of collarbone and blade-bone, upper foreleg and adjacent parts of butchered animal (COLD¹ *shoulder*); (in *pl.*) upper part of back, (fig.) body regarded as bearing burden, blame, etc.; **broad** ~**s**, ability to bear heavy load or responsibility; HEAD¹ *and shoulders*; **old head on young** ~**s**, (person displaying) youthful wisdom; RUB¹ *shoulders with*; ~ **to** ~, side by side, with closed ranks or united effort; **put** or **set** one's ~ **to the wheel**, make effort; **straight from the** ~ (of well-delivered blow or frank verbal attack). **2.** part of mountain, bottle, tool, etc., projecting like human shoulder; part of garment covering shoulder; strip of land adjacent to metalled surface of road. **3.** ~**-bag**, woman's handbag that can be hung from shoulder; ~**-belt**, bandolier or other band passing over one shoulder and under opposite arm; ~**-blade**, either large flat bone of upper back, scapula; ~**-high**, up to or as high as shoulders; ~**-holster** (in armpit); ~**-knot** (of ribbon, metal lace, etc., worn on shoulder by officer in full dress, livery servant, etc.); *~ **loop**, shoulder-strap of army, air-force, or marines officer; *~ **mark**, shoulder-strap of naval officer; ~**-note** (Print., at top corner of page); ~**-of-mutton sail**, = LEG-*of-mutton sail*; ~**-pad** (used to elevate shoulder of garment); ~**-strap**, (1) piece of cloth from shoulder to collar of military uniform, bearing indication of rank etc., similar piece on raincoat, (2) strip of fabric suspending garment or bag from wearer's shoulder. **4.** Hence (-)~ED² (-erd) *a.* **5.** *v.t.* & *i.* push with shoulder, jostle, make way thus. **6.** *v.t.* take (burden, lit. or fig.) on one's shoulders; ~ **arms**, (Mil.) hold rifle vertical with barrel against shoulder and butt in hand. [OE *sculdor*, = OFris *skuldere*, OHG *sculter(r)a* f. WG *skuldr-*]

shouldn't. See SHALL.

shout *v.* & *n.* **1.** *v.i.* make loud articulate or inarticulate cry or vocal sound, speak loudly, (*shouted to attract attention, with laughter, for joy*); ~ **at**, speak loudly to etc.; ~ **for**, call for by shouting; **all is over but** or **bar the** ~**ing**, contest is virtually decided. **2.** *v.t.* say loudly, call out, express in loud tones, (*shout approbation; shouted that the coast was clear; shouted to or for me to come*; '*Go back*', *he shouted*); ~ **down**, reduce to silence by shouting. **3.** *v.t.* & *i.* (Austral. & NZ colloq.) treat (another person, or abs.) to drinks etc. **4.** *n.* loud utterance or vocal sound from individual or group expressing joy, (dis)approval, defiance, etc., or calling attention; (Austral. & NZ colloq.) one's turn to order drink etc. for the company, free drink. [ME, perh. cogn. w. SHOOT¹; cf. ON *skúta* SCOUT²]

shove (-ŭv) *v.* & *n.* **1.** *v.t.* & *i.* push vigorously, cause to move along by hard or rough pushing; make one's way *along, past, through*, etc., by pushing, jostle (person); (colloq.) put somewhere (*shove it in the drawer*); ~**-halfpenny**, form of shovel board with coins etc. on table; ~ **off**, start from shore in boat, (colloq.) depart. **2.** *n.* act of shoving. [OE *scúfan*, =

MDu., MLG *schūven*, OHG *sciuban*, ON *skúfa*, Goth. -*skiuban* f. Gmc *skeubh-, *skaubh-, *skubh-]

sho′vel (-ŭ′v-) *n.*, & *v.t.* (‖-**ll**-). **1.** *n.* implement for shifting quantities of coal, earth, etc., often in form of spade with sides of blade turned up; machine (part) of similar form and function; ∼ **hat**, broad-brimmed hat as worn by some clergymen; ∼-**head**, (1) shark like hammerhead but with smaller head, (2) flat--headed species of catfish; hence ∼FUL 2 *n.* **2.** *v.t.* shift or clear (coal etc.) with or as with shovel; move roughly in large quantities (*shovel food into mouth*). [OE *scofl*, = MLG *schuffel*, cogn. w. OHG *scuvala*, f. Gmc *skuf-, *skubh- (see prec.)]

sho′velboard (-ŭ′v-) *n.* game played esp. on ship's deck by impelling discs with hand or long-handled shovel-like implement over marked surface. [earlier *shoveboard*, -*groat* f. SHOVE + BOARD[1], GROAT]

sho′veller, -**eler** (-ŭ′v-) *n.* **1.** In vbl senses. **2.** duck (*Anas clypeata*) with broad shovel-like beak. [f. SHOVEL + -ER[1]; sense 2 earlier *shovelard* f. -ARD, perh. after *mallard*]

show (arch.) **shew**, (-ō) *v.* (*p.p.* ∼**n**, *or* ∼**ed** *pr.* -ōd). **1.** *v.t.* allow or cause to be seen, disclose, manifest, offer (thing, thing *to* person) for inspection, exhibit, produce, give (treatment, treatment *to* person), reveal, (*clothes show signs of wear*; *white muslin shows the dirt*; *an aperture shows the inside*; *showed bad judgement in refusing*; *film was shown only once*; *show me, I was shown, a specimen*; *show your tickets, please*; *showed a profit on the year's business*; *show favour, mercy, to*; *showed me kindness*); indicate by one's behaviour the presence or extent of (one's feelings); exhibit (animal, flower, etc.) in show; ∼ one's **cards**, = show one's hand; show CAUSE[1], CLEAN[1] *pair of heels*, *cloven hoof* (see CLEAVE[1]), one's COLOUR[1]s, one's FACE[1], FIGHT[2]; ∼ thing **the fire**, heat it slightly; *show the* FLAG[4]; ∼ one's **hand**, reveal one's cards, (fig.) disclose one's plans; ∼ **a leg**, get out of bed; **nothing to** ∼ **for**, no visible result of (effort etc.); ∼ one**self**, be seen in public, let it be seen that one is (honest, a rogue, etc.); *show the white* FEATHER[1]. **2.** *v.i.* be visible or noticeable, come into sight, appear in public, have specified appearance, (*stain will never show*; *he dislikes me and it shows*; *buds are just showing*; *film now showing*; *shows white, like a disc, from here*); *finish third (or better) in horse-race. **3.** *v.t.* demonstrate, prove, expound, point out, cause (person) to understand (thing), (*has shown the falsity of the tale, that it is false, how false it is, it to be false*; *show person how to write, what to do, etc.*; *it only shows how little you know*; (abs.) *it all* or *just goes to show*); *show* person the DOOR; ∼ **the way** (by words, pointing, accompanying, or preceding, or by doing thing first). **4.** conduct (*showed us round the house*); ∼ person **out** or **in**, (esp.) open door for his exit or entrance; ∼ person **round**, take him to all points of interest. **5.** ∼-**down**, (Poker) laying down of cards with faces up, (fig.) final test, disclosure of achievements or possibilities; ∼ **forth**, (arch.) exhibit, expound; ∼ **off**, (*v.t.*) display to advantage, (*v.i.*) try to make impression by exhibiting one's wealth or skill (whence ∼-*off* n., person who shows off); ∼ **through**, be visible (lit. or fig.) although behind something else; ∼ **up**, make or be conspicuous or clearly visible, expose (fraud, impostor, inferiority of another), (colloq.) appear, be present. **6.** **shew′bread**, twelve loaves displayed in Jewish temple and renewed each sabbath; ∼-**card** (for advertising); ∼-**case**, glazed case for exhibiting goods, curiosities, etc.; ∼-**place** (that tourists etc. go to see); ∼′**room**, -**window**, (in which wares are kept, hung up, for inspection). [OE *scēawian*, = OS *skawon*, OHG *scouwōn* f. WG *skauwōjan (*skaubehold); cf. SHEEN]

show[2] (-ō) *n.* **1.** showing or being shown; DUMB *show*; ∼ **of force**, proof that one is prepared to use force; ∼ **of hands**, raising of hands to vote for or against. **2.** spectacle, exhibition, pageant, display (*a fine show of blossom*; *is on show today*), collection of things shown

esp. in competition or to entertain (*dog, flower, horse, motor, etc., -show*; ‖**Lord Mayor's Show**, procession of decorated vehicles etc. in London on day of Lord Mayor's coming into office); (colloq.) any public entertainment or performance; (sl.) concern, undertaking, business, (RUN[1], STEAL, *the show*; **give the** (**whole**) ∼ **away**, betray inadequacies or pretensions; **good** ∼!, that was well done, or fortunate; **poor** or **bad** ∼!, that was badly done or unfortunate). **3.** outward appearance, semblance, impression produced, parade, ostentation, pomp, mere display, (*pierce beneath the shows of things*; *there is a show of reason in it*; *made a good show in the high jump*; *good enough in outward show*; *made a (great) show of being reasonable about it*; *did it for show*; *is fond of show*). **4.** (sl.) opportunity of acting, defending oneself, etc., (*give him a fair show*). **5.** discharge of blood from vagina at approach of childbirth or onset of menstruation. [ME, f. prec.] ∼′**boat**, (river) steamboat in which theatrical performances are given; ∼ **business**, (sl.) ∼′**biz**, the entertainment (esp. theatrical) profession; ∼′**girl**, actress whose role is decorative rather than histrionic; ∼ **house** etc. (prepared as sample of rest of estate etc.); ∼-**jumping**, competitive jumping by horse-riders with points deducted for errors; ∼′**man**, proprietor or manager of menagerie or other such show, person skilled in showmanship; ∼′**manship**, the art of the showman, (fig.) capacity for exhibiting one's wares or capabilities to the best advantage; ∼-**piece**, excellent specimen used for show; ∼-**stopper**, (colloq.) performance receiving prolonged applause; ∼ **trial**, judicial trial allegedly designed to make a favourable impression on public opinion. [ME, f. prec.]

show′er *n.* & *v.* **1.** *n.* brief fall of rain, hail, sleet, or snow, or of arrows, bullets, water, dust, stones, etc., or (fig.) of incoming gifts, honours, letters, etc.; hence ∼-PROOF[2], ∼Y[2], *adjs.* **2.** ∼(-**bath**), bath or cubicle in which water is sprayed from above, apparatus or premises for this. **3.** *party for giving presents to prospective bride etc. **4.** group of meteors moving like a shower; group of particles initiated by cosmic-ray particle in earth's atmosphere; ‖(sl.) contemptible or unpleasant person(s). **5.** *v.t.* discharge (water, missiles, etc.) in a shower; lavishly bestow (gifts etc. *on* or *upon*). **6.** *v.i.* descend or come in a shower; use shower-bath. [OE *scūr*, = OS *skūr*, OHG *scūr*, ON *skúr*, Goth. *skūra* storm f. Gmc *skūr-]

show′ing (-ō′-) *n.* In vbl senses; quality of performance (*made a poor showing*; *on this showing he will fail*); evidence, putting of case, (*on present showing, on your own showing, it must be true*). [OE *scēawung* (as SHOW[1], -ING[1])]

shown. See SHOW[1].

show′|y (-ō′ĭ) *a.* striking, making good display; brilliant, gaudy; hence ∼ILY[2] *adv.*, ∼INESS *n.* [f. SHOW[2] + -Y[2]]

s.h.p. *abbr.* shaft horsepower.

shrank. See SHRINK.

shra′pnel *n.* fragments of bomb etc. thrown out by explosion; hollow projectile containing bullets or pieces of metal and timed to burst slightly short of objective and release them in shower. [f. Gen. H. *Shrapnel*, Brit. soldier d. 1842, inventor of the projectile]

shred *n.*, & *v.t.* (-**dd**-). **1.** *n.* scrap, fragment, rag, strip, torn or broken piece, small remains, least amount, (*tore it to shreds*; *without a shred of clothing on him*; *not a shred of evidence, reputation, etc.*); *tear* an argument etc. **to** ∼**s**, completely refute. **2.** *v.t.* tear or cut into shreds; hence ∼′**der**[1] (2) *n.* [OE *scrēad piece cut off (*scrēadian* v.), = OS *skrōd*, OHG *scrōt* f. WG *skraud-, *skreud-, *skrud-; see SHROUD]

shrew (-ōō) *n.* **1.** scolding woman; hence ∼′**ISH**[1] *a.* **2.** ∼(-**mouse**), small long-snouted mouselike insectivore of family Soricidae. [OE *scrēawa*, *scrēwa* shrew-mouse; cf. OHG *scrawaz* dwarf, MHG *schrawaz* etc. devil]

shrewd (-ŏŏd) *a.* **1.** sagacious, sensible, discriminating, astute, judicious, (*can make a shrewd guess*; *a shrewd observer*); (of face etc.) sagacious-looking. **2.** (arch. or literary). (Of pain, cold, etc.) sharp, biting; (of blow, thrust, etc.) severe, hard; mischievous, malicious. **3.** Hence ~**LY²** *adv.*, ~**NESS** *n.* [ME., = malignant, f. prec. in sense 'evil person or thing' + -ED², or p.p. of obs. *shrew* to curse, f. prec.]

shriek *v.i.* & *t.*, & *n.* (utter) shrill and usu. inarticulate cry of terror, pain, etc., screech, scream; (make) high--pitched piercing sound; ~ (**with laughter**), laugh uncontrollably; ~ (**out**), say in shrill agonized tones. [imit.; cf. dial. *screak*, ON *skrækja*, and SCREECH]

shrie'v|alty *n.* sheriff's office or jurisdiction; tenure of this; so ~**AL** *a.*, of sheriff. [f. *shrieve*, obs. var. of SHERIFF, + -*alty* as in *mayoralty* etc.]

shrift *n.* **1.** (arch.) confession to priest; confession and absolution. **2. short** ~, little time between condemnation and execution or punishment, (fig.) curt treatment. [OE *scrift*, = OHG *scrift*, ON *skrift*, vbl. n. f. SHRIVE]

shrīke *n.* bird of family Laniidae, with strong hooked and toothed bill and habit of impaling its prey of small birds and insects on thorns. [perh. cogn. w. OE *scric* thrush, MLG *schrīk* corncrake, imit.; cf. SHRIEK]

shrill *a.* & *v.* **1.** *a.* piercing and high-pitched in sound; (fig.) sharp, unrestrained; hence **shri'lLY²** *adv.*, ~**NESS** *n.* **2.** *v.i.* (Of cry etc.) sound shrilly. **3.** *v.t.* (Of person etc.) utter, send out, (song, complaint, etc.) shrilly. [ME, rel. to LG *schrell* sharp in tone or taste f. Gmc *skral-*, *skrel-*]

shrimp *n.*, & *v.i.* **1.** *n.* (*pl.* ~**s** or ~). small aquatic (esp. marine) edible decapod crustacean, grey-green when alive, pink when boiled. **2.** (usu. derog.) diminutive person. **3.** *v.i.* go catching shrimps; hence ~**ER¹** *n.* [ME, prob. cogn. w. MLG *schrempen* wrinkle, MHG *schrimpfen* contract, and SCRIMP]

shrīne *n.*, & *v.t.* **1.** *n.* casket, esp. one holding sacred relic; tomb (usu. sculptured or highly ornamented) of saint etc.; altar or chapel with special associations; Shinto place of worship; place hallowed by some memory. **2.** *v.t.* (poet.) enshrine. [OE *scrīn*, = OHG *scrīni*, ON *skrín*, Gmc f. L *scrinium* case for books etc.]

shrink *v.* (**shrank**; **shrunk** or, esp. as *a.*, **shru'nken**), & *n.* **1.** *v.i.* become of less dimensions, grow smaller, esp. by action of heat or cold or moisture; hence ~'**AGE** (3) *n.* **2.** recoil, retire from observation, (~ **into oneself**, become reserved), cower, flinch *from*, whence ~'**ingLY²** *adv.*; be averse *from doing*. **3.** *v.t.* make smaller (esp. in *pass.*; *his face has a shrunken look*), cause to shrink (esp. fabric etc., in order that it may not do so later); ~ (metal tyre etc.) **on**, slip it on while expanded with heat and let it tighten as it cools; ~**-wrap**, enclose (article) in material that shrinks tightly round it; hence ~'**ABLE** *a.* **4.** *n.* act of shrinking; shrinkage, whence ~**-PROOF²**, ~**-resistant**, *adjs.*; (sl.) psychiatrist, 'head-shrinker'. [OE *scrincan* (cf. *skrynka* to wrinkle]

shrīve *v.t.* (**shrove** *pr.* -ōv; **shriven** *pr.* -ĭ'ven). (arch.) hear confession of, assign penance to, and absolve; (of penitent) submit one*self* to priest for this purpose. [OE *scrīfan* impose as penance, = OS *skrīban*, OHG *scrīban* write, prescribe, WG f. L *scribere* write]

shri'vel *v.t.* & *i.* (||-ll-). contract or wither into wrinkled, folded, rolled-up, contorted, or dried-up, state. [perh. f. ON; cf. Sw. dial. *skryvla* to wrinkle]

shri'ven. See SHRIVE.

shrŏff *n.*, & *v.t.* (arch.) **1.** *n.* banker or money-changer in the East; (in Far East) native expert employed to detect base coin. **2.** *v.t.* examine (coin) for genuineness. [Anglo-Ind., ult. f. Arab. *ṣarrāf* (*ṣarafa* exchange)]

shroud *n.*, & *v.t.* **1.** *n.* winding-sheet, garment for the dead, whence ~'**LESS** *a.*; concealing agency (*wrapped in a shroud of mystery*); (in *pl.*) set of ropes forming part of standing rigging and supporting mast or topmast; ~**-laid,** (of rope) having four strands laid right--handed on a core. **2.** *v.t.* clothe (corpse) for burial; cover and conceal or disguise. [OE *scrūd*, = ON *skrúth* fittings, fabric, f. Gmc *skrūdh-*, *skreudh-* cut; see SHRED]

Shrŏve¹ *n.* ~ **Tuesday,** day before Ash Wednesday, on which and the two preceding days (~-**tide**) it was customary to be shriven. [ME, abnormally f. foll.]

shrŏve². See SHRIVE.

shrŭb¹ *n.* woody plant smaller than tree and usu. divided into separate stems from near the ground; hence ~'**by²** *a.*, ~'**bERY** (3) *n.* [ME, f. OE *scrubb*, *scrybb* shrubbery; cf. NFris. *skrobb* brushwood, W.Flem. *schrobbe* vetch, Norw. *skrubba* dwarf cornel, and SCRUB¹]

shrŭb² *n.* cordial made of sweetened fruit-juice and spirit (esp. rum). [f. Arab. *šurb*, *šarāb* (*šariba* to drink); cf. SHERBET, SYRUP]

shrŭg *v.* (-**gg**-) & *n.* **1.** *v.t.* & *i.* slightly and momentarily raise (shoulders), raise shoulders, to express indifference, helplessness, contempt, vexation, etc.; ~ **off**, dismiss as unimportant (as) by shrugging. **2.** *n.* this motion (*of the shoulders*, or abs.). [ME, of unkn. orig.]

shrŭnk('en). See SHRINK.

shtĭck *n.* (sl.) theatrical routine, gimmick, area of activity [Yiddish, f. G *stück* piece]

***shŭck** *n.*, & *v.t.* **1.** *n.* husk, pod; shell of oyster or clam; (in *pl.*, as *int.* of disgust or regret). **2.** *v.t.* remove shucks, of shell. [17th c., of unkn. orig.]

shŭ'dder *v.t.*, & *n.* (experience) sudden shivering due to fear, horror, repugnance, or cold; feel strong repugnance etc. (*I shudder to think what might happen*); (have) quivering or vibrating motion; **the** ~**s,** (colloq.) state of shuddering. [ME *shod(d)er* f. MDu. *schūderen*, MLG *schōderen* f. Gmc. *skūd-* shake; see -ER⁵]

shŭ'ffle *v.* & *n.* **1.** *v.t.* & *i.* move with scraping or sliding or dragging or difficult motion (*shuffles along rheumatically*; *shuffles his* or *with his feet*); ~**-board**, = SHOVELBOARD. **2.** *v.t.* slide or flick (cards etc., or abs.) over one another so as to change their relative positions; rearrange, intermingle, confuse; ~ **the cards,** (fig.) change the parts, try new policy, etc. **3.** slip (clothes, burden, etc., esp. clumsily or evasively) *off* or *on* (*shuffle off responsibility on to others*; *shuffled on his clothes*). **4.** *v.i.* keep shifting one's position (lit. or fig.); get out *of* evasively; fidget, vacillate, prevaricate; hence **shŭ'ffLER¹** *n.* **5.** *n.* shuffling movement; shuffling of cards, general change of relative positions; piece of equivocation or sharp practice; quick scraping movement of feet in dancing (**double** ~, this executed twice with one and then twice with the other foot) [f. or cogn. w. LG *schuffeln* walk clumsily f. Gmc *skuf-*; cf. SHOVE, -LE 3]

shŭ'ftĭ *n.* (sl.) a look (*at* thing). [f. Arab. *šaffa* try to see]

shŭn *v.t.* (-**nn**-). avoid, keep clear of, eschew, esp. by habit. [OE *scunian*, of unkn. orig.]

||**'shŭn!** *int.* (as Mil. word of command) = Attention! [abbr.]

shŭnt *v.* & *n.* **1.** *v.t.* & *i.* divert (train), ||(of train etc.) diverge, on to a side track, esp. to clear line for more important traffic, whence ~**ER¹** *n.* **2.** *v.t.* (Electr.) provide (current) with shunt. **3.** postpone or evade discussion of (subject), lay aside (project), leave (person) inactive. **4.** *n.* turning or being turned on to side track; (Electr.) conductor joining two points of circuit, through which more or less of current may be diverted; (Surg.) alternative path for circulation of blood; (sl.) collision of vehicles. [ME, perh. f. SHUN]

shŭsh *int.* & *v.* **1.** *int.* = HUSH² **2.** *v.i.* call for silence by saying *shush*; be silent. **3.** *v.t.* call or reduce to silence. [imit.]

shŭt *v.* (-**tt**-; **shut**). **1.** *v.t.* move (door, window, lid, lips, etc.) into position to block an aperture; ~ **the door on,** refuse to consider, make impossible; ~ **the stable door** etc. (see LOCK³). **2.** shut door etc. of (room, window, box, eye, mouth, etc.); bar access to (place etc.); ∼ one's **eyes** or (fig.) **ears** or **heart** or **mind to**, pretend not, or refuse, to see or hear or feel sympathy for or think about; ∼ **your face** or **head** or **mouth** or **trap**, (vulg.) stop talking; ∼**-eye**, (sl.) sleep. **3.** *v.i.* become or admit of being closed, swing or fall or contract into closed position, (*the door shut with a bang*; *what time do the shops shut?*; *lid shuts automatically, won't shut*; *pimpernels shut in rainy weather*). **4.** *v.t.* keep (person, sound, etc.) *out* or *in* by shutting door etc.; keep (person) *in* or *out of* room etc. by fastening door etc. **5.** (in *p.p.*, sl.) be or get rid *of* (person, thing). **6.** catch (finger, dress, etc.) by shutting something on it (*shut finger in door*, between it and jamb). **7.** bring (book, hand, telescope, etc.) into folded-up or contracted state. **8.** (w. *advs.*): ∼ **down**, push or pull (window-sash etc.) down into closed position, terminate operation of (factory, nuclear reactor, etc.), (of factory etc.) cease working, whence ∼-*down* n.; ∼ **in**, (of hills, houses, sea, etc.) encircle, prevent free prospect or egress from or access to (see also sense 4); ∼ **off**, stop flow of (water, gas, etc.) by shutting valve, separate *from* society etc.; ∼ **out**, exclude (landscape etc.) from view, *prevent (opponent) from scoring, prevent (possibility etc.) (see also sense 4); ∼-**out bid**, (Bridge) pre-emptive bid; ∼ **to**, close (door etc.), (of door etc.) close as far as it will go; ∼ **up**, close all doors and windows of or bolt and bar (house; *shut up shop*), close (box etc.) securely or decisively or permanently, imprison (person), put (thing) away in box etc., reduce to silence by rebuke or refutation, (colloq., esp. in *imper.*) stop talking. [OE *scyttan* f. WG **skuttjan* (**skut-* shoot¹)]

shŭ′tter *n.*, & *v.t.* **1.** *n.* In vbl senses; one of a set of wooden panels or iron plates, hinged, sliding, folding, or detachable, placed inside or outside glass of window to keep out light or burglars or ensure privacy (**put up the ∼s**, cease business for the day or permanently; structure of jointed laths or metal slats on rollers serving same purpose; blind of swell-box in organ for regulating loudness; device that opens and closes lens aperture of photographic camera; hence ∼ING¹ (3) *n.* (esp. = FORM¹ 15), ∼LESS *a.* **2.** *v.t.* provide with shutters; put up shutters of. [f. prec. +-ER¹]

shŭ′ttle *n.* & *v.* **1.** *n.* weaving-implement with two pointed ends by which weft-thread is carried or thrown across between threads of warp; carrier of lower thread in sewing-machine; train, bus, etc., going to and fro over short route on ∼ **service**; **space** ∼, rocket for repeated use, e.g. between earth and space station; ∼ **armature**, (Electr.) armature with single coil wound on elongated iron bobbin; ∼(**cock**), cork with ring of feathers, or similar device of plastic, struck to and fro in badminton and in battledore-and-shuttlecock [COCK¹, prob. f. flying motion], (fig.) thing passed repeatedly back and forth; ∼ **diplomacy**, negotiations conducted by mediator who travels to several countries at brief intervals. **2.** *v.t.* & *i.* (cause to) move to and fro like shuttle; move in shuttle. [OE *scytel* dart f. Gmc **skutilaz* (**skut-* shoot¹; see -LE 1)]

shȳ¹ *a.* (∼′er or shi′er, ∼′est or shi′est, pr. -ī′-). (Of animal, bird, fish, etc.) easily startled, timid, avoiding observation; diffident or uneasy in company; avoiding company *of* person, chary *of doing*, (FIGHT¹ *shy of*); (sl.) short (*of, on*), in the position of having lost (*I'm shy three quid*); (as *suf.*) showing fear of or distaste for (GUN-*shy*, WORK¹-*shy*); hence ∼′LY² *adv.*, ∼′NESS *n.* [OE *sceoh*, = MHG *schiech*, OHG **scīoh* f. Gmc **skeuh(w)az*]

shȳ² *v.i.*, & *n.* sudden(ly) start aside (*at* object or noise, or fig. *at* or *away from* proposal etc.) in alarm (usu. of horse, or fig. of person); hence ∼′ER¹ *n.* [f. prec.]

shȳ³ *v.t.*, & *n.* (colloq.) **1.** *v.t.* fling, throw, (stone etc., or abs.). **2.** *n.* act of shying (**have a ∼ at**, try to hit with missile, jeer at, make an attempt to get). [18th c., of unkn. orig.]

Shȳ′lŏck *n.* hard-hearted money-lender. [character in Shak. *Merchant of Venice*]

****shȳ′ster** *n.* (colloq.) person without professional honour, esp. tricky lawyer. [19th c.; orig. uncert.]

si (sē) *n.* (Mus.) = TE. [F f. It., perh. f. initials of *Sancte Iohannes*; see GAMUT]

SI *abbr.* (Order of the) Star of India; international system of units of measurement [f. F *Système International*]

Si *symb.* silicon.

si′al *n.* (Geol.) lighter upper layer of earth's crust. [f. SILICA + ALUMINA (main constituents)]

si′alagŏgue (-g) *n.* & *a.* (medicine) inducing flow of saliva. [F, f. Gk *sialon* saliva + *agōgos* leading]

si′amăng (sĭ′-, sē′-) *n.* large black gibbon of Sumatra and Malay peninsula. [Malay]

Siamē′se (-z) *a.* & *n.* (*pl.* same). (native or language) of Siam (Thailand); ∼ (**cat**), cream-coloured short-haired breed of cat with brown face etc.; ∼ **twins**, two Siamese men (d. 1874) joined by fleshy band at waist, any conjoined twins, any pair of very closely associated persons or things. [f. *Siam* + -ESE]

sĭb *a.* & *n.* **1.** *a.* (esp. Sc.) related, akin, (*to*). **2.** *n.* brother or sister; hence ∼′LING¹ *n.*, one of two or more children having one or both parents in common, ∼′SHIP *n.*, group of children having the same two parents. [OE *sib(b)*, = MDu. *sib(be)*, OHG *sibbi*, *sippi*, Goth. *-sibjis*]

Sĭ′bbald *n.* **∼′s rorqual**, blue whale. [f. Sir R. ∼, Sc. scientist d. 1722]

Sĭbē′rian *a.* & *n.* (native or inhabitant) of Siberia; ∼ **dog** (of breed much used for sledging). [f. *Siberia* + -AN]

si′bĭl|ant *a.* & *n.* **1.** *a.* hissing, sounded with a hiss (esp. of letter or set of letters, as *s*, *sh*); hence ∼ANCE, ∼ANCY, *ns.* **2.** *n.* sibilant letter(s). [f. L *sibilare* hiss; see -ANT]

si′bil|āte *v.t.* & *i.* pronounce with or utter hissing sound; hence ∼A′TION *n.* [f. as prec. + -ATE³]

si′bling, si′bship. See SIB.

si′bȳl *n.* one of the women who in ancient times acted in various places as reputed mouthpiece of a god, uttering oracles and prophecies; pagan prophetess; fortune-teller, witch. [ME, f. OF *Sibile* or f. med. L *Sibilla* f. L f. Gk *Sibulla*]

si′bylline *a.* issuing from an ancient sibyl, oracular, mysteriously prophetic; **the S∼ books**, collection of oracles belonging to ancient Roman State and often consulted by its magistrates for guidance. [f. L *Sibyllinus* (as prec.; see -INE¹)]

sic (sĭk) *adv.* (usu. parenth.) thus used, spelt, etc., (confirming, or calling attention to, form of quoted words). [L, = so, thus]

si′ccative *a.* & *n.* (substance etc.) having drying properties, esp. one mixed with oil-paint to dry it. [f. LL *siccativus* (*siccare* to dry; see -ATIVE)]

sīce¹ *n.* the six on dice. [ME, f. OF *sis* f. L *sex* six]

sīce². See SYCE.

Sicĭl′ian (-lyan, -lĭan) *a.* & *n.* (native or inhabitant) of Sicily. [f. L *Sicilia* Sicily, island in Mediterranean S. of Italy, + -AN]

sick¹ *a.*, *n.*, & *v.t.* **1.** *a.* ill, incapacitated by illness, feeling effects of some disease, (*a sick man*; *sick with* or arch. *of a fever*); **the ∼**, those who are ill; **go ∼**, (Mil.) report oneself as ill; **take ∼**, (colloq.) be taken ill. **2.** ||∼ (**at* or **to* one's **stomach**), vomiting or tending to vomit (*be, feel, make* person, *sick*; AIR¹*sick*, carsick, SEA*sick*); **look ∼**, (sl.) be unimpressive or discomfited. **3.** disordered, perturbed, suffering effects (of surfeit) *of*, disgusted, pining for, (*am sick at heart*; HEART*sick*; LOVE¹*sick*; *makes me sick to think of it*; colloq. *is awfully sick at being beaten*; *sick of the sight of home*; HOME¹*sick*; colloq. *am sick (to death of and tired) of being told off, of this bad weather*); (of humour) finding amusement in, or making fun of, misfortune and macabre things (*sick joke*). **4.** (Of ship) needing repair (esp. of specified kind; *nail-sick*, *paint-sick*). **5.** *sick*-BAY³; ∼-**bed**,

invalid's bed, state of being an invalid; ||**∼-benefit,**
allowance made to person absent from work through
illness; **∼-call,** visit to sick person by doctor etc.,
(Mil.) summons for sick men to attend; **∼-flag,**
yellow flag indicating presence of disease at quarantine station or on ship; ∼ **headache** (as in migraine);
∼-leave, leave of absence granted because of illness;
∼-list, list of those sick, esp. in regiment, ship, etc.,
(*on the* ∼-*list,* ill); **∼-making,** (colloq.) sickening;
the S∼ Man (of Europe), (Hist.) the Turkish
Empire; **∼-nurse,** = NURSE[1] 1; **∼-pay,** (to employee
etc. on sick-leave); **∼-room** (occupied by sick
person, or kept ready for the sick). **6.** Hence ∼*ISH*[1] *a.*
7. *n.* ||(colloq.) vomit. **8.** *v.t.* ∼ (**up**), (colloq.) vomit.
[OE *sēoc* = OS *siok,* OHG *sioh,* ON *sjūkr,* Goth. *siuks*
f. Gmc **seukaz*]

sick[2] *v.t.* (usu. in *imper.*) set upon; ∼ **him!** etc. (urging
dog to worry rat etc.). [19th c., dial. var. of SEEK]

si′cken *v.* **1.** *v.i.* begin to be ill, show symptoms of
illness (*child is sickening for measles* etc.); feel nausea or
disgust *at, to see,* etc. **2.** *v.t.* affect with inclination to
vomit, loathing, or disgust (*a sickening sight*) or with
weariness or despair *of* (*was sickened of trying to make
peace*). [ME, f. SICK[1] + -EN[6]]

si′ckle *n.* short-handled semicircular-bladed implement used for lopping and trimming, or for
cutting corn; sickle-shaped object (e.g. crescent
moon); HAMMER[1] *and sickle;* **∼bill,** bird with sickle-
-shaped bill, e.g. curlew; ∼ **cell,** sickle-shaped
erythrocyte, esp. as found in a severe hereditary
anaemia; **∼-feather,** one of long middle feathers of
cock's tail. [OE *sicol, sicel,* = MDu., MLG *sekele,*
OHG *sichila,* f. L *secula* (*secare* cut)]

si′ckly *a.,* & *v.t.* **1.** *a.* apt to be ill, chronically ailing, of
weak health; suggesting sickness, as of sick person,
languid, faint, pale, (*sickly colour, look, smile, complexion*); causing ill health (*sickly climate*); inducing or
connected with nausea (*sickly smell, taste*); mawkish,
weakly sentimental; hence ∼*INESS n.* **2.** *v.t.* (arch.)
cover over or o′er with a sickly hue, (w ref to Shak.
Hamlet III. i. 85). [ME, prob. after ON *sjúkligr* (as
SICK[1], -LY[1])]

si′ckness *n.* **1.** being ill, disease; *sickness* BENEFIT[1]. **2.**
a (specified) disease (FALL[1]*ing,* SLEEP[2]*ing,* SLEEPY,
sickness). **3.** vomiting or inclination to vomit. [OE
sēocnesse (as SICK[1], -NESS)]

side[1] *n.* **1.** one of the more or less flat surfaces bounding
an object (*cube has six sides; carry it with this side up*), esp.
more or less vertical outer or inner surface (*side of
house, cave, mountain,* etc.); such surface as dist. from
top and bottom, or front and back, or ends (*four,* or
two, sides of box; two sides of house). **2.** either surface of
thing that is regarded as having only two (*two sides of
sheet of paper, board, gramophone record,* etc.; *the inside and
outside of a bowl*); amount of writing filling one side of
sheet of paper; RIGHT[1], WRONG, *side;* BACK[1]*side.* **3.**
(Math.) bounding line of plane rectilinear figure
(*opposite sides of a parallelogram; hexagon has six sides*);
one of two quantities stated to be equal in an
equation. **4.** part of person or animal that is on his or
its right or left, esp. such part of trunk; corresponding
half of carcass (*side of mutton, bacon,* etc.); BLIND[1] *side;*
∼ **by** ∼, standing close together, esp. for mutual
support; **shake** or **split** one's **∼s,** laugh heartily. **5.**
part of object turned in same direction as observer's
right or left and not directly towards or away from
him, or turned in specified direction (*right, left, side;
north, south, seaward, side;* **debit, credit,** ∼, (in
account book); EPISTLE, GOSPEL, PROMPT[2], *side.* **6.**
part or region near margin and remote from centre or
axis of thing, subordinate or less essential or more or
less detached part, (*side of room, road, table,* etc.);
corner (of mouth); **from** ∼ **to** ∼, right across,
alternately each way from central line; **on one** ∼, not
in the main or central position; *set* or *take on one* ∼
(= ASIDE); **on the** ∼, as a sideline, in addition to
one's regular work or activity, secretly, as a side-bet,

*as a side-dish. **7.** region external but contiguous to,
specified direction with relation to, person or thing
(SEA*side, Merseyside; weeping at the grave-side; look on all
sides; came from all sides* or *every side; standing at my side;
on the north side of*); **by the** ∼ **of,** close to (and
compared with). **8.** partial aspect of thing, aspect
differing from or opposed to other aspects (*study all
sides of the question; has many sides to his character*);
department of school etc. (*the classical side*); **on the**
SAFE[2], high, fat, etc. ∼, fairly, somewhat. **9.** (cause
represented by, position in company with) one of two
sets of opponents in war, politics, games, etc., (*the Lord
is on my side; the side that bats first; there is much to be said,
there are faults, on both sides*); NO[1] *side,* ON[1]*side,* OFF*side;*
let the ∼ **down,** (fig.) frustrate one's colleagues'
efforts, cause them embarrassment or dishonour;
take ∼s, decide to espouse one or other cause. **10.**
position nearer or farther than, right or left of,
dividing line (*on this side of,* or *on this side, the Alps,
idolatry; on the other side of the road, the river*); **on this** ∼
the grave, in life; *on the* RIGHT[1], WRONG, *side of.* **11.**
line of descent through father or mother; DISTAFF or
spindle, SPEAR, *side.* **12.** ||(Bill. etc.) spinning motion
given to ball by striking it on one side, not centrally.
13. ||(sl.) assumption of superiority, swagger, (*puts on,
has too much, side*) **14. ∼-arms,** swords or bayonets or
pistols; **∼-band,** range of frequencies near carrier
frequency of radio wave, concerned in modulation;
∼-bet, bet between opponents, freq. in card-games,
over and above the ordinary stakes; **∼′board,** table
or flat-topped chest at side of dining-room for
supporting and containing dishes, decanters, etc., (in
pl., sl.) side-whiskers; **∼-bone,** (in carving fowls)
either small forked bone under wing; **∼′burns,** side-
-whiskers; **∼-car,** (1) jaunting-car, (2) car for
passenger(s) attachable to side of (motor) cycle, (3)
cocktail of orange liqueur, lemon juice, and brandy;
∼-chapel (in aisle or at side of church); **∼-dish,**
extra food subsidiary to main dish, **∼-door,** door in
or at side of building, (fig.) indirect means of access,
∼-drum, small double-headed drum in jazz or
military band or in orchestra (orig. hung at
drummer's side); **∼-effect,** secondary (usu. undesirable) effect; **∼-glance,** sideways or brief glance
(lit. or fig.); *∼**hill,** hillside; **∼-issue,** point that
distracts attention from what is important; **∼′kick,**
(colloq.) close associate; **∼′light,** light from side,
(fig.) incidental information etc., light at side of front
of motor vehicle to warn of its presence, (Naut.) red
port or green starboard light on ship under way;
∼′line, (*n.*) work etc. carried on in addition to one's
main activity, (in *pl.*) (space immediately outside)
lines bounding hockey-pitch, tennis-court, etc., at
sides, place for spectators as opp. participants, *(v.t.)*
remove (player) from team by injury, suspension,
etc.; **∼-note,** marginal note; **∼-road,** minor or
subsidiary road, road joining or diverging from main
road; **∼-saddle,** (*n.*) saddle for rider, esp. woman,
with both feet on same side of horse, (*adv.*) sitting thus
on horse; **∼-seat** (in vehicle etc., in which occupant
has back against side of vehicle); **∼-show,** minor
show attached to principal one, minor incident or
affair; **∼-slip** *v.i.,* & *n.,* skid(ding), (Aeron.) move,
motion, sideways instead of forward; *∼′sman* (-z-),
deputy churchwarden who shows worshippers to
seats, takes collection, etc.; **∼-splitting,** causing
violent laughter; **∼-step,** (*n.*) step taken sideways,
(*v.t.*) avoid by stepping sideways (esp. in football),
(fig.) evade; **∼-street,** street lying aside from main
streets or roads; **∼-stroke,** stroke towards or from a
side, incidental action, swimming action in which
swimmer lies on side; **∼-swipe,** (hit with) glancing
blow along side (also fig. of incidental criticism); **∼-
-table** (placed at side of room or apart from main
table); **∼-track,** (*n.*) siding, (*v.t.*) turn into siding,
shunt, (fig.) postpone or evade treatment or consideration of, divert from purpose; **∼-trip,** minor

excursion during a voyage; ∼ **valve** (in vehicle engine, operated from side of cylinder); ∼**-view,** view obtained sideways, profile; *∼'**walk,** path at side of road for pedestrians (∼*walk superintendent,* (joc.) spectator at building-site); *∼**-wheeler,** steamer with paddle-wheels; ∼**-whiskers** (growing on cheek); ∼ **wind,** wind from a side, (fig.) indirect agency or influence; *∼**-winder** (-wī-), (1) sideways blow, (2) small rattlesnake with lateral motion. **15.** Hence (-)**sī′**DED² *a.,* **-sī′dĕd**LY *adv.,* (-)**sī′dĕd**NESS *n.,* ∼′LESS (-dl-) *a.* [OE *sīde,* = OS *sīde,* OHG *sīta,* ON *sítha* f. Gmc **sīdhō,* prob. f. **sīdhaz* extending lengthways]

side² *v.i.* take part, be on same side, *with* disputant etc. [f. prec.]

sī′delŏng (-dl-) *adv.* & *a.* inclining to one side, oblique(ly), (*move sidelong; a sidelong glance*). [f. *sideling* (SIDE¹, -LING²); see -LONG]

sidēr′ĕal *a.* of the constellations or the fixed stars; ∼ **clock** (showing sidereal time); ∼ **day,** time between successive meridional transits of star or esp. of first point of Aries, about four minutes shorter than solar day; ∼ **time** (measured by apparent diurnal motion of stars); *sidereal* YEAR. [f. L *sidereus* (*sidus sideris* star) + -AL]

sī′derīte *n.* **1.** ferrous carbonate as mineral. **2.** meteorite consisting mainly of nickel and iron. [f. Gk *sidēros* iron + -ITE¹]

sī′derostăt *n.* (Astron.) instrument for keeping image of heavenly body in fixed position. [f. L (as SIDEREAL) after *heliostat*]

sī′deward(s) (-dwerd(z)) *adv.* & *a.* = foll. [f. SIDE¹ + -WARD(S)]

sī′de|ways (-dwāz) *adv.* & *a.* to or from a side (*moved sideways; sideways movement*); with one side facing forward (*sit sideways in the bus*); so ∼′WISE *adv.* & *a.* [f. SIDE¹ + -WAYS]

sī′ding *n.* short track by side of railway line and opening into it at one end or both for shunting purposes; *cladding material for outside of building. [f. SIDE¹ + -ING¹]

sī′dle *v.i.* walk obliquely (*along, up*), esp. in timid or furtive or cringing manner. [back-form. f. *sideling,* SIDELONG; cf. -LE 3]

siege *n.* operations of encamped attacking force to take, or compel surrender of, fortified place, period during which these last, (**raise the** ∼ **of,** abandon, or cause abandonment of, attempt to take by siege); **lay** ∼ **to,** conduct siege of); (fig.) persistent attack or attempt to persuade; ∼**-gun,** (Hist.) heavy gun used in sieges; *siege*-TRAIN 14. [ME, f. OF *sege* seat (*assegier* f. Rom. *assedicare* f. L **sedicum* siege)]

sie′mens (-z) *n.* (Electr.) unit of conductance, reciprocal of ohm. [f. W. von *Siemens,* Ger. electrical engineer d. 1892]

siĕ′nna *n.* ferruginous earth used raw or burnt as pigment of brownish-yellow (**raw** ∼) or reddish--brown (**burnt** ∼) colour. [f. It. (*terra di*) *Sienna* (earth of) Siena in Tuscany]

siĕ′rra *n.* long jagged mountain-chain esp. in Spain or Spanish America; Spanish mackerel. [Sp., f. L *serra* saw]

siĕ′sta *n.* afternoon nap or rest esp. in hot countries. [Sp., f. L *sexta* (*hora*) sixth hour]

sieve (sĭv) *n.,* & *v.t.* **1.** *n.* sorting utensil with meshed or perforated bottom through which liquids or fine particles can pass while solid or coarser matter is retained (**head like a** ∼, memory that retains little), or soft solid be passed to reduce it to uniform pulp etc. **2.** *v.t.* put through or sift with sieve; (fig.) (examine in order to) select or separate. [OE *sife,* = MDu., MLG *seve,* OHG *sib,* orig f. WG **sibhi*]

sifa′ka (-ah′-) *n.* long-tailed black and white lemur of genus *Propithecus.* [Malagasy]

sifflĕur (sēflĕr′) *n.* (*fem.* ∼**euse** pr. -ĕr′z). whistling artiste. [F (*siffler* whistle)]

sift *v.* **1.** *v.t.* separate into finer and coarser parts with

sieve, separate (finer parts) *from* material or its coarser parts or *out,* sprinkle (sugar etc.) from perforated spoon etc.; closely examine details of (evidence, facts, etc.) with regard to credibility or authenticity or relevance, analyse character of. **2.** *v.i.* (Of snow, light, etc.) fall as from sieve; ∼ **through,** examine with sifting. **3.** Hence (-)∼′ER¹ (1, 2) *n.* [OE *siftan,* = MDu., MLG *siften* f. WG **sibh-* (see SIEVE)]

Sig. *abbr.* Signor.

sīgh (sī) *v.* & *n.* **1.** *v.i.* emit long deep audible breath expressive of sadness, weariness, longing, relief from tension, cessation of effort, etc.; yearn *for* (person or thing desired or lost); (of wind etc.) make sound like sighing. **2.** *v.t.* utter or express with sighs. **3.** *n.* act of, sound made in, sighing (*a sigh of relief*). [ME *sihen* etc. prob. back-form. f. *sihte* past of *sīhen* f. OE *sīcan*]

sight¹ (sīt) *n.* **1.** faculty of perception through response of brain to action of light on eye; LONG¹, *near* or SHORT, *sight;* **know by** ∼, be familiar with appearance (only) of; **loss of** ∼, becoming blind; **second** ∼, power of mental vision by which future or distant occurrences are perceived; hence (-)∼′ED² *a.* **2.** seeing or being seen, way of looking at or considering thing; **catch, lose,** ∼ **of,** begin, cease, to see or (fig.) be aware of; **have lost** ∼ **of,** no longer know whereabouts of (person); **get a** ∼ **of,** manage to see; LINE² *of sight;* **at** or **on** ∼, as soon as person or thing has been seen (*plays music at* ∼, without preliminary study of score or practice of piece); **at first** ∼, on first glimpse or impression. **3.** range or unobstructed space within which person etc. can see or object be seen; **in** ∼, visible, (fig.) clearly near at hand; (**with**)**in** ∼ **of,** so as to see (lit. or fig.) or be seen from; **out of** ∼, not visible, (colloq.) excellent or delightful; **put out of** ∼, hide, ignore; **out of** ∼ **out of mind,** we forget the absent; **out of my** ∼! (rhetorical order to depart). **4.** thing seen, visible, or worth seeing, display, show, spectacle, (*a sad sight awaited us; the daffodils were a beautiful sight, a sight to see, a sight worth seeing;* **a** ∼ **for the gods** or **for sore eyes,** person or thing one is glad to see, esp. welcome visitor); (in *pl.*) noteworthy or attractive features of town etc. (*see the sights*); **a** (**perfect** etc.) ∼, (colloq.) person or thing of ridiculous, repulsive, dishevelled, etc., appearance; ∼ **unseen,** without previous inspection. **5.** (colloq.) great quantity (*will cost a sight of money; is a long sight better*). **6.** (device for assisting) precise aim with gun or observation with optical instrument; **lower one′s** ∼**s,** (fig.) become less ambitious; **set one′s** ∼**s on,** (fig.) aim at. **7.** ∼**-glass,** transparent device for observing interior of apparatus etc.; ∼**-line** (from person′s eye to what is seen); ∼**-reading, **-singing,** etc., reading music, singing, etc., at sight; ∼**-screen,** (Cricket) large movable white structure placed near boundary in line with wicket to help batsman see ball; ∼′**seer,** ∼′**seeing,** (person) visiting sights of town etc.; ||∼ **translation,** unseen; ∼′**worthy,** worth seeing. [OE (*ge*)*sihth,* = OS *gisicht,* OHG *sicht,* WG (as SEE¹)]

sight² (sīt) *v.t.* get sight of, esp. by coming near (*sight land, game*); observe presence of (esp. aircraft or unidentified flying object, or unusual species etc.); take observation of (star etc.) with instrument; provide (gun, quadrant, etc.) with sights; adjust sight of (∼′*ing shot,* experimental one to guide rifleman etc. in this); aim (gun etc.) with sights. [f. prec.]

sī′ghtlĕss (sī′t-) *a.* blind; (poet.) invisible; hence ∼LY² *adv.,* ∼NESS *n.* [ME, f. SIGHT¹ + -LESS]

sī′ghtlў (sī′t-) *a.* attractive to the sight, not unsightly; hence ∼iNESS *n.* [f. SIGHT¹ + -LY¹]

sī′gillate *a.* (Of pottery) with impressed patterns; (Bot.) having seal-like marks. [f. L *sigillatus* (*sigillum* seal dim. of *signum* sign; see -ATE²]

sī′gl|um *n.* (*pl.* ∼**a**). letter (esp. initial) or other character used to denote word, esp. for source of an edition of a text. [f. LL *sigla* pl., perh. f. *singula* neut. pl. of *singulus* single]

si'gma *n.* eighteenth Greek letter (Σ, σ or, when final, ς) = s. [L f. Gk]

si'gmate *a.* sigma-shaped; S-shaped. [f. prec. + -ATE²]

si'gmoid *a.* & *n.* **1.** *a.* curved like the uncial sigma (Ϲ) or like S; ∼ **flexure,** (Anat.) curved part of intestine between colon and rectum. **2.** *n.* sigmoid flexure. [f. Gk *sigmoeidēs* (as SIGMA; see -OID)]

sign¹ (sīn) *n.* **1.** mark traced on surface etc.; ∼ **of the cross** (made by Christian priest in blessing, or layman in reverence or prayer with finger between forehead and breast and across breast); ∼ **manual,** (arch. or Hist.) signature written with person's own hand, gesture of command etc. **2.** written mark conventionally used for word or phrase, symbol, thing used as representation of something, (*words are the signs of ideas; a sacrament is an outward and visible sign of an inward and spiritual grace*); **positive** or **plus** ∼, +; **negative** or **minus** ∼, −; ROAD¹ sign. **3.** (thing serving as) presumptive evidence or indication or suggestion or symptom of or that, distinctive mark, token, guarantee, password, miracle evidencing supernatural power, portent, (*violence is a sign of weakness or that one is weak; gave little or no sign of being aware of it; shows all the signs of decay; hands up in sign of surrender; by this sign ye shall know them; did signs and wonders;* *trail of wild animal; ∼ **and counter**∼, secret words etc. by which confederates recognize each other; ∼ **of the times,** thing showing the tendency of affairs. **4.** (Path.) objective symptom of disease (usu. w. defining word: *Babinski's, Oppenheim's, sign*). **5.** (Math.) positiveness or negativeness of a quantity. **6.** ∼('**board**), more or less fanciful device usu. painted on a board displayed formerly by all traders and still by many inns, board or other visible object giving name of business and placed in front of shop etc. **7.** natural or conventional motion or gesture used instead of words to convey information and esp. order or request (*conversed by signs; gave him a sign to withdraw*); ∼ **language,** esp. = DEAF-and-dumb *language*; **make no** ∼, seem unconscious, not protest, etc. **8.** any of twelve divisions of ZODIAC named from constellations formerly situated in them **9.** ∼**-painter, -writer,** (of signboards); ∼'**post** (at cross-roads etc. with arms showing names of places on each road, also fig. means of guidance), (*v.t.*) provide with signpost(s) (lit. or fig.). [ME f. OF *signe,* f. L *signum* mark, token]

sign² (sīn) *v.* **1.** *v.t.* mark with sign (esp. infant etc. *with the sign of the cross* in baptism). **2.** acknowledge or guarantee (letter, deed, picture, book, article, petition, bill, etc., or abs.) as one's own production or as having one's authority or consent by affixing or having affixed one's name or initials or recognized mark (*the will had never been signed; a signed masterpiece of Turner's; signed as usual with a double cross; does not sign his contributions to the press; nothing shall induce me to sign*); ∼ **for,** acknowledge receipt of by signing; hence ∼'**ABLE** *a.* **3.** write (one's name) to sign document etc.; convey (right, property, etc.) *away* by signing deed etc.; ∼ one**self,** write as one's name in signature (*signed himself 'Disgusted'*). **4.** *v.t.* & *i.* ∼ (on or up), engage, acknowledge being engaged, for some undertaking to which person binds himself by signature; ∼ **off,** end such engagement (of). **5.** communicate by gesture (*sign assent*); give order or make request by gesture *to* person to do (*signed to me to come*). **6.** ∼ **off,** (Bridge) indicate by conventional bid that one is seeking to end the bidding; so ∼-*off* n. **7.** ∼ **off, on,** end, begin, work, broadcasting, etc., esp. by writing, announcing, etc., one's name. [ME, f. OF *signer* f. L *signare* (*signum*; see prec.)]

si'gnal¹ *a.* remarkably good or bad, noteworthy, exemplary, (*signal victory, punishment, virtue, example*); hence ∼LY² *adv.* [f. F *signalé* f. It. p.p. *segnalato* distinguished (*segnale* SIGNAL²)]

si'gnal² *n.* & *v.* (||-ll-). **1.** *n.* intelligible (esp. pre-arranged) sign conveying information or direction esp. to person(s) at a distance (e.g. train-drivers), message made up of such signs, (*the signal was to be the dropping of a handkerchief; train stopped at the red signal; signals are made by day with flags and by night with lights; gave the signal for advance*); ∼ **of distress,** appeal for help, esp. from ship by firing guns; **code of** ∼**s,** ∼**-book,** body of signals arranged for sending complicated messages esp. in naval and mil. use; ∼s **department** etc. (concerned with arrangements for these). **2.** immediate occasion for some general movement (*the earthquake was the signal for an outbreak of the primitive instincts*); (Bridge) prearranged mode of bidding or play to convey information to one's partner; (Electr.) (sequence of) electrical impulse(s) or radio wave(s) transmitted as signal. **3.** ||∼**-box,** ∼**man** (responsible for display of naval, railway, etc., signals); *∼**-tower,** signal-box. **4.** *v.i.* make signals. **5.** *v.t.* make signals to; transmit (order, information) by signal; announce (event, *that*) by signal; direct (person *to* do) by signal. **6.** Hence ∼(l)ER¹ *n.* [ME f. OF, f. Rom. & med. L *signale* neut. (as n.) of LL *signalis* f. L *signum* SIGN¹; see -AL]

si'gnalize, -ise (-īz), *v.t.* make noteworthy or remarkable, lend distinction or lustre to, (*his accession was signalized by an amnesty*). [f. SIGNAL¹ + -IZE]

si'gnary *n.* list of signs constituting syllabic or alphabetic symbols of a language. [f. L *signum* SIGN¹ + -ARY¹, after *syllabary*]

si'gnatory *a.* & *n.* (party, esp. State) that has signed an agreement esp. a treaty (*the signatories,* or *signatory powers, to the Treaty of Rome*). [f. L *signatorius* of sealing (*signare -at-* mark; see -ORY)]

si'gnature *n.* **1.** act of signing document etc. **2.** person's name or initials or mark used in signing. **3.** (Print.) letter or figure placed at foot of one or more pages of each sheet of book as guide in making up for binding; such sheet after folding. **4.** (Mus.) **key** ∼, sharps or flats after clef at beginning of each staff; **time** ∼, fraction placed at beginning of composition, numerator giving number of beats in each bar and denominator duration of each beat. **5.** *directions to patient as part of medical prescription. **6.** (arch.) distinctive appearance or mark. **7.** ∼ **tune,** special tune used in broadcasting or theatre to announce a particular programme etc. [f. med. L *signatura* (LL = marking of sheep), as prec.; see -URE]

si'gnet *n.* private seal for use instead of or with signature as authentication (**the** ∼, royal seal formerly used for special purposes in England & Scotland, in Scotland later as seal of Court of Session; ||WRITER *to the* Signet); ∼**-ring,** finger-ring with seal set in it. [ME f. OF, or f. med. L *signetum* (as SIGN¹; see -ET¹)]

signi'ficance *n.* being significant (*with a look of deep significance*); covert or real import, what is meant to be or may be inferred, (*those were the words, but what is their significance?*); importance, noteworthiness, (*what he thinks about it is of no significance*). [OF, or f. L *significantia* (as SIGNIFY; see -ANCE)]

signi'ficancy *n.* expressiveness (*spoken with great force and significancy*); = prec. [f. as prec. + -ANCY]

signi'ficant *a.* having a meaning ('-*kin*' *is a significant termination*); expressive, suggestive, with unstated or secret sense, inviting attention; noteworthy, of considerable amount or effect or importance, not insignificant or negligible, (*a little man may be a very significant man*); ∼ **figure,** (Math.) digit conveying information about a number containing it, and not a zero used simply to fill vacant place at the beginning or end; hence ∼LY² *adv.* [f. L *significare* (see SIGNIFY) + -ANT]

significa'tion *n.* act of signifying; exact meaning or sense (*of,* esp. *of* word or phrase). [ME f. OF, f. L *significatio -onis* (as SIGNIFY; see -ATION)]

signi'ficative *a.* signifying; having a meaning; serving as sign or presumptive evidence *of.* [ME, f.

OF *significatif -ive*, or f. LL *significativus* (as foll.; see -ATIVE)]

si′gnify v. **1.** v.t. be a sign or indication or presage of (*a long upper lip signifies obstinacy*; *a lunar halo signifies rain*); mean, have as meaning, ('*DD*' signifies '*Doctor of Divinity*'); communicate, make known, (*he signified his agreement, that he could not consent*). **2.** v.i. be of importance, matter, (esp. w. neg.; *it does not signify*). - [ME, f. OF *signifier* f. L *significare* (as SIGN¹; see -FY)]

signor (*pl.* **signori**), **signora**, **signorina**, (sē′nyōr, sēnyōr′ē; sēnyōr′a; sēnyerē′na) ns. (Titles used of or to Italians corresponding to) Mr or sir, Mrs or madam, Miss or madam (to unmarried woman). [It., f. L SENIOR]

si′gnory (sē′nyerī) n. **1.** seigniory. **2.** (Hist.) governing body of medieval Italian republic. [ME f. OF *s(e)ignorie* (as SEIGNEUR)]

si′ka (sē′-) n. species of deer (*Cervus sika*) from Japan. [f. Jap. *shika*]

Sikh (sēk, sĭk) n. member of Indian monotheistic sect founded in 16th c.; hence ∿ISM n., the (religious) tenets of the Sikhs. [Hindi, = disciple, f. Skr. *sishya*]

si′lage n., & v.t. **1.** n. ensilage. **2.** v.t. put into silo. [alt. f. ENSILAGE after *silo*]

si′lence n., & v.t. **1.** n. abstinence from speech or noise, being silent, taciturnity, non-betrayal of secret etc., fact of not mentioning a thing, not communicating any message, etc., (*the silence of Scripture on the subject*; *silence gives consent*); ∿ **is golden,** saying nothing is often best; **keep, break,** ∿, abstain from speaking, speak; **pass over in** ∿, not mention; **put** or **reduce to** ∿, (esp.) refute in argument. **2.** absence of sound, stillness, (**in** ∿, without speech or other sound); **S**∿! (order to cease speech or noise); ||(**two minutes'**) ∿, ceremony observed at 11 a.m. on Remembrance Sunday. **3.** oblivion, state of not being mentioned, (*have passed into silence*); **tower of** ∿, structure on which Parsees place their dead. **4.** v.t. make silent by force, superior argument, etc., (*silenced the enemy's guns, the best debaters in the House, the voice of conscience*); hence **si′lenc**ER¹ n., device for reducing noise of escape of gas from gun, ||vehicle engine, etc., or of shutting of door etc. [ME f. OF, f. L *silentium* (as foll.; see -ENCE)]

si′lent a. **1.** not speaking, not uttering or making or accompanied by any sound; (of letter) written but not pronounced, e.g. *b* in *doubt*; (of film) without synchronized sound-track accompaniment; *∿ **butler,** device for gathering up crumbs, cigarette ash, etc.; ∿ **majority,** those of moderate opinions who rarely make themselves heard; *∿ **partner,** = SLEEP²*ing partner*; ∿ **system** (in prisons, by which prisoners are never allowed to speak). **2.** taciturn, speaking little; saying or recording nothing on some subject (*history is silent upon it*); (of spirits) un-flavoured. **3.** Hence ∿LY² adv. [f. L *silēre* be silent; see -ENT]

silē′n|us n. (pl. ∿i pr. ī). (Gk Myth.) bearded old man like satyr, sometimes with tail and legs of horse. [L, f. Gk *seilēnos*]

silē′sia (-sha) n. thin twilled cotton or linen cloth for dress-linings etc. [f. S∿ in E. Germany, where orig. made]

silhoue′tte (-lōōĕ′t) n., & v.t. **1.** n. picture of person in profile or of thing showing outline only, all inside the outline being usu. black, on white ground or cut out in paper; appearance of person or thing as seen against light so that outline only is distinguishable (**in** ∿, so seen or placed). **2.** v.t. represent or (usu. in *pass.*) exhibit in silhouette. [f. Étienne de *Silhouette*, Fr. author and politician d. 1767]

si′lica n. silicon dioxide, occurring as quartz etc. and as principal constituent of sandstone and other rocks; hence **sili′**CIC, ∿**i′**FEROUS, **sili′**CEOUS or **sili′**CIOUS (-shus), adjs., **sili′**CIFY v.t. & i. [f. L *silex -icis* flint, after *alumina* etc.]

si′licate n. one of many insoluble compounds of

metal(s), silicon, and oxygen, occurring widely in rocks of earth's crust. [f. prec. +-ATE¹ (3)]

si′lic|on n. non-metallic element occurring widely in silica and silicates; hence ∿o- *comb. form.* [f. L *silex -icis* flint (after *carbon, boron*), replacing earlier *silicium*]

si′licōne n. one of many polymeric organic compounds of silicon with high resistance to cold, heat, water, and passage of electricity. [f. prec. +-ONE]

silic|ō′sis n. (pl. ∿o′ses pr. -ō′sēz). lung fibrosis caused by inhalation of dust containing silica; hence ∿o′TIC a. [f. as SILICA +-OSIS]

si′liqu|a (pl. ∿ae), **sili′qu|e** (-ē′k), n. long narrow seed-vessel of cruciferous plants; so ∿OSE¹, ∿OUS, (sĭ′lĭkw-) adjs. [L]

silk n. **1.** fine strong soft lustrous fibre produced by silkworm in making cocoon; similar fibre spun by some spiders etc.; **artificial** ∿, rayon. **2.** thread or cloth made from silk fibre (||take ∿, become KC or QC and so have right to wear silk gown); (in *pl.*) kinds, or garments made, of such cloth, esp. jockey's cap and jacket in horse-owner's colours. **3.** ||(colloq.) KC or QC. **4.** silky styles of female maize-flower. **5.** (*attrib.*) made of silk (*silk stockings* etc.); **make a** ∿ **purse out of a sow's ear,** get better results than person's or thing's qualities admit of. **6.** ∿ **cotton,** kapok or similar substance; ∿**-fowl,** breed of fowl with silky plumage; ∿**-gland** (secreting the substance produced as silk); ∿ **hat,** tall cylindrical hat covered with silk plush; ∿**-screen printing,** = SCREEN-*printing*; ∿**′worm,** caterpillar of moth (esp. *Bombyx mori*) which spins its cocoon of silk. [OE *sioloc, seol(e)c* (cf. ON *silki*) f. LL *sericum* neut. (as n.) of L *sericus* (seres f. Gk *Sēres* an oriental people; see -IC)]

si′lken a. made of silk; clad in silk; soft or lustrous as silk; (of manner etc.) suave, insinuating. [OE *seol(o)cen* (as prec., -EN⁵)]

si′lk|y a. like silk in smoothness, softness, fineness, or lustre; (of manner etc.) suave, insinuating; hence ∿ILY² adv., ∿iNESS n. [f. SILK +-Y²]

sill n. shelf or slab of stone or wood or metal at foot of doorway or esp. window; horizontal timber at bottom of dock or lock entrance, against which gates close; (Geol.) sheet of igneous rock intruded between other rocks. [OE *syll(e)*, = MDu., MLG *sulle* cogn. w. ON *svill, syll,* OHG *swelli*]

si′llabŭb. See SYLLABUB.

si′ller n. (Sc.) silver; money. [=SILVER]

si′llimanīte n. (Min.) aluminium silicate in orthorhombic crystals, often fibrous. [f. B. *Silliman,* Amer. chemist d. 1864 +-ITE¹]

si′ll|y a. & n. **1.** (arch.) innocent, simple, helpless. **2.** foolish, imprudent, unwise; feeble-minded, imbecile; (Cricket) placed (dangerously) close to batsman (*silly mid-off, point,* etc.); ∿y-**billy,** (colloq.) foolish person; ||**the** ∿**y season,** August and September as season when newspapers start trivial discussions for want of important news. **3.** Hence ∿ILY² adv., ∿iNESS n. **4.** n. (colloq.) foolish person. [later form of ME *sely* (dial. *seely*) happy f. OE *∿sælig,* = OS, OHG *sālig* f. WG *∿sæliga* (*∿sæli* luck, happiness)]

si′lō n. (pl. ∿s), & v.t. **1.** n. pit or airtight structure in which green crops are pressed and kept for fodder, undergoing fermentation; pit or tower for storage of ||grain, cement, etc.; underground place where guided missile is kept ready for firing. **2.** v.t. make ensilage of. [Sp., f. L f. Gk *siros* pit for corn]

silt n. & v. **1.** n. sediment deposited by water in channel, harbour, etc.; ∿**stone,** rock of hardened silt; hence ∿′Y² a. **2.** v.t. & i. choke or be choked (*up*) with silt (*the channel has* or *is silted up*); hence ∿A′TION n. [ME, perh. cogn. w. Da., Norw. *sylt,* OLG *sulta,* OHG *sulza* salt marsh, f. as SALT]

Silūr′ian a. & n. **1.** a. of the Silures, a people of ancient SE Wales. **2.** a. & n. (Geol.) (of) Palaeozoic period or system above Ordovician and below Devonian. [f. L *Silures* +-IAN]

si′lva, sy̆′lva, n. (pl. ∿e or ∿s). trees of a region,

epoch, or environment; treatise on or list of these. [L (see foll.)]

si'lvan, sy'lvan, *a.* of the woods; having woods; rural. [f. F *sylvain,* obs. *silvain,* or f. L *Silvanus* woodland deity (*silva* a wood; see -AN)]

si'lver¹ *n.* & *a.* **1.** *n.* white lustrous malleable ductile precious metallic element used chiefly with admixture of harder metals for coin, plate, and ornaments, as subordinate monetary medium, and in compounds for photography etc., (GERMAN¹, NICKEL, *silver*; OXIDIZED *silver*); colour of silver. **2.** silver or cupro-nickel coins (*have you any silver on you?*); (esp. Sc.) money. **3.** silver vessels or implements (esp. cutlery); household cutlery of any material; = *silver medal.* **4.** *a.* made of silver; second-best (opp. *golden*); silvery; **every cloud has a ~ lining,** misfortune has its consolations or hopeful prospects. **5. ~ age,** period inferior to GOLDEN *age*, e.g. period of Latin literature corresp. to silver LATIN; ||**~ band** (playing silver-plated brass instruments); **~-bath,** (Photog.) solution of silver salt used for sensitizing; **~ birch,** common birch (*Betula alba*) with silver-coloured bark; **~ fir** (with silver-coloured under-sides of leaves); **~-fish,** (1) silver-coloured fish, esp. a colourless variety of goldfish, (2) silvery bristletail found in books and damp places; *silver* FOIL¹; **~ fox,** (variety of red fox with) black white-tipped fur; **~ gilt,** (1) gilded silver, (2) imitation gilding of yellow lacquer over silver leaf; **~-grey,** lustrous grey; **~ jubilee,** 25th anniversary of sovereign's accession or other event; *silver* LATIN, LEAF, **~ medal,** medal of silver usu. awarded as second prize; **~ paper,** (1) fine white tissue-paper for wrapping silver, (2) tin foil; **~ plate,** vessels, spoons, etc., of silver or of copper etc. plated with silver; **~-point,** (process of sketching on prepared paper with) silver-pointed stylus (*a head in silver-point*); **~ print,** photographic positive print on paper sensitized with silver salt; **~ salmon,** coho; **~ sand,** fine pure kind used in gardening; **~ screen,** motion pictures collectively; ||**~side,** upper (best) side of round of beef; **~smith,** worker in silver, manufacturer of silver articles; **~ solder,** solder containing silver; *silver* SPOON¹, STANDARD; ||**S~ Stick,** (1) field-officer of Life Guards when on palace duty, (2) official of Queen's bodyguard for Scotland; **~ thaw,** glassy coating of ice on the ground, exposed woodwork, etc., caused when rain freezes as it falls, or when a sudden thaw (after hard frost) is succeeded by a light frost; **~ tongue,** eloquence; **~-top,** disease of grasses with whitening caused by mites etc.; **~ware,** articles made of silver; **~ wedding,** 25th anniversary of wedding; **~weed,** plant with silvery leaves, esp. a potentilla with silver-coloured under-sides of leaves. [OE *seolfor,* = OS *silubar,* OHG *sil(a)bar,* ON *silfr,* Goth. *silubr* f. Gmc **silubr-,* of uncert. orig.]

si'lver² *v.* **1.** *v.t.* coat or plate with silver; provide (mirror-glass) with backing of tin amalgam etc.; (of moon or white light) give silvery appearance to; turn (hair) grey or white. **2.** *v.i.* (Of hair) turn grey or white. [ME, f. prec.]

si'lvern *a.* (arch. or poet.) = SILVER¹ 4. [OE *seolfren, silfren* (as SILVER¹, -EN⁵)]

si'lver|y *a.* resembling silver in whiteness, lustre, ringing sound, etc.; (of hair) white and lustrous; hence **~iNESS** *n.* [f. SILVER¹ + -Y²]

si'lviculture, sy'-, *n.* growing and tending of trees as branch of forestry. [F, f. L *silva* a wood + F CULTURE]

si'ma *n.* (Geol.) denser lower layer of earth's crust. [f. SILICA + MAGNESIA (main constituents)]

si'mian *a.* & *n.* **1.** (Zool.) (of) one of the anthropoid apes. **2.** ape(like), monkey(-like). [f. L *simia* ape (perh. f. *simus* flat-nosed f. Gk *simos*) + -AN]

si'milar *a.* & *n.* **1.** *a.* like, alike; having mutual resemblance or resemblance *to*; of the same kind, nature, or amount; (Geom.) shaped alike; hence or cogn. **~ITY** (-ă't-) *n.,* **~LY²** *adv.* **2.** *n.* (arch.) thing resembling another. [f. F *similaire* or f. med. L *similaris* f. L *similis* like; see -AR¹]

si'mile *n.* writer's or speaker's (use of) reference to thing or person with explicit comparison to it of what is being discussed, as illustration or ornament; words by which this is done (*the kingdom of heaven is like to a grain of mustard seed; as dead as a doornail; life, like a dome of many-coloured glass*). [ME f. L, neut. of *similis* like]

simi'litude *n.* likeness, guise, outward appearance, (*in, assume, the similitude of*); (expression of) comparison (*talks in similitudes*); (arch.) counterpart, facsimile, (*is the very similitude of*). [ME f. OF, or f. L *similitudo* (as prec.; see -TUDE)]

si'mmer *v.* & *n.* **1.** *v.i.* be on the point of boiling, boil very gently; (fig.) be in a state of suppressed anger, indignation, or laughter; **~ down,** calm oneself, become less agitated. **2.** *v.t.* keep simmering. **3.** *n.* simmering state. [alt. f. ME (now dial.) *simper,* perh. imit.; see -ER⁵]

||**si'mnel** *n.* **~ (cake),** rich ornamental cake baked esp. at Easter, Christmas, and Mid-Lent, often with marzipan layer and decoration. [ME, f. OF *simenel,* ult. f. L *simila* or Gk *semidalis* fine flour]

simō'niäc *n.* person guilty of simony. [ME, f. OF *simoniaque* or f. med. L *simoniacus* (as SIMONY; see -AC)]

simoni'acal *a.* guilty, or of the nature, of simony; hence **~LY²** *adv.* [f. prec. + -AL]

Simon Pūr'e *n.* & *a.* **1.** *n.* (**the real**) **~,** the real or genuine person or article. **2.** *a.* (*simon-pure*). real, genuine. [character in Centlivre's *Bold Stroke for a Wife* (1717)]

si'mony *n.* buying or selling of ecclesiastical preferment. [ME, f. OF *simonie* f. LL *simonia* f. *Simon Magus* (Acts 8:18); see -Y¹]

simōō'm, simōō'n, *n.* hot dry suffocating dust-laden wind blowing at intervals esp. in Arabian desert. [f. Arab. *samūm* (*samma* to poison)]

*simp *n.* (colloq.) simpleton. [abbr.]

simpatico (sĭmpă'tĭkō) *a.* congenial, likeable. [It. & Sp. (as SYMPATHY; see -IC)]

si'mper *v.* & *n.* **1.** *v.i.* smile affectedly, smirk. **2.** *v.t.* express by or with simpering (*simpered her consent*). **3.** *n.* affected or silly smile, smirk. [16th c.; cf. Da., Norw., Sw. dial. *semper, simper,* G *zimp(f)er* elegant, delicate]

si'mple *a.* & *n.* **1.** *a.* not compound, consisting of one element, all of one kind, involving only one operation or power, not divided into parts, not analysable; **~ eye** (of insect, having only one lens); **~ fracture** (of bone, only); (*simple*) HARMONIC *motion*; **~ idea** (not analysable into elements); *simple* INTEREST¹; **~ machine,** any of the mechanical powers; *simple* SENTENCE. **2.** (Bot.) **~ fruit** (formed from one pistil); **~ leaf** (of one blade); **~ pistil** (of one carpel). **3.** (Mus.) **~ interval** (of an octave or less); **~ time** (with two to four crotchets, quavers, etc., in the bar). **4.** not complicated or elaborate or adorned or involved or highly developed (*the style is simple and devoid of ornament; simple diet; a simple form of pump; the greatest works of art are the simplest*); **in ~ beauty,** unadorned; **the ~ life,** practice of doing without luxuries and artificial amusements, attempt to return to more primitive conditions; **~ forms of life,** creatures low in scale of evolution. **5.** absolute, unqualified, mere, neither more nor less than, (*tell the simple truth; a simple majority of votes decides; story was a simple invention; fee simple*; cf. PURE 3). **6.** plain in appearance or manner, unsophisticated, ingenuous, artless, (*a simple person; simple attire; a simple heart or mind*). **7.** foolish, ignorant, inexperienced, (*am not so simple as to suppose*); feeble-minded. **8.** easily understood or done, presenting no difficulty, (*gave a simple explanation; the problem is very simple; can be cured by a simple device*). **9.** of low rank, humble, insignificant, trifling, (*simple people; her simple efforts to please*). **10. ~-minded,** (1) natural, unsophisticated, (2) feeble-minded; **S~ Simon,** (fig.) foolish person [f. nursery-rhyme character]; hence or cogn. **~NESS** (-pĕln-), **simpli'ciTY,** *ns.*; **be simplicity itself,** be extremely easy to do etc. **12.** *n.* (arch.) herb used medicinally; medicine made from it. [ME f. OF, f. L *simplus*]

si′mpleton (-pelt-) *n*. foolish, gullible, or half-witted person. [f. prec. after surnames f. place-names in -*ton*]

si′mplèx *a*. & *n*. simple, uncompounded, (thing, esp. word). [L, = single, var. of *simplus* simple]

simpli′citer (sĭmplĭ′sĭter) *adv*. (esp. Sc. Law). universally, without limitation, not relatively or in certain respects only. [L]

si′mpli|fy *v.t*. make simple, make easy or easier to do or understand; so ~FICA′TION *n*. [f. F *simplifier* f. med. L *simplificare* (as SIMPLE; see -FY)]

si′mpl|ism *n*. affected simplicity; unjustifiable simplification of problem etc.; hence ~ĭ′stIC *a*. [f. SIMPLE + -ISM]

si′mply *adv*. In adj. senses; absolutely, without doubt or possibility of argument, (*he simply doesn't understand*; *I simply can't afford it*). [ME, f. SIMPLE + -LY²]

simŭlā′cr|um *n*. (*pl*. ~a). image of something; shadowy likeness, deceptive substitute, mere pretence. [L (as foll.)]

si′mŭl|āte *v.t*. feign, pretend to have or feel, put on, (*simulate virtue, indignation*); pretend to be, act like, resemble, mimic, (of word) take or have an altered form suggested by (word wrongly taken to be its source), (*actor simulates king* etc.; *art simulating nature*; *chameleon simulates its surroundings*; '*amuck*', *for* '*amok*', *simulates the English* '*muck*'); imitate conditions of (situation etc.) with model, for convenience or training; (in *p.p.*) made to resemble the real thing but not genuinely such (*simulated fur, pearl*); hence or cogn. ~A′TION, ~ātOR, *ns*. [f. L *simulare* (*similis* like) + -ATE³]

si′mulcast (-ah-) *n*. simultaneous transmission on radio and television. [f. foll. + BROADCAST]

simultā′néous *a*. occurring or operating at the same time (*with*); ~ **display**, playing of several games of chess at the same time; ~ **equations** (involving two or more variables that are to have same values in each equation); hence **simŭltanē′ITY**, ~NESS, *ns*., ~LY² *adv*. [f. med. L *simultaneus* f. L *simul* at the same time, prob. after *instantaneus* etc., + -OUS]

simū′r̄g *n*. monstrous bird of Persian myth, with power of reasoning and speech. [f. Pers. *sīmurg̣* f. Pahlavi *sīn* eagle + *murg̣* bird]

sin¹ *n*. & *v*. (-nn-). **1.** *n*. (act of) transgression (esp. wilful) against divine law or principles of morality; *ugly* etc. **as** ~, (colloq.) exceedingly; BESET*ting sin*; **deadly** or **mortal** ~ (such as causes death of the soul or is fatal to salvation); **the seven deadly** ~**s**, pride, covetousness, lust, anger, gluttony, envy, sloth; ~ **against the Holy Ghost,** worst possible offence [w. ref. to Matt. 12: 31–32]; **like** ~, (sl.) vehemently, forcefully; **live in** ~, (esp. colloq.) cohabit without marriage; **man of** ~, (1, arch. or joc.) reprobate, (2) Antichrist; **for my** ~**s**, (joc.) as a judgement on me for something or other; *sins of* OMISSION; ORIGINAL, VENIAL, *sin*. **2.** offence against good taste, propriety, etc. **3.** ~**-eater**, (Hist.) one hired to take on himself a dead person's sins by eating and drinking near the corpse; ~**-offering,** sacrifice etc. in expiation of sin. **4.** Hence ~*LESS a*. **5.** *v.i*. commit sin; offend *against*. **6.** *v.t*. commit (sin); ~ one's **mercies,** be ungrateful for good luck. **7.** Hence ~′**nEr¹** *n*. (lit., or joc. = rascal etc.). [OE *syn(n)*, rel. to OS *sundea*, OHG *sunt(e)a*, ON *synd*]

sin² *abbr*. sine.

Sināī′tic *a*. of Mount Sinai or the peninsula of Sinai. [var. of *Sinaic* (*Sinai* f. Heb. *sīnay*, -IC), w. euphonic *t*]

sinā′nthropus *n*. apelike man of extinct genus *Sinanthropus*. [mod. L, f. as SINO- (remains having been found near Peking) + Gk *anthrōpos* man]

si′napism *n*. mustard plaster. [f. F *sinapisme* or LL f. Gk *sinapismos* (*sinapi* mustard; see -ISM)]

since *adv.*, *prep.*, & *conj.* **1.** *adv.* after specified or implied past time, throughout or at some or any point in the period between such time and that which is present or being dealt with, (*has* or *had been healthy* (*ever*) *since*; *more flourishing at that time than ever before or*

since; *has since been cut down*; *have* or *had not seen him since*); ago (*happened many years since*; *how long since is it?*; *saw him not long since*). **2.** *prep.* after (specified past time or event), through or in period between (such time) and time present or being dealt with, (*has* or *had been going on, has happened, since 1960* or *Christmas*; *have eaten nothing since yesterday*; *since seeing you I have* or *had heard nothing*). **3.** *conj*. from the past time when, through or in the period before time present or being dealt with and after that when (*what have you been doing since we met?*; *nothing has happened since I have been watching, since we last met*). **4.** for the reason that, seeing that, inasmuch as, (*since it is so, there is no more to be said*); (ellipt.) as being (*a more dangerous, since unknown, foe*). [ME, reduced form of obs. *sithence* (or f. dial. *sin* (f. *sithen*) + -s³) f. OE *siththon*, earlier **sīth thon* after that (OS *sīth*, OHG *sīd*, ON *sīthr* less) + -s³]

sincēr′e *a*. (~r, ~st). free from pretence or deceit, the same in reality as in appearance or seeming or profession, not assumed or put on; hence or cogn. ~NESS (-ēr′n-), **sincĕ′rITY**, *ns*., ~LY² (-ēr′lǐ) *adv*. (**yours** ~**ly,** customary formula for closing letter to acquaintance or friend). [f. L *sincerus* clean, pure]

si′ncĭpŭt *n*. (Anat.) front of head from forehead to top. [L (*semi-* half, *caput* head)]

sīne *n*. (Math.) ~ (**of arc**), line drawn from one end of arc perpendicularly to radius through other end; ~ (**of angle**), ratio of sine of arc to radius; this quantity as generalized function of any argument; ~ **curve, wave,** (representing periodic oscillations of constant amplitude as given by sine function); **versed** ~, unity minus cosine. [f. L *sinus* curve, fold of toga, used in med. L as transl. of Arab. *jayb* bosom, sine]

si′nécūr|e *n*. office of profit or honour without duties attached, esp. benefice without cure of souls; hence ~ISM (3), ~IST (2), *ns*. [f. L *sine cura* without care]

sine die (sīnī dī′ē, sĭnā dē′ā) *adv*. (Of business adjourned indefinitely) with no appointed date. [L, = without day]

sine qua non (sīnī kwā nŏ′n, sĭnā kwah nō′n) *n*. indispensable condition or qualification. [L, = without which not]

si′new *n*., & *v.t*. **1.** *n*. (piece of) tough fibrous tissue uniting muscle to bone, tendon; (in *pl*.) muscles, bodily strength, wiriness, (fig.) what forms the strength or sustains or holds together, framework, resources, (**the** ~**s of war,** money); hence ~LESS *a*., ~Y² *a.*, having well-developed sinews, strong. **2.** *v.t*. (poet.) serve as sinews of, sustain, hold together. [OE *sin(e)we* etc., obl. forms of *sinu, seonu*, = MHG, MLG, MDu. *sene*, ON *sin* f. Gmc **senawō*]

sinfoni′a (-ē′a) *n*. (Mus.) symphony; (in early Italian opera) overture. [It., = SYMPHONY]

sinfoniē′ttä *n*. (Mus.) short or simple symphony; small symphony-orchestra. [It., dim. of prec.]

si′nful *a*. (Of person) full of sin, wicked; (of act) involving or characterized by sin; highly reprehensible; hence ~LY² *adv*., ~NESS *n*. [OE *synfull* (as SIN, -FUL)]

sing *v*. (**sang,** arch. **sung; sung**) & *n*. **1.** *v.i*. & *t*. utter words, utter (words), in tuneful succession, esp. in accordance with a set tune (*sing person's* PRAISES); (sl.) turn informer; hence ~′ABLE *a*. **2.** produce vocal melody, utter (song, tune), (*birds were singing*; *sing another song* or TUNE); ~ **small,** become more humble, be crestfallen. **3.** make inarticulate melodious or humming or buzzing or whistling sounds (*wind, kettle, bee, sings*; *singing* HINNY²); (of ears) be affected as with buzzing sound; ~**ing saw,** = MUSICAL *saw*. **4.** compose poetry; ~ (**of**), celebrate (hero, beauty, great event, etc.) in verse. **5.** usher (esp. old or new year) *out* or *in* with singing; put *to sleep, into good humour,* etc., with singing. **6.** ~ **out,** call out loudly, shout; ~ **up,** sing more loudly. **7.** Hence ~′**ER¹** *n*. **8.** *n*. *meeting for amateur singing. [OE *singan*, = OS, OHG *singan*, ON *syngva*, Goth. *siggwan* f. Gmc **sengwan*]

singe (-nj) v. (part. ∼**'ing** pr. -njĭ-) & n. **1.** v.t. & i. burn superficially or lightly (∼ person's **hair**, burn off tips as hairdressing operation; ∼ **pig, fowl**, burn off bristles, down, after killing, plucking; ∼ one's **wings**, take some harm esp. in venturesome attempt). **2.** n. superficial burn. [OE sencgan, = OS bisengian, MHG sengen, f. WG *sangjan]

Singh (-ng) n. (Title given to) great Indian warrior; title of member of warrior caste, esp. Rajput or Sikh. [Hind., f. Skr. siṅhá lion]

Singhalese. See SINHALESE.

si'ngle[1] (-nggel) a. & n. **1.** a. one only, not double or multiple, united, undivided, designed for or used or done by one person etc. or one set or pair; ||(of ticket) valid for outward journey only, not return. **2.** one by itself, not one of several (a single tree stands on the ridge; paid in a single sum); unmarried (single BLESSEDNESS); lonely, unaided. **3.** taken separately (every single thing); (w. neg. or interrog.) even one, not to speak of more (did not see a single one, a single person; can a single argument be advanced for it?). **4.** (arch.) free from duplicity, sincere, consistent, guileless, ingenuous, (a ∼ eye, devotion to one purpose; ∼ **heart** or **mind**, simplicity of character or devotion to one purpose). **5.** single ACROSTIC; ∼**-acting**, (of engine etc.) with steam admitted only to one side of piston; ∼ **bed** (for one person); ∼**breasted**, (of coat etc.) with only one set of buttons and buttonholes, not overlapping; single COMBAT; ∼**-cut,** (of file) with grooves cut in one direction only, not crossing; single-DECKER; single ENTRY, FILE[2]; ∼ **flower** (having only one set of petals); ∼**-handed** a. & adv., (1) (done etc.) without help from other persons (by his single-handed efforts; cannot be done single-handed), (2) with or for one hand (the men played single-handed against the women with both hands; two-handed and single handed swords); ∼**-line,** with movement of traffic in only one direction at a time; ∼**-loader,** breech-loading rifle without magazine; ∼**-minded,** having a single mind (in sense 4); ∼ **parent,** person bringing up child(ren) without marital partner; single RHYME[1]; ∼ **room,** bedroom for one person; ∼**-seater,** vehicle with one seat; ∼**stick,** (one-handed fencing with) basket-hilted stick of about sword's length; single TRACK[1]; *∼**-tree,** = SWINGLEtree; ∼ **wicket,** form of cricket in which only one batsman is in at one time. **6.** Hence ∼NESS n., **si'ngly**[2] adv., (-ngg-). **7.** n. single ticket; single issue of journal etc.; pop record with one piece of music etc. on each side; ||£1 note; *$1 note; hit for one run in cricket; (usu. in pl.) game with one player on each side; ∼**s bar** (for persons seeking social companions). [ME f. OF, f. L singulus, cogn. w. simplus simple]

si'ngle[2] (-nggel) v.t. choose out as an example or as distinguishable or to serve some purpose. [f. prec.]

si'nglet (-ngg-) n. **1.** ||garment worn under or instead of shirt, vest. **2.** single unresolvable line in spectrum. [f. SINGLE[1] + ET[1], after doublet, garment being unlined]

si'ngleton (-nggelt-) n. one card only of a suit (dealt to a player); single thing, only child, etc.; single child or animal born, not twin etc. [f. SINGLE[1], after simpleton]

si'ngsong a., n., & v. **1.** a. in or recited with monotonous rhythm. **2.** n. monotonous rhythm; monotonous cadence in speaking; ||impromptu vocal concert, meeting for amateur singing; ∼ **girl,** Chinese performer like geisha. **3.** v.t. & i. recite (verse etc.), speak, in singsong manner. [f. SING + SONG]

si'ngular (-ngg-) a. & n. **1.** (Gram.) ∼ (**number**), (form of noun, verb, etc.) denoting a single person or thing, not dual or plural. **2.** a. single, individual, (esp. **all and** ∼, all whether taken together or separately); unique; unusual, remarkable from rarity, much beyond the average in degree, extraordinary, surprising; eccentric, unconventional, strangely behaved; (Math.) possessing unique properties; hence ∼IZE (3) v.t. distinguish, individ-

ualize, ∼LY[2] adv. [ME f. OF singuler f. L singularis (as SINGLE[1]; see -AR[1])]

singula'rity (-ngg-) n. In adj. senses; uncommonness, being remarkable, odd trait or peculiarity. [ME, f. OF singularité f. LL singularitas (as prec.; see -ITY)]

sinh (shĭn, sĭnä'ch) abbr. hyperbolic sine.

Si'nhala (-nha-, -na-) n. & a. = foll. (esp. of language). [Sinh.]

Sinhale'se (-nhale'z, -na-), **Singhale'se** (-nggale'z), a. & n. (pl. same). (member or language) of an Aryan people deriving from N. India and now forming the majority of the population of Sri Lanka. [f. Skr. sinhalam Sri Lanka (Ceylon) + -ESE]

si'nister a. **1.** of evil omen; (usu. of person in regard to his appearance, or of his face or look) suggestive of evil, looking malignant or villainous; wicked, criminal, (a sinister motive); hence ∼LY[2] adv. **2.** (Her.) of or on left-hand side of shield etc. (i.e. to the spectator's right; BAR[1], BATON, BEND[1], sinister); (arch.) left(-hand). [ME, f. OF sinistre or f. L sinister left]

si'nistral a. & n. **1.** left-handed (person). **2.** a. of or on the left; (of flat-fish) with left side uppermost; (of spiral shell) with whorls rising to left and not as usu. to right. **3.** Hence ∼ITY (-ă'l-) n., ∼LY[2] adv. [f. prec. + -AL]

si'nistrórse a. rising towards the left (esp. Bot. of spiral stem). [f. L sinistrorsus (*sinistrovorsus f. sinister left + vertere turn)]

sink[1] v. (**sank** or **sunk; sunk** or, esp. as a. w. pass. sense, **sunken**). **1.** v.i. fall slowly downwards, disappear partly or wholly below surface of liquid or granular solid or below horizon, come gradually to lower level or pitch, droop, despond, gradually expire or perish or cease, (sun is sinking, sank; my heart, spirits, sank; sank under the burden; sink in the social scale; his head, chin, sank on his shoulder, chest; sink into feebleness, degradation, the grave, sleep, a quicksand, a chair (in weariness or luxury)); (of ship) go to bottom of sea etc.; (of eyes) be turned downwards, or shrink inwards; (of cheeks) shrink inwards, become hollow; (of voice) become lower-pitched or quieter; (of sick person) approach death; (of price etc.) become lower; (of storm or river) subside; (of ground) slope down, or reach lower level by subsidence; (of darkness) descend (up)on (place etc.); ∼ **in** person's **estimation,** become less highly esteemed by him; here goes, ∼ **or swim,** even at the risk of complete failure. **2.** penetrate, make way, in or into (bayonet sank in to the hilt); be absorbed in or into (mind etc.; paused to let his words sink in). **3.** v.t. cause or allow to sink, send below surface of liquid etc. or ground, lower level of, keep in obscurity or background, make no reference to, (would sooner sink the ship than surrender; sink one's head on one's chest; sank its teeth into my leg; sunk in thought; drought had sunk the streams; must sink our differences if we are to make progress); dig (well), bore (shaft); engrave (die), inlay (design); invest (money), lose (money) by investment; cause failure of (plan etc.) or discomfiture of (person); cause (ball) to enter pocket at billiards, hole at golf, etc., achieve this by (stroke etc.); sunk FENCE[1]; **sunken garden** (below general level of surroundings). **4.** Hence ∼**ABLE** a., ∼**AGE** (3) n. [OE sincan, = OS, OHG sinkan, ON sökkva, Goth. sigqan f. Gmc]

sink[2] n. **1.** place in which foul liquid collects; (fig.) place of rampant vice etc. **2.** basin or box of porcelain etc. with outflow pipe, esp. with water supply in KITCHEN etc. for washing-up. **3.** pool or marsh in which river's water disappears by evaporation or percolation. **4.** (Phys.) place of disappearance of flux-lines (cf. source); body used to absorb or dissipate heat. **5.** ∼(**-hole**), (Geol.) cavity in limestone etc. into which water disappears. [ME, f. prec.]

si'nker n. In vbl senses; weight used to sink fishing- or sounding-line (HOOK[1], line, and sinker); *doughnut; DIE[1]-sinker. [f. SINK[1] + -ER[1]]

si'nking n. In vbl senses; internal bodily sensation

caused by hunger or apprehension; ∿-fund, moneys set aside for the purpose of sinking or wiping out a State's or corporation's debt by degrees. [ME, f. SINK¹ + -ING¹]

si′nner. See SIN.

si′nnet. See SENNIT.

Sinn Fein (shĭn fā′n) n. patriotic movement (founded 1905) and party in Ireland aiming at political independence for the island; hence ∿ER¹ n. [f. Ir. *sinn féin* we ourselves]

Si′no- comb. form. Chinese (and), as: *Sino-Ame′rican*, ∿MA′NIA n., ∿PHIL(E), ∿PHOBE, ns. & adjs., ∿PHO′BIA n. [f. Gk *Sinai* the Chinese + -o-]

si′nologue (-g) n. person skilled in sinology. [F, f. as prec. + Gk -logos -speaking]

sino′log|ỹ n. study of Chinese language, history, customs, etc.; hence ∿IST (3) n. [f. SINO- + -LOGY]

si′nter n. & v. 1. n. siliceous or calcareous rock formed by deposit from springs; substance produced by sintering. 2. v.t. & i. (cause to) coalesce from powder into solid by heating. [G, = E *sinder* CINDER]

si′nuate a. (esp. Bot.) wavy-edged, with distinct inward and outward bends along edge. [f. L *sinuatus* p.p. of *sinuare* (SINUS) bend; see -ATE²]

sinŭŏ′sĭtỹ n. being sinuous; a bend, esp. in a stream or road. [f. F *sinuosité* or f. med. L *sinuositas* (as foll.; see -ITY)]

si′nŭous a. with many curves, serpentine, tortuous, undulating; hence ∿LY² adv. [f. F *sinueux* or f. L *sinuosus* (as SINUS; see -OUS)]

si′nus n. (Anat. & Zool.) cavity of bone or tissue, esp. in skull communicating with nostrils, whence ∿I′TIS n.; (Path.) fistula esp. to deep abscess; (Bot.) curve between lobes of leaf. [L, = bosom, recess]

si′nusoid n. curve having form of sine wave; hence ∿AL a. [f. F *sinusoïde* f. L SINUS; see -OID]

Si′on. Var. of ZION.

-sion (-shon or -zhon) suf. forming ns. (see -ION) from L p.p. stems in -s- (mansion, mission, persuasion).

Sioux (sōō) n. (pl. same) & a. (member or language) of a group of N. Amer. Indian tribes; hence **Siou′AN** (sōō′ǎn) a. [F, f. native name]

sip v. (-pp-) & n. 1. v.t. & i. drink in one or more small amounts or by spoonfuls. 2. n. act of sipping; small amount of liquid imbibed (a sip of brandy). [ME, perh. modification of SUP]

sīpe n. small groove or channel in tyre-tread to improve grip. [f. dial. *sipe* to ooze f. OE *sīpian*, MLG *sīpen*, of unkn. orig.]

si′phon n. & v. 1. n. pipe or tube shaped like inverted V or U with unequal legs for conveying liquid over edge of vessel and delivering it at lower level by utilizing atmospheric pressure; ∿(-bottle), aerated--water bottle from which liquid is forced out through tube by pressure of gas; (Zool.) canal or conduit esp. in cephalopods, sucking-tube of some insects etc. 2. ∿ **barometer** (with tube bent at bottom like inverted siphon). 3. Hence ∿AGE (3) n., ∿AL, **sīphŏ′nIC**, adjs. 4. v.t. & i. conduct or flow (as) through siphon (water is siphoning from vase on to tablecloth; money was siphoned off illegally from fund). [F, or f. L *sipho -onis* f. Gk *siphōn* pipe]

si′phonĕt n. honey-tube of aphis. [f. prec. + -ET¹]

sīphŏ′nophŏre n. compound usu. translucent marine animal of order Siphonophora, e.g. Portuguese man--of-war. [f. Gk *siphōno-* (as SIPHON, -o-) + -PHORE]

si′phŭncle n. (Zool.) = SIPHON. [f. L *siphunculus* dim. of *sipho* SIPHON]

si′ppĕt n. small piece of bread etc. soaked in liquid; piece of toast or fried bread as garnish; (fig.) fragment. [app. dim. of SOP; see -ET¹]

si quis (sī kwī′s) n. notice posted in ordination--candidate's parish church to give opportunity for objection. [L, = if anyone, opening wds of notice when in L]

sīr n., & v.t. (-rr-). 1. n. (Used esp. in sing. as voc. in addressing man who is superior in rank or age,

Speaker of legislative assembly either in his own person on point of order or as embodiment of the House in ordinary debate, whose name is or is to be understood as unknown to speaker, or inferior who is to be rebuked) please sir, may I go now?; excuse me, sir, have you the time?; you shall pay for this, sir!. 2. (S∿; usu. pr. ser). (Used as titular prefix to name of knight or baronet, always followed by Christian name, or its initial and surname, or the whole name) Sir John Moore, Sir J. Moore, (esp. as voc.) Sir John. 3. (**Dear**) **Sir(s)** (words used to begin formal letter). 4. person with title of, or addressed as, 'Sir'. 5. v.t. address as 'Sir' (don't sir me). [ME, reduced form of SIRE]

sīr′cár, sīr′kár, n. (Ind.) the Government; head of government or household; house-steward; Indian accountant. [f. Urdu *sirkar* f. Pers. *sarkār* (*sar* head, *kār* agent)]

sīr′dár n. (Ind. etc.) person in command, leader; Sikh. [f. Urdu *sardār* f. Pers. *sar* head + *dār* possessor]

sīre n., & v.t. 1. n. (poet.) father or male ancestor. 2. (arch., as voc. to king) = Your MAJESTY. 3. male parent of animal, esp. stallion kept for breeding. 4. v.t. (esp. of stallion) beget. [ME f. OF, f. Rom. *seior* f. L SENIOR]

sīr′en n. 1. (Gk Myth.) any of several women, or creatures half woman and half bird, living on rocky isle to which they lured unwary seafarers with enchanting singing. 2. sweet singer. 3. dangerously fascinating woman, temptress, a tempting pursuit etc.; (attrib.) irresistibly tempting, as of a siren. 4. eel--like tailed amphibian of family Sirenidae. 5. instrument used in acoustic experiments or for making loud sound for information, warning, etc., by revolution of perforated disc over jet of compressed air or steam; (instrument giving) warning of air raids or of approach of police etc. vehicle; ∿ **suit**, one-piece garment for whole body, easily put on or taken off. [ME, f. OF *sereine, sirene* f. LL *Sirena* fem. f. L f. Gk *Seirēn*]

sīrē′nian a. & n. (member) of the order Sirenia of large aquatic herbivorous mammals, e.g. manatee and dugong. [f. mod. L *Sirenia* (as prec.); see -IA², -AN]

sīr′găng n. green Asian bird with red wings (Kitta chinensis). [name in E. Indies]

sīr′kár. See SIRCAR.

sīr′loin n. ‖upper and choicer part of loin of beef; *rump steak. [f. OF *surloigne* var. of *surlonge* (as SUR-, LOIN)]

sirŏ′ccŏ n. (pl. ∿s). Sahara simoom reaching Italy etc.; warm sultry rainy wind in S. Europe. [F, f. It. *scirocco*, ult. f. Arab. *šaruḳ* east wind]

si′rrah (-a) n. (arch., as voc.) = SIR (in imperious or contemptuous use). [prob. f. ME *sīre* SIR]

***sirree′** n. (as voc.) = SIR (in emphatic use, esp. after yes or no). [f. SIR + emphatic suf.]

***si′rup.** See SYRUP.

sirvente (sērvah′nt) n. medieval usu. satirical lay of special metrical form. [F, f. Prov. *sirventes*, taken as pl.; of unkn. orig.]

sis n. (colloq.) sister. [abbr.]

***SIS** abbr. Secret Intelligence Service.

si′sal n. fibre prepared from leaves of an agave, used for cordage, ropes, etc.; plant (Agave sisalana) yielding this. [S∿, port of Yucatan]

si′skin n. olive-green songbird (Spinus spinus) allied to goldfinch. [f. MDu. *siseken* dim., rel. to MLG *sīsek*, MHG *zīse(c)*, of Slav. origin]

si′ssoō n. (valuable Indian timber from) tree of genus Dalbergia. [f. Urdu (Hindi) *sīsū*]

si′ssỹ n. & a. (typical of) effeminate or cowardly person. [f. SIS + -Y²]

si′ster n. 1. daughter of same parents or (also **half-∿**) same parent as another person; **the Fatal S∿s** or **S∿s three** or **three S∿s**, the Fates. 2. woman who is a close friend, female fellow member of class or sect or human race. 3. member of religious community of women; LAY² sister; **S∿ of Mercy,** member of educational or charitable order of women, esp. that founded in Dublin 1827. **4.** ||female hospital nurse in authority over others; (colloq.) any female nurse. **5.** personified quality or thing regarded as female that closely resembles another (*prose, younger sister of verse*); ∼ **ship** (built on same design as another). **6.** ∼ **german,** (having same parents); ∼ **uterine** (having same mother only); ∼**-in-law,** sister of one's husband or wife, wife of one's brother(-in-law). **7.** Hence ∼LY[1,2] *a.* & *adv.* [ME, f. ON *systir*; OE *sweoster* etc., = OS *swestar*, OHG *swester*, Goth. *swistar* f. Gmc **swestr* f. IE **swes(o)r-*]

si′sterhŏŏd *n.* relationship (as) between sisters; society of women bound by monastic vows or devoting themselves to religious or charitable work. [ME, f. prec. + -HOOD]

Si′stine (-ēn, -in) *a.* of one of the Popes called Sixtus, esp. Sixtus IV (∼ **chapel,** in Vatican, with frescoes by Michelangelo). [f. It. *Sistino* (*Sisto* Sixtus; see -INE[1])]

si′str|um *n.* (*pl.* ∼a). jingling metal instrument used by ancient Egyptians esp. in worship of Isis. [ME f. L, f. Gk *seistron* (*seiō* shake)]

Sisyphe′an *a.* everlastingly laborious. [f. L f. Gk *Sisupheios* (*Sisuphos* Sisyphus in Gk Myth., king of Corinth condemned in Hades to push a heavy stone up hill and begin again when it rolled down) + -AN]

sit *v.* (-tt-; **sat,** arch. **sate** *pr.* săt) & *n.* **1.** *v.i.* take or be in position in which body is supported more or less upright by buttocks resting on ground or floor or raised seat; *sit on the* FENCE[1]; ∼ **on** one's **hands,** take no action, not applaud; ∼ **tight,** (colloq.) remain firmly in one's place, not be shaken off or move away or yield to distractions; ∼ **well,** have good seat in riding. **2.** be engaged in some occupation in which this position is usual (∼ **in judgement,** assume right of judging others, be censorious); pose *for* portrait etc., *to* painter etc.; be candidate *for* (award by) examination; be member of Parliament etc. *for* (constituency); act as baby-sitter; (of Parliament, Courts, committee, etc.) be in session; ∼ **at** person's **feet,** be his pupil; ∼ **at home,** be inactive. **3.** (Of birds and some animals) rest with (hind) legs bent and body close to ground or perch; remain on nest to hatch eggs. **4.** be in more or less permanent position or condition (esp. of inactivity or being out of use or out of place); ∼**s the wind there?,** is it in that quarter?, is that the state of affairs?; *food* ∼**s heavy on the stomach,** is not soon digested; *her dress, imperiousness,* etc., ∼**s well on** *her,* suits, fits; *his principles* ∼ **loosely on him,** do not bind him much. **5.** *v.t.* keep or have one's seat on (horse etc.; *he could not sit his mule*). **6.** undergo, be candidate at, (examination etc.). **7.** cause to sit, place in sitting position. **8.** ∼ **back,** relax one's efforts; ∼ **by,** look on without interfering; ∼ **down,** take seat after standing, seat one*self,* cause to sit, (Mil.) encamp *before* place to besiege it; ∼-*down meal* etc. (eaten seated); ∼-*down strike,* one in which strikers refuse to leave the place where they were working; ∼ *down under,* submit tamely to (insult etc.); ∼ **in,** occupy place as protest esp. against (alleged) activities there (whence ∼-*in* n.), (colloq.) act as baby-sitter; ∼ *in on,* be present as guest etc. at (meeting etc.); ∼ **on,** (see also sense 4) (of jury etc.) hold session concerning, be member of (committee etc.), (colloq.) delay action concerning (*Government has been sitting on the matter*), (sl.) repress or rebuke or snub (*he wants sitting on*); ∼ **out,** take no part in something, esp. in particular dance (*decided to sit out*; *sat out the next dance*), sit outdoors, outstay (other visitors), stay till end of (performance, ordeal, etc.); ∼ **over,** (Cards) be (in advantageous position) on left of (player); ∼ **under,** be one of congregation preached to by (minister), (Cards) be on right of (player); ∼ **up,** rise from lying to sitting posture, remain (*late, nursing,* etc.) out of bed, sit erect without lolling; *make* person ∼ *up,* (colloq.) subject him to surprise, hard work, pain, etc.; ∼ *up and take notice,*

(colloq.) have one's interest (suddenly) aroused; ∼ **upon,** = *sit on*; ∼-*upon,* (colloq.) buttocks. **9.** ∼**′fast,** horny sore caused by saddle on horse's back. **10.** *n.* way dress etc. sits on person. [f. OE *sittan*, OS *sittian*, OHG *sizzen*, ON *sitja* (Goth. *sitan*), f. Gmc **sitjan*, **setjan* (**set-* f. IE **sed-* etc.)]

sitār (si′-, -ār′) *n.* long-necked Indian guitar-like instrument. [f. Hindi *sitār*]

si′tcŏm *n.* (colloq.) situation comedy. [abbr.]

sīte *n.,* & *v.t.* **1.** *n.* ground on which town or building stood, stands, or is to stand; place where some activity is or has been conducted (*camping site*; *caravan site*; *launching site*; *prehistoric burial site*). **2.** *v.t.* locate, place; provide with site. [ME f. AF, or f. L *situs* local position]

sith *conj.* (arch.) since. [OE *siththa* (as SINCE)]

Si′tka *n.* ∼ **cypress,** yellow cedar; ∼ **spruce,** tall spruce (*Picea sitchensis*) yielding valuable timber. [∼ in Alaska]

sītophō′bia *n.* morbid aversion to food. [f. Gk *sitos* food + -O- + -PHOBIA]

si′trep *n.* report on current military situation. [f. *situation report*]

si′tter *n.* In vbl senses; person sitting for portrait; sitting hen; ∼(-**i′n**), baby-sitter; (sl.) easy catch, shot, etc., thing easily done. [ME, f. SIT + -ER[1]]

si′tting[1] *n.* In vbl senses; time during which one sits continuously (*wrote, read, the whole poem at a sitting*; *all-night sitting of House of Commons*; *lunch is served in two sittings*); ||(Law) − TERM[1] 2; clutch of eggs; seat in church appropriated to a person; ∼-**room,** (1) space enough to accommodate seated persons, (2) room used for sitting in (opp. *bedroom*). [ME, f. SIT + -ING[1]]

si′tting[2] *a.* In vbl senses; (of game-bird) not flying (*shot a sitting pheasant*); (of animal) not running; (of hen) engaged in hatching; ∼ **duck, target,** person or thing easily attacked; ∼ **tenant,** one already in occupation of house etc. [f. SIT + -ING[2]]

si′tūate[1] *v.t.* place or put in (specified) position, situation, etc., (*is situated on the top of the hill*); (in *p.p.*) in (specified) circumstances (*am awkwardly situated at the moment*). [f. med. L *situare* f. L *situs* site + -ATE[3]]

si′tūate[2] *a.* (arch. or Law). situated. [f. LL *situatus* (as prec.; see -ATE[2])]

sītūā′tion *n.* place, with its surroundings, occupied by something (*house stands in a fine situation*); set of circumstances, position in which one finds oneself, (*came out of a difficult situation with credit*); critical point or complication in drama (*curtain falls on a strong situation*); employee's place or paid office (*cannot find a situation*); ∼ **comedy** (in which humour derives from characters' misunderstandings and embarrassments); ∼**s vacant, wanted,** (headings of lists of employment offered and sought); hence ∼AL *a.* [ME, f. F, or f. med. L *situatio* (as SITUATE[1]; see -ATION)]

si′tz-bath (-tsbahth; *pl. pr.* -ths, -dhz). hip-bath. [partial transl. of G *sitzbad* (*sitzen* sit, *bad* bath)]

Si′va (sē′-, shē′-) *n.* Hindu god held supreme by his special votaries, and by others associated as principle of destruction with Brahma and Vishnu in a triad; hence ∼ISM (3) *n.,* ∼ITE[1] (1) *n.* & *a.,* (-*a*-). [Skr. *Siva,* = propitious]

six *a.* & *n.* **1.** one more than five; symbol for this (6, vi, VI); card etc. with six pips; time of six o'clock; size etc. denoted by six; set of six; hit at cricket scoring six runs (**hit** or **knock for** ∼, (colloq.) utterly surprise or defeat); (in *pl.*) gloves, shoes, etc., of sixth size, candles weighing six to the pound; **it is** ∼ **of one and half-a-dozen of the other,** difference is merely nominal; **at** ∼**es and sevens,** in confusion or disagreement. **2.** **Six Counties** (of N. Ireland); ∼-**footer,** person 6 ft. in height, thing 6 ft. long; *∼-**gun,** = *six-shooter*; ||∼**′pence,** sum of 6p, (coin worth) 6d.; ||∼**′penny,** (*a.*) costing or worth 6p or 6d.; ∼*penny bit,* ∼*penny* (*n.*), the coin sixpence; ∼-**shooter,** six-chambered revolver. **3.** Hence ∼′FOLD *a.* & *adv.* [OE *siex* etc., = OS, OHG *sehs*, ON *sex*, Goth. *saihs* f. Gmc *seks* f. IE *s(w)eks*]

si'xain *n.* six-line stanza. [F (*six* six)]

si'xer *n.* hit for six runs in cricket; leader of group of six Brownies or Cubs. [f. SIX + -ER¹]

sixte *n.* sixth of eight parrying positions in fencing. [F, f. L *sextus* sixth]

sixteen (-ē'n, sī'-) *a.* & *n.* one more than fifteen; symbol for this (16, xvi, XVI); ~**mo**, sextodecimo; hence ~TH² *a.* & *n.* (*~th-note*, semiquaver). [OE *siextiene* (as SIX, -TEEN)]

sixth *a.* & *n.* **1.** *a.* next after fifth; ~ **part**, one of six equal parts into which thing is or may be divided. **2.** *n.* sixth part, thing, etc.; (Mus.) (note at) interval of which the span involves six alphabetical notes, harmonic combination of notes thus separated. **3.** ~ **day**, Friday; ||~ **form**, (usu.) highest form in secondary school (~-*form college*, one taking pupils only at this level); *sixth* SENSE. **4.** Hence ~'LY² *adv.*, in the sixth place. [f. SIX + -TH²]

Si'xtine (-ēn, -īn) *a.* = SISTINE. [f. mod. L *Sixtinus* (*Sixtus*; see -INE¹)]

si'xtȳ *a.* & *n.* **1.** six times ten; symbol for this (60, lx, LX); set of sixty persons or things; (in *pl.*) numbers etc., esp. years of a century or a life, from 60 to 69; hence ~FOLD *a.* & *adv.*, **si'xtiETH¹** *a.* & *n.* **2.** ~**one** etc., (arch.) **one-and-**~ etc., sixty plus one etc., w. corresp. ordinals ~**first** etc.; ~**four** (**thousand**) **dollar question**, difficult and crucial question [f. top prize in broadcast quiz shows]; ~**four'mo** (-fŏr'mō), (size of) book in which each leaf is 1/64 of printing-sheet [after *duodecimo* etc.]. [OE *siextig* (as SIX, -TY²)]

si'zable. Var. of SIZEABLE.

||**si'zar** *n.* student at Cambridge or at Trinity College, Dublin, paying reduced fees and formerly having certain menial duties; hence ~SHIP *n.* [f. foll. = ration + -AR³]

size *n.*, & *v.t.* **1.** *n.* relative bigness, dimensions, magnitude, (*is of vast, diminutive, size; size matters less than quality*); **cut down to** ~, (fig.) reduce to proper degree of (un)importance; **of a** ~, having the same size; **of some** ~, fairly large; *is* **the** ~ **of**, as big as; **the** ~ **of it**, (colloq.) a true account of the matter; **try** (thing) **for** ~, test to determine whether it fits (lit. or fig.); **what** ~?, how big?; OUTSIZE. **2.** one of the usu. numbered classes into which things, esp. garments, otherwise similar are divided in respect of size (*is made in several sizes; takes size 7 in gloves; is three sizes too big*). **3.** ~**-stick**, shoemaker's measure for taking length of foot. **4.** Hence (-)**sīzED²** (-zd) *a.* **5.** *v.t.* group or sort in sizes or according to size, whence **si'zER¹** (2) *n.*; ~ **up**, estimate size of, (colloq.) form judgement of (person etc.). [ME, f. OF *sise* f. *assise* ASSIZE, or f. ASSIZE]

sīze² *n.*, & *v.t.* **1.** *n.* gelatinous solution used in glazing paper, stiffening textiles, etc.; hence **si'zY²** *a.* **2.** *v.t.* glaze or stiffen or treat with size. [ME, perh. = prec.]

si'zeable (-za-) *a.* of (fairly) large size. [f. SIZE¹ + -ABLE]

si'zzl|e *v.i.*, & *n.* (make) sputtering sound as of frying; (colloq.) (be in) state of great heat or excitement or marked effectiveness; hence ~ING² *a.* & *adv.* (*sizzling hot*). [imit.]

SJ *abbr.* Society of JESUS.

||**SJA(A, B)** *abbr.* St. John Ambulance (Association, Brigade).

sjä'mbŏk (sh-) *n.*, & *v.t.* (S. Afr.) (flog with) rhinoceros-hide whip. [Afrik., f. Malay *samboq*, *chambok* f. Urdu *chābuk*]

***SJC** *abbr.* Supreme Judicial Court.

skald, scald², (-aw-, -ŏ-) *n.* composer and reciter of poems in ancient Scandinavia honouring heroes and their deeds; hence ~'IC *a.* [f. ON *skáld*, of unkn. orig.]

skat (-aht) *n.* three-handed card-game with bidding for contract. [G, f. It. *scarto* a discard (*scartare* discard)]

skāte¹ *n.* (*pl.* ~ or ~s). cartilaginous fish of family

Rajidae, esp. *Raja batis*, large flat rhomboidal food-fish. [ME, f. ON *skata*]

skāte² *n.* & *v.* **1.** *n.* one of pair of implements, each with steel blade or set of rollers, attached beneath boots or shoes and enabling wearer to glide over ice or (**roller-**~) hard floor or pavement etc.; ||**get** one's ~**s on**, (sl.) make haste; ~**'board**, (*n.*) short narrow board like large roller-skate on which person stands with both feet, (*v.i.*) travel on this. **2.** *v.i.* & *t.* move, perform (specified figure), on skates; pass lightly *over* (esp. fig.); ~ **on thin ice**, deal with subject needing tactful treatment; **ska'ting-rink**, piece of ice artificially made, or floor used, for skating; hence **skā'tER¹** *n.* [orig. *scates* pl. f. Du. *schaats* sing. f. ONF *escace*, OF *eschasse* stilt]

***skāte³** *n.* (sl.) (**cheap**) ~, contemptible, mean, or dishonest person. [20th c.; orig. uncert.]

skean, skēne, *n.* Gaelic dagger formerly used in Ireland and Scotland; ~**dhu'** (-dōō'), dagger worn in stocking as part of Highland costume. [f. Gael. *sgian* knife, *dubh* black]

skĕdă'ddle *v.i.*, & *n.* (colloq.) **1.** *v.i.* run away, disperse in flight. **2.** *n.* hurried flight or dispersal. [19th c., of unkn. orig.]

***skee'sicks** (-z-), **-zicks**, *n.* rascal, good-for-nothing. [19th c., of unkn. orig.]

skeet *n.* shooting sport in which clay target is thrown from trap to simulate flight of bird. [f. ON *skjóta* SHOOT¹]

skein (-ān) *n.* loosely coiled bundle of yarn or thread; flock of wild geese etc. in flight; (fig.) tangle, confusion. [ME, f. OF *escaigne*, of unkn. orig.]

skĕ'lĕton *n.* **1.** hard internal or external framework of bones, cartilage, shell, woody fibre, etc., supporting or containing animal or vegetable body; hence **skĕ'lĕtAL** *a.* **2.** dried bones of human being or other animal fastened together in same relative positions as in life (~ **at the feast**, something that spoils one's pleasure, intrusive worry; ~ **in the** ||**cupboard** or ***closet**, discreditable or humiliating fact concealed from strangers; very thin or emaciated person or animal; remaining part of anything after its life or usefulness is gone. **3.** framework or essential part of anything; ~ **crew** etc., permanent nucleus ready for supplementing; ~ **key** (fitting many locks by having interior of bit hollowed); ~ **staff** (minimum needed to do essential work). **4.** outline sketch, epitome, abstract. **5.** Hence ~IZE (3) *v.t.* [mod. L f. Gk, neut. (as n.) of *skeletos* dried-up (*skellō* dry up)]

skēne. See SKEAN.

skĕp *n.* wooden or wicker basket of various forms; quantity contained in this; straw or wicker beehive. [ME, f. ON *skeppa*, rel. to OHG *sceffil*]

***skĕ'psis, *skĕ'ptic**, etc. See SCEPSIS etc.

skĕ'rrick *n.* (Austral. & US colloq.) smallest bit (usu. w. neg.; *not a skerrick left*). [N. Engl. dial. wd]

skĕ'rrȳ *n.* reef, rocky isle. [Orkney dial., f. ON *sker*; cf. SCAR²]

skĕtch *n.* & *v.* **1.** *n.* preliminary, rough, slight, merely outlined, or unfinished drawing or painting often as experiment for or to assist in making of regular picture; brief account without many details conveying general idea of something, rough draft, general outline; slight usu. one-scene play often of comic kind; (colloq.) comical person or thing; short descriptive article; musical composition of single movement; ~**-block, -book**, arrangements of drawing-paper leaves for doing series of sketches on; ~**-map** (with outlines but little detail). **2.** *v.t.* make or give sketch of; ~ (**in, out**), indicate briefly or in outline. **3.** *v.i.* make sketches esp. of landscape (*went out sketching*). **4.** Hence ~'ER¹ *n.* [f. Du. *schets* or G *skizze* f. It. *schizzo* (*schizzare* make sketch f. Rom. *schediare* f. L f. Gk *skhedios* extempore)]

skĕ'tchȳ *a.* giving only slight or rough outline, like a sketch; (colloq.) unsubstantial or imperfect esp. through haste; hence ~ĭLY² *adv.*, ~ĭNESS *n.* [f. prec. + -Y²]

skew *a.*, *n.*, & *v.* **1.** *a.* oblique, slanting, sideways, distorted; ~ **arch, bridge,** (with line of arch not at right angles to abutment); ~ **chisel** (with oblique edge). **2.** (Math.) lying in three dimensions (*skew curve*); (of lines) not coplanar; (of statistical distribution) not symmetrical. **3.** ~'**back,** sloping face of abutment on which extremity of arch rests; ||~-**eyed,** squinting; ||~-**whi'ff,** (colloq. or dial.) askew; hence ~'NESS *n.* **4.** *n.* slant; **on the** ~, askew. **5.** *v.t.* make skew; distort. **6.** *v.i.* move obliquely; twist. [a. & n. f. v. f. ONF *eskiu(w)er* = OF *eschuer* (see ESCHEW)]

skew'bald (-awld) *a.* & *n.* (animal, esp. horse) with irregular patches of white and another colour (prop. not black; cf. PIEBALD). [f. ME *skued* (of uncert. orig.), after PIEBALD]

skew'er *n.*, & *v.t.* **1.** *n.* pin for holding meat compactly together while cooking. **2.** *v.t.* fasten together, pierce, (as) with skewer. [17th c., var. of dial. *skiver*, of unkn. orig.]

ski (skē) *n.* (*pl.* ~s *or* ~), & *v.i.* (~'d *or* ~ed, *pr.* skēd). **1.** *n.* one of pair of long narrow pieces of wood etc. usu. pointed and turned up at front, fastened under feet for travelling over snow; similar device under vehicle; WATER¹-*ski.* **2.** ~-**bob,** machine like bicycle with skis instead of wheels; ~ **boots, pants,** etc., (for wear when skiing); ~ **heil!** (hīl), good skiing!; ~-**jump,** (jump made from) steep slope levelling off before sharp drop to allow skier to leap through air; ~-**lift,** chair-lift or similar device for skiers; ~-**run,** slope suitable for skiing as sport. **3.** *v.i.* travel on skis. [Norw., f. ON *skíth* billet, snow-shoe]

skiä'graphy etc. See SCIAGRAPHY etc.

skid *n.* & *v.* (-**dd**-). **1.** *n.* piece of frame or timber serving as support, inclined plane, (Naut.) fender, etc.; **on the** ~s, (colloq.) ready for launching or discarding; **put the** ~s **under,** cause to hasten esp. to downfall. **2.** braking device, esp. wooden or metal shoe preventing wheel from revolving or used as drag; runner on aircraft for use when landing. **3.** slip or slide, esp. of wheel on slippery ground; ~-**lid,** (sl.) crash-helmet; ||~-**pan,** (1) slippery road surface prepared for vehicle-drivers to practise control of skids, (2) braking device (see sense 2); *~ **road,** (1) road for hauling logs along, (2) part of town frequented by loggers; hence *~ **row,** part of town frequented by vagrants, alcoholics, etc. **4.** *v.t.* support or move or protect or check with skid; cause (vehicle etc.) to skid. **5.** *v.i.* (Of wheel or vehicle, also of its driver) slide forwards or backwards or sideways on slippery ground; slip, slide. [17th c., of unkn. orig.]

*****skiddoo'** *v.t.* (sl.) go away, depart. [perh. f. SKEDADDLE]

ski'er¹ (skē'er) *n.* person using skis. [f. SKI + -ER¹]

ski'er². Var. of SKYER.

ski'ey. Var. of SKYEY.

skiff *n.* light rowing or sculling boat. [f. F *esquif* f. It. *schifo* f. Lombardic *skif* = OHG *skif* SHIP¹]

ski'ffle *n.* kind of folk music played by small group, mainly with rhythmic accompaniment to singing guitarist etc. [perh. imit.]

ski'-joring (skē'jŏr-, shēyĕr'-) *n.* winter sport in which skier is towed by horse or vehicle. [f. Norw. *skikjøring* (as SKI, *kjøre* drive, -ING¹)]

ski'lful, *****ski'llful,** *a.* having or showing skill (*at, in*); practised, expert, adroit, ingenious; hence ~LY² *adv.* [f. foll. + -FUL]

skill¹ *n.* expertness, practised ability, facility *in* an action or *in doing or to do* something; dexterity, tact. [ME, f. ON *skil* distinction, cf. foll.]

skill² *v.i. impers.* (arch.) avail; (w. neg. or interrog.) matter, make a difference, (*it skills not which*). [ME, f. ON *skila* give reason for, *skilja* distinguish]

skilled (-ld) *a.* having or showing skill, skilful, *in*; (of work) requiring skill; (of worker) highly trained or experienced. [f. SKILL¹ + -ED²]

ski'lless (-l-l-) *a.* (arch.) without skill; knowing nothing *of.* [f. SKILL¹ + -LESS]

ski'llet *n.* ||small metal pot with long handle and usu. legs used in cooking; *frying-pan. [ME, perh. f. OF *escuelete* dim. of *escuele* platter f. pop. L *scutella*]

*****ski'lful.** See SKILFUL.

||**ski'lly** *n.* thin broth or soup or gruel (usu. of oatmeal and water flavoured with meat). [abbr. f. *skilligalee*, prob. fanciful]

skim *v.* (-**mm**-) & *n.* **1.** *v.t.* take scum or cream or floating layer from surface of (liquid), take (cream etc.) from surface of liquid; ~ **the cream off,** (fig.) take the best part of; ~ **milk** (from which cream has been skimmed). **2.** keep touching lightly or nearly touching (surface) in passing over. **3.** *v.i.* go thus *over* or *along* surface, glide along in air. **4.** *v.t.* & *i.* read superficially (*through*), look over cursorily, gather salient facts contained (in). **5.** *n.* act of skimming; thin covering on liquid. [ME, back-form. f. foll.]

ski'mmer *n.* **1.** ladle etc. for skimming liquids. **2.** flat (straw) hat. **3.** long-winged marine bird of genus *Rynchops* that feeds by skimming over water with knifelike lower mandible immersed. [ME, f. OF *escumoir* (*escumer* f. *escume* scum f. Gmc; see SCUM); assim. to -ER¹]

ski'mmia *n.* E. Asian evergreen shrub of genus *Skimmia*, with red fruit. [mod. L, f. Jap.; see -IA¹]

skimp *a.* & *v.* **1.** *a.* scanty. **2.** *v.t.* supply meagrely, stint, (person with or *in* food, money, etc.; material, expenses, etc.). **3.** *v.i.* be parsimonious. [18th c.; orig. unkn. (cf. SCRIMP)]

ski'mpŷ *a.* meagre, not ample; hence ~ĭLY² *adv.*, ~iNESS *n.* [f. *skimp* a. + -Y²; cf. prec.]

skin¹ *n.* **1.** flexible continuous covering of human or other animal body; **change** one's ~, undergo impossible change of character etc.; **get under** person's ~, (colloq.) take strong hold on him, interest or annoy him intensely; **jump out of** one's ~, be startled, extremely delighted, etc.; **save** one's **skin,** avoid loss or injury; *is only* ~ **and bone,** very thin; **the** ~ **off your nose** (colloq. toasting formula); **no** ~ **off** one's **nose,** (colloq.) a matter of indifference or even benefit to one; *escape* **by** or **with the** ~ **of** one's **teeth,** narrowly; **thick, thin,** ~, imperviousness, sensitiveness, to affront or reproach; *wet* **to the** ~, through all one's clothing; **with a whole** ~, unwounded. **2.** colour of skin, complexion (*has a fair, dark, skin*). (Anat.) one layer of the skin (**true** or **inner** ~, dermis; **outer** ~, epidermis). **3.** skin of flayed animal with or without the hair etc.; material prepared from skins esp. of smaller animals (opp. *hide*); vessel for wine or water made of animal's whole skin. **4.** outer coating of plant, fruit, sausage, etc.; film like skin on surface of liquid etc. **5.** planking or plating of ship or boat inside or outside ribs; outer covering of aeroplane. **6.** = GOLD-*beater's skin*; thin sheet for use as typewriter stencil. **7.** ~-**deep,** of wound, or of emotion, impression, beauty, etc.) superficial, not deep or lasting; ~-**diver,** one who dives and swims under water, usu. in deep water with flippers and aqualung; ~ **effect,** (Electr.) tendency of high-frequency alternating current to flow through the outer layer only of a conductor; ~-**flick,** (sl.) explicitly pornographic film; ~-**food,** cosmetic intended to improve condition of skin; ~ **friction** (at surface of solid and fluid in relative motion); *~ **game,** (sl.) swindling game; ~-**graft,** (operation using) skin cut from another part or person and surgically substituted for damaged part; ~'**head,** ||young gangster esp. with close-cropped hair, *recruit in Marines; ~-**tight,** (of garment) very close-fitting. **8.** Hence ~'FUL 2 *n.*, (esp.) enough liquor to make one drunk, (-)~nED² (-nd), -'LESS, *adjs.* [OE *scin(n)* f. ON *skinn*; cf. OHG *scinden* flay]

skin² *v.* (-**nn**-). **1.** *v.t.* & *i.* ~ (**over**), cover (sore etc.) as with skin, (of wound etc.) form or become covered with new skin. **2.** *v.t.* strip off skin, withdraw or scrape skin from; flay; (sl.) fleece, swindle; *keep* one's EYE¹'s *skinned*; ~ **a flint,** be miserly or avaricious; ~'**flint,** niggard, miser. [f. prec.]

skink *n.* small lizard of family Scincidae. [f. F *scinc* or f. L f. Gk *skigkos*]

ski′nner *n.* In vbl. senses; dealer in skins, furrier. [ME, f. SKIN¹,² + -ER¹]

ski′nn|y *a.* made of or like skin; (of person) thin, emaciated; niggardly; *∼y-dipping, (sl.) bathing in the nude; hence ∼iness *n.* [f. SKIN¹ + -Y²]

skint *a.* (sl.) having no money. [= *skinned*, p.p. of SKIN²]

skip¹ *v.* (-pp-) & *n.* **1.** *v.i.* (Of young animal, child, etc.) jump about, gambol, caper, frisk, move lightly from one foot on to the other; use skipping-rope. **2.** shift quickly *from* or *off* one subject or occupation *to* another, be desultory; (sl.) make off, disappear. **3.** *v.t.* & *i.* omit, make omissions, in dealing with a series or in reading (*do them all without skipping any* or *skipping*; *always skips the small print*; *skips as he reads*; *skip every tenth row*); (colloq.) not participate in; (colloq.) flee, depart quickly (from); ∼ **it!**, (sl.) abandon topic etc. **4.** ∼'jack, (1) jumping toy made of bird's wishbone, (2) fish that jumps above water surface, (3) click beetle; ∼'ping-rope, *∼-rope, length of rope with handle·at each end, revolved over head and under feet during jumping as game or exercise; ∼ zone, annular region round broadcasting station where neither direct nor reflected waves are received. **5.** *n.* skipping movement, esp. quick shift from one foot to the other. [ME, prob. f. Scand.]

‖**skip²** *n.* college servant, esp. at Trinity College, Dublin. [prob. f. obs. *skip-kennel* lackey (as prec., KENNEL²)]

skip³ *n.*, & *v.t.* **1.** *n.* captain or director of side at bowls or curling. **2.** *v.t.* be skip of. [abbr. of SKIPPER²]

skip⁴ *n.* cage, bucket, etc., in which men or materials are lowered and raised in mines and quarries; large container for builder's refuse etc.; = SKEP. [var. of SKEP]

ski′pper *n.* In vbl senses; small dark thick-bodied butterfly. [ME, f. SKIP¹ + -ER¹]

ski′pper² *n.*, & *v.t.* **1.** *n.* sea captain, esp. master of small trading or fishing vessel; ∼'s daughters, tall white-crested waves. **2.** captain of an aircraft; captain of side in games. **3.** *v.t.* act as captain of. [ME, f. MDu., MLG *schipper* (*schip* SHIP¹; see -ER¹)]

ski′ppet *n.* small round wooden box to enclose and protect seal attached to document. [ME, of unkn. orig.]

skirl *v.i.*, & *n.* (make) shrill sound characteristic of bagpipes. [prob. Scand., ult. imit.]

skir′mish *n.*, & *v.i.* **1.** *n.* piece of irregular or unpremeditated fighting esp. between small or outlying parties, slight engagement; encounter of wit, argument, etc. **2.** *v.i.* engage in skirmish; hence ∼ER¹ *n.* [ME, f. OF *eskirmir*, *escremir*, f. Frank. *skirmjan* defend; see -ISH²]

skirr *v.i.* move rapidly esp. with whirring sound. [perh. rel. to SCOUR¹]

skir′ret *n.* perennial umbelliferous plant (*Sium sisarum*) formerly cultivated in Europe for its edible root. [ME *skirwhit(e)* perh. f. as SHEER¹, WHITE¹]

skirt *n.* & *v.* **1.** *n.* part of coat etc. that hangs below waist; woman's outer garment hanging from waist (divided ∼, culotte); (vulg. sl.) woman (esp. *bit of skirt*); ∼-dance (with graceful manipulation of full skirt). **2.** flap of saddle; hanging part round base of hovercraft. **3.** (in *sing.* or *pl.*) edge, border, extreme part; ∼ of beef etc., (1) diaphragm and other membranes as food, (2) ‖cut of meat from lower flank. **4.** Hence ∼'ED², ∼'LESS, *adjs.* **5.** *v.t.* go along or round or past the edge of; be situated along. **6.** *v.i.* go along coast, wall, etc.; ‖∼'ing(-board), board etc. along bottom of room-wall. [ME, f. ON *skyrta* shirt, corresp. to OE *scyrte*; see SHIRT]

skit¹ *n.* light piece of satire, burlesque, (*on*). [rel. to *skit* move lightly and rapidly, perh. f. ON *skyt-* cogn. w. *skjóta* SHOOT¹]

skit² *n.* (colloq.) a number, crowd (esp. in *pl.*, heaps, lots). [20th c.; cf. SCADS]

ski′tter *v.i.* move lightly or hastily *along* or *across*; fish by drawing bait jerkily along surface of water; hurry *about*, dart *off*. [app. frequent. of dial. *skite*, perh. f. as SKIT¹]

ski′ttish *a.* (Of horse etc.) nervous, inclined to shy, excitable, playful, fidgety; (of person, esp. woman) frivolous, coquettish, excessively lively; hence ∼LY² *adv.*, ∼NESS *n.* [ME, perh. f. as SKIT¹ + -ISH¹]

skittle *n.*, & *v.t.* **1.** *n.* (in *pl.*) game played with usu. nine wooden pins set up at end of alley to be bowled down usu. with wooden ball or disc (beer and ∼s, amusement; *life is not all beer and skittles*); (table) ∼s, game played with similar pins set up on board to be knocked down by swinging suspended ball; (colloq.) chess not played seriously. **2.** pin used in skittles. **3.** *v.t.* ∼ out, (Cricket) get (batsmen) out in rapid succession. [17th c. (also *kittle-pins*), of unkn. orig.]

skive *v.* **1.** *v.t.* split or pare (hide, leather); (sl.) evade (a duty). **2.** *v.i.* (sl.) evade a duty; ∼ off, depart evasively. [f. ON *skīfa*, rel. to ME *schīve* slice]

ski′ver *n.* In vbl senses; knife for skiving leather; thin leather got by skiving. [f. prec. + -ER¹]

ski′vvy *n.* **1.** ‖(colloq., derog.) female domestic servant. **2.** *thin high-necked long-sleeved garment; *(in *pl.*) underwear of vest and underpants. [20th c.; orig. unkn.]

skū′a *n.* large predatory sea-bird of genus *Stercorarius* etc. which pursues other birds and makes them disgorge the fish they have caught. [mod. L, f. Faroese *skúgvur*, ON *skúfr*]

skülldü′ggerÿ, -ülld-, (-g-) *n.* (joc.) trickery; unscrupulous behaviour. [earlier *sculduddery*, orig. Sc. = unchastity (18th c., of unkn. orig.)]

skülk¹ *v.i.* move stealthily, lurk, keep oneself concealed esp. in cowardice or because intending mischief; stay or sneak away in time of danger; shirk duty, avoid observation; hence ∼'ER¹ *n.* [ME, f. Scand.; cf. Norw. *skulka* lurk, Da. *skulke*, Sw. *skolka* shirk]

skülk² *n.* person who skulks; company of foxes. [ME, f. prec.]

skull *n.* bony case of brain of vertebrates; part of skeleton corresponding to head; (representation of) this with skin and soft internal parts removed; head as seat of intelligence; ∼ and cross-bones, representation of bare skull with two thigh-bones crossed below it as emblem of death, prison, or piracy; thick ∼, slowness of comprehension; ∼-cap, (1) small close-fitting peakless cap, (2) top part of skull, (3) plant of genus *Scutellaria* with helmet--shaped bilabiate flowers; hence (-)∼ED² (-ld) *a.* [ME *scolle*, of unkn. orig.]

skullduggery. See SKULDUGGERY.

skunk *n.*, & *v.t.* **1.** *n.* black white-striped bushy-tailed American carnivorous animal of genus *Mephitis* etc., about size of cat and able to emit powerful stench from liquid secreted by anal glands as defence; its fur; thoroughly contemptible person; *∼-bear, wolverine; *∼-cabbage, herb with offensive--smelling spathe. **2.** *(sl.) defeat; fail to pay (bill etc.). [f. Amer. Ind. *segankw*, *segongw*]

skÿ *n.*, & *v.t.* **1.** *n.* (in *sing.* or *pl.*) (the vault of) heaven, weather or climate evidenced by it, (blue, clear, cloudy, overcast, starry, etc., *sky* or *skies*); out of a clear ∼, as a complete surprise; the ∼ is the limit, there is practically no limit; to the skies, (1) very highly (*praised to the skies*), (2) into heaven (*raised to the skies*); under the open ∼, out of doors. **2.** ∼-blue *a.* & *n.* colour(ed) like clear sky; ∼-born, (poet.) of divine birth; ∼-diving, sport of falling freely from aircraft and opening parachute only at last safe moment; ∼--high *adv.* & *a.*, (as if) reaching the sky, very high(ly); ∼'jack *v.t.*, (sl.) hijack (aircraft); ∼'lark, (*n.*) lark that soars while singing, (*v.i.*) (w. pun on LARK¹,², and perh. of naut. orig. w. ref. to clambering about rigging), frolic, play tricks or practical jokes, ballyrag, etc.; ∼'light, window set in plane of roof or ceiling; ∼'**line,** outline of hills, buildings, etc., defined against sky, visible horizon; ∼ **marker,** parachute flare dropped to mark target area; ∼ **pilot,** (sl.) clergyman; ∼**-rocket** (*n.*) rocket exploding high in air, (*v.i.*, esp. fig. of prices etc.) rise steeply; ∼'**sail** (-sāl, -sal), light sail above royal in square-rigged ship; ∼'**scape,** picture chiefly representing sky; ∼'**scraper,** very tall building; ∼**-sign,** advertisement on roof of building; ∼ **wave,** radio wave reflected from ionosphere; ∼'**way,** (route in) sky as medium of transport; ∼**-writing,** legible smoke--trails made by aeroplane esp. for advertising. **3.** Hence ∼'**eY**², ∼'**LESS,** adjs., ∼WARD(s) adv. & *a.* **4.** *v.t.* hit (cricket etc. ball) high up; hang (picture) high on wall. [ME *ski(es)* cloud(s) f. ON *ský* (f. **skiuja*), rel. to OE *scēo,* OS *scio*]

Skȳe *n.* ∼ (**terrier**), small long-bodied short-legged long-haired slate or fawn coloured variety of Scotch terrier. [∼, island of Inner Hebrides]

skȳ'er *n.* high hit at cricket. [f. SKY + -ER¹]

slăb¹ *n.,* & *v.t.* (**-bb-**). **1.** *n.* flat broad fairly thick usu. square or rectangular piece of stone or other solid material; large flat piece of cake, chocolate, etc.; (of timber) outer piece sawn from log.; *∼**-sided,** long and lank; ∼**-stone,** (1) slab of stone, (2) kind of stone that splits readily into slabs. **2.** *v.t.* remove slabs from (log, tree) to prepare it for sawing into planks. [ME, of unkn. orig.]

slăb² *a.* (arch.) viscous, (of liquid) thick and sticky, (usu. *thick and slab* after Shak. *Macbeth* IV. i. 32). [rel. to *slab* ooze, sludge, prob. f. Scand.; cf. ODa. *slab* mud, Norw., Sw., Icel. *slabb* wet filth]

slăck¹ *a., adv., n.,* & *v.* **1.** *a.* sluggish; remiss; relaxed, languid; loose; inactive, negligent; (of rope etc.) not taut; (of trade, business, market) with little happening; (of weather) inclining one to indolence; (Phonet.) lax; ∼ **hand** or **rein,** lack of full control in riding or (fig.) governing; ∼ **lime,** slaked lime; *∼ **suit,** casual clothes of slacks and jacket or shirt; ∼ **water,** time near turn of tide, esp. at low tide; hence ∼'**LY**⁸ adv., ∼'**NESS** *n.* **2.** adv. slackly; (dry, bake, etc.) slowly or insufficiently. **3.** *n.* slack part of rope (haul in the slack); **take up the** ∼, (fig.) avoid undesirable lull; slack time in trade etc.; (colloq.) spell of inactivity or laziness; (in *pl.*) full-length loosely-cut trousers for informal wear. **4.** *v.t.* & *i.* slacken; loosen (rope etc.); (colloq.) take a rest, be indolent, whence ∼'ER¹ *n.*; slake (lime); ∼ **off,** loosen, (cause to) lose vigour; ∼ **up,** reduce speed of train etc. before stopping. [OE *slæc,* = OS *slak,* OHG *slah,* ON *slakr* f. Gmc *slakaz]

slăck² *n.* coal-dust. [ME, prob. f. LDu.]

slă'cken *v.t.* & *i.* make or become slack; ∼ **off,** = SLACK¹ *off.* [f. SLACK¹ + -EN⁶]

‖**SLADE** *abbr.* Society of Lithographic Artists, Designers, Engravers, and Process Workers.

slăg *n.,* & *v.i.* (**-gg-**). **1.** *n.* dross separated in fused state in reduction of ores, vitreous smelting-refuse, clinkers, (BASIC *slag*); volcanic scoria; ∼**-heap,** hill of refuse from mine etc; ∼**-wool,** = *mineral* WOOL; hence ∼'**gY**² (-gī) *a.* **2.** *v.i.* form slag; cohere into slaglike mass. [f. MLG *slagge,* perh. f. *slagen* strike, w. ref. to fragments formed by hammering]

slain. See SLAY¹.

slāke *v.t.* assuage, satisfy, (thirst, or fig. revenge etc.), whence ∼'LESS (-kl-) *a.* (poet.); disintegrate (LIME¹) by combining chemically with water. [OE *slacian* (*slæc* SLACK¹)]

sla'lom (-ah'-, -ā'-) *n.* ski-race down zigzag course defined by artificial obstacles (**giant** ∼, long--distance slalom); obstacle race in cars or canoes. [Norw., lit. 'sloping track']

slăm¹ *v.* (**-mm-**), *n.,* & *adv.* **1.** *v.t.* & *i.* shut with loud bang (*slammed the door; door slammed* to or *shut*); put down (object) with similar sound; move violently (*he slammed out of the room*); put or come into sudden action (*slam the brakes on*); (sl.) criticize severely; (sl.) hit,

beat, gain easy victory over; hence *∼'**mER**¹ *n.,* (sl.) prison. **2.** *n.* sound (as) of slammed door; shutting of door etc. with loud bang. **3.** *adv.* ∼(**ba'ng**), with sound of slam. [prob. f. Scand.; cf. ON *slam(b)ra*]

slăm² *n.* gaining of every trick at cards; **grand, little** or **small,** ∼, winning of 13, 12, tricks in bridge; **grand** ∼, (fig.) winning of all of a group of championships in tennis, golf, etc. [orig. name of card-game; perh. f. obs. *slampant* trickery]

sla'nder (-ah'-) *n.,* & *v.t.* **1.** *n.* false report maliciously uttered to person's injury; uttering of such reports, calumny; (Law) false oral defamation (cf. LIBEL); so ∼ous *a.* **2.** *v.t.* utter slander about, defame falsely; hence ∼ER¹ *n.* [ME *sclaundre* f. AF (OF) *escla(u)ndre,* alt. f. OF *escandle* f. LL *scandalum* (see SCANDAL)]

slăng *n.* & *v.* **1.** *n.* words and phrases, or particular meanings of these, that are in common informal use, but generally considered not to form part of standard English, and often used deliberately for picturesqueness or novelty or unconventionality; words etc. either entirely peculiar to or used in special senses by some class or profession, cant, (*racing, thieves', theatrical, schoolboy,* slang). **2.** *v.i.* & *t.* use abusive language (to); ∼'**ing-match,** prolonged exchange of insults. [18th c. cant, of unkn. orig.]

slă'ng¦ȳ *a.* of the character of slang; fond of using slang; hence ∼ILY⁸ *adv.,* ∼INESS *n.* [t. prec. + -Y²]

slant (-ah-) *v., a.,* & *n.* **1.** *v.i.* & *t.* slope, diverge from a line, (cause to) lie or go obliquely to a vertical or horizontal line; present (news etc.) from a particular angle esp. in biased or unfair way. **2.** *a.* sloping, inclined, oblique; ∼**-eyed,** having slanting eyes, esp. Mongoloid; ∼ **height** (of cone, from vertex to periphery of base); hence ∼'WAYS, ∼'WISE, advs. **3.** *n.* slope, oblique position, (**on the** or **on a** ∼, aslant); way of regarding a thing, point of view, aspect, bias. [1 later var. of ME (now dial.) *slent,* f. ON **slenta,* *sletta* dash, throw, prob. infl. by ASLANT; 2 f. ME *aslonte, o-slante* ASLANT *adv.*; 3 17th c. f. v.]

slantendi'cular (-ahnt-) *a.* (joc.) slanting, oblique. [f. prec. after *perpendicular*]

slăp *v.* (**-pp-**), *n.,* & *adv.* **1.** *v.t.* & *i.* strike (as) with palm of hand, smack; ∼ (**down**), (colloq.) reprimand; lay forcefully (*slapped the money on the table; slapped a writ, a large fine, on the offender*); put hastily or carelessly (*slap some paint on the walls*); ∼ **on the back,** congratulate. **2.** *n.* such stroke (∼ **in the face,** lit., or fig. rebuff, insult; ∼ **on the back,** congratulations; ‖∼ **and tickle,** (colloq.) boisterous esp. amorous amusement). **3.** *adv.* with the suddenness or effectiveness or true aim of a blow, suddenly, just, quite, full, (*ran slap into him; hit me slap in the eye*). **4.** ∼(**-bang**), violently, noisily, headlong; ∼'**dash,** (adv.) vehemently, recklessly, (a.) impetuous, random, careless, happy-go-lucky, (n.) (1) such action or work, (2) roughcast, (v.t.) roughcast; ∼**-happy,** (colloq.) (1) punch-drunk, (2) cheerfully casual; ∼**-up** *a.,* (sl.) excellent, done regardless of expense. [v. f. II. & adv. f. LG *slapp* (imit.)]

***slă'pjăck** *n.* kind of pancake cooked on a griddle, = FLAPJACK. [f. prec. 1 + JACK¹]

slă'pstick *n.* flexible divided lath used by clown; (fig.) boisterous knockabout comedy. [f. SLAP 1 + STICK²]

slăsh *v.* & *n.* **1.** *v.i.* make sweeping or random cut(s) with sword, knife, whip, etc.; (in *pres. part.,* fig.) vigorously incisive or effective. **2.** *v.t.* make long narrow gash(es) in (∼ed sleeve etc., with slits cut to show lining or puffing of other material); make (one's way) by slashing; reduce or cut drastically (prices etc.); lash (person etc.) with whip, crack (whip); censure vigorously. **3.** Hence ∼'ER¹ (1, 2) *n.* **4.** *n.* (wound or slit made by) slashing cut; (colloq.) = SOLIDUS 2; *debris resulting from the felling or destruction of trees; (vulg.) act of urinating. [ME, perh. f. OF **esclaschier, esclachier* break in pieces]

slăt *n.* thin narrow piece of wood or metal or plastic, esp. used in sets in Venetian blind, bedstead, etc.

[ME *s(c)lat* f. OF *esclat* splinter etc. (*esclater* split f. Rom. *EX¹*clatare*, imit.)]

slāte¹ *n., a., & v.t.* **1.** *n.* fine-grained grey, green, or bluish-purple metamorphic rock easily split into flat smooth plates; piece of such plate used as roofing- -material; piece of it usu. framed in wood used for writing on with ∼-**pencil** (small rod of soft slate); CLEAN¹ *slate*; **clean the** ∼, rid oneself of or renounce obligations; **wipe the** ∼ **clean,** forgive past offences; ‖**on the** ∼, recorded as debt to be paid. **2.** *list of nominees for office etc. **3.** ∼-**black, -blue, -grey,** modifications of these colours such as occur in slate; ‖∼-**club,** benefit society with small weekly contributions and accounts nominally kept on slate; ∼- -**colour(ed),** (of) dark bluish or greenish grey; hence **slā′ty²** *a.* **4.** *a.* (made) of slate. **5.** *v.t.* cover with slates esp. as roofing. **6.** *nominate, propose (for office etc.), make arrangements for (event etc.). [ME *s(c)late* f. OF *esclate*, fem. form of *esclat* SLAT]

‖**slāte²** *v.t.* (colloq.) criticize severely, scold. [app. f. prec.]

slā′ter *n.* one who slates roofs etc.; wood-louse or similar crustacean. [ME, f. SLATE¹ + -ER¹]

slā′ther (-dh-) *n., & v.t.* **1.** *n.* *(colloq., usu. in *pl.*) large amount. **2.** (Austral. & NZ sl.) **(open)** ∼, unrestricted scope for action. **3.** *v.t.* *(colloq.) spread thickly; squander. [19th c.; orig. unkn.]

slā′ttern *n.* sluttish woman; hence ∼LY¹ *a.* [17th c., rel. to *slattering* (woman etc.) slovenly, f. dial. *slatter* to spill, slop, waste, frequent. of *slat* strike; see -ER⁵]

slau′ghter (-aw′t-) *n., & v.t.* **1.** *n.* killing of animal(s) for food; killing of many persons or animals at once or continuously, carnage, massacre; ∼**house,** place for killing animals for food, place of carnage; hence ∼OUS *a.* (literary). **2.** *v.t.* kill (people) in ruthless manner or on great scale; butcher, (Hist.) (colloq.) defeat utterly; hence ∼ER¹ *n.* [ME *slahter* f. ON *slahtr (ON *slátr* butcher's meat), f. **slah-* (see SLAY¹)]

Slav (-ahv) *n. & a.* **1.** *n.* member of group of peoples in Central & Eastern Europe speaking languages of Slavonic group; hence ∼′OPHIL(E), ∼′OPHOBE, *ns. & adjs.,* ∼′ISM (2, 3) *n.* **2.** *a.* of the Slavs; Slavonic. [ME *Sclave* f. med. L *Sclavus,* late Gk *Sklabos,* & f. med. L *Slavus*]

slāve *n., & v.i.* **1.** *n.* person who is the legal property of another or others and is bound to absolute obedience, human chattel (WHITE¹ *slave*); helpless victim *to* or *of* some dominating influence (*is a slave to duty, to drink, the slave of his wife's caprices,* etc.; *the slaves of fashion*); drudge, person having no leisure; (arch.) contemptible person; part of machine directly dependent on another; ant captured by others and made to serve them. **2.** ∼-**bangle** (of gold, glass, etc., worn by woman usu. above elbow); ∼-**born** (in slavery, of slave parents); ∼-**driver,** overseer of slaves at work, (fig.) hard taskmaster; hence ∼-**drive** *v.t.*; ∼- -**hunter,** person who hunted esp. Blacks to sell them as slaves; ∼ **labour,** (fig.) forced labour; ∼-**ship** (employed in slave-trade); ∼ **state,** (Hist.) southern State of US in which slavery was legal before Civil War; ∼-**trade,** procuring, transporting, and selling as slaves, of human beings, esp. African Blacks. **3.** *v.i.* work like slave, drudge, (*at, over*). [ME, f. OF *esclave* = med. L *sclavus, sclava* Slav (captive); see prec.]

slā′ver¹ *n.* ship or person engaged in slave-trade. [f. prec. + -ER¹]

slā′ver² *v. & n.* **1.** *v.i.* let spittle flow from mouth; show excessive sentimentality *over.* **2.** *v.t.* (arch.) let one's spittle fall upon (garment etc., or another's cheek in kissing). **3.** *n.* spittle running from mouth, (fig.) fulsome or servile flattery. [ME, prob. f. LDu.; cf. SLOBBER]

slā′verȳ *n.* condition of a slave; existence of slaves as an institution; exhausting labour, drudgery. [f. SLAVE + -ERY]

slā′vey *n.* (colloq.) maid-servant, esp. hard-worked one. [f. SLAVE + -Y³]

Sla′vic (-ah′-) *a. & n.* (language-group) of the Slavs, Slavonic. [f. SLAV + -IC]

slā′vish *a.* as of or having the characteristics of slaves; abject, servile, base; showing no attempt at development or originality; hence ∼LY² *adv.,* ∼NESS *n.* [f. SLAVE + -ISH¹]

Slavō′nian *a. & n.* Slovene; (arch.) Slavic. [f. med. L *S(c)lavonia* country of Slavs (*Sclavus* SLAV) + -AN]

Slavŏ′nic *a. & n.* **1.** *a.* of the Slavs; ∼ **languages,** group of Indo-European languages including Russian, Polish, Czech, etc. **2.** *n.* Slavonic language- -group; **Church** or **Old** (**Church**) ∼, earliest written Slavonic language, surviving as liturgical language in Orthodox Church. [f. med. L *S(c)lavonicus* (as prec.; see -IC)]

slaw *n.* cole-slaw. [Du. *sla,* shortened f. *salade* SALAD]

slay¹ *v.t.* (**slew** *pr.* -ōō; **slain**). (esp. literary or joc.) kill; hence (-)∼ER¹ *n.* [OE *slēan,* = OS, OHG *slahan,* ON *slá,* Goth. *slahan,* f. Gmc **slah-,* **slag-*]

slay². Var. of SLEY.

SLBM *abbr.* submarine-launched ballistic missile.

slea′z|ȳ *a.* (Of textile etc.) flimsy; shoddy, slatternly, tawdry, squalid; hence ∼iLY² *adv.,* ∼iNESS *n.* [17th c., of unkn. orig.]

***slĕd**¹ *n. & v.* (**-dd-**) = foll. [f. MLG *sledde,* = MHG *slitte,* OHG *slito, slita,* ON *slethi,* cogn. w. SLIDE¹]

slĕdge¹ *n. & v.* **1.** *n.* vehicle on runners instead of wheels for conveying loads or passengers esp. over snow, drawn by horses or dogs or reindeer or pushed or pulled by person(s); toboggan. **2.** *v.i. & t.* travel, go, convey, in sledge. [f. MDu. *sleedse,* rel. to SLED]

slĕdge² *n.* ∼(-**hammer**), blacksmith's or labourer's large heavy hammer; ∼-**hammer** *a.,* (as if) given by or using this (*sledge-hammer blows, arguments, style*). [OE *slecg,* = MDu. *slegge,* ON *sleggja,* f. **slagj-* (as SLAY¹)]

sleek *a., & v.t.* **1.** *a.* (Of hair, fur, skin, or animal or person with such hair etc.) smooth and glossy; looking well-fed and comfortable; (fig.) ingratiating; (of thing) smooth and polished; hence ∼LY² *adv.,* ∼′NESS *n.* **2.** *v.t.* make sleek, esp. by stroking or pressing down. [later var. of SLICK]

sleep¹ *n.* bodily condition such as that which normally recurs for several hours every night, in which nervous system is inactive, eyes closed, postural muscles relaxed, and consciousness nearly suspended, (BEAUTY *sleep*); **fall on** ∼, (arch.) fall asleep (lit., or fig. = die); **get to** ∼, manage to fall asleep; **go to** ∼, enter state of sleep, (of limb) be numbed by pressure; **in** one's ∼, while asleep; **the** ∼ **of the just,** sound sleep; **last** ∼, death; **put to** ∼, anaesthetize, (euphem.) kill (animal) painlessly); *a period of* or single indulgence in sleep (*shall try to get a sleep*); prolonged inert condition of hibernating animals; (fig.) rest, quiet, negligence, death, etc.; ∼-**walker,** ∼- -**walking,** (person) walking or performing other actions during sleep. [OE *slēp, slæp,* = OS *slāp,* OHG *slāf,* Goth. *slēps* f. Gmc *slæpaz]

sleep² *v.* (**slept**). **1.** *v.i.* be in state of sleep, fall or be asleep, (**let** ∼**ing dogs lie,** avoid stirring up trouble; ∼ **like a log** or **top,** sleep soundly); ∼ **in,** (1) sleep by night at one's place of work, (2) sleep late (intentionally or not); ∼ **on, over,** not decide (question) till next day; ∼ **out,** sleep by night out of doors, not rest at one's place of work; ∼ **through,** fail to be woken by. **2.** *v.t.* spend in or affect by sleeping (*sleep the hours away; slept off his vexation, hangover*). **3.** *v.i.* be inactive or dormant (*sword sleeps in the scabbard; passed through the sleeping village*); (of top) spin so steadily as to seem motionless; ∼**ing partner** (not sharing in actual work of a firm). **4.** lie in the grave. **5.** spend the night *at, in,* etc.; have sexual intercourse in bed *together* or *with*; ∼ **around,** (colloq.) be sexually promiscuous. **6.** *v.t.* provide sleeping accommodation for (*lodging- -house sleeps 300 men*). **7.** ∼′**ing-bag** (for sleeping esp.

out of doors in); **S∼ing Beauty,** fairy-tale heroine who slept for 100 years; ∼'**ing-car(riage),** railway coach provided with beds or berths; ∼'**ing-draught,** ∼'**ing-pill,** (to induce sleep); ∼**ing sickness,** disease with extreme lethargy caused by trypanosome transmitted by tsetse-fly bite; ∼'**ing-suit,** child's one-piece night-garment. [OE *slēpan, slǣpan,* = OS *slāpan,* OHG *slāfan,* Goth. *slēpan* f. Gmc **slǣpan*]

slee'per *n.* In vbl senses; ‖wooden beam or piece of other material used as support for rails etc.; (berth in) SLEEP²*ing-car*; ring worn in place of ear-ring in pierced ear; thing that is suddenly successful after being undistinguished; *sleeping-suit. [ME, f. prec. +-ER¹]

slee'pless *a.* unable to sleep; such that sleep is absent (*a sleepless night*); continually active or moving; hence ∼LY² *adv.,* ∼NESS *n.* [ME, f. SLEEP¹ +-LESS]

slee'p|y *a.* drowsy, ready for sleep; habitually indolent, unobservant, etc.; without stir or bustle (*a sleepy little town*); (of fruit, esp. pear) insipid and dry with incipient decay; ∼**yhead,** sleepy or inattentive person (esp. in *voc.*); *S∼y **Hollow chair** (deeply upholstered); ∼**y sickness,** ENCEPHALITIS lethargica; hence ∼iLY² *adv.,* ∼iNESS *n.* [ME, SLEEP¹ +-Y²]

sleet *n.,* & *v.i. impers.* **l.** *n.* snow and rain together; hail or snow melting while falling; *thin coating of ice; hence ∼'Y² *a.* **2.** *v.i.* **it** ∼**s** or **is** ∼**ing,** sleet falls. [ME, prob. f. OE **slēte, *slīete,* rel. to MLG *slōten* pl. hail, MHG *slōz(e)* f. Gmc **slautan-*]

sleeve *n.* **1.** part of garment that (partly) covers arm; *wear* one's HEART *on* one's *sleeve*; LAUGH *in* or *up* one's *sleeve*; *have* (card, plan, etc.) **up** one's ∼, in reserve, concealed but ready for use; **roll up** one's ∼**s,** prepare to fight or work. **2.** tube enclosing rod or smaller tube. **3.** wind-sock; drogue towed by aircraft. **4.** cover of gramophone record. **5.** ∼**-board,** small ironing-board for pressing sleeves; ∼**-coupling,** tube for connecting shafts or pipes; ∼**-link,** cuff-link; ∼**-nut,** long nut with right-hand and left-hand screw-threads for drawing together pipes or shafts conversely threaded; ∼**-note,** descriptive matter on record-sleeve; ∼**-valve** (in the form of a cylinder with sliding movement). **6.** Hence **(-)sleeveD²** (-vd) *a.* [OE *slēfe, slīefe, slȳf,* = NFris. *slēv, slīv*]

slee'veless (-vl-) *a.* having no sleeves; futile, unprofitable, (*sleeveless errand*). [OE *slīeflēas* (as prec., -LESS)]

sleigh (slā) *n.* & *v.* = SLEDGE¹ (esp. for travelling over snow); ∼**-bell,** one of tinkling bells often attached to harness of sleigh-horse etc. [orig. US, f. Du. *slee,* = OHG *slito* (see SLED)]‖

sleight (slīt) *n.* **1.** (arch.) dexterity, cunning, deceptive trick or device or movement. **2.** ∼ **of hand,** conjuring, display of dexterity, quickness of hand in fencing etc. [ME *sleghth,* f. ON *slægth* (*slægr* SLY; see -TH¹)]

sle'nder *a.* of small girth or breadth, (gracefully) not stout, (*slender stem, waist, pillar,* LORIS, *girl, hand*); scanty, slight, meagre, inadequate, relatively small, (*slender hopes, means, store, income, acquaintance with subject, foundations for belief*); hence ∼IZE (3) *v.t.* & *i.* (esp. in regard to human body), ∼LY² *adv.,* ∼NESS *n.* [ME, of unkn. orig.]

slept. See SLEEP².

sleuth (slōō-) *n.,* & *v.i.* (act as) detective; ∼**-hound,** bloodhound (lit. or fig.). [orig. in ∼*-hound,* ME f. *sleuth* f. ON *slóth* track, trail (cf. SLOT²),+HOUND¹]

slew¹, slue, (slōō) *v.* & *n.* **1.** *v.t.* & *i.* turn or swing forcibly with effort out of the forward or ordinary position (*round, to the left,* etc.). **2.** *n.* such change of position. [18th c., Naut., of unkn. orig.]

slew². See SLAY¹.

*slew³ (slōō) *n.* (colloq.) large number or quantity. [f. Ir. *sluagh*]

sley (slā) *n.* weaver's REED¹. [OE *slege,* = OS *slegi,* cogn. w. SLAY¹]

slice *n.* & *v.* **l.** *n.* thin broad piece or wedge cut off or out esp. from meat, bread, large fruit, pie, or cake; share, part taken or allotted or gained, (*a slice of territory, of the profits, of luck,* etc.); implement with thin broad blade for serving fish etc. or for scraping or chipping; (Golf) slicing stroke; ∼ **of life,** realistic representation of everyday experience. **2.** *v.t.* cut (*up*) into slices; cut (piece) *off* thing or *off*; go through (air etc.) with cutting motion; (Golf) strike (ball, or abs.) so that it deviates away from the striker; ∼**d bread** (esp. sliced and wrapped before being sold); hence ∼ABLE (-sa-) *a.* **3.** *v.i.* cut (*into* or *through*) as if to remove slice. **4.** Hence **(-)sli'ceR¹** (1, 2) *n.* [ME, f. OF *esclice* n., *esclicier* v. splinter, f. Frank. *slītjan* = OHG *slīzan;* cf. SLIT]

slick *a., n.,* & *v.t.* **1.** *a.* (colloq.) dextrous, not marred by bungling, carried smoothly through; superficially or pretentiously smooth and dextrous; slippery; smooth, sleek; glib. **2.** *n.* smooth patch of oil etc. on road or sea. **3.** *v.t.* make sleek; flatten *down* (one's hair etc.). [ME *slike(n),* prob. f. OE **slice, -slician* polish; cf. SLEEK]

*sli'cker *n.* plausible rogue; = CITY *slicker;* raincoat of smooth material; = SILVER¹*-fish* (2). [f. prec. +-ER¹]

slid. See foll.

slide¹ *v.* (**slid**). **1.** *v.t.* & *i.* (cause to) progress along smooth surface with continuous friction on same part of object progressing (cf. ROLL²) (*slid in sitting position down a grass slope; piston slides noiselessly up and down; slide the drawer into place*). **2.** *v.i.* glide over ice on one or both feet without skates under gravity or with momentum got by running; move quietly, glide, go smoothly along; ∼ **over,** barely touch upon (delicate subject etc.). **3.** take its own course (*let it slide*); **let things** ∼, be negligent, allow deterioration. **4.** go unconsciously or by imperceptible degrees (*slide into sin; slide from one note to another* in music). **5.** *v.t.* cause to move (*into* position) quietly or unobtrusively. **6.** Hence **sli'deR¹** (1, 2) *n.* [OE *slīdan,* = LG *slīden,* MHG *slīten*]

slide² *n.* **1.** track on ice made by persons sliding; slope prepared with snow or ice for tobogganing. **2.** act of sliding. **3.** inclined plane down which children, goods, etc., slide to lower level, chute. **4.** ∼**(-way),** part(s) of machine on or between which sliding part works. **5.** part of machine or instrument that slides; ∼**-rule,** ruler with sliding central piece, graduated logarithmically to allow quick multiplication and division of numbers; ∼**(-valve),** sliding piece that opens and closes aperture by sliding across it. **6.** thing slid into place, esp. glass holding object for microscope; mounted picture placed usu. in projector for viewing on screen etc.; ‖ = HAIR-*slide;* *∼ **fastener,** zip-fastener. [f. prec.]

sli'ding *a.* In vbl senses; ∼ **door** (drawn across aperture on slide, not turning on hinges); ∼ **keel,** centre-board; ∼ **roof,** part of roof (esp. in motor car) made able to slide and so form aperture; ∼ **scale,** scale of fees, taxes, wages, etc., that varies as a whole in accordance with variation of some standard; ∼ **seat,** seat able to slide to and fro on runners etc., esp. in racing-boat to adjust length of stroke. [f. SLIDE¹ +-ING²]

slight (-īt) *a.* **1.** slender, frail-looking, (*saw a slight figure approaching; supported by a slight framework*). **2.** inconsiderable (*has a slight cold; have made a slight inquiry, some slight inquiries, into it; the damage is very slight*); perceptible but not great (*a or the slight smell of gas; I have some slight acquaintance with the matter*). **3.** not much or great or thorough, inadequate, scanty, (*after slight inquiry; did it well with but slight inconvenience to himself; a conclusion based on very slight observation; paid him slight attention*); (in *superl.,* w. neg. or interrog.) any whatever (*paid not the slightest attention;* **not in the**

~est, not at all). **4.** Hence ~ISH¹ 2 *a.*, ~'LY² *adv.*, ~'NESS *n.* [ME *slyght, sleght,* f. ON **slehtr, sléttr,* level, smooth, = OS *sliht,* OHG *sleht,* Goth. *slaihts* f. Gmc *slehtaz]

slight² (-īt) *v.t.,* & *n.* **1.** *v.t.* treat or speak of (person etc.) as not worth attention, fail in courtesy or respect towards, markedly neglect. **2.** *n.* marked piece of neglect, omission of due respect etc., (**put a ~ upon,** slight). [f. prec.]

sli'ly. Var. of SLYLY.

slim *a.* & *v.* (-mm-). **1.** *a.* of small girth or thickness, slenderly built (and graceful), of long narrow shape; small, insufficient, (*a slim chance of success*); clever, artful, crafty, unscrupulous; ~'line *a.*, of slender design; hence ~'LY² *adv.*, ~'mish¹ 2 *a.*, ~'NESS *n.* **2.** *v.i.* make oneself slimmer by dieting, exercise, etc.; hence ~'mER¹, ~'mING¹, *ns.* **3.** *v.t.* make slim(mer). [Du. or LG, = MLG *slim(m)* slanting, MHG *slimp* f. Gmc *slimbaz]

slime *n.,* & *v.t.* **1.** *n.* oozy mud or other substance of similar consistency, e.g. liquid bitumen or mucous exudation of fish etc.; ~ **mould,** spore-bearing micro-organism secreting slime. **2.** *v.t.* cover with slime. [OE *slīm,* = MDu., MLG, MHG *slīm,* ON *slím,* rel. to L *limus* mud, Gk *limnē* marsh]

sli'm|y *a.* of the consistency of slime; covered or smeared with or full of slime; slippery, hard to hold; disgustingly dishonest, meek, or flattering; hence ~iLY² *adv.,* ~iNESS *n.* [ME, f. prec. + -Y²]

sling¹ *v.t.* (**slung**), & *n.* **1.** *v.t.* hurl (stone etc., or abs.) from sling; (colloq.) throw (~ **ink,** be author, journalist, etc.); suspend with sling, allow to swing suspended, arrange so as to be supported from above, hoist or transfer with sling; *sling* one's HOOK¹; ~-**cart** (in which load is slung from axle-tree); *~-**shot,** boy's catapult; **slung shot,** metal ball attached by thong etc. to wrist and used esp. by criminals as weapon. **2.** *n.* strap or string used with the hand to give impetus to small missile; belt, strap, etc., used to support hanging weight, e.g. rifle, ship's boat, goods being transferred; bandage looped round neck to support injured arm; ~-**back,** shoe without quarters, held in place by strap above heel. [sense 1 ME, prob. f. ON *slyngva*; 2 ME, prob. f. LDu.]

sling² *n.* sweetened drink of spirits (esp. gin) and water. [18th c., of unkn. orig.]

sli'nger *n.* In vbl senses; user or operator of sling. [ME, f. SLING¹ + -ER¹]

slink¹ *v.i.* (**slunk**). go in stealthy manner or with guilty or ashamed or sneaking air (*off, away, by,* etc.); hence ~'Y² *a.*, gracefully slender, (of garment) close-fitting and flowing, sinuous. [OE *slincan* crawl, = MLG *slinken* subside]

slink² *v.t.,* & *n.* **1.** *v.t.* (Of animal) produce (young, or abs.) prematurely. **2.** *n.* animal, esp. calf, so born; its flesh; ~'**weed,** plant believed to cause slinking. [app. f. prec.]

slip¹ *v.* (-pp-). **1.** *v.i.* slide unintentionally esp. for short distance, lose footing or balance or place by unintended sliding, (*slipped in the mud* or *over the edge and fell*; *blanket slipped off bed*; *foot slips out of stirrup, ring slips off finger*). **2.** go with sliding motion (*as the door closes the catch slips into place*; *slipped into her night-dress*); *slipped* DISC. **3.** escape restraint or capture by being slippery or hard to hold or by not being grasped (*eel, opportunity, slipped through his fingers*; *let reins slip out of his hands*); **let ~,** release from leash, utter inadvertently, miss (opportunity); **let ~ the dogs of war,** (poet.) begin war. **4.** make one's way unobserved or quietly or quickly (*how time slips away!*; *slip by, past*; *slip out of the room*; *just slip across to the baker's*; *errors will slip in*); ~ **off** or **away,** depart without leave-taking etc. **5.** make careless mistake; fall below normal standard, deteriorate, lapse; ~ **up,** (colloq.) fail, make a mistake, whence ~-*up* n., (colloq.) failure, blunder. **6.** *v.t.* let go from restraint of some kind (*slip greyhounds from leash*); detach (anchor) from ship, ||(carriage)

from moving train; (of animal) produce (young) prematurely; release (clutch of motor vehicle) for a moment. **7.** pull (garment etc.) hastily *on, off.* **8.** insert or transfer stealthily or casually or with gliding motion (*slipped a coin into the porter's hand, a white powder into her glass, the papers into his pocket, a marker between the pages*); move (stitch) to the other needle without knitting it; ~ **something over on,** outwit. **9.** escape from, give the slip to, (*dog slips his collar, prisoner his guard*; *the point had slipped my mind, memory, attention*). **10.** ||~-**carriage, -coach,** railway carriage on express for detaching at station where rest of train does not stop; ~-**case,** close-fitting case for book; ~-**cover,** (1) calico etc. cover for furniture out of use, *LOOSE¹ cover, (2) jacket or slip-case for book; ~-**hook** (with contrivance for releasing it readily when necessary); ~-**knot,** (1) knot that can be undone by a pull, (2) = RUNNING² *knot*; ~-**on,** ~-**over,** (shoe, garment, etc.) that can be easily slipped on and off; ~-**ring** (for sliding contact in dynamo or electric motor); ||~-**road** (for entering or leaving motorway etc.); ~-**rope** (with both ends on board so that casting loose either end frees ship from moorings); ~'**shod,** having shoes down at heel, slovenly, (fig., of speech, writing, speaker, writer, method of work, etc.) careless, unsystematic, loose in arrangement; ~'**slop,** (*a.*) = *slipshod* (fig.), (*n.*) slipshod writing etc., (as redupl. of *slop*) washy stuff (lit. or fig.), weak drink, slops, sentimental talk or writing; ~-**stitch** (1) *n.,* & *v.t.,* (sew with) loose stitch joining layers of fabric and not visible externally, (2) = slipped stitch (see sense 8); ~'**way,** shipbuilding or landing slip. **11.** Hence ~'PAGE (3, 6) *n.* [ME, prob. f. MLG *slippen* = MHG *slipfen*; cf. SLIPPERY]

slip² *n.* **1.** act of slipping, blunder, accidental piece of misconduct; **there's many a ~ 'twixt the cup and the lip,** nothing is certain till it has happened; **give** person **the ~,** escape from or evade him; ~ **of the tongue, pen,** thing said, written, accidentally for something else. **2.** loose covering or garment, e.g. pillowcase, petticoat; GYM-*slip*. **3.** leash to slip dogs. **4.** (in *sing.* or *pl.*) artificial slope of stone as landing-stage; inclined structure on which ships are built or repaired. **5.** long narrow strip of thin wood, paper, etc.; printer's proof on such paper, galley proof; small piece of paper for making notes etc. **6.** cutting taken from plant for grafting or planting, scion; **a ~ of a,** slim (girl etc.). **7.** (Cricket). fieldsman stationed for balls glancing off bat to off side or (**leg ~**) leg side behind wicket; (in *sing.* or *pl.*) this part of ground (*was caught in the slips* or *at slip*). **8.** finely ground clay in creamy mixture with water for coating or making pattern on earthenware; ~-**ware,** ware coated with slip. **9.** loss of distance travelled by ship or aircraft arising from nature of medium in which its propeller revolves; loss of movement of pulley etc. due to slipping of belt; ~-**stream,** current of air or water driven backward by revolving propeller or moving vehicle. [ME, f. prec.; sense 8 f. OE *slipa, slyppe* slime (cf. COWSLIP); senses 5 & 6 prob. f. MDu., MLG *slippe* cut, strip, etc.]

sli'pper *n.,* & *v.t.* **1.** *n.* light loose comfortable indoor shoe (HUNT¹ *the slipper*), whence ~ED² (-erd) *a.*; light slip-on shoe for dancing etc.; skid or shoe placed under wagon-wheel as drag; ~ **animalcule,** paramoecium; ||~-**bath** (shaped like slipper, with covered end; also of any public bath); ~-**wort,** calceolaria. **2.** *v.t.* chastise (child etc.) with slipper; hence ~ING¹ (1) *n.* [ME f. SLIP¹ + -ER¹]

sli'pper|y *a.* (Of ground) difficult to stand on, causing slips by its smoothness or muddiness, (fig., of subject) requiring tactful handling; (of object or person) hard to hold firmly owing to polish or sliminess or elusive motion, (fig.) unreliable, incalculable, shifty, unscrupulous; ~y **elm,** (medicinal inner bark of) N. Amer. red elm; hence ~iLY² *adv.,* ~iNESS *n.* [prob. made by Coverdale (1535) after Luther's *schlipfferig,*

MHG *slipferig* (*slipfern*, *slipfen* f. Gmc *slip-); partly f. (now dial.) *slipper* slippery f. OE *slipor*, MLG *slipper* f. Gmc *slip-; see -Y²]

slı̌'ppy *a.* (colloq.) slippery; ||**look** or **be** ~, look sharp, make haste. [f. SLIP¹ + -Y²]

slit *v.t.* (-**tt**-; **slit**), & *n.* **1.** *v.t.* cut or tear lengthwise, make long straight narrow incision or rent in, cut into strips, (*slit hide into thongs, sheet of metal into strips or rods*; *slit the envelope* (open); *has slit my coat-sleeve from shoulder to wrist*). **2.** *n.* long straight narrow incision; long narrow opening comparable to cut (*a slit is provided for the coin to drop through*; *his eyes, the windows, are mere slits*; *light passes through slit into spectroscope*; *the slits on the neck are gill-openings*); ~-**eyed,** having long narrow eyes; ~-**pocket** (with vertical opening giving access to pocket or to garment beneath); ~ **trench,** narrow trench for soldier or weapon. [ME *slitte*, rel. to OE, OS *slītan*, OHG *slīzan*, ON *slíta*]

slı̌'ther (-dh-) *v.i.*, & *n.* **1.** *v.i.* slide unsteadily, go with irregular slipping motion; hence ~Y² *a.* **2.** *n.* act of slithering. [ME var. of (now dial.) *slidder* f. OE *slid(e)rian* frequent. f. *slid*-, weak grade of *slīdan* SLIDE¹]

slı̌'ver *n.* & *v.* **1.** *n.* long thin piece cut or split off; piece of wood torn from tree or timber, splinter (esp. of exploded shell); strip of loose textile fibres after carding. **2.** *v.t.* & *i.* break off as sliver; break up into slivers; form into slivers. [ME, cogn. w. (now dial.) *slive* cleave f. OE *slīfan]

slı̌'vovitz (-ts) *n.* Balkan plum brandy. [f. Serbo-Croatian *šljivovica* (*šljiva* plum)]

slŏb *n.* (colloq.) stupid or careless or fat person; (Ir.) muddy land. [f. Ir. *slab* mud f. SLAB²]

slŏ'bber *v.* & *n.* **1.** *v.i.* & *t.* slaver (*over*). **2.** *v.t.* do (task) badly, botch, bungle. **3.** *n.* = SLAVER²; hence ~Y² *a.* [ME, = Du. *slobbern*, of imit. orig.]

slōe *n.* (small bluish-black wild plum, fruit of) blackthorn; ~-**eyed,** (1) having eyes of this colour, (2) slant-eyed; ~-**gin,** liqueur of sloes steeped in gin. [OE *slā(h)*, ~ MDu., MLG *slē*, OHG *slēha*, *slēwa* f. Gmc *slaihwōn]

slŏg *v.* (-**gg**-) & *n.* **1.** *v.i.* & *t.* hit hard and freq. wildly esp. in boxing or at cricket; walk or work doggedly (*on*, *away*); hence ~'GER¹ (-g-) *n.* **2.** *n.* hard random hit; (spell of) hard steady work. [19th c., orig. unkn.; cf. SLUG²]

slō'gan *n.* Scottish Highland war-cry; party cry, watchword, motto; short catchy phrase used in advertising. [f. Gael. *sluagh-ghairm* (*sluagh* army, *gairm* shout)]

sloid, sloyd, *n.* system (orig. Swedish) of manual training, esp. by means of wood-carving. [f. Sw. *slöjd* f. ON *slægth* SLEIGHT]

slōop *n.* small one-masted fore-and-aft-rigged vessel with mainsail and jib; ||~ (**of war**), (Hist.) small warship with guns on upper deck only; ~-**rigged,** rigged like sloop. [f. Du *sloep(e)*, of unkn. orig.]

slōot. See SLUIT.

slŏp¹ *n.* & *v.* (-**pp**-). **1.** *n.* (in *pl.*) dirty water or liquid, waste contents of kitchen or bedroom or prison vessels; (in *pl.* or *sing.*) unappetizing weak liquid food. **2.** quantity of liquid spilled or splashed; weakly sentimental utterance. **3.** ||~-**basin** (for receiving dregs of cups at table); ~-**pail** (for removing bedroom or kitchen slops). **4.** *v.i.* & *t.* spill, (allow to) flow over or *over* edge of vessel; carry slops *out* (in prison etc.); make mess with slops, spill or splash liquid on, (clothes, floor, etc.); move *about* in slovenly manner; ~ **over,** (fig.) gush, be maudlin. [earlier sense 'slush', prob. repr. OE *sloppe, rel. to *slyppe*; cf. COWSLIP]

slŏp² *n.* **1.** (in *pl.*) workman's loose outer clothes; ready-made or cheap clothing; clothes and bedding supplied to sailors in navy; (arch.) wide baggy trousers esp. as worn by sailors. **2.** ~-**room** (from which slops are issued aboard ship); ~-**seller,** -**shop,** (of ready-made clothes). [ME; cf. OE *oferslop*

surplice, MDu. (*over*)*slop*, ON (*yfir*)*sloppr* f. Gmc *slup-]

||**slŏp³** *n.* (sl.) policeman. [f. *ecilop*, back sl. = *police*]

slōpe *n.* & *v.* **1.** *n.* inclined position or direction, state in which one end or side is at higher level than the other, difference in level between two ends or sides of thing, rate at which this increases with distance etc., position in a line neither parallel nor perpendicular to level ground or a line serving as standard, (*there is always a certain slope in a ship's deck*; *cut this side straight and the other with a slope to the right*; *the whole slope may amount to 2 ft.*); piece of rising or falling ground; skiing-ground on side of hill or mountain; *the* position of rifle when sloped (see sense 3); hence ~'WISE (-pwīz) *adv.* **2.** *v.i.* have or take slope; lie or tend obliquely esp. to ground level; slant esp. up or down; (sl.) make *off*, go away. **3.** *v.t.* place or arrange or make in or at a slope; ~ **arms,** place rifle at a slope over shoulder. [f. ASLOPE]

slŏ'pp|y *a.* **1.** (Of ground) wet with rain, full of puddles; (of food etc.) watery and disagreeable; (of floor, table, etc.) wet with slops, having water etc. spilt on it. **2.** (Of work) unsystematic, not thorough; (of garment) ill-fitting or untidy; ~**y Joe,** loose sweater. **3.** (Of sentiment or talk) weakly emotional, maudlin. **4.** Hence ~ILY² *adv.*, ~INESS *n.* [f. SLOP¹ + -Y²]

slŏsh *n.* & *v.* **1.** *n.* slush; ||(sl.) heavy blow; quantity of liquid; sound or act of splashing; hence ~'Y² *a.* **2.** *v.t.* & *i.* splash about, move with splashing sound; (colloq.) pour (liquid) clumsily, pour liquid on; ||(sl.) hit, beat; ||(in *p.p.*, colloq.) drunk. [var. of SLUSH]

slŏt¹ *n.*, & *v.t.* (-**tt**-). **1.** *n.* groove, channel, slit, or long aperture, made in machine etc. to admit some other part, esp. slit for coin to operate ~-**machine** (for automatic retail of small articles, allowing spell of play at pin-table, etc., * = FRUIT *machine*); (colloq.) place in hierarchy, in scheme, in regularly broadcast programme, etc. **2.** *v.t.* provide with slot(s). **3.** *v.t.* & *i.* place or be placed (as if) into slot. [ME, ~ hollow of the breast, f. OF *esclot*, of unkn. orig.]

slŏt² *n.* track of deer etc. esp. as shown by footprints; deer's foot. [f. *esclot* hoof-print of horse, prob. f. ON *slóth* trail; cf. SLEUTH]

slōth *n.* **1.** undue slowness to act; hence ~'FUL *a.* **2.** S. Amer. long-haired slow-moving arboreal edentate mammal with curved long-clawed feet. **3.** ~-**bear,** large lipped black shaggy honey-eating bear (*Melursus ursinus*) of India etc.; ~-**monkey,** slow LORIS. [ME, f. SLOW + -TH¹]

slouch *v.* & *n.* **1.** *v.i.* droop, hang down loosely; go or stand or sit with loose ungainly attitude. **2.** *v.t.* bend one side of brim of (hat) downwards (opp. *cock*). **3.** *n.* slouching attitude or walk, stoop, downward bend of hat-brim (opp. *cock*); (sl.) incompetent or slovenly worker or operator or performance (esp. neg., *is no slouch at etc.*), whence ~'Y² *a.*; ~ **hat** (with wide flexible brim). [v. f. *slouching* a. f. n. (+ -ING²), 16th c., of unkn. orig.]

slough¹ (-ow) *n.* quagmire, swamp, miry place; (**the S**~ **of Despond** [w. ref. to Bunyan's *Pilgrim's Progress*], state of hopeless depression). [OE *slōh*, *slō(g)*, of unkn. orig.]

slough² (slŭf) *n.* & *v.* **1.** *n.* snake's cast skin, any part that an animal casts or moults; dead tissue that drops off from living flesh etc.; (fig.) habit etc. abandoned. **2.** *v.t.* cast off as slough. **3.** *v.i.* drop off *off* as slough; cast off slough. [ME, perh. rel. to LG *slu(we)* husk]

slou'ghy¹ (-ow'ī) *a.* like a slough; miry, muddy. [f. SLOUGH¹ + -Y²]

slou'ghy² (slŭ'fī) *a.* (Path.) being or resembling a slough. [f. SLOUGH² + -Y²]

Slō'vǎk *n.* & *a.* (member or language) of Slavonic people inhabiting Slovakia etc. [f. Slovak etc. *Slovák*, rel. to SLOVENE]

slo'ven (-ŭ'v-) *n.* person who is untidy or dirty in personal appearance, careless and lazy, or unmethodical; hence ∼LY¹ *a.*, ∼LY² *adv.*, ∼RY (4) *n.* [ME, perh. f. Flem. *sloef* dirty, or Du. *slof* careless]

Slovēne (-ō'vēn, -ovē'n), **Slove'nian**, *adjs.* & *ns.* (member or language) of Slavonic people in Slovenia etc. [f. G *Slowene* f. Styrian etc. *Slovenec* f. OSlav. *Slov-*, perh. cogn. w. *slovo* word; -IAN]

slow (-ō) *a.*, *adv.*, & *v.* **1.** *a.* not quick, deficient in speed, taking a relatively long time to traverse a distance or do a thing, (*slow and steady wins the race*; *slow music*, *train*; ∼ **handclap** (by spectators as sign of boredom); ∼ **and sure,** haste is risky; ∼ **but sure,** successful in the end); done or obtained over a long time, gradual (*slow growth*, *progress*); not producing or allowing quick motion; hence ∼LY² *adv.* **2.** tardy, reluctant, lingering, (*was not slow to defend himself*); not hasty or easily moved (*is slow to anger*); (of clock etc.) showing time earlier than correct time; dull-witted, stupid, (*is slow of speech, of wit*); (of fire) burning feebly; (of oven) not very hot; deficient in interest or liveliness, dull, tedious, (*business is very slow today*); ∼(**-moving**), (of goods) not finding ready sale; (of photographic film) needing long exposure, (of lens) having small aperture; (of cricket-pitch, tennis-court, putting-green, etc.) on which ball bounces or runs slowly. **3.** ∼ **bowler** (not imparting quick motion to ball); ∼'**coach,** person slow in action, dull of wit, or behind the times in opinions etc.; *slow* LORIS; ∼ **march** (of troops in funeral procession etc.); ∼ **-match** (slow-burning, for igniting explosives); ∼ **motion,** operation or speed of film in which actions etc. appear much slower than usual because of more rapid exposure or slower projection, simulation of this in real action; ∼ **neutron** (with low kinetic energy, esp. after moderation); ∼ **poison** (of which repeated doses are eventually injurious); *∼'**poke,** = *slowcoach*; ∼ **puncture** (causing only slow deflation of tyre); ∼ **reactor,** nuclear reactor using slow neutrons. **4.** Hence ∼'NESS *n.* **5.** *adv.* at slow pace, slowly, (esp. where slow gives the essential point: *how slow he climbs!*; *please read* or *go slow* or *slower*; *watch goes slow*; *slow-moving traffic*); see GO¹ 2. **6.** *v.i.* & *t.* ∼ (**down, up**), reduce one's speed or one's pace of living, reduce speed of (train, ship, etc.); ∼-**down** *n.*, action of slowing down, go-slow. [OE *slāw*, = OS *slêu*, OHG *slêo*, ON *slær*, *sljár*, *sljór* f. Gmc *slæwaz f. IE *slēwos]

slow-worm (slō'-wẽrm) *n.* small European legless lizard (*Anguis fragilis*), blindworm. [OE *slā-wyrm*; first element of uncert. orig., cf. OSw. *slā*, Norw. *slo*, etc., slow-worm; see WORM¹]

sloyd. See SLOID.

slŭb¹ *n.* & *a.* **1.** *n.* thick place or lump in yarn or thread. **2.** *a.* (Of material etc.) with irregular appearance caused by uneven thickness of warp. [19th c., of unkn. orig.]

slŭb² *n.*, & *v.t.* (-**bb**-). **1.** *n.* wool slightly twisted as preparation for spinning. **2.** *v.t.* twist thus. [n. f. v., 18th c., of unkn. orig.]

slŭbberdĕgŭ'llion (-lyon) *n.* (arch.) worthless slovenly fellow. [f. *slubber* v. = SLOBBER, + fanciful ending]

slŭdge *n.* thick greasy mud; sewage (ACTIVATE*d sludge*); muddy or slushy sediment or deposit; accumulation of dirty oil, esp. in sump of internal combustion engine; sea-ice newly formed in small pieces; hence **slŭ'dgy²** *a.* [cf. SLUSH]

slue. See SLEW¹.

slŭg¹ *n.* **1.** shell-less gastropod often destructive to small plants. **2.** bullet esp. of irregular shape; missile for airgun; roundish lump of metal; (Print.) metal bar used in spacing; line of type in linotype printing. **3.** unit of mass, given acceleration of 1 ft. per sec. per sec. by force of 1 lb. **4.** *tot of liquor. [ME *slugg(e)* sluggard, prob. f. Scand.]

***slŭg²** *v.* (-**gg**-) & *n.* (strike with) hard blow. [19th c., orig. unkn.; cf. SLOG]

slŭ'gabĕd *n.* (arch.) lazy person who lies late in bed. [f. *slug* v. (see foll.) + ABED]

slŭ'ggard *n.* lazy sluggish person. [ME, f. *slug* v. be slothful (prob. f. Scand.; cf. SLUG¹) + -ARD]

slŭ'ggish (-gī-) *a.* inert, inactive, torpid, indolent, slow-moving, (*a sluggish stream, circulation, market, temper, person*); hence ∼LY² *adv.*, ∼NESS *n.* [ME, f. SLUG¹ or *slug* v. (see prec.) + -ISH¹]

sluice (-ōōs) *n.* & *v.* **1.** ∼(**-gate, -valve**), sliding gate or other contrivance for controlling volume or flow of water, floodgate; water above or below or issuing through floodgate; ∼(-**way**), artificial water-channel esp. for washing ore; (place for) rinsing. **2.** *v.t.* provide with sluice(s); flood with water from sluice; rinse; pour or throw water freely upon; wash *out* or *away* with flow of water. **3.** *v.i.* (of water) rush out etc. (as) from sluice. [ME, f. OF *escluse* f. Gallo-Rom. *exclusa (*aqua* water), fem. p.p. (as n.) of L *excludere* EXCLUDE]

sluit (-ōōt), **slōōt,** *n.* (S. Afr.) deep gully formed by heavy rain. [Afrik. *sluit* f. Du. *sloot* ditch]

slŭm *n.*, & *v.i.* (-**mm**-). **1.** *n.* overcrowded and squalid back street, district, etc., of city, inhabited by very poor people; ∼ **clearance,** demolition of slums and movement of their inhabitants to better housing; hence ∼'**my²** *a.* **2.** *v.i.* go about the slums to visit philanthropically or through curiosity or examine condition of inhabitants; behave like inhabitant of slums. [19th c. cant]

slŭ'mber *v.i.* & *t.*, & *n.* sleep (esp. with kind or manner specified or implied, or in poet. or rhet. or fig. use; *fell into a troubled slumber*; *his slumbers were interrupted by a knock*; *successors of Alaric had slumbered in a long peace*); ∼ **away,** spend (time) in slumber; ∼-**wear,** (Commerc.) night-clothes; hence ∼ER¹ *n.*, **slŭ'mb(e)rous** *a.* [ME *slumere* etc., f. *slŭmen* v. or *slŭme* n. (OE *slŭma*) + -ER⁵; -b- as in *number*]

slŭmp *n.*, & *v.i.* **1.** *n.* sudden or great and prolonged fall in prices or values, or diminution of demand for commodity or interest taken in subject or undertaking. **2.** *v.i.* undergo slump; fall in price; fall through, fail utterly; subside limply (*he slumped to the ground, into a chair*). [17th c., orig. 'sink in bog', imit.]

slŭng. See SLING¹.

slŭnk. See SLINK¹.

slŭr *v.* (-**rr**-) & *n.* **1.** *v.t.* & *i.* write or pronounce indistinctly with letters or sounds running into one another. **2.** *v.t.* (Mus.) perform (notes) legato; mark (notes) with slur. **3.** pass (fault, fact, etc.) lightly *over*, conceal or minimize; (arch. or US) put slur upon (person, character), make insinuations against. **4.** *n.* imputation, blame, stigma, (*he put a slur upon me*; *it is no slur on his reputation*); piece of slurring in handwriting, pronunciation, or singing; (Mus.) curved line to show that two or more notes are to be sung to one syllable or played or sung legato. [17th c., of unkn. orig.]

slŭrp *n.*, & *v.t.* (colloq.) eat(ing) or drink(ing) noisily. [f. Du. *slurpen, slorpen*]

slŭ'rry *n.* thin liquid cement; suspension of fine solid material in liquid, esp. water; thin mud; sticky muddy residue separated from coal at pit-head washing plants. [ME, rel. to dial. *slur* thin mud]

slŭsh *n.* watery mud or thawing snow; (fig.) silly sentiment; ∼ **fund,** money used to bribe public servants; hence ∼'y² *a.* [17th c., also *sludge* and *slutch* orig. unkn.]

slŭt *n.* slovenly woman, slattern; hussy; (arch., joc.) girl; hence ∼'tERY (4) *n.*, ∼'tISH¹ *a.* [ME; orig. unkn.]

slȳ *a.* (∼'er, ∼'est). cunning, wily, hypocritical, practising secrecy or stealth (∼ **dog,** person who keeps his peccadilloes or pleasures quiet), done etc. in secret (**on the** ∼, privately, covertly, without publicity); (Austral. & NZ sl.) illicit (liquor etc.); knowing, arch, bantering, insinuating, ironical; ∼'**boots,** (colloq.) sly person; hence ∼'LY² *adv.*, ∼'NESS *n.* [ME *sleh* etc. f. ON *slœgr* cunning, orig.

'able to strike' f. *slóg-* past stem of *slá* strike; cf. SLEIGHT]

slype *n.* covered way or passage between cathedral etc. transept and chapter-house or deanery. [perh. = *slipe* long narrow piece of ground, = SLIP² 5]

SM *abbr.* Sergeant-Major; short metre.

Sm *symb.* samarium.

smăck¹ *n.*, & *v.i.* **1.** *n.* flavour, taste that suggests presence of something; barely discernible amount *of* some food-material etc. or *of* a quality etc. present in dish or person's character, (*has a smack of ginger, of the cask, in it, of recklessness, of the old Adam, in him*). **2.** *v.i.* taste slightly *of*, suggest by taste or otherwise the presence or effects *of* (*wine smacking of the cork; his manner smacked of superciliousness*). [OE *smæc*, = MDu., MLG *smak*, OHG *-smac*]

smăck² *n.*, *v.*, & *adv.* **1.** *n.* slight sharp sound as of surface struck with palm of hand, of lips parted suddenly, or of whip cracked; blow with palm of hand or flat object, slap; hard hit at cricket; loud kiss (*gave her a hearty smack*); **have a ~ at**, (colloq.) attempt, attack; **~ in the eye** or **face**, (fig.) rebuff. **2.** *v.t.* slap (person's face etc., or abs.) with palm etc.; part (lips) noisily in eager anticipation or enjoyment of food or other delight; crack (whip). **3.** *v.t.* & *i.* move with sound of smack **4.** *adv.* (colloq.) with a smack; in sudden direct violent way, exactly (*went smack through windows, into ditch; hit it smack in the centre*). [f. MDu. *smack(en)*, of imit. orig.]

smăck³ *n.* single-masted sailing-boat for coasting or fishing. [f. Du. *smak*, earlier *smacke*, of unkn. orig.]

smă'cker *n.* (sl.) **1.** loud kiss; resounding blow. **2.** ||*£*1; *$*1. [f. SMACK² + -ER¹]

smăckeroo' *n.* (sl.) = prec. **2.** [alt. f. prec.]

small (-awl) *a.*, *n.*, & *adv.* **1.** *a.* not large, of deficient or comparatively little size or strength or power or number, (usu. without emotional implications of *little*); (of agent) not doing thing on large scale (*small farmer, shopkeeper*); consisting of fine particles (*small gravel, shot*); young, far from fully grown or developed; *small* DEER, FRY¹, HOURS; *small profits and quick* RETURN²*s*; **the ~est room**, (colloq.) lavatory in house; STILL¹ *small* voice; *in a small* WAY 12 **2.** (As distinctive epithet) of the smaller kind; **feel**, **look**, **~**, be humiliated; *small* ARM²*s*, BEER; **~-bore** (of firearm, esp. of .22 inch calibre); **~ capital**, letter shaped like capital but only about as high as lower--case letter; **~ change**, coins opp. notes, (fig.) trivial remarks; *small* CIRCLE¹; **~ claim** (as *small debt*); **~--clothes**, (arch.) knee-breeches; **~ craft**, boats; ||**~ debt** (not too large to be recovered by action in county or sheriff court); **~'goods**, (Austral.) delicatessen meats; **~ gross**, ten dozen; ||**~'holder**, owner or user of **~'holding**, agricultural holding smaller than farm; *small* INTESTINE¹; **~ letter** (not capital); *small* MERCY; **~'pox**, acute contagious virus disease, with fever and pustules usu. leaving permanent scars; **~ print**, matter printed in small type, (fig.) inconspicuous unfavourable limitations etc. in a contract; **~-scale**, made or occurring on a small SCALE³ or in small amounts; *small* SLAM²; **~-sword**, light tapering thrusting-sword, esp. for duelling; **~--time**, (colloq.) unimportant or petty; ||**~'wares**, haberdashery. **3.** not much (*paid small attention to etiquette*); **no ~**, considerable, a good deal of, (*there was no small excitement about it*); **has ~ Latin**, knows little of it; **~ wonder**, that is not very surprising. **4.** unimportant, trifling, (*grew from small beginnings; here is a small token of our esteem; is only a small matter*); **~ card** (of low rank in suit); **~ talk**, unimportant social conversations. **5.** socially undistinguished, poor, obscure, humble; **great and ~**, all classes; *in a small* WAY 12. **6.** morally mean, ungenerous, petty, paltry, (*his small spiteful nature; only a small man would think of that at such a time; I call it small of him to remind me of it*); **~-minded**, petty or rigid in one's views. **7.** Hence **~'ISH¹** 2 *a.*, **~'NESS** *n.* **8.** *n.* the slenderest part of

something, esp. **~ of the back**, hinder part of waist; ||(in *pl.*, colloq.) small articles of laundry, esp. underwear. **9.** *adv.* into small pieces (*chop it small*); SING *small.* [OE *smæl*, = OS, OHG *smal*, ON *smalr*, Goth. *smals* f. Gmc **smalaz*]

sma'llage (-aw'l-) *n.* wild celery. [ME, f. SMALL + obs. *ache* f. OF *ache* f. L f. Gk *apion* parsley]

smalt (-awlt, -ŏlt) *n.* glass coloured blue with cobalt; pigment made by pulverizing this. [F, f. It. *smalto* f. Gmc, cogn. w. SMELT¹]

sma̅rm *v.t.* (colloq.) smooth, plaster *down*; flatter fulsomely; hence **~'Y²** *a.* [orig. dial., also *smalm*, of uncert. orig.]

sma̅rt¹ *v.i.*, & *n.* **1.** *v.i.* (Of person or part of body, or of wound lit. or fig. or the missile or insult etc. that has inflicted it) feel or give acute pain or distress (*my finger smarts; smarting with nettle-stings, under disappointment,* etc.; *with the gibe yet smarting in his brain*); **~ for**, be paid out for, suffer consequences of, (esp. as threat; *you shall smart for this*). **2.** *n.* bodily or mental sharp pain, stinging sensation. **3.** **~-money** (paid or exacted as penalty or compensation); **~'weed**, the water-pepper. [v. f. OE *smeortan* = MDu. *smerten*, OHG *smerzan* f. WG **smert-*; n. ME, app. f. OE **smiortu* (as foll.)]

sma̅rt² *a.* & *adv.* **1.** *a.* severe enough to cause pain, sharp, vigorous, lively, brisk, (*gave him a smart rap over the knuckles; had a smart skirmish, walk, bout of toothache; went off at a smart pace*). **2.** clever, ingenious, showing quick wit or ingenuity, keen in bargaining, quick to take advantage, (*a smart talker, retort, saying, device, invention*); (of employee etc.) ready and intelligent; (of transaction) selfishly clever to verge of dishonesty; unscrupulously clever; **look ~**, make haste; **~ a'lec(k)**, **a'lick**, (ă'lǐk), **~'Y²**, **~'y-boots**, **~'y--pants**, (derog.) bumptious would-be clever person. **3.** bright and fresh in appearance, neat, in perfect order or repair, in gay or fashionable clothes, well groomed, showing bright colours or new paint, (*smart clothes; a smart garden; person, house, ship, looks very smart*). **4.** conspicuous in society, leading the fashion, stylish, (*smart people; the smart set*). **5.** *adv.* smartly. **6.** Hence **~'EN⁶** *v.t.* & *i.* (usu. *up*), **~'ISH¹** 2 *a.* & *adv.*, **~'LY²** *adv.*, **~'NESS** *n.* [OE *smeart*, rel. to *smeortan* (see prec.)]

smăsh *v.*, *n.*, & *adv.* **1.** *v.t.* & *i.* **~** (**up**), break utterly to pieces, shatter; break *in* with crushing blow; **~-and--grab** *a.*, (colloq.) (of robbery) by breaking shop--window and snatching goods etc.; **~-up** *n.*, complete smash, violent collision of vehicles. **2.** *v.t.* utterly rout and disorganize (enemy); hit (lawn--tennis etc. ball) downwards over net with great force; move with great force (*smashed his fist down on the table*); (in *p.p.*, sl.) drunk. **3.** *v.i.* (Of business firm) break, go bankrupt, come to grief; (of vehicle etc.) crash into another or an obstacle. **4.** Hence **~'ER¹** *n.*, **~'ING²** *a.*, (colloq.) unusually good, superlative, (person or thing). **5.** *n.* (sound of) breaking to pieces; violent fall or collision or disaster (**go to ~**, be spoilt or disorganized or ruined); smashing stroke in lawn tennis etc.; violent blow with fist etc.; bankruptcy, series of commercial failures; drink of spirit (esp. brandy) and water iced and flavoured; **~ hit**, ***~**, (sl.) notably successful play, film, song, etc. **6.** *adv.* (w. vbs. of motion) with a smash (*went smash into a goods train*). [18th c., prob. imit., after *smack, smite,* and *bash, mash,* etc.]

smătch *n.* = SMACK¹ *n.* [ME, app. f. OE *smæc* SMACK¹, infl. by *smatch* v. f. OE *smæccan*]

smă'tter, **smă'tter|ing**, *ns.* slight superficial knowledge of a language or subject; so **~ER¹** *n.* [ME *smatter* talk ignorantly, prate, of unkn. orig., + -ING¹]

smāze *n.* mixture of smoke and haze. [portmanteau wd; cf. SMOG.]

smear *v.t.*, & *n.* **1.** *v.t.* daub with greasy or sticky substance or with something that stains, (of grease etc.) make marks on; blot, obscure outline of, (writing, drawing); defame character of, (seek to) discredit publicly. **2.** *n.* blotch made by smearing; (specimen of) material smeared on microscope slide etc. for examination; attempt at defamation; hence ∿'y² *a.* [OE *smierwan*, = OHG *smirwen*, ON *smyrva*, *smyrja* f. Gmc **smerwjan*]

smĕ′gm|a *n.* sebaceous secretion in folds of the skin, csp. of the foreskin; hence ∿ᴬᵀɪᴄ *a.* [L, f. Gk *smēgma* -*atos* detergent (*smēkhō* cleanse)]

smĕll *n.* & *v.* (**smelt** or ∿**ed**). **1.** *n.* faculty of perception through response of brain to action of odour on nose (*smell is less acute in man than in most animals; has a fine sense of smell; is perceptible to smell as well as sight*); quality in substances that affects this sense, odour, (*has no, a sweet, pungent, disgusting, peculiar, smell; the smell of thyme, carrion*); unpleasant odour, whence ∿'ʏ² *a.*; act of inhaling in order to ascertain smell (*take a smell at it*); hence ∿-ʟᴇss *a.* **2.** *v.t.* perceive smell of, detect presence of by smell, (*am sure I smell gas; horses smelt the water a mile off; smell a* ʀᴀᴛ¹), whence ∿'ᴀʙʟᴇ *a.*; inhale smell of, set one's sense of smell to work at (*smelt it to see if it was high*); (of dog) hunt out by smell, (fig. of person) find *out* (secret, plotter, etc.) by investigation. **3.** *v.i.* perceive smells, have sense of smell; emit smell (usu. of kind specified by *a.* or *adv.*), suggest or recall the smell *of*, (*flowers that do not smell; smells sweet, nice, disgustingly, of garlic, of brandy*); (of dog or fig. of person) sniff or search *about*; ∿ **at**, inhale smell of; ∿ **of**, (fig.) be suggestive of (∿ **of the lamp**, seem to have been composed laboriously; ∿ **of the shop**, be over-anxious to sell one's wares, or over- -technical). **4.** stink, be rank, (*his breath smells*); seem from the smell to be (*food smells good; milk smells sour*). **5.** ∿'**ing-bottle**, small bottle of ∿'**ing-salts**, ammonium carbonate mixed with scent to be sniffed as restorative in faintness etc. [ME *smel(le)*, prob. f. OE, of unkn. orig.]

smĕ′ller *n.* In vbl senses; (sl.) nose. [f. prec. + -ᴇʀ¹]

smĕlt¹ *v.t.* extract metal from (ore) by melting; extract (metal) from ore by melting; hence ∿ᴇʀ¹ (1, 2), ∿'ᴇʀʏ (3), *ns.* [f. MDu., MLG *smelten*, = OHG *smelzan*, cogn. w. ᴍᴇʟᴛ²]

smĕlt² *n.* (*pl.* ∿s *or* ∿). small green and silver fish of genus *Osmerus* etc. allied to salmon and prized as food. [OE, of uncert. orig.; cf. �s ᴍᴏʟᴛ]

smĕlt³. See sᴍᴇʟʟ.

smew *n.* small species of merganser (*Mergus albellus*). [17th c., cogn. w. *smeath* & *smee* = smew, widgeon, etc.]

*smĭ′dgen, *smĭ′dgin, *n.* (colloq.) small bit or amount. [perh. f. syn. *smitch*; cf. dial. *smitch* wood- -smoke]

smĭ′lăx *n.* climbing shrub of genus, *Smilax*, root-stocks of some species of which yield sarsaparilla; climbing kind of asparagus much used in decoration. [L f. Gk, = bindweed]

smīle *v.* & *n.* **1.** *v.i.* relax features, often with parting of lips and upward turn of their ends, into pleased or kind or gently sceptical expression or forced imitation of these, look (*up*)*on* or *at* with such expression, (*smile sweetly, indulgently, cynically, bitterly*); ∿ **at**, (fig.) ridicule or show indifference to; **come up smiling**, (colloq.) recover from adversity and cheerfully face what is to come (like boxer rising at start of new round). **2.** be or appear propitious, have bright aspect (*the smiling countryside*); seem to look propitiously (*up*)*on* (*fortune smiled on us*). **3.** *v.t.* express by smiling (*smile a welcome*, one's *consent, appreciation*, etc.); give (smile) of specified kind (*smiled an ironical, a curious, smile*); drive (person's vexation etc.) *away*, bring (person) *into* or *out* of a mood, by smiling. **4.** *n.* act of smiling; smiling expression or aspect; hence **smĭ′lᴇʀ¹** *n.*, ∿-ʟᴇss (-l-l-) *a.* [ME, perh. f. Scand., cogn. w. sᴍɪʀᴋ; cf. OHG **smīlan* (part. *smīlenter*)]

smĭrch *v.t.*, & *n.* stain, soil, smear, spot, (lit., or fig., *a smirched reputation*). [ME, of unkn. orig.]

smĭrk *v.i.*, & *n.* (put on or wear) affected or conceited or silly smile. [OE *sme(a)rcian* f. **smar-*, **smer-* as in OE *smerian* laugh at]

smīte *v.* (**smote** *pr.* smōt; **smi′tten** or arch. **smit,** *pr.* smĭt-) & *n.* **1.** *v.t.* (arch., literary, or joc.) strike, hit, (*whosoever shall smite thee on thy right cheek; smote the harp- -strings; smite off his head; smote the first ball for four*); inflict severe defeat on (*smite person* ʜɪᴘ¹ *and thigh*); chastise (*God shall smite thee*); have sudden effect on (*an idea, his conscience, smote him*); (esp. in *p.p.*) strike or seize or infect or possess *with* disease or desire or emotion or fascination (*city, person, smitten with plague, palsy; am smitten with her charms or her* or abs.; *smitten with a desire to*). **2.** *v.i.* (arch., literary, or joc.) come forcibly or abruptly (*up*)*on* (*wave smote upon the cliff; sun's rays smiting upon him; sound smites upon the ear*). **3.** (arch. colloq.) blow, stroke, attempt. [OE *smītan* smear, = MDu., MLG *smīten*, OHG *smīzan*, Goth. -*smeitan* f. Gmc **smītan*]

smith *n.*, & *v.t.* **1.** *n.* worker in metal (esp. in comb., as ɢᴏʟᴅsmith, ᴛɪɴsmith); one who forges iron, black- smith; (fig.) one who creates (*song-smith*). **2.** *v.t.* make or treat by forging. [OE, = MDu. *smid*, *smit*, OHG *smid*, ON *smithr*, Goth. -*smitha* f. Gmc **smithaz*]

smitheree′ns (-dherē′nz), **smi′thers** (-dherz), *ns. pl.* small fragments (*smash* etc. *to* or *into smither(een)s*). [*smithereens* f. *smithers* (19th c., of unkn. orig.) + -ᴇᴇɴ]

smi′thery *n.* smith's work; ‖(esp. in naval dockyards) smithy. [f. sᴍɪᴛʜ + -ᴇʀʏ]

smi′thy (-dhǐ) *n.* blacksmith's workshop, forge, [ME, f. ON *smithja*, = OE *smiththe*, MLG *sme(d)e*, MDu. *smisse*, OHG *smidda*, *smitta*]

smi′tten. See sᴍɪᴛᴇ.

smŏck *n.*, & *v.t.* **1.** *n.* child's overall; ∿(-**frock**), (esp. European) field-labourer's former outer linen garment of shirtlike shape and with upper part closely gathered; similar garment worn by artists etc.; ∿-**mill**, windmill of which the cap only and not the body revolves. **2.** *v.t.* adorn with smocking. [OE *smoc*, = OHG *smoccho*, ON *smokkr*, prob. rel. to OE *smūgan* creep, ON *smjúga* put on a garment]

smŏ′cking *n.* honeycomb ornamentation on garment of which the basis is close gathers as on smock-frock. [f. prec. + -ɪɴɢ¹]

smŏg *n.* fog intensified by smoke; hence ∿'ɢʏ² (-gǐ) *a.* [portmanteau wd]

smōke¹ *n.* **1.** visible volatile products of burning, esp. with carbon etc. in suspension, (*a column, cloud, of smoke*); the (ʙɪɢ) *smoke*; **end, go up, in** ∿, come to nothing; *no smoke without* ꜰɪʀᴇ¹; **from** ∿ **into smother**, (arch.) from one evil to another or a worse; **like** ∿, (sl.) without hindrance or difficulty, rapidly, easily. **2.** spell of tobacco-smoking (*must have a smoke*); break for smoking during work. **3.** (sl.) cigar(ette). **4.** ∿ **abatement**, reduction of amount of smoke from chimneys etc. in towns; ∿-**ball**, (1) puff-ball, (2) projectile filled with material emitting dense smoke used to conceal military operations etc.; ∿-**bomb** (emitting dense smoke on bursting); ∿-**bush,** = *smoke-plant*; ∿-**dried**, cured in smoke; ∿-**ho**, (Austral. & NZ colloq.) = sᴍᴏᴋᴏ; ∿-**jack**, machine for turning roasting-spit by use of current of hot air in chimney; ∿-**plant, -tree**, ornamental shrub of genus *Cotinus* with feathery smokelike fruit-stalks; *smoke- -ring* ¹⁴; ∿-**rocket**, contrivance for injecting smoke into drain to discover leak; ∿-**screen**, cloud of smoke (lit. or fig.) diffused to hide operations; *smoke-* sᴛᴀᴄᴋ; ∿-**stone**, cairngorm; ∿-**tunnel**, form of wind- -tunnel using smoke filaments to detect motion of air. **5.** Hence ∿'ʟᴇss (-kl-) *a.* free from smoke, producing little or no smoke, (esp. of areas where smoke from chimneys is not allowed, or for fuel for use in such conditions). [OE *smoca*, f. weak grade of st. of *smēocan* emit smoke]

smōke² *v.* **1.** *v.i.* emit smoke or steam or visible vapour (*smoking ruins, horse*); (of lamp etc.) burn badly with the emission of smoke, (of chimney or fire) discharge smoke into room. **2.** *v.t.* colour or darken or obscure, spoil taste of in cooking, preserve or cure, suffocate, rid of insects etc., by action of smoke; (arch.) make fun of; **~d glass** (darkened with smoke for looking at sun etc.); **~ out**, discover by thorough investigation, destroy (wasps, their nest, etc.) by injecting smoke. **3.** breathe in and out smoke from (tobacco-pipe, cigar, cigarette, tobacco, opium, marijuana, etc.; *put that in your* PIPE¹ *and smoke it*); bring oneself into specified state by smoking; hence **smō′k**ABLE *a.* **4.** *v.i.* smoke tobacco (*smokes too much* or *like a chimney; do you, will you, smoke?*); ||**~-room,** smoking-room. [OE *smocian* (as prec.)]

smō′ker *n.* In vbl senses; person who habitually smokes tobacco (**~'s cough, heart, throat,** ailments due to excessive smoking); smoking--compartment on train; smoking-concert, men's informal entertainment. [f. prec.+-ER¹]

smō′king *n.* In vbl senses; **~-cap, -jacket,** (of ornamental kind formerly worn while one smoked); **~-compartment** (for smokers on railway-train); ||**~-concert** (at which smoking is allowed); **~-mixture,** blend of tobaccos for smoking in pipe; **~-room** (in hotel or house, kept for smoking in); **~-room** a., (of talk etc., esp.) such as is suited for men only. [f. SMOKE²+-ING¹]

smō′kō *n. (pl.* **~s).** (Austral. & NZ colloq.) stoppage of work for rest and smoke; tea break; smoking -concert. [f. SMOKE¹+-o]

smō′k|y *a.* emitting, veiled or filled with, obscured (as) with, stained with, coloured like, smoke (*smoky fire, city, room, ceiling, quartz*); hence **~**ILY² *adv.,* **~**INESS *n.* [ME, f. SMOKE¹+-Y²]

***smō′lder.** See SMOULDER.

smŏlt *n.* young salmon migrating to sea for first time. [ME, orig. Sc. & N. Engl.; of unkn. orig.]

smŏŏch *v.i.,* & *n.* (colloq.) (engage in) spell of kissing and caressing or slow dancing close together. [f. dial. *smouch,* imit.]

smōŏth¹ (-dh) *a.* & *adv.* **1.** *a.* having relatively even and regular surface, free from perceptible projections or lumps or indentations or roughness or (of liquid) undulations, not wrinkled or pitted or scored or hairy, that can be traversed without hindrance, (*smooth skin, surface, paste, tyre, lake, brow, chin, path*); **~ muscle** (without striations, usu. in thin sheet and performing involuntary functions); **in ~ water,** having passed obstacles or difficulties. **2.** not harsh in sound or taste (*smooth* BREATHING); (of verse) having easy and correct rhythm; (of movement etc.) not suddenly varying, not jerky; (of movement, journey, etc.) unaffected by difficulties or adverse conditions. **3.** equable, unruffled, polite, conciliatory, complimentary, flattering, (*smooth person, temper, manners, speech*); **~ face** hypocritically friendly); **~ things,** (esp.) flattery or insincere encouragement; **~ tongue,** insincerely flattering speech. **4.** **~-bore,** gun with unrifled barrel. **5.** Hence **~**ISH¹² *a.,* **~**'LY² *adv.,* **~**'NESS *n.* **6.** *adv.* smoothly (*course of true love never did run smooth*). [OE *smōth,* of unkn. orig.]

smōŏth² (-dh) *v.* & *i.* **1.** *v.t.* make or become smooth; remove accidental minor variations of (statistics etc.); free from impediments or discomforts (*smooth the way; will smooth his declining years*); **~ out** or **over** or **away,** reduce or get rid of (differences, perplexities, difficulties, faults, etc.) in fact or appearance; **~'ing-iron,** implement usu. heated to smooth linen etc.; **~'ing-plane,** small plane for finishing the planing of wood. **2.** *n.* smoothing touch or stroke (*gave his hair a smooth*). [ME, f. prec.]

smōŏ′thie (-dhī) *n.* (colloq.) person who is smooth (sense 3). [f. SMOOTH¹+-IE]

smŏr′gasbŏrd, smörgåsbord (smĕr′gŏsboord), *n.* Swedish hors-d'œuvres; buffet meal with variety of dishes. [Sw. (*smör* butter, *gås* goose, lump of butter, *bord* table)]

smŏrzȧ′ndō (-ts-) *a.* & *adv.* (Mus.) dying away. [It., gerund of *smorzare* extinguish]

smōte. See SMITE.

smo′ther (-ŭ′dh-) *n.* & *v.* **1.** *n.* smouldering ashes etc.;

cloud of dust, spray, smoke, etc., or obscurity caused by it (*from* SMOKE¹ *into smother*). **2.** *v.t.* suffocate, stifle, kill by stopping breath of or excluding air from; **~ed mate** (Chess, when king having no vacant square to move to is checkmated by knight). **3.** overwhelm *with* kisses, gifts, kindness, etc.; *defeat quickly; deaden or extinguish (fire) by heaping with ashes etc.; **~ (up),** suppress, conceal or secure concealment of, keep from notice or publicity, (*smother a yawn; with smothered curses; the facts, the recommendations of the committee, were smothered up*); cover entirely *in* (*strawberries smothered in cream*). **4.** *v.i.* perish of suffocation, have difficulty in breathing. [ME *smorther* f. st. of OE *smorian* suffocate, = MDu., MLG *smoren*]

smo′ther|y (-ŭ′dh-) *a.* tending to smother, stifling. [f. prec.+-Y²]

smou′lder (smō′l-), *smō′lder, v.i.,* & *n.* **1.** *v.i.* burn with smoke but without flame, burn inwardly or in suppressed way or unseen; (of feelings etc.) exist, operate, be nursed, undetected or without conspicuous effects (*smouldering discontent, hatred, rebellion*). **2.** *n.* smouldering combustion (*the smoulder will soon be a flame*). [ME, cogn. w. LG *smöln,* MDu. *smölen*]

smṛi′ti *n.* Hindu traditional religious etc. teachings. [f. Skr. *smṛti* what is remembered]

smŭdge¹ *v.* & *n.* **1.** *v.t.* smear or blur lines of (writing, drawing); make dirt-mark or confused blot or smear on (face, paper, surface); defile, sully, stain with disgrace, impair purity of, (person's record, fame, etc.). **2.** *v.i.* (Of ink, drawing, etc.) become smeared or blurred (*smudges easily*). **3.** *n.* dirt-mark, smear, blot, (lit. or fig.); smudged line or mark; hence **smŭ′dg**Y² *a.,* **~**NESS *n.* [ME, of unkn. orig.]

***smŭdge**² *n.* outdoor fire with dense smoke made to keep off insects, protect plants against frost, etc.; **~-pot** (containing burning material that produces smudge). [f. *smudge* v. cure (herring) by smoking, 16th c., of unkn. orig.]

smŭg *a.* consciously respectable, self-satisfied, unambitious, in character or appearance; hence **~**'LY² *adv.,* **~**'NESS *n.* [16th c., orig. 'neat', f. LG *smuk* pretty]

smŭ′gg|le *v.t.* import or export (goods, or abs.) illegally, esp. without payment of customs duties, whence **~**ER¹, **~**ING¹, *ns.;* convey secretly *in, out,* etc., or put *away* etc. into concealment. [17th c., also *smuckle,* f. LG *smukkeln, smuggelen*]

smŭt *n.* & *v.* (**-tt-**). **1.** *n.* (spot or smudge made by) small flake of soot; lascivious talk or pictures or stories; fungous disease of cereals in which parts of the ear change to black powder; fungus causing this; **~-ball,** grain affected by smut, **~-mill,** machine for freeing grain from smut; hence **~**'TY² *a.* **2.** *v.t.* mark with smut(s); infect (plant) with smut. **3.** *v.i.* (Of plant) contract smut. [rel. to LG *smutt,* MHG *smutz(en),* etc.; cf. OE *smitt(ian)* smear, and SMUDGE¹]

smŭtch. Var. (arch.) of SMUDGE¹.

Sn *symb.* tin. [f. L *stannum*]

snăck *n.* slight or casual or hurried meal (**~-bar,** place where snacks may be obtained); **go ~s,** (arch.) go shares. [ME, orig. a snap or bite, f. MDu. *snac(k)* (*snacken* v., var. of *snappen* SNAP]

snă′ffle *n.* bridle consisting of **~-bit,** or plain slender jointed bit without curb, and single rein; **ride** person **on the ~,** (fig.) manage him gently. [prob. f. LDu.; cf. MLG, MDu. *snavel* beak, snout]

snă′ffle² *v.t.* put snaffle on; (sl.) appropriate, steal, seize. [f. prec.]

***snă′fu** (-fōō′) *a.* & *n.* (sl.) (in state of) utter confusion. [acronym f. 'situation normal, all fouled up']

snăg *n.,* & *v.t.* (**-gg-**). **1.** *n.* jagged projecting point, e.g. irregular or broken tooth, stump of branch remaining on tree, pointed root or stump poking out of ground, piece of rough timber or rock embedded in river or sea bottom and impeding navigation; short tine of antler; tear in material caused by a snag; (fig.)

unexpected obstacle or drawback; hence ~**gED²** (-gd), ~**gY²** (-gī), *adjs.* **2.** *v.t.* catch on snag; tear on or pierce with snag; clear (land, waterway, tree-trunk) of snags; *catch by prompt action. [prob. f. Scand.; cf. Norw. dial. *snag(e)* sharp point]

snä'ggle-tōōth (-gel-) *n.* (*pl.* **-teeth**). irregular or projecting tooth; hence ~**ED²** (-tht) *a.* [f. prec. + -LE 1 + TOOTH]

snail *n.* **1.** gastropod with spiral shell able to enclose whole body, esp. slow-moving kind destructive in gardens; **Roman** ~, the chief edible kind; ~**'s pace**, (arch.) **gallop**, very slow movement. **2.** ~(-**wheel**), spiral cam in clock, resembling snail in outline; ~(-**clover**), plant like lucerne, with spiral pods; ~-**fish,** = *sea snail* (1); hence ~-**LIKE** *a.* [OE *snæg(e)l* etc., = OS, OHG *snegil,* ON *snigill* I. Gmc *snag-, *sneg-]

snäke *n.,* & *v.i.* **1.** *n.* limbless reptile of suborder *Ophidia;* limbless lizard or amphibian; ~ (**in** one's **bosom**), ungrateful or treacherous person; ~ **in the grass,** hidden danger or secret enemy; **see ~s,** have delirium tremens; ~**s and ladders,** game in which players move their counters along board towards goal with periodic sudden advances by 'ladders' or returns by 'snakes' depicted on the board; **the** ~, system of interconnected exchange rates for currencies of EEC countries. **2.** ~-**bird,** fish-eating bird of genus *Anhinga,* with long slender neck; **snake--charmer, -charming,** (person giving) exhibition of control of venomous snake by music etc.; *~-**fence** (of horizontal rails laid zigzag with overlapping ends); ~-**pit,** (fig.) scene of vicious behaviour; ~-**root,** plant having roots reputed to be snake-poison antidotes; ~'**s-head,** plant with some part resembling head of snake; ~-**weed,** bistort or other plant resembling snake; ~-**wood,** (1) (wood of) S. Amer. timber-tree (from its snakelike markings), (2) (wood of) E. Ind. plant of genus *Strychnos* (used as snake-poison antidote). **3.** *v.i.* move, twist, etc., like a snake. [f. OE *snaca* = MLG *snake,* ON *snákr, snókr*]

snä'k|ў *a.* infested with snakes; snakelike in appearance or in such attributes as venom, guile, coldness, ingratitude; composed of snakes (esp. of the hair of the Furies); (Austral. sl.) angry, irritable; hence ~**iLY²** *adv.,* ~**iNESS** *n.* [f. prec. + -Y²]

snäp *v.* (-**pp-**), *n.,* *adv.,* & *a.* **1.** *v.i.* make sudden audible bite (*dog snapped viciously*); ~ **at,** (1) try to bite, (2) speak irritably to, (3) accept (bait, offer, chance, etc.) eagerly; ~'**ping turtle,** large Amer. freshwater tortoise seizing prey with snap of jaws. **2.** *v.i.* & *t.* say ill-tempered or spiteful things; ~ **out,** say irritably. **3.** *v.t.* bite *off;* ~ person's **head** or **nose off,** (esp., fig.) interrupt him angrily or rudely. **4.** pick *up* (scraps, or fig. bargain, catch at cricket, etc.) hastily or smartly; take *up* (interlocutor) without letting him finish. **5.** *v.t.* & *i.* break with sharp crack (*snap the string, a stick; oar, wire, snaps*). **6.** produce report from, emit report or crack, (*snap pistol, whip*); ~ one's **fingers,** make audible fillip esp. *at* person etc. in contempt; ~ one's **fingers at,** (fig.) defy. **7.** close etc. with snapping sound (*snap the clasp,* one's *teeth together; the door snapped to*); move smartly (*snapped to attention;* ~ **out of,** (sl.) get rid of (mood, habit, etc.) by sudden effort. **8.** *v.t.* take snapshot of. **9.** (Amer. Footb.) put (ball) into play on ground by quick backward movement. **10.** *n.* act or sound of snapping. **11.** catch that fastens with a snap; small crisp brittle cake or biscuit (BRANDY-*snap,* GINGER-*snap*); snap-shot. **12.** ||card-game in which first player to call 'snap' when two cards of equal rank are exposed has right to take cards from other player(s) (also as *int.* at instance of unexpected similarity of two things). **13.** (**cold**) ~, sudden usu. brief spell of frost. **14.** crispness of style, fresh vigour or liveliness in action, zest, dash, spring. **15.** *(sl.) easy task. **16.** *adv.* with sound of snap. **17.** *a.* (Of decision etc.) taken on the spur of the moment, (Parl. etc.) taken unexpectedly, brought on

without notice, etc., (*a snap decision, election, vote,* etc.). **18.** *~ **bean** (eaten as young pods broken into pieces); ~-**bolt, -lock,** (going home automatically with spring on closing of door etc.); ~-**brim,** (of hat) with brim that can be turned up and down at opposite sides; ~'**dragon,** (1) plant of genus *Antirrhinum* with bag-shaped flower like dragon's mouth, (2) Christmas game of plucking raisins from dish of burning brandy; ~-**fastener,** = PRESS²-*stud;* ~-**hook, -link,** (with spring allowing entrance but barring escape of cord, link, etc.); ~ **shot,** shot taken with little or no delay in aiming; ~'**shot,** rapid casual photograph taken with small hand-camera. [prob. f. MDu. or MLG *snappen;* partly imit.]

snä'pper *n.* In vbl senses; carnivorous food-fish of family Lutjanidae; Australasian food-fish of genus *Pagrosomus;* snapping turtle; PRESS²-*stud;* *cracker (toy); ~-**up,** one who snaps up bargains etc. [f. prec. + -ER¹]

snä'ppish *a.* speaking, spoken, in ill-tempered or curt way; (of dog etc.) inclined to snap; hence ~**LY²** *adv.,* ~**NESS** *n.* [f. SNAP + -ISH¹]

snä'pp|ў *a.* (colloq.) brisk, full of zest; neat and elegant; **make it ~y,** be quick about it; hence ~**iLY²** *adv.* [f. SNAP + -Y²]

snäre *n.,* & *v.t.* **1.** *n.* trap for catching birds or animals, esp. one made with noose of wire or cord; (Surg.) wire loop for catching and extracting polyps etc.; device for tempting enemy or dupe to expose himself to capture, defeat, failure, disgrace, loss, etc.; thing that acts as a temptation (*popularity is often a snare*). **2.** (in *sing.* or *pl.*) twisted strings of gut or hide or wire stretched across lower head of side-drum to produce rattling sound; ~ (**drum**), drum thus fitted. **3.** *v.t.* catch (bird etc.) in snare, whence (-)**snär'ER¹** *n.;* get (person) into snare, ensnare. [OE *sneare* f. ON *snara,* = OS *snari,* OHG *snarahha;* sense 2 prob. f. MLG or MDu.]

snärk *n.* chimerical animal of ill-defined characteristics and potentialities. [from *The Hunting of the S*~ by Lewis Carroll (1876)]

snärl¹ *v.* & *n.* **1.** *v.i.* (Of dog) make high-pitched quarrelsome growl with bared teeth; (of person) speak cynically, make ill-tempered complaints or criticisms. **2.** *v.t.* ~ (**out**), utter in snarling tone, express (discontent etc.) by snarling. **3.** Hence ~**ER¹** *n.* **4.** *n.* act or sound of snarling; hence ~'**Y²** *a.* [earlier *snar,* f. (M)LG, MHG *snarren;* see -LE 3]

snärl² *v.* & *n.* **1.** *v.t.* & *i.* twist, entangle, become entangled; ~ **up,** confuse and hamper movement of (traffic etc.); hence ~-*up* n. **2.** *v.t.* adorn exterior of (narrow metal vessel) with raised work made by indirect internal hammering with ~'**ing-iron. 3.** *n.* knot, tangle. [ME, f. *snare* n. or v. (see -LE 3); sense 2 perh. f. n. in dial. sense 'knot in wood']

snätch *v.* & *n.* **1.** *v.t.* seize quickly, eagerly, or unexpectedly, esp. with suddenly outstretched hand(s) or by way of robbery, rescue narrowly *from,* secure with difficulty, carry suddenly *away* or *from,* (*snatched his gun up, down; wind snatched my cap off; child snatches its food; snatch a kiss, an early breakfast, an opportunity,* etc.; *handbag was snatched from its owner, baby from its pram; was snatched from the jaws of death; snatch half an hour's rest; snatch victory out of defeat; snatched away, from us, by premature death*). **2.** *v.i.* ~ **at,** shoot out hand(s) to seize, (fig.) take (offer etc.) eagerly. **3.** ~-**block,** (Naut.) block with hinged flap admitting rope to sheave. **4.** *n.* act of snatching (*made a snatch at it*) or robbery or (*sl.) kidnapping; (Weight-lifting) rapid raising of weight from floor to above head; (usu. in *pl.*) fragment(s) or short burst(s) of song or recitation or talk, short spell(s) of action (*only works in or by ~es,* in fits and starts), whence ~'**Y²** *a.* [ME *snecchen, sna(c)che,* of unkn. orig.; perh. rel. to SNACK]

snäth, snead, *n.* (US or dial.) pole of scythe. [OE *snæd,* of unkn. orig.]

snă′zz|ў *a.* (sl.) smart, attractive, excellent; hence ~**ĭLY²** *adv.* [20th c.; orig. unkn.]

sneak *v.*, *n.*, & *a.* **1.** *v.i.* & *t.* slink, go or take furtively, (*in*, *out*, *past*, *away*, etc.); hence ~**ER¹s** (-z) *n. pl.*, (sl.) soft-soled shoes. **2.** *v.i.* (in *pres. part.*) furtive, not avowed, (*have a sneaking affection for him*); persistent in one's mind (*have a sneaking feeling it is not right*). **3.** ||(school sl.) turn informer, tell tales. **4.** *v.t.* (sl.) make off with, steal unobserved. **5.** *n.* mean-spirited cowardly underhand person; ||(school sl.) informer, telltale; hence ~**Y²** *a.* **6.** *a.* acting or done without warning (*sneak attack*, *raider*); secret (~**thief**, one who steals without breaking in, using open doors or windows). [16th c., prob. dial.; perh. rel. to ME *snike*, OE *snīcan* creep]

snĕck *n.*, & *v.t.* (Sc. & N. Engl.) latch. [ME; cogn. w. SNATCH]

sneer *v.* & *n.* **1.** *v.i.* smile derisively (*at*); utter derisive words esp. of a covert or ironical kind (*at*); hence ~**ER¹** *n.* **2.** *v.t.* utter sneeringly. **3.** *n.* sneering look or remark. [16th c., perh. f. LDu.]

sneeze *v.i.*, & *n.* **1.** *v.i.* make explosive sound in sudden involuntary expiration to expel anything that irritates interior of nostrils (**not to be ~d at**, (colloq.) passable, not contemptible); ~**'wort**, kind of yarrow whose dried leaves are used to induce sneezing. **2.** act or sound of sneezing. [ME *snese*, app. alt. f. obs. *fnese* f. OE **fnēosan*, *-fnēsan*, ON *fnýsa*, & repl. earlier and less expressive *nese*]

Snĕll *n.* ~**'s law**, (Phys.) constancy of ratio of sines of angles of incidence and refraction between two given media. [f. W. ~, Du. mathematician d. 1626]

snĭb *n.*, & *v.t.* (-bb-). **1.** *n.* bolt, fastening, catch, of door, window, etc. **2.** *v.t.* bolt, fasten. [19th c.; orig. uncert.]

snick *v.t.*, & *n.* (cut) small notch (in), (make) small incision (in); (Cricket) (cause) slight deflection of course of (ball) with bat. [18th c., prob. suggested by SNICKERSNEE etc.]

snĭ′cker *v.i.*, & *n.* whinny, neigh; snigger [imit.]

snickersnee′ *n.* (joc.) large knife, esp. one usable as weapon. [alt. f. obs. *snick-or-snee* a fight with knives, earlier *stick or snee*, f. Du. *steken* thrust, *snij*(*d*)*en* cut]

snide *a.* & *n.* (colloq.) **1.** *a.* counterfeit, bogus; insinuating, sneering, slyly derogatory; **mean* (trick etc.). **2.** *n.* counterfeit jewellery or coin(s); snide person. [19th c. cant, of unkn. orig.]

sniff *v.* & *n.* **1.** *v.i.* draw up air audibly through nose to stop it from running or to detect smell or as expression of contempt; ~ **at**, (1) try the smell of, show interest in, (2) show contempt for or discontent with. **2.** *v.t.* draw up or *up* (air, liquid, scent, drug), draw up scent of (flower, brandy, meat, etc.), into nose; ~ **out**, (fig.) discover by investigation. **3.** *n.* act or sound of sniffing; amount of air etc. sniffed up. [ME; imit.]

snĭ′ffle *v.i.*, & *n.* **1.** *v.i.* sniff slightly or repeatedly. **2.** *n.* act of sniffling; (in *pl.*) cold in the head causing running nose and sniffling. [imit.; cf. SNIVEL]

snĭ′ff|ў *a.* (colloq.) inclined to sniff; disdainful, contemptuous; hence ~**ĭLY²** *adv.*, ~**ĭNESS** *n.* [f. SNIFF +-Y²]

snĭ′fter *n.* **1.** (sl.) small drink of intoxicating liquor; **balloon glass for brandy. **2.** ~**-valve**, **snĭ′fting- -valve**, (in steam-engine, to allow air in or out). [f. dial. *snift* sniff, perh. f. Scand.; imit.]

snĭ′gger (-g-) *v.i.*, & *n.* (utter) half-suppressed secretive laugh. [var. of SNICKER]

snĭ′ggle *v.i.* fish (for eels) by pushing bait into hole. [f. *snig* small eel, ME, of unkn. orig.]

snĭp *v.* (-pp-) & *n.* **1.** *v.t.* & *i.* cut with scissors or shears esp. in small quick strokes (*snip cloth, a hole*; *snip off the ends*; ~ **at**, make snipping strokes at); hence ~**pĭNG¹** (2) -Y². **2.** *n.* act of snipping; piece snipped off; ||(sl.) something easily done or cheaply acquired; (in *pl.*) hand-shears for metal-cutting. [f. LG & Du. *snippen* (imit.)]

snipe *n.* (*pl.* ~**s** or ~) & *v.* **1.** *n.* wading bird of genus *Gallinago*, with long straight bill, frequenting marshes; GUTTER*snipe*; ~**-eel** (with long slender snout); ~**-fish** (of family Macrorhamphosidae, with long tubular snout). **2.** *v.i.* go snipe-shooting. **3.** *v.i.* & *t.* (Mil.) fire shots from hiding usu. at long range into enemy's camp or at individuals; (fig.) make sly critical attack *at*; kill or hit by sniping; hence **snī′pER¹** *n.* [ME, prob. f. Scand.; cf. Icel. *mýrisnípa*, & MDu., MLG *snippe*, OHG *snepfa*]

snĭ′ppĕt *n.* small piece cut off, snipping; (in *pl.*) detached fragments *of* knowledge or information, short extracts from books, odds and ends, whence ~**Y²** *a.* [f. SNIP +-ET¹]

snitch *v.* (sl.) **1.** *v.i.* act as informer. **2.** *v.t.* steal. [17th c. in sense (fillip on) nose; orig. unkn.]

snĭ′vel *v.i.* (||-ll-), & *n.* **1.** *v.i.* run at the nose; make repeated sniffing sound; be tearful, show maudlin emotion; hence ~**ĭER¹** *n.*, ~**ĭ́ING²** *a.* **2.** *n.* running mucus; whining and weeping; hypocritical talk, cant. [ME, f. OE **snyflan* (*snofl* mucus); cf. SNUFFLE]

snŏb *n.* person with exaggerated respect for social position or wealth and a disposition to be ashamed of socially inferior connections, behave with servility to social superiors, and judge of merit by externals, person despising those whose attainments or tastes he considers inferior to his own, (*intellectual snob*; *the snob appeal of an address in Belgravia*; *has snob value but no more*; INVERT¹*ed snob*); hence ~**'bish¹** *a.*, ~**'bERУ** (4, 5), ~**ŏ′cRACY**, *ns.* [18th c. (now dial.) 'cobbler'; orig. unkn.]

snoek (-ōōk) *n.* (S. Afr.) barracouta. [Afrik., f. Du., = PIKE³, f. MLG *snōk*, prob. rel. to SNACK]

snŏg *v.i.* (-gg-). (sl.) (engage in) spell of kissing and caressing. [20th c., orig. unkn.]

*snŏ′llygŏster *n.* (sl.) shrewd unscrupulous person. [perh. f. *snallygaster*, a mythical creature]

snōōd *n.* **1.** (Sc. or literary). fillet worn by maidens in Scotland to confine hair. **2.** loose net for woman's back hair. **3.** short line attaching hook to a main line in sea fishing. [OE *snōd*, of unkn. orig.]

snōōk¹ *n.* = SERGEANT-fish. [f. Du. SNOEK]

snōōk² *n.* (sl.) contemptuous gesture with thumb to nose and fingers spread out (**cock a ~**, make this gesture, lit. or fig.). [19th c.; orig. unkn.]

snōō′ker (-ōō′-, -ōō′-) *n.*, & *v.t.* **1.** *n.* ~ (**pool**), form of POOL² 2, with 15 red and 6 other coloured balls; position in this game where direct shot would lose points. **2.** *v.t.* subject (player) to a snooker; (sl., esp. in *pass.*) thwart, defeat. [19th c.; orig. unkn.]

snōōp *v.i.*, & *n.* (colloq.) **1.** *v.i.* pry into matters one need not be concerned with; sneak *about* or *around* looking for infractions of the law; hence ~**'ER¹** *n.*, ~**'Y²** *a.*; **~'erscope*, device for revealing objects in the dark. **2.** *n.* act of snooping; snooper. [f. Du. *snoepen* eat on the sly]

snōōt *n.* (sl.) nose. [var. of SNOUT]

snōō′t|ў *a.* (colloq.) supercilious, conceited; hence ~**ĭLY²** *adv.*, ~**ĭNESS** *n.* [20th c.; orig. unkn.]

snōōze *v.i.*, & *n.* (colloq.) (take) short sleep esp. in daytime. [18th c. cant of unkn. orig.]

snōre *v.i.* & *t.*, & *n.* (make) hoarse rattling or grunting noise in breathing during sleep; pass (time) *away* in snoring; hence **snŏ′rER¹** *n.* [ME, prob. imit.; cf. SNORT]

snŏ′rkel, schnŏ′rkel (shn-), *n.*, & *v.i.* (||-ll-). **1.** *n.* device for supplying air to submerged submarine; breathing-tube for underwater swimmer. **2.** *v.i.* use snorkel. [f. G *schnorchel*]

snŏrt¹ *v.* & *n.* **1.** *v.i.* make explosive noise due to sudden forcing of breath through nose and usu. expressing anger or indignation or incredulity, or (of steam-engine etc.) noise resembling this. **2.** *v.t.* express (defiance etc.) by snorting; throw *out* (words) with snorting. **3.** *n.* noise made in snorting; (colloq.) small drink of liquor; (sl.) inhaled dose of powdered drug. [ME, prob. imit.; cf. SNORE]

||**snŏrt²** *n.* [substituted for SNORKEL]

snŏr′ter n. In vbl senses; (sl.) boisterous gale, performance etc. conspicuous for vigour or violence, difficult task. [f. SNORT¹ + -ER¹]

snŏt n. (vulg.) nasal mucus; contemptible person; ∼-rag, handkerchief. [prob. f. MDu., MLG snotte, MHG snuz, cogn. w. SNOUT]

snŏ′tt|ў a. & n. **1.** a. (vulg.) running or foul with nasal mucus; contemptible. **2.** (colloq.) annoyed, short-tempered; cheeky; supercilious. **3.** Hence ∼ĭLY² adv., ∼ĭNESS n. **4.** n. (Naval sl., arch.) midshipman. [f. prec. + -Y²]

snout n. projecting nose (and mouth) of animal; (derog.) human nose; pointed front of thing, nozzle, (snout of glacier, of battleship's ram, etc.); (sl.) tobacco, cigarette; ∼-beetle, weevil; hence (-)∼ED² a., ∼′Y² a., like a snout, having a (prominent) snout. [ME, f. MDu., MLG snūt(e)]

snow¹ (-ō) n. & v. **1.** n. atmospheric vapour frozen into ice crystals and falling to earth in light white flakes, or spread on it as a white layer after falling; (in pl.) falls or accumulations of snow (where are the snows of yester-year?). **2.** skin, hair, etc., resembling snow esp. in whiteness; dessert or other dish resembling snow; frozen carbon dioxide; (sl.) cocaine. **3.** ∼′ball, (n.) mass of snow pressed into hard ball esp. for use as missile, anything that grows or increases rapidly like snowball rolled on snow, (v.t. & i.) pelt or have pelting-match with snowballs, (fig.) increase rapidly; ∼′ball-tree, guelder rose; ∼-berry, garden shrub of genus Symphoricarpos, with white berries; ∼-bird, white or partly white bird, esp. the snow bunting, (sl.) cocaine addict; ∼-blind(ness), unable, inability, to see owing to effects on the eye of reflection of light endured in traversing snow-fields etc.; ∼-blink, reflection in sky of snow or ice fields; ∼-boot, overboot of rubber and cloth; ∼-bound, prevented by snow from going out or travelling; ∼-broth, melted or melting snow; ∼ bunting, mainly white species of finch; ∼-cap, white-crowned humming-bird; ∼-capped, (of mountain) covered at top with snow; ∼-drift, bank of snow heaped by wind; ∼′drop, bulbous plant (Galanthus nivalis) with white drooping flowers in early spring; ∼′fall, (esp.) amount of snow that falls on one occasion or on given area within given time; ∼-field, (esp.) permanent wide expanse of snow in mountainous or polar regions; ∼′flake, (1) one of the small collections of crystals in which snow falls; (2) (white flower of) plant of genus Leucojum; ∼-goggles, darkened spectacles worn by mountaineers etc. to prevent snow-blindness; ∼-goose, Arctic white goose with black-tipped wings; ∼-grouse, ptarmigan; ∼-ice, opaque white ice formed from melted snow; *∼ job, (sl.) attempt at deception by overwhelming with many details; ∼-leopard, OUNCE²; ∼-line, level above which snow lies permanently; ∼′man, figure made of snow esp. by children and set up; ABOMINABLE Snowman; *∼′mobile (-ēl), motor vehicle to travel over snow, esp. with skis and Caterpillar track; ∼ owl, = snowy owl; ∼-plant, microscopic alga growing in snow and colouring it red; ∼-plough, contrivance for clearing road or track by pushing snow aside; ∼-shoe, racket-head or ski attached to foot and enabling wearer to traverse snow without sinking in; ∼-shovel, large esp. wooden shovel for moving snow; ∼-slip, avalanche; ∼′storm, heavy fall of snow esp. with wind; ∼-white, white as snow. **4.** Hence ∼LESS, ∼′Y², adjs.; ∼y owl, large white owl (Nyctea nyctea). **5.** v.i. impers. it ∼s or is ∼ing, snow falls. **6.** v.t. & i. sprinkle or scatter or fall as or like snow. **7.** v.t. *(sl.) overwhelm, impress greatly. **8.** ∼ under, cover (as) with snow, overwhelm with numbers etc. (*esp. in pass. of election candidate defeated by huge majority). **9.** ∼ed up or in, snow-bound, blocked up with snow. [OE snāw, = OS, OHG snēo, ON snær etc., Goth. snaiws f. Gmc *snaiwaz]

snow² (-ō) n. small briglike sailing vessel with supplementary trysail mast. [f. Du. sna(a)uw or LG snau, of unkn. orig.]

SNP abbr. Scottish National Party.

Snr. abbr. Senior.

snŭb¹ v.t. (-bb-), & n. **1.** v.t. rebuff, reprove, humiliate, with sharp words or marked lack of cordiality; check movement of (boat, horse, etc.) esp. by rope wound round ∼′bing-post or bollard, tree, etc.; hence ∼′bER¹ n., (esp.) *shock absorber. **2.** n. act of snubbing, rebuff. [ME, f. ON snubba chide]

snŭb² a. & n. **1.** a. (Of nose) short and stumpy or turned up; ∼-nosed, having a snub nose. **2.** n. snub nose. [f. prec. in sense 'check growth of']

snŭff¹ v. & n. **1.** v.i. & t. = SNIFF; take snuff. **2.** n. = SNIFF. **3.** powdered tobacco taken by sniffing up nostrils (up to ∼, (sl.) ||not childishly ignorant or innocent, *reaching normal standard); medicinal powder taken by sniffing; ∼-box, small box to hold snuff; ∼-colour(ed), (of) dark yellowish-brown. [n. sense 2 f. v., sense 3 f. Du. snuf (tabak tobacco), both f. MDu. snuffen snuffle]

snŭff² n. & v. **1.** n. charred part of candle-wick, esp. when obscuring light. **2.** v.t. trim snuff from (candle) with fingers or scissors or snuffers; ∼ out, extinguish thus or with snuffer, (fig.) kill, put an end to, (I was nearly, his hopes were, snuffed out). **3.** v.i. ∼ it, ∼ out, (sl.) die. [ME snoffe, snuffe, of unkn. orig.]

snŭ′ffer n. **1.** person who takes snuff. **2.** small hollow cone with handle used to extinguish candle; (in pl.) implement like scissors used to snuff candle. [f. SNUFF¹,² + -ER¹]

snŭ′ffle v. & n. **1.** v.i. sniff; make sniffing sounds; speak nasally, whiningly, or like one with a cold; breathe noisily as through partly blocked nose; hence **snŭ′fflER¹** n. **2.** v.t. ∼ (out), utter with snuffling. **3.** n. sniff; snuffling sound, tone, or talk; (in pl.) partial blockage of nose causing snuffling. [prob. f. LG & Du. snuffelen (as SNUFF¹, -LE 3); cf. SNIVEL]

snŭ′ffУ a. like snuff in colour or substance. [f. SNUFF¹ + -Y²]

snŭ′ffУ² a. annoyed; irritable; supercilious, contemptuous. [f. SNUFF² + -Y²]

snŭg a. & n. **1.** a. protected from weather and cold, well enclosed or packed in or fixed in place, closely fitting, comfortably situated, cosy; (of income etc.) allowing comfort and comparative ease; hence ∼′LY² adv., ∼′NESS n. **2.** n. ||bar-parlour of inn. [16th c., orig. Naut.; prob. of LDu. orig.]

snŭ′ggerУ (-g-) n. snug place, esp. person's private room or den; || = prec. **2.** [f. prec. + -ERY]

snŭ′ggle v. **1.** v.i. shift one's position or lie close up to for warmth. **2.** v.t. draw (child etc.) close to one, cuddle. [f. SNUG¹, -LE 3]

sō¹ adv., conj., & pron. **1.** adv. to the extent or in the manner set forth by preceding or following as-clause or implied in context, thus, equally, similarly, analogously, (now used to express degree before as-clause only with negative: I am not so eager as you, I am as eager as you; as the time falls, so must it lie; occas. used twice correlatively: so many men so many minds; when he saw her so frightened; why are you panting so?; with a gesture, have known him since I was so high; so, and so only, can it be done; stand just so; could show me so divine a thing; did not expect to live so long; did not get it by force and ought not to be so deprived of it; can stand only so much of it; in sentence appended as explanation: I paid him double, I was so pleased; were it EVER or NEVER so bad etc.; MORE so; EVERY so often); so be it (expr. acceptance or being resigned); so far, to such an extent or distance, until now, (so far it has not happened; so far you are right); (in) so far as, to the extent that; so FAR¹ from; so far so good, progress has been satisfactory; and so forth, and so on, et cetera, and the like; so long!, (colloq.) goodbye till we next meet; so LONG² as; so many, nothing but (went down like so many skittles); so much, nothing but (rubbish etc.); so much for, that is all that need be done or said about; *so much* THE *worse* etc.; at **so much** *a week, a head,* etc., **so much** *of one ingredient and* **so much** *of another,* a definite but unspecified sum, quantity, etc.; **not so (very)** *difficult* etc. (as had been expected or predicted); **not so much as,** less . . . than (*is not so much discontented as unsatisfied*), not even (*did not so much as glance at it*); *so* SOON *as.* **2.** to the degree or in the manner or with the intent or result set forth by following *that*-clause or *but*-clause or *as* to (*so high that you cannot reach it*; *so run that ye may obtain*; **so much so that,** to such an extent that; *warned him so that,* or **so, he might avoid the danger*; *all precautions have been taken, so that we expect to succeed*; *not so deaf but he can, that he cannot, hear a gun*; *not so big a fool as to believe that*; *was so fortunate as to escape*; *put it so as not to offend him*; *it so happens that he was not there*). **3.** to a degree that demands exclamatory emphasis (*so many worlds, so much to do!*; *I am so glad, so tired!*; *she is so beautiful!*; *so kind of you!*; *cricket is so boring*); EVER *so easy* etc.; **so sorry!,** (colloq.) I beg your PARDON[1]. **4.** (arch.) on condition that or *that,* on condition set forth in *as*-clause or implied, (*so that or so it is done, it matters not how*; *so may you find forgiveness as now you forgive me!*); *so* HELP[1] *me* (*God*). **5.** *adv. & conj.* accordingly, consequently, therefore, as appears or results from preceding or implied statements or fact, (*he says he was not; so or and so he doubtless was not*; *so* or *and so I cannot come*; *so that's what he meant*; *so you are back again*); **so that's that** (colloq., concluding statement or discussion or piece of work); *so* (WHAT)?. **6.** *adv.* (accompanying emphasis on some later word) moreover, also, as well, in actual fact, (*well, so I did*; *you said it was good, and so it is*; *yes, I denied it, but or and so did you*; '*your birthday? yes, so it is*'). **7.** *adv. & pron.* (As substitute, often preceding v., for obj. of vbs. of saying, thinking, etc.) it, this, that, the same, this is what, (*so he said*; *do you think so?*; *and so say all of us*; *so saying, he departed*; *so spake Achilles,* i.e. what precedes, *and Patroclus so,* i.e. what follows; *she is ill and he thinks himself so*; arch., ellipt.: *So Satan, whom the archangel thus rebukes*); **I suppose so** (expr. hesitant agreement); **I told you so,** I warned you in vain; **so-called** (epithet calling attention to, or questioning accuracy of, description); **so to say** or **speak** (apology for exaggeration, metaphor, neologism, imprecision, bluntness, etc.); *you don't* SAY[2] *so.* **8.** in that state or condition, actually the case, (*he, it, is better so*; *God said Let there be light, and it was so*; *but perhaps it is not so*); EVER *so*; (with omission of *it is* etc.: *why so?*, *not so*; HOW *so?*, IF *so,* JUST[2] *so,* QUITE *so*). **9.** (arch.) **and so,** after which I, they, etc., proceeded (*and so to dinner, to bed,* etc.); **so please you,** by your favour, if you please. **10.** -so = -SOEVER. **11.** so-and-so (*pl.* **so-and-so's**), particular person or thing not needing to be specified (*never mind what so-and-so says*; *tells me to do so-and-so*), (colloq.) disliked or contemptible person; **so so, so- -so,** *pred. a.* or *adv.,* not more than passable, -bly, indifferent(ly), not very good or well; **or so,** or thereabouts (after expressions of quantity or numbers: *send me ten or so*; *a pound or so will do*). [OE *swā* etc., = OS, OHG *sō,* ON *svá,* Goth. *swa, swe*]

sō². See SOH.

‖SO *abbr.* Stationery Office.

*So. *abbr.* South.

soak *v. & n.* **1.** *v.t.* (Of absorbent substance) take *up* or suck in (liquid). **2.** *v.t. & i.* place or leave or lie in or *in* liquid for saturation, steep, (lit., or fig. in sunshine, one*self* in subject of study, etc.); make or be wet through, (of rain etc.) drench, whence ∼'ING[1] (1) *n.* **3.** (Of moisture or fig. of understanding etc.) make way *in*(*to*) or *through,* make its *way,* by saturation, whence ∼'AGE (3) *n.*; ‖∼**-away,** arrangement for disposal of rain-water by percolation through soil. **4.** *v.t.* (sl.) extract money from by extortionate charge, taxation, etc., (*soak the rich*). **5.** *v.i.* drink persistently, booze; (in *p.p.*) very drunk. **6.** *n.* soaking (*leave them in soak*); drinking-bout; (colloq.) hard drinker. [OE

socian cogn. w. *soc* sucking at breast, f. weak grade of *sūcan* SUCK]

soa'ker *n.* In vbl senses; hard drinker; drenching rain. [f. prec. + -ER[1]]

soap *n., & v.t.* **1.** *n.* cleansing agent that is compound of fatty acid with soda or potash or (**insoluble** ∼) another metallic oxide, of which the soluble kinds when rubbed in water yield a lather used in washing; **no** ∼, (colloq.) nothing doing; **soft** ∼, semifluid soap made with potash, (fig.) persuasive flattery (*soft*-∼ *v.t.,* treat thus). **2.** ∼**-bark, -berry, -nut, -plant, -pod, -root, -wort,** plants yielding substances serving purposes of soap. **3.** ∼**-boiler, -boiling,** manufacture(r) of soap; ∼**-box,** (packing-)box for holding soap, makeshift stand for street orator, crude vehicle; ∼**-bubble,** globe of air enclosed in iridescent film of soapy water made esp. by blowing through pipe or ring dipped in soapsuds; ∼**-dish,** holder for soap in bathroom etc.; ∼**-earth,** steatite; ∼**-flakes** (specially prepared for washing clothes etc.); ∼ **opera,** sentimental domestic broadcast serial [often sponsored by soap-makers]; ∼ **powder** (esp. with additives); ∼**'stone,** steatite; *soap*SUDS; ∼**-works,** place where soap is made. **4.** Hence ∼'LESS *a.* **5.** *v.t.* apply soap to; scrub or rub with soap. [OE *sāpe,* = MDu. *seepe,* OHG *seifa* f. WG *saipo]

soa'p|ȳ *a.* like, smeared or impregnated with, suggestive of, soap; (fig., of person or his manners or talk) unctuous, flattering; hence ∼ILY² *adv.,* ∼INESS *n.* [f. prec. + -Y²]

soar *v.i.* fly high (lit. or fig.), mount to or be at a great height above earth or normal position, hover or sail in the air without flapping of wings or use of engine, (*soaring eagle, spire, thoughts, prices, glider, ambition, ideals*). [ME, f. OF *essorer* f. Rom. *EX¹(*aurare* f. *aura* breeze)]

sŏb *v.* (-**bb-**) *& n.* **1.** *v.i.* draw breath in convulsive gasps usu. with weeping under mental distress or physical exhaustion. **2.** *v.t.* ∼ (**out**), utter with sobs. **3.** *n.* convulsive drawing of breath esp. in weeping; ∼**-sister,** writer of sentimental stories; ∼**-story,** narrative designed mainly to evoke sympathy; ∼**-stuff,** (colloq.) pathos, sentimental writing or behaviour. [ME *sobbe*(*n*), prob. imit.]

*SOB *abbr.* SON of a bitch (or *silly old bastard* etc.).

sō'ber *a.* (∼**er,** ∼**est**) *& v.* **1.** *a.* not drunk (**as** ∼ **as a judge,** entirely sober; **appeal from Philip drunk to Philip** ∼, suggest that opinion etc. represents passing mood only; temperate in regard to drink (*is a sober man*); moderate, well-balanced, tranquil, sedate, not vehement or passionate or excited or wayward or fanciful or exaggerated, (of colour) quiet and inconspicuous; **in** ∼ **fact,** in fact as opp. fancy; ∼**-sided,** sedate, solemn, earnest; ∼**-sides,** sedate person; hence ∼LY² *adv.* **2.** *v.t. & i.* ∼ (**down** or **up**), make or become sober or less wild, reckless, enthusiastic, visionary, etc. [ME, f. OF *sobre* f. L *sobrius*]

sobrī'etȳ *n.* being sober. [ME, f. OF *sobrieté* or L *sobrietas* (as SOBER; see -TY¹)]

sō'briquet (-kā), **sou'-** (sōō'-), *n.* nickname; assumed name. [F, orig. = 'tap under chin']

Soc. *abbr.* Socialist; Society.

sŏ'cage, sŏ'ccage, *n.* feudal tenure of land involving payment of rent or other non-military service to superior. [ME f. AF *socage* (*soc* f. OE *sōcn* SOKE; see -AGE)]

sŏ'ccer (-k-) *n.* (colloq.) Association football. [f. Assoc. + -ER¹]

sō'ciab|le (-sha-) *a. & n.* **1.** *a.* fitted for companionship, ready and willing to converse, not averse to society, communicative, liking company; (of meeting etc.) marked by friendliness, not stiff or formal; hence **sōci**ABI'LITY (-sha-) *n.,* ∼LY² *adv.* **2.** *n.* open carriage with facing side seats; S-shaped couch for two occupants partly facing each other; *social. [F, or f. L *sociabilis* (*sociare* to unite f. *socius* companion; see -ABLE)]

sō′cial (-shəl) *a.* & *n.* **1.** *a.* living in companies or organized communities, gregarious, (*man is a social animal*); not fitted for or not practising solitary life; interdependent, co-operative, practising division of labour; existing only as member of compound organism, (of insects) having shared nests etc., (of birds) building near each other in communities; (of plants) growing thickly together and monopolizing ground they grow on. **2.** concerned with the mutual relations of (classes of) human beings (*social problems, morality, students, philosophers*); **the ~ contract** or **compact,** agreement to co-operate for social benefits, e.g. to exchange individual freedom for uniform legal restriction, or to restrict pay-claims in return for more equitable laws; **~ credit,** economic theory that profits of industry should be distributed to the general public; **S~ Democrat,** politician aiming at improving condition of lower classes by gradual advance towards socialism; **~ disease,** venereal disease; **the ~ evil,** (arch.) prostitution; **~ history,** history of social behaviour; **~ order,** network of human relationships in society; **~ realism,** expression of social views in art etc.; **~ science,** scientific study of human society and social relationships, branch of this (e.g. politics, economics); **~ security,** State assistance to those lacking economic security and welfare; **~ service,** philanthropic activity; **~ services,** education, health, housing, insurance, pensions, etc., as State--provided welfare services; **~ worker,** person trained for social service(s). **3.** of or in or towards society (*social intercourse, life, etiquette, pleasures, duties*; one's *social superiors and inferiors*; *social rank, position, distinctions*; *has social tastes*; *a social club, evening, gathering*); **~ climber,** person seeking to gain higher rank in society; **~ secretary** (making arrangements for social activities of a group). **4.** (Rom. & Gk Hist.) of or with allies (*the Social War*). **5.** Hence or cogn. **sōciă′lITY** (-shĭ-) *n.,* **~LY²** *adv.* **6.** *n.* social gathering, esp. one organized by club, congregation, etc. [F, or f. L *socialis* allied (*socius* friend; see -AL)]

sō′cial|ism (-sha-) *n.* political and economic theory of social organization which advocates that community as a whole should own and control the means of production, distribution, and exchange; policy or practice based on this theory; **Christian S~ism,** attempt to apply Christian precepts in ordinary life resulting in some approximation to the aims of socialism; hence **~IST** (2) *n.,* **~ĭ′st**IC *a.* [f. F *socialisme* (as prec.; see -ISM)]

sō′cialīte (-sha-) *n.* person prominent in fashionable society. [f. SOCIAL + -ITE¹]

sō′cializ|e (-sha-), **-īs|e** (-īz), *v.* **1.** *v.t.* make social; arrange in socialistic manner; ***~ed medicine,*** provision of medical services for all from public funds; hence **~A′TION** *n.* **2.** *v.i.* act in sociable manner. [f. SOCIAL + -IZE]

soci′etў *n.* **1.** social mode of life, the customs and organization of an ordered community, (*the progress of society is an evolution*); hence **soci′et**AL *a.* **2.** a social community (*no society can retain members who flout its principles*); (Ecol.) plant community; ***~ finch,*** small white weaver-bird. **3.** members of a community whose movements and entertainments and other doings are more or less conspicuous, the socially distinguished, fashionable, leisured, well-to-do, and well-connected people, (*was welcomed by society*; *the customs of polite society*; *society does not approve*; *leaders of society*; *society people, gossip, news*). **4.** participation in hospitality, other people's homes or company, (*goes a great deal into, avoids, is at his best or embarrassed in, society*). **5.** companionship, company, (*society and solitude*; *always enjoy his society*; *seek, avoid, the society of*). **6.** association of persons united by a common aim or interest or principle (**S~ of Friends,** Quakers; **S~ of Jesus,** Jesuits; ||BUILDING *society*; ||FRIENDLY *Society*); **Royal S~ (of London,** founded 1662 to

promote scientific discussion). [f. F *société* f. L *societas -tatis* (*socius* companion; see -TY¹)]

Soci′nian *a.* & *n.* (holder) of the doctrine of the 16th-c. Italian rationalist theologians Laelius and Faustus Socinus, who denied the existence of the Trinity and the divinity of Christ; hence **~ISM** (3) *n.* [f. *Socinus,* Latinized f. *Sozzini,* + -IAN]

sōciŏ- (-sĭ-, -shĭ-) *comb. form.* of society or sociology (and), as: **~-bio′logy,** sociology studied from biological standpoint; **~-cu′ltural,** combining social and cultural factors; **~-econo′mic,** relating to social status and economic position; **~-lingui′stic,** pertaining to language in its social context; **~-linguis′tics,** study of language in relation to social factors. [f. L *socius* companion (cf. SOCIETY) + -O-]

sōciŏ′log|ў (-sĭ-, -shĭ-) *n.* science of the development and nature and laws of human (esp. civilized) society; study of social problems; hence **sōcioLO′GICAL** (-sĭ-, -shĭ-) *a.,* **~IST** (3) *n.* [f. F *sociologie* f. as prec. + -LOGY]

sōciŏ′mĕtr|ў (-sĭ-, -shĭ-) *n.* study of relationships within a group of people; hence **sŏciomĕ′tr**IC (-sĭ-, -shĭ-) *a.,* **~IST** (3) *n.* [f. SOCIO- + -METRY]

sŏck¹ *n.* **1.** (*pl.* **~s** or ***sox**). short stocking not reaching knee; ||**pull** one's **~s up,** (colloq.) make an effort; ||**put a ~ in it,** (sl.) be quiet. **2.** removable inner sole put into shoe for warmth etc. **3.** ancient comic actor's light shoe; (fig.) comic drama. **4.** white etc. **~** (of horse), = STOCKING. [OE *socc,* = OHG *soc,* ON *sokkr,* Gmc f. L *soccus* comic actor's shoe, light low-heeled slipper, f. Gk *sukkhos*]

sŏck² *v.t.,* & *n.* (sl.) **1.** *v.t.* hit (person) with fist or hand--flung missile; **~ it to,** attack or address (person) vigorously. **2.** *n.* blow inflicted by missile or fist; *power to deliver a blow. [*c.* 1700, cant, of unkn. orig.]

*sŏckdŏ′loger, -lager, *n.* (sl.) decisive blow or argument; remarkable thing. [19th c., prob. fanciful]

sŏ′ckĕt *n.,* & *v.t.* **1.** *n.* natural or artificial hollow for something to fit into or stand firm or revolve in (*socket of eye, hip, tooth*; *candle too large for socket*; BALL¹ *and socket*); (Electr.) device receiving plug, light-bulb, etc., to make connection; (Golf) part of iron club into which shaft is fitted. **2.** *v.t.* place in, fit with, socket; (Golf) hit (ball) with socket of club. [ME f. AF, dim. of OF *soc* ploughshare, prob. of Celt. orig.]

sŏ′ckeye (-kī) *n.* blue-backed salmon of Alaska etc. (*Oncorhynchus nerka*). [f. Salish *sukai* fish of fishes]

sŏ′cle *n.* (Archit.) plain low block or plinth serving as support for column, vase, statue, etc., or as foundation of wall. [F, f. It. *zoccolo* orig. 'wooden shoe' f. L *socculus* (*soccus* SOCK¹; see -ULE)]

Socră′t|ic *a.* & *n.* **1.** *a.* of, like, following, etc., Socrates, Gk philosopher d. 399 BC; *Socratic* ELENCHUS; **~ic irony,** pose of ignorance assumed in order to confute others by enticing them into display of supposed knowledge; **~ic method,** dialectic, procedure by questions and answer; hence **~IC**ALLY *adv.* **2.** *n.* follower of Socrates. [f. L f. Gk *Sōkratikos* (*Sōkratēs* Socrates; see -IC)]

sŏd¹ *n.,* & *v.t.* (**-dd-**). **1.** *n.* = TURF 1; **the old ~,** (colloq.) one's native land; **under the ~,** in the grave. **2.** *v.t.* cover (ground) with sods. [ME, f. MDu., MLG *sode,* = OFris. *sātha, sāda,* of unkn. orig.]

sŏd². See SEETHE.

sŏd³ *n.* & *v.* (**-dd-**). (vulg.) **1.** *n.* (derog. or joc.) person, fellow. **2.** *v.t.* = DAMN 2; (in *pres. part.*) = DAMNED 2. **3.** *v.i.* **~ off,** go away. [abbr. of SODOMITE]

sō′da *n.* **1.** compound of sodium in common use, esp. the carbonate (**washing-~**), bicarbonate (**baking--~**), or hydroxide (**caustic ~**). **2. ~(-water),** water made effervescent by impregnation with carbon dioxide under pressure and used alone or with spirits etc. as a drink (orig. made with sodium bicarbonate; *some soda-water*; *some or a brandy and soda*). **3. ~-bread** etc. (leavened with baking-soda); **~-fountain,** vessel in which soda-water is stored under pressure to be drawn out, shop etc. equipped with this

apparatus; *∼-**jerk**(**er**), (sl.) attendant at soda-
-fountain. [med. L, perh. f. *sodanum* glasswort (used as
remedy for headaches) f. *soda* headache f. Arab. *ṣudāʿ*
(*ṣadaʿa* split)]
soda'lity *n.* confraternity or association, esp. RC
religious guild or brotherhood. [f. F *sodalité* or f. L
sodalitas (*sodalis* comrade; see -ITY)]
so'dden *a.* & *v.* **1.** *a.* saturated with liquid, soaked
through; (of bread etc.) doughy, heavy and moist;
stupid or dull in fact or appearance with habitual
drunkenness; hence ∼LY² *adv.*, ∼NESS (-n-n-) *n.* **2.** *v.i.*
& *t.* become or make sodden. [p.p. of SEETHE]
so'dium *n.* soft silver-white metallic element, one of
the alkali metals, found in soda, salt, and other
compounds; ∼ **chloride,** common SALT; ∼ **lamp**
(using electrical discharge in sodium vapour and
giving yellow light); hence **so'dic** *a.* [f. SODA + -IUM]
So'dom *n.* (type of a) wicked town. [∼ in ancient
Palestine (Gen. 18, 19)]
so'domite *n.* person practising sodomy. [ME f. OF, f.
LL f. Gk *Sodomitēs* inhabitant of Sodom (*Sodoma*
Sodom; see -ITE¹)]
so'dom|y *n.* anal or other copulation-like act esp.
between male persons or between human being and
animal; hence ∼IZE (1) *v.t.* [ME, f. med. L *sodomia* f.
LL *peccatum Sodomiticum* sin of SODOM; see -Y¹]
soe'ver *adv.* (literary, or as *suf.* to *rel. prons.*, *advs.*, or
adjs.) of any possible kind or extent (*whosoever*,
howsoever, etc.; *how great soever it may be*). [f. SO¹ + EVER;
cf. WHATSOEVER]
so'fa *n.* long bedlike seat with raised ends and back, on
which several persons can sit or one lie; ∼ **bed,** piece
of furniture able to serve as either sofa or bed. [F, ult.
f. Arab. *ṣuffa*]
so'ffit *n.* under-surface of architrave, arch, balcony,
etc. [F *soffite* or It. *soffitta*, -*itto* f. Rom. *suffictus -a f. L
suffixus (as SUFFIX²)]
S. of S. *abbr.* Song of Songs (OT).
soft (sŏ-, ṣaw·) *a.*, *n.*, & *adv.* **1.** *a.* comparatively
lacking in hardness, yielding to pressure, malleable,
plastic, easily cut, (*soft as butter*; *soft toy*; *book in soft
cover*; *soft stone*, *iron*); *∼'**ball,** (modified form of
baseball using) ball like a baseball but softer and
larger; ∼-**boiled,** (of egg) boiled but not hard-
-boiled; ∼-**centred,** (of a chocolate, or fig.) with
centre having soft consistency; ∼ **coal** (bituminous);
∼ **corn,** moist thickening of skin between toes; ∼
currency (not convertible to gold or supported by
gold reserves, or not easily exchangeable for other
currencies, and therefore likely to depreciate); ∼
detergent (biodegradable); ||∼ **fruit,** small
stoneless fruit (strawberry, currant, etc.); ||∼
furnishings, curtains, rugs, etc.; ||∼ **goods,**
textiles; ∼ **palate,** rear part of palate; ∼ **roe** (of male
fish); *soft* SAWDER; ∼-**shell**(**ed**), (of crab etc.) having
soft shell esp. after recent moult, (fig.) moderate in
one's attitude; *soft* SOAP, SOLDER; ∼ **sugar**
(granulated or powdered); ∼ **tack,** bread or other
good fare (opp. HARD *tack*); ∼ **tissues** (of body, not
bony or cartilaginous); ∼'**ware,** programs etc. for
computer, or other interchangeable material for
performing operations, opp. HARD*ware*; ∼ **wicket**
(Cricket, with moist or sodden turf); ∼'**wood** (of
coniferous tree, easily sawn). **2.** having smooth
surface or fine texture, not rough or coarse, (*soft skin*,
hair, *raiment*). **3.** mellow, mild, balmy, not noticeably
cold or hot, (*soft air*; *a soft winter*). **4.** ||rainy or moist or
thawing (*soft weather*; *a soft day*). **5.** (Of water) free
from mineral salts and hence good for washing or
cooking. **6.** not crude or brilliant or dazzling (*soft
colours*, *light*, *eyes*); not sharply defined (*soft outline*);
not strident or loud, low-toned, *a soft voice*; *soft
whispers*, *murmurs*; *soft music*); ∼ **focus,** (Photog.)
slight deliberate blurring of picture; *soft* PEDAL¹; ∼-
-**pedal** *v.i.* & *t.*, play with soft pedal down, tone down,
refrain from emphasizing; ∼(-**core**) **pornography**
(not highly obscene).**7.** (Phonet.) sibilant (*c is soft in

'*ice*', *and g in* '*age*'); voiced or unaspirated. **8.** gentle,
quiet, conciliatory, complimentary or amorous, (*soft
rain*, *manners*); (of shares etc.) low-priced; ∼ **answer**
(esp. good-tempered one to abuse or accusation); ∼
drink (non-alcoholic); ∼ **drug** (not likely to cause
addiction); ∼ **landing** (in which spacecraft etc.
reaches ground without being destroyed); ∼
nothings, amorous talk; ∼ **on,** (colloq.) in love
with, unduly lenient to; ∼ **radiation** (with little
penetrating power); ∼ **sell,** gently persuasive
salesmanship; ∼-**spoken,** having a soft voice. **9.**
sympathetic, compassionate, (*has a soft heart*); ∼-
-**hearted,** easily affected by others' pain or grief; ∼
spot, sentimental affection *for*. **10.** tranquil (*soft
slumbers*). **11.** (sl.) easy (*has a soft job*; *a soft option*);
soft TOUCH² 9. **12.** flabby, feeble, effeminate, silly,
(*a soft luxurious people*; *soft muscles*); ∼-**headed,** ∼-
-**witted,** half idiotic. **13.** Hence ∼'ISH¹ 2 *a.*, ∼'LY²
adv., ∼'NESS *n.* **14.** *n.* silly weak person. **15.** *adv.* softly
(*play soft* or *softer*; *soft-whispering* etc.); (as *int.*, arch.)
wait a moment; hush! [OE *sōfte* agreeable, earlier
sēfte = OS *sāfti*, OHG *semfti* f. WG *samfti]
so'fta *n.* Muslim student of sacred law and theology.
[Turk., f. Pers. *sūḵta* burnt, afire]
so'ften (sŏ'fen, ṣaw·) *v.i.* & *t.* become or make soft or
softer; ∼ (**up**), reduce strength of (defences) by
bombing or other preliminary attack; ∼**ing**
(morbid, esp. senile, degeneration) **of the brain;**
hence ∼ER¹ (1, 2) *n.* [ME, f. SOFT + -EN⁶]
so'ftie, so'fty, (sŏ'-, saw'-) *n.* (colloq.) = SOFT 14. [f.
SOFT + -IE, -Y³]
||**SOGAT** (sŏ'găt) *abbr.* Society of Graphical and
Allied Trades.
so'gg|y (-gĭ) *a.* sodden, saturated, dank; hence ∼ĭLY²
adv., ∼iNESS *n.* [f. dial. *sog* a swamp + -Y²]
soh (sō), **so²,** *n.* (Mus.) fifth note of scale in movable-
-doh system; the note G in fixed-doh system. [f. *sol*,
ME, f. L *solve*; see GAMUT]
soho'¹ *int.* announcing discovery e.g. of hare or
unexpected event. [ME, f. AF hunting-cry]
So'ho² *n.* district of central London with many strip
clubs and foreign-style restaurants. [perh. f. prec.]
soi-disant (swahde'zahn) *a.* self-styled, pretended.
[F (*soi* oneself, *disant* saying)]
soigné (swah'nyā) *a.* (*fem.* ∼**e** *pr.* same). carefully
finished or arranged, well-groomed. [p.p. of F *soigner*
take care of (*soin* care)]
soil¹ *n.* upper layer of earth in which plants grow,
consisting of disintegrated rock usu. with admixture
of organic remains, mould, (*good*, *poor*, *clayey*, *alluvial*,
light, *rich*, etc., *soil*); ground belonging to (esp. one's
own) nation (*on British soil*); ∼ **science,** pedology;
hence ∼'LESS (-l-l-) *a.* [ME f. AF, perh. f. L *solium*
seat, taken in sense of L *solum* ground]
soil² *v.t.* & *n.* **1.** *v.t.* make dirty, smear or stain with
dirt, tarnish, defile, (*soiled linen*; (fig.) *would not soil my
hands with it*); so ∼'URE *n.* (arch.). **2.** *n.* dirty mark,
stain, smear, defilement; filth, refuse matter, (NIGHT-
-*soil*); ∼-**pipe,** discharge-pipe of water-closet. [ME, f.
OF *suill(i)er*, *soill(i)er*, etc., f. Rom. *suculare f. L *sucula*
dim. of *sus* pig]
soil³ *v.t.* feed (cattle) on fresh-cut green fodder (orig.
for purging). [perh. f. prec.]
soirée (swăr'ā) *n.* social evening, evening gathering
esp. for music, conversation, the advancement of
some society's objects, or the like. [F (*soir* evening)]
so'journ (-êrn, -ern) *v.i.*, & *n.* (make) temporary stay
in or *in* place or *with* or *among* person(s); hence ∼ER¹ *n.*
[ME, f. OF *so(r)jorn(er)* etc., f. Rom. *subdiurnare f. LL
SUB- + *diurnum* day]
||**soke** *n.* (Hist.) right of local jurisdiction; district
under a particular jurisdiction and administration
(*Soke of Peterborough*). [ME, f. AL *sōca* f. OE *sōcn*
prosecution, = ON *sókn* attack, Goth. *sōkns* inquiry f.
Gmc *sōkniz (*sōk- SEEK)]
Sŏl¹ *n.* (joc. or Rom. Myth.) the sun (personified).
[ME f. L]

sŏl². Var. of SOH.

sŏl³ *n.* liquid solution or suspension of a colloid. [abbr. of SOLUTION]

sō'la¹ *n.* pithy-stemmed E. Ind. swamp plant (~ **topi,** Indian sun-helmet made from its pith). [f. Urdu & Bengali *solā,* Hindi *sholā*]

sō'la². See SOLUS.

sŏ'lace *n.,* & *v.t.* comfort in distress or disappointment or tedium (~ oneself **with,** find compensation or relief in). [ME, f. OF (*solacier* f.) *solas* f. L *solatium* (*solari* CONSOLE¹)]

sō'lan *n.* ~ (**goose**), gannet. [prob. f. ON *súla* gannet + *önd* and- duck]

solā'nder *n.* book-shaped box for papers, specimens, etc. [f. D. C. *Solander,* Sw. botanist d. 1782]

sō'lar *a.* & *n.* **1.** *a* of, concerned with, determined by, the sun (*solar eclipse, spectrum, time,* YEAR); ~ **battery** or **cell,** device to convert solar radiation into electricity; ~ **constant,** quantity of heat reaching earth from sun; ~ **day,** interval between successive meridian transits of sun at a place; ~ **month,** one--twelfth of solar year; ~ **myth,** tale explained as symbolizing solar phenomena; ~ **plexus,** (complex of radiating nerves at) pit of stomach; ~ **system,** sun and the heavenly bodies whose motion is governed by it; ~ **wind,** continuous flow of charged particles from sun. **2.** *n.* solarium; upper chamber in medieval house. [ME, f. L *solaris* (*sol* sun; see -AR¹)]

sō'lar|ism *n.* belief in solar myths as chief source of mythology; so ~IST (2) *n.* [f. prec. + -ISM]

solā'ri|um *n.* (*pl.* ~a). place, often enclosed in glass, for enjoyment, or esp. medical use, of sun's rays. [L, = sundial, sunning-place, (as SOLAR; see -ARIUM)]

sō'lariz|e, -īs|e (-īz), *v.i.* & *t.* (Photog.) cause or undergo change in relative darkness of parts of image by long exposure; hence ~A'TION *n.* [f. SOLAR + -IZE]

solā'ti|um (-shī-) *n.* (*pl.* ~a). thing given as compensation or consolation. [L, = SOLACE]

sōld. See SELL.

sŏldanĕ'lla *n.* dwarf Alpine plant of genus *Soldanella,* often with fringed leaves. [mod. L, f. It.]

sŏ'lder *n.,* & *v.t.* **1.** *n.* fusible alloy used to join edges of less fusible metals (**hard, soft,** ~, fusible at higher, lower, temperature and serving for different metals); (fig.) cementing agency. **2.** *v.t.* join with solder; ~**ing-iron,** tool used hot for applying solder. [ME, f. OF *soudure* (*souder* f. L *solidare* fasten f. *solidus* SOLID; see -URE)]

sō'ldier (-ljer) *n.,* & *v.i.* **1.** *n.* member of army (lit. or fig.; *soldiers and sailors; children play at soldiers;* TIN, TOY, *soldier*); OLD *soldier;* ~ **of Christ,** active or proselytizing Christian; ~ **of fortune,** adventurous person ready to take service under any State or person that will hire him; ~**'s wind,** (Naut.) fair wind for going in either direction; UNKNOWN *Soldier.* **2.** (**common**) ~, private or NCO in army (*both officers and soldiers*); PRIVATE *soldier.* **3.** military commander of specified ability (*a great, fine, poor, soldier; no soldier*); hence ~SHIP (3) *n.* **4.** Hence ~-LIKE *a.,* ~LY¹,² *a.* & *adv.* **5.** ~ (**ant**), (1) one of fighting section of ant or termite colony, (2) large red Austral. ant; ~ (**beetle**), reddish-coloured insect of family Cantharidae, with carnivorous larvae; ~ **course** (of bricks placed upright in wall); ~ (**crab**), hermit--crab; ~ (**fish**), (Austral.) small red fish of genus *Apogon;* ~ **orchis,** military orchis. **6.** *v.i.* serve as soldier (*go soldiering*); (arch. sl.) shirk one's work; ~ **on,** (colloq.) persevere doggedly. [ME *souder* etc., f. OF *soud(i)er, so(l)dier* (*sou(l)de* pay f. L SOLIDUS; see -ARY¹)]

sō'ldiery̆ (-ljerī) *n. the* soldiers (of a State, in a district, etc.); *a* set of troops of specified character (*a wild, licentious,* etc., *soldiery*). [f. prec. + -Y¹; cf. -ERY]

sōle¹ *n.,* & *v.t.* **1.** *n.* lower surface of human or other foot that rests flat on ground in walking or standing; part of shoe, sock, etc., below foot, esp. part other than heel; bottom or foundation or lower surface of plough, carpenter's plane, wagon, golf-club head, etc.; floor of ship's cabin; ~**-plate,** bedplate of engine etc.; hence **-sōlED²** (-ld) *a.* **2.** *v.t.* provide (shoe etc.) with sole. [OE **solu, *sole,* = OS, OHG *sola* f. pop. L **sola* f. L *solea* sandal]

sōle² *n.* flat-fish of genus *Solea,* much esteemed as food; LEMON² *sole.* [ME f. OF, f. Prov. *sola* f. Rom. **sola* f. L *solea* (as prec., named from its shape)]

sōle³ *a.* one and only, exclusive, (*his sole reason is this; he is the sole heir, has the sole right; on my own sole responsibility*); (arch. or Law, esp. of woman) unmarried (FEME *sole*); (arch.) alone, unaccompanied, (*went forth sole*); CORPORATION *sole;* hence ~LY² (-l-lī) *adv.* [ME, f. OF *soule* f. L *sola* fem. of *solus* alone]

sŏ'lĕc|ism *n.* offence against grammar or idiom, blunder in the manner of speaking or writing; piece of bad manners or incorrect behaviour; so ~IST (1) *n.,* ~ĭ'stIC *a.* [f. F *solécisme* or f. L f. Gk *soloikismos* (*soloikos* speaking incorrectly; see -ISM)]

sŏ'lemn (-m) *a.* accompanied with religious or other ceremony, done etc. in due form, formally regular, (*solemn feast-day, sacrifice, oath; the Solemn League and Covenant; probate in solemn form*); mysteriously impressive (*solemn silence, cathedral*); full of importance, weighty, (*a solemn occasion, truth, warning*); grave, sober, deliberate, slow in movement or action, (*solemn music; a solemn promise, solemn looks; a solemn pace*); pompous, pretending to gravity or importance, dull, (*put on a solemn face; a solemn fool*); ~ **mass,** = high MASS¹; hence ~LY² *adv.* [ME f. OF *solem(p)ne,* f. L *so(l)lemnis* customary, celebrated at fixed date (*sollus* entire)]

sŏle'mnĭty̆ *n.* rite, celebration, festival, piece of ceremony; being solemn, solemn character or feeling or behaviour. [ME, f. OF *solem(p)nité* f. L *sollem(p)nitas -tatis* (as prec.; see -ITY)]

sŏ'lemnīz|e, -īs|e (-īz), *v.t.* celebrate (festival etc.); duly perform (marriage ceremony); make solemn; so ~A'TION *n.* [ME, f. OF *solem(p)niser* f. med. L *solem(p)nizare* (as SOLEMN; see -IZE)]

sō'len *n.* razor-shell esp. of genus *Solen.* [L, f. Gk *sōlēn* tube, shellfish]

sō'lēnoid *n.* cylindrical coil of wire which, when an electric current is passed through it, behaves as a bar magnet. [f. F *solénoïde* (as prec.; see -OID)]

sŏl-fa' (-ah') *v.i.* & *t.* (~**ed** or ~**'d,** *pr.* -ah'd), & *n.* = SOLMIZATE, SOLMIZATION; TONIC *sol-fa.* [f. SOL² + FA]

sŏlfatā'ra *n.* volcanic vent emitting only sulphurous and other vapours. [name of volcano near Naples, f. It. *solfo* sulphur]

sŏlfĕ'gg|iō (-jō) *n.* (*pl.* ~i *pr.* -jē). solmization, sol-fa; sol-fa exercise for voice. [It., (as SOL-FA)]

sŏli. See SOLO.

sŏli'cit *v.* **1.** *v.t.* invite, make appeals or requests to, importune, ask importunately or earnestly for, (*events solicit his attention; we solicit your custom, you for your custom; was known to have solicited the judges*); approach (person, or abs.) for immoral purpose. **2.** *v.i.* make request or petition (*for*). **3.** So ~A'TION *n.* [ME, f. OF *solliciter* f. L *sollicitare* agitate (*sollicitus* anxious f. *sollus* entire + *citus* p.p. set in motion)]

sŏli'citor *n.* **1.** one who solicits; **canvasser.* **2.** ‖member of the legal profession qualified to advise clients and instruct barristers but not to appear as advocate except in certain lower courts; **law officer of city etc.;* S~-Ge'neral, ‖Crown law officer below Attorney-General (in Scotland below Lord Advocate), **law officer below Attorney-General.* [ME, f. OF *solliciteur* (as prec.; see -OR)]

sŏli'citous *a.* eager *to* do; desirous *of;* anxious, troubled, (*about, for,* etc., or abs.); hence ~LY² *adv.* [f. L *sollicitus* (see SOLICIT, -OUS)]

sŏli'citūde *n.* being solicitous; anxiety, concern. [ME, f. OF *sollicitude* f. L *sollicitudo* (as prec.; see -TUDE)]

sŏ'lĭd *a.* (~**er,** ~**est**) & *n.* **1.** *a.* of stable shape, not liquid or fluid, having some rigidity, (*solid food*; *water becomes solid at 0°C*); ∼ **solution,** solid material containing one substance uniformly distributed in another; ∼ **state,** state of matter that retains its boundaries without support; ∼-**state** *a.*, (esp.) using electronic properties of solids to replace those of valves. **2.** of solid substance throughout, not hollow, without internal cavities or interstices, uninterrupted, whole, (*solid sphere* or *ball*); (of tyre) without central tube; (of printing) without spaces or hyphens between words or without leads between lines; (colloq., of time) complete, uninterrupted, (*worked for two solid hours at it*); ∼-**drawn,** (of tube etc.) pressed or drawn out from solid bar of metal. **3.** strongly constructed, not flimsy, (*solid house, pier, furniture; man of solid build*). **4.** homogeneous, alike all through, (*of solid silver* etc.); (fig.) staunch, reliable, (*a solid Tory*); *(colloq.) on good terms *with*; ∼ **colour** (covering the whole of an object, without pattern etc.); ∼ **vote** etc. (unanimous, undivided); **go** or **be** ∼ **for,** be united in favour of. **5.** well grounded, sound, reliable, real, genuine, not fancied or pretended or showy, (*solid reasons, arguments, sense, comfort*); (of person or his work) sensible but not brilliant; of sound financial position. **6.** of three dimensions; cubic (foot etc.); ∼ **angle** (formed by planes etc. meeting at point). **7.** concerned with solids (*solid geometry; solid measure*). **8.** Hence or cogn. **solī′dĭfy** *v.t.* & *i.*, **solĭdĭfĬCA′TION,** **solĭ′dĬTY,** *ns.*, ∼LY² *adv.* **9.** *n.* solid substance or body; (Geom.) body or magnitude having three dimensions (REGULAR *solid*); (in *pl.*) solid food. [ME; a. f. OF *solide* or f. L *solidus* rel. to *salvus* safe, *sollus* entire; n. f. F *solide* f. L *solidum* neut. (as n.) of *solidus*]

sŏlĭdă′rĭtў *n.* holding together, mutual dependence, community of interests, feelings, and action. [f. F *solidarité* f. *solide* = prec.; see -ARY¹, -ITY)]

sŏlĭdŭ′ngŭlate (-ngg-) *a.* (Zool.) solid-hoofed, of horse family. [f. L *solidus* solid + *ungulatus* ungulate; see -ATE²]

sŏ′lĭd|us *n.* (*pl.* ∼**i** *pr.* -ī). **1.** (Hist.) gold coin introduced by Roman Emperor Constantine. **2.** oblique stroke / used in writing fractions (*3/4*), or to denote alternatives (*and/or*), ratios (*miles/day*), shillings (*7/6*), etc. **3.** ∼ (curve) curve in graph of temperature and composition of a mixture, below which the substance is entirely solid. [ME, f. L (see SOLID)]

sŏlĭfĭ′dĭan *a.* & *n.* (holder) of doctrine that faith by itself suffices for salvation. [f. mod. L *solifidius* f. L *solus* alone + -I- + *fides* faith, + -IAN]

sŏlĭflŭ′ction *n.* gradual movement of wet soil etc. down slope. [f. L *solum* soil + -I- + L *fluctio* flowing (*fluere fluct-* flow; see -ION)]

sŏlĭ′loqu|ў *n.* talking without, or regardless of the presence of, hearers; piece of this esp. by character in play; hence ∼IST (1) *n.*, ∼IZE (2) *v.i.* [f. LL *soliloquium* f. L *solus* alone + -I- + *loqui* speak]

sŏ′lĭpĕd *a.* & *n.* solidungulate (animal). [f. F *solipède* or mod. L *solipes -pedis* f. L *solidipes* (*solidus* solid, *pes* foot)]

sŏ′lĭps|ĭsm *n.* (Metaphys.) view that the self is the only knowable, or the only existent, thing; so ∼IST (2) *n.* [f. L *solus* alone + *ipse* self + -ISM]

sŏlĭtair′e *n.* diamond or other gem set by itself; ear-ring etc. having a single gem; game played on special board by one person with marbles etc. removed one at a time by jumping others over them; * = PATIENCE 2; extinct bird like dodo; Amer. thrush of genus *Myadestes*; (arch.) = foll. 2. [F, f. L *solitarius* (see foll.)]

sŏ′lĭtar|ў *a.* & *n.* **1.** *a.* living alone, not gregarious, without companions, unfrequented, secluded, single, lonely, sole, (*a solitary life, walk, valley, instance*); (of insect) not living in communities; (Bot.) growing singly, not in cluster; ∼**y confinement,** isolation in separate cell as punishment; hence ∼ĭLY² *adv.*, ∼ĭNESS *n.* **2.** *n.* recluse, anchorite. **3.** (sl.) solitary confinement. [ME, f. L *solitarius* (*solus* alone; see -ARY¹)]

sŏ′lĭtūde *n.* being solitary; lonely place. [ME f. OF, or f. L *solitudo* (*solus* alone; see -TUDE)]

sŏlmĭzā′tion *n.* (Mus.) system of associating each note of scale with particular syllable, now usu. *doh ray me fah so lah te*, in fixed-doh system C always being doh and other syllables accordingly, in movable-doh or tonic sol-fa system key-note always being doh and other syllables accordingly; so **sŏ′lmĭzATE³** *v.i.* & *t.* [f. F *solmisation* (as SOL², MI, -IZE, -ATION)]

sŏ′lō *n.* (*pl.* ∼**s** or, *in sense 1*, **so′li** *pr.* -ē), *a.*, & *adv.* **1.** *n.* vocal or instrumental piece or passage, or dance, performed by one person with or without subordinate accompaniment; hence ∼IST (1) *n.* **2.** ∼ (whist), card-game like whist in which one player may oppose the others; declaration or playing to win five tricks at this. **3.** an unaccompanied flight by pilot in aircraft. **4.** *a.* performed as solo; ∼ **stop,** organ-stop especially suitable for imitating solo performance on another instrument. **5.** *a.* & *adv.* unaccompanied, alone, (*for solo flute; solo flight; flying solo*); ∼ **motor cycle** (without side-car). [It., f. L *solus* alone]

Sŏ′lomon *n.* **1.** profoundly wise person; **is no** ∼, (iron.) is stupid; hence **Sŏlomŏ′nĬC** *a.* **2.** judgement **of** ∼ (see 1 Kgs. 3:16–28); ∼**'s seal,** (1) figure like Star of David, (2) plant of genus *Polygonatum*, esp. one with drooping green and white flowers; SONG *of Solomon*. [∼, king of Israel in 10th c. BC, famed for his wisdom]

Sŏ′lon *n.* sage; wise legislator. [f. *Solon*, Athenian lawgiver d. *c.* 558 BC]

sŏ′lstĭce *n.* either time (**summer, winter,** ∼, about 21 June, 22 Dec.) at which sun is farthest from equator and appears to pause before returning. **2.** point in ecliptic reached by sun at solstice. **3.** So **sŏlstĬ′tIAL** (-shal) *a.* [ME f. OF, f. L *solstitium* (*sol* sun, *sistere stit-* make stand)]

sŏ′lūbĭlĭz|e, -ĭs|e (-īz), *v.t.* make (more) soluble; hence ∼A′TION *n.* [f. SOLUBILITY + -IZE, after *stabilize*]

sŏ′lūble *a.* that can be dissolved (*in* liquid etc., esp. in water), that can be solved; ∼ **glass,** = WATER¹-*glass* (2); hence **sŏlUBI′LITY** *n.* [ME f. OF, f. LL *solubilis* (as SOLVE; see -UBLE)]

sō′l|us *pred. a.* (*fem.* ∼**a**). alone, unaccompanied, (esp. in stage direction: *enter king, solus*, or joc.: *found myself solus*). [L]

sŏ′lūte *n.* dissolved substance. [f. L *solutum*, neut. (as n.) of *solutus* (see SOLVE)]

solū′tion (-lōō′-, -lū′-) *n.* **1.** dissolving or being dissolved, esp. conversion of solid or gas into liquid form by mixture with liquid solvent; state resulting from this (*held in solution*); liquid etc. and solid or gas so mixed (*a solution of alum*); = RUBBER² *solution*; SOLID *solution.* **2.** resolution, solving, explanation, method for the solving, *of, for, to,* a problem, puzzle, question, doubt, difficulty, etc. **3.** separating, breaking; ∼ **of continuity,** breach, interruption, (Med.) separation of normally contiguous parts. [ME f. OF, f. L *solutio -onis* (as SOLVE; see -ION)]

Solu′trèan, -ian, (-lū′-, -lōō′-) *a.* & *n.* (culture) of the palaeolithic period in Europe following the Aurignacian and preceding the Magdalenian. [f. *Solutré* in E. France, where remains of it were found, + -AN, -IAN]

sŏ′lvāte *v.t.* & *i.* (cause to) enter into combination with solvent; hence ∼A′TION *n.* [f. foll. + -ATE³]

sŏlve *v.t.* find answer to (problem, puzzle) or way out of (difficulty); (arch.) loosen, unravel, dissolve, (knot, tangle, cohesion, etc.); hence **sŏ′lvABLE** *a.*, **sŏ′lvER¹** *n.* [ME, = loosen, f. L *solvere solut-* unfasten, release]

sŏ′lv|ent *a.* & *n.* **1.** *a.* having the power of dissolving or forming a solution with something; (fig.) weakening the hold of traditions or beliefs; having money enough to meet all pecuniary liabilities, whence ∼ENCY *n.* **2.** *n.* solvent liquid etc. (*water is the commonest solvent; alcohol is a solvent of resinous substances*); dissolving or weakening agent (*science as a solvent of superstition*). [f. as prec.; see -ENT]

-som. See -SOME[1].

Som. *abbr.* Somerset.

sō′ma[1] *n.* body as opp. soul; body other than germ--cells. [f. Gk *sōma -atos* body]

sō′ma[2] *n.* intoxicating drink used in Vedic ritual; plant yielding it. [f. Skr. *sōma*]

Soma′li (-ah′-) *a.* & *n.* (member or language) of Hamitic Muslim people of Somalia. [native name]

somă′tic *a.* of the body, corporeal, physical, (opp. *mental, spiritual, psychic*); ∼ **cell,** body cell as opp. germ-cell; ∼ **death** (of the body as a whole). [f. Gk *sōmatikos* (as SOMA[1]; see -IC)]

sō′mato- *comb. form.* (the human) body, as: ∼GE′NIC, originating in the body; ∼LOGY (-ŏ′l-), science of living bodies physically considered; ∼**to′nic,** like mesomorph in temperament, with predominantly physical interests; ∼**type,** physique expressed in relation to various extreme types. [f. as SOMA[1]+-O-]

‖**sŏ′mbre** (-ber), *****sŏ′mber,** *a.* dark, gloomy, dismal, (*a sombre sky, prospect; man of sombre character*); hence ∼LY[2] *adv.,* ∼NESS *n.,* **sŏ′mbr**OUS *a.* (literary). [F *sombre* f. OF *sombre* n. f. Rom. *subombrare* f. L SUB-+*umbra* shade]

sŏmbrer′ō (-ār′ō) *n.* (*pl.* ∼s). broad-brimmed felt or straw hat worn esp. in SW of US. [Sp. (*sombra* shade, f. as prec.)]

some (sŭm, sum) *a., pron.,* & *adv.* **1.** *a.* & *pron.* particular but unknown or unspecified (person or thing), (*some fool has locked the door; saw it in some book (or other); will tell you some day; is true to some extent; ask some experienced person; some (people) say yes and some (or others or other people) say no*). **2.** a certain quantity or number of (thing) (*drink some water; buy some apples; I have some already; have some more; some (but not all) of it is spoilt; some (but not all) of them were late; if I find some I will send them*); **and the′n** ∼, (sl.) and (plenty) more than that. **3.** *a.* ∼ (**little, small,** etc.), an appreciable or considerable quantity of (*went some miles out of our way; had some (little) trouble in arranging it; have been waiting (for) some time; some years ago; that is some help*); some FEW. **4.** such to a certain extent (*that is some guide, test, proof*); (US or sl.) such in the fullest sense, truly worthy of the name, (*this is some war; I call that some poem*). **5.** (Usu. stressed). at least a small amount of (*do have some mercy on our nerves; has after all some sense of decency*). **6.** approximately so many or much of (thing) (*waited some 20 minutes; weighs some 15 stone; we were some dozen, 60, in all*). **7.** *adv.* (colloq.) in some degree (*we talked some; do it some more*). [OE *sum,* = OS, OHG *sum,* ON *sumr,* Goth. *sums* f. Gmc **sumaz* f. IE **sm̥mos*]

-some[1], **-som,** *suf.* forming *adjs.* (1) f. *ns.,* w. sense 'adapted to, productive of' (*gamesome, cuddlesome, quarrelsome, fearsome*), (2) f. *adjs.,* w. sense 'characterized by being' (*lithesome, lissom, blithesome, fulsome*), (3) f. *vbs.,* w. sense 'apt to' (*meddlesome, tiresome, winsome, wearisome*). [OE -*sum,* = OS, OHG -*sam,* ON -*samr,* Goth. **-sams*]

-some[2] *suf.* forming *ns.* f. numerals w. sense 'group of' (*foursome*). [OE *sum* (see prec.) after numerals in gen. pl.]

-sōme[3] *suf.* (Biol.) denoting portion of a body, esp. of a cell, (*chromosome, ribosome*). [f. Gk *sōma* body]

so′mebody (sŭ′mb-) *n.* & *pron.* some person; a person of importance. [ME, f. SOME+BODY (= person)]

*****someday.** See DAY 9.

so′mehow (sŭ′mh-) *adv.* in some unspecified or unexplained manner, for some reason or other, (*he somehow dropped behind; somehow or other I never liked him*); no matter how (*must get it finished somehow*). [f. SOME+HOW]

*****so′meone** (sŭ′mwŭn, -un) *n.* & *pron.* somebody. [ME, f. SOME+ONE]

*****so′meplāce** (sŭ′mp-) *adv.* somewhere. [f. SOME+PLACE[1]]

so′mersault (sŭ′-; -awlt, -ŏlt) *n.,* & *v.i.* **1.** *n.* acrobatic movement in which person turns head over heels in the air or on the ground and lands on feet; **turn a** ∼,

perform this. **2.** *v.i.* perform somersault. [f. OF *sombresau(l)t* alt. f. *sobresault* f. Prov. **sobresaut* f. L *supra* above+*saltus* leap (*salire* to leap)]

so′mething (sŭ′mth-) *n., pron.,* & *adv.* **1.** *n.* & *pron.* some thing (*have something to tell you; has lost something; his temper is something awful*); ∼ (**or other**) (as substitute for unknown or forgotten description: *she is a lecturer in something or other; he is something in the City*); some quantity etc. of thing expressed or understood (*have seen something of his work; there is something (of truth etc.) in what you say; take a drop of something (liquor); has something (impressive) about him; it is something (praiseworthy etc.) to have got so far; you have something (a valid point) there*); an important thing (*thinks himself something; the party was quite something*). **2.** *adv.* (arch.) in some degree (*was something impatient, troubled*). **3.** **or** ∼, or some unspecified alternative possibility (*has lost a glove or something; is called a 'strike-out' or something; must have run away or something*); **see** ∼ **of,** meet (person) for short time or occasionally; ∼ **else,** thing that is different (colloq., and better); ∼ **like,** approximately (*he left something like a million*), a thing like, somewhat like (*it is something like a cross between a rabbit and a cat; shaped something like a cigar*); ∼ **li′ke,** (colloq.) impressive, a fine specimen of; ∼ **of,** to some extent, in some sense, (*is something of an expert on dogs*). [OE *sum thing* (as SOME, THING)]

so′metime (sŭ′mt-) *adv.* & *a.* former(ly) (*was sometime mayor of this city; the sometime sheriff*); at some time. [f. SOME+TIME[1]]

so′metimes (sŭ′mtīmz) *adv.* at some times (*have sometimes thought about it; is sometimes hot and sometimes cold*). [f. SOME+TIME[1]+-s[1]]

so′mewhat (sŭ′mwŏt) *n., pron.,* & *adv.* **1.** *n.* & *pron.* (arch.) something (*loses somewhat of its force*). **2.** *adv.* in some degree (*it is somewhat difficult; answered somewhat hastily*); **more than** ∼, (colloq.) very (*was more than somewhat perplexed*). [ME, f. SOME+WHAT]

so′mewhen (sŭ′mw-) *adv.* at some time. [ME, f. SOME+WHEN]

so′mewhere (sŭ′mwār) *adv.* & *pron.* (in or to) some place; (euphem.) in hell etc. (*will see him somewhere first*); ∼ **about,** approximately; **get** ∼, (sl.) achieve success. [ME, f. SOME+WHERE]

sō′mīte *n.* each body-division of a segmented animal; hence **sōmī′t**IC *a.* [f. Gk *sōma* body+-ITE[1] (2)]

sŏmnă′mbūl|ism *n.* sleep-walking; condition of brain inducing this; so ∼ANT *a.,* ∼IST (3) *n.* [f. L *somnus* sleep+*ambulare* walk+-ISM]

sŏmni′ferous *a.* inducing sleep, soporific. [f. L *somnifer* (*somnium* dream; see -FEROUS)]

sŏ′mnol|ent *a.* sleepy, drowsy; inducing drowsiness; (Path.) in state between sleeping and waking; hence or cogn. ∼ENCE, ∼ENCY, *ns.,* ∼ent**LY**[2] *adv.* [ME, f. OF *sompnolent* or f. L *somnolentus* (*somnus* sleep; see -LENT)]

son (sŭn) *n.* **1.** male child in relation to his parents; ∼ **and heir,** (esp.) eldest son; ∼**-in-law,** daughter's husband; *he is* **his father's** ∼, like, or worthy of, his father. **2.** **the Son of Man,** (NT) Christ, the Messiah, (OT) descendant of Adam, esp. as form of address in Ezekiel; the ∼s of men, mankind; **the Son (of God),** Second Person of the Trinity; ∼ **of God,** (1) angel, (2) person spiritually attached to God. **3.** ∼ **of a bitch,** (vulg.) disliked person or thing; *son of a* GUN; (*every*) MOTHER[1]'s *son.* **4.** male descendant, male member of family, nation, etc. **5.** (**my**) ∼ (as form of address esp. by old man to young man, confessor to penitent, etc.). **6.** person viewed as inheriting an occupation, quality, etc., (*sons of toil, freedom, darkness,* etc.); ∼ **of the soil,** native of a district, worker on the land, dweller in the country. **7.** Hence ∼LESS *a.,* ∼′SHIP *n.* [OE *sunu,* = OS, OHG *sunu,* ON *sunr, sonr,* Goth. *sunus* f. Gmc **sunuz*]

sŏ′n|ant *a.* & *n.* (Phonet.) voiced (sound); hence ∼ANCY *n.* [f. L *sonare* sound; see -ANT]

sō′năr *n.* system for underwater detection of objects

by reflected or emitted sound; apparatus for this. [f. *sound n*avigation (and) *r*anging, after *radar*]

sona'ta (-nah'-) *n.* (Mus.) composition for one instrument (e.g. piano) or two (e.g. piano and violin), normally with three or four movements (one or more being usu. in sonata form) contrasted in rhythm and speed but related in key; ~ **form,** type of composition in which two themes ('subjects') are successively set forth, developed, and restated. [It., fem. p.p. of *sonare* sound]

sŏnati'na (-tē'-) *n.* simple or short sonata. [It., dim. of prec.]

sŏnde *n.* device sent up to obtain information about atmospheric conditions, esp RADIO*sonde.* [F, = sounding(-line)]

sŏne *n.* unit of subjective loudness, equal to 40 phons. [f. L *sonus* sound]

son et lumière (sŏn ā lōō'myār) *n.* entertainment given by night at historic building etc. with recorded sound and lighting effects to give dramatic narrative of its history. [F, = sound and light]

sŏng *n.* **1.** singing, vocal music, (*burst forth into song*); musical cry of some birds. **2.** short poem set to music or meant to be sung; short poem in rhymed stanzas; (arch.) poetry, verse, (*renowned in song*); (Mus.) composition suggestive of a song (*Mendelssohn's 'Songs without Words'*). **3. for a ~** or (arch.) **an old ~,** very cheaply; **nothing to make a ~ about,** (colloq.) of very trifling importance; ~ **and dance,** (colloq.) rigmarole, commotion; S~ **of Degrees** or **Ascents** (in OT, Psalms 120–134, name variously explained); S~ **of S~s,** S~ **of Solomon,** poetic OT book traditionally attributed to Solomon. **4.** ~'**bird** (with musical cry); ~**-book,** collection of songs; *song*-CYCLE; ~**-smith,** composer of songs; ~**-sparrow,** N. Amer. sparrow of genus *Melospiza*; *song*-THRUSH[1]. **5.** Hence ~'LESS *a.* [OE *sang,* = OS *sang,* OHG *sanc,* ON *songr,* Goth. *saggws* f. Gmc **sangwaz* f. as SING]

sŏ'ngst|er *n.* singer; song-bird; poet; *song-book; hence ~ɌESS[1] *n.* [OE *sangestre* (as prec., -STER)]

sŏ'nic *a.* of or relating to or using sound or sound-waves; ~ **bang** or **boom,** loud noise heard when shock wave from supersonic aircraft reaches hearer; ~ **barrier,** – SOUND[2] *barrier*; ~ **mine** (exploded by sound of ship). [f. L *sonus* sound + -IC]

sŏ'nnet *n.* poem of 14 lines with lengths and rhymes in accordance with one of various definite schemes, in English usu. having 10 syllables per line and rhyming *abbaabba*+varying sestet of 3 rhymes, or *ababcdcdefefgg,* or *ababbcbccdcdee*; ~ **sequence,** set of sonnets on one theme; so ~EER', (usu. derog.) (*n.*) composer of sonnets, (*v.i.*) compose sonnets, (*v.t.*) celebrate in sonnets, address sonnets to. [F, or f. It. *sonetto* dim. of *suono* SOUND[2]; see -ET[1]]

so'nny (sŭ'-) *n.* (colloq., as familiar form of address to) boy or younger man. [f. SON+-Y[3]]

sŏ'nobuoy (-boi) *n.* buoy for detecting underwater sounds and transmitting them by radio. [f. L *sonus* sound +-o-+BUOY[1]]

sonofabitch. Var. of SON *of a bitch.*

sonŏ'meter *n.* instrument for measuring vibration frequency of string etc.; audiometer. [f. L *sonus* sound +-o-+-METER]

sonorous (sonŏr'-, sŏ'ner-) *a.* resonant; loud-sounding; (of speech, style, etc.) full and rich, imposing; hence or cogn. sonŏ'rITY, ~NESS, *ns.,* ~LY[2] *adv.* [f. L *sonorus* (*sonor* sound) +-OUS]

sŏ'nsy, sŏ'nsie, *a.* (Sc.) plump, buxom; of cheerful disposition (*sonsy lass*); bringing good fortune. [ult. f. Ir. & Gael. *sonas* good fortune (*sona* fortunate); see -Y[2]]

sool *v.t.* (Austral.) set (dog) to attack; (of dog) worry (animal). [f. (now dial.) *sowl,* 17th c., of unkn. orig.]

soon *adv.* **1.** not long after the present time or time in question or *after* specified time, in a short time, (*shall soon know the result; was soon convinced of his error; arrived soon after the gate was closed; least said soonest mended*). **2.**

as (or **so,** esp. after neg. or when causality or other close connection is suggested) ~ **as,** at the moment that, not later than, as early as, (*came as* (or *so*) *soon as I heard of it; he will get there as soon as they* (do); *did not arrive so* (or *as*) *soon as I expected; as soon as* (*ever*) *there is any talk of paying he cools down*). **3.** (With expressed or implied comparison) willingly (*I would just as soon stay at home* (*as go*); *would sooner die than let him* (or *than that he should*) *find it out; which would you sooner or soonest do?*). **4.** early (*what makes you come so soon?; how soon will it be ready?; you spoke too soon*); **no ~er . . . than,** at the very moment that (*no sooner said than done,* it was done the moment it was proposed etc.); ~ **or late,** ~**er or later,** at some future time, eventually. **5.** Hence ~'ISH[1] 2 *adv.* [OE *sōna,* = OS, OHG *sān* f. WG **sæno*]

soot *n.,* & *v.t.* **1.** *n.* black carbonaceous substance rising in fine flakes in the smoke of wood, coal, oil, etc., and deposited on sides of chimney etc. **2.** *v.t.* cover with soot. [OE *sōt,* = MLG *sōt,* MDu. *soet,* ON *sót* f. Gmc **sōtam* that which settles]

soo'terkin *n.* (arch.) Dutch woman's afterbirth allegedly produced by sitting over stove; (fig.) abortive scheme, imperfect literary composition. [perh. f. prec.; cf. obs. *sooterkin* sweetheart, app. f. archaic Du. **soetekijn* (*soet* sweet)]

sooth *n.* (arch.) truth, fact; **in** (**good**) ~, really, truly. [OE *sōth,* orig. a. = true, = OS *sōth,* ON *sannr, sathr* f. Gmc **santhaz* f. IE **sontos*]

soothe (-dh) *v.t.* calm (person, nerves, passions); soften, mitigate, (pain); (arch.) flatter, humour, (person, his vanity). [OE *sōthian* verify (*sōth* true; see prec.)]

soo'thfast (-ah-) *a.* (arch.) truthful; true; loyal, steadfast. [OE *sōthfæst* (as SOOTH, FAST[3])]

soo'thsayer *n.* **1.** one who foretells the future; diviner; hence **soo'thsay** *v.i.* **2.** mantis. [ME, f. SOOTH+*sayer* (SAY[2], -ER[1])]

soo't|y *a.* covered with or full of soot; (esp. of animal or bird) coloured like soot, brownish-black, (*sooty albatross, kangaroo, tern*); hence ~ILY[2] *adv.,* ~INESS *n.* [ME, f. SOOT+-Y[2]]

sŏp *n.* & *v.* (-pp-). **1.** *n.* piece of bread etc. dipped or steeped in liquid before being eaten or cooked; MILK[1]*sop;* something given (*to* formidable or troublesome animal, person, etc., esp. *to* CERBERUS) to pacify, bribe. **2.** *v.t.* soak (bread etc. in liquid); take *up* (water etc.) by absorption in towel etc.; wet thoroughly. **3.** *v.i.* be drenched (*am sopping with rain; clothes are sopping wet*). [OE *sopp,* corresp. to MLG *soppe,* OHG *sopfa* bread and milk, prob. f. weak grade of base of OE *sūpan,* SUP]

*sŏph *n.* (colloq.) sophomore. [abbr.]

sŏ'phism *n.* false argument, esp. one intended to deceive (cf. PARALOGISM). [ME, f. OF *sophime* f. L f. Gk *sophisma* clever device (*sophizomai* become wise f. *sophos* wise; -ISM)]

sŏ'phist *n.* **1.** captious or fallacious reasoner, quibbler. **2.** (Gk Ant.) paid teacher of philosophy and rhetoric. **3.** So sophi'stIC(AL) *adjs.,* ~RY (4, 5) *n.* [f. L f. Gk *sophistēs* (*sophizomai;* see prec., -IST)]

sŏ'phister *n.* = prec. 1; (esp. Hist.) student of varying seniority at some English and American universities. [ME, f. OF *sophistre* f. L (as prec.)]

sophi'stic|āte[1] *v.* **1.** *v.t.* involve (subject) in sophistry; mislead (person) thus. **2.** deprive (person, thing) of natural simplicity, make artificial by worldly experience etc.; (in *p.p.,* of person) worldly-wise, cultured. **3.** tamper with (text etc.) for purposes of argument etc.; adulterate (wine etc.). **4.** (in *p.p.*) (Of equipment, techniques, etc.) elaborate, using advanced methods, highly developed or complicated. **5.** *v.i.* use sophistry. **6.** So ~A'TION *n.* [f. med. L *sophisticare* tamper with (*sophisticus* f. *sophista;* see SOPHIST, -ATE[3])]

sophi'sticate[2] *a.* & *n.* sophisticated (person). [f. med. L *sophisticatus* p.p. of *sophisticare* (as prec.; see -ATE[2])]

*sŏ'phomŏr|e *n.* second-year university or high-

-school student; hence ∼IC (-ŏ′r-) *a*. [app. f. *sophom* obs. var. of SOPHISM + -OR]

Sō′phy *n*. (Hist.) ruler of Persia in 16th-17th c. [f. Pers. *ṣafī* surname of dynasty, f. Arab. *ṣafī-ud-dīn* pure of religion, title of founder's ancestor]

sōpor|i′fĭc *a*. & *n*. (drug) tending to produce sleep; so ∼i′FEROUS *a*. [f. L *sopor* sleep + -i- + -FIC]

sŏ′pp|y̆ *a*. soaked with water; ||(colloq.) mawkishly sentimental (∼ **on**, foolishly enamoured of); hence ∼INESS *n*. [f. SOP + -Y²]

sōprani′nō (-nē′-) *n*. (*pl*. ∼s). (Mus.) instrument higher than soprano, occas. added to group of recorders etc. [It., dim. of foll.]

sopra′n|ō (-rah′-) *n*. (*pl*. ∼os, or ∼i *pr*. -ē). (Mus.) highest female or boy's voice, treble; singer with soprano voice; part written for soprano voice; (usu.) highest-pitched member of a group of similar instruments; ∼o **clef** (placing middle C on lowest line of staff); hence ∼IST (3) *n*., (esp.) male adult singer retaining boy's soprano voice. [It. (*sopra* above f. L *supra*)]

sŏr′a *n*. ∼ (**rail**), bird frequenting marshes of N. & S. Carolina etc. in autumn and used as food. [prob. native name]

sŏrb¹ *n*. = SERVICE² *tree*; ∼(-**apple**), its fruit. [f. F *sorbe* or f. L *sorbus* service tree, *sorbum* service-berry]

Sŏrb² *n*. = WEND²; hence ∼′IAN *a*. & *n*. [f. G *Sorbe* var. of *Serbe* SERB]

sŏrbĕfā′cient (-shent) *a*. & *n*. (Med.) (drug etc.) causing absorption. [f. L *sorbēre* suck in + -FACIENT]

sŏr′bĕt *n*. water-ice; sherbet. [F, f. It. *sorbetto* f. Turk. *şerbet*, f. Arab *šarba* drink; cf. SHERBET]

||Sŏr′bō *n*. (*pl*. ∼s). (P) ∼ (**rubber**), sponge rubber. [f. ABSORB + -O]

sŏr′cer|er *n*. user of magic arts, wizard, enchanter (lit. or fig.); so ∼ESS¹, **sŏr′**CERY (4, 5), *ns*. [f. obs. *sorcer* f. OF *sorcier* f. Rom. *sortiarius caster of lots (*sors sortis* lot; see -ARY¹), + -ER¹]

sŏr′did *a*. mean, niggardly; ignoble, base; mercenary; dirty, squalid; dull-coloured; hence ∼LY² *adv*., ∼NESS *n*. [f. F *sordide* or f. L *sordidus* (*sordēre* be dirty; see -ID¹)]

sŏrdi′n|ō (-ē′-) *n*. (*pl*. ∼i *pr*. -ē). (Mus.) mute for bowed or wind instrument. [It. (*sordo* mute f. L *surdus*)]

sŏr′dor *n*. sordidness. [f. SORDID after *squalor*]

sōre *a*., *n*., & *adv*. **1.** *a*. (Of part of body) causing pain from injury or disease (*has a sore arm*; FOOT¹-*sore*; FOOT¹-*sore*; THROAT; *touched him on a sore place*, lit. or fig.); (of person) suffering pain; *a* SIGHT¹ *for sore eyes*; *like a* BEAR¹ *with a sore head*; *∼′**head**, grumpy person; STICK¹ *out like a sore thumb*. **2.** irritated, aggrieved, touchy, (*is very sore about his defeat*); *vexed (*at*); arousing painful feelings, irritating, (*a sore point*, *subject*). **3.** (arch. or poet.) distressing, grievous, severe, (*in sore distress*; *a sore struggle*; *affliction sore long time he bore*). **4.** Hence ∼′NESS (sōr′n-) *n*. **5.** *n*. sore place on body e.g. where skin or flesh is bruised or inflamed; (fig.) sore subject, painful memory, (*reopen old sores*). **6.** *adv*. (arch.) grievously, severely, (*sore oppressed*, *afflicted*). [OE *sār*, *n*. & *a*., *sāre* adv., = OS, OHG *sēro*, ON *sár* n., *sárr* a., Goth. *sair* n., f. Gmc *sairam, *sairaz*]

||sŏ′rel *n*. male fallow deer in third year. [var. of SORREL²]

sŏr′ely (sōr′li) *adv*. severely, grievously, (*sorely tempted*, *in need of*). [OE *sārlīce* (as SORE, -LY²)]

sŏr′ghum (-gum) *n*. tropical cereal grass of genus *Sorghum*, e.g. durra. [mod. L, f. It. *sorgo*, perh. f. Rom. *syricum (*gramen*) Syrian (grass)]

sŏr′ī. See SORUS.

sori′tēs (-z) *n*. (*pl*. same). series of propositions in which predicate of each is subject of next; form of sophism leading by gradual steps from truth to absurdity and based on the absence of precise, esp. numerical, limits to terms such as 'heap'; hence **sori′**TICAL *a*. [L f. Gk *sōreitēs* in heaps (*sōros* heap)]

sŏrn *v.i*. (Sc.) obtrude oneself *on* (person) for bed and board; hence ∼′ER¹ *n*. [f. *sorren* free hospitality given to one's lord, f. obs. Ir. *sorthan* free quarters]

sorŏ′ptimist *n*. member of an international association of women's clubs. [app. f. L *soror* sister + OPTIMIST]

sorŏ′ricid|e *n*. killing of one's sister; one who kills his sister; hence ∼AL *a*. [f. LL *sororicidium*, L *sororicida*, (*soror* sister; see -CIDE)]

sorŏ′rity *n*. devotional sisterhood; *women's society in university or college. [f. med. L *sororitas* or f. L *soror* sister, after *fraternity*]

sorŏ′s|is *n*. (*pl*. ∼es *pr*. -ēz). (Bot.) fleshy compound fruit, e.g. pineapple, mulberry. [mod. L, f. Gk *sōros* heap + -OSIS]

sŏr′ption *n*. absorption and adsorption considered jointly. [f. ab*sorption*, ad*sorption*]

sŏ′rra *n*. (Sc. & Ir.) Var. of SORROW 4.

sŏ′rrel¹ *n*. acid-leaved herb of genus *Rumex*, used in salads etc. [ME, f. OF *surele*, *sorele* (*sur* f. Gmc *sūraz SOUR; see -LE 1)]

sŏ′rrel² *a*. & *n*. (of) light reddish-brown colour; sorrel animal, esp. horse; ||sorel. [ME, f. OF *sorel* (*sor* yellowish f. Frank. *saur dry; see -LE 2)]

sŏ′rrow (-ō) *n*., & *v.i*. **1.** *n*. mental distress caused by loss of good or occurrence of evil. **2.** occasion of sorrow, misfortune, trouble, (*has had many sorrows*, *much sorrow*); **the Man of S∼s**, Christ. **3.** lamentation (*his sorrow was loud and long*). **4.** (Sc. & Ir.) (**the**) ∼, not at all, never (*sorrow a one*, *a bit*, etc.). **5.** *v.i*. feel sorrow (*at*, *over*, *for*, person etc.); mourn (*after*, *for*, lost person or thing); hence ∼ER¹ *n*., ∼ING² *a*. [OE *sorh*, *sorg*, = OS, OHG *sorga*, ON *sorg*, Goth. *saurga*]

sŏ′rrowful (-ŏf-, -of-) *a*. showing or feeling sorrow; distressing, lamentable; hence ∼LY² *adv*., ∼NESS *n*. [OE *sorhful* (as prec., -FUL)]

sŏ′rry *a*. **1.** (*pred*.) feeling regret (*am sorry to hear it*, *that you must go*, *about your accident*); ∼ **for**, regretful concerning (thing) or concerning unhappiness etc. or (iron.) inadequacy of (person); ∼ **for** oneself, (colloq.) dejected; ∼!, (colloq.) I beg your PARDON¹. **2.** (literary). wretched, paltry, shabby, of poor quality, (*a sorry fellow*, *nag*; *in a sorry plight*; *a sorry excuse*); hence **sŏ′rri**LY² *adv*., **sŏ′rri**NESS *n*. [OE *sārig*, = OS, OHG *sērag*, f. WG **sairag-*, *-ig-* (as SORE, -Y²)]

sŏrt¹ *n*. **1.** group of things etc. with common attributes, class, kind, species, variety, (*biscuits of several sorts*; *a new sort of bicycle*; *people of every sort and kind*; *all sorts and conditions of men*). **2.** = KIND¹ (*nothing of the sort*; *what sort of tree?*; *she's not the sort to make a fuss*; (colloq.) *these sort of men*, *a sort of stockbroker* etc., *I sort of expected it*). **3. a** ∼ **of** war etc., *a war* etc. **of a** ∼ or (colloq.) **of** ∼**s**, not fully deserving the name. **4.** (colloq.) person of specified sort (*a good sort*). **5.** (arch.) manner, way, (*in seemly*, *courteous*, etc., *sort*); **after** or **in a** ∼ (= FASHION); **in some** ∼, to a certain extent. **6.** (Print.) any letter or piece in fount of type. **7. out of** ∼**s**, slightly unwell, in low spirits, or irritable. [ME, f. OF *sorte* f. Rom. *sorta alt. f. L *sors sortis* lot, condition]

sŏrt² *v*. **1.** *v.t*. ∼ (**out**, **over**), separate into sorts according to size, quality, destination, etc. **2.** ∼ **out**, disentangle (lit. or fig.), select (things of one or more sorts) from miscellaneous group (*sorted out those of largest size*), (sl.) deal with, punish. **3.** Hence ∼′ABLE *a*., ∼′ER¹, ∼′ING¹, *ns*. **4.** *v.i*. (arch.) correspond or agree *with* (*his actions sort ill*, *well*, *with his protestations*). [ME, f. OF *sortir* or f. L *sortiri* divide or obtain by lot (as prec.), or f. prec. or f. ASSORT]

sortes (sōr′tēz) *n*. *pl*. divination by chance selection of passages: ∼ **Biblicae** (bĭ′blīsē) from the Bible, ∼ **Homericae** (hŏmĕ′rĭsē) from Homer, etc. [L, pl. of *sors* lot]

sŏr′tie (-ē, -ĭ) *n*. **1.** sally esp. of beleaguered garrison. **2.** operational flight by a military aircraft. [F, fem. p.p. (as *n*.) of *sortir* go out]

sŏr′tilège *n*. divination by lots. [ME f. OF, f. med. L *sortilegium* sorcery f. L *sortilegus* sorcerer (as SORT¹, *legere* choose)]

sŏrti'tion n. casting of lots. [f. L *sortitio* (*sortiri* cast lots; see SORT², -ITION)]

sŏr'|us n. (*pl.* ~**i** pr. -ī). (Bot.) heap, cluster, esp. of spore-cases on under-surface of fern-leaf, or in fungus or lichen. [mod. L, f. Gk *sōros* heap]

SOS (ĕsōĕ's) n. international code-signal of extreme distress; ||broadcast appeal to (otherwise untraceable) person (to visit dying relative etc.); urgent appeal for help. [chosen as being easily transmitted and recognized in Morse code]

sō-sō. See so¹ 11.

sŏstenu'tō (-nŏo'-) adv., a., & n. (*pl.* ~**s**). (Mus.) (passage performed) in sustained or prolonged manner. [It., p.p. of *sostenere* SUSTAIN]

sŏt n., & v.i. (-**tt**-). **1.** n. confirmed drunkard, person stupefied by habitual drunkenness; hence ~'**tish**¹ a. **2.** v.i. tipple. [OE *sott* & OF *sot* foolish, f. med. L *sottus*, of unkn. orig.]

sotēriŏ'logy n. (Theol.) doctrine of salvation. [f. Gk *sōtēria* salvation +-o-+-LOGY]

Sō'thic a. of the dog-star; ~ **year**, ancient Egyptian year of 365¼ days, fixed by heliacal rising of dog-star; ~ **cycle** (of 1460 Sothic years, after which 365-day calendar year gives same date for this rising). [f. Gk *Sōthis* f. Egypt. name of dog-star +-IC]

sotto voce (sŏtō vō'chĭ) adv. in an undertone, aside. [It. (*sotto* under, *voce* voice)]

sou (sōo) n. (Hist.) French coin of various values; (colloq.) very small amount of money (**not a** ~, no money at all). [F, orig. pl. *sous* f. OF *sout* f. L SOLIDUS]

soubrĕ'tte (sōo-) n. maidservant or similar character (esp. w. implication of pertness, coquetry, intrigue, etc.) in comedy. [F, f. Prov. *soubreto* fem. of *soubret* coy (*sobrar* f. L *superare* be above)]

soubriquet. See SOBRIQUET.

sou'chŏng (sōo'sh-) n. fine black kind of China tea. [f. Chin. *xiao* small +*zhong* sort]

Soudanese. Var. of SUDANESE.

souffle (sōo'fĕl) n. (Med.) low murmur heard in auscultation of various organs etc. [F (*souffler* blow f. L SUFflare)]

soufflé (sōo'flā) a. & n. **1.** a. made light and frothy (*omelette soufflé*); (of pottery) decorated with small spots. **2.** n. light spongy dish usu. made with flavoured egg yolks added to stiffly beaten whites of eggs and baked. [F, p.p. (as prec.)]

soufrière (sōofriăr') n. solfatara. [F (*soufre* sulphur)]

sough (sŭf, sow) n., & v.i. (make) moaning, whistling, or rushing sound as of wind in trees etc. [f. OE *swōgan* resound]

sought. See SEEK.

souk (sōok) n. market-place in Muslim countries. [f. Arab. *sūḵ*]

soul (sōl) n. **1.** spiritual or immaterial part of man, held to survive death (*immortality of the soul*; ALL Souls' *Day*; COMMEND one's *soul* to God); *lost soul* (see LOSE); *sell* one's ~ *for*, make any sacrifice to get; **upon my** ~ (form of asseveration or expr. of surprise). **2.** moral and emotional part of man (*his whole soul revolted from it*; CURE¹ *of souls*; *has a soul above such trivialities*); ~ *kiss*, deep kiss; ~ **mate**, person ideally suited to another; ~-**searching**, examination of one's own conscience. **3.** intellectual part of man, vital principle and mental powers of animals including man, (*keep* BODY¹ *and soul together*); **cannot call his** ~ **his own**, is dominated by another; ~-**destroying**, deadeningly monotonous etc. **4.** animating or essential part, person viewed as this, (*he was the* (*life and*) *soul of the enterprise, of the party*). **5.** person viewed as embodying moral or intellectual qualities (*the greatest souls of antiquity*; *left that to meaner souls*). **6.** emotional or intellectual energy e.g. as revealed in work of art (*the fellow has no soul*; *his pictures lack soul*). **7.** (Of person) personification or pattern *of*; **the** ~ **of honour**, person incapable of dishonourable conduct. **8.** person (*not a soul to speak to for miles around*; *ship went down*

with 200 souls); person regarded with familiarity, patronage, pity, contempt, etc., (*my, good soul*; *there's a good soul*; *the poor little soul had lost her way*; *a simple soul*). **9.** American Negrohood or Black culture; ~ **brother**, fellow Negro; ~ **food**, traditional food of American Negroes; ~ **music**, style of jazz or rock playing with strong emotional fervour; ~ **sister**, fellow Negress. **10.** Hence (-)~ED² (sōld) a. [OE *sāwol*, *sāw*(*e*)*l*, = Goth. *saiwala* f. Gmc **saiwalō*; cf. OS *sēola*, OHG *sē*(*u*)*la*)*la*]

sou'lful (sōl'-) a. having, expressing, appealing to, the (esp. higher) emotional or intellectual qualities; (colloq.) over-emotional; hence ~LY² adv., ~NESS n. [f. prec. +-FUL]

sou'lléss (sōl-l-) a. having no soul; destitute of noble qualities; dull, uninteresting; hence ~LY² adv., ~NESS n. [f. SOUL +-LESS]

sound¹ a. & adv. **1.** a. healthy, not diseased or injured or rotten, (*a sound mind in a sound body*; *sound fruit*, *timbers*, *ship*); correct, orthodox, logical, well-founded, judicious, (*sound doctrine*, *theologian*, *argument*, *views*, *policy*); financially secure (*sound company*, *investment*); undisturbed (*sound sleep*, *sleeper*); thorough (*sound thrashing*); hence ~LY² adv., ~NESS n. **2.** adv. soundly (*will sleep the sounder for it*); fast *asleep*. [ME *sund*, *isund* f. OE *gesund*, – OS *gisund*, OHG *gisunt* f. WG **gasunda*]

sound² n. & v. **1.** n. sensation caused in ear by vibration of surrounding air; what is or may be heard; vibrations causing sensation of sound; similar vibrations whether audible or not; (**musical**) ~ (produced by continuous and regular vibrations, opp. *noise*); any of a series of articulate utterances (*vowel and consonant sounds*); music, speech, etc., accompanying film or other visual presentation; mere words (*sound and fury*); (fig.) mental impression produced by oral or other statement etc., (*will have a strange sound*; *don't like the sound of it*). **2.** ~ **barrier**, high resistance of air to objects moving at speeds near that of sound; ~-**board**, = SOUNDING²-*board*; ~-**bow**, thick edge of bell against which tongue strikes; ~-**box** (carrying a recording or reproducing acoustic gramophone-stylus); ~ **broadcasting**, ~ **radio**, (opp. television); ~ **effect**, sound other than speech or music made artificially for use in play, film, etc.; ~ **engineer** (dealing with acoustics etc.); ~-**film**, cinema film with audible dialogue, songs, etc., recorded on sound-track; ~-**hole**, -**post**, aperture in belly, small prop between belly and back, of some stringed instruments; *sound*-PROOF² a., & v.t.; ~-**ranging**, determination of position by timing arrival of sounds from known points; ~ **shift** (see SHIFT² 8); ~ **spectrograph**, instrument for analysing sound into frequency components; ~-**track**, narrow strip on side of cinema film for recording sound; ~-**wave** (of condensation and rarefaction, by which sound is propagated in elastic medium e.g. air). **3.** Hence ~'LESS a. **4.** v.i. give forth sound (*the trumpet shall sound*); convey an impression by sound (lit. or fig.; *sounds to me like something cracking*; *sounds as if a tap were running*; *sounds as if he wanted to give it up*; *will sound very strange to say you hadn't time*; *that* (*excuse* etc.) *sounds very hollow*); ~ **in**, (Law) be concerned with (*damages* etc.); ~ **off**, (colloq.) talk loudly, express one's opinions forcefully. **5.** v.t. cause to sound; utter (*sound a note of alarm*); pronounce (*the h in 'hour' is not sounded*); give notice of (*an alarm*, *the retreat*, etc.) with bell, trumpet, etc.; cause to resound, make known, (*sound his praises far and wide*); test (*railway-carriage wheel* etc., *lungs* etc.) by noting sound produced by hammer, on auscultation, etc. [ME; n. f. AF *s*(*o*)*un*, OF *son* f. L *sonus* (-*d* as in ROUND⁵), v. f. AF *suner*, OF *soner* f. L *sonare* (*sonus*)]

sound³ v. & n. **1.** v.t. test depth or quality of bottom of (sea, channel, pond, etc., or abs.) with ~'**ing-line** etc.; find depth of water in (ship's hold) with ~'**ing-rod**; get records of temperature, humidity, pressure, etc., from (upper atmosphere) with ∿**ing-balloon** or sonde; (Med.) examine (bladder etc.) with probe; ∿ (**out**), inquire esp. in cautious or reserved manner into sentiments or inclination of (person *about* etc.). **2.** *v.i.* (Of whale or fish) dive to the bottom. **3.** *n.* surgeon's probe. [ME, f. OF *sonder* f. Rom. *subundare, f. L SUB-+*unda* wave]

sound[4] *n.* **1.** narrow passage of water connecting two seas or sea with lake etc.; arm of sea. **2.** fish's air-bladder. [OE *sund*, = ON *sund* swimming, strait, f. Gmc *sundam (as SWIM)]

sou'nder[1] *n.* (arch.) herd of wild swine. [ME, f. OF *sonre, sundre* f. Gmc]

sou'nder[2] *n.* In vbl senses; telegraphic receiving instrument for reading message by sound. [f. SOUND[2]+-ER[1]]

sou'nder[3] *n.* In vbl senses; ECHO-*sounder*. [f. SOUND[3]+-ER[1]]

sou'nding[1] *n.* measurement of depth of water; (in *pl.*) region near enough to shore to admit of this; (fig.) cautious investigation; ∿-**balloon, -line, -rod,** (see SOUND[3]). [ME, f. SOUND[3]+-ING[1]]

sou'nding[2] *n.* In vbl senses; ∿-**board,** (1) canopy over pulpit etc. to direct sound towards audience, (2) thin plate of wood increasing sound from musical instrument, (3, fig.) means of causing opinions etc. to be more widely known. [ME, f. SOUND[2]+-ING[1]]

sou'nding[3] *a.* giving forth (esp. loud or resonant) sound (*sounding brass*); (fig.) having more sound than sense or truth (*sounding rhetoric, promises*), imposing (*sounding titles*). [ME, f. SOUND[2]+-ING[2]]

soup (sōōp) *n.,* & *v.t.* **1.** *n.* liquid food made of stock from stewed meat etc. and other ingredients; **in the ∿,** (sl.) in difficulties. **2.** *(sl.) nitro-glycerine, esp. for safe-breaking. **3.** ∿ **and fish,** (sl.) evening dress; ∿-**kitchen,** public establishment for supplying soup free to the poor or in times of distress; ∿ **maigre** (-*ger*), (arch.) thin soup chiefly of vegetables; ∿-**plate,** ∿-**spoon,** (large and deep for soup). **4.** Hence ∿'Y[2] *a.* **5.** *v.t.* ∿ (**up**), (colloq.) increase power of (engine), supercharge. [f. F *soupe* sop, broth, f. LL *suppa* (*suppare soak f. Gmc; cf. SOP, SUP)]

sou'pçon (sōō'psawṅ) *n.* very small quantity, dash, (*of* flavouring, quality, etc.; *add a soupçon of garlic; a soupçon of grey in his hair*). [F, f. OF *sou*(*s*)*peçon* f. LL *suspectio -onis* (see SUSPICION)]

sour *a., n.,* & *v.* **1.** *a.* of acid taste like lemon or vinegar, esp. as result of unripeness (*sour apples*, GRAPES) or of fermentation (*sour milk, bread*); (of smell) suggestive of fermentation; (of soil) deficient in lime and usu. dank; (of person or temper) harsh, peevish, morose; (of thing) unpleasant, distasteful; **go** or **turn** ∿, (fig.) turn out badly, lose one's keenness *on*. **2.** ∿ **cream** (deliberately fermented by adding bacteria); *∿'**dough,** old-timer in Alaska etc. [dial., = leaven]; *∿ **mash,** brewing- or distilling-mash made acid to promote fermentation; ∿'**puss,** (sl.) sour-tempered person [*puss* = face]; ∿-**sop,** (large succulent fruit of) W. Ind. tree, *Anona muricata.* **3.** Hence ∿'ISH[1] [2] *a.,* ∿'LY[2] *adv.,* ∿'NESS *n.* **4.** *n.* acid solution used in bleaching etc.; *acid drink esp. of whisky with lemon-juice or lime-juice. **5.** *v.t.* & *i.* make or become sour (lit., or fig.; *soured by misfortune*). [OE *sūr*, = OS, OHG *sūr*, ON *súrr* f. Gmc *sūraz]

source (sōrs) *n.* spring, fountain-head, from which stream issues (*the sources of the Nile*); body emitting radiation etc.; (Phys.) place where flux-lines begin; origin, place or person from which thing comes or is got, (*the source of all our woes; reliable sources of information*); document etc. providing evidence; **at** ∿, at point of origin or issue; ∿-**book** [transl. of G *quellenbuch*], book or collection of original documents serving as material for the historical study of a subject; ∿-**criticism** [transl. of G *quellenkritik*], evaluation of different (esp. successive) literary or historical sources. [ME, f. OF *sors, sourse,* p.p. (as n.) of *sourdre* rise f. L *surgere*]

sou'saphōne (sōō'z-) *n.* large brass wind instrument

shaped like French horn. [f. J. P. *Sousa*, Amer. bandmaster d. 1932, after *saxophone*]

souse[1] *n.* & *v.* **1.** *n.* pickle made with salt; *food in pickle, esp. pig's head, feet, and ears; dip, plunge, drenching, in water; drinking-bout. **2.** *v.t.* put in pickle (*soused mackerel*). **3.** *v.t.* & *i.* plunge into liquid; soak (thing in liquid), throw (liquid *over* thing); (in *p.p.,* sl.) drunk. [ME, f. OF *sous, souz* pickle f. OS *sultia,* OHG *sulza* brine f. Gmc **sult-, *salt-* SALT]

souse[2] *adv.* (arch. or dial.) with swift descent, headlong, (*came souse into our midst*). [f. obs. *souse* swoop of hawk on rising bird, alt. f. SOURCE in obs. sense 'rising of hawk etc.']

sou'tache (sōō'tahsh) *n.* narrow flat ornamental braid. [F, f. Magyar *sujtás*]

soutā'ne (sōōtah'n) *n.* cassock of RC priest. [F, f. It. *sottana* (*sotto* under f. L *subtus*)]

souteneur (sōōtenēr') *n.* man living on earnings of prostitute(s). [F, = protector]

sou'ter (sōō'-) *n.* (Sc. & N. Engl.) shoemaker, cobbler. [OE *sūtere* f. L *sutor* (*suere* sut- sew)]

sou'terrain (sōō'-) *n.* (esp. Archaeol.) underground chamber or passage. [F (*sous* under, *terre* earth)]

south *adv., n., a.,* & *v.i.* **1.** *adv., n.,* & *a.* (towards, at, near) point of horizon to right of person facing east; (**to the**) ∿ (**of**), in a southward direction (from); compass point opposite NORTH 3; ∿ **wind,** wind blowing from the south; *south* BY[1] *east* or *west.* **2.** (w. uses & derivs. like those of *south*) ∿-**east,** ∿-**west,** compass point midway between south and east or west; ∿-∿-**east, -west,** compass point midway between south and south-east or south-west. **3.** (usu. *S*∿). part of world or country or town lying to the south; *the Southern STATE[1]s (**Deep S**∿), States bordering Gulf of Mexico); card-player occupying position designated 'south'. **4. S**∿ **African,** (native or inhabitant) of Republic of South Africa; ∿'**bound,** travelling southwards; **S**∿'**down,** (one of) breed of sheep raised esp. for mutton, orig. on South Downs of Hampshire and Sussex; ∿'**paw** *n.* & *a.,* (colloq.) left-handed (person) esp. in sport; *South* POLE[2]; **S**∿ **Sea,** southern Pacific Ocean; **S**∿ **Sea Bubble,** scheme for trading in southern hemisphere to repay British national debt, started and collapsed 1720. **5.** Hence ∿'WARD *a.* & *n.,* ∿'WARD(s) *adv.* **6.** *v.i.* move towards south; (of heavenly body) cross meridian. [OE *sūth*, = OS *suth,* OHG *sunt,* ON *suthr*]

southea'ster, sou'ther, *ns.* wind from SE, from S. [f. SOUTH(-*east*)+-ER[1]]

sou'therly (sŭ'dh-) *a., adv.,* & *n.* in a southern position or direction; (wind) blowing (nearly) from the south; ∿ (**buster**), (Austral. & NZ) cool southerly gale. [f. SOUTH, as *easterly* etc.]

sou'thern (sŭ'dh-) *a.* & *n.* **1.** *a.* of or (dwelling) in south; lying or directed towards the south; *Southern* CROSS[1], HEMISPHERE; ∿ **lights,** aurora australis; *Southern* STATE[1]s; ∿**wood,** species of wormwood (*Artemisia abrotanum*) with scented leaves; hence ∿ER[1] (4) *n.,* ∿MOST *a.* **2.** *n.* inhabitant of the south, esp. of the Southern States. [OE *sūtherne* (as SOUTH, -ERN)]

sou'thing *n.* In vbl senses; (Naut. etc.) distance travelled or measured southward, southerly direction. [f. SOUTH+-ING[1]]

sou'thron (sŭ'dh-) *a.* & *n.* (arch. Sc.) English(man). [Sc. var. of SOUTHERN]

southwě'ster *n.* SW wind. [f. SOUTH-*west* +-ER[1]]

souvenir (sōōvenēr') *n.* thing given, bought, kept, etc., to recall the past, memento (of occasion, place, etc.). [F, inf. (as n.) of *souvenir* f. L SUB(*venire* come) occur to the mind]

sou'wě'ster *n.* SW wind; waterproof hat with broad flap at back. [f. SOUTHWESTER]

‖**sov.** *abbr.* sovereign.

sŏ'vereign (-vrĭn) *a.* & *n.* **1.** *a.* supreme (*sovereign power;* **the** ∿ **good,** *summum bonum*); unmitigated (*with sovereign contempt*). **2.** possessing sovereign power (*sovereign States*); royal (*our sovereign* LORD); *sovereign*

PONTIFF; so ∿TY¹ *n.* **3.** very good or effective (*a sovereign remedy*). **4.** Hence ∿LY² *adv.* **5.** *n.* supreme ruler, esp. monarch; ‖British gold coin (now rarely used) worth nominally £1. [ME, f. OF *so(u)verain* f. Rom. *SUPER(*anus* -AN); -*g*- by assoc. w. *reign*]

sö′viet *n.* & *a.* **1.** *n.* council elected in district of USSR; **Supreme S∿,** governing council of USSR or one of its constituent republics; **S∿ Union, Union of S∿ Socialist Republics, the S∿(s),** the Russian nation since 1922. **2.** *a.* (*S∿*). Russian; of the Soviet Union. **3.** Hence ∿IZE (3) *v.t.*, ∿ö′LOGIST *n.*, one who makes a special study of the Soviet Union. [f. Russ. *sovet* council]

sö′vran. Var. (poet.) of SOVEREIGN.

sow¹ (sō) *v.t.* (∿ed *pr.* söd; ∿n *or* ∿ed). **1.** scatter (seed, or abs.) on or in the earth for purpose of growth; (fig.) initiate, arouse, (*must reap what you have sown*); *sow* the SEED(*s*) *of*; ∿ **the wind** (see WHIRL*wind*). **2.** plant (field etc. *with* seed) by sowing; (fig.) cover thickly *with*. **3.** Hence ∿ER¹ (1, 2), ∿′ING¹, *ns.* [OE *sāwan*, = OS *sāian*, OHG *sāwen* etc., ON *sá*, Goth. *saian* f. Gmc *sǣjan f. IE **sē(j̄)-*]

sow² *n.* **1.** adult female pig (esp. after farrowing) or guinea-pig; **get the wrong ∿ by the ear,** fix on wrong person or thing, reach wrong conclusion; **as drunk as a ∿,** completely drunk; SILK *purse out of sow's ear.* **2.** ∿(-bug), wood-louse. **3.** main trough through which molten iron runs into side channels to form pigs; large block of iron that solidifies in this. **4.** ∿′back, low ridge of sand etc.; ∿′bread, kind of cyclamen whose roots are eaten by pigs; ∿′thistle, plant of genus *Sonchus* with thistle-like leaves and milky juice. [OE *sugu*, = OS *suga*, MDu., MLG *soge*, rel. to OE, OHG *sū*, ON *sýr*, f. IE *su-]

sown. See SOW¹.

söx. See SOCK¹.

soy *n.* sauce made in Japan and China from pickled soya beans; ∿ (**bean**), soya bean. [Jap. *shō-yu* f. Chin. *shi-you* (*shi* salted beans, *you* oil)]

söy′a *n.* ∿ (**bean**), (seed of) widely cultivated leguminous plant (*Soja hispida*) orig. of SE Asia, yielding edible oil and flour. [f. Du. *soja* f. Malay *soi* f. as prec.]

sö′zzled (-zəld) *a.* (sl.) very drunk. [p.p. of dial. *sozzle* mix sloppily (prob. imit.)]

SP *abbr.* starting price.

spa (-ah) *n.* (place where there is a) curative mineral spring. [f. *Spa* in Belgium]

space¹ *n.* **1.** continuous extension viewed with or without reference to the existence of objects within it. **2.** interval between points or objects viewed as having one, two, or three dimensions (*separated by a space of 10 ft.; clear a space in that corner; box occupies too much space*); amount of paper used in writing etc. (*would take too much space to discuss in detail; bought space in the newspapers to advertise the idea*); large region (*the wide open spaces*). **3.** = OUTER *space*; ∿ **age,** era when space travel has become possible; ∿′**craft,** vehicle travelling in space; ∿ **flight,** (1) journey through space, (2) = *space travel*; ∿′**man,** = *space traveller*; ∿ **medicine** (dealing with effects of space travel on human body); *∿ **opera,** science-fiction drama etc. dealing with interplanetary travel; *space* PROBE; ∿ **rocket** (used to launch spacecraft); ∿′**ship,** spacecraft (esp. controlled by its crew); *space* SHUTTLE; ∿ **station,** artificial satellite used as base for operations in space; ∿′**suit,** garment designed to allow wearer to breathe etc. in space; ∿ **travel**(l**er**), (person) going from one place to another through space; ∿ **vehicle,** = *spacecraft*; ∿ **walk,** physical activity by astronaut in space outside spacecraft. **4.** blank between printed, typed, or written words etc.; piece of metal providing this. **5.** Interval of time (*in the space of an hour, after a short space; let us rest a space*). **6.** ∿**-bar,** bar in typewriter for making space between words etc.; ∿**-heater,** self-contained unit for heating room etc. in which it is; ∿**-saving,** occupying little space;

∿**-time,** fusion of concepts of space and time, esp. as a four-dimensional continuum in which the existent exists. [ME, f. OF *espace* f. L *spatium*]

space² *v.t.* set or arrange at intervals, put spaces between (esp. words, letters, lines, or abs., in printing, typing, or writing); ∿ **out,** put more or wider spaces or intervals between; hence **spā′cING¹** (1, 6) *n.* [f. prec.]

spacial. Var. of SPATIAL.

spā′cious (-shus) *a.* enclosing a large space; having ample space, roomy; hence ∿LY² *adv.*, ∿NESS *n.* [ME, f. OF *spacios* or f. L *spatiosus* (as SPACE¹; see -IOUS)]

spāde¹ *n.*, & *v.t.* **1.** *n.* tool for digging or cutting ground, turf, etc., with sharp-edged broad metal blade and wooden handle used with both hands; **call a ∿ a ∿,** call things by their names, speak plainly or bluntly; hence ∿′FUL 2 (-df-) *n.* **2.** tool of similar shape for various purposes, e.g. for removing blubber from whale; ∿ **beard** (of more or less oblong shape); ∿ **foot,** square spadelike enlargement at end of chair-leg; ∿′**work,** (fig.) hard preparatory work. **3.** *v.t.* dig over (ground) with spade. [OE *spadu*, *spada*, = OFris. *spada*, OS *spado*]

spāde² *n.* **1.** playing-card of suit (∿s) denoted by black figures shaped like inverted heart with small handle; ∿ **guinea** (of George III with spade-shaped shield on reverse); **in ∿s,** (sl.) to a high degree, with great force. **2.** *(sl.; R) a Black. [f. It. *spade* pl. of *spada* sword f. L *spatha* f. Gk *spathē*, cogn. w. prec.; assoc. w. shape of pointed SPADE¹]

‖**spā′dger** *n.* (sl.) sparrow. [fanciful alt.]

spadi′lle *n.* (highest trump, esp.) ace of spades in ombre and quadrille. [F, f. Sp. *espadilla* dim. of *espada* sword; see SPADE²]

spā′d|ix *n.* (*pl.* ∿ices *pr.* -īsēz). (Bot.) spike of flowers closely arranged round fleshy axis and usu. enclosed in a spathe; hence or cogn. ∿′**i**′CEOUS (-shus), ∿**i**COSE¹, *adjs.* [L, f. Gk, = palm-branch]

spā′dō *n.* (*pl.* ∿s). castrated or otherwise sexually impotent man. [ME f. L, f. Gk *spadōn* eunuch]

spae (spā) *v.i.* & *t.* (Sc.) foretell, prophesy; ∿′**wife,** female fortune-teller. [ME, f. ON *spá*]

spaghe′tti (-gĕ′-) *n.* pasta made in solid strings, between macaroni and vermicelli in thickness. [It., pl. of dim. of *spago* string]

spahi (spah′hē) *n.* (Hist.) member of Turkish irregular cavalry; member of native Algerian cavalry in French service. [f. Turk. *sipāhī* f. as SEPOY]

spāke. See SPEAK.

spall (-awl) *v.t.* & *i.*, & *n.* splinter, chip; (Mining) prepare (ore) for sorting by breaking it up; hence ∿A′TION *n.*, (Phys.) break-up of bombarded nucleus into several parts. [ME, also *spale*, of unkn. orig.]

spälpee′n *n.* (Ir.) mean fellow, rascal; youngster. [f. Ir. *spailpín*, of unkn. orig.; cf. -EEN]

Spăm *n.* (P) tinned meat product made mainly from ham. [f. *spiced ham*]

spăn¹ *v.* (-nn-). **1.** *v.t.* (Of bridge, arch, etc., fig. of memory etc.) stretch from side to side of, extend across, (river etc., fig. period etc.), (of builder etc.) bridge (river etc.); measure, cover, the extent of (thing) with one's hand with fingers stretched. **2.** *v.i.* *move in distinct stretches like span-worm. [f. foll.]

spăn² *n.* **1.** full extent from end to end (*span of a bridge, of an arch, our brief span* (*of life*), *the whole span of Roman history*). **2.** each part of a bridge etc. between piers or supports. **3.** maximum lateral extent of aeroplane or its wing. **4.** maximum distance between tips of thumb and little finger, esp. as a measure = 9 in. **5.** short distance or time (*our life is but a span*). **6.** ∿ **roof** (with two inclined sides, opp. *penthouse* or *lean-to*); *∿**-worm,** caterpillar of geometer moth. [OE *spun*(*n*), – MDu. *spanne*, OHG *spanna*, ON *spann-* or f. OF *espan*]

spăn³ *n.* **1.** (Naut.) rope with both ends fastened to take purchase in loop. **2.** *matched pair of horses, mules, etc. **3.** (S. Afr.) team of two or more pairs of oxen. [f. LG & Du. *span* (*spannen* unite = OE, OHG *spannan*)]

spän⁴. See SPICK.

spän⁵. See SPIN¹.

spä′ndrel *n.* space between curve of arch and surrounding rectangular moulding or framework, or between shoulders of adjoining arches and moulding above; ∼ **wall** (built on curve of arch, filling in spandrel). [perh. f. AF *spaund(e)re*, or f. *espaundre* EXPAND]

****späng** *adv.* (colloq.) exactly, completely, (*spang in the middle*). [20th c.; orig. unkn.]

spä′ngle (-nggel) *n.*, & *v.t.* **1.** *n.* small thin piece of glittering material esp. one of many as ornament of dress etc.; small sparkling object; spongy excrescence on oak-leaves; hence **spä′ngly**² (-ngg-) *a.* **2.** *v.t.* cover with spangles (esp. in *p.p.*: STAR¹-*spangled*). [ME, f. *spang* (f. MDu. *spange*, OHG *spanga*, ON *spöng* brooch f. Gmc **spangō*) +-LE 3]

Spä′niard (-yerd) *n.* native of Spain; (NZ) species of spear grass. [ME, f. OF *Espaignart* (*Espaigne* Spain; see -ARD)]

spä′niel (-yel) *n.* (breed of) dog with long silky coat, drooping ears, and docile and affectionate disposition, used by sportsmen or kept as pet; (fig.) fawning or cringing person. [ME, f. OF *espaigneul* Spanish (dog) f. Rom. **(hi)spaniolus* f. *Hispania* Spain]

Spä′nish *a.* & *n.* **1.** *a.* of Spain or the Spaniards or their language; ∼ **America**, parts of America orig. settled by Spaniards, incl. most of S. America and part of W. Indies; *Spanish* ARMADA; ∼ **bayonet**, yucca with stiff sharp-pointed leaves; *Spanish* CHESTNUT; ∼ **fly**, bright green beetle (*Lytta vesicatoria*) dried and used for raising blisters, as aphrodisiac, etc.; ∼ **Main**, (Hist.) NE coast of S. America between Orinoco river and Panama, and adjoining part of Caribbean Sea; ∼ **omelette** (with chopped vegetables and often not folded); ∼ **onion** (large and mild-flavoured); *Spanish* POTATO; ∼ **windlass**, use of stick as lever for tightening ropes etc. **2.** *n.* language of the Spaniards. [ME (*Spain*; see -ISH¹)]

spänk *v.* & *n.* **1.** *v.t.* slap on buttocks with open hand or slipper etc. **2.** *v.i.* (Of horse etc.) move briskly, esp. at step between trot and gallop. **3.** *n.* slap, blow with open hand etc., on buttocks. [perh. imit.]

spä′nker *n.* In vbl senses; fast horse; (colloq.) person or thing of notable size or quality; (Naut.) fore-and--aft sail set on after side of mizen-mast. [f. prec. +-ER¹]

spä′nking *a.* & *adv.* In vbl senses; (colloq.) striking(ly), excellent(ly), (*had a spanking time*; *a spanking fine woman*), moving quickly (*a spanking trot, breeze*), lively, brisk. [f. SPANK +-ING²; perh. partly symbolic (cf. *whacking, thumping*)]

spä′nner *n.* **1.** ‖instrument for turning nut on screw etc.; **a** ∼ **in the works**, (fig.) upsetting element or influence. **2.** cross-brace of bridge etc. [G *spannen* draw tight; see SPAN³, -ER¹)]

spär¹ *n.* stout pole esp. such as is used for mast, yard, etc., of ship; main longitudinal beam of aeroplane wing; ∼**-buoy** (made of a spar with one end moored so that the other stands up); ∼**-deck**, light upper deck in vessel. [ME *sparre, sperre,* f. OF *esparre* or ON *sperra* or direct f. Gmc; cf. MDu., MLG *sparre,* OS, OHG *sparro*]

spär² *n.* crystalline easily cleavable and non-lustrous mineral, e.g. calcite, FLUORSPAR, ICELAND *spar.* [MLG, cogn. w. OE *spæren* of plaster, *spærstān* gypsum]

spär³ *v.i.* (-rr-), & *n.* **1.** *v.i.* make motions of attack and defence with closed fists, use the hands (as) in boxing, (*at* opponent); (of gamecock) fight with feet or spurs; (fig.) engage in argument (*they are always sparring*); ∼**′ring partner**, boxer employed to practise with another in training for a fight, (fig.) person with whom one enjoys arguing. **2.** *n.* sparring motion; boxing-match; cock-fight. [ME, f. OE *sperran, spyrran,* of unkn. orig.; cf. ON *sperrask* kick out]

spä′rable *n.* headless nail for soles and heels of shoes. [f. SPARROW-*bill*]

sparä′xis *n.* S. Afr. iridaceous plant of genus *Sparaxis,* with showy flowers and jagged spathes. [mod. L f. Gk, = laceration (*sparassō* tear)]

spāre¹ *a.* & *n.* **1.** *a.* scanty, frugal, (*spare diet*); lean, thin, (*man of spare frame*); not copious (*a spare style of prose*); hence ∼′LY² (-ār′li) *adv.,* ∼′NESS (-ār′n-) *n.* **2.** that can be spared, not required for ordinary use, (*how to use your spare time; have no spare cash*); (colloq.) not wanted by others (*is this seat going spare?*); reserved for emergency or occasional use (*always take a spare cap; visitors sleep in the spare room*); ‖**go** ∼, (sl.) become very annoyed or baffled; ∼ **part**, duplicate part to replace lost or damaged part of machine etc.; ‖ ∼ **tyre**, (fig., colloq.) obesity just above waist. **3.** *n.* ‖spare part. **4.** (Bowling). knocking-down of all pins with first two balls. [OE *spær,* = OHG *spar,* ON *sparr,* cogn. w. foll.]

spāre² *v.* **1.** *v.t.* be frugal or grudging of (*spare the rod and spoil the child; must not spare expense*); **not** ∼ oneself, exert one's utmost efforts. **2.** dispense with, afford to give, do without, (*cannot spare him just now; can you spare me a moment, a pound?; could have spared the explanation*); **to** ∼, left over, additional to what is needed, (*arrived with an hour to spare;* ENOUGH *and to spare*). **3.** abstain from inflicting, relieve of the necessity of doing etc., (w. double obj.; *spare me these protestations, this task*); abstain from killing, hurting, wounding, etc., (*spare me, my life, my feelings;* **if I am** ∼**d,** if I live so long); abstain from causing (*spare his blushes*). **4.** *v.i.* be frugal. [OE *sparian,* = OS, OHG *sparōn,* ON *spara* f. Gmc **sparōjan*]

spär′e-rib *n.* part of closely-trimmed ribs of meat, esp. pork. [prob. f. MLG *ribbesper,* by transposition and assoc. w. SPARE¹]

spärg|e *v.t.* moisten by sprinkling (esp. in brewing); hence ∼′ER¹ (2) *n.* [app. f. L *spargere* sprinkle]

spär′ing *a.* inclined to save, economical; restrained, limited; hence ∼LY² *adv.,* ∼NESS *n.* [f. SPARE² +-ING²]

spärk¹ *n.* **1.** fiery particle thrown off from burning substance, or still visibly alight in ashes, or struck out by impact from flint etc., (**as the** ∼**s fly upward,** with the certainty of a law of nature). **2.** small bright object or point e.g. in gem. **3.** (fig.) flash of wit etc.; **strike** ∼**s out of** person, provoke him to lively or original conversation. **4.** (usu. w. neg.) particle of fire or (fig.) of a quality etc. (*not a spark of life remained; if you had a spark of generosity in you*). **5.** (Electr.) luminous effect of sudden disruptive discharge through air etc.; such discharge serving to fire explosive mixture in internal combustion engine; **advance, retard, the** ∼ (in cycle of engine operation); *spark* CHAMBER; ∼**-gap**, space between electric terminals where sparks occur; ∼**-plug**, = SPARK²*ing-plug,* ***(fig.) person providing impetus in an undertaking. **6.** S∼s, (colloq. nickname for) radio operator on ship. **7.** Hence ∼′LESS *a.,* ∼′LET *n.,* (1) small spark, (2) capsule of compressed carbon dioxide for siphons (**P**). [OE *spærca, spearca,* = MDu., MLG *sparke,* of unkn. orig.]

spärk² *v.* **1.** *v.i.* emit sparks of fire or electricity; ‖∼′**ing-plug**, device for firing explosive mixture in internal combustion engine. **2.** (Electr.) produce sparks at point where circuit is interrupted. **3.** *v.t.* ∼ (**off**), stir into activity, initiate (process) suddenly. [ME, f. prec.]

spärk³ *n.,* & *v.i.* **1.** *n.* = BLADE 3; gallant; hence ∼′ISH¹ *a.* **2.** *v.i.* play the gallant. [prob. fig. use of SPARK¹]

spär′kl|e *v.i.,* & *n.* **1.** *v.i.* (seem to) emit sparks, (of gem, star, eye, water, etc. and fig. of wit etc.) glitter, glisten, scintillate; ∼**ing wine** (giving off carbon dioxide in small bubbles, opp. *still*). **2.** *n.* sparkling; gleam, spark. [ME, f. SPARK¹ +-LE 1, 3]

spär′kler *n.* In vbl senses; sparkling firework; (sl.) diamond. [f. prec. +-ER¹]

spär′ling *n.* European species of smelt, *Osmerus eperlanus.* [ME, f. OF *esperlinge,* of Gmc orig.]

spă′roid *a.* & *n.* (fish) of family Sparidae, e.g. porgy. [f. mod. L *Sparoides* f. L f. Gk *sparos* sea-bream; see -OID]

spă′rrow (-ō) *n.* small brownish-grey bird, of genus *Passer*; bird of similar appearance (HEDGE¹-*sparrow*), ∼-**bill**, sparable; ∼-**grass**, (dial. or vulg.) asparagus; ∼-**hawk**, small hawk (*Accipiter nisus*) preying on small birds. [OE *spearwa*, = OHG *sparo*, ON *spörr*, Goth. *sparwa* f. Gmc **sparwon*, **sparwaz*]

spăr′rў *a.* of, like, rich in, SPAR². [f. SPAR² + -Y²]

spărse *a.* (Of population etc.) thinly scattered, not dense; (Bot. & Zool.) placed or occurring at wide or irregular intervals; hence ∼′LY² (-slī) *adv.*, **spăr′sITY**, ∼′NESS (-sn-), *ns.* [f. L *sparsus* p.p. of *spargere* scatter]

Spăr′tacist *n.* member of extreme socialist party in Germany in 1918. [f. *Spartacus*, pen-name of leader, after leader of slave revolt against Rome 73–71 BC, + -IST]

Spăr′tan *a.* & *n.* (native or inhabitant) of Sparta in ancient Greece (esp. w. allus. to supposed characteristics of Spartans: *Spartan endurance, frugality, simplicity*). [ME, f. L *Spartanus* (*Sparta* f. Gk *Sparta*, -tē; see -AN)]

spă′sm *n.* excessive muscular contraction (CLONIC, TONIC, *spasm*), sudden convulsive movement, wrench, or strain, (*a spasm of coughing*; (fig.) *spasms of grief* etc.); (colloq.) brief spell *of* an activity. [ME, f. OF *spasme* or f. L f. Gk *spasmos, spasma* (*spaō* pull)]

spăsmŏd′[i]c (-z-) *a.* of, caused by, subject to, spasm(s) (*a spasmodic jerk*; *spasmodic asthma*); occurring or done by fits and starts (*spasmodic efforts*); hence ∼ICALLY *adv.* [f. mod. L *spasmodicus* f. Gk *spasmōdēs* (as prec.; see -ODE, -IC)]

spă′st[i]c *a.* & *n.* (Med.) 1. (person) suffering from cerebral palsy, with tonic spasm of muscles. 2. *a.* = prec. 3. Hence ∼ICALLY *adv.*, ∼i′CITY *n.* [f. L f. Gk *spastikos* pulling (*spaō* pull; see -IC)]

spăt¹ *n.* & *v.* (-tt-). 1. *n.* spawn of shellfish esp. oyster. 2. *v.i.* & *t.* (Of oyster etc.) spawn; shed (spawn). [AF, of unkn. orig.]

spăt² *n.* (usu. in *pl.*) short gaiter covering instep and reaching little above ankle; cover for aircraft wheel. [abbr. of SPATTERdash]

spăt³. See SPIT².

*spăt⁴ *n.*, & *v.i.* (-tt-). (colloq.) 1. *n.* petty quarrel; slight amount. 2. *v.i.* quarrel pettily. [prob. imit.]

spă′tchcŏck *n.*, & *v.t.* 1. *n.* fowl killed and then plucked, dressed, split open, and cooked immediately. 2. *v.t.* treat (fowl) thus; (colloq.) insert, interpolate, esp. incongruously. [orig. in Ir. use, expl. by Grose (1785) as f. *dispatch-cock*, but cf. SPITCHCOCK]

spăte *n.* river-flood (*river is in spate*); (fig.) large or excessive amount (*a spate of inquiries, of words*). [ME, Sc. & N. Engl., of unkn. orig.]

spăthe (-dh) *n.* (Bot.) large bract or pair of bracts enveloping spadix or flower-cluster; hence **spatha′CEOUS**, **spă′th**OSE¹, *adjs.* [f. L f. Gk *spathē* broad blade etc.]

spă′th[i]c *a.* of SPAR²; like spar esp. in cleavage; ∼ **iron ore**, = SIDERITE 1. [f. *spath* spar f. G *spath*, + -IC]

spă′tial (-shal) *a.* of space (*spatial relations, extent*); hence **spătiă′l**ITY (-shī-) *n.*, ∼IZE (3) *v.t.*, ∼LY² *adv.* [f. L *spatium* space f. + -AL]

spătio-tĕ′mporal (-shī-) *a.* belonging to both space and time or to space-time; hence ∼LY² *adv.* [f. as prec. + -O- + TEMPORAL]

spă′tter *v.* & *n.* 1. *v.t.* scatter (liquid, mud, etc.) here and there in small drops; splash (person *with* mud, slander, etc.) thus. 2. *v.i.* (Of liquid) fall here and there in drops. 3. *n.* spattering, splash (*of* mud etc.); quick succession of light sounds, pattering. 4. ∼**dash**, *roughcast, (usu. in *pl.*) cloth or other legging to protect stocking etc. from mud etc. [frequent. f. base as in Du., LG *spatten* burst, spout; see -ER⁵]

spă′tŭla *n.* broad-bladed instrument for working pigments, picking up powder, etc.; surgeon's

instrument for pressing tongue down or to one side. [L, var. of *spathula*, dim. of *spatha* SPATHE]

spă′tŭlate *a.* spatula-shaped; having broad rounded end. [f. prec. + -ATE²]

spă′vin *n.* disease of horse's hock with hard bony tumour or excrescence; **blood, bog,** ∼, distension of the joint by effusion of lymph or fluid; **bone** ∼, deposit of bony substance uniting the bones; hence ∼ED² (-nd) *a.* [ME, f. OF *espavin*, var. of *esparvain* f. Gmc **spadwāni*]

spawn *v.* & *n.* 1. *v.t.* (Of fish, frog, mollusc, crustacean) produce (eggs, or abs.); (derog.) produce (offspring), (fig.) produce or generate esp. in large numbers. 2. *v.i.* (Of eggs or young of fish etc.) be produced, issue. 3. *n.* eggs of fish, frogs, etc.; (derog.) human or other offspring; white fibrous matter from which fungi are produced, mycelium, (*mushroom spawn*). [ME, f. AF *espaundre* shed roe, OF *espandre* EXPAND]

spay *v.t.* remove ovaries of (female animal). [ME, f. AF *espeier*, OF *espeer* cut with a sword (*espee* sword f. L *spatha*; see SPATHE)]

SPCK *abbr.* Society for Promoting Christian Knowledge.

speak *v.* (**spoke** *pr.* ōk, arch. **spake** *pr.* -āk; **spo′ken** *pr.* ō′k-, arch. or joc. **spoke**) 1. *v.i.* use articulate utterance in ordinary (not singing-) voice (*unable to speak after his stroke*; *wish you would speak distinctly*; (on telephone) *hallo, Grose speaking*). 2. hold conversation (*with* or *to* person; *of* or *about* thing; *so¹ to speak*; *have heard him speak of it*); make mention in writing *of*. 3. make oral address, deliver speech, before assembly, magistrate, tribunal, etc., (*Prime Minister spoke for an hour*; *shall speak for* or *against the resolution*; *has a good speaking voice*). 4. (Of hound) bark, bay; (of musical instrument, gun, etc.) sound. 5. *v.t.* utter (words); make known (one's opinion, the truth, etc.) thus; use (specified language) in speaking (*cannot speak French*; ∼ one's **mind** (bluntly, frankly, etc.). 6. hail and hold communication with (ship). 7. (arch.) (Of conduct, circumstance, etc.) show (person) to be (*his conduct speaks him generous*); be evidence of (*the loud laugh that speaks the vacant mind*). 8. (Of fact etc.) ∼ **volumes**, be very significant; ∼ **volumes** etc. **for**, ∼ **well for**, be abundant evidence of, place in favourable light, (*speaks volumes for his forbearance*); ∼ **for itself**, need no supporting evidence. 9. *speak by the*, *like a, without*, BOOK¹; *speak person* FAIR³; ∼ **for**, (1) act as spokesman of, state the sentiments of, (2) bespeak; ∼ **for** oneself, give one's own opinions (only); **not** or **nothing to** ∼ **of**, not or nothing worth mentioning, practically not or nothing; ∼ **out**, speak loudly or freely, give one's (whole) opinion; ∼ **to**, address, converse with, (person etc.), speak in confirmation of or in reference to, (*I can speak to his having been there*; *will speak to that point later*), (colloq.) reprove; ∼ **up**, = *speak out*. 10. FAIR³, smooth, SOFT, ill, well, etc., **-spoken** [as if *-speech*ED²], (given to) using such language. 11. *∼**easy**, (sl.) illicit liquor shop. [OE *sprecan*, later *specan*, = OS *sprekan*, OHG *sprehhan*]

spea′ker *n.* one who speaks esp. in public; one who speaks specified language (*speaker of French*, *French-speaker*); (S∼) presiding officer in legislative assembly charged with preservation of order etc. (CATCH¹ *Speaker's eye*), whence ∼SHIP *n.*; = LOUDspeaker. [ME, f. prec. + -ER¹]

spea′king¹ *n.* In vbl senses; ∼ **acquaintance**, person one knows well enough to exchange conversation with him, this degree of familiarity; **not on** ∼ **terms**, not, esp. no longer, having speaking acquaintance with (usu. implying estrangement); ∼-**trumpet**, instrument for conveying voice to a distance; ∼-**tube**, tube for conveying voice from one room, building, etc., to another. [ME, f. SPEAK + -ING¹]

spea′king² *a.* In vbl senses; ||∼ **clock**, telephone service giving correct time in words; ∼ **likeness**, lifelike portrait; **strictly, roughly, generally,** ∼, in the strict etc. sense of the word(s) (*am not strictly speaking a member of the staff*); **legally** etc. ~, from the legal etc. point of view. [ME, f. SPEAK + -ING²]

spear *n.*, & *v.t.* **1.** *n.* hunter's or foot-soldier's thrusting or hurling weapon consisting of long shaft with point usu. of steel; (arch.) spearman; sharp-pointed and barbed instrument for stabbing fish etc.; pointed stem of asparagus etc.; ~ (long stiff) **grass**; ~ **gun** (used to propel spear in underwater fishing); ~'**head**, (*n.*, fig.) individual or group chosen to lead a thrust or attack, (*v.t.*) act as spearhead of (attack etc.); ~'**man**, person esp. soldier who uses spear; ~'**mint**, a common garden mint (*Mentha spicata*), used in cookery and to flavour chewing-gum; ~ **side**, male branch of family; ~'**wort**, ranunculus with hastate leaves. **2.** *v.t.* pierce or strike (as if) with spear. [OE *spere*, = OS, OHG *sper*, ON *spjör* pl.]

spĕc¹ *n.* (colloq.) speculation, speculative enterprise, (*it turned out a good spec*); *did it* **on** ~ (in hope of success). [abbr. of SPECULATION]

spĕc² (-s) *n.* (colloq.) specification (of patent etc.). [abbr.]

spe'cial (-shal) *a.* & *n.* **1.** *a.* of a particular kind, peculiar, not general, (*lacks the special qualities required*; *word used in a special sense*; *what is your special work?*; *its special charm did not appeal to him*). **2.** for a particular purpose (*appointed special agents*; *received special instructions*). **3.** especial, exceptional in amount, degree, intensity, etc., (*took special trouble*; *find no special excellence in his work*). **4.** ‖~ **area,** district for which special provision is made in legislation, because of depression etc.; ‖S~ **Branch,** police department dealing with political security; ~ **case,** (1) written statement of facts submitted by litigants to court, (2) exceptional or peculiar case; ‖~ **constable** (sworn in to assist in maintaining public peace in time of emergency); ~ **correspondent** (appointed by newspaper to report on special event or facts); ~ **delivery** (of mail in advance of regular delivery); ~ **drawing rights** (to purchase extra foreign currency from International Monetary Fund); ~ **edition** (including later news than ordinary edition of newspaper); *special* INTENTION, JURY; ‖~ **licence** (allowing marriage to take place without publication of banns or at time or place other than those usually required by law); *special* PLEA; ~ **pleader,** counsel employed to give verbal or written opinions on matters submitted to him and to deal with various proceedings out of usual course; ~ **pleading,** (Law) pleading with reference to a particular case, (pop.) specious but unfair argument, statement of case designed to favour speaker's point of view rather than to discover the truth; *special* VERDICT. **5.** Hence ~LY² *adv.* **6.** *n.* special constable, train, examination, edition of newspaper, dish on menu, etc. [ME, f. OF *especial* (ESPECIAL) or f. L *specialis* (as SPECIES; see -AL)]

spe'cial|ist (-sha-) *n.* one who devotes himself to work *in* a particular branch of a profession (esp. of medicine), science, etc.; hence or cogn. ~ISM (1) *n.*, ~i'stIC *a.* [f. prec. + -IST]

spĕciă'litӯ (-shǐ-) *n.* **1.** special feature or characteristic. **2.** special pursuit, product, operation, etc., thing to which a person or firm gives special attention. [ME, f. OF *especialité* or f. LL *specialitas* (as SPECIAL; see -ITY)]

spe'cializ|e (-sha-), **-īs|e** (-īz), *v.* **1.** *v.t.* make specific or individual; modify, limit, (idea, statement); (Biol.) adapt, set apart, (organ etc.) for particular purpose, differentiate. **2.** *v.i.* be differentiated, become individual in character; (be(come) a specialist. **3.** Hence ~A'TION *n.* [f. F *spécialiser* (as SPECIAL; see -IZE)]

spe'cialty (-shal-) *n.* **1.** (Law). instrument under seal, sealed contract. **2.** = SPECIALITY 2. [ME, f. OF (*e*)*specialté* (as SPECIAL; see -TY¹)]

spĕciă'tion (-sĭ-, -shĭ-) *n.* (Biol.) (cause of) formation of new species by evolutionary process. [f. SPECIES + -ATION]

spē'cie (-shē, -shǐ) *n.* coin as opp. to paper money. [L, abl. of foll. in phr. *in specie*]

spē'cies (-shēz, -shǐz) *n.* (*pl.* same). **1.** (Biol.) group of animals or plants subordinate in classification to genus and having members that can interbreed and that differ only in minor details; **the** or **our** ~, mankind. **2.** class of individuals having common qualities or characteristics; (Logic) group subordinate to genus and containing individuals agreeing in some common attribute(s) and called by a common name. **3.** kind, sort, (*has a species of cunning*; *a species of dogcart*). **4.** (Law). form or shape given to materials. **5.** (Eccl.) visible form of each of the elements of consecrated bread and wine used in the Eucharist. [L, = appearance, kind, beauty, (*specere* look)]

specǐ'fic *a.* & *n.* **1.** *a.* definite, distinctly formulated, (*a specific statement*; *has no specific aim*). **2.** of a species (*the specific name of a plant* etc.); ~ **difference,** what differentiates a species. **3.** possessing, or concerned with, the properties that characterize a species (*the specific forms of animals*; *draws a specific distinction between them*). **4.** relating to particular subject; peculiar (*has a specific style*; *a style specific to that school of painters*); (of a duty or tax) assessed by quantity or amount, not by value of goods. **5.** ~ **cause** (producing a particular form of disease); ~ **disease** (caused by one identifiable agent); *specific* GRAVITY, HEAT¹; ~ **medicine** (having distinct effect in curing a certain disease); ~ **performance** (of contractual duty, as ordered in cases where damages would not be adequate remedy). **6.** Hence **spĕcǐ'fICALLY** *adv.*, **spĕcǐfi'cITY**, ~NESS, *ns.* **7.** *n.* specific medicine or remedy; specific aspect or factor. [f. LL *specificus* (as SPECIES; see -FIC)]

spĕcǐfică'tion *n.* specifying or being specified; specified detail, esp. (in *pl.*) detailed description of construction, workmanship, materials, etc., of work (to be) undertaken, prepared by architect, engineer, etc.; description by applicant for patent of the construction and use of his invention; (Law) conversion of materials into a new product not held to be the property of the owner of the materials. [f. med. L *specificatio* (as foll.; see -FICATION)]

spĕ'cif|ӯ *v.t.* name expressly, mention definitely, (items, details, ingredients, etc., or abs.); include in (e.g. architect's) specifications (*a French window was not specified*); hence ~IABLE *a.* [ME, f. OF *specifier* or f. LL *specificare* (as SPECIFIC; see -FY)]

spĕ'cimen *n.* individual or part taken as example of a class or whole, esp. individual animal or plant or piece of a mineral etc. used for investigation or scientific examination, (*specimens of copper ore*; *fine specimen of the swallow-tail*; *of mosaic work*; *a specimen of his handwriting, skill, generosity*); (Med.) sample of urine etc. for testing; (colloq., usu. derog.) person of specified sort; ~ **page** (of book, printed in prospectus etc.). [L (*specere* look)]

spĕcǐ|ŏ'logӯ (-shǐ-) *n.* science of (origin etc. of) species; hence ~OLO'GICAL *a.* [f. SPECIES + -O- + -LOGY]

spē'cious (-shŭs) *a.* of good appearance, plausible, fair or right on the surface but not in reality, (*specious argument, tale, pretence, person, appearance*); hence or cogn. **spēcio'sITY** (-shǐ-), ~NESS, *ns.*, ~LY² *adv.* [ME, = beautiful, f. L *speciosus* (as SPECIES; see -IOUS)]

spĕck *n.*, & *v.t.* **1.** *n.* small spot, dot, stain; particle (*of dirt* etc.); spot of rottenness in fruit; hence ~ LESS *a.* **2.** *v.t.* (esp. in *p.p.*) mark with specks. [OE *specca*; cf. foll.]

spĕ'ckle *n.*, & *v.t.* **1.** *n.* small spot or stain, esp. one of many irregular natural markings of skin etc. **2.** *v.t.* (esp. in *p.p.*) mark with speckles or patches. [ME, f. MDu. *spekkel*]

spĕcktioneer' *n.* chief harpooner on whaling-ship. [f. Du. *speksnijder*, for *-snijder* (*spek* blubber, *snijden* cut; see -ER¹)]

spĕcs *n. pl.* (colloq.) (pair of) spectacles; specifications. [abbr.]

spĕ'ctacle *n.* **1.** public show. **2.** object of sight, esp. of public attention, (*a charming spectacle*; *a drunken woman is a deplorable spectacle*); **make a** ∼ (= EXHIBITION) **of** oneself. **3. (pair of)** ∼s, pair of lenses to correct or assist defective sight, or to protect eyes, set in springless frame constructed to rest on nose and ears (ROSE¹-*coloured spectacles*); frame containing a green and a red piece of glass in railway signal; ‖**pair of** ∼s, (Cricket) batsman's score of 0 in each innings of match. [ME f. OF, f. L *spectaculum* (*spectare* frequent. of *specere* look).]

spe'ctacled (-kəld) *a.* wearing spectacles; (of animal) marked in a way that suggests spectacles; ∼ **bear,** S. Amer. bear (*Tremarctos ornatus*); ∼ **cobra,** INDIAN cobra. [f. prec. + -ED²]

spĕctā'cūlar *a. & n.* **1.** *a.* of or like a public show; striking, amazing, lavish; hence ∼LY² *adv.* **2.** *n.* spectacular performance etc. [f. SPECTACLE, after *oracular* etc.]

spĕctā'tor *n.* one who looks on esp. at a show, game, incident, etc.; ∼ **sport** (attracting many spectators). [f. F *spectateur* or f. L *spectator* (*spectare*; see SPECTACLE, -OR)]

***spě'cter.** See SPECTRE.

spě'ctral *a.* **1.** ghostlike, of ghosts. **2.** of spectra or the SPECTRUM (*spectral colours, analysis*). **3.** Hence ∼LY² *adv.* [f. foll. + -AL]

‖**spě'ctre** (-ter), ***spě'cter,** *n.* **1.** ghost, thing that is thought to be seen but has no material existence; haunting presentiment (*of* ruin, war, madness, etc.); ∼ **of the Brocken,** huge shadowy image of the observer projected on mists about mountain-top, first observed on the Brocken in Germany. **2.** (In names of animals compared to spectres from thinness of body etc.) *spectre-bat, -crab, -shrimp*. [F, or f. L SPECTRUM]

spě'ctro- *comb. form.* spectrum, as: ∼**che'mistry,** chemistry based on the study of spectra of substances; ∼**he'liograph,** instrument for taking photographs of the sun in light of one wavelength only; ∼**he'lioscope,** similar device for visual observation; ∼**photo'meter,** instrument for measuring intensity of light in various parts of the spectrum. [f. SPECTRUM + -O-]

spě'ctro|grăm *n.* record obtained with ∼GRAPH (2), apparatus for photographing or otherwise reproducing spectra; so ∼GRA'PHIC *a.*, ∼GRAPHY (-ŏ'g-) *n.* [f. prec. + -GRAM]

spĕctrŏ'|mĕter *n.* spectroscope that can be used for measurement of observed spectra; hence ∼**mě'trIc** *a.*, ∼METRY *n.* [f. G *spektrometer* or F *spectromètre* (as SPECTRO-, -METER)]

spě'ctro|scōpe *n.* instrument for producing and examining spectra; hence ∼**scŏ'pIc**(AL) *adjs.*, ∼**scopIST** (3), ∼**scopY¹,** (-ŏ's-) *ns.* [f. G *spektroskop* or F *spectroscope* (as SPECTRO-, -SCOPE)]

spě'ctr|um *n.* (*pl.* ∼a). **1.** image formed by rays of light or other radiation or sound in which the parts are arranged in a progressive series according to their refrangibility, i.e. according to wavelength; this as characteristic of a body or substance when emitting or absorbing radiation; similar arrangement of component parts according to mass etc.; ∼**um** (or ∼**al**) **analysis,** chemical analysis by means of spectroscope. **2.** (**ocular**) ∼**um,** after-image. **3.** entire range of wavelengths of electromagnetic radiation; (fig.) entire range of anything arranged by degree, quality, etc. [L, = image, apparition (*specere* look)]

spě'cūlar *a.* of (the nature of) a speculum; reflecting (*specular surface*); ∼ **iron** (**ore**), lustrous haematite. [f. L *specularis* (as SPECULUM; see -AR¹)]

spě'cūl|āte *v.i.* **1.** pursue an inquiry, meditate, form theory or conjectural opinion, (*on, upon, about,* subject, the nature, cause, etc., of a thing, or abs.). **2.** make investment, engage in commercial operation, that involves risk of loss, (*has been speculating in stocks, in rubber*; esp. w. implication of rashness: *is believed to speculate a good deal*); so ∼**ātOR** (3). [f. L *speculari* spy out, observe, (*specula* watch-tower f. *specere* look) + -ATE³]

spĕcūlā'tion *n.* **1.** meditation on, inquiry into, theory or conjecture about, a subject (*much given to speculation*). **2.** speculative investment or enterprise, practice of speculating, in business (*ruined by* (*a single unlucky*) *speculation; bought it as a speculation*). **3.** game in which trump cards are bought and sold. [ME f. OF, or f. LL *speculatio* (as prec.; see -ATION)]

spě'cūlative *a.* of or based on speculation; given to or engaging in speculation; involving risk of loss; hence ∼LY² (-vlĭ) *adv.*, ∼NESS (-vn-) *n.* [ME, f. OF *speculatif -ive* or f. LL *speculativus* (as SPECULATE; see -ATIVE)]

spě'cūl|um *n.* (*pl.* ∼a). **1.** (Surg.) instrument for dilating cavities of human body for inspection. **2.** mirror, usu. of polished metal e.g. ∼**um-metal** (alloy of copper and zinc, esp. in reflecting telescope. **3.** (Ornith.) lustrous coloured area on wing of some birds. [L, = mirror (*specere* look)]

spĕd. See SPEED.

speech *n.* **1.** faculty of speaking (*recover one's speech*); act of speaking (**have** ∼ **with,** speak with); **freedom of** ∼, right to express one's views freely. **2.** thing said, remark (*after this unlucky speech he remained silent*); manner of speaking (*a man of blunt speech*). **3.** public address (*after-dinner, impromptu,* MAIDEN, SET³, *speech; speech for the defence*); **make** (**deliver**) **a** ∼; ‖**Queen's** or **King's** (**gracious**) ∼, ∼ **from the throne,** brief statement on foreign and domestic affairs and on the chief measures to be considered by Parliament, prepared by Government and read by sovereign in person or by commission at opening of Parliament. **4.** language of a nation, region, group, etc. **5.** act of sounding in organ-pipe etc. **6.** FIGURE¹ *of* speech; PART's *of* speech; ‖∼**-day,** annual day for presenting prizes in schools usu. marked by speeches etc.; ∼**-reading,** lip-reading; ∼ **therapy,** treatment to improve defective speech; ∼**-writer** (esp. of public speeches for statesman etc.). **7.** Hence ∼'FUL *a.*, talkative. [OE *sprǣc,* later *spēc,* = OS *sprāka,* OHG *sprāhha* f WG (*see* SPEAK)]

spee'chi|fȳ *v.i.* (joc. or derog.) make speeches, hold forth in public; hence ∼FICA'TION, ∼fīER¹, *ns.* [f. prec. + -I- + -FY]

spee'chless *a.* dumb; temporarily deprived of speech by emotion etc. (*speechless with rage*); hence ∼LY² *adv.*, ∼NESS *n.* [OE *spǣclēas* (as SPEECH, -LESS)]

speed *n. & v.* (**sped** exc. in senses 8 & 9). **1.** *n.* rapidity of movement (*with all speed; more haste less speed; at full speed*); rate of progress or motion, rate of change of distance with time (*attains a high speed; depends on the speed required*); gear appropriate to a range of speeds of bicycle, (US or arch.) motor car, etc.; (Photog.) sensitivity of film to light, light-gathering power of lens, duration of exposure; **at** ∼, moving quickly; AIR∼, GROUND¹, *speed*. **2.** (arch.) success, prosperity, (*send me good speed*). **3.** (sl.) methamphetamine. **4.** ∼'**ball,** (sl.) mixture of cocaine with heroin or morphine; ∼'**boat,** motor boat designed for high speed; ∼ **limit,** maximum permitted speed of vehicle on road etc.; ∼**-merchant,** (colloq.) motorist etc. who travels at high speed; ∼'**way,** (1) (arena for) motor-cycle racing, (2) *road or track reserved for fast motor traffic. **5.** *v.i.* go fast (*sped down the street*). **6.** *v.t.* send fast, send on the way, (*speed an arrow from the bow; speed the parting guest*). **7.** *v.i. & t.* (arch.) be or make prosperous, succeed, give success to, (*how have you sped? God speed you!*). **8.** *v.t.* regulate speed of (engine etc.), cause to go at fixed speed; ∼ **up,** cause to work at greater speed (*the service wants speeding up*); ∼**-up** *n.,* increase in rate of working, esp. by employees without corresponding additional pay. **9.** *v.i.* (Of motorist etc.) travel at illegal or dangerous speed; ∼'**up,** move at greater speed. [n. f. OE *spēd,* earlier *spōd,* = OS *spōd,* OHG *spuot* f. Gmc *spōan* prosper; v. f. OE *spēdan,* = OS *spodian,* OHG *spuoten* f. Gmc st. *spōd-*]

spee'dō *n.* (*pl.* ∼s). (colloq.) = foll. [abbr.]

speedŏ'mĕter *n.* appliance indicating speed of vehicle. [f. SPEED + -O- + -METER]

spee'dster *n.* person who travels at high speed, esp. illegally. [f. SPEED + -STER]

spee'dwĕll *n.* small herb of genus *Veronica*, with creeping or ascending stem and small usu. bright--blue flowers. [app. f. SPEED 7 + WELL³]

spee'dlў *a.* moving quickly, rapid; expeditious, prompt, coming without delay, (*speedy answer, vengeance*); hence ∼ĬLY² *adv.*, ∼ĬNESS *n.* [ME, f. SPEED + -Y²]

speiss (-īs) *n.* compound of arsenic, iron, etc., formed in smelting some lead ores. [f. G *speise* food, amalgam]

spĕlĕŏ'log|ў *n.* scientific study of caves; hence **spĕleŏlŏ'g**ICAL *a.*, ∼IST (3) *n.* [f. F *spéléologie* f. L f. Gk *spēlaion* cave; see -LOGY]

spe'lican. Var. of SPILLIKIN.

spĕll¹ *n.* words used as charm, incantation or its effect (**break the** ∼, make it ineffectual; **under a** ∼, mastered by or as by a spell); attraction, fascination, exercised by person, activity, quality, etc.; ∼'**bind**, bind (as) by a spell; ∼'**binder**, (esp.) political speaker who can hold audiences spellbound; ∼'**bound**, bound (as) by a spell. [OE *spel*(*l*), = OS, OHG *spel* tale, ON *spjall*, Goth. *spill*, f. Gmc **spellam*]

spĕll² *v.t.* (||**spelt** or ∼**ed** *pr.* -lt). **1.** write or name (in correct sequence) the letters that form (a word, or abs.; *how do you spell 'analyse'?; 'surprise' must not be spelt with a z; can't spell his own name; wish you would learn to spell* (*correctly*)); ∼ **out** or **over**, make out (words, writing) letter by letter, (fig.) explain in detail. **2.** (Of letters) make up, form, (word; *what does c a t spell?*); (fig., of circumstances, scheme, etc.) have as necessary result, involve, (*these changes spell ruin to the farmer*). [ME, f. OF *espel*(*l*)*er*, **espeldre* f. Frank. **spellōn* discourse (as prec.)]

spĕll³ *n.*, & *v.t.* **1.** *n.* turn of work (*did a spell of carpentering*); short or fairly short period (*wait* (*for*) *a spell; had a spell of hay fever; a cold spell in April*); (Austral.) period of rest from work. **2.** *v.t.* relieve, take the place of, (person) in work etc.; allow to rest briefly. [n. f. v., later form of dial. *spele* take place of f. OE *spelian*, of unkn. orig.]

spĕll⁴ *n.* splinter of wood etc.; trap in game of **knur and** ∼ (N. Engl. game like trap-ball). [perh. f. obs. *speld*]

spĕ'ller *n.* In vbl senses; spelling-book. [ME, f. SPELL² + -ER¹]

spĕ'llican. Var. of SPILLIKIN.

spĕ'lling *n.* In vbl senses (*his spelling is weak; not sure of the spelling of 'aneurysm'; another spelling of the same word*); ∼-**bee**, competition in spelling; ∼-**book** (for teaching spelling); ∼-**pronunciation**, artificial pronunciation based on spelling, e.g. *forehead* pr. fŏr'hĕd instead of fŏ'rĭd. [ME, f. SPELL² + -ING¹]

spĕlt¹ *n.* species of wheat (*Triticum spelta*). [OE f. OS *spelta* (OHG *spelza*), ME f. MLG, MDu. *spelte*]

||**spĕlt².** See SPELL².

spĕ'lter *n.* (esp. commercial) zinc. [corresp. to OF *espeautre*, MDu. *speauter*, G *spialter*, rel. to PEWTER]

*spĕlŭ'nk|er *n.* one who explores caves for sport; so ∼ING¹ *n.* [f. obs. *spelunk* cave (f. L *spelunca*) + -ER¹]

spĕnce *n.* (arch.) buttery, larder. [ME, f. OF *despense* f. L *dispensa* fem. p.p. (as n.) of *dispendere* (see DISPENSE)]

spĕ'ncer¹ *n.* short close-fitting jacket; thin jumper worn under dress etc. [prob. f. 2nd Earl *Spencer*, Engl. politician d. 1834]

spĕ'ncer² *n.* (Naut.) trysail. [perh. f. K. *Spencer* (early 19th c.)]

Spĕncēr'ian *a.* & *n.* (follower) of the doctrines of continual mechanical evolution of the universe, propounded by Spencer; hence ∼ISM (3) *n.* [f. H. *Spencer*, Engl. philosopher d. 1903 + -IAN]

spĕnd *v.t.* (**spent**). **1.** pay out (money, or abs.; *on* or **for a thing; on person or thing so as to improve etc.*) in making a purchase etc.; ∼ **a penny**, (colloq.) urinate or defecate [f. coin-operated lock of public water-

-closet]; ***∼'**ing money,** pocket-money. **2.** use, use up, consume (*our ammunition was all spent; shall spend no more effort on him; how do you spend your time?; spent a pleasant day; night is far spent*); exhaust, wear out, (*his anger will soon spend itself*); (in *p.p.*) having lost its original force or strength (*storm is spent; spent cannon--ball, tan, fish after spawning*). **3.** ∼'**thrift,** extravagant person, prodigal. **4.** Hence ∼'ABLE *a.*, ∼'ER¹ *n.* [OE *spendan*, = OHG *spentōn*, ON *spenna*, f. L *expendere* (see EXPEND); in ME perh. also f. obs. *dispend* f. OF *despendre* expend f. L *dispendere* (see DISPENSE)]

Spĕnsēr'ian *a.* (in the style) of Spenser; ∼ **stanza,** that used by Spenser in the *Faerie Queene*, with eight iambic pentameters and an alexandrine, rhyming *ababbcbcc*. [f. E. *Spenser*, Engl. poet d. 1599 + -IAN]

spĕnt. See SPEND.

spĕrm¹ *n.* (*pl.* ∼s or ∼). male generative fluid; (Biol.) spermatozoon. [ME, f. LL f. Gk *sperma -matos* seed (*speirō* sow)]

spĕrm² *n.* ∼ (**whale**), large whale (*Physeter catodon*) yielding spermaceti; = SPERMACETI; ∼-**oil,** lubricant found together with spermaceti. [abbr. of foll.]

spĕrmacĕ'ti *n.* white waxy substance contained in head of sperm whale etc., used for candles and ointments. [ME f. med. L, f. LL *sperma* SPERM¹ + *ceti* of whale (*cetus* f. Gk *kētos*), it being regarded as whale--spawn]

spĕr'marў *n.* organ in which spermatozoa are generated. [f. mod. L *spermarium* (as SPERM¹; see -ARY¹)]

spĕrmă'tic *a.* of SPERM¹ or the spermary; ∼ **cord** (supporting testicle within scrotum). [f. LL f. Gk *spermatikos* (as SPERM¹; see -IC)]

spĕr'matid *n.* (Biol.) cell that develops into spermatozoon. [f. as SPERM¹ + -ID²]

spĕr'mato- *comb. form.* seed, SPERM¹, as: ∼**blast,** spermatid; ∼**cyte,** cell that is ancestor of spermatozoa; ∼**ge'nesis,** development of spermatozoa; ∼**go'nium,** cell from which male gametes are ultimately formed; ∼**phore,** capsule containing spermatozoa; ∼**phyte,** plant producing seeds; ∼**zo'on** (*pl.* ∼*zo'a*), male fertilizing element contained in semen of animals, (or ∼**zo'id**) similar element in lower plants. [f. as SPERM¹ + -O-]

spĕr'micīd|e *n.* substance able to kill spermatozoa; hence ∼AL *a.* (irreg. f. SPERM¹ + -I- + -CIDE (1)]

spĕr'mo-. Var. of SPERMATO-.

spew, (arch.) **spūe,** *v.t.* & *i.* vomit (lit. or fig.). [OE *spīwan, spēowan*, = OS, OHG *spīwan*, ON *spýja*, Goth. *speiwan*, Gmc f. IE **spjūj-*, imit.]

sp. gr. *abbr.* specific gravity.

sphă'gn|um *n.* (*pl.* ∼**a**). moss of genus *Sphagnum*, growing in bogs and peat, and used as packing etc. [mod. L, f. Gk *sphagnos* a moss]

sphă'lerīte *n.* = BLENDE. [f. Gk *sphaleros* deceptive (cf. BLENDE) + -ITE¹]

sphē'no- *comb. form.* of the sphenoid bone and (*spheno--ethmoidal*). [Gk (*sphēn* wedge; see -O-)]

sphē'noid *a.* & *n.* wedge-shaped, esp. ∼ (**bone**), compound bone between temporal bone and eye; hence **sphēnoi'd**AL *a.* [f. mod. L f. Gk *sphēnoeidēs* (*sphēn* wedge; see -OID)]

sphēre *n.*, & *v.t.* **1.** *n.* (surface of) solid figure generated by revolution of semicircle about its diameter, every point on whose surface is equidistant from its centre. **2.** ball, globe; (poet.) the heavens, the sky; any heavenly body, globe representing the earth; globe representing the surface on which heavenly bodies appear to lie (**oblique, right, parallel,** ∼, sphere of apparent heavens at place where there is oblique angle, right angle, zero angle, between equator and horizon). **3.** each of the revolving globe-shaped shells in which the heavenly bodies were formerly supposed to be set; **music** or **harmony of the** ∼s (supposed to be produced by movements of these shells). **4.** one's field of action, influence, or existence, one's natural surroundings, one's place in society, (*has done much within his own sphere; great mistake to take him out of his sphere; moves in quite another sphere*); ~ **of influence,** claimed or recognized area of State's interests. **5.** Hence **sphēr'y²** *a.* (poet.). **6.** *v.t.* (arch.) enclose (as) in sphere; make sphere-shaped; (poet.) exalt to the (celestial) spheres. [ME *sper(e)* f. OF *espere* f. LL *sphera,* L f. Gk *sphaira* ball]

sphē'r|ic *a.* = foll., whence ~**i'cITY** *n.*; (poet.) of the heavens, celestial, exalted. [f. LL f. Gk *sphairikos* (as prec.; see -IC)]

sphē'rical *a.* shaped like a sphere, globular, whence ~**LY²** *adv.*; of spheres (*spherical geometry, trigonometry*); (of triangle etc.) bounded by arcs of great circles of sphere; ~ **aberration** (due to spherical form of lens or mirror). [f. as prec.; see -ICAL]

sphē'roid *n.* spherelike but not perfectly spherical body, solid generated by half-revolution of ellipse about its major axis (PROLATE *spheroid*) or minor axis (OBLATE² *spheroid*); hence **spheroid'AL** (-ĕr'-, -ĕr-) *a.,* ~**i'cITY** *n.* [f. L f. Gk *sphairoeidēs* (as SPHERE; see -OID)]

spherŏ'meter *n.* instrument for finding radius of sphere and for exact measurement of thickness of small bodies. [f. F *sphéromètre* (as SPHERE, -O-, -METER)]

sphē'rul|e (-ool) *n.* small sphere; hence ~**AR¹** *a.* [f. LL *sphaerula* dim. of L *sphaera* (see SPHERE, -ULE)]

sphē'rulite (-ōō-) *n.* vitreous globule as constituent of volcanic rocks. [f. as prec. + -ITE¹]

sphi'ncter *n.* ring of muscle surrounding and serving to guard or close an opening or tube; hence ~**AL,** **sphinctĕ'ric,** *adjs.* [L, f. Gk *sphigktēr* (*sphiggō* bind tight)]

sphi'ngid (-ngg-) *a.* & *n.* (member) of the hawk-moth family Sphingidae. [f. foll. + -ID³]

sphinx *n.* **1.** (Gk Myth.; S~) winged monster of Thebes with woman's head and lion's body who proposed a riddle to the Thebans, killed all who could not guess it, and on Oedipus's solving it threw herself from the rock on which she sat, and died. **2.** (Egypt. Ant.) figure with lion's body and man's or animal's head, esp. (**the S~**) colossal one near the Pyramids at Giza. **3.** enigmatic or inscrutable person. **4.** hawk-moth; species of baboon (*Papio sphinx*). [L, f. Gk *Sphigx,* app. f. *sphiggō* draw tight]

sphragi'stics *n. pl.* (also treated as *sing.*) study of engraved seals. [f. F *sphragistique* n. & a. f. Gk *sphragistikos* (*sphragis* seal; see -IC)]

sphȳ'gmo- *comb. form.* (Physiol.) pulse, pulsation, as: ~**graph,** instrument for showing character of pulse in series of curves; ~**gram,** record so produced; ~**mano'meter,** instrument for measuring blood pressure. [f. Gk *sphugmo-* (*sphugmos* pulse f. *sphuzō* to throb)]

spī'c|a *n.* **1.** (Bot.) spike; hence ~**ATE²,** ~**ātED¹,** *adjs.* **2.** (Surg.) spiral bandage with reversed turns, suggesting ear of corn. [L, = spike, ear of corn, rel. to *spina* SPINE; in sense 2 after Gk *stakhus*]

spice *n.,* & *v.t.* **1.** aromatic or pungent vegetable substance used to flavour food, e.g. cloves, pepper, mace; spices collectively (*dealer in spice; sugar and spice and all that's nice*), so **spī'cERY** (1) *n.*; (fig.) interesting or piquant quality, slight flavour (*of* malice etc. in person's character, writings, etc.); ~**bush,** aromatic Amer. shrub of genus *Lindera* or *Calycanthus.* **2.** *v.t.* flavour with spice (lit. or fig.). [ME, f. OF *espice(r)* f. L *species* specific kind, in LL pl. = merchandise]

spick *a.* ~ **and span,** smart and new, brand-new, very neat. [16th c. *spick and span new,* emphatic extension of ME *span new* f. ON *spán-nýr* (*spánn* chip, *nýr* new)]

spi'cknel *n.* baldmoney. [var. of SPIGNEL]

spi'cūl|e *n.* small sharp-pointed body; (Zool.) small hard calcareous or siliceous body esp. in framework of sponge; (Bot.) small or secondary spike; (Astron.) spikelike prominence; hence ~**AR¹,** ~**ATE²,** *adjs.* [f. mod. L *spicula, spiculum,* dims. of SPICA; see -ULE]

spī'c|ȳ *a.* of, flavoured or fragrant with, spice; (fig.) piquant, pungent, sensational, improper (*spicy story*),

(sl.) showy, smart; hence ~**iLY²** *adv.,* ~**iNESS** *n.* [f. SPICE + -Y²]

spī'der *n.* **1.** eight-legged arthropod of the order Araneida, many species of which spin webs esp. for capture of insects as food (~ **and fly,** (fig.) ensnarer and ensnared); kinds of arachnid like spider (RED *spider*). **2.** thing compared to spider esp. as having prominent legs or radiating spokes etc.; *iron frying-pan (orig. with legs or feet). **3.** high-built cart etc. with very large light wheels. **4.** ~**crab,** crab of superfamily Oxyrhyncha, with long thin legs; ~**line,** thread of spider's web substituted for wire in reticle etc.; ~**man,** one who works at great height in construction of buildings; ~ **monkey,** Amer. monkey with long limbs and long prehensile tail; ~ **plant** (with long narrow striped leaves); ~**wasp,** wasp that stores its nest with spiders as food for its young; ~**wort,** plant of genus *Tradescantia,* whose flowers have slender hairy stamens. **5.** Hence ~**y²** *a.,* (esp. of handwriting, legs, spokes, etc.) very thin. [OE *spīthra* (as SPIN¹)]

spie'geleisen (-gelīzen) *n.* kind of pig-iron containing manganese, used in Bessemer process of steel-making. [G (*spiegel* mirror, *eisen* iron)]

***spiel** *n.* & *v.* (sl.) **1.** *n.* speech, story, esp. glib or persuasive one. **2.** *v.i.* hold forth, orate. **3.** *v.t.* reel off (patter, yarn, tale of misfortune). [G, = play, game]

spie'ler *n.* (sl.) *one who spiels; (Austral.) gambler, swindler. [G (as prec.; see -ER¹)]

spi'ffȳ, spi'ffing, *adjs.* (arch. colloq.) smart, handsome; excellent. [19th c.; orig. unkn.]

spi'f(f)licāte *v.t.* (usu. joc.) trounce, castigate, destroy. [18th c.; fanciful]

spī'gnel *n.* baldmoney. [perh. f. ME *spigurnel,* plant-name, f. med. L *spigurnellus,* of unkn. orig.]

spī'got *n.* small peg or plug, esp. one for insertion into vent-hole of cask; (similar device controlling flow of liquor in) faucet; plain end of pipe-section fitting into socket of next one. [ME, perh. f. Prov. *espigou(n)* f. L *spiculum* dim. of *spicum* = SPICA]

***spīk** *n.* (derog.; R) Spanish American, esp. Mexican. [f. SPEAK as allegedly used in 'no spik English' etc.]

spīke¹ *n.,* & *v.t.* **1.** *n.* sharp point; pointed piece of metal e.g. one of set forming top of iron fence etc. or worn on bottom of running shoe to prevent slipping; (in *pl.*) running-shoes fitted with spikes; large stout nail esp. as used for railways; pointed metal rod standing upright on base and used e.g. to hold postponed matter in newspaper office; (sl.) hypodermic needle; ~ **heel** of shoe (high and tapering to narrow base). **2.** *v.t.* fasten with or furnish with spikes; fix on or pierce with spikes; (Hist.) plug up vent of (gun) with spike (~ person's **guns,** spoil his plans), (fig.) make useless, *put an end to (idea etc.); (colloq.) add alcohol to (drink). [ME, perh. f. MLG, MDu. *spiker,* rel. to SPOKE¹]

spīke² *n.* (Bot.) flower-cluster of many sessile flowers arranged closely on long common axis; separate sprig of any plant in which flowers form spikelike cluster; hence ~**LET** (-kl-) *n.* [ME, = ear of corn, f. L SPICA]

spī'kenard (-kn-) *n.* (ancient costly aromatic ointment made chiefly from) Indian plant (*Nardostachys jatamansi*); **ploughman's** ~, composite fragrant plant (*Inula squarrosa*) with purplish-yellow flower-heads. [ME, (ult.) f. med. L *spica nardi* (as SPIKE², NARD), after Gk *nardostakhus*]

spī'k|ȳ¹ *a.* like a spike; having spike(s); (colloq.) easily offended, (derog.) holding rigid high-church or ritualistic views; hence ~**iLY²** *adv.,* ~**iNESS** *n.* [f. SPIKE¹ + -Y²]

spī'kȳ² *a.* having spikes or ears. [f. SPIKE² + -Y²]

spīle *n.,* & *v.t.* **1.** *n.* wooden peg, spigot; large timber for driving into ground, pile; *small spout for conducting sap from sugar-maple etc. **2.** *v.t.* make spike-hole in (cask etc.). [MDu., MLG, = wooden peg etc.; in sense 'pile' app. alt. f. PILE¹]

spill¹ *v.* (**spilt** or ~**ed**) & *n.* **1.** *v.t.* allow (liquid, substance in small particles) to fall or run out from vessel esp. accidentally or wastefully (*spilt the salt; no use crying over spilt* MILK[1]); ~ **blood,** be guilty of bloodshed; ~ **the blood of,** kill; ~'**way,** passage for surplus water from dam; hence ~'AGE (3, 6) *n.* **2.** (Naut.) empty (sail) of wind; lose (wind) from belly of sail. **3.** (sl.) disclose (information etc.); ~ **the beans,** give the show away, divulge information indiscreetly. **4.** throw from saddle or vehicle (*horse spilt him*). **5.** *v.i.* (Of liquid etc.) be spilt, fall or run out from vessel; ~ **over** (of surplus population of towns; cf. OVERSPILL). **6.** *n.* spilling or being spilt; throwing or being thrown from saddle etc. (*had a nasty spill*); tumble, fall. [OE *spillan* kill, = MDu., MLG *spillen,* rel. to OE *spildan* destroy = OS *spildian,* OHG *spilden,* ON *spilla,* of unkn. orig.]

spill[2] *n.* thin strip of wood, folded or twisted paper, for lighting candles, pipe-tobacco, etc. [ME, rel. to SPILE]

spi'likin *n.* splinter of wood, bone, etc.; (in *pl.*) game in which heap of these is to be removed by taking one at a time without disturbing others. [f. prec. + -KIN]

spilt. See SPILL[1].

spilth *n.* what is spilt; act of spilling; excess, surplus. [f. SPILL[1] + -TH[1]]

spin[1] *v.* (**-nn-;** *spun or* arch. **span; spun**). **1.** *v.t.* draw out and twist (wool, cotton, or abs.) into threads; make (yarn) thus. **2.** (Of spider, silkworm, etc.) make (web, gossamer, cocoon, or abs.) by extrusion of fine viscous thread; make (artificial fibre) thus. **3.** (fig.) produce, compose, (narrative, literary article, etc.); ~ **a yarn,** (orig. Naut.) tell a story. **4.** ~ **out,** spend, consume, (time, one's life, etc., *by* discussion etc., *in* occupation etc.), prolong (discussion etc.), make (story, money, etc.) last as long as possible, (Cricket) dismiss (batsman, side) by spin bowling. **5.** cause (top etc.) to whirl round; shape (metal) on mould in lathe etc.; turn (person, thing) quickly round; toss (coin); impart spin to (cricket ball); ~**-dry,** dry (washed articles) in rapidly rotating drum (~**-drier,** machine for doing this). **6.** fish in (stream, pool) with spinner or spinning bait. **7.** (in *p.p.*) converted into threads for subsequent use (*spun glass, gold, silver*); **spun silk,** cheap material of short-fibred and waste silk often mixed with cotton; **spun yarn,** (Naut.) line formed of rope-yarns twisted together. **8.** ~ **off,** throw off by centrifugal force in spinning; ~**-off** *n.,* incidental result(s), esp. as benefit from industrial or technological development. **9.** *v.i.* (Of top etc.) whirl round; (of person or thing) turn *round* quickly, e.g. as result of being struck; (of person's head etc.) be in a whirl through dizziness or astonishment. [OE *spinnan,* = OHG, Goth. *spinnan,* ON *spinna*]

spin[2] *n.* spinning motion, whirl; aircraft's diving descent combined with rotation (FLAT[2] *spin*); secondary revolving motion esp. as developed in rifle bullet, or in billiard or tennis ball struck aslant; (Cricket) twisting motion given to ball when bowled (~ **bowler,** expert at this); brisk or short run or spell of driving, rowing, cycling, etc., (*went for a spin*); (Phys.) intrinsic angular momentum of elementary particle; (Austral. colloq.) piece of good or bad luck. [f. prec.]

spina bi'fida *n.* congenital defect of spine allowing meninges to protrude. [mod. L (as SPINE, BIFID)]

spi'nach (-nij) *n.* garden vegetable (*Spinacia oleracea*) with succulent leaves cooked as food; other plant similarly used; *(colloq.)* unwanted or unnecessary thing; ~ **beet,** kind of beet grown for its leaves and used like spinach; hence **spin**A'CEOUS *a.* [prob. f. MDu. *spinaetse, spinag(i)e,* f. OF *espinage, espinache* f. med. L *spinac(h)ia* etc. f. Arab. *'isfānāḵ* f. Pers. *ispānāḵ;* perh. assim. to L *spina* SPINE, w. ref. to prickly seeds]

spi'nal *a.* of the spine, (*spinal curvature, disease*); ~ **canal,** cavity between vertebrae containing spinal cord; ~ **column,** spine; ~ **cord,** cylindrical structure within spine, a part of the central nervous system; *spinal* MARROW. [f. LL *spinalis* (as SPINE; see -AL)]

spi'ndle *n.,* & *v.i.* **1.** *n.* pin in spinning-wheel used for twisting and winding the thread; small bar with tapered ends serving same purpose in hand-spinning; pin bearing bobbin of spinning-machine; pin or axis that revolves or on which a thing revolves; (Biol.) spindle-shaped configuration in mitosis; slender thing or person; varying measure of length for yarn. **2.** ~ **berry,** fruit of spindle-tree; ~**-shanked,** with long thin legs; ~**-shanks,** person with such legs; ~**-shaped,** of circular cross-section and tapering towards each end; ~ **side,** = DISTAFF *side;* ~**-tree,** shrub or small tree of genus *Euonymus,* esp. *E. europaeus* with greenish-white flowers, pink or red berries, and hard wood used for spindles. **3.** Hence **spi'ndly**[2] *a.,* slender, attenuated. **4.** *v.i.* have, or grow into, long slender form. [OE *spinel,* = OS *spinnila,* OHG *spin(n)ila,* f. as SPIN[1] + -LE 1]

spi'ndrift *n.* spray blown along surface of sea. [Sc. var. of *spoondrift* (*spoon* run before wind or sea, DRIFT[1])]

spine *n.* **1.** series of vertebrae extending from skull, backbone; central feature, main support or source of strength. **2.** (Bot. & Zool.) stiff sharp-pointed process; (Anat.) sharp-pointed slender process of bone; hence **spin**ED[2] (-nd), **spi'n**OSE[1], **spi'n**OUS, *adjs.* **3.** sharp ridge or projection. **4.** part of book's cover or jacket that encloses its page-fastening part and usu. faces outwards on shelf. **5.** ~**-chiller, -chilling,** (book, film, etc.) causing thrill of terror. [ME, f. OF *espine* or f. L *spina* thorn, backbone]

spi'nel *n.* hard crystalline mineral of various colours consisting chiefly of magnesia and alumina; substance of similar composition or properties; ~ **ruby,** valuable deep-red variety of spinel. [f. F *spinelle,* f. It. *spinella* dim. of *spina* (as prec.; see -LE 2)]

spi'neless (-nl-) *a.* having no spine, invertebrate; (of fish) having no fin-spines; (fig.) lacking energy or resolution, weak, having no backbone, whence ~LY[2] *adv.,* ~NESS *n.* [f. SPINE + -LESS]

spinet (spine't, spi'nit) *n.* (Hist.) small harpsichord with oblique strings. [f. obs. F. *espinette* f. It. *spinetta* virginal, spinet, dim. of *spina* thorn etc. (as SPINE), both instruments having plucked strings]

spi'nifex *n.* coarse spiny-leaved Austral. grass of genus *Spinifex.* [mod. L, f. L *spina* spine + -I- + -*fex* maker (*facere* make).]

spi'nnaker *n.* large triangular sail carried opposite mainsail of racing-yacht running before wind. [fanciful f. *Sphinx,* name of yacht first using it, perh. after *spanker*]

spi'nner *n.* In vbl senses; manufacturer engaged in (esp. cotton-)spinning; (arch.) spider; real or artificial fly for (esp. trout-)fishing, revolving bait; (Cricket) spin bowler, ball given spin; spin-drier; spinneret. [ME, f. SPIN[1] + -ER[1]]

spi'nneret *n.* spinning-organ in spider, silkworm, etc.; device for forming filaments of synthetic fibre. [f. prec. + -ET[1]]

‖**spi'nney** *n.* small wood, thicket. [f. OF *espinei* f. Rom. **spineta* f. L *spinetum* thicket (*spina* thorn)]

spi'nning *n.* In vbl senses; ~**-house,** (Hist.) house of correction for prostitutes; ~**-jenny,** early machine for spinning with more than one spindle at a time; ~**-machine,** (esp.) machine that spins fibres continuously; ~**-top,** = TOP[3]; ~**-wheel,** household implement for spinning yarn or thread, with spindle driven by wheel driven by crank or treadle. [ME, f. SPIN[1] + -ING[1]]

spi'nose, spi'nous. See SPINE.

Spino'zism *n.* doctrine of Spinoza that there is one sole and infinite substance of which extension and thought are attributes and individual beings are changing forms; so ~IST (2) *n.,* ~**i'st**IC *a.* [f. B. de *Spinoza,* Du. philosopher d. 1677 + -ISM]

spi'nster *n.* unmarried woman; (elderly) woman thought unlikely to marry; hence ~HOOD *n.* [ME, orig. = woman who spins, f. SPIN[1] + -STER]

spinthā'riscope *n.* instrument with fluorescent

screen showing incidence of alpha particles by flashes. [irreg. f. Gk *spintharis* spark + -SCOPE]

spi′nŭl|e *n.* (Bot. & Zool.) small spine; hence ∼OSE¹, ∼OUS, *adjs.* [f. L *spinula* dim. of *spina* spine; see -ULE]

spi′nÿ *a.* **1.** full of spines, prickly; ∼ **eel,** eel-shaped fish with dorsal fin of free spines; ∼ **lobster,** lobster--like crustacean with spiny shell and no claws; ∼ **rat,** bristly rat of S. America. **2.** (fig.) perplexing, troublesome, thorny. **3.** Hence **spi′niNESS** *n.* [f. SPINE + -Y²]

spir′acle *n.* (Zool.) external respiratory orifice in insects; blow-hole of whale etc.; hence **spīrä′cŭlAR¹** *a.* [f. L *spiraculum* (*spirare* breathe)]

spīrä′cŭl|um *n.* (*pl.* ∼a). = prec. [L; see prec.]

spīrae′a *n.* shrub or plant of genus *Spiraea,* with small white or pink flowers. [L, f. Gk *speiraia* (*speira* coil)]

spīr′al *a., n.,* & *v.* (||-ll-). **1.** *a.* coiled; winding continually about and constantly receding from or moving towards a centre, whether remaining in same plane like watch-spring or rising in a cone; winding continually and advancing as if along cylinder, like thread of screw; ∼ **balance** (measuring weight by torsion of spiral spring); ∼ **nebula** (in which matter is mainly in one or more spiral arms); ∼ **staircase** (rising circularly round central axis). **2.** Hence ∼ITY (-ă′l-) *n.,* ∼LY⁹ *adv.* **3.** *n.* plane or other spiral curve, spiral spring; spiral formation in shell etc.; spiral nebula; (fig.) gradual but progressive rise or fall of two or more interdependent quantities alternately (*the vicious spiral of rising prices and wages*). **4.** *v.t.* make spiral. **5.** *v.i.* move in a spiral course. [F, or f. med. L *spiralis* (as SPIRE²; see -AL)]

spīr′ant *a.* & *n.* (Phonet.) (consonant) uttered with continuous expulsion of breath, esp. fricative. [f. L *spirare* breathe; see -ANT]

spīre¹ *n.* & *v.* **1.** *n.* tapering structure in form of tall cone or pyramid rising above tower; continuation of tree trunk above point where branching begins; any tapering body, e.g. spike of flower; hence **spīr′Y²** *a.* **2.** *v.i.* shoot up. **3.** *v.t.* furnish with spire. [OE *spīr,* = MLG, MDu. *spīer, spīr,* MHG *spīr*]

spīre² *n.* spiral, coil; single twist of this; upper part of spiral shell. [F, f. L f. Gk *speira* coil]

spīrī′ll|um *n.* (*pl.* ∼a). bacterium of genus *Spirillum* characterized by a spiral structure. [mod. L, irreg. dim. of L *spira* (see prec.)]

spi′rĭt *n.* **1.** animating or vital principle of person or animal; intelligent or immaterial part of person, soul; **in** (**the**) ∼, inwardly (*groaned in spirit; was vexed in spirit; shall be with you in* (*the*) *spirit*). **2.** person viewed as possessing this, esp. w. ref. to particular mental or moral qualities, (*one of the most ardent spirits of his time; a meeting of choice spirits*); KINDRED *spirit.* **3.** rational or intelligent being not connected with material body (*God is a spirit;* HOLY *Spirit; spirit* MOVE²s *person*); disembodied soul, incorporeal being, elf, fairy, (*spirits must have been at work;* FAMILIAR *spirit; peace to his departed spirit*). **4.** person's mental or moral nature or qualities (*a man of unbending spirit*); **the poor in** ∼, (arch.) the meek. **5.** (high) ∼, courage, self-assertion, vivacity, energy, dash, (*if you had the spirit of a mouse; went at it, played the waltz, with spirit; infused spirit into his men*). **6.** person viewed as supplying this (= SOUL 4, but usu. w. adj.; *was the animating spirit of the rebellion*). **7.** mental or moral condition or attitude, mood, (*took it in a wrong spirit; depends on the spirit in which it is done; did it in a spirit of mischief; enter into the spirit of the thing;* PUBLIC *spirit; objections made in a captious spirit*). **8.** real meaning opp. to verbal expression (*must consider the spirit of the law, not the letter; have followed out the spirit of his instructions*). **9.** animating principle or influence, mental or moral tendency (*cannot resist the spirit of the age* or *times*). **10.** immaterial principle formerly thought to govern vital phenomena; ANIMAL *spirits*; high or great ∼s, cheerfulness and buoyancy; poor or low ∼s, depression. **11.** volatile liquid got by distillation (||MOTOR *spirit;* WOOD *spirit*); purified

alcohol (METHYLATED *spirit*); (usu. in *pl.*) strong distilled liquor esp. alcohol, e.g. brandy, whisky, gin, rum, (*a glass of spirits and water;* ARDENT *spirits; touches no spirit but gin*). **12.** solution (*of* volatile principle) in alcohol, tincture; ∼s **of salt,** (arch.) hydrochloric acid; ∼(s) **of wine,** (arch.) purified alcohol. **13.** ∼ **blue,** blue aniline dye soluble in alcohol; ∼ **duck,** bufflehead or golden-eye (diving rapidly at flash of gun etc.); ∼ **duplicator** (using alcoholic solution to produce copies from master sheet); ∼ **gum,** quick--drying solution of gum used esp. for attaching false hair; ∼-**lamp** (burning methylated or other volatile spirit instead of oil); ∼-**level,** glass tube nearly filled with alcohol, used to test horizontality by position of air-bubble; ∼-**rapper,** person professing to converse with departed spirits by means of their raps on table etc.; so ∼-**rapping.** [ME, f. AF (*e*)*spirit,* OF *esp*(*e*)*rit,* f. L *spiritus* breath, spirit (*spirare* breathe)]

spi′rĭt *v.t.* convey (*away, off,* etc.) rapidly and secretly (as) by agency of spirits; ∼ **up,** animate, cheer, (person). [f. prec.]

spi′rĭtĕd *a.* full of spirit, animated, lively, brisk, courageous, (*a spirited translation, attack, reply*); having specified spirit(s) (*high, low, mean, proud, -spirited*); hence (-)∼LY² *adv.,* ∼NESS *n.* [f. SPIRIT¹ + -ED²]

spi′rĭtĭsm *n.* = SPIRITUALISM 1. [f. SPIRIT¹ + -ISM]

spi′rĭtlĕss *a.* lacking courage, vigour, or vivacity; hence ∼LY² *adv.* [f. SPIRIT¹ + -LESS]

spi′rĭtūăl *a.* & *n.* **1.** *a.* of spirit as opp. to matter; of the soul esp. as acted on by God (*spiritual life*); of or proceeding from God, holy, divine, inspired, (*spiritual songs; the spiritual law*); concerned with sacred or religious things (*our spiritual interests*); ∼ (ecclesiastical) **courts;** ||**lords** ∼, bishops and archbishops in House of Lords (cf. TEMPORAL). **2.** having the higher qualities of the mind; concerned with or based on the spirit (*spiritual relationship;* one's *spiritual home*). **3.** Hence ∼LY² *adv.,* ∼NESS *n.* **4.** *n.* religious song characteristic of Amer. Blacks. [ME, f. OF *spirituel* f. L *spiritualis* (as SPIRIT¹; see -AL)]

spi′rĭtūăl|ĭsm *n.* **1.** belief that departed spirits communicate with and show themselves to the living, esp. through mediums; system of doctrines or practices founded on this. **2.** (Philos.) doctrine that spirit exists as distinct from matter or that spirit is the only reality (cf. MATERIALISM). **3.** Hence or cogn. ∼IST (2) *n.,* ∼I′STIC *a.* [f. prec. + -ISM]

spĭrĭtŭā′lĭtÿ *n.* spiritual quality, (Hist., usu. in *pl.*) what belongs or is due to the Church or to an ecclesiastic as such (*the spiritualities of his office*). [ME, f. OF *spiritualité* or LL *spiritualitas* (as SPIRITUAL; see -ITY)]

spi′rĭtŭălĭz|e, -īs|e (-īz), *v.t.* make spiritual, elevate, (character, person, thoughts); attach spiritual as opp. to literal meaning to; hence ∼A′TION *n.* [f. SPIRITUAL + -IZE, or f. F *spiritualiser*]

spĭrĭtŭĕ′l(le) *a.* marked by refinement and sprightliness of mind. [f. F *spirituel,* fem. -*elle* (as SPIRITUAL)]

spi′rĭtŭous *a.* containing much alcohol, distilled and not only fermented (*spirituous liquor*); hence ∼NESS *n.* [f. L *spiritus* spirit + -OUS, or f. F *spiritueux*]

spi′rĭtus *n.* (Gk Gram.; arch.). ∼ **a′sper, le′nis** (lē′nĭs), = rough, smooth, breathing. [L]

spīr′ivălve *a.* (Esp. of gastropod) having spiral shell; (of shell) spiral. [F, f. L *spira* SPIRE² + *valva* (see VALVE)]

spīr′kĕtĭng *n.* (Naut.) inside planking between top of waterways and lower sills of ports. [f. obs. *spirket, spurket,* space between timbers of ship's side, of unkn. orig., + -ING¹ (6)]

spīr′o-¹ *comb. form.* coil, as: ∼**chaete,** *∼**chete,** (-kēt), spiral-shaped bacterium; ∼**gyr′a** (-jīr′a), freshwater alga with spiral bands of chlorophyll. [f. L *spira,* Gk *speira* coil + -o-]

spīr′o-² *comb. form.* breath, as: ∼**graph,** instrument for recording breathing movement; ∼**meter** (-ŏ′m-), instrument for measuring lung capacity. [irreg. f. L *spirare* breathe + -o-]

spirt. See SPURT[2].

spir′y. See SPIRE[1].

spit[1] *n.*, & *v.t.* (-tt-). **1.** *n.* slender bar on which meat that is to be roasted is fixed before fire etc.; skewer; small point of land projecting into sea; long narrow underwater bank. **2.** *v.t.* thrust spit through (meat etc.); (fig.) pierce or transfix with sword etc. [OE *spitu*, = MDu., MLG *spit*, *spet*, OHG *spiz* f. WG **spitu*]

spit[2] *v.* (-tt-; **spat** *or* **spit**) & *n.* **1.** *v.i.* eject saliva; do this as sign of hatred or contempt; ∼ **and polish**, cleaning and polishing work of soldier etc., (fig.) exaggerated neatness and smartness. **2.** *v.t.* eject (saliva, blood, food, etc. *out*) from mouth; (fig.) utter (oaths, threats, etc.) vehemently; ∼ **it out**, (colloq.) speak louder or without further delay. **3.** *v.i.* (Of cat etc., or fig. of person) make noise as of spitting as sign of anger or hostility; (of rain) fall lightly (*it is only spitting*); (of fire, candle, pen) send out sparks, stray ink, etc. **4.** ***∼′**ball** (of chewed paper as missile, or baseball moistened by pitcher to impart spin); ∼′**fire**, person of fiery temper; ∼**ting cobra** (ejecting venom without striking); ∼**ting image**, (colloq.) = sense 7. **5.** *n.* spitting (esp. of cat). **6.** spittle; saliva-like secretion of some insects; CUCKOO--*spit*. **7. the** (**dead** or **very**) ∼ (**and image**), (colloq.) exact counterpart *of*, likeness *of*, (*he is the very spit of his father*). [OE *spittan* = G dial. *spützen*, of imit. orig.; cf. SPEW]

spit[3] *n.* spade-depth of earth (*dig it two spit(s) deep*). [MDu. & MLG, = OE *spittan* dig with spade, prob. rel. to SPIT[1]]

spi′tchcŏck *n.*, & *v.t.* **1.** *n.* eel split and broiled. **2.** *v.t.* prepare thus (eel, fish, bird). [16th c., of unkn. orig.; cf. SPATCHCOCK]

spīte *n.*, & *v.t.* **1.** *n.* ill will, malice, (*did it from pure spite* or *in* or *out of spite*); grudge (*has a spite against me*); **in** ∼ **of,** (arch.) ∼ **of,** notwithstanding; **in** ∼ **of** oneself, though one would rather have done otherwise. **2.** *v.t.* thwart, mortify, annoy, (*does it to spite me*); **cut off** one's **nose to** ∼ one's **face,** injure oneself by vindictive or resentful conduct. [ME, f. OF *despit* DESPITE]

spi′teful (-tf-) *a.* animated by spite, malevolent; hence ∼LY[2] *adv.*, ∼NESS *n.* [ME, f. prec.+-FUL]

spi′ttle *n.* saliva esp. as ejected from mouth. [alt. f. ME (now dial.) *spattle* (OE *spātl* f. *spātan* to spit) after SPIT[2]]

spittoo′n *n.* vessel to spit into, usu. round metal or earthenware vessel with funnel-shaped top. [f. SPIT[2]+-OON]

spitz (-ts) *n.* small dog with pointed muzzle, esp. Pomeranian. [G *spitz*(*hund*) (*spitz* pointed, *hund* dog)]

||**spiv** *n.* (sl.) person living by his wits without regular work; one who engages in petty black-market dealings etc.; hence ∼′VERY (5) *n.*, ∼′ISH[1] *a.* [20th c.; orig. unkn.]

splă′nchn|ic (-ngk-) *a.* of the viscera, intestinal; so ∼o- *comb. form*, ∼ŏ′LOGY, ∼ŏ′TOMY, *ns.* [f. mod. L f. Gk *splagkhnikos* (*splagkhna* entrails; see -IC)]

splăsh *v.* & *n.* **1.** *v.t.* cause to be struck by small drops (person etc. *with* water, mud, etc.); throw small drops of (liquid *about, on,* or *over* person etc.); decorate with scattered colour (*white robe splashed with red*); display (news) prominently; spend (money) ostentatiously. **2.** *v.i.* (Of liquid) fly about in drops or scattered portions; (of person) cause liquid to do this, move *across, along,* etc., thus; step, fall, plunge, etc., *into* (water etc.) so as to splash it; ∼ **out,** (colloq.) spend money freely. **3.** *n.* splashing; quantity of liquid splashed; resulting noise (*we heard a splash*; **make a** ∼, attract much attention); prominent display of news etc.; WATER[1]-*splash*; ||(colloq.) small quantity of soda--water etc. (diluting whisky etc.); spot of dirt etc. splashed on to thing; daub or patch of colour esp. on animal's skin. **4.** ∼′**back,** panel behind sink etc. to protect wall from splashes; ∼**-board,** guard in front of vehicle or over or beside wheel of vehicle to keep

mud etc. off occupants; ∼**-down,** alighting of space-craft on sea. **5.** Hence ∼′Y[2] *a.* [alt. f. PLASH[2]]

splăt *n.* flat piece of thin wood in centre of chair-back. [f. *splat* v. split up, rel. to SPLIT[1]]

splă′tter *v.i.* & *t.*, & *n.* splash esp. with continuous and noisy action; ***spatter. [imit.]

splay *v.*, *n.*, & *a.* **1.** *v.t.* construct (aperture) with divergent sides; make (window, doorway) wider at one side of wall; spread (elbows, feet, etc., *out*). **2.** *v.i.* (Of aperture or its sides) be divergent in shape or position. **3.** *n.* surface making oblique angle with another, e.g. splayed side of window, embrasure. **4.** *a.* wide and flat, turned outward; ∼**-foot** *n.* & *a.*, ∼--**footed** *a.*, (having) broad flat foot turned outward. [ME, f. DISPLAY[1]]

spleen *n.* **1.** abdominal organ involved in maintaining proper condition of blood in most vertebrates, situated in mammals at left of stomach. **2.** lowness of spirits, moroseness, ill temper, spite, (*a fit of spleen*; *vented his spleen*); hence ∼′FUL, ∼′Y[2], *adjs.* **3.** ∼′**wort,** fern of genus *Asplenium*, formerly used as remedy for spleen disorders. [ME, f. OF *esplen* f. L f. Gk *splēn*]

splēn- *comb. form.* = prec. 1, as: ∼e′ctomy, excision of spleen; ∼i′tis, inflammation of spleen; ∼o′logy (-ŏ′l-), study of spleen; ∼ome′galy, enlargement of spleen; ∼o′tomy (-ŏ′t-), incision into, or dissection of, spleen. [Gk (as prec.)]

splĕ′ndent *a.* shining, lustrous; illustrious. [ME, f. L *splendēre* to shine; see -ENT]

splĕ′ndid *a.* magnificent, gorgeous, sumptuous, glorious, brilliant, (*a splendid palace, gift, achievement, victory*); dignified, impressive, (*splendid isolation*); (colloq.) excellent, very fine, (*here is a splendid chance of escape*); hence ∼LY[2] *adv.* [f. F *splendide* or f. L *splendidus* (as prec.; see -ID[1])]

splĕ′ndiferous *a.* (colloq.) splendid. [irreg. f. foll.+-FEROUS]

||**splĕ′ndour** (-der), *****splĕ′ndor,** *n.* great or dazzling brightness; magnificence, grandeur; **sun in** ∼ (Her., with rays and human face). [ME, f. AF *splendeur* or f. L *splendor* (as SPLENDENT; see -OR)]

splĕnĕ′t|ic *a.* & *n.* **1.** ill-tempered, peevish, (person); hence ∼ICALLY *adv.* **2.** *a.* of the spleen. [f. LL *spleneticus* (as SPLEEN; see -ETIC)]

splĕ′nic *a.* of or in the spleen; ∼ **fever,** anthrax; so **splĕ′noid** *a.* [f. F *splénique* or f. L f. Gk *splēnikos* (as SPLEEN; see -IC)]

splĕ′ni|us *n.* (*pl.* ∼**i** *pr.* -ī). (either section of) muscle on back and sides of neck serving to draw back the head; hence ∼AL *a.* [mod. L, f. Gk *splēnion* bandage]

splīce *v.t.*, & *n.* **1.** *v.t.* join ends of (ropes) by interweaving strands; join (pieces of timber, magnetic tape, film, etc.) in overlapping position; (colloq., esp. in *pass.*) join in marriage; *splice the MAIN brace*. **2.** *n.* junction of two ropes or pieces of wood etc. (e.g. handle and blade of cricket-bat) made by splicing; **sit on the** ∼, (Cricket sl.) play a cautious defensive game, stonewall. [prob. f. MDu. *splissen*, of uncert. orig.]

splīne *n.*, & *v.t.* **1.** *n.* rectangular key fitting into grooves in hub and shaft of wheel and allowing longitudinal play; slat; flexible wood or rubber strip, e.g. used in drawing large curves esp. in railway work. **2.** *v.t.* fit with spline. [orig. E. Anglian dial., perh. rel. to SPLINTER]

splint *n.*, & *v.t.* **1.** *n.* strip of rigid or flexible material to protect part of body (e.g. for holding broken bone when set) or for basketwork etc.; tumour or bony excrescence on inside of horse's leg; ∼(-**bone**), (1) either of two small bones in horse's foreleg lying behind and close to cannon-bone, (2) human fibula; ∼**-coal,** hard bituminous laminated coal burning with great heat. **2.** *v.t.* secure (broken limb etc.) with splint(s). [ME *splent*(*e*), f. MDu. *splinte* or MLG *splinte*, *splente* metal plate or pin, rel. to foll.]

spli′nter *v.* & *n.* **1.** *v.t.* & *i.* break into splinters; = SHIVER[2]. **2.** *n.* sharp-edged or thin piece broken off from wood, stone, etc.; ||∼-**bar,** crossbar in vehicle to which traces are attached, swingle-tree; ∼ (**group** or **party),** (esp. Polit.) party (esp. one that is very small in numbers) that has broken away from a larger one; ∼-**proof** (against splinters e.g. of bursting shells or bombs). **3.** Hence ∼Y² *a.* [ME, f. MDu. (= LG) *splinter, splenter;* rel. to prec.]

split¹ *v.* (**-tt-; split**). **1.** *v.t.* & *i.* break forcibly, be broken into parts esp. longitudinally or with the grain or plane of cleavage; (of ship) be wrecked; cause fission (of atom). **2.** divide into parts (*split it into three layers; the job, sum,* etc., *was split* (*up*) *among 6 of us; the three of them split a bottle of wine, split up after ten years together*); *dilute (whisky etc.) with water; remove or be removed by breaking or dividing (*off* or *away*); *split the* DIFFERENCE; ∼ **hairs,** draw over-subtle distinctions; ∼ *the **ticket** or one's **vote,** vote for opposed candidates; ||∼ **the vote,** (of candidate) attract votes from another so that both are perhaps defeated by a third. **3.** divide into disagreeing or hostile parties (*on* or *over* question etc.); ∼ **with,** (colloq.) = *break with* (BREAK¹ 3). **4.** ∼ (one's **sides),** be convulsed with laughter; so SIDE¹-*splitting.* **5.** *v.i.* (Of headache etc., in *pres. part.*) acute; **my head is** ∼**ting** (feels acute pain). **6.** (sl.) betray secrets, inform *on* (accomplice etc.); depart. **7.** (in *p.p.*) ∼ **gear, pulley, wheel,** (made in halves for removal from shaft); ∼ **infinitive** (with adverb etc. inserted between *to* and verb, e.g. *seems to partly correspond*); ∼**-level,** (of building) having some room(s) a fraction of a storey higher than the adjacent part; ∼ **mind,** schizophrenia; ∼ **moss** (of genus *Andreaea,* of which capsules split at maturity); ∼ **pea** (dried and split in half for cooking); ∼ **personality,** alteration or dissociation of personality such as may occur in some mental illnesses esp. schizophrenia and hysteria; *split* PIN¹; ∼ **ring** (usu. of steel with two helical turns, on the pattern of those used for bunches of keys); ∼ **second,** a very brief moment of time; ∼ **shift** (comprising two or more separate periods of duty); ∼ **shot, stroke,** stroke at croquet driving two touching balls in different directions. **8.** Hence (∼)∼'tER¹ (1, 2) *n.* [orig. Naut., f. MDu. *splitten,* rel. to *spletten, spliten,* MHG *splizen*]

split² *n.* **1.** splitting or being split; fissure, rent, crack, cleft. **2.** separation into parties, schism, rupture, breach. **3.** split osier etc. for parts of basketwork; each strip of steel, cane, etc., of reed in loom; single thickness of split hide. **4.** turning up of two cards of equal value in faro, so that stakes are divided. **5.** half bottle of mineral water; half glass of liquor. **6.** (||in *pl.*) feat of sitting down or leaping with legs widely spread out at right angles to body. **7.** sweet dish of split fruit, ice cream, etc., (*banana split*). [f. prec.]

||**splŏdge.** Var. of SPLOTCH.

splŏsh *n.* & *v.* (colloq.) **1.** *n.* a quantity of water suddenly dropped or thrown down. **2.** *v.t.* & *i.* move with splashing. [imit.]

splŏ′tch *n.,* & *v.t.* daub, blot, smear; (make) large irregular spot or patch (on); hence ∼'Y² *a.* [perh. f. SPOT¹+obs. *plotch,* BLOTCH]

splŭrge *n.,* & *v.i.* (make) noisy or ostentatious display or effort. [19th c. US; prob. imit.]

splŭ′tter *v.* & *n.* = SPUTTER (esp. of speech); hence ∼ER¹ *n.* [f. SPUTTER by assoc. w. *splash*]

Spŏde *n.* type of fine pottery or porcelain. [f. J. ∼, Engl. maker of china d. 1827]

spoil¹ *n.* **1.** (in *pl.* or collect. *sing.*) plunder taken from enemy in war, or seized by force; (fig.) profit, advantage accruing from success in contest etc., (joc.) emoluments of public office etc.; *∼s **system,** practice of giving public offices to adherents of successful party; *∼'**sman** (-z-), advocate of, one who seeks to profit by, this. **2.** earth etc. thrown up or brought up in excavating, dredging, etc. [ME, f. OF *espoille* (*espoillier;* see foll.)]

spoil² *v.* (∼t (exc. sense 1), or ∼ed *pr.* -ld *or* -lt). **1.** *v.t.*

(arch. or literary). plunder, deprive (person *of* thing), by force or stealth; ∼ **the Egyptians** (persons regarded as one's natural enemies etc.; Exod. 12: 36). **2.** damage, diminish the good qualities of, reduce person's enjoyment of, (*was quite spoilt by the rain; will spoil all the fun; always spoils a joke in the telling; the news spoilt his dinner*). **3.** injure character of (person etc.) by indulgence (*spare the rod and spoil the child; are determined to spoil me; is the spoilt child* or *darling of fortune*). **4.** *v.i.* (Of fruit, fish, etc., fig. of joke etc.) become unfit for use, decay, go bad, (*will not spoil with keeping*); be ∼**ing for,** desire eagerly (*a fight* etc.). **5.** ∼-**five,** card-game in which deal is 'spoilt' if no player takes three of the five tricks; ∼-**sport,** one who spoils others' sport or enjoyment. [ME, f. OF *espoillier* f. L *spoliare* (*spolium* spoil, plunder), or f. DESPOIL]

spoi′lage *n.* paper spoilt in printing; spoiling of food by decay. [f. prec. + -AGE]

spoi′ler *n.* In vbl senses; device on aircraft or vehicle to retard it by interrupting air flow; similar device on vehicle to prevent it from being lifted off road at speed. [f. SPOIL²+-ER¹]

spŏke¹ *n.,* & *v.t.* **1.** *n.* each of the bars running from hub to rim of wheel, whence ∼'WISE (-kw-) *adv.;* rung of ladder; each radial handle or steering-wheel of vessel; **put a** ∼ **in** person's **wheel,** thwart or hinder his purposes; ∼-**bone,** radius of forearm; ∼'**shave,** blade set between two handles, used for spokes and other esp. curved work where ordinary plane is not suitable. **2.** *v.t.* furnish with spokes; obstruct (wheel etc.) by thrusting spoke in. [OE *spāca,* = OS *spēca,* OHG *speihha* f. WG **spaika,* Gmc **spaik-* (cf. SPIKE¹)]

spŏke², (-)**spŏ′ken.** See SPEAK.

spŏ′kes|man (-ks-) *n.* (*pl.* ∼**men,** *fem.* ∼**woman**). one who speaks on behalf of others; person deputed to express a group's views. [irreg. f. SPOKE² after *craftsman* etc.]

spŏliā′tion *n.* plunder, pillage, esp. of neutral vessels by belligerent; (fig.) extortion; (Eccl.) taking of fruits of benefice under pretended title etc.; (Law) destruction, mutilation, alteration of document to prevent its being used as evidence; so **spŏ′liātor** *n.,* **spŏ′liatory** *a.* [ME, f. L *spoliatio* (as SPOIL²; see -ATION)]

spŏnda′ic *a.* of spondees; (of hexameter) having spondee as fifth foot. [f. F *spondaïque* or LL *spondaicus* = LL f. Gk *spondeiakos* (as foll.; see -AC, -IC)]

spŏ′ndee (-dē, -dĭ) *n.* (Pros.) foot consisting of two long syllables. [ME f. OF, or f. L f. Gk *spondeios* (*pous* foot) f. *spondē* libation, as being characteristic of music accompanying libations]

spŏndū′licks *n. pl.* (sl.) money. [19th c.; orig. unkn.]

spŏ′ndyl- *comb. form.* vertebra(e), as ∼'TIS *n.* [f. L f. Gk *spondulos* vertebra]

sponge¹ (-ŭnj) *n.* **1.** aquatic animal of phylum Porifera, with pores in body-wall and tough elastic skeleton. **2.** skeleton of a sponge or colony of sponges, esp. soft light elastic kind used as absorbent in bathing, cleansing surfaces, etc.; piece of porous rubber etc. used similarly; **throw in** or **up the** ∼, (of boxer or his attendant) throw into the air as token of defeat the sponge used between rounds, (fig.) abandon contest, admit oneself beaten; **pass the** ∼ **over,** (arch.) agree to forget (offence etc.). **3.** thing of spongelike absorbency or consistency, e.g. piece of leavened dough, sponge-cake, absorbent pad used in surgery, kind of mop for cleaning bore of big gun, iron or other metal in finely divided condition. **4.** (fig.) parasite, person who contrives to live at another's expense; one who drinks heavily. **5.** ||∼-**bag,** waterproof bag for toilet articles; ||∼-*bag trousers* (of checked material); ∼ **biscuit,** ∼-**cake,** (light, of sponge like consistency); ∼ **cloth,** soft loosely woven cotton fabric with wrinkled surface; ∼ **cucumber, -gourd, vegetable** ∼, loofah; ∼ **pudding,** light pudding of spongelike consistency; ∼ **rubber** (made porous like a sponge); ∼-**tree,** spiny tropical acacia with globose heads of fragrant yellow flowers yielding a perfume. [OE, f. L f. Gk *spoggia, spoggos*]

sponge² (-ŭnj) *v.* & *n.* **1.** *v.t.* wipe or cleanse with sponge; sluice water over (parts of body etc., or abs.; *down, over*) with sponge; wipe *out* or efface (writing, fig. memory of thing etc.) (as) with sponge; absorb, take *up*, (water etc.) with sponge; obtain (food etc., or abs.) by mean or parasitic behaviour. **2.** *v.i.* gather sponges; ~ **on**, live as the parasite of, be meanly dependent on (person *for* thing). **3.** Hence **spo'ngER¹** (1, 2) (-ŭ'nj-) *n.* **4.** *n.* sponging, bath with sponge, (*had a sponge down*). [ME, f. prec., or OF *esponger* (*esponge* f. L *spongia*, as prec.)]

spo'nging (-ŭ'nj-) *n.* In vbl senses; ~**house**, (Hist., f. arch. sense 'extortion') bailiff's house for initial confinement of arrested debtor. [f. prec. + -ING¹]

spo'ng|y (-ŭ'nji) *a.* like sponge; porous, compressible, elastic, absorbent, as sponge; (of metal) finely divided and loosely coherent; hence ~INESS *n.* [f. SPONGE¹ + -Y²]

spo'nsion (-shŏn) *n.* being surety for another; engagement made on behalf of State by agent not authorized to do so. [f. L *sponsio* (*spondēre spons-* promise solemnly; see -ION)]

spo'nson *n.* projection from side of warship or tank to enable gun to be trained forward and aft; triangular platform before and abaft paddle-box; short subsidiary wing to stabilize seaplane. [19th c.; orig. unkn.]

spo'nsor *n.,* & *v.t.* **1.** *n.* person who makes himself responsible for another; person who presents candidate for baptism and makes responses on behalf of infant etc. being baptized; person who introduces proposal for legislation; person who subscribes to charity in return for specified activity by another; advertiser who pays for a broadcast programme into which advertisements of his wares are introduced; organization lending support to election candidate; hence **spŏnsŏr'IAL** *a.,* ~**SHIP** *n.* **2.** *v.t.* be sponsor for. [L (as SPONSION; see -OR)]

spŏntā'neous *a.* **1.** acting, done, occurring, without external cause; voluntary, without external incitement, (*made a spontaneous offer of his services*); (of sudden movement, etc.) involuntary, not due to conscious volition; growing naturally without cultivation; (Biol., of structural changes in plants, muscular activity in esp. young animals) instinctive, automatic, prompted by no motive; (of bodily movement, literary style, etc.) gracefully natural and unconstrained. **2.** ~ **combustion,** ignition of mineral or vegetable substance (e.g. heap of rags soaked with oil, mass of wet coal) from heat engendered by rapid oxidation; ~ **generation,** supposed production of living from non-living matter as inferred from appearance of life (due in fact to bacteria etc.) in some infusions; ~ **suggestion** (from association of ideas without conscious volition). **3.** Hence or cogn. **spŏntanē'ITY,** ~NESS, *ns.,* ~LY² *adv.* [f. LL *spontaneus* (*sponte* of one's own accord; see -ANEOUS)]

spŏntōō'n *n.* (Hist.) kind of halberd used by some British infantry officers. [f. obs. F *sponton* f. It. *spuntone* (*spuntare* to blunt f. *s-* EX-¹ + *punto* POINT¹; see -OON)]

spoof *v.t.,* & *n.* (colloq.) swindle, hoax; parody; hence ~'ER¹ *n.* [invented by A. Roberts, Engl. comedian d. 1933]

spook *n.* (joc.) ghost; hence ~'ISH¹, ~'Y², *adjs.* [Du., = MLG *spōk*, of unkn. orig.]

spool *n.,* & *v.t.* **1.** *n.* reel for winding yarn, *thread, photographic film, etc., on; quantity thus wound; revolving cylinder of angler's reel. **2.** *v.t.* wind on spool. [ME, f. OF *espole* or f. MLG *spōle,* MDu. *spoele,* OHG *spuolo,* of unkn. orig.]

spoon¹ *n.* & *v.* **1.** *n.* utensil consisting of round or usu. oval bowl and a handle for conveying esp. liquid food to mouth, or for stirring, usu. of silver or plated metal for table use (**tea**~, **dessert-**~, **table**~, of small, medium, large size, also as recognized measure for

medicine, culinary ingredients, etc.; APOSTLE *spoon;* EGG¹, SALT, -*spoon*) or of wood or iron for cooking etc.; **born with a silver** ~ **in** one's **mouth,** destined to be wealthy; **wooden** ~, (Hist.) (wooden spoon given to) last man in Cambridge mathematical tripos, (fig.) booby prize; EGG¹-*and-spoon race;* hence (-)~'FUL 2 *n.* **2.** spoon-shaped thing, esp. (oar with) broad curved blade, wooden-headed golf-club with more loft than driver and brassie. **3.** ~(-**bait**), bright revolving spoon-shaped piece of metal used as lure in fishing; ~'**beak,** shoveller duck; ~'**bill,** (1) shoveller duck, (2) wading-bird of family Plataleidae, with very broad flat tip of bill; *~-**bread,** soft maize bread; ~-**feed,** feed by means of esp. liquid food from spoon, (fig.) artificially encourage (industry) by bounties or import duties, provide information etc. to without requiring any effort on recipient's part; ~-**meat,** liquid food, food for infants (lit. or fig.). **4.** *v.t.* take (liquid etc., *up, out*) with spoon; hit (ball) feebly upwards. **5.** *v.i.* fish with spoon-bait. [OE *spōn* chip of wood, = MLG *spān,* OHG *spān,* ON *spánn, spónn*]

spoon² *n.* & *v.* (sl.) **1.** *n.* simpleton; silly or demonstratively fond lover. **2.** *v.i.* behave in silly amorous way. **3.** *v.t.* woo in silly or sentimental way. [f. prec.]

spoo'nerism *n.* accidental or deliberate transposition of initial letters etc. of two or more words (*you have hissed the mystery lectures*). [f. Revd W. A. Spooner, Engl. scholar d. 1930, reputed to make such errors in speaking, + -ISM]

spoo'n|y *a.* & *n.* (sl.) **1.** *a.* foolish, silly; sentimental, amorous, sweet (*up*)*on*; hence ~ILY² *adv.,* ~INESS *n.* **2.** *n.* simpleton. [f. SPOON² + -Y²]

spoor *n.* & *v.* **1.** *n.* track or scent of animal. **2.** *v.t.* & *i.* follow by spoor; hence ~'ER¹ *n.* [Afrik., f. MDu. *spo*(*o*)*r,* = OE, OHG, ON *spor*]

spora'd|ic *a.* occurring only here and there, separate, scattered; hence ~ICALLY *adv.* [f. med. L f. Gk *sporadikos* (*sporas -ados* scattered, cf. *speirō* to sow; see -IC)]

spora'ngi|um (-nj-) *n.* (*pl.* ~a). (Bot.) receptacle in which spores are formed. [mod. L, f. Gk *spora* SPORE + *aggeion* vessel]

spore *n.* (Bot.) minute reproductive cell of cryptogamous plants; resistant form of bacterium etc. [f. mod. L f. Gk *spora* sowing, seed (*speirō* sow)]

spor'o- *comb. form.* spore, as: ~**ge'nesis,** spore-formation; ~**genous** (-ŏ'j-), producing spores; ~**phyte** (-fīt), spore-producing form of plant with alternation of generations; hence ~**phy'tic** (-fī't-) *a.* [f. Gk *spora* (as prec.) + -O-]

spo'rran *n.* pouch, usu. of leather or sealskin covered with fur etc., worn by Highlander in front of kilt. [f. Gael. *sporan* f. med. L *bursa* PURSE¹]

sport *n.* & *v.* **1.** *n.* amusement, diversion, fun; **in** ~, jestingly; **make** ~ **of,** turn into ridicule, make fun of; **be the** ~ (plaything, butt) of *Fortune* etc. **2.** pastime, game; outdoor pastime, e.g. hunting, fishing, racing, cricket, football; these collectively (*the world of sport*); **have good** ~, (esp.) make good bag or basket when shooting etc.; || (**athletic**) ~**s,** (1) running, jumping, throwing discus, etc., (2) meeting of athletes to compete in these (*school sports*); ~**s car** (of low-built fast type); ~**s coat,** *~ **coat,** (suitable for outdoor sports or informal wear); ~**s writer,** one who writes (esp. as journalist) on sports. **3.** (colloq.) good fellow, sportsman; *playboy. **4.** animal or plant deviating suddenly or strikingly from normal type. **5.** *v.i.* divert oneself, take part in pastime; (Biol.) become or produce a sport. **6.** *v.t.* wear, exhibit, produce, esp. ostentatiously, (*sported a gold tie-pin*); || *sport* one's OAK. [ME, f. DISPORT]

spor'ting *a.* interested in sport (*a sporting man*); sportsmanlike (*a sporting offer; will give you* **a** ~ **chance,** some possibility of success); concerned in sport (*sporting dog, news*); *~ **house,** brothel; hence ~LY² *adv.* [f. prec. + -ING¹,²]

spŏr'tive *a.* playful; hence ∼LY² (-vlĭ) *adv.*, ∼NESS (-vn-) *n.* [f. SPORT + -IVE]

spŏr'tsman *n.* (*pl.* **spor'tsmen**, *fem.* **spor'ts-woman**). person fond of sports, esp. of hunting etc.; person who behaves fairly and generously; hence ∼LIKE *a.*, ∼SHIP *n.* [f. SPORT + MAN¹]

spŏr'tl̇y̆ *a.* (colloq.) fond of sport; gay, rakish, showy; hence ∼ĭLY² *adv.*, ∼ĭNESS *n.* [f. SPORT + -Y²]

spö'rūl̇|e *n.* spore; small spore; hence ∼AR¹ *a.* [F, or f. mod. L *sporula* (as SPORE; see -ULE)]

spŏt¹ *n.* **1.** particular place, definite locality, (*dropped it on this precise spot*; *the spot where William III landed*); place used for a particular activity (NIGHT-*spot*); particular part of one's body or (fig.) character (TOUCH¹ *the spot*; SOFT, TENDER³, *spot*); (fig., colloq.) one's (regular) position in an organization, pro-gramme of events, etc. **2.** small part of the surface of a thing distinguished by colour, texture, etc., usu. round or less elongated than a streak or stripe (*a blue tie with pink spots*; *can the* LEOPARD *change his spots?*); small mark or stain; pimple; small circle, SPADE², etc., used in various numbers to distinguish faces of dice, playing-cards in suit, etc.; (fig.) moral blemish, stain, (*without a spot on his reputation*); SUN*spot*; **knock** ∼**s off**, defeat easily. **3.** fish of various species with noticeable spot on skin. **4.** ||(colloq.) small quantity of anything (*a spot of leave, lunch, whisky, culture*); drop (*of* rain etc.); a drink. **5.** (Bill. etc.) small round black patch to mark position where ball is placed at certain times; ||∼**-stroke**, pocketing red ball from spot where it is usually placed after previous pocketing; ||∼**-barred game** (in which successive spot-strokes are not allowed); ∼(**-ball**), white ball distinguished from the other by two black spots. **6. on the** ∼, without delay or change of place, then and there, at scene of action or event, (of person) wide awake, equal to the situation, in good form at game etc., (colloq.) in difficult position, compelled to take some action; **put on the** ∼, *(sl.) decide to murder; **running on the** ∼, raising feet alternately as in running but without moving forwards or backwards; **in a** (**tight** etc.) ∼, (colloq.) in difficulties; ∼**-o'n**, (colloq.) precise(ly). **7.** (Commerc.) money paid or goods delivered im-mediately after sale (usu. attrib.: *spot cash*, *spot silver*). **8.** ∼('**light**, (*n.*) (projector giving) beam of light on particular part of theatre stage or on particular part of road in front of vehicle, (fig.) receiving of full attention or publicity; ∼'*light*, (*v.t.*) illuminate with spotlight (lit. or fig.). **9.** ∼ **check**, test made on the spot or on randomly selected subject; ∼ **height**, (figure on map showing) altitude of a point; ∼ **welding** (between points of metal surfaces in con-tact). [ME, perh. f. MDu. *spotte*, LG *spot*, ON *spotti* small piece]

spŏt² *v.* (**-tt-**). **1.** *v.t.* mark, stain, soil, with spot(s) (lit., or fig. of character etc.); (Bill. etc.) place (ball) on spot. **2.** (colloq.) single out beforehand (winner of race etc., horse etc. as winner *for* event), detect, recognize identity, nationality, etc., of, (*spotted him at once as the murderer, as an American*); catch sight of; (Mil.) locate (enemy's position), esp. from the air; watch for and take note of (trains, talent, etc.); hence (-)∼'ter¹ *n.* **3.** (in *p.p.*, Zool.) marked or decorated with spots; ∼**ted Dick or dog**, Dalmatian dog, ||(sl.) plum duff; ∼**ted fever**, (1) cerebro-spinal meningitis, (2) typhus. **4.** *v.i.* make spots (*it's spotting with rain*). [ME, f. prec.]

spö'tl̇ĕss *a.* free from spot or stain (lit. or fig.); hence ∼LY² *adv.*, ∼NESS *n.* [ME, f. SPOT¹ + -LESS]

spö'tt̊|y̆ *a.* marked with (many) spots; patchy, irregu-lar; hence ∼ĭLY² *adv.*, ∼ĭNESS *n.* [ME, f. SPOT¹ + -Y²]

spouse (-z) *n.* husband or wife. [ME *spūs(e)* f. OF *sp(o)us(e)* masc., *sp(o)use* fem., vars. of *espous(e)* f. L *sponsus sponsa* p.p. of *spondēre* betroth]

spout *v.* & *n.* **1.** *v.t.* & *i.* discharge or issue forcibly in a jet (*blood spouts from wound*; *wound spouts blood*; *whale spouts water*); utter (verses etc., or abs.) in declamatory

---

manner, speechify. **2.** *n.* projecting tube through which liquid etc. is poured from teapot, kettle, roof--gutter, etc., or issues from fountain, pump, etc.; sloping trough down which thing may be shot into receptacle; (Hist.) lift serving pawnbroker's store--room; **up the** ∼, (sl.) (1) in pawn, (2) useless, hopeless, (3) pregnant. **3.** jet or column of liquid or grain etc.; WATER*spout*; ∼(**-hole**), whale's blow--hole. **4.** Hence ∼'ER¹ *n.*, ∼'LESS *a.* [ME, f. MDu. *spouten*, f. imit. base **spūt-*; cf. ON *spýta* SPIT²]

SPQR *abbr.* Roman Senate and people [f. L *Senatus Populusque Romanus*]; small profits and quick RETURN²s.

||**Spr.** *abbr.* Sapper.

sprăg *n.* billet of wood or similar device for braking wheel of car etc.; support-prop in coal-mine. [19th c.; orig. unkn.]

sprain *v.t.*, & *n.* **1.** *v.t.* wrench (ankle, wrist, etc.) violently so as to cause pain and swelling but not dislocation. **2.** *n.* such wrench; resulting inflammation and swelling. [17th c.; orig. unkn.]

spraints *n. pl.* otter's dung. [ME, f. OF *espreintes* f. *espraindre*, *espriembre squeeze out f. Rom. *expremere f. L EX¹(*primere = premere* press)]

sprăng. See SPRING¹.

sprăt *n.*, & *v.i.* (**-tt-**). **1.** *n.* small European herring--like fish (*Sprattus sprattus*) much used as food; other similar fish, e.g. sand-eel, young herring; **a** ∼ **to catch a herring or mackerel or whale**, a little risked to gain much. **2.** *v.i.* fish for sprats; hence ∼'ter¹, ∼'ting¹, *ns.* [earlier *sprot*, OE. = MDu., MLG *sprot*, of unkn. orig.]

sprawl *v.* & *n.* **1.** *v.i.* & *t.* spread oneself, spread (one's limbs), out in careless or ungainly way; (of writing, plant, town, etc.) be of irregular or straggling form. **2.** *n.* sprawling movement or attitude; straggling group or mass; URBAN *sprawl*. [OE *spreawlian*; cf. NFris. *spraweli*, Da. *sprelle* kick about]

spray¹ *n.* branch of tree with branchlets or flowers, esp. slender or graceful one, sprig of flowers or leaves; ornament in similar form (*a spray of diamonds* etc.); ∼-**drain**, drain in field etc. made by filling trench with branches; hence ∼'**ey¹** *a.* [-Y²]. [ME, f. OE *sprǣg, of unkn. orig.]

spray² *n.*, & *v.t.* **1.** *n.* water or other liquid flying in small drops from force of wind, dashing of waves, or action of atomizer etc.; medical or other liquid preparation to be applied in this form with atomizer etc.; instrument or apparatus for such application. **2.** *v.t.* throw (liquid, or abs.) in form of spray; sprinkle with small drops or particles, esp. (fruit-trees etc.) with insecticides. **3.** ∼-**dry**, dry (milk etc.) by spraying into hot air etc.; ∼-**gun**, gunlike device for spraying paint etc. **4.** Hence ∼'ER¹ (1, 2) *n.*, ∼'**ey²** *a.* [-Y²]. [earlier *spry*, perh. rel. to MDu. *spra(e)yen*, MHG *spræjen* sprinkle]

spread¹ (-ĕd) *v.* (**spread**). **1.** *v.t.* ∼ (**out**), extend surface of, cause to cover larger surface, by unrolling, unfolding, smearing, flattening out, etc., (fig.) dis-play thus to eye or mind, (*peacock spreads its tail*; *spread one's* WINGs; *spread out a rug on the grass*; *spread butter on bread*; *map lay spread out on the table*; *the view spread out before us*); ∼**oneself**, be lavish or discursive; hence ∼'ER¹ (2) *n.* **2.** *v.i.* ∼ (**out**), show or acquire extended or extensive surface (*river here spreads out to a width of half a mile*; *on every side spread a vast desert*; *spreading yews*; *spreads like butter*). **3.** *v.t.* & *i.* (cause to) become widely felt, known, etc., (*his name spread fear in every quarter*; *rumour spread from mouth to mouth*; *why not spread a little happiness?*). **4.** *v.t.* cover surface of (*slices of bread spread with jam*; *a table spread with every luxury*; *meadow spread with daisies*). **5.** ∼ **eagle**, (1) figure of eagle with legs and wings extended as emblem; (2, Naut.) person lashed in rigging with arms and legs spread out as punishment; ∼**-ea'gle**, (*v.t.*) lash (man) thus, spread out, defeat utterly, (*a.*) *bombastic, esp. noisily patriotic. [OE -*sprǣdan*, = OS -*spreidan*, MDu., MLG *sprēden*, OHG *spreitan* f. WG **spraidjan* causative of **sprīdan* be extended]

spread[2] (-ĕd) *n*. **1.** spreading; capability of expanding (*inferior to the eagle in spread of wings*); span of aeroplane's wings; increased bodily girth (*middle--age(d) spread*); breadth, compass, (*arches of equal spread*); diffusion (*of* education etc.). **2.** = BED[1]*spread*; (colloq.) feast, meal; difference between two rates, prices, etc.; sweet or savoury paste for spreading on bread; printed matter spread across two facing pages or across more than one column. [f. prec.]

spree *n.*, & *v.i.* (colloq.) **1.** *n.* lively frolic, bout of drinking etc.; **on the ~**, engaged in this; **buying, shopping, spending, ~**, bout of lavish spending. **2.** *v.i.* have a spree. [19th c.; orig. unkn.]

sprĕnt *a.* (arch.) sprinkled, overspread, (*with* drops, particles, etc.). [p.p. of obs. *sprenge* f. OE *sprengan* f. Gmc **sprangjan* causative of **springan* SPRING[1]]

sprig[1] *n.*, & *v.t.* (-gg-). **1.** *n.* small branch, (off)shoot; ornament of sprig form, esp. on fabric (*sprig muslin*); (usu. derog.) youth, young man, (*a sprig of (the) nobility*); **~'tail**, pintail; hence **~'gy**[2] (-gi) *a.* **2.** *v.t.* ornament with sprigs (*sprigged muslin*). [ME, f. or cogn. w. LG *sprick*]

sprig[2] *n.* small tapering headless tack. [ME, of unkn. orig.]

spri'ghtl|y̆ (-ī't-) *a.* vivacious, lively, gay; hence **~ĭNESS** *n*. [f. *spright* var. of SPRITE +-LY[1]]

spring[1] *v.* (**sprang** or ***sprung; sprung**). **1.** *v.i.* jump, move rapidly or suddenly, (*up, down, out, over, through, away, back*, etc.; *sprang (up) from his seat; sprang through the gap, at his throat, to their assistance; blood sprang to her cheeks*). **2.** move rapidly as from constrained position or by action of a spring (*branch sprang back; door sprang to*). **3.** come (*up*) into being, originate or arise (*from* source), appear, (*a breeze sprang up; the piers from which the arches spring; is sprung from or of a royal stock; the buds are springing; the belief has sprung up; his actions spring from a false conviction*); **where did you ~ from?** (to person arriving suddenly or unexpectedly or whose presence is only now realized). **4.** become warped or split. **5.** *v.t.* rouse (game) from earth or covert; (sl.) contrive escape of (person *from* prison etc.). **6.** split, crack, (wood or wooden implement). **7.** cause to act suddenly by means of a spring, produce or develop or make known suddenly or unexpectedly, (*spring a trap; has sprung a new theory; loves to spring surprises on us*); (colloq.) spend (money). **8.** (usu. in *p.p.*) provide (motor vehicle etc.) with springs. **9.** cause (mine) to explode. **10. ~ a leak**, develop leak (orig. Naut., from straining of timbers). **11. sprung rhythm**, poetic metre approximating to speech, each foot having one stressed syllable followed by a varying number of unstressed. [OE *springan*, = OS, OHG *springan*, ON *springa* f. Gmc **sprengan*]

spring[2] *n.* **1.** jump (*took a spring; rose with a spring*). **2.** season in which vegetation begins to appear, first season of the year, in N. hemisphere March–May (Astron., from vernal equinox to summer solstice); (fig.) early stage of life etc.; = *spring* TIDE[1]. **3.** place where water, oil, etc., wells up from earth, basin or flow so formed, (*hot, mineral, springs*). **4.** backward movement from constrained position, recoil, e.g. of bow. **5.** elasticity (*these mattresses have no spring in them*). **6.** elastic contrivance usu. of bent or coiled metal used esp. as motive power in clockwork etc. or for preventing vibration or sudden impact. **7.** (fig.) motive actuating person etc., source, origin, (*the springs of human action*). **8.** upward curve of beam etc. from horizontal line. **9.** splitting or yielding of plank etc. under strain. **10. ~ balance** (measuring weight by tension of spring); **~ bed** (with spring mattress); **~'board**, elastic board giving impetus in leaping, diving, etc., (fig.) source of impetus in any activity; **~ chicken**, young fowl for eating (orig. available only in spring), (fig.) young person; **~-clean** *n.*, & *v.t.*, clean(ing) (house, room) thoroughly, esp. in spring; **~**

gun (contrived to go off when trespasser or animal stumbles on it or on wire attached to it); **~-halt**, spasmodic movement of horse's hind leg; **~ mattress** (containing or consisting of springs); **~ onion** (taken from ground before bulb has formed, and eaten raw in salad); **~'tail**, wingless insect of order Collembola, leaping by means of springlike caudal part; *spring* TIDE[1]; **~'tide** (poet.), **~'time**, season of spring, time compared to this; **~ water** (from spring, opp. to river or rain water). **11.** Hence **~'LESS, ~'LIKE**, *adjs.*, **~'LET** *n*. [OE, f. as prec.]

spri'ngal(d) *n.* (arch.) youngster, stripling. [ME, perh. f. SPRING[1]]

spri'ngbŏk *n.* S. Afr. gazelle (*Antidorcas marsupialis*) with habit of springing in play or when alarmed; **S~s**, (nickname for) S. Africans, S. African Rugby football etc. touring team etc. [Afrik., f. Du. *springen* SPRING[1] + *bok* antelope]

springe (-nj) *n.* noose or snare for catching small game. [ME, repr. OE **sprencg*, rel. to obs. *sprenge* (see SPRENT)]

spri'nger *n.* In vbl senses; (Archit.) part of arch where curve begins, lowest stone of this, bottom stone of coping of gable, rib of groined roof or vault; small spaniel used to spring game; springbok. [f. SPRING[1] + -ER[1]]

spri'ng|y̆ *a.* (Of movement or substance) elastic; hence **~ĭNESS** *n*. [f. SPRING[1,2] + -Y[2]]

spri'nkle *v.t.*, & *n.* **1.** *v.t.* scatter (liquid, ashes, crumbs, etc.) in small drops or particles, whence **spri'nkl**ER[1] (2) *n.* (esp. as lawn-waterer or fire--extinguisher); (fig.) distribute in small amounts; subject (ground, object) to sprinkling (*with* liquid etc., or fig.); (of liquid etc.) fall thus on; hence **spri'nkl**ING (2) *n.*, (esp., fig.) *a* few or *a* little here and there *of.* **2.** *n.* light shower (*of* rain etc.); a sprinkling *of.* [ME, perh. f. MDu. *sprenkelen*]

sprint *v.* & *n.* **1.** *v.i.* & *t.* run short distance, run (specified distance), at full speed; hence **~'ER**[1] *n.* **2.** *n.* such run; similar short spell of maximum effort in cycling, swimming, car-racing, etc. [f. ON **sprinta*, of unkn. orig.]

sprit *n.* small spar reaching diagonally from mast to upper outer corner of sail; **~'sail** (-sāl, -sal), sail extended by sprit, (formerly) sail extended by yard set under bowsprit. [OE *sprēot* pole; = MDu., MLG *spr(i)et*, cogn. w. SPROUT]

sprite *n.* elf, fairy, goblin. [ME, f. *sprit* var. of SPIRIT[1]]

spro'ckĕt *n.* each of several teeth on wheel engaging with links of chain; **~-wheel**, such wheel, e.g. for engaging bicycle chain. [16th c., of unkn. orig.]

sprout *v.* & *n.* **1.** *v.i.* begin to grow, shoot forth, put forth shoots; spring up, grow to a height. **2.** *v.t.* produce by sprouting (lit., or fig.: *has sprouted horns, a moustache*). **3.** *n.* shoot of plant; (in *pl.*, colloq.) = BRUSSELS *sprouts*. [OE **sprūtan*, = OS *sprūton*, MLG *sprūten* f. WG **sprūtan*]

spruce[1] (-ōōs) *a.*, & *v.t.* **1.** *a.* neat in dress and appearance, trim, smart; hence **~'LY**[2] (-slī) *adv.*, **~'NESS** (-sn-) *n.* **2.** *v.t.* smarten (one*self* etc., usu. *up*). [perh. f. foll. in obs. sense 'Prussian', in the collocation *spruce* (*leather*) *jerkin*]

spruce[2] (-ōōs) *n.* conifer of genus *Picea*, with dense foliage in conical shape; its wood; **~-beer** (made from leaves and small branches of spruce). [alt. f. obs. *Pruce* Prussia; cf. PRUSSIAN]

sprue[1] (-ōō) *n.* passage through which metal is poured into mould; metal filling sprue. [19th c., of unkn. orig.]

sprue[2] (-ōō) *n.* tropical deficiency disease with ulcerated mucous membrane of mouth and chronic enteritis. [f. Du. *spruw* THRUSH[2]; cf. Flem. *spruwen* sprinkle]

spruit (-rāt) *n.* (S. Afr.) small watercourse, usu. almost dry except in the wet season. [Du., cogn. w. SPROUT]

sprŭng. See SPRING[1].

sprȳ *a.* (∼'er, ∼'est). active, lively; hence ∼'LY² *adv.*, ∼'NESS *n.* [18th c., dial. & US, of unkn. orig.]

spŭd *n.* & *v.* (-dd-). **1.** *n.* small narrow spade for cutting roots of weeds etc.; (sl.) potato; ∼-**bashing**, (Services' sl.) task of peeling potatoes. **2.** *v.t.* remove (weeds *up* or *out*) with spud. **3.** *v.i.* make initial drilling for oil-well. [ME; orig. unkn.]

spūe. See SPEW.

spūm|e *n.,* & *v.i.* froth, foam; hence or cogn. ∼'OUS, ∼'Y², *adjs.* [ME, f. OF (*e*)*spume* or f. L *spuma*]

spŭn. See SPIN¹.

spunge. Var. (arch.) of SPONGE.

spŭnk *n.* touchwood; (colloq.) courage, mettle, spirit, whence ∼'Y² *a.*; (sl.) semen. [16th c., of unkn. orig.; cf. PUNK²]

spŭr *n.* & *v.* (-rr-). **1.** *n.* pricking instrument with point or rowel worn on rider's heel and used to urge horse (**put** or **set** ∼**s to,** = sense 5; **win** one's ∼**s,** (Hist.) gain knighthood, (fig.) gain distinction, make a name for oneself); (fig.) stimulus, incentive; **on the ∼ of the moment,** impromptu, on a momentary impulse. **2.** spur-shaped thing, e.g. hard projection on cock's leg, steel point fastened to leg of gamecock, projection from mountain (range), branch road or railway, climbing-iron; (Bot.) slender hollow projection from some part of flower, group of fruit-buds. **3.** ∼ **royal,** 15-shilling coin of James I bearing spurlike sun with rays; ∼-**wheel,** ∼-**gear,** cog-wheel with radial teeth; ∼'**wort,** plant with whorls of leaves like rowel of spur. **4.** Hence ∼'LESS *a.* **5.** *v.t.* prick (horse) with spurs; incite (person *on* to effort, *to* do, etc.); stimulate (interest etc.); (esp. in *p.p.*) furnish (person, boots, gamecock) with spurs. **6.** *v.i.* ride horse hard (*on, forward,* etc.; lit. or fig.). [OE *spora, spura,* = OS, OHG *sporo,* ON *spori* f. Gmc **spuron* f. IE **sper-* strike with foot; cf. SPURN]

spŭrge *n.* plant of genus *Euphorbia,* with acrid milky juice; ∼ **laurel,** shrub of genus *Daphne,* esp. yellow-flowered *D. laureola.* [ME, f. OF *espurge* (*espurgier* f. L EX¹*purgare* PURGE)]

spŭr'ious *a.* not genuine, not being what it pretends to be, not proceeding from the pretended source, (*spurious pregnancy, coin,* (*reading in*) *MS, anger*); (of offspring) illegitimate; having outward similarity of form or function only; hence ∼LY² *adv.,* ∼NESS *n.* [f. L *spurius* false +-OUS]

spŭrn *v.* & *n.* **1.** *v.t.* repel, thrust back, with foot; reject with disdain, treat with contempt, (offer, advances, person, etc.). **2.** *v.i.* (arch.) ∼ **at,** spurn. **3.** *n.* (arch.) spurning, contemptuous rejection. [OE *spurnan, spornan,* = OS, OHG *spurnan,* ON **spurna,* cf. SPUR]

spŭ'rrier *n.* spur-maker. [ME, f. SPUR+-IER]

spŭ'rry, -rey, *n.* slender plant of genus *Spergula,* esp. **corn-**∼, white-flowered weed in cornfields etc. [f. Du. *spurrie,* prob. rel. to med. L *spergula*]

spŭrt² *v.i.,* & *n.* (make) short sudden violent effort esp. in racing. [= foll.]

spŭrt², spȳrt, *v.* & *n.* **1.** *v.i.* gush out in a jet or stream. **2.** *v.t.* cause (liquid etc.) to do this. **3.** *n.* sudden gushing out, jet. [16th c., of unkn. orig.]

spu'tnik (-ōō't-, -ŭ't-) *n.* Russian artificial earth satellite. [Russ., = travelling companion]

spŭ'tter *v.* & *n.* **1.** *v.t.* emit with spitting sound; speak, utter, (words, threats, a language, etc.) rapidly or incoherently; (Phys.) deposit (metal) by using fast ions etc. to eject particles of it from target. **2.** *v.i.* speak in hurried or vehement fashion (*at* person etc.); (of thing) emit spitting sounds, esp. when being heated (*sausages sputtered in the pan*). **3.** Hence ∼ER¹ *n.* **4.** *n.* sputtering speech. [f. Du. *sputteren* (imit.)]

spŭ't|um *n.* (*pl.* ∼a). saliva, spittle; expectorated matter esp. as diagnostic of disease. [L, neut. p.p. (as *n.*) of *spuere* spit]

spȳ *n.* & *v.* **1.** *n.* person who goes secretly into enemy's or rival's territory to observe activities, watch movements, etc., and report the result; person who keeps (esp. secret) watch on movements of others (*refuse to be*

a spy on his conduct). **2.** *v.t.* discern, make out, esp. by careful observation, (*spied a horseman approaching*); **I** ∼, children's game of guessing visible object from initial letter of its name; ||*I spy* STRANGERS; ∼ **out,** explore esp. secretly, discover by this means. **3.** *v.i.* play the spy, keep close and secret watch (*on* person, movements, etc.); pry (*into* secret etc.). **4.** ∼'**glass,** small telescope; ∼'**hole,** peep-hole. [ME, f. OF (*espie* *n.* f.) *espier* espy f. Gmc **spekh-* f. IE **spek-*]

sq. *abbr.* square.

Sqn. Ldr. *abbr.* Squadron Leader.

squab (-ŏb) *a.* & *n.* **1.** *a.* short and fat, squat. **2.** *n.* short fat person, whence ∼'bY² *a.*; young esp. unfledged pigeon or other bird; stuffed cushion, esp. ||as part of seat in motor car; sofa, ottoman. **3.** ∼-**chick,** unfledged bird; ∼ **pie,** (1) pigeon pie, (2) pie of mutton, pork, onions, and apples. [17th c., of unkn. orig.; cf. obs. *quab* shapeless thing, Sw. dial. *sqvabba* fat woman]

squa'bbl|e (-ŏ'-) *v.i.,* & *n.* (engage in) petty or noisy quarrel (*with* person *about* thing); hence ∼ER¹ *n.* [prob. imit.; cf. Sw. dial. *sqvabbel* a dispute]

squă'ccŏ *n.* (*pl.* ∼s). small crested heron of S. Europe, Africa, and Asia. [f. It. dial. *sguacco*]

squad (-ŏd) *n.* **1.** (Mil.) small number of men assembled for drill etc.; **awkward** ∼ (of raw recruits not yet competent to take place in regimental line, or fig.); hence ∼'dIE, ∼'dY², ||(sl.) recruit, private. **2.** small party of persons with common task etc.; FLYING² *squad;* *∼ **car,** police car having radio link with headquarters. [f. F *escouade* var. of *escadre* f. It. *squadra* SQUARE¹]

squa'dron (-ŏ'd-) *n.* **1.** *n.* principal division of cavalry regiment or armoured formation, consisting of two troops. **2.** organized body of persons. **3.** detachment of warships employed on particular service; FLYING² *squadron.* **4.** unit of Royal Air Force (10 to 18 aircraft); ∼ **leader,** officer commanding this. [f. It. *squadrone* (as prec.; see -OON)]

squail *v.* (in *pl.*) game with small wooden discs (∼s) propelled across table or board (∼-**board**). [19th c., of unkn. orig.; cf. dial. *kayles* skittles]

squa'lid (-ŏ'l-) *a.* dirty; repulsively filthy; mean or poor in appearance; (fig.) wretched; hence or cogn. ∼ITY (-ĭ'd-), ∼NESS, **squa'lor** (-ŏ'l-), *ns.,* ∼LY² *adv.* [f. L *squalidus* (*squalēre* be rough or dirty; see -ID¹)]

squall (-awl) *v.* & *n.* **1.** *v.i.* cry out, scream, violently as in fear or pain. **2.** *v.t.* utter in screaming or discordant voice. **3.** *n.* sudden or violent gust or successive gusts of wind, esp. with rain or snow or sleet; **arched** ∼ (occurring near equator with sudden collection of black clouds in form of arch and sun violent thunderstorm); **black** ∼ (with dark cloud); **line** ∼ (occurring along cold front); **white** ∼ (arising in fair weather without formation of clouds); **look out for** ∼**s,** (fig.) be on one's guard against danger or trouble; hence ∼'Y² *a.* **4.** discordant cry, scream (esp. of baby). [prob. f. SQUEAL, assoc. w. *bawl*]

squa'loid *a.* & *n.* (fish) like shark, esp. of suborder Squaloidea. [f. L *squalus,* a sea-fish +-OID]

squalor. See SQUALID.

squā'm|a *n.* (*pl.* ∼ae). (Bot. & Zool.) scale; scalelike feather or part of bone; hence ∼OSE¹, ∼OUS, *adjs.,* ∼ULE *n.* [L]

squa'nder (-ŏ'n-) *v.t.* spend (money, time, etc.) wastefully; dissipate (fortune etc.) thus; hence ∼ER¹ *n.,* ∼MANIA *n.,* craze for extravagant expenditure. [16th c., of unkn. orig.]

squāre¹ *n.* **1.** equilateral rectangle; object of (approximately) this shape; square scarf; small square area on game-board; **back to** ∼ **one,** (colloq.) back to starting-point with no progress made. **2.** open area in town at meeting of streets or ||(usu. quadri-lateral) planted with trees etc. and surrounded with buildings esp. dwelling-houses, (*Berkeley, Trafalgar, Times, Square*); *block of buildings bounded by four streets; area of cricket-field suitable for use as wicket;

area within barracks etc. for drill; ∼-**bashing,** (Services' sl.) drill on barrack-square. **3.** L-shaped or T-shaped instrument for obtaining or testing right angles; **out of** ∼, not at right angles; SET³ *square*. **4.** (arch., usu. fig.) standard, pattern. **5. on the** ∼, fair(ly), honest(ly), (*can be trusted to act on the square*); **is on the** ∼, is a Freemason. **6.** product of a number multiplied by itself (*the square of 9 is 81, of x² is x⁴*); INVERSE *square law; 9* **is a perfect** ∼, has integral square root. **7.** body of infantry drawn up in rectangular form; **hollow** ∼, (Hist.) body so drawn up with space in middle. **8.** square arrangement of letters, figures, etc., (MAGIC *square*; WORD¹-*square*). **9.** (sl.) conventional or old-fashioned person, one ignorant of or opposed to current trends. **10.** unit of 100 sq. ft. as measure of flooring etc. [ME, f. OF *esquire, esquar(r)e* f. Rom. **exquadra* (*exquadrare*; see SQUARE³)]

square² *a.* & *adv.* **1.** *a.* of square shape; ∼ **foot, metre, mile,** etc., (area equal to that of) square whose side is one foot etc.; ∼ **measure** (expressed in square feet etc.). **2.** rectangular (*table with square corners*); at right angles *to*; (Cricket) on line through stumps at right angles to the wicket. **3.** ∼ **number,** square of an integer e.g. 1, 4, 9, 16, etc.; ∼ **root** *of a given number,* number of which it is the square (*the square root of 9 is 3, of x⁶ is x³, of 2 is irrational*). **4.** ∼ **dance, game** (in which four couples, players, face inwards from four sides). **5.** having the breadth more nearly equal to the length or height than is usual (*a man of square frame*). **6.** of square section (*square peg in round HOLE¹; has a square jaw*). **7.** properly arranged, in good order, (*must tidy up and get things square*). **8.** thorough, uncompromising, (*was met with a square refusal*). **9.** fair, honest, (*his dealings are not always quite square*); **a** ∼ **deal,** fair bargain, fair treatment. **10.** (sl.) conventional or old-fashioned, unsophisticated, conservative, (cf. SQUARE¹ 9). **11.** on a proper footing, even, quits, (*am now square with all the world*); **get** ∼ **with,** pay, compound with, (creditor); **(all)** ∼, with no debit remaining, (Golf) having won same number of holes as opponent. **12.** ∼ **brackets** (of [ ] shape); ∼-**built,** of comparatively broad shape; *∗∼head,* (derog.; R) Scandinavian, German, or Dutch immigrant; ∼ **leg,** (Cricket) (position of) fieldsman at some distance on batsman's leg-side and nearly opposite stumps; ∼ **meal** (substantial and satisfying); ∼ **piano** (early type with low oblong shape like clavichord); ∼-**rigged,** with principal sails at right angles to length of ship and extended by horizontal yards slung to mast by middle, opp. to *fore--and-aft rigged*; ∼ **sail,** four-cornered sail extended on yard slung to mast by middle; ∼-**shouldered,** with broad and not sloping shoulders, esp. opp. to *round--shouldered*; ∼-**toed,** (having boots or shoes) with square toes, (fig.) formal, prim; ∼ **wave** (Phys., with periodic sudden alternations between only two values of quantity). **13.** Hence ∼'LY² (-ār'lĭ) *adv.*, ∼'NESS (-ār'n-) *n.*, **squar'**ISH¹ 2 *a.* **14.** *adv.* squarely (*sat square on his seat; hit him square on the jaw*); fairly (*do you think he plays square?*); FAIR² *and square.* [ME, f. OF *esquarré* p.p. (as foll.)]

square³ *v.* **1.** *v.t.* make rectangular, give rectangular cross-section to (timber etc.); mark out in squares (∼**d paper,** esp. for plotting graphs); place (shoulders etc.) squarely facing forwards; ∼ **the circle,** construct square equal in area to given circle (problem incapable of purely geometrical solution), (fig.) do what is impossible. **2.** multiply (number) by itself (*3 squared is 9; x squared is written x²*). **3.** *v.t.* & *i.* adjust, make or be suitable *to* or consistent *with*, reconcile, (*decline to square my conduct to* or *with his interests; his practice does not square, he does not square his practice, with his principles*). **4.** *v.t.* settle, pay, (bill etc., or abs. *up*); *square* ACCOUNT²s *with*. **5.** (colloq.) pay, esp. bribe, (*can you square the porter?; has been squared to hold his tongue,* (*can you square the porter?; has been squared to hold his tongue,*) secure acquiescence etc. of (person) thus. **6.**

(Golf). make score of (match, or abs.) all square. **7.** (Naut.) lay (yards) at right angles with keel making them at same time horizontal, get (dead-eyes) horizontal, get (ratlines) horizontal and parallel to one another. **8.** *v.i.* ∼ (*∗off*), assume attitude of boxer; ∼ **up to,** move towards (person) in this attitude, face and tackle (difficulty etc.) resolutely. **9.** *∗*∼ **away,** tidy up. [ME, f. OF *esquarrer* f. Rom. **EX¹*(*quadrare* f. *quadra* square)]

squa'rrōse (-ŏ'r-) *a.* (Bot. & Zool.) rough with scalelike processes. [f. L *squarrosus* scurfy, scabby; see -OSE¹]

∥squar'son *n.* (arch., joc.) squire and parson in one. [portmanteau wd]

squash¹ (-ŏ-) *v.* & *n.* **1.** *v.t.* crush, squeeze flat or into pulp; pack tight, crowd; quash (rebellion); (colloq.) dismiss (proposal etc.), silence (person) with crushing retort. **2.** *v.i.* make one's way (*into*) by squeezing. **3.** *n.* squashed thing or mass, whence ∼'Y² *a.*; crowd, crowded assembly; (sound of) fall of soft body; ∼ (**rackets**), game played with rackets and small fairly soft ball in closed court; drink made of crushed fruit; ∼ **hat** (of soft felt etc.). [alt. f. QUASH]

squash² (-ŏ-) *n.* (gourd, used as vegetable etc., of) trailing herbaceous annual plant of genus *Cucurbita*. [f. obs. (*i*)*squoutersquash* f. Narraganset *asquutasquash* (*asq* uncooked)]

squat (-ŏt) *v.* (**-tt-**), *a.*, & *n.* **1.** *v.i.* sit on ground etc. with knees drawn up and heels close to or touching hams, crouch with hams resting on backs of heels; (of animal) crouch close to ground; (colloq.) sit (*down, on,* etc.); (colloq.) act as squatter. **2.** *v.t.* put (one*self,* person) into squatting position. **3.** *a.* in squatting posture; (of person etc.) short and thick, dumpy. **4.** *n.* squatting posture; being squatter; place occupied by squatter(s). [ME, f. OF *esquatir* flatten (*es-* EX-¹ + *quatir* press down, crouch f. Rom. **coactire* f. L *coactus* p.p.; see COGENT)]

squa'tter (-ŏ't-) *n.* In vbl senses; person who settles on new esp. public land without title; person who takes unauthorized possession of unoccupied premises; (Austral.) (1, Hist.) person who gets right of pasturage from government on easy terms, (2) sheep-farmer esp. on large scale. [f. prec. +-ER¹]

squaw *n.* N. Amer. Ind. woman or wife; ∼-**man,** white married to squaw; *∗*∼ **winter,** brief wintry spell before Indian summer. [f. Narraganset *squaws,* Massachusetts *squaw* woman]

squawk *v.i.*, & *n.* **1.** *v.i.* make squawk. **2.** *n.* (usu. bird's) loud harsh cry; loud complaint; ∼-**box,** (colloq.) loudspeaker. [imit.]

squeak *v.* & *n.* **1.** *v.i.* utter short shrill cry as of mouse; make slight high-pitched sound as of unoiled hinge; (colloq.) pass narrowly *by, through,* etc.; (sl.) turn informer. **2.** *v.t.* utter (words) shrilly. **3.** *n.* short shrill sound, whence ∼'Y² *a.*; (**narrow**) ∼, narrow escape, success barely attained; BUBBLE¹ *and* squeak. [ME; imit., cf. *squeal, shriek,* and Sw. *skväka* croak]

squea'ker *n.* In vbl senses; young bird, esp. pigeon. [f. prec. +-ER¹]

squeal *v.* & *n.* **1.** *v.i.* utter shrill cry as of child from pain, fear, anger, joy, etc.; (sl.) protest excitedly e.g. against taxation; (sl.) turn informer. **2.** *v.t.* utter (words) with squeal. **3.** Hence ∼'ER¹ *n.* **4.** *n.* shrill prolonged cry of child, pig, etc. [ME; imit.]

squea'mish *a.* easily nauseated; fastidious, overscrupulous in questions of propriety, honesty, etc.; hence ∼LY² *adv.*, ∼NESS *n.* [ME var. of (now dial.) *squeamous,* f. AF *escoymos,* of unkn. orig.]

squeegee' *n.*, & *v.t.* **1.** *n.* rubber-edged implement for sweeping wet deck, road, etc.; small similar instrument or roller used in photography. **2.** *v.t.* treat with squeegee. [f. *squeege,* strengthened form of foll.]

squeeze *v.* & *n.* **1.** *v.t.* exert pressure on (sponge, lemon, etc.) esp. in order to extract moisture or reduce size, compress with hand or between two bodies; bring (moisture) *out* thus; ∼ person's **hand** (as sign of sympathy, affection, etc.); ∼d **orange**, (fig.) person or thing from whom or which no more is to be had. **2.** thrust (one*self*, person, thing, *into* vehicle, room, etc., *out of*, etc.) by pressure. **3.** harass by exactions, extort money etc. from; constrain, bring pressure to bear on; (Bridge) subject (player) to squeeze; get (money etc. *out of* person etc.) by extortion, entreaty, etc. **4.** ∼ (**out**), produce with effort (*a tear* etc.). **5.** Hence **squee′z**ABLE *a.*, **squee′z**ER[1] (1, 2) *n.* **6.** *v.i.* & *t.* make one's way or *way* by pressure (*into* etc.). **7.** *n.* application of pressure by squeezing (lit. or fig.); small quantity produced by squeezing; (pressure of) crowd, crush, (*we all got in, but it was a* (*tight*) *squeeze*); ‖close embrace; impression of coin etc. taken by pressing damp paper, wax, etc., against it; (Econ.) restriction imposed on borrowing, investment, etc.; forced exaction by Asian official, illicit commission, percentage on goods purchased extorted by native servant. **8.** ∼ **bottle,** flexible container whose contents are extracted by squeezing it; ∼ (**play**), (Bridge) leading winning cards until opponent is forced to discard important card, (Baseball) hitting ball short to infield to enable runner on third base to start for home as soon as ball is pitched. [earlier *squise*, intensive of obs. *queise*, of unkn. orig.]

squĕlch *v.* & *n.* **1.** *v.t.* stamp on, crush flat, put an end to; disconcert, silence. **2.** *v.i.* make sucking sound as of treading in thick mud. **3.** *n.* act or sound of squelching. [imit.]

squib *n.* & *v.* (**-bb-**). **1.** *n.* small firework burning with hissing sound and usu. with final explosion (**damp** ∼, unsuccessful attempt to impress etc.); short satirical composition, lampoon. **2.** *v.i.* & *t.* (arch.) write, attack with, lampoons. [16th c., of unkn. orig., perh. imit.]

squid *n.*, & *v.i.* (**-dd-**). **1.** *n.* ten-armed cephalopod esp. of genus *Loligo* used as bait or food, artificial bait imitating this. **2.** *v.i.* fish with squid as bait. [17th c., of unkn. orig.]

squiffed (-ft), **squi′ffy**, *adjs.* (sl.) slightly drunk. [19th c., of unkn. orig.]

squi′ggle *n.* short curly line, esp. in handwriting; hence ∼Y[2] *a.* [imit.]

squill *n.* **1.** bulbous plant of genus *Scilla.* **2.** sea-shore plant (*Urginea maritima*) whose bulbs are dried and used as diuretic, purgative, etc. **3.** crustacean of genus *Squilla.* [ME, f. L *squilla*, *scilla* f. Gk *skilla*]

squinch *n.* straight or arched structure across interior angle of square tower to carry dome etc. [var. of obs. *scunch* abbr. f. SCUNCHEON]

squint *v.*, *n.*, & *a.* **1.** *v.i.* have the eyes turned in different directions, have squint; look obliquely or with half-closed eyes (*at* etc.). **2.** *v.t.* close (eyes) quickly, hold (eyes) half-shut. **3.** *n.* abnormality of an eye which does not turn to match the other's direction; stealthy or sidelong glance; (colloq.) glance, look, (*let's have a squint at it*); leaning, inclination, (*to*, *towards*, policy etc.). **4.** oblique opening through wall of church affording view of altar. **5.** *a.* squinting; looking different ways; ∼**-eyed**, (fig.) malignant. [f. ASQUINT; adj. perh. f. *squint-eyed* f. obs. *squint* adv. f. *asquint*]

squire *n.*, & *v.t.* **1.** *n.* country gentleman, esp. *the* chief landed proprietor in a district; *magistrate or lawyer; woman's escort or gallant (∼ **of dames**, man who is attentive to or frequents company of women); ‖(colloq., as *voc.*) sir; (Hist.) attendant on knight; hence ∼DOM (-īr′d-), ∼HOOD (-īr′h-), ∼LET, ∼LING, (-īr′l-), ∼SHIP (-īr′sh-), *ns.*, ∼LY[1] (-īr′li) *a.* **2.** (Austral.) young snapper fish. **3.** *v.t.* (Of man) attend upon, escort, (woman). [ME, f. OF *esquier* ESQUIRE]

squir(**e**)**′archy** (-īr′ärki) *n.* the class of landed proprietors, esp. as having political or social influence; hence [by back-form. after *monarch*] ∼**arch** (-k) *n.*,

∼**ărch**AL, ∼**ar′ch**ICAL, (-k-) *adjs.* [f. prec., after *hierarchy* etc.]

‖**squiree′n** *n.* owner of small landed property esp. in Ireland. [f. SQUIRE + -EEN]

squirm *v.i.*, & *n.* **1.** *v.i.* wriggle, writhe; (fig.) show or feel embarrassment or discomfiture. **2.** *n.* wriggling movement. [imit., prob. assoc. w. WORM[1]]

squi′rrel *n.*, & *v.t.* (‖**-ll-**). **1.** *n.* rodent of family Sciuridae, usu. of arboreal habits, with bushy tail carried over back, and pointed ears; its fur; **barking** ∼, prairie-dog; GREY, GROUND[1]-, RED, *squirrel*; ∼**-cage** (for squirrel etc., with revolving cylinder resembling treadmill; fig. of similar structure in electric motor or of monotonous repetition); *∼-hawk,** large hawk preying on squirrels; ∼**-monkey,** small soft-haired S. Amer. monkey of genus *Saimiri*; ∼**(-tail) grass** (of barley genus, with bushy spikelets). **2.** *v.t.* hoard away. [ME, f. AF *esquirel*, OF *esquireul*, f. Rom. *scuriolus,* dim. of L f. Gk *skiouros,* f. *skia* shade + *oura* tail]

squirt *v.* & *n.* **1.** *v.t.* eject (liquid, powder) in a jet as from syringe. **2.** *v.i.* (Of liquid etc.) be discharged thus. **3.** *n.* syringe; jet of water etc.; small quantity produced by squirting; ∼(**-gun**), kind of toy syringe; (colloq.) insignificant self-assertive person. [ME, imit.]

squish *v.i.*, & *n.* (move with) slight squelching sound; hence ∼Y[2] *a.* [imit.]

‖**squit** *n.* (sl.) small or insignificant person. [cf. dial. *squit* in same sense, and *squit* to squirt]

squitch *n.* = COUCH[3]-*grass.* [alt. f. QUITCH]

Sr. *abbr.* Senior; Señor; Sister (sense 3).

sr *abbr.* steradian(s).

Sr *symb.* strontium.

‖**SRC** *abbr.* Science Research Council.

SRN *abbr.* State Registered Nurse.

SRO *abbr.* *standing room only; ‖Statutory Rules and Orders.

SS *abbr.* Saints; steamship; (Hist.) Nazi special police force [f. G *Schutz-Staffel*]

‖**SSAFA** *abbr.* Soldiers', Sailors', and Airmen's Families Association.

SSC *abbr.* (Sc.) Solicitor to the Supreme Court.

SSE *abbr.* south-south-east.

‖**SSRC** *abbr.* Social Science Research Council.

SSS *abbr.* *Selective Service System; (Golf) standard scratch score.

SST *abbr.* supersonic transport.

SSW *abbr.* south-south-west.

-st. See -EST[2].

St. *abbr.* Saint; stokes; Street.

st. *abbr.* stone; (Cricket) stumped by.

Sta. *abbr.* Station.

stăb *v.* (**-bb-**) & *n.* **1.** *v.t.* & *i.* pierce, wound, with (usu. short) pointed tool or weapon e.g. knife or dagger; aim blow with such weapon (*at*); (fig.) inflict sharp pain on (person, his feelings, conscience, etc.), aim blow *at* (reputation, person, etc.); ∼ **in the back,** slander or betray; hence ∼′b**ER**[1] *n.* **2.** *n.* act of stabbing; blow or thrust with knife etc., wound thus made, blow or pain inflicted on person's feelings; (colloq.) attempt, try; ∼**-culture** (of bacteria inoculated by deep-thrust needle). [ME; cf. dial. *stob* in first sense]

Sta′bat Mater (stah′-; mah-) *n.* (musical setting for) Latin hymn on agony of the Virgin Mary at the Crucifixion. [f. the opening wds, L *Stabat mater dolorosa* 'Stood the Mother, full of grief']

stǎ′bile *n.* abstract sculpture or structure of wire, sheet metal, etc. [f. L *stabilis* STABLE[1]]

stǎ′biliz|**e, -is**|**e** (-īz), *v.t.* & *i.* make or become stable; hence ∼A′TION *n.*, ∼ER[1] (1, 2) *n.* (esp. gyroscope device to prevent rolling of ship, or *horizontal tailplane of aircraft). [f. STABILITY (see foll.) + -IZE]

stǎ′ble[1] *a.* firmly fixed or established, not easily to be moved or changed or unbalanced or destroyed or altered in value, (*doubt whether the building, the govern-*

ment, is stable; *element forms stable compounds, has no stable isotope)*; firm, resolute, not wavering or fickle, *(a stable and steadfast friend)*; stable EQUILIBRIUM; hence or cogn. **stabi′lIty**, ∼NESS (-beln-), *ns.*, **stā′bLY**[2] *adv.* [ME f. AF; OF *estable* f. L *stabilis* (*stare* stand; see -ABLE)]

stā′ble[2] *n.* & *v.* **1.** *n.* building set apart and adapted for lodging and feeding (and training) horses; racehorses of particular stable; (fig.) (persons, products, etc., having) common origin or affiliation; ∼**-boy**, ∼**-lad**, ∼**-man**, person employed in stable; ∼**-companion**, ∼**-mate**, horse of same stable, (fig.) member of same school, club, etc.; **lock the ∼-door** etc. (see LOCK[3].) **2.** *v.t.* put or keep (horse) in stable. **3.** *v.i.* (Of horse etc., or fig. of person) be stabled. [ME, f. OF *estable* f. Rom. **stabula* & L *stabulum* (*stare* stand)]

stā′bling *n.* In vbl senses; accommodation for horses etc. [f. prec. + -ING[1]]

stā′blish *v.t.* (arch.) fix firmly, establish, set up. [var. of ESTABLISH]

stacca′to (-ah′tō) *a.*, *adv.*, & *n.* (*pl.* ∼s). **1.** (Mus.) *a.* & *adv.* (to be played) in abrupt sharply detached manner (cf. LEGATO, TENUTO); ∼ **mark**, dot or stroke above or below staccato note in score. **2.** *a.* & *n.* (uttered etc. with) delivery or presentation in separate short bursts. [It., p.p. of *staccare* = *distaccare* DETACH]

stack *n.*, & *v.t.* **1.** *n.* circular or rectangular pile of grain in sheaf or of hay, straw, etc., usu. with sloping thatched top, rick; ∼**-yard**, enclosure for these. **2.** ‖(As measure of wood) pile of 108 cu. ft. **3.** pile or heap of anything, esp. in orderly arrangement; (colloq.) large quantity, *(has stacks of money, a whole stack of work to get through)*; stacked group of aircraft; pyramidal group of rifles, pile; ∼(**-room**), part of library where books are compactly stored and to which public does not have direct access. **4.** (**chimney-**)∼, number of chimneys standing together. **5.** isolated tall factory chimney; (**smoke-**)∼, chimney or funnel to discharge smoke of locomotive or steamer; **BLOW[1]* one's *stack*. **6.** ‖high detached rock esp. off coast of Scotland and Orkneys. **7.** *v.t.* pile in stack(s); arrange (cards, or fig. circumstances etc.) secretly for cheating; instruct to fly round same point at different levels (aircraft waiting to land at airport); ∼ (= PILE[3]) **arms**. [ME, f. ON *stakkr* haystack, f. Gmc **stakkaz*]

stā′ctē *n.* sweet spice used by ancient Jews in making incense. [ME, f. L f. Gk *staktē* (*stazō* drip)]

stā′ddle *n.* platform or framework supporting rick etc.; ∼**-stone** (used similarly). [OE *stathol* base, = OS *stathal*, OHG *stadal*, ON *stöthull* f. Gmc **stathlaz* (**sta-STAND[1]*)]

stā′di∣um *n.* **1.** (Gk Ant.; *pl. also* ∼a). measure of length, about 185 metres; course for foot-race and chariot-race. **2.** enclosed athletic or sports ground with tiers of seats for spectators. **3.** stage or period of development etc. [ME f. L, f. Gk *stadion*]

sta′d(t)hōlder (stah′d-, stah′t-, stä′-) *n.* (Hist.) viceroy or governor of province or town in Netherlands; chief magistrate of United Provinces of Netherlands; hence ∼**SHIP** *n.* [f. Du. *stadhouder* deputy (*stad* STEAD, *houder* HOLDER, after med. L LOCUM TENENS)]

staff[1] (-ahf) *n.* (*pl.* ∼s *or* (arch. exc. Mus.) **staves** *pr.* stävz), & *v.t.* **1.** *n.* stick or pole for use in walking or climbing or as weapon (lit., or fig.: *bread is the staff of life; you are the staff of his old age)*; QUARTER[1]*staff*. **2.** this as sign of office or authority; *pastoral* ∼, crosier. **3.** shaft, pole, as support or handle (FLAG[4]*staff*); spindle in watch. **4.** rod for measuring distances, heights, etc., in surveying. **5.** token given to engine-driver on single-line railway as authority to proceed over a given section of line (∼ **system**, this method of working). **6.** (Mil. etc.) body of officers assisting officer in high command and concerned with army or regiment or fleet or air force as a whole; GENERAL *staff*; ‖∼ **college** (in which officers are prepared for staff duties); ∼ **officer** (serving on staff); ∼ **sergeant**, ‖senior sergeant of non-infantry company, **NCO*

ranking just above sergeant. **7.** body of persons carrying on work under manager etc. *(editorial staff of newspaper; diplomatic staff*; ‖∼ **nurse**, nurse ranking just below a sister); those in authority within an organization, opp. students, pupils, etc.; hence (-)∼ED[2] (-ft) *a.*, **∼′ER[1]* *n.*, member of staff esp. of newspaper. **8.** (Mus.) set of usu. five parallel lines on any one or between any adjacent two of which a note is placed to indicate its pitch; ∼ **notation** (by means of staff, esp. opp. to TONIC *sol-fa*). **9.** *v.t.* provide (institution etc.) with staff. [OE *stæf*, = OS *staf*, OHG *stap*, ON *stafr* f. Gmc **stabhaz*]

staff[2] (-ahf) *n.* mixture of plaster of Paris, cement, etc., as temporary building-material. [19th c.; orig. unkn.]

staffa′ge (-ah′zh) *n.* accessory items in painting, esp. figures in landscape picture. [G (*staffieren* decorate, perh. f. OF *estoffer*; see STUFF, -AGE)]

Staffs. *abbr.* Staffordshire.

stag *n.* **1.** male of red deer or of other large kinds of deer, esp. in fifth year. **2.** ‖(St. Exch.) person who applies for shares of new issue with a view to selling at once at a profit. **3.** **man* who attends social gathering unaccompanied by woman. **4.** ∼**-beetle** (with branched mandibles like stag's antlers); ∼**-horn**, (1) horn of stag used for knife-handle etc., (2) club-moss or coral resembling antlers; ∼′**hound**, large hound hunting deer by sight or scent; ∼ **film**, **∼ **movie**, (suitable for men only); ∼**-party** (of men only). [ME f. OE **stacga*, **stagga*; cf. *docga* dog, *frogga* frog, **picga* pig]

stāge[1] *n.* **1.** raised floor or platform, e.g. scaffold for workmen's use in building; LANDING-*stage*. **2.** surface on which object is placed for inspection through microscope. **3.** platform on which plays etc. are performed before an audience; (fig.) the drama, dramatic art or literature, actor's profession; **go on the** ∼, become actor or actress. **4.** scene of action *(quitted the stage of politics)*; **hold the** ∼, dominate conversation etc. **5.** point or period in development, process, etc., *(reached a critical stage; at this stage an interruption occurred; passed through a long stage of inactivity; is in the tomboy stage, the larval stage)*. **6.** (regular) stopping-place on route, distance between two of these, *(travelled by easy stages)*; (**fare-**)∼, section of bus etc. route for which fixed fare is charged, stopping-place at end of this. **7.** (Geol.) range of strata forming subdivision of series. **8.** (Electr.) single amplifying transistor or valve with associated equipment. **9.** section of rocket with separate engine, jettisoned when its propellant is exhausted. **10.** ∼**-coach**, (Hist.) large closed coach running regularly by stages between places; ∼′**craft**, skill or experience in writing or staging plays; ∼ **direction**, instruction in text of play as to movement, position, tone, etc., of actor, or sound effects etc.; ∼ **door**, actors' and workmen's entrance from street to theatre behind stage; ∼ **effect**, effect produced in acting or on the stage, artificial or theatrical effect produced in real life; ∼ **fever**, inordinate desire to go on the stage; ∼ **fright**, nervousness on facing audience esp. for first time; ∼**-hand**, person handling scenery etc. during performance on stage; ∼**-manage**, be stage-manager of, (fig.) arrange and control for effect in manner of stage-manager; ∼**-manager**, person responsible for lighting and other mechanical arrangements, costumes, etc. of play; ∼ **play** (opp. broadcast etc.); ∼ **rights**, exclusive rights to perform particular play; ∼**-struck**, struck with stage fever; ∼**-wait**, hitch or delay in theatrical performance; ∼ **whisper**, aside, whisper meant to be heard by others than the person addressed. [ME, f. OF *estage* dwelling f. Rom. **staticum* standing-place (*stare* stand); see -AGE]

stāge[2] *v.t.* present (play) on stage; arrange occurrence of, esp. dramatically *(stage a come-back)*. [f. prec.]

stā′ger *n.* old ∼, experienced person, old hand. [f. STAGE[1] + -ER[1]]

stä′gey. Var. of STAGY.

stägflā′tion n. (Econ.) state of inflation without corresponding increase of demand and employment. [f. STAGNATION + INFLATION]

stä′ggard n. (arch.) stag in fourth year. [ME, f. STAG + -ARD]

stä′gger (-g-) v. & n. **1.** v.i. walk or stand unsteadily, totter; hesitate, waver in purpose. **2.** v.t. cause to totter (was staggered by the blow); cause to hesitate or waver (the question, the news, staggered him, his resolution; was staggered at the suggestion). **3.** arrange in zigzag order, esp. set (spokes of wheel) to incline alternately to right and left; arrange (holidays, hours of work, etc.) so that they do not coincide with those of others; arrange (road-crossing) so that side roads are not in line. **4.** Hence ∼ER¹ n. **5.** n. tottering movement; overhanging or slantwise or zigzag arrangement of like parts in a structure etc. **6.** (in pl.) disease of brain and spinal cord esp. in horses and cattle; giddiness. [alt. of ME (now dial.) stacker f. ON stakra frequent. of staka push, stagger]

stä′ggering (-g-) a. In vbl senses; bewildering, astonishing; hence ∼LY² adv. [f. prec. + -ING²]

stä′ging n. In vbl senses; driving or running stage-coaches; scaffolding, temporary platform or support; shelves for plants in greenhouse; ∼ area, intermediate assembly point for troops in transit; ∼ post, regular stopping-place, esp. on air route. [ME, f. STAGE²,¹ + -ING¹]

Stä′girite n. the ∼, Aristotle. [f. L f. Gk Stag(e)irītēs native of Stagira in Macedonia, birthplace of Aristotle; see -ITE¹]

stägn|ā′te v.i. (Of liquid) be(come) motionless, have no current, cease to flow; (of life, action, mind, business, person) be(come) dull or sluggish; hence or cogn. ∼ANCY, ∼A′TION, ns., ∼ANT a. [f. L stagnare (stagnum pool) + -ATE³]

stägni′colous a. living in swamps or stagnant water. [f. mod. L stagnicolus f. L stagnum pool + colere inhabit, + -OUS]

stä′g|ŷ a. theatrical in manner, style, appearance, etc.; hence ∼ĬLY² adv., ∼ĬNESS n. [f. STAGE¹ + -Y²]

staid a. of steady and sober character; of quiet and serious demeanour; sedate; hence ∼′LY² adv., ∼′NESS n. [= stayed, p.p. of STAY¹]

stain v.t., & n. **1.** v.t. discolour, soil, (cigarettes stain the fingers; wine will stain the cloth; guaranteed not to stain clothes); (fig.) sully, blemish, (reputation, name, person); colour (wood, glass, etc.) by process other than painting or covering the surface; impregnate (substance) for microscopic examination with colouring matter that makes structure visible by being deposited in some parts more than in others; print colours on (wallpaper); hence ∼′ABLE a., ∼′ER¹ n. **2.** n. discoloration, spot or mark caused esp. by contact with foreign matter and not easily removed (cloth is covered with tea-stains); staining-material; (fig.) blot, blemish, (without a stain on his character); hence ∼′LESS a. (esp. of reputation); ∼less steel, chrome steel not liable to rust or tarnish under ordinary conditions. [ME, f. distain f. OF desteindre desteign- f. Rom. *distingere (as DIS-, TINGE)]

stair n. **1.** each of a set of fixed indoor steps (on the top stair but one). **2.** (in pl. exc. arch. or Sc.) set of these (passed him on the stairs; down a winding stair); FLIGHT¹ or PAIR¹ of stairs; BACK¹ stairs; **below ∼s**, in basement of house esp. as part occupied by servants; DOWNSTAIRS; UPSTAIRS. **3.** (in pl.) landing-stage. **4.** ∼′case, (part of building containing) flight(s) of stairs (MOVING, SPIRAL, staircase); ∼head, level space at top of stairs; ∼rod (for securing stair-carpet in angle between two steps); ∼′way, (1) way up a flight of stairs, (2) staircase. [OE stæger f. Gmc *staig-, *stig- to climb; cf. (M)Du., (M)LG steiger landing-stage]

||**staithe** (-dh) n. wharf, esp. waterside coal depot equipped for loading vessels. [ME, f. ON *stathwō,

stöth landing-stage, = OS stath, OHG stad bank, shore f. Gmc *stathaz, *-am (*sta- STAND¹)]

stäke n., & v.t. **1.** n. stout stick or post sharpened at one end and driven into ground as support, boundary mark, etc.; post to which person was tied to be burnt alive, (fig.) punishment of death by burning, (was condemned to, suffered at, the stake); long vertical rod in basket-making; *pull (up) ∼s, depart, go to live elsewhere. **2.** metal-worker's small anvil fixed on bench by pointed prop. **3.** money etc. wagered on an event, esp. deposited with third party (∼′holder) by each of those who make a wager; (in pl.) money to be contended for esp. in horse-race, such race (maiden, trial, stakes); **have a ∼ in the country**, be materially concerned in its welfare, e.g. as land-owner; **at ∼**, at issue, in question, risked, (life itself is at stake). **4.** ∼-boat (anchored to mark course for boat race etc.); ∼-net, fishing-net hung on stakes. **5.** v.t. fasten, secure, or support with stake(s); mark off, out, (area) with stakes (stake (out) a claim, lit. or fig.); *(colloq.) give financial or other support to; *∼ out, (colloq.) place under, or for purpose of, surveillance; *∼-out n., (colloq.) (area under) surveillance. **6.** wager, risk, (money etc. on event etc.). [OE staca, = MDu., (M)LG stake, f. WG *stak, *stek- pierce, cogn. w. STICK²; senses 3 and 6 16th c., perh. of different orig.]

Stäkha′nov|īte (-kah′n-) n. (Esp. Russian) worker who increases his output to an exceptional extent, and so gains special awards; hence ∼ISM (3) n. [f. A. G. Stakhanov, Russ. coal-miner d. 1977 + -ITE¹ (1)]

stä′lactīte n. deposit of calcium carbonate, usu. in form like large icicle, hanging from roof of cave etc. and formed by trickling of water; hence **stalä′ct**IC, **stalä′ctī**FORM, **stälacti′t**IC, adjs. [f. mod. L stalactites f. Gk stalaktos dripping (stalassō drip; see -ITE¹)]

Stä′läg n. (Hist.) German prison camp, esp. for non-commissioned officers and privates. [G (stamm base, main stock, lager camp)]

stä′lagmīte n. deposit like stalactite standing on floor of cave etc. and often uniting with stalactite; hence **stälagmi′t**IC a. [f. mod. L stalagmites f. Gk stalagma dripping (as STALACTITE)]

stäle¹ a. & v. **1.** a. musty, insipid, or otherwise the worse for age or use, not fresh; ∼ **bread** (musty, or not quite new: stale bread is best for toast). **2.** lacking novelty, trite, (stale joke, news, tricks); (of athlete or other performer) having ability impaired by over-exertion; (Law, esp. of claim) having been left dormant for an unreasonably long time. **3.** Hence ∼′LY² (-l-lī) adv., ∼′NESS (-ln-) n. **4.** v.t. & i. make or become stale or common [ME, prob. f. AF & OF *estalo (estaler halt; cf. STALL¹)]

stäle² v.i. (arch. or dial.), & n. **1.** v.i. (Esp. of horses and cattle) urinate. **2.** n. urine of horses and cattle. [ME, perh. f. OF estaler adopt position (cf. prec.)]

stä′lemäte (-lm-) n., & v.t. **1.** n. (Chess) drawn position resulting from player's having no move available, his king not being in check; (fig.) deadlock, drawn contest. **2.** v.t. bring (player) to stalemate; (fig.) bring to a standstill. [f. obs. stale (f. AF estale f. estaler be placed; cf. STALE¹) + MATE¹]

Sta′lin|ism (-ah′-) n. policy followed by Stalin in government of USSR; so ∼IST (2) n. [f. J. V. Stalin (Dzhugashvili), Soviet statesman d. 1953 + -ISM]

stalk¹ (-awk) v. & n. **1.** v.i. stride, walk in stately or imposing manner (along etc.); steal up to game under cover. **2.** v.t. pursue (game, enemy) stealthily; ∼′ing-horse, horse behind which hunter conceals himself, (fig.) pretext concealing one's real actions or intentions; hence (-)∼′ER¹ n. **3.** n. stalking of game; imposing gait. [OE *stealcian f. Gmc *stalkōjan, frequent. of *stal-, *stel- STEAL]

stalk² (-awk) n. main stem of herbaceous plant; slender attachment or support of leaf, flower, fruit, etc.; similar support of organ etc. in animals or of device; stem of wineglass etc.; tall chimney of factory etc.; ∼-eyed, (of crab etc.) having the eyes mounted on stalks; hence (-)~ED² (-kt), ~LESS, *adjs.*, ~LET *n.* [ME *stalke*, prob. dim. of (now dial.) *stale* rung of ladder, long handle, f. OE *stalu*]

stall¹ (-awl) *n. & v.* **1.** *n.* (single compartment for one animal in) stable, cow-house; ~-**feed,** fatten (cattle) in stall. **2.** trader's STAND² 5 in bazaar, market, etc., or out of doors, compartment in a building for sale of goods, table in this on which goods are exposed; ‖BOOK¹*stall.* **3.** fixed seat in choir or chancel of church, more or less enclosed at back and sides and often canopied, esp. one appropriated to clergyman (*canon's, dean's, stall*); (fig.) office, dignity, of canon etc. (*how long has he had his stall?*). **4.** ‖each of a set of seats in theatre, esp. on ground floor. **5.** compartment for occupation by one person in shower-baths etc.; compartment for one horse at start of race. **6.** receptacle for one object (FINGER-*stall*). **7.** (condition resulting from) stalling of engine or aircraft. **8.** *v.t.* put or keep (cattle etc.) in stall esp. for fattening (*a stalled ox*); furnish (stable etc.) with stalls. **9.** cause (engine, vehicle, aircraft) to stall. **10.** *v.i.* (of horse or cart) stick fast as in mud or snow; *be snow-bound; (of motor vehicle or its engine) stop because of overload on engine or inadequate supply of fuel to it; (of aircraft or its pilot) reach condition where speed is too low to allow effective operation of controls. [OE *steall,* = MDu., OHG *stal,* ON *stallr* f. Gmc **stalla*- prob. f. **stadhlaz* (**sta*- STAND¹); partly f. OF *estal* f. Frank. **stal*]

stall² (-awl) *v.* **1.** *v.i.* play for time when being questioned etc. **2.** *v.t.* block, delay, obstruct; ~ **off,** evade or deceive. [f. *stall* pickpocket's confederate, orig. 'decoy' f. AF *estal(e)*, prob. cogn. w. prec.]

‖**sta'llage** (-aw'l-) *n.* space for, rent for, right to erect, stall(s) in market etc. [ME, f. OF *estalage* (*estal* STALL¹; see -AGE)]

sta'llion (-yon) *n.* uncastrated male horse, esp. one kept for breeding. [ME, f. OF *estalon* thr. Rom. f. Gmc **stall*- STALL¹]

sta'lwart (-aw'l-) *a. & n.* **1.** *a.* strongly built, sturdy; courageous, resolute, determined, (*stalwart supporters*); hence ~LY² *adv.*, ~NESS *n.* **2.** *n.* (esp. Polit.) resolute uncompromising partisan. [Sc. var. of obs. *stalworth* f. OE *stælwierthe* (*stæl* place, WORTH¹)]

sta'men (-ĕn, -en) *n.* male fertilizing organ of flowering plants, including anther containing pollen; hence **sta'mini'FEROUS** *a.* [L *stamen staminis* warp in upright loom, thread]

sta'mina *n.* staying-power, power of endurance; ability to undergo prolonged strain on body or mind. [L, pl. of prec., in sense warp, threads spun by the Fates]

sta'minal *a.* of stamens or stamina. [f. as STAMEN + -AL]

sta'minate *a.* having stamens but no pistils; having stamens. [f. as STAMEN + -ATE²]

sta'mmer *v. & n.* **1.** *v.i.* speak (habitually, or on occasion from embarrassment etc.) with halting articulation esp. with pauses or rapid repetitions of same syllable; hence ~ER¹ *n.* **2.** *v.t.* ~ (**out**), utter (words) thus (*stammered out an excuse*). **3.** *n.* stammering speech; tendency to stammer. [OE *stamerian,* = OS *stamaron,* MLG, MDu. *stameren* f. WG **stamrōjan*]

sta'mp *v. & n.* **1.** *v.t.* impress pattern, mark, etc., upon (metal, butter, paper, etc.) with die or similar instrument of metal, wood, rubber, etc.; impress (pattern etc.) thus; produce by cutting *out* with die etc.; impress *on* the memory etc.; affix postage or other stamp to (envelope, document); crush, pulverize, (ore etc.). **2.** *v.i. & t.* bring down one's foot, bring down (foot), heavily on ground; bring into specified state thus (*stamp down earth around plant*); ~ **on,** suppress; ~ **out,** put an end to, crush, destroy; ~'**ing-ground,** favourite place of resort or action. **3.** *v.t.* assign a character to, characterize, (*this alone stamps the story* (*as*) *an invention, stamps him as a genius*). **4.** Hence (-)~'ER¹ (1, 2) *n.* **5.** *n.* instrument for stamping

pattern or mark; mark made by this; impression of official mark required to be made for revenue purposes on deeds, bills of exchange, etc., as evidence of payment of tax; piece of paper impressed with official mark as evidence of payment of tax or fee and meant to be affixed to letter, postcard, deed of transfer of property, etc. (‖INSURANCE *stamp,* POSTAGE *stamp*); mark impressed on, label etc. affixed to, commodity as evidence of quality etc. **6.** (fig.) characteristic mark, impress, (*bears the stamp of genius*); character, kind, (*avoid men of that or his stamp*). **7.** block that crushes ore in stamp-mill; (sound made by) heavy downward blow with foot. **8.** S~ **Act,** act concerned with stamp-duty, esp. that imposing duty on American colonies in 1765 and repealed in 1766; ~-**collecting,** ~-**collector,** (of postage stamps as objects of interest or value); ~-**duty** (imposed on certain kinds of legal instrument); *stamp*-HINGE; ~-**machine** (for selling postage stamps); ~-**mill** (for crushing ore etc.); ~-**office** (for issue of government stamps and receipt of stamp-duty etc.); ~-**paper,** (1) paper with government revenue stamp, (2) gummed marginal paper of sheet of postage stamps. [vb. prob. f. OE **stampian,* OHG *stampfōn* pound, ON *stappa* f. Gmc **stampōjan* (**stamp*-, prob. cogn. w. **stap*STEP²); n. partly f. v., partly f. OF *estampe* f. same Gmc source]

stampe'de *n. & v.* **1.** *n.* sudden fright and scattering or a number of horses, cattle, etc.; sudden flight or hurried movement of people due to interest or panic; *(Polit.) unconcerted movement of many persons by common impulse. **2.** *v.i. & t.* (cause to) take part in stampede or act hurriedly or unreasonably. [f. Sp. *estampida* crash, uproar, fem. a.p. (as n.) f. Rom. **stampire* f. Gmc **stampjan* (as prec.)]

stance (-ă-, -ah-) *n.* (Golf, Cricket, etc.) position taken for stroke; (fig.) attitude of body or mind. [F, f. It. STANZA]

stanch¹, staunch², (-ah-, -aw-) *v.t.* restrain the flow of (esp. blood); restrain the flow from (esp. wound). [ME, f. OF *estanchier* f. Rom. **stancare* f. *stancus* dried up, of unkn. orig.)]

stanch² etc. See STAUNCH¹ etc.

sta'nchion (-ah'nshon) *n., & v.t.* **1.** *n.* post, pillar, upright support, vertical strut; upright bar, pair of bars, or frame, for confining cattle in stall. **2.** *v.t.* supply with stanchion; fasten (cattle) to stanchion. [ME, f. AF *stanchon,* OF *estanchon, -son* (*estance* prop, f. Rom. **stantia;* see STANZA)]

stand¹ *v.* (**stood** *pr.* -ŏŏd). **1.** *v.i.* have or take or maintain upright position, esp. on feet or base, be set upright, (*stood there till I was tired; was too weak to stand; chair will not stand on two legs; hair stood on end with fright; stand at* EASE¹, ‖EASY, (Mil.); *stand in* person's LIGHT¹, *in the* BREACH¹, *on* one's HEAD¹, *in the* WAY *of*. **2.** be of specified height (*stands six foot three*). **3.** be situated, be, (*on each side stand two pillars; a stranger stood in the doorway; the cups stand on the top shelf; here once stood a village, a huge oak*). **4.** assume stationary position, cease to move, (*now stand still; was commanded to stand*); ~ (**and deliver**)! (highwayman's order); ~'**still,** stoppage, inability to proceed. **5.** maintain position, avoid falling or moving or being moved, (*don't stand there arguing; house will stand for another century; stand on* one's *own feet* (FOOT¹ 12); *stand fast; stand firm*); *not a* LEG *to stand on; stand* PAT³. **6.** hold good, remain valid or unaltered, (*the former conditions may stand; the wording must stand*). **7.** be, find oneself, in specified situation, rank, etc., (*stands convicted of treachery, in need of help, under heavy obligations; thermometer stood at 90°; the matter stands thus; he stands first on the list, in the same relation to both parties; I stand prepared to dispute it, in awe of*); act in specified capacity (*stand proxy for*); (Cricket) act as umpire; be certain or likely to (win, lose, etc.). **8.** ~ **alone,** be unequalled; *stand at* BAY⁴; *stand* CORRECT³*ed;* ~ **high,** be high in status, price, etc.; *stand person in good* STEAD; ~ **well,** be on good terms or in good repute *with*; **as it** ~**s,** in its present condition, unaltered. **9.** move to and remain in specified position (lit. or fig.; *stand back, clear, aside, aloof, away, *from under*); (Naut.) hold specified course (*stand in for the shore; you are standing into danger*); (of dog) point, set. **10.** *v.t.* place or set in upright or specified position (*stand the jug on the table; stand it against the wall; shall stand you in the corner as punishment*). **11.** endure without yielding or complaining, tolerate, (*her nerves could not stand the strain; how does he usually stand pain?; could never stand the fellow; shall stand no (more) nonsense; stood the enemy's fire; failed to stand the test*); ~ one's **ground,** maintain one's position (lit., or fig. in argument etc.). **12.** undergo (trial); *stand a* CHANCE[1]. **13.** provide for another or others at one's own expense (*stood him a drink; stood a bottle to the company; who is going to stand* TREAT?). **14.** Hence ~EE' *n.,* (colloq.) one who stands, esp. when all seats are occupied. **15.** (w. *preps.*): ~ **by,** uphold, support, side with, (person), adhere to, abide by, (terms, promises), (Naut.) stand ready to take hold of or operate (anchor etc.); ~ **for,** represent, signify, imply, (*US stands for 'Unitied States'*; *Liberalism stands for a great deal more than that*), ||be candidate for (office), ||be candidate for representation of (constituency) in Parliament, espouse the cause of (free trade etc.), (colloq.) endure, tolerate, acquiesce in; ||~ (person) **in,** (arch.) cost (specified sum); ~ **on,** insist on, observe scrupulously, (*stand on ceremony,* one's *dignity,* one's *rights*); ~ **over,** stand close to person to watch, control, threaten, etc.; ~ **to,** = *stand by; it stands to* REASON[1]; ~ **upon,** = *stand on.* **16.** (w. *advs.*): ~ **by,** stand near, be a bystander, look on without interfering (*will not stand by and see him ill-treated*), stand ready, be on the alert; ~by n. (pl. *-bys*), thing or person that one can depend on, equipment kept for emergency; ~ **down,** *v.t.* & *i.,* retire from team, witness-box, or similar position, ||cease to be candidate etc., ||(Mil.) go off duty; ~ **in,** deputize *for*; ~-*in* n., deputy, substitute, esp. for actor when latter's acting ability is not needed; ~ **in with,** be in league with; ~ **off,** move or keep away, keep one's distance, ||dispense with services of (employee) temporarily, ~-*off* n., *deadlock; ~-**off** (**half**), (Rugby Footb.) half-back who forms link between scrum-half and three-quarters; ~-**o'ffish,** cold or distant in manner; ~ **on,** (Naut.) continue on same course; ~ **out,** hold out, persist in opposition (*against*) or support (*for*) or endurance, be prominent or conspicuous or outstanding; *~-*out* n., remarkable person or thing; ~ **over,** be postponed, be left for later settlement etc.; ~ **to,** (arch.) fall to, set to work, (Mil.) take post in preparation for an attack (esp. before dawn or after dark); ~ **up,** rise to one's feet from sitting or other position, maintain erect position (*have only the clothes I stand up in*), be valid (*that argument does not stand up on examination*), (colloq.) fail to keep appointment with; ~ **up for,** side with, maintain, support, (person, cause); ~ **up to,** meet, face, (opponent) courageously, (of thing) remain unimpaired despite the effects of (hard wear etc.); ~-*up* a., (of collar) upright, high, opp. to *turn-down,* (of meal) eaten standing, (of fight) thorough, fair and square. [OE *standan,* = OS, Goth. *standan,* OHG *stantan,* ON *standa* f. Gmc *standan (**sta-,* **sto-,* f. IE **sth'-,* **sthā-* (cause to) stand)]

stand[2] *n.* **1.** cessation from motion or progress, stoppage, (*came, was brought, to a stand*); **be at a** ~, (arch.) be unable to proceed, be in perplexity. **2.** stationary condition assumed for purpose of resistance, esp. **make a** ~ (*against* enemy, *for* or *against* principle, etc.), (Cricket) prolonged stay at wicket by two batsmen. **3.** position taken up (*took his stand near the door*); **take** one's ~, base argument etc., rely, *on.* **4.** table, set of shelves, rack, etc., on or in which things may be placed, (*music, hat, umbrella, -stand;* HALL-*stand;* INK*stand;* ||WASH[1]-*hand stand*); ~ **camera** (for use on tripod, not hand-held). **5.** small open-fronted structure for trader outdoors or in market etc. (*fruit-stand,*

NEWS-*stand*) or at exhibition. **6.** standing-place for vehicles etc. (*cab-stand*). **7.** raised structure for persons to sit or stand on (BAND[1]*stand*; GRAND*stand*); *witness--box (*take the stand*). **8.** standing growth (*of* trees, clover, etc.). **9.** (Theatr. etc.) each halt made on a tour to give performances (ONE-*night stand*). **10.** ||(Mil.) ~ **of arms,** complete set of weapons for one man; ~ **of colours,** regiment's flags. [ME, f. prec.]

stǎ'ndard *n.* **1.** distinctive flag, esp. flag of cavalry regiment, opp. *to colours* of infantry; (fig.) rallying principle (*raise the standard of revolt*). **2.** weight or measure to which others conform or by which the accuracy or quality of others is judged (*by present-day standards*; DOUBLE[1] *standard*; *standard pound, yard,* etc.; **S~ English,** form of English speech used, with local variations, by majority of educated English-speaking people); thing serving as basis of comparison; document specifying (inter)nationally agreed properties for manufactured goods etc. (*British Standard*); *standard* DEVIATION. **3.** degree of excellence etc. required for particular purpose (*does not come up to (the) standard*; *set a low standard*; ~ **of living,** degree of material comfort available to person or class or community); thing recognized as model for imitation etc. (~ **book** etc., one recognized as meritorious or authoritative); ||grade of classification in primary schools. **4.** average quality (*work was of a low standard*); ordinary procedure, or quality or design of a product, without added or novel features. **5.** prescribed proportion of weight of fine metal, establishment of monetary basis, in gold or silver coin (**gold, silver,** ~) or in both (DOUBLE[1] *standard*); **multiple, tabular,** ~, standard of value obtained by averaging prices of a number of products. **6.** measure (165 cu. ft.) of timber. **7.** upright support; upright water or gas pipe; tree or shrub that stands alone without support; shrub grafted on upright stem and trained in tree form (*standard rose*). **8.** ~-**bearer,** soldier who bears standard, (fig.) prominent leader in cause; *S~-**bred,** (member of) breed of race-horses able to attain a specified speed; ||~ **lamp** (set on tall pillar standing on floor); ~ **time** (uniform for places in approximately same longitude, and established in a country or region by law or custom). [ME, f. AF *estaundart,* OF *estendart* (*estendre,* as EXTEND; see -ARD); in sense 7 affected by assoc. w. STAND[1]]

stǎ'ndardīz|**e, -is**|**e** (īz), *v.t.* make conform to standard; determine properties of by comparison with a standard; hence ~A'TION n. [f. prec. + -IZE]

stǎ'nding[1] *n.* In vbl senses; estimation in which one is held, repute, position, (*men of high standing; is of no standing;* **in good** ~, fully paid-up as member etc.); length of service, membership, etc.; duration (*a dispute of long standing*); ~-**room,** space to stand in. [ME, f. STAND[1] + -ING[1]]

stǎ'nding[2] *a.* In vbl senses; established, permanent, (*a standing rule; has become a standing* JOKE[1]; **long-**~, that has long existed, not recent); (= *at* STUD[2]) not made, raised, etc., for the occasion (*a standing army,* COMMITTEE; ~ **order,** instruction to banker to make regular payments, or to bookseller etc. for regular supply of a periodical; ~ **orders,** those governing manner in which all business shall be conducted in Parliament, council, society, etc.); (of race, jump, start, etc.) performed from rest, without run-up; **all** ~, (Naut. or transf.) without time to lower sails, taken by surprise; **leave** person ~, make far more rapid progress than he; ~ **corn** (unreaped); ~ **ovation** (by audience risen from their seats); ~ **rigging** (fixed in position); ~ **type** (Print., not yet distributed after use); ~ **water** (stagnant); ~ **wave,** vibration of system in which some particular points remain fixed while others between them vibrate with the maximum amplitude. [ME, f. STAND[1] + -ING[2]]

stǎ'ndish *n.* (arch.) inkstand. [ME, prob. f. STAND[1]]

*stǎndpǎ'tter *n.* (esp. Polit.) one who opposes changes in policy. [f. *stand* PAT[3] + -ER[1]]

stã'nd-pīpe *n.* vertical pipe for fluid to rise in. [f. STAND¹ + PIPE¹]

stã'ndpoint *n.* point of view (lit. or fig.). [f. STAND¹ + POINT¹, after G *standpunkt*]

stã'nhope (-nɒp) *n.* light open carriage for one, with 2 or 4 wheels. [f. Hon. & Rev. Fitzroy *Stanhope*, Engl. clergyman d. 1864, for whom first made]

stã'niel (-yel) *n.* kestrel. [OE *stāngella* (*stān* stone, *gella yeller f. *gellan* YELL)]

stãnk. See STINK.

||**stã'nnarў** *n.* tin-mine; (usu. in *pl.*) tin-mining district of Cornwall and Devon; ~ **court** (for regulation of tin-mines in the stannaries). [f. med. L *stannaria* n. pl. f. LL *stannum* tin; see -ARY¹]

stã'nn|ic *a.* (Chem.) of tin esp. in its higher valence (*stannic acid*); so ~ATE¹ (3) *n.* [f. LL *stannum* tin + -IC]

stã'nn|ous *a.* (Chem.) of tin esp. in its lower valence (*stannous salts*); so ~ITE¹ (2) *n.* [f. as prec. + -OUS]

stã'nza *n.* group of (usu. four or more) usu. rhymed lines occurring as repeated metrical unit (SPENSERIAN *stanza*); group of four lines in some Greek and Latin metres (SAPPHIC *stanza*); hence (-)~'D², ~ED² (-ad), **stãnzã'**IC, *adjs.* [It., = standing-place, chamber, stanza, f. Rom. *stantia abode f. L *stare* stand; see -ANCE]

stãp *v.t.* (-pp-). (arch.) = STOP¹ (~ **my vitals, me,** excl. of surprise or anger). [affected pronunc. in Vanbrugh's *The Relapse* (1697)]

stape'lia *n.* S. Afr. plant of genus *Stapelia*, with evil-smelling flowers. [mod. L, f. J. B. van *Stapel*, Du. botanist d. 1636 + -IA¹]

stã'pēs (-z) *n.* (*pl.* same). small stirrup-shaped bone in ear of mammal. [mod. L, f. med. L *stapes* stirrup]

stãph *n.* (colloq.) = foll. [abbr.]

stãphÿlocō'cc|us *n.* (*pl.* ~i *pr.* -kī). form of pus-producing bacterium characterized by forming grapelike clusters; hence ~AL *a.* [mod. L, f. Gk *staphulē* bunch of grapes + *kokkos* berry]

stã'ple¹ *n.*, & *v.t.* **1.** *n.* U-shaped piece of metal bar or wire with ends designed for driving into or fastening to wood etc. to take hasp of padlock or hook or bolt, or for driving through and clenching, to secure papers, netting, electric wire, etc. **2.** *v.t.* furnish or fasten with staple; hence **stã'pl**ER¹ (1, 2) *n.* [OE *stapol*, = OHG *staffal* foundation, ON *stöpull* pillar f. Gmc *stapulaz; see -LE 1]

stã'ple² *n.*, *a.*, & *v.t.* **1.** *n.* important or principal article of commerce (*the staples of that country, of British industry*); raw material; (fig.) chief element or material (*formed the staple of conversation*); fibre of cotton, wool, etc., regarded as determining its quality, (*cotton of fine, short, long, staple*). **2.** *a.* principal (*staple commodities*); important as product or export. **3.** *v.t.* sort, classify, (wool etc.) according to fibre; WOOL-stapler. [ME, f. OF *estaple* market f. MLG, MDu. *stapel* market, f. as prec.]

stãr¹ *n.* **1.** celestial body appearing as luminous point in night sky; (**fixed**) ~, such body so far from earth as to appear motionless except for diurnal revolution of the heavens (opp. *planet, comet*, etc.); this as subject of astronomical study; large self-luminous gaseous ball such as the sun is; BINARY, DOUBLE¹, MULTIPLE, *star*; DAY-*star*; EVENING, MORNING, *star*; FALL¹*ing*, SHOOT¹-*ing*, *star*; POLE²-*star*. **2.** thing suggesting star by its shape, esp. figure or object with radiating points e.g. as insignia of an order or mark of rank (S~s and Stripes, US national flag; S~s and Bars, flag of Confederate States); asterisk; star-shaped mark esp. as indicating category of excellence; white spot on forehead of horse etc.; (Electr.) Y-shaped arrangement of three-phase windings; SEE¹ *stars*. **3.** famous actor or actress or other performer (**the ~ system,** that of relying on stars to make film or play attractive; ~ **turn,** principal item in an entertainment or performance), whence ~'DOM *n.*; brilliant or prominent person, (*literary star; star pupil*; **bright particular ~,** object of one's devotion); ||convict serving first prison

sentence. **4.** heavenly body regarded as influencing person's fortunes etc. (*born under an unlucky star; his star was in the ascendant; you may thank your* (lucky) *stars you were not there*; ILL-*starred*); **my ~s!** (colloq. excl. of surprise). **5.** ~-**apple,** edible purple apple-like fruit (with starlike cross-section) of a tropical evergreen tree (*Chrysophyllum cainito*); **S~ Chamber,** ||(Hist.) court of civil and criminal jurisdiction primarily concerned with offences affecting crown interests, noted for summary and arbitrary procedure, and abolished 1640, (fig.) arbitrary oppressive tribunal; ~-**crossed,** (arch.) ill-fated; ~-**dust,** a multitude of stars looking like dust, (fig.) twinkling mass, romantic mystical sensation; ~'**fish,** echinoderm of class Asteroidea with five or more radiating arms; ~-**gazer,** (joc.) astronomer or astrologer; ~'**light,** (*n.*) light of stars (*walked home by starlight*), (*a.*) with stars visible, lighted by the stars, (*a starlight night*); ~'**lit,** = starlight (*a.*); ~ **of Bethlehem** [f. Matt. 2:9], starlike flower, esp. of *Ornithogalum umbellatum* with white starlike flowers striped with green on outside; **S~ of David,** figure of two interlaced equilateral triangles used as Jewish and Israeli symbol; **S~ of India,** (Hist.) order instituted 1861 to commemorate assumption of direct government of India; ||~ **prisoner** (see sense 3); *~ **route,** postal delivery route served by private contractors; ~ **sapphire** (cabochon); ~ **shell,** kind designed to burst in air and light up enemy's position; ~-**spangled,** spangled with stars (esp. of US flag); ~-**stone,** = star sapphire; ~-**stream,** systematic drift of stars; ~-**studded,** containing many stars (esp. in sense 3); ~'**wort,** plant of genus *Stellaria*, with star-like flowers. **6.** Hence ~'LET*n.*, little star, esp. young film actress who shows promise of becoming a star, ~'LESS, ~'LIKE, ~'RY², *adjs.*; ~**ry-eyed,** (colloq.) visionary, enthusiastic but impractical. [OE *steorra*, = OS, OHG *sterro* f. WG *sterro; cf. OHG *sterno*, ON *stjarna* Goth. *stairnō* f. Gmc *sternōn f. IE **ster-*]

star² *v.* (-rr-). **1.** *v.t.* (esp. in *p.p.*) set or adorn (as) with stars. **2.** affix asterisk or star symbol to (name in list etc.); present as theatrical, film, etc., star. **3.** *v.i.* appear as star actor. [f. prec.]

stãr'board (-berd) *n.*, & *v.t.* (Naut. & Aeron.) **1.** *n.* right-hand side of ship or boat or aircraft looking forward (cf. PORT⁵); starboard TACK¹, WATCH¹. **2.** *v.t.* turn (helm, or abs.) to starboard. [OE *stēorbord* (*stēor* rudder, as STEER¹, *bord* BOARD¹), early Teut. ships being steered with a paddle over the right side]

stãrch *n.*, *v.t.*, & *a.* **1.** *n.* white odourless tasteless carbohydrate obtained chiefly from cereals and potatoes but found in all plants except fungi, an important constituent of human food (~-**reduced,** containing less than normal proportion of starch). **2.** preparation of this for stiffening linen etc. before ironing; (fig.) stiffness of manner, formality. **3.** *v.t.* stiffen with starch (lit., or fig. esp. in *p.p.*); whence ~ER¹ *n.* **4.** *a.* (arch.) precise, prim; hence ~'LY² *adv.*, ~'NESS *n.* [n. f. v., ME *sterche* f. OE *stercan stiffen; = OS *sterkian*, OHG *sterken* f. WG *starkjan f. Gmc *starkaz; cf. STARK]

stãr'ch|ÿ *a.* of or like starch; containing much starch; (of person) precise, prim; hence ~iLY² *adv.*, ~iNESS *n.* [f. prec. + -Y²]

stãre *v.* & *n.* **1.** *v.i.* look fixedly with eyes wide open (*at, upon,* etc., or abs.) from or *with* surprise, admiration, bewilderment, stupidity, horror, impertinent curiosity, etc.; (of eyes) be wide open and fixed (*staring mad*); be unpleasantly prominent or striking. **2.** *v.t.* reduce (person) to specified condition by staring (*stared him out of countenance, into silence*); ~ **down,** outstare; ~ **person in the face,** be evident or imminent, (*the facts stare us, ruin stared him, in the face*). **3.** *n.* staring gaze. [OE *starian*, = OHG *starēn*, ON *stara* f. Gmc **star-* be rigid]

stãrk¹ *a.* & *adv.* **1.** *a.* stiff, rigid, (*lies stark in death*); desolate, bare; sharply evident (*in stark contrast*);

downright, sheer, (*stark madness*); stark naked; (arch.) strong; hence ∼LY² *adv.*, ∼'NESS *n*. **2.** *adv.* quite, wholly, (*stark mad, naked*). [OE *stearc*, = OS, OHG *stark*, ON *sterkr*, Goth. **starks* f. Gmc **starkaz*; *stark naked* f. earlier *start-naked* f. obs. *start* tail (cf. REDstart)]

Stärk² *n*. ∼ **effect**, (Phys.) splitting of spectrum line into several components by electric field. [f. J. ∼, Ger. physicist d. 1957]

‖**stär′kers** (-z) *a*. (sl.) stark naked. [f. STARK¹; see -ER¹ (5)]

stär′ling¹ *n*. small gregarious partly migratory bird (*Sturnus vulgaris*) with blackish-brown speckled lustrous plumage inhabiting chiefly cultivated areas; bird of family Sturnidae or *Icteridae. [OE *stærlinc* (*stær* starling = OHG *star(a)*, ON *stari* f. Gmc **staraz*, **starōn*; see -LING¹)]

stär′ling² *n*. protective piling round pier of bridge. [perh. corrupt. of (now dial.) *staddling* (STADDLE, -ING¹)]

stär′rў. See STAR¹ 6.

start¹ *v*. **1.** *v.i.* make sudden movement from pain, surprise, etc., (*started in his seat*; *started at the sound of my voice*); change position abruptly from shock or sudden impulse (*start aside, from one's chair*). **2.** (Of thing) move suddenly (*out* etc.; *tears started to her eyes*); (of eyes, usu. w. exagg.) burst *from* (their sockets etc.); (of timbers etc.) spring from proper position, give way. **3.** set out, begin journey (*we start at six*); make a beginning (*on* journey, undertaking, book, meal, etc.); (of engine etc.) begin running; ∼ **at** or **with**, have as initial member of sequence etc. (*prices start at ten dollars*; *we started with prawn cocktail*); **to** ∼ **with**, in the first place, before anything else is considered (*you have no right to be here, to start with*), at the beginning (*had six members to start with*). **4.** *v.t.* begin, commence, (work etc., doing, *to* do); ∼ **life**, be born, begin one's career, etc.; ∼ **school**, attend it for first time. **5.** rouse (game) from lair etc.; *start a* HARE. **6.** originate, set going, (undertaking, business, publication, fire, quarrel, race, etc.); cause (engine, clock, etc.) to begin operating; cause (person) to make a beginning (*on*); cause to begin doing (*the smoke started me coughing*); conceive (baby), cause (baby) to be conceived; cause or enable (person) to commence business etc.; give signal to (persons) to start in race; ∼ **something**, (colloq.) cause trouble. **7.** cause or experience the starting or loosening of (timbers etc.). **8.** (Naut.) pour out (liquor) from cask. **9.** ∼ **in**, (colloq.) begin (*to* do), *make a beginning on*; ∼ **off**, begin to move; ∼ **out**, (colloq.) proceed as intending (*to* do), begin journey; ∼ **up**, rise suddenly e.g. from seat, arise, come into existence or action, occur to the mind, (*many difficulties, rivals, have started up*), originate (undertaking etc.), start (engine). [OE **stiertan*, **styrtan*, etc., = OHG *sturzen* overthrow, rush f. Gmc **sturt-, *start-, *stert-*]

start² *n*. **1.** sudden movement of surprise, pain, etc., (*give* person **a** ∼, cause him to move thus); (in *pl.*) intermittent or spasmodic efforts or movements (esp. *by* (*fits and*) *starts*). **2.** beginning of journey or action or race (*shall make an early start for town*; *is difficult work at the start*; *the start is fixed for 3 p.m.*; *saw it from start to finish*); starting or starting-place of race; **for a** ∼, (colloq.) to start with. **3.** advantage conceded in race (*will give you 60 yards start, 15 seconds start*); advantageous initial position gained in business etc. (*got a good start in life*); **get the** ∼ **of**, gain advantage over. **4.** (colloq.) surprising occurrence (*queer, rum, start*). [ME, f. prec.]

stär′ter *n*. In vbl senses; one who gives signal to start in race; horse or competitor starting in race (*list of probable starters*); (esp. automatic) apparatus for starting engine of motor vehicle etc.; initial action etc., first course of meal; **for** ∼**s**, (sl.) to start with; **under** ∼'**s orders**, (of racehorses etc.) in position to start race and awaiting starting-signal. [f. START¹ + -ER¹]

stär′ting *n*. In vbl senses; ∼**-block**, shaped rigid block for bracing feet of runner at start of race; ∼**-**

-gate, movable barrier for securing fair start in horse--races; ‖∼**-handle**, crank for starting motor engine; ∼**-pistol** (used to give signal for start of race); ∼**-point** (from which a journey, process, argument, etc., begins); ∼**-post** (from which competitors start in race); ∼ **price**, final odds before start of horse-race etc.; *starting-*PUNCH¹; *starting-*STALL¹. [ME, f. START¹ + -ING¹]

stär′tle *v.t.* cause (person etc.) to start with surprise or sudden alarm, give shock to, take by surprise. [OE *steartlian* (as START¹, -LE 3)]

stär′tling *a*. surprising, alarming, (*startling news, discovery, development*); hence ∼LY² *adv.* [f. prec. + -ING²]

stärve *v*. **1.** *v.i.* die of hunger; suffer from lack of food; suffer extreme poverty; (colloq.) feel very hungry (*am simply starving*); (arch. or dial.) perish with or suffer from cold; (fig.) suffer mental or spiritual want, feel strong craving *for* (sympathy, amusement, knowledge, etc.). **2.** *v.t.* cause to perish with hunger; deprive *of*, keep scantily supplied with, food (lit. or fig.); compel (garrison etc. *into* surrender, *out*, etc.) thus; (arch.) cause to perish, affect severely, with cold; cause to starve mentally or spiritually (SEX--*starved*). **3.** hence **stärvā′TION** *n*. [OE *steorfan* die, = OS, OHG *sterban* f. Gmc **sterbh-*, perh. – 'be rigid']

stär′veling (-vl-) *n*. & *a*. **1.** *n*. starving or ill-fed person or animal. **2.** *a*. starving; (fig.) meagre. [f. prec. + -LING¹]

stäsh *v.t.*, & *n*. (sl.) **1.** *v.t.* conceal, put *away* in safe place. **2.** *n*. *house; hiding-place; thing hidden. [18th c.; orig. unkn.]

stä′s|is *n*. (*pl.* ∼**es** *pr.* -ēz). **1.** state of stopped flow, stagnation, (lit. or fig.). **2.** (Path.) stoppage of circulation of any of the fluids of the body. [mod. L f. Gk (*sta-* STAND¹)]

-stä′s|is *suf*. (*pl.* ∼**es** *pr.* -ēz), forming *n*s. w. sense 'slowing or stopping of flow of or growth of or deviation from' (*haemostasis, bacteriostasis, homoeostasis*). [f. prec.]

-stät *suf*. forming *n*s. w. ref. to keeping fixed or stationary (*coelostat, rheostat, thermostat*). [first in *heliostat*; f. Gk *statos* stationary and agent-suf. *statēs* (*sta-*stand)]

stä′tal *a*. pertaining to State(s). [f. foll. + -AL]

stäte¹ *n*. & *a*. **1.** *n*. condition in which a thing is, mode of existence as determined by circumstances, (*precarious state of health*; *found him in a state of deep depression*; *things were in an untidy state*; *in a bad state of repair*); ∼ **of the art**, current stage of development or knowledge of a subject; *state of* GRACE; ∼ **of life**, rank and occupation; *in a state of* NATURE; ∼ **of things** or **affairs** or (fig.) **play**, conditions existing for the time being; ∼ **of war** (when war has been declared or hostilities are in progress); CIVIL *state*; **in a** ∼, (colloq.) untidy, excited, anxious, etc. **2.** (Often *S*∼). organized political community under one government, commonwealth, nation; such community forming part of federal republic, esp. **the** (**United**) **S**∼**s** (of America); **of S**∼, = sense 11 (‖MINISTER¹, SECRETARY, *of* State); **State's* EVIDENCE; FREE¹, POLICE, SLAVE, *state*; **Northern S**∼**s** (in N. of US); **Papal** *States*; **Southern S**∼**s** (in S., esp. SE, of US); **S*∼**s' Rights**, rights and powers not assumed by United States but reserved to its individual states. **3.** (in *pl.*) legislative body in Jersey, Guernsey, and Alderney; **S**∼**s General**, legislative body in Netherlands, and in France before 1789. **4.** civil government (*Church and State*). **5.** rank, dignity, (*in a style befitting his state*). **6.** pomp (*arrived in great state*); **keep** ∼, maintain one's dignity, be difficult of access; **in** ∼ (with all due ceremony); **lie in** ∼, (of deceased great personage) be laid in public place of honour before burial. **7.** (Bibliog.) one of two or more variant forms within a single edition of a book. **8.** (impression taken from) an etched or engraved plate at a particular stage of its progress. **9.** ~'**craft,** art of conducting affairs of State; *~-**house,** building where legislature of a state meets; ~ **house,** (NZ) private house built at government's expense; ~'**room,** (1) state apartment, (2) private compartment in passenger ship or *train; ***S**~'**side,** (colloq.) of, in, or towards the US; *~'**wide,** so as to include or cover a whole State. **10.** Hence ~'HOOD (-t-h-) *n.,* ~'LESS (-tl-) *a.* (esp. of person having no nationality or citizenship). **11.** *attrib. a.* of, for, concerned with, the State (*state documents, service*); **S**~ **capitalism,** policy of State control of use of capital; ***S**~ **Department** (of foreign affairs); *state* PRISONER; **S**~ **socialism,** policy of State control of industries and services in order to benefit all equally; ||**S**~ **school** (managed by public authorities); ~ **trial,** prosecution by State esp. for political offence; *~ **university** (managed by public authorities for a State of US). **12.** reserved for or done on occasions of ceremony (*state apartments, carriage, visit*); involving ceremony (*state opening of Parliament*). [ME; partly f. ESTATE, partly f. L STATUS]

state[2] *v.t.* express, esp. fully or clearly, in speech or writing (*have stated my opinion; must state full particulars; this condition was expressly stated; no precise time was stated; did not state why; states that arrangements are complete*); fix, specify, (date, etc.; *at stated intervals*), whence **stā'tedLY**[2] *adv.*; (Law) specify facts of (case) for consideration by court; (Mus.) play (theme etc.) so as to make it known to the listener; hence **stā'tABLE** *a.* [f. prec.]

stā'telÿ (-tlĭ) *a.* (of manner, language, person, literary style, rhythm, building, proportions, etc.) dignified, imposing, grand; ||~**y home,** large magnificent house, esp. one open to visits by public; hence ~**iNESS** *n.* [ME, f. STATE[1] + -LY[1]]

stā'tement (-tm-) *n.* stating or being stated, expression in words; thing stated (*that statement is unfounded*); formal account of facts, e.g. of liabilities and assets (*the Bank issues monthly statements to each customer*) or of amount due to tradesman. [f. STATE[2] + -MENT]

stā'ter *n.* ancient-Greek coin of one of various values, esp. gold coin worth 20 drachmas or silver coin worth 4 drachmas. [ME f. LL, f. Gk *statēr*]

stā'tesman (-ts-) *n.* (*pl.* -**men**). person skilled, esp. one taking prominent part, in management of State affairs; sagacious far-sighted practical politician; **elder** ~, (1) one of the Japanese statesmen who mainly directed the evolution of Japan between the re-establishment of the Mikado (1868) and the end of the 19th c., (2) person of ripe years and experience whose counsel is therefore sought and valued; hence ~LIKE, ~LY[1], *adjs.*, ~SHIP (3) *n.* [= *state's man,* after F *homme d'état*]

stā'tic *a.* & *n.* **1.** *a.* concerned with bodies at rest or forces in equilibrium (opp. *dynamic*); of statics; acting as weight but not moving (*static pressure*); passive, not acting or changing. **2.** ~ **electricity,** electric charges at rest, not flowing as current; ~ **line,** length of cord attached to aircraft etc. and releasing parachute without use of rip-cord. **3.** *n.* atmospherics; static electricity. [f. mod. L f. Gk *statikos* (*sta*- stand; see -IC)]

-stā'tĭc *suf.* forming *adjs.*, esp. corresp. to *ns.* in -STASIS (*bacteriostatic*). [f. as prec.]

stā'tĭcal *a.* = STATIC 1; hence ~LY[2] *adv.* [f. as STATIC + -ICAL]

stā'tĭcĕ *n.* sea lavender; sea-pink. [L f. Gk, fem. of *statikos* STATIC (w. ref. to stanching of blood)]

stā'tĭcs *n. pl.* (usu. treated as *sing.*) science of bodies at rest or forces in equilibrium (opp. *dynamics*); = STATIC 3. [f. STATIC n. in same senses + -ICS]

stā'tion *n.,* & *v.t.* **1.** *n.* place, building, etc., in which person or thing stands or is placed esp. habitually or for definite purpose (*was assigned a station in the valley; took up a convenient station; Oxford won the toss and chose the Surrey station;* ACTION *stations*). **2.** establishment where a public service is provided (*broadcasting, coastguard,* FILLING, FIRE[1], POLICE, *polling, station*) or which is used as a base for some activity (*air, lifeboat, naval, research, station*); POWER-, SERVICE[1], *station*; *subsidiary post office. **3.** stopping-place on railway with buildings for temporary accommodation of passengers and goods or ||of goods only; buildings of railway station; **bus** ~, **coach** ~, similar stopping-place for a number of buses etc. **4.** position in life, (high) rank, status, employment, (*occupied a humble station; men of* (*exalted*) *station; she married beneath, has ideas above, her station; the duties of his station*). **5.** (Surv.) point from which measurements are made. **6.** military or naval post esp. (Hist.) in India; officers or society residing there. **7.** (Austral.) large pastoral or mixed farming estate; sheep-run or its buildings. **8.** (Eccl.) ~ (**of the Cross**), each of series of usu. 14 images or pictures representing events in Christ's passion before which devotions are performed in some churches etc., such devotions; church esp. in Rome to which pilgrims etc. go for devotions. **9.** (Bot. & Zool.) nature of the habitat of plant or animal in respect of climate, soil, etc. **10.** (arch.) standing, being still; (place of) halting. **11.** ~-**bill,** (Naut.) list of appointed emergency posts of ship's company; *~ **break,** pause between broadcast programmes for identification of station transmitting them; *~-**house,** police station; ~-**keeping,** maintenance of one's proper relative position in a moving body of ships etc.; ~-**master,** official in charge of railway-station; ~-**pointer,** three-armed protractor for locating place on chart from certain data; ||~ **sergeant** (in charge of police station); ~-**wagon,** estate car. **12.** *v.t.* assign station to; place (person, one*self*) in specified location. [ME, = standing, f. OF, f. L *statio -onis* (*stare* stand; see -ATION)]

stā'tionarÿ *a.* remaining in one place, not moving, (*balloon was now stationary*); not meant to be moved, not portable, (*stationary engine, troops*); (of planet) having no apparent motion in longitude; not changing in magnitude, number, quality, efficiency, etc., (*stationary temperature, population*); ~ **air** (remaining in lungs during ordinary respiration); ~ **wave,** = STANDING[2] *wave;* hence **stā'tionariNESS** *n.* [ME, f. L *stationarius* (as prec.; see -ARY[1])]

stā'tioner *n.* one who sells writing-materials etc.; ||**S**~**s' Hall** (of Stationers' Company in London, at which book was formerly *entered,* i.e. registered, for purposes of copyright). [ME, = bookseller (as prec. in med. L sense 'shopkeeper' (esp. bookseller) as opp. pedlar)]

stā'tionerÿ *n.* articles sold by stationer; materials for writing on or with; CONTINUOUS *stationery;* ||**S**~ **Office,** Government's publishing house (also providing Government offices with stationery). [f. prec. + -Y[1]]

stā'tism *n.* State administration and control of social and economic affairs. [f. STATE[1] + -ISM]

stā'tist *n.* statistician; supporter of statism. [orig. 'politician', f. It. *statista* (as STATE[1], -IST)]

stati'stic *a.* & *n.* **1.** *a.* = foll. **2.** *n.* statistical fact or item. [f. G *statistisch, statistik,* (*statist,* as prec.)]

stati'stical *a.* of or pertaining to statistics; ~ **physics** (concerned with systems of large numbers of particles etc., to which statistics is applicable); hence ~LY[2] *adv.* [f. prec. + -AL]

stati'stics *n. pl.* **1.** numerical facts systematically collected (*statistics of population, crime;* VITAL *statistics*). **2.** (usu. treated as *sing.*) science of collecting, classifying, and using statistics, esp. in or for large quantities or numbers. **3.** So **stātĭsti'**CIAN *n.* [f. STATISTIC + -ICS]

stā'tor *n.* (Electr.) stationary part of machine, esp. of electric generator or motor. [f. STATIONARY after ROTOR]

stā'toscōpe *n.* aneroid barometer for showing minute variations of pressure, esp. to indicate altitude of aircraft. [f. Gk *statos* fixed (*sta*- stand) + -SCOPE]

stā'tuarÿ *a.* & *n.* **1.** *a.* of or for statues (*statuary art*); ~ **marble,** fine-grained white kind. **2.** *n.* sculptor; (art of making) statues. [f. L *statuarius* (as foll.; see -ARY¹)]

stǎ'tu|e (-chōō, -tū) *n.* sculptured or cast or moulded figure of person or animal (esp. one not much below life size, opp. to ∿ᴇ´ᴛᴛᴇ *n.*); hence ∿ᴇᴅ² (-ūd) *a.* [ME, f. OF, f. L *statua* (*stare* stand)]

stǎtuě'sque (-tūě'sk, -chōō-) *a.* like, or having the dignity or beauty of, a statue; hence ∿ʟʏ² (-klǐ) *adv.*, ∿ɴᴇss (-kn-) *n.* [f. prec. + -ᴇsǫᴜᴇ, after *picturesque*]

stǎ'tur|e (-yer) *n.* height of (esp. human) body; (fig.) stage of advancement, degree of eminence; hence (-)∿ᴇᴅ² (-yerd) *a.* [ME f. OF, f. L *statura* (*stare* stat-stand; see -ᴜʀᴇ)]

stǎ'tus *n.* **1.** social position, rank, relation to others, relative importance, (*his status is a matter of doubt; their status is wholly different; his status among novelists*); superior social etc. position (∿ **symbol**, possession etc. indicating person's high status). **2.** (Law). person's relation to others as fixed by law. **3.** position of affairs; ∿ **quo,** *the* unchanged position; ∿ **quo (ante),** *the* previous position. [L, = standing (*stare* stand) (*quo* in which, *ante* before)]

stǎ'tūtable *a.* = sᴛᴀᴛᴜᴛᴏʀʏ, esp. in amount or value; hence ∿ʟʏ² *adv.* [f. foll. + -ᴀʙʟᴇ]

stǎ'tūte *n.* **1.** a written law of a legislative body, e.g. Act of Parliament (∿s **at large** (in full as originally enacted, regardless of later modifications); ∿ **law,** a statute, (collect.) the statutes (opp. to ᴄᴀsᴇ¹-*law* and ᴄᴏᴍᴍᴏɴ¹ *law*); statute ᴍɪʟᴇ. **2.** ordinance of corporation, founder, etc., intended to be permanent (*University Statutes*). **3.** (Bibl.) divine law (*kept, teach me, thy statutes*). **4.** ∿**-barred,** barred by the statute of ʟɪᴍɪᴛᴀᴛɪᴏɴs; ∿**-book,** book(s) containing the statute law; ∿**-roll,** (1) engrossed statute, (2) statute-book. [ME, f. OF *statut* f. LL *statutum* neut. p.p. (as n.) of L *statuere* set up (sᴛᴀᴛᴜs)]

stǎ'tūtor|y̌ *a.* enacted, required, permitted, by statute (*statutory provisions, minimum*; **statutory* ʀᴀᴘᴇ¹); hence ∿ɪʟʏ² *adv.* [f. prec. + -ᴏʀʏ]

staunch¹, stanch², (-aw-, -ah-) *a.* trustworthy, loyal, (*staunch friend, supporter*); (of ship, joint, etc.) water-tight, airtight, hence ∿'ʟʏ⁸ *adv.*, ∿'ɴᴇss *n.* [ME, f. OF *estanche* fem. of *estanc* f. Rom. **stancus*; see sᴛᴀɴᴄʜ¹]

staunch². See sᴛᴀɴᴄʜ¹.

stǎve¹ *n.* each of the curved pieces of wood forming sides of cask, pail, etc.; rung of ladder; stanza, verse; (Mus.) = sᴛᴀFF¹ 8; ∿**-rhyme,** alliteration esp. in old Gmc poetry. [ME, var. of sᴛᴀFF¹, due to pl. *staves*]

stǎve² *v.t.* (∿d *or*, esp. Naut., stove *pr.* -ōv). **1.** ∿ (**in**), break a hole in (cask, boat), crush or bash (hat, ribs, box) out of shape. **2.** furnish, fit, (cask etc.) with staves. **3.** ∿ **off,** avert, ward off, defer, (ruin, exposure, etc.). [f. prec.]

staves. See sᴛᴀFF¹.

stǎ'vesācre (-vzāker) *n.* species of larkspur (*Delphinium staphisagria*) whose emetic seeds are used as poison for vermin. [ME, f. L *staphisagria* f. Gk *staphis agria* wild raisin]

stay¹ *v.* & *n.* **1.** *v.t.* (arch. or literary). check, stop, (progress, inroads of disease, etc.); ∿ one's **hand,** (arch.) cease action. **2.** appease hunger of (person, his stomach), appease (hunger), esp. for short time. **3.** postpone (judgement, decision). **4.** (literary). support, prop (*up*) as or with buttress etc. **5.** *v.i.* continue to be in same place or state, not depart or change, (*stay here till I return; will not stay where it is put* or (colloq.) *stay put; will not stay clean; stayed away from the meeting; stayed behind* or *on when others left*); **has come to** ∿, **is here to** ∿, (colloq.) must be regarded as permanent; ∿**-at-home** *a.* & *n.*, (person) remaining habitually at home; ∿ **for** or **to,** (colloq.) wait long enough to partake of (*can you stay for* or *to supper?*); ∿ **in,** remain indoors, esp. in school after hours as punishment; ∿**-in strike,** = sɪᴛ-*down strike*; ∿ **up,** not go to bed. **6.** dwell temporarily (*at hotel etc.*, in town etc., *with* person). **7.** (arch.) pause in movement, action, speech (esp. in *imper.*), etc. (*stay! you forget one thing*). **8.** *v.i.* & *t.*

show endurance (to end of) esp. in race; ∿'**ing--power,** endurance; ∿ **the course,** be able to reach end of race, (fig.) struggle, etc.; hence ∿'ᴇʀ¹ *n.* **9.** *n.* staying, esp. dwelling, in one place, duration of this, (*made a long stay in London; your stay has been very short*). **10.** suspension of judicial proceedings; ∿ **of execution,** postponement of carrying out judgement given. **11.** (arch. or literary). check, restraint, (*will endure no stay; a stay upon his activity*). **12.** endurance, staying--power. **13.** prop, support, (*you have been the stay of my old age*). **14.** (in *pl.*) corset, esp. with whalebone etc. stiffening and laced. **15.** ∿**-bar, -rod,** support in building or machinery; ∿**-maker,** (of corsets). [f. AF *estai*- st. of OF *ester* f. L *stare* stand; sense 'support' (4, 13-15) f. OF *estaye(r)* prop, f. as foll.]

stay² *n.*, & *v.t.* (Naut.) **1.** *n.* rope supporting mast or spar; **in** ∿**s,** (of ship) going about from one tack to another; **miss** ∿**s,** fail in endeavour to go about in tacking; ∿'**sail** (-sāl, -sal), sail extended on stay. **2.** guy or rope supporting flagstaff etc.; tie-piece in aircraft etc. **3.** *v.t.* support (mast etc.) by stays; put (ship) on other tack. [OE *stæg*, = MLG *stach*, ON *stag* f. Gmc **staga*- (**stag-*, **stah*- be firm; cf. sᴛᴇᴇʟ.)]

STC *abbr.* short-title catalogue.

STD *abbr.* Doctor of Sacred Theology [f. L *Sanctae Theologiae Doctor*]; subscriber trunk dialling

stead (stěd) *n.* **stand** (person) **in good** ∿, be advantageous or serviceable to; **in** person's or thing's ∿, instead of him or it, as substitute. [OE *stede*, = OS *stad, stedi*, OHG *stat*, ON *stathr*, Goth. *staths* f. Gmc **stadhiz* f. IE **st(h)'tis* (**st(h)'-*, **st(h)a-* sᴛᴀɴᴅ¹)]

stea'dfast (stě'dfast, -ahst) *a.* constant, firm, unwavering; hence ∿ʟʏ² *adv.*, ∿ɴᴇss *n.* [OE *stedefæst* (as prec., FᴀsT³)]

‖**stea'ding** (stě'd-) *n.* farmstead. [f. sᴛᴇᴀᴅ + -ɪɴɢ¹]

stea'dy (stě'dǐ) *a.*, *adv.*, *n.*, & *v.* **1.** *a.* firmly fixed or supported or standing or balanced, not tottering or rocking etc., (*is steady on his legs; must level table's legs to make it steady*); firmly directed, not faltering, (*steady eye, hand*). **2.** done, moving, acting, happening, in uniform and regular manner (*went off at a steady pace; had a steady wind behind us; requires a steady light; observe a steady increase in the numbers*); ∿, (as command or warning) be steady, abstain from erratic or boisterous behaviour, premature action, hasty inference, etc.; (**keep her**) ∿!, (Naut.) keep direction of ship's head unchanged; ∿ **on!**, go slower! or stop!; ∿ **state,** unvarying condition (esp. in physical process, e.g. of universe not created by any past event). **3.** constant in mind or conduct, not changeable, (*steady in his principles, allegiance*); of industrious and temperate habits **4.** Hence **stea'di**ʟʏ² *adv.*, **stea'di**ɴᴇss *n.*, (stě'd-). **5.** *adv.* steadily; **go** ∿ **with,** (colloq.) be regular sweetheart of; ∿**-going,** staid, sober. **6.** *n.* (colloq.) regular sweetheart. **7.** *v.t.* & *i.* make or become steady (*steady the boat; boat steadied; adversity will steady him; he will soon steady* (*down*)). [f. sᴛᴇᴀᴅ + -ʏ²]

steak (stāk) *n.* thick slice of meat (esp. beef) or fish, cut for grilling, frying, etc.; beef from front of animal, cut for stewing or braising; ∿**-house,** restaurant specializing in serving beefsteaks; ∿**-knife** (with serrated steel blade). [ME, f. ON *steik*, cogn. w. *steikja* roast on spit, *stikna* be roasted]

steal *v.* (stole; sto'len; *pr.* stō-) & *n.* **1.** *v.t.* take away (thing, or abs.) esp. secretly for one's own use without right or leave, take feloniously; ∿ **the show,** unexpectedly outshine other performers; *steal* person's ᴛʜᴜɴᴅᴇʀ. **2.** obtain surreptitiously or by surprise (*stole a kiss; a stolen interview*); (Baseball) reach (base) by deceiving fielders. **3.** ∿ (**away**), win, get possession of, (esp. person's *heart* fig.) by insidious arts, attractions, etc.; ∿ **a march on,** get an advantage over by surreptitious means, anticipate. **4.** *v.i.* move (in, out, away, up, etc.) secretly or silently (*stole out of the room; mist stole over the valley*); (of sound etc.) become gradually perceptible. **5.** Hence (-)∿'ᴇʀ¹ *n.* **6.** *n.* ***(colloq.) stealing; (unexpectedly) easy task or good bargain. [OE *stelan*, = OS, OHG *stelan*, ON *stela*, Goth. *stilan* f. Gmc **stel-*]

stealth (stĕl-) *n.* secrecy, secret procedure; **by** ∼, surreptitiously. [ME, f. OE **stælth* (as prec., -TH¹)]

stea′lth|ў (stĕ′l-) *a.* (Of action) done with stealth, proceeding imperceptibly; (of person or thing) moving with stealth; hence ∼ĭLУ² *adv.*, ∼ĭNESS *n.* [f. prec. +-У²]

steam¹ *n.* **1.** invisible gas into which water is changed by boiling, used as motive power by virtue of its elasticity; **saturated** ∼ (in contact with, and at same temperature as, boiling water); **superheated** ∼ (having higher temperature at given pressure than saturated steam); **wet, dry,** ∼ (containing, not containing, suspended particles of water). **2.** visible particles of water resulting from condensation of steam; any vaporous exhalation. **3.** energy or power provided by or (colloq.) as if by steam (FULL¹ *steam ahead*); **get up** ∼, generate enough power to work steam-engine, (fig.) work oneself into energetic or angry state; **let off** ∼, (fig.) relieve one's pent-up energy or feelings; **run out of** ∼, lose one's impetus; **under** one's **own** ∼, without external motive power (lit. or fig.). **4.** ∼**-bath** (in which bather or substance to be heated is immersed in steam); ∼′**boat,** boat propelled by steam; ∼**-boiler,** vessel in which water is boiled to generate steam esp. for working an engine; ∼**-box, -chest,** (through which steam passes from engine boiler to cylinder); ∼**-coal** (used in heating steam-boilers); ∼**-cylinder** (in which piston of steam-engine moves); ∼**-engine,** locomotive or stationary engine in which the motive power depends on elasticity and expansion or rapid condensation of steam; ∼**-gauge** (attached to boiler to show pressure of steam); ∼**-hammer,** forging-hammer worked by steam; ∼**-heat,** heat given out by steam from radiators etc.; ∼ **iron,** electric iron emitting steam from its flat surface; ∼**-jacket,** casing round cylinder etc. with space between to be filled by steam for heating the cylinder etc.; ‖∼ **navvy,** = *steam-shovel*; ∼**-organ,** set of steam whistles producing musical notes, played by keyboard like that of organ; ∼**-power,** force of steam applied to machinery etc.; ∼ **radio,** (colloq.) radio broadcasting regarded as antiquated by comparison with television; ∼′**roller,** (*n.*) heavy slow-moving locomotive engine with wide wheels and roller used in road-making, (fig.) a crushing power or force, (*v.t.*) crush or move along as with a steamroller; ∼′**ship** (propelled by steam); ∼**-shovel,** excavator worked by steam; ∼**-tight,** capable of resisting passage of steam; ∼ **train** (esp. opp. electric or diesel train); ∼ **tug,** steamer for towing ships etc.; ∼ **turbine** (in which a high-velocity jet of steam rotates a bladed disc or drum); *steam* WHISTLE. **5.** Hence ∼′У² *a.,* of, like, full of, steam, (colloq.) erotic. [OE *stēam* = WFris. *steam,* Du. *stoom* f. Gmc **staumaz*]

steam² *v.* **1.** *v.t.* cook (food) by steam; treat with steam, soften (timber) for bending by steam, get (envelope) *open* by treating its gum with steam; ∼ **up,** cover with condensed steam, (sl., esp. in *p.p.*) make (person) excited or angry. **2.** *v.i.* give out steam or vapour (*kettle steaming on the hob; horses steaming after a gallop; water steaming hot*); rise as or like vapour; move by agency of steam (*we, the vessel, steamed down the river*); ∼ (**up**), become covered with condensed steam; (colloq.) work vigorously, make great progress, (*steam ahead, away*). [OE *stỹman, stēman,* f. Gmc **staumjan* (as prec.)]

stea′mer *n.* In vbl senses; vessel or vehicle propelled by steam; vessel in which things are steamed, esp. cooked by steam; ***∼ **rug,** travelling-rug. [f. prec. +-ER¹]

stèa′ric *a.* derived from stearin; ∼ **acid,** white crystalline fatty acid obtained from animal or vegetable fats; hence **stē′ar**ATE¹ (3) *n.* [f. F *stéarique* f. Gk *stear steatos* tallow; see -IC]

stē′arĭn *n.* ester of glycerol and stearic acid, esp. white crystalline constituent of tallow etc.; mixture of fatty acids used for candles. [f. F *stéarine* f. as prec. +-IN]

stē′atīte *n.* kind of usu. grey talc, soapstone; hence **stēati′t**ĬC *a.* [f. L f. Gk *steatitēs* (as STEARIC; see -ITE¹)]

stēatopў′g|ĭa *n.* excessive development of fat on the buttocks, esp. of Hottentot women; hence ∼OUS (-opī′g-, -ŏ′pĭg-) *a.* [mod. L, f. as STEARIN +Gk *pugē* rump + -IA¹]

steed *n.* (poet., rhet., or joc.) horse, war-horse; hence ∼′LESS *a.* [OE *stēda* stallion, cogn. w. STUD²]

steel *n., a.,* & *v.t.* **1.** *n.* malleable alloy of iron and carbon much used as material for tools, weapons, etc., and capable of being tempered to many different degrees of hardness; **cold** ∼, cutting or thrusting weapons; **pressed** ∼ (moulded under pressure); *a grip, muscles, a heart,* **of** ∼, very tight, strong, hard, etc. **2.** rod of steel, usu. tapered and roughened, for sharpening knives; FLINT *and* steel; strip of steel for stiffening corset or expanding skirt; (poet. or rhet.; not in *pl.*) sword (*foemen worthy of their steel*). **3.** *a.* of or like steel. **4.** ∼ **band** (of W. Ind. musicians with instruments made from oil-drums); ∼**-clad,** wearing armour; ∼ **engraving,** engraving on, impression taken from, steel plate; ∼′**head,** large N. Amer. rainbow trout; ∼ **plate,** sheet of steel for engraving, armour of warships, etc.; ∼ **wool,** fine shavings of steel massed together, used as abrasive; ∼′**work,** steel articles; ∼′**works,** place where steel is manufactured. **5.** *v.t.* harden, make resolute, (one*self,* one's heart, etc., *to do, to action,* for disappointment etc., *against* compassion etc.). [OE *stȳle, *stēle, stēli,* = OS *stēhli,* WG **stahlja* a. f. Gmc **stahla-* prob. f. **stah-, *stag-* be rigid; see STAY²]

stee′l|ў *a.* of, or hard as, steel; inflexibly severe (*steely glance, composure*); hence ∼ĬNESS *n.* [f. prec. +-У²]

stee′lyārd *n.* kind of balance with short arm to take the thing weighed and long graduated arm along which a weight is moved till it balances this. [f. STEEL +YARD¹]

stee′nbŏk (stē′n-, stā′n-) *n.* small African antelope (*Raphicerus campestris*). [Du. (*steen* STONE, *bok* BUCK¹)]

stee′ning *n.* stone lining of well. [f. *steen* v. f. OE *stǣnan* to stone, +-ING¹]

stee′nkĭrk, stei′nkĭrk, (stē′n-k-) *n.* (Hist.) man's or woman's neck-cloth with long lace ends. [f. F (*cravate à la*) *Steinkerke* in Belgium, named after French defeat of English at *Steenkerke* in Belgium (1692)]

steep¹ *a.* & *n.* **1.** *a.* having a marked slope, almost perpendicular, (*steep hill, stairs*); (of rise or fall) rapid, (colloq., of demand, price, etc.) exorbitant, unreasonable, (*seems a bit steep that we should have both the trouble and the expense*), (of story etc.) exaggerated, incredible; hence ∼′EN⁶ *v.i.* & *t.,* ∼′ISH¹ 2 *a.,* ∼′LУ² *adv.,* ∼′NESS *n.,* ∼′У² (poet.) *a.* **2.** *n.* steep slope, precipice. [OE *stēap* f. WG **staupa-,* rel. to STOOP¹]

steep² *v.t.,* & *n.* **1.** *v.t.* soak in liquid; bathe with liquid; ∼ **in,** (fig.) impregnate with, pervade with, (*steeped in the classics, misery, slumber*). **2.** *n.* process of steeping (*barley in steep*); liquid in which thing is steeped. [ME, f. OE **stīepan, *stēpan* f. Gmc **staupjan* (as STOUP)]

stee′ple *n.* lofty structure, esp. tower surmounted by spire, rising above roof of church; ∼**chase,** (1) horse-race (orig. with steeple as goal) across tract of country or on racecourse with ditches, hedges, etc., to jump, (2) cross-country foot-race; ∼**chaser,** rider or runner in, or horse trained for, steeplechase; ∼**chasing,** the sport of riding in steeplechases; ∼**-crowned,** (of hat) with tall pointed crown; ∼**jack,** man who climbs tall chimneys, steeples, etc., to do repairs etc.; hence ∼**-top,** Greenland whale, with spout-holes ending in one point; hence **stee′pl**ED² (-pĕld) *a.* [OE *stēpel, stȳpel* f. Gmc **staupilaz* (as STEEP¹; see -LE 1)]

steer¹ *v.t.* & *i.,* & *n.* **1.** guide (vessel) by rudder or helm, guide vessel in specified direction, guide (motor vehicle, aircraft, etc.) by wheel etc.; ∼′**ing-wheel,** (1) vertical wheel with handles along rim for controlling rudder, (2) wheel for controlling front wheels of motor vehicle, mounted on ∼**'ing-column,** (3) wheel of cycle etc. by which it is steered. **2.** direct (one's course), direct one's course, in specified direction (*steered his flight heavenwards; we steered (our course) for the railway station*); guide movement or trend of (*steer them into the garden*; *steer him* or *the conversation away from that subject*); ∼ **clear of,** take care to avoid; ∼**'ing committee** (deciding order of dealing with business, or priorities and general course of operations). **3.** ∼**'sman** (-z-), one who steers vessel. **4.** Hence ∼**ABLE** *a.,* ∼**ER¹** (1, 2) *n.,* ∼**ING¹** (1, 4) *n.* **5.** *n.* *steering, guidance (BUM² steer). [OE stieran, = OHG stiuren, ON stýra, Goth. stiurjan settle f. Gmc *steurjan (*steurō rudder)]*

steer² *n.* young male of bovine animal, esp. one castrated and raised for beef. [OE *stēor,* = OHG *stior,* ON *stjórr,* Goth. *stiur,* f. Gmc **steuraz*]

steer'age *n.* act of steering; (Naut.) effect of helm on ship (*ship went with easy steerage*); (arch.) part of ship allotted to passengers travelling at cheapest rate; (Hist., in warship) quarters assigned to midshipmen etc. just forward of wardroom; ∼**-way,** amount of headway required by vessel to enable her to be controlled by helm [ME, f. STEER¹ + -AGE]

steeve¹ *v.* & *n.* (Naut.) **1.** *n i* (Of bowsprit) make angle with horizontal. **2.** *v.t.* cause (bowsprit) to do this. **3.** *n.* such angle. [17th c.; orig. unkn.]

steeve² *n.,* & *v.t.* (Naut.) **1.** *n.* long spar used in stowing cargo. **2.** *v.t.* stow with steeve. [ME, f. OF *estiver* or f. Sp. *estivar* f. L *stipare* pack tight]

*stein (stīn) *n.* large earthenware mug esp. for beer. [G, lit. 'stone']

stei'nböck (stī'n-) *n.* Alpine ibex; steenbok. [G. (*stein* STONE, *bock* BUCK¹)]

steinkirk. See STEENKIRK.

stē'la *n.* (*pl.* ∼**e**). (Archaeol.) upright slab or pillar usu. with inscription and sculpture, esp. as gravestone. [L, f. as foll.]

stele (stēl, stē'lĭ) *n.* **1.** (Bot.) axial cylinder in stem or root of vascular plant. **2.** (Archaeol.) = prec. [f. Gk *stēlē* standing block]

stē'llar *a.* of star(s); so ∼**ĭFORM** *a.* [f. LL *stellaris* f. L *stella* star; see -AR¹]

stē'llate, stĕllā'ted, *adjs.* arranged like a star, radiating; (Bot., of leaves) surrounding stem in a whorl. [f. L *stellatus* (*stella* star; see -ATE², -ED¹]

||**stē'llenbösch** (-sh) *v.t.* (arch. Mil. sl.) supersede without formal disgrace by appointing to unimportant command. [f. S∼ in S. Africa, military base so utilized]

stē'llŭlar *a.* shaped like, or with, small stars. [f. LL *stellula* dim. of L *stella* star + -AR¹]

stĕm¹ *n.* & *v.* (-mm-). **1.** *n.* main body or stalk (usu. rising into light and air but occas. subterranean) of tree, shrub, or plant; slender stalk supporting fruit, flower, or leaf, and attaching it to main stalk or branch or twig. **2.** stem-shaped part, e.g. slender part of wineglass between body and foot, vertical line upwards or downwards from head of note in music, upright stroke of written or printed letter, winding-shaft of watch (*∼**-winder,** watch wound by turning head on end of stem, not by key); tubular part of tobacco-pipe. **3.** (Gram.) part of noun, verb, etc., to which case-endings etc. are added, part that appears or would originally appear unchanged throughout the cases and derivatives of a noun, persons of a tense, etc. **4.** line of ancestry, branch of family, (*descended from an ancient, a collateral, stem*). **5.** curved timber or metal piece to which ship's sides are joined at fore end, piece joined to and forming upright continuation of keel at fore end; **from** ∼ **to stern,** from end to end of ship. **6.** ∼ **cell,** (Biol.) undifferentiated cell from which specialized cells develop; ∼ **stitch,** embroidery stitch used for narrow stems etc.; *∼**'ware,** glasses with stems. **7.** Hence ∼**LESS,** (-)∼**mED²** (-md), *adjs.,* ∼**LET** *n.* **8.** *v.t.* remove

stem(s) from (tobacco etc.); make headway against (tide etc.). **9.** *v.i.* spring *from,* (arch.) originate *in.* [OE *stemn, stefn,* f. Gmc **stamniz* (cogn. w. OHG *stam,* ON *stamn, stafn*) f. root **sta-* STAND¹]

stĕm² *v.* (-mm-) & *n.* **1.** *v.t.* check, dam up, (stream etc., lit. or fig.). **2.** *v.i.* retard oneself by forcing heel of ski(s) outwards. **3.** *n.* act of stemming on skis; ∼**-turn,** turn on skis made by stemming with one ski. [f. ON *stemma* = OHG *stemmen,* f. Gmc **stamjan* (*stam-check; cf. STAMMER)]

stĕ'mma *n.* (*pl.* ∼**ta**). family tree, pedigree; line of descent e.g. of variant texts of a work; (Zool.) simple eye, facet of compound eye. [L, f. Gk *stemma* wreath (*stephō* wreathe)]

stĕ'mple *n.* each of several crossbars in shaft of mine serving as supports or steps. [17th c., of uncert. orig.; cf. MHG *stempfel*]

Stĕn *n.* ∼ (**gun**), type of lightweight sub-machine-gun. [f. *S* and *T* (initials of inventors' surnames Shepherd and Turpin), + *-en* after BREN]

stĕnch *n.* offensive or foul smell; ∼**-trap** (in sewer etc., to prevent upward passage of gas). [OE *stenc* (any) smell, = OS *stanc,* OHG *stank* f. Gmc **stankw-* var. of **stinkw-* STINK]

stĕ'ncil *n.,* & *v.t.* (||-ll-). **1.** *n.* ∼(-**plate,** thin sheet of metal etc. in which lettering or other pattern (interrupted when necessary by thin bar of material left to prevent piece from falling out) is cut out, used to produce corresponding pattern on a surface beneath it by applying paintbrush etc.; decoration, lettering, etc., produced by stencil; waxed sheet etc. from which stencil is made by means of typewriter. **2.** *v.t.* produce (pattern) on or *on* surface, ornament (surface) with pattern, by brushing paint etc. over a stencil-plate laid on the surface. [n. f. v. in sense 'ornament', ME, f. OF *estanceler* sparkle, cover with stars, (*estencele* spark f. pop. L **stincilla* for L *scintilla*)]

*stĕ'nŏ *n.* (*pl.* ∼**s**). (colloq.) stenographer. [abbr.]

stĕnŏ'graph|y *n.* shorthand writing; hence ∼**ER¹** *n.,* **stĕnogrā'phĭc** *a.* [f. Gk *stenos* narrow + -GRAPHY]

stĕnō'sļis *n.* (*pl.* -**es** *pr.* -ēz). (Path.) narrowing of a passage in the body. [mod. L, f. Gk *stenōsis* narrowing (*stenoō* make narrow f. as prec.; see -OSIS)]

stĕ'notyp|e *n.* letter(s) representing syllables or phonemes; machine like typewriter for writing these; hence ∼**IST** (3) *n.* [f. STENOGRAPHY + TYPE¹]

||**stĕ'nter** *n.* = TENTER². [f. *stent* v. perh. f. *stend,* = EXTEND]

Stĕ'ntor *n.* person with powerful voice; hence **stĕntō'rIAN** *a.* [f. Gk *Stentōr,* herald in Trojan War (Homer, *Iliad* v. 785)]

stĕp¹ *v.* (-**pp**-). **1.** *v.i.* lift and set down foot or alternate feet as in walking; ∼ **out,** quicken pace, walk long, short, steps; ∼ **out,** (fig.) be active socially; ∼ **through a dance,** perform its steps; ∼ **high,** (esp. of trotting horse) lift feet high. **2.** go short distance or progress in some direction (as) by stepping or steps (lit. or fig.; *step aside, back, forward, up, across the road, into the boat, into the breach, into a fortune*); ∼ **down,** (fig.) resign high position; ∼ **in, out,** enter, leave, room or house; ∼ **in,** (fig.) intervene to help or hinder; *step on the GAS¹* or (colloq.) *on it;* ∼ **this way** (deferential formula for 'come this way, follow me'). **3.** *v.t.* perform (dance); ∼ **it,** dance. **4.** measure (distance *off* or *out*) by stepping. **5.** (Naut.) set up (mast) in step. **6.** ∼ **up,** increase rate, volume, etc., of; ∼ **up, down,** (Electr.) increase, decrease, (voltage) by transformer. **7.** ∼**-in** *n.* & *a.,* (garment, esp. arch. of woman's undergarment) put on by being stepped into without unfastening; ∼**'ping-stone,** raised stone usu. as one of set in stream or muddy place to help in crossing, (fig.) means or stage of progress to an end. [OE *stæppan, steppan,* = OS **steppian,* OHG *stepfen* f. Gmc **stap-* (as foll.)]

stĕp² *n.* **1.** complete movement of one leg in walking or running or unit of movement in dancing (*took a step back;* ONE*step,* TWO-*step*); distance gained by stepping (*a long step towards success*; *do not move a step*); short distance (*but a step from my door*). **2.** mark left by foot on ground; sound made by setting foot down (*do you hear a step?*), manner of stepping as seen or heard (*recognized her step*; *walks with a rapid step*). **3.** simultaneous stepping with corresponding legs by two or more persons or animals; **in**, **out of**, ∼, stepping, not stepping, in time with others or with drum-beat etc., (fig.) conforming, not conforming, to what others are doing; **break** ∼, get out of step; **change** ∼, begin to keep step with opposite leg; **keep** ∼, remain in step (*with* person, *to* drum, etc.). **4.** measure taken esp. as one of a series in some course of action (*must take steps in the matter, to prevent it*, etc.; *a rash, prudent*, FALSE, *step*). **5.** ∼ **by** ∼, gradually, cautiously, by degrees; in person's ∼**s**, following his example; **turn** one's ∼**s**, go in specified direction; *mind* or WATCH[2] one's *step*. **6.** surface provided or utilized for placing foot on in ascending or descending, e.g. tread, or rise and tread, of staircase, block of stone or other platform before door or altar etc., rung of ladder, notch cut for foot in ice-climbing, attached piece of vehicle for stepping up or down by; **(pair of)** ∼**s**, ∼**-ladder**, short ladder with flat steps and prop used without being leant against wall etc. **7.** (fig.) one of the degrees in some scale of precedence or advancement, going from one of these to another e.g. by promotion or increase of pay; *(Mus.) interval of one tone. **8.** (Naut.) block or socket or platform supporting mast; (Carpentry) piece of timber with another fixed upright in it; (Mech.) lower socket or bearing for shaft. **9.** ∼**-cut**, (of gem) cut in straight facets round centre; ∼**-dance** (in which the steps are peculiar or difficult or of more importance than the figure, usu. danced as display by one performer). **10.** Hence ∼**pED**[2] (-pt) *a.*, ∼'**WISE** *adv.* [OE *stæpe, stepe*, f. WG **stapiz* f. Gmc **stap-*]

stĕ'p- *pref.* denoting nominal relationship analogous to one specified, resulting from remarriage of a parent: ∼'**child**, ∼'**daughter**, ∼'**son**, one's wife's or husband's child by previous marriage; ∼'**father**, STEPMOTHER, ∼**parent**, one's parent's later husband or wife; ∼'**brother**, ∼'**sister**, child of one's step-parent; ∼'**dame**, (arch.) stepmother. [OE *stēop-*, = OS, OHG *stiof-*, ON *stjúp-*, cogn. w. OHG *stiufen* bereave]

stĕphanō'tis *n.* climbing tropical plant of genus *Stephanotis*, with fragrant white waxy flowers. [mod. L, f. Gk fem. adj. = fit for a wreath (*stephanos*)]

stĕ'pmother (-mŭdh-) *n.* one's father's later wife; harsh or neglectful mother (lit. or fig.); hence ∼LY[1] *a.* [OE *stēopmōdor* (as STEP-, MOTHER[1])]

stĕppe *n.* level grassy plain devoid of forest esp. in SE Europe and Siberia. [f. Russ. *step'*]

-ster *suf.* forming *ns.* denoting agents, orig. fem. (*spinster*) & f. *vbs.* (*brewster*), now often f. *ns.* (*gangster, maltster*) or *adjs.* (*youngster*) & w. *fem.* in -*stress* (*seamstress, songstress*); occas. derog. (*rhymester, trickster*). [OE -*estre* etc., = MLG, MDu. -*ster* f. WG **-strja* f. Gmc **-astrijōn*]

sterā'dian *n.* unit of solid angle, equal to angle at centre of sphere subtended by part of surface whose area is equal to square of radius. [f. as STEREO- + RADIAN]

stĕrcorā'ceous (-shŭs), **stĕr'coral,** *adjs.* of, produced by, living in, dung or faeces. [f. L *stercus -oris* dung + -ACEOUS, -AL]

stēre *n.* unit of volume equal to one cubic metre. [f. F *stère* f. Gk *stereos* solid]

ste'rĕō (-ĕ'r-, -ēr'-) *n.* (*pl.* ∼**s**) & *a.* stereophonic (record-player etc.), stereophony; stereoscope, stereoscopic; stereotype. [abbr.]

stĕreō- (-ĕ'r-, -ēr'-) *comb. form.* solid, having three dimensions, as: ∼**che'mistry**, branch of chemistry dealing with composition of matter as affected by relations of atoms in space; ∼**graphy** (-ŏ'g-), art of depicting solid bodies in a plane; ∼**i'somer**, (Chem.) one of two or more compounds differing only in spatial arrangement of atoms; ∼**metry** (-ŏ'mĭ-), measurement of solid bodies. [f. Gk *stereos* solid + -o-]

stĕ'rĕobāte *n.* (Archit.) solid mass of masonry as foundation for building. [f. F *stéréobate* f. L f. Gk *stereobatēs* (as prec., *bainō* walk)]

stĕreŏphŏ'n|**ic** (-ĕr-, -ēr-) *a.* (Of sound-reproduction) using two or more transmission channels so that sound reaches listener from more than one direction and thus seems more realistic; hence ∼**ICALLY** *adv.*, ∼Y[1] (-ŏ'fonĭ) *n.* [f. STEREO- + PHONIC]

stĕreŏscōp|**e** (-ĕ'r-, -ēr'-) *n.* device for viewing pair of photographs etc. taken at slightly different angles, looking at each with one eye, the combined images giving an impression of depth and solidity; hence ∼**IC** (-ŏ'p-) *a.*, ∼Y[1] (-ŏ'skopĭ) *n.* [f. STEREO- + -SCOPE]

stĕreŏtype (-ĕ'r-, -ēr'-) *n.*, & *v.t.* **1.** *n.* printing-plate cast from mould of piece of printing composed in type; making or use of such plates; (fig.) unduly fixed mental impression. **2.** *v.t.* make stereotype(s) of; print by use of stereotypes; (fig., esp. in *p.p.*) make unchangeable, impart monotonous regularity to, fix in all details, formalize. [f. F *stéréotype* a. (as STEREO-, TYPE[1])]

stĕ'ric *a.* (Chem.) pertaining to arrangement in space of atoms in a molecule; ∼ **hindrance** (of chemical reaction because of spatial arrangement of reacting atoms). [irreg. f. Gk *stereos* solid + -IC]

stĕ'rīle *a.* unfruitful, unproductive, barren, not producing crop or fruit or young or complete seed or result (*sterile land, cow, plant, year, effort, discussion*); free from living germs esp. bacilli or bacteria or microbes; mentally barren, lacking originality or emotive force; hence or cogn. ∼LY[2] (-l-lĭ) *adv.*, **steri'lITY** *n.* [f. F *stérile* or f. L *sterilis*]

stĕ'rĭlīz|**e**, -**īs**|**e** (-īz) *v.t.* make sterile; deprive of power of reproduction by removal etc. of organs; make free from micro-organisms, whence ∼ER[1] (2) *n.*; hence ∼A'TION *n.* [f. prec. + -IZE]

stĕr'let *n.* small sturgeon (*Acipenser ruthenus*) found in Caspian Sea area and yielding fine caviare. [f. Russ. *sterlyad'*]

stĕr'ling *a.* & *n.* **1.** *a.* (Of coin or precious metal) genuine, of standard value or purity; ∼ **silver** (of 92½ per cent purity). **2.** of solid worth, not showy, that is what it seems to be, (*is a sterling fellow*; *sterling sense, qualities, character*), whence ∼NESS *n.* **3.** *n.* British money, as dist. from foreign money (*pound sterling*); ∼ **area**, (Hist.) countries with currency tied to British pound and reserves mainly in sterling and not in gold or dollars, transferring money freely between themselves; ∼ **balance** etc. (repayable in sterling). [prob. f. OE **steorling* coin with a star (*steorra*; see -LING[1]), some of the early Norman pennies having on them a small star]

stĕrn[1] *a.* severe, grim, rigid, strict, enforcing discipline or submission, not compassionate or indulgent or yielding, (*stern countenance, ruler, treatment, rebuke, virtue, father, tutor*; *ambition should be made of sterner stuff*; **the** ∼**er sex**, men); hence ∼LY[2] *adv.*, ∼NESS (-n-n-) *n.* [OE *styrne*, **stierne* f. WG **sternja*, prob. f. **ster-*, **star-* be rigid (cf. STARE)]

stĕrn[2] *n.* **1.** hind part of ship or boat (opp. *bow, head, stem*; *from* STEM[1] *to stern*), esp. part projecting behind stern-post; ∼**-chase**, pursuit of ship by another straight behind it; ∼ **foremost**, moving backwards; ∼ **on**, with stern presented; BY[1] *the* ∼ *the stern*. **2.** buttocks, rump; tail esp. of foxhound. **3.** ∼**-fast**, rope or chain securing stern to quay etc.; ∼**-post**, central upright timber or iron of stern usu. bearing rudder; ∼ **sheets**, space in boat aft of rowers' thwarts often with seats for passengers; ∼**-way**, backward motion or impetus of ship; ∼**-wheeler**, steamer propelled by one large paddle-wheel at stern. **4.** Hence (-)∼ED[2] (-nd), ∼MOST, *adjs.*, ∼WARD *a.* & *adv.*, ∼WARDS *adv.* [ME, prob. f. ON *stjórn* steering (*stýra* STEER[1])]

stĕr'n|**um** *n.* (*pl.* ∼**ums** *or* ∼**a**). = BREAST[1]*bone*; hence

∼AL *a.* (*sternal* RIB), ∼o- *comb. form.* [mod. L, f. Gk *sternon* chest]

stĕr̄nūtā′tion *n.* (Med. or joc.) sneezing, sneeze. [f. L *sternutatio* (*sternutare* frequent. of *sternuere* sneeze; see -ATION)]

stĕr̄′nūtător *n.* substance (esp. poison gas) causing irritation of nose. [f. as prec. +-OR]

sternū′tatorў *a.* & *n.* (substance, e.g. snuff) causing sneezing. [f. as STERNUTATION + -ORY]

steroid (-ēr̄′-, -ē′r-) *n.* (Chem.) one of large group of organic compounds with four carbon rings, incl. some hormones and other physiological substances; hence **steroi′d**AL *a.* [f. foll. + -OID]

ster′ŏl (-ēr̄′-, -ĕ′r-) *n.* (Chem.) one of group of complex solid alcohols important in vitamin synthesis. [f. CHOLESTEROL, ERGOSTEROL, etc.]

stĕr̄′torous *a.* (Of breathing or breather, esp. in apoplexy etc.) making snorelike sounds; hence ∼LY[2] *adv.*, ∼NESS *n.* [f. *stertor*, mod. L f. L *stertere* snore + -OR, + -OUS]

stĕt *v.* (-tt-). **1.** *v.i.* (as *imper.*, written in margin of proof or MS) ignore correction or alteration, let original form stand. **2.** *v.t.* write 'stet' against, cancel correction of. [L, = let it stand, 3 sing. pres. subj. of *stare* stand]

stĕ′thⱷscŏpe *n.*, & *v.t.* **1.** *n.* instrument used in auscultation esp. of heart and lungs. **2.** *v.t.* examine with stethoscope. **3.** Hence ∼scopIST (1), ∼scopY[1], (-ŏ′s-) *ns.*, ∼scŏ′pIC *a.* [f. F *stéthoscope* f. Gk *stēthos* breast; see -SCOPE]

stĕ′tson *n.* slouch hat with very wide brim and high crown. [f. J. B. *Stetson*, Amer. hat-maker d. 1906]

stĕ′vedŏre *n.* man employed in loading and unloading ships. [f. Sp. *estivador* (*estivar* stow a cargo f. L *stipare*; see STEEVE[2])]

stĕ′vengraph (-n-grahf) *n.* colourful woven silk picture. [f. T. *Stevens*, Engl. weaver d. 1888, whose firm made them, + -GRAPH]

stew[1] *n.* (arch.) hot bath; (esp. in *pl.*) brothel. [ME, f. OF *estuve*, rel. to foll.]

stew[2] *v.* & *n.* **1.** *v.t.* & *i.* cook by long simmering in closed vessel with liquid; ∼ **in** one's **own juice,** (be left unaided to) undergo consequences of one's own actions etc., (in *p.p.*, of tea) bitter or strong with too long infusing; (in *p.p.*, sl.) drunk. **2.** *v.i.* (fig.) be oppressed by close or moist warm atmosphere; (sl.) study hard; *(colloq.)* be worried or anxious (*over*). **3.** *n.* dish of meat etc. made by stewing (Irish ∼, of mutton, potato, and onion); **in a** ∼, (colloq.) agitated with perplexity, anxiety, or anger; ∼-**pan,** ∼-**pot,** shallow saucepan, covered crock, used for stewing. [ME, f. OF *estuver* f. Rom. *extupare, *extufare* prob. f. EX-[1] + *tūfus* f. Gk *tuphos* smoke, steam]

stew[3] *n.* ‖fish-pond, tank for keeping fish alive in; artificial oyster-bed. [ME, f. F *estui (estoier* confine f. Rom. *studiare* take care of f. as STUDY[1])]

stew′ard *n.* & *v.* **1.** *n.* person entrusted with management of another's property, esp. paid manager of great house or estate. **2.** purveyor of provisions etc. for a college, club, guild, ship, etc. **3.** passengers' attendant and waiter on ship or aircraft or train. **4.** any of the officials managing race-meeting, ball, show, etc.; SHOP *steward.* **5.** ‖**Lord High S**∼ **of England,** high officer of State presiding at coronations; ‖**Lord S**∼ **of the Household,** high court officer in charge of kitchen etc. and presiding at Board of GREEN[1] Cloth; **High S**∼, judicial officer at Oxford and Cambridge Universities; (**Lord High**) **S**∼ **of Scotland,** (Hist.) chief officer of Scottish royal court. **6.** Hence ∼ESS[1], ∼SHIP, *ns.* **7.** *v.t.* & *i.* act as steward (of). [OE *stīweard* (*stig* (prob.) house, hall, *weard* WARD[1])]

stg. *abbr.* sterling.

Sth. *abbr.* South.

sthĕ′nic *a.* (Path.) (Of disease etc.) with morbid increase of vital action esp. of heart and arteries. [f. Gk *sthenos* strength + -IC, after *asthenic*]

stichomў′thia (-k-) *n.* dialogue in alternate lines of

verse esp. in ancient Greek plays. [mod. L, f. Gk *stikhomuthia* (*stikhos* line of verse, *muthos* speech)]

stick[1] *v.* (**stuck**). **1.** *v.t.* thrust point of *in*(*to*) or through (*stick the spurs in; stick bayonet, pin, into* or *through*); **get stuck into,** (sl.) make serious start on (job etc.). **2.** insert pointed thing(s) into, stab, (*will pull out a knife and stick you; tipsy-cake stuck over,* or *stuck, with almonds; pincushion stuck full of pins*); ∼ **pigs,** engage in PIG-sticking. **3.** fix (*up*)*on* pointed thing, be fixed (as) by point *in*(*to*) or *on* (*to*), (colloq.) put in specified position, (*heads were stuck on spikes of gateway; arrows stick in target; piece of needlework with needle sticking in it; stick feather, rose, in cap, buttonhole; stick pen behind one's ear; stick up a target; have stuck their prices up, I see; stick it on the bill; stick your cap on; stick them in your pocket; stick a few commas in it*); *just stick it on the table, down anywhere*). **4.** *v.i.* & *t.* ∼ **out** or **up,** protrude, (cause to) project, be or make erect, (*stick one's head out of window; his hair sticks straight up; stick out one's chest; how his stomach sticks out!*); ∼ one's **chin** (or **neck**) **out,** (colloq.) ask for trouble, expose oneself to danger; ∼ **out a mile** (sl.), ∼ **out like a sore thumb** (colloq.), be very obvious or incongruous; ∼ **up,** (sl.) rob (person etc.) by threatening with gun (∼ **'em up!,** (sl.) hands up!; ∼-**up** *n.*, (sl.) hold up); **stuck-up,** conceited, insolently exclusive, [prob. f. carriage of head]; ∼ **up to,** not humble oneself before, offer resistance to; ∼ **up for,** maintain cause or character of (esp. absent person). **5.** fix or become or remain fixed (as) by glue, suction, or other means of adhesion of surfaces (*stick label, postage stamp, on; this envelope will not stick; was referred to as 'Winnie' and the nickname stuck; memory of it sticks in my mind; friends should stick together; limpet sticks to rock; stick photographs in album*); (colloq.) remain in same place (*are you going to stick indoors all day?*); ‖post (*bill*) as placard on wall; (colloq., of accusation etc.) be regarded as valid (*could not make the charges stick*); ‖(sl.) endure, tolerate (*cannot stick that fellow; could not stick it* (*out*) *any longer*); ∼ **around,** (colloq.) linger, remain near same place; ∼ **at it,** (colloq.) be persistent; ∼ **it on,** (sl.) make high charges, tell exaggerated story; **stuck on,** (sl.) captivated by; ∼ **out for,** insist on (price etc., refusing anything less); ∼ **to,** remain fixed on or to, remain faithful to (friend, promise, etc.), abide by, (∼ *to business,* avoid distractions; ∼ *to the point,* not digress); ∼ to person's **fingers,** (of money) be embezzled etc. by him; *stick to one's* GUNS, one's LAST[1]; ∼ **to it,** persist, not cease trying (*∼-to-it-ive,* persistent); ∼ **with,** (colloq.) remain in touch with or faithful to; **stuck with,** (colloq.) unable to get rid of. **6.** lose or deprive of power of motion through friction, jamming, suction, difficulty, or other impediment, (*is stuck on a sandbank; got through some ten lines, and then stuck*); ∼ **at nothing,** allow nothing, esp. no scruples, to deter one; ∼ **fast,** be hopelessly bogged etc.; **stuck for,** at a loss for, unable to think of; ∼ **in the mud,** lit. or fig. be unprogressive; ∼-**in-the-mud,** slow, unprogressive, (person); ∼ **in** one's **throat** etc., be unable to be swallowed (lit. or fig.) or spoken. **7.** *v.t.* provide (plant) with stick as support or to climb up. **8.** ‖∼**'ing-piece,** beef from lower part of neck; ∼**'ing-place, -point,** (at which screw becomes jammed; usu. fig. w. ref. to Shak. *Macbeth* I. vii. 60, or denoting point at which progress becomes impossible); ∼**'ing-plaster,** (piece of) adhesive fabric to cover small cuts etc.; ∼**'jaw,** toffee etc. hard to masticate because it makes jaws stick together; *∼**pin,** tie-pin; *∼**weed,** = RAG[1]*weed* (2). [OE *stician,* = OHG *stehhan* prick f. Gmc *stik-* f. IE *st*(*e*)*ig-*; sense 7 f. foll.]

stick[2] *n.* **1.** shoot of tree cut to convenient length for use in walking or as bludgeon (BIG *stick*) or as fuel or to support plant; staff, wand, rod; piece of wood etc. (whether as part of something or separate) more or less resembling these in shape and size (BROOM*stick,* DRUM[1]*stick,* FIDDLE*stick,* ‖GOLD *Stick,* JOY[1]*stick,* SHOOTING-*stick,* ‖SILVER[1] *Stick,* SINGLE[1]*stick,* SWORD-

-*stick*, WALKING[1]-*stick*); (colloq.) such piece of wood as part of house or furniture (*house pulled down and not a stick left standing*; *has only a few sticks of furniture*; **up ~s**, (sl.) go to live elsewhere); implement used to propel ball in hockey, polo, etc.; gear-lever, conductor's baton; cane used in punishing; (**the**) **~**, (caning as) punishment (lit. or fig.; **get** or **take ~**, be severely criticized); compositor's instrument with compartment of adjustable width for setting type before transfer to galley; (in *pl.*) raising of stick above shoulder in hockey; (in *pl.*, sl.) remote rural areas, hurdles, football goal; (Naut., joc.) mast or spar; (colloq.) person, esp. one lacking vigour or intelligence or social qualities; slender more or less cylindrical piece of sealing--wax, shaving-soap, rhubarb, celery, chocolate, or dynamite; number (of bombs or paratroops) released in rapid succession from aircraft. **2.** *in a cleft stick* (see CLEAVE[1]); *as* CROSS[3] *as two sticks*; HOP[2] *the stick*; *the* DIRTY, WRONG, *end of the stick*. **3. ~ figure**, drawing of human figure with single straight lines for body and limbs; **~-insect**, (usu. wingless) insect of family Phasmidae with twiglike body; **~lac** (in natural state, encrusting insects and small twigs). [OE *sticca*, = OHG *stecko* f. WG **stikka* (**stik-*stek*-pierce; see prec.)]

sti′cker *n.* In vbl senses; adhesive label; difficult problem; wooden rod transmitting motion between ends of levers in piano or organ; persistent person; BILL[4]*sticker*, PIG-STICK. [f. STICK[1] + -ER[1]]

sti′ckit *a.* (Sc.) not proceeding with one's intended profession; **~ minister**, licentiate who has failed to get a pastoral charge. [Sc. form of p.p. of STICK[1]]

sti′ckleback (-kelb-) *n.* small fish of family Gasterosteidae, with sharp spines on back. [ME, f. OE *sticel* thorn, sting (as STICK[2], -LE 1) + *bæc* BACK[1]]

sti′ckler *n.* **~ for**, person who insists on or pertinaciously supports or advocates (*is a great, am no, stickler for authority, precision*, etc.). [f. obs. *stickle* be umpire, ME *stightle* control, frequent. of *stight* f. OE *stiht(i)an* set in order]

sti′cky *a.* tending or intended to stick to what is touched; glutinous, viscous; (of weather) humid; (colloq.) unbending, critical, making or likely to make objections (*he was very sticky about giving me leave*); (sl.) highly unpleasant and painful (*he'll come to a sticky end*); **~ybeak**, (Austral. sl.) inquisitive person; **~y wicket**, (colloq.) **~y dog**, (Cricket, or fig.) pitch drying after rain and difficult for batsmen; hence **~ILY**[2] *adv.*, **~INESS** *n.* [f. STICK[1] + -Y[2]]

stiff *a.* & *n.* **1.** *a.* rigid, not flexible, unbending, unyielding, uncompromising, obstinate, (*stiff collar*; *lies stiff in death*; *put up a stiff resistance*; *answered with a stiff refusal*); (of leg) incapable of bending at knee; (of ship) heeling little under sail; (of market) with prices remaining firm; *stiff upper LIP*; **~-necked**, obstinate or haughty; **~ with**, (sl.) abundantly provided with. **2.** lacking ease or grace or graciousness or spontaneity, constrained, reserved, haughty, formal, (*stiff manners*; *a stiff reception, bow*; *stiff movement, attitude*; *writes in a stiff style*). **3.** not working freely, sticking, offering resistance, (*a stiff hinge, piston*, etc.); **~ neck**, rheumatic affection in which head cannot be turned without pain. **4.** (Of muscle, limb, etc., or person in regard to them) aching when in action, as result of previous exertion. **5.** hard to cope with, calling for strength or effort of some kind, trying, (*stiff examination, climb, slope, breeze*); (of price or penalty) high; (of an alcoholic or medicinal drink) strong. **6.** (Of moist clay, batter, etc.) thick and viscous, not fluid, in or approaching plastic state. **7.** (*pred.*, colloq.) to the point of exhaustion, almost to death, (*bore, scare, stiff*). **8.** Hence **~ISH**[1] 2 *a.*, **~LY**[2] *adv.*, **~NESS** *n.* **9.** *n.* (sl.) corpse; (**big**) **~**, hopeless or intractable or incorrigible person. [OE *stif*, = MLG, MDu. *stīf*, ON *stīfr* f. Gmc **stīfaz* f. IE **stīpos*]

sti′ffen *v.t.* & *i.* make or become stiff(er); (Mil.) bring in better soldiers to improve quality of (a force); hence **~ER**[1] (2), **~ING**[1] (1, 4), *ns.* [f. prec. + -EN[6]]

sti′fle[1] *v.t.* & *i.* smother; constrain breathing or suppress utterance of, be thus constrained. [perh. alt. of ME *stuff(l)e* f. OF *estouffer* f. Rom. **extuffare*]

sti′fle[2] *n.* **~(-joint)**, joint of horse's, dog's, etc., leg between hip and hock; **~-bone**, bone of stifle-joint, like knee-cap. [ME; orig. unkn.]

sti′gma *n.* (*pl.* **~s** or **~ta**). **1.** (arch.) mark branded on slave, criminal, etc. **2.** imputation attaching to person's reputation; stain on one's good name. **3.** characteristic feature *of*; (Path.) definite characteristic of some disease; (Anat. & Zool.) spot, pore, small natural mark on skin etc.; insect's spiracle. **4.** small red spot on person's skin that bleeds periodically or under mental stimulus. **5.** (Bot.) part of style or ovary-surface that receives pollen in impregnation. **6.** (Eccl., usu. in *pl.* **~ta**). mark(s) corresponding to those left on Christ's body by the nails and spear at the Crucifixion, said to have been impressed on the bodies of St. Francis of Assisi and others and attributed to divine favour. [L, f. Gk *stigma -atos* mark made by pointed instrument, brand (**stig-*, cogn. w. STICK[2])]

stigma′t|ic[1] *a.* pertaining to stigma(s); [by back--form.] anastigmatic, not astigmatic; hence **~ICALLY** *adv.* [f. as prec. + -IC]

stigma′tic[2], **sti′gmatist**, *ns.* (Eccl.) person bearing stigmata. [f. as prec., -IST]

sti′gmatīz|e, **-īs|e** (-īz) *v.t.* use opprobrious terms against, describe opprobriously *as*, (*shall not stigmatize him as he deserves*; *stigmatize him, it, as a coward, cowardice*); (Eccl.) produce stigmata on; hence **~A′TION** *n.* [f. F *stigmatiser* or med. L f. Gk *stigmatizō* (as STIGMA; see -IZE)]

sti′lbēne *n.* (Chem.) aromatic hydrocarbon forming phosphorescent crystals. [f. Gk *stilbō* glitter + -ENE]

stilboe′strol (-ē′s-), ***-ē′strol**, *n.* powerful synthetic oestrogen derived from stilbene. [f. prec. + OESTRUS + -OL]

stile *n.* steps, rungs, etc., arranged to allow person to get over or through fence or hedge or wall but excluding cattle etc.; *help lame* DOG[1] *over stile*. [OE *stigel*, = OS, OHG *stigilla* f. Gmc **stig-* climb]

stile[2] *n.* vertical piece (cf. RAIL[1]) in frame of panelled door, wainscot, etc. [prob. f. Du. *stijl* pillar, door--post]

stile′tto *n.* (*pl.* **~s** or **~es**). **1.** short thick-bladed dagger. **2.** pointed implement for making eyelets etc.; **~ heel** of shoe (long and pointed); see -ET[1] dagger (as STYLUS); see -ET[1]]

still[1] *a.*, *n.*, *v.*, & *adv.* **1.** *a.* without or almost without motion (*keep still*); (of water) without surface movement (*still waters run* DEEP[3]). **2.** without or almost without sound (*still as the grave*; *a still evening*; *how still everything is!*); (of sounds) hushed, stilled; **~ small voice**, that of conscience (w. ref. to 1 Kgs. 19:12). **3.** (Of wine etc.) not sparkling or effervescing (*still hock, lemonade*). **4. ~ birth**, birth of dead child; **~′born**, born dead, (fig.) abortive; ***~-hunt**, silent pursuit of quarry (lit. or fig.); **~ life** (*pl. ~ lifes* or *lives*), (a) painting of inanimate things such as fruit and cut flowers; **~ picture**, = sense 6. **5.** Hence **~′NESS** *n.* **6.** *n.* ordinary static photograph (as distinct from a motion picture), esp. single shot from cinema film. **7.** deep silence (*in the still of night*). **8.** *v.t.* (literary). quiet, calm, appease, assuage, silence. **9.** *v.i.* (literary). grow calm (*when the tempest stills*). **10.** *adv.* without or almost without moving (*stand, sit, lie, still*). **11.** then or now or for the future as before, even to this or that past or present or future time, (*Pyramids are still standing*; *what, are you still here so late?*; *had still not realized the truth*); nevertheless, for all that, on the other hand, all the same; (w. *compar.* etc.) even, yet, (*still greater efforts*; *still* LESS; *greater efforts still*; *still another possible explanation*); (arch.) constantly, habitually. [OE *stille a.* & *adv.*, *stillan v.*, = OS, OHG *stilli* f. WG **stillja*, **stellja* (**stel-* be fixed)]

still[2] *n.* distilling-apparatus, esp. for making spirituous liquors, consisting essentially of a closed boiler and a condensing chamber; ||~-room, (1) room for distilling, (2) housekeeper's store-room in large house. [f. *still* v., ME f. DISTIL]

sti'llage *n.* bench, frame, etc., for keeping articles off floor while draining, drying, waiting to be packed, etc. [app. f. Du. *stellagie* scaffold (*stellen* to place + F *-age*; see -AGE)]

sti'llicïde *n.* (Law). (right or duty relating to) dropping of water from eaves on to another's land. [f. L *stillicidium* (*stilla* drop, *cid-* f. *cadere* fall)]

sti'lly¹ (-l-lĭ) *adv.* In adj. senses. [OE *stillīce* (as STILL¹, -LY²)]

sti'lly² *a.* (poet.) still, quiet. [f. STILL¹ after *vasty* etc.]

stilt *n.* 1. pole with rest for foot used generally in pairs with upper part of pole bound to leg or held with hand or arm, enabling user to walk at a distance above the ground (on ~s lit., or fig. = bombastic, stilted). 2. one of set of piles or posts supporting building etc. 3. long-legged slender-billed marsh bird of genus *Himantopus*; ~-petrel, -sandpiper, (long-legged kind). [ME & LG *stilte* f. Gmc *steltjōn, cogn. w. MDu., MLG *stelte*, OHG *stelza* f. *steltōn; cf. STOUT]

sti'ltĕd *a.* (as) on stilts; (of literary style etc.) artificially lofty, pompous, bombastic, whence ~LY² *adv.*, ~NESS *n.*; (of arch) with pieces of upright masonry between imposts and springers. [f. prec. + -ED²]

Sti'lton *n.* rich blue-veined cheese with added cream. [~ in Cambridgeshire, where originally sold]

sti'lus. Var. of STYLUS.

sti'mŭlant *a.* & *n.* 1. *a.* stimulating (esp. Med., producing increase of activity in the body or some part of it). 2. *n.* stimulant agent or substance, as warmth, electricity, joy, etc., or quickening drug or article of food esp. alcoholic drink. [f. L (as foll.; see -ANT)]

sti'mŭl|ate *v.t.* apply stimulus to, act as stimulus upon, animate, spur on, excite (person etc., or abs.) to (more vigorous) action; hence or cogn. ~A'TION, ~ātor, *ns.*, ~ATIVE *a.* [f. L *stimulare* (as foll.) + -ATE³]

sti'mŭl|us *n.* (*pl.* ~i *pr.* -ī). 1. thing that rouses to activity or energy (*so lethargic that no stimulus affects him*); rousing effect (*under the stimulus of hunger*). 2. (Physiol.) thing that evokes specific functional reaction in organ or tissue. [L, = goad, spur, incentive]

sti'my. Var. of STYMIE.

sting *v.* (stung) & *n.* 1. *v.t.* wound with sting (*a bee, nettle, stung him, his finger*); affect with tingling physical or sharp mental pain (*pepper stings one's tongue; the cane, the blow, his conscience, the imputation, stung him; stung by reproaches, with envy or desire; a stinging insult*); incite by such mental effect (*was stung into replying*); (sl.) charge heavily, involve in expense, swindle. 2. *v.i.* (Of part of one's body) feel or be seat of acute pain (*my hand stings*); be able to sting, have a sting, (*some bees do not sting;* ~'ing-nettle, opp. DEAD nettle). 3. *n.* sharp-pointed wounding organ often tubular and connected with poison-gland of insect etc.; snake's poison-fang; stiff sharp hair of nettle etc. causing rash or inflammation on contact with skin; infliction of wound with sting, wound so made, pain caused by it, wounding quality or effect, rankling or acute pain of body or mind, keenness or vigour, (*was hurt by a sting; face covered with stings; the sting of hunger; stings of remorse; this air, bowling, has no sting in it*); (sl.) swindle, robbery; ~ in the tail, (fig.) unexpected final pungency. 4. ~-moth, (Austral.) moth with stinging larva; ~-nettle, stinging-nettle; ~-ray, esp. of family Dasyatidae, with long tapering tail having sharp serrated projecting spine(s) used by it as weapon; ~-winkle, beaked shellfish that bores holes in other shellfish. 5. Hence ~'LESS *a.* [OE *stingan* v., *sting* n., = ON *stinga* f. Gmc *steng-* pierce]

sti'ngaree (-ngg-) *n.* (US & Austral.) = STING-ray. [corrupt.]

sti'nger *n.* In vbl senses; smart painful blow. [f. STING + -ER¹]

||sti'ngö (-nggō) *n.* (arch. sl.) strong beer. [f. STING, w. ref. to sharp taste, + -o]

sti'ng|y̆ (-njĭ) *a.* meanly parsimonious, niggardly; hence ~ILY² *adv.*, ~iNESS *n.* [perh. f. dial. *stinge* sting + -Y²]

stink *v.* (stank or stunk; stunk) & *n.* 1. *v.i.* emit strong offensive smell (*stink in the* NOSTRILS *of*); (fig.) be or seem very unpleasant or unattractive or unsavoury; ~ of money, (sl.) be notoriously rich. 2. *v.t.* drive (person) *out* etc. by stink; fill (place) with stink; (sl.) perceive stink of (*can stink it a mile off*). 3. *n.* strong offensive smell, stench; ||(in *pl.*, sl.) chemistry or natural science as subject of study; (colloq.) loud complaint (*kick up, raise, a stink about*); like ~, (sl.) intensely. 4. ~-alive, the BIB¹ [from rapid putrefaction after death]; ~-ball, ~-bomb, small bomb emitting nauseating smell on exploding; ~-horn, ill-smelling fungus of order Phallales; ~'pot, (1) any receptacle containing something that stinks, (2) objectionable person or thing; ~-stone, kind of limestone giving off fetid smell when quarried; ~-trap, stench-trap; ~'weed, plant akin to wall-rocket; ~'wood, (ill-smelling timber of) Afr. tree (*Ocotea bullata*). [OE *stincan* = MDu., MLG *stinken*, OHG *stinkan* f. WG *stinkwan*, cf. STENCH]

sti'nkard *n.* stinking person or animal, esp. teledu [f. prec. + -ARD]

sti'nker *n.* stinkard, stinkpot; petrel feeding on carrion; (sl.) anything peculiarly offensive, irritating, or severe, (esp. of a letter: *I wrote him a stinker*), difficult task. [f. STINK + -ER¹]

sti'nking *a.* & *adv.* 1. In vbl senses; having typical usu. disagreeable smell (~ badger, teledu; ~ cedar or yew, evergreen Amer. tree of genus *Torreya*, with yewlike leaves stinking when bruised; ~ weed or wood, a rank-scented cassia); (sl.) objectionable; cry ~ fish, condemn one's own products etc. 2. *adv.* (sl.) extremely and objectionably (*stinking rich*). [OE *stincende* (as STINK, ING²)]

sti'nko *a.* (sl.) drunk. [f. STINK + -o]

stint *v.t.*, & *n.* 1. *v.t.* keep on limited allowance (*stint oneself* or person or animal *of* food etc.); supply or give in niggardly manner or grudgingly (*stint food, money, service*, etc.). 2. *n.* limitation of supply or effort (usu. *without, no, stint*); hence ~'LESS *a.* 3. fixed or allotted amount of or of work (*do one's daily stint*). 4. small sandpiper, esp. dunlin. [OE *styntan* to blunt, dull, f. Gmc *stuntjan* (*stunt-*; cf. STUNT¹)]

stīpe *n.* (Bot. & Zool.) stalk or stem (esp. support of carpel, stalk of frond, stem of fungus, eye-stalk); hence sti'pïFORM, sti'pïtATE², stïpï'tïFORM, *adjs.* [F, f. L STIPES]

sti'pel *n.* (Bot.) secondary stipule at base of leaflets of compound leaf; hence ~lATE² *a.* [f. F *stipelle* f. mod. L *stipella* dim. (as STIPULE)]

sti'pĕnd *n.* fixed money allowance at regular intervals for work done, salary, esp. clergyman's official income. [ME, f. OF *stipend(i)e* or f. L *stipendium* (*stips* wages, *pendere* to pay)]

stïpĕ'ndiary *a.* & *n.* (person) receiving stipend, paid, not serving gratuitously; ||~ (magistrate), paid professional magistrate in large provincial town. [f. L *stipendiarius* (as prec.; see -ARY¹)]

sti'p|ēs (-z) *n.* (*pl.* ~ites *pr.* sti'pïtēz). stipe. [L, = log, tree-trunk]

sti'ppl|e *v.* & *n.* 1. *v.t.* engrave (plate, thing portrayed), paint or draw, in stipple, not lines; roughen smooth surface of (paint, cement, etc.). 2. *v.i.* use such method. 3. Hence ~ER¹ (1, 2), ~ING¹, *ns.* 4. *n.* dotted engraving, painting, etc., having gradation of shade etc.; effect (as) of this. [f. Du. *stippelen* frequent. of *stippen* to prick (*stip* point)]

sti'pŭlate¹ *a.* (Bot.) having stipules. [f. L *stipula* (as STIPULE) + -ATE²]

sti'pŭl|ate² *v.* 1. *v.i.* ~ate for, mention or insist upon as essential condition. 2. *v.t.* demand or specify as part of bargain or agreement; (in *p.p.*) laid down as part of the terms of an agreement (*is not of the stipulated quality*). **3.** *v.i.* & *t.* *agree *to*, agree on, (evidence etc. to figure in legal proceedings). **4.** So ∼A'TION, ∼ātor, *ns.* [f. L *stipulari* + -ATE²]

sti'pūl|e *n.* small leaflike appendage to leaf usu. at base of leaf-stem; hence ∼AR¹ *a.* [F, or f. L *stipula* straw]

stīr¹ *v.* (-**rr**-) & *n.* **1.** *v.t.* & *i.* set, keep, or (begin to) be, in motion (*not a breath of wind stirs the lake, the leaves; sit without stirring a finger* etc. or *stirring; if you stir, I shoot*); rise from bed (*is not stirring yet*), go out (*of house* etc.). **2.** *v.t.* use poker etc. to ventilate and assist burning of (fire etc.); arouse, excite, stimulate, (person, his wrath etc.); move spoon etc. round and round in (tea, porridge, soup, etc.) to mix ingredients, keep from burning in pot, etc.; ∼ **the blood,** inspire enthusiasm etc.; ∼ **in,** add (ingredient) and mix with rest by stirring; ∼ one's **stumps,** (colloq.) make haste, walk etc. faster; ∼ **up,** mix well by stirring, make (mud, sediment, etc.) rise from bottom of liquid by stirring, (fig.) rouse, excite, animate, inspirit, (*stir up strife, mutiny, curiosity*). **3.** ∼-**about,** (1) porridge made by stirring oatmeal etc. in boiling water or milk, (2) bustling person. **4.** Hence ∼'RER¹ (1, 2) *n.* **5.** *n.* commotion, bustle, disturbance, excitement, sensation, (*full of stir and movement*; **make a great** ∼, be much discussed etc.); slightest movement (*not a stir*), whence ∼LESS *a.*; act of stirring (*give the fire a stir*). [OE *styrian*, = OS -*sturian*, MHG *stürn* f. Gmc *sturjan*]

stīr² *n.* (sl.) prison; ∼-**crazy,** mentally abnormal from being imprisoned (lit. or fig.). [19th c.; orig. unkn.]

‖**stīrk** *n.* (prov.) yearling bullock or heifer. [OE *stirc*, perh. dim. of *stēor* STEER²; see -OCK]

stīr'picŭlture *n.* breeding of special stocks or strains. [f. as foll. + -I- + CULTURE]

stīrp|s *n.* (*pl.* ∼**es** *pr.* stēr'pēz). **1.** (Law). (progenitor of) branch of family. **2.** (Zool.) classificatory group. [L, = stock]

stīr'ring *a.* In vbl senses; actively occupied (*lead a stirring life*); exciting, stimulating, inspiring, (*stirring events, music, tales*), whence ∼LY² *adv.* [OE *styrende* (as STIR¹, -ING²)]

stī'rrup *n.* horse-rider's foot-rest usu. consisting of metal or leather loop with flattened base hung by ∼--**strap** or ∼-**leather** from ∼-**bar,** iron attachment let into saddle; part of garment etc. passing under instep; (Naut.) rope with eye giving hold in reefing; ∼(-**bone**), stapes; ∼-**cup** (of wine etc. presented to person about to depart, orig. on horseback); ∼-**iron,** metal loop of stirrup; ∼-**jar,** ancient Greek jar with arched supported handle at top; ∼-**pump,** hand--operated pump with stirrup-shaped foot-rest and nozzle for producing either jet or spray of water, used to extinguish small fires. [OE *stigrāp* (*stigan* climb f. as STILE¹, ROPE)]

stitch *n.* & *v.* **1.** *n.* sudden acute pain in side of body. **2.** single pass of needle in sewing (*a stitch in time* SAVE¹*s nine*); result of it or of single complete movement in knitting, crocheting, embroidery, etc., (*if one stitch gives the rest will*); thread etc. between two successive needle-holes; least bit of material, esp. of clothing; **drop a** ∼, let loop fall off end of knitting-needle; **in** ∼'**es,** (colloq.) laughing uncontrollably. **3.** fastening through sheets of book etc.; (Surg.) movement of needle, loop of material formed, in sewing up a wound with gut, silk, wire, etc. **4.** method followed in making stitches or kind of work produced (*am learning a new stitch*; LOCK²-*stitch*, CROSS-*stitch*, etc.). **5.** ∼-**wheel,** harness-maker's notched wheel for pricking leather in places where stitches are to go; ∼'**wort,** plant of genus *Stellaria*, esp. one with erect stem and white starry flowers, named as curing stitch in side. **6.** *v.t.* & *i.* sew, make stitches (in), join or close with stitches; ∼ **up,** join or mend by sewing; hence ∼'ER¹, ∼'ERY (1), *ns.* [OE *stice*, = OS *stiki*, OHG *stih*, Goth *stiks* f. Gmc *stikiz* (*stik*- STICK¹)]

sti'thy (-dhǐ) *n.* (arch. or poet.) smith's shop, forge. [ME, f. ON *stethi* (*stathjon* f. Gmc *sta*- STAND¹)]

sti'ver *n.* even the smallest coin (usu. *don't care, has not, a stiver*). [f. Du. *stuiver* small coin, prob. cogn. w. STUB]

stŏ'a *n.* (*pl.* ∼s *or* ∼e). portico or roofed colonnade in ancient-Greek architecture; **the S**∼, = *the* PORCH (cf. STOIC). [Gk]

stoat *n.* ermine, esp. when in its brown summer coat. [ME, of unkn. orig.]

stochǎ'st|ic (-k-) *a.* governed by the laws of probability; hence ∼ICALLY *adv.* [f. Gk *stokhastikos* (*stokhazomai* aim at, guess f. *stokhos* aim; see -IC)]

stŏck *n.*, *a.*, & *v.* **1.** *n.* stump, butt, main trunk, (∼s **and stones,** inanimate things. lethargic persons; LAUGHING¹-*stock*); plant into which graft is inserted; body-piece serving as base or holder or handle for working parts of implement or machine (e.g. for barrel of rifle or for ploughshare); headstock or tailstock; cross-bar of anchor; LOCK², *stock, and barrel*. **2.** (source of) family or breed, raw material of manufacture (e.g. of paper or cinema film), quantity ready for drawing on, equipment for trade or pursuit, (*renew one's stock, lay in a stock, has a great stock, of information, of hardware*); * = (performances of) *stock company*; ROLL²*ing-stock*; **in** ∼, ready without needing to be procured specially; **out of** ∼, not thus available; **comes of** (*a*) good, Puritan, treacherous, etc., ∼ (family of distinct character); **take** ∼, review one's stock for accurate knowledge of what one has, (fig.) observe with a view to estimating character etc. of. **3.** (Zool.) aggregate organism of polyp etc. **4.** liquor made by stewing bones, meat, fish, vegetables, etc., as basis for soup, stew, sauce, or gravy. **5.** farm animals (*livestock*) and implements (*deadstock*); FAT-*stock*. **6.** cruciferous fragrant-flowered plant of genus *Matthiola*; NIGHT-*scented*, TEN-*week*, VIRGINIA, *stock* [orig. ∼-*gillyflower*, named as having stronger stem than clove-gillyflower]. **7.** (in *pl.*, Hist.) timber frame with holes for feet and occas. hands in which petty offenders were confined in sitting position in public. **8.** (in *pl.*) timbers on which ship rests during building; **on the** ∼s, in construction or preparation. **9.** stiff wide band of leather or other material worn round neck esp. in riding-kit; piece of black or purple silk etc. worn below clerical collar. **10.** ‖money lent to a government and involving payment of fixed interest to lenders or their successors in title; right to receive such interest (*buy, hold, stock*); ‖**the** ∼s, State's funded debts as a whole; **take** ∼ **in,** (fig.) concern oneself with. **11.** capital of corporation or company contributed by individuals for prosecution of some undertaking and divided into shares entitling holders to proportion of profits (DEFER¹*red*, ‖ORDINARY, ‖PREFERENCE or *preferred stock*); *share(s) of stock; one's ∼ **rises, falls,** (fig.) one is more, less, popular or highly regarded. **12.** ‖hard solid brick pressed in a mould. **13.** ‖∼-**account, -book,** (showing amount of goods laid in and amount disposed of); ∼-**breeder,** raiser of livestock; ∼'**broker,** ∼'**broking,** (person engaged in) buying and selling for clients stocks held by stockjobbers; ∼-**car,** (1) *railway cattle-truck, (2) racing car with basic chassis of ordinary commercial model, but sometimes partly made from old cars, used in racing where deliberate bumping is allowed; ∼ **company,** one semi-permanently engaged at a particular theatre; ∼'**dove,** European wild pigeon (*Columba oenas*) smaller and darker than ring-dove [prob. named from breeding in stocks of trees]; ∼-**exchange,** place where stocks and shares are publicly bought and sold; **the S**∼ **Exchange,** (building occupied by) association of dealers in stocks conducting business according to fixed rules (*on the S*∼ *Exchange*, a member of this association); ∼'**fish,** cod or similar fish split and dried in open air without salt; ∼'**holder,** holder of stock or shares; ∼--**in-trade,** all requisites for a trade (lit. or fig.: *the politician's stock-in-trade of a dozen catchwords*):

∼'**jobber,** ∼'**jobbing,** ‖(person engaged in) dealing in stocks so as to profit by fluctuations in price; ∼'**jobber,** *(unscrupulous) stockbroker; ∼'**list,** daily or periodical publication giving current prices of stocks etc. or stating dealer's stock of goods; ∼ **lock** (enclosed in wooden case, usu. on outer door); ∼'**man,** (Austral.) man in charge of livestock, *owner of livestock, *person in charge of stock of goods in warehouse etc.; ∼-**market,** stock exchange or transactions on it; ∼'**pile,** accumulate(d) stocks of commodities, raw materials, nuclear weapons, etc., to be held in reserve; ∼-**pot** (for making or keeping stock, sense 4); ∼'**rider,** (Austral.) herdsman on unfenced station; ∼-**room** (for storage of goods kept in stock); ∼ **saddle,** cowboy's (ornamental) saddle; ∼-**still,** motionless; ∼-**taking,** review of stock in shop etc. or fig.; ∼-**whip** (with short handle and long lash for herding cattle); ∼'**yard,** enclosure with pens etc. for sorting or temporary keeping of cattle. **14.** Hence ∼'LESS *a.* **15.** *a.* kept in stock and regularly available (*a stock item, size*); (fig.) always available and perpetually repeated without fresh thought or originality (*stock argument, comparison, joke, response, role*). **16.** *v.t.* fit (gun etc.) with stock. **17.** (Hist.) confine in the stocks. **18.** provide (shop, farm, etc.) with goods or livestock or requisites (*a well-stocked larder, library*, etc.); keep (goods) in stock. **19.** *v.i.* ∼ (**up**), take in stocks of goods (*stock up with coal for the winter*). [OE *stoc(c)*, = OS *stok*, ON *stokkr* trunk f. Gmc **stukkaz*]

stŏckā'de *n.*, & *v.t.* (fortify with) breastwork or enclosure of upright stakes. [f. obs. F *estocade*, alt. of *estacade* f. Sp. *estacada* (rel. to STAKE)]

Stŏ'ckhōlm (-hōm) *n.* ∼ **pitch, tar,** (prepared from resinous pinewood, used esp. in shipbuilding. [∼ in Sweden]

stŏckǐně't, -ě'tte, *n.* elastic knitted material used esp. for bandages. [prob. f. *stocking net*]

stŏ'cking *n.* tight covering usu. knitted or woven of wool or cotton or silk or nylon for foot and (part of) leg (*pair of stockings*); *is or stands six feet* **in** one's ∼s or ∼(**ed**) **feet** (when measured) without shoes; **elastic** ∼, surgical appliance of elastic webbing like stocking or part of it worn for varicose veins, strained muscles, etc.; **white** etc. ∼, lower part of leg of horse etc. differently coloured from rest of leg; ∼ **cap,** knitted usu. conical cap; ∼-**filler,** small present for adding to stocking hung up for Santa Claus; ∼-**frame, -loom, -machine,** knitting-machine; ∼ **mask,** nylon stocking worn over head as criminal's disguise; ∼-**stitch** (of alternate rows plain and purl, giving uniform surface); hence ∼LESS *a.* [f. STOCK, in (now dial.) sense 'stocking' +-ING[1]]

‖**stŏ'ckist** *n.* one who stocks (certain) goods for sale. [f. STOCK +-IST]

stŏ'ck|**ў** *a.* (of person, plant, or animal) thickset, relatively short and strongly built; hence ∼ĭLY² *adv.*, ∼ĭNESS *n.* [f. STOCK + -Y²]

stŏdge *n.* & *v.* (colloq.) **1.** *n.* food esp. of thick heavy kind; unimaginative person or work. **2.** *v.i.* eat greedily; trudge through mud etc. **3.** *v.t.* stuff with food etc. [n. f. v., imit., after *stuff* and *podge*]

stŏ'dg|**ў** *a.* (Of food) heavy, filling, indigestible; (of book, style, etc.) over-full of facts or details, lacking lightness or originality or interest; dull, drab; hence ∼ĭLY² *adv.*, ∼ĭNESS *n.* [f. prec. + -Y²]

stoep (-ōōp) *n.* (S. Afr.) terraced veranda in front of house. [Du. Du. cogn. w. STEP¹,²]

*****stŏ'gў, -gie,** (-gĭ) *n.* rough heavy boot; long narrow roughly-made cigar. [orig. *stoga*, short for *Conestoga* in Pennsylvania]

stŏ'ic *n.* & *a.* (S∼). (typical of) philosopher of the school founded at Athens *c.* 308 BC by Zeno making virtue the highest good, concentrating attention on ethics, and inculcating control of the passions and indifference to pleasure and pain (*Stoic doctrines, indifference*); hence S∼ISM (2, 3) *n.* **2.** (person) having

great self-control or fortitude or austerity; hence ∼AL *a.*, ∼ALLY² *adv.*, ∼ISM (2, 3) *n.* [ME, f. L f. Gk *stōïkos* (STOA, w. ref. to Zeno's teaching in the *Stoa Poikilē* or Painted Porch at Athens; see -IC)]

stoichiŏ'|**mètrў,** ‖-**cheiŏ'**|-, (-kī-) *n.* determination of equivalent weights of substances in chemical reactions; quantitative relationship between reacting substances; hence ∼mě'trIC (-kĭo-) *a.* [f. Gk *stoikheion* element + -O- + -METRY]

stōke *v.* **1.** *v.t.* ∼ (**up**), feed with fuel and tend (furnace or colloq. fire), feed furnace or fire-box of (engine etc.). **2.** *v.i.* act as stoker; ∼ (**up**), (colloq.) take food esp. steadily and in large quantity. **3.** ∼'**hold,** compartment in which steamer's fires are tended; ∼'**hole,** space for stokers in front of furnace. [back-form. f. foll.]

stō'ker *n.* one who feeds and tends furnace or fire-box esp. that of steamer or steam-engine; machine for doing this. [Du. f. *stoken* stoke f. MDu. *stoken* push cogn. w. STICK¹, f. -ER¹]

stōkes (-ks) *n.* (*pl.* same). unit of kinematic viscosity, corresponding to dynamic viscosity of 1 poise and density 1 gram per cc. [f. Sir G. G. *Stokes*, British physicist d. 1903]

STOL *abbr.* short take-off and landing (aircraft).

stō'la *n.* (*pl.* ∼e). = foll. 1. [L, f. Gk *stolē* equipment, clothing (*stellō* put, array)]

stōle[1] *n.* **1.** (Rom. Ant.) woman's long loose outer dress. **2.** (Eccl.) strip of silk or other material hanging from back of neck over shoulders and down to knees (worn by deacon over left shoulder only). **3.** woman's wrap of similar shape. [OE *stol(e)* f. as prec.]

stōle², stō'len. See STEAL.

stō'lid *a.* phlegmatic, unemotional, lacking or seeming to lack animation, not easily excited, obstinate, apparently stupid; hence or cogn. **stoli'd**ITY *n.*, ∼LY² *adv.* [f. obs. F *stolide* or f. L *stolidus*]

stō'lon *n.* (Bot.) reclined or prostrate branch that strikes root and develops new plant; (Zool.) rootlike creeping growth; hence ∼ATE², ∼i'FEROUS, *adjs.* [f. L *stolo -onis*]

stō'ma *n.* (*pl.* ∼s *or* ∼**ta**). **1.** (Zool.) small mouthlike opening of lower animals. **2.** (Bot.) minute orifice in epidermis of leaf etc. [mod. L, f. Gk *stoma -atos* mouth]

stō'mach (-ŭ'mak) *n.*, & *v.t.* **1.** *n.* internal organ in which first part of digestion occurs, in man a pear-shaped enlargement of the alimentary canal extending from end of gullet to beginning of gut (**on an empty** ∼, not having recently eaten; **on a full** ∼, after large meal); one of several digestive organs of animal, esp. ruminant, either of similar character or differing in action or function (*ruminant's* **first** ∼ or paunch or rumen, **second** ∼ or honeycomb or reticulum, **third** ∼ or psalterium or omasum or manyplies, **fourth** or **true** ∼ or reed or maw or abomasum); **muscular** ∼ (acting by grinding or squeezing, as the gizzard). **2.** belly, abdomen, lower front of body, (PIT¹ *of the stomach*); protuberant belly (*what a stomach he has got!*). **3.** appetite for or *for* food (STAY¹ one's *stomach*). **4.** taste or readiness or sufficient spirit *for* (or arch. *to*) controversy, conflict, danger, or an undertaking (*had no stomach for the fight*). **5.** ∼-**ache,** pain in belly, esp. in bowels; ∼-**pump,** syringe for emptying stomach or forcing liquid into it; ∼-**tooth,** lower canine milk-tooth in infants, cutting of which often disorders stomach; ∼-**tube** (for introducing through gullet into stomach to wash it out or empty it by siphon action); ∼ **upset, upset** ∼, temporary slight disorder of digestive system. **6.** Hence ∼AL, ∼LESS, *adjs.*, ∼FUL 2 *n.* **7.** *v.t.* eat with relish or toleration, find sufficiently palatable to swallow or keep down, (fig.) submit to or put up with (affront etc.), (usu. w. neg.; *cannot stomach it*). [ME *stomak* f. OF *stomaque, estomac* f. L f. Gk *stomakhos* gullet (*stoma* mouth)]

stō'macher (-ŭ'mak-) *n.* ornament worn on bodice-front; (Hist.) front-piece of 15th-17th-c. woman's dress covering breast and pit of stomach, ending downwards in point often lapping over skirt, and often set with gems or richly embroidered. [ME, prob. f. OF *estomachier* (as prec.; see -ER²)]

stoma'chic (-k-) *a.* & *n.* **1.** *a.* of the stomach; aiding stomach action, promoting digestion or appetite. **2.** *n.* stomachic medicine or stimulant. [f. F *stomachique* or f. L f. Gk *stomakhikos* (as STOMACH; see -IC)]

stōmati'tis *n.* inflammation of the mucous membrane of the mouth. [f. as STOMA + -ITIS]

stōmatŏ'log|y̆ *n.* science of (diseases of) the mouth; hence **stōmato**LO'GICAL *a.*, ∿IST (3) *n.* [f. as STOMA + -O- + -LOGY]

stŏmp *n.,* & *v.i.* **1.** *n.* lively jazz dance with heavy stamping. **2.** *v.i.* dance stomp; tread heavily; *stamp one's feet. [US dial. var. of STAMP]

stōne *n., a.,* & *v.t.* **1.** *n.* piece of rock of any shape usu. detached from earth's crust and of no great size, esp. a pebble, a cobble, or a single piece used or usable in building or road-making or as missile (*built of great stones; as hard as a stone;* ROCK³*ing*-stone; ROLL²*ing stone*; SERMONS *in stones*; STOCKS *and stones*); ∿s will cry out, wrong is great enough to move inanimate things; **give a ∿ for bread,** offer a mockery of help; **mark with a white ∿,** record as a joyful day [w. ref. to ancient-Roman use of chalk]; METEORIC *stone*; **leave no ∿ unturned,** try every possible means (*to do*); **break ∿s,** get living by preparing road-metal, (fig.) be reduced to extremities; **cast** or **throw ∿s** or **a ∿ at,** or **the first ∿,** lit., or fig. = make aspersions on character etc. (of); **those who live in glass houses should not throw ∿s,** aspersion by the vulnerable provokes damaging retort; *kill two* BIRDS *with one stone*; ∿'s **thrŏw,** distance stone can be thrown, short or moderate distance. **2.** = PRECIOUS *stone* (*no stone in it worth less than £100*). **3.** stones or rock as a substance or material (LIME¹*stone,* SAND*stone;* HOLYSTONE; PHILO-SOPHERS' *stone*), esp. for building (PORTLAND *stone*); ∿ **jar** etc. (of stoneware); **has a heart of ∿,** is hard-hearted; **harden into ∿,** petrify (lit. or fig.). **4.** piece of stone of definite and designed shape (often with purpose specified by word in comb. or by context: GRAVE¹*stone,* GRIND*stone,* HEARTH*stone,* MILL¹*stone,* OIL¹*stone,* TOMB*stone,* WHET*stone*); (Print.) smooth flat surface on which type is imposed in pages. **5.** thing resembling stone in hardness or pebble in shape, e.g. hard morbid concretion in the body (or disease in which these occur), hard case of kernel in stone-fruit, seed of grape, pellet of hail, (arch. or vulg.) testicle. **6.** (*pl.* same). ||weight of 14 lb. (or of other amounts varying with the commodity) esp. as unit weighing person or large animal; **give a ∿ and a beating to,** (orig. Racing sl.) surpass easily. **7.** S∿ **Age,** stage of civilization in which tools and weapons were of stone not metal; ∿-**axe** (with two blunt edges for hewing stone); ∿-**blind,** completely blind; *∿ **boat,** flat sledge carrying stones; ∿-**boiling,** primitive method of boiling by putting heated stones into water; ∿-**borer,** mollusc of genus *Lithophaga;* ∿-**brash,** subsoil of broken stones; *∿-**broke,** = STONY 2; ∿-**cast,** = *stone's throw* (see sense 1); ∿'**chat,** small black and white European song-bird (*Saxicola torquata*), with alarm-note like knocking of pebbles; ∿-**coal,** anthracite; ∿-**cold,** completely cold; ∿'**crop,** plant of genus *Sedum,* esp. yellow-flowered plant growing on walls and rocks; ∿-**curlew,** large-headed bird of family Burhinidae; ∿-**dead, -deaf,** completely so; ∿-**eater,** = *stone-borer;* *∿-**fence,** (sl.) whisky and cider, or similar mixed drink; ∿-**fern,** ceterach; ∿-**fish,** venomous tropical fish with erect dorsal spines; ∿-**fly,** insect of order Plecoptera, with aquatic larvae found under stones, used as bait; ∿-**fruit,** drupe; ∿-**ground** *a.,* ground with millstones; ||∿'-**hatch,** ring-plover; *stone* JUG¹; ∿-**lily,** fossil crinoid; ∿-**marten,** = BEECH-*marten;* ∿'**mason,** dresser of or builder in stone; ∿-**parsley,** umbelliferous hedge plant with aromatic seeds; ∿-**pine,** S. European pine-tree with

branches at top spreading like umbrella; ∿-**pit, quarry;** ∿-**plover,** = *stone-curlew;* ∿-**saw,** untoothed iron blade stretched in saw-frame for cutting stone with aid of sand; ∿-**snipe,** (1) = *stone-curlew,* (2) large N. Amer. snipe; ∿'**wall** *v.i.* & *t.,* obstruct by stonewalling; ∿**wa'lling,** (Cricket) excessively cautious batting, ||(Polit. etc.) obstruction of discussion; ∿'**ware,** pottery made from very siliceous clay or from composition of clay and flint; ∿'**weed,** gromwell; ∿'**work,** masonry; ∿'**wort,** (1) = *stone-parsley,* (2) plant of genus *Chara,* with calcareous deposit on stem. **8.** Hence (-)stōnED² (-nd), ∿'LESS (-nl-), *adjs.* **9.** *a.* made of stone. **10.** *v.t.* pelt with stones; ∿ **the crows** (sl. excl. of surprise or disgust). **11.** remove stones from (fruit). **12.** face, pave, etc., with stone. **13.** (sl.; esp. in *p.p.*) stupefy or stimulate with drink, drug, etc. [OE *stān,* = OS *stēn,* OHG *stein,* ON *steinn,* Goth. *stains* f. Gmc **stainaz*]

stŏnk *v.t.,* *n.* bombard(ment) with artillery. [20th c.; cf. dial. *stonk* game of marbles]

stŏ'nker *v.t.* (Austral. & NZ sl.) baffle, tire, defeat. [20th c.; orig. unkn.]

stō'n|y̆ *a.* & *adv.* **1.** *a.* full of, covered with, having many, stones; hard, rigid, fixed, as stone; (of stare etc.) refusing response or recognition; (of fear, grief, etc.) stupefying; ∿y **heart,** (1) obdurate or unfeeling heart, (2) hard core or interior; hence ∿ILY² *adv.,* ∿INESS *n.* **2.** *a.* & *adv.* ∿y(-**broke**), (sl.) entirely without money. [OE *stānig* (as STONE, -Y²)]

stŏŏd. See STAND¹.

stŏŏge *n.* & *v.i.* (sl.) **1.** *n.* butt, foil, esp. for a comedian; deputy, subordinate, esp. for routine or unpleasant work; compliant person, puppet. **2.** *v.i.* move, esp. fly, *about, around,* etc.; act as stooge *for.* [20th c., orig. US; of unkn. orig.]

stook (-ŏŏk, -ōŏk) *n.,* & *v.t.* (chiefly Sc. & N. Engl.) = SHOCK³. [ME *stouk,* f. or cogn. w. MLG *stūke*]

stŏŏl *n.,* & *v.i.* **1.** *n.* (usu. movable) seat for one, having no back or arms and often consisting of wooden slab on three or four legs; CAMP¹-*stool;* MUSIC-*stool;* ∿ **of repentance,** that on which fornicators etc. were set to receive rebuke in churches in Scotland, (fig.) humble position of repentance; **fall between two ∿s,** fail from vacillation between two courses etc. **2.** = FOOT¹*stool;* low bench for kneeling on; seat as symbol of authority; (Archit.) window-sill. **3.** (place for) evacuation of bowels (*go to stool*); faeces evacuated. **4.** root or stump of felled tree or dormant or cut plant, from which shoots spring. **5.** *decoy-bird. **6.** ∿-**ball,** old game resembling cricket still played in Sussex etc. esp. by girls; ∿-**pigeon,** pigeon (fixed to stool) used, person acting, as decoy, police informer. **7.** *v.i.* throw up shoots from root; (arch.) evacuate bowels; *(sl.) act as stool-pigeon. [OE *stōl,* = OS *stōl,* OHG *stuol,* ON *stóll,* Goth. *stōls* chair, throne f. Gmc **stōlaz* (**stō-, *stā-,* STAND¹)]

*stŏŏ'lie *n.* (sl.) person acting as stool-pigeon. [f. prec. + -IE]

stŏŏp *v.* & *n.* **1.** *v.i.* bring one's head nearer the ground by bending forwards and down from standing position, (fig.) deign or condescend *to* do, descend or lower oneself *to* (some conduct, or abs.); ∿ **to conquer,** gain power or one's end by preliminary self-abasement). **2.** carry one's head and shoulders bowed forward. **3.** (of hawk etc., or fig.) swoop, pounce, (*on*). **4.** *v.t.* incline (head, neck, shoulders) forwards and down. **5.** *n.* stooping carriage of body; (arch.) swoop of hawk etc. [OE *stūpian,* = MDu. *stūpen,* ON *stúpa* f. Gmc **stūp-,* rel. to STEEP¹]

stŏŏp². Var. of STOUP.

*stŏŏp³ *n.* porch or small veranda or steps in front of house. [f. Du. STOEP]

stŏp *v.* (-pp-). **1.** *v.t.* close or almost close up or *up* by plugging, obstructing, etc., prevent or forbid passage through, make impervious or impassable, (*stop a leak, hole,* etc.); plug upper end of (organ-pipe), giving note an octave lower; (Bridge) be able to prevent opponents from taking all tricks in (suit); ‖FILL (tooth) with ∼'p**ING**¹ n. of gold, amalgam, cement, etc.; ∼ one's **ears,** put one's fingers in them to avoid hearing, (fig.) refuse to listen; ∼ **a gap,** serve to meet a temporary need; ∼ person's **mouth,** (fig.) induce him by bribery or other means to keep silence about something; ∼ **the way,** be or act as obstruction, prevent progress. **2.** put an end to (motion etc.), completely check progress or motion or operation of, effectively hinder or prevent, discontinue (one's action), (*stop cricket-ball, runaway horse, progress; stop person's doing, person from doing; stop me if I talk for too long; stop that noise!; shall stop their misbehaviour at once; shall stop playing, subscribing, my visits, my endeavours; do stop grumbling, your complaints, that noise;* ∼ **it!,** desist from your action; ∼ **thief!,** cry of pursuer); (Boxing) parry (blow), knock out (opponent); (sl.) receive (blow, bullet, etc.); make (sound) inaudible; (Hort.) pinch back (plant); make (clock, factory, etc.) cease working; **enough to** ∼ **a clock,** (colloq., of face etc.) very ugly. **3.** cut off, suspend, decline customary giving of or permission for, (*shall stop your wages, holidays, meetings; the cost must be stopped out of his salary*); ∼ (**payment of**), direct one's banker not to honour (cheque); ∼ **payment,** declare oneself insolvent. **4.** obtain desired pitch from (string of violin etc.) by pressing at appropriate point with finger, so shortening vibrating length; DOUBLE¹-*stopping*. **5.** *v.i.* cease, come to an end, (*noise, annuity, stops;* ∼ **dead** or **short,** cease abruptly); cease from motion or speaking or action, make a halt or pause, (*car stopped outside the house; he stopped in the middle of a sentence; my watch, his heart, has stopped; train does not stop at* or *before Exeter; he never stops to think*); ∼ **at nothing,** be ruthless; ‖∼'**ping train** (stopping at many intermediate stations). **6.** (colloq.) remain, stay, sojourn, (*shall stop in bed, at home; are you going to stop for the sermon?; have been stopping in Cornwall with friends*). **7.** *v.t.* ‖provide with *stops,* punctuate, (*a badly spelt and stopped letter*). **8.** (Naut.) make fast, stopper, (cable etc.). **9.** *∼ by,* call at (place, or abs.); ∼ **down,** (Photog.) reduce aperture of (lens, or abs.) with diaphragm; ∼ **off,** fill in (part of mould not to be used) with sand; ∼ **off,** ∼ **over,** break one's journey; ∼'**off,** ∼'**over,** a break in one's journey; ∼ **out,** cover (part of area) to prevent printing, etching, etc., there. **10.** Hence ∼'**p**AGE (3) n. **11.** ∼'**cock,** externally-operated valve inserted in pipe to regulate passage of contents; ∼'**gap,** temporary substitute; ∼'**go,** alternate cessation and recommencement of progress; ∼**-lamp,** light on rear of motor vehicle showing when brakes are applied; ∼ **light,** (1) red traffic-light, (2) = *stop-lamp;* ‖∼**-press,** (late news) inserted in newspaper after printing has begun; ∼ **valve** (closing pipe against passage of liquid); ∼**-volley,** (Lawn Tennis) checked volley close to net, dropping ball dead on other side; ∼**-watch** (with mechanism for instantly starting and stopping it at will, used in accurate timing of races etc.). [ME, f. OE *-stoppian* = MLG *stoppen,* OHG *stopfōn,* WG f. LL *stuppare* STUFF 5 (see ESTOP)]

stŏp² n. **1.** stopping or being stopped, pause, check, (*put a stop to; make, come to, bring to, a stop; train runs from London to Edinburgh without a stop*); place of regular stopping of bus, train, etc. **2.** sign used to clarify meaning in written matter, punctuation-mark, esp. comma, semi-colon, colon, or FULL¹ stop; (in telegrams etc.) = PERIOD 5. **3.** (Mus.) change of pitch effected by stopping (see prec. 4), (in organ) row of pipes of one character, knob etc. by which these are brought into action; (fig.) manner of speech adopted to produce particular effect (*can put on* or *pull out the pathetic, blustering, virtuous,* etc., *stop at will;* **with all the** ∼**s out,** exerting extreme effort). **4.** batten, peg, or the like, meant to stop motion of something at fixed point; (Bridge) card(s) stopping suit. **5.** (Opt. & Photog.) diaphragm, (device reducing) effective diameter of lens; (Phonet.) consonant sound made by

closure of organs followed by audible release of air, as *g, k, t, p;* (Naut.) small line used as lashing. **6.** ∼**-drill** (with shoulder limiting depth of penetration); ∼**-knob** (controlling organ-stop); ∼**-order** (to stockbroker to buy or sell on stock's reaching specified price, or preventing payment of funds in custody of lawcourt). **7.** Hence ∼'LESS *a.* [ME, f. prec.]

stŏpe n. steplike part of mine where ore etc. is being extracted. [app. cogn. w. STEP²]

stŏ'ppage. See STOP¹ 10.

stŏ'pper n., & *v.t.* **1.** n. In vbl senses; plug for closing bottle etc. usu. of same material as the vessel (**put a** ∼ **on,** bring about cessation of); implement for pressing down tobacco in pipe-bowl; (Naut.) rope, clamp, double claw, etc., for checking and holding rope cable or chain cable; (Bridge) = prec. 4. **2.** *v.t.* close or secure with stopper. [ME, f. STOP¹ + -ER¹]

stŏ'pple n., & *v.t.* **1.** n. stopper of bottle or other vessel; **ear-plug.* **2.** *v.t.* close with stopple. [ME; partly f. STOP¹ + -LE 1, partly f. ESTOPPEL]

stŏr'age n. storing of goods, data, etc., method of doing this (COLD¹ *storage*); space available for it; cost of warehousing; ∼ **battery, cell,** apparatus for storing electrical energy in a chemical form, accumulator; ∼ **heater,** electric heater accumulating heat outside peak hours, for later release. [f. STORE + -AGE]

stŏr'ax n. (tree of genus *Styrax* yielding) fragrant resin formerly used as perfume; (liquid) ∼, balsam got from oriental tree of genus *Liquidambar.* (L f. Gk, var. of STYRAX)

store n., a., & *v.t.* **1.** n. abundance, provision, stock of something ready to be drawn upon, (*has a store, a good store, stores, of wine, wit, anecdotes, wisdom*); **in** ∼, kept in readiness, about to come, destined or intended *for* (*I have, tomorrow has, a surprise in store for you*). **2.** place where things are kept for sale, **shop,* ‖large commercial establishment selling goods of many different kinds, (DEPARTMENT *store;* ‖**the** ∼**s,** such establishment(s) opp. ordinary shops); warehouse for temporary keeping of furniture etc. **3.** ‖device in computer for storing and retrieving data or instructions. **4.** (in *pl.*) articles of particular kind or for special purpose accumulated for use, supply of things needed, (*military, naval,* etc., *stores;* MARINE *stores*). **5. lay, put,** or **set** ∼ **by** or **on,** reckon precious or important (esp. *set no great store by*). **6.** *a.* kept for future use; (of cattle etc.) not yet (being) fattened; **bought at shop, esp.* (of clothes) ready-made. **7.** **∼-front,* (rooms etc. at) street front of a store; ∼'**house,** place where things are stored up, granary etc., (esp. fig.; *person, book, is a storehouse of information* etc.); ∼'**keeper,** person in charge of store(s), **shopkeeper;* ∼'**man** (in charge of, or employed to handle, stored goods); ∼**-room** (in which household or other supplies are kept); ∼**-ship** (carrying stores for fleet, garrison, etc.). **8.** *v.t.* stock or furnish adequately with or *with* something useful (usu. with knowledge or the like; *store your mind with facts; a well-stored memory*). **9.** put in store, lay up or *up* or *away* for future use; deposit (furniture etc.) in a warehouse for temporary keeping. **10.** (Of receptacle) hold, keep, contain, have storage-accommodation for (*a single cell can store enough energy for 12 months' operation*). **11.** Hence **stŏr'ABLE** *a.* [ME, f. obs. *astore* n. & v. f. OF (*estore* f.) *estorer* v. f. L *instaurare* renew; cf. RESTORE]

stŏr'ey, stŏr'ȳ², n. any of the parts into which a house or building is divided horizontally, the whole of the rooms etc. having a continuous floor, (*fell from a third-storey window; a house of five storeys*); thing forming horizontal division; **upper** ∼, (joc.) the brain or intellect; hence **(-)stŏr'eyED**², **(-)stŏr'ȳED**², **(-**rĭd) *a.* [ME, f. AL *historia* HISTORY (perh. orig. meaning a tier of painted windows or sculpture)]

stŏr'iāted *a.* decorated with artistic historical, legendary, or emblematic designs; hence ∼A'TION n. [f. HISTORIATED]

stŏr'ied¹ (-rĭd) *a.* (literary). celebrated in legend,

associated with legends or stories or history; adorned with legendary or historical representations. [f. STORY[1] and *story* v. adorn thus + -ED[1,2]]

storied[2]. See STOREY.

stork n. tall stately wading bird of family Ciconiidae, the best-known species pure white except for black wing-tips, long reddish bill, and red feet, sometimes nesting on buildings, and in the nursery the pretended bringer of babies; KING[1] *Stork*; ∼'s-bill, plant of genus *Pelargonium* or *Erodium*. [OE *storc*, = OS *stork*, OHG *stor(a)h*, ON *storkr* f. Gmc **sturkaz* (prob. rel. to STARK[1], from its rigid posture)]

storm n. & v. **1.** n. violent disturbance of the atmosphere with thunder (THUNDER*storm*), strong wind, or heavy rain or snow (SNOW[1]*storm*) or hail (HAIL[1]*storm*); ∼ **in a teacup**, great excitement over trivial matter. **2.** (Meteorol.) wind intermediate between gale and hurricane (on Beaufort scale, of 55–72 m.p.h.). **3.** violent disturbance of the established order in human affairs, tumult, agitation, war, invasion, dispute, etc. (∼ **and stress**, period of fermenting ideas and unrest in person's or nation's life [f. G. *sturm und drang*, used as title of a play characteristic of the literary movement in Germany *c.* 1770–82]). **4.** violent shower *of* missiles or outbreak *of* hisses, applause, indignation, etc. **5.** direct assault by troops on fortified place, capture *of* place by such assault; **take by** ∼, capture thus, (fig.) rapidly captivate (audience or person). **6.** ∼**-belt**, tract in which storms are frequent or regular; ∼**-bird**, storm PETREL; ∼**-bound**, prevented by storms from leaving port or continuing voyage; ∼**-centre**, point to which wind blows spirally inward in cyclonic storm, (fig.) subject etc. upon which agitation or disturbance is concentrated; ∼**-cloud**, heavy rain-cloud, (fig.) state of affairs that threatens disturbances; ∼**-cock**, missel-thrush; ∼**-collar**, high coat-collar that can be turned up and fastened; ‖∼**-cone**, tarred-canvas cone hoisted as warning of high wind, upright for north and inverted for south; ∼**-door**, additional outer door for protection in bad weather or winter; ‖∼**-finch**, storm PETREL; ∼**-glass**, sealed tube containing a solution of which the clarity is thought to change when storms approach; ‖∼**-lantern**, hurricane lamp; *storm* PETREL; ∼**-sail** (of smaller size and stouter canvas than the corresponding one used in ordinary weather); ∼**-signal**, device warning of an approaching storm; ∼**-troops**, (1) shock-troops, (2) Nazi political militia (∼**-trooper**, member of this); ∼**-window**, additional outer sash-window used like storm-door; ∼**-zone**, = *storm-belt*. **7.** Hence ∼'LESS, ∼'PROOF[2], adjs. **8.** v.i. (Of wind, rain, etc.) rage, be violent; move violently or angrily (*stormed out of the meeting*). **9.** talk violently, rage, bluster, (*at* or *against*). **10.** v.t. & i. attack or capture by storm (∼'**ing-party**, detachment ordered to begin assault). [OE, = OS *storm*, OHG *sturm*, ON *stormr* f. Gmc **sturmaz* prob. f. **stur*- STIR[1]]

storm'm|y a. of marked violence, raging, vehement, boisterous, (*stormy wind, sea, passions, temper, abuse*); subject to or troubled with storms (lit. or fig.; *a stormy coast, night, debate, life*); associated with or threatening storms (*a stormy sunset; stormy* PETREL); hence ∼ILY[2] adv., ∼INESS n. [ME, f. prec. + -Y[2]]

stor'y[1] n. **1.** past course of person's or institution's life (*his story is an eventful one; in our rough island-story*). **2.** account given of an incident or series of events (*they all tell the same story; according to his own story, which may or may not be true*); **the** (**old,**) **old** (or **same old**) ∼, (fig.) the very familiar course of events; **to cut** or **make a long** ∼ **short** (formula excusing omission of details); **it is quite another** ∼ **now,** (fig.) things have greatly changed; **the** ∼ **goes,** it is said. **3.** piece of narrative, tale of any length told or printed in prose or verse of actual or fictitious events, legend, myth, anecdote, novel, romance, (*tell me a story; but is the story true?*); narrative or descriptive item of news; **good** or **funny** ∼, amusing anecdote often embodying witticism or ludicrous situation; SHORT *story*; **but that is another** ∼ (formula for breaking off and tantalizing reader with allusion). **4.** main facts or plot of novel or epic or play (*reads only for the story; the story is the least part of the book*). **5.** facts or experiences that deserve narration (*that face must have a story belonging to it*). **6.** (colloq. or childish). lie, fib; liar (*oh, you story!*). **7.** ∼**-book** (containing story or stories); ∼**-book ending** etc. (romantically happy); ∼**-line,** = sense 4; ∼**-teller,** (1) person esp. in Orient making a living by telling stories to audiences, person who tells stories to audience of children, (2) writer of stories, (3) retailer of anecdotes in society, (4, colloq.) liar. [ME *storie* f. AF *estorie* (OF *estoire*) f. L (as HISTORY)]

stor'y[2]. See STOREY.

stoup (-ōōp) n. flagon, beaker, drinking-vessel; holy-water basin. [ME, f. ON *staup* = OE *stēap*, OHG *stouf* f. Gmc **staupaz, -am*, cogn. w. STEEP[2]]

stout a. & n. **1.** a. brave, doughty, resolute, vigorous, sturdy, stubborn, staunch, (*made a stout resistance; a stout opponent*); ∼ **fellow,** (arch. or colloq.) brave fighter etc.; **a** ∼ **heart,** courage; ∼**-hear'ted,** courageous. **2.** of considerable thickness or strength (*a stout stick, ship,* etc.); corpulent, bulky, tending to fatness. **3.** Hence ∼ISH[1] 2 a., ∼'LY[2] adv., ∼'NESS n. **4.** n. strong dark beer brewed with roasted malt or barley. [ME, f. AF & dial. OF (*e*)*stout* f. WG **stult-*, perh. rel. to STILT]

stove[1] n., & v.t. **1.** n. closed apparatus in which heat is produced by combustion of fuel or electrically for use in warming rooms, cooking, etc.; ‖(Hort.) hothouse with artificial heat; ∼**-enamel** (heat-proof kind produced by treatment of enamelled objects in stove); ∼**-pipe** (conducting smoke and gases from stove to chimney); ∼**-pipe hat,** (colloq.) tall silk hat. **2.** v.t. ‖force or raise (plants) in stove. [ME = sweating-room, f. MDu., MLG *stove*, OHG *stuba* f. Gmc **stubh-*, perh. rel. to STEW[2]]

stove[2]. See STAVE[2].

stow (-ō) v.t. pack (goods etc.) in right or convenient places without waste of room; (Naut.) place (cargo, provisions) in proper place and order; fill (receptacle) with articles compactly arranged; (sl., esp. in *imper.*) abstain from, cease to indulge in (∼ **it,** cease talking etc.); ∼ **away,** place (thing) where it will not cause obstruction, conceal oneself on board ship etc. so as to travel without charge or escape unseen; ∼'**away,** (1) person who does this, (2) place where things may be stowed away; hence ∼'AGE (1, 3, 4) n. [ME, f. *bestow*; in Naut. use perh. infl. by Du. *stouwen*]

STP abbr. Professor of Sacred Theology [f. L *Sanctae Theologiae Professor*]; standard temperature and pressure.

str. abbr. strait; stroke (oar).

strabi'sm|us (-z-) n. (Path.) squinting, squint; hence ∼AL, ∼IC, adjs. [mod. L, f. Gk *strabismos* (*strabizō* squint f. *strabos* squinting; see -ISM)]

Strad n. (colloq.) Stradivarius. [abbr.]

strad'dle v. & n. **1.** v.i. take or be in attitude with legs wide apart, (of legs) be wide apart. **2.** v.t. stand or sit across (thing) thus (*cannot straddle his horse; stood straddling the ditch*); part (one's legs) widely; drop shots or bombs short of and beyond (target etc.); (fig.) vacillate between two policies etc. regarding (an issue). **3.** n. act of straddling (lit. or fig.); doubling of stakes in poker; (St. Exch.) option giving holder the right of either calling for or delivering stock at fixed price. [alt. of *striddle*, back-form. f. *striddlings* astride f. *strid-* = STRIDE; see -LE 3]

Stradivar'ius (-ār'-, -ār'-) n. violin or other stringed instrument made by Antonio Stradivari of Cremona (d. 1737) or his followers. [Latinized f. *Stradivari*]

strafe (-ahf) v.t. & n. (sl.) **1.** v.t. bombard, harass with shells, bombs, sniping, etc.; reprimand; abuse; thrash. **2.** n. piece of strafing. [joc. adaptation of G 1914 catchword *Gott* ∼ (God punish) *England*]

strä′ggl|e *v.i.*, & *n.* **1.** *v.i.* stray from the main body, fail to remain compact (*straggling village*), get dispersed, proceed in scattered irregular order (*crowd straggled along*), be sporadic, occur here and there, (of plant, beard, etc.) grow long and loose; hence ∼ER¹ *n.*, ∼Y² *a.* **2.** *n.* body or group of straggling or scattered persons or things. [ME, perh. alt. f. *strackle* frequent. of dial. *strake* go, rel. to STRETCH; see -LE 3]

straight (-āt) *a.*, *n.*, & *adv.* **1.** *a.* without curve or bend, extending uniformly in same direction, (of line, Geom.) lying evenly between any two of its points; (of arch) flat-topped; (of person's back) not bowed; (of hair) not curly or wavy; (of knee) not bent; (of legs) not bandy or knock-kneed; (of skirt) not flared; coming direct from its source; undiluted, unmodified; successive (*ten straight wins; beaten in straight sets*). **2.** (Of aim, look, blow, course) going direct to the mark; upright, honest, candid, not evasive, (*straight dealings, answer, speaking; is perfectly straight, straight as a die, in all his dealings*); (of thinking) logical, not swayed by emotion; (of drama etc.) without music and not portraying abnormal behaviour etc.; (colloq., of music) not jazzlike. **3.** in proper order or place or condition, duly arranged, level, symmetrical, (*are the pictures, is my tie, hair, straight?*); (sl.) conventional, respectable, heterosexual; **put things** ∼, get rid of disorder; *get, keep, put, set, the facts* or RECORD² *straight*. **4.** ∼ **and narrow**, the path of rectitude; ∼ **bat**, (Cricket) bat held vertically, (fig.) honourable behaviour; ∼-**edge**, bar with one edge accurately straight, used for testing; ∼-**eight**, motor vehicle with eight cylinders in line; ∼ **eye**, ability to detect deviation from the straight; ∼ **face** (intentionally expressionless, esp. avoiding smile though amused); ||∼ **fight**, (Polit.) direct contest between two candidates; *straight* FLUSH⁵ (cf. sense 6); ∼ **man**, person who says things so that comedian can make jokes about them; *∼ **razor** (cut-throat); *∼ **ticket**, (voting for) party programme or candidate-list without modification; ∼ **tip**, hint (esp. as to likely winner of race or prospects of investment) got from good authority; ∼′**way**, (arch.) at once, immediately. **5.** Hence ∼EN¹ *v.t.* & *i.* (∼**en up**, stand erect after bending), ∼′LY² *adv.*, ∼′NESS *n.* **6.** *n.* straight condition (**on the** ∼, opp. *on the* BIAS¹; **out of the** ∼, crooked); straight part of something, esp. concluding stretch of racecourse (*they were level as they reached the straight*); (sl.) straight person; sequence of five cards in poker. **7.** *adv.* in a straight line, direct, without deviation or hesitation or circumlocution, (*comes straight from Paris; is making straight for a precipice; I told him straight, told it him straight out*); **go** ∼, (fig.) not be dishonest or criminal; *straight from the* SHOULDER. **8.** in right direction, with good aim, (*shoot straight*); correctly (*does not see straight*); (arch.) at once, immediately. **9.** ∼ **away**, (colloq.) immediately; *∼′**away**, straight (course etc.), straightforward; ∼ **off**, (colloq.) without hesitation, deliberation, etc., (*cannot tell you straight off*). **10.** ∼-**bred**, not cross-bred; ∼-**cut**, (of tobacco) cut lengthwise into long silky fibres; *∼-**out**, (Polit. etc.) uncompromising. [ME, p.p. of STRETCH]

straightfor′ward (-āt) *a.* honest, open, frank; (of task etc.) presenting no complications; hence ∼LY² *adv.*, ∼NESS *n.* [f. prec. (f + FORWARD¹]

strain¹ *v.* **1.** *v.t.* stretch tightly, make taut; exercise to greatest possible or beyond legitimate extent, press to extremes, wrest or distort from true intention or meaning; = STRETCH 2; *strain every* NERVE; ∼ one's **ears, eyes, voice,** etc., listen etc. to best of one's power (see also sense 4); ∼ one's **authority, powers, rights,** etc., apply them beyond their province or in violation of their true intention. **2.** hug (person) *to* oneself or one's breast etc. **3.** (in *p.p.*) produced under compulsion or by effort, artificial, forced, constrained, not spontaneous or natural, (*strained manner, laugh, cordiality,* etc.); ∼ed

interpretation etc. (involving unreasonable assumption as to grammar etc.). **4.** overtask, injure or try or imperil by over-use or making of excessive demands, (*take care not to strain your eyes, voice,* etc.; *for fear of straining his followers' loyalty; has strained a muscle, his leg, his heart,* etc.); ∼ one**self**, injure oneself by effort, (fig.) make undue exertions; ∼**ed relations,** dangerous or unpleasant tension between parties who have tried each other's forbearance too far. **5.** *v.i.* make intense effort, strive intensely *after,* tug *at,* hold out with difficulty under or *under* pressure, (*the straining horses, masts; plants straining upwards to the light; dogs, horses, rowers, strain at the leash, collar, oar; porter straining under his load; strains too much after epigram, effect,* etc.). **6.** *v.t.* & *i.* clear (liquid) of solid matter by passing through sieve or other ∼′ER¹ (2) *n.*; filter (solids) *out* from liquid; (of liquid) percolate; ∼ **at a gnat,** be unduly scrupulous or fussy about trifles (w. ref. to Matt. 23:24, where sense is prop. 'strain a liquid if it contains even a gnat'). **7.** Hence ∼′ABLE *a.* [ME, OF *estreindre estrei(g)n-* f. L *stringere strict-* draw tight]

strain² *n.* **1.** pull, stretching force, tension, demand upon or force that tries cohesion or strength or stability of resources, exertion required to meet such demand or to do something difficult, injury or change of structure resulting from such exertion or force, (*the strain on the rope was tremendous; was a great strain on my resources, attention, credulity; could not stand* or *take the strain,* lit. or fig.; *the strains of modern life; has a strain in his leg; is suffering from strain* or *overstrain*); **at** (**full**) ∼ or **on the** ∼, exerted to the utmost. **2.** (Phys.) condition of a body subjected to stress, molecular displacement; quantity measuring this, equal to amount of deformation usu. divided by original dimension. **3.** (in *sing.* or *pl.*) burst or snatch or spell of music or poetry (*martial, inspiriting, pathetic,* etc., *strains; heard strains of 'Tosca' from the bathroom*). **4.** tone or style adopted in talking or writing, tendency of discourse, (*he went on in another strain; and much more in the same strain*). [ME, f. prec.]

strain³ *n.* **1.** breed of animals, plants, cells, etc.; human stock or family (*comes of a good strain*). **2.** moral tendency forming part of a character (*there is a strain of weakness, ferocity, mysticism, in him*). [ME, 'progeny', f. OE *∗strēon* gain, procreation]

strait *a.* & *n.* **1.** *a.* (arch.) narrow, limited, confined or confining. **2.** ∼ **gate,** limitation of access (w. ref. to Matt. 7:14); ∼-**jacket** or ||-**waistcoat,** (*n.*) strong garment put on violent person to confine arms, (fig.) restrictive measures, (*v.t.*) confine thus (lit. or fig.); ∼-**laced,** (fig.) severely virtuous, morally scrupulous, puritanic. **3.** (arch.) strict, rigorous, (*straitest sect,* w. ref. to Acts 26:5). **4.** Hence ∼′LY² *adv.*, ∼′NESS *n.,* (arch.). **5.** *n.* (in *sing.* or *pl.*) narrow passage of water connecting two seas or large bodies of water; (usu. in *pl.*) difficult position, need, distress, (*in desperate, dire, straits*). [ME *streit,* f. OF *estreit* tight, narrow (place), f. L *strictus* STRICT]

strai′ten *v.t.* & *i.* **1.** (arch.) make or become narrow. **2.** *v.t.* restrict in range or scope; ∼ed **circumstances,** inadequate means of living, poverty; ∼ed **for** or **in,** (arch.) not amply supplied with. [f. prec. + -EN⁶]

strāke *n.* continuous line of planking or plates from stem to stern of ship (GARBOARD *strake*); section of iron rim of wheel. [ME, app. f. *∗strak-,* cogn. w. OE *streccan* STRETCH]

stramō′nium *n.* (drug, much used in treatment of asthma, from dried leaves of) datura. [mod. L, perh. f. Tartar *turman* horse-medicine]

strānd¹ *n.* & *v.* **1.** *n.* (rhet. or poet.) margin of sea, lake, or river, esp. foreshore. **2.** *v.t.* & *i.* run aground; (in *p.p.*) in difficulties, unable to get along esp. for want of funds or other resources, left behind while others advance. [OE, = MLG *strand-,* ON *strönd*]

strānd² *n.,* & *v.t.* **1.** *n.* one of the strings or wires that are twisted together to make a rope etc.; constituent filament in necklace, hair, DNA, etc.; (fig.) element or strain in any composite whole. **2.** *v.t.* break a strand in (rope); arrange in strands. [ME; orig. unkn.]

strānge (-nj) *a.* **1.** foreign, alien, (*in a strange land*), not one's own (*worship strange gods*), not familiar or well known (*to*), (*cannot play on a strange ground, with a strange racket*; *the place, work, handwriting, is strange to me*). **2.** novel, peculiar, eccentric, surprising, unaccountable, (*it is a strange thing, story*; *how strange that you should not have heard!*; *wears the strangest clothes*; *truth is stranger than fiction*; *repeating the question with strange persistence*); **feel** ∼, not be in one's usual condition, esp. feel dizzy etc. (see also sense 4); **it feels** ∼, it is an unaccustomed sensation; ∼ **particle**, (Phys.) elementary particle classified as unusual according to a property conserved in strong interactions; ∼ **to say**, (parenth.) it is surprising that. **3.** Hence ∼**LY**² (-njlĭ) *adv.* **4.** fresh or unaccustomed *to*, unacquainted, bewildered, (*am strange to the work*); **am quite** ∼ **here**, do not know my way about or the people etc.; **feel** ∼, feel not at home, out of one's element etc. (see also sense 2). **5.** Hence ∼**NESS** (-njn-) *n.* [ME, f. OF *estrange* f. L *extraneus* EXTRANEOUS]

strā'nger (-nj-) *n.* **1.** foreigner, person in a country or town or company that he does not belong to, person unknown to or *to* oneself or another; person entirely unaccustomed *to* some feeling or practice or experience; floating tea-leaf etc. held to foretell arrival of a visitor. **2. am a** ∼ **here, to the town,** etc., do not know my way about etc.; ||**I spy** ∼**s**, (in House of Commons) I demand withdrawal of all but members and officials; **make a, no,** ∼ **of,** treat distantly, cordially; **you are quite a** ∼, you are seldom seen here now; **he is no, a,** ∼ **to me,** I know, do not know, him; **is a, no,** ∼ **to,** has had no, much, experience of; **the little** ∼, (joc.) new-born child. [ME, f. OF *estranger* f. Rom. *extranearius* f. L (as prec.; see -ER² (2))]

strā'ngle (-nggel) *v.t.* throttle, kill by external compression of throat; (of collar etc.) squeeze (neck); (fig.) hamper or suppress (movement, impulse, cry, etc.); ∼**hold,** wrestling hold that throttles opponent, deadly grip (lit. or fig.). [ME, f. OF *estrangler* f. L *strangulare* f. Gk *straggalaō* (*straggalē* halter; cf. *straggos* twisted)]

strā'ngler *n.* In vbl senses; ||throttle of petrol engine. [f. prec. + -ER¹]

strā'ngles (-nggelz) *n. pl.* (usu. treated as *sing.*) infectious streptococcal fever of horse, ass, etc. [pl. of *strangle* n. f. STRANGLE]

strā'ngūl|āte (-ngg-) *v.t.* (Path. & Surg.) prevent circulation through (vein, intestine, etc.) by compression; remove (tumour) etc. by binding with cord; ∼**ated hernia** (in which constriction arrests circulation in protruding part). [f. L (as STRANGLE) + -ATE³]

strāngūlā'tion (-ngg-) *n.* strangling or being strangled; strangulating. [f. L *strangulatio* (as prec.; see -ATION)]

strā'ngūrӯ (-ngg-) *n.* disease in which urine is passed painfully and in drops; so **strāngūr'ĭous** (-ngg-) *a.* [ME, f. L f. Gk *straggouria* (*stragx -ggos* drop squeezed out, *ouron* urine; see -Y¹)]

străp *n.,* & *v.t.* (-pp-). **1.** *n.* strip of leather; strip of leather or other flexible material with buckle or other fastening for holding things together or other purpose (CHIN-*strap,* SHOULDER-*strap*); loop for grasping to steady oneself in moving vehicle; strip of metal used to secure or connect, leaf of hinge, etc.; (Bot.) tongue-shaped part in floret; (**the**) ∼, chastisement with a strap. **2.** ∼**'hanger,** bus or train passenger who has to stand and hold strap for lack of sitting-space; ∼ **hinge** (with long extensions to be screwed to door and wall etc.); ∼**laid,** (of rope) made by laying ropes side by side and joining them into a flat band; ∼**-oil,** (sl.) beating given with strap; ∼**-work,** ornamentation imitating plaited straps. **3.** Hence

∼'**LESS** *a.,* (of garment) without (shoulder-)straps. **4.** *v.t.* secure with strap (*up, down,* etc.); (colloq., esp. in *p.p.*) subject to dearth; close (wound), bind (part), up or *up* with adhesive plaster or ∼'**PING**¹ (4) *n.*; flog with strap; (in *pres. part.* as *a.*) big, tall, sturdy, (*a strapping girl, fellow*), whence ∼'**PER**¹ *n.* [dial. form of STROP]

strappā'dō *n.* (*pl.* ∼**s**), & *v.t.* (Hist.) **1.** *n.* torture inflicted by securing person's hands or other part in ropes, raising him, and letting him fall till brought up with jerk by taut rope. **2.** *v.t.* subject to strappado. [f. F (*e*)*strapade* f. It. *strappata* (*strappare* snatch)]

strǎss *n.* = PASTE¹ 6. [G, f. name of inventor, Josef *Strasser* (18th c.)]

strata(l). See STRATUM.

strǎ'tagem *n.* (an) artifice, trick(ery), device(s) for deceiving enemy, (*devised a stratagem*; *must be effected by stratagem*). [ME, f. F *stratagème* f. L *stratagema* f. Gk *stratēgēma* f. *stratēgeō* be a general (*stratēgos,* f. *stratos* army + *agō* lead)]

stratē'g|ĭc *a.* of, dictated by, serving the ends of, strategy (*strategic skill, considerations, movement, position*); (of materials) essential in war; (of bombing) designed to disorganize the enemy's internal economy and to destroy morale (opp. *tactical*); hence ∼**ICAL** *a.,* ∼**ICALLY** *adv.,* ∼**ICS** *n.* [f. F *stratégique* f. Gk *stratēgikos* (as prec.; see -IC)]

strǎ'tĕg|ӯ *n.* generalship, the art of war, (lit. or fig.); management of an army or armies in a campaign, art of so moving or disposing troops or ships or aircraft as to impose upon the enemy the place and time and conditions for fighting preferred by oneself, (cf. TACTICS); instance of, or plan formed according to, this; hence ∼**IST** (3) *n.* [f. F *stratégie* f. Gk *stratēgia* generalship (*stratēgos*; see STRATAGEM, -Y¹)]

strǎth *n.* (Sc.) broad mountain valley; ∼**spey'** (-ā'-), (music for) a slow Scottish dance (named f. *Strathspey* valley of the river Spey). [f. Gael. *srath*]

stratǐ'cŭlate *a.* (Geol.) arranged in thin layers. [f. STRATUM, after *vermiculate* etc.]

strǎ'tǐ|fӯ *v.t.* (esp. in *p.p.*) arrange in strata; construct in layers, social grades, etc.; so ∼**FICA'TION** *n.* (∼**ficational grammar,** treating language as comprising several structural layers with different syntactic rules). [f. F *stratifier* (as STRATUM; see -FY)]

stratǐ'graphӯ *n.* (Geol. etc.) (study of) order and relative position of strata; hence **strǎtǐ**GRA'PHIC(AL) *adjs.* [f. STRATUM + -I- + -GRAPHY]

strǎ'tō- *comb. form.* **1.** stratus, as: ∼**ci'rrus,** ∼**cu'mulus,** clouds combining features of stratus and cirrus or cumulus. **2.** stratosphere, as: ∼**-cruiser,** jet air-liner travelling in stratosphere; ∼**pause,** interface between stratosphere and ionosphere. [f. STRATUS or STRATUM + -O-]

stratǒ'cracӯ *n.* military government, domination by soldiers. [f. Gk *stratos* army + -CRACY]

strǎ'tosph|ēre *n.* layer of atmospheric air above troposphere, in most of which the temperature ceases to fall with increasing height, remaining constant; hence ∼**ĕ'rǐc** *a.* [f. foll. + -O- + SPHERE, after *atmosphere*]

strā't|um (-ah'-, -ā'-) *n.* (*pl.* ∼**a**). (Geol. etc.) layer, or set of successive layers, of any deposited substance; layer of atmosphere, biological tissue, or other structure; social grade (*the various strata of society*); hence ∼**AL** *a.* [L, = something spread or laid down, neut. p.p. (as n.) of *sternere* strew]

strā't|us (-ā'-, -ah'-) *n.* (*pl.* ∼**i** *pr.* -ī). continuous horizontal sheet of cloud. [L, p.p. of *sternere* (see prec.)]

straw¹ *n.* **1.** dry cut stalks of grain as material for bedding, thatching, packing, hats, fodder, etc., (*made of, thatched* etc. *with, straw*; *a load of straw*; *straw mattress, hat, rope,* etc.; **in the** ∼, (arch.) in parturition); **make bricks without** ∼, try to work without adequate means (w. ref. to Exod. 5: 7); **man of** ∼, stuffed effigy, imaginary person set up as opponent, surety, etc., person undertaking financial commitment without adequate means, sham argument set up for demolition); straw hat. **2.** single stalk or piece of straw; insignificant trifle (*is not worth a straw; don't care a straw*); hollow tube orig. of straw for sucking drink through; CHEESE[1] *straw*; **catch** or **grasp at a** ∼, resort to utterly inadequate expedient, like a drowning man; **the last** ∼, slight addition that makes something no longer bearable (as with camel's load), limit of tolerance or controllable vexation; ∼ **in the wind**, slight hint that suggests much. **3.** ∼**-board**, coarse cardboard made of straw pulp; *∼ **boss**, assistant foreman; ∼**-colour(ed)**, (of) pale yellow; ∼ **poll** or **vote**, unofficial balloting as test of strength of support; ∼**-worm**, caddis-worm. **4.** Hence ∼Y[2] *a*. [OE *strēaw*, = OS, OHG *strō*, ON *strá* f. Gmc *strawam, cogn. w. STREW]

straw[2] *v.t.* (arch.) strew. [f. var. of OE *stre(o)wian* STREW]

straw'berry *n*. (plant of genus *Fragaria*, with white flowers, trifoliate leaves, and) pulpy red fruit having surface studded with yellow seeds; **crushed** ∼, dull crimson colour; ∼ **blonde**, (woman with) yellowish-red (hair); ||**the** ∼ **leaves**, nobility of high rank, w. ref. to ornamentation of duke's, marquis's, and earl's coronet; ∼**-mark**, soft reddish birthmark; ∼ **pear**, (fruit of) W. Ind. cactaceous plant (*Hylocereus undatus*); *strawberry* ROAN[1]; ∼ **tongue**, red swollen tongue as in scarlet fever; ∼**-tree**, (1) evergreen tree (*Arbutus unedo*) bearing strawberry-like fruit, (2) Amer. spindle-tree with crimson pods. [OE *strēa(w)berige, strēowberige* (as STRAW[1], BERRY[1]; reason for name unknown)]

stray *v.i., n., & a.* **1.** *v.i.* wander, go aimlessly, deviate from the right way or from virtue, lose one's way, get separated from flock or companions or proper place; (in *p.p.*) that has gone astray. **2.** *n.* strayed domestic animal; strayed thing or person (WAIFS *and strays*); (esp. in *pl.*) electrical phenomena interfering with radio reception. **3.** *a.* strayed; scattered, sporadic, occurring or met with now and then or casually or unexpectedly, (*a few stray instances, a stray customer or two came in; hit by a stray bullet; lucky enough to find a stray taxi*); (Phys.) wasted or unwanted (*eliminate stray magnetic fields*). [ME, f. AF & OF *estrayer* v., AF (*a*)*strey* n. & *a.* f. OF *estraié* (as ASTRAY)]

streak *n. & v.* **1.** *n.* long narrow irregular line or band or layer-edge, esp. one distinguished by colour or substance and visible on a surface (*black with red streaks; a streak of light above the horizon*); line of bacteria etc. placed on culture medium; ∼ **of lightning**, flash (*like a* ∼ *of lightning, like a* ∼, swiftly). **2.** (fig.) strain, element, (*has a streak of humour, superstition,* etc., *in him*); spell, series, (*had a long winning streak*). **3.** Hence ∼'Y[2] *a.*; ∼**y bacon** (having alternate streaks of fat and lean). **4.** *v.t.* (usu. in *p.p.*) mark with streak(s). **5.** *v.i.* move very rapidly (like a streak of lightning); (colloq.) run through public place while indecently unclothed, whence ∼'ER[1], ∼'ING[1] (1), *ns.* [OE *strica* pen-stroke, = OHG *strich*, Goth. *striks* f. Gmc **strik-* STRIKE]

stream *n. & v.* **1.** *n.* body of water flowing in bed, river or (esp.) brook, (*on the banks of a stream;* UPSTREAM, DOWNSTREAM); hence ∼'LESS *a.*, ∼'LET *n.* **2.** flow of any liquid, onward moving fluid mass or crowd, (in *sing.* or *pl.*) large quantity of or *of* something that flows or moves along, (*saw a stream of lava; came out, went by, in a stream* or *streams; a stream* or *streams of blood, tears, people*); ||group of schoolchildren selected as being of similar ability for a given age; ∼ **of consciousness,** (literary style depicting) continuous flow of person's thoughts and conscious reactions to events; **on** ∼, (of factory etc.) in operation. **3.** current, direction of flow, (*with, against, the stream; the stream of tendency, thought, is the other way*); **go with the** ∼, do as others do. **4.** ∼**-anchor** (intermediate in size between bower and kedge esp. for use in warping); ∼'**line**, (*n.*) natural course of water or air currents, shape of aircraft, motor car,

etc., calculated to cause least resistance to motion, (*v.t.*) give a streamline form to, (fig.) simplify, make more efficient or better organized. **5.** *v.i.* flow or move as a stream; run with liquid (*streaming eyes, cold, windows*); (of banner, loose hair, etc.) float or wave in the wind. **6.** *v.t.* emit stream of (blood etc.); ||arrange (pupils of school) in streams. [OE *strēam*, = OS *strōm*, OHG *stroum*, ON *straumr* f. Gmc *straumaz f. IE **srou-* flow]

strea'mer *n*. pennon, ribbon attached at one end and floating or waving at the other; narrow strip of paper thus used; banner headline; (in *pl.*) aurora borealis. [ME, f. prec. + -ER[1]]

street *n*. **1.** town or village road that has (mainly) contiguous houses on one side or both, this with the houses; (*go down, across, the street; lives in the next street; window looks on the street; in Oxford Street,* **on 57th Street;* HIGH, MAIN[3], SIDE[1]-, etc., *street*); **in the** ∼, outside the houses, (of St. Exch. business) done after closing-time; KEY[1] *of the street;* MAN[1] *in* or **on the street;* **not in the same** ∼ **with,** (colloq.) utterly inferior to in ability etc.; **on the** ∼**s**, living by prostitution; ∼**s ahead (of)**, (colloq.) much superior (to); (**right**) **up** one's ∼, (colloq.) familiar or acceptable; WALK[1], WOMAN *of, the streets*. **2.** persons who live or work in a street; **the S**∼, street or district associated with particular occupation etc., esp. ||FLEET[2] Street or *WALL STREET. **3.** *street* ARAB; *∼'**car**, tram; ||∼ **cries** (of hawkers); ∼ **door**, main outer house-door opening on street; ∼**-sweeper**, person, or machine with revolving brush, employed for cleaning streets; ∼**-walker**, prostitute seeking customers in street. **4.** Hence (-)∼'ED[2] *a.*, ∼'WARD *adv. & a.* [OE *strǣt*, = OS *strāta*, OHG *strāz(z)a*, f. LL *strāta (via)* paved (way), fem. p.p. of *sternere* lay down]

strength (-ngth, -ngkth) *n*. **1.** being strong, degree or respect in which person or thing is strong, (*the strength of a man, rope, fortress, current, magnetic field, argument,. fleet; the strength of wine, acid, tea, evidence; strength of body, mind, will, judgement; his strength is in endurance; tensile, compressive, strength of a beam; has not the strength to lift a cup, to walk upstairs; that is beyond human, too much for my, strength*); argue etc. **from** ∼, from a strong position; **from** ∼ **to** ∼, with ever-increasing success, MEASURE[2] one's *strength with*, **on the** ∼ **of**, encouraged by or relying on or arguing from (*I did it on the strength of your promise*). **2.** what makes strong (*God is our strength; his strength is patience*). **3.** proportion of whole number present (*were there in great, full, strength*); full complement (*up to, below, strength*); **in** ∼, in large numbers; **on the** ∼, (Mil. etc.) on the muster-roll. **4.** Hence ∼'LESS *a.* [OE *strengþu*, = OHG *strengida* f. Gmc *strangiþō (as STRONG; see -TH[1])]

stre'ngthen (-ngth-, -ngkth-) *v.t. & i.* make or become stronger; ∼ person's **hand**(s), (fig.) encourage him to vigorous action. [ME, f. prec. + -EN[6]]

stre'nuous *a*. energetic, unrelaxing, ardently persistent; requiring exertion; hence ∼LY[2] *adv.*, ∼NESS *n.* [f. L *strenuus* brisk + -OUS]

strep *n*. (colloq.) = foll. [abbr.]

streptoco'cc|us *n*. (*pl.* ∼**i** *pr.* -kī). bacterium of genus *Streptococcus* that remains attached after fission and is usu. found in chains; hence ∼AL *a.* [f. Gk *streptos* twisted (*strephō* turn) + COCCUS]

streptomy'cin *n*. antibiotic produced by *Streptomyces griseus* bacteria, effective against some groups of disease-producing bacteria. [f. Gk *streptos* (as prec.) + *mukēs* fungus + -IN]

Stre'pyan *a. & n.* (of) a palaeolithic culture of N. Europe. [f. *Strépy* in Belgium, where remains of it were found, + -AN]

stress *n., & v.t.* **1.** constraining or impelling force of (*under, driven by, stress of weather, poverty,* etc.). **2.** effort, demand upon physical or mental energy, (STORM *and stress; subjected to great stress; times of slackness and times of stress*); ∼ **disease** (suffered by managers etc. sub-

jected to continual stresses); hence ∼'FUL *a*. **3.**
emphasis (**lay** ∼ **on,** convey that one attaches
importance to); accentuation, emphasis laid on
syllable or word, *a* or the accent, (*stress and quantity are
different metrical principles; the stress is on the first syllable,
on the adjective*). **4.** (Mech.) force per unit area exerted
between contiguous bodies or parts of a body. **5.**
Hence ∼'LESS *a*. **6.** *v.t.* lay (the) stress on, accent,
emphasize; subject to mechanical or physical or
mental stress. [ME, f. DISTRESS¹ or partly f. OF *estresse*
narrowness, oppression, f. Rom. **strictia* f. L *strictus*
STRICT]

stretch *v*., *n*., & *a*. **1.** *v.t.* make taut, tighten, straighten,
place somewhere in tight-drawn or outspread state,
(*the rope must be stretched tight; stretch a wire across the
road; with a canopy stretched over them*); (in *p.p.*) lying at
full length; ∼ (one**self,** or abs.), tighten muscles after
sleeping etc. by extending limbs etc. in various directions; ∼ one's **legs,** straighten them by walking as
relief from sitting etc.; *stretch* one's WINGS; ∼ person
on the ground, knock him sprawling; ∼ **out,** extend
(hand, foot, etc., or abs.) by straightening arm or leg,
make (money etc.) last for sufficient time. **2.** strain,
exert to utmost or beyond legitimate extent, make the
most of, do violence to, exaggerate, (*stretch a principle,
one's powers, one's credit*); ∼ **a point,** agree to
something beyond the limit normally allowed; ∼ (**the
truth,** or abs.), exaggerate, lie. **3.** *v.i.* have specified
length or extension, be continuous between points or
to or from a point, (*stretches from end to end, across the sky,
to infinity; road stretches away, memory stretches down, from
or to place, period*). **4.** *v.t.* & *i.* draw, be drawn or
admit of being drawn, out into greater length or
extension or size (*gloves, shoes, need stretching; it stretches
like elastic*). **5.** *n.* stretching or being stretched (*by a
stretch of authority, the imagination, language, etc.; with
every faculty on the stretch*); ∼ **marks** (esp. on abdomen
after pregnancy); hence ∼'Y² *a*. (colloq.). **6.** continuous expanse or tract or spell (*a stretch of road, open
country, etc.; works ten hours at a stretch*); (Naut.)
distance covered on one tack; (sl.) imprisonment for
a year or other term, period of service; *straight
side of race-track. **7.** *a.* able to stretch, elastic,
(*stretch fabric*). [OE *streccan,* = OHG *strecken,* f. WG
*strakkjan; cf. STRAIGHT]

stre'tcher *n.* In vbl senses; brick or stone laid with side
in face of wall (cf. HEADER); board in boat against
which rower presses feet; appliance, often of canvas
stretched on oblong frame, for carrying disabled or
dead person on; rod or bar as tie between chair-legs
etc.; wooden frame over which canvas of picture is
stretched; (arch. sl.) exaggeration, lie; ∼**-bearer,**
person who helps to carry stretcher; ∼**-bond,**
method of building in which all bricks are stretchers
but joints of contiguous courses do not coincide. [ME,
f. prec. + -ER¹]

stretto (stre'tō) *adv.* (Mus.) in quicker time. [It., =
narrow]

strew (-ōō) *v.t.* (*p.p.* ∼**n** or ∼**ed**). scatter (sand,
flowers, small objects) over a surface; (partly) cover
(surface, object) *with* small objects scattered. [OE
stre(o)wian, = OS *strōian,* OHG *strewen,* ON *strá,*
Goth. **straujan,* prob. f. IE **ster-* spread]

'strewth. Var. of 'STRUTH.

strī'|a *n.* (*pl.* ∼**ae**). **1.** (Anat., Zool., Bot., & Geol.)
linear mark on surface, slight ridge or furrow or score.
2. (Archit.) fillet between flutes of column. **3.** Hence
∼ATE² *a.*, ∼ATE³ *v.t.*, ∼A'TION, ∼ature, *ns.* [L]

strī'cken *a.* struck, esp. so as to afflict, (lit. or fig.);
stricken with fever; PANIC²-*stricken*); levelled with
strickle; *deleted (from etc.); ∼ **field,** (scene of)
pitched battle; ∼ **heart** (afflicted by strokes of grief);
∼ **in years,** (arch.) enfeebled by age. [arch. p.p. of
STRIKE]

stri'ckle *n.* rod used in strike-measure; whetting tool.
[OE *stricel* (cogn. w. STRIKE)]

strict *a.* precisely limited or defined, accurate, tense,

without irregularity or exception or deviation,
requiring or giving implicit obedience or exact
performance, not lax, (*in the strict sense; keep strict watch;
lives in strict seclusion; was told me in strict confidence; gave
strict orders; a strict code of laws or customs; strict parents,
schoolmaster, Muslim, discipline, morals*); hence ∼'LY²
adv. (∼**ly speaking,** if one uses words in their strict
sense), ∼'NESS *n.* [f. L *strictus* p.p. of *stringere* tighten]

stri'ctur|e *n.* **1.** (usu. in *pl.*) piece of censure, critical
remark (*on or upon*). **2.** (Path.) morbid narrowing of
some canal or duct in the body; hence ∼ED² (-kcherd)
a. [ME, f. L *strictura* (as prec.; see -URE)]

stride *v.* (**strode** *pr.* -ōd; **stri'dden** *pr.* -ĭ'd-) & *n.* **1.**
v.i. & *t.* walk with long steps. **2.** *v.t.* pass over (ditch
etc.) with one step; bestride, straddle. **3.** *n.* single step
esp. in respect of length, gait as determined by length
of stride, (*walks with vigorous strides or a vigorous stride*);
(fig., usu. in *pl.*) progress (*has made great strides towards
self-sufficiency*); (in *pl.*, sl.) trousers; **take in** (one's) ∼,
clear (obstacle) without changing gait to jump, (fig.)
find no serious impediment in; **get into** one's ∼,
(fig.) settle down steadily to the job in hand; **be
thrown out of** one's ∼, (fig.) be disconcerted. **4.**
distance between feet parted either laterally or as in
walking. [OE *strīdan,* = MLG *strīden* straddle]

stri'dent *a.* loud and harsh in sound; hence
stri'dENCY *n.*, ∼LY² *adv.* [f. L *stridere* creak; see -ENT]

stri'dul|āte *v.i.* (Esp. of cicada, grasshopper, etc.)
make shrill jarring sound; so ∼ANT *a.*, ∼A'TION *n.* [f. F
striduler f. L *stridulus* creaking (as prec.) + -ATE³]

strife *n.* contention, state of conflict, struggle between
opposed persons or things. [ME, f. OF *estrif;* cf. OF
estriver STRIVE]

stri'gil *n.* **1.** (Gk & Rom. Ant.) skin-scraper used by
bathers or after exercise. **2.** structure used by insect to
clean antennae etc. [f. L *strigilis* (*stringere* graze)]

stri'gōse *a.* **1.** (Bot.) with short stiff hairs or scales. **2.**
(Entom.) streaked. [f. L *striga* swath, furrow + -OSE¹]

strike *v.* (**struck; struck** or arch. STRICKEN) & *n.* **1.**
v.t. & *i.* bring into sudden contact with something
resistant, hit upon or (*up*)*on,* deliver stroke(s), come
sharply into contact with, (*struck me in the mouth, with
his fist, with a dart; strike* one's *foot against a stone,* one's
hand on the table, while the IRON¹ *is hot; struck by lightning;
lightning never strikes twice in same place; strike a blow,
strike, for freedom; hammer strikes on or strikes bell; ship
strikes rock or on rock or strikes; his head struck the kerb*);
send by striking (*strike ball out of court*); divert by
striking (*strike weapon up, down, aside*); jerk tackle in
order to secure hook in (fish, or abs.); discover (track
etc.); encounter (unusual thing etc.); (of serpent)
wound with fangs; ∼ **hands,** (arch.) touch or clasp
hands in sign of agreement made; ∼ **lucky,** have
lucky success; *strike* OIL¹; *strike it* RICH; ∼ **at,** seek to
strike; *strike at the* ROOT¹(*s*) *of*; ∼ **back,** strike or attack
in return, (of gas-burner) burn from internal point
before gas has become mixed with air; ∼ **home,** get
blow right to target; ∼ **out,** (1) hit from the shoulder
or violently, (2) use arms and legs in swimming, (3)
take vigorous action; ∼ **upon,** have (idea etc.)
luckily occur to one, (of light) illuminate; **struck on,**
(sl.) infatuated with. **2.** produce or record or bring
into specified state by stroke(s) or striking (*strike
sparks, fire, light, out of flint* or fig. *out of* person); (of
clock) indicate (time, or abs.), (of time) be indicated,
by sounding of bell etc. (*clock strikes, strikes the hour, five,
etc.; the hour has struck*); produce (musical note) by
touching key etc.; make (coin) by stamping; make
(bargain) as if by striking hands; ignite (match) by
rubbing against something; make (person *blind, deaf,*
etc.) at one stroke; ∼ **me dead!** (vulg. form of
asseveration); *strike* (arrive at) *the* HAPPY *medium*; ∼ **a
light,** produce light by striking match, (sl., as int.
expr. disgust etc.); ∼ **me pink!** (vulg. int. expr.
surprise); *strike the right* NOTE¹; ∼ **all of a heap,**
(colloq.) dumbfound; ∼ **down,** fell by striking (lit.,
or fig. of illness etc.); ∼ **off,** remove (head etc.) with

stroke, delete (name etc., esp. from register of solicitors etc. because of misconduct), produce (copies of document), = DASH¹ 2 *off*; ~ **out**, forge or devise (plan etc.), delete (item, name, etc.), (Baseball) dismiss (batter) by means of three strikes, be dismissed thus; ~ **through,** delete (word etc.) with stroke of pen; ~ **up,** start (acquaintance, conversation, etc.) rapidly or casually, (of band or performer) begin playing or singing (tune etc., or abs.). **3.** attract attention of, occur to mind of, produce mental impression on, impress *as*, (*what struck me was the generosity of the offer; struck my eye as I glanced over the letter; it strikes me that he may have misunderstood; an idea suddenly struck me; it strikes me as ridiculous*); **how does it** ~ **you?,** what do you think about it?. **4.** lower or take down (flag, sail, mast, tent); signify surrender by striking flag, surrender; ~ one's **flag,** surrender ship or fortress to enemy, (of admiral) resign command; ~ **tents,** break up camp. **5.** cease (work), cease work, (of employees) enter upon or be on a strike (sense 12; *strike for higher pay* etc.), *act thus against (employer). **6.** (cause to) penetrate (*struck a knife, terror, into his heart; ink strikes through paper in printing; cold struck through his clothes,* (in)*to his marrow; the wind strikes cold; rays strike through fog; plant strikes its roots into the soil, strikes root, or strikes*); (of oysters), attach themselves to bed; suddenly fill (person) *with* (terror, panic, dizziness, etc.); insert (cutting of plant) in soil to take root. **7.** direct one's course somewhere, take specified direction, diverge *to,* start *into,* (*then strike to the right; strike into or out of a track, subject,* etc.); ~ **in,** intervene in talk, often *with* suggestion etc., (of disease) attack interior of body from surface. **8.** level (grain etc. or the measure) in *strike-measure* (see sense 13). **9.** ascertain (balance) by deducting credit or debit from the other; arrive at (average, state of balance) by equalizing all items; compose (jury) esp. by allowing both sides to reject same number. **10.** suddenly and dramatically assume (attitude). **11.** Hence **strī́kABLE** *a.* **12.** *n.* employees' concerted refusal to work till some grievance is remedied; similar refusal to participate in other expected activity; **on** ~, acting on such refusal; ~'**bound,** immobilized by strike; ~**breaker,** employee brought in to replace striker; ~**pay,** allowance for subsistence made by trade union to employees on strike; GENERAL, HUNGER¹-, LIGHTNING, SIT-*down* or *stay-in,* SYMPATHETIC, UNOFFICIAL, *strike.* **13.** strickle; ~**measure** (when grain etc. is measured by passing a rod across top of heaped vessel to secure that it shall be full and no more). **14.** sudden success at finding petroleum, gold, etc., or in financial operations; sudden success or good luck. **15.** (Baseball). batter's unsuccessful attempt to hit pitched ball, or other event counting equivalently against him. **16.** act of striking (*lightning strike*; BIRD-*strike*); knocking-down of all bowling-pins with first ball; horizontal direction in geological structure; attack, esp. from the air. [OE *strīcan* go, stroke, = OHG *strīhhan,* f. WG *strīk-*]

strī́ker *n.* In vbl senses; player who is (next) to strike the ball in games; (Footb. etc.) player whose main function is to seek to score goals; device striking primer in gun. [ME, f. prec. + -ER¹]

strī́king¹ *n.* In vbl senses; ~**circle,** (Hockey) elongated semicircle in front of goal from within which ball must be hit in order to score; **within** ~**distance,** near enough to strike (lit. or fig.); ~**force,** (esp.) military body ready to attack at short notice; ~**plate** (against which end of spring-lock bolt strikes in closing). [ME, f. STRIKE + -ING¹]

strī́king² *a.* In vbl senses; sure to be noticed, arresting, impressive; (of clock) making sound to indicate hours etc.; hence ~LY² *adv.,* ~NESS *n.* [f. STRIKE + -ING²]

Strine *n.* comic transliteration of (alleged) Australian speech, e.g. *Emma Chissitt* = 'How much is it?'; (esp. uneducated) Australian English. [= *Australian* in Strine]

string *n.* & *v.* (**strung**). **1.** *n.* narrow cord; piece of this or of leather, ribbon, webbing, or other material, used for tying up, lacing, drawing or holding together, actuating puppet, etc., (*want some string and brown paper*; APRON-*strings*; BOW¹*string*); *two strings to* one's BOW¹, hence **first, second,** ~, person or thing that one's chief, alternative, reliance is set on; *have* person **on a** ~, entirely under one's influence; **pull (some)** ~**s,** exert (esp. hidden) influence; **pull the** ~**s,** be the real actuator of what another does; SHOE¹-*string*; **without** ~**s, with no** ~**s attached,** not subject to conditions. **2.** tough fibrous piece connecting two halves of pod in bean etc. **3.** piece of catgut etc. interwoven with others to form head of tennis etc. racket; piece of catgut, cord, wire, etc., yielding musical tone(s) when stretched and caused to vibrate in piano, harp, violin, or other instrument (**harp on one** ~, dwell on single subject; **touch the** ~**s,** play; **touch a** ~, (fig.) excite particular feeling in person's heart); (in *pl.*) stringed instruments in a band or orchestra; (*attrib.*) relating to or consisting of or imitative of stringed instruments (*string quartet, orchestra, tone*); hence (-)~ED² (-ngd) *a.* **4.** set of or usu. *of* objects strung together or persons or things of one kind coming one after another (*a string of heads, onions, symbols; filed past in a long string; a string of porters, cars, oaths, lies*); string-course; racehorses, collectively, under training at a particular stable. **5.** ~ **bag** (esp. for carrying parcels etc.); ~ **band** (esp. of stringed instruments only); ~**bark,** stringy-bark; ~ **bass,** double-bass; *~ **bean,** French or kidney bean with strings, (fig.) tall thin person; ~(-**board**), supporting timber in which ends of staircase steps are set; ~**course,** raised horizontal band or course of bricks etc. on a building; ~**halt,** = SPRING²-*halt*; ~**piece,** long timber supporting and connecting the parts of a framework; ~ **tie,** very narrow necktie; ~ **vest** (made of large meshes). **6.** Hence ~'LESS *a.* **7.** *v.t.* supply with string(s); tie with string. **8.** secure (bow) in state ready for use by bending it and slipping loop of string into notch, (fig., esp. in *p.p.*) tighten up or make ready or sensitive or excited (senses, nerves, resolution, or person in regard to them; *was strung up to do the deed*); HIGH(*ly*)-*strung.* **9.** thread (beads etc.) on a string; arrange in or as a string; remove strings from (beans). **10.** *(colloq.)* hoax. **11.** *v.t.* & *i.* (colloq.) ~ **along,** deceive (person); ~ **along with,** accompany; ~ **up,** (1) kill by hanging, (2) make tense. **12.** *v.i.* (of glue etc.) become stringy. **13.** (Bill.) make the preliminary strokes that decide which player shall begin. [OE *streng,* OHG *stranc,* ON *strengr* f. Gmc *strangiz*; cf. STRONG]

stringĕ'ndō (-nj-) *adv.* (Mus.) with increasing speed. [It. (*stringere,* f. as foll.)]

strī́ng|ent (-nj-) *a.* (Of rule, stipulation, etc.) strict, precise, requiring exact performance, leaving no loophole or discretion; (of money-market etc.) tight, hampered by scarcity, unaccommodating, hard to operate in; hence ~ENCY *n.,* ~entLY² *adv.* [f. L *stringere* draw tight; see -ENT]

strī́nger *n.* In vbl senses; string-board; longitudinal structural member in framework esp. of ship or aircraft; newspaper correspondent not on regularly paid staff. [f. STRING + -ER¹]

strī́ng|y *a.* **1.** fibrous, like string; ~**y-bark,** (Austral.) eucalyptus with tough fibrous bark. **2.** (Of liquid) viscous, ropy. **3.** Hence ~iNESS *n.* [f. STRING + -Y²]

strip¹ *v.* (-pp-) & *n.* **1.** *v.t.* denude, lay bare, deprive of or *of* covering or (all) clothing or appurtenance or property or rank (~**ped to the waist,** wearing nothing above waist); deprive (house) of furniture, (bed) of bedclothes, (ship) of rigging, (tree) of bark and branches; ~ (**down),** remove accessory fittings of or take apart (machine etc.) to inspect or adjust it; milk (cow) to last drop; remove the old hair from (dog); remove stems from (tobacco); tear thread from (screw), cogs from (gearwheel), etc.; remove (paint),

remove paint from, with solvent; DIVIDEND *stripping*.
2. pull or tear (covering lit. or fig., appurtenance,
property) off or *off* from or *from* something. **3.** *v.i.* take
off or *off* one's clothes, undress; ~**tease** *n.*, & *v.i.*,
(perform in) entertainment in which woman or
occas. man gradually undresses before an audience.
4. (of screw) lose thread; (of bullet) issue from rifled
gun without spin owing to loss of surface. **5.** *n.* act of
stripping, esp. of undressing in strip-tease; ~ **club** (at
which strip-tease performances are given); *~ **mine**
(worked by removing material that overlies ore etc.).
[ME, f. OE *strȳpan, -strīepan despoil, = MDu.
stroopen, OHG *stroufen* f. WG *straupjan]

strip[2] *n.* long narrow piece (*a strip of card, paper, cloth,
garden, territory*); narrow flat bar of iron or steel; ~
(**cartoon**), sequence of small drawings telling comic
or serial story in newspaper etc; ‖(colloq.) clothes
worn by members of football etc. team; AIR[1]-,
LANDING-, *strip*; **tear** person **off a** ~, (sl.) rebuke him
angrily; ~ **light**, tubular fluorescent lamp; ~ **mill**
(in which steel slabs are rolled into strips). [ME, f. or
cogn. w. MLG *strippe* strap, thong, prob. rel. to foll.]

strïpe *n.* **1.** long narrow band usu. of uniform breadth
on a surface from which it differs in colour or texture
(*black with a red stripe*; STAR[1]s *and Stripes*; *stripes on
soldier's trousers; zebra's stripes*); (Mil.) chevron etc. on
sleeve denoting rank (**get, lose, a** ~, be promoted,
demoted); *category of character, opinion, etc., (*a
man of that stripe; men of all political stripes*); hence
(-)**strïpED**[2] (-pt), **strï'pY**[2], *adjs.* **2.** (arch., usu. in
pl.) blow with scourge or lash. **3.** (in *pl.*, treated as
sing.; colloq.) tiger. [perh. back-form. f. *striped*; cf.
MDu., MLG *strīpe*, MHG *strīfe*; sense 2 ME, of
unkn. orig.]

strï'pling *n.* youth approaching manhood. [ME,
prob. f. STRIP[2]+-LING, in sense of having figure not
yet filled out]

strï'pper *n.* In vbl senses; device or solvent for
removing paint etc.; strip-tease performer. [f. STRIP[1]
+-ER[1]]

strïve *v.i.* (**strove** *pr.* -ōv; **strï'ven** *pr.* -ĭ'ven). struggle,
endeavour, try hard, make efforts, contend, (*to do,
for* or *after* desired end, *with* or *against* opponent or
temptation or difficulty); ~ **together,** or **with each
other,** quarrel, dispute pre-eminence etc. [ME, f. OF
estriver rel. to *estrif* STRIFE]

strö'be *n.* (colloq.) stroboscope; stroboscopic lamp.
[abbr.]

strobï'la *n.* (*pl.* ~e). = foll. 2. [mod. L, f. Gk *strobilē*
twisted lint-plug (*strephō* twist)]

strö'bile *n.* **1.** cone of pine etc.; imbricated flower of
hop. **2.** chain of segments in tapeworm; section of
jellyfish larva developing into new individual. [F, or
f. LL f. Gk *strobilos* (*strephō* twist)]

strö'bil|us *n.* (*pl.* ~**i** *pr.* -ī). = prec. 1. [LL (as prec.)]

strö'bo|scöpe *n.* instrument for determining speeds of
rotation etc. by intermittent vision with intervals
adjusted to make the rotating object appear stationary; lamp made to flash intermittently esp. for this
purpose; hence ~**scö'p**ıc *a.* [f. Gk *strobos* whirling +
-O-+-SCOPE]

strö'de. See STRIDE.

Strö'ganöff *a.* (Of meat) cut into strips and cooked in
sour-cream sauce (*beef Stroganoff*). [f. P. ~, 19th-c.
Russ. diplomat]

strö'ke[1] *n.*, & *v.t.* **1.** *n.* act of striking, shock given by
being struck, (*to receive 20 strokes of the birch; with one
stroke of his sword; killed by a stroke of lightning* or *lightning
stroke*); **at a** ~, by a single action; **finishing** ~, *coup de
grâce*, final and fatal stroke. **2.** sudden disabling attack
esp. of apoplexy; SUNstroke. **3.** single effort put forth,
one complete performance of a recurrent action or
movement, time or way in which such movements are
done; slightest such action (*has not done a stroke of work*);
whole of motion (of wing, oar, etc.) till starting-
-position is regained; whole motion (of piston) in
either direction; (Golf) action of hitting (at) ball with

club, as unit of scoring; (Rowing) mode or action of
moving oar (*row a fast, slow, long, etc., stroke; second boat
is gaining at every stroke*); mode of moving arms and legs
in swimming (BACK[1]*stroke*, BREAST[1]-*stroke*); **off** one's
~, not performing as well as usual. **4.** method of
striking in games etc., specially successful or skilful
effort, (*invented a new stroke in cricket; stroke of wit,
diplomacy, etc.; ~ **of business,** profitable transaction;
~ **of genius,** original or strikingly successful idea;
~ **of** (good) **luck,** unforeseen opportune occurrence;
MASTER[1]-*stroke*. **5.** mark made by movement in one
direction of pen or pencil or paintbrush, similar
mark printed, detail contributing to general effect
in description, (UP, DOWN[5], HAIR, -*stroke; thick,
thin, horizontal, oblique, etc., stroke; dash off picture
with a few strokes; description is full of strokes from the life*);
with a ~ **of the pen,** merely by writing signature
etc.; **finishing** ~**s,** finishing touches. **6.** sound
made by a striking clock (**it is on the** ~ **of nine,**
clock is about to strike 9; *was there* **on the** ~, punctually). **7.** ~ (**oar**), oar or oarsman nearest stern,
setting time of stroke. **8.** *v.t.* act as stroke of (boat,
crew). [ME, f. OE *strāc* f. Gmc *straikaz*, cogn. w.
STRIKE]

strö'ke[2] *v.t.*, & *n.* **1.** *v.t.* pass the hand gently, and usu.
repeatedly in same direction, along surface of (~
person or **his hair the wrong way,** irritate him; ~
person **down,** appease his anger etc.). **2.** *n.* act or spell
of stroking. [OE *strācian,* = MDu., MLG *strēken*,
OHG *streihhōn* f. Gmc *straik-* (as prec.)]

ströll *v.i.*, & *n.* **1.** *v.i.* saunter, go for short leisurely
walk; go from place to place giving performances etc.
(*strolling players*). **2.** *n.* short leisurely walk (*go for, take,
a stroll*). [orig. of vagrant, prob. f. G *strollen, strolchen*
(*strolch* vagabond, of unkn. orig.)]

ströl'ler *n.* In vbl senses; *push-chair. [f. prec. +-ER[1]]

strö'ma *n.* (*pl.* ~**ta**). (Biol.) framework of an organ or
cell, usu. of connective tissue; fungous tissue containing spore-producing bodies; hence **stromä'tic** *a.*
[mod. L, f. LL f. Gk *strōma* coverlet]

ströng *a.* & *adv.* (~'**er,** ~'**est,** *pr.* -ngg-). **1.** *a.* having
power of resistance, not easily broken or torn or worn
or injured or captured, tough, healthy, firm, solid,
(*strong china, stick, cloth, fortress, conviction, faith, character, foundation*); (of constitution) able to overcome, or
not liable to, disease; (of nerves) proof against fright,
irritation, etc.; (of patient) restored to health; (of
market) having steadily high or rising prices. **2.**
capable of exerting great force or of doing much,
muscular, powerful by size or numbers or resources or
quality or ability, well equipped (*in*), convincing,
striking, powerfully affecting the senses, (*strong to
suffer, save, etc.; is strong enough to lift a horse; strong in
judgement, Greek, numbers, health; strong eyes, memory,
army; strong evidence, argument, case; strong light, perfume,
cigar, colour;* **as** ~ **as a horse** or **an ox,** able to do or
stand much work); (of company) numerous, having
specified number (*we were 200 strong*); capable of doing
much when united (*a strong combination*); formidable,
likely to win, (*a strong candidate*); (of tea etc.) made
with large proportion of the flavouring element; (of
solution) containing relatively little solvent; (of situation in play or story) calculated to move audience
deeply; (of voice) loud or penetrating; (of food or its
flavour) pungent; (of breath) ill-smelling. **3.** energetic, effective, vigorous, decided, (*a strong tide,
attraction, influence, inclination to, suspicion; strong feelings,
support(er)*); (of literary style) vivid and terse; (of
wind) very fresh; (of measure) drastic. **4.** (Gmc
Gram.) (Of verb) forming inflexions by vowel-
-change within stem rather than by addition of suffix
(e.g. *swim swam, give gave, break broke; cf. float floated*),
(of noun or adjective declension) corresponding to
original vowel-stems, opp. WEAK 7; ~ **grade,** stressed
ablaut-form. **5.** ~ **arm,** use of force or sheer strength
(so ~-*arm a.*); ~**box,** strongly made small chest for
valuables; *strong* DRINK[2]; ~'**hold,** fortified place,

secure refuge, centre of support for a cause etc.; ∼ **interaction,** (Phys.) interaction between certain elementary particles that is very strong but is effective only at short distances; ∼ **language,** forcible (esp. profane or abusive) expressions; ∼ **man,** muscular person, masterful or capable person; ∼ **meat,** doctrine or action acceptable only to vigorous or instructed minds; ∼**-mi′nded,** having a vigorous or determined mind; ∼ **point,** specially fortified defensive position, (fig.) thing at which one excels; ∼**-room** (designed to protect valuables against fire and theft); ∼ **stomach** (not easily affected by nausea); ∼ **suit,** suit at cards in which one can take tricks, (fig.) thing at which one excels; ∼ **waters,** (arch.) alcoholic liquor. **6.** Hence ∼ISH¹ (2) a., ∼LY² adv. **7.** adv. strongly (tide is running strong), **come it** ∼, (sl.) go to great lengths, use exaggeration; **come it too** ∼, (sl.) overdo it, use too much exaggeration; GO¹ it strong; **going** ∼, (colloq.) continuing action vigorously, in good health or trim. [OE, = OS strang, ON strangr f. Gmc *strangaz; cf. STRING]

stro′ntia (-sha) n. strontium oxide. [f. strontian native strontium carbonate f. Strontian in Highland Region of Scotland, where it was discovered; see -IA¹]

stro′ntium n. (Chem.) soft silver-white metallic element; ∼ **90,** radioactive isotope of strontium concentrated selectively in bones when ingested. [f. prec. + -IUM]

strop n., & v.t. (-pp-). **1.** n. strip of leather on which razor is sharpened, implement or machine serving same purpose; (Naut.) collar of leather or spliced rope or iron used for handling cargo. **2.** v.t. sharpen on or with strop. [ME f. MDu., MLG; OHG strupf, WG f. L stroppus, struppus]

strophä′nthin n. white crystalline poisonous glucoside extracted from various species of the genus Strophanthus of tropical plants and used as a heart--tonic. [f. mod. L strophanthus f. Gk strophos twisted cord + anthos flower, + -IN]

stro′phè n. (lines recited during) turn made in dancing by ancient-Greek chorus (∼, **antistrophe, epode,** three sections of a choral ode or of one division of it, strophe and antistrophe exactly corresponding in metre), group of lines forming section of lyric poem; hence **stro′phic** a. [f. Gk strophē, lit. turning (strephō turn)]

∥**stro′ppy** a. (sl.) bad-tempered, awkward to deal with. [20th c.; orig. unkn.]

strove. See STRIVE.

strow (-ō) v.t. (p.p. ∼n or ∼ed). (arch.) strew. [var. of STREW]

struck. See STRIKE.

stru′ctural (-kcher-) a. of structure; ∼ **engineering,** design and construction of dams, bridges, etc.; ∼ **formula,** (Chem., showing arrangement of atoms in the molecule of a compound); ∼ **linguistics,** study of language as system of interrelated elements; ∼ **psychology,** study of arrangement and composition of mental states and conscious experiences; ∼ **steel,** strong mild steel in shapes suited to construction work; hence ∼LY² adv. [f. STRUCTURE + -AL]

stru′cturalⅼism (-kcher-) n. doctrine that structure rather than function is important; structural linguistics or psychology; hence ∼IST (2) n. [f. prec. + -ISM]

stru′cturⅼe n., & v.t. **1.** n. manner in which a building or organism or other complete whole is constructed, supporting framework or whole of the essential parts of something, (the structure of a house, machine, animal, poem, sentence, society; a sentence of loose, a rock of columnar, structure; its structure is ingenious; demanded a new wages structure); hence ∼•LESS (-kcherl-), (-)∼ED² (-kcherd), adjs. **2.** thing constructed, complex whole, a building, (a fine marble structure; a lumbering structure pulled by six horses). **3.** v.t. give structure to, organize. [ME f. OF, or f. L structura (struere struct- build; see -URE)]

stru′del (-ōō′-) n. confection of thin pastry rolled up round a filling and baked (apple strudel = APFEL-STRUDEL). [G]

stru′ggle v.i., & n. **1.** v.i. throw one's limbs or body about in violent effort to get free or escape grasp (child struggled and kicked); make violent or determined efforts under difficulties, strive hard to do or for thing, contend with or against opponent or obstacle or difficulty, (struggled to express himself, to control his feelings, for supremacy; struggling with his infirmity, against superior numbers or the forces of nature); make one's way with difficulty through, up, along, in, etc., (light struggled in through dirty panes; struggled to his feet); (esp. in pres. part.) experience difficulty in making a living or getting recognition (a struggling artist etc.); hence **stru′gglⅼER¹** n. **2.** n. spell of struggling, confused wrestle or jostling, hard contest, determined effort under difficulties; **the** ∼ **for existence** or **life,** the competition between organisms esp. as an element in natural selection, or between persons seeking livelihood. [ME strugle, strogel, etc., frequent. (see -LE 3) of uncert. orig.; perh. imit.]

strŭm v. (-mm-) & n. **1.** v.i. touch keys or twang strings of piano or other stringed instrument (esp. carelessly or unskilfully). **2.** v.t. strum on (piano, guitar, etc.). **3.** n. sound made by strumming (the strum of a guitar). [imit.; cf. THRUM²]

stru′mⅼa (-ōō′-) n. (pl. ∼ae). scrofula; goitre; (Bot.) cushion-like dilatation of an organ; so ∼OSE¹, ∼OUS, adjs. [L., = scrofulous tumour]

stru′mpèt n. (arch. or rhet.) prostitute. [ME, of unkn. orig.]

strŭng. See STRING.

strŭt¹ v.i. (-tt-), & n. (walk with) pompous or affected stiff erect gait. [ME 'bulge, swell, strive', earlier ˙stroute f. OE strūtian be rigid (?)]

strŭt² n., & v.t. (-tt-). **1.** n. bar of wood or iron inserted in a framework and intended to bear weight or pressure in the direction of its length, brace, e.g. one set obliquely from rafter to king-post or queen-post. **2.** v.t. brace with strut(s). [16th c., prob. f. prec.]

'struth (-ōō-) int. (colloq., used as mild oath). [f. God's truth]

stru′thious (-ōō′-) a. of or like an ostrich. [f. L struthio ostrich + -OUS]

strȳ′chnⅼine (-knēn) n. vegetable alkaloid got from plants of genus Strychnos (esp. nux vomica), very bitter to the taste and highly poisonous, used as stimulant and tonic; hence ∼IC a., ∼**(in)**ISM (5) ns. [F, f. L f. Gk strukhnos kind of nightshade; see -INE⁵]

Sts. abbr. Saints.

Stŭ′art n. & a. (member) of the royal family of England and Scotland from James I to Anne. [name of royal house of Scotland from accession (1371) of Robert II, a hereditary STEWARD of Scotland]

stŭb n., & v.t. (-bb-). **1.** n. stump of tree, tooth, etc.; remnant of pencil, cigar, or similar object after use; stunted tail etc.; counterfoil of cheque, receipt, etc.; ∼**-axle** (supporting only one wheel of a pair); ∼**-mortise, -tenon,** (going only part of the way through); hence ∼**by²** a. **2.** v.t. grub up by the roots; clear (land) of stubs; ∼ one's **toe,** hurt it by striking against something; ∼ **(out),** extinguish (cigar, cigarette) by pressing lighted end against some hard object. [OE stub(b) = MDu., MLG stubbe, ON stubbr, stubbi f. Gmc *stubbaz, *stubbon]

stŭ′bble n. cut stalks of cereal plants left sticking up after harvest; cropped hair or beard, hair on unshaven chin or cheek; hence **stŭ′bbly²** a. [ME, f. AF stuble, OF estuble f. L stup(u)la var. of stipula straw]

stŭ′bborn a. unreasonably obstinate; unyielding, obdurate, inflexible; refractory, intractable, (facts are ∼ things, will not adapt themselves to theory); hence ∼LY² adv., ∼NESS (-n-n-) n. [ME stiborn, stoburn, etc., of unkn. orig.]

stŭ′cco n. (pl. ∼es), & v.t. **1.** n. plaster or cement used for coating wall surfaces or moulding into architectural decorations. **2.** v.t. coat with stucco. [It., of Gmc orig.]

stŭck. See STICK¹.

stŭd¹ n., & v.t. (-dd-). **1.** n. large-headed nail, boss, or knob, projecting from a surface esp. for ornament; small object projecting slightly from road-surface as marker etc.; rivet, cross-piece in each link of chain--cable. **2.** double button esp. for use with two button-holes in shirt-front (||COLLAR¹-*stud*); ||PRESS²-*stud*. **3.** post to which laths are nailed; *height of room as indicated by length of this; hence ∼′dING¹ n., wood-work of lath-and-plaster wall. **4.** v.t. set with studs to strengthen or usu. to decorate; (in *p.p.*) thickly set or strewn *with* (*door, lawn, sea, sky, studded with nails, daisies, islands, stars*); be scattered over or about (surface). [OE *studu, stuthu* post, prop, = MHG *stud*, ON *stoth*, cogn. w. G *stützen* to prop]

stŭd² n. number of horses kept for breeding etc.; place where these are kept; (sl.) young man, esp. one noted for sexual prowess; **at** ∼, (of male horse) publicly available for breeding on payment of fee; ∼**-book** (containing pedigrees of horses); ∼**-farm**, place where horses are bred; ∼(**-horse**), stallion; ∼ (**poker**), form of poker with betting after dealing of successive rounds of cards face up. [OE *stōd*, = OHG *stuot*, ON *stóth* f. Gmc **stōdh-* (**stō-*, **sta-* STAND¹)]

stŭ′dding-sail (stŭ′nsal) n. sail set on small extra yard and boom beyond leech of square sail in light winds. [16th c., of uncert. orig.; perh. f. MLG, MDu. *stötinge* a thrusting]

stŭ′dent n. **1.** person studying in order to qualify himself for some occupation, or devoting himself to some branch of learning or investigation, or observa-tion, or under instruction at university or other place of higher education or technical training or *at school (*medical, theological, historical, theology, history, student; a student of archaeology, law, botany, manners, society; numbers its students in thousands*); (*attrib.*) study-ing in order to become (*student teacher*). **2.** person of studious habits. **3.** ||graduate recipient of stipend from foundation of college, esp. fellow of Christ Church, Oxford; hence ∼SHIP n. [ME, f. L *studēre* (*studium* STUDY¹); see -ENT]

stŭ′dio n. (*pl.* ∼s). **1.** working-room of painter, sculptor, photographer, etc., often with skylights or windows specially designed to secure suitable light. **2.** room in which cinema-film is made; (in *pl.*) such premises of a film company with auxiliary buildings. **3.** room used for making recordings or in broadcast-ing station for transmissions. **4.** ∼ **couch**, couch that can be converted into a bed; ∼ **flat** (containing room suitable as artist's studio, or only one main room). [It., f. L (as STUDY¹)]

stŭ′dious a. assiduous in study, much occupied with reading; taking care *to do* or *in doing*; anxiously desirous *of doing*; studied, deliberate, intended, zealous, anxious, painstaking, (*with studious care, attention, politeness*); hence ∼LY² adv., ∼NESS n. [ME, f. L *studiosus* (as foll.; see -OUS)]

stŭ′dy¹ n. **1.** (in *sing.* or *pl.*) devotion of time and thought to acquiring information esp. from books, pursuit of some branch of knowledge, (*gives his time to study; my studies have convinced me of its truth; the study of mathematics, morals; continued his studies abroad; Institute of Advanced Studies*); **make a** ∼ **of**, investigate carefully (see also sense 3); (Theatr.) memorizing or memorizer of roles; ∼**-group** (of persons meeting from time to time to study a particular subject or topic). **2.** thing that is or deserves to be investigated or carefully examined (*the proper study of mankind is man; his face was a study*). **3.** (arch.) thing to be secured by pains or attention (*it shall be my study to please*); **make a** ∼ **of**, try to secure (see also sense 1). **4. in a brown** ∼, in a reverie, too intent on one's thoughts to observe what is passing. **5.** drawing etc. made for practice in technique or as preliminary experiment for picture or part of it (*his studies are exquisite, but his finished work disappointing; a study of a head*); (Mus.) composition designed to develop skill in some

particular branch of execution; literary or dramatic portrayal of an aspect of behaviour, character, etc. **6.** room used for literary occupation, transaction of business, etc., (*you will find him in his or the study*). [ME, f. OF *estudie* f. L *studium* zeal, study]

stŭ′dy² v. **1.** v.t. make a study of, take pains to investigate or acquire knowledge of (subject), scrutinize or earnestly contemplate (visible object), (*study law, French, philosophy; study person's face or character, a map, the stars*); read (book) attentively; try to learn (role) by heart; take pains to achieve (result) or pay regard to (*studies others' convenience, his own interests*). **2.** v.i. apply oneself to study esp. reading (∼ **for the Bar,** cf. READ 11). **3.** v.t. (arch.) be on the watch, try constantly to manage, *to do* (*studies to avoid disagreeable topics*). **4.** (in *p.p.*) deliberate, intentional, affected, (*a studied insult; with studied politeness, rudeness, unconcern*); hence **stŭ′died**LY² (-dĭd-) adv. [ME, f. OF *estudier* f. med. L *studiare* f. L (as prec.)]

stŭff n. & v. **1.** n. material that thing is made of or that is or may be used for some purpose (*such stuff as dreams are made on; the stuff that heroes are made of; Conrad's books are good stuff; always eating sweet stuff; lots of stuff about it in the newspapers*); **the** ∼, (colloq.) available supply of something, esp. drink or drugs or (sl.) money; BIT² of *stuff*. **2.** woollen fabric (opp. silk, cotton, linen); ||∼ **gown** (worn by barrister who has not taken silk). **3.** valueless matter, refuse, trash, nonsense, (*take that stuff away; stuff and nonsense! ; what stuff he writes!*). **4.** (sl.) **do** one's ∼, perform one's tricks, get on with one's assigned task; HOT¹ *stuff*; **know** one's ∼, be a master of one's subject, trade, etc.; ROUGH *stuff*; *that's* **the** ∼ (**to give 'em** or **to give the troops**), the absolutely correct way to proceed etc. **5.** v.t. pack, cram, stop up, fill, distend, (*stuff one's ears with wool, cushion with feathers, doll with padding; head stuffed with romantic ideas*); fill out skin of (animal, bird, etc.) with material to restore original shape (∼**ed shirt,** (colloq.) pompous but incompetent person; **get** ∼**ed,** (sl.) take oneself away); fill (fowl, rolled meat, vegetable marrow, etc.) with minced seasoning etc. before cooking; make (person, goose, etc.) eat to repletion (∼ one**self,** gorge, eat greedily); (usu. in *pass.*) block *up* (nose etc. with secretions); *place bogus votes in (ballot-box); (vulg.) copulate with (woman). **6.** ram or press into receptacle (*stuffed his things into a small bag, his fingers into his ears, the food into his mouth*), push hastily (*stuffed the note behind the cushion*), (sl.) dispose of as unwanted (*you can stuff the job so far as I'm concerned*). **7.** v.i. stuff oneself. **8.** Hence (-)∼ER¹ n. [ME *stoffe* f. OF (estoffe n. f.) *estoffer* equip, furnish f. Gk *stuphō* draw together]

stŭ′ffing n. In vbl senses; material used for stuffing (sense 5); ∼**-box** (in machinery, packed with material to allow working of axle while remaining airtight); **knock** or **take the** ∼ **out of,** (colloq.) make feeble or weak, defeat utterly. [f. prec.+-ING¹]

stŭ′ff|** y** a. (Of room etc., or atmosphere in it) lacking fresh air or ventilation, close, hard to breathe in, fusty; dull uninteresting; (of nose etc.) stuffed up; (colloq.) angry, sulky; (colloq.) narrow-minded, prim; hence ∼iLY² adv., ∼iNESS n. [f. STUFF+-Y²]

stŭ′lti|**fy** v.t. (Of act, statement, agent, speaker) reduce (previous act etc.) to foolishness or absurdity; make (act etc.) of no effect, neutralize (one*self*) as agent, by later inconsistent act etc.; impair, render inefficient through frustration etc.; hence ∼FICA′-TION n. [f. LL *stultificare* f. L *stultus* foolish; see -FY]

stŭm n., & v.t. (-mm-). **1.** n. unfermented grape-juice, must. **2.** v.t. prevent from fermenting, secure (wine) against further fermentation in cask, by use of sulphur etc.; renew fermentation of (wine) by adding stum. [f. Du. (*stommen* v. f.) *stom* n. f. *stom* a. dumb]

stŭ′mble v. & n. **1.** v.i. lurch forward, have partial fall, from catching or striking or misplacing foot (∼ **along,** go with frequent stumbles); make blunder(s) in doing something (*stumbles in his speech; stumble through a recitation*); (arch.) be offended, feel scruples, at; come accidentally (*up*)*on* or *across*; *∼**bum**, (colloq.) clumsy person; **stumbling-block,** obstacle, circumstance that causes difficulty or hesitation or scruples. **2.** *v.t.* (arch.) cause to stumble or pause, nonplus. **3.** *n.* act of stumbling. [ME *stomble, stumble,* (w. euphonic *b*) corresp. to Norw. *stumla,* cogn. w. STAMMER]

‖**stü′mer** *n.* (sl.) worthless cheque, counterfeit coin or note; sham, fraud; failure. [19th c.; orig. unkn.]

stŭmp *n.* & *v.* **1.** *n.* projecting remnant of cut or fallen tree, corresponding remnant of broken branch or tooth or amputated limb, stub of cigar or pencil, worn-down brush or other implement, (***up a** ∼, in difficulties); (in *pl.,* joc.) legs (STIR¹ one's *stumps*). **2.** stump of tree, or other place, used by orator to address meeting from; **on the** ∼, (colloq.) engaged in political speech-making or agitation; ∼ **oratory** (of kind suitable for such speeches); ∼ **speech** (thus made). **3.** (Cricket). one of the three uprights of a wicket (*off, middle, leg, stump*; DRAW¹ *stumps*). **4.** cylinder of rolled paper or other material with conical ends for softening pencil-marks and other uses in drawing. **5.** *v.i.* walk stiffly or noisily as on wooden leg. **6.** *v.t.* (Of question etc., colloq.) be too hard for; (in *p.p.*) at a loss, at one's wit's end; hence ∼ER¹ (2) *n.* **7.** (Cricket). (Of wicket-keeper) put (batsman who is not in his ground and not running) out by dislodging bail(s) with ball or while holding ball; hence ∼ER¹ (1) *n.,* (colloq.) wicket-keeper. **8.** *v.i.* & *t.* *make stump speeches (see sense 2); traverse (district) doing this. **9.** *v.t.* use stump on (drawing, line, etc.). **10.** *v.i.* & *t.* ‖∼ **up,** (sl.) pay over the money required, produce (sum). [ME *stompe,* f. MDu. *stomp,* OHG *stumpf* n. & a.; sense 4 prob. thr. F *estompe*]

stŭ′mp∣ў *a.* thickset, stocky, of small height or length in proportion to girth, (*stumpy man, book, tail, pencil*); hence ∼iLY² *adv.,* ∼iNESS *n.* [f. prec. + -Y²]

stŭn *v.t.* (-nn-). (Of sound) deafen temporarily, bewilder; (of blow, lit. or fig.) knock senseless, reduce to insensibility or stupor, benumb, overwhelm. [ME, f. OF *estoner* ASTONISH]

stŭng. See STING.

stŭnk. See STINK.

stŭ′nning *a.* In vbl senses; (colloq.) extremely attractive, delightful, splendid; hence or cogn. **stŭ′nn**ER¹ *n.,* ∼LY² *adv.* [f. STUN + -ING²]

stŭ′nsail, stŭ′ns'l, (-sal) *n.* = STUDDING-SAIL. [repr. pronunc.]

stŭnt¹ *v.t.* (esp. in *p.p.*) retard growth or development of, dwarf, cramp. [f. (now dial.) *stunt* foolish, MHG *stunz,* ON *stuttr* short f. Gmc **stuntaz,* perh. rel. to STUMP]

stŭnt² *n.,* & *v.i.* (colloq.) **1.** *n.* special effort, feat, show performance (∼ **man,** man employed to take actor's place in performing dangerous stunts), display of concentrated energy; advertising device. **2.** *v.i.* perform stunts, esp. aerobatics. [orig. unkn.; first in 19th-c. US college athletics]

stŭ′pa *n.* round usu. domed building erected as Buddhist shrine. [f. Skr. *stūpa*]

stūpe¹ *n.,* & *v.t.* (treat with) flannel etc. soaked in hot water, wrung out, and applied as fomentation. [ME, f. L f. Gk *stup(p)ē* tow]

stūpe² *n.* (sl.) foolish person. [f. STUPID]

stū′pe∣fÿ *v.t.* make stupid or torpid, deprive of sensation, (*stupefied with drink, narcotics, grief,* etc.); hence or cogn. ∼FA′CIENT *a.* & *n.,* ∼FA′CTION, ∼FIER¹ (1, 2), *ns.,* ∼**făctive** *a.* [f. F *stupéfier* f. L *stupefacere* (*stupēre* be amazed; see -FY)]

stūpe′ndous *a.* amazing, prodigious, astounding, esp. by size or degree (*a stupendous structure, error, achievement; stupendous folly*); hence ∼LY² *adv.,* ∼NESS *n.* [f. L *stupendus* gerundive of *stupēre* be amazed at, + -OUS]

stū′pid *a.* (∼er, ∼est) & *n.* **1.** *a.* in a state of stupor or lethargy; slow-witted, lacking in sensibility, obtuse, characteristic of persons of this nature, (*a stupid person,*

joke, idea, book; *what a stupid place to put it in!*), so **stūpi′d**ITY *n.*; uninteresting, dull; hence ∼LY² *adv.* **2.** *n.* (colloq.) stupid person. [f. F *stupide* or f. L *stupidus* (as prec.; see -ID¹)]

stū′por *n.* dazed state, torpidity, whence ∼ous *a.*; helpless amazement. [ME f. L (as STUPENDOUS; see -OR)]

stŭr′d∣ў¹ *a.* robust, hardy, vigorous, lusty, strongly built, (*sturdy child, opponent, legs, frame, resistance, courage*); ∼**y beggar,** (arch.) able-bodied but idle beggar; hence ∼iLY² *adv.,* ∼iNESS *n.* [ME 'reckless, violent', f. OF *est(o)urdi* p.p. of *estourdir* stun, daze f. Rom. *exturdire f. L *ex-* EX-¹ + *turdus* thrush (taken as type of drunkenness)]

stŭr′d∣ў² *n.* vertigo in sheep caused by tapeworm in brain; hence ∼iED² (-id) *a.* [f. prec.]

stŭr′geon (-jon) *n.* large anadromous fish of genus *Acipenser* etc., resembling shark in general shape, having mailed body and head, yielding caviare and isinglass, and esteemed as food. [ME f. AF; OF *esturgeon* f. Rom. *sturio -onis f. Gmc *sturjon]

Sturm und Drang (shtoorm ŏont drah′ng) *n.* = STORM *and stress.* [G]

stŭ′tter *v.* & *n.* **1.** *v.i.* stammer; involuntarily repeat parts, esp. initial consonants, of words in effort to articulate. **2.** *v.t.* ∼ (**out**), utter (words) thus. **3.** Hence ∼ER¹ *n.* **4.** *n.* act or habit of stuttering. [frequent. of (now dial.) *stut,* ME f. Gmc **stut-* knock; see -ER⁵]

stŷ¹ *n.* & *v.* **1.** *n.* pen or enclosure for pig(s); filthy abode or dwelling; place of debauchery. **2.** *v.t.* & *i.* lodge in sty. [OE *stī,* prob. = *stig* hall (cf. STEWARD), f. Gmc *stijam]

stŷ², **stŷe,** *n.* inflamed swelling on edge of eyelid. [f. (now dial.) *styany = styan* eye f. OE *stīgend* sty, lit. riser (*stīgan* rise) + EYE¹, shortened as though = *sty on eye*]

Stŷ′gian *a.* (as) of the Styx or Hades; murky, gloomy. [f. L f. Gk *Stugios* (STYX) + -AN]

stŷle *n.,* & *v.t.* **1.** *n.* ancient writing-implement, small rod with pointed end for scratching letters on wax-covered tablets and blunt end for obliterating; thing of similar shape esp. for engraving, tracing, etc.; gnomon of sundial; (Bot.) narrow extension of ovary supporting stigma. **2.** manner of writing, speaking, or doing, esp. as contrasted with the matter to be expressed or thing done (*the style is better than the matter; written in a florid, cumbrous, lucid,* or *delightful style; different styles of rowing, swimming; slashed about him in fine style;* CRAMP³ person's *style;* **good, bad,** ∼, = *good, bad,* FORM¹). **3.** collective characteristics of the writing or diction or way of presenting things or artistic expression or decorative methods (in painting, architecture, furniture, dress, etc.) proper to a person or school or period or subject, manner exhibiting these characteristics, (*in the style of Shakespeare, Raphael, Wagner; the epic, lyric, dramatic, classical, style; buildings in Romanesque, Early English, Tudor, style; fried chicken Southern style; flattery is not his style*); ***old** ∼, = OLD *face;* (as *suf.*) = -WISE (*dressed cowboy-style*). **4.** descriptive formula, designation of person or thing, full title, (*is entitled to the style of 'Right Honourable'; did not recognize him under his new style; my style is plain John Smith; regret that I am not acquainted with your proper style*); **old, new,** ∼, (of date) reckoned by the Julian, Gregorian, calendar. **5.** noticeably superior quality or manner esp. in regard to breeding or fashion, distinction, (*let us do the thing in style if we do it at all*); **has no** ∼, is commonplace. **6.** kind, sort, esp. with regard to appearance (*what style of house do you require?; a gentleman of the old style*). **7.** make, shape, pattern, (*in all sizes and styles*). **8.** *v.t.* design, arrange, make, etc., in (esp. fashionable) style; hence ***stŷ′l**ER¹ *n* **9.** (usu. in *pass.*) use specified designation of (*is styled king, folly*). [ME f. OF *stile, style* f. L *stilus;* sp. *style* due to assoc. w. Gk *stulos* column]

stŷ′lèt *n.* slender pointed instrument, stiletto; (Surg.) stiffening wire of catheter, probe. [f. F *stilet* f. It. STILETTO]

stȳ'lish a. noticeable for (fashionable) elegance or superior quality or manner; hence ∼LY² adv., ∼NESS n. [f. STYLE + -ISH¹]

stȳ'list n. person with or aiming at good literary style; person who designs fashionable styles or makes things according to these. [f. STYLE + -IST]

stȳli'st|ic a. of literary style; hence ∼ICALLY adv., ∼ICS n., study of literary style. [f. as prec. + -IC, after G stilistisch]

stȳ'lite n. medieval ascetic living on top of a pillar. [f. eccl. Gk stulitēs (stulos pillar; see -ITE¹)]

stȳ'lize, -ise (-īz), v.t. (usu. in p.p.) make (artistic representation) conform to the rules of a conventional style. [f. STYLE + -IZE, after G stilisieren]

stȳ'lo n. (pl. ∼s). (colloq.) = STYLOGRAPH. [abbr.]

stȳ'lobate n. (Archit.) continuous base supporting row of columns. [f. L f. Gk stulobatēs (stulos pillar, bainō walk)]

stȳ'lo|graph (-ahf) n. kind of pen containing reservoir of ink and marking with point instead of split nib; hence ∼grä'phIC a. [f. STYLUS + -O- + -GRAPH]

stȳ'loid a. & n. (Anat.) ∼ (process), spine of bone, esp. that projecting from base of temporal bone. [f. mod. L styloides f. Gk stuloeidēs (stulos pillar; see -OID)]

stȳ'l|us n. (pl. ∼i pr. -ī, or ∼uses). **1.** = STYLE 1. **2.** tracing-point producing indented groove in gramophone record, or following such groove in reproducing sound. [erron. sp. of L stilus; cf. STYLE]

stȳ'mie n., & v.t. **1.** n. (Golf). situation on putting-green when one ball lies between the other ball and the hole, formerly a possible obstruction to the play of the farther ball (lay a stymie); (fig.) difficult situation. **2.** v.t. (Golf). put (opponent, his ball, oneself) into position of having to negotiate a stymie; (fig.) obstruct, thwart. [19th c.; orig. unkn.]

stȳ'ptic a. & n. (substance) that checks bleeding. [ME, f. L f. Gk stuptikos (stuphō contract; see -IC)]

stȳr'ax n. storax resin; tree or shrub of genus Styrax, e.g. storax-tree. [L, f. Gk sturax; cf. STORAX]

stȳr'ene n. liquid hydrocarbon easily polymerized and used in making plastics etc. [f. prec. + -ENE]

Stȳx n. (Gk Myth.) river encompassing Hades (**cross the** ∼, die; black as Styx). [ME f. L, f. Gk Stux -ugos (stugnos hateful, gloomy)]

su|'able (sū'-, soo'-) a. that can be sued; hence ∼ABI'LITY n. [f. SUE + -ABLE]

sua'sion (swā'zhŏn) n. persuasion as opposed to force (moral suasion); so **sua'sive** (sw-) a. [ME f. OF, or f. L suasio (suadēre suas- urge; see -ION)]

suav|e (swahv) a. bland, soothing, mollifying, (superficially) polite, (suave wine, person, speech, manners); hence or cogn. ∼ELY² (-vlī) adv., ∼ITY n. [F, or f. L suavis agreeable, cogn. w. SWEET]

sŭb n. & v. (-bb-). (colloq.) **1.** n. subaltern; sub-editor; submarine; subscription; substitute. **2.** v.i. act as substitute for someone. **3.** v.t. sub-edit. [abbr.]

sub- (sŭb, sub) pref. denoting: **1.** Lower position (subordinate, subscribe); to lower position (submerge, subside); from lower position (subtract). **2.** Covertness, secrecy, (suborn). **3.** Inclusion (subsume). **4.** Closeness (subsequent, suburb). **5.** Inferiority (subserve). **6.** Support (subsidy, subvention). **7.** (forming adjs.) Under as regards (1) position (esp. Anat.; subabdominal), (2) degree (subnormal), or (3) quality (subhuman); (4) somewhat (subacid), more or less (subaquatic), (5) approximately (subcylindrical), (6) incipiently (subdelirious), (7) nearly (suberect), (8) immediately adjacent in space or time (subalpine; subapostolic). **8.** (forming ns.) (1) subordinate, secondary, deputy, (sub-editor, subheading, subdean); (2) secondary part of (subculture, subsection); (3) incipient (subdelirium); (4) lying below (subsoil); (5) (Chem., of salt) basic (subacetate); (6) smaller than or inferior to (subshrub, sub-man). **9.** (forming vbs.) subordinately, secondarily, (subdivide, sublet). [f. or after L sub- (sub under, close to, towards)]

sŭbăbdŏ'minal a. See SUB- 7(1).

sŭbă'cid a. moderately acid or tart (lit. or fig.); hence **sŭbaci'd**ITY n. [f. L subacidus (see SUB- 7 (4), ACID¹)]

sŭbacū'te a. (Med.) between acute and chronic. [f. SUB- 7 (2) + ACUTE]

sŭbā'gencў, sŭbā'gent, ns. See SUB- 8 (1).

subahdār' (sŏoba-) n. (Hist.) chief native officer of company of sepoys. [f. Urdu ṣūba ᵸdār (ṣūbah province + Pers. dār master)]

sŭbā'lpīne a. of higher slopes of mountains just below timber-line. [f. SUB- 7 (8) + ALPINE]

sŭ'baltern a. & n. **1.** a. of inferior rank; (Logic, of proposition) particular, not universal. **2.** n. ||(Mil.) officer below rank of captain, esp. second lieutenant. [f. LL SUB(alternus ALTERNATE¹)]

sŭbăpostŏ'lic a. of period immediately after that of the Apostles. [f. SUB- 7 (8) + APOSTOLIC]

sŭbă'qua a. (Of sport etc.) taking place under water. [f. SUB- 1 + L aqua water]

sŭbaquă'tic a. of more or less aquatic habits or kind; underwater. [f. SUB- 7 (4, 1) + AQUATIC]

sŭbā'quĕous a. underwater. [f. SUB- 7 (1) + AQUEOUS]

sŭbār'ctic a. of or like regions somewhat south of Arctic Circle. [f. SUB- 7 (8) + ARCTIC]

sŭbā'stral a. terrestrial. [f. SUB- 7 (1) + ASTRAL]

sŭbato'mic a. occurring in or smaller than an atom. [f. SUB- 7 (3) = ATOMIC]

sŭbaudi'tion n. mental supplying of omitted word(s), understanding of what is not expressed, reading between the lines. [f. LL subauditio f. SUB(audire hear) understand; cf. AUDITION]

sŭbā'xillarў a. See SUB- 7 (1).

sŭb-bā'sement (-sm-) n. storey below basement. [f. SUB- 8 (4) + BASEMENT]

sub-branch (-ah-), **sŭ'b-breed,** ns., see SUB- 8 (1); **sŭ'bcătègorў** n., SUB- 8 (2); **sŭbcau'dal** a., SUB- 7 (1); **sŭ'bclass** (-ahs) n., SUB- 8 (2).

subclā'vian a. & n. (artery etc.) lying or extending under collar-bone. [f. mod. L subclavius (as SUB- 7 (1), clavis key; cf. CLAVICLE) + -AN]

subcli'nical a. (Med., of disease) not yet presenting definite symptoms. [f. SUB- 7 (6) + CLINICAL]

sŭ'bcommission(er) (-shŏn-), **sŭ'bcommittee** (-tǐ), ns., see SUB- 8 (1); **sŭbcō'nical** a., SUB- 7 (5).

subcō'nscious (-shus) a. & n. (of) part of mind that is not fully conscious but is able to influence actions etc.; hence ∼LY² adv., ∼NESS n. [f. SUB- 7 (7) + CONSCIOUS]

subcō'ntinent n. land-mass that is large, but smaller than those usually called continents; large geographically or politically independent part of a continent. [f. SUB- 8 (2) + CONTINENT²]

subcō'ntrăct¹ n., **subcontră'ct²** v.i. & t., **subcontrā'ctor** n. See SUB- 8 (1), 9.

subcō'ntrarў a. & n. (Logic). (proposition) that cannot be false at the same time as another. [f. LL SUB(contrarius CONTRARY), transl. Gk hupenantios]

subcŏr'dāte a., see SUB- 7 (5); **subcŏr'tical, subcŏ'stal, subcrā'nial,** adjs., SUB- 7 (1).

subcrī'tical a. (Phys.) of less than critical mass etc. [f. SUB- 7 (2) + CRITICAL]

sŭ'bcŭlture n. (Sociol.) cultural group within a larger culture; hence **sŭ'bcŭltural** (-cher-) a. [f. SUB- 8 (2) + CULTURE]

subcŭtā'nĕous, subcŭtī'cular, adjs., see SUB- 7 (1); **subcȳli'ndrical** a., SUB- 7 (5).

sŭbdea'con n. (Eccl.) minister of order next below deacon; epistoler; so **sŭb**DIA'CONATE n. [f. SUB- 8 (1) + DEACON²]

sŭbdea'n n. official ranking next below, or acting as deputy for, dean; so **sub**DEA'NERY n., **sub**DECA'NAL a. [f. SUB- 8 (1) + DEAN¹]

***sŭ'bdĕb** n. (colloq.) = foll. [abbr.]

***sŭbdĕ'butante** (-ahnt) n. girl who is about to become a débutante, or one of corresponding age. [f. SUB- 8 (3) + DÉBUTANTE]

sŭbdĕcā'nal. See SUBDEAN.

sŭbdĕli'rious a., **sŭbdĕli'rium** n. See SUB- 7 (6), 8 (3).

sŭbdīvīde (sŭ'-, -ī'd) *v.t. & i.* divide again after first division. [ME, f. L *subdividere* (as SUB- 9, DIVIDE¹)]

sŭbdivision (-zhon; sŭ'-, -vī'-) *n.* subdividing; subordinate division; *area of land divided into plots for sale. [f. LL *subdivisio* (as SUB- 8 (1), DIVISION)]

sŭbdŏ'minant *n.* (Mus.) fourth note of diatonic scale of any key. [f. SUB- 8 (1) + DOMINANT]

subdŭ'ct *v.t.* (arch.) withdraw, remove; deduct, subtract; hence **subdŭ'ction** *n.* [f. L SUB(*ducere* duct- draw)]

subdūe' *v.t.* conquer, subjugate, (*subdue enemies, nature, rough land*); tame, bring into subjection, discipline, (*subdue one's passions; subdued by kindness*); (esp. in *p.p.*) soften, make gentle or less intense, tone down, mitigate, (*subdued colours, light, mood, manners, satisfaction*); hence **subdū'ABLE** *a.*, **subdū'AL** *n.* [ME *sodewe* f. AF *soduer, *su(*b*)*duer* = OF *so*(*u*)*duire* deceive, seduce, f. L *subducere*, (see prec.), used w. sense of SUB(*dere* = *dare* put) conquer]

sŭb-ĕ'dĭtor *n.* assistant editor; ‖person who prepares material for printing in book, newspaper, etc.; hence **sŭb-ĕditō'r**IAL *a.*, (as back-form.) **sŭb-ĕ'dĭt** *v.t.* [f. SUB- 8 (1) + EDITOR]

sŭbĕrĕ'ct *a.* (Bot.) See SUB- 7 (7).

sŭbē'rĭc, **sŭbē'rĭc**, **sŭ'berōse**, *adjs.* corky, of or like cork. [t. L *suber* cork(-oak) + -EOUS, -IC (F *subérique*), -OSE¹]

sŭ'hfămilў *n.* taxonomic category between family and tribe or genus. [f. SUB- 8 (2) + FAMILY]

sŭbfē'brīle *a.* See SUB- 7 (4).

sub fīnem (sŭb fī'nem, sŏŏb fē'něm) *adv.* towards the end (of specified chapter etc.). [L]

sŭ'bflŏŏr (-ōr) *n.* foundation for floor in building. [f. SUB- 8 (4) + FLOOR]

sŭ'bfōrm *n.* See SUB- 8 (1).

sŭ'bfŭsc *a. & n.* dusky, dull-coloured (formal clothing in some universities). [f. L *subfuscus* (as SUB- 7 (4), *fuscus* dark brown)]

sŭ'bgēnus *n.* (*pl.* **su'bgenera**). taxonomic category between genus and species. [f. SUB- 8 (2) + GENUS]

sŭbglā'cial (*or* -shal) *a.*, see SUB- 7 (8); **sŭ'bgroup** (-ōŏp) *n.*, SUB- 8 (2).

sŭ'bhead, **sŭ'bheading**, (-ĕd-) *ns.* subordinate division in classification; subordinate heading or title in chapter, article, etc. [f. SUB- 8 (1) + HEAD¹, HEADING]

sŭbhĕpă'tic *a.*, see SUB- 7 (1); **sŭb-Himalay'an** *a.*, SUB- 7 (8)

sŭbhū'man *a.* less than human; not fully human. [f. SUB- 7 (3) + HUMAN]

‖**sŭbinfeudā'tion** *n.* See SUB- 8 (1).

subjā'cent *a.* underlying, situated below. [f. L SUB(*jacēre* lie); see -ENT]

sŭ'bject¹ (-ĭ-, -ĕ-) *a. & adv.* **1.** *a.* under government, not independent, in subjection, owing obedience *to*, (*a subject province, tribe; is held subject*; *has long been subject to France*; *States subject to foreign rule*; *we are all subject to the laws of nature, the law of the land*). **2.** liable or exposed or prone *to* (thing; *persons subject to gout*; *is very subject to damage, envy,* etc.). **3.** *a. & adv.* ~ **to**, conditional(ly) upon (for validity etc.), on the assumption of, without precluding, (*the arrangement is made, or is, subject to your approval*; *subject to your consent, I propose to try again*; *subject to correction, these are the facts*). [ME f. OF *suget* etc., f. L *subjectus* p.p. of SUB(*icere* = *jacĕre* throw)]

sŭ'bject² (-ĭ-, -ĕ-) *n.* **1.** person subject to political rule, any member of a State except the Sovereign, any member of a subject State, (*rulers and subjects*; *the subjects of the Crown, of the Sultan*; *the LIBERTY of the subject*); person owing obedience to another. **2.** (Logic & Gram.) member of a proposition about which something is predicated, noun or noun-equivalent with which verb of sentence is made to agree in number etc., (*subject and predicate are the essential parts of a sentence*; *every verb has a subject expressed or understood*). **3.** (Philos.) thinking or feeling entity, the mind, the ego, the conscious self, as opp. all that is external to the mind (~ **and object**, the ego and the non-ego,

self and not-self, the consciousness and what it is or may be conscious of); substance or substratum of anything as opp. its attributes. **4.** what is (to be) discussed or described or represented, matter (to be) treated of or dealt with, (*never talks on serious subjects*; *proposed a subject for the debate*; *a difficult, interesting, dull, subject*; *what is the subject of the poem, story, picture?*; *constantly wanders from the subject*; *he, it, was made the subject of an experiment*; *cannot think of a subject to write about*); department of study (*was examined in six subjects*); (Mus.) theme of fugue or sonata, leading phrase, motif; ~ (**for dissection**), dead body; **change the ~**, talk of something else, esp. as way out of embarrassment; **on the ~ of**, concerning, about. **5.** circumstance, person, or thing, that gives occasion *for* specified feeling or action (*is a subject for ridicule, pity, congratulation*). **6.** (esp. Med.) person of specified usu. undesirable bodily or mental tendencies (*a sensitive, bilious, hysterical, subject*). **7.** ~ **catalogue** etc. (arranged according to subjects treated); ~**-heading** (in index, collecting references to a subject); ~**-matter**, matter treated of in book, lawsuit, etc.; ~**-object**, (Philos.) object of sense or thought as it is conceived of (opp. *object-object*). **8.** Hence ~LESS *a.* [ME f. OF *suget* etc. f. L *subjectus -um* masc. and neut. p.p. (as prec.)]

subjĕ'ct³ *v.t.* subdue (nation etc. usu. *to* one's sway etc.); expose, make liable, treat, *to* (*rudeness subjects one to retorts in kind*; *must be subjected to great heat*; *shall subject it to criticism, to chemical analysis*); so **subjĕ'ct**ION *n.* [ME, f. OF *subjecter* or f. L *subjectare* frequent. (as SUBJECT¹)]

subjĕ'ctive *a. & n.* **1.** *a.* (Philos.) belonging to, of, due to, the consciousness or thinking or perceiving subject or ego as opp. real or external things; due to one's own feelings or capacities rather than being actually existent; imaginary. **2.** (Of art, artists, literature, or history) giving prominence to or depending on personal idiosyncrasy or individual point of view, not producing the effect of literal and impartial transcription of external realities; hence ~NESS (-vn-), **subjĕcti'v**ITY, *ns.* **3.** (Gram.) of the subject; ~ **case**, nominative; ~ **genitive** (as in 'by the act of God'; cf. OBJECTIVE). **4.** Hence ~LY² (-vlī) *adv.* **5.** *n.* subjective case. [ME, f. L *subjectivus* (as SUBJECT¹; see -IVE)]

subjĕ'ctiv|**ism** *n.* doctrine that knowledge is merely subjective and that there is no external or objective test of truth; so ~IST (2) *n.* [f. prec. + -ISM]

subjoi'n *v.t.* add at the end, append, (illustration, anecdote, etc.). [f. obs. F *subjoindre* f. L SUB(*jungere junct-* join)]

sŭ'bjoint *n.* secondary joint (e.g. in insect's leg). [f. SUB- 8 (1) + JOINT¹]

sub judice (sŭb jōō'dĭsī, sŏŏb ū'dĭkā) *a.* under judicial consideration (*newspaper comment on cases sub judice is prohibited*); not yet decided, still debatable, (*the matter is still sub judice*). [L, ~ under a judge]

sŭ'bjug|**āte** (-jŏŏ-) *v.t.* subdue, vanquish, bring under bondage or into subjection; hence or cogn. ~ABLE *a.*, ~A'TION, ~ātor, *ns.* [ME, f. LL SUB(*jugare* f. *jugum* yoke) bring under the yoke + -ATE³]

subjū'nctive *a. & n.* ~ (**mood**), (Gram.) mood of verbs used esp. to denote what is imagined or wished or possible (*if I were you*; *God help you*; *suffice it to say*; *be that as it may*), in some languages also in subordinate clauses; hence ~LY² (-vlī) *adv.* [f. F *subjonctif -ive* or f. LL *subjunctivus* f. L (as SUBJOIN; see -IVE), transl. Gk *hupotaktikos*, as being used in subjoined clauses]

sŭ'bkingdom *n.* taxonomic category below kingdom; phylum. [f. SUB- 8 (2) + KINGDOM]

sŭblăpsā'rian *a. & n.* = INFRALAPSARIAN. [f. mod. L *sublapsarius* (as SUB- 7 (1), *lapsus* LAPSE¹; see -ARIAN)]

sŭ'blease¹ *n.*, **sŭblea'se²** *v.t.*, **sŭblĕ't** *v.t.* (-tt-; **suble't**). lease to subtenant. [f. SUB- 8 (1), 9 + LEASE, LET²]

‖**sŭb-lieutĕ'nant** (see LIEUTENANT) *n.* officer ranking next below lieutenant. [f. SUB- (1) + LIEUTENANT]

sŭ′blĭm|āte[1] *v.t.* **1.** convert (substance) from solid state directly to its vapour by heat (and usu. allow to solidify again). **2.** (fig.) refine, purify, idealize; (Psych.) divert energy of (primitive impulse) into culturally higher activity. **3.** Hence ∼A′TION *n.* [f. as foll. + -ATE[3]]

sŭ′blimate[2] *a.* & *n.* sublimated (substance); CORROSIVE sublimate. [f. L *sublimare* SUBLIME[2] + -ATE[2]]

subli′me[1] *a.* (∼r, ∼st). of the most exalted kind, so distinguished by elevation or size or nobility or grandeur or other impressive quality as to inspire awe or wonder, aloof from and raised far above the ordinary, (*sublime mountain, ɜcenery, ambition, virtue, love, thought, beauty, genius, poet*); (of indifference, impudence, etc.) like that of one too exalted to fear consequences; *Sublime* PORTE; hence or cogn. ∼LY[2] (-mlĭ) *adv.*, **subli′mity** *n.* [f. L *sublimis*]

subli′me[2] *v.t.* & *i.* **1.** = SUBLIMATE[1] 1; undergo sublimation. **2.** purify or elevate, become pure, as by sublimation; make sublime. [ME, f. OF *sublimer* or f. L *sublimare* lift up, in med. L sublimate, f. as prec.]

subli′minal *a.* (Psych.) below the threshold of sensation or consciousness; ∼ **advertising** (presented by very brief television picture etc. so as to influence opinion or behaviour without being consciously perceived); ∼ **self,** part of one's personality outside conscious awareness. [f. SUB- 7 (1) + L *limen -inis* threshold + -AL]

subli′ngual (-nggwal) *a.* under the tongue. [f. SUB- 7 (1) + L *lingua* tongue + -AL]

subli′ttoral *a.* See SUB- 7 (8).

‖**Sub-Lt.** *abbr.* Sub-Lieutenant.

sublu′nary (-lōō′-, -lū′-) *a.* beneath the moon; within the moon's orbit; subject to the moon's influence; of this world, earthly. [f. LL *sublunaris* (as SUB- 7 (1), LUNAR); see -ARY[2]]

sub-machi′ne-gŭn (-shē′) *n.* lightweight machine-gun held by hand for firing. [f. SUB- 8 (1) + MACHINE- -*gun*]

sŭ′b-|măn *n.* (*pl.* ∼**men**). markedly inferior man; brutal or stupid man. [f. SUB- 8 (6) + MAN[1]]

submarin|e (sŭ′bmɛrēn, -ē′n) *a.* & *n.* **1.** *a.* existing, occurring, done, or used, under the surface of the sea, (*submarine plant, earthquake, travel, cable*). **2.** *n.* submarine vessel, esp. warship capable of operating either on or under the water surface, equipped with torpedo-tubes, guns, and periscope; hence ∼ER[1] (4) *n.* [f. SUB- 7 (1) + MARINE]

sŭ′bmaster (-mah-) *n.* assistant (head)master in school. [f. SUB- 8 (1) + MASTER[1]]

submăxi′llary *a.* under the lower jaw. [f. SUB- 7 (1) + MAXILLARY]

submē′diant *n.* (Mus.) sixth note of diatonic scale of any key. [f. SUB- 8 (1) + MEDIANT]

submē′ntal *a.* under the chin. [f. SUB- 7 (1) + MENTAL[2]]

submer′ge *v.* **1.** *v.t.* place below water, flood with water, inundate (lit. or fig.); **the ∼d tenth,** the part of the population that is sunk in poverty or permanently in distress. **2.** *v.i.* (Of submarine or its crew or commander) dive, go below surface. **3.** Hence or cogn. **submer′gence, submer′sion** (-shon), *ns.* [f. L SUB(*mergere mers-* dip)]

submer′sible *a.* & *n.* (vessel) capable of being submerged. [f. *submerse* v. = prec., + -IBLE]

submicrosco′pic *a.* too small to be seen by an ordinary microscope. [f. SUB- 7 (3) + MICROSCOPIC]

submi′niature (-nĭcher) *a.* of greatly reduced size; (of camera) miniature and using 16-mm. film. [f. SUB- 7 (2) + MINIATURE]

submi′ssion (-shon) *n.* **1.** submitting or being submitted (*shall be satisfied with nothing short of complete submission*; *demands the submission of the signature to an expert*). **2.** (Law). theory etc. submitted by counsel to judge or jury. **3.** humility, meekness, resignation, acceptance of authority, obedient conduct or spirit. [ME f. OF, or f. L *submissio* (as SUBMIT; see -ION)]

submi′ssive *a.* willing to submit; yielding to power or authority; humble, obedient; hence ∼LY[2] (-vlĭ) *adv.*, ∼NESS (-vn-) *n.* [f. prec. after *remissive* etc.]

submi′t *v.* (-tt-). **1.** *v.t.* surrender one*self* for control etc. *to* (*submit ourselves entirely to the Divine Will*); subject *to* operation or process. **2.** present for consideration or decision (*should like to submit it to your inspection*; *fifteen entries were submitted*; *submit a case to court*); urge or represent deferentially (*I submit that a material fact has been overlooked*; *that, I submit, is a false inference*). **3.** *v.i.* give way, resign oneself, yield, cease or abstain from resistance, (*to*; *will never submit, submit to indignity, submit to being parted from you*; *had to submit to defeat*). [ME, f. L SUB(*mittere miss-* send)]

submŭ′ltiple *n.* & *a.* (number) that is an aliquot part of another specified number. [f. SUB- (3) + MULTIPLE]

subnor′mal *a.* less than normal; below normal (esp. as regards intelligence); hence ∼ITY (-ă′l-) *n.* [f. SUB- 7 (2) + NORMAL]

subnū′clear *a.* (Phys.) occurring in or smaller than an atomic nucleus. [f. SUB- 7 (3) + NUCLEAR]

subō′cūlar, suboesophageal (-ēsofă′jī-, -ēsŏfajē′-), *adjs.* See SUB- 7 (1).

subor′bital *a.* **1.** situated below the orbit of the eye. **2.** not completing a full orbit round the earth etc. [f. SUB- 7 (1), (2) + ORBITAL]

sŭ′border *n.* taxonomic category between order and family; so **subor′DINAL** *a.* [f. SUB- 8 (2) + ORDER[1]]

subor′dinary *a.* (Her.) charge that is common but less so than ordinaries. [f. SUB- 8 (1) + ORDINARY]

subor′dinate[1] *a.* & *n.* **1.** *a.* of inferior importance or rank, secondary, subservient, (*to*); ∼ **clause,** sentence made by inclusion of a conjunction or by position to serve as *n.* or *a.* or *adv.* in another sentence; hence ∼LY[2] (-tlĭ) *adv.* **2.** *n.* person working under another's control or orders. [f. med. L SUB(*ordinatus* p.p. f. L *ordinare* ordain); see -ATE[2]]

subor′din|āte[2] *v.t.* make subordinate, treat or regard as of minor importance, bring or put into subservient relation, (*to*); hence or cogn. ∼A′TION *n.*, ∼ATIVE *a.* [f. med. L *subordinare* (as prec.) + -ATE[3]]

subor′n *v.t.* induce by bribery or otherwise to commit perjury or other unlawful act; hence or cogn. **subōrn**A′TION, ∼ER[1], *ns.* [f. L SUB(*ornare* equip) incite secretly]

subō′xide *n.* (Chem.) oxide containing smallest proportion of oxygen. [f. SUB- 8 (1) + OXIDE]

sŭ′bphȳl|um *n.* (*pl.* ∼**a**). taxonomic category between phylum and class. [f. SUB- 8 (2) + PHYLUM]

sŭ′b-plŏt *n.* subordinate plot in play etc. [f. SUB- 8 (1) + PLOT[1]]

subpoe′na (subpē′-, sup-) *n.*, & *v.t.* (∼ed or ∼'d, *pr.* -ad). **1.** *n.* writ commanding person's attendance in lawcourt. **2.** *v.t.* serve subpoena on. [ME, f. L *sub poena* under penalty (first wds in the writ)]

subprī′or *n.* prior's assistant or deputy. [f. SUB- 8 (1) + PRIOR[1]]

sŭ′brēgion (-jon) *n.* division of faunal region; hence ∼AL (-ē′-) *a.* [f. SUB- 8 (2) + REGION]

subrē′ption *n.* obtaining of thing by surprise or misrepresentation. [f. L *subreptio* purloining f. SUB(*ripere rept-* = *rapere* snatch); see -ION]

subrogā′tion *n.* (Law). substitution of one party for another as creditor, with transfer of rights and duties. [f. LL *subrogatio* f. SUB(*rogare* ask) choose as substitute; see -ATION]

sub rosa (sŭb rō′za) *a.* & *adv.* (Of communication, consultation, etc.) in confidence, under express or implied pledge of secrecy. [L, lit. under the rose, as emblem of secrecy]

sŭ′broutine (-rōōtēn) *n.* (Computers). routine designed to perform a frequently used mathematical operation within a program. [f. SUB- 8 (1) + ROUTINE]

subsă′turātèd (-cher-, -tūr-) *a.*, **subsătūrā′tion** *n.* See SUB- 7 (2).

subscrī′b|e *v.* **1.** *v.t.* write (esp. one's name) at foot of document etc. (*the subscribed names carry weight*; *someone has subscribed a motto); write one's name at foot of, sign, (document, picture, etc.); **~e** one**self**, sign one's name as. **2.** v.i. express one's adhesion *to* an opinion or resolution (*cannot subscribe to that*). **3.** v.i. & t. enter one's name in a list of contributors, make or promise a contribution, contribute (specified sum), to or *to* a common fund or *for* a common object, raise or guarantee raising of by subscribing thus; **~e for,** engage before publication to take copy or copies of (book); **~e to,** engage to take (newspaper etc.) for specified time. **4.** Hence or cogn. **~ER¹** *n.*, (esp.) person paying regular sum for hire of telephone line operated by commercial company (**~er trunk dialling,** making of trunk-calls by subscriber without assistance of operator). [ME, f. L SUB(*scribere* script- write)]

sŭ′bscrĭpt *a.* & *n.* **1.** *a.* (Gk Gram.) iota **~,** small ι written below ᾱ, η, or ω. **2.** *a.* & *n.* (Math. etc.) (symbol) written below and to the right of another symbol. [f. L *subscriptus,* p.p. of *subscribere* (see prec.)]

subscrī′ption *n.* thing, esp. money, subscribed; act of subscribing; fee for membership of society etc.; offering of reduced price to those ordering book before publication; **~ concert** etc. (paid for mainly by those who subscribe (sense 3) for tickets to attend). [ME, f. L *subscriptio* (as SUBSCRIBE; see -ION)]

sŭ′bsĕction *n.* See SUB- 8 (2).

subsĕ′lli|um *n.* (*pl.* **~a**). = MISERICORD 3. [L. (as SUB-1, *sella* seat)]

sŭ′b-sēquence *n.* sequence forming part of a larger one. [f. SUB- 8 (2) + SEQUENCE]

sŭ′bsĕqu|ent *a.* that follow(s) or followed a specified event etc., of later time or date than something, posterior in time *to*; hence **~ENCE** *n.,* **~entLY²** *adv.* [ME f. OF, or f. L SUB(*sequi* follow); see -ENT]

subsĕr′ve v.t. serve as means in furthering (purpose, action, etc.). [f. L SUB(*servire* SERVE)]

subsĕr′vi|ent *a.* serving as means, having merely instrumental relation, (*to*); subordinate *to*; cringing, obsequious; hence **~ENCE, ~ENCY,** *ns.,* **~entLY** *adv.* [f. L (as prec.; see -ENT)]

sŭ′bsĕt *n.* See SUB- 8 (2).

sŭ′bshrŭb *n.* low-growing or small shrub. [f. SUB- 8 (6) + SHRUB¹]

subsī′d|e v.i. **1.** (Of water, esp. flood) sink to low(er) level; (of ground) cave in, sink; (of building, ship, etc.) settle down lower in ground or water; (of suspended matter) fall to bottom, be precipitated; (of swelling etc.) become less; (of person, usu. joc.) sink into sitting or kneeling or lying posture (*subsided into an armchair*). **2.** cease from activity or agitation, become tranquil, abate, (*storm, tumult, apprehension, excitement, subsides*). **3.** So **~ENCE** (subsī′-, sŭ′bsī-) *n.* [f. L SUB(*sidere* settle cogn. w. *sedēre* sit)]

subsī′diar|y *a.* & *n.* **1.** *a.* serving to assist or supplement, auxiliary, supplementary; hence **~iLY²** *adv.* **2.** (Of company) controlled by another on basis of voting power or issued share capital. **3.** (Of troops) paid for by subsidy, hired by another nation. **4.** *n.* subsidiary thing or person, accessory; subsidiary company. [f. L *subsidiarius* (as SUBSIDY; see -ARY¹)]

sŭ′bsidīz|e, -ĭse (-īz), v.t. pay subsidy to; reduce cost of by subsidy; hence **~A′TION** *n.* [f. foll. + -IZE]

sŭ′bsĭdy *n.* **1.** (Hist.) parliamentary grant of money to the sovereign for State needs; tax levied on particular occasion. **2.** money grant from one State to another in return for military or naval aid or other equivalent. **3.** money contributed by State or public body to keep down price of commodities etc. (*food, housing, subsidy*) or to expenses of commercial undertaking, charitable institution, etc., held to be of public utility. [ME, f. AF *subsidie,* OF *subside* f. L *subsidium* assistance; see -Y¹]

subsī′st v. **1.** v.i. exist, continue to exist, remain in being; keep oneself alive, support life, be kept alive, find sustenance, (*on vegetables, charity,* etc., *by begging* etc.). **2.** v.t. (arch.) provide sustenance for. [f. L SUB(*sistere* set, stand) stand firm]

subsī′stence *n.* subsisting; means of supporting life, livelihood, what one lives on or by; **~ allowance** or **money,** allowance or advance of pay granted for maintenance esp. while travelling on business; **~ farming** (in which almost all produce is consumed by farmer's household); **~ level, ~ wage,** (merely enough to provide the bare necessities of life). [f. LL *subsistentia* substance (as prec.; see -ENCE)]

sŭ′bsoil *n.* soil lying immediately under surface soil. [f. SUB- 8 (4) + SOIL¹]

subsŏ′n|ic *a.* relating to speeds less than that of sound; hence **~ICALLY** *adv.* [f. SUB- 7 (2) + SONIC]

sŭ′bspēcies (-shēz, -shĭz) *n.* (*pl.* same). (Biol.) taxonomic category below species, usu. a more or less permanent variety geographically isolated; so **subSPECI′FIC** *a.* [f. SUB- 8 (2) + SPECIES]

sŭ′bstance *n.* **1.** particular kind of material having more or less uniform properties (*a heavy, porous, yellow, transparent, substance; the small number of substances that make up the world*). **2.** reality, solidity, (arch.) wealth and possessions, (*sacrifice the substance for the shadow; there is no substance in him; an argument of little substance*); *a man of* **~,** with much property, wealthy; *waste* one's **~,** be spendthrift. **3.** theme, subject, material as opposed to form, (*the substance is good, but the style is repellent*). **4.** essential nature (*the Son being of one substance with the Father*); essence or most important part of anything, pith, purport, real meaning, (*can give you the substance of his remarks*); *I agree with you in* **~,** generally, apart from details. **5.** (Metaphys.) the substratum that the cognizable properties or qualities or attributes or accidents of things are conceived as inhering in or affecting, the essential nature underlying phenomena, (*substance and accidents in metaphysics correspond to subject and predicate in logic*). [ME f. OF, f. L SUB(*stantia* essence f. *stare* stand; see -ANCE)]

substă′ndard *a.* of less than required or normal quality or size; inferior; (of language usage) existing in a community but not accepted in the standard language. [f. SUB- 7 (3) + STANDARD]

substă′ntial (-shal) *a.* having substance, actually existing, not illusory, (*the ghost proved substantial after all*); of real importance or value, of considerable amount, (opp. *nominal, verbal; a substantial argument, point; awarded substantial damages; made a substantial contribution; made substantial progress, concessions*); of solid material or structure, not flimsy, stout, (*a substantial house; a man of substantial build*); possessed of much property, well-to-do, commercially sound, (*a substantial yeoman; deal only with substantial firms*); deserving the name in essentials, virtual, practical, (*substantial truth, agreement, success, performance of contract*); hence or cogn. **~ITY** (-shiā′l-) *n.,* **~LY²** *adv.* [ME, f. OF *substantiel* or LL *substantialis* (as SUBSTANCE; see -AL)]

substă′ntialism (-sha-) *n.* (Philos.) doctrine that behind phenomena there are substantial realities; so **~IST** (2) *n.* [f. prec. + -ISM]

substă′ntialize (-sha-), **-ise** (-īz), v.t. & i. invest with or acquire substance or actual existence. [f. SUB-STANTIAL + -IZE]

substă′nti|āte (-shĭ-) v.t. prove the truth of, give good grounds for, (charge, statement, claim); hence **~A′TION** (-shĭ-, -sĭ-) *n.* [f. med. L *substantiare* give substance to, f. as SUBSTANCE; + -ATE²]

sŭ′bstantīve (or, in sense 2, substă′-) *a.* & *n.* **1.** *a.* expressing existence (**the ~ verb,** 'to be'). **2.** having separate and independent existence, not merely inferential or implicit or subservient or parasitic; (of enactment, motion, etc.) made in due form as such; (of dye) not needing mordant; (of law) relating to rights and duties; (Mil., of rank etc.) permanent (not brevet, honorary, acting, or temporary). **3.** (arch.) denoting a substance (NOUN *substantive*). **4.** Hence **~LY²** (-vlĭ) *adv.,* (esp. Gram., as a substantive). **5.** *n.* = NOUN 1; hence **sŭbstantī′VAL** *a.* [ME, f. OF *substantif -ive,* or f. LL *substantivus* (as SUBSTANCE; see -IVE)]

sŭ′bstātion n. subordinate station, esp. reducing high voltage of electric power transmission to that suitable for supply to consumers. [f. SUB- 8 (1)+STATION]

substĭ′tŭent a. & n. (Chem.) (group of atoms) replacing another atom or group in a compound. [f. L (as foll.; see -ENT)]

sŭ′bstit|ūte n., a., & v. **1.** n. & a. (person or thing) acting or serving in place of another; artificial food used in place of a natural food (butter substitute); (Sc. Law) deputy (sheriff substitute). **2.** v.t. make (person or thing) fill a place or discharge a function for or for another; (vulg.) replace (person or thing) by or with another; put in exchange (for). **3.** v.i. act as substitute (for). **4.** Hence or cogn. ∼ūtABLE a., ∼ū′tION n., ∼ū′tionAL, ∼ū′tionARY¹, ∼ūtIVE, adjs. [ME, f. L substitutus p.p. of SUB(stituere = statuere set up)]

sŭ′bstrāte n. = foll.; surface to be painted, printed, etc., on; nutrient medium for bacteria culture. [Anglicized f. foll.; see -ATE¹]

sŭ′bstrat|um (-ah-, -ā-) n. (pl. ∼a). underlying layer or substance; foundation, basis, (lit., or fig.; there is a substratum of truth in it). [mod. L, p.p. (as n.) of L SUB(sternere strew); cf. STRATUM]

sŭ′bstrŭctur|e n. underlying or supporting structure; hence ∼AL a. [f. SUB- 8 (4)+STRUCTURE]

subsŭ′me v.t. include (instance etc.) under a rule or class; hence **subsŭ′mpt**ION n. [f. med. L SUB(sumere sumpt- take)]

sŭ′btĕnancy̆, sŭ′btĕnant, ns. See SUB- 8 (1).

subtĕ′nd v.t. (Geom.) (Of line, arc, figure, etc.) form (angle) at a point when its extremities are joined to that point; (of angle or chord) have bounding lines or points that meet or coincide with those of (line or arc). [f. L SUB(tendere stretch); cf. TEND¹]

sŭ′bterfŭge n. attempt to escape censure or defeat in argument by evading the issue or using deception; statement etc. resorted to for such purpose; use of such statements etc. [F, or f. LL subterfugium f. L subterfugere escape secretly (subter beneath, fugere flee)]

subtĕr′minal a. nearly at the end. [f. SUB- 7 (7)+ TERMINAL]

sŭbterrā′nean a. existing, occurring, or done under the earth's surface; underground. [f. L SUB(terraneus f. terra earth)+-AN]

subtil(e), subtilty. Vars. (arch.) of SUBTLE(TY).

sŭ′btiliz|e, -īs|e, (sŭ′tĭlīz) v. **1.** v.t. make subtle; elevate, refine. **2.** argue or reason subtly (upon). **3.** Hence ∼A′TION n. [f. F subtiliser or f. med. L subtilizare (as SUBTLE; see -IZE)]

sŭ′btītle n., & v.t. (provide with) subordinate or additional title of book etc., or caption of cinema film (esp. translating dialogue). [f. SUB- 8 (1)+TITLE]

sŭ′btle (sŭ′tel) a. (∼r, ∼st). pervasive or elusive owing to tenuity (the subtle air; a subtle vapour, perfume); evasive, mysterious, hard to grasp or trace, (subtle magic, charm, power, art, poison; a subtle distinction); making fine distinctions, having delicate perception, acute, (subtle senses, perception, insight; a subtle observer, philosopher, intellect, mind); ingenious, elaborate, clever, (a subtle device, fancy, workman, explanation, policy; subtle fingers); crafty, cunning (now the serpent was more subtle than any beast of the field; a subtle enemy); hence **sŭ′bt**LY² (sŭ′t-) adv. [ME f. OF sotil, f. L subtilis]

sŭ′btlety̆ (sŭ′teltĭ) n. In adj. senses; a fine distinction, piece of hair-splitting. [ME, f. OF s(o)utilté f. L subtilitas -tatis (as prec.; see -TY¹)]

subtō′nic n. (Mus.) note below tonic, seventh note of diatonic scale of any key. [f. SUB- 8 (4)+TONIC]

‖sŭbtō′pi|a n. (derog.) suburban and rural areas disfigured by ill-planned and ugly building development; unsightly suburbs regarded as encroaching upon the natural scene; hence ∼AN a. [f. SUBURB+ UTOPIA]

sŭ′btōtal n. total of part of a group of figures to be added. [f. SUB- 8 (2)+TOTAL]

subtră′ct v.t. deduct (part, quantity, number) from or from whole or greater quantity or number, esp. in arithmetic or algebra; hence or cogn. ∼ION n., ∼IVE a. [f. L SUB(trahere tract- draw)]

sŭ′btrahĕnd (-a-h-) n. (Math.) quantity or number to be subtracted. [f. L subtrahendus gerundive of subtrahere (see prec.)]

sŭbtrŏ′pical a. (characteristic) of regions bordering on the tropics. [f. SUB- 7 (8)+TROPICAL]

sŭ′bŭlate a. (Bot. & Zool.) slender and tapering. [f. L subula awl+-ATE²]

sŭ′bŭrb n. outlying district of city. [ME, f. OF suburbe or f. L SUB(urbium f. urbs urbis city)]

subŭr′ban a. of suburb(s); (derog.) provincial in outlook; hence ∼ITE¹ (1) n., ∼IZE (3) v.t. [f. L suburbanus (as prec.; see -AN)]

Subŭr′bia n. (usu. derog.) the suburbs (esp. of London) and their inhabitants. [f. SUBURB+-IA¹]

subvĕ′ntion n. grant of money from government etc., subsidy. [ME f. OF, f. LL subventio -onis f. L SUB(venire vent- come) assist; see -ION]

subvĕr′sive a. & n. (person) seeking to subvert (esp. government); hence ∼LY² (-vlĭ) adv., ∼NESS (-vn-) n. [f. med. L subversivus (as foll.; see -IVE)]

subvĕr′t v.t. overturn, upset, effect destruction or overthrow of, (religion, monarchy, the constitution, principles, morality); so **subvĕr′s**ION (-shon) n. [ME, f. OF subvertir or f. L SUB(vertere vers- turn)]

sŭ′bway n. underground passage for pipes etc. or for pedestrians to cross below road(s) etc.; *under-ground railway. [f. SUB- 8 (4)+WAY]

subzēr′ō a. less than zero (esp. on scale of temperature). [f. SUB- 7 (2)+ZERO]

suc- pref., assim. form of SUB- 1-6 before c.

sŭccĕdā′nĕ|um (-ks-) n. (pl. ∼a). substitute, thing (or occas. person) that one falls back on in default of another; so ∼OUS a. [mod. L, neut. (as n.) of L succedaneus (as foll.; see -ANEOUS)]

succee′d (-ks-) v. **1.** v.i. have success (in doing etc.); be successful, prosper, accomplish one's purpose; (of plan etc.) be brought to successful outcome. **2.** v.t. & i. follow in order, come next to or to, ensue, be subsequent (to), come by inheritance or in due order to or to office or title or property, (day succeeds day or to day; agitation succeeded calm; succeeding ages will reverence his memory; Elizabeth I succeeded Mary, succeeded to the throne, succeeded). **3.** v.t. take the place previously filled by. [ME, f. OF succeder or f. L SUC(cedere cess- go)]

succĕ′ntor (-ks-) n. precentor's deputy in some cathedrals; hence ∼SHIP n. [LL, f. L SUC(cinere cent- = canere sing); see -OR]

succès de scandale (sŏoksā de skahṅdah′l) n. eager reception given to work because of its scandalous nature or associations. [F]

succès d'estime (sŏoksā dĕstē′m) n. passably cordial reception given to performance or work from respect for performer or author rather than appreciation of its merits; *cordial reception by the critics but not by the general public. [F]

succès fou (sŏoksā fŏo′) n. success marked by wild enthusiasm. [F]

succĕ′ss (-ks-) n. **1.** outcome of undertaking (ill success); favourable outcome, accomplishment of what was aimed at, attainment of wealth or fame or position, (have inquired for it without success; military successes; spoilt by success); nothing succeeds like ∼, one success leads to others; ∼ story, person's rise from poverty etc. to fame; hence ∼FUL a., ∼FULLY adv. **2.** thing or person that turns out well (the experiment is a success; was a great success as a bishop). [f. L successus (as SUCCEED)]

succĕ′ssion (-ksĕ′shon) n. **1.** a following in order; **in** ∼, one after another, without intervention of anything else; **in quick** ∼, following one another at short interval(s). **2.** series of things in succession (a succession of defeats). **3.** (right of) succeeding to the throne or any office or inheritance, set or order of persons having such right, (laws regulating the succession; the *succession must not be broken; is second in the succession*); **in ~ to**, as successor of; **apostolic ~**, uninterrupted transmission of spiritual authority through successive Popes and other bishops from the Apostles; **law of ~** (regulating inheritance esp. in cases of intestate's decease); **settle the ~**, determine who shall succeed; **S~ State** (resulting from partition of previously existing country). **4.** (Biol.) order of development of species or community; = SERE³. **5.** Hence ~AL *a*. [ME f. OF, or f. L *successio* (as SUCCEED; see -ION)]

succe'ssive (-ks-) *a*. following one after another, in uninterrupted succession, running, consecutive; hence ~LY² (-vlǐ) *adv*. [ME, f. med. L *successivus* (as SUCCEED; see -IVE)]

succe'ssor (-ks-) *n*. person or thing that succeeds to another (*successor of* or *to his father*; *his immediate successor*). [ME, f. OF *successour* f. L *successor* (as SUCCEED; see -OR)]

succi'nct (-ks-) *a*. terse, concise, briefly expressed; hence ~LY² *adv*., ~NESS *n*. [ME, f. L *succinctus* p.p. of SUC(*cingere* gird) tuck up]

succi'n|ic (-ks-) *a*. (Chem.) ~**ic acid**, crystalline dibasic acid derived from amber etc.; hence ~ATE¹ (3) (sŭ'ks-) *n*. [f. F *succinique* f. L *succinum* amber; see -IC]

su'ccory *n*. CHICORY plant. [alt. f. *cicoree* etc., early forms of CHICORY]

*****su'ccotăsh** *n*. dish of green maize and beans boiled together. [f. Narraganset *msiquatash*]

Su'ccôth (sŏŏ'kŏt) *n*. Jewish autumn thanksgiving festival commemorating sheltering in the wilderness. [f. Heb. *sukkôt* pl. of *sukkāh* thicket, hut]

||**su'ccour** (-ker), *****su'ccor**, *v.t.* & *n*. (literary). **1.** *v.t.* come to the assistance of, give aid to, (person in danger or difficulty). **2.** *n*. aid given at time of need; (in *pl*., arch.) reinforcements, troops coming to the rescue; hence ~LESS *a*. [ME, f. OF *socorre* v., *socours* n. f. med. L *succursus*, f. L SUC(*currere* curs- run)]

su'ccub|a *n*. (*pl.* ~ae), **su'ccub|us** *n*. (*pl.* ~**i** *pr*. -ī). female demon supposed to have sexual intercourse with sleeping men. [f. LL *succuba* prostitute, med. L *succubus*, f. SUC(*cubare* lie)]

su'ccul|ent *a*. & *n*. **1.** *a*. juicy (of food, lit. or fig.); (Bot.) thick and fleshy, having such leaves or stems; hence ~ENCE *n*., ~entLY² *adv*. **2.** *n*. (Bot.) succulent plant. [f. L *succulentus* (*succus* juice; see -ULENT)]

succu'mb (-m) *v.i.* be overcome, have to cease from resistance or competition or other effort, be forced to give way *to*, die owing *to*, die, (*succumb to superior numbers, grief, temptation, one's injuries*). [ME, f. OF *succomber* or f. L SUC(*cumbere* lie)]

succu̱r'sal *a*. (esp. Eccl., of chapel etc.) subsidiary. [f. F *succursale* f. med. L *succursus* (as SUCCOUR; see -AL)]

sŭch *a*. (no *compar.* or *superl*.; placed not between *a* or *an* and *n*. but before or after them), & *pron*. **1.** *a*. of the same kind or degree *as* (*such people, people such, as these; such beauty as yours; there is such a thing as divorce, you know; experiences such as this are rare; such grapes as you never saw*); **~ as**, (1) of the or a kind that (*a scarlet such as makes the eyes ache*), (2) for example (*insects, such as moths and bees*); **~ as it is**, if indeed it is good etc. enough to be called that. **2.** so great, having a quality in so high a degree, *as to do* or *that* (*is such as to make one despair; had such a fright that she hardly survived it; not such a fool as to believe that*). **3.** of the kind or degree already described or implied in context (*never had such sport; there are no such things now; it is no such thing; such things make one despair; such is life; no such* LUCK; *don't be in such a hurry; how could you leave him at such a time?; saw just such* ANOTHER *yesterday; long may he continue such!*); (colloq. preceding *a*. & *n*. w. effect of so modifying the adjective: *don't use such horrid language; was it such a long time ago?; don't want such a big one or such big ones*); (occas. used twice correlatively = LIKE¹ 1:) **~ master ~ man**, the servant is such as the master is. **4.** (Law or formal), the aforesaid, of the aforesaid kind (*whoever shall make such return falsely*). **5.** so great!,

of a kind that demands exclamatory description, (*we have had such sport!*; (EVER) *such an enjoyable evening!*; *house has such a lot of windows*). **6.** of a kind or degree sufficient to explain the preceding or following statement (*he cannot come too often, he gives such pleasure; there was such a draught, it is no wonder she caught cold*). **7. ~(-and-~)**, (person or thing) of particular kind but not needing to be specified (*will be in such-and-such a place at such-and-such a time*); **~-and-~ a person**, someone, so-and-so. **8. ~ a one**, such a person or thing (*as*), (arch.) some person or thing unspecified. **9.** *pron*. **~ as**, those who, persons such as. **10.** that, the thing or action referred to, (*such were his words; such being the case, we can do nothing; I may have offended, but such was not my intention*). **11. as ~**, as being what has been named (*in country places a stranger is welcome as such*); **all ~**, all persons of such character (*so perish all such!*). **12. ~'like**, (colloq.) (things) of such kind. **13.** (vulg. or Commerc.) the aforesaid thing(s), it, they or them, (*those who leave parcels in the train cannot expect to recover such*). [OE *swilc, swylc*, = OS *sulīk*, OHG *solīh*, ON *slīkr*, Goth. *swaleiks* f. Gmc **swa* so¹ + **līk* form (cf. LIKE¹)]

sŭck *v*. & *n*. **1.** *v.t.* draw (milk or other fluid) into mouth by making partial vacuum with muscles of lips etc., (fig.) imbibe or gain (*knowledge, advantage*, etc. *from; suck in knowledge; suck advantage out of*). **2.** draw milk or liquid or sustenance or advantage from (*suck the breast, the mother; ~ dry*, exhaust of contents thus; *suck* EGG¹s); roll the tongue round, squeeze in the mouth, (*suck sweets, one's teeth*, etc.); **~ (off)**, (sl.) perform fellatio on. **3.** (Of substance) **~ in** or **up**, absorb; (of whirlpool etc.) **~ in**, engulf. **4.** *v.i.* suck the breast or udder; suck something, use sucking action, make sucking sound, (*sat sucking at his pipe*); (of pump etc.) make gurgling or drawing sound; **~ up**, (sl.) play toady (*to*). **5.** *n*. opportunity of sucking the breast; **give ~** (arch.) of mother or nurse or dam). **6.** drawing action of whirlpool etc., spell of sucking with lips or in mouth (*take a suck at it*); small draught of or of liquor; (sl., esp. in *pl*.) disappointment, fiasco, (**~s!**, *int*. expr. derision or amusement at another's failure after confidence). [OE *sūcan*, = L *sugere* f. IE **sūg-*]

su'cker *n*. & *v*. **1.** *n*. person or thing that sucks, esp. sucking-pig or new-born whale; (sl.) person easily deceived, greenhorn, (**be a ~ for**, be unable to resist attractions of); fish that has mouth suggesting suction or adheres by suction; ***lollipop. **2.** piston of suction-pump; pipe through which liquid is drawn by suction. **3.** flat or concave animal organ or artificial device of rubber etc. that adheres by suction and atmospheric pressure to what it is placed against. **4.** (Bot.) shoot springing from subterranean part of stem, from part of root remote from main stem, from axil, or abnormally from bole or branch. **5.** *v.t.* & *i.* (Bot.) remove suckers from; produce suckers. [ME, f. prec. + -ER¹]

su'cking *a*. In vbl senses; not yet weaned (*sucking child, sucking-pig*), unfledged (*sucking dove*); **~-disc**, = prec. 3; **~-fish**, remora. [f. SUCK + -ING²]

su'ckle *v*. **1.** *v.t.* give suck to; (fig.) nourish. **2.** *v.i.* feed by sucking at breast or udder. [ME, prob. back-form. f. foll.]

su'ckling *n*. unweaned child or animal; BABEs and sucklings. [ME, f. SUCK + -LING¹]

su'crôse (sŏŏ'-, sū'-) *n*. (Chem.) sugar obtained from sugar-cane, sugar-beet, etc. [f. F *sucre* SUGAR + -OSE²]

su'ction *n*. sucking; production of partial vacuum by removal of air etc. for purpose of enabling external atmospheric pressure to force in liquid or produce adhesion of surfaces; **~-pump** (drawing liquid through pipe into chamber exhausted by piston). [f. LL *suctio* f. L *sugere* suct- SUCK; see -ION]

sŭctōr'ial *a*. (Zool.) adapted for or capable of sucking; having sucker for feeding or adhering; so **~IAN** *n*. [f. mod. L *suctorius* (as prec.; see -ORY) + -AL]

Sudane′se (sōōdanē′z) *a.* & *n.* (*pl.* same). (native or inhabitant) of (the) Sudan. [f. *Sudan*, republic in NE Africa, or the *Sudan*, region of Africa S. of Sahara desert, + -ESE]

sudār′i|um (sū-, sōō-) *n.* (*pl.* ∼a). cloth for wiping face, esp. St. Veronica's legendary handkerchief miraculously impressed with face of Christ; = VERONICA 2. [L, = napkin (*sudor* sweat; see -ARY¹)]

sudatōr′i|um (sū-, sōō-) *n.* (*pl.* ∼a). (esp. Rom. Ant.) hot-air or steam bath taken in order to induce sweating. [L, neut. of *sudatorius* (see foll.)]

su′datory (sū′-, sōō′-) *a.* & *n.* **1.** *a.* promoting perspiration. **2.** *n.* sudatory drug; = prec. [f. L *sudatorius* (*sudare* sweat; see -ORY)]

sŭdd *n.* floating plants, trees, etc., impeding navigation of White Nile. [Arab., = obstruction]

sŭ′dden *a.* & *n.* **1.** *a.* occurring or come upon or made or done unexpectedly or without warning, abrupt, abnormally rapid, hurried, (*sudden need, fear; a sudden resolve, departure, change, turn of the wrist, bend in the road; is very sudden in his movements*); ∼ **death**, (fig., colloq.) decision by a single toss of a coin, decision of draw or tie by result of next game, next hole won, etc.; hence ∼LY² *adv.*, ∼NESS (-n-n-) *n.* **2.** *n.* (**all**) **of a** (or arch.) **on a** ∼, suddenly. [ME, f. AF *sodein, sudein*, OF *soudain* f. LL *subitanus* f. L *subitaneus* (*subitus* sudden; see -ANEOUS)]

sudori′ferous (sū-, sōō-) *a.* (Of gland etc.) secreting sweat. [f. LL *sudorifer* f. L *sudor* sweat; see -FEROUS]

sudori′fic (sū-, sōō-) *a.* & *n.* (drug) causing sweating. [f. mod. L *sudorificus* f. L *sudor* sweat; see -FIC]

Su′dra (sōō′-) *n.* lowest of four great Hindu castes, with menial occupations. [f. Skr. *śūdra*]

sŭds (-z) *n.*, & *v.i.* **1.** *n. pl.* (**soa′p**) ∼, froth of soap and water; hence ∼Y² *a.* **2.** *(sl.)* beer. **3.** *v.i.* form suds. [orig. = fen waters etc., of uncert. orig.; cf. MDu., MLG *sudde*, MDu. *sudse* marsh, bog, prob. rel. to SEETHE]

sue (sū, sōō) *v.t.* & *i.* **1.** institute legal proceedings against (person, or abs.); make application to or *to* lawcourt *for* redress; ∼ (**out**), make petition in lawcourt for and obtain (writ, pardon, etc.). **2.** entreat (person, or abs.); make entreaty *to* (person, *for* a favour. [ME, f. AF *suer, siwer*, etc. f. OF *siu-* etc. st. of *sivre* f. Rom. **sequere* f. L *sequi* follow]

suede (swād) *n.* kid or other skin with flesh side rubbed to a nap; ∼(-**cloth**), woven fabric with short nap imitating this. [f. F (*gants de*) *Suède* (gloves of) Sweden]

su′et (sū′-, sōō′-) *n.* hard fat of kidneys and loins of oxen, sheep, etc.; ∼ **pudding** (made with suet and usu. boiled or steamed); hence ∼Y² *a.* [ME, f. AF **suet, *sewet* f. OF *seu* f. L *sebum* tallow; see -ET¹]

suf- *pref.*, assim. form of SUB- 1-6 before *f*.

sŭ′ffer *v.* **1.** *v.t.* undergo, experience, be subjected to, (pain, loss, grief, defeat, change, punishment, wrong, etc.). **2.** *v.i.* undergo pain or grief or damage or disablement (*suffers acutely; suffering mortals; was suffering from neuralgia; your reputation will suffer; the engine suffered severely; trade is suffering from the war*); undergo martyrdom; hence ∼ER¹, ∼ING¹ (1), *ns.* **3.** *v.t.* put up with, tolerate, (*does not suffer fools gladly*); (arch.) permit *to* do, allow to be done. Hence ∼ABLE *a.* [ME, f. AF *suffrir, soeffrir*, OF *sof(f)rir* f. Rom. **sufferire* f. L SUF(*ferre* bear)]

sŭ′fferance *n.* tacit consent, permission or toleration implied by abstinence from objection, (**on** ∼, in virtue of such toleration); (arch.) submissiveness. [ME, f. AF, OF *suffraunce* f. LL *sufferentia* (as prec.; see -ENCE)]

suffi′ce *v.* **1.** *v.i.* be enough (*to do, for* person or purpose, or abs.), be adequate, (*your word will suffice; that suffices to prove it*); ∼ **it to say**, I will content myself with saying that. **2.** *v.t.* satisfy, meet the needs of, (*half a dozen sufficed him*). [ME, f. OF *suffire* (*suffis-*) f. L SUF(*ficere* = *facere* make)]

suffi′ciency (-shen-) *n.* adequate resources, a competence, a sufficient amount of or *of* something; (arch.) being sufficient, ability, efficiency. [f. LL *sufficientia* (as foll.; see -ENCY)]

suffi′cient (-shent) *a.* & *n.* **1.** *a.* sufficing, adequate esp. in amount or number to the need, enough, (*is sufficient to feed a hundred men; had not sufficient courage for it; has impudence sufficient for anything; have you sufficient provisions?*); SELF-*sufficient*; hence ∼LY² *adv.* **2.** (arch.) competent, of adequate ability or resources. **3.** *n.* enough, a sufficient quantity, (*have you had sufficient?; am not sufficient of an expert to decide*). [ME f. OF, or f. L *sufficiens* (as SUFFICE; see -ENT)]

sŭ′ffix¹ (sū′-, -i′x) *v.t.* append, esp. as suffix; hence ∼A′TION *n.* [f. foll. & L *suffixus* p.p. (see foll.)]

sŭ′ffix² *n.* verbal element added at end of word to form derivative (e.g. -*ation*, -*fy*, -*ing*, -*itis*); (Math.) = SUBSCRIPT 2. [f. mod. L *suffixum* neut. p.p. (as n.) of L SUF(*figere* fasten)]

sŭ′ffoc|āte *v.* **1.** *v.t.* (Of person, overlying mass, fumes, etc.) choke or kill by stopping breathing; produce choking sensation in, impede breath or utterance of, (*suffocated by* or *with grief, excitement*, etc.). **2.** *v.i.* be or feel suffocated, gasp for breath. **3.** So ∼A′TION *n.* [f. L SUF(*focare* f. *fauces* throat) + -ATE³]

Sŭ′ffolk (-ok) *n.* breed of black-faced sheep; = *Suffolk* PUNCH⁴. [∼ in England]

sŭ′ffragan *a.* & *n.* ∼ (**bishop**), **bishop** ∼, (1) bishop appointed to help diocesan bishop in administration of diocese, (2) bishop in relation to his archbishop or metropolitan; ∼ **see** etc. (of suffragan bishop); hence ∼SHIP *n.* [ME f. AF & OF, repr. med. L *suffraganeus* assistant (bishop) f. L *suffragium* (see foll., -AN); orig. of bishop summoned to vote in synod]

sŭ′ffrage *n.* **1.** vote, view expressed by voting, (*the electors gave their suffrages for and against*); opinion in support of proposal etc. **2.** right of voting in political elections; **manhood** ∼ (extended to all adult males other than those disqualified e.g. as being criminals, without property tests etc.); **female** or **women** ∼ (extended to women as well as men); **universal** ∼ (extended to all adults with minor exceptions). **3.** (Eccl., esp. in *pl.*) intercessory petition of priest in liturgy; short petition of congregation, esp. one said in response to priest; (arch.) an intercessory prayer. [ME, f. L *suffragium*, partly thr. F *suffrage*]

sŭ′ffrage′tte *n.* (Hist.) woman who agitated, esp. with violence, for woman suffrage. [f. prec. + -ETTE, after foll.]

sŭ′ffragist *n.* one who advocates extension of the suffrage, esp. to women. [f. SUFFRAGE + -IST]

suffu′se (-z) *v.t.* (Of colour or moisture) well up from within and colour or moisten (*a blush, tears, suffused her cheeks, eyes*); (fig.) overspread with colour etc.; so **suffu′sion** (-zhon) *n.* [f. L SUF(*fundere fus-* pour)]

Su′fi| (sōō′-) *n.* Muslim ascetic (and pantheistic) mystic; hence ∼IC *a.*, ∼ISM (3) *n.* [f. Arab. *ṣūfī*, perh. f. *ṣūf* wool (from his woollen garment)]

sug- *pref.*, assim. form of SUB- 1-6 before *g*.

su′gar (shōō′-) *n.*, & *v.t.* **1.** *n.* sweet crystalline substance obtained from various plants, esp. the sugar-cane and sugar-beet, for use in cookery, confectionery, brewing, etc.; **cane, beet, maple,** etc., ∼ (named from plant of origin); BROWN¹, WHITE¹, CASTOR², LUMP¹, *sugar*. **2.** sweet words, flattery, anything comparable to sugar put round pill in reconciling person to what is unpalatable; **(sl.)* money; ***(as colloq. term of address) dear, darling. **3.** (Chem.) soluble usu. sweet-tasting simple crystalline carbohydrate of group found esp. in plants, e.g. glucose; ∼ **of lead**, lead acetate. **4.** ‖∼-**basin** (holding sugar for table use); ∼-**beet** (from which sugar is extracted); ∼-**bird** (of kind that sucks nectar from flowers); ∼-**bowl**, = *sugar-basin; sugar-*CANDY; ∼-**cane**, a perennial tropical grass with stout jointed stems 18-20ft. high from which sugar is made; ∼-**coated**, (of food) enclosed in sugar, (fig.) made superficially attractive; ∼-**daddy**, (sl.) elderly man who lavishes gifts on a young woman; ∼-**gum,** Australian gum-tree with sweet foliage eaten by cattle; ∼-**house,** establishment in which raw sugar is made; *sugar*-LOAF[1]; ∼-**maple,** *Acer saccharum* etc. (from sap of which sugar is made); ∼-**mite** (infesting unrefined sugar); ∼-**pea,** kind of pea eaten with pod; ∼**plum,** (arch.) sweetmeat, esp. small ball of boiled sugar; ∼-**refiner**(**y**), (establishment of) manufacturer who refines raw sugar; ∼-**shaker,** ∼-**sifter,** (for sprinkling powdered sugar); ∼ **soap,** alkaline compound for cleaning or removing paint; ∼-**tongs,** small tongs for picking up lump sugar at table. **5.** Hence ∼LESS *a.* **6.** *v.t.* sweeten with sugar (lit. or fig.); coat with sugar (*sugar the pill*); spread sugar mixture on (tree) to catch moths. [ME, f. OF *çukre, sukere* f. It. *zucchero* prob. f. med. L *succarum* f. Arab. *sükkar*]

su′gar|ỹ (shŏŏ′-) *a.* containing or resembling sugar; (fig.) attractively or excessively sweet or pleasant; hence ∼iNESS *n.* [f. prec. +-Y[2]]

sugge′st (suj-) *v.t.* **1.** cause (idea) to present itself, call up the idea of by mention or association; (of thing) ∼ **itself,** come into the mind. **2.** propose (theory, plan, *that*) for acceptance or rejection, set up the hypothesis *that,* (*suggested a retreat, that they should retreat, that the calculation was incorrect*); **I** ∼ **that** (formula of examining counsel in imputing motives etc.: *I suggest that you had a secret understanding with them*). [f. L sug(*gerere gest* bring)]

sugge′st|ible (suj) *a.* that may be suggested; open to (esp. hypnotic) suggestion; hence ∼IBI′LITY *n.* [f. prec. +-IBLE]

suggestio falsi (sujĕstiō fă′lsī) *n.* positive misrepresentation not involving direct lie but going beyond concealment of the truth (cf. SUPPRESSIO VERI). [L]

sugge′stion (suje′schon) *n.* suggesting or being suggested; theory or plan suggested; suggesting of lewd ideas; insinuation of a belief or impulse into the mind, such belief or impulse; hint, slight trace, (*not a suggestion of condescension about her*); ∼-(**s**)-**book,** ∼(**s**)-**box,** (to receive written suggestions for improvements etc.). [ME f. OF, f. L *suggestio -onis* (as SUGGEST; see -ION)]

sugge′stive (suj-) *a.* conveying a suggestion (*of*); suggesting something indecent; hence ∼LY[2] (-vlĭ) *adv.,* ∼NESS (-vn-) *n.* [f. SUGGEST +-IVE]

suicidal (sŭ′isidal, sŏŏ′-, -ĭ′d-) *a.* pertaining to suicide; (of person) tending to commit suicide; (fig.) destructive or fatal to one's own interests etc.; hence ∼LY[2] *adv.* [f. foll. +-AL]

su′icide (sŭ′-, sŏŏ′-) *n.,* & *v.i.* **1.** *n.* person who intentionally kills himself. **2.** intentional self--slaughter; **commit** ∼, kill oneself intentionally; ∼ **pact,** agreement between persons to commit suicide together; ∼ **pilot** etc. (on dangerous mission in war, or undertaking a mission involving his own death). **3.** action destructive to one's own interests or continuance in some capacity; **commit political** ∼, ruin one's prospects as a politician, political party, etc.; RACE[3] *suicide.* **4.** *v.i.* commit suicide. [f. mod. L *suicida, suicidium,* f. L *sui* of oneself; see -CIDE]

sui generis (sŭī jĕ′nerĭs, sŏŏē g-) *a.* of its own kind, peculiar, unique. [L]

sui juris (sŭī joor′ĭs, sŏŏē ūr′-) *a.* of full age and capacity, independent. [L]

su′illine *a.* of the pig family. [f. L *suillus* (*sus* pig) +-INE[1]]

su′i-mate. See MATE[1].

suint (swĭ-) *n.* natural grease in sheep's wool. [F (*suer* sweat)]

suit (sŏŏt, sūt) *n.* & *v.* **1.** *n.* suing, petition, seeking of woman's hand in marriage, (*pay suit to; press* one's *suit; prosper in* one's *suit*). **2.** ∼ (**at law**), lawsuit (*criminal, civil,* etc., *suit*). **3.** any of the four sets (spades, hearts, diamonds, clubs) into which pack of cards is divided (**follow** ∼, play card of suit that was led, fig. conform to another's actions); player's holding in it (LONG[1], SHORT, STRONG, *suit*); (Bridge) one of the suits as

proposed trumps in bidding, opp. no trumps. **4.** set of outer clothes esp. when of same cloth, consisting usu. of jacket (and for men sometimes waistcoat) and trousers or skirt; costume for use in particular circumstances (PLAY[2]-*suit,* SPACE[1]*suit,* SWIM-*suit*); ∼′**case,** oblong case for carrying clothes etc., usu. with handle and flat hinged lid; hence ∼′ING[1] (3) *n.* **5.** set *of* sails, set *of* armour, for simultaneous use. **6.** *v.t.* accommodate, adapt, make fitting or appropriate, *to* (*suit* one's *style to* one's *audience*; ∼ **the action to the word,** carry out promise or threat at once); (in *p.p.*) appropriate *to,* well adapted or having the right qualities *for,* (*is not suited to be or for an engineer*). **7.** satisfy, meet the demands or requirements or interests of, (*does not suit all tastes; it suits me* or *my* BOOK[1] *to put up with him*; ∼ **yourself,** (1) do as you choose, (2) find something that satisfies you); (of climate, food, etc.) improve or not impair the health of, agree with, (*cold, asparagus, does not suit me*). **8.** *v.t.* & *i.* go well with or *with* appearance or character of, become, (*red does not suit with, suits, her complexion; the part suits him admirably; mercy suits a king*). **9.** *v.i.* be convenient (*that date will suit*). [ME, f. AF *siute,* OF *si(e)ute* f. Gallo-Rom. *sequita* fem. p.p. (as n.) of Rom. *sequere* follow; see SUE]

suit′|able (sŏŏ′t-, sū′t-) *a.* suited *to* or *for,* well fitted for the purpose, appropriate to the occasion; hence ∼ABI′LITY, ∼**able**NESS (-beln-), *ns.,* ∼ABLY *adv.* [f. prec. I -ABLE, after *agreeable*]

suite (swēt) *n.* retinue, set of persons in attendance; set of things, esp. rooms or furniture, belonging together; (Mus.) set of instrumental compositions (orig. of movements in dance style) to be played in succession. [F (as SUIT)]

sui′tor (sŏŏ′t-, sū′t-) *n.* plaintiff or petitioner in lawsuit; wooer, man who seeks to marry a (specified) woman. [ME, f. AF *seutor, suitour,* etc., f. L *secutor -oris* (*sequi secut-* follow; see -OR)]

suk(h). Vars. of SOUK.

sukiya′ki (sŏŏ-; -ah′-) *n.* Japanese dish of sliced meat simmered with vegetables and sauce. [Jap.]

su′lcāte *a.* (Bot. & Anat.) grooved, fluted, channelled. [f. L *sulcatus* p.p. of *sulcare* furrow (as foll.); see -ATE[2]]

su′lc|us *n.* (*pl.* ∼**i** *pr.* -sī). groove, furrow, esp. between two convolutions of brain. [L]

su′lfa. See SULPHA.

*su′lfur etc. See SULPHUR etc.

sulk *n.,* & *v.i.* **1.** *n.* (usu. in *pl.*) sulky fit. **2.** *v.i.* be sulky. [n. f. v., perh. back-form. f. foll.]

su′lk|y *a.* & *n.* **1.** *a.* sullen, morose, silent or inactive or unsociable from resentment or ill temper; (of thing) sluggish; hence ∼iLY[2] *adv.,* ∼iNESS *n.* **2.** *n.* light two--wheeled one-horse vehicle for single person, esp. as used in trotting-races. [perh. f. obs. *sulke* hard to dispose of +-Y[2]]

su′llage *n.* filth, refuse, sewage. [perh. f. AF *s*(**o*)*uillage* (*souiller* SOIL[2]; see -AGE)]

su′llen *a.* & *n.* **1.** *a.* passively resentful, unforgiving, gloomy-tempered, unsociable, not responding to friendliness or encouragement or urging, stubbornly ill-humoured, morose; dismal, melancholy; hence ∼LY[2] *adv.,* ∼NESS (-n-n-) *n.* **2.** *n.* (in *pl.,* arch.) sullen frame of mind, ill temper, depression. [16th c. alt. f. ME *solein* f. AF **solein* (*sol* SOLE[2])]

su′lly *v.t.* diminish the purity or splendour of (reputation, character, victory, etc.), disgrace; (poet.) soil, tarnish. [perh. f. F *souiller* (as SOIL[2])]

su′lpha, su′lfa, *a.* sulphonamide (*sulpha drug*). [abbr. of SULPHANILAMIDE]

sulpha′mic, *sulf-, *a.* ∼ **acid,** strong acid used as weed-killer, an amide of sulphuric acid; hence **su′lpham**ATE[1] (3) *n.* [f. SULPHUR +AMIDE +-IC]

sulphani′lamide, *sulf-, *n.* colourless sulphonamide drug with anti-bacterial properties. [f. *sulphanilic* (SULPHUR, ANILINE, -IC) +AMIDE]

su′lphāte, *sulf-, *n.* salt of sulphuric acid. [f. F *sulfate,* f. L *sulphur;* see -ATE[3]]

sŭ'lphīde, *sŭ'lf-, *n.* binary compound of sulphur. [f. SULPHUR + -IDE]

sŭ'lphīte, *sŭ'lf-, *n.* salt of sulphurous acid. [f. F *sulfite* alt. of *sulfate* SULPHATE; cf. -ITE¹ (2)]

sŭlphŏ'namīde, *sŭlf-, *n.* & *a.* ~ **(drug),** substance derived from amide of a sulphonic acid, able to prevent multiplication of some pathogenic bacteria. [f. foll. + AMIDE]

sŭ'lphōne, *sŭ'lf-, *n.* organic compound containing SO_2 group united directly to two carbon atoms; hence **sŭ'lphon**ATE¹ (3), **sŭlphon**A'TION, *ns.,* **sŭlphŏ'n**IC *a.* [f. G *sulfon* (as SULPHUR, -ONE)]

sŭ'lphur, *sŭ'lfur, *n., a.,* & *v.t.* **1.** *n.* pale-yellow non-metallic element having crystalline and amorphous forms, burning with blue flame and suffocating smell, and used in making gunpowder, matches, and sulphuric acid, in vulcanizing, and in medical treatment of skin-diseases; FLOWERs, LIVER¹, MILK¹, of *sulphur.* **2.** yellow butterfly of family Pieridae. **3.** material of which hell-fire and lightning were held to consist. **4.** ~**-bottom (whale),** Pacific rorqual with yellow belly; ~ **candle** (burnt to produce sulphur dioxide for fumigating); ~**-spring** (of water impregnated with sulphur or its compounds); ~**-wort,** a yellow-flowered herb. **5.** Hence ~Y² *a.* **6.** *a.* containing or like sulphur; of pale slightly greenish yellow. **7.** *v.t.* apply sulphur to; fumigate with sulphur. [ME, f. AF *sulf(e)re,* OF *soufre* f. L *sulfur, sulp(h)ur*]

sŭ'lphūr|āte, *sŭ'lf-, *v.t.* impregnate or fumigate or treat with sulphur, esp. in bleaching; hence ~A'TION, ~ātor, *ns.* [f. prec. + -ATE³]

sŭlphūr'ĕous, *sŭlf-, *a.* of, like, suggesting, sulphur; sulphur-coloured. [f. L *sulphureus* (SULPHUR); see -EOUS]

sŭlphūrě'ttĕd, *sŭlfŭrě'tĕd, *a.* containing sulphur in combination; ~ **hydrogen,** hydrogen sulphide. [f. *sulphuret* sulphide f. mod. L *sulphuretum* (cf. -URET), + -ED²]

sŭlphūr'ĭc, *sŭlf-, *a.* (Chem.) containing sulphur in a higher valency (cf. SULPHUROUS); ~ **acid,** H_2SO_4, dense oily colourless highly acid and corrosive fluid much used in chemical industry; ~ **ether,** = ETHER 3. [f. F *sulfurique* (as SULPHUR; see -IC)]

sŭ'lphūrīz|e, -īs|e (-īz), *sŭ'lf-, *v.t.* = SULPHURATE; hence ~A'TION *n.* [f. F *sulfuriser* (as SULPHUR; see -IZE)]

sŭ'lphūrŏus, *sŭ'lf-, *a.* **1.** = SULPHUREOUS. **2.** (or -ūr'-) (Chem.) containing sulphur in a lower valency (cf. SULPHURIC); ~ **acid,** H_2SO_3, unstable weak acid used as reducing and bleaching agent. [f. L SULPHUR(*osus* -OUS), or f. SULPHUR + -OUS]

sŭ'ltan *n.* **1.** Muslim sovereign; **the S~,** (Hist.) sultan of Turkey; hence ~ATE¹ *n.* **2.** gorgeously coloured bird like *Porphyrio;* variety of white domestic fowl from Turkey; **(sweet)** ~, sweet-scented plant, *Centaurea moschata* or *C. suaveolens.* [F, or f. med. L *sultanus,* f. Arab. *sulṭān* power, ruler (*saluṭa* sultān)]

sŭltā'na (-tah'-) *n.* **1.** sultan's mother, wife, concubine, or daughter. **2.** mistress of king etc. **3.** sultan-bird. **4.** seedless raisin used in puddings and cakes; small pale yellow grape yielding it. [It., fem. of *sultano* = prec.]

sŭ'ltanèss *n.* (arch.) = prec. 1. [f. SULTAN + -ESS¹]

sŭ'ltr|y̆ *a.* (Of atmosphere or weather) hot and close or oppressive; (of temper etc. or person) passionate, sensual; hence ~iLY² *adv.,* ~iNESS *n.* [f. obs. *sulter* swelter prob. f. **swulter* cogn. w. SWELTER + -Y²]

sŭm *n.* & *v.* **(-mm-). 1.** *n.* ~ **(total),** total amount resulting from addition of items, brief expression that includes but does not specify details, substance, summary, (*the sum of two and three is five; the sum of all my wishes is happiness; the sum of his objections is this*); **in ~,** briefly but comprehensively put. **2.** particular amount of money (*what sum would you give for it?; for the sum of £15; a good, round, considerable, sum;* LUMP¹ *sum*). **3.** (working out of) an arithmetical problem (*good at sums; did a rapid sum in his head*). **4.** *v.t.* find sum of; ~

(up), collect into or express or include as one total or whole; gather *up* (evidence, points of argument etc., already treated in detail) into brief review; ~ **up,** form or express idea of character of (person or situation). **5.** *v.i.* ~ **up,** (esp. of judge after both sides have been heard) make recapitulation of evidence or argument, whence ~mING¹-*u'p n.* [ME, f. OF *summe, somme,* f. L *summa* main part, fem. of *summus* highest; v. f. OF *sommer* or f. med. L *summare* f. L *summa*]

su'măc, -ăch, (sū'măk, soo'-, shoo'-) *n.* (dried and ground leaves, used in tanning and dyeing, of) shrub of genus *Rhus.* [ME f. OF *sumac* or f. med. L *sumac(h)* f. Arab. *summāk*]

Sūmēr'ian *a.* & *n.* (Archaeol.) **1.** *a.* of the early and non-Semitic element in the civilization of ancient Babylonia. **2.** *n.* Sumerian person or language. [f. *sumérien* (*Sumer* in Babylonia; see -IAN)]

su'mma *n.* (*pl.* ~e). summary of what is known of a subject. [ME, f. L (see SUM)]

su'mmar|īze, -īse (-īz), *v.t.* make or be a summary of, sum up; so ~IST (1) *n.* [f. foll. + -IZE]

su'mmar|y̆ *a.* & *n.* **1.** *a.* compendious, brief, dispensing with needless details or formalities, done with despatch or (Law) without formalities required by common law, (*a summary account; summary methods*); ~**y jurisdiction,** authority of a court to use summary proceedings and arrive at judgement or conviction; ~**y offence** (within scope of summary court); hence ~iLY² *adv.* **2.** *n.* brief account, abridgement, epitome. [ME, a. f. med. L *summarius,* n. f. L *summarium,* f. L *summa* SUM; see -ARY¹]

summā'tion *n.* addition, finding of total or sum; summing-up; hence ~AL *a.* [f. SUM + -ATION]

su'mmer¹ *n., a.,* & *v.* **1.** *n.* warmest season of the year, in N. hemisphere June–August (Astron., from summer solstice to autumnal equinox); warmer part of year; INDIAN *summer;* ||**St. Luke's ~,** ||**St. Martin's ~,** period of fine weather expected about 18 Oct., 11 Nov. **2.** weather typical of summer; (fig.) mature stage of life etc. **3.** (literary, usu. in *pl.* with number etc.) year of life or age (*a child of ten summers*). **4.** *a.* characteristic of or fit for summer; ~**-house,** light building in garden etc. providing cool shade in summer; *summer* LIGHTNING; ~ **pudding** (of chopped usu. soft fruit in bread or sponge-cake); ~ **school,** long-vacation meeting for lectures etc., esp. at university; *summer* SOLSTICE; ~**-time** or ~**time,** the weather or season of summer; ||~ **time** (shown by clocks advanced in summer for DAYLIGHT saving); ~**-weight,** (of clothes) suitable in weight for use in summer. **5.** Hence ~LESS, ~LY¹, ~Y², *adjs.* **6.** *v.i.* pass the summer (*at or in* place). **7.** *v.t.* pasture (cattle) *at or in.* [OE *sumor,* = OS, OHG, ON *sumar*]

su'mmer² *n.* ~**(-tree),** horizontal bearing beam, esp. one supporting joists or rafters. [ME, a. AF *sumer, somer* pack-horse, beam, OF *somier* f. Rom. **saumarius* f. LL *sagmarius* (*sagma* f. Gk *sagma* pack-saddle)]

summersault, -set. Vars. of SOMERSAULT.

su'mmĭt *n.* highest point, top, apex, highest degree, (*the icy summits of the Alps; at the summit of power; the summit of my ambition is*); ~ **(meeting, talks, etc.),** discussion taking place between heads of governments, whence ~RY (5) *n.*; hence ~LESS *a.* [ME, f. OF *somet, som(m)ete,* (*som* top f. L *summum* neut. of *summus;* see -ET¹)]

su'mmon *v.t.* demand the presence of, call upon to appear, esp. as defendant or witness in lawcourt; so ~ER² (4) *n.* (Hist.); call together by authority for action or discussion; call upon (*to do,* esp. town etc. *to surrender*); ~ **up,** gather (courage, spirit, etc.) usu. to do or for undertaking. [ME, f. OF *somondre* f. pop. L **summonere* f. L *summonēre* (as SUB- 2, *monēre* warn)]

su'mmons (-z) *n.,* & *v.t.* **1.** *n.* authoritative call or urgent invitation to attend on some occasion or do something. **2.** call to appear before judge or magistrate. **3.** *v.t.* serve with summons. [ME, f. OF *somonce,* *sumunse* f. Gallo-Rom. *summonsa f. L *summonita* fem. p.p. (as n.) of *summonēre* (see prec.)]

summum bonum (sŭmum bō'num, soō- bŏ-) *n*. the chief good, esp. as the end or ultimate determining principle in an ethical system. [L]

su'mō (soō'-) *n*. (*pl.* ~s). (participant in) Japanese wrestling where defeat follows touching of ground except with soles of feet, or failure to keep within marked area. [Jap.]

sŭmp *n*. pit or well for the reception of (esp. superfluous) water, oil, or other liquid in mines, machines, etc.; cesspool. [ME = marsh, f. MDu., MLG *sump*, or (mining) G *sumpf*, rel. to SWAMP]

sŭ'mpter *n*. (arch.) pack-horse; pack-animal (*sumpter-horse*, *-mule*, *-pony*). [ME, f. OF *som(m)etier* f. Rom. *saumatarius f. LL f. Gk *sagma -atos* pack-saddle; cf. SUMMER², -ER² (2)]

sŭ'mptüary *a*. regulating expenditure; (of law, edict, etc.) limiting private expenditure, in the interests of the State. [f. L *sumptuarius* (*sumptus* cost f. *sumere sumpt-* take)]

sŭ'mptüous *a*. rich and costly; suggesting lavish expenditure; hence ~LY² *adv*., ~NESS, **sŭmptüo'sity**, *ns*. [ME, f. OF *somptueux* f. L *sumptuosus* (as prec.; see -OUS)]

sŭn *n*. & *v*. (**-nn-**). **1.** *n*. the star that the earth travels round and receives warmth and light from, such light or warmth or both (*keep out, let in, the sun*). **2.** ~ **rises, sets,** (is brought above, below, the horizon by earth's rotation; *his, its*, etc., ~ **is set,** time of prosperity or existence is over; **rise with the** ~, get up early; **hail** or **adore the rising** ~, curry favour with new or coming power; *empire* etc. **on which the** ~ **never sets,** world-wide; **let not the** ~ **go down upon your wrath,** limit it to one day. **3. against the** ~, counter-CLOCK¹*wise*; **catch the** ~, (1) be in sunny position, (2) become sunburnt; *make* HAY¹ *while the sun shines*; **in the** ~, exposed to sun's rays (*place in the* ~, (fig.) favourable situation or condition); MIDNIGHT, MOCK², *sun*; S~ **of Righteousness,** Christ; **see the** ~, be alive; **take the** ~, expose oneself to sun's light and heat; **take,** (sl.) **shoot, the** ~, (Naut.) ascertain its altitude in order to fix latitude; **touch of the** ~, slight attack of sunstroke; **beneath** or **under the** ~, anywhere in the world; **with the** ~, = CLOCK¹*wise*. **4.** ~ **and planet,** system of gearing in which cogged wheel on reciprocating rod both rotates on its axis and travels round the wheel that it engages and communicates motion to. **5.** any fixed star with or without planets. **6.** (poet.) day or year. **7.** ~**-bath,** exposure of body to sun; ~'**bathe,** take sun-bath; ~'**beam,** ray of sun; ~**-bear,** small black bear of SE Asia; ~**-bird,** small bright-plumaged Old-World bird of family Nectariniidae, with resemblance to humming-birds; ‖~**-blind,** window awning; ~**-bonnet** (of cotton etc., with projection and pendent back to shade face and neck); ~**-bow,** effect like rainbow given by sunlight on spray etc.; ~'**burn** *n.*, & *v.i.*, (undergo) tanning or inflammation of skin by exposure to sun; so ~'**burnt** or ~'**burned** *a.*; ~'**burst,** firework or ornament or piece of jewellery imitating sun and rays; ~**-dance** (of N. Amer. Indians in honour of sun); ~**-deck,** upper deck of steamer; ~**-dew,** small insectivorous bog-plant of genus *Drosera*, with hairs secreting drops of moisture; ~'**dial,** instrument showing time by shadow of pointer, cast by sun on graduated plate; ~**-disc,** winged disc emblematic of sun-god; ~**-dog,** parhelion; ~'**down,** sunset; ~'**downer,** (Austral.) tramp who times his arrival at a station for the evening, ‖(colloq.) a drink at sunset; ~**-dress** (allowing arms, shoulders, and back to be exposed to sunlight); ~'**dried,** dried by sun and not by artificial heat; *~'**fast,** (of dye) not subject to fading by sunlight; ~'**fish,** fish of almost spherical shape, esp. a large ocean fish (*Mola mola*); ~'**flower,** tall garden-plant of genus *Helianthus* with showy golden-rayed

flowers, grown also for its seeds which yield an edible oil; **Sunflower State,* Kansas; ~**-glasses** (tinted to protect the eyes from direct sunlight or glare); ~**-god,** the sun worshipped as a deity; ~**-hat,** ~**-helmet,** (adapted by material or shape to keep sun off); ~**-lamp,** (1) large lamp with parabolic reflector used in film-making, (2) lamp giving ultra-violet rays for therapy or artificial sun-tan; ~'**light,** ~'**lit,** (illuminated by) light from the sun; ~ **lounge,** room designed to receive much sunlight; ~**-myth,** solar myth; *~ **parlor,** sun lounge; ~**-rays,** (1) sunbeams, (2) ultra-violet rays used therapeutically as substitute for sunlight; ~'**rise,** (moment of) sun's rising; ~**-roof,** = *sunshine roof*; ~'**set,** (moment of) sun's setting, western sky with colours characterizing sunset, (fig.) declining period of life; ~'**shade,** (1) parasol, (2) awning; ~'**shine,** light of sun (~*shine recorder*, instrument recording duration of sunshine; ~*shine roof,* sliding roof of saloon motor car; **Sunshine State,* Florida), area illuminated by it, fair weather, (fig.) cheerfulness or bright influence (also joc. as form of address), hence ~'**shiny** *a.*; ~'**spot,** one of the dark patches, changing in shape and size and lasting for varying periods, observed on sun's surface; ~**-star,** red starfish with many rays, ~**-stone,** cat's eye gem, feldspar with embedded flecks of haematite etc.; ~'**stroke,** acute prostration or collapse from excessive heat of sun; ~**-suit,** play-suit suitable for sunbathing; ~**-tan** *n.*, & *v.i.*, tan(ning of) skin by exposure to sun; ~**-trap,** place (esp. sheltered from wind) suitable for catching the sunshine; *~**-up,** sunrise; ~ **visor,** = VISOR 3. **8.** Hence ~'**LESS,** ~'**LIKE,** ~'**PROOF²,** *adjs.*, ~'**WARD** a. & *adv.*, ~'**WARDS** *adv.*, ~'**WISE** *adv.* (opp. WITHERSHINS). **9.** *v.t.* expose to the sun; ~ *one*self, bask in sunlight (lit. or fig.). **10.** *v.i.* sun oneself. [OE *sunne, sunna,* = OS, OHG *sunna, sunno,* f. Gmc *sunnōn f. IE **su-*]

Sun. *abbr.* Sunday.

sŭ'ndae (-dā, -dĭ) *n*. confection of ice-cream topped or mixed with crushed fruit, nuts, syrup, etc. [perh. f. SUNDAY, w. ref. to sale of left-over ice-cream during the week]

Sŭndanē'se (-z) *n*. & *a*. (member or language) of a people of Western Java. [f. *Sunda* name of W. Java + -ESE, after *Chinese*]

Sŭ'nday (-dā, -dĭ) *n*. & *adv*. **1.** *n*. day of week, following Saturday, Lord's day, observed by Christians as day of rest and worship; newspaper published on Sundays; **month of** ~s, indefinite long period; ~ **best,** ~ **(go-to-meeting) clothes,** (usu. joc.) best clothes (kept for Sunday use); ~ **letter,** dominical letter; ~ **painter,** one who paints purely for pleasure; ~ **school** for religious instruction of children on Sundays). **2.** *adv*. (cf. FRIDAY 2). [OE *sunnandæg,* = OS *sunnundag,* OHG *sunnuntag,* ON *sunnudagr,* transl. of L *dies solis,* Gk *hēmera hēliou* day of the sun]

sŭ'nder *v*. & *a*. (arch. or literary). **1.** *v.t.* & *i*. separate, sever. **2.** *a*. **in** ~, apart. [v. f. OE *sundrian,* f. *āsundrian* etc.,= OHG *sund(e)rōn,* ON *sundra;* a. ME, f. *o(n)sunder* ASUNDER]

sŭ'ndry *a.* & *n.* **1.** *a.* various, several; ALL *and sundry.* **2.** *n.* (Austral.) an extra in cricket; (in *pl.*) oddments, accessories or items not needing special mention; ‖**su'ndriesman** (-rĭzm-), dealer in sundries. [OE *syndrig* separate, = OHG *sunt(a)ric,* cogn. w. prec.; see -Y²]

sŭng. See SING.

sŭnk('en). See SINK¹.

sŭnn *n.* ~ **(hemp),** E. Ind. hemplike fibre. [f. Urdu & Hindi *san* f. Skr. *śāṇá* hempen]

Sŭ'nn|a *n.* traditional portion of Muslim law based on Muhammad's words or acts, but not written by him, accepted as authoritative by the orthodox (~ITE¹, ~I, *ns.*) but rejected by the Shiites. [Arab., = form, way, course, rule]

sŭ'nn|ȳ *a.* bright with or as sunlight; exposed to, warm with, the sun (**the** ~**y side,** side of house etc. that gets sun, (fig.) the more cheerful aspect of circumstances etc.); cheery, bright in disposition, diffusing cheerfulness; hence ∼ı̆LY² *adv.*, ∼ı̆NESS *n.* [ME, f. SUN + -Y²]

sŭp *v.* (-**pp**-) & *n.* **1.** *v.t.* & *i.* take (soup, tea, etc.) by sips or spoonfuls. **2.** *v.i.* take supper (*on* or *off* specified food). **3.** *n.* mouthful of liquid (esp. *neither bite nor sup*). [senses 1 and 3 f. OE *sūpan*, = MLG *sūpen*, OHG *sūfan*, ON *súpa*; sense 2 ME, f. OF *soper*, *super* f. Gmc *sup-* (as SOP, SOUP, and sense 1)]

sup- *pref.*, assim. form of SUB- 1-6 before *p*.

su'per (sōō'-, sū'-) *n.* & *a.* **1.** *n.* (colloq.) supernumerary actor, (fig.) extra or unwanted or unimportant person etc.; superintendent; superphosphate; (Commerc.) superfine cloth or manufacture. **2.** *a.* (Commerc.) superfine; (of measure) superficial, in square (not lineal or solid) measure (*120 super ft.*, or *120 ft. super*). **3.** ∼(-**duper**), (sl.) exceptional, splendid. [abbr.]

su'per- (sōō'-, sū'-) *pref.* denoting: **1.** (forming *adjs.*) (1) situated directly over (*superincumbent*), (2) not in or under but above (*superaqueous, supernatant*), (3) exceeding, going beyond, more than, transcending, too exalted for contact or connection with, (*superfine, superhuman, supernatural*). **2.** (forming *vbs.*) (1) on the top of something (*superimpose, superscribe*), (2) observation from above (*superintend*), (3) besides, in addition, (*superadd*), (4) to a degree beyond what is usual or right (*supersaturate*). **3.** (forming *ns.*) (1) upper or outer (*superstratum, superstructure*), (2) of higher kind, higher in degree, superior in quality, expressing addition, in higher than the ordinary sense, esp. in names of classificatory divisions (*superclass*). [f. or after L *super-* (*super* on top (of), above, beyond)]

su'perable (sōō'-, sū'-) *a.* that can be overcome. [f. L *superabilis* (*superare* overcome; see -ABLE)]

superabou'nd (sōō-, sū-) *v.i.* be very or too abundant. [f. LL *superabundare* (as SUPER- 2 (4), ABOUND)]

superabŭ'nd|ant (sōō-, sū-) *a.* abounding beyond what is normal or right; hence or cogn. ∼ANCE *n.*, ∼ant LY² *adv.* [ME, f. LL *superabundare* (see prec., -ANT)]

super|ă'dd (sōō-, sū-) *v.t.* add over and above; hence ∼ADDI'TION *n.* [ME, f. L *superaddere* (as SUPER- 2 (3), ADD)]

su'peraltar (sōō'perawl-, sū'-, -öl-) *n.* (Eccl.) slab of stone consecrated for use on unconsecrated altar etc. [ME, f. med. L *superaltare* (as SUPER- 3 (1), ALTAR)]

superă'nnŭ|āte (sōō-, sū-) *v.t.* declare too old for work or use or continuance, dismiss or discard as too old; send into retirement with pension; (in *p.p.*) too old for work or use; hence ∼ABLE *a.*, ∼A'TION *n.*, (esp.) (payment made to obtain) pension granted to superannuated person. [back-form. f. *superannuated* f. med. L *superannuatus* f. L SUPER- + *annus* year; see -ATE², -ED¹]

superā'quĕous (sōō-, sū-) *a.* above water. [f. SUPER- 1 (2) + AQUEOUS]

supe̊r'b (sōō-, sū-) *a.* of the most impressive or splendid or exalted kind, grand, majestic, (*superb beauty, courage, impudence; a superb view, display, specimen, voice, binding*); (colloq.) of very high quality, excellent; hence ∼LY² *adv.* [f. F *superbe* or f. L *superbus* proud]

supercă'lender (sōō-, sū-) *v.t.* give highly glazed finish to (paper) by extra calendering. [f. SUPER- 2 (4) + CALENDER¹]

su'percārgō (sōō'-, sū'-) *n.* (*pl.* ∼es). person in merchant ship managing sales etc. of cargo. [earlier *supracargo* f. Sp. *sobrecargo* (*sobre* over, CARGO)]

supercēlē'stial (sōō-, sū-) *a.* above the heavens; more than heavenly. [f. LL *supercaelestis* (as SUPER- 1 (2, 3), CELESTIAL)]

su'perchārge (sōō'-, sū'-) *v.t.* charge to excess (*with* energy, emotion, etc.); use supercharger on. [f. SUPER- 2 (4) + CHARGE²]

su'perchārger (sōō'-, sū'-) *n.* device supplying air or

fuel to internal combustion engine at above normal pressure to increase efficiency. [f. prec. + -ER¹]

superci'liary (sōō-, sū-) *a.* of the eyebrow; over eye. [f. L *supercilium* eyebrow (SUPER-, *cilium* eyelid) + -ARY¹]

superci'lious (sōō-, sū-) *a.* contemptuous, showing haughty indifference; assuming an air of superiority; hence ∼LY² *adv.*, ∼NESS *n.* [f. L *superciliosus* (as prec.) + -OUS]

su'perclass (sōō'-, sū'-; -ahs) *n.* See SUPER- 3 (2).

super|colŭ'mnar *a.* (sōō-, sū-) (Archit.) having one order or set of columns above another; so ∼colŭmnA'TION *n.* [f. SUPER- 1 (1) + COLUMNAR]

super|cŏndŭcti'vity (sōō-, sū-) *n.* (Phys.) property of zero electrical resistance in some substances at temperatures near absolute zero; hence ∼condŭ'ctıVE, *adjs.*, ∼condŭ'ctor *n.*, (substance) having this property. [f. SUPER- 3 (2) + CONDUCTIVITY]

superco'nscious (sōō-, sū-; -shus) *a.* transcending human consciousness; hence ∼LY² *adv.*, ∼NESS *n.* [f. SUPER- 1 (3) + CONSCIOUS]

su'percool (sōō'-, sū'-) *v.t.* cool (liquid) below its freezing-point without solidification or without crystallization. [f. SUPER- 2 (4) + COOL²]

supercri'tical (sōō-, sū-) *a.* (Phys.) of more than critical mass etc. [f. SUPER- 1 (3) + CRITICAL]

super-ĕ'gō (sōō-, sū-) *n.* (*pl.* ∼s). (Psych.) part of mind that exerts conscience and responds to social rules. [f. SUPER- 3 (2) + EGO]

superĕlĕvā'tion (sōō-, sū-) *n.* amount by which outer edge of curve on road or railway is above inner edge. [f. SUPER- 3 (2) + ELEVATION]

superĕ'min|ent (sōō-, sū-) *a.* supremely eminent or remarkable; hence or cogn. ∼ENCE *n.*, ∼ent LY² *adv.* [f. L *supereminēre* rise above (as SUPER- 2 (4), EMINENT)]

super|ĕrogā'tion (sōō-, sū-) *n.* doing of more than duty requires; **works of** ∼**erogation,** (RC Theol.) actions such as form a reserve fund of merit that can be drawn on in favour of sinners; so ∼ĕrŏ'gatory *a.* [f. LL *supererogatio* f. SUPER(*erogare* pay out, orig. public money after formal request for permission, f. as E- + *rogo* ask); see -ATION]

superĕ'xcell|ent (sōō-, sū-) *a.* very or supremely excellent; hence ∼ENCE *n.*, ∼ent LY² *adv.* [f. LL *superexcellens* (as SUPER- 1 (3), EXCELLENT)]

su'perfămily (sōō'-, sū'-) *n.* taxonomic category between family and order. [f. SUPER- 3 (2) + FAMILY]

superfă'tted (sōō-, sū-) *a.* (Of soap) containing extra fat. [f. SUPER- 2 (4) + FAT + -ED²]

superfēcŭndā'tion (sōō-, sū-) *n.* = foll. 1. [f. SUPER-3 (2) + FECUNDATION]

superfētā'tion (sōō-, sū-) *n.* **1.** (Med. & Zool.) second conception during gestation. **2.** (Bot.) fertilization of same ovule by different kinds of pollen. **3.** accretion of one thing on another. [f. F *superfétation* or f. mod. L *superfetatio* f. L SUPER(*fetare* f. *fetus* FOETUS); see -ATION]

superfi'cial (sōō-, sū-; -shal) *a.* of or on the surface only, not going deep, without depth, (*superficial colour, resemblance, knowledge, wound, accomplishments*); (of person) having no reserve of knowledge or feeling beyond what he shows; (of measure) square (cf. SUPER 2); hence ∼ıTY (-shiǎ'l-) *n.*, ∼LY² *adv.* [f. LL *superficialis* f. L (as foll.; see -AL)]

superfi'ciĕs (sōō-, sū-; -shiĕz) *n.* (*pl.* same). (Geom. etc.) surface. [L (as SUPER- 3 (1), *facies* face)]

su'perfīne (sōō'-, sū'-) *a.* affecting great refinement; (Commerc.) of extra quality. [f. med. L *superfinus* (as SUPER- 1 (3), FINE²)]

superflu'ity (sōō-, sū-; -lōō'-) *n.* being superfluous; superfluous amount or thing. [ME, f. OF *superfluité* f. LL *superfluitas -tatis* f. L *superfluus* (see foll., -ITY)]

supe̊r'fluous (sōō-, sū-; -lōō-) *a.* more than enough, redundant, needless; hence ∼LY² *adv.*, ∼NESS *n.* [ME, f. L SUPER(*fluus* f. *fluere* to flow) + -OUS]

For other words in *super-* **see** SUPER-.

su′pergīant (soō′-, sū′-) *n.* (Astron.) star of very great luminosity and size. [f. SUPER- 3 (2) +GIANT]

super|hea′t (soō-, sū-) *v.t.* heat (liquid) above its boiling-point without vaporization; heat (vapour) above the boiling-point (*superheated* STEAM¹); hence ⁓HEA′TER *n.* [f. SUPER- 2 (4) +HEAT²]

superhě′t (soō-, sū-) *n.* (colloq.) = foll. [abbr.]

superhě′terodȳne (soō-, sū-) *n.* & *a.* (using) system of radio reception in which a local variable oscillator is tuned to beat at a constant ultrasonic frequency with carrier-wave frequencies, thus making it unnecessary to vary the amplifier tuning and securing great selectivity. [f. SUPERSONIC + HETERODYNE]

*su′perhighway (soō′-, sū′-; -īwā) *n.* broad main road for fast traffic. [f. SUPER- 3 (2) +HIGHWAY]

superhū′man (soō-, sū-) *a.* beyond (normal) human capacity or power; higher than man; hence ⁓LY² *adv.* [f. LL *superhumanus* (as SUPER- 1 (3), HUMAN)]

superhū′meral (soō-, sū-) *n.* (Eccl.) vestment worn over shoulders, e.g. amice, ephod, or pallium. [f. LL *superhumerale* (as SUPER- 1 (1), HUMERAL)]

super|impō′se (soō-, sū-; -z) *v.t.* lay (thing) on or on something else; so ⁓IMPOSI′TION *n.* [f. SUPER- 2 (1) +IMPOSE]

superincū′mbent (soō-, sū-; -n-k-) *a.* lying on something else. [f. SUPER- 1 (1) +INCUMBENT²]

superindū′ce (soō-, sū-) *v.t.* introduce or induce in addition [f. L SUPER(*inducere*, as INDUCE) cover over, bring from outside]

superinte′nd (soō-, sū-) *v.t.* & *i.* have the management (of), arrange and inspect working (of); so ⁓ENCE, ⁓ENCY, *ns.* [f. eccl. L SUPER(*intendere*, as INTEND), transl. Gk *episkopō*]

superinte′ndent (soō-, sū-) *n.* person who superintends; director of institution etc.; ‖police officer above rank of inspector, *head of police department; *caretaker of building. [f. eccl. L (as prec.); see -ENT]

super′ior (soō-, sū-, sư-) *a.* & *n.* **1.** *a.* upper, in higher position, of higher rank, (*superior officer, rank, court*); (of planet) having orbit outside the earth's; (of insect's wings) folding over others; (of figures or letters) written or printed above the line; (Bot., of calyx) above ovary, (of ovary) above calyx. **2.** better or greater in some respect, related as the better or greater to, (*by superior wisdom, cunning*, etc.; *is superior in speed to any other machine*); ⁓ *numbers*, (esp.) more men or their strength (*was overcome by superior numbers*). **3.** of quality or qualities above the average, having or showing consciousness of such qualities, (*made of superior leather; he remarked with a superior air*); ⁓ *persons*, the better educated etc., (iron.) prigs. **4.** above giving attention or yielding or making concessions *to* (*superior to bribery, temptation, revenge, fortune*); *rise* ⁓ *to*, be unaffected by. **5.** Hence or cogn. **superio′rity** (soō-, sū-, sư-) *n.* (⁓*ity complex*, undue conviction of one's own superiority to others, (colloq.) aggressive behaviour to compensate for one's supposed inferiority to others), ⁓LY² *adv.* **6.** *n.* one's better, person superior to another, in rank or in some respect (*is deferential to his superiors; has no superior in courage*). **7.** head of monastery or other religious house (esp. *Father, Mother, Lady, Superior*); hence ⁓ESS¹ *n.* **8.** superior letter or figure. [ME, f. OF *superiour* f. L *superior -oris*, compar. of *superus* that is above (*super* above)]

superjā′cent (soō-, sū-) *a.* overlying, superincumbent. [f. L SUPER(*jacēre* lie); see -ENT]

super′lative (soō-, sū-) *a.* & *n.* **1.** *a.* of the highest quality or degree (*superlative wisdom, beauty*, etc.); (Gram.) ⁓ *adjective, adverb*, one in the ⁓ *degree*, expressing the highest or a very high degree of a quality (*bravest; most absurdly*); hence ⁓LY² (-vlī) *adv.*, ⁓NESS (-vn-) *n.* **2.** *n.* superlative degree or form (*not used in the superlative; what is the superlative of 'shy'?*); word in the superlative or expressing high degree (**his talk is all ⁓s**, he expresses extreme opinions or exaggerates). [ME, f. OF *superlatif -ive* f. LL *superlativus* f. L SUPER(*latus* p.p. of *ferre* take); see -IVE]

superlū′nary (soō-, sū-; -loō′-, -lū′-) *a.* beyond the moon; celestial. [f. med. L *superlunaris* (as SUPER- 1 (2), LUNAR); see -ARY²]

su′per|măn (soō′-, sū′-) *n.* (*pl.* ⁓men). ideal superior man of the future; man of superhuman powers or achievement. [f. SUPER- 3 (2) +MAN¹, formed by G. B. Shaw after Nietzsche's G *übermensch*]

su′permàrkét (soō′-, sū′-) *n.* large self-service store selling foods and some household requirements. [f. SUPER- 3 (2) +MARKET¹]

supermǔ′ndāne (soō-, sū-) *a.* superior to earthly things. [f. med. L *supermundanus* (as SUPER- 1 (2), MUNDANE)]

superna′cūlum (soō-, sū-) *adv.* & *n.* **1.** *adv.* to the last drop (*drink supernaculum*). **2.** *n.* wine etc. of high quality. [mod. L, tr. G *auf den nagel* on to the nail, w. ref. to upturning of glass on thumb to prove emptiness]

supér′nal (soō-, sū-) *a.* (poet. or rhet.) heavenly, divine; of the sky; lofty. [ME f. OF, or f. med. L *supernalis* f. L *supernus* (*super* above); see -AL]

superna′tant (soō-, sū-) *a.* & *n.* (substance) floating on surface of liquid. [f. SUPER- 1 (2) +*natant* swimming (as NATATION; see -ANT)]

superna′tural (soō-, sū-; -cher-) *a.* due to or manifesting some agency above the forces of nature; outside the ordinary operation of cause and effect; hence ⁓ISM (2, 3), ⁓IST (2), *ns.*, ⁓IZE (2) *v.t.*, ⁓LY² *adv.*, ⁓NESS *n.* [f. med. L *supernaturalis* (as SUPER- 1 (3), NATURAL)]

supernō′rmal (soō-, sū-) *a.* beyond what is normal or natural. [f. SUPER- 1 (3) +NORMAL]

supernō′va (soō-, sū-) *n.* (*pl.* ⁓e or ⁓s). (Astron.) star that suddenly increases very greatly in brightness because of explosion ejecting most of its mass. [f. SUPER- 3 (2) +NOVA]

supernū′meràry (soō-, sū-) *a.* & *n.* (person or thing) in excess of normal number, (person) engaged for extra work, (actor) who appears on stage but does not speak. [f. LL *supernumerarius* (soldier) added to legion already complete, f. L *super numerum* beyond the number; see -ARY¹]

su′per|ōrder (soō′-, sū′-) *n.* taxonomic category between order and class; so ⁓OR′DINAL *a.* [f. SUPER- 3 (2) +ORDER¹]

superōr′dinate (soō-, sū-) *a.* of superior importance or rank (*to*). [f. SUPER- 1 (2), after *subordinate*]

superphŏ′sphāte (soō-, sū-) *n.* fertilizer made by treating phosphate rock with sulphuric or phosphoric acid. [f. SUPER- 3 (2) +PHOSPHATE]

superphȳ′sical (soō-, sū-; -z-) *a.* beyond what is physical; unexplainable by physical causes. [f. SUPER- 1 (3) +PHYSICAL]

super|pō′se (soō-, sū-; -z) *v.t.* place (thing) on or *on* or above something else; bring into same position so as to coincide; so ⁓POSI′TION *n.* [f. F *superposer* (as SUPER- 2 (1), *poser* place, POSE¹)]

su′perpower (soō′-, sū′-) *n.* extremely powerful nation, esp. one of only a few such. [f. SUPER- 3 (2) + POWER]

supersā′tur|āte (soō-, sū-; -cher-, -tūr-) *v.t.* add to (esp. solution) beyond saturation point; hence ⁓A′TION *n.* [f. SUPER- 2 (4) +SATURATE]

su′per|scrībe (soō′-, sū′-) *v.t.* write (inscription) at top of or on outside of document etc.; write inscription over or on (thing); so ⁓scrī′ptION *n.*, (esp.) words superscribed. [f. L SUPER(*scribere* script-write)]

su′perscript (soō′-, sū′-) *a.* & *n.* (Math. etc.) (symbol) written above and to the right of another symbol. [f. L *superscriptus* p.p. of *superscribere* (see prec.)]

super|se′de (soō-, sū-) *v.t.* set aside, cease to employ, adopt or appoint another person or thing in place of, (of such person or thing) take the place of; hence or cogn. ~sĕ'dence, ~sĕ'dure, ~se'ssion, *ns*. [f. OF *superseder* f. L super(*sedēre sess-* sit) be superior to]

supersŏ'n|ic (sōō-, sū-) *a.* relating to speeds greater than that of sound; (arch.) ultrasonic; hence ~ically *adv.* [f. super- 1 (3) +sonic]

su'perstăr (sōō'-, sū'-) *n.* performer surpassing even the stars (star[1] 3). [f. super- 3 (2) +star[1]]

supersti'ti|on (sōō-, sū-) *n.* credulity regarding the supernatural, irrational fear of the unknown or mysterious; misdirected reverence; religion or practice or particular opinion based on such tendencies; widely held but unjustified idea of the effects or nature of a thing; so ~ious (-shus) *a.* [ME f. OF, or f. L *superstitio* f. super(*stare stat-* stand); see -ion]

su'perstŏre (sōō'-, sū'-) *n.* hypermarket; large supermarket. [f. super- 3 (2) +store]

su'perstrat|um (sōō'-, sū'-; -ah-, -ā-) *n.* (*pl.* ~a). overlying stratum. [f. super- 3 (1) +stratum]

su'perstrŭctur|e (sōō'-, sū'-) *n.* building with respect to its foundation; structure resting on something else; upper part of building etc.; concept etc. based on others; hence ~al *a.* [f. super- 3 (1) +structure]

supersubstă'ntial (sōō-, sū-; -shal) *a.* transcending material substance or all substance. [f. eccl. L super(*substantialis* f. *substantia* substance; see -al)]

super|sŭ'btle (sōō-, sū-; -ŭ'tel) *a.* excessively subtle; so ~su'btlety *n.* [f. super- 1 (3) +subtle]

su'pertănker (sōō'-, sū'-) *n.* very large tanker ship. [f. super- 3 (2) +tanker]

su'pertăx (sōō'-, sū'-) *n.*, & *v.t.* = surtax. [f. super- 2 (3), 3 (2) +tax[1,2]]

supertĕ'mporal (sōō-, sū-) *a.* **1.** above the temples of the head. **2.** transcending time. [f. super- 1 (1, 3) + temporal]

superterrā'nĕan (sōō-, sū-) *a.* existing or dwelling on the earth's surface. [f. super- 1 (2), after subterranean]

supertĕrrĕ'ne (sōō-, sū-) *a.* **1.** = foll. **2.** = prec. [f. super- 1 (2), after *subterrene* f. L sub(*terrenus* terrene]

superterrĕ'strial (sōō-, sū-) *a.* belonging to a region above the earth, celestial. [f. super- 1 (3) +terrestrial]

supertŏ'nic (sōō-, sū-) *n.* (Mus.) note above tonic, second note of diatonic scale of any key. [f. super- 3 (2) +tonic]

super|vĕ'ne (sōō-, sū-) *v.i.* occur as interruption to or change from some condition or process; so ~vĕ'ntion *n.* [f. L super(*venire vent-* come)]

su'per|vīse (sōō'-, sū'-; -z) *v.t.* oversee, superintend execution or performance of (thing) or actions or work of (person); hence ~vi'sion (-zhon) *n.*, ~vīsory (-z-) *a.* [f. med. L super(*vidēre vis-* see)]

su'pervisor (sōō'-, sū'-; -z-) *n.* person who supervises; *administrative or advisory official in town, school, etc. [med. L (as prec.; see -or), or f. prec. +-or]

su'pin|āte (sū'-, sōō'-) *v.t.* put (hand, foreleg) into supine position (cf. pronate); so ~a'tion *n.*, ~ā'tor *n.* (esp. muscle effecting this). [back-form. f. supination f. L *supinatio* (*supinare* f. *supinus*; see foll., -ate[3]]

supine[1] (sū'-, sōō'-, -ī'n) *a.* having front or ventral part upwards, (of hand) with palm upwards, lying face upwards (cf. prone); disinclined for moral or mental action, indolent, lethargic; hence ~ly[2] (-nlĭ) *adv.*, ~ness (-n-n-) *n.* [f. L *supinus* (st. of *super* above; see -ine[1]]

su'pine[2] (sū'-, sōō'-) *n.* (L Gram.) verbal noun comprising accusative in *-um* and ablative in *-u* formed from stem of past participle and used to denote purpose or make adj. specific (e.g. *mirabile dictu* wonderful to relate). [f. LL *supinum* neut. (as n.) of *supinus* (see prec.); reason for name unknown]

sŭ'pper *n.* meal taken at the end of the day, esp. evening meal less formal and substantial than dinner; Last[3] *Supper*; Lord's *Supper*; **sing for** one's ~, (be required to) do something in return before or im-

mediately after receiving a benefit; hence ~less *a.* [ME, f. OF *soper, super, (soper* sup; see -er[4])]

suppla'nt (-ah'-) *v.t.* dispossess and take the place of, esp. by underhand means; hence ~er[1] *n.* [ME, f. OF *supplanter* or f. L sup(*plantare* f. *planta* sole) trip up]

sŭ'pple *a.* (~r, ~st) & *v.* **1.** *a.* easily bent, pliant, flexible; compliant, avoiding overt resistance, artfully or servilely submissive; ~-jack, (walking-cane of) strong twining tropical shrub; hence ~ly[2] (-pel-lĭ, -plĭ) *adv.*, ~ness (-peln-) *n.* **2.** *v.t.* & *i.* make or become supple. [ME f. OF *souple*, f. Rom. *supples* f. L sup(*plex -plicis* f. *plic-* bend) submissive]

sŭ'pplĕment[1] *n.* thing added to remedy deficiencies; part added to book etc. with further information, or to periodical for treatment of particular matter(s); ~ **of an angle**, (Math.) its deficiency from 180° (cf. complement[1]); hence ~al, ~ary[1], (-mĕ'n-) *adjs.* (*supplementary* benefit[1]). [ME, f. L sup(*plementum* f. *-plēre* fill; see -ment]

sŭpplĕmĕnt[2] (sŭ'-, -ĕ'nt) *v.t.* make supplement to; hence ~a'tion *n.* [f. prec.]

supplĕ'ti|on *n.* supplementing, esp. (Ling.) occurrence of unrelated forms as part of same conjugation etc. (*go, went*); so ~ive *a.* [ME f. OF, f. med. L *suppletio -onis* (as supply[1]; see -ion)]

sŭ'ppliant *a.* & *n.* (literary). **1.** *a.* supplicating, expressive of supplication; hence ~ly[2] *adv.* **2.** *n.* humble petitioner. [ME f. F (*supplier* f. L as foll.; see -ant)]

sŭ'pplic|āte *v.t.* & *i.* make humble petition to or *to* person, for or *for* thing; so ~ant *a.* & *n.*, ~a'tion *n.*, ~atory (-at-, -āt-) *a.* [ME, f. L sup(*plicare* f. *plic-* bend) +-ate[3]]

supply'[1] *v.t.*, *n.*, & *a.* **1.** *v.t.* furnish, provide, (thing needed, or person, receptacle, etc., with or *with* thing needed); hence **suppli'**er[1] *n.* **2.** make up for, meet, serve to obviate, (deficiency, need, loss); fill (place, vacancy, pulpit) as substitute. **3.** *n.* providing of what is needed (**Committee of S~**, House of Commons discussing details of estimates for public service). **4.** stock, store, amount of something provided or available or accessible, (*an inexhaustible supply of fish*; *water-supply*); in short *supply*; ~ **and demand** (Econ., regarded as factors regulating price of commodities). **5.** (in *pl.*) collected necessaries for army etc.; grant of money by Parliament for cost of government; money allowance to person. **6.** person, esp. clergyman or schoolteacher, who acts as temporary substitute for another; **on** ~, acting thus. **7.** *a.* providing supply or supplies (*supply officer, pipe, teacher*). [ME, f. OF *so(u)pleer* etc. f. L sup(*plēre* fill)]

sŭ'pply'[2] *adv.* supplely. [f. supple +-ly[2]]

suppŏ'rt *v.t.*, & *n.* **1.** *v.t.* carry (part of) weight of, hold up, keep from falling or sinking, (*foundation, buttress, supports house, wall*; *supported by a lifebelt*; *had to be supported home*). **2.** enable to last out, keep from failing, give strength to, encourage, (*what supported him* or *his strength was a glass of brandy, a good conscience, hope, your approval*; *too little food to support life*). **3.** endure, tolerate, (*supports fatigue well*; *I can support life, such insolence, no longer*); hence ~able *a.*, ~ably *adv.* **4.** supply with necessaries, provide for, (*support oneself, a family*). **5.** lend assistance or countenance to, back up, second, further, (*support a cause, policy, team, leader, candidate*); take secondary part to (actor or other performer); speak in favour of (resolution etc.); assist (lecturer etc.) by one's presence; subscribe to funds of (institution); ~ing **film, picture**, etc., less important part of cinema programme. **6.** bear out, tend to substantiate or corroborate, bring facts to confirm, (statement, charge, theory, etc.). **7.** keep up or represent (part, character) adequately. **8.** Hence ~ive *a.* **9.** *n.* supporting or being supported (*give support to*; *needs support*; *gets no support*; *troops stationed in support*); ~ **price**, minimum price guaranteed to farmers etc. by Government subsidy; **in** ~ **of**, in order to support, advocate, etc. **10.** person or thing that supports (*shelf must have another support*; *he is the chief support of the cause*). **11.** Hence ∼LESS *a*. [ME, f. OF *supporter* f. L SUP(*portare* carry)]

suppor'ter *n*. In vbl senses; (Her.) representation of living creature holding up or standing beside an escutcheon (usu. as one of pair on either side); one who takes an interest in a particular team or sport. [ME, f. prec. + -ER¹]

suppo's|e (-z) *v.t.* **1.** assume (as true) for purposes of argument (*let us suppose it to be true*; *well, suppose it was so*); (in *pres. part.* or *imper.*, with conjunctional force =) if (*supposing white were black you would be right*; *suppose your father saw you what would he say?*); (in *imper.* as formula of proposal: *suppose we went for a walk*; *suppose we try another*). **2.** (Of theory, result, etc.) involve or require as a condition, presuppose, (*that supposes a mechanism without flaws*; *design in creation supposes a creator*). **3.** take for granted, presume, assume in default of knowledge, be inclined to think, accept as probable, (*I suppose we shall be back in an hour*; *you cannot suppose, it is not to be supposed, that*; *I suppose he won't come* or *I don't suppose he will come*; *what do you suppose he meant?*); *I suppose so¹* 7; (abs. in parenth.: *you will not be there, I suppose*). **4.** (in *pass.*) have as a duty (*he is supposed to clean the shoes*); **not be** ∼**ed,** (1) not have as a duty, (2, colloq.) have duty not (*you are not supposed to kick people*). **5.** (in *p.p.*) believed to exist, believed to have specified character, (*the supposed music of the spheres*; *his supposed brother, generosity*; *he is supposed to be very rich*); hence ∼**éd**LY² *adv*. **6.** Hence or cogn. ∼ABLE *a.*, **suppos**i'TION *n.*, **supposi'tion**AL *a.*, (-z-). [ME, f. OF SUP(*poser* POSE¹)]

supposi'tious (-zi'shus) *a*. hypothetical, assumed; = foll.; hence ∼LY² *adv.*, ∼NESS *n*. [partly f. foll., partly f. SUPPOSITION + -OUS]

supposi'tious (-zĭtĭ'shus) *a*. substituted for the real, spurious, (*supposititious child, writings*); hence ∼LY² *adv.*, ∼NESS *n*. [f. L *supposititius, -icius* f. SUP(*ponere* posit-place) substitute; see -ITIOUS¹]

suppo'sitory (-z-) *n*. (Med.) cone or cylinder of medicinal substance introduced into rectum or vagina or urethra and left to melt. [ME, f. med. L *suppositorium*, neut. (as n.) of LL *suppositorius* placed underneath (as prec.; see -ORY)]

suppre'ss *v.t.* use force or authority to make cease, put an end to activity or existence of, (rebellion, sedition, agitators, haemorrhage, conscience, piracy, monasteries, etc.); restrain, keep in, not give vent to, withhold or withdraw from publication, keep secret, not reveal, (groan, yawn, feelings, name, book, evidence, facts); (Psych.) keep out of one's consciousness; (Electr.) partly or wholly eliminate (unwanted frequencies, interference); equip (device) so as to reduce interference due to it; hence or cogn. ∼IBLE, ∼IVE, *adjs.*, ∼ION (-shon), ∼OR, *ns*. [ME, f. L SUP(*primere* press- = *premere* press)]

suppressio veri (supresio verĭ) *n*. suppression of truth, misrepresentation by concealment of facts that ought to be made known (cf. SUGGESTIO FALSI). [L]

su'ppur|āte *v.i.* form pus, fester; so ∼A'TION *n.*, ∼ATIVE *a.* [f. L SUP(*purare* f. PUS) + -ATE³]

supra (sōō'pra, sū'-) *adv*. above; previously, before (in a book or writing). [L, = above]

su'pra- (sōō'-, sū'-) *pref*. above (opp. INFRA-, SUB-). **1.** (Anat.) = SUPER- 1 (1) (∼**or'bital,** above the orbit of the eye; ∼**re'nal,** = ADRENAL); upper (∼**maxi'llary,** (of) the upper jaw). **2.** over, beyond; ∼**lapsar'ian(ism),** (holder of, holding) Calvinist doctrine that predestination preceded the Creation and the Fall; ∼**mu'ndane,** above or superior to the world; ∼**na'tional,** transcending national limits; ∼**segme'ntal,** (Phonet.) relating to features of phonemes as assembled in an utterance. [f. or after L *supra-* (*supra* above, beyond, before in time)]

supre'mac|y (sōō-, sū-) *n*. being supreme, highest authority; **Act of S**∼**y** (securing ecclesiastical supremacy to the Crown and excluding the authority

of the pope); hence ∼IST *n.*, advocate of some group's (esp. WHITE¹) supremacy. [f. foll. + -ACY]

supre'me (sōō-, sū-) *a.* & *n.* **1.** *a*. highest in authority or rank; **the S**∼ **(Being),** God; **S**∼ **Court,** highest judicial court in State etc. (cf. JUDICATURE); ∼ **end** or **good,** *summum bonum*; **supreme** PONTIFF; *Supreme* SOVIET. **2.** greatest possible, uttermost, extreme, last and greatest or most important, (*supreme wisdom, courage,* etc.; *the supreme test of fidelity*; *a* or *the supreme hour, moment,* etc.); (of penalty, sacrifice, etc.) involving one's death. **3.** *n.* (dish served in) rich cream sauce. **4.** Hence ∼LY² (-mlĭ) *adv*. [f. L *supremus* superl. of *superus* that is above (*super* above)]

suprême (suprě'm) *n.* = prec. 3. [F]

supre'mō (sōō-, sū-) *n.* (*pl.* ∼s). supreme leader or ruler. [Sp., = SUPREME]

Supt. *abbr.* Superintendent.

suq. Var. of SOUK.

sur- *pref*. **1.** Assim. form of SUB- 1–6 before *r* (*surreptitious, surrogate*). **2.** = SUPER- (*surcharge, surface, surprise, surrealism, surrender*) [OF].

sur'a, sur'ah¹, (soor'a) *n*. chapter or section of Koran. [f. Arab. *sūra*]

sūr'ah² (-a) *n*. soft twilled silk for scarves etc. [f. F pr. of SURAT]

sur'al *a*. of the calf of the leg (*sural artery* etc.). [f. mod L *suralis* f. L *sura* calf; see -AL]

surä't *n*. (Hist.) kind of cotton grown, kind of coarse cotton cloth made, in the Bombay Presidency. [f. S∼ in India]

surcea'se *n.* & *v.* (arch.) **1.** *n.* cessation. **2.** *v.i.* & *t.* cease. [ME, f. OF *sursis, -ise* (cf. AF *sursise* omission), p.p. of OF *surseoir* refrain, delay f. L (as SUPERSEDE), w. assim. to CEASE¹, ²]

sur'charge¹ *n*. excessive or additional load or burden or amount of money charged; additional charge made by assessors as penalty for false returns of taxable property; mark printed on postage stamp changing its value; ‖amount in official account not passed by auditor and having to be refunded by person responsible; showing of omission in account for which credit should have been given. [f. foll.]

surchär'ge² *v.t.* overload, fill or saturate to excess; (of assessor or auditor) exact surcharge from, exact (sum) as surcharge, fine (person sum) as surcharge; show omission of credit in (account); print surcharge on (postage stamp). [ME, f. OF SUR(*charger* CHARGE⁴)]

sur'cingle *n*. band round horse's body usu. to keep pack etc. in place. [ME, f. OF SUR(*cengle* girth f. L *cingula* f. *cingere* gird)]

sur'coat *n*. **1.** (Hist.) loose robe worn over armour. **2.** similar sleeveless garment worn as part of insignia of order of knighthood. **3.** (Hist.) outer coat of rich material. **4.** man's belted jacket. [ME, f. OF SUR(*cot* coat)]

sur'culōse *a*. (Bot.) producing suckers. [f. L *surculosus* (*surculus* twig; see -OSE¹)]

sürd *a.* & *n.* **1.** (Math.) irrational (number, esp. root of integer). **2.** (Phonet.) voiceless (sound). [f. L *surdus* deaf, mute; sense 1 by mistransl. into L of Gk *alogos* irrational, speechless, thr. Arab. *jadr aṣamm* deaf root]

sure (shoor) *a.* & *adv.* **1.** *a*. having or seeming to have adequate reason for belief, convinced *of* or (*that*), having certain prospect or confident anticipation or satisfactory knowledge *of*, free from doubts *of*, (*you may be sure of his honesty, he is* or *that he is honest*; *he feels* or *is sure of success*; *I did not feel sure of my position, could not feel sure about it*; *if one could be sure of living to 70*); **I'm** ∼ *I didn't mean to hurt you* (form of asseveration); **well, I'm** ∼! (excl. of surprise). **2.** safe, reliable, trusty, unfailing, (*there is only one sure way*; *put it in a sure place*); ∼ **card,** scheme etc. certain to succeed; ∼**footed,** never stumbling or making false step (lit. or fig.); ∼ **shot,** marksman who never misses; SLOW *and, but, sure*. **3.** to be relied on, certain, *to do* (*is sure to turn out well*; *would be sure to dislike him*) or to happen (*as sure as*

FATE); **be** ~ (in *imper.* or *inf.*) take care, not fail, (*be sure you* or *to* or *and finish it*); *~-**fire**, (colloq.) certain (to succeed); *~ **thing**, (*n.*) a certainty, (*int.*) certainly!. **4.** undoubtedly true or truthful (*one thing is sure*); **to be** ~, (formula of concession =) to avoid overstatement (*to be sure she is not perfect, is pretty*), (as excl. of surprise: or *so it is, to be sure!*; *well, to be sure!*); **for** ~, (colloq.) without doubt; **make** ~, ascertain absolutely that something is as supposed, take measures to secure that something is as desired, establish the truth or ensure the existence or happening *of*, (in *past*) have confident (but often false) anticipation *of* or *that* (*he suspected nothing, and made sure of succeeding*); hence ~'NESS (shoor'n-) *n.* **5.** adv. (arch.) undoubtedly, with certainty. **6.** *(colloq.) certainly (*it sure was cold*). **7.** as certainly as (*as sure as* EGG¹*s are eggs, as sure as I stand here*, etc., colloq. forms of asseveration); ~ **enough,** in fact as well as in prospect (*I said it would be, and sure enough it is*), with practical certainty (*he will come sure enough*). [ME, f. OF *sur sure*, earlier *seür* f. L *securus* SECURE]

sure'ly (shoor'li) *adv.* with certainty or safety (*will diminish slowly but surely*; *mule plants its feet surely*); if strong belief or experience or probability or right is to count for anything (*it surely cannot have been he*; *surely I have met you before*; *there is no truth in it, surely*; *surely you will not desert me*); (as answer) certainly, undoubtedly, ('*May I use your telephone?* '*Surely*'). [ME, f. prec. +-LY²]

surety (shoor'eti, shoor'ti) *n.* **1.** person who makes himself responsible for another's appearance in court or payment of debt or performance of undertaking (**stand** ~, become so responsible, go bail, *for* another); hence ~SHIP *n.* **2.** (arch.) certainty; **for** or **of a** ~, certainly. [ME, f. OF *surté, seürté* f. L *securitas -tatis* SECURITY].

surf *n.,* & *v.i.* **1.** *n.* foam and swell of sea breaking on shore or reefs; ~-**bird,** Pacific coast-bird related to sandpiper; ~-**board,** long narrow board used in surf-riding; ~-**boat** (of buoyant build for use in surf); ~-**man** (skilled in managing surf-boats); ~-**riding,** sport of being carried over surf to shore on boards etc.; hence ~'ER¹ *n.* **2.** *v.i.* go surf-riding; hence ~'ER¹ *n.* [app. f. obs. *suff,* perh. assim. to *surge*; orig. applied to the Indian coast]

sur'face (-is) *n., a.,* & *v.* **1.** *n.* the outside of a material body, area of this, (any of) the limits that terminate a solid, the upper boundary of soil, water, etc., outward aspect of material or immaterial thing, what is apprehended of something on casual view or consideration, (*has a smooth, uneven, surface; presents a large surface to view; its upper surface is as cold as ice; looks only at the surface of men and things; his politeness is only of or on the surface; one never gets below the surface with him*); **come to the** ~, (fig.) become perceptible after being hidden; hence (-)**sur'fac**ED² (-fist) *a.* **2.** (Geom.) that which has length and breadth but no thickness. **3.** *attrib. a.* of the surface only (*surface plausibility, impressions*); of the surface of the sea, opp. the air above or the water beneath; of the surface of the earth, opp. underground. **4.** ~-**active,** (of substance) able to affect wetting properties of a liquid; *~-**car** (running on road, opp. underground or elevated transport); ~ **craft,** ship travelling only on surface of sea (opp. *submarine*); ~ **density,** amount of mass etc. per unit area of surface; ~ **mail** (carried by sea or *land and not by air); ~ **noise** (in playing gramophone record, due to roughness of groove); ~-**printing** (from raised surface such as letterpress type, not from incised plate); ~ **tension,** (Phys.) tension of surface-film of liquid tending to minimize its surface area; ~-**water** (that collects on and runs off from surface of ground etc.). **5.** *v.t.* put special surface on (paper etc.); bring (submarine) to the surface. **6.** *v.i.* come to the surface; (colloq.) wake, become visible or known. [F (as SUR-, FACE¹)]

surfa'ctant *n.* surface-active agent. [abbr.; see -ANT]

sur'feit (-fit) *n.* & *v.* **1.** *n.* excess esp. in eating or drinking; oppression or satiety resulting. **2.** *v.t.* & *i.* overfeed, (cause to) take too much of something; cloy, satiate *with.* [ME, f. OF *sorfe(i)t, surfe(i)t,* f. Rom. *superfactum neut. p.p. (as n.) of *superficere (as SUPER-, L *facere* fact- do); cf. LL *superficiens* excessive]

surfi'cial (-shal) *a.* (Geol.) of the earth's surface; hence ~LY² *adv.* [f. SURFACE after *superficial*]

surge *v.i.,* & *n.* **1.** *v.i.* (Of sea, crowd, standing corn, emotion, etc.) move up and down or to and fro (as) in waves; (Naut., of rope or chain or windlass) slip back with a jerk; move suddenly and powerfully *forwards, upwards,* etc.; (of electric current etc.) increase suddenly. **2.** *n.* waves, a wave; surging motion, (fig.) impetuous onset; ~ **tank** (to neutralize sudden changes of pressure in flow of liquid). [f. OF *sourdre sourge-,* or *sorgir* f. Cat., f. L *surgere* rise]

sur'geon (-jon) *n.* person skilled in surgery; medical practitioner qualified to practise (esp. one who specializes in) surgery (~ **dentist,** dentist thus qualified for dental surgery); medical officer in navy or army or military hospital; TREE *surgeon*; ~-**fish,** fish of genus *Acanthurus* with movable lancet-shaped spines on each side of tail; *~ **general,** head of public health service or of medical service in army etc.; ~'s **knot,** reef-knot with double twist. [ME, f. AF *surgien,* etc., f. OF *serurgien, sirurgien (sirurgie* f. L *chirurgia* f. Gk *kheirourgia* handiwork, surgery f. *kheir* hand, -o-, *-ergo* to work; see -Y¹)]

sur'gery *n.* **1.** manual or instrumental treatment of injuries or disorders of the body, (*antiseptic, clinical, plastic,* etc., *surgery*). **2.** ||place where or time when doctor, dentist, etc., gives advice and treatment; (colloq.) place where MP, lawyer, etc., is available for discussion of person's problems; period during which doctor etc. is present at surgery. [ME, f. OF *surgerie,* contr. f. *sirurgerie (sirurgien;* see prec., -ERY)]

sur'gical *a.* of surgeons or surgery (*surgical skill, operations, instruments*); resulting from surgery (*surgical fever*); used for surgery or in conditions suitable for surgery (*surgical boot*); || ~ **spirit,** methylated spirits used in surgery for cleansing etc.; hence ~LY² *adv.* [f. earlier *chirurgical* f. *chirurgy* f. OF *sirurgie* (see SURGEON)]

sur'icate (soor'-) *n.* S. Afr. burrowing mammal (*Suricata suricatta*) like mongoose, grey with black stripes. [F, f. S. Afr. native name]

Surina'm (soor-) *n.* ~ **toad,** pipa. [~ in S. America]

sur'ly *a.* uncivil, given to making rude answers, showing unfriendly temper, churlish; hence ~iLY² *adv.,* ~iNESS *n.* [alt. sp. of obs. *sirly* haughty f. SIR +-LY¹]

surmi'se (-z) *n.* & *v.* **1.** *n.* conjecture, suspicion of the existence or guess at the nature of something. **2.** *v.t.* infer doubtfully, suspect the existence of. **3.** *v.i.* make a guess, try to divine something. [ME f. AF & OF fem. p.p. of *surmettre* accuse f. LL SUPER(*mittere* miss-send)]

surmou'nt *v.t.* **1.** (esp. in *pass.*) cap, be on the top of, (*peaks surmounted with snow*). **2.** overcome, get over, (difficulty, obstacle); hence ~ABLE *a.* [ME, f. OF SUR(*monter* MOUNT²)]

surmu'llet *n.* red mullet. [f. F *surmulet* f. OF *sor red* + *mulet* MULLET]

sur'name *n.* & *v.t.* **1.** *n.* name common to all members of a family; (Rom. Ant.) cognomen; (arch.) additional name of descriptive or allusive kind attached to a person and occas. becoming hereditary. **2.** *v.t.* give surname to; give (person surname); (in *p.p.*) called by way of additional name, having as family name. [ME, alt. of *surnoun* f. AF (as SUR-, NOUN name)]

surpa'ss (-ah's) *v.t.* go beyond (another, or oneself previously) in degree, amount, or quality; be or do more or better than; hence ~ING² *a.,* greatly excelling or exceeding others, of very high degree. [f. F SUR(*passer* PASS¹)]

sūr'plic|e n. loose full-sleeved white-linen vestment descending usu. to knees or ankles and worn usu. over cassock by clergy and choristers at divine service; ||~e-fee (paid to clergy for marriages, funerals, etc.); hence ~ED² (-st) a. [ME, f. AF surplis, OF sourpelis, f. med. L superpellicium (as SUPER-, pellicia PELISSE)]

sūr'plus n. & a. **1.** n. what remains over, what is not required for the purpose in hand, esp. excess of public revenue over expenditure for the financial year, (opp. deficit); so ~AGE (1) n. **2.** a. that is in excess of what is taken, used, needed, or acceptable (surplus to my needs); ~ value, difference between value of work done and wages paid. [ME f. AF; OF s(o)urplus f. med. L SUPER(PLUS)]

surprī'se (-z) n., & v.t. **1.** n. catching of person(s) unprepared (the fort was taken, the truth must be elicited, by surprise; determined to attempt a surprise); **a ~ visit** (without notice). **2.** emotion excited by the unexpected (full of surprise; his surprise was visible); **to my great ~,** much against my expectations; ||~ **package, packet,** (with unexpected contents, e.g. sweets with coin; often fig.). **3.** event etc. that excites surprise (was a great surprise to me); piece of unexpected news, unexpected gift, etc.; ~, ~! (excl. of ironical surprise). **4.** v.t. capture (place, person) by surprise; attack without warning; come upon (person) off his guard (surprised him in the act). **5.** affect with surprise, turn out contrary to expectations of, be a surprise to, (it may surprise you to learn of this; more surprised than frightened; surprised that, to find etc.); **~d at,** scandalized by (I am surprised at you, your behaviour); hence **surprī'sING²** a., **surprī'singLY²** adv., (-z-). **6.** hurry (person) by surprise into conduct or act or doing (surprised me into rudeness, consent, dropping the reins); discover (secret etc.) by unexpected action. **7.** Hence **surprī'sAL** 2 (-z-) n. (arch.). [OF, fem. p.p. (as n.) of SUR(prendre f. L praehendere seize)]

surra (sū'ra, soor'a) n. febrile disease affecting horses and cattle in the tropics. [Marathi]

surre'al|ism n. (twentieth-century movement in) art and literature purporting to express the subconscious mind by phenomena of dreams etc.; so ~ a., ~IST (2) a. & n., ~i'stIC a. [f. F SUR(réalisme REALISM)]

sŭrrebū'tter n. (Law). plaintiff's reply to defendant's rebutter. [f. SUR- 2+REBUTTER, after foll.]

sŭrrejoi'nder n. (Law). plaintiff's reply to defendant's rejoinder. [f. SUR- 2+REJOINDER]

surrĕ'nder v. & n. **1.** v.t. hand over, give into another's power or control, relinquish possession of, esp upon compulsion or demand, (surrender fortress, army, freedom, hopes, chastity, privilege, office); give up rights under (insurance policy) in return for smaller sum payable immediately; give oneself over to habit, emotion, influence, etc. **2.** v.i. (Of fortress, ship, or force, or its commander) accept enemy's demand for submission; give oneself up, cease from resistance, submit; ||~ **to** one's **bail,** duly appear in court after being released on bail. **3.** n. surrendering or being surrendered; ~ **value,** amount payable to one who surrenders insurance policy. [ME f. AF, f. OF SUR(rendre RENDER)]

sŭrrepti'tious (-shus) a. underhand, kept secret, done by stealth, clandestine; hence ~LY² adv. [ME, f. L surrepticius -itius f. SUR(ripere rept- = rapere seize); see -ITIOUS¹]

*sŭ'rrey n. light four-wheeled carriage with two seats facing forwards. [f. S~ in England, where first made]

sŭ'rrogate n. deputy, substitute; ||deputy of bishop or his chancellor for granting licences for marriages without banns; *judge in charge of probate, inheritance, and guardianship; hence ~SHIP (-tsh-) n. [f. L surrogatus p.p. of SUR(rogare ask) elect as substitute; see -ATE²]

surrou'nd v.t., & n. **1.** v.t. come or be all round, invest, enclose, encompass, encircle, environ; ~ed **by** or **with,** having on all sides; **the ~ing country,** the neighbouring district. **2.** n. ||border, edging, esp.

(floor-covering for) area between walls and carpet; *driving of wild animals into place of no escape. [ME = overflow, f. AF sur(o)under, OF s(o)uronder f. LL SUPER(undare flow f. unda wave)]

surrou'ndings (-z) n. pl. sum total of things or conditions in the neighbourhood of a person or thing (picturesque, healthy, degraded, cultured, surroundings). [f. prec. +-ING¹ +-s¹]

sūr'tăx n., & v.t. (impose) additional tax (on) (esp. of graduated tax on incomes above a certain figure in addition to ordinary income tax). [f. F SUR(taxe TAX²)]

sūrtou't (-ōō't, -ōō', sĕr'-) n. (Hist.) greatcoat; frock--coat. [F (sur over, tout everything)]

survei'llance (-vā'l-) n. supervision, close observation, invigilation, esp. of suspected person. [F, f. SUR(veiller f. L vigilare keep watch)]

survey'¹ (-vā') v.t. let the eyes pass over, take general view of, form general idea of the arrangement and chief features of, make or present survey of; examine condition of (building etc.); determine boundaries, size, position, shape, contour, etc., of (land, coast, district, estate, etc.) by measuring distances and angles. [ME, f. AF survei(e)r, OF so(u)rveeir -vey- f. med. L SUPER(vidēre see)]

sŭr'vey' (-vā) n. general view, casting of eyes or mind over something; inspection or investigation of the condition, amount, etc., of something, account given of result of this; department carrying on, operations constituting, piece of, surveying of land etc.; map or plan setting forth results of such work; ||ORDNANCE survey. [f. prec.]

survey'or (-vā'-) n. official inspector of (surveyor of weights and measures etc.), official in charge of a department, whence ~SHIP n.; person professionally engaged in surveying (QUANTITY surveyor); *exciseman. [ME, f. AF & OF surve(i)our (as SURVEY¹; see -OR)]

survi'val n. **1.** surviving (~ **of the fittest,** process or result of natural selection); ~ **kit,** emergency rations etc. carried by airmen. **2.** person or thing that has remained as a relic of an earlier time. [f. foll. +-AL 2]

survi've v. **1.** v.t. outlive, be still alive or in existence after the passing away of, (survive one's children, contemporaries, etc.; survive one's usefulness); come alive through or continue to exist in spite of (survive all perils). **2.** v.i. continue to live or exist, be still alive or existent. **3.** Hence **survi'vOR** n., one who survives, (Law) joint tenant who has right to whole estate on other's death. [ME, f. AF survivre, OF sourvivre f. L SUPER(vivere live)]

sŭs n., & v.t. (**-ss-**). (sl.) suspect; suspicion; ~ **out,** reconnoitre. [abbr.]

sus- pref., assim. form of SUB- 1–6 before c, p, or t.

Sus. abbr. Susanna (Apocrypha).

suscĕptibi'lity n. being susceptible; (in pl.) sensitive feelings of a person; (Phys.) ratio of magnetization to magnetizing force. [f. foll. +-ITY; see -IBILITY]

suscĕ'ptib|le a. **1.** (pred.) admitting of (words are susceptible of another interpretation; facts not susceptible of proof), open or liable or accessible or sensitive to (very susceptible to pain, injury, kindness, women's charms). **2.** impressionable, sensitive, readily touched with emotion, touchy. **3.** Hence ~LY² adv. [f. LL susceptibilis f. L SUS(cipere cept- = capere take); see -IBLE]

suscĕ'ptive a. concerned with the receiving of emotional impressions or ideas, receptive; = prec. [f. LL susceptivus (as prec.; see -IVE)]

su'shi (sōō'-) n. Japanese snack of cold rice flavoured and garnished. [Jap.]

sŭ'slik n. E. European & Asian rodent like gopher, of genus Citellus. [Russ.]

suspĕ'ct¹ v.t. **1.** have an impression of the existence or presence of (danger, a plot, foul play, collusion, a causal relation); believe without adequate proof to be (suspect him to be my brother, a liar, dying); be inclined to think that or that (I suspect you once thought otherwise; you, I *suspect, don't care*). **2.** incline to mentally accuse *of* or inculpate, doubt the innocence of, distrust, (*I suspect him of lying, of deep designs; suspected persons; the ignorant suspect everybody*); ∼**ed** *criminal, connection*, etc., person or thing suspected of being (such). **3.** hold to be uncertain, mistrust, doubt the genuineness or truth of, (*suspect the authenticity of the evidence*). [ME, f. L *suspicere* (see foll.)]

sŭ′spĕct² *a.* & *n.* **1.** *a.* of suspected character, subject to suspicion or distrust, not unimpeachable, (*the statement of an interested party is naturally suspect*). **2.** *n.* suspected person (*political suspects are kept under surveillance*). [ME, f. L *suspectus* p.p. of *suspicere* (as SUB- 1, 2, *specere* look)]

suspĕ′nd *v.t.* **1.** hang up; (in *p.p.*, of solid particles or body in fluid medium) sustained somewhere between top and bottom (*a balloon suspended in mid-air; suspended particles of dust*); **suspĕ′ns**IBLE *a.* **2.** keep in undecided or inoperative state for a time, defer, temporarily annul, adjourn, debar temporarily from office or function or privilege or membership, (*suspend judgement, hostilities, the rules, the proceedings, a player, a clergyman*); ∼ **payment,** (of company) fail to meet financial engagements, admit insolvency; ∼**ed animation,** state of cessation of vital functions without death; ∼**ed sentence** (Law, remaining unenforced subject to good behaviour during specified period). [ME, f. OF *suspendre* or L SUS(*pendere pens-* hang)]

suspĕ′nder *n.* In vbl senses; (in *pl.*) *pair of braces, ‖pair of (sets of) attachments to hold up socks or stockings by their tops; ‖∼ **belt,** woman's undergarment carrying suspenders for holding up stockings. [f. prec.+-ER¹]

suspĕ′nse *n.* **1.** state of usu. anxious uncertainty or expectation or waiting for information; ∼ **account** (in which items are temporarily entered till proper place is determined); **keep** person **in** ∼, delay telling him what he is eager to know; hence ∼FUL (-sf-) *a.* **2.** (Law). suspension, temporary cessation of right etc. [ME, f. AF & OF *suspens,* f. p.p. (as n.) of L *suspendere* SUSPEND]

suspĕ′nsion (-shon) *n.* suspending or being suspended; substance consisting of particles suspended in a medium; means by which vehicle is supported on its axles; (Mus.) prolongation of note of chord to form discord with following chord; ∼ **bridge** (in which roadway is hung across river etc., usu. on wire or chain cables passing over towers and anchored, without support from below). [F, or f. L *suspensio* (as SUSPEND; see -ION)]

suspĕ′nsive *a.* having the power or tendency to suspend or postpone; causing suspense; *suspensive* VETO; hence ∼LY² (-vlĭ) *adv.,* ∼NESS (-vn-) *n.* [f. F *suspensif -ive* or f. med. L *suspensivus* (as SUSPEND; see -IVE)]

suspĕ′nsorў *a.* (Of ligament, muscle, bandage, etc.) holding (organ etc.) suspended. [f. F *suspensoire* (as SUSPENSION; see -ORY)]

suspi′cion (-shon) *n.* feeling or state of mind of one who suspects (*have a suspicion that all is not well*); suspecting or being suspected (**above** ∼, too obviously good etc. to be suspected; **under** ∼, suspected); partial or unconfirmed belief esp. that something is wrong or someone guilty; soupçon *of*; hence ∼LESS *a.* [ME, f. AF *suspeciun* (OF *sospeçon*) f. med. L *suspectio -onis* f. L *suspicere* (see SUSPECT¹, -ION), assim. to F *suspicion* & L *suspicio*)]

suspi′cious (-shus) *a.* prone to, feeling, indicating, suggesting or justifying, suspicion (*the ignorant are suspicious of everybody; his silence made me suspicious; with a suspicious glance; under suspicious circumstances*); hence ∼LY² *adv.,* ∼NESS *n.* [ME f. AF & OF, f. L *suspiciosus* (as prec.; see -OUS)]

suspīr′e *v.i.* (esp. poet.) sigh (*for*); breathe; so **sŭspirA′TION** *n.* [f. L *suspirare* (as SUB- 1, *spirare* breathe)]

sŭss. Var. of SUS.

Sŭ′ssèx *n.* speckled or red domestic fowl of English breed; ∼ **spaniel** (dark golden breed with short legs and neck). [∼ in England]

sustai′n *v.t.* **1.** carry weight of, hold up, keep from falling or sinking, esp. for prolonged period. **2.** = SUPPORT 2; ∼**ing food** (that keeps up one's strength); ∼**ing member** (making regular contributions to funds of institution etc.); *∼**ing programme,** broadcast programme without commercial sponsor. **3.** endure without giving way, stand, bear up against, (*sustained the shock of the enemy's attack; will not sustain comparison with*). **4.** undergo, experience, suffer, (*sustain a defeat, a broken leg, severe bruises, loss,* etc.). **5.** (Of court or other authority) allow validity of, give decision in favour of, uphold, (*sustain the objection, the applicant in his claim,* etc.). **6.** = SUPPORT 6. **7.** keep up or represent (part, character) adequately. **8.** keep (sound, effort, etc.) going continuously (*a sustained note, effort; the interest is well sustained*). **9.** Hence ∼ABLE *a.,* ∼MENT *n.* [ME, f. AF *sustein-,* OF *so(u)stein-* stressed st. of *so(u)stenir* f. L SUS(*tinēre tent- = tenēre* hold)]

sŭ′stĕnance *n.* nourishing, nourishment; nourishing quality, subsistence, food (lit. or fig.; *there is no sustenance in it; lived a week without sustenance of any kind*); means of support. [ME, f. AF *sustenaunce,* OF *so(u)stenance* (as prec.; see -ANCE)]

sŭstentā′tion *n.* support of life; maintenance; ∼ **fund** (collected to support indigent clergy, esp. in Church of Scotland). [ME f. OF, or f. L *sustentatio* (*sustentare* frequent. of *sustinēre* SUSTAIN; see -ATION)]

susurrā′tion, susŭ′rrus, (sū-, sŏŏ-) *ns.* (literary). whispering, rustling. [(ME, f. LL *susurratio* f. L *susurrare* f.) L *susurrus* a. or n.; see -ATION]

sŭ′tler *n.* (Hist.) camp-follower selling provisions etc. to soldiers. [f. obs. Du. *soeteler* (*soetelen* befoul, perform mean duties f. Gmc **sudh-*; cf. SUDS)]

Su′tra (sŏŏ′-) *n.* (set of) aphorism(s) in Hindu literature; narrative part of Buddhist literature; Jainist scripture. [f. Skr. *sūtra* thread, rule (*siv* SEW)]

suttee′, sati′, (-ē′) *n.* (Hist.) Hindu widow who immolated herself on her husband's funeral pyre; (custom requiring) such immolation. [Hindi & Urdu, f. Skr. *satī* faithful wife (*sat* good)]

su′tur|e (sŏŏ′-) *n.,* & *v.t.* **1.** *n.* (Anat.) seamlike line of junction of two bones at their edges, esp. in the skull; (Bot. & Zool.) similar junction of parts; (Surg.) uniting of edges of wound by stitching, thread or wire used for this; hence ∼AL (-cher-), ∼ED² (-cherd), *adjs.* **2.** *v.t.* stitch (wound). [F, or f. L *sutura* (*suere sut-* sew; see -URE)]

su′zerain (sŏŏ′-, sū′-) *n.* feudal overlord; sovereign or State having some control over another State that is internally autonomous; hence ∼TY¹ *n.* [F, app. f. *sus* above f. L *su(r)sum* upward, after *souverain* SOVEREIGN]

s.v. *abbr.* side valve; under the word (*for 'span' see s.v. 'spick'*) [f. L *sub voce* or *sub verbo*].

svĕlte *a.* (Of human figure) slim, slender, lissom; graceful. [F, f. It. *svelto*]

SW *abbr.* South-West(ern).

swab (-ŏb) *n.,* & *v.t.* (**-bb-**). **1.** *n.* mop or other arrangement of absorbent material on handle for cleaning or mopping up; absorbent pad used in surgery; specimen of morbid secretion etc. taken with a swab for bacteriological examination. **2.** (sl.) contemptible person. **3.** *v.t.* clean with swab; take up (moisture) with swab. [n. f. v., back-form. f. *swabber* f. early mod. Du. *zwabber* f. Gmc base = 'splash, sway']

swă′cked (-kt) *a.* (sl.) drunk. [p.p. of Sc. *swack* drink heavily]

swa′ddl|e (-ŏ′-) *v.t.,* & *n.* **1.** *v.t.* swathe in bandages or many or thick wraps or garments; ∼**ing-bands, -clothes,** (in which infants were formerly wrapped to restrain them, (fig.) influences that restrain freedom of action or thought). **2.** *n.* *swaddling-clothes. [ME, f. SWATHE²+-LE 3]

swad̆dy (-ŏ'-) *n.* (sl.) soldier. [f. dial. *swad* soldier, bumpkin, perh. of Scand. orig., + -Y³]

Swade'shi (-ahdā'-) *n.* (Hist.) movement in India for production of home-manufactured, and boycott of foreign, goods. [Bengali, = own-country things]

swăg¹ *n.* **1.** ornamental festoon of flowers etc.; carved or moulded representation of this; drapery of similar appearance. **2.** (sl.) booty carried off by burglars etc., gains made by political or other jobbery; large quantity. **3.** (Austral. & NZ) tramp's, miner's, or bush-traveller's bundle; ∼'**man**, tramp. [f. foll.]

swăg² *v.* (-gg-). **1.** *v.i.* sway from side to side; hang heavily. [f. *v.t.* cause to sway or sag; arrange (curtain etc.) in swags; (Austral.) carry in swag. [16th c., prob. f. Scand.]

swăge *n.,* & *v.t.* **1.** *n.* die or stamp for shaping wrought iron etc. by hammering or pressure; tool for bending metal etc.; ∼-**block** (with variety of perforations, grooves, etc., for shaping metal). **2.** *v.t.* shape with swage. [f. F *s(o)uage* decorative groove, of unkn. orig.]

swă'gger¹ (-g-) *v.i., n.,* & *a.* **1.** *v.i.* walk like a superior among inferiors; show self-confidence or self-satisfaction by gait; go *about, in, out,* etc., with such walk; behave in domineering or defiant way; talk boastfully (*about* thing) or in hectoring manner; hence ∼ER¹ *n.* **2.** *n.* swaggering gait or manner or talk; dashing or confident air or way of doing something, freedom from tameness or hesitancy, smartness; || ∼-**cane**, ∼-**stick**, short cane carried by soldiers in town etc. or by officers. **3.** *a.* (colloq.) smart, fashionable, (*swagger clothes, society,* etc.); (of coat) cut with loose flare from shoulders. [app. f. SWAG² + -ER⁵]

swă'gger², **swă'ggie**, (-g-) *n.* (Austral.) tramp travelling with swag. [f. SWAG¹ + -ER, -IE]

Swahi'li (swahhē'-, swa-h-) *n.* Bantu people of Zanzibar and the adjacent coasts; their language, widely used in E. Africa. [f. Arab. *sawāhil* pl. of *sāhil* coast; see -I]

swain *n.* (arch or poet.) young rustic; bucolic lover; lover, suitor. [ME *swein* f. ON *sveinn* lad = OE *swān* swine-herd, OHG *swein* f. Gmc **swainaz*]

swa'llow¹ (-ŏ'lō) *v.* & *n.* **1.** *v.t.* cause or allow (food etc.) to pass down one's throat; = EAT (one's *words*); repress (tears, resentment, etc.); pronounce (sounds) indistinctly or not at all; ∼ **a camel**, make no difficulty about something incredible or impossible or outrageous (w. ref. to Matt. 23:24). **2.** ∼ (**up**), engulf, absorb, exhaust, draw in, make away with, (*the earth swallowed them up; the expenses more than swallow up the earnings; death is swallowed up in victory*). **3.** accept (*statement*) with ready credulity (*will swallow anything you tell him*); accept meekly, put up with, (affront, insult). **4.** Hence ∼ABLE *a.* **5.** *v.i.* perform muscular action (as) of swallowing something. **6.** *n.* act of swallowing; amount swallowed at once; gullet; || ∼(-**hole**), = SINK²-*hole.* [OE *swelg* n., *swelgan* v., = OHG *swel(a)han,* ON *svelga* f. Gmc **swelg-* etc.]

swa'llow² (-ŏ'lō) *n.* **1.** bird of genus *Hirundo* etc., esp. migratory, long-winged, swift-flying, wide-gaped, weak-legged, fork-tailed, insectivorous bird associated with summer; **one** ∼ **does not make a summer** (warning against hasty inference from one instance). **2.** || ∼-**dive** (with arms outspread till close to water); ∼-**hawk,** = *swallow-tailed kite;* ∼-**tail,** deeply forked tail, butterfly etc. having this, two-pointed end of flag, (in *sing.* or *pl.,* colloq.) swallow-tailed coat; ∼-**tailed,** (of bird etc.) with deeply forked tail (∼-*tailed coat,* tailcoat; ∼-*tailed kite,* Amer. white kite (*Elanoides forficatus*) with black deeply forked tail), dovetailed; ∼-**wort,** (1) milkweed, (2) greater celandine. [OE *swealwe,* = OS *swala,* OHG *swal(a)wa,* ON *svala* f. Gmc **swalwōn*]

swăm. See SWIM.

swa'mi (-ah'-) *n.* Hindu idol; Hindu religious teacher (esp. as form of address to Brahmin); (fig.) = PUNDIT 2. [f. Hindi *swāmī* master, prince, f. Skr. *svāmin*]

swamp (-ŏ-) *n.* & *v.* **1.** *n.* piece of wet spongy ground,

bog, marsh, (*attrib.,* in many names of plants and animals found in swamps); hence ∼Y² *a.* **2.** *v.t.* (Of water) overwhelm, flood, soak, (boat or its crew or contents, house, provisions, etc.); make helpless with excessive supply of something (*am swamped with* or *in letters, applications, work*); (of greater quantity or numbers) swallow up, make invisible etc., prevent from being noticed or taking effect; *defeat decisively. **3.** *v.i.* become swamped. [17th c.; usu. referred to Gmc root **swamp-, *swamb-, *swamm-* sponge, fungus]

swan (-ŏn) *n.,* & *v.i.* (-nn-). **1.** *n.* large water-bird of genus *Cygnus* etc. with long flexible neck, webbed feet, and in most species snow-white plumage, formerly supposed to sing melodiously at point of death; **black** ∼, (1) something extremely rare, (2) Australian swan with mainly black plumage; *all his geese are swans* (see GOOSE). **2.** (fig., w. ref. to sweetness of swan's dying song.) poet (esp. S∼ **of Avon,** Shakespeare). **3.** *∼-**dive,** = SWALLOW²-*dive;* ∼-**flower,** S. Amer. orchid with flower shaped like swan's neck; ∼-**goose,** long-necked China goose, esp. = CHINESE *goose;* ∼-**herd,** (esp. royal) officer having charge of swans; ∼-**maiden** (in Gmc Myth., able to change herself into swan); ∼-**mark** (cut in skin of swan's beak to show ownership); ∼-**neck,** curved structure shaped like swan's neck; ∼'**sdown** (-z-), (1) down of swan used in trimmings and esp. in powder-puffs, (2) kind of thick cotton cloth with soft nap on one side; ∼-**shot** (of large size for shooting swans); ∼-**skin,** kind of fine twilled flannel; ∼-**song,** fabled song of dying swan, (fig.) person's last composition, performance, etc.; || ∼-**upping,** annual taking up and marking of Thames swans. **4.** Hence ∼LIKE *a.* & *adv.,* ∼NERY (3) *n.* **5.** *v.i.* (sl.) move aimlessly or majestically (*around*) like swan. [OE, = OS, OHG *swan,* ON *svanr* f. Gmc **swanaz*]

swănk *n.,* & *v.i.* (colloq.) **1.** *n.* ostentation, swagger, bluff; || ∼'**pot,** person behaving with swank; hence ∼'Y² *a.,* marked by swank, ostentatiously smart. **2.** *v.i.* behave with swank. [orig. 19th c. Midland Engl. wd]

swap (-ŏp), **swŏp,** *v.* (-pp-) & *n.* (colloq.) **1.** exchange by way of barter (lit. or fig.; *swapped my knife for bread; swap blows, jokes; will you swap places* etc.*?, will you swap?, shall we try a swap?*); **never** ∼ **horses while crossing the stream,** leave changes till crisis is past. **2.** *n.* thing suitable for swapping. [ME, orig. = 'hit', prob. imit.]

SWAPO *abbr.* South West Africa People's Organization.

swara'j (-ah'j) *n.* (Hist.) self-government, independence, for India; hence ∼IST (2) *n.* [Skr., = self-ruling (cf. RAJ)]

sward (-ôrd) *n.* (literary). expanse covered with short grass, lawnlike ground; turf, whence ∼ED² *a.* [OE *sweard* skin, = MDu., MLG *swarde,* MHG *swarte,* ON *svörthr,* of unkn. orig.]

swäre. See SWEAR.

swarf (-ôrf) *n.* fine chips or filings of stone, metal, etc.; wax etc. removed in cutting gramophone record. [f. ON *svarf* file-dust]

swarm¹ (-ôrm) *n.,* & *v.i.* **1.** *n.* large number or dense group of insects, birds, small animals, persons, etc., moving about in a cluster or irregular body esp. round prey or enemy; (in *pl.*) great numbers *of* children, stars, people, bills, etc.; cluster of honey-bees emigrating from hive with queen bee to establish new home; group of zoospores (∼-**cell, -spore,** zoospore or other mobile spore). **2.** *v.i.* move in a swarm (*round, about, over* etc., thing or person, *in, out*); (of bees) cluster for emigration; congregate in large numbers, be very numerous; (of place) be overrun, be crowded, abound, *with* (road, hills, house, swarming with beggars, rebels, fleas*). [OE *swearm,* = OS *swarm,* OHG *swar(a)m,* ON *svarmr* f. Gmc **swarmaz*]

swarm² (-ôrm) *v.* **1.** *v.i.* ∼ **up,** climb (rope or tree or pole) by clasping with arms and legs alternately, climb (steep slope) by clinging with hands and knees. **2.** *v.t.* swarm up (rope etc.). [16th c., of unkn. orig.]

swart (-ört) *a.* (arch.) dark-hued, swarthy. [OE *sweart*, = OS *swart*, OHG *swarz*, ON *svartr*, Goth. *swarts* f. Gmc **swartaz*]

swar'thĭy̆ (-ör'dhĭ) *a.* dark, esp. dark-complexioned; hence ∼ĭLY² *adv.*, ∼ĭNESS *n.* [var. of obs. *swarty* (as prec.; see -Y²)]

swash¹ (-ŏ-) *v.* & *n.* **1.** *v.t.* (arch.) strike violently. **2.** *v.i.* (Of water etc.) wash about, make sound of washing or rising and falling; (arch.) swagger. **3.** ∼'buckler, ∼'buckling, swaggering (bully or ruffian). **4.** *n.* motion or sound of swashing water. [imit.]

swash² (-ŏ-) *a.* **1.** inclined obliquely; ∼-plate, inclined disc revolving on axle and giving reciprocating motion to part in contact with it. **2.** (Typogr., of letter) having flourished stroke(s). [17th c., of unkn. orig.]

swa'stĭka (swŏ's-) *n.* ancient symbol formed by cross with equal arms when all arms are continued as far again at right angles clockwise (esp. as symbol of Nazis) or counter-clockwise. [f. Skr. *svastika* (*svastí* well-being f. *sú* good + *astí* being)]

swat (-ŏt) *v.t.* (-tt-). hit hard; crush (fly etc.) with blow, whence ∼'tER¹ (2) *n.* [17th c. in sense 'sit down', N. Engl. dial. & US var. of SQUAT]

swatch (-ŏ-) *n.* sample (esp. of cloth or fabric); a collection of samples. [17th c., of unkn. orig.]

swath (-aw-; *pl. pr.* -ths, -dhz), **swāthe¹** (-dh), *n.* ridge of grass, corn, etc., lying after being cut; space left clear after one passage of mower etc.; broad strip; **cut a wide** ∼, (fig.) be effective in destruction. [OE *swæth, swathu*, = MHG *swade*]

swāthe² (-dh) *v.t.*, & *n.* **1.** *v.t.* bind with bandages; enclose in wraps or cloths or warm garments or many garments n. **2.** *n.* bandage, wrapping. [OE *swathian* (**swæth* n.; cf. SWADDLE)]

sway *v.* & *n.* **1.** *v.i.* lean unsteadily to one side or in different directions by turns, have unsteady swinging motion, oscillate irregularly; waver, vacillate; ∼-back(ed), (with) back (esp. of horse) abnormally hollowed, (having) lordosis. **2.** *v.t.* give swaying motion to (*wind sways trees*); govern the motion of; wield, control direction of, have influence over, govern, (poet.) rule over, (*his speech swayed votes; is too much swayed by the needs of the moment*; *sways a fifth of mankind*). **3.** *n.* swaying motion or position; rule, government, (*hold sway*). [ME; cf. LG *swājen* be blown to and fro, Du. *zwaaien* swing, wave]

swear (swār) *v.* (**swore**, arch. **sware; sworn**) & *n.* **1.** *v.t.* & *i.* state something on oath, take oath (*to, that or that*), promise (conduct, to do) on oath, take (oath), (*will you swear, swear it, swear to it,* (*that*) *you were not there?; swear eternal fidelity; had sworn,* or *sworn a solemn oath, to return*); (colloq.) say emphatically that (*swore he hadn't touched it*); ∼ **by** or **to,** appeal to as witness and guarantee of oath; ∼ **by,** (colloq.) profess or have great belief in, regularly resort to or recommend; ∼ **off,** take oath to abstain from (drink etc.); ***∼ **out,** obtain (warrant etc.) by making charge on oath; **cannot** ∼ **to it,** (colloq.) am not fully certain that it is so. **2.** *v.i.* use profane or obscene oaths to express anger or as expletives (*at* person etc.); ∼ **at,** (of colours etc.) fail to harmonize with. **3.** *v.t.* cause to take oath, administer oath to, (*swear a witness* etc.; *swear person to* (maintain) *secrecy*); **sworn brothers** or **friends,** intimates; **sworn enemies** (open and irreconcilable); ∼ **evidence** etc. (given on oath); ∼ **in,** induct into office or membership by administering oath. **4.** make sworn affirmation of (offence) *against* (*swear treason against*); ∼ **the peace against,** make oath that one is in danger of bodily harm from. **5.** Hence ∼'ER¹ *n.* **6.** *n.* ∼(-word), (colloq.) a profane or obscene oath. [OE *swerian*, = OS *swerian*, OHG *swer(i)en*, ON *svetja* f. Gmc **swarjan* (**swar-,* cogn. w. ANSWER¹)]

sweat (-ĕt) *n.* & *v.* (∼'ed *or* ***∼). **1.** *n.* moisture exuded from the skin esp. when one is hot or anxious; **in** or **by the** ∼ **of** one's **brow** or **face,** by dint of toil; **bloody** ∼, exudation of blood mixed with sweat. **2.** sweating state, spell of sweating, piece of exercise that induces sweat (*in a,* (colloq.) *all of a, sweat*; *night sweats; a sweat will do him good*); **a cold** ∼ (as in death, fainting, terror, etc.). **3.** (colloq.) state of anxiety (*in a sweat*); drudgery, toil, effort, laborious task or undertaking; **no** ∼, there is no need to worry; ||**old** ∼, old soldier, person with much experience. **4.** drops exuding from or condensing on any surface. **5.** ∼-**band,** leather or other lining of hat or cap, band round wrist, head, etc., for wiping away or absorbing sweat; ∼-**cloth,** (esp.) thin blanket under horse's saddle or collar; ∼-**duct** (by which sweat exudes from ∼-**gland,** spiral tubular gland secreting sweat below skin); ∼-**house,** ∼-**lodge,** Amer. Ind. steam-bath; ∼-**shirt,** sleeved cotton sweater worn esp. by athletes before or after exercise; ∼-**shop** (in which sweated workers are employed); ∼-**suit** (of sweat-shirt and close-fitting trousers). **6.** Hence ∼'LESS, ∼'Y², *adjs.* **7.** *v.i.* exude sweat, perspire; (fig.) be in state of terror or suffering or repentance (∼ **it out,** (colloq.) endure to the end; (of wall etc.) exhibit surface moisture; toil, drudge. **8.** *v.t.* emit (blood, gum, etc.) like sweat; make (horse, athlete, etc.) sweat by exercise; ∼ **blood,** (fig.) work strenuously, be extremely anxious. **9.** *v.t.* & *i.* employ (labour, workers) at starvation wages for long hours under poor conditions; (in *p.p.,* of clothes etc.) made by sweated workers; (of workers) work on such terms. **10.** *v.t.* subject (hides, tobacco) to fermentation in manufacturing; fasten (metal part) *on* or *in* by partial fusion of metal or solder. **11.** ∼'ing-bath (for producing sweat); ∼'ing-room (in Turkish bath, or for drying cheeses); ∼'ing-sickness, epidemic fever with sweating prevalent in England in 15th–16th c. [ME *swet(e)*, alt. (after *swete* v. f. OE *swǣtan*, OHG *sweizzen* roast) f. *swote* f. OE *swāt*, OS *swēt*, OHG *sweiz* f. Gmc **swait-*]

swea'ter (-ĕ't-) *n.* In vbl senses; employer who sweats workers; jersey or other pullover worn during or before or after exercise to prevent chills, or as informal garment; ∼ **girl,** (colloq.) girl or woman with well-developed bust and wearing sweater to emphasize it. [f. prec. + -ER¹]

swēde *n.* **1.** (*S*∼). native of Sweden. **2.** ∼ (**turnip**), large yellow-fleshed turnip brought from Sweden to Scotland in 18th c. [f. MLG & MDu. *Swēde,* prob. f. ON *Svíthjóth* (*Svíar* Swedes, *thjóth* people)]

Swēdenbŏr'gĭan *a.* & *n.* (adherent) of the 'New Church' and religious doctrines of E. Swedenborg, Sw. philosopher d. 1772; hence ∼ISM (3) *n.* [f. *Swedenborg* + -IAN]

Swē'dish *a.* & *n.* (language) of Sweden or its inhabitants; ∼ **drill,** system of therapeutic muscular exercises. [f. SWEDE or *Sweden* + -ISH¹]

*swee'nÿ *n.* atrophy of muscle, esp. of shoulder, in horse. [prob. f. G dial. *schweine* atrophy]

sweep¹ *v.* (**swept**) & *n.* **1.** *v.i.* glide swiftly, speed along with impetuous unchecked motion, go majestically, extend in continuous curve or line or slope, (*eagle sweeps past; wind sweeps along; cavalry sweeps down on the enemy; she swept out of the room; his glance sweeps from right to left; with a sweeping stroke; coast sweeps northward; plain sweeps away to the sea*). **2.** *v.t.* impart sweeping motion to, carry *along* or *down* or *away* or *off* in impetuous course or forceful action, clear *off* or *away* or *out of* existence etc. or *from,* (*swept his hand across; flood sweeps away bridge; waves logs down with it; was swept away by an avalanche; the plague swept off thousands*); ∼ **away,** (fig.) abolish swiftly. **3.** traverse swiftly or in all directions (*wind sweeps the hillside; epidemic, new fashion, sweeps America*); pass lightly across or along, pass eyes or hand quickly along or over (∼ **the strings** etc., play musical instrument); drag (river-bottom etc.) to find something. **4.** (Of artillery etc.) include in line of fire, cover whole of, (*battery sweeps the approaches, glacis, street*). **5.** ~ (**up**), clear everything from, clear of dust or litter or soot with broom or sweeper or brush, (*sweep floor, carpet, chimney; sweep up the room*); **swept and garnished**, generally renovated, w. ref. to Luke 11:25; ~ **the board**, win all cards or money on gaming-table, (fig.) win all possible prizes etc.; ~ **a constituency** etc., receive nearly all votes, have large majority; ~ **the seas**, drive all enemies from them. **6.** gather *up* or collect (as) with broom or brush, push *aside, away*, etc., thus; *sweep under the* CARPET; ~ **everything into** one's **net**, seize all that comes; **swept-back**, (of aircraft wing) having outer part aft of inner part; **swept-up**, (of hair) = UPSWEPT; **swept-wing**, (of aircraft) having swept-back wings; hence ~ING¹ (2) *n.* (usu. in *pl.*; lit. or fig.). **7.** propel (barge etc.) with sweeps. **8.** ~**back**, angle at which aircraft's wing is set back from position at right angles to body; ~**-net**, ~**-seine**, large fishing-net; ~**-second hand** (on clock or watch, moving on same dial as other hands); ~**stake**(**s**), (prize won in) race or contest in which all competitors' stakes are taken by winner(s), form of gambling on horse-races etc. in which whole of participators' stakes goes to drawer(s) of winning or placed horse(s) etc. [ME *swepe*, earlier *swope* f. OE *swāpan*]

sweep² *n.* **1.** sweeping motion or extension, curve in road etc., piece of curving road etc., (*with a sweep of his arm, eyes, scythe; a sweep of mountain country; river makes a great sweep to the left; house is approached by a fine sweep*). **2.** range or compass of something that has sweeping motion (lit. or fig.; *within or beyond the sweep of the scythe, net, telescope, eye, human intelligence*). **3.** act of sweeping (as) with broom (*give it a thorough sweep, sweep-up, sweep-out*; **make a clean** ~, (1) have complete riddance of old or outdated material, staff, etc., (2) win all prizes etc.); sortie by aircraft. **4.** long oar worked by rower(s) standing on barge, becalmed sailing-ship, etc.; sail of windmill. **5.** long pole mounted as lever for raising buckets from well. **6.** = CHIMNEY-*sweep*. **7.** (colloq.) sweepstake. **8.** movement of beam across screen of cathode-ray tube. [f. prec.]

swee'per *n.* In vbl senses; = CARPET-*sweeper*, MINE¹-*sweeper*; person whose work is to clean a place by sweeping; (Footb. etc.) player positioned just in front of goalkeeper. [f. SWEEP¹ + -ER¹]

swee'ping *a.* In vbl senses; of wide range regardless of limitations or exceptions, (*sweeping condemnation, generalization,* etc.); far-reaching, comprehensive, (*sweeping changes, success,* etc.); hence ~LY² *adv.*, ~NESS *n.* [f. SWEEP¹ + -ING²]

sweet *a.* & *n.* **1.** *a.* tasting like sugar or honey (*sweet apples* etc.); ~**-and-sour**, cooked in sauce containing sugar and vinegar or lemon; ~ **stuff**, sweetmeats; ~ **tea** etc. (with much sugar); **a ~ tooth**, liking for sweet things; ~ **wine** (opp. DRY¹); **tastes** ~, has sweet taste. **2.** smelling pleasant like roses or perfumes, fragrant, (*smells sweet; has a sweet scent; air is sweet with jasmine; sweet breath*). **3.** melodious or harmonious in sound (*has a sweet voice; sounds sweet; sweet song, singer*). **4.** fresh and sound, not salt or salted or sour or bitter or rancid or high or stinking, (*is the milk, butter, still sweet?; keep the room clean and sweet*); (of water) fresh and drinkable. **5.** highly agreeable or attractive or gratifying, inspiring affection, dear, beloved, amiable, gentle, easy, (colloq.) pretty or charming or delightful, ('*tis sweet to hear one's own praises; a sweet nature, face, girl; sweet* SEVENTEEN; *sweet love, dalliance, idleness, dreams, sleep; what a sweet blouse, moustache, collie!*; *how sweet of you to bring me a present!*); **keep** person ~, ingratiate oneself with him; ~ **on**, (colloq.) fond of or in love with. **6.** pleasing to oneself merely; **at** one's **own** ~ **will**, just as or when one pleases, arbitrarily, at random. **7.** *sweet* BASIL; ~ **bay**, (1) = BAY¹ 1, (2) N. Amer. magnolia (*M.*

virginiana); ~**bread**, pancreas or thymus gland of animal, esp. as food; *sweet*-BRIER¹; *sweet* CHESTNUT; ~ **cicely**, white-flowered plant (*Myrrhis odorata*); ~ **corn**, kind of maize with sweet-flavoured grains; ~ **flag**, = *sweet rush*; *sweet*-GALE¹; ~**heart**, *n.*, & *v.t.* (act as) one of pair of lovers; ~ **herb**, fragrant culinary herb; ~**meal**, sweet wholemeal (biscuit etc.); ~**meat**, small shaped piece of confectionery usu. consisting chiefly of sugar or chocolate with flavouring or filling, or of fruit preserved in sugar; ~ **oil**, (esp.) olive oil; ~ **pea**, climbing garden annual (*Lathyrus odoratus*) with showy variously-coloured sweet-scented flowers; *sweet* PEPPER¹ 2, POTATO; ~**-root**, liquorice; ~ **rush**, ~ **sedge**, kind of sedge with thick creeping aromatic rootstock used in medicine and confectionery; ||~**-shop**, (where sweetmeats are sold); ~**-sop**, (sweet-pulped green-rinded fruit of) a tropical Amer. evergreen shrub (*Annona squamosa*); *sweet* SULTAN; ***~**-talk**, blandish-(ment); ~**-tempered**, amiable; *sweet* VIOLET; ~**-wi'lliam**, cultivated species of pink with close-clustered sweet-smelling flowers often particoloured in zones. **8.** Hence ~ISH¹ 2 *a.*, ~LY² *adv.*, ~NESS *n.* (~**ness and light**, display of mildness and reason). **9.** *n.* sweet part (*the sweet and the bitter or sweets and bitters of life*); *sweetmeat* (COUGH²-*sweet*); ||sweet dish such as pudding, tart, ice cream, jelly, forming course of meal; (arch., usu. in *pl.*) fragrance; (in *pl.*) delights, gratifications, pleasures, (*the sweets of office, flattery, success*); (esp. in *voc.*) darling. [OE *swēte*, = OS *swōti*, OHG *s(w)uozi*, ON *sœtr*, f. Gmc **swōtja-*, **swōti-*, f. IE **swād-*]

swee'ten *v.t.* & *i.* make or become sweet(er); make agreeable or less painful; hence ~ER¹ *n.*, (esp.) bribe, substitute for sugar, ~ING¹ (4) *n.* [f. prec. + -EN⁶]

swee'tie *n.* (colloq.) ||sweetmeat; ~(**-pie**), sweetheart. [f. SWEET + -IE]

swee'ting *n.* sweet-flavoured variety of apple; (arch.) darling. [ME, f. SWEET + -ING³]

swell *v.* (*p.p.* swo'llen *pr.* swō'-, or ~**ed**), *n.*, & *a.* **1.** *v.i.* & *i.* (cause to) grow bigger or louder, dilate, expand, rise or raise up from surrounding surface, bulge out, increase in volume or force or intensity, (*river swollen with melted snow; the injured wrist began to swell or swell up; the swelling sails, wind swells the sails; the swelling tide; expenditure swollen by extravagance; items swell the total; frog swelled himself to size of ox; a thousand voices swell the sound; sound swells on the breeze; murmur swelled into a roar; ground swells into an eminence*); (of heart) feel like bursting with emotion; ~ **with** *pride, indignation*, etc., be or seem hardly able to restrain; ~ **like a turkey-cock**, put on blustering air; ~**ed** or **swollen head**, (colloq.) conceit. **2.** *n.* act or condition of swelling; heaving of sea with waves that do not break, after storm etc.; protuberant part of column etc. **3.** (Mus.) gradual increase of loudness, with or without subsequent gradual decrease; mechanism in organ etc. for obtaining crescendo or diminuendo by opening or closing slats in front of ~**-box** containing pipes of the ~**-organ. 4.** (colloq.) person of distinction or ability; person of good social standing; person of dashing or fashionable appearance; hence ~**'DOM** *n.* **5.** ~**-fish**, globe-fish; ~**-rule**, (Print.) rule or dash widening in middle and tapering towards ends. **6.** *a.* (colloq.) that is a swell (sense 4); fine, splendid; ||~ **mob**(**sman**), (arch. sl.) (class of) criminal dressing fashionably as disguise; hence ~ISH¹ 2 *a.* [OE *swellan*, = OS **swellan*, OHG *swellan*, ON *svella* f. Gmc **swellan*]

swe'lling *n.* In vbl senses; protuberance, esp. abnormal enlargement of part of body. [f. prec. + -ING¹]

swe'lter *v.i.*, & *n.* **1.** *v.i.* (Of atmosphere etc., or of thing or person suffering from it) be faint or sweating or languid or oppressive with heat. **2.** *n.* sweltering atmosphere or condition. [f. base of (now dial.) *swelt*, f. OE (= OS) *sweltan* perish, = OHG *swelzan*, ON *svelta*, Goth. *swiltan* f. Gmc **swelt-* etc.]

swĕpt. See SWEEP¹.

swĕrve v. & n. **1.** v.i. diverge from regular line of motion, go off in changed direction, dodge, (*never swerves an inch from the path, from his duty; bird, ball, swerves in the air; horse, right-half, swerved suddenly*). **2.** v.t. cause to swerve, esp. cause (ball) to swerve in the air. **3.** n. divergence from course, swerving motion; hence ∼′LESS (-vl-) a. [ME, repr. OE *sweorfan* SCOUR, = OS, OHG *swerban* wipe etc., ON *sverfa* file, Goth. -*swairban*]

SWG abbr. standard wire gauge.

swift a., adv., & n. **1.** a. (literary). rapid, QUICK 3, soon coming or passing, not long delayed, (*swift runner, movement, feet, retribution, anger, laughter, response, riddance*). **2.** prompt, quick to do, (*has a swift wit; swift to anger; be swift to hear, slow to speak*). **3.** Hence ∼′LY² adv., ∼′NESS n. **4.** adv. (arch. exc. in comb.) swiftly (*swift-coming, -passing*). **5.** n. very long-winged and swift-flying insectivorous bird of family Apodidae with superficial resemblance to swallow; hence ∼′LET n., small swift of genus *Collocalia*. **6.** swift-running small lizard. **7.** revolving frame for winding yarn etc. from. [OE, cogn. w. *swī̆fan* move in a course]

swig v. (-gg-) & n. (colloq.) **1.** v.t. & i. take deep draughts (of). **2.** n. (act of taking) a (deep) draught of liquor. [v. f. n. (16th c.) in obs. sense 'liquor', of unkn. orig.]

swill v. & n. **1.** v.t. rinse, pour water over or through, flush, (*out*). **2.** v.t. & i. drink greedily. **3.** n. rinsing (*give it a swill or swill out*); inferior liquor; (partly) liquid refuse as pig-food. [OE *swillan, swilian*, of unkn. orig.]

swim v. (-mm-; swam; swum) & n. **1.** v.i. float on or at surface of liquid (SINK¹ *or swim; vegetables swimming in butter; with bubbles swimming on it*). **2.** progress at or below surface of water by working legs, arms, tail, webbed feet, fins, flippers, wings, body, etc.; (fig.) go with gliding motion; ∼ **with the tide** or **stream**, act with the majority. **3.** v.t. traverse or accomplish (stream, distance, etc.) thus, compete in (race) thus, compete in with thus, cause (horse, dog, etc.) to progress thus. **4.** Hence ∼′mER¹ n. **5.** v.i. appear to undulate or reel or whirl, have dizzy effect or sensation, (*everything swam before his eyes; my head swims*). **6.** be flooded or overflow with or with or in moisture (*eyes, deck, swimming with tears, water; swimming eyes; floor swimming in blood*). **7.** ‖∼′ming-bath, indoor swimming-pool; ∼′ming-bell, bell-shaped swimming-organ of jellyfish etc.; ∼′ming-bladder, fish's air-bladder; ∼′ming-pool, artificial pool for swimming in; ∼′ming-stone, float-stone. **8.** n. spell of swimming; deep pool frequented by fish in river; (fig.) main current of affairs (**in the** ∼, engaged in or acquainted with what is going on); ∼-**suit**, bathing-suit. [OE *swimman*, = OS, OHG *swimman*, ON *svim(m)a* f. Gmc. *swemjan*]

swi′mmeret n. swimming-foot in crustaceans. [f. SWIMMER + -ET¹]

swi′mmingly adv. with easy and unobstructed progress (*going on swimmingly*). [f. SWIM + -ING² + -LY²]

swi′ndl|e v.t., & n. **1.** v.t. cheat (person, money *out of* person, person *out of* money etc., or abs.); so ∼ER¹ n. **2.** n. fraudulent scheme, imposition, piece of swindling, person or thing represented as what it is not; ∼e-**-sheet**, (colloq.) expense account. [back-form. f. *swindler* f. G *schwindler* extravagant maker of schemes, swindler (*schwindeln* be dizzy)]

swine n. (*pl.* same). **1.** (US, formal, or Zool.) = PIG 1, whence **swi′nery**³ n.; PEARL¹s *before swine*. **2.** person of greedy or bestial habits; (colloq.) unpleasant thing. **3.** ∼-**fever**, infectious intestinal virus disease of pigs; ∼-**herd**, one who tends pigs; ∼-**plague**, infectious bacterial lung-disease of pigs. **4.** Hence **swi′nish** a. (esp. of persons or their habits). [OE *swin*, = OS, OHG *swīn*, ON *svin*, Goth. *swein* f. Gmc *swīnam*, neut. (as n.) of a. f. IE *suw-* pig]

swing v. (swung *or rarely* swang; swung) & n. **1.** v.t. & i. move with to-and-fro or curving motion as of object having fixed point(s) or side but otherwise free; sway, hang so as to be free to sway, like a pendulum or door or branch of tree or hammock or anchored ship; oscillate, revolve (propeller etc.), rock, wheel, ∼ **at**, attempt to hit by moving fist etc. in curve; ∼ **round**, suddenly turn to face different direction. **2.** v.t. suspend (hammock) by its ends; have decisive influence on (voting, *jury*, etc.); *∼ (sl.) be competent to deal with; *not room to swing a* CAT¹; ‖∼ **the lead**, (sl.) malinger, shirk duty; **swung dash**, (Typogr.) dash (∼) with alternate curves. **3.** v.i. go with swinging gait (*he swung out of the room; swing along, past, by*); move by gripping something and leaping etc. (*swing from bough to bough*); (sl.) be executed by hanging; (sl.) be lively or up-to-date or promiscuous. **4.** v.t. & i. (music) with swing rhythm; (Cricket etc.) (cause ball to) deviate from straight flight in the air. **5.** Hence ∼′ER¹ n. **6.** n. act of swinging, oscillation, swinging movement; *circular tour; **in full** ∼, at height of activity; *swing of the* PENDULUM. **7.** swinging gait or rhythm (*goes with a swing; get into the swing of things*); vigorous continued action. **8.** ∼ (**music**), easy rhythmic jazz, esp. with freely varied melody and simple harmonic accompaniment in strict rhythm. **9.** seat slung by ropes or chains for swinging in (‖*swings and* ROUND³*abouts*); spell of swinging in this. **10.** extent to which thing swings; amount by which votes, points scored, etc., change from one side to the other. **11.** ∼-**boat**, boat-shaped carriage hung from frame for swinging in at fair etc.; ∼ **bridge** (that can be swung aside as a whole or in sections to let ships etc. pass); ∼-**door** (able to open in either direction and close itself when released); ∼ **plough** (without wheels); ∼-**wing**, aircraft wing that can be moved backwards and forwards. [OE *swingan* to beat, = OHG *swingan* f. Gmc *sweng-, *swang-]

swinge (-nj) v.t. (*part.* ∼′ing *pr.* -njĭ-). **1.** (arch.) strike hard, beat. **2.** (in *pres. part.*) ‖(of blow) forcible; huge, daunting; (majority, lie, taxation, damages). [alt. f. ME *swenge* f. OE *swengan* shake, shatter, f. Gmc *swangwjan*]

swi′nging a. In vbl senses; (of gait, melody, etc.) vigorously rhythmical; (sl.) lively, up to date, excellent, or promiscuous; hence ∼LY² adv. [f. SWING + -ING²]

swi′ngle (-nggl) n., & v.t. **1.** n. wooden instrument for beating flax and removing woody parts from it; swinging part of flail; ‖∼**tree**, crossbar pivoted in middle, to ends of which traces are fastened in cart, plough, etc. **2.** v.t. clean (flax) with swingle; **swi′ngling-tow**, coarse part of flax. [ME, f. MDu. *swinghel* (as SWING; see -LE¹)]

swink v.i., & n. (arch.) toil. [OE *swinc* n. f. *swincan* v., parallel form. to *swingan* SWING]

swipe v. & n. **1.** v.i. & t. (colloq.) hit *at* or hit (cricket-ball etc., or fig.) hard and recklessly; (sl.) steal esp. by snatching; hence **swi′pER¹** n. **2.** n. (colloq.) reckless hard hit or attempt to hit (at cricket etc., or fig.). [perh. var. of SWEEP¹]

‖**swipes** (-ps) n. *pl.* (sl.) poor weak or otherwise inferior beer. [f. prec. in sense 'drink off']

swi′pple n. swingle of flail. [ME, prob. f. as SWEEP¹ + -LE 1]

swirl v. & n. **1.** v.i. & t. eddy, carry (object) or be carried with eddying motion. **2.** n. eddying motion of water, air, etc., commotion made by fish etc. rushing through water; twist, curl. [ME, v. f. n., orig. Sc., perh. of LDu. orig.]

swish¹ v. & n. **1.** v.t. & i. audibly cut the air with (cane etc.); cut (flower etc.) *off* thus; make such audible cut *with* cane etc.; flog with birch or cane. **2.** v.i., & n. (make, move with) sound as of cane or lash or swift bird cutting the air or of scythe cutting grass. **3.** Hence ∼′Y² a. [imit.]

swish² a. (colloq.) smart, fashionable. [perh. f. prec.]

Swiss *a.* & *n.* (*pl.* same). (native) of Switzerland; ~ **French, German,** dialects of French and German spoken in Switzerland; ~ **chard,** = CHARD; ~ **cheese** (esp. with internal holes); ~ **cheese plant,** climber *Monstera deliciosa,* with holes in leaves; ~ **guards,** body of soldiers at Vatican serving the Pope; ~ **milk** (condensed and sweetened); ~ **roll,** thin flat sponge-cake spread with jam or butter-cream and rolled up. [f. F *Suisse* f. MHG *Swīz*]

switch *n.* & *v.* **1.** *n.* flexible shoot cut from tree; tapering rod or whip resembling this. **2.** tress of detached or false hair tied at one end used in hairdressing. **3.** mechanism for making and breaking connection between corresponding parts of a system, by which railway trains are diverted from one line to another, electric circuits completed or interrupted, etc. **4.** switching of positions, roles, tactics, etc.; deviation from usual procedure. **5.** ~'**back,** zigzag railway or road for ascending or descending steep slopes, ||road with alternate ascents and descents, ||railway (chiefly used for amusement at fairs etc.) in which train's ascents are effected solely by momentum acquired in previous descents; ~**blade,** pocket-knife with blade released by spring; ~'**board,** arrangement for varying the connections between a number of electric circuits, esp. in telephony; ~('**ing)-engine,** shunting-engine; ~-**man** (in charge of railway switches); ~-**signal,** flag or lantern or semaphore board indicating position of railway signal; *~*~-**tower,** signal-box; *~*~-**yard,** area where railway--carriages are switched between lines. **6.** *v.t.* whip with switch. **7.** swing (thing, or abs.) round quickly, snatch suddenly, whisk, (*cow switches her tail; I switched my head round; he switched it out of my hand*). **8.** transfer (train, current, etc.) with switch, (fig.) direct (thoughts, talk) to another subject; ~ (**over**), change or exchange (positions, roles, tactics, etc., or abs.), whence ~-**over** *n.* **9.** turn (electric light, current, radio or television set, or abs.) *off* or *on* by switch; ~**ed on,** (sl.) (1) under the influence of marijuana etc., (2) aware of what is going on, up to date. **10.** *v.i.* (Bridge). change to another suit in bidding or play. [early forms *swits, switz,* prob. f. LG; cf. Hanoverian dial. *swutsche,* LG *swukse* long thin stick]

*****swi'tcheroo** *n.* (sl.) unexpected change of behaviour etc. [fanciful f. prec.; cf. SMACKEROO]

swi'ther (-dh-) *v.i.,* & *n.* (Sc.) **1.** *v.i.* hesitate, be uncertain. **2.** *n.* flurry, doubt, uncertainty. [16th c., of unkn. orig.]

Swi'tzer (-ts-) *n.* (||arch.) a Swiss. [f. MHG *Switzer,* or MDu. *Switser,* (*Swīz* Switzerland)]

swi'vel *n.* & *v.* (||-ll-). **1.** *n.* coupling between two parts enabling one of them to revolve without turning the other; ~ **chain, (gun),** etc., (provided with swivel); ~ **chair** (with seat turning horizontally); ~-**eye(d),** (with) squinting eye. **2.** *v.t.* & *i.* turn (as) on swivel (*swivelled the gun, his eyes, round*). [ME, f. weak grade *swif-* of OE *swīfan* sweep + -LE 1; cf. SWIFT]

||**swiz(z)** *n.* (*pl.* -**zzes**). (sl.) swindle, disappointment. [20th c.; orig. unkn.]

swi'zzle *n.* (colloq.) compounded intoxicating drink esp. of rum or gin and bitters made frothy; ||(sl.) = prec.; ~-**stick** (used for frothing or flattening drinks). [19th c.; orig. unkn.]

swŏb. Var. of SWAB.

swŏ'llen. See SWELL.

swoon *v.i.,* & *n.* (literary). (have) fainting-fit (*swooned for joy, with pain,* etc.); (of sound) die languidly away. [ME *swoune* perh. back-form. f. *swogning n.* (*iswogen* f. OE *geswogen* overcome p.p. of *swogan* suffocate, of unkn. orig.); see -ING[1]]

swoop *v.i.* & *n.* **1.** *v.i.* come down or *down* with the rush of a bird of prey, make sudden attack from a distance, (*on prey, place,* etc.). **2.** *v.t.* (colloq.) snatch (*up*) the whole of at one swoop. **3.** *n.* sudden attack or downward plunge (as) of bird of prey; snatching action carrying off many things at once; *at one* FELL[3] *swoop.* [perh. dial. var. of obs. *swōpe* f. OE *swāpan;* see SWEEP[1]]

swōōsh *v.i.,* & *n.* (make, move with) noise of sudden rush of liquid, air, etc. [imit.]

swŏp. See SWAP.

sword (sōrd) *n.* **1.** offensive weapon consisting of long variously shaped blade for cutting or thrusting or both and hilt with hand-guard, also worn with court dress; **the** ~, war, military power, war as means of deciding disputes; *sword of* DAMOCLES; **the** ~ **of justice,** judicial authority; ||**S**~ **of State** (borne before sovereign on state occasions); CROSS[2] *swords;* **draw, sheathe, the** ~, begin, cease from, war; FIRE[1] *and sword;* MEASURE[2] *swords;* **put to the** ~, (esp. of victor or captor) kill; **throw** one's ~ **into the scale,** back claim etc. with arms. **2.** ~-**arm,** (usu.) right arm; ~-**bayonet** (with short sword-blade and hilt); ||~-**bearer,** person carrying sovereign's or other great person's sword on some occasions; ~-**belt** (to which scabbard is attached); ~-**bill,** long-billed humming-bird; ~-**cane,** = *sword-stick;* ~-**cut,** wound given with sword-edge, scar left by it; ~-**dance,** in which swords are brandished, or performer treads about swords laid on ground); ~-**fish,** sea fish (*Xiphias gladius*) with upper jaw prolonged into sharp swordlike weapon; ~-**flag,** yellow iris; ~-**grass,** (1) gladiolus, (2) grass or sedge with swordlike leaves; ~-**guard,** part of sword-hilt that protects hand; ~-**hand,** (usu.) right hand; ~-**knot,** ribbon or tassel attached to sword-hilt orig. for securing it to wrist; ~-**law,** military domination; ~-**lily,** gladiolus; ~-**play,** fencing, (fig.) repartee, cut-and-thrust argument; ~'**sman** (-z-), person of (usu. specified) skill with sword; ~'**smanship** (-z-), swordsman's art; ~-**stick,** hollow walking-stick containing blade that can be used as sword; ~-**swallower,** one who (ostensibly) swallows a sword-blade as entertainment; ~-**tail,** (1) = KING[1]-*crab* (1), (2) tropical fish of genus *Xiphophorus.* **3.** Hence (-)~'**ED**[2], ~'**LESS,** ~'**LIKE,** ~'**PROOF**[2], *adjs.* [OE *sw(e)ord,* = OS *swerd,* OHG *swert,* ON *sverth* f. Gmc **swerdham*]

swŏre, swŏrn. See SWEAR.

||**swŏt** *v.* (-tt-) & *n.* (sl.) **1.** *v.i.* work hard esp. at books. **2.** *v.t.* ~ (subject) **up,** study it hurriedly. **3.** *n.* hard study; (thing that demands) effort; person who works hard esp. at learning. [dial. var. of SWEAT]

swound *n.,* & *v.i.* (arch.) swoon. [f. MF *snoune* SWOON]

swŭm. See SWIM.

swŭng. See SWING.

swȳ *n.* (Austral.) two-up [f. G *zwei* two]

sȳ- *pref.,* assim. form of SYN- before *s* + consonant & before *z.*

SY *abbr.* steam yacht.

sȳ'bar|īte *n.* & *a.* luxurious and voluptuous (person); hence ~i'**TIC**(AL) *adjs.,* ~**ītISM** (2) *n.* [orig. native or inhabitant of Sybaris in S. Italy, noted for luxury, f. L f. Gk *Subarītēs* (*Subaris* Sybaris; see -ITE[1])]

sȳ'bil. Var. of SIBYL.

sȳ'camine *n.* (Bibl.) the black mulberry-tree. [f. L f. Gk *sukaminos* mulberry-tree f. Heb. *šikmāh* sycamore, assim. to Gk *sukon* fig]

sȳ'camŏre *n.* **1.** ~ (**maple**), large maple (*Acer pseudoplatanus*) grown for its shade and timber; its wood. **2.** *plane-tree or its wood. **3.** (Bibl.) species of fig-tree (*Ficus sycomorus*) growing in Egypt, Syria, etc. [var. of SYCOMORE]

sȳce, sīce[2], *n.* (Anglo-Ind.) groom. [f. Hind. f. Arab. *sā'is, sāyis*]

sȳ'comŏre *n.* = SYCAMORE 3. [ME, f. OF *sic(h)amor* f. L f. Gk *sukomoros* (*sukon* fig, *moron* mulberry)]

sȳcō'ni|um *n.* (*pl.* -**a**). (Bot.) fleshy hollow receptacle developing into multiple fruit as in fig. [mod. L, f. Gk *sukon* fig]

sȳ'coph|ant (-ănt, -ant) *n.* servile flatterer, toady, parasitic person; so ~**ANCY** *n.,* ~**ă'ntIC** *a.* [f. F *sycophante* or f. L f. Gk *sukophantēs* informer (*sukon* fig; *phainō* show; reason for name uncert.)]

sȳcō's|is *n.* (*pl.* ∼es *pr.* -ēz). skin-disease of bearded part of face, with inflammation of hair-follicles. [mod. L, f. Gk *sukōsis* (*sukon* fig; see -OSIS); orig. of figlike ulcer]

sȳ'ĕn|īte *n.* grey crystalline rock of feldspar and hornblende with or without quartz; hence ∼ĭ'TIC *a.* [f. F *syénite* f. L *Syenites* (*lapis* stone) of *Syene* in Egypt; see -ITE[1]]

sȳl- *pref.*, assim. form of SYN- before *l*.

sȳ'llabarȳ *n.* list of characters representing syllables and serving the purpose, in some languages or stages of writing, of an alphabet. [f. mod. L *syllabarium* (as SYLLABLE; see -ARY[1])]

sȳllǎ'b|ic *a.* of syllable(s); (Pros.) based on number of syllables; (of symbol) representing a whole syllable; articulated in syllables; hence ∼ICALLY *adv.*, ∼ĭ'CITY (-*a*-) *n.* [f. F *syllabique* or f. LL f. Gk *sullabikos* (as SYLLABLE; see -IC)]

sȳllǎbi(fi)cā'tion *ns.* division into or articulation by syllables. [f. (med. L *syllabicatio* f. *syllabicare* f.) L *syllaba*; see SYLLABLE, -ATION, -FICATION]

sȳ'llabīze, -īse (-īz), *v.t.* divide into or articulate by syllables. [f. med. L *syllabizare* f. Gk *sullabizō* (as foll.; see -IZE)]

sȳ'llabl|e *n.*, & *v.t.* **1.** *n.* unit of pronunciation uttered without interruption as word or part of word and containing usu. one vowel sound with or without consonant(s) preceding or following ('*inferno*' *has three syllables*); character(s) representing syllable; (transf.) so much as a word, the least amount of speech (*did not utter a syllable*); **in words of one** ∼e, expressed plainly or bluntly; hence (-)∼ED[2] (-bĕld) *a.* **2.** *v.t.* pronounce by syllables, articulate distinctly; (poet.) utter (name, word). [ME, f. AF *sillable* f. OF *sillabe* f. L f. Gk *sullabē* (as SYL-, *lambanō* take)]

sȳ'llabŭb, sĭ'-, *n.* dish made of cream or milk flavoured, sweetened, and whipped to thicken it. [16th c., of unkn. orig.]

sȳ'llab|us *n.* (*pl.* ∼uses, *or* ∼i *pr.* -ī). **1.** concise statement of main subjects of lecture, course of teaching, etc.; conspectus or programme of hours of work etc. **2.** (RC Ch.) summary of points decided by an ecclesiastical decree, esp. catalogue of 80 heretical doctrines or practices or institutions condemned by Pius IX in 1864, or of 65 heretical doctrines condemned by Pius X in 1907. [mod. L, orig. misreading of L *sittybas* acc. pl. of *sittyba* f. Gk *sittuba* title-slip or label]

sȳllĕ'ps|is *n.* (*pl.* ∼es *pr.* -ēz). figure of speech applying a word to two others in different senses (e.g. *took the oath and his seat*) or to two others of which it grammatically suits one only (e.g. *neither you nor he knows*); cf. ZEUGMA; so **sȳllĕ'ptic** *a.* [LL, f. Gk *sullēpsis* taking together (*sullambanō*; see SYLLABLE)]

sȳ'llog|ism *n.* **1.** form of reasoning in which from two given or assumed propositions called the premisses and having a common or middle term a third is deduced called the conclusion, from which the middle term is absent; **false** ∼**ism,** one whose conclusion does not necessarily follow from its premisses because it fails to fulfil the rules of logic. **2.** deductive reasoning as opp. induction. **3.** So ∼ĭ'stIC *a.* [ME, f. OF *silogi(s)me* or f. L f. Gk *sullogismos* f. *sullogizomai* (as SYL-, *logizomai* to reason f. *logos* reason); see -ISM]

sȳ'llogīze, -īse (-īz), *v.* **1.** *v.i.* use syllogisms. **2.** *v.t.* put (facts, argument) in syllogistic form. [ME, f. OF *sil(l)ogiser* or LL *syllogizare* f. Gk *sullogizomai* (as prec.; see -IZE)]

sȳlph *n.* elemental spirit of the air in Paracelsus's system; slender graceful woman or girl; humming-bird with long forked tail; hence ∼'LIKE *a.* [f. mod. L *sylphes,* G *sylphen* (pl.), perh. based by Paracelsus on L *sylvestris* of the woods + *nympha* nymph]

sȳ'lva(n). See SILVA(N).

sȳ'lvicŭlture. See SILVICULTURE.

sȳm- *pref.*, assim. form of SYN- before *b, m, p,* as: **sympe'talous,** having petals united, **symphy'l-lous,** having leaves united.

sȳ'mbĭŏnt *n.* organism living in symbiosis. [f. Gk *sumbiōn -ountos* part. of *sumbioō* live together (as foll.)]

sȳmbi|ō'sǐs *n.* (*pl.* ∼o'ses *pr.* -ō'sēz). association of two different organisms living attached to each other or one within the other, e.g. fungus and alga in lichen; (fig.) co-operation of persons; hence ∼o'TIC *a.* [mod. L, f. Gk *sumbiōsis* a living together (*sumbioō* live together, *sumbios* companion f. as SYM- + *bios* life; see -OSIS)]

sȳ'mbol *n.*, & *v.t.* (||-ll-). **1.** *n.* thing regarded by general consent as naturally typifying or representing or recalling something (esp. an idea or quality) by possession of analogous qualities or by association in fact or thought (*white, the lion, the thunderbolt, the cross, are symbols of purity, courage, Zeus, Christianity*). **2.** mark or character taken as the conventional sign of some object or idea or process, e.g. the astronomical signs for the planets, the letters standing for chemical elements, musical notation, the mathematical signs for addition and infinity, the asterisk. **3.** (Eccl.) creed. **4.** Hence or cogn. **sȳmbŏ'lIC**(AL) *adjs.* (∼**ic logic,** use of symbols to denote propositions etc. in order to assist reasoning; ∼**ic theology,** study of the creeds of various churches), **sȳmbŏ'lical**LY[2] *adv.*, **sȳmbŏ'lics,** **sȳmb(ol)ŏ'LOGY,** *ns.* **5.** *v.t.* symbolize. [ME in sense 3, f. L f. Gk *sumbolon* mark, token, (as SYM-, *ballō* throw)]

sȳ'mbol|ism *n.* use of symbols to represent things; symbols collectively; school of painters and of (esp. French) poets seeking special symbols to express essence of things by suggestion; hence ∼IST (2) *n.* [f. prec. + -ISM]

sȳ'mbolīz|e, -īs|e (-īz), *v.t.* be symbol of; represent by means of symbols; so ∼A'TION *n.* [f. F *symboliser* (*symbole* SYMBOL; see -IZE)]

sȳ'mmĕtr|ȳ *n.* **1.** (beauty resulting from) right proportion between the parts of the body or any whole, balance, congruity, harmony. **2.** such structure as allows of an object's being divided by a point or line or plane or radiating lines or planes into two or more parts exactly the same in size and shape and similar in position relatively to the dividing point etc., repetition of exactly similar parts facing each other or a centre; RADIAL *symmetry*; hence (in Art) ∼OPHO'BIA *n.* **3.** approximation to such structure, possession by a whole of corresponding parts correspondingly placed; (Bot.) possession by flower of sepals and petals and stamens and pistils in (multiples of) the same number. **4.** Hence or cogn. **sȳmmĕ'trIC**(AL) *adjs.*, **sȳmmĕ'trical**LY[2] *adv.*, ∼IZE (3) *v.t.* [f. obs. F *symmétrie* or f. L f. Gk *summetria* (as SYM-, *metron* measure)]

sȳmpathĕ'ctomȳ *n.* surgical removal of sympathetic ganglion etc. [f. foll. + -ECTOMY]

sȳmpathĕ'tic *a.* & *n.* **1.** *a.* of, full of, exhibiting, expressing, due to, effecting, sympathy (*to* or *towards*; *sympathetic heart, person, conduct, words*); (of landscape etc.) that touches the feelings by association etc.; (of pain etc.) caused by pain or injury to someone else or in another part of the body; (of sound, resonance, string) sounding by vibration communicated through the air or other medium from vibrating object; ∼ **ganglion,** ∼ **nerve,** parts of a system of nerves uniting viscera and blood-vessels and passing along vertebral column; ∼ **ink,** invisible ink; ∼ **magic** (seeking to affect person etc. by means of associated thing); ∼ **strike** (by workers in support of other strikers). **2.** capable of evoking sympathy, likeable, appealing to reader etc.; ∼ **to,** inclined to favour (proposal etc.). **3.** Hence **sȳmpathĕ'tic**ALLY *adv.* **4.** *n.* sympathetic nerve or system. [f. SYMPATHY, after *pathetic*]

sȳ'mpathīz|e, -īs|e (-īz), *v.i.* feel or express sympathy, share feeling or opinion *with* person etc., agree *with* sentiment; hence ∼ER[1] *n*. [f. F *sympathiser* (as foll.; see -IZE)]

sȳ'mpathȳ *n*. (capacity for) being simultaneously affected with the same feeling as another; ∼ (*with* person, thing, or state etc.), tendency to share or state of sharing another person's or thing's emotion or sensation or condition; (in *sing.* or *pl.*) mental participation *with* another in his trouble or *with* another's trouble; compassion or approval (*for*); (in *sing.* or *pl.*) agreement (*with*) in opinion or desire; **in** ∼, having, or as a result of, sympathy with another, by way of sympathetic action. [f. L f. Gk *sumpatheia* f. SYM(*pathēs* f. *pathos* feeling) sympathetic; see -Y[1]]

symphŏ'nˌic *a*. pertaining to or like a symphony or symphonies; ∼**ic ballet** (danced to symphony); ∼**ic dance**, orchestral piece in dance style; ∼**ic poem**, orchestral piece usu. in one movement and usu. descriptive or rhapsodic; hence ∼ICALLY *adv*. [f. SYMPHONY + -IC]

symphŏ'nious *a*. (literary). harmonious, concordant; hence ∼LY[2] *a*. [f. L *symphonia* (see SYMPHONY) + -OUS]

sȳ'mphonist *n*. composer of symphonies. [f. foll. + -IST]

sȳ'mphony *n*. (Mus.) elaborate composition for full orchestra, usu. in sonata form; passage for instruments alone in vocal work; *symphony orchestra; ∼ orchestra (playing symphonies and other serious orchestral works). [ME, = harmony of sound, f. OF *symphonie* f. L f. Gk *sumphōnia* f. SYM(*phōnos* f. *phōnē* sound) harmonious]

sȳ'mphȳsˌis *n*. (*pl*. ∼es *pr*. -ēz). growing together; (place or line of) union between two bones esp. in median plane of body; hence ∼eAL, ∼IAL, (-fī'z-) *adjs*. [mod. L, f. Gk SYM(*phusis* growth)]

sympŏ'diˌum *n*. (*pl*. ∼a). (Bot.) apparent main axis or stem made up of successive secondary axes, as in vine; hence ∼AL *a*. [mod. L, f. as SYM-+ Gk *pous podos* foot; see -IUM]

sympŏ'siärch (-z-; -k) *n*. president of symposium. [f. Gk *sumposiarkhos* (as SYMPOSIUM, *arkhos* ruler f. *arkhō* rule)]

sympŏ'slăst (-zĭ-) *n*. participant in symposium. [f. Gk *sumposiazō* drink together (as foll.), after *enthusiast* etc.]

sympŏ'siˌum (-z-) *n*. (*pl*. ∼a). **1.** drinking-party, esp. of ancient Greeks with conversation etc. after banquet. **2.** philosophical or other friendly discussion; set of contributions on one subject from various authors and points of view at meeting or in magazine etc. **3.** Hence ∼AC, ∼AL, *adjs*. [f. L f. Gk *sumposion* f. SYM(*potēs* drinker); see -IUM]

sȳ'mptom *n*. **1.** perceptible change in the body or its function indicating injury or disease; **subjective, objective,** ∼ (directly perceptible to patient only, to others). **2.** sign or token of the existence of something. **3.** Hence or cogn. ∼A'TIC *a*. (*of*), ∼atŏ'LOGY *n*. [ME *synthoma*, f. med. L *sinthoma*, & f. LL f. Gk *sumptōma* *-atos* chance, symptom, f. SYM(*piptō* fall) happen]

sȳn- *pref*. with, together, alike, as: **synallagma'tic,** (of treaty or contract) imposing reciprocal obligations [f. Gk *allassō* exchange]; **syna'ntherous,** having stamens joined by anthers; **syna'nthous,** with flowers and leaves appearing simultaneously; **sy'ncarp** (-n-k-), compound fruit from flower with several carpels, e.g. blackberry; **synda'ctyl(ous)** *adjs*., **synda'ctylism, synda'ctyly,** *ns*., having digits united as in webbed feet etc.; **syndesmo'sis,** articulation by ligaments; **syneco'logy,** study of ecological communities in their environment; **sy'ngamy** (-ngg-), (Biol.) fusion of gametes or nuclei in reproduction; **synge'nesis** (-nj-), sexual reproduction from combined male and female elements; **sy'ngnathous,** (of fish) with jaws united in tubular snout; **synosto'sis,** joining of bones by ankylosis etc. [f. or after Gk *sun-* (*sun* with)]

sӯnaer'ĕsˌis (-cī'-), *sȳnēr'ĕsˌis, n. (pl. ∼es *pr*. -ēz). contraction of two vowels into diphthong or single vowel. [LL, f. Gk SYN(*airesis* f. *haireō* take)]

sȳnaesˌthē'sïa (-nĭ-), *-ĕsˌth-, (-zïa) *n*. sensation produced in part of body by stimulus elsewhere; production of mental sense-impression by stimulation of another sense; hence ∼thē'tIC *a*. [mod. L, f. SYN- after *anaesthesia*]

sȳ'nagŏgˌue (-ŏg) *n*. (meeting-place of) Jewish assembly or congregation for religious observance and instruction; hence ∼AL, ∼ICAL (-gŏ'g-, -gŏ'j-), *adjs*. [ME, f. OF *sinagoge* f. LL f. Gk *sunagōgē* f. SYN(*agō* bring)]

sȳ'napse *n*. place where nerve-cells join. [f. as foll.]

sȳnä'psˌis *n*. (*pl*. ∼es *pr*. -ēz). **1.** = prec. **2.** (Biol.) fusion of chromosome-pairs at start of meiosis. **3.** Hence **sȳnä'ptIC** *a*. [f. Gk SYN(*apsis* = *hapsis* f. *haptō* join)]

sȳnär'thrŏ'sˌis *n*. (*pl*. ∼es *pr*. -ēz). (Anat.) articulation with bones immovably fixed, e.g. sutures of skull. [f. SYN- + Gk *arthrōsis* jointing (*arthron* joint; see -OSIS)]

sȳnc, sȳnch (-ngk), *n*. & *v*. (colloq.) **1.** *n*. synchronization. **2.** *v.t.* & *i*. synchronize. [abbr.]

sȳnchŏndrŏ'sˌis (-ngk-) *n*. (*pl*. ∼es *pr*. -ēz). nearly immovable articulation of bones by layer of cartilage, as in spinal vertebrae. [f. SYN- + Gk *khondros* cartilage + -OSIS]

sȳ'nchrō- (-ngkr-) *comb. form*. synchronized, synchronous, as: ∼cy'clotron, cyclotron reaching higher energies by decreasing electric field frequency with increasing particle energy and mass. [abbr.]

sȳ'nchromĕsh (-ngkr-) *a*. & *n*. (system of gear--changing, esp. in motor vehicles) in which the sliding gear-wheels are provided with small friction clutches which make contact with the non-sliding wheels before engagement, thus facilitating gear-changing by making both wheels revolve at meshing speed during engagement. [abbr. of *synchronized mesh*]

sȳnchrŏ'nˌic (-ngkr-, -n-kr-) *a*. describing a subject (esp. a language) as it exists at one point in time (opp. *diachronic*); hence ∼ICALLY *adv*. [f. LL *synchronus* (see SYNCHRONOUS) + -IC]

sȳ'nchronism (-ngkr-) *n*. synchrony; synchronizing of sound and picture in cinematography, television, etc. [f. Gk *sugkhronismos* (as SYNCHRONOUS; see -ISM)]

sȳ'nchronīzˌe (-ngkr-), **-īsˌe** (-īz), *v*. **1.** *v.i.* occur at the same time, be simultaneous (*with*). **2.** *v.t.* make occur at same time; carry out synchronism of (film); ascertain or set forth the correspondence in date of (events). **3.** *v.t.* & *i*. cause (clocks etc.) to show, (of clocks etc.) show, a standard or uniform time. **4.** Hence ∼A'TION *n* [f. prec. + -IZE]

sȳ'nchronous (-ngkr-) *a*. existing or occurring at same time (*with*); ∼ **motor**, (Electr.) motor having speed exactly proportional to current frequency; hence ∼LY[2] *adv*. [f. LL *synchronus* f. Gk *sugkhronos* (as SYN-, *khronos* time) + -OUS]

sȳ'nchronȳ (-ngkr-) *n*. being synchronic or synchronous; treatment of events etc. as being synchronous. [f. Gk *sugkhronos* (see prec., -Y[1])]

sȳ'nchrotrŏn (-ngkr-) *n*. (Phys.) cyclotron in which magnetic field strength increases with energy of particles to keep their orbital radius constant. [f. SYNCHRO- + -TRON]

sȳ'nclīnˌe *n*. (Geol.) rock-bed forming a trough; so ∼AL (-ī'n-, sī'-) *a*. [f. SYN(*clinal* f. Gk *klinō* lean; see -AL)]

sȳ'ncopˌāte *v.t.* shorten (word) by dropping interior letter(s) or syllable(s), as *symbology* for *symbolology*, *Gloster* for *Gloucester* (Mus.) displace beats or accents in (passage) so that what was 'strong' becomes 'weak', and vice versa; so ∼A'TION *n*. [f. LL *syncopare* swoon (as foll.) + -ATE[3]]

sȳ'ncopˌe *n*. (Gram.) syncopated spelling or pronunciation; (Path.) temporary loss of consciousness from fall of blood-pressure, whence ∼AL *a*. [ME, f. LL f. Gk *sugkopē* (as SYN-, *koptō* strike, cut off)]

For other words in *syn-* see SYN-.

sy̆'ncrĕt|ism *n*. **1.** (Philos. & Theol.) attempt to unify or reconcile differing schools of thought, sects, etc.; (derog.) inconsistency of accepting incompatible principles or beliefs. **2.** (Philol.) merging of inflected forms of a word. **3.** Hence or cogn. **sy̆ncrĕ'tic** *a*., ∿ɪsᴛ (2) *n*., ∿ɪ'stɪc *a*., ∿ɪᴢᴇ (2, 3) *v.i.* & *t*. [f. mod. L *syncretismus* f. Gk *sugkrētismos* (*sugkrētizō* combine as two parties against a third; see -ɪsᴍ)]

sy̆ncy̆'ti|um *n*. (*pl*. ∿a). mass of protoplasm with several nuclei but forming one cell; hence ∿ᴀʟ *a*. [f. as sʏɴ-+-ᴄʏᴛᴇ+-ɪᴜᴍ]

sy̆'ndĕs|is *n*. (*pl*. ∿es *pr*. -ēz). = sʏɴᴀᴘsɪs 2. [mod. L, f. Gk sʏɴ*desis* binding together (*sundeō* bind together)]

sy̆ndĕ'tic *a*. (Gram.) of or using conjunctions. [f. Gk sʏɴ*detikos* (as prec.); see -ɪᴄ)]

sy̆'ndic *n*. government official, esp. chief magistrate in Andorra etc.; ||(Camb. Univ.) member of special committee of senate. [F, f. LL f. Gk sʏɴ(*dikos* f. *dikē* justice) advocate]

sy̆'ndical|ism *n*. movement among industrial workers (esp. in France) aiming at transfer of means of production and distribution from their present owners to unions of workers; so ∿ɪsᴛ (2) *n*. [f. F *syndicalisme* (*syndical* f. as prec., -ᴀʟ; see -ɪsᴍ)]

sy̆'ndicate¹ *n*. **1.** combination of commercial firms etc. associated to promote some common interest; combination of persons for the acquisition of literary articles etc., and their simultaneous publication in a number of periodicals; group of people who combine to buy or rent property, gamble, organize crime, etc. **2.** body of syndics. [f. F *syndicat* f. med. L *syndicatus* f. LL *syndicus* (see sʏɴᴅɪᴄ, -ᴀᴛᴇ¹)]

sy̆'ndic|āte² *v.t.* form into syndicate; publish (material) through syndicate; hence ∿ᴀ'ᴛɪᴏɴ *n*. [f. prec.; see -ᴀᴛᴇ³]

sy̆'ndrom|e (-drōm, -dromĭ) *n*. concurrent symptoms in disease; characteristic combination of opinions, behaviour, etc.; hence ∿ɪᴄ (-ŏ'm-) *a*. [mod. L, f. Gk sʏɴ(*dromē* f. *dramein* to run)]

sy̆ne. See ᴀᴜʟᴅ.

sy̆nĕ'cdochĕ (-kĭ) *n*. figure of speech in which part is named but whole is understood (*50 sail* for *50 ships*) or whole is named but part is understood (*England beat Australia at cricket*). [ME f. L, f. Gk sʏɴ(*ekdokhē* f. *ekdekhomai* take up)]

sy̆'nerg|ism, sy̆'nerg|y̆, *ns*. combined effect of drugs, organs, etc. that exceeds the sum of their individual effects; hence or cogn. ∿ᴇ'ᴛɪᴄ, **sy̆nĕr'gic,** ∿ɪ'stɪc, *adjs*. [f. Gk sʏɴ*ergos* working together (-*ergō* to work)+-ɪsᴍ, -ʏ¹]

sy̆nizē's|is *n*. (*pl*. ∿es *pr*. -ēz). (Gram. & Pros.) coalescence of two vowels into one syllable other than as recognized diphthong. [L, f. Gk *sunizēsis* f. sʏɴ(*izanō* = *hizanō* settle down f. *hizō* sit)]

sy̆'nod *n*. ecclesiastical council attended by delegated clergy and sometimes laity (**General S∿**, highest governing body in Church of England); Presbyterian ecclesiastical court above presbyteries and subject to General Assembly; any meeting for debate; so ∿ᴀʟ *a*. [ME, f. LL f. Gk *sunodos* (as sʏɴ-, *hodos* way) meeting]

sy̆nŏ'dic(al) *adjs*. synodal; (Astron.) pertaining to conjunction of planets etc. (**∿ period,** time between successive conjunctions of planet with sun). [f. LL f. Gk *sunodikos* (as prec.; see -ɪᴄ, -ɪᴄᴀʟ)]

sy̆noe'cious (-ē'shʊs) *a*. (Bot.) with male and female organs in same inflorescence or receptacle; (Biol.) symbiotic with benefit to one partner. [f. sʏɴ- after *dioecious* etc.]

sy̆'nonym *n*. word or phrase identical and coextensive in sense and usage with another of the same language (as *caecitis* with *typhlitis*); word denoting the same thing(s) as another but suitable to different context (as *serpent, slay,* cf. *snake, kill*) or containing different emphasis (as *blindworm,* cf. *slow-worm*); word equivalent to another in some only of either's senses (as *ship* to *vessel*); hence or cogn. **sy̆nony̆'mic** *a*., **sy̆nony̆'mity** *n*., **sy̆nŏ'ny̆mous** *a*. (*with*). [ME, f. L f.

Gk *sunōnumon* neut. (as n.) of *sunōnumos* (as sʏɴ-, -ōnum- name; cf. ᴀɴᴏɴʏᴍᴏᴜs)]

sy̆nŏ'ny̆my̆ *n*. synonymity; collocation of synonyms for emphasis (as *in any shape or form*); system or collection of, treatise on, synonyms. [f. LL f. Gk *sunōnumia* (as prec.; see -ʏ¹)]

sy̆nŏ'ps|is *n*. (*pl*. ∿es *pr*. -ēz). summary; brief general survey. [LL, f. Gk sʏɴ(*opsis* seeing)]

sy̆nŏ'ptic *a*. & *n*. **1.** *a*. of or forming a synopsis; taking or affording a comprehensive mental view; of the Synoptic Gospels; giving a general view of weather conditions; **S∿ Gospels,** those of Matthew, Mark, and Luke, describing events from same point of view; hence ∿ᴀʟ *a*., ∿**al**ʟʏ² *adv.* **2.** *n*. (writer of) a Synoptic Gospel. [f. Gk *sunoptikos* (as prec.); see -ɪᴄ)]

sy̆nŏ'ptist *n*. writer of a Synoptic Gospel. [f. prec.+ -ɪsᴛ]

sy̆nŏ'vi̇|a *n*. (Physiol.) viscous fluid lubricating joints and tendon sheaths; hence ∿ᴀʟ *a*. (∿**al membrane,** dense membrane of connective tissue secreting synovia), **sy̆novi̇'tis** *n*., inflammation of synovial membrane. [mod. L, formed prob. arbitrarily by Paracelsus]

sy̆ntǎ'ctic *a*. of, according to, syntax; hence ∿ᴀʟ *a*., ∿ᴀʟʟʏ *adv.* [f. Gk *suntaktikos* (as sʏɴᴛᴀx; see -ɪᴄ)]

sy̆ntǎ'gm|a *n*. word or phrase forming syntactic unit; orderly collection of statements; hence ∿ᴀ'ᴛɪᴄ, ∿ɪᴄ, *adjs*. [LL, f. Gk *suntagma* (as foll.)]

sy̆'ntǎx *n*. sentence-construction, (analysis of) the grammatical arrangement of words in speech or writing to show their connection and relation; set of rules governing this arrangement. [f. F *syntaxe* or f. LL f. Gk sʏɴ(*taxis* f. *tassō* arrange) marshalling, syntax]

sy̆'nthĕs|is *n*. (*pl*. ∿es *pr*. -ēz). combination, composition, putting together, (opp. *analysis*); building up of separate elements esp. of conceptions or propositions or facts, into a connected whole, esp. a theory or system; (Chem.) artificial production of compounds from their constituents as opp. extraction from plants etc.; (Gram.) making of compound and derivative words, preference of composition and inflexion to use of prepositions etc.; (Surg.) joining of divided parts; hence ∿ɪsᴛ (1) *n*., ∿ɪᴢᴇ (1) *v.t.*, ∿ɪᴢᴇʀ¹ *n*., (esp.) electronic device for combining sounds. [L, f. Gk *sunthesis* (as sʏɴ-, ᴛʜᴇsɪs)]

sy̆nthĕ'tic *a*. & *n*. **1.** *a*. made by synthesis (*synthetic drugs*), esp. to imitate a natural product (*synthetic cream, rubber*); synthetic ʀᴇsɪɴ; (colloq.) artificial, affected, insincere; (Philos.) having truth or falsity determinable by recourse to experience; ∿ **philosophy,** Spencerianism. **2.** Hence ∿ᴀʟ *a*., ∿ᴀʟʟʏ *adv.* **3.** *n*. synthetic substance. [f. F *synthétique* or mod. L *syntheticus* f. Gk *sunthetikos* f. *sunthetos* f. sʏɴ(*tithēmi* put); see -ɪᴄ]

sy̆'nthĕtist, sy̆'nthĕtize. Vars. of sʏɴᴛʜᴇsɪsᴛ, sʏɴᴛʜᴇsɪᴢᴇ.

sy̆'phil|is *n*. contagious venereal disease affecting first some local part (**primary ∿is**), secondly the skin and mucous membrane (**secondary ∿is**), and thirdly the bones and muscles and brain (**tertiary ∿is**); **congenital ∿is** (contracted by unborn child from mother's blood); hence ∿ɪ'ᴛɪᴄ, ∿ᴏɪᴅ, *adjs.*, ∿ɪᴢᴇ (5) *v.t.* [mod. L, f. title (*Syphilis, sive Morbus Gallicus*) of L poem (1530), f. *Syphilus,* a character in it, supposed first sufferer from the disease]

sy̆'phon, sy̆r'en. Vars. of sɪᴘʜᴏɴ, sɪʀᴇɴ.

Sy̆'riǎc *n*. & *a*. (in) the language of ancient Syria, western Aramaic. [f. L f. Gk *Suriakos* (*Suria* Syria; see -ᴀᴄ)]

Sy̆'rian *a*. & *n*. (native or inhabitant) of Syria in SW Asia. [ME, f. OF *sirien* f. L f. Gk *Surios*; see -ᴀɴ]

sy̆ri̇'nga (-ngga) *n*. **1.** mock ᴏʀᴀɴɢᴇ¹. **2.** (Bot.) plant of genus *Syringa,* lilac. [mod. L, f. as sʏʀɪɴx (w. ref. to use of stems cleared of pith as pipe-stems)+-ᴀ]

sy̆ringe (sĭ'rĭnj, -rĭ'-) *n*., & *v.t.* **1.** *n*. tube with nozzle and piston or bulb for drawing in liquid by suction

For other words in syn- see sʏɴ-.

and then ejecting it in fine stream, used in surgery, gardening, etc.; HYPODERMIC *syringe.* **2.** *v.t.* sluice or spray (ear, plant, etc.) with syringe. [ME, f. med. L *syringa* (as foll.)]

sȳ′rin|x *n.* (*pl.* ∼xes, *or* ∼ges *pr.* -ĭ′njĕz). pan-pipe; (Archaeol.) narrow gallery cut in rock in ancient Egyptian tomb; lower larynx or song-organ of birds, whence **sȳrī′ngè**AL (-nj-) *a.* [L *syrinx -ngis,* f. Gk *surigx suriggos* pipe, channel]

Sȳro- *comb. form.* Syrian (and), as: ∼-*Ara′bian,* ∼- -*Phoeni′cian.* [f. Gk *Suro-* (*Suros* a Syrian; see -O-)]

sȳ′rup, *sĭ′rup, *n.* **1.** water (nearly) saturated with sugar; this combined with flavouring as beverage or with drug(s) as medicine. **2.** condensed sugar-cane juice, part of this remaining uncrystallized at various stages of refining, molasses, treacle; ‖**golden** ∼, trade name for pale kind; **maple** ∼ (made by evaporating maple sap or dissolving maple sugar). **3.** (fig.) excessive sweetness of literary style etc. **4.** Hence ∼Y[2] *a.* [ME, f. OF *sirop* or med. L *siropus* f. Arab. *šarāb* beverage; cf. SHERBET, SHRUB[2]]

sȳssárcō′s|is *n.* (*pl.* ∼es *pr.* -ēz). connection between bones by intervening muscle. [mod. L, f. Gk *sussarkōsis* (as SYN-, *sarx sarkos* flesh, -OSIS)]

sȳstá′ltic *a.* contracting and dilating by turns, having systole and diastole, pulsatory. [f. LL f. Gk *sustaltikos* (as SY-, *staltos* f. *stello* put; see -IC)]

sȳ′stem *n.* **1.** complex whole, set of connected things or parts, organized body of material or immaterial things; *the* established political or social order; **mountain** ∼, range or connected ranges; **river, railway,** ∼, (1) river, railway, with its tributaries or branches, (2) rivers, railways, of a country, continent, etc.; ∼s **analysis,** technique of analysing an operation etc. in order to use a computer in seeking ways to improve its efficiency etc. **2.** (Phys.) group of associated bodies moving under mutual gravitation etc.; SOLAR *system;* ∼ **of pulleys** (several arranged to work together). **3.** (Biol.) set of organs or parts in animal body with common structure or function (*digestive, muscular, nervous, reproductive, system*); **the** ∼, animal body as a whole; **get thing out of** one's ∼, (fig.) be rid of its effects. **4.** method, organization, considered principles of procedure, (principle of) classification; body of theory or practice pertaining to a particular form of government, religion, etc.; method of choosing one's procedure in gambling etc.; one of six general types of crystal structure; METRIC *system;* **Ptolemaic** etc. ∼, set of hypotheses or principles composing Ptolemy's etc. theory; (Geol.) **Devonian** etc. ∼, major group of strata etc. so named; ∼ **of philosophy,** set of co-ordinated doctrines; hence ∼LESS *a.* **5.** (Mus.) braced staves of score. [f. F *système* or f. LL f. Gk *sustēma -atos* (as SY-, *histēmi* set up)]

sȳstemă′t|ic *a.* methodical, according to a plan, not casual or sporadic or unintentional, classificatory, (*systematic worker, liar, insolence, nomenclature*); ∼**ic theology** (arranging religious truths in a self--consistent whole); hence or cogn. ∼ICALLY *adv.,* ∼ICS *n.,* taxonomy, **sȳ′stemat**ISM (1), **sȳ′stemat**IST (1), *ns.,* **sȳ′stemat**IZE (3) *v.t.* [f. F *systématique* f. LL f. late Gk *sustēmatikos* (as prec.; see -IC)]

sȳstě′m|ic *a.* (Physiol.) of the bodily system as a whole, not confined to a particular part, (of blood circulation) other than pulmonary; (of insecticide, fungicide, etc.) entering the plant via roots or shoots and passing through the tissues; hence ∼ICALLY *adv.* [irreg. f. SYSTEM + -IC]

sȳ′stole *n.* (Physiol.) contraction of heart rhythmically alternating with DIASTOLE; hence **sȳstŏ′l**IC *a.* [LL, f. Gk *sustolē* (*sustellō* contract, as SYSTALTIC)]

sȳ′zȳgȳ *n.* **1.** (Astron.) conjunction or opposition, esp. of moon with sun. **2.** pair of connected or correlated things. [f. LL f. Gk *suzugia* (*suzugos* yoked, paired, f. as SY- + *zugon* yoke; see -Y[1])]

T

T, t, (tē) *n.* (*pl.* **Ts** *or* **T's**). twentieth letter of alphabet; T-shaped thing (esp. *attrib.*: *T-bandage, -bar, -bolt, -joint, -junction, -pipe*); *suits me, hit it off*, etc., **to a T,** exactly, to a nicety; **cross the t's,** (fig.) be minutely accurate, emphasize details; **T-bone,** T-shaped bone esp. in steak from thin end of loin; **T-shirt,** short--sleeved informal shirt having shape of T when spread out flat; **T-square,** T-shaped SQUARE¹ 3.

't *pron.* = IT¹ ('*tis*). [contr.]

-t¹ *suf.* = ED¹ (*bought, crept, sent*).

-t² *suf.* = -EST² (*shalt, wert*).

T *abbr.* tera-; tesla.

t. *abbr.* ton(s); tonne(s).

T *symb.* tritium.

‖**ta** (tah) *int.* (childish or colloq.) thank you. [infantile form]

‖**TA** *abbr.* Territorial Army.

Ta *symb.* tantalum.

taal (tahl) *n.* **the** ~, (Hist.) early form of Afrikaans. [Du., = language, cogn. w. TALE]

tăb *n.,* & *v.t.* (**-bb-**). **1.** *n.* small flap, strip, tag, or tongue, as appendage for grasping, suspending, fastening, or identifying garment etc.; similar object as part of garment etc.; ‖(Mil.) mark on collar distinguishing staff officer; (loop for suspending) stage-curtain; (colloq.) account, tally, *bill, *price; **keep** ~(**s**) or **a** ~ **on,** keep account of, have under observation or in check. **2.** *v.t.* provide with tab(s). [prob. f. dial.; cf. TAG¹]

TAB *abbr.* typhoid-paratyphoid A and B vaccine; (Austral.) Totalizator Agency Board.

tă'bard *n.* **1.** (Hist.) knight's short emblazoned garment worn over armour. **2.** herald's official coat emblazoned with arms of sovereign. [ME, f. OF *tabart*, of unkn. orig.]

tă'barèt *n.* upholstery fabric of alternate satin and plain stripes. [prob. f. TABBY]

tabă'scō *n.* (*pl.* ~**s**). pungent pepper made from fruit of *Capsicum annuum*; (*T*~; **P**) sauce made from tabasco pepper. [f. *T*~ in Mexico]

tă'bby̆ *n.* plain weave; watered fabric, esp. of silk; ~ (**cat**), brindled or mottled or streaked cat, esp. of grey or brownish colour with dark stripes; cat, esp. female; (derog.) gossiping woman, ‖esp. old maid. [f. F *tabis* f. Arab. *al-'attabiya* quarter of Baghdad where tabby was manufactured; connection of remaining senses uncert.]

‖**tă'berdar** *n.* scholar of Queen's College, Oxford; hence ~SHIP *n.* [f. L *tabardarius* (as TABARD; see -AR²; from former dress)]

tă'bernăcl|e *n.* & *v.* **1.** *n.* (Bibl.) fixed or movable habitation usu. of light construction; **Feast of T~es,** Succoth. **2.** (Jewish Hist.) tent used as sanctuary before final settlement of Jews in Palestine. **3.** place of public worship other than church. **4.** (Eccl.) ornamented receptacle for pyx or Eucharistic elements; canopied niche; ~**e-work,** ornamental carving or tracery over pulpit etc.; hence ~ED² (-kèld) *a.* **5.** socket or double post for hinged mast that requires lowering to pass under bridges. **6.** *v.t.* place in tabernacle. **7.** *v.i.* dwell temporarily. [ME f. OF, or f. L *tabernaculum* tent dim. of *taberna* hut; see -CULE]

tă'bēs (-z) *n.* (Med.) emaciation; ~ **dorsalis,** locomotor ATAXY; hence **tabĕ'tic** *a.* [L, = wasting away]

tă'bĭnĕt *n.* watered fabric of silk and wool. [app. f. TABBY]

ta'bla (tă'-, tah'-) *n.* (Ind. Mus.) pair of small drums played with hands. [Hind., f. Arab. *ṭabla* drum]

tă'blature *n.* (Mus.) early form of notation indicating point of string etc. to be stopped; (arch.) mental picture. [F, f. It. *tavolatura* (*tavolare* set to music; see -URE)]

tă'ble *n.,* & *v.t.* **1.** *n.* piece of furniture consisting of flat top of wood, marble etc. and one or more usu. vertical supports esp. one on which meals are laid out, articles of use or ornament kept, work done, or games played; **breakfast, dinner, tea,** etc., ~, table used for such meals or on which such meal is laid out; **at** ~, while taking meal at table (see also SERVE, WAIT¹); **under the** ~, (esp.) drunken after dinner. **2.** company seated at table for dinner etc.; (quantity and quality of) food provided at table (*keeps a good table*; *expenses of his table*). **3.** part of machine tool on which work is put to be operated on. **4.** slab of wood, stone, etc.; matter written on this; **the two** ~**s** or **the** ~**s of the law** etc., the Ten COMMANDMENTS; **the Twelve T~s,** laws promulgated in Rome 451–450 BC, principal source of Roman jurisprudence. **5.** = *tableland*. **6.** (Archit.) flat usu. rectangular vertical surface; horizontal moulding esp. cornice. **7.** flat surface of gem; cut gem with two flat faces. **8.** each half or quarter of folding board for backgammon; (Bridge) *the* dummy hand. **9.** list of facts, numbers, etc., systematically arranged esp. in columns (MULTIPLICATION *table*; *tables of weights and measures*; *table of contents*); matter contained in this; **learn** one's ~**s** (of multiplication, weights and measures, etc.); **mathematical** ~**s** (of logarithms, trigonometrical ratios, etc.). **10.** lay (measure, report, etc., in Parliament etc.) **on the** ~, (1) postpone indefinitely, (2) ‖submit for discussion; **on the** ~, offered for discussion; **turn the** ~**s** (**on** person, or abs.), reverse relations (with), esp. pass from inferior to superior position [f. interchange of positions at backgammon; see sense 8]. **11.** ~**-cloth** (of white linen etc. for use at meals, or of coloured material esp. for use at other times); ~**-cut,** (of gem) cut with large flat top; ~**-flap,** hinged end of table-top, lowered when not in use; ~**-knife** (for use at meals, esp. for cutting meat small); ~**land,** extensive elevated region with level surface, plateau; ~**-leaf,** (1) piece that may be inserted in top of table to increase its length, (2) = *table-flap*; ~ **licence** (to serve alcoholic liquor with meals only); ~**-lifting, -rapping, -turning,** lifting etc. of table apparently without physical force, as spiritualistic phenomenon; ~**-linen,** table-cloths, napkins, etc.; ~ **manners,** ability to behave properly while eating at table; ~**-mat** (to protect surface of table from hot dishes etc.); ~**-money,** allowance to higher officers in army etc. for official hospitality, charge to members of club for use of dining-room; *table*-NAPKIN; **T~ Round,** = ROUND¹ *Table*; *table* SALT; *table*SPOON¹, whence ~*spoonful* 2 *n.*; ~**-talk,** miscellaneous informal talk at table; ~ **tennis,** game like lawn tennis with net across table; ~**-tomb,** flat--topped chestlike tomb; ~**-top** *a.,* for use on table; ~**ware,** dishes etc. for use at table; ~**-water,** mineral water bottled for use at table; ~ **wine** (for drinking with meal). **12.** Hence ~FUL (2) (-bèlf-) *n.* **13.** *v.t.* lay (measure etc.; see sense 10) on the table; strengthen (sail) with wide hem; hence **tă'blING¹** (1, 2) *n.* [ME f. OF, f. L *tabula* plank, tablet, list]

tă'bleau (-lō) *n.* (*pl.* ~**x** *pr.* -ōz). **1.** picturesque presentation; ~ (**vivant** *pr.* vē'vahn̄; *pl.* ~x *vivants pr.* same; lit. 'living picture'), silent and motionless group of persons etc. arranged to represent a scene. **2.** dramatic or effective situation suddenly brought about; ~ **curtains,** (Theatr.) pair of curtains drawn open by diagonal cord. [F, = picture, dim. of *table* see (prec.)]

table d'hôte (tahbl dō't) *n.* meal at fixed time and price for guests at hotel; ~ **dinner** etc. (served in hotel etc. at fixed price, with less choice of dishes than à la carte). [F, = host's table]

tă'blĕt *n.* **1.** thin sheet of ivory, wood, etc., for writing on, esp. each of a set fastened together; (usu. in *pl.*) such set; * = PAD³ 3. **2.** small slab esp. with or for inscription (*votive tablet*). **3.** small flat piece of prepared substance, e.g. soap; small fixed weight or measure of a drug compressed into convenient shape. **4.** (Archit.) = TABLE 6. [ME, f. OF *tablete* f. Rom., dim. of L *tabula* TABLE; SEE -ET¹]

tă'blier (-lyā) *n.* (Hist.) apron-like part of woman's dress. [F]

tă'bloid *n.* newspaper, usu. popular in style, printed on sheets of half size; anything in compressed or concentrated form. [orig. **P,** name of compressed and concentrated drug-preparation; see TABLET, -OID]

taboō', tabu' (-ōō'), *n., a.,* & *v.t.* **1.** *n.* (among Polynesians etc.) system or act of setting apart person or thing as accursed or sacred; ban, prohibition. **2.** *a.* prohibited, consecrated; avoided or prohibited by social custom (*taboo word*). **3.** *v.t.* put (thing, practice, etc.) under taboo; exclude or prohibit by authority or social influence (*the subject was tabooed*). [f. Tongan *tabu*]

ta'bor *n.* (Hist.) small drum, esp. one used to accompany pipe. [ME, f. OF *tab*(*o*)*ur;* cf. TABLA, Pers. *tabīra* drum]

tă'bourĕt (-bər-), ****tă'borĕt,** *n.* low seat usu. without arms or back. [F, = stool, dim. as prec.]

tabu. See TABOO.

tă'būlar *a.* **1.** of, arranged in, computed etc. by means of, tables (*tabular statement, values, results, computations*); *tabular* STANDARD. **2.** broad and flat like a table (*tabular surface*); (of crystal) with two broad flat faces; (formed) in thin plates. **3.** Hence ~LY² *adv.* [f. L *tabularis* (as TABLE; see -AR¹)]

tabula rasa (tăbŭla rä'sa, -za, -ah'-) *n.* erased tablet, (fig.) human mind (esp. at birth) viewed as having no innate ideas. [L, = scraped tablet]

tă'būlāte *v.t.* arrange (figures, facts) in tabular form, hence ~A'TION *n.* [f. LL *tabulare* (*tabula* table) + -ATE³]

tă'būlātor *n.* person who tabulates; device on typewriter for advancing to sequence of set positions in tabular work; machine that tabulates data. [f. prec. + -OR]

tă'camahăc (-amah-) *n.* gum resin from tropical Amer. tree esp. of genus *Bursera* or *Protium;* (resin of) balsam poplar. [f. obs. Sp. *tacamahaca* f. Aztec *tecomahyac*]

tă'c-au-tăc (-ō-) *n.* (Fencing). parry combined with riposte. [F, imit.]

tacet (tā'sĭt) *v.i.* (as *imper.* in Mus. score). be silent (of voice or instrumental part). [L, = is silent]

tă'chĭsm(e) (-shĭzm) *n.* = ACTION *painting.* [F *tachisme* (*tache* stain; see -ISM)]

tachi'sto|scōpe (-k-) *n.* instrument for very brief measured exposure of objects to the eye; hence ~scō'pic *a.* [f. Gk *takhistos* swiftest + -o- + -SCOPE]

tă'chō (-kō) *n.* (*pl.* ~s). (colloq.) tachometer. [abbr.]

tă'chograph (-kŏgrahf) *n.* device in motor vehicle for automatic recording of its speed and travel-time. [f. Gk *takhos* speed + -o- + -GRAPH]

tachŏ'mĕter (-k-) *n.* instrument for measuring velocity or speed of rotation (esp. of vehicle engine). [f. Gk *takhos* speed + -o- + -METER]

tăchўcăr'dĭa (-kĭ-) *n.* (Path.) abnormally rapid heart-action. [f. Gk *takhus* swift + *kardia* heart]

tachў'graph|ў (-k-) *n.* **1.** stenography, esp. that of ancient Greeks and Romans; hence ~ER¹ *n.,* **tăchў-gră'ph**IC(AL) (-k-) *adjs.* **2.** abbreviated medieval writing of Greek and Latin. [f. Gk *takhus* swift + -GRAPHY]

tachў'mĕter (-k-) *n.* surveyor's instrument for rapid location of points; speed-indicator. [f. as prec. + -METER]

tă'cĭt *a.* understood, implied, or existing, without being stated, (*tacit consent, agreement, understanding*); hence ~LY² *adv.* [f. L *tacitus* silent (*tacēre* be silent)]

Tăcĭtē'an *a.* like the style of Tacitus, terse and sententious. [f. Cornelius *Tacitus,* Roman historian d. AD 117 + -EAN]

tă'cĭtŭrn *a.* reserved in speech, saying little, uncommunicative; so ~ITY (-ĕr'-) *n.* [f. F *taciturne* or f. L *taciturnus* (as TACIT)]

tăck¹ *n.* & *v.* **1.** *n.* small sharp broad-headed easily removed nail of iron, copper, etc., for securing carpet etc.; * = THUMB*tack;* BRASS *tacks.* **2.** long stitch as slight or temporary fastening, or as marker, in sewing. **3.** (Naut.) rope for securing corner of some sails, corner to which this is fastened; direction in which vessel moves as determined by position of sails (**port, starboard,** ~, with wind on port, starboard, side); temporary change of direction in sailing to take advantage of side wind etc., esp. each of several alternate movements to port and starboard. **4.** (fig.) course of action or policy (*must change our tack; is on the right or wrong tack; try another tack*). **5.** ||extraneous clause appended to bill in Parliament. **6.** sticky condition of varnish etc. **7.** ~**-driver,** machine that automatically places and drives tacks; ~**-hammer,** light hammer for driving tacks, usu. with claw for extracting them. **8.** *v.t.* fasten (carpet etc. *down*) with tacks; stitch (pieces or parts of cloth etc.) lightly together; (fig.) annex, append, (thing *to* or *on to* another); ||append (clause, see sense 5). **9.** *v.i.* change ship's course (*about*) by turning head to wind (cf. WEAR²); make sequence of such changes; (fig.) change one's conduct, policy, etc. **10.** Hence ~'ER¹ (1, 2) *n.* [ME *tak* etc., of uncert. orig.; cf. Bibl. *tache* clasp, link f. OF *tache*]

tăck² *n.* riding-harness, saddles, etc.; ~**-room** (where this is kept). [f. TACKLE]

tăck³ *n.* food (HARD, SOFT, *tack*); (derog.) stuff, rubbish. [19th c.; orig. unkn.]

tă'ckle *n.,* & *v.t.* **1.** *n.* (**block and**) ~, mechanism esp. of ropes, pulley-blocks, hooks, etc., for lifting weights, managing sails or spars, etc.; windlass with its ropes and hooks; requisites for a task or sport (*fishing-tackle*). **2.** act of tackling in football etc.; (Amer. Footb.) (player in) position next to end of forward line. **3.** ~**-block,** pulley over which rope runs; ~**-fall,** rope for applying force to blocks of a tackle. **4.** *v.t.* grapple with, grasp with endeavour to hold or manage or overcome, (opponent, awkward thing or problem); enter into discussion with (person esp. *about* or *on* awkward matter); (Footb. etc.) obstruct, intercept, or seize and stop (player running with ball); secure by means of tackle. **5.** Hence **tă'ckl**ING¹ (1, 3, 6) *n.* [ME, prob. f. MLG *takel* (*taken* lay hold of; see -LE 1)]

tă'ck|ў¹ *a.* (Of varnish etc.) slightly sticky, not quite dry; hence ~INESS *n.* [f. TACK¹ + -Y²]

***tă'ckў²** *a.* showing poor taste or style; tatty, seedy. [19th c.; orig. unkn.]

ta'cō (tah'-) *n.* (*pl.* ~s). Mexican food of meat etc. in folded or rolled tortilla. [Mex. Sp.]

tăct *n.* intuitive perception of what is fitting esp. of the right thing to do or say in order to avoid giving offence or to gain goodwill, adroitness in dealing with persons or circumstances; hence ~'FUL, ~'LESS, *adjs.* [F, f. L *tactus* (sense of) touch (*tangere tact-* touch)]

tă'ctic *n.* (piece of) tactics. [f. mod. L *tactica* f. Gk *taktikē* (*tekhnē* art), f. as TACTICS]

tă'ctical *a.* of tactics; (of bombing) carried out in immediate support of (esp. brief or local) military or naval operations (opp. *strategic*); adroitly planning or planned; hence ~LY² *adv.* [f. Gk *taktikos* (as foll.) + -AL]

tă'ctics *n. pl.* (also treated as *sing.*) art of disposing military or naval or air forces esp. in actual contact with enemy (cf. STRATEGY); procedure calculated to gain some end, skilful device(s), (*cannot approve of these tactics*); hence **tăcti'**CIAN *n.* [f. mod. L f. Gk *taktika* neut. pl. (*taktos* ordered f. *tassō* arrange; see -IC)]

tă′ctile *a.* **1.** of, perceived by, connected with, the sense of touch, (*tactile impression, organ*); so **tă′ctŭ**AL *a.* **2.** tangible; (Paint.) producing or having to do with the effect of solidity (*tactile values* etc.). **3.** Hence **tăctī′l**ITY *n.* [f. L *tactilis* (*tangere tact-* touch; see -IL)]

tă′dpōle *n.* larva of amphibian, esp. frog or toad from time it leaves egg till loss of gills and tail. [ME *taddepolle* (as TOAD, POLL[1], f. size of head)]

taedium vitae (tēdĭum vī′tē, vē′tī) *n.* weariness of life (with tendency to suicide). [L]

tae′nǐ|a *n.* (*pl.* ∼ae *or* ∼as). (Archit.) fillet between Doric architrave and frieze; (Anat.) ribbon-like part esp. of brain or colon; (Zool.) tapeworm of genus *Taenia*; (Gk Ant.) fillet, headband; hence ∼OID *a.* [L, f. Gk *tainia* ribbon]

tă′ffeta *n.* fine plain-woven silk or silklike fabric. [ME, f. OF *taffetas* or med. L *taffata*, ult. f. Pers. *tāfta* p.p. (as n.) of *tāftan* twist]

tă′ffrail (-rāl, -rǐl) *n.* (Naut.) rail round stern of vessel. [f. earlier *tafferel* f. Du. *taffereel* panel, dim. of *tafel* (as TABLE); assim. to RAIL[1]]

Tă′ffy[1] *n.* (colloq.) (Nickname for) Welshman. [supposed W pronunc. of *Davy* = *David*]

*****tă′ffy**[2] *n.* sweetmeat like toffee; insincere flattery. [19th c., of unkn. orig.]

tă′fia *n.* (W. Ind.) rum distilled from molasses etc. [18th c.; orig. uncert.]

tăg[1] *n.* & *v.* (-gg-). **1.** *n.* metal or plastic point at end of lace etc. to assist insertion. **2.** loop at back of boot used in pulling it on. **3.** label, esp. one for tying on, to show address, price, etc.; *****motor-vehicle licence-plate. **4.** loose or ragged end of anything; ragged lock of wool on sheep. **5.** appendage; (Theatr.) closing speech addressed to audience; trite quotation, stock phrase; refrain of song. **6.** (tip of) animal's tail. **7.** *****∼ day, = FLAG[4]-*day* (but with tags not flags); ∼-**end,** last remnant of anything; ∼′**rag,** = RAG[1]*tag.* **8.** *v.t.* furnish (lace etc., literary composition) with tag(s); label with radioactivity. **9.** join (thing, esp. piece of writing, *to* or *on to* another, things *together*), find rhymes for (verses), string (rhymes) together. **10.** shear away tags from (sheep). **11.** *v.t.* & *i.* (colloq.) follow closely; trail behind; go *along with.* [ME, of unkn. orig.]

tăg[2] *n.,* & *v.t.* **1.** *n.* children's game in which one chases the rest until he touches another, who then becomes pursuer; (Baseball) tagging of runner. **2.** *v.t.* touch in game of tag; (Baseball) put (runner) out or *out* by touching with ball or with hand holding ball. [18th c.; orig. unkn.]

Taga′log (-ah′-) *n.* (member or language) of principal people of Philippine Islands. [Tagalog (*taga* native, *ilog* river)]

tagē′tēs (-z) *n.* plant of genus *Tagetes*, with showy yellow or orange flowers. [mod. L, f. L *Tages*, Etruscan divinity]

tagliatĕ′llè (tahlyah-), **-lli** (-ē), *n.* ribbon-shaped form of pasta. [It.]

Tahi′tian (ta-hē′shan) *a.* & *n.* (native, inhabitant, or language) of Tahiti. [f. *Tahiti* in S. Pacific + -AN]

tahr. Var. of THAR.

tahsi′l (-ē′l) *n.* territorial subdivision in India for revenue purposes; hence ∼**dăr** *n.*, native collector of revenue in tahsil. [f. Hind. *taḥsīl* f. Arab., = collection; Pers. *dār* holder]

tai′ga (tī′gah) *n.* coniferous forest lying between tundra and steppe esp. in Siberia. [Russ.]

tail[1] *n.* & *v.* **1.** *n.* hindmost part of animal esp. when prolonged beyond (rest of) body; **on** person's ∼, closely following him; **with** ∼ **between legs,** showing dejection; **with** ∼ **up,** (of person, fig.) in good spirits; **turn** ∼, turn one's back, run away; *twist the* LION's *tail*; *put* SALT *on tail of*; cf. WAG[1]. **2.** thing like or suggesting tail in shape or position, hind or lower or subordinate or inferior part, slender part or prolongation; luminous train of comet, outer corner *of the eye*, rear part of aeroplane containing rudder etc., part of shirt below waist, hanging part of back of coat,

end of procession etc., weaker batsmen of cricket team, foot of page, long train of attendants etc., back of a cart, appendage at lower end of kite, stem of musical note, part of letter *g* etc. below line, exposed end of slate or tile in roof, unexposed end of brick or stone in wall, slender backward prolongation of butterfly's wing, comparative calm at end *of a gale*, calm stretch following rough water in a stream, (sl.) person following or shadowing another. **3.** (in *pl.*, colloq.) (evening dress with) tailcoat. **4.** (usu. in *pl.*) reverse of coin turned upwards after toss (cf. HEAD[1] 5). **5.** ∼′**back,** queue of traffic unable to proceed freely; ∼-**bay,** part of canal lock between tail-gate and lower pond; ∼-**board,** hinged or removable back of cart, lorry, etc.; ∼′**coat,** man's morning or evening coat with long skirt divided at back into tails and cut away in front; *tail-*COVERT[2]; ∼-**end,** hindmost or lowest or last part; ∼-**gate,** (1) lower end of canal lock, (2) = *tail-board*, (3) hatchback door of estate car, (4)***** (*v.i.*) drive too close behind another vehicle; ∼-**lamp,** ∼-**light,** (carried at back of train, car, bicycle, etc.); ∼′**piece,** (1) decoration in blank space at end of chapter etc., (2) triangular piece of wood to which lower ends of strings are fastened in some musical instruments, (3) appendage at the end of a thing; ∼′**pipe,** suction-pipe of pump, exhaust-pipe of motor vehicle; ∼′**plane,** horizontal stabilizing surface of aeroplane tail; ∼-**race,** part of mill-race below water-wheel; ∼-**skid,** support for tail of aeroplane when on ground; ∼-**spin,** spin of aircraft, (fig.) state of panic; ∼′**stock,** adjustable part of lathe holding fixed spindle; ∼ **wind** (blowing in direction of one's travel). **6.** Hence (-)∼ED[2] (-ld), ∼′LESS (-l-l-), *adjs.* **7.** *v.t.* furnish with tail; remove stalks of (fruit); dock tail of (lamb etc.). **8.** (sl.) shadow, follow closely. **9.** join (thing *on to* another). **10.** ∼ **after,** follow closely; ∼ **away** or **off,** fall behind or away in scattered line, become fewer or smaller or slighter, end inconclusively; ∼ **in,** fasten (timber) by one end into wall etc. [OE *tæg(e)l,* = OHG *zagal,* ON *tagl,* Goth. *tagl* hair, f. Gmc **taglaz*]

tail[2] *n.* & *a.* (Law). **1.** *n.* limited ownership, esp. of estate limited to a person and heirs of his body; **in** ∼, under such limitation. **2.** *a.* so limited (esp. *estate tail*, FEE-*tail*). [ME, f. OF *taille* notch, cut, tax, (*taillier* cut f. Rom. **tal(l)iare* f. L *talea* twig)]

tai′ling *n.* In vbl senses; (in *pl.*) refuse or inferior part of grain, ore, etc. [f. TAIL[1] + -ING[1]]

tai′lor *n.* & *v.* **1.** *n.* maker of (esp. men's) outer garments esp. to order; ∼-**bird,** small Asian etc. bird sewing leaves together to form nest; ∼-**made,** (*a.*, esp. of woman's dress) made by tailor usu. with little ornament and with special attention to exact fit, (fig.) perfectly suited for purpose, (*n.*) tailor-made garment; ∼′**s chair** (without legs, for sitting cross-legged like tailor at work); ∼′**s twist,** fine strong silk thread used by tailors. **2.** Hence ∼ESS[1] *n.* **3.** *v.i.* be, work as, a tailor; hence ∼ING[1] (1, 2) *n.* **4.** *v.t.* make (esp. tailor-made clothes) as tailor; (in *p.p.*) tailor-made; (esp. in *p.p.*) make clothes for. [ME & AF *taillour*, OF *tailleur* cutter f. Rom. **tal(l)iator -oris* (**tal(l)iare*; see TAIL[2], -OR)]

taint *n.* & *v.* **1.** *n.* spot or trace of decay or corruption or disease (lit. or fig.), corrupt condition, infection, (*taint was a taint of insanity in the family; the moral taint had spread among all classes; without taint of commercialism*); hence ∼′LESS *a.* **2.** *v.t.* introduce corruption or disease into, infect, (*tainted meat*); affect slightly *with.* **3.** *v.i.* be infected or corrupted (*meat will taint readily in hot weather*). [ME, partly f. OF *teint(e)* f. L *tinctus, tincta* masc. & fem. p.p. (as n.) of *tingere* dye, partly f. ATTAINT]

tai′păn[1] (tī′-) *n.* head of a foreign business in China. [Chin.]

tai′păn[2] (tī′-) *n.* largest venomous snake in Australia. [Aboriginal]

taj (tahj) *n.* tall conical cap of dervish. [f. Arab. *tāj*]

tā′kable. See TAKE¹ 21.

ta′kahė (tah′ka-hĭ) n. notornis. [Maori]

tāke¹ v. (**took** pr. tŏŏk; **ta′ken**). **1.** v.t. lay hold of with the hand(s) or other part of the body or with any instrument (lit. or fig.), grasp, seize, capture, catch by pursuit or surprise, captivate, win, gain, (take it between your finger and thumb; took him by the throat; take the BULL¹ by the horns; the devil take it, him! ; take the BIT¹ between one's teeth; take a fortress; take by STORM; took 113 prisoners, six wickets; was taken prisoner or captive; the woman taken in adultery; rabbit taken in trap; took him in the act, at a disadvantage; took rook with pawn, king with ace, first five tricks; takes £100 a week in fees, in salary, at the box-office; take person's FANCY¹; took the first set 6–3; took first prize; taken ABACK, SHORT); ~ **the biscuit** or **bun** or **cake**, (sl.) surpass all; ~**n** ill or (colloq.) **bad**, suddenly affected by illness; ~**n by** or **with**, attracted or charmed by. **2.** v.i. be successful or effective (novel, inoculation, skin-graft, did not take); (of plant, seed, etc.) begin to grow. **3.** v.t. assume possession of, acquire, avail oneself of, use, (takes whatever he can lay his hands on; wish you would not take my bicycle; quotation taken from Pope; take the first road on the left; shall take a bath, a holiday; (in recipe) take a dozen eggs and beat them well; has taken a partner, a wife; take LEAVE¹ to, take the LIBERTY; take ADVANTAGE¹ of; take the opportunity to do, of doing; ~ one's **time**, not hurry; ~ person **all his time**, (colloq.) tax his powers); occupy (position) esp. as one's right (take a or the CHAIR; take one's seat, a BACK¹ seat); copulate with (woman); obtain after fulfilling necessary conditions (take a degree, ORDER¹s, ‖SILK); regularly buy (periodical etc.); obtain use of by purchase etc. (took tickets, seats, for the ballet; must take lessons, lodgings, a taxi, a train to London; will take two pairs of these socks, please; took the cure at Bath); use as instance (take Hitler, now); consume (will take some food, a cup of tea; takes too much alcohol; took poison; do you take sugar?); have as necessary condition or accompaniment or part (these things take time, it will only take me an hour; it takes a poet to translate Virgil; transitive verbs take an object; this cake takes six eggs; takes a large size in hats, ~ **a lot of** or **some doing**, be hard to do; **have what it** ~**s**, possess necessary qualities esp. for success). **4.** cause to come or go with one, carry with one, conduct, convey, remove, dispossess person etc. of, (take the letters to the post, the dog for a walk, the children to the pantomime, the corkscrew from the shelf; take for a RIDE; my business often takes me abroad; route, bus, takes you past the station; took him into partnership; takes all the fun out of it; take to TASK; was taken from us by a stroke); ~ **in hand,** undertake, start doing or dealing with, undertake the control or reform of (the boy wants taking in hand); you can't ~ **it with you,** (colloq.) your possessions will pass to others when you die; ~ **to pieces,** separate component parts of; take APART, ASIDE. **5.** catch, be infected with or affected by, (cold, fever, fire, etc.; ~ **ill** or *sick, (colloq.) be taken ill); conceive, experience, indulge, give play to, exert, (take comfort, courage, offence, umbrage, a dislike to, EXCEPTION to, a FANCY¹ to, FRIGHT; take one's revenge, takes a pride in his work, a pleasure in contradicting; take pity on him; take no notice; take heed, pains, trouble). **6.** ascertain and record (person's measure, height, temperature, name, address, etc.) by inquiry, measurement, etc. **7.** apprehend, grasp mentally, infer, conclude, understand, interpret, (I take your meaning or (arch.) you; I take this to be ironical; I take it that we are to wait here; took his reply as a denial, him to be or for a fool; would you take this passage literally?); take person at his WORD¹; take it for GRANTED; I ~ **your point,** I grant the validity of what you say. **8.** treat or regard in specified manner, adopt specified attitude towards, (take things coolly; take it easy; take to HEART¹); ~**n all in all,** taking one thing with another, when the matter is viewed as a whole; ~ **it badly,** be very upset; ~ **it ill,** resent it; ~ **as read,** dispense with the actual reading of (minutes etc.); ~ **it well,** not be upset or resentful. **9.** accept, put up with, submit to, adopt, choose, receive, accommodate, derive, (take the offer; take what you can get; took a risk in doing that; I took his bet or him; took a beating from his opponent; cannot take a joke in good part; cannot take coffee without suffering from insomnia; must take us as you find us; will take no nonsense; will not take this treatment; took it like a lamb; will not take a hint; takes its name from the inventor; (you may) ~ it from me or ~ my word for it, I, a well-informed person, assure you; ~ it, (colloq.) endure adversity, punishment, etc., bravely; ~ it or leave it, please yourself, I do not care whether you accept it or not; ~ sides, join one of two parties; ~ that! (accompanying a blow etc.); ~ (hold, adopt) a different view. **10.** perform, execute, make, undertake, negotiate, deal with, (take notes, dictation; took a decision, a sudden leap; horse will not take the fence; take a walk; take a look at this, around you; took a deep breath; take a BOW¹, an oath; took the corner too fast); be taught or examined in (subject), be teacher of (subject) in school etc.; conduct (religious service). **11.** make (photograph); photograph (person etc.). **12.** take (no) ACCOUNT² of; take into ACCOUNT²; take ACTION; take ADVICE; take AIM²; take CARE¹ (of); take a CHANCE¹, one's CHANCE¹; take into CONSIDERATION; take EFFECT¹; take HEART¹ (of grace); take HOLD²; ~-**home,** (of pay etc.) available to employee after deduction of taxes etc.; take one's HOOK¹; take LEAVE¹ (of); take LIFE, take LIFE (in one's hands); ~ person's (esp. God's) name in vain, use it lightly or profanely, (joc.) mention it; take PART¹; take PLACE¹, the PLACE¹ of, one's PLACE¹; take POSSESSION; take PRECEDENCE; take STOCK (of, in); take the WALL, (the) WIND¹. **13.** (w. advs.): ~ **away,** subtract (number), remove, buy (food etc.) at restaurant for eating elsewhere; ~-**away** n., restaurant selling food thus; ~ **back,** retract (statement etc.), (Print.) transfer to previous line, carry (person) back in thought to past time; ~ **down,** write down (spoken words), humiliate (take person down a PEG¹), remove (building, structure) by taking it to pieces. **14.** ~ **in,** admit, receive, (lodger, guest, etc.); conduct (esp. lady) to dinner; undertake (work) to be done at one's home; include, comprise, (colloq.) visit (place) en route; make (garment) smaller; furl (SAIL¹); understand, digest mentally; deceive, cheat; ‖regularly buy (newspaper etc.); ~-in n., deception. **15.** ~ **off,** remove (clothes, HAT, etc.) from the body; remove, lead away; deduct (part of price); ridicule by imitation, mimic; jump, spring, (from or at place); (of aircraft or pilot) became airborne from ground etc.; regard (day etc.) as holiday; ~oneself off, depart; ~ off n., caricature, place from which one jumps, act of becoming airborne. **16.** ~ **on,** undertake (work, responsibility); acquire (takes on a new meaning); engage (employee); agree to oppose (person at golf etc.); (colloq.) show violent emotion, make a fuss. **17.** ~ **out,** cause to come out, bring or convey out, (take him out for a walk; books must not be taken out of the library); * = take away (food); remove (stain etc.); (Bridge) remove (partner or his call) from suit by bidding a different one or two trumps; procure, get issued, (patent, summons, etc.); ~ **it out of,** have revenge on, exhaust strength of; ~ **it out on,** work off one's frustration etc. by attacking or maltreating; ~ person **out of himself,** make him forget his worries etc. **18.** ~ **over,** succeed to management or ownership of (business), assume control, (Print.) transfer to next line; ~-over n., assumption of control (esp. of business etc.). **19.** ~ **up,** lift up; absorb, occupy, engage (sponges take up water; takes up all my time, my attention); take (person) into vehicle (train stops to take up passengers); adopt as protégé or pursuit; begin (residence etc.); interrupt or correct or question (speaker); pursue (matter, idea, inquiry) further; shorten (garment); accept (offer etc.); ~ **person up on,** accept his (offer, bet, etc.); ~ **up with,** begin to consort with; take up the CUDGELS, GAUNTLET¹, GLOVE.

20. (w. *preps.*): ∼ **after,** resemble (ancestor etc., esp. parent) in character, features, etc.; ∼ **against,** oppose, begin to dislike; ∼ **from,** subtract (*take 4 from 6*), diminish, weaken, detract from; ∼ (person) **into** one's **confidence,** confide in him; ∼ **it into** one's **head,** get the idea *that,* resolve *to* do; ∼ **to,** begin, have recourse to, fall into the habit of (using), begin to busy oneself with, adapt oneself to, conceive liking for (person); *take to* one's HEEL[1]'s; ∼ **it (up)on** one(**self**), venture or presume *to.* **21.** Hence **tā′kABLE** *a.* [OE *tacan* f. ON *taka*]

take² *n.* amount (*of* fish, game, etc.) taken or caught; (Print.) amount of copy set up at one time; takings, esp. money received at theatre for seats; (Cinemat.) scene or sequence of actions photographed at one time without interruption. [f. prec.]

tā′ker *n.* In vbl senses; one who takes a bet etc. (*there were no takers*). [ME, f. TAKE¹ + -ER¹]

ta′kin (tah′-) *n.* Tibetan horned ruminant (*Budorcas taxicolor*). [Mishmi]

tā′king¹ *n.* In vbl senses; (in *pl.*) money taken in business, receipts; (arch.) state of agitation (*was in a great taking*). [ME, f. TAKE¹ + -ING¹]

tā′king² *a.* In vbl senses; attractive, captivating; catching, infectious; hence ∼LY² *adv.,* ∼NESS *n.* [ME, ⸢ TAKE¹ + -ING²]

ta′la (tah′-) *n.* rhythmic pattern of Indian music. [Skr.]

tă′lapoin *n.* **1.** Buddhist monk or priest. **2.** small W. Afr. monkey (*Cercopithecus talapoin*). [f. Port. *talapão* f. Talaing *tala põi* my lord]

talār′ia *n. pl.* (Rom. Myth.) winged sandals as attribute of Mercury, Iris, and others. [L, neut. pl. of *talaris* (*talus* ankle; see -AR¹)]

ta′lbot (taw′-, tŏ′-) *n.* extinct breed of large white hunting-hound. [perh. f. family name *Talbot*]

tălc *n.,* & *v.t.* (**-ck-**). **1.** *n.* a magnesium silicate usu. found in flat smooth often transparent plates and used as lubricator etc.; talcum powder; mica esp. as glazing-material; hence **tă′lcky²,** ∼′OSE¹, ∼′OUS, *adjs.* **2.** *v.t.* treat with talc. [F, or f. med. L *talcum,* f. Arab. f. Pers. *ṭalḳ*]

tă′lcum *n.* = prec.; ∼ (**powder**), powdered talc for toilet use, usu. perfumed. [med. L; see prec.]

tāle *n.* **1.** true or usu. fictitious narrative esp. one imaginatively treated, story, (*tell me a tale; a true tale of the Crusades; marvellous legendary tales*); THEREby hangs a *tale;* ∼ **of a tub,** idle fiction; TELL¹ *a* or *the tale;* TELL¹ one's or *its own tale; old wives' tale* (see WIFE). **2.** malicious report whether true or false (*all sorts of tales will get about*); TELL¹ *tales* (*out of school*); ∼′**bearer,** person who maliciously gossips or reveals secrets; so ∼′**bearing** *a.* & *n.;* ∼′**teller,** one who tells tale(s) (in either sense). **3.** (arch. or literary). number, total, (*the tale is complete*); *shepherd tells his* ∼ (of sheep). [OE *talu,* = OS, ON *tala,* OHG *zala,* f. Gmc *talō* (**tal-;* cf. TELL¹)]

tă′lent *n.* **1.** special aptitude, faculty, gift, (*for music* etc.; *for doing;* see Matt. 25:14–30); high mental ability; hence ∼ED², ∼LESS, *adjs.* **2.** persons of talent (*all the talent of the country; looking out for local talent; ministry of all the talents*); ∼-**scout,** ∼-**spotter,** seeker-out of talent esp. for entertainment industries. **3.** ancient weight and money of account among Assyrians, Greeks, Romans, etc., of varying value. [OE *talente* & OF *talent* f. L *talentum* inclination of mind f. Gk *talanton* balance, weight, sum of money]

tales (tā′lēz) *n.* (Law). writ for summoning jurors, list of persons who may be so summoned, to supply deficiency; **pray a** ∼, plead for completion of jury thus; ∼′**man** (tā′lēz-, tā′lz-), person so summoned. [ME f. L ∼ (*de circumstantibus*) such (of the by-standers), first wds of writ]

Tăliacŏ′tian (-shan) *a.* ∼ **operation,** formation of new nose by means of flap taken from upper arm but severed only after union has taken place. [f. *Taliacotius,* Latinized f. *Tagliacozzi,* It. surgeon d. 1599 + -AN]

tă′lion *n.* = LEX TALIONIS. [ME f. OF, f. L *talio -onis* (*talis* such)]

tă′lipēs (-z) *n.* club-foot(edness). [mod. L f. L *talus* ankle + *pes* foot]

tă′lipŏt *n.* very tall S. Ind. fan palm with huge leaves used as sunshades etc. [f. Malayalam *tālipat,* Hindi *tālpāt* f. Skr. *tālapattra* (*tāla* palm, *pattra* leaf)]

tă′lisman (-z-) *n.* charm, amulet, thing supposed capable of working wonders; inscribed stone or ring supposed to ensure safety or good fortune; hence ∼IC (-ă′n-) *a.* [F & Sp., = It. *talismano,* f. med. Gk *telesmon,* Gk *telesma* completion, religious rite (*teleō* complete f. *telos* end)]

talk (tawk) *v.* & *n.* **1.** *v.i.* converse, communicate ideas, by spoken words (*was talking with* or *to a friend; what are you talking about?*); communicate by radio; *talk* BIG; *talk* TALL; **people will** ∼, there will be gossip or scandal; **now you're** ∼′**ing,** (sl.) I welcome that offer etc.; **you can** or **can't** ∼, (colloq.) you are just as bad yourself; **do the** ∼′**ing,** be spokesman; **know what one is** ∼′**ing about,** be expert; **money** ∼s (has influence). **2.** have the power of speech (*child is learning to talk; this parrot can talk*); betray secrets (*we have ways of making you talk*). **3.** *v.t.* express, utter, discuss, in words, (*you are talking nonsense; talk treason, scandal, philosophy,* SHOP, *cricket*); ***∼ **turkey,** (colloq.) be straightforward and realistic. **4.** use (language) in speech (*they were talking French*). **5.** bring into specified condition etc. by talking (*talked himself hoarse; talk* one*self out of a difficulty; talked him out of his resolution, into his grave*); *talk the hind leg off a* DONKEY. **6.** ∼ **about,** discuss, make subject of gossip, (∼ **about** *trouble* etc.!, (colloq.) there was a great deal of it); ∼ **at,** address to one of a company remarks covertly hostile and meant to be heard by (another), address pompously; ∼ **away,** consume (time) in talking; ∼ **back,** (1) reply defiantly, (2) respond on two-way radio system; ∼ **down,** silence (person) by superior loudness or persistence, bring (pilot or aircraft) to a landing by radio instructions from the ground, speak patronizingly or condescendingly *to;* ∼ **of,** (1) discuss, mention, (2) express some intention of (*doing*); ∼ **out,** get rid of (bill in Parliament etc.) by prolonging discussion till time of adjournment; ∼ **over,** discuss at some length; ∼ **person over** or **round,** win him over by talking; ∼ **round,** discuss (subject) at length without reaching conclusion; *talk through* one's HAT, one's NECK¹; ∼ **to,** converse with, (colloq.), reprove (*gave him a talking-to*); ∼ **to** one**self,** soliloquize; ∼ **up,** discuss (subject) in order to rouse interest in it. **7.** Hence ∼′ER¹ *n.* **8.** *n.* conversation (*let us have some talk*); discussion (*talks were held*); SMALL, TABLE-, TALL, *talk;* **it will end in** ∼, nothing will be done; ∼ **show** (of interviews on television). **9.** short address or lecture in conversational style (esp. when broadcast). **10.** (theme of) gossip (*there is talk of a new appointment; they, their quarrels, are the talk of the town*). **11.** mode of speech (BABY-, *sailors', talk*). [ME *talk(i)en* frequent. v. f. TALE or TELL¹]

ta′lkathon (tawk-) *n.* (colloq.) prolonged public oral discussion. [f. prec. + MARATHON]

ta′lkative (tawk′-) *a.* fond of talking; hence ∼LY² (-vlĭ) *adv.,* ∼NESS (-vn-) *n.* [ME, f. TALK + -ATIVE]

ta′lkee-talkee (taw′kĭtawkĭ) *n.* incessant chatter; broken English of W. Ind. Blacks etc. [redupl. & dim. f. TALK]

ta′lkfĕst (tawk′-) *n.* (colloq.) talkfest; informal meeting for general discussion. [f. TALK + FEST]

ta′lkie (taw′kĭ) *n.* (sl.) = SOUND²-*film.* [f. *talking film,* after *movie*]

ta′lking¹ (taw′k-) *n.* In vbl senses; ∼ **point,** topic for discussion or argument; ∼-**shop,** (derog.) Parliament etc. regarded as place of argument rather than action. [ME, f. TALK + -ING¹]

ta′lking² (taw′k-) *a.* In vbl senses; having the power of speech (*talking parrot*); expressive (*talking eyes*); ∼ **book,** recorded reading of book esp. for the blind; ∼

film or **picture**, = SOUND²-*film*; ~ **head**, (colloq.) speaker's head shown on television; ~ **of**, while we are discussing (*talking of food, what time is dinner?*). [f. TALK + -ING²]

tall (tawl) *a.* & *adv.* **1.** *a.* (Of person) of more than average height, or of specified height (*he is six feet tall*); (of tree, steeple, mast, ship, stag, etc.) higher than the average or than surrounding objects; ~**'boy**, tall chest of drawers sometimes in lower and upper sections or mounted on legs; ~ **drink** (served in tall glass); ~ **hat**, = TOP¹ *hat*; hence ~'NESS *n.* **2.** (sl.) extravagant, boastful, excessive, (*a tall story; tall talk*); **a** ~ **order**, an exorbitant or unreasonable demand. **3.** Hence ~'ISH (2) *a.* **4.** *adv.* in a tall way; **talk** ~, boast; **walk** ~, be proud. [ME, repr. OE *getæl* swift, prompt, = OS *gital*, OHG *gizal* quick]

tä'llage *n.* (Hist.) form of taxation on towns etc., abolished in 14th c.; tax on feudal dependants etc. [ME f. OF *taillage* (*tailler* cut; see TAIL², -AGE)]

tä'llith *n.* scarf worn by Jews esp. at prayer. [f. Rabbinical Heb. *ṭallīt* (*ṭillel* to cover)]

tä'llow (-ō) *n.*, & *v.t.* **1.** *n.* substance got by melting the harder and less fusible kinds of (esp. animal) fat, used for making candles and soap, greasing machinery, etc.; **vegetable** ~, vegetable fat similarly used; ~**-chandler**, maker or vendor of tallow candles; ~**-drop**, style of cutting precious stones with dome on one or both sides; ~**-tree**, tree esp. of genus *Stillingia* yielding vegetable tallow; hence ~ISH¹, ~Y², *adjs.* **2.** *v.t.* grease with tallow. [ME *tal*(*u*)*g*, f. MLG *talg*, *talch*, of unkn. orig.]

tä'lly *n.* & *v.* **1.** *n.* (Hist.) piece of wood scored across with notches for the items of an account and then split into halves of which each party kept one; account so kept. **2.** score, reckoning; mark made to register a fixed number of objects delivered or received, such number used as unit. **3.** ticket, label of wood or metal or paper with name etc. attached to thing for identification. **4.** corresponding thing, counterpart, duplicate, (*of*). **5.** ~ **clerk**, one who keeps a tally of goods, esp. those loaded or unloaded in docks; ||~**man**, one who keeps a tally or tally-shop, one who sells goods on credit; ~**-sheet**, paper on which tally is kept; ||~**-shop** (conducted on tally system); ||~ **system**, **trade**, (of sales on short credit or instalments with account kept by tally). **6.** *v.t.* record or reckon by tally. **7.** *v.i.* agree, correspond, (*with; goods do not tally with invoice*). **8.** Hence **tä'lli̇er¹** *n.* [ME, f. AF *tallie*, AL *tal*(*l*)*ia* f. L *talea*; cf. TAIL²]

tä'lly-hō' *int.*, *n.* (*pl.* ~s), & *v.* **1.** *int.* & *n.* huntsman's cry to hounds on viewing fox. **2.** *v.i.* & *t.* utter, indicate (fox) or urge (hounds) with, this. [cf. F *taïaut*]

Tä'lmud (-ŏŏd, -ud) *n.* body of Jewish civil and ceremonial law and legend comprising the Mishnah and the Gemara; hence **Tälmu̇'di̇c**(AL) *adjs.*, ~IST (2, 3) *ns.* [f. late Heb. *talmūḍ* instruction f. Heb. *lāmaḍ* learn]

tä'lon *n.* **1.** claw esp. of bird of prey. **2.** cards left after deal; last part of dividend-coupon sheet, entitling to new sheet on presentation. **3.** shoulder of bolt against which key presses in shooting it; ogee moulding. **4.** Hence (-)~ED² (-nd) *a.* [ME, f. OF, = heel, f. Rom. *talo -onis* f. L (see foll.)]

tä'l|us¹ *n.* (*pl.* ~i *pr.* -ī). (Anat.) ankle(-bone). [L, = ankle, heel]

tä'lus² *n.* slope of wall that tapers to top or rests against bank; (Geol.) sloping mass of fragments at foot of cliff. [F, of unkn. orig.]

täm *n.* tam-o'-shanter. [abbr.]

TAM *abbr.* television audience measurement.

tä'mable Var. of TAMEABLE.

tama'le (-ah'-) *n.* Mexican food of seasoned meat and maize flour steamed or baked in maize husks. [f. Mex. Sp. *tamal*, pl. *tamales*]

tamä'ndua *n.* arboreal ant-eater (*Tamandua*

tetradactyla) of Central & S. America. [Port., f. Tupi *tamanduá*]

tä'manoir (-nwär) *n.* great ant-eater (*Myrmecophaga jubata*) of S. America. [F, f. Carib *tamanoâ* (cf. prec.)]

tä'maräck *n.* Amer. larch, esp. *Larix laricina*; its wood. [Amer. Ind.]

tä'marin *n.* S. Amer. marmoset of genus *Leontocebus*. [F, f. Carib]

tä'marind *n.* (tropical tree, *Tamarindus indica*, with) fruit whose acid pulp is used in making cooling or medicinal drinks etc. [f. med. L *tamarindus* f. Arab. *tamr-hindī* DATE¹ of India]

tä'marisk *n.* plant of genus *Tamarix*, esp. **common** or **French** ~, evergreen shrub (*T. gallica*) with feathery branches, tiny leaves, and small white or pink flowers, often planted near sea. [ME, f. LL *tamariscus*, L *tamarix*]

tä'mbour (-oor) *n.*, & *v.t.* **1.** *n.* drum; circular frame on which silk etc. is stretched to be embroidered, material so embroidered; (Archit.) cylindrical stone in shaft of column, circular part of various structures, lobby with ceiling and folding doors in church porch etc. to obviate draught; drum-fish or globe-fish; sloping buttress or projection in fives-court etc. **2.** *v.t.* decorate, embroider, (material, or abs.) on tambour. [F, f. *tabour* TABOR]

tämbour'a (-oor'a) *n.* Indian stringed instrument used as drone. [f. Arab. *ṭanbūra*]

tä'mbourin (-ber-) *n.* long narrow drum used in Provence; (music for) dance accompanied by this. [F, dim. of TAMBOUR]

tämbouri'ne (-berē'n) *n.* **1.** small musical instrument made of wooden or metal hoop with parchment stretched over one side and loose jingling metal discs. **2.** Afr. pigeon with tambourine-like note. [f. as prec.]

täme *v.t.*, & *a.* **1.** *v.t.* make gentle and tractable, domesticate, (wild animal, bird, etc.); subdue, curb, reduce to submission, humble, (person, spirit, courage, ardour, etc.); hence ~'LESS (ml : literary) *a.*, (-)**tä'mer¹** *n.* **2.** *a.* made tractable, domesticated, not wild; (joc., of person) kept available for one's domestic or private use; ~ **cat**, (fig.) person tolerated as useful hanger-on. **3.** * (Of land or plant) cultivated, produced by cultivation. **4.** submissive, spiritless, inert, unexciting, insipid, (*tame acquiescence, scenery, description*). **5.** Hence ~'LY² (-mlī) *adv.*, ~'NESS (-mn-) *n.* [v. f. a., f. OE *tam*, = OHG *zan*, ON *tamr* f. Gmc *tamaz* f. IE *dom*-]

tä'meable (-ma-) *a.* capable of being tamed; hence **täme**ABI'LITY (-ma-), ~NESS (-heln-), *ns.* [f. prec. + -ABLE]

Tä'mil *n.* & *a.* (language or member) of a Dravidian people inhabiting S. India and Sri Lanka; hence **Tami̇'li̇an** *a.* [f. native name *Tamil*, cogn. w. DRAVIDIAN]

***Tä'mmany̆** *n.* organization of Democratic party notorious in 19th c. for political corruption; hence ~ISM (3) *n.* [orig. name of benevolent society in New York, f. 17th-c. Indian chief friendly to whites]

täm-o'-shä'nter, (colloq.) **tä'mmy̆**, *ns.* round woollen or cloth cap fitting closely round brows but large and full above. [f. hero of Burns's *Tam o' Shanter*]

tämp *v.t.* pack (blast-hole) full of clay etc. to get full force of explosion, whence ~'ING¹ (3) *n.*; ram down (road material etc.); hence ~'ER¹ (1, 2) *n.* [perh. back-form. f. *tampin* (var. of TAMPION) taken as = *tamping*]

tä'mpän *n.* venomous S. Afr. tick. [perh. f. Tswana]

tä'mper *v.i.* & *n.* ~ **with**, meddle with, make unauthorized changes in (will, MS, etc.), exert secret or corrupt influence upon, bribe, **2.** Hence ~ER¹ *n.*, ~-PROOF² *a.* [var. of TEMPER¹]

tä'mpion *n.* wooden stopper for muzzle of gun; plug e.g. for top of organ-pipe. [ME, f. F *tampon*, nasalized var. of *tapon* f. Frank. **tappo* (as TAP¹)]

tä'mpon *n.*, & *v.t.* **1.** *n.* plug used to stop haemorrhage or absorb secretions. **2.** *v.t.* plug (wound etc.) with tampon. [F; see prec.]

tampona'de, tä'mponage, *ns.* use of tampon for wound etc. [f. prec. + -ADE, -AGE]

tä'm-täm *n.* large metal gong. [Hindi; see TOM-TOM]

tän[1] *v.* (-nn-), *n.*, & *a.* **1.** *v.t.* convert (raw hide) into leather by soaking in liquid containing tannic acid or by use of mineral salts etc., whence ∿'**nable** *a.*, ∿'**nage** (3), ∿'**ner**[1], ∿'**nery** (2, 3), *ns.* **2.** *v.t.* & *i.* make or become brown by exposure to sun; (sl.) beat, thrash. **3.** Hence ∿'**ning**[1] (1) *n.* **4.** *n.* bark of oak or other tree bruised and used for tanning hides (FLOWERs *of tan*); colour of this, yellowish-brown; bronze of sunburnt skin; **the** ∿, (sl.) (1) the circus, (2) floor of riding-school; (**spent**) ∿, tan from which tannic acid has been extracted, used for covering roads etc. **5.** ∿-**liquor, -ooze, -pickle,** liquid used in tanning; ∿-**pit,** ∿-**vat,** (for containing tan-liquor); ∿-**yard,** tannery. **6.** *a.* of tan colour; BLACK[1] *and Tans.* [OE *tannian,* prob. f. med. L *tan(n)are,* perh. f. Celt.]

tän[2] *abbr.* tangent.

tä'nager *n.* Amer. bird of family Thraupidae, the males mostly with brilliant plumage. [f. mod. L *tanagra* f. Tupi *tangara*]

Tanagra (tä'năg-, tanä'g-) *n.* ∿ (**statuette, figurine**), terracotta statuette found in ancient tombs near Tanagra. [∿, town in ancient Greece]

‖**T. & A.V.R.** *abbr.* Territorial and Army Volunteer Reserve.

tä'ndem *adv.* & *n.* **1.** *adv.* (Of horses in harness) one behind another; **drive** ∿ (with horses so harnessed). **2.** *n.* (carriage with) horses tandem; bicycle or tricycle with seats for two or more one behind another; group of two or more persons, machines, etc., with one behind or following another; **in** ∿, thus arranged. [L, = at length (of time), used punningly]

tä'ndoor *n.* (Ind.) clay oven; ∿**i** *n.*, food cooked over charcoal in tandoor. [Hind.]

täng[1] *n.*, & *v.t.* **1.** *n.* projecting point; part of chisel, knife, sword, etc., by which blade etc. is held firm in handle. **2.** strong taste or flavour or smell, characteristic property, whence ∿'y[2] *a.* **3.** *v.t.* furnish or affect with a tang. [ME, f. ON *tange* point, tang of knife]

täng[2] *n.* large coarse seaweed, esp. of genus *Fucus.* [f. Scand., = Norw. & Da. *tang,* Icel. *tháng*]

täng[3] *v.* & *n.* **1.** *v.t.* & *i.* ring, clang, sound loudly. **2.** *n.* tanging sound. [imit.]

tä'ngelö (-nj-) *n.* (*pl.* ∿s). hybrid of tangerine and grapefruit. [f. TANGERINE + POMELO]

tä'ngent (-nj-) *a.* & *n.* **1.** *a.* (Of line or surface) meeting a curved line or surface at a point and having same direction there, thus touching it but not (usually) intersecting it; (of surface) meeting a curved surface along a curve or line of such points; hence **tä'ngENCY** (-nj-) *n.* **2.** *n.* line etc. that is tangent (**fly, go, off at a** ∿, diverge impetuously from matter in hand or from normal line of thought or conduct); ∿ **of an angle,** (Math.) ratio of the perpendicular subtending it in any right-angled triangle to the base; ∿ **galvanometer** (for which strength of current measured is proportional to tangent of angle of deflection). **3.** upright piece that strikes string of clavichord. [f. L *tangere* touch; see -ENT]

täng̈e'ntial (-një'nshal) *a.* of or along a tangent; divergent; peripheral; hence ∿LY[2] *adv.* [f. prec. + -IAL]

Tängeri'ne (-njerē'n) *a.* & *n.* **1.** (native) of Tangier. **2.** t∿ (**orange**), small flattened kind, its deep orange-yellow colour. [f. *Tanger, Tangier* + -INE[1]]

tä'nghin (-nggĭn) *n.* Madagascar tree, the large purple fruit of which has poisonous kernel formerly used in ordeals; this poison. [F, f. Malagasy *tangena*]

tä'ng|ible (-nj-) *a.* perceptible by touch; definite, clearly intelligible, not elusive or visionary, (*tangible advantages, scheme, distinction*); (Law) corporeal; hence ∿IBI'LITY, ∿**ibleNESS** (-beln-), *ns.*, ∿**ibLY**[2] *adv.* [F, or f. LL *tangibilis* (*tangere* touch; see -IBLE)]

tä'ngle[1] (-nggel) *v.* & *n.* **1.** *v.t.* & *i.* intertwine (threads, hair, etc.), become involved, in confused mass; entrap, entangle; complicate (*a tangled affair*); become involved (esp. in conflict) *with.* **2.** *n.* confused mass of intertwined threads etc.; confused state (*skein, business, is in a tangle*); hence **tä'ngly**[2] (-ngg-) *a.* [ME var. of obs. *tagle,* of uncert. orig.]

tä'ngle[2] (-nggel) *n.* = TANG[2]; leathery seaweed of genus *Laminaria.* [prob. f. Norw. *taangel* f. ON *thöngull*]

tä'ngō[1] (-nggō) *n.* (*pl.* ∿s), & *v.i.* **1.** *n.* S. Amer. slow ballroom dance of Central Afr. origin; music for it. **2.** *v.i.* dance the tango. [Amer. Sp.]

tä'ngō[2] *n.* tangerine colour. [abbr. after prec.; see -O]

tä'ngräm (-ngg-) *n.* Chinese puzzle square cut into seven pieces to be combined into various figures. [19th c.; orig. unkn.]

tanh (thǎn, tǎnsh, tǎnä'ch) *abbr.* hyperbolic tangent.

tä'nist *n.* (Hist.) successor-apparent to Celtic chief, usu. most vigorous adult of his kin, chosen by election; hence ∿RY (5) *n.* [f. Ir. & Gael. *tánaiste* heir]

tänk *n.*, & *v.i.* **1.** *n.* large metal, wooden, glass etc., vessel for liquid, gas, etc.; part of locomotive tender containing water for boiler; (Ind.) storage-pond, artificial lake, reservoir for water. **2.** (Mil.) armoured motor vehicle carrying guns and moving on Caterpillar tracks. **3.** ∿-**car,** railway truck with large tank for carrying liquids; ∿ **drama,** sensational drama in which water is used for representing rescue from drowning etc.; ∿-**engine,** railway engine carrying fuel and water receptacles on its own frame, not in tender; ∿ **farm,** area where petroleum is stored in tanks; ∿-**farming,** growing plants in tanks of water without soil; ∿ **top,** short tight sleeveless scoop-necked upper garment; ∿-**trap,** obstacle able to stop a military tank. **4.** Hence ∿'FUL (2) *n.* **5.** *v.i.* ∿ (**up**), fill tank of vehicle etc., (sl.) drink heavily. [f. Gujarati *tānkh* etc., perh. f. Skr. *tadāga* pond]

tä'nka *n.* Japanese poem in five lines and 31 syllables giving complete picture of event or mood. [Jap.]

tä'nkage *n.* (charge for) storage in tanks; cubic content of tank(s); kind of fertilizer got from refuse bones etc. [f. TANK + -AGE]

tä'nkard *n.* large one-handled drinking-vessel usu. of silver or pewter and often with cover; contents of, amount held by, this (*a tankard of ale*). [ME, of unkn. orig.; cf. MDu. *tanckaert*]

tä'nker *n.* ship or aircraft with tank(s) for carrying liquids, esp. mineral oils, in bulk; road vehicle with large tank for conveying milk etc. in bulk. [f. TANK + -ER[1]]

tä'nner. See TAN[1].

tä'nn|ic *a.* of tan; ∿**ic acid,** tannin; so ∿ATE[1] (3) *n.* [f. F *tannique* (as foll.; see -IC)]

tä'nnin *n.* any of several astringent substances got from oak-galls and various tree-barks, used in preparing leather and in making ink etc. [f. F *tanin* (as TAN[1]; see -IN)]

Tännoy *n.* (P) type of public-address loudspeaker system. [20th c.; orig. uncert.]

tä'nrec. See TENREC.

tä'nsy (-zī) *n.* herb of genus *Tanacetum,* esp. common species with yellow flowers and finely-toothed bitter aromatic leaves formerly used in medicine and cookery. [ME, f. OF *tanesie* f. med. L f. Gk *athanasia* immortality (a- not, *thanatos* death)]

tä'ntalīte *n.* rare heavy black mineral, principal source of tantalum. [f. G & Sw. *tantalit* (as TANTALUM; see -ITE[1])]

tä'ntalīz|e, -īs|e (-īz) *v.t.* torment, tease, (person etc.) by sight or promise of desired thing withheld or kept just out of reach; hence ∿A'TION *n.* [f. as TANTALUS + -IZE]

tä'ntalum *n.* rare hard white metallic element highly resistant to heat and to action of acids; hence **täntä'l**IC *a.* [f. as foll. w. ref. to its non-absorbent quality; see -IUM]

tă′ntalus *n.* spirit-stand in which decanters are locked up but visible; wood ibis. [L, f. Gk *Tantalos* mythical king of Phrygia, condemned to stand in Tartarus surrounded by inaccessible water and fruit]

tă′ntamount *pred. a.* equivalent *to* (*his message was tantamount to a flat refusal*). [f. obs. v. f. It. *tanto montare* amount to so much]

tănti′vў *n.* & *a.* (arch.) **1.** *n.* hunting cry; swift movement, gallop, rush; (*T~*; Hist.) English High Churchman or Tory of 1660-88. **2.** *a.* swift; of Tantivies. [perh. imit. of hoof-beats]

tant pis (tahṅ pē′) *adv.* so much the worse. [F]

tă′ntr|a *n.* each of a class of Hindu or Buddhist mystical and magical writings; hence ~ic *a.*, ~ism (3), ~ist (2), *ns.* [Skr., = loom, groundwork, doctrine (*tan* stretch)]

tă′ntrum *n.* outburst of bad temper or petulance (*is in a tantrum; went into her tantrums*). [18th c., of unkn. orig.]

Taoiseach (tē′shaχ) *n.* Prime Minister of Irish Republic. [Ir., = chief, leader]

Tao|ism (tah′ō-, tow′-) *n.* religious doctrine orig. based on writings attributed to Laoze, Chinese philosopher (*c.* 500 BC); hence ~ist (2) *n.* [f. Chin. *dao* (right) way + -ISM]

tăp¹ *n.*, & *v.t.* (-pp-). **1.** *n.* device through which liquid or gas flows from pipe or vessel in controllable manner; plug used to close opening in cask; liquor of a particular brewing etc. w. ref. to quality; taproom; act of tapping telephone etc.; **on ~**, ready to be drawn, (fig.) ready for immediate use, (of government bonds etc.) freely available. **2.** instrument for cutting thread of female screw. **3.** ~ **bill, issue,** etc., (available on tap); ~**-borer,** auger for boring tapering hole in cask; ~**′room** (in which liquor on tap is sold and drunk); ~**-root,** chief descending root of plant; ~**-water** (esp. supplied through pipes to taps in house etc.). **4.** *v.t.* furnish (cask) with tap; pierce (cask etc.) to let out liquid, let out thus; (Surg.) release (fluid accumulated in body), operate thus on (person); draw sap from (tree) by cutting into it; penetrate to, get into communication with, establish trade etc. in, (district etc.); apply to, solicit, (person *for* subscription etc.); broach (subject); (usu. secretly) draw current from (telegraph or telephone wires etc.) to detect message; make female screw-thread in. [OE *tæppian* v. t.) *tæppa*, = OHG *zapho*, ON *tappi* f. Gmc **tappon*]

tăp² *v.* (-pp-) & *n.* **1.** *v.t.* strike lightly (*tap the door with your knuckles, the pavement with your stick; tapped his forehead knowingly*); cause (thing) to strike lightly *against* etc. (*tapped his stick against the window*); **apply leather to (heel or sole of shoe). **2.** *v.i.* strike gentle blow, rap, (*at* or *on door etc.*). **3.** *n.* light blow, rap; sound of this (*heard a tap at the door*); **(in *pl.*, usu. treated as *sing.*) signal on drum or bugle for lights to be put out in soldiers' quarters, similar signal at military funeral; ~**dance, -dancer, -dancing,** (on stage, characterized by rhythmical tapping of the feet). [ME *tappe*, imit., perh. thr. F *taper*]

ta′pa (tah′-) *n.* bark of paper-mulberry tree, used in Pacific islands for clothes, mats, etc.; cloth made from it. [Polynesian]

tāpe *n.*, & *v.t.* **1.** *n.* narrow woven cotton etc. strip used for tying up parcels or papers, fastening or labelling garments, etc., (RED *tape*); such strip stretched across racing-track at finishing-line (**breast the ~,** win race); narrow band of strong fabric rotating on pulleys etc. in machinery; (**adhesive**) ~, strip of paper, transparent film, etc., coated with adhesive for fastening packages etc.; continuous strip of paper on which messages are printed in tape-machine; (**magnetic**) ~, impregnated or coated plastic strip or ribbon for electromagnetic recording and reproduction of signals; (**paper**) ~, (esp. PUNCH²ed) long strip of paper; tape-measure; tape recording; tapeworm. **2.** ~**-machine** (for receiving and recording telegraph messages); ~**-measure,** strip of tape or thin flexible metal marked for use as distance--measure, and often coiled up in cylindrical case; ~ **recorder,** apparatus for recording sounds etc. on magnetic tape and afterwards reproducing them; ~**-record** *v.t.*, ~ **recording,** (make) such record or reproduction; ~**′worm,** tapelike many-jointed cestode of genus *Taenia* etc. parasitic in alimentary canal in man and most vertebrates. **3.** Hence ~**′LESS,** ~**′LIKE,** (-pl-) *adjs.* **4.** *v.t.* furnish, tie up, with tape; join sections of (book) with bands of tape; record on magnetic tape; fasten with adhesive tape; ||**have** person or thing ~**d,** (sl.) have summed him up, fully understand it. [OE *tæppa, -e,* of unkn. orig.]

tā′per *n., a.,* & *v.* **1.** *n.* slender candle, wick coated with wax etc. (~**-stick,** holder for this). **2.** *a.* (esp. poet. or rhet.) growing gradually smaller towards one end like cone or pyramid (*taper fingers*). **3.** *v.t.* & *i.* ~ (**off**), make or become taper, (cause to) grow gradually less, (*the upper part tapers* or *is tapered* (*off*) *to a point*). [OE *tapur, -or, -er* wax candle, f. L PAPYRUS, whose pith was used for candle-wicks]

tă′pĕstr|ў *n.* thick hand-woven textile fabric in which design is formed by weft stitches across parts of warp, used for covering walls, furniture, etc.; machine--made fabric imitating or resembling this; hence (-)~ied² (-rĭd) *a.* [ME, alt. f *tapissery* f OF *tapisserie* (*tapissier* tapestry-worker or *tapisser* to carpet, f. TAPIS; see -RY)]

tăpiŏ′ca *n.* starchy substance in hard white grains got from cassava and used for puddings etc. [f. Tupi--Guarani *tipioca* (*tipi* dregs, *og, ok* squeeze out)]

tā′pir (-ĕr, -ēr) *n.* hoofed piglike mammal of tropical America and Malaya, with short proboscis, allied to rhinoceros; hence ~OID *a.* & *n.* [f. Tupi *tapira*]

tapis (tă′pē) *n.* **on the ~,** (of subject) under consideration or discussion. [ME, a kind of cloth, f. OF *tapiz* f. Rom. **tappetium* f. LL f. Gk *tapētion* dim. of *tapēs -ētos* tapestry]

tapō′tement (-tm-) *n.* (Med.) percussing as part of massage treatment. [F (*tapoter* to tap; see -MENT)]

tă′ppet *n.* arm, collar, cam, etc., used in machinery to impart intermittent motion; ~ **loom** (in which hammers are worked by tappets); ~ **rod** (carrying tappet, e.g. to open or close valve). [app. f TAP² + -ET¹]

tă′ppit *a.* (Sc.) topped; ~ **hen,** crested hen, large drinking-vessel with knob on lid. [= *topped*, p.p. of TOP²]

tă′pster *n.* person employed at a bar to draw and serve liquor. [OE *tæppestre,* orig. fem. (as TAP¹, -STER)]

tapu (tah′pŏŏ) *n.* & *a* (NZ.) = TABOO. [Maori]

tär¹ *n.,* & *v.t.* (-rr-) **1.** *n.* thick dark inflammable liquid got by dry distillation of wood, coal, etc., and used as preservative of timber and iron, antiseptic, etc.; similar substance formed in combustion of tobacco etc.; ***beat the ~ out of,** (colloq.) knock the STUFFING out of; **a touch of the ~-brush,** admixture of Negro or Indian blood as shown by colour of skin; **~′heel, native of N. Carolina; ~ **macadam,** road--materials of stone or slag bound with tar; ~**-paper,** tar-coated thick paper as building-material; ~**-seal,** (NZ & Austral.) surface (a road) with tar macadam, road thus surfaced; ~**-water,** cold infusion of tar formerly used as medicine. **2.** *v.t.* cover with tar; ~ **and feather,** smear with tar and then cover with feathers as punishment; ~**red with the same brush** or **stick,** having the same faults. [OE *te(o)ru,* = MLG *ter(e),* ON *tjara* f. Gmc **terw- (*trew-* TREE)]

tär² *n.* (colloq.) sailor. [abbr. of TARPAULIN]

tă′r(r)adĭddle *n.* (colloq.) petty lie; pretentious nonsense. [18th c.; cf. DIDDLE]

taraki′hi (tārakē′hē), **tĕrakihi** (tĕrakē′), *n.* (NZ). species of morwong widely used as food. [Maori]

tărantă′ss *n.* springless four-wheeled Russian vehicle. [f. Russ. *tarantas*]

tărantĕ′lla, -ĕ′lle, *n.* (music for) rapid whirling S. Ital. dance once held to be a cure for or effect of

tarantism. [(F *tarantelle* f.) It. *tarantella* dim. f. as foll.]

tǎ′rantism *n.* (Hist.) dancing mania, esp. that originating in S. Italy among those who (thought they) had been bitten by the tarantula. [f. mod. L *tarantismus*, It. *tarantismo* (*Taranto* in S. Italy f. L *Tarentum*; see -ISM)]

tarǎ′ntūla *n.* large black spider of S. Europe whose bite was formerly held to cause tarantism; large hairy tropical spider. [med. L, f. It. *tarantola* (as prec.)]

tarǎ′xacum *n.* herb of genus *Taraxacum*, e.g. dandelion; drug prepared from dried roots of dandelion. [med. L, f. Arab. *ṭaraḵṣaḵūk* f. Pers. *talḵ* bitter + *chakūk* purslane]

tarbōō′sh *n.* cap like fez, worn alone or as part of turban. [f. Egypt. Arab. *ṭarbūš*, ult. f. Pers. *sar-būš* head cover]

Tárdenoi′sian (-z-) *a.* & *n.* (Archaeol.) (of) a mesolithic culture using small flint implements. [f. *Tardenois* in NE France, where remains of it were found, + -IAN]

tǎ′digrāde *a.* & *n.* (Zool.). **1.** slow-moving (animal). **2.** (minute aquatic arthropod) of order Tardigrada. [F, or f. L *tardigradus* (*tardus* slow, *gradi* walk)]

tǎ′r|d|ẙ *a.* slow-moving, slow, sluggish; late, coming or done late, (*tardy retribution, amends, reform*, *to school); (of person etc.) reluctant, hanging back; hence ∼ILY² *adv.*, ∼iNESS *n.* [f. F *tardif -ive* f. Rom. *tardivus f. L *tardus* slow; see -IVE]

tāre¹ *n.* vetch, esp. as corn-weed or fodder; (Bibl., in *pl.* in Matt. 13:25, 36) an injurious corn-weed. [ME, of unkn. orig.]

tāre² *n.*, & *v.t.* **1.** *n.* allowance made for weight of box etc. in which goods are packed; weight of motor vehicle without fuel etc.; ∼ **and tret**, arithmetical rule for computing tare etc. **2.** *v.t.* ascertain weight of (box etc.). [ME f. F, = deficiency, tare, f. med. L *tara* f. Arab. *ṭarḥa* what is rejected (*ṭaraḥa* reject)]

tāre³. See TEAR¹.

tárge *n.* (arch.) = foll. 4. [ME f. OF; see foll.]

tar′ġet (-g-) *n.* **1.** circular stuffed pad with concentric circles painted on surface as mark in archery; similar usu. rectangular mark for firearms; anything that is fired at or made an objective of warlike operations; substance bombarded with particles, e.g. to generate X-rays; (fig.) objective, (minimum) result aimed at, (*export, fuel, savings, target; our target date is next July*); (fig.) person or thing serving as object *for* (scorn etc.). **2.** *circular railway signal e.g. at a switch. **3.** neck and breast of lamb as joint. **4.** shield, buckler, esp. small round one. **5.** ∼**-card** (coloured like target, for keeping archer's score); ∼**practice** (in shooting at target). [ME, dim. of ME and OF *targe* f. Frank. *targa shield, cogn. w. OE *targe, -a*, OHG *zarga*, ON *targa*]

Tár′gum *n.* any of various ancient Aramaic paraphrases or interpretations of the Hebrew scriptures; hence ∼IST (3) *n.* [f. Chald. *trgūm* interpretation (*trgēm* interpret)]

tǎ′riff *n.*, & *v.t.* **1.** *n.* list of duties or customs to be paid on imports or exports; such duties collectively; law imposing these; duty on particular class of goods; **preferential** ∼, reduced duties on imports from favoured country; **retaliatory** ∼, import duties levied by a nation to balance foreign duties imposed on its exports; ∼ **reform**, (Hist.) removal of inequalities etc. in tariff, esp. with general aim of ||increasing or *decreasing import duties; ∼ **wall**, tariff-created national trade barrier. **2.** list of charges (*railway, postal, hotel, tariff*); standard charges agreed between insurers etc. **3.** *v.t.* make tariff of duties on (goods). [f. F *tarif* f. It. *tariffa* f. Turk. *tarife* f. Arab. *ta'rīf(a)* ('*arrafa* notify)]

tar′latan *n.* thin stiff open kind of muslin. [f. F *tarlatane*, earlier *tarn-*; prob. of Ind. orig.]

Tár′măc, t-, *n.*, & *v.t.* (-ck-). **1.** *n.* (P) = TAR¹ *macadam*; part of airfield surface made of Tarmac. **2.** *v.t.* apply Tarmac to. [abbr.]

tǎrn *n.* small mountain lake. [ME *terne, tarne* f. ON **tarnu, tjörn*]

***tár′nal, *tárnā′tion,** *adjs.* & *advs.* (sl.) = DAMNED 2, 3. [dial. pr. of ETERNAL, DAMNATION]

tǎr′nish *v.* & *n.* **1.** *v.t.* lessen or destroy the lustre of (*has been tarnished by damp*; (fig.) *a tarnished reputation*); hence ∼ABLE *a.* **2.** *v.i.* lose lustre (*will tarnish if exposed*). **3.** *n.* loss of lustre, blemish, stain; film of colour formed on exposed surface of mineral. [f. F *ternir* (*terne* dark); see -ISH²]

tǎr′ō *n.* (*pl.* ∼s). tropical plant (*Colocasia esculenta*) of arum family with tuberous root used as food esp. in Pacific islands. [Polynesian]

tǎ′rŏc, tǎ′rōt (-ō), *n.* **1.** (in *sing.* or *pl.*) game played with pack of 78 cards used also for fortune-telling. **2.** card, esp. one of 22 trumps, in this. [f. It. *tarocchi*, *tarot*, of unkn. orig.]

tárp *n.* (US & Austral. colloq.) tarpaulin. [abbr.]

tár′pǎn *n.* wild horse of central Asia. [Kirghiz Tartar]

tárpau′lin *n.* waterproof cloth esp. of tarred canvas; sheet of this as covering; sailor's tarred or oilskin hat; (arch.) sailor. [prob. f. TAR¹ + PALL¹ + -ING¹ (3)]

Tárpei′an (-pē′an) *a.* ∼ **rock**, cliff from which ancient-Roman criminals were hurled. [f. L *Tarpeius* (*Tarpeia*, who was said to be buried at foot of the rock) + -AN]

tár′pon *n.* large silvery game-fish (*Megalops atlanticus*) common in Gulf of Mexico. [f. Du. *tarpoen*; orig. unkn.]

tǎ′rradiddle. See TARADIDDLE.

tǎ′rragon *n.* plant (*Artemisia dracunculus*) allied to wormwood, with leaves used for flavouring salads etc. and in making a vinegar. [= med. L f. med. Gk *tarkhōn*, perh. thr. Arab. f. Gk *drakōn* dragon]

Tárragō′na *n.* Spanish wine like port. [∼ in Spain]

tarrā′s. See TRASS.

tǎ′rriance *n.* (arch.) tarrying; sojourn.

tár′rẙ¹ *a.* of, like, smeared with, tar. [f. TAR¹ + -Y²]

tǎ′rrẙ² *v.* (literary). **1.** *v.i.* remain, stay, lodge, (*at, in*, etc.); wait (*for*); delay in coming or appearing, be late. **2.** *v.t.* wait for. [ME; orig. uncert.]

tár′sal. See TARSUS.

tár′sia *n.* = INTARSIA. [It.]

tár′sier *n.* small large-eyed arboreal nocturnal E. Ind. animal like lemur. [F (as foll., from structure of foot)]

tár′s|us *n.* (*pl.* ∼i *pr.* -ī). **1.** collection of bones between lower leg and metatarsus, ankle; shank of bird's leg; (Entom.) terminal segment of limb. **2.** plate of connective tissue in eyelid. **3.** Hence ∼AL *a.*, ∼I-, ∼O-, *comb. forms.* [mod. L, f. Gk *tarsos* flat of the foot, rim of eyelid]

tárt¹ *a.* sharp-tasting, acid; cutting, biting, (*a tart rejoinder*); hence ∼′LY² *adv.*, ∼′NESS *n.* [OE *teart*, of unkn. orig.]

tárt² *n.* & *v.* **1.** *n.* ||pie containing fruit or sweet filling (*apple, cherry, tart*); piece of pastry with jam etc. on top; so ∼′LET *n.* **2.** (sl.) girl or woman, esp. of immoral character; hence ∼′Y² *a.* **3.** *v.t.* & *i.* (colloq.) ∼ **up**, dress up like a tart (sense 2), deck gaudily, (fig.) smarten up. [ME f. OF *tarte*, = med. L *tarta*, of unkn. orig.; sense 2 prob. abbr. of *sweetheart*]

tár′tan¹ *n.* & *a.* woollen fabric with stripes of various colours crossing at right angles esp. as worn by Scottish Highlanders; (other fabric) so striped; (Scottish plaid with) distinctive pattern of a clan. [perh. f. OF *tertaine, tiretaine*]

tár′tan² *n.* lateen-sailed single-masted vessel used in Mediterranean. [f. F *tartane* f. It. *tartana*, perh. f. Arab. *ṭarīda*]

tár′tar¹ *n.* **1.** pink or red deposit of acid potassium tartrate from completely fermented wine, forming hard crust on side of cask, whence ∼IZE (5) *v.t.*; ∼ **emetic**, potassium antimony tartrate used as mordant and in medicine (formerly as emetic); CREAM¹ *of tartar*. **2.** incrustation of saliva, calcium phosphate, etc., forming on the teeth. [ME, f. med. L f. med. Gk *tartaron*]

Tăr′tar² *a.* & *n.* **1.** (native) of Central Asia E. of Caspian Sea; (member) of a group of peoples including Turks, Mongols, etc.; ∼ **fox, corsac;** t∼ **sauce** (of mayonnaise, chopped gherkins, etc.); so **Tărtār′ian** *a.* **2.** *n.* Turkic language of Tartars. **3.** violent-tempered or intractable or savage person (catch a ∼, meet with person who is unexpectedly more than a match for one). [ME *tartre* f. OF *Tartare* or f. med. L *Tartarus*]

tăr′tăre *a.* ∼ **sauce,** = TARTAR² *sauce*. [F, = prec.]

tărtă′ric *a.* (Chem.) of TARTAR¹ 1; ∼ **acid,** organic acid present in numerous plants, esp. unripe grapes. [f. F *tartarique* f. med. L *tartarum*; see TARTAR¹, -IC]

Tăr′tarus *n.* (Gk Myth.) abyss below Hades where Titans were confined; place of punishment in Hades; so **Tărtār′ean** *a.* [L, f. Gk *Tartaros*]

tăr′trăte *n.* salt of tartaric acid. [F (as TARTAR¹, -ATE¹)]

Tărtu′f(f)|e (-ōō′f) *n.* religious hypocrite; hence ∼IAN *a.*, ∼ISM (3) *n.* [character in Molière]

Tăr′zan *n.* man of great agility and powerful physique. [name of white man reared by African apes, in stories by E. R. Burroughs, Amer. writer d. 1950]

Tas. *abbr.* Tasmania.

task (tah-) *n.,* & *v.t.* **1.** *n.* piece of work imposed; lesson to be learnt at school; piece of work voluntarily undertaken (*undertook the task of classification*); **take person to** ∼, accuse him of fault, rebuke him *for* (doing); ∼ **force,** ∼ **group,** specially organized unit for a special task; ∼′**master,** ∼′**mistress,** one who imposes task or burden. **2.** *v.t.* assign task to; exact labour from, put strain upon, tax, (person's powers, intellect, etc.). [ME, f. ONF *tasque* = OF *tasche* f. med. L *tasca,* perh. f. *taxa* f. L *taxare* TAX¹]

Tăsmā′nian (-z-) *a.* & *n.* (inhabitant or native) of Tasmania; ∼ **devil,** savage-looking nocturnal carnivorous marsupial now confined to Tasmania; ∼ **wolf,** wolflike nocturnal carnivorous marsupial now confined to Tasmania. [f. *Tasmania* f. A. J. *Tasman,* Du. navigator d. 1659 who discovered the island, + -IA¹, + -AN]

tăss¹ *n.* (Sc.) small draught (*of brandy* etc.). [ME, f. OF *tasse* f. Arab. *ṭāsa* basin f. Pers. *tast*]

Tăss² *n.* telegraphic news-agency of the Soviet Union. [f. initials of Russ. title]

tă′ssel¹ *n.* & *v.* (‖-ll-). **1.** *n.* tuft of loosely hanging threads or cords as ornament for cushion, cap, etc.; tassel-like head of some plants, esp. staminate inflorescence at top of maize stalk. **2.** *v.t.* furnish with tassel. **3.** *v.i.* *(Of maize etc.)* form tassels. [ME, f. OF *tas(s)el* clasp, of unkn. orig.]

tă′ssel² *n.* small piece of stone, wood, etc., supporting end of beam or joist. [OF, f. pop. L *tassellus* f. L *taxillus* small die & *tessella* (see TESSELLATE)]

tă′ssie *n.* (Sc.) small cup. [f. TASS¹ + -IE]

tāste¹ *v.* **1.** *v.t.* learn flavour of (food etc., or abs.) by taking it into the mouth (*do taste this cheese*); examine (teas, wines, etc.) thus. **2.** (esp. w. neg.) eat or drink (even a) small portion of (*has not tasted food for days*). **3.** perceive the flavour of (*can taste nothing when you have a cold; fancy I taste garlic*). **4.** (arch.) relish, enjoy, (*cannot taste a joke against himself*). **5.** experience, have experience of, (*shall not taste death; has never tasted success*). **6.** Hence ∼′ABLE (-ta-) *a.* **7.** *v.i.* have specified flavour (*tastes sour*); ∼ **of,** (of food etc., or fig.) have flavour or smack of (*tastes of mint*), (arch.) = sense 2 or 5. [ME, = touch, taste, f. OF *taster* touch, try, taste, f. Rom. *taxtare,* perh. f. L *tangere* touch + *gustare* taste]

tāste² *n.* **1.** sensation caused in tongue etc. by contact of some soluble things, flavour, (*cannot endure the taste of onions; white of egg has no taste*); **bad** or **nasty** ∼ **in the mouth,** (fig.) unpleasant after-feeling. **2.** faculty of perceiving this sensation; ∼-**bud,** group of cells in epithelium of tongue etc. through which this faculty operates. **3.** small portion (*of* food, or fig.) taken as sample; slight sensation or experience thus received (**a** ∼ *of the whip* etc., enough to show how it feels). **4.**

liking, predilection, (*has no taste for sweet things; a taste for drawing, scenery, argument; is not to my taste; tastes differ; there is no accounting for tastes*); add pepper, garnish, **to** ∼, in the amount that gives the desired result. **5.** faculty of discerning and enjoying beauty or other excellence esp. in art and literature, or appropriateness of conduct, (*a man of taste; good, bad, taste*). **6.** disposition or execution of work of art, choice of language, conduct, etc., dictated by or seen in the light of this faculty, (*composed in admirable taste; the remark was in bad taste*). [ME, f. OF *tast* (*taster;* see prec.)]

tā′steful (-tf-) *a.* (Of person, work of art, etc.) having, showing, done in, good taste; hence ∼LY² *adv.,* ∼NESS *n.* [f. prec. + -FUL]

tā′stelèss (-tl-) *a.* having no flavour; uninteresting; lacking artistic taste; (of language, conduct, etc.) not in good taste; hence ∼LY² *adv.,* ∼NESS *n.* [f. TASTE² + -LESS]

tā′ster *n.* In vbl senses; person employed to judge teas, wines, etc., by taste (COPY¹-*taster*); (Hist.) person employed to taste food before it was touched by his employer, esp. as precaution against poison; small shallow cup used by wine-taster; instrument for extracting small sample from within a cheese. [ME, f. AF *tastour,* OF *tastour* (*taster;* see TASTE¹)]

tā′st|ў *a.* (colloq.) savoury, of pleasant flavour, appetizing; hence ∼ILY² *adv.,* ∼INESS *n.* [f. TASTE² + -Y²]

tăt¹ *v.* (-tt-). **1.** *v.i.* do tatting. **2.** *v.t.* make by tatting. [19th c.; orig. unkn.]

tăt² *n.* (colloq.) tattiness; tatty thing(s) or person. [back-form. f. TATTY²]

tăt³. See TIT².

ta-ta′ (tătah′) *int.* (childish or colloq.) goodbye. [19th c.; orig. unkn.]

tata′mi (-ah′-) *n.* Japanese standard-sized mat; unit of room-size in Japan. [Jap.]

Tatar. Var. of TARTAR² 1.

tā′ter *n.* (vulg.) potato. [abbr.]

tā′tler. Var. (arch.) of TATTLER 1.

ta′tou (tah′tōō) *n.* armadillo. [Tupi]

tă′tter *n.* (usu. in *pl.*) rag, irregularly torn piece of cloth, paper, etc.; (fig.) useless remains (*left his argument in tatters*); ∼ **dema′lion** (-dimā′lion), ragamuffin; hence ∼ED² (-erd), ∼Y², *adjs.* [ME, f. ON *taturr,* pl. *tötrar* rags]

Tă′ttersall *n.* ∼ (**check**), pattern of coloured lines forming squares like tartan. [f. R. ∼, Engl. horseman d. 1795]

tă′tting *n.* kind of knotted lace made by hand with small shuttle and used for trimming etc. [19th c.; orig. unkn.]

tă′ttle *v.* & *n.* **1.** *v.i.* prattle, chatter, gossip idly. **2.** *v.t.* utter (words) idly; ∼-**tale,** telltale. **3.** *n.* trivial talk. [ME, f. MFlem. *tatelen, tateren,* imit.]

tă′ttler *n.* **1.** prattler, gossip, (arch. **tatler,** esp. (*T*∼) as name of periodical). **2.** vociferous sandpiper of genus *Totanus* etc. [f. prec. + -ER¹]

tattōō′¹ *n.,* & *v.i.* **1.** *n.* evening drum or bugle signal recalling soldiers to quarters; elaboration of this with music and marching as entertainment; drumming or rapping; **devil's** ∼, idle drumming or tapping with fingers etc. **2.** *v.i.* rap quickly and repeatedly; beat the devil's tattoo (*on*). [17th c. *tap-too* f. Du. *taptoe,* lit. 'close the tap' (of the cask)]

tattōō′² *v.t.,* & *n.* **1.** *v.t.* mark (skin etc.) with indelible patterns by inserting pigments in punctures; make (pattern) thus; hence ∼ER¹, ∼IST (3), *ns.* **2.** *n.* such mark. [v. f. n. f. Polynesian]

tattōō′³ *n.* (Anglo-Ind.) native-bred pony. [f. Hindi *ṭaṭṭū*]

tă′ttў¹ *n.* (Anglo-Ind.) matting of cuscus-grass roots hung and kept wet to cool and perfume the air. [f. Hindi *ṭaṭṭī* wicker frame]

tă′tt|ў² *a.* (colloq.) ragged, untidy, shabby; tawdry, fussily ornate; inferior; hence ∼ILY² *adv.,* ∼INESS *n.* [orig. Sc., = shaggy, app. rel. to OE *tættec* rag, TATTER]

tau (-aw, -ow) *n.* nineteenth Greek letter (T, τ) = t; ∼ **cross** (T-shaped). [ME f. Gk]

taught. See TEACH.

taunt v.t., & n. **1.** v.t. reproach, upbraid, (person etc. *with* conduct etc.) contemptuously. **2.** n. contemptuous reproach. [16th c., in phr. *taunt for taunt* f. F *tant pour tant* tit for tat, hence smart rejoinder]

taupe (tōp) n. grey colour with brownish or other tinge. [F, = MOLE²]

taur´ine a. bull-like, bovine. [f. L *taurinus* (*taurus* bull; see -INE¹)]

tauro´machy (-kĭ) n. (arch.) bullfight(ing). [f. Gk *tauromakhia* (*tauros* bull, *makhē* fight); see -Y¹]

Taur´|us n. (person born under) sign of the ZODIAC, the Bull; hence ⌒EAN a. & n., (person) born under Taurus. [ME f. L, = bull]

taut a. (Of rope etc.) tight, not slack; (of ship etc.) in good order or condition; (of nerves etc.) tense; strict or severe as regards duty; hence ⌒EN⁶ v.t. & i., ⌒LY² adv., ⌒NESS n. [ME *touht*, *togt*, perh. = TOUGH, infl. by *tog-* p.p. st. of obs. *tee* (OE *tēon*) pull]

tau´to- comb. form. the same, as: ⌒chrone (-krōn) [f. Gk *khronos* time], curve on which body starting from state of rest under given force will reach fixed point in same time from whatever point it starts; ⌒phony (-ŏ´f-), repetition of same sound. [Gk, f. *tauto, to auto* the same]

tautŏ´g n. food and game fish (*Tautoga onitis*) of Atlantic coast of N. America. [f. Narraganset *taut--auog* pl.]

tautŏ´log|y n. saying of the same thing twice over in different words, esp. as fault of style, (e.g. *arrived one after the other in succession*); statement necessarily true; hence **tautŏlŏ´g**IC(AL) adjs., ⌒IST (1) n., ⌒IZE (2) v.i., ⌒OUS a. [f. LL f. Gk TAUTO(*logia* -LOGY)]

tau´tomēr n. (Chem.) organic compound reacting as if its molecule had more than one structure; hence ⌒IC (-mĕ´r-) a., ⌒ISM (2) (-ŏ´m-) n. [f. TAUTO- + -MER]

tä´vern n. (literary). inn or public house. [ME, f. OF *taverne* f. L *taberna* hut, tavern]

‖TAVR. Var. of T. & A.V.R.

taw¹ v.t. make (hide) into leather without use of tannin, esp. by soaking in solution of alum and salt; hence ⌒ER¹, ⌒ERY (3), ns. [OE *tawian*, = MDu., MLG *touwen*, OHG *zouwen*, Goth. *taujan* do, f. Gmc *taw(ō)jan*]

taw² n. large streaked etc. marble for shooting in game of marbles; game played with taws; line from which players propel marbles. [18th c.; orig. unkn.]

taw´dr|y a. & n. **1.** a. showy but worthless, gaudy, having too much or ill-judged ornament; hence ⌒ILY² adv., ⌒INESS n. **2.** n. cheap or excessive or tasteless finery. [a. f. n., short for *tawdry lace*, orig. *St. Audrey's lace* (*Audrey* = *Etheldrida*, patron saint of Ely)]

taw´n|y a. brownish-yellow, brownish-orange, tan--coloured; ⌒y **eagle,** brownish Afr. & Asian eagle (*Aquila rapax*); ⌒y **owl,** reddish-brown European owl; hence ⌒INESS n. [ME, f. AF *tauné*, OF *tané* (*tan* TAN¹)]

taws, tawse, (-z) n. *sing.* or *pl.* (Sc.) thong with slit end for chastising children. [app. pl. of obs. *taw* tawed leather, f. TAW¹]

täx¹ v.t. **1.** impose tax on (subjects, citizens, etc., commodity, land, etc.), pay tax on (*income taxed at source*); ⌒ed **cart,** (Hist.) type of open cart for trade etc., on which little or no tax was payable. **2.** make demands upon, demand exertion from, (person's resources, powers, ingenuity, etc.). **3.** (Law). examine and (dis)allow items of, assess, (costs etc.); ‖⌒´ing-master, law court official who taxes costs. **4.** charge (person *with* fault, *with doing*); call to account. **5.** Hence ⌒ABI´LITY, ⌒ABLENESS (-bǝln-), ns., ⌒´ABLE a. [ME, f. OF *taxer* f. L *taxare* censure, charge, compute, perh. f. Gk *tassō* fix]

täx² n. contribution levied on or *on* persons, property, or business, for support of national or *local government (DIRECT², INCOME, INDIRECT, POLL¹-, ‖PURCHASE¹, VALUE-added, tax)*; oppressive or burdensome obligation; strain, heavy demand, (*up*)*on* (person, his energies etc.); ⌒-collector, (colloq.) ⌒´man, official who collects taxes; ⌒-deductible, (of expenses) that may be paid out of income before deduction of income tax; ⌒-dodger, (colloq.) one who evades paying taxes; ⌒-farmer, one who buys from government the right to collect certain taxes; ⌒-free, exempt from taxes; ⌒-gatherer, (arch.) tax-collector; ⌒ haven, country etc. where income tax is low; ⌒´payer, one who pays taxes; ⌒ return, declaration of income for taxation purposes; *tax* YEAR; hence ⌒LESS a. [ME, f. prec.]

täxā´tion n. imposition or payment of tax(es); taxing of costs. [ME, f. AF *taxacioun*, OF *taxation* f. L *taxatio -onis* (*taxare*; see TAX¹, -ATION)]

tä´xï n. & v. (⌒ing or **ta´xying**). **1.** n. ⌒(-cab), motor car plying for hire and usu. fitted with taximeter; other motor car of similar pattern; boat etc. similarly used; ⌒-dancer, dance-partner whose services may be hired; ⌒-driver, ⌒-man, driver of taxi. **2.** v.i. & t. go or convey in taxi. **3.** v.i. (Aeron., of aircraft or pilot) go along ground or water under machine's own power before or after flying. [abbr. of *taximeter cab*]

tä´xidērm|y n. art of preparing and mounting skins of animals with lifelike effect; hence **täxidēr´m**AL, **täxidēr´m**IC, adjs., ⌒IST (3) n. [f. Gk TAXIS + *derma* skin; see -Y¹]

tä´ximēter n. automatic device fitted to taxi-cab etc. and indicating fare due for distance travelled up to present moment in journey. [f. F *taximètre* (*taxe* tariff, TAX²; see -METER)]

tä´xïs n. (Surg.) manual pressure applied to restore parts to their place; (Gk Ant.) variously sized division of troops; (Gram. & Rhet.) arrangement; (Biol.) movement of organism in particular direction in response to external stimulus. [Gk (*tassō* arrange)]

tä´x|on n. (*pl.* ⌒a). taxonomic group, esp. genus or smaller group. [back-form. f. foll.]

täxŏ´nom|y n. (principles of) classification, esp. in biology; hence or cogn. ⌒IST (3) n., **täxonŏ´m**IC(AL) adjs. [f. F *taxonomie* f. as TAXIS + Gk *-nomia* distribution]

ta´zza (tah´tsa) n. saucer-shaped cup, esp. one mounted on a foot. [It.]

TB abbr. torpedo-boat; tubercle bacillus, hence (colloq.) tuberculosis.

Tb symb. terbium.

T-bone. See T.

tbsp. abbr. tablespoonful.

Tc symb. technetium.

TCD abbr. Trinity College, Dublin.

TD abbr. Territorial (Officer's) Decoration; (Ir.) Teachta Dála, Member of the Dáil.

tē, ti² (tē), n. (Mus.) seventh note of scale in movable--doh system; the note B in fixed-doh system. [alt. f. *si*, F f. It., perh. f. *Sancte Iohannes*; see GAMUT]

Te symb. tellurium.

tea n. & v. (⌒ed or ⌒'d, *pr.* tēd). **1.** n. ⌒(-plant), evergreen shrub or small tree of camellia genus with fragrant white flowers grown in China, India, etc. **2.** leaves of this dried and prepared for use in various ways; (sl.) marijuana. **3.** infusion of tea-leaves as beverage; infusion etc. of leaves of other plants or of other substance (*camomile, beef, tea*); ⌒ **and sympathy,** (colloq.) friendly treatment of the unhappy. **4.** (**afternoon**) ⌒, light afternoon meal with tea; (**early morning**) ⌒ (usu. drunk before getting up); ‖(**high**) ⌒, evening meal with tea and usu. meat etc. **5.** ⌒-bag, small permeable bag of tea-leaves for infusion; ⌒-ball (of perforated metal, to contain tea for infusion); ⌒-bread, light or sweet bread for eating at tea; tea-BREAK²; tea-CADDY¹; ⌒´cake, ‖light flat usu. sweet bun eaten at tea, often toasted, *small sweet cake; ⌒ ceremony, elaborate Japanese ritual of serving and drinking tea; ⌒-chest, light cubical wooden box lined with sheets of lead or tin, in which tea is exported; ⌒-cloth, (1) cloth for tea-table, (2) tea-towel; tea-COSY; ⌒´cup, cup from which tea is

drunk (STORM *in a teacup*), whence ∼*cup*FUL 2 *n.*; ∼
dance, *thé dansant*; ∼-**fight,** (colloq.) tea-party;
∼-**garden** (in which tea is grown, or served to the
public); ∼-**gown,** woman's long loose ornamental
gown worn at tea etc.; ∼-**house** (in which tea etc. is
served in China and Japan); ∼-**kettle** (used in
making tea); ∼-**lady,** woman employed to make tea
in offices etc.; ∼-**leaf,** leaf of tea esp. (in *pl.*) after
infusion or soaking, (rhyming sl.) thief; ∼-**party** (at
which tea is served); ∼-**planter,** proprietor or
cultivator of tea plantation; ∼'**pot,** spouted vessel in
which tea is made and from which it is poured;
∼-**room** (for serving tea etc. to the public); ∼-**rose**
(with scent compared to that of tea); *tea*-SERVICE[1] or
∼-**set;** ∼-**shop,** (1) = *tea-room,* (2) shop selling tea
(sense 2); *tea*SPOON[1], whence ∼'*spoon*FUL 2 *n.*; *tea*-
-TABLE; ∼-**things,** things used for serving tea;
∼-**time** (at which tea is served); ∼-**towel** (for drying
washed crockery etc.); ∼-**tray** (on which tea-set is
used or carried); ∼-**tree,** (Austral.) tree of genus
Leptospermum etc. whose leaves are used as substitute
for tea; ∼-**trolley,** small wheeled table to carry tea-
-things; ∼-**urn** (for boiling or holding water for tea);
∼-**wagon,** = *tea-trolley.* 6. *v.i.* take tea. 7. *v.t.* give tea
to (person). [17th c. *tay, tey,* prob. f. Du. *tee* f. Chin.
(Amoy dial.) *te,* = Mandarin dial. *cha*]

teach *v.* (**taught** *pr.* tawt). 1. *v.t.* enable or induce
(person etc. to do) by instruction and training (*teach
him to swim; dog was taught to beg; misfortune has taught him
to be thankful for small mercies*); compel (person) by
punishment etc. to do (*this will teach you to speak the
truth*); (colloq.) make (person) disinclined (*to offend
etc.; I will teach him to meddle in my affairs*). 2. give
lessons at school or elsewhere in or on (subject, game,
instrument, etc., *to* person; *taught him Greek; teaches
Greek for a living; teaches the violin; teach me bridge; was
never taught music; music was never taught to a more
unwilling pupil*); *∼ **school,** be a teacher in a school.
3. give instruction to, educate; ∼-**in,** series of lectures
and discussions on subject of public interest. 1.
explain, show, state by way of instruction, (fact etc.,
how, that, etc., *to* person; *taught that we must forgive our
enemies; teach him how to swim; I was taught that two sides
of a triangle were greater than the third; was taught
otherwise; was never taught this; who taught you that?*). 5.
v.i. be a teacher, give lessons esp. at school. 6. Hence
∼'ER[1] *n.* [OE *tǣcan* f. Gmc *taikjan (*t(a)ik*- show f. IE
d(e)ig-)]

tea'ch|able *a.* apt to learn, docile; (of subject etc.) that
can be taught; hence ∼ABI'LITY, ∼ableNESS (-bəln-),
ns. [ME, f. prec. + -ABLE]

tea'ching *n.* In vbl senses; what is taught, doctrines,
(*the teachings of the Church*); profession of teacher; ∼
hospital (where medical students are taught); ∼
machine, mechanical device for giving instruction. [ME, f. TEACH + -ING[1]]

teak *n.* (orig. E. Ind. tree, *Tectona grandis,* with)
heavy durable timber that does not warp or shrink,
much used in shipbuilding. [f. Port. *teca* f. Malayalam
tēkka]

teal *n.* (*pl.* same). small freshwater duck of genus *Anas*
etc. [rel. to MDu. *tēling,* of unkn. orig.]

team *n.* & *v.* 1. *n.* two or more draught animals
harnessed together; one animal or more with harness
and vehicle. 2. set of players forming one side in game
(*cricket, golf, team*); set of persons working together;
∼-**mate,** fellow member of a team; ∼ **spirit,** willingness to act for group rather than individual benefit;
∼-**work,** combined effort, organized co-operation.
3. *v.t.* harness (horses etc.) in team; ∼ (**up**), join (one)
as team *with* (another). 4. *v.i.* ∼ (**up**), join in team or
in common action (*with*). [OE *tēam* offspring, = OS
tōm, OHG *zoum,* ON *taumr* bridle, f. Gmc *taumaz*
prob. f. *taug-* pull; cf. TOW[1]]

tea'mster *n.* driver of a team; *lorry-driver. [f. prec.
+ -STER]

tea'poy *n.* small three- or four-legged table esp. for tea.

[f. Hindi *tīn, tir*- three + Pers. *pāī* foot; sense and
spelling infl. by TEA]

tear[1] (tār) *v.* (**tore** *or* arch. **tare; torn**) & *n.* 1. *v.t.* pull
apart with some force (*tore up the letter; has torn his coat;
tear it in half, in two, in pieces; torn to pieces by a tiger;* (fig.)
*country was torn by factions, heart torn by conflicting
emotions, was torn* (distracted at having to make a
choice) *between love and duty*); make (hole, rent) thus;
∼ **it,** (sl.) spoil one's chances, foil one's plans, (*that's
torn it*). 2. pull violently or with some force (lit. or fig.)
esp. *down, off,* etc., (*tore down the notice; tear out a page;
tear off the cover; tree torn up by the roots*); remove (person)
forcibly *from;* ∼ one**self away,** go away despite
strong allurement to stay; ∼ one's **hair,** pull it in
anger or perplexity or despair. 3. *v.i.* pull violently or
with some force *at* etc.; run or walk or travel hurriedly
or impetuously (*tore down the hill*); undergo tearing
(*tore down the middle*). 4. ∼'**away,** (*a.*) impetuous, (*n.*)
hooligan, ruffian; ∼-**sheet,** sheet torn from magazine etc. to provide copy of one page. 5. *n.* hole made
or damage caused by tearing; torn part of cloth etc.
[OE *teran,* = OHG *zeran,* Goth. -*tairan* f. Gmc *teran* f.
IE *der-*]

tear[2] *n.* 1. ∼(-**drop**), drop of clear saline liquid
ordinarily serving to moisten and wash the eye but
falling from it as result of grief or other emotion or of
coughing or laughter, (*the tears fell or rolled down her
cheeks; wept bitter tears of remorse; laughed till the tears
came; a tear-stained face*); in ∼s, weeping; without ∼s,
(fig.) presented so as to be easily learned etc.;
CROCODILE *tears.* 2. tearlike thing, e.g. drop of fluid,
solid drop of resin etc. 3. ∼-**duct** (carrying tears to
eye or from eye to nose); ∼-**gas,** lachrymatory gas
used in warfare etc. to disable opponents or make
crowds disperse; ∼-**jerker,** (colloq.) song, story,
film, etc., calculated to evoke sadness or sympathy.
[OE *tēar,* = OHG *zah(h)ar,* ON *tár,* Goth. *tagr* f. IE
dakru-]

tear'ful *a.* shedding tears; (of event, news, etc.)
mournful, sad; hence ∼LY[2] *adv.,* ∼NESS *n.* [f. prec. +
-FUL]

tear'ing (tār'-) *a.* in vbl senses; violent, overwhelming, (*tearing hurry, pace, rage*). [f. TEAR[1] + -ING[1]]

tear'less *a.* not shedding tears; hence ∼LY[2] *adv.,*
∼NESS *n.* [f. TEAR[2] + -LESS]

tear'y *a.* (colloq.) tearful. [ME, f. TEAR[2] + -Y[1]]

tease (-z) *v.t.,* & *n.* 1. *v.t.* irritate playfully or
maliciously with jests, questions, or petty annoy-
ances; *importune (person *for* thing, *to* do); pick into
separate fibres, comb, card, (wool, flax, etc.); dress
(cloth etc.) with teasels, ∼ **out,** separate by disentangling (lit. or fig.). 2. *n.* (colloq.) person fond of
teasing others. [OE *tǣsan,* = MDu., MLG *tēzen,*
OHG *zeisan* f. WG *taisjan*]

tea'sel (-z-), **tea'zel, tea'zle,** *n.,* & *v.t.* 1. *n.* plant of
genus *Dipsacus* with large prickly heads that are dried
and used in dressing cloth to form nap; such head;
device used as substitute for teasels. 2. *v.t.* dress
(cloth) with teasels; hence **tea'sel**ER[1] (-z-) *n.* [OE
tǣs(e)l = OHG *zeisala* (as prec.; see -LE 1)]

tea'ser (-z-) *n.* In vbl senses; teasing person; (colloq.)
difficult question or problem or task, thing hard to
deal with. [ME, f. TEASE + -ER[1]]

teat *n.* mammary nipple esp. of animal; thing resembling this, esp. device of rubber etc. for sucking milk
from bottle. [ME f. OF *tete,* prob. of Gmc orig.,
replacing TIT[3]]

tea'zel, -zle. See TEASEL.

těc[1] *n.* (sl.) detective (novel). [abbr.]

Těch (-k), **Těc**[2], *n.* (colloq.) technical college, institute, or school. [abbr.]

těchně'tium (-knē'shum) *n.* (Chem.) artificially
produced radioactive metallic element. [mod. L, f.
Gk *technētos* artificial (*teknē*) art) + -IUM]

tě'chnic (-k-) *n.* technique; (usu. in *pl.*) technology;
(in *pl.*) technical terms, details, methods, etc.; hence
∼IST (3) *n.* [f. L f. Gk *teknikos* (*teknē* art; see -IC)]

tĕ′chnical (-kn-) *a.* of or in a particular art, science, handicraft, etc., (*technical terms, skill, difficulty*); of, for, in, applied science or vocational training (*technical college, education, school*); (of book etc.) (1) dealing with applied science, (2) using technical terms; legally such, in the strict legal interpretation, (*technical assault*); ∼ **hitch,** interruption or breakdown due to mechanical failure; ∼ **knock-out,** (Boxing) referee's termination of fight on grounds of boxer's inability to continue, his opponent being declared winner; hence ∼LY² *adv.,* ∼NESS *n.* [f. as prec.+-AL]

tĕchnĭcă′litў (-kn-) *n.* technicalness; technical expression, (merely) technical distinction, etc., (*legal technicalities; was acquitted on a technicality*). [f. prec.+ -ITY]

tĕchni′cian (-knĭ′shan) *n.* person skilled in technique of an art or craft; person expert in practical application of science. [f. TECHNIC+-IAN]

Tĕ′chnicolor (-knĭkŭl-) *n.* (*P) process of colour cinematography in which colours are separately but simultaneously recorded and then transferred to a single positive print; (fig.) vivid colour, artificial brilliance; hence ∼ED² (-erd) *a.* [f. TECHNICAL+COLOR¹]

tĕchni′que (-knē′k) *n.* mode of artistic execution in music, painting, etc.; mechanical skill in art; means of achieving one's purpose, esp. skilfully. [F, as TECHNIC]

tĕchnŏ′cracў (-kn-) *n.* government or control of society or industry by technical experts; hence **tĕ′chno**CRAT (-kn-) *n.,* advocate of this, **tĕchno- cră′**TIC (-kn-) *a.* [f. Gk *tekhnē* art+-o-+-CRACY]

tĕchnŏ′logЇ̆у (-k-) *n.* (science of) practical or industrial art(s); ethnological study of development of such arts; application of science; hence **tĕchno**LO′GICAL (-kn-) *a.,* ∼IST (3) *n.* [f. Gk *tekhnologia* systematic treatment (*tekhnē* art; see -LOGY)]

tĕ′chў. See TETCHY.

tĕctŏ′n|ic *a.* of building or construction; (Geol.) relating to deformation of earth's crust or to structural changes caused thereby; hence ∼ICALLY *adv.,* ∼ICS *n.,* whole art of producing useful and beautiful buildings, (Geol.) structural features as a whole. [f. LL f. Gk *tektonikos* (*tektōn -onos* carpenter; see -IC)]

tĕctŏ′rial *a.* forming a covering, esp. ∼ **membrane** (of inner ear, covering organ of CORTI). [f. L *tectorium* a cover (as foll.)+-AL]

tĕ′ctri|x *n.* (*pl.* ∼ces *pr.* -ĭsēz, -ī′sēz). (Ornith.), = COVERT². [mod. L, f. L *tegere tect-* cover; see -TRIX]

tĕd¹ *v.t.* (-dd-). turn over and spread out (grass, hay) to dry; hence ∼′dER¹ (1, 2) *n.* [ME, f. ON *tethja* spread manure, (*tad* dung, *toddi* small piece)]

∥Tĕd² *n.* (colloq.) Teddy boy. [abbr.]

Tĕ′ddy *n.* 1. ∥∼ (**boy**), (colloq.) youth affecting Edwardian (sense 2) style of dress. 2. t∼ **bear,** child's toy bear. [f. pet-name *Teddy* for (sense 1) *Edward,* or (sense 2) *Theodore* Roosevelt, US President d. 1919 famous as bear-hunter]

Te Deum (tē dē′ŭm, tā dā′ŭm) *n.* (music for) hymn beginning *Te Deum laudamus,* 'Thee, God, we praise', sung at matins, or on special occasions as thanksgiving; expression of thanksgiving or exultation. [L]

tĕ′dious *a.* wearisome, irksome, tiresomely long; hence ∼LY² *adv.,* ∼NESS *n.* [ME, f. OF *tedieus* or f. LL *taediosus* (as foll.; see -OUS)]

tĕ′dium *n.* tediousness. [f. L *taedium* (*taedēre* to weary)]

tee¹. Var. of T.

tee² *n.* & *v.* 1. *n.* mark aimed at in quoits, bowls, curling. 2. (Golf). cleared space from which ball is struck at beginning of play for each hole; small pile of sand or small appliance of wood, rubber, etc., on which ball is placed before being thus struck. 3. *v.t.* place (ball) on golf tee. 4. *v.i.* ∼ **off,** play ball from tee, (fig.) start, begin; ∼ **up,** place ball on tee, (fig., colloq.) organize. [sense 1 perh.=prec.; sense 2 f. obs. *teaz,* of unkn. orig.]

tee³ *n.* umbrella-shaped usu. gilded ornament crowning stupa or pagoda. [f. Burm. *h′ti* umbrella]

teehee′. Var. of TEHEE.

teem¹ *v.i.* be prolific, be stocked to overflowing *with,* (*forests teem with snakes; book teems with blunders*); be abundant (*fish teem in these waters*). [OE *tēman* etc. give birth to f. *taumjan* f. Gmc *taumaz* TEAM]

teem² *v.* 1. *v.t.* (dial. or tech.) empty, discharge, pour out, (vessel, cart, coal, molten metal, etc.); hence ∼′ER¹ *n.* 2. *v.i.* (Of water etc.) flow copiously, pour. [ME *tēmen* f. ON *tœma* (*tómr* a. empty)]

teen *n.* (arch.) grief, misfortune. [OE *tēon(a),* = OS *tiono,* ON *tjón*]

-teen *suf.* = TEN, added to (modified) numerals 3 to 9 to form the names of those from 13 to 19. [OE *-tīene, -tēne, -tўne,* = OS *-tein,* OHG *-zehan,* Goth. *-taihun*]

tee′n-āg|e *a.* pertaining to or characteristic of teenagers; so ∼ED¹ (-jd) *a.* [f. TEENS+AGE¹]

tee′nāger *n.* person in teens. [f. as prec.+-ER¹]

teens (-z) *n. pl.* years of one's age from 13 to 19 (*boy in his teens*). [f. -TEEN+-S¹]

tee′nsў(-weensў), tee′nў(-weenў), adjs. (childish or colloq.) tiny. [var. of TINY]

tee′nў-bŏpper *n.* (colloq.) teen-age girl who follows latest fashions in clothes, pop music, etc. [f. TEENS+ -Y³+BOPPER]

tee′pee. See TEPEE.

tee′ter *v.i.,* & *n.* 1. *v.i.* totter; move unsteadily; *see-saw. 2. n. *see-saw. [var. of dial. *titter*]

teeth. See TOOTH.

teeth|e (-dh) *v.i.* grow or cut (esp. milk-) teeth; hence ∼′ING¹ *n.* (∼ing-ring, small ring for infant to bite on while teething; ∼ing **troubles,** initial difficulties in an enterprise etc.). [ME, f. prec.]

teetō′tal *a.* of or advocating total abstinence from intoxicants, whence ∼ISM (3) *n.;* (US colloq., or dial.) total, entire, whence ∼LY² *adv.* [redupl. of TOTAL]

teetō′taller, *-aler, *n.* total abstainer, advocate of total abstinence from intoxicants. [f. prec.+-ER¹]

teetō′tum *n.* children's four-sided top with sides lettered to determine gain or loss by the spinner; any top spun with the fingers (**like a ∼,** spinning). [f. *T* (the letter on one side)+L *totum* the whole (stakes), for which this letter stood]

tĕff *n.* African cereal (*Eragrostis abyssinica*). [f. Amh. *țēf*]

tĕg *n.* sheep in its second year. [ME *tegge* (in place-names), f. OE *tegga,* OSw. *takka* ewe]

tĕ′gūlar *a.* of or (arranged) like tiles; hence ∼LY² *adv.* [f. L *tegula* tile (*tegere* cover)+-AR¹]

tĕ′gūment *n.* natural covering of (part of) animal body; hence ∼AL, ∼ARY¹, (-č′n-) *adjs.* [f. L *tegumentum* (*tegere* cover; see -MENT)]

tĕhee′ *n.,* & *v.i.* 1. *n.* restrained or contemptuous laugh. 2. *v.i.* laugh thus, titter. [imit.]

tehsil. Var. of TAHSIL.

teind (tēnd) *n.* (Sc. & N. Engl.) tithe; (Sc., usu. in *pl.*) portion of laity's estates assessable for clergy stipend. [ME *tende* = TENTH]

tĕknŏ′nўm|ў *n.* (Anthrop.) practice of naming parent from child; hence ∼OUS *a.* [f. Gk *teknon* child+-ōnumos -named (cf. ANONYMOUS)+-Y¹]

tĕ′ktīte *n.* small roundish glassy body of unknown origin such as occur in various regions of the earth. [f. G *tektit* f. Gk *tēktos* molten (*tēkō* melt); see -ITE]

Tel. *abbr.* Telegraph(ic); Telephone.

tĕlaesth|ē′sia (-lĭ-), *tĕlesth|ē′sia,* (-zĭa), *n.* (Psych.) direct perception of distant occurrences or objects that is not effected by the recognized senses; so ∼ē′tIC *a.* [mod. L, f. as TELE-+Gk *aisthēsis* perception+-IA¹]

tĕlamon *n.* (*pl.* ∼es *pr.* -ō′nēz). (Archit.) male figure used as pillar to support entablature. [f. L f. Gk *telamōnes* pl. of *Telamōn,* name of a mythical hero]

tĕ′lĕ- *comb. form.* 1. far (esp. in names of instruments producing or recording results etc. at a distance; *telemeter, telethermo′meter*). 2. television, as: ∼**cast,** (transmit) television broadcast programme or item; ∼**caster,** television broadcaster; ∼**cine,** ∼**film,** cinema film transmitted by television; ∼**ge′nic,**

suitable for being televised; ~**prompter,** device that slowly unrolls (television) speaker's text, in large print, out of view of audience; ~**record** *v.t.*, record (item or programme to be televised), whence ~*recording* n.; ~**vi'sual,** pertaining to television. [sense 1 f. Gk *tēlē-* (*tēle* far off); sense 2 f. TELEVISION]

te'lecámera *n.* television camera; telephotographic camera. [f. TELE-+CAMERA]

telecommunica'tion *n.* communication over long distances by cable, telegraph, telephone, or broadcasting; (usu. in *pl.*) branch of technology concerned with this. [f. F *télécommunication* (as TELE-, COMMUNICATION)]

te'ledu (-oo) *n.* stinking badger of Java and Sumatra. [Jav.]

tele'gony *n.* (Biol.) supposed influence of previous sire seen in subsequent sire's progeny by same dam; hence **telego'nic** *a.* [f. TELE-+Gk *-gonia* begetting]

te'legram *n.* message sent by telegraph and usu. then written etc. for delivery to addressee. [f. TELE-+-GRAM, after foll.]

te'legraph[1] (-ahf) *n.* **1.** (apparatus for) transmitting messages or signals to a distance esp. by making and breaking electrical connection; BUSH[1] *telegraph.* **2.** semaphore apparatus. **3.** newspaper (used in titles, as *Daily Telegraph*). **1.** ~(-**board**), board on which numbers of horses running in race, cricket scores, etc., are put up so as to be visible at distance; ~-**key,** device for making and breaking electric circuit of telegraph; ~-**line, -pole** or **-post, -wire,** (used in providing telegraphic connection); ~ **money order,** money ORDER[1] for which authority to pay is transmitted by telegraph; ~-**plant,** E. Ind. plant (*Desmodium gyrans*) whose leaves have spontaneous jerking motion. [f. F *télégraphe* (as TELE-, -GRAPH)]

te'legraph[2] (-ahf) *v.* **1.** *v.t.* send (message *to* person, or abs.) by telegraph. **2.** *v.i.* make signals (*to* person *to do, that,* etc.). [f. prec.]

telegraph|**er** (tĭlĕ'gra-, tĕ'lĭgrah-) *n.* person skilled in, or employed in, telegraphy; so ~IST (3) *n.* [f. prec.+-ER[1]]

telegraphe'se (-z) *n.* (colloq. or joc.) elliptical style usual in telegrams. [f. TELEGRAPH[1]+-ESE]

telegra'ph|**ic** *a.* of telegraphs or telegrams; of telegraphic brevity, economically worded, with unessential words omitted; ~**ic address,** abbreviated or other registered address for use in telegrams; hence ~ICALLY *adv.* [f. TELEGRAPH[1]+-IC]

tele'graphy *n.* art of construction of, practice of communicating by, telegraph; WIRELESS *telegraphy.* [f. TELEGRAPH[1]+-Y[1]]

telekine'sis *n.* (*pl.* ~es *pr.* -ēz). (Psych.) movement at a distance from the motive cause or agent without material connection. [mod. L, f. as TELE-+Gk *kinēsis* motion (*kineō* move)]

te'lemark *n.,* & *v.i.* (make) swing turn in skiing used to change direction or to stop short. [f. *T*~ in Norway]

telemeter (tĕ'lĭmē-, tĭlĕ'mĭ-) *n.* & *v.* **1.** *n.* apparatus to record readings of an instrument at a distance usu. by means of radio. **2.** *v.i.* record readings thus. **3.** *v.t.* transmit (readings etc.) to a receiving set or station. **4.** So **tele'metry** *n.* [f. TELE-+-METER]

teleo'log|**y** *n.* doctrine of final causes, view that developments are due to the purpose or design that is served by them; hence **teleolo'gic**(AL) *adjs.,* ~ISM (3), ~IST (2), *ns.* [f. mod. L *teleologia* f. Gk *telos teleos* end+-O-+-LOGY]

te'leost *n.* (Zool.) fish of order Teleostei, with skeleton (usu.) completely ossified. [f. Gk *teleo-* complete (*telos;* see prec.)+*osteon* bone]

te'lepath *n.,* & *v.i.* **1.** *n.* telepathic person. **2.** *v.i.* practise telepathy. [back-form. f. foll.]

tele'path|**y** *n.* communication from one mind to another at a distance other than through known senses; hence **telepa'thic** *a.,* ~IST (2) *n.,* ~IZE (1, 2) *v.t.* & *i.* [f. TELE-+-PATHY]

te'lephone *n.* & *v.* **1.** *n.* apparatus for transmitting sound (esp. speech) to a distance by wire or cord or radio, esp. by converting acoustic vibrations to electrical signals for transmission; (transmitting and) receiving instrument used in this, with bell to indicate incoming call, (*the telephone is ringing; pick up the telephone*); the ~, system of communication by a network of telephones; **on the ~,** (1) having an instrument connected to this, (2) by use of or (while) using the telephone; **over the ~,** by use of the telephone. **2.** ~ **book, directory,** (listing names and numbers of telephone subscribers); ~ **booth,** ||~-**box,** ~ **kiosk,** (containing telephone for public use); *telephone* CALL[2]; *telephone* EXCHANGE[1] 5; ~ **number** (assigned to a particular subscriber and used in making connections to his telephone). **3.** *v.t.* send (message etc.), by telephone; speak to (person) by telephone. **4.** *v.i.* make telephone call. **5.** Hence **telepho'nic** *a.,* **tele'phon**IST (3) (esp. operator in telephone exchange), **tele'phony**[1], *ns.* [f. TELE-+-PHONE]

telepho'to *a.* telephotographic; ~ **lens** (for telephotography). [abbr.]

telephoto'graphy *n.* photographing of distant objects by means of a combination of telescopic and ordinary photographic lens giving large image, so **telephotogra'phic** *a.* [f. TELE-+PHOTOGRAPHY]

te'leport *v.t.* move by telekinesis; hence ~A'TION *n.* [f. TELE-+PORT[4]]

te'leprinter *n.* telegraph instrument for transmitting messages by typing. [f. TELE-+PRINTER]

te'lergy *n.* (Psych.) force conceived as operating on the brain in telepathy. [f. TELE-+ENERGY]

te'lescope *n.* & *v.* **1.** *n.* optical instrument using lenses or mirrors or both to make distant objects appear nearer and larger; **radio ~,** directional aerial system for collecting radio waves from celestial objects and recording their intensity etc. **2.** *v.t.* press, drive, (sections of tube, colliding trains, etc.) together so that one slides into another like sections of small telescope; compress (lit. or fig.) forcibly. **3.** *v.i.* close, be driven, be capable of closing, thus. [f. It. *telescopio* or mod. L *telescopium* (as TELE-, -SCOPE)]

telesco'p|**ic** *a.* of, or made with, a telescope (*telescopic observations*); visible only through telescope (*telescopic stars*); consisting of sections that telescope (*telescopic umbrella*); ~**ic sight,** telescope used for sighting on rifle etc.; hence ~ICALLY *adv.* [f. prec.+-IC]

*telesthesia, etc. See TELAESTHESIA, etc.

*te'lethon *n.* (colloq.) very long television programme, esp. to raise money for a fund. [f. TELE-+MARATHON]

Te'letype (P), ***telety'pewriter** (-prī-) *ns.* teleprinter. [f. TELE-+TYPE[1](WRITER)]

te'leview (-vū) *v.t.* watch by means of television; hence ~ER[1] *n.* [f. TELE-+VIEW]

te'levis|**e** (-z) *v.t.* transmit by television; hence ~OR *n.,* apparatus for televising. [back-form. f. foll.]

television (tĕ'lĭvĭzhon, -vĭ'-) *n.* system for reproducing actual or recorded scene at a distance on a screen etc. by radio transmission, usu. with appropriate sounds; vision of distant objects obtained thus; televised programmes etc.; ~ (**set**), apparatus for displaying pictures transmitted thus. [f. TELE-+VISION]

te'lex, Te'lex, *n.,* & *v.t.* **1.** *n.* system of telegraphy in which printed signals or messages are sent from and to teleprinters connected to public telecommunication network. **2.** *v.t.* send, communicate with, by telex. [f. TELEPRINTER+EXCHANGE[1]]

tell[1] *v.* (**told** *pr.* tō-). **1.** *v.t.* give detailed account of (as) in spoken or written words (*tell me a tale; every picture tells a story*); ~ **a tale,** be significant or revealing; ~ **the tale,** (sl.) relate marvellous or incredible story, esp. tale of woe to evoke sympathy; ~ **its own tale,** be significant, explain itself, need no comment; ~ one's **own tale,** give one's own account of the matter; ~ **tales (out of school),** report esp. maliciously what is meant to be secret. **2.** make known, divulge, state, express in words, (*tell me your name, what you want, what to do; tell me all about it; will tell you a secret, that he has failed, my candid opinion; cannot tell you how glad I was*); *tell* FORTUNE[1]*s*; ∼ **it not in Gath,** (usu. joc.) let this news not reach and gladden the enemy [w. ref. to 2 Sam. 1:20]; *∼ (person) **goodbye,** say goodbye to; *tell that to the* (*horse*) MARINES; **don't ∼ me** *it's here already* (expr. incredulity); **you're** ∼**ing me,** (sl.) I am fully aware of that; **I ∼ you, let me ∼ you,** (emphatic or impatient assurance); *I told you* so[1] 7; *I'll tell you* WHAT; ∼ **the world,** announce openly, assert emphatically. **3.** utter (*you told me a lie; are you telling the truth?*). **4.** *v.i.* give information or description (*of* or *about*); reveal a secret; HEAR *tell* (*of*); **time will ∼,** we shall know eventually; ∼ **on,** (colloq.) inform against (person). **5.** *v.t.* & *i.* decide, determine, (*how do you tell which button to press?*); ∼ **the time,** read it from face of clock etc.; **as far as** one **can ∼,** judging from the available evidence; **you never can ∼,** appearances and probabilities are deceptive. **6.** distinguish (*cannot tell them apart, him from his brother*). **7.** assure (*it is not easy, I can tell you;* cf. sense 2). **8.** *v.i.* produce marked effect (*every blow tells; strain began to tell on him*); have influence *in favour of* or *against*. **9.** *v.t.* count (votes esp. in House of Commons, one's BEAD[1]*s; we were 18 men all told*); ∼ **off,** count off or detach for duty (*six of us were, I was, told off to get fuel*), reprimand, scold, (person). **10.** direct, order, (person) *to* do something (*tell him to wait for me*). **11.** Hence ∼'ABLE *a.* [OE *tellan,* = OS *tellian,* OHG *zellen,* ON *telja* f. Gmc *taljan* (*talō̆* TALE)]

tĕll[2] *n.* artificial mound in Middle East etc. formed by accumulated remains of ancient settlements. [f. Arab. *tall* hillock]

tĕ'ller *n.* In vbl senses; any of four persons appointed (two for each side) to count votes in House of Commons; person appointed to receive or pay out money in bank etc.; hence ∼SHIP *n.* [ME, f. TELL[1] + -ER[1]]

tĕ'lling *a.* having marked effect, striking; hence ∼LY[2] *a.* [f. TELL[1] + -ING[2]]

tĕ'll-tāle *n.* one who tells about another's private affairs, tattler; (fig.) thing, circumstance, that reveals person's thoughts, conduct, etc., (esp. *attrib.:* *tell-tale blushes; the tell-tale clay on his shoes*); mechanical device for recording person's attendance at specified time etc., giving warning that cistern is full, etc.; (Naut.) index near wheel to show position of tiller, compass hung usu. in captain's cabin for checking ship's course. [f. TELL[1] + TALE]

tĕllū'rian *a.* & *n.* (inhabitant) of the earth. [f. L *tellus -uris* earth + -IAN]

tĕllū'ric *a.* **1.** of the earth as a planet; of the soil. **2.** (Chem.) of tellurium, esp. in its higher valency; hence **tĕ'llūr**ATE[1] (3) *n.* [sense 1 f. as prec.; sense 2 f. foll.]

tĕll|ūr'ium *n.* (Chem.) rare brittle lustrous silver-white element; hence ∼'ūrIDE, ∼'ūrITE[1] (Chem., Min.), *ns.,* ∼'ūrOUS *a.* [f. L *tellus -uris* earth + -IUM, prob. named in contrast to *uranium*]

||**tĕ'llÿ** *n.* (colloq.) television (set). [abbr.]

tĕ'lpher *a.* & *n.* (container) serving to transport (esp. goods) by electric power; so ∼AGE (1, 2) *n.* [f. *telephore* f. TELE- + -PHORE]

tĕ'lson *n.* last segment in abdomen of Crustacea etc. [Gk, = limit]

Tĕ'lugu (-ōō) *n.* language or member of Dravidian people in SE India. [Telugu]

*****tĕ'mblor** *n.* earthquake. [Sp.]

tĕmĕrar'ious *a.* (literary). reckless, rash. [f. L *temerarius* (*temere* rashly) + -OUS]

tĕmĕ'rĭtÿ *n.* rashness. [f. L *temeritas* (*temere* rashly; see -ITY)]

tĕmp *n.* (colloq.) temporary employee. [abbr.]

temp. abbr. in the time of (*temp. Henry I*) [f. L *tempore* abl. of *tempus* time]; temperature.

tĕ'mper *v.* **1.** *v.t.* bring (clay etc.) to desired consistency by moistening, mixing, and kneading. **2.** *v.t.* & *i.* bring (metal, esp. steel), (of metal) come, to

proper hardness and elasticity by heating after quenching. **3.** *v.t.* modify, mitigate, (justice etc.) by blending *with* (mercy, etc.); moderate, restrain, tone down. **4.** (Mus.) tune, modulate, (piano, organ) in particular temperament. **5.** Hence ∼ABLE, ∼ATIVE, *adjs.,* ∼ER[1] *n.* [OE *temprian* f. L *temperare* mingle; infl. by OF *temprer, tremper*]

tĕ'mper[2] *n.* **1.** mixture, esp. suitable combination of ingredients (*of* mortar etc.); resulting condition or consistency. **2.** condition of metal as regards hardness and elasticity. **3.** habitual or temporary disposition of mind (*person of a saturnine, fiery, placid, temper; persons of congenial temper*); **in a good ∼,** in amiable mood, not irritable or angry; **in a bad ∼,** peevish, angry; **lose** one's ∼, become angry; **keep, control,** one's ∼, not lose it; **out of ∼,** angry. **4.** irritation, anger, (*fit of temper; what a temper he is in!*); **have a ∼,** be prone to become angry; **show ∼,** be petulant. **5.** Hence (-)∼ED *a.,* (-)∼edLY[2] *adv.,* (-erd-). [ME, f. prec.]

tĕ'mpera *n.* method of painting like DISTEMPER[3], esp. as technique of fine art on canvas etc. [It.]

tĕ'mperament *n.* **1.** individual character of one's physical constitution permanently affecting the manner of acting, feeling, and thinking, (*a nervous temperament; the artistic temperament*); SANGUINE, **lymphatic** or **phlegmatic, choleric** or **bilious, melancholic** or **atrabilious,** ∼ (formerly attributed to predominance of blood, lymph or phlegm, yellow bile, black bile). **2.** (Mus.) adjustment of intervals in tuning of piano etc. so as to fit the scale for use in all keys, esp. **equal ∼** (in which the 12 semitones are at equal intervals). **3.** Hence ∼AL (-ĕ'n-) *a.,* (esp., of person) liable to peculiar moods, having or giving way to erratic or neurotic temperament, behaving unpredictably. [ME, f. L *temperamentum* (as TEMPER[1]; see -MENT)]

tĕ'mperance *n.* moderation, self-restraint, in speech, conduct, etc., esp. in eating and drinking; moderation in use of, or total abstinence from, alcoholic liquors as beverages; ∼ **hotel** (not supplying alcoholic drinks); ∼ **society** etc. (for restriction or abolition of use of alcoholic drinks). [ME, f. AF *temperaunce* f. L *temperantia* (as TEMPER[1]; see -ANCE)]

tĕ'mperate *a.* moderate; self-restrained, abstemious; of mild temperature; *temperate* ZONE; hence ∼LY[2] (-tlĭ) *adv.,* ∼NESS (-tn-) *n.* [ME, f. L *temperatus,* p.p. of *temperare* (see TEMPER[1], -ATE[2])]

tĕ'mperature (-pr-) *n.* degree or intensity of heat of a body in relation to others, esp. as shown by thermometer or perceived by touch etc.; (Med.) degree of internal heat of the body (**take** person's ∼, ascertain any variation from normal value, in illness etc.); (colloq.) body temperature above normal (**have,** RUN[1], *a temperature*); (fig.) degree of excitement in discussion etc.; ∼**-humidity index,** quantity giving measure of discomfort due to combined effects of temperature and humidity of air. [f. F *température* or f. L *temperatura* (as TEMPER[1]; see -URE)]

tĕ'mpersome *a.* having a quick temper. [f. TEMPER[2] + -SOME[1]]

tĕ'mpest *n.* violent storm of wind often with rain, snow, etc.; (fig.) violent tumult or agitation; *****∼ **in a teapot,** = STORM *in a teacup.* [ME, f. OF *tempest(e)* f. Rom. *****tempesta,* *****tempestum* f. L *tempestas* season, storm (*tempus* time)]

tĕmpĕ'stŭous *a.* (Of weather, time, etc., or fig. of person or mood) stormy, violent; hence ∼LY[2] *adv.,* ∼NESS *n.* [f. LL *tempestuosus* (as prec.; see -OUS)]

Tĕ'mplar *n.* **1.** member of religious and military order (**Knights T∼s**) for protection of pilgrims to Holy Land, suppressed in 1312. **2.** lawyer or law student with chambers in the Temple, London. [ME, f. AF *templer,* OF *templier,* = med. L *templarius* (as TEMPLE[1]; see -AR[2])]

tĕ'mplate (-ĭt), **tĕ'mplĕt,** *n.* pattern, gauge, usu. thin board or metal plate, used as guide in cutting or drilling metal, stone, wood, etc.; timber or plate used to distribute weight in wall or under beam etc.; molecular pattern governing assembly of protein etc. [orig. *templet*, prob. f. TEMPLE³+-ET¹, alt. after *plate*]

te'mple¹ *n.* **1.** edifice dedicated to accommodation or service of (esp. ancient Egyptian, Greek, Roman, or modern Hindu, Buddhist, etc.) god(s) or other objects of religious reverence. **2.** any of three successive religious buildings of the Jews in Jerusalem; *synagogue. **3.** place of Christian public worship, esp. Protestant church in France. **4.** (fig.) place in which God is regarded as residing, esp. Christian's person or body. **5. Inner, Middle, T∼,** two Inns of Court on site of the Temple (establishment of Knights Templars) in London; **T∼ Bar,** gateway (removed 1879) that marked westward limit of City Corporation's jurisdiction, at junction of Fleet Street and Strand in London. [OE *temp(e)l*, reinforced in ME by OF *temple*, f. L *templum* open or consecrated space]

te'mple² *n.* flat part of either side of head between forehead and ear. [ME f. OF, f. Rom. **temp(u)la*, f. L *tempora* pl. of *tempus*]

te'mple³ *n.* device in loom for keeping cloth stretched. [ME f. OF, orig. same wd as prec.]

te'mplet. See TEMPLATE.

te'mp|o *n.* (*pl.* ∼os, or ∼i *pr.* -ē). **1.** (Mus.) time, rapidity of movement; characteristic speed and rhythm of movement (*waltz tempo*). **2.** (fig.) rate of motion or activity (*the tempo of the war is quickening*). [It., f. L *tempus* time]

te'mporal *a.* **1.** of this life, secular, esp. opp. to *spiritual* (*temporal affairs, interests*); ||∼ **lords** or **lords ∼,** peers of realm (cf. SPIRITUAL); ∼ **power** (of ecclesiastic esp. Pope in temporal matters); hence ∼LY² *adv.* **2.** of or in or denoting time; ∼ **conjunction,** *when* etc. **3.** of the temple(s) of the head (*temporal artery, bone*). [ME, f. OF *temporel* or f. L *temporalis* (*tempus -oris*; see TEMPORARY, TEMPLE², -AL)]

tempora'lity *n.* temporariness; (usu. in *pl.*) a secular possession, esp. properties and revenues of religious corporation or ecclesiastic. [ME, f. LL *temporalitas* (as prec.; see -ITY)]

te'mporalty *n.* (arch.) the laity. [ME, f. TEMPORAL+-TY¹]

te'mporar|y *a.* & *n.* **1.** *a.* lasting, meant to last, only for a time, (*temporary buildings, relief, possession, office*); hence ∼iLY² *adv.,* ∼iNESS *n.* **2.** *n.* person employed temporarily. [f. L *temporarius* (*tempus -oris* time; see -ARY¹)]

te'mporiz|e, -īs|e (-īz), *v.i.* adopt indecisive or time-serving policy; avoid committing oneself, act so as to gain time; comply temporarily with requirements of occasion; hence ∼A'TION, ∼ER¹, *ns.* [f. F *temporiser* bide one's time f. med. L *temporizare* delay (*tempus -oris* time; see -IZE)]

tempt *v.t.* **1.** entice, incite esp. to sin, (*to do, to action* esp. evil one); *I am* ∼**ed** (strongly disposed) *to question this.* **2.** allure, attract. **3.** (arch.) make trial of, try the resolution of, (*God did tempt Abraham*). **4.** provoke, defy, (*shalt not tempt the Lord; would be tempting Providence* or *fate to try it*). **5.** Hence or cogn. ∼ABI'LITY *n.,* ∼ABLE *a.* [ME, f. OF *tenter, tempter* test, f. L *temptare* handle, test, try]

tempta'tion *n.* tempting or being tempted (**the T∼,** esp. of Christ, see Matt. 4); incitement esp. to sin; thing that attracts, attractive course of action. [ME, f. OF *tentacion, temptacion* f. L *temptatio -onis* (as prec.; see -ATION)]

te'mpt|er *n.* one who tempts; **the T∼er,** the Devil; so ∼**ress¹** *n.* [ME, f. OF *tempteur,* f. eccl. L *temptator -oris* (as TEMPT; see -OR)]

te'mpting *a.* enticing to evil; attractive, inviting; hence ∼LY² *adv.* [f. TEMPT+-ING²]

te'mpura (-oora) *n.* Japanese dish of fish or shellfish or vegetables, fried in batter. [Jap.]

ten *a.* & *n.* **1.** one more than nine; symbol for this (10,

x, X); card with ten pips; time of ten o'clock; size etc. denoted by ten; set of ten; (as round number: *ten times as easy; ten to one he forgets it*); HART *of ten;* UPPER *ten.* **2.** *Ten* COMMANDMENTS; ∼**-gallon hat,** cowboy's large broad-brimmed hat; ∼**pins** (usu. treated as *sing.*), game similar to ninepins; *Ten* TRIBES; ∼**-week stock,** garden flower (*Matthiola incana annua*) said to bloom ten weeks after sowing of seed. **3.** Hence ∼**FOLD** *a.* & *adv.,* ∼TH² *a.* & *n.* (∼**th-rate,** of extremely poor quality), ∼**thLY²** *adv.* [OE *tīen, tēn,* = OS *tehan,* OHG *zehan,* ON *tíu,* Goth. *taihun* f. Gmc **tehan, -un* f. IE *dekm]

ten. *abbr.* tenuto.

te'nable *a.* that can be maintained or defended against attack (*a tenable position, fortress, theory*); (of office etc.) that can be held *for* specified time, *by* class of person, etc.; hence **tēn**ABI'LITY, ∼NESS (-beln-), *ns.* [F (*tenir* hold f. L *tenēre*; see -ABLE)]

te'nace *n.* (holding of) two cards, one ranking next above, the other next below, card held by opponent. [F f. Sp. *tenaza,* lit. pincers]

tenā'cious (-shus) *a.* holding fast; keeping firm hold (*of* property, principles, life, etc.), not readily relinquishing; persistent, resolute; (of memory) retentive; adhesive, sticky; strongly cohesive; hence or cogn. ∼LY² *adv.,* ∼NESS, **tenā'city,** *ns.* [f. L *tenax -acis* (*tenēre* hold; see -ACIOUS)]

tenā'cul|um *n.* (*pl.* ∼a). surgeon's sharp hook for picking up arteries etc. [L, = holding instrument (*tenere* hold)]

te'nant *n.,* & *v.t.* *n.* one who occupies land or tenement under a landlord; (Law) person holding real property by private ownership; occupant (*of* any place); ∼ **farmer** (cultivating farm he does not own); ||∼ **right,** right of tenant to continue tenancy at termination of lease; hence or cogn. **te'n**ANCY *n.,* ∼LESS *a.,* ∼RY (1, 2) *n.* **2.** *v.t.* occupy as tenant; hence ∼ABLE *a.* [ME f. OF, part. of *tenir* hold f. L *tenēre*; see -ANT]

tench *n.* (*pl.* same). European freshwater fish (*Tinca tinca*) of carp family. [ME, f. OF *tenche* f. LL *tinca*]

tend¹ *v.i.* be moving, be directed, hold a course, (lit. or fig.; *tends in our direction, downwards, this way, towards the coast, to the same conclusion*); be apt or inclined, serve, conduce, (*to* action, quality, etc.; *to* do). [ME, f. OF *tendre* stretch f. L *tendere tens-* or *tent-*]

tend² *v.* **1.** *v.t.* take care of, look after, (sheep, invalid, machine). **2.** *v.i.* wait (*up*)*on*; *give attention to.* **3.** So ∼'ANCE *n.* (arch.). [ME, f. ATTEND]

te'ndency *n.* way of TEND¹ing, leaning, inclination, (*towards, to,* thing; *to* do). [f. med. L *tendentia* (as TEND¹, see ENCY)]

tendě'ntious (-shus) *a.* (derog.) (Of writing etc.) having an underlying purpose, calculated to promote a particular cause or viewpoint; hence ∼LY² *adv.,* ∼NESS *n.* [f. as prec.+-OUS]

te'nder¹ *n.* In vbl senses; vessel or vehicle attending larger one to supply stores, convey passengers or orders, etc.; carriage attached to steam-locomotive and carrying fuel, water, etc. [ME, f. TEND²+-ER¹, or f. ATTENDER]

te'nder² *v.* & *n.* **1.** *v.t.* offer, present, (one's services, apologies, resignation, etc.); offer (money etc.) as payment. **2.** *v.i.* make a tender (*for* supply of thing or execution of work). **3.** *n.* offer, esp. offer in writing to execute work or supply goods at fixed price; **put out to ∼,** seek tenders in respect of (work etc.). **4. plea of ∼** (that defendant has always been ready to satisfy plaintiff's claim and now brings the sum into court); **legal ∼,** currency that cannot legally be refused in payment of debt (usu. up to limited amount for baser coins etc.). [f. OF *tendre* (see TEND¹); for *-er* cf. RENDER and -ER⁴]

te'nder³ *a.* **1.** soft, not tough or hard, (*tender steak*). **2.** easily touched or wounded, susceptible to pain or grief, (*a tender heart, conscience*); ∼ **place** (on skin etc.); ∼ **spot,** (fig.) subject on which one is touchy. **3.**

delicate, fragile, (lit., or fig. of reputation etc.); **of ~ age,** immature, young. **4.** loving, affectionate, fond, (*tender parents*; *wrote tender verses*); solicitous, considerate, (*of* one's honour, good name, etc.). **5.** requiring careful handling, ticklish, (*a tender subject*). **6. ~ -eyed,** (1) having gentle eyes, (2) weak-eyed; **~foot,** newcomer in bush etc., novice (esp. in Scouts); **~-hearted,** having tender heart, easily moved by pity etc.; **~loin,** ||middle part of pork loin, *undercut of sirloin, *(*T~loin*) district of city where vice and corruption are prominent. **7.** Hence **~IZE** (3) *v.t.,* **~LY²** *adv.,* **~NESS** *n.* [ME, f. OF *tendre* f. L *tener*]

te'ndon *n.* strong band or cord of tissue forming termination and attachment of fleshy part of muscle; **Achilles ~** (connecting heel [where alone Achilles was vulnerable] with calf muscles; in quadruped, = HAMSTRING); so **tĕndĭnı'TIS** *n.,* **tĕ'ndĭnous** *a.* [F, or f. med. L *tendo -dinis* f. Gk *tenōn* sinew (*teinō* stretch)]

te'ndrĭl *n.* slender leafless plant-organ attaching itself to or round another body for support; (fig.) slender curl of hair etc. [prob. f. obs. F *tendrillon* dim. of obs. *tendron* young shoot f. Rom. *tenerumen* f. L *tener* TENDER³]

Te'nĕbrae *n. pl.* (RC Ch.) matins and lauds for last three days of Holy Week, at which candles are successively extinguished. [L, = darkness]

tĕnĕbrĭ'fĭc *a.* (arch.) causing darkness. [f. as prec.; see -FIC]

te'nĕbrous *a.* (arch.) dark, gloomy. [ME, f. OF *tenebrus* f. L *tenebrosus* (as TENEBRAE; see -OUS)]

te'nĕment *n.* piece of land held by an owner; (Law) any kind of permanent property, e.g. lands or rents, held from a superior; dwelling-place; dwelling-house, esp. (Sc.) containing several dwellings; set of apartments used by one family; *~(-house),* house containing several such tenements; so **~AL,** **~ARY¹,** (-mĕ'n-) *adjs.* [ME f. OF, f. med. L *tenementum* (*tenēre* hold; see -MENT]

tĕnĕ'smus (-z-) *n.* (Path.) continual inclination to evacuate bowels or bladder accompanied by painful straining. [med. L, f. Gk *teinesmos* straining (*teinō* stretch)]

tĕnĕt *n.* principle, dogma, doctrine, of a person or school. [L, = he holds (*tenēre* hold)]

tĕ'nfōld. See TEN.

***tĕ'nia.** See TAENIA.

Tenn. *abbr.* Tennessee.

tĕ'nné (-nĭ), **tĕ'nnӯ,** *n.,* & *a.* (usu. placed after *n.*) (Her.) orange-brown. [obs. F, var. of *tanné* TAWNY]

tĕ'nner *n.* (colloq.) ||ten-pound or *ten-dollar note. [f. TEN + -ER¹]

tĕ'nnĭs *n.* **1.** indoor game (**real** or **royal** or *court ~**) for 2 or 4 persons played by striking ball with rackets over net stretched across walled court. **2.** = LAWN² *tennis*. **3.** ~ **arm, elbow,** sprain caused (as) by playing tennis; **~-ball, -court, -racket,** (used in playing tennis). [ME *tenetz, tenes,* etc., app. f. OF *tenez* 'take, receive', called by server to his opponent, imper. of *tenir* take]

tĕ'nnō *n.* (*pl.* ~s). Emperor of Japan viewed as divinity. [Jap.]

tĕ'nnӯ. See TENNÉ.

Tĕnnӯsō'nian *a.* & *n.* **1.** *a.* (in the style of) Tennyson. **2.** *n.* student or admirer of Tennyson. [f. Alfred (Lord) *Tennyson,* Engl. poet d. 1892 + -IAN]

tĕ'non, *n.,* & *v.t.* **1.** *n.* projecting piece of wood made for insertion into corresponding cavity (esp. MORTISE) in another piece; **~-saw** (small, with strong brass or steel back, for fine work). **2.** *v.t.* cut as tenon; join by means of tenon; hence **~ER¹** (1, 2) *n.* [ME f. F (*tenir* hold f. L *tenēre;* see -OON)]

tĕ'nor *n.* **1.** settled or prevailing course or direction, esp. fig. of one's *life,* way, etc.; general purport, drift, (*of* speech, writing, etc.); (Law) (1) actual wording, (2) exact copy. **2.** (Mus.) highest ordinary adult male voice, between baritone and alto or counter-tenor; singer with this voice; part written for tenor voice;

instrument, esp. viola, of which range is roughly that of tenor voice; **~ bell** (largest of peal or set); **~ clef** (placing middle C on second highest line of staff). [ME, f. AF *tenur,* OF *tenour* f. L *tenor -oris* (*tenēre* hold; see -OR)]

tenŏ'tomӯ *n.* tendon-cutting, esp. as remedy for club-foot. [f. F *ténotomie,* irreg. f. Gk *tenōn -ontos* tendon; see -TOMY]

tĕ'nrĕc, tă'nrĕc, *n.* hedgehog-like tailless insectivorous mammal of Madagascar. [F *tanrec,* f. Malagasy *t(r)àndraka*]

tĕnse¹ *n.* (Gram.) form taken by verb to indicate the time (also continuance or completeness) of the action etc. (*present, future, past, imperfect, perfect, tense;* PRIMARY, HISTORIC, *tense*); set of such forms for the various persons and numbers; SEQUENCE *of tenses;* hence **~'LESS** (-sl-) *a.* [ME, f. OF *tens* f. L *tempus* time]

tĕnse² *a.* & *v.* **1.** *a.* (Of cord, membrane, or fig. of nerve, mind, emotion) stretched tight, strained to stiffness; causing tenseness (*a tense moment*); (Phonet.) pronounced with vocal muscles tense; hence **~'LY²** (-slĭ) *adv.,* **~'NESS** (-sn-), **tĕ'nsITY,** *ns.* **2.** *v.t.* & *i.* make or become tense; ~ **up,** become tense. [f. L *tensus* p.p. of *tendere* stretch (TEND¹)]

tĕ'nsĭle *a.* **1.** of tension (*tensile force, stress*); ~ **strength,** resistance to breaking under tension. **2.** capable of being drawn out or stretched; hence **tĕnsĭ'lITY** *n.* [f. med. L *tensilis* (as prec.; see -IL)]

tĕnsĭ'mĕter *n.* instrument for measuring vapour pressure; manometer. [f. foll. + -METER]

tĕ'nsion (-shon) *n.,* & *v.t.* **1.** *n.* stretching, being stretched; tenseness; mental strain or excitement; strained (political, social, etc.) state or relationship. **2.** (Mech.) stress by which bar, cord, etc. is pulled when it is part of a system in equilibrium or motion; expansive force of gas or vapour; SURFACE *tension;* electromotive force (*high, low, tension*). **3.** Hence **~AL** *a.* **4.** *v.t.* subject to tension. [F, or f. L *tensio* (as TEND¹; see -ION)]

tĕ'nson, tĕ'nzon, *n.* contest in verse-making between troubadours; piece of verse composed for this. [F *tenson,* = Prov. *tenso*]

tĕ'nsor *n.* **1.** (Anat.) muscle that tightens or stretches a part. **2.** (Math.) generalized form of vector involving two or more directions for each of its components. [mod. L (as TEND¹; see -OR)]

tĕnt¹ *n.* & *v.* **1.** *n.* portable shelter or dwelling of canvas, cloth, etc., supported by pole(s) and stretched by cords secured to **~-pegs** driven into ground; (Med.) tentlike enclosure for control of air supply to patient. **2.** **~-bed** (with tentlike canopy, or for patient in tent); **~ coat, dress,** (cut very full); **~-fly,** (1) flap at entrance of tent, (2) piece of canvas stretched over ridge-pole of tent leaving open space but keeping off sun and rain; **~-pegging,** cavalry exercise or sport in which rider tries at full gallop to carry off on point of lance tent-peg fixed in ground; **~-stitch,** (one of) series of parallel diagonal stitches [perh. f. another wd]. **3.** *v.t.* cover (as) with tent. **4.** *v.i.* encamp in tent; dwell temporarily. [ME f. OF *tente* f. Rom. *tenta* neut. pl. p.p. (as fem. n.) of L *tendere* stretch]

tĕnt² *n.,* & *v.t.* **1.** *n.* (Surg.) piece, bunch, roll, of lint, linen, etc., inserted into wound or natural opening to keep it open. **2.** *v.t.* (arch.) keep open thus. [ME f. OF *tente* (*tenter* probe, as TEMPT)]

tĕnt³ *n.* deep red sweet wine chiefly from Spain, used esp. as sacramental wine. [f. Sp. *tinto* deep-coloured f. L *tinctus* p.p. (see TINGE)]

tĕ'ntacl|e *n.* long slender flexible process or appendage of (esp. invertebrate) animal, used for feeling, grasping, or moving; (Bot.) sensitive hair or filament; (fig.) thing used like tentacle as feeler etc.; so (-)**~ED** (-keld), **tĕntă'cŭlAR¹, tĕntă'cŭlATE²,** *adjs.* [f. mod. L *tentaculum,* f. L *tentare = temptare* (TEMPT) + -*culum* -CULE]

tĕ'ntative *a.* & *n.* **1.** *a.* done by way of trial, experimental; hesitant, not definite, (*tentative suggestion,* *acceptance*); hence ∼LY² (-vlĭ) *adv.* **2.** *n.* experimental proposal or theory. [f. med. L *tentativus* (as prec.; see -IVE)]

‖**tĕ'nter¹** *n.* person in charge of something, esp. of machinery in factory; workman's unskilled attendant. [f. obs. and Sc. *tent* pay attention perh. f. *tent* attention f. INTENT¹ or obs. *attent* (as ATTEND), +-ER¹]

tĕ'nter² *n.* machine for stretching cloth to dry in shape; ∼(**hook**), each of the hooks that hold the cloth; **on** ∼**hooks**, (arch.) **on the** ∼**hooks**, in state of suspense or mental agitation due to uncertainty. [ME, f. AF **tentur* f. med. L *tentorium* (as TEND¹; see -ER², -OR)]

tĕnth. See TEN.

tĕ'nŭ|is *n.* (*pl.* ∼es *pr.* -ēz). (Phonet.) voiceless stop, e.g. *k, p, t.* [L, = thin, transl. Gk *psilos* smooth]

tĕnŭ'itȳ *n.* slenderness; (of air, fluid) rarity, thinness. [f. L *tenuitas* (as prec.; see -ITY)]

tĕ'nŭous *a.* thin, slender, small; rarefied; (of distinction etc.) subtle, over-refined; hence ∼LY² *adv.*, ∼NESS *n.* [f. L *tenuis* +-OUS]

tĕ'nure (-nyer) *n.* condition, form of right or title, under which (esp. real) property is held; (period of) holding, possession, enjoyment, (*during his tenure of office*); **permanent appointment as teacher etc.; hence **tĕnŭr'IAL** *a.* [ME f. OF (*tenir* hold f. L *tenēre*; see -URE)]

tenu'tō (-ōō'-) *a.* & *adv.* (Mus., of note etc.) sustained, given its full time-value (cf. STACCATO). [It., — held]

tŏ'nzon. See TENSON.

tĕocă'lli *n.* temple of Aztec or other Mex. aborigines, usu. on truncated pyramid. [Nahuatl (*teotl* god, *calli* house)]

tĕ'pee, tee'pee, *n.* conical tent of Amer. Indians, made of skins, cloth, or canvas, on frame of poles. [f. Dakota *tīpī*]

tĕ'pĭd *a.* slightly warm, lukewarm (lit. or fig.); hence or cogn. **tĕpĭ'dITY,** ∼NESS, *ns.*, ∼LY² *adv.* [f. L *tepidus* (*tepēre* be lukewarm; see -ID¹)]

tĕqui'la (-kē'-) *n.* mescal (sense 1) or redistilled mescal. [f. *T*∼ in Mexico]

ter- *pref.* thrice, threefold, (*tercentary; tervalent*). [f. L *ter* thrice]

tĕ'ra- *pref.* denoting factor of 10¹², as ∼METRE². [f. Gk *teras* monster]

terai' (-ī') *n.* wide-brimmed felt hat, often with double crown, worn by travellers etc. in subtropical regions. [f. *T*∼, belt of marshy jungle between Himalayan foothills and plains, f. Hindi *tarāī* moist (land)]

terakihi. See TARAKIHI.

tĕ'raph *n.* (*pl.* ∼im, also used as *sing.*) small image as domestic deity or oracle of ancient Hebrews. [ME, f. LL *theraphim,* Gk *theraphin* f. Heb. *t'rāpīm*]

tĕrato- *comb. form.* monster, as: ∼ge'nic *a.,* ∼geny (-ŏ'j-) *n.,* (of) production of monstrosities; ∼logy (-ŏ'l-), tale(s) of the marvellous, (Biol.) study of animal or vegetable monstrosities; so ∼LO'GICAL *a.,* ∼LOGIST (-ŏ'l-) *n.;* ∼ma (-ŏ'-), tumour of heterogeneous tissues. [f. Gk *teras -atos* monster +-o-]

tĕr'bium *n.* (Chem.) metallic element of lanthanide series. [mod. L, f. *Ytterby* in Sweden +-IUM]

tĕrce *n.* (Eccl.) (office of) canonical hour of prayer appointed for third daytime hour (i.e. 9 a.m.). [var. of TIERCE]

tĕr'cel, tier'cel, *n.* male of hawk, esp. peregrine or goshawk; **tercel-gentle,** male falcon. [ME, f. OF *tercel* etc., f. Rom. **tertiolus* dim. of L *tertius* third, perh. because believed to come from third egg of clutch]

tĕrcĕntenarȳ (-sĕntē'-, -sĕ'ntĭ-) *a.* & *n.* (festival) of the three-hundredth anniversary. [f. TER- + CENTENARY]

tĕrcĕntĕ'nnial *a.* & *n.* **1.** *a.* lasting, occurring every, three hundred years. **2.** *n.* = prec. [f. TER- +CENTENNIAL]

tĕr'cĕt, tier'cĕt, *n.* (Pros.) = TRIPLET. [F, f. It. *terzetto* dim. of *terzo* third f. L *tertius*; see -ET¹]

tĕ'rĕbēne *n.* mixture of terpenes prepared by treating

oil of turpentine with sulphuric acid, used as expectorant etc. [f. foll. + -ENE]

tĕ'rĕbinth *n.* small S. Eur. tree (*Pistacia terebinthus*) yielding turpentine. [ME, f. OF *t(h)erebinte* or f. L f. Gk *terebinthos*]

tĕrĕbi'nthine *a.* of the terebinth; of turpentine. [f. L f. Gk *terebinthinos* (as prec.; see -INE²)]

tĕrĕbr|a *n.* (*pl.* ∼ae). boring ovipositor of Hymenoptera; so ∼ANT *a.,* having a terebra. [L, = borer]

terĕ'dō *n.* (*pl.* ∼s). ship-worm of genus *Teredo,* mollusc that bores ships etc. [L, f. Gk *terēdōn (teirō* rub hard, wear away, bore)]

terĕ'te *a.* (Biol.) smooth and rounded. [f. L *teres -etis*]

tĕr'gal *a.* of the back, dorsal. [f. L *tergum* back + -AL]

tĕr'givĕrs|āte *v.i.* turn one's back on something; be apostate, change one's party or principles; equivocate, make conflicting or evasive statements; hence or cogn. ∼A'TION, ∼ātor, *ns.* [f. L *tergiversari* turn one's back (*tergum* back, *vertere vers-* turn) +-ATE³]

-tĕr'ia *suf.* forming *ns.* denoting self-service establishments. [f. CAFETERIA]

tĕrm¹ *n.* **1.** (arch.) boundary, limit, esp. of time, (*set a term to his encroachments, his existence*); hence ∼LESS *a.* **2.** limited period (*for a term of 5 years; his term of office expired*); (**full**) ∼, completion of (normal) pregnancy; period of tenure; period of some weeks, alternating with holiday or vacation, during which instruction is given in school or university, or ‖during which lawcourt holds sessions (‖EAT one's *terms*), whence ∼'LY¹ *a.,* ∼'LY² *adv.;* period of imprisonment; period over which operations are conducted or results contemplated (*in the short, medium, long, term*). **3.** appointed day, esp. Scottish QUARTER¹-*day.* **4.** (Law). ∼ (**of or for years,** estate or interest in land to be enjoyed for fixed period. **5.** = TERMINUS. **4. 6.** (Math.) each of two quantities in ratio; each quantity in a series; part of expression joined to the rest by + or − ($3x^2 − b + cz$ has three terms). **7.** (Logic). word(s) that may be subject or predicate of a proposition (MAJOR¹, MIDDLE¹, MINOR, *term*). **8.** word used to express a definite concept esp. in particular branch of study etc., (*technical, scientific, law, term*); **in** ∼**s of,** in the language peculiar to, using as basis of expression or thought; CONTRADICTION *in terms;* **in set** (definite) ∼**s. 9.** (in *pl.*) language employed, mode of expression, (*in the most flattering, no* UNCERTAIN, *terms*); *state* etc. **in** ∼**s,** explicitly. **10.** (in *pl.*) conditions, stipulations, (*cannot accept his terms; do it on your own terms; surrendered on terms*); (esp.) charge, price, (*his terms are £5 a lesson; hire-purchase on easy terms;* INCLUSIVE *terms*); **bring** person **to** ∼**s,** cause him to accept conditions; **come to** ∼**s,** yield, give way; **come to** or **make** ∼**s,** conclude agreement (*with*), reconcile oneself *with* difficulties etc.; **on** ∼**s** (fig. of friendship or equality); ‖∼**s of reference,** points referred to an individual or body of persons for decision or report, (definition of) scope of inquiry etc.; ∼**s of trade,** ratio between prices paid for imports and received for exports. **11.** (in *pl.*) relation, footing, (*am on good, bad, familiar, terms with him; not on* SPEAKING¹ *terms*). [ME f. OF *terme* f. L TERMINUS]

tĕrm² *v.t.* denominate, call, (*the music termed plainsong; I forget how or what he terms it*). [f. prec.]

tĕr'magant *n.* & *a.* **1.** *a.* (Hist.; *T*∼). imaginary deity of violent and turbulent character, often appearing in morality plays. **2.** brawling overbearing woman, shrew. **3.** *a.* violent, turbulent, shrewish. [ME *Tervagant* f. OF *Tervagan* f. It. *Trivigante*]

tĕr'minable *a.* that may be terminated; coming to an end after certain time (*terminable annuity*); hence ∼NESS (-bln-) *n.* [f. TERMINATE¹ +-ABLE]

tĕr'minal *a.* & *n.* **1.** *a.* of or forming a limit or terminus (*terminal station*); (Med.) forming or undergoing last stage of fatal disease; (Bot.) borne at end of stem etc.; (Zool. etc.) ending a series (*terminal joints*); of, done etc., each term (*terminal accounts, examinations*); ∼ **figure,** = TERMINUS 4; ∼ **velocity** (of falling body, such that resistance of air etc. prevents further increase of speed under gravity); hence ∼LY² *adv.* **2.** *n.* terminating thing, extremity, esp. point of connection for closing electric circuit; terminus for railway trains or long-distance buses; departure and arrival building for air passengers; ornament at end of column etc.; apparatus for transmission of messages to and from computer, communications system, etc. [f. L *terminalis* (as TERMINUS; see -AL)]

tĕr′mĭnāte *v.* **1.** *v.t.* bound, limit. **2.** *v.t. & i.* bring or come to an end; end (pregnancy) before term by artificial means. **3.** *v.i.* (Of word) end *in* (specified letter(s) or syllable). [f. L *terminare* (as TERMINUS) + -ATE³]

tĕrmĭnā′tion *n.* In vbl. senses; word's final syllable or letter(s) esp. as element in inflexion or derivation, whence ∼AL *a.*; **put a** ∼ **to, bring to a** ∼, make an end of. [ME, f. OF, or f. L *terminatio* (as prec.; see -ATION)]

tĕr′mĭnātor *n.* person or thing that terminates; dividing line between light and dark part of heavenly body. [f. TERMINATE + -OR, or f. LL *terminator*]

tĕr′mĭner. See OYER.

tĕr′mĭn|ĭsm *n.* doctrine that everyone has limited term for repentance; = NOMINALISM; so ∼IST (2) *n.* [f. L TERMINUS + -ISM]

tĕrmĭnŏlŏ′gĭcal *a.* of terminology; ∼ **inexactitude,** (joc.) a lie; hence ∼LY² *adv.* [f. foll. + -ICAL]

tĕrmĭnŏ′log|ў *n.* science of proper use of terms; system of terms used in a science, art, etc.; hence ∼IST (3) *n.* [f. G *terminologie* f. med. L TERMINUS term; see -LOGY]

tĕr′mĭn|us *n.* (*pl.* ∼i *pr.* -ī, *or* ∼uses). **1.** final point, goal; starting-point. **2.** point at end of railway or bus route, pipeline, etc. **3.** (Math.) end-point of vector etc. **4.** figure of human bust ending in square pillar, orig. as boundary-marker. **5.** ∼ **us ad que′m, a quo′** (ahkwō′), finishing-, starting-, point (of argument, policy, period, etc.). [L, = end, limit, boundary]

tĕrmĭtâr′ĭum, tĕr′mĭtarў, *ns.* nest of termites. [f. foll. + -ARIUM, -ARY¹]

tĕr′mĭte *n.* social insect of order Isoptera, chiefly tropical and very destructive to timber, white ant. [f. LL *termes -mitis* alt. f. L *tarmes* after *terere* rub]

tĕr′mor *n.* (Law.) one who holds lands etc. for a term of years, or for life. [ME, f. AF *termer* (as TERM¹; see -ER², -OR)]

tĕrn¹ *n.* sea-bird of genus *Sterna*, like gull but usu. smaller and with long forked tail. [of Scand. orig.; cf. Da. *terne*, Sw. *tärna* f. ON *therna*]

tĕrn² *n.* set of three, esp. three lottery numbers that when drawn together win large prize; such prize. [f. F *terne* f. L *terni* three each]

tĕr′narў *a.* composed of three parts; (Math.) using three as base (*ternary* SCALE³); ∼ **form,** (Mus., of movement) having subject repeated after interposed second subject in related key. [ME, f. L *ternarius* (*terni* three each; see -ARY¹)]

tĕr′nate *a.* arranged in threes, esp. (Bot., of leaf) having three leaflets, whorled in threes; hence ∼LY² (-tlĭ) *adv.* [f. mod. L *ternatus* (as prec.; see -ATE²)]

tĕrne *n.* ∼(-plate), inferior tin-plate alloyed with much lead. [prob. f. F *terne* dull; cf. TARNISH]

terŏtĕchnŏ′logў (tĕr-, tēr-; -k-) *n.* branch of technology dealing with installation and maintenance of equipment. [f. Gk *tēreō* take care of + -O- + TECHNOLOGY]

tĕr′pēne *n.* (Chem.) any of large group of hydrocarbons found in essential oils esp. from conifers and oranges. [f. *terpentin* obs. var. of TURPENTINE + -ENE]

Tĕrpsĭchorē′an (-k-) *n.* pertaining to dancing. [f. *Terpsichore* Muse of dancing + -AN]

terra (tĕ′ra) *n.* ∼ **alba** (ă′lba), pipeclay or similar white mineral [L *albus* white]; ∼ **firma** (fĕr′ma), dry land, firm ground [L *firmus* firm]; ∼ **incognita** (ĭn--kŏ′gnĭta), unknown or unexplored region [L *incognitus* unknown]; ∼ **sigillata** (sĭjĭlā′ta), (1) astringent

clay from Lemnos, (2) Samian ware, [med. L *sigillatus* sealed]. [L, = earth]

tĕ′rrace (-as, -ĭs) *n.*, & *v.t.* **1.** *n.* raised level space, natural or artificial, esp. for walking or standing or cultivation; (Geol.) raised beach, or similar formation beside river etc. **2.** row of housing along top or face of slope, row of contiguous uniform houses; ∼-**house,** one of row of houses joined by party-walls. **3.** *v.t.* form into or furnish with terrace(s); ∼**d house,** = *terrace--house*; ∼**d roof,** flat roof esp. of an Indian or Eastern house. [OF, f. Rom. **terracea* (as prec.; see -ACEOUS)]

tĕrracŏ′tta *n.* unglazed usu. brownish-red fine pottery used as ornamental building-material and in statuary, pottery, etc.; statuette of this; its colour. [It. *terra cotta* baked earth]

terrae filĭ|us (tĕrĭ fĭ′lĭus) *n.* (*pl.* ∼i *pr.* -ī). person of humble or obscure parentage; (Hist.) satirical orator at Oxford Univ. [L, = son of the earth]

tĕrra′in *n.* tract of land as regarded by the physical geographer or the military tactician. [F, f. Rom. **terranum*, f. L *terrenum* neut. (as *n.*) of *terrenus* TERRENE]

tĕrramâr′|a *n.* (*pl.* ∼e *pr.* -ā). = foll. [It. dial.; see foll.]

tĕrramare (-âr′ĭ, -âr′) *n.* (ammoniacal earthy deposit found in mounds in) prehistoric lake-dwelling or -settlement esp. in Italy. [F, f. It. dial. *terra* (*mara* = *marna* marl)]

tĕ′rrapin *n.* N. Amer. edible freshwater tortoise of family Emydidae; (*T*∼; **P**) type of prefabricated one--storey building. [Algonquian]

tĕrra′quĕous *a.* (Of the earth) comprising both land and water; living in or extending over land and water. [f. L *terra* earth + AQUEOUS]

tĕrrâr′ĭ|um *n.* (*pl.* ∼a *or* ∼ums). **1.** vivarium for terrestrial animals. **2.** sealed transparent globe etc. containing growing plants. [mod. L, f. L *terra* earth, after *aquarium*]

tĕrrä′zzō (-tsō) *n.* (*pl.* ∼s). flooring-material of stone chips set in concrete and given a smooth surface. [It., = terrace]

tĕrrē′ne *a.* of earth, earthy; terrestrial. [ME f. AF, f. L *terrenus* (TERRA)]

terr′eplein (tār′plān) *n.* level space where battery of guns is mounted. [orig. = talus behind rampart, f. F *terre-plein* f. It. *terrapieno* (*terrapienare* fill with earth f. *terra* earth + *pieno* f. L *plenus* full)]

terrĕ′strial *a.* & *n.* **1.** *a.* of the earth, esp. opp. to *celestial*; **the** ∼ **globe,** the earth; **a** ∼ **globe** (representing the earth); *terrestrial* MAGNETISM; ∼ **planet,** Mercury, Venus, Earth, or Mars; ∼ **telescope** (giving erect image for observation of terrestrial objects). **2.** of this world, worldly, (*terrestrial aims, interests*). **3.** of land opp. to water; (Zool.) living on the ground, (Bot.) growing in the soil, opp. to *aquatic, arboreal* or *epiphytic, aerial*. **4.** Hence ∼LY² *adv.* **5.** *n.* inhabitant of earth. [ME, f. L *terrestris* (*terra* earth) + -IAL]

tĕ′rrĕt, -ĭt, *n.* each of loops or rings on harness-pad for driving-reins to pass through. [ME, var. of (now dial.) *toret* f. OF *to(u)ret* dim. of TOUR]

terre-verte (tārvâr′t) *n.* soft green earth used as pigment. [F, = green earth]

tĕ′rrĭble *a.* causing terror, fit to cause terror, awful, dreadful, formidable; (colloq.) very great or bad (*he is a terrible bore*); (colloq.) incompetent (*I'm terrible at tennis*); ENFANT TERRIBLE; hence ∼NESS (-bĕln-) *n.* [ME f. F, f. L *terribilis* (*terrēre* frighten; see -IBLE]

tĕ′rrĭblў *adv.* In adj. senses; (sl.) very, extremely, (*he was terribly nice about it*). [f. prec. + -LY²]

tĕrrĭ′colous *a.* living on or in the earth. [f. L *terricola* earth-dweller (*terra* earth, *colere* inhabit) + -OUS]

tĕ′rrier¹ *n.* **1.** small active hardy dog able to pursue fox etc. into earth. **2.** (*T*∼; colloq.) ‖member of Territorial Army etc. [ME, f. OF (*chien*) *terrier* f. med. L *terrarius* f. L *terra* earth; see -ER² (2)]

tĕ′rrier² *n.* book recording site, boundaries, etc.,

of land of private persons or corporations; rent-roll; (Hist.) collection of acknowledgements of vassals or tenants of a lordship. [ME, f. OF *a.* (as *n.*) = med. L *terrarius* (*liber* book); see prec.]

terri′f|ic *a.* causing terror; (colloq.) of great size, excellent (*did a terrific job*), excessive (*making a terrific noise*); hence ~ICALLY *adv.* [f. L *terrificus* (*terrēre* frighten; see -FIC)]

te′rrify *v.t.* fill with terror, frighten (q.v. for constructions). [f. L *terrificare* (as prec.; see -FY)]

te̅rri′genous *a.* produced by the earth or land (*terrigenous deposits*). [f. L *terrigenus* earth-born + -OUS]

terri′ne (-ē′n) *n.* (earthenware vessel, esp. containing and sold with) table delicacy such as pâté. [orig. form of TUREEN]

te′rrit. See TERRET.

te̅rritō̅′ial *a.* & *n.* **1.** *a.* of territory (*territorial possessions*); limited to a district (*the right was strictly territorial*); (*T*~) of (any of) the US Territories; ||**T**~ **Army,** volunteer force organized 1908–67 according to localities to provide reserve of trained and disciplined manpower for use in emergency, now **T**~ **and Army Volunteer Reserve;** ~ **waters,** marginal waters under the jurisdiction of a State, esp. that part of the sea within three (or other number of) miles of shore measured from low-water mark; hence ~IZE (3) *v.t.*, ~LY² *adv.* **2.** *n.* ||member of Territorial Army etc. [f. LL *territorialis* (as TERRITORY; see -AL)]

te̅rritō̅′ialism *n.* system of Church government in which civil power has supreme authority. [f. prec. + -ISM]

te′rritory *n.* extent of land under jurisdiction of sovereign, State, city, etc.; (fig.) sphere, province; area over which goods-distributor or commercial traveller operates; large tract of land; (*T*~) organized division of a country, esp. (US etc.) one not yet admitted to full rights of a State; (Zool.) area held by animal(s) against others of same species; area defended by team etc. in game. [ME, f. L *territorium* (*terra* land; see -ORY)]

te′rror *n.* **1.** extreme fear; ~-**stricken,** ~-**struck,** affected with terror. **2.** person or thing that causes terror; (holy) ~, (colloq.) formidable person, troublesome child, etc.; **king of** ~**s,** Death (Job 18:14); **Reign of T**~, **the T**~, period of French Revolution 1793–4, similar period marked by remorseless sanguinary excesses of revolutionaries (also **Red T**~) or reactionaries (also **White T**~). [ME f. OF *terrour* f. L *terror -oris* (*terrēre* frighten; see -OR)]

te′rror|ist *n.* one who favours or uses terror-inspiring methods of governing or of coercing government or community; hence or cogn. ~ISM (2, 3) *n.,* ~i′stic *a.* [f. F *terroriste* (as prec.; see -IST)]

te′rrorize, -ise (-īz), *v.t.* fill with terror; coerce by terrorism; hence ~A′TION *n.* [f. TERROR + -IZE]

te′rry *n.* & *a.* (pile fabric) with the loops uncut, used esp. for towels. [18th c., of unkn. orig.]

Tersa′nctus *n.* (Eccl.) = SANCTUS. [L (*ter* thrice, SANCTUS)]

te̅rse *a.* (Of speech, written matter, style, writer) free from cumbrousness and superfluity, smooth and concise; curt; hence ~′LY² (-slĭ) *adv.,* ~′NESS (-sn-) *n.* [f. L *tersus* p.p. of *tergēre* wipe, polish]

te̅r′tian (-shan) *a.* & *n.* (fever) recurring every other (by inclusive reckoning every third) day. [ME (*fever*) *tersiane* f. L (*febris*) *tertiana* (as foll.; see -AN)]

te̅r′tiary (-sherĭ) *a.* & *n.* **1.** *a.* of the third order, rank, formation, etc.; next after secondary. **2.** *n.* bird's flight-feather of third row, borne on humerus; (*T*~) member of third order of monastic body, (Geol.) period or system subsequent to Secondary. [f. L *tertiarius* (*tertius* third; see -ARY¹)]

tertium quid (tĕ̅′shĭum kwĭ′d) *n.* a third something, esp. intermediate between mind and matter or between opposite things. [L, app. transl. Gk *triton ti*]

te̅r′valent (tĕr′va-, -vā′-) *a.* (Chem.) = TRIvalent. [f. TER- + *valent-* part. st. f. as VALENCE²]

Te̅′rȳle̅ne, t-, *n.* (P) synthetic polyester used as textile fibre. [f. *terephthalic* acid (f. *terebic* f. TEREBINTH, + PHTHALIC) + ETHYLENE]

terza rima (tārtsa rē′ma) *n.* (Pros.) arrangement of (esp. iambic pentameter) triplets rhyming *aba bcb cdc* etc. as in Dante's *Divina Commedia*. [It., = third rhyme]

terzett|o (tārtsĕ′tō) *n.* (pl. ~i pr. -ē, or ~os). (Mus.) vocal trio. [It.; see TERCET]

Te̅′sla *n.* **1.** ~ **coil,** form of induction coil for producing high-frequency alternating currents. **2.** (*t*~). unit of magnetic induction, = 10,000 gauss. [f. N. ~, Amer. scientist d. 1943]

te′ssell|ate *v.t.* (esp. in *p.p.*) make from tesserae (*tessellated pavement*); (Bot. & Zool., in *p.p.*) regularly chequered; hence ~A′TION *n.* [f. L *tessellare* (*tessella* dim. of foll.) + -ATE³]

te′sser|a *n.* (pl. ~ae). small square usu. cubical block used in mosaic, whence ~AL *a.*; (Rom. & Gk Ant.) small square of bone etc. used as token, ticket, etc. [L f. Gk, neut. of *tesseres, tessares* four]

tessitura (tĕsĭtoor′a) *n.* (Mus.) range within which most tones of a voice-part fall. [It., = TEXTURE]

te̅st¹ *n.* **1.** critical examination or trial of person's or thing's qualities (ACID¹ *test*; BLOOD¹ *test*; BREATH *test*; MEAN¹s *test*; MOT *test*); **put to the** ~, cause to undergo this; STAND¹ *the test.* **2.** means of so examining, standard for comparison or trial, circumstances suitable for this, (*success is not a fair test*). **3.** ground of admission or rejection (*is excluded by our test*). **4.** (Chem.) reagent, substance employed to reveal presence of another in a compound. **5.** ||movable hearth in reverberating furnace with cupel used in separating gold or silver from lead. **6.** (colloq.) test match. **7.** **T**~ **Act** (of 1672–1828, requiring all persons before holding office in Britain to **take the** ~, i.e. the oaths of supremacy and allegiance or equivalent test, or act of 1871 relaxing conditions for university degrees); ~ **bed,** equipment for testing aircraft engines before acceptance for general use; ~ **case,** (Law) case whose decision is taken as settling other cases involving same question of law; ~ **drive** (to determine qualities of motor vehicle with view to regular use; so *test-drive v.t.*); ~ **flight** (to determine performance of aircraft); ~ **match** (in cricket tour etc., usu. between different countries and as one of series); ~ **meal** (of specified quantity and composition, eaten to assist tests of gastric secretion); ~ **paper,** minor examination-paper, (Chem.) paper impregnated with substance changing colour under known conditions; ~-**piece** (performed by entrant in musical etc. competition); ~ **pilot** (undertaking test flights); ~-**tube** (of thin glass closed at one end, for tests or other chem. purposes); ~-*tube baby,* (colloq.) one conceived by artificial insemination, or developing elsewhere than in a mother's body. [ME f. OF, f. L *testu(m)* earthen pot, collateral form of *testa* TEST³; in mod. use mainly f. foll.]

te̅st² *v.t.* put to the test or a test, make trial of, (person, thing, quality); try severely, tax, (one's powers of endurance etc.); ||refine or assay (metal); (Chem.) examine by means of reagent; ~ **out,** put (theory etc.) to practical test; hence ~ABI′LITY *n.*, ~′ABLE *a.*, ~EE′ *n.* [f. prec.]

te̅st³ *n.* external shell etc. of invertebrate, esp. tunicate. [f. L *testa* tile, jug, shell, etc.; cf. TEST¹]

te̅′sta *n.* (pl. ~e). (Bot.) seed-coat. [L (as prec.)]

testa′ceous (-shus) *a.* of shells or shellfish; with hard continuous shell; (Bot. & Zool.) of brick-red colour. [f. L *testaceus* (as TEST³; see -ACEOUS)]

te̅′stacy *n.* being testate. [f. TESTATE, after *intestacy*]

te̅′stament *n.* **1.** = WILL² 8; so ~ARY¹ (-ĕ′n-) *a.* **2.** (Bibl.) covenant, dispensation; **the Old, New, T**~, portion of the Bible dealing with Mosaic, Christian, dispensation; (*T*~) copy of the NT. **3.** (colloq.) (written) statement of one's beliefs, principles, etc. [ME, f. L *testamentum* will (as TESTATE; see -MENT); in early Christian L rendering Gk *diathēkē* covenant]

tĕ′state (-āt, -at) *a*. & *n*. (person) who has left a valid will at death. [f. L *testatus* p.p. of *testari* testify, make will, (*testis* witness); see -ATE²]

tĕstā′|tor *n*. one who has made a will, esp. one who dies testate; so ∼TRIX *n*. [ME, f. AF *testatour* f. L *testator* (as prec.; see -OR)]

tĕ′ster¹ *n*. In vbl senses. [f. TEST² + -ER¹ (1, 2)]

tĕ′ster² *n*. canopy, esp. over four-poster bed. [ME, f. med. L *testerium, testrum, testura* f. Rom. *testa head f. L *testa* tile]

‖**tĕ′ster³** *n*. (Hist.) shilling of Henry VIII, esp. depreciated one; sixpence. [var. of earlier & F *teston* f. Rom. (as prec.; see -OON)]

tĕ′sticle *n*. male organ that secretes spermatozoa etc., esp. one of ovoid pair enclosed in scrotum behind penis of man and most mammals; so **tĕsti′cŭl**AR¹ *a*. [ME, f. L *testiculus* dim. of *testis* witness (of virility)]

tĕsti′cŭlate *a*. having or shaped like testicles; (Bot., esp. of orchid) having pair of tubers so shaped. [f. LL *testiculatus* (as prec.; see -ATE²)]

tĕ′stifȳ *v*. 1. *v.i.* (Of person or thing) bear witness (*to* fact, state, assertion, *against* person etc., (arch.) *of* or *concerning* matter); (Law) give evidence. 2. *v.t.* affirm, declare, (one's regret etc., *that, how*, etc.); (of thing) be evidence of, evince. [ME, f. L *testificari* (*testis* witness; see -FY)]

tĕstimō′nïal *n*. certificate of character, conduct, or qualifications; gift or money presented to person, esp. in public, as mark of esteem, in acknowledgement of services, etc. [ME, f. OF *testimoignal* a. f. *tesmoin* or f. LL *testimonialis* (as foll.; see -AL)]

tĕ′stimonȳ *n*. evidence, demonstration, (*called him in testimony; produce testimony* (to or *of*); *we have his testimony for that; in testimony whereof*); (Law) oral or written statement under oath or affirmation; declarations, statements, (*must rely on the testimony of history, of historians*); (arch.) solemn protest or confession; (Bibl.) the decalogue, esp. *the tables of the testimony*; (in *sing*. or *pl*.) the Scriptures. [ME, f. L *testimonium* (*testis* witness; see -MONY)]

tĕ′st|is *n*. (*pl*. ∼es *pr*. -ēz). (Anat. & Zool.) testicle. [L, = witness (cf. TESTICLE)]

tĕstŏ′sterōne *n*. steroid androgen formed in testicles. [f. TESTIS + -O- + STEROL + -ONE]

tĕstŭ′dinal *a*. of or shaped like a tortoise. [f. as foll. + -AL]

tĕstu′d|ō (-ū′-, -ōō′-) *n*. (*pl*. ∼os, or ∼ines *pr*. -īnēz). (Rom. Ant.) screen formed by body of troops in close array with overlapping shields; movable screen to protect besieging troops. [L *testudo -dinis* tortoise etc. (as TEST³)]

tĕ′st|ȳ *a*. irritable, touchy; hence ∼iLY² *adv*., ∼iNESS *n*. [ME f. AF *testif*, f. OF *teste* head (as TEST³); see -IVE]

tĕtă′n|ic *a*. of, such as occurs in, tetanus (*tetanic spasm*); hence ∼ICALLY *adv*. [f. L f. Gk *tetanikos* (as foll.; see -IC)]

tĕ′tan|us *n*. bacterial disease marked by tonic spasm of voluntary muscles, e.g. lockjaw; prolonged contraction of muscle caused by rapidly repeated stimuli; hence ∼IZE (3) *v.t.*, ∼OID *a*. [ME f. L, f. Gk *tetanos* muscular spasm (*teinō* stretch)]

tĕ′tanȳ *n*. disease with intermittent muscular spasms caused by malfunction of parathyroid glands and consequent deficiency of calcium. [f. F *tétanie* (as prec.; see -Y¹)]

tĕ′(t)ch|ȳ *a*. peevish, irritable; hence ∼iLY² *adv*., ∼iNESS *n*. [prob. f. *tecche, tache* blemish, fault, f. OF *teche, tache*, + -Y²]

tête-à-tête (tātahtā′t) *adv*., *a*., & *n*. 1. *adv*. & *a*. together in private. 2. *a*. private, confidential; concerning only two persons. 3. *n*. private interview or conversation usu. between two; sofa for two face to face. [F, lit. head-to-head]

tête-bêche (tātbā′sh) *a*. (Of postage stamp) printed upside down or sideways relative to another. [F (*tête* head, *bêche* f. *béchevet* double bed-head)]

tĕ′ther (-dh-) *n*., & *v.t.* 1. *n*. rope, chain, halter, by

which grazing animal is confined; (fig.) scope, extent of one's knowledge, authority, etc.; **at the end of** one's ∼, having reached the limit of one's abilities, resources, patience, etc. 2. *v.t.* tie (esp. grazing animal) with tether. [ME, f. ON *tjóthr*, = OHG *zeotar* wagon-pole f. Gmc *teudr- (*teu- fasten)]

tĕ′tra- *comb. form*. 1. four, as: ∼**chord** (-k-), scale series of four notes in half-octave (esp. in ancient music), musical instrument with four strings; ∼**cy′clic**, (Bot.) having four circles or whorls; ∼**da′ctyl** *a*. & *n*., ∼**da′ctylous** *a*., four-toed (animal); ∼**gon**, plane figure with four angles and four sides; ∼**gram**, **T**∼**gra′mmaton**, word of four letters, esp. Hebrew name of God written in four letters; ∼**gynous** (tĭtră′jĭ-), having four pistils; ∼**logy** (tĭtră′l-), group of four related literary or operatic works, esp. (Gk Ant.) three tragedies (trilogy) and satyric drama; ∼**merous** (tĭtră′m-), having four parts; ∼**meter** (tĭtră′m-), (Pros.) verse of four measures; ∼**morph**, (Christian Art) union of attributes of four evangelists in one winged figure; **tetra′ndrous** (tĭtră′-), having four stamens; ∼**ploid**, having four times the haploid set of chromosomes; ∼**pod** *a*. & *n*., ∼**podous** (tĭtră′p-) *a*., (animal or structure) with four feet; ∼**pterous** (tĭtră′p-), having four wings; ∼**stich** (-k), (Pros.) group of four lines of verse; ∼**style** *a*. & *n*., (building) with four pillars esp. forming portico in front or supporting ceiling; ∼**sy′llable**, word of four syllables (so ∼*sylla′bic a*.); **tetrato′mic**, (Chem.) having four atoms (of a specified kind) in the molecule; ∼**va′lent**, (Chem.) having a valence of four. 2. (Chem., forming names of compounds) containing four atoms or groups of a specified kind (*tetroxide*; ∼**cy′clin**, an antibiotic with molecule of four rings; ∼**e′thyl lead**, liquid added to petrol as antiknock). [Gk (*tettares* four)]

tĕ′trăd *n*. the number four; group of four. [f. Gk *tetras -ados* (as prec.; see -AD 1)]

tĕtră′gonal *a*. of a TETRAGON; (Cryst.) having three axes at right angles, two of them equal; hence ∼LY² *adv*. [f. TETRAGon + -AL]

tĕtrahē′dr|on (-a-h-) *n*. (*pl*. ∼a or ∼ons). four-sided solid, triangular pyramid; so ∼AL *a*. [f. late Gk *tetraedron* neut. (as n.) of TETRA(*edros* f. *hedra* base) four-sided; cf. -HEDRON]

tĕ′trărch (-k) *n*. one of four joint rulers; (Rom. Hist.) governor of fourth part of country or province, subordinate ruler; hence or cogn. ∼ATE¹ (1), ∼Y¹, *ns*., ∼ICAL (-ā′rk-) *a*. [ME, f. LL *tetrarcha* f. L *tetrarches* f. Gk *tetrarkhēs* (as TETRA-, *arkhō* rule)]

tĕ′trōde *n*. thermionic valve having four electrodes. [f. TETRA- + Gk *hodos* way]

tĕ′tter *n*. (arch. or dial.) pustular skin-eruption, e.g. eczema; ∼**wort**, greater celandine (supposed to cure tetters). [OE *teter*; cf. OHG *zittaroh*, G dial. *zitteroch*, Skr. *dadru*]

Teut. *abbr*. Teutonic.

Teuto- *comb. form*. = foll., as: ∼MANIA(C), ∼PHIL(E), ∼PHOBE, ∼PHOBIA, *adjs*. & *ns*. (irreg. f. foll. + -O-]

Teu′ton *n*. member of a Teutonic nation, esp. a German; (Hist.) member of a N. Eur. tribe mentioned in 4th c. BC and attacking Roman republic *c*. 110 BC. [f. L *Teutones, Teutoni*, f. IE base meaning 'people' or 'country']

Teutŏ′nic *a*. & *n*. 1. *a*. of the Teutons; of the Germanic peoples or their languages; having characteristics attributed to these peoples; German; hence ∼ISM (4), **Teu′ton**ISM (2, 4), *ns*., **Teu′ton**IZE (3) *v.t*. 2. *n*. Germanic language. [f. F *teutonique* f. L *Teutonicus* (as prec.; see -IC)]

Tex. *abbr*. Texas.

Tĕ′xan *a*. & *n*. (native or inhabitant) of Texas. [f. *Texas* in US + -AN]

tĕxt *n*. 1. original words of author esp. opp. to paraphrase of or commentary on them (*there is nothing about this in the text; the text is hopelessly corrupt*). 2. passage of Scripture quoted as authority or esp. chosen as subject of sermon etc.; subject, theme. **3.** main body of book opp. to notes, pictures, etc.; *textbook; (in *pl.*) books prescribed for study. **4.** ~(-hand), fine large kind of handwriting esp. for manuscripts. **5.** ~book, (*n.*) standard book in a branch of study, (*a.*) = COPY¹- -*book* (2), instructively typical. [ME f. ONF *texte*, *texte* f. L *textus* tissue, literary style (in med. L = Gospel) f. L *texere* text- weave]

te'xtīle *a.* & *n.* **1.** *a.* of weaving (*the textile art, industry*); woven, suitable for weaving, (*textile fabrics, materials*). **2.** *n.* textile material; any cloth. [f. L *textilis* (as prec.; see -IL)]

te'xtūal *a.* of or in the text (*textual* CRITICISM, *errors*); hence ~LY² *adv.* [ME, f. med. L *textualis* (as TEXT; see -AL)]

te'xtūal|ist *n.* one who adheres strictly to the letter of the text; person learned in scriptural texts; so ~ISM (3) *n.* [f. prec. +-IST]

te'xtur|e *n.*, & *v.t.* **1.** *n.* arrangement of threads etc. in textile fabric, characteristic feel due to this; arrangement of small constituent parts, perceived structure, (*of* skin, rock, soil, organic tissue, literary work, etc.); representation of structure and detail of objects in art; (Mus.) quality of sound formed by combining parts; hence ~AL (-scher-, -tūr-), ~eLESS (-cher-), *adjs.* **2.** *v.t.* make by weaving; provide with texture. [ME, f. L *textura* weaving (as TEXT; see -URE)]

||**TGWU** *abbr.* Transport & General Workers' Union.

-th¹ *suf.* forming *ns.* (a) f. *vbs.* (*hirth, growth, tilth*) [f. or after OE & ON, f. IE * *tos* etc.], (b) f. *adjs.* (*breadth, filth, length*) [f. or after OE -*thu*, -*tho*, -*th* f. Gmc *-*ithō* f. IE *-*ttā*].

-th², **-éth¹** (after -*ty*), *suf.* forming ordinal and fractional numbers with all simple numbers from *four* onwards (*4th, fifth, twentieth*). [OE -*tha*, -*the*, or -*otha*, -*othe*, f. IE *-*tos*]

-th³. See -ETH².

Th. *abbr.* Thursday.

Th *symb.* thorium.

Thai (tī) *a.* & *n.* (native, inhabitant, or language) of Thailand; (member) of a Mongolian people in SE Asia or the group of languages spoken by them. [Thai, = free]

thă'lam|us *n.* (*pl.* ~i *pr.* -ī). (Gk Ant.) inner room, women's apartment; (Anat.) interior region of brain where sensory nerves originate, esp. *optic thalamus*; (Bot.) receptacle of flower. [l., f. Gk *thalamos*]

thală'ssic *a.* of sea(s), esp. small or inland seas. [f. F *thalassique* f. Gk *thalassa* sea; see -IC]

tha'ler (tah'-) *n.* (Hist.) German silver coin. [G *t(h)aler*; see DOLLAR]

thali'domide *n.* sedative drug found in 1961 to cause malformation of limbs of foetus when taken by mother early in pregnancy; ~ **baby** or **child** (born deformed, esp. without limb(s), through effects of this drug). [f. ph*thalimidoglutarimide*]

thă'll|ium *n.* rare soft white metallic element; hence ~IC, ~OUS, *adjs.* [f. as THALLUS (from green line in its spectrum) +-IUM]

thă'llogen, thă'llophȳte, *ns.* (Bot.) plant having thallus, e.g. alga or fungus or lichen. [f. mod. L *Thallophyta* (as foll., -GEN, -PHYTE)]

thă'll|us *n.* (*pl.* ~i *pr.* -ī). plant-body without vascular tissue and not differentiated into root, stem, and leaves; hence ~OID *a.* [L, f. Gk *thallos* green shoot (*thallō* bloom)]

tha'lweg (tah'lv-) *n.* **1.** (Geog.) line where opposite slopes meet at bottom of valley or river or lake. **2.** (Law). boundary between States along centre of river etc. [G (*thal, tal* valley, *weg* way)]

Thames (tĕmz) *n.* ||*set the Thames on* FIRE¹; FATHER¹ *Thames*. [river ~ in England]

than (dhan *or, when stressed*, dhăn) *conj.* (& quasi-*prep.*) introducing second member of comparison (*you are taller than he* (*is*), (colloq.) *taller than him*; *I know you better than he* (*does*), *better than* (*I know*) *him*; *it is better to use hot water than cold*; *would do anything rather than let him get hurt, rather than this*; *would do anything rather than that he* *should get hurt*; *a man than whom no one is better able to judge*) or statement of difference (*any person other than himself*; *not known elsewhere than in Britain*). [OE *thanne* etc., orig. same wd as THEN]

thă'nage *n.* (Hist.) rank of or land granted to thane. [ME, f. AF *thanage* (as THANE; see -AGE)]

thănato- *comb. form.* death, as: ~logy (-ŏ'l-), scientific study of phenomena accompanying and practices relating to death. [f. Gk *thanatos* death +-o-]

thāne *n.* (Engl. Hist.) one holding land from king etc. by military service, ranking between ordinary freemen and hereditary nobles; (Sc. Hist.) one holding land from king, ranking with earl's son, chief of clan; hence ~DOM (-nd-), ~SHIP (-nsh-), *ns.* [OE *theg(e)n* servant, soldier, = OS *thegan*, OHG *degan*, ON *thegn* freeman, liegeman f. Gmc *thegnaz f. IE *teknos]

thănk *v.t.* express gratitude to (person *for* thing); ~ **God, goodness, heaven(s)**, etc., (expr. pious gratitude, or (colloq.) pleasure or relief); (I) ~ **you**, (colloq.) ~'**ing you**, (polite formula acknowledging gift, service, offer accepted or refused); ~ **you for nothing** (as contempt. denial that any thanks are due from one); ~ **you for,** (anticipatory) please give me etc.; **I will** ~ **you** (as polite formula, now usu. iron. implying reproach; *I will thank you to shut the door, wipe your shoes, leave my affairs alone*); **he can** ~ **himself, has only himself to ~, for that,** it is his own fault; ~-**you** *n.*, (colloq.) expressing of thanks. [OE *thancian*, = OS *thankon*, OHG *dankōn* f. Gmc *thankōjan (as THANKS)]

thă'nkful *a.* grateful; (of words or act) expressive of thanks; hence ~LY² *adv.*, ~NESS *n.* [OE *thancful* (as THANKS, -FUL)]

thă'nklèss *a.* not feeling or expressing gratitude; (of task etc.) not likely to win thanks, unprofitable; hence ~LY² *adv.*, ~NESS *n.* [f. as foll. +-LESS]

thănks *n. pl.* **1.** (expression of) gratitude (*give thanks to Heaven; expressed his heartfelt thanks; she smiled her thanks; small, iron. much, thanks I got for it; many thanks for your help*); say grace ~, say grace at meal; RETURN¹ *thanks*; **thank-offering**, offering made as act of thanksgiving; ~ **to** (as the good or bad result of) *my foresight, your obstinacy*; **small** or **no** ~ **to,** despite. **2.** (As formula) thank you (esp. colloq., *thanks awfully, very much*, etc.). [pl. of obs. *thank* f. OE *thanc*, = OS *thank*, OHG *danc*, Goth. *thagks* f. Gmc *thankaz, cogn. w. THINK]

thă'nksgiving (-g-) *n.* expression of gratitude esp. to God; form of words for this (**General T~**, in Book of Common Prayer); ***T~** (**Day**) (set apart for giving thanks to God, fourth Thursday in November in US, usu. second Monday in October in Canada). [f. prec. | GIVE¹ |-ING¹]

thăr (tär) *n.* goat-antelope of Nepal; Himalayan wild goat. [native name in Nepal]

that¹ *a., pron.,* & *adv.* **1.** *dem. a.* & *pron.* (*pr.* dhăt; *pl.* **those** *pr.* dhōz). the (person, thing), the person or thing, pointed to or drawn attention to or observed by the speaker at the time, or already named or understood or in question or familiar, (*observe that dog in the next field; who is that* (*woman*) *in the garden?; what was that* (*noise*)?; *what bird is that?; don't roll your eyes in that imbecile fashion; I knew all that before; that* (action of yours or of which you speak) *is not fair; I use that term in a special sense; much to the disgust of that monarch; things were easier in those days*); (expr. strong feeling: *I will not see that boy bullied; when you have done thumping that piano; shall not easily forget that day; 'Are you glad?' 'I am that'*); (coupled or contrasted with THIS, and applied esp. to the farther, less immediate or obvious, etc., of two; *this poker is much heavier than that* (one)); (on telephone) ||the person spoken to (*who is that?*); **and** (**all**) **that,** and all or various things associated with or similar to what has been mentioned, and so forth; AT *that*; **wouldn't give** ~ (a snap of the fingers) **for** it; HOW's *that?*; **like** ~, of that kind, in that manner, as you are doing, as he has been doing, etc., (*don't roll your eyes like that; wish he would not talk like that*), without effort (*did *the job just like tha′t*), of that character (*he wouldn't accept any payment—he is like that*); TAKE[1] *that!*; THIS *and that*; THIS, *that, and the other*; WITH *that*; ∼ **is** (**to say**) (introducing explanation of preceding word or words); *that's* IT[1]; ∼**'s more like it,** you are improving; ∼**'s right!** (expr. approval or (colloq.) assent); ∼**'s** *a dear, a good boy,* etc., (colloq.) you are (by virtue of present or future obedience etc.); (so[1]) ∼**'s** ∼ (concluding a narrative or discussion, or completing a task); ∼ **there,** (vulg.) = *that* a.; ∼ **will do,** no more is needed or desirable. **2.** *pron.* (replacing *the* w. noun, w. sense completed by *rel. pron.* expressed or omitted: *those who drink water think water; those may try it who choose; hold fast that which is good; had that in his eye which forbade further trifling; all those (that) I saw; all those specimens that I saw;* or by *a.* or equivalent: *those unfit for use; those below the standard; a tunic like that described above; those persons most affected by the tax; like most of those coming from abroad; cost of oil is more than that of gas*); (arch. or colloq., foll. by THAT[2]) such, such a, (*has that confidence in his theory that he would put it into practice tomorrow; was wounded to that degree that he resigned*). **3.** *adv.* (colloq.) to such a degree, so, (*will go that far; have done that much*); (**all**) ∼, very (*not all that expensive*). **4.** *rel. pron.* (*pr.* dhat; *pl.* same; used, exc. arch., rhet., or poet., only to introduce defining-clause essential or rhet. viewed as essential to identification; often omitted esp. after antecedent in obj. case; cf. WHICH, WHO: *the book* (*that* or *which*) *I sent you; the box* (*that* or *which*) *you put them in; the man* (*that* or *whom*) *you saw; the people* (*that*) *you got it from* or *from whom you got it; the meanest flower that blows; the best* (*that*) *you can do; no one* (*that*) *I ever heard of could see any difference; what is it* (*that*) *makes you sad?; this is all* (*that*) *I have; there is nothing here that matters*). **5.** *rel. adv.* = *prep.* + sense 4 (*the day* (*that*) *I first met her; at the speed* (*that*) *he was going he could not stop*). [OE *þæt,* nom. & acc. sing. neut. of dem. pron. & a. *se, sēo, þæt* (see THE); *those* f. OE *þās* pl. of *þes* THIS]

that[2] (dhæt, *or, when stressed,* dhăt) *conj.* (introducing subord. clause; often omitted): (statement or hypothesis) *they say* (*that*) *he is better; there is no doubt* (*that*) *he meant it; it is suggested that the mistake was intentional; it is monstrous that he should expect further help;* (result was that the handle fell off; (purpose) *he lives that he may eat; he withdrew (in order) that the dispute might cease;* (result) *am so sleepy* (*that*) *I cannot keep my eyes open; his language was such that we refused to see him again; what have I done that you should treat me like this?; where is he, that you come without him?;* (reason or cause) *it is rather that he has not the time;* (wish) (*Oh!) that we two were maying;* IN[1] *that;* NOT *that;* NOW *that.* [uses of THAT[1] dem. or rel. pron., in which it becomes a mere rel. or conj. particle]

thătch *n.,* & *v.t.* **1.** *n.* roof-covering of straw, reeds, palm-leaves, etc.; (colloq.) hair of the head. **2.** *v.t.* cover (roof, house, or abs.) with thatch; hence ∼ *ER*[1] *n.* [n. late collateral form of (now dial.) *thack* (OE *þæc,* = OHG *dach* roof f. Gmc **thakam*), after v. f. OE *theccan* = OS *thekkian,* OHG *decchen,* ON *thekja* f. Gmc **thakjan,* assim. to *thack*]

thau′matrōpe *n.* disc etc. with two different pictures on its two sides, which combine into one by persistence of visual impressions when disc is rapidly rotated; zoetrope. [irreg. f. Gk *thauma* marvel + *-tropos* -turning]

thau′matūrg|e, thau′matūrg|ist, *ns.* worker of miracles, wonder-worker; hence or cogn. **thaumatū′r′g**IC(AL) *adjs.,* ∼Y[1] *n.* [f. med. L f. Gk *thaumatourgos* a. (*thauma -matos* marvel + *-ergos* -working)]

thaw *v.* & *n.* **1.** *v.i.* (Of ice, snow, frozen thing) pass into liquid or unfrozen state; (of weather, *it*) become warm enough to melt ice etc.; become warm enough to lose numbness etc.; (fig.) become less cold or stiff in manner, become genial. **2.** *v.t.* cause to thaw (lit. or fig.) **3.** *n.* thawing; warmth of weather that thaws (*a thaw has set in*); hence ∼ LESS, ∼Y[2] *adjs.* [OE *thawian,* = OHG *douwen* f. WG **thawōjan,* of unkn. orig.]

the (*before vowel* dhĭ, *before consonant* dhe, *when stressed* dhē) *a.* & *adv.* **1.** *a.* (Called the *definite article;* placed before *ns.* to denote person(s) or thing(s)) already mentioned or under discussion, or from the nature of the case actually or potentially existent, or unique (as class or individual), or familiar, or otherwise sufficiently identified, (*tried to soothe the child; gave the man a tip; shall let the matter drop; called on everyone in the building; got there and back in the day, within the week; how is the game or score?, what is the score, the time?; depends on the weather; the Devil, sun, moon, stars, Himalayas, Thames; inflammation of the lungs; pulled the trigger; what was the result?; generally correct, but there is the occasional error; you will be the loser; revised by the author; flowers that bloom in the spring; came into the garden; find their way to the sea; went to the baths, the theatre, *is in the hospital with a broken leg; the Queen, President, Prime Minister, Earl of Norfolk; the difficulty is to avoid slipping; if you want a quick survey, this is the book; story does not lose in the telling*); ||(colloq.) *my, our,* (*the wife, the dog*). **2.** (w. *sing. n.* as repr.) species, class, etc., (*the lion, domestic cat, philosopher, cucumber, gavotte, general reader, man in the street; was quite the philosopher about his misfortunes; has the novel a future?; the pen is mightier than the sword; plays the harp superbly; we have the television;* (rhet., esp. Bibl.) *the oppressor, years that the locust hath eaten*). **3.** (w. *n.* as fig. repr.) occupation, pursuit, etc., (*the stage, theatre, platform, pulpit, hustings, table, bottle*); **the Macnab** etc., chief of clan of that name; (w. names of diseases etc.) *the itch, the fidgets,* (colloq.) *the measles, the toothache,* (arch.) *the smallpox;* (w. names of units) = a, per, (£5 *the square foot; allow 8 minutes to the mile; 16 ounces go to the pound*); (w. units of time) present, current, (*man of the moment, hero of the hour, questions of the day, book of the month, best-dressed woman of the year, painter of the century*). **4.** (w. sense completed by *a.* or rel. clause or equivalent: *the book* (*that*) *you borrowed; the best* (*that*) *I can do for you; wonder you have the impudence* (*to ask it*), (excl.) *the impudence of the fellow!; the cup on the top shelf; the one with a broken handle; the England of today; the best way; the only way; the way out; the upper classes; the better man of the two*). **5.** (w. *adjs.* used abs.) that which is, those who are, etc., (*from the sublime to the ridiculous; none but the brave deserve*(s) *the fair; your letter of the ninth* (day of the month)). **6.** (w. *adjs.* used rhet. etc. as part of definition) which is, who are, etc., (*gave details of the shocking disaster; scored past the unsighted Smith; Alfred the Great, Edward the Seventh, the Honourable James Jones;* ||*the High Street*). **7.** (Stressed; of person or thing) best known or best entitled to the name (*no relation to the Kipling*). **8.** *adv.* (a) *rel.,* only in comb. w. (b). in whatever degree. (b) in that degree, by that amount, on that account, (*the more he gets, the more he wants; I play the worse, the more I practise; am not* (or *none*) *the more inclined to help him because he is poor, on that account, for what you tell me; none the better for seeing you*); *that makes it* **all** ∼ **worse** (in the full degree to be expected from what you say etc.); (tautologically) **so much** ∼ *worse for him,* the worse (*or* so much worse) for him. [a. OE, replacing *se, sēo, þæt,* (= THAT[1]), = ON *sá, sú, that,* OHG *der, diu, daz,* Goth. *sa, sō, thata,* f. Gmc **sa, *so, *that;* adv. f. OE *thȳ, thē,* instrumental case]

thēā′ndric *a.* of union, or by joint agency, of divine and human nature in Christ. [f. eccl. Gk *theandrikos* (*theos* god, *anēr andros* man; see -IC)]

thēanthrō′pic *a.* both divine and human; tending to embody deity in human form. [f. eccl. Gk *theanthrōpos* god-man (*theos* god, *anthrōpos* man) + -IC]

thē′archy (-kĭ) *n.* government by god(s); system or order of gods (*the Olympian thearchy*). [f. eccl. Gk *thearkhia* rule of god (*theos* god, *-arkhia* f. *arkhō* rule)]

thē′atre (-ter), *****thē′ater,** *n.* **1.** building or outdoor area for dramatic representations; cinema; ∼**-going,** frequenter of, frequenting, theatres; ∼**-in--the-round,** dramatic performance on stage surrounded by spectators. **2.** room or hall for lectures etc. with seats in tiers; || = *operating theatre* (see

OPERATE; ～ **sister,** nurse assisting in this). **3.** dramatic literature or art; effective material for stage (makes good theatre). **4.** scene or field of action (the theatre of war; so theatre weapons). **5.** natural land- -formation in gradually rising part-circle like ancient Gk & Rom. theatres. [ME, f. OF t(h)eatre or f. L f. Gk theatron (theaomai behold)]

theā′tric a. = foll. [f. as foll.; see -IC]

theā′trical a. & n. **1.** a. (Of manner, speech, gesture, person) calculated for effect, showy, artificial, affected; of or suited to the theatre, of acting or actors; hence ～ISM (2, 4), ～ITY (-ă′l-), ns., ～IZE (3) v.t., ～LY² adv. **2.** n. (in pl.) theatrical actions; theatrical performances, esp. private or amateur theatricals. [f. LL f. Gk theatrikos (theatron THEATRE) + -ICAL]

Thē′ban a. & n. (inhabitant or native) of Thebes in ancient Egypt or ancient Greece. [ME, f. L Thebanus (Thebae Thebes f. Gk Thēbai)]

thē′ca n. (pl. ～e pr. -sē). (Bot.) part of plant serving as receptacle; (Zool.) case or sheath enclosing organ or part. [L, f. Gk thēkē case]

thé dansant (tā dahnsah′n) n. afternoon tea with dancing. [F]

thee. See THOU.

theft n. (act or instance of) stealing; (Law) dishonest appropriation of another's property with intent to deprive him of it permanently. [OE thiefth, theofth, later theoft, = ON thyft(h) f. Gmc *thiuhhithō (as THIEF, -TH¹)]

thegn (-ān) n. (Engl. Hist.) = THANE. [OE; see THANE]

thē′ine n. = CAFFEINE. [f. mod. L thea tea + -INE⁵]

their (dhār) poss. pron. attrib. of them(selves); for phrs. see HER², OUR. [ME, f. ON their(r)a of them, gen. pl. of sá THE, that]

theirs (dhārz) poss. pron. pred. (& abs.) = prec.; for phrs. see HERS. [ME, f. prec. + -s³]

thē′ism n. belief in existence of gods or a god, esp. a God supernaturally revealed to man (cf. DEISM) and sustaining a personal relation to his creatures; so ～IST (2) n., ～i′stic(AL) adjs. [f. Gk theos god + -ISM]

them. See THEY.

themă′t|ic a. **1.** (Mus.) of themes (thematic treatment); ～ic catalogue (giving opening themes of works as well as names etc.). **2.** (Gram.) of or belonging to a theme (thematic vowel, form); (of form of verb) having thematic vowel. **3.** Hence ～ICALLY adv. [f. Gk thematikos (as foll.; see -IC)]

thēme n. subject on which one speaks, writes, or thinks; *school composition, essay, on given subject; (Gram.) stem of noun or verb, part to which inflexions are added, esp. composed of root and added vowel; (Mus.) melodic subject usu. developed with variations (～ song, recurrent melody in musical play or film; ～ song or tune, signature tune of performer etc.); (Hist.) any of 29 provinces in Byzantine empire. [ME teme f. OF *teme f. L f. Gk thema -matos (tithēmi set, place)]

themse′lves (dhemsĕ′lvz) pron. Emphat. & refl. form corresp. to THEY or THEM (for uses cf. HERSELF, ITSELF). [f. THEM + pl. of SELF]

thĕn (dh-) adv., a., & n. **1.** adv. at that time (was then too much occupied; then comes the trouble; the then existing laws; Sir Winston, then Mr., Churchill); NOW and then; ～ **and there,** immediately and on the spot. **2.** next, after- wards, after that, and also, (it must then soak for two hours; and then the operation is complete; then (again,) there are the children to consider); it is a problem, but then (after all) that is what he is here for. **3.** in that case, therefore, it follows that, (then you should have said so; then it is no use your going); (but) then (if what you say is true) why did you take it?; (of grudging or impatient concession) if you must have it so (take it then; 'Between you and I' . . . 'me', then); (resumptively, not as first word) accord- ingly (the new Governor, then, came prepared); NOW then; WELL⁴ then; WHAT then?. **4.** a. existing etc. at that time (the then Duke, secretary). **5.** n. that time (before, till, by,

from, then); every NOW and then. [OE thanne, thonne, etc., = OS than(na), OHG danne, denne, adv. form. f. dem. root *tha-; cf. THAT¹, THE]

thē′nar n. (Anat.) palm of hand, sole of foot; ball of thumb. [mod. L f. Gk]

thĕnce (dh-) adv. & n. (arch. or literary). (from) ～, from that place or source, for that reason, (a dis- crepancy thence results; it thence appears); (from) ～for′th, ～for′ward, from that time onward. [ME thannes, thennes, (thanne, thenne adv. f. OE thanon(e) etc., = OS & OHG danan(a) f. WG *thanana) + -s³]

thē′o- comb. form. God or god, as: ～ce′ntric, having God as its centre; ～cracy (thĭŏ′k-), form of govern- ment by God or god directly or through a priestly order etc. (the Theocracy, Jewish commonwealth from Moses to the monarchy), so ～CRAT n.; ～crasy (thē′okrăsĭ, thĭŏ′krasĭ), (1) mingling of deities into one personality, (2) union of soul with God through contemplation (among Neoplatonists, Buddhists, etc.), [f. Gk krasis mingling]; ～dicy (thĭŏ′d-), vindication of divine providence in view of existence of evil [f. Gk dikē justice], whence ～dice′AN a.; ～gony (thĭŏ′g-), (account of) genealogy of the gods; ～machy (thĭŏ′makĭ), strife against or among the gods [f. Gk makhe fight]; ～ma′nia, (1) insane belief that one is God, (2) religious insanity; ～phany (thĭŏ′f-), visible manifestation of god to man; ～phor′ic, bearing the name of god; ～pneust, divinely inspired. [Gk (theos god; see -O-)]

thēobrō′mine (-ĭn, -ēn) n. bitter white alkaloid from cacao seeds, related to caffeine. [f. Theobroma cacao genus, mod. L f. Gk theos god + brōma food, + -INE⁵]

theŏ′dol|ite n. surveying-instrument for measuring horizontal and vertical angles by means of rotating telescope; hence ～i′tic a. [16th c. theodelitus, of unkn. orig.]

thēolō′gian n. person skilled in theology. [ME, f. OF theologien (as foll.; see -IAN)]

theŏ′log|y n. study of or system of (esp. Christian) religion; rational analysis of a religious faith; hence or cogn. **thēolō′g|ICAL** a. (theological VIRTUES), ～IST (3) n., ～IZE (1, 2) v.t. & i. [ME f. OF theologie f. L f. Gk THEO(logia -LOGY)]

thēophy′lline (-ĭn, -ēn) n. alkaloid similar to theobromine, found in tea-leaves. [irreg. f. mod. L thea tea + Gk phullon leaf + -INE⁵]

theŏr′bo n. (pl. ～s). two-necked musical instrument of lute class much used in 17th c. [f. It. tiorba, of unkn. orig.]

thē′orem n. (Math.) proposition not self-evident but to be proved by chain of reasoning, a truth to be established by means of accepted truths, (cf. PROBLEM); algebraical or other rule, esp. one ex- pressed by symbols or formulae, (BINOMIAL theorem); so ～A′TIC a. [f. F théorème or f. LL f. Gk theōrēma speculation, proposition (theōreō look at)]

theŏrĕ′tic a. & n. **1.** a. = foll. **2.** n. (in sing. or pl.) speculative part of a science etc. [f. LL f. Gk theōrētikos (as THEORY; see -ETIC)]

theŏrĕ′tical a. concerned with knowledge but not with its practical application, speculative; based on mere theory, not dealing with facts as presented by experience; hence ～LY² adv. [f. as prec. + -AL]

theŏrĕti′cian (-shạn) n. person concerned with theoretical part of a subject. [f. THEORETIC + -IAN]

thē′or|y n. supposition or system of ideas explaining something, esp. one based on general principles independent of the facts, phenomena, etc., to be explained, opp. to HYPOTHESIS, (atomic theory; theory of gravitation, evolution); speculative (esp. fanciful) view (one of my pet theories); the sphere of abstract know- ledge or speculative thought (this is all very well in theory, but how will it work in practice?); exposition of the principles of a science etc. (the theory of music); (Math.) collection of propositions to illustrate principles of a subject (probability theory; theory of equations); hence

∼IST (3) *n.*, ∼IZE (2) *v.i.* [f. LL f. Gk *theōria* (*theōros* spectator f. *theōreō* look at)]

thĕŏ'soph|ў *n.* any of various philosophies professing to achieve a knowledge of God by spiritual ecstasy, direct intuition, or special individual relations, esp. a modern movement following Hindu and Buddhist teachings and seeking universal brotherhood; hence or cogn. **thĕ'osŏph**, ∼ER¹, ∼IST (2), *ns.*, **thĕo-sŏ'phIC**(AL), **thĕosophi'stIC**(AL), *adjs.*, ∼IZE (2) *v.i.* [f. med. L f. late Gk *theosophia* f. THEO(*sophos* wise) wise concerning God]

thĕrapeu't|ic *a.* & *n.* **1.** *a.* curative; of the healing art; hence ∼ĭCAL *a.*, ∼ĭcalLY² *adv.*, ∼IST (3) *n.* **2.** *n.* (in *pl.*, usu. treated as *sing.*) branch of medicine concerned with treatment of disease and action of remedial agents in disease or health. [orig. n., f. F *thérapeutique* or f. LL f. Gk *therapeutika* neut. pl. (as *n.*) of *therapeutikos* (*therapeuō* wait on, cure; see -IC)]

thĕ'rap|ў *n.* medical treatment of disease; hence ∼IST (3) *n.* [f. mod. L f. Gk *therapeia* healing]

Thĕrava'da (-ah'-) *n.* = HINAYANA. [f. Pali *theravāda* (*thera* elder, old, *vāda* speech, doctrine)]

there (dhār; in sense 3 usu. dh*er*) *adv.*, *n.*, & *int.* **1.** *adv.* in or at that place or position (*put it there*; *put it down, in, out, over, through, under, up, there*; *what is that dog doing there?*; *lived there for some years*; ALL *there*; **have been** ∼ **before**, (sl.) know all about it; HERE *and there*; *neither* HERE *nor there*; ∼ **and then**, = THEN *and there*; (calling attention) **hallo** ∼!, **you** ∼!, **move along** ∼!, ∼ **goes the bell**, *there's courage* etc. FOR *you*, ∼ (= THAT¹)'s *a dear* etc.); in that respect, at that point in argument, progress of affairs, situation, etc., (*there I agree with you*; *there you go misquoting me again*; *ay, there's the* RUB¹)'s *a dear* etc.); *that is my final decision* (whether you like it or not); ∼ **it is**, (1) that is the trouble, (2) nothing can be done about it; ∼ **you are**, this is what you wanted etc. (& see sense 5). **2.** to that place or position (*goes there every day*; *got there, there and back, in two hours*); **get** ∼, (sl.) succeed, understand what is meant; ∼ **or** ∼**abouts**, about that place, amount, time, etc., ('*Was it two years ago?*' '*There or thereabouts*'). **3.** (Merely expletive or introductory, preceding, or in interrog. or neg. or quasi-neg. sentence following, vb., which normally precedes its subject, esp. *be*; in poet. or excl. use, subject may stand first: *there was a cart close by*; *was there anything in it?*; *there will be plenty to eat*; *what is there for supper?*; *not a sound was there to indicate their presence*; *seldom has there been more fuss*; *there fell a deep silence*; *a fool there was*; *a nice mess there is or seems to be!*). **4.** *n.* that place (*was brought from there*; *lives somewhere near there*; *tide comes up to there*; *passed by there*). **5.** *int.* expr. confirmation, triumph, dismay, etc., (*there (you are)! what did I tell you?*) or used to soothe child etc. (*there, there, never mind*). **6.** ∼**abou't(s** (cf. sense 2), near that place (*ought to be somewhere thereabouts*), near that number, quantity, etc., (*two litres or thereabouts*); ∼**a'fter**, (formal) after that; ∼**ane'nt**, (Sc.) about that matter; ∼**a't**, (arch.) at that place, on that account, after that; ∼**by** (dharbī', dhar'bī), by that means, as result of that (∼*by hangs a tale*, in which connection there is something to be told); ∼**for'**, (arch.) for that object or purpose; ∼**'fore**, for that reason, accordingly, consequently, [= *therefor*]; ∼**fro'm**, (arch.) from that or it; ∼**i'n**, (formal) in that place, in that respect; ∼**ina'fter**, ∼**inbefor'e**, later, earlier, in same document etc.; ∼**i'nto**, (arch.) into that place; ∼**o'f**, (formal) of that or it; ∼**o'n**, (arch.) on that or it (of motion or position); ∼**ou't**, (arch.) out of that, from that source; ∼**throu'gh**, (arch.) through that; ∼**to'**, (formal) to that or it, in addition, to boot; ∼**tofor'e**, (formal) before that time; ∼**u'nto**, (arch.) to that or it; ∼**upo'n**, in consequence of that, soon or immediately after that, (arch.) upon that (of motion or position); ∼**wi'th**, (arch.) with that, thereupon; ∼**witha'l**, (arch.) in addition, besides. [OE *thǣr, thēr*, = OS *thār*, OHG *dār*, ON, Goth. *thar* f. dem. root **tha-* (cf. THAT¹, THE)]

thĕr'iac *n.* (arch.) antidote to bites of poisonous animals, esp. snakes. [f. L f. Gk *thēriakē* antidote, fem. (as n.) of *thēriakos* (as foll.; see -AC)]

thĕriänthrŏ'pic *a.* of or worshipping beings represented in combined form of man and animal. [f. Gk *thērion* dim. of *thēr* wild beast + *anthrōpos* man + -IC]

thĕriomŏr'phic *a.* (Esp. of deity) having animal form. [f. as prec. + Gk *morphē* form + -IC]

thĕrm *n.* unit of heat, esp. ||statutory unit of calorific value in gas-supply (100,000 British THERMAL units). [f. Gk *thermē* heat]

thĕr'mae *n. pl.* (Gk & Rom. Ant.) public baths. [L, f. Gk *thermai* pl. (as prec.)]

thĕr'mal *a.* & *n.* **1.** *a.* of heat; ∼ **capacity**, number of heat units needed to raise temperature of a body by one degree; ∼ **reactor**, nuclear reactor using ∼ **neutrons** (in thermal equilibrium with surroundings); ∼ **springs** (of naturally hot water); ∼ **unit** (for measuring heat); *British* ∼ **unit**, amount of heat needed to raise 1 lb. of water at maximum density one degree F; hence ∼LY² *adv.* **2.** *n.* rising current of heated air (used by gliders to gain height). [F (as THERM; see -AL)]

thĕr'mic *a.* = prec. [f. as THERM + -IC]

thĕr'midôr *n.* **lobster** ∼, mixture of lobster meat, mushrooms, cream, egg yolks, and sherry, cooked in lobster shell. [*T*∼, name of eleventh month of Fr. revolutionary calendar, f. as THERM + Gk *dōron* gift]

thĕr'mïon *n.* ion or electron emitted by incandescent substance; hence **thĕrmïŏ'nIC** *a.* (∼ic ||valve or **tube, device giving flow of thermionic electrons in one direction, used esp. in rectification of current and in radio reception). [f. THERMO- + ION]

thĕrmi'stor *n.* (Electr.) resistor whose resistance is greatly reduced by heating, used for measurement and control. [f. *thermal resistor*]

thĕr'mïte, thĕr'mit, *n.* mixture of finely powdered aluminium and oxide of iron that produces a very high temperature on combustion (used in welding and for incendiary bombs). [G *thermit* (as foll.; see -ITE¹)]

thĕr'mŏ- *comb. form.* heat, as: ∼**che'mistry**, branch of chemistry dealing with the quantities of heat evolved or absorbed during chemical reactions; ∼**electri'city**, electricity produced by difference of temperature, so ∼**ele'ctric** *a.*; ∼**ge'nesis**, production of heat esp. in human or animal body; ∼**gram**, record made by ∼**graph** (self-registering thermometer); ∼**la'bile**, unstable when heated; ∼**lumine'scent**, luminescent when heated; ∼**lysis** (-ŏ'l-), decomposition by action of heat; ∼**nu'clear**, relating to nuclear reactions that occur only at very high temperatures, (of bomb etc.) using such reactions; ∼**phil(e)**, (bacterium etc.) growing at high temperatures; ∼**pile**, set of thermocouples esp. arranged for measuring small quantities of radiant heat; ∼**pla'stic**, (substance) becoming plastic on heating, hardening on cooling, and able to repeat these processes; ∼**se'tting**, (of plastics) setting permanently when heated; ∼**sphere**, region of atmosphere beyond mesosphere; ∼**sta'ble**, stable when heated; ∼**ta'xis**, regulation of heat or temperature esp. in warm-blooded animals, so ∼**ta'ctic**, ∼**ta'xic**, *adjs.*; ∼**tropism** (-ŏ't-), involuntary movement of animal or plant towards or away from source of heat, so ∼**tro'pic** *a.* (*thermos* hot, *thermē* heat)]

thĕr'mocouple (-kŭ-) *n.* pair of different metals in contact at a point, generating thermoelectric voltage that can serve as measure of temperature at this point relative to their other parts. [f. THERMO- + COUPLE¹]

thĕrmodynã'm|ics *n. pl.* (usu. treated as *sing.*) science of relations between heat and other (mechanical, electrical, etc.) forms of energy; so ∼IC(AL) *adjs.*, ∼**ical**LY² *adv.* [f. THERMO- + DYNAMICS]

thermŏ'meter *n.* instrument for measuring temperature, esp. graduated glass tube with small bore containing mercury or alcohol which expands when heated; **clinical** ~ (small, with range of 25° or less, for taking temperature of esp. patient's body); MAXI-MUM, MINIMUM, *thermometer*; hence **thermome′TRI-**c(AL) *adjs.*, **thermo′**METRY *n.* [f. F *thermomètre* or mod. L *thermometrum* (as THERMO-, -METER)]

Ther′mŏs, t-, *n.* (P) ~ (**flask** etc.), (brand of) vacuum flask. [Gk (as THERMO-)]

ther′mostät *n.* device which automatically main-tains constant temperature or actuates appropriate equipment when temperature varies beyond fixed limit; hence ~IC (-ă′t-) *a.* [f. THERMO- + Gk *statos* standing]

thesaur′|us *n.* (*pl.* ~i *pr.* -ī). storehouse of informa-tion, esp. dictionary or encyclopaedia; list of concepts or words arranged according to sense or chosen for use in indexing etc. [L, f. Gk *thēsauros* treasure]

these. See THIS.

thē′s|is (*or* thĕ′- in sense 2) *n.* (*pl.* ~es *pr.* -ēz). **1.** proposition to be maintained or proved; dissertation, esp. by candidate for degree. **2.** unstressed syllable in or part of metrical foot (opp. ARSIS). [ME f. LL f. Gk, = putting, placing, a proposition etc., f. the- root of *tithēmi* place]

Thē′spian *a.* & *n.* **1.** *a.* of tragedy or the drama. **2.** *n.* actor or actress. [f. Gk *Thespis* traditional originator of Gk tragedy + -AN]

Thess. *abbr.* Thessalonians (NT).

thē′ta *n.* eighth Greek letter (Θ, θ) = th. [Gk]

the′urg|y *n.* supernatural or divine agency esp. in human affairs; art of securing this; magical science of Neoplatonists; hence **theur′**GIC(AL) *adjs.*, ~IST (3) *n.* [f. LL f. Gk *theourgia* (*theos* god, *-ergos* working; see -Y¹)]

thew *n.* (usu. in *pl.*) bodily strength; sinew, muscle; (fig.) mental or moral vigour. [OE *thēaw* usage, conduct, = OS *thau*, OHG *dau* discipline, of unkn. orig.]

they (dhā) *pron.* (*obj.* **them** *pr.* dhem or, when stressed, dhem) *refl.* **themselves** or *arch.* **them;** *poss.* **THEIR,** **THEIRS**). Pl. of HE¹, SHE, IT¹; he and she etc.; the or any persons *who;* people in general (*they say*); those in authority (*they have raised the fees;* WE *and they*); **them** (*colloq.,* cf. HER¹ 2); (joc.) **them′s** (those are) **my** SENTIMENTS; (vulg.) *not like* **them** (those) *Pharisees* etc. [ME *thei,* obj. *theim,* f. ON *their* nom. pl. masc., *theim* dat. pl., of *sá* THE, that]

*THI *abbr.* temperature-humidity index.

thi′amine (-īn, -ēn) *n.* vitamin B₁, aneurin. [f. THIO- + VITAMIN*e*]

Thibetan. Var. of TIBETAN.

thick *a., n.,* & *adv.* **1.** *a.* of great or specified depth (between opposite surfaces) or diameter (*bread is (cut) too thick; spread the butter thick; a board, a rope, two inches thick; how thick was it?*); (of line etc.) broad, not fine; (of script, type, etc.) consisting of thick lines. **2.** arranged closely, crowded together, dense, (*thick hair, forest, fog; crowd grew thicker*); numerous (*fell thick as peas*); abounding, packed *with* (*trees thick with leaves; air thick with snow*); of firm consistency (*thick paste*); containing much solid matter (*thick soup*); turbid, muddy, cloudy, not clear, (*thick puddles, weather*); im-penetrable by the sight (*thick darkness*). **3.** stupid, dull; (of voice) muffled, indistinct. **4.** (colloq.) intimate (esp. *thick as thieves*). **5. lay it on** ~, (sl.) flatter or exaggerate grossly; ||**a bit** ~, (sl.) going beyond what is reasonable, excessive in some disagreeable quality; ||~ **ear,** (sl.) external ear swollen as result of blow (esp. *give person a thick ear*); ~ **end of the stick,** the worst of a bargain etc. **6.** ~ **head,** (1) stupidity, (2) muzziness; ~′**head,** blockhead; ~**-headed,** stupid; ~**-knee,** stone-curlew; ~′**set,** (*a.*) set or growing close together, heavily or solidly built, (*n.*) thicket; ~**-skinned,** (fig.) not sensitive to reproach or rebuff, stolid; ~**-skulled, -witted,** stupid; hence ~′ISH¹ 2 *a.,* ~′LY *adv.* **7.** *n.* thick part of anything (**in the** ~ **of it** or **of things,** in busiest part of fight, activity, etc.;

through ~ **and thin,** under all conditions, in spite of all difficulties, resolutely). **8.** *adv.* thickly (*snow was falling thick; blows came thick and fast*). [OE *thicce* a. & adv., = OS *thikki, thikko,* OHG *dicki, diccho,* ON *thykkr* f. Gmc **theku-,* of unkn. orig.]

thi′cken *v.t.* & *i.* make or become thick(er); give (gravy etc.) more solid consistency, whence ~ING¹ (3) *n.; plot* ~s (becomes more intricate). [ME, f. prec. + -EN⁶]

thi′cket *n.* number of shrubs, trees, etc., growing close together. [OE *thiccet* (as THICK, + -ET¹ denominative suf.)]

thi′ckness *n.* being thick; dimension other than length and breadth; layer of material of known thick-ness (*three thicknesses of cardboard will suffice*); part that is thick or lies between opposite surfaces (*steps cut in the thickness of the wall*). [OE *thicnes* (as THICK, -NESS)]

thie|f *n.* (*pl.* ~**ves** *pr.* -vz). **1.** one who steals esp. secretly and without violence; *thieves'* LATIN; hence ~′VERY (4), ~′VISH¹ *a.* **2.** ~**f ant** (stealing food from others); ||~**f-taker,** (Hist.) member of group under-taking to arrest thieves. [OE *thēof,* = OS *thiof,* OHG *diob,* ON *thjófr,* Goth. *thiubs* f. Gmc *theubhaz]

thieve *v.* **1.** *v.i.* be a thief, engage in stealing. **2.** *v.t.* steal (thing). [OE *thēofian* (as prec.)]

thigh (thī) *n.* part of human leg between hip and knee; corresponding part in other animals; *smite* HIP¹ *and thigh;* ~**-bone,** bone of thigh, femur; ~**-boot** (reach-ing to thigh); hence (-)~ED² (-ıd) *a.* [f. OE *thē(o)h, thīoh,* OHG *dioh,* ON *thjó* f. Gmc *theuham]

thill *n.* shaft of cart or carriage, esp. one of pair; ~**-horse,** ~′ER¹ *n.,* (put between thills). [ME, of unkn. orig.]

thi′mble *n.* metal or plastic cap with closed or open end, worn to protect finger and push needle in sewing; (Mech.) short metal tube, ferrule, etc.; (Naut.) metal ring concave on outside and fitting in loop of spliced rope to prevent chafing; hence ~FUL 2 (-belf-) *n.,* (esp.) small quantity (*of brandy etc.*) to drink; ~**rig** *n.,* & *v.i.* (-gg-), (play) swindling sleight--of-hand trick with three thimble-shaped cups and pea, and bystanders betting which cup covers pea; ~**rigger,** one who conducts this, sharper. [OE *thymel* (as THUMB, see -LE 1)]

thin¹ *a.* & *adv.* **1.** *a.* having opposite surfaces close together, of small thickness or diameter, slender, (*thin board, sheet,* ICE¹, *wire, string*); not dense or copious (*thin haze, hair*); not full or closely packed (*a thin audience*); of slight consistency (*thin paste, gruel*); lacking an im-portant ingredient (*thin beer, blood, voice, humour, eloquence*); (fig.) shallow, transparent, scanty, flimsy, (*thin disguise, excuse, patience is wearing thin*); lean, not plump; (of line) narrow, fine, (of script, type, etc.) consisting of thin lines; (sl.) uncomfortable, wretched, (*have a thin time*); *through* THICK *and thin;* ~ **air,** (fig.) condition of invisibility or non-existence (*appear out of, disappear into, thin air*); ~ **on the ground,** few in number; ~ **on top,** balding; *thin end of the* WEDGE; ~**-skinned,** (fig.) sensitive to reproach or rebuff; hence ~′LY² *adv.,* ~′NESS (-n-n-) *n.,* ~′NISH¹ 2 *a.* **2.** *adv.* thinly (*cut the bread very thin*). [OE *thynne,* = OS *thunni,* OHG *dunni,* ON *thunnr* f. Gmc *thunnuz f. IE **tn-,* **ten-* stretch]

thin² *v.t.* & *i.* (-nn-). make or become thin(ner), reduce in bulk or numbers (*his hair is thinning; crowd began to thin out*); remove some young fruit from (vine, tree) to improve growth of rest; ~ **out,** treat (seedlings etc.) similarly; hence ~′ER¹ *n.,* (esp., also in *pl.* treated as *sing.*) volatile liquid used to make paint etc. thinner. [OE *thynnian* (as prec.)]

thine (dhīn) *poss. pron.* See THY. [OE *thīn,* = OS *thīn,* OHG *dīn,* ON *thinn,* Goth. *theins* f. Gmc *thīnaz f. IE **t(w)einos* (as THOU; cf. MINE³)]

thing *n.* **1.** whatever is or may be thought about or perceived (including or opp. to *person*), as: (of ani-mate object, esp. person, expr. contempt, pity, affection, etc.) *poor thing, you spiteful thing, a dear old* *thing, dumb things,* (sl.) OLD *thing;* (of inanimate material object) *take those things off the table, platinum is a costly thing;* (of act, fact, idea, course of action, task, affair, circumstance) *a foolish thing to do, it is a strange thing that you cannot understand that, the only thing now is to shout for help, it is a big thing to undertake, is likely to achieve great things, a reputation for getting things done, things begin to look brighter, has made a mess of things, takes things too seriously, asked me how things were);* (of specimen or type of work etc.) *the latest thing in hats, a little thing of mine I should like to read to you;* one's special interest or concern (esp. colloq. *do* one's *own thing);* (colloq.) something remarkable *(now* there's *a thing!);* (in *pl.)* personal belongings *(pack up your things),* (esp. outer) clothing, equipment, (Law) property *(things personal, real),* the world in general *(is impossible in* or *by the nature of things),* (w. following *a.,* often joc.) all that is so describable *(things Japanese, political, feminine);* **and** ∼**s,** (colloq.) and the like; **do** ∼**s to,** (colloq.) affect remarkably; **(just) one of those** ∼**s,** (colloq.) something ordained by fate or unavoidable; SEE[1] *things.* **2. the** ∼, (1) what is conventionally proper or fashionable, (2) what is to be aimed at *(the thing is to get orders),* (3) what is needed *(your suggestion was just the thing),* (4) what is in question *(for the fun, the look, of the thing),* (5) what is most important *(the thing about him is his complete integrity; the thing is, will she come?);* am not feeling **the** ∼, quite well. **3. and another** ∼, moreover; **do the decent** etc. ∼ **by,** treat decently etc.; *(the)* FIRST *thing;* **for one** ∼, as one of several reasons; GOOD *thing;* **have a** ∼ **about,** (colloq.) be obsessed or prejudiced about; **know a** ∼ **or two,** be experienced or shrewd; LAST[3] *thing(s);* **make a** ∼ **of,** regard as essential, get excited about; **not a** ∼, nothing *(did not mean a thing to me);* *SURE *thing;* ∼ **in itself** (viewed in the abstract, not in relation to others). [OE, = OS *thing,* OHG *ding* deliberative assembly, ON *thing* f. Gmc *thingam]*

thi′ngamў,   thi′ngumajïg,   thi′ngum(a)bŏb, thi′ngummў, thi′ngў, *ns.* (colloq.) person or thing whose name one forgets or does not know or does not wish to mention; what's-his-name, what-d'you-call-it. [f. prec., w. meaningless suf.]

think *v.* (**thought** *pr.* thawt) & *n.* **1.** *v.t.* consider, be of opinion, *(we think (that) he will come; we do not think it probable; I think it a shame; thinks himself very fine; to think (that) he should treat me like this!; it is not thought proper; is thought to be a fraud; what do you think of* or *about my idea?);* **I do′n't** ∼ (sl. addition to ironical statement; *you are a model of tact, I don't think).* **2.** intend, expect, *(thinks to deceive us);* (colloq.) remember *(did not think to lock the door).* **3.** form conception of *(cannot think the infinite;* (colloq.) *I can't think how you do it).* **4.** recognize presence or existence of *(the child thought no harm).* **5.** reduce to specified condition etc. by thinking *(cannot think away a toothache).* **6.** *v.i.* exercise the mind otherwise than by passive reception of another's ideas; ∼ **for** one**self,** have independent mind; **let me** ∼ (appeal for time before answering etc.). **7.** have half-formed intention *(I think I'll try).* **8.** ∼ **about,** consider, esp. consider the practicability of (scheme, doing); ∼ **again,** change one's mind; ∼ **aloud,** utter one's thoughts immediately as they occur; ∼ **back to,** recall (past event or time); ∼ **big,** be ambitious; *think* FIT[3]; ∼ **of,** consider, be aware of in the mind, imagine, propose to oneself, entertain the idea of, hit upon, *(have many things to think of; think of you constantly; must be thinking of going; couldn't think of (doing) such a thing; think of a word beginning with B; would have telephoned if I had thought of it);* **(just** or **to)** ∼ **of it!,** one can hardly imagine it; ∼ **better of,** (1) decide on second thoughts to abandon (intention), (2) have higher opinion of (person, esp. than to believe etc.); ∼ **little** or **nothing of,** consider insignificant or contemptible, *(thinks nothing of walking 30 miles a day; I think nothing of your friend Jones);* ∼ **much, a lot, well, highly, of,** esteem; *think no small* BEER *of;*

∼ **on,** (arch.) think of or about; ∼ **out,** consider carefully, devise (plan etc.); ∼ **over,** reflect upon in order to reach decision *(think over what I have said; will think it over);* ∼ **through,** reflect fully upon (problem etc.); ∼ **twice,** use careful consideration, avoid hasty action etc.; ∼ **up,** (colloq.) devise, produce by thought; ∼ **upon,** (arch.) think of or about. **9.** Hence ∼′ABLE *a.* **10.** *n.* (colloq.) act of thinking *(must have a think about that);* ∼**-piece,** piece of writing dealing with general assessment and interpretation of news etc.; ∼**-tank,** organization providing advice and ideas on national and commercial problems, *(sl.) the brain. [OE *thencan thōhte gethōht,* = OS *thenkian,* OHG *denken,* ON *thekkja,* Goth. *thagkjan,* factitive f. Gmc *thank-* f. IE *teng-* etc.]

thi′nker *n.* In vbl senses; one who thinks in a specified way *(original thinker);* person with skilled or powerful mind. [ME, f. prec. + -ER[1]]

thi′nking[1] *n.* In vbl senses; opinion, judgement, *(the best, to my thinking; what is your thinking on this question?);* **put on** one's ∼**-cap,** meditate on a problem. [ME, f. THINK + -ING[1]]

thi′nking[2] *a.* In vbl senses; thoughtful, intellectual. [f. THINK + -ING[2]]

thi′nner. See THIN[2]; *compar.* of THIN[1].

thi′ō- *comb. form.* sulphur, as: ∼**-acid,** ∼**-su′lphate,** ∼**ure′a,** etc., compounds in which (some) oxygen is replaced by sulphur. [f. Gk *theion* sulphur + -o-]

third *a.* & *n.* **1.** *a.* next after second; ∼ **part,** one of three equal parts into which thing is or might be divided. **2.** *n.* third part, thing, etc.; (person having) place in third class in examination; third gear; (Mus.) (note at) interval of which the span involves three alphabetical notes, harmonic combination of notes thus separated; (Hist., in *pl.)* third of deceased husband's property falling to widow. **3.** *third* BASE[1] 9; ∼**-best,** (what is) of third quality; ∼ **class,** next after second class in accommodation, examination-list, etc.; ∼ **day,** Tuesday; *third* DEGREE; *third* ESTATE; *third* FLOOR; ∼ **force,** party etc. acting as check on conflict between two others; ∼ **gear,** next above second gear in motor vehicle or bicycle; ∼ **man,** (Cricket) fieldsman near boundary behind slip(s), his place; ∼ **party,** another party besides the two principals, bystander etc., *(∼-party insurance,* against damage or injury suffered by person other than the insured); ∼ **person,** (1) = *third party,* (2) see PERSON 5, 6; ∼ **rail** (carrying current to electric train); ∼**-reading,** aj inferior, poor; *third* READING; T∼ **World,** the countries of Asia, Africa, and Latin America not politically aligned with Communist or with Western nations. **4.** Hence ∼′LY[2] *adv.,* in the third place. [OE *third(d)a, thridda,* = OS *thriddio,* OHG *dritto,* ON *thrithi,* Goth. *thridja* f. Gmc *thridhjaz* f. IE *tritjós]*

thirst *n.,* & *v.i.* **1.** *n.* suffering caused by lack of drink; desire for a drink; (fig.) ardent desire, craving, *(of, for, after,* glory, person's blood, etc.). **2.** *v.i.* feel thirst, be thirsty, (fig. *for, after)* (or arch. lit.). [OE *thurst, thyrstan* = OS *thurst(ian)* f. WG *thurstu (*thurs-* f. IE **t(o)rs-)]*

thir′stўȳ *a.* feeling thirst *(am very thirsty);* (of country or season) dry, parched; (fig.) eager *(for, after);* (colloq.) causing thirst *(this is thirsty work);* hence ∼iLY[2] *adv.,* ∼iNESS *n.* [OE *thyrstig, thyrstig* (as prec., -Y[2])]

thirteen (-ē′n, thēr′-) *a.* & *n.* one more than twelve; symbol for this (13, xiii, XIII); size etc. denoted by thirteen; hence ∼TH[2] *a.* & *n.* [OE *thrēotiene,* = OS *thriutein,* OHG *drīzehan,* ON *threttán* (as THREE, -TEEN)]

thir′tў *a.* & *n.* **1.** three times ten; symbol for this (30, xxx, XXX); (in *pl.)* numbers, esp. years of a century or life, from 30 to 39; hence ∼FOLD *a.* & *adv.,* **thir′tiETH**[1] *a.* & *n.* **2.** ∼**-one** etc., (arch.) **one-and-**∼ etc., thirty plus one etc., w. corresp. ordinals ∼**-first** etc.; T∼**-nine Articles** (assented to by those taking orders in Church of England); *∼**-second-note,** demisemiquaver; ∼**-two-mo,** book with 32 leaves to the printing-sheet. [OE *thrītig*, = OS *thrītig*, OHG *drīzzug*, ON *thrírtegr* (as THREE, -TY²)]

this (dh-) *dem. a. & pron.* (*pl.* **these** *pr.* dhēz), & *adv.* **1.** *dem. a. & pron.* the (person, thing), the person or thing, close at hand or touched or pointed to or drawn attention to or observed by the speaker at the time, or already named or understood or in question or familiar (seldom idiomatically interchangeable with THAT¹, but often only equally applicable to the facts, the implication of greater nearness, familiarity, etc., being purely idiomatic: *observe this dog on the hearth-rug; who are these people in the next room?; what is all this (noise)?; what flower is this?; fold it like this; I knew all this before; this* (action of yours or of which I speak) *is not fair; this term is liable to much abuse; at this time Caesar was in Gaul; things are easier* (in) *these days; am not going to leave this house, this country*); (of time) the present (*day,* etc.; *this day* FORTNIGHT, WEEK, *month; shall be* or *have been busy all this week; ought to be ready by this* (*time*), *before this* (*time*)), of today (*this morning, this evening*), just past or to come (*have been asking for it these three weeks; will not be wanted these ten years*); (on telephone) ||the person speaking, *the person spoken to, (who is this?);* (colloq., in narrative) a previously unspecified (*yesterday I was arguing with this bus-conductor, when . . .*); ~ **and that,** various ones, various things, (*went to this doctor and that* or *to this and that doctor; talked of this and that*); ~, **that, and the other,** various things; ~ **here,** (vulg.) *– this* a.; ~ **much,** this amount, esp. = what I am about to state (*I know this much, that the thing is absurd*); *this* WORLD. **2.** *adv.* (colloq.) to such a degree, so, (*knew him when he was this high*); so as to correspond to the present time, place, etc., (*not likely to get this far*). [OE, neut. of *thes,* = OS *these,* OHG *dese,* WG (**tha-* THE, THAT¹, **-se* dem. suf.)]

thi′sness (dh-) *n.* quality of being this, = HAECCEITY. [f. prec. + -NESS]

thi′stle (-sel) *n.* prickly composite herbaceous plant of genus *Carduus* etc. usu. with globular heads of purple flowers; (figure of this as) Scottish national emblem; **Order of the T~,** Scottish order of knighthood; ~**down,** DOWN² of thistle, esp. w. ref. to its lightness or flimsiness; hence **thi′stly²** (-slī) *a.* [OE *thistel,* = OS *thistil,* OHG *distil,* ON *thistill* f. Gmc **thistilaz, -ilõ*]

thi′ther (dhī′dh-) *adv.* (arch.) to that place; ~**to,** up to that time; hence ~**WARD**(S) *adv.* [OE *thider,* alt. (after HITHER) f. *thæder* f. root **tha-* (THAT¹, THE) +suf. *-ther* denoting motion towards; cf. HITHER, WHITHER]

thixo′tropy *n.* property of becoming temporarily liquid when shaken, stirred, etc., and returning to gel state on standing; so **thixotro′pic** *a.* [f. Gk *thixis* touching + -o- + *tropē* turning + -Y¹]

tho′. See THOUGH.

||**thōle¹** *v.t.* (arch. or Sc.) undergo, endure, suffer, (pain, grief, etc., or abs.); permit, admit of. [OE *tholian,* = OS *tholon, tholian,* OHG *dolōn, dolēn,* ON *thola,* Goth. *thulan* f. Gmc **thul-* f. IE **tol-* etc. raise]

thōle² *n.* & ~ **(-pin),** pin in gunwale of boat as fulcrum for oar; each of two such pins forming rowlock, between which oar works. [OE *thol(l),* = MDu., MLG *dolle,* ON *thollr* fir-tree, peg]

thō′l|os *n.* (*pl.* ~**oi**). (Gk Ant.) dome(-shaped tomb). [Gk]

Thŏ′mas (t-) *n.* ~ (**Atkins**), = TOMMY 1; DOUBT²*ing Thomas.* [OE f. L, f. Gk *Thõmas*]

Thŏ′m|ism (tō′-) *n.* doctrine of Thomas Aquinas, It. scholastic philosopher and theologian d. 1274, or of his followers; so ~IST (2) *n.,* ~**i′stic**(AL) *adjs.* [f. prec. + -ISM]

thŏng *n.,* & *v.t.* **1.** *n.* narrow strip of hide or leather used as halter, reins, lash of whip, etc. **2.** *v.t.* furnish with thong; strike with thong. [OE *thwang, thwong,* = OHG *dwang* rein f. Gmc **thwang-* restrain]

thŏr′ă|x *n.* (*pl.* ~**ces** *pr.* -asēz, or ~**xes**). **1.** (Anat. & Zool.) part of trunk between neck and abdomen; hence **thŏră′cic** *a.* **2.** (Gk Ant.) breastplate, cuirass. [L, f. Gk *thõrax -akos*]

thōr′ium *n.* radioactive metallic element, the oxide of which (**thor′ia**) is used in gas-mantles. [f. *Thor,* Scand. god of thunder + -IUM]

thōrn *n.* **1.** stiff sharp-pointed process on plant, esp. abortive branch; thorn-bearing shrub or tree; **a** ~ **in** one's **flesh** or **side,** constant source of annoyance; **on** ~**s,** continuously uneasy esp. in expectation of being detected etc. at any moment. **2.** name of OE & Icel. runic letter, = th. **3.** ~**apple,** (prickly fruit of) *Datura stramonium;* ~**back,** (1) ray with spines on back and tail, (2) Eur. spider crab (*Maia squinado*); ~**bill,** S. Amer. humming-bird of genus *Ramphomicron;* ~**bush,** bush bearing thorns, e.g. haw-thorn; ~**lizard,** moloch; ~**tail,** Amer. humming-bird of genus *Popelairia;* ~**tree,** tree bearing thorns, esp. hawthorn or (S. Afr.) spiny acacia; hence ~**LESS,** ~′**PROOF²,** ~′**Y²** (often fig. of affair, = hard to handle), *adjs.* [OE, = OS, ON *thorn,* OHG *dorn,* Goth. *thaurnus* f. Gmc **thurnuz* f. IE **trnus*]

thŏ′rough (thŭ′rō) *a., n., prep., & adv.* **1.** *a.* complete, unqualified, not superficial, out-and-out, (*his work is seldom thorough; has caught a thorough chill; want a thorough change; a thorough scoundrel*). **2.** *n.* (Hist.) uncompromising policy of Strafford and Laud under Charles I. **3.** *prep. & adv.* (arch.) through (*thorough hush, thorough brier*). **4.** thorough BASS³; **~***brace,** leather strap supporting body of vehicle; ~**bred** *a.* & *n.,* (animal, esp. horse, or fig. person) of pure breed, high-spirited, mettlesome, (*T~*) (member of) breed of racehorses originating from Engl. mares and Arab stallions; ~**fare,** road or street or path open at both ends, esp. one through which much traffic passes; *no* ~*fare,* (as notice in obstructed or private road) no public right of way; ~**going,** not superficial, uncompromising, extreme, out-and-out; ~**paced,** (lit., of horse) trained to all paces, (fig.) complete, unqualified, (*a thoroughpaced rascal*); ~**pin,** swelling in hollow of horse's hock; ~**wax,** umbelliferous herb with stem appearing to grow through leaves [f. WAX²]. **5.** Hence ~**LY²** *adv.,* ~**NESS** *n.* [orig. prep., f. OE *thuruh, thurh,* var. of *thurh* THROUGH]

thōrp, thōrpe, *n.* (arch.) village, hamlet. [OE *thorp, throp,* = OS, ON *thorp,* OHG *dorf,* Goth. *thaurp* land f. Gmc **thurpam*]

Thos. *abbr.* Thomas.

those. See THAT¹.

thou¹ (dh-) *pron.* (*obj.* **thee** *pr.* dhē; *poss.* THY, THINE; *pl.* YE¹, YOU) & *v.* **1.** Sing. *pron.* of 2nd pers. (arch. or poet. or dial. exc. in addressing God and (usu. *thee* as subj. w. 3rd pers. v.) as formerly used by Quakers). **2.** *v.t.* address (person) as *thou.* **3.** *v.i.* use *thou* instead of *you.* [OE *thu,* = acc. & dat. *thē,* OS *thu, thī,* OHG *du, dih, dir,* ON *thú, thik, thér,* Goth. *thu, thuk, thus* f. Gmc **thu, *theke, *thez* f. IE **tu, *te(s)*]

thou² *n.* (*pl.* ~**s** or ~). (colloq.) thousand(th). [abbr.]

though, thō′, (dhō) *conj. & adv.* **1.** *conj.* notwithstanding the fact that (*he finished first though he began last; though it was late, late though it was, we decided to go*); (ellipt.) though annoyed, *I consented*); but nevertheless (*ready though unwilling*). **2.** (even) on the supposition that (*it is better to ask him (even) though he (should) refuse or refuses*); **as** ~, as IF; **what** ~, (arch.) what does it matter if (*the way is* or *be long?*). **3.** (Introducing what is virtually an independent sentence) and yet, nevertheless, (*I have no doubt he will understand—though you never know; she read on, though not to the very end*). **4.** *adv.* (colloq.) however (*I wish you had told me, though*). [ME *thoh* etc. f. ON **thóh, thó, *thauh,* corresp. to OE *thēah,* OS *thoh,* OHG *doh,* Goth. *thauh* or, yet, f. Gmc **thauh* (**tha-* THAT¹, THE)]

thought¹ (thawt) *n.* **1.** process or power of thinking; way of thinking characteristic of a person or class; faculty of reason; sober reflection (**in** ~, meditating); consideration (*after serious thought; acts without thought*); **give** ~ **to,** consider; **take** ~, consider matters; **have** or **take no** ~ **for,** neglect, not heed; TRAIN of thought. **2.** idea, conception, chain of reasoning, etc., produced by thinking (*an essay full of striking thoughts;* **a**

(**happy**) ∼, a well-timed or apposite idea or suggestion); half-formed intention (*had (some) thoughts of resigning; had no thought of offending him*); (usu. in *pl.*) what one thinks, one's opinion, (*will tell you my thoughts on the matter*); subject of one's thinking (*his one thought is how to get away; a* PENNY *for your thoughts*); **in** person's ∼s, thought of by him. **3. a** ∼, a little, somewhat, (*seems to me a thought arrogant*); **quick as** ∼, very quick; SECOND *thoughts*; ∼ **police** (attempting totalitarian control over thoughts as well as over actions); ∼--provoking, giving rise to serious thought; ∼--reader, -reading, (person capable of) direct perception of what another is thinking; ∼-transference, telepathy; ∼-wave, undulation of the supposed medium of thought-transference. **4.** Hence (-)∼ED² *a.* [OE *thōht*, = OS *githāht*, OHG *gidāht* f. Gmc *gathanht-* (*thankjan; cf. THINK)]

thought². See THINK.

thou′ghtful (-aw′t-) *a.* engaged in or given to meditation; (of book, writer, remark, etc.) giving signs of original thought; (of person or conduct) considerate (*of*), not haphazard or unfeeling; hence ∼LY² *adv.*, ∼NESS *n.* [ME, f. THOUGHT¹ +-FUL]

thou′ghtless (-aw′t-) *a.* careless of consequences or of others' feelings; due to lack of thought; hence ∼LY² *adv.*, ∼NESS *n.* [f. THOUGHT¹ +-LESS]

thou′sand (-z-) *a. & n.* (*pl.* ∼ *or* ∼s; for pl. usage see HUNDRED). ten hundred; symbol for this (1,000, m, M); set of 1,000, £1,000, etc.; very many (*a thousand times easier*; see PITY); **one in a** ∼, (fig.) a rare or excellent one; (**a**) ∼ **and one** etc., one thousand plus one etc., w. corresp. ordinals ∼-and-first etc.; (**a**) ∼ **and one**, myriad, numberless, (*the thousand and one small worries of life*; *made a thousand and one excuses*); **a** ∼ thanks, pardons, apologies, etc., (forms of polite exaggeration); UPPER *ten thousand*; hence ∼FOLD *a., adv., & n.*, (-)∼TH² *a. & n.* [OE *thūsend,* = OS *thūsundig,* OHG *dūsunt,* ON *thúsund,* Goth. *thūsundi* f. Gmc *thūsundi*]

thrall (-awl) *n., a., & v.t.* (literary). **1.** *n.* slave (*of, to,* person or thing, lit. or fig.); bondage (*in thrall*); hence **thra′l**DOM (-aw′l-), *∼*∼DOM, *n.* **2.** *a.* (arch.) enslaved (*to*). **3.** *v.t.* enslave. [OE *thrǣl* f. ON *thrǽll,* perh. f. *thrahilaz* (Gmc *thrah-* run)]

thrash *v.* **1.** *v.t.* = THRESH 1; ∼ **out**, arrive at, obtain, (truth etc.) by repeated trial, discuss (problem etc.) exhaustively. **2.** *v.i.* (Of paddle-wheel, branch, etc.) act like flail, deliver repeated blows, (of ship) keep striking the waves, make way against wind or tide (*thrash to windward*), move violently *about* or *around* (*in* water etc.). **3.** *v.t.* beat esp. with stick or whip, conquer, surpass; hence ∼′ING¹ (1) *n.* [OE *therscan,* later *threscan,* = OHG *dreskan,* ON *threskja,* Goth. *thriskan* f. Gmc *thersk-* f. IE *tersk-*]

thrä′sher¹ *n.* In vbl senses; = THRESHER. [f. prec. +-ER¹]

thrä′sher² *n.* long-tailed N. Amer. thrushlike bird of family Mimidae. [perh. f. E dial. *thrusher* = THRUSH¹]

thrasö′nical *a.* bragging; hence ∼LY² *adv.* [f. L *Thraso -onis,* braggart soldier in Terence's 'Eunuchus', f. Gk *thrasus* bold, +-ICAL]

thrawn *a.* (Sc.) perverse, ill-tempered; misshapen. [Sc. form of THROW′*n,* in obs. senses]

thread¹ (-rĕd) *n.* **1.** spun-out filament of cotton, flax, silk, wool, glass, etc., yarn, (**has not a dry** ∼ **on him,** is wet through); piece of this; (*in pl.,* sl.) clothes; thin cord of twisted yarns; **gold** ∼ (of silk etc. with gold wire wound round it); *thread and* THRUM¹. **2.** thread-shaped thing, long slender body, e.g. spiral ridge of screw, or one turn of this; thin seam or vein of ore. **3.** (fig.) the ∼ (course) **of life; hang by a** ∼, (of person's life etc.) be in a precarious state, (of momentous issue etc.) be determinable either way by something still in doubt; **lose the** ∼ (sequence, connection) *of an argument*; **resume** or **take up the** ∼ **of,** proceed with after interruption; **gather up the** ∼s, bring divisions of subject etc. into relation after separate treatment. **4.** ∼′bare, (of cloth) worn so

that nap is lost and thread visible, (of person) wearing such clothes, (fig.) well-worn, hackneyed; ∼′fish, small tropical fish with long streamers from fins; ∼ **lace** (made of linen etc. thread, not silk); ∼-mark, mark made in bank-note paper with highly coloured silk fibres to prevent photographic counterfeiting; ∼--paper, (strip of) soft thin paper used for rolling up thread, (fig.) slender person; ∼′worm, threadlike nematode worm, esp. one infesting rectum of children. **5.** Hence ∼′Y² *a.,* (esp., of person's pulse) scarcely perceptible. [OE *thrǣd,* = OS *thrād,* OHG *drāt,* ON *thráthr* f. Gmc *thrǣdhuz* (*thrǣ-* twist, THROW¹)]

thread² (-rĕd) *v.t.* pass thread through eye of (needle); arrange (material in strip form, e.g. film, recording--tape) in proper position in camera, recorder, etc.; string (beads etc.) on thread, make (chain etc.) thus; pick one's way through (maze, streets, crowded place, etc.), make one's *way* thus; streak (hair etc.) as with threads; form screw-thread on. [ME, f. prec.]

threat (-rĕt) *n.* declaration of intention to punish or hurt; (Law) menace of bodily hurt or injury to reputation or property, such as may restrain person's freedom of action; indication of something undesirable coming (*there is a threat of rain*). [OE *thrēat* affliction etc., f. Gmc *threut-, *thraut-, *thrut-*]

threa′ten (-rĕ′t-) *v.t.* use threats towards (person etc., or abs., *with* harm etc.; *threatened me with death; am threatened with a visit*); give warning of the infliction of (harm etc., or abs.), announce one's intention (*to do*), as punishment or in revenge etc., (*threatens every kind of torment; threaten to resign,* (fig.) *clouds threaten* (rain, an interruption, to interrupt us), *the practice threatens to become general*). [OE *thrēatnian* (as prec.; see -EN⁶)]

three *a. & n.* **1.** one more than two; symbol for this (3, iii, III); card etc. with three pips; time of three o'clock; size etc. denoted by three; set of three; (in *pl.*) gloves, shoes, etc., of third size; (Rugby Footb.) = *three-quarter; three* CHEER¹s; ∼ **parts** (quarters); ∼ **times** ∼, three cheers thrice repeated; *the three* Rs; RULE *of three.* **2.** ∼-ball, golf match between three players each with his own ball; ∼-card **trick** (in which bets are made on which is the face among three cards lying face downwards); ∼-colour **process** (of reproducing natural colours by combining photographs in red, blue, and yellow or other primary colours); ∼-cornered, triangular, (of contest etc.) between three parties each for himself; ∼--decker, warship with three gun-decks, novel in three volumes, sandwich with three slices of bread, three--tiered pulpit; ∼-dimensional, having or appearing to have length, breadth, and depth; ∼-handed, with three hands, (of card-game) played by three persons; ||∼ **halfpence,** 1½p or 1¾d.; **T**∼ **in One,** the Trinity; ∼-lane, (of road) marked out for three lines of traffic; ∼-legged **race** (-gd-, -gĭd-), race between pairs having one runner's right leg tied to other's left leg; ||*three-line* WHIP²; ∼-ma′ster, vessel (esp. schooner) with three masts; ||∼′pence (thrĕ′p-, thrĭ′p-), sum of three pence; ||∼′penny (same pr.), costing or worth 3p or 3d.; ||∼′penny (**bit**) (same pr.), former coin worth three pence; ||∼-per-ce′nts, (Hist.) (government) bonds bearing interest at 3%; *three*-PHASE; ∼--piece (of suit of clothes or suite of furniture comprising three separate parts); ∼-ply, (*a.*) of three strands, webs, or thicknesses, (*n.*) three-ply wool, three-ply wood made by gluing together three layers with grain in different directions; ∼-point landing, (Aeron.) landing of an aircraft on the two main wheels and the tail wheel or skid simultaneously; ||∼-point turn, method of turning vehicle round in narrow space by moving forwards, backwards, and forwards; ∼--quarter(s), of three-fourths of normal size or numbers, (of portrait) going down to hips or showing three-fourths of face (between full face and profile); ∼-quarter (**back**), (Rugby Footb.) any of 3 or 4 players just behind half-backs; ∼-quarter (**length**), (of coat etc.) having three-fourths of normal length;

∼**-ring circus**, circus having three rings, (fig.) extravagant performance; ∼'**score**, (arch.) sixty (∼*score and ten*, age of 70 as normal limit of life); ∼**-way**, involving three ways or participants (*resulted in a three-way tie*); ∼**-wheeler**, vehicle with three wheels. **3.** Hence ∼'**FOLD** *a. & adv.* [OE *thrī*, = OS *thria*, OHG *drī*, ON *thrír* f. Gmc *thrijiz f. IE *trejes]

three'some *n. & a.* **1.** *n.* set of three persons; game etc. for three, esp. (Golf) of one against two. **2.** *a.* of three. [f. prec. +-SOME²]

thrĕmmató'logy *n.* science of breeding animals and plants. [f. Gk *thremma -matos* nursling +-O-+-LOGY]

thrĕ'n|ōde, thrĕ'n|odỹ, *n.* (song of) lamentation esp. on person's death; hence or cogn. ∼**ō'dIAL,** ∼**ō'dIC,** *adjs.,* ∼**odIST** (3) *n.* [f. Gk *thrēnōidia* (*thrēnos* wailing, *ōidē* ODE)]

thrĕsh *v.* **1.** *v.t.* beat out or separate grain from (corn etc.) on threshing-floor or in threshing-machine; go *over* (problem etc.) in search of solution; ∼ **out**, = THRASH *out*; ∼'**ing-floor**, hard level floor for threshing; ∼'**ing-machine**, power-driven machine for separating grain from straw or husk. **2.** *v.i.* = THRASH 2. [var. of THRASH]

thrĕ'sher *n.* In vbl senses; shark lashing at enemies with very long upper lobe of tail. [f. prec. +-ER¹]

thrĕ'shōld *n.* plank or stone at bottom of door in dwelling-house, church, etc.; (fig.) point of entry (*on the threshold of a revolution, of a new century*); (Physiol. & Psych.) limit below which a stimulus ceases to be perceptible; (Phys.) limit below which no reaction etc. occurs, esp. minimum dose of radiation producing a specified effect. [OE *therscold, threscold,* etc., = ON *thresk(j)öldr,* OHG *thriscūfti,* cogn. w. THRASH in sense 'tread']

threw. See THROW¹.

thrīce *adv.* (arch. or literary). three times; (esp. in comb.) highly (*thrice-blessed*). [ME *thries* (*thrie adv.* f. OE *thrīwa, thrīga* f. as THREE, -s³)]

thrid *v.t.* (**dd**-). (arch.) = THREAD⁹.

thrift *n.* **1.** frugality, economical management; *∼ **account**, deposit account; hence ∼'LESS *a.* **2.** *n.* plant of genus *Armeria*, esp. sea-pink. [ME f. ON (as THRIVE)]

thri'ft|ỹ *a.* frugal, economical; thriving, prosperous; hence ∼ILY² *adv.,* ∼INESS *n.* [ME, f. prec. +-Y²]

thrill *v.* & *n.* **1.** *v.t.* penetrate (person etc.) with thrill of emotion or sensation (*his voice thrilled the listeners*); hence ∼'ER¹ (2) *n.* (esp. sensational or exciting play, story, etc.), ∼'ING² *a.* **2.** *v.i.* be thus penetrated or agitated (*with* horror, excitement, etc.); (of emotion etc.) pass *through, over, along*, (*fear thrilled through my veins*); quiver, throb, (**as**) with emotion. **3.** *n.* wave or nervous tremor of emotion or sensation, (*a thrill of joy, of recognition*); throb, pulsation; (Med.) vibratory movement or resonance observed in auscultation. [f. (now dial.) *thirl* f. OE *thyrlian* pierce (*thyrel* hole f. *thurh* THROUGH; see -LE 1)]

thrips *n.* insect of order Thysanoptera, esp. pest injurious to plants. [L f. Gk, = woodworm]

thrīve *v.i.* (**throve** *pr.* -ōv, or ∼**d; thri'ven** *pr.* -ǐ'ven, or ∼**d**). prosper, flourish; grow rich; (of animal or plant) grow vigorously. [ME, f. ON *thrífask* refl. of *thrífa* grasp]

thro'. See THROUGH.

throat *n.* **1.** front of neck between chin and collar-bone, corresponding part of animal, (**cut** person's ∼, slash this esp. with intent to kill him; **cut** one's **own** ∼, (fig.) bring about one's own defeat; **cut one another's** ∼**s**, compete ruinously; **take by the** ∼, try to throttle); windpipe (*the words* STICK¹ *in one's throat*; LIE² *in one's throat*; **give** person **the lie in his** ∼, accuse him of lying grossly); (literary) voice esp. of song-bird; gullet (CLEAR² one's throat; JUMP² *down* person's *throat*; **ram** or **thrust down** person's ∼, force (thing) on his attention; **sore** ∼, inflammation of lining membrane of gullet etc.; **clergyman's** (**sore**) ∼, chronic form of this affecting those who

speak much in public); ∼ **lozenge** etc. (sucked to alleviate sore throat); ∼ **microphone** (suspended at neck of speaker etc. and actuated by vibrations of larynx). **2.** throat-shaped thing, e.g. narrow part of chimney or blast-furnace, narrow part of river between rocks, narrow passage esp. in or near an entrance; (Naut.) forward upper corner of fore-and-aft sail. **3.** Hence (-)∼'ED² *a.* [OE *throte, throtu,* = OHG *drozza,* f. Gmc **thrut-*, **thrūt-* swell]

throa'tỹ *a.* guttural, uttered in the throat; hoarse; having prominent or capacious throat; hence ∼ILY² *adv.,* ∼INESS *n.* [f. prec. +-Y²]

thrŏb *v.i.* (**-bb**-), & *n.* **1.** *v.i.* (Of heart, bosom, temples, etc.) palpitate, pulsate esp. with more than usual force or rapidity; (fig.) quiver, vibrate, (as) with emotion or with persistent rhythm. **2.** *n.* throbbing; palpitation, (esp. violent) pulsation, (HEART-*throb; throbs of pleasure*). [ME, app. imit.]

thrōe *n.* (usu. in *pl.*) violent pang(s), esp. of childbirth or death, or fig. of authorship etc.; anguish; **in the** ∼**s**, (colloq.) struggling with the task *of* (*spring-cleaning* etc.). [ME *throwe* perh. f. OE *thrēa, thrawu* calamity, alt. perh. by assoc. w. *woe*]

thrŏ'mbin *n.* enzyme promoting clotting of blood. [f. as THROMBUS | -IN]

thrŏ'mbocȳte *n.* blood platelet, small plate of protoplasm concerned in coagulation of blood. [f. as THROMBUS +-O-+-CYTE]

thrŏmbō'se *v.t.* & *i.* affect with or undergo thrombosis. [back-form. f. foll.]

thrŏmb|ō'sis *n.* (*pl.* ∼**oses** *pr.* -ō'sēz). coagulation of blood in blood-vessel or organ during life; hence ∼**o'TIC** *a.* [mod. L, f. Gk *thrombōsis* curdling (as foll.; see -OSIS)]

thrŏ'mb|us *n.* (*pl.* ∼**i** *pr.* -ī). blood-clot formed in vascular system and obstructing circulation. [mod. L, f. Gk *thrombos* lump, blood-clot]

thrōne *n.,* & *v.t.* **1.** *n.* chair of state for sovereign, pope, bishop, etc., usu. decorated and raised on dais; sovereign power (*came to the throne; lost his throne*); (in *pl.*) third ORDER¹ of ninefold celestial hierarchy; hence ∼'LESS (-nl-) *a.* **2.** *v.t.* enthrone (lit. or fig.). [ME f. OF *trone* f. L f. Gk *thronos* high seat]

thrŏng *n.* & *v.* **1.** *n.* crowd of people; multitude (*of* people or things in small space. **2.** *v.i.* come, go, press, (*round* etc.) in multitudes. **3.** *v.t.* fill (street etc.) with a crowd or as crowd does; (arch.) crowd round, press hard upon, (person). [ME *thrang(e), throng(e)*, OE *gethrang,* f. vbl st. *thring-, thrang-*]

thrŏ'stle (-sel) *n.* **1.** song-THRUSH¹. **2.** ∼**(-frame)**, machine for continuously spinning wool, cotton, etc. [OE; OS *throsla,* OHG *drōscala* f. Gmc **thrau(d)st-*, cogn. w. THRUSH¹]

thrŏ'ttle *n.,* & *v.t.* **1.** *n.* throat, gullet, windpipe; ∼**(-valve)**, valve controlling flow of steam, fuel, etc., in engine; ∼**(-lever)**, lever etc. operating this valve. **2.** *v.t.* choke, strangle; prevent utterance etc. of; control (steam etc., engine) with throttle-valve; ∼ **back** or **down**, reduce speed of (engine, vehicle) thus. [v. ME, perh. f. THROAT +-LE 3; n. perh. dim. of THROAT (see -LE 1)]

through, thro', *thru, (-rōō) *prep., adv., & a.* **1.** *prep.* from end to end or side to side of, between the sides or walls or parts of, (*marched through the town; arrow went through his arm; see through a telescope; look through the window; pass through the doorway; swam through the waves; pushes his fingers through his hair; read through the whole book*; (fig.) *went through many trials, got through his examinations, bill passed through Parliament, I saw through his hypocrisy, wait through ten long years, flashed through his mind*). **2.** by reason of, by agency, means, or fault of, (*it all came about through his not knowing the way; concealed it through shame; it was all through you that we were late*). **3.** *up to and including (*Friday through Tuesday*). **4.** *adv.* through a thing, from side to side, from end to end, from beginning to end, (*let us stroll through; would not let us through* (the gate etc.); *ice gave and I went through; read* *it carefully through*); ∼ **and** ∼, through again and again, thoroughly, completely; **be** ∼, have finished (*with*), be connected to desired telephone etc., cease to have dealings (*with*), have no further prospects. **5.** *a.* going or concerned with going through (*a through bolt*; ∼-**stone,** = BOND¹*stone*); (of travel by rail, ship, air, etc.) going or concerned with going all the way without change of line or vehicle etc., going over different companies' lines with same ticket (*through carriage, train, passenger, ticket*); (of traffic) passing through a place to another destination; **no** ∼ **road,** = *no* THOROUGH*fare*. **6.** ∼-**composed,** (Mus.) durchkomponiert; ∼'**put,** amount of material put through a manufacturing etc. process; ∼'**way,** thoroughfare, esp. motorway. [OE *thurh,* = OS *thurh, thuru,* OHG *duruh* f. WG **thurh*]

throu'ghly (-ōō'lĭ) *adv.* (arch.) thoroughly. [ME, f. prec. + -LY²]

throughou't (-rōō-ow't) *adv. & prep.* **1.** *adv.* right through, in every part, in all respects, (*timber was rotten throughout; followed a sound policy throughout*). **2.** *prep.* right through, from end to end of, (*throughout the length and breadth of the land; throughout the 18th century*). [ME, f. THROUGH + OUT]

thrō've. See THRIVE.

throw¹ (-ō) *v.* (**threw** *pr.* -ōō; ∼**n**). **1.** *v.t.* release (thing) after imparting motion, propel through space, send forth or dismiss esp. with some violence, (fig.) compel to be in specified condition, (*threw the ball at the stumps, over his head, to him; mortars throw shells; hose throws water; threw himself down, on his knees; ship was thrown upon the coast; thrown from his horse; was thrown out of work, into prison, into a dilemma, upon his own resources*); project (rays, light; *throw* LIGHT¹ *on*); (Cricket) bowl (ball) with illegitimate sudden straightening of elbow; cast (line etc. in fishing, shadow, spell); *throw cold* WATER¹ *on, dust*¹ *in* person's *eyes;* ∼ **good money after bad,** incur further loss in hopeless attempt to recoup previous loss; ∼ one**self at,** blatantly seek as spouse, friend, etc.; *throw a* SOP *to;* ∼'**ing-stick,** = THROW²-*stick* (2); ∼ **stones,** (fig.) cast aspersions. **2.** (Of wrestler) bring (antagonist) to the ground; (of horse) unseat (rider); (colloq.) disconcert (*his question threw me for a moment*). **3.** put (clothes etc.) carelessly or hastily *on, off, over* one's *shoulders* etc.; (of snake) cast (skin). **4.** (Of animal, e.g. bitch, rabbit, pigeon) give birth to (young). **5.** cause (dice) to fall on table etc., obtain (specified number) thus. **6.** twist (silk etc.) into thread or yarn. **7.** shape (round pottery) on potter's wheel; turn (wood etc.) on lathe. **8.** turn, direct, move esp. quickly (esp. part of body), (*threw his eyes to the ground, a glance backwards, his arms up, his head back*); cause to pass or extend suddenly to another state or position (*threw army or bridge across river; threw switch to 'on'; throw* OPEN¹); put into a form or *into* another form, language, etc. **9.** *lose (contest, race, etc.) intentionally. **10.** have (fit, tantrum, etc.); (sl.) give (a party). **11.** ∼ **about** or **around,** throw in various directions, spend (one's money) ostentatiously, make vigorous use of (one's WEIGHT¹, lit. or fig.); ∼ **away,** (fig.) part with as unwanted, part with needlessly or recklessly, lose by neglect (*threw away all his advantages, an excellent chance*), discard (card), (Theatr.) speak (lines) with deliberate under-emphasis, (in *p.p.*) wasted (*the advice was thrown away on him*); ∼-*away* a. & n., (1) (thing) to be thrown away after (one) use, (2) deliberately under-emphasized; ∼ **back,** revert to ancestral character, (usu. in *pass.*) compel to rely *on*; ∼-*back* n., (instance of) reversion to ancestral character; ∼ **down,** cause to fall; *throw down the* GAUNTLET¹ *or* GLOVE; ∼ **in,** add (thing) to a bargain without extra charge, interpose (word, remark) by way of parenthesis or casually, (Footb. etc.) throw (ball) from edge of pitch etc. after it has gone out of play there, (Cricket etc.) return (ball) from outfield, (Cards) give (player) the lead (to his disadvantage); ∼ one's **hand in,** (lit.)

abandon one's chances in card game esp. poker, (fig.) give up, withdraw from a contest; *throw in* one's LOT *with, the* TOWEL; ∼ one**self into,** engage vigorously in; ∼ **off,** discard (acquaintance etc.), contrive to get rid of (illness, troublesome companion), abandon (disguise), produce, deliver, (poem, epigram) in offhand manner, (of hounds or hunt) begin hunting, make a start, (and see sense 3); ∼-*off* n., start in hunt or race; ∼ one**self on** or **upon,** attack, place one's reliance on (*the mercy of the court* etc.); ∼ **out,** put out forcibly or suddenly, part with as unwanted (∼-*out* n., what is discarded thus), expel (trouble-maker etc.), build (wing of house, pier, projecting or prominent thing), put forward tentatively, reject (proposal, bill in Parliament), confuse or distract (person speaking, thinking, or acting) from the matter in hand so that he blunders or stops, (Cricket & Baseball) put out (opponent) by throwing ball to wicket or base; ∼ **over,** desert, abandon; ∼ **together,** (1) assemble hastily, (2) bring into casual contact; ∼ **up,** lift (sash-window) quickly, erect (building), bring to notice, renounce (task), resign (office), (*v.t. & i.*) vomit; ∼ **up** one's **eyes** (as sign of horror or outraged propriety); *throw up the* SPONGE¹. **12.** Hence (∼)∼'ER¹ *n.* [OE *thrāwan* twist, turn, = OS *thrāian,* OHG *drāen,* WG f. IE **ter-*]

throw² (-ō) *n.* **1.** throwing; cast of dice; cast of fishing-line etc.; distance a missile is or may be thrown (*record throw with the hammer; a* STONE's *throw*); being thrown in wrestling; (Cricket) bowler's illegitimate delivery by throwing; *a ∼, (sl.) each (*sold at £5 a throw*). **2.** (Geol. & Mining.) fault in strata; amount of vertical displacement so caused. **3.** machine or device giving rapid rotary motion; (extent of) movement of crank, cam, etc.; distance moved by pointer of instrument etc. **4.** *∼ (**rug**), light cover for furniture, light wrap; ∼-**stick,** (1) club or stick meant to be whirled from the hand (e.g. boomerang), (2) device for throwing spear etc. more forcibly. [f. prec.]

throw'ster (-rō'-) *n.* one who throws silk. [ME, f. THROW¹ + -STER]

*thru. See THROUGH.

thrŭm¹ *n.,* & *v.t.* (**-mm-**). **1.** *n.* fringe of warp-threads remaining on loom when web has been cut off; single thread of this; any loose thread or tuft; **thread and** ∼, all alike, good and bad; hence ∼'**MY²** *a.* **2.** *v.t.* make of or cover with thrums. [OE, = OHG *drum* remnant, end-piece, f. Gmc **thrum-, *thram-* f. IE **trm-*]

thrŭm² *v.* (**-mm-**) & *n.* **1.** *v.t. & i.* play monotonously or unskilfully on or *on* (stringed instrument); drum, tap, idly on or *on* (table etc.). **2.** *n.* such playing; resulting sound. [imit.]

thrush¹ *n.* small or medium-sized bird of family Turdidae, e.g. blackbird, nightingale, or esp. **song-**∼ (*Turdus philomelos*) or MISSEL-*thrush.* [OE *thrysce* f. Gmc **thruskjōn;* cf. THROSTLE]

thrush² *n.* disease, esp. of children, marked by whitish fungous vesicles in mouth and throat; similar disease of vagina; inflammation affecting frog of horse's foot. [17th c., of unkn. orig.]

thrŭst *v.* (**thrust**) & *n.* **1.** *v.t.* push with sudden impulse or with force (lit. or fig.; *thrust his fist into my face, the letter into his pocket; thrust a pin into the cushion; I thrust out my hand; some have greatness thrust upon them; was thrust from his rights; my objections were thrust aside*); ∼ one**self** or one's **nose in,** obtrude, interfere. **2.** pierce (person etc.) *through;* make one's *way* by force. **3.** *v.i.* make sudden push *at* (person etc. *with* dagger etc.); force oneself *through, past,* etc. **4.** Hence ∼'ER¹ *n.* (esp.) ‖foxhunter who endangers others or the hounds in securing a forward place, pushing person, reaction-propulsion system. **5.** *n.* sudden or forcible push; forward force exerted by propeller, jet, etc.; strong attempt to penetrate enemy's line or territory; attack with point of weapon; chief theme, gist, (of remarks etc.); remark aimed at person; stress between two contiguous bodies esp. parts of structure, e.g. arch, rafters. **6.** ∼-**block,** (esp.) casting or frame carrying or containing bearings on which collars of propeller-shaft press; ∼-**hoe** (worked by thrust, not pull); ∼ **stage** (Theatr., extending into audience). [ME *thruste* etc. f. ON *thrýsta*]

***thruway.** See THROUGH*way.*

thŭd *v.i.* (-dd-), & *n.* (make, fall with) low dull sound as of blow on non-resonant thing. [prob. f. OE *thyddan* thrust]

thŭg *n.* **1.** (*T*∼; Hist.). member of religious organization of robbers and assassins in India suppressed about 1825. **2.** vicious or brutal ruffian. **3.** Hence ∼′**gERY** (5) (-g-) *n.* [f. Hindi & Marathi *thag* swindler]

thŭg′ge|**e** (-gē) *n.* (Hist.) the practice of the Thugs; so ∼ISM (3) (-g-) *n.* [f. Hindi *thagī* (as prec.)]

thū′ja, thū′ya, *n.* coniferous tree of genus *Thuja* or *Thuya,* arbor vitae. [mod. L, f. Gk *thu(i)a,* an Afr. tree]

thū′lium *n.* (Chem.) metallic element of lanthanide series. [mod. L, f. L *Thule* name of a region in the uttermost north + -IUM]

thŭmb (-m) *n.* & *v.* **1.** *n.* short thick finger set apart from and opposable to the others on human hand; digit of other animals corresponding to this; part of glove etc. that holds thumb; ∼**s down,** gesture of rejection; ∼**s up!** (sl. excl. of satisfaction); RULE *of thumb;* STICK[1] *out like a sore thumb;* **he has ten** ∼**s,** his FINGERS are all thumbs; **under** person's ∼ (influence, domination). **2.** ∼-**index** *n.,* & *v.t.,* (provide with) set of lettered grooves cut or tabs fixed in fore-edges of book's leaves to facilitate reference; ∼-**mark** (made by thumb, esp. dirty thumb on leaf of book); ∼-**nail,** nail of thumb; ∼-*nail sketch,* portrait of small size or hastily made, brief word-picture; ∼-**nut** (Mech.), shaped for thumb to turn); ∼-**pot,** flower-pot of smallest size; ∼-**print,** impression of thumb esp. as used for identification; ∼′**screw,** instrument of torture for squeezing thumbs, (Mech.) screw with flattened head for thumb to turn; ∼-**stall,** cover like finger-stall to protect thumb; ∼-**sucking,** infantile habit of sucking one's thumb; *∼′**tack,** drawing-pin. **3.** Hence (-)∼ED[2] (-md), ∼′LESS, *adjs.* **4.** *v.t.* wear, soil, (pages etc.) with thumb; (try to) get (a lift in a vehicle) by signal with thumb to indicate movement in desired direction; ∼ one's **nose,** cock a SNOOK[2] (*at*). **5.** *v.i.* turn over pages (as if) with thumb (*thumbed through the directory*). [OE *thūma,* = OS *thūma,* OHG *dūmo* f. WG *thōmo f. IE **tum-* swell]

thŭ′mmim. See URIM.

thŭmp *v.* & *n.* **1.** *v.t.* & *i.* beat or strike heavily esp. with fist; deliver blows *at, on,* etc., esp. to attract attention; ∼(**out**), play (tune) on piano etc. with thumping of keys. **2.** *n.* heavy blow, bang. [imit.]

thŭ′mp|**er** *n.* In vbl senses; (colloq.) large, striking, or impressive person or thing, esp. lie, so ∼ING[2] *a.* [f. prec. + -ER[1]]

thŭ′nder *n.* & *v.* **1.** *n.* loud noise heard after flash of lightning and due to disturbance of air by discharge of electricity; (rhet. or fig.) thunderbolt; (fig.) resounding loud deep noise (*thunders of applause*); (in *sing.* or *pl.*) authoritative censure or threats; BLOOD[1]-*and- -thunder;* (sl.) = HELL (*what the or in thunder* . . . *?*); **steal** person's ∼, (fig.) forestall him (by telling the story he meant to tell, making profitable use of his invention before he can, and the like) [f. remark of John Dennis (*c.* 1710) when stage thunder he had intended for his own play was used for another]. **2.** ∼-**bolt,** flash of lightning with crash of thunder, imaginary bolt or shaft viewed as destructive agent in lightning esp. as attribute of god, stone or fossil supposed to be such bolt, formidable threat etc.; ∼-**box,** primitive lavatory; ∼**clap,** crash of thunder (esp. fig., or in simile, of sudden terrible event or news); ∼-**cloud,** storm-cloud charged with electricity and producing thunder and lightning; ∼ **egg,** rounded concretion of chalcedony; ∼-**head,** rounded cumulus cloud projecting upwards and heralding thunder; ∼-**shower**

(accompanied by thunder); ∼**storm** (with thunder and lightning and usu. heavy rain or hail); ∼**struck,** struck by lightning, (fig.) amazed. **3.** Hence ∼LESS, ∼OUS, ∼Y[2], *adjs.* **4.** *v.i.* give forth thunder (esp. *it thunders, is thundering*); make noise like thunder, sound very loudly, (*voice thundered in my ears*); move with loud noise (*train thundered past*); make violent threats etc. *against* etc. **5.** *v.t.* utter (threats etc.) in loud or impressive manner. [OE *thunor,* = OS *thunar,* OHG *donar,* ON *thórr* f. Gmc f. IE *t(*o*)*n-*]

thŭ′nderer *n.* In vbl senses; **the** *T*∼, Jupiter (Tonans), ||(arch. or joc.) *The Times* newspaper. [ME, f. prec. + -ER[1]]

thŭ′ndering *a.* & *adv.* In vbl senses; (colloq.) unusual(ly), remarkable, remarkably, decided(ly), (*a thundering nuisance; a thundering great fish*); hence ∼LY[2] *adv.* [f. THUNDER + -ING[2]]

thŭr′ible *n.* censer. [ME f. OF, or f. L *t*(*h*)*uribulum* (as foll.)]

thŭr′i|fer *n.* acolyte carrying censer; so ∼FEROUS (-ĭ′f-) *a.,* incense-bearing, ∼FICA′TION *n.,* burning of incense. [LL (*thus thuris* incense f. Gk *thuos* sacrifice, *-fer* -bearing)]

Thur(s). *abbr.* Thursday.

Thŭr′sday (-zdā, -zdĭ) *n.* & *adv.* **1.** *n.* day of week, following Wednesday; HOLY *Thursday.* **2.** *adv.* (cf. FRIDAY 2). [OE *thunres-, thur*(*e*)*sdæg,* day of thunder, representing LL *Jovis dies* day of Jupiter]

thŭs (dh-) *adv.* (formal). in this way, in the way (to be) indicated; accordingly; as a result or inference; to this extent, so, (*thus far; thus much*). [OE, = OS *thus,* of unkn. orig.]

thŭs′nèss (dh-) *n.* (joc.) state of being thus. [f. prec. + -NESS]

thū′ya. See THUJA.

thwăck *v.t.,* & *n.* = WHACK 1, 2. [imit.]

||**thwaite** *n.* (dial.) piece of wild land made arable. [f. ON *thveit(i)* paddock (*thvīta = OE *thwītan* to cut)]

thwart (-ôrt) *v.t., n., a., adv.,* & *prep.* **1.** *v.t.* frustrate, foil, (person, wish, purpose). **2.** *n.* oarsman's bench placed across boat. **3.** *a.* (arch.) lying across, transverse. **4.** *adv.* & *prep.* (arch.) across, athwart; (Naut.) ∼-**ship** *a.,* -**ships** *adv.,* (Naut.) (lying) across ship. [ME *thwert* adv. f. ON *thvert* neut. of *thverr* transverse = OE *thwe*(*o*)*rh,* OHG *twerh,* Goth. *thwairhs* angry f. Gmc *thwerhwaz f. IE **twerk-,* **twork-*]

thy (dhī) *poss. pron. attrib.* (arch. or poet. or dial. exc. as described at THOU). of thee (in *pred.* & *abs.* use, & usu. before vowel, **thine;** *thy lips; the fault is thine; thine eyes*); for phrs. see HER[2], HERS. [ME *thī,* reduced f. *thīn* THINE]

thȳ′lacine *n.* = TASMANIAN *wolf.* [F, f. mod. L *thylacinus* f. Gk *thulakos* pouch; see -INE[1]]

thȳme (tīm) *n.* herb of genus *Thymus* with aromatic leaves; **garden** ∼, shrub with pungent aromatic leaves used in cookery; **lemon** ∼, lemon-scented wild thyme; **wild** ∼ (species with mildly aromatic leaves); hence **thȳ′m**Y[2] (tī′-) *a.* [ME, f. OF *thym* f. L f. Gk *thumon* (*thuō* burn sacrifice)]

thȳ′mine (-ēn) *n.* (Chem.) crystalline base found as constituent of DNA or derived from thymus gland. [f. *thymic* (as THYMUS; see -IC) + -INE[5]]

thȳ′mŏl *n.* (Chem.) a white crystalline phenol obtained from oil of thyme and used as antiseptic. [f. as THYME + -OL]

thȳ′m|us *n.* (*pl.* ∼i *pr.* -ī). ∼**us** (**gland**), (Anat.) lymphoid organ situated near base of neck (in man becoming much smaller at approach of puberty). [mod. L, f. Gk *thumos*]

thȳr′oid *n.* & *a.* (Anat. & Zool.) shield-shaped (∼ **cartilage,** large cartilage of larynx, projection of which in man forms Adam's apple); connected with the thyroid cartilage (*thyroid artery*); ∼ (**gland**), (1) large ductless gland lying near larynx and trachea secreting hormone which regulates growth and development through rate of metabolism, (2) extract prepared from the thyroid gland of animals and

used in treating goitre, cretinism, etc.; hence **thȳr′e͞o-, thȳr′o-**, *comb. forms.* [f. obs. F *thyroide* or mod. L *thyroides*, irreg. f. Gk *thureoeidēs* (*thureos* oblong shield; see -OID)]
thȳr′ŏ′xine *n.* white crystalline active principle of thyroid gland. [f. prec. + OX- + -INE⁶]
thȳr′s|us *n.* (*pl.* ∿i *pr.* ī). (Gk & Rom. Ant.) staff tipped with ornament like pine-cone, an attribute of Bacchus; (Bot.) inflorescence as in lilac, with primary axis racemose and secondary axis cymose. [L, f. Gk *thursos*]
thȳsĕ′lf (dh-) *pron.* Emphat. & refl. form corresp. to THOU or THEE (for uses cf. HERSELF). [ME, f. THY + SELF]
ti¹ (tē) *n.* tree or shrub of genus *Cordyline*, esp. *C. terminalis* with edible roots. [Tahitian, Maori, etc.]
ti². See TE.
Ti *symb.* titanium.
tiār′a *n.* ancient-Persian turban worn erect by king, depressed by others; pope's diadem pointed at top and surrounded by three crowns, (fig.) the papal office; jewelled ornamental band worn on front of woman's hair; hence ∿ED² (-rad), ∿′D², *adjs.* [L f. Gk, of unkn. orig.]
Tibĕ′tan *a.* & *n.* (native, inhabitant, or language) of Tibet. [f. *Tibet* + -AN]
ti′bi|a *n.* (*pl.* ∿ae). (Anat.) inner and usu. larger of two bones from knee to ankle; tibiotarsus of bird; fourth segment of leg in insects; so ∿AL *a.* [L, = shin-bone, flute]
tibiotār′s|us *n.* (*pl.* ∿i *pr* -ī). bone in bird corresponding to tibia, fused at lower end with some bones of tarsus. [f. prec. + -O- + TARSUS]
tic *n.* habitual spasmodic contraction of muscles esp. of face; ∿ (**douloureux** *pr.* d͞o͞olerĕr′, d͞oler͞o͞o′), trigeminal neuralgia. [F, f. It. *ticchio*]
tice *n.* (Cricket) = YORKER; (Croquet) stroke tempting opponent to aim at one's ball. [f. (now dial.) *tice* v. (= ENTICE)]
tick¹ *v.* & *n.* **1.** *v.i.,* & *n.* (make) slight recurring click, esp. that of watch or clock (||**to** or **on the** ∿, with exact punctuality; **what makes** person ∿, his motivation; ∿ **over**, (of engine, or fig.) idle); ||(colloq.) moment, instant; ∿-**tack**, pulsating sound resp. of the heart, kind of manual semaphore signalling practised by racecourse bookmakers; *∿-**tack-toe**, noughts and crosses; ∿-**tick**, ticking of watch etc.; ∿-**tock**, ticking of large clock etc. **2.** *n.* small mark set against items in list etc. in checking, esp. to note correctness. **3.** *v.t.* mark (item, usu. *off*) with tick. **4.** (Of clock etc.) ∿ **away** (the time etc.); ∿ **off**, (sl.) reprimand; (of tape-machine) ∿ **out** (news etc.) [n. ME; cf. Du. *tik*, LG *tikk* touch, tick; v. 16th c.; cf. Du. *tikken*, OHG *zekōn* pluck]
tick² *n.* arachnid parasitic on dogs, cattle, etc.; insect parasitic on sheep, birds, etc.; (colloq.) unpleasant or despicable person; ∿ **bean** (shaped like tick); ∿ **fever** (transmitted by bite of tick). [OE *tīca, *ticca, ME *teke, tyke; cf. MDu., MLG *tēke, OHG *zēcho*]
tick³ *n.* cover or case of mattress or pillow; = TICKING. [ME *tikke, tēke = MDu., MLG *tēke, OHG *ziehha, f. WG *teka, *tika, f. L f. Gk *thēkē case]
tick⁴ *n.* (colloq.) credit (*buy goods on tick*). [app. abbr. of TICKET in phr. *on the ticket*]
ti′cker *n.* In vbl senses; (colloq.) watch, tape--machine; (joc.) the heart; *∿-**tape**, paper strip from tape-machine, this or similar material thrown from windows to greet a celebrity. [f. TICK¹ + -ER¹]
ti′ckėt *n.,* & *v.t.* **1.** *n.* written or printed piece of card or paper entitling holder to admission to place of entertainment etc., participation in event, conveyance by train etc., or other right, (*concert, theatre, library, lottery, railway, bus, cloakroom, pawn, -ticket*); (Mil.) certificate of discharge; certificate of qualification as ship's master, pilot, etc.; label attached to thing and giving price or other particulars; official notification of traffic offence etc. (*parking ticket*);

*(Polit.) list of candidates put forward by a party, (fig.) principles of a party, (SPLIT¹ *the ticket;* STRAIGHT *ticket*); **the** ∿, (sl.) the correct or desirable thing. **2.** ∿-**collector**, railway official who takes or checks passengers' tickets; ||∿-**day**, (St. Exch.) day before settling day, when names of actual purchasers are handed to stockbrokers; ∿-**office**, place where tickets for transport, entertainment, etc., are sold; ||∿ **of leave** (Hist., allowing liberty with certain restrictions to ∿-*of-leave man,* i.e. prisoner or convict who had served part of his time); ∿-**porter**, (Hist.) licensed London porter identified by badge; ∿--**punch** (for making hole in ticket to show that it has been used). **3.** *v.t.* put ticket on (article for sale etc.). [f. obs. F *étiquet* E. OF *estiquet*(*e*) (*estiquier, estechier* fix f. MDu. *steken;* see -ET¹)]
||**tickety̆-b͞o͞o′** *a.* (sl.) all right, satisfactory. [perh. f. prec. + -Y² + BOO]
ti′cking *n.* stout usu. striped linen or cotton material for bed-ticks. [f. TICK³ + -ING¹]
ti′ckle *v.* & *n.* **1.** *v.t.* apply light touches or stroking to (person, part of his body, or abs.) so as to excite the nerves and usu. produce laughter and spasmodic movement (*tickle him with a feather; tickle the soles of her feet; don't tickle*); ∿ person's **ribs**, (fig.) cause him great amusement. **2.** *v.i.* feel this sensation (*my foot tickles*). **3.** *v.t.* excite agreeably, amuse, divert, (person, his sense of humour, vanity, etc.; *I was highly tickled at the idea; this will tickle his palate;* ∿**d pink** or **to death,** (colloq.) extremely amused etc.); catch (trout etc.) by stroking with the hand. **4.** *n.* act or sensation of tickling; so **ti′ckly²** *a.* [ME, prob. frequent. of TICK¹ touch lightly; see -LE 3]
ti′ckler *n.* In vbl senses; puzzling or delicate question or matter; *memorandum book. [f. prec. + -ER¹]
ti′cklish *a.* easily tickled, sensitive to tickling; (of person or question or thing to be dealt with) difficult, critical, requiring careful handling; hence ∿LY² *adv.,* ∿NESS *n.* [f. TICKLE + -ISH¹]
ticpolo′nga (-ngga) *n.* venomous serpent of India and Sri Lanka. [f. Sinh. *titpolongā* spot-viper]
ti′c-tăc. Var. of TICK¹-*tack.*
ti′dal *a.* of tide(s); actuated by tide(s); ∿ **air** (passing in and out of lungs at each respiration); ∿ **basin, dock,** etc., (subject to rise and fall of tide); ∿ **flow** (of traffic moving mainly in opposite directions at different times of day); ∿ **friction** (of tide wave, retarding diurnal rotation of earth); ∿ **river** (affected by tide to considerable distance from mouth); ∿ **wave,** (1) exceptionally large ocean wave e.g. one attributed to earthquake, (2) widespread manifestation of feeling etc., (3) tidal wave; hence ∿LY² *adv.* [f. TIDE¹ + -AL]
*** ti′dbit.** See TITBIT.
***tiddledy-wink.** See TIDDLY-WINK.
||**ti′ddler** *n.* (childish or colloq.). small fish, esp. minnow or stickleback; unusually small thing. [perh. rel. to *tiddly* 'little' and TITTLEBAT]
ti′ddly̆, ti′ddley, (-lī) *a.* (sl.) slightly drunk. [earlier sense 'a drink', 19th c.; orig. unkn.]
ti′ddly̆-wink, *ti′ddledy̆-** (-deld-), *n.* counter flicked into cup or other receptacle on centre of table in game of ∿s. [19th c., perh. rel. to prec.]
tide¹ *n.* **1.** time, season, (arch. exc. in *Whitsuntide, Christmas-tide, eventide,* etc.). **2.** periodical rise (**flood--**∿) and fall (**ebb-**∿) of sea due to attraction of moon and sun; water as moved by this (*tide* TURN¹*s*; ∿ **is in, out,** water is at high, low, level); **high, low,** ∿, completion of flood, ebb, -tide; **spring, neap,** ∿, tide of maximum, minimum, height when solar and lunar attractions are combined or at right angles; **work double** ∿s (twice normal time, or as hard as possible); **meteorological** ∿ (due to regular alternations of wind etc.). **3.** (fig.) trend of opinion or fortune or events (*go with, against, the tide;* TURN¹,² (*of*) *the tide; roll back the tide of war*). **4.** ∿-**gate** (opened to admit water or let vessels pass during rising tide, closed to keep water in during ebb); ∿-**gauge**

(showing extremes or present level of tide); ~-**lock** (between tidal harbour etc. and basin or canal behind it); ~-**land** (submerged at high tide); ~-**mark,** mark made by tide at high water, (colloq.) line on body to which person has washed, or on bath to which water has risen when person was in it; ~-**mill** (with water-wheel driven by tide); ~-**rip(s),** rough water caused by opposing tides; ~-**table,** list of times of high tide at a place; ~-**waiter,** (Hist.) customs officer who boarded ship on arrival to enforce customs regulations; ~ **water** (brought by or affected by tides); ~ **wave,** undulation of water passing round earth and causing high and low tides; ~'**way,** channel where tide runs, tidal part of river, ebb or flow in such channel. **5.** Hence ~'LESS (-dl-) *a.* [OE *tīd* time, = OS *tīd*, OHG *zīt*, ON *títh* f. Gmc *tīdiz* (*tī̆-*; cf. TIME¹)]

tide² *v.* **1.** *v.i.* drift with tide, esp. work in or out of harbour with help of tide. **2.** *v.t.* & *i.* (enable or assist to) get *over* (difficulty etc., or abs.). [f. prec.]

ti'dings (-z) *n.* (literary; treated as *sing.* or *pl.*) (piece of) news, information. [OE *tīdung,* prob. f. ON *títhindi* events (*títhr* occurring)]

ti'd|y *a., n.,* & *v.t.* **1.** *a.* (Of dress, room, person, habits) neatly arranged, neat, orderly; (colloq.) pretty large, considerable, (*left a tidy sum when he died; a tidy day's work*); hence ~iLY² *adv.,* ~iNESS *n.* **2.** *n.* detachable usu. ornamental cover for chair-back etc.; receptacle for odds and ends, e.g. in kitchen sink. *v.t.* ~y (**up**), make (room, table, etc., one*self*, or abs.) neat, put in good order. [ME, = timely etc., f. TIDE¹ + -y²]

tie¹ *v.* (*part.* **ty'ing** *pr.* tī'ĭ-). **1.** *v.t.* attach or fasten with cord or the like (*tie the dog to the railings;* HAND¹*s are tied;* RIDE *and tie; tie his legs together; tie on a label*); secure (shoe etc.) by tightening and knotting its strings; arrange (string, ribbon, tie, etc.) to form knot, bow, etc. (**and dye,** method of producing dyed patterns by tying string etc. to protect parts of fabric from dye), form (knot, bow) thus; bind (rafters etc.) by cross-piece etc.; restrict, bind, (person etc. *to, down to,* conditions, occupation, place, etc.); **fit to be** ~**d,** (sl.) very angry; ~ **in** or **up,** (cause to) agree or be closely associated *with;* ~ **up,** fasten with cord etc., obstruct, make (money etc.) not immediately available e.g. by investment, restrict, esp. annex conditions to (bequest etc.) to prevent its being sold or diverted from its purpose; hence ~-*up n.* **2.** (Mus.) unite (notes) by tie. **3.** *v.t.* & *i.* make tie with or *with* (competitor; *for* place or prize), equal (feat etc.). [OE *tīgan, tēgan* f. Gmc *taugian,* as foll.]

tie² *n.* **1.** cord, chain, etc., used for fastening. **2.** = NECK¹*tie;* ‖OLD *school tie* **3.** (fig.) thing that unites or restricts persons, bond, obligation, (*ties of blood, friendship*). **4.** rod or beam holding parts of a structure together; *rail sleeper. **5.** (Mus.) curved line above or below two notes of same pitch that are to be joined as one. **6.** equality of score or draw or dead heat among competitors in game or contest; **play, shoot,** etc., **off a** ~, play further game etc. to decide between such competitors. **7.** match between any pair of several competing players or teams; **cup**~, match in competition for a cup. **8.** *laced shoe. **9.** ~-**bar,** metal rod holding parts of building together; ~-**beam,** horizontal beam connecting rafters; ~-**break(er),** means of) deciding winner as between competitors tying; ~-**clip,** ~-**pin,** ~-**tack,** (to hold necktie in place); ~-**line,** direct telephone line between two subscribers; ~-**piece,** ~-**rod,** connecting member; ~-**wig** (tied at back with ribbon). [OE *tēah, tēg,* = ON *taug* rope f. Gmc *taugō* (*tauh-;* cf. TEAM, TOW¹)]

‖**tied** (tīd) *a.* (Of public house etc.) bound to supply only a particular brewer's liquor; (of dwelling-house) occupied subject to tenant's working for house's owner. [p.p. of TIE¹]

tier *n.* row or rank, esp. one of several placed one above another as in theatre; one of several units of a

structure placed one above another; (Naut.) circle of coiled cable, place for coiled cable; hence (-)~ED² (-ērd) *a.* [earlier *tire* f. F (*tirer* draw, elongate f. Rom. *tirare*)]

tierce *n.* **1.** (arch.) one third of a pipe as wine-measure; cask containing certain quantity (varying with the goods) esp. of provisions. **2.** (Mus.) interval of two octaves and a major third. **3.** sequence of three cards; third of eight parrying positions in fencing, or corresponding thrust. **4.** (Eccl.) = TERCE. **5.** So ~ED² (-st) *a.* (Her.), divided into three parts of different tinctures. [ME, f. OF *t(i)erce* f. L *tertia* fem. (as n.) of *tertius* third]

tier'cel. See TERCEL.

tier'cet. See TERCET.

tiers état (tyārz ātah') *n.* (Fr. Hist.) = *third* ESTATE. [F]

tiff¹ *v.i.* = TIFFIN. [abbr.]

tiff² *n.* fit of peevishness; slight or petty quarrel. [18th c.; orig. unkn.]

ti'ffany *n.* thin gauze muslin. [orig. (dress for) Twelfth-night, f. OF *tifanie* f. eccl. L *theophania* f. Gk THEO*phaneia* manifestation of God, Epiphany]

ti'ffin *n.,* & *v.i.* (Ind.) (take) light meal esp. of curried dishes and fruit, lunch. [app. f. *tiffing* taking slight drink]

tig *n.* game of TAG². [var. of TICK¹]

ti'ger *n.* **1.** large Asian yellow-brown black-striped carnivorous maneless feline (*Panthera tigris*); **American** ~, jaguar; **paper** ~, person or thing threatening in appearance but ineffectual. **2.** fierce or energetic person; (colloq.) formidable opponent in a game; ‖dissolute swaggerer or bully; ‖(arch.) groom accompanying master in light vehicle; *(sl.) yell supplementary to three cheers, final burst. **3.** ~-**beetle,** carnivorous beetle of family Cicindelidae, with spotted or striped wing-covers; ~-**cat,** any moderate-sized feline resembling the tiger, e.g. ocelot, serval, margay, (Austral.) carnivorous marsupial of genus *Dasyurus;* ~('s) **eye,** yellow brown gem of brilliant lustre, *pottery-glaze of similar appearance; ~-**lily,** tall garden lily with flowers of dull orange spotted with black or purple; ~-**moth** (with richly spotted and streaked wings suggesting tiger's skin); ~-**wood,** striped or streaked wood for cabinet-making. **4.** Hence ~ISH¹ *a.,* **ti'grESS¹** *n.* [ME, f. OF *tigre* f. L f. Gk *tigris*]

tight (tīt) *a., n.,* & *adv.* **1.** *a.* closely and firmly put together (*tight joint, ship*); impermeable, impervious, esp. (in *comb.*) to specified thing (*airtight, watertight*). **2.** closely held, drawn, fastened, fitting, etc., (*tight knots; cork is too tight*); (of shoe) too closely fitting; (of control etc.) strictly imposed. **3.** tense, stretched so as to leave no slack, (*tight cord*); ~'**rope,** one on which acrobats, rope-dancers, etc., perform). **4.** (colloq.) drunk; stingy. **5.** (Of money or materials) not easily obtainable; (of money-market) in which money is tight. **6.** produced by or requiring great exertion or pressure (*a tight squeeze*); (of precautions, programme, etc.) stringent, demanding; ~ **corner** or **place** or (colloq.) **spot,** (fig.) difficult situation. **7.** ~-**fisted,** stingy; ~-**lipped,** with lips compressed to restrain emotion or speech; ~'**wad,** (sl.) close-fisted or stingy person. **8.** Hence ~EN⁶ *v.t.* & *i.,* (~*en* one's *belt,* go without food, lit. or fig.), ~'LY² *adv.,* ~'NESS *n.* **9.** *n.* (in *pl.*) close-fitting elastic garments as worn by dancers, acrobats, etc.; woman's one-piece stretchable undergarment covering legs and body up to waist, worn in place of stockings. **10.** *adv.* tightly (*squeeze it tight; hold me tight*); SIT *tight;* ~-**fitting,** (of garment) fitting (too) close to body. [prob. alt. f. *thight* f. ON *théttr,* *théttr* watertight, of close texture]

ti'gon *n.* offspring of tiger and lioness. [portmanteau wd f. TIGER + LION]

ti'gress. See TIGER.

tike. See TYKE.

ti′ki *n.* (NZ). large wooden or small ornamental greenstone image of creator of man or of an ancestor. [Maori]

til (tēl) *n.* Portuguese tilde. [Port.]

ti′lbury̆ *n.* (Hist.) light open two-wheeled carriage. [f. inventor's name]

ti′lde (*-e, -ā*) *n.* mark (∼) put over letter, e.g. Spanish *n* when pronounced *ny* (so *señor*) or Portuguese *a* or *o* when nasalized (so *São Paulo*). [Sp., var. of *tidlo* f. L *titulus* TITLE]

tile *n.*, & *v.t.* **1.** *n.* thin slab of baked clay for roof, pavement, drain, etc.; similar slab glazed and often decorated for hearth, fireplace, wall, etc.; such slabs collectively; thin flat piece used in game; **have a** ∼ **loose,** (sl.) be slightly crazy; **on the** ∼**s,** (sl.) on a debauch. **2.** (sl.) hat, esp. silk hat. **3.** ∼′**stone,** flagstone suitable to be split for use instead of tiles. **4.** *v.t.* cover (roof etc., or abs.) with tiles; ∼ **in,** enclose in tiles. **5.** (Freemasonry). guard (lodge, meeting) against intrusion by placing tiler at door. **6.** Hence **ti′l**ING¹ (1, 2, 6) *n.* [OE *tigule, -ele,* = OS *tiegla,* OHG *ziagal(a),* ON *tigl,* f. L *tegula* f. IE *teg-* cover]

ti′ler *n.* **1.** one who makes or lays tiles. **2.** (Freemasonry). door-keeper of lodge. [ME, f. prec. + -ER¹]

till¹ *v.t.* prepare and use (land) for crops; hence ∼′ABLE *a.,* ∼′AGE (3) *n.* [OE *tilian* strive for, cultivate, = OS *tilian, tilon* obtain, OHG *zilōn,* Goth. *gatilon* f. Gmc *tilōjan* (*tilam* aim, goal)]

till² *prep.* & *conj.* **1.** *prep.* up to, as late as, (specified time; *wait till evening, four o'clock, then, Monday, next week*); up to the time of (event expected to happen sooner or later; *was true till death; waited till the end, till his return, arrival, departure*). **2.** *conj.* up to the time when (*ring till you get an answer; do not turn off till you come to the gate*); so long that (*laughed till I cried*). [f. OE & ON *til* to, prob. orig. f. Gmc *tilam* n. (see prec.) used as adv.]

till³ *n.* money-receptacle behind counter in shop, bank, etc. [ME, of unkn. orig.]

till⁴ *n.* stiff clay containing boulders, sand, etc., boulder clay; hence ∼′y² *a.* [17th c. Sc.; orig. unkn.]

tiller¹ *n.* (literary or arch.) one who tills. [ME, f. TILL¹ + -ER¹]

ti′ller² *n.* horizontal bar fitted to head of rudder for steering; ∼**-chain, -rope,** (connecting tiller with wheel). [ME, f. AF *telier* weaver's beam f. med. L *telarium* f. L *tela* web; see -ER² (2)]

ti′ller³ *n.,* & *v.i.* **1.** *n.* shoot of plant springing from bottom of original stalk; sapling; sucker. **2.** *v.i.* put forth tillers. [app. repr. OE *telgor* extended (*telga* bough)]

tilt¹ *v.* & *n.* **1.** *v.i.* & *t.* (cause to) assume sloping position from vertical or horizontal, heel over, (*table is apt to tilt; don't tilt the table; tilt the cask so as to drain it*); (Geol. of strata, in *act.* or *pass.*) turn *up* at steep angle. **2.** *v.i.* strike, thrust, run, *at* with weapon; engage in contest *with*; ∼ **at the ring** (suspended for horseman to carry off on point of lance); *tilt at* WINDMILLS. **3.** *v.t.* forge or work (steel etc.) with tilt-hammer. **4.** Hence ∼ER¹ (1, 2) *n.* **5.** *n.* tilting; sloping position. **6.** charging on horseback with lance etc. against opponent across barrier, or at mark (∼**-yard,** place used for this); encounter between opponents; **full** ∼**,** at full speed, with full force, (*come* or *run full tilt against*). **7.** ∼(**-hammer**), heavy pivoted hammer used in forging. [ME *tilte* perh. f. OE *tyltan, *tieltan* (*tealt* unsteady) f. Gmc *taltjan*; sense 2 f. 6, of unkn. orig.]

tilt² *n.,* & *v.t.* **1.** *n.* covering of canvas etc. esp. for cart. **2.** *v.t.* furnish with tilt. [ME, var. of *telde,* OE *teld,* OHG *zelt,* perh. infl. by TENT¹]

tilth *n.* tillage, cultivation (lit. or fig.); depth of soil affected by this; condition of soil under cultivation. [OE *tilth(e)* (as TILL¹, -TH¹)]

Tim. *abbr.* Timothy (NT).

ti′mbal *n.* (arch.) kettledrum. [f. F *timbale,* earlier *tamballe* f. Sp. *atabal* f. Arab. *aṭ-ṭabl* the drum]

timbale (tăṅbah′l) *n.* drum-shaped dish of minced meat or fish in pastry shell. [F; see prec.]

ti′mber *n.* **1.** wood prepared for building, carpentry, etc.; trees suitable for this; woods, forest; piece of wood, beam, esp. (Naut.) any of the curved pieces forming ribs of vessel, (SHIVER² *my timbers*); (esp. as *int.*) tree about to fall. **2.** ||∼**-cart** (high-wheeled, with tackle for lifting timber); ∼**-head,** top end of timber rising above deck and used for belaying ropes etc.; ∼**-hitch,** knot used in attaching rope to log or spar; *∼**land,** land covered with forest yielding timber; ∼**-line** (above which no trees grow); ∼**-toe(s),** (sl.) (person with) wooden leg; ∼**-wolf,** large N. Amer. grey wolf. **3.** Hence (-)∼ED² (*-erd*) *a.,* ∼ING¹ (2, 3) *n.* [OE, = building; OS *timbar,* OHG *zimbar,* ON *timbr* f. Gmc *timram* f. IE *dem-* build]

timbre (tăṅbr, tă′*mber*) *n.* characteristic quality of sounds produced by a particular voice or instrument, depending on the number and character of the overtones. [F, f. Rom. *timbano* f. med. Gk *timbanon* f. Gk *tumpanon* drum]

ti′mbrel *n.* (arch.) tambourine or similar instrument. [dim. of ME *timbre* f. OF (as prec.; see -LE 2)]

Timbŭctoō′ *n.* very remote place. [f. *Timbuktu* in W. Africa]

time¹ *n.* **1.** duration, indefinitely continued existence, progress of this viewed as affecting persons or things, (*time will show who is right; will stand for all time; has stood the test of time; time and tide wait for no man; take time by the* FORELOCK); (**Father**) T∼ (personified esp. as old man with scythe and hourglass). **2.** more or less definite portion of time associated with particular events or circumstances, historical or other period, (*the times of the Stuarts; the time of the Black Death; for the time* (BEing); *will last for a time; at different times of the year; prehistoric times; the good old times; things have changed since those times; the scientists of the time*); **the** ∼(**s**), the age now (or then) present (BEHIND *the times*); ∼ **was,** there has been a time *when.* **3.** allotted or available portion of time, the time at one's disposal, (*had no time to discuss it; spend, lose, waste, time; gave a lot of his time to relief work; cannot find the time to write; give me time and I will pay; the cure is bound to take (some) time*); one's lifetime (*will last my time*); prison sentence (*is doing time*); period of apprenticeship (*served his time*); duration of boxing-round, drinking-hours, etc. (*time is up; referee* or *landlord called* '*Time!*'). **4.** moment or definite portion of time destined or suitable for a purpose etc. (*there is a time for everything; will fix a time for seeing him; now is the time (to buy, to press your point); I must* BIDE *my time; it is* (HIGH) *time to go, time for lunch, time for a change, time* (*that*) *I was going* or *for me to go;* BEHIND *time; till such time as they return home*); period of gestation (*is far on in her time*), date of childbirth (*is near her time*) or death (*my time is drawing near*). **5.** (in *sing.* or *pl.*) conditions of life, prevailing (esp. economic) circumstances, of a period (*hard, bad, good, times; at the* BEST¹ *of times;* (*the*) *times have changed*); **have a** ∼ (**of it**), undergo trouble or difficulty; **have a good** ∼**,** enjoy oneself. **6.** occasion (*the first time (that) I saw him; admitted at twopence a time; cannot do it this time, wait till next time; have told you a dozen times; for the last time of asking*); ∼**s out of number,** ∼ **and** (∼) **again,** **many a** ∼**,** ∼ **after** ∼**,** on many occasions, in many instances; (expressing multiplication: *three times four is twelve, one-and-a-half times four is six; is three times the size of mine; ten times easier* or *as easy*). **7.** (amount of) time as reckoned by conventional standards (*the time allowed was four months; did a mile in record time*); point of time esp. stated in hours and minutes of the day (*the time fixed was 4.30; what is the time? what time is it?; is that the correct time?*); measured time spent in work etc. (*workmen on* SHORT *time*); ∼ **and a half,** DOUBLE¹ *time,* etc., (paid at that much more than the normal rate); (GREENWICH, MEAN², SIDEREAL, STANDARD, SUMMER¹(-), *time.* **8.** (Mus.) duration of note as indicated by semibreve, minim, etc.; style of movement depending on number and accentuation of beats in a bar (*time* SIGNATURE); rate of execution; = *tempo*; DOUBLE¹ *time*. **9. against ∿,** with utmost speed so as to reach a goal by a specified time (*working, riding, against time*); **ahead of ∿,** earlier than expected or promised; **ahead of** one's **∿,** having ideas too enlightened to be accepted by one's contemporaries; **all the ∿,** during the whole of the time referred to (*they were laughing all the time; I thought you were serious, but all the time you were only teasing me*), at all times (*is a business man all the time*); one, two, etc., **at a ∿,** in such groups (separately); **at the same ∿,** at a time which is the same for both or all, simultaneously, notwithstanding, all the same; **at ∿s,** intermittently; **at one ∿,** during a known but unspecified past period (*at one time we met frequently*), simultaneously (*ran three businesses at one time*); BEAT¹ *time*; **before** (one's) **∿,** = *ahead of* (one's) *time*; **before** one's **∿,** prematurely (*old* etc.); **between ∿s,** in the intervals between other actions, occasionally; EVERY *time*; **from ∿ to ∿,** occasionally; GAIN² *time*; (*all*) *in* GOOD *time*; **half the ∿,** (colloq.) as often as not; **have no ∿ for,** not wish or be able to spend time on, dislike; **have the ∿,** (1) be able to spend time needed, (2) know from watch etc. what time it is; **in ∿,** not late, early enough (*to do, for* thing), eventually, sooner or later, in accordance with or following the time of music etc.; **in** (**less than**) **no ∿,** rapidly, in an instant; **in** one's **∿,** at some previous period of one's life (*in his time he was the world's greatest hurdler*); **in** one's **own ∿,** outside working hours; **in** one's **own** (**good**) **∿,** at a rate decided by oneself only; **keep ∿,** walk, dance, sing, etc., in time; **keep good** or **bad ∿,** (of clock etc.) record time accurately or not; KILL¹ *time*; **lose no ∿,** (1) not waste time *in doing, on* thing, (2) act immediately; MAKE¹ *time; in the* NICK¹ *of time;* **no ∿,** (colloq.) a very short interval (*it was no time before she was back*); **on ∿,** in accordance with timetable etc., *on hire-purchase; **out of ∿,** unseasonable, unseasonably, too late, (of singing etc.) not in time; **play for ∿,** seek to gain time by delaying etc.; TAKE¹ (one's, *all* one's) *time;* ∿ immemorial or out of mind, (for, from) a longer time than anyone can remember or trace; **the ∿ of day,** hour by clock; **at this ∿ of day,** (fig.) at this late stage in history, in the negotiations, etc.; **know the ∿ of day,** be well informed; **pass the ∿ of day,** (colloq.) exchange greeting or casual remarks (*with* person); *so that's the* ∿ **of day!** (sl., the state of affairs, your little game, etc.), **the ∿ of** one's **life,** a period of exceptional enjoyment or pleasant or unpleasant excitement (*have the time of one's life; give* person *the time of his life*); ∿ **off** or **∿ out,** time used for rest or for a different activity, *brief intermission in game; **what ∿,** (poet., arch., or joc.) while, when; **T∿s** (in title of newspaper or magazine: *The Times, Oxford Times, Church Times*); **The T∿s,** esp. *The Times* of London, *The New York Times,* or the *Financial Times.* **10. ∿-and-motion** *a.*, concerned with measuring efficiency of industrial etc. operations; **∿-ball** (dropped from top of pole at observatory to indicate fixed moment of mean time); **∿-bargain,** a contract for sale of stock etc. at future time (often a form of gambling); **∿ bomb** (designed to explode at a set time after being dropped or put in position); **∿-book, -card, -clock,** (for recording workmen's hours of work); **∿ capsule** (buried in foundations of new building etc. and containing objects typical of the present time, for discovery in the future); **∿-consuming** *a.*, using much time, wasteful of time; *∿ **deposit,** bank deposit not repayable before set date; **∿-expired,** (of soldier) having completed period of military service; **∿ exposure** (of photographic film for longer than an instant); **∿ factor,** passage of time as limitation on what can be achieved; **∿-fuse** (calculated to burn for or explode at a given time); **∿-honoured,** venerable because of antiquity, traditional, customary; **∿'keeper,** one

who records time esp. of workmen or in game (*watch* etc. *is good, bad, ∿keeper,* keeps good, bad, time); **∿-lag,** interval of time between cause etc. and result or consequence; **∿-lapse** *a.,* (of film etc.) containing frames taken at long intervals but shown at normal pace to accelerate view of events; **∿-limit** (within which something must be done); **∿'piece,** time-measuring instrument, esp. non-striking portable but stationary clock; **∿-scale,** sequence of events as measure of historical etc. duration; **∿-server,** one who, esp. for selfish ends, adapts himself to opinions of the times or of persons in power; **∿-sharing,** operation of computer by several users simultaneously; **∿-sheet** (for recording hours of work etc.); **∿-signal,** visible or audible announcement of exact time of day; **∿-switch** (acting automatically at set time); **∿'table,** scheme of school work, etc., table showing times of public transport services; **∿-travel,** hypothetical movement through time; **∿-work** (paid for by time, not piece-work); **∿-worn,** impaired by age; *time* ZONE. [OE *tīma,* = ON *tími,* f. Gmc root **tī-* extend]

time² *v.* **1.** *v.t.* choose the time for, do at chosen or correct time, (*must time your blows; time the opening of the valves; remark was ill, well, timed*); arrange time of arrival of, regulate rate of travelling of, (train etc.); ascertain the time taken by (race, runner, process, etc.), whence **ti'mer¹** (1, 2), **ti'ming¹,** *ns.* **2.** *v.i.* keep time, harmonize, *with.* [ME, f. prec.]

ti'meless (-ml-) *a.* (rhet. or poet.) not subject to or affected by the passage of time; (arch.) untimely; hence **∿LY²** *adv.,* **∿NESS** *n.* [f. TIME¹ +-LESS]

ti'mely (-mli) *a. & adv.* **1.** *a.* seasonable, opportune; hence **∿iNESS** *n.* **2.** *adv.* (arch.) opportunely. [ME, f. TIME¹ +-LY¹]

||**ti'meous** (-mɐs), ||**ti'mous,** *a.* (chiefly Sc.) timely; hence **∿LY²** *adv.* [f. TIME¹ +-OUS]

ti'mer. See TIME².

ti'mid *a.* (∿er, ∿est). easily alarmed; indicating fear; shy; hence *or* cogn. **timi'dity,** **∿NESS,** *ns.,* **∿LY²** *adv.* [f. F *timide* or f. L *timidus* (*timēre* fear; see -ID¹)]

ti'ming. See TIME².

timǒ'cracy *n.* form of government in which there is a property qualification for office; form of government in which rulers are motivated by love of honour; hence **timocrǎ'tic** *a.* [f. OF *timocracie* f. med. L f. Gk *timokratia* (*timē* honour, worth, value; see -CRACY)]

ti'morous *a.* frightened; timid, easily alarmed; hence **∿LY²** *adv.,* **∿NESS** *n.* [ME, f. OF *temoreus* f. med. L *timorosus,* f. L *timor* (*timēre* fear; see ∿OR, -OUS)]

ti'mothy *n.* **∿** (**grass**) a fodder-grass, *Phleum pratense.* [f. *T∿* Hanson, who introduced it in Carolina *c.* 1720]

||**ti'mous.** See TIMEOUS.

ti'mpanǀo *n.* (usu. in *pl.* ∿**i** *pr.* -ē). kettledrum; hence **∿IST** *n* , one who plays the timpani in an orchestra. [It., = TYMPANUM]

tin *n.,* & *v.t.* (**-nn-**). **1.** *n.* silvery-white malleable metallic element, taking high polish and resisting corrosion, used mainly in alloys with lead, copper, or antimony to form solder, white-metal, pewter, bronze, etc., or in plating thin iron or steel sheets to form tin plate for containers, kitchen utensils, toys, etc.; CRY¹ *of tin.* **2.** vessel etc. of tin or tinned iron esp. ||for preserving meat, fish, fruit, etc., or to support food being cooked; tinned iron as material for this; ||(sl.) money. **3. ∿ fish,** (Naut. sl.) torpedo; **∿ foil,** FOIL¹ of tin or aluminium or tin alloy for wrapping etc.; **∿ god,** object of unjustified veneration; **∿ hat,** (Army sl.) modern soldier's steel helmet; *∿'horn *n.* & *a.,* pretentious but unimpressive (person); ||*put the tin LID on;* **∿ Lizzie,** small cheap motor car; **∿'man,** tinsmith; ||**∿-opener,** tool for opening tins; **∿-pan alley,** (fig.) the world of the composers and publishers of popular music; **∿ plate,** sheet iron or sheet steel coated with tin; **∿-plate** *v.t.,* coat with tin;

∼'pot *a*., (derog.) cheap, inferior; ∼'smith, worker in tin and tin plate; ∼ soldier, toy soldier made of tin etc.; ∼'stone, cassiterite; ∼-tack, tinned iron tack; ∼'ware, vessels etc. of tin or tin plate; *tin* WHISTLE. 4. *v.t.* cover or coat with tin; ||pack (meat etc.) in a tin for preservation. [OE, = OHG *zin*, ON *tin*, f. Gmc *tinam*, of unkn. orig.]

ti'namou (-ōō) *n*. S. Amer. bird of family Tinamidae, resembling grouse but related to rhea. [F, f. Galibi *tinamu*]

tinct *a*. (poet.) coloured, tinted. [f. L *tinctus* p.p. (see TINGE)]

tinctō̆r'ial *a*. of colour or dyeing; producing colour. [f. L *tinctorius* (*tinctor* dyer); see TINGE, -ORY, -AL]

ti'ncture *n*., & *v.t.* 1. *n*. alcoholic solution of some (usu. vegetable) principle used in medicine (*tincture of quinine*); slight flavour, spice, smack, (*of* thing, fig. *of* moral quality etc.); tinge (*of* colour); (Her.) inclusive term for the metals, colours, and furs used in coats of arms. 2. *v.t.* colour slightly, tinge, flavour; (fig.) affect slightly (*with* quality). [ME, f. L *tinctura* dyeing (as TINGE; see -URE)]

ti'ndal *n*. (Ind.) native petty officer of Lascars. [f. Hind. *tandel* f. Malayalam *taṇḍal*]

ti'nder *n*. dry substance readily taking fire from spark, esp. charred linen etc. used in ∼-box (containing tinder, flint, and steel, for kindling fire); hence ∼y² *a*. [OE *tynder*, *tyndre* f. Gmc *tund-* etc. kindle]

tīne *n*. point, prong, e.g. of antler, harrow, or fork; hence (-)tīnED² (-nd) *a*. [OE *tind*, = OHG *zint*, ON *tindr*]

ti'nèa *n*. (Path.) ringworm. [L, = moth, worm]

ting *n*., & *v.i.* & *t.* (make, cause to make) tinkling sound as of bell. [imit.]

tinge (-nj) *v.t.* (*part.* ∼ing *pr.* -njĭ-), & *n*. 1. *v.t.* colour slightly (*with* red etc.); (fig.) modify by mixture (*with* envy etc.). 2. *n*. tint, slight colouring or admixture, flavour (lit. or fig.). [ME, f. L *tingere tinct-* dye, stain]

ti'ngle (-nggel) *v*. & *n*. 1. *v.i.*, & *n*. (feel) slight prickling or stinging or throbbing sensation esp. in ears or hands; cause this (*the reply tingled in his ears*). 2. *v.t.* make (ear etc.) tingle. [ME, perh. var. of TINKLE]

ti'nker *n*. & *v*. 1. *n*. mender (esp. itinerant) of kettles, pans, etc. (*don't care* a ∼'s damn or cuss, at all); (Sc. & Ir.) gypsy; rough-and-ready worker, botcher; act of tinkering (*had an hour's tinker at it*); *small mackerel. 2. *v.t.* repair (metal-work), patch (anything, lit. or fig.) roughly or temporarily. 3. *v.i.* work in amateurish or clumsy or desultory fashion *at* or *with* (thing) in the way of repair or alteration. [ME, of unkn. orig.]

ti'nkle *v*. & *n*. 1. *v.i.*, & *n*. (make) succession of short light ringing sounds; ||give person a ∼, (colloq.) telephone him. 2. *v.t.* make (small bell etc.) tinkle. [ME, f. obs. *tink* to chink (imit.) + -LE 3]

ti'nner *n*. In vbl senses; tin-miner; tinsmith. [f. TIN + -ER¹]

tinnī'tus *n*. (Med.) ringing in the ears. [L (*tinnire* -*it*-ring, tinkle, of imit. orig.)]

ti'nn|ў *a*. of or like tin; having metallic taste or thin metallic sound; hence ∼ĭLY² *adv.*, ∼iNESS *n*. [f. TIN + -Y²]

ti'nsel *n*., *a*., & *v.t.* (||-ll-). 1. *n*. glittering metallic substance made in thin sheets and used in strips, threads, etc., to give inexpensive sparkling effect; fabric adorned with tinsel; (fig.) superficial brilliancy or splendour. 2. *a*. showy, gaudy, cheaply splendid. 3. *v.t.* adorn with tinsel (lit. or fig.). [prob. f. AF *(satin) estincelé* f. OF (*estincele* spark f. pop. L *stincilla* for L *scintilla*)]

tīnt *n*., & *v.t.* 1. *n*. a variety of a colour, esp. one made lighter by admixture of white; tendency towards, admixture of, a different colour (*red of* or *with a blue* or *bluish tint*); background of faint colour for printing on; set of parallel engraved lines to give uniform shading; ∼-block, block bearing design to be printed in faint colour as background; hence ∼'LESS *a*. 2. *v.t.* apply

tint to, colour (lit. or fig.); hence ∼'ER¹ *n*. [alt. f. earlier *tinct* f. L *tinctus* dyeing (as TINGE), perh. infl. by It. *tinto*]

tintinnăbŭlā'tion *n*. ringing or tinkling of bells. [f. as foll. + -ATION]

tintinnă'bŭl|um *n*. (*pl.* ∼a). bell, esp. small tinkling one; hence ∼AR(Y)¹, ∼OUS, *adjs.* [L, = bell (*tintinnare* redupl. form, as TINNITUS)]

Tīntō'mēter *n*. (P) instrument for determining tints. [f. TINT + -O- + -METER]

ti'n|ў *a*. very small or slight; hence ∼ĭLY² *adv.*, ∼iNESS *n*. [f. obs. *tine*, *tyne* (*a*. & *n*., small, a little); ME, of unkn. orig.) + -Y²]

-tion (-shun) *suf.* forming *ns.* of action, condition, etc.; cf. -ATION, -ITION, -UTION, and -ION. [F. or after F, or f. L -*tio* -*tionis* f. p.p. stems in -*t*- + as -ION]

tip¹ *n*., & *v.t.* (-pp-). 1. *n.* extremity, end, esp. of small or tapering thing (*the tips of the fingers*; *walk on the tips of your toes*; *tip of a cigarette*, *of a bird's* or *aeroplane's wing*; on the ∼ of one's tongue, just about to be said, or on the point of being remembered and spoken); leaf-bud of tea, whence ∼'pY² *a.*; thin flat brush used in gilding; small piece or part attached to end of thing, e.g. ferrule, leather cap on billiard-cue, filter on cigarette. 2. ∼'staff (*pl.* ∼staffs or ∼staves), (metal-tipped staff as badge of) sheriff's officer; ∼-tilted, (of nose) turned up at tip; ∼'toe, (*n.*) the tips of the toes, (*adv.*) on tiptoe, with heels off the ground, (*v.i.*) walk (as if) on tiptoe; ∼top (-ĭ'-, -ŏ'-), (*n.*) highest point of excellence, (*a*. & *adv.*) excellent(ly). 3. *v.t.* furnish with tip; paste (sheet as part of book) *in* at inside edge of page. [ME, f. ON *typpi* n., *typpa* v., *typptr* tipped f. Gmc *tupp-* TOP¹; prob. reinforced by MDu. & MLG *tip*]

tip² *v.* (-pp-) & *n*. 1. *v.t.* & *i.* (cause to) lean or slant, tilt, topple, (*over*, *up*, etc.) esp. with slight effort; ∼ the balance or SCALE²(*s*); ∼ one's *hat* or ||(sl.) lid, raise one's hat. 2. *v.t.* strike or touch lightly; ||∼ and run, form of cricket in which batsman must run if bat touches ball (∼*-and-run raid*, one in which the raider appears suddenly and makes off immediately after attacking; cf. HIT¹ 5); ∼ off, (Basketball) start play by throwing ball up between two opponents. 3. overturn, cause to overbalance, (person *into* pond etc.); ||discharge (contents of truck, jug, etc. *out*, *into*, etc.) thus. 4. (sl.) throw lightly, hand, give, communicate, in informal manner; mention as likely winner of horse-race or other contest; ∼ (= SHOW¹) one's hand; ∼ person the wink, give him private warning or information, ∼ off, give (person) warning, hint, or inside information, so ∼-*off* n., a hint. 5. make usu. small present of money to (esp. for service given or expected; *must tip the porter*, *the waiter*). 6. Hence ∼'pER¹ (1, 2) *n.* 7. *n.* small money present (cf. sense 5). 8. private or special information about horse-racing, stock-market, etc., (STRAIGHT *tip*); piece of advice, good way of doing something; miss one's ∼, fail in one's object. 9. slight push or tilt; light stroke esp. in baseball; ||place where material, esp. refuse, is tipped. 10. ∼-cart (pivoted for tipping); ∼'cat, (game with) short piece of wood tapering at ends and struck with stick; ∼-up, able to be tipped, (of seat) as used in theatres etc. to allow of free passing. [ME, perh. f. Scand.; partly f. prec.]

ti'ppèt *n*. cape or muffler of fur etc. covering shoulders and coming down some distance in front, worn by women (arch.) and as part of official costume by judges, clergy, etc.; (Hist.) long narrow strip of cloth as part of or attachment to hood etc. [ME, prob. f. TIP¹; see -ET¹]

ti'ppl|e *v*. & *n*. 1. *v.i.* drink intoxicating liquor habitually. 2. *v.t.* drink (liquor) repeatedly in small amounts. 3. So ∼ER¹ *n.* 4. *n.* (colloq.) (esp. strong) drink. [ME, back-form. f. *tippler*, of unkn. orig.]

ti'pster *n.* one who gives tips about horse-races etc. [f. TIP² + -STER]

ti'ps|ў *a.* slightly intoxicated; caused by or showing intoxication (*a tipsy lurch*); ∼y-cake, sponge-cake soaked in wine or spirits and served with custard; hence ~ify *v.t.*, ~ily² *adv.*, ~iness *n.* [prob. f. TIP², = inclined to lean, unsteady; cf. *tricksy, flimsy*]

||**TIR** *abbr.* Transport International Routier (F, = international road transport).

tirā′de (tĭr-, tīr-) *n.* long vehement speech esp. of censure; long passage of declamation etc. [F, = long speech, f. It. *tirata* volley (*tirare* f. Rom. *tirare draw; see -ADE)]

tirailleur (tĭralēr′, tērahyēr′) *n.* sharpshooter, skirmisher. [F (*tirailler* shoot independently f. *tirer* shoot, draw f. Rom. *tirare draw)]

tīre¹ *v.t. & i.* make or grow weary; exhaust patience or interest of, bore; (in *p.p.*) having had enough *of*, sick *of*, (thing, doing), exhausted *with*, (fig.) hackneyed; hence ~′less (tīr′l-) *a.*, untiring. [OE *tēorian*, of unkn. orig.]

tīre² *n.*, & *v.t.* **1.** *n.* band of metal placed round rim of wheel to strengthen it. **2.** *v.t.* place tire on (wheel). [ME, perh. = TIRE⁴]

***tīre³**. See TYRE.

tīre⁴ *n.*, & *v.t.* (arch.) **1.** *n.* head-dress; attire; ~′woman (employed to dress another woman). **2.** *v.t.* adorn (one's hair or head); **tir′ing-room**, dressing-room (esp. in theatre). [ME, f. ATTIRE]

tīr′esome (tīr′s-) *a.* wearisome, tedious; (colloq.) annoying (*how tiresome!* – *I have left my watch behind*); hence ~LY² (-mlĭ) *adv.*, ~NESS (-mn-) *n.* [f. TIRE¹ + -SOME¹]

tīr′o, tȳr′o. *n.* (*pl.* ~s). beginner, novice [L *tiro*, med. L *tyro*, recruit]

′tis (-z) (arch. or poet.) it is. [contr.]

tisā′ne (-z-) *n.* ptisan; infusion of dried herbs etc. [F, f. as PTISAN]

ti′ssue (-sū, -shū, -shoō) *n.* fine woven esp. gauzy fabric; (Biol.) substance of animal or plant body, mass of cells of one kind (*adipose, connective, muscular, nervous, tissue*); (fig.) interwoven series, set, collection, (*of* lies, absurdities, etc.); ~(-**paper**), thin soft unsized paper for wrapping or protecting delicate articles, engravings in book, etc.; (**paper**) ~, disposable piece of thin soft absorbent paper for wiping, drying, etc., with. [ME, f. OF *tissu* rich material, p.p. (as n.) of *tistre* f. L *texere* weave]

tit¹ *n.* small bird of family Paridae; **bearded** ~, similar but unrelated bird (*Panurus biarmicus*), the male having black face-tufts; **blue** ~, *Parus caeruleus*, with bright blue tail, wings, and top of head. [prob. f. Scand.]

tit² *n.* ~ **for tat**, blow for blow, retaliation. [= earlier TIP² *for tap*]

tit³ *n.* (vulg.) nipple (esp. of woman); (in *pl.*) woman's breasts. [OE, cf. MLG *titte*]

Tit. *abbr.* Titus (NT).

Tī′tan *n.* **1.** (Gk Myth.) member of a gigantic family of early gods, the children of Heaven and Earth; sun-god. **2.** person of superhuman size, strength, intellect, etc. **3.** Hence ~E′SQUE *a.*, ~ESS¹ *n.* [ME f. L f. Gk]

titā′n|ic¹ *a.* of or like the Titans; gigantic, colossal; hence ~ICALLY *adv.* [f. Gk *titanikos* (as prec.; see -IC)]

titā′nic² *a.* (Chem.) of titanium, esp. in tetravalent form; hence **ti′tan**ATE¹ (3) *n.* [f. foll. + -IC]

titā′nium *n.* grey metallic element occurring in many clays etc.; ~ (**di**)**oxide**, a white pigment. [f. Gk (as TITAN) + -IUM, after *uranium*]

ti′tbit, *ti′dbit, *n.* delicate bit, choice morsel (of food, news, etc.). [perh. f. dial. *tid* tender + BIT²]

***ti′tfer**. See TITRE.

||**ti′tfer** *n.* (sl.) hat. [abbr. of *tit for tat*, rhyming sl.]

tithe (-dh) *n.*, & *v.t.* **1.** *n.* (Hist.) tax of one-tenth, esp. tenth part of annual produce of land or labour taken for support of clergy and church; hence ~**barn** (built to hold tithes paid in kind). **2.** (rhet.) tenth part (esp. *not a tithe of*). **3.** *v.t.* subject to tithes; hence **ti′th**ABLE (-dh-) *a.* [OE (*teogothian, tēothian* v. f.) *teogotha, tēotha* TENTH]

ti′thing (-dh-) *n.* taking tithe; (Hist.) (area occupied by) ten householders living near together and bound over as sureties for each other's peaceable behaviour. [f. as prec. + -ING¹]

ti′ti (tē′tē) *n.* S. Amer. monkey of genus *Callicebus*. [Tupi]

ti-ti (tē′tē) *n.* (NZ). mutton-bird. [Maori]

Tī′tian (-shan) *a.* ~ (**red**), (esp. of hair) bright golden auburn; so ~E′SQUE *a.*, in the style of Titian. [name of *Tiziano* Vecelli, It. painter d. 1576]

ti′till|āte *v.t.* tickle, excite pleasantly; so ~A′TION *n.* [f. L *titillare* + -ATE³]

ti′t(t)iv|āte *v.t.* (colloq.) adorn, smarten, put finishing touches to, (one*self* etc., or abs.); hence ~A′TION *n.* [earlier *tid-*, perh. f. TIDY after *cultivate*]

ti′tlark *n.* pipit, ||esp. meadow pipit. [f. TIT¹ + LARK¹]

ti′tle *n.*, & *v.t.* **1.** *n.* distinguishing appellation placed at head of chapter, poem, etc.; contents of title-page of book, short essential part of these used in reference (e.g. *Gone with the Wind, Shakespeare's Plays*); book or publication as distinguished from others; HALF-*title*. **2.** formula at head of legal document, statute, etc.; division of statute etc.; caption or CREDIT¹ title in film. **3.** distinctive name; personal appellation, hereditary or not, denoting or implying office (e.g. *king, queen, judge, mayor, rector, professor, captain*) or nobility (e.g. *duke, duchess, marquis, earl, viscount, baron, lord*; COURTESY *title*) or distinction or merit (e.g. *baronet, knight*) or (usu. degree) qualification (e.g. *DD, MA*), or used in addressing or referring to person (e.g. *Lord, Lady, Sir, Miss, Herr, Madame, Doctor, Professor*, prefixed to name; *Your* or *Her* or *His Majesty, Grace*, etc.). **4.** (Law) right to ownership of property with or without possession, the facts constituting this; ~(-**deed**), legal instrument as evidence of right; just or recognized claim (*to*); service, merit, etc., that constitutes this. **5.** championship in sport. **6.** (Eccl.) fixed sphere of work and source of income as condition to ordination; parish church in Rome under cardinal. **7.** ~-**deed** (see sense 4); ~-**page**, page at beginning of book giving particulars of subject, authorship, publication, etc.; ~-**piece**, essay etc. with same title as book that contains it and others; ~-**role**, part in a play etc. that gives it its name (e.g. *Othello*). **8.** Hence ~LESS (-tĕl-l-) *a.* **9.** *v.t.* give title to; (esp., in *p.p.*) having title of nobility. [ME f. OF, f. L *titulus* placard, title]

ti′tling¹ *n.* titlark or titmouse. [ME, f. TIT¹ + -LING¹]

ti′tling² *n.* impressing of title in gold leaf etc. on cover of book. [f. TITLE + -ING¹]

ti′t|mouse *n.* (*pl.* ~**mice**) tit esp. of genus *Parus*. [ME *titmōse* (TIT¹, OE *māse* titmouse, – OHG *meisa* f. WG *maisō); assim. to MOUSE¹]

Tī′tō|ism (tē′-) *n.* independent form of Communism e.g. as initiated by President Tito in Yugoslavia, as dist. from that of USSR and its satellite countries; so ~IST (2) *n.* [f. *Tito*, assumed name of Josip Broz d. 1980 + -ISM]

ti′tr|āte *v.t.* (Chem.) determine quantity of given constituent (in solution) by observing volume of a standard solution necessary to convert this constituent entirely into another form; hence ~A′TION *n.* [f. F *titrer* (as foll.) + -ATE³]

ti′tre (-ter), ***ti′ter,** *n.* (Chem.) strength of solution or quantity of constituent as determined by titration. [F, = TITLE]

ti′tter *v.i.*, & *n.* **1.** *v.i.* laugh or giggle in restrained or covert manner. **2.** *n.* such laugh. [imit.]

ti′ttivāte. See TITIVATE.

ti′ttle *n.* small written or printed stroke or dot; particle, whit, (esp. *not one jot or tittle*). [ME, f. L (as TITLE)]

||**ti′ttlebăt** (-telb-) *n.* stickleback. [var., of childish orig.]

ti′ttle-tāttle *n.*, & *v.i.* (engage in) petty gossip. [redupl. f. TATTLE]

ti′ttup *v.i.* (-p- or -pp-), & *n.* **1.** *v.i.* go *along* etc., move, conduct oneself, in lively or frisky fashion; prance or canter. **2.** *n.* canter; spring, prance; hence ～(p)Y² *a.* [perh. imit. of hoof-beats]

ti'tty *n.* (vulg.) = TIT³; (childish) teat, breast. [f. TEAT + -Y³]

titūbā'tion *n.* (Med.) unsteadiness esp. as caused by nervous disease. [f. L *titubatio* (*titubare* totter; see -ATION)]

ti'tular *a.* & *n.* **1.** *a.* held by virtue of a title (*titular possessions*); relating to a title (*titular hero of book*); existing, that is such, only in name (*titular sovereign(ty)*); ～ **bishop**, (RC Ch.) bishop bearing name of a former Christian see esp. in Muslim countries; ～ **saint**, patron saint of church; hence ～LY² *adv.* **2.** *n.* holder of office etc. esp. benefice without corresponding functions or obligations; titular saint. [f. F *titulaire* or mod. L *titularis* (*titulus* TITLE; see -AR¹)]

ti'zzy *n.* (sl.) state of nervous agitation (*in a tizzy; all of a tizzy*). [20th c.; orig. unkn.]

T-junction. See T.

TKO *abbr.* technical knock-out.

Tl *symb.* thallium.

TLS *abbr.* *Times Literary Supplement*; typed letter signed.

TM *abbr.* (*P) Transcendental Meditation.

Tm *symb.* thulium.

tmē'sis *n.* (*pl.* ～es *pr.* -ēz). (Gram.) separation of parts of compound word by intervening word(s) (e.g. *what things soever*, sl. *abso-bloody-lutely*). [Gk *tmēsis* cutting (*temnō* cut)]

TMO *abbr.* telegraph money order.

TN *abbr.* Tennessee.

tn *abbr.* *ton(s); town.

TNT *abbr.* trinitrotoluene.

to¹ (*before vowel* tŏŏ, *before consonant* tŏ, *when stressed* tŏŏ) *prep.* **1.** in the direction of (place, person, thing, condition, quality, etc.; with or without implication of intention or of arrival; *was walking over to the town; on his way to his station; fled to Rome; throw it to me; got to the house by four; to bed with you!; fluttered to the ground; was committed to the flames; invited them to dinner; house looks to the south; held it (up) to the light; to arms!; fought hand to hand; back to back; told him to his face; was carried to destruction; letter has come to hand; fell to work; fell to musing; tends to, has a tendency to, indolence; slow to anger; appointed to the post; born to a great fortune; all to no purpose; to his shame be it said*). **2.** as far as, not short of, (*true to the end; cut him to the heart; a patriot to the core; rooted to the spot; goods to the value of £10; increased from 10 to 20*, cf. FROM; *fought to the last gasp; to a MAN¹; hit it to the boundary; correct to a hair's breadth; suits him to a T; much to my surprise; loves her to distraction; acted his part to perfection; might run to £5; drank himself to death; might argue to all eternity; don't know to this day how it ended; and so on to the end of the chapter*). **3.** (Of comparison, ratio, adaptation, reference, etc.: *this is nothing to what it might be; won by 3 goals to 2; 3 is to 4 as 6 is to 8; ten to one he will find out; two to one is not fair play;* ||*it is five minutes to two; 100 miles to London; not up to the mark; equal to the occasion; made to order; drawn to scale;not to the point; true to life; will speak to that question later; sang to a small guitar; cannot do it to his liking; corresponding, compared, inferior,* etc., *to*). **4.** (arch.) for, by way of, (*took her to wife*). **5.** (Introducing indirect object of verb, recipient, possessor, etc., or person or thing affected by the action, quality, etc.: *lend it or this or your knife to John or to him; write to me; explain it to me; talking to oneself; this does not apply to the secretary; please apply to the secretary; seems to me absurd; to my mind or thinking, I object to that remark; secretary to the governor; pleasant to the taste; impervious to weather; caverns measureless to man; obedient to command; duty to one's neighbour; unkind to him; has been a good father to them; a room to myself; what's that to you?; game to Borg; drink to me only with thine eyes;* HERE's *to you; to goods* etc., in debit entries; *broken in to the saddle; accustomed to it; next door to us; ready to his hand; has not a shilling to his name; weigh four to the pound; there is a moral to it; there is

no end to it; that is all there is to it; I wish to God he would stop*). **6.** (Before vb. as sign of infinitive, expressing purpose, consequence, etc., limiting meaning of adj., or forming vbl n.: *he proposes to stay, declines to go, wants to know, began to sing, failed to understand, does it to annoy; shoot to kill; the rubber floor is to prevent noise; the matter is difficult to explain; it is useless to rebel, to rebel is useless; allow me to remind you; was seen to fall; was heard to complain; I'm not one to complain; floor was felt to tremble; was never known or found to fail; have sometimes known or found it (to) fail; he was made to repeat it; help me (to) lift this; you are pleased to be facetious; I prefer to go; lived to be 100; had my work to do, had to do my work; was about to protest; awoke to find her gone; for a year, in years, to* COME; *the first to arrive; to be honest, I can't face it; to hear him talk, you would think he invented it; to* WIT¹); cf. BE 3. **7.** (As substitute for infinitive: *meant to call but forgot to, had no time to, did not promise to*). [OE *tō* adv. & prep., = OS *tō*, OHG *zō, zuo* f. WG *tō adv.]

to² (tŏŏ) *adv.* to or in the normal or required position or condition, esp. to a standstill, (COME, FALL¹, GO¹, HEAVE¹, *to*); (of door) just not shut; **to and fro,** backwards and forwards, repeatedly between same places. [f. prec.]

toad *n.* **1.** amphibian of genus *Bufo*, like frog but with clumsy and usu. warty body and not aquatic except when breeding; detestable or disgusting person; HORN¹*ed toad.* **2.** ～**-eater,** toady; ～**-fish,** Amer. fish of family Batrachoididae, with large head; ～'**flax,** perennial plant with flaxlike leaves and spurred yellow flowers marked with orange spot (*ivy-leaved ～flax,* related plant with lilac flowers and ivy-shaped leaves); ～**-in-the-hole,** beef or sausages baked in batter; ～'**stone,** stone, occas. precious, supposed to resemble or to have been formed in body of toad, formerly used as amulet etc.; intrusive volcanic rock in limestone; ～'**stool,** (esp. poisonous) fungus with round top and slender stalk. **3.** Hence ～'ISH¹ *a.* [OE *tādige, tādde, tāda,* of unkn. orig.]

toa'dy *n.* & *v.* **1.** *n.* sycophant, obsequious hanger-on; hence ～ISH¹ *a.,* ～ISM (2) *n.* **2.** *v.t.* & *i.* ～ (to), behave servilely to, fawn upon, (person, or abs.). [f. TOAD--eater + -Y³]

toast *n.,* & *v.t.* **1.** *n.* bread slice(s) browned on each side before fire or by electric etc. heat (FRENCH, FALL¹, Melba, *toast;* sardines etc. **on** ～, laid on this and served at table; **have** person **on** ～, (sl.) have him at one's mercy; **as warm as (a)** ～, glowing with warmth). **2.** person (Hist. esp. woman) or thing in whose honour company is requested to drink; call to drink or instance of drinking thus. **3.** ～**-list,** ～**-master,** (person who announces) toasts at public dinner; ～**-rack** (for holding slices of toast at table); ～ **and water,** = ～**-water** (arch., in which toast has stood, used as cooling drink). **4.** *v.t.* brown, cook, (bread, teacake, cheese, bacon) before fire or by electric etc. heat; warm (one's feet, one*self*) thus. **5.** drink to the health or in honour of. **6.** Hence ～'ER¹ (1, 2) *n.,* (esp.) electrical device for toasting bread. [ME, n. f. v. f. OF *toster* roast f. Rom. *tostare* f. L *torrēre tost-* parch; sense 2 f. notion that woman's name flavours drink as spiced toast would]

toa'sting *n.* In vbl senses; ～**-fork,** long-handled fork for making toast, (arch., joc.) sword. [f. prec. + -ING¹]

toba'cco *n.* (*pl.* ～s). **1.** ～(-**plant**), plant of genus *Nicotiana,* of Amer. orig. with narcotic leaves used for smoking, chewing, or snuff; its leaves esp. as prepared for smoking etc. **2.** ～ **heart,** disorder of heart caused by excessive use of tobacco; ～ **mosaic virus** (causing mosaic disease in tobacco, etc., and much used in biochemical research); *tobacco-*PIPE¹; ～-**pouch** (for carrying small quantity of tobacco); ～-**stopper,** instrument for pressing down tobacco in pipe. [f. Sp. *tabaco,* of Amer. Ind. orig.]

toba'cconist *n.* dealer in tobacco, esp. by retail. [f. prec. + -IST, w. euphonic *n*]

tobŏ'ggan *n.,* & *v.i.* **1.** *n.* long light narrow sledge curved upwards at front, used for going downhill esp. over prepared snow or ice. **2.** *v.i.* ride on toboggan; hence ∼ER¹, ∼ING¹, *ns.* [f. Can. F *tabaganne* f. Algonquian]

to′bў *n.* ∼ (jug), jug or mug for ale etc. usu. in form of old man with three-cornered hat; ||∼ **collar,** broad turned-down goffered collar like the frill of Punch's dog Toby. [familiar form of name *Tobias*]

tocca′ta (-kah′-) *n.* (Mus.) composition for piano, organ, etc., designed to display performer's technique. [It., fem. p.p. (as n.) of *toccare* touch]

||**Tŏc H** (-ā′ch) *n.* society of (orig. ex-service)men and women for Christian fellowship and social service. [*toc* = signallers' former name for letter *T*, + *H*, for *Talbot House*, soldiers' club started by Revd P. T. B. Clayton (d. 1972) in Ypres Salient in 1915 in memory of Gilbert Talbot]

Tochār′ian (-k-) *a.* & *n.* (of or in) extinct Indo-European language of central Asian people in first millennium AD. [f. F *tocharien* f. L *Tochari* f. Gk *Tokharoi* a Scythian tribe]

tŏ′cher (-χ-) *n.* (Sc.) marriage portion, dowry. [f. Ir. & OGael. *tochar*]

||**tō′cō** *n.* (*pl.* ∼s). (arch. sl.) a thrashing; chastisement. [f. Hind. *ṭhōkō*, imper. of *ṭhoknā* thrash]

tocŏ′pherŏl *n.* oily liquid compound of vitamin E group, found in seed and fish oils. [f. Gk *tokos* offspring + *pherō* bear + -OL]

tŏ′csin *n.* (bell rung as) alarm-signal (lit. or fig.). [F, f. OF *touquesain, toquassen* f. PROV. *tocasenh* (*tocar* TOUCH¹, *senh* signal-bell)]

||**tŏd¹** *n.* (arch.) bush; mass of foliage; weight of wool, usu. 28 lb. [ME; cf. LG *todde* bundle, pack, ON *toddi* bit, piece]

||**tŏd²** *n.* (Sc. & N. Engl.) fox. [ME, of unkn. orig.]

||**tŏd³** *n.* (sl.) **on** one's ∼, alone, on one's own. [perh. f. *on* one's *Tod Sloan* (Amer.-born jockey d. 1933), rhyming sl.]

today′, to-day′, *adv.* & *n.* (on) this present day, (*saw or shall see him today; today is her birthday*); nowadays; *today* WEEK; HERE *today, gone tomorrow.* [OE *tō dæg* on (this) day (as TO¹, DAY)]

tŏ′ddle *v.* & *n.* **1.** *v.i.* walk with short tottering steps, as child learning to walk; (colloq.) take casual or leisurely walk (*round, to,* etc.); (colloq.) depart; hence **tŏ′ddler¹** *n.* **2.** *v.t.* make (one's *way*), perform (distance), thus. **3.** *n.* toddling walk. [16th c., orig. Sc. & N. Engl. *todle,* of unkn. orig.]

tŏ′ddy *n.* sap of some kinds of palm, fermented to produce arrack; sweetened often spiced drink of spirits and hot water. [f. Hind. *tāṛī* (*tār* palm f. Skr. *tāla* palmyra)]

to-do′ (-dōō′) *n.* bustle, fuss. [f. to DO¹, = 'to be done', as in *What's to do?*]

tŏ′dy *n.* small insectivorous W. Ind. bird of genus *Todus,* related to kingfisher. [f. F *todier* f. L *todus,* a small bird]

toe *n.* & *v.* (*part.* ∼′ing *pr.* tō′ĭ-). **1.** *n.* one of five terminal members of foot; part of stocking, shoe, or boot, that covers the toes. **2.** fore part of hoof; piece of iron under front of horseshoe to prevent slipping. **3.** toelike object; projection from foot of buttress etc. to give stability; outer end of head of golf-club. **4.** BALL¹ *of* (big) *toe;* BIG *toe* or great *toe;* **the light fantastic** ∼, (joc.) dancing; LITTLE *toe;* **on** one's ∼**s,** alert, eager; *from* TOP¹ *or* HEAD¹ *to toe;* TREAD¹ *on* person's *toes;* **turn up** one's ∼**s,** (sl.) die; *heel-and-toe* WALKING¹. **5.** ∼**-cap,** outer covering of toe in boot or shoe; ∼**-clip** (on bicycle pedal, to prevent foot from slipping); ∼**-dance** (performed on tiptoe); ∼**-hold,** slight foothold (lit. or fig.); ∼**-nail,** nail of human toe, metal nail driven obliquely through end of board etc. **6.** Hence (-)**tōED²** (tōd), ∼′LESS (tō′l-), *adjs.* **7.** *v.t.* furnish with toe, mend toe of, (stocking, shoe); touch (*the line, mark*) with toe before starting in race (∼ **the line** or ***mark,** (fig.) conform esp. under pressure to the requirements of one's party); (Golf) strike (ball)

with part of club too near toe. **8.** *v.i.* ∼ **in, out,** turn toes in, out, in walking, (of vehicle wheels) be set with slight convergence forwards, backwards. [OE *tā,* = ON *tá,* OHG *zēha* f. Gmc **taih(w)ōn*]

||**tŏff** *n.,* & *v.t.* (sl.). **1.** *n.* distinguished or well-dressed person. **2.** *v.t.* dress *up* like a toff. [perh. perversion of TUFT 3]

tŏ′ffee (-fĭ), **tŏ′ffў,** *n.* sweetmeat made with sugar, butter, etc., often with nuts; ||small piece of this; **can′t** *shoot* etc. **for** ∼, (sl.) is incompetent at shooting etc.; ∼**-apple,** toffee-coated apple on stick; ||∼**-nose(d),** (sl.) snob(bish), pretentious (person). [f. TAFFY²]

||**tŏft** *n.* homestead; land once occupied by this. [OE, f. ON *topt*]

tŏg *n.,* & *v.t.* (**-gg-**). (sl.) **1.** *n.* (usu. in *pl.*) garment. **2.** *v.t.* dress (person, one*self, out* or *up*); hence ∼′**gERY** (5) (-g-) *n.* [app. abbr. of 16th-c. cant *togeman(s), togman,* f. F *toge* or L TOGA]

tō′ga *n.* ancient Roman citizen's loose flowing outer garment; ∼ **praetexta** (prĕtĕ′-) (with wide purple border, worn by boys, magistrates, etc.); ∼ **virilis** (vĭrī′lĭs), white toga donned as sign of manhood (at age of 14); hence ∼′D², ∼ED² (-ad) *a.* [L, cogn. w. *tegere* cover]

toge′ther (-gĕ′dh-) *adv.* in company or conjunction (*walking together; lived together; were at school together*); simultaneously (*both together exclaimed*); one with another (*compared together; fighting together*); into conjunction, so as to unite, (*sew them together; tied together; put* TWO *and two together*); into company or companionship; (colloq.) well organized or controlled; uninterruptedly (*he would talk for hours together*); ∼ **with,** as well as, and also; hence ∼NESS *n.,* (esp.) feeling of belonging together. [OE *tōgædere* (*tō* TO¹, *gædre* together f. **gad-*; cf. GATHER)]

tŏ′ggle *n.,* & *v.t.* **1.** *n.* device for fastening with cross-piece which can pass through hole or loop in one position but not in another; pin or other cross-piece through eye of rope, link of chain, etc., to keep it in place; pivoted barb of harpoon; ∼(-joint), device for exerting pressure along two rods hinged together by transverse force at the hinge; ∼**-switch,** electric switch with projecting lever to be moved usu. up and down. **2.** *v.t.* furnish, or fasten, with toggle. [18th c. Naut., of unkn. orig.]

Tōgōlě′se (-z) *a.* & *n.* (*pl.* same). (native or inhabitant) of Togo. [f. *Togo,* republic in W. Africa; cf. CONGOLESE]

toil *v.i.,* & *n.* **1.** *v.i.* work long or laboriously (*at, on, through, task*); move painfully or laboriously (*up* hill etc., *along*). **2.** *n.* hard or continued labour, drudgery; ∼**-worn,** worn (out) by toil. **3.** Hence ∼′ER¹ *n.,* ∼′FUL, ∼′SOME¹, *adjs.* [ME, f. AF *toiler* v., *toil* n., dispute, OF *tooilier, tooil,* f. L *tudiculare* stir about (*tudicula* machine for bruising olives, cogn. w. *tundere* beat)]

toile (twahl) *n.* cloth esp. for garments; pattern of garment in muslin etc. for fitting or for use in making copies; ∼ **de Jouy** (-dezhwē′), cotton or linen printed fabric with light-coloured background. [F, f. as TOILS]

toi′lĕt *n.* **1.** process of washing, dressing, arranging the hair, etc., (*make* one's *toilet*); (arch.) (style of) dress, costume, (*an elaborate toilet; a toilet of white satin*). **2.** ∼(-**table,** dressing-table usu. with looking-glass. **3.** (room containing) lavatory. **4.** (Med.) cleansing of part after an operation or at time of childbirth. **5.** ∼**-cover,** (for toilet-table); ∼**-paper,** thin soft paper for use in lavatory; ∼ **powder,** dusting powder used in making one's toilet; ∼**-roll** (of toilet-paper); ∼**-set** (of utensils for making one's toilet); ∼**-soap** (mild and usu. perfumed and coloured); ∼**-training** (of child, to control urination and defecation and use lavatory); ∼ **water,** scented liquid used after washing oneself. [f. F *toilette* cloth, wrapper, dim. of prec.]

toi′lĕtry *n.* article(s) used in making one's toilet. [f. prec. + -RY]

toilĕ'tte (twah-) *n.* = TOILET 1. [F; see TOILET]

toils (-z) *n. pl.* net, snare, (lit. or fig.; *taken in the toils*). [pl. of *toil* f. OF *toile* cloth, f. L *tela* web]

to'ing (tōō'-) *n.* ∼ **and froing** (-ŏ'ĭ-), movement to and fro. [f. TO² + -ING¹]

Tokay' *n.* sweet aromatic dessert wine made near *Tokaj* in Hungary; similar Californian wine.

tō'ken *n.* & *a.* **1.** *n.* sign, symbol, evidence, (*of affection* etc.; *as a* or *in token of my esteem*); memorial of friendship, keepsake; ring, coin, etc., serving as proof of authenticity; voucher that can be exchanged for specified kind of goods or at specified shop(s) (‖BOOK¹ *token*). **2.** (Hist.) piece of metal like and used instead of coin, but worth much less than nominal value and issued by tradesmen, bank, etc., without sanction of government; device like coin bought for use with machines etc. or for other payments where money itself is not to be handled. **3.** **by** (**this** or **the same**) ∼, (arch.) **more by** ∼, (1) similarly, (2) moreover, (3) in corroboration of what I say. **4.** *a.* serving as token(s) or as sample; perfunctory; ∼ **money,** coins of higher nominal than intrinsic value but exchangeable for full-standard money at the higher rate; ∼ **payment,** (1) payment of small proportion of sum due as indication that debt is not repudiated, (2) nominal payment; ∼ **resistance,** ∼ **strike,** (brief, to demonstrate strength of feeling only); ∼ **vote,** Parliamentary vote of money in which the amount stated pro forma to allow discussion is not meant to be binding; hence ∼ISM *n.*, policy of making only a token effort or of doing no more than is minimally necessary. [OE *tāc(e)n*, = OS *tēcan*, OHG *zeihhan*, ON *teikn* f. Gmc **taiknam* (**taik-* TEACH)]

‖tō'kō. Var. of TOCO.

tolbooth. See TOLL¹.

tōld. See TELL¹.

Tolĕ'dō *n.* (*pl.* ∼s). fine sword(-blade) made at *Toledo* in Spain.

tō'lerab|le *a.* endurable; fairly good, not bad, (*am in tolerable health*); hence ∼leNESS (-b*ě*ln-) *n.*, ∼LY² *adv.* [ME f. OF, f. L *tolerabilis* (as TOLERATE; see -ABLE)]

tō'ler|ance *n.* willingness to tolerate, forbearance; (esp. Med.) capacity to tolerate; permissible variation in dimensions, weight, etc.; REMEDY of coinage; so ∼ANT *a.* [ME f. OF, f. L *tolerantia* (as foll.; see -ANCE)]

tō'ler|āte *v.t.* endure, permit, (practice, action, person's doing); allow (person, religious sect, opinion) to exist without interference or molestation; endure with forbearance; sustain, endure, (suffering etc.), esp. (Med.) sustain use of (drug, radiation, etc.) without harm; so ∼A'TION *n.*, (esp.) allowing of differences in religious opinion without discrimination. [f. L *tolerare* endure + -ATE³]

tōll¹ *n.* **1.** tax or duty paid for use of market, public road, etc., or for service rendered; *charge for long--distance telephone call. **2.** (Law). ‖∼ **thorough** (taken by town for use of highway, bridge, etc.), ‖∼ **traverse** (for passing over private land). **3.** cost or damage necessarily and regrettably caused by disaster or incurred in achieving something; **take its** ∼, be accompanied by loss, injury, etc. **4.** ∼-**bar,** -**gate,** bar or usu. gate across road to prevent passage of person, vehicle, etc., until toll is paid; **to'l(l)booth,** (arch., Sc.) town hall, town gaol; ∼-**bridge** (at which toll is charged for passage); ∼-**call,** (‖Hist.) telephone call for which charge is higher than for local call; ∼-**house** (occupied by collector at toll--gate or toll-bridge); ∼-**road** (maintained by means of tolls collected on it). [OE, = OHG *zol*, ON *tollr* f. med. L *toloneum* f. LL *teloneum* f. Gk *telōnion* toll-house (*telos* tax)]

tōll² *v.* & *n.* **1.** *v.t.* cause (bell, or abs.) to ring with slow uniform strokes; (of bell or clock) give out (stroke, knell, hour of day) thus, be tolled on account of (person, his death, etc.). **2.** *v.i.* (Of bell) give out slow measured sounds. **3.** *n.* tolling or stroke of bell. [ME,

spec. use of (now dial.) *toll* entice, pull, f. OE **tollian*]

Tŏ'ltĕc *n.* member or language of Amer. Ind. people that flourished in Mexico before the Aztecs; hence ∼AN *a.* [Amer. Ind.]

tolu (tolū', tō'lū) *n.* fragrant brown balsam got from a S. Amer. tree (*Myroxylon balsamum*) and used in perfumery and medicine. [f. (Santiago de) *T*∼ in Colombia]

tŏ'lū|ēne *n.* colourless aromatic liquid hydrocarbon derivative of benzene, orig. got from tolu; so ∼IC *a.*, ∼OL *n.*, commercial grade of toluene. [f. prec. + -ENE]

Tŏm *n.* **1.** ∼, **Dick, and Harry,** (usu. derog.) persons taken at random, ordinary people, *every* ordinary person; PEEP²ing *Tom*. **2.** (*tom*). male animal, esp. tom(-**cat**); male turkey. **3.** ∼ **o' Bedlam,** (Hist.) deranged beggar released from hospital of St. Mary (see BEDLAM); **to'mboy,** wild romping girl who behaves like boy; *to'mcod, small fish of genus *Microgadus*, ∼ **Collins,** Collins made with gin; **tomfoo'l,** (*n.*) fool, trifler, (*a.*) extremely foolish, (*v.i.*) play the fool, act in trifling manner; **tomfoo'lery,** foolish trifling, foolish ornaments etc.; ∼ **and Jerry,** drink of hot rum, water, and beaten eggs; **tomno'ddy,** stupid person, fool; ∼ **Thumb,** a legendary dwarf, any diminutive person, dwarf variety of various plants; ∼ **Tiddler's ground,** children's game, place where money can be had for the picking up; **to'mtit,** small bird, esp. blue tit. [abbr. of name THOMAS]

tŏ'mahawk (-a-h-) *n.*, & *v.t.* **1.** *n.* war-axe of N. Amer. Indian, with head of horn, stone, or iron (*BURY *the tomahawk*); (Austral.) hatchet. **2.** *v.t.* strike, cut, or kill, with tomahawk; criticize savagely in reviewing. [f. Renape *tämähāk* (*tämäham* he cuts)]

tomă'lley *n.* fat (called 'liver') in lobster, cooked to make a green sauce. [Carib]

tomă'tō (-ah'-) *n.* (*pl.* ∼es). (plant, *Lycopersicon esculentum*, with) glossy red or yellow pulpy edible fruit; **currant** ∼, plant of same genus with small fruit about size of currant; **tree-**∼, S. Amer. shrub of same family with lemon-shaped red fruit. [17th c. *tomate*, = F (2 syl.) or Sp. & Port. (3 syl.), f. Mex. *tomatl*]

tomb (tōōm) *n.* hole (made) in earth or rock to receive dead (esp. human) body, grave; subterranean or other vault for the dead; sepulchral monument; **the** ∼, state of death; ∼'**stone,** monumental stone placed over grave; hence ∼'LESS *a.* [ME *t(o)umbe* f. AF *tumbe*, OF *tombe* f. LL *tumba* f. Gk *tumbos*]

tŏ'mbäc *n.* alloy of copper and zinc used esp. as material for cheap jewellery. [F, f. Malay *tambāga* copper]

tŏ'mbola (tŏ'mbola, tŏmbō'la) *n.* kind of lottery resembling lotto. [F or f. It. (*tombolare* tumble)]

tōme *n.* book, volume, esp. large heavy one. [F, f. L f. Gk *tomos* section, volume (*temnō* cut)]

-tōme *suf.* forming *ns.* w. sense (1) section, segment [f. Gk *tomē* a cutting], (2) instrument for cutting (*microtome*), esp. (Surg.) for operation w. name in -TOMY [f. Gk *-tomos* -cutting]

tomĕ'nt|um *n.* (*pl.* ∼a). (Bot.) kind of pubescence composed of matted woolly hairs; (Anat.) flocculent inner surface of pia mater; hence ∼OSE¹ (tomĕ'-, tō'mĕ-), ∼OUS, *adjs.* [L, = cushion-stuffing]

tŏ'mmў *n.* **1.** (usu. *T*∼). British private soldier [f. *T*∼ *Atkins*, orig. *Thomas Atkins*, name randomly chosen and used in specimens of completed official forms 1815-]. **2.** (Mech.) spanner or screw-driver; ∼(-**bar),** short bar for use with box-spanner. **3.** ‖bread, provisions, esp. as carried by workman or given to workman in lieu of wages; truck system of payment. **4.** ∼-**gun,** (type of) sub-machine-gun [f. co-inventor J. T. *Thompson* US Army officer d. 1940]; ∼-**rot,** = ROT¹ 3. [f. TOM + -Y³]

tomŏ'graphў *n.* method of radiography displaying details in a selected plane within the body. [f. Gk *tomē* a cutting + -o- + -GRAPHY]

tomŏr'row, to-mŏr'rrow, (-ō) *adv. & n.* (on) the day after today (*will write tomorrow; tomorrow is her birthday*); the (near) future; **like there's no** ∿, (sl.) with complete disregard of future needs; ∿ **come never,** a day that will never arrive; ∿ **morning, afternoon,** etc., (*ns. & advs.*) (in) the morning etc. of tomorrow; *tomorrow* WEEK. [f. TO¹ + MORROW; cf. TODAY]

tŏ'mpĭon. Var. of TAMPION.

tŏ'm-tŏm *n.,* & *v.i.* (-mm-). **1.** *n.* Indian, African, etc., hand-beaten drum; tall jazz drum. **2.** *v.i.* beat tom-tom. [f. Hindi *tamtam,* imit.]

-tomỹ *suf.* forming *ns.* w. sense 'cutting' (*anatomy, dichotomy*) and esp. names of surgical operations of incision (*laparotomy*). [f. (mod. L f.) Gk *-tomia* cutting (*temnō* cut)]

ton¹ (tŭn) *n.* **1.** measure of weight, (**long**) ∿ of 2,240 or (**short**) ∿ of 2,000 lb. avoirdupois; **metric** ∿, **tonne. 2.** measure of capacity for various materials, esp. 40 cu. ft. of timber; ∿**-mile,** one ton of goods carried one mile, as unit of traffic. **3.** unit of volume in shipping (**deadweight, displacement,** ∿, 2,240 lb. of total load, 35 cu. ft. of total water displaced, with load-line just immersed; **freight** ∿, 40 cu. ft. of cargo; **gross, net** or **register,** ∿, 100 cu. ft. of gross, net, internal capacity). **4.** unit of refrigerating power able to freeze 2,000 lb. of ice at 0°C in 24 hours. **5,** (colloq.) large number or amount (*tons of money; bag* **weighs (half) a** ∿, is very heavy); ∿**s of,** very many (*tons of people; have asked him tons of times*). **6.** ||(sl.) £100; speed of 100 m.p.h. (∿**-up boys,** motor-cyclists who travel at high speed); (Cricket) century. [different. f. TUN in 17th c.]

ton² (tawn) *n.* prevailing mode, fashion; fashionable style or society. [F]

tŏ'nal *a.* of tone or tones; of tonality; (of fugue etc.) having repetitions of subject at different pitches in same key; hence ∿LY² *adv.* [f. med. L *tonalis* (as TONE¹; see -AL).]

tonǎ'litỹ *n.* (Mus.) character of tone, (relationships constituting) key; colour scheme of picture. [f. prec. + -ITY]

tŏ'nd|ō *n.* (*pl.* ∿**i** *pr.* -ē). painting, or relief, of circular form. [It., = round (plate), f. *rotondo* f. L *rotundus* round]

tōne¹ *n.* **1.** sound, esp. w. ref. to pitch, quality, and strength. **2.** modulation of voice to express emotion, sentiment, etc., (*impatient, lively, imploring, despondent, bantering, suspicious, tone*); corresponding style in writing etc. **3.** (Phonet.) accent on one syllable of word; way of pronouncing word to distinguish it from others of similar sound (*Mandarin Chinese has four tones*). **4.** (Mus.) musical sound, esp. of definite pitch and character; ||interval of major second, e.g. C–D, E–F sharp (**whole-**∿ **scale,** scale consisting entirely of tones, with no semitones); FUNDAMENTAL *tone;* GREGORIAN *tones.* **5.** (Med.) proper firmness of the bodily organs; state of health in which natural functions are duly performed. **6.** prevailing character of morals, sentiments, etc., in a group (*raise* or *lower the tone of the nation* etc.; *tone of the market is confident; gave a flippant tone to the debate; set the tone with a dignified speech*). **7.** general effect of colour or of light and shade in picture; tint, shade of colour; degree of luminosity of colour; (Photog.) colour of monochrome picture. **8.** ∿**-arm,** tubular arm connecting sound-box of gramophone to horn, or pick-up of record-player to amplifier; ∿ **control,** variation of proportion of high and low frequencies in reproduced sound; ∿**-deaf,** unable to perceive accurately differences of musical pitch; ∿**-poem,** (1) musical composition for orchestra illustrating or translating a poetic idea, (2) painting in which the tones are harmonized poetically; ∿**-row, =** SERIES 8. **9.** Hence ∿LESS (-nl-) *a.* [ME, f. (OF *ton* f.) L f. Gk *tonos* tension, tone (*teinō* stretch)]

tōne² *v.* **1.** *v.t.* give tone or quality (of sound or colour) to; ∿**d paper** (having slight, esp. pale amber, tint).

2. (Photog.) give (monochrome picture) altered colour in finishing by means of chemical solution. **3.** *v.i.* undergo change in colour by toning; harmonize (*does not tone (in) with the wallpaper*). **4.** ∿ **down,** (*v.t.*) soften colouring of (picture), render (statement, expression of views, etc.) less pronounced or confident, (*v.i.*) become softer, less pronounced, etc.; ∿ **up,** provide with or receive higher tone or pitch or character or greater vigour. **5.** Hence **tō'nER¹** (1, 2) *n.* [ME, f. prec.]

tō'nēme *n.* (Phonet.) phoneme distinguished from another only by its tone; hence **tōnē'mIC** *a.* [f. TONE¹ after *phoneme*]

tŏng *n.* a Chinese guild, association, or secret society. [f. Chin. *tang* meeting-place]

tŏ'nga (-ngga) *n.* (Ind.) light two-wheeled vehicle. [f. Hindi *tāngā*]

tŏngkä'ng *n.* junklike boat used in E. Indies. [Malay]

tŏngs (-z) *n. pl.* (**pair of**) ∿, instrument for more conveniently grasping and holding usu. with two limbs pivoted together near either end or connected by spring piece, esp. **fire-**∿ (for grasping coal etc.); LAZY, SUGAR, *-tongs;* HAMMER¹ *and tongs;* **would not touch** (repulsive person or thing) **with a pair of** ∿ (still less without). [pl. of *tong* f. OE *tang(e),* = OS *tanga,* OHG *zanga,* ON *töng,* f. Gmc **tang-* f. IE **dank-*]

tongue¹ (tŭng) *n.* **1.** fleshy muscular organ in the mouth, serving purposes of tasting, licking, swallowing, and (in man) of speech; **put out** one's ∿, protrude it from mouth as grimace, or for doctor's inspection; **with** one's ∿ **hanging out,** thirsty or (fig.) expectant. **2.** this organ of ox etc. as article of food. **3.** faculty of, tendency in, speech (*has a ready* or *fluent tongue; sharp, LONG¹, caustic, dangerous, tongue*); **have, speak with,** one's ∿ **in** one's **cheek,** speak insincerely or with sly irony; **keep a civil** ∿ in one's **head,** avoid rudeness; **have lost, find,** one's ∿, be too bashful or surprised to speak, recover power of speech after this; **give** ∿, (of hounds) bark esp. on finding scent, speak so as to be widely heard; **hold** one's ∿, be silent; *on the* TIP¹ *of* one's *tongue;* **wag** one's ∿, talk indiscreetly or volubly. **4.** language of a nation etc. (*the German tongue*); MOTHER¹ *tongue*); CONFUSION *of tongues;* **gift of** ∿**s,** power of speaking in unknown languages, esp. as claimed by some modern sects or as miraculously conferred on early Christians (Acts 2). **5.** thing like tongue in shape (esp. tapering) or function, e.g. long low promontory, strip of leather closing gap under laces or buckle of shoe, clapper of bell, pin of buckle, projecting edge of matchboard, slip connecting two grooved boards etc., index or scale or balance, vibrating slip in reed of some musical instruments, jet of flame, pointed movable rail in railway-switch. **6.** ∿**-bit** (with plate preventing horse from getting tongue over mouthpiece); ∿**-bone,** hyoid; ∿**-lashing,** severe rebuke; ∿**-tie,** impediment in speech due to shortness of fraenum of tongue; ∿**-tied,** having this, (fig.) debarred from speaking out esp. through shyness; ∿**-twister,** sequence of words difficult to pronounce quickly and correctly, e.g. *she sells sea shells.* **7.** Hence **(-)tongue**D² (tŭngd), ∿LESS, *adjs.,* ∿LET *n.* [OE *tunge* = OS, ON *tunga,* OHG *zunga,* Goth. *tuggō* f. Gmc **tungōn,* cogn. w. L *lingua* (f. **dingua*)]

tongue² (tŭng) *v.t. & i.* produce staccato etc. effects with (flute etc.) by use of tongue, use tongue thus (**double-tonguing,** use of two tongue movements for rapid passages); ∿ **and groove,** furnish (matchboard etc.) with tongue and groove. [f. prec.]

tŏ'nĭc *a. & n.* **1.** *a.* (Of medicine, medical treatment, etc., or fig. of success, misfortune, punishment) serving to invigorate, bracing; producing tension, esp. of muscles, or normal tone of organs etc.; ∿ **spasm,** continuous muscular contraction (cf. CLONIC); ∿ **water,** non-alcoholic carbonated drink with quinine. **2.** (Mus.) of tones, esp. of the keynote;

∼ **accent,** accent on syllable; ∼ **major** and **minor,** keys with same keynote; ∼ **sol-fa,** system of sight--singing and notation in which keynote of all major keys is doh and keynote of all minor keys is lah, with time-values shown by vertical lines, colons, etc. **3.** Hence **tŏ′nically** *adv.* **4.** *n.* tonic medicine etc. (lit. or fig.); tonic water; (Mus.) keynote. [f. F *tonique* f. Gk *tonikos* (as TONE[1]; see -IC)]

toni′city *n.* being tonic; healthy elasticity of muscles etc. [f. prec. + -ITY]

toni′ght, to-nī′ght, (-nī′t) *adv.* & *n.* (on) the present evening or night, (on) the evening or night of today. [f. TO[1] + NIGHT; cf. TODAY]

tŏ′nish *a.* fashionable, stylish. [f. TON[2] + -ISH[1]]

tŏ′nka bean *n.* black fragrant seed of S. Amer. tree of genus *Dipteryx,* used in perfumery etc. [*tonka,* name in Guyana + BEAN]

to′nnage (tŭ′-) *n.* internal cubic capacity, or freight--carrying capacity, of ship in TON[1]s; total carrying capacity etc. of country's mercantile marine; charge per ton on cargo or freight; ∼ **and poundage,** (Hist.) customs duties on each tun of wine and pound's-worth of merchandise imported or exported, usu. granted as subsidies and levied unconstitutionally by Charles I without consent of Parliament; ∼**-deck** (second upwards from keel). [in Hist. sense ME f. OF (*tonne* TUN); otherwise f. TON[1] + -AGE]

tonne (tŭn, tŭ′nĭ) *n.* metric ton of 1000 kg. [F (see TUN)]

tŏ′nneau (-nō) *n.* part of motor car that contains the back seats. [F, lit. cask, tun]

tonŏ′mèter *n.* tuning-fork or other instrument for measuring pitch of tones; instrument for measuring pressure of fluid. [f. as TONE[1] + -O- + -METER]

tŏ′nsil *n.* either of two small organs on each side of root of tongue; hence **tŏ′nsillar**[1] *a.,* ∼le′ctomy, ∼li′tis, *ns.* [f. F *tonsilles* or f. L *tonsillae* pl.]

tŏnsŏr′ial *a.* (joc.) of a barber or his work. [f. L *tonsorius* f. *tonsor* barber (*tondēre tons-* shave; see -OR) + -AL]

tŏ′nsure (-sher) *n.,* & *v.t.* **1.** *n.* rite of shaving the crown (RC Ch. until 1972) or whole head (Orthodox Ch.) esp. of person entering priesthood or monastic order; shaved part of monk's or priest's head. **2.** *v.t.* shave head of; give tonsure to. [ME f. OF, or f. L *tonsura* (as prec.; see -URE)]

tŏntine (tŏntē′n, tŏ′ntēn) *n.* annuity shared by subscribers to loan, the shares increasing as subscribers die till last survivor gets all, or till specified date when remaining subscribers share the proceeds. [F, f. name of Lorenzo *Tonti* of Naples, originator of tontines in France *c.* 1653]

*****Tŏ′nÿ**[1] *n.* (*pl.* ∼**s**). annual award for outstanding theatrical performance. [f. nickname of Antoinette Perry, Amer. actress d. 1946]

*****tŏ′nÿ**[2] *a.* stylish, fashionable. [f. TONE[1] + -Y[2]]

tŏo *adv.* **1.** in a higher degree than is admissible or desirable for a specified or understood purpose, standard, etc., (*too ripe for cooking; too good to be true; allows too long an interval, too long intervals; too large for me, my taste, my purpose; the rumour was all too true;* is too fond of *comfort*); too MANY *for;* ∼ **much (of a good thing),** intolerable; *too* MUCH *for;* **none** ∼, rather less than (*good* etc.); ONLY[2] *too;* ∼**-too** *a.* & *adv.,* extreme, excessive(ly). **2.** (colloq.) very (*you are too kind; he is not too well today; they did not perform too well*). **3.** also, as well, (*take the others too; mean to do it too* (as well as threaten)). **4.** moreover (*achieved, too, at small cost*). [stressed form of TO[1], f. 16th-c. sp. *too*]

tŏŏk. See TAKE[1].

tŏol[1] *n.* **1.** mechanical implement, usu. held in hand, for working upon something (*carpenter's, gardener's, mason's, tools*); simple machine, e.g. lathe; (cutting part of) MACHINE tool; EDGE[1]- or *edged tool.* **2.** (fig.) thing used in an occupation or pursuit (*literary tools; the tools of* one's *trade; the computer as a research tool*); person used as mere instrument by another, cat's-paw.

3. separate figure in tooling of book; small stamp or roller to make this. **4.** (sl.) penis. **5.** ∼**-bag, -box,** (to hold workman's tools); ∼**-holder,** (1) device for holding tool in lathe, (2) handle for use with different tools; ∼**-post, -rest,** devices to support cutting-tool in lathe; ∼**-pusher,** worker directing drilling on oil rig; ∼**-shed** (in which garden etc. tools are kept). [OE *tōl,* = ON *tól* pl., f. GMC **tōwlam* (**tōw-;* cf. TAW[1])]

tŏol[2] *v.* **1.** *v.t.* dress (building-stone) with chisel; ornament (sides and back of book-cover) with tooling; ∼ **(up),** equip with tools. **2.** *v.i.* work with tool. **3.** *v.t.* & *i.* (sl.) drive (vehicle), drive, ride, (*along* etc.), esp. in casual or leisurely manner. **4.** Hence ∼′ER[1] *n.* [f. prec.]

tŏo′ling *n.* **1.** stone-dressing with chisel. **2.** ornamentation of book-cover with designs impressed by heated tools; BLIND[1] *tooling.* [f. prec. + -ING[1]]

tŏon *n.* E. Ind. tree (*Cedrela toona*) with close-grained red wood used for furniture etc. [f. Hindi *tūn*]

tŏot *v.* & *n.* **1.** *v.t.* sound, esp. produce short sound with, (horn, cornet, whistle, etc.); ∼ one's **own horn,** praise oneself. **2.** *v.i.* sound horn etc. thus; (of horn etc.) give out such sound; (of grouse) call. **3.** *n.* sound of tooted horn, trumpet, etc. [prob. f. MLG *tūten,* or imit.]

tŏoth *n.* (*pl.* **teeth**) & *v.* **1.** *n.* each of several hard dense structures growing in rows in jaws of most vertebrates and used for biting and chewing; **false, artificial,** ∼ (made by or for dentist to replace missing one). **2.** tooth-shaped projection or thing, e.g. cog, point, etc., of gear-wheel, saw, comb, rake; pointed part of leaf--margin. **3.** sense of taste, liking (*for* a food); SWEET *tooth.* **4. armed to the teeth** (completely, elaborately); **cast** or **fling** thing in person's *teeth,* reproach him with it; *cut* one's EYE[1]-*teeth;* **escape by** or **with the skin of** one's **teeth** (narrowly); **fight** ∼ **and nail** (fiercely, with utmost effort); **get** one's **teeth into,** begin serious work upon; **in the teeth of,** in spite of (opposition etc.), in opposition to (instructions etc.), directly against (the wind etc.); **kick in the teeth,** (colloq.) treat(ment) with brutal contempt; LIE[2] *in* one's *teeth;* **long in the** ∼, old (orig. of horses, from recession of gums with age); **put teeth into** (law, regulation, etc.), make it effective; SET[1] one's *teeth; set* person's *teeth on* EDGE[1]; **show** one's **teeth,** adopt threatening manner; *take the* BIT[1] *between* one's *teeth.* **5.** ∼′**ache,** pain in tooth or teeth; ∼**-billed,** (of bird) having toothlike process(es) on cutting edges of bill; ∼**-brush** (for cleaning teeth); ∼*-brush moustache* (bristly); ‖∼**-comb** (with fine close-set teeth; prop. FINE[2]*-tooth comb,* taken as *fine tooth-comb*); ∼**-glass, -mug,** (used when cleaning teeth); ∼′**paste, -powder,** (for cleaning teeth); ∼′**pick,** small sharp instrument of quill, wood, etc., for removing food etc. lodged between teeth; ∼**-shell,** (long tubular tusk-shaped shell of) mollusc of class Scaphopoda; ∼′**wort,** (1) parasitic plant with toothlike root-scales, (2) plant of genus *Dentaria,* with toothed root-stock. **6.** Hence (-)∼ED[2] (-tht), ∼′LESS *adjs.,* ∼′LET *n.* **7.** *v.t.* furnish with teeth. **8.** *v.i.* (Of cog--wheels) interlock. [OE *tōth,* pl. *tēth,* = OS *tand,* OHG *zan(d),* ON *tŏnn,* Goth. *tunthus* f. GMC **tanthuz* f. IE **dont-, *dent-*]

tŏo′thful (-ŏol) *n.* small draught of spirit etc., thimbleful. [f. prec. + -FUL 2]

tŏo′thing *n.* In vbl senses; projecting bricks or stones left at end of wall to provide for continuation; ∼**-plane** (with serrated blade for roughening surface). [f. TOOTH + -ING[1]]

tŏo′thsome *a.* pleasant to eat; hence ∼LY[2] (-mlĭ) *adv.,* ∼NESS (-mn-) *n.* [f. TOOTH + -SOME[1]]

tŏo′thÿ *a.* having numerous, large, or prominent teeth. [f. TOOTH + -Y[2]]

tŏo′tle *v.i.* toot gently or repeatedly esp. on flute; (colloq.) move casually *along, around,* etc. [f. TOOT + -LE 3]

tōō'tsy̆(-wōō'tsy̆) *n.* (joc. or childish). foot. [cf. FOOTSIE]

tŏp¹ *n.* & *a.* **1.** *n.* highest point or part; **at the ~** (of the tree), (fig.) in highest rank in profession etc.; **come to the ~**, win distinction; **from ~ to toe**, from head to foot, completely; **on ~**, above, in superior position, in addition, on upper part of head (*going bald on top*); **on ~ of**, (fig.) (1) fully in command of, (2) in close proximity to, (3) in addition to; **on ~ of the world**, exuberant; **over the ~**, over parapet of trench, (fig.) into final or decisive state or state of excess. **2.** (usu. in *pl.*) leaves etc. of plant grown mainly for its root (*turnip-tops*); bundle of long wool fibres prepared for spinning. **3.** surface (of ground), upper surface (of table etc.). **4.** upper part of shoe; cover of carriage; folding roof of car or pram; lid of saucepan etc. (BLOW¹ one's *top*); stopper of bottle; creamy part of milk; upper part of page in book; upper edges of book's leaves (*gilt top*); garment worn on upper part of body; turned-down part of leg of sock or stocking, (broad band of light-coloured material on) corresponding part of high boot. **5.** (person occupying) highest rank, foremost place, (*came out (at the) top of the school or form*); upper or more honourable end, head, (*top of the table*). **6.** utmost degree, height, (*realized the top of my ambition; called at the top of his voice*); **the ~ of the morning (to you)** (Irish morning greeting); (in *pl.*, *pred.*) person or thing of very best quality. **7.** (Naut.) platform round head of lower mast, serving to extend topmast rigging or carry guns. **8.** (in *pl.*) two or three highest cards of a suit in bridge etc. **9.** || = *top* GEAR in motor vehicle (*climbed the hill in top*). **10.** *a.* highest in position or degree or importance (*the top rail; at top speed; top prices paid; the country's top chess--player; was given top priority; singer reached her top note*); hence **~MOST** *a.* **11.** **~-boot**, boot with high top usu. of different material or colour and made to look as if turned down; *top* BRASS; **~'coat**, overcoat, outer coat of paint etc.; **~ copy** (in typing, opp. *carbon copy* etc.); **~ dog**, (sl.) victor, master; **~ drawer**, uppermost drawer in a chest etc., (fig.) high social position or origin; **~-dress**, apply manure or fertilizer on the top of (earth) instead of ploughing it in; **~-dressing**, this process, manure so applied, (fig.) superficial show; **~-flight**, in highest rank of achievement; || **~ fruit** (grown on trees, not bushes); **~ga'llant** (tŏpg-, tŏg-), mast, sail, yard, rigging, immediately above topmast and topsail; || *top* GEAR; **~-hamper**, encumbrance on top, esp. upper sails and rigging; **~ hat**, tall silk hat; **~-heavy**, overweighted at top so as to be in danger of falling (lit., or fig. of scheme etc.); || **~-hole**, (sl.) first-rate; **~'knot**, (1) knot, bow, of ribbon etc., tuft, crest, worn or growing on head, (2) kind of small flounder; *****~lo'fty**, (colloq.) haughty; **~'man**, top-sawyer, (Naut.) man doing duty in a top; **~'mast** (next above lower mast); **~-notch**, (colloq.) first-rate; **~'sail** (-sāl, -sal), square sail next above lowest, fore-and-aft sail on gaff; **~-sawyer**, sawyer in upper position in saw-pit; **~ secret**, of the highest secrecy; **~'side**, cut from upper side of round of beef, side of ship above water-line; **~'soil**, top layer of soil, opp. *subsoil*. [OE *topp*, = OHG *zopf* plait, ON *toppr* f. Gmc **toppaz*]

tŏp² *v.t.* (**-pp-**). **1.** furnish with top or cap (*cake topped with icing*). **2.** remove top of (plant) to improve growth etc.; remove withered calyx of (fruit); (sl.) execute by hanging. **3.** reach top of (hill etc.). **4.** be higher than; be superior to, surpass; be at top of (*top the list*; **~** one's *part*, act or discharge it to perfection. **5.** (Golf). hit (ball) above centre; make (stroke) thus. **6.** **~** (off *or* up), put an end or a finishing touch to (thing, or abs.); **~ out**, put highest stone on (building); **~ up**, fill up (partly empty container). [ME, f. prec.]

tŏp³ *n.* wooden or metal toy, usu. conical, spherical, or pear-shaped, rotating on sharp point at bottom when set in motion by hand, spring, or string; SLEEP² *like a*

top; ||**old ~**, (sl.) old chap, old fellow, (see OLD 5); **~-shell**, shellfish of family Trochidae with short conical shell. [OE, of uncert. orig.]

tō'păz *n.* **1.** transparent or translucent aluminium silicate mineral, yellow, white, green, blue, or colourless, used as gem; **false ~**, transparent yellow variety of quartz; **oriental ~**, yellow sapphire. **2.** S. Amer. humming-bird of genus *Topaza*. [ME, f. OF *topace*, *topaze* f. L f. Gk *topazos*, *-zion*]

topă'zolīte *n.* yellow or green kind of garnet. [f. prec. **+-O-+-LITE**]

tōpe¹ *v.i.* (arch. or literary). drink intoxicating liquor to excess, esp. habitually; hence **tō'pER¹** *n.* [perh. f. obs. *top* quaff]

tōpe² *n.* (Ind.) grove, esp. of mangoes. [f. Telugu *tōpu*, Tamil *tōppu*]

tōpe³ *n.* = STUPA. [f. Punjabi *tōp* f. Prakrit & Pali *thūpo* f. Skr. STUPA]

tōpe⁴ *n.* small shark of genus *Galeorhinus*. [perh. f. Corn.]

topee. See TOPI.

Tō'phĕt *n.* Hell. [name of place in Valley of Hinnom near Jerusalem used for idolatrous worship and later for depositing refuse, for consumption of which fires were kept burning, f. Heb. *tōpet*]

tō'ph|us *n.* (*pl.* **~i** *pr.* -ī). **1.** gouty deposit of calcareous matter round teeth and at surface of joints; dental tartar. **2.** tufa. [L, name of loose porous stones]

tō'pĭ, tō'pee, (-ĭ) *n.* (Anglo-Ind.) hat, esp. SOLA¹ *topi*. [f. Hindi *tōpī*]

tō'piar|ў *a.* & *n.* **1.** *a.* concerned with or formed by clipping shrubs etc. into ornamental shapes; hence **tōpiā'rIAN** *a.*, **~IST** (3) *n.* **2.** *n.* topiary art. [f. F *topiaire* f. L *topiarius* landscape-gardener (*topia opera* fancy gardening f. Gk *topia* pl. dim. of *topos* place + OPERA¹)]

tŏ'pĭc *n.* theme for discussion, subject of conversation or discourse. [f. L f. Gk (*ta*) *topika* topics, as title of a treatise by Aristotle (*topos* a place, a commonplace, see -IC)]

tŏ'pĭcal *a.* of topics; dealing with esp. current or local topics (*topical allusion, song*); local, esp. (Med.) affecting a part of the body; hence **~ITY** (-ă'l-) *n.*, **~LY²** *adv.* [f. as prec. **+-AL**]

tŏ'plĕss *a.* (seemingly) without a top; (of clothes) having no upper part, (of person) wearing such clothes, bare-breasted. [f. TOP¹ **+-LESS**]

topō'graph|ў *n.* detailed description, representation on map etc., of natural and artificial features of a town, district, etc.; such features; (Anat.) mapping of surface of body with reference to the parts beneath; hence **~ER¹** *n.*, **tŏpogră'phIC(AL)** *adjs.* [ME, f. LL f. Gk *topographia* (*topos* place; see -GRAPHY)]

topō'log|ў *n.* (Math.) study of geometrical properties and spatial relations unaffected by continuous change of shape or size of figures; hence **tŏpolō'gICAL** *a.*, **~IST** (3) *n.* [f. G *topologie* f. Gk *topos* place; see -LOGY]

topŏ'nymy̆ *n.* study of the place-names of a region; so **tŏ'ponym** *n.*, place-name, **tŏponý'mIC** *a.* [f. Gk *topos* place + *onoma* name + -Y¹]

tŏ'p|os *n.* (*pl.* **~oi**). stock theme in literature etc. [Gk, = commonplace]

tŏ'pper *n.* in vbl senses; (colloq.) = TOP¹ *hat*; (colloq.) a good fellow, good sort. [f. TOP² **+-ER¹**]

tŏ'pping¹ *a.* pre-eminent in position, rank, etc.; ||(sl.) excellent. [f. TOP² **+-ING²**]

tŏ'pping² *n.* In vbl senses, esp. decorative substance on top of cake etc. [f. TOP² **+-ING¹**]

tŏ'pple *v.i.* & *t.* (cause to) fall headlong or as if top--heavy, or to totter and fall (*over, down*; lit. or fig.). [f. TOP² **+-LE** 3]

tŏpsў-tû'r'v|ў *adv., a., & n.* upside down; (in) utter confusion; hence **~ĭLY²** *adv.*, **~ĭNESS**, **~ў̆DOM**, *ns.* [app. f. TOP¹ + obs. *terve* overturn]

tōque (-k) *n.* **1.** woman's small hat with little or no or turned-up brim; (Hist.) small cap or bonnet for man or woman. **2.** bonnet-monkey; small macaque with caplike arrangement of hair. [F, app. = It. *tocca*, Sp. *toca*, of unkn. orig.]

toqui'lla (-kē'ya) *n.* (fibre from leaves of) S. Amer. palmlike tree (*Carludovica palmata*). [Sp., = small gauze head-dress, dim. of *toca* toque]

tŏr *n.* hill, rocky peak, esp. in Devon and Cornwall. [OE *torr*; cf. Gael. *tòrr* bulging hill]

Tŏr'ah (*-a*) *n.* revealed will of God, esp. Mosaic law; the Pentateuch; scroll containing this. [f. Heb. *tōrāh* instruction]

tŏrc. Var. of TORQUE 1.

tŏrch *n.* piece of resinous wood or twisted flax etc. soaked in tallow etc. for carrying lighted in hand; other appliance for this purpose, e.g. oil-lamp on pole; ‖(**electric**) ∼, electric lamp with battery etc. in portable case; *blowlamp; *arsonist; (fig.) source of heat or illumination; **carry a ∼ for,** have (esp. unreturned) admiration of; **hand on the ∼,** keep tradition of knowledge etc. alive; ∼**-fishing,** catching fish by torchlight at night; ∼**'light,** (light of) torch; ∼**-race,** (Gk Ant.) festival performance of runners handing lighted torches to others in relays; ∼**-singer,** woman who sings ∼**-songs** (sentimental songs of unrequited love); ∼**-thistle,** cactus of genus *Cereus*. [ME, f. OF *torche* f. Rom. *torca* f. L *torqua* (*torquēre* twist)]

tŏrchère (-shār') *n.* tall stand with small table for candlestick etc. [F (as prec.)]

tŏr'chon (-shŏn, -shawn) *n.* ∼ (**lace**), coarse bobbin lace with geometrical designs. [F, = duster, dishcloth (*torcher* wipe)]

tŏre¹. See TEAR¹.

tŏre² *n.* = TORUS 1, 4. [F, f. L TORUS]

tŏ'reădŏr *n.* bullfighter, esp. on horseback. [Sp. (*torear* fight bulls f. *toro* bull f. L *taurus*)]

torer'ō (-ār'ō) *n.* (*pl.* ∼**s**). bullfighter. [Sp. (*toro*; see prec.)]

toreu't‖ic (-rōō'-) *a.* of chasing, carving, and embossing, esp. metal; hence ∼ICS *n.* [f. Gk *toreutikos* (*toreuō* work in relief; see -IC)]

tŏr'gŏch (-χ) *n.* red-bellied CHAR¹ in Welsh lakes. [W (*tor* belly, *coch* red)]

tŏr'ic *a.* having form of (part of) torus. [f. TORUS + -IC]

tŏ'rii *n.* (*pl.* same). gateway of Shinto shrine, with two uprights and two cross-pieces. [Jap.]

tŏrn. See TEAR¹.

tŏrnă'dō *n.* (*pl.* ∼**es**). violent storm of small extent with whirling winds, esp. in W. Africa at beginning and end of rainy season and in US etc. over narrow track often accompanied by funnel-shaped cloud; (fig.) outburst or volley *of* cheers, hisses, missiles, etc.; hence **tŏrnă'dIC** *a.* [app. assim. of Sp. *tronada* thunderstorm (*tronar* to thunder) to Sp. *tornar* to turn; see -ADO]

tŏr'oid *n.* figure of toroidal shape. [f. TORUS + -OID]

tŏroi'dal *a.* of or resembling torus; hence ∼LY² *adv.* [f. as prec. + -AL]

tŏr'ōse *a.* (Bot.) cylindrical with bulges at intervals; (Zool.) knobby. [f. L *torosus* (TORUS; see -OSE¹)]

tŏrpĕ'dō *n.* (*pl.* ∼**es**), & *v.t.* **1.** *n.* (Zool.) electric ray. **2.** cigar-shaped self-propelled submarine missile that can be aimed at a ship etc. and explodes on impact with it; **aerial** ∼, similar missile discharged from aircraft. **3.** *explosive device, e.g. petard or detonator. **4.** ∼**-boat,** small fast lightly armed warship for

carrying or discharging torpedoes; ∼**-net(ting)** (of steel wire, hung round ship to intercept torpedoes); ∼**-tube** (from which torpedoes are discharged). **5.** *v.t.* destroy or attack with torpedo; (fig.) paralyse, make (policy, institution, etc.) ineffective. [L, = numbness, electric ray (*torpēre* be numb)]

tŏr'pĕfy *v.t.* make numb or torpid. [f. L *torpefacere* (*torpēre* be numb; see -FY)]

tŏr'pid *a.* & *n.* **1.** *a.* (Of hibernating animal) dormant; numb; sluggish, inactive, dull, apathetic; hence ∼ITY (-ĭ'd-), ∼NESS, *ns.*, ∼LY² *adv.* **2.** *n.* (*T*∼; in *pl.*) ‖Hilary-term boat-races at Oxford between (orig. second crews of) colleges; (in *sing.*) boat or crew in these. [f. L *torpidus* (as foll.; see -ID¹)]

tŏr'por *n.* torpidity; hence ∼i'FIC *a.* [L (*torpēre* be sluggish; see -OR)]

tŏr'quăte *a.* (Zool.) with ring of peculiar colour or texture of hair or plumage round neck. [f. L *torquatus* (as foll.; see -ATE²)]

tŏrque (-k) *n.* **1.** necklace of twisted metal, esp. of ancient Gauls and Britons. **2.** (Mech.) moment of system of forces tending to cause rotation; ∼ **converter,** device to transmit correct torque from engine to axle in motor vehicle. [(sense 1 F f. L *torques*) f. L *torquēre* to twist]

tŏrr *n.* (*pl.* same). unit of pressure in measuring partial vacuum, equal to 1/760 of standard atmosphere. [f. *Torricelli* (see TORRICELLIAN)]

tŏ'rrĕ‖fy *v.t.* parch or scorch with heat; roast, dry, (metallic ore, drug); hence ∼FA'CTION *n.* [f. F *torréfier* f. L *torrefacere* (*torrēre* scorch; see -FY)]

tŏ'rrent *n.* rushing stream of water, lava, etc.; (in *pl.*) great downpour of rain (*rain came down in torrents*); (fig.) violent flow (*of* abuse, grief, questions); hence **torrĕ'ntIAL** (-shǎl) *a.* [F, f. It. *torrente* f. L *torrens* *-entis* scorching, boiling, roaring (*torrēre* scorch; see -ENT)]

Tŏrricĕ'llian (-sĕ'-, -chĕ'-) *a.* ∼ **experiment** (with mercury in tube, leading to principle on which barometer is made); ∼ **tube** (used for this); ∼ **vacuum** (above liquid in Torricellian tube). [f. E. *Torricelli*, It. physicist (d. 1647 + -AN)]

tŏ'rrid *a.* (Of land etc.) parched by sun, very hot; (fig.) intense, zealous; torrid ZONE; hence ∼ITY (-ĭ'd-), ∼NESS, *ns.*, ∼LY² *adv.* [f. F *torride* or f. L *torridus* (*torrēre* parch; see -ID¹)]

tŏrse *n.* (Her.) = WREATH. [obs. F *torse*, *torce* wreath f. Rom. **torsa* for L *torta* fem. p.p. (as TORT)]

tŏr'sel. Var. of TASSEL 2.

tŏr'sion (-shon) *n.* twisting, esp. of one end of body while other end is held fixed; (Math.) departure of curve from planar form; (Bot.) state of being spirally twisted; (Med.) twisting of cut end of artery after operation etc. to stop haemorrhage; ∼ **balance** for measuring minute horizontal forces by means of fine twisted wire; ∼ **pendulum** (rotating, not swinging); hence ∼AL, ∼LESS, *adjs.* [ME f. OF, f. LL *torsio* *-onis* f. L *tortio* (as TORT; see -ION)]

tŏrsk *n.* fish of cod family. [Norw. *to(r)sk* f. ON *tho(r)skr* prob. cogn. w. *thurr* dry]

tŏr'sō *n.* (*pl.* ∼**s**). trunk of human statue apart from head and limbs; human trunk; (fig.) unfinished or mutilated work. [It., = stalk, stump, torso, f. L THYRSUS]

tŏrt *n.* (Law). breach of duty (other than under contract) leading to liability for damages; so ∼'feasor (-z-), person guilty of tort. [ME f. OF, f. med. L *tortum* wrong, neut. p.p. (as n.) of L *torquēre* tort- twist]

tŏr'te (-te) *n.* (*pl.* ∼**n** *or* ∼**s**). large flat confection of pastry covered with chocolate etc. [G]

tŏrticŏ'llis *n.* (Path.) rheumatic etc. disease of muscles of neck, causing twisting and stiffness. [mod. L, f. *tortus* crooked (see TORT) + *collum* neck]

tŏrti'lla (-ēlya) *n.* thin flat maize cake eaten hot in Latin America. [Sp. dim. of *torta* cake f. LL]

tŏr'tious (-shus) *a.* (Law). constituting a tort,

wrongful; hence ∼LY² *adv.* [f. AF *torcious* (*torcion* extortion f. LL *tortio* torture; see TORSION, -OUS)]

tŏr′toise (-tus) *n.* **1.** land (or freshwater) slow-moving reptile of order Chelonia, encased in two scaly or leathery shields forming a box and having retractile head and legs; ALLIGATOR *tortoise*; (Rom. Ant.) = TESTUDO. **2.** ∼(**shell**) (-tus-sh-, -tush-), yellowish--brown mottled and clouded outer shell or scale of some sea-turtles used for combs etc.; ∼**shell butter-fly, cat,** (with black and yellow markings suggesting tortoiseshell). [ME *tortuce* etc., OF *tortue*, f. med. L *tortuca*, of uncert. orig.]

tŏr′trix *n.* moth of genus *Tortrix*, rolling leaves up to make its nest. [mod. L, fem. of L *tortor* twister (see TORT, -OR, -TRIX)]

tŏr′tŭous *a.* full of twists and turns; (fig., of policy etc.) devious, circuitous, crooked, not straightforward; hence or cogn. ∼′SITY, ∼NESS, *ns.*, ∼LY² *adv.* [ME f. OF, f. L *tortuosus* (*tortus* a twist f. as TORT; see -OUS)]

tŏr′tŭr|e *n.*, & *v.t.* **1.** *n.* infliction of severe bodily pain e.g. as punishment or means of persuasion (*was put to the torture*; *instruments of torture*); severe physical or mental pain. **2.** *v.t.* subject to torture (*tortured to extract a confession*; *tortured with neuralgia or anxiety*); (fig.) force out of natural position or state, pervert meaning of (words). **3.** Hence ∼ABLE, ∼OUS, *adjs.*, ∼ER¹ *n.* [F, f. L.L. *tortura* twisting (as TORT; see -URE)]

tŏ′rūla *n.* (*pl.* ∼e). yeast or yeastlike fungus without spores and not causing alcoholic fermentation. [mod. L, dim. of TORUS; see -ULE]

tŏr′|us *n.* (*pl.* ∼i *pr.* -ī). **1.** large moulding of convex semicircular profile esp. as lowest member of base of column. **2.** (Bot.) receptacle of flower. **3.** (Anat.) smooth ridge of bone or muscle. **4.** (Geom.) surface or solid formed by rotating closed curve, esp. circle, about line in its plane but not intersecting it. [L, = swelling, bulge, cushion, etc.]

Tŏr′y *n.* & *a.* **1.** (colloq. or derog.) = CONSERVATIVE 2, 5. **2.** (Hist.) (member) of party that opposed the exclusion of the Duke of York (James II), inclined to the Stuarts after 1689, but after 1760 accepted George III and the established order in Church and State, opposed Reform Bill of 1832, and gave rise to Conservative party (opp. WHIG); *loyal colonist during American Revolution. **3.** Hence ∼ISM (3) *n.* [orig. = Irish outlaw, prob. f. Ir. *tóraighe* pursuer (*tár* pursue)]

tŏsh *n.* (sl.) rubbish, nonsense. [19th c., of unkn. orig.]

toss (tŏs, taws) *v.* (∼ed, arch. or poet. **tost**) & *n.* **1.** *v.t.* throw up (ball etc.) with the hand; (of bull etc.) throw (person etc.) up with the horns. **2.** throw (thing *to* person, *away*, *aside*, *out*, etc.) lightly or carelessly. **3.** throw (coin) into air to decide choice etc. by way it falls; settle question or dispute with (person *for* thing) thus (*will toss you for* (or *who has*) *the armchair*). **4.** ∼ (person) **in blanket,** jerk him upwards out of it by pulling suddenly on all corners; *toss the* CABER; ∼ one's **head,** throw it back esp. in contempt or impatience; ∼ **oars,** raise them to upright position in salute; ∼ **a pancake,** jerk it up so that it returns upside-down to pan; ∼′**pot,** (arch.) toper. **5.** *v.t.* & *i.* throw (thing, one*self*) about from side to side, throw oneself about thus in bed etc., roll about restlessly; (of sea, ship, branch, etc.) roll or swing with fitful to-and--fro motion. **6.** *v.t.* coat (food) with dressing etc. by gentle shaking. **7.** ∼ **off,** (*v.t.*) drink off at a draught, dispatch (work) rapidly or without apparent effort, (sl., *v. refl.* & *i.*) masturbate; ∼ **up,** toss coin (see sense 3), prepare (food) hastily; ∼-*up* n., tossing of coin, doubtful matter (*it is a toss-up whether he comes or not*). **8.** *n.* tossing of coin, head, etc., (**win, lose, the** ∼, have, not have, its decision in one's favour; **argue the** ∼, dispute about a choice); **full** ∼, a full pitch at cricket; PITCH²-*and-toss*. **9.** ||throw from horseback etc. (**take a** ∼, be thrown). [16th c., of unkn. orig.]

tŏt¹ *n.* (colloq.) small child, esp. *a tiny tot*; dram of liquor; small drinking-vessel. [18th c., of dial. orig.]

tŏt² *n.* & *v.* (-tt-). (colloq.) **1.** *n.* ||set of figures to be added. **2.** *v.t.* add (usu. *up*); ∼**ting-u′p,** adding of separate items (||esp. of convictions for driving offences to cause disqualification). **3.** *v.i.* (Of items) mount up (∼ **up to,** amount to). [abbr. of TOTAL or of L *totum* the whole]

||**tŏt³** *n.* (sl.) bone or other article retrieved from refuse--heap etc.; hence ∼′tING¹ *n.*, collecting of valuable items from among refuse. [19th c., of unkn. orig.]

tō′tal *a.*, *n.*, & *v.* (||-ll-). **1.** *a.* complete, comprising the whole, (*the total number of persons*, *total population*, SUM *total*); absolute, unqualified, (*was in total ignorance of it*; *resulted in total loss of his fortune*; *total* ABSTINENCE, *abstainer*); ∼ **eclipse** (in which whole disc etc. is obscured); ∼ **internal reflection** (without refraction, of light-ray meeting interface between two media at more than a certain critical angle to the normal); ∼ **recall,** ability to remember every detail of one's experience clearly; ∼ **war** (in which all available weapons and resources are employed); hence or cogn. **totā′l**ITY *n.* (e.g. time for which an eclipse is total), ∼LY² *adv.* **2.** *n.* total number or amount. **3.** *v.t.* find the total of (things, set of figures; amount in number to (*the visitors totalled 131*); *(sl.) wreck completely. **4.** *v.i.* amount *to*, mount *up to*. [ME f. OF, f. med. L *totalis* (*totus* entire; see -AL)]

tōtälitār′ian *a.* relating to a form of government that permits no rival loyalties or parties, usu. demanding entire subservience of the individual to the State; hence ∼ISM (3) *n.* [f. TOTALITY + -ARIAN]

tō′talizātor *n.* device showing number and amount of bets staked on race with a view to dividing the total among those betting on winner; system for dealing with bets in this way. [f. foll. + -ATE³ + -OR]

tōtaliz|e, -īs|e (-īz), *v.t.* collect into a total, find the total of; hence ∼A′TION *n.*, ∼ER¹ *n.* = prec. [f. TOTAL + -IZE]

tōte¹ *n.* (sl.) totalizator. [abbr.]

tōte² *v.t.* (colloq.) convey, carry as load, (gun, supplies, timber, etc.); ∼ **bag,** woman's large bag for carrying parcels etc.; *∼ **box,** small container for goods. [17th c. US, prob. of dial. orig.]

tō′tem *n.* natural object esp. animal adopted among N. Amer. Indians as emblem of clan or individual on ground of kinship; image of this; ∼-**pole,** pole on which totems are carved or hung, often in tall vertical array, (fig.) hierarchy; hence **totĕ′m**ıc, ∼′st**ıc,** *adjs.*, ∼ISM (3), ∼IST (2), *ns.* [Algonquian]

t′other, t′other, (tŭ′dh-) *a.* & *pron.* the other; **tell** ∼ **from which,** (joc.) tell one from the other. [ME *the tother*, for earlier *thet other* 'the other'; now understood as = *the other*]

tŏties quŏties (tōtĭēz kwō′ŭēz, tōshĭēz kwō′shĭēz) *adv.* on each occasion, every time. [L, = as often as]

tōtō caelo (tōtō sē′lō, kī′lō) *adv.* by an immense amount (*differ toto caelo*). [L, = by the whole heaven]

tŏ′tter¹ *v.i.*, & *n.* **1.** *v.i.* stand or walk unsteadily or feebly (esp. of child learning to walk); (of tower etc., or fig. of State, system, etc.) be shaken, be on the point of falling; hence ∼ER¹ *n.*, ∼Y² *a.* **2.** *n.* unsteady or shaky movement or gait. [ME, f. MDu. *touteren* to swing, f. OS *taltron*]

||**tŏ′tter²** *n.* (sl.) rag-and-bone man. [f. TOT³ + -ER¹]

tŏ′tting See TOT².³.

tou′can (tōō′-) *n.* tropical Amer. fruit-eating bird of family Ramphastidae, with immense beak. [f. Tupi *tucana*, Guarani *tucâ*]

touch¹ (tŭch) *v.* **1.** *v.t.* be placed or move so as to meet (thing etc.) at one or more points without intervening space or object, be in or come into contact with; bring part of body esp. hand into contact with, establish this relation towards (thing *with* one's hand, stick, etc.), cause (two things) to come into contact; (w. neg.) move or harm in any degree; *touch* BOTTOM¹; ∼ one's **hat** (as salutation); ∼ **pitch,** (fig.) have to do with shady transaction or person; ∼ **the spot,** find out or do exactly what was needed; *wouldn't touch him* (unpleasant person) *with a* BARGE-*pole or a pair of* TONGS; *touch* WOOD. **2.** *v.i.* (Of two things etc.) be in or come into contact with one another. **3.** *v.t.* (Geom.) be tangent to (circle etc.). **4.** apply slight force to; strike (keys, strings, of musical instrument), strike keys or strings of. **5.** delineate, mark lightly, put *in*, (*features etc.*) with brush, pencil, etc. **6.** reach, rise as far as (*thermometer touched 90°*); (fig.) approach in excellence etc. (*no one can touch him in light comedy, for purity of style*). **7.** affect with tender feeling, soften, (*it touched me to the heart; was visibly touched by her appeal*); rouse painful or angry feelings in (*touched him to the quick*). **8.** deal with (subject) lightly or in passing; (arch.) concern (*the matter touches you closely*). **9.** (usu. w. neg.) have to do with, (*dare not touch alcohol; has not touched her breakfast; is forbidden to touch the money for ten years; never touches his violin now*). **10.** injure slightly (*blossom is a little touched by the frost*). **11.** (in *p.p.*) slightly crazy. **12.** affect slightly, modify, (*morality touched with emotion*); (w. neg.) produce slightest effect on, cope with, (*brass polish won't touch these candlesticks; couldn't touch the algebra paper*). **13.** (Hist., of monarch) lay hand on (person) as supposed cure for scrofula. **14.** (sl.) ~ person **for**, get (sum of money) from him as loan or gift (*touched me for £5*). **15.** ~ **at**, (Naut.) call at (port etc.); ~**down**, (Rugby & Amer. Footb.) touch ground with ball behind either one's own or the opponent's goal, (of aircraft) alight; ~'*down* n., act of touching down; ~ **off**, represent exactly, explode by touching with match etc., (fig.) initiate (process) suddenly; ~ **on** or **upon**, treat (subject) briefly, refer to or mention casually, verge on; ~ **up**, correct, give finishing touches to or retouch (picture, writing, etc.), strike (horse) lightly with whip, jog (memory). **16.** ~**-and- -go**, (*a.*) uncertain as regards result, risky, (*n.*) touch- -and-go situation; ~**-me-not**, plant of genus *Impatiens* with ripe seed-capsules jerking open when touched. **17.** Hence ~'ABLE *a*. [ME, f. OF *tochier, tuchier*, f. Rom. ******toccare*, prob. imit., f. ******toc* imitating a knock]

touch² (tŭch) *n*. **1.** act or fact of touching, contact, (*felt a touch on my arm; goalkeeper got a touch to the ball*); game of TAG²; **at a** ~, if touched, however lightly; **to the** ~, when touched. **2.** faculty of perception through response of brain to contact esp. with fingers or lips. **3.** light stroke with pencil, brush, etc., in drawing etc. (*added a few touches*); **finishing** ~**es** (lit., or fig. of writing, management of affairs, etc.); *touch of the* SUN. **4.** small amount, slight tinge or trace, (*wants a touch of salt; has a touch of flu; a touch of colour in her cheeks, of frost in the air, of the* SUN; *an occasional touch of irony*); = SHAVE² 2; **a** ~, (*adv.*) slightly. **5.** performer's manner of touching keys or strings of musical instrument, manner or degree in which keys etc. respond to this, manner or style of workmanship in carving etc. or in writing, (*has a light or firm touch on piano; writer has light touch*); **the Nelson** ~, Nelson's or a Nelson-like masterly handling of a situation; **personal** ~, way of treating a matter characteristic of or designed for an individual. **6.** mental correspondence, sympathy, communication; **keep in** ~, (1) remain in sympathy, (2) continue correspondence or personal relations, (*with*); **get, put, in(to)** ~ **with**, come, cause to come, into communication with; **out of** ~, no longer in touch (*with*). **7.** (arch.) test (as) with touchstone (*put it to the touch*). **8.** (Footb.) part of field outside the side limits (~**-lines**) and between continuations of goal- -lines (~**-in-goal**, each of the four corners enclosed by continuations of touch-lines and goal-lines. **9.** (sl.) act of getting money from person; **easy** or **soft** ~, person readily parting with money. **10.** ~**-body, -corpuscle**, (concerned in sense of touch); ***** ~ **foot- ball** (with touching in place of tackling); ~**-hole**, small hole in gun for igniting the charge; ~**-judge**, linesman in Rugby football; ~**-line** (see sense 8); ~**-mark**, maker's mark on pewter; ~**-needle**, needle of gold or silver alloy of known composition used as standard in testing other alloys on touchstone;

~ **of nature**, natural trait, (pop.) exhibition of feeling with which others sympathize (f. misinter- pretation of Shak. *Troilus & Cressida* III. iii. 175); ~- **-paper** (impregnated with nitre, for firing gunpowder etc.); ~'**stone**, fine-grained dark schist or jasper used for testing alloys of gold etc. by marking it with them, (fig.) standard, criterion; ~**-typing**, use of typewriter without looking at keys; ~'**wood**, readily inflammable wood, esp. soft substance into which wood is changed by some fungi, used as tinder. [ME, f. OF *touche* (*tochier*; see prec.); partly f. prec.]

touché (tōō'shā) *int*. acknowledging hit by fencing- -opponent or justified accusation or valid point made by another person in discussion. [F, p.p. of *toucher* TOUCH¹]

tou'cher (tŭ'-) *n*. In vbl senses; (Bowls) wood that touches jack. [ME, f. TOUCH¹ + -ER¹]

tou'ching (tŭ'-) *a*. & *prep*. **1.** *a*. affecting, pathetic, (*a touching incident; shows the most touching confidence in us*); hence ~LY² *adv.*, ~NESS *n*. **2.** *prep*. (arch. or literary). (**as**) ~, concerning, about. [ME, f. TOUCH¹ + -ING¹; in sense 2 f. OF *touchant* part. (as TOUCH¹)]

tou'ch|**ÿ** (tŭ'-) *a*. apt to take offence, over-sensitive; hence ~iLY² *adv.*, ~iNESS *n*. [perh. alt. f. TETCHY after TOUCH²]

tough (tŭf) *a*. & *n*. **1.** *a*. hard to break or cut or tear or chew, not brittle or tender; (of clay etc.) stiff, tenacious; able to endure hardship, hardy; un- yielding, stubborn, difficult, (*he's a tough customer; found it a tough job*); (colloq.) acting sternly or vigorously (*get tough with*); (colloq., of luck etc.) hard, severe, unpleasant; *****ruffianly, violent and criminal; ~**guy**, (colloq.) person not easily injured or thwarted; ~**-minded**, realistic, not sentimental; hence ~'EN⁶ *v.t. & i.*, *****~'IE *n.*, tough person or problem, ~'ISH¹ 2 *a.*, ~'LY² *adv.*, ~'NESS *n*. 2. tough person, esp. ruffian. [OE *tōh*, = OHG *zāh* f. Gmc ******tanhuz*]

tou'pee, toupet, (tōō'pā) *n*. wig or artificial patch of hair worn to cover bald spot. [F *toupet* hair-tuft dim. of OF *toup* tuft (as TOP¹); see -ET¹]

tour (toor) *n*. & *v*. **1.** *n*. journey through a country from place to place; GRAND *tour*; **on** ~, going from place to place to give performances, play matches, etc. **2.** rambling excursion, journey, walk, (*a tour of observation through the town*); spell of duty on military or diplomatic service, time to be spent at a station. **3.** ~ **de force** (-de fŏr's), feat of strength or skill [F]. **4.** *v.i.* make tour (*through* etc.); ~'**ing-car** (with room for passengers and much luggage). **5.** *v.t.* make tour of, travel through, (country etc.). **6.** Hence ~'ER¹ *n*., touring-car. [ME, f. OF *to(u)r*, f. L f. Gk *tornos* lathe]

tour'aco (toor'-) *n*. (pl. ~s). large Afr. bird of family Musophagidae, with crimson and green plumage and prominent crest. [F, f. native name in W. Africa]

tour'ism (toor'-) *n*. organized touring; operation of tours as a business; provision of things and services that attract tourists. [f. TOUR + -ISM]

tour'ist (toor'-) *n*. & *a*. **1.** *n*. person who makes a tour, traveller, esp. for recreation; ~ **trap**, place that exploits tourists; hence ~Y² *a.*, (derog.) suitable for or visited by tourists. **2.** *a*. of or for tourists; ~ **class**, low class of passenger accommodation in ship, aircraft, etc. **3.** Hence ~IC (-ĭ's-) *a*. [f. TOUR + -IST]

tour'maline (toor'malĭn, -ēn) *n*. boron aluminium silicate mineral of various colours possessing unusual electric properties and used as gem. [F, f. Sinh. *toramalli* cornelian]

tour'nament (toor'-) *n*. **1.** (Hist.) pageant in which two parties of mounted and armed men contended with usu. blunted weapons; appointed meeting for jousting etc. **2.** modern display of military exercises, contests, etc., (*Royal Tournament*); any contest of skill between a number of competitors (*chess, lawn-tennis, tournament*). [ME, f. OF *torneiement* (*torneier* TOURNEY; see -MENT]

tour'nedos (toor'nedō) *n*. (pl. same). small fillet of beef with strip of suet round it. [F]

tour'ney (toor'-) *n.*, & *v.i.* (take part in) tournament (esp. sense 1). [ME, f. (OF *tornei* n. f.) OF *torneier* v. f. Rom. *torniare* f. L *tornus* a turn]

tour'niquet (toor'nĭkā) *n.* bandage etc. for stopping flow of blood through artery by compression effected with screw or twisted bar. [F, prob. f. OF *tournicle* coat of mail, TUNICLE, infl. by *tourner* TURN¹]

tou'sle (-zel) *v.t.* handle roughly or rudely; make (esp. hair) untidy. [frequent. of (now dial.) *touse*, ME f. OE *tūsian* cogn. w. OHG *-zuson*; see -LE 3]

tous-les-mois (tōōlāmwah') *n.* food starch got from tubers of species of canna. [F, lit. = every month, prob. corrupt. of W. Ind. *toloman*]

tout *v.* & *n.* **1.** *v.i.* solicit custom, pester possible customers with requests (*for* orders); ||spy out movements and condition of racehorses in training; *offer racing tips for share of resulting gains. **2.** *v.t.* solicit custom of (person) or for (thing). **3.** *n.* person employed in touting. [ME *tūte* look out (OE *tūtian*) = ME (now dial.) *toot* (OE *tōtian*) f. Gmc *tūt-*, *tōt-* project]

tout court (tōō koor') *adv.* (Of name etc.) without addition of title or explanation. [F, lit. quite short]

tout ensemble (tōōt ahnsah'nbl) *n.* See ENSEMBLE. [F (*tout* whole, ENSEMBLE)]

tovăr'ish *n.* comrade. [f. Russ. *tovarishch*]

tow¹ (to) *v.t.*, & *n.* **1.** *v.t.* (Of vessel, horse on bank, etc.) pull (boat, barge, etc.) along in water by rope or chain; (of vehicle) pull another running behind it; pull (person, thing) along behind one. **2.** *n.* towing or being towed; **have in** or **on** ∼, be towing, (fig.) be accompanied by, assume direction of, take possession of, (person). **3.** ∼('ing)-line,-rope, (used in towing); ∼('ing)-net (for dragging through water to collect specimens); ∼('ing)-path (along river or canal for use in towing); hence ∼'ABLE *a.*, ∼'AGE (3, 4) (tō'ĭj) *n.* [OE *togian*, = OHG *zogōn*, ON *toga* f. Gmc *togōjan* (*tog-* pull; cf. TUG)]

tow² (tō) *n.* coarse and broken part of flax or hemp prepared for spinning; loose bunch of rayon etc. strands; ∼-coloured, (of hair) light in colour; ∼-head, tow-coloured or unkempt hair; hence ∼'Yª (tō'ĭ) *a.* [ME, f. MLG *touw*, f. OS *tou*, rel. to ON *tó* wool f. *tāw-* (cf. TOOL¹)]

tow'ard¹ (tō'erd) *a.* (arch.) docile, apt; promising, auspicious; about to take place, being planned; hence ∼LY¹ *a.*, docile, promising, ∼NESS *n.* [as foll.]

towards, toward², (tŏrd(z), twŏrd(z), towŏr'd(z)) *prep.* in the direction of (*looks towards the sea*; *set out towards town*); as regards, in relation to, (*felt some animosity toward him*; *his attitude towards death*); for, for the purpose of, (*saved something towards his education*); near (*towards noon*; *toward the end of our journey*). [OE *toweard* a. future, = OS *tōward*, OHG *zuowart* (as TO¹, -WARD; see -s³)]

tow'el *n.* & *v.* (||-ll-). **1.** *n.* absorbent cloth, paper, etc., for drying oneself or thing after washing; || = SANITARY *towel*; **throw in the** ∼, (Boxing or fig.) admit defeat; ROLLER, TEA-, *towel*; ∼-horse, -rail, frame for hanging towels on. **2.** *v.t.* wipe or dry (one*self* etc.) with towel; || (sl.) thrash. **3.** *v.i.* wipe or dry oneself with towel. **4.** Hence ∼lING¹ (1, 3) *n.* [ME, f. OF *toail(l)e* f. Gmc *thwahljō* (*thwaham* to wash)]

tow'er *n.* & *v.i.* **1.** *n.* tall usu. equilateral (esp. square) or circular structure, often forming part of church or other large building; similar structure housing machinery, apparatus, operators, etc., (*control, cooling, tower*); ∼ (**block**), tall building containing offices or dwelling-places; fortress etc. comprising or including a tower; (fig.) place of defence, protector, (∼ **of strength**, champion, comforter, etc.); IVORY *tower*; MARTELLO *tower*; WATER¹-*tower*; *tower of SILENCE*; ||**the T**∼ (**of London**), assemblage of buildings now used as repository of crown jewels etc., orig. fortress, palace, and State prison; hence ∼ED² (-erd), ∼Y², *adjs.* **2.** *v.i.* reach high (*above* or *over* surroundings, lit., or fig. of eminent person: *towers*

above his contemporaries), (of eagle etc.) soar or be poised aloft, (of wounded bird) shoot straight up; (in *pres. part.*) high, lofty, (fig., of rage etc.) violent. [OE *torr*, & ME *tūr*, AF & OF *tur* etc., f. L f. Gk *turris*]

town *n.* **1.** considerable collection of dwellings etc. (larger than *village*), esp. one not created a city. **2.** densely populated settlement, esp. opp. country or suburbs. **3.** the people of a town (*the whole town knows of it*); **the talk of the** ∼, what is being talked about generally in the town. **4.** London or the chief city or town in one's neighbourhood, (*went up to town from York*; *is not in town, is out of town*; *the best coffee in town*); central business area of one's neighbourhood (*went into town today*). **5.** * = TOWNSHIP 2. **6. go to** ∼, act or work with energy and enthusiasm; **man about** ∼, fashionable idler; *woman etc.* **of the** ∼, belonging to the disreputable side of town life; **on the** ∼, in carefree pursuit of urban pleasures; PAINT² *the town red*; *town and* GOWN. **7.** ∼ **clerk**, officer of corporation of a town, in charge of records, etc., ||(until 1974) secretary and legal adviser of town corporation; ||∼ **council**(lor), (member of) elective governing body in municipality; *town* CRIER; ∼ **gas**, manufactured gas for domestic and commercial use; ∼ **hall**, building for transaction of official business of town, often also used for public entertainment etc.; ∼ **house**, (1) one's town (as opp. to country) residence, (2) ||town hall, (3) house in planned group in town, (4) terrace-house; ∼-**major**, (Hist.) chief executive officer in garrison-town or fortress; ||∼ **mayor**, chairman of town council; *∼ **meeting** (of voters of town for transaction of public business); ∼ **planning**, preparation of plans for regulated growth and improvement of towns; ∼'**scape**, (1) picture of a town, (2) visual appearance of town(s); ∼'**sfolk** (-z-), inhabitants of particular town(s); ∼'**sman**, ∼'**swoman**, (-z-), inhabitant of town, fellow citizen; ∼'**speople** (-z-), the people of a town; ∼ **talk**, (arch.) the talk of the town (see sense 3). **8.** Hence ∼'LESS, ∼'WARD, *adjs.*, ∼'LET *n.*, ∼'WARD(s) *adv.* [OE *tun* enclosure, = OS *tūn*, ON *tún*, OHG *zūn* fence, hedge f. Gmc *tunaz*, *tunam*, rel. to Celt. *dun-*]

townee', *tow'nie, *tow'nỹ, *n.* (derog.) townsman, esp. opp. countryman or (in university town) member of the university. [f. prec. + -EE, -IE, -Y³]

tow'nship *n.* **1.** (Hist.) community inhabiting a manor, parish, etc.; manor or parish as territorial division; small town or village forming or having formed part of a large parish. **2.** (US & Can.) division of county with some corporate powers; district six miles square. **3.** (Austral. & N.Z.). small town, town-site. [OE *tūnscipe* (as TOWN, -SHIP)]

towy. See TOW².

tŏxae'm|ia, *-ē'm|ia, *n.* blood-poisoning; condition in pregnancy with increased blood-pressure; hence ∼IC *a.* [f. as foll. + -AEMIA]

tŏ'x|ic *a.* of poison (*toxic symptoms*); poisonous; caused by poison (*toxic anaemia*); hence ∼ICALLY *adv.*, ∼I'CITY, ∼ICOMA'NIA, *ns.*, ∼I-, ∼ico-, ∼o-, *comb. forms*. [f. med. L *toxicus* poisoned f. L *toxicum* f. Gk *toxikon pharmakon* poison for arrows (*toxa* arrows; see -IC)]

tŏxico'log|ỹ *n.* science of poisons; hence **tŏxico-lŏ'g**ICAL *a.*, ∼IST (3) *n.* [f. prec. + -o- + -LOGY]

tŏ'xin *n.* poison esp. of animal or vegetable origin; (Path.) poison formed in body by pathogenic organism. [f. TOXIC + -IN]

tŏxŏ'phil|ite *n.* & *a.* (student or lover) of archery; hence ∼Y¹ *n.* [f. Ascham's *Toxophilus* (1545) f. Gk *toxon* bow + *-philos* -PHIL, + -ITE¹]

toy *n.*, *a.*, & *v.i.* **1.** *n.* thing to play with, esp. for child; thing meant rather for amusement than for serious use; occupation followed in trifling or unpractical manner. **2.** ∼-**box** (for keeping one's toys in); ∼'**man**, dealer in toys; ∼ **soldier** (of lead etc., or of an army that has no fighting to do). **3.** *a.* that is a toy; (of dog etc.) of diminutive breed or variety. **4.** *v.i.* trifle, amuse oneself; ∼ **with**, deal with or handle in trifling or fondling or careless manner. [16th c.; earlier = dallying, fun, jest, whim, trifle; orig. unkn.]

Tpr. *abbr.* Trooper.

trăbĕā′tion *n.* use of beams (not arches or vaulting) in construction; so **trā′bĕ**ATE² *a.* [f. L *trabs trabis* beam + -ATION]

trabĕ′cŭl|a *n. (pl. ~ae).* (Anat.) supporting band or bar of connective tissue etc.; (Bot.) beamlike projection or process; so ~AR¹, ~ATE², *adjs.* [L, dim. of *trabs* beam; see -CULE]

tracă′sserie *n.* state of annoyance; fuss, petty quarrel. [F (*tracasser* bustle; see -ERY]

trāce¹ *v.t.,* & *n.* **1.** *v.t.* ~ (out), delineate, mark out, sketch, write esp. laboriously, (*traced (out) a plan of the district; traced the words with a shaking hand*; (fig.) *the policy he traced (out) was never followed*). **2.** ~ (over), copy (drawing etc.) by following and marking its lines on superimposed sheet (esp. of transparent **tracing-paper**) through which they are visible or on sheet placed below with carbon paper etc. between; hence **trā′c**ING¹ (1, 2) *n.* **3.** follow or mark track or path of (person, animal, footsteps, etc., *along, through, to,* etc.). **4.** ascertain position and dimensions etc. of (ancient road, wall, etc.) by its remains. **5.** observe or find vestiges or signs of (*his resentment can be clearly traced in many passages; cannot trace any letter of that date*). **6.** ~ back, go back over the course of (*have traced my genealogy back to (the time of) William I; the report has been traced back to you*). **7.** pursue one's way along (path etc.). **8.** Hence ~ABLE (-sa-) *a.* **9.** *n.* track left by person or animal walking or running or by moving pen of instrument etc.; (esp. in *pl.*) footprints or visible signs of a course pursued; line on screen of cathode-ray tube showing path of moving spot; curve's projection on or intersection with plane etc. **10.** visible or other sign of what has existed or happened (*of these buildings no trace remains; sorrow has left its traces on her face; has vanished, sunk, without trace*); change in the brain as result of learning; small quantity (*contains traces of soda*); amount of substance, rainfall, etc., too small to be measured; ~ **element** (occurring or required, esp. in soil, only in minute amounts). **11.** Hence ~′LESS (-sl-) *a.* [ME; (n. f. OF *trace*) f. OF *tracier* f. Rom. *tractiare* f. L *tractus* drawing (see TRACT¹)]

trāce² *n.* each of the two side-straps or chains or ropes by which horse draws vehicle; **kick over the ~s,** (fig., of person) become insubordinate or reckless; ~-horse (that draws in traces or by single trace, esp. one hitched on to help up hill etc.). [ME f. OF *trais,* pl. of TRAIT]

trā′cer *n.* In vbl senses; (Mil.) projectile whose course is made visible by flame etc. emitted; artificially produced radioactive isotope capable of being followed in its course in the human body etc. by the radiation it produces. [f. TRACE¹ + -ER¹]

trā′cer|ў *n.* stone ornamental open-work esp. in head of Gothic window; decorative pattern or natural outline (e.g. in insect's wing) suggesting this; **bar ~y** (with strips of stone across aperture); **geometric ~y** (with openings of geometrical form); **plate ~y** (with perforations in otherwise continuous stone); hence ~IED² (-ĭd) *a.* [f. TRACE¹ + -ERY]

trachea (trakē′a, trā′kĭa) *n. (pl. ~e).* principal air-passage of body from larynx to bronchial tubes; (Zool.) each of the passages by which air is conveyed through body of insect, arachnid, etc.; (Bot.) duct, vessel; hence **trā′chĕ**AL, **trā′chĕ**ATE², *adjs.,* **trachĕ′o-** *comb. form,* (-k-). [ME f. med. L., = LL *trachia* f. Gk *trakheia (artēria)* 'rough artery', f. *trakhus* rough]

trāchĕŏ′tomў (-k-) *n.* incision of trachea; ~ **tube,** breathing-tube inserted in opening so made. [f. TRACHEO- + -TOMY]

trach|ŏ′ma (-k-) *n.* contagious disease of eye with inflamed granulation on inner surface of lids; hence ~ŏ′matOUS *a.* [f. mod. L f. Gk *trakhōma (trakhus* rough; see -OMA)]

trā′chўte (-k-) *n.* light-coloured volcanic rock

rough to the touch; hence **trachў′t**IC (-k-) *a.* [F, f. Gk *trakhutēs* roughness (as prec.) + -ITE¹]

trăck¹ *n.* & *v.* **1.** *n.* mark or series of marks left by person, animal, or thing, in passing along; (in *pl.*) such marks, esp. footprints; **in** one's ~s, (sl.) where one stands, there and then; **off the** ~, (fig.) away from subject; **on** person's ~, in pursuit of him, (fig.) in possession of clue to his conduct, plans, etc.; **on the wrong** ~, following wrong line of inquiry etc.; **cover** one's ~s, conceal evidence of what one has done; **keep, lose,** ~ **of,** follow, fail to follow, the course or development of; **make ~s,** (sl.) go or run away; **make ~s for,** (sl.) go in pursuit of or towards. **2.** course taken (*followed in his track; track of ionizing particle, of comet*); ONE-*track mind.* **3.** path, esp. one beaten by use, (fig.) course of life or routine, (*a rough track round the hillside; road has only a single track;* BEATEN *track*). **4.** prepared racing-path (*grass track; running-track*); racecourse for horses etc. **5.** continuous line of railway; **single, double,** ~, one pair, two pairs, of rails; ***across, *on the wrong side of, the** ~s, in socially inferior part of town; hence *~′AGE (1) *n.* **6.** band round wheels of tank, tractor, etc.; hence ~-laying, (of vehicle) having caterpillar tread. **7.** transverse distance between a vehicle's wheels. **8.** = SOUND²-*track*; groove on gramophone record; section of gramophone record with a recorded sequence; lengthwise strip of magnetic tape containing one sequence of signals. **9.** ~ **events,** (Athletics) running-races as opp. throwing etc. (FIELD *events*); *~′layer, ~′man, platelayer; ~ **record,** (fig.) person's past achievements; ~ **shoe,** spiked shoe worn by runner; ~ **suit** (worn by athlete etc. during training); *~ **system,** streaming in education; ~′way, beaten path, ancient roadway. **10.** Hence ~′LESS *a.* (*~less trolley, trolleybus). **11.** *v.t.* follow the track of (animal, person, to lair etc.; spacecraft etc.); ~ **down,** reach or capture by tracking. **12.** trace, make out, (course, development, etc.) by vestiges. **13.** *make track with (dirt etc.) from feet; *leave such track on (floor etc.). **14.** *v.i.* (Of wheels) run so that the hinder is exactly in the first's track; (of gramophone stylus) follow groove; (of cine-camera) move along set path while taking picture. [ME, f. OF *trac,* perh. f. LDu. *tre(c)k* draught etc.]

trăck² *v.* **1.** *v.t.* tow (boat) by rope etc. from bank. **2.** *v.i.* travel by being towed. [app. f. Du. *trekken* to draw etc., assim. to prec.]

trā′cker *n.* In vbl senses; wooden connecting-rod in organ mechanism; police dog tracking by scent; BLACK¹ *tracker.* [f. TRACK¹,² + -ER¹]

trăct¹ *n.* region or area of indefinite (usu. large) extent, (*a tract of sand; pathless tracts*); (Anat.) area of organ or system (*olfactory, respiratory, tract*); ||(arch.) period (*of time* etc.). [f. L *tractus* drawing (*trahere* tract-draw, pull)]

trăct² *n.* short treatise or discourse or pamphlet esp. on religious subject; **T~s for the Times,** Oxford T~s, (see TRACTARIANISM). [app. abbr. of L *tractatus* TRACTATE]

trăct³ *n.* (RC Ch.) anthem replacing alleluia in some masses. [f. med. L *tractus (cantus)* drawn-out (song), p.p. of L *trahere* draw]

tră′ct|able *a.* (Of person, material, etc.) easily handled, manageable, pliant, docile, malleable; hence ~ABI′LITY, ~ableNESS (-beln-), *ns.,* ~ABLY *adv.* [f. L *tractabilis (tractare* handle, frequent. of *trahere tract-* draw; see -ABLE)]

Trăctār′ian *a.* & *n.* (adherent or promoter) of ~ISM (3) *n.,* 19th-c. English High-Church movement towards an earlier sacramental Catholicism and against liberalism, voiced by Newman, Pusey, Keble, Froude, etc., in 90 tracts (*Tracts for the Times*) published at Oxford 1833–41. [f. TRACT² + -ARIAN]

tră′ctāte *n.* treatise. [f. L *tractatus (tractare;* see TRACTABLE, -ATE²)]

tră′ction *n.* drawing of a body along a surface, esp. of vehicle along road or track (*electric, steam, traction*);

grip of tyre on road, wheel on rail, etc.; (Med.) sustained pull on limb etc. for therapeutic purpose; contraction e.g. of muscle; *public transport service; ~-engine, steam or diesel engine for drawing heavy load on ordinary road or across fields etc.; ~-wheel, driving-wheel of locomotive etc.; hence or cogn. ~AL, trä′ctIVE, adjs. [F, or f. med. L tractio f. L trahere tract-draw; see -ION]

trä′ctor n. traction-engine; stationary or movable engine for hauling; self-propelled vehicle for hauling other vehicles, farm machinery, etc. [f. as prec. + -OR]

träd a. & n. (colloq.) traditional (jazz). [abbr.]

träde n. & v. **1.** n. business, esp. mechanical or mercantile employment opp. to *profession*, carried on as means of livelihood or profit (*a carpenter, a butcher, by trade*); skilled handicraft (*learn a trade*); **be in ~**, be a retailer, keep a shop; JACK[1] *of all trades*; **trick of the ~**, device for attracting custom, gaining advantage over rival by special technique, etc. **2.** exchange of commodities for money or other commodities, commerce; business done with specified class or at specified time (*tourist, Christmas, trade*); *a transaction; **foreign ~**, exportation and importation of goods from and to home country or exchange of commodities of different countries; **domestic** or **home ~** (carried on within a country); **is good, bad, for ~**, induces, discourages, buying; **carrying-~**, transportation of goods from one country to another by water or air as a business. **3.** *the* persons engaged in one trade (*the trade will never agree to it*; *is unpopular with the book trade*), esp. ||(colloq.) *the* licensed victuallers, (Nav. sl.) *the* submarine service. **4.** BALANCE[1] *of trade*; ||BOARD[1] *of Trade*; FREE[1] *trade*; TERM[1]s *of trade.* **5.** (usu. in *pl.*) trade wind. **6.** ||T~ **Board,** (Hist.) statutory body for the settlement of disputes, wage claims, etc., in certain industries; ||~ **cycle,** recurring succession of trade conditions alternating between prosperity and depression; ~ **journal** (containing articles and information on a particular trade); ~ **mark,** device or word or words legally registered (or established by use) as distinguishing a manufacturer's or trader's goods, (fig.) distinctive feature of person's activities etc.; ~ **name,** (1) that by which a thing is called in the trade, (2) name given by manufacturer to proprietary article, (3) name under which business is carried on; ~ **paper,** = *trade journal*; ~ **plates,** number-plates used by dealer etc. on various unlicensed cars; ~ **price** (charged by manufacturer etc. to dealer for goods that are to be sold again); ~ **secret,** device or technique used in trade and giving advantage because not generally known; ~'**sman** (-z-), person engaged in trade, esp. shopkeeper or craftsman; ~'**speople** (-z-), tradesmen (and their families); **T~s Union Congress,** official representative body of British trade unions, meeting annually; ~ **union,** ~s **union,** organized association of workers in a trade or group of allied trades or a profession, formed for protection and promotion of their common interests; ~-u′**nionism,** this system of association; ~-u′**nionist,** advocate of this or member of trade union; ~ **wind,** wind blowing continually towards equator within parallels 30° N. and 30° S. and deflected westwards by rotation of earth [f. obs. *blow trade* = blow regularly]. **7.** *v.i.* buy and sell, engage in trade (*in* commodity or (fig.) *in* favours etc., *with* person); have a transaction (*with* person *for* thing); carry merchandise (*to* place); ~ **on,** take (esp. unscrupulous) advantage of (person's credulity, one's reputation, etc.). **8.** *v.t.* exchange in commerce, barter, (goods); ~ **(in),** give (used car etc.) in (part) payment or exchange *for*; ~-*in* n., (thing given in) such transaction; *~-**last,** compliment from a third person to be reported in exchange for one to the reporter; ~ **off,** exchange esp. by way of compromise, so ~-*off* n. **9.** Hence trä′dABLE a. [ME, f. MLG *trade* track, f. OS *trada*, OHG *trata* (*trad-* TREAD)]

trä′der n. person engaged, vessel regularly employed, in trade. [f. prec. + -ER[1]]

trädèscä′ntia n. perennial herb of genus *Tradescantia*, with large blue, white, or pink flowers. [mod. L, f. J. Tradescant, Engl. naturalist d. 1638 + -IA[1]]

trä′ding n. In vbl senses; ~ **estate,** area designed to be occupied by a group of industrial and commercial firms; *trading-*POST[4]; ~ **stamp** (given by tradesman to customer and exchangeable in quantity for various articles). [f. TRADE + -ING[1]]

tradi′tion n. **1.** opinion or belief or custom handed down, handing down of these, from ancestors to posterity esp. orally or by practice. **2.** (Theol.) doctrine etc. supposed to have divine authority but not committed to writing, esp. (1) laws held by Pharisees to have been delivered by God to Moses, (2) oral teaching of Christ and Apostles not recorded in writing by immediate disciples, (3) words and deeds of Muhammad not in Koran. **3.** artistic or literary principle(s) based on accumulated experience or continuous usage (*stage tradition*; *the traditions of the Dutch School*). **4.** (Law). formal delivery. **5.** Hence ~ARY[1] a., ~IST (2) n., = TRADITIONALIST. [ME, f. OF *tradicion* or f. L *traditio* f. *tradere* (*tra-* = TRANS-, *dare* give) hand on, betray; see -ION]

tradi′tional a. of or based on or obtained by tradition; (of jazz) in style resembling that of the early period of jazz history; hence ~LY[2] adv. [f. prec. + -AL]

tradi′tional|ism n. (excessive) respect for tradition esp. in religion; philosophical system referring all religious knowledge to divine revelation and tradition; so ~IST (2) n. [f. F traditionalisme or f. prec. + -ISM]

trä′ditor n. (pl. ~s, or ~es pr. -ōr′ēz). early Christian who to save his life surrendered copies of Scripture, or Church property, to persecutors. [L (see TRAITOR)]

tradü′ce v.t. calumniate, misrepresent; hence tradü′CER[1], ~MENT (-sm-), ns. [f. L *traducere* disgrace (*tra-* = TRANS-, *ducere duct-* lead)]

tradü′cian|(ist) ns. one who believes that soul as well as body is propagated; so ~ISM (3) n. [f. LL *traducianus* transmitting f. L *tradux -ucis* vine-shoot trained for propagation; see -IAN]

trä′ffic v. (-ck-) & n. **1.** *v.i.* trade (*in* commodity, lit. or fig.), esp. deal or bargain in something that should not be the subject of a trade. **2.** *v.t.* deal in, barter. **3.** Hence ~KER[1] n. **4.** n. trade, esp. trafficking (*in* commodity; *the traffic in drugs*; *unscrupulous traffic in lucrative appointments*); transportation of goods, coming and going of persons or goods by road, rail, air, sea, etc.; number or amount of persons or goods conveyed; (amount of) use of a service (*telephone traffic*); dealings or communication between persons etc. **5.** *~ **circle,** roundabout; *~ **cop,** (colloq.) policeman controlling road traffic; ~ **island,** paved etc. area in road to direct the traffic and provide refuge for pedestrians crossing; ~ **jam,** condition in which road traffic cannot proceed freely and comes to a standstill; ~**-light,** ~**-signal,** (usu. automatic) signal controlling road traffic (esp. at junctions) by coloured lights; ~ **sign** (conveying information, warning, etc., to vehicle-drivers); ||~ **warden,** person appointed to assist police in controlling movement of road traffic and esp. parking of vehicles. **6.** Hence ~LESS a. [f. F *traf(f)ique(r)*, Sp. *traficar*, *tráfico*; It. *trafficare*, *traffico*, of unkn. orig.]

||trä′fficator n. device on road vehicle to indicate intended change of direction of travel. [f. prec. + INDICATOR]

trä′gacänth n. white or reddish gum from plants of genus *Astragalus*, used in pharmacy, calico-printing, etc. [f. F *tragacante* f. L f. Gk *tragakantha*, name of shrub (*tragos* goat, *akantha* thorn)]

tragė′dian n. writer of tragedies; actor in tragedy. [ME, f. OF *tragediane* (as TRAGEDY; see -IAN)]

tragėdie′nne n. actress in tragedy. [F, fem. f. as prec.]

trä′gėdy̆ n. **1.** drama in prose or verse of elevated theme and diction and with unhappy events or ending (cf. COMEDY). **2.** sad event, calamity; serious accident or crime. [ME, f. OF *tragedie* f. L f. Gk *tragōidia* app. goat-song (*tragos* goat, *ōidē* song)]

trăˈgˌic *a.* **1.** of, in the style of, tragedy (*tragic drama; in a tragic voice; tragic actor*); ∼**ic irony** (orig. in Gk tragedy, of words having an inner esp. prophetic meaning for audience, unsuspected by speaker). **2.** sad, calamitous, distressing, (*a tragic tale, event, scene*). **3.** Hence ∼ICALLY *adv.* [f. F *tragique* f. L f. Gk *tragikos* (*tragos* goat; see prec., -IC)]

trăˈgical *a.* = prec. **2.** [f. as prec.+-AL]

trăgˌicŏˈm|ĕdy *n.* drama of mixed tragic and comic elements; so ∼IC *a.*, ∼ICALLY *adv.* [f. F *tragicomédie* or f. It. *tragicomedia* f. LL *tragicomoedia* f. L *tragico-comoedia* (as TRAGIC, COMEDY)]

trăˈgopăn *n.* Asian horned pheasant of genus *Tragopan*. [L f. Gk (*tragos* goat, *Pan* the god Pan)]

trahison des clercs (trahīzawn dā klār´) *n.* betrayal (of standards) by the intellectuals. [F, title of book by J. Benda (1927)]

trail *n.* & *v.* **1.** *n.* part drawn behind or in the wake of a thing, long (real or apparent) appendage, (*engine left a trail of smoke behind it*; CONDENSATION trail; *the trail of a meteor*); hinder end of gun-carriage stock; track left by what has moved or has been drawn over surface (*vandals left a trail of wreckage; slimy trail of a slug*). **2.** track, scent followed in hunting, (*on, off, the trail*); beaten path esp. through wild region (BLAZE⁴ *a trail*, whence ∼-**blazer**, esp. fig.); **at the** ∼, (Mil.) with arms trailed; ∼-**net**, drag-net. **3.** *v.t.* draw along behind one esp. on the ground, (*trailed her dress through the mud; trailing clouds of glory*); drag (one*self*, one's limbs) along wearily etc.; follow the trail of, pursue, shadow; (Mil.) ∼ **arms**, let rifle etc. hang balanced in one hand and ||parallel to ground; *trail* one's COAT. **4.** *v.i.* be drawn along behind (*skirt trails on the ground*); hang loosely; walk wearily, lag, straggle; be losing in game or other contest; tail *away* or *off*; (of plant) grow to some length over ground, wall, etc. **5.** ∼**ˈing edge**, rear edge of aircraft's wing etc., (Electr.) part of pulse in which amplitude diminishes, (opp. *leading edge*); ∼**ˈing wheel** (not given direct motive power). [ME, n. f. v. f. OF *traillier* to tow, or f. MLG *treilen* haul, f. Rom. *tragulare* f. L *tragula* drag-net]

traiˈler *n.* In vbl senses; trailing plant; set of short extracts from cinema or television film, exhibited to advertise it in advance; wheeled vehicle (esp. caravan) drawn by another. [f. prec.+-ER¹]

train *v.* & *n.* **1.** *v.t.* & *i.* bring (person, animal, etc.) or come to desired state or standard of efficiency etc. by instruction and practice (*train up a child in the way he should go; he trained, was trained, for the ministry; a trained nurse, soldier; did not escape his trained eye*). **2.** *v.t.* teach and accustom (person, animal, *to do, to* action; *dog is trained to jump through hoop; trained to obey or obedience*). **3.** *v.t.* & *i.* bring (horse, athlete, one*self*) or come to physical efficiency by exercise and diet (*is training for the boat race; trains horses; is only half-trained*); ∼ **down** (to lower weight). **4.** *v.t.* cause (plant) to grow in required shape (*up* or *over wall* etc.). **5.** point, aim, (gun, camera, on object etc.). **6.** (arch.) entice, lure, (*away* etc.); draw along (esp. heavy thing). **7.** *v.i.* & *t.* (colloq.) go by train; perform (journey) thus. **8.** Hence ∼ˈABLE *a.*, ∼EEˈ *n.* **9.** *n.* thing drawn along behind or forming hinder part, esp. elongated part of woman's skirt trailing on ground or of official robe, long or conspicuous tail of bird. **10.** body of attendants, retinue, (*formed part of his train; a train of admirers*); **in the** ∼ **of**, as a sequel of. **11.** succession or series of persons or things (*long train of sightseers, of camels; wagon train; by an unlucky train of events; suggested a whole train of ideas; train of thought*); **in** ∼, properly arranged or directed. **12.** series of railway carriages or trucks drawn by same engine(s). **13.** line of combustible material to lead fire to charge of explosive. **14.** (Mil.) artillery and other equipment for siege or battle, with their vehicles and attendants. **15.** series of connected wheels or parts in machinery. **16.** ∼ˈ**band**, (Hist.) each division of London citizen soldiery esp. in Stuart period; ∼-**bearer**, (1) person employed to hold up train of another's robe, (2) long-tailed S. Amer. humming-bird; ∼-**ferry**, vessel that conveys a railway train across a piece of water; ∼-**mile**, one mile travelled by one train, as unit of traffic; ∼ˈ**sick**, affected with nausea caused by motion of train; ∼-**spotter**, collector of locomotive numbers. **17.** Hence ∼ˈLESS *a.* [ME, (n. f. OF *train*(*e*)) f. OF *traïner, trahiner*, f. Rom. **traginare*, ult. f. L *trahere* draw]

traiˈner *n.* In vbl senses; one who trains horses, athletes, etc., for races etc., or sees to physical fitness of footballers etc.; aircraft or device simulating it used to train pilots. [f. prec.+-ER¹]

traiˈning *n.* In vbl senses; PHYSICAL *training*; **in** ∼, (1) undergoing physical training (so **go into** ∼), (2) physically fit as result of this, opp. **out of** ∼; ∼-**college, -school,** (for training persons, formerly esp. teachers); ∼-**ship** (on which boys are taught seamanship etc.). [ME, f. TRAIN +-ING¹]

traiˈn-oil *n.* oil got from blubber of whale (esp. of the right whale). [f. obs. *train, trane* train-oil f. MLG *trān*, MDu. *traen*, app. = TEAR²]

traipse *n.*, & *v.i.* (colloq. or dial.) **1.** *n.* slattern; tedious journey on foot. **2.** *v.i.* tramp or trudge wearily; go *about* on errands. [16th c. *trapes* v.; orig. unkn.]

trait (trā) *n.* distinguishing feature in character, appearance, habit, or portrayal. [F, f. L *tractus* (as TRACT¹)]

traiˈtor *n.* one who is false to his allegiance or acts disloyally (*to* country, king, cause, religion, principles, him*self*, etc.); so ∼OUS *a.*, **traiˈtrESS**¹ *n.* [ME, f. OF *traït*(*o*)*ur* f. L *traditor -oris* (*tradere*; see TRADITION, -OR)]

trajectorˈy (trăˈjĭ-, trajēˈ-) *n.* path described by projectile moving or object developing under given forces; (Geom.) curve or surface cutting system of curves or surfaces at constant angle. [orig. *a.*, f. med. L *trajectorius* f. L *traicere traject-* (*tra-* = TRANS-, *jacere* throw); see -ORY]

tra-laˈ (-ah´) *int.* expr. joy or gaiety. [imit. of song]

trăm¹ *n.* ||∼(ˈ**car**), passenger car running on rails laid in public road; four-wheeled car used in coal-mines; ||∼**lines**, rails for tramcar, (fig.) immovable principle etc., (colloq.) either pair of long parallel lines at side of lawn-tennis doubles court, similar lines at side or back of badminton court; ∼-**road**, (Hist.) road with wooden, stone, or metal wheel-tracks; ∼ˈ**way**, (1) tram-road, (2) ||rails for tramcar. [f. MLG & MDu. *trame* balk, beam, barrow-shaft]

trăm² *n.* ∼ (**silk**), double silk thread used for weft of some velvets and silks. [f. F *trame* f. L *trama* weft]

trăˈmmel *n.*, & *v.t.* (||-ll-). **1.** *n.* triple drag-net for fish, which are trapped in a pocket formed when they attempt to swim through; *hook in fireplace for kettle etc.; instrument for drawing ellipses etc. with bar sliding in perpendicular grooves; beam-compass; (usu. in *pl.* and fig.) impediment(s) to free movement or action (*trammels of etiquette, of official routine*). **2.** *v.t.* (usu. fig.) confine, hamper, with trammels. [in sense 'net' ME, f. OF *tramail* f. med. L *tramaculum, tremaculum,* perh. f. as TRI-+*macula* (MAIL¹); later history uncert.]

tramontaˈna (trah-; -ah´-) *n.* cold north wind in Adriatic. [It.; see foll.]

tramŏˈntāne *a.* & *n.* **1.** *a.* (situated or living) on other side of mountains, esp. the Alps; (fig., from It. point of view) foreign, barbarous. **2.** *n.* tramontane person; = prec. [ME, f. It. *tramontano* f. L TRANS- (*montanus* f. *mons montis* mountain) beyond the mountains; cf. -ANE]

trămp *v.* & *n.* **1.** *v.i.* walk heavily and firmly (*heard him tramping about overhead*); walk, go on foot; be a tramp. **2.** *v.t.* perform (journey), traverse (country), on foot (usu. reluctantly, wearily, etc.); stamp (*down* etc.), tread on, or trample. **3.** *n.* sound of person(s) walking or marching or of horse's steps. **4.** journey on foot, walk. **5.** iron plate protecting sole of boot from wear and tear of spade in digging; part of spade that it strikes. **6.** person who tramps the roads as vagrant; this mode of life; (sl.) dissolute woman. **7.** (**ocean**) ~, freight--vessel, esp. steamer, running on no regular line. [ME *trampe* f. Gmc *tremp-*, *tramp-*]

trä′mpl|e v. & n. **1.** v.t. tread under foot, press down or crush thus, (*trampled to death by elephants*). **2.** v.i. ~**e on,** tread heavily on, (fig.) treat roughly or with contempt, show no consideration for, (person, feelings, etc.). **3.** n. sound or act of trampling. [ME, f. prec. + -LE 3]

trä′mpoline (-ēn) n., & v.i. **1.** n. canvas sheet connected by springs to horizontal frame, used by acrobats etc. **2.** v.i. use trampoline. [f. It. *trampolino* (*trampoli* stilts)]

trance (-ah-) n., & v.t. **1.** n. sleeplike state without response to stimuli; half-conscious state; ecstasy, rapture, extreme exaltation; catalepsy; hypnotic state. **2.** v.t. (poet.) = ENTRANCE². [ME, f. OF *transe* (*transir* depart, fall into trance f. L *transire*; see TRANSIT)]

tranche (-ahnsh) n. portion, esp. of income, or of block of shares. [F, = slice (as TRENCH)]

trä′nny n. (sl.) transistor radio. [abbr.; see -Y³]

trä′nquil a. calm, serene, unruffled, not agitated, (*preserved a tranquil mind; tranquil surface of pond*); hence or cogn. ~lITY (-ĭ′l-) n., ~LY² adv. [f. F *tranquille* or f. L *tranquillus*]

trä′nquilliz|e, -is|e (-īz), *-**ïlī-,** v.t. make tranquil, esp. by drug etc.; hence ~ER¹ n., drug used to diminish anxiety. [f. prec. + -IZE]

trans- (-ă-, -ah-; -s-, -z-) *pref.* w. sense 'across, beyond' (*transcontinental, transgress, trans-Siberian*), 'on or to the other side of' (*transatlantic*; opp. *cis-*), 'through' (*transonic, transpierce*), 'into another state or place' (*transcribe, transform, transliterate*), 'surpassing, transcending' (*transfinite*); (Chem.) (1) having two atoms or groups on opposite sides of plane of symmetry, (2) having higher atomic number than (*transuranic*). [f. or after L *trans* across]

transä′ct (trä-, trah-; -s-, -z-) v.t. perform, carry through, (business); hence ~OR n. [f. L TRANS(*igere act-* = *agere* do)]

transä′ction (trä , trah-; -s-, -z-) n. management of business (*left the transaction of the matter to him*); piece of esp. commercial business done (*the transactions of a firm; the transaction will not bear looking into*); (in *pl.*) reports of discussions, papers read etc., at meetings of learned society (*Philosophical Transactions of the Royal Society*). [ME, f. LL *transactio* (as prec.; see -ION)]

transä′lpīne (trä-, trah-; -s-, -z-) a. beyond the Alps (usu. from It. point of view). [f. L TRANS(*alpinus* ALPINE)]

transatlä′ntic (trä-, trah-; -s-, -z-) a. beyond the Atlantic, ||American, *European; crossing the Atlantic (*transatlantic flight, line, steamer*). [f. TRANS- +ATLANTIC]

transcei′ver (-ănsē′-, -ahnsē′-) n. combined radio transmitter and receiver. [f. TRANSMITTER + RECEIVER]

transcě′nd (-ă-, -ah-) v.t. be beyond the range or domain or grasp of (human experience, reason, description, belief, etc.); excel, surpass. [ME, f. OF *transcendre* or f. L *transcendere* (TRANS-, *scandere* climb)]

transcě′nd|ent (-ă-, -ah-) a. & n. **1.** a. excelling, surpassing, (*transcendent merit, genius*); transcending human experience. **2.** (Scholastic Philos.) higher than, not included under any of, Aristotle's ten categories. **3.** (Kantian Philos.) not realizable in experience. **4.** (Esp. of God) existing apart from, not subject to limitations of, the material universe, opp. *immanent.* **5.** Hence or cogn. ~ENCE, ~ENCY, ns., ~entLY² adv. **6.** n. (Philos.) transcendent thing. [as prec.; see -ENT]

transcendě′ntal (trä-, trah-) a. & n. **1.** a. = prec. **2.** (Kantian Philos.) of a priori character, presupposed in and necessary to experience; ~ **cognition,** a priori knowledge; ~ **object,** real (unknown and unknowable) object; ~ **unity** (brought about by cognition). **3.** explaining matter and objective things as products of the subjective mind (esp. in Schelling's philosophy); regarding the divine as guiding principle in man (esp. in Emerson's philosophy). **4.** (pop.) abstruse, vague, obscure, visionary, abstract; T~ **Meditation** (*P; seeking to induce detachment from problems and relief from anxiety etc.). **5.** (Math.) (Of function) not capable of being produced by the algebraical operations of addition, multiplication, and involution, or the inverse operations. **6.** Hence ~LY² adv. n. transcendental term, conception, etc. [f. med. L *transcendentalis* (as prec.; see -AL)]

transcendě′ntal|ism (trä-, trah-) n. transcendental philosophy; exalted or visionary language; so ~IST (2) n., ~IZE (3) v.t. [f. prec. + -ISM]

transcŏ′ntině′ntal (trä-, trah-; -s-, -z-) a. (Of railway etc.) extending across a continent. [f. TRANS-+ CONTINENTAL]

transcrī′be (-ă-, -ah-) v.t. make copy of, esp. in writing; transliterate; write out (shorthand) in ordinary characters; record for subsequent reproduction; broadcast in this form; arrange (music) for different instrument etc.; hence or cogn. ~I′bER¹, ~i′ptION, ns., ~i′ptION|AL, ~i′ptIVE, adjs. [f. L *transcribere* (TRANS-, *scribere* script- write)]

tra′nscript (-ă′-, -ah′-) n. (written or recorded) copy. [ME f. OF *transcrit* f. L *transcriptum* neut. p.p. (as n.); see prec.]

transdū′cer (-ă-, -ah-; -s-, -z-) n. device that converts variations of one quantity into those of another (e.g. pressure into voltage). [f. L TRANS(*ducere* lead) + -ER¹]

transě′ct (-ă-, -ah-; -s-, -z-) v.t. cut across or transversely; so ~ION n. [f. TRANS-+L *secare sect-* cut]

tra′nsept (-ă′-, -ah′-) n. transverse part of cruciform church; either arm (**north, south,** ~) of this, hence ~AL (-ĕ′p-) a. [f. mod. L *transeptum* (as TRANS-, *septum*)]

transexual. Var. of TRANSSEXUAL.

transfēr′¹ (-ă-, -ah-) v. (-**rr-**). **1.** v.t. convey, remove, hand over, (thing etc. *from* person or place *to* another); make over possession of (property, ticket, rights, etc., *to* person). **2.** convey (drawing etc.) from one surface to another esp. to lithographic stone by means of transfer-paper; remove (picture) from one surface to another esp. from wood or wall to canvas. **3.** move (person) to another group, (esp. Footb.) club, etc.; change (sense of word etc.) by extension or metaphor. **4.** v.i. change from one station, route, etc., to another to continue journey; change or be moved to another group, club, etc. **5.** Hence ~EE′, ~OR, ~ER¹, ns. [ME, f. F *transférer* or f. L TRANS(*ferre* latbear)]

tra′nsfer² (-ă′-, -ah′-) n. **1.** transferring or being transferred; conveyance of property or right, document effecting this; *ticket allowing journey to be continued on another route etc. **2.** design etc. (to be) conveyed from one surface to another; small usu. coloured picture or design on paper from which it is transferable to other surface. **3.** ~**book,** register of transfers of property, shares, etc.; *~ **company** (conveying passengers or luggage between usu. nearby stations); ~ **fee** (paid for transfer esp. of professional footballer); ~**ink** (for making designs on lithographic stone or transfer-paper); ~ **list** (of footballers available for transfer); ~**paper** (specially coated to receive impression of transfer-ink and transfer it to stone); ~ **RNA** (conveying amino--acid molecule from cytoplasm to ribosome for use in protein synthesis); *~ **table,** railway traverse-table. [f. prec.]

transfer|able (-ă′-, -ah′-; -er-, -ēr′-) a. capable of being transferred; ~**able vote,** indication on ballot--paper of candidate to whom vote shall be transferred if candidate for whom it is first cast is eliminated in one of successive counts or has more votes than are needed for election; hence ∿ABI′LITY *n*. [f. TRANS-FER¹+-ABLE]

tra′nsference (-ă′-, -ah′-) *n*. action of transferring; (Psych.) redirection of desires etc. to new object. [f. TRANSFER¹+-ENCE]

transfě′rrin (-ă-, -ah-) *n*. protein transporting iron in blood of animals. [f. TRANS-+L *ferrum* iron+-IN]

transfigurā′tion (tră-, trah-) *n*. change of form or appearance, esp. that of Christ (Matt. 17:2, Mark 9:2-3); (7∿) festival of Christ's transfiguration, 6 Aug. [ME f. OF, or f. L *transfiguratio* (as foll.; see -ATION)]

transfi′gure (-ă-, -ah-; -ger) *v.t.* change in form or appearance, esp. so as to elevate or idealize. [ME, f. OF *transfigurer* or f. L TRANS(*figurare* FIGURE²)]

transfi′nite (-ă-, -ah-) *a*. beyond or surpassing what is finite; (Math., of number) exceeding all finite numbers. [f. TRANS-+FINITE]

transfi′x (-ă-, -ah-) *v.t.* pierce with lance etc.; (of horror etc.) root (person) to the spot, paralyse faculties of; hence ∿ION (-kshon) *n*. [f. L TRANS(*figere fix-* fix)]

transfōr′m¹ (-ă-, -ah-) *v*. **1.** *v.t.* make (esp. considerable) change in the form, outward appearance, character, disposition, etc., of (*caterpillar is transformed into butterfly; a year in the army has transformed him* (in character or physique); *a beard may transform a man beyond recognition*); (Electr.) change voltage etc. of (current); hence ∿ABLE, ∿ATIVE, *adjs*. **2.** *v.i.* undergo transformation (*to, into*). [ME, f. OF *transformer*, or f. L TRANS(*formare* FORM²)]

tra′nsfōrm² (-ă′-, -ah′-) *n*. (Math. & Ling.) product of transformation. [f. prec.]

transformā′tion (tră-, trah-) *n*. transforming or being transformed (*has undergone a great transformation*); (Zool.) change of form esp. of insects; change from solid to liquid or from liquid to gaseous state or vice versa; (Math.) change from one (geometrical) figure or expression or function to another of same magnitude, value, etc.; (Phys.) transmutation of element; (Ling.) statement of basic equivalence of differently-structured sentences; woman's wig; ∿ **scene,** elaborate spectacular scene in pantomime with scenery etc. changing in sight of audience; hence ∿AL *a*. [ME f. OF, or f. LL *transformatio* (as TRANSFORM¹; see -ATION)]

transfōr′mer (-ă-, -ah-) *n*. In vbl senses; apparatus for reducing or increasing voltage of alternating current. [f. TRANSFORM¹+-ER¹]

transfū′s|e (-ă-, -ah-; -z) *v.t.* cause (fluid, or fig. quality etc.) to pass from one vessel etc. to another; permeate (lit. or fig.); (Med.) transfer (blood) from veins of person or animal to those of another, inject (liquid) into blood-vessel to replace lost fluid; so ∿ION (-zhon) *n*. [ME, f. L TRANS(*fundere fus-* pour)]

transgrě′ss (-ă-, -ah-; -s-, -z-) *v.t.* violate, infringe, go beyond bounds set by, (commandment, law, limitation, or abs.); so ∿ION (-shon), ∿OR, *ns*., ∿IVE *a*. [f. F *transgresser* or f. L TRANS(*gredi gress-* = *gradi* go)]

tranship. Var. of TRANS-SHIP.

transhū′mance (tră-, trah-; -s-h-) *n*. seasonal moving of livestock to another region. [F (*transhumer* f. L TRANS-+ *humus* ground; see -ANCE)]

tra′nsi|ent (-ă′-, -ah′-; -s-, -z-) *a*. & *n*. **1.** *a*. not permanent (*the transient affairs of this life*); quickly passing away, fleeting; of short duration, momentary, hasty, (*a transient gleam of hope*); (Mus.) unessential, serving only to connect (*transient chord, note*); hence ∿ENCE, ∿ENCY, *ns*., ∿entLY² *adv*. **2.** *n*. temporary visitor, worker, etc.; (Electr.) brief current etc. [f. L TRANS(*ire* go); see -ENT]

transillu′min|āte (tră-, trah-; -ōō′-) *v.t.* pass strong light through in order to inspect, esp. for diagnosis; so ∿A′TION *n*. [f. TRANS-+ILLUMINATE]

‖**tränsī′e** *n*. custom-house permit for passage of goods. [L TRANS(*ire* go) go across]

transi′stor (-ă-, -ah-; -ns-, -nz-) *n*. semiconductor device with three electrodes, performing same functions as thermionic valve but smaller, stronger, and consuming less power; ∿ (**radio**), portable radio set equipped with transistors; hence ∿IZE *v.t.*, design with transistors (rather than valves). [portmanteau wd, f. TRANSFER¹+RESISTOR]

tra′nsĭt (-ă′-, -ah′-; -s-, -z-) *n*. & *v*. **1.** *n*. going, conveying, being conveyed, across or over or through (*allowed 2 days for the transit of the lake; improved methods of transit by rail; goods delayed in transit*); passage, route, (*the overland transit*); *local conveying of passengers on public routes; apparent passage of heavenly body across meridian of place; apparent passage of heavenly body across disc of sun or planet. **2.** ∿ **camp** (for temporary accommodation of soldiers, refugees, etc.); ∿-**circle, -instrument,** (for observing transit of heavenly body across meridian); ∿-**compass, -theodolite,** surveyor's instrument for measuring horizontal angle; ∿-**duty** (paid on goods passing through a country); ∿ **lounge** (at airport, for passengers who will take off again soon after disembarking); ∿ **visa** (allowing only passage through country); **3.** *v.t.* & *i.* make transit (across). [ME, f. L *transitus* f. TRANS(*ire it-* go)]

transi′tion (-ă-, -ah-; -sī′zhon, -zī′shon) *n*.·passage or change from one place or state or act or set of circumstances to another (*came by an abrupt transition into hilly country; we live in an age of transition; is subject to frequent transitions from high spirits to depression*); (Mus.) momentary modulation; (Art) change from one style to another, esp. (Archit.) from Norman to Early English; ∿ **point** (Phys., at which different phases of same substance can be in equilibrium); hence ∿AL, ∿ARY¹, *adjs*. [F, or f. L *transitio* (as prec.; see -ION)]

tra′nsitĭv|e (-ă′-, -ah′-; -s-, -z-) *a*. **1.** (Gram.) taking a direct object expressed or understood (e.g. *pick* in: *pick peas, pick till you are tired*; opp. to *intransitive* as in *picked at the hole to make it bigger*). **2.** (Logic, of relation) such as to be valid for any two members of a sequence if it is valid for every pair of successive members. **3.** Hence ∿eLY² (-vlī) *adv*., ∿eNESS (-vn-), ∿ITY (-ĭ′v-), *ns*. [LL *transitivus* (as TRANSIT; see -ITIVE)]

tra′nsitor|ý (-ă′-, -ah′-; -s-, -z-) *a*. not permanent, lasting only a short time; ∿y **action,** (Law) one that can be brought in any country irrespective of where the transaction etc. occurred; hence ∿iLY² *adv*., ∿īNESS *n*. [ME, f. AF *transitorie*, OF *transitoire* f. L *transitorius* (as TRANSIT; see -ORY)]

translā′te (tră-, trah-; -s-, -z-) *v.t.* **1.** express the sense of (word, sentence, speech, book, poem, etc., or abs.) in or *into* another language; in or *to* another form of representation, in plainer words, etc. **2.** infer or declare the significance of, interpret, (signs, movements, conduct, hint, etc.; *I translated this as a protest; translated his gestures to the bystanders*). **3.** move from one person, place, or condition to another; (Eccl.) remove (bishop) to another see, (saint's relics etc.) to another place; (Bibl.) convey to heaven without death; transform. **4.** (Mech.) cause (body) to move so that all its parts travel in the same direction, impart motion without rotation to. **5.** Hence or cogn. ∿ā′tABLE, ∿ā′tionAL, *adjs*., ∿A′TION, ∿ā′tOR, *ns*. [ME, f. L *translatus*, p.p. of *transferre* (see TRANSFER¹)+-ATE³]

translĭ′ter|āte (tră-, trah-; -s-, -z-) *v.t.* represent (word etc., or abs.) in the more or less corresponding characters of a different alphabet or language; hence ∿A′TION, ∿ātOR, *ns*. [f. TRANS-+L *littera* letter+-ATE³]

translocā′tion (tră-, trah-; -s-, -z-) *n*. movement from place to place, esp. (Bot.) of substances in a plant. [f. TRANS-+LOCATION]

translu′c|ent (-ă-, -ah-; -s-, -z-; -ū′-, -ōō′-) *a*. transmitting light but not transparent; transparent; hence ∿ENCE, ∿ENCY, *ns*., ∿entLY² *adv*. [f. L TRANS(*lucēre* shine); see -ENT]

For other words in *trans*- see TRANS-.

translu′narў (-ă-, -ah-; -s-, -z-; -ū′-, -ōō′-) *a.* lying beyond the moon; (fig.) insubstantial, visionary. [f. TRANS-, after *sublunary*]

transmari′ne (tră-, trah-; -s-, -z-; -ē′n) *a.* situated or going beyond the sea. [f. L TRANS(*marinus* MARINE)]

transmīgr|āte (tră-, trah-; -s-, -z-; -ī′-) *v.i.* (Of soul) pass into, become incarnate in, a different body, undergo metempsychosis; migrate; hence or cogn. ∿ANT *a.* & *n.* (esp. alien passing through one country on way to another), ∿A′TION, ∿ātor, *ns.*, ∿atory *a.* [ME, f. L TRANS(*migrare* MIGRATE)]

transmi′ssion (-ă-, -ah-; -s-, -z-; -shon) *n.* transmitting or being transmitted; broadcast programme; mechanism by which power is transmitted from engine to axle in motor vehicle; ∿ **line**, conductor(s) carrying electricity over large distances with minimum losses. [f. L TRANS(*missio*; see MISSION)]

trans|mi′t (-ă-, -ah-; -s-, -z-) *v.t.* (**-tt-**). **1.** pass on, hand on, transfer, communicate, (*will transmit the message, the parcel, the title, the disease, the faculty; his writings have transmitted the principle to posterity*). **2.** allow to pass through, be a medium for, serve to communicate, (heat, light, sound, electricity, emotion, signal, news). **3.** Hence or cogn. ∿mi′ssIBLE, ∿mi′ssIVE, ∿mi′ttABLE, *adjs.*, ∿mi′ttAL *n.* [ME, f. L TRANS(*mittere* miss- send)]

transmi′tter (-ă-, -ah-; -s-, -z-) *n.* In vbl senses; equipment used to transmit message, signal, etc.; substance transferring message at junction of nerve fibre. [f. prec. + -ER¹]

transmö′gri|fў (-ă-, -ah-; -s-, -z-) *v.t.* (joc.) transform esp. in magical or surprising manner; hence ∿FICA′TION *n.* [17th c., of unkn. orig.]

transmö′ntāne (tră-, trah-; -s-, -z-) *a.* tramontane. [f. L *transmontanus* (see TRAMONTANE)]

transmūtā′tion (tră-, trah-; -s-, -z-) *n.* transmuting; change into another form, nature, or substance; (Alch.) supposed change of baser metals into gold etc.; (Phys.) change of one element into another by nuclear bombardment etc.; (Geom.) change of figure or body into another of same area or volume; (Biol.) Lamarck's theory of change of one species into another, whence ∿IST (2) *n.* [ME f. OF, or f. LL *transmutatio* (as foll.; see -ATION)]

transmū′t|e (-ă-, -ah-; -s-, -z-) *v.t.* change the form, nature, or substance of; subject to transmutation; hence or cogn. ∿ABI′LITY, ∿ER¹, *ns.*, ∿ABLE, ∿ATIVE, *adjs.* [ME, f. L TRANS(*mutare* change)]

transnā′tional (tră-, trah-; -s-, -z-) *a.* extending beyond national boundaries. [f. TRANS- + NATIONAL]

transōcĕä′nic (-tră-, trah-; -s-, -z-; -ōsĭ-, -ōshĭ-) *a.* situated beyond the ocean; (concerned with) crossing the ocean (*transoceanic flight of birds*). [f. TRANS- + OCEANIC]

tră′nsom *n.* **1.** horizontal (cf. MULLION) bar of wood or stone across window or top of door; ∿ **window** (divided by transom, or placed above transom of door or larger window). **2.** each of several beams fixed across stern-post of ship; beam across saw-pit; strengthening crossbar. **3.** Hence ∿ED² (-md) *a.* [ME *traversayn, transyn, -ing,* f. OF *traversin* (TRAVERSE)]

transö′nic (-ă-, -ah-; -s-, -z-) *a.* relating to speeds close to that of sound. [f. TRANS- + SONIC, after *supersonic* etc.]

transpaci′fic (tră-, trah-; -ns-, -nz-) *a.* beyond the Pacific; crossing the Pacific. [f. TRANS- + PACIFIC]

tra′nspadāne (tră′-, trah′-) *a.* situated beyond (usu. = north of) the Po. [f. L TRANS(*padanus* f. *Padus* river Po in N. Italy; see -ANE)]

transparence. Var. of foll. 1.

transparencў (tră-, trah-; -ă′r-, -ār′-) *n.* **1.** being transparent. **2.** picture, inscription, etc., made visible by light behind it; (Photog.) positive picture on glass as ornament or lantern-slide, or otherwise to be viewed by light from behind it; **his** etc. **T**∿ (arch. burlesque title = G *Durchlaucht*; cf. SERENITY). [f. med. L *transparentia* (as foll.; see -ENCY)]

transparent (tră-, trah-; -ă′r-, -ār′-) *a.* **1.** transmitting rays of light without diffusion so that bodies behind can be distinctly seen (cf. *translucent*); transmitting heat or other electromagnetic rays without distortion. **2.** (fig.) (Of disguise, pretext, etc.) easily seen through, (of motive, quality, etc.) easily seen through attempted disguise; evident, obvious, (*transparent sincerity*); easily understood; free from affectation or disguise, frank. **3.** Hence ∿LY² *adv.*, ∿NESS *n.* [ME f. OF, f. med. L *transparens* f. L TRANS(*parēre* appear) shine through; see -ENT]

transpier′ce (-ă-, -ah-) *v.t.* pierce through. [f. TRANS- + PIERCE]

transpīr′|e (-ă-, -ah-) *v.* **1.** *v.t.* emit through skin or lungs; send off in vapour. **2.** *v.i.* be emitted thus; pass off as perspiration; (Bot., of plant or leaf) exhale watery vapour. **3.** (fig.) (Of secret etc.) leak out, come to be known; (colloq.) occur, happen. **4.** Hence or cogn. ∿ABLE, ∿atory, *adjs.*, **transpir**A′TION (tră-, trah-) *n.* [f. F *transpirer* or f. med. L *transpirare* f. L TRANS- + *spirare* breathe]

transpla′nt¹ (tră-, trah-; -lah′-) *v.t.* plant in another place; remove and establish, esp. cause to live, in another place; (Surg.) transfer (living tissue or organ) and implant in another part of body or in another (human or animal) body; hence or cogn. ∿ABLE *a.*, ∿A′TION, ∿ER¹ (1, 2), *ns.* [ME, f. LL TRANS(*plantare* PLANT²)]

tra′nsplant² (tră′-, trah′-: -lah-) *n.* transplanting of tissue or organ; thing transplanted. [f. prec.]

transpö′nder (-ă-, -ah-; -s-, -z-) *n.* device for receiving radio signal and automatically transmitting a different signal. [f. TRANSMIT + RESPOND¹ + -ER¹]

transpö′ntine (-ă-, -ah-; -s-, -z-) *a.* on the other side of a bridge, esp. on south side of Thames; cheaply melodramatic, like the plays in 19th-c. Surrey-side theatres. [f. TRANS- + L *pons pontis* bridge + -INE¹]

transpö′r′t¹ (-ă-, -ah-) *v.t.* **1.** take (person, goods, troops, baggage, etc.) from one place to another, whence ∿ER¹ *n.*; ∿er **bridge** (carrying vehicles etc. across water on suspended moving platform). **2.** (Hist.) take (criminal) to penal colony; deport. **3.** (esp. in *p.p.*) affect with strong emotion (*transported with joy, anger, fear*). [ME, f. OF *transporter*, or f. L TRANS(*portare* carry)]

tra′nspört² (-ă′-, -ah′-) *n.* **1.** conveyance or transportation from place to place, means of this (*the transport has arrived*); ∿ **café** (providing meals for (esp. commercial) motor-vehicle drivers). **2.** ship or aircraft used to carry soldiers, stores, etc., to destination. **3.** (Hist.) transported convict. **4.** vehement emotion (*in a transport of rage; was in transports* (of joy etc.)). [ME, f. prec.]

transpör′t|able (tră-, trah-) *a.* **1.** that may be transported; hence ∿ABI′LITY *n.* **2.** (Hist.) (Of offender or offence) punishable by transportation. [f. TRANSPORT¹ + -ABLE]

transportā′tion (tră-, trah-) *n.* conveying or being conveyed from place to place; *means of this; (Hist.) removal to penal colony. [f. TRANSPORT¹ + -ATION]

transpö′s|e (-ă-, -ah-; -z) *v.t.* cause (two or more things) to change places; change position of (thing) in series; (Alg.) transfer (term) with changed sign to other side of equation; change natural or existing order or position of (words, a word) in sentence; (Mus.) write or play in different key; ∿ing **instrument** (producing notes different in pitch from the written notes); ∿ing **piano** etc. (on which transposition may be effected mechanically); hence ∿AL, ∿ER¹, *ns.* [ME, = transform, f. OF TRANS(*poser*, see COMPOSE)]

transposi′tion (-ă-, -ah-; -zĭ′-) *n.* transposing, being transposed; hence or cogn. ∿AL, **transpö′sit**IVE (-ă-, -ah-; -zī-), *adjs.* [F, or f. LL TRANS(*positio*; see POSITION)]

transsĕ′xual (tră-, trah-; -zs-; -ksū-, -kshōō-) *a.* & *n.* (person) having physical characteristics of one sex and psychological characteristics of the other; hence ∿ISM (2) *n.* [f. TRANS- + SEXUAL]

trans-shi′p (-ă-, -ah-; -nsh-, -ns-sh-, -nzsh-) *v.t. & i.* (**-pp-**). transfer from one ship or conveyance to another; hence ∿MENT *n.* [f. TRANS- + SHIP²]

trans-sonic. Var. of TRANSONIC.

transubstă′nti|āte (tră-, trah-; -shĭ-) *v.t.* change from one substance into another, esp. (Theol.) convert whole substance of Eucharistic elements into body and blood of Christ by consecration; so ∿A′TION (shĭ-, -sĭ-) *n.* [f. med. L *transubstantiare* (as TRANS-, SUBSTANCE) + -ATE³]

transū′d|e (-ă-, -ah-) *v.i.* (Of fluid) pass through pores or interstices of membrane etc.; so ∿A′TION *n.*, ∿atORY *a.* [f. F *transsuder* f. OF *tressuer* f. Gallo-Rom. *TRANS(sudare sweat)*]

transūrā′nic (tră-, trah-) *a.* (Chem.) (Of element) having higher atomic number than uranium. [f. TRANS- + URANIC]

Transvaa′l (tră-, trah-; -s-, -z-; -ah′l) *n.* ∿ **daisy,** orange-flowered S. Afr. herb (*Gerbera jamesoni*). [∿ in S. Afr.]

transvê̂r′sal (tră-, trah-; -nz-) *a. & n.* **1.** *a.* (Of line) cutting a system of lines; hence ∿ITY (-ă′l-) *n.*, ∿LY² *adv.* **2.** *n.* transversal line. [ME, f. med. L *transversalis* (as foll.; see -AL)]

tra′nsvêrse (-ă′-, -ah′-; -z-; *or* -êr′-) *a.* situated, arranged, acting, in crosswise direction (*transverse artery, ligament, section, stress*); ∿ **magnet** (whose poles are at sides and not ends); ∿ **wave** (vibrating at right angles to direction of propagation); hence ∿LY² (-slĭ) *adv.* [f. L TRANS(*vertere vers-* turn)]

transvê′st (-ă-, -ah-; -ns-, -nz-) *v.t.* (Psych.) clothe (usu. one*self*) in other garments esp. those of opposite sex; hence or cogn. ∿ISM (3), ∿IST (2), ∿ITE¹ (1), *ns.* [f. TRANS- + L *vestire* clothe]

tră′nter *n.* (dial.) carrier; hawker. [app. f. AF *traventer*, AL *trave(n)tarius*, of unkn. orig.]

trăp¹ *n., & v.t.* (**-pp-**). **1.** *n.* pitfall or enclosure or mechanical structure for catching animals, affording entrance but not exit and often baited and having door or lid actuated by spring; device for pigeons to enter but not leave loft; arrangement to measure speed of motorist without his knowledge, for detecting infringement of speed limit; golf bunker; (fig.) trick or arrangement for betraying person into speech or act (*is always setting traps for me; is this (question etc.) a trap?*). **2.** device for suddenly releasing bird, or throwing ball etc. into air, to be shot at; compartment from which greyhound is released at start of race; shoe-shaped wooden device with pivoted bar that sends ball from its heel into air on being struck at other end with bat (∿**-ball,** game played with this). **3.** device for preventing passage of steam etc.; U--shaped or other section of pipe so arranged as to prevent return flow of gas by means of permanent barrier of liquid. **4.** two-wheeled carriage with springs, e.g. dogcart. **5.** = *trapdoor*; (sl.) mouth (*shut your trap*). **6.** (colloq., esp. in *pl.*) percussion instrument esp. in jazz band. **7.** ∿′**door,** door flush with surface of floor or roof (∿*door spider,* kind that makes hinged trapdoor at top of nest); ∿**-shooting,** sport of shooting at objects released from trap. **8.** *v.t.* catch (animal, fig. person) in trap; furnish (place) with traps; stop and retain (as) in trap. [OE *treppe, træppe*; cf. syn. MDu. *trappe,* med. L *trappa;* ult. orig. uncert.]

trăp² *n.* (Min.) ∿(**-rock**), dark-coloured igneous rock of often columnar structure. [f. Sw. *trapp* (*trappa* stair, the rock freq. presenting a stairlike appearance]

trăp³ *v.t.* (**-pp-**). furnish with trappings. [f. obs. *trap* n., ME f. OF *drap;* see DRAPE]

trăp⁴ *n.* **1.** (Sc.) ladder leading to a loft. **2.** ∿**-cut,** = STEP²*-cut.* [app. = Du., MFlem. *trap* flight of steps]

trapes. Var. of TRAIPSE.

trapē′ze *n.* crossbar(s) suspended by cords used as swing for acrobatics etc. [f. F *trapèze* f. LL *trapezium* (see foll.)]

trapē′zi|um *n.* (*pl.* ∿**a** *or* ∿**ums**). ‖quadrilateral with one pair but not two pairs of sides parallel; *trapezoid. [LL, f. Gk *trapezion* (*trapeza* table)]

tră′pĕzoid *n.* ‖quadrilateral with no two sides parallel; *trapezium; hence ∿AL (-oi′d-) *a.* [f. mod. L *trapezoides* f. Gk *trapezoeidēs* (as prec.; see -OID)]

tră′ppĕan *a.* of the nature of the rock TRAP². [f. TRAP² + -EAN]

tră′pper *n.* one engaged in trapping wild animals esp. for furs. [f. TRAP¹ + -ER¹]

tră′ppĭngs (-z) *n. pl.* harness of horse esp. when ornamental; (fig.) ornamental accessories (*of* office etc.). [ME, f. as TRAP³ + -ING¹ + -s¹]

Tră′ppist *n.* member of branch of Cistercian order founded 1664 at La Trappe noted for silence and other austerities; hence ∿INE³ (-ĭn) *n.*, member of affiliated order of nuns. [f. F *trappiste* (La *Trappe* in Normandy; see -IST)]

tră′pp|ȳ *a.* (colloq., esp. of things). tricky, treacherous; hence ∿ĭNESS *n.* [f. TRAP¹ + -Y²]

trăps *n. pl.* (colloq.) personal belongings, baggage. [perh. contr. f. TRAPPINGS]

trăsh *n., & v.t.* **1.** *n.* worthless or waste stuff, rubbish, refuse; fragments or loppings of trees etc.; (cane-)∿, (W. Ind.) refuse of crushed sugar-canes and dried stripped leaves and tops of sugar-cane used as fuel. **2.** thing, e.g. literary production, of bad workmanship or material; nonsensical talk; worthless person(s). **3.** *∿**-can,** dustbin; ∿**-ice,** broken ice mixed with water; *white ∿, (derog.) the POOR white population in the Southern States. **4.** Hence ∿′ERY (1) *n.*, ∿′Y² *a.* **5.** *v.t.* strip (sugar-canes) of outer leaves to hasten ripening; discard as worthless; wreck. [16th c., of unkn. orig.]

trăss, tarră′s, *n.* light-coloured tuff used as cement-material. [f. Du. *trass,* earlier *terras, tiras* f. Rom.; cf. TERRACE]

trăttori′a (-ē′*a*) *n.* Italian eating-house. [It.]

trau′ma *n.* (*pl.* ∿**ta** *or* ∿**s**). (morbid condition of body produced by) wound or external violence; (Psych.) emotional shock. [Gk *trauma -matos* wound]

traumă′t|ic *a.* of or for wounds; or or causing trauma, (colloq.) unpleasant (*a traumatic experience*). [f. LL f. Gk *traumatikos* (as prec.; see -IC)]

trau′matism *n.* (condition produced by) action of trauma. [f. as TRAUMA + -ISM]

tră′vail *n., & v.i.* **1.** (arch.) (suffer) pangs of childbirth. **2.** (literary). (make) painful or laborious effort. [ME, f. OF (*travail* n. f.) *travaillier* f. Rom. *trepaliare f. med. L *trepalium* instrument of torture f. L *tres* three + *palus* stake]

tră′vel *v.* (‖**-ll-**) *& n. v.i.* make a journey esp. one of some length to distant countries (*ordered to travel for his health*); (colloq.) withstand long journey (*wines that travel badly*); act as COMMERCIAL traveller (*for* firm, *in* commodity); (of machine or part) move (*along* bar etc., *in* groove etc.); pass esp. in deliberate or systematic manner from point to point (*his eye travelled over the scene*); (of deer etc.) move onwards in feeding; move or proceed in specified manner or at specified rate (*horse travels slowly; light travels faster than sound, travels at thousands of miles per second;* ∿ **out of the record,** (fig.) wander from subject); (colloq.) move quickly along road etc. **2.** *v.t.* journey along or through; travel over, traverse, (distance). **3.** (in *p.p.*) experienced in travelling. **4.** ∿ling-bag, small bag carried in hand, for traveller's requisites; ∿ling-cap, -rug, etc., (of form suitable for travelling); ∿ling clock, small clock in a case; ∿ling crane (moving on esp. overhead support); ∿ling fellowship etc. (enabling holder to travel in order to study); *∿ling salesman, commercial traveller; ∿ling wave (in which particles of medium move in direction of propagation). **5.** *n.* travelling esp. in foreign countries (*has returned from his travels; do not like travel books*); range, rate, or mode of motion of part in machinery; ∿ **agency, agent, bureau,** (making arrangements for travellers); ∼-**sick**(**ness**), suffering from nausea induced by motion of vehicle etc.; ∼-**stained** etc. (as result of travel). [ME, orig. = prec.]

‖**trä′veller**, *-eler*, *n*. In vbl senses; moving mechanism (esp. TRAVELling crane); = COMMERCIAL *traveller*; ∼'s **cheque** or *check** (for fixed amount, encashable on signature usu. in many countries); ∼'s **joy**, wild clematis; ∼'s **tale**, incredible and probably untrue story. [ME, f. prec. + -ER¹]

trä′velŏgue (-g) *n*. film or illustrated lecture with narrative of travel. [f. TRAVEL, after *monologue* etc.]

travers|e *n*. & *v*. (trä′vers, travĕr′s). **1.** *n*. thing, esp. part of structure, that crosses another; gallery from side to side of church etc.; single line of survey (usu. plotted from compass bearings and chained or paced distances between angular points); tract thus surveyed; (Naut.) zigzag line taken by ship owing to contrary winds or currents; skier's similar movement on slope; sideways movement of part in machine; sideways motion across face of precipice from one practicable line of ascent or descent to another, place where this is necessary; (Mil.) pair of right-angle bends in trench to avoid enfilading fire; (Law) denial esp. of allegation of matter of fact; horizontal turning of large gun to required direction; ∼e-**table**, (1) nautical table for computing distance in traverses, (2) platform for shifting engine etc. from one line of rails to another. **2.** *v.t.* travel or lie across (*must traverse a vast extent of country; district traversed by canals*); (fig.) consider, discuss, the whole extent of (subject); turn (large gun) horizontally; deny esp. (Law) in pleading; thwart, frustrate, oppose, (plan, opinion). **3.** *v.i.* (Of needle of compass etc.) turn (as) on pivot; (of horse) walk obliquely; make traverse in climbing. **4.** Hence ∼ABLE *a*., **travĕr′sal** 2 *n*. [n. f. OF *travers(e)*, v. f. OF *traverser*, f. LL *traversare, transversare* (as TRANSVERSE)]

trä′verser *n*. In vbl senses; railway traverse-table. [f. prec. + -ER¹]

trä′vertine (-ĭn, -ēn) *n*. white or light-coloured calcareous rock deposited from springs. [f. It. *travertino, tivertino* f. L *tiburtinus* of Tibur (Tivoli), near Rome, see -INE¹]

trä′vèsty *v.t.*, & *n*. **1.** *v.t.* make (person or thing) ridiculous (intentionally or not) by grotesque representation. **2.** *n*. such treatment or imitation (*of*), esp. in literature. [orig. a., f. F *travesti* p.p. of *travestir* disguise, change the clothes of, f. It. *travestire* (*tra*-TRANS-, *vestire* clothe)]

travoi′s (-oi′) *n*. (*pl*. same *pr*. -oi′z). N. Amer. Ind. vehicle of two joined poles pulled by horse etc. and carrying burden. [f. earlier *travail* f. F, perh. same wd as TRAVAIL]

trawl *v*. & *n*. **1.** *v.i*. fish with trawl-net or seine-net. **2.** *v.t.* catch by trawling. **3.** *n*. act of trawling (lit. or fig.); ∼(-**net**), large bag-net with wide mouth held open, dragged along the bottom by boat; *∼(-**line**), long sea-fishing line buoyed and supporting short lines with baited hooks. [prob. f. MDu. *traghelen* to drag, cf. *traghel* drag-net, perh. f. L *tragula*]

traw′ler *n*. person who trawls; boat for use with trawl-net or trawl-line. [f. prec. + -ER¹]

tray *n*. flat utensil usu. of wood or metal and usu. with raised edge, for placing or carrying esp. small articles on; metal or other container on desk for correspondence (*in, out, pending, -tray*); shallow lidless box forming compartment in trunk; hence ∼′FUL 2 *n*. [OE *trīg, *trīeg* f. Gmc *traujam* (*trau-, *treu-* wood; see TREE)]

trea′cherous (-ĕ′ch-) *a*. violating faith or allegiance, betraying trust, perfidious; not to be relied on, deceptive, likely to fail or give way when used; hence or cogn. ∼LY² *adv.*, ∼NESS, **trea′cherv¹** (-ĕ′ch-), *ns*. [ME, f. OF *trecherous* (*trecheor* a cheat f. *trechier, trichier*; see TRICK, -OUS)]

trea′cle *n*. ‖syrup got in process of refining sugar; molasses; (fig.) cloying blandishments etc.; hence

trea′cly² *a*. [ME *triacle*, in sense 'theriac', f. OF f. L *theriaca* THERIAC]

tread (-ĕd) *v*. (**trod** *pr*. -ŏd, arch. **trode** *pr*. -ōd; **tro′dden** or **trod**) & *n*. **1.** *v.i*. set down one's foot, walk, step, (of foot) be set down, (*do not tread on the grass, in the mud; trod on a snake; fools rush in where angels fear to tread*); *tread in* person's FOOT¹*steps*; ∼ **lightly**, (fig.) deal cautiously with delicate subject; ∼ **on air** (of buoyant or jubilant person); ∼ **on** person's **corns** or **toes**, (fig.) offend against his feelings or privileges; ∼ **on eggs** (of person who needs to be very tactful); ∼ **on the heels of**, (fig., of event etc.) come closely or immediately after; ∼ (set one's foot lit. or fig. as sign of supremacy) **on the neck of** person. **2.** *v.t.* walk on, press or crush with the feet, (*treads a perilous path; trod the room from end to end*); *tread grapes* (in making wine); make track with (dirt etc.) from feet. **3.** perform, execute, in walking etc. (*trod a dozen hurried paces*); make (hole etc.) by treading; ∼ **a measure**, (arch.) execute a dance. **4.** (Of male bird) copulate with (hen, or abs.). **5.** ∼ **down**, press down with feet, trample on, crush, destroy; ∼ **in**, press in or into earth etc. with feet; ∼ **out**, stamp out (fire, fig. insurrection etc.), press out (wine, grain) with feet; ∼ **the stage** or **boards**, be an actor, appear on stage; ∼ **under foot**, trample on, destroy, treat contemptuously; ∼ **water**, maintain upright position in water with head above surface by action as if walking upstairs. **6.** *n*. manner or sound of walking (*recognized his heavy tread; approached with cautious tread*). **7.** (Of male bird) copulation; chalaza. **8.** ∼(-**board**), top surface of step or stair. **9.** part of wheel that touches ground or rails, thick moulded part of vehicle tyre, part of rail that wheels touch; CATERPILLAR *tread*; part of sole that rests on ground. **10.** ∼′**mill**, appliance for producing motion by stepping of man or horse etc. on movable steps on revolving cylinder, esp. kind formerly used in prisons as punishment, (fig.) monotonous routine; ∼-**wheel**, treadmill or similar appliance. [OE *tredan*, - OS *tredan*, OHG *tretan*, f. WG *tredhan*]

trea′dl|e (-ĕ′d-) *n*., & *v.t.* **1.** *n*. lever moved by foot and imparting motion to machine, e.g. lathe, sewing-machine, bicycle, reed-organ. **2.** *v.i.* work treadle. [OE *tredel* stair (as prec.; see -LE 1)]

trea′son (-z-) *n*. **1.** (**high**) ∼, violation by subject of allegiance to sovereign or to chief authority of State (e.g. by plotting sovereign's death or engaging in war against him); (**petit** or **petty**) ∼, (Hist.) similar offence against a subject, e.g. murder of one's master or husband. **2.** breach of faith, disloyalty, (*to cause, friend*, etc.). **3.** ‖∼-**felony**, attempt (regarded as felony or misdemeanour, not treason) to depose sovereign or make war in order to compel change of policy etc. **4.** Hence ∼OUS *a*. [ME, f. AF *treisoun* etc., OF *traïson*, f. L (as TRADITION)]

trea′sonab|le (-z-) *a*. involving the crime of treason; guilty of treason; hence ∼le**NESS** (-beln-) *n*., ∼LY² *adv*. [ME, f. prec. + -ABLE]

trea′sure (-ĕ′zher) *n*., & *v.t.* **1.** *n*. (literary) precious metals or gems, hoard of these, accumulated wealth, (*buried treasure; had amassed great treasure(s); a voyage in quest of treasure*). **2.** thing valued for rarity, workmanship, associations, etc., (*art treasures*); (colloq.) beloved or highly valued person. **3.** *v.t.* store (*up*) as valuable; receive or regard as valuable, store (*up*) in memory, (person's words, looks, etc.). **4.** ∼-**house**, place where treasures (esp. fig.) are kept; ∼-**hunt**, search for treasure, game in which players seek hidden object(s); ∼ **trove** [f. AF *trové* p.p. of TROVER], gold etc. found hidden of unknown ownership, (fig.) valuable object(s) found or collected. [ME, f. OF *tresor* f. Rom. *tresaurus* f. L THESAURUS]

trea′surer (-ĕ′zher-) *n*. person in charge of funds of municipality, society, company, club, etc.; officer authorized to receive and disburse public revenues; **Lord High T**∼, (Hist.) Crown officer controlling sovereign's revenues; ||T∼ **of the Household**, official ranking next to Lord Steward; HONORARY *treasurer*; hence ∼SHIP *n*. [ME, f. AF *tresorer*, OF -*ier* (*tresor*; see prec., ∼ARY[1], ∼ER[2]), after LL *thesaurarius*] **trea′sury** (-ĕ′zherĭ) *n*. **1**. place or building where treasure (lit. or fig.) is stored; (fig.) book, person, etc., viewed as repository of information etc. **2**. place where public revenues are kept; department managing public revenue of a country, officers of this; ||**Lords of the T**∼, board in charge of British public revenue, viz. Prime Minister (*First Lord of the T*∼), Chancellor of the Exchequer, and 5 junior lords; ||**T**∼ **bench**, front bench on right hand of Speaker in House of Commons, occupied by Prime Minister, Chancellor of Exchequer, and other ministers. **3**. ∼ **bill**, bill of exchange issued by the government to raise money for temporary needs; ∼ **note**, (||Hist.) note issued by Treasury for use as currency. **4**. Hence ∼SHIP *n*., treasurership. [ME, f. OF *tresorie* (as TREASURE; see -Y[1])]

treat *v*. & *n*. **1**. *v.t*. act towards, behave to, (*treated me abominably, kindly, as if I were a child; better treat it as a joke*). **2**. deal with or act upon (person, thing) with view to obtaining particular result, apply process to, subject to chemical agent etc., (*treated him for sunstroke; how would you treat a sprained ankle?; must next be treated with acid*). **3**. handle, deal with, (subject) in literature or art or speaking. **4**. give (person, or abs.) access to or to food and drink or entertainment (lit. or fig.) at one's own expense (*I will treat you all; think you might treat me to an ice cream; treated myself to a new hat*); (of candidate for election) give food etc. or cause these to be given to (electors) in order to influence election. **5**. *v.i*. negotiate terms (*with person*); ∼ **of**, = sense 3. **6**. Hence or cogn. ∼′ABLE *a*., ∼′ER[1], ∼′ING[1], *ns*. **7**. *n*. thing that gives great pleasure (*what a treat it is not to have to get up early*); entertainment designed to do this, e.g. picnic etc. for schoolchildren; treating of others to food etc. (**stand** ∼, bear expense of entertainment). [ME, f. AF *treter*, OF *traitier* f. L *tractare* handle frequent. of *trahere, tract*- draw, pull]

trea′tise (-s, -z) *n*. literary composition dealing more or less formally and methodically with definite subject. [ME, f. AF *tretis*, OF **traitiz* (*traitier*; see prec.)]

trea′tment *n*. (mode of) dealing with or behaving towards a person or thing (*received rough treatment from him; must follow the prescribed treatment; is now ready for treatment with acid*); mode of treating a subject in literature or art or speaking; **the** (**full** etc.) ∼, (colloq.) the customary way of dealing with a particular type of person etc. [f. TREAT + -MENT]

trea′tẙ *n*. formally concluded and ratified agreement between States; agreement between persons (*to do* etc.), esp. for purchase of property at price agreed by them alone, not by auction; **in** ∼, negotiating *with* (person *for* purchase etc.); ∼ **port**, (Hist.) one that a country was bound by treaty to keep open to foreign trade (esp. in Far East). [ME, f. AF *treté* f. L *tractatus* TRACTATE; see -Y[4]]

tre′ble *a*., *n*., & *v*. **1**. *a*. threefold, triple, whence **tre′bLY**[2] *adv*.; three times as much or many (*treble the amount*); (esp. ||of boy's voice or boy, or of instrument) = SOPRANO; (of voice etc.) high-pitched; ∼ **chance**, method of competing in football pool in which there are (orig.) three different possible scores from one's forecast of each match; ∼ **clef** (placing G above middle C on second lowest line of staff); *treble* RHYME[1]. **2**. *n*. treble quantity or thing; (Darts) throw on narrow ring enclosed between two middle circles of dartboard, scoring treble; (Racing) bet on three horses etc. as in DOUBLE[2]; = SOPRANO (see sense 1); high-pitched voice etc. **3**. *v.t*. & *i*. multiply, be multiplied, by three (*has trebled its value; its value has trebled*). [ME f. OF, f. L *triplus* TRIPLE]

tre′büchĕt (-sh-), **tre′bückĕt**, *n*. (Hist.) military machine for throwing stones etc.; tilting balance for

accurately weighing light articles. [ME f. OF (*trebucher* overthrow f. pop. L *TRANS*bucare* f. Frank. *buk belly)]

trece′nt|ō (-āchĕ′-) *n*. Italian style of art and literature of the 14th c.; hence ∼IST (2, 3) *n*. [It., = 300, used w. ref. to years 13—]

tree *n*., & *v.t*. **1**. *n*. perennial plant with single woody self-supporting stem or trunk usu. unbranched (cf. SHRUB[1]) for some distance above ground (CHRISTMAS *tree*); piece or framework of wood for various purposes; e.g. AXLE, ROOF, SHOE[1], SWINGLE, -*tree*; (arch. or poet.) gibbet, cross used for (esp. Christ's) crucifixion; (Math.) diagram of branching connecting lines; = *family* or GENEALOGICAL *tree*; **grow on** ∼**s**, (fig.) be plentifully available without effort; **up a** ∼, (fig.) cornered, nonplussed; *at the* TOP[1] *of the tree*. **2**. ∼ **agate** (with treelike markings); ∼ **calf**, calf binding for books stained with treelike design; ∼**-creeper**, bird of family Certhiidae feeding on insects in tree-bark; ∼**-dozer**, bulldozer for felling trees; ∼**-fern**, fern with upright stem attaining size of tree; ∼**-frog**, = *tree-toad*; ∼**-goose**, BARNACLE 1; ∼**-hopper**, insect of family Membracidae, living in trees; ∼**-house**, structure in tree for children to play in; ∼**-line**, = TIMBER-*line*; ∼**-milk**, juice of tree or shrub used instead of milk; ∼′**nail**, pin of hard wood for securing planks etc.; ∼ **of heaven**, ornamental Asian tree of genus *Ailanthus*, with ill-scented flowers; ∼ **of knowledge**, branches of knowledge as a whole; ∼ **of life**, arbor vitae; ∼ **onion** (producing bulbs on stems, not flowers); ∼**-ring**, ANNUAL ring in tree; ∼**-shrew**, squirrel-like arboreal mammal of family Tupaiidae; ∼ **sparrow**, ||small sparrow (*Passer montanus*), large sparrow (*Spizella arborea*), found among trees; ∼ **surgeon**, one who treats decayed trees in order to preserve them; so ∼ **surgery**; ∼**-toad**, arboreal amphibian climbing by means of adhesive discs on digits; *tree-*TOMATO; ∼**-top**, topmost branches of tree. **3**. Hence ∼′LESS *a*. **4**. *v.t*. force (animal, fig. person) to take refuge in tree; put into difficult position; stretch on shoe-tree. [OE *trēow*, = OS *treo*, ON *tré*, Goth. *triu* f. Gmc *trewam f. weak grade of IE **deru-*, **doru-*]

treen *n*. small domestic wooden object(s), esp. antiques. [f. *treen* a. wooden f. OE *trēowen* (as prec., -EN[5])]

tre′fa (-ā′-) *a*. not kosher. [f. Heb. *ṭerēpāh* flesh of animal torn (*ṭāraḥ* rend)]

tre′foil *n*. & *a*. 1. *n*. leguminous plant of genus *Trifolium* with leaves of three leaflets and flowers of various colours, clover; plant with similar leaves; three-lobed ornamentation in tracery etc. **2**. *n*. & *a*. (thing) arranged in three lobes; whence ∼ED (-ld) *a*. [ME, f. AF *trifoil* f. L TRI(*folium* leaf)]

trèha′la (-ah′-) *n*. manna-like substance of cocoon formed by a beetle of Asia Minor. [f. Turk. *tgala*]

trĕk *v.i*. (-kk-), & *n*. (orig. S. Afr.) **1**. *v.i*. (Of ox) draw vehicle, pull load; travel by ox-wagon or similarly with animals; travel arduously; migrate. **2**. *n*. such journey, each stage of it; organized migration, esp. of Boers 1835-7. [f. S. Afr. Du. (*trek* n. f.) *trekken* draw, travel]

trĕ′llis *n*., & *v.t*. **1**. *n*. (∼-**work**), lattice or grating of light wooden crossbars nailed together where they cross, similar structure of wire or metal, as screen or to support climbing plants, etc. **2**. *v.t*. furnish, support (vine etc.), with trellis. [ME, f. OF *trelis, trelice* f. Rom. *trilicius f. L TRI(*lix* f. *licium* warp-thread) three-ply]

trĕ′matōde *n*. parasitic flatworm of class Trematoda, e.g. fluke. [f. mod. L *Trematoda* f. Gk *trēmatōdēs* perforated (*trēma* hole; see -ODE[1])]

trĕ′mble *v.i*. & *n*. **1**. *v.i*. shake involuntarily from fear, agitation, physical weakness, etc., (*he was trembling with anger; voice trembled with excitement*); (fig.) be in state of extreme agitation, fear, suspense, etc., (*I tremble for his safety, to think what has become of him; tremble at the thought; no cause to tremble before his judge*); move in quivering manner (*leaves tremble in the breeze*);

(fig., of person's fate, life, etc.); ∼ **in the balance**, have reached a critical point, be in extreme danger. **2.** Hence or cogn. ∼MENT (-belm-) *n.*, **tre'mbl**y² *a.* (colloq.). **3.** *n.* trembling, quiver, (*there was a tremble in her voice*); **all of a** ∼, (colloq.) trembling all over. **4.** (in *pl.*) disease (esp. of cattle) marked by trembling. [ME, f. OF *trembler* f. med. L *tremulare* f. L *tremulus* TREMULOUS]

tre'mbler *n.* In vbl senses; automatic vibrator for making and breaking electric circuit; W. Ind. bird with continually shaking tail. [f. prec. + -ER¹]

tre'mbling *a.* In vbl senses; ∼ **bog** (formed over water etc. and shaking at every step); ∼ **poplar**, aspen. [f. TREMBLE + -ING²]

treme'ndous *a.* awe-inspiring, fearful, overpowering, (colloq.) remarkable, considerable, excellent, (*a tremendous explosion; makes a tremendous difference; gave a tremendous performance*); hence ∼LY² *adv.*, ∼NESS *n.* [f. L *tremendus* gerundive of *tremere* tremble + -OUS]

tre'molō *n.* (*pl.* ∼s). (Mus.) tremulous effect in singing or playing bowed instruments etc.; rapid continuous change of pitch during singing of note; device in organ producing tremulous effect; cf. VIBRATO. [It., as TREMULOUS]

tre'mor *n.*, & *v.i.* **1.** *n.* (Of leaf, part of body, voice, person) shaking, quivering; thrill (of fear, exultation, etc.); (**earth**) ∼, slight earthquake; **intention** ∼ (in part of body when it moves to do something). **2.** *v.i.* undergo tremor(s). [ME, f. OF *tremour* & f. L *tremor* (*tremere* tremble; see -OR)]

tre'mulous *a.* trembling, quivering, (*tremulous leaves, voice, hand*); (of line etc.) drawn by tremulous hand; timid, vacillating; hence ∼LY² *adv.*, ∼NESS *n.* [f. L *tremulus* (*tremere* tremble) + -OUS]

tre'nail. Var. of TREE*nail.*

trench *v.* & *n.* **1.** *v.t.* dig ditch(es) or trench(es) in (ground); turn over earth of (field etc.) by digging succession of contiguous ditches. **2.** *v.i.* (arch.) encroach (*up*)*on* (person's rights, privacy, etc.); verge or border closely (*up*)*on* (heresy, vulgarity, etc.). **3.** *n.* long narrow usu. deep depression or ditch, (Mil.) ditch with earth thrown up to form parapet, (in *pl.*) defensive system of these; long narrow deep area in ocean. **4.** ∼**-cart**, handcart on low wheels for use in trenches; ∼ **coat**, (soldier's) lined or padded waterproof coat, *loose belted raincoat; ∼ **fever**, form of fever affecting soldiers in trenches, spread by lice; ∼ **foot**, disease of feet caused by much standing in water; ∼ **mortar**, light simple mortar throwing bomb from one's own into enemy trenches; ∼ **warfare**, hostilities carried on from more or less permanent trenches. [ME, f. OF *trenchier* v., *trenche* n., cut f. Rom. *trincare* for L *truncare* TRUNCATE]

tre'nchant *a.* **1.** (arch. or poet.) sharp, keen, (*trenchant sword*). **2.** (Of style, language, policy, etc.) penetrating, incisive, decisive, vigorous; hence **tre'nch**ANCY *n.*, ∼LY² *adv.* [ME f. OF, part. of *trenchier* (see prec.)]

tre'ncher *n.* (arch.) wooden platter for serving food; ∼ (**cap**), stiff square academic cap, mortar-board; ‖∼**-fed**, (of hound) kept by a member of the hunt, not as one of a pack; **good, poor**, etc., ∼**man**, one who eats much, little, etc. [ME, f. AF *trenchour*, OF -*eoir* (*trenchier*; see TRENCH, -ER²)]

trend *v.i.*, & *n.* **1.** *v.i.* have specified general direction, bend or turn away in specified direction; (fig.) be chiefly directed, have general and continued tendency, (*towards* etc.). **2.** *n.* general direction and tendency (esp. fig. of events, opinion, etc.); ∼**-setter**, person who leads the way in fashion etc. [ME 'revolve' etc. f. OE *trendan* f. Gmc *trend-*, *trand-*, *trund-*; cf. TRUNDLE]

‖**tre'nd**y *a.* & *n.* (colloq., usu. derog.) **1.** *a.* fashionable, following the latest trend of fashion; hence ∼iLY² *adv.*, ∼iNESS *n.* **2.** *n.* trendy person. [f. prec. + -Y²]

tre'ntal *n.* (RC Ch.) set of 30 successive usu. daily masses for the dead. [ME, f. OF *trentel* & med. L *trentalis* f. pop. L *trenta* for L *triginta* thirty + -AL]

trente-et-quarante (trahṅtākārah'ṅt) *n.* = ROUGE-*et-noir.* [F, = 30 and 40]

trepa'n¹ *n.*, & *v.t.* (-nn-). **1.** *n.* surgeon's cylindrical saw for removing part of bone of skull; borer for sinking shafts. **2.** *v.t.* perforate (skull) with trepan; hence **trepan**A'TION, ∼NING¹, *ns.* [ME, (f. OF *trepaner* v. f. *trepan* n.) f. med. L *trepanum* f. Gk *trupanon* (*trupaō* bore f. *trupē* hole)]

trepa'n² *v.t.* (-nn-), & *n.* trap, snare, lure. [17th c., earlier *trapan* n., prob. thieves' sl. f. TRAP¹]

trepa'ng *n.* = BÊCHE-DE-MER 1. [f. Malay *trīpang*]

trephi'ne (-ī'n, -ē'n) *n.*, & *v.t.* **1.** *n.* improved form of trepan with guiding centre-pin. **2.** *v.t.* operate on (skull, cornea, person) with this; hence **trephin**A'-TION *n.* [orig. *trafine*, f. L *tres fines* three ends, app. formed after TREPAN¹]

trepida'tion *n.* alarm, flurry; tremulous agitation; trembling of limbs e.g. in paralysis. [f. L *trepidatio* (*trepidare* be agitated, tremble, f. *trepidus* alarmed; see -ATION)]

tre'spass *v.i.*, & *n.* **1.** *v.i.* make unlawful or unwarrantable intrusion (*on* or *upon* land, rights, etc., or abs.); ∼ **on** person's **preserves**, (fig.) meddle in a matter that he has made his own); make unwarrantable claim *on* (*shall trespass on your hospitality; may I trespass on your valuable time?*); (literary or arch.) offend (*against* person, law, principle, rights; *forgive them that trespass against us*); hence ∼ER¹ *n.* **2.** *n.* transgression of law or right; (Law) any transgression that is not (misprision of) treason or felony, wrongful entry on another's land with damage, tort against person or property, action arising from this. [ME, f. (OF *trespas* n. f.) *trespasser* pass over, trespass, f. med. L TRANS(*passare* PASS¹)]

tress *n.*, & *v.t.* **1.** *n.* portion, lock, plait, of hair of human (esp. woman's or girl's) head; (in *pl.*) hair of (esp. woman's or girl's) head; hence (-)∼ED² (-st), ∼'Y², *adjs.* **2.** *v.t.* (esp. in *p.p.*) arrange (hair) in tresses. [ME, f. OF *tresce, tresse* n., *tresser* v., perh. ult. f. Gk *trikha* threefold]

tre'ssure (-sher) *n.* (Her.) narrow orle. [ME, orig. = hair-ribbon, f. OF *tressour* etc. (as prec.; see -URE)]

tre'stle (-sel) *n.* supporting structure for table etc., consisting of bar supported by two divergent pairs of legs or of two frames fixed at an angle or hinged; ∼(**-table**), table of board(s) laid on trestles or other supports; ∼(**-work**), open braced framework of wood or metal or concrete for supporting bridge etc.; ∼(**-tree**), (Naut.) each of a pair of horizontal pieces on lower mast supporting topmast etc. [ME, f. OF *trestel* f. Rom. *transtellum* beam, dim. of L *transtrum*; see -LE 2]

tret *n.* (Hist.) allowance of extra weight formerly made to purchasers of some goods for waste in transportation; TARE² *and* tret. [ME f. AF & OF, var. of *trait* draught; see TRAIT]

trevă'lly *n.* Austral. food-fish of genus *Caranx.* [app. f. CAVALLY]

‖**trews** (-ōoz) *n. pl.* close-fitting usu. tartan trousers. [f. Ir. *trius*, Gael. *triubhas* (sing.); cf. TROUSER]

trey (trā) *n.* the three on dice or (arch.) cards. [ME, f. OF *trei*(*s*) three f. L *tres*]

TRH *abbr.* Their Royal Highnesses.

tri- *comb. form.* three, triple, thrice, (Chem., forming names of compounds) containing three atoms or groups of a specified kind, as: ∼**a'cetate** (containing 3 acetate groups, esp. as base for fabrics); ∼**ade'l-phous**, (Bot.) with stamens united in 3 bundles; ∼**a'ndrous**, having 3 stamens; ∼**a'xial**, having 3 axes; ∼**ba'sic**, (Chem.) having 3 replaceable hydrogen atoms; ∼**centenary** (-tē'-, -sē'-), = TER-CENTENARY; ∼**chlor'ide**, compound of element or radical with 3 atoms of chlorine; ∼'**chord** (-k-) *a.* & *n.*, 3-stringed (instrument esp. lute), (of piano) with 3 strings to most notes; ∼**chroma'tic**, having or using 3 colours (∼*chromatic photography*, THREE-colour process), (of vision) having the normal

3 colour-sensations, i.e. red, green, and purple; so ⁓*chro′matism* n.; ⁓**cor′poral**, ⁓**cor′porate**, (Her.) having 3 bodies and one head; ⁓**cotyle′donous**, with 3 cotyledons; ⁓**cro′tic** (-ŏ′t-), (of pulse) with triple beat; ⁓**cu′spid**, (tooth) with 3 cusps or points, heart-valve formed of 3 triangular segments; ⁓**da′ctyl(ous)**, with 3 fingers or toes; ⁓**de′ntate**, with 3 teeth or prongs; ⁓**di′gitate**, = *tridactyl*; ⁓**dime′nsional**, of 3 dimensions; ⁓**fa′cial**, = TRIGEMINAL; ⁓**fo′cal**, (of lens) having 3 parts with different focal lengths; ⁓**fo′liate**, (of compound leaf) with 3 leaflets, (of plant) having such leaves; ⁓**fo′liated**, (Bot.) trifoliate, (Archit.) trefoiled; ⁓**′form(ed)**, formed of 3 parts, having 3 forms or bodies; ⁓**fur′-cate**[1] (-at) *a.*, divided into 3 branches; ⁓**furcate**[2] (-āt) *v.t. & i.*, divide into 3 branches; ⁓**goneu′tic**, (Entom.) having 3 broods in a year; ⁓**′gram**, ⁓**′graph**, group of 3 letters representing one sound, figure of 3 lines; ⁓**′gynous** (trī′j-), having 3 pistils; ⁓**he′dral**, with 3 surfaces; ⁓**he′dron**, figure of 3 intersecting planes; ⁓**hy′dric**, (Chem.) containing 3 hydroxyl groups; ⁓**la′biate**, 3-lipped; ⁓**la′minar**, of 3 layers; ⁓**la′teral** *a. & n.*, (figure) having 3 sides, affecting or between 3 parties; ⁓**le′mma**, choice between 3 (unwelcome) things; ⁓**li′near**, of 3 lines; ⁓**li′ngual**, using, or in, 3 languages; ⁓**li′teral**, of 3 letters, (of Semitic language) having (most) roots with 3 consonants; ⁓**lo′bate**, 3-lobed; ⁓**lo′cular**, with 3 cells or compartments; ⁓**me′str(i)al**, occurring every 3 months; ⁓**′merous** (-ĭ′-), having 3 parts; ⁓**mor′phism**, ⁓**mor′phic** *or* ⁓**mor′phous**, (Bot., Zool., & Cryst.) existence, existing, in 3 distinct forms; ⁓**no′mial** *a. & n.*, (scientific name, algebraic expression) consisting of 3 terms; ⁓**no′mialism**, use of 3 terms in scientific naming of objects; ⁓**oe′cious** (-ē′sh-), (Bot.) with male, female, and hermaphrodite organs each on separate plants; ⁓**o′xide**, (Chem.) oxide containing 3 oxygen atoms; ⁓**pe′talous**, having 3 petals; ⁓**phy′llous**, three-leaved; ⁓**pi′nnate**, thrice pinnate; ⁓**′stichous** (-ĭ′stĭk-), (Bot.) arranged in 3 vertical rows; ⁓**stigma′tic**, ⁓**sty′lous**, (Bot.) having 3 stigmas, styles; ⁓**su′lcate**, (Bot.) 3-grooved, (Zool.) divided into 3 digits or hoofs; ⁓**ter′nate**, (Bot.) thrice ternate, having 27 leaflets; ⁓**′tone**, (Mus.) interval of 3 tones, augmented fourth; ⁓**valent** (-ā′-, -ă′-), (Chem.) having a valence of 3; ⁓**-wee′kly** *a.*, produced or occurring 3 times in a week or every 3 weeks. [L & Gk, f. L *tres*, Gk *treis* three]

tri′able *a.* that may be tried. [ME f. AF (as TRY; see -ABLE)]

tri′ad (-ăd, -ad) *n.* the number three; group of three; (Mus.) chord of three notes, esp. common chord; Welsh form of literary composition with arrangement in groups of three; (esp. criminal) tong; hence **triă′dic** *a.* [f. F *triade* or LL f. Gk *trias -ados* (*treis* three; see -AD)]

tri′age *n.* sorting according to quality; assignment of degrees of urgency to decide order of treatment of wounded etc. [F (*trier*; cf. TRY, -AGE)]

tri′al *n.* **1.** process or mode of testing the qualities of a thing, experimental treatment, investigation by means of experience, test, attempt, (*was found on trial to be incompetent; shall subject or put it to further trial; trial of the PYX*); *bicycle is hired, clerk employed*, **on** ⁓ (to be retained only if efficient); *will give you or it* **a** ⁓ (employ on trial); ⁓ **and error,** process of succeeding by repeated trying with or without improvement of method by learning from failures; ⁓ **of strength** (to find who is the stronger). **2.** trying thing or experience or person, esp. hardship, trouble, (*old age has many trials; fear you will find the boy, the piano next door, a great trial*). **3.** judicial examination and determination of issues between parties by judge with or without jury or by referee etc. (*was (put) on (his) trial or stood or was brought to or underwent trial for murder*). **4.** = *trial match*; test of individual ability on motor cycle over rough ground or on road; hence ⁓IST (3) *n.*

5. ⁓ **balance** (of ledger in double-entry bookkeeping), comparison of totals on either side, inequality of which reveals error in posting; ⁓ **balloon,** *ballon d'essai*; ⁓ **court** (opp. appellate court); ⁓ **eights,** two experimental rowing crews tried against each other with a view to selection of crew for boat race; *trial* HEAT[1]; *trial* JURY; ⁓ **match,** game of cricket, football, etc., in which players who may be selected for an important team take part; ⁓ **run,** ⁓ **trip,** new vessel's or vehicle's trip to test its performance, (fig.) experiment. [AF *trial, triel* (*trier* TRY; see -AL 2)]

tri′ångle (-nggel) *n.* **1.** figure (esp. plane) bounded by three (esp. straight) lines (SPHERICAL *triangle*); any three points not in one straight line, together with the imaginary lines joining them; ETERNAL *triangle*. **2.** implement etc. of this shape; right-angled triangle of wood etc. as drawing-implement; (Naut.) device of three spars for raising weights; (Mus.) steel rod in form of triangle open at one angle sounded by striking with small steel rod; (Hist.) frame of three halberds joined at top to which soldier was bound for flogging; ⁓ **of forces,** triangle whose sides represent in magnitude and direction three forces in equilibrium. [ME f. OF, or f. L *triangulum* neut. (as n.) of TRI(*angulus* ANGLE[1]) three-cornered]

triă′ngular (-ngg-) *a.* of the shape of a triangle, three-cornered, (of contest, treaty, etc.) between three persons or parties; ⁓ **compasses** (with three legs, for marking out triangles); ⁓ **numbers,** sums of the series 1, 6, 28, 55 [w. ref. to arrangement of such numbers of points in equilateral triangle]; ⁓ **pyramid** (with triangular base); hence ⁓ITY (-ă′r-) *n.*, ⁓LY[2] *adv.* [f. LL *triangularis* (as prec.; see -AR[1])]

triă′ngul|āte[1] (-ngg-) *v.t.* make triangular; divide (area etc.) into triangles for surveying; measure and map (area) by use of triangles with known base length and base angles, determine (height, distance, etc.) thus; hence ⁓A′TION *n.* [f. L (as TRIANGLE) + -ATE[3]]

triă′ngulate[2] (-ngg-) *a.* (Zool.) marked with triangles; hence ⁓LY[2] (-tlĭ) *adv.* [f. med. L *triangulatus* (as prec.; see -ATE[2])]

triă′ntelōpe *n.* large flat-bodied Austral. spider. [corrupt. of TARANTULA]

Tri′as *n.* (Geol.) earliest Mesozoic period or system, above Permian and below Jurassic; hence **Triă′ss**IC *a. & n.* [f. LL (as TRIAD); f. threefold subdivision in Germany]

triatō′mic *a.* (Chem.) having three atoms (of a specified kind) in the molecule; having three replaceable atoms or radicals. [f. TRI- + ATOM + -IC]

tri′bad|e *n.* woman who engages with another in simulation of sexual intercourse; hence ⁓ISM (2) *n.* [F, or f. L f. Gk *tribas* (*tribō* rub)]

tri′bal *a.* of tribe(s); hence ⁓LY[2] *adv.* [f. TRIBE + -AL]

tri′bal|ism *n.* tribal organization; so ⁓IST (2) *n.*, ⁓i′st**IC** *a.* [f. prec. + -ISM]

tribe *n.* **1.** group of (primitive) families under recognized chief and usu. claiming common ancestor; (Rom. Hist.) each of the political divisions (orig. three, probably representing clans, ult. 35) of the Romans; any similar division whether of natural or political origin, e.g. **the Twelve T**⁓**s** of the Israelites **the Ten T**⁓**s,** these without Judah and Benjamin; **the Lost T**⁓**s,** the Ten Tribes after deportation by Shalmaneser). **2.** (Biol.) group of plants or animals usu. ranking between genus and subfamily. **3.** (in *pl.*) large numbers. **4.** (usu. derog.) set, number, of persons esp. of one profession etc. or family (*the whole tribe of parasites, actors; the scribbling tribe*). **5.** ⁓**′sman** (-z-), member of a tribe or of one's own tribe. [ME, orig. in pl. form *tribuz, tribus* f. OF or f. L *tribus* sing. & pl.]

tri′blĕt *n.* mandrel used in making tubes, rings, etc. [f. F *triboulet* of unkn. orig.]

For other words in *tri-* see TRI-.

trĭ'bō- *comb. form.* rubbing, friction, as: ∿**electri'city,** generation of electric charge by friction; ∿**logy** (-ŏ'l-), study of friction, wear, lubrication, and design of bearings, science of interacting surfaces in relative motion; ∿**lumine'scence,** emission of light from a substance when rubbed, scratched, etc.; ∿**meter** (-ŏ'm-), instrument for measuring friction in sliding. [f. Gk *tribos* rubbing + -o-]

trĭ'brăch[1] (-k) *n.* (Pros.) foot of three short syllables; hence **trĭbră'ch**IC (-k-) *a.* [f. L f. Gk TRI(*brakhus* short)]

trĭ'brăch[2] (-k) *n.* object with three arms, esp. prehistoric flint implement. [f. TRI- + Gk *brakhiōn* arm]

tribūlā'tion *n.* great affliction or oppression (*trials and tribulations*); cause of this. [ME f. OF, f. eccl. L *tribulatio -onis* f. L *tribulare* press, oppress, (*tribulum* sledge for threshing, f. *terere trit-* rub); see -ATION]

tribū'nal *n.* judgement-seat, seat or bench for judge(s) or magistrate(s); court of justice; (fig.) place of judgement, judicial authority (*before the tribunal of public opinion*); board appointed to adjudicate regarding fair rents, exemption from military service, etc. [F, or f. L (as foll.; see -AL)]

trĭ'būn|**e** *n.* **1.** (Rom. Hist.) ∿**e** (**of the people**), each of origin. two, ultimately ten) officers chosen by the people to protect their liberties against senate and consuls; (**military**) ∿**e**, officer commanding legion for two-month periods. **2.** popular leader or demagogue. **3.** Hence or cogn. ∿ATE[1] (1), ∿eSHIP (-nsh-), *ns.*, ∿i'ciAL, ∿i'tiAL, (-shal), ∿i'ciAN, *adjs.* [ME, f. L *tribunus*, prob. f. *tribus* tribe]

trĭ'būne[2] *n.* raised floor for magistrate's chair in apse of Roman basilica; bishop's throne, apse containing this, in basilica; platform, stage, pulpit, esp. that used by speakers in French Chamber of Deputies; raised area with seats. [F, f. It. f. med. L *tribuna* for L TRIBUNAL]

trĭ'būtar|**y** *a.* & *n.* **1.** *a.* paying or subject to tribute (*tributary States*); contributory, auxiliary; (of river) flowing into larger river or into lake; hence ∿iLY[2] *adv.*, ∿iNESS *n.* **2.** *n.* tributary State, person, or stream. [ME, f. L *tributarius* (as foll.; see -ARY[1])]

trĭ'būte *n.* **1.** money or equivalent paid periodically by one State or ruler to another in acknowledgement of submission or as price of peace or protection, or by virtue of treaty; obligation to pay this (*was laid under tribute*). **2.** (fig.) contribution, esp. thing done, said, given, etc., as mark of respect, affection, etc., (*paid tribute to his great services; many floral tributes to actress, at funeral*); **a** ∿ **to,** an indication of (some praiseworthy quality). **3.** (Mining). proportion of ore or its equivalent paid to miner for his work, or to owner of mine. [ME, f. L *tributum* neut. p.p. (as n.) of *tribuere -ut-* assign, orig. divide between tribes (*tribus*)]

||**trĭ'cȧr** *n.* three-wheeled motor car. [f. TRI- + CAR]

trīce[1] *v.t.* (Naut.) ∿ (**up**), haul up (and secure in place); tie up. [ME, f. MDu. & MLG *trīsen*]

trīce[2] *n.* **in a** ∿, in an instant. [ME, f. prec.]

trī'ceps *a.* & *n.* **1.** *a.* (Of muscle) having three heads or points of attachment. **2.** *n.* triceps muscle, esp. large muscle at back of upper arm. [L, = three-headed, f. TRI- + -*ceps* (*caput* head)]

trĭchī'asis (-k-) *n.* (Path.) introversion of eye-lashes. [LL, f. Gk *trikhiasis* (*trikhiaō* be hairy; see -ASIS)]

trĭchī'n|**a** (-k-) *n.* (*pl.* ∿**ae**). hairlike nematode worm parasitic in body of man and carnivores; hence ∿IZE (3) *v.t.*, ∿o'sIS (-kī-) *n.*, disease caused by eating meat containing trichinae, **trĭ'chin**OUS (-k-) *a.* [mod. L, f. Gk *trikhinos* of hair (as foll.; see -INE[2])]

trĭ'cho- (-k-) *comb. form.* hair, as: ∿**genous** (-ŏ'j-), causing or promoting growth of hair; ∿**logy** (-ŏ'l-), study of the structure, functions, and diseases of hair; ∿**pa'thic** *a.*, ∿**pathy** (-ŏ'p-) *n.*, (treatment) of diseases of hair. [f. Gk *thrix trikhos* hair + -o-]

trĭ'chōme (-k-) *n.* (Bot.) hair, scale, prickle, or other outgrowth from epidermis of plant. [f. Gk *trikhōma* (*trikhoō* cover with hair f. as prec.; see -OMA)]

trĭchōmŏ'n|**ăd** (-k-) *n.* flagellate protozoan of genus *Trichomonas*; ∿**i'**ASIS *n.*, disease caused by this as parasite in man, cattle, or fowls. [f. TRICHO- + MONAD]

trĭchŏ'tom|**y** (-k-) *n.* division (esp. sharply defined) into three, esp. of human nature into body, soul, and spirit; so **trĭchotŏ'm**IC (-k-), ∿OUS, *adjs.*, ∿IZE (1, 3) *v.t.* & *i.* [f. Gk *trikha* threefold (*treis* three), after *dichotomy*]

trĭchrō'|**ic** (-k-) *a.* (Esp. of crystal viewed in different directions) showing three colours; so ∿ISM (2) *n.* [f. Gk TRI(*khroos* f. *khrōs* colour) + -IC]

trick *n.*, & *v.t.* **1.** *n.* fraudulent device or stratagem (*I suspect some trick; trick of the* TRADE); optical or other illusion (*misled by a trick of vision*). **2.** feat of skill or dexterity, trained animal's unusual action; knack, precise or best mode of doing or dealing with a thing; (*attrib.*) skilfully made to deceive or mystify (*trick photograph*); BAG[1] *of tricks*; **do the** ∿, (sl.) accomplish one's purpose, achieve desired result; **a** ∿ **worth two of that,** a better expedient; **how's** ∿**s?**, (sl.) how are you?, how are things? **3.** peculiar or characteristic practice, habit, mannerism, (*has a trick of repeating himself*). **4.** mischievous or foolish or discreditable act, practical joke, prank, (*is always playing mad tricks; a dirty or shabby trick to play*); **up to** one's ∿**s,** misbehaving; **up to** person's ∿**s,** aware of what he is likely to do by way of mischief. **5.** (Cards). the cards played in a round, one from each player; such round, point gained as result of this; hence ∿'LESS *a.* **6.** (Naut.) man's turn at helm, usu. two hours. **7.** ∿ **cyclist,** cyclist who performs tricks, (sl.) psychiatrist; *∿ **or treat,** Hallowe'en children's game of calling at houses with threat of pranks if sweets etc. are not given them; ∿ **wig** (of which hair can be made to stand on end). **8.** *v.t.* deceive by trick, cheat, (person; *out of* thing, *into* doing, etc.); (of thing) foil, baffle, disappoint the calculations of, take by surprise; ∿ (**out** or **up**), dress, decorate, deck. **9.** Hence ∿'ER[1], ∿'FRY (4, 5), ∿'STER, *ns.*, ∿'ISH[1] *a.* [ME, f. OF dial. *trique*, OF *triche* (*trichier* deceive, of unkn. orig.)]

trĭ'ckle *v.* & *n.* **1.** *v.i.* (Of liquid) flow in drops or in small stream (*tears trickled down her cheeks; water trickles through crevice*); (fig.) come or go slowly or gradually (*ball trickled into hole; audience, information, trickled out*). **2.** *v.t.* cause (liquid etc.) to trickle; pour out in drops. **3.** *n.* trickling stream; ∿ **charger,** accumulator-charger that works at a steady low rate from the mains. [ME *trekel, trikle*, prob. imit.; see -LE 3]

trĭ'cks|**y** *a.* playful, frolicsome; full of tricks; hence ∿iLY[2] *adv.*, ∿iNESS *n.* [f. TRICK; for -*sy* cf. *tipsy*]

trĭ'ck|**y** *a.* crafty, deceitful; skilful at evasion, resourceful, adroit; (of task etc.) requiring caution or adroitness, full of pitfalls, ticklish; hence ∿iLY[2] *adv.*, ∿iNESS *n.* [f. TRICK + -Y[2]]

trĭcli'nic *a.* (Cryst.) having three unequal oblique axes. [f. Gk TRI- + *klinō* incline + -IC]

trĭcli'ni|**um** *n.* (*pl.* ∿**a**). (Rom. Ant.) dining-table with couches along three sides; room containing this. [L, f. Gk TRI(*klinion* f. *klinē* couch)]

trī'colour, *-or, (-ŭler) *a.* & *n.* **1.** *a.* having three colours. **2.** *a.* flag of three colours, esp. French national standard of blue, white, and red, adopted during Revolution. [f. F *tricolore* f. LL TRI(*color* COLOUR[1])]

trī'coloured (-kŭlerd) *a.* = prec. [f. TRI- + COLOURED]

trī'cȯrn, -ne, *a.* & *n.* (imaginary animal) with three horns; (cocked hat) with brim turned up on three sides. [f. F *tricorne* or f. L TRI(*cornis* f. *cornu* horn)]

trī'cȯt (-ī'kō, -ē'ko) *n.* hand-knitted woollen fabric; imitation of this; ribbed woollen cloth. [F, = knitting (*tricoter* knit, of unkn. orig.)]

trī'cȳcl|**e** *n.*, & *v.i.* (ride on) three-wheeled pedal-driven road vehicle; three-wheeled motor vehicle for disabled driver; hence ∿IST (1) *n.* [f. TRI- + CYCLE]

trī'dent *n.* three-pronged implement e.g. fish-spear or gladiator's weapon; such spear or sceptre as attribute of Poseidon (Neptune) or Britannia. [f. L TRI(*dens dentis* tooth)]

Tridĕ'ntīne *a.* & *n.* **1.** *a.* of the Council of Trent (1545–63) esp. as basis of Roman Catholic doctrine and practice. **2.** *n.* strictly orthodox Roman Catholic. [f. med. L *Tridentinus* (*Tridentum* Trent = Trento in N. Italy; see -INE¹)]

tri'dūum *n.* (RC Ch.) three days' prayer in preparation for saint's day or other religious occasion. [L, neut. of **TRI(duus f. dies day)]

tri'dȳmīte *n.* (Min.) form of silica occurring in cavities of igneous rocks. [f. G *tridymit* f. Gk *tridumos* threefold (as TRI-, *didumos* twin), f. its occurrence in groups of three crystals, + -ITE¹]

tried. See TRY.

triĕ'nnial *a.* & *n.* **1.** *a.* lasting, recurring every, three years; hence ∼LY² *adv.* **2.** *n.* visitation of diocese by Anglican bishop every three years. [f. LL TRI(*ennis* f. *annus* year) + -AL]

triĕ'nni|um *n.* (*pl.* ∼ums *or* ∼a). period of three years. [L (as prec.)]

tri'er *n.* In vbl senses; person appointed to decide whether challenge to juror is well founded; tester esp. of foodstuffs; one who perseveres in his attempts. [ME, f. TRY + -ER¹]

tri'erȧr̄chȳ (-kǐ) *n.* (Gk Ant.) (Athenian formation of fleet at expense of) body of citizens compelled to provide triremes at their own expense. [f. Gk *triērar-khia* (*triērarkhos* such citizen f. *triērēs* trireme + *-arkhos* ruler)]

tri'fid *a.* (esp. Biol.) partly or wholly cleft into three divisions or lobes. [f. L TRI(*fidus* f. root of *findere* split)]

tri'fle *n.* & *v.* **1.** *n.* thing, fact, circumstance, of only slight value or importance (*wastes time on trifles; the merest trifle puts him out*; (iron.) *shall probably break our necks, but that is a trifle*); small amount esp. of money (*was sold for a mere trifle*); **a** ∼ *adv.*, somewhat (*seems a trifle angry*). **2.** ||confection of sponge-cake with custard or cream or white of eggs and fruit, jam, jelly, wine, almonds, etc. **3.** *v.i.* talk or act frivolously; ∼ **with**, treat (person, thing, matter) with flippancy or derision, refuse to take seriously, occupy oneself carelessly with, toy with, (novel, cigarette, etc.). **4.** *v.t.* throw or fool *away* (time, energies, money, etc., on object). **5.** Hence **tri'flER¹** *n.* [ME f. OF *truf(f)le* by-form of *truf(f)e* deceit, of unkn. orig.]

tri'fling *a.* In vbl senses; frivolous; unimportant, petty; hence ∼LY² *adv.* [f. prec. + -ING²]

trifor'i|um *n.* (*pl.* ∼a). gallery or arcade above arches of nave and choir (and transepts) of church. [AL, of unkn. orig.]

trig *a.*, & *v.t.* (-gg-). (arch. or dial.) (make) trim, spruce, smart. [ME, = trusty, f. ON *tryggr*, = Goth. *triggws* TRUE]

tri'gam|ous *a.* **1.** thrice married or having three wives or husbands at once; so ∼IST (3), ∼Y¹, *ns.* **2.** (Bot.) having male, female, and hermaphrodite flowers in same head. [f. Gk TRI(*gamos* -married) + -OUS]

trigĕ'minal *a.* & *n.* (of) cranial nerve of fifth pair, dividing into three branches (ophthalmic, maxillary, mandibular); ∼ **neuralgia** (involving one or more of these branches, and often causing severe pain). [f. as foll. + -AL]

trigĕ'min|us *n.* (*pl.* ∼i *pr.* -ī). trigeminal nerve. [L, = born as a triplet (TRI-, *geminus* born at same birth)]

tri'gger (-g-) *n.*, & *v.t.* **1.** *n.* movable device for releasing spring or catch and so setting mechanism in action, esp. projecting tongue in firearm that liberates hammer of lock; agent that sets off a chain reaction; HAIR-*trigger*; **pull the** ∼, initiate a process; **quick on the** ∼, (fig.) quick to respond; ∼-**fish** (whose first dorsal fin-spine can be depressed by pressing on second); ∼-**happy**, apt to shoot on slight provocation; hence (-)∼ED² (-erd) *a.* **2.** *v.t.* fire (gun) by use of trigger; ∼ (**off**), set in action, initiate or precipitate (process). [17th c. *tricker* f. Du. *trekker* (*trekken* pull; cf. TREK, -ER¹)]

tri'glȳph *n.* (Archit.) each of the three-grooved tablets alternating with metopes in Doric frieze; hence **trigly'ph**IC(AL) *adjs.* [f. L f. Gk TRI(*gluphos* f. *gluphē* carving)]

tri'gon *n.* triangle; ancient triangular lyre or harp; cutting region of upper molar tooth. [f. L f. Gk *trigōnon* neut. (as n.) of TRI(*gōnos* -cornered); cf. -GON]

tri'gonal *a.* of a triangle; (Biol.) triangular in cross-section; (Cryst.) having axis with threefold symmetry; hence ∼LY² *adv.* [f. med. L *trigonalis* (as prec.; see -AL)]

trigon|ŏ'metrȳ *n.* branch of mathematics dealing with relations of sides and angles of a triangle, and with relevant functions of any angles; hence ∼omĕ'tr**IC(AL)** *adjs.* [f. mod. L *trigonometria* (as TRIGON, -O-, -METRY)]

trīke *n.*, & *v.i.* (colloq.) tricycle. [abbr.]

tri'lbȳ *n.* **1.** ||∼(**hat**), soft felt hat with lengthwise dent in crown and narrow brim. **2.** (sl., in *pl.*) feet. [f. name of fair-footed heroine of G. du Maurier's novel *Trilby*, in stage version of which such a hat was worn]

tri'lith, tri'lithon, *n.* monument of three stones, esp. two uprights and a lintel; hence **trili'th**IC *a.* [Gk *trilithon* neut. of TRI(*lithos* stone)]

trill *v.* & *n.* **1.** *v.i.* (Of person or thing) give forth sound with tremulous vibration (*trilling laughter*). **2.** *v.t.* & *i.* sing in quavering manner, esp. (Mus.) with trill. **3.** *n.* quavering or tremulous sound, esp. (Mus.) quick alternation of two notes a (semi)tone apart, shake; (consonant pronounced with) vibration of tongue etc. [f. It. (*trillo* n. f.) *trillare*]

tri'lling *n.* compound crystal of three individuals. [f. TRI- + -LING¹, app. after Da., Sw. *trilling*, Du. *drieling*]

tri'llion (-lyon) *a.* & *n.* (for *pl.* usage see HUNDRED). ||a million million million; **a million million; hence ∼TH² *a.* & *n.* [F, or It. *trilione* (as TRI-, MILLION, after *billion*)]

tri'lobīte *n.* fossil marine arthropod of Palaeozoic times, characterized by a three-lobed body. [f. mod. L *Trilobites* (TRI-, Gk *lobos* lobe; see -ITE¹)]

tri'logȳ *n.* group of three related literary or operatic works, esp. (Gk Ant.) set of three tragedies to be performed in immediate succession. [f. Gk TRI(*logia* -LOGY)]

trim *a.*, *v.* (-mm-), & *n.* **1.** *a.* in good order, well arranged or equipped, neat, spruce; hence ∼LY² *adv.*, ∼'NESS *n.* **2.** *v.t.* set in good order, make neat or tidy, remove irregular or superfluous or unsightly parts from (lamp or strictly its wick, hedge, beard, folded sheets of book, etc.); remove (such parts; *off, away*) by clipping, pruning, planing, etc.; ∼ (**up**), make (person, one*self*) neat in dress and appearance; ornament (dress etc. *with* ribbon, lace, etc.); adjust balance of (ship, boat, aircraft) by distribution of ballast, cargo, or passengers, arrange (yards, sails) to suit wind (lit. or fig.), (*trim* BY¹ *the head, stern*); (colloq.) rebuke sharply, thrash, cheat out of money, worst in bargain etc. **3.** *v.i.* hold middle course in politics or opinion; attach oneself to temporarily prevailing views, or to neither of contesting parties; be time-server. **4.** *n.* state or degree of adjustment or readiness or fitness (*found everything in perfect trim*); **in** ∼, suitably dressed, healthy, etc., (Naut.) in good order; **in fighting** ∼, (of ship, or fig.) ready for battle. **5.** adornment; dress, equipment; decorative material on furniture, vehicle, etc. **6.** trimming of hair etc. **7.** inclination of aircraft to horizontal. [as n. & *v.* f. v., formally repr. OE *trymman, trymian* make firm, arrange; but there is no clear evidence for the verb from OE to 1500]

tri'marăn *n.* vessel like catamaran, with three hulls side by side. [f. TRI- + CATAMARAN]

tri'mer *n.* (Chem.) compound like DIMER but with three times the monomer atoms; hence **trīme'r**IC *a.* [f. TRI + -MER]

trimĕ'ster *n.* period of three months. [f. F *trimestre* f. L TRI(*mestris* f. *mensis* month)]

tri'mēter *n.* (Pros.) verse of three measures; hence

For other words in tri- see TRI-.

trīmě′trɪc(al) *adjs*. [f. L f. Gk TRI(*metros* f. *metron* measure)]

trï′mmer *n*. In vbl senses; one who trims articles of dress; person who trims in politics etc., time-server; instrument for clipping etc.; (Archit.) short piece of timber across opening (e.g. for hearth) to carry ends of truncated joists; small capacitor etc. used to tune radio set. [f. TRIM + -ER¹]

trï′mming *n*. In vbl senses; ornamentation of lace, braid, etc., on dress etc.; (in *pl*.) pieces cut off in trimming, (colloq.) usual accompaniments esp. of meat-joint etc. [f. TRIM + -ING¹]

trīne *a*. & *n*. **1.** *a*. threefold, triple, made up of three parts; ~ **aspersion** or **immersion**, thrice sprinkling in baptism; hence **trī′nal** *a*. **2.** *a*. & *n*. (Astrol.) (of) aspect of two heavenly bodies 120° (one-third of zodiac) apart; **in** ~, so related (*to*). [ME, f. OF *trin* *trine* f. L *trinus* threefold (*tres* three)]

trīnītrotŏ′lūēne, -ŭŏl, *n*. high explosive formed from toluene by substitution of nitro (NO₂) groups for three hydrogen atoms. [f. TRI- + NITRO- + TOLUENE]

trï′nĭtӯ *n*. being three; group of three; **the (Holy) T~,** (Theol.) union of three Persons (Father, Son, Holy Spirit) in one Godhead, doctrine of this, whence **Trīnĭtar′ian(ism)** *ns*.; **T~ (Sunday),** Sunday next after Whit Sunday; ‖**T~ Brethren,** members of **T~ House,** association concerned with licensing of pilots, erection and maintenance of lighthouses, buoys, etc., in England, Wales, etc.; ‖**T~ term** (in university etc., beginning after Easter). [ME, f. OF *trinité* f. L *trinitas -tatis* triad f. as TRINE; see -ITY]

trï′nkĕt *n*. trifling ornament, jewel, etc., worn on the person; small fancy article; hence ~RY (1, 5) *n*. [16th c., of unkn. orig.]

trī′ō (-ē′ŏ) *n*. (*pl*. ~s). **1.** (Mus.) (performers of) composition for three voices or instruments (**piano** ~, violin, violoncello, and piano); second division of minuet, scherzo, march, etc. (perh. orig. performed by trio of instruments). **2.** set of three; three aces, kings, queens, or jacks, in one hand at piquet. [F & It., f. L *tres* three, after *duo*]

trī′ōde *n*. thermionic valve having three electrodes; semiconductor rectifier having three terminals. [f. TRI- + ELECTRODE]

trī′ŏlĕt (-ē′-, -ī′-) *n*. poem of 8 (usu. 8-syllabled) lines rhyming *abaaabab*, first line recurring as fourth and seventh and second as eighth. [F (as TRIO; see -LET)]

trī′or. Var. of TRIER (Law).

trĭp *v*. (-pp-) & *n*. **1.** *v.i.* walk or dance with quick light steps; (fig., of rhythm etc.) run lightly. **2.** take a trip (*to* a place, or esp. (colloq.) with drugs); hence ‖~′per¹ *n*., person who goes on a trip esp. for a day's pleasure. **3.** ~ (**up**), make false step, stumble, (*on* or *over* obstacle, difficulty, etc.); make mistake, commit inconsistency or inaccuracy or moral delinquency. **4.** *v.t.* ~ (**up**), (of person or obstacle) cause (person) to stumble by entangling or suddenly catching his feet, (fig.) detect (person) in blunder. **5.** release and raise (anchor) from bottom by means of cable, turn (yard etc.) from horizontal to vertical position for lowering; release (part of machine) suddenly by knocking aside catch etc. **6.** *n*. journey, voyage, excursion esp. for pleasure (ROUND¹ *trip*); (colloq.) visionary experience caused by drug, EGO-trip. **7.** nimble step. **8.** stumble (lit. or fig.); tripping or being tripped up. **9.** contrivance for tripping mechanism etc. **10.** ~**hammer,** large TILT¹-*hammer* operated by tripping; ~**wire** (stretched near ground to trip up enemy etc. and often operating warning device, mine, etc.). [ME, f. OF *treper, trip(p)er,* f. MDu. *trippen* skip, hop]

trĭpär′tīte *a*. consisting of three parts; (Bot., of leaf) divided into three segments almost to the base; shared by or involving three parties; ~ **indenture** (with three corresponding parts or copies); hence ~LY² (-tlĭ) *adv.,* **trĭpärtī′tion** *n*. [ME, f. L TRI(*partitus* p.p. of *partiri* divide)]

trīpe *n*. first or second stomach of ox etc. as food; (in *pl.,* vulg.) entrails, belly; (sl.) worthless or trashy thing(s); ~**-de-roche** (trĕpderŏ′sh) [F, lit. rock-tripe], bitter slightly nutritive vegetable substance obtained from some lichens and used at a pinch by Canadian hunters etc. as food; ~′**man,** man who prepares and sells tripe; hence **trī′pery** (3) *n*. [ME f. OF, of unkn. orig.]

trĭphī′bious *a*. (Of military operations) on land, on sea, and in the air. [irreg. f. TRI- after *amphibious*]

trĭ′phthŏng *n*. union of three vowels (letters or sounds) pronounced in one syllable (as in *fire*); three vowel characters representing sound of single vowel (as in *beau*); hence ~AL (-ŏ′ngg-) *a*. [f. F *triphtongue* (as TRI-, DIPHTHONG)]

trī′plāne *n*. aeroplane with three sets of wings. [f. TRI- + PLANE³]

trī′ple *a*. & *v*. **1.** *a*. threefold, consisting of three parts or involving three parties (*triple entente*); *triple* ACROSTIC; **T~ Alliance,** alliance of three States etc.; ~ **crown,** (1) Pope's tiara, (2) winning of all three of group of important events in horse-racing, rugby football, etc.; ~ **fugue** (with three subjects); ~ **jump,** athletic exercise or contest comprising hop, step, and jump; ~ **play,** (Baseball) putting out three runners; *triple* RHYME¹; ~ **time** (Mus., with three beats to the bar). **2.** amounting or equivalent to three times the amount or number of; hence **trī′pLy²** *adv*. **3.** *n*. set of three; number or amount three times greater than another; (in *pl*.) peal of changes on seven bells. **4.** *v.t.* & *i.* multiply by three. [OF, or f. L *triplus* f. Gk *triplous*; v. ME, f. LL *triplare* f. L *triplus*]

trī′plĕt *n*. set of three things; three verses rhyming together; (Mus.) group of three notes performed in the time of two; one of three children or animals born at a birth. [f. prec. + -ET¹, after *doublet*]

trī′plĕx *a*. triple, threefold; **T~ (glass), (P)** toughened or laminated safety glass for car windows etc. [L TRI(*plex -plicis* f. *plic-* fold)]

trī′plĭcate¹ *a*. & *n*. **1.** *a*. threefold; (esp.) of which three copies are made. **2.** *n*. each of a set of three copies or corresponding parts; state of being triplicate (*document drawn up in triplicate*). [ME, f. L *triplicatus* p.p. of *triplicare* (as prec.; see -ATE²)]

trī′plĭcāte² *v.t.* treble, make triplicate; so ~A′TION *n*. [f. as prec. + -ATE³]

trĭplĭ′cĭtӯ *n*. state of being triple; group of three things; (Astrol.) set of three zodiacal signs 120° apart. [ME, f. LL *triplicitas* f. L TRIPLEX; see -ITY]

trī′ploid *a*. & *n*. (Biol.) (organism or cell) having three times the haploid set of chromosomes; hence ~Y¹ *n*., condition of being triploid. [f. mod. L *triploides* f. Gk (as TRIPLE; see -OID)]

trī′pŏd *n*. stool, table, utensil, resting on three feet or legs; three-legged stand for supporting camera etc.; (Gk Ant.) bronze altar at Delphi on which priestess sat to utter oracles; hence **trī′pod**AL *a*. [f. L *tripus tripodis* f. Gk TRI(*pous podos* foot)]

trī′pŏli *n*. = ROTTEN-stone. [F, f. T~ in N. Africa or in Syria]

‖**trī′pŏs** *n*. (Camb. Univ.) honours examination for degree of Bachelor of Arts. [as TRIPOD, w. ref. to stool on which BA sat to deliver satirical speech at Commencement]

‖**trī′pper.** See TRIP 2.

trĭ′ptych (-k) *n*. picture or carving on three panels with sides able to fold over centre, set of three associated pictures so placed, esp. as altar-piece; set of three writing-tablets hinged or tied together; set of three artistic works. [f. TRI- after *diptych*]

trĭptӯ′que (-ē′k) *n*. customs permit serving as passport for motor vehicle. [F, as prec. (orig. having three sections)]

trĭquĕ′tr|**a** *n*. (*pl*. ~ae). symmetrical ornament of three interlaced arcs; so ~AL, ~OUS, *adjs*., (esp. Biol.) triangular in cross-section etc. [L, fem. of *triquetrus* three-cornered]

trī′rēme *n*. ancient esp. Greek warship with three

banks of oars. [f. F *trirème* or f. L TRI(*remis* f. *remus* oar)]

Trĭsă′gĭŏn (-g-) *n*. hymn esp. in Eastern Churches with triple invocation of God as holy. [ME f. Gk, neut. of *trisagios* (*tris* thrice, *hagios* holy)]

trĭsĕ′ct *v.t.* cut or divide into three (usu. equal) parts; hence or cogn. ⌒ION, ⌒OR, *ns*. [f. TRI- + L *secare sect-* cut]

trī′shaw *n*. light three-wheeled pedalled vehicle used in Far East. [f. TRI- + RICKSHAW]

trĭskĕ′lion *n*. symbolic figure of three legs or lines from common centre. [f. Gk TRI- + *skelos* leg]

trī′smus (-z-) *n*. (Path.) = LOCK³*jaw*. [mod. L, f. Gk *trismos* = *trigmos* a scream, grinding]

triste (-ē-) *a*. sad, melancholy, dreary. [F, f. L *tristis*]

trī′stful *a*. (arch.) = prec. [f. obs. *trist* a. (as prec.) + -FUL]

trĭsy̆′llable *n*. word or metrical foot of three syllables; so **trĭsy̆′llă′bĭc** *a*. [f. TRI- + SYLLABLE]

trĭtă′gonĭst *n*. third actor in Greek play (cf. DEUTERAGONIST). [f. Gk *tritagōnistēs* (*tritos* third, *agōnistēs* actor)]

trīte *a*. (Of expression, sentiment, quotation, etc.) commonplace, hackneyed, worn out by constant repetition; hence ⌒LY² (-tlī) *adv.*, ⌒NESS (-tn-) *n*. [f. L *tritus* p.p. of *terere* rub]

trī′thē|ĭsm *n*. doctrine that there are (esp. that Father, Son, and Holy Spirit are) three Gods; hence ⌒IST (2) *n.*, ⌒i′stIC(AL) *adjs.* [f. TRI- + THEISM]

trī′tĭ|āte *v.t.* replace ordinary hydrogen in (substance) by tritium; hence ⌒A′TION *n*. [f. foll. + -ATE³]

trī′tium *n*. (Chem.) heavy radioactive isotope of hydrogen with mass about three times that of ordinary hydrogen. [mod. L, f. Gk *tritos* third + -IUM]

trī′tŏ- *comb. form.* third, as: T⌒Isaiah, supposed later author of Isaiah 56–66. [f. Gk *tritos* third + -o-]

Trī′ton¹ *n*. **1.** (Gk Myth.) minor sea-god usu. represented as man with fish's tail and carrying trident and shell-trumpet; *Triton among the* MINNOWS. **2.** (*t*⌒). marine gastropod of family Cymatiidae, with long conical shell; newt. [L, f. Gk *Trĭtōn*]

trī′ton² *n*. nucleus of tritium atom, consisting of proton and two neutrons. [f. TRITIUM + -ON]

trī′tŭr|āte *v.t.* grind to fine powder; masticate thoroughly; hence or cogn. ⌒ABLE *a.*, ⌒A′TION, ⌒ātor, *ns*. [f. L *triturare* thresh corn (*tritura* rubbing, as TRITE; see -URE) + -ATE³]

trī′umph *n.*, & *v.i.* **1.** *n*. state of being victorious or successful, signal success, great achievement, thing that constitutes this, (*returned home in triumph*; *has achieved great triumphs*; *the triumphs of science*); (at success, manifestation of this, exultation, (*great was his triumph on hearing this*; *could detect no triumph in his eye*). **2.** (Rom. Ant.) procession into Rome and ceremony in honour of victory and victorious general. **3.** *v.i.* gain victory, be successful, prevail, (*over* enemy, opposition, obstacles, etc.); (Rom. Ant.) enjoy a triumph; exult (*over* fallen enemy etc., or abs.). [ME; n. f. OF *triumphe*, v. f. OF *triumpher* f. L *triumphare*, f. L *triump(h)us*, prob. f. Gk *thriambos* hymn to Bacchus]

trĭŭ′mphal *a*. of, used in, celebrating, a triumph (*triumphal car, progress, hymn*); ⌒ **arch** (built to commemorate victory etc.). [ME f. OF, or f. L *triumphalis* (as prec.; see -AL)]

trĭŭ′mphant *a*. victorious, successful, (CHURCH¹ *triumphant*); (of person, speech, voice, etc.) exulting; hence ⌒LY² *adv*. [ME f. OF, or f. L *triumphare*; see TRIUMPH, -ANT]

trĭŭ′mvir *n*. (*pl.* ⌒s, or ⌒i *pr.* -ī). (Rom. Hist. etc.) each of three men united in office; each member of first or second triumvirate; hence ⌒AL *a*. [L, orig. in pl. *triumviri*, back-form. f. *trium virorum* gen. of *tres viri* three men]

trĭŭ′mvirate *n*. office of a triumvir; set of triumvirs or of any three persons (esp. in authority); (Rom. Hist.) first ⌒, (coalition 60 BC between) Pompey, Julius Caesar, and Crassus, second ⌒, (that in 43 BC

between Mark Antony, Octavian, and Lepidus. [f. L *triumviratus* (as prec.; see -ATE¹)]

trī′ūne *a*. three in one (*triune God head*); hence **trĭū′nĭTY** *n*. [f. TRI- + L *unus* one]

trī′vĕt *n*. iron tripod for holding cooking-vessels over heat; iron bracket designed to hook on to bars of grate for similar purposes; *metal plate on three feet for hot dish; **as right** (orig. = steady) **as a** ⌒, (*a*. & *adv.*, colloq.) in perfectly good health or position or circumstances; ⌒ **table** (with three feet). [ME *trevet*, app. f. L TRI(*pes pedis* foot) three-footed]

trī′via *n. pl.* trifles, trivialities. [mod. L, pl. of TRIVIUM, infl. by foll.]

trī′vial *a*. of small value or importance, trifling, (*trivial matters, offence, loss*; *raised trivial objections*); (of person) concerned only with trivial things; (arch.) commonplace, humdrum, (*the trivial round of daily life*); (Biol. & Chem., of name) (1) popular, not scientific, (2) specific, opp. to generic; (Math.) giving rise to no difficulty or interest; hence ⌒ITY (-ă′l-), ⌒NESS, *ns.*, ⌒IZE (3) *v.t.*, ⌒LY² *adv*. [f. L *trivialis* commonplace (*trivium*; see foll., -AL)]

trī′vium *n*. (Hist.) medieval university course of grammar, rhetoric, and logic. [L, = place where three roads meet (as TRI-, *via* road)]

-trix *suf.* (*pl.* **-trices** *pr.* -trīsĭz -or -trī′sēz, *or* **-trixes**), forming *fem.* agent *ns.* corresp. to masc. *ns.* in -*tor*, esp. in Law (*executrix, administratrix*) & Geom. = straight line (*directrix*). [f. L -*trix -tricis*]

troat *v.i.*, & *n*. (make) cry of rutting buck. [cf. OF *tr(o)ut*, int. for urging on hunting dogs etc.]

trŏ′cär *n*. (Surg.) instrument used in dropsy etc. for withdrawing fluid from body. [f. F *trois-quarts, trocart* (*trois* three + *carre* side, face of instrument), f. its triangular form]

trochā′ic (-k-) *a*. & *n*. (Pros.) **1.** *a*. of or using trochees (*trochaic dimeter, tetrameter*). **2.** *n*. (usu. in *pl.*) trochaic verse. [f. L f. Gk *trokhaikos* (as TROCHEE; see -IC)]

trŏ′chal (-k-) *a*. (Zool.) wheel-shaped; ⌒ **disc**, flattened end of rotifer serving to draw in food or to propel. [f. Gk *trokhos* wheel + -AL]

trochā′nter (-k-) *n*. (Anat. & Zool.) each of several bony processes for attachment of muscles on upper part of thigh-bone; second segment of leg in insects. [F, f. Gk *trokhantēr* (*trekhō* run)]

trŏche (-sh) *n*. small usu. circular medicated tablet or lozenge. [f. obs. *trochisk* f. OF *trochisque* f. LL f. Gk *trokhiskos* dim. of *trokhos* wheel]

trŏ′chee (-kē, -kī) *n*. (Pros.) foot consisting of one long followed by one short syllable. [f. L f. Gk *trokhaios* (*pous*) running (foot) (*trekhō* run)]

trŏ′chilus (-k-) *n*. small Egyptian bird mentioned by ancient writers as picking crocodiles' teeth. [f. L f. Gk *trokhilos* (*trekhō* run)]

trŏ′chle|a (-k-) *n*. (*pl.* ⌒ae). (Anat.) pulley-like part or arrangement; hence ⌒AR¹ *a*. [L, = pulley, f. Gk *trokhilia*]

trŏ′choid (-k-) *a*. & *n*. **1.** *a*. (Anat.) rotating on its own axis; (of curve) generated by a point moving with one curve that rolls on another; (of shell) top-shaped. **2.** *n*. trochoid joint or curve; top-shell. **3.** Hence ⌒AL (-koi′-) *a*. [f. Gk *trokhoeidēs* wheel-like (*trokhos* wheel; see -OID)]

trŏ′chus (-k-) *n*. top-shell, esp. of genus *Trochus*. [L, f. Gk *trokhos* wheel]

trŏd(′den), trŏde. See TREAD.

trŏ′glody̆t|e *n*. cave-dweller, esp. of prehistoric times; (fig.) hermit; anthropoid ape; hence or cogn. **trŏ́glo-dy̆t**IC(AL) *adjs.*, ⌒ISM (2) *n*. [f. L f. Gk *trōglodutēs* f. name of Ethiopian people, after *trōglē* hole]

trŏ′gŏn *n*. tropical bird of genus *Trogon*, with brilliantly coloured plumage. [mod. L, f. Gk *trōgōn* (*trōgō* gnaw)]

troi′ka *n*. (Russian vehicle with) team of three horses abreast; group of three persons, esp. as administrative council. [Russ. (*troe* three)]

For other words in *tri*- see TRI-.

troi'lism *n.* sexual activity in which three persons take part simultaneously. [perh. f. F *trois* three; see -ISM]

Trō'jan *a.* & *n.* **1.** (inhabitant) of Troy; ∼ **War** (legendary ten years' struggle between Greeks under Agamemnon and Trojans under Priam); ∼ **Horse**, hollow wooden horse used by Greeks to enter Troy, (fig.) person or device that is insinuated to bring about enemy's downfall. **2.** *n.* (fig.) person who works or fights or endures courageously (*like a Trojan*). [ME, earlier *Troyan, Troian,* f. L *Troianus* (*Troia* Troy, ancient city in NW Asia Minor)]

trōll[1] *v.* & *n.* **1.** *v.t.* & *i.* sing out in carefree jovial spirit; fish for, fish in (water), fish, with rod and running line and dead bait or with spoon-bait drawn along behind boat. **2.** *n.* trolling for fish; line or bait used in this. [ME 'stroll, roll'; cf. OF *troller* to quest, MHG *trollen* stroll]

trōll[2] *n.* (Scand. & Gmc Myth.) supernatural being, giant or (now usu.) friendly but mischievous dwarf. [f. ON & Sw. *troll*, Da. *trold*]

trō'lley, trō'lly, *n.* ‖low truck running on rails; ‖small table or stand on wheels or castors for use in serving food, transporting light objects, luggage, etc.; ∼(-**wheel**), wheel attached to pole etc. used for collecting current from overhead electric wire to drive vehicle (‖∼**bus,** electric bus running on road and using trolley; *∼***-car,** electric tram using trolley, *= trolley-car.* [of dial. orig., perh. f. TROLL[1]]

trō'llop *n.* slatternly woman, slut; prostitute; hence ∼ISH[1], ∼Y[2], *adjs.* [17th c.; perh. rel. to TRULL]

trŏmbōn|e (-ō'n, -ŏ'm-) *n.* large brass wind instrument with sliding tube, whence ∼IST (3) *n.*; its player; organ reed-stop of similar quality. [F or f. It. (*tromba* trumpet; see TRUMP[1], -OON)]

trō'mmel *n.* (Mining.) revolving cylindrical sieve for cleaning ore. [G, = drum]

tromŏ'mĕter *n.* instrument for measuring very slight earthquake shocks. [f. Gk *tromos* trembling + -METER]

trŏmpe *n.* apparatus for producing blast in furnace by using falling water to displace air [F, = trumpet, see TRUMP[1]]

trompe-l'œil (trŏmp lŭ'ē) *n.* & *a.* (still-life painting etc.) designed to make spectator think objects represented are real. [F, lit. 'deceives the eye']

-trŏn *suf.* forming *ns.* w. sense (1) thermionic valve etc. (*dynatron, klystron*), (2) elementary particle (*positron*), (3) particle accelerator (*betatron, cyclotron, synchrotron*). [f. ELECTRON]

trōŏp *n.* & *v.* **1.** *n.* assembled company, assemblage of persons or animals, (*a troop of children, of antelopes; surrounded by troops of friends*); (in *pl.*) soldiers, armed forces, (‖HOUSEHOLD *troops*); cavalry unit commanded by captain; unit of artillery and armoured formation; grouping of three or more Scout patrols. **2.** ∼**-carrier,** large aircraft, *or armoured vehicle, for transporting troops; ∼**-ship,** = TRANSPORT[2] 2. **3.** *v.i.* assemble, flock together; move in a troop (*along, in, out,* etc.); (colloq.) go, walk, *off* or *away.* **4.** *v.t.* form (regiment) into troops; ‖∼**ing the colour**(**s**), ceremony of transferring flags and carrying them along ranks of soldiers at public mounting of garrison guards. [F, f. *troupe*, back-form. f. *troupeau* dim. of med. L *troppus* flock, prob. of Gmc orig.]

trōŏ'per *n.* **1.** cavalry soldier; private soldier in cavalry or armoured unit; **swear like a** ∼ (extensively or forcefully). **2.** cavalry horse; troop-ship; (Austral. Hist. & US) mounted or motor-borne policeman. [f. prec. + -ER[1]]

tropae'olum *n.* S. Amer. trailing or climbing plant of genus *Tropaeolum*, with spurred yellow or scarlet flowers. [mod. L, f. L *tropaeum* TROPHY, w. ref. to likeness of flower and leaf to helmet and shield]

trōpe *n.* figurative (e.g. metaphorical or ironical) use of a word. [f. L f. Gk *tropos* turn, way, trope, (*trepō* turn)]

trō'phic *a.* concerned with nutrition (*trophic nerves*);

(as *suf.*) relating to nutrition (*autotrophic*). [f. Gk *trophikos* (*trophē* nourishment f. *trephō* nourish; see -IC)]

trō'pho- *comb. form.* nourishment, as: ∼**blast,** layer of tissue on outside of mammalian blastula thought to nourish embryo; ∼**neuro'sis,** defective nutrition due to derangement of nerves. [f. Gk *trophē* (see prec.) + -O-]

trō'ph|y *n.* **1.** thing made or kept or awarded as memorial of victory (lit. or fig.); memorial or token of valour, skill, etc.; ornamental group or symbolic or typical objects arranged on wall etc. **2.** (Gk & Rom. Ant.) arms etc. of vanquished enemy set up on field of battle or elsewhere to commemorate victory. **3.** Hence (-)∼IED[2] (-īd) *a.* [f. F *trophée* f. L *trop(h)aeum* f. Gk *tropaion* (*tropē* rout f. *trepō* turn)]

trō'pic *n.* & *a.* **1.** *n.* parallel of latitude 23° 27′ north (∼ **of Cancer**) or south (∼ **of Capricorn**) of the equator (**the** ∼**s,** region between these); each of the two corresponding circles on celestial sphere where sun appears to turn after reaching greatest declination; ∼**-bird,** ternlike sea-bird of genus *Phaethon.* **2.** *a.* = foll. 1; of tropism. **3.** (as *suf.*) = -TROPHIC; turning towards (*heliotropic*). [ME, f. L f. Gk *tropikos* (*tropē* turning f. *trepō* turn; see -IC)]

trō'pical *a.* **1.** of, peculiar to, suggestive of, the tropics, (*tropical fish, diseases, heat; tropical* YEAR); (fig.) very hot, passionate, luxuriant. **2.** of trope(s), figurative. **3.** Hence ∼LY[2] *adv.* [f. as prec. + -AL]

trō'pism *n.* (Biol.) turning of (part of) organism in particular direction in response to external stimulus. [f. second element of *heliotropism* etc.]

tropo'logy *n.* figurative use of words; figurative interpretation esp. of the Scriptures; hence **trŏpolŏ'gICAL** *a.* [f. LL f. Gk *tropologia* (as TROPE; see -LOGY)]

trō'popause (-z) *n.* interface between troposphere and stratosphere. [f. foll. + PAUSE]

trō'posph|ēre *n.* layer of atmospheric air extending about seven miles upwards from earth's surface, in which temperature falls with increasing height (cf. STRATOSPHERE); hence ∼**.ĕ'rIC** *a.* [f. Gk *tropos* turning + -O- + SPHERE]

trō'ppō *adv.* (Mus.) too; *andante* etc. **ma non** ∼, but not too much so. [It.]

trŏt[1] *v.* (-tt-) & *n.* **1.** *v.i.* (Of horse etc.) proceed at steady pace faster than walk lifting each diagonal pair of legs alternately, often with brief intervals during which body is unsupported; (of person) run at moderate pace esp. with short strides (*along* etc.), (colloq.) walk, go. **2.** *v.t.* cause (horse, person) to trot; traverse (distance) by trotting; ∼ **out,** cause (horse) to trot to show his paces, (fig.) produce, introduce, (person, thing, information, subject) for or as if for inspection and approval. **3.** *n.* action or exercise of trotting (*proceed at a trot; went for a trot*); (fig.) brisk steady movement or occupation; *(sl.)* student's crib; in *pl.*, Austral. colloq.) (meeting for) trotting-races; **the** ∼**s,** (sl.) diarrhoea; **on the** ∼, (colloq.) (1) continually busy (*kept him on the trot*), (2) in succession (*for five weeks on the trot*). [ME, f. OF (*trot* n. f.) *troter* f. Rom. & med. L *trottare,* of Gmc orig.]

Trŏt[2] *n.* (sl.) Trotskyist. [abbr.]

trŏth *n.* (arch.) **1.** truth; (**in**) ∼, **by my** ∼, truly, upon my word. **2.** faith, loyalty, (*pledge* one's *troth*); **plight** one's ∼, pledge one's word esp. in betrothal. [ME *trowthe,* for OE *trēowth* TRUTH]

Trŏ'tsky|ism *n.* political or economic principles of Trotsky, esp. as urging world-wide socialist revolution; so ∼IST (2), ∼ITE[1], *ns.* [f. L. *Trotsky* (L. D. Bronstein), Russ. politician d. 1940 + -ISM]

trŏ'tter *n.* In vbl senses; horse of special breed trained for trotting; (usu. in *pl.*) animal's foot used as food (*pigs' trotters*), (joc.) human foot. [ME, f. TROT + -ER[1]]

trŏ'tting *n.* in vbl senses; harness racing for trotting horses. [f. TROT + -ING[1]]

trottoir (trŏtwär') *n.* pavement at side of street. [F (*trotter* TROT)]

trō'tȳl *n.* trinitrotoluene. [f. trinitro*toluene* + -YL]

trou'badour (-ōō'badoor) *n.* lyric poet in S. France etc. in 11th–13th c., singing in Provençal mainly of chivalry and gallantry. [F, f. Prov. *trobador* (*trobar* find, invent, compose in verse)]

trou'ble (trŭ'b-) *v. & n.* **1.** *v.t. & i.* agitate, disturb, be disturbed or worried, (FISH[2] *in troubled waters*; *don't let it trouble you, don't trouble about it*; *has been troubled about* or *with money matters*); (in *p.p.*) expressing worry (*a troubled countenance*). **2.** *v.t.* afflict, cause pain etc. to, (*am troubled with neuralgia*; *how long has it been troubling you?*). **3.** *v.t. & i.* subject or be subjected to inconvenience or unpleasant exertion (esp. in polite or ironically polite speech: *may I trouble you to shut the door?*, *to mind your own business?*; *sorry to trouble you*; *don't trouble* (*to explain* etc., or abs.)). **4.** *n.* vexation, affliction, (*has been through much trouble*; *am having trouble with the ignition, with my teeth*); (in *pl.*) continuing public disturbances; faulty operation (*engine trouble*); disease (*suffers from kidney trouble*); cause of vexation etc. (*the trouble with him is that he always wants to win*); **ask for** or **look for** ∼, (colloq.) meddle, be rash, etc.; **in** ∼, subject to censure, punishment, etc., (colloq.) pregnant but unmarried; so **get** (*v.t. & i.*) **into** ∼; **make** ∼, cause disturbance or disagreement. **5.** inconvenience or unpleasant exertion (*did it to spare you trouble*; *shall not put you to any trouble in the matter*; *might have saved myself the trouble*; **give** oneself (**the**) ∼, **go to the, some,** etc., ∼, **take** (**the**) ∼, exert oneself to do something, cause of this (*fear that the child is a great trouble to you*; **be no** ∼, cause no inconvenience etc.). **6.** ∼ **and strife,** ||(rhyming sl.) wife; ∼**-maker,** troublesome person, esp. deliberate fomenter of disagreement; ∼**-shooter,** (1) person who traces and corrects faults in machinery etc., (2) mediator in diplomatic, industrial, etc., disputes; ∼**-spot,** place where trouble frequently occurs. [ME, f. OF (*truble* n. f.) *trubler, turbler* f. Rom. **turbulare* (**turbulus* for L *turbidus* TURBID)]

trou'blesome (trŭ'bels-) *a.* (Of person or thing) causing trouble, vexatious; hence ∼LY[2] (-mlĭ) *adv.,* ∼NESS (-mn-) *n.* [f. prec. + -SOME[1]]

trou'blous (trŭ'b-) *a.* (arch. or literary). full of troubles, agitated, disturbed, (*troublous times*). [ME, f. OF *troubleus* (as TROUBLE; see -OUS)]

trough (-ŏf, -awf) *n.* long narrow open wooden or other receptacle for holding water or food for sheep etc., kneading dough, washing ore, etc. (BOOK[1]-, PNEUMATIC, *trough*); wooden or other channel for conveying liquid; hollow between two waves; (Meteorol.) elongated region of low barometric pressure; region near minimum on curve of variation of a quantity. [OE *trog,* = OS, ON *trog,* OHG *troc* f. Gmc **trugaz* f. IE **drukós* (**dru-* wood, tree)]

trounce *v.t.* beat severely, castigate, (lit. or fig.). [16th c. 'afflict', of unkn. orig.]

troup|e (-ōōp) *n.* company of actors, acrobats, etc.; hence ∼ER[1] *n.,* member of a theatrical troupe, (fig.) staunch colleague. [F, = TROOP]

trou'ser (-z-) *n.* **1.** (**pair of**) ∼**s,** two-legged outer garment reaching from waist usu. to ankles; WEAR[1] *the trousers.* **2.** ∼**-clip,** = BICYCLE-*clip*; ∼(**s**) **pocket** (esp. as holding one's money, or hand when idle); ∼**-press** (to make or keep crease in legs of trousers); ∼**-suit,** woman's suit of trousers and jacket. **3.** Hence ∼ED[2] (-zerd) *a.,* ∼ING[1] (3) *n.* [in pl. as extended pl. form, after *drawers,* of arch. *trouse* sing., f. Ir. (& Gael.) *triubhas* TREWS]

trousseau (trōō'sō, trōōsō') *n.* (*pl.* ∼s or ∼x *pr.* -z). bride's outfit of clothes etc. to begin married life. [F, lit. bundle, dim. of *trousse* TRUSS]

trout *n.* (*pl.* usu. same). small fish of genus *Salmo* in northern rivers and lakes, esteemed as food and game; similar fish of family Salmonidae (SALMON or *sea trout*); (sl., derog.) *old* etc. woman; hence ∼'LET, ∼'LING[1] *ns.,* ∼'Y[2] *a.* [OE *truht* f. LL *tructa*]

trouvaille (trōō'vīl) *n.* lucky find, windfall. [F (*trouver* find)]

trouvère (trōōvār') *n.* epic poet in N. France in 11th–14th c. [f. OF *trovere* (*trover* find); cf. TROUBADOUR]

tröve *n.* = TREASURE *trove.*

trö'ver *n.* (Law). finding and keeping personal property; common-law action to recover value of personal property wrongfully taken or detained. [AF, f. OF *trover* to find; see -ER[4]]

trow (-ō, -ow) *v.t.* (arch.) think, believe. [OE *truwian, trēowian,* cogn. w. TRUCE]

trow'el *n., & v.t.* (||-ll-). **1.** *n.* mason's or bricklayer's flat-bladed short-handled tool for spreading mortar etc.; **lay it on with a** ∼, (fig.) flatter lavishly. **2.** gardener's short-handled scoop for lifting plants etc. **3.** *v.t.* apply (plaster etc.), dress (wall etc.), with trowel. [ME, f. OF *truele* f. med. L *truella* f. L *trulla* scoop dim. of *trua* ladle etc.]

troy *n.* ∼ (**weight**), system of weights used for precious metals and gems, with pound of twelve ounces or 5,760 grains. [ME, prob. f. *Troyes* in France]

trs. *abbr.* transpose.

tru'ant (-ōō'-) *n., a., & v.i.* **1.** *n.* one who absents himself from place of work, esp. child who stays away from school without leave; **play** ∼, stay away thus. **2.** *a.* (Of person, conduct, character, thoughts, etc.) shirking, idle, loitering, wandering. **3.** *v.i.* play truant. **4.** Hence **tru'ANCY** (-ōō'-) *n.* [ME f. OF, f. Gallo-Rom. **truant-* prob. f. Celt. (W *truan,* Gael. *truaghan* wretched)]

truce (-ōōs) *n.* (agreement for) temporary cessation of hostilities (FLAG[4] *of truce*); respite from pain etc., rest from work etc. (**a** ∼ **to,** (arch.) let us have done with); ∼ **of God,** (Hist.) suspension of war or of private feuds esp. during certain church festivals etc.; hence ∼'LESS (-sl-) *a.* [ME *trew(e)s* etc. pl. of *tru(w)e* f. OE *trēow,* OS *treuwa,* OHG *triuwa,* Goth. *triggwa* covenant]

tru'cial (-ōō'shal) *a.* (Hist.) of or bound by truce of 1835 between Britain and Arab sheikhs of Oman Peninsula. [f. prec. + -IAL, app. after *fiducial*]

trŭck[1] *v. & n.* **1.** *v.i.* (arch.) make an exchange, trade, bargain, (*with* person *for* thing). **2.** *v.t.* (arch.) exchange, barter, (thing *for* another). **3.** *n.* exchange, barter, traffic, (**have no** ∼ **with,** avoid dealing with); small wares; **market-garden produce (truck farm, garden*); (colloq.) odds and ends. **4.** ∼ (**system**), (Hist.) practice of paying workmen in goods instead of money or in money on the understanding that they will buy provisions etc. in ∼ **shop** from their employers. [ME, f. AF **truquer,* OF **troquer,* = med. L *trocare,* of unkn. orig.]

trŭck[2] *n. & v.* **1.** *n.* strong usu. four- or six-wheeled vehicle for heavy goods, lorry; ||open railway wagon; motor vehicle for transporting goods, troops, etc.; porter's two-, three-, or four-, wheeled barrow for luggage at railway station etc.; railway bogie; wheeled stand for transporting goods; (Naut.) wooden disc at top of mast with holes for halyards; small solid wheel. **2.** *v.t.* convey on or in truck. **3.** *v.i. *drive truck.* **4.** Hence ∼'AGE (1, 3, 4) *n.* [perh. short for TRUCKLE in sense 'wheel, pulley']

*trŭ'cker *n.* **1.** market-gardener. **2.** driver of truck. [TRUCK[1,2] + -ER[1]]

trŭ'ckle *v.i., & n.* **1.** *v.i.* submit obsequiously, cringe, (*to*); hence **trŭ'ckl**ER[1] *n.* **2.** *n.* ∼(**-bed**), low bed on wheels that may be pushed under another for storage, esp. as formerly used by servants etc. [n. ME f. AF *trocle* f. L TROCHLEA; v. orig. = to sleep in truckle-bed]

trŭ'cül|ent *a.* fierce, cruel; aggressive, savage; pugnacious; hence or cogn. ∼ENCE, ∼ENCY, *ns.,* ∼entLY[2] *adv.* [f. L *truculentus* (*trux trucis* fierce; see -ULENT)]

trŭdge *v. & n.* **1.** *v.i.* walk esp. laboriously. **2.** *v.t.* traverse (distance) by trudging. **3.** *n.* trudging walk. [16th c., of unkn. orig.]

trŭ'dgen *n.* swimming stroke like crawl with scissors

movement of legs. [f. J. *Trudgen*, 19th-c. Engl. swimmer]

true (-ōō) *a.*, *adv.*, & *v.t.* **1.** *a.* in accordance with fact or reality, not false or erroneous, (*his story is true*; *that is only too true*; *is it true that he refused?*); **come** ~, be realized in fact; (**it is**) ~, certainly, admittedly, (*true, it would cost more*). **2.** in.accordance with reason or correct principles or accepted standard, rightly so called, genuine, not spurious or hybrid or counterfeit or merely apparent, having all the attributes implied in the name, (*could not form a true judgement*; *frog is not a true reptile*; *is a true benefactor*, *the true heir*); *true* HORIZON, RIB, SKIN[1]; ~ **north** etc. (geographical, not magnetic). **3.** accurately conforming *to* (type etc.); ~ **to life**, showing life as it really is. **4.** (Of voice etc.) in good tune. **5.** loyal, constant, adhering faithfully, (*to one's word*, *friend*, *one*self, *etc.*) **6.** (Of wheel, post, beam, etc.) in correct position, balanced or upright or level; **out of (the)** ~, not in correct or exact position. **7.** (arch.) not given to lying, veracious; honest (*true men*). **8.** ~ **bill,** (Hist. & US) bill of indictment endorsed by grand jury as being sustained by evidence, (fig.) true statement or allegation; ~**-blue** *a.* & *n.*, (person, esp. ||Conservative or Presbyterian) of uncompromising orthodoxy or loyalty; ~**-born,** of genuine or legitimate birth, truly such by birth (*a true-born Englishman*); ~**-breed,** of genuine or good breed, ~**-hearted,** faithful, loyal; ~**-love,** (1) person truly loved or loving, sweetheart, (2) herb Paris, with four leaves arranged like ~**-love(r's) knot** (kind of double knot with interlacing bows on each side, symbolizing true love); ~**'penny,** (arch.) honest fellow. **9.** Hence ~'NESS *n.* **10.** truly (*tell me true*; RING[2] *true*); accurately (*aim true*); without variation (*breed true*). **11.** *v.t.* bring (tool, wheel, frame, etc.) into exact position or form required. [OE *trēowe*, *trȳwe*, = OS, OHG *triuwi*, ON *tryggr*, Goth. *triggws*, f. n. repr. by TRUCE]

trü'ffle *n.* edible subterranean fungus of genus *Tuber*, esteemed for its rich flavour; globular sweetmeat of chocolate mixture covered with cocoa etc., ~**-dog, -pig,** (trained to discover truffles) [prob. f. Du. *truffel*, f. obs. F *truffle* perh. f. pop. L *tufera* for L *tubera* pl. of TUBER]

||**trüg** *n.* wooden milk-pan; shallow garden basket made of wood strips. [perh. dial. var. of TROUGH]

tru'ism (-ōō'-) *n.* a self-evident or indisputable truth; proposition that states nothing not already implied in one of its terms (e.g. *I don't like my tea too hot* = *I don't like it hotter than I like it*); hackneyed truth, platitude. [f. TRUE + -ISM]

trüll *n.* (arch.) prostitute. [16th c.; cf. G *trulle*, TROLLOP]

tru'ly (-ōō'-) *adv.* sincerely, genuinely, (*am truly grateful*, *a truly alarming state of affairs*; YOURS *truly*); (usu. parenth.) really, indeed, (*truly, I should be puzzled to say*); faithfully, loyally, (*has served his master truly*); accurately, truthfully, (*it has been truly stated*; *is not truly represented*); rightly, properly, (WELL[3] *and truly*) [OE *trēowlīce* (as TRUE, -LY[2])]

trumeau' (trōōmō') *n.* (*pl.* ~**x** *pr.* -z). piece of wall, pillar, between two openings, e.g. pillar dividing large doorway. [F]

trümp[1] *n.* (arch. or poet.) (sound of) trumpet (LAST[3] *trump*; *trump of doom*). [ME f. OF *trompe*, f. Frank. *trumpa*, prob. imit.]

trümp[2] *n.* & *v.* **1.** *n.* playing-card of a suit temporarily ranking above others; (colloq.) person of great excellence; ~ **card,** card turned up to determine which suit shall be trumps, any card of this suit, (fig.) valuable resource; NO[1] *trump(s)*; **play a** ~, gain advantage esp. by surprise move; ||**turn up** ~**s,** (colloq.) turn out better than was expected, have a stroke of luck. **2.** *v.t.* take (card, trick) with a trump; ~ **up,** fabricate, invent, (story, excuse, accusation, etc.). **3.** *v.i.* play trump card when another suit has been led. [corrupt. f. TRIUMPH in same (now obs.) sense]

trü'mpery *n.* & *a.* **1.** *n.* worthless finery; rubbish; nonsense. **2.** *a.* showy but worthless, delusive, shallow, (*trumpery jewels*, *arguments*). [ME, f. OF *tromperie* (*tromper* deceive; see -ERY)]

trü'mpĕt *n.* & *v.* **1.** *n.* metal tubular or conical wind instrument with flared mouth and bright penetrating ringing tone, used for military etc. signals, by heralds, and in orchestral form having valves etc. to give additional notes; organ reed-stop with similar tone; trumpeter, esp. (Hist.) one sent as envoy; EAR[1], SPEAKING[1], *-trumpet*; trumpet-shaped thing, e.g. tubular corona of daffodil; sound (as) of trumpet; BLOW[1] one's *own trumpet*; **Feast of T**~**s,** Jewish festival celebrating beginning of year; FLOURISH[2] *of trumpets*; **marine** ~, large single-stringed viol with trumpet--like tone. **2.** ~**-call,** call by sound of trumpet, (fig.) urgent summons to action; ~**-creeper, -vine,** N. Amer. creeper with large red trumpet-shaped flowers; ~**-flower, -leaf,** plant with trumpet-shaped flowers, leaves; ~**-major,** head trumpeter of cavalry regiment; ~**-shell,** = TRITON[1] 2, esp. of genus *Triton*. **3.** *v.t.* proclaim (as) by sound of trumpet, (fig.) celebrate. **4.** *v.i.* blow trumpet; (of enraged elephant etc.) make loud sound as of trumpet. [ME, f. OF *trompette* dim. (as TRUMP[1]; see -ET[1])]

trü'mpĕter *n.* **1.** one who sounds a trumpet, esp. cavalry soldier giving signals with trumpet; **be one's own** ~, = BLOW[1] one's *own trumpet*. **2.** bird making trumpet-like sound, esp. variety of domestic pigeon, or large S. Amer. cranelike bird of genus *Psophia*; ~ (**swan**), large N. Amer. wild swan. **3.** fish making trumpet-like sound when taken from water, esp. Austral. & NZ food-fish of genus *Latris*. [f. prec. + -ER[1] or f. F *trompeteur*]

trü'ncal *a.* of the trunk of a body or tree. [f. TRUNK + -AL]

trü'nc|āte *v.t.*, & *a.* **1.** *v.t.* (or -ā't). cut top or end from (tree, body, screw-thread, cone, pyramid, (fig.) sequence, quoted passage, etc.), (Cryst.) replace (edge or angle) by plane; hence ~A'TION *n.* **2.** *a.* truncated; (Bot. & Zool., of leaf, feather, etc.) ending abruptly as if cut off at tip, whence ~āteLY[2] (-tlī) *adv.* [f. L *truncare* maim + -ATE[2,3]]

trü'ncheon (-shon) *n.* short club or cudgel e.g. that carried by policeman; baton, staff of authority, esp. (Her.) that of Earl Marshal. [ME, f. OF *tronchon* stump f. Rom. *truncio -onis f. L *truncus* trunk]

trü'ndle *n.* & *v.* **1.** *n.* small broad wheel, e.g. castor; set of parallel rods between two discs, serving as pinion; ~(**-bed**), truckle-bed. **2.** *v.t.* roll, move on wheel(s), (esp. heavily or noisily; hoop, truck, etc., along, down, etc.). **3.** *v.i.* (of hoop etc.) move thus. [var. of obs. or dial. *trendle*, *trindle*, f. OE *trendel* circle (as TREND)]

trünk *n.* **1.** main stem of tree opp. to branches and roots; human or animal body apart from head and limbs (and tail); main part of any structure. **2.** main body of artery, nerve, etc.; ~(**-line**), main line of railway or canal or air transport, main telephone line (esp. from town to town). **3.** large box with hinged lid, for carrying clothes etc. on journey (WARDROBE *trunk*); *boot of motor car. **4.** shaft, conduit, or trough, usu. rectangular of wood, for ventilation, separation of ores, etc. **5.** long flexible nose of elephant etc. **6.** (in *pl.*) short breeches worn with tights etc.; close-fitting shorts worn by men for swimming, boxing, etc.; men's short underpants. **7.** ~**-call,** telephone call on trunk-line with charges according to distance; ~ **hose,** 16th–17th-c. puffed breeches from waist to middle of thigh; ~**-nail,** nail with large ornamental head for trunk, coffin, etc.; ||~**-road,** important main road. **8.** Hence ~'FUL 2 *n.*, ~'LESS *a.* [ME f. OF *tronc* f. L *truncus*]

trü'nnion (-yon) *n.* supporting cylindrical projection on each side of cannon or mortar; hollow gudgeon supporting cylinder in steam-engine and giving passage to steam. [f. F *trognon* core, tree-trunk, of unkn. orig.]

truss 1152 **tryst**

trüss *v.t.*, & *n*. **1.** *v.t.* support (roof, bridge, etc.) with truss (sense 3). **2.** fasten (wings of fowl etc.), fasten wings etc. of (fowl etc.), before cooking; ∼ (**up**), tie arms of (person) to his sides; ∼ (**up**), (arch.) fasten, tighten, (garment), hang (criminal). **3.** *n*. supporting structure or framework of roof, bridge, etc., e.g. pair of rafters with tie-beam, king-post, and struts. **4.** ||bundle of old (56 lb.) or new (60 lb.) hay or (36 lb.) straw. **5.** compact terminal cluster of flowers or fruit. **6.** large corbel supporting monument etc. **7.** (Naut.) heavy iron ring securing lower yards to mast. **8.** padded belt or encircling spring used to support hernia. [ME, f. OF *trusser* v., *trusse* n., of unkn. orig.]

trüst *n*. & *v*. **1.** *n*. firm belief in reliability, honesty, veracity, justice, strength, etc., of person or thing, (*our trust is in God*; *I have* or *place* or *put considerable trust in him*; *put no trust in him*); confident expectation (*that*). **2.** person or thing confided in (*he is our sole trust*). **3.** reliance on truth of statement etc. without examination; **take on** ∼, accept without evidence. **4.** commercial credit (*obtained goods on trust*). **5.** responsibility arising from confidence reposed in one (*am in a position of trust*). **6.** (Law). confidence reposed in person by making him nominal owner of property to be used for another's benefit; right of the latter to benefit by such property; property so held, legal relation between holder and property so held; **in** ∼, so held. **7.** thing or person committed to one's care, resulting obligation, (*would not desert his trust*; *have fulfilled my trust*). **8.** (organization managed by) body of trustees; organized association of several companies for purpose of reducing or defeating competition etc., esp. one in which all or most stock is transferred to central committee and shareholders lose voting power while remaining entitled to profits, whence ∼**iFICA′TION** *n*., ∼**′iFY** *v.t.* **9.** **BRAIN**(*s*) *trust*; ∼ **company** (formed to act as trustee or deal with trusts); ∼**-deed**, deed by debtor conveying property to trustee for payment of creditor, deed conveying property to creditor to sell and pay himself and restore the residue, any instrument of conveyance that creates a trust; ∼ **territory**, one under trusteeship of (State designated by) United Nations; ||**UNIT** *trust*. **10.** *v.t.* place trust in, believe in, rely on the character or behaviour of, (*have never trusted him*; *if we may trust this account*; *can trust him to do his best*; (in *imper.*, colloq., iron.) *trust him to get it wrong*); ∼ **person with,** allow him to use (thing) because one is confident that he will not misuse it; hence ∼**ING²** *a*. **11.** consign (thing *to* person etc.), place or leave (thing *with* person etc., *in* place etc.), without misgivings. **12.** allow credit to (customer *for* goods). **13.** entertain an earnest or (occas.) confident hope (*I trust he is not hurt(?)*; *I trust to hear better news*). **14.** *v.i.* place reliance *in*; ∼ **to,** place (esp. undue) reliance on (*we must trust to meeting someone who knows*; *decided to trust to luck*; *does not do to trust to memory for these things*). [ME *troste*, trun. f. ON *traust* (*traustr* strong); v. f. ON *treysta* w. assim. to n.]

trüstee′ *n*. person who holds property in trust for another (||**the Public T**∼, State official executing wills and trusts when invited); each of a body of persons, often elective, managing affairs of institution; State made responsible for government of an area; one who is responsible for preservation and administration of a thing; hence ∼**SHIP** *n*. [f. prec. + -EE]

trü′stful *a*. full of trust, unsuspicious, confiding; hence ∼**LY²** *adv.*, ∼**NESS** *n*. [f. TRUST + -FUL]

trü′stworth|**y** (-ĕrdhī) *a*. worthy of trust, reliable; hence ∼**iLY²** *adv.*, ∼**iNESS** *n*. [f. TRUST + -WORTHY]

trü′st|**y** *a*. & *n*. **1.** *a*. (arch.) trustworthy (*trusty steed, sword, servant*), whence ∼**iLY²** *adv.*, ∼**iNESS** *n*.; ||∼**y and well-beloved** (in sovereign's epistolary form of address to subjects). **2.** *n*. well-behaved and privileged convict. [ME f. TRUST + -Y²]

truth (-ōō) *n*. (*pl. pr.* -dhz *or* -ths). quality or state of being true or accurate or honest or sincere or loyal or accurately shaped or adjusted (*the truth of the rumour is doubted*; *there is (some) truth in what he says*; *wheel is out of truth*); what is true (*have told you the (whole) truth*; *the truth is that I forgot*; *am a lover of truth*; *fundamental truths*); GOD's, GOSPEL, HALF-, HOME¹, *truth*; **in** ∼ (literary), **of a** ∼ (arch.), truly, really; MOMENT *of truth*; **to tell the** ∼, ∼ **to tell,** (introducing a confession); ∼ **drug,** substance administered in supposition that it will make person tell the truth; ∼ **table,** list indicating truth or falsity of various propositions in logic etc.; hence ∼ **LESS** *a*. [OE *trīewth*, *trēowth* (as TRUE; see -TH¹)]

tru′thful (-ōō′-) *a*. habitually speaking the truth, veracious; (of tale etc.) true; hence ∼**LY²** *adv.*, ∼**NESS** *n*. [f. prec. + -FUL]

trȳ *v*. & *n*. **1.** *v.t.* test (quality), test the qualities of (person, thing), by experiment, subject (person etc.) to suffering or hard treatment (as if) for this purpose, (*try your skill, strength*; *try it on the* DOG¹; *rope must be tried before it is used*; *try for* SIZE¹; *this will try his courage*; *my patience has been sorely tried*; *should not try your eyes with that small print*); examine the effectiveness or usefulness of for a purpose (*try soap and water, Woolworths, our ginger ale, quinine, the top shelf, the back door, shaking it*); ascertain state of fastening of (door, window, etc.); ∼ one's **hand,** see how skilful one is, esp. at first attempt. **2.** make experiment in order to find out (*let us try which takes longest, whether it will break*); *try* CONCLUSIONS, *a* FALL². **3.** investigate and decide (case, issue) judicially; subject (person) to trial (*for murder*, etc., or *for his life*); (arch.) settle (question) by investigation; ***(of lawyer) submit (case) for judgement. **4.** *v.t.* & *i*. attempt to achieve or perform (*tried a jump and fell*; *better try something easier*); use exertion (*to do,* or abs.; *do try to be in time*; *must try to get it finished tonight*; *if at first you don't succeed try, try, try again*; *no use trying to persuade him*; *try harder next time*; *tried my best* or *hardest*; *don't try to excuse yourself*; *have often tried to mend it*); ∼ **and,** (colloq.; rarely w. neg. or in past tense) = *try to do*. **5.** *v.t.* ∼ (**out**), extract (oil) from fat by heating, treat (fat) thus, render (fat); ∼ (**up**), smooth (roughly-planed board) with ∼**′ing-plane** to give accurately flat surface. **6.** ∼ **back** *v.i.*, = HARK *back* (lit. or fig.); ∼ **for,** apply or compete for (appointment etc.), seek to reach or attain; ∼ **on,** put (clothes etc.) on to test fit, ||begin (*it, one's games, tricks,* etc., *with* person) experimentally to see how much will be tolerated (*no use trying it on with me*); ∼**-on** *n*., (colloq.) act of trying (it) on, an attempt to deceive; ∼ **out,** put to the test, test thoroughly; ∼**-out** *n*., experimental test of efficiency, popularity, etc. **7.** ∼**-sail** (-sal), small strong fore-and-aft sail set with gaff in heavy weather on mainmast or foremast or supplementary mast instead of mainsail or foresail [f. obs. naut. sense of v. = LIE³ (or fig.)]; ∼**-square,** carpenter's square usu. with one wooden and one metal limb. **8.** *n*. attempt (*made a good try*; *have a try at it, for it, to catch it*). **9.** (Rugby Footb.) (points scored for) touching-down of ball by player behind opponents' goal-line, entitling his side to a kick at goal; (Amer. Footb.) attempt to score extra point in various ways after touchdown. [ME 'separate', 'distinguish', f. OF *trier* sift, of unkn. orig.]

trȳ′ing *a*. In vbl senses, esp. severely testing, hard to endure; hence ∼**LY²** *adv.* [f. prec. + -ING²]

trȳ′panosōm|**e** *n*. flagellate protozoan parasite infesting blood etc. and causing ∼**ī′ASIS** *n*., disease of group including sleeping sickness, kala-azar, etc. [f. Gk *trupanon* borer + -SOME³]

trȳ′psin *n*. chief digestive enzyme present in pancreatic juice. [f. Gk *tripsis* friction (*tribō* rub; because first obtained by rubbing down the pancreas with glycerine) + -IN]

trȳst *n*. & *v*. (arch. or literary). **1.** *n*. appointed meeting, appointment, (*keep, break, tryst*). **2.** *v.t.* engage to meet (person), appoint (time, place) for meeting. **3.** *v.i.* make a tryst (*with*). [ME, = obs. *trist* (= TRUST) f. OF *triste* appointed station in hunting]

tsar, czar (z-), *n.* **1.** (Hist.) emperor of Russia; hence ∼ism (3), ∼ist (2), *ns.* **2.** person with great authority. [f. Russ. *tsar'*, ult. f. L *Caesar*]

tsar′evich, cz- (z-), *n.* (Hist.) eldest son of emperor of Russia. [Russ. *tsarevich* son of a tsar]

tsari′na, czari′na (z-), (-ē′na) *n.* (Hist.) Empress of Russia. [It. & Sp. (*c*)*zarina* f. G (*c*)*zarin* fem. of (*c*)*zar* TSAR; cf. -INA]

tse′tse *n.* Afr. fly of genus *Glossina* carrying disease (esp. sleeping sickness) to man and animals by biting. [Tswana]

TSH *abbr.* Their Serene Highnesses; thyroid-stimulating hormone.

T-shirt, T-square. See T.

tsp. *abbr.* teaspoonful.

tsuna′mi (tsōonah′mĭ) *n.* series of long, high sea waves caused by disturbance of ocean floor or seismic movement; = TIDAL *wave* (1). [Jap. (*tsu* harbour, *nami* wave)]

Tswa′na (-ah′-) *n.* (Bantu language, member, of) Negroid people between Orange and Zambezi rivers. [native name]

TT *abbr.* teetotal(ler); ‖Tourist Trophy; tuberculin-tested.

TU *abbr.* Trade Union.

Tu. *abbr.* Tuesday.

tua′n (tōōah′n) *n.* (As respectful term of address by Malay-speakers) sir, master. [Malay *tu*(*w*)*an*]

tuatar′a (tōōa-) *n.* large iguana-like reptile, peculiar to New Zealand, having dorsal row of yellow spines. [Maori (*tua* on the back, *tara* spine)]

tub *n.* & *v.* (-bb-). **1.** *n.* open flat-bottomed usu. round vessel of wooden staves held together by hoops, or of metal or plastic, used for washing (WASH-*tub*) or holding butter, liquids, soil for plants, etc.; varying measure of capacity for butter, corn, tea, etc. **2.** (‖colloq.) bath (vessel or process; *jumped into his tub*; *seldom has a tub*). **3.** (Mining). bucket or wheeled box for conveying ore, coal, etc. **4.** (derog. or joc.) clumsy slow boat. **5.** boat (esp. stout roomy one) for practice rowing. **6.** ∼ **chair** (with solid arms continuous with usu. semicircular back); ∼**-thumper,** (derog. or joc.) ranting preacher or orator. **7.** Hence ∼′FUL 2 *n.* **8.** *v.t.* & *i.* plant, row, coach (oarsmen), bathe, wash, in tub; line (mine-shaft) with wooden or iron casing; hence ∼′bABLE *a.*, ∼′bING[1] (1, 2) *n.* [ME, prob. f. LDu. (MDu., MLG *tubbe*)]

tu′ba *n.* brass wind instrument in bass range of saxhorn family; its player; sonorous organ reed-stop. [It., f. L, = trumpet]

tu′bal *a.* (Anat.) of (esp. bronchial or Fallopian) tube(s). [f. mod. L *tubalis* (as TUBE) or f. TUBE; see -AL]

tu′bby *a.* tub-shaped, short and fat, corpulent; (of violin etc.) dull-sounding, lacking resonance; so ∼ISH[1] *a.* [f. TUB +-Y[2]]

tube *n.*, & *v.t.* **1.** *n.* long hollow cylinder esp. for conveying or holding liquids etc.; cylinder of thin flexible metal with screw cap for holding semi-liquid substance ready for use; cylindrical body of wind instrument; (Anat. & Zool.) hollow cylindrical vessel or organ; = INNER *tube*, whence ∼′LESS (-bl-) *a.* **2.** *thermionic valve; cathode-ray tube, e.g. in television set; *the ∼, television. **3.** (colloq.) cylindrical tunnel of some electric railways in London etc.; railway system of this kind. **4.** CROOKES, PNEUMATIC, TEST[1]-, *tube.* **5.** ∼**-flower,** ornamental E. Ind. shrub (*Clerodendron siphonanthus*) with long tubular corolla; ∼**-foot,** tubular grasping projection of starfish etc.; ∼**-shell,** bivalve forming shelly tube; ∼**-well,** hollow iron pipe with sharp point and perforations at bottom for getting water from underground. **6.** *v.t.* furnish with or enclose in tube(s); ∼d **horse** (that has had a metallic tube inserted to help breathing). **7.** Hence **tu′bING**[1] (2) *n.* [F, or f. L *tubus*]

tube′ctomy *n.* (Surg.) removal of Fallopian tube(s). [f. prec. + -ECTOMY]

tu′ber *n.* short thick rounded part of stem or rhizome, usu. underground, covered with modified buds, e.g. in potato; similar root of dahlia etc.; (Anat.) swelling part, prominence. [L, = hump, swelling]

tu′bercle *n.* small rounded projection esp. of bone; (Path.) small rounded swelling on body or in organ, esp. as characteristic of tuberculosis in lungs etc.; (Bot.) wartlike excrescence, small tuber; ∼ **bacillus** (causing tuberculosis); so **tubér′cul**ATE[2], **tubér′cul**ous, *adjs.* [f. L *tuberculum* dim. of TUBER; see -CULE]

tubér′cular *a.* & *n.* **1.** *a.* of or having tubercle(s); of tuberculosis. **2.** *n.* tuberculosis patient. [f. L (as prec.) + -AR[1]]

tubércula′tion *n.* formation, or a growth, of tubercles. [f. L (as TUBERCLE) + -ATION]

tubér′culin *n.* sterile liquid from cultures of tubercle bacillus, used in diagnosis (and treatment) of tuberculosis; ∼ **test,** hypodermic injection of tuberculin to detect tubercular infection; ∼**-tested,** (of milk) from cows giving negative response to tuberculin test. [f. L (as TUBERCLE) + -IN]

tubérculo′sis *n.* infectious bacterial disease marked by tubercles, esp. in lungs (**pulmonary** ∼). [mod. L, f. as TUBERCLE; see OSIS]

tu′berōse[1] *a.* covered with tubers, knobby; of nature of a tuber; bearing tubers; so ∼o′SITY *n.* [f. L *tuberosus* (TUBER; see -OSE[1])]

tu′berōse[2] (-z) *n.* tropical tuberose plant (*Polianthes tuberosa*) with creamy-white fragrant funnel-shaped flowers. [f. L *tuberosa* fem. (as prec.), pop. regarded as = TUBE + ROSE[1]]

tu′berous *a.* = TUBEROSE[1]; ∼ **root** (thick and fleshy like tuber but without buds). [f. F *tubéreux* or f. L *tuberosus* (TUBER; see -OUS)]

tu′bi- *comb. form.* tube, as: ∼**colous** (-bī′-), (of worm, spider, etc.) living in or constructing tubes; ∼**corn** *a.* & *n.*, (ruminant) with hollow horns; ∼FORM *a.*; ∼**li′ngual,** (of bird) with tubular tongue. [f. L *tubus* tube + -I-]

tu′bular *a.* tube-shaped; having, consisting of, contained in, tube(s); (of furniture etc.) made of tubular pieces; ∼ **boiler** (in which heat or water to be heated passes through many tubes); ∼ **bridge,** rectangular hollow bridge through which railway etc. passes; so **tu′bul**ous *a.* [f as foll. + -AR[1], but without dim. force]

tu′bule *n.* small tube; hence **tu′buli-** *comb. form.* [f. L *tubulus* dim. of *tubus* tube; see -ULE]

‖**TUC** *abbr.* Trades Union Congress.

tuck[1] *v.* & *n.* **1.** *v.t.* put tuck(s) in (material), shorten or tighten or ornament with tuck(s); draw or thrust or roll the outer parts of (cloth etc. *up, in*) close together or so as to be held in place (*tuck in the blankets, the loose ends*; *tucked up his shirt-sleeves, her petticoats*); draw together into small compass (*tucked his legs under him like a tailor*; *bird tucks head under wing*); cover (person, oneself) snugly and compactly up or in, (*tucked him, himself, up in bed*); stow away (thing in corner etc., away, out of sight, etc.); empty (seine) by means of smaller one. **2.** *v.i.* & *t.* ∼ in or into, ∼ away, (sl.) eat heartily. **3.** *n.* flat fold, often one of several parallel folds, in fabric fixed in place by stitches for shortening or tightening or ornament; = *tuck-net*; (Naut.) part of vessel's hull where planks meet under stern. **4.** ‖(sl.) eatables etc. pastry and sweets; ∼**-box,** ∼**-shop,** (where tuck is kept esp. for schoolchildren). **5.** ∼**-in,** (part) that can be tucked in (e.g. of blouse to be tucked inside top of skirt); ‖∼**-in, -out,** (sl.) large meal; ∼**-net, -seine,** small net for taking fish from larger one; ∼**-pointing,** method of pointing brickwork with coloured mortar, a central groove in which is filled with fine white line putty, projecting slightly. [ME *tukke, tokke,* f. MDu., MLG *tucken,* = OHG *zucchen* pull, pluck, cogn. w. TUG]

tuck[2] *n.* (arch.) beat (*tuck of drum*). [f. ME (now dial.) *tuck* v. f. ONF *toquer,* OF *toucher* TOUCH[1]]

tŭ′cker[1] *n.* In vbl senses; piece of lace, linen, etc., in or on woman's bodice in 17th–18th c. (*best* BIB[2] *and tucker*); (Austral. colloq.) food. [ME, f. TUCK[1]+-ER[1]]

*tŭ′cker[2] *v.t.* ~ (out), (colloq.) tire, weary. [f. TUCK[1]+-ER[5]]

tŭ′cket *n.* (arch.) flourish on trumpet. [f. as TUCK[2]+ -ET[1]]

tu′cum (tōō′-) *n.* Brazilian palm with fibre used for cordage etc. [f. Tupi *tucumá*]

-tŭde *suf.* forming abstract *ns.* (*altitude, attitude, desuetude, exactitude, solitude*). [f. or after F *-tude* f. L *-tudo -tudinis*]

Tŭ′dor *n.* & *a.* (member) of the royal family of England from Henry VII to Elizabeth I; ~ **arch,** flattened four-centred arch; ~ **flower,** ornament of upright stalked trefoil; ~ **rose,** conventional five--lobed figure of rose, esp. combination of red and white roses; ~ **style** (late Perpendicular, or half--timbered elaborately decorated design of houses). [f. Owen ~ of Wales, grandfather of Henry VII]

Tue(s). *abbr.* Tuesday.

Tŭe′sday (tū′zdā, tū′zdǐ) *n.* & *adv.* **1.** *n.* day of week, following Monday; SHROVE[1] *Tuesday.* **2.** *adv.* (cf. FRIDAY 2). [OE *Tīwesdæg* (transl. of L *dies Martis* day of Mars) f. *Tīwes* gen. of *Tīw* Gmc god identified w. Roman Mars]

tŭ′f|a *n.* porous rock formed round mineral springs; = foll.; hence ~A′CEOUS *a.* [It., var. of *tufo* (see foll.)]

tŭff *n.* rock formed by consolidation of volcanic ashes; hence ~A′CEOUS *a.* [f. F *tuf(fe)* f. It. *tufo* f. LL *tofus,* L TOPHUS]

tŭ′ffet *n.* = foll. 1; *low seat. [var. of foll.]

tŭft *n.* & *v.* **1.** *n.* bunch or collection of threads, grass, feathers, hair, etc., held or growing together at the base; hence ~′Y[2] *a.* **2.** (Anat.) bunch of small blood--vessels; (arch.) imperial (beard). **3.** ||(arch.) titled undergraduate [from gold tassel formerly worn on cap]. **4.** ~**-hunter, -hunting,** one who seeks, practice of seeking, society of titled persons, snob(bery). **5.** *v.t.* furnish with tuft(s); make depressions at regular intervals in (mattress etc.) by passing thread through. **6.** *v.i.* grow in tufts. [ME, prob. f. OF *tof(f)e,* of unkn. orig.; for *-t* cf. GRAFT[1]]

tŭ′fted *a.* having or growing tuft(s); (of bird) with tuft of feathers on head. [f. prec.+-ED[1,2]]

tŭg *v.* (-gg-) & *n.* **1.** *v.t.* pull with great effort or violently (lit. or fig.); tow (vessel) by means of tugboat. **2.** *v.i.* make vigorous pull *at.* **3.** *n.* tugging, violent pull, (*gave a tug at the bell*); violent or painful effort (esp. fig.; *felt a great tug at parting*). **4.** ~ ('boat), small powerful steam-vessel for towing others. **5.** aircraft towing glider; loop from saddle supporting shaft or (in double harness) trace. **6.** ~ **of love,** (colloq.) dispute over custody of child; ~ **of war,** contest in which each of two teams holding same rope tries to pull the other across line marked between them, decisive or severe contest. [ME *togge, tugge,* intensive f. Gmc **teuh-;* see TOW[1]]

tu′i (tōō′ǐ) *n.* (NZ). bird with dark plumage and white throat-tuft, parson-bird. [Maori]

tüi′tion *n.* teaching, instruction, esp. as a thing to be paid for; fee for this; hence ~AL, ~ARY[1], *adjs.* [ME f. OF, f. L *tuitio -onis* (*tuēri tuit-* watch, guard; see -ITION)]

tŭlarae′m|ĭa, *-ē′m|ĭa, *n.* severe infectious bacterial disease of man and domestic animals, carried by contact or by insect bites; hence ~IC *a.* [mod. L, f. *Tulare* County, California (where first observed)+ -AEMIA]

tŭ′lchan (-χ-) *n.* (Sc.) calf-skin stuffed with straw or spread on mound beside cow to make her give milk; ~ **bishops,** (Hist.) titular bishops in whose names revenues of Scottish sees were drawn by lay barons after Reformation. [Gael., = mound]

tŭ′lip *n.* (flower of) bulbous spring-flowering plant of genus *Tulipa,* esp. one of many cultivated forms with showy cup-shaped flowers of various colours and markings; ~**-root,** disease of oats etc. causing base of stem to swell; ~**-tree,** (1) N. Amer. tree (*Liriodendron tulipifera*) with flowers like large greenish--yellow tulips and soft white wood (~**-wood**), (2) similar tree of genus *Magnolia* etc. [orig. *tulipa(n)* f. mod. L *tulipa* f. Turk. *tul(i)band* f. Pers. *dulband* TURBAN (f. shape of expanded flower)]

tŭlle *n.* fine silk etc. net used for veils and dresses. [f. *T*~ in SW France, where first made]

tŭ′lwâr *n.* sabre of N. India etc. [f. Hindi *talwār*]

tŭm[1] *n.* sound of banjo or similar instrument. [imit.]

tŭm[2] *n.* (childish or joc.) stomach. [abbr. of TUMMY]

tŭ′mble *v.* & *n.* **1.** *v.i.* fall esp. helplessly (*down, over, off, from,* etc.) suddenly or violently; (of waves, sick person, etc.) roll, toss, irregularly up and down or from side to side or over and over; move, walk, run, in headlong or blundering fashion (*came tumbling along; tumbled up the stairs; tumbled into* or *out of bed*); turn rapidly in amount etc.; (of pigeon) turn over backwards in flight; perform acrobatic feats. **2.** *v.t.* cause to tumble; pull about, disorder, rumple, (clothes, hair, etc.); overturn, fling headlong, throw or push (*down, out, in,* etc.) roughly or carelessly; dry in tumbler--drier; clean in tumbling-barrel. **3.** ~ **home** or **in,** (Naut.) of ship's sides) incline inwards above extreme breadth, whence ~*-home* n., amount of this inclination; ~ **to,** (colloq.) understand, grasp, (hidden idea etc.). **4.** *n.* fall (*had a slight, nasty,* etc. *tumble*); somersault or other acrobatic feat; untidy or confused state (*things were all in a tumble*). **5.** ~**-bug,** dung--beetle rolling up balls of dung; ~**down,** falling or fallen into ruin, dilapidated; ~**-drier,** = TUMBLER--drier; *~**-weed,** plant forming globular bush that breaks off in late summer and is rolled about by the wind. [ME *tumbel,* f. MLG *tummelen,* OHG *tumalōn,* frequent. of *tūmōn;* see -LE 3]

tŭ′mbler *n.* in vbl senses; one who turns somersaults etc., acrobat; variety of pigeon that tumbles; flat--bottomed drinking-glass without handle or foot (formerly with rounded bottom so as not to stand upright), whence ~FUL (2) *n.;* electrical switch worked by pushing small sprung lever; pivoted piece in lock that holds the bolt until lifted by key; notched pivoted plate in gun-lock; toy figure that rocks when touched; tumbling-barrel etc.; ~(-drier), machine for drying washing in heated drum rotating on horizontal axis. [ME, f. prec.+-ER[1]]

tŭ′mbling *n.* in vbl senses; ~**-barrel, -box,** etc., revolving device containing abrasive substance, in which castings etc. are cleaned by friction against each other or the walls of the box; ~**-bay,** (pool receiving) outfall of river, reservoir, etc. [ME, f. TUMBLE+-ING[1]]

tŭ′mbrel, -il, *n.* (Hist.) two-wheeled covered cart for carrying tools, ammunition, etc.; tip-cart, esp. dung--cart; open cart used in French Revolution to convey victims to the guillotine; instrument of punishment, usu. = cucking-stool. [ME, f. OF *tumbrel, tomberel* (*tomber* fall)]

tŭ′me|fy *v.t.* & *i.* (cause to) swell, inflate, be inflated, (lit. or fig.); so (Path.) ~FA′CIENT *a.,* ~FA′CTION *n.* [f. F *tuméfier* f. L *tumefacere* (*tumēre* swell; see -FY)]

tŭmé′sc|ent *a.* becoming tumid, swelling; showing such response to sexual stimulation; hence ~ENCE *n.* [f. L *tumescere* (as prec.; see -ESCENT)]

tŭ′mid *a.* (Of parts of the body etc.) swollen, inflated; (fig., of style etc.) inflated, bombastic; hence or cogn. ~ITY (-ĭ′d-) ~NESS, *ns.,* ~LY[2] *adv.* [f. L *tumidus* (*tumēre* swell; see -ID[1])]

tŭ′mmy *n.* (childish or colloq.) stomach; ~**-button,** (colloq.) navel. [childish pr.; see -Y[3]]

tŭ′mour (-mer), ***tŭ′mor,** *n.* local swelling esp. from morbid or abnormal growth; so **tŭ′mor**OUS *a.* [f. L *tumor* (*tumēre* swell; see -OR)]

tŭ′mtum[1] *n.* (Anglo-Ind.) light vehicle, dog-cart. [19th c.; orig. unkn.]

tŭ′mtum[2]. Var. of TUM[1,2].

tŭ′mult *n.* commotion of a multitude esp. with confused cries etc.; public disturbance, riot; din, uproar; confused and excited state of mind. [ME, f. OF *tumulte* or f. L *tumultus*]

tŭmŭ′ltŭarў *a.* (Of troops) hastily brought together, undisciplined; done hurriedly, haphazard; = foll. [f. L *tumultuarius* (as prec.; see -ARY¹)]

tŭmŭ′ltŭous *a.* full of or making tumult; disorderly, agitated; hence ∼LY² *adv.*, ∼NESS *n.* [OF, or f. L (as TUMULT; see -OUS)]

tŭ′mŭl|us *n.* (*pl.* ∼i *pr.* -ī). ancient sepulchral mound, barrow; so ∼AR(Y)¹ *adjs.* [L (*tumēre* swell)]

tŭn *n.*, & *v.t.* (-nn-). 1. *n.* large cask for wine, beer, etc.; measure of capacity (252 wine gallons); brewer's fermenting-vat; ∼′dish, wooden funnel esp. in brewing, intermediate reservoir in metal-founding. 2. *v.t.* store (liquor) in tun. [OE *tunne*, = OHG, ON *tunna*, f. med. L *tunna*, prob. of Gaulish orig.]

tŭ′na¹ *n.* (*pl.* ∼s *or* same). tunny; ∼(-fish), its flesh as food. [Amer. Sp., perh. f. Sp. *atún* tunny]

tŭ′na² *n.* prickly pear, esp. (fruit of) *Opuntia tuna*. [Sp. f. Haitian]

tŭ′na³ (*or* tōō′-) *n.* (NZ). common species of eel (*Anguilla sucklandii*). [Maori]

tu′ndra (tŭ′-, tōō′-) *n.* vast level treeless Arctic region where subsoil is frozen. [Lappish]

tūne *n.* & *v.* 1. *n.* melody with or without harmony (call the ∼, have control of events; see PIPER); correct pitch or intonation in singing or playing (*sings in, out of, tune*); due adjustment of instrument to obtain this (*piano is out of tune*). 2. agreement, concord, harmonious relation (*in, out of, tune with* one's *surroundings or company*); *in, out of,* proper condition; suitable mood (*for* purpose etc.). 3. change one's ∼, sing another *or* a different ∼, assume a different style of language or manner, e.g. change from insolent to respectful tone; to the ∼ (considerable or exorbitant amount) of £500 etc.; to some ∼, to a remarkable degree. 4. *v.t.* put (violin, piano, etc.) in tune; adjust (radio receiver etc.) to particular wavelength of signals; adjust (engine etc.) to run smoothly and efficiently; hence tŭ′nER¹ (1, 2) *n.* 5. (fig.) adjust, adapt, (thing *to* standard, purpose, circumstances, etc.); (poet.) produce music from (instrument), produce (music) (*lark tunes his song*), express, celebrate, in music. 6. *v.i.* be in harmony (lit. *or* fig., *with*). 7. ∼ in, set radio receiver to right wavelength to receive transmitted signal; ∼ out, cut out (radio etc. signal) by tuning; ∼ up, (of orchestra) bring instruments to proper or uniform pitch, begin to play or sing, bring to most efficient condition. 8. Hence tŭ′nABLE, (-na-) *a.* [ME; unexpl. var. of TONE¹]

tŭ′neful (-nf-) *a.* melodious, musical; hence ∼LY² *adv.*, ∼NESS *n.* [f. prec. + -FUL]

tŭ′neless (-nl-) *a.* not in tune; unmelodious, unmusical; (arch.) making no (musical) sound; hence ∼LY² *adv.*, ∼NESS *n.* [f. TUNE + -LESS]

tŭng *n.* ∼(-tree), Chinese tree of genus *Aleurites*, esp. a species whose seeds yield ∼ oil used for varnishing etc. [f. Chin. *tong*]

tŭ′ngst|en *n.* steel-grey heavy metallic element with very high melting-point, used for the filaments of electric lamps and for alloying steel etc.; hence ∼ATE¹ (3) *n.*, ∼IC, ∼OUS, *adjs.* (Chem.) [Sw. (*tung* heavy, *sten* stone)]

tŭ′nic *n.* 1. ancient Greek or Roman short-sleeved body-garment reaching about to knees; loose blouse or coat gathered or belted at waist; close-fitting short coat of uniform of soldier, policeman, etc.; GYM-*tunic*. 2. (Zool.) leathery envelope of ascidian etc.; (Anat.) membrane enclosing or lining an organ; (Bot.) any of the layers of a bulb, integument of a part; (Eccl.) tunicle. [f. F *tunique* or f. L *tunica*]

tŭ′nica *n.* (*pl.* ∼e) (Zool. & Anat.) = prec. [L]

tŭ′nicate *a.* & *n.* 1. *a.* (Zool.) enclosed in tunic; (Bot.) having concentric layers. 2. *a.* & *n.* (member) of subphylum Urochorda of marine animals with hard

outer coat. [f. L *tunicatus* p.p. of *tunicare* clothe with tunic (as prec.; see -ATE²)]

tŭ′nicle *n.* (Eccl., esp. RC Ch.) short vestment of bishop or subdeacon at Eucharist etc. [ME f. OF, or f. L *tunicula* dim. of TUNICA]

tŭ′ning *n.* In vbl senses; ∼-fork, two-pronged steel fork designed to give particular note (esp. middle C) when struck; ∼-peg, -pin, (attached to strings in piano etc. and turned to alter their tension in tuning). [f. TUNE + -ING¹]

Tŭni′sian (-z-) *a.* & *n.* (native or inhabitant) of Tunisia or Tunis. [f. *Tunisia* in N. Afr. or its capital *Tunis* + -IAN]

tŭ′nnel *n.* & *v.* (‖-ll-). 1. *n.* artificial subterranean passage through hill etc. or under road or river etc., esp. for railway or road; subterranean passage dug by burrowing animal; tube containing propeller-shaft etc.; WIND¹-*tunnel*; ∼-net, fishing-net wide at mouth and narrow at other end; ∼ vision (defective in lateral directions). 2. *v.t.* make a tunnel through (hill etc.); furnish with tunnel; make one's *way* by tunnelling. 3. *v.i.* make one's way by tunnelling (*through, into,* etc.); (Phys.) pass through potential barrier. [ME, f. OF *tonel* dim. of *tonne* TUN; see -LE 2]

tŭ′nnў *n.* large marine scombroid fish esp. of genus *Thunnus*, used as food-fish and game fish. [f. F *thon* f. Prov. *ton*, f. L f. Gk *thunnos*]

tŭp *n.*, & *v.t.* (-pp-). 1. *n.* male sheep, ram; striking-head of steam-hammer, pile-driver, etc. 2. *v.t.* copulate with (ewe). [ME *toje, tupe,* of unkn. orig.]

Tupamǎr′ō (tōō-) *n.* (*pl.* ∼s). left-wing urban guerrilla in Uruguay. [f. *Tupac Amaru,* name of two Inca leaders]

tu′pelō (tōō′-) *n.* (*pl.* ∼s). large N. Amer. swamp tree of genus *Nyssa*; its wood. [Creek (*ito* tree, *opilwa* swamp)]

Tu′pi (tōō′-) *n.* & *a.* (member or language) of Amer. Ind. people in Amazon valley etc. [Tupi]

‖**tŭ′ppence, tŭ′ppennў.** Vars. of TWOpence, TWOpenny.

tŭque (-k) *n.* Canadian stocking cap. [Can. F form of TOQUE]

tu quoque (tū kwō′kwi, tōō kwō′kwä) *n.* the retort *So are* (*or did etc.*) *you.* [L, = you too]

turaco(u), turako. Vars. of TOURACO.

Tŭrā′nian *a.* & *n.* (the group) of Asian languages that are neither Semitic nor Indo-European, esp. the Ural-Altaic family of languages. [f. Pers. *Tūrān* region beyond Oxus + -IAN]

tŭr′ban *n.* man's head-dress of scarf wound round cap, worn esp. by Muslims and Sikhs; modification of this, esp. (1) woman's head-dress resembling turban, (2) woman's or child's close-fitting hat with narrow or no brim; ∼ lily (with deep-red spotted turban-shaped flowers); ∼-shell, mollusc of genus *Turbo* with thick spiral shell; ∼-stone, Muslim pillar tombstone with turban carved on top; hence ∼ED² (-nd) *a.* [16th c. also *tulbant* etc., ult. f. Turk. *tülbent* f. Pers. *dulband;* cf. TULIP]

‖**tŭr′barў** *n.* right of digging turf on common or on another's ground; place where turf or peat is dug. [ME, f. AF *turberie,* OF *tourberie* (*tourbe* TURF; see -ARY¹)]

tŭrbĕllǎr′ian *a.* & *n.* (flatworm) of class Turbellaria, with external cilia causing eddies in water. [f. mod. L *Turbellaria* f. L *turbella* dim. of *turba* crowd (see foll., -ARY¹) + -AN]

tŭr′bid *a.* (Of liquid or colour) muddy, thick, not clear; (fig.) confused, disordered; hence ∼ITY (-ĭ′d-), ∼NESS, *ns.*, ∼LY² *adv.* [f. L *turbidus* (*turba* crowd, disturbance; see -ID¹)]

tŭr′bin|ate *a.* shaped like a top or inverted cone; (of shell) with whorls decreasing rapidly in size; (Anat., esp. of some nasal bones) of scroll-like formation; whirling like a top; so ∼AL *a.,* ∼A′TION *n.* [f. L *turbinatus* (as foll.; see -ATE²)]

tŭr′bīne *n.* water-wheel driven by impact or reaction or both of a stream of water; similar machine driven by flow of gas (esp. *gas turbine, steam turbine*); ∼ **boat** etc. (driven by turbines). [F, f. L *turbo -binis* spinning- -top, whirlwind]

tur′bit *n.* variety of domestic pigeon with stout build, neck frill, and short beak. [app. f. L *turbo* top, from its figure]

tur′bo- *comb. form.* turbine, as: ∼-**charger,** super- charger driven by turbine(s) using exhaust gases; ∼- -**fan,** = FAN¹-*jet*; ∼-**jet (engine),** (aircraft with) jet engine in which jet gases also operate turbine-driven compressor for supplying compressed air to com- bustion chamber; ∼-**prop (engine),** (aircraft with) jet engine in which turbine is used as in turbo-jet and also to drive propeller. [f. TURBINE + -O-]

tur′bot *n.* large Eur. flat-fish (*Scophthalmus maxi- mus*) esteemed as food; similar fish, e.g. halibut. [ME f. OF, f. OSw. *törnbut* (*törn* thorn, *but* BUTT²)]

tur′bul|ent *a.* disturbed, in commotion; tumultuous; insubordinate, riotous; (Phys., of flow) having irregu- lar variations in the course of time; hence or cogn. ∼ENCE *n.*, ∼ent**LY²** *adv.* [f. L *turbulentus* (*turba* crowd; see -ULENT]

Tur′cō (*pl.* ∼s). (Hist.) Algerian soldier in French army. [Sp., Port., & It., = TURK]

Tur′cō-, Tur′kō-, *comb. form.* Turkish (and); hence ∼PHIL(E), ∼PHOBE, *ns.* & *adjs.* [f. med. L (as TURK) + -O-]

Tur′coman. See TURKOMAN.

turd *n.* (vulg.) ball or lump of excrement; con- temptible person. [OE *tord,* = ON *tord*(*ýfill*) dung(-beetle) f. Gmc *turdam*]

tur′doid *a.* thrushlike. [f. L *turdus* THRUSH¹ + -OID]

tūree′n *n.* deep covered dish from which soup, gravy, etc., is served at table. [earlier *terrine, -ene* f. F *terrine* large circular earthenware dish, fem. (as n.) of OF *terrin* earthen f. Rom. *terrinus* f. L *terra* earth; see -INE¹]

turf *n.* (*pl.* ∼s, *or* **turves** *pr.* -vz), & *v.t.* **1.** *n.* covering of grass etc. with earth and matted roots as surface layer of grassland; piece of this cut from ground; **the** ∼, the racecourse, occupation or profession of horse- -racing; hence ∼′Y² *a.* **2.** slab or block of peat for fuel. **3.** ∼ **accountant,** bookmaker; ∼ **drain** (covered with turf); ∼′ITE¹, ∼′**man,** person interested in horse-racing. **4.** *v.t.* plant (ground) with turf; (sl.) throw (person or thing) *out.* [OE, = OS *turf,* ON *torf*(*a*), OHG *zurf, zurba,* f. Gmc *turbh-* f. IE *drbh-*]

tur′g|id *a.* swollen, inflated, enlarged; (fig., of language) pompous, bombastic; hence or cogn. ∼E′SCENCE, ∼i′**dITY,** *ns.*, ∼E′SCENT *a.*, ∼id**LY²** *adv.* [f. L *turgidus* (*turgēre* swell; see -ID¹)]

tur′gor *n.* (Bot.) rigidity of cells due to uptake of water. [LL (as prec.; see -OR)]

tur′ion *n.* (Bot.) young scaly shoot rising from under- ground bud as in asparagus etc. [F, f. L *turio -onis* shoot]

Turk *n.* **1.** native of Turkey; native or inhabitant of Ottoman empire; member of the Central Asian people from whom the Ottomans derived, speaking Turkic languages; (**R**) ferocious, wild, or unmanage- able person; (arch.) Muslim; Turkish horse; see YOUNG 2. **2.** ∼′s **cap,** martagon lily or other plant with turban-like flowers; ∼′s **head,** turban-like ornamental knot. [ME, = F *Turc,* It. etc. *Turco,* med. L *Turcus,* Pers. & Arab. *Turk,* of unkn. orig.]

tur′key¹ *n.* **1.** large (esp. domestic) orig. Amer. gallinaceous bird of genus *Meleagris,* esteemed as food and associated with festivities of ||Christmas or *Thanksgiving; *TALK *turkey.* **2.** flesh of turkey as food; COLD¹ *turkey.* **3.** ∼ **buzzard, vulture,** Amer. carrion vulture (*Cathartes aura*); ∼**cock,** male of turkey (*red as a* ∼*cock,* flushed with anger etc.), (fig.) pompous or self-important person. [16th c., short for *turkeycock, -hen,* orig. applied to the guinea-fowl, as imported through Turkey, and then erron. to the Amer. bird]

Tur′key² *n.* ∼ **carpet** (made of wool with thick pile and bold design); ||∼ **leather** (treated with oil before hair side is removed); ∼ **oak,** a S. Eur. oak (*Quercus cerris*); ∼ **red,** (cotton cloth dyed with) scarlet pigment from madder or alizarin. [∼ in Asia Minor & SE Europe, country of the Turks]

Tur′k|i *a.* & *n.* (of) a group of Ural-Altaic (incl. Turkish) languages and peoples; so ∼IC *a.* [f. Pers. *turkī* (as TURK; see -I)]

Tur′kish *a.* & *n.* **1.** *a.* of Turkey or the Turks or their language. **2.** ∼ **bath,** hot-air or steam bath followed by washing, massage, etc., (in *sing.* or *pl.*) building used for this; ∼ **carpet,** TURKEY² carpet; ∼ **coffee,** strong usu. sweet black coffee made from very finely ground beans; ∼ **delight,** sweetmeat in flavoured gelatinous lumps coated with powdered sugar; ∼ **tobacco** (aromatic kind grown mainly in Turkey and Greece); ∼ **towel,** towel of cotton terry. **3.** *n.* language of the Turks. [f. TURK + -ISH¹]

Tur′kō-. See TURCO-.

Tur′koman, Tur′coman, Tur′kmen, *n.* member or language of any of various Turkic tribes in Turk- menistan etc.; ∼ **carpet,** rich-coloured kind with soft long nap. [f. Pers. *Turkumān* (as TURK, *mānistan* resemble)]

tur′meric *n.* E. Ind. plant (*Curcuma longa*) of ginger family; its large aromatic root powdered as dyestuff, stimulant, and condiment esp. in curry-powder; ∼-**paper** (saturated with turmeric and used as test for alkalis). [16th-c. forms *tarmaret* etc., perh. f. F *terre mérite* and mod. L *terra merita,* of unkn. orig.]

tur′moil *n.*, & *v.t.* **1.** *n.* agitation, tumult, trouble. **2.** *v.t.* (arch.; esp. in *p.p.*) agitate, trouble. [16th c., of unkn. orig.]

turn¹ *v.* **1.** *v.t.* & *i.* move round so as to keep at same distance from a centre or axis, give rotary motion to, receive such motion, (*crank turns wheel; wheel turns; turn the key in the lock; turn the tap; tap will not turn; make person turn in his* GRAVE¹; *turn on one's* HEEL¹). **2.** *v.t.* execute (somersault etc.) with rotary motion. **3.** *v.t.* & *i.* change from one side to another, invert, reverse, (fig.) revolve mentally, (*turn upside down, inside out, back to front; whole world has turned topsy-turvy; turned the body with its face upwards; have turned the matter over and over in my mind*); (Print.) invert (type) so that it appears upside down (∼**ed comma,** inverted comma; ∼**ed period,** ˙); make (profit); convert less soiled inside of (dress etc.) to serve as outside; *turn one's* COAT; *not turn a* HAIR; *turn an* HONEST *penny,* the SCALE²(*s*), *the* TABLES (*on*), TURTLE². **4.** give new direction to, take new direction, adapt, be adapted, (*turn your face this way; river turns to the right; turned his flight northwards; turn into a side-road; turned the hose on them; cricket-ball turns on pitching; turned to God in her trouble; turn your attention to this; have often turned my thoughts, thoughts have often turned, to the subject*); (Golf) begin second half of round; resist or divert (bullet); blunt (edge of knife etc. or fig. of remark etc.); *turn to* ACCOUNT²; *turn one's* BACK¹ *on, a* DEAF *ear* (*to*), one's HAND¹ *to*; *turn* TAIL¹; ∼ **the tide,** (fig.) reverse trend of events, so **tide** ∼**s** (also lit.); *not know* **where** or **which way to** ∼, (fig.) what course to follow, how to proceed, where to seek help; *a* WORM¹ *will turn.* **5.** *v.t.* move to other side of, go round, flank, (*turn the* CORNER); ∼ (**the flank** or **position of**) **an army,** pass round so as to attack it from flank or rear; ∼ person's **flank,** outwit him, defeat him in argument etc. **6.** pass age or time of (*is or has turned 40, noon*). **7.** cause to go, send, put, (*was turned into a field, adrift in the world; turn it out into a basin; never turned* (*away*) *a beggar from his door*). **8.** *v.t.* & *i.* change in nature, form, condition, etc., change for the worse, (cause to) become, (*turned water into wine; has been turned into a theatre, a frog, a millionaire; fear he will turn awkward; has turned traitor, informer,* ||Queen's EVIDENCE, Muslim, botanist; *joy is or has turned to bitterness; my luck has turned at last; turned pale at the thought; very thought turns me pale*); (of leaves, hair, etc.) change colour;

translate (*turn it into French*); make or become sour (of milk), nauseated (of stomach), giddy (of head); ~ person's **brain** or **head**, make him vain or silly. **9.** shape (object) in lathe; give (esp. elegant) form to (*can turn a compliment; could turn a Latin verse in my day*; WELL-*turned phrase, leg*). **10.** (w. *advs.*): ~ **about**, turn so as to face in new direction; *~ **around** = turn round*; ~ **away**, turn to face in another direction, refuse to look (at) or accept; ~ **back**, (cause to) cease advance and begin retreat, fold back; ~ **down**, fold down, fold down corner of sheet of (bed, page), place (playing-card) face downwards, reduce volume of (sound etc.) by turning knob etc., reduce flame of (gas, lamp, etc.) by turning tap etc., reject (proposal, its maker, etc.); ~ **in**, fold inwards, hand in, surrender, register (score, performance, etc.), deliver, incline inwards (*his toes turn in*), (colloq.) go to bed, (colloq.) abandon (plan etc.); ~ **off**, enter side-road, stop flow or working of (water, radio, etc.) by means of tap, switch, etc., operate (tap etc.) thus, (colloq.) cause to lose interest, dismiss (servant etc.) from employment; ~ **on**, start flow or working of (water, radio, etc.) by means of tap, switch, etc., operate (tap etc.) thus, (colloq.) arouse interest of, stimulate, (person sexually, with drugs, etc.); ~ **out**, expel, extinguish (electric light etc.), incline outwards (*turn out your toes*), equip, dress (*well turned out*), produce (manufactured goods etc.), ||empty (room etc. for cleaning), expose contents of (*made him turn out his pockets*), (colloq.) get out of bed, (colloq.) go out of doors or to vote etc., (Mil.) call (guard) from guard-room, be found, prove to be the case, (*this turns out to be true; he turned out a humbug; it turns out that he was never there; we shall see how things turn out, whether it turns out well*); ~ **over**, (cause to) fall over, upset, expose or bring uppermost the other side of (page etc., *a new* LEAF, or abs.), cause (engine etc.) to revolve, consider thoroughly, transfer the conduct of (thing to person), do business to the amount of (*turns over £5,000 a week*); ~ **round** – *turn about*, adopt new opinions or policy, unload and reload (ship etc.); ~ **to**, begin work; ~ **up**, disinter (*plough turns up mouse's nest*), make one's appearance (*turned up an hour late, unexpectedly*), (of event, opportunity, etc.) happen, present itself, (colloq.) cause to vomit (*the sight turned me up*), give upward turn to (NOSE, TOES, etc.), increase volume of (sound etc.) by turning knob etc., increase flame of (gas, lamp, etc.) by turning tap etc., place (playing-card) face upwards. **11.** (w. *preps.*): ~ **against**, make or become hostile to; ~ **on**, depend on, face hostilely, become hostile to; ~ **to**, apply oneself to, set about (work, *doing*), go on to consider next; ~ **upon**, = *turn on*. **12.** ~-**about**, turning about, (fig.) abrupt change of policy etc.; ~-**bench**, watchmaker's portable lathe; ~-**buckle**, device for tightly connecting parts of metal rod or wire; ~-**cap**, revolving chimney-top; ~'**coat**, one who turns his COAT; ~'**cock**, person employed to turn on water for mains etc.; ~-**down**, (of collar) doubled down; ~'**key**, (n.) person in charge of prison keys, (a., of contract etc.) providing for supply of equipment ready for operation; ~-**off**, side-road; ~-**out**, turning out esp. for duty, strike of employees, number of persons who go to vote, set spectacle, etc., equipage, quantity of goods manufactured etc. in given time; ~'**over**, turning over, semicircular or triangular pie or tart made by turning half of pastry over filling, amount of money turned over in business, numbers of persons etc. entering and leaving employment etc.; ~'**pike**, (Hist.) defensive frame of spikes, (Hist.) toll-gate, (Hist. & US) road on which toll is or was collected at gates; ~-**round**, (of ship etc.) process of arriving at destination, unloading, reloading, and leaving; ~-**screw**, screwdriver; ~'**sick**, = STURDY²; ~'**side**, giddiness in dogs and cattle; ~'**sole**, plant supposed to turn with the sun (ult. f. L *sol* sun); ~'**spit**, person or long-bodied

short-legged dog, formerly used to turn spit; ~'**stile**, post at entrance of building esp. where admission fee is charged or numbers entering are counted, with arms that move round as person passes through; ~'**stone**, bird of genus *Arenaria*, allied to plover, seeking small animals under stones as food; ~'**table**, circular revolving platform for reversing a locomotive etc., circular revolving support for gramophone record being played; ~-**up**, thing turned up, ||esp. lower end of trouser leg, (colloq.) commotion, (colloq.) unexpected event. [OE *tyrnan, turnian*, in ME reinforced f. OF *turner, torner*, f. L *tornare* turn in lathe (*tornus* f. Gk *tornos*)]

turn² *n.* **1.** turning, rotary motion, changed or change of direction or position or tendency, deflection, deflected part, bend, (*a single turn of the handle; with a neat turn of the wrist; took a sudden turn to the left; his illness, events, took a favourable turn; gave a new turn to the argument; path is full of twists and turns; walked along a turn of the river*); turning of road; point at which turning or change occurs; change of tide (lit. or fig.) from ebb to flow or vice versa; **at every** ~, continually; HAND¹'s turn; **on the** ~, changing, (of milk) becoming sour, at the turning-point; ||THREE-*point turn*; **to a** ~, (roasted etc.) precisely right. **2.** character, tendency, disposition, formation, (*was of a humorous turn, a mechanical turn of mind; do not like the turn of the sentence; the turn of an ankle*); ~ **of speed**, ability to go very fast on occasion. **3.** short walk, stroll, drive, ride, (*take a turn in the garden, on a bicycle*); short performance on stage, in circus, etc. **4.** opportunity, occasion, privilege, obligation, coming successively to each of several persons etc. (*it is your turn to watch; it was now my turn to be angry; you must wait your turn; be patient, your turn will come*); **by** ~**s**, in rotation of individuals or groups, alternately; **in** ~, in succession; **in** one's ~, when one's turn comes; **out of** ~, before or after one's turn, (fig.) at an inappropriate moment; **take** ~**s**, work etc. alternately; (~ **and**) ~ **about**, alternately. **5.** purpose (*did not serve my, its turn*); service of specified kind (*did me a good, an ill, turn; one good turn deserves another*). **6.** (Mus.) grace consisting of principal note with those above and below it, in various sequences. **7.** each round in coil of rope, wire, etc. **8.** (Print.) inverted type as temporary substitute for missing letter; letter turned wrong side up. **9.** (colloq.) momentary nervous shock (*gave me quite a turn*). **10.** (profit made by) difference between the buying and selling prices of stocks etc. [ME, partly f. AF **torn, *turn*, = OF *torn* f. L *tornus* (see prec.); partly f. prec.]

tur'n|er *n.* In vbl senses; one who works with lathe, so ~ERY (1, 2, 3) *n.*; ***member of society of gymnasts. [ME, f. OF *tornere -eor* f. LL *tornator* (as TURN¹; see -ER²)]

tur'ning *n.* In vbl senses; use of lathe, (in *pl.*) chips or shavings formed by this; place where road meets another, such road, (*stop at the next turning; take the second turning to the left*); ~-**circle**, smallest circle in which vehicle can be turned round without reversing; ~-**point**, point in place, time, development, etc., at which decisive change occurs (*has reached the turning-point; this may be the turning-point of his life*). [ME, f. TURN¹ + -ING¹]

tur'nip *n.* (biennial plant of genus *Brassica* with) fleshy globular white root used as vegetable and for feeding cattle etc.; (sl.) large thick old-fashioned watch; ~-**top**, sprouting leaves of turnip used as vegetable; hence ~Y² *a.*, (esp.) tasting of turnips. [earlier *turnep(e)*, f. NEEP; first element of uncert. orig.]

tur'pentine *n.*, & *v.t.* **1.** *n.* oleo-resin secreted by several coniferous trees and (**Chian** ~) by terebinth; (**oil of**) ~, volatile pungent oil distilled from this, used in mixing paints and varnishes and in medicine; ~-**tree**, terebinth or other tree yielding turpentine. **2.** *v.t.* apply turpentine to. [ME f. OF *ter(e)bentine* f. L *ter(e)binthina* (*resina* resin) (as TEREBINTH; see -INE²)]

tŭr'pĕth *n.* cathartic root of an E. Ind. jalap; ∼ (**mineral**), yellow basic mercury sulphate. [ME, f. med. L *turbit(h)um* f. Arab. & Pers. *turbid*]

tŭr'pitŭde *n.* baseness, depravity, wickedness. [F, or f. L *turpitudo* (*turpis* disgraceful, base; see -TUDE)]

tŭrps *n.* (colloq.) oil of turpentine. [abbr.]

tŭr'quoise (-kwoiz, -koiz, -kwahz) *n.* opaque or translucent sky-blue or greenish-blue precious stone, hydrated copper aluminium phosphate; ∼ **blue, green,** colours between green and blue. [ME *turkeis* etc., f. OF *turqueise*, later *-oise* Turkish (stone) (*Turc* TURK; f. being orig. known in Turkestan or coming through Turkish dominions)]

tŭ'rrĕt *n.* small tower connected with main building whether rising from ground or projecting from wall or corbels esp. at angle of main building; low flat usu. revolving armoured tower for gun and gunners in ship or aircraft or fort or tank; (Mech.) rotating holder for various dies and cutting tools in ∼ **lathe,** drill, etc.; hence ∼ED² *a.,* having turret(s), (of shell) having long conical spiral part. [ME, f. OF *to(u)rete* dim. of *to(u)r* TOWER; see -ET¹]

tŭr'tle¹ *n.* (arch.) = ∼-**dove,** wild dove of genus *Streptopelia,* esp. *S. turtur,* noted for soft cooing and affection for mate and young. [OE *turtla, turtle,* = OHG *turtulo, -la,* & OE *turtur,* = ON *turturi,* & ME *turture,* OF *turtre,* all f. L *turtur*]

tŭr'tle² *n.* marine or *freshwater reptile of order Chelonia with structure of tortoise and with flippers used in swimming; flesh of turtle, much used for soup; MOCK² *turtle soup;* **turn** ∼, capsize; ∼-**neck,** high close-fitting neck of knitted garment, *polo-neck; ∼-**shell,** (1) tortoise-shell, esp. dark kind used for inlaying, (2) large handsome kind of cowrie. [app. alt. of *tortue* (see TORTOISE), assim. to prec.]

Tŭ'scan *a.* & *n.* (classical Italian language, inhabitant) of Tuscany; (Archit.) of a simple unornamented ORDER¹; ∼ **straw,** fine yellow wheat-straw used for hats etc. [ME f. F, f. L *Tuscanus* (*Tuscus* Etruscan; see -AN)]

tŭsh¹ *int.* (arch.) = PSHAW. [ME; imit.]

tŭsh² *n.* long pointed tooth, esp. canine tooth of horse; elephant's short tusk. [OE *tusc* TUSK]

tŭ'sherÿ *n.* (literary). use of affected archaisms such as TUSH¹. [-ERY; wd made by R. L. Stevenson]

tŭsk *n.,* & *v.t.* **1.** *n.* long pointed tooth, esp. protruding from closed mouth as in elephant, walrus, etc.; tusklike tooth or other object; hence (-)∼ED² (-kt), ∼'Y², *adjs.* **2.** *v.t.* gore, thrust, tear up, with tusk(s). [ME alt. of OE *tux* var. of *tusc;* cf. TUSH²]

tŭ'sker *n.* elephant or wild boar with developed tusks. [f. prec. + ER¹]

tŭ'sser, tŭ'ssŏre, *tŭ'ssah (-*a*), *n.* Indian or Chinese silkworm yielding strong but coarse brown silk; ∼(-**silk**), silk of this and of some other silkworms. [f. Urdu f. Hindi *tasar* f. Skr. *tasara* shuttle]

tŭ'ssive *a.* (Med.) of a cough. [f. L *tussis* cough + -IVE]

tŭ'ssle *n.,* & *v.i.* struggle, scuffle, (*with person,* *for* thing). [orig. Sc. & N. Engl., perh. dim. of *touse;* see TOUSLE]

tŭ'ssock *n.* clump, hillock, of grass etc.; ∼(-**moth**) (of genus *Orgyia* etc., with tufted larvae); ∼-**grass** (growing in tussocks, esp. *Poa flabellata* from Patagonia etc.); hence ∼Y² *a.* [16th c., perh. alt. f. dial. *tusk* tuft; see -OCK]

tŭ'ssŏre. See TUSSER.

tŭt¹(-tŭ't) *int., n.,* & *v.i.* (-tt-). **1.** *int.* expr. impatience, contempt, or rebuke. **2.** *n.* such exclamation. **3.** *v.i.* exclaim thus. [imit. of click of tongue against teeth]

∥tŭt² *n.* (Mining). job; ∼-**work,** piece-work. [18th c. in Cornwall, of unkn. orig.]

tŭ'tĕlage *n.* guardianship; (period of) being under this; instruction, tuition. [f. L *tutela* (*tuēri tuit-* or *tut-* watch) + -AGE]

tŭ'tĕlarÿ, tŭ'tĕlar, *adjs.* serving as guardian, protective, (*tutelary saint, god*); of a guardian (*tutelary authority*). [f. LL *tutelaris,* L *-arius* (*tutela;* see prec., -AR¹, -ARY¹)]

tŭ'tĕnăg *n.* zinc imported from China and E. Indies; white alloy like German silver. [f. Marathi *tuttināg* perh. f. Skr. *tuttha* copper sulphate + *nāga* tin, lead]

tū'tor *n.* & *v.* **1.** *n.* private teacher, esp. one having general charge of person's education; ∥university graduate, usu. a college fellow, supervising studies and welfare of assigned undergraduates; *college teacher below instructor; (Law) guardian of minor; ∥book of instruction in a subject; hence or cogn. ∼AGE (2), ∼ESS¹, ∼SHIP, *ns.* **2.** *v.t.* act as tutor to, instruct; discipline, school. **3.** *v.i.* work as tutor; *study under tutor. [ME, f. AF, OF *tutour* or f. L *tutor* (*tuēri tut-* watch; see -OR)]

tūtŏr'ial *a.* & *n.* **1.** *a.* of a tutor; hence ∼LY² *adv.* **2.** *n.* period of individual instruction given by college tutor. [f. L *tutorius* (as prec.) + -AL]

tŭ'tsan *n.* a St. John's wort once thought to heal wounds etc. [ME, f. AF *tutsaine* all healthy]

tu'tti (tōō'tē) *adv.* & *n.* (Mus.) all voices or instruments together; passage thus performed. [It., pl. of *tutto* all]

tutti-fru'tti (tōōtēfrōō'tē) *n.* confection, esp. icecream, of or flavoured with mixed fruits. [It., = all fruits]

tŭ'ttÿ *n.* impure zinc oxide used as polishing-powder. [ME, f. OF *tutie* f. med. L *tutia* f. Arab. *tūtiyā*]

tu'tu¹ (tōō'tōō) *n.* ballet dancer's skirt, esp. short projecting skirt of stiff frills in layers. [F]

tu'tu² (tōō'tōō) *n.* (NZ). shrub of genus *Coriaria,* with black berries containing poisonous seeds. [Maori]

tuum. See MEUM.

tu-whi't (tōō-), **tu-whoō'** (-tōō-), *n.,* & *v.i.* (-tt-). (make) cry of owl. [imit.]

***tŭx** *n.* (colloq.) = foll. [abbr.]

***tŭxē'dō** *n.* (*pl.* ∼s or ∼es). dinner-jacket; man's evening dress including this. [f. country club at *T*∼ Park, NY]

tuyère, -ere, (twēyār', tōōyār', twēr') *n.* nozzle through which air is forced into furnace etc. [F (*tuyau* pipe)]

TV *abbr.* television (set).

TVA *abbr.* Tennessee Valley Authority.

twa'ddl|e (-ŏ'-) *v.i.,* & *n.* (indulge in) senseless, feeble, or prosy talk or writing; hence ∼ER¹ *n.,* ∼Y² *a.* [alt. f. earlier *twattle,* alt. of TATTLE]

twain *a.* & *n.* (arch. or poet.) two; two persons or things; *cut* etc. **in** ∼, in two. [OE *twegen,* masc. nom. & acc. of *twā* TWO]

twăng *v.* & *n.* **1.** *v.i.* & *t.* (cause to) make sharp ringing sound as of string of musical instrument or bow when plucked, (derog.) play *on* or on (fiddle etc.) thus; hence ∼'LE 3 (-ă'nggel) *v.i.* & *t.* **2.** speak or utter with nasal sound. **3.** *n.* sound of tense string when plucked; nasal tone of voice. [imit.]

'twas (-ŏz, -oz) (arch. or poet.) it was. [contr.]

twat (-ăt, -ŏt) *n.* (vulg.) female genitals; (derog.) unpleasant or stupid person. [17th c.; orig. unkn.]

tway'blāde *n.* orchid of genus *Listera* etc., with green or purple flowers and single pair of leaves. [f. *tway* var. of TWAIN + BLADE]

tweak *v.t.,* & *n.* **1.** *v.t.* pinch and twist sharply, pull with sharp jerk, twitch. **2.** *n.* twitch, sharp pull, pinch. [prob. alt. f. dial. *twick* & TWITCH¹]

∥twee *a.* (**tweer** *pr.* twē'er; **tweest** *pr.* twē'īst). (esp. affectedly) dainty or quaint. [f. childish pr. of SWEET]

tweed *n.* twilled woollen or wool-and-cotton fabric with roughish surface and usu. two colours combined in the yarn, used esp. for men's clothes and orig. made in S. Scotland; (in *pl.*) cloths or clothes of tweed; hence ∼'Y² *a.,* (colloq.) fond of wearing tweed, (fig.) heartily informal. [orig. a misreading of *tweel,* Sc. form of TWILL, helped by assoc. w. the river *Tweed*]

twee'dle *n.* sound as of fiddle; ∼**du'm and** ∼**dee'** (-deld-), persons or things differing only or chiefly in name (orig. of rival musicians). [imit.]

'tween *prep.* between, esp. ∼-**decks,** (space) between decks. [ME, f. BETWEEN]

∥twee'nÿ *n.* (colloq.) between-maid. [f. as prec. + -Y³]

tweet n., & v.i. chirp (of small bird); hence ∼'ᴇʀ¹ n., small loudspeaker for accurately reproducing high-frequency signals (cf. ᴡᴏᴏꜰ²ᴇʀ). [imit.]

twee'zer n., & v.t. **1.** n. (pair of) ∼s, small pair of tongs for taking up small objects, plucking out hairs, etc. **2.** v.t. extract (hair, thorn, etc.) with tweezers. [extended form of tweezes (cf. pincers etc.) pl. of obs. tweeze case for small instruments, f. etweese = étuis, pl. of ÉTUI]

twĕlfth a. & n. **1.** a. next after eleventh; ‖the ∼ (of August, as beginning of legal grouse-shooting); ∼ man, reserve member of cricket team; ∼ part, one of twelve equal parts. **2.** T∼-day (after Christmas, festival of Epiphany); T∼-night, night before this, formerly celebrated with various festivities etc.; T∼-cake (prepared for Twelfth-night, often with bean or coin to determine 'ruler' of the feast). **3.** Hence ∼ʟʏ² adv. **4.** n. twelfth part, thing, etc.; (Mus.) (note at) interval of an octave and a fifth. [OE twelfta, = OHG zwelifto, ON tólfti (as foll.; see -ᴛʜ²)]

twĕlve a. & n. **1.** one more than eleven; symbol for this (12, xii, XII); time of twelve o'clock; size etc. denoted by twelve; set of twelve; the T∼ (Apostles); Twelve Tables, Tribes; (in pl.) duodecimo sheet of book; hence ∼'ꜰᴏʟᴅ (-vf-) a. & adv. **2.** ∼'mo, duodecimo; ∼'month, period of twelve months, year (today etc. ∼month, a year before or esp. after today etc.); ∼-note, ∼-tone, (Mus.) using twelve chromatic notes of octave arranged in chosen order without conventional key; ‖∼'penny a., (Hist.) costing or worth a shilling. [OE twelf(e), = OS twelif, OHG zwelif, ON tólf, Goth. twalif f. Gmc, prob. f. *twa ᴛᴡᴏ + *lif- as in ᴇʟᴇᴠᴇɴ]

twĕ'nty a. & n. twice ten; symbol for this (20, xx, XX); set of twenty persons or things; (in pl.) numbers, esp. years of a century or life, from 20 to 29; large indefinite number (have told him twenty times); ∼-one etc., (arch.) one-and-∼ etc., twenty plus one etc., w. corresp. ordinals ∼-first etc.; ∼-five, (Rugby Footb. & Hockey) line drawn across ground 25 yards (23 metres) from either goal, ground between this and goal-line; ∼mo, ∼fourmo, leaf of sheet folded into 20, 24, equal parts, book made up of such leaves; hence twĕ'ntiᴇᴛʜ¹ a. & n., ∼ꜰᴏʟᴅ a. & adv. [OE twentig, = OS twēntig, OHG zweinzug, perh. f. as ᴛᴡᴏ + -ᴛʏ²]

'twere (-ĕr, -er) (arch. or poet.) it were. [contr.]

twĕrp n. (sl.) stupid or objectionable person. [20th c.; orig. unkn.]

twi-, twy-, comb. form. (arch.) two, double, twice, as: ∼'bill, double-bladed battle-axe; ∼'fold a. & adv., twofold; ∼'formed, having two forms or parts. [OE, = OHG zwi-, ON tvi-, cogn. w. L ʙɪ-, Gk ᴅɪ-²]

twice adv. two times (esp. of multiplication), on two occasions, (twice 3 is 6; told him twice; ᴛʜɪɴᴋ twice); doubly, in double degree or quantity, (twice as strong; has twice the strength); is ∼ the man he was (twice as strong etc.); did it at or in ∼, (colloq.) in two attempts or instalments; ∼-laid, (of rope) made from yarns of old rope; ∼-told, (fig.) trite. [ME twiges, f. OE twige f. as ᴛᴡᴏ, -s³]

‖**twi'cer** n. (sl.) double-dealing person, cheat. [f. prec. + -ᴇʀ¹]

twi'ddle v. & n. **1.** v.t. twirl randomly or idly, esp. ∼ one's thumbs (for lack of occupation). **2.** v.i. trifle with (object); move twirlingly. **3.** n. slight twirl; twirled mark or sign; hence twi'ddlʏ² a. [app. imit., after twirl, twist, and fiddle, piddle]

twig¹ n. small shoot or branch of tree or plant; (Anat.) small branch of artery etc.; divining-rod, esp. work the twig; hop the ∼, (colloq.) die; hence (-)∼ɢᴇᴅ² (-gd), ∼'ʟᴇss, ∼'ɢʏ² (-gĭ), adjs. [OE twigge, rel. to OE twig, twī; cf. OHG zwīg f. Gmc as ᴛᴡɪ-]

twig² v.t. (-gg-). (colloq.) understand, catch the meaning of, (person, words, plan, that etc., or abs.); perceive, observe. [18th c., of unkn. orig.]

twi'light (-īt) n. light from sky when sun is below horizon in morning or (usu.) evening; period of this; faint light; (fig.) state of imperfect knowledge, understanding, etc.; ∼ arc(h) or curve (dividing the earth's shadow from part of sky lit by direct rays of sun); ∼ of the gods, (Norse Myth.) conflict in which gods and giants destroy each other; ∼ sleep, partial narcosis esp. as means of making childbirth less painful; ∼ zone, (1) area between two others in position and character, (2) urban area becoming decrepit. [ME (ᴛᴡɪ-, ʟɪɢʜᴛ¹)]

twi'lightĕd (-īt-), **twi'lit**, adjs. dimly illuminated (as) by twilight. [p.p. of twilight v., f. prec.]

twill n., & v.t. **1.** n. textile fabric in which weft-threads pass alternately over one warp-thread and under (not one as in plain weaving but) two or more thus producing diagonal lines. **2.** v.t. (esp. in p.p.) weave (material) thus. [N. Engl. var. of obs. twilly, OE twili = OHG zwilīh, f. ᴛᴡɪ- after L ʙɪ(lix f. licium thread)]

'twill (arch. or poet.) it will. [contr.]

twin n., a., & v. (-nn-). **1.** a. forming, or being one of, a closely related or associated pair esp. of children or animals born at a birth (twin children, brother(s), sister(s)); (Bot.) growing in pairs; consisting of two closely connected and similar parts; ∼ bed, one of a pair of single beds; ∼-engined, having two engines, *∼'flower, plant of genus Linnaea with paired flowers; ∼-screw, (steamer) with two propellers on separate shafts having opposite twists; ∼ set, woman's matching cardigan and jumper; ∼ towns, two towns (usu. in different countries) establishing special links. **2.** n. each of a closely related or associated pair esp. of children or animals born at a birth; exact counterpart of person or thing; compound crystal one part of which is in a reversed position with reference to the other; the T∼s, zodiacal sign Gemini; hence ∼'ʟɪɴɢ¹, ∼'sʜɪᴘ, ns. **3.** v.t. & i. join intimately together, couple, pair, (with); hence ∼'ɴɪɴɢ¹ n., formation of twin crystals. **4.** v.i. bear twins; grow as twin crystal. [OE twinn double, f. ᴛᴡɪ-; cf. ON tvinnr]

twine n. & v. **1.** n. strong thread or string of two or more strands of hemp, cotton, etc., twisted together; coil, twist; interlacing, tangle. **2.** v.t. form (garland etc.) by twisting strands together; form (garland etc.) of interwoven material, garland (brow etc.) with; interweave; coil, wind, (thing about, round, another). **3.** v.i. & refl. (Of plant, snake, etc.) coil or twist itself or itself (round). [OE twīn, twigin linen, ult. f. stem of ᴛᴡɪ-]

twinge (-nj) n. sharp momentary local pain (lit. or fig.; a twinge of toothache, rheumatism, conscience, remorse). [f. twinge v. pinch, wring f. OE twengan, = MLG twengen, OHG zwengen f. Gmc *twang-]

twink v.i., n., & n. **1.** twinkle, sparkle. **2.** n. in a ∼, in an instant. [ME, f. OE *twincan; cf. MHG zwinken, and foll.]

twi'nkle v. & n. **1.** v.i. (Of light, star, etc.) shine with rapidly intermittent gleams, sparkle; (of feet in dancing, etc.) move rapidly up and down or to and fro; (of eyes) sparkle (at jest etc.). **2.** v.t. blink, wink, (one's eyes); emit (light, signal) in quick gleams. **3.** n. twitching of eyelid, blink, wink, (in a ∼, in an instant); sparkle, gleam, of the eyes, (a humorous, mischievous, twinkle); short rapid movement e.g. of feet in dancing; quick tremulous light, glimmer. [OE twinclian, frequent. of *twincan; see prec., -ʟᴇ 3]

twi'nkling n. in vbl senses; in a ∼, in the ∼ of an eye, (joc.) of a teacup, etc., in an instant. [ME, f. prec. + -ɪɴɢ¹]

twirl v. & n. **1.** v.t. & i. revolve rapidly, spin, whirl, twist, (round). **2.** v.t. turn (one's thumbs etc.) round and round in purposeless way, twiddle. **3.** n. twirling, rapid or idle circular motion; twirling thing, flourish or curl made with pen etc.; hence ∼'ʏ² a. [16th c., prob. alt., after whirl, f. obs. tirl ᴛʀɪʟʟ]

twirp. Var. of ᴛᴡᴇʀᴘ.

twist n. & v. **1.** n. thread, rope, etc., made by winding two or more strands etc. about one another; fine strong silk thread used by tailors etc.; roll of bread, tobacco, etc. in form of twist; ‖paper packet with screwed-up ends; curled piece of lemon etc. peel to flavour a drink. **2.** act of twisting, condition of being twisted, (*give it a twist; full of twists and turns*); dance with vigorous bodily contortions; unexpected development of events in story etc.; *change from usual procedure. **3.** manner or degree in which thing is twisted, e.g. inclination of rifle-grooves, spinning motion given to ball in cricket etc. to make it take special curve. **4.** peculiar tendency of mind, character, etc., (freq. derog.); **round the ∼,** (sl.) crazy. **5.** twisting strain; (angle showing) amount of twisting of rod etc.; forward motion combined with rotation about an axis. **6.** ‖(sl.) drink made of two ingredients mixed. **7.** ‖(colloq.) hearty appetite; swindle. **8.** (sl.) young woman, esp. disreputable one. **9.** *v.t.* wind (strands etc.) one about another; form (rope etc.) thus; interweave (thing *with* or *in with* another). **10.** give spiral form to (rod, column, cord, etc.) as by rotating the ends in opposite directions; break *off* thus; *twist* person *round* one's (*little*) FINGER. **11.** cause (ball, esp. in billiards) to rotate while following curved path. **12.** twine (flowers etc. *into* garland etc.); make (garland etc.) thus. **13.** make one's *way* (*through* crowd, etc., *along*, etc.) in winding manner. **14.** pull out of natural shape, distort, (*fell and twisted her ankle; features twisted with pain*; (fig.) *wants to twist my words into an admission of error*; **∼** person's **arm,** force his hand or wrist round as torture, (fig.) coerce him by moral pressure); ‖(colloq.) cheat; (in *p.p.*, of mind etc.) warped, (Geom., of curve) extending in three dimensions. **15.** *v.i.* **∼**ABLE *a.* **16.** *v.i.* be given, grow in, spiral form; move (*along, through*, etc.) in winding manner; take twisted position (*twisted round in his seat*); dance the twist. [ME; cogn. w. TWIN, TWINE]

twi′ster *n.* In vbl senses; untrustworthy person, swindler; twisting ball in cricket or billiards; *tornado, waterspout, etc.; TONGUE¹-*twister*. [f. prec. + -ER¹]

twi′sty *a.* full of twists; (fig.) dishonest. [f. TWIST + -Y²]

twit¹ *v.t.* (-tt-). reproach, taunt, (usu. good-humouredly) (person *with* or *about* fault etc.). [16th c. *twite*, f. *atwite* f. OE *ætwītan* reproach with (*æt* at, *wītan* blame)]

twit² *n.* (sl.) ‖foolish or insignificant person; state of jumpiness. [orig. dial., perh. f. prec.]

twitch¹ *v. & n.* **1.** *v.t.* pull (thing *off* etc.) with light jerk; pull sharply at, jerk at, (person's sleeve etc.) esp. to call attention. **2.** *v.i.* pull sharply, jerk, *at*; (of features, muscles, limbs) move or contract spasmodically. **3.** *n.* sudden involuntary contraction or movement, sudden pull or jerk; (colloq.) state of nervousness, whence **∼′**Y² *a.*; noose and stick for quietening horse during veterinary operation. [ME, = LG *twikken*, MHG *zwicken* f. Gmc **twik-*; cf. OE *twiccian*, dial. *twick*]

twitch² *n.* **∼**(-**grass**), = COUCH³-*grass*. [var. of QUITCH]

twite *n.* mountain linnet (*Acanthis flavirostris*). [imit. of its note]

twi′tter *v. & n.* **1.** *v.i.* (Of bird, or fig. of person) utter succession of light tremulous sounds, chirp. **2.** *v.t.* utter or express thus. **3.** *n.* twittering; (colloq.) tremulously excited state. [ME, imit.; cf. -ER⁵]

'twixt *prep.* (poet. or arch.) = BETWIXT. [abbr.]

two (tōō) *a. & n.* **1.** one more than one; symbol for this (2, ii, II); card etc. with two pips; time of two o'clock; size etc. denoted by two; (in *pl.*) gloves, shoes, etc., of second size; **a . . . or ∼,** one or two . . .s, a few . . .s; *two* CHEER²*s; cut divide,* etc., **in ∼,** into two parts; *in two* SHAKE²*s,* ‖**in ∼ ticks,** ‖**in ∼ s,** (colloq.) in a very short time; ONE *or* two; **∼ can play at that game,** cf. GAME¹ *that two can play;* **∼ and ∼, ∼ by ∼,** in pairs; **put ∼ and ∼ together,** make inference from known facts; **that makes ∼ of us,** (colloq.) that is true of myself also; *two a* PENNY; *two* TABLES; hence **∼**′FOLD *a.* & *n.,* **∼**′NESS *n.* **2.** ***∼-bit,** costing 25 cents, (fig.) petty;

∼-by-four, (*n.*) timber with cross-section 2″ by 4″, *(*a.*, fig.) petty; **∼-dimensional,** having or appearing to have length and breadth but no depth; **∼-edged,** double-edged; **∼-faced,** having two faces, (fig.) insincere; **∼-fisted,** ‖clumsy, *vigorous; **∼-handed,** having two hands, (of sword) requiring to be used with both hands, (of saw, game, etc.) to be worked, played, etc., by two persons; **∼-line(d),** (Print.) having a depth double that of the normal size of letters; ‖(**∼pence** (tŭ′pens), sum of two pence (**∼***pence coloured,* cheap and, as opp. *penny plain,* gaudy), thing of little value (*don't care twopence*); ‖**∼penny** (tŭ′penǐ), costing or worth 2p or 2d., cheap, worthless; ‖(**∼penny-halfpenny** (tŭpnǐhǎ′pnǐ), contemptible, insignificant, trumpery; **∼-piece,** suit of clothes or woman's bathing-suit comprising two separate parts; **∼-ply,** (wool etc.) of two strands, layers, or thicknesses (*two-ply rope, carpet*); **∼-seater,** vehicle or aircraft with two seats; **∼-sided,** having two sides, aspects, etc.; **∼-step,** round dance with sliding step in march or polka time; **∼-stroke,** (of internal combustion engine) having power cycle completed in one up-and-down movement of piston; **∼-sui′ter,** (Bridge) hand containing two long suits; **∼-time** *v.t.,* (sl.) swindle, deceive (esp. spouse by infidelity); **∼-tone,** having two colours or sounds; **∼-up,** gambling game with tossing of two coins; **∼-way,** involving two ways or participants, (Electr., of switch) permitting current to be switched on or off from either of two points, (of tap etc.) permitting fluid etc. to flow in either of two channels or directions, (of traffic etc.) moving in two esp. opposite directions; **∼-whee′ler,** vehicle with two wheels. [OE *twā* fem. & neut., *tū* neut. (cf. TWAIN), = OS *twā, twō,* OHG *zwā, zwō,* ON *tvær,* Goth. *twōs,* cogn. w. Skr. *dwau, dwe,* Gk & L *duo*]

***two′fer** (tōō′-) *n.* free ticket entitling holder to buy theatre-tickets at half price. [f. *two for* one]

two′some (tōō′-) *a. & n.* (game, dance, etc.) for two persons; pair or couple of persons. [f. TWO + -SOME²]

'twould (-ood) (arch. or poet.) it would. [contr.]

twy-. See TWI-.

twy′er. Var. of TUYÈRE.

TX *abbr.* Texas.

-ty¹ *suf.* forming *n*s. denoting quality or condition (*bounty, cruelty, faculty, plenty, puberty, safety, subtlety*). [ME *-tie, -tee, -te* f. OF *-té, -tet* f. L *-tas -tatis;* cf. -ITY]

-ty² *suf.* = tens (*twenty, thirty, ninety,* etc.). [OE *-tig,* = OS *-tig,* OHG *-zug;* cf. ON *tigr,* Goth. *tigus* ten]

ty′chism (-k-) *n.* theory that chance controls the universe. [f. Gk. *tukhē* chance + -ISM]

Tȳchō′nǐan, Tȳchŏ′nic, (-k-) *adjs.* of the (astronomical system) of Tycho Brahe. [f. *Tycho -onis* Latinized name of *Tyge* Brahe, Da. astronomer d. 1601 + -IAN, -IC]

tȳcōō′n *n.* Title applied by foreigners to shogun of Japan 1854–68; business magnate. [f. Jap. *taikun* great prince]

tȳ′ing. See TIE¹.

tȳke, tīke, *n.* cur; ‖low fellow; (**Yorkshire**) **∼,** Yorkshireman; *small child. [ME, f. ON *tík* bitch]

tyle(r). Var. of TILE 5, TILER 2.

tȳ′lopŏd *a. & n.* (animal) with padded not hoofed digits, e.g. camel; hence **tȳlŏ′pod**OUS *a.* [f. Gk *tulos* knob or *tulē* callus, cushion + -o- + *pous podos* foot]

tȳ′mpan *n.* (Print.) apparatus to equalize pressure between platen etc. and printing-sheet; (Archit.) tympanum. [F, or f. L TYMPANUM]

tȳmpă′nic *a.* (acting) like a drumhead; (Anat.) of the tympanum (*tympanic membrane*); **∼ (bone),** bone of ear supporting tympanic membrane. [f. TYMPANUM + -IC]

tȳ′mpanist, tȳ′mpanō *n.* Var. of TIMPANIST, TIMPANO.

tȳmpan|ī′tēs (-z) *n.* swelling of abdomen caused by gas in intestine etc.; hence **∼ī′t**IC *a.* [LL, f. Gk *tumpanītēs* of drum (as TYMPANUM; see -ITE¹)]

tȳ′mpan|um *n.* (*pl.* **∼a** *or* **∼ums**). **1.** (Anat.) middle ear; ear-drum; hence ∿ɪ'ᴛɪs *n*. **2.** (Zool.) bony labyrinth at base of trachea in some ducks; membrane covering hearing-organ on leg etc. of insect. **3.** (Archit.) vertical triangular space forming centre of pediment; (carving on) similar space over door between lintel and arch. **4.** drum-wheel for raising water from stream. [L, f. Gk *tumpanon* drum (*tuptō* strike)]

Ty̆'nwald (-ŏld) *n*. Isle of Man annual assembly proclaiming newly enacted laws. [f. ON *thing-völlr* place of assembly (*thing* assembly, *völlr* field)]

type[1] *n*. **1.** person, thing, event, serving as illustration, symbol, prophetic similitude, or characteristic specimen, of another thing or of a class (*water may serve as a type of instability; paschal lamb is a type of Christ; the treatment he received is but a type of what patriots must expect; he is an admirable type of modern athleticism or of the modern athlete*); (colloq.) person, esp. of a specified character. **2.** class of things etc. having common characteristics (*her beauty was of* or *belonged to another type; dislike men of that type*); (as *suf.*) made of, resembling, functioning by or as, (*ceramic-type materials; Cheddar-type cheese*). **3.** (Biol. etc.) plan of structure (*deviates from the type;* TRUE *to type*); main division of animal or vegetable kingdom characterized by this (*the vertebrate type*); organism (chosen as) having the essential characteristics of its group (∿ **genus**, genus giving its name to and having the characteristics of a higher group, e.g. a family); ∿ **site**, (Archaeol.) site where objects are found as defining the characteristics of a period etc. are found. **4.** Biblical event regarded as symbolic or foreshadowing a later one (cf. ANTITYPE). **5.** object, conception, work of art serving as model for subsequent artists. **6.** device on either side of medal or coin. **7.** (Print.) piece of metal or wood having on its upper surface a raised letter or character for use in printing, a kind or size of such pieces, (collect. *sing.*) set or supply of these, (*wooden types* or *type is now used only for posters; ran short of type; short of certain types; printed in large type*); in ∿, composed and ready for printing. **8.** ∿-**bar**, (1) bar in typewriter carrying one pair of letters etc., (2) line of types in solid bar as cast in some typesetting machines; *type* BASKET; ∿-**cast** *v.t.*, cast (actor) in role appropriate to his nature or of a kind in which he has been successful; ∿-**face**, (impression made by) inked part of type, set of types (or letters etc. otherwise printed) in one design; ∿-**founder**, one who designs and makes metal type for printing; ∿-**high**, (of block etc.) set at proper height to print with accompanying type; ∿-**metal**, alloy of lead etc. used for printing-types; ∿**'script** *a*. & *n.*, (state of being) typewritten (document); ∿**'setter**, (1) compositor, (2) composing-machine; ∿**'setting**, setting of types in proper order for printing; ∿-*setting machine* (for simplifying this process, now usu. including the making of types as they are needed); ∿-**wheel**, wheel bearing letters in relief as used in some typewriters and telegraphs. **9.** Hence **ty̆'**ᴘᴀʟ *a*. [ME f. F, or f. L f. Gk *tupos* impression, figure, type (*tuptō* strike)]

type[2] *v.t.* & *i*. be a type or example of; write with typewriter; assign to type; type-cast. [f. prec.]

ty̆'pewrite (-prīt) *v.t.* & *i*. (-wrote; -written; usu. in *p.p.*) write with typewriter. [back-form. f. foll.]

ty̆'pewriter (-prī-) *n*. machine for writing in characters like those used in printing, by pressing keys to actuate steel types that strike paper through inked ribbon; (arch.) typist. [f. TYPE[1]+WRITER]

typhli'tis *n*. inflammation of caecum; hence ∿ɪ'ᴛɪᴄ *a*. [mod. L, f. Gk *tuphlon* caecum or blind gut (*tuphlos* blind)+-ITIS]

ty̆'phoid *a*. & *n*. like typhus; ∿ (**fever**), infectious bacterial fever with eruption of red spots on chest and abdomen and severe intestinal irritation, similar disease of animals; ∿ **condition** or **state** (of depressed vitality, occurring in many acute diseases); hence **ty̆phoi'd**ᴀʟ *a*. [f. TYPHUS+-OID]

typhōo'n *n*. violent hurricane in E. Asian seas; so **ty̆phō'n**ɪᴄ *a*. [partly f. Port. *tufão* f. Arab. *ṭūfān* perh.

f. Gk *tuphōn* whirlwind; partly f. Chin. dial. *tai fung* big wind]

ty̆'ph|us *n*. rickettsial infectious fever with eruption of purple spots, great prostration, and usu. delirium; hence ∿ous *a*. [mod. L, f. Gk *tuphos* smoke, stupor (*tuphō* to smoke)]

ty̆'pic *a*. (arch. or poet.) = foll. 1. [f. F *typique* f. LL f. Gk *tupikos* (as TYPE[1]; see -IC)]

ty̆'pical *a*. **1.** serving as a type or characteristic example, representative, symbolical, emblematic, (*of*), (*a typical genus, plant, Scotsman, shingles rash; is typical of the genus*). **2.** characteristic of, serving to distinguish, a type (*typical markings, structure, phraseology*). **3.** Hence ∿ʟʏ[2] *adv.*, ∿ɪᴛʏ (-ă'l-), ∿ɴᴇss, *ns*. [f. med. L *typicalis* f. LL *typicus* (see prec., -AL)]

ty̆'pi|fy *v.t.* represent by a type, foreshadow; be a type or example of, embody the characteristics of; hence ∿ꜰɪᴄᴀ'ᴛɪᴏɴ, ∿ꜰɪᴇʀ[1], *ns*. [f. L *typus* TYPE[1]+-FY]

ty̆'pist *n*. one who uses a typewriter, esp. professionally; **shorthand** ∿ (who can also write shorthand). [f. TYPE[1]+-IST]

ty̆'pō *n*. (*pl.* ∿s). (colloq.) typographer; *typographical error. [abbr.]

typō'graph|y *n*. **1.** art of printing; so ∿ᴇʀ[1] *n*. **2.** style or appearance of printed matter (*faults of typography; the typography was admirable*). **3.** Hence **typŏgrǎ'ph**ɪᴄ(ᴀʟ) *adjs*. [f. F *typographie* or mod. L *typographia* f. as TYPE[1]+-O-+-GRAPHY]

typō'log|y *n*. study and interpretation of (esp. biblical) types; hence **typŏlō'g**ɪᴄᴀʟ *a.*, ∿ɪsᴛ (3) *n*. [f. Gk *tupos* TYPE[1]+-O-+-LOGY]

ty̆'ponym *n*. (Biol.) name based on a type. [f. as prec.+Gk *onum-* = *onoma* name]

ty̆rǎ'nnical *a*. acting like, characteristic of, a tyrant; arbitrary, imperious, despotic; hence ∿ʟʏ[2] *adv*. [f. OF *tyrannique* f. L f. Gk *turannikos* (as TYRANT; see -IC)+-AL]

ty̆rǎ'nni|cīde *n*. killer or killing of a tyrant; hence ∿cī'dᴀʟ *a*. [F, f. L *tyrannicida, -cidium* (as TYRANT; see -CIDE)]

ty̆'rannize, -ise (-īz) *v*. **1.** *v.i.* play the tyrant, rule despotically or cruelly (*over* person etc.). **2.** *v.t.* rule (person etc.) despotically. [f. F *tyranniser* (as TYRANT; see -IZE)]

ty̆rǎ'nnosaur *n*. fossil biped dinosaur (*Tyrannosaurus rex*), largest known carnivore. [f. as TYRANT, after *dinosaur*]

ty̆'rann|y *n*. **1.** despotic or cruel exercise of power; instance of this, tyrannical act or behaviour; hence ∿ous *a*. **2.** rule of (Greek) tyrant; State thus ruled; period of this. [ME, f. OF *tyrannie* f. med. L *tyrannia* f. Gk *turannia* (as foll.; see -Y[1])]

ty̆r'ant *n*. **1.** oppressive or cruel ruler; person exercising power or authority arbitrarily or cruelly. **2.** (Gk Hist.) absolute ruler who seized power without legal right; one of 30 oligarchs ruling Athens 404-403 BC. **3.** ∿-**bird**, ∿ **flycatcher**, Amer. bird of genus *Tyrannus*, driving all other birds from near its nest. [ME *tyran, -ant*, f. OF *tiran, tyrant* f. L f. Gk *turannos*]

‖**tȳre, *tīre**[3], *n*. hollow inflated, or solid, rubber ring placed round wheel of vehicle to prevent jarring; ∿-**chain** (fastening over tread of tyre to improve grip on ice etc.); ∿-**gauge**, portable device for measuring air-pressure in tyre. [var. of TIRE[2]]

Ty̆'rian *a*. & *n*. (native or inhabitant) of ancient Tyre in Phoenicia; *Tyrian* PURPLE. [f. L *Tyrius* (*Tyrus* Tyre)+-AN]

tȳr'ō. See TIRO.

Ty̆rol|ē'an *a*. of or characteristic of the Tyrol; so ∿ᴇ'sᴇ *a*. & *n*. [f. *Tyrol*, Tirol, Alpine province of W. Austria+-EAN]

Ty̆'rrhēne, Tȳrrhē'nian, (-rē-) *adjs*. & *ns*. Etruscan. [f. L *Tyrrhenus*+-IAN]

tzar. Var. of TSAR.

tziga'ne (tsĭgah'n) *a*. & *n*. **1.** *a*. of the Hungarian gypsies or their music. **2.** *n*. Hungarian gypsy. [F, f. Magyar *c(z)igány*]

U

U¹, u, (ū) *n.* (*pl.* **Us** *or* **U's**). twenty-first letter of alphabet; **U-bolt, -tube,** etc., (shaped like U); **U--turn,** driving of vehicle so as to face in opposite direction without reversing, (fig.) complete reversal of policy etc.

U² (ōō) *n.* Burmese title of respect before man's name. [Burm.]

U³ (ū) *a.* (colloq.) upper-class; supposedly characteristic of the upper class. [abbr.]

U. *abbr.* universal (of cinema film open to all persons); university.

u *pref.* = μ (symbol for MICRO- 2).

U *symb.* uranium.

ŭbī'etỹ *n.* being in definite place, local relation. [f. med. L *ubietas* f. L *ubi* where; see -TY¹]

-ŭbī'lĭtỹ *suf.* forming *ns.* f. *adjs.* in -UBLE (*dissolubility*). [f. L *-ubilitas*; see -ITY]

ūbĭquitār'ĭan *a.* & *n.* (Theol.) of, believer in, the omnipresence of Christ's body; hence ∼ISM (3) *n.* [f. mod. L *ubiquitarius* (as foll.; see -ARIAN)]

ŭbī'quĭtỹ *n.* being everywhere or in an indefinite number of places at same time; (joc., of person) being frequently encountered; ‖∼y of the king, (Law) his official presence in all courts in the person of his judges; hence ∼OUS *a.* [f. mod. L *ubiquitas* f. L *ubique* everywhere (*ubi* where; see -ITY)]

-ūble *suf.* forming *adjs.* w. senses as -ABLE (*soluble, voluble*); hence **-ūbLY²** *adv. suf.* [F, f. L -*u-* of vbs. in *-vere* + *-bilis* (see -BLE)]

U'-boat (ū'b-) *n.* (Hist.) German submarine. [f. G *U--boot* (*Unterseeboot* under-sea boat)]

UC *abbr.* University College.

u.c. *abbr.* upper case.

‖**UCATT** *abbr.* Union of Construction, Allied Trades, and Technicians.

‖**UCCA** *abbr.* Universities Central Council on Admissions.

ū'dal *n.* kind of freehold right based on uninterrupted possession prevailing in N. Europe before feudal system and still in Orkney and Shetland; ∼**ler,** ∼**man,** holder of property by udal. [f. ON *óthal*, = OE *ēthel, ēthel, ōthel,* OS *ōthil,* OHG *uodal* f. Gmc **ōth-*]

UDC *abbr.* Universal Decimal Classification; ‖(Hist.) Urban District Council.

ŭ'dder *n.* mammary glands of cattle etc. in pendulous baggy organ having more than one teat; hence (-)∼**ED²** (-erd), ∼**LESS,** *adjs.* [OE *ūder,* = OS *ūder,* OHG *ūter* f. WG **ūdhr-*]

UDI *abbr.* unilateral declaration of independence.

ūdŏ'mèter *n.* rain-gauge. [f. F *udomètre* f. L *udus* damp; see -O-, -METER]

UDR *abbr.* Ulster Defence Regiment.

UEFA *abbr.* Union of European Football Associations.

UFO *abbr.,* **ū'fō** *n.* (*pl.* ∼**s**), unidentified flying object, esp. 'flying saucer'.

ugh (ūh, ōōh) *int.* expr. disgust or horror, or sound of cough or grunt. [imit.]

ŭ'glī *n.* mottled green and yellow citrus fruit, hybrid of grapefruit and tangerine. [f. foll.]

ŭ'glỹ *a.* & *n.* **1.** *a.* unpleasing or repulsive to sight or hearing (*an ugly beast of a bulldog; must not make ugly faces; the ugliest house I have seen; has an ugly scar on his forehead; produced an ugly discord*); morally repulsive, vile, discreditable, unpleasant, unpleasantly suggestive, threatening, unpromising, (*ugly vices; his conduct has an ugly look; ugly rumours are about; cloud has an ugly look; have had ugly weather; an ugly gash*); ∼ **customer,** unpleasantly formidable person; ∼ **duckling,** person who turns out to be the genius etc. of the family after

being thought the dullard etc. [w. ref. to cygnet in brood of ducks in tale by Andersen]; hence **ŭ'glĭFY** *v.t.,* **ŭ'glĭLY²** *adv.,* **ŭ'glĭNESS** *n.* **2.** *n.* = prec.; silk shade worn as appendage to bonnet about middle of 19th c. [ME, f. ON *uggligr* to be dreaded (*ugga* to dread; see -LY¹)]

U'grian, U'gric, (ōō'-) *adjs.* & *ns.* (language or member) of (orig.) E. branch of Finnic peoples, esp. Magyar. [f. Russ. *Ugry* name of race dwelling E. of Urals + -IAN, -IC]

UHF *abbr.* ultra-high frequency.

uh'lan (ōō'-, ū'-) *n.* (Hist.) cavalryman armed with lance in some European armies, esp. former German army. [F & G, f. Pol. (*h*)*ulan* f. Turk. *oğlan* youth, servant]

Ui'gur (wē'goor) *n.* member or language of a Turkic people in W. China. [E. Turk. *uighur* (*ui* follow)]

Ui'tlander (ā'tlŏndĕr) *n.* (S. Afr.) foreigner, alien, esp. before Boer War. [Afrik., f. Du. *uit* out + *land* land; see -ER¹]

UK *abbr.* United Kingdom.

UKAEA *abbr.* United Kingdom Atomic Energy Authority.

ūkā'se (-z) *n.* edict of Tsarist Russian government; any arbitrary order. [f. Russ. *ukaz* ordinance, edict (*ukazat'* show, decree)]

ukiyŏ-e' (ōōkēyōyā') *n.* school of Japanese art using subjects from everyday life and simple treatment. [Jap., = genre picture]

Ukrai'nian (ū-) *a.* & *n.* (native or language) of the Ukraine, a constituent republic of USSR. [f. *Ukraine* f. Russ. *ukraina* frontier region (*u* at, *krai* edge) + -IAN]

ūkule'lè (-lā'-) *n.* small four-stringed Hawaiian (orig. Portuguese) guitar. [Hawaiian]

-ūlar *suf.* forming *adjs.,* sometimes corresp. to *ns.* in -ULE (*pustular*) but often without dim. force (*angular, cellular, globular, granular, tubular*); so **-ūlā'rĭTY** *n. suf.,* ∼LY² *adv. suf.* [f. or after L -*ularis* (as -ULE, -AR¹)]

ŭ'lcer *n.* open sore on external or internal surface of body with suppuration etc.; (fig.) moral blemish, corroding or corrupting influence, etc.; hence or cogn. ∼ED² (-erd), ∼OUS, *adjs.* [ME, f. L *ulcus -eris,* rel. to Gk *helkos*]

ŭ'lcer|āte *v.i.* & *t.* form, convert or be converted into, affect with, an ulcer (lit. or fig.); hence or cogn. ∼ABLE, ∼ATIVE, *adjs.,* ∼A'TION *n.* [ME, f. L *ulcerare* (as prec.) + -ATE³]

-ūle *suf.* forming dim. *ns.* (*capsule, globule, granule, pustule*). [f. or after L -*ulus, -ula, -ulum*]

u'lèma (ōō'-) *n.* (member of) body of Muslim doctors of sacred law and theology. [f. Arab. *'ulamā* pl. of *'ālim* learned (*'alama* know)]

-ūlent *suf.* forming *adjs.* w. sense 'abounding in, full of' (*flatulent, fraudulent, turbulent*); so **-ūlENCE** *n. suf.,* ∼LY² *adv. suf.* [f. L -*ulentus*]

ūlĭ'ginōse, -ous, *adjs.* (Bot.) growing in wet or swampy places. [f. L *uliginosus* (*uligo -ginis* moisture; see -OSE¹, -OUS)]

ŭ'llage *n.* amount by which cask etc. falls short of being full, loss by evaporation or leakage. [ME, f. AF *ulliage,* OF *ouillage* (*ouiller* fill up f. Gallo-Rom. **oculare* f. L *oculus* eye, w. ref. to bung-hole; see -AGE)]

ŭ'ln|a *n.* (*pl.* ∼**ae**). large thinner bone of forearm in man (cf. RADIUS); corresponding bone in animal's foreleg or bird's wing; hence ∼AR¹ *a.* [L, rel. to Gk *ōlenē* and ELL]

ūlŏ'trichan *a.* & *n.,* **-chous** *a.,* (-k-). woolly-haired; (member) of the crisp- or woolly-haired division of mankind. [f. mod. L *Ulotrichi* f. Gk *oulos* woolly, crisp + *thrix trikhos* hair + -AN, -OUS]

-ūlous *suf.* forming *adjs.* (*fabulous, garrulous, populous,* *tremulous*); hence ∼LY² *adv. suf.*, ∼NESS *n. suf.* [f. L *-ulosus* & *-ulus* + -OUS]

ŭ'lster *n.* long loose overcoat of rough cloth, often with belt, [orig. sold in Belfast]; U∼ **custom,** form of tenant right in Ireland; U∼**man,** U∼**woman,** native or inhabitant of Ulster. [f. U∼ in Ireland]

ult. *abbr.* ultimo.

ŭltēr'ior *a.* situated beyond; more remote, not immediate, in the future; in the background, beyond what is seen or avowed, (*ulterior motive, plans*); hence ∼LY² *adv.* [L, compar. of *ulter; cf. ULTRA-]

ŭ'ltĭma *n.* last syllable of word. [L *ultima* (*syllaba*), fem. of *ultimus* last]

ŭ'ltĭmate *a.* last, final, beyond which no other exists or is possible, (*ultimate result, analysis*); fundamental, primary, (*ultimate basis, principles, truths*); maximum (*ultimate tensile strength*); ∼ **cause** (beyond which no other can be found); **the** ∼ **facts of nature** (beyond reach of analysis); hence ∼LY² (-tlĭ) *adv.*, ∼NESS (-tn-) *n.* [f. LL *ultimatus* p.p. of *ultimare* come to an end (*ultimus* last); see -ATE²]

ultima Thule (ŭltĭma thū'lē) *n.* far-away unknown region. [L, = farthest Thule (as prec., THULIUM)]

ŭltimā't|um *n.* (*pl.* ∼ums *or* ∼a). final proposal or statement of terms, rejection of which by opposite party may lead to end of harmonious relations, declaration of war, etc.; final point; fundamental principle. [neut. p.p. (as n.); see ULTIMATE]

ŭ'ltĭmŏ *a.* (Commerc.) of last month (*the 28th ultimo*). [L, = in the last (*mense* month)]

ŭltĭmogĕ'nĭture *n.* system in which youngest son (cf. PRIMOGENITURE) has right of inheritance. [f. L *ultimus* last, after *primogeniture*]

ŭ'ltra *a.* & *n.* (person) favouring extreme views or measures, esp. in religion or politics. [orig. as abbr. of F *ultra-royaliste*; see foll.]

ŭ'ltra- *pref.* beyond, on the other side of; extreme(ly), excessive(ly), (*ultra-conservative, ultra-fashionable, ultra-modern*). [f. L *ultra* beyond]

ŭltrace'ntrĭfuge *n.* high-speed centrifuge to deter mine size of small particles and large molecules by their rate of sedimentation. [f. ULTRA- + CENTRIFUGE]

ŭ'ltra-high (-hī) *a.* (Of frequency) in range 300 to 3000 megahertz. [f. ULTRA- + HIGH]

ŭ'ltra|ĭst *n.* holder of extreme opinions in politics, religion, etc.; so ∼ISM (3) *n.* [f. ULTRA + -IST]

ultramari'ne (-ē'n) *a.* & *n.* **1.** *a.* (arch.) situated beyond the sea. **2.** *n.* (colour of) blue pigment got from lapis lazuli; imitation of this from powdered fired clay, sodium carbonate, sulphur, and resin. [f. obs. It. *oltramarino* & med. L ULTRA(*marinus* MARINE); sense 2 from fact that lapis lazuli was brought from beyond sea]

ŭltrami'croscōpe *n.* instrument revealing, by scattered light, objects too small to be seen with ordinary microscope. [f. ULTRA- + MICROSCOPE]

ŭltramĭcroscŏ'pĭc *a.* of ultramicroscope; too small to be seen with ordinary microscope. [f. ULTRA- + MICROSCOPIC]

ŭltramŏ'nt|āne *a.* & *n.* **1.** *a.* situated south of the Alps; Italian; favourable to absolute authority of Pope in matters of faith and discipline, whence ∼**an**ISM (3), ∼**an**IST (2), *ns.* **2.** *n.* one who resides south of the Alps; person holding ultramontane views. [f. med. L ULTRA(*montanus* f. L *mons montis* mountain; see -ANE)]

ŭltramŭ'ndāne *a.* lying beyond the world or the solar system. [f. L ULTRA(*mundanus* f. *mundus* world; see -ANE)]

ŭltrasŏ'n|ĭc *a.* of sound waves with pitch above upper limit of human hearing; hence ∼ICALLY *adv.*, ∼ICS *n.*, (science and application of) ultrasonic waves. [f. ULTRA- + SONIC]

ŭ'ltrasound *n.* sound having ultrasonic frequency; ultrasonic waves. [f. ULTRA- + SOUND²]

ŭ'ltrastrŭcture *n.* (Biol.) structure not visible with optical microscopes. [f. ULTRA- + STRUCTURE]

ŭltravī'olet *a.* (Phys.) having wavelength (just)

beyond violet end of visible spectrum; of or using such radiation. [f. ULTRA- + VIOLET]

ultra vires (ŭltra vīr'ēz, ōōltrah vēr'āz) *adv.* & *pred. a.* beyond one's (legal) power or authority. [L]

ŭ'lŭl|āte *v.i.* howl, wail; give prolonged cry of joy; hoot; so ∼ANT *a.*, ∼A'TION *n.* [f. L *ululare* (imit.) + -ATE³]

-um. See -IUM.

ŭ'mbel *n.* (Bot.) flower-cluster in which stalks nearly equal in length spring from common centre and form a flat or curved surface as in parsley; so ∼LAR¹, ∼LATE², *adjs.*, **ŭmbĕ'll**ULE *n.* [f. obs. F *umbelle* or f. L *umbella* sunshade dim. of UMBRA]

ŭmbĕ'llifer *n.* plant of order Umbelliferae, bearing umbels; hence **ŭmbelli'fer**OUS *a.* [f. obs. F *umbellifère* f. L (as prec., *-fer* bearing)]

ŭ'mber *n.*, *a.*, & *v.t.* **1.** *n.* natural pigment like ochre but darker and browner (**raw** ∼, this in natural state, of dark yellow colour; **burnt** ∼, redder and deeper in colour); ∼**bird,** dark-brown Afr. bird allied to stork and heron. **2.** *a.* of umber colour; dark, dusky. **3.** *v.t.* colour (as) with umber. [f. F (*terre d'*)*ombre* or It. (*terra di*) *ombra* = shadow (earth), f. L UMBRA or *Umbra* fem. of *Umber* Umbrian]

ŭmbĭlical (-ĭ'lĭ-, -ĭ'kal) *a.* **1.** of, situated near, affecting, the umbilicus; ∼ **cord,** ropelike structure attaching foetus to placenta, (fig.) essential connecting-line in various technologies. **2.** centrally placed. [obs. F, or f. UMBILICUS + -AL]

ŭmbĭ'lĭcate *a.* shaped like a navel; having an umbilicus. [f. foll. + -ATE²]

ŭmbĭlĭcus (-ĭ'lī-, -ĭ'kus) *n.* navel; (Bot. & Zool.) navel-like formation; (Geom.) point in a surface through which all cross-sections have same curvature. [L, rel. to Gk *omphalos* and NAVEL]

ŭ'mbles (-belz) *n. pl.* edible offal of deer etc. (cf. HUMBLE *pie*). [ME var. of NUMBLES]

ŭ'mbō *n.* (*pl.* ∼s, *or* ∼nes *pr.* -ō'nēz) boss of shield, esp. in centre; (Bot. & Zool.) boss, knob, protuberance; hence **ŭ'mbon**AL, **ŭ'mbon**ATE², *adjs.* [L *umbo* umbo]

ŭ'mbr|a *n.* (*pl.* ∼ae *or* ∼as). **1.** (Astron.) total shadow (cf. PENUMBRA) cast by earth or moon in eclipse; dark central part of sunspot (cf. PENUMBRA). **2.** (Rom. Ant.) uninvited guest brought by an invited guest. **3.** Hence ∼AL *a.* [L, = shade]

ŭ'mbrage *n.* **1.** sense of slight or injury, offence, (*give, take, umbrage (at)*). **2.** (arch. or poet.) shade; what gives shade. **3.** So **ŭmbrā'ge**OUS (*jus*) *a.* [ME f. OF, f. Rom. *umbraticum* neut. (as n.) of L *umbraticus* (UMBRA; see -AGE)]

ŭmbrĕ'lla *n.* **1.** light usu. circular screen of silk etc. in collapsible form raised on radial ribs attached to central stick, used for protection against sunshine or as portable protection against rain or as symbol of authority in some Oriental and African countries; (fig.) screen of fighter aircraft or curtain of fire put up as protection against enemy aircraft; protection, patronage, co-ordinating or unifying agency (often *attrib.*); gelatinous disc of jellyfish etc. by contraction and expansion of which it swims; ∼(-**shell**), gastropod with umbrella-like shell. **2.** ∼**bird,** S. Amer. bird of genus *Cephalopterus*, with radiating crest; ∼**pine,** (1) = STONE-*pine*, (2) tall Japanese evergreen with leaves in umbrella-like whorls; ∼**stand** (for holding closed umbrellas, usu. with pan at bottom to catch drippings); ∼-**tree,** small magnolia with leaves in umbrella-like whorl at end of branch. **3.** Hence ∼ED² (-ad) *a.* [f. It. *ombrella, -ello,* dim. of *ombra* shade f. L UMBRA]

ŭmbrĕ'tte *n.* = UMBER-*bird.* [f. mod. L *umbretta* n. f. F *ombrette* (*ombre* shade f. L UMBRA); see -ETTE]

U'mbr|ian (ŭ'-) *a.* & *n.* **1.** *a.* of (ancient or modern) Umbria in central Italy; ∼ **school,** Renaissance school of painting to which Raphael and Perugino belonged. **2.** *n.* language (allied to Latin) or inhabitant of ancient Umbria. [f. L *Umber* Umbrian or *Umbria* + -IAN]

ŭmbrī'ferous *a.* affording shade. [f. L *umbrifer* (UMBRA; see -FEROUS)]

u'miăk (ōō'myăk) *n.* Eskimo skin-and-wood open boat worked by women with paddles. [Eskimo]

u'mlaut (ōō'mlowt) *n.*, & *v.t.* **1.** *n.* (In Gmc languages) vowel change due to *i*, *j*, etc., (now usu. lost or altered) in following syllable (e.g. German *mann männer*, *fuss füsse*, English *man men*); diaeresis used to mark this in German etc. **2.** *v.t.* modify (form, sound) by umlaut. [G (*um* about, *laut* sound)]

u'mpīre *n.* & *v.* **1.** *n.* third person called in to decide between arbitrators who disagree; person chosen to give final decision on disputed question; person chosen to enforce rules and settle disputes in cricket, hockey, baseball, etc.; hence **u'mpīrAGE** (3), ∼SHIP (-īrsh-), *ns.* **2.** *v.i.* act as umpire (*for* persons, *in* game etc.). **3.** *v.t.* act as umpire in (game). [ME, later form of *noumpere* f. OF *nonper* not equal (*non* NON-, *per* PEER¹); for loss of *n-* cf. ADDER]

ŭmpteen (-ē'n, ŭ'-) *a.* (sl.) indefinitely many, a lot of; hence or cogn. ∼TH², **ŭ'mpTY²**, *adjs.* [joc. form. on -TEEN]

'un *pron.* (colloq.) one (*that's a good 'un*; *he's a tough 'un*); WRONG *'un*. [dial. var.]

---

un-. This prefix has limitless applications in English, and only a selection of the existing words formed by it is given here. Its two broad categories of use are described under UN-¹ and UN-², which convey the respective senses of contrary action and absence of a quality, and which are not identical in etymology. Within each of these, more than one narrower category of use is explained. Many vbl adjs. in *-able*, *-ed*, and *-ing* can be formed from either prefix; for example, *undressed* may mean 'having had the clothes removed (after being dressed)' or 'not having been dressed', and *unbending* may mean 'that unbends' or 'that does not bend'. Usually only the form with *un-²* is listed here, the form with *un-¹* being implied as a derivative of the corresponding verb. The stress shown for *un-* words is the normal one, but the prefix is sometimes stressed for emphasis or in attrib. use (*an u'nmasked villain*; *u'ntold wealth*). Words in *un-* are rarely hyphened except when they are formed from a capitalized word (*un-American*) or when they are made for the occasion (*un-suburban*).

ŭn-¹ *pref.* w. neg. sense, usu. denoting a contrary or annulling or depriving or removing action. **1.** To *vbs.*, forming *vbs.* w. contrary sense (*unlock*; cf. COME 13); occas. w. intensified sense (*unloose, unrip*). **2.** To *ns.* forming *vbs.*, w. sense 'deprive (oneself) of' (*unfrock, unmask*), 'separate from' (*unlimber*). **3.** To *ns.* forming *vbs.*, w. sense 'release from' (*uncage*), 'take out of' (*unearth*), 'displace from' (*unhorse*). **4.** To *ns.* forming *vbs.*, w. sense 'cause to be no longer' (*unman*), 'degrade from position of' (*unking*). (Words in 2, 3, and 4 may sometimes be regarded as formed from a verb, e.g. *cage*, and thus as belonging in 1.) [OE *un-*, *on-*, = OS *ant-*, OHG *ant-*, *int-*, Goth. *and-*]

ŭn-² *pref.* w. neg. sense, usu. denoting absence of a quality. **1.** To *adjs.* & *advs.*, either simply w. sense 'not (at all)' (*unconscious, undoubted, unmistakable, unofficial, unsuspecting*), or often w. sense 'the reverse of', implying praise or blame (*unfair, ungracious, unremitting, unselfish, untimely* a. & adv., *untrue*); cf. IN-², NON-. A few such as *unsplinterable* are included here even though their rare positive forms have not been listed elsewhere. Most *adjs.* in UN-² can form *advs.* in -LY² and *ns.* in -NESS, even where these are not listed. **2.** To *ns.*, w. similar senses to those given in 1 (*unrest, untruth*). These may sometimes be regarded as derivs. of a word in 1 (*unchastity*). [OE, = OS,

OHG, Goth. *un-*, ON *ú-*, *ó-* f. IE *-n*, ablaut var. of *ne* not]

UN *abbr.* United Nations.

UNA *abbr.* United Nations Association.

ŭnabā'shed (-sht), **ŭnabā'tĕd**, *adjs.* See UN-² 1.

ŭnā'ble *a.* not able (*to* do), lacking ability. [ME, f. UN-² 1 + ABLE]

ŭnabri'dged (-jd), **ŭnabsōr'bed** (-sōr'bd, -z-), **ŭnăccĕ'ntĕd** (-ks-), **ŭnaccĕ'ptable** (-ks-), **ŭnaccō'mmodāting**, *adjs.* See UN-² 1.

ŭnacco'mpaniĕd (-ŭ'mpanĭd) *a.* not accompanied; (Mus.) without accompaniment. [f. UN-² 1; see ACCOMPANY]

ŭnacco'mplĭshed (-ŭ'-, -ŏ'-; -sht) *a.* not accomplished or completed; lacking accomplishments. [f. UN-² 1 + ACCOMPLISHED]

ŭnaccou'nt|able *a.* that cannot be explained; strange in behaviour; not responsible; hence ∼ABI'LITY, ∼ableNESS (-beln-), *ns.*, ∼ABLY *adv.* [f. UN-² 1 + ACCOUNTABLE]

ŭnaccou'ntĕd *a.* of which no account is given; ∼ for, unexplained, not included in account. [f. UN-² 1; see ACCOUNT¹]

ŭnaccŭ'stomed (-md) *a.* not accustomed (*to*); not usual (*his unaccustomed silence*). [f. UN-² 1 + ACCUSTOMED]

ŭnacknow'lĕdged (-nŏ'lijd), **ŭnacquai'ntĕd**, *adjs.* See UN-² 1.

ŭnadŏ'ptĕd *a.* not adopted; ||(of road) not taken over for maintenance by local authority. [f. UN-² 1; see ADOPT]

ŭnadōr'ned (-nd) *a.* See UN-² 1.

ŭnadŭ'lterātĕd *a.* not adulterated, pure, (fig.) sheer (nonsense etc.). [f. UN-² 1; see ADULTERATE²]

ŭnadvĕ'nturous (-cher-) *a.* See UN-² 1.

ŭnadvī'sable (-z-) *a.* not open to advice; (of thing) inadvisable. [f. UN-² 1 + ADVISABLE]

ŭnadvi's|ed (-zd) *a.* indiscreet, rash; not having had advice; hence ∼ĕdLY² *adv.* [ME, f. UN-¹ 1 + ADVISED]

ŭnaffĕ'ctĕd *a.* not affected (*by*); free from affectation, genuine, sincere; hence ∼LY² *adv.*, ∼NESS *n.* [f. UN-² 1 + AFFECTED]

ŭnaffī'liātĕd, ŭnafrai'd, ŭnai'dĕd, ŭnā'lienable, ŭnallow'able, *adjs.* See UN-² 1.

ŭnalloyed (-ă'loid, -aloi'd) *a.* not alloyed; (fig.) pure, unmixed, (*unalloyed joy*). [f. UN-² 1; see ALLOY²]

ŭna'lterable (-aw'-, -ŏ'-), **ŭnaltered** (-aw'ltĕrd, -ŏ'-), **ŭnama'zed** (-zd), **ŭnămbī'gŭous, ŭnămbī'tious** (-shŭs), **ŭnamĕ'nable**, *adjs.* See UN-² 1.

ŭn-Amĕ'rican (-am-) *a.* not in accordance with American characteristics; contrary to the interests of the US. [f. UN-² 1 + AMERICAN]

ŭnā'miable, ŭnă'nalȳsable (-z-), **ŭnă'nalȳsed** (-zd), *adjs.*, see UN-² 1 + ADVISABLE & *i*., UN-¹ 1.

ŭnanĕ'led (-ld) *a.* (arch.) not having received extreme unction. [f. UN-² 1; see ANELE]

ŭnā'nimous *a.* all agreeing in opinion (*we were, the meeting was, unanimous (for reform, as to the policy to be pursued, in protesting*, etc.)); (of opinion, vote, etc.) formed, held, given, by general consent; hence or cogn. **ŭnanī'mITY**, ∼NESS, *ns.*, ∼LY² *adv.* [f. LL *unanimis*, L *unanimus* (*unus* one, *animus* mind) + -OUS]

ŭnannou'nced (-st) *a.* See UN-² 1.

ŭna'nswerab|le (-ah'nser-) *a.* that cannot be answered; that cannot be refuted; hence ∼LY² *adv.* [f. UN-² 1 + ANSWERABLE]

ŭna'nswered (-ah'nserd), **ŭnăntī'cipātĕd**, *adjs.* See UN-² 1.

ŭnăpostŏ'lic *a.* contrary to apostolic usage; not having apostolic authority. [f. UN-² 1 + APOSTOLIC]

ŭnappă'rent *a.* See UN-² 1.

ŭnappea'lable *a.* that cannot be appealed against. [f. UN-² 1 + APPEALABLE]

ŭnappea'ling, ŭnappea'sable (-z-), **ŭnappea'sed** (-zd), **ŭnă'ppĕtīzing, ŭnapprĕ'ciātĕd** (-shī-), **ŭnapprĕ'ciative** (-shī-), **ŭnapproa'chable, ŭnapprō'priātĕd, ŭnappro'ved** (-ōō'vd), *adjs.* See UN-² 1.

ŭnă'pt *a.* not suitable (*for*); not apt (*to* do); hence ∼LY², ∼NESS *n.* [ME, f. UN-² 1 + APT]

ŭnăr'guable *a.* See UN-² 1.

ŭnăr'm *v.t.* deprive or free of arms or armour. [ME, f. UN-¹ 2 + ARM²]

ŭnăr'med (-md) *a.* See UN-² 1.

ŭnărti'stic *a.* not artistic, esp. not concerned with art. [f. UN-² 1 + ARTISTIC]

ŭnăscertai'nable, ŭnăscertai'ned (-nd), **ŭnashā'med** (-md), *adjs.*, **ŭnashā'mĕdlў** *adv.* See UN-² 1.

ŭna'sked (-ah'skt) *a.* not asked (*for*), requested, or invited. [ME, f. UN-² 1; see ASK]

ŭnassai'lab|le *a.* that cannot be attacked or questioned; hence ∼LY² *adv.* [f. UN-² 1 + ASSAILABLE]

ŭnassi'gnable (-ī'n-), **ŭnassi'gned** (-ī'nd), **ŭnassi'stĕd,** *adjs.* See UN-² 1.

ŭnassū'ming *a.* not pretentious or arrogant; modest; hence ∼LY² *adv.* [f. UN-² 1 + ASSUMING]

ŭnattă'ched (-cht) *a.* not attached (*to*); not attached to a particular regiment, church, college, club, etc.; not engaged or married. [f. UN-² 1; see ATTACH]

ŭnattai'nable, ŭnattĕ'mptĕd, *adjs.* See UN-² 1.

ŭnattĕ'ndĕd *a.* not attended (*to*); (of person, vehicle, etc.) having no person accompanying; (of thing) not accompanied or followed by. [f. UN-² 1; see ATTEND]

ŭnattră'ctive *a.* See UN-² 1.

ū'nau *n.* Brazilian two-toed sloth. [Tupi]

ŭnau'thorized (-zd), **ŭnavai'lable,** *adjs.* See UN-² 1.

ŭnavai'ling *a.* achieving nothing, ineffectual; hence ∼LY² *adv.* [f. UN-² 1; see AVAIL¹]

ŭnavoi'dable, ŭnavow'ed (-ow'd), *adjs.* See UN-² 1.

ŭnawār'e (-aw-) *a.* & *adv.* **1.** *a.* not aware, ignorant, (*of, that*); hence ∼NESS (-ār'n-) *n.* **2.** *adv.* = foll. [f. UN-² 1 + AWARE]

ŭnawār'es (-awār'z) *adv.* unexpectedly (*came upon them unawares*); inadvertently (*must have dropped it unawares*); **at** ∼, unexpectedly. [f. earlier *unware(s)* f. OE *unwær(es)*; see UN-², WARE², -s³]

ŭnbă'cked (-kt) *a.* not supported; having no backers in betting etc.; having no back(ing). [f. UN-² 1, see BACK²]

ŭnbă'g *v.t.*, see UN-¹ 3; **ŭnbă'lance** *v.t.*, UN-¹ 1.

ŭnbălanced (-st) *a.* not balanced; (of mind or person) unstable or deranged. [f. UN-² 1; see BALANCE²]

ŭnbăr' *v.t.* (-rr-). remove bar from (gate etc.); unlock, open, (lit. or fig.). [f. UN-¹ 1 + BAR²]

ŭnbear'able (-ār'-), **ŭnbea'table,** *adjs.* See UN-² 1.

ŭnbea'ten *a.* not beaten; (of record etc.) not surpassed. [f. UN-² 1 + BEATEN]

ŭnbĕco'ming (-kŭ'-) *a.* indecorous (*an unbecoming speech*); not befitting (person, *to* or *for* person); not suited to the wearer (*an unbecoming hat*); hence ∼LY² *adv.*, ∼NESS *n.* [f. UN-² 1 + BECOMING]

ŭnbĕ'd *v.t.*, see UN-¹ 3; **ŭnbĕfi'tting, ŭnbĕfrie'ndĕd** (-ĕ'-), **ŭnbĕgŏ'tten,** *adjs.*, UN-² 1.

ŭnbĕknow'n(st) (-īnō'-) *a.* (colloq.) not known; ∼ to, without the knowledge of. [f. UN-² 1 + BEknown (arch.) = UNKNOWN]

ŭnbĕlie'f *n.* incredulity, disbelief esp. in divine revelation or in a particular religion; so **ŭnBELIE'VER** *n.*, **ŭnBELIE'VING** *a.* [f. UN-² 2 + BELIEF]

ŭnbĕlie'vable, ŭnbĕlo'ved (-ŭ'vd), *adjs.*, see UN-² 1; **ŭnbĕ'lt** *v.t.*, UN-¹ 2.

ŭnbĕ'nd *v.t.* & *i.* (**unbe'nt**). change from bent position, straighten; relax from strain or exertion or constraint or severity; become affable; (Naut.) unfasten (sails) from yards and stays, cast (cable) loose, untie (rope). [f. UN-¹ 1 + BEND²]

ŭnbĕ'nding *a.* relaxing from one's exertion or constraint. [f. prec. + -ING²]

ŭnbĕ'nding² *a.* not bending, inflexible; firm; austere; hence ∼LY² *adv.*, ∼NESS *n.* [f. UN-² 1; see BEND³]

ŭnbĕ'nt *a.* See UN-² 1.

unberufen (ŏŏnberŏŏ'fen) *int.* deprecating Nemesis after boastful remark etc. [G, = unsummoned]

ŭnbĕsee'm *v.t.* (arch.) (impers.) be unbecoming to. [f. UN-¹ 1 + BESEEM]

ŭnbĕsee'ming, ŭnbĕsou'ght (-saw't), **ŭnbĕspō'ken, ŭnbī'as(s)ed** (-st), *adjs.* See UN-² 1.

ŭnbi'blical *a.* not in or authorized by the Bible. [f. UN-² 1 + BIBLICAL]

‖**ŭnbi'ddable** *a.* disobedient, not docile. [f. UN-² 1 + BIDDABLE]

ŭnbi'dden *a.* not commanded or invited. [f. UN-² 1 + BIDDEN]

ŭnbī'nd *v.t.* (**unbou'nd**). release from bonds or binding. [f. UN-¹ 1 + BIND¹]

ŭnbī'rthday *a.* (joc., of a present) given other than on a birthday. [f. UN-² 1 + BIRTHday]

ŭnbi'tt *v.t.* (Naut.), see UN-¹ 3 and BITTS; **ŭnblea'ched** (-cht), **ŭnblĕ'mished** (-sht), **ŭnblĕ'ssed** (-st), **ŭnblĕ'st, ŭnbli'nking,** *adjs.*, UN-² 1.

ŭnblŏ'ck *v.t.* remove obstruction from; (Cards) allow later unobstructed play of (suit, or abs.) by playing high card. [f. UN-¹ 1 + BLOCK²]

ŭnblow'n (-ō'n) *a.*, see UN-² 1 and BLOW¹,³; **ŭnblŭ'shing,** UN-² 1.

ŭnbō'lt *v.t.* release (door etc.) by drawing back the bolt. [f. UN-¹ 1 + BOLT²]

ŭnbō'ltĕd *a.*, see UN-² 1 and BOLT²,⁵.

ŭnbŏ'nnĕt *v.* **1.** *v.i.* (arch.) remove one's bonnet esp. as mark of respect. **2.** *v.t.* remove bonnet from. [f. UN-¹ 2 + BONNET]

ŭnbŏŏ'kish *a.*, see UN-² 1; **ŭnboo't** *v.t.* & *i.*, UN-¹ 2; **ŭnbŏr'n** *a.*, UN-² 1.

ŭnbo'som (-ŏŏ'z-) *v.t.* disclose (thoughts etc.); ∼ oneself, disclose one's thoughts, secrets, etc. [f. UN-¹ 3 + BOSOM]

ŭnbou'nd *a.*, see UN-¹ 1, UN-² 1, BIND¹, and UN-BIND.

ŭnbou'ndĕd *a.* not bounded (*by*, or abs.); infinite. [f. UN-² 1; see BOUND²]

ŭnbrā'ce *v.t.* remove brace(s) of, free from tension, relax (nerves etc.). [f. UN-¹ 1 + BRACE²]

ŭnbrea'kable (-ā'-), **ŭnbri'bable,** *adjs.* See UN-² 1.

ŭnbri'dle *v.t.* remove bridle from (horse, or fig. person, tongue, etc.). [f. UN-¹ 1 + BRIDLE²]

ŭnbri'dled (-deld) *a.* not bridled (esp. fig. of insolence, tongue, etc.) [f. UN-² 1; see BRIDLE²]

ŭnbrō'ken *a.* not broken; not subdued (*unbroken horse*); not interrupted (*unbroken sleep, peace*); not surpassed (*unbroken record*); hence ∼LY² *adv.*, ∼NESS (-n-n-) *n.* [f. UN-² 1 + BROKEN]

ŭnbŭ'ckle *v.t.* release the buckle of (strap, shoe, etc.). [f. UN-¹ 1 + BUCKLE²]

ŭnbui'ld (-bĭ'-) *v.t.* (**unbui'lt**). demolish, destroy, (building, or fig.). [f. UN-¹ 1 + BUILD¹]

ŭnbui'lt (-bĭ'-) *a.* not (yet) built (on). [f. UN-² 1; see BUILD¹]

ŭnbŭr'den *v.t.* relieve of burden; relieve (oneself, one's conscience, etc.) by confession etc. *to* person. [f. UN-¹ 1 + BURDEN²]

ŭnbŭr'dened (-nd), **ŭnbu'ried** (-ĕ'rĭd), **ŭnbu'sinĕsslīke** (-bĭzn-), *adjs.* See UN-² 1.

ŭnbu'rў (-bĕ'-) *v.t.* remove from ground etc. after burial (lit. or fig.). [f. UN-¹ 1 + BURY]

ŭnbŭ'tton *v.t.* open (coat etc.), open coat etc. of (person), by taking buttons out of buttonholes.[f. UN-¹ 1 + BUTTON²]

ŭnbŭ'ttoned (-nd) *a.* not buttoned; (fig.) communicative, informal. [f. UN-² 1; see BUTTON²]

ŭncă'ge (ŭn-k-) *v.t.* See UN-¹ 3.

ŭnca'lled (ŭn-kaw'ld) *a.* not summoned or invited; ∼-for, impertinently or unnecessarily offered or intruded. [f. UN-² 1; see CALL¹]

ŭncă'ndid (ŭn-k-) *a.* See UN-² 1.

ŭncă'nn|ў (ŭn-k-) *a.* seemingly supernatural; mysterious; hence ∼iLY² *adv.*, ∼iNESS *n.* [orig. Sc. & N. Engl., f. UN-² 1 + CANNY]

ŭncano'nical (ŭn-k-), **ŭncă'nonīzed** (ŭn-k-; -zd), *adjs.*, see UN-² 1; **ŭncă'p** (ŭn-k-) *v.t.*, UN-¹ 2.

ŭncăr'ed-fŏr (ŭn-kār'd-) *a.* disregarded, neglected. [f. UN-² 1; see CARE²]

ŭncă'se (ŭn-k-) *v.t.* & *i.* remove from cover or case; (arch.) undress. [f. UN-¹ 3 + CASE²]

ŭncau'sed (ŭn-kaw'zd) *a.* having no cause; not created. [f. UN-² 1; see CAUSE²]

ŭncea'sing *a.* See UN-² 1.

ŭncĕrĕmō'nious *a.* lacking ceremony or formality; abrupt in manner, discourteous; hence ~LY² *adv.*, ~NESS *n.* [f. UN-² 1+CEREMONIOUS]

ŭncĕr'tain (-tən, -tĭn) *a.* not certainly knowing or known (*am uncertain which he means, whether I should go or not; is of uncertain age; result is uncertain*); not to be depended on (*his aim is uncertain*), changeable (*uncertain temper, weather*); **in no ~ terms**, clearly and forcefully; hence ~LY² *adv.*, ~TY¹ *n.*; ~**ty principle**, (Phys.) principle that momentum and position of a particle cannot both be precisely determined at same time, or one of other similar restrictions on accuracy of measurement. [ME, f. UN-² 1+CERTAIN]

ŭncerti'ficatĕd, ŭncĕr'tĭfied (-ĭd), *adjs.*, see UN-² 1; **ŭnchai'n** *v.t.*, UN-¹ 1; **ŭnchă'llengeable** (-nja-), **ŭnchă'llenged** (-njd), *adjs.*, UN-² 1.

ŭncha'ncў (-ah'-) *a.* (Sc.) ill-omened; dangerous. [f. UN-² 1+CHANCY]

ŭnchă'ngeable (-nja-), **ŭnchā'nged** (-njd), **ŭnchā'nging** (-nj-), **ŭnchăracterī'stic** (-n-kărĭk-), **ŭnchăr'ged** (-jd), *adjs.* See UN-² 1.

ŭnchă'ritab|le *a.* not charitable; severe in judgement; hence ~le**NESS** (-bəln-) *n.*, ~LY² *adv.* [f. UN-² 1+CHARITABLE]

ŭnchăr'tĕd, ŭnchăr'tered (-ərd), **ŭnchā'ste**, *adjs.*, see UN-² 1; **ŭnchā'stitў** *n.*, UN-² 2; **ŭnchĕ'cked** (-kt), **ŭnchī'valrous** (-sh-), *adjs.*, UN-² 1.

ŭnchri'stian (ŭn-krī'styən) *n.* not Christian; contrary to Christian principles; (colloq.) outrageous. [f. UN-² 1+CHRISTIAN]

ŭnchŭr'ch *v.t.* excommunicate; deprive of status as church. [f. UN-¹ 3, 4+CHURCH¹]

ŭ'ncial (-sĭal, -shal) *a.* & *n.* **1.** *a.* of or written in majuscule writing with rounded unjoined letters found in MSS of 4th-8th c., from which modern capitals are largely derived. **2.** *n.* uncial letter or style or MS. [f. L *uncialis* (*uncia* inch; see -AL), in LL sense (Jerome, of uncert. orig.)]

ŭ'ncinate, ŭ'ncifōrm, *adjs.* (Anat. etc.) hooked, crooked. [f. L (*uncinatus* f. *uncinus* hook f.) *uncus* hook; see -INE¹, -ATE², -FORM]

ŭncĭr'cumcised (-zd) *a.* not circumcised; (fig.) spiritually impure, heathen. [ME, f. UN-² 1; see CIRCUMCISE]

ŭncĭr'cumcī'sion (-zhon) *n.* state of being uncircumcised; **the ~**, (NT) the Gentiles. [f. UN-² 2+CIRCUM-CISION]

ŭnci'vil *a.* ill-mannered, impolite; contrary to civic well-being; hence ~LY² *adv.* [f. UN-² 1+CIVIL]

ŭnci'vilized (-zd), **ŭnclā'd** (ŭn-k-), **ŭnclai'med** (-n-klā'md), *adjs.* See UN-² 1.

ŭncla'sp (ŭn-klah'-) *v.t.* loosen clasp(s) of, release grip of (hand etc.). [f. UN-¹ 1+CLASP²]

ŭnclă'ssified (ŭn-k-; -īd) *a.* See UN-² 1.

ŭ'ncle *n.* **1.** father's or mother's brother; aunt's husband; (colloq.) unrelated man friend of children; ||BOB⁵'s *your uncle*; *****cry ~**, (colloq.) admit defeat; DUTCH¹ *uncle*; **U~ Sam**, (colloq.) federal government or citizens of US; *****U~ Tom**, Negro subservient to Whites [f. hero of Mrs Stowe's *Uncle Tom's Cabin*]. **2.** (sl.) pawnbroker. [ME f. AF; OF *oncle* f. LL *aunculus*, f. L *avunculus* maternal uncle (see AVUNCULAR)]

-ŭncle *suf.* forming *ns.* usu. dim. (*carbuncle*). [f. OF *-uncle, -oncle* or f. L *-unculus, -la*, a special form of *-ulus* -ULE]

ŭnclea'n (ŭn-k-) *a.* not clean; foul; unchaste; (Bibl., of spirit) wicked; unfit to be eaten, ceremonially impure; hence ~NESS (-n-n-) *n.* [OE *unclǣne* (as UN-² 1, CLEAN¹)]

ŭnclea'nlў (ŭn-klĕ'-) *a.*, see UN-² 1; **ŭnclĕ'nch, ŭncli'nch**, (ŭn-k-) *vbs. t.* & *i.*, UN-¹ 1; **ŭncloa'k** (ŭn-k-) *v.t.*, UN-¹ 2; **ŭnclō'g** (ŭn-k-) *v.t.*, UN-¹ 1; **ŭncloi'ster** (ŭn-k-) *v.t.*, UN-¹ 3.

ŭnclō'se (ŭn-klō'z) *v.t.* & *i.* open. [ME, f. UN-¹ 1+CLOSE³]

ŭnclō'the (ŭn-klō'dh) *v.t.*, see UN-¹ 1; **ŭnclō'thed** (ŭn-klō'dhd), **ŭnclou'dĕd** (ŭn-k-), **ŭnclŭ'ttered** (ŭn-k-; -erd), *adjs.*, UN-² 1.

ŭ'ncō *a.*, *n.* (*pl.* ~**s**), & *adv.* (Sc.) **1.** *a.* strange, unusual; notable. **2.** *n.* stranger; (in *pl.*) news. **3.** *adv.* remarkably, very; **the ~ guid**, (usu. derog.) rigidly religious people. [ME, var. of UNCOUTH]

ŭncoi'l (ŭn-k-) *v.t.* & *i.* See UN-¹ 1.

ŭnco'loured, ***-ored**, (ŭn-kŭ'lerd) *a.* having no colour(s); not exaggerated; not influenced *by*. [f. UN-² 1+COLOURED]

ŭncome-ā't-able (ŭn-kŭm-) *a.* (colloq.) inaccessible, unattainable. [f. UN-² 1+COME-*at-able*]

ŭnco'melў (ŭn-kŭ'mlĭ) *a.* improper, unseemly; not pleasant in appearance. [ME, f. UN-² 1+COMELY]

ŭnco'mfortable (ŭn-kŭ'-) *a.* See UN-² 1.

ŭncommĕr'cial (ŭn-k-; -shal) *a.* not commercial; contrary to commercial principles. [f. UN-² 1+COMMERCIAL]

ŭncommi'ttĕd (ŭn-k-) *a.* See UN-² 1.

ŭnco'mmon (ŭn-k-) *a.* & *adv.* **1.** *a.* not common, unusual, remarkable; remarkably great etc.; hence ~LY² *adv.*, ~NESS (-n-n-) *n.* **2.** *adv.* (arch., colloq., or dial.) uncommonly. [f. UN-² 1+COMMON¹]

ŭncommū'nicative (ŭn-k-) *a.* not inclined to give information, taciturn, reserved; hence ~LY² (-vlĭ) *adv.*, ~NESS (-vn-) *n.* [f. UN-² 1+COMMUNICATIVE]

ŭncompā'nionable (ŭn-k-; -nyo-), **ŭncomplai'ning, ŭncomplē'tĕd, ŭncŏ'mplicātĕd, ŭncomplimĕ'ntarў, ŭncompou'ndĕd**, (ŭn-k-) *adjs.* See UN-² 1.

ŭncŏ'mpromīsing (ŭn-k-; -z-) *a.* not allowing or seeking compromise; unyielding, stubborn; hence ~LY² *adv.* [f. UN-² 1; see COMPROMISE²]

ŭnconcea'led (ŭn-k-; -ld) *a.* See UN-² 1.

ŭnconcĕr'n (ŭn-k-) *n.* freedom from anxiety, indifference, apathy. [f. UN-² 2+CONCERN²]

ŭnconcĕr'n|ed (ŭn-k-; -nd) *a.* not concerned (*in* or *with*); free from anxiety or agitation; hence ~ĕdLY² *adv.* [f. UN-² 1; see CONCERN¹]

ŭncondi'tional (ŭn-k-) *a.* not subject to conditions (*unconditional refusal, surrender*); hence ~ITY (-ă'l-) *n.*, ~LY² *adv.* [f. UN-² 1+CONDITIONAL]

ŭncondi'tioned (ŭn-k-; -nd) *a.* not subject to conditions; not determined by previous conditions; ~ **reflex**, instinctive response to stimulus. [f. UN-² 1; see CONDITION²]

ŭnconfī'ned (ŭn-k-; -nd), **ŭnconfĭr'med** (ŭn-k-; -md), *adjs.* See UN-² 1.

ŭnconfōr'mab|le (ŭn-k-) *a.* not conformable or conforming, esp. (Hist.) to provisions of Act of UNIFORMITY; (Geol.) not having same direction of stratification, whence **ŭnconfōr'mITY** (ŭn-k-) *n.*; hence ~le**NESS** (-bəln-) *n.*, ~LY² *adv.* [f. UN-² 1+CONFORMABLE]

ŭncongē'nial (ŭn-konj-), **ŭnconnĕ'ctĕd** (ŭn-k-), **ŭncŏ'nquerable** (ŭn-kŏ'ngk-), **ŭncŏ'nquered** (ŭn-kŏ'ngkerd), *adjs.* See UN-² 1.

ŭncŏ'nscionab|le (ŭn-kŏ'nshon-) *a.* **1.** having no conscience; contrary to the dictates of conscience. **2.** not right or reasonable; unreasonably excessive. **3.** Hence ~le**NESS** (-bəln-) *n.*, ~LY² *adv.* [f. UN-² 1+obs. *conscionable* (*conscions* obs. var. of CONSCIENCE, -ABLE)]

ŭncŏ'nscious (ŭn-kŏ'nshus) *a.* & *n.* **1.** *a.* not conscious (*was unconscious of any change; lay unconscious for some hours; has an unconscious prejudice; examples of unconscious humour*); hence ~LY² *adv.*, ~NESS *n.* **2.** *n.* part of mind whose content is not normally accessible to consciousness but which is found to affect behaviour; COLLECTIVE *unconscious*. [f. UN-² 1+CONSCIOUS]

ŭnconsi'dered (ŭn-k-; -erd) *a.* disregarded; not based on consideration. [f. UN-² 1; see CONSIDER]

ŭnconstitū'tional (ŭn-k-) *a.* not in accordance with the political constitution or with procedural rules; hence ~ITY (-ă'l-) *n.*, ~LY² *adv.* [f. UN-² 1+CONSTITUTIONAL]

For other words in *un-* see UN-, UN-¹, UN-².

ŭnconstrai′ned (ŭn-k-; -nd) *a*. See UN-² 1.

ŭnconstrai′nt (ŭn-k-) *n*. freedom from constraint. [f. UN-² 2 + CONSTRAINT]

ŭnconsū′med (ŭn-k-; -md), **ŭncontai′nable, ŭncontă′mināted, ŭncontĕ′stĕd, ŭncŏntradi′ctĕd, ŭncontrō′llable,** (ŭn-k-), **ŭncontrō′lled** (ŭn-k-; -ld); **ŭncŏntrovē̆r′sial** (ŭn-k-; -shal), **ŭncŏntrovē̆rtĕd, ŭncŏntrovē̆rtĭble,** (ŭn-kŏ′-, -ēr′-) *adjs*. See UN-² 1.

ŭnconvĕ′ntional (ŭn-k-) *a*. not bound by convention or custom; unusual; hence ∼ITY (-ă′l-) *n*., ∼LY² *adv*. [f. UN-¹ 1 + CONVENTIONAL]

ŭnconvē̆r′tĕd (ŭn-k-), **ŭnconvi′nced** (ŭn-k-; -st), **ŭnconvi′ncing** (ŭn-k-), **ŭncoŏ′ked** (ŭn-koŏ′kt), *adjs*. See UN-² 1.

ŭncoŏ′l (ŭn-k-) *a*. (sl.) not cool (in Jazz sense); unrelaxed; unpleasant. [f. UN-² 1 + COOL¹]

ŭncoŏ′perative, ŭncoŏ′dināted, (ŭn-k-) *adjs*., see UN-² 1; **ŭncor̄′d** (ŭn-k-) *v.t.*, UN-¹ 1.

ŭncor̄′k (ŭn-k-) *v.t*. draw cork from (bottle); (fig.) give vent to (feelings etc.). [f. UN-¹ 1 + CORK]

ŭncorrŏ′borātĕd, ŭncorrŭ′ptĕd, ŭncou′ntable, ŭncou′ntĕd (ŭn-k-) *adjs*. See UN-² 1.

ŭncou′ple (ŭn-kŭ′-) *v.t*. release (dogs, wagons, etc.) from couples or couplings. [ME, f. UN-¹ 2 + COUPLE¹]

ŭncou′pled (ŭn-kŭ′peld), **ŭncour′tlў** (ŭn-kōr′-), *adjs*. See UN-² 1.

ŭncou′th (ŭn-koŏ′th) *a*. **1.** (Of person, conduct, etc.) strange, awkward, clumsy, uncultured, (of language) harsh, rugged. **2.** (arch.) not known, unfamiliar, unusual, (of place) unfrequented, desolate, wild, (of life) uncivilized, comfortless. **3.** Hence ∼LY² *adv*., ∼NESS *n*. [OE *uncūth* unknown (as UN-² + *cūth* p.p. of *cunnan* know, CAN²)]

ŭnco′venantĕd (ŭn-kŭ′-) *a*. not promised by or based on (esp. God's) covenant; not bound by covenant. [f. UN-² 1 + COVENANTED]

ŭnco′ver (ŭn-kŭ′-) *v*. **1.** *v.t*. remove cover(ing) from; lay bare, disclose, make known. **2.** *v.i*. remove one's hat, cap, etc. [ME, f. UN-¹ 1, 3 + COVER¹,²]

ŭnco′vered (ŭn-kŭ′verd) *a*. not covered by roof, clothing, etc.; wearing no hat. [ME, f. UN-² 1; see COVER¹]

ŭncreā′te¹ (ŭn-k-) *v.t*. annihilate. [f. UN-¹ 1 + CREATE]

ŭncreā′te² (ŭn-k-) *a*. (arch.) = foll. [f. UN-² 1 + obs. *create* f. L *creatus* p.p. of *creare*; see CREATE, -ATE²]

ŭncreā′tĕd (ŭn-k-) *a*. existing without having been created; not created. [f. UN-² 1; see CREATE]

ŭncri′tical (ŭn-k-) *a*. not critical, disinclined or not competent to criticize; not in accordance with principles of criticism; hence ∼LY² *adv*. [f. UN-² 1 + CRITICAL]

ŭncrŭ′pped (ŭn-krŏ′pt) *a*. See UN-² 1.

ŭncro′ss (ŭn-krŏ′s, -aw′s) *v.t*. remove (legs, arms, knives, etc.) from crossed position. [f. UN-¹ 1 + CROSS²]

ŭncro′ssed (ŭn-krŏ′st, -aw′st) *a*. not wearing a cross; not thwarted; ||(of cheque) not crossed. [f. UN-² 1; see CROSS²]

ŭncrow′n (ŭn-k-) *v.t*. deprive (king etc.) of crown (lit. or fig.). [f. UN-¹ 2 + CROWN¹]

ŭncrow′ned (ŭn-k-; -nd) *a*. not crowned; having power but not name of (*king* etc.). [f. UN-² 1; see CROWN²]

ŭncrŭ′shable (ŭn-k-) *a*. See UN-² 1.

UNCSTD *abbr*. United Nations Conference on Science and Technology for Development.

UNCTAD *abbr*. United Nations Conference on Trade and Development.

ŭ′nction *n*. anointing with oil or unguent for medical purposes or as religious rite or ceremonial (EXTREME *unction*); thing used in anointing, unguent, (fig.) soothing or flattering words or thought or circumstance (see FLATTER); fervent or sympathetic quality in words or tone caused by or causing deep religious or other emotion; simulation of this, affected enthusiasm; keen enjoyment of a situation or activity. [ME, f. L *unctio* (*ung*(*u*)*ere* *unct*- anoint; see -ION)]

ŭ′nctūous *a*. full of (esp. simulated) unction; greasy, oily, esp. (of minerals) having a soapy feel when touched; hence ∼LY² *adv*., ∼NESS *n*. [ME, f. med. L *unctuosus* f. L *unctus* anointing (as prec.); see -OUS]

ŭncŭ′lled (ŭn-kŭ′ld), **ŭncŭ′ltured** (ŭn-kŭ′lcherd), *adjs.*, see UN-² 1; **ŭncŭ′rb** (ŭn-k-) *v.t.*, UN-¹ 1; **ŭncŭr′bed** (ŭn-kēr′bd), **ŭncŭr′ed** (ŭn-kūr′d), *adjs.*, UN-² 1; **ŭncŭr′l** (ŭn-k-) *v.t.*, UN-¹ 1; **ŭncŭrtai′led** (ŭn-k-; -ld), **ŭncŭr′tained** (ŭn-kēr′tand), *adjs.*, UN-² 1.

ŭncŭ′stomed (ŭn-k; -md) *a*. not liable to customs duty; on which no duty has been paid. [ME, f. UN-² 1 + p.p. of obs. *custom* v. pay duty on, f. OF *costumer* (as CUSTOM)]

ŭncŭ′t (ŭn-k-) *a*. not cut; (of book) with leaves not cut open or with untrimmed margins; (of book, film, etc.) not shortened, e.g. by censor; (of diamond) not shaped by cutting; (of fabric) having pile-loops intact. [ME, f. UN-² 1; see CUT²]

ŭndă′maged (-ijd), **ŭndā′tĕd, ŭndau′ntĕd,** *adjs*. See UN-² 1.

ŭndĕ′cagon *n*. hendecagon. [f. L *undecim* eleven, after *decagon*]

ŭndĕcei′ve (-sē′v) *v.t*. free (person) from deception or *of* error. [f. UN-¹ 1 + DECEIVE]

ŭndĕci′dĕd *a*. not settled or certain (*the point is still undecided*); hesitating, irresolute, (*he stood undecided*); hence ∼LY² *adv*. [f. UN-² 1 + DECIDED]

ŭndĕci′pherable, ŭndĕclăr′ed (-ār′d), *adjs*. See UN-² 1.

ŭndĕfĕ′ndĕd *a*. not defended (esp. of lawsuit where no defence is entered). [f. UN-² 1; see DEFEND]

ŭndĕfī′led (-ld), **ŭndĕfī′ned** (-nd), *adjs.*, see UN-² 1; **ŭndĕ′ify** *v.t.*, UN-¹ 1; **ŭndĕli′vered** (-erd), **ŭndĕma′nding** (-ah′-), **ŭndĕmocră′tic, ŭndĕ′monstrātĕd,** *adjs.*, UN-² 1.

ŭndĕmŏ′nstrative *a*. not given to or making outward expression of one's feelings; hence ∼LY² (-vlĭ) *adv*., ∼NESS (-vn-) *n*. [f. UN-² 1 + DEMONSTRATIVE]

ŭndĕnī′able *a*. that cannot be denied or disputed; unexceptionable, excellent; hence ∼LY² *adv*. [f. UN-² 1 + DENIABLE]

ŭ′nder *prep.*, *adv.*, & *a*. **1.** *prep*. in or to a position lower than, below, (*it lay or fell under the table*; *struck him under the left eye*); at foot of (high wall etc.), sheltered by (island etc.); *under* CANVAS, the COUNTER¹, COVER² (*of*), FOOT¹, one's HAT, HATCH¹*es*, the LEE of, person's NOSE, the ROSE¹; ∼ **the sun**, anywhere in the world; ∼ **water** (in and covered by it); *take under one's* WING. **2.** within, on the inside of, (surface etc.; *inserted a knife-blade under the bark*; *was seen to blush under his dusky skin*); *under* one's ARM¹, BELT¹; ∼ **separate cover,** in another envelope. **3.** inferior to, less than, (*no one under a bishop*; *did it in under an hour*; *incomes under £4000*; *those under 18 cannot vote*; *total is under what was expected*); at lower cost than; *under* AGE¹, one's BREATH. **4.** in the position or act of supporting or sustaining, subjected to, undergoing, liable to, on condition of, subject to, governed or controlled or bound by, in accordance with, in the form of, in the reign of, (*sank under the load* (lit. or fig.); *groaning under tyranny*; *is now under repair*; *under examination*; *forbidden under pain of death*; *a criminal under* SENTENCE *of death*; *born under Saturn, Aries*; *fought under Wellington*; *country prospered under him or his rule*; *under the patronage of the Royal Society*; *sent to prison under guard*; *might succeed under other conditions*; *is under a delusion*; *was under the impression that*; *under the circumstances*; *is permissible under the agreement*; *was under a vow*; *is classified under biology*; *known under an assumed name*; *appears under various forms*; *under pretence of ignorance*; *lived under the Stuarts*); *planted with* (crop); propelled by (power, sail, etc.); attested by (one's *hand*, i.e. signature, *and seal*); following (quoted phrase in turn at cards); *under* ARM²*s*, a CLOUD, CONTROL¹, FIRE¹, WAY, *the* WEATHER¹. **5.** *adv*. in or to a lower position or subordinate condition; in or into state of unconsciousness; BRING, GO¹, KEEP¹, KNUCKLE, SNOW¹, *under*; DOWN³ *under*. **6.** lower (*under jaw, layers, servants*);

hence ∿MOST *a*. [OE, = OS *undar*, OHG *untar*, ON *undir*, Goth. *undar* f. Gmc *undher-* f. IE *ndhero-*]

ŭ′nder- *pref.* = prec. **1.** As *prep.* to *ns.*, forming *adjs.* w. sense 'below' (*underground*). **2.** As *adv.* or *prep.* to *vbs.* & vbl derivs., w. sense 'beneath, lower than, below' (*underseal*, *undersell*, *undersigned*). **3.** As *adv.* to *adjs.*, *vbs.*, & vbl derivs., w. sense 'insufficiently, incompletely' (*undercook*, *underdeveloped*, *underfeed*, *undernourished*, *undernourishment*, *underpay*, *underpopulated*, *underripe*, *understock*, *underuse*). **4.** As *a.* to *ns.*, w. sense 'situated beneath, subordinate', often equivalent to UNDER *a.* (*undercarriage*, *underfelt*, *under-king*, *underlip*, *under--secretary*, *undersoil*). [OE (as prec.)]

ŭnderachie′v|e *v.i.* do less than was expected (esp. scholastically); hence ∿ER[1] *n.* [f. UNDER- 3 + ACHIEVE]

ŭnderă′ct *v.t.* & *i.* act (part etc.), act part, with insufficient force. [f. UNDER- 3 + ACT[2]]

ŭ′nderârm *a.* & *adv.* under one's ARM[1]; in armpit(s); (Cricket etc.) with hand below shoulder (*underarm bowling, service*). [f. UNDER- 1 + ARM[1]]

ŭ′nderbĕllÿ *n.* under surface of animal or thing, esp. as area vulnerable to attack. [f. UNDER- 4 + BELLY[1]]

ŭnderbi′d[1] *v.t.* (-dd-; underbi′d). **1.** make lower bid than (person); hence ∿DER[1] *n.*, person who makes the bid next below the highest. **2.** (Bridge etc.) bid less on (hand, or abs.) than is justified. [f. UNDER- 2 + BID[1]]

ŭ′nderbid[2] *n.* act of underbidding; bid thus made. [UNDER- 4 + BID[2]]

ŭ′nderbŏdÿ *n.* under surface of body of animal, vehicle, etc. [f. UNDER- 4 + BODY[1]]

ŭnderbrĕ′d *a.* ill-bred, vulgar; not of pure breeding. [f. UNDER- 3 + BRED]

***ŭ′nderbrŭsh** *n.* undergrowth in forest. [f. UNDER- 4 + BRUSH[1]]

ŭ′ndercărriage (-rĭj) *n.* **1.** supporting frame of vehicle. **2.** structure beneath aircraft, usu. retractable when not in use, to receive impact on landing and support aircraft on ground etc. [f. UNDER- 4 + CARRIAGE]

‖**ŭ′ndercârt** *n.* (colloq.) = prec. 2. [f. UNDER- 4 + CART]

ŭnderchâr′ge *v.t.* charge too little for (thing) or to (person); give less than proper charge to (gun, electric battery, etc.). [f. UNDER- 3 + CHARGE[2]]

ŭ′nderclay *n.* clay bed under coal seam. [f. UNDER- 4 + CLAY]

ŭ′ndercliff *n.* terrace or lower cliff formed by landslip. [f. UNDER- 4 + CLIFF]

ŭ′nderclōthes (-ōdhz, -ōz), **ŭ′nderclōthing** (-dh-), *ns.* clothes worn under others, esp. next to skin. [f. UNDER- 4 + CLOTHES, CLOTHING]

ŭ′ndercoat *n.* coat worn under another; animal's under layer of hair or down; layer of paint under finishing coat; paint thus used, so ∿ING[1] (3) *n.* [f. UNDER- 4 + COAT]

ŭnderco′ver (-kŭ′-) *a.* surreptitious; engaged in spying esp. by working with or among those to be observed. [f. UNDER- 1 + COVER[2]]

ŭ′ndercroft (-ŏft, -awft) *n.* crypt. [ME, f. UNDER- 4 + *croft* crypt f. MDu. *crofte* cave f. med. L *crupta* for L *crypta*; see CRYPT]

ŭ′ndercŭrrent *n.* current below the surface; (fig.) unperceived influence or feeling of different or contrary tendency, suppressed or underlying activity. [f. UNDER- 4 + CURRENT[2]]

ŭndercŭt[1] *v.t.* (-tt-; undercu′t). cut away material to show (carved design etc.) in relief; (Golf etc.) strike (ball) so as to make it rise high; sell or work at lower price or wages than. [f. UNDER- 2 + CUT[2]]

ŭ′ndercŭt[2] *n.* *notch cut in tree-trunk to guide its fall when felled; ‖under-side of sirloin. [f. UNDER- 4 + CUT[1]]

ŭnderdĕvě′lop|ed (-pt) *a.* not fully developed; (Photog.) not developed enough to give a normal image; (of country etc.) below its potential economic level; so ∿MENT *n.* [f. UNDER- 3; see DEVELOP]

ŭ′nderdŏg *n.* dog, or usu. (fig.) person, losing a fight; one who is in a state of inferiority or subjection. [f. UNDER- 4 + DOG[1]]

ŭnderdo′ne (-ŭ′n, ŭ′-) *a.* not thoroughly done; (of meat etc.) lightly or insufficiently cooked. [f. UNDER- 3 + DONE]

ŭnderdrĕ′ss *v.t.* & *i.* dress too plainly or too lightly. [f. UNDER- 3 + DRESS[1]]

ŭnderĕ′mphas|is *n.* (*pl.* ∿es *pr.* -ēz). insufficient degree of emphasis; so ∿IZE (1) *v.t.* [f. UNDER- 3 + EMPHASIS]

ŭnderĕmploy′|ed (-oi′d) *a.* not fully employed; so ∿MENT *n.* [f. UNDER- 3; see EMPLOY]

ŭnderĕ′stimate[1] *n.* estimate that is too low. [f. UNDER- 3 + ESTIMATE[1]]

ŭnderĕ′stim|āte[2] *v.t.* form too low an estimate of; hence ∿A′TION *n.* [f. UNDER- 3 + ESTIMATE[2]]

ŭnderĕxpo′s|e (-z) *v.t.* (esp. Photog.) expose for too short a time; so ∿URE (-zh*er*) *n.* [f. UNDER- 3 + EXPOSE]

ŭ′nderfĕlt *n.* felt for laying under carpet. [f. UNDER- 4 + FELT[1]]

ŭ′nderfloor (-ōr) *a.* situated beneath the floor (esp. of source of domestic heating). [f. UNDER- 1 + FLOOR]

ŭ′nderflow (-ō) *n.* undercurrent. [f. UNDER- 4 + FLOW]

ŭnderfoo′t *adv.* under one's feet; on the ground; (fig.) in state of subjection; (fig.) so as to obstruct one's progress. [ME, f. UNDER- 1 + FOOT[1]]

ŭ′ndergârment *n.* piece of underclothing. [f. UNDER- 4 + GARMENT]

ŭndergîr′d *v.t.* make secure underneath; (fig.) strengthen, support. [f. UNDER- 2 + GIRD[1]]

ŭ′nderglāze *a.* (Of painting on porcelain etc.) done before the glaze is applied. [f. UNDER- 1 + GLAZE]

ŭndergō′ *v.t.* (**underwe′nt**; undergo′ne *pr.* -gŏ′n, -gaw′n; cf. GO[1]). be subjected to, suffer, endure esp. with firmness, (*has undergone many trials*; *underwent a rapid change, an operation*). [OE UNDER(*gān* GO[1])]

ŭndergrā′d *n.* (colloq.) = foll. [abbr.]

ŭndergrā′du|ate *n.* member of university who has not taken the first degree; hence ∿E′TTE *n.*, (joc.) female undergraduate. [f. UNDER- 1 + GRADUATE[1]]

ŭndergrou′nd[1] *adv.* beneath surface of ground; in or into secrecy or hiding. [f. UNDER- 1 + GROUND[1]]

ŭ′nderground[2] *a.* & *n.* (railway) situated underground; (fig.) secret, hidden, (group or activity), esp. aiming to subvert the established order; ∿ **press**, production of unconventional and experimental publications. [f. prec.]

ŭ′ndergrowth (-ōth) *n.* shrubs or small trees growing under larger ones. [f. UNDER- 4 + GROWTH]

ŭ′nderhănd[1] *a.* clandestine, secret, not above-board; crafty, deceptive; (Cricket etc.) = UNDERARM. [f. foll.]

ŭnderhă′nd[2] *adv.* in underhand manner. [OE (as UNDER-, HAND[1])]

ŭnderhă′ndĕd *a.* & *adv.* = UNDERHAND[1],[2]. [f. UNDER-HAND[1] + -ED[1]]

ŭ′nderhŭng *a.* (Of lower jaw) projecting beyond upper jaw; having underhung jaw. [f. UNDER- 2 + HUNG]

ŭnderlay′[1] *v.t.* (**underlai′d**). lay something under (thing) as support or to raise it. [OE UNDER(*lecgan* LAY[3])]

ŭ′nderlay[2] *n.* thing laid under another, esp. paper under types, (material for) sheet under carpet or mattress as protection or support. [f. UNDER- 2 + LAY[3]]

ŭnderlay′[3]. See UNDERLIE.

ŭ′nderlease *n.*, & *v.t.* sublease. [f. UNDER- 2, 4 + LEASE]

ŭnderlĕ′t *v.t.* (-tt-; underle′t). sublet; let at less than the true value. [f. UNDER- 2, 3 + LET[2]]

ŭnderlī′e *v.t.* (**underly′ing; underlay′; underlai′n**). lie, be situated, under (stratum etc., or abs.); (arch.) be subject to (challenge etc.); (fig., of

For other words in *un-* see UN-, UN-[1], UN-[2].

principle, reason, etc.) be the basis of (doctrine, law, conduct, etc., or abs., esp. in part.); exist beneath the superficial aspect of. [OE UNDER(*ligcan* LIE³)]

ŭnderlī′ne¹ *v.t.* draw line under (word etc.) to give emphasis or draw attention or indicate italic or other special type; stress, emphasize. [f. UNDER- 2 + LINE³]

ŭ′nderlīne² *n.* line drawn under word etc.; caption below illustration. [f. UNDER- 4 + LINE²]

ŭ′nderlinen *n.* underclothes of linen etc. [f. UNDER- 4 + LINEN]

ŭ′nderling *n.* (usu. derog.) subordinate. [ME, f. UNDER- 5 + -LING¹]

ŭnderly′ing. See UNDERLIE.

ŭndermǎ′nned (-nd) *a.* (Of ship etc.) having too few men to operate it properly; understaffed. [f. UNDER- 3; see MAN²]

‖**ŭndermĕntioned** (-ĕ′nshond, ŭ′-) *a.* mentioned at later place in book etc. [f. UNDER- 2; see MENTION²]

ŭndermī′ne *v.t.* make mine or excavation under, wear away base or foundation of, (*rivers undermine their banks*); injure (person, reputation, influence, etc.) by secret or insidious means; weaken, injure, wear out, (health etc.) insidiously or imperceptibly. [ME, f. UNDER- 2 + MINE²]

ŭndernea′th *adv., prep., a.,* & *n.* **1.** *adv.* & *prep.* at or to a lower place (than), below; within, on the inside (of), (surface etc.), **2.** *a.* & *n.* lower (surface, part). [OE *underneothan* (as UNDER, *neothan*; cf. BENEATH)]

ŭ′nderpants *n. pl.* undergarment covering lower part of body and part of legs. [f. UNDER- 4 + PANTS]

ŭ′nder-part *n.* lower or under part; subordinate part in play etc. [f. UNDER- 4 + PART¹]

ŭ′nderpass (-ahs) *n.* (crossing that has) road etc. passing under another. [f. UNDER- 4 + PASS²]

ŭnderpi′n *v.t.* (-nn-). support from below with masonry etc.; (fig.) support, strengthen. [f. UNDER- 2 + PIN²]

ŭ′nderplŏt *n.* subordinate plot in play etc. [f. UNDER- 4 + PLOT¹]

ŭnderpri′vileged (-jd) *a.* less privileged than others; not enjoying the normal standard of living or rights in a society. [f. UNDER- 3; see PRIVILEGE]

ŭnderprodŭ′ction *n.* production of less than is usual or required. [f. UNDER- 3 + PRODUCTION]

ŭ′nderprōŏf *a.* containing less alcohol than proof spirit does. [f. UNDER- 1 + PROOF¹ 5]

ŭnderprŏ′p *v.t.* (-pp-). support with prop; (fig.) support, sustain. [f. UNDER- 2 + PROP¹]

ŭnderquō′te *v.t.* quote lower price than (person); quote lower price than others for (goods etc.). [f. UNDER- 2 + QUOTE]

ŭnderrā′te (-er-r-) *v.t.* = UNDERESTIMATE². [f. UNDER- 3 + RATE²]

ŭnderscōr′e¹ *n.t.* = UNDERLINE¹. [f. UNDER- 2 + SCORE]

ŭ′nderscōre² *n.* = UNDERLINE². [f. UNDER- 4 + SCORE]

ŭ′ndersea *a.* below (surface of) the sea, submarine. [f. UNDER- 1 + SEA]

ŭ′nderseal *v.t.* seal under-part of (esp. motor vehicle) against dirt etc.). [f. UNDER- 2 + SEAL²]

ŭndersĕ′ll *v.t.* (underso′ld). sell at lower price than; sell at less than the true value. [f. UNDER- 2, 3 + SELL]

ŭndersĕ′t¹ *v.t.* (-tt-; **underse′t**). underprop; place something under (thing). [ME, f. UNDER- 2 + SET¹]

ŭ′ndersĕt² *n.* (Naut.) undercurrent. [f. UNDER- 4 + SET²]

ŭnder-sĕ′xed (-kst) *a.* having less than the normal degree of sexual desire. [f. UNDER- 3 + SEX + -ED²]

ŭ′ndershirt *n.* undergarment worn under shirt, vest. [f. UNDER- 1 + SHIRT]

ŭndershōō′t *v.t.* (undersho′t). (Of aircraft) land short of (runway); shoot short of or below. [f. UNDER- 3 + SHOOT¹]

*****ŭ′ndershorts** *n.* short underpants. [f. UNDER- 4; see SHORT]

ŭ′ndershŏt *a.* (Of water-wheel) turned by water flowing under it; = UNDERHUNG. [f. UNDER- 2 + SHOT²]

ŭ′nder-shrŭb *n.* subshrub. [f. UNDER- 4 + SHRUB¹]

ŭ′nder-sīde *n.* lower or under side or surface. [f. UNDER- 4 + SIDE¹]

ŭndersīgned (-īnd) *a.* whose signature is appended in document etc. (*we, the undersigned, wish to state . . .*). [f. UNDER- 2; see SIGN²]

ŭ′ndersized (-zd; ŭ′-, -ī′-) *a.* of less than the usual size; dwarfish. [f. UNDER- 3 + SIZE¹ + -ED²]

ŭ′nderskirt *n.* skirt worn under another, petticoat. [f. UNDER- 4 + SKIRT]

ŭ′nderslung *a.* supported from above; (of vehicle chassis) hanging lower than axles. [f. UNDER- 2 + SLUNG]

ŭnderspĕ′nd *v.* (-spe′nt). **1.** *v.t.* spend less than (specified amount). **2.** *v.i.* & *refl.* spend too little. [f. UNDER- 3]

ŭndersta′ffed (-ah′ft) *a.* having less than the necessary number of staff. [f. UNDER- 3; see STAFF¹]

ŭndersta′nd *v.* (understoo′d, arch. *p.p.* understa′nded). **1.** *v.t.* perceive the meaning of (words, person, language, etc.; *does not understand what you say, you, French*); ∼ **each other,** know each other's views or feelings, be in agreement or collusion; **tongue not** ∼**ed of the people,** (arch.) foreign language. **2.** grasp mentally, perceive the significance or explanation or cause or nature of, know how to deal with, (*do not understand why he came, what the noise is about, the point of his remark; quite understand your difficulty; cannot understand him, his conduct, his wanting to go; thoroughly understands children; could never understand mathematics*). **3.** infer esp. from information received, take as implied, take for granted, (*I understand that it begins at noon, that they are almost destitute, him to be or that he is a distant relation; but I understood that expenses were to be paid; no one could understand that from my words*); (expr. uncertainty or surprise or indignation: *do I understand* (*you to say*) *that or am I to understand that you refuse?*); GIVE¹ person *to understand.* **4.** supply (word) mentally (*the verb may be either expressed or understood*). **5.** Hence ∼ABLE *a.* **6.** *v.i.* have understanding (in general or particular); believe or assume from knowledge or inference (*he is coming tomorrow, I understand*). [OE UNDER(*standan* STAND¹)]

understa′nding¹ *a.* having understanding or insight or good judgement; able to be sympathetic to others' feelings; hence ∼LY² *adv.* [ME, f. prec. + -ING²]

understa′nding² *n.* In vbl senses; intelligence (*has an excellent understanding*); power of apprehension, power of abstract thought, (often opp. to *reason*); agreement, harmony, convention, thing agreed upon, (*must come to an understanding with him; disturbed the* (*good*) *understanding between them; had a secret understanding with other firms; consented only on this understanding, on the distinct understanding that*). [OE (as UNDERSTAND, -ING¹)]

understa′te *v.t.* express in (unduly) restrained terms; represent as being less than it actually is; so ∼MENT (-tm-) *n.* [f. UNDER- 3 + STATE²]

ŭ′ndersteer *v.i.,* & *n.* (Of motor vehicle) (have) tendency to turn less sharply than was intended. [f. UNDER- 3 + STEER¹]

ŭ′nderstrapper *n.* underling, subordinate agent. [f. UNDER- 4 + STRAP + -ER¹; cf. dial. *strapper* groom]

ŭ′nderstŭdy *n.,* & *v.t.* **1.** *n.* one who studies another's theatrical etc. role or duties in order to act at short notice in absence of the other. **2.** *v.t.* study (role etc.) thus; act as understudy to (person). [n. f. v., f. UNDER- 2 + STUDY²]

ŭ′nder-sŭrface (-ĭs) *n.* lower or under surface. [f. UNDER- 4 + SURFACE]

ŭndertă′ke *v.t.* (undertoo′k; underta′ken). bind oneself to perform, make oneself responsible for, engage in, enter upon, (work, enterprise, responsibility); accept an obligation, promise, (*to* do); guarantee, affirm, (*I will undertake that he has not heard a word, that you shall or will not be the loser by it*). [ME, f. UNDER- 2 + TAKE¹]

ŭ′ndertāker *n.* In vbl senses; one whose business is

For other words in *under-* **see UNDER-.**

to carry out arrangements for funerals; (Hist.) influential person in 17th-c. England who undertook to procure particular legislation, esp. to obtain supplies from House of Commons if king would grant some concession. [ME, f. prec. + -ER¹]

ŭ'ndertāking (*or* -ā'-) *n.* In vbl senses; work etc. undertaken (*a serious undertaking*); pledge, promise; management of funerals. [ME, f. UNDERTAKE + -ING¹]

ŭ'ndertĕn|ant *n.* subtenant; so ∼ANCY *n.* [f. UNDER-4 + TENANT]

ŭ'nderthings (-z) *n. pl.* (colloq.) underclothes. [f. UNDER- 4 + THING + -s¹]

ŭ'ndertint *n.* subdued tint. [f. UNDER- 4 + TINT]

ŭ'ndertōne *n.* subdued tone of sound or colour; underlying quality; undercurrent of feeling. [f. UNDER-4 + TONE¹]

ŭ'ndertow (-ō) *n.* current below sea-surface moving in opposite direction to surface current. [f. UNDER-4 + TOW¹]

ŭ'ndertrick *n.* (Bridge). trick by which declarer falls short of contract. [f. UNDER- 4 + TRICK]

ŭndervǎ'lū|e *v.t.* rate at too low a value; underestimate; hence ∼A'TION *n.* [f. UNDER- 3 + VALUE]

ŭ'ndervĕst *n.* = VEST¹ 2. [f. UNDER- 4 + VEST¹]

ŭ'nderwa'ter (-aw'-) *a.* & *adv.* (situated, carried on, etc.) under water. [f. UNDER- 1 + WATER¹]

ŭ'nderwear (-ār) *n.* underclothes. [f. UNDER- 4 + WEAR²]

ŭ'nderweight (-wāt) *n.* & *a.* **1.** *n.* insufficient weight. **2.** *a.* (-wā't) weighing less than is normal or desirable. [f. UNDER- 3 + WEIGHT¹]

ŭnderwĕ'nt. See UNDERGO.

ŭnderwhĕ'lm *v.t.* (joc.) be far from overwhelming. [f. UNDER- 2, after *overwhelm*]

ŭ'nderwing *n.* moth with conspicuous markings on under-side of wings. [f. UNDER- 1 + WING]

ŭ'nderwŏŏd *n.* undergrowth. [f. UNDER- 4 + WOOD]

ŭ'nderworld (-wēr-) *n.* mythical abode of the dead under the earth; antipodes; part of society comprising those who live by (organized) crime and immorality. [f. UNDER- 4 + WORLD]

ŭnderwrī'te (-erī't) *v.* (**underwro'te; underwri'tten**). **1.** *v.t.* sign, and accept liability under, (policy of insurance esp. on marine property), accept (liability) thus; engage to buy all stock in (company etc.) not bought by the public; undertake to finance or support; write below (*the underwritten names*). **2.** *v.i.* practise (marine) insurance. **3.** Hence **ŭ'nderwrītER¹** (-erī-) *n.* [ME, f. UNDER- 2 + WRITE]

ŭndĕscĕ'ndĕd *a.* not having descended; (of testicle) remaining in abdomen instead of descending normally into scrotum. [f. UN-² 1 + DESCENDED]

ŭndĕsēr'v|ed (-zēr'vd) *a.* not deserved (as reward or punishment); hence ∼ĕdLY² *a.* [ME, f. UN-² 1; see DESERVE]

ŭndĕsēr'ving (-z-) *a.* See UN-² 1.

ŭndĕsī'gn|ed (-zī'nd) *a.* unintentional; hence ∼ĕdLY² *adv.* [f. UN-² 1; see DESIGN²]

ŭndĕsīr'|able (-z-) *a.* & *n.* **1.** *a.* not desirable, objectionable, unpleasant; hence ∼ABI'LITY, ∼ableNESS (-beln-), *ns.*, ∼ABLY *adv.* **2.** *n.* undesirable person, esp. drunkard etc. [f. UN-² 1 + DESIRABLE]

ŭndĕsīr'ed (-zīr'd) *a.*, **ŭndĕsīr'ous** (-z-), **ŭndĕtě'ctable, ŭndĕtě'ctĕd,** *adjs.* See UN-² 1.

ŭndĕtēr'mined (-nd) *a.* = UNDECIDED. [ME, f. UN-² 1 + DETERMINED]

ŭndĕtēr'red (-ēr'd) *a.*, **ŭndĕvĕ'loped** (-pt), **ŭndē'viāting, ŭndī'agnōsed** (-zd), *adjs.* See UN-² 1.

ŭ'ndies (-diz) *n. pl.* (colloq.) (esp. women's) underclothing. [abbr.; cf. -Y³]

ŭndiffĕrĕ'ntiātĕd (-shĭ-), **ŭndĭgĕ'stĕd, ŭndĭ'gnĭfīed** (-īd), **ŭndĭlū'tĕd, ŭndimĭ'nished** (-sht), **ŭndĭ'mmed** (-md), *adjs.* See UN-² 1.

ŭ'ndĭne (-ēn) *n.* female water-spirit. [f. mod. L *undina* (wd invented by Paracelsus) f. L *unda* wave; see -INE¹]

ŭndĭplomǎ'tic, ŭndĭschǎr'ged (-jd), *adjs.*, see UN-² 1; **ŭndĭ'scĭpline** *n.*, UN-² 2; **ŭndĭ'scĭplined** (-nd),

ŭndĭsclō'sed (-zd), **ŭndĭsco'verable** (-kŭ'-), **ŭndĭsco'vered** (-kŭ'verd), **ŭndĭscrī'mĭnāting,** **ŭndĭsguī'sed** (-gī'zd), **ŭndĭsmay'ed,** (-ā'd), **ŭndĭspū'tĕd, ŭndĭssō'lved** (-zŏ'lvd), **ŭndĭsti'nguished** (-nggwĭsht), *adjs.*, UN-² 1.

ŭndĭstrī'būtĕd *a.* not distributed; ∼ **middle,** (Logic) fallacy resulting from failure of middle term to refer to all members of a class. [ME, f. UN-² 1; see DISTRIBUTE]

ŭndĭstūr'bed (-bd), **ŭndĭvī'dĕd, ŭndĭvŭ'lged** (-jd), *adjs.* See UN-² 1.

ŭndo' (-ōō') *v.t.* (**undi'd**; UNDONE; cf. DO¹). unfasten, untie, (coat, button, parcel); unfasten garment(s) of (person); annul, cancel, (*cannot undo the past, our past actions*); ruin prospects or reputation of; hence ∼ING¹ *n.* [OE *undōn* (as UN-¹, DO¹)]

ŭndŏ'ck *v.t.* See UN-¹ 1, 3 and DOCK⁴.

ŭndo'ne (-ŭ'n) *a.* not done (up) (*left the job, the buttons, undone*). [ME, f. UN-² 1 + DONE]

ŭndou'btĕd (-ow't-) *a.* not regarded as doubtful, unaffected by doubt; hence ∼LY² *adv.*, without any doubt. [ME, f. UN-² 1; see DOUBT²]

ŭndrā'ped (-pt) *a.* See UN-² 1.

ŭndrea'med (-ē'md, -ĕmt), **ŭndrea'mt** (-ĕ'mt), *a.* not (even) dreamed; not thought *of.* [f. UN-² 1; see DREAM²]

ŭndrĕ'ss¹ *v.* **1.** *v.t.* take off the clothes of. **2.** *v.i.* take off one's clothes. [f. UN-¹ 1 + DRESS¹]

ŭndrĕ'ss² *n.* ordinary dress opp. full dress or uniform; informal dress, négligé. [f. UN-² 2 + DRESS²]

ŭndrĕ'ssed (-st), **ŭndrĭ'nkable,** *adjs.* See UN-² 1.

UNDRO *abbr.* United Nations Disaster Relief Organization.

ŭndūe' *a.* not owed or suitable; excessive, disproportionate; ∼ **influence** (Law; by which person is induced not to act of his own free will); so **ŭndū'LY²** *adv.* [ME, f. UN-² 1 + DUE¹]

ŭ'ndŭlant *a.* moving like waves; ∼ **fever,** brucellosis in humans. [f. foll. + -ANT]

ŭ'ndŭlāte¹ *v.i.* & *t.* (cause to) have wavy motion or look. [f. as foll. + -ATE³]

ŭ'ndŭlate² *a.* wavy, going alternately up and down or in and out (*leaves with undulate margins*); hence ∼LY² (-tlĭ) *adv.* [f. LL *undulatus* f. L *unda* wave; see -ULE, -ATE²]

ŭndŭlā'tion *n.* wavy motion or form, gentle rise and fall, each wave of this; set of wavy lines. [f. mod. L *undulatio* or UNDULATE²; see -ATION]

ŭ'ndŭlātorў *a.* undulating, wavy; of or due to undulation; ∼ **theory** (that light is propagated through the ether by wave-motion imparted to the ether by molecular vibrations of the radiant body). [f. UNDULATE¹ + -ORY]

ŭndū'tiful, ŭndy̆'ing, *adjs.* See UN-² 1.

ŭnear'ned (-ēr'nd) *a.* not earned; ∼ **income** (from interest payments etc., opp. wage or salary or fees); ∼ **increment,** increase in value of property not due to owner's labour or outlay. [ME, f. UN-² 1; see EARN]

ŭnear'th (-ēr'-) *v.t.* drive (fox etc.) from earth; dig up; (fig.) bring to light, find by searching. [f. UN-¹ 3 + EARTH¹]

ŭnear'thl|ў (-ēr'-) *a.* not earthly; supernatural, mysterious; (colloq.) absurdly early or inconvenient (*getting up at this unearthly hour?*); hence ∼ĭNESS *n.* [f. UN-² 1 + EARTHLY]

ŭnea'se (-z) *n.* lack of ease, discomfort, distress. [f. UN-² 2 + EASE¹]

ŭnea's|ў (-zĭ) *a.* disturbed or uncomfortable in body or mind (*passed an uneasy night*); disturbing (*had an uneasy suspicion*); hence ∼ĭLY² *adv.*, ∼ĭNESS *n.* [ME, f. UN-² 1 + EASY]

ŭnea'table *a.* not able to be eaten, esp. because of its condition (cf. INEDIBLE). [f. UN-² 1 + EATABLE]

ŭnea'ten *a.* See UN-² 1.

ŭnea'th *adv.* (arch.) with difficulty; scarcely. [OE *unēathe* (as UN-², *ēathe* easily, = OS *ōtho*, OHG *ōdo*, ON *auth*-]

For other words in *un-* see UN-, UN-¹, UN-².

ŭnĕconŏ'm|ĭc *a.* not economic, incapable of being profitably operated etc.; hence ~ICALLY *adv.* [f. UN-² 1 + ECONOMIC]

ŭnĕconŏ'mical *a.* See UN-² 1.

ŭnĕ'dĭfȳing *a.* not edifying, esp. uninformative or degrading. [f. UN-² 1; see EDIFY]

ŭnĕ'dĭtĕd, ŭnĕ'dūcātĕd, ŭnĕmbă'rrassed (-st), **ŭnĕmō'tional, ŭnĕmphă'tic,** *adjs.* See UN-² 1.

ŭnĕmploy'able *a. & n.* (person) unfitted by character, age, etc., for paid employment. [f. UN-² 1 + EMPLOYABLE]

ŭnĕmploy'ed (-oi'd) *a.* not in use; having no employment; temporarily out of work. [f. UN-² 1; see EMPLOY]

ŭnĕmploy'ment *n.* lack of employment; inability to find paid work; ~ **benefit** (paid by State or *trade union to unemployed worker). [f. UN-² 2 + EMPLOYMENT]

ŭnĕnclō'sed (-n-klō'zd) *a.* See UN-² 1.

ŭnĕncŭ'mbered (-n-k-; -erd) *a.* having no encumbrance; (of estate) free from mortgage etc. [f. UN-² 1; see ENCUMBER]

ŭnĕ'ndĭng *a.* having (apparently) no end; hence ~LY² *adv.,* ~NESS *n.* [f. UN-² 1; see END²]

ŭnĕndow'ed (-ow'd), **ŭnĕndūr'able, ŭnĕngā'ged** (-n-gā'jd), *adjs.* See UN-² 1.

ŭn-E'nglish (-ĭ'ngg-) *a.* not (characteristic of the) English. [f. UN-² 1 + ENGLISH¹]

ŭnĕnjoy'able, ŭnĕnlī'ghtened (-ī'tend), **ŭnĕ'nterprising** (-z-), **ŭnĕnthusiă'stic** (-ūz-, -ōŏz-), **ŭnĕ'nviable, ŭnĕ'nvied** (-īd), *adjs.* See UN-² 1.

ŭnĕ'qual *a.* not equal (*to*); of varying quality; not with equal advantage to both sides (*unequal bargain, contest*). [f. UN-² 1 + EQUAL¹]

ŭnĕ'qualize *v.t.,* see UN-¹ 1; **ŭnĕ'qualled** (-ld), UN-² 1.

ŭnĕqui'vocal *a.* not ambiguous, plain, unmistakable; hence ~LY² *adv.,* ~NESS *n.* [f. UN-² 1 + EQUIVOCAL]

ŭnĕr'ring *a.* not erring or failing or missing the mark; hence ~LY² *adv.,* ~NESS *n.* [f. UN-² 1; see ERR]

ŭnĕscā'pable *a.* See UN-² 1.

UNESCO, Unĕ'scō, (ūnĕ'skō) *abbr.* United Nations Educational, Scientific, & Cultural Organization.

ŭnĕspī'ed (-ī'd) *a.* See UN-² 1.

ŭnĕssĕ'ntial (-nshǎl) *a. & n.* 1. *a.* not essential; not of the first importance. 2. *n.* unessential part or thing. [f. UN-² 1 + ESSENTIAL]

ŭnĕstă'blished (-sht) *a.* See UN-² 1.

ŭnĕ'thical *a.* not ethical, esp. unscrupulous in business or professional conduct; hence ~LY² *adv.* [f. UN-² 1 + ETHICAL]

ŭnĕvăngĕ'lical (-nj-) *a.* See UN-² 1.

ŭnĕ'ven *a.* not level or smooth; not uniform or equable; (of contest) unequal; hence ~LY² *adv.,* ~NESS (-n-n-) *n.* [OE *unefen* (as UN-², EVEN²)]

ŭnĕvĕ'ntful, ŭnĕxă'mined (-gz-; -nd), *adjs.* See UN-² 1.

ŭnĕxa'mpled (-gzah'mpeld) *a.* having no precedent or parallel. [f. UN-² 1; see EXAMPLE]

ŭnĕxcĕ'lled (-ld) *a.* See UN-² 1.

ŭnĕxcĕ'ptionab|le *a.* with which no fault can be found; entirely satisfactory; hence ~leNESS (-beln-) *n.,* ~LY² *adv.* [f. UN-² 1 + EXCEPTIONABLE]

ŭnĕxcĕ'ptional *a.* not out of the ordinary; hence ~LY² *adv.* [f. UN-² 1 + EXCEPTIONAL]

ŭnĕxcī'ting, ŭnĕ'xĕcūted, ŭnĕxĕ'mplified (-gz-, -īd), **ŭnĕxhau'sted** (-gzaw'-), **ŭnĕxpĕ'cted, ŭnĕ'xpiātĕd, ŭnĕxpīr'ed** (-ī'd), **ŭnĕxplai'nable, ŭnĕxplai'ned** (-nd), **ŭnĕxplōr'ed** (-ōr'd), **ŭnĕxpō'sed** (-zd), **ŭnĕxprĕ'ssed** (-st), **ŭnĕ'xpurgātĕd, ŭnfā'dĭng,** *adjs.* See UN-² 1.

ŭnfai'ling *a.* not failing; never ending; constant; reliable; hence ~LY² *adv.,* ~NESS *n.* [ME, f. UN-¹ 2; see FAIL²]

ŭnfai'r *a.* not equitable or honest or impartial or according to rules (*an unfair advantage; procured by unfair means; unfair play*); hence ~LY² *adv.,* ~NESS *n.* [OE *unfæger* (as UN-² 1, FAIR²)]

ŭnfai'th *n.* See UN-² 2.

ŭnfai'thful *a.* not loyal; treacherous; adulterous; hence ~LY² *adv.,* ~NESS *n.* [ME, f. UN-² 1 + FAITHFUL]

ŭnfa'ltering (-aw'l-, -ŏ'l-), **ŭnfami'liar** (-lyer), **ŭnfā'shionable** (-shon-), *adjs.* See UN-² 1.

ŭnfā'shioned (-shond) *a.* not wrought into shape. [f. UN-² 1; see FASHION]

ŭnfa'sten (-ah'sen) *v.t. & i.* make or become loose; detach; open fastening(s) of. [ME, f. UN-¹ 1 + FASTEN]

ŭnfa'stened (-ah'send) *a.* See UN-² 1.

ŭnfa'thered (-ah'dherd) *a.* fatherless; (fig.) of unknown origin (*unfathered rumours*). [f. UN-² 1; see FATHER²]

ŭnfa'therly (-ah'dh-), **ŭnfā'thomable** (-dh-), **ŭnfā'thomed** (-dhomd), **ŭnfā'vourable** (-ver-), **ŭnfea'sible** (-z-), *adjs.,* see UN-² 1; **ŭnfea'ther** (-ĕ'dh-) *v.t.,* UN-¹ 2; **ŭnfĕ'd** *a.,* UN-² 1.

ŭnfee'd *a.* paid no fee. [f. UN-² 1 + FEED³]

ŭnfee'ling *a.* lacking sensation or sensitivity; unsympathetic, harsh, not caring about others' feelings; hence ~LY² *adv.,* ~NESS *n.* [OE *unfelende* (as UN-², FEELING²)]

ŭnfei'gned (-ā'nd), **ŭnfĕ'lt, ŭnfĕ'minine, ŭnfĕ'nced** (-st), **ŭnfermĕ'ntĕd, ŭnfĕr'tilized** (-zd), *adjs.,* see UN-² 1; **ŭnfĕ'tter** *v.t.,* UN-¹ 1; **ŭnfĕ'ttered** (-erd), **ŭnfī'lial, ŭnfī'lled** (-ld), **ŭnfī'ltered** (-erd), **ŭnfī'nished** (-sht), *adjs.,* UN-² 1.

ŭnfī't¹ *a.* not fit (*to do, for* purpose); hence ~LY² *adv.,* ~NESS *n.* [f. UN-² 1 + FIT³]

ŭnfī't² *v.t.* (-tt-). make unsuitable (*for*). [f. UN-¹ 1 + FIT⁴]

ŭnfī'ttĕd *a.* not fit; not fitted; not furnished with fittings. [f. UN-² 1; see FIT⁴]

ŭnfī'tting *a.,* see UN-² 1; **ŭnfī'x** *v.t.,* UN-¹ 1; **ŭnfī'xed** (-kst), **ŭnflā'gging** (-g-), *adjs.,* UN-² 1.

ŭnflă'pp|able *a.* (colloq.) imperturbable; remaining cool in a crisis; hence ~ABI'LITY *n.* [f. UN-² 1 + FLAP + -ABLE]

ŭnflă'ttering, ŭnflā'voured (-erd), *adjs.* See UN-² 1.

ŭnflĕ'dged (-jd) *a.* not yet fledged; (of person) inexperienced. [f. UN-² 1; see FLEDGE]

ŭnflĕ'shed (-sht), **ŭnfli'nching,** *adjs.* See UN-² 1.

ŭnfō'ld¹ *v.t. & i.* open folds (of), spread out, develop; (fig.) reveal (thoughts etc.); hence *~MENT n.* [OE *unfealdan* (as UN-¹, FOLD²)]

ŭnfō'ld² *v.t.* release (sheep) from fold(s). [f. UN-¹ 3 + FOLD¹]

ŭnfor'ced (-st), **ŭnfor'dable, ŭnfōresee'n** (-ōrs-), **ŭnforgĕ'ttable** (-g-), **ŭnforgi'vable** (-g-), **ŭnforgĕ'tten,** *adjs.* See UN-² 1.

ŭnfor'med (-md) *a.* not formed; not developed; shapeless. [ME, f. UN-² 1; see FORM²]

ŭnfor'mulated, ŭnforthco'ming (-kŭ'-), **ŭnfor'tified** (-īd), *adjs.* See UN-² 1.

ŭnfor'tunate (-chōō-) *a. & n.* 1. *a.* having bad fortune, unlucky; disastrous; regrettable; hence ~LY² (-tlĭ) *adv.,* (also, qualifying whole sentence) it is unfortunate that. 2. *n.* unfortunate person. [f. UN-² 1 + FORTUNATE]

ŭnfou'ndĕd *a.* having no foundation (esp. fig.: *unfounded hope, rumours*). [f. UN-² 1; see FOUND¹]

ŭnfree'ze *v.t. & i.* (**unfro'ze; unfro'zen**). (cause to) thaw. [f. UN-¹ 1 + FREEZE]

ŭnfrĕquĕ'ntĕd *a.* See UN-² 1.

ŭnfrie'ndĕd (-rĕ'n-) *a.* without friends. [f. UN-² 1 + FRIEND + -ED²]

ŭnfrie'ndly (-rĕ'n-) *a.* See UN-² 1.

ŭnfrŏ'ck *v.t.* deprive (priest etc.) of frock or ecclesiastical rank. [f. UN-¹ 2 + FROCK]

ŭnfrui'tful (-ōō't-), **ŭnfulfī'lled** (-ōōlfī'ld), **ŭnfū'ndĕd,** *adjs.* See UN-² 1.

ŭnfu'nny *a.* not amusing (though meant to be). [f. UN-² 1 + FUNNY]

ŭnfūr'l *v.t. & i.,* see UN-¹ 1; **ŭnfūr'nished** (-sht) *a.,* UN-² 1.

ŭngai'nl|ȳ (ŭn-g-) *a.* (Of person or animal, or movements thereof) awkward-looking, clumsy;

hence ∼ɪɴᴇss n. [f. ᴜɴ-² 1 + obs. *gainly* ME f. obs. *gain* a., OE f. ON *gegn* straight, + -ʟʏ¹]

ŭngă′llant (ŭn-g-), ŭngăr′bled (ŭn-gär′beld), ŭn-gĕ′nerous (ŭnj-), ŭngē′nial (ŭnj-), ŭngē′ntle (ŭnj-), ŭngĕ′ntlemanly (ŭnjĕ′ntelm-), *adjs.* See ᴜɴ-² 1.

ŭnget-ă′t-able (ŭn-g-) *a.* (colloq.) inaccessible. [f. ᴜɴ-² 1 + ɢᴇᴛ¹-*at-able*]

ŭngĭ′ld (ŭn-g-) *v.t.*, see ᴜɴ-¹ 1; ŭngĭ′mmicky (ŭn-g-) *a.*, ᴜɴ-² 1; ŭngĭr′d (ŭn-g-) *v.t.*, ᴜɴ-¹ 1; ŭnglā′zed (ŭn-glā′zd) *a.*, ᴜɴ-² 1.

ŭnglo′ve (ŭn-glŭ′v) *v.t.* & *i.* remove gloves (of). [ME, f. ᴜɴ-¹ 2 + ɢʟᴏᴠᴇ]

ŭnglo′ved (ŭn-glŭ′vd) *a.* See ᴜɴ-² 1.

ŭngŏ′dll|y (ŭn-g-) *a.* impious, wicked; (colloq.) outrageous; hence ∼ɪɴᴇss n. [f. ᴜɴ-² 1 + ɢᴏᴅʟʏ]

ŭngo′vernab|le (ŭn-gŭ′-) uncontrollable, violent; hence ∼ʟʏ² *adv.* [f. ᴜɴ-² 1 + ɢᴏᴠᴇʀɴᴀʙʟᴇ]

ŭngrā′ceful (ŭn-grā′sf-) *a.* See ᴜɴ-² 1.

ŭngrā′cious (ŭn-grā′shus) *a.* not kindly or courteous or attractive; hence ∼ʟʏ² *adv.*, ∼ɴᴇss n. [ME, = graceless, unlucky, f. ᴜɴ-² 1 + ɢʀᴀᴄɪᴏᴜs]

ŭngrammă′tical (ŭn-g-) *a.* contrary to rules of grammar; hence ∼ʟʏ² *adv.* [f. ᴜɴ-² 1 + ɢʀᴀᴍᴍᴀᴛɪᴄᴀʟ]

ŭngrā′teful (ŭn-grā′tf-), ŭngrŭ′dging (ŭn-g-), *adjs.* See ᴜɴ-² 1.

ŭ′ngual (ŭ′nggw-) *a.* of, like, bearing, a nail or hoof or claw. [f. L ᴜɴɢᴜɪs + -ᴀʟ]

ŭnguăr′d (ŭn-gär′d) *v.t.* deprive of guard or defence; (Cards) discard a low card that was protecting (a high card) from capture. [f. ᴜɴ-² 2 + ɢᴜᴀʀᴅ¹]

ŭnguăr′dĕd (ŭn-gär′-) *a.* not guarded; incautious; thoughtless; hence ∼ʟʏ² *adv.* [f. ᴜɴ-² 1; see ɢᴜᴀʀᴅ²]

ŭ′nguent (ŭ′nggw-) n. soft substance used as ointment or for lubrication. [f. L *unguentum* (*unguere* anoint)]

ŭnguĭ′culate (ŭnggw-) *a.* having nail(s) or claw(s). [f. mod. L *unguiculatus* (*unguiculus* dim. of ᴜɴɢᴜɪs; see -ᴄᴜʟᴇ, -ᴀᴛᴇ²)]

ŭ′ngu|is (ŭ′nggw-) n. (*pl.* ∼es *pr.* -ēz). (Bot.) narrow base of petal; (Zool.) nail, claw. [L]

ŭ′ngŭl|a (ŭ′ngg-) n. (*pl.* ∼ae). hoof, claw, talon; so ∼ᴀᴛᴇ² (2) *a.* & n., (Zool.) hoofed (mammal). [L, dim. of ᴜɴɢᴜɪs]

ŭngŭ′m (ŭn-g-) *v.t.*, see ᴜɴ-¹ 2; ŭnhă′ckneyed (-nĭd) *a.*, ᴜɴ-² 1; ŭnhair′ *v.t.*, ᴜɴ-¹ 2.

ŭnhă′llowed (-ōd) *a.* not consecrated; not sacred, unholy, wicked. [f. ᴜɴ-² 1; see ʜᴀʟʟᴏᴡ²]

ŭnhă′mpered (-erd) *a.* See ᴜɴ-² 1.

ŭnhă′nd *v.t.* (rhet.) take one's hands off; release from one's grasp. [f. ᴜɴ-¹ 3 + ʜᴀɴᴅ¹]

ŭnhă′ndsome (-ns-), ŭnhă′ndy, *adjs.* See ᴜɴ-² 1.

ŭnhă′ng *v.t.* (unhu′ng). take down from a hanging position. [ME, f. ᴜɴ-¹ 1 + ʜᴀɴɢ¹]

ŭnhă′nged (-ngd) *a.* See ᴜɴ-² 1.

ŭnhă′pp|y *a.* not happy, miserable; causing misfortune; disastrous; inauspicious; unsuccessful; hence ∼ʟʏ² *adv.*, ∼ɴᴇss n. [ME, f. ᴜɴ-² 1 + ʜᴀᴘᴘʏ]

||ŭnhâr′bour (-ber) *v.t.* dislodge (deer) from covert. [f. ᴜɴ-¹ 3 + ʜᴀʀʙᴏᴜʀ]

ŭnhâr′med (-md) *a.*, see ᴜɴ-² 1; ŭnhâr′ness, ŭnha′sp (-ah′-), *vbs. t.*, ᴜɴ-¹ 1; ŭnhea′lthful (-č′l-) *a.*, ᴜɴ-² 1.

ŭnhea′lth|y (-č′l-) *a.* not in good health; unwholesome; (of place etc.) harmful to health, (sl.) dangerous to life; hence ∼ɪʟʏ² *adv.*, ∼ɪɴᴇss n. [f. ᴜɴ-² 1 + ʜᴇᴀʟᴛʜʏ]

ŭnhear′d (-ĕr′d) *a.* not heard; ∼(-of), unknown, unprecedented. [ME, f. ᴜɴ-² 1 + ʜᴇᴀʀᴅ]

ŭnhee′dĕd, ŭnhee′dful, ŭnhee′ding, *adjs.* See ᴜɴ-² 1.

ŭnhĕ′lm *v.t.* & *i.* (arch.) remove helmet (of). [ME, f. ᴜɴ-¹ 2 + ʜᴇʟᴍ¹]

ŭnhĕ′lpful, ŭnhĕ′raldĕd, ŭnhĕrō′ĭc, ŭnhĕ′sitāt-ing (-z-), *adjs.* See ᴜɴ-² 1.

ŭnhĭ′nge (-nj) *v.t.* take (door etc.) off its hinges; (fig., esp. in *p.p.*) unsettle or disorder (person's mind etc.). [f. ᴜɴ-¹ 1 + ʜɪɴɢᴇ]

ŭnhistō′ric(al) *adjs.*, see ᴜɴ-² 1; ŭnhĭ′tch *v.t.*, ᴜɴ-¹ 1.

ŭnhō′l|y (-ŭ) *a.* not holy; impious, profane, wicked; (colloq.) dreadful, outrageous, (*made an unholy row about it*); hence ∼ɪɴᴇss n. [OE *unhálig* (as ᴜɴ-², ʜᴏʟʏ)]

ŭnhŏ′noured (ŭnŏ′nerd) *a.* See ᴜɴ-² 1.

ŭnhŏŏ′k *v.t.* detach from hook(s); unfasten by releasing hook(s). [f. ᴜɴ-¹ 3 + ʜᴏᴏᴋ¹]

ŭnhō′ped (-pt) *a.* ∼ for, not hoped for or expected. [ME, f. ᴜɴ-² 1; see ʜᴏᴘᴇ³]

ŭnhŏr′se *v.t.* throw or drag from horse; (of horse) throw (rider); (fig.) dislodge, overthrow. [ME, f. ᴜɴ-² 3 + ʜᴏʀsᴇ¹]

ŭnhou′se (-z) *v.t.* deprive of shelter, turn out of house. [ME, f. ᴜɴ-¹ 3 + ʜᴏᴜsᴇ¹]

ŭnhou′seled (-zeld) *a.* (arch.) not having received the Eucharist. [f. ᴜɴ-² 1 + obs. *housel* v. & n. (give) consecrated elements f. OE *húsl*(*ian*), of unkn. orig., + -ᴇᴅ¹]

ŭnhū′man *a.* = ɪɴʜᴜᴍᴀɴ 1; superhuman; non-human. [f. ᴜɴ-² 1 + ʜᴜᴍᴀɴ]

ŭnhū′manize *v.t.*, see ᴜɴ-¹ 1; ŭnhŭ′ng, ŭnhŭ′rried (-īd), ŭnhŭr′t, *adjs.*, ᴜɴ-² 1; ŭnhŭ′sk *v.t.*, ᴜɴ-¹ 3.

ū′ni- *comb. form.* one, having or consisting of one, as: ∼a′xial, having a single axis; ∼ca′meral, of only one (legislative) chamber; ∼ce′llular, one-celled; ∼co′lour(ed), of one colour; ∼cu′spid *a.* & n., (tooth) with one cusp; ∼cycle, single-wheeled vehicle esp. as used by acrobats; ∼dime′nsional, having (only) one dimension; ∼dire′ctional, having only one direction of motion, operation, etc.; ∼li′ngual, of only one language; ∼li′teral, consisting of one letter; ∼lo′cular, (Bot. & Zool.) single-chambered; ∼nu′cleate, having one nucleus; ∼parous (-ï′-), producing one at a birth, (Bot.) having one axis or branch; ∼ped n. & *a.*, single-footed (person); ∼per′sonal, (of Deity) existing only as one person; ∼pla′nar, lying in one plane; ∼pod, one-legged support; ∼po′lar, (Biol., of cell etc.) having only one pole, (Electr.) showing only one kind of polarity; ∼ser′ial, set in one row; ∼valent (-ī′-), (Chem.) having a valence of one; ∼valve *a.* & n., (mollusc) with one valve; ∼vocal (-ï′-) *a.* & n., (word) of only one proper meaning. [L *unus* one; see -ɪ-)]

U′niat, -ate, (ū′-) n. & *a.* (member) of any community of Christians in E. Europe and Near East that acknowledge papal supremacy but retain own liturgy etc. [f. Russ. *uniyat* (*uniya* f. L *unio* ᴜɴɪᴏɴ)]

UNICEF (ū′nĭsĕf) *abbr.* United Nations Children's (orig. International Children's Emergency) Fund.

ū′nicŏrn n. **1.** fabulous animal with horse's body and single straight horn in OT transl. Heb. *rᵉem*, a two-horned animal); heraldic representation of this, with twisted horn, deer's feet, goat's beard, and lion's tail. **2.** ∼(-fish), ∼ whale, sea-∼, narwhal. **3.** ∼ moth (having caterpillar with hornlike prominence on back). **4.** pair of horses with third horse in front; equipage with these. **5.** ∼(-shell), gastropod with spine on lip of shell. [ME, f. OF *unicorne* f. L ᴜɴɪ(*cornis* f. *cornu* horn), transl. Gk *monocerōs*]

ŭnĭde′a′d *a.* having no ideas. [f. ᴜɴ-² 1 + ɪᴅᴇᴀ′ᴅ]

ŭnĭde′al, ŭnĭdĕ′ntified (-īd), *adjs.* See ᴜɴ-² 1.

UNIDO (ūnē′dō) *abbr.* United Nations Industrial Development Organization.

ŭnĭfĭcā′tion etc. See ᴜɴɪꜰʏ.

ū′nifŏrm *a.*, n., & *v.t.* **1.** *a.* not changing in form or character, the same, unvarying, (*present a uniform appearance; all of uniform size and shape; keeps a uniform temperature; behaved with uniform moderation*); constant in the course of time (*uniform acceleration*); (of tax, law, etc.) not varying with time or place; conforming to same standard or rules or pattern; hence ∼ʟʏ² *adv.* & n. uniform distinctive dress worn by members of same body, e.g. by soldiers, sailors, policemen, nurses, schoolchildren. **3.** *v.t.* make uniform; clothe in uniform (*a uniformed officer*). [f. F *uniforme* or f. L ᴜɴɪ(*formis* f. *forma* ꜰᴏʀᴍ¹)]

ūnifŏrmitār′ian *a.* & n. (holder) of theory that

geological processes are always due to continuously and uniformly operating forces; hence ∿ISM (3) *n*. [f. foll. +-ARIAN]

ūnifŏr′mĭtў *n*. being uniform, sameness, consistency; **Act of U∿** (for securing uniformity in public worship and use of a particular Book of Common Prayer, esp. that of 1662). [ME, f. OF *uniformité* or f. LL *uniformitas* (as UNIFORM; see -ITY)]

ū′nĭ|fў *v.t.* reduce (things, or abs.) to unity or uniformity; hence or cogn. ∿FICA′TION, ∿fīER¹, *ns*. [f. F. *unifier* or f. LL UNI(*ficare*; see -FY)]

ūnĭlă′teral *a*. one-sided; performed by or affecting only one person or party (*unilateral declaration of independence, disarmament*); (of parking of vehicles) restricted to one side of street; (of leaves) all on same side of stem; hence ∿LY² *adv*. [f. UNI- + LATERAL]

ūnĭllu′mĭnātĕd (-ōō′-), **ūnĭmă′gĭnable, ūnĭmă′gĭnātive, ūnĭmpair′ed** (-āī′d), **ūnĭmpă′ssioned** (-shond), *adjs*. See UN-² 1.

ūnĭmpea′chab|le *a*. giving no opportunity for censure; beyond reproach or question; hence ∿LY² *adv*. [f. UN-² 1 + IMPEACHABLE]

ūnĭmpĕ′dĕd *a*., see UN-² 1; **ūnĭmpŏr′tance** *n*., UN-² 2; **ūnĭmpŏr′tant, ūnĭmpō′sing** (-z-), **ūnĭmprĕ′s-sionable** (-shon-), **ūnĭmprĕ′ssive**, *adjs*., UN-² 1.

ūnĭmpro′ved (-ōō′vd) *a*. not made better; not made use of; (of land) not used for agriculture or building. [f. UN-² 1; see IMPROVE]

ūnĭmpū′gned (-ū′nd), **ūnĭ′ndĕxed** (-kst), **ūnĭnflŏ′ctĕd, ūnĭ′nfluenced** (-ōōenst), *adjs*. See UN-² 1.

ūnĭnfŏr′med (-md) *a*. not informed or instructed; uneducated, ignorant. [f. UN-² 1 + INFORMED]

ūnĭnhă′bĭtable, ūnĭnhă′bĭted, ūnĭnhĭ′bĭted, ūnĭnĭ′tiātĕd (-shī-), **ūnĭ′njured** (-jerd), *adjs*. See UN-² 1.

ūnĭnspīr′ed (-īr′d) *a*. not inspired; (of oratory etc.) commonplace. [f. UN-² 1; see INSPIRE]

ūnĭnspīr′ing, ūnĭnstrŭ′ctĕd, ūnĭnsur′able (-shoor′-), **ūnĭnsur′ed** (-shoor′d), **ūnĭntĕ′lligent, ūnĭntĕ′lligible, ūnĭntĕ′ntĭonal,** *adjs*. See UN-² 1.

ūnĭ′nterĕstĕd (-tr-, -ter-) *a*. not interested, esp. unconcerned, indifferent; hence ∿LY² *adv*., ∿NESS *n*. [f. UN-² 1; see INTEREST]

ūnĭ′nterĕsting (-tr-, -tər), **ūnĭnterrŭ′ptĕd, ūnĭnvĕ′ntive, ūnĭnvĕ′stĭgātĕd, ūnĭnvī′tĕd,** *adjs*. See UN-² 1.

ūnĭnvī′ting *a*. not inviting, unattractive, repellent; hence ∿LY² *adv*. [f. UN-² 1 + INVITING]

ūnĭnvŏ′ked (-kt), **ūnĭnvŏ′lved** (-vd), *adjs*. See UN-² 1.

ū′nion (-ĭon, -yon) *n*. 1. uniting, being united, coalition, junction, (*the union of the parts was imperfect; union by first or second* INTENTION), **the U∿** (of English and Scottish crowns in 1603 or parliaments in 1707, or of Great Britain and Ireland in 1801). 2. matrimony, marriage. 3. concord, agreement, (*lived together in perfect union*). 4. a whole resulting from combination of parts or members, esp. (1) the US, (2) the UK, (3) South Africa, (4) the Union of SOVIET Socialist Republics; (Math.) totality of members of two or more sets; = TRADE *union*; ∿ **catalogue** (showing combined holdings of several libraries). 5. ||(Hist.) two or more parishes consolidated for administration of poor-laws; ∿ (**workhouse**), workhouse erected by this. 6. ||association of independent (esp. Congregational or Baptist) churches for purposes of co-operation. 7. (*U∿*). general social club and debating society at some universities and colleges; buildings of such society. 8. part of flag with device emblematic of union normally occupying upper corner next to staff; ∿ **down**, hoisted with union below as signal of distress; **U∿ Jack** or **flag**, national ensign of United Kingdom formed by union of crosses of St. George, St. Andrew, and St. Patrick; *∿ **jack**, JACK³ comprising union from national flag. 9. joint or coupling for pipes etc. 10. fabric of mixed materials, e.g. cotton with linen or silk or jute. 11. *∿ **suit**, single

undergarment for body and legs, combinations. [ME f. OF, or f. eccl. L *unio* unity f. L *unus* one; see -ION]

ū′nion|ĭst (-ĭo-, -yo-) *n*. 1. member of a trade union; advocate of trade unions. 2. (Polit.) one who supports union, esp. one opposed to rupture of parliamentary union between Great Britain and (Northern) Ireland; (arch.) Conservative; *(Hist.) one who during the civil war opposed secession. 3. one who supports union of churches. 4. So ∿ISM (3) *n*., ∿ĭ′stĭc *a*. [f. prec. +-IST]

ū′nionīz|e, -īs|e, (-ĭonīz, -yo-), *v.t.* bring under trade-union organization or rules; hence ∿a′TION *n*. [f. UNION + -IZE]

ūn-ĭ′onīzed, -īsed, (-zd) *a*. See UN-² 1.

ūnī′que (-ē′k) *a*. & *n*. 1. *a*. of which there is only one, unequalled, having no like or equal or parallel, (*his position was unique; this vase is so far as is known unique*); (colloq.; D) remarkable, unusual, (*the most unique man I ever met*); hence ∿LY² (-klĭ) *adv*., ∿NESS (-kn-) *n*. 2. *n*. unique thing or person. [F, f. L *unicus* (*unus* one; see -IC)]

ū′nĭsĕx *n*. & *a*. 1. *n*. tendency of human sexes to become indistinguishable in dress etc. 2. *a*. (Of clothes) designed to be worn by either sex. [f. UNI- + SEX]

ūnĭsĕ′xŭal *a*. of one sex; (Bot.) having stamens or pistils but not both; hence ∿ITY (-ă′l-) *n*., ∿LY² *adv*. [f. UNI- + SEXUAL]

ū′nison *a*. & *n*. 1. *a*. (Mus.) coinciding in pitch; hence or cogn. ∿AL, ∿ANT, ∿OUS, (-ĭ′s-) *adjs*.; ∿ **string** (tuned in unison with another string and meant to be sounded with it). 2. *n*. (Mus.) coincidence in pitch of sounds or notes, this regarded as an interval; state of sounding at same pitch or at pitches differing by octave(s) (esp. *in unison*). 3. concord, agreement, (*acted in perfect unison*). [OF, or f. LL UNI(*sonus* SOUND²)]

ū′nĭssued (-shōōd, -sūd) *a*. See UN-² 1.

ū′nĭt *n*. 1. individual thing or person or group regarded for purposes of calculation etc. as single and complete, each of the (smallest) separate individuals or groups into which a complex whole may be analysed, (*the family as the unit of society*). 2. the number 'one'; quantity chosen as a standard in terms of which other quantities may be expressed; quantity of elec tricity etc. for which stated charge is made; ||smallest share in unit trust. 3. device with specified function forming element in complex mechanism; piece of furniture for fitting with others like it or made of complementary parts; group with special function in an organization. 4. ||∿-**holder**, person with holding in unit trust; ∿ **price** (charged for each unit of goods supplied); ||∿ **trust**, investment company investing combined contributions from many persons in various securities and paying them dividends in proportion to their holdings; ∿ **volume** (etc.), volume taken as unit in calculation or expression of other quantities. [1570 (J. Dee's preface to Billingsley's transl. of Euclid), f. L *unus* repl. UNITY, prob. after *digit*]

ūnĭtār′ian *n*. & *a*. 1. *n*. (*U∿*). one who, member of a religious body that, maintains against the doctrine of the Trinity that God is one person; advocate of general freedom of belief; hence **U∿**ISM (3) *n*., **U∿**IZE (3) *v.t.* 2. advocate of unity or centralization esp. in politics. 3. *a*. (*U∿*). of the Unitarians. 4. = foll. 2. [f. mod. L *unitarius* f. L *unitas* UNITY; see -ARIAN]

ū′nĭtarў *a*. 1. of a unit or units. 2. marked by unity or uniformity. [f. UNIT or UNITY + -ARY¹]

ūnī′te *v*. 1. *v.t.* & *i*. join together, make or become one, combine, consolidate, amalgamate, (*unite the parts with cement; give the parts time to unite; the two nations gradually (became) united; oil will not unite with water*); **U∿d Brethren**, (the sect of) MORAVIANS; **U∿d Kingdom**, Great Britain and (since 1922 Northern) Ireland; **U∿d Nations**, (orig., in 1942) those united against the Axis powers in the war of 1939–45, (later) a peace-seeking organization of these and many other

States; **U∼d Provinces,** (Hist.) (1) seven provinces united in 1579 and forming basis of republic of Netherlands, (2) major Indian administrative division, comprising Agra and Oudh; **U∼d Reformed Church** (formed 1972 from English Presbyterian and Congregational Churches); *United* STATE*¹s*. **2.** *v.i.* agree, combine, co-operate, (*in* sentiment, conduct, doing). **3.** Hence **ū′nĭtIVE** *a*. [ME, f. L *unire -it- (unus* one) +-ITE²]

ū′nĭtў *n*. **1.** oneness, being one or single or individual, being formed of parts that constitute a whole, due interconnection and coherence of parts, (*disturbs the unity of the idea; pictures lack unity; national unity*). **2.** thing showing such unity, thing that forms a complex whole, (*a person regarded as a unity*); (Math.) the number 'one', factor that leaves unchanged the quantity on which it operates; **the dramatic unities, the unities of time, place, and action,** limitation of supposed time of drama to that occupied in acting it or to a single day, use of same scene throughout, and abstention from all that is irrelevant to development of single plot. **3.** harmony, concord, between persons etc., (*dwell together in unity; at unity with*). [ME, f. OF *unité* f. L *unitas -tatis (unus* one; see -ITY)]

Univ. *abbr.* University.

ūnivêr′sal *a*. & *n*. **1.** *a*. of or belonging to or done etc. by all persons or things in the world or in the class concerned, applicable to all cases, (*the terror was universal; met with universal applause; has the universal sanction of philosophers; the rule does not pretend to be universal*). **2.** ∼ **agent** (empowered to do all that can be delegated); ∼ **compass** (with legs that may be extended for large circles); ∼ **coupling** or **joint** (transmitting power by a shaft at any selected angle); ∼ **language,** artificial language intended for use by all nations; ∼ **proposition** (in which predicate is affirmed or denied of the entire subject; opp. *particular proposition*); universal SUFFRAGE; ∼ **time** (used for astronomical reckoning at all places). **3.** Hence or cogn. ∼ITY (-ă′l-) *n*., ∼IZE (3) *v.t.*, ∼LY² *adv*. **4.** *n*. (Logic). universal proposition; (Philos.) general notion or idea, thing that by its nature may be predicated of many. [ME f. OF, or f. L *universalis* (as UNIVERSE; see -AL)]

ūnivêr′sal|ist *n*. one who holds, esp. member of an organized body of Christians who hold, that all mankind will eventually be saved; hence or cogn. ∼ISM (3) *n*., ∼i′stIC *a*. [f. prec.+-IST]

ū′nivêrse *n*. all existing things; the whole creation; the COSMOS¹; the world, all mankind; ∼ (**of discourse**), (Logic) all the objects under consideration; (Statistics) = POPULATION 3. [f. F *univers* f. L *universum* neut. (as n.) of UNI(*versus* p.p. of *vertere* turn) combined into one, whole]

ūnivêr′sĭtў *n*. educational institution designed for instruction or examination or both of students in all or many of the more important branches of advanced learning, conferring degrees in various faculties, and often embodying colleges and similar institutions; members of this collectively; team, crew, etc., representing a university; **at** ∼, studying there; *university* EXTENSION. [ME, f. OF *université* f. L *universitas -tatis* the whole (world), in LL college, guild (as prec.; see -ITY)]

ŭnjau′ndiced (-st) *a*., see UN-² 1; **ŭnjoi′n** *v.t.*, UN-¹ 1; **ŭnjoi′ned** (-nd) *a*., UN-² 1.

ŭnjoi′nt *v.t.* separate joints of; (fig.) disunite. [f. UN-¹ 1+JOINT³]

ŭnjŭ′st *a*. not just, contrary to justice or fairness; hence ∼LY² *adv*. [ME, f. UN-² 1+JUST¹]

ŭnjŭ′stifiable *a*. See UN-² 1.

ŭnkĕ′mpt (ŭn-k-) *a*. uncombed, dishevelled; untidy, of neglected appearance. [f. UN-² 1+arch. *kempt* p.p. of *kemb* COMB² f. OE *cemban* (as COMB¹)]

ŭnkĕ′nnel (ŭn-k-) *v.t.* (||-ll-). dislodge (fox) from its hole; (fig.) bring to light. [f. UN-¹ 3+KENNEL¹]

ŭnkī′nd (ŭn-k-) *a*. not kind; harsh, ungentle, unpleasant; hence ∼LY² *adv*., ∼NESS *n*. [ME, f. UN-² 1+KIND²]

ŭnkī′ng (ŭn-k-) *v.t.*, see UN-¹ 4; **ŭnkī′nglў** (ŭn-k-) *a*., UN-² 1.

ŭnkī′nk (ŭn-k-) *v.t.* remove kinks from, straighten. [f. UN-¹ 1+KINK]

ŭnknī′ghtlў (ŭn-nī′t-) *a*., see UN-² 1; **ŭnknī′t, ŭnknŏ′t,** (ŭn-n-) *vbs. t.*, UN-¹ 1.

ŭnknow′able (ŭn-nō′-) *a*. & *n*. **1.** *a*. that cannot be known. **2.** *n*. unknowable thing; **the U∼,** postulated absolute or ultimate reality. [ME, f. UN-² 1+KNOWABLE]

ŭnknow′ing (ŭn-nō′-) *a*. not knowing; unconscious or ignorant (*of*, or abs.); hence ∼LY² *adv*. [ME, f. UN-² 1+KNOWING²]

ŭnknow′n (ŭn-nō′n) *a*., *n*., & *adv*. **1.** *a*. not known, unfamiliar, (*to*, *his purpose, what he wanted, that district, was unknown to me*); *unknown* COUNTRY, QUANTITY; **U∼ Soldier** or **Warrior,** unidentified representative member of a country's armed forces killed in war, given burial with special honours in national memorial. **2.** *n*. unknown thing or person; unknown quantity (*equation in two unknowns*). **3.** *adv*. ∼ **to,** without the knowledge of. [ME, f. UN-² 1+KNOWN]

ŭnlā′belled (-ld), **ŭnlā′boured** (-êrd), *adjs*. See UN-² 1.

ŭnlā′ce *v.t.* undo laces of; unfasten or loosen thus. [ME, f. UN-¹ 1+LACE²]

ŭnlā′de *v.t.* See UN-¹ 1.

ŭnlā′den *a*. not laden; ∼ **weight** (of vehicle without goods etc.). [f. UN-² 1; see LADE]

ŭnlā′dўlīke, ŭnlai′d, ŭnlamĕ′ntĕd, *adjs*. See UN-² 1.

ŭnlā′sh *v.t.* unfasten (thing lashed down etc.). [f. UN-¹ 1+LASH¹]

ŭnlā′tch *v.t.* & *i*., see UN-¹ 1; **ŭnlaw′ful** *a*., UN-² 1.

ŭnlay′ *v.t.* (unlai′d). (Naut.) untwist (rope). [f. UN-¹ 1+LAY³]

ŭnlea′ded (-lĕ′-) *a*. See UN-² 1.

ŭnlear′n (-êr′n) *v.t.* (for forms see LEARN). cause to be no longer in one's knowledge or memory. [ME, f. UN-¹ 1+LEARN]

ŭnlear′nĕd¹ (-êr′-) *a*. not LEARNED, untaught, ignorant; hence ∼LY² *adv*. [ME, f. UN-² 1+LEARNED]

ŭnlear′ned² (-êr′nd), **ŭnlear′nt** (-êr′-), *adjs*. that has not been learnt. [f. UN-² 1; see LEARN]

ŭnlea′sh *v.t.* release from leash or restraint; set free to engage in pursuit or attack (lit. or fig.). [f. UN-¹ 1+LEASH]

ŭnlea′vened (-lĕ′vend) *a*. See UN-² 1.

ŭnlĕ′ss *conj*. if not except when, (*shall go, shall not go, unless I hear from him, unless absolutely compelled; always walked unless I had a bicycle*). [f. LESS preceded by *on* or *in*, unstressed & assim. to UN-²]

ŭnlĕ′ttered (-êrd) *a*. not instructed in learning got from books; illiterate. [ME, f. UN-² 1+LETTER+-ED²]

ŭnli′censed (-st) *a*. See UN-² 1.

ŭnli′cked (-kt) *a*. not licked into shape; unpolished, rude. [f. UN-² 1; see LICK]

ŭnli′ghted (-ī′t-) *a*. See UN-² 1.

ŭnlī′ke *a*. & *prep*. not like, different(ly) (from), dissimilar, (*is unlike both his parents; the two are unlike; portrait is utterly unlike; sings quite unlike anyone I have heard before*); not characteristic of (*such behaviour is unlike him*); ∼ **signs,** (Math.) plus and minus; hence ∼NESS (-kn-) *n*. [perh. f. ON *úlíkr*, OE *ungelic* as UN-², LIKE¹]

ŭnli′kel|ў (-klĭ) *a*. improbable (*unlikely tale*); not to be expected to do; unpromising (*unlikely errand*); hence ∼ĭHOOD, ∼ĭNESS, *ns*. [ME, f. UN-² 1+LIKELY]

ŭnli′mber *v.t.* remove (gun, or abs.) from limber for action. [f. UN-¹ 1+LIMBER¹]

ŭnli′mĭted *a*. without limit, unrestricted, very great in number or quantity, (*has unlimited scope, possibilities; unlimited expanse of sea; drinks unlimited coffee*); hence ∼LY² *adv*., ∼NESS *n*. [ME, f. UN-² 1; see LIMIT²]

ŭnli′ned¹ (-nd) *a*. without lining. [f. UN-² 1; see LINE⁴]

For other words in *un-* see UN-, UN-¹, UN-².

unlined (-nd) a. without lines; (of face etc.) without wrinkles. [f. UN-² 1; see LINE³]

unli'nk v.t., see UN-¹ 1; **unli'quidated** a., UN-² 1.

unli'sted a. not included in (published) list, esp. of Stock Exchange prices or of telephone numbers. [f. UN-² 1; see LIST¹]

unli't a. See UN-² 1.

unloa'd v.t. remove load from (ship, cart, etc., or abs.); remove (load) from ship etc.; (fig.) get rid of; remove charge from (firearm etc.). [f. UN-¹ 1 + LOAD²]

unlo'ck v.t. release lock of (door, box, etc., or fig.); release (thing) by unlocking (lit. or fig.). [ME, f. UN-¹ 1 + LOCK³]

unlo'cked (-kt) a. See UN-² 1.

unloo'ked (-kt) a. ~ for, unexpected, unforeseen. [f. UN-² 1; see LOOK]

unloo'se v.t. = LOOSE² 1. [ME, f. UN-² 1 + LOOSE²]

unloo'sen v.t. = LOOSE² 1. [ME, f. UN-² 1 + LOOSEN]

unlo'vable (-ŭ'-), **unlo'ved** (-ŭ'vd), adjs. See UN-² 1.

unlo'vel|y (-ŭ'vlĭ) a. not attractive, unpleasant, ugly; hence ~iNESS n. [ME, f. UN-² 1 + LOVELY]

unlo'ving (-ŭ'-) a. See UN-² 1.

unlu'ck|y a. not fortunate or successful; wretched; bringing bad luck; ill-judged; hence ~iLY² adv. [f. UN-² 1 + LUCKY¹]

unmā'dc, unmai'denly, adjs. See UN-² 1.

unmā'ke v.t. (unma'de). undo the making of, destroy, depose, annul. [ME, f. UN-¹ 1 + MAKE¹]

unmā'n v.t. (-nn-). deprive (ship etc.) of men; deprive of manly qualities, discourage, (person). [f. UN-¹ 2, 4 + MAN¹]

unmā'nageab|le (-nĭja-). not (easily) managed or manipulated or controlled; hence ~leNESS (-beln-) n., ~LY² adv. [f. UN-² 1 + MANAGEABLE]

unmā'nly, unmā'nned (-nd), adjs. See UN-² 1.

unmā'nnerl|y a. without good manners; showing lack of good manners; hence ~iNESS n. [ME, f. UN-² 1 + MANNERLY]

unmā'rked (-kt) a. not marked; not noticed. [f. UN-² 1; see MARK²]

unmā'rkètable, unmā'rriageable (-rĭja-), **unmā'rried** (-id), **unma'sculine** (-mă'-, -mah'-), adjs. See UN-² 1.

unma'sk (-ah'-) v. 1. v.t. remove mask from; (fig.) expose true character of. 2. v.i. remove one's mask. [f. UN-¹ + MASK²]

unmā'tchable, unmā'tched (-cht), adjs. See UN-² 1.

unmea'ning a. having no significance, meaningless; hence ~LY² adv., ~NESS n. [f. UN-² 1 + MEANING²]

unmea'nt (-ĕ'-), **unmea'surable** (-ĕ'zher-), adjs. See UN-² 1.

unmea'sured (-ĕ'zherd) a. not measured; limitless. [ME, f. UN-² 1 + MEASURED]

unmee't a. (arch.) not suitable (to do, for a purpose); hence ~LY² adv., ~NESS n. [OE unmǣte (as UN-², MEET³)]

unmēlō'dious, unmē'ltèd, unmē'morable, adjs. See UN-² 1.

unmē'ntionable a. & n. 1. a. that cannot (properly) be mentioned. 2. n. (in pl., arch., joc.) trousers; undergarments. [f. UN-² 1 + MENTIONABLE]

unmēr'chantable, unmēr'ciful, unmē'rited, ||unmē'talled (-ld), **unmethō'dical, unmē'trical, unmi'litary, unmi'ndful**, adjs. See UN-² 1.

unmistā'kab|le a. that cannot be mistaken or doubted, quite clear; hence ~LY² adv. [f. UN-² 1 + MISTAKABLE]

unmi'tigātèd a. not mitigated or modified; absolute, unqualified, (an unmitigated scoundrel). [f. UN-² 1; see MITIGATE]

unmi'xed (-kst), **unmō'difīed** (-īd), **unmō'dūlātèd, unmolē'stèd**, adjs. See UN-² 1.

unmoor' (-oor', -ōr) v.t. release moorings of (vessel, or abs.); weigh all but one anchor of (vessel). [f. UN-¹ 1 + MOOR³]

unmō'ral a. not concerned with morality; hence **unmorā'lITY** n. [f. UN-² 1 + MORAL]

unmōr'tise v.t., see UN-¹ 1; **unmo'therly** (-ŭ'dh-), **unmou'ntèd, unmour'ned** (-ōr'nd), adjs., UN-² 1.

unmo'ved (-ōō'vd) a. not moved; not changed in one's purpose; not affected by emotion. [ME, f. UN-² 1; see MOVE²]

unmow'n (-ō'n) a. See UN-² 1.

unmu'ffle v.t. remove muffler from (face, bell, etc.). [f. UN-¹ 1 + MUFFLE³]

unmu'rmuring a. not complaining; hence ~LY² adv. [f. UN-² 1; see MURMUR²]

unmu'sical (-z-) a. not pleasing to the ear; unskilled in or indifferent to music; hence ~LY² adv., ~NESS n. [f. UN-² 1 + MUSICAL]

unmu'tilātèd a. See UN-² 1.

unmu'zzle v.t. remove muzzle from; (fig.) relieve of obligation to remain silent. [f. UN-¹ 2 + MUZZLE¹]

unnai'l (ŭn-n-) v.t. see UN-¹ 2.

unnā'meable (ŭn-nā'ma-) a. that cannot be named, esp. too bad to be named. [f. UN-² 1 + NAMEABLE]

unnā'med (ŭn-nā'md), **unnā'tional** (ŭn-n-), adjs. See UN-² 1.

unnā'tural (ŭn-nă'cher-) a. contrary to (the usual course of) nature; extremely cruel or wicked; lacking natural feelings; artificial; hence ~LY² adv., ~NESS n. [ME, f. UN-² 1 + NATURAL]

unnē'cessar|y (ŭn-n-) a. not necessary; more than is necessary (with unnecessary care); hence ~iLY² adv. [f. UN-² 1 + NECESSARY]

unnei'ghbourly (ŭn-na'ber-) a. See UN-² 1.

unner've (ŭn-n-) v.t. deprive of strength or resolution. [f. UN-¹ 1 + NERVE]

unnō'ticed (ŭn-nō'tist) a. See UN-² 1.

unnu'mbered (ŭn-n-; -erd) a. not marked with a number; not counted; not able to be counted. [ME, f. UN-² 1; see NUMBER²]

UNO (ū'nō) abbr. United Nations Organization.

unobjē'ctionable, unobscūr'ed (-ūr'd), **unobsēr'vant** (-z-), **unobsēr'ved** (-zēr'vd), **unobstrū'ctèd, unobtai'nable, unobtru'sive** (-ōō'-), **unō'ccūpied** (-ĭd), adjs. See UN-² 1.

unoffē'nding a. not offending; harmless, innocent. [f. UN-² 1; see OFFEND]

unoffi'cial (-shal) a. not having official character or authorization; ~ strike (not formally approved by trade union of those striking); hence ~LY² adv. [f. UN-² 1 + OFFICIAL]

unoi'led (-ld), **unō'pened** (-nd), **unoppō'sed** (-zd), **unor'dinary, unor'ganized** (-zd), adjs. See UN-² 1.

unori'ginal a. not having originality, derivative; hence ~ITY (-ă'l-) n., ~LY² adv. [f. UN-² 1 + ORIGINAL]

unor'namentèd, unor'thodox, unostentā'tious (-shus), **unow'ned** (-ō'nd), adjs. See UN-² 1.

unpă'ck v.t. open and remove contents of (package, luggage, etc., or abs.); take out (thing) from package etc. [f. UN-¹ 1 + PACK²]

unpā'ged (-jd) a. with pages not numbered. [f. UN-² 1; see PAGE²]

unpai'd a. (Of debt or person) not (having been) paid; ||the great ~, unpaid magistrates or justices. [ME, f. UN-² 1 + PAID]

unpair'ed (-ār'd), **unpā'latable**, adjs. See UN-² 1.

unpā'ralléled (-ld) a. having no parallel or equal. [f. UN-² 1; see PARALLEL²]

unpār'donable a. See UN-² 1.

unpār'liame'ntary (-lam-) a. contrary to parliamentary usage; ~ language, oaths or abuse. [f. UN-² 1 + PARLIAMENTARY]

unpā'tentèd, unpătriŏ'tic, unpā'ved (-vd), **unpee'led** (-ld), adjs., **unpe'g** v.t., UN-¹ 2; **unpeo'ple** (-ē'-) v.t., UN-¹ 2; **unperce'ived** (-sē'vd), **unpercē'ptive, unperfor'med** (-md), adjs., UN-² 1.

u'npēr'son n. person whose name or existence is denied or ignored. [f. UN-² 2 + PERSON]

unpersua'dèd (-sw-), **unpersua'sive** (-sw-), **unpertūr'bed** (-bd), adjs. See UN-² 1.

unphiloso'phic(al) adjs. not according to philosophical principles; lacking philosophy. [f. UN-² 1 + PHILOSOPHIC(AL)] ŭnphy̆siŏlŏ'gic(al) (-z-) a. not in accordance with normal physiological functioning. [f. UN-² 1 + PHYSIOLOGIC(AL)]

ŭnpi'ck v.t. undo sewing of (stitches, garment, etc.). [f. UN-¹ 1 + PICK²]

ŭnpi'cked (-kt) a. not selected; (of flower) not plucked. [f. UN-² 1; see PICK²]

ŭnpicturĕ'sque (-kcherĕ'sk) a. See UN-² 1.

ŭnpi'n v.t. (-nn-). unfasten or detach by removing pins; (Chess) make (man) no longer pinned. [ME, f. UN-¹ 1 + PIN²]

ŭnpi'tied (-īd), ŭnpi'tyĭng, adjs. See UN-² 1.

ŭnplā'ced (-st) a. not placed, esp. in race etc. [f. UN-² 1; see PLACE²]

ŭnplā'nned (-nd), ŭnpla'ntĕd (-ah'-), ŭnpla'stered (-ah'sterd), ŭnplau'sĭble (-z-), adjs. See UN-² 1.

ŭnplay'able a. (Esp. of ball in games) that cannot be played, returned, etc. [f. UN-² 1 + PLAYABLE]

ŭnplea'sant (-ĕ'z-) a. not pleasant, disagreeable; hence ∼LY² adv., ∼NESS n. (the late ∼ness, a recent war). [f. UN-² 1 + PLEASANT]

ŭnplea'sing (-z-) a., see UN-² 1; ŭnplea'sure (-ĕ'zher) n., UN-² 2; ŭnplĕ'dged (-jd), ŭnplou'ghed (-ow'd), ŭnplŭ'cked (-kt), adjs., UN-² 1; ŭnplŭ'g v.t., UN-¹ 1; ŭnplŭ'mbed (-md), ŭnpŏĕ'tic(al), adjs., UN-² 1.

ŭnpoi'ntĕd a. having no point(s); not punctuated; (of written Hebrew etc.) having no vowel points marked; (of brickwork etc.) not pointed. [f. UN-² 1 + POINTED]

ŭnpŏ'lished (-sht) a. See UN-² 1.

ŭnpoli'tical a. not concerned with politics. [f. UN-² 1 + POLITICAL]

ŭnpŏ'lled (-ld), ŭnpollu'tĕd (-ōō'-), adjs. See UN-² 1.

ŭnpŏ'pŭlar a. not popular, not liked by the public or by people in general; hence ∼ITY (-ă'r-) n., ∼LY² adv. [f. UN-² 1 + POPULAR]

ŭnpossĕ'ssed (-zĕ'st) a. not possessed; not in possession of. [f. UN-² 1; see POSSESS]

ŭnpŏ'sted a. See UN-² 1.

ŭnprā'ctical a. not practical; (of person) not having practical skill; hence ∼ITY (-ă'l-) n., ∼LY² adv. [f. UN-² 1 + PRACTICAL]

ŭnprā'ctised, *-iced, (-st) a. not experienced or skilled; not put into practice. [f. UN-² 1; see PRACTISE]

ŭnprĕ'cĕdĕntĕd a. for which there is no precedent, unparalleled; novel; hence ∼LY² adv. [f. UN-² 1 + PRECEDENTED]

ŭnprĕdi'ctable, ŭnprĕ'judiced (-jōōdĭst), adjs. See UN-² 1.

ŭnprĕmĕ'ditātĕd a. not previously thought over, not deliberately planned, unintentional; hence ∼LY² adv. [f. UN-² 1; see PREMEDITATE]

ŭnprepār'ed (-ār'd) a. not prepared (in advance), not ready; hence ∼NESS n. [f. UN-² 1; see PREPARE]

ŭnprĕposse'ssing (-zĕ'-), ŭnprĕsĕ'ntable (-z-), ŭnprĕsŭ'ming (-z-), ŭnprĕsŭ'mptuous (-z-), adjs. See UN-² 1.

ŭnprĕtĕ'ndĭng, ŭnprĕtĕ'ntious (-shus), adjs. not making a great display; hence ∼LY² adv., ∼NESS n. [f. UN-² 1; see PRETEND, PRETENTIOUS]

ŭnpri'ced (-st) a. not having price(s) fixed or marked or stated. [f. UN-² 1 + PRICED]

ŭnpri'se't v.t., see UN-¹ 4; ŭnpri'med (-md) a., UN-² 1.

ŭnpri'ncipled (-peld) a. not having or based on good moral principles of conduct. [f. UN-² 1 + PRINCIPLED]

ŭnpri'ntable a. that cannot be printed, esp. because too blasphemous, indecent, etc. [f. UN-² 1 + PRINTABLE]

ŭnpri'ntĕd, ŭnpri'vilĕged (-jd), ŭnprocūr'able, ŭnprodŭ'ctive, adjs. See UN-² 1.

ŭnprofĕ'ssional (-shon-) a. not belonging to one's or a profession; contrary to professional standards of behaviour etc. [f. UN-² 1 + PROFESSIONAL]

ŭnprŏ'fitable, ŭnprogrĕ'ssive, ŭnprŏ'mising, ŭnprŏ'mptĕd, ŭnpronou'nceable (-nsa-), ŭnprophĕ'tic, ŭnpropi'tious (-shus), ŭnprŏ'sperous, ŭnprotĕ'ctĕd, ŭnpro'vable (-ōō'-),

ŭnpro'ved (-ōō'vd), ŭnpro'ven (-ōō'-), ŭnprovī'dĕd, adjs. See UN-² 1.

ŭnprovŏ'ked (-kt) a. (Of person or act) having no provocation. [f. UN-² 1; see PROVOKE]

ŭnpŭ'blished (-sht), ŭnpŭ'nctual, ŭnpŭ'nctūātĕd, ŭnpŭ'nishable, ŭnpŭ'nished (-sht), ŭnpūr'ifīed (-īd), adjs. See UN-² 1.

ŭnputdow'nable (-pŏŏ-) a. (colloq.) (Of book) so engrossing that reader cannot put it down. [f. UN-² 1 + PUT¹ down + -ABLE]

ŭnqua'lifīed (ŭn-kwŏ'lifīd) a. not competent (am unqualified to serve); not legally or officially qualified (an unqualified practitioner); not modified or restricted (gave his unqualified assent; was an unqualified success). [f. UN-² 1; see QUALIFY]

ŭnquee'n (ŭn-kw-) v.t., see UN-¹ 4; ŭnquĕ'nchable (ŭn-kw-), ŭnquĕ'nched (ŭn-kwĕ'ncht), adjs., UN-² 1.

ŭnquĕ'stionab|le (ŭn-kwĕ'schon-) a. that cannot be disputed or doubted; hence ∼LY² adv. [f. UN-² 1 + QUESTIONABLE]

ŭnquĕ'stioned (ŭn-kwĕ'schond) a. that is not disputed or doubted; not interrogated. [f. UN-² 1; see QUESTION²]

ŭnquĕ'stioning (ŭn-kwĕ'schon-) a. asking no questions; done etc. without asking questions. [f. as prec.]

ŭnqui'et (ŭn-kw-) a. restless, agitated, stirring; perturbed, anxious. [f. UN-² 1 + QUIET²]

ŭnquŏ'table (ŭn-kw-) a. See UN-² 1.

ŭnquŏ'te (ŭn-kw-) v.i. terminate passage placed within quotation-marks (esp. in imper. in dictation etc.). [f. UN-¹ 1 + QUOTE]

ŭnquŏ'tĕd (ŭn-kw-), ŭnrā'nsomed (-md), adjs. See UN-² 1.

ŭnră'vel v. (||-ll-). 1. v.t. cause to be no longer ravelled, tangled, or intertwined, (lit. or fig.); undo (fabric, esp. knitted one). 2. v.i. become disentangled or unknitted. [f. UN-¹ 1 + RAVEL]

ŭnrā'vished (-sht), ŭnrā'zored (-erd), ŭnrea'chable, adjs. See UN-² 1.

ŭnrea'd (-ĕ'd) a. not read; (of person) not well-read. [f. UN-² 1; see READ]

ŭnrea'dable a. See UN-² 1.

ŭnrea'd|y¹ (-ĕ'-) a. not ready; not prompt in action; hence ∼iNESS n. [f. UN-² 1 + READY]

ŭnrea'dy² (-ĕ'-) a. lacking good advice, rash, (Ethelred the Unready). [f. UN-² 1 + REDE¹ + -Y², assim. to prec.]

ŭnrĕ'al a. not real; imaginary; hence ∼ITY (-iă'l-) n. [f. UN-² 1 + REAL²]

ŭnrĕāli'stic, ŭnrĕ'alīzable, ŭnrĕ'alīzed (-zd), ŭnrea'ped (-pt), adjs. See UN-² 1.

ŭnrea'son (-z-) n. lack of reasonable thought or action. [ME, = injustice, f. UN-² 2 + REASON¹]

ŭnrea'sonab|le (-z-) a. not reasonable; going beyond the limits of what is reasonable or equitable; hence ∼leness (-beln-) n., ∼LY² adv. [ME, f. UN-² 1 + REASONABLE]

ŭnrea'soned (-zond), ŭnrea'soning (-z-), ŭnrĕcĕ'ptive, ŭnrĕci'procātĕd, ŭnrĕ'ckoned (-nd), ŭnrĕclai'med (-md), ŭnrĕ'cognizable, ŭnrĕ'cognized (-zd), ŭnrĕ'compĕnsed (-st), ŭnrĕ'concīled (-ld), ŭnrĕdee'med (-md), ŭnrĕdrĕ'ssed (-st), adjs. See UN-² 1.

ŭnree'l v.t. & i. unwind from reel. [f. UN-¹ 1 + REEL¹]

ŭnree've v.t., see UN-¹ 1; ŭnrĕfi'ned (-nd), ŭnrĕflĕ'cting, ŭnrĕfōr'med (-md), ŭnrĕ'gal, ŭnrĕgār'dĕd, ŭnrĕgĕ'nerate, ŭnrĕ'gistered (-erd), ŭnrĕgrĕ'ttĕd, ŭnrĕ'gŭlātĕd, ŭnrĕhear'sed (-ĕr'st), adjs., UN-² 1; ŭnrei'n (-ā'n) v.t., UN-¹ 3; ŭnrĕlā'tĕd, ŭnrĕlā'xed (-kst), ŭnrĕlĕ'nting, ŭnrĕli'able, ŭnrĕli'eved (-vd), adjs., UN-² 1.

ŭnrĕli'gious (-jus) a. irreligious; not concerned with religion. [ME, f. UN-² 1 + RELIGIOUS]

ŭnrĕmār'kable, ŭnrĕmĕ'mbered (-erd), adjs. See UN-² 1.

ŭnrĕmi'tting a. never relaxing or slackening, incessant; hence ∼LY² adv. [f. UN-² 1; see REMIT¹]

For other words in un- see UN-, UN-¹, UN-².

ŭnrĕmū'nerǎtive *a.* bringing no, or not enough, profit; hence ∼LY² (-vlĭ) *adv.*, ∼NESS (-vn-) *n.* [f. UN-² 1 + REMUNERATIVE]

ŭnrénou'nced (-st), **ŭnrĕpea'led** (-ld), *adjs.* See UN-² 1.

ŭnrĕpea'table *a.* that cannot be done again; too foul etc. to be said again. [f. UN-² 1 + REPEATABLE]

ŭnrĕpĕ'ntant, ŭnrĕpŏr'tĕd, ŭnrĕprĕsĕ'ntative (-z-), **ŭnrĕprĕsĕ'ntĕd** (-z-), **ŭnrĕpro'ved** (-ōō'vd), *adjs.* See UN-² 1.

ŭnrĕquī'tĕd *a.* (Of love etc.) not returned. [f. UN-² 1; see REQUITE]

ŭnrĕsĕr've (-z-) *n.* See UN-² 2.

ŭnrĕsĕr'ved (-zĕr'vd) *a.* not reserved (*unreserved seats*); without reservations (*unreserved confidence*); free from reserve (*an unreserved nature*); hence ∼LY² (-vĭdlĭ) *adv.*, ∼NESS *n.* [f. UN-² 1; see RESERVE]

ŭnrĕsī'stĕd (-zī'-), **ŭnrĕsī'sting** (-zī'-), **ŭnrĕsŏ'lved** (-zŏ'lvd), **ŭnrĕspŏ'nsive**, *adjs.* See UN-² 1.

ŭnrĕ'st *n.* lack of rest; restlessness, disturbance, agitation. [ME, f. UN-² 2 + REST²]

ŭnrĕ'stful, ŭnrĕ'sting, ŭnrĕstŏr'ed (-ŏr'd), **ŭnrĕstrai'ned** (-nd), **ŭnrĕstrĭ'ctĕd, ŭnrĕtŭr'ned** (-nd), **ŭnrĕvea'led** (-ld), **ŭnrĕvĕr'sed** (-st), **ŭnrĕvī'sed** (-zd), **ŭnrĕvŏ'ked** (-kt), **ŭnrĕwar'dĕd** (-ŏr'-), **ŭnrhĕtŏ'rical** (-ĭt-), **ŭnrhȳ'med** (-rī'md), **ŭnrhȳ'thmical** (-rĭ'dh-, -th-), **ŭnrī'dable**, **ŭnrī'dden**, *adjs.* See UN-² 1.

ŭnrī'ddle *v.t.* solve, explain, (mystery etc.). [f. UN-¹ 1 + RIDDLE¹]

ŭnrī'g *v.t.* (-gg-). remove rigging from (ship); undress. [f. UN-¹ 2 + RIG¹]

ŭnrī'ght (-ī't) *n.* (arch.) injustice, wrong. [OE *unriht* (as UN-² 2, RIGHT³)]

ŭnrī'ghteous (-ī'chŭs) *a.* not righteous, unjust, wicked, dishonest; hence ∼LY² *adv.*, ∼NESS *n.* [OE *unrihtwīs* (as UN-² 1, RIGHTEOUS)]

ŭnrī'p *v.t.* (-pp-). open by ripping. [f. UN-¹ 1 + RIP⁸]

ŭnrī'pe, ŭnrī'sen (-z-), *adjs.* See UN-² 1.

ŭnrī'valled, *-aled, (-ald) *a.* having no equal, peerless. [f. UN-² 1; see RIVAL]

ŭnrī'vĕt *v.t.* See UN-¹ 1.

ŭnrō'be *v.t.* & *i.* disrobe; undress. [f. UN-¹ 2 + ROBE]

ŭnrō'll *v.t.* & *i.* open out from rolled-up state; display or be displayed thus. [ME, f. UN-¹ 1 + ROLL³]

ŭnromă'ntic *a.* See UN-² 1.

ŭnrōō'f *v.t.* remove roof of. [f. UN-¹ 2 + ROOF]

ŭnrōō'fed (-ft) *a.*, see UN-² 1; **ŭnrōō'st** *v.t.*, UN-¹ 3.

ŭnrōō't *v.t.* uproot; (fig.) eradicate. [ME, f. UN-¹ + ROOT²]

ŭnrō'pe *v.t.* & *i.*, see UN-¹ 3, **ŭnroy'al, ŭnru'ffled** (-fěld), **ŭnru'led** (-ōō'ld), *adjs.*, UN-² 1.

ŭnru'ly (-ōō'-) *a.* not easily controlled or disciplined, disorderly; *unruly* MEMBER; hence ∼ĭNESS *n.* [ME, f. UN-² 1 + *ruly* (RULE, -Y²)]

UNRWA (ŭ'nrah) *abbr.* United Nations Relief and Works Agency.

ŭnsă'ddle *v.t.*, see UN-¹ 1, 3; **ŭnsă'fe, ŭnsai'd** (-ĕ'd), **ŭnsă'laried** (-ĭd), **ŭnsă'leable** (-la-), **ŭnsa'ltĕd** (-aw'-, -ŏ'-), **ŭnsă'nctĭfīed** (-ĭd), **ŭnsă'nctioned** (-nd), **ŭnsă'nitarȳ, ŭnsătisfă'ctorȳ, ŭnsă'tisfīed** (-ĭd), **ŭnsă'tisfȳing**, *adjs.*, UN-² 1.

ŭnsă'turā'tĕd (-chər-, -tūr-) *a.* not saturated; (Chem.) able to combine with another substance, esp. hydrogen, to form a third by addition of molecules with elimination of double or triple bonds. [f. UN-² 1; see SATURATE]

∥ŭnsă'vour|ȳ (-erĭ), ***-or|ȳ,** *a.* disagreeable to taste, smell, or feelings; disgusting; distasteful; morally offensive; hence ∼ĭLY² *adv.*, ∼ĭNESS *n.* [ME, f. UN-² 1 + SAVOURY]

ŭnsay' *v.t.* (for forms see SAY²). retract (statement). [ME, f. UN-¹ 1 + SAY²]

ŭnsay'able, ŭnscā'lable, *adjs.*, see UN-² 1; **ŭnscā'le** *v.t.*, UN-¹ 2; **ŭnscăr'red** (-ăr'd) *a.*, UN-² 1.

ŭnscā'thed (-dhd) *a.* without suffering any injury. [ME, f. UN-² 1; see SCATHE]

ŭnscĕ'ntĕd, ŭnschĕ'dŭled (-shĕ'dŭld), **ŭnschŏ'larlȳ** (-sk-), **ŭnschōō'led** (-skōō'ld), *adjs.* See UN-² 1.

ŭnscĭentī'f|ic *a.* not familiar with science; not in accordance with scientific principles; hence ∼ICALLY *adv.* [f. UN-² 1 + SCIENTIFIC]

ŭnscră'mble *v.t.* restore from scrambled state, esp. interpret (scrambled conversation etc.). [f. UN-¹ 1 + SCRAMBLE]

ŭnscree'ned (-nd) *a.* not provided with a screen; not shown on a screen; not passed through a screen (lit. or fig.). [f. UN-² 1; see SCREEN]

ŭnscrew' (-ōō') *v.t.* & *i.* unfasten by turning or removing screw(s) or by twisting like screw; loosen (screw). [f. UN-¹ 1 + SCREW]

ŭnscrī'ptĕd *a.* (Of speech etc.) delivered without a prepared script. [f. UN-² 1 + SCRIPT + -ED²]

ŭnscrī'ptural (-cher-, -choor-) *a.* not in accordance with Scripture; hence ∼LY² *adv.* [f. UN-² 1 + SCRIPTURAL]

ŭnscru'pŭlous (-ōō'-) *a.* not having scruples, shameless, unprincipled; hence ∼LY² *adv.*, ∼NESS *n.* [f. UN-² 1 + SCRUPULOUS]

ŭnsea'l *v.t.* break seal of, open, (letter etc.) [ME, f. UN-¹ 1 + SEAL²]

ŭnsea'led (-ld) *a.* See UN-² 1.

ŭnsea'm *v.t.* unfasten seams of (garment). [f. UN-¹ 1 + SEAM]

ŭnsear'chable (-ĕr'-), **ŭnsear'ched** (-ĕr'cht), **ŭnsea'sonable** (-zo-), **ŭnsea'soned** (-zond), *adjs.* See UN-² 1.

ŭnsea't *v.t.* remove from (esp. parliamentary) seat; dislodge from seat, esp. on horseback. [f. UN-¹ 3 + SEAT]

ŭnsea'worthȳ (-ĕrdhĭ), **ŭnsĕ'condĕd, ŭnsĕcūr'ed** (-ūr'd), *adjs.* See UN-² 1.

ŭnsee'dĕd *a.* (Of tennis-player etc.) not seeded. [f. UN-² 1; see SEED]

ŭnsee'ing *a.* blind; unobservant; hence ∼LY² *adv.* [f. UN-² 1; see SEE¹]

ŭnsee'mlȳ *a.* See UN-² 1.

ŭnsee'n *a.* & *n.* 1. *a.* not seen; (of translation) done without previous preparation. 2. *n.* ∥unseen translation. [ME, f. UN-² 1 + SEEN]

ŭnsĕ'gregātĕd, ŭnsĕlĕ'ct, ŭnsĕlfcŏ'nscious (-shŭs), **ŭnsĕ'lfish, ŭnsĕ'nsā'tional, ŭnsĕnti'mĕntal, ŭnsĕ'parātĕd, ŭnsĕr'viceable** (-sab-), *adjs.* See UN-² 1.

ŭnsĕ'ttle *v.* 1. *v.t.* disturb settled state or arrangement of; derange. 2. *v.i.* become unsettled. [f. UN-¹ + SETTLE²]

ŭnsĕ'ttled (-tĕld) *a.* not (yet) settled; liable to or open to change or further discussion; (of bill etc.) unpaid. [f. UN-² 1; see SETTLE²]

ŭnsĕ'x *v.t.* deprive (esp. woman) of qualities of her or his sex. [f. UN-¹ 2 + SEX]

ŭnsĕ'xed (-kst) *a.*, see UN-² 1; **ŭnshă'ckle** *v.t.*, UN-¹ 1; **ŭnshă'dĕd, ŭnshă'keable** (-ka-), **ŭnshă'ken, ŭnshă'pelȳ** (-plĭ), **ŭnshăr'ed** (-ăr'd), **ŭnshā'ved** (-vd), **ŭnshā'ven,** *adjs.*, UN-² 1; **ŭnshea'the** (-dh) *v.t.*, UN-¹ 2; **ŭnshĕ'd** *a.*, UN-² 1; **ŭnshĕ'll** *v.t.*, UN-¹ 3; **ŭnshĕ'ltered** (-erd) *a.*, UN-² 1.

ŭnshi'p *v.t.* (-pp-). remove or discharge (cargo, passenger) from ship; remove (esp. Naut.: mast, oar, etc.) from fixed position. [ME, f. UN-¹ 3, 1 + SHIP¹,²]

ŭnshŏ'ckable, ŭnshŏ'd, *adjs.*, see UN-² 1; **ŭnshoe'** (-ōō') *v.t.*, UN-¹ 2; **ŭnshŏr'n, ŭnshrĭ'nkable, ŭnshri'nking,** *adjs.*, UN-² 1.

ŭnsī'ghtĕd (-ī't-) *a.* not sighted or seen; prevented from seeing. [f. UN-² 1; see SIGHT²]

ŭnsī'ghtlȳ (-ī't-) *a.* unpleasing to the sight, ugly; hence ∼ĭNESS *n.* [ME, f. UN-² 1 + SIGHTLY]

ŭnsī'gned (-īnd) *a.* See UN-² 1.

ŭnsī'zed¹ (-zd) *a.* not made to a size; not sorted by size. [f. UN-² 1; see SIZE¹]

ŭnsī′zed[2] (-zd) *a.* not treated with size. [f. UN-[2] 1; see SIZE[2]]

ŭnskī′lful *a.* See UN-[2] 1.

ŭnskī′lled (-ld) *a.* not having or needing skill or special training. [f. UN-[2] 1 +SKILLED]

ŭnskī′mmed (-md), **ŭnslee′ping**, *adjs.*, see UN-[2] 1; **ŭnslī′ng** *v.t.*, UN-[1] 1; **ŭnsmī′ling, ŭnsmō′ked** (-kt), *adjs.*, UN-[2] 1.

ŭnsnār′l *v.t.* disentangle. [f. UN-[1] 1 +SNARL[2]]

ŭnsō′ciable (-sha-) *a.* See UN-[2] 1.

ŭnsō′cial (-shal) *a.* not social; not seeking or suitable for or conforming to society; antisocial. [f. UN-[2] 1 + SOCIAL]

ŭnsoi′led (-ld), **ŭnsō′ld**, *adjs.*, see UN-[2] 1; **ŭnsō′lder** *v.t.*, UN-[1] 1; **ŭnsō′ldierlỹ** (-jerlĭ), **ŭnsolī′cited, ŭnsō′lvable, ŭnsō′lved** (-vd), *adjs.*, UN-[2] 1.

ŭnsophī′stĭcātĕd *a.* natural, ingenuous, innocent; not adulterated or artificial; hence ∼LY[2] *adv.*, ∼NESS *n.* [f. UN-[2] 1; see SOPHISTICATE]

ŭnsōr′dĭd, ŭnsōr′tĕd, ŭnsou′ght (-aw′t), *adjs.* See UN-[2] 1.

ŭnsou′nd *a.* not sound; diseased, unhealthy, rotten, wicked, ill-founded, fallacious, unreliable; **of** ∼ **mind,** insane; hence ∼LY[2] *adv.*, ∼NESS *n.* [ME, f. UN-[2] 1 +SOUND[1]]

ŭnsou′ndĕd, ŭnsour′ed (-owr′d), **ŭnsow′n** (-ō′n), *adjs.* See UN-[2] 1.

ŭnspār′ing *a.* profuse, lavish; merciless. [f. UN-[2] 1 + SPARING]

ŭnspea′kab|le *a.* that cannot be expressed in words; indescribably bad or objectionable. [ME, f. UN-[2] 1 +SPEAK +-ABLE]

ŭnspē′cifīed (-īd), **ŭnspĕctā′cŭlar**, *adjs.*, see UN-[2] 1; **ŭnspĕ′ll** *v.t.*, UN-[1] 3; **ŭnspĕ′nt, ŭnspī′lled** (-ld), **ŭnspī′lt, ŭnspī′ritŭal, ŭnsplī′ced** (-st), **ŭnsplī′nterable, ŭnspoi′led** (-ld), **ŭnspoi′lt, ŭnspō′ken, ŭnspŏr′ting, ŭnspŏr′tsmanlīke,** *adjs.*, UN-[2] 1.

ŭnspŏ′ttĕd *a.* not marked with spot(s); (fig.) morally pure; unnoticed. [ME, f. UN-[2] 1; see SPOT[2]]

ŭnsprŭ′ng *a.* See UN-[2] 1.

ŭnstā′b|le *a.* not stable; changeable; showing tendency to sudden mental or emotional changes; *unstable* EQUILIBRIUM; hence ∼LY[2] *adv.* [ME, f. UN-[2] 1 +STABLE[1]]

ŭnstai′ned (-nd), **ŭnstă′mped** (-pt), **ŭnstār′ched** (-cht), **ŭnstā′tĕd, ŭnstā′tesmanlīke** (-ts-), *adjs.* See UN-[2] 1.

ŭnstā′tūtab|le *a.* contrary to statute(s); hence ∼LY[2] *adv.* [f. UN-[2] 1 +STATUTABLE]

ŭnstea′dfast (-ĕ′-) *a.* See UN-[2] 1.

ŭnstea′d|ỹ (-ĕ′-) *a.* not steady or firm; changeable, fluctuating, not uniform or regular; hence ∼ĭLY[2] *adv.*, ∼ĭNESS *n.* [f. UN-[2] 1 +STEADY]

ŭnstī′ck *v.t.* (unstu′ck). separate (thing stuck to another); (colloq.) cause (aircraft) to leave ground; **come unstuck,** (colloq.) come to grief, fail. [f. UN-[1] 1 +STICK[1]]

ŭnstī′ntĕd, ŭnstī′nting, ŭnstīr′red (-ēr′d), *adjs.*, see UN-[2] 1; **ŭnstī′tch** *v.t.*, UN-[1] 1.

ŭnstŏ′p *v.t.* (-pp-). free from obstruction; remove stopper from. [ME, f. UN-[1] 1 +STOP[1]]

ŭnstŏ′ppable *a.*, see UN-[2] 1; **ŭnstŏ′pper** *v.t.*, UN-[1] 2; **ŭnstrai′ned** (-nd), **ŭnstrā′tifīed** (-īd), **ŭnstrea′med** (-md), *adjs.*, UN-[2] 1.

ŭnstrĕ′ssed (-st) *a.* not subjected to stress; not pronounced with stress. [f. UN-[2] 1; see STRESS]

ŭnstrī′ng *v.t.* (unstru′ng). remove or relax string(s) of (bow, harp, etc.); remove from string; (esp. in *p.p.*) unnerve. [f. UN-[1] 2 +STRING]

ŭnstrŭ′ctured (-kcherd) *a.* not structured; informal. [f. UN-[2] 1; see STRUCTURE]

ŭnstŭ′dīed (-īd) *a.* easy, natural, spontaneous. [f. UN-[2] 1; see STUDY[2]]

ŭnstŭ′ffed (-ft) *a.* See UN-[2] 1.

ŭnstŭ′ffỹ *a.* not stuffy; informal, casual. [f. UN-[2] 1 + STUFFY]

ŭnsubdūe′d (-ū′d), **ŭnsŭ′bjugātĕd** (-jōō-), *adjs.* See UN-[2] 1.

ŭnsubstă′ntial (-shal) *a.* having little or no solidity or reality or factual basis; hence ∼ITY (-shĭă′l-) *n.*, ∼LY[2] *adv.* [ME, f. UN-[2] 1 +SUBSTANTIAL]

ŭnsubstă′ntiātĕd (-shĭ-) *a.*, see UN-[2] 1; **ŭnsuccĕ′ss** (-ks-) *n.*, UN-[2] 2; **ŭnsuccĕ′ssful** (-ks-), **ŭnsu′gared** (-shōō′gerd), **ŭnsuggĕ′stive** (-suj-), **ŭnsui′table** (-sōō′-, -sū′-), **ŭnsui′tĕd** (-sōō′-, -sū′-), **ŭnsŭ′llied** (-īd), **ŭnsŭ′mmoned** (-nd), *adjs.*, UN-[2] 1.

ŭnsŭ′ng *a.* not sung; not celebrated in song. [ME, f. UN-[2] 1 +SUNG]

ŭnsŭ′nned (-nd) *a.* not reached by or affected by or exposed to sunlight. [f. UN-[2] 1; see SUN]

ŭnsupplī′ed (-īd), **ŭnsuppŏr′table, ŭnsuppŏr′tĕd, ŭnsur′e** (-shoor′), **ŭnsurpa′ssable** (-ah′-), **ŭnsurpa′ssed** (-ah′st), **ŭnsurvey′ed** (-ā′d), **ŭnsuscĕ′ptible, ŭnsuspĕ′ctĕd, ŭnsuspĕ′cting, ŭnsuspī′cious** (-shus), **ŭnsustai′ned** (-nd), *adjs.*, see UN-[2] 1; **ŭnswā′the** (-dh) *v.t.*, UN-[1] 1; **ŭnsway′ed** (-ā′d) *a.*, UN-[2] 1.

ŭnswear′ (-ār′) *v.t.* (**unswor′e; unswor′n**). retract (thing sworn). [f. UN-[1] 1 +SWEAR]

ŭnswee′tened (-nd), **ŭnswĕ′pt,** *adjs.* See UN-[2] 1.

ŭnswēr′ving *a.* not turning aside; steady, constant; hence ∼LY[2] *adv.* [f. UN-[2] 1; see SWERVE]

ŭnswōr′n, ŭnsymmĕ′trical, ŭnsympathĕ′tic, ŭnsystemā′tic, *adjs.*, see UN-[2] 1; **ŭntă′ck** *v.t.*, UN-[1] 1; **ŭntai′ntĕd, ŭntă′lentĕd, ŭntă′meable** (-ma-), **ŭntā′med** (-md), *adjs.*, UN-[2] 1; **ŭntă′ngle** (-nggel) *v.t.*, UN-[1] 1; **ŭntă′nned** (-nd), **ŭntă′pped** (-pt), **ŭntār′nished** (-sht), **ŭntā′stĕd,** *adjs.*, UN-[2] 1.

ŭntau′ght (-aw′t) *a.* not taught; not instructed by teaching, ignorant; not acquired by teaching, natural, spontaneous. [ME, f. UN-[2] 1 +TAUGHT]

ŭntă′xed (-kst) *a.*, see UN-[2] 1; **ŭntea′ch** *v.t.*, UN-[1] 1; **ŭntea′chable, ŭntear′able** (-tār′-), **ŭntĕ′chnical** (-kn-), **ŭntĕ′mpered** (-erd), **ŭntĕ′nable, ŭntĕ′nantĕd, ŭntĕ′ndĕd, ŭntĕ′stĕd,** *adjs.*, UN-[2] 1; **ŭntĕ′ther** (-dh-) *v.t.*, UN-[1] 3; **ŭntĕ′thered** (-dherd), *adjs.*, UN-[2] 1.

ŭnthă′nked (-kt), **ŭnthă′nkful, ŭnthă′tched** (-cht), *adjs.*, UN-[2] 1; **ŭnthī′nk** *v.t.*, UN-[1] 1.

ŭnthī′nkab|le *a.* that cannot be conceived in thought or grasped by the mind; (colloq.) highly unlikely or undesirable; hence ∼LY[2] *adv.* [ME, f. UN-[2] 1 + THINKABLE]

ŭnthī′nking *a.* thoughtless; unintentional, inadvertent; hence ∼LY[2] *adv.* [f. UN-[2] 1 +THINKING[2]]

ŭnthou′ght (-aw′t), **ŭnthou′ghtful** (-aw′t-), *adjs.* See UN-[2] 1.

ŭnthrea′d (-rĕ′d) *v.t.* take thread out of (needle); find one's way out of (maze). [f. UN-[1] 1 +THREAD[2]]

ŭnthrĕ′shed (-sht) *a.*, see UN-[2] 1; **ŭnthrī′ft** *n.*, UN-[2] 2; **ŭnthrī′ftỹ** *a.*, UN-[2] 1; **ŭnthrō′ne** *v.t.*, UN-[1] 3; **ŭntī′dỹ** *a.*, UN-[2] 1.

ŭntie′ *v.t.* (*part.* **unty′ing**). unfasten (knot etc.); unfasten cords etc. of (package etc.); release from bonds or attachment. [OE *untīgan* (as UN-[1], TIE[1])]

ŭntie′d (-ī′d) *a.* See UN-[2] 1.

untī′l *prep.* & *conj.* = TILL[2] (used esp. when its clause or phrase stands first: *until you told me, I had no idea of it,* and in formal style: *resided there until his decease*). [orig. north. ME *untill* f. ON (= OE, OS) *und* as far as +TILL[2]]

ŭntī′llable, ŭntī′lled (-ld), *adjs.* See UN-[2] 1.

ŭntī′melỹ (-mlī) *a.* & (arch.) *adv.* inopportune(ly), (of death) premature(ly). [f. UN-[2] 1 +TIMELY]

ŭntī′nged (-njd), **ŭntīr′ing, ŭntī′tled** (-teld), *adjs.* See UN-[2] 1.

ŭ′nto (-ōō, -o) *prep.* (arch.) = TO[1] (in all uses except as sign of infinitive; *do unto others; sick, faithful, unto death; a* LAW[1], *take, unto oneself*). [ME; formed f. UNTIL, w. TO[1] repl. north. TILL[2]]

ŭntō′ld *a.* not told; not (able to be) counted (*untold wealth*). [OE *unteald* (as UN-[2], TOLD)]

ŭntou′chable (-ŭ′-) *a.* & *n.* **1.** *a.* that cannot or must not be touched. **2.** *n.* member of hereditary Hindu

For other words in *un-* see UN-, UN-[1], UN-[2].

group held to defile members of higher caste on contact. [f. UN-² 1 + TOUCHABLE]

ŭntou′ched (-ŭ′cht) a. See UN-² 1.

ŭntoward′ (-towŏr′d, -tō′werd) a. perverse, refractory; awkward; unlucky; unseemly; hence ∼LY² adv., ∼NESS n. [f. UN-² 1 + TOWARD¹]

ŭntrā′ceable (-sa-), **ŭntrā′ced** (-st), **ŭntrai′ned** (-nd), **ŭntră′mmelled** (-ld), **ŭntranslā′table** (-tră-, -trah-; -s-, -z-), **ŭntranspŏr′table** (-tră-, -trah-), adjs. See UN-² 1.

‖**ŭntră′velled, *-eled,** (-eld) a. that has not travelled; that has not been travelled over or through. [f. UN-² 1; see TRAVEL]

ŭntri′ed (-ī′d) a. not tried or tested, inexperienced; not tried by a judge. [f. UN-² 1 + TRIED]

ŭntrŏ′dden a. See UN-² 1.

ŭntrou′bled (-rŭ′beld) a. not troubled; calm, tranquil. [ME, f. UN-² 1; see TROUBLE]

ŭntrue′ (-ōō′) a. not true; contrary to what is the fact; not faithful or loyal (to); deviating from accepted standard; hence **ŭntru′**LY² (-ōō′-) adv. [OE untrēowe etc. (as UN-², TRUE)]

ŭntru′ss, see UN-¹ 1; **ŭntrŭ′ssed** (-st), **ŭntrŭ′st-worthy** (-ĕrdhĭ), adjs., UN-² 1.

ŭntru′th (-ōō′-) n. (pl. pr. -dhz or -ths). being untrue; false statement (told me an untruth). [OE untrēowth etc. (as UN-² 2, TRUTH)]

ŭntru′thful (-ōō′-) a., see UN-² 1; **ŭntŭ′ck** v.t., UN-¹ 1; **ŭntū′ned**, **ŭntū′neful** (-nf-), **ŭntŭr′ned** (-nd), **ŭntu′tored** (-erd), adjs., UN-² 1; **ŭntwī′ne**, **ŭntwi′st**, vbs. t. & i., UN-¹ 1; **ŭnū′sed** (-zd or -st) a., UN-² 1.

ŭnū′sual (-zhōōal) a. not usual; exceptional, remark-able; hence ∼LY² adv., ∼NESS n. [f. UN-² 1 + USUAL]

ŭnŭ′tterab|le a. inexpressible; beyond description (unutterable torment, joy, fool); hence ∼LY² adv. [f. UN-² 1 + UTTER² + -ABLE]

ŭnŭ′ttered (-erd), **ŭnvă′ccinātĕd** (-ks-), adjs. See UN-² 1.

ŭnvă′lūed (-ūd) a. not regarded as valuable. [f. UN-² 1; see VALUE]

ŭnvār′ied (-īd) a. See UN-² 1.

ŭnvăr′nished (-sht) a. not varnished; (fig., of state-ment or person) plain and straightforward. [f. UN-² 1; see VARNISH]

ŭnvār′ying a. See UN-² 1.

ŭnveil′ (-ā′l) v. 1. v.t. remove veil from; remove concealing drapery from (statue etc.) as part of ceremony of first public display; (fig.) disclose, reveal, make publicly known. 2. v.i. remove one's veil. [f. UN-¹ 2 + VEIL]

ŭnvĕ′ntilātĕd, ŭnvĕ′rifīable, ŭnvĕ′rifīed (-īd), adjs. See UN-² 1.

ŭnvĕr′sed (-st) a. not versed or experienced (in). [f. UN-² 1 + VERSED¹]

ŭnvī′olātĕd, ŭnvī′sĭtĕd (-z-), **ŭnvī′tiātĕd** (-shĭ-), adjs. See UN-² 1.

ŭnvoi′ced (-st) a. not spoken; (Phonet.) not voiced. [f. UN-² 1; see VOICE]

ŭnwa′ntĕd (-ŏ′-), **ŭnwar′līke** (-ŏr′-), **ŭnwar′med** (-ŏr′md), adjs. See UN-² 1.

ŭnwa′rrantab|le (-wŏ′-) a. indefensible, un-justifiable; hence ∼leNESS (-beln-) n., ∼LY² adv. [f. UN-² 1; see WARRANTABLE]

ŭnwa′rrantĕd (-wŏ′-) a. unauthorized; unjustified. [f. UN-² 1 + WARRANT²]

ŭnwār′y a. See UN-² 1.

ŭnwa′shed (-ŏ′sht) a. not washed; not usually washed or clean (**the great** ∼, the rabble). [f. UN-² 1; see WASH¹]

ŭnwa′tched (-ŏ′cht), **ŭnwa′tchful** (-ŏ′-), **ŭn-wa′tered** (-aw′terd), **ŭnwā′vering, ŭnwea′ned** (-nd), **ŭnwear′able** (-ār′-), **ŭnwear′ied** (-īd), **ŭnwear′y, ŭnwear′ying**, adjs., see UN-² 1; **ŭn-wea′ve** v.t., UN-¹ 1; **ŭnwĕ′d, ŭnwĕ′ddĕd, ŭn-wee′dĕd, ŭnwei′ghed** (-ā′d), **ŭnwĕ′lcome**, adjs., UN-² 1.

ŭnwĕ′ll a. not in good health; (somewhat) ill. [ME, f. UN-² 1 + WELL³]

ŭnwĕ′pt a. not wept (for). [f. UN-² 1 + WEPT]

ŭnwĕ′ttĕd, ŭnwhī′pped (-pt), **ŭnwhī′tened** (-nd), **ŭnwhō′lesome** (ŭnhō′ls-), adjs. See UN-² 1.

ŭnwie′ld|ў a. slow or clumsy of movement, difficult to use or manage, owing to size or weight or shape; hence ∼iLY² adv., ∼iNESS n. [ME, f. UN-² + (now dial.) wieldy active f. WIELD + -Y²]

ŭnwi′lling a. not willing or inclined (to do, for thing, for thing to be done, that, or abs.); hence ∼LY² adv., ∼NESS n. [OE unwillende (as UN-², WILLING²)]

ŭnwī′nd v.t. & i. (**ŭnwou′nd**). (cause to) become drawn out at length after having been wound; (colloq.) relax. [ME, f. UN-¹ 1 + WIND³]

ŭnwī′nking a. not winking; watchful, vigilant; hence ∼LY² adv. [f. UN-² 1; see WINK]

ŭnwī′sdom (-z-) n. being unwise; folly; imprudence. [OE unwīsdōm (as UN-² 2, WISDOM)]

ŭnwī′se (-z) a. foolish, imprudent; injudicious; hence ∼LY² adv. (-zlī) adv. [OE unwīs (as UN-², WISE¹)]

ŭnwī′shed (-sht) a. not wished for or for. [f. UN-² 1; see WISH]

ŭnwī′thered (-dherd), **ŭnwī′tnĕssed** (-st), adjs. See UN-² 1.

ŭnwi′tting a. not aware or conscious; unintentional; hence ∼LY² adv. [OE unwitende (as UN-², WIT¹, -ING²)]

ŭnwo′manly (-wŏŏ′-), **ŭnwŏ′ntĕd, ŭnwŏŏ′dĕd, ŭnwŏŏ′ed** (-ōō′d), **ŭnwor′kable** (-ĕr′-), **ŭn-wor′ked** (-ĕr′kt), **ŭnwor′kmanlīke** (-ĕr′-), adjs. See UN-² 1.

ŭnwor′ldl|ў (-ĕr′-) a. not worldly; spiritually-minded; hence ∼iNESS n. [f. UN-² 1 + WORLDLY]

ŭnwor′n a. that has not been worn or impaired by wear. [f. UN-² 1 + WORN]

ŭnwor′shipped (-ĕr′shĭpt) a. See UN-² 1.

ŭnwor′th|ў (-ĕr′dhĭ) a. not worthy or befitting the character (of); discreditable, unseemly; con-temptible, base; hence ∼iLY² adv., ∼iNESS n. [ME, f. UN-² 1 + WORTHY]

ŭnwou′nd, ŭnwou′ndĕd (-ōō′-), **ŭnwō′ven**, adjs., see UN-² 1; **ŭnwră′p** (ŭnr-) v.t., UN-¹ 1; **ŭnwri′nkled** (ŭnrĭ′ngkeld), **ŭnwri′table** (ŭnr-), adjs., UN-² 1.

ŭnwri′tten (ŭnr-) a. not written; (of law etc.) resting originally on custom or judicial decision, not on statute. [ME, f. UN-² 1 + WRITTEN]

ŭnwrou′ght (ŭnraw′t), **ŭnwrŭ′ng** (ŭnr-), adjs. See UN-² 1.

ŭnyle′lding a. not yielding to pressure etc.; hence ∼LY² adv., ∼NESS n. [f. UN-² 1; see YIELD]

ŭnyo′ke, ŭnzī′p, vbs. t. See UN-¹ 1.

ŭp adv., prep., a., n., & v. (**ŭpp-**). 1. adv. to or in high(er) place, position, degree, amount, value, etc., ‖to or in capital or university, to or in place farther north or otherwise regarded as high(er), (bird flew up to the eaves; high up in the air; what is he doing up there?; lives four floors up; a few feet farther up; flames mount up, total mounts up; tide is coming up; water came up to his chin; roll your sleeves up; lift up your head; up in Scotland, up to Scotland from London, up to London or town from the country; is high up in the school; went up three places in class); (colloq.) yonder at the front, top, etc.; to earlier time; towards source of river; inland; (of jockey) in the saddle; (of sword, arch.) in scabbard; (of points etc. in game) registered on score-board, forming total score for the time being, constituting one player's or team's lead over another, (of player etc.) holding such lead; before magistrate etc. (was had up or brought up for speeding); in position of gain (£5 up on the transaction); at or to high(er) price (meat is up, has gone up, this week; prices $3 and up); (of theatre-curtain) raised etc. to reveal stage; ALL-up. 2. to the place or time in question or in which the speaker etc. is (child came up and asked me the time; went straight up to the door; all the time up till now; sure to TURN¹ up late). 3. to or in erect or vertical or inflated position (lit. or fig.) esp. as favourable to activity, out of bed or from lying or sitting or kneeling posture, in(to) condition of efficiency or activity, (*sprang up from his seat*; *stand up*; *turn your collar up*; *put your umbrella up*; *pump up the tyres*; *was (already) up early this morning*; *was (still) up late last night*; *must be up and doing*; *matter is up for discussion*; *house is up for sale*; *stir up sedition*; *screw up your courage*; *wind up your courage*; *radio takes a long time to warm up*); (as *int.*) get, stand, etc., up (**up with you,** get up; **up with it,** put it up; *up with the revolution!*, may it succeed); instructed (*is well up in mathematics*); advanced (*is up with the leaders*); (of ship's helm) with rudder to leeward; in rebellion (*up in* ARM²s); (of hunt etc.) in progress; (of sun etc.) having risen; (of road etc.) with surface broken or removed during repairs; *up and* ABOUT; *his* BLOOD¹ *is up*; **something is up,** (colloq.) something unusual or undesirable is happening; **what's up?** (colloq.) what is going on? what is the matter? **4.** (Expr. complete or effectual result etc.; *eat, drink, burn, dry, tear, use, up*; *sawn up into logs*); into compact or accumulated state (*pack, bind, store, save, up*); securely (*lock, chain, tie, fasten, fix, nail, seal, up*); *the* GAME¹ *is up*; **time is up,** allowance of time is exhausted; CHEER², CLEAR², FOLLOW, HUNT¹, HURRY², SPEAK, WASH¹, *up*; HARD *up*; **it is all up with him,** his case is hopeless. **5.** See BEAR³ *up,* BRING *up,* COME *up,* GET¹ *up,* GIVE¹ *up,* GO¹ *up,* KEEP¹ *up,* MAKE¹ *up,* PUT¹ *up,* RUN¹ *up,* SEND¹ *up,* SET¹ *up,* TURN¹ *up.* **6.** up against, close to, in(to) contact with, (colloq.) confronted with (*up against a problem*); *up against it,* in great difficulties; **up and down,** (fig.) to and fro (*marching up and down*), in every direction (*have looked for it up and down*); **up to,** until (*up to the present*), not exceeding in number (*can take up to six guests*), less than or equal to (*sums up to £5*), comparable with (*not up to your usual standard*), incumbent on (*it is up to us to do something*), capable of or fit for (*am not up to walking 20 miles*), up to DATE², ||*up to the* KNOCKER, *up to the* MARK¹, *up to the* MINUTE¹, *up to* SNUFF¹, *up to* one's or person's TRICKS. **7.** *prep.* upwards along, through, or into, from bottom to top of, (*climbed up the ladder, up the hill*; *smoke goes up chimney*); towards source of (river); along (*walk up the street*); **up and down,** (fig.) to and fro along; *up* COUNTRY; **up hill and down dale,** up and down in every direction, taking the country or (fig.) the situation as it comes; *up*-MARKET¹; **up stage,** at or to back of theatre stage. **8.** at or in a higher part of (*lives farther up the road*; *somewhere up (the) river*; *some dust up my nose*; *sitting up a tree*); *up the* POLE¹; *up the* SPOUT. **9.** *a.* directed upwards; **up beat, draught, grade, platform, -stroke, train** (in senses opposite to those of DOWN⁵); **up-and-coming,** (colloq.) enterprising, alert, and likely to succeed; **up-and-over,** (of door etc.) opened by being raised and turned into horizontal position. **10.** *n.* on the up-and-up, (colloq.) (1) steadily improving, (2) on the level, honest(ly); **ups and downs,** rises and falls, undulating ground, alternately good and bad fortune. **11.** *v.i.* (colloq.) start up, begin abruptly to say or do something (*he ups and says*); ∼ with, raise, pick up, (*he upped* (or *up*) *with his fist, with his stick*). **12.** *v.t.* (colloq.) raise, esp. abruptly; *up* STICK²s. [OE *up(p), uppe,* = OS *up(pa),* ON *upp(i),* rel. to OHG *ūf*]

ŭp- *pref.* **1.** As *adv.* to *vbs.* & vbl *derivs.,* = prec. 1, 3: **upbear´,** (arch.) sustain aloft; **u´pheaped,** accumulated, piled up; **uphea´ve,** lift forcibly; **uprai´se,** raise to higher level; **upri´se,** rise (to standing position, to higher level etc.). **2.** As *prep.* to *ns.,* forming *adjs.* & *advs.,* = prec. 7, 8; **up-country,** towards the interior, inland; **u´pfield,** in or to a position farther along a football etc. field. **3.** As *a.* to *ns.,* = prec. 9: UPBEAT, UPLAND; **up-stroke** (see UP 9). [OE *up(p)-,* = MDu. *op-,* OS *up-,* OHG *ūf-,* ON *upp-,* = OE *up*]

UP *abbr.* (sl.) = UP 4 (*it is all UP with him*); Uttar Pradesh (formerly United Provinces), India.

u.p. *abbr.* underproof.

Upă´nĭshăd (oo-) *n.* each of a series of philosophical compositions concluding exposition of the Vedas. [Skr. (*upa* near, *ni-ṣad* sit down)]

ū´pas *n.* ∼(-tree), (Bot.) Javanese tree yielding milky sap used as arrow-poison, (Myth.) Javanese tree thought to be fatal to whatever came near it, (fig.) pernicious influence, practice, etc.; poisonous sap of upas and other trees. [Malay *ūpas* poison]

ŭ´pbeat *a.* optimistic, cheerful. [f. UP- 3 + BEAT²]

ŭpbrai´d *v.t.* chide, reproach (person etc. *with* or *for* fault etc., or abs.); hence ∼ING¹ *n.* [OE UP(*brēdan = bregdan* BRAID² in obs. sense 'brandish')]

ŭ´pbringing *n.* bringing up (of child), education. [f. obs. *upbring* to rear (UP- 1, BRING) + -ING¹]

ŭpca´st¹ (-ah´-) *v.t.* (*upca´st*). cast up. [ME, f. UP- 1 + CAST¹]

ŭ´pcast² (-ah-) *n.* casting up, upward throw; (Mining) shaft through which air leaves a mine; (Geol.) = UPTHROW. [f. UP- 1 + CAST²]

ŭpdā´te *v.t.* bring up to date. [f. UP- 1 + DATE³]

ŭp-ĕ´nd *v.t.* & *i.* set or rise up on end. [f. UP- 1 + END²]

ŭ´pfōld *n.* (Geol.) anticline. [f. UP- 1 + FOLD²]

ŭpgrā´de *v.t.* raise in rank etc. [f. UP- 1 + GRADE]

ŭ´pgrowth (-ōth) *n.* process or result of growing upwards. [f. UP- 1 + GROWTH]

ŭphea´val (ŭp-h-) *n.* heaving up; (Geol.) upward displacement of part of earth's crust; (fig.) violent social etc. change. [f. UP*heave* + -AL 2]

ŭphĭll (ŭp-h-) *n., a.,* & *adv.* **1.** *n.* (ŭ´-). upward slope. **2.** *a.* (ŭ´-). sloping up, ascending, (fig.) arduous, difficult, (*uphill work*). **3.** *adv.* (-ĭ´l). in ascending direction, on an upward slope. [f. UP- 2 + HILL]

ŭphō´ld (ŭp-h-) *v.t.* (uphe´ld). hold up, keep erect, support; give support or countenance to (person, practice, etc.); maintain, confirm, (decision, verdict). [ME, f. UP- 1 + HOLD¹]

ŭphō´lder (ŭp-h-) *n.* In vbl senses; (as guild-name) upholsterer. [ME, f. prec. + -ER¹]

ŭphō´lster (ŭp-h-) *v.t.* furnish (room etc.) with hangings, carpets, furniture, etc.; provide (chair etc.) with textile covering, padding, springs, etc., cover (chair etc. *with* or *in* tapestry etc.); **well-∼ed,** (joc., of person) fat. [back-form. f. foll.]

ŭphō´lsterer (ŭp-h-) *n.* one whose trade it is to upholster; ∼-bee (that furnishes its nest with cut leaves etc.); so **ŭphō´lst**ERY (1, 2) (ŭp-h-) *n.* [f. obs. *upholster* to f. UPHOLD (in obs. sense 'keep in repair') + -STER, + -ER¹]

ŭ´phrōe *n.* (Naut.) long wooden block with holes through which ropes of crowfoot are rove. [f. Du. *juffrouw* young lady, (Naut.) dead-eye (*jong young, vrouw* woman)]

ŭ´pkeep *n.* (cost or means of) maintenance in good condition. [f. UP- 1 + KEEP¹]

ŭ´pland *n.* & *a.* (of) higher or inland parts of a country. [f. UP- 3 + LAND¹]

ŭpli´ft¹ *v.t.* raise (in rank, moral elevation, etc.); one's voice in praise etc.). [ME, f. UP- 1 + LIFT]

ŭ´plift² *n.* being raised; (Geol.) raising of part of earth's surface; (colloq.) morally or intellectually elevating influence. [f. UP- 1 + LIFT 4]

ŭ´pmōst. See UPPERMOST.

upŏ´n *prep.* (more formal, but usu. idiomatically interchangeable with) ON¹; idiomatic preferences are *once upon a time*; *upon my word*; *on the whole*; *tier upon tier of seats*; *fell upon him unawares*; *had him on toast*; *came at once on receiving your message*; *take it on trust*; *will go on the chance*; *went on the spree*; *Christmas is almost upon us*. [ME, f. UP + ON¹, after ON *upp á*]

ŭ´pper *attrib. a.,* & *n.* **1.** *a.* higher in place, situated above another part, (*upper lip, arm, atmosphere, circle* in theatre, *Jurassic,* etc.), situated on higher land (*Upper Egypt*; *upper* CASE²; ∼-cut *n.,* & *v.t.,* (hit with) blow delivered upwards with arm bent; *have* or *get* or *gain* the ∼ hand, mastery, control, dominance; *upper* JAW, PARTIALS; ∼ regions, the sky, heaven; *upper* STOREY; ∼ works, part of ship that is above water when laden for voyage. **2.** higher in rank, dignity, etc., (the *upper class, servants*); **the U∼ Bench,** (Hist.) King's BENCH during Commonwealth in England; **the U∼**

For other words in *up-* **see** UP-.

House, (in legislature, esp.) House of Lords, bishops in Convocation; **the ~ ten (thousand),** (colloq.) **the ~ crust,** the aristocracy, the highest social group. **3.** *n.* part of boot or shoe above sole; **on one's ~s,** (colloq.) in financial difficulties. [ME, f. UP 9 + -ER³]

u′ppermŏst *a.* & *adv.* **1.** (*or* **u′pmŏst**) *a.* highest in place or rank. **2.** *adv.* on or to the top or front or most prominent position (lit. or fig.). [ME, f. prec. + -MOST]

u′ppïsh *a.* self-assertive; putting on airs; hence ~LY² *adv.,* ~NESS *n.* [f. UP + -ISH¹]

u′ppïty *a.* (colloq.) arrogant, snobbish. [fanciful f. UP]

u′prïght (-rīt; *or* ŭprī′t in pred. use) *a.* & *n.* **1.** *a.* erect, vertical, (*an upright post, posture; stood upright; set it upright*); (of book, picture, etc.) greater in height than breadth; ~ **piano** (with vertical strings). **2.** righteous, strictly honourable or honest; hence ~LY² *adv.,* ~NESS *n.* **3.** *n.* post or rod fixed upright esp. as support to some structure; upright piano. [OE UP(*riht* RIGHT¹)]

uprï′sïng (-z-) *n.* insurrection; (arch.) rising from bed. [ME, f. UP- 1 + RISING¹]

u′proar *n.* tumult, violent disturbance, clamour; hence **uproar′ious** *a.* (often of laughter, high spirits, etc.). [f. Du *oproer* (*op* up, *roer* confusion), assoc. w. ROAR]

upröö′t *v.t.* pull from ground etc. together with roots; (fig.) displace (person) from accustomed location; eradicate, destroy. [f. UP- 1 + ROOT²]

u′prŭsh *n.* upward rush, (esp., Psych.) from the subconscious. [f. UP- 1 + RUSH² 7]

ups-a-daisy. Var. of UPSY-DAISY.

ŭpsë′t *v.* (**upse′t**). **1.** *v.t.* & *i.* overturn, be overturned, (*carriage (was) upset*). **2.** *v.t.* disturb composure or temper or digestion of (*the news quite upset him; ate something that upset him; was upset that you refused*); disorganize. **3.** shorten and thicken (metal, esp. tire) by hammering or pressure. [f. UP- 1 + SET¹]

ŭ′psĕt² *n.* & *a.* **1.** *n.* upsetting or being upset (*stomach upset*); surprising result in game etc. **2.** *a.* ~ **price,** lowest acceptable selling price of property in auction etc., reserve price. [f. UP- 1 + SET²]

ŭ′pshŏt *n.* final issue, conclusion; general effect, the long and the short, (*of a matter*). [f. UP- 1 + SHOT¹]

ŭpside-dow′n *adv.* & *a.* with the upper part under, with top where bottom should be, inverted; in total disorder (*everything was turned upside-down*). [ME, orig. *up so down,* perh. = 'up as if down']

‖ŭpsi′des (-dz) *adv.* (colloq.) ~ **with,** equal with (person) by retaliation etc. [f. *upside* = top part (UP- 3, SIDE¹) + -s³]

ŭpsi′lon *n.* twentieth Greek letter (Υ, υ) = u. [Gk, = slender U (*psilos* slender), w. ref. to its later coincidence in sound with Gk *oi*]

ŭpstā′ge *a., adv.,* & *v.t.* **1.** *a.* & *adv.* nearer back of theatre stage; (fig.) snobbish(ly). **2.** *v.t.* move upstage from (actor) to make him face away from audience, (fig.) divert attention from (person) to oneself, put at a disadvantage, outshine. [f. UP- 2 + STAGE¹; cf. UP 7]

ŭpstair′s *adv.* & *n.,* **ŭ′pstair(s)** *a.,* (-z). up the stairs; (to, on, of) upper floor of house etc.; KICK² person *upstairs.* [f. UP- 2 + STAIR]

ŭpstă′nding *a.* standing up; well set up; honest, straightforward. [ME, f. UP- 1 + STANDING²]

ŭ′pstărt *n.* & *a.* (person) who has risen suddenly from humble position; (person) who assumes arrogant tone. [f. UP- 1 + START¹]

***ŭ′pstāte** *a., adv.,* & *n.* (pertaining to, in) part of state remote from large cities, esp. northern part. [f. UP- 2 + STATE¹]

ŭ′pstream *a.* & *adv.* in the direction opposite to that in which a stream or river flows. [f. UP- 2 + STREAM]

ŭ′psŭrge *n.* upward surge, rise. [f. UP- 1 + SURGE]

ŭ′pswĕpt *a.* (Of hair) combed up and arranged on top of head; curved or sloped upwards. [f. UP- 1 + SWEPT]

ŭ′pswing *n.* upward movement or trend. [f. UP- 1 + SWING]

ŭ′psў-daisў (-zī) *int.* expr. encouragement to child rising after fall or being lifted. [f. earlier *up-a-daisy* f. UP; cf. LACKADAISICAL]

ŭ′ptāke *n.* lifting; understanding, apprehension, (*quick on* or *in the uptake*). [f. UP- 1 + TAKE²]

ŭ′pthrow (-ō) *n.* throwing upwards; (Geol.) upward dislocation of strata. [f. UP- 1 + THROW²]

ŭ′pthrŭst *n.* upward thrust, e.g. of fluid on immersed body; (Geol.) = UPHEAVAL. [f. UP- 1 + THRUST]

ŭptïght (-ī′t, ŭ′-) *a.* (colloq.) nervously tense; angry; *rigidly conventional. [f. UP- 1 + TIGHT]

ŭ′ptown *a., adv.,* & *n.* (pertaining to, in, into) higher or *residential part of town or city. [f. UP- 2 + TOWN]

ŭptŭr′n¹ *v.t.* turn upwards; turn up (ground in ploughing etc.); (in *p.p.*) turned upside-down. [f. UP- 1 + TURN¹]

ŭ′ptŭrn² *n.* upheaval; improvement, upward trend. [f. UP- 1 + TURN²]

UPU *abbr.* Universal Postal Union.

ŭ′pward *a.* & *adv.,* **ŭ′pward|s** (-z) *adv.* **1.** (moving, extending, pointing, leading) towards what is higher, superior, more important, larger in amount, or earlier; hence ~LY² *adv.* **2.** ~ **(s) of,** more than (*found upward(s) of 40 specimens*). [OE *upweard(es)* (as UP, -WARD(S))]

ŭ′pwarp (-ôrp) *n.* (Geol.) broad surface elevation, anticline. [f. UP- 1 + WARP²]

ŭ′pwïnd *a.* & *adv.* in the direction opposite to that in which the wind is blowing. [f. UP- 2 + WIND¹]

ur- (ʊʊr) *pref.* primitive, original, earliest. [G]

ūr′acïl *n.* (Chem.) crystalline compound formed by hydrolysis of RNA. [f. UREA + ACETIC + -IL]

ūrae′m|ïa, *-ē′m|ïa, *n.* (Path.) morbid condition due to presence in blood of urinary matter normally eliminated by kidneys; hence ~IC *a.* Gk *ouron* urine + *haima* blood; see -AEMIA]

ūrae′us *n.* serpent (emblem of power) as represented on head-dress of Egyptian divinities and sovereigns. [mod. L, f. Gk *ouraios,* repr. the Egypt. wd for 'cobra']

Ũral-Alta′ïc (ũral āl) *a.* of (the people of) the *Ural* and *Altaic* mountain ranges; (Philol.) of a family of Finno-Ugric, Turkic, Mongolian, and other agglutinative languages of N. Europe and Asia.

ūr′anïsm *n.* homosexuality, esp. of males. [f. G *uranismus* f. Gk *ouranios* heavenly, taken as 'spiritual'; see -ISM]

ūrā′nium *n.* radioactive grey heavy metallic element, capable of nuclear fission and hence used as a source of nuclear energy; hence **ūrā′nic,** **ūr′anous,** *adjs.* [mod. L, f. URANUS + -IUM; cf. *tellurium*]

ūrano-¹ *comb. form.* the heavens, as: ~ **graphy** (-ŏ′g-), descriptive astronomy; ~**metry** (-ŏ′m), measurement of stellar distances, map showing positions and magnitudes of stars. [f. Gk *ouranos* heaven(s) + -o-]

ūrano-² *comb. form.* uranium. [f. URANIUM + -o-]

Uranus (ūr′an-, ūrā′n-) *n.* planet discovered by Herschel in 1781, outermost of solar system except Neptune and Pluto. [L, f. Gk *Ouranos* heaven, Uranus, in Gk Myth. the son of Gaea (Earth) and father of Kronos (Saturn), the Titans, etc.]

ūr′āte. See URIC.

ūr′ban *a.* of, living or situated in, a city or town (*urban districts, population;* opp. *rural*); ‖~ **district,** (Hist.) group of urban communities governed by elected council; ~ **guerrilla** (operating in towns by kidnapping etc.); ~ **renewal,** slum clearance; ~ **sprawl,** uncontrolled expansion of urban areas. [f. L *urbanus* (*urbs urbis* city; see -AN)]

ūrbā′ne *a.* courteous, suave, elegant or refined in manner; hence ~LY² (-nlī) *adv.* [f. F *urbain* or f. L *urbanus* (see prec.)]

ūr′ban|ïsm *n.* urban character; study of urban life, whence ~IST (3) *n.* [f. URBAN + -ISM]

ūr′banïte *n.* dweller in city or town. [f. URBAN + -ITE¹]

ūrbă′nïtў *n.* courtesy, polished manners; urban life. [f. F *urbanité* or f. L *urbanitas* (as URBAN; see -ITY)]

ūr′banïz|e, -ïs|e (-īz), *v.t.* make urban; remove rural character of (district); hence ∼A'TION n. [f. F *urbaniser* (as URBAN; see -IZE)]

ur'ceolate a. (Bot.) pitcher-shaped, with large body and small mouth. [f. L *urceolus* dim. of *urceus* pitcher + -ATE²]

ur'chin n. **1.** roguish or mischievous boy; boy, youngster; ∼ **cut**, cut-short hair-style for women. **2.** = SEA-urchin; (arch.) hedgehog, goblin. [ME *hirchon*, *urcheon* f. ONF *herichon*, OF *heriçon* f. Rom. *hericio* f. L (*h*)*ericius* hedgehog]

Ur'du (oor'doo, er'-) n. Indic language, allied to Hindi but with large admixture of Persian, and usu. written in Persian script, an official language of Pakistan. [f. Hind. (*zabān i*) *urdū* (language of the) camp, f. Pers. *urdū* f. Turki *ordū* (see HORDE)]

-ure suf. forming ns. w. sense (1) (result of) action or process (*composure*, *enclosure*, *failure*, *figure*, *scripture*, *seizure*), (2) function, state, rank, dignity, office, (*judicature*, *prefecture*), (3) collective body of agents (*legislature*), (4) that by which the action is effected (*closure*, *ligature*). [f. or after OF *-ure* f. L *-ura*]

urea (ūr'-, -i'a) n. (Chem.) soluble colourless crystalline compound contained esp. in urine of mammals. [mod. L, f. F *urée* f. Gk *ouron* urine]

-uret suf. (Chem.) forming names of binary compounds, now for the most part replaced by -IDE. [f. mod. L *-uretum* first applied to F wds in *-ure*]

ureter n. duct by which urine passes from kidney to bladder or cloaca; hence ∼AL, **urete'ric**, adjs., ∼i'TIS, ∼o'TOMY, ns. [f. F *uretère* or mod. L *ureter* f. Gk *ourētēr* (*oureō* urinate)]

urethane (-ē'-, ūr'-) n. (Chem.) crystalline amide, ethyl carbamate. [f. F *uréthane* (as UREA, ETHANE)]

urethr|a n. (pl. ∼ae or ∼as). duct by which urine is discharged from bladder; hence ∼AL a., ∼i'TIS, ∼o'TOMY, ns. [LL, f. Gk *ourēthra* (as URETER)]

urge v.t., & n. **1.** v.t. drive forcibly, impel, hasten, cause to proceed with effort, (*urged his horse forward*; *urged him on*; *urged our flight northwards*); entreat earnestly or persistently (*urge him to action, to take steps, his going, that he should go*); advocate (measure etc.) pressingly (*on* or *upon* person); ply (person etc.) hard with argument or entreaty; dwell earnestly or emphatically upon, esp. as reason or justification, (*urged his youth, the difficulty of getting supplies*; *argument was urged in vain*). **2.** n. urging impulse or tendency; yearning. [f. L *urgēre* press, drive]

urg|ent a. pressing, calling for immediate action or decision or attention, (*am in urgent need*; *the matter is urgent*; *an urgent demand*); importunate, earnest and persistent in demand; hence ∼ENCY n., ∼entLY² adv. [ME f. F (as prec.; see -ENT)]

URI abbr. upper respiratory infection.

-uria suf. forming ns. denoting that a substance is (excessively) present in the urine (*albuminuria*, *pyuria*). [mod. L, f. Gk *-ouria* (as URINE; see -IA¹)]

ur'ic a. of urine; ∼ **acid** (found in small quantities in healthy urine of man and mammals, chief constituent in that of birds and reptiles); hence **ur'ATE¹** (3) n. [f. F *urique* (as URINE; see -IC)]

-urient suf. forming adjs. w. sense 'desiring (to do something)' (*esurient*). [f. L *-urient-* part. st. of desiderative vbs.; see -ENT]

ur'im n. ∼ **and thummim**, objects of now unknown nature worn in or on breastplate of Jewish high priest (Exod. 28:30). [Heb. '*ûrîm* pl. of '*ôr* a light, *tummîm* pl. of *tōm* completeness]

urinal (ūr'i-, -ī'-) n. vessel or receptacle for use in urination, e.g. by invalid in bed; structure containing such receptacles. [ME f. OF, f. LL *urinal* neut. (as n.) of *urinalis* (as URINE; see -AL)]

urina'lys|is n. (pl. ∼es pr. -ēz). chemical analysis of urine esp. for diagnostic purposes. [f. URINE + ANALYSIS]

ur'inary a. of or relating to urine (*urinary organs*, *diseases*). [f. med. L *urinarius* (as URINE; see -ARY¹)]

ur'in|āte v.i. discharge urine; hence ∼A'TION n. [f. med. L *urinare* (as foll.) + -ATE³]

ur'in|e n. pale-yellow fluid secreted from the blood by the kidneys and (in man and higher animals) stored in bladder and discharged at intervals; hence ∼OUS a. [ME f. OF, f. L *urina*]

urn n., & v.t. **1.** n. vase with foot and usu. with rounded body, esp. as used for storing the ashes of the cremated dead or as vessel or measure; (poet.) anything in which dead body or its remains are preserved, e.g. grave. **2.** large vessel with tap, in which tea, coffee, etc., is made or kept hot. **3.** ∼-**flower**, S. Amer. bulbous plant of genus *Urceolina*, with yellow and green urn-shaped flower. **4.** Hence ∼'FUL 2 n. **5.** v.t. enclose in urn. [ME, f. L *urna*, rel. to *urceus* pitcher]

ur'ning n. homosexual (usu. male). [G, f. *Urania*; cf. URANISM]

ur'o-¹ comb. form. urine, as: ∼**ge'nital**, pertaining to urinary and genital products or organs; ∼**logy** (-ŏ'l-), study of urinary system. [f. Gk *ouron* urine + -o-]

ur'o-² comb. form. tail, as: ∼**chord**, notochord of tunicate; ∼**dele** [f. Gk *dēlos* evident], amphibian with adult tail, e.g. newt; ∼**py'gium**, rump of bird. [f. Gk *oura* tail + -o-]

Ur'sa (er'-) n. ∼ **Major, Minor**, Great, Little, BEAR¹. [L, = (she-)bear]

ur'sine a. of or like a bear. [f. L *ursinus* (*ursus* bear; see -INE¹)]

Ur'suline (-er'-) a. & n. (nun) of an order founded by St. Angela in 1537 for nursing the sick and teaching girls. [f. St. *Ursula*, founder's patron saint, + -INE¹]

urticar'ia n. (Path.) nettle-rash. [mod. L, f. L *urtica* nettle (*urere* burn)]

ur'tic|āte v.t. sting like a nettle; so ∼A'TION n. [f. med. L *urticare* (L *urtica*; see prec.) + -ATE³]

ur'us n. = AUROCHS 1. [L, f. Gmc **ūrus*]

us. See WE.

US abbr. Under-Secretary; United States (of America); unserviceable.

USA abbr. *United States Army; United States of America.

usable. See USE².

USAF abbr. United States Air Force.

u'sage (ū'z-, ū's-) n. manner of using or treating, treatment, (*met with harsh usage*; *damaged by rough usage*); habitual or customary practice esp. as creating a right or obligation or standard (*sanctified by usage*; *ancient usage*; *contrary to the usage of the best writers*; *modern English usage*); (Law) habitual but not necessarily immemorial practice. [ME f. OF (*us* USE¹; see -AGE)]

u'sance (ū'z-) n. time allowed by commercial usage for payment of foreign bills of exchange. [ME f. OF, f. Rom. **usantia* (**usare*; see USE², -ANCE)]

||USDAW abbr. Union of Shop, Distributive, and Allied Workers.

use¹ n. **1.** using, employment, application to a purpose, (*should recommend the use of a saw*; *for external use only*; *put it to good use*; *is meant for use not ornament*; *has passed out of use*; *is in daily use*; *becomes easier with use*; *worn and polished with use*); **make ∼ of**, employ, apply, benefit from. **2.** right or power of using (*requested the use of the piano*; *lost the use of his left arm*). **3.** availability, utility, purpose for which thing can be used, (*a blunt knife is of use, of no use, for this work*; *a torch will be found of* (*great*) *use*; *it is* (*of*) *no use talking or to talk*; *what is the use of talking?*; *talking is no use*; *find a use for banana-skins*); **have no ∼ for**, be unable to find a use for, (fig.) dislike, be impatient with. **4.** custom, familiarity, (*long use has reconciled me to it*; *use and* WONT³). **5.** ritual and liturgy of a church, diocese, etc., (SARUM, *Anglican*, *Roman*, *use*). **6.** (Law). benefit or profit of lands and tenements, esp. in the possession of another who holds them solely for the beneficiary. [ME f. OF *us*, f. L *usus* (as foll.)]

use² (ūz) v. **1.** v.t. cause to act or serve for a purpose, handle as instrument, consume as material, exercise, put into operation, avail oneself of, (*seldom uses a knife*; *should use oil for frying*; *we seem to use a great deal of butter*;

never uses a dictionary; learn to use your hands, your wits; must use the services of an agent; shall use every means; must use your opportunities; use your discretion; should at least use some moderation); apply (name, title, etc.) to oneself; ~ person's **name**, quote him as authority, reference, etc.; **could** ~, (colloq.) would be glad to have, would be improved by having. **2.** treat in specified manner (has used me shamefully; how is the world using you?). **3.** (in past, usu. pr. ūst, esp. when followed immediately by to; neg. **used not, did not use,** (colloq.) **use(d)n't** pr. ū'sent, or **didn't use**). had as one's or its constant or frequent practice or state (I used to take the bus, be the manager; does not come as often as he used (to); there used to be a law against it). **4.** ~ **up,** consume the whole of (material etc.), find use for (remaining material etc.), exhaust, wear out e.g. with overwork. **5.** Hence **ū'SABLE** (ū'z-) a. [ME, f. OF user f. Rom. *usare frequent. of L uti us- use]

ūsed a. **1.** (ūzd). In vbl senses; (of clothes, vehicles, etc.) second-hand. **2.** (ūst). ~ **to,** having become familiar with by habit or custom (am not used to this sort of thing, to being called a liar; become used to eating horse-flesh). [p.p. of prec.]

ū'seful (ū'sf-) a. **1.** of use, serviceable, producing or able to produce good results (to person, for thing; gave me some useful hints); ~ **load** (carried by aircraft etc. in addition to its own weight); **make** oneself ~, perform services. **2.** (colloq.) highly creditable or efficient (a useful performance). **3.** Hence ~LY² adv., ~NESS n. [ME, f. USE¹ + -FUL]

ū'seless (ū'sl-) a. serving no useful purpose, unavailing, (useless erudition; contents were rendered useless by damp; protest is useless); hence ~LY² adv., ~NESS n. [f. USE¹ + -LESS]

ū'ser¹ (ū'z-) n. In vbl senses; drug addict. [f. USE² + -ER¹]

ū'ser² (ū'z-) n. (Law). continued use or enjoyment of a right etc.; **right of** ~, (1) right to use, (2) presumptive right arising from user. [inferred f. NON-USER]

ū'sher n., & v.t. **1.** n, officer or servant acting as door-keeper of court etc., showing persons to seats in public hall etc., (for walking before person of rank, as (gentleman usher of the) BLACK¹ Rod; ||(arch. or joc.) under-teacher, assistant schoolmaster; hence ~ETTE (3) (esp. in cinema), ~SHIP, ns. **2.** v.t. act as usher to, precede (person) as usher; announce, show in etc. (lit. or fig.). [ME, f. AF usser, OF u(i)ssier, var. of huissier f. med. L ustiarius for L ostiarius (ostium door; see -ARY¹, -ER²)]

USIA, USIS, abbrs. United States Information Agency, Service.

USN abbr. United States Navy.

***USO** abbr. United Service Organization.

ū'squebaugh (-aw) n. whisky. [f. Ir. & Sc. Gael. uisge beatha water of life; cf. WHISKY¹]

USS abbr. United States Ship; ||Universities Superannuation Scheme.

USSR abbr. Union of SOVIET Socialist Republics.

ū'sual (ū'zhŏŏal) a. such as commonly occurs or is observed or done, customary, habitual, (asked the usual questions; with his usual disregard of convention; the courtesy usual with him; it is usual to tip the waiter; came earlier than (was) usual; have forgotten something as (is) usual or (vulg. or joc.) as per usual); **the** ~, **my** ~, (drink etc.); hence ~LY² adv., ~NESS n. [ME, f. OF usual, usuel or f. LL usualis (as USE¹; see -AL)]

ūsūcā'ption, ūsūcā'pion, (ūz-) n. (Law). acquisition of title or right to property by uninterrupted and undisputed possession for prescribed term. [f. OF usucap(t)ion or f. L usucap(t)io f. usucapere acquire by prescription (usu by USE¹, capere capt- take); see -ION]

ū'sūfrŭct (ū'z-) n., & v.t. **1.** n. right of enjoying the use and advantages of another's property short of destruction or waste of its substance; so ~ŪARY¹ (-ū'k-) a. & n. **2.** v.t. hold in usufruct. [f. med. L usufructus f. L usus (et) fructus (usus USE¹, fructus FRUIT)]

ū'surer (ū'zher-) n. one who lends money at exorbitant

interest. [ME f. AF; OF usureor (usure f. L usura; see USURY)]

ūsū̆r'p (ūz-) v. **1.** v.t. seize, assume, (throne, office, power, property, etc.) wrongfully. **2.** v.i. encroach (up)on. **3.** Hence or cogn. ~A'TION (-zer-), ~ER¹, ns. [ME, f. OF usurper f. L usurpare seize for use]

ū'surу̇ (ū'zher̄) n. **1.** practice of lending money at exorbitant interest, esp. at higher interest than is legal; hence **ūsū̆r'ious** (ūz-, ūzh-) a. **2.** such interest; (usu. fig.) interest (the service was repaid with usury). [ME, f. AF *usurie or f. med. L usuria f. L usura (as USE¹; see -URE, -Y¹)]

UT abbr. universal time; Utah.

ūtĕ'nsil n. instrument, implement, esp. one in working or domestic use (writing, cooking, utensils) or in religious use. [ME, f. OF utensile f. med. L, neut. (as n.) of L utensilis usable (as USE²; see -IL)]

ū'terine a. of or relating to the uterus; born of same mother but not same father (brother, sister, uterine). [ME, f. LL uterinus (as foll.; see -INE¹)]

ū'ter|us n. (pl. ~**i** pr. -ī). womb; hence ~I'TIS n. [L]

ū'tile a. having utility, useful. [ME f. OF, f. L utilis (uti use; see -IL)]

ūtĭlĭtār'ian a. & n. of, consisting in, based on, utility; (holder) of utilitarianism. [f. UTILITY + ARIAN]

ūtĭlĭtār'ianism n. doctrine that actions are right because they are useful; doctrine that greatest happiness of greatest number should be guiding principle of conduct. [f. prec. + -ISM]

ūtĭl'ĭtу̇ n. & a. **1.** n. usefulness, profitableness; useful thing; = PUBLIC utility. **2.** a. made or serving for utility; severely practical and (e.g. in wartime) standardized (utility clothes, furniture); ~ **man,** actor of the smallest speaking parts in plays, footballer etc. who can play in various positions, *odd-job man; ~ **room** (containing large fixed domestic appliances, e.g. washing-machine); ~ **vehicle** (serving various functions). [ME, f. OF utilité f. L utilitas -tatis (as UTILE; see -ITY)]

ū'tĭlīz|e, -īs|e (in), v.t. make use of, turn to account, use; hence ~ABLE a., ~A'TION n. [f. F utiliser f. It. utilizzare (as UTILE; see -IZE)]

-ū'tion (-ū'-, -ōō'-) suf. forming ns. w. senses as -ATION (solution). [F, f. L -u- of vbs. in -vere]

ūti possidētis (ūtī pŏsĭdē'tĭs) n. principle that leaves belligerents in possession of what they have acquired. [L, = as you possess]

ū'tmost (-ōst, -ost) a. & n. **1.** a. furthest, extreme, (the utmost limits); that is such in the highest degree (showed the utmost reluctance). **2.** n. the utmost point, degree, etc.; **do** one's ~ (all that one can do). [OE ūt(e)most (as OUT, -MOST)]

Utō'pia (ū-) n. imaginary place with perfect social and political system; ideally perfect place or state of things. [title of book by More (1516), mod. L, = nowhere, f. Gk ou not + topos place; see -IA¹]

Utō'pian (ū-), **ū-,** a. & n. (inhabitant) of Utopia; (characteristic of an) ardent but unpractical reformer, etc., whence **ūtō'pianISM** (3) n. [f. mod. L Utopianus (as prec.; see -AN)]

U'trĕcht (ū'trĕkt) n. ~ **velvet,** mohair plush for furniture. [~ in Holland]

ū'trĭcle n. small cell or sac of animal or plant, esp. one in the inner ear; hence **ūtrĭ'cūl**AR¹ a. [f. L utricule or f. L utriculus dim. of uter leather bag; see -CULE]

ū'tter¹ attrib. a. complete, total, unqualified, (utter misery; saw the utter absurdity of it; an utter denial); ||~ **barrister** (junior, addressing court from outside bar within which QC pleads); hence ~LY² adv., ~MOST a., ~NESS n. [OE ūter(r)a, ūttra, compar. adj. f. ūt OUT; cf. OUTER]

ū'tter² v.t. emit audibly (cry, groan, sigh, etc.); express in spoken or written words (one's sentiments, a lie, the truth, etc.); put (forged bank notes, base coin, etc.) into circulation. [ME, f. MDu. ūteren make known, assim. to prec.]

ū'tterance¹ n. uttering, expressing in words, (gave

utterance to his rage); power of speech (*defective utterance*); spoken words (*his pulpit utterances*); (Ling.) spoken or written words forming complete expression of a thought. [ME, f. prec. + -ANCE]

ŭ'tterance[2] *n.* (literary). *fight* etc. **to the** ~, to the bitter end. [ME, f. OF *outrance* (*outrer* surpass, f. L ULTRA; see -ANCE)]

UV *abbr.* ultraviolet.

ŭ'vūl|a *n.* (*pl.* ~ae). pendent fleshy part of soft palate; similar process in bladder or cerebellum; hence ~AR[1] *a.* [ME f. LL, dim. of L *uva* grape]

ŭxŏr'icīd|e *n.* killing of one's wife; one who kills his wife; hence ~AL *a.* [f. L *uxor* wife; see -CIDE]

ŭxŏr'ious *a.* (excessively) fond of one's wife; (of action etc.) showing such fondness; hence ~LY[2] *adv.*, ~NESS *n.* [f. L *uxoriosus* (*uxor* wife) + -OUS]

U'zbĕk, U'zbĕg, (ŭ'-) *n.* member or language of a Turkic people in central Asia. [Uzbek]

V

V, v, (vē) *n.* (*pl.* **Vs** *or* **V's**). twenty-second letter of alphabet; V-shaped thing, e.g. joint, aircraft formation; (as Roman numeral) 5 (**vi** 6, **vii** 7, **viii** 8); **V1, V2,** weapons used by Germany near end of war of 1939–45 [f. G. *vergeltungswaffe* reprisal weapon]; **V8,** (vehicle having) engine with eight cylinders in V form; **V neck** (of garment, with straight sides meeting at acute angle); **V sign** (made by hand with fingers clenched except the first and second outspread in V shape, as gesture symbolizing victory, approval, or vulgar derision).

V *abbr.* volt(s).

v. *abbr.* verse; verso; versus; very; *vide.*

V *symb.* vanadium.

VA *abbr.* *Veterans' Administration; Vicar Apostolic; Vice-Admiral; Virginia; ||Order of Victoria and Albert.

Va. *abbr.* Virginia.

||**văc** *n.* (colloq.) vacation; vacuum cleaner. [abbr.]

va'cancў *n.* being vacant or empty or unoccupied; emptiness of mind, idleness, listlessness; unoccupied post or place (*has a vacancy on his staff; no vacancies at present in this hotel*). [f. foll. +-ANCY, or f. LL & med. L. *vacantia*]

va'cant *a.* **1.** empty, not filled or occupied, (*house is still vacant; have no vacant space; will amuse your vacant hours; applied for a vacant post*); ||∼ **possession,** ownership of house etc. without prior occupant. **2.** not mentally active, not rationally occupied, empty-headed, thoughtless, listless, stupid, (*his mind seems completely vacant; received the news with a vacant stare*); hence ∼LY² *adv.* [ME f. OF, or f. L *vacare* (as foll.; see -ANT)]

vaca'tｅ|e *v.t.* go away from so as to leave empty or unoccupied, give up occupation or possession of, (military position, place, house, throne, office); (Law) annul (judgement, contract, etc.); hence ∼ABLE *a.* [f. L *vacare* be empty +-ATE³]

vaca'tion *n.,* & *v.i.* **1.** *n.* vacating (of house, post, etc.); part of year constituting fixed period of cessation from work, esp. in ||lawcourts and universities, (Christmas, Easter, Whitsun, long or summer vacation); *∼**land,** area providing recreations for holiday-makers. **2.** *n.,* & *v.i.* *(take) holiday; hence ∼IST (1) *n.* [ME f. OF, or f. L *vacatio* (as prec.; see -ATION)]

va'ccinｌāte (ks) *v.t.* inoculate with vaccine to procure immunity from smallpox or with vaccine of any disease in order to produce it in mild form and so prevent serious attack; hence ∼A'TION, ∼ātoR, *ns.* [f. foll. +-ATE³]

va'ccine (-ksēn, -ksĭn) *a.* & *n.* **1.** *a.* of cows or cowpox or vaccination. **2.** *n.* virus of cowpox as used in vaccination; modified micro-organism of any disease similarly used; hence **va'ccin**AL (-ks-) *a.* [f. L *vaccinus* (*vacca* cow; see -INE¹)]

vaccï'nia (-ks-) *n.* (Med.) cowpox, esp. inoculated. [mod. L, f. as prec. +-IA¹]

va'cill�|āte *v.i.* move from side to side, oscillate, waver; fluctuate in opinion or resolution; so ∼A'TION *n.* [f. L *vacillare* sway +-ATE³]

va'cūｌōle *n.* (Biol.) minute cavity in organ or cell, containing air, fluid, etc.; hence ∼olAR¹ *a.,* ∼olA'TION *n.,* formation of vacuoles. [F, dim. of L *vacuus* empty]

va'cūous *a.* empty; evacuated; unintelligent, expressionless, (*vacuous remark, stare*); hence or cogn. **vacū'**ITY, ∼NESS, *ns.,* ∼LY² *adv.* [f. L *vacuus* empty (as VACATE) +-OUS]

va'cūum *n.* (*pl.* **va'cua** *or* **va'cuums**), & *v.* **1.** *n.* space entirely devoid of matter; space or vessel from which air has been partly or completely removed by pump etc. (TORRICELLIAN *vacuum*); decrease of pressure below normal atmospheric value; (fig.) absence of normal or previous content of a place, environment, etc.; (colloq., *pl.* ∼s) vacuum cleaner. **2.** ∼ **brake** (in which pressure is caused by exhaustion of air); ∼-**clean** *v.t.* & *i.,* clean by use of ∼ **cleaner,** apparatus for removing dust etc. from carpets etc. by suction; ||∼ **flask,** vessel with double wall enclosing vacuum so that liquid in inner receptacle retains its temperature; ∼-**gauge** (for testing pressure after production of vacuum); ∼-**packed,** sealed after partial removal of air; ∼ **pump** (for production of vacuum); ∼ **tube,** sealed tube with almost perfect vacuum for free passage of electric current. **3.** *v.t.* & *i.* (colloq.) use vacuum cleaner (on). [mod. L, neut. (as *n.*) of L *vacuus* empty]

VAD *abbr.* (member of) Voluntary Aid Detachment.

vade-mecum (vădīmē'kum, vahdīmā'kum) *n.* handbook or other thing carried constantly about the person. [F f. mod. L, = go with me]

va'gabönd *a., n.,* & *v.t.* **1.** *a.* having no fixed habitation, wandering; driven or drifting to and fro, straying. **2.** *n.* wanderer, vagrant, esp. idle and worthless one; (colloq.) scamp, rascal; hence ∼vAGE (2), ∼ISM (2), *ns.,* ∼ISH¹ *a.,* ∼IZE (2) *v.i.* **3.** *v.i.* wander about as vagabond. [ME f. OF, or f. L *vagabundus* (*vagari* wander)]

va'gal. See VAGUS.

vagary (vā'geri, vagār'ĭ) *n.* whimsical or extravagant notion or action; caprice; hence **vagār'**IOUS *a.* [f. L *vagari* wander]

vagī'n|a *n.* (*pl.* ∼ae *or* ∼as). **1.** canal between womb and external genital orifice of woman or other female mammal; similar canal in insect etc.; hence **vagĭn**ｉ'TIS *n.* **2.** (Bot.) sheath formed round stem by base of leaf. **3.** Hence ∼AL *a.* [L, = sheath, scabbard]

vagĭnĭ'smus (-z-) *n.* painful spasmodic contraction of vagina. [mod. L (as prec.; see -ISM)]

va'gr|ant *a.* & *n.* **1.** *a.* wandering, roving, straggling, itinerant, (*vagrant musician*); indulging in vagrant speculations); being a vagrant; hence ∼ANCY *n.,* ∼antLY² *adv.* **2.** *n.* wanderer, idle rover, vagabond; idle disreputable person without settled home or regular work. [ME f. AF *vag(a)raunt,* perh. alt. f. AF *wakerant* etc. by assoc. w. F *vagari* wander]

va'grom *a.* = prec. [illit. alt. of prec.; see Shak. *Much Ado* III. iii. 26]

vague (-g) *a.* indistinct, not clearly expressed or identified, of uncertain or ill-defined meaning or character, (*returned only a vague answer; has some vague idea of going to Canada; have not the vaguest notion of his reasons; heard a vague rumour to that effect*); (of person or mind) imprecise, inexact in thought or expression or understanding; hence ∼LY² (-glī) *adv.,* ∼NESS (-gn-) *n.,* **vā'gu**ISH¹ (-gī-) *a.* [F, or f. L *vagus* wandering, uncertain]

vā'g|us *n.* (*pl.* ∼i *pr.* -gī). (Anat.) pneumogastric nerve, either of tenth pair of cranial nerves with branches to heart etc.; hence ∼AL *a.* [L (see prec.)]

vail¹ *v.* (arch. or poet.) **1.** *v.t.* lower or doff (one's plumes, pride, crown, etc.) esp. in token of submission. **2.** *v.i.* yield, give place, remove hat as sign of respect etc. [ME f. obs. *avale* f. OF *avaler* (*a val* down, f. *val* VALE¹) to lower]

vail² *n.* (arch.; usu. in *pl.*). gratuity, tip; occasional profit from office. [ME, f. obs. *vail* AVAIL¹]

vain *a.* **1.** unsubstantial, empty, trivial, (*vain boasts, triumphs, distinctions*); useless, unavailing, followed by no good result, (*in the vain hope of dissuading him; resistance is vain, it is vain to resist*); **in** ∼, with no result, to no purpose, uselessly, (*we protested in vain, it was in* *vain that we protested*; TAKE[1] *person's name in vain*). **2.** conceited (*of* one's beauty etc.). **3.** Hence ∼LY[2] *adv.*, ∼'NESS (-n-n-) *n.* [ME f. OF, f. L *vanus* empty, without substance]

vainglŏr'|y̆ (-n-g-) *n.* boastfulness, extreme vanity; so ∼ĭous *a.* [ME, after OF *vaine gloire*, L *vana gloria*]

vair *n.* **1.** (arch.) squirrel-fur widely used for medieval linings and trimmings. **2.** (Her.) fur represented by small shield-shaped or bell-shaped figures usu. alternately azure and argent. [ME f. OF, f. L (as VARIOUS)]

Vai'sya (vī'-) *n.* (member of) third of four great Hindu castes, comprising the merchants and agriculturalists. [f. Skr. *vaiśya* peasant, labourer]

vă'lanc|e, vă'lenc|e[1], *n.* short curtain round frame or canopy of bedstead, above window, or under shelf; hence ∼ED[2] (-st) *a.* [ME, perh. f. AF *valance (*valer* = OF *avaler* descend; see VAIL[1], -ANCE)]

vāle[1] *n.* (arch. or poet. exc. in place-names). valley (*o'er field and vale*; *Vale of the White Horse*); **this ∼, the ∼ of tears**, etc., the world as scene of life, trouble, etc.; **∼ of years**, old age. [ME, f. OF *val* f. L *vallis*, *valles*]

va'le[2] (vā'lĭ, vah'lā) *int.* & *n.* farewell. [L, imper. of *valēre* be well or strong]

vălĕdĭ'ction *n.* (words used in) bidding farewell. [f. L VALE[2](*dicere dict-* say) bid farewell, after *benediction*]

vălĕdĭ'ct|orȳ *a.* & *n.* **1.** *a.* serving as valediction. **2.** *n.* *valedictory oration, esp. as given by (usu. highest-ranking) member of graduating class (the ∼ŏr'ĭAN *n.*). [f. prec. +-ORY]

vă'lence[1]. See VALANCE.

vă'lence[2] *n.* **1.** (Chem.) combining or replacing power of an atom as compared with hydrogen atom as standard (*hydrogen, carbon, has a valence of one, four*); *valency; ∼ **electron** (in outermost shell of atom). **2.** (Biol. etc.) ability to interact. [f. LL *valentia* power, competence (as VALE[2]; see -ENCE)]

Vălen'cĭe'nnes (vălahṅsy̆e'n) *n.* rich kind of lace. [∼ in NE France, where made in 17th & 18th c.]

||vă'lency *n.* (Chem.) unit of combining power (*carbon has four valencies*); = VALENCE[2]. [f. as VALENCE[2]; see -ENCY]

vă'lentīne *n.* **1.** (St.) V∼'s day, 14 Feb., feast of St. Valentine, on which birds were supposed to pair. **2.** sweetheart chosen on this day; amatory or satirical letter or card or picture sent, often anonymously, to person of opposite sex on this day.[ME, f. OF *Valentin* f. L *Valentinus*, name of two saints]

valēr'ian *n.* herb of genus *Valeriana*, esp. **common ∼**, with pink or white flowers and strong smell liked by cats; root of this used as medicinal stimulant. [ME, f. OF *valeriane* f. med. L *valeriana* (*herba*), app. fem. of L *Valerianus* of Valerius; see -IAN]

vălĕ'rĭc *a.* (Chem.) derived from valerian (∼ **acid**, fatty acid occurring in valerian root; hence **vă'ler**ATE[1] (3) *n.*). [f. prec. +-IC]

vă'let (-lĭt, -lī, -lā) *n.* & *v.* **1.** *n.* gentleman's personal attendant who looks after clothes etc.; hotel etc. employee with similar duties. **2.** *v.t.* & *i.* act as valet (to). [F, = OF *valet*, *vaslet*, VARLET, f. Rom. *vassellittus dim. of *vassus (see VASSAL)]

valē'ta. See VELETA.

vălĕtūdĭnār'ian *a.* & *n.* **1.** *a.* of infirm health; seeking to recover health; unduly anxious about one's own health. **2.** *n.* valetudinarian person. **3.** Hence or cogn. ∼ISM (2) *n.*, **vălĕtū'dĭn**ARY[1] *a.* & *n.* [f. L *valetudinarius* in ill health (*valetudo -dinis* health f. *valēre* be well; see -TUDE, -ARIAN, -ARY[1])]

vă'lgus *n.* deformity involving outward turning of foot. [L, = bandy-legged]

Vălhă'lla *n.* (Norse Myth.) palace in which souls of slain heroes feasted; building used for honouring the illustrious. [mod. L, f. ON *Valhöll* (*valr* the slain, *höll* HALL)]

vă'liant (-lya-) *a.* (Of person or conduct) brave, courageous; hence ∼LY[2] *adv.* [ME, f. AF *valiaunt*, OF *vail(l)ant* f. Rom. *valiens f. L *valēre* be strong; see -ANT]

vă'lid *a.* (Of reason, objection, argument, etc.) sound, defensible, well-grounded; (Law) sound and sufficient, executed with proper formalities, (*valid contract*; *the marriage was held to be valid*); legally acceptable (*valid passport*); hence or cogn. **vali'd**ITY *n.*, ∼LY[2] *adv.* [f. F *valide* or f. L *validus* strong (as prec.; see -ID[1])]

vă'lid|āte *v.t.* make valid, ratify, confirm; hence ∼A'TION *n.* [f. med. L *validare* f. L (as prec.) +-ATE[3]]

vali'se (-ē's, -ē'z) *n.* kitbag; *kind of small portmanteau. [F, f. It. *valigia* corresp. to med. L *valisia*, of unkn. orig.]

Vălkyrie (vălkēr'ĭ, vă'lkĭrĭ) *n.* (Norse Myth.) each of Odin's 12 handmaidens who selected those destined to be slain in battle. [f. ON *Valkyrja* lit. chooser of the slain (*valr* the slain + **kur-*, **kuz-* cogn. w. CHOOSE)]

văllĕ'cūl|a *n.* (*pl.* ∼ae). (Anat. & Bot.) groove, furrow; hence ∼AR[1], ∼ATE[2], *adjs.* [LL, dim. of L *vallis* valley]

vă'lley *n.* **1.** low area more or less enclosed by hills and usu. with stream flowing through it; any depression compared to this; **∼ of the shadow of death**, (period of) close approach to death, extreme affliction (Ps. 23:4, prob. orig. meaning 'valley of deep shadows'). **2.** (Archit.) internal angle formed by intersecting planes of roof. [ME, f. AF *valey*, OF *valee* f. Rom. *vallata f. L *vallis, valles*; cf. VALE[1], -Y[4]]

vă'llum *n.* (Rom. Ant.) rampart and stockade as defence. [L, collect. f. *vallus* stake]

valō'nia *n.* acorn-cups of the Levantine evergreen ∼ **oak** (*Quercus aegilops*), used in tanning, dyeing, and making ink. [f. It. *vallonia* ult. f. Gk *balanos* acorn]

*vă'lor. See VALOUR.

vă'loriz|e, -īs|e (-ĭz), *v.t.* raise or fix price of (commodity etc.) by artificial means, esp. by government action; so ∼A'TION *n.* [back-form. f. *valorization* f. F *valorisation* (as foll.; see -IZE, -ATION)]

||vă'lour (-lẽr), ***vă'lor, n.** (poet., formal, or joc.) personal courage esp. as shown in fighting, prowess; so **vă'lor**OUS *a.* [ME f. OF, f. LL *valor -oris* (*valēre* be strong; see -OR)]

valse (vahls, vawls) *n.* waltz. [F. f. G (as WALTZ)]

vă'lŭable *a.* & *n.* **1.** *a.* of great value or price or worth (*valuable property, land, furniture, information, assistance*). **2.** *n.* (usu. in *pl.*) valuable thing(s), esp. small article(s) of personal property, (*sent all her valuables to the bank*). [f. VALUE 9 +-ABLE]

vălŭā'tion *n.* estimation (esp. by professional valuer) of a thing's worth, worth so estimated, price set on a thing, (*valuation of land*; *disposed of at a low valuation*; *sets too high a valuation on his abilities*). [f. VALUE 9 +-ATION]

vă'lŭător *n.* one who makes valuations, valuer. [f. prec. +OR]

vă'lūe *n.*, & *v.t.* **1.** *n.* worth, desirability, utility, qualities on which these depend, (*now learnt the value of fresh water, a friend, quinine, accuracy, regular exercise*). **2.** worth as estimated, valuation, (*sets a high value on his time*). **3.** purchasing power, power of a commodity to purchase others, amount of money or (Econ.) other commodities for which thing can be exchanged in open market. **4.** equivalent of a thing, what represents or is represented by or may be substituted for a thing, (*paid him the value of his lost property*); ability of a thing to serve a purpose or cause an effect (*news value*); (in *pl.*) one's principles or standards, one's judgement of what is valuable or important in life; meaning of word etc.; quality of a spoken sound; (Mus.) duration of sound signified by note; relative rank or importance of playing-card, chess piece, etc., according to rules of game; (Paint.) relation of one part of picture to others in respect of light and shade, part characterized by a particular tone. **5.** (Math.) amount or quantity denoted by algebraical term or expression. **6.** (Biol.) rank in classification. **7.** (Phys. etc.) numerical measure of a quantity (*value of gravity at the equator*); (Chem. etc.) number giving content etc. of a substance expressed on some conventional scale (*iodine value as measure of unsaturated fats*). **8.** ∼ **a'dded tax**, tax on amount by which value of an article has been increased at each stage of its production; ∼ **(for money),** something well worth the money spent; ∼-**judgement,** subjective estimate of quality etc.; ∼ **received,** money or its equivalent given for bill of exchange. **9.** *v.t.* estimate the value of, appraise (professionally, whence ‖**vă′lūer¹** *n.,* or otherwise), (*should value the whole at £2,000*); have high or specified opinion of, attach importance to, prize, esteem, appreciate, pride one*self,* (*value sincerity (beyond all things*); *a valued friend*; *values himself on* or *for his conversational powers*). [ME f. OF, fem. p.p. of *valoir* be worth f. L *valēre*]

vă′lūelèss (-ŭl-) *a.* having no value, worthless; hence ∼NESS *n.* [f. prec. + -LESS]

valū′ta *n.* value of a currency with respect to another; a currency thus considered. [It., = VALUE]

vălv|e *n.* **1.** automatic or other device for controlling passage of liquid or gas or the like through pipe etc., usu. to allow movement in one direction only; SAFETY-*valve;* ‖ = THERMIONIC *valve.* **2.** (Anat. & Zool.) membranous part of organ etc. allowing flow of blood etc. in one direction and not in another (*valves of the heart, of the veins*). **3.** (Conch.) each of two or more separable pieces of which shell consists, whole shell in one piece. **4.** (Bot.) each of the segments into which a capsule dehisces; lidlike part of anther. **5.** (Mus.) device for varying length of tube in brass wind instrument. **6.** (arch.) leaf of folding door. **7.** Hence or cogn. ∼′ATE² (Bot.), (-)∼ED² (-vd), ∼′ELESS (-vl-), *adjs.,* ∼′ULE *n.* [ME, f. L *valva* leaf of folding door]

vă′lvŭl|ar *a.* having (form or function of) valve(s); so ∼ɪ′TIS *n.,* inflammation of valves of heart. [f. mod. L *valvula,* dim. of L *valva* (see prec.) + -AR¹]

vă′mbrāce *n.* (Hist.) defensive armour for forearm. [ME, f. AF *vaunt-bras,* OF *avant-bras* (*avant* before, see AVAUNT; *bras* arm)]

*vamōō′se *v.i.* & *t.* (sl.) depart hurriedly (from). [f. Sp. *vamos* let us go]

vămp¹ *n.* & *v.* **1.** *n.* upper front part of boot or shoe; vamped or patched-up article; improvised musical accompaniment. **2.** *v.t.* put new vamp to (boot, shoe); repair, furbish usu. *up;* make *up* by patching or from odds and ends. **3.** *v.t.* & *i.* improvise musical accompaniment (to); improvise (musical accompaniment). [ME, f. AF **vaumpé,* OF *avantpié* (*avant* before, see AVAUNT; *pied* foot)]

vămp² *n.* & *v.* (colloq.) **1.** *n.* adventuress, woman who exploits men; unscrupulous flirt. **2.** *v.t.* (of woman) allure, exploit, (man). **3.** *v.i.* act as vamp. [abbr. of foll.]

vă′mpīre *n.* **1.** ghost or reanimated body (usu. of wizard, heretic, criminal, etc.) supposed to leave grave at night and suck blood of sleeping persons; person who preys ruthlessly on others; = prec. **2.** ∼ **(bat),** S. Amer. etc. bat actually or supposedly biting horses, cattle, and sleeping persons, and lapping their blood. **3.** (Theatr.) small spring trapdoor used for sudden disappearances. **4.** Hence **vămpī′ʀɪc** *a.* [F, or G *vampir,* f. Magyar *vampir* perh. f. Turk. *uber* witch]

vă′mpīrism *n.* belief in existence of vampires; action of a vampire (lit. or fig.). [f. prec. + -ISM]

vă′mplāte *n.* (Hist.) iron plate protecting hand when lance was couched. [ME, f. AF *vauntplate* (as VAM-BRACE, PLATE¹)]

văn¹ *n.* testing of ore quality by washing on shovel or by machine; (arch.) winnowing fan; (arch. or poet.) wing. [ME, southern & western var. of FAN¹, perh. partly f. OF *van* or L *vannus*]

văn² *n.* vanguard (lit. or fig.; *in the van of civilization*). [abbr.]

văn³ *n.* covered vehicle for conveying furniture or other goods or horses etc. or prisoners; ‖railway carriage for luggage (**luggage** ∼) or goods or for use of guard (**guard's** ∼); ‖gypsy caravan. [abbr. of CARAVAN]

‖**văn⁴** *n.* (Tennis colloq.) = ADVANTAGE¹ 3. [abbr.]

vanā′dium *n.* hard grey metallic element used in small quantities for strengthening some steels; hence **vă′nad**ATE¹ (3) *n.,* **vană′d**ɪC, **vă′nad**OUS, *adjs.* (Chem.). [mod. L, f. ON *Vanadis* name of the Scand. goddess Freyja + ɪUM]

Văn A′llen (ă′-) *n.* ∼ **(radiation) belt** or **layer,** one of two regions partly surrounding earth at heights of several thousand kilometres, containing intense radiation and many high-energy charged particles. [f. J. A. ∼, Amer. physicist b. 1914]

‖**V. & A.** *abbr.* Victoria & Albert Museum.

Vă′ndal *a.* & *n.* **1.** (member) of a Germanic people that in 4th-5th c. ravaged Gaul, Spain, N. Africa, and Rome, destroying many books and works of art. **2.** (*v*∼). wilful or ignorant destroyer or damager of works of art or other property; hence **v**∼ɪSM (2) *n.,* **v**∼ɪZE (1) *v.t.* **3.** Hence ∼ɪC (-ă′l-) *a.* [f. L *Vandalus* f. Gmc **Wandal-* etc.]

vă′ndy′ke *n., a.,* & *v.t.* **1.** *n.* each of a series of large points forming border to lace, cloth, etc.; cape, collar, etc., with these. **2.** *a.* (*V*∼). in the style of dress, esp. with pointed borders, common in portraits by Van Dyck; **V**∼ **(neat pointed) beard; V**∼ **brown,** deep rich brown. **3.** *v.t.* cut (cloth, edge of lawn, etc.) in vandykes. [f. Sir A. *Van Dyck,* Anglicized *Vandyke,* Flem. painter d. 1641]

vāne *n.* weathercock; similar device exposed to current of water etc.; blade of windmill, turbine, screw propeller, etc.; sight of surveying instruments, sight of quadrant etc.; flat part of bird's feather formed by barbs; hence **vān**ED² (-nd), ∼′LESS (-nl-), *adjs.* [ME, southern & western var. of obs. *fane* f. OE *fana* banner, = OS, OHG *fano,* ON *fani,* Goth. *fana* f. Gmc *fanon]

vané′ssa *n.* butterfly of genus *Vanessa,* e.g. red admiral, painted lady. [mod. L]

văng *n.* (Naut.) each of two guy-ropes running from end of gaff to deck. [earlier *fang* = gripping-device, OE f. ON *fang* grasp f. Gmc *fang-]

vă′nguărd (-n-gärd) *n.* foremost part of army or fleet advancing or ready to do so; (fig.) leaders of movement, of opinion, etc. [earlier *vandgard,* (*a*)*vantgard,* f. OF *avan*(*t*)*garde* (*avant* before, see AVAUNT; *garde* GUARD¹)]

vani′lla *n.* tropical climbing orchid of genus *Vanilla,* with fragrant flowers; ∼(-**pod**), fruit of this; extract obtained from vanilla-pod or synthetically and used for flavouring ice cream, chocolate, etc. [f. Sp. *vainilla* pod dim. of *vaina* sheath, f. L VAGINA]

vani′llin *a.* fragrant principle of vanilla. [f. prec. + IN]

vă′nish *v.* & *n.* **1.** *v.i.* disappear suddenly; disappear gradually, fade away; cease to exist; (Math.) become zero; ∼**ing-cream,** emollient that leaves no visible trace when rubbed into skin; ∼**ing-point,** point at which receding parallel lines viewed in perspective appear to meet, (fig.) state of complete disappearance. **2.** *v.t.* cause to disappear. **3.** *n.* (Phonet.) slight sound with which a principal sound ends (e.g. ōō, ĭ, at end of ō, ā). [ME, f. OF *e*(*s*)*vaniss-* stem of *e*(*s*)*vanir;* see EVANISH]

Vă′nitory, v-, *n.* (P) wash-basin surrounded by flat top for use as a dressing-table. [perh. f. foll. + -ORY]

vă′nity *n.* **1.** futility, unsubstantiality, unreality, emptiness, unsubstantial or unreal thing, (*the vanity of worldly wealth, of human achievements; these things are vanity* or *vanities; pomps and vanity of this wicked world*); **V**∼ **Fair,** the world (allegorized in Bunyan's *Pilgrim's Progress*) as scene of vanity. **2.** empty pride, desire for admiration, based on personal attainments or attractions or qualities; ∼ **bag, case,** (carried by woman and containing small mirror, cosmetics, etc.). **3.** ostentatious display. **4.** *dressing-table. [ME, f. OF *vanité,* f. L *vanitas -tatis* (as VAIN; see -ITY)]

vă′nquish *v.t.* (literary). conquer, overcome, (lit. or fig.); hence ∼ABLE *a.,* ∼ER¹ *n.* [ME *venkus, -quis,* etc., f. OF *vencus* p.p., and *-quis* past tense, of *veintre* f. L *vincere;* assim. to -ISH²]

va'ntage (vah'-) *n.* = ADVANTAGE¹ (esp. in Tennis, cf. VAN⁴; COIGN *of vantage*; ~**-ground, -point,** advantageous position for defence or attack). [ME f. AF, f. OF *avantage* ADVANTAGE¹]

vă'pĭd *a.* insipid, flat, (*vapid beer, conversation, remark, pleasures, moralizings*); hence **vapĭ'd**ITY, ~NESS, *ns.*, ~LY² *adv.* [f. L *vapidus*; see -ID¹]

*vă'por. See VAPOUR.

vă'por|ize, -ise (-īz), *v.t.* & *i.* convert or be converted into vapour; hence or cogn. ~īzA'TION, ~īzER¹ (2), *ns.*, ~(**iz**)ABLE *adjs.* [f. foll. + -IZE]

vă'pour (-per), ***vă'por,** *n.*, & *v.i.* **1.** *n.* moisture or other substance diffused or suspended in air, e.g. mist, smoke; (Phys.) gaseous form of a normally liquid or solid substance (cf. GAS¹), present above it and into which it is entirely converted when heated above boiling-point, whence **vāporĭ'**FIC, **vă'porĭ-**FORM, *adjs.*, **vāporĭ'**METER *n.*; medicinal agent to be inhaled; unsubstantial thing, vain imagination; (in *pl.*, arch.) depression, melancholy, hypochondria, hysteria, or similar nervous disorder, whence ~ISH¹ *a.* **2.** ~ **bath,** bath in vapour or steam, apparatus for apartment for this; ~**-burner,** apparatus for vaporizing and burning a hydrocarbon for producing light or heat; ~ **density** (of gas or vapour relative to hydrogen etc.); ~**-engine** (driven by steam or other vapour); ~ **pressure** (of vapour in contact with its liquid or solid form); ~ **trail,** condensation trail. **3.** Hence or cogn. **vă'por**OUS, ~Y², *adjs.* **4.** *v.i.* rise as vapour; utter idle boasts or empty talk, whence ~ER¹ *n.* (~er moth, tussock-moth), ~ING¹ *n.* [ME f. OF, or f. L *vapor* steam, heat]

vaquer'o (-kā'rō) *n.* (*pl.* ~s). (Sp. Amer. etc.) herdsman. [Sp. (*vaca* cow)]

var. *abbr.* variant; variety.

vară'ctor *n.* semiconductor diode with capacitance dependent on applied voltage. [f. *varying reactor*]

Vară'ngian (-nj-) *n.* Norse rover, esp. one of those who penetrated into Russia in 9th–10th c.; ~ **guard,** bodyguard of Byzantine emperors formed of Varangians. [f. med. L *Varangus* f. med. Gk *varaggos* f. ON *Væringi* lit. confederate (*várar* oaths) + -IAN]

vă'rĕc *n.* seaweed; = KELP 2. [f. F *varec*(*h*) f. ON **wrek* WRECK]

vār'iable *a.* & *n.* **1.** *a.* that can be varied or adapted, (*rod of variable length; the pressure is variable*); (of gear) designed to give varying speeds, e.g. slow advance and quick return; apt to vary, not constant, fickle, unsteady, (*variable mood, temper, fortune*); (of wind, currents) tending to change direction; (Astron., of star) periodically varying in brightness; (Math., of quantity) indeterminate, able to assume different numerical values; (Bot. & Zool., of species) including individuals or groups that depart from the type; (Biol., of organism) tending to change in structure or function; hence **vāriabĭ'**LITY, ~NESS (-beln-), *ns.*, **vār'iab**LY² *adv.* **2.** *n.* variable thing (esp. quantity or star); (Naut.) shifting wind, (in *pl.*) region between NE and SE trade winds. [ME f. OF, f. L *variabilis* (as VARY; see -ABLE)]

vār'iance *n.* disagreement, difference of opinion, dispute, lack of harmony, (*on that point we are at variance (among ourselves); at variance with the authorities; have had a slight variance with him; this theory is at variance with all that is known on the subject*); (Law) discrepancy between statements or documents; (Statistics) quantity equal to square of standard deviation; *permission to depart from usual rules. [ME f. OF, f. L *variantia* difference (as VARY; see -ANCE)]

vār'iant *a.* & *n.* **1.** *a.* differing in form or in details from the one named or considered, differing thus among themselves, (*a variant reading in some MSS; 40 variant types of pigeon*); variable, changing. **2.** *n.* variant form, spelling, type, reading, etc., ('*enure*' *is a variant of* '*inure*'; *difficult to choose between these variants*). [ME f. OF (as VARY; see -ANT)]

vār'iate *n.* (Statistics). quantity having a numerical

value for each member of a group; variable quantity, esp. one whose values occur according to a frequency distribution. [f. p.p. of L *variare*; see VARY, -ATE¹]

vāriā'tion *n.* **1.** varying, departure from a former or normal condition or action or amount or from a standard or type, extent of this, (*prices are subject to variation; repeated variations of temperature; is subject to a variation of several degrees*); (Astron.) deviation of heavenly body from mean orbit or motion (**periodic, secular,** ~, compensated in short, in very long, period); (of magnetic needle) declination; (Biol.) structural or functional deviation from type; (Math.) change in a function etc. due to small changes in values of constants etc. (*calculus of variations*). **2.** thing that varies from a type; (Mus.) tune or theme repeated in a changed or elaborated form; (Ballet) solo dance. **3.** Hence ~AL *a.* [ME f. OF, or f. L *variatio* (as VARY; see -ATION)]

vărĭcě'lla *n.* chicken-pox. [mod. L, irreg. dim. of VARIOLA]

vă'ricocēle *n.* tumour composed of varicose veins of spermatic cord. [f. as VARIX + -O- + -CELE]

vār'icoloured, *-ored, (-kŭlerd) *a.* variegated in colour; of various or different colours. [f. L *varius* VARIOUS + COLOURED]

vă'ric|ōse *a.* of or affected with varix (*varicose ulcer, vein*); hence ~o'sITY *n.* [f. L *varicosus* (VARIX; see -OSE¹)]

varied. See VARY.

vār'ieg|āte (-rĭg-) *v.t.* diversify in appearance, esp. in colour; mark with irregular patches of different colours; (in *p.p.*, Bot.) having two or more colours of leaves; hence ~A'TION *n.* [f. L *variegare* (*varius* VARIOUS) + -ATE³]

vari'etist *n.* one whose habits etc. differ from what is normal. [f. foll. + -IST]

vari'ety *n.* **1.** being various, diversity, absence of monotony or uniformity, many-sidedness, (*was struck by the variety of his attainments, of his conversation, of the scene; London has for me the charm of variety; cannot live without variety*). **2.** quantity or collection of different things (*looked over a variety of books; for a variety of reasons*); ~ (**entertainment** or **show**), mixed series of dances, songs, comedy acts, acrobatic feats, etc.; *~ **meat,** edible offal of animals; *~ **store** (selling many kinds of small items); ~ **theatre** (for variety shows etc.). **3.** (specimen or member of a) class of things differing in some common qualities from the rest of a larger class to which they belong; different form *of* thing, quality, etc. **4.** (Biol.) individual or group usually fertile within the species to which it belongs but differing from the species type in some qualities capable of perpetuation; sub-species; cultivar; hence **vari'et**AL *a.* [f. F *variété* f. L *varietas* (as VARIOUS; see -TY¹)]

vār'ifôrm *a.* having various forms. [f. L (as VARIOUS) + -FORM]

vari'ol|a *n.* smallpox; hence ~AR¹, **vār'iol**OID, ~OUS, *adjs.* [med. L, = pustule, pock (as VARIOUS)]

vār'iōle *n.* shallow pit like smallpox mark; spherule in variolite. [f. med. L (see prec.)]

vār'iol|īte *n.* rock with embedded spherules causing on surface an appearance like smallpox pustules; hence ~i'tIC *a.* [f. as prec. + -ITE¹]

vāriō'meter *n.* device for varying the inductance in an electric circuit, or for indicating aircraft's rate of change of altitude. [f. as VARIOUS + -O- + -METER]

vāriōr'um *a.* & *n.* **1.** *a.* with notes of various editors or commentators (*a variorum (edition of) Horace*). **2.** *n.* variorum edition. [L, gen. pl. masc. of *varius* VARIOUS, short for *cum notis variorum*]

vār'ious *a.* **1.** different, diverse, (*the modes of procedure were various; types so various as to defy classification*). **2.** separate, several, more than one, (*came across various people; for various reasons*). **3.** Hence ~LY² *adv.*, ~NESS *n.* [f. L *varius* changing, diverse + -OUS]

vari′stor *n.* semiconductor diode with resistance dependent on applied voltage. [f. *varying resistor*]

vār′ĭ|x *n.* (*pl.* ∼ces *pr.* vă′risēz). (Path.) permanent abnormal dilation of vein or artery; vein etc. thus dilated; (Conch.) each of the ridges across the whorls of a univalve shell. [ME f. L *varix -icis*]

vār′lĕt *n.* (arch. or joc.) menial, low fellow, rascal; (Hist.) knight's attendant; hence ∼RY (1) *n.* [ME f. OF, var. of *vaslet*; see VALET]

vār′mint *n.* (dial. or US). mischievous or discreditable person or animal, esp. fox. [var. of *varmin*, VERMIN]

vār′na *n.* any of the four great Hindu castes. [Skr., = colour, class]

vār′nish *n.*, & *v.t.* **1.** *n.* resinous solution in oil or spirit applied to wood, metal, etc., to give hard shiny transparent coating; other preparation for similar purpose, e.g. ‖NAIL¹ varnish. **2.** artificial or natural glossiness; superficial polish of manner; external appearance or display without underlying reality; ∼-tree (from which varnish-resin is obtained). **3.** *v.t.* apply varnish to (wood, picture, etc.; (fig.) character, person, action, account; or abs.); gloss over (fact); ∼ing-day, day before exhibition of pictures on which exhibitors may retouch and varnish their pictures already hung. [ME, f. OF *verniss(i)er* v. f.) *vernis* n. f. L *veronix* BANDARAC 2 or med. Gk *bereniké* prob. f. *Berenice* in Cyrenaica]

vār′sĭty *n.* **1.** ‖(colloq., esp. w. ref. to sports) university. **2.** *university etc. first team in a sport. [abbr.]

vārsovĭĕ′nne (-vyĕ′n), **vărsovia′na** (-vyah′-), *n.* (music for) dance resembling mazurka. [F & It., = (dance) of Warsaw (*Varsovie, Varsovia*) in Poland]

vār′us *n.* deformity involving inward turning of foot. [L, = knock-kneed]

vārv|e *n.* annually deposited layers of clay and silt in lake used to determine chronology of glacial sediments; hence ∼ED² *a.* [f. Sw. *varv* layer]

vār′y *v.* **1.** *v.t.* change, make different, modify, diversify, (*can vary the pressure at will; seldom varies the routine, varies the treatment according to circumstances; style is not sufficiently varied*); (in *p.p.*) showing variety (*a varied career, scene*). **2.** *v.i.* undergo change, be(come) different in degree or quality, be of different kinds, (*he, his mood, varies from day to day; temperature varies from 30° to 70°; tried with varying success; varies from the type; opinions vary on this point*). **3.** ∼ (directly) **as,** ∼ inversely **as,** be in direct, inverse, proportion to (*attraction of bodies varies* (directly) *as their masses and inversely as the square of their distance*). [ME, f. OF *varier* or f. L *variare* (as VARIOUS)]

văs *n.* (*pl.* ∼a *pr.* vā′sa). (Anat.) vessel, duct; ∼ de′ferens (*pl.* ∼a defere′ntia*), spermatic duct of testicle; hence vă′SAL *a.* [L, = vessel]

vă′scŭlar *a.* of, made up of, containing, vessels or ducts for conveying blood, sap, etc., (*vascular functions, tissue, system*); ∼ **plant** (with woody conducting elements); hence ∼ITY (-ă′r-) *n.*, ∼IZE (3) *v.t.*, ∼LY² *adv.* [f. mod. L *vascularis* f. L VASCULUM; see -AR¹]

vă′scŭl|um *n.* (*pl.* ∼a). botanist's (usu. metal) collecting-case with lengthwise opening. [L, dim. of VAS]

vase (vahz) *n.* vessel of earthenware, metal, etc., usu. tall and circular, used as ornament or container (*flower-vase*); ∼-**painting,** decoration of vases with pigments esp. among ancient Greeks, instance of this; hence ∼′FUL 2 (-zf-) *n.* [F, f. L VAS]

vasĕ′ctom|y̆ *n.* (Surg.) removal of part of each vas deferens esp. for sterilization of patient; hence ∼IZE (1) *v.t.* [f. VAS + -ECTOMY]

Vă′seline, v-, (-ēn) *n.,* & *v.t.* **1.** *n.* (P) type of petroleum jelly used as ointment etc. **2.** *v.t.* treat with Vaseline. [irreg. f. G *wasser* water + Gk *elaion* oil + -INE⁵]

vă′sĭform (-z-) *a.* duct-shaped; vase-shaped. [f. L *vasi-* (VAS; see -I-) + -FORM]

vāsō- *comb. form.* vessel, esp. blood-vessel, as: ∼-a′ctive,

∼-mo′tor, causing constriction or dilatation of blood-vessels; so ∼-constri′ctive, ∼-dila′ting; ∼pre′ssin, pituitary hormone acting to reduce diuresis and increase blood pressure. [f. L VAS + -O-]

vă′ssal *n.* (Hist.) holder of land by feudal tenure on conditions of homage and allegiance (**great, rear,** ∼, holding directly from king, holding from great vassal); (rhet.) slave, humble dependant; so ∼AGE (1, 2) *n.* [ME f. OF, f. med. L *vassallus* retainer, of Celt. orig., the simplex *vassus* corresp. to OBret. *uuas*, W *gwas*, Ir. *foss*; cf. VAVASOUR]

vast (vah-) *a.* & *n.* **1.** *a.* immense, huge, very great, (*a vast expanse of water; vast plains; shook his vast frame; a vast multitude, scheme*); (colloq.) great (*gave him vast satisfaction; makes a vast difference*); hence ∼′ĭTUDE *n.*, ∼′LY² *adv.*, ∼′NESS *n.* ∼′y² *a.* (rhet.). **2.** *n.* (poet. or rhet.) vast space (*the vast of heaven*). [f. L *vastus* void, immense]

văt *n.*, & *v.t.* (-tt-). **1.** *n.* large tub, cistern, tank, or other vessel, esp. for holding liquids or holding something in liquid in process of manufacture, as in brewing, tanning, dyeing; dyeing liquor in which textile is soaked to take up colourless soluble dye afterwards coloured by oxidation in air; hence ∼′FUL 2 *n.* **2.** *v.t.* place or treat in vat. [ME, southern & western var. of *fat*, OE *fæt*, = OS, ON *fat*, OHG *fuʒ* f. Gmc *fatam* vessel]

VAT (vēātē′, văt) *abbr.* value added tax.

vă′tic *a* prophetic, inspired. [f. L *vates* prophet + -IC]

Vă′tican *n.* Pope's palace and official residence in Rome; (fig.) papal government; ∼ **City,** independent papal state in Rome 1929–; ∼ **Council,** (1) ecumenical council of RC Ch. held 1869–70 and proclaiming infallibility of Pope when speaking *ex cathedra*, whence ∼ISM (3), ∼IST (2), *ns.*, (2) similar council held 1962–5. [F, or f. L *Vaticanus* name of hill in Rome]

vati′cin|āte *v.t.* & *i.* prophesy; so ∼AL *a.*, ∼A′TION, ∼āTOR, *ns.*, ∼āTORY *a.* [f. L *vaticinari* (*vates* prophet) + -ATE³]

vau′devill|e (vō′, vaw′-) *n.* variety entertainment; satirical or topical song with refrain; light stage-play with interspersed songs; hence ∼IAN (-ĭ′l-) *a.* & *n.* [F, orig. of convivial song esp. any of those composed by O. Basselin, 15th-c. poet born at *Vau de Vire* in Normandy]

Vaudois¹ (vōdwah′) *a.* & *n.* (*pl.* same). (inhabitant or dialect) of Vaud in Switzerland. [F (*Vaud, -ois* -ESE)]

Vaudois² (vōdwah′) *a.* & *n.* (*pl.* same). (member) of the WALDENSES. [F, repr. med. L *Valdensis*; see WALDENSES]

vault¹ (vaw-, vŏ-) *n.,* & *v.t.* **1.** *n.* (Archit.) arched roof, continuous arch, set or series of arches whose joints radiate from central point or line. **2.** vaultlike covering (*the vault of heaven*); arched apartment; arched or over cellar or subterranean chamber as place of storage (*bank vaults,* WINE-*vault,* etc.), of interment beneath church or in cemetery (*family vault*), etc. **3.** (Anat.) arched roof of a cavity. **4.** *v.t.* (in *p.p.*). make in form of, furnish with, vault(s). **5.** Hence ∼′ING¹ (6) *n.* [ME f. OF (*vouter* v. f.) *voute, vaute,* f. Rom. **vol(u)ta* for *voluta* fem. p.p. of L *volvere* roll]

vault² (vaw-, vŏ-) *v.* & *n.* **1.** *v.i.* leap, spring, esp. while resting on the hand(s) or with help of pole, (*vault over the gate, from the saddle, on to a horse*); ∼′ing-horse, gymnast's wooden block for use in vaulting. **2.** *v.t.* spring over (gate etc.) thus. **3.** Hence ∼′ER¹ *n.* **4.** *n.* leap so performed. [f. OF *vo(u)lter* leap, f. Rom. **vol(u)tare* frequent. of L *volvere* roll, assim. to prec.]

vaunt *v.i.* & *t.,* & *n.* (literary). boast, brag; boast of, extol boastfully, so ∼′ER¹ *n.* (arch.). [ME, f. AF *vaunter,* OF *vanter* f. LL *van(i)tare* f. L *vanus* VAIN; partly obs. *avaunt* v. f. *avanter* (*a* intensive, *vanter*)]

vau′nt-courier (-kōō-) *n.* (arch.) forerunner. [f. *avant- -courier* f. F *avant-courier* (*avant* before; see AVAUNT, COURIER)]

vă′vasory *n.* (Hist.) estate of vavasour. [f. OF *vavasorie* or f. med. L *-oria* (as foll.; see -Y¹)]

vă′vasour (-oor) *n.* (Hist.) vassal holding from great lord and having other vassals under him. [ME, f. OF *vavas(s)our* f. med. L *vavassor*, perh. f. *vassus vassorum* VASSAL of vassals]

vaw′ard. Var. (arch.) of VANGUARD.

VC *abbr.* Vice-Chairman, -Chancellor, -Consul; Victoria Cross.

VD *abbr.* venereal disease; Volunteer (Officer's) Decoration.

VDU *abbr.* visual display unit (for computer output).

've *v.* (colloq., chiefly after pronouns). = HAVE¹. [abbr.]

VE *abbr.* Victory in Europe; ~ **day,** 8 May 1945.

veal *n.* calf's flesh as food; hence ~′y² *a.*, like veal, (fig.) immature. [ME, f. AF *ve(e)l*, OF *veiaus veel* f. L *vitellus* dim. of *vitulus* calf]

vĕ′ctor *n.*, & *v.t.* **1.** *n.* (Math.) quantity having both magnitude and direction, esp. as determining position of one point in space relative to another (RADIUS *vector*); course to be taken by aircraft; hence **vĕc-tŏr′IAL** *a.* **2.** carrier of disease or infection from one organism to another. **3.** *v.t.* direct (aircraft in flight) to desired point. [L, = carrier (*vehere vect-* convey; see -OR)]

Ve′da (vā′-, vē′-) *n.* (in *sing.* or *pl.*) most ancient Hindu scriptures, esp. **Rig, Sāma, Yajur, Atharva,** ~~, four collections of hymns etc. [f. Skr. *vēda*, lit. (sacred) knowledge]

Veda′nta (vĕdah′-, vĭdă′-) *n.* **1.** Upanishads. **2.** monistic Hindu philosophy founded on the Upanishads. **3.** Hence ~IC *a.*, ~IST (3) *n.* [f. Skr. *vēdānta* (as VEDA, *anta* end)]

Vĕ′dda *n.* aboriginal of Sri Lanka. [f. Sinh. *veddā* hunter]

vĕdĕ′tte *n.* mounted sentry placed in advance of an outpost. [F, = scout, f. It. *vedetta, veletta* f. Sp. *vela(r)* watch f. L *vigilare*]

Ve′dic (vā′-, vē′-) *a.* & *n.* **1.** *a.* of Veda(s). **2.** *n.* language of the Vedas, old form of Sanskrit. [f. F *védique* or G *vedisch*; see VEDA, -IC]

vee *n.* (thing shaped like) letter V. [name of the letter]

*Veep *n.* (colloq.) Vice-President. [f. abbr. VP]

veer¹ *v.t.* (Naut.) slacken, let out, (rope, cable, etc.); ~ **and haul,** tighten and slacken (rope etc.) alternately, (fig.) deal with problem by skilful manœuvres. [ME, f. MDu. *vieren*]

veer² *v.* & *n.* **1.** *v.i.* change direction esp. (of wind; cf. BACK²) clockwise; (Naut.) = WEAR³. **2.** *v.i.* & *t.* (fig.) change in course or opinion or conduct or language. **3.** *n.* change of direction, shifting round. [f. F *virer* f. Rom. **virare*, perh. alt. f. L *gyrare* GYRATE²]

vĕg (-j) *n.* (colloq.) vegetable(s). [abbr.]

vĕ′gan *n.* & *a.* (person) eating no animals or animal products; strict(ly) vegetarian. [f. VEGETARIAN]

vĕ′getable *a.* & *n.* **1.** *a.* of (the nature of), derived from, concerned with, comprising, plants, esp. opp. *animal* or *mineral* (*vegetable* BUTTER¹, IVORY, *kingdom,* MARROW, OYSTER, PARCHMENT, SPONGE¹, TALLOW, WAX¹); (of life etc.) like that of vegetable, uneventful, monotonous. **2.** *n.* plant, esp. herbaceous plant or part of one used for food, e.g. cabbage, potato, turnip, bean, pumpkin, yam; person living vegetable life through injury or lack of ambition. [ME f. OF, or f. LL *vegetabilis* animating (as VEGETATE; see -ABLE)]

vĕ′gĕtal *a.* of (the nature of) plants; vegetative; **the ~ functions** (of growth, circulation, nutrition, etc.). [f. med. L *vegetalis* f. L *vegetare* animate; see -AL]

vĕgĕtār′ian *n.* one who abstains from animal food, esp. that obtained by killing animals, and whose diet includes roots, green vegetables, cereals, seeds, fruit, and nuts, with or without eggs and dairy products; hence ~ISM (3) *n.* [irreg. f. VEGETABLE + -ARIAN]

vĕ′gĕtate *v.i.* grow as plants do, fulfil vegetal functions; (fig.) live an uneventful or monotonous life. [f. L *vegetare* animate (*vegetus* f. *vegēre* be active) + -ATE³]

vĕgĕtā′tion *n.* vegetating (lit. or fig.); plants collectively, plant life, (*luxuriant vegetation; no sign of vegetation*

for miles round); (Path.) abnormal plantlike growth on surface of body. [f. med. L *vegetatio* growth (as VEGETATE; see -ATION)]

vĕ′gĕtātive *a.* concerned with growth and development, opp. (sexual) reproduction; of vegetation; hence ~LY² (-vlĭ) *adv.*, ~NESS (-vn-) *n.* [ME, f. OF *vegetatif -ive* or f. med. L *vegetativus* (as VEGETATE; see -IVE)]

vĕ′hĕm|ent (vē′ĭ-) *a.* showing or caused by strong feeling, impetuous, ardent, passionate, (*a vehement desire, protest; man of vehement character*); (arch.) acting with great force, violent, (*a vehement wind, onset*); hence or cogn. ~ENCE *n.*, ~ently² *adv.* [ME, f. F *véhément* or f. L *vehemens -entis*, perh. f. **vemens* deprived of mind, assoc. w. *vehere* carry]

vĕ′hicle (vē′ĭ-) *n.* carriage or conveyance of any kind used on land or in space; liquid etc. used as medium for suspending pigments, drugs, etc.; thing or person used as medium for thought or feeling or action (*used the pulpit, the press, as a vehicle for his political opinions; will not be used as the vehicle of your resentment*); so **vĕhĭ′cūlAR¹** *a.* [f. F *véhicule* or f. L *vehiculum* (*vehere* carry; see -CULE)]

vehm|gericht (fā′mgerĭ̄χt) *n.* German system of secret tribunals prevailing esp. in Westphalia *c.* 1200–1550; such tribunal; so ~IC *a.* [G (*vehm* punishment, *gericht* tribunal)]

veil (vāl) *n.*, & *v.t.* **1.** *n.* piece of usu. more or less transparent material attached to woman's hat or otherwise forming part of head-dress, esp. one serving to conceal the face or as protection against sun, dust, etc.; piece of linen etc. as part of nun's head-dress, falling over head and shoulders (**take the** ~, become nun); curtain, esp. that separating sanctuary in Jewish Temple, (**beyond the** ~, in the unknown state of life after death); (fig.) disguise, pretext, (*under the veil of religion*); **draw a** ~ **over,** avoid discussing or calling attention to. **2.** = VELUM; (Photog.) slight fogging. **3.** slight huskiness of voice, natural or due to a cold etc. **4.** Hence ~′ING³ (3) *n.* ~′LESS (-l-l-) *a.* **5.** *v.t.* cover (one's face, one*self,* or abs.) with veil; (fig.) partly conceal, disguise, mask, (*veiled threat, resentment*). [ME, f. AF *veil(e)*, OF *voil(e)* f. L *vela* pl. of VELUM]

vein (vān) *n.*, & *v.t.* **1.** *n.* membranous tube forming part of system by which blood is conveyed to heart (cf. ARTERY). **2.** (pop.) any blood-vessel (*has royal blood in his veins*). **3.** nervure of insect's wing; slender bundle of tissue forming part of framework of leaf; (Geol. & Mining) fissure in rock filled with deposited material, e.g. ore (~′stone, gangue). **4.** streak or stripe of different colour in wood, marble, cheese, etc. **5.** distinctive character or tendency, cast of mind or disposition, mood, (*was of an imaginative vein; said this in a humorous vein; other remarks in the same vein*). **6.** Hence ~′LESS, ~′LIKE, ~′Y², *adjs.*, ~′LET *n.* **7.** *v.t.* (esp. in *p.p.*) fill or cover (as with vein(s)); hence ~′ING³ (6) *n.* [ME, f. OF *veine* f. L *vena*]

vē′la. See VELUM.

vēlā′|men *n.* (*pl.* ~mina). enveloping membrane esp. of aerial root of orchid. [L (*velare* cover)]

vē′lar *a.* of a veil or velum; (Phonet., of sound) pronounced with back of tongue near soft palate. [f. L *velaris* (VELUM; see -AR¹)]

vĕld, vĕldt, (vĕld, vĕlt, fĕlt) *n.* (S. Afr.) open country neither cultivated nor true forest; ~′schoen (fĕ′l-skōŏn), shoe of untanned hide. [Afrik., = FIELD]

vele′ta, valē′ta, *n.* ballroom dance in triple time. [Sp., = weather-vane]

vĕlitā′tion *n.* (arch.) slight skirmish, controversy. [f. L *velitatio* (*velitari* skirmish f. *veles velitis* light-armed skirmisher; see -ATION)]

vĕllē′itý *n.* low degree of volition not prompting to action; slight wish or inclination. [f. med. L *velleitas* f. L *velle* to wish; see -ITY]

vĕ′llum *n.* fine parchment orig. from skin of calf; manuscript written on this; smooth writing-paper imitating vellum. [ME, f. OF *velin* (as VEAL; see -INE¹)]

vělō′cǐpēd|e *n.* **1.** (Hist.) light vehicle propelled by rider, esp. early form of bicycle; hence ∿IST (3) *n.* **2.** *child's tricycle. [f. F *vélocipède* f. L *velox -ocis* swift +*pes pedis* foot]

vělō′cǐtý *n.* quickness or rate of motion or action usu. of inanimate things; (Mech.) speed in a given direction; ∿ **of escape,** = ESCAPE¹ *velocity;* ∿ **of light,** constant rate (about 300,000 km. per sec.) at which radiation travels in vacuum; so **věloci′METER** *n.* [f. F *vélocité* or f. L *velocitas* (as prec.; see -ITY)]

velour′, velours′, (-oor′) *n.* plushlike woven fabric or felt; hat of such felt. [F *velours* velvet f. OF *velour, velous* f. L *villosus* hairy (*villus*; see VELVET)]

velouté (-ōō′tā) *n.* sauce of white stock mixed with cooked butter and flour. [F, = velvety]

velskoon. Var. of VELDschoen.

vē′l|um *n.* (*pl.* ∿**a**). (Anat., Bot., & Zool.) membrane or membranous covering, esp. the soft palate. [L, = sail, curtain, covering, veil]

vělū′tǐnous *a.* (Bot. & Entom.) velvety. [perh. f. It. *vellutino* (*velluto* VELVET)]

vě′lvĕt *n.* & *a.* **1.** *n.* closely woven fabric (orig. of silk) with thick short pile on one side; furry skin covering a growing antler; profit, gain; **on** ∿, in an advantageous or prosperous position; hence ∿ED⁹, ∿Y², *adjs.* **2.** *a.* of, like, soft as, velvet; ∿ **bean,** annual bean of southern US used as fodder; ∿ **glove,** outward gentleness or suavity cloaking inflexibility (*with an iron hand in a velvet glove*). [ME, f. OF *veluotte* (*velu* velvety f. med. L *villutus* f. L *villus* down)]

vě′lvĕtee′n *n.* cotton fabric with pile like velvet; (in *pl.*) trousers etc. made of this. [f. prec.]

Ven. *abbr.* Venerable (as title of archdeacon).

vēna cā′va *n.* (*pl.* **-ae -ae**). each of usu. two veins conveying blood into heart. [L, = hollow vein]

vě′nal *a.* (Of person) that may be bribed, ready to sell one's influence or services to or sacrifice principles from sordid motives; (of conduct etc.) characteristic of venal person; hence or cogn. **vena′lITY** *n.,* ∿LY² *adv.* [f. L *venalis* (*venum* thing for sale; see -AL)]

věnā′tion *n.* arrangement of veins in leaf, insect's wing, etc.; hence ∿AL *a.* [f. L *vena* vein +-ATION]

věnd *v.t.* **1.** (Law). sell; hence ∿EE′ *n.* **2.** offer (small wares) for sale; hence (-)∿ER¹ *n.;* ∿**ing-machine** (for automatic retail of small articles). **3.** Hence ∿IBLE *a.* [f. F *vendre* or f. L *vendere* sell (as VENAL, *dare* give)]

vě′ndăce *n.* small delicate fish (*Coregonus albula*) found in some British lakes. [f. OF *vendese, -oise* f. Gaulish *vindesia* (*vindos* white)]

věndě′tta *n.* blood feud in which family of injured or murdered man seeks vengeance on offender or his family; this practice as prevalent in Corsica etc.; prolonged bitter hostility. [It., f. L *vindicta;* see VINDICTIVE]

vendeuse (vahṅdĕr′z) *n.* saleswoman, esp. in fashionable dress-shop. [F]

vě′ndor *n.* **1.** (esp. Law). one who sells. **2.** = VENDing- -machine. [AF *vendo(u)r* (as VEND, -OR)]

***věndūe′** *n.* public auction. [f. Du. *vendu(e)* f. F *vendue* sale (*vendre* VEND)]

věneer′ *v.t.,* & *n.* **1.** *v.t.* cover (wood, furniture, etc.) with thin coating of finer wood; (fig.) disguise (character etc.) under superficial polish of manner etc.; so ∿ING¹ (1, 2, 4) *n.* **2.** *n.* thin outer coating, veneering (lit. or fig.); layer in plywood; ∿**moth,** moth of subfamily Crambidae, whose colouring suggests veneer. [earlier *fineer* f. G *furni(e)ren* f. F *fournir* FURNISH]

vě′něpǔncture, vě′nǐ-, *n.* (Med.) puncture of vein esp. with hypodermic needle to withdraw blood or for intravenous injection. [f. L *vena* vein + PUNCTURE]

vě′ner|able *a.* entitled to veneration on account of character, age, associations, etc., (*venerable priest, relics, beard, ruins;* in Ch. of Engl. as title of archdeacon, in RC Ch. as title of one who has attained

a certain degree of sanctity but is not fully beatified or canonized); hence ∿ABI′LITY, ∿ableNESS (-bɜln-), *ns.,* ∿abLY² *adv.* [ME f. OF, or L *venerabilis* (as foll.; see -ABLE)]

vě′nerāt|e *v.t.* consider worthy of and regard with deep respect or warm approbation; revere; so ∿OR *n.* [f. L *venerari* adore, revere +-ATE³]

věnerā′tion *n.* deep respect, reverence; venerating or being venerated. [ME, f. OF, or f. L *veneratio* (as prec.; see -ATION)]

věner′ēal *a.* of sexual desire or intercourse; relating to ∿ **disease** (contracted chiefly by sexual intercourse with person already infected); hence ∿LY² *adv.* [ME, f. L *venereus* (*venus veneris* sexual love) +-AL]

věněrēŏ′logý *n.* study of venereal diseases; hence **věněrēŏlŏ′gICAL** *a.,* ∿IST (3) *a.* [f. as prec. + o- +-LOGY]

vě′nerÿ¹ *n.* (arch.) hunting. [ME, f. OF *venerie* (*vener* to hunt f. Rom. *venare* for L *venari;* see -ERY)]

vě′nerÿ² *n.* (arch.) sexual indulgence. [f. med. L *veneria* (as VENEREAL; see -Y¹)]

vě′nēsĕction, vě′nǐ-, *n.* phlebotomy. [f. med. L *venae sectio* cutting of VEIN; see SECTION]

Věnē′tian (-shan) *a.* & *n.* **1.** *a.* of Venice; **v∿ blind,** window blind of horizontal slats that may be adjusted so as to admit or exclude light and air; ∿ **carpet** (with worsted warp and usu. with striped pattern); ∿ (= FRENCH) **chalk;** ∿ **glass,** delicate glassware made at Murano near Venice; ∿ **pearl,** imitation pearl of solid glass, ∿ **red,** reddish pigment of ferric oxides; ∿ **sumac,** Eur. smoke-tree with large panicles of flowers; ∿ **window** (with three separate openings, central one being arched and highest). **2.** *n.* native or dialect of Venice. **3.** (*v∿*). venetian blind, whence **v∿**ED² (-nd) *a.* [ME, f. OF *Venicien,* assim. to med. L *Venetianus* (*Venetia* Venice; see -AN)]

vě′ngeance (-njans) *n.* punishment inflicted or retribution exacted for wrong to oneself or to person etc. whose cause one supports; **with a** ∿, in a higher degree than was expected or desired, in the fullest sense of the word(s), and no mistake, (*this is punctuality with a vengeance*). [ME f. OF (*venger* avenge f. L, as VINDICATE; see -ANCE)]

vě′ngeful (-njf-) *a.* disposed to revenge, vindictive; hence ∿LY² *adv.,* ∿NESS *n.* [f. obs. *venge* avenge (as prec.) +-FUL]

vě′nial *a.* (Of sin or fault) pardonable, excusable, not very wrong, (Theol.) not mortal; hence ∿ITY (-ǎ′l-), ∿NESS, *ns.,* ∿LY² *adv.* [ME f. OF, f. LL *venialis* (*venia* forgiveness; see -AL)]

vě′nǐpǔncture, -sĕction. See VENEPUNCTURE etc.

věnī′r′e *n.* (Law). **1.** ∿ (**facias** *pr.* fā′shiǎs), (Hist. or US) writ directing sheriff to summon jury. **2.** *panel of persons thus summoned; ∿**man,** member of this. [f. L *venire facias* make or cause to come]

vě′nison (-nz-, -nǐs-) *n.* deer's flesh as food. [ME, f. OF *veneso(u)n* f. L *venatio -onis* hunting (*venari* to hunt; see -ATION, -ISON)]

Věnī′tē *n.* canticle consisting of Ps. 95. [ME f. L, = come ye, its first word]

Věnn *n.* ∿ **diagram,** set of circles etc. representing logical classes which may or may not coincide, intersect, etc. [f. J. ∿, Engl. logician d. 1923]

vě′nom *n.* poisonous fluid secreted by serpents, scorpions, etc., and introduced into system of victim by bite or sting; (fig.) malignity, virulence of feeling or language or conduct; hence ∿ED² (-md) *a.* [ME, f. OF *venim,* var. of *venin* f. Rom. *venimen* f. L *venenum* poison]

vě′nomous *a.* containing or full of venom; secreting venom, inflicting poisonous wounds by this means; (fig.) virulent like venom, spiteful, malignant; hence ∿LY² *adv.,* ∿NESS *n.* [ME, f. OF *venimeux* (*venim;* see prec., -OUS)]

vě′nōse *a.* having many or very marked veins. [f. L *venosus* (*vena* vein; see -OSE¹)]

vě′nous *a.* (Anat., Zool., & Bot.) of, full of, contained in, veins; hence or cogn. **vĕn**o′sITY *n.*, ∼LY² *adv.* [f. L as prec., or f. L *vena* vein + -OUS]

vĕnt¹ *n.* & *v.* **1.** *n.* ∼(-hole), hole or opening allowing motion of substance out of or into confined space, e.g. touch-hole of gun, hole in top of barrel to admit air while liquid is being drawn out, finger-hole in musical instrument (also ∼′AGE *n.*), flue of chimney, fumarole of volcano. **2.** anus esp. of lower animal, serving for both excretion and reproduction. **3.** (fig.) outlet, free passage, free play, (*gave vent to his indignation; impatience found a vent*). **4.** venting of otter etc.). **5.** ∼-peg, ∼-plug, (for stopping vent of barrel etc.). **6.** Hence ∼LESS *a.* **7.** *v.t.* make vent in (gun, cask, etc.); give vent or free expression to (one's SPLEEN; *vented his disgust in an epigram, with a snort, on the office-boy*). **8.** *v.i.* (Of otter or beaver) come to surface for breath. [partly f. F *vent* f. L *ventus* wind, partly f. F *évent* f. *éventer* expose to air f. OF *esventer* f. Rom. *EX¹(ventare* f. L *ventus* wind)]

vĕnt² *n.* slit made in garment, esp. in lower edge of back of coat. [ME, var. of *fent* f. OF *fente* slip f. Rom. *findita* fem. p.p. (as n.) f. L *findere* cleave]

vĕ′ntidŭct *n.* (Archit.) air-passage, esp. for ventilation. [f. L *ventus* wind + -I- + *ductus* DUCT]

vĕ′ntifăct *n.* stone shaped by wind-blown sand. [f. L *ventus* wind + -I- + *factum* neut. p.p. of *facere* make]

vĕ′ntil *n.* (Mus.) valve in wind instrument; shutter for regulating air-flow in organ. [G, f. It. *ventile*, f. med. L *ventile* sluice f. L *ventus* wind]

vĕ′ntil|āte *v.t.* cause air to circulate freely in (room etc.); purify by air, oxygenate, (blood); submit (question, subject, grievance, etc.) to public consideration and discussion; hence or cogn. ∼A′TION, ∼ātOR (esp., appliance or aperture for ventilating room, compartment, mine, etc.), *ns.*, ∼ātIVE *a.* [f. L *ventilare* blow, winnow (*ventus* wind) + -ATE³]

vĕ′ntral *a.* & *n.* (Anat. & Zool.) of or on the abdomen (opp. DORSAL); (Bot.) of the front or lower surface; ∼ (fin), either of the ventrally placed fins; hence ∼LY² *adv.* [f. *venter* abdomen f. L + -AL]

ventre à terre (vahntr ah tār′) *adv.* at full speed. [F, lit. with belly to ground]

vĕ′ntricle *n.* (Anat.) cavity in the body, hollow part of organ, esp. one of four in the brain or two in the heart; hence **vĕntrī′cŭlAR**¹ *a.* [ME, f. L *ventriculus* dim. of *venter* belly; see -CULE]

vĕ′ntricōse *a.* having a protruding belly; (Bot.) distended, inflated. [irreg. f. prec. + -OSE¹]

vĕntrī′loqu|ism *n.* act or art of speaking or uttering sounds in such a manner that the voice appears to come from some source other than the speaker; so ∼IST (1), ∼Y¹, *ns.*, **vĕntrilŏ′qui**AL, ∼i′stIC, ∼OUS, *adjs.*, ∼IZE (2) *v.i.* [ult. f. L *ventriloquus* ventriloquist (*venter* belly, *loqui* speak)]

vĕntrī′potent *a.* (literary). large-bellied; gluttonous. [F, f. med. L *ventripotens* (*venter*, POTENT)]

vĕ′nture *n.* & *v.* **1.** *n.* undertaking of a risk, risky undertaking, (*declined the venture; ready for any venture*); commercial speculation (*one lucky venture made his fortune*); (arch.) thing at stake, property risked; **at a** ∼, at random, without previous consideration; **V**∼ **Scout**, senior Scout. **2.** *v.i.* dare, not be afraid, (*did not venture to stop him; I venture to differ from you*); dare to go out. (*shall not venture out*); take risks; ∼ (**up**)**on**, dare to engage in, make, etc. **3.** *v.t.* dare to make or advance or put forward, hazard, (*would not venture an opinion, a guess, a step*); expose to risk, stake, (*will venture a small bet on it; venture nothing, nothing gain or have or win*). **4.** Hence **vĕ′ntur**ER¹ (-cher-) *n.*, (esp. Hist.) one who undertakes or shares in a trading venture, ∼SOME¹ (-chers-) *a.* [f. *aventure* = ADVENTURE¹,²]

vĕntūr′i *n.* short piece of tube between wider sections for measuring flow-rate or exerting suction. [f. G. B. Venturi, It. physicist d. 1822]

vĕ′nūe *n.* **1.** (Law). country etc. within which jury must be gathered and cause tried (orig. neighbourhood of crime etc.); **change the** ∼ (to avoid riot, prejudiced jury, etc.). **2.** appointed place of meeting

esp. for match etc., rendezvous. [F, = coming, fem. p.p. (as n.) of *venir* come f. L *venire*]

vĕ′nūle *n.* (Anat.) small vein adjoining capillaries. [f. L *venula* dim. of *vena* vein; see -ULE]

Vē′nus *n.* **1.** (Rom. Myth.) goddess of love. **2.** planet second from sun in solar system; hence **Vĕnŭ′s**IAN (-z-) *a.* & *n.* **3.** sexual love, amorous influences or desires. **4.** beautiful woman. **5.** ∼′s **comb**, = SHEPHERD'*s needle*; ∼(′s) **fly-trap**, herb *Dionaea muscipula*, with leaves that close on insects etc.; ∼'s **girdle**, ribbon-like ctenophore; ∼'s **slipper**, = LADY'*s slipper*. [OE, f. L *Venus Veneris*]

verā′cious (-shus) *a.* speaking, disposed to speak, the truth; (of statement etc.) true, not (meant to be) false; hence ∼LY² *adv.*, **verā′c**ITY *n.* [f. L *verax veracis* (*verus* true; see -ACIOUS)]

verā′nda, -dah (-*a*) *n.* open portico or gallery along side of house with roof supported on pillars. [f. Hindi *varandā* f. Port. *varanda*]

vĕ′ratrine (-īn, -ēn) *n.* poisonous compound from sabadilla etc. used esp. as local irritant in treatment of neuralgia and rheumatism. [f. F *vératrine* f. L *veratrum* hellebore; see -INE⁵]

vĕrb *n.* (Gram.) part of speech that predicates, word or phrase whose function is predication (e.g. italicized words in Time *flies*, Salt *is* good, You *surprise* me). [ME, f. OF *verbe* or f. L *verbum* word, verb]

vĕr′bal *a.* & *n.* **1.** *a.* of or concerned with words (*verbal distinctions, subtleties, critic(ism), accuracy*, INSPIRATION). **2.** oral, not written (*a verbal communication, contract; verbal evidence*). **3.** (of translation) literal, word for word. **4.** (Gram.) (of the nature of) a verb (*verbal inflexions*); ∼ **noun**, noun derived from verb and partly sharing its constructions (e.g. E nouns in -ING¹); ∼ **senses**, those of a corresponding verb. **5.** Hence ∼LY² *adv.* **6.** *n.* verbal noun; verbal statement, esp. one made to police. [ME f. F, or f. LL *verbalis* (as prec.; see -AL)]

vĕr′bal|ism *n.* minute attention to words, verbal criticism; (merely) verbal expression; so ∼IST (2) *n.*, ∼i′stIC *a.* [f. prec. + -ISM]

vĕr′baliz|e, -is|e (-īz), *v.* **1.** *v.t.* make (noun etc.) into a verb; express in words. **2.** *v.i.* be verbose. **3.** Hence ∼A′TION *n.* [f. F *verbaliser*, or f. VERBAL + -IZE]

verbā′tim *adv.* & *a.* in exactly the same words, word for word (*copied it verbatim; a verbatim reprint*). [ME f. med. L (adv.), f. L *verbum* word; cf. LITERATIM]

verbē′na *n.* plant of genus *Verbena*, vervain; **lemon** ∼, similar plant (*Lippia citriodora*) with lemon-scented leaves. [L, = sacred bough of olive etc., in med. L vervain]

vĕr′biage *n.* needless accumulation of words, verbosity. [F (obs. *verbeier* chatter f. *verbe* word; see VERB, -AGE)]

vĕr′bicide *n.* (joc) destruction of, or one who destroys, sense or value of a word. [f. as VERB + -I- + -CIDE]

verbō′se *a.* using or expressed in more words than are wanted, prolix; hence or cogn. ∼LY² (-slī) *adv.*, ∼NESS (-sn-), **verbo′s**ITY, *ns.* [[f. L *verbosus* (*verbum* word; see -OSE¹)]

verboten (ferbō′ten) *a.* forbidden, esp. by authority. [G]

vĕrb. să′p. *int.* expr. absence of need for further explicit statement. [abbr. of L *verbum sapienti sat est* a word is enough for the wise person]

vĕr′dant *a.* (Of grass etc.) green, fresh-coloured; (of field etc.) covered with green grass etc.; (of person) unsophisticated, raw, green; hence **vĕr′d**ANCY *n.*, ∼LY² *adv.* [perh. f. OF *verdeant* part. of *verdoier* be green f. L *viridiare* (*viridis* green)]

vĕrd-ănti′que (-ē′k) *n.* ornamental usu. green serpentine; green incrustation on ancient bronze; green porphyry. [obs. F, = antique green]

||**vĕr′derer** *n.* judicial officer of royal forests. [AF, earlier *verder*, OF *verdier* f. Gallo-Rom. *viridarius* f. L *viridis* green; see -ER²]

vĕr'dict n. **1.** decision of jury on issue of fact in civil or criminal cause (*brought in a verdict of not guilty, a verdict for the plaintiff*); **open** ~ (affirming commission of crime but not specifying criminal, or occurrence of violent death but not specifying cause); **partial** ~ (finding person guilty of part of the charge); **sealed** ~ (written, and delivered to clerk of court when court has adjourned during deliberation of jury); **special** ~ (stating facts as proved but leaving court to draw conclusion from them). **2.** decision, judgement, (*the verdict of the public was in his favour; does not dispute your verdict*). [ME f. AF *verdit*, OF *voirdit* (*voir, veir* true f. L *verus, dit* f. L DICTUM saying)]

vĕr'digris (-ĭs, -ēs) n. green crystallized substance formed on copper by action of acetic acid and used in medicine and as pigment etc.; green rust on copper or brass. [ME, f. OF *verte-gres, vert de Grece* green of Greece]

vĕr'diter n. basic copper carbonate as blue or green pigment. [f. OF *verd de terre* green of earth]

vĕr'dur|e (-dyer) n. greenness of vegetation, green vegetation, whence ~ED[2] (-dyerd), ~OUS, *adjs.*; (fig.) freshness. [ME f. OF (*verd* green f. L *viridis*; see -URE)]

Verey. Var of VERY[2].

vĕrge[1] n. **1.** extreme edge, brink, border, (usu. fig.; *drew near to the very verge of the stream; on the verge of 70, destruction, tears, betraying his secret*). **2.** grass edging of flower-bed, road, etc.; (Archit.) edge of tiles projecting over gable (~**-board,** = BARGE-BOARD). **3.** wand or rod carried before bishop, dean, etc., as emblem of office. **4.** (Hist.) area of jurisdiction of Lord High Steward. [ME f. OF, f. L *virga* rod]

vĕrge[2] v.i. incline downwards or in specified direction (*the now verging sun; verge towards old age, to a close*); ~ **on,** border on, approach closely, (*path verges on the edge of a precipice; a solemnity verging on the tragic*). [f. L *vergere* bend, incline]

vĕr'ger n. official in a church who shows persons to their seats etc.; ||officer who bears staff before bishop, (vice-)chancellor of university, etc.; hence ~SHIP n. [ME, f. AF *verger* (as VERGE[1]; see -ER[2]]

ver'glas (vār'glah) n. thin coating of ice or sleet. [F]

vĕri'dical a. truthful; (Psych., of visions etc.) coinciding with realities; hence ~LY[2] adv. [f. L *veridicus* (*verus* truc, *dicere* say) + -AL]

vĕ'riĕst. See VERY[1].

vĕ'ri|fy̆ v.t. establish the truth or correctness of by examination or demonstration (*must verify the statement, his figures; always verify your references*); (of event, action, etc.) bear out, make good, fulfil, (prediction, promise); (Law) append affidavit to (pleadings), support (statement) by testimony or proofs; hence or cogn. ~FICA'TION, ~fIER[1], ns., ~fIABLE a. [ME, f. OF *verifier* f. med. L *verificare* (*verus* true; see -FY)]

vĕ'rily adv. (arch.) really, truly, in very truth. [ME, f. VERY[1] + -LY[2], after OF & AF]

vĕrisimi'litūde n. appearance of being true, semblance of actuality, (*the verisimilitude of the tale; verisimilitude is not proof*); statement etc. that seems true; so **vĕrisi'milar[1]** a. [f. L *verisimilitudo* f. *verisimilis* probable (*veri* gen. of *verus* true, *similis* like); see -TUDE]

vĕr'ism n. realism in literature or art; so **vĕr'ist** (2) n. [f. L *verus* or It. *vero* true + -ISM]

vĕri'smō n. (*pl.* ~s). = prec. (esp. of opera). [It. (as prec.)]

vĕ'ritab|le a. real, rightly so called, (*a veritable boon*); hence ~LY[2] adv. [OF (as foll.; see -ABLE)]

vĕ'rity̆ n. truth (of statement etc.); true statement, esp. one of fundamental import; really existent thing; **of a** ~, (arch.) in truth, really. [ME, f. OF *ver(i)té* f. L *veritas -tatis* (*verus* true; see -ITY)]

vĕr'juice (-ōōs) n. acid liquor got from crab-apples, sour grapes, etc., and formerly used in cooking and medicine; (fig.) bitterness. [ME, f. OF *vertjus* (VERT[1] green, *jus* JUICE)]

verkrampte (ferkrǎ'mpte) a. (S. Afr.) regarded as relatively reactionary or unprogressive, esp. towards Blacks. [Afrik.]

verligte (ferli'χte) a. (S. Afr.) regarded as relatively progressive or enlightened, esp. towards Blacks. [Afrik.]

vĕr'meil (-māl, -mĭl) n. silver gilt; orange-red garnet; (poet.) vermilion. [ME f. OF; see VERMILION]

vĕr'mi- *comb. form.* worm, as; ~**cide,** drug that kills worms; ~**form,** worm-shaped (*vermiform* APPENDIX); ~**fuge,** (drug) that expels intestinal worms; ~**vorous** (-ĭ'v-), feeding on worms. [f. L *vermis* worm; see -I-]

vĕr'mian a. of worms, wormlike. [f. L *vermis* worm + -AN]

vĕrmicĕ'lli (-s-, -ch-) n. pasta made in long slender threads. [It., pl. of *vermicello* dim. of *verme* f. L *vermis* worm]

vermi'cŭlar a. like a worm in form or movements, vermiform; (Med.) of or caused by intestinal worms; marked with close wavy lines. [f. med. L *vermicularis* f. L *vermiculus* dim. of *vermis* worm; see -AR[1]]

vermi'cŭlate a. = prec. (usu. fig.); worm-eaten. [f. L *vermiculatus* p.p. of *vermiculari* be full of worms (as prec.; see -ATE[2])]

vermicŭlā'tion n. being eaten or infested by or converted into worms; vermicular marking; worm-eaten state. [f. L *vermiculatio* (as prec.; see -ATION)]

vermi'cŭlite n. hydrous silicate mineral usu. resulting from alteration of mica, and expandable into sponge by heating. [f. as VERMICULATE + -ITE[2] (2)]

vermi'lion (-yon) n., a., & v.t. **1.** n. cinnabar; brilliant red pigment made by grinding this or artificially. **2.** n. & a. (of) this colour. **3.** v.t. colour (as) with vermilion. [ME, f. OF *vermeillon* (*vermeil* f. L *vermiculus* dim. of *vermis* worm; see -OON)]

vĕr'min n. (usu. treated as *pl.*) mammals and birds injurious to game, crops, etc., e.g. foxes, weasels, rats, mice, moles, owls; noxious insects, e.g. fleas, bugs, lice; parasitic worms or insects; (fig.) vile persons, so ~OUS a. [ME f. OF *vermin, -ine* f. Rom. *verminum, -ina* collect. f. L *vermis* worm]

vĕr'min|āte v.i. breed vermin, become infested with parasites; so ~A'TION n. [f. L *verminare* (*vermis* worm) + -ATE[3]]

vĕr'mouth (-ōōth, -uth) n. white wine flavoured with wormwood or other aromatic herbs; **French, Italian,** ~, dry, sweet, kind. [f. F *vermout* f. G *wermut* WORMWOOD]

verna'cŭlar a. & n. **1.** a. (Of language, idiom, word) of one's native country, native, indigenous, not of foreign origin or of learned formation; ~ **architecture** (concerned with ordinary buildings, not cathedrals etc.). **2.** n. the language or dialect of the country (*Latin gave place to the vernacular*); language of a particular class or group; homely speech. **3.** Hence ~ISM (4), ~ITY (-ă'r-), ns., ~IZE (3) v.t., ~LY[2] adv. [f. L *vernaculus* domestic, native (*verna* home-born slave) + -AR[1]]

vĕr'nal a. of or like, appearing or occurring or done in, appropriate to, spring, (*vernal breezes, flowers,* EQUINOX, *migration, fancies*); ~ **grass,** sweet-scented Eur. grass grown for hay; hence ~LY[2] adv. [f. L *vernalis* (*vernus* f. *ver* spring; see -AL)]

vĕrnalizā'tion n. cooling of seed before planting, in order to accelerate flowering; hence **vĕr'nal**IZE (1) v.t. [(transl. of Russ. *yarovizatsiya*) f. prec. + -IZE + -ATION]

verna'tion n. (Bot.) arrangement of leaves in leaf-bud (cf. AESTIVATION). [f. mod. L *vernatio* f. L *vernare* bloom (as VERNAL; see -ATION)]

Vĕr'ner n. ~**'s law** (relating to voicing of orig. fricatives in Germanic languages, giving e.g. *sodden* as p.p. of *seethe*). [f. K.A. ~, Da. philologist d. 1896]

vĕr'nicle n. = VERONICA 2. [ME f. OF, earlier *ver(o)nique* f. med. L VERONICA]

vĕr'nier n. small movable graduated scale for obtaining fractional parts of the subdivisions on fixed scale of barometer, sextant, etc.; ∼ **engine,** auxiliary engine for slight changes in motion of space rocket etc. [f. P. *Vernier*, Fr. mathematician d. 1637]

ve′ronal *n.* sedative drug, derivative of barbituric acid. [G, f. *Verona* in Italy]

verŏ′nica *n.* **1.** plant of genus *Veronica* or *Hebe*; speedwell. **2.** cloth with representation of Christ's face, esp. one miraculously so impressed after being used by St. Veronica to wipe sweat from Christ's face as he went to Calvary; any similar picture of Christ's face. **3.** matador's movement of cape away from charging bull. [med. L, f. woman's Christian name *Veronica*]

verru′c|a (-rōō′-) *n.* (*pl.* ∼ae *pr.* -sē). (Path., Zool., & Bot.) wart, wartlike elevation; so **ve′rruc**OSE[1], **ve′rruc**OUS, (-rōō-) *adjs.* [L]

ver′sant *n.* extent of land sloping in one direction; general slope of land. [F (*verser* f. L *versare* frequent. of *vertere* vers- turn; see -ANT)]

ver′satile *a.* turning easily or readily from one subject or occupation to another, capable of dealing with many subjects, having many uses, (*versatile author, mind, material*); (Bot. & Zool.) moving freely about or up and down on a support (*versatile anther, antennae*); changeable, inconstant; hence or cogn. ∼LY[2] (-l-lī) *adv.*, **versati′lity** *n.* [F, or f. L *versatilis* (as prec.; see -IL)]

vers de société (vār de sōsĭātā′) *n.* light witty topical verse. [F]

vĕrse *n.* & *v.* **1.** *n.* metrical line in accordance with rules of prosody (*quoted some verses of the Iliad*; CAP[2] *verses*); group of definite number of such lines, stanza with or without refrain; metrical composition in general, particular type of this, (*wrote pages of verse*; *expressed in indifferent verse*; *what is not prose is verse*; *a prize for Latin verse*). **2.** each of the short divisions of chapter in Bible (CHAPTER *and verse*); versicle; solo part of anthem etc. **3.** Hence ∼′LET (-sl-) *n.* **4.** *v.t.* express in verse. **5.** *v.i.* compose verses. [OE *fers* (OHG, ON *vers*) f. L *versus* (*vertere vers-* turn) turn of plough, furrow, line (of writing); in ME reinforced by OF *vers* f. L *versus*]

vĕrsed[1] (-st) *a.* experienced, practised, skilled, proficient, (*in* subject, occupation, etc.). [f. F *versé* or f. L *versatus* p.p. of *versari* be engaged in (as VERSANT; see -ED[1])]

vĕrsed[2] (-st) *a.* reversed (*versed* SINE). [f. mod. L (*sinus*) *versus* turned (sine) f. as VERSE]

vĕr′set *n.* (Mus.) short prelude or interlude for organ. [F, dim. of *vers* VERSE; see -ET[1]]

vĕr′sicle *n.* short sentence, esp. of each series of short sentences in liturgy said or sung alternately by minister or priest (opp. *response*) and people. [ME, f. OF *versicule* or f. L *versiculus* dim. of *versus* (see VERSE, -CULE)]

vĕr′sicoloured (-kŭlerd) *a.* variegated; changing from one colour to another in different lights. [f. L *versicolor* (*versus* p.p. of *vertere* turn, *color* colour)]

versi′cular *a.* of (esp. Biblical) verses or versicles. [f. L (AS VERSICLE) +-AR]

vĕr′si|fy *v.* **1.** *v.t.* turn (prose) into verse; express in verse. **2.** *v.i.* compose verses. **3.** So ∼FICA′TION, ∼fIER[1], *ns.* [ME, f. OF *versifier* f. L *versificare* (as VERSE; see -FY)]

vĕr′sīn(e) *n.* = *versed* SINE. [f. VERSED[2] *sine*]

vĕr′sion (-shon) *n.* **1.** book etc. when put into another language or form; AUTHORIZED, REVISED (*∗Standard*), *Version*. **2.** piece of translation, esp. into foreign language, as school exercise. **3.** account of a matter from particular person's point of view (*now let me have your own version of the affair*); special form or variant of a thing, e.g. as performed, adapted, etc. **4.** (Obstet.) turning of foetus in womb to improve presentation. **5.** Hence ∼AL *a.* [F, or f. med. L *versio* f. L *vertere* vers-turn; see -ION]

vers libre (vār lē′br) *n.* verse composition in which different metres are mingled, or prosodic restrictions disregarded, or variable rhythm substituted for

definite metre; hence **versli′br**IST (vārlē′) *n.*, writer of *vers libre*. [F, = free verse]

vĕr′sŏ *n.* (*pl.* ∼s). left-hand page of open book; back of leaf (opp. RECTO); reverse of coin. [f. L *verso* (*folio*) = turned (leaf), abl. p.p. as VERSE]

vĕrst *n.* Russian measure of length, about ⅔ mile. [f. Russ. *versta*]

vĕr′sus *prep.* (esp. Law & Sport, abbr. *v.* or *vs.*) against (*Rex versus Crippen*; *Surrey v. Kent*). [L, = towards, in med. L against]

vĕrt *n.* & *a.* **1.** *n.* (Law, Hist.) all that bears green leaves in forest; right to cut this. **2.** *n.,* & *a.* (usu. placed after *n.*) (Her.) green. [ME f. OF, f. L *viridis* green]

vĕr′tebr|a *n.* (*pl.* ∼ae). each segment of backbone; (in *pl.*) backbone; so ∼AL *a.* [L (*vertere* turn)]

vĕr′tebrate (-at, -āt) *a.* & *n.* (animal) having spinal column or notochord, esp. (member) of the (sub)phylum Vertebrata, including mammals, birds, reptiles, amphibians, and fishes. [f. L *vertebratus* jointed (as prec.; see -ATE[2])]

vĕrtebrā′tion *n.* division into vertebrae or similar segments; (fig.) firmness. [f. VERTEBRA +-ATION]

vĕr′t|ex *n.* (*pl.* ∼ices *pr.* -ĭsēz, *or* ∼exes). **1.** highest point, top, apex; (Anat.) crown of head. **2.** (Geom.) each angular point of triangle, polygon, etc.; point at which axis meets curve or surface; meeting-point of lines that form an angle. [L, *vertex* -*ticis* whirlpool, crown of head, vertex (*vertere* turn)]

vĕr′tical *a.* & *n.* **1.** *a.* of or at the vertex or highest point; at, or passing through, the zenith; perpendicular to plane of horizon; in direction from top to bottom of picture etc.; (Anat.) of the crown of the head; combining all stages in hierarchy (sense 3), or in production of a class of goods (*vertical* INTEGRA-TION); ∼ **angles,** each pair of opposite angles made by two intersecting lines; ∼ **fin** (dorsal, anal, or caudal); ∼ **plane** (perpendicular to the horizon); ∼ **take-off** of aircraft (directly upwards); hence ∼ITY (-ă′l-) *n.,* ∼LY[2] *adv.* **2.** *n.* vertical line, plane, or circle; **out of the** ∼, not vertical. [F, or f. LL *verticalis* (as prec.; see -AL)]

vĕr′ticil *n.* (Bot. & Zool.) whorl, set of parts arranged in circle round axis; hence **verti′cill**ATE[2] *a.* [f. L *verticillus* whorl of spindle, dim. of VERTEX]

vertigŏ (vĕr′tĭ-, vertĭ′-) *n.* (*pl.* ∼s). giddiness, dizziness; condition with sensation of whirling and tendency to lose balance; so **verti′gin**OUS *a.* [L *vertigo -ginis* whirling (*vertere* turn)]

vertu. See VIRTU.

vĕr′vain *n.* herbaceous plant of genus *Verbena*, esp. one with small blue, white, or purple flowers, formerly believed to have various virtues and used as amulet etc. [ME, f. OF *verveine* f. L VERBENA]

verve (vĕrv, vārv) *n.* enthusiasm, energy, vigour, esp. in artistic or literary work. [F, earlier = form of expression, f. L *verba* words]

vĕr′vĕt *n.* small greyish Afr. monkey. [F]

vĕ′rў *a.* & *adv.* **1.** *attrib. a.* (arch.) real, true, genuine, that is such in the truest or fullest sense, (*very God of very God*; *the veriest simpleton knows that*; *in very truth*; *must consent from very shame*). **2. the, this, that, his,** etc., ∼ (emphasizing identity, coincidence, significance, or extreme degree; *this is the very spot where I found it*; *the very SAME*; *those were his very words*; *speaking in this very room*; *did it that very day*; *the very fact of his presence is enough*; *you are the very man I am looking for*; *a needle is the very thing* (*for our purpose*); *come here this very minute*; *grieves me to the very heart*; *the very stones cry out*; *at the very edge of the cliff*; *a very little more will do*; *give me only a very little*). **3.** *adv.* (w. superl. *adjs.* or *own*). in the fullest sense (*drink it to the very last drop*; *the very last thing I expected*; *did the very best I could*; *did my very utmost*; *may keep it for your very own*). **4.** (w. *adjs.,* adjectival participles, & *advs.*) in a high degree (*that is very easy*, *very annoying*, *very easily done*; *a very trying time*; *very often fails*; *find very few instances*; *gives very little trouble*; *Very*

REVEREND; *very much better*; *very much annoyed*); **not** ∼, (1) in a low degree, (2) far from being; *not so*[1] *very;* ∼ **high frequency** (in range 30 to 300 megahertz); ∼ **good,** ∼ **well,** (formula of consent or approval). [ME, f. OF *verai* f. Gallo-Rom. *veraius f. L *verus* true]

Verÿ[2] (vĕ'rĭ, vēr'ĭ) *n.* ∼ **light,** coloured flare projected from ∼ **pistol** for signalling or temporarily illuminating part of battlefield etc. [f. E. W. ∼, Amer. inventor d. 1910]

vĕsī'ca *n.* **1.** (Anat. & Zool.) bladder, esp. urinary bladder. **2.** ∼ (**piscis** or **piscium** = fish's or fishes'), pointed oval used as aureole in medieval sculpture and painting. **3.** Hence **vĕ'sicAL** *a.* [L]

vĕ'sic͞āte *v.t.* raise blisters on; hence ∼ANT, ∼ātORY, *adjs.* & *ns.,* ∼A'TION *n.* [f. LL *vesicare* (as prec.) +-ATE[3]]

vĕ'sicle *n.* (Anat., Zool., Bot., & Geol.) small bladder, cell, bubble, or hollow structure; (Bot.) blister; so **vĕsī'cŭlAR**[1], **vĕsī'cŭlATE**[2], *adjs.,* **vĕsĭcŭlA'TION** *n.* [f. F *vésicule* or f. L *vesicula* dim. of VESICA; see -ULE]

vĕ'sper *n.* **1.** (*V*∼). Venus as evening star; (poet.) evening. **2.** (Eccl., in *pl.*) (office of) sixth of the canonical hours of prayer; evensong; ∼(-**bell**), bell that calls to vespers. [f. L *vesper* evening (star), or f. OF *vespres* f. eccl. L *vesperas* f. L *vespera* evening]

vĕ'spertine *a.* of or occurring in the evening; (Bot., of flower) opening, (Zool.) flying, in the evening; (Astron.) setting near the time of sunset. [f. L *vespertinus* (VESPER; 3CC -INE[1])]

vĕ'spiary *n.* nest of wasps. [irreg. f. L *vespa* wasp, after *apiary*]

vĕ'spine *a.* of wasps. [f. L *vespa* wasp +-INE[1]]

vĕ'ssel *n.* **1.** hollow receptacle esp. for liquid, e.g. cask, cup, pot, bottle, dish. **2.** ship, boat, esp. large one. **3.** (Anat.) duct, canal, holding or conveying blood or other fluid, esp. BLOOD[1]*-vessel*; (Bot.) woody duct carrying or containing sap etc. **4.** (Bibl., or allus. esp. joc.). person viewed as recipient or exponent of a quality; **weak** ∼, unreliable person; **weaker** ∼, woman (1 Pet. 3:7); *vessels of* WRATH. **5.** Hence ∼FUL 2 *n.* [ME, f. AF *vessel(e)*, OF *vaissel(le)* f. LL *vascellum,* (pl.) *-ella,* dim. of VAS]

vĕst[1] *n.* **1.** (‖Commerc.) waistcoat. **2.** ‖knitted or woven undergarment worn on upper part or whole of trunk. **3.** piece, usu. V-shaped, on front of body of woman's dress, esp. to fill opening at neck. **4.** (arch.) clothing, dress. **5.** ∼-**pocket,** of a size suitable for the (waistcoat-)pocket, very small. [f. F f. It. *veste* f. L *vestis* garment]

vĕst[2] *v.* **1.** *v.t.* (esp. in *pass.*) furnish (person *with* authority, powers, property, etc.); ∼ (property, power) **in** (person), confer formally on him an immediate fixed right of present or future possession of; ∼**ed interests, rights,** etc., (possession of which is established in a person by right or by long association and usu. gives rise to expectation of gain). **2.** (poet.) clothe. **3.** *v.i.* ∼ **in,** (of property, right, etc.) come into the possession of (person); ∼'**ing day** (on which this takes place). [ME, orig. p.p.f. OF *vestu* (*vestir* f. L *vestire -it-* clothe, as prec.)]

vĕ'sta *n.* short wooden or (**wax** ∼) wax match. [f. *Vesta,* Rom. goddess of hearth and household, L = Gk *Hestia*]

vĕ'stal *a.* & *n.* of the Roman goddess Vesta or the vestal virgins; ∼ (**virgin**), virgin consecrated to Vesta, vowed to chastity, who shared charge of sacred fire perpetually burning on the altar, (fig.) chaste woman, esp. nun. [ME, f. L *vestalis* a. & n. (as prec.; see -AL)]

vĕstee' *n.* = VEST[1] 3. [f. VEST[1] +-EE]

vĕ'stiary *n.* & *a.* **1.** *n.* vestry, robing-room, or cloakroom. **2.** *a.* relating to clothes or dress. [ME, f. OF *vestiarie, vestiaire;* see VESTRY]

vĕ'stibŭle *n.* **1.** antechamber, hall, lobby, next to outer door of house and from which more rooms are reached by door(s); porch of church etc. **2.** *enclosed entrance to railway-carriage; ∼ **train** (with corri-

dor). **3.** (Anat.) chamber or channel communicating with others; part of mouth outside teeth; central cavity of labyrinth of inner ear. **4.** *∼ **school** (for training new industrial employees). **5.** Hence **vĕstī'-bŭlAR**[1] *a.* [F, or f. L *vestibulum* entrance-court]

vĕ'stige *n.* trace, evidence, sign, (*vestiges of an earlier civilization; found no vestiges of his presence*); slightest amount, particle, (*without a vestige of clothing; has not a vestige of evidence for this assertion*); (Biol.) part or organ now degenerate and of little or no utility but well developed in ancestors; hence **vĕstī'gIAL** *a.* (esp. Biol.). [F, f. L *vestigium* footprint]

vĕ'stiture *n.* investiture; clothing; (Zool.) hair, scales, etc., covering a surface. [ME, f. med. L *vestitura* f. L *vestire* (see VEST[2], -URE)]

vĕ'stment *n.* garment, esp. official or state robe; any of the official garments of clergy, choristers, etc., worn during divine service, esp. chasuble. [ME, f. OF *vestiment, vestement* f. L *vestimentum* (as VEST[2]; see -MENT)]

vĕ'stry *n.* **1.** room or building attached to church and in which vestments are kept and put on. **2.** ‖(Hist.) meeting of parishioners usu. in vestry for parochial business; body of parishioners meeting thus; ∼-**clerk,** officer chosen by vestry to keep parish accounts etc.; ∼**man,** member of a vestry; hence **ve'strAL** *a.* [ME, f. AF **vest(e)rie* alt. of OF *vestiarie, vestiaire,* f. L *vestiarium* (as VEST[1]; see -ARIUM, -ERY)]

vĕ'sture *n.,* & *v.t.* (poet. or rhet.) **1.** *n.* garments, dress, clothes; covering. **2.** *v.t.* clothe. [ME f. OF, f. med. L *vest(it)ura* (as VEST[2]; see -URE)]

vĕt[1] *n.,* & *v.t.* (-**tt**-). (colloq.) **1.** veterinary surgeon. **2.** *v.t.* examine and pass fit, treat, (animal); (fig.) make careful examination of (scheme, work, candidate, etc.). [abbr.]

*vĕt[2] *n.* (colloq.) veteran. [abbr.]

vĕtch *n.* plant of pea family esp. of genus *Vicia,* largely used, wild or cultivated, for forage; **common** ∼, tare; **kidney**-∼, perennial herb (*Anthyllis vulneraria*) with red or yellow flowers; hence ∼'y[5] *a.* [ME, f. AF & ONF *veche* f. L *vicia*]

vĕ'tchling *n.* plant of genus *Lathyrus,* allied to vetch. [f. prec. +-LING[1]]

vĕ'teran *n.* & *a.* **1.** *n.* person who has grown old in or had long experience of (esp. military) service or occupation (*a veteran of two world wars; a veteran golfer*); *ex-service man (*V∼s' **Day,** usu. 4th Mon. in Oct.). **2.** *a.* of a veteran; composed of veterans; [∼ **car** (made before 1916, or before 1905). [f. F *vétéran* or f. L *veteranus* a. & n. (*vetus -eris* old; see -AN)]

vĕterinār'ian *n.* veterinary surgeon. [f. L *veterinarius* (as foll.) +-AN]

vĕ'terinarÿ *a.* & *n.* **1.** *a.* of or for (treatment of) diseases and injuries of farm and domestic animals; ∼ **surgeon,** one skilled in such treatment. **2.** *n.* veterinary surgeon. [f. L *veterinarius* (*veterinae* cattle)]

vĕ'tiver *n.* = CUSCUS[1]. [f. F *vétiver* f. Tamil *veṭṭivēru* (*vēr* root)]

vē'tō *n.* (*pl.* ∼es), & *v.t.* **1.** *n.* constitutional right of sovereign, president, governor, upper house of legislature, etc., to reject a legislative enactment (*POCKET[1] *veto;* **suspensive** ∼, one suspending but not necessarily preventing completion of measure); right of permanent member of UN Security Council to reject a resolution; (official message conveying) such rejection; prohibition (*put a or his veto on the proposal*). **2.** *v.t.* exercise veto against (bill etc.); forbid authoritatively. [L, = I forbid, w. ref. to its use by Roman tribunes of the people in opposing Senate's measures]

vĕx *v.t.* anger by slight or petty annoyance, irritate, (*this would vex a saint; how vexing!*); (arch.) grieve, afflict; (poet. or rhet.) put (sea etc.) into state of commotion; **a** ∼**ed** (difficult and much discussed) **question.** [ME, f. OF *vexer* f. L *vexare* shake, disturb]

vĕxā'tion *n.* vexing, being vexed; harassing by means of malicious or trivial litigation; state of irritation or distress; annoying or distressing thing (*subjected to many vexations*). [ME f. OF, or f. L *vexatio -onis* (as prec.; see -ATION)]

vĕxā'tious (-shŭs) *a.* causing or tending to cause vexation; (Law) not having sufficient grounds for action and seeking only to annoy defendant; hence ∼LY² *adv.*, ∼NESS *n.* [f. prec. + -OUS]

vĕxillŏ'logy̆ *n.* study of flags. [f. as foll. + -O- + -LOGY]

vĕxi'll|um *n.* (*pl.* ∼a). (Rom. Ant.) military standard esp. of maniple, body of troops under this; (Bot.) large upper petal of papilionaceous flower; vane of a feather; (Eccl.) flag on or wound round bishop's staff, processional banner or cross. [L (*vehere vect-* carry)]

VG *abbr.* very good; Vicar-General.

VHF *abbr.* very̆ high frequency.

*VI *abbr.* Virgin Islands.

vī'a *prep.* by way of, through, (*from Exeter to York via London; sent it via his secretary*). [L, abl. of *via* way, road]

vī'able *a.* (Of foetus or new-born child) capable of maintaining life; (of plant, animal, etc.) able to live or exist in particular climate etc.; (of seed) able to germinate; (of plan etc.) feasible, practicable esp. from economic standpoint; so **vīABI'LITY** *n.*, **vī'ABLY** *adv.* [F (*vie* life f. L *vita*; see -ABLE)]

vī'adŭct *n.* long bridgelike structure, esp. series of arches, for carrying road or railway over valley or dip in ground; such road or railway. [f. L *via* way, after *aqueduct*]

vī'al *n.* small (usu. cylindrical glass) vessel for holding liquid medicines etc.; **pour out** ∼s **of wrath**, take vengeance (Rev. 16:1), (colloq.) give vent to anger; hence ∼FUL (2) *n.* [ME, var. of *fiole* etc.; see PHIAL]

via media (vīa mē'dĭa, vēa mē'dĭa) *n.* middle way or course between extremes. [L]

vī'and *n.* (formal; usu. in *pl.*) article(s) of food, victual(s). [ME, f. OF *viande* food f. Rom. **vi(v)anda* for L *vivenda*, neut. pl. gerundive of *vivere* live]

viā'tic|um *n.* (*pl.* ∼a). provisions or official allowance of money for journey; Eucharist as given to person (in danger of) dying. [L, neut. (as n.) of *viaticus* (*via* road; see -ATIC)]

vī'bes (-bz) *n. pl.* (colloq.) vibraphone; vibrations. [abbr.]

vī'brā'cŭl|um *n.* (*pl.* ∼a). whiplike appendage of bryozoans, serving to bring food within reach by lashing movements; hence ∼AR¹ *a.* [mod. L (as VIBRATE; see -CULE)]

vī'brant *a.* vibrating; thrilling *with* (action etc.); responding readily to emotions etc.; (of sound) resonant. [f. L *vibrare* (see VIBRATE, -ANT)]

vī'braphōn|e *n.* percussion instrument of metal bars with motor-driven resonators and metal tubes giving vibrato effect; hence ∼IST (3) *n.* [f. VIBRATO + -PHONE]

vī'brā'te *v.* **1.** *v.i.* & *t.* move to and fro like pendulum, (cause to) oscillate. **2.** *v.i.* (Of sound) throb (*on ear, in memory,* etc.); (Phys.) move unceasingly to and fro, esp. rapidly; thrill, quiver, (*with* passion etc.). **3.** *v.t.* (Of pendulum) measure (seconds etc.) by vibrating. **4.** Hence **vī'bratIVE, vī'bratORY, adjs.** [f. L *vibrare* shake, swing + -ATE³]

vī'bratile *a.* capable of vibrating; (of cilia etc.) used in vibratory motion. [f. VIBRATORY (see prec.) after *pulsatile* etc.]

vī'brā'tion *n.* vibrating, oscillation; (Phys.) (rapid) motion to and fro esp. of the parts of a fluid or an elastic solid whose equilibrium has been disturbed or of electromagnetic wave; (in *pl.*) mental (esp. occult) influence; hence ∼AL *a.* [f. L *vibratio* (as VIBRATE; see -ATION)]

vī'brā'tō (-ah'-) *n.* (*pl.* ∼s). (Mus.) tremulous effect in singing or of playing stringed or wind instrument by rapid slight variation of pitch; cf. TREMOLO. [It., p.p. of *vibrare* VIBRATE]

vī'brā'tor *n.* person or thing that vibrates; (Mus.) reed in reed-organ; (Med.) electric or other instrument used in massage. [f. VIBRATE + -OR]

vī'brī'ssae *n. pl.* stiff coarse hairs near mouth of most mammals (e.g. cat's whiskers) and in human nostril; bristle-like feathers near mouth of insectivorous birds. [L (as VIBRATE)]

vī'bŭr'num *n.* shrub of genus *Viburnum* w. usu. white flowers, e.g. guelder rose and wayfaring-tree. [L, = wayfaring-tree]

Vic. *abbr.* Victoria.

vī'car *n.* **1.** (In Ch. of England) incumbent of parish where tithes formerly belonged to chapter or religious house or layman (cf. RECTOR); Episcopal clergyman deputizing for another. **2.** ∼ **of Bray,** systematic turncoat [w. ref. to 18th-c. song]; **lay** ∼, cathedral officer singing some parts of service; ||∼ **choral,** clerical or lay assistant in some (esp. musical) parts of cathedral service; ∼**-general,** Anglican official assisting (arch) bishop in ecclesiastical causes etc., RC bishop's assistant in matters of jurisdiction etc.; **cardinal** ∼, Pope's delegate acting as bishop of diocese of Rome; ∼ **apostolic,** RC missionary or titular bishop; ∼ **forane** (fōrā'n) [= FOREIGN], dignitary appointed by RC bishop to exercise limited local jurisdiction; V∼ **of (Jesus) Christ,** the Pope. **3.** Hence **vicār'iATE¹** (1), ∼**SHIP,** *ns.* [ME, f. AF *viker(e)*, OF *vicaire* f. L *vicarius* substitute f. *vicis* (see VICE⁴, -ARY¹)]

vī'carage *n.* benefice or residence of vicar. [ME, f. prec. + -AGE]

vicār'ial *a.* of, or serving as, a vicar. [f. VICAR + -IAL]

vicār'ious *a.* deputed, delegated, (*vicarious authority*); acting or done for another (*vicarious work*); ∼ **suffering** esp. of Christ in place of sinner); experienced imaginatively through another person (*vicarious pleasure*); hence ∼LY² *adv.*, ∼NESS *n.* [f. L *vicarius* (see VICAR, -IOUS)]

vīce¹ *n.* **1.** evil (esp. grossly immoral) habit or conduct, (particular form of) depravity, serious fault, (*has the vice of gluttony; drunkenness is not among his vices; vice is duly punished and virtue rewarded in fifth act*); **has no redeeming** ∼ (to relieve overpowering rectitude). **2.** defect, blemish, (*of* character, literary style, etc.); fault(s) or bad habit(s) in horse etc.; ∼ **squad,** police department enforcing laws against prostitution etc. **3.** (Hist.) character in a morality play representing a vice. [ME f. OF, f. L *vitium*]

||vīce², *vīse, *n.,* & *v.t.* **1.** *n.* instrument with two jaws between which thing may be gripped usu. by operation of screw so as to leave the hands free for working upon it, esp. attached to carpenter's or metal-worker's bench; hence ∼**LIKE** (-sl-) *a.* **2.** *v.t.* secure (material to be worked upon, or fig.) in vice. [ME, = winding stair, screw, f. OF *vis* f. L *vitis* vine]

vīce³ *n.* (colloq.) = VICE-*president* etc. [abbr.]

vīce⁴ (vī'sĭ, vīs) *prep.* in the place of, in succession to, (*gazetted as captain vice Captain Jones promoted*). [L, abl. of **vix vicis* change]

vice- *pref.* forming *ns.* w. sense 'person acting or qualified to act in place of, or next in rank to', and derivs. of these, as: ∼**a'dmiral,** ADMIRAL of third grade; ∼**a'dmiralty,** office of vice-admiral (||∼**-admiralty courts,** tribunals with admiralty jurisdiction in British colonial possessions); *vice-chair'man*(*ship*); ||∼**-cha'mberlain** (esp. deputy of Lord Chamberlain); ∼**-cha'ncellor,** deputy chancellor (esp. of university, discharging most of the administrative duties); *vice-cha'ncellorship; vice-co'mmodore; vice-co'nsul*(*ship*); *vice-co'nsulate; vice-go'vernor;* ∼**-ki'ng,** = VICEROY; *vice-ma'ster;* ∼**-pre'sident**(*ship*), *-pre'sidency, -preside'ntial; vice-pri'ncipal;* ∼**-quee'n,** = VICEREINE; *vice-re'gent; vice-she'riff; vice-war'den.* [f. prec.]

vīceger|ent (-sjē'r-, -sjē') *a.* & *n.* (person) exercising delegated power, deputy, (*of* God, king, etc.); hence ∼ENCY *n.* [f. med. L *vicegerens* (as VICE⁴ + L *gerere* carry on; see -ENT)]

vīce'nnial *a.* lasting, occurring every, twenty years. [f. LL *vicennium* period of 20 years (*vicies* 20 times f. *viginti* 20, *annus* year) + -AL]

vi′cereine (-srān) *n.* viceroy's wife; woman viceroy. [F (as VICE-, *reine* queen)]

vi′ceroy (-sr-) *n.* ruler exercising authority on behalf of sovereign in colony, province, etc.; hence **vīce-re′g**AL, **viceroy′**AL, *adjs.*, **viceroy′al**TY[1], ∼SHIP, *ns.*, (-ST-). [F (as VICE-, *roy* king)]

vīce′simal *a.* vigesimal. [f. L *vicesimus* twentieth +-AL]

vice ver′sa *adv.* with the order of terms changed, the other way round: *the man blames his wife and* ∼ (she him); *the cat stole the dog's dinner and* ∼ (he hers); *calls black white and* ∼ (white black). [L, = the position being reversed (as VICE[4], *versa* abl. fem. p.p. of *vertere* turn)]

Vi′chy (vē′shē) *n.* ∼ (**water**), effervescent mineral water from Vichy freq. bottled. [∼ in central France]

vichyssoi′se (-shīswah′z) *n.* creamy soup of leeks and potatoes, served chilled. [f. F *vichyssois -oise* of Vichy (cf. prec.)]

vi′cinage *n.* neighbourhood, surrounding district; relation of neighbours. [ME, f. OF *vis(e)nage* f. Gallo--Rom. *vecinatus* (*vecinus* for L *vicinus* neighbour)]

vicinal (vī′sī-, -sī′-) *a.* neighbouring, adjacent; of a neighbourhood, local. [F, or f. L *vicinalis* (*vicinus* neighbour; see -AL)]

vici′nity *n.* surrounding district; nearness in place (*to*); close relationship (*to*); **in the** ∼ (**of**), near. [f. L *vicinitas* (as prec.; see -ITY)]

vi′cious (-shŭs) *a.* **1.** of the nature of vice, morally evil or injurious, (*vicious tendencies, habits, life*); addicted to vice (*vicious companions*); (of horse etc.) having vices. **2.** (Of language, document, reasoning, etc.) incorrect, faulty, unsound, corrupt, (*vicious* CIRCLE[1]; so ∼ **spiral**, continual interaction causing e.g. steady increases of both prices and wages). **3.** bad-tempered, spiteful, (*vicious dog, mood, remarks*); violent, severe, (*vicious attack, weather*). **4.** Hence ∼LY[2] *adv.*, ∼NESS *n.* [ME f. OF, or f. L *vitiosus* (as VICE[1]; see -OUS)]

vici′ssi|tūde *n.* change of circumstances esp. of fortune; (arch. or poet.) regular change, alternation; hence ∼tū′di**n**ous *a.* [F, or f. L *vicissitudo -dinis* f. *vicissim* by turns (as VICE[4]; see -TUDE)]

vi′ctim *n.* living creature sacrificed to a deity or in performance of religious rite; person or thing injured or destroyed in seeking to attain an object, in gratification of a passion etc., or as result of event or circumstance, (*the victims of his relentless ambition; fell a victim to his own avarice; the victims of disease, of a railway accident, of an earthquake*); prey, dupe, (*the numerous victims of the confidence trick*). [f. L *victima*]

vi′ctimiz|e, -īs|e (-īz), *v.t.* make (person etc.) a victim; cheat (person); make (striker etc.) suffer by dismissal or other exceptional treatment; hence ∼A′TION *n.* [f. prec. +-IZE]

vi′ctor *n.* (rhet.) conqueror in battle or contest; ∼ **ludor′um**, most successful competitor in school etc. sports; so **vi′ctr**ESS[1] *n.* [ME, f. AF *victo(u)r* or f. L *victor* (*vincere vict-* conquer; see -OR)]

victor′ia *n.* **1.** low light four-wheeled carriage with seat for two and raised driver's seat and with collapsible top. **2.** gigantic S. Amer. water-lily of genus *Victoria*. **3.** species of crowned pigeon; variety of domestic pigeon. **4.** large red luscious variety of plum. **5.** V∼ **Cross**, decoration awarded to members of the Commonwealth armed services for conspicuous act of bravery, founded by Queen Victoria in 1856. [f. Queen *Victoria* of England d. 1901]

Victor′ian *a. & n.* of, (person, esp. author) living in, characteristic of, the reign of Queen Victoria (1837–1901); ||**Royal** ∼ **Chain** (order founded by Edward VII in 1902 and conferred by sovereign on special occasions); ||**Royal** ∼ **Order** (founded by Queen Victoria in 1896 and conferred usu. for service rendered to sovereign); so **Victōri**A′NA *n. pl.* [f. as prec. +-AN]

victōr′ious *a.* conquering, triumphant; marked by victory (*victorious day*); hence ∼LY[2] *adv.*, ∼NESS *n.* [ME f. AF; OF *victorieux*, f. L *victoriosus* (as foll.; see -OUS)]

vi′ctory *n.* defeating one's enemy in battle or war or one's opponent in contest (lit. or fig.; *battle ended in a decisive victory for him; fought hard for victory; hero of many victories; gained a* ∼ *for the victory over his passions*); Cadmean or PYRRHIC[2], MORAL, *victory*. [ME, f. AF *victorie*, OF *victoire*, f. L *victoria* (as VICTOR; see -Y[1])]

vi′ctual (vī′tal) *n. & v.* (||-ll-). (formal). **1.** *n.* (usu. in *pl.*) food, provisions, esp. as prepared for use; hence ∼LESS (-l-l-) *a.* **2.** *v.t.* supply with victuals. **3.** *v.i.* obtain stores; eat victuals. [ME, f. OF (*vitaillier* v. f.) *vitaille* f. LL. *victualia*, neut. pl. of L *victualis* (*victus* food, cogn. w. *vivere* live; see -AL)]

vi′ctualler, (vī′tler) *n.* one who furnishes victuals, ||esp. **licensed** ∼, innkeeper licensed to sell alcoholic liquor etc.; ship employed to carry stores for other ships. [ME, f. OF *vitaill(i)er, vitaillour* (as prec.; see -ER[2])]

vicu′ña (-kyo̅o̅′na, -ko̅o̅′-) *n.* S. Amer. mammal allied to llama, with fine silky wool; (imitation of) cloth made from its wool. [Sp., f. Quechua]

vide (vī′dī, vī′dā, vē′dā) *v.t.* (*imper.*, in reference to passage in book etc.). see, consult; QUOD[2] *vide*. [L, imper. of *vidēre* see]

vide′licet *adv.* = VIZ. [ME f. L (*vidēre* see, *licet* it is permissible)]

vi′děŏ *n.* (*pl.* ∼**s**) *& a.* **1.** *n.* television. **2.** *a.* relating to (recording for) broadcasting of photographic images; ∼ **frequency** (in the range used for video signals in television); ∼**phone**, telephone transmitting picture of person speaking; ∼ **signal** (containing information for producing television signal); ∼**tape** *n.* & *v.t.*, (make recording of, by use of) magnetic tape suitable for records of television pictures and sound. [L, = I see]

vi′dimus *n.* inspection or certified copy of accounts etc. [L, = we have seen (*vidēre* see)]

vie *v.i.* (*part.* **vying** *pr.* vī′-). strive for superiority, carry on rivalry, (*with* another in quality, *in* doing). [prob. f. ME, as ENVY[2]]

vie′lle *n.* hurdy-gurdy. [F, f. OF *viel(l)e*; see VIOL]

Vie′nna *n.* Vienna SCHNITZEL; ∼ **steak**, fried rissole of minced meat; hence **Vienne′se** *a. & n.* [∼ in Austria]

Viĕtname′se (-z) *a. & n.* (*pl.* same). (native, inhabitant, or language) of Vietnam in SE Asia. [f. *Vietnam* +-ESE]

vieux jeu (vyer zher′) *a.* old-fashioned, hackneyed. [F, lit. 'old game']

view (vū) *n. & v.* **1.** *n.* inspection by eye or mind, survey, (*of* surroundings, subject, etc.); (Law) inspection by jury of place, property, etc., concerned in a case, or of dead body; PRIVATE *view*. **2.** power of seeing, range of vision, (*came into view; passed from our view; house has a view of the sea*); what is seen, scene, prospect, (*a superb view*); picture etc. representing this. **3.** manner of considering a subject, opinion, mental attitude, (*takes a different view; his view is that we are the aggressors; takes a* DIM *or* POOR, *a favourable, view of her conduct; holds extreme views* (in politics etc.)); take the LONG[1] *view*. **4.** (arch.) intention, design, (*will this meet your views?*). **5. in** ∼ **of**, able to see, or to be seen by or from, (*came in view of the church; stood in full view of the audience*), having regard to, considering, (*in view of recent developments we do not think this step advisable*), (arch.) in anticipation of, (on ∼, being shown (for inspection); **with a** ∼ **to, with the** or **a** ∼ **of**, for the purpose of, as a step towards; **with a** ∼ **to**, with the aim of attaining; **to the** ∼, openly, in public. **6. have in** ∼, have as one's object, bear (circumstance) in mind in forming judgement etc.; POINT[1] *of view*; ∼**finder**, part of camera showing extent of picture; ∼ **halloo′**, huntsman's shout on seeing fox break cover; ∼**point**, point of view, standpoint. **7.** *v.t.* survey with the eyes; survey mentally, form mental impression or judgement of, (*subject may be viewed in different ways; does not view the matter in the same light*); inspect (house etc.); see (fox break cover. **8.** *v.i.* watch television. **9.** Hence ∼′ABLE *a.* [ME f. AF *v(i)ewe*, OF *vēue* fem. p.p. (as n.) f. *vêoir* see f. L *vidēre*]

view′er (vū′-) *n.* In vbl senses; television-watcher; device for looking at film transparencies etc. [f. prec. + -ER¹]

view′less (vū′-) *a.* having no opinions; (poet, or rhet.) invisible. [f. VIEW + -LESS]

view′y (vū′ĭ) *a.* (colloq.) holding odd or fanciful opinions. [f. VIEW + -Y²]

vigĕ′simal *a.* of twentieths or twenty; reckoning or reckoned by twenties; hence ∼LY² *adv.* [f. L *vigesimus* (*viginti* twenty) + -AL]

vi′gil *n.* keeping awake during the time usually given to sleep, watchfulness, (*keep vigil*); (usu. in *pl.*) nocturnal devotions; eve of a festival, esp. eve that is a fast. [ME, f. OF *vigile* f. L *vigilia* (*vigil* awake)]

vi′gil|ance *n.* watchfulness, caution, circumspection; *∼ance committee*, self-appointed body for maintenance of order etc. in imperfectly organized community; so ∼ANT *a.* [F, or f. L *vigilantia* (*vigilare* keep awake f. as prec.; see -ANCE)]

vigilă′nte *n.* member of a vigilance committee or similar body. [Sp., = vigilant]

vi′gneron (vē′nyerawn) *n.* vine-grower. [F (*vigne* VINE)]

vignĕ′tt|e (vēnyĕ′t) *n.*, & *v.t.* **1.** *n.* ornament round capital letter etc. or in blank space; illustration, esp. on title-page of book, not enclosed in definite border; photograph or portrait showing only head and shoulders with background gradually shaded off; (fig.) character sketch, short description. **2.** *v.t.* make portrait of (person) in vignette style, shade off (photograph or portrait); hence ∼ER¹, ∼ING¹, ∼IST (3), *ns.* [F, dim. of *vigne* VINE; see -ETTE]

vi′gorous *a.* strong and active, robust; (of plant) growing strongly; full of vigour, showing or requiring physical strength or activity; forceful, acting or done with vigour; hence ∼LY² *adv.*, ∼NESS *n.* [ME f. OF, f. med. L *vigorosus* f. L *vigor* (see foll., -OUS)]

‖vi′gour (-ger), *vi′gor, n.* active physical strength or energy; flourishing physical condition; healthy growth, vitality, vital force; mental strength or activity as shown in thought or speech or literary style, forcibleness, trenchancy, animation; hence ∼LESS *a.* [ME f. OF *vigour* f. L *vigor -oris* (*vigēre* be lively; see -OR)]

vihā′ra *n.* Buddhist temple or monastery. [Skr.]

Vī′king *n.* Scandinavian trader and pirate of 8th–10th c. [f. ON *víkingr*, perh. f. OE *wīcing* (*wīc* camp; see -ING³)]

vila′yĕt (-ah′-) *n.* province of Turkey. [Turk., f. Arab. *wilāya* district]

vile *a.* morally base, depraved, shameful, abject, disgusting; (arch.) worthless; (colloq.) abominably bad (*vile weather*); hence ∼LY² (-l-lĭ) *adv.*, ∼NESS (-ln-) *n.* [ME, f. OF *vil vile*, f. L *vilis* cheap, base]

vi′li|fy *v.t.* defame, traduce, speak evil of; hence ∼FICA′TION, ∼fIER¹, *ns.* [ME in sense 'lower in value', f. LL *vilificare* (as prec.; see -FY)]

vi′lipĕnd *v.t.* (arch.) treat contemptuously, disparage. [ME, f. OF *vilipender* or f. L *vilipendere* (as VILE, *pendere* consider)]

vill *n.* (Hist.) feudal township. [AF, f. OF *vil(l)e* farm f. L (as foll.)]

vi′lla *n.* **1.** country residence; ‖detached or semi-detached house in suburban or residential district, whence ∼DOM *n.*, Suburbia; house for holiday-makers at seaside etc. **2.** (Rom. etc. Hist.) country estate. [It. & L]

vi′llag|e *n.* group of houses etc., larger than hamlet and smaller than town; *small municipality with limited corporate powers*; inhabitants of a village; hence ∼ER¹ (4) (-ĭj-) *n.* [ME f. OF, f. L *villa*; see -AGE]

vi′llain (-ăn) *n.* person guilty or capable of great wickedness, scoundrel; ∼ (*of the piece*), character in play whose evil actions or motives are important in the plot; (colloq., playfully) rascal (without serious imputation of badness); (arch.) rustic, boor; hence

∼ESS¹ *n.* [ME f. OF *vilein, vilain* f. Rom. **villanus* f. L *villa*; see -AN]

vi′llainous (-lan-) *a.* **1.** worthy of a villain, vile, wicked; so **vi′llainy¹** (-lanĭ) *n.* **2.** (colloq.) abominably bad (*villainous weather*). **3.** Hence ∼LY² *adv.*, ∼NESS *n.* [ME, f. prec. + -OUS]

villanĕ′lle *n.* form of poem of 19 lines on two rhymes with some lines repeated. [F, f. It. *villanella* fem. of *villanello* rural, dim. of *villano* (as VILLAIN)]

-ville *suf.* (colloq.) forming names of fictitious places w. ref. to particular quality etc. (*they must come from Squaresville*). [f. F *ville* town, as in many US town-names]

villeggiatura (vĭlĕjatoor′a) *n.* stay or retirement in the country. [It. (*villeggiare* live at VILLA or in the country)]

vi′llein (-ĭn) *n.* (Hist.) feudal serf, tenant entirely subject to lord or attached to manor; so ∼AGE *n.*, tenure or status of villein. [ME, var. of VILLAIN]

vi′ll|us *n.* (*pl.* ∼i *pr.* -ī). (Anat.) each of the short hair-like processes on some membranes, esp. on mucous membrane of small intestine; (Bot., in *pl.*) long soft hair covering fruit, flowers, etc.; hence or cogn. ∼iFORM, ∼OSE¹, ∼OUS, *adjs.*, ∼o′SITY *n.* [L, = shaggy hair]

vim *n.* (colloq.) vigour. [perh. f. L, acc. of *vis* energy]

vimi′nĕous *a.* (Bot.) of or producing twigs or shoots. [f. L *vimineus* (*vimen viminis* osier; see -EOUS)]

vi′na (vē′-) *n.* Indian four-stringed musical instrument with fretted finger-board and a gourd at each end. [f. Skr. & Hindi *viṇā*]

vinā′ceous (-shus) *a.* wine-red. [f. L *vinaceus* (*vinum* wine; see -ACEOUS)]

vinaigrĕ′tte (-nĭg-) *n.* small ornamental bottle for holding aromatic salts etc., smelling-bottle; ∼ (*sauce*), salad dressing of oil and wine vinegar. [F, dim. of *vinaigre* VINEGAR; see -ETTE]

vi′ncible *a.* that can be overcome or conquered; ∼ **ignorance** (that can be overcome by the ignorant person himself). [f. L *vincibilis* (*vincere* overcome; see -IBLE)]

vi′ncul|um *n.* (*pl.* ∼a). (Alg.) line drawn over several terms to show that they have a common relation to what follows or precedes (e.g. $a + b \times c = ac + bc$, but $a + b \times c = a + bc$; $a - b + c = a - b - c$); (Anat.) ligament, fraenum. [L, = bond (*vincire* bind)]

vi′ndic|āte *v.t.* justify (person, religion, etc.) by evidence or argument; clear of suspicion etc.; establish the existence or merits or justice of (one's veracity, courage, conduct, character, assertion); hence or cogn. ∼A′TION, ∼ātOR, *ns.*, ∼ABLE, ∼ATIVE, *adjs.* [f. L *vindicare* claim, avenge (*vindex -dicis* claimant, avenger) + -ATE³]

vi′ndicatory *a.* tending to vindicate; (of laws) punitive. [f. prec. + -ORY]

vindi′ctive *a.* revengeful, tending to seek revenge; ∼ **damages** (exceeding simple compensation and awarded as punishment of defendant); hence ∼LY² (-vlĭ) *adv.*, ∼NESS (-vn-) *n.* [f. L *vindicta* vengeance (as VINDICATE) + -IVE]

vine *n.* climbing or trailing woody-stemmed plant of genus *Vitis*, whose fruit is the grape; (*any plant* with) slender stem that trails or climbs; ∼**-borer**, beetle or moth whose larva destroys vines; ∼**-dresser**, one who prunes, trains, and cultivates vines; hence **vi′ny²** *a.* [ME f. OF *vi(g)ne* f. L *vinea* vineyard (*vinum* wine)]

vi′negar *n.* sour liquid got from wine, cider, etc., by fermentation and used as condiment or for pickling; (fig.) sour behaviour or character; **aromatic** ∼ (containing camphor etc. in solution); MOTHER³ of *vinegar*; RASPBERRY *vinegar*; V∼ **Bible**, 1717 ed. with *parable of the vinegar* (for *vineyard*) in heading above Luke 20; hence ∼ISH¹, ∼Y², *adjs.* [ME, f. OF *vyn egre* f. Rom. **vinum acrum* sour wine f. L *vinum* wine + *acer acre* sour]

vi′nery *n.* vine greenhouse. [f. VINE + -ERY]

vī′neyard (-ny-) *n.* plantation of grape-vines, esp. for wine-making; (fig.) sphere of action or labour. [ME, f. VINE + YARD²]

vingt(-et)-un (vănt(ā)ĕr′n̄) *n.* card-game in which the object is to reach as nearly as possible the number of 21 pips on one's cards without exceeding it; hand of 21 pips in this. [F, = 21]

vī′ni- *comb. form.* wine, as: ~**culture**, cultivation of vines; ~**fica′tion,** conversion of grape-juice etc. into wine. [f. L *vinum* wine + -I-]

vin ordinaire (văn̄ ōrdīnār′) *n.* cheap (usu. red) wine as drunk in France mixed with water. [F, = ordinary wine]

vī′nous *a.* of, like, due to, addicted to, wine, (*vinous flavour, fermentation, eloquence*); hence **vīno′sITY** *n.* [f. L *vinum* wine + -OUS]

vin rosé (văn̄ rōză′) *n.* = ROSÉ. [F]

vint¹ *v.t.* make (wine). [back-form. f. VINTAGE]

vint² *n.* Russian card-game like auction bridge. [Russ., = screw]

vī′ntage *n.* & *a.* **1.** *n.* (season of) gathering grapes for wine-making; (wine made from) season's produce of grapes, (fig.) (thing made etc. in) a particular year etc.; (poet. or rhet.) wine; wine of high quality kept separate from others. **2.** *a.* of high quality esp. from the past; of a past season; ||~ **car** (made 1917-30). [alt. (after *vintner*) f. ME *vendage, vindage* f. OF *vendange* f. L *vindemia* (*vinum* wine, *demere* remove)]

vī′ntager *n.* grape-gatherer. [f. prec. + -ER¹]

vī′ntner *n.* wine-merchant. [ME, f. AL *vintenarius, vinetarius* f. AF *vineter,* OF *vinetier,* f. med. L *vinetarius* f. L *vinetum* vineyard (*vinum* wine; see -ER³)]

vī′nȳ. See VINE.

vī′nȳl *n.* plastic made by polymerizing a compound containing the ~ **group,** CH₂CH; (esp.) POLYvinyl chloride. [f. L *vinum* wine + -YL]

vī′ol *n.* medieval (usu. 6-)stringed musical instrument, similar to violin etc. but held vertically; BASS³ *viol.* [ME *viel* etc. f. OF *viel(l)e,* alt. f. *viole* (whence mod. E sp.) f. Prov. *viola, viula,* prob. f. Rom. **vitula* f. L *vitulari* be joyful; cf. FIDDLE]

viō′la¹ *n.* **1.** kind of large violin, alto or tenor violin; its player. **2.** viol; ~ **da bra′ccio** (brah′chō), viol corresponding to modern viola; ~ **da ga′mba,** viol held between player's legs, esp. corresponding to modern violoncello; ~ **d'amor′e** (dămōr′ă), sweet-toned tenor viol. [It. & Sp., prob. f. Prov. (see prec.)]

vi′ola² *n.* plant of genus *Viola,* e.g. pansy and violet; (esp.) cultivated hybrid of this genus. [L, ~ violet]

violā′ceous (-shŭs) *a.* of violet colour; (Bot.) of violet family Violaceae. [f. L *violaceus* (as prec.; see -ACEOUS)]

vī′ol∥āte *v.t.* disregard, fail to comply with, act against the dictates or requirements of, (oath, treaty, law, terms, conscience); treat profanely or with disrespect (sanctuary etc.); break in upon, disturb, (person's privacy etc.); rape; so ~**ABLE** *a.,* ~**A′TION,** ~**ātOR,** *ns.* [ME, f. L *violare* treat violently + -ATE³]

vī′olence *n.* quality of being violent; violent conduct or treatment, outrage, injury, (**do** ~ **to,** act contrary to, outrage); (Law) unlawful exercise of physical force, intimidation by exhibition of this. [ME f. OF, f. L *violentia* (as foll.; see -ENCE)]

vī′olent *a.* **1.** involving great physical force (*a violent storm; came into violent collision*); ~ **death** (resulting from external force or from poison; cf. NATURAL). **2.** involving unlawful exercise of force (*laid violent hands on him*). **3.** intense, vehement, passionate, furious, impetuous, vivid, (*violent pain, abuse, controversy, discrepancy, revulsion, contrast, dislike, shock, colours; is of or was in a violent temper*). **4.** Hence ~**LY²** *adv.* [ME f. OF, f. L *violentus;* see -LENT]

vī′olet *n.* & *a.* **1.** *n.* plant of genus *Viola* etc. with blue, purple, white, or other flowers, esp. **sweet**(-scented) ~; DOG¹-*violet;* **shrinking** ~, shy person. **2.** *n.* & *a.* (of) the colour seen at end of spectrum opposite red, produced by slight admixture of blue with red. **3.** *n.*

violet pigment; violet clothes or material. [ME, f. OF *violet(te)* dims. of *viole* f. L VIOLA²]

vīoli′n *n.* musical instrument with 4 strings of treble pitch played with bow; violinist (FIRST, SECOND, *violin*); hence ~**IST** *n.,* player of violin. [f. It. *violino* dim. of VIOLA¹]

vī′olist¹ *n.* player of viol. [f. VIOL + -IST]

viō′list² *n.* player of viola. [f. VIOLA¹ + -IST]

violoncĕ′ll∥ō (-chĕ′-) *n.* (*pl.* ~**os**). cello; hence ~**IST** (3) *n.* [It., dim. of *violone* (see foll.)]

violō′nĕ *n.* double-bass viol. [It., augment. of VIOLA¹; see -OON]

VIP *abbr.* very important person.

vī′per *n.* venomous snake of family Viperidae, esp. **common** ~ or adder, the only poisonous snake in Gt. Britain; (fig.) malignant or treacherous person (~ **in** one's **bosom,** person who betrays those who have helped him); ~**'s bugloss,** stiff bristly blue-flowered plant (*Echium vulgare*); ~**'s grass,** scorzonera; hence or cogn. ~**iFORM,** ~**INE¹,** ~**ISH¹** (fig.), ~-**LIKE,** ~**OUS** (fig.), *adjs.* [f. F *vipère* or f. L *vipera* (**vivipera* f. *vivus* alive + *parere* bring forth)]

virā′gō (-ah′-, -ā′-) *n.* (*pl.* ~**s**). turbulent woman, termagant; (arch.) woman of masculine strength or spirit. [OE, f. L = female warrior (*vir* man)]

vīr′al. See VIRUS.

vī′relay *n.* short (esp. old French) lyric poem with two rhymes to a stanza variously arranged. [ME, f. OF *virelai*]

vir′ement (vīr′ment, vēr′mahn) *n.* power to transfer items from one financial account to another. [F (*virer* turn; see VEER², -MENT)]

vī′rĕō *n.* (*pl.* ~**s**). small greenish Amer. songbird of family Vireonidae. [L, perh. = greenfinch]

virĕ′sc∥ence *n.* greenness; (Bot.) abnormal greenness in petals etc. normally of some bright colour; so ~**ENT** *a.* [f. L *virescere,* incept. of *virēre* be green; see -ESCENCE]

vīr′gate¹ *a.* (Bot. & Zool.) slim, straight, and erect. [f. L *virgatus* (*virga* rod; see -ATE²)]

vīr′gate² *n.* (Hist.) varying measure of land, esp. 30 acres. [f. med. L *virgata* (rendering OE *gierd-land* yard land) f. L *virga* rod + -ATE¹]

Virgī′lian *a.* of, or in the style of, the Roman poet Virgil (d. 19 BC). [f. L *Vergilianus* (P. *Vergilius* Maro, Virgil; see -AN)]

vīr′gin *n.* & *a.* **1.** *n.* person (esp. woman) who has had no sexual intercourse; ~**'s bower,** clematis; hence or cogn. ~**HOOD,** **virgi′nITY,** *ns.* **2.** member of any order of women under a vow to remain virgins. **3.** **the** (**Blessed**) **V**~ (**Mary**), mother of Christ. **4.** picture or statue of the Virgin. **5.** female insect producing eggs without impregnation. **6.** (*V*~). *the* zodiacal sign Virgo. **7.** *a.* that is a virgin; of or befitting a virgin (*virgin modesty*); undefiled, spotless; not yet used or penetrated or tried (*virgin soil*); (of clay) not fired; (of metal) made from ore by smelting; (of wool) not yet, or only once, spun or woven; (of insect) producing eggs without impregnation. **8.** ~ **birth,** (1) doctrine of Christ's birth without human father, (2) parthenogenesis; ~ **comb** (that has been used only once for honey and never for brood); ~ **forest** (in its untouched natural state); ~ **honey** (taken from virgin comb, or drained from comb without heat or pressure); ~ **queen,** unfertilized queen bee; **the V**~ **Queen,** Queen Elizabeth I of England. [ME, f. AF & OF *virgine* f. L *virgo -ginis*]

vīr′ginal *a.* & *n.* **1.** *a.* that is or befits or belongs to a virgin; hence ~**LY²** *adv.* **2.** *n.* ~, (**pair of**) ~**s,** legless early form of spinet in box, used in 16th-17th c. [ME f. OF, or L *virginalis* (as prec.; see -AL); n. perh. because intended for use by young women]

Virgī′ni∥a *n.* tobacco from Virginia; ~**a creeper,** N. Amer. vine cultivated for ornament; *~**a reel,** a country dance; ~**a stock,** branching plant with white or pink flowers; so ~**AN** *n.* & *a.* [f. ~ in US, orig. the first English settlement (1607), f. VIRGIN *Queen* + -IA¹]

Vīr′gō *n.* **1.** (*pl.* ∿s). (person born under) sign of the ZODIAC, the Virgin; hence ∿AN (-ōan) *a.* & *n.*, (person) born under Virgo. **2.** v∿ **inta′cta**, virgin with hymen intact. [OE, f. L, = virgin]

vīr′gŭle *n.* slanting line to mark division of words or lines; = SOLIDUS 2. [F, = comma, f. L *virgula* dim. of *virga* rod; see -ULE]

vĭridĕ′sc|ent *a.* greenish, tending to become green; hence ∿ENCE *n.* [f. LL *viridescere* f. L *viridis* (see foll., -ESCENT)]

vĭri′dĭan *a.* & *n.* (chromium oxide pigment of) bluish-green (colour). [f. L *viridis* green (*virēre* be green)]

vĭri′dĭtў *n.* greenness, verdancy. [ME, f. OF *viridité* or f. L *viriditas* (*viridis* green; see prec., -ITY)]

vi′rĭle *a.* **1.** of man as opp. to woman or child; ∿ **member**, (arch.) penis. **2.** of or having procreative power. **3.** (of mind, character, literary style, etc.) having masculine vigour or strength. **4.** So **virĭ′lĬTY** *n.* [ME, f. F *viril* or f. L *virilis* (*vir* man; see -IL.)]

vi′rĭlism *n.* (Path.) development of secondary male characteristics in female or precociously in male. [f. prec. + -ISM]

vīrŏ′log|ў *n.* scientific study of viruses; hence **vīro-lŏ′gICAL** *a.*, ∿IST (3) *n.* [f. VIRUS + -O- + -LOGY]

vîrtu′, vèrtu′, (-ōō′) *n.* **1.** love of fine arts; **article** or **object of** ∿ (interesting from workmanship, antiquity, rarity, etc.). **2.** virtuosity. [f. It. *virtù* VIRTUE, virtu]

vīr′tŭal *a.* **1.** that is such for practical purposes though not in name or according to strict definition, (*is the virtual manager of the business; take this as a virtual promise; constitutes a virtual exculpation*). **2.** (Opt.) relating to points at which rays would meet if produced backwards (*virtual focus, image*). **3.** (Mech.) relating to infinitesimal displacement of point in system. **4.** Hence ∿ITY (-ă′l-) *n.*, ∿LY² *adv.* [ME, f. med. L *virtualis* f. L *virtus* after LL *virtuosus*; see -AL]

vīr′tŭe *n.* **1.** moral excellence, uprightness, goodness, (*virtue is its own reward; make a virtue of* NECESSITY); particular moral excellence (*patience is a virtue*); **the** (**seven**) **cardinal** ∿s (**natural** ∿s, justice, prudence, temperance, fortitude; **theological** ∿s, faith, hope, charity). **2.** chastity esp. of woman (EASY *virtue*); good quality (*has the virtue of being adjustable, of resisting heat*); inherent power, efficacy, (*no virtue in such drugs*); one of seventh ORDER¹ of ninefold celestial hierarchy; **by** or **in** ∿ **of**, on the strength of, on the ground of, (*claims it in virtue of his long service; is entitled to it by virtue of his prerogative*). **3.** Hence ∿LESS (-ūl-) *a.* [ME, f. OF *vertu* f. L *virtus -tutis* (*vir* man)]

vîrtŭō′s|ō *n.* (*pl.* ∿i *pr.* -ē, *or* ∿os). person with special knowledge of or taste for works of art or virtu; person skilled in the technique of a fine art, esp. performance of music; hence ∿IC *a.*, **vîrtŭō′sITY**, ∿ōSHIP, *ns.*, [It., = learned, skilful, f. LL (as foll.)]

vīr′tŭous *a.* possessing or showing moral rectitude; chaste; hence ∿LY² *adv.*, ∿NESS *n.* [ME, f. OF *vertuous* f. LL *virtuosus* (*virtus* VIRTUE; see -OUS)]

vi′rul|ent (-ryŏŏ-, -rŏŏ-) *a.* poisonous; (of disease) malignant or violent; (fig.) malignant, bitter, (*virulent animosity, tone, abuse*); hence ∿ENCE *n.*, ∿entLY² *adv.* [ME, orig. of poisoned wound, f. L *virulentus* (as foll.; see -ULENT)]

vīr′|us *n.* any of numerous kinds of very simple organisms smaller than bacteria, mainly of nucleic acid in protein coat, multiplying only in living cells and often able to cause diseases; (arch. or fig.) poison, source of disease; hence ∿AL *a.* [L, = slimy liquid, poison]

vis (vĭs) *n.* (Mech.) ∿ *inertiae* (ĭnēr′shĭē), inertia; ∿ *viva* (vī′va), 'living force' (= mass × square of velocity) of moving body, twice its kinetic energy. [L, = strength, force]

Vis. *abbr.* Viscount.

vi′sa (vē′za) *n.*, & *v.t.* (∿ed *or* ∿′d, *pr.* -ad). **1.** *n.* endorsement on passport etc. showing that it has been found correct, esp. as allowing holder to enter or

leave a country. **2.** *v.t.* mark with visa. [F, f. L *visa* neut. pl. p.p. of *vidēre* see]

vi′sag|e (-z-) *n.* (literary). face, countenance; hence (-)∿ED² (-zĭjd) *a.* [ME f. OF, f. L *visus* sight (as prec.); see -AGE]

vis-à-vis (vēzahvē′) *adv.*, *prep.*, & *n.* (*pl.* same). **1.** *adv.* in a position facing one another. **2.** *prep.* opposite to; in relation to. **3.** *n.* person or thing facing another, esp. in some dances; person occupying corresponding position in another group; *social partner. [F, = face to face (*vis* face f. L, as prec.)]

Visc. *abbr.* Viscount.

viscă′cha *n.* S. Amer. burrowing rodent with valuable fur. [Sp., f. Quechua (*h*)*uiscacha*]

vi′scera *n. pl.* the interior organs in the great cavities of the body (e.g. brain, heart, liver), esp in the abdomen (e.g. the intestines). [L, pl. of VISCUS]

vi′sceral *a.* of the viscera; relating to inward feelings; ∿ (= SYMPATHETIC) **nerve**. [f. prec. + -AL]

viscerotŏ′nic *a.* like endomorph in temperament, with predominantly social interests. [f. VISCERA + -O- + TONIC]

vi′scid *a.* sticky, glutinous; semifluid; hence ∿ITY (-ĭ′d-) *n.* [f. LL *viscidus* f. L *viscum* birdlime; see -ID¹]

vi′scōse *n.* (In the manufacture of rayon etc.) cellulose in highly viscous state (suitable for drawing into yarn) formed by treatment with sodium hydroxide solution and carbon disulphide. [f. LL *viscosus* (as VISCOUS; see -OSE¹)]

viscō′sitў *n.* **1.** quality or degree of being viscous. **2.** (Phys., of fluid) internal friction, power of resisting a change in the arrangement of the molecules; quantity expressing this (**dynamic** ∿, measuring the force needed to overcome internal friction; **kinematic** ∿, measuring the force per unit density); hence **viscō′-METER, viscosi′METER**, *ns.* [ME, f. OF *viscosité* or f. med. L *viscositas* (as VISCOUS; see -ITY)]

vi′scount (vī′k-) *n.* British nobleman between earl and baron; hence ∿CY, ∿SHIP, ∿Y⁴, *ns.* [ME, f. AF *viscounte*, OF *vi*(*s*)*conte* f. med. L *vicecomes -mitis* (as VICE-, COUNT³)]

vi′scountess (vī′k-) *n.* viscount's wife or widow; woman holding rank of viscount in her own right. [ME, f. prec. + -ESS¹]

vi′scous *a.* sticky, glutinous; (Phys.) having high viscosity; semifluid; hence ∿NESS *n.* [ME f. AF, or f. LL *viscosus* (as VISCID; see -OUS)]

vi′scus *n.* (Anat.) any of soft internal organs of body (usu. in *pl.* VISCERA). [L]

***vīse.** See VICE².

visé (vē′zā) *n.*, & *v.t.* (∿d *or* ∿′d, *pr.* -ād). (arch.) = VISA. [F, p.p. of *viser* scrutinize f. Rom. *visare for L *vidēre vis-* see]

Vĭ′shnu (-ōō) *n.* Hindu god regarded by his worshippers as supreme deity and saviour, by others as second member of triad including Brahma and Siva; hence ∿ISM (3) *n.*, ∿ITE¹ (1) *n.* & *a.* [f. Skr. *Vishṇu*]

vĭsĭbĭ′litў (-z-) *n.* being visible; (Meteorol. etc.) possibility of seeing, range of vision, as determined by conditions of light and atmosphere. [f. F *visibilité* or f. LL *visibilitas* f. L *visibilis* (see foll., -ITY)]

vi′sĭble (-z-) *a.* **1.** that can be seen by the eye; (of light) within the range of wavelengths to which the eye is sensitive; that can be perceived or ascertained, apparent, open, (*has no visible means of support; spoke with visible impatience*); prepared to receive callers; (of exports etc.) consisting of actual goods (cf. INVISIBLE). **2. the Church** ∿, whole body of professed Christian believers; visible HORIZON. **3.** Hence ∿NESS (-bəln-) *n.*, **vi′sĭbLY²** (-z-) *adv.* [ME f. OF, or f. L *visibilis* (*vidēre vis-* see; see -IBLE)]

Vĭ′sĭgŏth (-z-) *n.* West Goth, member of branch of Goths who settled in France and Spain in 5th–8th c. [f. LL *Visigothus*]

vi′sion (-zhon) *n.*, & *v.t.* **1.** *n.* act or faculty of seeing, sight, (*has impaired his vision*); **field of** ∿, all that comes into view when the eyes are turned in some direction. **2.** thing or person seen in dream or trance (SEE[1] *visions*); supernatural or prophetic apparition, phantom; thing seen vividly in the imagination (*the romantic visions of youth; had visions of roast beef and plum pudding*); person etc. of unusual beauty; hence ∿AL *a.*, ∿IST (3) *n.* **3.** imaginative insight; statesmanlike foresight, sagacity in planning. **4.** what is seen on television screen. **5.** *v.t.* see, present, (as) in a vision. [ME f. OF, f. L *visio -onis* (as VISIBLE; see -ION)]

vi'sionar|y̆ (-zho-) *a. & n.* **1.** *a.* given to seeing visions or to indulging in fanciful theories; existing only in a vision or in the imagination; imaginary, fanciful, unpractical; hence ∿iNESS *n.* **2.** *n.* visionary person. [f. prec. + -ARY[1]]

vi'sit (-z-) *v. & n.* **1.** *v.t.* go or come to see (person, place, etc., or abs.) as act of friendship or ceremony, on business or for a purpose, or from interest; go or come to see for purpose of official inspection or supervision or consultation or correction; hence ∿ABLE *a.* **2.** (Of disease, calamity, etc.) come upon, attack, (*be visited by* or *with the plague*); (Bibl.) punish (person, sin), inflict punishment for (his sins etc.) *upon* person, (arch.) comfort, bless, (person *with* salvation etc.). **3.** *v.i.* be visitor; *∿ with,* visit, converse with; ∿ing *professor* (spending some time at another university). **4.** *n.* act of visiting, call on a person or at a place, temporary residence with person or at place, (*was on a visit to some friends; paid him a long visit; during his second visit to the East*); *chat*; occasion of going to doctor, dentist, etc.; formal or official call for purpose of inspection etc., DOMICILIARY *visit*; *right of visit* (see VISITATION). [ME, f. OF *visiter* or f. L *visitare* go to see, frequent. of *visare* view f. *vidēre* vis- see; n. f. v., or perh. f. F *visite*]

vi'sitant (-z-) *a. & n.* **1.** *a.* (arch. or poet.) visiting. **2.** *n.* migratory bird temporarily in a particular locality; visitor, esp. supposedly supernatural one. [F, or f. L *visitare* (as prec.; see -ANT)]

visita'tion (-z-) *n.* **1.** official visit of inspection or the like, esp. bishop's examination of the churches of his diocese; (colloq.) unduly protracted visit or social call; boarding of vessel belonging to another State to learn her character and purpose (**right of** ∿ or **visit,** right to do this, not including right of search). **2.** divine dispensation of punishment or reward, notable experience compared to this; (Eccl.) festival on 2 July in honour of visit of the Virgin Mary to Elizabeth (Luke 1:39); **Nuns of the V**∿, RC order founded 1610, now concerned esp. with education. **3.** (Zool.) unusual and large migration of animals. [ME f. OF, or f. LL *visitatio* (as VISIT; see -ATION)]

visitatorial. See VISITOR.

vi'siting (-z-) *n.* paying visit(s), making call(s); **have a** ∿ **acquaintance with, be on** ∿ **terms with,** know well enough to visit; ∿-**book** (for names of persons calling or to be called upon); *visiting*-CARD[2]. [ME, f. VISIT + -ING[1]]

vi'sitor (-z-) *n.* one who visits a person or place; migratory bird (cf. VISITANT); ||(in college etc.) official with right or duty of occasionally inspecting and reporting, whence or cogn. **visit(at)ŏr'IAL** (-z-) *adjs.*; ∿**s' book** (in which visitors to church, embassy, etc., write their names and addresses and occas. remarks). [ME, f. AF *visitour*, OF *visiteur* (as VISIT; see -OR)]

vi'sor (-z-), **vi'zor,** *n.* **1.** movable part of helmet covering face. **2.** projecting front part of cap; (Hist.) mask. **3.** shield (fixed or movable) at top of vehicle windscreen to protect eyes from bright sunshine etc. **4.** Hence ∿ED[2] (-zerd), ∿LESS, *adjs.* [ME f. AF *viser*, OF *visiere* (*vis* face f. L *visus*; see VISAGE)]

vi'sta *n.* long narrow view as between rows of trees; long succession of remembered or anticipated events etc., mental prospect or retrospect, (*opened up new vistas* or *a new vista to his ambition*); hence ∿ED[2] (-ad) *a.* [It., = view (*visto* seen, p.p. of *vedere* see f. L *vidēre*)]

vi'sual (-zhyoō-, -zyoō-) *a.* of, concerned with, or used in, seeing (*visual nerve, organ*); ∿ **aid,** film etc. as aid to learning; ∿ **angle** (formed at the eye by rays from the extremities of an object viewed); ∿ **field** (of vision); ∿ **point,** effective position of eye in optical analysis; ∿ **purple,** light-sensitive pigment in retina; ∿ **ray,** line from object to eye; hence ∿ITY (-ă'l-) *n.*, ∿LY[2] *adv.* [ME, f. LL *visualis* (*visus* sight f. *vidēre* see; see -AL)]

vi'sualiz|e (-zhyŏŏ-, -zyŏŏ-), **-is|e** (-īz), *v.t.* make visible esp. to the mind (thing not visible to the eye); make visible to the eye; hence ∿A'TION *n.* [f. prec. + -IZE]

vi'tal *a. & n.* **1.** *a.* of or concerned with or essential to organic life (*vital energies, functions; wounded in a vital part*); ∿ **power** (to sustain life). **2.** essential to existence of a thing or to the matter in hand (*a vital question; question of vital importance; secrecy is vital to the success of the scheme*). **3.** affecting life; fatal to life or to success etc., (*a vital wound, error*); full of life or activity. **4.** ∿ **capacity,** volume of air that can be expelled from lungs after taking deepest possible breath; ∿ **force, élan vital;** ∿ **statistics,** number of births, marriages, deaths, etc., (colloq.) measurements of woman's bust, waist, and hips. **5.** Hence ∿LY[2] *adv.* **6.** *n.* (in *pl.*) vital parts, e.g. lungs, heart, brain. [ME f. OF, f. L *vitalis* (*vita* life; see -AL)]

vi'tal|ism *n.* (Biol.) doctrine that life originates in a vital principle distinct from chemical and other physical forces; hence ∿IST (2) *n.*, ∿i'stIC *a.* [f. F *vitalisme*, or f. prec. + -ISM]

vită'lity *n.* vital power, ability to sustain life; animation, liveliness, (fig., of institution, language, etc.) ability to endure and to perform its functions. [f. L *vitalitas* (as VITAL; see -ITY)]

vi'taliz|e, -is|e (-īz), *v.t.* endow with life; infuse with vigour; hence ∿A'TION *n.* [f. VITAL + -IZE]

vi'tamin *n.* any of a number of accessory food factors present in many foodstuffs and essential to normal growth and nutrition of man and other animals; ∿ **A** (found in fish-liver oils etc.); ∿ **B₁, B₂, B₁₂, H,** members of group found in yeast etc.; ∿ **C** (found in fruit and vegetables, and preventing scurvy); ∿ **D,** group of several vitamins (D₁, D₂, etc.) found in fish-liver oils and egg-yolk, and preventing rickets; ∿ **E** (found in wheat-germ and green leaves, and preventing sterility); ∿ **H** (see above); ∿ **K** (found in green leaves etc., and assisting blood-clotting); hence ∿IZE (1) *v.t.* [orig. *vitamine* f. G *vitamin* f. L *vita* life + G *amin* AMINE, because orig. thought to contain an amino-acid]

vĭtĕ'llin *n.* (Chem.) chief protein constituent of yolk of egg. [f. foll. + -IN]

vĭtĕ'll|us *n.* (*pl.* ∿i *pr.* -ī). yolk of egg; protoplasmic contents of ovum; hence ∿ARY[1], ∿INE[1], *adjs.* (∿ine **membrane,** yolk-sac). [L, = yolk]

vi'ti- *comb. form.* vine, as: ∿**culture,** grape-growing. [f. L *vitis* vine]

vi'ti|āte (-shī-) *v.t.* impair the quality or efficiency of, corrupt, debase, contaminate, (*person's constitution vitiated by intemperance; vitiated air, blood, mind, judgement*); make invalid or ineffectual (*a single word may vitiate a contract*); so ∿A'TION, ∿ātOR, *ns.* [f. L *vitiare* (*vitium* VICE[1] + -ATE[3]]

vi'treous *a.* of (the nature of) glass; like glass in hardness, brittleness, transparency, structure, etc. (*vitreous enamel*); ∿ **body** or **humour,** (Anat.) transparent jelly-like tissue filling eyeball; hence or cogn. ∿NESS, *n.* [f. L *vitreus* (*vitrum* glass) + -OUS]

vitre'scence, *ns.,* **vitre'scent, vi'triform,** *adjs.* [f. L *vitrum* glass]

vi'trify *v.t. & i.* convert or be converted into glass or glasslike substance esp. by heat; hence or cogn. ∿FA'CTION, ∿FICA'TION, *ns.,* ∿**f**iADLE *a.* [f. F *vitrifier* or f. med. L *vitrificare* (as prec.; see -FY)]

vi'triol *n.* sulphuric acid or a sulphate, orig. one of glassy appearance, (fig.) caustic speech, criticism, feeling, etc.; **blue** or **copper** ∿, copper sulphate; **green** ∿, iron sulphate; **white** ∿, zinc sulphate; **oil**

of ∼, concentrated sulphuric acid; ∼-**throwing**, throwing oil of vitriol in person's face as act of vengeance etc.; hence **vitrĭŏ'lɪc** a., ∼ɪᴢᴇ (1) v.t. [ME f. OF, or f. med. L vitriolum f. L vitrum glass]

Vitru'vian (-ōō'-) a. ∼ **scroll**, convoluted scroll pattern in frieze decorations etc. [f. M. Vitruvius Pollio, Roman architect of 1st c. ʙᴄ+-ᴀɴ]

vi'tt|a n. (pl. ∼ae). (Bot.) oil-tube in fruit of some plants; (Zool.) stripe of colour; so ∼ᴀᴛᴇ² a. [L, = band, chaplet]

vĭtŭ'per|āte v.t. & i. revile, abuse; hence or cogn. ∼ᴀ'ᴛɪᴏɴ, ∼ᴀᴛᴏʀ, ns., ∼ᴀᴛɪᴠᴇ a. [f. L vituperare (vitium VICE¹)+-ᴀᴛᴇ³]

viva¹ (vē'va) int. & n. (the cry) 'long live' as salute etc. [It., 3 sing. pres. subj. of vivere live f. L]

∥vī'va² n., & v.t. (∼ed or ∼'d, pr. -ad). (colloq.) = ᴠɪᴠᴀ ᴠᴏᴄᴇ 2, 3. [abbr.]

viva'ce (vēvah'chā) adv. (Mus.) in a lively brisk manner. [It., f. L (as foll.)]

vǐvā'cious (-shus) a. lively, sprightly, animated; hence or cogn. ∼ʟʏ² adv., **vǐvǎ'cɪᴛʏ** n. [f. L vivax -acis (vivere live; see -ᴀᴄɪᴏᴜs)]

vivandière (vīvahṅdyāɪ') n. (Hist.) woman attached to continental esp. French regiment and selling provisions and liquor. [F]

vivār'i|um n. (pl. ∼a). place artificially prepared for keeping animals in (nearly) their natural state. [L, = warren, fishpond (vivus living f. vivere live; see -ᴀʀɪᴜᴍ)]

vi'văt (vī'-, vē'-) int. & n. = ᴠɪᴠᴀ¹. [L, 3 sing. pres. subj. of vivere live]

vīva vō'cě (vō'sǐ, vō'chǐ) adv., a., n., & v.t. **1.** adv. & a. oral(ly). **2.** n. oral examination. **3.** v.t. (w. hyphen). examine viva voce. [med. L, = with the living voice]

vī'văx n. malaria parasite (Plasmodium vivax) causing tertian fever. [mod. L, f. L (see ᴠɪᴠᴀᴄɪᴏᴜs)]

vǐvě'rrĭne a. of the civet family or subfamily. [f. mod. L viverrinus f. L viverra ferret; see -ɪɴᴇ¹]

vī'vers (-z) n. pl. (Sc.) food, victuals. [f. F vivres (vivre live f. L vivere)]

vi'vid a. (Of light or colour) strong, intense, glaring, (a vivid flash of lightning; of a vivid green); (of person) lively, vigorous; (of mental faculty or impression) clear, vigorous, strongly marked, (has a vivid imagination; gave a vivid description; have a vivid recollection of the scene); hence ∼ʟʏ² adv., ∼ɴᴇss n. [f. L vividus (vivere live; see -ɪᴅ¹)]

vi'vi|fy v.t. (esp. fig.) give life to, enliven, animate; so ∼ғɪᴄᴀ'ᴛɪᴏɴ n. [f. F vivifier f. LL vivificare f. L vivus living (vivere live; see -ғʏ)]

vǐvǐ'parous a. (Zool.) bringing forth young alive, not hatching by means of egg, (cf. ᴏᴠɪ¹parous); (Bot.) producing bulbs or seeds that germinate while still attached to parent plant; hence **vivǐpā'rɪᴛʏ**, ∼ɴᴇss, ns., ∼ʟʏ² adv. [f. L viviparus (vivus, see prec., -ᴘᴀʀᴏᴜs)]

vi'vǐsect v.t. perform vivisection on. [back-form. f. foll.]

vivǐsě'ction n. dissection or other painful treatment of living animals for purposes of scientific research; (fig.) unduly detailed or ruthless criticism; hence ∼ᴀʟ a., ∼ɪsᴛ (2, 3), **vi'vǐsěctᴏʀ**, ns. [f. L vivus living (see ᴠɪᴠɪғʏ), after dissection]

vi'xen n. female fox; quarrelsome woman, termagant; hence ∼ɪsʜ¹, ∼ʟʏ¹, adjs. [ME fixen f. OE *fyxen (= MHG vühsinne) fem. of ғᴏx; see -ᴇɴ³]

viz. (vǐz, nā'mlǐ) adv. that is to say, in other words, namely, (usu. following words that promise or more or less clearly require explanation etc. as; as: under the following conditions, viz. that etc.; a permanent board of three, viz. etc.). [abbr. of ᴠɪᴅᴇʟɪᴄᴇᴛ, z being med. L symbol for abbr. of -et]

vi'zard n. (arch.) = ᴠɪsᴏʀ 2. [f. ᴠɪsᴏʀ+-ᴀʀᴅ]

vizcă'cha. Var. of ᴠɪsᴄᴀᴄʜᴀ.

vizier (vǐzēɪ', vǐ'zǐer) n. high official, esp. State minister, in some Muslim countries; **grand** ∼, prime minister in former Turkish empire and other Muslim countries; hence ∼ᴀᴛᴇ¹ (1), ∼sʜɪᴘ, ns., ∼ɪᴀʟ (-ēɪ'-)

a. [ult. f. Arab. wazīr caliph's chief counsellor]

vī'zor. See ᴠɪsᴏʀ.

vi'zsla (-zhla) n. Hungarian hunting-dog with deep--red coat. [f. V∼ in Hungary]

VJ abbr. Victory over Japan; ∼ **day**, ∥15 August 1945, *2 September 1945.

v.l. abbr. variant reading. [f. L varia lectio]

Vlăch (-k) a. & n. (member) of a Romanian-speaking people in SE Europe. [Bulg., f. OSlav. Vlachŭ Romanian etc. f. Gmc *Walh foreigner]

vlei (flā) n. (S. Afr.) hollow in which water collects during rainy season. [Du. dial., f. Du. vallei valley]

∥VO abbr. Royal Victorian Order.

vō'cable n. word, esp. w. ref. to form rather than meaning. [F, or f. L vocabulum (vocare call)]

vocǎ'būlarў n. (list, arranged alphabetically with definitions or translations, of) the (principal) words used in a language or usu. in a particular book or branch of science etc., or by a particular author, (a Livy with notes and vocabulary; a word not found in the Chaucerian vocabulary; the ever-increasing scientific vocabulary; person's range of language (his vocabulary is limited); set of artistic or stylistic forms or techniques, esp. range of set movements in ballet etc. [f. med. L vocabularius, -um (as prec.; see -ᴀʀʏ¹)]

vō'cal a. & n. **1.** a. of, concerned with, uttered by, the voice, (a vocal communication); ∼ **cords**, folds of lining membrane of larynx about the opening of the glottis, with edges vibrating in air-stream to produce voice; ∼ **music** (written for or produced by the voice with or without accompaniment); ∼ **score**, musical score showing voice parts in full. **2.** expressing one's feelings freely in speech (was very vocal about his rights); (poet., of trees, water, etc.) endowed (as) with a voice; (Phonet.) voiced. **3.** Hence or cogn. **vocǎ'ʟɪᴛʏ** n., ∼ʟʏ² adv. **4.** n. musical performance with singing; (in sing. or pl.) sung part; (RC Ch.) person entitled to vote in certain elections. [ME, f. L vocalis (as ᴠᴏɪᴄᴇ; see -ᴀʟ)]

vocǎ'lic a. of or consisting of vowel(s). [f. prec.+-ɪᴄ]

vō'calism n. use of voice in speaking or singing; vowel sound or system. [f. ᴠᴏᴄᴀʟ+-ɪsᴍ]

vō'calist n. singer (opp. to instrumentalist). [f. ᴠᴏᴄᴀʟ +-ɪsᴛ]

vō'caliz|e, -īs|e (-īz), v. **1,** v.t. form (sound), utter (word), with the voice; (as vbl. a.) esp. make sonant, (f is vocalized into ᴠ); write (Hebrew etc.) with vowel points. **2.** v.i. (joc.) speak, sing, hum, shout, etc. **3.** (Mus.) sing florid passage to vowel(s). **4.** Hence ∼ᴀ'ᴛɪᴏɴ n. [f. ᴠᴏᴄᴀʟ+-ɪᴢᴇ]

vocā'tion n. **1.** divine call to, or sense of fitness for, a career or occupation, (felt no vocation (for the ministry); has never had the sense of vocation; little or no vocation to literature). **2.** employment, trade, profession, (all vocations are overcrowded). **3.** Hence ∼ᴀʟ a. [ME f. OF, or f. L vocatio (vocare call; see -ᴀᴛɪᴏɴ)]

vō'cative a. & n. (Gram.) ∼ (**case**), case of nouns etc. esp. in inflected languages, used in addressing or invoking person or thing. [ME, f. OF vocatif -ive or f. L vocativus (vocare call; see -ᴀᴛɪᴠᴇ)]

vocǐ'fer|āte v.t. & i. utter (words etc., or abs.) noisily; shout, bawl; hence or cogn. ∼ᴀɴᴄᴇ, ∼ᴀ'ᴛɪᴏɴ, ∼ ātᴏʀ, ns., ∼ᴀɴᴛ a. & n. [f. L vociferari (vox voice, ferre bear)]

vocǐ'ferous a. (of person, his speech, etc.) noisy, clamorous; insistently and forcibly expressing one's views; hence ∼ʟʏ² adv., ∼ɴᴇss n. [f. as prec.+-ᴏᴜs]

vŏ'dka n. alcoholic spirit made esp. in Russia by distillation of rye etc. [Russ., dim. of voda water]

vōe n. small bay, creek, in Orkney and Shetland. [f. Norw. vaag, ON vágr]

vōgue (vōg) n. the prevailing fashion (the vogue for large hats; large hats are the vogue); popular use or reception (has had a great vogue); **in** ∼, in fashion, generally current; ∼-**word**, word currently fashionable; hence **vō'guɪsʜ¹** (-gǐ-) a. [F, f. It. voga rowing, fashion (vogare row, go well)]

voice *n.*, & *v.t.* **1.** *n.* sound formed in larynx etc. and uttered by mouth, esp. human utterance in speaking, shouting, singing, etc., (*heard a voice*; *spoke in a low voice*; *did not recognize her voice*; *the voice of the cuckoo*; *has such a loud voice*); ability to produce this (*has laryngitis and has lost her voice*); **in** (**good**) ∼, in proper vocal condition for singing or speaking; *at the* TOP[1] *of* one's *voice*; hence **-voic**ED[2] (-st) *a.* **2.** use of the voice, utterance esp. in spoken or (fig.) written words, opinion so expressed, right to express opinion, (*gave voice to his indignation in a pamphlet*; *dog gave voice to his joy*; *I have no voice in the matter*); agency by which opinion is expressed; **the** ∼ **of God**, expression of God's will, wrath, etc.; **with one** ∼, unanimously. **3.** (Phonet.) sound uttered with resonance of vocal cords, not with mere breath. **4.** (Gram.) set of forms of a verb showing relation of the subject to the action (ACTIVE, PASSIVE, MIDDLE[1], *voice*); verb in this form. **5.** (Mus.) vocal part in composition; constituent part of fugue. **6.** ∼**-box**, larynx; ∼**-over**, narration in film not accompanied by picture of speaker; ∼**-print**, visual record of speech, analysed with respect to frequency, duration, and amplitude; *∼vote (taken by noting relative strength of calls of ay and no). **7.** *v.t.* give utterance to, express, (*believe I am voicing the general sentiment when I say*; *letter voices our opinion*); (Mus.) regulate tone-quality of (organ-pipes), whence **voi'**cER[1] *n.*, (Phonet., esp. in *p.p.*) utter with vocal vibration (e.g. *b, d, g, v, z*; cf. sense 3). [ME, f. AF *voiz*, OF *vois* f. L *vox vocis*]

voi'ceful (-sf-) *a.* (poet. or rhet.) vocal; sonorous. [f. prec. + -FUL]

voi'celess (-sl-) *a.* speechless, dumb, mute; (Phonet.) uttered with breath and not voice (e.g. *f, k, p, s, t*); hence ∼NESS *n.* [f. VOICE + -LESS]

void *a., n.,* & *v.t.* **1.** *a.* empty, vacant; (of office) vacant (*bishopric fell void*); (of hand) having no cards *in* a suit. **2.** (esp. Law, of deed, promise, contract, etc.) invalid, not binding, (*null and void*); (poet. or rhet.) ineffectual; useless. **3.** ∼ **of**, lacking, free from, (*a proposal wholly void of sense*, *his style is void of affectation*). **4.** Hence ∼'NESS *n.* **5.** *n.* empty space (*vanished into the void*); (fig.) *cannot fill the void made by death*); unfilled space in wall or building; (Bridge etc.) absence of cards in a particular suit. **6.** *v.t.* render invalid; evacuate (excrement etc., or abs.); hence ∼'ABLE *a.* [ME, f. OF dial. *voide*, OF *vuide, vuit* f. Rom. **vocitus* cogn. w. L *vacare* VACATE; v. partly f. AVOID, partly f. OF *voider* f. Rom. **vocitare* (**vocitus*)]

voi'dance *n.* vacancy in benefice; voiding. [ME f. OF (as prec.; see -ANCE)]

voi'děd *a.* In vbl senses; (Her., of bearing) having the central area cut away so as to show the field. [p.p. of VOID]

voile (voil, vwahl) *n.* thin semitransparent cotton, woollen, or silken dress-material. [F, = VEIL]

voir dire (vwār dēr′) *n.* (Law.) oath to give true answers to questions affecting one's competence as juror etc. [OF (*voir truth, dire* say)]

vol. *abbr.* volume.

vō'lant *a.* (Zool.) flying, able to fly; (Her.) represented as flying; (literary) nimble, rapid. [F (*voler* f. L *volare* fly; see -ANT)]

vō'lar *a.* (Anat.) of the palm or sole. [f. L *vola* hollow of hand or foot + -AR[1]]

vŏ'latīle *a.* & *n.* **1.** *a.* evaporating rapidly (*volatile salts*); ∼ (= ESSENTIAL) **oil.** **2.** (fig.) lively, gay, changeable, (*volatile wit, writer, disposition*); transient; apt to break out into violence. **3.** Hence or cogn. ∼NESS (-ln-), **vŏlati'**lITY, ∼s. *n.* **4.** *n.* volatile substance. [f. OF *volatil* or f. L *volatilis* (*volare -at-* fly; see -IL)]

vŏla'tīlīz|e, -īs|e (-iz), *v.t.* & *i.* (cause to) evaporate; hence ∼ABLE *a.*, ∼A'TION *n.* [f. prec. + -IZE]

vŏ'l-au-vent (-ō-vahn) *n.* (usu. small) case of puff pastry filled with meat, fish, etc., and sauce. [F, lit. 'flight in the wind']

vŏlcă'n|ic *a.* of, like, produced by, a volcano; ∼ic **bomb,** mass of ejected lava usually rounded and

sometimes hollow; ∼ic **glass,** obsidian; hence ∼ICALLY *adv.*, **vŏlcani'**cITY *n.* [f. F *volcanique* (*volcan* volcano f. as foll.; see -IC)]

vŏlcā'nō *n.* (*pl.* ∼es). mountain or hill having opening(s) in earth's crust through which lava, cinders, steam, gases, etc., are or have been expelled continuously or at intervals (*active, dormant, extinct, volcano*); (fig.) violent esp. suppressed feeling, state of things likely to cause violent outburst. [It., f. L *Volcanus* Vulcan, Rom. god of fire]

vŏlcanŏ'logy. Var. of VULCANOLOGY.

vōle[1] *n.* (arch.) winning of all tricks at cards. [F (*voler* fly f. L *volare*)]

vōle[2] *n.* small ratlike or mouselike herbivorous rodent of family Cricetidae. [orig. *vole-mouse* f. Norw. **vollmus* (*voll* field, *mus* mouse)]

vō'let (-lā) *n.* panel or wing of triptych. [F (*voler* fly f. L *volare*)]

vō'litant *a.* (Zool.) = VOLANT. [f. L *volitare* frequent. of *volare* fly; see -ANT]

voli'tion *n.* exercise of the will; power of willing (**of** or **by** one's **own** ∼, voluntarily); hence ∼AL, **vŏ'lit**IVE, *adjs.* [F, or f. med. L *volitio* (*volo* I wish; see -ITION)]

vŏlkerwanderung (fĕr'lkervahnderŏŏng) *n.* migration of peoples, esp. of Germanic and Slavic peoples into Europe in 2nd–11th c. [G]

vŏ'lley *n.* & *v.* **1.** *n.* simultaneous discharge of missiles, missiles so discharged; (fig.) noisy emission (*of oaths* etc.) in quick succession; (Lawn Tennis etc.) return of ball in play before it touches ground; (Football) kicking of ball in play before it touches ground; (Cricket) pitching of ball, ball pitched, right up to batsman or stumps without bouncing; **half-**∼, (Lawn Tennis, Football) playing of ball as soon as it touches ground, (Cricket) ball so pitched that batsman may hit it as it bounces, hit so made; ∼**-ball,** game for two teams of six volleying large ball by hand over net. **2.** *v.t.* return or send (ball, or abs.) by volley, whence ∼ER[1] *n.*, discharge (missiles, abuse, etc., or abs.) in volley. **3.** *v.i.* (Of missiles) fly in a volley, (of guns etc.) sound together; make sound like volley of artillery. [f. F *volée* f. Rom. **volata* fem. p.p. (as n.) of L *volare* fly; see -Y[4]]

vŏ'lplāne *n.*, & *v.i.* (Aeron.) glide. [f. F *vol plané* (*vol* flight, *plané* p.p. of *planer* hover); see PLANE[3]]

vols. *abbr.* volumes.

vōlt[1] *v.i.*, & *n.* **1.** *v.i.* make a volte. **2.** *n.* Var. of VOLTE. [f. F *volter* (VOLTE)]

vōlt[2] *n.* unit of electromotive force, difference of potential that would carry one ampere of current against one ohm resistance. [f. as VOLTAIC]

vō'ltage *n.* electromotive force expressed in volts. [f. prec. + -AGE]

vŏltā'ic *a.* (arch.) of electricity from a primary battery, galvanic, (*voltaic battery,* PILE[2]). [f. A. *Volta,* It. physicist d. 1827 + -IC]

Vŏltair'ean, -ian, *adjs.* & *ns.* (follower) of Voltaire; critical(ly) sceptic(al); hence ∼ISM (3) *n.* [f. de *Voltaire,* later surname of F. M. Arouet, Fr. author d. 1778 + -EAN, -IAN]

vŏltă'mēter *n.* instrument for measuring electric currents by their electrolytic effects. [f. as VOLTAIC + -METER]

vŏlte *n.* (Fenc.) quick movement to escape thrust; sideways circular movement of horse. [F, f. It. *volta* turn, fem. p.p. (as n.) of *volgere* turn f. L *volvere* roll]

vŏlte-fa'ce (-tfah's) *n.* turning round, esp. (fig.) complete change of front in argument, politics, etc. [F, f. It. *voltafaccia* (*voltare* to turn f. Rom. **volvitare* frequent. of L *volvere* to roll; as FACE[1])]

vō'ltmēter *n.* instrument for measuring electric potential in volts. [f. VOLT[2] + -METER]

vŏ'lūb|le *a.* **1.** (of speech, speaker) fluent, glib; hence or cogn. **vŏlubi'**lITY, ∼leNESS (-bln-), *ns.*, ∼LY[2] *adv.* **2.** (arch.) revolving, rotating. **3.** (Bot.) twisting round a support, twining. [F, or f. L *volubilis* (*volvere* roll; see -UBLE)]

vŏ′lūme n. **1.** set of (written or usu. printed) sheets of paper bound together and forming part or the whole of a work or comprising several works (*issued in 3 volumes; an odd volume of 'Punch'; library of 12,000 volumes;* SPEAK *volumes*); (Hist.) scroll of papyrus etc., ancient form of book. **2.** (usu. in *pl.*) wreath, coil, rounded mass, *of* smoke etc. **3.** solid content, bulk; space occupied by gas or liquid; amount or quantity *of* (business etc.). **4.** (Mus. etc.) quantity or power of sound; fullness of tone. **5.** Hence (-)**vŏ′lūm**ED² (-md) *a.* [ME f. OF *volum(e)*, f. L *volumen -minis* roll (*volvere* to roll)]

vŏlūmĕ′tr|ic *a.* of or pertaining to measurement by volume; hence ∼ICALLY *adv.* [f. prec. + METRIC]

volu′min|ous (-lū′-, -lōō′-) *a.* consisting of many volumes; (of writer) producing many books etc.; of great volume, bulky, (of drapery etc.) loose and ample; hence ∼o′SITY, ∼OUSNESS, *ns.*, ∼OUSLY² *adv.* [f. LL *voluminosus* (as VOLUME; see -OUS)]

vŏ′luntar|ism n. **1.** doctrine of independence of Church etc. (see foll. 5). **2.** (Philos.) doctrine that the will is a fundamental or dominant factor. **3.** principle of relying on voluntary action rather than compulsion. **4.** So ∼IST (2) n. [irreg. f. foll. + -ISM]

vŏ′luntar|y *a.* & n. **1.** *a.* done, acting, able to act, of one's own free will, not constrained or compulsory, intentional, (*a voluntary gift; there was no voluntary misstatement; was a voluntary agent in the matter; voluntary service, army*); ∼y **confession** (of criminal, not prompted by promise or threat); (Law) ∼y **conveyance** or **disposition** (made without compensation in money or other consideration). **2.** brought about, produced, etc., by voluntary action; (of institution) supported by voluntary contributions; ||∼y **Aid Detachment,** group of organized voluntary first-aid and nursing workers; ||∼y **school** (built by voluntary institution but maintained by LEA). **3.** (Of limb, muscle, movement) controlled by the will. **4.** Hence ∼iLY² *adv.*, ∼iNESS n. **5.** n. organ solo played before, during, or after church service; music for this; (arch.) extempore performance esp. as prelude to other music; (arch.) one who holds that the Church or the schools should be independent of the State and supported by voluntary contributions; (in competitions) special performance left to performer's choice. [ME, f. OF *volontaire* or f. L *voluntarius* (*voluntas* will; see -ARY¹)]

vŏ′luntar|yism n. = VOLUNTARISM 1, 3; so ∼IST (2) n. [f. prec. + -ISM]

vŏlunteer′ n. & v. **1.** n. person who spontaneously undertakes task etc.; person who voluntarily enters military or other service, esp. member of any of the corps of voluntary soldiers formerly organized in UK and provided with instructors, arms, etc., by the State; (*attrib.*, of vegetation) growing spontaneously. **2.** v.t. undertake, offer, (one's services, remark, explanation, etc.; *to* do) voluntarily. **3.** v.i. make voluntary offer of one's services (*for* campaign, purpose); be a volunteer. [f. F *volontaire* (as VOLUNTARY), assim. to -EER]

volŭ′ptūary *a.* & n. concerned with, (person) given up to, luxury and sensual pleasure. [f. L *volupt(u)arius* (as foll.; see -ARY¹)]

volŭ′ptūous *a.* of, tending to, occupied with, derived from, sensuous or sensual pleasure; hence ∼LY² *adv.*, ∼NESS n. [ME, f. OF *voluptueux* or f. L *voluptuosus* (*voluptas* pleasure; see -OUS)]

volū′t|e n. & *a.* **1.** n. spiral scroll characteristic of Ionic, Corinthian, and Composite capitals; hence ∼ED² *a.* **2.** (spiral shell of) gastropod of genus *Voluta.* **3.** *a.* (Bot. etc.) rolled up. [F, or f. L *voluta* fem. p.p. (as n.) of *volvere* to roll]

volu′tion (-lū′-, -lōō′-) n. rolling motion; spiral turn; whorl(s) of spiral shell; (Anat.) convolution. [f. as prec., after *revolution* etc.]

vŏ′lva n. (Bot.) membranous covering enclosing immature fungus. [L (*volvere* wrap)]

vŏ′mer n. (Anat.) small thin bone separating nostrils in man and most vertebrates. [L, = ploughshare]

vŏ′mit *v.t.*, & n. **1.** *v.t.* eject (matter, or abs.) from stomach through mouth; (fig., of volcano, chimney, etc.) eject violently, belch forth. **2.** n. matter vomited from stomach; (arch.) emetic; **black** ∼, (black substance vomited in) yellow fever. [ME, f. (OF *vomite* n. or L *vomitus* f.) L *vomere -it-*, or f. frequent. L *vomitare*]

vŏmitŏr′i|um n. (*pl.* ∼a). = foll. 2. [L; see foll.]

vŏ′mitŏry *a.* & n. **1.** *a.* emetic. **2.** n. (Rom. Ant.) each of a series of passages for entrance and exit in (amphi)theatre. [f. L *vomitorius* a., *-um* n., (as VOMIT; see -ORY)]

vŏō′dōō n., & *v.t.* **1.** n. use of, belief in, religious witchcraft as prevalent among W. Ind. etc. Blacks; person skilled in this; voodoo spell; hence ∼ISM (3), ∼IST (2, 3), *ns.* **2.** v.t. affect by voodoo, bewitch. [f. Dahomey *vodu*]

-vora. See -VOROUS.

vorā′cious (-shus) *a.* greedy in eating, ravenous, (lit. or fig.; *voracious schoolboy, readers*); hence or cogn. ∼LY² *adv.*, ∼NESS, **vorā′c**ITY, *ns.* [f. L *vorax* (*vorare* devour; see -ACIOUS)]

-vŏre. See foll.

-vorous *suf.* forming *adjs.* (usu. w. intermediate -I-) w. sense 'feeding on' (*carnivorous*); so **-vora,** forming names of groups of animals classified by their food (*Insectivora*), **-vore** (vŏr), forming name of individual of such group (*herbivore*). [f. L *-vorus* (*vorare* devour) + -OUS]

vŏr′t|ĕx n. (*pl.* ∼**ices** *pr.* -ĭsēz, or ∼**exes**). mass of whirling fluid, esp. whirlpool or whirlwind; (Phys.) portion of fluid whose particles have rotatory motion; any whirling motion or mass, esp. (fig.) system, occupation, pursuit, etc., viewed as swallowing up or engrossing those who approach it (*the vortex of society*); ∼**ex-ring,** vortex whose axis is a closed curve, e.g. smoke-ring puffed from smoker's lips or pipe; hence ∼iCAL, ∼iCOSE¹, ∼i′cŭLAR¹, *adjs.*, ∼i′cITY n. [L *vortex -icis* eddy, var. of VERTEX]

vŏrtĭcĕ′lla n. bell-shaped animalcule of family Vorticellidae found in stagnant water etc. [f. mod. L *vorticella,* dim. of prec.]

vŏr′tic|ist n. **1.** (Metaphys.) person regarding the universe, with Descartes, as a plenum in which motion propagates itself in circles. **2.** (Art) painter etc. of futurist school using 'vortices' of modern civilization as basis. **3.** So ∼ISM (3) n. [f. as VORTEX + -IST]

vŏrtĭ′ginous *a.* (arch.) whirling, vortical. [f. L *vortigo -ginis,* var. of VERTIGO, + -OUS]

vŏ′tar|y n. person vowed to the service *of* (God etc.); ardent follower, devoted adherent or advocate, (*of* person, system, occupation, etc.); hence ∼ESS¹, ∼IST (1), *ns.* [f. L *vot-* (as foll.) + -ARY¹]

vōte n. & v. **1.** n. formal expression of will or opinion in regard to election of officer etc., sanctioning law, passing resolution, expressing thanks, etc., signified by ballot, show of hands, voice, or otherwise, (*shall give my vote to or for the Labour candidate; was put to the vote and passed without a dissentient vote; let us take a vote on it*). **2.** opinion expressed, ||money granted, by majority of votes; the collective votes (that may be) given by a party etc. (*will lose the Labour, Conservative, vote*); the right to vote (*Swiss women now have the vote*); ticket etc. used for recording vote; ∼ **of confidence** (showing that majority support policy of governing body etc.); hence ∼′LESS (-tl-) *a.* **3.** v.i. give a vote (*for* or *against* person or measure, *to* do). **4.** v.t. enact, resolve, (*that*), grant (sum), cause to be (*in* = elected, *on* to or *off* committee, etc.), by majority of votes; (colloq.) pronounce, declare, by general consent (*was voted a failure*); (colloq.) announce one's proposal (*that*); ∼ **down,** defeat (proposal etc.) by votes. **5.** Hence **vŏ′t**ABLE *a.*, **vŏ′t**ER¹ n. [ME, (n. f. L *votum*) f. p.p. st. *vot-* of L *vovēre* vow]

vŏ′ting n. In vbl senses; ∼**-machine** (for automatic

registering of votes); ∼-**paper** (used in voting by ballot in election of MP etc.); ∼ **stock** (entitling holder to a vote). [f. prec. +-ING¹]

vō′tive *a.* offered or consecrated in fulfilment of a vow, (*votive offering, tablet, picture*); ∼ **mass** (Eccl., for special purpose or occasion). [f. L *votivus* (as VOTE; see -IVE)]

vouch *v.* **1.** *v.t.* (arch.) confirm, uphold, (statement) by evidence or assertion; cite as authority. **2.** *v.i.* answer *for*, be surety *for*, (*will vouch for the truth of this, for him* or *his honesty*). [ME, f. OF *vo*(*u*)*cher* summon etc., ult. f. L *vocare* call]

vou′cher *n.* In vbl senses; document, receipt, etc., establishing the payment of money or the truth of accounts; document which can be exchanged for goods or services as token of payment made or promised by holder or another (‖LUNCHEON *voucher*). [AF (as prec.; see -ER⁴), or f. prec. +-ER¹]

vouchsā′fe *v.t.* condescend to give or grant (*vouchsafed me no answer*); condescend (*to* do). [ME, f. VOUCH in sense 'warrant' +SAFE²]

vou′ssoir (vōō′swär) *n.* each of the wedge-shaped or tapered stones forming an arch. [f. OF *vossoir* etc., f. pop. L *volsorium*, ult. f. L *volvere* roll]

vow *n.*, & *v.t.* **1.** *n.* solemn promise or engagement esp. in the form of an oath to God or other deity or to saint; **baptismal** ∼**s** (given at baptism by baptized person or by sponsors); **monastic** ∼**s** (by which monk binds himself or nun herself to poverty, chastity, and obedience); **lovers′** or **marriage** ∼**s** (promises of fidelity); **under a** ∼, having made a vow. **2.** *v.t.* promise solemnly (thing, conduct; *vowed a temple to Apollo; vow obedience, vengeance against oppressor*). **3.** (arch.) declare, esp. solemnly, (*that*, or abs.). [ME, f. AF *v*(*o*)*u*, OF *vo*(*u*), f. L (as VOTE); v. f. OF *vouer*, in sense 3 partly f. AVOW]

vow′el *n.* each of the more open sounds uttered in speaking, sound capable of forming a syllable, made with vibration of vocal cords but without audible friction, (opp. to, but not sharply divided from, CONSONANT); letter(s) representing this, as *a, e, i, o, u, aw, ah*; **indeterminate** or **neutral** or **obscure** ∼ (heard in second syllable of *cousin, reason, haddock*; cf. SCHWA); ∼ **gradation,** = ABLAUT; ∼ **mutation,** = UMLAUT; ∼-**point,** each of a set of marks indicating vowels in Hebrew etc.; hence (-)∼LED² (-ld), ∼LESS (-l-l-), ∼LY², *adjs.* [ME, f. OF *vouel, voiel* f. L *vocalis* (*littera*) VOCAL (letter)]

vow′elize, -ise (-īz) *v.t.* insert the vowels in (Hebrew etc., shorthand). [f. prec. +-IZE]

vox (vŏks) *n.* ∼ **angelica,** organ-stop with soft tremulous tone; ∼ **humana** (hūmah′na), organ--stop with tone supposed to resemble human voice; ∼ **populi** (pŏ′pūlī), the people's voice (i.e. public opinion, the general verdict, popular belief, or rumour). [L, = voice]

voy′ag|e *n.* & *v.* **1.** *n.* journey, esp. long one by sea or water or air or ship; account of this. **2.** *v.i.* & *t.* travel or traverse by water or air, or fig.; hence ∼EABLE (-ija-) *a.*, ∼ER¹ *n.* [ME, f. AF & OF *veiage, voiage* f. L *viaticum*; see -AGE; v. f. F *voyager*, or f. n.]

voyageur′ (vwahyahzhēr′) *n.* man employed in transportation of goods and passengers between trading posts; Canadian boatman. [F, = VOYAGER]

voyeur′ (vwahyēr′) *n.* one who obtains sexual gratification from looking at others' sexual actions or organs; hence ∼ISM (2) *n.* [F (*voir* see)]

VP *abbr.* Vice-President.

VR *abbr.* Queen Victoria [f. L *Victoria Regina*]; variant reading.

‖**vraic** *n.* seaweed found in Channel Islands, used for fuel and manure. [F dial.; cf. VAREC]

‖**VRD** *abbr.* Volunteer Reserve Decoration.

VRI *abbr.* Victoria, Queen and Empress. [f. L *Victoria Regina Imperatrix*]

vs. *abbr.* versus.

VS *abbr.* Veterinary Surgeon.

‖**VSO** *abbr.* Voluntary Service Overseas.

VSOP *abbr.* Very Special Old Pale (brandy).

VT, Vt., *abbr.* Vermont.

VTO(L) *abbr.* vertical take-off (and landing).

vŭg *n.* rock-cavity lined with crystals. [f. Corn. *vooga*]

vŭlcā′nic etc. Var. of VOLCANIC etc.

Vŭ′lcanist *n.* (Geol.) holder of PLUTONIC theory. [f. F *vulcaniste, volcaniste* (as VOLCANO; see -IST)]

vŭ′lcanīte *n.* hard black vulcanized rubber, ebonite. [f. as foll. +-ITE¹]

vŭ′lcaniz|e, -īs|e (-īz), *v.t.* treat (rubber or rubberlike material) with sulphur etc. esp. at high temperature to increase elasticity and strength; hence ∼ABLE *a.*, ∼A′TION, ∼ER¹ (1, 2), *ns.* [f. *Vulcan*, Rom. god of fire and metal-working +-IZE]

vŭlcanŏ′log|y *n.* scientific study of volcanoes; hence **vŭlcanolŏ′g|ICAL** *a.*, ∼IST (3) *n.* [f. as prec. +-O- +-LOGY; see VOLCANO]

vŭ′lgar *a.* **1.** of or characteristic of the common people, plebeian, coarse in manners, low, (*vulgar expressions, mind, tastes, finery*). **2.** in common use, generally prevalent, (*vulgar errors*); the ∼ (Christian) **era;** ∼ **fraction** (expressed by numerator and denominator, not decimally); *vulgar* LATIN; the ∼ (national, vernacular, esp. formerly as opp. to Latin) **tongue. 3.** Hence or cogn. ∼ISM (4, 2), ∼ITY (-ă′r-), *ns.*, ∼LY² *adv.* [ME, f. L *vulgaris* (*vulgus* common people; see -AR¹)]

vŭlgār′ian *n.* vulgar (esp. rich) person. [f. prec. +-IAN]

vŭ′lgariz|e, -īs|e (-īz), *v.t.* make (person, manners, etc.) vulgar, infect with vulgarity; spoil (scene, sentiment, etc.) by making too common or frequented or well known; popularize, hence ∼A′TION *n.* [f. VULGAR +-IZE]

Vŭ′lgate (-āt, -at) *n.* **1.** Latin version of the Bible prepared mainly by St. Jerome in late 4th c.; official RC text as revised 1592. **2.** (*v*∼) traditionally accepted text of any author; common speech. [f. L *vulgata* (*editio* edition), fem. p.p. of *vulgare* make public (*vulgus*; see VULGAR)]

vŭ′lner|able *a.* that may be wounded (lit. or fig.); susceptible of injury, exposed to damage by weapon, criticism, etc.; (Contract Bridge) having won one game towards rubber and therefore being liable to higher penalties; hence ∼ABI′LITY, ∼**able**NESS (-běln-), *ns.*, ∼**abl**Y² *adv.* [f. LL *vulnerabilis* f. L *vulnerare* to wound (*vulnus -eris* wound); see -ABLE]

vŭ′lnerarȳ *a.* & *n.* (drug, plant, etc.) useful or used for healing of wounds. [f. L *vulnerarius* (*vulnus*; see prec. and -ARY¹)]

vŭ′lpīne *a.* of (the nature of) a fox; crafty, cunning. [f. L *vulpinus* (*vulpes* fox; see -INE¹)]

vŭ′ltur|e *n.* large bird of prey of order Raptores with head and neck more or less bare of feathers, feeding chiefly on carrion and reputed to gather with others in anticipation of a death; (fig.) rapacious person; cognate or cogn. ∼INE¹, ∼ISH¹, ∼OUS, (-cher-) *adjs.* [ME, f. AF *vultur*, OF *voltour* etc., f. L *vulturius*]

vŭ′lv|a *n.* (Anat. & Zool.) external female genitals, esp. external orifice of vagina; hence ∼AR¹ *a.*, ∼I′TIS *n.* [L, = womb]

vv. *abbr.* verses; volumes.

vȳ′ing. See VIE.

W

W, w, (dŭ'belyoo) *n.* (*pl.* **Ws** *or* **W's**). twenty-third letter of alphabet.
W. *abbr.* watt(s); Welsh; west(ern); women's (size).
w. *abbr.* wicket; wide; wife; with.
W *symb.* tungsten. [f. mod. L *wolframium*]
WA *abbr.* Washington (state); Western Australia.
Waac (wăk) *n.* member of Women's Army Auxiliary Corps (||1914–18 or *1942–48). [f. initials *WAAC*]
||Waaf (wăf) *n.* member of Women's Auxiliary Air Force (1939–48). [f. initials *WAAF*]
wabble. See WOBBLE.
***WAC** *abbr.* Women's Army Corps.
wă'cke (-ke) *n.* greyish-green or brownish rock resulting from decomposition of basaltic rock. [G, f. MHG *wacke* large stone, OHG *wacko* pebble]
wă'ckў *a.* & *n.* (sl.) crazy (person). [orig. dial., = left--handed, f. WHACK + -Y²]
wad (wŏd) *n.*, & *v.t.* (-dd-). **1.** *n.* lump or bundle of soft material used esp. to keep things apart or in place or to stuff up opening, esp. disc of felt etc. keeping powder or shot in place in gun; roll of notes, money; (in *sing.* or *pl.*) large quantity esp. of money; ||(sl.) bun, sandwich, etc. **2.** *v.t.* press (cotton etc.) into wad or wadding; line or stuff (garment, coverlet), protect (person, walls, etc.), with wadding; stop up (aperture, gun-barrel), keep (powder etc.) in place, with wad. [perh. rel. to Du. *watten*, F *ouate* padding, cotton wool]
wa'dding (wŏ'd-) *n.* soft pliable material usu. of cotton or wool used to line or stuff garments, quilts, etc., or to pack fragile articles in, cotton wool; material from which gun-wads are made. [f. prec. + -ING¹]
wa'ddle (wŏ'-) *v.i.*, & *n.* **1.** *v.i.* walk with the rocking motion natural to stout short-legged person or to bird with short legs set far apart as duck or goose. **2.** *n.* waddling gait. [perh. frequent. of WADE; see -LE 3]
wa'ddў (wŏ'-) *n.* Australian Aboriginal's war-club. [Aboriginal wd, perh. f. WOOD]
wāde *v.* & *n.* **1.** *v.i.* walk through water or other impeding medium e.g. snow, mud, sand; make one's way with difficulty or by force; (fig.) ∼ **in,** (colloq.) intervene, make vigorous attack on one's opponent; ∼ **into,** (colloq.) attack (person, task) vigorously; ∼ **through,** read (book etc.) in spite of its dullness etc. **2.** *v.t.* ford (stream) on foot; hence **wā'dABLE** *a.* **3.** **wading bird,** long-legged water-bird that wades (opp. short-legged web-footed swimmers). **4.** *n.* spell of wading. [OE *wadan*, = OHG *watan*, ON *vatha* f. Gmc *wadhan* go (through) f. IE *wadh-]
wā'der *n.* In vbl senses; wading bird; (in *pl.*) high waterproof boots, or waterproof garment for body and legs, worn in fishing etc. [f. prec. + -ER¹]
wa'di (wah-, wŏ'-) *n.* rocky watercourse dry except in rainy season (in N. Africa etc.). [f. Arab. *wādī*]
***WAF** *abbr.* Women in the Air Force.
w.a.f. *abbr.* with all faults.
wā'fer *n.*, & *v.t.* **1.** *n.* very thin sweet crisp biscuit now chiefly eaten with ice cream; thin disc of unleavened bread used in Eucharist; small disc of dried paste formerly used for fastening letters, holding papers together, etc.; disc of red paper stuck on legal document instead of seal; ∼**thin,** very thin; hence ∼Y² *a.* **2.** *v.t.* attach or seal with wafer. [ME f. AF *wafre*, ONF *waufre*, OF *gaufre* (cf. GOFFER) f. MLG *wāfel* waffle; cf. foll.]
wa'ffle¹ (wŏ'-) *n.* small crisp batter cake baked in ∼**iron** usu. of two shallow metal pans hinged together. [f. Du *wafel, waefel* f. MLG *wāfel*; cf. prec.]
wa'ffle² (wŏ'-) *v.i.*, & *n.* (indulge in) verbose but

---

aimless or ignorant talk or writing. [orig. dial., frequent. of *waff* = yelp, yap; imit.]
waft (wah-, wŏ-) *v.* & *n.* **1.** *v.t.* & *i.* convey or travel easily (as) through air or over water; sweep smoothly and lightly along. **2.** *n.* whiff of odour; transient sensation of peace, joy, etc. **3.** (Naut.) distress signal, e.g. ensign rolled or knotted or garment flown in rigging. [orig. 'convoy (ship etc.)', back-form. f. obs. *waughter, wafter* armed convoy-ship, f. Du. or LG *wachter* (*wachten* to guard)]
wăg¹ *v.* (-gg-) & *n.* **1.** *v.t.* & *i.* shake to and fro, oscillate; *dog* ∼s *tail,* shows pleasure thus: **tail** ∼s **dog,** less or least important member of society or section of party or part of structure has control; *wag* one's FINGER *at*; ∼ one's **head** (in derision or amusement); **beards, chins, jaws, tongues, are** ∼**ging,** talk is going on. **2.** *v.i.* (arch.) (Of the world, times, etc.) go along with varied fortune or characteristics. **3.** ∼'**tail,** small bird of genus *Motacilla* (*grey, pied, yellow,* etc., *wagtail*) with long tail in frequent motion. **4.** *n.* single wagging motion (*with a wag of his tail, head,* etc.). [ME *waggen* f. root of OE *wagian* sway, = OHG *wagōn*, ON *vaga*]
wăg² *n.* facetious person, one given to jesting or practical jokes; ||(sl.) truant (esp. *play wag* or the *wag*); hence, ∼'**gERY** (4) *n.,* ∼'**gISH¹** *a.,* (-g-). [prob. f. obs. *waghalter* one likely to be hanged (as prec., HALTER)]
wāge¹ *n.* (in *sing.* or *pl.*) amount paid at regular intervals esp. by the day or week or month, for time during which workman or servant is at employer's disposal (*gets good wages; brings his wages home; at a wage* or *at wages of £40 a week*; **living** ∼, wages that allow earner and family to live without fear of privation; SUBSISTENCE *wage*); (fig.) requital (*the wages of sin is death*); (Econ., in *pl.*) part of total production that rewards labour rather than remunerating capital; ∼**claim,** = PAY¹-*claim*; ∼(**s**) **council,** board of workers' and employers' representatives determining wages where there is not collective bargaining; ∼**-earner,** one who works for wages; *wage* FREEZE; ∼ **slave,** person dependent on income from labour in conditions like slavery; ∼ **stop,** limitation of supplementary benefit at level of normal wage. [ME f. AF & ONF; OF *g(u)age* f. Gmc *wadhjam* (cf. GAGE¹, WED)]
wāge² *v.t.* carry on (war, conflict, contest). [ME, = pledge, gage, f. AF *wager*, ONF *wagier*, OF *guagier* (*guage*; see prec.)]
wā'ger *n.*, & *v.t.* & *i.* **1.** = BET. **2.** *n.* (Hist.) ∼ of **battle,** ancient form of trial by personal combat between the parties or their champions; ∼ of **law,** trial by evidence of witnesses on oath. [ME, f. AF *wageure* (*wager*; see prec.)]
wă'ggle *v.i.* & *t.*, & *n.* (colloq.) = WAG¹; (Golf) swing (of) club-head to and fro over ball before playing shot; hence **wă'gglY²** *a.,* unsteady. [f. WAG¹ + -LE 3]
Wagnēr'ian (vah-) *a.* & *n.* (admirer) of the music of Wagner; like Wagner's grandly-planned dramatic operas. [f. R. *Wagner,* Ger. composer d. 1883 + -IAN]
wă'gon, ||wă'ggon, *n.* four-wheeled vehicle for drawing heavy loads, often with removable semi-cylindrical top or cover, usu. drawn by two or more horses, (**hitch** one's ∼ **to a star,** utilize powers higher than one's own); trolley for conveying tea etc.; ||open railway vehicle or railway van for goods; *small vehicle or cart, van, motor car; (**water-**)∼, vehicle for carrying water, whence *on the* (*water-*)∼, (sl.) teetotal; *wagon* TRAIN 11; ∼**-roof, -vault,** (shaped like wagon-tilt). [earlier *wagon, wag(h)en,* f. Du. *wag(h)en,* cogn. w. OE *wægn* WAIN]

wăg(g)oner n. driver of wagon. [f. Du. *wagenaar* (as prec., -ER¹)]

wăg(g)onĕ'tte n. four-wheeled horse-drawn pleasure vehicle (open or with removable cover) with facing side-seats. [f. WAGON + -ETTE]

wagon-lit (văgawn̄lē') n. sleeping-car on Continental railway. [F]

Waha'bi, Wahha'bi, (wahah'-) n. one of a sect of Muslim puritans following strictly the original words of the Koran. [f. Muhammad ibn Abd-el-*Wahhab*, founder in 18th c. + -I]

wahi'nė (wah-hē'nī) n. (NZ) woman, wife. [Maori]

waif n. **1.** ownerless object or animal, thing cast up by or drifting in sea or brought by unknown agency. **2.** homeless and helpless person, esp. unowned or abandoned child. **3.** ⁓s **and strays,** odds and ends, homeless or neglected children. [ME, f. AF *waif, weif,* ONF *gaif,* prob. of Scand. orig.]

wail v. & n. **1.** v.i. lament with wail or with words suggesting wail; (of wind etc.) make sound like person wailing; **W⁓ing Wall,** high wall in Jerusalem said to stand on site of Herod's temple, where Jews traditionally pray and lament on Fridays. **2.** v.t. (poet. or rhet.) bewail, wail over. **3.** n. prolonged plaintive inarticulate loud high-pitched cry; sound like or suggestive of this; hence ⁓'FUL a. (poet.). [ME, f. ON *veila* (*vei* int = WOE)]

wain n. (poet. or dial.) wagon; **the ⁓, =** CHARLES's WAIN; ⁓'**wright,** wagon-builder. [OE *wæg(e)n, wān,* = OHG *wagan,* ON *vagn,* f Gmc *wagnoz,* *wegnaz* f. IE *wogh-, *wegh-* carry; cf. WAY, WEIGH]

wai'nscot n., & v.t. **1.** wooden panelling or boarding on lower part of room-wall; ||(Hist.) imported oak of fine quality. **2.** v.t. line with wainscot; hence ⁓ING¹ (3) n. [ME, f. MLG *wagenschot,* app. f. *wagen* WAGON + *schot* of uncert. meaning]

waist n. **1.** part of human body below ribs and above hips, usu. of smaller circumference than these; its circumference. **2.** narrower middle part of normal human figure, similar narrow part in middle of long object, e.g. violin or hour-glass or wasp. **3.** middle part of ship, between forecastle and quarterdeck. **4.** part of garment encircling or covering waist; narrow middle part of woman's dress etc.; part of garment between neck and waist; *blouse or bodice. **5.** ⁓'**band,** ⁓-**belt,** (worn round waist); ⁓-**cloth,** = LOIN*cloth;* ⁓-**dee'p, -hi'gh,** adjs. & advs., up to waist; ⁓'**line,** outline of size of person's waist, e.g. as indicator of fatness. **6.** Hence (-)⁓ED² a. [ME *wast,* perh. repr. OE *wæst,* *weahst* (= Goth. *wahstus* growth), f. root of WAX²]

||**wai'stcoat** (-sk-, -stk-) n. man's garment for upper part of body, usu. buttoned and sleeveless, normally worn under jacket but partly visible in front; woman's similar garment. [f. prec. + COAT]

wait v. **1.** v.i. defer action or departure for specified time or until some expected event occurs, be expectant or on the watch, (*for, till; wait a minute; waited (for) an hour; shall not wait here any longer; kept me waiting or made me wait; have a month to wait yet; will do it for you while you wait; wait till I come, for high water or a fine day; waited to see what would happen*); ⁓ **and see,** await progress of events; ⁓ **for it!,** (colloq.) do not begin before the proper moment; ⁓ **for me!,** do not go so fast that I am left behind; **cannot ⁓,** is impatient; *that can ⁓,* need not be dealt with at present, since it is unimportant; **you ⁓!** (as threat of retribution). **2.** v.t. await, bide, (*is waiting his opportunity; you must wait your turn, my convenience*); defer (meal etc.) till another's arrival. **3.** v.i. ⁓ (**at** or *on table*), act as waiter or as servant with similar functions; act as attendant. **4.** ⁓-**a-bit,** plant with hooked thorns etc. that catch the clothing; ⁓ (**up**)**on,** await convenience of, serve as attendant to, pay respectful visit to; ⁓ **up,** not go to bed but wait (*for someone to arrive*). [ME, f. ONF *waitier* = OF *guaitier,* f. Gmc **wahtan (*wak-* WAKE¹)]

wait² n. **1.** ||(in pl.) street singers of Christmas carols; (Hist.) official bands of musicians maintained by a city or town. **2.** act or time of waiting (*had a long wait for the train*); watching for enemy, ambush, (*lie in or lay wait,* usu. *for*). [ME, partly f. ONF **wait, wet (waitier;* see prec.), partly f. prec.]

wai'ter n. In vbl. senses; man who takes orders, brings food, changes plates, etc., at hotel or restaurant tables, whence **wai'tr**ESS¹ n.; tray, salver; DUMB *waiter;* TIDE¹-*waiter.* [f. WAIT¹ + -ER¹]

wai'ting n. In vbl. senses; stopping of motor vehicle at side of road even without leaving it (*no waiting*); (period of) official attendance at court (LADY, LORD, etc., *-in-waiting*); ⁓ **game,** abstention from early action in contest etc. so as to act more effectively later; ⁓-**list** (of persons waiting for vacancy, next chance to obtain thing, etc.); ⁓-**room** (provided for persons to wait in, esp. by doctor, dentist, etc., or at railway or bus station). [ME, f. WAIT¹ + -ING¹]

waive v.t. refrain from insisting on or using, tacitly or implicitly relinquish or forgo, (right, claim, opportunity, legitimate plea, etc.); hence **wai'v**ER⁴ n. (Law). [ME, f. AF *weyver,* OF *gaiver* allow to become a 'WAIF', abandon]

wāke¹ v. (*past* **woke** pr. wōk, *or* ⁓**d;** *p.p.* ⁓**d, wo'ken,** *or* **woke). 1.** v.i. & t. ⁓ (**up**), cease to sleep, cause to cease sleeping, (lit. or fig.: *spring wakes all nature; nature wakes; shouting woke the echoes; woke up to the fact that he meant it*). **2.** v.i. be awake (*arch exc.* in part. or gerund: *in his waking hours; waking or sleeping; waking* DREAM¹). **3.** v.i. & t. ⁓ (**up**), cease or rouse from sloth, torpidity, inactivity, or inattention (*needs something to wake him up*); rise or raise from the dead. **4.** v.t. disturb (silence, place) with noise, make re-echo. **5.** ⁓-**robin,** ||arum, esp. cuckoo-pint, *plant of genus *Trillium.* [goes back to two OE forms: (a) strong v. **wacan wōc *wacen,* (b) weak v. *wacian* (cf. OS *wakon,* OHG *wahhēn, -ōn*), f. Gmc **wak-,* cf. WATCH²]

wāke² n. **1.** (Hist.) vigil commemorating church dedication, merry-making or fair on the occasion. **2.** (usu. in pl.) annual holiday in (industrial) northern England. **3.** (Ir.) watch beside corpse before burial, lamentations and merry-making in connection with it. [partly f. OE **wacu* (= OHG *wahha,* ON *vaka*), rel to prec.; in ME partly f. prec.; sense 'vigil' perh. f. ON]

wāke³ n. strip of smooth-looking water left behind moving ship (**in the ⁓ of,** behind, following, as result of, after the example of); turbulent air left behind moving aircraft etc. [prob. f. MLG, f. ON **vaku, vök* hole or opening in ice]

wā'keful (-kf-) a. unable to sleep, (of night etc.) passed with little or no sleep; vigilant; hence ⁓LY² adv., ⁓NESS n. [f. WAKE¹ + -FUL]

wā'ken v.t. & i. cause to be, become, awake (lit. or fig.). [f. ON *vakna* = OE *wæcnan,* Goth. *-waknan* f. Gmc **wak-* WAKE¹; cf. -EN⁶]

Wa'lach (wŏ'lak) n. = VLACH; hence ⁓IAN (-lā'k-) a. & n. [f. as VLACH]

Waldĕ'ns|ēs (wŏ-; -z) n. pl. puritan religious sect orig. in S. France, now chiefly in Italy and America, founded c. 1170 and much persecuted; hence ⁓IAN a. & n. [med. L, f. Peter *Waldo* of Lyons, founder]

wāle n. & v.t. **1.** n. = WEAL²; ridge on woven fabric, e.g. corduroy; specially woven strong band round woven basket; (Naut.) broad thick timber along ship's side; ⁓-**knot** or **wall-knot** (made at end of rope by intertwining strands to prevent unravelling or act as stopper). **2.** v.t. provide or mark with wales. [OE *walu* stripe, ridge, = LG *wāle,* ON *vala* knuckle]

Wā'ler n. horse imported (esp. Hist. for Indian army) from New South Wales. [f. *Wales* + -ER¹]

walk¹ (wawk) v. **1.** v.i. (Of person or other biped) progress by advancing each foot alternately, never having both feet off ground at once; go *backwards, sideways,* on one's *hands,* etc., with similar movements; go with gait usual except when speed is desired; (of quadruped) go with slowest gait, always having at least two feet on ground at once; *be released from suspicion or charge; (Baseball) reach first base on BALL[1]s; (Cricket) leave wicket after being put out. **2.** travel or go on foot (*walk into shop, down hill*); take exercise thus (*walks for two hours each day*); (of GHOST) be visible. **3.** (arch.) live with or in specified principle or manner, conduct oneself, (*walk in love, humbly, with God*). **4.** *v.t.* perambulate, traverse on foot at walking speed, tread floor or surface of; ∼ **the boards,** be actor or actress; ∼ **the hospitals** or **wards,** be medical student; *walk the* PLANK[1]; ∼ **the streets,** (1) traverse streets esp. in search of work etc., (2) be prostitute; hence ∼'ABLE *a.* **5.** cause to walk with one; accompany in walking; ride or lead (horse, dog, etc.) at walking pace; take charge of (hound-puppy at walk); (Baseball) allow to reach first base on BALL[1]s; ∼ person **off his feet** or **legs,** exhaust him with walking. **6.** ∼ **about,** stroll; ∼'**about** *n.,* Austral. Aboriginal's period of wandering in bush, informal stroll among crowd by royal person etc.; ∼ **away from,** easily outdistance; ∼ **away with,** = *walk off with*; ∼ **in,** enter; ∼ **into,** (colloq.) encounter through unwariness (*walked into the trap*), (sl.) attack forcefully, eat (meal etc.) heartily; ∼ **it,** (1) perform journey on foot, not ride, (2) have easy victory; ∼ **off,** depart (esp. abruptly); ∼ **off with,** (colloq.) steal, win easily; ∼**-on,** = WALKING[1]-*on part* or its player; ∼ (= TREAD) **on air;** ∼ **out,** ‖go for walks (*with*) in courtship, depart suddenly and angrily, whence ∼*-out n.* (esp. as protest or strike); ∼ **out on,** desert, leave in the lurch; ∼ **over,** (1) treat contemptuously, (2) traverse (racecourse, or abs.) at walk if one wishes or with little effort, owing to absence or inferiority of competitors, whence ∼*-over* n., easy victory or achievement; ∼ **tall,** be proud; ∼ **up!** (showman's invitation to circus etc.); ∼ **up to,** approach (person) for talk etc.; *∼-**up** *n.* & *a.,* (building) with access to upper floors only by stairs. [OE *wealcan* roll, toss, wander, corresp. to MDu. & MLG *walken* to full, cudgel, ON *valka* drag about f. Gmc **walk-*]

walk[2] (wawk) *n.* **1.** walking gait or pace, person's action in walking, (*go at, never gets beyond, a walk; know him by his walk; win* etc. **in a** ∼, without effort). **2.** traversing of distance by walking (*is only ten minutes' walk from here*); excursion on foot, stroll, constitutional, (*go for, take, take person for, a walk; to the castle and back is a good walk*); journey on foot completed to earn money promised for charity etc.; (Math.) sequence of distinct movements from point to point; SPACE[1] *walk.* **3.** person's favourite walking-ground; round of hawker, postman, etc.; place or track or route intended or suitable for strollers or foot-passengers, promenade, colonnade, footpath; place where hound-puppy is sent to accustom it to various surroundings; place where gamecock is kept (COCK[1] *of the walk*); part of forest under one keeper; ROPE-*walk*; ‖SHEEP-*walk*; ∼ **of life,** calling, profession, occupation. **4.** ∼'**way,** passage for walking along (esp. one connecting different sections of a building), wide path in garden etc. [ME, f. prec.]

wa'lker (waw'k-) *n.* In vbl senses; wheeled or footed framework for person (e.g. baby or cripple) unable to walk unaided; bird of kind that walks instead of hopping or swimming. [ME, f. WALK[1] + -ER[1]]

wa'lkie-talkie (waw'kĭtawkĭ, -taw'-) *n.* radio transmitting- and receiving-set carried on the person to provide two-way communication as one walks about. [f. WALK[1] + TALK + -IE]

wa'lking[1] (waw'k-) *n.* In vbl senses; **heel-and-toe** ∼ (in which both heel and toe are used, as required in walking-races); ∼-**o'n part** (in which actor or actress appears on stage but does not speak); ∼ **papers,** (colloq.) dismissal; ∼-**stick,** (1) stick carried when walking, esp. as added support, (2) *STICK[2]-insect; ∼-**tour,** pleasure-journey of some days on foot. [ME, f. WALK[1] + -ING[1]]

wa'lking[2] (waw'k-) *a.* In vbl senses; ∼ **delegate,** trade-union official who visits members and their employers for discussions; ∼ **dictionary** or **encyclopaedia,** person able to provide much miscellaneous information; ∼ **fern,** Amer. evergreen fern of genus *Camptosorus,* whose fronds take root at their ends; ∼ **gentleman** or **lady,** theatrical performer without speaking part, needed for appearance only; ∼ **leaf,** (1) = *walking fern,* (2) = leaf-insect; ∼ **wounded** (able to walk despite injuries). [ME, f. WALK[1] + -ING[2]]

wall (wawl) *n.,* & *v.t.* **1.** *n.* continuous and usu. vertical and solid structure of stones, bricks, concrete, timber, etc., narrow in proportion to length and height, serving to enclose (partly) or protect or divide off town, house, room, field, etc.; surface of inner side(s) of room, esp. as place for display of pictures etc.; *with* one's BACK[1] *to the wall;* **blank** ∼ (without door or gate or window, or without decoration); **bang** or **run** one's **head against a** (**brick**) ∼, attempt the impossible; **see through a brick** ∼, have miraculous insight; ∼**s have ears,** eavesdroppers are or may be present; PARTY[1]-*wall;* RETAINING *wall;* (*drive* or *send* person) **up the** ∼, (colloq.) crazy or furious; WRITING *on the wall.* **2.** thing resembling wall in appearance or effect; steep side of mountain; protection or obstacle consisting of weapons etc.; vertical outermost part of hollow structure; (Anat., Zool., & Bot.) outermost layer of organ, cell, etc.; (Mining) rock enclosing lode or seam. **3.** (arch.) (position next to) wall as opp. gutter side of street footpath (**give** person **the** ∼, allow him cleaner and safer part in passing; **take the** ∼ **of,** refuse this courtesy to). **4.** side as opp. centre of road (*the weakest* **goes to the** ∼, is pushed aside, gets the worst in competition). **5.** ∼-**barley,** wild barley as weed; ∼-**board** (made from wood-pulp etc. and used to cover walls); ∼-**cress,** plant of genus *Arabis* growing in stony places; ∼-**fern,** common polypody; ∼'**flower,** yellow-flowered plant of genus *Cheiranthus* growing wild on old walls, fragrant spring garden-plant (*C. cheiri*) with usu. orange or brown or yellow clustered flowers, (colloq.) woman sitting out dances for lack of partners; ∼-**fruit** (of trees fastened against wall for protection and warmth); ‖∼ **game,** Eton form of football played beside a wall; ∼-**painting** (on wall usu. of room, esp. fresco); ∼'**paper** (for pasting over room-walls, freq. with decorative printed patterns); ∼-**pepper,** pungent kind of stonecrop; ∼-**plate,** timber laid in or on wall to distribute pressure of girder etc.; *wall*-ROCKET[1]; ∼-**rue,** small fern with leaves like rue, growing on walls and rocks; ∼-**to**∼, (of carpet) covering whole floor of room. **6.** Hence ∼-LESS *a.* **7.** *v.t.* (esp. in *p.p.*) provide or protect with wall; hence ∼'ING[1] (2) *n.* **8.** block up (aperture etc.), seal *off* (space), with wall; shut *up* (person) within wall. [OE, = OS *wal,* f. L *vallum* rampart (*vallus* stake)]

wa'llaby (wŏ'-) *n.* **1.** small species of kangaroo; **on the** ∼ (**track**), (Austral.) vagrant, unemployed. **2.** (*W*∼; in *pl.,* colloq.) Australians, esp. Australian international Rugby Union team. [f. Aboriginal *wolabā*]

Wallach. Var. of WALACH.

wallah (wŏ'la) *n.* (orig. Anglo-Ind., now sl.) person employed about or concerned with something, -man; BOX[2]-*wallah;* **competition-**∼, Indian civil servant appointed by competitive examination. [f. Hindi *-wālā* suf. = -ER[1] (3)]

wallaroo' (wŏ-) *n.* large brownish-black kangaroo (*Macropus robustus*). [f. Aboriginal *wolarū*]

wa'llet (wŏ'-) *n.* **1.** (arch.) bag for carrying personal necessaries, food, etc., on journey, esp. as used by pilgrim or beggar. **2.** flat case for holding banknotes etc. [ME *walet,* prob. f. AF **walet,* perh. f. Gmc **wall-*roll]

wa'll-eye (waw'lī) *n.* eye with iris showing whitish opacity or streaking, or turned outwards in squint;

Amer. pike with large prominent eyes. [back-form. f. foll.]

wa'll-eyed (waw'līd) a. having wall-eye; *(of fish) having large prominent eyes. [ME, f. ON *vagleygr (*vagl, cf. Icel. vagl film over eye; auga EYE¹)]

wa'll-knòt (waw'ln-) n. See WALE. [perh. rel. to Norw. & Sw. valknut double or secure knot]

Wallōo'n (wŏ-) n. & a. **1.** n. member or language (a French dialect) of a Gaulish people in S. Belgium and neighbouring parts of France. **2.** a. of the Walloons or in their language. [f. F Wallon f. med. L Wallo -onis f. Gmc *walhaz foreign; cf. WELSH¹]

wa'llop (wŏ'-) v.t., & n. (sl.) **1.** v.t. thrash, beat; hit hard; (in pres. part.) big, strapping, thumping; hence ~ING¹ (1) n. **2.** n. heavy resounding blow; beer or other drink. [earlier senses 'gallop', 'boil', f. ONF (walop n. f.) waloper, OF galoper f. Frank. *wala hlaupan (*wala well, *hlaupan run, LEAP¹; cf. GALLOP)]

wa'llow (wŏ'lō) v.i., & n. **1.** v.i. roll about in mud, sand, water, etc.; take gross or unrestrained delight in sensuality etc. **2.** n. act of wallowing; place to which buffaloes etc. resort to wallow, resulting depression in ground. [OE walwian roll f. WG *walwōjan f. Gmc *walw-, *welw- roll f. IE *wolw-, *welw-]

Wa'll Street (waw'l-) n. American financial interests or money-market. [street in New York City]

wa'lnut (waw'l-) n. (tree of genus Juglans yielding) nut containing delicate-flavoured kernel in pair of boat-shaped shells; timber of walnut-tree used in cabinet making. [OE walh-hnutu f. Gmc *walhaz foreign + *hnut- NUT]

Walpur'gis night (vahlpoor'gis-nīt) n. eve of 1 May, when (acc. to G legend) witches meet on the Brocken or elsewhere and hold revels with the Devil. [f. G Walpurgisnacht (Walpurgis gen. of Walpurga 8th-c. Engl. woman saint, nacht NIGHT)]

wa'lrus (waw'l-, wŏ'l-) n. large amphibious carnivorous arctic long-tusked mammal (Odobenus rosmarus) related to seal and sea-lion; ~ moustache (long, thick, and hanging down at sides). [prob. f. Du. walrus, -ros, perh. by metath. after walvisch 'whale-fish' f. wd repr. by OE horschwæl 'horse-whale']

waltz (wawlts, wawls, wŏ-) n. & v. **1.** n. (music for) dance in triple time with graceful flowing melody, performed by couples who progress and rotate simultaneously. **2.** v.i. dance waltz; dance in, out, round, etc., in joy etc.; move easily or casually. **3.** v.t. move easily or casually. **3.** v.t. move (person) in or as in waltz; waltz MATILDA. **4.** Hence ~ER¹ n.; ~'ing mouse (of breed unable to walk straight). [f. G walzer (walzen revolve)]

wa'mpum (wŏ'-) n. beads made from shells and string for money or decoration or as mnemonic patterns by N. Amer. Indians. [f. Algonquin wampumpeag (wap white, umpe string, -ag pl. suf.)]

wan (wŏn) a. (Of person or his complexion or look) pale, looking worn or exhausted; (of heavenly body or its light) faint, partly obscured; (arch., of night, water, etc.) dark, black; hence ~'LY² adv., ~'NESS (-n-n-) n. [OE wann dark, black, of unkn. orig.]

wand (wŏ-) n. slender rod for carrying in hand or setting in ground as temporary mark; magician's or music-conductor's baton; staff symbolizing some officials' authority. [ME, f. ON *vandur, vöndr, = OE wandus, prob. f. Gmc *wanduz (*wend-, *wand-; cf. WEND¹, WIND³)]

wa'nder (wŏ'-) v. & n. **1.** v.i. go from country to country or from place to place without settled route or destination; go aimlessly in, off, etc.; (of river or road) wind, meander; ~ing Jew, (1) legendary person supposed to be still living from when Christ said 'Thou shalt wander on the earth till I return' as punishment for an insult, (2) person who never settles down, (3) climbing plant of genus Tradescantia etc.; ~ing sailor, moneywort; ~-plug (to be fitted into any of various sockets in electrical device); hence

~ER¹ n. **2.** stray, diverge from the right way (lit. or fig.), get lost, depart from home. **3.** talk or think irrelevantly or disconnectedly or incoherently, stray from subject in hand, be inattentive or delirious, (his mind wandered; wanders in his talk). **4.** v.t. traverse in wandering (you may wander the world (through) and not find such another). **5.** Hence ~ING¹ (1) n. (esp. in pl.). **6.** n. act of wandering. [OE wandrian = MLG, MDu. wanderen, f. WG *wandrōjan (as WEND¹; see -ER⁵)]

wa'nderlust (wŏ'nderlŭst, vah'nderlŏost) n. eager desire or fondness for travelling or wandering. [G]

wanderoō (wŏ-) n. langur or macaque of Sri Lanka. [f. Sinh. wanderu monkey]

wa'ndoō (wŏ'-) n. W. Austral. eucalyptus with white bark and durable brown wood. [Aboriginal]

wāne v.i., & n. **1.** v.i. decrease in brilliance, size, or splendour; (of moon) decrease in apparent size after the full (cf. WAX²); lose power or vigour or importance or repute, decline. **2.** n. process of waning; on the ~, waning, declining. **3.** defect of plank etc. that lacks square corners; hence wā'ney² a. [OE wanian lessen, = OS wanon, OHG wanōn, wanēn, ON vana, Goth. *wanan f. Gmc *wanōjan (*wana- lacking f. IE *wa-)]

wā'ngle (-nggel) v.t., & n. (sl.) **1.** v.t. secure (favour, desired result) by scheming or contrivance, show in the desired light, fake, (report etc.). **2.** n. act of wangling. [19th-c. printers' sl.; orig. unkn.]

wa'nion (wŏ'nyon) n. (arch.) with a ~ (to), with a curse (on), with a vengeance. [var. of waniand part. of WANE (waning moon = unlucky hour)]

wänk n., & v.i. (vulg.) (engage in) masturbation; hence ~'ER¹ n. (also, contemptible person). [20th c.; orig. unkn.]

Wä'nkel (w-, v-) n. ~ engine, rotary internal combustion engine with continuously rotated and eccentrically pivoted nearly triangular shaft. [f. F. ~, Ger. engineer b. 1902]

want¹ (wŏ-) n. **1.** lack, absence, deficiency, of (ship rotting for want of paint; took this for want of anything better; shows great want of thought, care, sense, judgement). **2.** need of, need of sustenance, poverty, (is in want of money, a gardener; living in great want). **3.** desire for thing held necessary to life or happiness or success or completion, thing so desired, (a man of few wants; meets a long-felt want; can supply your wants); *~ ad, newspaper advertisement by person seeking to obtain employee or thing. [ME, f. ON vant neut. of vanr lacking = OE wana, f. as WANE]

want² (wŏ-) v. **1.** v.t. be without or deficiently supplied with; fall short by (specified amount) of specified limit. **2.** v.i. be in want (for; let him want for nothing; must not be allowed to want). **3.** v.t. require, need, (thing, doing, to be done, to do). **4.** desire, wish for possession or presence of, (to do, thing, person; I want some sugar, it done, you to try; call me if I am wanted); do not ~ to, (1) am unwilling to, (2) ought not to (you don't want to overdo it); ~ed (by the police), suspected to be criminal etc. **5.** v.i. (US & Sc. colloq.) desire to come or go or get (want out). [ME, f. ON vanta (as prec.)]

wa'nting (wŏ'-) a. lacking in quality or quantity; unequal to requirements; absent; deficient (is wanting in judgement); be found ~, not meet requirements. [ME, f. prec.+-ING²]

wa'nton (wŏ'-) a., n., & v.i. **1.** a. sportive, gambolling, playful, irresponsible, capricious, (wanton child, kid, wind, mood); luxuriant, unrestrained, wild, (wanton growth, ringlets, profusion). **2.** licentious, unchaste, lewd, (a wanton woman; wanton thoughts). **3.** motiveless, serving no purpose, random, arbitrary, (wanton mischief, destruction). **4.** Hence ~'LY² adv., ~'NESS (-n-n-) n. **5.** n. licentious person. **6.** v.i. sport, gambol, move capriciously; behave licentiously (with). [ME wantowen (wan- UN-², towen f. OE togen p.p. of tēon discipline, cogn. w. TEAM)]

||wa'pentake (wă'-, wŏ'-) n. (Hist.) hundred or division of shire (in areas of England that had large

Danish population). [OE *wǣpen(ge)tæc* f. ON *vápnatak* (*vápn* weapon, *tak* taking f. *taka* TAKE[1]); perh. w. ref. to voting in assembly by show of weapons]

wa'piti (wŏ'-) *n*. N. Amer. elk, resembling red deer but larger. [f. Cree *wapitik* white deer]

war[1] (wôr) *n*. **1.** strife usu. between nations conducted by force; state of open hostility and suspension of ordinary international law prevalent during such strife, military or naval or air attack or series of attacks; period of such strife (TROJAN *War*; *Wars of the* ROSE[1]*s*; **the War**, one in progress or recently ended); (fig.) hostility or contention between persons, efforts to combat crime, disease, poverty, etc., natural conflict compared to war (∼ **of the elements**, storms and catastrophes in nature). **2. art of** ∼, strategy and tactics; **at** ∼, engaged in hostilities (*with* enemy); **carry the** ∼ **into the enemy's camp** or **country**, (fig.) make counter-accusations etc., not confine oneself to defence; CIVIL *war*; **cold** ∼, unfriendly relations between nations (esp. USSR and West after Second World War), with hostile propaganda but not fighting; COUNCIL *of war*; **declare** ∼, announce imposition of hostilities (*on* nation or fig. institution, practice, etc.); **dogs of** ∼, (poet.) havoc accompanying war; **gang** ∼, fighting between members of rival gangs of criminals etc.; **go to** ∼, begin hostile operations; **go to the** ∼**s**, (arch.) serve as soldier; **a good** ∼, (colloq.) an enjoyable time during a war; **holy** ∼ (waged in support of a religious cause); HOT[1] *war*; **have been in the** ∼**s**, (colloq.) show signs of injury or rough usage; **laws of** ∼, limitations on belligerents' action recognized by civilized nations; MAN[1]-*of-war*; **private** ∼, feud between persons or families disregarding law of murder etc., or hostilities against members of another State without sanction of one's own government; **rights of** ∼ (permitting belligerents certain acts illegitimate in peace); SHOOTING *war*; TOTAL *war*; **trade of** ∼, soldier's profession; TUG *of war*; *war of* ATTRITION; ∼ **to the knife**, relentless struggle to the bitter end esp. between persons; ∼ **of nerves**, attempt to wear down opponent by gradual destruction of morale; WORLD *war*. **3.** ∼ **baby**, (esp. illegitimate) child born in wartime; ∼ **bride**, woman who marries soldier etc. met as result of war; ∼ **chest**, funds for war or other campaign; ∼**-cloud**, state of international affairs that threatens war; ∼ **correspondent** (employed to send reports from scene of war); ∼ **crime, criminal**, (perpetrator of) action violating laws of war; ∼**-cry**, phrase or name shouted in charging or rallying to attack, party catchword; ∼ **damage** (caused by events resulting from war); ∼**-dance** (performed by primitive peoples before war or after victory); ∼ **department**, State office in charge of army; ∼**-game**, kriegspiel, or similar exercise testing tactical knowledge; ∼**-gaming**, conduct of battles with toy soldiers; ∼**-god**, one worshipped as giving victory in war, esp. the Greek Ares or Roman Mars; ∼ **grave** (of person killed in fighting); ∼**'head**, explosive head of missile, torpedo, or similar weapon; ∼**-horse**, knight's or trooper's powerful horse, (fig.) veteran soldier or politician; ||∼ **loan**, stock issued by Government to raise funds in wartime; ∼**-lord**, military commander(-in-chief); ∼ **memorial**, monument etc. commemorating those killed in a war; ∼**'monger**, one who seeks to bring about war; ||**War Office**, (Hist.) State department in charge of army; ∼**-paint**, paint put on body esp. by N. Amer. Indians before battle, (colloq.) ceremonial costume, full fig, cosmetics; ∼**-path**, (route of) warlike expedition of N. Amer. Indians (*be, go, on the* ∼*-path*, (fig.) be engaged in, enter upon, any conflict, have taken, take, hostile attitude); ∼**-plane**, military aircraft; ∼ **poet** (writing on topics relating to wars, esp. the two world wars); ∼**'ship** (for use in war); ∼**-song** (inciting to war, or celebrating martial deeds);

∼**'time**, period when war is being waged; ∼**-weary**, dejected by prolonged war; ∼**-whoop**, yell esp. of N. Amer. Indians in charging; ∼**-widow**, woman whose husband has been killed in war; ∼**-work**, work done on account of a war; ∼**-worn**, experienced in or damaged or exhausted by war. [ME *werre* f. AF, ONF, var. of OF *guerre* f. WG **werra* (cf. OHG *werra* confusion, strife, OS, OHG *werran* embroil), f. Gmc **werz-, *wers-* (cf. WORSE)]

war[2] (wôr) *v*. (**-rr-**). **1.** *v.i*. (arch.) make war. **2.** *v.t*. bring or beat *down* by war. **3.** (in *pres. part*.) rival, competing, inconsistent, (*warring creeds, factions, principles*). [ME, f. prec.]

War. *abbr*. Warwickshire.

wa'ratah (wŏ'-) *n*. Austral. crimson-flowered shrub of genus *Telopea*. [Aboriginal]

war'ble[1] (wôr'-) *v*. &. *n*. **1.** *v.i*. & *t*. (Esp. of bird, also fig. of person or sound) sing in gentle continuous trilling manner. **2.** *v.t*. speak or utter in manner suggestive of warbling bird's song; express in song or verse. **3.** *n*. warbled song or utterance. [ME, f. ONF *werble(r)* f. Frank. *hwirbilōn* whirl, trill]

war'ble[2] (wôr'-) *n*. hard lump on horse's back from galling of saddle; (tumour on cattle etc. produced by) larva of ∼ **fly** beneath skin. [16th c.; orig. uncert.]

war'bler (wôr'-) *n*. In vbl senses; small bird of family Sylviidae or *Parulidae, e.g. blackcap, whitethroat, and chiff-chaff, sometimes not remarkable for song. [f. WARBLE[1]+-ER[1]]

ward[1] (wôrd) *n*. **1.** (arch.) act of guarding or defending place etc. (cf. WATCH[1] 2); bailey of castle. **2.** (arch.) confinement, custody, guardian's control. **3.** minor under care of guardian; ∼ (**of court**), minor, insane person, etc., under protection of court such as Court of Chancery. **4.** administrative division esp. for elections. **5.** separate room or division in prison (*condemned* etc. *ward*) or hospital (ISOLATION etc. *ward*; WALK[1] *the wards*) ||or (Hist.) workhouse (CASUAL etc. *ward*). **6.** (in *pl*.) notches and projections in key and lock designed to prevent opening of lock by wrong key. **7.** **ward*-HEEL[2]*er*; ∼**-maid**, woman employed to clean etc. in hospital ward; ||∼**-mote**, (Hist.) meeting of citizens or liverymen of ward [f. as MOOT]; ∼**'room** (in warship, for commissioned officers). [OE *weard*, = OHG *warta* watch, ON *vartha* cairn f. Gmc **wardho* (**wardh-* extended form of **war-* WARE[2,3]; cf. GUARD[1])]

ward[2] (wôrd) *v.t*. ∼ ∼ (**off**), parry (blow), avert (danger, poverty, etc.). **2.** (arch.) guard, protect. [OE *weardian*, = OS *wardon*, OHG *wartēn*, ON *vartha* f. Gmc **wardhōjan* (as prec.)]

-ward *suf*. forming *adjs*. w. sense 'having specified direction or tendency' (*backward, downward, eastward, homeward, onward, toward*), also used as *advs*. (= -WARDS) and *ns*. (*to the eastward*); **to usward**, (arch.) towards us. [f. or after OE *-weard* f. Gmc **-wardha* (**wardh-* var. of **werth-* turn)]

war'den[1] (wôr'-) *n*. **1.** president or governor (*of* some colleges, schools, hospitals, *prisons, youth hostels, etc.). **2.** official appointed to perform supervisory duties (CHURCH[1]*warden*, GAME[1]-*warden*, ||TRAFFIC *warden*), esp. (**air-raid**) ∼ (helping civilian population in air raids). **3.** Hence ∼SHIP *n*. [ME, f. AF & ONF *wardein*, var. of OF *g(u)arden* GUARDIAN]

war'den[2] (wôr'-) *n*. kind of cooking pear. [ME, of unkn. orig.]

war'der (wôr'-) *n*. **1.** ||gaoler, whence **war'dress**[1] (wôr'-) *n*. **2.** (Hist.) staff of authority carried by commander and used to give signals. **3.** (arch.) sentinel, watchman. [ME, f. AF *wardere, -our* f. ONF *warder*, OF *garder* (see GUARD[1], -ER[2]); sense 2 partly f. *warderer* perh. f. obs. *warderere* look out behind!]

War'dour Street (wôr'der-) *n*. antique and imitation-antique furniture trade (∼ **English**, affectedly archaic); cinema film trade. [name of street in London]

war'drobe (wôr'-) *n*. place where clothes are kept,

esp. large cabinet or movable cupboard with pegs, shelves, etc.; person's or persons' stock of clothes; department of royal household in charge of garments; ∼ **bed,** bed that can be folded up into wardrobe; ∼ **dealer,** dealer in second-hand clothes; ∼ **master,** ∼ **mistress,** one who has charge of professional wardrobe of an actor, actress, or theatrical company; ∼ **trunk** (fitted with separate drawers, coat-hangers, etc., and designed to stand on end, serving as wardrobe). [ME, f. ONF *warderobe*, OF *garderobe* (as GUARD², ROBE)]

-wards (-z) *suf.* forming *advs.* (and *adjs.*) w. sense 'to or in the direction of' (*backwards, downwards, eastwards, homewards, onwards, towards*). [f. as -WARD + -s³]

war′dship (wȯr′-) *n.* tutelage, guardian's care, (*under wardship; has the wardship of*). [ME, f. WARD¹ + -SHIP]

wāre¹ *n.* **1.** things manufactured for sale, esp. pottery of any kind, or in comb. (HARDware, IRON¹ware, ‖SMALLwares). **2.** (usu. in *pl.*) articles that person etc. has for sale (usu. *his* etc. *wares*). **3.** (With distinctive epithet) kind of manufactured material, esp. pottery (*Wedgwood, Delft, biscuit,* etc., *ware*), named from inventor, place of manufacture, or some characteristic. **4.** ∼**′house** *n.,* building in which goods are stored, repository, wholesale or large retail store; ∼**′house** (or -z) *v.t.,* store (esp. furniture or bonded goods) temporarily in repository; ∼**′houseman,** worker in or owner of repository; cf. ITALIAN. [OE *waru,* = MDu., MLG *ware,* ON *vara* f. Gmc **warō,* perh. orig. = 'object of care', cogn. w. foll.]

wāre² *pred. a.* (poet.) aware. [OE *wær,* = OS *war,* OHG *giwar,* Goth. **wars* f. Gmc **war-;* cf. WARD¹]

ware³, ′ware, (wār, wȯr) *v.t.* (esp. in *imper.*) look out for, be cautious about, avoid, (*ware hounds, wire, traps!,* esp. in hunting-field). [OE *warian,* = OS *waron,* OHG *-warōn,* ON *vara* f. Gmc **war-* (as prec.), & f. ONF *warer* f. Gmc]

war′fare (wȯr′-) *n.* state of war, campaigning, being engaged in war, (*after long warfare; bacteriological, chemical, warfare; his warfare is over*). [ME, f. WAR¹ + FARE¹]

war′like (wȯr′-) *a.* martial, fond of or skilful in war; military, of or for war, (*warlike preparations*); bellicose, threatening war. [ME, f. WAR¹ + -LIKE]

war′lock (wȯr′-) *n.* (arch.) sorcerer, wizard. [OE *wær-loga* traitor (= OS *wār-logo*) f. *wǣr* covenant + **log* cogn. w. LIE²]

warm¹ (wȯrm) *a. & n.* **1.** *a.* of or at fairly high temperature (*hot, warm, tepid, cool, cold; warm water, weather, countries*); (of blood) remaining at temperature generally well above that of the surroundings as in mammals and birds; (of person etc.) (1) at natural temperature, not cold, (2) having temperature of skin raised by exercise or excitement or external heat; **keep a place** ∼, occupy it temporarily on behalf of another. **2.** (Of clothes etc.) serving to keep one warm; (of exertion etc.) making one warm. **3.** (Of friendly relations or actions or agents) sympathetic, hearty, zealous, (*a warm partisan, friend,* WELCOME, RECEPTION; *warm thanks*). **4.** animated, heated, exciting or excited, in or resulting from sanguine or offended or indignant or unreserved mood, (*when warm with wine; the dispute or disputants grew warm*). **5.** (Of position etc.) difficult or dangerous to maintain or meet (*warm* RECEPTION *or* WELCOME; **make it or things** ∼ **for** person, create strong feeling against him). **6.** (Of feelings etc.) sympathetic, cordial, affectionate, susceptible, (*has a warm heart, smile*); (of temperament) amorous, prone to sexual desire; (of description etc.) intended to appeal to erotic feelings. **7.** (Of colour) suggestive of warmth, esp. containing rich reds or yellows. **8.** (Of scent in hunting) fresh and strong, indicating recent passage of quarry; (of seeker in children's hiding games etc.) near the object sought, on verge of finding. **9.** ‖(arch., colloq.) (Of person) comfortably off, rich. **10.** ∼**-blooded,** having warm blood, (fig.) ardent, passionate; ∼

front (of advancing mass of warm air); ∼**-hearted,** affectionate, cordial; ∼ **work,** keen or dangerous conflict (and cf. sense 2). **11.** Hence ∼′ISH¹ 2 *a.,* ∼′LY² *adv.,* ∼′TH¹ *n.* **12.** *n.* warmth of atmosphere; warm thing, esp. BRITISH *warm.* [OE *wearm,* = OS, OHG *warm,* ON *varmr* f. Gmc **warmaz,* prob. f. IE **ghworm-* etc.]

warm² (wȯrm) *v. & n.* **1.** *v.t.* make warm, excite, (*fire warms room, person,* etc.; *wine to warm the heart; warm oneself at fire* etc.). **2.** *v.i.* warm oneself at fire etc.; ∼ **(up),** become warm or animated or sympathetic (*room is warming up; he warmed up as he got into his subject, warmed to his subject; my heart warms to him*). **3.** ∼ **up,** (of radio, engine, etc.) reach temperature of efficient working; (of athlete etc.) prepare for contest by exercise or practice; hence ∼*-up n.;* ∼**-ed-up** or **-over,* (of food, lit. or fig.) reheated, stale. **4.** ∼**′ing-pan,** flat closed long-handled usu. brass vessel for holding live coals formerly used for warming inside of bed before it was occupied, (fig.) person holding office temporarily to keep it for another not yet ready. **5.** Hence (-)∼′ER¹ (2) *n.* **6.** *n.* warming or being warmed (*must have, give it, another warm first*). [OE *werman* v.t. (= OS *wermian,* OHG *wermen,* ON *verma,* Goth. *warmjan,* f Gmc **warmjan*), & OE *wearmian* v.i. (= OHG *war(a)mēn*) f. Gmc **warmējan,* cf. prec.]

warn (wȯrn) *v.t.* give notice to, put on guard, admonish, (person or abs.); *of* danger or consequences or future or unknown present circumstance, *against* person or thing or doing, *that* something impends or must be reckoned with, *that* he is neglecting or has neglected to do something, *to* (= that he must) do); ∼ **off,** tell (person) to keep away (from), (Racing) prohibit from attending races (at); ∼**′ing coloration,** (Biol.) conspicuous colouring that warns an enemy against attacking. [OE *war(e)nian, wearnian,* = OHG *warnēn, warnōn,* f. WG **warnōjan, -ǣjan* f. Gmc **war-;* cf. WARE²]

war′ning (wȯr′) *n.* In vbl senses (**take** ∼, change one's course of action when warned of its danger); thing that serves to warn (*palpitation is a warning of heart trouble; let this be a warning to you*); **give** ∼, (arch.) give notice, announce that employment, tenancy, etc., is to terminate in specified (e.g. a month's) time. [OE *war(e)nung* etc. (as prec., -ING¹)]

warp¹ (wȯrp) *v.t. & i.* **1.** make or become crooked or perverted, change from straight or right or natural state, bias, (*sun had warped the boards; seasoned timber does not warp; hardship warped his disposition; judgement warped by self-interest; has a somewhat warped sense of humour*). **2.** (Naut.) haul (ship) in some direction by rope attached to fixed point; progress thus. **3.** *v.t.* fertilize by inundating with warp; choke *up* (channel) with alluvial deposit; arrange (threads) as warp. [OE *weorpan* throw, = OS *werpan,* OHG *werfan,* ON *verpa,* Goth. *wairpan,* f. Gmc **werp-, *warp-*]

warp² (wȯrp) *n.* **1.** threads stretched lengthwise in loom to be crossed by weft. **2.** rope used in towing or warping, or attached to trawl-net. **3.** state of being warped, esp. crooked state produced in timber etc. by uneven shrinkage or expansion; (fig.) perversion or perverse inclination in mind. **4.** sediment or alluvial deposit, esp. that left by turbid water kept standing on poor land. [OE *wearp,* = OHG *warf,* ON *varp,* f. Gmc **warp-* (cf. prec.), or f. prec.]

warragal. Var of WARRIGAL.

wa′rrant¹ (wǒ′-) *n.* **1.** thing or person that authorizes (person in) action (*have no warrant for this action; his promise or order, our strength, is our warrant; I will be your warrant; with the warrant of a good conscience*). **2.** voucher, written authorization to receive money (*dividend warrant*), obtain or supply goods or services (*travel warrant;* ROYAL *warrant*), carry out arrest or search (DISTRESS¹-, SEARCH-, *warrant*), represent principal in lawsuit (*warrant of attorney*), etc. **3.** certificate of service rank held by ∼**-officer** (between commissioned officers and NCOs). [ME f. ONF *warant, -and,* var. of

OF *guarant, -and*, f. Frank. *werēnd* (*giwerēn* be surety for)]

wa′rrant[2] (wŏ′-) *v.t.* **1.** serve as warrant for, justify, (*nothing can warrant such insolence*); hence ∿ABLE *a.*, that can be warranted, (of stag) old enough to be hunted (5 or 6 years). **2.** = GUARANTEE 2, (esp.) answer for genuineness etc. of; **I** or **I'll** ∿ (**you**), (usu. parenth.) I am certain, no DOUBT[1]; hence ∿ER[1], ∿OR, ∿EE′ (one to whom warranty is given), *ns.* [ME, f. OF *warantir, -dir*, vars. of *g(u)arantir, -dir*, (as prec.)]

wa′rranty (wŏ′-) *n.* authority or justification (usu. *for* doing or saying or supposing); (Law) express or implied undertaking on vendor's part that thing sold is vendor's and is fit for use or fulfils specified conditions, often accepting responsibility for necessary repairs over a specified period; undertaking by insured person of truth of statement or fulfilment of condition. [ME, f. AF *warantie*, var. of *garantie* (as WARRANT[1]; see -Y[1])]

wa′rren (wŏ′-) *n.* piece of ground in which rabbits abound or are preserved or (Hist.) game is preserved; (fig.) densely populated district, region with many narrow winding streets etc.; so ∿ER[2] *n.*, person in charge of rabbit-warren or game-warren. [ME, f. AF & ONF *warenne*, OF *garenne* game-park f. Gaulish *varrenna* fenced-off area (*varros* post)]

wa′rrigal (wŏ′-) *n.* & *a.* (Austral.) **1.** *n.* dingo dog; untamed horse; wild Aboriginal. **2.** *a.* wild, untamed. [Aboriginal]

wa′rrior (wŏ′-) *n.* fighting man; (rhet. or poet.) distinguished or veteran soldier; member of any of the fighting services (UNKNOWN *Warrior*); COLD[1] *warrior*; (*attrib.*, of nation etc.) martial; ∿ **ant** (that makes slaves of other species). [ME, f. ONF *werreior* etc., OF *guerreior* etc. (*werreier, guerreier*, make WAR[1]; see -ER[2], -OR)]

wart (wôrt) *n.* **1.** small hardish roundish excrescence on skin caused by virus-induced abnormal growth of papillae and thickening of epidermis (∿**s and all**, without concealment of blemishes or unattractive parts). **2.** similar lump on stem etc. of plant; (colloq.) objectionable person. **3.** ∿**-cress**, creeping weed of genus *Coronopus*; ∿**-grass, -weed, -wort**, kind of spurge with juice thought to cure warts; ∿**-hog**, large-headed Afr. wild pig of genus *Phacocoerus*, with warty lumps on face and large curved tusks. **4.** Hence ∿′Y[2] *a.* [OE *wearte*, = OS *warta*, OHG *warza*, ON *varta* f. Gmc *wartōn*]

war′ily *a.* given to caution, habitually on the look-out, circumspect; cautious in the matter *of* person, thing, or do*ing*; showing, or done with, caution; hence ∿ILY[2] *adv.*, ∿INESS *n.* [f. WARE[2] + -Y[2]]

was. See BE.

wash[1] (wŏ-) *v.* **1.** *v.t.* cleanse with liquid esp. water (*wash* one's *face* etc., one*self*, or any object); ∿ thing **out**, (1) clean its inside by washing, (2) clean it by brief washing of its fabric; *wash* one's *dirty* LINEN; ∿ one's **hands**, (fig.) decline responsibility etc. *of*, (euphem.) go to lavatory. **2.** (fig.) purify (*wash me throughly from mine iniquity*). **3.** take (stain, dirt, etc.) *out* or *off* or *away* by washing. **4.** ∿ **up**, *wash one's face and hands, ‖wash (table utensils etc.; usu. abs.) after use. **5.** *v.i.* wash oneself or esp. one's (face and) hands (*must wash before dinner*); wash clothes. **6.** (Of coloured material or dye) bear washing without loss of colour; (of stain etc.) be taken *off* or *out* by washing; **won't** ∿, (colloq., of argument etc.) will not stand examination; ∿**ed out**, faded by washing, (fig.) enfeebled, limp, demoralized; hence ∿′ING[2] *a.* (*washing prints*). **7.** *v.t.* moisten (*roses washed with dew*); (of river, sea, etc.) touch (coast, bank, country) with its waters. **8.** (Of moving liquid) carry along in specified direction (*a wave washed him overboard; was washed up* (*by the sea*) (= on to shore); *beef washed down with ale*); erode, denude, (*sea-washed cliffs*); scoop out (*water had washed a channel*); ∿ **out**, cause wash-out of (road etc.), rain off (event etc.); ∿**ed up**, (sl.)

defeated, having failed. **9.** *v.i.* go splashing or sweeping *over, along, out, in*, or *into*. **10.** *v.t.* sift (ore) by action of water. **11.** brush thin coating of watery colour over (paper in water-colour or sepia painting, wall), coat (inferior metal) thinly *with* gold etc.; ∿ **out**, (colloq.) cancel. **12.** ∿**-and-wear** *a.*, (of garment) easily washed, quickly dried, and needing no ironing; ∿**-basin** (for washing one's hands etc.); ∿**-boiler**, clothes-washing cauldron, copper; ∿**-bottle**, apparatus for purifying gases etc. by passage through liquid; ∿**-bowl**, = wash-basin; ∿**-cloth**, = ‖DISH[1]*cloth*, * = FACE[1]-*cloth* (1); ‖∿**-hand** *a.*, for use in washing one's hands (*wash-hand basin*; ∿**-hand stand**, piece of furniture to hold basin, jug, soap, etc.); ∿**-house**, (esp. out)building where clothes are washed; ∿**-leather**, chamois or similar leather; ∿**-out**, breach in railway or road track caused by flood, heavy rainfall, etc., (sl.) complete failure, fiasco, (sl.) useless or inefficient person; ∿**-pot**, (arch. w. ref. to Ps. 60:8) vessel for washing one's hands; *∿**-rag**, = FACE[1]-*cloth* (1); *∿**-room**, = LAVATORY 1 & 2; ∿**-stand**, = *wash-hand stand*; ∿**-tub**, tub for washing clothes; *∿**-woman**, washerwoman. **13.** Hence ∿′ABLE *a.*, (esp.) that can be washed without damage. [OE *wæscan* = OS, OHG *wascan*, ON *vaska* f. Gmc **wa(t)skan* (**wat-* WATER[1])]

wash[2] (wŏ-) *n.* **1.** washing or being washed (*give it a good wash; must get or have a wash*); **the** ∿, treatment at laundry (*send the clothes to the wash*); **come out in the** ∿, (fig.) eventually reach satisfactory state); quantity of clothes just (to be, being) washed. **2.** visible or audible motion of agitated water, esp. waves caused by passage of vessel; turbulent air behind moving aircraft. **3.** soil swept off by water, alluvium; sandbank exposed only at low tide. **4.** kitchen slops and scraps given to pigs. **5.** malt etc. fermenting before distillation; thin or weak or inferior liquid food (*this soup, tea, claret, is mere wash*); liquid food for animals; (fig.) twaddle, wish-wash. **6.** liquid for spreading over surface to cleanse or heal or disinfect or colour; lotion, cosmetic (EYE[1]*wash*); thin coating of water-colour, wall-colouring, or metal. **7.** ∿′**board**, board of ribbed wood or sheet of corrugated zinc for use when scrubbing clothes in washing, (fig.) road surface worn to similar shape; ∿**-day** (on which clothes are washed); ∿**-drawing** (made with washes of esp. black or grey water-colour; ∿′**land** (periodically flooded by stream). [ME, f. prec.]

Wash. *abbr.* Washington.

wa′sher (wŏ′-) *n.* In vbl senses (DISH[1]*washer*); flat ring or perforated piece of leather, rubber, metal, etc., used to give tightness to joint, nut, fastening, etc.; ∿**woman**, laundress. [ME, f. WASH[1] + -ER[1]]

wa′shery (wŏ′-) *n.* place where coal etc. is washed. [f. WASH[1] + -ERY]

wa′shing (wŏ′-) *n.* In vbl senses (BOND[1]-*washing*; BRAIN*washing*); clothes etc. sent to the wash; **get on with the** ∿, (sl.) stop wasting time; ∿**-day**, = WASH[2]-*day*; ∿**-machine** (for the washing of clothes etc.); ∿**-powder** (of soap or detergent for washing clothes etc.); ∿**-soda**, sodium carbonate, used dissolved in water for washing and cleaning; ‖∿**-u′p**, (washing of) table utensils after use (∿**-up** *machine*, = DISH[1]*washer* (2)). [ME, f. WASH[1] + -ING[1]]

Washingto′nia (wŏ-) *n.* Californian fan palm of genus *Washingtonia*. [f. G. *Washington*, Amer. statesman d. 1799 + -IA[1]]

wa′shy (wŏ′-) *a.* (Of liquid food etc.) too watery, weak, thin, insipid; (of colour) faded-looking, thin; (of style, sentiment, etc.) diffuse, feeble, lacking vigour or compression; hence ∿ILY[2] *adv.*, ∿INESS *n.* [f. WASH[1,2] + -Y[2]]

wasn't. See BE.

wasp (wŏ-) *n.* hymenopterous social or solitary often carnivorous insect of superfamily Vespoidea, esp. common kind (of genus *Vespa*) with black and yellow transverse stripes, very slender waist, liking for fruit and sweets, and formidable sting; ∿-bee, -beetle, -fly, kinds having some resemblance to wasps; ∿--waist, (esp. woman's) very slender waist. [OE *wæfs*, *wæps*, *wæsp* = OS *wepsia* etc., OHG *wafsa*, *wefsa*, f. WG **wabhis-*, **waps-* f. IE **wobhes-*, **wops-*, perh. cogn. w. WEAVE (from weblike form of nest)]

WASP (wŏsp) *abbr.* (usu. derog.) White Anglo-Saxon Protestant.

wa′spish (wŏ′-) *a.* irritable, petulant, ill-tempered, sharp in retort; hence ∿LY² *adv.*, ∿NESS *n.* [f. WASP + -ISH¹]

wa′ssail (wŏsäl, -sal) *n.*, & *v.i.* (arch.) **1.** *n.* festive occasion, drinking-bout; kind of liquor drunk on such occasion; ∿-bowl etc. (from which healths were drunk, esp. on Twelfth Night and Christmas Eve). **2.** *v.i.* make merry, hold carousing festivities. [ME *wæs hæil* etc., f. ON *ves heill*, corresp. to OE *wes hál* 'be in good health', form of salutation (cf. HALE¹)]

Wa′ssermann (vah′-) *n.* ∿ (test), test for syphilis using reaction of patient's blood serum. [f. A. von ∿, Ger. pathologist d. 1925]

wast. See BE.

wā′stage *n.* amount wasted or that runs to waste, loss by use, wear, decay, leakage, etc.; loss of employees other than by dismissal. [f. WASTE² + -AGE]

wāste¹ *a.* **1.** (Of district etc.) desolate, desert, uninhabited, uncultivated, as result of natural barrenness etc. or of ravages or catastrophe; **lay** ∿, ravage; **lie** ∿, be uncultivated; ∿ **land** (not used for cultivation or building). **2.** (fig.) monotonous, presenting no features of interest, (*the waste periods of history*). **3.** superfluous, refuse, no longer serving a purpose, left over after use; ∿ **paper**, paper regarded as spoiled or valueless; ∿-**paper basket**, basket for temporary storage of waste paper; ∿ **products**, useless by-products of manufacture or of physiological process. [ME, f. ONF *wast*, var. of OF *g(u)ast* f. Rom. **wasto* f. L *vastus*]

wāste² *v.* **1.** *v.t.* ravage; treat (documents etc.) as waste paper. **2.** expend or employ to no purpose or for inadequate result, use extravagantly or ineffectually; squander (*waste money, time, food,* etc., or *abs.*; ∿ **not**, **want not**, extravagance leads to poverty); give (advice etc.) without effect (*on* person); ∿ **breath** or **words**, talk uselessly. **3.** *v.t.* & *i.* wear gradually away, wither, (cause to) lose substance, make or become weak, (*his resources were wasted, were rapidly wasting; a wasting asset; a wasted arm, a wasting disease; is wasting away for lack of food*). **4.** *v.i.* run to waste (*that water is wasting*). **5.** Hence **wā′stABLE** *a.* [ME, f. ONF *waster*, var. of OF *g(u)aster* f. Rom. **wastare* for L *vastare* (*vastus* = prec.)]

wāste³ *n.* **1.** desert, waste region, dreary scene, (**a** ∿ **of waters**, unbroken expanse of sea or floods). **2.** being used up, diminution by wear and tear; hence ∿ LESS (-tl-) *a.* **3.** waste material or food, useless remains or by-products, refuse, scraps, shreds; = COTTON¹ *waste*. **4.** act of wasting, throwing away or extravagant or ineffectual use of money, time, food, etc.; **go to** ∿, **run to** ∿, (of liquid or fig. of affection etc.), be wasted. **5.** (Law). injury to estate caused by act or neglect esp. by a life-tenant. **6.** ∿-basket, = (esp.) WASTE¹-*paper basket*; ∿(-pipe) (to carry off waste material, esp. from washing etc.). [ME, f. ONF *wast(e)*, var. of OF *g(u)ast(e)* f. L *vastum* neut. of *vastus* WASTE¹; partly f. ONF *waster* (see prec.)]

wā′steful (-tf-) *a.* extravagant; causing or exhibiting waste; hence ∿LY² *adv.*, ∿NESS *n.* [ME, f. prec. + -FUL]

wā′ster *n.* In vbl senses; article spoilt or flawed in manufacture; (sl.) good-for-nothing person. [ME, f. AF *wastere* (as WASTE², -ER²), & f. WASTE² + -ER¹]

wā′strel *n.* thing spoilt in making; neglected child, waif; good-for-nothing person; wasteful person. [f. WASTE² + -REL]

watch¹ (wŏ-) *n.* **1.** period of wakefulness at night; ancient division of night-time; **in the** ∿**es of the**

night, while one lies awake, in the night-time; **pass as a** ∿ **in the night**, be soon forgotten. **2.** alert state, being on the look-out, vigilance, constant observation or attention, (*keep watch* or *a watch, good* or *a good watch*); ∿ **and ward**, (orig.) guard by night and day (now merely emphatic for *watch*); **on the** ∿, waiting usu. for expected or desired or feared occurrence; SET¹ *a watch*. **3.** (Hist.) man or body of men charged with patrolling streets at night, guard. **4.** (Hist.) irregular Highland troops in 18th c.; BLACK¹ *Watch*. **5.** four--hour spell of duty on board ship (DOG¹-*watch*; SET¹ *the watch*); one of the halves (**starboard** and **port** ∿ from position of men's bunks) into which ship's crew is divided to take alternate duty; ∿ **and** ∿, such arrangement; ∿ **below**, time when one is off duty. **6.** small portable spring-driven or battery-powered timepiece usu. worn on wrist or carried in pocket; STOP¹-*watch*. **7.** ∿-**case**, outer metal case enclosing works of watch; ∿-**chain**, metal watch-guard; ||W∿ **Committee**, (Hist.) committee of a county borough council dealing with policing etc.; *∿ **crystal**, = *watch-glass* (1); ∿-**dog**, dog kept to guard property etc., (fig.) guardian against infringement etc.; ∿-**fire** (at night in camps etc.); ∿-**glass**, (1) glass disc covering dial of watch, (2) similar piece of glass used as receptacle for experimental material; ∿-**guard**, chain etc. for securing watch when worn on the person; ∿-**key** (for winding up works of watch); ∿′**man**, man employed to look after empty building etc. at night, (arch. or Hist.) sentinel or member of night-watch; ∿-**night**, last night of year, religious service then celebrated; ∿ **oil**, thin kind for lubricating works of watches and clocks; ∿-**pocket** (in garment esp. waistcoat, or separate for attachment to bed etc., holding watch); ∿-**spring**, mainspring of watch; ∿-**strap** (for fastening watch on wrist); ∿-**tower**, post for observation of approaching danger; ∿′**word**, phrase expressing briefly the principles of a party etc. (e.g. *Equal pay for equal work*), (Hist.) military password. [OE *wæcce* (**wæccan*; see foll.)]

watch² (wŏ-) *v.* **1.** *v.i.* be on the watch, keep watch, vigilant, take heed, look out for opportunity etc., exercise protecting care *over*; ∿′**ing brief** (of barrister who follows case for client not directly concerned, or fig.); ∿ **out**, be on one's guard. **2.** (arch.) remain awake for devotions etc. **3.** *v.t.* keep eyes fixed on, keep under observation, follow observantly, (*had him watched by detectives; was watching the television; boy was paid to watch sheep; shall watch your career with interest; am having to watch my weight; watch him do it* or *doing it*); *watch the* CLOCK¹; ∿ **one's step**, (colloq.) ∿ **it** or one**self**, take care or precautions; ∿**ed pot never boils**, strained waiting makes time seem long. **4.** look out for, await, (opportunity; ∿ one's **chance**, wait for right moment). **5.** Hence (-)∿ER¹ *n.* [OE **wæccan*, doublet of *wacian* (WAKE¹), repr. WG **wakæjan*]

wa′tchful (wŏ′-) *a.* accustomed to or engaged in watching, vigilant, (*about, against, for, of, over, to* do); showing vigilance; (arch.) wakeful; hence ∿LY² *adv.*, ∿NESS *n.* [f. WATCH¹ + -FUL]

wa′ter (waw′-) *n.* **1.** colourless transparent tasteless odourless compound of oxygen and hydrogen in liquid state convertible by heat into steam and by cold into ice, liquid consisting chiefly of this (in seas, lakes, streams, springs, rain, tears, sweat, saliva due to appetite, urine, serum, amniotic fluid (usu. in *pl.*), morbid accumulation of fluid, etc.), body of this as sea or lake or river (*across* or *over the water*), (HOT¹ and *cold, salt* and *fresh* or *sweet*, SMOOTH¹ or *still* and *rough* or *troubled*, HARD and SOFT, *aerated, saline, chalybeate, thermal*, BLUE¹, HEAVY, HOLY, MINERAL, RUNNING², TABLE-, *water; the upper waters of the Thames*); water as supplied (esp. through pipes) for domestic use; (in *pl.*) part of sea etc. (*in Icelandic waters; cross the waters*), mineral water at spa etc. (*take* or *drink the waters*);

STRONG *waters*. **2.** BACK² *water*; BACK¹*water*; *between* WIND¹ *and water*; **by** ∼, using ship, barge, etc., for travel or transport; **cast** one's **bread upon the** ∼**s**, do good without expecting gratitude or immediate or definite reward; **in deep** ∼(**s**), floundering, in great difficulties, in affliction; *still waters run* DEEP³; FIRE¹ *and water*; FISH¹ *out of water*, FISH² *in troubled waters*; *keep* one's HEAD¹ *above water*; HOLD¹ *water*; *spend money, shed blood*, etc., **like** ∼, lavishly or recklessly; **make** ∼, (1) urinate, (2, of ship) leak; *pour* OIL¹ *on the waters*; **on** the ∼, (fig.) in boat or ship; **pass** ∼, urinate; **pour** or **throw cold** ∼ **on**, disparage or discourage (scheme etc.); TREAD *water*; UNDER *water*; UNDERWATER; ∼**s of forgetfulness**, Lethe, oblivion, death; ∼ **of life**, spiritual enlightenment; ∼ **under the bridge** or **over the dam**, irrevocable past; **writ(ten) in** ∼, (of achievements etc.) transient. **3.** state of tide (HIGH, LOW¹, *water*). **4.** solution of specified substance in water, e.g. LAVENDER-, ROSE¹-, etc., *water*, SODA-*water*, DILL-*water*. **5.** transparency and brilliance of gem esp. diamond; **of the first** ∼, of finest quality or extreme degree (*diamond, genius, blunder, of the first water*). **6.** (Finance). amount of nominal capital added by WATER²*ing*. **7.** *attrib.* (in compounds, of which those especially that distinguish varieties of plants and animals are too numerous to be given separately). found in or near, growing in, used or employed on, etc., the water; of, for, worked or effected by, made with, containing, using, yielding, etc., water. **8.** ‖∼-**bailiff**, (1, Hist.) custom-house officer at port, (2) official enforcing laws on shipping or on fishing; ∼-**bath**, bain-marie, (Chem.) vessel containing heated water for evaporation etc. of substances; ∼-**bear**, = TARDIGRADE 2; W∼-**bearer**, = *Water-carrier*; ∼-**bed**, rubber mattress filled with water (esp. for invalid to avoid bedsores); ∼-**biscuit**, unsweetened biscuit made from flour and water; ∼-**blister** (containing colourless fluid, not blood or pus); *water*-BLOOM¹; ∼-**boatman**, aquatic bug of genus *Notonecta*, swimming upside-down on water; ∼-**borne**, (of goods) conveyed by water, (of disease) communicated or propagated by use of contaminated drinking-water; ∼-**bottle** (for drinking-water, esp. of glass for dining-table, bedroom, etc., or of metal etc. in soldier's kit); ∼-**brain**, = STURDY²; ∼**brash**, pyrosis; *water*-BREAKER²; ∼-**buck**, Afr. antelope of genus *Kobus*, frequenting river-banks; ∼-**buffalo**, the common domestic Indian buffalo; ∼ **bus**, river or lake boat carrying passengers on regular run; ∼-**butt**, barrel used to catch rain-water; ∼-**cannon**, device for shooting powerful jet of water to disperse crowd etc.; ∼-**carriage**, conveyance of goods etc. by water; W∼-**carrier**, *the* zodiacal sign Aquarius; ∼-**cart**, (esp.) cart carrying water for sale or for sprinkling roads; ∼-**clock** (measuring time by flow of water); ∼-**closet**, (room etc. containing) lavatory with arrangement for flushing bowl with water; ∼-**colour**, artists' paint made of pigment diluted with water and not oil, picture painted with such colours, art of painting such pictures, whence ∼-*colour*IST (3) *n.*; *water* COMPRESS¹; ∼-**cooled** (by circulating water); ∼-**cooler**, tank of cooled drinking-water; ∼**course**, (1) brook, stream, artificial channel for flow of water, (2) its bed; ∼-**craft**, (1) skill in sailing etc., (2) vessel(s) travelling on water; *water*-CRANE¹ 2; ∼**cress**, hardy perennial cress growing in springs etc., with pungent leaves used as salad; ∼-**cure**, hydropathy; ∼-**diviner**, dowser (see DOWSE²); ∼-**dog** (trained to retrieve waterfowl, etc.); ∼-**drinker**, (esp.) total abstainer from alcohol; ∼-**fall**, stream falling over precipice or down steep hillside; ∼-**finder**, dowser (see DOWSE²); ∼-**flea**, small aquatic crustacean hopping like flea; ∼-**fowl** (usu. collect. as *pl.*), birds frequenting water, esp. swimming game-birds; ∼**front**, part of town adjoining river, lake, etc.; ∼-**gas** (got by decomposing steam with red-hot coke,

mainly hydrogen and carbon monoxide); ∼-**gate**, (1) flood-gate, (2) gate giving access to river etc.; ∼-**gauge**, (1) glass tube etc. indicating height of water inside reservoir, boiler, etc., (2) pressure expressed in terms of head of water; ∼-**glass**, (1) tube with glass bottom enabling objects under water to be observed, (2) solution of sodium or potassium silicate used as a vehicle for fresco-painting, for hardening artificial stone, or for preserving eggs; ∼-**guard**, Customs officer(s) watching ships to prevent smuggling; ∼-**hammer**, percussion made by water in pipe when tap is turned off, or by water in steam-pipe when live steam is admitted; ∼-**heater**, device for heating (esp. domestic) water; ∼-**hemlock**, poisonous herb of genus *Cicuta*, found in marshes etc.; ∼-**hen**, bird of family Rallidae, esp. a gallinule (*Gallinula chloropus*); ∼-**hole**, shallow depression or cavity in which water collects (esp. in the bed of a river otherwise dry); ∼-**hog**, capybara; ∼ **hyacinth**, tropical river-weed (*Eichhornia crassipes*); ∼-**ice**, confection of flavoured and frozen water and sugar; ∼-**jacket**, case filled with water and enclosing part of machine that is to be heated or (esp.) kept cool; ∼-**jump**, place where horse in steeplechase etc. must jump over water; ∼-**laid**, (of rope) = CABLE¹-*laid*; ∼-**lens**, magnifying lens made of transparent cell filled with water; ∼-**level**, (1) (height of) surface of water in reservoir etc., (2) plane below which ground is saturated with water, (3) level using water to determine horizontal; ∼-**lily**, aquatic plant of family Nymphaeaceae, with broad flat floating leaves and white or blue or yellow or red flowers; ∼-**line**, (1) line along which surface of water touches ship's side (marked on ship for certain specified conditions of loading; cf. LOAD¹ *line*), (2) linear watermark; ∼-**logged**, (of wood) so saturated, (of vessel) so filled, with water as barely to be able to float, (of ground) made useless by saturation with water; ∼-**main**, main pipe in water-supply system; ∼**man**, (1) boatman plying for hire, (2) oarsman, *good, bad*, etc., at keeping boat truly balanced etc.; ∼**mark**, (*n.*) faint design visible in some paper when viewed by transmitted light, indicating name of maker etc., (*v.t.*) impress such mark on (paper) in making; ∼-**meadow** (kept fertile by being flooded periodically by stream); ∼-**melon**, (plant bearing) elliptical melon with smooth green skin, red pulp, and watery juice; ∼ **meter**, apparatus registering amount of water supplied to house etc.; ∼ **milfoil**, milfoil-like plant of genus *Myriophyllum* growing in water; ∼-**mill** (worked by water-wheel); ∼-**mole**, (Austral.) platypus; ∼-**monkey**, jar with long narrow neck for water, used in hot countries; ∼-**moth**, caddis-fly; ∼-**nymph** (inhabiting or presiding over water); *water* OUZEL; *∼-**parting** = WATERSHED 1; ∼-**pepper**, acrid plant found in wet places; ∼-**pheasant**, jacana, pintail, or goosander; ∼-**pipe**, (1) pipe for conveying water, (2) hookah; ∼-**pistol**, toy pistol shooting jet of water etc.; ∼-**plane** (passing through ship's water-line); ∼-**plantain**, ditch-plant of genus *Alisma*, with plantain-like leaves; ∼-**platter**, = VICTORIA 2; ∼ **polo**, game played by swimmers with ball like football; ∼-**power**, (1) mechanical force got from weight or motion of water, (2) fall in stream capable of being utilized as force; ∼-**proof**, (*a.*) impervious to water; (*n.*) waterproof garment or material, (*v.t.*) make waterproof; ∼ **purslane**, creeping plant (*Peplis portula*) growing in damp places; ∼-**rail**, bird of genus *Rallus*; ∼-**ram**, hydraulic ram; ∼-**rat**, = *water-vole*; ∼-**rate**, charge made for use of public water-supply; ∼-**repellent**, not easily penetrated by water; ∼-**sail** (below lower studding-sail close over water); ∼-**scorpion**, aquatic bug of family Nepidae; ∼-**seal**, body of water used in bent pipe etc. to prevent passage or escape of gas; ∼-**shoot**, pipe or trough for overflow of water; ∼**side**, margin of sea, lake, or river; ∼-**skater**, insect moving on surface of water; ~-**ski** (on pair of which a person towed by a motor boat can travel skimming surface of water; so as *v.i.*); ~-**skin**, skin bag for carrying water; ~-**softener**, apparatus for softening hard water; ~-**soldier**, aquatic plant with plumelike flowers above surface; ~-**soluble**, soluble in water; ~ **souchy** (sōō´shĭ), fish boiled and served in its own liquor [Du. *zootje* boiling]; ~-**spaniel**, large spaniel of variety used for retrieving waterfowl; ~-**splash**, part of road submerged by stream or pool; ~**spout**, (1) gyrating column of water and spray formed by whirlwind between sea and cloud, (2) sudden violent fall of rain; ~ **starwort**, slender plant of genus *Callitriche* growing in still water; ~-**supply**, providing and storing of water, or amount of water stored, for use of town, house, etc.; ~-**table**, (1) string-course arranged to throw water off building, (2) = *water-level* (2); ~-**tiger**, larva of water-beetle *Dytiscus*; ~**tight**, (of joint, shoes, cask, compartment in ship, etc.) tightly enough fastened or fitted to prevent ingress or egress of water, (fig., of argument etc.) unassailable; ~*tight compartment*, part of ship separated by watertight partitions for safety, (fig.) place for subject etc. kept entirely separate; ~ **torture** (by exposing victim to incessant sound of dripping water; ~-**tower** (supporting elevated tank to secure pressure for distributing water-supply, or for delivering water at great height in fire-fighting; ~-**vole**, vole frequenting water, esp. *Arvicola amphibius*; *water-*WAGON; ~ **wagtail**, common pied wagtail; ~-**wave**, wave in the hair produced by the use of water; ~**way**, (1) route for travel by water, navigable channel, (2) thick plank at outer edge of deck along which channel is hollowed for water to run off by; ~-**weed**, aquatic plant without special use or beauty; ~-**wheel**, wheel driven by water to work machinery, or used to raise water; ~-**wings**, inflated floats fixed behind shoulders of person learning to swim; *~-**witch**, (1) dowser (see DOWSE[2]), (2) quick-diving water-bird; ~**works**, establishment for managing water-supply, (sl.) urinary system. **9.** Hence ~LESS *a.* [OE *wæter*, = OS *watar*, OHG *wazzar*, f. WG *watar* f. Gmc *wat-*, f. IE *wod-*, cogn. w. WET]

wa´ter[2] (waw´-) *v.* **1.** *v.t.* sprinkle (road, plants, etc.), adulterate (milk, beer, etc.), (of river etc.) supply (place), with water. **2.** give drink of water to (horse etc.). **3.** *v.i.* (of animal) go to pool etc. to drink; (of ship, engine, etc., or person in charge of it) take in supply of water. **4.** (Of smarting eyes) secrete tears; (of mouth when food is seen or food or pleasure eagerly anticipated) run with saliva (**makes** one's **mouth** ~, excites desire or envy), whence *mou´th-* ~ING[2] *a.* **5.** (esp. in *p.p.*) produce irregular wavy damask-like markings on (material) by moistening and pressing in manufacture (*watered silk*). **6.** (Finance). increase (company's debt, or nominal capital) by issue of new shares without corresponding addition to assets. **7.** ~ **down**, dilute, make (story, doctrine, etc.) less vivid or forceful or horrifying. [OE *wæterian* (as prec.)]

Wa´terford (waw´-) *n.* ~ **glass**, clear colourless flint glass. [~ in Ireland]

wa´tering (waw´-) *n.* In vbl senses; ~-**can**, ~-**pot**, portable vessel for watering plants, with long tubular spout often ending in perforated sprinkler; ~-**cart**, = WATER[1]-*cart*; ~-**place**, (1) pool etc. at which animals water, (2) place where water is obtained, (3) spa or seaside resort. [OE *wæterung* (as WATER[2], -ING[1])]

Waterlōō' (waw-) *n.* crushing blow, decisive contest, (*meet* one's *Waterloo*). [~ in Belgium, where Napoleon was finally defeated in 1815]

wa´tershĕd (waw´-) *n.* **1.** line of separation between waters flowing to different rivers or basins or seas. **2.** (fig.) turning-point e.g. in history. **3.** (pop.) catchment area. [f. WATER[1] +

shed ridge of high ground (cogn. w. SHED[1]), after G *wasserscheide*]

wa´ter|ў (waw´-) *a.* (consisting) of water (~**y grave**, place where person lies drowned); containing too much water, over-moist, sodden, (esp. of cooked vegetables or fish); (of eyes or lips) suffused or running with water; (of liquid) too thin, actually or apparently diluted, resembling water; (fig., of expression, talk, style, etc.) vapid, insipid, uninteresting, feeble, (of colour) pale, washed out; suggestive of rain (*a watery moon, sky*); hence ~**INESS** *n.* [f. OE *wæterig* (as WATER[1], -Y[2])]

Wa´tson (wŏ´-) *n.* stolid person acting as foil to genius. [f. Dr. ~, character in SHERLOCK Holmes stories]

watsō´nia (wŏ-) *n.* S. Afr. plant of genus *Watsonia*, resembling gladiolus. [f. W. *Watson*, Engl. botanist d. 1787, +-IA[1]]

watt (wŏt) *n.* unit of power, rate of working of one joule per second, corresponding to electric circuit where electromotive force is one volt and current one ampere; ~-**hour**, energy used when one watt is applied for one hour; hence ~'**AGE** *n.*, amount of electrical power expressed in watts; ~'**METER** *n.* [f. J. *Watt*, Sc. engineer d. 1819]

Wa´tteau (wŏ´tō) *n.* ~ **back** (of woman's dress with broad pleat from neck to hem without girdle); ~ **bodice** (with square neck-opening and short ruffled sleeves); ~ **hat** (shallow, with wide brim, and flowers as decoration). [f. A. ~, Fr. painter d. 1721]

wa´ttle[1] (wŏ´-) *n.*, & *v.t.* **1.** *n.* interlaced rods and twigs as material of fences, walls, or roofs, (~ **and daub**, this plastered with mud or clay to make huts etc.); (in *sing.* or *pl.*) rods and twigs for such use. **2.** Austral. acacia with long pliant branches supplying such twigs, having bark used in tanning, and bearing golden flowers adopted as national emblem; (dial.) wicker hurdle. **3.** *v.t.* construct of wattle; interlace (twigs etc.); enclose or fill up with wattles. [OE *watul*, of unkn. orig.]

wa´ttle[2] (wŏ´-) *n.* fleshy appendage on head or throat of turkey and other birds; BARB[1] of fish; hence ~ED[2] (-tĕld) *a.* [16th c.; orig. unkn.]

waul *v.i.* give loud harsh cry like cat. [imit.]

wāve *v.* **1.** *v.i.* vibrate or be stirred with sinuous or sweeping motions like those of flag or tree or field of corn in wind, flutter, undulate. **2.** *v.t.* impart waving motion to; brandish (sword) as encouragement to followers etc.; ~ one's **hand** (*to* person), move hand to and fro in greeting or as signal. **3.** *v.i.* wave hand or thing held in it (*to* person); give direction thus to person to do. **4.** *v.t.* tell (person) thus to go *away, on,* etc.; direct (person) thus *to* do; express *farewell* etc. thus; ~ **aside**, dismiss as intrusive or irrelevant; ~ **down**, wave as signal to (vehicle or its driver) to stop. **5.** give undulating surface or course or appearance to (hair of head, lines in drawing, etc.), make wavy. **6.** *v.i.* (Of hair, line, etc.) have such appearance, be wavy. [OE *wafian* = MHG *waben*, f. Gmc *wabh-* move to and fro; cf. WAVER]

wāve[2] *n.* **1.** ridge of water between two depressions; long body of water curling into arched form and breaking on shore, breaker; **the** ~(**s**), (poet. or rhet.) the sea, water. **2.** body of attackers, immigrants, etc., coming in one of successive groups advancing like sea-waves. **3.** (Phys.) disturbance of particles of a fluid medium into a ridge-and-trough oscillation by which motion is propagated or sound etc. conveyed in some direction without corresponding advance or without any advance of the particles in that direction; single curve in the course of such motion; similar variation of electromagnetic field in propagation of radiation through medium or vacuum. **4.** temporary heightening of some influence or condition or feeling (*a wave of enthusiasm, prosperity, depression*; **heat, cold,** ~, spell of hot, cold, weather, rise or fall of temperature travelling over large area). **5.** undulating line or outline or surface, waviness. **6.** gesture of

waving; waving of hair (COLD[1] wave; PERMANENT wave). **7.** ~'**band,** range of wavelengths between specified limits; ~ **equation,** differential equation expressing properties of motion in waves; ~-**form,** curve showing shape of wave at given time; ~-**front,** surface containing points affected in same way by a wave at given time; ~ **function** (satisfying wave equation and describing properties of wave); ~'**guide,** metal tube etc. confining and conveying electromagnetic waves; ~'**length,** distance from one crest of wave to the next, corresponding distance between points in sound wave or electromagnetic wave, this as distinctive feature of radio waves from a particular transmitter or (fig.) of an individual's line of thought; ~ **mechanics,** method of analysis of behaviour esp. of atomic phenomena with particles represented by wave equations; ~ **number,** number of waves in unit distance; ~ **theory,** undulatory theory of light etc.; ~ **train,** sequence of similar waves. **8.** Hence ~'LESS (-vl-) *a.*, ~'LET (-vl-) *n.* [alt. f. ME *wawe, wage* cogn. w. WAG[1], after prec., or f. prec.]
wā′ver *v.i.* falter, become unsteady, begin to give way; be irresolute or undecided *between* different courses or opinions, be shaken in resolution or belief; (of light etc.) flicker; hence ~'ER *n.* [ME, f. ON *vafra* flicker, = MHG *waberen,* f. Gmc *wabh-*; see WAVE[1]]
wā′vey. See WAVY².
wā′v|y|y¹ *a.* undulating, (of line or surface) consisting of or showing alternate contrary curves, (*wavy hair*); ‖W~y **Navy,** (colloq., Hist.) RNVR (from wavy gold stripes or rings on sleeve); hence ~ĭLY² *adv.*, ~ĭNESS *n.* [f. WAVE¹,² +-Y²]
wā′vy², wā′vey, *n.* the snow-goose. [f. *wawa* f. Cree *wehweh,* Ojibwa *wēwe* goose]
wa′-wa (wah′wah) *n.* sound of trumpet etc. with mute moved in and out of bell. [imit.]
wawl. Var. of WAUL.
wăx¹ *n.*, & *v.t.* **1.** *n.* sticky plastic yellowish substance secreted by bees as material of honeycomb cells, beeswax; white translucent odourless tasteless material got from this by bleaching and purifying and used for candles, in modelling, as basis of polishes, and for other purposes; **be ~ in** person's **hands,** be entirely subservient to him; **lost ~,** *cire perdue*; **mould** person **like ~,** mould his character on desired lines or induce him to act just as desired. **2.** substance resembling wax in some respect, e.g. secretion of some other insects (esp. scale-insect), EAR¹-wax, fossil resin (**mineral ~**) esp. ozocerite, bee-bread, PARAFFIN wax, **vegetable ~** (exudation of certain plants such as sumac), SEAL²*ing-wax,* COBBLER's *wax.* **3.** (colloq.) (material for manufacture of) gramophone record. **4.** *attrib.* made of wax. **5.** ~'**berry,** (fruit of) candleberry-myrtle; ~'**bill,** small weaver-bird with translucent bill; ~-**chandler,** maker or seller of wax candles; ~'**cloth,** oilcloth; ~ **doll** (with face etc. of wax); ~-**insect** (that secretes wax); ~-**light,** taper or candle of wax; ~-**myrtle,** candleberry-myrtle; ~-**painting,** encaustic; ~-**palm,** (1) S. Amer. palm with stem coated in mixture of resin and wax, (2) carnauba; ~-**paper** (waterproofed with layer of wax); ~-**pocket,** bee's abdominal sac to store wax; ~-**pod,** yellow-podded bean; ~-**tree** (yielding vegetable or insect wax); *wax* VESTA; ~'**wing,** bird of genus *Bombycilla* with small tips like red sealing-wax to some wing-feathers; ~'**work,** (making of) objects modelled in wax, esp. dummies of persons with face and hands of coloured wax clothed to look as in life and be exhibited, (in *pl.*) such exhibition. **6.** *v.t.* smear, polish, encrust, treat surface of, with wax; (colloq.) record for the gramophone. [OE *wæx, weax,* = OS, OHG *wahs,* ON *vax* f. Gmc *wahsam*]
wăx² *v.i.* **1.** (Of moon between new and full) have progressively larger part of visible surface illuminated (cf. WANE); ~ **and wane,** (fig., of influence etc.) undergo alternations of increase and decrease. **2.**

(arch. or poet.) grow, increase; (w. adj. compl.) pass into specified condition or esp. mood or tone (*wax fat, old, merry, facetious, indignant, pathetic, wroth, angry*). [OE *weaxan,* = OS, OHG *wahsan,* ON *vaxa,* Goth. *wahsjan* f. Gmc *wahs-* f. IE *woks-, *auks-*]
wăx³ *n.* (sl.) fit of anger (*is in, got into, put him in, a wax*). [19th c., of uncert. orig.; perh. f. WAX² *wroth* etc.]
wă′xen *a.* (arch.) made of wax; having smooth pale translucent surface as of wax; able to receive impressions like wax, plastic. [f. WAX¹ + -EN⁵]
wă′x|y|ў *a.* resembling wax in some way, esp. easily moulded or having smooth pale translucent surface; (of tissue) degenerated to consistency resembling wax; (sl.) angry, quick-tempered; hence ~ĭLY² *adv.*, ~ĭNESS *n.* [f. WAX¹,³ + -Y²]
way *n.* & *adv.* **1.** *n.* road, track, path, (lit. or fig.) provided for passing along; place of passage through door etc.; (in *pl.*) structure of timber etc. down which new ship is slid when launched, parallel rails etc. as track for movement of machine; (as name of road or street, ancient: *Appian Way, Icknield Way,* or modern); *the house* **across** *or* **over** *the* ~, opposite; MILKY *Way;* PARTING *of the ways;* PAVE *the way for;* ‖PERMANENT *way;* **go the ~ of all the earth, of all flesh, of nature,** die (see also FLESH¹); **go the ~ of all good things,** be inevitably lost; **the Way of the Cross,** series of paintings of stations of the Cross in church or along road. **2.** best route, or route taken or contemplated, between two places or to place, method or plan for attaining object, person's desired or chosen course of action, (*ask the* or one's *way; there is a right way and a wrong way of using the tool; that is not the way to do it; do it this way, my way; don't like the way she smiles; the way the* COOKIE *crumbles; where there's a* WILL² *there's a way*); BOTH *ways;* **by ~ of,** through, by means of, (see also sense 12); ‖EACH *way;* FEEL *one's way;* **find a ~,** (fig.) discover means of attaining object; **find its** or one's or **the ~,** reach destination, arrive at specified point; **get** or **have** one's (**own**) ~, **have it** one's (**own**) ~, get what one wants, see one's orders carried out or one's desires gratified; **go** one's ~ or (now dial.) ~**s,** depart; **go** one's **own ~,** act independently esp. against others' advice; **go** person's ~, (colloq.) accompany him, (of things) be favourable to him; **lead the ~,** act as guide or leader, show how to do something; **lose** one's or **the ~,** go astray; **no ~,** it is impossible; **not, nothing, out of the ~,** common or unremarkable (thing); **one ~ and another,** taking various aspects of the matter jointly; **one ~ or another,** by some means; **out of the ~,** remote, inaccessible, (see also sense 4); **out of** one's ~, not on one's intended route; **go out of the** or one's ~, make special effort, act gratuitously or without compulsion (*to be rude, to be helpful*); **put** oneself **out of the ~,** inconvenience oneself to serve another; *out of* HARM's *way;* SEE¹ one's *way to;* **take its** or one's ~, go usu. *to* or *towards;* **the Way,** the Christian religion; ~**s and means,** methods of achieving something, esp. (Parl.) means of providing money. **3.** (in *sing.* or *colloq.* in *pl.*) travelling-distance, length of road etc. (to be) traversed, (*India is a long way away* or *off; went a little, a good, a long, some, way with* or *to meet him,* lit. or fig.; ‖ONCE *in a way; is still a long way off perfection, from being perfect*); **all the ~,** the whole distance, completely; HALF-*way.* **4.** unimpeded opportunity of advance, space free of obstacles, region or ground over which advance is desired or would naturally take place; **clear the ~,** remove obstacles, stand aside; **give ~,** fail to resist, be dislodged or broken under load, make concessions, allow precedence (*to*), abandon oneself (*to grief* etc.), (see also sense 9); *give ~ to,* be superseded by; **in** one's or **the ~,** forming obstacle or impediment; LION *in the way;* **make ~,** allow room (*for* others) to proceed, (see also sense 9); **out of** one's or **the ~,** no longer an obstacle or impediment; disposed of, settled, (of person) imprisoned or killed, (see also sense 2); **put** person **in the ~,** give him

opportunity *of*; RIGHT[3] *of way*. **5.** being engaged, or time spent, in movement from place to place (lit. or fig.; *with songs to cheer the way*; *met him on the way out* or *back* or *home*); **by the** ~, during journey, (fig.) incidentally, as a more or less irrelevant comment; *in a* FAIR[2] *way*; **on the** or one's ~, travelling, approaching, having progressed (*is well on the* or *its way to completion*), (colloq., of child) conceived but unborn; **on the** ~ **out**, (colloq.) about to disappear, fail, or perish; (**be**) **on your** ~!, begone!. **6.** specified direction (usu. in adv. phr. without prep.; *which way is he looking, going?*; STEP[1] *this way*; *will call next time I'm your way*; (colloq.) *lives somewhere Brighton way*); *(in pl.)* parts into which thing is divided (*split it three ways*); **come** person's ~, (fig.) fall to his lot, become available; **look the other** ~, avoid looking at person who is looking at one, deliberately ignore something one should notice; **the other** ~ **about** or **round**, reversed, inverted. **7.** custom, manner of behaving, habit, personal peculiarity, (*is not my way to deceive people*; *has a way of leaving his bills unpaid*; *these bright ideas have a way of turning out badly*); *the* normal course of events (*that is always the way*); ability to attain one's object (*has a way with him*; *the way of a man with a maid*); specific manner of life or procedure (*I soon got into his ways, into the way of it* or *things*); **in its** ~, if regarded from a particular standpoint appropriate to it; **only this** etc. ~, unseemly or unpleasing behaviour having no special significance; ~ **of life**, principle(s) or habit(s) governing all one's actions etc.; (to one's) ~ **of thinking**, (according to one's) customary opinion of matters; ~ **of the world**, conduct no worse than is customary. **8.** scope, sphere, range, line of occupation, branch of business, (*hunting is not, does not lie* or *come* or *fall in my way*; *is in the grocery way*; *want a few things in the stationery way*). **9.** advance in some direction, impetus, progress, (*fight, push,* etc. one's *way* to or *through* place); movement of ship etc. (*gather, lose, way*; *have way on*; **under** ~, not made fast, (usu.) in motion, (fig.) in progress); **give** ~, (of oarsmen) row hard, (see also sense 4); **make** ~, advance (lit. or fig.) (see also sense 4); **make** one's ~, go (*home* etc.); **make** one's (**own**) ~ (**in the world**), progress, prosper; **make** or **pay its** ~, be profitable; **pay** one's ~, not get into debt. **10.** respect (*not a bad fellow in some ways*; *is satisfactory in one* or *a way*); **in a** ~, to a limited extent, not altogether, (see also sense 12); **in more** ~**s than one** (calling attention to multiple meaning etc.); **in no** ~, not at all. **11.** ordinary course (*did it in the way of business*). **12.** condition, state, degree, (*things are in a bad way*; *we are all in the same way*); **any** ~, = ANYWAY; **by** ~ **of**, as substitute for or form of, with intention of, (*carries a stick by way of weapon*; *did it by way of apology, of discovering the truth*), imagining or representing oneself as doing (*is by way of making a great effort, of being a humorist*), habitually doing, (see also sense 2); **either** ~, in either case or event; ||**in a** (**great** ~, (colloq.) agitated; *in a* BIG *way*; *in a* or *the* FAMILY *way*; **in a small** ~, unambitiously, on a small scale. **13.** ~**-bent**, wall-barley; ~**-bill**, list of passengers or parcels on vehicle; ~'**farer**, ~'**faring**, traveller, travelling, esp. on foot; ~'**faring-tree**, white-flowered Eur. & Asian shrub (*Viburnum lantana*) common along roadsides, with berries turning from green through red to black; ~**lay**', lie in wait for, wait for or stop to rob or interview; ~**leave**, right of way rented to mine-owner, electricity company, etc.; ~'**mark**, natural or artificial object as guide to traveller; ~'**side**, (land at) side of road (esp. *attrib.*: *wayside flowers, inn*); *~ **station**, minor station on railway; *~ **train** (stopping at way stations); ~**-worn**, tired with travel. **14.** *adv.* (colloq.) to a considerable extent, far, (*way off the target*); ~ **back**, long ago; ~**-out**, unusual, eccentric, avant-garde, progressive, excellent. [OE *weg*, = OS, OHG *weg*, ON *vegr*, Goth. *wigs* f. Gmc *wegaz (*weg-move, carry, cf. WAIN, WEIGH); in sense 14 f. AWAY]

-way *suf.* = -WAYS. [f. prec.]

||**way'bread** (-ĕd) *n.* broad-leaved PLANTAIN[1]. [OE *wegbrǣde* (as WAY, BROAD)]

-ways (-z) *suf.* forming *adjs.* & *advs.* indicating direction or manner (*crossways, lengthways, sideways*); cf. -WISE. [f. WAY + -'s 1]

way'ward *a.* childishly self-willed or perverse, capricious, unaccountable, freakish; hence ~LY[2] *adv.*, ~NESS *n.* [ME, f. obs. *awayward* turned away (AWAY, -WARD); cf. FROWARD]

way'zgōōse *n.* printing-house's annual festivity. [earlier *waygoose*, 17th c., of unkn. orig.]

Wb *abbr.* weber(s).

WC *abbr.* water-closet; West Central.

WCC *abbr.* World Council of Churches.

W/Cdr. *abbr.* Wing Commander.

WD *abbr.* ||War Department; Works Department.

wē (*or, when unstressed,* wĭ) *pron.* (*obj.* **us** *pr.* us *or, when stressed,* ŭs; *also* 's; *poss.* OURSELF, OURSELVES, *arch.* **us**; *poss.* OUR, OURS). Pl. of I[2] (used also for *I* by royal person in proclamations etc. and by writer of editorial article in newspaper etc.); I and other person(s), = ONE 7; I and you; (colloq.) I (*give us a chance*); (colloq.) you (*how are we feeling today?*); ~ **and they, us and them**, the group including, and the group regarded as opposed to, our social class etc. [OE, = OS *wī, wē*, OHG *wir*, ON *vér, vær* f. Gmc *wiz; *us* f. OE *ūs*, = OS *ūs*, OHG *uns*, ON *oss* f. Gmc *uns f. IE *ņs, *nes]

||**WEA** *abbr.* Workers' Educational Association.

weak *a.* **1.** deficient in strength or power or number, fragile, easily broken or bent or defeated, (*weak barrier, rope*; *candidate weak in algebra*; *weak resistance, team*); (of crew) short-handed; (of syllable etc.) unstressed; ~'**er brethren**, less able members of a group; ~ **ending**, unstressed syllable in normally stressed place at end of verse-line; ~ **hand** (deficient in high cards); ~ **knees**, (usu. fig.) inability to stand firm, lack of resolution, so ~*-kneed* *a.*; **the** ~**er sex**, women; ~ **sister**, ineffective person; *weak* VESSEL; *weaker* VESSEL. **2.** deficient in vigour, not acting strongly, sickly, feeble, (*weak health, imagination, intellect*; *weak demand for goods, market is weak*); ~ **constitution**, lack of power to resist disease etc.; ~ **eyes** or **sight** (easily tired, or not seeing well); ~ **heart** (acting feebly); ~ **interaction**, (Phys.) weakest form of interaction between elementary particles (cf. STRONG *interaction*); ~ **mind** or **head** (below average in intelligence, verging on idiocy); ~**-mi'nded**, (1) having weak mind, (2) lacking resoluteness; ~ **nerves**, nervousness; ~ **stomach** (easily upset); ~ **voice** (easily tired or not reaching far). **3.** deficient in resolution or power of resisting temptation, easily led, (*weak character, man*; *weak side* or *point*); (of action or features) indicating lack of resolution (*a weak surrender, compliance, smile, chin*); **in a** ~ **moment**, at a time when one is unusually compliant or temptable. **4.** unconvincing, logically deficient, (*weak logic, evidence*; *a weak case, argument*). **5.** (Of mixed liquid or solution) watery, thin, dilute, (*weak tea, brandy-and-water, brine*). **6.** (Of style etc.) not vigorous or well-knit, diffuse, slipshod. **7.** (Gmc Gram.) (Of verb) forming inflexions by addition of suffix to, not only by vowel-change in, stem, (of noun or adjective declension) corresponding to original stems in -*n*, (opp. STRONG 4); ~ **grade**, unstressed ablaut-form. **8.** Hence ~'EN[6] *v.t.* & *i.*, ~'ISH[1] 2 *a.* [ME, f. ON *veikr*, = OE *wāc* pliant, insignificant, OS *wēk*, OHG *weih* f. Gmc *waikaz (*waik- yield)]

***wea'kfish** *n.* (*pl.* usu. same). marine food-fish of genus *Cynoscion*. [f. obs. Du. *weekvisch* (*week* soft f. as prec.; *visch* FISH[1])]

weak'ling *n.* feeble person etc. [f. WEAK + -LING[1]]

wea'kly[1] *adv.* In adj. senses. [ME, f. WEAK + -LY[2]]

wea'kly[2] *a.* sickly, not robust, ailing. [f. WEAK + -LY[1]]

wea'kness *n.* In adj. senses; weak point, defect; inability to resist a particular temptation; self-

-indulgent liking or inclination *for*. [ME, f. WEAK +
-NESS]

weal¹ *n*. (literary). welfare, prosperity, good fortune,
(esp. *weal and* WOE, *weal or woe*, *for the public* or *general
weal*). [OE *wela*, = OS *welo* f. WG *welon (as WELL³)]

weal² *n*., & *v.t.* (mark with) ridge raised on flesh by
stroke of rod or whip. [var. of WALE, infl. by obs. *wheal*
suppurate]

‖**weald** *n*. the ~, formerly wooded district including
parts of Kent, Surrey, and East Sussex; ~**-clay**, beds
of clay, sandstone, limestone, and ironstone, forming
top of wealden strata, with abundant fossil remains.
[OE, = *wald* WOLD]

‖**wea'lden** *a*. & *n*. **1**. *a*. of the weald; resembling the
weald geologically. **2**. *n*. series of lower-Cretaceous
freshwater deposits above oolite and below chalk,
best exemplified in the weald. [f. prec. + -EN⁵]

wealth (wĕl-) *n*. riches, large possessions, opulence;
being rich; abundance, *a* profusion or great quantity
or display, of (*a wealth of illustration, wit, fruit; wealth of
words is not eloquence*); (arch.) welfare, prosperity; ~
tax (on personal capital); hence ~'Y² *a*. [ME *welthe*, f.
WELL³ or WEAL¹ + -TH¹, after *health*]

wean¹ *v.t.* accustom (infant or other young mammal)
to food other than milk; (fig.) disengage or cure
(*away*) *from* habit, specified company, etc., by
enforced abstinence or counter-attractions; hence
~'ER¹ *n*., young animal recently weaned. [OE *wenian*
accustom, = OS *wennian*, OHG *-wennen*, ON *venja*, f.
Gmc *wanjan (*wanaz accustomed; cf. WONT¹)]

wean² *n*. (Sc.) child. [contr. of *wee ane* little one]

wea'nling *n*. newly-weaned child etc. [f. WEAN¹ +
-LING¹]

wea'pon (wĕ'p-) *n*. thing designed or used or usable as
instrument for inflicting bodily harm, e.g. gun,
bomb, rifle, sword, spear, stick, hammer, poker,
horn, claw; action or procedure or means used to get
the better in a conflict (*irony is a double-edged weapon; use
the weapon of a general strike; tears, the woman's weapon*);
hence ~LESS *a*., ~RY (1) *n*. [OE *wǣp*(*e*)*n*, = OS
wāpan, OHG *waf*(*f*)*an*, ON *vápn*, Goth. *wēpn f. Gmc
*wǣpnam, of unkn. orig.]

wear¹ (wār) *v*. (**wore**; **worn**). **1**. *v.t.* be dressed
habitually or on some occasion in (*wears green, serge,
shorts*, as usual colour etc.; *is wearing* or *wore* or *intends to
wear diamonds*, on this occasion); ~'**ing apparel**,
clothes; **worn clothes** (that have been put on at
least once; see also sense 5); ~ **the crown, sword,
gown, willow, breeches** or **trousers**, be a
monarch or martyr, soldier, lawyer, desolate lover,
husband-ruling wife. **2**. have on, or as part of, one's
person (*wear a beard, glasses, perfume; wear* one's *hair
long; wear a joyful face, a sour look*); *wear* one's HEART on
one's *sleeve*; ~ **in** one's **heart**, be devoted to (person
or principle); ~ one's **years well**, remain young-
-looking. **3**. (Of ship) fly (flag); (colloq., usu. w. neg.)
accept, tolerate. **4**. Hence ~'ABLE *a*., ~'ER¹ *n*. **5**. *v.t.*
& *i*. injure surface of, partly consume or obliterate,
damage, attenuate, or alter, by rubbing or stress or
use, suffer such injury or consumption or change,
come or bring into specified state by use, rub or be
rubbed or (fig.) pass *off* or *out* or *away* or *down*, (*step
worn with pilgrims' knees; inscription has been worn*, or *has
worn, away; wear the freshness, the nap, off; impression,
novelty, soon wears off; wear* one's *trousers, trousers have been
worn, into holes* or *bagginess; seams wear threadbare; care-
-worn, toil-worn; is worn to a shadow with care; stick wears
down to a stump*); (**well-**)**worn**, (of joke etc.) stale, (of
clothes) damaged by use; ~ **out**, use or be used till
usable no longer (see also sense 6); ~ **thin**, (fig., of
patience etc.) be over-used. **6**. exhaust, tire or be tired
out, put *down* by persistence, (*worn with travel; a wearing
occupation, companion; wear out* one's WELCOME; *his
patience wore*, or *was worn, out at last; succeeded in wearing
down the opposition*). **7**. *v.i.* endure continued use *well,
badly*, etc., remain for specified time in working order
or presentable state, last long; person ~s **well**,

retains youthful strength or esp. look. **8**. *v.i.* & *t*. (Of
time) go slowly or tediously, (of time) pass, pass
(time) gradually away, (*winter, time, day, wears on* or
away; wear away or *out* one's *life* or *time* or *youth* in
trifles); ~ **through the day**, survive it somehow. **9**.
v.t. (Of water etc.) make (hole, groove, channel) by
rubbing or attrition (usu. of incidental or undesigned
action). [OE *werian*, = OHG *werien*, ON *verja*, Goth.
wasjan clothe, f. Gmc *wazjan (**was-* clothing)]

wear² (wār) *n*. **1**. wearing or being worn on person,
use as clothes, (*the best materials for Sunday, working,
spring, seaside*, etc., *wear*); **in general** ~, fashionable;
in ~, being regularly worn by person. **2**. thing to
wear, fashionable or suitable apparel (*sportswear*),
(collect.) things to wear in or on specified part or
place (*footwear, underwear, beach wear*). **3**. ~ (**and
tear**), damage sustained as result of ordinary use; **the
worse for** ~, damaged by use, (fig.) injured. **4**.
capacity for resisting wear and tear (*there is a great deal
of, no, wear* (*left*) *in it*). [ME, f. prec.]

wear³ (wār) *v.t.* & *i*. (**wore**). bring (ship), (of ship)
come, about by turning head away from wind (cf.
TACK¹ 9). [17th c., of unkn. orig.]

wear'|y *a*. & *v*. **1**. *a*. unequal to or disinclined for
further exertion or endurance; ~**y Willie**, (sl.)
habitually weary person, tramp. **2**. disgusted at the
continuing *of*; impatient *of*. **3**. tiring, tedious,
irksome. **4**. Hence ~iLY² *adv.*, ~iNESS *n*. **5**. *v.t.* make
weary (esp. *of* or *with* importunity or monotony);
hence ~iSOME¹ *a*. **6**. *v.i.* grow weary (*of* importunity
or importunate person); hence ~iLESS *a*. **7**. (chiefly
Sc.) long *to* do or *for*. [OE (*wēr*(*i*)*gian* v. f.) *wērig,
wǣrig*, = OS *-wōrig*, OHG *wuarag* drunk, f. WG
*wōriga, *wōraga]

wea'sand (-z-) *n*. (arch. or dial.) windpipe, gullet,
throat. [OE *wāsend*, = OS *wāsend*(*i*), OHG *weisant*,
perh. orig. pres. part.]

wea'sel (-z-) *n*., & *v.i.* **1**. *n*. small nimble reddish-
-brown white-bellied slender-bodied ferocious
carnivorous quadruped (*Mustela nivalis*) allied to
stoat and ferret; stoat; tracked vehicle for use in snow,
bog, etc.; ~**-faced**, with thin sharp features; *~
word (used to remove any real force from expression
containing it). **2**. **v.i.* equivocate, quibble; default *on*,
get *out* of obligation. [OE *wes*(*u*)*le*, = OHG *wisula* f.
WG *wisulōn, of unkn. orig.]

wea'ther¹ (wĕ'dh-) *n*. & *a*. **1**. *n*. atmospheric conditions prevailing at a place and time, combination
produced by heat or cold, clearness or cloudiness,
dryness or moisture, wind or calm, high or low
pressure, and electrical state, of local air and sky,
(*favourable, seasonable, good*, FAIR², FINE², *bad*, FOUL,
cold, dull, rainy, windy, weather; goes out in all weathers);
under stress of ~, owing to storms etc.; CLERK *of the
weather*; **make good** or **bad** ~ **of it**, (Naut., of ship)
behave well or badly in storm; **make heavy** ~ **of**,
(fig.) find trying or needlessly difficult; **above the** ~,
(Aeron.) in calm region above clouds; **under the** ~,
(colloq.) indisposed, out of sorts. **2**. ~**-beaten**,
seasoned by or bearing the marks of exposure to
storms; ~**-board**, (*n*.) sloping board attached at
bottom of door to keep out rain, (*v.t.*) supply with
~**-boarding** or **-boards**, horizontal boards of which
each overlaps the next below to throw off rain as
protective casing to wall etc.; ~**-bound**, unable to
proceed owing to bad weather; ~**-box**, indicator
with figures of man and woman, one issuing to foretell
rain, the other fine weather; ~**-chart**, diagram
showing state of weather over wide area; ~**cock**,
revolving pointer often in shape of cock mounted in
high place esp. on church spire to show whence wind
blows, (fig.) inconstant person; ~**-contact** or
-cross, leakage from one telegraph wire to another
due to wet weather; ~ **forecast**, prediction of
weather for next few hours or longer period;
~**-glass**, barometer; ~**-house**, = *weather-box*;
~**man**, (1) meteorologist, esp. one who broadcasts

a weather forecast, (2) *member of violent revolutionary group; ∼-**map**, = *weather-chart*; ∼-**moulding**, dripstone; *weather*PROOF[2]; ∼-**prophet**, person who foretells weather; ∼-**service**, -**ship**, -**station**, organization, ship, post, for meteorological observations; ∼-**strip**, piece of material used to make door or window proof against rain or wind; ∼-**tiles** (arranged to overlap like weather--boarding); ∼-**vane**, = *weathercock*; ∼-**wise**, able to forecast weather; ∼-**worn**, damaged by storms etc. **3.** *a.* (Naut.) windward (*on the weather side, quarter, beam, bow*); *weather gage* or GAUGE[1]; **keep a** or one's ∼ **eye open**, (fig.), be watchful; *weather* HELM[2]; hence ∼MOST *a.* [OE *weder*, = OS *wedar*, OHG *wetar*, ON *vethr* f. Gmc *wedhram, prob. f. root **we-* to blow (WIND[1])]

wea'ther[2] (wĕ'dh-) *n.* **1.** *v.t.* expose to atmospheric changes, esp. deliberately to dry, season, etc.; (usu. in *pass.*) discolour or partly disintegrate (rock, stones) by exposure to air. **2.** *v.i.* be discoloured or worn thus. **3.** *v.t.* (Of ship or its crew) get to windward of (cape etc.); come safely through (storm, lit. or fig.). **4.** make (boards, tiles) overlap downwards; hence ∼ING[1] (2) *n.* [ME, f. prec.]

wea'therl|y (wĕ'dh-) *a.* (Naut.) (Of ship) making little leeway, capable of keeping close to wind; hence ∼iNESS *n.* [WEATHER[1] + -LY[1]]

weave[1] *v.* (**wove** or **wōv; wo'ven** or WOVE[1]) & *n.* **1.** *v.t.* form (thread etc.) into fabric, (fabric) out of thread etc., by interlacing long threads running in two directions. **2.** *v.i.* make fabric thus, work at loom. **3.** *v.t.* make (basket, wreath, etc.) by interlacing rods, flowers, etc.; work up (facts etc.), introduce (details), *into* story or connected whole, fashion (poem, tale, etc.); contrive (plot). **4.** *n.* style of weaving. [OE *wefan*, = OHG *weban*, ON *vefa* f. Gmc *webhan f. IE **webh-*]

weav|e[2] *v.i.* move repeatedly from side to side; take devious course esp. to avoid obstructions; (RAF sl.) manœuvre aircraft thus, take evasive action; get ∼ing, (sl.) hurry, begin action. [prob. f. ME *weve*, var. of *waive* f. ON *veifa* WAVE[1]]

wea'ver *n.* In vbl. senses; one whose occupation is weaving; ∼(-bird), tropical bird of family Ploceidae remarkable for elaborate or dextrously made woven nests; ∼'s knot, SHEET[3]-*bend* using in weaving. [ME, f. WEAVE[1] + -ER[1]]

wea'zen. See WIZENED.

wĕb *n.* & *v.* (-bb-). **1.** *n.* woven fabric, amount woven in one piece, (lit., or fig.: *a web of lies*); (spider's) ∼, cobweb; similar product of any spinning creature, gossamer, etc. **2.** membrane filling spaces between toes esp. of swimming bird or animal, connective tissue; vane of feather. **3.** (large roll of paper used esp. in newspaper-printing, made on) endless wire-mesh on rollers. **4.** thin flat part connecting more solid parts in machinery etc., e.g. part of railway-carriage wheel between hub and rim. **5.** ∼-**fingered**, ∼-**toed**, having ∼-**fingers** or -**toes** (abnormally or normally connected with web); ∼-**foot** (with web--toes), whence ∼-**footed**; ∼-**offset**, offset printing on web of paper; ∼-**wheel** (with plate or web instead of spokes, or with rim, spokes, and centre, in one piece as in watch-wheels); *∼-**worm**, gregarious caterpillar spinning large web in which to sleep or to feed on enclosed foliage. **6.** Hence ∼BED[2] (-bd) *a.* **7.** *v.t.* & *i.* weave web (on). [OE *web*(*b*), = OS *webbi*, OHG *weppi, wappi*, ON *vefr*, f. Gmc *wabhjam (**wabh-* var. of **webh-* WEAVE)]

wĕ'bbing *n.* strong narrow closely-woven fabric such as is used to support upholstery, for belts, etc. [f. prec. + -ING[1]]

we'ber (vā'-) *n.* unit of magnetic flux, causing electromotive force of one volt in circuit of one turn when generated or removed in one second. [f. W. E. Weber, Ger. physicist d. 1891]

wĕd *v.t.* & *i.* (-dd-; *p.p.* occas. **wed**). **1.** (rhet.) (Of party to marriage, priest, or parent etc.) = MARRY[1]; unite (qualities often separated; *wed efficiency to economy*). **2.** (in *p.p.*) married (*wedded pair*, WIFE; **newly-**∼s, newly wedded pair); of marriage (*wedded life, bliss*); so devoted *to* opinion, occupation, etc., as to be unable to abandon it. [OE *weddian* to pledge, = OHG *wettōn*, ON *vethja*, Goth. *gawadjōn* f. Gmc *wadhjōjan (*wadhjam a pledge; cf. GAGE[1])]

Wed. *abbr.* Wednesday.

wĕ'dding *n.* marriage ceremony (and festivities); anniversary of this (DIAMOND, GOLDEN, RUBY, SILVER[1], *wedding*); ∼ **breakfast**, meal etc. usual between wedding ceremony and departure for honeymoon; ∼-**cake**, rich decorated cake of which portions are distributed to guests at wedding and sent to absent friends; ∼-**card** (with names of bride and bridegroom sent to friends as announcement of wedding); ∼-**day**, day or anniversary of wedding; ∼-**favour**, (arch.) white rosette or knot of ribbons worn in honour of wedding; ∼ **garment**, (fig.) qualification for participating in feast of some kind (ref. to Matt. 22:11); ∼ **march**, march (esp. by Mendelssohn) played at wedding; ∼-**ring** (put on bride's finger at wedding-ceremony and usu. worn there constantly as distinctive mark of married woman, or similarly worn by married man). [OE *weddung* (as WED, -ING[1])]

wĕdge *n.*, & *v.t.* **1.** *n.* piece of wood, metal, etc., one end of which is an acute-angled edge formed by two converging planes used to split wood or rock or widen opening or tighten structure or exert force in various ways, a form of inclined plane; **thin end of the** ∼, change, measure, action, etc., that will open the way to further changes or developments and is therefore of more importance than it seems. **2.** thing resembling wedge in being chiefly outlined by two planes or lines converging at acute angle (*a wedge of cake; the seats are arranged in wedges*); (shoe with) wedge-shaped heel; golf-club with wedge-shaped head used for approach shots. **3.** ∼ **shaped**, (1) shaped like solid wedge, (2) V-shaped; ∼-**tailed**, (of bird) having middle tail--feathers longest. **4.** Hence ∼'WISE (-jw-) *adv.* **5.** *v.t.* tighten or fasten by use of wedge; thrust or pack (*in*) tightly like a wedge between other things or persons, or *together*; push *off* or *away* like a wedge. [OE *wecg*, = OS *weggi*, OHG *weggi, wecki*, ON *veggr* f. Gmc *wagjaz]

Wĕ'dgwood (-jw-) *n.* (P) kind of fine pottery esp. with white cameo design, made by Wedgwood and his successors; blue colour therefrom of this. [f. J. ∼, Engl. potter d. 1795]

wĕ'dlock *n.* the married state; **born in, out of,** ∼ (legitimately, illegitimately). [OE *wedlac* (*wed* pledge, cogn. w. WED, *-lāc* suf. denoting action) marriage vow]

Wĕ'dnesday (wĕ'nzdā, -dī) *n.* & *adv.* **1.** *n.* day of week, following Tuesday; ASH[2] *Wednesday.* **2.** *adv.* (cf. FRIDAY 2). [f. ME *wednesdei*, OE *wōdnesdæg* day of (the god) Odin, transl. of LL *Mercurii dies* day of planet Mercury]

wee[1] *a.* (**weer** *pr.* wē'er; **weest** *pr.* wē'ist). **1.** (Esp. childish or Sc.) little, very small. **2.** (colloq.) extremely small, tiny, (*a wee bit*). **3.** Wee Frees, (nickname for) minority of Free Church of Scotland that refused inclusion in the United Free Church in 1900. [orig. Sc. n., f. north. ME *wei* (small) quantity f. Anglian *wēg*(*e*) = West Saxon *wǣg*(*e*); cf. WEY]

wee[2]. Var. of WEE-WEE.

weed *n.* & *v.* **1.** *n.* wild herb growing where it is not wanted; **the** (**Indian, soothing,** etc.) ∼, (arch.) tobacco; (**the**) ∼, (sl.) marijuana. **2.** lanky and weakly horse or person. **3.** ∼-**grown**, overgrown with weeds; ∼-**killer**, substance used to destroy weeds or other plants. **4.** Hence ∼'LESS, ∼'Y[2], *adjs.* **5.** *v.t.* clear (ground etc.) of weeds (lit. or fig.); sort *out* (inferior parts or members of a quantity or company) for removal, rid (quantity or company) of inferior members etc. **6.** *v.i.* cut off or uproot weeds. **7.** Hence

∼ER¹ (1, 2) *n.* [OE (*wēodian* v. f.) *wēod*, = OS *wiod*, of unkn. orig.]

weeds (-z) *n. pl.* (**widow's**) ∼, deep mourning worn by widow. [OE *wǣd*(*e*) garment, = OS *wād*(*i*), OHG *wāt*, *giwāti*, ON *váth* f. Gmc **wǣdhiz, *gawǣdhjam*]

week *n.* **1.** period of seven days reckoned usu. from and to midnight on Saturday-Sunday (**day of the** ∼, Sunday, Monday, etc.); ∼ **of Sundays**, ∼ **of** ∼**s**, seven weeks, indefinite long period; **feast of** ∼**s**, = PENTECOST 1; KNOCK¹ *into the middle of next week.* **2.** period of seven successive days reckoned from any point (*can you come to us for a week?*; *have not seen you for weeks*; *did it weeks ago*); **a** ∼ (**from**) **today**, or **today, this day, Monday**, etc., ∼, 7 days before or esp. after today etc.; *week* IN²*, week out.* **3.** the six days between Sundays, or the five days between Sunday and Saturday (*never go there in the week*); period of work done during these (*42-hour week*). **4.** ∼'**day**, any day other than (Saturday or) Sunday; ∼'**end**, (*n.*) Sunday and (part of) Saturday (occas. longer period) as time for holiday or visit, (*v.i.*) make weekend visit etc.; ∼**-long** *a.* & *adv.*, (lasting) for whole week; ∼**-night**, evening or night of weekday. [OE *wice*, = OS -*wika*, OHG *wehha*, *wohha*, ON *vika*, Goth. *wikō* f. Gmc **wikōn*, prob. orig. = sequence]

wee′kly *a.*, *adv.*, & *n.* **1.** *a.* & *adv.* (produced or occurring) once every week; of or for or lasting a week. **2.** *n.* weekly newspaper or periodical. [f. prec. +-LY¹,²]

ween *v.t.* (arch. or poet.) **1.** be of opinion; I ∼ (*that*, or abs.), I think or suppose. **2.** expect to get etc. [OE *wēnan*, = OS *wānian*, OHG *wan*(*n*)*ēn*, ON *væna*, Goth. *wēnjan* f. Gmc **wænjan* (**wæniz* hope)]

wee′ny *a.* (childish or colloq.) tiny; ∼**-bopper**, girl like teeny-bopper but younger. [f. WEE¹ after *tiny, teeny*]

weep *v.* (**wept**) & *n.* **1.** *v.i.* shed tears (*for* or *over* person or thing; *at* event etc.; *for* or *with* pain, joy, etc.). **2.** *v.t.* shed (tears); shed tears for, lament over, bewail; ∼ **out**, utter with tears; ∼ one's **eyes** or **heart out**, weep excessively or for a long time. **3.** *v.i.* & *t.* send forth or be covered with drops; come or send forth in drops, exude, drip; ∼**ing eczema** (with exudation); **W**∼**ing Cross**, (Hist.) wayside cross for penitents to pray at (*come home by W*∼*ing Cross*, be made to repent one's conduct etc.). **4.** *v.i.* (Of tree) have drooping branches (chiefly in *pres. part.* as distinctive epithet of variety or species: *weeping birch, willow*, etc.). **5.** *n.* fit or spell of weeping. [OE *wēpan*, = OS *wōpian*, OHG *wuofan*, ON *œpa*, Goth. *wōpjan* f. Gmc **wōp-*, prob. imit.]

wee′per *n.* In vbl. senses; hired mourner at funeral; small image on monument, representing mourner; (in *pl.*, Hist.) crape hatband worn by men at funerals, widow's black crape veil or white cuffs; capuchin monkey. [ME, f. prec.+-ER¹]

wee′pie *n.* (colloq.) sentimental or mournful film, play, etc. [f. WEEP+-IE]

wee′py *a.* & *n.* (colloq.) **1.** *a.* inclined to weep, tearful. **2.** *n.* = prec. [f. WEEP+-Y²,³]

wee′ver *n.* sea-fish of genus *Trachinus*, with sharp venomous dorsal spines. [perh. f. OF *wivre, guivre*, serpent, dragon, f. L *vipera* VIPER]

wee′vil *n.* beetle of family Curculionidae, with head extended into a proboscis, feeding on grain, nuts, fruit, and bark; any insect damaging stored grain; hence ∼Y² *a.* [ME, f. MLG *wevel* = OE *wifel* beetle, OS -*wivil*, OHG *wibil*, ON **vifill* f. Gmc **webhilaz* (**webh-* move about briskly; cf. WAVE¹, WEAVE¹)]

wee-wee *n.*, & *v.i.* (sl.) **1.** *n.* urination; urine. **2.** *v.i.* urinate. [20th c.; orig. unkn.]

w.e.f. *abbr.* with effect from.

wĕft¹ *n.* transverse threads woven into warp to make web; yarn for these; something woven (lit. or fig.); filling-strips in basket-weaving. [OE *weft*(*a*), = ON *veptr, vipta*, MHG *wift* fine thread, f. Gmc **weft-* (**webh-* WEAVE¹)]

wĕft². Var. of WAFT 3.

Wehrmacht (vār′mahχt) *n.* (Hist.) German armed forces. [G, = defensive force]

weigh (wā) *v.* & *n.* **1.** *v.t.* find weight of with scales or other machine; balance in hands (as if) to guess weight of (*meditatively weighed his stick in his hand*); ∼ **out**, take a definite weight of, take specified weight from larger quantity, distribute in definite quantities by aid of scales, (*weigh out butter, portions or 3 lb. of butter*). **2.** *v.i.* & *t.* ∼ **out, in**, (of jockey weighed with saddle etc. before, after, race); ∼ **in** (of boxer etc., weighed before contest); ∼ **in with** argument etc., (colloq.) introduce with some confidence. **3.** *v.t.* estimate relative value or importance of, compare (*with* or *against*, or abs.) consider with a view to choice or rejection or preference, (*weigh the consequences, pros and cons, argument with* or *against* another; *weigh claims* or *merits of candidates*); ∼ **up**, (colloq.) appraise, form estimate of; ∼ one's **words**, select such as express neither more nor less than one means. **4.** *v.t.* & *i.* be equal to (specified weight), balance in the scales, (fig.) have specified importance, exercise pressure or influence, have weight or importance, be heavy or burdensome, (*weighs a* TON¹*, very little, light, heavy, heavily*); ∼ (**heavy** etc.) (**up**)**on**, be burdensome or depressing to; ∼ **with**, be regarded as important by (*the point that weighs with me*). **5.** *v.t.* bring down by weight lit. or fig., (of counterweight) force *up*, (*fruit weighs down branch; branches weighed down by fruit; weighed down with cares*). **6.** raise from below water (*weigh* ANCHOR¹). **7.** ∼**-beam**, portable steelyard suspended in frame; ∼'**bridge**, weighing-machine with plate set in road on to which vehicles etc. can be driven to be weighed; ∼**-house**, building in which goods can be weighed officially; ∼'**ing-machine** (usu. for greater weights or of more complicated mechanism than simple balance); ∼**-lock**, canal lock with provision for weighing barges; ∼'**man**, man employed to weigh goods, esp. mined coal at colliery. **8.** Hence ∼'ABLE *a.* **9.** *n.* process or occasion of weighing; **under** ∼, (D) = *under* WAY 9. [OE *wegan*, = OS, OHG *wegan*, ON *vega* lift, weigh, Goth. **wigan* shake, f. Gmc **wegan* (**weg-*, **wag-*, **wǣg-*, f. IE **wegh-* etc.; cf. WAG¹, WAIN, WAY)]

weight (wāt) *n.* **1.** force with which body tends to centre of attraction, esp. (of terrestrial things) degree of downward tendency in body produced as resultant of earth's gravitation and centrifugal force (*the weight of a body varies with latitude and altitude but its mass does not*). **2.** relative mass or quantity of matter contained and giving rise to downward force, heaviness, regarded as a property of bodies (*superior both in size and in weight; he is twice your weight; kept in position by its weight*); surface density of cloth etc. as measure of its suitability for particular season, garment, etc.; ATOMIC *weight*; DEAD *weight*; ∼ **of metal**, total amount that can be thrown by ship's gun(s) at one discharge; **throw** one's ∼ **about** or **around**, (colloq.) act with (unpleasant) self-assertiveness. **3.** body's mass numerically expressed in some recognized scale (*what is your weight?*; *goods sold by weight not quantity*); scale or notation for expressing weights (TROY, AVOIRDUPOIS, body); BOX²*ing- -weights*; PULL¹ one's *weight*. **4.** heavy body (*keep papers down with a weight; clock is worked by weights; must not lift weights*); piece of metal etc. of known mass used in scales for weighing articles (*where is the ounce weight?*); heavy object thrown or PUT¹ by athletes, e.g. SHOT¹. **5.** load to be supported (*the pillars have a great weight to bear*); force to which LEVER is applied; heavy burden of care, responsibility, etc. **6.** importance, convincing effect, influence, preponderance, (*considerations without weight; men of weight; has great weight with me; the weight of evidence is against him*); relative value assigned to an observation etc. **7.** ∼, be influential or important. **7.** ∼**-cloth**, lead-weighted saddle-cloth to make up difference between weight horse is to carry and weight of jockey; ∼**-lifter,** one who engages in ∼**-lifting,** athletic sport or exercise of lifting heavy objects; ∼**-watcher,** one who takes care not to become unduly fat. **8.** Hence ∼′LESS *a.* (esp. in free-falling spacecraft etc.). [OE *(ge)wiht,* = ON *vétt, vætt* f. Gmc -*wehtiz* (*weg-; cf. prec.)]

weight² (wāt) *v.t.* attach a weight to, hold down with a weight or weights; impede or burden with load (lit. or fig.); assign handicap weight to (horse); treat (fabric) with mineral etc. to make it seem stouter; (Statistics) multiply components of (average) by factors to take account of their importance; hence ∼′ING¹ *n.,* (esp.) extra pay or allowances given in special cases, e.g. to allow for higher cost of living in London. [f. prec.]

wei′ght|ÿ (wā′tĭ) *a.* weighing much, heavy; momentous, important; well-weighed, giving evidence of earnest thought, deserving of consideration; influential, authoritative; hence ∼ĭLY² *adv.,* ∼ĭNESS *n.* [ME, f. WEIGHT¹ +-Y²]

Weimara′ner (wī-, vī-; -ah′-) *n.* (usu. grey) variety of pointer used as gun dog. [G, f. *Weimar* in Germany (where developed)]

weir (wēr) *n.* dam across river to raise level of water upstream or regulate flow; enclosure of stakes etc. set in stream as trap for fish. [OE, *wer* (- OS *weri*) f. *werian* dam up]

weird¹ (wērd) *n.* (Esp. Sc.) fate, destiny; DREE one's *weird.* [OE *wyrd* destiny, = OS *wurd,* OHG *wurt,* ON *urthr* f. Gmc *werth-, *warth, *wurth-* become; cf. WORTH²]

weird² (wērd) *a.* connected with fate (**the** ∼ **sisters,** (1) the Fates, (2) witches); supernatural, uncanny, unearthly; (colloq.) queer, odd, old-fashioned, strange, incomprehensible; hence ∼′IE, ∼′O (pl. ∼os), ∼′LY² *adv.,* (colloq.) eccentric person; ∼′LY² *adv.,* ∼′NESS *n.* [ME, attrib. use of prec., in *weird sister(s)*]

Wei′smannism (vī′-) *n.* theory of heredity assuming continuity of germ-plasm and non-transmission of acquired characteristics [f. A. *Weismann,* Ger. biologist d. 1914 + -ISM]

Welch¹. Var. of WELSH¹ (now only in *Royal Welch Fusiliers*).

welch²(er). See WELSH².

we′lcome *int., n., v.t.,* & *a.* **1.** *int.* of greeting = know that your coming here gives pleasure (often w. *adv.:* *welcome home, to England!*). **2.** *n.* saying 'welcome' to person; kind or glad reception or entertainment of person or acceptance of offer, gift, etc.; **bid** person ∼, assure him he is welcome; **wear out** or **outstay** or **overstay** one's ∼, go too often or stay too long as visitor etc.; **give a warm** ∼ **to,** (1) show great joy at arrival of, (2) make vigorous resistance to. **3.** *v.t.* say 'welcome' to, greet on arrival (*home* etc.), receive (guest, arrival, news, opportunity, gift, event) with pleasure or signs of it; greet or receive *with* (embrace, gunfire, etc.). **4.** *a.* gladly received (*a welcome guest, interruption, gift, rest, denial, sight*); **make** person ∼, let him feel so; hence ∼NESS (-mn-) *n.* **5.** *pred. a.* ungrudgingly permitted *to* do or given right *to* thing, absolved of thanking or recompensing, (*you are welcome to take it, you may have it and welcome; any one is welcome to my share, to any service I can do*); **you are** ∼, no thanks are required. [orig. OE *wilcuma* (*wil-* desire, pleasure, *cuma* comer) one whose coming is pleasing, w. later change to *wel-* = WELL³ after OF *bien venu* (or ON *velkominn*)]

weld¹ *n.* (plant, *Reseda luteola,* yielding) yellow dye formerly used. [ME, f. OE *w(e)alde* = MDu. *woude,* MLG *walde*]

weld² *v.t.,* & *n.* **1.** *v.t.* unite (pieces of metal, esp. iron) into homogeneous mass by hammering or pressure (usu. when iron is softened by heat but not melted), or by fusion with electric arc etc.; make by welding; (fig.) unite closely, bring (recruits, parts, arguments, etc.) into or *into* homogeneous whole. **2.** Hence ∼′ABLE *a.,* ∼′ER¹ *n.* **3.** *n.* joint made by welding. [alt.

f. WELL² in obs. sense melt or weld (heated metal), prob. infl. by p.p.]

we′lfare *n.* satisfactory state, health and prosperity, (usu. *of* person, society, etc.); maintenance of members of community in such condition, esp. by statutory procedure or social effort; money etc. thus received by those in need; W∼ **State,** country seeking to ensure welfare of all citizens by means of government-operated social services; ∼ **work,** organized efforts to improve conditions of living for the poor, the disabled, etc. [ME, f. WELL³ + FARE²]

we′lkin *n.* (poet. or literary). sky, upper air. [OE *wolcen* cloud, sky, = OS, OHG *wolkan*]

well¹ *n.* **1.** (poet. or arch.) spring or fountain, (fig.) source; ∼ **of English undefiled,** Chaucer. **2.** mineral spring; (in *pl.*) spa. **3.** shaft sunk in ground and lined with stone or other protection for obtaining subterranean water, oil, etc., (ARTESIAN *well*). **4.** enclosed space more or less resembling well-shaft; space in middle of building from basement to roof containing stairs or lift or surrounded by stairs or open for light and ventilation; ||railed space for solicitors etc. in lawcourt; (Phys.) region of minimum potential etc.; = INK-*well*; depression for gravy etc. in dish or tray, or for mat in floor. **5.** ∼**-deck,** space on main deck of ship, enclosed by bulwarks and higher decks; ∼**-head,** (1) source, fountain-head, (2) top of well; ∼**-spring,** = *well-head* (1). [OE *wella,* = OHG *wella* wave, ON *vella* boiling heat f. Gmc *wall-*; cf. foll.]

well² *v.i.* (literary). spring (as) from fountain (*up, out, forth*). [OE *wællan, wellan* boil, melt, causative of *weallan,* = OS, OHG *wallan* boil, gush forth, f. WG *wallan*]

well³ *adv.* & *a.* (BETTER¹, BEST¹). **1.** *adv.* in good manner or style, satisfactorily, rightly, (*the work is well done; that is well said; a well situated house; you did well to come; is eating well now; well begun is half done*); ∼ **done!,** **run!,** etc., (cry of commendation); ∼ **met!** (arch. greeting to person one has been wanting to meet); **come off** ∼, have good luck, distinguish oneself; DO¹ oneself well; DO¹ *well for oneself;* DO¹ *well (out of);* LIVE² *well;* ∼ **out of it,** ∼ **rid of them,** disengaged without disaster etc. **2.** thoroughly, with care or completeness, sufficiently, to a considerable distance or extent, with margin enough to justify description, quite, (*look well to it; judge well and truly; thrash him, polish it, well; is well up in the list, well on in life, well over retiring age, well past forty, well among the leaders of thought, well in the lead;* PRETTY *well*); ∼ **away,** having started or made considerable progress; ∼ **and truly,** decisively (*beaten* etc.). **3.** heartily, kindly, laudatorily, approvingly, on good terms, (*love* or *like* person *well; treat* person *well; think* or *speak well of*); SPEAK *well for;* **stand** ∼ **with** person, be approved by him; **wish** person ∼, hope that he prospers. **4.** probably, not incredibly, easily, with reason, wisely, advisably, (*it may well be that you are right; cannot very well refuse the offer; you may well ask; we might well make the experiment*). **5. as** ∼, (1) in addition, to an equal extent, not less truly, (2) with equal reason, preferably, without worse consequences, (*we* MAY¹ *as well go; that is just as* ∼, need not be regretted), (3) advisable (*it would be as well to inquire*); **as** ∼ **as,** in addition to (*gave me clothes as well as food; you were there as well as I; as well as helping,* colloq. *help, me she continued her own work*). **6.** *pred. a.* in good health (*is she well or ill?; will soon be better; is best in the winter; quite well thank you; am perfectly well;* in satisfactory state or position, satisfactory, advisable, (*am very well where I am; all's well; it would be well to inquire*); ALL *very well; let* or **leave** ∼ **(enough) alone,** not meddle needlessly; ∼ **enough,** tolerably good or attractive; ∼ **and good** (formula of dispassionate acceptance of decision; *if you choose to take my advice, well and good*); ∼ **off,** fortunately situated, fairly rich; ∼**-to-do,** fairly rich; VERY¹ *well.* **7.** *attrib. a.* in good health (*a well man should not be dawdling in bed*;

the well are impatient of the sick). [OE *wel(l)*, = OS *wel(a)*, OHG *wela, wola,* ON *vel,* Goth. *waila,* prob. f. same st. as WILL¹]

wĕll⁴ *int.* expr. great astonishment (*well, who would have thought it?*; *well, I* NEVER!), relief (*well, here we are at last*), concession (*well, come if you like*; *well, perhaps you are right*; *well then, say no more about it*), resumption or continuation of talk (*well, who was it?*; *well, he says he must see you*; *well, that's a difficult question*); qualified recognition of point (*well, but what about Jones?*), expectation (*well then?*), resignation (*oh well, it can't be helped*), etc.; **ah** ~, (expr. resignation); ~, ~! (expr. surprise). [ellipt. uses of prec. adv.]

wĕll(-) *pref.* = WELL³ *adv.* **1.** To *ns.* & *adjs.*: ~-**being,** welfare; ~-**doer,** virtuous person; -**doing,** virtuous conduct; ~'**nigh,** (rhet.) almost; ~-**wisher,** person who wishes well to another. **2.** To participles in -ED¹, -ING², etc., and to *adjs.* in -ED², (usu. w. hyphen except in pred. use of past participles in -ED¹ etc. not having restricted force: *my watch is well regulated*; *I do not think his action was well-advised*; cf. *he is not well advised by his friends*): ~-**advi'sed,** (of person or action) prudent, wise; ~-**affected,** favourably disposed *to(wards),* loyal; ~-**appointed,** having all necessary equipment; ~-**balanced,** sane, sensible, equally matched; *well*-BEHAVED; ~-**beloved** *a.* & *n.,* dearly loved (person); ~-**born,** of noble family; ~-**bred,** having good breeding or manners, (of horse etc.) of good or pure stock; ~ **chosen** (esp. of words or phrases); ~-**condi'tioned,** in good physical or moral condition; ~-**conducted,** characterized by good conduct or organization; *well* CONNECTED; ~-**defined,** clearly indicated or determined; ~-**disposed,** having good disposition or friendly feeling (*towards*); ~ **done,** (of meat) cooked thoroughly; ~ **earned,** fully deserved; ~-**favoured,** good-looking; ~-**found,** = *well-appointed*; ~ **founded,** (of suspicion or other belief or sentiment) having foundation in fact or reason; ~-**groomed,** (of person) having carefully tended hair, skin, clothes, etc.; ~ **grounded,** (1) = *well founded,* (2) well trained in rudiments; ~-**heeled,** (colloq.) wealthy; ~-**informed,** having well-stored mind or access to reliable information; ~-**intentioned,** having or showing good intentions; ~-**judged,** (of action) showing good judgement or tact or good aim; ~-**knit,** (esp. of person) compact, not loose-jointed or sprawling; ~-**known,** (1) known to many, (2) known thoroughly; ~-**liking,** (arch.) with well-fed prosperous look (*fat and well-liking*); ~-**looking,** of attractive appearance; ~ **made,** (of person or animal) having good build, (of thing) skilfully manufactured; ~-**mannered,** having good manners; ~ **marked,** distinct, easy to detect; *well* MATCH²*ed*; ~-**meaning,** ~ **meant,** = *well-intentioned* (but ineffective or unwise); ~ **oiled,** (fig., of expression) complimentary, (sl.) very drunk; ~ **ordered,** arranged in orderly manner; ~ **paid,** liberally rewarded for work, service, etc.; *well* PRESERVE²*d*; ~-**read,** having read much [cf. -ED¹ (2)], with mind well stored by reading; ~-**rounded,** complete and symmetrical, (of sentence) complete and well expressed; ~-**seen,** (arch.) accomplished *in*; ~ **set,** skilfully placed or adjusted, (of batsman) accustomed to the bowling and unlikely to be out; ~ **set up,** (of person) compact, firmly knit; ~ **spent** (esp. of money, time, or effort); ~-**spo'ken,** ready or refined in speech; ~-**thought-out,** carefully devised; ~ **thumbed,** bearing marks of frequent handling; ~ **timed,** opportune, timely; ~-**tried,** often tested with good result; ~-**trodden,** (of path etc.) frequented; ~ **turned,** (of compliment, phrase, verse) neatly expressed; *well*-UPHOLSTER*ed*; *well-worn* (see WEAR¹).

wĕ'lladay, wĕ'llaway (-*a*-wā), *ints.* (arch. or joc.) of grief. [OE *wei lā wei* alt. f. *wā lā wā* (woe, lo! woe) after OScand. *wei*; *welladay* 16th c. alt. after *lackaday* (see LACKADAISICAL)]

‖**wĕ'llies** (-ĭz) *n.* (colloq.) wellingtons. [abbr.; see -IE]

wĕ'llington *n.* rubber waterproof boot usu. reaching knee; high boot covering knee in front. [f. 1st Duke of *Wellington,* Brit. general and statesman d. 1852]

wĕllingtō'nia *n.* = SEQUOIA. [f. as prec. + -IA¹]

Wĕ'lsian (-z-) *a.* characteristic of Wells's writings, esp. in predicting conditions of the future. [f. H. G. *Wells,* Engl. writer d. 1946 + -IAN]

wĕls *n.* sheat-fish. [G]

Wĕlsh¹ *a.* & *n.* (Celtic language, (as *pl.*) people) of Wales; *Welsh* CORGI; ~ **dresser** (with open shelves above cupboard); ~ **harp** (with three rows of strings); ~'**man,** ~'**woman,** native of Wales; ~ **lamb** or **mutton** (from small Welsh mountain sheep; ~ **onion,** species (*Allium fistulosum*) forming clusters of bulbs; ~ **rabbit** or by pop. etym. **rarebit,** dish of melted or toasted cheese on toast. [OE *Welisc, Wælisc,* etc., = OHG *wal(a)hisc, walesc* Roman, Italian, French, ON *valskr* Gaulish f. Gmc **walhaz* foreign f. L *Volcae,* name of a Celtic people]

welsh², **wĕlch²,** *v.i.* (Of loser of bet, esp. bookmaker) decamp without paying; evade an obligation; ~ **on,** fail to carry out one's promise to (person), fail to honour (obligation); hence ~ER¹ *n.* [19th c.; orig. unkn.]

wĕlt *n.,* & *v.t.* **1.** *n.* strip of leather sewn round edge of boot or shoe upper to serve as attachment to sole; WEAL²; heavy blow; ribbed etc. border or edging of garment etc., trimming. **2.** *v.t.* provide with welt; raise weals on, beat, flog. [ME *welte, walt,* of unkn. orig.]

Weltanschauung (vĕltahnshow'ŏŏng) *n.* philosophy of life; conception of the universe. [G (*welt* world, *anschauung* perception)]

wĕ'lter *v.i.,* & *n.* **1.** *v.i.* roll, wallow, be washed about, lie prostrate or be soaked or steeped *in* blood etc. **2.** *n.* general confusion, disorderly mixture or aimless conflict *of* creeds, policies, errors, etc. [ME, f. MDu., MLG *welteren*]

wĕ'lter² *n.* **1.** heavy rider or boxer; ~ (**race** etc.), race etc. for heavyweight riders; ~**weight,** (1) heavyweight rider, (2) weight carried in addition to weight assigned according to age, (3) see BOX⁵*ing*-*weights*. **2.** (colloq.) heavy blow; big person or thing. [19th c.; orig. unkn.]

Weltpolitik (vĕltpŏlĭtē'k) *n.* participation (esp. in leading role) in international politics. [G (*welt* world, *politik* politics)]

Weltschmerz (vĕ'ltshmārts) *n.* apathetic or vaguely yearning outlook on life. [G (*welt* world, *schmerz* pain)]

wĕn¹ *n.* more or less permanent benign sebaceous tumour on skin esp. of scalp; (arch.) goitre; (fig.) abnormally large or congested city (**the great** ~, London). [OE *wen(n), wæn(n),* of unkn. orig.; cf. Du. *wen,* MLG *wene,* LG *wehne* tumour, wart]

wĕn² *n.* runic letter in OE & ME, later replaced by *w.* [OE, var. of *wyn* joy (see WINSOME), used as beginning with this letter; cf. THORN]

wĕnch *n.,* & *v.i.* **1.** *n.* (dial. or joc.) girl or young woman. **2.** (arch.) prostitute. **3.** *v.i.* (arch.) (Of man) consort with prostitutes; hence ~'ER¹ *n.* [ME *wenche(l)* f. OE *wencel* child; cf. OE *wancol* weak, tottering]

wĕnd¹ *v.* (literary) **1.** *v.t.* ~ one's **way,** go. **2.** *v.i.* (arch.) go. [OE *wendan* turn, = OS *wendian,* OHG *wentan,* ON *venda,* Goth. *wandjan,* causative of Gmc **windan* WIND²]

Wĕnd² *n.* one of a Slavic people formerly spread over N. Germany, and now inhabiting E. Saxony; hence ~'IC, ~'ISH¹, *adjs.* [f. G *Wende* f. OHG *Winida,* of unkn. orig.]

Wĕ'ndў ~ **house,** children's small houselike structure for playing in. [character in Barrie's *Peter Pan*]

Wĕ'nsleydāle (-zlĭ-) *n.* variety of white or blue cheese; breed of long-woolled sheep. [~ in North Yorkshire]

wĕnt. See GO¹.

wĕn′tletrăp (-telt-) *n.* shellfish of genus *Scalaria* with spiral shell of many whorls. [f. Du. *wenteltrap* winding stair, spiral shell]

wĕpt. See WEEP.

were(n't). See BE.

wer′ewol∣f, wer′wol∣f, (wēr′wŏŏlf, wĕr′-) *n.* (*pl.* ∼ves *pr.* -vz). (Myth.) human being able to be turned at times into wolf. [OE *werewulf,* = MDu. *weerwolf,* MHG *werwolf;* first element perh. f. OE *wer* man = L *vir*]

wert. See BE.

Werthē′r∣ian (vertēr′-) *a.* morbidly sentimental; so ∼ISM (3) *n.* [f. *Werther,* hero of Goethe's 'Sorrows of Werther' (1774) + -IAN]

Wĕsleyan (wĕ′zlian, wĕ′s-, arch. wĕzlē′an) *a.* & *n.* (Hist.) (member) of the Protestant denomination founded by Wesley; hence ∼ISM (3) *n.* (cf. METHODISM). [f. J. *Wesley,* Engl. evangelist d. 1791 + -AN]

wĕst *adv., n.,* & *a.* **1.** (towards, at, near) point of horizon where sun sets at the equinoxes (cardinal point 90° to left of North); (**to the**) ∼ (**of**), in a westward direction (from); EAST *and west;* ∼ **wind,** wind blowing from the west; **go** ∼, (sl.) be killed, lost, wrecked, etc. **2.** *n.* (usu. **W**∼). part of world or country or town lying to the west (***the W**∼, part of US lying west of originally settled areas or of the Mississippi; ***Far W**∼, region beyond Great Plains; **Middle W**∼, region adjoining the northern Mississippi; WILD *West*); western part of late-Roman world; European in contrast to Oriental civilization; non-Communist States of Europe and America; card-player occupying position designated 'west'. **3.** ∼′**about,** westwards; ∼′**bound,** travelling westwards; *west* BY[1] *north* or *south;* **W**∼ **Country,** south-western counties of England; ∥**W**∼ **End,** fashionable part of London incl. Mayfair and Piccadilly; *West* INDIAN; *West* INDIES; ∼**-north-**∼, compass point midway between west and north-west (so ∼**-south-**∼); ***W**∼ **Side,** western part of Manhattan. **4.** Hence ∼′WARD *a.* & *n.,* ∼′WARD(s) *adv.* [OE, = OS, OHG *west,* ON *vestr* f. Gmc. **westaₓ* f. IE **wes-*]

wĕ′stering *a.* (Esp. of sun) tending towards the west. [f. *wester* v. ME f. prec. + -ER⁵]

wĕ′sterlỹ *a., adv.,* & *n.* in a western position or direction; (wind) blowing (nearly) from the west. [f. *wester* a. f. OE *westra* (WEST) + -LY¹]

wĕ′stern *a.* & *n.* **1.** *a.* of or (dwelling) in the west; lying or directed towards the west; (*W*∼) of the (**Far, Middle*) West; **W**∼ **Church,** part of Christian Church that continued to acknowledge popes after schism, Latin Church; **W**∼ **Empire** (cf. ROMAN² *Empire*); *Western* HEMISPHERE; **W**∼ **roll,** high-jumper's technique of turning body over bar; hence ∼ER¹ (4) *n.,* ∼IZE (3) *v.t.,* make (Oriental person etc.) more like the West in ideas, institutions, etc., ∼MOST *a.* **2.** *n.* film or novel dealing with cowboys etc. in western N. America. [OE *westerne* (as WEST, -ERN)]

wĕ′sting *n.* (Naut. etc.) distance travelled or measured westward; westerly direction. [f. WEST + -ING¹]

∥**Wĕ′stminster** *n.* (Houses of) Parliament in London; past or present member of Westminster School. [∼ in London, where Houses of Parliament (*Palace of* ∼) are]

wĕt *a., v.t.* (-tt-; wet *or* we′tted), & *n.* **1.** *a.* soaked, covered, splashed, moistened, or supplied, with or *with* water or other liquid (*wet sponge, land, road, table, clothes, feet;* ∼ **behind the ears,** immature, inexperienced; ∼ **to the skin,** ∼ **through,** with clothes soaked through); used with or using water; (of day, weather, etc.) rainy; comprising or supplying, or allowing the sale of, alcoholic liquor; (of paint, ink, etc.) recently applied and not yet dry; (sl.) mistaken, stupid, inept. **2.** *****∼′**back,** (colloq.) illegal immigrant from Mexico to US; ∼ **bargain** (closed with drink); *wet* BLANKET¹; ∥*wet*-BOB⁵; ∼ **bulb** (of

thermometer, covered with wet muslin etc. to give measure of air humidity by its lower temperature due to evaporation of water from it into the air); ∼ **dock** (in which ship can float); ∼ **dream,** erotic dream with involuntary emission of semen; ∼ **fly,** artificial fly used under water by angler; ∼′**lands,** swamps and other damp areas of land; ∼ **look,** shiny surface of fabric; ∼**-nurse,** (*n.*) woman employed to suckle another's child, (*v.t.*) act as wet-nurse to (child), (fig.) treat as if helpless; ∼ **pack,** therapeutic wrapping of body in wet cloths etc.; ∼ **plate,** (Photog.) sensitized collodion plate exposed while wet; *wet* STEAM¹; ∼ **suit,** porous garment worn by skin-diver etc. **3.** Hence ∼′NESS *n.,* ∼′TISH¹ 2 *a.* **4.** *v.t.* make wet (∼ **bargain,** close it with drink; ∼ **the baby's head,** (sl.) celebrate birth by drinking; ∼ one's **whistle,** (colloq.) drink); urinate in or on; ∼′**ting agent,** substance that helps water etc. to spread or penetrate; hence ∼t′ABLE *a.,* ∼′TING¹ (1) *n.* **5.** *n.* moisture, liquid that wets something, rainy weather or season; (sl.) a drink; *****one who favours sale of alcoholic liquor; (sl.) stupid or inept person. [OE (*wǣtan* v. f.) *wǣt* a. & n., = ON *vátr,* superseded in ME by p.p. of the v.; cogn. w. WATER¹]

wĕ′ta *n.* (NZ) large wingless horned grasshopper whose grubs bore in wood. [Maori]

wĕ′ther (-dh-) *n.* castrated ram. [OE, = OS *withar,* OHG *widar,* ON *vethr,* Goth. *withrus* f. Gmc **wethruz*]

WEU *abbr.* Western European Union

wey (wā) *n.* former unit of weight or volume varying with different kinds of goods, e.g. 3 cwt. of cheese. [f. OE *wǣg(e),* balance, weight, OS, OHG *wāga,* ON *vág* f. Gmc **wǣg-* WEIGH]

w.f. *abbr.* (Print.) wrong fount.

WFTU *abbr.* World Federation of Trade Unions.

Wg. Cdr. *abbr.* Wing Commander.

whăck *v.t., & n.* **1.** *v.t.* (colloq.) strike heavily with stick etc., thwack, whence ∼′ING¹ (1) *n.;* ∥(in *p.p.*) tired out; bring *up* etc. by vigorous action. **2.** *n.* (colloq.) heavy resounding blow esp. with stick; attempt at. **3.** *v.t.,* & *n.* (sl.) share; ***out of** ∼, out of order. [imit. or alt. f. THWACK]

whă′cker *n.* (sl.) thing (esp. a lie) or person big of its kind. [f. prec. + -ER¹; cf. *whopper* etc.]

whă′cking *a.* & *adv.* (sl.) **1.** *a.* big of its kind. **2.** *adv.* very (*big* etc.). [f. as prec. + -ING¹; cf. *whopping* etc.]

∥**whă′ckō** *int.* (sl.) expr. joy. [f. WHACK + -O]

whă′ckỹ. Var. of WACKY.

whāle *n.* (*pl.* ∼s *or* ∼) & *v.* **1.** *n.* fishlike marine mammal of order Cetacea, esp. large one hunted for oil, spermaceti, whalebone, ambergris, etc., (**right** ∼, kind yielding best whalebone); **very like a** ∼ (ironical assent to absurd statement; see Shak. *Hamlet* III. ii. 399). **2. a** ∼ **of a,** (colloq.) an exceedingly (great); **a** ∼ **at, for, on,** very good at or keen on; ∼**-back,** structure shaped like whale's back; ∼**-boat,** double-bowed boat (like those) used in whaling; ∼′**bone,** elastic horny substance growing in thin parallel plates in upper jaw of some whales, used as stiffening etc.; ∼**-head,** Afr. bird allied to herons and storks; ∼**-oil,** train-oil or sperm oil got from whales; ∼**-shark,** huge tropical shark. **3.** *v.i.* be engaged in whale-hunting; **wha′ling-gun** (for firing harpoon etc. at whales); **wha′ling-master,** captain of a whaler. **4.** *v.t.* & *i.* *(colloq.) beat, thrash. [OE *hwæl,* = OHG *wal,* ON *hvalr*]

whā′ler *n.* whaling ship or man; whale-boat; Austral. shark of genus *Carcharhinus.* [f. prec. + -ER¹]

*whā′ling *a.* (sl.) = WHACKING. [f. WHALE + -ING²]

whăm *int., n.,* & *v.* (-**mm**-). **1.** *int.* expr. sound of forcible impact. **2.** *n.,* & *v.i.* & *t.* (make, strike with) such sound. [imit.]

*whă′mmỹ *n.* (thing with) supernatural power, esp. one bringing bad luck. [20th c., of unkn. orig.]

whăng *v.* & *n.* (colloq.) **1.** *v.t.* strike heavily and loudly, whack. **2.** *v.i.* (Of drum etc.) sound (as) under blow. **3.** *n.* whanging sound or blow. [imit.]

whăngee' (-nggē') n. (cane made from) Chinese or Japanese bamboo of genus *Phyllostachys*. [f. Chin. *huang* old bamboo-sprouts]

wha'rė (wŏ'-) n. Maori hut or house. [Maori]

whar|f (-ôrf) n. (pl. ∿fs, or ∿ves pr. -vz), & v.t. **1.** n. wooden or stone platform beside which ship may be moored for (un)loading etc.; hence ∿'FAGE (1, 4) n. **2.** v.t. moor (ship) at, store (goods) on, wharf. [OE *hwearf*, = MLG *warf*, *werf* mole, dam, wharf]

whar'finger (-ôr'fĭnj-) n. wharf-owner. [app. f. earlier *wharfager*, f. WHARFAGE + -ER¹; cf. *messenger*]

what (-ŏt) a., pron., & adv. **1.** interrog. a. (asking for selection from indefinite or (colloq.) definite number: *what books have you read?*; *don't know what plan he will try*; (colloq.) *what book have you chosen?*; or asking for statement of amount or number or kind: *what men, money, abilities, has he?*; *what news?*; *what kind of man is he?*; *I know what time to start, what difficulties there are*); ∿ **matter?**, what does it matter?; ∿ **good** or **use is it?**, what purpose will it serve?; ||*what* PRICE?. **2.** excl. a. how great or strange or otherwise remarkable (*what a fool you are!*; *what impudence!*; *what luck!*; *what a swindle!*; *what an idea!*; *what genius he has!*); (before a. & n.) = HOW 3 (*what partial judges we are!*). **3.** rel. a. the ...that, any ...that, as much or many ...as, (*dispose of what difficulties there are*; *lend me what money* or *men you can*; *will give you what help is possible*); *what* TIME¹. **4.** interrog. pron. what thing(s)? (*what is your name?*; *how I wonder what you are*; *cannot guess what he meant*; *don't know what she said*; *what followed is unknown*); (in rhet. questions equiv. to neg. statement: *what is the use of trying?*); (asking for repetition or confirmation of something not properly heard or understood, or for agreement: *what?*; *you did what?*; *what, do you really mean it?*; *what, are you stepping westward?*; ||(colloq.) *nice day, what?*); ∿ **about**, what is the news concerning, how do you dispose of the question of, what do you think of, I suggest (*what about a game of chess?*); ∿**-d'you** (or **d'ye**)-**call-it** etc., ∿**'s-its** (or **his**)-**name**, ∿ **is it**, ∿ **you may call it**, (substitutes for name that cannot be recalled); ∿ **for?**, for what reason or purpose? (GIVE¹ person *what for*); ∿ **have you**, anything else (similar) that there may be or that one can think of; ∿ **ho!** (excl. of greeting or hailing); ∿ (would result, does it matter) **if**; ∿ **is he**, what is his occupation, character, social status, etc.?; ∿ **is it** etc. **like** (asking for description etc.); ∿ **next?**, (fig.) what more absurd or impudent or strange or novel thing is possible?; ∿ **not**, and many other similar things; ∿**'not**, (1) indefinite or trivial thing, (2) 19th-c. stand with shelves for small objects; ∿ **of**, what is the news concerning; ∿ **o'f it?**, = so WHAT? (1); ∿ **do you say**, *∿ say, (colloq.) I suggest that (*what do you say we have a rest*); ∿ **will people say?**, is it a respectable thing to do?; (**I'll**) **tell you** ∿, my assertion or proposal is this; ∿ **then?**, what would happen next or be the consequence?; *what* THOUGH; *I* or *you* KNOW¹ *what* (*he or it is*); KNOW¹ *what's what*; **or** ∿ (indefinite alternative following question: *are you trying to kill me, or what?*); **so** ∿**?**, (1) that fact has no immediate relevance or interest, (2) there is no obvious solution or procedure. **5.** excl. pron. what thing(s)!, how much!, etc., (*what he must have suffered!*). **6.** rel. pron. that or those which, the thing(s) that, anything that, a thing that, (*what followed was unpleasant*; *this is what I mean*; *did what he was attempting*; *what I have written I have written*; *what I don't know isn't knowledge*; *give me what you can*; *what is called 'the general reader'*; COME *what may*; *tell me what you remember of it*; *but, what even you must condemn, he was lying*; *will do what 'I can for you*; *use no arguments but what you yourself believe in*); (vulg.) who, which, (*it's the poor what gets the blame*); BUT¹ *what*; NOT *but what*; ∿ **is more**, and as an additional point, moreover. **7.** adv. to what extent or degree (*what do we care?*; *what does it matter?*); ∿ **with**, on account of (usu. more than one thing). [OE *hwæt* = OS *hwat*, OHG (*h*)*waz*,

ON *hvat*, Goth. *hwa* f. Gmc **hwat* f. IE **q "od* neut. of **q "os* WHO]

whatě'ver (-ŏt-), **whate'er'** (poet.; -ōtāī'), a. & pron. **1.** = prec. 3, 6 (with addition of or emphasis on indefinite sense: *whatever I have is yours*; *whatever measures are considered necessary*; *do whatever you like*). **2.** (In indef. concessive clause) though any(thing) (*whatever results follow, whatever happens, whatever friends we may offend, we shall have done our duty*). **3.** (w. neg. or interrog.) at all, whatever it, he, etc., may be, (*there is no doubt whatever*; *is there any chance whatever?*; *no one whatever would accept*; *cannot see anyone whatever*); **or whatever**, or anything similar. **4.** (colloq.) = *what* EVER. [ME, f. prec. + EVER]

wha'tsō (-ŏ't-) a. & pron. (arch.) = prec. 1, 2. [ME, = WHAT + SO¹. f. OE *swā hwæt swā*]

whatsŏě'ver (-ŏt-), **whatsŏe'er'** (poet.; -ōtsōār'), a. & pron. = WHATEVER 1, 2, 3. [ME, f. prec. + EVER]

wheal. Var. of WEAL².

wheat n. (highly nutritious seeds of) cereal plant of genus *Triticum* bearing dense four-sided spike of grain, an important source of flour for bread; *separate wheat from* CHAFF; ∿**-belt**, region where wheat is chief agricultural product; ∿**-grass**, couch-grass; ||∿**-meal**, (esp. wholemeal) wheat-flour; hence ∿'EN⁵ a. [OE *hwæte*, = OS *hwēti*, OHG *wei*(*z*)*zi*, ON *hveiti*, Goth. *hwaiteis* f. Gmc **hwaitjaz* (**hwit-* WHITE¹)]

whea'tear n. small bird of genus *Oenanthe*, esp. species with white belly and rump. [app. f. *wheatears*, **whiteeres* (as WHITE¹, ARSE¹)]

Whea'tstōne n. ∿ **bridge**, apparatus for measuring electrical resistances by equalizing potential at two points of circuit. [f. C. *Wheatstone*, Engl. physicist d. 1875]

whee int. expr. joy or excitement. [imit.]

whee'dl|e v.t. coax *into* doing or *into* good temper etc., persuade by flattery or endearments, cajole; get (thing) *out of* person by wheedling; cheat (person) *out of* thing by wheedling; hence ∿ER¹ n., ∿ING² a. [perh. f. G *wedeln* fawn, cringe (*wedel* tail)]

wheel¹ n. **1.** circular frame or disc arranged to revolve on axle and used to facilitate motion of vehicle or for various mechanical purposes; machine etc. of which a wheel is an essential part; object resembling a wheel (CATHERINE *wheel*); = POTTER¹'S, SPINNING-, STEER¹-ing-, wheel (**at the** ∿, driving a vehicle or directing a ship, (fig.) in control of affairs); **bicycle*; set of short lines concluding stanza; * = BIG *wheel*; **break on the** ∿, maim (and kill) on medieval instrument of torture that revolved with victim bound to it and beaten; *break* BUTTERFLY *on wheel*; FLY¹ *on wheel*; (**Fortune's**) ∿, wheel which Fortune is depicted as turning, (symbol of) vicissitudes; *go on* (**oiled**) ∿**s**, smoothly; OIL² *the wheels*; SHOULDER *to the wheel*; *put a* SPOKE¹ *in* person's *wheel*; ∿ **and axle**, machine using leverage given by difference in circumference between wheel and its axle; ∿ **of life**, (1) zoetrope, (2) endless sequence of individual's lives in Buddhism; ∿**s of life**, vital processes etc.; ∿**s within** ∿**s**, intricate machinery, (fig.) indirect or secret motives or agencies. **2.** motion as of wheel, circular motion, motion of line as on pivoted end esp. as military movement (**right, left**, etc., ∿, words of command to company etc. in line to swing round on right, left, flank as pivot). **3.** ∿**-animal**(**cule**), rotifer; ∿**-back**, chair with back shaped like, or containing design of, wheel; ∿'**barrow**, shallow open box with shafts and one wheel for carrying loads etc. (∿*barrow race*, between pairs in which one person holds feet of other person walking on hands); ∿'**base**, distance between front and rear axles of vehicle; ∿'**chair**, invalid's chair on wheels; ∿**-horse**, wheeler, *** (fig.) steady worker; ∿**-house**, steersman's shelter; ∿**-lock**, (gun with) antiquated lock having steel wheel to rub against flint etc.; ∿'**man**, cyclist;

*steersman; ∼**-race,** part of mill-race where mill-
-wheel is placed; *∼'**sman** (-z-), steersman; ∼**-spin,**
rotation of vehicle wheels without traction; ∼**-tree,**
Austral. tree with circular flower-clusters; ∼
window (circular with spokelike tracery); ∼'-
wright, maker or repairer of (esp. wooden) wheels.
4. Hence (-)∼ED² (-ld), ∼'LESS (-l-l-), adjs., ∼'IE n.,
(in pl., sl.) travelling short distance with front
wheel(s) off ground. [OE hwēo(go)l, = MDu. wiel,
MLG wēl, ON hjól, hvél f. Gmc *hwe(g)ula f. IE
*qʷeqʷlo- (*qʷelo- move around)]

wheel² v. **1.** v.t. turn on axis or pivot, swing round
in line on one flank as pivot; ∼ (**about** or **round),**
(cause to) change direction (lit. or fig.) or face
another way. **2.** v.t. push or pull (wheeled thing esp.
wheelbarrow or pram or wheelchair or bicycle or its
load or occupant, or furniture on castors) in some
direction. **3.** v.i. go in circles or curves; travel in
wheeled vehicle; ride on bicycle; *∼ **and deal,**
engage in political or commercial scheming. [ME, f.
prec.]

whee'ler n. In vbl senses; horse harnessed next to
wheels and behind another (cf. LEADER); wheelwright; *∼**-dealer,** one who wheels and deals. [ME,
f. WHEEL¹,² +-ER¹]

wheez|e v. & n. **1.** n i. breathe with audible whistling
sound. **2.** v.t. ∼**e out,** utter with wheezing. **3.** n. sound
of wheezing; hence ∼'Yº a. **4.** (sl.) joke, anecdote, etc.,
interpolated by actor during performance; catch-
-phrase; clever expedient; scheme, plan. [prob. f. ON
hvæsa to hiss]

whelk¹ n. marine spiral-shelled gastropod mollusc of
genus Buccinum etc., esp. species used as food. [OE
wioloc, weoloc, of unkn. orig.; perh. infl. by foll.]

whelk² n. pimple. [f. OE hwylca (hwelian suppurate)]

whelm v.t. (poet. or rhet.) engulf, submerge, overwhelm. [OE *hwelman = hwylfan overturn, whence
dial. whelve]

whelp n. & v. **1.** n. young dog, pup; (arch.) cub, young
lion, tiger, bear, wolf, etc.; disagreeable or ill-bred
child or youth; (Naut., esp. in pl.) projection on
barrel of capstan or windlass. **2.** v.i. produce whelp(s)
or (derog.) child. **3.** v.t. give birth to (esp. derog. of
human mother); originate (evil scheme etc.). [OE
hwelp, = OS hwelp, OHG (h)welf, ON hvelpr]

when adv., conj., pron., & n. **1.** interrog. adv. at what
time?, on what occasion?, how soon?, how long ago?,
in what circumstances?, (when did, shall, you see him?;
don't know when it was; when do you use 'an'?); (in rhet.
question equiv. to neg. statement: when shall we see his
like again?); **say** ∼ (process is to begin or stop, esp.
when enough drink has been poured). **2.** rel. pron.
(With ref. to time) at which (the time when such things
could happen is past; there are occasions when one must yield;
have seen the day when that would not have been allowed). **3.**
conj. at the or any time that, on the or any occasion
that, at whatever time, as soon as, (he exclaimed when he
saw me; when it rains he stays at home; shall have it when you
ask politely); (ellipt.) he looked in when passing, when found
make a note of, myself when young); (introducing excl.
clause without main clause: when I think what I have
done for that man!). **4.** although, considering that,
(walks when he might ride; how could you, when you knew it
might kill him?; how convince him when he will not listen?).
5. after or upon which, but just then, and then, (the
conflict began, when it soon stopped and which was stronger; we
were just coming to the point when the bell interrupted us). **6.**
pron. what time?, which time, (till when can you stay?;
from when does it date?; since when things have been better).
7. n. time, date, occasion, (told me the when and the how of
it; and have they fixed the where and when?). [OE hwanne,
hwenne, etc., = OS hwan(na), OHG wanne, wenne,
Goth. hwan, f. interrog. st. *hwa- (WHO, WHAT); cf.
THEN f. *tha-]

whence adv., conj., pron., & n. (arch. or literary). **1.**
interrog. adv. from what place or source? from where?
(no one knows whence she comes). **2.** rel. adv., & conj. (With

ref. to place) from which (the source whence these evils
spring); to the place from which (return whence you
came); = and thence; ∼**soe'ver** (-s-s-), from whatever
place or source. **3.** pron. what place?, which place,
(from whence does it come?; the source from whence it
springs). **4.** n. source (we know neither our whence nor our
whither). [ME whannes, whennes, (whanne, whenne f. OE
hwanon(e) whence, f. as prec., + -sª; cf. THENCE)]

wheně'ver, whěne'er' (poet.; -âr'), conj. & adv. **1.** at
whatever time, on whatever occasion; (Sc. & Ir.) as
soon as; every time that; **or whenever,** or at any
similar time. **2.** (colloq.) = when EVER. [ME, f.
WHEN + EVER]

whěnsöě'ver, whěnsoe'er' (poet.; -âr'), conj. & adv.
= WHENEVER 1. [ME, f. whenso f. OE *swā hwanne swā;
cf. WHATSOEVER]

where (-âr) adv., conj., pron., & n. **1.** interrog. adv. in or to
what place or position (lit. or fig.)?, in what direction?, in what respect?, (where is Dorothy?; where are you
going?; showed me where they were; where does it concern us?;
where are you looking?; cf. COME in); in what book etc.?
(where did you read that?); in what situation or condition? (where will you be if that happens?); (in rhet.
question equiv. to neg. statement: where is the sense of
it?). **2.** rel. adv., & conj. (With ref. to place) in which or
to which (places where they sing; (ellipt.) where he is
weakest is in his facts); in or to the or any place, in the
direction or part or respect, in which (where your
treasure is; go where you like; is, send where he will he
taken care of; that is where you are wrong; where the ancients
knew nothing we know a little; (ellipt.) delete where
inapplicable); and there (reached Crewe, where the car
broke down). **3.** pron. what place? (where do you come from,
are you going to?); (colloq.) which (place) (the town
where he comes from). **4.** n. place, scene of something,
(cf. WHEN 7; ANYWHERE, EVERYWHERE, NOWHERE,
SOMEWHERE). **5.** ∼**abou'ts** adv., where? (within
considerable limits or vaguely; whereabouts is he?; don't
know even whereabouts to look); ∼'**abouts** n. (as sing. or
pl.), person's or thing's location roughly defined;
∼**a'fter,** (formal) after which; ∼**a's** conj., taking into
consideration or having as premiss the fact that (esp.
in legal preambles), in contrast or comparison with
the fact that, but (in contrast with what has been
said); ∼**a't,** (arch.) at which place, for which reason;
∼**by',** (formal) by what means?, by which means, in consequence of which; ∼'**fore,** (adv.) for what reason?,
why?, for which reason, (n.) reason (the whys and
wherefores); ∼**fro'm,** (arch.) from which; ∼**i'n,**
(formal) in what place or respect?, in which place or
respect; ∼**i'nto,** (arch.) into which; ∼**o'f,** (formal) of
what?, of which; ∼**o'n,** (arch.) on what?, on which;
∼**ou't,** (arch.) out of which; ∼**throu'gh,** (arch.)
through which; ∼**to',** (formal) to what?, to which;
∼**u'nder,** (arch.) under which; ∼**u'nto,** (arch.) to
what?, to which; ∼**upo'n** (or wār'-), immediately
after which, in consequence of which, (arch.) upon
which; ∼**wi'th,** (arch.) with what?, with which;
∼'**withal** n., (colloq.) money etc. needed for a
purpose (has not the wherewithal to do it); [OE hwār,
hwār = OS hwār, OHG (h)wār, wā, ON hvar, Goth.
hwar f. st. *hwa- (see WHEN); cf. HERE, THERE]

wherě'ver, (-ārs-), **whereso'e'er'** (poet.;
-ārsoār'), conj. & adv. = foll. 1. [ME, f. whereso f. OE
*swā hwār swā; cf. WHATSOEVER]

wherě'ver (-âr'-), **where'er'** (poet.; -ārâr'), conj. &
adv. **1.** in or to whatever place; or wherever, or any
place; **or wherever,** or in any similar place. **2.** (colloq.) =
where EVER. [ME, f. prec. + EVER]

whě'rrÿ n. light shallow rowing-boat usu. for carrying
passengers; ||large light barge; ||∼**man** (employed
on wherry). [ME, of unkn. orig.]

whět v.t. (-tt-), & n. **1.** v.t. sharpen by rubbing on or
with stone etc.; stimulate (appetite, interest, desire);
∼'**stone,** shaped stone for tool-sharpening, (fig.)
thing that sharpens the wits. **2.** n. sharpening; small
quantity taken to create or creating appetite for

more; dram of liquor. [OE *hwettan*, = OHG *wezzan*, ON *hvetja* f. Gmc **hwatjan* (**hwattaz* sharp)]

whe′ther[1] (-dh-) *a.*, & *interrog.* & *rel. pron.* (arch.) which of the two. [OE *hwæther*, *hwether*, = OS *hwethar*, OHG (*h*)*wedar*, ON *hvatharr*, Goth. *hwathar* f. Gmc **hwa-*, **hwe-*; cf. WHEN, WHO, EITHER, OTHER]

whe′ther[2] (-dh-) *conj.* **1.** (Introducing indirect question expr. doubt or choice between alternatives: *don't know whether he will be here* (or not), *whether or not he will be here, don't know whether he is here or* (whether he is) *in London; am doubtful, must decide, the question is, whether to go* (or not); DOUBT[2] *whether; whether or* NO[2]). **2.** (With following *or* or *or whether*, introducing alternative conditions in conditional sentence, = *if . . . and likewise if . . .*: *the result will be bad whether we stay or whether we go, whether we stay or go, whether we stay or not, whether or* NO[2]). [OE, = prec.]

whew (hwū, *or* a whistle) *int.* expr. surprise, consternation, or relief. [imit.]

whey (-ā) *n.* watery part of milk that remains liquid when the rest forms curds; **~-faced**, (arch.) pale esp. with fear. [OE *hwæg, hweg*, = MDu. *wey*, f. LG **hwaja-*.]

which *a.* & *pron.* (*poss.* in sense 4 **of which**, *or* **whose**). **1.** *interrog. a.* (asking for selection from alternatives conceived as limited in number or known: *which Jones do you mean?; which way shall we go?; say which book you prefer*). **2.** *rel. a.* and, now, although, since, etc., this or these (usu. w. n. serving to sum up details of compound or vague antecedent: *a smile and a shilling, which equipment is within most people's reach, will suffice; for ten years, during which time he spoke to nobody; which things are an allegory*). **3.** *interrog. pron.* which person(s) or thing(s)? (*which of you am I to thank for this?; say which* (*of these books*) *you would like best*); **~ is ~?**, which of two etc. given persons etc. corresponds to one of given descriptions etc., and which to another?; T'OTHER *from which*. **4.** *rel. pron.* (cf. THAT[1] 4, WHO; used to convert what would in the simplest grammar be an independent sentence into a subordinate clause by taking the place of a noun expressed in that sentence and expressed or implied in another sentence; (arch.) of things and (arch.) of persons; used esp. to introduce a clause not essential for identification: *the meeting, which was held in the Park, was a failure; Our Father, which art in Heaven; he said he saw me there, which* (statement) *was a lie*; occas. in clause preceding antecedent: *moreover, which you will hardly credit, he was not there himself*); **the ~**, (arch.) = *which* rel. (a. or pron.). [OE *hwilc*, = OS (*h*)*wilik*, OHG (*h*)*welih*, ON *hvílíkr*, Goth. *hwileiks* f. Gmc. **hwa-*, **hwe-*, **hwi-* + **líkam* body, form; cf. LIKE[1], -LY[1], SUCH]

whiche′ver *a.* & *pron.* **1.** any (of a definite set of persons or things) which; that or those which. **2.** (colloq.) = *which* EVER. [ME, f. prec. + EVER]

whichsoe′ver *a.* & *pron.* (arch.) = prec. 1. [ME; cf. WHATSOEVER]

whi′dah (-da) *n.* small Afr. weaver-bird of genus *Vidua*, the male having mainly black plumage and tail-feathers of great length. [orig. WIDOW-*bird*, altered f. assoc. w. *Whidah* (now Ouidah) in Benin]

whiff *n.* & *v.* **1.** *n.* puff of air, smoke, odour, (fig.) scandal, etc. (*want a whiff of fresh air*); minor discharge *of grape-shot* etc.; small cigar; ||light narrow outrigged sculling-boat. **2.** *v.t.* & *i.* blow or puff lightly. **3.** *v.i.* smell (unpleasant). [imit.]

whi′ffl|**e** *v.* & *n.* **1.** *v.i.* & *t.* (Of wind) blow lightly, shift about. **2.** *v.i.* be variable or evasive, whence **~ER**[1] *n.*; (of flame, leaves) flicker, flutter; make the sound of a light wind in breathing etc. **3.** *n.* slight movement of air. [f. WHIFF + -LE 3]

*whi′ffletree (-felt-) *n.* = SWINGLE*tree*. [var. of WHIPPLETREE]

Whig *n.* & *a.* (Hist.) **1.** 17th-c. Scottish Presbyterian. **2.** ||(member) of political party that, after the Revolution of 1688, aimed at subordinating the power of the Crown to that of Parliament and the upper

classes, passed the Reform Bill of 1832, and in the mid-19th c. was succeeded by the Liberals (opp. TORY). **3.** *supporter of American Revolution; (member) of political party 1834–56, succeeded by the Republicans. **4.** Hence **~′gERY** (4), **~′gISM** (3), *ns.*, **~′gISH**[1] *a.*, (-g-). [prob. abbr. of *whiggamer*, *-more*, Scottish rebel of 1648, f. *whig* to drive + MARE[2]]

while[1] *n.*, & *v.t.* **1.** *n.* space of time, time occupied by or spent in some action etc., (*have been waiting all this while*; *happened a* (long) *while ago or back*; *go away for a while*); **in a little ~**, soon; **once in a ~**, occasionally, at long intervals; (**for**) **a ~**, for some time; *have not seen him* **for a long ~**, for a long time past; **a good** or **great ~**, a considerable time; **between ~s**, in the intervals between other actions; **worth ~** or one's **~**, repaying the time spent in doing it etc.; **the ~**, during some other process, (poet.) during the time that; **all the ~**, during the whole time (that). **2.** *v.t.* pass (time, hour, etc.) *away* in leisurely or interesting manner. [OE *hwíl* = OS, OHG *hwíla*, ON *hvíla*, Goth. *hweila* f. Gmc **hwílô* f. IE **qwi-*]

while[2] *conj.* **1.** during the time that, for as long as, at the same time as, (*please write while I dictate*; *Jones got 98 runs while Smith at the other end was making 15*; *while there is life there is hope*; (w. ellipsis of pron. subj. and BE) *while reading I fell asleep*; *we are safe while in his care; he retained the consciousness of it while asleep*). **2.** in more or less marked contrast with the fact that simultaneously, although, whereas, (*Nero fiddling while Rome burns*; *while I have no money to spend, you have nothing to spend money on*; *while I admit his good points I can see his bad*; *while convinced it is true, I cannot prove it*). **3.** (N. Engl.) until. [abbr. of OE *thá hwíle the*, ME the WHILE[1] *that*]

whiles (-lz) *conj.* (arch.) = prec. [f. WHILE[1] + -s[3], orig. in *somewhiles*, *otherwhiles*, advs.]

whi′lom *adv.* & *a.* (arch.) **1.** *adv.* once, formerly. **2.** *a.* former (*his whilom friend*). [OE *hwílum*, dat. pl. of *hwíl* WHILE[1]]

||whilst *conj.* = WHILE[2]. [ME, f. WHILES; cf. AGAINST]

whim *n.* **1.** sudden fancy, caprice, freakish idea; capriciousness. **2.** kind of windlass for raising ore or water from mine. [17th c.; orig. unkn.]

whi′mbrel *n.* small curlew, esp. *Numenius phaeopus*. [f. foll. (imit.); cf. *dotterel*]

whi′mper *v.* & *n.* **1.** *v.i.* make feeble querulous or frightened sounds, cry and whine softly. **2.** *v.t.* utter whimperingly. **3.** Hence **~ER**[1] *n.* **4.** *n.* sound of whimpering. [imit., f. dial. *whimp* + -ER[5]]

whi′msical (-z-) *a.* capricious; odd-looking, fanciful; hence **~ITY** (-ă′l-) *n.*, **~LY**[2] *adv.* [f. foll. + -ICAL]

whi′msy, whi′msey, (-zĭ) *n.* = WHIM 1. [rel. to foll.; cf. *flimsy*]

whi′m-whām *n.* (arch.) plaything, toy; = WHIM 1. [redupl., of uncert. orig.]

whin[1] *n.* (in *sing.* or *pl.*) gorse, furze; **~′chat**, small brownish sweet-singing bird (*Saxicola rubetra*). [prob. Scand.; cf. Norw. *hvine*, Sw. *hven*]

whin[2], **whi′nsill**, **whi′nstone**, *n.* (piece of) hard dark (esp. basaltic) rock or stone. [ME, of unkn. orig.; see SILL, STONE]

whin|**e** *v.i.* & *t.*, & *n.* (make) long-drawn complaining cry (as) of child or dog; (make) shrill prolonged sound like this; (utter) querulous talk or petty complaint; utter in whining tone; hence **~ER**[1] *n.*, **~′Y**[2] *a.* [OE *hwínan*, = ON *hvína* whiz]

whinge (-nj) *v.i.* (dial. or Austral.) whine, grumble peevishly. [OE *hwinsian*, OHG *win*(*i*)*sôn* f. Gmc **hwinisôjan*]

whi′nny *v.i.*, & *n.* (give) gentle or joyful neigh. [imit.; cf. WHINE]

whip[1] *v.* (-pp-). **1.** *v.t.* & *i.* (w. adv. or *prep.*) move with sudden or unexpected or rapid motion, snatch, dart, (*whip behind the door*; *whipped up her toy terrier*; *whip out sword, knife*; *whip off* one's *coat*); **~-graft**, graft with tongue of scion in slit in stock and vice versa; **||~-round**, appeal for contributions from a group to charitable cause. **2.** *v.t.* bind (cord, stick) with close covering of twine, overcast (hem etc.). **3.** flog, lash, (horse, body, etc.); use whip to bring hounds in, *off*, *together*; strike or reprove vigorously; fish (stream) with whipping motion; urge *on* with whip; bring (fault, etc.) *out of* person by flogging; beat (cream or eggs) into froth; spin (top) with whip; (sl.) excel, defeat; ~ **up**, summon (attendance), generate (attack, feeling), by vigorous action. **4.** Hence ~'ᴘɪɴɢ¹ (1, 4) *n*.; ~**ping-boy**, (Hist.) boy educated with and chastised instead of young prince, (fig.) scapegoat; ~**ping-cream** (suitable for whipping); ~**ping-post** (to which persons were tied to be whipped, usu. in public); ~**ping-top** (kept spinning by blows of lash). [ME (*h*)*wippen*, prob. f. MLG & MDu. *wippen* swing, leap, dance, f. Gmc **wip-* move quickly]

whip² *n*. **1.** instrument for urging on or punishing with lash attached to short or long stick (*fair* CRACK¹ *of the whip*); coachman (*good, poor*, etc., *whip*). **2.** hunt official subordinate to huntsman and charged with management of hounds; ||(Parl. etc.) (1) official appointed to maintain discipline among, secure attendance of, and give necessary information to, members of his party, (2) written notice (variously underlined with number of lines representing degrees of urgency, as **three-line** ~) requesting attendance on particular occasion, (3) party discipline and instructions (*ask for, take, the Liberal whip*). **3.** rope-and-pulley hoisting apparatus. **4.** sweet dish made with whipped cream etc. **5.** ~**-bird**, Austral. bird with cry like crack of whip; ~'**cord**, tightly twisted cord such as is used for making whiplashes, close-woven worsted fabric; ~**-crane**, light derrick with tackle for hoisting; ~**-fish** (with dorsal fin elongated into filament like whiplash); ~**-gin**, = sense 3; ~ **hand**, hand that holds whip; *have the* ~ *hand* (*of or over*), be in position to control; ~'**lash**, lash of whip, flagellum; ~*lash injury* (to neck, caused by sudden jerk of head in collision of vehicle etc.); ~**-ray**, sting-ray; ~**-saw**, (*n*.) narrow saw-blade with ends held by frame, *(v.t. & i.)* cheat, be cheated, by joint action on or by two others; ~**-scorpion**, arachnid with long slender abdomen; ~**-snake** (slender); ~**-stitch** (made by whipping); ~'**stock**, handle of whip. [ME, partly f. prec., partly f. MLG *wip(pe)* quick movement]

whi'pper *n*. In vbl senses; ~**-in**, (Hunting) = WHIP² 2; ~**-snapper**, small child, young and insignificant but presumptuous or intrusive person [perh. for *whipsnapper*, implying noise and unimportance]. [f. WHIP¹ +-ER¹]

whi'ppet *n*. cross-bred dog of modified greyhound type used for racing. [prob. f. obs. *whippet* move briskly, f. *whip it*]

whi'ppletree (-pĕl-) *n*. = SWINGLE*tree*. [app. f. WHIP¹ + TREE]

whi'ppoorwill *n*. Amer. nightjar (*Caprimulgus vociferus*). [imit. of cry]

whi'pp|ў *a*. flexible, springy; hence ~ɪɴᴇss *n*. [f. WHIP² +-ʏ²]

whi'pster *n*. = WHIPPER-*snapper*. [app. f. WHIP¹ + -STER]

whir. See WHIRR.

whirl *v. & n.* **1.** *v.t. & i.* swing round and round, revolve rapidly (*whirling* DERVISH). **2.** send (missile etc.), (of moving body) travel, swiftly in orbit or curve; convey or go rapidly *away* etc. in wheeled conveyance. **3.** *v.i.* (Of brain, senses, etc.) be giddy, seem to spin round, (of thoughts etc.) follow each other in bewildering succession. **4.** *n.* whirling movement (lit. or fig.; *my thoughts are in a whirl*); bustling activity (*the social whirl*); ***(sl.) attempt (*give it a whirl*). **5.** ~'**pool**, circular eddy in sea, river, etc., often causing suction to its centre; ~'**wind**, mass of air whirling rapidly round and round in cylindrical or funnel shape (*sow the wind and reap the* ~*wind*, suffer worse results of bad action), (fig.) confused tumultuous

process, (attrib.) very rapid (*whirlwind courtship, tour*); ~'**ybird**, (sl.) helicopter. [ME; v. f. ON *hvirfla*, n. f. MLG & MDu. *wervel* spindle & ON *hvirfill* circle f. Gmc **hwerbhilaz* (**hwerbh-* turn)]

whi'rligig (-g-) *n*. spinning or whirling toy; (fig.) revolving motion (~ **of time**, changes of fortune); merry-go-round; water-beetle of family Gyrinidae that circles about on surface. [ME, f. prec. + obs. *gig* whipping-top]

whirr, whir, *v.i.* (-**rr**-), & *n.* (make) continuous buzzing or softly clicking sound as of bird's wings quickly flapping or cog-wheels in rapid action. [ME, prob. Scand.; cf. Da. *hvirre*, Norw. *kvirra*, perh. rel. to WHIRL]

whisht. (Ir.) Var. of WHIST¹.

whisk *n. & i.* **1.** *n.* bunch of grass, hair, twigs, etc., to flap dust off, flies away, etc., with; instrument for beating up eggs or cream; quick movement (as) of whisk or of animal's tail. **2.** *v.t.* flap (dust, fly, etc.) *away* or *off*; beat (eggs etc.) into a froth; take *away* or *off* with sudden motion (*waiter whisked my plate away*). **3.** *v.t. & i.* convey or go lightly and quickly esp. out of sight (*was whisked away in a helicopter; mouse whisks into its hole*). **4.** *v.t.* brandish lightly or flip or wave about (*went whisking a cane, her tail*). [ME *wisk*, prob. Scand. cf. ON *visk* wisp, Sw. *viska* to whisk (off)]

whi'sker *n*. **1.** (usu. in *pl.*) hair of man's face, esp. cheek (cf. MOUSTACHE, BEARD¹); SIDE¹-*whiskers*. **2.** bristle growing from upper lip of cat etc., set of such bristles on one side; CAT¹'*s whiskers*. **3.** (colloq.) small distance (*within a whisker of*). **4.** strong hairlike crystal of metal etc. **5.** Hence (-)~ᴇᴅ² (-erd), ~ʏ², *adjs.* [f. prec. +-ᴇʀ¹]

whi'skey *n*. Var. of foll. (esp. US and of Irish whisky.)

whi'sk|ў¹ *n*. spirit distilled from malted barley, other grains, or potatoes etc.; drink of this; ~**ified**, (joc.) affected by whisky-drinking; ~**y-jack**, Canadian jay. [abbr. of obs. *whiskybae*, var. of USQUEBAUGH]

whi'sky² *n*. (Hist.) kind of light gig or chaise. [f. WHISK, w. ref. to lightness of motion]

whi'sper *v. & n.* **1.** *v.i.* speak without vibration of vocal chords; talk with intention of being audible only close at hand or to confidant; converse privately, indulge in slander or plotting; (of leaves, stream, etc.) rustle; ~**ing-gallery**, gallery, dome, etc., in which some acoustic peculiarity causes least sound made at a particular point to be audible at another far off. **2.** *v.t.* convey (statement etc. to person), inform or order (person *that* or *to* do), by whispering; covertly make known (tale, *that*). **3.** Hence ~ᴇʀ¹, ~ɪɴɢ¹ (1), *ns.* **4.** *n.* whispering speech (*always talks in a whisper or in whispers*); whispered remark (STAGE¹ *whisper*); rumour of unknown origin, insinuation, mysterious hint; rustling sound. [OE *hwisprian*, early Flem. *wisperen*, f. Gmc **hwis-* (imit.)]

||**whist¹** (arch. or dial.) *int.* enjoining silence. [ME, imit.; cf. HIST, HUSH²]

||**whist²** *a.* (arch.) silent. [ME, f. prec.]

whist³ *n.* card-game of mingled skill and chance for four or exceptionally three or two persons; **long, short,** ~, with ten, five, points to game; RUBBER³ *of whist;* ~ **drive,** PROGRESSIVE whist party usu. with prizes. [f. earlier *whisk*, perh. f. WHISK; infl. by WHIST¹ (w. ref. to the silence usual in the game)]

whi'stle (-sel) *v. & n.* **1.** *v.i.* make—with the lips or with instrument for the purpose, or (of bird etc.) with the voice, or (of missile, wind, etc.) by rapid motion— clear shrill sound (as) of breath forced through small orifice formed with lips; make such sound as signal (*to* person, *for* thing; *becalmed superstitious sailors* ~ **for a wind**, whence ~ **for,** (colloq.) seek in vain; **let** person **go** ~, disregard his wishes) or expr. surprise, derision, etc.; ~ **in the dark** (lit. or fig.; to overcome one's fears). **2.** *v.t.* give (tune) etc. by whistling; ~ (**up**), summon or give signal to (dog, attendant) by whistling; ~ **down the wind,** turn (hawk) loose, (fig.) let go, abandon. **3.** *n.* whistling sound or note. **4.** instrument for producing such sound; **penny** or **tin** ~, tin pipe with six holes giving different notes; **steam** ~, whistle sounded by jet of steam; **pay for** one's ~, pay high for a caprice [w. ref. to story of B. Franklin]; **as clean, clear, dry, as a** ~ (prov. similes); ***~-stop,** small unimportant town on railway, politician's brief pause for electioneering speech on tour, rapid superficial visit. **5.** (colloq.) throat (WET one's *whistle*). [OE *(h)wistlian* v., *(h)wistle* n., of imit. orig.; cf. ON *hvīsla* whisper, MSw. *hvisla* whistle]

whi′stler (-sl-) *n.* In vbl senses; kind of marmot; bird that whistles. [OE *hwistlere* (as prec., -ER¹)]

whi′stling (-sl-) *a.* In vbl senses; (of bird or animal) characterized by uttering clear shrill sound; **~-buoy** (fitted with whistle sounded by movement of waves); ~ **kettle** (fitted with whistle sounded by steam when contents are boiling). [f. WHISTLE + -ING²]

whit¹ *n.* (arch. or literary). particle, least possible amount, (**every** ~, the whole, wholly; **no** ~, **not** or **never a** ~, not at all). [earlier *w(h)yt*, app. alt. f. WIGHT in phr. *no wight* etc.]

Whit² *a.* ~ **Sunday,** seventh Sunday after Easter, commemorating descent of Holy Spirit at Pentecost (Acts 2); ~ **Monday, Tuesday,** those following, ~ **week(-end),** that containing, Whit Sunday. [OE *Hwīta Sunnandæg,* lit. white Sunday, prob. f. white robes of newly-baptized at Pentecost]

white¹ *a.,* & *v.t.* **1.** *a.* resembling a surface reflecting sunlight without absorbing any of the visible rays, of the colour of milk or fresh snow or common salt or the common swan's plumage; approaching such colour, pale esp. in face (*white as a sheet*; *white with rage*; so in *a white rage*); that is an albino (*white mouse*); less dark than other things of the same kind; (of hair) having lost its colour esp. in old age; **bleed** ~, (fig.) drain of wealth etc. [w. ref. to hanging of killed calf to whiten veal]. **2.** characterized by presence of some white (in many -ED² compounds used esp. in describing animals etc., as *white-bellied, -crowned, -eyed, -faced, -headed, -rumped, -tailed, -throated, -winged*); (of plant) having white flowers, light-coloured bark, etc. **3.** (Of water, air, glass) transparent, colourless; (fig.) innocent, unstained, of harmless kind. **4.** of (the class of) or reserved for white men (see *white man* below; *white culture, civilization, woman*; *the White Australia policy*). **5.** (Polit.) of royalist or counter-revolutionary or reactionary tendency (opp. *red*). **6.** *white* ADMIRAL; ~ **ant,** termite; ~′**bait,** small silvery-white fish prob. the young of herring, sprat, etc., eaten fried in quantities, (NZ) young inanga; ~′**beam,** tree (*Sorbus aria*) with silvery downy under-side of leaf, and red berries; ~ **bear,** polar bear, *grizzly bear; **W**~**boy,** member of 19th-c. illegal agrarian association in Ireland wearing white shirts at nightly meetings and outrages; ~ **bread** (made from fine bolted flour); ~ **bronze** (containing much tin); ~-**caps,** breakers far out at sea; ~ **cell,** leucocyte; ~ **coal,** = WATER¹-*power* (1) [F *houille blanche*]; ~ **Christmas** (with snow); ||~-**coffee** (with milk or cream); ~-**collar** (of worker) not engaged in manual labour; **W**~ **Continent,** Antarctica; ~ **corpuscle,** leucocyte; *white* CROW¹, CURRANT; *white* **dwarf,** (Astron.) small very dense faint star; *white* ELEPHANT, ||ENSIGN; ~-**eye,** bird with white ring round eye; ~**face,** white make-up of actor etc.; **W**~ **Father,** member of an order of missionaries in Africa [f. their white habits]; *white* FEATHER¹; ~ **fish,** (1) light-coloured esp. silver fish, e.g. cod, haddock, (2) lake-fish of genus *Coregonus* etc.; *white* FLAG⁴; ~ **fly,** small insect of family Aleyrodidae attacking shrubs etc.; **W**~ **Friar,** Carmelite [f. their white cloaks]; *white* FROST; ||~ **gloves** (Hist.) presented to assize judge finding no criminal cases to try); ~ **gold,** pale alloy of gold with nickel etc.; *~ **goods,** white household fabrics or goods (refrigerators etc.); ~ **grouse,** ptarmigan; ~-**haired** or ~-**headed**

boy, highly favoured person; ~ **hands,** (fig.) innocence or integrity; ~-**heart cherry** (orig. ~ heart-cherry), pale cultivated heart-shaped kind; ~ **heat,** temperature at which metal emits white light, (fig.) state of intense passion or activity; ~ **hope,** person who is expected to attain renown; ~ **horses,** (fig.) white-crested waves at sea; ~-**hot,** at white heat; **W**~ **House,** official residence of US president in Washington; ||~ **land** (restricted to agricultural use); *white* LEAD¹; ~ **leather,** = WHIT-LEATHER; ~ **leg,** MILK¹-*leg*; *white* LIE¹; ~ **light** (colourless, e.g. ordinary daylight); ~-**lipped** (esp. with fear); ~-**livered,** cowardly, dastardly; *white* MAGIC; ~ **man,** member of one of the human groups with relatively pale complexion, chiefly inhabiting or having inhabited Europe, and characterized by a certain type of civilization (*the* ~ *man's burden,* supposed task of leading the coloured peoples forward), (colloq.) person of honourable character, good breeding, etc.; ~ **matter,** fibrous part of brain and spinal cord; ~ **meat,** poultry, veal, rabbit, pork; ~ **metal,** white or silvery alloy; ~ **monk,** Cistercian [f. their white habits]; ~ (sleepless) **night** [F *nuit blanche*]; ~ **noise** (containing many frequencies with about equal energies); ~-**out,** atmospheric condition, esp. in polar regions, marked by dense snow-cloud and total obscuration of physical features [after BLACK³-*out*]; ||**W**~ **Paper,** report issued by Government to give information; *white* PEPPER¹; *~ **ribbon,** badge of temperance; ~ **rose,** emblem of Yorkshire, or of House of York in Wars of the Roses; **W**~ **Russian,** Belorussian; ~ **sale** (of household linen); *white* SAUCE; ~ **sheet,** penitent's garb (in *stand in a* ~ *sheet,* confess sin etc.); ~ **slave,** woman entrapped (and sent abroad) into prostitution (*the* ~-*slave traffic,* ~ *slavery*); ~′**smith,** (1) worker in tin, (2) polisher or finisher of metal goods; ~ **spirit,** light petroleum fraction used as solvent etc.; *white* SQUALL; ~ **stock,** STOCK (sense 4) made from veal, chicken, etc., and uncoloured; ~ **sugar** (purified); ~ **supremacy,** doctrine based on supposed inherent inferiority of Negroes and other non-white races; *White* TERROR; ~′**thorn,** hawthorn (cf. BLACK¹-*thorn*); ~-**throat,** species of warbler or Amer. sparrow with white patch on throat; ~ **tie,** man's white bow-tie worn as part of full evening dress; **white* TRASH; *white* VITRIOL; ~ **war,** war without bloodshed, economic warfare; ~ **water,** shallow or foamy water; ~ **whale,** northern cetacean, white when adult; ~ **wine** (of amber or golden or pale yellow colour, opp. *red wine*); ~ **witch** (using power for beneficent purposes only); ~′**wood,** light-coloured wood esp. prepared for staining etc. **7.** Hence ~′LY² (-tlĭ) *adv.,* ~′NESS (-tn-) *n.,* **whi′tish** 1,2 *a.* **8.** *v.t.* (arch.) make white (*whited* SEPULCHRE). [OE *hwīt,* = OS *hwīt,* OHG *(h)wīz,* ON *hvítr,* Goth. *hweits* f. Gmc *hwītaz* f. IE *kwitnos*]

white² *n.* **1.** white or nearly white colour; white pigment (CHINESE etc. *white*); white clothes or material (*dressed in white*); blank space in printing. **2.** albuminous part round yolk of egg; visible part of eyeball round iris; (freq. *W*~) white person (*mean* or *poor white*); white butterfly; (colloq., in *pl.*) leucorrhoea; white ball in billiards etc.; (player of) white men in chess etc. [OE; f. prec.]

Whi′techapel (-t-ch-) *n.* **1.** ~ (**cart**), light two-wheeled sprung cart used by shopkeepers etc. **2.** (Cards). lead of singleton with a view to subsequent trumping. **3.** (Bill.) pocketing of opponent's ball. [~ in London]

||**Whi′tehall** (-t-hawl) *n.* British Government; its offices or policy. [street in London where there are many Government offices]

whi′ten *v.i.* & *t.* make or become white(r) (lit. or fig.); hence ~ER¹,² (1, 2) *n.* [ME, f. WHITE¹ + -EN⁶]

whi′tening (-tn-) *n.* In vbl senses; = WHITING¹. [f. prec. + -ING¹]

whi′tewash (-twŏ-) *n.*, & *v.t.* **1.** *n.* solution of quick-lime or of whiting and size for brushing over walls, ceilings, etc., to give clean appearance, (fig.) means employed to conceal faults etc. in order to clear person or institution of imputations. **2.** *v.t.* cover with whitewash, (fig.) attempt by concealment to clear reputation of, (in *pass.*, of insolvent) get fresh start by passage through bankruptcy court; *defeat (opponent) without allowing any opposing score. [n. f. v., f. WHITE¹ + WASH¹]

Whi′tey *n.* (usu. derog.) white person; white persons collectively. [f. WHITE¹ + -Y³]

whi′ther (-dh-) *adv.*, *conj.*, & *n.* (arch. or rhet.) **1.** *interrog. adv.* to what place or position (lit. or fig.); what is the future of (*Whither Democracy?*). **2.** *rel. adv.*, & *conj.* (With ref. to place) to which; to the, or (also ∼soe′ver) any, place to which, = *and thither.* **3.** Hence ∼WARD(s) *adv.* **4.** *n.* destination (cf. WHENCE 4). [OE *hwider* f. Gmc *hwi-*; cf. WHICH, HITHER, THITHER]

whi′ting¹ *n.* chalk prepared by drying, grinding, etc., for use in whitewashing, plate-cleaning, etc. [ME, f. WHITE¹ + -ING¹]

whi′ting² *n.* small white-fleshed food-fish (*Merlangus merlangus*). [ME, f. MDu. *wijting*, app. f. as WHITE¹ + -ING³]

whi′tish. See WHITE¹ 7.

whi′tleather (-lědh-) *n.* tawed leather. [ME, f. WHITE¹ + LEATHER]

‖**Whi′tley** *n.* ∼ **Council** (of representatives of employers and workers for discussion and settlement of industrial or civil-service relations and conditions); hence ∼ISM (-ĭĭ-) *n.*, use of such methods for dealing with industrial problems. [f. J. H. ∼, chairman of committee (1916) that recommended creation of such councils]

whi′tlow (-ō) *n.* inflammatory sore on finger esp. near the nail, usu. with suppuration. [ME *whitflaw, -flow*, app. = WHITE¹ + FLAW¹ in sense 'crack', but perh. of LG orig.; cf. Du. *fijt*, LG *fit* whitlow]

Whi′tsun *n.* ∼**day**, (1) = WHIT Sunday, (2, Sc.) 15 May, a quarter-day; ∼(**tide**), Whit Sunday and following days; ∼ **week**, Whit week. [ME, f. *Whitsun Day* = WHIT² *Sunday*]

whi′ttle¹ *n.* (arch. or dial.) long knife, esp. such as is used by butchers. [var. of ME *thwitel* f. OE *thwītan* to cut off + -LE 1]

whi′ttle² *v.t.* trim, carve, slice off pieces from, (wood, or abs.: *whittle at*) with knife; ∼ (**down, away**), reduce amount or effect of by repeated subtraction. [f. prec.]

Whi′tworth *n.* ∼ **thread**, standard screw-thread for metal [f. Sir J. ∼, Engl. engineer d. 1887]

whi′ty *a.* inclining to white (usu. in comb. with other colour-name, esp. *whity-brown*); cf. WHITEY. [f. WHITE¹ + -Y²]

whiz, whizz, *v.i.* (**-zz-**), & *n.* (make) sound given by friction of body moving at great speed through air; move quickly; ∼**-bang**, (sl.) high-velocity shell from a small-calibre gun, whose passage is heard before the gun's report; ∼**-kid**, (colloq.) exceptionally brilliant or successful young person. [imit.]

who (hōō *or, when unstressed*, hŏŏ) *pron.* (*obj.* **whom** *pr.* hōōm, colloq. **who;** *poss.* **whose** *pr.* hōōz). **1.** *interrog.* what person(s)?, which person(s)?, what sort of person(s) in regard to position or authority?, (*who said so?; whom,* colloq. *who, do you mean?; told him who they were, whom* or colloq. *who to look out for; whose son is he?*); (in rhet. questions equiv. to neg. statement: *who would have thought it?; it was Jones, of course—who else?; who am I that I should object?*); (asking for repetition of person's name not properly heard; *you saw whom?,* colloq. *who?, it was Mr. who?*); *know* ∼**'s** ∼, who or what each person is; *a* ∼**'s** ∼, list with facts relating to notable persons; ∼**-does-what dispute** or **strike**, one about which of the trade unions is to do a particular job; ∼ **goes there?** (see GO¹ 6); ∼ **is it** (substitute for name that cannot be recalled). **2.** *rel.* (person or persons) WHICH or THAT¹ (*the man whom,* colloq. *who, you saw; those for whose benefit it was done; anyone who chooses can apply; there is no one who we can believe is, whom we can believe to be, competent*). **3.** (arch.) the or any person(s) that (*who steals my purse, steals trash; whom the gods love die young*); **as ∼ should say,** like a person who said, as though one said. **4.** = and, but, though, since, if, etc., he or him or they, etc. (*sent it to Jones, who passed it on to Smith; is flirting with Dick, whom she actually detests*). [OE *hwā*, = OS *hwē,* OHG (*h*)*wer,* Goth. *hwas* f. Gmc *hwas, *hwes* f. IE *q^wos, *q^wes; whom* f. OE dat. *hwām, hwǣm; whose* f. gen. *hwæs*]

WHO *abbr.* World Health Organization.

whoa *int.* (To horse etc.) expr. command to stop or stand still. [var. of HO]

whodu′(n)nit (hōō-) *n.* (colloq.) detective or mystery story, play, etc. [= *who done* (illiterate for *did*) *it?*]

whoe′ver (hōō-), **whoe′er′** (poet.; hōōār′), *pron.* (*obj.* **whomever, whome′er,** colloq. **whoever;** *poss.* **whosever;** *pr.* as at WHO). **1.** the or any person(s) that (*whoever comes will be welcome*). **2.** (In indef. concessive clause) though anyone (*whoever else objects, I do not; whosever it is, I mean to have it*). **3.** (colloq.) = *who* EVER. [ME, f. WHO + EVER]

whōle (hōl) *a.* & *n.* **1.** *a.* (arch.) in good health, well, (*thy faith hath made thee whole*). **2.** in sound condition, uninjured, not broken, intact, (*hope you will come back whole; got off with a whole skin; there is not a plate left whole; has swallowed a plum whole*). **3.** integral, consisting of one or more units, without fractions; ∼ **number** (that can be got from zero by adding or subtracting units). **4.** undiminished, without removal of part (*whole milk; whole blood; was talking the whole time*); bread made of ∼ **meal** (of wheat or other cereal, not deprived of some constituents by bolting). **5.** not less than (*spent whole years of misery; went up a whole foot; lasted three whole days; whole regiments were cut down; talked a whole lot of nonsense*); all that there is of (*the whole truth, world, duty of man; do thing* **with** one's ∼ **heart,** heartily, with concentrated effort, etc., without doubts etc.); all members etc. of (*the whole priesthood*). **6.** ∼ **cloth** (of full size as manufactured; *out of* ∼ *cloth,* entirely fabricated and false); ∼**-coloured,** all of one colour; ∼ **foods** (not artificially processed or refined); ∼**-hearted,** (of person) completely devoted, (of action) done with one's whole heart (see sense 5); ∼**-ho′gger,** one who goes the *whole* HOG¹; ∼ **holiday,** day taken entirely as holiday (opp. *half holiday*); ∼**-hoofed,** with undivided hoofs; ∼**-length,** (of portrait) representing person from head to foot; ∼ **life insurance** (for which premiums are payable throughout life of insured person); ∼′**meal** *a.*, made from ∼ *meal* (see sense 4); *∼ **note,** semibreve; ∼ **number** (cf. sense 3); ∼ **plate,** photographic plate or film 16.5 × 21.6 cm; ∼**-souled,** = *whole-hearted;* *∼ **step,** = *whole tone,* ∼**-time,** full time; ∼ **tone,** (Mus.) interval of one TONE¹; ∼**-tone** *a.*, (Mus.) using intervals composed of whole tones without semitones; ∼ **wheat** (not separated into parts by bolting; cf. sense 4). **7.** Hence ∼′NESS (-ln-) *n.* **8.** *n.* thing complete in itself; all that there is of or of something (*the golden rule contains the whole of morality*); all members etc. of (*the whole of London knows it*); **as a** ∼, (considered etc.) as a unity, not as separate parts; **on the** ∼, taking into consideration everything that bears on the question, after weighing pros and cons etc. **9.** organic unity, complete system, total made up of parts, (*nature is a whole; the whole and the parts*). [OE *hāl,* = OS *hēl,* OHG *heil,* ON *heill,* Goth. *hails* f. Gmc *hailaz*]

who′lesal|e (hō′ls-) *n.*, *a.*, *adv.*, & *v.t.* **1.** *n.* selling of articles in large quantities to be retailed by others. **2.** *a.* & *adv.* by or relating to wholesale, at wholesale price (*I can get it for you wholesale*), (transf.) on a large scale (*a wholesale slaughter took place; sends out Christmas* *cards wholesale*). **3.** *v.t.* sell wholesale; hence ∼ER¹ *n.* [ME, orig. *by whole sale*]

whō'lesome (hō'ls-) *a.* promoting physical or moral health, salubrious, prudent, not morbid, (*wholesome food, air, exercise, advice, respect, excitement*); hence ∼LY² (-mlĭ) *adv.*, ∼NESS (-mn-) *n.* [ME, f. OE **hālsum* (as WHOLE, -SOME¹)]

whō'lly (hō'l-lĭ) *adv.* entirely, without limitation or diminution, (*I am wholly at a loss*); exclusively, without admixture, (*a wholly bad example*). [ME, f. OE **hāllīce* (as WHOLE, -LY²)]

whom, whomever, etc. See WHO, WHOEVER, etc.

whōop (hōōp) *v.i.*, & *n.* (utter) loud cry (as) of excitement etc.; **∼-de-do'* (-dĭdōō´) *n.*, excitement, bustle, noisy activity; ∼'ing **cough,** infectious bacterial disease, esp. of children, with short violent cough followed by long sonorous inspiration; ∼'ing **crane, swan,** (species that make whooping or whistling sound); ∼ **it up,** (colloq.) engage in revelry, **make a stir. [ME; imit.]

whoōpee (-ōō´-, -ē´) *int.* & *n.* **1.** *int.* expr. exuberant joy. **2.** *n.* (colloq.) **make** ∼, rejoice noisily or hilariously. [f. prec.]

whoō'per (h-) *n.* In vbl senses; whooping swan. [f. WHOOP + -ER¹]

whoōps *int.* Var. of OOPS.

whŏp *v.t.* (sl.) (-**pp-**). (sl.) thrash, (fig.) defeat, overcome; (in *pres. part.*) very large or remarkable of its kind (esp. *a whopping lie*), whence ∼'pER¹ *n.* [ME, var. of (dial.) *wap*, of unkn. orig.]

whŏre (hōr) *n.*, & *v.i.* **1.** *n.* prostitute; sexually immoral woman; ∼-**house,** brothel; ∼-**master,** -**monger,** fornicator; ∼'**son,** (arch.) disliked person. **2.** *v.i.* (arch.) (Of man) commit fornication; (fig.) commit idolatry or iniquity (esp. *go a-whoring after strange gods* etc.). [OE *hōre,* = OHG *huora,* ON *hóra,* f. Gmc **hōrōn* f. IE **qār-*]

whŏrl *n.* ring of leaves or other organs round stem etc. of plant; complete circle in fingerprint; one turn of a spiral; small wheel on spindle steadying its motion; hence ∼ED² (-ld) *a.* [ME *wharwyl, whorwil,* app. var. of WHIRL, infl. by *wharve* n. = whorl of spindle]

whor'tleberry (wēr'telb-) *n.* = BILBERRY. [16th c., SW Engl. dial. form of *hurtleberry,* ME, of unkn. orig.]

whose. See WHO and WHICH.

whosever, whoseso(ever). See WHOEVER, WHOSO-(EVER).

who'sō (hōō'-) *pron.* (*obj.* whomso, *poss.* whoseso; *pr.* as at WHO). (arch.) = WHOEVER 1, 2. [ME, = WHO + SO¹, f. OE *swā hwā swā*]

whosoē'ver (hōō-), **whosōe'er** (poet.; hōōsōār´), *pron.* (*obj.* whomso-, *poss.* whoseso-; *pr.* as at WHO). = WHOEVER 1, 2. [ME, f. prec. + EVER]

whȳ¹ *adv.* & *n.* (*pl.* ∼s). **1.** interrog. *adv.* on what ground?, for what reason?, with what purpose?, (*why did you do it?; why not take it?; cannot think why you came;* (often ellipt.) *You are late; why?*); ∼ **so?** (demand for grounds of statement or view). **2.** *rel. adv.* on account of which (*the reasons why he did it are obscure*). **3.** *n.* reason, explanation, (cf. WHEREfore). [OE *hwī, hwȳ* instr. of *hwæt* WHAT, f. Gmc **hwī,* IE **q ʷei,* locative of **q ʷo-* WHO]

whȳ² *int.* expr. surprised discovery or recognition (*why, it is surely Jones!; why, what a bruise you have got!; why, of course, that was it*), protest at simplicity of question etc. ('*What is twice two?' 'Why, four.'; why, a child could answer that*), pause for reflection ('*Is it true?' 'Why, yes, I think so'*), objection (*why, what is the harm?*), introduction of apodosis (*if silver will not do, why, we must try gold*), etc. [ellipt. uses of prec. 1]

whydah. Var. of WHIDAH.

WI *abbr.* West Indies; Wisconsin; ‖Women's Institute.

wich-. See WYCH-.

wick¹ *n.* (piece of) fibrous or spongy material by which flame is kept supplied with liquid fuel or illuminant; (Surg.) gauze strip inserted in wound to drain it; **get on** person's ∼, (sl.) annoy him. [OE

wēoce, -wēoc, = MDu. *wiecke,* MLG *wēke,* OHG *wiohha,* of unkn. orig.]

wick² *n.* town, hamlet, district, (now dial. exc. in compounds e.g. *bailiwick,* and in place-names e.g. *Hampton Wick, Warwick*); (dial.) dairy farm. [OE *wīc,* = OS *wīc,* OHG *wīh,* Goth. *weihs,* prob. f. L *vicus* street, village]

wi'ckėd *a.* (∼**er,** ∼**est**). **1.** sinful, iniquitous, vicious, given to or involving immorality (∼ **Bible,** edition of 1631 with *not* omitted in seventh commandment), offending intentionally against what is right; **the** ∼, (abs.) wicked persons. **2.** spiteful, ill-tempered, intending or intended to give pain; playfully mischievous, roguish; (colloq.) very bad or formidable. **3.** Hence ∼LY² *adv.*, ∼NESS *n.* [ME, f. obs. *wick* in same senses (perh. adj. use of OE *wicca* wizard) + -ED¹ as in *wretched*]

wi'cker *n.* plaited twigs or osiers as material of baskets, chairs, mats, protective covers, etc.; ∼**work,** (things made of) wicker. [ME, f. E. Scand.; cf. Sw. *viker* willow cogn. w. *vika* bend]

wi'ckėt *n.* **1.** ∼ (**-door, -gate**), small door or gate, esp. one beside or within larger one and used when latter is not open. **2.** **aperture in door or wall usu. closed with sliding panel; **croquet hoop. **3.** (Cricket). set of three stumps and two bails defended by batsman (**keep** ∼, be ∼**-keeper,** fieldsman stationed close behind batsman's wicket; **at the** ∼, batting; *catch at* **the** ∼, by wicket-keeper); batsman's avoidance of being out (∼ **is down** or **lost** or **taken,** ∼ **falls,** batsman is out (in any manner); **third** ∼, period between second and third dismissals of batsmen in side's innings; **win by two** ∼**s,** score necessary runs with three batsmen not out); = PITCH³ 4 (*went down the wicket to drive*); state of pitch (**on a good,** STICKY, ∼, (fig.) in advantageous, unfavourable, position). [ME, f. AF & ONF *wiket,* OF *guichet,* of uncert. orig.]

wi'ckiup *n.* Amer. Indian hut of frame covered with grass etc. [f. Fox *wikiyap*]

widdershins. See WITHERSHINS.

wide *a.*, *adv.*, & *n.* **1.** *a.* measuring much or more than other things of same kind or across from side to side, broad, not narrow, (*wide door, road, river, brim, sleeve, margin, cloth, angle, interval*); ∼ **margin,** (fig.) a good deal more allowed than is (likely to be) needed; ∼ **screen,** cinema screen much greater in width than in height. **2.** (Appended to measurement) in width (*a strip 3 ft. wide*); (as *suf.*) extending over the whole of (*nation-wide*). **3.** extending far, embracing much, of great extent, (*has a wide range; a wide domain; has wide experience; reached a wide public; a man of wide reading; there is a wide difference between*); **of** ∼ **distribution,** occurring in many places; **of** ∼ **fame,** known to many; ∼ **generalization** (covering many particulars); **the** ∼ **world,** all the world great as it is; hence ∼LY² (-dlĭ) *adv.* **4.** not tight or close or restricted, loose, free, liberal, unprejudiced, not specialized, general, (*wide trousers; takes wide views*); ∼ **guess,** one allowing margin for errors of detail; **give** ∼ **berth to,** not go too near, keep clear of, avoid. **5.** open to full extent (*staring with wide eyes*). **6.** at considerable distance from a point or mark, not within reasonable distance *of;* ∼ **ball,** (Cricket) ball judged by umpire to pass wicket beyond batsman's reach and counting one to his side; ∼ **of the mark,** (fig.) quite incorrect. **7.** ‖(sl.) shrewd, skilled in sharp practice (*wide boy*). **8.** Hence **wi'dEN⁶** *v.t.* & *i.*, **wi'dISH¹ 2** *a.* **9.** *adv.* widely (*ranges FAR¹ and wide*); to full extent (*open your mouth wide; wide awake*); far from target etc. (*is shooting wide; arrow fell wide of target*); ∼ **open,** (fig.) exposed (*to attack etc.*), **(of town etc.) lenient in enforcing regulations. **10.** *n.* wide ball; **the** ∼, the wide world; *broke* etc. **to the** ∼, completely; **dead to the** ∼, unconscious. **11.** ∼-**angle,** (of lens) having short focal length and field covering wide angle; ∼**-awake,** (colloq., fig.) wary, knowing; ∼'**awake,** soft wide-brimmed low-crowned felt hat; ∼**-eyed,** surprised or naïve; ∼**-ranging**, covering an extensive range; ∼**'spread**, widely disseminated or distributed. [OE *wīd* a., *wīde* adv., = OS *wīd*, OHG *wīt*, ON *vīthr* f. Gmc **wīdaz*]

wi'(d)geon (wi'jon) *n*. wild duck, esp. *Anas penelope* or **Anas americana*. [perh. f. imit. **wi-*, after *pigeon*]

wi'dget *n*. (colloq.) gadget, (unspecified) device. [perh. alt. of GADGET]

wi'dow (-ō) *n*., & *v.t.* **1.** *n.* woman who has lost her husband by death and not married again (GRASS *widow*; **golf** etc. ∼, woman whose husband often leaves her and plays golf etc.); ∼**'s cruse**, supply that looks small, but seems or is inexhaustible (see 1 Kgs. 17:10-16); ∼**'s mite**, small money contribution (see Mark 12:42); ∼**'s peak**, V-shaped growth of hair towards centre of forehead; *widow's* WEEDS. **2.** extra cards dealt separately and taken by highest bidder; (Print.) break-line at top of page or column; BLACK[1] *widow*; **the** ∼, (sl.) champagne [f. the Veuve (F = widow) Cliquot brand]. **3.** ∼**-bird**, whidah. **4.** Hence ∼HOOD *n*. **5.** *v.t.* (usu. in *p.p.*) kill husband or mate of, deprive of husband or wife or mate, make into widow or widower, (fig.) deprive *of*. [OE *widewe* etc., = OS *widowa*, OHG *wituwa*, Goth. *widuwō*, f. IE **widhewo* a.]

wi'dower (-ōĕr) *n*. man who has lost his wife by death and not married again; GRASS *widower*. [ME, f. prec. +-ER[1]]

width *n*. measurement from side to side; large extent; comprehensiveness or liberality *of* mind, views etc.; piece of material of full width as woven (*shall want three widths of it*); hence ∼'WAYS, ∼'WISE, *advs*. [17th c. (WIDE, -TH[1]), repl. *wideness*]

wield *v.t.* (literary). control, command, hold and use, manage with the hands or otherwise, (*wield power, the sceptre, a kingdom* etc. chiefly poet., *weapon* lit. or fig.). [OE *wealdan*, *wieldan* = OS, Goth. *waldan*, OHG *waltan*, ON *valda* f. Gmc **waldh-*]

wie'n|er (vē'-) *n*. **frankfurter; Wiener* SCHNITZEL; hence **∼*IE *n*. (sl.) [G, = Viennese]

wife *n*. (*pl.* **wives** *pr.* -vz). **1.** old and rustic or uneducated woman (esp. in **old wives' tale**, foolish or superstitious tradition); (in *comb.*) woman engaged in selling etc. (FISH[1]*wife*, HOUSEWIFE, MIDWIFE). **2.** married woman esp. in relation to her husband (*his wife; the wife of the President; will make a good wife*); **wedded, lawful,** ∼, (emphatic phrs. in contrast w. *mistress, concubine*, etc.); THE *wife; all the* WORLD *and his wife; have, take,* **to** ∼, (arch.) as wife; ∼**-swapping**, (colloq.) sexual activity of various men with one another's wives. **3.** Hence ∼HOOD (-fh-), *ns.*, ∼'LESS, ∼'LIKE, ∼'LY[1], (-fl-) *adjs*. [OE *wīf* woman, = OS *wīf*, OHG *wīp*, ON *vīf*; ult. orig. unkn.]

wig[1] *n*. artificial head of hair worn to conceal baldness or to change or disguise appearance, or as part of official dress esp. of judge or lawyer or of servant's livery, or (Hist.) as part of fashionable costume; ∼**s on the green**, (arch.) a free fight; hence (-)∼GED[2] (-gd), ∼'LESS, *adjs*. [abbr. of PERIWIG; cf. WINKLE]

wig[2] *v.t.* (-gg-). rebuke sharply, rate; hence (esp.) ∼'GING[1] (1) (-g-) *n*. [app. f. prec. in sl. or colloq. sense 'rebuke' (19th c.)]

wigeon. See WIDGEON.

wi'ggle *v*. & *n*. (colloq. or dial.) **1.** *v.t.* cause (thing) to move repeatedly from side to side. **2.** *v.i.* move from side to side; ∼ **out of**, extricate oneself from by wiggling. **3.** *n*. act of wiggling; **get a** ∼ **on**, **(sl.)* make haste; hence **wi'ggly**[2] *a.*, showing wiggles, having small irregular undulations. [ME, f. MLG & MDu. *wiggelen*, frequent. of **wig-*; cf. WAG[1], WAGGLE, -LE[3]]

wight (wīt) *n*. (arch. or joc. or dial.) person (esp. *luckless, wretched,* etc., *wight*). [OE *wiht* thing, creature, = OS, OHG *wiht*, ON *vættr* fem., Goth. *waihts* fem.; orig. unkn.]

wi'gwag *v.i.* (-gg-). (colloq.) move lightly to and fro; wave flags thus in signalling. [redupl. f. WAG[1]]

wi'gwam (-ăm, -ŏm) *n*. N. Amer. Indian's tent or hut of skins or mats or bark on poles; similar structure for children etc.; ***headquarters of political organization. [f. Ojibwa *wigwaum*, Algonquin *wikiwam* their house]

wi'lco *int*. (colloq.) expr. compliance or agreement. [abbr. of *will comply*]

wild *a., adv.,* & *n*. **1.** (Of animal or plant) not domesticated or cultivated (esp. of species or varieties allied to others that are not wild; *wild beast, plant; wild ass, duck, rose, vine*); not civilized, barbarous; (of scenery etc.) having conspicuously desolate appearance; ∼ **and woolly**, lacking refinement(s), barbarous. **2.** (Of horse, game-bird, etc.) shy, given to shying, easily startled, hard to get near. **3.** unrestrained, wayward, disorderly, irregular, out of control, unconventional, (*a wild fellow; settled down after a wild youth; hair hanging in wild locks; living in wild times; room is in wild disorder*); (of playing-card) having any rank chosen by player holding it; **run** ∼, grow or stray unchecked or undisciplined or untrained. **4.** tempestuous, violent, (*a wild wind, night*). **5.** intensely eager, excited, frantic, passionate, distracted, mad, (*is wild with excitement, to try it; wild delight, excitement, enthusiasm, grief, rage*); (of looks, appearance, etc.) indicating distraction; (colloq.) angry, infuriated; ∼ **about**, enthusiastically devoted to (person or subject); **drive** ∼, madden. **6.** haphazard, rash, ill--considered, ill-aimed, disturbed by excitement, (*a wild guess, shot, blow, venture; wild opinions, bowling*). **7.** ∼ **boar**, tusked wild pig (*Sus scrofa*) from which domestic pigs are descended; ∼ **cat**, medium-sized wild feline, esp. European species (*Felis sylvestris*); ∼'**cat**, (fig.) hot-tempered or violent person; ∼'**cat** *a.*, reckless, financially unsound, (of strike) sudden and UNOFFICIAL, (of well) drilled for oil etc. where there is only a possibility of success; ∼'**fire**, = *Greek* FIRE[1], will-o'-the-wisp, (fig.) thing that spreads rapidly; ∼'**fowl**, game-bird(s); ∼**-goo'se chase**, foolish or hopeless or fruitless quest; ∼ **horse**, horse not domesticated or broken in (∼ *horses would not drag etc. it from me*, I refuse to disclose the secret); *wild* HYACINTH; ∼'**life**, wild animals collectively; ∼ **man**, (1) savage, (2) political extremist; ∼ *man of the woods*, orang-utan; *wild* OATS; ∼ **rice**, tall grass of genus *Zizania* yielding edible grains; ∼ **silk**, silk from wild silkworms, or imitation of this from short silk fibres; *wild* THYME; **W**∼ **West**, western US in time of lawlessness; ∼'**wood**, (poet.) uncultivated or un-frequented woodland. **8.** Hence ∼'ISH[1] 2 *a.*, ∼'LY[2] *adv.*, ∼'NESS *n*. **9.** *adv*. in wild manner (*shooting wild*). **10.** *n*. desert, wild tract; (out) **in the** ∼, (colloq.) far from towns etc. [OE *wilde* = OS, OHG *wildi*, ON *villr*, Goth. *wiltheis*, f. Gmc **wilthijaz*]

wi'ldebeest (w-, v-) *n*. gnu. [Afrik. (as prec., BEAST)]

wi'lder *v.t.* (arch. or poet.) lead astray; bewilder. [perh. based on foll.]

wi'lderness *n*. **1.** desert, uncultivated and uninhabi-ted tract; **voice (crying) in the** ∼ etc., unregarded advocate of some reform, w. ref. to Matt. 3:3 etc.; **in the** ∼, (of political party) out of office, w. ref. to Num. 14:33 etc. **2.** part of garden left with uncultiva-ted appearance. **3.** confused assemblage *of*. [f. OE *wild(d)ēornes*, f. *wild(d)ēor* wild deer; see -NESS]

wi'lding *n*. plant sown by natural agency, esp. wild crab-apple; fruit of such plant. [f. WILD +-ING[3]]

wile *n.*, & *v.t.* **1.** *n*. (usu. in *pl.*) trick, cunning procedure, artifice. **2.** *v.t.* lure or entice away, into, etc.; = WHILE[1] 2. [ME *wil*, perh. f. Scand. (ON *vél* craft)]

wi'lful, *wi'llful, *a.* (Of action or state) for which compulsion or ignorance or accident cannot be pleaded as excuse, intentional, deliberate, due to perversity or self-will, (*wilful murder, waste, ignorance, disobedience*); obstinate, self-willed, headstrong, refractory; hence ∼LY[2] *adv.*, ∼NESS *n*. [ME, f. WILL[2] +-FUL]

wi'lga *n*. (Austral.) small white-flowered drought--resistant tree of genus *Geijera*. [Aboriginal]

wī′lĭnėss. See WILY.

will[1] *v.t.* & *aux.* (*pres.* **will,** *or* **'ll** (after pers. pron., or colloq.), exc. 2 *sing.* (arch.) **wilt** *or* **'lt**, *neg.* **will not, 'll not,** (colloq.) **won't** *pr.* wŏnt; *past* **would** *pr.* wŏŏd *or* wud, *or* **'d** (after pers. pron., or colloq.), exc. 2 *sing.* (arch.) **wouldst** *pr.* wŏŏdst, *or* **wouldest** *pr.* wŏŏ′dĭst, *or* **'dst,** *neg.* **would not, 'd not,** (colloq.) **wouldn't** *pr.* wŏŏ′dĕnt; no other parts used). **1.** *v.t.* (In all persons, with more or less of orig. sense of volition). desire (thing; arch.; *what wilt thou?*; *what would they?*); want or desire or choose to (*the haven where I would be; come when you will; I will* or *would have you know that I am the one who gives the orders here;* **would-be** *a.* & *adv.,* as (unachieved) aspiration or intention: *a would-be gentleman, smart saying*); wish that or *that* (esp. (*I*) *would* expr. unfulfilled wish: *it shall be as you will; said it should be as we would; would* or *I would I were a bird!; would it were otherwise!;* **would** God *that I had died!,* if only God had wished, or perh. ellipt. for 'I would to God'; *I would to heaven I was dead*); consent or be persuaded to (*will* or *would not go any farther; wound would not heal; this window won't open; would you pass the salt?; would not do it for £100*); have habitual or inevitable tendency to (*boys will be boys; accidents will happen; you will have your way; you* would *do that!; he will* or *would get in my light*); be accustomed or observed from time to time to (*will sit there for hours; now and then a blackbird would call; will succeed once in ten times*); be likely to turn out to (*this will be Reading, I suppose; I don't know who it would be*). **2.** *v. aux.* In 2nd and 3rd person (1st having **shall, should,** exc. colloq.) forming simple future or conditional statement or order or question (*you,* colloq. *I, will hear soon enough; the battalion will attack at dawn; would have been killed if they had let go; will* or *would you, they, be able to hear at such a distance?,* but cf. SHALL 6). **3.** In 1st person (others having **shall, should**) forming future or conditional statement expressing speaker's will or intention (*I will not be caught again;* ∼ **do,** (colloq.) I will do that; *we would have come if you had given us longer notice*). **4.** (Less often than **shall, should**) in sentences of type 2 changed in reporting to 1st from other person (*you say I will, said I would, never manage it, reporting you will never*). **5.** Replacing **shall** or **should** in sentences of type 2 changed in reporting from 1st to other person (*he said he would never manage it, reporting I shall never*). **6.** In reporting 1st pers. sentences of type 3 (*you promised you would not be caught again*). **7.** (colloq.) = SHALL 8 (*I would like to disagree;* **I wouldn't know,** (as is to be expected) I do not know). [OE **willan, wyllan* = OS *willian,* ON *vilja,* Goth. *wiljan* f. Gmc **wel(l)jan* f. IE **wel-, *wol-*]

will[2] *n.* **1.** faculty by which person decides or conceives himself as deciding upon and initiating action (*mind consists of the understanding and the will*); **freedom of the ∼, free ∼,** power of determining one's choice of action independently of causation or fate; **a ∼ of** one's **own,** (euphem.) obstinacy, wilfulness of character. **2.** ∼(**-power**), control exercised by deliberate purpose over impulse, self-control, (*has a strong, weak, will; overcame her shyness by will-power*). **3.** deliberate or fixed desire or intention (*the patient's will to live is the surgeon's best ally; did it against my will*); **free ∼,** inclination to act without suggestion from others (*did it of my own free will*); **where there's a ∼ there's a way,** determination will overcome any obstacle. **4.** energy of intention, power of effecting one's intentions or dominating other persons; *do* thing **with a ∼,** energetically or resolutely. **5.** (arch.) contents of the will, what is desired or ordained by person, (*thy will be done*); **what is your ∼?,** what do you wish done?; **have** one's ∼, get thing desired. **6.** arbitrary discretion; **at ∼,** whenever one pleases; *tenant* **at ∼,** who can be turned out without notice. **7.** disposition towards others, wishing of good or ill, (GOOD or ILL *will*; cf. GOODWILL); **with the best ∼ in the world,** however good one's intentions. **8.** directions (usu.

written) in legal form for disposition to be made of person's property after his death (often *last will and testament; make one's will*). **9.** Hence (-)∼ED[2] (-ld), ∼-LESS, *adjs.* [OE *willa,* = OS *willio,* OHG *will(i)o,* ON *vili,* Goth. *wilja* f. Gmc **wiljon, *weljon* (**wel-* be pleasing; cf. prec.)]

will[3] *v.t.* **1.** have as object of one's will, intend unconditionally, (*God wills, willeth, willed, that man should be happy; he who wills success is half-way to it*). **2.** (abs.) exercise will-power (*has no power to will; willing and wishing are not the same*). **3.** instigate or impel or compel by exercise of will-power (*you can will yourself into contentment; willed the genie into his presence*). **4.** bequeath by will (*shall will my money to a hospital*). [OE *willian* (as prec.)]

wī′llėt *n.* (*pl.* same). large N. Amer. shore-bird like snipe. [f. *pill-will-willet,* imit. of its cry]

wi′llies (-ĭz) *n. pl.* (sl.) nervous feeling of discomfort or fear (*gives me the willies*). [19th c.; orig. unkn.]

wi′lling[1] *n.* In vbl senses; cheerful intention (*show willing*). [f. WILL[1],[3] + -ING[1]]

wi′lling[2] *a.* disposed to consent or undertake (*to do, or* abs.; *do not spur a willing horse; am willing to admit he is right*); of, given etc. by, willing person (*willing hands, help,* etc.); hence ∼LY[2] *adv.,* ∼NESS *n.* [ME, f. OE **willende* (as WILL[1], -ING[2])]

will-o'-the-wi′sp (-dh-) *n.* **1.** phosphorescent light on marshy ground perh. due to combustion of methane. **2.** person of uncertain whereabouts or appearances. **3.** delusive hope or plan. [orig. *Will with the wisp; wisp* = handful of (lighted) hay etc.]

wi′llow (-ō) *n.* **1.** tree or shrub of genus *Salix,* with pliant branches, growing usu. near water in temperate climates, many kinds of which yield osiers or timber used for cricket bats and other purposes; WEAR[1] *the willow,* ∼**-pattern,** conventional design of Chinese type done in blue on white china etc., introduced in England 1780. **2.** cricket-bat. **3.** ∼**-herb,** plant of genus *Epilobium* etc., esp. one with leaves like willow and pale purple flowers; ∼**-warbler,** ∼**-wren,** bird of genus *Phylloscopus.* [OE *welig,* = OS *wilgia,* MLG *wilge*]

wi′llowy (-ŏĭ) *a.* abounding in willows; bordered by willows; lithe and slender. [f. prec. + -Y[2]]

wi′lly-ni′lly *adv.* & *a.* (existing or occurring) whether one likes it or not. [= *will I, nill I* (WILL[1], NILL)]

wi′lly-willy *n.* (Austral.) cyclone or dust-storm. [Aboriginal]

wilt[1]. See WILL[1].

wilt[2] *v.* & *n.* **1.** *v.i.* (Of plant, leaf, flower) wither; lose vigour, droop. **2.** *v.t.* cause to wilt. **3.** *n.* disease of plants that causes wilting. [orig. dial., perh. alt. f. *wilk, welk,* of LDu. orig.]

Wi′lton *n.* kind of carpet like Brussels, with loops cut into thick pile, first made at Wilton. [∼ in Wiltshire]

Wilts. *abbr.*

wī′lÿ *a.* full of wiles, crafty, cunning; hence ∼ĭLY[2] *adv.,* ∼ĭNESS *n.* [ME, f. WILE + -Y[2]]

wi′mple *n.* & *v.* **1.** *n.* covering of linen or silk worn by nuns and formerly by other women, arranged in folds about head, cheeks, chin, and neck. **2.** *v.t.* put wimple on, veil; arrange in folds. **3.** *v.i.* fall in folds. [OE *wimpel,* = OS *wimpal,* OHG *winfila,* ON *vimpill*]

Wi′mpÿ *n.* (colloq.) hamburger served in plain bun. [P]

Wi′mshŭrst (-z-h-) *n.* ∼ **machine,** device for generating electric charge by turning glass discs in opposite directions. [f. J. ∼, Engl. engineer d. 1903]

win *v.* (-**nn**-; **won** *pr.* wŭn) & *n.* **1.** *v.t.* secure as result of fighting, competition, betting etc., or effort, (*win victory, fortress, prize, honour, fame, fortune, wager, game; win one's confidence; won £5 from me at cards*); get (ore etc.) from mine; (sl.) steal; *win* one's SPURS, ∼ one's **way,** progress by struggle etc. **2.** be victorious in (*win battle, game, bet, race*); ∼ **the day** or (arch.) **field,** be victorious in battle (lit. or fig.); *win the* TOSS. **3.** *v.i.* win race, contest, money, etc., (*win by a* HEAD[1], *in a* CANTER, HAND[1]*s down, by two* etc. *lengths, easily,* etc.; *usually wins at cards; let those laugh who win*); **you can't** ∼ (**them all**), (colloq.) there is no way of achieving (universal) success. **4.** *v.t.* (arch.) make one's way to (*win the shore, summit*). **5.** *v.i.* make one's way, or (w. compl.) become by successful effort, (*win home; win through,* (colloq.) *out, through all difficulties; win free, clear,* etc.). **6.** *v.t.* persuade, induce to do, gain over (*soon won his audience over*). **7.** *v.i.* (arch.) exercise increasing attraction *upon* (*a theory that wins upon one by degrees*). **8.** *n.* a success or victory in a game (*has had three wins and no defeats*). [OE *winnan* toil, endure, = OS, OHG, Goth. *winnan,* ON *vinna*]

wince[1] *v.i.,* & *n.* **1.** *v.i.* show bodily or mental pain or distress by slight start or loss of composure, flinch, (*under* or *at*). **2.** *n.* act of wincing. [ME, f. AF *wencir* = OF *guenchir* turn aside, f. WG *wenkjan*; cf. WINCH, WINK]

||**wi'nce**[2] *n.* roller for moving textile fabric through dyeing-vat. [var. of WINCH]

wi'ncey *n.* strong material of wool and cotton or wool and linen used for shirts etc.; hence ||∼E'TTE (2) (-iē'-) *n.,* lightweight napped flannelette formerly used for night-clothes etc. [orig. Sc.; app. f. *woolsey* in LINSEY-WOOLSEY]

winch *n.,* & *v.t.* **1.** *n.* crank of wheel or axle; ||reel or fishing-rod; hoisting-machine, windlass; = WINCE[2]. **2.** *v.t.* lift with winch. [OE *wince* f. Gmc **winkjōn* (**wenk*; cf. WINCE[1])]

Wi'nchester *n.* ∼ (**quart**), (bottle holding) standard quart as orig. deposited at Winchester, about half a gallon. [∼ in Hampshire]

wind[1] (poet. also wī-) *n.* **1.** air in more or less rapid natural motion, breeze or gale, (*hot, cold, whistling, variable,* etc., *wind*); **north** etc. ∼, wind blowing from the north etc.; **fair** ∼ (helping ship's course); CONTRARY *wind*; ILL *wind*; **before the** ∼, helped by its force; **between** ∼ **and water,** at a vulnerable point; **close to the** ∼, (sailing) as nearly against it as is consistent with using its force, (fig.) close to indecency or dishonesty; **down the** ∼, in the direction in which it is blowing (WHISTLE *down the wind*; DOWNWIND); **how the** ∼ **blows** or **lies,** (fig.) what developments are likely, what is the state of opinion; **in the** ∼, (fig.) happening or about to happen; **like the** ∼, swiftly; **near the** ∼, – *close to the wind*; **off the** ∼, (Naut.) with the wind on the quarter; **on a** ∼, (Naut.) against a wind on either bow; **on the** ∼, (of sound or scent) carried by the wind; RAISE *the wind*; **to the** (**four**) ∼**s,** in all directions, into state of abandonment or neglect; *in the teeth of the wind* (see TOOTH); UPWIND; WHIRL*wind*; ∼ **and weather,** exposure to influence of wind, rain, etc.; ∼(**s**) **of change,** force or tendency for reform; **in the** ∼'**s eye,** directly against it; ∼ **is in that quarter,** (fig.) things are in that (particular) state; **take the** ∼ **out of** person's **sails,** frustrate him by anticipating his arguments, etc. **2.** windward position or *weather* GAUGE[1] (*take* or *get the wind of*). **3.** mere empty words, meaningless rhetoric. **4.** artificially produced air--current (esp. for sounding an organ or other wind instrument), air stored for use or used as current, (collect.) part of orchestra or band consisting of wind instruments, (*organ fails when the wind is exhausted; was knocked down by the wind of the missile; the strings were drowned by the wind,* and the WOOD-*wind by the brass*). **5.** smell carried by the wind, indication of thing's whereabouts or existence, commencing publicity; **get** ∼ **of,** smell out, begin to suspect, hear rumour of; **take** or **get** ∼, be rumoured, become known. **6.** gas generated in bowels etc. by indigestion, flatulence; **break** ∼, release it by anus; **get** or **have the** ∼ **up,** (sl.) become or be frightened; **put the** ∼ **up,** (sl.) frighten. **7.** breath as needed in exertion or speech, power of breathing without difficulty while running or making similar continuous effort, spot below

centre of chest where blow temporarily paralyses breathing, (*have lost, let me recover* or *get, my wind; has a good, bad,* LONG[1], SHORT, *wind*); **broken** ∼, condition of being BROKEN-winded; **second** ∼, recovery of wind in course of exercise after initial breathlessness, (fig.) renewed energy for effort; **sound in** ∼ **and limb,** in full physical health; **have** one's ∼ **taken,** be paralysed by blow in the wind. **8.** ∼'**bag,** wordy orator; ∼ **band,** wind instruments as band or part of orchestra; ∼'**bound,** unable to sail because of contrary winds; ∼-**break,** row of trees, fence, shrubs, etc., or temporary wall, serving to break force of wind; *∼'**breaker,** ||∼-**cheater,** jacket for protecting person from cold wind; ∼-**chest,** (Mus.) box for compressed air supplied to pipes or reeds in organ; ∼-**chill,** cooling effect of wind blowing on a surface; ∼-**cone,** = *wind-sock*; ∼-**egg,** soft-shelled unfertilized or imperfect egg incapable of producing chicken; ∼'**fall,** fruit blown down, (fig.) unexpected good fortune, esp. legacy; ∼-**flower,** anemone; ∼-**force** (esp. stated on Beaufort etc. scale); ∼-**gall,** (1) soft tumour on horse's fetlock-joint, (2) coloured sun--halo; ∼-**gauge,** (1) anemometer, (2, Mus.) instrument showing amount of wind in organ, (3) apparatus attached to sights enabling allowance to be made for wind in shooting; ||∼'**hover,** kestrel; ∼ **instrument,** musical instrument in which sound is produced by current of air, e.g. organ, & esp. by breath, e.g. flute, trumpet; ∼-**jammer,** merchant sailing-ship; ∼ **machine** (Theatr., for producing blast of air or sound of wind); ∼'**pipe,** breathing--tube from throat to lungs, trachea; ∼-**rose,** diagram of relative frequency of wind directions at a place; ∼-**row,** line of raked hay, corn-sheaves, peats, etc., made to allow drying by wind; ∼-**sail,** canvas funnel conveying air to lower parts of ship; ||∼'**screen,** *∼'**shield,** (of glass in front of motor-vehicle driver); ∼-**sleeve,** ∼-**sock,** canvas cylinder or cone flying from masthead to show direction of wind at airfield etc.; ∼-**sucker, -sucking,** (horse with) bad habit of noisily drawing in and swallowing breath; ∼-**swept,** exposed to or affected by (high) winds; ∼-**tunnel,** tunnel-like apparatus for producing air-stream of known velocity past model of aircraft etc. to investigate flow or effect of wind pressure on structure. **9.** Hence ∼'LESS *a.* [OE, = OS *wind,* OHG *wint,* ON *vindr,* Goth. *winds* f. Gmc **windaz* f. IE **went-* blowing]

wind[2] (in sense 1 wī-) *v.t.* (in sense 1 also **wound**). **1.** sound (horn, bugle, blast, call) by blowing. **2.** detect presence of by scent (*hounds, deer, wind the fox, stalkers*). **3.** make breathe quick and deep by exercise, exhaust wind of by exertion or blow, renew wind of by rest, (*give horse a gallop to wind him; am quite winded by the climb; rested to wind the horses*). [ME, f. prec.]

wind[3] *v.* (**wound**) & *n.* **1.** *v.i.* go in circular, spiral, curved, or crooked course, meander, (*path, river, winds; herd wind slowly o'er the lea; creeper winds round pole*); ∼**ing staircase** (spiral). **2.** *v.t.* make one's or its way circuitously, insinuate one*self into,* (*brook winds its way; wound himself* or *his way into my affections*). **3.** *v.t.* & *i.* coil, wrap closely, (*wind cotton on reel, wool into ball,* etc.); provide (reel etc.) with coiled cotton etc.; coil (wool) into ball from skein; ∼ **off** (*adv.* or *prep.*), unwind; *wind round* one's FINGER. **4.** *v.t.* surround (as) with coil, embrace, (*wound the blanket round him, her arms round the child, the child in her arms*); coil string round (TOP[3]). **5.** hoist or draw by use of windlass etc. (*wind ship out of harbour, men* or *ore up from mine, window of vehicle down*); wind up (clock etc.). **6.** ∼ **down,** unwind (lit. or fig.); ∼ **up,** coil the whole of (*wind up piece of string*), tighten coiling or coiled spring or fig. tension or intensity or efficiency of (*wind up* (*spring* or *weights of*) *clock* etc.; *is winding himself up for an effort to do it; person is wound up to fury; expectation was wound up to a high pitch*), bring to a conclusion, conclude, (*wound up his speech,* or *wound up, by declaring*);

shot his wife and child and wound up by stabbing himself), arrange affairs of and dissolve (company), (of company) cease business and go into liquidation, (colloq.) arrive finally (*he'll wind up in prison*); ∼**-up** *n.*, conclusion, finish. **7.** Hence ∼'ER¹ (1, 2) *n.* **8.** *n.* bend or turn in course; single turn in winding clock, string, etc. [OE *windan*, = OS *windan*, OHG *wintan*, ON *vinda*, Goth. *-windan* f. Gmc **windan* rel. to WANDER, WEND¹]

wi'ndage *n.* difference between projectile's and gun-bore's diameter allowing escape of gas; (allowance for) influence of wind in deflecting missile; friction of air against moving part of machine. [f. WIND¹+-AGE]

wi'nding *n.* In vbl senses; (Electr.) coils of wire round armature etc.; ∼**-engine** (for hoisting); ∼**-sheet** (in which corpse is wrapped for burial). [OE *windung* (as WIND³, -ING¹)]

wi'ndlass *n.*, & *v.t.* **1.** *n.* machine for hauling or hoisting on wheel-and-axle principle, with horizontal axle. **2.** *v.t.* hoist or haul with windlass. [alt. (perh. by assoc. w. dial. *windle* to wind) f. obs. *windas* f. AF, = OF *guindas* f. ON *vindáss* (*vinda* WIND³, *áss* pole)]

||**wi'ndlestraw** (-dels-) *n.* old dry stalk of grass. [OE *windelstrēaw* grass for plaiting (*windel* basket f. as WIND³, -LE 1; *strēaw* STRAW¹)]

wi'ndmill (-nm-, -ndm-) *n.* mill worked by action of wind on sails (**fight** or **tilt at** ∼**s**, battle with imaginary enemy or grievance, w. ref. to Don Quixote; **throw** one's **cap over the** ∼, act recklessly or unconventionally); toy of stick with revolving light card etc. [ME, f. WIND¹+MILL¹]

wi'ndow (-ō) *n.* **1.** opening in wall or roof of building, ship, vehicle, etc., usu. filled with glass in fixed or sliding or hinged frames to admit light and often air to room etc. and allow occupants to look out or objects within to be seen; glass filling such opening (*broke*, *cleaned*, *the window*), (fig.) opportunity to observe; space for display behind window of shop etc. (**have all** one's **goods in the** (**front** or **shop-**)∼, be superficial; aperture in wall for issue of tickets etc.; **blank, blind, false,** ∼, moulding or recess as for window but without aperture; FRENCH *window*; **out of the** ∼, (colloq.) no longer taken into account. **2.** opening or transparent part in envelope to show address written on letter; range of electromagnetic spectrum for which a medium is transparent; interval during which positions of planets etc. allow specified journey by spacecraft; ||strips of metal foil in air to obstruct radar detection. **3.** ∼**-box,** box on outside window-sill in which flowers are grown; ∼**-cleaner, -cleaning,** (esp. as occupation); ∼**-dressing,** art of arranging goods attractively in shop-window, (fig.) adroit presentation of statistics etc.; ∼ **envelope** (with opening or transparent part allowing address to show); ∼**-ledge,** sill of window; ∼**-seat,** usu. upholstered seat against window in room; ∼**-shopping,** looking (for pleasure or for comparison of prices etc.) at goods displayed in shop-windows without buying; ||∼**-tax,** (Hist.) tax on any windows or window-like openings (1695–1851). **4.** Hence (-)∼ED² (-ōd), ∼LESS, *adjs.* [ME, f. ON *vindauga* (as WIND¹, EYE¹)]

Wi'ndsor (-nz-) *n.* **House of** ∼, name of British Royal Family since 1917; ∼ **chair** (all of wood with curved frame and upright rods as support for back); ∼ **soap** (brown or white scented kind); ||∼ **uniform,** blue coat with red collar and cuffs sometimes worn at Windsor by the royal household and guests having royal permission. [∼ in Berkshire, site of royal residence at ∼ Castle]

wi'ndward *a.*, *adv.*, & *n.* **1.** *a.* & *adv.* on or towards the side from which the wind blows, exposed to the wind, (opp. *leeward*). **2.** *n.* this side or direction (*to windward*); **get to** ∼ **of,** avoid smell of, (fig.) gain advantage over. [f. WIND¹+-WARD]

wi'ndỹ *a.* wind-swept (*windy hill-top*, *plain*, *situation*); in which wind is high (*windy night*, *weather*, *crossing*); wordy, verbose, empty (*windy eloquence*, *logic*, *speaker*); generating or characterized by flatulence; (arch.) windward (**on the** ∼**y side of,** safely away from); (sl.) nervous, frightened; hence ∼iLY² *adv.*, ∼iNESS *n.* [OE *windig* (as WIND¹, -Y²)]

wine *n.* & *v.* **1.** *n.* fermented grape-juice as alcoholic drink (DRY¹ and *sweet*, STILL¹ and *sparkling*, WHITE¹ and RED, *wine*); SPIRIT¹(*s*) *of wine*; *good wine needs no* BUSH¹; **new** ∼ **in old bottles,** new principle too powerful to be restrained by ancient forms; **take** ∼ **with,** pledge and be pledged by at table; **in** ∼, exhilarated or drunk with wine. **2.** fermented drink resembling wine made from specified fruit etc. (*cowslip*, *currant*, *ginger*, *palm*, *wine*). **3.** dark red colour of red wine. **4.** ∼**-apple,** large red apple with winy flavour; ∼'**berry,** = MAKO²; ∼'**bibber,** tippler, drunkard, [f. *bib* to tipple]; ∼**-biscuit** (served with or flavoured with wine); ∼'**bottle,** glass bottle for wine; *wine*-CELLAR; ∼**-coloured,** having colour of wine (see sense 3); ∼**-cooler,** vessel in which winebottles are cooled with ice; ∼'**fat,** (arch.) = *winepress* [*fat* = VAT]; *wine* GALLON; ∼'**glass,** any glass for drinking wine from; ∼'**glass(ful),** this as measure of liquid, esp. of size used for sherry, = four tablespoons; ∼**-grower,** cultivator of grapes for wine; so ∼**-growing** *n.*; ∼**-palm,** kind from which palm wine is made, e.g. coquito; ∼'**press** (in which grapes are squeezed); ∼'**sap,** large red American winter apple; ∼'**skin,** whole skin of goat etc. sown up and used to hold wine; ∼**-stone,** = TARTAR¹ 1; ∼**-tasting,** judging quality of wine by tasting it; ∼**-vault,** (1) cellar in which wine is kept, (2) bar etc. where wine is retailed. **5.** Hence ∼'LESS (-nl-), ∼iNY², *adjs.* **6.** *v.i.* drink wine. **7.** *v.t.* entertain to wine; ∼ **and dine,** entertain to dinner with wine. [OE *wīn*, = OS, OHG *wīn*, ON *vín*, Goth. *wein* f. Gmc **wīnam* f. L *vinum*]

wi'nery *n.* establishment for making wine. [f. prec. + -ERY]

wing *n.* & *v.* **1.** *n.* one of the limbs or organs by which the flight of a bird, bat, insect, angel, etc., is effected; part in non-flying bird or insect corresponding to this; winglike supporting part of aircraft; **clip** person's ∼**s,** limit his movements or ambitions or expenditure; *come* **on the** ∼**s of the wind,** swiftly; **lend** ∼**s to,** accelerate; **on the** ∼, flying; SINGE one's *wings*; **spread** or **stretch** one's ∼**s,** (fig.) develop one's full powers; **take under** one's ∼, treat as protégé; **his** ∼**s are sprouting** etc., his virtues are too great for a being below the degree of an angel; **take** ∼, fly away; *money* **takes to itself** ∼**s,** disappears. **2.** more or less separate projecting part of something, esp. of building or battle array (*north wing was added in 17th century*; *cavalry were massed on left wing*); (in *pl.*) sides of theatre stage, pieces of side scenery (**waiting in the** ∼**s,** (fig.) holding oneself in readiness); ||mudguard of motor vehicle; extreme section of political party. **3.** (Footb., Hockey, etc.) forward etc. whose place is at either end of the line; side part of playing-area. **4.** air-force unit of several ||squadrons or **groups.* **5.** (in *pl.*) pilot's badge in RAF etc. **6.** (Anat. & Bot.) lateral part or projection of organ or structure. **7.** ∼**-beat,** one complete set of motions with wing in flying; ∼**-case,** horny cover, a modified fore-wing, protecting some insects' flying wing; ∼**-chair** (with side-pieces projecting forwards at top of high back); ∼**-collar,** man's high stiff collar with upper corners turned down; ||∼ **commander,** RAF officer commanding wing (sense 4); *wing*-COVERT²; ∼**-footed,** (poet.) swift; ||∼**-game,** game-birds; ∼**-nut** (with projections for thumb and fingers to turn it on screw); ∼**-span, ∼-spread,** measurement across wings when extended, or between tips of aircraft's wings; ∼**-stroke,** = *wing-beat*; ∼**-tip,** outer end of wing of bird, aircraft, etc. **8.** Hence ∼ED² (-ngd), ∼'LESS, *adjs.*, ∼'LET *n.* **9.** *v.t.* equip with wings, enable to fly or mount, send in flight, lend speed to, (*wing arrow with eagle's feathers*, or *at the mark*; *vengeance winged the shaft*;

ambition wings his spirit; fear winged his steps); ~**ed god,** Mercury; ~**ed horse,** Pegasus, poetry; **W~ed Victory,** statue of Greek goddess of victory with wings; ~**ed words** (going swiftly like arrows to mark, significant). **10.** wound (bird) in wing or (person) in arm. **11.** *v.i.* & *t.* travel or traverse on wings (*bird wings its way, wings to its mate, wings the air*). [ME pl. *wenge, -en, -es* f. ON *vængir*, pl. of *vængr*]

*****wi'ngding** *n.* (sl.) wild party; drug addict's real or feigned seizure. [20th c.; orig. unkn.]

wi'nger *n.* wing forward etc. (see WING 3); LEFT[1], RIGHT[1], *-winger.* [f. WING + -ER[1]]

wink *v.* & *n.* **1.** *v.i.* close and open eye(s), blink, (of eye) close and open; **as easy as** ~'**ing,** very easy; **like** ~'**ing,** (sl.) very quickly or vigorously. **2.** momentarily close one eye to awaken attention of or convey private intimation to (or *at*) person. **3.** (Of light, star, etc.) twinkle, shine intermittently. **4.** ~ **at,** (fig.) shut one's eyes to, purposely avoid seeing, pretend not to notice, connive at, (abuse, transgression, etc.). **5.** *v.t.* close and open (eye or eyes); give (signal etc.) by flashing lights. **6.** *n.* act of winking, esp. as signal etc. (TIP[2] person *the wink;* **in a** ~, very quickly); short sleep (**not a** ~, no sleep at all; FORTY *winks*). [OE *wincian,* = OS *wincon,* OHG *winchan* stagger, nod, f. Gmc **wink* etc.; cf. WINCE[1], WINCH]

wi'nker *n* In vbl senses; (usu. in *pl.*) horse's blinker; motor vehicle's flashing light to indicate intended change of direction of travel. [f. prec. + -ER[1]]

wi'nkle *n.,* & *v.t.* **1.** *n.* edible gastropod of genus *Littorina,* periwinkle; ~-**picker,** (sl.) long pointed shoe. **2.** *v.t.* ~ **out,** extract or eject (as a winkle from its shell with a pin). [abbr. of PERIWINKLE[2]; cf. WIG[1]]

wi'nner *n.* In vbl senses; successful thing (*her new book is a winner*). [ME, f. WIN + -ER[1]]

wi'nning[1] *n.* In vbl senses; (in *pl.*) money won in betting etc.; ~-**post** (marking end of race). [ME, f. WIN + -ING[1]]

wi'nning[2] *a.* In vbl senses; persuasive, attractive, (*a winning smile*); that brings victory or advantage (*winning hit,* HAZARD, *card*); hence ~LY[2] *adv.* [f. WIN + -ING[2]]

wi'nnow (-ō) *v.t.* blow (grain) free of chaff etc. in wind or air-current, blow (chaff etc.) *away* or *out* or *from;* sift, separate, clear of refuse or inferior specimens or falsehood, clear (refuse etc.) *out* or *away,* examine, sort, weed out; (poet.) fan (air with wings), flap (wings), stir (hair etc.); hence ~ER[1] (1, 2) *n.* [OE *windwian* (as WIND[1])]

wi'nō *n.* (*pl.* ~s). (sl.) alcoholic. [f. WINE + -O]

wi'nsome *a.* (Of person or his or her appearance, manner, smile, etc.) charming, attractive, bright; hence ~LY[2] (-mli) *adv.,* ~NESS (-inn-) *n.* [OE *wynsum* (*wyn* joy; see -SOME[1])]

wi'nter *n., a.,* & *v.* **1.** coldest season of the year, in N. hemisphere Dec.-Feb. (Astron., from winter solstice to vernal equinox); colder part of year. **2.** (poet. or rhet., usu. in *pl.* with number etc.) year of life or age (*a man of fifty winters*). **3.** *a.* characteristic of or used etc. in or lasting for the winter; (of fruit) ripening late or keeping until or during winter; (of wheat or other crop) sown in autumn and reaped in spring; *winter* ACONITE; ~ **cress,** cress of genus *Barbarea* formerly cultivated for winter salad; ~-**fallow,** (land) lying fallow during winter; ~ **garden,** garden or conservatory of plants flourishing in winter; ~**green,** plant (esp. of genus *Pyrola* or *Gaultheria*) remaining green through winter; *winter* JASMINE; *Winter* OLYMPICS; ~ **quarters** (esp. to which troops retire for winter); ~ **sleep,** hibernation; *winter* SOLSTICE; ~ **sports,** open-air sports on snow or ice esp. in winter (e.g. skiing); ~-**tide** (poet.), ~-**time,** season of winter; ~-**weight,** (of clothes) suitable in weight for use in winter. **4.** Hence ~LESS, ~LY[1], *adjs.* **5.** *v.i.* pass the winter (*at* or *in* place). **6.** *v.t.* keep or feed (plants, cattle) during winter. [OE, = OS, OHG *wintar,* ON *vetr,* Goth. *wintrus* f. Gmc **wentrus,* prob. rel. to WET]

wi'nterīz|e, -īs|e (-īz), *v.t.* adapt for operation, or for use, in cold weather. [f. prec. + -IZE]

wi'ntr|y *a.* having the temperature, storminess, or appearance appropriate to winter, cold, windy, cheerless, (*wintry weather, day, sun, scene*); (of smile, greeting, etc.) lacking warmth or interest or vivacity; hence ~iNESS *n.* [OE *wintrig,* or f. WINTER + -Y[2]]

wi'nȳ. See WINE.

wīpe *v.t.,* & *n.* **1.** *v.t.* clean or dry surface of by rubbing with cloth, paper, hand, etc., (*wipe table, dish, face, hands*); ~ one's **eyes,** dry tears, cease weeping; ~ person's **eye,** (sl.) get advantage by anticipating him; ~ **the floor with,** (sl.) inflict humiliating defeat on; ~ **out** (bath or other hollow utensil); *wipe the* SLATE[1] *clean.* **2.** get rid of, clear *away* or *off* (*the* MAP[1]) or *up,* take *up,* wash *out,* by wiping (*wipe your tears* (*away*)); ~ **off,** annul (debt etc.); ~ **out,** remove (disgrace) by atonement, (insult etc.) esp. by vengeance, utterly destroy, annihilate, (*the whole army was wiped out*); ~-**out** *n.,* (1) obliteration of one radio signal by another, (2, sl.) fall from surf-board. **3.** spread (substance) over surface in thin layer. **4.** *n.* act of wiping (*give this plate a wipe*); (sl.) sweeping blow; (sl.) handkerchief. [OE *wīpian;* cf. OHG *wifan* wind round, Goth. *weipan* crown; rel. to WHIP]

wi'per *n.* In vbl senses; cam or tappet, (Electr.) moving contact; rubber strip mechanically moved to and fro across windscreen to remove rain etc. [f. prec. + -ER[1]]

WIPO *abbr.* World Intellectual Property Organization.

wīre *n.* & *v.* **1.** *n.* (piece of) metal drawn out into form of thread or slender flexible rod; quantity of this as barrier, framework, etc.; **pull** (**the**) ~**s,** operate puppets etc., (fig.) exert hidden influence. **2.** piece of wire used to carry electric current esp. of telegraph or telephone; **by** ~, by telegraph; **private** ~ (reserved for person's exclusive use); **get** one's or **the** ~**s crossed,** (fig.) become confused and misunderstand. **3.** (colloq.) telegram or cablegram (*sent me a wire*). **4.** ~-**bird,** St. Helena plover living on wire-grass; ~-**brush** (for cleaning rusty metal, or making hissing sound with cymbal etc.); ~-**cloth** (woven from wire); ~-**cutter,** tool for cutting wire; ~'**draw,** draw (metal) out into wire, elongate, protract unduly, (fig., esp. in *p.p.*) refine or apply or press (argument, point, etc.) with idle or excessive subtlety; ~-**edge,** turned-back edge formed when blade is badly sharpened; ~ **gauge,** (1) gauge for measuring diameter of wire etc., (2) standard series of sizes in which wire etc. is made; ~**gauze** (woven from wire); ~-**grass** (with wiry stems); ~ **gun** (made by coiling flat wire round tube); ~-**haired,** (esp. of dog) with stiff or wiry hair; ~'**man,** installer or repairer of electric wires; ~ **mattress,** wires stretched in frame as support for canvas etc. mattress; ~ **netting** (of wire twisted into meshes); ~'**puller,** politician etc. who pulls wires; ~ **rope** (made by twisting wires together as strands); ~'**scape,** obtrusive electric wires spoiling natural scenery; ~-**tapping,** eavesdropping on telephone conversations by tapping (TAP[1] 4); ~-**walker,** acrobat performing feats on wire rope; ~ **wheel,** vehicle-wheel with spokes of wire; ~ **wool,** mass of fine wire used esp. for cleaning kitchen utensils; ~-**worm,** destructive larva of click beetle; ~-**wove,** (of paper) = WOVE. **5.** *v.t.* provide, fasten, strengthen, etc., with wire(s); snare (bird, rabbit, etc.) with wire; (Electr.) install circuits for lighting in (a house etc.); (Croquet, usu. in *pass.*) obstruct (ball, shot, player) by hoop. **6.** *v.t.* & *i.* (colloq.) telegraph (*wire me the result; wired to him; was wired for*). [OE *wīr,* = MLG *wīre,* ON **vírr,* prob. cogn. w. WITHE]

wīr'elĕss (wīr'l-) *a., n.,* & *v.* **1.** *a.* without wire(s) (~ **telegraphy,** radio, transmission of signals by electromagnetic waves); ||of or pertaining to radio (~ **set,** radio receiver). **2.** *n.* wireless telegraphy or telegram;

||radio receiving set or broadcast or programme. **3.** *v.i.* send radio message. **4.** *v.t.* send (message), inform (person), by radio. [f. prec. + -LESS]

wīr'ing *n.* In vbl senses; electrical circuit(s) esp. in a building. [f. WIRE + -ING¹]

wīr'| y̆ *a.* made of wire; tough and flexible as wire, (of person) sinewy, untiring, whence ∼iLY² *adv.*, ∼īNESS *n.* [f. WIRE + -Y²]

wis *v.i. pres.* (pseudo-arch., parenth.) *I*, *you*, etc., know well. [orig. *I wis* = obs. *iwis* 'certainly' f. OE *gewis* (Y-, WIT¹), erron. taken as 'I know' and as pres. tense of *wist* (WIT¹)]

Wis. *abbr.* Wisconsin.

Wisd. *abbr.* Wisdom of Solomon (Apocrypha).

wi'sdom (-z-) *n.* being wise; (possession of) experience and knowledge together with the power of applying them critically or practically; sagacity, prudence, common sense; wise sayings (W∼ **of Solomon, W∼ of Jesus the Son of Sirach** = Ecclesiasticus, books of Apocrypha); **W∼ literature,** (1) books of philosophical reflections of life written in ancient Babylonia or Egypt, (2) biblical books of Job, Proverbs, Ecclesiastes, Wisdom of Solomon, Ecclesiasticus, Epistle of James; ∼ **tooth,** hindmost molar usu. cut at about 20 years of age (*cut one's* ∼ *teeth,* gain discretion). [OE *wīsdōm* = OS *wīsdōm,* OHG *wīstuom,* ON *vísdómr* (as WISE¹; see -DOM)]

wīse¹ (-z) *a.* & *v.* **1.** *a.* (Of person) having, (of action, course of action, speech, opinion, etc.) dictated by or in harmony with or showing, experience and knowledge judiciously applied; sagacious, prudent, sensible, discreet; having knowledge; ∼ **after the event,** (of person) who explains but has failed to foresee; *came away* **none the** or **not much** or **no** ∼**r** or **as** ∼ **as he went,** knowing no more than before; **without anyone's being the** ∼**r,** undetected. **2.** (arch.) having occult power or knowledge of mysterious things; ∼ **man,** wizard, esp. one of the Magi; ||∼ **woman,** (1) witch, fortune-teller, (2) midwife. **3.** suggestive of wisdom, oracular, (*with a wise shake of the head*); ∼**'crack** *n.,* & *v.i.,* (colloq.) (make) smart pithy remark or witticism; ∼ **guy,** (colloq.) know-all; ∼ **saw,** proverbial saying. **4.** *(sl.)* **be** or **get** ∼ **to,** be or become aware of; **put** person ∼ **(to),** inform him (of), enlighten him (concerning). **5.** Hence ∼'LY² (-zlī) *adv.* **6.** *v.t.* & *i.* *∼*∼ **up,** (sl.) = *put* or *get wise.* [OE *wīs,* = OS, OHG *wīs*(*i*), ON *víss,* Goth. *-weis* f. Gmc *wīsaz* (*wīttos* f. IE *weid-,* cogn. w. WIT¹)]

wīse² (-z) *n.* (arch.) way, manner, guise, (*in solemn* etc. *wise;* esp. *in some, no, any, wise; on this wise*). [OE *wīse* = OS, OHG *wīsa,* ON *vísa* f. Gmc *wīsōn,* *wīsō* f. *wit*- WIT¹]

-wise (-z) *suf.* forming *adjs.* & *advs.* of manner (*clockwise, crosswise, lengthwise, nowise*) or respect (*moneywise*); cf. -WAYS. [f. as prec.]

wi'seācre (-zāker) *n.* one who pretends to, or affects an air of, wisdom. [f. MDu. *wijsseggher* soothsayer, prob. f. OHG *wīssago,* *wīzago,* w. assim. to WISE¹, SAY²*er,* ACRE]

wi'sent (wē'z-) *n.* European bison (*Bison bonasus*). [G; cf. BISON]

wish *v.* & *n.* **1.** *v.t.* have as a desire or aspiration (*that*- -clause with *that* usu. omitted, or obj. and compl.: *wish (to God that) I had never been born, were* or *was a bird, may live to see it; wish you would be quiet; could not wish it better; wish* one*self dead, home,* etc.; *wish person happy, miles away,* etc.); *it is* **to be** ∼**ed** *that,* desirable; *I* ∼ **it may not** *prove true,* fear it will. **2.** want with the kind of desire that tends to affect result (*to do,* person or thing *to do,* person or thing and p.p., or w. simple obj. esp. pron.: *I wish to go, you to do it, it finished* or *to be finished; what do you wish?; they say they wish peace, an interview*). **3.** have desire that succeeding *well* or *ill* may befall or happen to (*wishes me well,* to all men, *nobody ill*), whence (-)∼'ER¹ *n.* **4.** say one hopes for (joy, luck, pleasant journey, sorrow, etc.) to happen to person

(*I wish you joy, wish success to each and all*); ∼ person **'good day'** etc., greet him thus; ∼ person **joy of,** (iron.) hope he will enjoy. **5.** (colloq.) foist (*up*)*on* person. **6.** *v.i.* have desire or aspiration; ∼ **for,** desire to have, express wish that one may have. **7.** ∼**'bone,** forked bone between neck and breast of bird (longer part of it from cooked bird when it is broken between two persons being said to entitle holder to magic fulfilment of any wish), object of similar shape. **8.** *n.* (expression of) desire or aspiration, request, implied command, (**the** ∼ **is father to the thought,** we believe thing because we wish it true; *if wishes were horses beggars would ride; has a great wish to go to sea; cannot grant your wish; has disregarded my wishes in the matter*), whence ∼'FUL *a.,* desiring (*to do;* ∼**ful thinking,** belief founded on wishes rather than facts); **best** or **good** ∼**es,** hopes felt or expressed for another's happiness etc.; ∼**-fulfilment,** tendency of subconscious desire to be satisfied in fantasy etc. **9.** thing desired (*have got my wish*). [OE *wy̆scan,* OHG *wunsken,* = ON *œskja* f. Gmc *wunskjan,* ult. cogn. w. WEEN, WONT¹]

wi'sh-wash (-ŏsh) *n.* washy drink or talk or writing. [redupl. of WASH²]

wi'shy̆-washy̆ (-wŏ-) *a.* (Of tea, soup, etc.) weak, sloppy; feeble or poor in quality or character. [redupl. of WASHY]

wisp *n.* small bundle or twist of straw etc.; small separate quantity *of* smoke, hair, etc.; small thin person etc.; hence ∼'Y² *a.* **2.** flock (of snipe). [ME, of uncert. orig.; cf. WFris. *wisp,* and WHISK]

wist. See WIT¹.

wistār'ia, wistēr'ia, *n.* climbing plant of genus *Wistaria,* with pendulous racemes of blue, purple, or white flowers. [f. C. *Wistar* (or *Wister*), Amer. anatomist d. 1818 + -IA¹]

wi'stful *a.* (Of person or looks etc.) affected with or betraying vague yearnings or mournfulness or unsatisfied desire to understand; hence ∼LY² *adv.,* ∼'NESS *n.* [app. assim. of obs. *wistly* adv. intently (cf. WHIST¹.²) to *wishful,* w. corresp. change of sense]

wit¹ *v.* (*sing. pres.* I, 3 **wot,** 2 **wo'ttest;** *past* & *p.p.* **wist;** *inf.* **wit;** *part.* WITTING; no other parts used). **1.** (arch.) know (*of*); **God wot** (knows); **I wot** (know well). **2.** **to** ∼, that is to say, namely. [OE *witan,* = OS *witan,* OHG *wizzan,* ON *vita,* Goth. *witan,* f. Gmc *wait*-, *wit*-, f. IE *woid-* etc.]

wit² *n.* **1.** (in *sing.* or *pl.*) intelligence, understanding, (*has not the wit, the wits, wit enough, to see; remedy is past the wit of man to devise; has quick, slow,* etc., *wits, a nimble wit,* whence (-)∼'tED² *a.*); **out of** one's ∼**s,** mad, distracted; **have** or **keep** one's ∼**s about** one, be alert or observant or of lively intelligence; **at** one's ∼'s or **wits' end,** utterly at a loss; **live by** one's ∼**s** (by ingenious or crafty expedients, without settled occupation); SET¹ one's **wits to;** **the five** ∼**s,** (arch.) the senses or the mind. **2.** (power of giving sudden intellectual pleasure by) unexpected combining or contrasting of previously unconnected ideas or expressions (*possessed of both wit and humour; pages sparkling with wit*). [OE *wit*(*t*), *gewit*(*t*), = OS *wit,* OHG *wizzi,* ON *vit,* Goth. *-witi* f. as prec.]

wit³ *n.* **1.** (arch.) person of great mental ability. **2.** witty person; person who talks wittily; hence ∼'LING¹ 2 *n.* [f. prec.]

witch *n.,* & *v.t.* **1.** *n.* woman practising sorcery (WHITE *witch; witches'* SABBATH); (fig.) fascinating or bewitching woman; ugly old woman, hag; flat-fish resembling the lemon sole. **2.** ∼ **ball,** coloured glass ball as formerly hung to repel witches; ∼'**craft,** sorcery, use of magic; ∼**-doctor,** tribal magician of primitive people; ∼**es' broom,** tufted gall caused by mites on birch etc.; ∼**-hunt,** search for witch(es), (fig.) search for suspected Communists or other persons with unorthodox views. **3.** *v.t.* bewitch (the ∼**ing time of night** [Shak. *Hamlet* III. ii. 406], time when witches are active, midnight); (fig.) fascinate, charm, whence ∼'ERY (4, 5) *n.*, ∼'ING² *a.* [OE *wicca* masc., *wicce* fem. (*wiccian* v., of unkn. orig.)]

witch-. See WYCH-.

wi'tchettў, -etў, *n.* (Austral.) large white larva of beetle or moth, eaten as food by Aborigines. [Aboriginal]

witenagĕmō't (-g-) *n.* (Hist.) Anglo-Saxon national council or parliament. [OE, f. *witena* gen. pl. of *wita* wise man (as WIT¹) + *gemōt* meeting (cf. MOOT)]

with (-dh) *prep.* **1.** in antagonism to, against, (*fight, quarrel, struggle, dispute, argue, compete, vie, with*). **2.** in or into company of or relation to, among, beside, (*come, go, walk, eat, live, spend the day or night with; king is expected with or together with queen and court; numbered with the transgressors*; (un)*connected with; associate one*self *with; our frontier with Canada;* COMPARE¹ *with;* have *a* WORD¹, WORD¹*s,* (*nothing*) *to* DO¹, *with;* DEAL² *with;* SLEEP² *with*); employed by (*he is with Shell*); ∼ **God,** dead and in heaven; **have** ∼ **you,** (arch.) I accept your offer or challenge; ∼ **it,** (colloq.) up to date, progressive, following latest fashions; **not** ∼ **you,** (colloq.) unable to follow your meaning. **3.** agreeably or in harmonious relations to (*I feel, think, sympathize, with you; am with you on that point;* w. neg. wds in opp. sense: *I disagree with you; he that is not with me is against me; vote with the Liberals; blue does not* GO¹ *with green*); **one** ∼, part of same whole as. **4.** having, carrying, possessed of, characterized by, (*vase with handles; man with sinister expression; walking with a gun; went out with no hat on;* ∼ **child** or **young,** pregnant. **5.** in the care or charge or possession of (*have no money with me; leave child, parcel, with nurse, porter; it rests with you to decide; the deal, decanter, next move, is with you*). **6.** by use of as instrument or means (*cut it with a knife; have no pen to write with; walks with a crutch; damn with faint praise*). **7.** by addition or supply or acquisition or possession of as material (*fill it, overflowing, with water; crawling with vermin; laden with baggage; threaten with dismissal; blessed with beauty; adorn with frescos*). **8.** in same way or direction or degree or at the same time as (*changes with the seasons; believes with Locke that; quantity varies directly or inversely, increases, with another; rise with the sun; with his death the barony becomes extinct*); ∼ **that,** thereupon, simultaneously, saying or having just said that; BEGIN *with.* **9.** because or by operation of, owing to, (*trembles with fear; is down with measles;* STIFF *with cold*). **10.** displaying or so as to display, under favourable or unfavourable circumstances of, (*heard it with calmness; fought with courage; handle with care; won with ease, difficulty, a good deal to spare; shot well with a good, wretched, light*); under accompanying conditions of (*sleep with the window open; speak with one's mouth full; holiday with all expenses paid; with a song in my heart; with a cold east wind blowing*). **11.** in regard to, concerning, in the sphere of, in the mind or view of, (*be patient with him; with God all things are possible; it is holiday time with us; has great influence with the President; my dealings with the plaintiff; what do you want with me?; can be dispensed with*); **away, down, in,** OFF, OUT, **on, up, to the devil,** etc., ∼ **him** or **it,** take or send or put him or it, he may go, away etc. **12.** despite, notwithstanding, the presence of (*with all his learning, he is the simplest of men; with many admirable qualities, the best of intentions, he failed completely*). [OE, = OS *with,* prob. shortened f. Gmc prep. corresp. to OE *wither,* OHG *widar* against]

witha'l (-dhaw'l) *adv. & prep.* (arch.) **1.** *adv.* with it, in addition, moreover, as well, at the same time. **2.** *prep.* (esp. at end of rel. clause or question). with (*what shall he fill his belly withal?*). [ME, f. prec. + ALL]

withdraw' (-dh-) *v.* (**withdrew'**; ∼**n**). **1.** *v.t.* pull aside or back (*withdraw curtain,* one's *hand*); take away, remove, (*child from school, coins from circulation, money from bank, horse from race, troops from position, favour etc. from person*); retract (*offer, statement, promise,* or *abs.*; in *imper.,* as demand that a speaker shall retract something as unparliamentary etc.); (in *p.p.*) mentally detached,

unsociable. **2.** *v.i.* retire from presence or place, go aside or apart; adopt detached mental attitude; ∼**ing-room,** (arch.) drawing-room. [ME, f. *with-away* (as WITH) + DRAW¹]

withdraw'al (-dh-) *n.* act of withdrawing; process of ceasing to take addictive drugs, often with unpleasant physical reaction (*withdrawal symptoms*). [f. prec. + -AL 2]

withe (with, widh), **wi'thў** (-dhi), *n.* tough flexible branch esp. of willow or osier used for binding bundles etc. [OE *withthe, withig,* = OHG *wit(hi)* etc., ON *vith(ja)* f. Gmc *withōn,* cogn. w. WIRE]

wi'ther (-dh-) *v.t. & i.* make or become dry and shrivelled (*up*), deprive of or lose vigour or vitality or freshness or importance (*away*), decline, languish, decay, (*has a withered arm; flowers and beauty wither; age cannot wither her*); blight with scorn etc., put out of action with gun-fire etc., whence ∼ING² *a.* [ME, app. var. of WEATHER², different. for certain senses]

wi'thers (-dherz) *n. pl.* ridge between horse's shoulder-blades (**my** ∼ **are unwrung,** imputation etc. does not affect me, f. Shak. *Hamlet* III. ii. 252). [app. reduced f. (16th c.) *widersome* or *-sone,* f. *wider-, wither-* against (cf. WITH), as the part that resists strain of collar; second element obscure]

wi'thershins (-dh-; -z), **wi'dder-,** *adv.* (esp. Sc.) in a direction contrary to apparent course of sun (considered as unlucky), anticlockwise. [f. MLG *wedder-sins* f. MHG *widdersinnes* (*wider* against, *sin* direction)]

withhō'ld (-dh-h-) *v.t.* (**withhe'ld**). refrain from putting into action, refuse to grant, (*withhold* one's *consent, support*); hold back, restrain, (*from*); *∼*∼**ing tax** (deducted from income at source). [ME, f. *with-away* (as WITH) + HOLD¹]

withi'n (-dh-) *adv. & prep.* **1.** *adv.* (arch. or literary). inside, to or at or on the inside, in(to) house or room, internally, (*clean within and without; as seen from within; beauty without and foulness within*); in spirit (*make me pure within*); Bishopsgate ∼, inside the city walls. **2.** *prep.* to or on or in the inside of, enclosed by, (∼ **doors,** in or into house; WHEEL¹*s within wheels*). **3.** not beyond, not too far for, not transgressing, so as not to pass or exceed, subject to, (*live or keep within one's income; acting within one's rights; keep it within bounds; a task well within his powers*); ∼ **the meaning of the Act** etc., covered by it; ∼ **the law,** not illegal; ∼ one*self,* not putting forth whole power; *within* REASON¹. **4.** not too far for, near enough to affect or be affected by, not farther off than (*of* w. sense 'from', or abs.; *is within three miles of a station; was within an ace of destruction*); ∼ **reach,** SIGHT¹, **call,** near enough to reach or be reached etc. (*within sight of port*). **5.** in a time no longer than, before expiration or since beginning of, (*of* w. sense 'from', or abs.; *shall have it within an hour; within a year of his death, within the or a year, all was changed; have seen him within these last three days*). [OE *withinnan* on the inside (as WITH, *innan* adv. & prep. within, f. as IN²)]

withou't (-dh-) *adv., prep., & conj.* **1.** *adv.* (arch. or literary). outside, to or at or on the outside, out of or outside house or room, externally, (*white within and without; as seen from without; stands disconsolate without; listening to the wind without*); in outward appearance (*a prince without but a beggar within*); Bishopsgate ∼, outside the city walls. **2.** *prep.* not having, not with, with no, devoid of, lacking, in want of, free from, with freedom from, not feeling or showing, in or with absence of, (*came without a hat; a rose without a thorn; am without friends or money; did it without difficulty or being discovered or anyone's noticing; act without hesitation; cannot live without her, go away without thanking you; is absolutely without fear, anxiety; times without* NUMBER¹; *train left without us; one cannot make an* OMELETTE *without breaking eggs; without health happiness is impossible*); DO¹ or GO¹ *without* (thing expressed or implied); *without* (*a*) DOUBT¹; ∼ **end,** infinite, eternal; *without* FAIL¹, PREJUDICE, RESERVE²; *go without* SAYING. **3.** (arch.) on the outside of, outside, (*met us without the gates; is* *without the pale of civilization*); **things ~ us,** all that is not ourselves. **4.** *conj.* (arch. or vulg.) unless. [OE *withūtan* (as WITH, *ūtan* from outside f. as OUT)]

withstǎ'nd (-dh-) *v.* (**withstoo'd**). **1.** *v.t.* resist, oppose, (person, force, hardship, wear, etc.). **2.** *v.i.* make opposition, offer resistance. [OE *withstandan* (*with-* against, cf. WITH; STAND¹)]

withy. See WITHE.

wi'tlĕss *a.* foolish; crazy; stupid; lacking wit; hence ~LY² *adv.,* ~NESS *n.* [OE *witlēas* (as WIT², -LESS)]

wi'tling. See WIT³.

wi'tloof (-ōf) *n.* chicory plant; its salad leaves. [Du., = white leaf]

wi'tnĕss *n.* & *v.* **1.** *n.* testimony, evidence, (**bear ~ to** or **of,** state one's belief in, state or be fact(s) tending to establish); confirmation (*stands there in witness of the event*; **call to ~,** appeal to for confirmation); thing or person whose existence, position, state, etc., serves as testimony *to* or proof of (*is a living witness to my clemency*). **2.** = EYE¹*witness*; person present at event. **3.** person giving sworn testimony in lawcourt or for legal purpose; person attesting genuineness of signature to document by adding his own signature; ||**~-box,** **~* **stand,** enclosure in lawcourt from which witnesses give evidence. **4.** *v.t.* (arch.) state in evidence (thing, *that,* etc.); indicate, serve as evidence of, (*a deathly pallor witnessed his agitation*). **5.** see, be spectator of; act as witness of (document, signature, etc.). **6.** *v.i.* give evidence (*against, for*); serve as evidence (*against, for, to*); (**as**) **~ my poverty,** of which let my poverty be proof. [OE *witnes* (as WIT², -NESS)]

wi'tter *v.i.* (colloq.) **~ (on),** speak with annoying lengthiness on trivial matters. [20th c.; prob. imit.]

wi'tticǐsm *n.* (usu. derog.) witty remark, jest. [coined by Dryden (1677) f. WITTY, after *criticism*]

wi'tting *a.* aware, intentional; hence ~LY² *adv.* [ME, f. WIT¹ + -ING²]

wi'ttol *n.* (arch.) acquiescent cuckold. [ME *wetewold,* app. formed by substitution of *wete* WIT¹ for first syllable of *cokewold* CUCKOLD]

wi'tt|ȳ *a.* full of WIT² (sense 2); capable of or fond of saying things that are brilliantly or sparklingly amusing; hence ~ĭLY² *adv.,* ~ĭNESS *n.* [OE *wit(t)ig* (as WIT², -Y²)]

wīve *v.t.* & *i.* (arch.) provide with, take, wife. [OE *wīfian* (as WIFE)]

wī'vern. Var. of WYVERN.

wives. See WIFE.

wiz *n.* & *a.* (sl.) wizard. [abbr.]

wi'zard *n.* & *a.* **1.** *n.* magician, sorcerer; person who effects seeming impossibilities; conjurer; hence ~RY (4, 5) *n.* **2.** *a.* (sl.) wonderful, excellent. [ME, f. WISE¹ + -ARD)]

wi'zened (-nd), **wi'zen, wea'zen,** *a.* of shrivelled or dried-up appearance (chiefly of person or his face or look). [p.p. of *wizen* shrivel f. OE *wisnian,* = OHG *wesanēn,* ON *visna* f. Gmc **wis-*]

wk. *abbr.* weak; week; work.

Wm. *abbr.* William.

WMO *abbr.* World Meteorological Organization.

WNW *abbr.* west-north-west.

wō *int.* = WHOA. [var. of *who* int., HO]

WO *abbr.* Warrant Officer.

w.o. *abbr.* walk-over.

woad *n.,* & *v.t.* **1.** *n.* (plant, *Isatis tinctoria,* yielding) kind of blue dye now superseded by indigo. **2.** *v.t.* dye with woad. [OE *wād,* = OHG *weit* f. Gmc **waida-, *waisda-*]

wǒ'bbĕgŏng *n.* (Austral.) = CARPET-*shark.* [Aboriginal]

wǒ'bbl|e, wa'bbl|e (wǒ'-), *v.i.,* & *n.* **1.** *v.i.* (Of top or revolving body) revolve with changing inclinations, rock; (of person, missile, etc.) go unsteadily, vibrate or tilt from side to side, swerve, stagger; (fig.) vacillate, waver, act inconsistently, be inconstant; (of voice or sound) quaver, pulsate; hence ~ER¹ *n.,*

~Y² *a.* **2.** *n.* wobbling movement, change of direction or policy, swerve, piece of vacillation. [corresp. to LG *wabbeln,* ON *vafla* waver f. Gmc **wabh-*; cf. WAVE¹, WAVER, -LE 3]

||**wǒdge** *n.* (colloq.) chunk, lump. [alt. f. WEDGE]

wōe *n.* (arch., literary, or joc.) affliction, bitter grief, distress, (*tale of woe*; **weal and ~,** prosperity and adversity; **~ is me,** alas; **~ be (un)to,** a curse upon; **woe** WORTH² *the day*); (in *pl.*) calamities, troubles; **~'begone,** dismal-looking [*begone* p.p. of *bego* f. OE BE(*gān* GO¹) surround]. [OE *wā, wē,* = OS, OHG *wē,* ON *vei, væ,* Goth. *wai,* f. Gmc **wai,* natural excl. of lament]

wō'eful (wō'f-) *a.* afflicted with distress; bad, unpleasant, wretched; hence ~LY² *adv.* [ME, f. prec. + -FUL]

wǒg¹ *n.* (sl., derog.; **R**) native of Middle East; foreigner. [20th c.; orig. unkn.]

wǒg² *n.* (Austral. sl.) (micro-organism causing) infectious illness. [20th c.; orig. unkn.]

wǒ'ggle *n.* loop of leather round Scout's neckerchief. [20th c.; orig. unkn.]

woke(n). See WAKE¹.

wōld *n.* piece of open uncultivated esp. elevated country, downland or moorland. [OE *wald,* = OS, OHG *wald* forest, ON *völlr* field f. Gmc **walthus,* perh. rel. to WILD; cf. WEALD]

wolf (wŏŏ-) *n.* (*pl.* **wolves** *pr.* -vz), & *v.t.* **1.** *n.* erect- -eared straight-tailed coarse-furred tawny-grey fierce usu. gregarious carnivorous doglike mammal of genus *Canis,* esp. *Canis lupus,* preying on sheep etc. in combining in packs to hunt larger animals; **cry ~** (**too often**), raise false alarm (till genuine one is disregarded); **have** or **hold a ~ by the ears,** be in a precarious situation; **keep the ~ from the door,** avert hunger or starvation; **lone ~,** person who prefers to act alone; **~ in sheep's clothing,** malicious person who pretends friendship; **throw to the wolves,** sacrifice without compunction. **2.** rapacious or greedy person; (sl.) man who aggressively seeks women for sexual purposes. **3.** (Mus.) jarring sound from some notes in bowed instrument; out-of-tune effect when playing certain chords on old organs (before present 'equal temperament' was in use). **4. ~-cub,** (1) young wolf, (2) ||(former name for) Cub Scout; **~-dog,** (1) dog kept to guard sheep from or hunt wolves, (2) dog-and-wolf hybrid; **~-fish,** large voracious blenny of genus *Anarhichas*; **~'hound,** borzoi or other dog used (orig.) to hunt wolves; **~-pack,** attacking-group of submarines or aircraft; **~'sbane,** aconite, esp. *Aconitum lycoctonum*; **~'s-claw, ~'s-foot,** club-moss; **~'skin,** (mat, cloak, etc., made of) wolf's skin; **~'s-milk,** spurge; **~ spider** (of family Lycosidae, chasing instead of netting prey); **~-tooth,** supernumerary premolar in horse; **~-whistle,** whistle of a man admiring sexually, and trying to attract the attention of, a woman. **5.** Hence ~ISH¹ *a.* **6.** *v.t.* devour or swallow greedily (*down*). [OE *wulf,* = OS *wulf,* OHG *wolf,* ON *ulfr,* Goth. *wulfs* f. Gmc **wulfaz* f. IE **wlq ⁰os*]

wo'lfram (wŏŏ'-) *n.* **1. ~(ite),** ore yielding tungsten, native tungstate of iron and manganese. **2.** tungsten. [G, perh. f. *wolf* WOLF + *rahm* cream, or MHG *rām* dirt, soot]

wo'lverine (wŏŏ-; -ēn), **-ēne,** *n.* Amer. GLUTTON 2; its fur; ***W~ State,** Michigan. [16th c. *wolvering,* somehow derived f. *wolv-,* st. of WOLF]

wolves. See WOLF.

wo'man (wŏŏ'-) *n.* (*pl.* **women** *pr.* wĭ'mĭn), & *v.t.* **1.** *n.* adult human female; *make an* HONEST *woman of*; INNER *woman*; LITTLE *woman*; OLD *woman*; **the other ~** (who attracts married man so that he deserts or neglects his wife); OUTER *woman*; **play the ~,** weep or show fear; *woman with a* PAST¹; SCARLET *woman*; **~ of the streets,** prostitute; *woman of the* WORLD 6; ||**Women's Institute,** organization of women in rural areas to meet regularly and engage in crafts etc.; **Women's**

Lib(eration), movement urging liberation of women from domestic duties and subservient status; ~'s or **women's rights,** position of legal and social equality with men. **2.** the average or typical woman, the female sex, any woman, (*how does woman differ from man?*); (in *pl.*) women as partners in illicit sexual activity; **man born of** ~, mortal man; ~'s **wit,** instinctive insight or resource. **3.** (colloq.) charwoman; (arch.) queen's or great lady's female attendant, lady-in-waiting; ||~ **of the bedchamber** (ranking below LADY *of the bedchamber*). **4.** man with feminine characteristics (*is a woman in tenderness*); OLD *woman.* **5.** the feminine emotions (*all the woman in her rose in rebellion*; *stirred the woman in him*). **6.** *attrib.* female (*woman driver, doctor, friend*; *women doctors*); *woman* SUFFRAGE. **7.** *suf.* (chiefly in terms correl. to compounds in *-man*). woman concerned or dealing or skilful with or describable as (*countrywoman,* HORSE¹-*woman,* NEEDLE*woman,* GENTLEWOMAN). **8.** ~**-hater,** misogynist; ~**kind,** wo'**menkind,** women in general (one's ~*kind,* the women of one's family); wo'**menfolk,** women, one's womankind. **9.** Hence ~HOOD *n.* (= female maturity, womanly instinct, womankind), ~LESS, ~LIKE, *adjs.* **10.** *v.t.* (arch.) make behave like a woman, cause to weep etc. **11.** equip with staff of women; address or speak of as 'woman' (not 'lady'). [OE *wīfmon(n), -man(n)* (as WIFE, MAN¹), a formation peculiar to English, the ancient wd being WIFE]

wo'manish (wŏŏ'-) *a.* (Of a man or his feelings, conduct, looks, etc.) like women or their ways etc. (usu. derog.), effeminate; hence ~LY² *adv.,* ~NESS *n.* [ME, f. prec. + -ISH¹]

wo'manize (wŏŏ'-), **-ise** (-īz), *v.* **1.** *v.t.* make womanish. **2.** *v.i.* (Of a man) philander, consort illicitly with women. [f. WOMAN + -IZE]

wo'manl|ȳ (wŏŏ'-) *a.* (Of a woman or her feelings, conduct, etc.) having or showing the qualities befitting a woman, not masculine or girlish, (*womanly modesty, compassion, tact, etc.*); hence ~INESS *n.* [ME, f. WOMAN + -LY¹]

womb (wŏŏm) *n.* organ in woman and other female mammals in which child or young is conceived and nourished till birth, uterus, (FRUIT *of the womb*); (fig.) place of conception and development (*future events in the womb of time*). [OE *wamb, womb,* = OHG *wamba,* ON *vǫmb,* Goth. *wamba*]

wo'mbat *n.* Australian herbivorous marsupial mammal esp. of genus *Phascolomis,* like small bear. [Aboriginal]

women. See WOMAN.

won. See WIN.

wo'nder¹ (wŭ'-) *n.* **1.** miracle, prodigy, strange or remarkable thing or specimen or performance or event, (**do** or **work** ~**s,** do miracles, succeed remarkably; ~**s will never cease,** (iron.) this is indeed surprising); marvellously successful thing, precocious child, etc.; NINE *days'* wonder; **the seven** ~**s of the world,** seven remarkable structures so called in antiquity; **the** ~ **is,** what is surprising is; **for a** ~, (esp.) by way of welcome exception (*you are punctual for a wonder*); **what** ~, **small** ~, **it is no** ~, **no** ~, (that), naturally, inevitably, of course, one cannot be surprised or might have guessed that. **2.** emotion excited by what surpasses expectation or experience or seems inexplicable, surprise mingled with admiration or curiosity or bewilderment, (*were filled with wonder; looked at him in silent* or *open-mouthed wonder*). **3.** ~**land,** fairyland, land full of surprises or marvels; ~**-stricken, -struck,** filled with or made dumb by wonder; ~**-worker,** one who performs miracles. [OE *wundor,* = OS *wundar,* OHG *wuntar,* ON *undr,* of unkn. orig.]

wo'nder² (wŭ'-) *v.* **1.** *v.i.* be filled with wonder, feel surprise, (*at, to see* etc., or abs.); **I shouldn't** ~ **if,** (colloq.) I think it likely that; hence ~ING² *a.,* ~MENT

n. **2.** *v.t.* be surprised to find (*that*). **3.** feel curiosity about, desire to know (*wonder what the time is, how to proceed,* etc.); express tentative inquiry (*I wonder whether I might open the window*); **I** ~, (as excl.) I very much doubt it. [OE *wundrian* (as prec.)]

wo'nderful (wŭ'-) *a.* marvellous, surprising, exceeding (esp. better than) what was expected, remarkable, admirable; hence ~LY² *adv.* [OE *wunderfull* (as WONDER¹, -FUL)]

wo'ndrous (wŭ'-) *a.* & *adv.* (poet. or rhet.) **1.** *a.* wonderful; hence ~LY² *adv.,* ~NESS *n.* **2.** *adv.* (qualifying *adjs.* only). wonderfully (*wondrous kind*). [alt. f. obs. *wonders* a. & adv. (gen. of WONDER¹; cf. -s³), after *marvellous*]

wŏ'nga(-wŏnga) *n.* large Austral. pigeon. [Aboriginal]

||**wŏ'nký** *a.* (sl.) shaky, groggy; unreliable. [fanciful formation]

wŏnt¹ *pred. a.* (arch. or literary). accustomed *to* do (*as he was wont to say*). [OE *gewunod* p.p. of *gewunian* (*wunian* dwell)]

wŏnt² *v.* (3 *sing.* *pres.* *ind.* ~s or ~; *past* ~ or ~'ed). (arch.) **1.** *v.t.* accustom *to.* **2.** *v.i.* be accustomed. [ME, f. prec. or as back-form. f. WONTED]

wŏnt³ *n.* (arch. or literary). what is customary or general or habitual to a person (*according to his wont; it is my wont to,* **use and** ~, established custom). [16th c., of doubtful orig., perh. f. obs. *wone* habit and WONT¹]

won't. See WILL¹.

wo'nted *attrib. a.* habitual to person, accustomed, usual, (*heard me with his wonted courtesy; met with the wonted obstacles*). [either f. WONT³ + -ED², or an extension of WONT¹ with -ED¹]

woo *v.t.* (literary). **1.** ask in marriage, court, (woman, or abs.); hence ~'ER¹ *n.* **2.** pursue, seek to win, (fame, fortune, etc.); coax, importune, try to persuade, (person usu. *to* do or *to* compliance etc.). [OE *wōgian* v.i., *āwōgian* v.t., of unkn. orig.]

wŏŏd *n.* **1.** (in *sing.* or *pl.*) growing trees occupying fairly densely a considerable tract of ground; one **cannot see the** ~ **for the trees,** details impede general view; **out of the** ||~ or *~s,* out of danger etc.; **don't halloo till you are out of the** ||~ or *~s,* do not assume too soon that difficulties are over; hence (-)~'ED³ *a.* **2.** hard compact fibrous substance between pith and bark of trunks and branches of tree, whether growing or cut for timber or fuel or use in arts and crafts; timber, fuel, etc., of this; **touch** ~, *knock* (on) ~, put hand etc. against something wooden (as superstition to avert ill luck, or to avoid capture in children's game). **3.** the cask or unbottled storage of wine etc. (*in, from, the wood*). **4.** (Bowls) = BOWL² 1; (Golf) wooden-headed club. **5.** ~ **alcohol,** methyl alcohol; ~ **anemone,** wild spring-flowering anemone; ~'**bine** or ~'**bind,** wild honeysuckle, *Virginia creeper; ~'**block** (from which woodcuts are made); ~'**cock,** game-bird related to snipe; ~'**craft,** (1) knowledge of forest conditions esp. as applied in hunting etc., (2) skill in woodwork; ~'**cut,** (print, usu. as illustration in book, taken from) piece of wood carved in relief; ~'**cutter,** (1) man who cuts wood, (2) maker of woodcuts; ~**-engraver,** (1) maker of woodcuts, (2) beetle that bores in wood; ~**-fibre,** fibre got from wood esp. as material for paper; ~**-gas** (from distillation of wood, used for lighting etc.); ||~ **grouse,** capercaillie; *wood* HYACINTH; ~ **ibis,** Amer. wading bird frequenting wooded swamps; ~'**land,** wooded country, woods, (often attrib.: *woodland scenery*); ~'**lark,** lark (*Lullula arborea*) perching on trees; ~**-leopard,** spotted moth whose larva bores into trees; ~**-louse,** small isopod land crustacean of genus *Oniscus* etc. found in old wood, often able to roll itself into a ball; ~'**man,** forester, woodcutter; ~**-notes,** spontaneous bird--song or poetry; ~**-nymph,** (1) dryad or hamadryad, (2) species of humming-bird and moth; ~ **paper**

(made of wood-pulp); ~'**pecker,** bird of family Picidae that clings to tree-trunks and taps them to discover insects; ~'**pie,** greater spotted woodpecker; ~-**pigeon,** ring-dove; ~'**pile,** stack of wood esp. for fuel (NIGGER *in the woodpile*); ~-**pulp,** wood-fibre reduced chemically or mechanically to pulp as material for paper; ~'**ruff,** white-flowered plant of genus *Asperula,* esp. *sweet* ~*ruff* grown esp. for fragrance of its whorled leaves when dried or crushed; ~'**rush,** grassy herb of genus *Luzula; wood--SCREW;* ~-**shed** (where wood is stored esp. for fuel); ~'**sman** (-z-), dweller in or frequenter of woods, person skilled in woodcraft; ~-**smoke** (from burning of wood); ~ **sorrel,** plant of genus *Oxalis* with trifoliate leaves and white or pink flowers; ~ **spirit,** crude methyl alcohol got from wood; ~-**spurge,** species of spurge with greenish-yellow flower--clusters; ~ **tar** (got from wood); ~-**warbler,** bird *Phylloscopus sibilatrix,* ***warbler;** ~-**wasp,** wasp that hangs nests in tree or burrows in rotten wood; ~'**waxen,** dyer's broom [OE *weaxe* (as WAX²)]; ~-**wind,** orchestral wind instruments made (orig.) of wood; ~-**wool,** fine pine etc. shavings used as surgical dressing or for packing; ~'**work,** (1) work done in wood, (2) things made of wood, esp. the wooden part of a house etc.; ~'**worm,** wood-boring larva of furniture beetle; ~-**yard** (where wood is used or stored). **6.** Hence ~ LESS *a.* [OE *wudu, wi(o)du,* = OHG *witu,* ON *vithr* f. Gmc *widuz]

Woŏ'dburȳtype *n.* (process of making) print from metal plate to which gelatine film from photographic negative is transferred. [f. W. B. *Woodbury,* Engl. inventor d. 1885, + TYPE¹]

woŏ'dchŭck *n.* reddish-brown and grey N. Amer. marmot. [f. Amer. Ind. name; cf. Cree *wuchak, otchock*]

woŏ'den *a.* **1.** made of wood (*wooden stool, leg*); ~ **horse** (by use of which Troy was taken; cf. TROJAN); *wooden* SPOON¹; ~ **walls,** ships as defence. **2.** like wood, stiff, clumsy, without animation or flexibility, inexpressive, (*wooden movements, manners, stare, face*); ~**head(ed),** stupid (person); hence ~LY² *adv.,* ~NESS (-n-n-) *n.* [f. WOOD + -EN⁵]

***woŏ'dsȳ** (-zī) *a.* silvan. [irreg. f. WOODS + -Y²]

woŏ'dlȳ *a.* (Of region) abounding in woods, well--wooded; of the nature, consisting, of wood (*the woody parts of a plant; woody stem, tissue*); (of plant) forming stem and branches of wood (*woody* NIGHTSHADE); hence ~iNESS *n.* [ME, f. WOOD + -Y²]

woŏ'er. See WOO.

woŏf¹ *n.* = WEFT¹. [OE *ōwef,* alt. f. *ōwebb* (after *wefan* WEAVE¹) f. as A- 1, WEB; *w*- f. assoc. w. *warp*]

woŏf² *n.,* & *v.i.* (give) gruff bark of dog; hence ~'ER¹ *n.,* loudspeaker for accurately reproducing low--frequency signals (cf. TWEETER). [imit.]

woŏl *n.* **1.** kind of hair distinguished by fineness, softness, wavy structure, and scaly surface, forming fleece of sheep, goat, alpaca, etc., and occurring mixed with ordinary hair in coat of some other animals; DYE²*d in the wool; much cry and little* ~, much talk or effort but disappointing result, fiasco; **go for** ~ **and come home shorn,** have tables turned on one; **pull the** ~ **over** person's **eyes,** deceive him; hence (-)~(I)ED² (-Id) *a.* **2.** woollen yarn, worsted; woollen garments or cloth (*safest to wear wool*). **3.** soft short under-fur or down. **4.** Negro's short curly hair, (joc.) any person's hair; **lose** one's ~, (sl.) show anger. **5.** kinds of wool-like substance (COTTON¹, GLASS, LEAD¹, STEEL, WIRE, WOOD~, *wool*); **mineral** ~ (made from molten slag subjected to strong blast, and used for packing walls etc.). **6.** ~-**carding, -combing,** processes by which short, long, wool is prepared for spinning; ~-**dyed,** DYE²*d* in the wool; ~-**fat,** lanolin; ||~-**fell,** skin of sheep etc. with fleece still on; ~-**gathering,** absent--minded(ness), dreamy or inattentive (mood); ||~-**grower,** one who breeds sheep for wool; ~-**oil,**

suint; ~-**pack,** fleecy cumulus cloud, (Hist.) bale of wool; ||W~'**sack,** large wool-stuffed cushion on which Lord Chancellor sits in House of Lords (*reach* etc. *the W*~*sack,* become Lord Chancellor; *take seat on the W*~*sack,* open proceedings in House of Lords); ~-**skin,** = *wool-fell;* ~-**sorters' disease,** anthrax; ~-**stapler,** one who grades producer's wool and sells to manufacturer; ~-**work,** embroidery with wools on canvas etc. [OE *wull,* = OHG *wolla,* ON *ull,* Goth. *wulla* f. Gmc *wullō f. IE **wl̥na*]

woŏ'llen, *woŏ'len, *a.* & *n.* **1.** *a.* made (partly) of wool, esp. from short fibres. **2.** *n.* woollen fabric, as blanket, flannel, cloth; (in *pl.*) woollen garments; ~-**draper,** (Hist.) retailer of woollens. [OE *wullen* (as prec., -EN⁵)]

woŏ'llȳ *a.* & *n.* **1.** *a.* bearing or naturally covered with wool or wool-like hair; (Bot.) downy; ~-**bear,** large hairy caterpillar esp. of tiger-moth. **2.** resembling or suggesting wool (*woolly hair, clouds*). **3.** (Of sound) indistinct; (Paint.) lacking in definition or luminosity or incisiveness; (of mind or thought) confused and hazy; WILD *and woolly.* **4.** Hence **woŏ'lliNESS** *n.* **5.** *n.* (colloq.) woollen garment, ||esp. knitted one or *undergarment. [f. WOOL + -Y²]

woŏ'mera *n.* (Austral.) Aboriginal throwing-stick for dart or spear, or club used as missile. [Aboriginal]

***woŏ'z|ȳ** *a.* (colloq.) dizzy, unsteady; dazed or slightly drunk; vague; hence ~ĭLY² *adv.,* ~ĭNESS *n.* [19th c., of unkn. orig.]

wŏp¹. Var. of WHOP.

***wŏp**² *n.* (sl., derog.) Italian or other S. European, esp. as immigrant in US. [20th c.; orig. unkn.]

Worcester (woŏ'ster) *n.* ~(shire) **sauce,** pungent sauce first made in Worcester. [~ in England]

Worcs. *abbr.* Worcestershire (former county in England).

word¹ (wêrd) *n.* **1.** any sound or combination of sounds (or its written or printed symbol, customarily shown with a space on either side of it but none within it) forming meaningful element of speech, conveying an idea or alternative ideas, and capable of serving as a member of, the whole of, or a substitute for, a sentence; basic unit of expression of data and instructions in computer; **at a** ~, as soon as requested; **have no** ~**s for,** be unable to express; **in a** or **one** ~, briefly, to sum up; **in other** ~**s,** expressing the same thing differently; **not a** ~ **of it,** no part whatever (of story etc.); *is* **not the** ~ **for it,** not an adequate description; **put into** ~**s,** express in speech or writing as well as in thought; ~ **for** ~, *repeat* etc. in exactly the same words, *translate* literally; **a** ~ **to the wise,** = VERB. SAP. **2.** speech (*honest in word and deed; bold in word only*); **by** ~ **of mouth,** in speech (only). **3.** (in *sing.* or *pl.*) thing said, saying, remark, conversation; (in *pl.*) text of song, actor's part, etc.; (**hard, high,** etc.) ~**s,** angry talk (*have* ~*s,* quarrel *with*); thing (merely) said (and not done); BIG *words;* EAT one's *words;* **of few** ~**s,** taciturn; GOOD *word;* **have a** ~ **to say,** know something worth hearing; **have a** ~, converse briefly (*with*); HOUSEHOLD *word;* LAST³ *word;* **of many** ~**s,** talkative; (**not) in so many** ~**s,** (not) explicitly or bluntly; **say the** ~, give the order etc.; **say a few** ~**s,** make a short speech; **suit the action to the** ~, do at once what has been threatened etc.; **take** person **at his** ~, act on assumption that he means what he says; **too** *funny* etc. **for** ~**s** (inexpressibly); WASTE² *words;* ~ **of command,** word or phrase giving instruction (esp. in drill etc.); *words* FAIL² *me;* W~ (of God), (1) Bible or part of it, (2) title of Second Person, incarnate in Christ, = LOGOS; *a word in* SEASON; **not have a** ~ **to throw at a dog,** be unsociably or superciliously taciturn. **4.** news, intelligence, a message, (*send* or *leave word that* or *of; word came that* or *of; the word got round that; the word is, word has it, that*); **send** ~, have message taken (*that,* to do, etc.). **5.** one's promise, assurance, or responsible statement; **give** person, **give, pledge,** one's ~, make promise; **keep, break,** one's ∼, do, fail to do, what one has promised; **I give you my ∼ for it,** promise it shall be or state that it is so; **take** person's ∼ **for it,** accept his statement that it is so; **upon my ∼** (form of asseveration); **(upon) my ∼** (excl. at something that shocks or surprises); ∼ **of honour,** promise or statement made upon one's HONOUR¹; **a man of his ∼,** one who keeps his promises; **be as good as, better than,** one's ∼, fulfil, exceed, what one has promised; **his ∼ is (as good as) his bond** (may be relied on). **6.** command, order, password, motto, *(his word is law; give the word to do or for; act promptly at the word; must give the word before you can pass);* SHARP¹*'s the word.* **7.** ∼**-blind, -deaf,** incapacitated by kinds of brain defect from attaching meaning to words seen or heard; ∼'**book,** book with list(s) of words, vocabulary; ∼**-game** (in which words are thought of, guessed, etc.); ∼ **order,** arrangement of words in sentence etc.; ∼**-painter, -painting,** vivid descriptive writer, writing; ∼**-per'fect,** knowing part, lesson, etc., by heart; ∼**-picture,** piece of word--painting; ∼**-play,** joke using features of words, pun, etc.; ∼ **processor,** device recording and displaying typed words for editing and automatically printing in desired format; ∼'**smith,** skilled user or maker of words; ∼**-square,** set of words of equal length so chosen that when they are written under each other the letters read downward in columns give the same words, e.g. *too old ode.* **8.** Hence ∼'AGE (1) *n.,* ∼'LESS *a.* [OE, = OS *word,* OHG *wort,* ON *orth,* Goth. *waurd* f Gmc *wordam]

word² (werd) *v.t.* put into words, phrase, select words to express; hence ∼'ING¹ (1, 2, 6) *n.* [ME, f. prec.]

wor'di̧y (wer'-) *a.* tending to use, expressed in, (too) many words; in, consisting of, words *(wordy warfare);* hence ∼ī̧LY² *adv.,* ∼ī̧NESS *n.* [OE *wordig* (as WORD¹, -Y²)]

wore. See WEAR¹,³.

work¹ (werk) *n.* **1.** expenditure of energy, striving, application of effort or exertion to a purpose, *(all work and no play, never does a stroke of work; never liked, will do no, work);* **at** ∼, engaged in work, operating; **set to** ∼, (cause to) begin operations; ∼**-to-rule,** act of WORK²ing to rule. **2.** (Phys.) exertion of force overcoming resistance or producing molecular change *(convert heat into work);* **internal** ∼ (exerted on molecules of a body). **3.** task (to be) undertaken, materials (to be) used in task, *(the work of converting the heathen);* **have** one's ∼ **cut out (for** one), have a hard task, have as much as one can do; *all in the* DAY*'s work;* **the** ∼ **of** *a moment* etc., a task occupying (only) a specified time. **4.** thing done by work, result of action, achievement, thing made; book or piece of literary or musical composition, (in *pl.)* all such compositions by author, composer, etc.; literary or other product *of;* (Theol., usu. in *pl.)* meritorious act as opposed to faith or grace; **a good day's** ∼, much accomplished; GOOD *works;* PIECE *of work;* **a** ∼ **of art,** fine picture, building, poem, etc.; ∼**s of mercy,** charitable actions; *works of* SUPEREROGATION. **5.** doings or experiences of specified kind *(sharp, bloody, wild, work; thirsty, dry, work);* DIRTY, NICE, *work; make* SHORT *work of.* **6.** employment, esp. the opportunity of earning money by labour, laborious occupation, *(is out of, is in regular, wants, is looking for, work; many hands make light work).* **7.** (usu. in *pl.* or in *comb.)* piece of fortification, structure for defence, *(the works are impregnable; advanced, detached, defensive, work(s);* EARTH¹*work).* **8.** (in *pl.)* operations of building etc. (CLERK *of (the) works;* **public** ∼**s,** such operations done by or for the State). **9.** (in *pl.)* acting or operative part of machine *(of* clock etc.; *something must be wrong with the works);* (sl.) all that is available **(give** person **the** ∼**s,** give him or tell him everything, (esp.) kill him). **10.** (in *pl.,* often treated as *sing.)* place where manufacture etc. is carried on *(ironworks, gasworks; the works is or are closed next week);* ∼**s council,** group of employees representing those employed in a works etc. in discussions with employer. **11.** (articles having) ornamentation of specified kind, things or parts made of specified material or with specified tools etc., *(covered with elaborate work; rustic, embossed, beaten, frosted, work;* WOOD*work,* IRON¹*work,* STONE*work;* FANCY¹*-work,* NEEDLE*work,* POKER¹*-work);* needle-work, knitting, etc.; (Naut.) UPPER *works.* **12.** ∼'**aday,** fit for or used or seen on workdays, ordinary, everyday, practical, *(this workaday world);* ∼**-bag, -basket, -box,** (holding materials and implements for work, esp. for needlework); ∼**-bench** (for mechanical work, esp. carpentry); ∼**-camp** (for work esp. by volunteers helping a community); ∼'**day,** day on which work is usu. done; ∼**-force,** (number of) workers engaged or available in an industry etc.; ∼**-horse,** horse (or fig. person or machine etc.) that performs arduous labour; ∼'**house,** ‖(Hist.) public institution for reception of paupers in parish or union of parishes, *house of correction for petty offenders; ∼**-load,** amount of work to be done by particular employee etc.; ∼'**man,** man hired to do manual labour, person *good, bad, skilled,* etc., at his job *(a bad workman blames, quarrels with, his tools);* ∼'**manlike,** characteristic of a good workman; ∼'**manship,** person's relative skill in doing task, relative finish or execution seen in manufactured article or work of art, thing made *(the world is God's workmanship);* ∼'**mate,** one engaged in same work as another; ∼'**people,** people employed in labour for wages; ∼'**piece,** thing worked on with tool or machine; ∼**-room** (in which work is done); ∼'**sheet,** paper for recording work done, calculations in progress, etc.; ∼'**shop,** (1) room or building in which manufacture is carried on, (2) meeting of several persons for intensive discussion etc.; ∼**-shy,** disinclined to work; ∼ **study,** system of examining performance of jobs so that they can produce the best results for employees and employers; ∼**-table** (with drawers for sewing-materials etc.); ∼'**woman,** female worker or operative. **13.** Hence ∼'LESS *a.* [OE *weorc* etc., = OS *werk,* OHG *werc,* ON *verk* f. Gmc *werkam f. IE *wergon]

work² (werk) *v.* (∼**ed;** *or* **wrought** *pr.* rawt, arch. exc. in formal use in senses 1, 4, 5, and 8). **1.** *v.i.* engage in bodily or mental work, carry on operations *(at or on* thing), make efforts *(for or against* cause), be craftsman in some material *(worked or wrought in brass* etc.); ∼ **away** *or* **on,** continue to work; *work double* TIDE¹*s;* ∼ **to rule,** follow rules of one's occupation pedantically to reduce efficiency, usu. as protest; ∼ **with,** work jointly with (person), be workmate of. **2.** (Of machine, plan, etc.) operate, act, do its appointed work, *(charm, drug, pump, scheme, works or will not work);* (of part of machine) run, revolve, go through regular motions, *(wheel works on axle, works freely, stiffly).* **3.** *v.t.* (Of person) put or keep (machine etc.) in operation, keep (person, horse, machine, etc.) going or at work, exact toil from, *(work ship, typewriter, lift,* ‖*the* ORACLE; *works his men too hard, that idea to death; work one's fingers to the* BONE¹); carry on, manage, control, *(work mine, scheme; my partner works the Liverpool district; is worked by wires, electricity,* etc.). **4.** *v.i.* have influence or effect, exercise influence *(up)on, (work upon person, his mind,* etc.; *all these things have worked together for good; the appeal wrought powerfully upon him;* OVERWROUGHT). **5.** *v.t.* bring about, effect, accomplish, produce as result, *(work wonders, cures, mischief, a change);* ∼ one's **will,** accomplish one's purpose *(upon* person or thing); *will* ∼ **it** *if I can,* (sl.) bring it about, achieve desired result. **6.** *v.i.* be in motion, be agitated, cause agitation, ferment (lit. or fig.), *(face, features, worked violently; waves work to and fro; thoughts, conscience, working within him; yeast began to work).* **7.** *v.i.* & *t.* make way or make (way etc.) or cause to make way slowly or with difficulty or by shifting motions (usu. w. *adv.* or *prep.),* gradually become (loose, free, tight, etc.) by motion, (*socks work down, shirt works up; needle worked out eventually from her arm; ferrule has worked off, loose; work your knife through the card; was trying to work round to that question; angler working upstream; grub works its way into or out of; wind has worked round*); (Naut.) sail against wind (*ship is working eastwards*). **8.** *v.t.* knead, hammer, fashion, into shape or desired consistency (*work dough, clay; work flour and butter into a paste; butter should be thoroughly worked*); **wrought iron** (that has been or can be forged or rolled, not cast). **9.** artificially and gradually excite into (*worked his audience into enthusiasm, himself into a rage*). **10.** *v.i.* & *t.* do, make by, needlework or the like (*reads to them while they work; work pattern, initials, on linen* etc.; *is working a shawl*). **11.** *v.t.* solve (sum) by mathematical processes. **12.** purchase (one's PASSAGE¹ etc.) with labour instead of money (lit. or fig.); obtain by labour the money for (one's way through university etc.). **13.** ~ **in**, find place for (illustration, subject, etc.; *will work it in somewhere*); ~*-in* n., take-over by workers etc. of factory threatened with closure; ~ **off**, get rid of, get over, find customers etc. for, by work or activity; ~ **out**, find (amount etc.) or solve (sum) by calculation, (of amount etc.) be calculated *at* (*works out at £6.50*), (of sum) give definite result (*will not work out*), exhaust with work (person, *a mine*, etc., *is quite worked out*), accomplish or attain with difficulty (*work out one's salvation*), have result (*plan did not work out well*), provide for or plan all details of (*has worked out a scheme of invasion*); ~*-out* n., (esp. in Boxing etc.) a practice or test; ~ **over**, examine thoroughly, (colloq.) treat with violence; ~ **up**, bring gradually into efficient state, elaborate in description, advance gradually *to* (climax), excite (person, expectations, etc.) by degrees, mingle (materials) into whole, acquire familiarity with (subject) by study. [OE *wyrcan* (Gmc **wurkjan*), *wircan* (Gmc **werkjan*), & *we*(*o*)*rcan* (f. *we*(*o*)*rc* n.); see prec.]

wor'k|able (wĕr'-) *a*. that can be worked, that will work, that is worth working, practicable, feasible; hence ~ABI′LITY, ~ableNESS (-beln-), *ns.*, ~ABLY *adv.* [f. prec. + -ABLE]

workahŏ'lic (wĕrka-h-) *n.* (colloq.) person addicted to working. [f. WORK¹ + ALCOHOLIC]

wor'ker (wĕr'-) *n.* In vbl senses; employee esp. in manual or industrial work; neuter or undeveloped female of various social insects (bee, ant, etc.); ~ **priest**, French RC, or Anglican, priest who engages in non-religious (esp. industrial) work for part of his time. [ME, f. WORK² + -ER¹]

wor'king¹ (wĕr'-) *n.* In vbl senses; way thing works or result of its working; mine, quarry, etc., or part of it in which work is being or has been done (*was found in a disused working*); ~ **capital** (used in actual carrying on of business); ~ **day**, (1) = WORK¹*day*, (2) portion of the day devoted to work; ~ **drawing** (to scale, serving as guide for building or construction); ~ **hours**, those normally devoted to work; ~ **hypothesis** (used as basis for action); ~ **knowledge** (adequate to work with); ~ **lunch** etc., meal at which business, policy, etc., are discussed as main topic; ~ **order**, condition in which machine etc. works (satisfactorily); ~**-out**, calculation of results, elaboration of details. [ME, f. WORK² + -ING¹]

wor'king² (wĕr'-) *a.* In vbl senses; engaged in manual or industrial labour (*working man; the working class*); ~ **model** (of machine etc., able to operate though on reduced scale); ~ **party**, (esp.) ||committee etc. appointed to advise on improving efficiency in an industry etc. or to investigate and report on some question. [ME, f. WORK² + -ING²]

world (wĕr-) *n.* **1.** time or state or scene of human existence; **the** or **this** ~, mortal life; **out of this** ~, (colloq.) incredibly good etc., indescribable; **the other** or **next** ~, **the** ~ **to come**, life after death; *the* LOWER³ *world; the* PRINCE *of this world;* **bring into the** ~, (1) possess at one's birth, (2) deliver (child) at

birth, (3) beget or bear (child); **come into the** ~, be born; **get** etc. **the best of both** ~**s**, benefit from both secular and spiritual (or other partly conflicting) interests; **the end of the** ~, cessation of all mortal life by destruction of universe or otherwise; ~ **without end**, for ever. **2.** secular interests and occupations (**the** ~, **the flesh, and the devil**, kinds of temptation). **3.** the universe, all creation, everything, (*the best of all possible worlds*); **in the** ~, at all, that exists, etc., (*who, how, what, in the world was it?*; *nothing in the world*); **for all the** ~, precisely *like* or *as if*; **carry the** ~ **before** one, have rapid and complete success. **4.** everything that exists outside oneself (**the external** ~, all phenomena; DEAD *to the world*; **the** ~ **of dreams**, things as they seem in dreams); anything however valuable (*would not do it for the, to gain the whole, world; she is all the world to me; think the world of her; would give the world to know*). **5.** the earth, heavenly body supposed to resemble it, its countries and their inhabitants, all people, the earth as known or in some respect limited, (*go round the world; a universe of worlds; are there other worlds than ours?*; *all the world's a stage; make a* NOISE *in the world;* **all the** ~ **knows**, it is generally known; (**all**) **the** ~ **over**, throughout the world; **the** ~**'s end**, farthest attainable point of travel; **the wise old** ~, general experience and custom; **give to the** ~, publish; *on* TOP¹ *of the world;* **the Old W**~, Europe, Asia, and Africa, part known by ancients to exist (OLD-*world*); **the New W**~, America; **the Roman** etc. ~, as much of the world as concerned Rome etc.; *the* THIRD *World*); (*attrib.*) affecting many nations (*world politics, tendency*), of all nations (*world champion, record*). **6.** human affairs, their course and conditions, active life, (*so wags the world; how goes the world with you?*); **know, see, the** ~, have, acquire, experience; **man** or **woman of the** ~, practical tolerant person experienced in life or society; **all's right with the** ~ (expression of optimism); **take the** ~ **as it is, as one finds it**, be adaptable. **7.** average or respectable or fashionable society or people or their customs or opinions; **the great** ~, fashionable society; **all the** ~ **and his wife**, (1) all with pretensions to fashion, (2) any miscellaneous large assembly; **what will the** ~ **say?**, dare we defy public opinion?. **8.** all that concerns or all who belong to specified department or class, sphere, domain, (*the literary, scientific, sporting, animal, ancient, world; the world of letters, art, sport*); (as newspaper or magazine title) *Wireless World*. **9.** a vast or infinite number or amount or extent (*a world of meaning, trouble, faults; will do him a or the world of good*); **a** ~ or ~**s too wide** etc., by far. **10. W**~ **Bank**, (colloq.) International Bank for Reconstruction and Development; ~**-beater**, person or thing surpassing all others; **W**~ **Cup**, quadrennial competition between association football teams representing various countries; ~**-famous**, known throughout the world; ~ **language**, (1) artificial language for universal use, (2) language spoken in many countries; ~**-line**, (Phys.) curve in space-time joining positions of a particle throughout its existence; ~ **power**, nation having influence in world politics; **W**~ **Series**, US championship for baseball teams; ~**-shaking**, important enough to affect the whole world; ~**-view**, *Weltanschauung*; ~ **war**, war involving many important nations (*First, Second, W*~ *War*, of 1914–18, 1939–45); ~**-weary**, weary of (the life of) the world; ~**-wide**, covering, occurring in, known in, all parts of the world. [OE *w*(*e*)*orold, world*, = OS *werold*, OHG *weralt*, ON *veröld* f. Gmc **weraz* man + **aldh-* age (see OLD)]

wor'ldling (wĕr'-) *n.* worldly person. [f. prec. + -LING¹]

wor'ldl|ÿ (wĕr'-) *a.* temporal, earthly, (~y **goods**, property); exclusively or mainly concerned with or devoted to the affairs of this life, esp. to pursuit of wealth or pleasure (~y **wisdom**, esp. prudence in advancing one's own interests); OTHER-*worldly*;

∼**y-minded,** intent on worldly things; ∼**y-wise,** having worldly wisdom; hence ∼**iNESS** *n.* [OE *woruldlic* (as WORLD, -LY¹)]

worm¹ (wẽrm) *n.* **1.** invertebrate limbless or apparently limbless slender burrowing or creeping animal, esp. segmented in rings or parasitic in intestines or tissues; wormlike larva of insect, esp. one feeding on fruit, timber, etc.; SHIP¹-*worm*; blindworm or SLOW-WORM; maggot supposed to eat dead bodies in the grave (**food for** ∼**s,** dead person); (fig.) inward torment; (in *pl.*) internal (esp. intestinal) parasites; (**even**) **a** ∼ **will turn,** the meekest will resist or retaliate if pushed too far. **2.** abject or insignificant or contemptible person. **3.** spiral part of screw; short screw working in worm-gear; spiral pipe of still in which vapour is cooled and condensed. **4.** ligament under dog's tongue. **5.** ∼-**cast,** convoluted tubular mass of earth voided by earthworm on surface of ground; ∼'**eaten,** eaten into by worms, full of worm-holes, (fig.) antiquated; ∼-**fishing** (with worm for bait); ∼-**gear,** arrangement of toothed wheel worked by revolving spiral; ∼-**hole** (left in wood, fruit, etc., by passage of worm); ∼-**seed,** (plant e.g. santonica bearing) seed used to expel intestinal worms; ∼'**s-eye view,** (joc.) view as seen from below or from humble position (opp. *bird's-eye view*); ∼-**wheel,** wheel of worm-gear. **6.** Hence ∼'**y**² *a.* [OE *wyrm,* = OS, OHG *wurm,* ON *ormr* serpent, Goth. *waurms* f. Gmc **wurmiz, *wurmaz*]

worm² (wẽrm) *v.* **1.** *v. refl.* & *t.* insinuate one*self* or oneself *into* (favour, person's confidence, etc.). **2.** *v.t.* & *i.* convey one*self,* progress, make one's way, with crawling motion (*wormed himself or his way or wormed through the bushes*). **3.** *v.t.* draw (secret etc.) by crafty persistence *out* (*of* person) or *from* (person). **4.** cut worm of (dog's tongue). **5.** rid (plant, dog, etc.) of worms. **6.** (Naut.) make (rope etc.) smooth by winding thread between strands. [f. prec.]

wor'mwŏŏd (wẽr'-) *n.* perennial herb of genus *Artemisia* with bitter, tonic, and stimulating qualities used in preparation of vermouth and absinth and in medicine; bitter mortification or its cause. [ME, alt. f. obs. *wormod* f. OE *wormōd, wermōd,* (OS *wer(i)moda,* OHG *wer(i)muota,* of unkn. orig.), after *worm, wood;* cf. VERMOUTH]

wŏrn. See WEAR¹.

wo'rrit (wŭ'-) *n.* & *n.* (colloq.) – foll. [orig. vulg. alt. f. foll.]

wo'rry (wŭ'-) *v.* & *n.* **1.** *v.t.* (Of dog) bite or seize esp. at throat (rat, sheep, dog) repeatedly, shake or pull about with the teeth; attack repeatedly; ∼ **out,** obtain (solution to problem etc.) by dogged effort. **2.** tease, harass, importune, be continuously or intermittently troublesome to, allow no rest or peace of mind to (∼ one**self,** take needless trouble); (in *p.p.*) uneasy (*worried about, that, to find* etc.; **much** or **very worried,** full of uneasiness; **wears a worried look,** looks anxious or troubled). **3.** *v.i.* give way to anxiety, let the mind dwell on troubles, fret; **I should** ∼, (colloq.) it doesn't trouble or concern me at all; **not to** ∼, (colloq.) do not worry, there is no need to worry; ∼ **along** or **through,** manage to advance by persistence in spite of obstacles. **4.** Hence **wo'rriMENT** *n.,* **wo'rriSOME**¹ *a.,* (wŭ'-). **5.** *n.* dog's worrying of quarry; (usu. in *pl.*) care(s), thing(s) that worry person; cares, worried state, over-anxiety; ∼ **beads,** string of beads for fiddling with to occupy one's hands or calm oneself; ∼-**guts,** ∼-**wart,** (colloq.) person who habitually worries unduly. [OE *wyrgan* strangle, = OHG *wurgan* f. WG **wurgjan*]

worse (wẽrs) *a., adv.,* & *n.* **1.** *a.* & *adv.* more bad or badly or evil or ill; (as *pred. a.*) in or into less good health (*is worse today; is getting worse*), in less good condition or circumstances (*is none the worse for it; the worse for* LIQUOR¹, *for* WEAR²); *for* BETTER¹ (or) *for worse;* ∼ **luck!,** excl. of disappointment at unlucky event; *worse* OFF; ∼ **and** ∼, increasingly worse; hence

wor'sEN⁶ (wẽr'-) *v.t.* & *i.* **2.** *n.* worse thing(s) (*have worse to tell; but worse followed; you might do worse than* (to) *accept*); **from bad to** ∼, into even worse state; **or** ∼, or as an even worse alternative; **the** ∼, defeat in contest, worse condition (*a change for the worse*); **if worse comes to* WORST. [OE *wyrsa, wiersa,* = OS *wirsa,* OHG *wirsiro,* ON *verri,* Goth. *wairsiza* f. Gmc **wersizon* (**wers-;* cf. WAR¹)]

wor'ship (wẽr'-) *n.* & *v.* (-**pp-** or **-*p-). **1.** (arch.) worthiness, merit, recognition given or due to these, honour and respect, (**men of** ∼, persons of repute). **2. Your, His, W**∼ (title used to or of certain magistrates, or to show respect for person of higher station or ironical pretence of this). **3.** reverence paid to God or god, esp. in church service (*public worship; do worship;* **freedom of** ∼, = *freedom of* RELIGION; **place of** ∼, church etc.); adoration or devotion comparable to this felt or shown towards person or principle (*an object of worship; regarding her with worship in his eyes; the worship of wealth, intellect, athletics*). **4.** *v.t.* adore as divine, pay religious homage to; idolize, regard with adoration, (*worships the ground she walks on*). **5.** *v.i.* take part in (public) worship; be full of adoration. **6.** Hence ∼(**p**)**ER**¹ *n.* [OE *weorthscipe* (as WORTH¹, -SHIP)]

wor'shipful (wẽr'-) *a.* **1.** (arch.) entitled to honour and respect. **2.** ‖(Title given to justices of the peace, recorders, London City companies and Freemasons' lodges and their masters). **3.** imbued with spirit of veneration. **4.** Hence ∼LY² *adv.,* ∼NESS *n.* [ME, f. prec. +-FUL]

worst (wẽrst) *a., adv., n.,* & *v.t.* **1.** *a.* & *adv.* most bad or badly or evil or ill. **2.** *n.* worst part, feature, state, possible assumption, event, possible issue, or action (*the worst of the storm is over; that is the worst of being clever; saw him at his worst; if the worst happens; prepare for the worst; when things are at the or their worst*); **at (the)** ∼, in the worst possible case; **get** or **have the** ∼ **of it,** be worsted; ‖**if the** ∼ **comes to the** ∼, **if worse comes to* ∼, if the worst happens; **do your, let him** etc. **do his** etc., ∼, (expression of defiance). **3.** *v.t.* get the better of, defeat, outdo. [OE *wierresta, wyrresta a., wyr(re)st adv.,* = OS *wirsista,* OHG *wirsisto,* ON *verst(r)* f. Gmc **wersistaz* (**wers-* WORSE; see -EST¹)]

wor'stĕd (wŏŏs'-) *n.* fine smooth yarn spun from combed long-staple wool; fabric woven from this. [f. *Worste(a)d* in Norfolk]

wort (wẽrt) *n.* **1.** plant, herb, (arch. exc. in names of plants: *St. John's wort; woundwort; liverwort*). **2.** infusion of malt before it is fermented into beer. [sense 1 f. OE *wyrt,* = OS *wurt,* OHG *wurz,* ON *urt,* Goth. *waurts;* sense 2 f. OE *wyrt,* = OS *wurtja* spicery, MHG *würze;* both cogn. w. ROOT¹]

worth¹ (wẽrth) *pred. a.* (governing *n.* like *prep.*) & *n.* **1.** *a.* of value equivalent to (*is worth much, little, nothing, about £1;* BIRD in the hand is worth two in the bush; *what is the house worth?; the rarer it is the more it is worth*). **2.** deserving, worthy of, bringing compensation for, (*worth doing, hearing, notice, the trouble,* (one's) WHILE¹, one's SALT, *an effort*); ∼ **it,** (colloq.) worth while; **well** ∼, certainly worth (*doing* etc.); *I give you, you must take, this* **for what it is** ∼, without guarantee of its truth, wisdom, etc. **3.** possessed of, having property amounting to, (*is, died, worth a million pounds; spent all he was worth on it*); **for all one is** ∼, (colloq.) with one's utmost efforts, without reserve. **4.** ∼'**while,** that is worth WHILE¹ (*a worthwhile undertaking*). **5.** *n.* what a person or thing is worth, value, merit, high merit or excellence, (*of great, little, no, worth; persons of worth; true worth often goes unrecognized*); hence ∼'LESS² *a.* **6.** equivalent of money etc. in commodity (*ten pounds' worth of petrol;* MONEY¹*s-worth;* PENNY*worth;* SHILLINGS*worth.* [OE *w(e)orth* etc. a. & n., = OS *werth,* OHG *werd,* ON *verth(r),* Goth. *wairth(s)*]

worth² (wẽrth) *v.t.* 3 *sing. pres. subj.* (arch.) woe ∼, cursed be (*the day* etc.). [OE *weorthan* become, = OS *werthan,* OHG *werdan,* ON *vertha,* Goth. *wairthan* f. Gmc **werthan* f. IE **wert-*]

wor'th|ȳ (wẽr'dhĭ) *a.* & *n.* **1.** *a.* estimable, having some moral worth, of a fair degree of merit, respectable, (*a grave and worthy man; has lived a worthy life*); (with patronizing effect, cf. HONEST) no more than moderately estimable (*I asked the worthy rustic whether*). **2.** deserving *of* or *to* be or do, (arch.) deserving of, (*is worthy of* or *worthy remembrance* or *being remembered; is worthy to be remembered, to take the lead*). **3.** corresponding to the worth *of* or (arch.) of, adequate, appropriate, of sufficient worth or merit, (*in words worthy of* or *worthy the occasion; he is not worthy of her; a foeman worthy of your steel; has found a worthy opponent; received a worthy reward*). **4.** Hence ∼ILY² *adv.*, ∼INESS *n.* **5.** *n.* worthy person; person of some distinction in his country, time, etc.; (joc.) person. [ME *wurthi* etc., f. WORTH¹ 5 + -Y²]

-worthȳ (wẽrdhĭ) *suf.* forming *adjs.*, w. sense 'deserving of' (*blameworthy, noteworthy, praiseworthy*), 'suitable or fit for' (*newsworthy, roadworthy, seaworthy*). [f. prec.]

wŏt(′tĕst). See WIT¹.

∥**wŏ′tcher** *int.* (sl.) of greeting. [f. *what* CHEER¹?]

would, would-be, wouldn't, would(e)st. See WILL¹.

Woulfe, Woulff, (wōolf) *n.* ∼ **bottle,** (Chem.) jar with more than one neck, used for passing gas through liquid etc. [f. P. *Woulfe*, Engl. chemist d. 1803]

wound¹ (wōo-) *n.*, & *v.t.* **1.** *n.* injury done by (deliberate) cut or stab or blow or tear to animal or vegetable tissues including and usu. going beyond the cutting or piercing or breaking or tearing of the skin or bark or other integument, (fig.) injury done to person's reputation etc. or pain inflicted on his feelings, (poet.) pangs of love, (*receive, inflict, make, heal, a wound; open, incurable, festering, mortal, wound*); ∼′wort, plant formerly supposed to have healing properties, esp. kidney-VETCH or plant of genus *Stachys*; hence ∼LESS *a.* **2.** *v.t.* inflict wound on (lit. or fig.; *wounded soldiers, feelings*). [(v. f. OE *wundian*) f. OE *wund* = OS *wunda*, OHG *wunta*, ON *und*]

wound². See WIND².,³.

wou′nd|ȳ *a.* & *adv.* (arch.) **1.** *a.* very great, extreme; hence ∼ILY² *adv.* **2.** *adv.* extremely, excessively. [f. *wounds* int. of asseveration (cf. ZOUNDS) + -Y²]

wōve¹ *a.* (Of paper) made on wire-gauze frame and so having uniform unlined surface. [var. of *woven*, p.p. of WEAVE¹]

wōve², wō′ven. See WEAVE¹.

wow¹ *int.*, *n.*, & *v.t.* **1.** *int.* expr. astonishment or admiration. **2.** *n.* (sl.) a sensational success. **3.** *v.t.* (sl.) impress or excite greatly. [orig. Sc.; imit.]

wow² *n.* slow pitch-fluctuation in sound-reproduction, perceptible in long notes. [imit.]

wow′ser (-z-) *n.* (Austral.) puritanical fanatic; spoil-sport; teetotaller. [20th c.; orig. unkn.]

WP *abbr.* weather permitting.

w.p.b. *abbr.* waste-paper basket.

∥**WPC** *abbr.* woman police CONSTABLE.

w.p.m. *abbr.* words per minute.

WR *abbr.* West RIDING².

∥**WRAC** *abbr.* Women's Royal Army Corps.

wrăck *n.* wreck(age); = RACK¹,⁷; seaweed cast up or growing below high-water mark, and used for manure etc. [ME f. MDu. *wrak* or MLG *wra(c)k*, a parallel form. to OE *wræc*, rel. to *wrecan* WREAK; cf. WRECK, RACK¹]

∥**WRAF** *abbr.* Women's Royal Air Force.

wraith *n.* person's double or apparition supposedly seen shortly before or after his death; ghost, apparition. [16th c., orig. Sc.; of unkn. orig.]

wrā′ngle (ră′nggĕl) *v.i.*, & *n.* brawl, (engage in) loud or angry argument or altercation or quarrel; *herd (cattle). [ME, prob. f. LDu.; cf. LG *wrangelen*, frequent. of *wrangen* to struggle, cogn. w. WRING]

wrā′ngler (-ngg-) *n.* In vbl senses; *cowboy; (Camb. Univ.) person placed in first class of mathematical

tripos (**senior** ∼, first in the class when it was arranged in order of merit), whence ∼SHIP *n.* [f. prec. + -ER¹]

wrăp *v.* (-pp-) & *n.* **1.** *v.t.* ∼ (**up**), enfold, enclose or pack or conceal in folded or soft encircling material, (*wrap it in paper, cotton wool; wrap up parcel; mountain, affair, is wrapped in mist, mystery; wraps up his meaning in tortuous sentences, in allegory*); ∼ **up,** finish off, settle, (dealings etc.); ∼**ped up,** engrossed or involved (*mother, country's prosperity, is wrapped up in her child, its shipping*); ∼**ping-paper,** strong or decorative paper for parcels. **2.** *v.i.* ∼ **over,** (of garment) overlap itself when worn; ∼ **up,** put on wraps (*mind you wrap up well if you go out*), (in *imper.*, sl.) be quiet; ∼′**around** *a.* & *n.*, (object) that extends round a thing. **3.** *v.t.* arrange or draw (flexible covering) *round* or *about* person or thing (*wrapped her shawl closer about her*); hence ∼′**ping¹** (3) *n.* **4.** *n.* (usu. in *pl.*) shawl(s), rug(s), coat(s), cloak(s), neckerchief(s), etc., as addition to ordinary indoor clothes; **take the ∼s off,** disclose; **under ∼s,** in concealment or secrecy. [ME, of unkn. orig.]

wră′ppage *n.* wrapping(s). [f. prec. + -AGE]

wrā′pper *n.* In vbl senses; (loose indoor garment resembling) dressing-gown; paper enclosing newspaper or similar packet for posting; paper enclosing sweet, chocolate, etc.; (freq. detachable) paper cover of book; tobacco-leaf of superior quality enclosing cigar. [ME, f. WRAP + -ER¹]

wrăsse *n.* thick-lipped strong-toothed bright--coloured rock-haunting sea-fish of family Labridae. [f. Corn. *wrach*, mutated f. *gwrach*, = W *gwrach*, lit. 'old woman']

wrath (rŏ-, raw-) *n.* (poet., rhet., or joc.) anger, indignation; **vessels** or **children of** ∼, persons destined to undergo divine chastisement; VIALS *of wrath*; **slow to** ∼, not irascible; hence ∼′FUL, *∼′Y², adjs.* [OE *wrǣththu* (*wrǎth* WROTH + *-ithō* -TH¹)]

wreak *v.t.* **1.** give play or satisfaction to, put in operation, (*vengeance, rage,* etc., usu. (*up*)*on* enemy etc.; *effort* etc.); cause (damage etc.). **2.** (arch.) avenge (wrong, wronged person). [OE *wrecan* drive, avenge, etc., = OS *wrekan*, OHG *rehhan*, ON *reka*, Goth. *wrikan* persecute, f. Gmc *wrekan* (*wrek-*, cf. WRACK, WRECK, WRETCH, f. IE *wreg-*)]

wreath *n.* (*pl. pr.* -dhz *or* -ths). flowers or leaves strung or woven or wound together into ring for wearing on head or for decorating statue, building, etc., or placing as mark of respect on coffin etc.; carved imitation of this; similar ring of soft twisted material such as silk, (Her.) representation of this below crest; curl *of* smoke, circular or curved band of cloud, light drifting mass of snow etc. [OE *writha* f. weak grade of *wrīthan* WRITHE]

wreathe (-dh) *v.* **1.** *v.t.* encircle as or (as) with wreath (*face wreathed in smiles*); form (flowers, silk, etc.) into wreath; wind (one's arms etc. or (of snake etc.) it*self*) *round* person etc.; make (garland). **2.** *v.i.* (Of smoke etc.) move in shape of wreaths. [partly back-form. f. *wrethen* (see foll.); partly f. prec.]

wrea′then (-dh-) *a.* (arch.) wreathed, intertwined. [ME *wrethen,* wrythen, with. p.p. of WRITHE]

wrĕck *n.* & *v.* **1.** *n.* ruin, destruction, disablement, esp. of ship (cf. SHIP¹*wreck; save ship, one's fortunes, from wreck; gale caused many wrecks; the wreck of the Hesperus, of his happiness*). **2.** ship that has suffered wreck, greatly damaged or disabled building or vehicle or person, disorganized remains or wretched remnant *of*, (*shores are strewn with wrecks; person is a physical* or *mental wreck; is but a* or *the wreck of his former self*). **3.** (Law). goods etc. cast up by the sea (*wreck of the sea belongs to the Crown*). **4.** ∼**-master,** officer appointed to take charge of goods etc. cast up from wrecked ship. **5.** *v.t.* cause wreck of (ship, train, hopes, undertaking, person or his fortunes); (in *p.p.*) involved in shipwreck (*wrecked sailors, goods*). **6.** *v.i.* suffer wreck; *deal with wrecked vehicle(s) etc. [ME, f. AF *wrec* etc. (cf.

VAREC), f. ON *_wrek_ f. Gmc *_wrekan_ to drive; cf. WREAK]

wrĕ′ckage _n._ wrecked material, remnants, fragments; action or process of wrecking. [f. prec. + -AGE]

wrĕ′cker _n._ In vbl senses; one who tries from shore to bring about shipwreck with view to profiting by wreckage, or who steals such wreckage; person employed in demolition, or in recovering wrecked ship or its contents; *person who repairs damaged vehicles; *vehicle or train used in recovering damaged one. [f. WRECK + -ER¹]

wrĕn¹ _n._ small usu. brown short-winged song-bird of family Troglodytidae, esp. European species with erect tail. [OE _wrenna_, rel. to OHG _wrendo, wrendilo_, Icel. _rindill_]

‖**Wrĕn**² _n._ member of the Women's Royal Naval Service; hence ∼′**nery** (3) _n._ (joc.). [orig. in pl., f. abbr. WRNS]

wrĕnch _n., & v.t._ **1.** _n._ violent twist or oblique pull or tearing off, (fig.) pain caused by parting, (_gave a wrench to his ankle, at the door-handle; leaving home was a great wrench_). **2.** implement like spanner (usu. adjustable) made to grip and turn nuts, bolts, etc. **3.** (Phys.) combination of couple with force along its axis. **4.** _v.t._ twist or pull (thing, or abs.) violently round or sideways, injure or pull _off_ or _away_ by twisting, (_wrenched the door open, at the handle, his horse's head round, his ankle, fool's head off, opponent's sword from him_); pervert, distort, (facts etc.). [n. f. v., f. OE _wrencan_ twist, = OHG _renchen_, of unkn. orig.]

wrĕst _v.t., & n._ **1.** _v.t._ twist, deflect, distort, pervert, (_wrests the law to suit himself; wrest the facts, sense_ or _words of a passage_, etc.); obtain by effort or with difficulty; force or wrench away from person's grasp (_wrested his sword from him_). **2.** _n._ (arch.) key for tuning harp, piano, etc.; ∼-**block** or -**plank,** part of piano holding ∼-**pins,** to which strings are attached. [OE _wrǣstan_, = ON *_wreista_ f. Gmc *_waristjan_, rel. to WRIST]

wrĕ′stl|e (-sel) _v. & n._ **1.** _v.i._ grapple with and try to throw adversary esp. in sporting contest under code of rules (_with_, or abs.); contend, grapple, do one's utmost to deal, _with_ evil, temptation, duty, task, problem, etc.; ∼**e with God** or **in prayer,** pray fervently; hence ∼**er**¹, ∼**ing**¹, (rĕ′sl-) _ns._ **2.** _v.t._ have wrestling-match with; move with efforts as if wrestling. **3.** _n._ wrestling-match; hard struggle. [OE *_wrǣstlian_; cf. MLG _wrostelen_, OE _wraxlian_]

wrĕtch _n._ very unfortunate or miserable person; despicable person, person without conscience or shame (often as term of playful depreciation). [OE _wrecca_, = OS _wrekkio_, OHG _reccho_ exile, adventurer, f. WG *_wrakjo_ f. Gmc *_wrak-_ (cf. WREAK)]

wrĕ′tchĕd _a._ (∼**er,** ∼**est**). miserable, unhappy, afflicted; inferior, of bad quality or no merit, contemptible, unsatisfactory, causing discontent or discomfort or nuisance, confounded, (_wretched weather, health, horse, inn, accommodation, poetry, poet_, etc.); **feel** ∼, be much embarrassed or very unwell; hence ∼**ly**² _adv._, ∼**ness** _n._ [ME, irreg. f. prec. + -ED¹; cf. WICKED]

‖**wrick.** See RICK².

wri′ggle _v. & n._ **1.** _v.i._ (Of worm etc.) move body with short twistings, (of animal or person) make wormlike motions, (fig.) be slippery, practise evasion; make way _along, through, out, in_, etc., by wriggling (lit. or fig.; _wriggle out of a garment, a difficulty_). **2.** _v.t._ move oneself, one's _body, tail, hand_, etc., with wriggling motion; make one's _way_ by wriggling. **3.** _n._ wriggling movement. [ME, f. MLG _wriggelen_ frequent. of _wriggen_; see -LE 3]

wright (rīt) _n._ craftsman, maker, (arch. exc. in comb., as _shipwright, wheelwright, playwright_). [OE _wryhta, wyrhta_, = OS _wurhtio_, OHG _wurhto_ f. WG *_wurhtjo_ (*_wurk-_; cf. WORK²)]

wring _v.t._ (**wrung**), _& n._ **1.** _v.t._ squeeze, squeeze and twist esp. to remove liquid (_out_), twist forcibly, break by twisting; distress, torture; ∼ person's **hand,** press it with emotion; ∼ one's **hands,** squeeze them

together in sign of great distress; ∼**ing wet,** (colloq.) ∼**ing,** so wet that moisture can be removed by wringing; ∼ **neck of,** kill chicken etc. by twisting its head round. **2.** extract by squeezing, get _out_ by pressure or importunity, extort, (_wring water, groan, consent, money, from_ or _out of_ or _out_). **3.** Hence (-)∼′**er**¹ (2) _n._ (esp. device for squeezing wet clothes etc. between rollers). **4.** _n._ squeeze (_gave my hand, give those clothes, a wring_). [OE _wringan_, = OS -_wringan_, OHG _ringan_, rel. to WRONG]

wri′nkle _n. & v._ **1.** _n._ furrow-like crease or depression or ridge in the skin (esp. of the kind produced by age) or other flexible surface; hence **wri′nkly**² _a._ **2.** (colloq.) piece of serviceable information not generally known, tip, dodge, (_is full of wrinkles; gave me, put me up to, a wrinkle or two_). **3.** _v.t._ produce wrinkles in (_he wrinkled his forehead; wrinkled with age_). **4.** _v.i._ form wrinkles; become marked with wrinkles. [orig. repr. OE _gewrinclod_ sinuous]

wrist _n._ joint connecting hand with forearm; corresponding part in animal; part of garment covering wrist; (effect got in fencing, ball-games, sleight-of-hand, etc., by) ∼(-**work**), working of the hand from the wrist alone; ∼(-**pin**), (Mech.) stud projecting from crank etc. as attachment for connecting-rod; ∼′**band,** band forming or concealing end of shirt-sleeve, cuff; ∼-**drop,** inability to extend hand through paralysis of forearm muscles; ∼-**watch** (worn on strap etc. round wrist). [OE, = MHG _rist_, ON _rist_ instep f. Gmc *_wristiz_, prob. f. *_wridh-_, weak grade of base of WRITHE]

wri′stlĕt _n._ band or ring worn on wrist to strengthen or guard it or as ornament, bracelet, handcuff, etc.; ‖∼ **watch,** = WRIST-_watch_. [f. prec. + -LET]

writ¹ _n._ **1.** form of written command in name of sovereign, State, court, etc., issued to official or other person and directing him to act or abstain from acting in some way (_writ of attachment, habeas corpus, subpoena_, etc.); **serve** ∼ **on** person, deliver it to him; ∼ **runs** _in district_ etc., is theoretically valid or is actually respected. **2.** Crown document summoning peer to Parliament or ordering election of member(s) of Parliament. **3.** HOLY or _Sacred_ Writ. [OE, = OHG _riz_ written stroke, ON _rit_, Goth. _writs_ f. as WRITE]

writ². See foll.

write _v._ (**wrote** _pr._ rōt, arch. **writ; wri′tten,** usu. arch. **writ**). **1.** _v.i._ form or mark symbols representing word(s) esp. with pen or pencil or typewriter on paper or parchment or other surface (_write legibly, in ink; cannot_ or _does not read_ or _write_). **2.** _v.t._ form or mark (such symbols), form or mark the symbols that represent or constitute (word, special script, etc.), (_writes a good_ etc. HAND¹ 7; _write one's name; writes his name with a final 'e'; notice is written on wall; can write his alphabet, the Greek letters, Greek, shorthand_); enter (data) in computer store, esp. on magnetic tape. **3.** (fig., esp. in _p.p._) indicate (quality or condition) by appearance on etc. person's _face_ etc. (_has honesty written in his face; guilt was written all over her_); cause to be recorded (_name written in_ BOOK¹ _of life; writ(ten) in_ WATER¹); **writ large,** on a large scale, in a magnified or emphasized form. **4.** fill, draw up or fill in, with writing (_has written three sheets; paper written all over; write cheque, certificate, application_); underwrite (insurance policy). **5.** _v.t. & i._ compose for written or printed reproduction or publication, put into literary form. form and set down in writing, be engaged temporarily or permanently in such composition, compose books etc. well etc., (_is writing a book, an article, his life, poetry, a novel, report, letter, play, symphony, opera; New Testament was written in Greek; writes a little, in_ or _for the papers, for a living_); bring (character, episode) _into_ or _out of_ story by suitable changes of text. **6.** write and send letter (_to_ person, or abs.), (US, Commerc., or colloq.) write and send letter _to_ (person), (_writes home once a week; nothing to write_ HOME¹ _about; have written to him; we wrote you last week; will write (off) for a fresh supply_). **7.** _v.t._ send or convey (_to_ person news, _that, how_, etc.) by letter (_write me all the news, the result, how you got home; wrote to his mother that he was bullied). **8.** state in writing or print (Herodotus writes, it is written, that). **9.** (arch.) describe in writing as (writes himself esquire). **10.** ~ **down,** (1) record or take note of in writing, (2) write as if for those considered inferior, (3) disparage in writing, (4) reduce nominal value of (stock, goods, etc.); ~ **in,** (1) send letter to firm etc., (2) *add (extra name) on list of candidates when voting (so ~-in n.); ~ **off,** write and send letter, compose with facility, cancel, recognize in writing the non-existence or annulment of, (bad debts, sums absorbed by depreciation, lost or destroyed goods, etc.; so ~-off n., esp. vehicle etc. so badly damaged as to be not worth repairing); ~ **out,** write the whole of, exhaust oneself by writing (has written himself out, has no ideas etc. left); ~ **up,** (1) praise in writing, (2) write full account of (incident etc.; so ~-up n.), (3) make entries to bring (diary etc.) up to date. **11.** Hence **wrī′t**ABLE a. [OE wrītan scratch, score, write, = OS wrītan cut, write, OHG rīzan tear, draw, ON ríta score, write, f. Gmc *wrītan; orig. of symbols inscribed with sharp tools on stone or wood]

wrī′ter n. In vbl senses; clerk, esp. in Navy or in government offices; scribe; author; **the (present)** ~, myself; **W~ to the Signet,** Scottish solicitor conducting cases in Court of SESSION; ~'**s cramp,** muscular spasm due to excessive writing. [OE wrītere (as prec.; see -ER¹)]

writhe (rīdh) v. & n. **1.** v.i. twist or roll oneself about (as) in acute pain, squirm; shrink mentally, be stung or bitterly annoyed, (under, at, insult etc.; with shame etc.). **2.** v.t. twist (one's body etc.) about. **3.** n. act of writhing. [OE wrīthan, = OHG rīdan, ON rítha, rel. to WREATHE]

wrī′then (-dh-) a. (arch.) writhing, twisting, intertwined. [ME, p.p. of prec.]

wrī′ting n. In vbl senses; handwriting; written document; piece of literary work done, book, article, etc., (the writings of Plato; W~s, Hagiographa); **at this (present)** ~, at the time when this is being written; **put thing in** ~, write it down; ~-**case** (holding writing-materials); ~-**desk,** desk for writing at, esp. with compartments for papers etc.; ~-**ink** (opp. printing-ink); **the** ~ **on the wall,** ominously significant event etc. (Dan. 5:5, 25-28); writing-PAD³; ~-**paper,** paper for writing on, esp. cut to size usual for letters; ~-**table,** table for writing at, usu. with drawers etc. [ME, f. WRITE + -ING¹]

wrī′tten. See WRITE.

‖**WRNS** abbr. Women's Royal Naval Service.

wrŏng a., n., adv., & v.t. **1.** a. out of order, in(to) bad or abnormal condition, (something is wrong with him, with the engine; my watch has gone wrong); **what's** ~ **with . . .?,** (colloq.) surely no alternative or substitute for . . . is wanted. **2.** contrary to law or morality, wicked, (knows the right from the wrong; lying is wrong). **3.** other than the right or suitable or the more or most desirable (always does the wrong thing; backed the wrong horse; took the wrong road; the wrong answer, move); **in the** ~ **box,** unsuitably or awkwardly placed, in a difficulty, at a disadvantage; **get hold of the** ~ **end of the stick,** (fig.) be quite mistaken in attempt to understand; ~-**footed,** (colloq.) caught unprepared; ~ **fount,** (of printed letter etc.) size, shape, etc., other than what is wanted; ~ **side,** side (of fabric etc.) not meant to be exposed or used (~ side out, inside out), less good or undesired side (of door, the BLANKET¹, specified age, etc.; out of BED¹ on the wrong side; cf. LAUGH 1, TRACK¹ 1, 5); get wrong SOW² by ear; BARK⁵ up wrong tree; ~ 'un, (colloq.) person of bad character, (Cricket) googly; **go down the** ~ **way,** (of food) enter windpipe instead of gullet; **(the)** ~ **way round,** in opposite of proper or usual orientation. **4.** mistaken, in error, (a wrong opinion, guess, decision, hypothesis; clock is wrong by ten minutes; I think you are, can prove you, wrong); ~-**headed,** perverse and obstinate. **5.** Hence ~′LY² adv., ~′NESS n. **6.** n. what is morally

wrong, wrong action, (the difference between right and wrong; can two wrongs make a right?); **do** ~, sin, offend, transgress. **7.** injustice, unjust action or treatment, (do wrong to; suffer wrong; has done me a great wrong); **do** person ~, malign or mistreat him. **8. in the** ~, in position of or responsibility for having caused quarrel, made the mistake, been the offender, etc., (you were, they are both, in the wrong); **put** person **in the** ~, show or make it appear that he was the offender. **9.** adv. (usu. placed last). in wrong direction or manner, with incorrect result, (aim, guess, answer, do sum, sort things, wrong; you told, led, me wrong); **get** person ~, misunderstand him; *(colloq.) **get in** ~ **with** person, incur his dislike; **get** person **in** ~, bring him into disfavour; **go** ~, take wrong path, (fig.) depart from virtuous or suitable behaviour, get out of working order. **10.** v.t. treat unjustly, do wrong to, (his deeply wronged wife); mistakenly attribute bad motives etc. to (I assure you you wrong me). [OE wrang f. ON *wrangr, rangr awry, unjust, rel. to WRING]

wrŏ′ngdo|er (-dōō-) n. person who violates law or morality; so ~ING¹ n. [f. prec. 6 + DOER]

wrŏ′ngful a. characterized by unfairness or injustice; contrary to law; (of person) not entitled to position etc. occupied; hence ~LY² adv., ~NESS n. [ME, f. WRONG + -FUL]

wrŏ′ngous a. **1.** (arch.) wrongful. **2.** (Sc. Law). illegal, unjust. **3.** Hence ~LY² adv. [alt. f. ME wrangwīs (wrang wrong + -wīs, after rihtwīs RIGHTEOUS]

wrŏte. See WRITE.

wrŏth pred. a. (rhet., poet., or joc.; no compar. or adv.) angry. [OE wrāth, = OS wrēth, OHG reid, ON reithr f. Gmc *wraith-, *wrīth-; cf. WRITHE]

wrought. See WORK².

wrŭng. See WRING.

‖**WRVS** abbr. Women's Royal Voluntary Service.

wrȳ a. (~'er or wri'er, ~'est or wri'est, pr. rī′-). distorted, turned to one side, skew, (~ **face, mouth, smile,** grimace expressing disgust or disapprobation or mockery); ~'**bill,** NZ plover with sharply deflected bill; ~'**mouth,** blenny of genus Cryptacanthodes; ~'**neck,** (1) torticollis, (2) bird of genus Jynx allied to woodpeckers, able to turn head over shoulder; hence ~'LY² adv., ~'NESS n. [f. wry v. f. OE wrīgian tend, incline, in ME deviate, swerve, contort; cf. OFris. wrīgia bend]

WS abbr. Writer to the Signet.

WSW abbr. west-south-west.

wt. abbr. weight.

Wu (wōō) n. Chinese dialect of Yangzi valley. [Chin.]

wu′nderkind (vōō′nderkĭnt) n. person who achieves great success while relatively young. [G (wunder wonder, kind child)]

WV, W.Va., abbrs. West Virginia.

***WW** abbr. World War (I, II, etc.).

WX abbr. women's extra large size.

WY abbr. Wyoming.

wȳ′andŏtte n. American breed of fowl, usu. black and white. [name of Amer. Ind. tribe]

wych-, wich-, witch-, pref. in names of trees with pliant branches; ~-**alder,** Amer. plant akin to witch-hazel, with alder-like leaves; ~-**elm,** species of elm (Ulmus glabra); ~-**hazel,** (1) Amer. shrub of genus Hamamelis whose bark yields astringent lotion, (2) = wych-elm. [OE wic(e) app. f. Gmc *wik- bend, cogn. w. WEAK]

Wȳ′kehamist (-kam-) a. & n. (past or present member) of Winchester College. [f. mod. L Wykehamista f. William of Wykeham, bishop of Winchester & founder (d. 1404) + -IST]

wȳn. Var. of WEN².

wȳnd n. (Sc.) narrow street, alley. [ME, app. f. st. of WIND³]

Wyo. abbr. Wyoming.

wȳ′vern n. (Her.) winged two-legged dragon with barbed tail. [f. ME wyver, f. OF wivre, guivre, f. L vipera; for -n cf. BITTERN]

X

X, x, (ĕks) *n.* (*pl.* **Xs** *or* **X's,** *pr.* ĕ′ksīz). twenty-fourth letter of alphabet; (Alg., usu. *x*) first unknown quantity; (Geom.) first coordinate; unknown or unspecified person, number, etc.; (as Roman numeral) 10 (**xi** 11, **xv** 15, **xx** 20, **xl** 40, **xc** 90); cross-shaped symbol esp. used to indicate position (*X marks the spot*) or incorrectness or to symbolize a kiss or vote, or as signature by person unable to write his name.

-x (-z) *suf.* equiv. to -s¹, retained in *pl.* of many *ns.* in *-u* taken from French (*beaux, jeux d'esprit, tableaux*). [F]

‖X *symb.* (Of films) not suitable for persons under 18.

xä′nth|ic (z-) *a.* yellowish; **∼ic acid,** colourless unstable acid; hence **∼ATE¹** (3) *n.*, yellow salt of xanthic acid. [f. Gk *xanthos* yellow + -IC]

Xänt(h)ï′ppé (zăntĭ′-) *n.* shrewish woman or wife. [name of Socrates' wife]

xänthō′ma (z-) *n.* (*pl.* **∼s** *or* **∼ta**). (Path.) skin disease with irregular yellow patches on neck etc. [f. as XANTHIC + -OMA]

xä′nthophÿll (z-) *n.* dark brown compound associated with chlorophyll and causing yellow colour of leaves in autumn. [f. as XANTHIC + -O- + Gk *phullon* leaf]

X-chrōmosōme (ĕ′kskr-) *n.* chromosome of which number in female cells is twice that in male cells. [f. *X* as arbitrary label + CHROMOSOME]

x.d. *abbr.* EX² dividend.

Xe *symb.* xenon.

xē′bĕc (z-) *n.* small three-masted Mediterranean vessel with lateen and usu. some square sails. [alt. (after Sp. *xabeque*) f. F *chebec* f. It. *sciabecco* f. Arab. *šabāk*]

xē′no- (z-) *comb. form.* foreign(er), other, as: **∼gamy** (-ŏ′g-), cross-fertilization; **∼lith,** (Geol.) stone or rock occurring in a system to which it does not belong; **∼phobe, ∼pho′bia,** (person with) morbid dislike of foreigners. [f. Gk *xenos* strange(r), foreign + -O-]

xē′nŏn (z-) *n.* (Chem.) heavy inert gaseous element. [Gk, neut. of *xenos* strange]

xērä′nthemum (z-) *n.* annual herb of genus *Xeranthemum,* with everlasting composite flowers. [mod. L, f. Gk *xēros* dry + *anthemon* flower]

xero- (zēr′o, zĕ′ro) *comb. form.* dry, as: **∼graphy** (-ŏ′g-), dry copying process in which black or coloured powder adheres to parts of surface remaining electrically charged when it is exposed to light from bright parts of image of what is to be copied; so **∼graph,** copy thus produced, **∼gra′phic** *a.*; **∼philous** (-ŏ′f-), (of plant) adapted to extremely dry conditions; **∼phile, ∼phyte,** plant able to grow in very dry conditions, e.g. in desert. [f. Gk *xēros* dry + -O-]

Xerŏx, x-, (zēr′-, zĕ′r-) *n.*, & *v.t.* (**P**) (reproduce by) a certain process of xerography; copy so made. [f. prec.]

Xho′sa (kŏ′-, kaw′-) *a.* & *n.* (member or language) of a Bantu people of Cape Province, S. Africa. [native name]

xī (*or* gzī *or* zī) *n.* fourteenth Greek letter (Ξ ξ) = x. [Gk]

x.i. *abbr.* EX² interest.

-xion (-kshon) *suf.* forming *ns.* (see -ION) from L *p.p.* stems in -x- (*fluxion, inflexion*).

xī′phoid (z-) *a.* sword-shaped; **∼ process** (at lower end of sternum). [f. Gk *xiphoeidēs* (*xiphos* sword; see -OID)]

Xmas (krĭ′smas) *n.* = CHRISTMAS. [abbr., with X for initial chi of Gk *Khristos* Christ]

xo′an|ŏn (z-) *n.* (*pl.* **∼a**). (Gk Ant.) primitive usu. wooden image of deity supposed to have fallen from heaven. [Gk (*xeō* carve)]

X-ray (ĕ′ks-) *n.*, & *v.t.* **1.** *n.* (in *pl.*) electromagnetic radiation of short wavelength, able to pass through opaque bodies. **2.** picture made by effect of X-rays on photographic plate, esp. showing position of bones etc. by their greater absorption of the rays. **3.** *v.t.* photograph, examine, or treat with X-rays. [transl. of G *x-strahlen* pl., so called by their discoverer (see ROENTGEN) from their then unknown nature]

Xt(ian) *abbrs.* Christ(ian). [cf. XMAS]

xÿ′lĕm (z-) *n.* (Bot.) woody tissue (opp. PHLOEM). [f. Gk *xulon* wood]

xÿ′lēne (z-) *n.* (Chem.) one of three isomeric hydrocarbons formed from benzene by substitution of two methyl groups, obtained from wood etc. [f. as prec. + -ENE]

xÿ′lo- (z-) *comb. form.* wood, as: **∼carp(ous),** (having) hard woody fruit; **∼graph,** (esp. early) wood-engraving; **∼graphy** (-ŏ′g-), (esp. early or primitive) engraving on wood, use of wood blocks in printing; **∼phagous** (-ŏ′f-), (of insect) eating, or boring into, wood. [f. Gk *xulon* wood + -O-]

xÿ′lonīte (z-) *n.* celluloid. [irreg. f. *xyloidin* (as prec., -OID, -IN) + -ITE¹]

xÿ′lophōn|e (z-) *n.* musical instrument of flat wooden bars graduated in length and struck with small wooden hammer(s); hence **∼IST** (3) *n.* [f. Gk *xulon* wood + -O- + -PHONE]

xÿ′st|us (z-) *n.* (*pl.* **∼i** *pr.* -ī). covered portico used by ancient-Greek athletes for exercise; (Rom. Ant.) garden walk or terrace. [L, f. Gk *xustos* smooth (*xuō* scrape)]

Y

Y, y, (wī) *n.* (*pl.* **Ys** *or* **Y's**). twenty-fifth letter of alphabet; (Alg., usu. *y*) second unknown quantity; (Geom.) second coordinate; Y-shaped arrangement of lines, piping, roads, etc., forked clamp or support; **Y-cross,** Y-shaped cross esp. on chasuble, suggesting figure of crucified Christ; **Y-moth** (of genus *Plusia*, with mark like Y on wings).

y̆- *pref.* (arch.) of *p.p.*, collective *ns.*, etc., (*yclept*); cf. AMONG, ENOUGH, HANDIWORK. [OE *ge-* f. Gmc **ga-*]

-y̆¹ *suf.* forming *ns.* denoting (1) state, condition, or quality, (*courtesy, fury, glory, synchrony*); (2) action or its result (*colloquy, remedy, subsidy*); (3) object formed (*company, library*); (4) name of country etc. (*Italy*). [f. or after F *-ie* f. Rom. f. L *-ia*, Gk *-(e)ia*, or L *-ium*; cf. -ACY, -ERY, -GRAPHY, etc.]

-y̆² *suf.* forming *adjs.* f. *ns.* & *adjs.*, w. sense 'full of', 'having the quality of', 'addicted to', (*gluey, horsy, icy, messy, slangy, thorny*), & f. *vbs.* w. sense 'inclined to', 'apt to', (*preachy, runny, sticky*). [f. or after OE *-ig* f. Gmc **-iga, *-aga*]

-y̆³ *suf.* forming dim. *ns.*, pet names, etc., (*granny, jenny, Sally*). [ME; orig. Sc. (cf. -IE)]

-y̆⁴ *suf.* forming *ns.*, & *adjs.* (esp. Her.), (*army, county, easy, paly*). [f. AF & OF *-e(e)* f. L *-atu-, -ata-*; cf. -ATE¹,²]

Y. *abbr.* yen; Yeomanry; * = YMCA or YWCA.

y. *abbr.* year(s).

Y *symb.* yttrium.

yă′bby̆, yă′bbie, *n.* (Austral.) small freshwater crayfish often used as bait. [Aboriginal]

yacht (yŏt) *n.*, & *v.i.* **1.** *n.* light sailing-vessel kept, and usu. specially built and rigged, for racing; similar vessel for travel on sand or ice; vessel propelled by sails, steam, electricity, or motive power other than oars, and used for private pleasure excursions, cruising, travel, etc.; ∼-**club** (esp. for yacht-racing); ∼′**sman,** person who yachts. **2.** *v.i.* race or cruise in yacht; hence ∼′ING¹ (1) *n.* [f. early mod. Du. *jaghte* = *jaghtschip* fast pirate-ship f. *jag(h)t* chase (*jagen* to hunt) + *schip* SHIP¹]

yăck(etў-yă′ck) *n.*, & *v.i.* (sl., derog.) (engage in) trivial or unduly persistent conversation. [imit.]

yă′ffle *n.* (dial.) green woodpecker. [imit. of its laughing cry]

yager. Var. of JAEGER¹.

yah *int.* expr. derision or defiance. [imit.]

yahōō′ (ya-h-) *n.* brute in human shape; coarse person of bestial passions and habits. [name of imaginary race of brutish men in Swift's *Gulliver's Travels*]

Yah′veh, Yah′weh, Yah′vist, etc. See JEHOVAH, JEHOVIST.

yăk *n.* long-haired humped grunting wild or domesticated ox of Tibet. [f. Tibetan *gyag*]

Yāle *n.* (**P**) ∼ **lock,** type of lock for doors etc., with revolving barrel. [f. L. ∼, Amer. inventor d. 1868]

yăm *n.* (edible starchy tuber of) tropical or subtropical climbing plant of genus *Dioscorea*; *sweet POTATO. [f. Port. *inhame* or Sp. *iñame*, of unkn. orig.]

yă′mmer *v.i.*, & *n.* (colloq. or dial.) lament, wail, grumble; (utter) voluble talk. [OE *geōmrian* (*geōmor* sorrowful)]

yăng *n.* (Chin. Philos.) active male principle of universe (opp. *yin*). [Chin.]

yănk¹ *v.t.*, & *n.* (colloq.) **1.** *v.t.* pull (lever etc., or abs.) with a jerk. **2.** *n.* sudden hard pull. [19th c.; orig. unkn.]

Yănk² *n.* (colloq.) = foll. [abbr.]

Ya′nkee (-kĭ) *n.* *inhabitant of New England; *inhabitant of northern States, Federal soldier in Civil War; ‖(colloq.) inhabitant of US, American; type of bet on four or more horses to win (or be placed) in different races; (*attrib.*) of or as of the Yankees; ∼ **Doodle,** (1) American tune and song regarded as a national air, (2) = *Yankee*; hence ∼DOM, ∼ISM (2, 4), *ns.*, ∼FY *v.t.* [perh. f. Du *Janke* dim. of *Jan* John used derisively (1683), or perh. orig. pl. f. *Jengees*, Amer. Ind. pronunc. of *English*]

yaourt. See YOGHURT.

yăp *v.i.* (-**pp**-), & *n.* **1.** *v.i.* bark shrilly or fussily; (colloq.) talk noisily or foolishly or complainingly. **2.** *n.* sound of yapping. [imit.]

yă′pŏck *n.* S. Amer. water-opossum, with webbed hind feet. [f. *Oyapok, Oiapoque*, N. Brazilian river]

‖**yăpp** *n.* kind of bookbinding with limp leather cover projecting to fold over edges of leaves. [name of London bookseller *c.* 1860, for whom first made]

yâr′borough (-ro) *n.* whist or bridge hand with no card above a 9. [f. Earl of *Yarborough* (d. 1897), said to have betted against its occurrence]

yârd¹ *n.* **1.** unit of linear measure, = 3 feet or 0.9144 metre; = SQUARE² or CUBIC yard (*of* sand etc.); yard-length of material (*a yard and a half of cloth*); (in *pl.*, colloq.) great length *of*; **by the** ∼, (fig.) at great length; ‖∼ **of ale,** (contents of) deep slender glass for liquor; ‖∼ **of clay,** long clay pipe; ‖ **of tin,** coachman's horn. **2.** cylindrical spar tapering to each end slung horizontally (*square yard*) or slantwise (*lateen yard*) across mast to support sail (*lower topsail, topgallant, royal, yard, according to sail supported*); **man the** ∼**s,** place men, stand, along yards as form of salute. **3.** ∼-**arm,** (either end of) yard (sense 2); ∼ **measure,** rod, tape, etc., a yard long and usu. divided into feet, inches, and quarters or fifths; ∼′**stick,** rigid yard-measure, (fig.) standard of comparison. [f. OE *gerd*, **gierd, gyrd*, = OS *gerdia* twig, OHG *gart(e)a, gerta* f. WG **gazdjō*; cf. GADFLY]

yârd² *n.*, & *v.t.* **1.** *n.* piece of enclosed ground, especially one surrounded by or attached to building(s) or used for some manufacturing or other purpose (BOAT¹, BRICK¹, CHURCH¹, COURT¹, DOCK¹, FARM¹, GRAVE¹, SHIP¹, STOCK, *-yard,* VINEYARD); *garden of house; ‖**the Y**∼, (colloq.) SCOTLAND YARD; ∼-**man,** man working in railway-yard or timber-yard, *gardener or one who does various outdoor jobs; ∼-**master,** manager of railway-yard. **2.** *v.t.* put (cattle) into stockyard. [OE *geard* enclosure, region, = OS *gardo*, OHG *gart(o)*, ON *garthr* (cf. GARTH), Goth. *gards* house, *garda* enclosure, f. Gmc **gardaz*; cf. GARDEN]

yâr′dage *n.* total number of yards; (payment for) use of a stockyard etc. [f. YARD¹,² + -AGE]

yâr′mulka *n.* skull-cap worn by Jewish men. [Yiddish]

yârn *n.*, & *v.i.* **1.** *n.* any spun thread esp. of kinds prepared for weaving, knitting, or rope-making. **2.** (colloq.) story, traveller's tale, anecdote, rambling discourse, (SPIN¹ *a yarn*). **3.** *v.i.* (colloq.) tell yarns. [OE *gearn* = OHG, ON *garn*]

yă′rrow (-ō) *n.* perennial herb of genus *Achillea*, esp. milfoil. [OE *gearwe*, = OHG *gar(a)wa*, of unkn. orig.]

yă′shmăk *n.* veil worn in public by Muslim women of some countries, concealing whole of face except eyes. [f. Arab. *yašmak*, Turk. *yaşmak*]

yă′taghăn (-găn) *n.* sword without guard and often with double-curved blade, used in Muslim countries. [f. Turk. *yātāğan*]

yaw *v.i.*, & *n.* (Naut. & Aeron.) **1.** *v.i.* (Of ship, aircraft, spacecraft, etc.) fail to hold straight course, fall off, go unsteadily (esp. turning from side to side). **2.** *n.* yawing of ship etc. from course. [16th c., of unkn. orig.]

yawl *n.* **1.** (Hist.) ship's jolly-boat with four or six oars.

2. two-masted fore-and-aft sailing-boat with mizen-mast stepped far aft; small kind of fishing-boat. [f. MLG *jolle* or Du. *jol*, of unkn. orig.; cf. JOLLY²-*boat*]

yawn *v.* & *n.* **1.** *v.i.* (Of chasm etc.) gape, be wide open, (*a yawning gulf, rent,* etc.). **2.** (Of person or animal) open the mouth wide and inhale as effect of drowsiness, boredom, etc. **3.** *v.t.* utter or say with a yawn. **4.** *n.* act of yawning; (sl.) something boring. [OE *ginian*, *geonian*, = OHG *ginōn*]

***yawp** *v.i.*, & *n.* (utter) harsh or hoarse cry, or foolish talk. [ME; imit.]

yaws (-z) *n. pl.* (usu. treated as *sing.*) contagious bacterial skin-disease of tropical countries, with raspberry-like excrescences. [17th c.; orig. unkn.]

Yb *symb.* ytterbium.

Y-chromosome (wī′kr-) *n.* chromosome occurring in only male cells, whose presence or absence in zygote determines sex of new individual formed in reproduction. [f. *Y* as arbitrary label + CHROMOSOME]

yclě′pt *a.* (arch. or joc.) called (by the name of). [OE *gecleopod* p.p. of *cleopian* call f. Gmc **klipōjan*]

yd(s). *abbr.* yard(s).

ye¹ *pron.* (arch.) YOU, occas. **ye,** *refl.* YOURSELVES or **you** *or* ye, *poss.* YOUR, YOURS). (poet., arch., religious, dial., or joc.) Pl. of THOU¹ (*blessed are ye; ye zephyrs gay; how d'ye do?*); **ye gods (and little fishes)!** (joc. int. of astonishment). [OE *ge*, = OS *gi, ge,* OHG *ir,* ON *ér,* forms assim. to *we* etc. ult. f. Gmc **juz* (cf. YOU)]

ye² (*or as* THE) *a.* (pseudo-arch.) = THE (*ye olde tea-shoppe*). [var. sp. due to use of *y*-shaped letter THORN in 14th c.]

yea (yā) *adv.* & *n.* (arch.) **1.** *adv.* yes (*let your communication be* ∼, ∼, **nay, nay,** yes and no without oaths); indeed, nay, (*ready, yea eager*). **2.** *n.* the word 'yea'; ∼**s and nays,** ayes and noes, affirmative and negative votes; ∼ **and nay,** shilly-shally. [OE *gea, ge,* = OS, OHG *jā,* ON *já,* Goth. *ja, jai* f. Gmc **ja, *je*]

yeah (yĕa) *adv.* (colloq.) yes; (**oh**) ∼? (expr. incredulity). [casual pronunc. of YES]

yean *v.t.* & *i.* (arch.) bring forth (lamb or kid). [perh. f. OE **geēanian* (as Y-, *ēanian* to lamb)]

yea′nling *n.* (arch.) young lamb or kid. [f. prec. + -LING¹]

year (yēr, yĕr) *n.* **1.** time occupied by the earth in one revolution round the sun (**astronomical, equinoctial, natural, solar, tropical,** ∼, 365d. 5h. 48m. 46s. in length) or (**sidereal** ∼, longer by 20m. 23s. because of precession) by the sun in returning to the same position in relation to the fixed stars; **great** or **Platonic** ∼, period (estimated by ancient astronomers at about 26,000 years) occupied by the celestial bodies in returning to same relative positions. **2.** (**calendar** or **civil**) ∼, period of days (esp. **common** ∼ of 365 or LEAP¹ ∼ of 366 reckoned from 1 Jan.) used for time-reckoning in ordinary affairs, commencing on a certain day and corresponding more or less exactly in length to the astronomical year; **lunar** ∼ (of 12 lunar months); LUNISOLAR *year*; *year of* GRACE, *of Our* LORD; ||**in the** ∼ **dot** or **one,** (colloq.) very long ago; FROM *year to year, year* BY¹ *year; year* IN² *year out;* **of the** ∼, chosen as outstanding in a particular year (*award to Sportsman of the Year*). **3.** period of same length as civil year commencing at any day; group of students entering college etc. in same academic year; **Christian, Church, ecclesiastical,** ∼, round of sacred seasons reckoned from and to Advent; **financial** or **fiscal year** or **tax** ∼ (reckoned from ||1 or 6 Apr. or ***1 Jan. or July for taxing and accounting purposes); SABBATICAL *year*; **academic** or **school** ∼ (usu. reckoned from beginning of autumn term); **a** ∼ **and a day,** period specified in some legal matters to ensure completion of a full year; **a** ∼ (**from**) **today** etc., 12 months before or esp. after today etc. **4.** (in *pl.*) age, time of life; **young for his** ∼**s,** not showing much sign of his age; (**getting on**) **in** ∼**s,** old. **5.** (in *sing.* or *pl.*) very long time. **6.** ∼**-book,** annual publication bringing information on some subject up to date; ∼**-long,** lasting a year, lasting the whole year; ∼**-round,** existing etc. throughout the year. [OE *gē(a)r,* = OS, OHG *jār,* ON *ár,* Goth. *jēr* f. Gmc **jǣram* f. IE **jēr-, *jōr-*]

year′ling (yēr′-, yĕr′-) *n.* & *a.* **1.** *n.* animal more than one and less than two years old; racehorse in calendar year after year of foaling. **2.** *a.* a year old, having existed or been such for a year, (*yearling heifer, bride*); intended to terminate after one year (*yearling bonds*). [f. prec. + -LING¹]

year′ly (yēr′-, yĕr′-) *a.* & *adv.* (produced or occurring) once every year, annual(ly); of or for or lasting a year. [OE *gēarlic, -lice* (as YEAR, -LY¹,²)]

yearn (yern) *v.i.* be filled with longing or compassion or tenderness (*for* or *after* rest, home, affection, etc.; *to* do; *towards* or *to* person etc.); hence ∼′ING¹ *n.,* ∼′ING² *a.* [OE *giernan,* = OS *girnean,* ON *girna,* Goth. *gairnjan* f. Gmc **gernjan* (**gernaz* eager)]

yeast *n.* yellowish frothy viscous substance consisting of fungous cells developed by germination in contact with saccharine liquids and producing alcoholic fermentation, used in brewing beer, making wine, distilling spirit, and raising bread etc.; dried form of this used in baking; ∼ **cake, pastry,** (made light with yeast). [OE **g(i)est, gist,* = MDu. *ghist,* MHG *jist,* ON *jöstr*]

yea′st|y *a.* frothy like yeast; in a ferment, working like yeast; wordy, superficial; hence ∼**iLY²** *adv.,* ∼**iNESS** *n.* [f. prec. + -Y⁰]

***yĕgg** *n.* (sl.) ∼(′**man**), travelling burglar or safe-breaker. [said to be a surname]

yĕll *v.* & *n.* **1.** (make, utter with) sharp loud cry of pain or anger or fright or delight or derision (*yelled with pain, fury, laughter;* yelled curses, my name, a refusal, defiance; with yells of horror); shout. **2.** *n.* *organized cry used by students e.g. in encouraging their representatives in athletic contests. [OE *g(i)ellan,* = OHG *gellan,* ON *gjalla* f. Gmc **gel-, *gal-;* cf. NIGHTINGALE]

yě′llow (-ō) *a., n., a.* & *v.* **1.** *a.* of the colour between green and orange in the spectrum, coloured like buttercup or primrose or lemon or egg-yolk or gold, (as distinguishing epithet of plants, animals, etc.: *yellow* RATTLE², ROCKET¹, *wagtail, ochre;* often also in comb. with parts of body etc.: *yellow-bill, -legs, -root, -rump, -seed, -shank, -tail, -throat, -top, -wood,* forming animal and plant names); of the colour of faded leaves, ripe wheat, etc.; having yellow skin or complexion. **2.** ∼**back,** cheap novel etc. in yellow cover; ∼**-belly,** (1) a coward, (2) fish with yellow underparts; ∼ **cedar,** evergreen ornamental tree from NW America (*Chamaecyparis nootkatensis*); ***∼ **dog,** mongrel; ***∼**-dog** *a.,* antagonistic to trade unions; ∼ **fever,** tropical virus disease with fever and jaundice; *yellow* FLAG⁴; ∼**hammer,** bunting of which the male has yellow head, neck, and breast [*-hammer* of uncert. orig.]; ∼ **Jack,** = *yellow fever* or *flag;* the SEAR¹, the *yellow leaf;* ||∼ **lines** (painted on road beside pavement to indicate restriction on parking of vehicles); ∼ **metal,** brass of 60 parts copper and 40 parts zinc; ∼ **pages,** section of telephone directory on yellow paper and listing business subscribers according to goods or services they offer; **the** ∼ **peril,** supposed danger that the yellow races may overwhelm the white or overrun the world; **the** ∼ **press,** unscrupulously sensational newspapers; ∼ **soap,** common household soap; ∼ **spot,** point of acutest vision in retina; ∼ **streak,** trait of cowardice. **3.** (fig.) (Of looks, mood, feelings, etc.) jealous, envious, suspicious; (colloq.) cowardly. **4.** Hence ∼**iSH¹** 2, ∼**Y²,** *adjs.,* ∼**iLY²** *adv.,* ∼**iNESS** *n.* **5.** *n.* yellow colour; yellow pigment; yellow clothes or material (*dressed in yellow*); yellow ball in snooker etc.; (colloq.) cowardice; yellow moth or butterfly; **the** ∼**s,** jaundice of horses etc.; ***a peach-disease with yellowed leaves. **6.** *v.t.* & *i.* make or become yellow (*paper yellowed with age; the yellowing leaves*). [OE *geolu, geolo,* = OS, OHG *gelo* f. WG **gelwa* f. IE **ghelwo-,* rel. to GOLD]

yělp *v.i.*, & *n.* (utter) sharp shrill cry (as) of dog in pain or excitement; hence ∼'ER¹ *n.* [OE *gielp*(*an*) boast, imit.; cf. YAWP]

yěn¹ *n.* (*pl.* same). Japanese monetary unit. [Jap., f. Chin. *yuan* round, dollar]

yěn² *n.*, & *v.i.* (-nn-). (sl.) **1.** *n.* longing, yearning. **2.** *v.i.* yearn. [Chin. dial.]

yeo'man (yō'-) *n.* (*pl.* yeo'men). **1.** man holding and cultivating small landed estate; (Hist.) person qualified by possessing free land of annual value 40 shillings to serve on juries, vote for knight of shire, etc.; (Hist.) servant in royal or noble household. **2.** ||member of the yeomanry force; ||∼ (**of signals**), petty officer in Navy, concerned with visual signalling; *petty officer performing clerical duties on board ship. **3.** ∼('s) **service**, efficient or useful help in need; ||Y∼ **of the Guard**, member of sovereign's bodyguard, (pop.) warder in Tower of London; ||Y∼ **Usher**, deputy of Black Rod. **4.** Hence ∼LY¹ *a.* [ME *yoman*, *yeman*, etc. prob. f. YOUNG + MAN¹]

yeo'manrỹ (yō'-) *n.* body of yeomen; ||(Hist.) volunteer cavalry force raised chiefly from yeoman class (1794–1908). [ME, f. prec. + -RY]

*yěp. Var. (colloq.) of YES.

-yer *suf.* var. of -IER, esp. after *w* (*bowyer*, *lawyer*, *sawyer*).

yěr'ba *n.* ∼ **maté**, = MATÉ. [Sp., = herb]

yěs *adv.* & *n.* **1.** the answer to your question is affirmative, it is as you say or as I have said, your request or command will be complied with, the statement made or course intended is correct or satisfactory, the negative statement etc. made is not correct ('*It isn't ready*'—'*Yes, it is*'); ∼ **and, or,** (forms for introducing stronger phr.: *I could endure, yes, and enjoy it*; *he would beat me, yes, and you too*); ∼?, indeed?, is that so?, what do you want?; ∼, ∼ (emphat.); OH¹ *yes*; ∼ **and no**, that is partly true and partly untrue. **2.** (In answer to summons or address) I am here, I hear or am attending to you. **3.** *n.* the word or answer *yes* (say ∼, grant request, accept proposal, confirm statement); ∼**-man** (colloq.) characterless, obedient, weakly acquiescent person. [OE *gēse*, *gīse*, prob. f. **gīa* YEA + *sīe* 3 sing. pres. subj. of *bēon* BE]

yěster- *comb. form.* (poet. or arch.) of yesterday, that is last past, (*yester-eve, yestermorn, yesternight*); ∼**-year**, (1) last year, (2) the recent past. [OE *geostran*, = OHG *gestaron*]

yě'sterday (-dā, -dĭ) *n.* & *adv.* (on) the day before today (*arrived yesterday*; *yesterday was her birthday*); (in) the recent past (*is but of yesterday*; *not* BORN *yesterday*); ∼ **morning, afternoon,** etc., (*ns.* & *advs.*) (*in*) the morning etc. of yesterday. [OE *giestran dæg* (as prec., DAY)]

yět *adv.* & *conj.* **1.** *adv.* as late as now or then, with continuance to this or to that time, still, (*there is yet time; is he yet living?; there is life in the old dog yet; much yet remains to be done; his greatest achievement yet; his yet unfinished task; I seem to see him yet; while it was yet morning*); AS¹ *yet*. **2.** (w. neg. or interrog.) so soon as now or then, by this or by that time, so far, in the immediate future, (*it is not time yet; is he dead yet?; they have not yet heard; I have never yet lied; need you go (just) yet?; it will not happen just yet; these things are not yet*). **3.** again, in addition, (*yet once more; another and another and yet another; yet again; more and yet more*); **nor** ∼, and also not (*won't listen to me nor yet to her*). **4.** before the matter is done with, before all is over, in the time that still remains (though not hitherto), (*he will win, I will be even with you, yet*). **5.** (w. compar.) even (*a yet more difficult, easier, task*). **6.** nevertheless, and in spite of that, but for all that, (*it is strange, and yet it is true; strange and yet true; the logic seems sound, but or and yet it does not convince me*). **7.** *conj.* but at the same time, but nevertheless, (*the work is done, yet what is the use of it all?; faint yet pursuing*). [OE *gīet*(*a*), = OFris. *iēta*, of unkn. orig.]

yě'tĭ *n.* = ABOMINABLE Snowman. [Tibetan]

yew *n.* ∼(-**tree**), slow-growing dark-leaved evergreen coniferous tree of genus *Taxus* often planted in churchyards; its wood, used formerly as material for bows and still in cabinet-making. [OE *īw, ēow,* = OS *īh*, OHG *īwa*, ON *ȳr* bow f. Gmc **īhw-, *īgw-*]

Y'ggdrasil (ĭ'-) *n.* (Scand. Myth.) ash-tree whose roots and branches join heaven and earth and hell. [f. ON *yg*(*g*)*drasill* (*Yggr* Odin, *drasill* horse)]

||**YHA** *abbr.* Youth Hostels Association.

Yĭd *n.* (sl., derog.; R) Jew. [back-form. f. foll.]

Yĭ'ddish *a.* & *n.* (of) language used by Jews in or from central and eastern Europe, orig. a Middle Rhine dialect, with words from Hebrew and several modern languages; hence ∼ER¹ *a.* & *n.*, (person) speaking Yiddish. [f. G *jüdisch* Jewish]

yield *v.* & *n.* **1.** *v.t.* give or return or bring as fruit or result (*earth yields her increase; land yields good crops; investment yields 15%; betting tax yields a large revenue*); (abs., of land etc.) repay cultivation etc. *well, poorly,* etc. **2.** give up, deliver over, surrender, resign, comply with demand for, concede, (*yield fortress*, one*self prisoner; yield possession*, one's *pride of place; yield precedence to; yield the* PALM¹; *yield up the* GHOST; ∼ **the point,** concede it in argument). **3.** *v.i.* surrender, make submission to, give consent or change one's course of action in deference *to*, comply with demand, respond as desired *to*, be inferior or confess inferiority *to*, (*town yielded without awaiting assault; yield to superior force, persuasion, treatment, seducer; courage never to submit or yield; I yield to none in appreciation of his merits*); give right of way (*to* other traffic); *allow another the right to speak in debate etc. **4.** *n.* amount yielded or produced, output, return; ∼ **point**, (Phys.) stress beyond which material becomes plastic. [OE *g(i)eldan* pay, = OS *geldan*, OHG *geltan*, ON *gjalda*, Goth. *-gildan* f. Gmc **geldhan* pay]

yĭn *n.* (Chin. Philos.) passive female principle of universe (opp. *yang*). [Chin.]

*yĭp *v.i.* (-pp-), & *n.* = YELP. [imit.]

yĭ'ppee *int.* expr. delight or excitement. [cf. HIP⁵]

yĭ'ppie, yĭ'ppỹ, *n.* politically active Amer. hippie. [f. *Y*outh *I*nternational *P*arty, after HIPPIE]

-ỹl *suf.* (Chem.) forming *ns.* denoting a radical (*amyl, ethyl, phenyl*). [f. F *-yle* f. Gk *hūlē* wood, substance]

y'lăng-ylăng (ē'l-; -ēl-) *n.* Malayan tree (*Cananga odorata*) from the fragrant yellow flowers of which a perfume is distilled; the perfume itself. [f. Tagalog *ĕlang-ilang*]

YMCA *abbr.* Young Men's Christian Association.

-ỹne *suf.* (Chem.) forming names of unsaturated compounds containing a triple bond (*ethyne* = acetylene). [alt. f. -INE⁵]

yŏb('bō) *n.* (*pl.* ∼s). (sl.) lout, hooligan. [back sl. for BOY; see -O]

yŏd *n.* tenth and smallest letter of Hebrew alphabet; the sound (y). [f. Heb. *yōd* (*yad* hand)]

yō'del *v.* (||-ll-) & *n.* **1.** *v.t.* & *i.* sing with melodious inarticulate sounds and frequent changes between falsetto and normal voice in the manner of Swiss and Tyrolean mountain-dwellers. **2.** *n.* yodelling cry. [f. G *jodeln*]

yō'g|a *n.* Hindu system of philosophic meditation and asceticism designed to effect reunion with the universal spirit; = HATHA YOGA; hence ∼IC (-g-) *a.* [Hind. f. Skr., = union]

yŏgh (-g, -χ) *n.* Middle-English letter used for certain values of *g* and *y*. [ME]

yō'ghurt (-gert), **yō'gurt, yaourt** (yah'oort), *n.* semi-solid sourish junket-like or curd-like food prepared from milk fermented by added bacteria. [f. Turk. *yoğurt*]

yō'g|i (-gĭ) *n.* devotee of yoga; hence ∼ISM (3) *n.* [Hind. (YOGA)]

yō'-heave-hō *int.* & *n.* = HEAVE¹ *ho.*

yō-(hŏ-)hō' *int.* used to attract attention, or = prec. [cf. prec. & HO]

yoicks int. fox-hunter's halloo. [orig. unkn.; cf. *hyke* call to hounds, HEY¹]

yōke n. & v. **1.** n. wooden cross-piece fastened over necks of two oxen etc. and attached to the plough or wagon that they are to (help to) draw; (Rom. Hist.) uplifted yoke or arch of three spears symbolizing it under which defeated enemy was made to march (*army passed under the yoke*); (fig.) sway or dominion or servitude (*submitted to his yoke; had never endured the yoke*); (fig.) bond of union, esp. the marriage tie. **2.** pair of oxen etc. (*pl.* often same after numeral); (arch.) amount of land that one yoke of oxen can plough in a day. **3.** piece of timber shaped to fit person's shoulders and support pail etc. at each end. **4.** separately made shoulder-piece of shirt or coat or blouse, or piece fitted to top part of skirt, from which the rest hangs. **5.** object shaped like yoke; crossbar on which bell swings; crossbar of rudder to whose ends ropes are fastened; bar of soft iron between poles of electromagnet. **6.** ∼-**bone,** cheek-bone connecting bones of head and face; ∼'**fellow,** ∼'**mate,** partner in marriage, work, etc. **7.** v.t. put yoke on; couple or unite (esp. pair) in marriage or otherwise, link (one *to* another). **8.** v.i. match or work together. [OE *geoc*, = OS *juc*, OHG *joh*, Goth. *juk*, ON *ok* f. Gmc **jukam* f. IE **jugom*]

yō'kel n. rustic, country bumpkin. [perh. f. dial. *yokel* green woodpecker]

yōlk¹ (yōk) n. yellow internal part of egg, nourishing the young before hatching, (Biol.) corresponding part of any animal ovum; ∼-**bag, -sac,** membrane enclosing yolk of egg; hence (-)∼ED² (-kt), ∼'Y², adjs. [OE *geol(o)ca* (*geolu* YELLOW)]

yōlk² (yōk) n. = SUINT. [OE **eowoca*]

Yŏm Ki'ppur n. = Day of ATONEMENT. [Heb.]

yŏn a., adv., & pron. (arch. or poet. or dial.) **1.** a. & adv. yonder; HITHER *and yon*. **2.** pron. yonder person or thing. [OE *geon*, = OHG *jenēr*, ON *enn*, Goth. *jains* that]

yŏ'nder a. & adv. (literary) (situated) over there, at some distance in the direction towards which I am looking or pointing, within or conceived as within view but distant. [ME; cf. OS *gendra*, Goth. *jaindrē*]

yō'ni n. symbol of female genitals venerated by Hindus etc. [Skr.]

yoō'-hoō int. expr. desire to attract person's attention. [spontaneous utterance]

yōre n. (literary) **of** ∼, formerly, in or of old days. [OE *geāra*, *geāre*, etc., adv. forms of uncert. orig.]

York¹ n. ∼ **and Lancaster,** rival parties in the Wars of the Roses (∼*-and-Lancaster rose,* red and white particoloured kind); **House of** ∼, English kings from Edward IV to Richard III. [f. 1st Duke of ∼ (cf. YORKIST), f. ∼ in England f. OE *Eoforwīc* f. L *Eboracum* + *wīc* dwelling]

york² v.t. (Cricket). bowl with yorker. [back-form. f. foll.]

yŏr'ker n. (Cricket). ball so bowled as to pitch immediately in front of batsman's block. [prob. f. YORK¹, as having been introduced by Yorkshire players, +-ER¹]

Yŏr'kist a. & n. (adherent) of family descended from 1st Duke of York (d. 1402, 5th son of Edward III) or of the White Rose party supporting it in the Wars of the Roses. [f. YORK¹ +-IST]

Yorks. abbr. Yorkshire.

Yŏr'kshire (-er, -ĕr) n. ∼**man,** ∼**woman,** (born or living in Yorkshire); ∼ **pudding,** batter baked and eaten with or before roast meat, esp. beef; ∼ **terrier,** small shaggy blue and tan toy kind; *Yorkshire* TYKE. [∼, former county in England]

Yŏ'ruba n. member or language of a Black people on W. Afr. coast, esp. in Nigeria. [native name]

you (ū, yoō) pron. (obj. you; refl. YOURSELF, YOURSELVES, arch. you; poss. YOUR, YOURS). **1.** Sing. (w. pl. vb.) and pl. pron. of 2nd pers.; the person(s) or thing(s) addressed; (as voc. w. n. in excl. statement:

you fool(s)!; you darling!; you idiot, you!); **∼-all,* (colloq.) you; ∼'**re another** (colloq. phr. retorting accusation on person who makes it); ∼-**know-what** or -**who,** something or someone unspecified but understood; *you and* YOURS; *not quite you* (cf. HER¹ 2). **2.** (In general statements) one, any one, all concerned, every one, a person, (*you never can tell; what are you to do with a child like this?; it is bad at first, but you soon get used to it; there's a shot for you!*). [OE *ēow* acc. & dat. of *gē* YE¹, = OS *ju,* OHG *iu(h)* f. WG **iwwi(z)*; supplanting *ye* f. more frequent use of obj. case, and *thou* and *thee* as more courteous form]

young (yŭ-) a. (∼'**er,** ∼'**est,** pr. -ngg-) & n. **1.** a. not far advanced in life or growth or development or existence, of recent birth or origin or formation, not yet old, still vigorous, immature, youthful, inexperienced, (*a young child, man, animal, plant, wine, nation, institution; young for his* YEARS); (of night, year, century, etc.) still near its beginning; (w. surname etc.) son as dist. f. father (*young Jones; the Young* PRE-TENDER), (in compar.) person as dist. f. older one of same name (*the younger Pitt; Teniers the younger*), (Sc.) heir of landed commoner (*younger of Mackintosh*); felt in or characteristic of youth (*young love, ambition,* etc.); **the** ∼, young people; ∼ **and old,** everyone. **2.** *young* BLOOD¹; one's ∼ **day(s)** (when one was young); Y∼ England, Liberals, etc., political group claiming to speak for younger members of the population; ∼ **family** (of young children); *young* RUSTIC; ∼ **girl,** unmarried adolescent girl or young woman; ∼**er hand,** (Cards) second player of two; *young* HOPEFUL; *young* IDEA; ∼ **lady** or **man** (sweetheart, girl- or boy-friend; or lit., esp. as voc.); *young* MARRIEDS; ∼ **person** (arch., esp. as viewed by the respectable elderly; ∥in Law, usu. between 14 and 17 years old); **you** ∼ **rascal** etc. (usu. playfully to child); *old head on young* SHOULDERS; ∼ **thing** (arch., indulgent description of young person); Y∼ **Turk,** (1) member of revolutionary party in Turkey 1908, (2, R) member of rebellious group in political party; ∼ **turk,** (R) violent child or youth; ∼ '**un,** (colloq., usu. as voc.) youngster; ∼ **woman** (sweetheart or girl-friend; or lit., esp. as voc.). **3.** Hence ∼'ISH¹ 2 a., ∼'LING¹ n. (arch.) **4.** n. (collect.) offspring esp. of animals before or soon after birth (**with** ∼, pregnant). [OE *g(e)ong,* = OS *jung,* OHG *junc,* ON *ungr,* Goth. *juggs* f. Gmc **ju(wu)ngaz* f. IE **juwnkos*]

you'ngster (yŭ'-) n. child, esp. active or lively boy; young person. [f. prec. +-STER, after foll.]

you'nker (yŭ'-) n. (arch.) = prec. [f. MDu. *jonckher* (*jonc* YOUNG, *hēre* lord); cf. JUNKER]

your (ŭr, yŏr, *when unstressed,* yer) *poss. pron. attrib.* **1.** of you(rself or -selves) (for phrs. see HER², OUR). **2.** (colloq., usu. derog.) much talked of, well known, familiar, (*no one so fallible as your expert in handwriting; your facetious bore is the worst of all*). [OE *ēower* gen. of *gē* YE¹, = OS *iuwar,* OHG *iuwēr,* & OE *ēower* poss. adj., = OHG *iuwar*]

yours (ūrz, yŏrz) *poss. pron.* & *pred.* a. **1.** *pron.* the one(s) belonging to or of you (for phrs. see HERS); your letter; **you and** ∼, you together with your family, property, etc. **2.** a. belonging to you, at your service, (*it is yours if you will accept it*); ∼, or ∼ EVER, FAITHFULLY, *obediently,* SINCERELY, *truly,* or COMMAND¹, or EVER etc. ∼, (formulae preceding signature of letter); ∼ **truly,** (joc.) I (the speaker or writer); **what's** ∼**?,** (colloq.) what would you like to drink? [ME, f. prec. +-s³]

yourse'lf (ūr- etc., as YOUR) *pron.* Emphat. & refl. form corresp. to YOU sing. (for uses cf. HERSELF); **how's** ∼**?,** (sl.) how are you? (esp. after answering similar inquiry). [ME, f. YOUR +SELF]

yourse'lves (ūr- etc. as YOUR; -vz) *pron.* Emphat. & refl. form corresp. to YOU pl. (for uses cf. HERSELF). [f. prec. +-s¹]

youth (ūth) n. (*pl. pr.* ūdhz). **1.** being young, adolescence, (the vigour or enthusiasm or weakness or inexperience or other characteristic of) the period between childhood and full manhood or woman-hood, (*has all the appearance of extreme youth*; *in my hot, raw, vigorous*, etc., *youth; from youth onwards; youth's a stuff will not endure; the secret of perpetual, of keeping* one's, *youth*); early stage of development etc. **2.** young man (*as a youth of 16*). **3.** (as *pl.*) young people collectively (*the youth of the country; loves to be surrounded by youth*); ∼ **centre** or **club,** place or organization provided for leisure-time activities of young people; ∼ **hostel,** place where (esp. young) holiday-makers, hikers, etc. (∼ *hostellers*) can put up cheaply for the night. [OE *geoguth*, = OS *juguth*, OHG *jugund* f. WG **jugunth-*, *juwunth-* f. Gmc **juwung-* (see YOUNG)]

you'thful (ū'-) *a.* (still) young; characteristic of the young (*youthful impatience*); having the freshness or vigour of youth (*youthful complexion*); hence ∼LY² *adv.*, ∼NESS *n.* [f. prec. + -FUL]

yowl *n.*, & *v.i.* (utter) loud wailing cry (as) of cat or dog in distress, pain, etc. [imit.]

yō'-yō *n.* (*pl.* ∼s). **1.** (*Yo-Yo*; **P**). toy consisting of pair of discs with deep groove between them in which string is attached and wound, and which can be made to fall and rise by its weight and momentum. **2.** thing which repeatedly and rapidly falls and rises again. [20th c., of unkn. orig.]

yr. *abbr.* year(s); younger; your.

yrs. *abbr.* years; yours.

ÿttér'bium *n.* (Chem.) metallic element of lanthanide series. [mod. L, f. *Ytterby* in Sweden + -IUM]

ÿ'ttrium *n.* (Chem.) trivalent metallic element, resembling those of lanthanide series. [f. as prec.]

yua'n (yōōah'n) *n.* (*pl.* same). monetary unit of China. [Chin.; see YEN¹]

yu'cca *n.* American white-flowered plant of genus *Yucca*, with swordlike leaves. [Carib]

Yu'goslav, Ju'goslav, (ū'goslahv) *a.* & *n.* (native or inhabitant) of Yugoslavia; hence ∼IAN (-ah'-) *a.* & *n.* [Austrian G. *Jugoslav* f. Serb. *jugo-* (*jug* south) + SLAV]

yule (ūl) *n.* ∼(-tide), (arch.) the Christmas festival; ∼-log (large, burnt in hearth on Christmas Eve). [OE *gēol(a)*; cf. ON *jól*; ult. orig. unkn.]

yu'mmÿ *a.* (colloq.) tasty, delicious. [f. foll. + -Y²]

yŭm-yŭ'm *int.* expr. pleasure from (prospect of) eating. [imit.]

*yŭp. Var. of YEP.

yurt (yoort) *n.* Mongolian nomads' circular skin- or felt-covered tent, with collapsible frame. [f. Russ. *yurta*]

YWCA *abbr.* Young Women's Christian Association.

Z

Z, z, (zĕd) *n.* (*pl.* **Zs** *or* **Z's**). twenty-sixth letter of alphabet; (Alg., usu. *z*) third unknown quantity; (Geom.) third coordinate; *from A to Z* (see A).

zabaglio'ne (zahbahlyō'nā) *n.* Italian sweet of whipped and heated egg yolks, sugar, and (esp. Marsala) wine. [It.]

zä'ffre (*-er*), *****zä'ffer, *n.* impure cobalt oxide used as blue pigment. [f. It. *zaffera* or f. F *safre*]

zäg *n.* sharp change of direction in zigzag course. [f. ZIGZAG]

zä'mbō *n.* (*pl.* ∼s). = SAMBO 1. [Sp.; see SAMBO]

zamī'ndār. See ZEMINDAR.

ZANU (zah'nōō) *abbr.* Zimbabwe African National Union.

zä'nў *n.* & *a.* **1.** *n.* (Hist.) attendant clown awkwardly mimicking chief clown in shows, merry andrew. **2.** person given to buffoonery, foolish jester. **3.** *a.* characteristic of a zany; comically idiotic, crazily ridiculous. [f. F *zani*, or f. It. *zan(n)i*, Venetian form of *Gianni, Giovanni* John]

zäp *v.t.* (**-pp-**). (sl.) hit, attack, knock out, kill. [imit.]

zapatea'dō (zah-; -ah'-) *n.* (*pl.* ∼-s). (Sp. dance with) rhythmic stamping of feet. [Sp. (*zapato* shoe)]

ZAPU (zah'pōō) *abbr.* Zimbabwe African People's Union.

zarape. See SERAPE.

Zarathustrian. See ZOROASTRIAN.

zari'ba (-rē'-), **zarē'ba,** *n.* hedged or palisaded enclosure for protection of camp or village in the Sudan etc. [f. Arab. *zarība* cattle-pen]

zäx. See SAX[1].

zeal *n.* earnestness or fervour in advancing a cause or rendering service; hearty and persistent endeavour; so ∼'OUS (zē'l-) *a.* [ME *zele* f. eccl. L f. Gk *zēlos*]

zea'lot (zē'l-) *n.* zealous person; uncompromising or extreme partisan, fanatic; (Z∼) one of a Jewish sect aiming at world Jewish theocracy and resisting the Romans until AD 70; hence ∼RY (4) *n.* [f. eccl. L f. Gk *zēlōtēs* (as prec.; see -OT²)]

ze'bĕc(k). Var. of XEBEC.

zē'bra *n.* **1.** striped Afr. quadruped of genus *Equus* allied to ass and horse. **2.** *attrib.* striped like zebra (*zebra finch*); ||∼ (**crossing**), striped street-crossing where pedestrians have precedence over vehicles; ∼ **wolf,** = TASMANIAN *wolf.* **3.** Hence **zē'brINE**[1] *a.* [It or Port., f. Congolese]

zē'bū *n.* humped ox (*Bos indicus*) of India, E. Asia, and Africa. [f. F *zébu*, of unkn. orig.]

Zech. *abbr.* Zechariah (OT).

||**zĕd** *n.* letter Z. [f. F *zède* f. LL f. Gk ZETA]

zĕ'dōarў *n.* aromatic ginger-like substance made from rootstock of E. Ind. plants of genus *Curcuma* and used in medicine, perfumery, and dyeing. [ME, f. med. L *zedoarium* f. Pers. *zidwār*]

*****zee** *n.* letter Z. [17th c., var. of ZED]

Zee'man (zā'-) *n.* ∼ **effect,** (Phys.) splitting of spectrum line into several components by magnetic field. [f. P. ∼, Du. physicist d. 1943]

zē'in *n.* principal protein of maize. [f. *Zea* generic name of maize + -IN]

Zeitgeist (tsī'tgīst) *n.* spirit of the times; trend of thought and feeling in a period. [G (*zeit* time, *geist* spirit)]

zĕmi'ndār, zamī'ndār, *n.* (Ind. Hist.) district governor and revenue-farmer under Mogul empire; Indian landed proprietor paying land-tax to British Government. [Hind., f. Pers. *zamindār* (*zamīn* earth, *dār* holder)]

Zĕn *n.* form of Buddhism emphasizing value of

meditation and intuition; hence ∼'(**n**)IST (3) *n.* [Jap., = meditation]

zĕna'na (-ah'-) *n.* that part of house in which women of high-caste families are secluded in India and Iran; ∼ **mission** (Hist., of women visiting zenanas to spread medical and other reform among inmates). [f. Hind. *zenāna* f. Pers. *zanāna* (*zan* woman)]

Zĕnd *n.* interpretation of the Avesta, each Zend being part of the ∼-**Avesta,** Zoroastrian scriptures of Avesta or text and Zend or commentary. [f. Pers. *zand* interpretation]

Zĕ'ner *n.* ∼ **cards,** set of 25 cards with 5 different symbols, used in ESP research. [f. K. E. ∼, Amer. psychologist b. 1903]

zē'nith *n.* **1.** point of heavens directly above observer (opp. NADIR); ∼-**distance,** arc intercepted between celestial body and zenith, complement of body's altitude. **2.** highest point, time or place of greatest power or prosperity or happiness, (*is at his, its, the, zenith*). **3.** Hence ∼AL *a.*; ∼**al projection** (of part of globe on plane tangent at centre of the part, showing correct directions of all points from centre). [ME, f. OF or med. L *cenit* ult. f. Arab. *samt* (*ar-ra's*) path (over the head)]

zē'olite *n.* one of a number of minerals consisting mainly of hydrous silicates of calcium, sodium, and aluminium, able to act as cation exchangers. [f. Sw. & G *zeolit* f. Gk *zeō* boil + -LITE (from their characteristic swelling and fusing under the blowpipe)]

Zeph. *abbr.* Zephaniah (OT).

zĕ'phyr *n.* **1.** soft mild gentle wind or breeze. **2.** athlete's thin gauzy jersey for running, rowing, boxing, etc. in; light dress-material. [f. F *zephyr* or f. L f. Gk *zephuros* (god of the) west wind]

Zĕ'ppelin *n.* large dirigible airship of type built, orig. for military use in Germany, in early 20th c. [f. Count F. von ∼, Ger. airman d. 1917, first constructor]

zēr'ō *n.* (*pl.* ∼s) & *v.* **1.** *n.* figure 0, nought, cipher; no quantity or number, nil; starting-point of scale from which positive or negative quantity is reckoned; temperature of freezing-point of water or other point selected to graduate thermometer-scale from (**absolute** ∼, temperature at which the particles whose motion constitutes heat would have least possible energy, −273.15°C); GROUND[1] *zero.* **2.** ∼ (**hour**), (orig. & esp. Mil.) hour at which timed programme is to begin. **3.** lowest point, nullity, nonentity. **4.** Hence ∼TH² *a.*, coming next before what is regarded as 'first' in series. **5.** *v.t.* adjust (instrument etc.) to zero point. **6.** *v.i.* set gun-sights for firing; ∼ **in on,** take aim at (target etc.), focus attention on. [f. F. *zéro* or f. It. f. OSp. *zero* f. Arab. *ṣifr* (CIPHER¹)]

zĕst *n.* piquancy, stimulating flavour, (esp. fig.; *adds a zest to*); keen enjoyment or interest, relish (*for*) gusto, (*entered into it with zest*); piece of orange or lemon peel as flavouring; hence ∼'FUL, ∼'Y², *adjs.* [f. F *zeste* orange or lemon peel, of unkn. orig.]

zē'ta *n.* sixth Greek letter (Z, ζ) = z. [f. Gk *zēta*]

zētē'tic *a.* proceeding by inquiry. [f. Gk *zētētikos* (*zēteō* seek; see -IC)]

zeu'gma *n.* figure of speech using a verb or adjective with two nouns, to one of which it is strictly applicable while the word appropriate to the other is not used (e.g. *kill the boys and* [sc. *destroy*] *the luggage, with weeping eyes and* [sc. *grieving*] *hearts*); cf. SYLLEPSIS; hence **zeugmä'tic** *a.* [L, f. Gk *zeugma -atos* (*zeugnumi* to yoke, *zugon* yoke)]

Zeus *n.* (Gk Myth.) supreme god of Olympus; **by** ∼**!,** = *by* JOVE. [Gk]

zhō. Var. of DZHO.

zi'bet, *zi'beth (-t), *n.* Asian or Indian civet (*Viverra zibetha*); its perfume. [f. med. L *zibethum* (see CIVET)]

zi'ggurat *n.* pyramidal tower in ancient Mesopotamia, surmounted by temple. [f. Assyr. *ziqquratu* pinnacle]

zi'gzag *a., adv., n.,* & *v.i.* (-gg-). **1.** *a.* & *adv.* with abrupt alternate right and left turns, with alternating salient and re-entrant angles, with motion as of tacking ship, (*a zigzag line, course, road, fence, trench, flash of lightning*). **2.** *n.* zigzag line or (esp. for ascending steep hill) road or (in sieges) set of trenches. **3.** *v.i.* move in zigzag course. [F, f. G *zickzack*, symbolic form.]

zi'llah (-*a*) *n.* administrative district in India, containing several pergunnahs. [f. Hind. *dilah* division]

*zi'llion (-lyon) *n.* indefinite large number. [f. z (perh. = unknown quantity) + MILLION]

zinc *n.,* & *v.t.* (-c- *or* -k- *or* -ck-, *pr.* -k-). **1.** *n.* white metallic element used as component of brass and German silver, as roofing material, as coating for sheet iron (cf. GALVANIZE), in electric batteries, and in printing-plates; (*zinc*) BLENDE; **flowers of** ~ or ~ **oxide,** powder used as white pigment and in ~ **ointment;** hence ~'IC *a.*, ~'IFY *v.t.*, ~'Y² *a.* (*or* -k- *or* -ck-; *pr.* -k-). **2.** *v.t.* coat or treat with zinc. [f. G *zink*, of unkn. orig.]

zi'nco *n.* (*pl.* ~s) & *v.* = foll. [abbr.]

zi'nco|graph (-ahf) *n.* & *v.* **1.** *n.* zinc plate with design etched in relief on it for printing from; print taken from this. **2.** *v.t.* & *i.* etch on zinc; reproduce (design) thus. **3.** So ~GRAPHY (-ŏ'g-) *n.*, ~TYPE¹ *n.* = *zinco-graph.* [f. ZINC + -O- + -GRAPH]

zing *n.,* & *v.i.* (colloq.) **1.** *n.* vigour, energy; hence ~'Y² *a.* **2.** *v.i.* move swiftly or shrilly. [imit.]

Zi'ngar|o (-ngg-) *n.* (*pl.* ~i). gypsy. [It.]

zink-. See ZINC.

zi'nnia *n.* composite plant of genus *Zinnia*, with showy rayed flowers of deep red and other colours. [f. J. G. *Zinn*, Ger. physician and botanist d. 1759 + -IA¹]

Zi'on *n.* (holy hill of) ancient Jerusalem; the Jewish religion; the Christian Church; the Heavenly Jerusalem or kingdom of heaven; ||nonconformist chapel. [OE, f. eccl. L *Sion* f. Heb. *şīyôn*]

Zi'on|ism *n.* movement founded 1897 that has sought and achieved the re-establishment of a Jewish nation in Palestine; so ~IST (2) *n.* [f. prec. + -ISM]

zip *n.* & *v.* (-pp-). **1.** *n.* light sharp sound, as of bullet passing through air, the sudden tearing of cloth, etc. **2.** (fig.) energy, vigour; hence ~'PY² *a.* **3.** ~(-fastener), fastening device consisting of two flexible strips with interlocking projections closed or opened by sliding clip pulled along them; ~-bag etc. (equipped with zip-fastener for closing). **4.** *Zip code, system of five-figure numbers used to identify postal delivery areas [f. *zone improvement plan*]. **5.** *v.t.* & *i.* fasten (*up*) with zip-fastener; hence ~'pER¹ *n.*, zip-fastener. **6.** *v.i.* move with zip or at high speed. [imit.]

zir'con *n.* zirconium silicate of which some translucent varieties (HYACINTH, JARGON²) are cut into gems. [f. G *zirkon*; cf. JARGON²]

zirco'nium *n.* grey metallic element found chiefly in zircon and used in various industrial applications. [f. prec. + -IUM]

zi'ther (-dh-) *n.* (Mus.) flat many-stringed instrument placed horizontally and played partly with fingers of left hand and partly with plectrum on right thumb and with fingers of right hand; hence ~IST (1) *n.* [G (as CITHERN)]

zlŏ'tỷ *n.* (*pl.* ~s or same). monetary unit of Poland. [Pol., lit. 'golden']

Zn *symb.* zinc.

zŏ'diăc *n.* belt of the heavens limited by lines about 8° from the ecliptic on each side, including all apparent positions of the sun, moon, and planets as known to the ancients, and divided into 12 equal parts called **signs of the** ~ (Aries, Taurus, Gemini, Cancer, Leo,

Virgo, Libra, Scorpio, Sagittarius, Capricorn(us), Aquarius, Pisces), each formerly containing the similarly named constellation but now by precession of equinoxes coinciding with the constellation that bears the name of the preceding sign; diagram of these signs; (fig.) complete cycle, circuit, or compass. [ME, f. OF *zodiaque* f. L *zodiacus* f. Gk *zōidiakos* (*zōidion* sculptured animal-figure, dim. of *zōion* animal); see -AC]

zodi'acal *a.* of or in the zodiac; ~ **light,** luminous area of sky shaped like tall triangle occas. seen in east before sunrise or in west after sunset, esp. in tropics. [F (as prec.; see -AL)]

zŏ'étrŏpe *n.* optical toy in form of cylinder with series of pictures on inner surface which give impression of continuous motion when viewed through slits with cylinder rotating. [irreg. f. Gk *zōē* life + -*tropos* turning]

zŏ'ic *a.* of animals; (Geol., of rock etc.) containing fossils, with traces of animal or plant life. [prob. back-form. f. AZOIC]

Zö'llner (tsĕr'-) *n.* ~'s **lines,** parallel lines made to appear not parallel by short oblique intersecting lines. [f. J. K. F. ~, Ger. physicist d. 1882]

zollverein (tsŏ'lferīn) *n.* customs union, esp. of German states in 19th c. [G]

zŏ'mbie, *zŏ'mbi, *n.* corpse said to be revived by witchcraft; (colloq.) person resembling this, dull or apathetic person. [W. Afr.]

zŏ'nda *n.* hot dusty N. wind in Argentina. [Amer. Sp.]

zŏne *n.,* & *v.t.* **1.** *n.* area enclosed between two exact or approximate concentric circles; part of surface of sphere enclosed between two parallel planes, or of cone, cylinder, etc., between such planes cutting it perpendicularly to axis. **2.** any well-defined region of more or less beltlike form; (time) ~, range of longitudes where a common standard time is used; (Geol. etc.) region between specified limits of depth. **3.** area having particular features, properties, purpose, or use, (*danger, demilitarized, erogenous, smokeless, zone*). **4.** (Geog.) any of five divisions of the earth bounded by circles parallel to the equator; **frigid** ~s (N. of Arctic, S. of Antarctic, Circle); **torrid** ~ (between the tropics of Cancer and Capricorn); **temperate** ~s (between frigid and torrid zones). **5.** encircling band or stripe distinguishable in colour or texture or character from rest of object encircled. **6.** (arch.) belt or girdle worn round the body. **7.** Hence **zŏ'nal, zŏ'nary¹, zŏ'nate²** (Bot. & Zool.), *adjs.* **8.** *v.t.* encircle as or with zone; arrange or distribute by zones; assign as or to zone (sense 6), whence **zŏ'nING²** *n.* [F, or f. L f. Gk *zōnē* girdle]

zŏŏ *n.* zoological garden. [abbr.]

zŏ'o- *comb. form.* of animals, of animal life, as: ~**geo'graphy,** zoology dealing with local distribution of animals; ~**graphy** (-ŏ'g-), descriptive zoology; ~**latry** (ŏ'l-), worship of animals; ~**mancy,** divination from appearances or behaviour of animals; ~**mor'phic,** (1) dealing with or represented in animal forms, (2) having gods of animal form; so ~**mor'phism;** ~**phyte,** plantlike animal, esp. coral, jellyfish, sea anemone, or sponge; so ~**phy'tic** (-fĭ'-) *a.*; ~**pla'nkton,** plankton consisting of animals; ~**spore,** spore capable of motion; ~**tomy** (-ŏ't-), dissection or anatomy of animals. [f. Gk *zōio-* (*zōion* animal; see -O-)]

zŏ'oid *n.* organic body or cell resembling but not being animal or plant; more or less independent organism given by gemmation or fission; member of compound organism; hence **zŏoi'dAL** *a.* [f. as prec. + -OID]

zŏö'log|ỷ *n.* science of animal structure, physiology, classification, habits, and distribution; hence or cogn. **zŏolo'gICAL** *a.* (~**ical garden**(s), public garden or park with collection of animals for exhibition and study), ~**IST** (3) *n.* [f. mod. L *zoologia* (as ZOO-, -LOGY)]

zoom *v.i.*, & *n.* **1.** *v.i.* cause aeroplane to mount at high speed and steep angle; move quickly, esp. with buzzing sound; (of camera) change (esp. quickly) from long shot to close-up. **2.** *n.* aeroplane's steep climb; ∼ **lens**, (Photog. etc.) lens which by variation of focal length allows (esp. quick) transition from long shot to close-up. [imit.]

zoot *a.* ∼ **suit**, (colloq.) man's suit with long loose jacket and high-waisted tapering trousers. [rhyming on SUIT]

zo'ri *n.* Japanese straw etc. sandal. [Jap.]

zo'ril *n.* carnivorous Afr. quadruped allied to skunk and weasel. [f. F *zorille* f. Sp. *zorrilla* dim. of *zorro* fox]

Zoroä'strian, Zärathu'strian (-thōō'-), *a.* & *n.* (follower) of Zoroaster or Zarathustra, (adherent) of the dualistic religious system taught by him and his followers in the Zend-Avesta based on the conflict between Ormuzd or (Ahura) Mazda god of light and good and Ahriman spirit of darkness and evil (the religion of the magi and ancient Persia still followed by Parsees); hence ∼ISM (3) *n.* [f. (L f. Gk *Zōroastrēs* f.) Avestan *Zarathustra*, Persian founder of the religion 6th c. BC + -IAN]

zou'ave (zōō'ahv, zwahv) *n.* member of French light-infantry corps orig. formed of Algerians and retaining their oriental uniform. [F, f. *Zouaoua*, name of tribe]

‖**zounds** (-z) *int.* (arch.) expr. indignation. [= (God)'s *wounds* (i.e. those of Christ on the Cross)]

ZPG *abbr.* zero population growth.

Zr *symb.* zirconium.

zucchě'ttō (tsŏŏk-) *n.* (*pl.* ∼s). RC ecclesiastic's skull-cap, black for priest, purple for bishop, red for cardinal, and white for pope. [f. It. *zucchetta* dim. of *zucca* gourd, head]

zucchi'ni (zŏŏkē'-) *n.* (*pl.* same *or* ∼s). courgette. [It., pl. of *zucchino* dim. of *zucca* gourd]

zu'gzwang (tsŏŏ'ktsvahng) *n.* (Chess). obligation to move in one's turn even when this must be disadvantageous. [G (*zug* move, *zwang* compulsion)]

Zu'lu (zōō'lōō) *n.* & *a.* (member or language) of a S. Afr. Bantu people. [native name]

zwie'back (zwē'bǎk, tsvē'bahk) *n.* kind of biscuit rusk or sweet cake toasted in slices. [G, = twice baked]

Zwi'nglian (zwĭ'ngg-, tsv-) *a.* &. *n.* (follower) of Zwingli. [f. U. *Zwingli*, Swiss religious reformer d. 1531 + -IAN]

zwi'tterïon (zw-, tsv-) *n.* molecule or ion having separate positively and negatively charged groups. [G (*zwitter* a hybrid); see ION]

zy'gal *a.* H-shaped (esp. of brain-fissures). [f. as foll. + -AL]

zy'go- *comb. form.* joining, pairing, as: ∼**da'ctyl** *a.* & *n.*, ∼**da'ctylous** *a.*, (bird) with two toes pointing forward and two backward; ∼**mor'phic**, ∼**mor'phous**, (of flower) divisible into similar halves only by one plane; ∼**spore**, spore formed by conjugation of two similar gametes. [f. Gk *zugo-* (*zugon* yoke; see -O-)]

zygo'ma *n.* (*pl.* ∼ta). bony arch of cheek, yoke-bone; hence **zygomä'tic** *a.* [f. Gk *zugōma -atos* (*zugon* yoke; see -OMA)]

zygo's|is *n.* (*pl.* ∼es *pr.* -ēz). (Biol.) conjugation. [mod. L, f. Gk *zugōsis* joining (*zugoō* to yoke f. *zugon* yoke; see -OSIS)]

zy'gōte *n.* (Biol.) cell formed by union of two gametes. [f. Gk *zugōtos* yoked (*zugoō*; see prec.)]

zy'mäse *n.* enzyme of group orig. found in yeast, causing breakdown of glucose. [F, f. Gk *zumē* leaven; see -ASE]

zymo's|is *n.* (*pl.* ∼es *pr.* -ēz). fermentation; zymotic disease. [mod. L, f. Gk *zumōsis* f. as prec.; see -OSIS]

zymo'tic *a.* (of fermentation; ∼ **disease**, epidemic, endemic, contagious, infectious, or sporadic disease regarded as caused by multiplication of germs introduced from outside. [f. Gk *zumōtikos* (as prec.; see -OTIC)]

zy'murgy *n.* branch of applied chemistry dealing with use of fermentation in brewing etc. [f. Gk *zumē* leaven, after *metallurgy*]

APPENDIX I

WEIGHTS AND MEASURES

Note. The conversion factors are not exact unless so marked. They are given only to the accuracy likely to be needed in everyday calculations.

I. BRITISH AND AMERICAN, WITH METRIC EQUIVALENTS

Linear Measure

1 inch	= 25.4 millimetres exactly
1 foot = 12 inches	= 0.3048 metre exactly
1 yard = 3 feet	= 0.9144 metre exactly
1 (statute) mile = 1,760 yards	= 1.609 kilometres

Square Measure

1 square inch	= 6.45 sq. centimetres
1 square foot = 144 sq. in.	= 9.29 sq. decimetres
1 square yard = 9 sq. ft.	= 0.836 sq. metre
1 acre = 4,840 sq. yd.	= 0.405 hectare
1 square mile = 640 acres	= 259 hectares

Cubic Measure

1 cubic inch	= 16.4 cu. centimetres
1 cubic foot = 1,728 cu. in.	= 0.0283 cu. metre
1 cubic yard = 27 cu. ft.	= 0.765 cu. metre

Capacity Measure

British

1 pint = 20 fluid oz.	= 0.568 litre
= 34.68 cu. in.	
1 quart = 2 pints	= 1.136 litres
1 gallon = 4 quarts	= 4.546 litres
1 peck = 2 gallons	= 9.092 litres
1 bushel = 4 pecks	= 36.4 litres
1 quarter = 8 bushels	= 2.91 hectolitres

American dry

1 pint = 33.60 cu. in.	= 0.550 litre
1 quart = 2 pints	= 1.101 litres
1 peck = 8 quarts	= 8.81 litres
1 bushel = 4 pecks	= 35.3 litres

American liquid

1 pint = 16 fluid oz.	= 0.473 litre
= 28.88 cu. in.	
1 quart = 2 pints	= 0.946 litre
1 gallon = 4 quarts	= 3.785 litres

Avoirdupois Weight

1 grain	= 0.065 gram
1 dram	= 1.772 grams
1 ounce = 16 drams	= 28.35 grams
1 pound = 16 ounces	= 0.4536 kilogram
= 7,000 grains	(0.45359237 exactly)
1 stone = 14 pounds	= 6.35 kilograms
1 quarter = 2 stones	= 12.70 kilograms
1 hundredweight = 4 quarters	= 50.80 kilograms
1 (long) ton = 20 hundredweight	= 1.016 tonnes
1 short ton = 2,000 pounds	= 0.907 tonne

See also APOTHECARY and TROY in the dictionary.

2. METRIC, WITH BRITISH EQUIVALENTS

Linear Measure

1 millimetre	= 0.039 inch
1 centimetre = 10 mm	= 0.394 inch
1 decimetre = 10 cm	= 3.94 inches
1 metre = 10 dm	− 1.094 yards
1 decametre = 10 m	= 10.94 yards
1 hectometre = 100 m	= 109.4 yards
1 kilometre = 1,000 m	= 0.6214 mile

Square Measure

1 square centimetre	= 0.155 sq. inch
1 square metre	= 1.196 sq. yards
1 are = 100 sq. metres	= 119.6 sq. yards
1 hectare − 100 ares	− 2.471 acres
1 square kilometre	= 0.386 sq. mile

Cubic Measure

1 cubic centimetre	= 0.061 cu. inch
1 cubic metre	= 1.308 cu. yards

Capacity Measure

1 millilitre	= 0.002 pint (British)
1 centilitre = 10 ml	= 0.018 pint
1 decilitre = 10 cl	− 0.176 pint
1 litre = 10 dl	= 1.76 pints
1 decalitre = 10 l	= 2.20 gallons
1 hectolitre = 100 l	= 2.75 bushels
1 kilolitre = 1,000 l	= 3.44 quarters

Weight

1 milligram	= 0.015 grain
1 centigram = 10 mg	= 0.154 grain
1 decigram = 10 cg	= 1.543 grain
1 gram = 10 dg	= 15.43 grain
1 decagram = 10 g	= 5.64 drams
1 hectogram = 100 g	= 3.527 ounces
1 kilogram = 1,000 g	= 2.205 pounds
1 tonne (metric ton) = 1,000 kg	= 0.984 (long) ton

3. TEMPERATURE

Fahrenheit: Water boils (under standard conditions) at $212°$ and freezes at $32°$.
Celsius or Centigrade: Water boils at $100°$ and freezes at $0°$.
Kelvin: Water boils at 373.15 K and freezes at 273.15 K

$F = 9C/5 + 32$ or $F + 40 = 9(C + 40)/5$
$C = 5(F - 32)/9$ or $C + 40 = 5(F + 40)/9$
$K = C + 273.15$

4. THE POWER NOTATION

This expresses concisely any power of ten (any number that is composed of factors 10), and is sometimes used in the dictionary. 10^2 or ten squared = $10 \times 10 = 100$; 10^3 or ten cubed = $10 \times 10 \times 10 = 1,000$. Similarly, $10^4 = 10,000$, and $10^{10} = 1$ followed by ten noughts = 10,000,000,000. Proceeding in the opposite direction, dividing by ten and subtracting one from the index, we have $10^2 = 100$, $10^1 = 10$, $10^0 = 1$, $10^{-1} = \frac{1}{10}$, $10^{-2} = \frac{1}{100}$, and so on; $10^{-10} = 1/10^{10} = 1/10,000,000,000$. See also POWER 9 in the dictionary.

5. THE METRIC PREFIXES

	Abbreviations	Factors
deca	da	10
hecto	h	10^2
kilo	k	10^3
mega	M	10^6
giga	G	10^9
tera	T	10^{12}
peta	P	10^{15}
exa	E	10^{18}
deci	d	10^{-1}
centi	c	10^{-2}
milli	m	10^{-3}
micro	μ	10^{-6}
nano	n	10^{-9}
pico	p	10^{-12}
femto	f	10^{-15}
atto	a	10^{-18}

Pronunciations and derivations of these are given at their alphabetical places in the dictionary. They may be applied to any units of the metric system: hectogram (abbr. hg) = 100 grams; kilowatt (abbr. kW) = 1,000 watts; megahertz (MHz) = 1 million hertz; centimetre (cm) = $\frac{1}{100}$ metre; microvolt (μV) = one millionth of a volt; picofarad (pF) = 10^{-12} farad, and are sometimes applied to other units (megabit, microinch).

6. CHEMICAL NOTATION

The symbol for a molecule (such as H_2O, CH_4, H_2SO_4) shows the symbols for the elements contained in it (C = carbon, H = hydrogen, etc.), followed by a subscript numeral denoting the number of atoms of each element in the molecule where this number is more than one. For example, the water molecule (H_2O) contains two atoms of hydrogen and one of oxygen.

APPENDIX II

THE GREEK ALPHABET

Capital	Lower-case	Name*	English transliteration in this dictionary
A	α	alpha	a
B	β	beta	b
Γ	γ	gamma	g
Δ	δ	delta	d
E	ε	epsilon	e
Z	ζ	zeta	z
H	η	eta	ē
Θ	θ	theta	th
I	ι	iota	i
K	κ	kappa	k
Λ	λ	lambda	l
M	μ	mu	m
N	ν	nu	n
Ξ	ξ	xi	x
O	ο	omicron	o
Π	π	pi	p
P	ρ	rho	r
Σ	σ, (at end of word)ς	sigma	s
T	τ	tau	t
Υ	υ	upsilon	u
Φ	φ	phi	ph
X	χ	chi	kh
Ψ	ψ	psi	ps
Ω	ω	omega	ō

‘ (rough breathing) over vowel = prefixed h (ἁ = ha)
over rho = suffixed h (ῥ = rh)

’ (smooth breathing) over vowel or rho: not transliterated

. (iota subscript) under vowel = suffixed i (ᾳ = ai)

*Pronunciations are given in the dictionary entries for these words.

THE RUSSIAN ALPHABET

Capital	Lower-case	Approx. Pronunciation of Name	English transliteration in this dictionary
А	а	(ah)	a
Б	б	(bĕ)	b
В	в	(vĕ)	v
Г	г	(gĕ)	g
Д	д	(dĕ)	d
Е	е	(yĕ)	e
Ё	ё	(yŏ)	ë
Ж	ж	(zhĕ)	zh
З	з	(zĕ)	z
И	и	(ē)	i
Й	й	(ēkră′tkŏyĕ)	ĭ
К	к	(kah)	k
Л	л	(ĕl)	l
М	м	(ĕm)	m
Н	н	(ĕn)	n
О	о	(ŏ)	o
П	п	(pĕ)	p
Р	р	(ĕr)	r
С	с	(ĕs)	s
Т	т	(tĕ)	t
У	у	(ōō)	u
Ф	ф	(ĕf)	f
Х	х	(χah)	kh
Ц	ц	(tsĕ)	ts
Ч	ч	(chĕ)	ch
Ш	ш	(shah)	sh
Щ	щ	(shchah)	shch
Ъ	ъ	(tvyōr′dĭznahk)	” ('hard sign')
Ы	ы	(ĭ)	y
Ь	ь	(myah′k-kĭznahk)	' ('soft sign')
Э	э	(ĕŏberŏ′tnŏyĕ)	é
Ю	ю	(ū)	yu
Я	я	(yah)	ya

ABBREVIATIONS AND SYMBOLS USED

Norm./an
north./ern
Norw./egian
ns. nouns
num./eral

O Old (with languages)
obj. object; objective
obl./ique
OBret. Old Breton
OBrit. Old British
obs./olete
Obstet./rics etc.
OBulg. Old Bulgarian
occas./ional(ly)
OCelt. Old Celtic
ODa. Old Danish
ODu. Old Dutch
OE Old English
OF Old French
OFrank. Old Frankish
OFris. Old Frisian
OGael. Old Gaelic
OHG Old High
   German
OIcel. Old Icelandic
OIr. Old Irish
OIt. Old Italian
OL Old Latin
OLG Old Low German
ON Old Norse
ONF Old Northern
   French
ONorw. Old
   Norwegian
OPers. Old Persian
OPort. Old Portuguese
opp. (as) opposed (to);
   opposite
OProv. Old Provençal
Opt./ics etc.
ord./inary etc.
orig. origin; original(ly)
Ornith./ology etc.
OS Old Saxon
OScand. Old
   Scandinavian
OSlav. Old Slavonic
OSp. Old Spanish
OSw. Old Swedish

P: see note below
Paint./ing
Palaeog./raphy etc.
parenth./etic etc.
Parl./iament(ary)

part. (present)
   participle
pass./ive(ly)
Path./ology etc.
pej./orative
perf./ect (tense)
perh./aps
Pers./ian
pers./on(al)
Peruv./ian
Pharm./acy etc.
Philol./ogy etc.
Philos./ophy etc.
Phoen./ician
Phonet./ics etc.
Photog./raphy etc.
phr./ase
Phren./ology etc.
phrs. phrases
Phys./ics
Physiol./ogy
pl./ural
poet./ical etc.
Pol./ish
Polit./ics etc.
pop. popular etc., not
   technical
pop. L popular Latin,
   informal spoken Latin
Port./uguese
poss. possessive;
   possible etc.
p.p. past participle
pr./onounced etc.
prec./eding entry
pred. predicate;
   predicative(ly)
pref./ix
prep./osition
pres./ent (tense)
pret./erite
Print./ing
prob./able etc.
pron./oun etc.
pronunc./iation
prop./er(ly)
Pros./ody etc.
Prov./ençal (medieval
   if not otherwise
   described)
prov. proverb etc.;
   provincial etc.
Psych./ology etc.

R: see note below
redupl./icated etc.

ref./erence
refash./ioned
refl./exive(ly)
rel. related; relative
repl./acing etc.
repr./esenting etc.
Rhet./oric etc.
rhet./orical(ly)
Rom. Roman; (in
   etymologies)
   Romanic
Russ./ian

S. Afr. South Africa(n)
S. Amer. South
   America(n)
Sc./ottish etc.
Scand./inavia(n)
sent./ence
Shak./espeare
sim./ilar(ly)
sing./ular
Sinh./alese
Skr. Sanskrit
sl./ang
Slav./onic
Sociol./ogy etc.
Sp./anish
sp./elling etc.
spec./ial(ly)
st./em
St. Exch. Stock
   Exchange
subj. subject etc.;
   subjunctive
subord./inate
subst./antive
suf./fix
superl./ative
Surg./ery etc.
Surv./eying etc.
Sw./edish
syl./lable etc.
symb./ol
syn./onym etc.

t. transitive
tech./nical(ly)
Teleph./ony etc.
Telev./ision etc.
Teut./onic
Theatr./ical etc.
Theol./ogy etc.
thr./ough
transf. in transferred
   sense